Stanley Gibbons
SIMPLIFIED CATALOGUE

Stamps of the **World**

This popular catalogue is a straightforward listing of the stamps that have been issued everywhere in the world since the very first–Great Britain's famous Penny Black in 1840.

This edition, in which both the text and the illustrations have been captured electronically, is arranged completely alphabetically in a four-volume format. Volume 1 (Countries A–D), Volume 2 (Countries E–J), Volume 3 (Countries K–R) and Volume 4 (Countries S–Z).

Readers are reminded that the Catalogue Supplements, published in each issue of **Gibbons Stamp Monthly**, can be used to update the listings in **Stamps of the World** as well as our 22-part standard catalogue. To make the supplement even more useful the Type numbers given to the illustrations are the same in the Stamps of the World as in the standard catalogues. The first Catalogue Supplement to this Volume appeared in the September 2003 issue of **Gibbons Stamp Monthly**.

Gibbons Stamp Monthly can be obtained through newsagents or on postal subscription from Stanley Gibbons Publications, Parkside, Christchurch Road, Ringwood, Hants BH24 3SH.

The catalogue has many important features:

- The vast majority of illustrations are now in full colour to aid stamp identification.
- All Commonwealth miniature sheets are now included.
- As an indication of current values virtually every stamp is priced. Thousands of alterations have been made since the last edition.
- By being set out on a simplified basis that excludes changes of paper, perforation, shade, watermark, gum or printer's and date imprints it is particularly easy to use. (For its exact scope see "Information for users" pages following.)
- The thousands of colour illustrations and helpful descriptions of stamp designs make it of maximum appeal to collectors with thematic interests.
- Its catalogue numbers are the world-recognised Stanley Gibbons numbers throughout.
- Helpful introductory notes for the collector are included, backed by much historical, geographical and currency information.
- A very detailed index gives instant location of countries in this volume, and a cross-reference to those included in the other volumes.

Over 4,690 stamps and miniature sheets and 740 new illustrations have been added to the listings in this volume. This year's four-volumes now contain over 406,730 stamps and 97,315 illustrations.

The listings in this edition are based on the standard catalogues: Part 1, Commonwealth & British Empire Stamps 1840–1952, Part 2 (Austria & Hungary) (6th edition), Part 3 (Balkans) (4th edition), Part 4 (Benelux) (5th edition), Part 5 (Czechoslovakia & Poland) (6th edition), Part 6 (France) (5th edition), Part 7 (Germany) (6th edition), Part 8 (Italy & Switzerland) (6th edition), Part 9 (Portugal & Spain) (4th edition), Part 10 (Russia) (5th edition), Part 11 (Scandinavia) (5th edition), Part 12 (Africa since Independence A-E) (2nd edition), Part 13 (Africa since Independence F-M) (1st edition), Part 14 (Africa since Independence N-Z) (1st edition), Part 15 (Central America) (2nd edition), Part 16 (Central Asia) (3rd edition), Part 17 (China) (6th edition), Part 18 (Japan & Korea) (4th edition), Part 19 (Middle East) (5th edition), Part 20 (South America) (3rd edition), Part 21 (South-East Asia) (3rd edition) and Part 22 (United States) (5th edition).

This edition includes major repricing for all Western Europe countries in addition to the changes for Benelux Part 4, Italy and Switzerland Part 8 and Czechoslovakia & Poland Part 5. Also Rumania, Rumanian Occupation of Hungary and Turkey, together with all thematic Bird issues have been revised for this volume.

Acknowledgements

A wide-ranging revision of prices for Western European countries has been undertaken for this edition with the intention that the catalogue should be more accurate to reflect the market for foreign issues.

Many dealers in both Great Britain and overseas have participated in this scheme by supplying copies of their retail price lists on which the research has been based.

We would like to acknowledge the assistance of the following for this edition:

ALMAZ CO
of Brooklyn, U.S.A.

AMATEUR COLLECTOR LTD, THE
of London, England

E. ANGELOPOULOS
of Thessaloniki, Greece

AVION THEMATICS
of Nottingham, England

J BAREFOOT LTD
of York, England

BELGIAN PHILATELIC SPECIALISTS INC
of Larchmont, U.S.A.

Sir CHARLES BLOMEFIELD
of Chipping Camden, England

T. BRAY
of Shipley, West Yorks, England

CENTRAL PHILATELIQUE
of Brussels, Belgium

JEAN-PIERRE DELMONTE
of Paris, France

EUROPEAN & FOREIGN STAMPS
of Pontypridd, Wales

FILATELIA LLACH SL
of Barcelona, Spain

FILATELIA RIVA RENO
of Bologna, Italy

FILATELIA TORI
of Barcelona, Spain

FORMOSA STAMP COMPANY, THE
of Koahsiung, Taiwan

FORSTAMPS
of Battle, England

ANTHONY GRAINGER
of Leeds, England

HOLMGREN STAMPS
of Bollnas, Sweden

INDIGO
of Orewa, New Zealand

ALEC JACQUES
of Selby, England

M. JANKOWSKI
of Warsaw, Poland

D.J.M. KERR
of Earlston, England

H. M. NIELSEN
of Vejle, Denmark

LEO BARESCH LTD
of Hassocks, England

LORIEN STAMPS
of Chesterfield, England

MANDARIN TRADING CO
of Alhambra, U.S.A.

MICHAEL ROGERS INC
of Winter Park, U.S.A.

PHILATELIC SUPPLIES
of Letchworth, England

PHIL-INDEX
of Eastbourne, England

PHILTRADE A/S
of Copenhagen, Denmark

PITTERI SA
of Chiasso, Switzerland

KEVIN RIGLER
of Shifnal, England

ROLF GUMMESSON AB
of Stockholm, Sweden

R. D. TOLSON
of Undercliffe, England

JAY SMITH
of Snow Camp, U.S.A.

R. SCHNEIDER
of Belleville, U.S.A.

ROBSTINE STAMPS
of Hampshire, England

SOUTHERN MAIL
of Eastbourne, England

STAMP CENTER
of Reykjavik, Iceland

REX WHITE
of Winchester, England

Western European countries will now be repriced each year in Stamps of the World and where there is no up-to-date specialised foreign volume in a country these will be the new Stanley Gibbons prices.

It is hoped that this improved pricing scheme will be extended to other foreign countries and thematic issues as information is consolidated.

Stanley Gibbons
SIMPLIFIED CATALOGUE

Stamps of the World

2004 Edition

IN COLOUR

An illustrated and priced four-volume guide to the postage stamps of the whole world, excluding changes of paper, perforation, shade and watermark

VOLUME 3

COUNTRIES K–R

STANLEY GIBBONS LTD
Lo

By Appointment to
Her Majesty the Queen
Stanley Gibbons Limited
London
Philatelists

69th Edition

Published in Great Britain by
Stanley Gibbons Ltd
Publications Editorial, Sales Offices and Distribution Centre
Parkside, Christchurch Road,
Ringwood, Hampshire BH24 3SH
Telephone 01425 472363

ISBN: 085259-552-2

Published as Stanley Gibbons Simplified Stamp Catalogue from 1934 to 1970, renamed Stamps of the World in 1971, and produced in two (1982-88), three (1989-2001) or four (from 2002) volumes as Stanley Gibbons Simplified Catalogue of Stamps of the World.
This volume published November 2003

S.G. Item No. 2883 (04)

Printed in Great Britain by Unwin Brothers Ltd, Old Woking, Surrey

Information for users

Aim

The aim of this catalogue is to provide a straightforward illustrated and priced guide to the postage stamps of the whole world to help you to enjoy the greatest hobby of the present day.

Arrangement

The catalogue lists countries in alphabetical order and there is a complete index at the end of each volume. For ease of reference country names are also printed at the head of each page.

Within each country, postage stamps are listed first. They are followed by separate sections for such other categories as postage due stamps, parcel post stamps, express stamps, official stamps, etc.

All catalogue lists are set out according to dates of issue of the stamps, starting from the earliest and working through to the most recent.

Scope of the Catalogue

The *Simplified Catalogue of Stamps of the World* contains listings of postage stamps only. Apart from the ordinary definitive, commemorative and airmail stamps of each country – which appear first in each list – there are sections for the following where appropriate:

- postage due stamps
- parcel post stamps
- official stamps
- express and special delivery stamps
- charity and compulsory tax stamps
- newspaper and journal stamps
- printed matter stamps
- registration stamps
- acknowledgement of receipt stamps
- late fee and too late stamps
- military post stamps
- recorded message stamps
- personal delivery stamps

We receive numerous enquiries from collectors about other items which do not fall within the categories set out above and which consequently do not appear in the catalogue lists. It may be helpful, therefore, to summarise the other kinds of stamp that exist but which we deliberately exclude from this postage stamp catalogue.

We do *not* list the following:

Fiscal or revenue stamps: stamps used solely in collecting taxes or fees for non-postal purposes. Examples would be stamps which pay a tax on a receipt, represent the stamp duty on a contract or frank a customs document. Common inscriptions found include: Documentary, Proprietary, Inter. Revenue, Contract Note.

Local stamps: postage stamps whose validity and use are limited in area, say to a single town or city, though in some cases they provided, with official sanction, services in parts of countries not covered by the respective government.

Local carriage labels and Private local issues: many labels exist ostensibly to cover the cost of ferrying mail from one of Great Britain's offshore islands to the nearest mainland post office. They are not recognised as valid for national or international mail. Examples: Calf of Man, Davaar, Herm, Lundy, Pabay, Stroma. Items from some other places have only the status of tourist souvenir labels.

Telegraph stamps: stamps intended solely for the prepayment of telegraphic communication.

Bogus or "phantom" stamps: labels from mythical places or non-existent administrations. Examples in the classical period were Sedang, Counani, Clipperton Island and in modern times Thomond and Monte Bello Islands. Numerous labels have also appeared since the War from dissident groups as propaganda for their claims and without authority from the home governments. Common examples are labels for "Free Albania", "Free Rumania" and "Free Croatia" and numerous issues for Nagaland, Indonesia and the South Moluccas ("Republik Maluku Selatan").

Railway letter fee stamps: special stamps issued by railway companies for the conveyance of letters by rail. Example: Talyllyn Railway. Similar services are now offered by some bus companies and the labels they issue likewise do not qualify for inclusion in the catalogue.

Perfins ("perforated initials"): numerous postage stamps may be found with initial letters or designs punctured through them by tiny holes. These are applied by private and public concerns as a precaution against theft and do not qualify for separate mention.

Information for users

Labels: innumerable items exist resembling stamps but – as they do not prepay postage – they are classified as labels. The commonest categories are:

- propaganda and publicity labels: designed to further a cause or campaign;
- exhibition labels: particularly souvenirs from philatelic events;
- testing labels: stamp-size labels used in testing stamp-vending machines;
- Post Office training school stamps: British stamps overprinted with two thick vertical bars or SCHOOL SPECIMEN are produced by the Post Office for training purposes;
- seals and stickers: numerous charities produce stamp-like labels, particularly at Christmas and Easter, as a means of raising funds and these have no postal validity.

Cut-outs: items of postal stationary, such as envelopes, cards and wrappers, often have stamps impressed or imprinted on them. They may usually be cut out and affixed to envelopes, etc., for postal use if desired, but such items are not listed in this catalogue.

Collectors wanting further information about exact definitions are referred to *Philatelic Terms Illustrated,* published by Stanley Gibbons and containing many illustrations in colour.

There is also a priced listing of the postal fiscals of Great Britain in our *Commonwealth & British Empire Stamps 1840–1952* Catalogue and in Volume 1 of the *Great Britain Specialised* Catalogue (5th and later editions).

Prices are shown as follows:

10 means 10p (10 pence);
1.50 means £1.50 (1 pound and 50 pence);
For £100 and above, prices are in whole pounds.

Our prices are for stamps in fine condition, and in issues where condition varies we may ask more for the superb and less for the sub-standard.

The minimum catalogue price quoted is 10p. For individual stamps prices between 10p and 45p are provided as a guide for catalogue users. The lowest price charged for individual stamps purchased from Stanley Gibbons is 50p.

The prices quoted are generally for the cheapest variety of stamps but it is worth noting that differences of watermark, perforation, or other details, outside the scope of this catalogue, may often increase the value of the stamp.

Prices quoted for mint issues are for single examples. Those in se-tenant pairs, strips, blocks or sheets may be worth more.

Where prices are not given in either column it is either because the stamps are not known to exist in that particular condition, or, more usually, because there is no reliable information as to value.

All prices are subject to change without prior notice and we give no guarantee to supply all stamps priced. Prices quoted for albums, publications, etc. advertised in this catalogue are also subject to change without prior notice.

Due to different production methods it is sometimes possible for new editions of Parts 2 to 22 to appear showing revised prices which are not included in that year's *Stamps of the World.*

Catalogue Numbers

Stanley Gibbons catalogue numbers are recognised universally and any individual stamp can be identified by quoting the catalogue number (the one at the left of the column) prefixed by the name of the country and the letters "S.G.". Do not confuse the catalogue number with the type numbers which refer to illustrations.

Prices

Prices in the left-hand column are for unused stamps and those in the right-hand column for used. Prices are given in pence and pounds:

100 pence (p) 1 pound (£1).

Unused Stamps

In the case of stamps from *Great Britain* and the *Commonwealth,* prices for unused stamps of Queen Victoria to King George V are for lightly hinged examples; unused prices of King Edward VIII to Queen Elizabeth II issues are for unmounted mint. The prices of unused Foreign stamps are for lightly hinged examples for those issued before 1946, thereafter for examples unmounted mint.

Used Stamps

Prices for used stamps generally refer to fine postally used examples, though for certain issues they are for cancelled-to-order.

Information for users

Guarantee

All stamps supplied by us are guaranteed originals in the following terms:

If not as described, and returned by the purchaser, we undertake to refund the price paid to us in the original transaction. If any stamp is certified as genuine by the Expert Committee of the Royal Philatelic Society, London, or by B.P.A. Expertising Ltd., the purchaser shall not be entitled to make any claim against us for any error, omission or mistake in such certificate.

Consumers' statutory rights are not affected by the above guarantee.

Currency

At the beginning of each country brief details give the currencies in which the values of the stamps are expressed. The dates, where given, are those of the earliest stamp issues in the particular currency. Where the currency is obvious, e.g. where the colony has the same currency as the mother country, no details are given.

Illustrations

Illustrations of any surcharges and overprints which are shown and not described are actual size; stamp illustrations are reduced to $\frac{3}{4}$ linear, *unless otherwise stated.*

"Key-Types"

A number of standard designs occur so frequently in the stamps of the French, German, Portuguese and Spanish colonies that it would be a waste of space to repeat them. Instead these are all illustrated on page xiv together with the descriptive names and letters by which they are referred to in the lists.

Type Numbers

These are the bold figures found below each illustration. References to "Type **6**", for example, in the lists of a country should therefore be understood to refer to the illustration below which the number **"6"** appears. These type numbers are also given in the second column of figures alongside each list of stamps, thus indicating clearly the design of each stamp. In the case of Key-Types – see above – letters take the place of the type numbers.

Where an issue comprises stamps of similar design, represented in this catalogue by one illustration, the corresponding type numbers should be taken as indicating this general design.

Where there are blanks in the type number column it means that the type of the corresponding stamps is that shown by the last number above in the type column of the same issue.

A dash (–) in the type column means that no illustration of the stamp is shown.

Where type numbers refer to stamps of another country, e.g. where stamps of one country are overprinted for use in another, this is always made clear in the text.

Stamp Designs

Brief descriptions of the subjects of the stamp designs are given either below or beside the illustrations, at the foot of the list of the issue concerned, or in the actual lists. Where a particular subject, e.g. the portrait of a well-known monarch, recurs frequently the description is not repeated, nor are obvious designs described.

Generally, the unillustrated designs are in the same shape and size as the one illustrated, except where otherwise indicated.

Surcharges and Overprints

Surcharges and overprints are usually described in the headings to the issues concerned. Where the actual wording of a surcharge or overprint is given it is shown in bold type.

Some stamps are described as being "Surcharged in words", e.g. **TWO CENTS**, and others "Surcharged in figures and words", e.g. **20 CENTS**, although of course many surcharges are in foreign languages and combinations of words and figures are numerous. There are often bars, etc., obliterating old values or inscriptions but in general these are only mentioned where it is necessary to avoid confusion.

No attention is paid in this catalogue to colours of overprints and surcharges so that stamps with the same overprints in different colours are not listed separately.

Numbers in brackets after the descriptions of overprinted or surcharged stamps are the catalogue numbers of the unoverprinted stamps.

Note – the words "inscribed" or "inscription" always refer to wording incorporated in the design of a stamp and not surcharges or overprints.

Coloured Papers

Where stamps are printed on coloured paper the description is given as e.g. "4 c. black on blue" – a stamp printed in black on blue paper. No attention is paid in this catalogue to difference in the texture of paper, e.g. laid, wove.

Information for users

Watermarks

Stamps having different watermarks, but otherwise the same, are not listed separately. No reference is therefore made to watermarks in this volume.

Stamp Colours

Colour names are only required for the identification of stamps, therefore they have been made as simple as possible. Thus "scarlet", "vermilion", "carmine" are all usually called red. Qualifying colour names have been introduced only where necessary for the sake of clearness.

Where stamps are printed in two or more colours the central portion of the design is in the first colour given, unless otherwise stated.

Perforations

All stamps are perforated unless otherwise stated. No distinction is made between the various gauges of perforation but early stamp issues which exist both imperforate and perforated are usually listed separately.

Where a heading states "Imperf. or perf". or "Perf. or rouletted" this does not necessarily mean that all values of the issue are found in both conditions.

Dates of Issue

The date given at the head of each issue is that of the appearance of the earliest stamp in the series. As stamps of the same design or issue are usually grouped together a list of King George VI stamps, for example, headed "1938" may include stamps issued from 1938 to the end of the reign.

Se-tenant Pairs

Many modern issues are printed in sheets containing different designs or face values. Such pairs, blocks, strips or sheets are described as being "se-tenant" and they are outside the scope of this catalogue, although reference to them may occur in instances where they form a composite design.

Miniature Sheets

As an increasing number of stamps are now only found in miniature sheets, Stamps of the World will, in future, list these items. This edition lists all Commonwealth countries' miniature sheets, plus those of all non-Commonwealth countries which have appeared in the catalogue supplement during the past year. Earlier miniature sheets of non-Commonwealth countries will be listed in future editions.

"Appendix" Countries

We regret that, since 1968, it has been necessary to establish an Appendix (at the end of each country as appropriate) to which numerous stamps have had to be consigned. Several countries imagine that by issuing huge quantities of unnecessary stamps they will have a ready source of income from stamp collectors – and particularly from the less-experienced ones. Stanley Gibbons refuse to encourage this exploitation of the hobby and we do not stock the stamps concerned.

Two kinds of stamp are therefore given the briefest of mentions in the Appendix, purely for the sake of record. Administrations issuing stamps greatly in excess of true postal needs have the offending issues placed there. Likewise it contains stamps which have not fulfilled all the normal conditions for full catalogue listing.

These conditions are that the stamps must be issued by a legitimate postal authority, recognised by the government concerned, and are adhesives, valid for proper postal use in the class of service for which they are inscribed. Stamps, with the exception of such categories as postage dues and officials, must be available to the general public at face value with no artificial restrictions being imposed on their distribution.

The publishers of this catalogue have observed, with concern, the proliferation of 'artificial' stamp-issuing territories. On several occasions this has resulted in separately inscribed issues for various component parts of otherwise united states or territories.

Stanley Gibbons Publications have decided that where such circumstances occur, they will not, in the future, list these items in the SG catalogue without first satisfying themselves that the stamps represent a genuine political, historical or postal division within the country concerned. Any such issues which do not fulfil this stipulation will be recorded in the Catalogue Appendix only.

Stamps in the Appendix are kept under review in the light of any newly acquired information about them. If we are satisfied that a stamp qualifies for proper listing in the body of the catalogue it is moved there.

Information for users

"Undesirable Issues"

The rules governing many competitive exhibitions are set by the Federation Internationale de Philatelie and stipulate a downgrading of marks for stamps classed as "undesirable issues".

This catalogue can be taken as a guide to status. All stamps in the main listings and Addenda are acceptable. Stamps in the Appendix should not be entered for competition as these are the "undesirable issues".

Particular care is advised with Aden Protectorate States, Ajman, Bhutan, Chad, Fujeira, Khor Fakkan, Manama, Ras al Khaima, Sharjah, Umm al Qiwain and Yemen. Totally bogus stamps exist (as explained in Appendix notes) and these are to be avoided also for competition. As distinct from "undesirable stamps" certain categories are not covered in this catalogue purely by reason of its scope (see page viii). Consult the particular competition rules to see if such are admissable even though not listed by us.

Where to Look for More Detailed Listings

The present work deliberately omits details of paper, perforation, shade and watermark. But as you become more absorbed in stamp collecting and wish to get greater enjoyment from the hobby you may well want to study these matters.

All the information you require about any particular postage stamp will be found in the main Stanley Gibbons Catalogues.

Commonwealth countries before 1952 are covered by the Commonwealth & British Empire Stamps 1840–1952 published annually.

For foreign countries you can easily find which catalogue to consult by looking at the country headings in the present book.

To the right of each country name are code letters specifying which volume of our main catalogues contains that country's listing.

The code letters are as follows:

Pt. 2 Part 2
Pt. 3 Part 3 etc.

(See page xiii for complete list of Parts.)

So, for example, if you want to know more about Chinese stamps than is contained in the *Simplified Catalogue of Stamps of the World* the reference to

CHINA Pt. 17

guides you to the Gibbons Part 17 *(China)* Catalogue listing for the details you require.

New editions of Parts 2 to 22 appear at irregular intervals.

Correspondence

Whilst we welcome information and suggestions we must ask correspondents to include the cost of postage for the return of any stamps submitted plus registration where appropriate. Letters should be addressed to The Catalogue Editor at Ringwood.

Where information is solicited purely for the benefit of the enquirer we regret we cannot undertake to reply.

Identification of Stamps

We regret we do not give opinions as to the genuineness of stamps, nor do we identify stamps or number them by our Catalogue.

Users of this catalogue are referred to our companion booklet entitled *Stamp Collecting – How to Identify Stamps.* It explains how to look up stamps in this catalogue, contains a full checklist of stamp inscriptions and gives help in dealing with unfamiliar scripts.

Stanley Gibbons would like to complement your collection

At Stanley Gibbons we offer a range of services which are designed to complement your collection.

Our modern stamp shop, the largest in Europe, together with our rare stamp department has one of the most comprehensive stocks of Great Britain in the world, so whether you are a beginner or an experienced philatelist you are certain to find something to suit your special requirements.

Alternatively, through our Mail Order services you can control the growth of your collection from the comfort of your own home. Our Postal Sales Department regularly sends out mailings of Special Offers. We can also help with your wants list—so why not ask us for those elusive items?

Why not take advantage of the many services we have to offer? Visit our premises in the Strand or, for more information, write to the appropriate address on page x.

The Stanley Gibbons Group Addresses

Stanley Gibbons Limited, Stanley Gibbons Auctions

339 Strand, London WC2R 0LX
Telephone 020 7836 8444, Fax 020 7836 7342,
E-mail: enquiries@stanleygibbons.co.uk
Internet: www.stanleygibbons.com for all departments.

Auction Room and Specialist Stamp Departments. Open Monday–Friday 9.30 a.m. to 5 p.m.

Shop. Open Monday–Friday 9 a.m. to 5.30 p.m. and Saturday 9.30 a.m. to 5.30 p.m.

Fraser's
(a division of Stanley Gibbons Ltd)

399 Strand, London WC2R 0LX
Autographs, photographs, letters and documents

Telephone 020 7836 8444, Fax 020 7836 7342,
E-mail: info@frasersautographs.co.uk
Internet: www.frasersautographs.com

Monday–Friday 9 a.m. to 5.30 p.m. and Saturday 10 a.m. to 4 p.m.

Stanley Gibbons Publications

Parkside, Christchurch Road, Ringwood, Hants BH24 3SH.
Telephone 01425 472363 (24 hour answer phone service), Fax 01425 470247,
E-mail: info@stanleygibbons.co.uk

Publications Mail Order. FREEPHONE 0800 611622 Monday–Friday 8.30 a.m. to 5 p.m.

Stanley Gibbons Publications Overseas Representation

Stanley Gibbons Publications are represented overseas by the following sole distributors (*), distributors (**) or licensees (***).

Australia
Lighthouse Philatelic (Aust.) Pty. Ltd.*
Locked Bag 5900 Botany DC, New South Wales, 2019 Australia.

Stanley Gibbons (Australia) Pty. Ltd.***
Level 6, 36 Clarence Street, Sydney, New South Wales 2000, Australia.

Belgium and Luxembourg**
Davo c/o Philac, Rue du Midi 48, Bruxelles, 1000 Belgium.

Canada*
Lighthouse Publications (Canada) Ltd., 255 Duke Street, Montreal Quebec, Canada H3C 2M2.

Denmark**
Samlerforum/Davo, Ostergade 3, DK 7470 Karup, Denmark.

Finland**
Davo c/o Kapylan Merkkiky Pohjolankatu 1 00610 Helsinki, Finland.

France*
Davo France (Casteilla), 10, Rue Leon Foucault, 78184 St. Quentin Yvelines Cesex, France.

Hong Kong**
Po-on Stamp Service, GPO Box 2498, Hong Kong.

Israel**
Capital Stamps, P.O. Box 3769, Jerusalem 91036, Israel.

Italy*
Ernesto Marini Srl, Via Struppa 300, I-16165, Genova GE, Italy.

Japan**
Japan Philatelic Co. Ltd., P.O. Box 2, Suginami-Minami, Tokyo, Japan.

Netherlands*
Davo Publications, P.O. Box 411, 7400 AK Deventer, Netherlands.

New Zealand***
Mowbray Collectables. P.O. Box 80, Wellington, New Zealand.

Norway**
Davo Norge A/S, P.O. Box 738 Sentrum, N-0105, Oslo, Norway.

Singapore**
Stamp Inc Collectibles Pte Ltd., 10 Ubi Cresent, #01-43 Ubi Tech Park, Singapore 408564.

Sweden*
Chr Winther Soerensen AB, Box 43, S-310 Knaered, Sweden.

Switzerland**
Phila Service, Burgstrasse 160, CH 4125, Riehen, Switzerland.

Abbreviations

Anniv.	denotes	Anniversary
Assn.	,,	Association
Bis.	,,	Bistre
Bl.	,,	Blue
Bldg.	,,	Building
Blk.	,,	Black
Br.	,,	British or Bridge
Brn.	,,	Brown
B.W.I.	,,	British West Indies
C.A.R.I.F.T.A.	,,	Caribbean Free Trade Area
Cent.	,,	Centenary
Chest.	,,	Chestnut
Choc.	,,	Chocolate
Clar.	,,	Claret
Coll.	,,	College
Commem.	,,	Commemoration
Conf.	,,	Conference
Diag.	,,	Diagonally
E.C.A.F.E.	,,	Economic Commission for Asia and Far East
Emer.	,,	Emerald
E.P.T. Conference	,,	European Postal and Telecommunications Conference
Exn.		Exhibition
F.A.O.	,,	Food and Agriculture Organization
Fig.	,,	Figure
G.A.T.T.	,,	General Agreement on Tariffs and Trade
G.B.	,,	Great Britain
Gen.	,,	General
Govt.	,,	Government
Grn.	,,	Green
Horiz.	,,	Horizontal
H.Q.	,,	Headquarters
Imperf.	,,	Imperforate
Inaug.	,,	Inauguration
Ind.	,,	Indigo
Inscr.	,,	Inscribed or inscription
Int.	,,	International
I.A.T.A.	,,	International Air Transport Association
I.C.A.O.	,,	International Civil Aviation Organization
I.C.Y.	,,	International Co-operation Year
I.G.Y.	,,	International Geophysical Year
I.L.O.	,,	International Labour Office (or later, Organization)
I.M.C.O.	,,	Inter-Governmental Maritime Consultative Organization
I.T.U.	,,	International Telecommunication Union
Is.	,,	Islands
Lav.	,,	Lavender
Mar.	,,	Maroon
mm.	,,	Millimetres
Mult.	,,	Multicoloured
Mve.	denotes	Mauve
Nat.	,,	National
N.A.T.O.	,,	North Atlantic Treaty Organization
O.D.E.C.A.	,,	Organization of Central American States
Ol.	,,	Olive
Optd.	,,	Overprinted
Orge. or oran.	,,	Orange
P.A.T.A.	,,	Pacific Area Travel Association
Perf.	,,	Perforated
Post.	,,	Postage
Pres.	,,	President
P.U.	,,	Postal Union
Pur.	,,	Purple
R.	,,	River
R.S.A.	,,	Republic of South Africa
Roul.	,,	Rouletted
Sep.	,,	Sepia
S.E.A.T.O.	,,	South East Asia Treaty Organization
Surch.	,,	Surcharged
T.	,,	Type
T.U.C.	,,	Trades Union Congress
Turq.	,,	Turquoise
Ultram.	,,	Ultramarine
U.N.E.S.C.O.	,,	United Nations Educational, Scientific Cultural Organization
U.N.I.C.E.F.	,,	United Nations Children's Fund
U.N.O.	,,	United Nations Organization
U.N.R.W.A.	,,	United Nations Relief and Works Agency for Palestine Refugees in the Near East
U.N.T.E.A.	,,	United Nations Temporary Executive Authority
U.N.R.R.A.	,,	United Nations Relief and Rehabilitation Administration
U.P.U.	,,	Universal Postal Union
Verm.	,,	Vermilion
Vert.	,,	Vertical
Vio.	,,	Violet
W.F.T.U.	,,	World Federation of Trade Unions
W.H.O.	,,	World Health Organization
Yell.	,,	Yellow

Arabic Numerals

As in the case of European figures, the details of the Arabic numerals vary in different stamp designs, but they should be readily recognised with the aid of this illustration:

٠	١	٢	٣	٤
0	1	2	3	4
٥	٦	٧	٨	٩
5	6	7	8	9

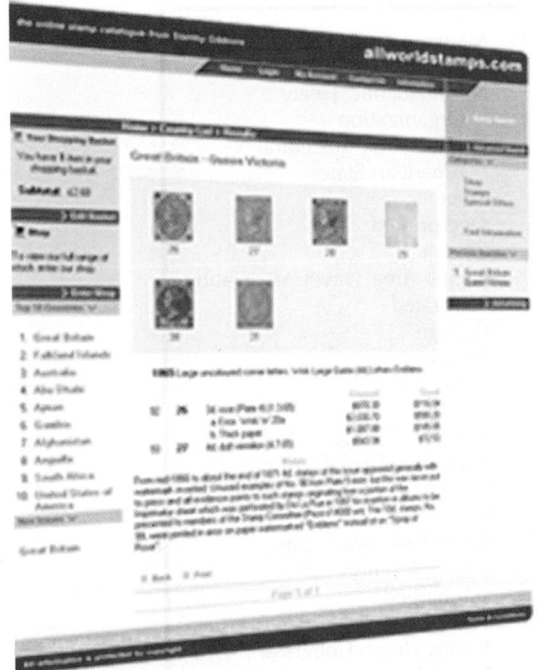

Stanley Gibbons Stamp Catalogue
Complete List of Parts

1 Commonwealth & British Empire Stamps 1840–1952 (Annual)

Foreign Countries

2 Austria & Hungary (6th edition, 2002)
Austria · U.N. (Vienna) · Hungary

3 Balkans (4th edition, 1998)
Albania · Bosnia & Herzegovina · Bulgaria · Croatia · Greece & Islands · Macedonia · Rumania · Slovenia · Yugoslavia

4 Benelux (5th edition, 2003)
Belgium & Colonies · Luxembourg · Netherlands & Colonies

5 Czechoslovakia & Poland (6th edition, 2002)
Czechoslovakia · Czech Republic · Slovakia · Poland

6 France (5th edition, 2001)
France · Colonies · Post Offices · Andorra · Monaco

7 Germany (6th edition, 2002)
Germany · States · Colonies · Post Offices

8 Italy & Switzerland (6th edition, 2003)
Italy & Colonies · Liechtenstein · San Marino · Switzerland · U.N. (Geneva) · Vatican City

9 Portugal & Spain (4th edition, 1996)
Andorra · Portugal & Colonies · Spain & Colonies

10 Russia (5th edition, 1999)
Russia · Armenia · Azerbaijan · Belarus · Estonia · Georgia · Kazakhstan · Kyrgyzstan · Latvia · Lithuania · Moldova · Tajikistan · Turkmenistan · Ukraine · Uzbekistan · Mongolia

11 Scandinavia (5th edition, 2001)
Aland Islands · Denmark · Faroe Islands · Finland · Greenland · Iceland · Norway · Sweden

12 Africa since Independence A-E (2nd edition, 1983)
Algeria · Angola · Benin · Burundi · Cameroun · Cape Verdi · Central African Republic · Chad · Comoro Islands · Congo · Djibouti · Equatorial Guinea · Ethiopia

13 Africa since Independence F-M (1st edition, 1981)
Gabon · Guinea · Guinea-Bissau · Ivory Coast · Liberia · Libya · Malagasy Republic · Mali · Mauritania · Morocco · Mozambique

14 Africa since Independence N-Z (1st edition, 1981)
Niger Republic · Rwanda · St. Thomas & Prince · Senegal · Somalia · Sudan · Togo · Tunisia · Upper Volta · Zaire

15 Central America (2nd edition, 1984)
Costa Rica · Cuba · Dominican Republic · El Salvador · Guatemala · Haiti · Honduras · Mexico · Nicaragua · Panama

16 Central Asia (3rd edition, 1992)
Afghanistan · Iran · Turkey

17 China (6th edition,1998)
China · Taiwan · Tibet · Foreign P.O.s · Hong Kong · Macao

18 Japan & Korea (4th edition, 1997)
Japan · Korean Empire · South Korea · North Korea

19 Middle East (5th edition, 1996)
Bahrain · Egypt · Iraq · Israel · Jordan · Kuwait · Lebanon · Oman · Qatar · Saudi Arabia · Syria · U.A.E. · Yemen

20 South America (3rd edition, 1989)
Argentina · Bolivia · Brazil · Chile · Colombia · Ecuador · Paraguay · Peru · Surinam · Uruguay · Venezuela

21 South-East Asia (3rd edition, 1995)
Bhutan · Burma · Indonesia · Kampuchea · Laos · Nepal · Philippines · Thailand · Vietnam

22 United States (5th edition, 2000)
U.S. & Possessions · Marshall Islands · Micronesia · Palau · U.N. (New York, Geneva, Vienna)

Thematic Catalogues

Stanley Gibbons Catalogues for use with **Stamps of the World.**
Collect Aircraft on Stamps (out of print)
Collect Birds on Stamps (5th edition, 2003)
Collect Chess on Stamps (2nd edition, 1999)
Collect Fish on Stamps (1st edition, 1999)
Collect Fungi on Stamps (2nd edition, 1997)
Collect Motor Vehicles on Stamps (in preparation)
Collect Railways on Stamps (3rd edition, 1999)
Collect Shells on Stamps (1st edition, 1995)
Collect Ships on Stamps (3rd edition, 2001)

Key-Types

(see note on page vii)

French Group

A. "Blanc."

B. "Mouchon."

C "Merson."

D. "Tablet."

E.

F.

G.

H.

"International Colonial Exhibition."

I. "Faidherbe."

J. "Palms."

K. "Balay."

L. "Natives."

M. "Figure."

German Group

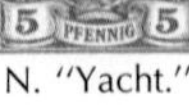
N. "Yacht."

O. "Yacht."

Spanish Group

X. "Alfonso XII."

Y. "Baby."

Z. "Curly Head"

Portuguese Group

P. "Crown."

Q. "Embossed."

R. "Figures."

S. "Carlos."

T. "Manoel."

U. "Ceres."

V. "Newspaper."

W. "Due."

STANLEY GIBBONS SIMPLIFIED CATALOGUE OF STAMPS OF THE WORLD—VOLUME 3 COUNTRIES K–R

KAMPUCHEA Pt. 21

Following the fall of the Khmer Rouge government, which had terminated the Khmer Republic, the People's Republic of Kampuchea was proclaimed on 10 January 1979.
Kampuchea was renamed Cambodia in 1989.

100 cents = 1 riel.

105 Soldiers with Flag and Independence Monument, Phnom Penh

106 Moscow Kremlin and Globe

1980. Multicoloured. Without gum.

402	0.1r. Type **105**	1·90	1·90
403	0.2r. Khmer people and flag	3·75	3·75
404	0.5r. Fisherman pulling in nets	5·00	5·00
405	1r. Armed forces and Kampuchean flag	8·25	8·25

1982. 60th Anniv of U.S.S.R. Multicoloured.

406	50c. Type **106**	15	10
407	1r. Industrial complex and map of U.S.S.R.	30	10

107 Arms of Kampuchea

1983. 4th Anniv of People's Republic of Kampuchea. Multicoloured.

408	50c. Type **107**	25	10
409	1r. Open book illustrating national flag and arms (horiz)	50	15
410	3r. Stylized figures and map	1·40	40

108 Runner with Olympic Torch

109 Orange Tiger

1983. Olympic Games, Los Angeles (1984) (1st issue). Multicoloured.

412	20c. Type **108**	10	10
413	50c. Javelin throwing	15	10
414	80c. Pole vaulting	20	10
415	1r. Discus throwing	35	15
416	1r.50 Relay (horiz)	50	20
417	2r. Swimming (horiz)	85	30
418	3r. Basketball	1·25	45

See also Nos. 526/32.

1983. Butterflies. Multicoloured.

420	20c. Type **109**	15	10
421	50c. "Euploea althaea"	20	15
422	80c. "Byasa polyeuctes" (horiz)	40	20
423	1r. "Stichophthalma howqua" (horiz)	70	25
424	1r.50 Leaf butterfly	1·25	45
425	2r. Blue argus	1·75	60
426	3r. Lemon migrant	2·75	80

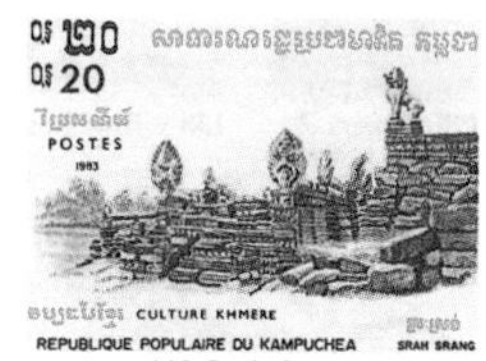
110 Srah Srang

1983. Khmer Culture. Multicoloured.

427	20c. Type **110**	10	10
428	50c. Bakong	15	10
429	80c. Ta Som (vert)	25	10
430	1r. North gate, Angkor Thom (vert)	40	15
431	1r.50 Kennora (winged figures) (vert)	70	25
432	2r. Apsara (carved figures), Angkor (vert)	75	25
433	3r. Banteai Srei (goddess), Tevoda (vert)	1·25	40

111 Dancers with Castanets

1983. Folklore. Multicoloured.

434	50c. Type **111**	25	10
435	1r. Dancers with grass headdresses	55	20
436	3r. Dancers with scarves	1·25	40

112 Detail of Fresco

1983. 500th Birth Anniv of Raphael (artist).

438	**112**	20c. multicoloured	10	10
439	–	50c. multicoloured	15	10
440	–	80c. multicoloured	25	10
441	–	1r. multicoloured	50	15
442	–	1r.50 multicoloured	85	25
443	–	2r. multicoloured	1·10	25
444	–	3r. multicoloured	1·40	40

DESIGNS: Nos. 439/44, different details of frescoes by Raphael.

113 Montgolfier Balloon

1983. Bicentenary of Manned Flight. Mult.

446	20c. Type **113**	10	15
447	30c. "La Ville d'Orleans", 1870	20	10
448	50c. Charles's hydrogen balloon	30	15
449	1r. Blanchard and Jeffries crossing Channel, 1785	50	20
450	1r.50 Salomon Andree's balloon flight over Arctic	85	35
451	2r. Auguste Piccard's stratosphere balloon "F.N.R.S."	90	40
452	3r. Hot-air balloon race	1·50	50

114 Cobra

116 Sunflower

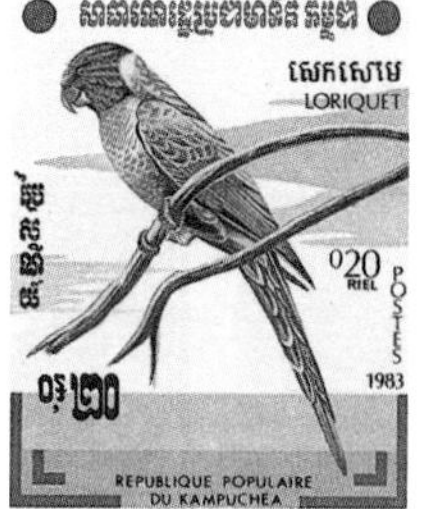
115 Rainbow Lory

1983. Reptiles. Multicoloured.

454	20c. Crested lizard (horiz)	15	10
455	30c. Type **114**	20	10
456	80c. Trionyx turtle (horiz)	25	10
457	1r. Chameleon	45	15
458	1r.50 Boa constrictor	75	25
459	2r. Crocodile (horiz)	90	25
460	3r. Turtle (horiz)	1·40	40

1983. Birds. Multicoloured.

461	20c. Type **115**	20	10
462	50c. Barn swallow	30	10
463	80c. Golden eagle (horiz)	50	15
464	1r. Griffon vulture (horiz)	85	25
465	1r.50 Javanese collared dove (horiz)	1·25	40
466	2r. Black-billed magpie	1·60	55
467	3r. Great Indian hornbill	2·50	95

1983. Flowers. Multicoloured.

468	20c. Type **116**	10	10
469	50c. "Caprifoliaceae"	15	10
470	80c. "Bougainvillea"	25	10
471	1r. "Ranunculaceae"	40	15
472	1r.50 "Nyctagynaeceae"	75	25
473	2r. Cockscomb	90	25
474	3r. Roses	1·40	40

117 Luge

1983. Winter Olympic Games, Sarajevo (1984) (1st issue). Multicoloured.

475	1r. Type **117**	40	15
476	2r. Biathlon	90	25
477	4r. Ski-jumping	1·75	50
478	5r. Two-man bobsleigh	1·90	60
479	7r. Ice hockey	2·75	85

See also Nos. 496/502.

118 Cyprinid

1983. Fishes. Multicoloured.

481	20c. Type **118**	20	10
482	50c. Loach	30	10
483	80c. Bubblebee catfish	35	10
484	1r. Spiny eel	80	15
485	1r.50 Cyprinid (different)	1·25	30
486	2r. Cyprinid (different)	1·50	30
487	3r. Aberrant fish	2·25	60

119 Factory and Gearwheel

1983. Festival of Rebirth. Multicoloured.

488	50c. Type **119**	20	10
489	1r. Tractor and cow (horiz)	35	15
490	3r. Bulk carrier, diesel locomotive, car and bridge	2·75	60

120 Red Cross and Sailing Ship

1984. 5th Anniv of Liberation. Multicoloured.

492	50c. Type **120**	20	10
493	1r. Three soldiers, flags and temple	35	15
494	3r. Crowd surrounding temple	1·00	35

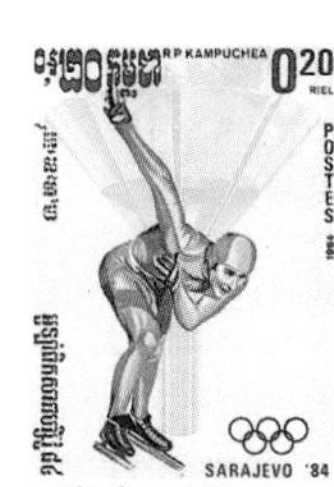
121 Speed Skating

122 Ilyushin Il-62M Jet over Angkor Vat

1984. Winter Olympic Games, Sarajevo (2nd issue). Multicoloured.

496	20c. Type **121**	10	10
497	50c. Ice hockey	15	10
498	80c. Skiing	20	10
499	1r. Ski jumping	50	15
500	1r.50 Skiing (different)	75	25
501	2r. Cross-country skiing	90	25
502	3r. Ice skating (pairs)	1·25	40

1984. Air.

504	**122**	5r. multicoloured	2·50	75
505		10r. multicoloured	4·75	1·50
506		15r. multicoloured	7·25	2·25
507		25r. multicoloured	12·25	3·75

For design as Type **122** but inscribed "R.P. DU KAMPUCHEA", see Nos. 695/8.

123 Cattle Egret

124 Doves and Globe

1984. Birds. Multicoloured.

508	10c. Type **123**	15	10
509	40c. Black-headed shrike	40	15
510	80c. Slaty-headed parakeet	75	20
511	1r. Golden-fronted leafbird	1·25	20
512	1r.20 Red-winged crested cuckoo	1·40	30
513	2r. Grey wagtail	2·25	75
514	2r.50 Forest wagtail	2·75	85

1984. International Peace in South-East Asia Forum, Phnom Penh. Mult, background colour given.

515 **124**	50c. green	20	10
516	1r. blue	40	15
517	3r. violet	1·25	35

125 "Luna 2"

1984. Space Research. Multicoloured.

518	10c. "Luna 1"	10	10
519	40c. Type **125**	15	10
520	80c. "Luna 3"	25	10
521	1r. "Soyuz 6" and cosmonauts (vert)	40	15
522	1r.20 "Soyuz 7" and cosmonauts (vert)	65	20
523	2r. "Soyuz 8" and cosmonauts (vert)	75	25
524	2r.50 Book, rocket and S. P. Korolev (Russian spaceship designer) (vert)	1·25	40

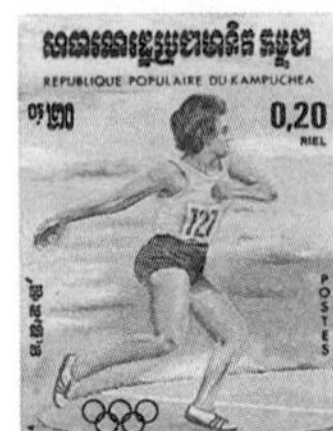

126 Throwing the Discus

1984. Olympic Games, Los Angeles (2nd issue). Multicoloured.

526	20c. Type **126**	10	10
527	50c. Long jumping	15	10
528	80c. Hurdling	25	10
529	1r. Relay	50	15
530	1r.50 Pole vaulting	75	25
531	2r. Throwing the javelin	90	25
532	3r. High jumping	1·25	40

128 Coyote

1984. Dog Family. Multicoloured.

535	10c. Type **128**	10	10
536	40c. Dingo	15	10
537	80c. Hunting dog	25	10
538	1r. Golden jackal	45	15
539	1r.20 Red fox	75	20
540	2r. Maned wolf (vert)	1·25	25
541	2r.50 Wolf	1·75	40

129 Class BB 1002 Diesel Locomotive, 1966, France

1984. Railway Locomotives. Multicoloured.

542	10c. Type **129**	10	10
543	40c. Class BB 1052 diesel locomotive, 1966, France	15	10
544	80c. Franco-Belgian-built steam locomotive, 1945, France	25	15
545	1r. Steam locomotive No. 231-505, 1929, France	50	20
546	1r.20 Class 803 diesel railcar, 1968, Germany	90	25
547	2r. Class BDE-405 diesel locomotive, 1957, France	1·40	40
548	2r.50 Class DS-01 diesel railcar, 1925, France	2·00	50

130 Magnolia

1984. Flowers. Multicoloured.

549	10c. Type **130**	10	10
550	40c. "Plumeria"		
551	80c. "Himenoballis" sp.	25	15
552	1r. "Peltophorum roxburghii"	45	20
553	1r.20 "Couroupita guianensis"	70	25
554	2r. "Lagerstroemia" sp.	1·10	30
555	2r.50 "Thevetia perubiana"	1·75	50

131 Mercedes Benz

1984. Cars. Multicoloured.

556	20c. Type **131**	10	10
557	50c. Bugatti	15	10
558	80c. Alfa Romeo	35	15
559	1r. Franklin	50	20
560	1r.50 Hispano-Suiza	85	25
561	2r. Rolls Royce	1·25	30
562	3r. Tatra	1·50	50

132 Sra Lai (Rattle) **133** Gazelle

1984. Musical Instruments. Multicoloured.

564	10c. Type **132**	10	10
565	40c. Skor drum (horiz)	15	10
566	80c. Skor drums (different)	35	15
567	1r. Thro khmer (stringed instrument) (horiz)	40	20
568	1r.20 Raneat ek (xylophone) (horiz)	70	25
569	2r. Raneat kong (bells) (horiz)	75	30
570	2r.50 Thro khe (stringed instrument) (horiz)	1·25	50

1984. Mammals. Multicoloured.

571	10c. Type **133**	10	10
572	40c. Roe deer	15	10
573	80c. Hare (horiz)	25	15
574	1r. Red deer	50	20
575	1r.20 Indian elephant	75	30
576	2r. Genet (horiz)	90	40
577	2r.50 Kouprey (horiz)	1·25	60

134 "Madonna and Child"

1984. 450th Death Anniv of Correggio (artist). Multicoloured.

578	20c. Type **134**	10	10
579	50c. Detail showing man striking monk	15	10
580	80c. "Madonna and Child" (different)	25	15
581	1r. "Madonna and Child" (different)	40	20
582	1r.50 "Mystical Marriage of St. Catherine"	70	30
583	2r. "Pieta"	75	40
584	3r. Detail showing man descending ladder	1·25	60

135 Bullock Cart

1985. National Festival (6th Anniv of People's Republic). Multicoloured.

586	50c. Type **135**	40	10
587	1r. Horse-drawn passenger cart	65	25
588	3r. Elephants	1·60	50

136 Footballers **138** Glistening Ink Cap

137 Eska-Mofa Motor Cycle, 1939

1985. World Cup Football Championship, Mexico (1986) (1st issue). Designs showing footballers.

590 **136**	20c. multicoloured	10	10
591 –	50c. multicoloured	25	10
592 –	80c. multicoloured	45	15
593 –	1r. multicoloured (horiz)	55	25
594 –	1r.50 mult (horiz)	80	35
595 –	2r. multicoloured	1·00	45
596 –	3r. multicoloured	1·60	70

See also Nos. 680/6.

1985. Centenary of Motor Cycle. Multicoloured.

598	20c. Type **137**	10	10
599	50c. Wanderer, 1939	25	10
600	80c. Premier, 1929	45	15
601	1r. Ardie, 1939	55	25
602	1r.50 Jawa, 1932	80	35
603	2r. Simson, 1983	1·00	45
604	3r. "CZ 125", 1984	1·60	70

1985. Fungi. Multicoloured.

606	20c. "Gymnophilus spectabilis" (horiz)	15	10
607	50c. Type **138**	40	15
608	80c. Panther cap	70	20
609	1r. Fairy cake mushroom	90	35
610	1r.50 Fly agaric	1·40	45
611	2r. Shaggy ink cap	1·60	60
612	3r. Caesar's mushroom	2·75	95

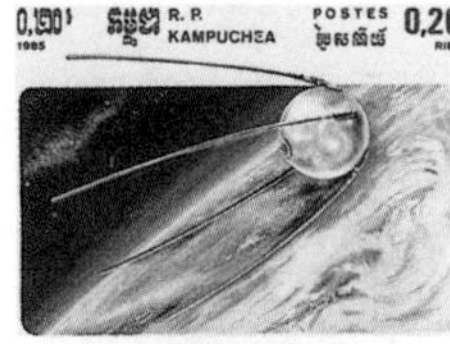

139 "Sputnik 1"

1985. Space Exploration. Multicoloured.

613	20c. Type **139**	10	10
614	50c. "Soyuz" rocket on transporter and Yuri Gagarin (first man in space)	40	10
615	80c. "Vostok 6" and Valentina Tereshkova (first woman in space)	45	15
616	1r. Space walker	55	25
617	1r.50 "Salyut"–"Soyuz" link	80	35
618	2r. "Lunokhod 1" (lunar vehicle)	1·00	45
619	3r. "Venera" (Venus probe)	1·60	70

140 Absara Dancer **140a** Captured Nazi Standards, Red Square, Moscow

1985. Traditional Dances. Multicoloured.

621	50c. Absara group (horiz)	35	10
622	1r. Tepmonorom dance (horiz)	70	25
623	3r. Type **140**	1·75	75

1985. 40th Anniv of End of Second World War. Multicoloured.

623a	50c. Rejoicing soldiers in Berlin	30	10
623b	1r. Type **140a**	55	25
623c	3r. Tank battle	1·75	75

141 Tortoiseshell Cat **142** "Black Dragon" Lily

1985. Domestic Cats. Multicoloured.

624	20c. Type **141**	10	10
625	50c. Tortoiseshell (different)	25	10
626	80c. Tabby	45	15
627	1r. Long-haired Siamese	60	25
628	1t.50 Sealpoint Siamese	1·00	35
629	2r. Grey cat	1·25	45
630	3r. Black cat	2·00	70

1985. Flowers. Multicoloured.

631	20c. Type **142**	10	10
632	50c. "Iris delavayi"	25	10
633	80c. "Crocus aureus"	45	15
634	1r. "Cyclamen persicum"	60	25
635	1r.50 Fairy primrose	90	35
636	2r. Pansy "Ullswater"	1·10	45
637	3r. "Crocus purpureus grandiflorus"	1·75	70

143 "Per Italiani" (Antoine Watteau) **144** Lenin and Arms

1985. International Music Year. Multicoloured.

638	20c. Type **143**	10	10
639	50c. "St. Cecilia" (Carlos Saraceni)	25	10
640	80c. "Still Life with Violin" (Jean Baptiste Oudry) (horiz)	45	15
641	1r. "Three Musicians" (Fernand Leger)	55	25
642	1r.50 Orchestra	80	35
643	2r. "St. Cecilia" (Bartholomeo Schedoni)	1·00	45
644	3r. "Harlequin with Violin" (Christian Caillard)	1·60	70

1985. 115th Birth Anniv of Lenin. Multicoloured.

646	1r. Type **144**	60	25
647	3r. Lenin on balcony and map	1·60	70

145 Saffron-cowled Blackbird

1985. "Argentina '85" International Stamp Exhibition, Buenos Aires. Birds. Multicoloured.

648	20c. Type **145**	10	10
649	50c. Saffron finch (vert)	25	15
650	80c. Blue and yellow tanager (vert)	45	25
651	1r. Scarlet-headed blackbird	65	30
652	1r.50 Amazon kingfisher (vert)	1·25	40
653	2r. Toco toucan (vert)	1·75	50
654	3r. Rufous-bellied thrush	2·40	80

146 River Launch, Cambodia, 1942

1985. Water Craft. Multicoloured.

655	10c. Type **146**	15	10
656	40c. River launch, Cambodia, 1948	25	15
657	80c. Tug, Japan, 1913	45	20
658	1r. Dredger, Holland	65	25
659	1r.20 Tug, U.S.A.	1·10	35
660	2r. River freighter	1·50	45
661	2r.50 River tanker, Panama	2·00	70

147 "The Flood" (Michelangelo) **148** Son Ngoc Minh

1985. "Italia '85" International Stamp Exhibition, Rome. Paintings. Multicoloured.

662 20r. Type **147** 10 10
663 50r. "The Virgin of St. Marguerite" (Mazzola) 25 10
664 80r. "The Martyrdom of St. Peter" (Zampieri Domenichino) 45 15
665 1r. "Allegory of Spring" (detail) (Sandro Botticelli) 55 25
666 1r.50 "The Sacrifice of Abraham" (Caliari) 80 35
667 2r. "The Meeting of Joachim and Anne" (Giotto) 1·00 45
668 3r. "Bacchus" (Michel Angelo Carravaggio) 1·60 70

1985. Festival of Rebirth.

670 **148** 50c. multicoloured 15 10
671 1r. multicoloured 40 15
672 3r. multicoloured 1·10 45

149 Tiger Barbs

1985. Fishes. Multicoloured.

673 20c. Type **149** 15 10
674 50c. Giant snakehead 40 15
675 80c. Veil-tailed goldfish 75 20
676 1r. Pearl gourami 90 35
677 1r.50 Six-banded tiger barbs 1·25 45
678 2r. Siamese fighting fish 1·60 60
679 3r. Siamese tigerfish 2·75 90

150 Footballers **152** "Mir" Space Station and Spacecraft

151 Cob

1986. World Cup Football Championship, Mexico (2nd issue).

680 **150** 20c. multicoloured 10 10
681 – 50c. multicoloured 25 10
682 – 80c. multicoloured 45 15
683 – 1r. multicoloured 55 25
684 – 1r.50 multicoloured 80 35
685 – 2r. multicoloured 1·00 45
686 – 3r. multicoloured 1·60 70

DESIGNS: 50c. to 3r. Various footballing scenes.

1986. Horses. Multicoloured.

688 20c. Type **151** 10 10
689 50c. Arab 25 10
690 80c. Australian pony 45 15
691 1r. Appaloosa 55 25
692 1r.50 Quarter horse 80 35
693 2r. Vladimir heavy draught horse 1·00 45
694 3r. Andalusian 1·60 70

1986. 27th Russian Communist Party Congress. Multicoloured.

694a 50c. Type **152** 25 10
694b 1r. Lenin 55 25
694c 5r. Statue and launch of space rocket 2·50 1·00

1986. Air. As Nos. 504/7 but inscr "R.P. DU KAMPUCHEA".

695 **122** 5r. multicoloured 2·75 95
696 10r. multicoloured 5·75 1·60
697 15r. multicoloured 8·50 2·50
698 25r. multicoloured 15·00 4·25

153 Edaphosaurus (⅔-size illustration)

1986. Prehistoric Animals. Multicoloured.

699 20c. Type **153** 10 10
700 50c. Sauroctonus 25 10
701 80c. Mastodonsaurus 45 15
702 1r. Rhamphorhynchus (vert) 60 25
703 1r.50 "Brachiosaurus brancai" (vert) 90 35
704 2r. "Tarbosaurus bataar" (vert) 1·10 45
705 3r. Indricotherium (vert) 1·75 70

154 "Luna 16"

1986. 25th Anniv of First Man in Space. Multicoloured.

706 10c. Type **154** 10 10
707 40c. "Luna 3" 25 10
708 80c. "Vostok" 45 15
709 1r. Cosmonaut Leonov on space walk 55 25
710 1r.20 "Apollo" and "Soyuz" preparing to dock 80 35
711 2r. "Soyuz" docking with "Salyut" space station 1·00 45
712 2r.50 Yuri Gagarin (first man in space) and spacecraft 1·60 75

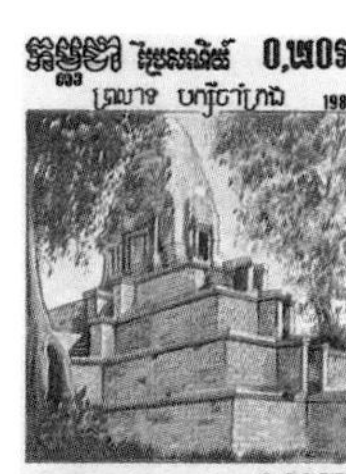

155 Baksei Chmkrong Temple, 920

1986. Khmer Culture. Multicoloured.

713 20c. Type **155** 10 10
714 50c. Buddha's head 25 10
715 80c. Prea Vihear monastery, Dangrek 45 15
716 1r. Fan with design of man and woman 55 25
717 1r.50 Fan with design of men fighting 80 35
718 2r. Fan with design of dancer 1·00 45
719 3r. Fan with design of dragon-drawn chariot 1·60 70

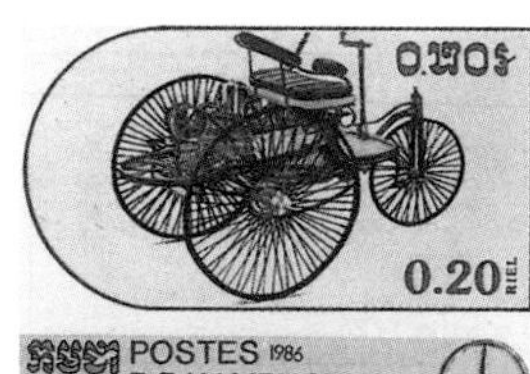

156 Tricar, 1885

1986. Centenary (1985) of Motor Car. Mercedes Benz Models. Multicoloured.

720 20c. Type **156** 10 10
721 50c. Limousine, 1935 25 10
722 80c. Open tourer, 1907 45 15
723 1r. Light touring car, 1920 55 25
724 1r.50 Cabriolet, 1932 80 35
725 2r. "SKK" tourer, 1938 1·00 45
726 3r. "190", 1985 1·60 70

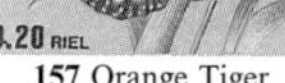

157 Orange Tiger **159** Solar System, Copernicus, Galileo and Tycho Brahe (astronomers)

158 English Kogge of Richard II's Reign

1986. Butterflies. Multicoloured.

727 20c. Type **157** 15 10
728 50c. Five-bar swallowtail 35 15
729 80c. Chequered swallowtail 65 20
730 1r. Chestnut tiger 75 35
731 1r.50 "Idea blanchardi" 1·10 45
732 2r. Common mormon 1·40 60
733 3r. "Dabasa payeni" 2·25 95

1986. Medieval Ships.

734 20c. Type **158** 10 10
735 50c. Kogge 25 10
736 80c. Knarr 45 15
737 1r. Galley 55 25
738 1r.50 Norman ship 80 35
739 2r. Mediterranean usciere 1·10 45
740 3r. French kogge 1·75 70

1986. Appearance of Halley's Comet. Multicoloured.

741 10c. Type **159** 10 10
742 20c. "Nativity" (Giotto) and comet from Bayeux Tapestry 10 10
743 50c. Comet, 1910, and Mt. Palomar observatory, U.S.A. 25 10
744 80c. Edmond Halley and "Planet A" space probe 45 15
745 1r.20 Diagram of comet's trajectory and "Giotto" space probe 60 25
746 1r.50 "Vega" space probe and camera 80 35
747 2r. Thermal pictures of comet 1·00 45

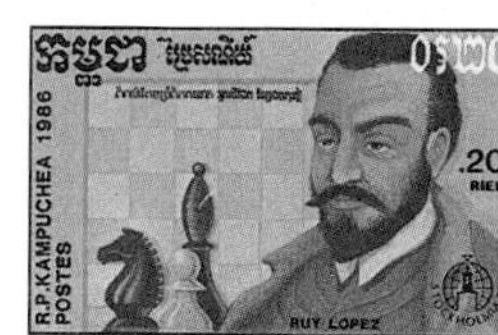

160 Ruy Lopez

1986. "Stockholmia 86" International Stamp Exhibition. Chess. Multicoloured.

749 20c. Type **160** 10 10
750 50c. Francois-Andre Philidor 25 10
751 80c. Karl Anderssen and Houses of Parliament, London 45 15
752 1r. Wilhelm Steinitz and Charles Bridge, Prague 60 25
753 1r.50 Emanuel Lasker and medieval knight 90 35
754 2r. Jose Raul Capablanca and Morro Castle, Cuba 1·10 45
755 3r. Aleksandr Alekhine 1·75 70

161 "Parodia maassii" **162** Bananas

1986. Cacti. Multicoloured.

757 20c. Type **161** 10 10
758 50c. "Rebutia marsoneri" 25 10
759 80c. "Melocactus evae" 45 15
760 1r. "Gymnocalycium valnicekianum" 55 25
761 1r.50 "Discocactus silichromus" 80 35
762 2r. "Neochilenia simulans" 1·00 45
763 3r. "Weingartia chiquichuquensis" 1·60 70

1986. Fruit. Multicoloured.

764 10c. Type **162** 10 10
765 40c. Papaya 20 10
766 80c. Mangoes 45 15
767 1r. Breadfruit 55 35
768 1r.20 Lychees 60 25
769 2r. Pineapple 1·00 45
770 2r.50 Grapefruit (horiz) 1·40 55

163 Concorde (⅔-size illustration)

1986. Aircraft. Multicoloured.

771 20c. Type **163** (wrongly inscr "Concord") 10 10
772 50c. Douglas DC-10 25 10
773 80c. Boeing 747SP 45 15
774 1r. Ilyushin Il-62M 55 25
775 1r.50 Ilyushin Il-86 80 35
776 2r. Antonov An-24 (wrongly inscr "AN-124") 1·10 45
777 3r. Airbus Industrie A300 1·75 70

164 Elephant and Silver Containers on Tray

1986. Festival of Rebirth. Silverware. Mult.

778 50c. Type **164** 25 10
779 1r. Tureen 55 20
780 3r. Dish on stand 1·60 45

165 Kouprey

1986. Endangered Animals. Cattle. Mult.

781 20c. Type **165** 10 10
782 20c. Gaur 10 10
783 80c. Bateng cow and calf 45 15
784 1r.50 Asiatic water buffalo 90 30

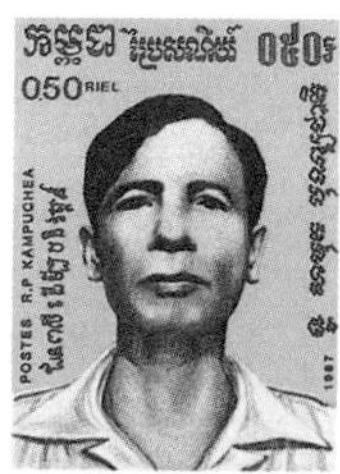

166 Tou Samuth (revolutionary)

1987. National Festival. 8th Anniv of People's Republic.

785 **166** 50c. multicoloured 20 10
786 1r. multicoloured 40 15
787 3r. multicoloured 1·10 35

167 Biathlon

1987. Winter Olympic Games, Calgary (1988) (1st issue). Multicoloured.

788 20c. Type **167** 10 10
789 50c. Figure skating 25 10
790 80c. Speed skating 45 15
791 1r. Ice hockey 55 25
792 1r.50 Two-man luge 80 35
793 2r. Two-man bobsleigh 1·00 45
794 3r. Cross-country skiing 1·60 70

See also Nos. 864/70.

168 Weightlifting

1987. Olympic Games, Seoul (1988) (1st issue). Designs showing ancient Greek and modern athletes. Multicoloured.

796 20c. Type **168** 10 10
797 50c. Archery (horiz) 25 10
798 80c. Fencing (horiz) 45 15
799 1r. Gymnastics 55 25
800 1r.50 Throwing the discus (horiz) 80 35
801 2r. Throwing the javelin . . . 1·00 45
802 3r. Hurdling . . . . 1·60 70

See also Nos. 875/81.

169 Papillon

1987. Dogs. Multicoloured.

804 20c. Type **169** 10 10
805 50c. Greyhound 25 10
806 80c. Great Dane 45 15
807 1r. Dobermann 55 25
808 1r.50 Samoyed 80 35
809 2r. Borzoi . . . . 1·00 45
810 3r. Rough collie . . . . . . 1·60 70

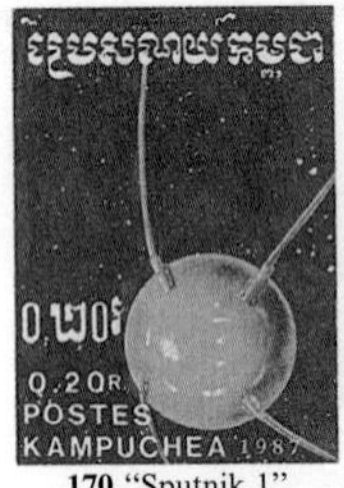

170 "Sputnik 1"

171 Flask

1987. Space Exploration. Multicoloured.

811 20c. Type **170** 10 10
812 50c. "Soyuz 10" 25 10
813 80c. "Proton" 45 15
814 1r. "Vostok 1" 55 25
815 1r.50 "Elektron 2" 80 35
816 2r. "Kosmos" . . . . 1·00 45
817 3r. "Luna 2" . . . . 1·60 70

1987. Metalwork. Multicoloured.

819 50c. Type **171** 20 10
820 1r. Repousse box (horiz) . . 50 25
821 1r.50 Teapot and cups on tray (horiz) 75 35
822 3r. Ornamental sword . . . 1·50 70

172 Carmine Bee Eater

1987. "Capex'87" International Stamp Exhibition, Toronto. Birds. Multicoloured.

823 20c. Type **172** 15 10
824 50c. Hoopoe (vert) 30 10
825 80c. South African crowned crane (vert) 50 10
826 1r. Barn owl (vert) 65 15
827 1r.50 Grey-headed kingfisher (vert) 85 20
828 2r. Red-whiskered bulbul . . 1·10 30
829 3r. Purple heron (vert) . . . 2·00 45

173 Horatio Phillip's "Multiplane" Model, 1893

1987. Experimental Aircraft Designs. Mult.

831 20c. Type **173** 10 10
832 50c. John Stringfellow's steam-powered model, 1848 25 10
833 80c. Thomas Moy's model "Aerial Steamer", 1875 . . 45 15
834 1r. Leonardo da Vinci's "ornithopter", 1490 . . . 55 25
835 1r.50 Sir George Cayley's "convertiplane", 1843 . . . 80 35
836 2r. Sir Hiram Maxim's "Flying Test Rig", 1894 . . 1·00 45
837 3r. William Henson's "Aerial Steam Carriage", 1842 . . 1·60 70

174 Giant Tortoise

1987. Reptiles. Multicoloured.

839 20c. Type **174** 10 10
840 50c. African spiny-tailed lizard 25 10
841 80c. Iguana 45 15
842 1r. Coast horned lizard . . . 55 25
843 1r.50 Northern chuckwalla 80 35
844 2r. Glass lizard . . . . . . 1·00 45
845 3r. Common garter snake . . 1·60 70

175 Kamov Ka-15

1987. "Hafnia 87" International Stamp Exhibition, Copenhagen. Helicopters. Multicoloured.

846 20c. Type **175** 10 10
847 50c. Kamov Ka-18 . . . . . 25 10
848 80c. Westland Lynx 45 15
849 1r. Sud Aviation Gazelle . . 55 25
850 1r.50 Sud Aviation SA 330E Puma 80 35
851 2r. Boeing-Vertol CH-47 Chinook . . . . 1·00 45
852 3r. Boeing UTTAS . . . . . 1·60 70

176 Revolutionaries

178 Earth Station Dish Aerial

177 Magirus-Deutz No. 21

1987. 70th Anniv of Russian October Revolution. Multicoloured.

853a 2r. Revolutionaries on street corner (horiz) 95 40
853b 3r. Type **176** . . . . 1·25 50
853c 5r. Lenin receiving ticker-tape message (horiz) . . . 2·50 1·00

1987. Fire Engines. Multicoloured.

854 20c. Type **177** 10 10
855 50c. "SIL-131" rescue vehicle 25 10
856 80c. "Cas-25" fire pump . . 45 15
857 1r. Sirmac Saab "424" . . . 60 25
858 1r.50 Rosenbaum-Falcon . . 85 35
859 2r. Tatra "815-PRZ" . . . . 1·10 45
860 3r. Chubbfire "C-44-20" . . 1·60 70

1987. Telecommunications. Multicoloured.

861 50c. Type **178** 10 10
862 1r. Technological building with radio microwave aerial (27 × 44 mm) . . . 55 25
863 3r. Intersputnik programme earth station (44 × 27 mm) 1·60 70

179 Speed Skating

1988. Winter Olympic Games, Calgary (2nd issue). Multicoloured.

864 20c. Type **179** 10 10
865 50c. Ice hockey 25 10
866 80c. Slalom 45 15
867 1r. Ski jumping 55 25
868 1r.50 Biathlon 80 35
869 2r. Ice dancing . . . . 1·00 45
870 3r. Cross-country skiing . . . 1·60 70

180 Irrigation Canal Bed

1988. Irrigation Projects. Multicoloured.

872 50c. Type **180** 10 10
873 1r. Dam construction 50 20
874 3r. Dam and bridge . . . . 1·50 65

181 Beam Exercise

1988. Olympic Games, Seoul (2nd issue). Women's Gymnastics. Multicoloured.

875 20c. Type **181** 10 10
876 50c. Bar exercise (horiz) . . . 25 10
877 80c. Ribbon exercise 45 15
878 1r. Hoop exercise 55 25
879 1r.50 Baton exercise 80 35
880 2r. Ball exercise (horiz) . . . 1·00 45
881 3r. Floor exercise (horiz) . . 1·60 70

182 Abyssinian

1988. "Juvalux 88" 9th Youth Philately Exhibition, Luxembourg. Cats. Multicoloured.

883 20c. White long-haired (horiz) 10 10
884 50c. Type **182** 25 10
885 80c. Ginger and white long-haired 45 15
886 1r. Tortoiseshell queen and kitten (horiz) 55 25
887 1r.50 Brown cat 80 35
888 2r. Black long-haired cat . . 1·00 45
889 3r. Grey cat . . . . 1·60 70

183 "Emerald Seas" (liner)

1988. "Essen 88" International Stamp Fair. Ships. Multicoloured.

891 20c. Type **183** 10 10
892 50c. Car ferry 20 10
893 80c. "Mutsu" (nuclear-powered freighter) 35 10
894 1r. "Kosmonavt Yury Gagarin" (research ship) 50 15
895 1r.50 Tanker 55 20
896 2r. Hydrofoil 75 30
897 3r. Hovercraft . . . . 1·25 35

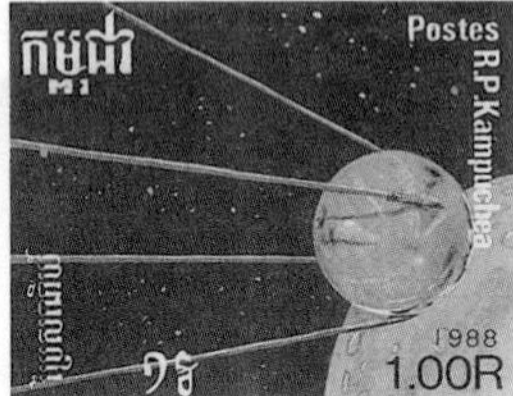

184 Satellite

1988. Space Exploration. Designs showing different satellites.

899 – 20c. multicoloured (vert) 10 10
900 – 50c. multicoloured (vert) 20 10
901 – 80c. multicoloured (vert) 35 10
902 **184** 1r. multicoloured 50 15
903 – 1r.50 multicoloured . . . 55 20
904 – 2r. multicoloured 75 30
905 – 3r. multicoloured . . . . 1·25 35

185 Swordtail

1988. "Finlandia 88" International Stamp Exhibition, Helsinki. Tropical Fish. Multicoloured.

907 20c. Type **185** 15 10
908 50c. Head-and-taillight tetra 30 10
909 80c. Paradise fish 55 15
910 1r. Black moor goldfish . . . 85 20
911 1r.50 Cardinal tetra 90 30
912 2r. Sword-tailed characin . . 1·25 45
913 3r. Sail-finned molly . . . . 2·10 60

186 Flowery Helicostyla

188 "Cattleya aclandiae"

187 Seven-spotted Ladybird

1988. Sea Shells. Multicoloured.

915 20c. Type **186** 10 10
916 50c. Changing helicostyla . . 20 10
917 80c. Shining helicostyla . . . 35 10
918 1r. Marinduque helicostyla 50 15
919 1r.50 Siren chlorena 55 20
920 2r. Miraculous helicostyla . . 75 30
921 3r. "Helicostyla limansauensis" . . . . . . 1·25 35

1988. Insects. Multicoloured.

922 20c. Type **187** 10 10
923 50c. "Zonabride geminata" (blister beetle) 20 10
924 80c. "Carabus auronitens" (ground beetle) 35 10
925 1r. Honey bee 50 15
926 1r.50 Praying mantis 55 20
927 2r. Dragonfly 75 30
928 3r. Soft-winged flower beetle 1·25 35

1988. Orchids. Multicoloured.

929 20c. Type **188** 10 10
930 50c. "Odontoglossum" "Royal Sovereign" . . . 20 10
931 80c. "Cattleya labiata" . . . 35 10
932 1r. Bee orchid 50 15
933 1r.50 "Laelia anceps" 55 20
934 2r. "Laelia pumila" 75 30
935 3r. "Stanhopea tigrina" (horiz) . . . . 1·25 35

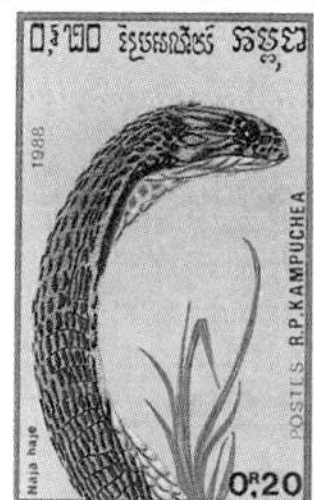
189 Egyptian Banded Cobra

190 Walking Dance

1988. Reptiles. Multicoloured.

936	20c. Type **189**	10	10
937	50c. Common iguana	20	10
938	80c. Long-nosed vine snake (horiz)	35	10
939	1r. Common box turtle (horiz)	50	15
940	1r.50 Iguana (horiz)	55	20
941	2r. Viper (horiz)	75	30
942	3r. Common cobra	1·25	35

1988. Festival of Rebirth. Khmer Culture. Multicoloured.

943	50c. Type **190**	20	10
944	1r. Peacock dance (horiz)	50	15
945	3r. Kantere dance (horiz)	1·25	35

191 Bridge

1989. Multicoloured.

946	50c. Type **191**	25	10
947	1r. More distant view of bridge	50	20
948	3r. Closer view of bridge	1·60	65

192 Cement Works

1989. National Festival. 10th Anniv of People's Republic of Kampuchea. Multicoloured.

949	3r. Bayon Earth Station (horiz)	20	10
950	12r. Electricity generating station 4 (horiz)	75	30
951	30r. Type **192**	2·10	85

193 Footballers

1989. World Cup Football Championship, Italy (1990).

952	**193** 2r. multicoloured	10	10
953	– 3r. multicoloured	20	10
954	– 5r. multicoloured	30	10
955	– 10r. multicoloured	65	25
956	– 15r. multicoloured	1·00	40
957	– 20r. multicoloured	1·25	50
958	– 35r. multicoloured	2·40	95

DESIGNS: 3r. to 35r. Various footballing scenes.

194 Tram

1989. Trams and Trains. Multicoloured.

960	2r. Type **194**	10	10
961	3r. ETR 401 Pendolino express train, 1976, Italy	20	10
962	5r. High speed train, Germany	35	15
963	10r. Theme park monorail train	80	25
964	15r. German Trans Europe Express (TEE) train	1·25	35
965	20r. "Hikari" express train, Sanyo Shinkansenline, Japan	1·50	50
966	35r. TGV express train, France	3·00	85

195 Fidel Castro

196 Scarlet Macaw

1989. 30th Anniv of Cuban Revolution.

968	**195** 12r. multicoloured	90	40

1989. Parrots. Multicoloured.

969	20c. Type **196**	10	10
970	80c. Sulphur-crested cockatoo	10	10
971	3r. Rose-ringed parakeet	25	15
972	6r. Blue and yellow macaw	50	20
973	10r. Brown-necked parrot	90	35
974	15r. Blue-fronted amazon	1·40	50
975	25r. White-capped parrot (horiz)	2·10	80

197 Skiing

1989. Winter Olympic Games, Albertville (1992). Multicoloured.

977	2r. Type **197**	10	10
978	3r. Biathlon	20	10
979	5r. Cross-country skiing	30	10
980	10r. Ski jumping	65	25
981	15r. Speed skating	1·00	40
982	20r. Ice hockey	1·25	50
983	35r. Two-man bobsleighing	2·40	95

198 "Nymphaea capensis" (pink)

1989. Water Lilies. Multicoloured.

985	20c. Type **198**	10	10
986	80c. "Nymphaea capensis" (mauve)	10	10
987	3r. "Nymphaea lotus dentata"	25	10
988	6r. "Dir. Geo. T. Moore"	50	15
989	10r. "Sunrise"	90	30
990	15r. "Escarboncle"	1·40	45
991	25r. "Cladstoniana"	2·10	70

199 Wrestling

1989. Olympic Games, Barcelona (1992). Multicoloured.

993	2r. Type **199**	10	10
994	3r. Gymnastics (vert)	20	10
995	5r. Putting the shot	30	10
996	10r. Running (vert)	65	25
997	15r. Fencing	1·00	40
998	20r. Canoeing (vert)	1·40	50
999	35r. Hurdling (vert)	2·40	95

200 Downy Boletus

1989. Fungi. Multicoloured.

1001	20c. Type **200**	10	10
1002	80c. Red-staining inocybe	10	10
1003	3r. Honey fungus	35	15
1004	6r. Field mushroom	70	25
1005	10r. Brown roll-rim	1·25	45
1006	15r. Shaggy ink cap	1·90	65
1007	25r. Parasol mushroom	3·00	1·00

201 Shire Horse

1989. Horses. Multicoloured.

1008	2r. Type **201**	10	10
1009	3r. Brabant	20	10
1010	5r. Bolounais	30	10
1011	10r. Breton	65	25
1012	15r. Vladimir heavy draught horse	1·00	40
1013	20r. Italian heavy draught horse	1·25	50
1014	35r. Freiberger	2·40	95

KATANGA Pt. 14

The following stamps were issued by Mr. Tshombe's Government for independent Katanga. In 1963 Katanga was reunited with the Central Government of Congo.

1960. Various stamps of Belgian Congo optd **KATANGA** and bar or surch also. (a) Masks issue of 1948.

1	1f.50 on 1f.25 mauve and blue	80	20
2	3f.50 on 2f.50 green and brown	80	25
3	20f. purple and red	2·75	85
4	50f. black and brown	6·50	3·00
5	100f. black and red	48·00	21·00

(b) Flowers issue of 1952. Flowers in natural colours; colours given are of backgrounds and inscriptions.

6	10c. yellow and purple	20	20
7	15c. green and red	20	20
8	20c. grey and green	35	25
9	25c. orange and green	35	25
10	40c. salmon and green	35	25
11	50c. turquoise and red	45	35
12	60c. purple and green	35	25
13	75c. grey and lake	45	35
14	1f. lemon and red	55	45
15	2f. buff and olive	65	55
16	3f. pink and green	90	65
17	4f. lavender and sepia	1·25	95
18	5f. green and purple	1·25	95
19	6f.50 lilac and red	1·25	85
20	7f. brown and green	1·75	1·25
21	8f. yellow and green	1·75	1·25
22	10f. olive and purple	28·00	17·00

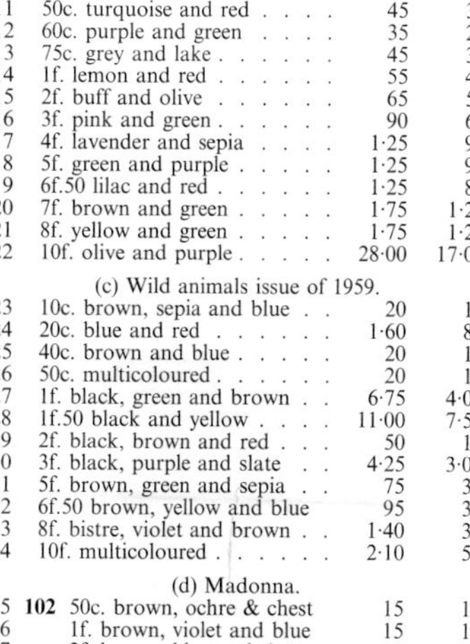

(c) Wild animals issue of 1959.

23	10c. brown, sepia and blue	20	10
24	20c. blue and red	1·60	80
25	40c. brown and blue	20	10
26	50c. multicoloured	20	10
27	1f. black, green and brown	6·75	4·00
28	1f.50 black and yellow	11·00	7·50
29	2f. black, brown and red	50	10
30	3f. black, purple and slate	4·25	3·00
31	5f. brown, green and sepia	75	30
32	6f.50 brown, yellow and blue	95	30
33	8f. bistre, violet and brown	1·40	35
34	10f. multicoloured	2·10	50

(d) Madonna.

35	**102** 50c. brown, ochre & chest	15	15
36	1f. brown, violet and blue	15	15
37	2f. brown, blue and slate	20	20

(e) African Technical Co-operation Commission. Inscr in French or Flemish.

38	**103** 3f. salmon and slate	7·00	7·00
39	3f.50 on 3f. salmon & slate	2·10	2·10

1960. Independence. Independence issue of Congo optd **11 JUILLET DE L'ETAT DU KATANGA**.

40	**106** 20c. bistre	10	10
41	50c. red	10	10
42	1f. green	10	10
43	1f.50 brown	10	10
44	2f. mauve	10	10
45	3f.50 violet	15	10
46	5f. blue	15	10
47	6f.50 black	15	10
48	10f. orange	25	20
49	20f. blue	45	30

5

1961. Katanga Art.

50	**5** 10c. green	10	10
51	20c. violet	10	10
52	50c. blue	10	10
53	1f.50 green	10	10
54	2f. brown	10	10
55	– 3f.50 blue	10	10
56	– 5f. turquoise	10	10
57	– 6f. brown	10	10
58	– 6f.50 blue	10	10
59	– 8f. purple	15	10
60	– 10f. brown	15	10
61	– 20f. myrtle	25	20
62	– 50f. brown	50	40
63	– 100f. turquoise	85	70

DESIGNS: 3f.50 to 8f. "Preparing food"; 10f. to 100f. "Family circle".

6 Pres. Tshombe

1961. 1st Anniv of Independence. Portrait in brown.

64	**6** 6f.50+5f. red, green & gold	1·25	1·00
65	8f.+5f. red, green and gold	1·25	1·00
66	10f.+5f. red, green and gold	1·25	1·00

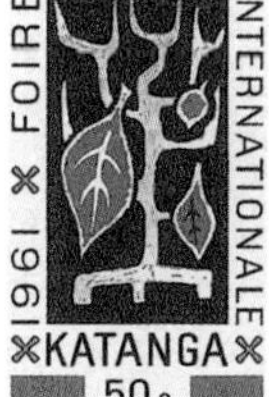
7 "Tree"

8 Early Aircraft, Steam Train and Safari

1961. Katanga International Fair. Vert symbolic designs as T **7**.

67	**7** 50c. red, green and black	10	10
68	– 1f. black and blue	10	10
69	– 2f.50 black and yellow	15	15
70	**7** 3f.50 red, brown and black	15	15
71	– 5f. black and violet	25	25
72	– 6f.50 black and yellow	30	30

1961. Air.

73	**8** 3f.50 multicoloured	3·00	3·25
74	– 6f.50 multicoloured	65	65
75	**8** 8f. multicoloured	3·00	3·25
76	– 10f. multicoloured	65	65

DESIGNS: 6f.50, 10f. Tail of Boeing 707.

9 Gendarme in armoured Vehicle

1962. Katanga Gendarmerie.

77	**9** 6f. multicoloured	2·25	2·25
78	8f. multicoloured	35	35
79	10f. multicoloured	45	45

POSTAGE DUE STAMPS

1960. Postage Due stamps of Belgian Congo handstamped **KATANGA**. (a) On Nos. D270/4.

D50	D **86** 10c. olive	80	80
D51	20c. blue	80	80
D52	50c. green	1·00	1·00
D53	1f. brown		
D54	2f. orange		

(b) On Nos. D330/6.

D55	D **99** 10c. brown	3·25	3·25
D56	20c. purple	3·25	3·25
D57	50c. green	3·25	3·25
D58	1f. blue	1·00	1·00
D59	2f. red	2·00	2·00
D60	4f. violet	2·75	2·75
D61	6f. blue	3·25	3·25

KATHIRI STATE OF SEIYUN Pt. 1

The stamps of Aden were used in Kathiri State of Seiyun from 22 May 1937 until 1942.

1937. 16 annas = 1 rupee.
1951. 100 cents = 1 shilling.
1966. 1000 fils = 1 dinar.

1 Sultan of Seiyun

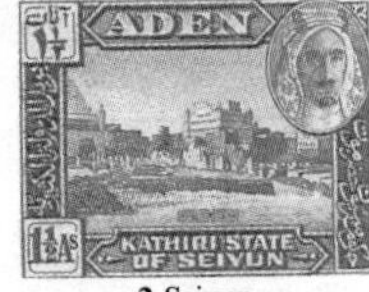

2 Seiyun

1942.
1 1 ½a. green 20 50
2 ¾a. brown 40 80
3 1a. blue 70 50
4 2 1½a. red 70 70
5 – 2a. brown 40 70
6 – 2½a. blue . . . . 1·25 1·00
7 – 3a. brown and red . . . . . 1·75 1·75
8 – 8a. red . . . . 1·25 50
9 – 1r. green . . . . 3·75 1·50
10 – 2r. blue and purple . . . . . 7·00 10·00
11 – 5r. brown and green . . . . 22·00 16·00
DESIGNS—VERT: 2a. Tarim; 2½a. Mosque at Seiyun; 1r. South Gate, Tarim; 5r. Mosque entrance, Tarim. HORIZ: 3a. Fortress at Tarim; 8a. Mosque at Seiyun; 2r. A Kathiri house.

1946. Victory. Optd **VICTORY ISSUE 8TH JUNE 1946.**
12 2 1½a. red 10 65
13 – 2½a. blue (No. 6) 10 10

1949. Royal Silver Wedding. As T **4b/c** of Pitcairn Islands.
14 1½a. red . . . . 30 2·00
15 5r. green . . . . 15·00 9·00

1949. 75th Anniv of U.P.U. As T **4d/g** of Pitcairn Islands surch with new values.
16 2½a. on 20c. blue 15 50
17 3a. on 30c. red . . . . 1·00 80
18 8a. on 50c. orange 25 75
19 1r. on 1s. blue 30 90

1951. 1942 stamps surch in cents or shillings.
20 1 5c. on 1a. blue 15 65
21 – 10c. on 2a. brown 30 50
22 – 15c. on 2½a. blue 15 75
23 – 20c. on 3a. brown and red . . . 20 1·25
24 – 50c. on 8a. red 20 50
25 – 1s. on 1r. green . . . . . . 30 1·50
26 – 2s. on 2r. blue and purple . . 3·00 18·00
27 – 5s. on 5r. brown and green . . 18·00 32·00

1953. Coronation. As T **4h** of Pitcairn Islands.
28 15c. black and green . . . . . 30 1·75

14 Sultan Hussein

29 "Telstar"

1954. As 1942 issue and new designs, but with portrait of Sultan Hussein as in T **14**.
29 14 5c. brown 10 10
30 10c. blue 15 10
31 2 15c. green 15 10
32 – 25c. red 15 10
33 – 35c. blue 15 10
34 – 50c. brown and red 15 10
39 – 70c. black . . . . 2·00 1·00
35 – 1s. orange 15 10
40 – 1s.25 green . . . . 2·00 7·50
41 – 1s.50 violet . . . . 2·00 7·50
36 – 2s. green . . . . 4·00 2·25
37 – 5s. blue and violet . . . . . 7·50 6·50
38 – 10s. brown and violet . . . 7·50 6·50
DESIGNS—VERT: 35c. Mosque at Seiyun; 70c. Qarn Adh Dhabi; 2s. South Gate, Tarim; 10s. Mosque entrance, Tarim. HORIZ: 50c. Fortress at Tarim; 1s. Mosque at Seiyun; 1s.25, Seiyun; 1s.50, Gheil Omer; 5s. Kathiri house.

1966. Nos. 29 etc surch **SOUTH ARABIA** in English and Arabic, with value and bar.
42 14 5f. on 5c. 15 10
43 5f. on 10c. 15 50
44 2 10f. on 15c. 15 50
45 – 15f. on 25c. 20 60
46 – 20f. on 35c. 15 30
47 – 25f. on 50c. 15 75
61 – 35f. on 70c. . . . . 1·75 80
49 – 50f. on 1s. 20 20
50 – 65f. on 1s.25 . . . . 20 20
51 – 75f. on 1s.50 . . . . 20 30
65 – 100f. on 2s. . . . . 3·00 2·50
53 – 250f. on 5s. . . . . 1·40 3·75
54 – 500f. on 10s. . . . . 1·75 3·75
Each value has two similar surcharges.

1966. Nos. 57, 59, 61/7 variously optd as given below, together with Olympic "rings".
68 10f. on 15c. (**LOS ANGELES 1932**) 35 35
69 20f. on 35c. (**BERLIN 1936**) . . . 45 45
70 35f. on 70c. (**INTERNATIONAL COOPERATION**, etc) 45 45
71 50f. on 1s. (**LONDON 1948**) . . . 50 55
72 65f. on 1s.25 (**HELSINKI 1952**) 50 1·00
73 75f. on 1s.50 (**MELBOURNE 1956**) . . . . 60 1·50
74 100f. on 2s. (**ROME 1960**) . . . . 70 1·75
75 250f. on 5s. (**TOKYO 1964**) . . .1·00 3·50
76 500f. on 10s. (**MEXICO CITY 1968**) . . . . .1·25 4·00

1966. World Cup Football Championship. Nos. 57, 59, 61/2, 65/7 optd **CHAMPIONS ENGLAND** (10f., 50f. and 250f.) or **FOOTBALL 1966** (others). Both with football symbol.
77 10f. on 15c. 70 30
78 20f. on 35c. 90 40
79 35f. on 70c. . . . . 1·25 40
80 50f. on 1s. . . . . 1·40 40
81 100f. on 2s. . . . . 3·75 2·00
82 250f. on 5s. . . . . 7·50 5·00
83 500f. on 10s. . . . . 9·50 8·00

1966. Centenary of I.T.U. (1965).
84 29 5f. green, black and violet . . 1·25 15
85 – 10f. purple, black and green . . 1·40 20
86 – 15f. blue, black and orange . . 1·75 20
87 29 25f. green, black and red . . 2·50 20
88 – 35f. purple, black and yellow . . . . 2·75 20
89 – 50f. blue, black and brown . . 3·25 25
90 29 65f. green, black and yellow . 3·75 30
DESIGNS: 10, 35f. "Relay"; 15, 50f. "Ranger".

32 Churchill at Easel

1966. Sir Winston Churchill's Paintings. Mult.
91 5f. Type **32** . . . . 1·75 15
92 10f. "Antibes" . . . . 2·00 15
93 15f. "Flowers" (vert) . . . . 2·00 20
94 20f. "Tapestries" . . . . . . 2·00 35
95 25f. "Village, Lake Lugano" . . 2·00 35
96 35f. "Church, Lake Como" (vert) . . . . 2·00 40
97 50f. "Flowers at Chartwell" (vert) . . . . 2·25 65
98 65f. Type **32** . . . . 2·75 90

1967. "World Peace". Nos. 57, 59, 61/7 optd **WORLD PEACE** and names as given below.
99 10f. on 15c. (**PANDIT NEHRU**) . . . . 1·25 1·00
100 20f. on 35c. (**WINSTON CHURCHILL**) . . . . . 4·50 2·25
101 35f. on 70c. (**DAG HAMMARSKJOLD**) . . . 50 80
102 50f. on 1s. (**JOHN F. KENNEDY**) 60 90
103 65f. on 1s.25 (**LUDWIG ERHARD**) . . . . 70 1·10
104 75f. on 1s.50 (**LYNDON JOHNSON**) . . . . 80 1·25
105 100f. on 2s. (**ELEANOR ROOSEVELT**) . . . . . 1·00 2·00
106 250f. on 5s. (**WINSTON CHURCHILL**) . . . . . 13·00 10·00
107 500f. on 10s. (**JOHN F. KENNEDY**) . . . . . 5·00 11·00

40 "Master Crewe as Henry VIII" (Sir Joshua Reynolds)

1967. Paintings. Multicoloured.
108 5f. Type **40** 30 25
109 10f. "The Dancer" (Degas) . . 35 30
110 15f. "The Fifer" (Manet) . . . 40 35
111 20f. "Stag at Sharkey's" (boxing match, G. Bellows) . 45 40
112 25f. "Don Manuel Osorio" (Goya) 50 45
113 35f. "St. Martin distributing his Cloak" (A. van Dyck) . 70 65
114 50f. "The Blue Boy" (Gainsborough) 85 75
115 65f. "The White Horse" (Gauguin) . . . . 1·10 1·00
116 75f. "Mona Lisa" (Da Vinci) (45 × 62 mm) . . . . . . 1·40 1·25

1967. American Astronauts. Nos. 57, 59, 61/2 and 65/6 optd as below, all with space capsule.
117 10f. on 15c. (**ALAN SHEPARD JR.**) . . . . . 55 1·25
118 20f. on 35c. (**VIRGIL GRISSOM**) . . . . . . 70 1·25
119 35f. on 70c. (**JOHN GLENN JR.**) . . . . 95 1·50
120 50f. on 1s. (**SCOTT CARPENTER**) . . . . . 95 1·50
121 100f. on 2s. (**WALTER SCHIRRA JR.**) . . . . . 2·25 3·75
122 250f. on 5s. (**GORDON COOPER JR.**) . . . . . 3·50 7·00

50 Churchill Crown

1967. Churchill Commemoration.
123 50 75f. multicoloured . . . . 9·00 6·50

APPENDIX

The following stamps have either been issued in excess of postal needs or have not been made available to the public in reasonable quantities at face value.

1967.

Hunting. 20f.

Olympic Games, Grenoble. Postage 10, 25, 35, 50, 75f.; Air 100, 200f.

Scout Jamboree, Idaho. Air 150f.

Paintings—Renoir. Postage 10, 35, 50, 65, 75f.; Air 100, 200, 250f.

Paintings—Toulouse-Lautrec. Postage 10, 35, 50, 65, 75f.; Air 100, 200, 250f.

The National Liberation Front is said to have taken control of Kathiri State of Seiyun on 1 October 1967.

KAZAKHSTAN Pt. 10

Formerly a constituent republic of the Soviet Union, Kazakhstan declared its independence on 16 December 1991.

1992. 100 kopeks = 1 rouble.
1994. 100 tyin (ty.) = 1 tenge (t.).

1 "Golden Warrior"

КАЗАКСТАН
(2)

1992. "Golden Warrior" (from 5th-century B.C. tomb).
1 1 50k. multicoloured 15 15

1992. Nos. 6079/80 of Russia optd as T **2**, in Cyrillic (2, 4) or English (3, 5) capitals.
2 12k. purple . . . . 2·75 2·25
3 12k. purple . . . . 2·75 2·25
4 13k. violet . . . . 2·75 2·25
5 13k. violet . . . . 2·75 2·25

(3)

4 Saiga

1992. Russian–French Space Flight. Nos. 6072/4 of Russia surch as T **3**.
6 30k. on 2k. brown 50 20
7 75k. on 3k. green 35 35
8 1r. on 1k. brown 45 45

1992.
9 4 75k. multicoloured 15 15

5 "Turksib" (E. K. Kasteev)

1992. Kazakh Art.
10 5 1r. multicoloured 25 25

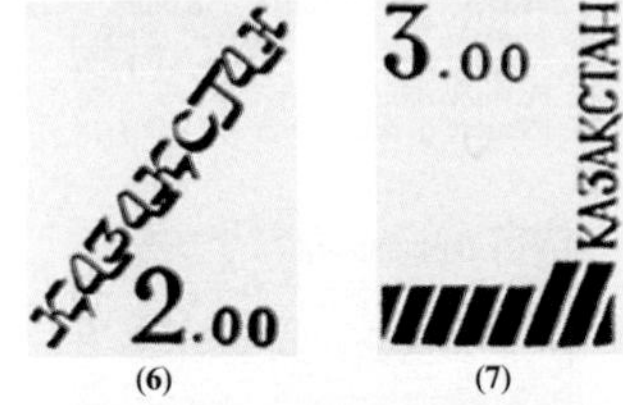

(6) (7)

(8)

9 National Flag and Arms

1992. Various stamps of Russia surch as T **6** (11/12), **7** (13/14) or **8** (15/16).
11 1r.50 on 1k. brown (No. 5940) 15 10
12 2r. on 2k. brown (No. 6073) 40 20
13 3r. on 6k. blue (No. 4673) . . 25 20
14 5r. on 6k. blue (No. 4673) . . 25 20
15 10r. on 1k. brown (No. 5940) 40 30
16 24r.50 on 1k. brown (No. 5940) 40 30

1992. Republic Day.
17 9 5r. multicoloured 25 15

10 Rocket Launch

11 National Flag

1993.
18 10 1r. green 10 10
19 3r. red 10 10
20 10r. bistre 15 10
21 25r. violet 30 15
22 11 50r. yellow, blue and deep blue 60 30
See also Nos. 45 etc.

12 Rocket and Earth

1993. Space Mail.
23 12 100r. multicoloured 35 30

13 Cock

1993. New Year. Year of the Cock.
24 13 60r. black, red and yellow 35 30

14 Space Station

1993. Cosmonautics Day.

No.	Type	Description	Mint	Used
25	**14**	90r. multicoloured	35	30

15 Nazarbaev and Flag on Map

1993. President Nursultan Nazarbaev (1st series).

No.	Type	Description	Mint	Used
26	**15**	50r. multicoloured	35	25

See also No. 28.

16 Kalkaman-Uly

1993. 325th Birth Anniv of Bukar Zhyrau Kalkaman-Uly (poet).

No.	Type	Description	Mint	Used
27	**16**	15r. multicoloured	35	25

17 Arms, Flag on Map and Nazarbaev

1993. President Nursultan Nazarbaev (2nd series).

No.	Type	Description	Mint	Used
28	**17**	100r. multicoloured	35	25

18 Desert Dormouse

1993. Mammals. Multicoloured.

No.	Type	Description	Mint	Used
29		5r. Type **18**	10	10
30		10r. Porcupine	10	10
31		15r. Marbled polecat	20	10
32		20r. Asiatic wild ass	25	15
33		25r. Mouflon	30	15
34		30r. Cheetah	35	20

19 Ice Hockey 20 Skiers

1994. Winter Olympic Games, Lillehammer, Norway (1st issue). Multicoloured.

No.	Type	Description	Mint	Used
35		15t. Type **19**	10	10
36		25t. Skiing	10	10
37		90t. Ski jumping	35	15
38		150t. Speed skating	60	30

1994. Winter Olympic Games, Lillehammer, Norway (2nd issue). Multicoloured.

No.	Type	Description	Mint	Used
39		2t. Type **20**	20	10
40		6t.80 Vladimir Smirnov (Kazakh skier)	55	20

See also No. 42.

21 Dog 22 Smirnov

1994. New Year. Year of the Dog.

No.	Type	Description	Mint	Used
41	**21**	30t. black, blue and green	25	10

1994. Vladimir Smirnov, Winter Olympic Games Medals Winner. As No. 40 but face value changed and with additional inscription in Kazakh.

No.	Type	Description	Mint	Used
42	**22**	12t. multicoloured	75	35

23 Launch of "Soyuz TM16" at Baikonur

1994. Cosmonautics Day.

No.	Type	Description	Mint	Used
43	**23**	2t. multicoloured	25	10

1994.

No.	Type	Description	Mint	Used
45	**10**	15ty. blue	10	10
76		20ty. orange	10	10
77		25ty. yellow	10	10
78		50ty. grey	10	10
46		80ty. purple	15	10
79		1t. green	20	10
80		2t. blue	35	15
81		4t. mauve	60	25
82		6t. green	90	40
83		12t. mauve	1·90	90

25 Mt. Abay

1994. 5th "Asia Dauysy" International Music Festival, Almaty. Multicoloured.

No.	Type	Description	Mint	Used
47		10t. Type **25**	50	25
48		15t. Medeo Ice Stadium, Almaty	85	45

26 Horsfield's Tortoises

1994. Reptiles. Multicoloured.

No.	Type	Description	Mint	Used
49		1t. Type **26**	10	10
50		1t.20 Toad-headed agamas	10	10
51		2t. Halys vipers	10	10
52		3t. Turkestan plate-tailed geckos	15	10
53		5t. Steppe agamas	25	15
54		7t. Glass lizards	35	20

27 National Arms

1994. Republic Day.

No.	Type	Description	Mint	Used
56	**27**	2t. multicoloured	15	10

28 "Why does the Swallow have a Forked Tail?" (dir. Amen Khaidorov)

1994. Children's Fund. Kazakh Children's Films. Multicoloured.

No.	Type	Description	Mint	Used
57		1t.+30ty. Type **28**	10	10
58		1t.+30ty. "The Calf and Hare seek a Better Life" (E. Abdrakhmanov)	10	10
59		1t.+30ty. Asses ("Lame Kulan" dir. Amen Khaidarov)	10	10

29 Entelodon

1994. Prehistoric Animals. Multicoloured.

No.	Type	Description	Mint	Used
60		1t. Type **29**	10	10
61		1t.20 Saurolophus	10	10
62		2t. Plesiosaurus	10	10
63		3t. "Sordes pilosus"	15	10
64		5t. Mosasaurus	25	15
65		7t. "Megaloceros giganteum"	35	20

1995. Nos. 45/6 surch.

No.	Type	Description	Mint	Used
67	**24**	1t. on 15ty. blue	10	10
68		2t. on 15ty. blue	15	10
69		3t. on 80ty. purple	25	10
70		4t. on 80ty. purple	35	15
71		6t. on 80ty. purple	45	20
72		8t. on 80ty. purple	50	25
73		12t. on 80ty. purple	1·10	50
74		20t. on 80ty. purple	2·10	85

31 Pig 32 Kunanbaev

1995. New Year. Year of the Pig.

No.	Type	Description	Mint	Used
75	**31**	10t. blue, black and light blue	50	50

1995. 150th Birth Anniv of Abai Kunanbaev (writer). Multicoloured.

No.	Type	Description	Mint	Used
86		4t. Type **32**	25	25
87		9t. Kunanbaev holding pen and book	50	50

33 Flight Path of "Soyuz" Spacecraft

1995. Cosmonautics Day. Multicoloured.

No.	Type	Description	Mint	Used
88		2t. Type **33**	80	40
89		10t. Yuri Malenchenko, Talgat Musabaev and Ulf Merbold (cosmonauts)	7·50	7·50

34 Manshuk Mametova and Battle Scene

1995. 50th Anniv of End of Second World War. Multicoloured.

No.	Type	Description	Mint	Used
90		1t. Type **34**	35	20
91		3t. Aliya Moldafulova and tank	1·00	75
92		5t. Wheat field, dove and eternal flame	3·75	3·25

35 "Spring" (S. Membeev)

1995. Paintings. Multicoloured.

No.	Type	Description	Mint	Used
93		4t. Type **35**	50	50
94		9t. "Mountains" (Zh. Shardenov)	1·00	1·00
95		15t. "Kulash Baiseitova in role of Kyz Zhibek" (G. Ismailova) (vert)	2·00	2·00
96		28t. "Kokpar" (K. Telzhanov)	4·00	4·00

1995. "Asia Dauysy" International Music Festival, Almaty. Nos. 47/8 optd **KAZAKSTAN '95 1995**.

No.	Type	Description	Mint	Used
97		10t. multicoloured	1·00	80
98		15t. multicoloured	1·50	1·25

37 Dauletkerei

1995. 175th Birth Anniv of Dauletkerei (composer and poet).

No.	Type	Description	Mint	Used
99	**37**	2t. multicoloured	35	25
100		28t. multicoloured	4·25	3·75

38 Gandhi, Temple and Spinning Wheel

1995. 125th Birth Anniv (1994) of Mahatma Gandhi.

No.	Type	Description	Mint	Used
101	**38**	9t. red and black	1·00	80
102		22t. red and black	4·00	3·50

39 Anniversary Emblem 40 Cathedral of the Ascension

1995. 50th Anniv of U.N.O.

No.	Type	Description	Mint	Used
103	**39**	10t. gold and blue	1·00	80
104		36t. gold and blue	4·00	3·50

1995. Buildings in Almaty.

No.	Type	Description	Mint	Used
105	**40**	1t. green	15	15
106	–	2t. blue	20	10
107	–	3t. red	30	15
108	–	48t. brown	5·50	5·50

DESIGNS: 2t. Culture Palace; 3t. Opera and Ballet House; 48t. Theatre.

See also Nos. 124/5.

41 White-tailed Sea Eagle

1995. Birds of Prey. Multicoloured.

No.	Type	Description	Mint	Used
109		1t. Type **41**	10	10
110		3t. Osprey	20	10
111		5t. Lammergeier	35	15
112		6t. Himalayan griffon	40	20
113		30t. Saker falcon	2·10	1·00
114		50t. Golden eagle	3·50	1·75

42 Rat and Lunar Cycle 43 Baikonur Launch Pad highlighted on Globe

1996. Chinese New Year. Year of the Rat.

No.	Type	Description	Mint	Used
115	**42**	25t. red, black and lilac	1·40	1·00

1996. Cosmonautics Day. Multicoloured.

No.	Type	Description	Mint	Used
116		6t. Type **43**	80	60
117		15t. Yuri Gagarin	1·90	1·50
118		20t. Proposed "Alpha" space station	3·00	2·50

45 Cycling 46 Zhabaev (after embroidery by G. Atknin)

1996. Olympic Games, Atlanta. Multicoloured.
120 4t. Type **45** 35 20
121 6t. Wrestling 55 25
122 30t. Boxing 2·75 1·40

1996. As T **40** but smaller, size 24 × 19 mm.
124 1t. green 10 10
125 6t. green 20 10
DESIGNS: 1t. Circus; 6t. Academy of Sciences (50th anniv).

1996. 150th Birth Anniv of Zhambil Zhabaev (writer).
126 **46** 12t. multicoloured 70 50

47 Tomb, Dombauyl

1996. Ancient Buildings. Multicoloured.
127 1t. Type **47** 20 10
128 3t. Mausoleum, Aisha Biy 50 30
129 6t. Mausoleum, Syrly Tam 2·50 2·00

48 "Soyuz TM-13" docked with "Mir" Space Station

49 Map of Kazakhstan and Dove with Letter

1996. 5th Anniv of Toktar Aubakirov's (cosmonaut) Service on "Mir". Multicoloured.
131 46t. Type **48** 1·90 1·50
132 46t. Aubakirov 1·90 1·50
Nos. 131/2 were issued together, se-tenant, forming a composite design.

1996. World Post Day.
133 **49** 9t. blue 35 20
134 – 40t. orange 3·50 3·00
DESIGN: 40t. Dove with letter and Universal Postal Union emblem.

1996. Republic Day. No. 56 surch **KAZAKSTAN 1. 1996.**
135 **27** 21t. on 2t. multicoloured 1·00 75

51 "Saturnia schenki"

1996. Butterflies. Multicoloured.
136 4t. Type **51** 15 10
137 6t. "Parnassius patricius" 20 10
138 12t. "Parnasssius ariadne" 40 20
139 46t. "Colias draconis" 1·50 1·10

52 Borzois giving Chase

1996. Hunting Dogs.
140 **52** 5t. multicoloured 20 10

53 Bride before Yurte

54 Writing Materials and Books

1996. Traditional Costumes and Dwelling. Multicoloured.
142 10t. Type **53** 20 10
143 16t. Bridegroom before yurte 45 25
144 45t. Yurte interior 1·25 65
Nos. 142/4 were issued together, se-tenant, Nos. 142/3 forming a composite design.

1996. Bicentenary of National Archive.
145 **54** 4t. brown 15 10
146 – 68t. violet 2·50 2·10
DESIGN: 68t. Book and documents.

56 Head

1997. The Marbled Polecat. Multicoloured.
148 6t. Type **56** 15 10
149 10t. Adult with tail down 25 15
150 32t. Two polecats 80 45
151 46t. Adult with tail raised 1·10 70

57 Ox

58 Aries

1997. New Year. Year of the Ox.
152 **57** 40t. brown, black and green 1·00 70

1997. Star Signs. Each violet and purple.
153 1t. Type **58** 10 10
154 2t. Taurus 10 10
155 3t. Gemini 10 10
156 4t. Cancer 10 10
157 5t. Leo 10 10
158 6t. Virgo 10 10
159 7t. Libra 10 10
160 8t. Scorpio 10 10
161 9t. Sagittarius 10 10
162 10t. Capricorn 10 10
163 12t. Aquarius 25 20
164 20t. Pisces 40 30

59 Saturn and Automatic Transfer Vehicle

60 Emblem

1997. Cosmonautics Day. Multicoloured.
166 10t. Type **59** 25 20
167 10t. Space shuttle and "Mir" space station 25 20
168 10t. "Sputnik 1" and Earth 25 20
Nos. 166/8 were issued together, se-tenant, forming a composite design.

1997. World Book and Copyright Day.
169 **60** 15t. yellow and green 30 20
170 60t. yellow and green 1·10 85

61 Auezov Museum, Almaty

1997. Birth Centenary of Mukhtar Auezov (philologist). Multicoloured.
171 25t. Type **61** 45 35
172 40t. Auezov at table (after Shcherkassky) 80 55

62 Order of Bravery

63 "Tulipa alberti"

1997. Orders and Medals. Multicoloured.
173 15t. Type **62** 30 20
174 15t. Medal of Honour 30 20
175 20t. Order of Victory 40 30
176 30t. National Order of Merit 55 40

1997. Tulips. Multicoloured.
177 15t. "Tulipa regelii" 30 20
178 35t. Type **63** 70 45
179 35t. "Tulipa greigii" 70 45

64 "Shepherd" (Sh. Sariev)

65 Moss Agate

1997. Paintings. Multicoloured.
180 25t. Type **64** 45 35
181 25t. "Fantastic Still Life" (S. Kalmykov) 45 35
182 25t. "Capturing Horse" (M. Kenbaev) (horiz) 45 35

1997. Minerals. Multicoloured.
183 15t. Type **65** 30 20
184 15t. Chalcedony 30 20
185 20t. Azurite 40 30
186 20t. Malachite 40 30

66 "Gylippus rickmersi"

1997. Arachnidae. Multicoloured.
188 30t. Type **66** 60 40
189 30t. "Latrodectus pallidus" 60 40
190 30t. "Oculicosa supermirabilis" 60 40
191 30t. "Anomalobuthus rickmersi" 60 40

68 Horse Race

1997. National Sports. Multicoloured.
193 20t. Type **68** 40 30
194 20t. Tearing goatskin ("Koknar") 40 30
195 20t. Wrestling 40 30
196 20t. Two-horse race 40 30

69 Ice Dancing

70 "Little Girl" (A. Ashkiyazara)

1998. Winter Sports. Multicoloured.
197 15t. Type **69** 30 20
198 30t. Biathlon 55 40

1998. Children's Paintings. Multicoloured.
199 15t. Type **70** 30 20
200 15t. "My House" (M. Tarakara) (horiz) 30 20

71 Tiger and Lunar Cycle

72 Kurmangazy

1998. New Year. Year of the Tiger.
201 **71** 30t. brown, black and yellow 55 40

1998. 175th Birth Anniv of Kurmangazy (composer).
202 **72** 30t. yellow, brown & black 55 40

73 Baitursynov

75 "Apollo 8" Spacecraft and Moon

74 Winged and Horned Beasts, Issyk Kurgan

1998. 125th Birth Anniv of Akhmet Baitursynov (writer).
203 **73** 30t. light brown, brown and black 55 40

1998. Archaeological Finds. Multicoloured.
204 15t. Type **74** 35 25
205 30t. Pendants, Aktasty (vert) 70 50
206 40t. Gold and jewel-studded open-work ornament depicting animals, Kargaly 95 65

1998. Cosmonautics Day. Multicoloured.
207 30t. Type **75** 55 40
208 30t. "Apollo 8", Earth and Moon 55 40
209 50t. "Vostok 6" orbiting Earth 90 60
Nos. 207/8 were issued together, se-tenant, forming a composite design.

76 Mosque

77 State Arms

1998. Astana. New Capital of Kazakhstan.
210 **76** 10t. brown 20 15
211 – 15t. blue (inscr "Akmola") 30 20
212 – 15t. blue (inscr "Astana") 1·00 90
213 – 20t. blue 40 30
214 – 25t. violet 30 20
DESIGNS—VERT: 15t. Petroleum Ministry; 20t. Parliament. HORIZ: 25k. President's Palace.

1998.
216 **77** 1t. green 10 10
217 2t. blue 10 10
218 3t. red 10 10
219 4t. purple 10 10
220 5t. yellow 10 10
221 8t. orange 10 10
225 20t. orange 15 10
229 50t. blue 25 15

79 Black Stork

1998. Birds. Multicoloured.
231 15t. Type **79** 30 20
232 30t. Greater flamingoes 55 40
233 50t. Great white crane 90 60

80 Lynx

82 Stamp and U.P.U. Emblem

1998. Wild Cats. Multicoloured.
234 15t. Type **80** 30 20
235 30t. Sand dune cat 55 40
236 50t. Snow leopard 90 60

1998. World Post Day.
238 **82** 30t. bistre 35 25

83 Anniversary Emblem

84 Warrior with Sword

1998. 5th Anniv of the Tenge (currency unit).
239 **83** 40t. orange 50 30

1998. Kazakh Horsemen. Multicoloured.
240 20t. Type **84** 25 20
241 30t. Using bow and arrow . . 35 25
242 40t. With spear and shield . . 65 50

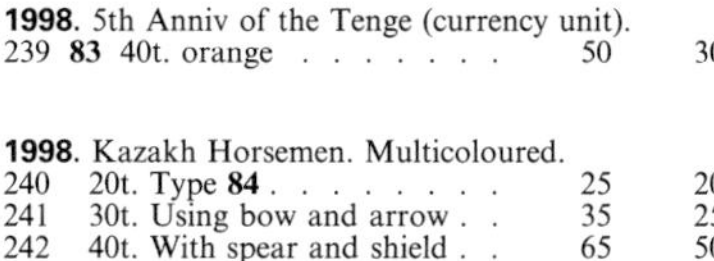

86 Family (census)

87 Rabbit and Lunar Cycle

1999.
244 **86** 1t. green 10 10
245 – 3t. red 10 10
246 – 9t. green 10 10
247 – 15t. red 25 15
248 – 20t. brown 30 20
249 – 30t. brown 40 25
DESIGNS—HORIZ: 15t. Kanyish Sambaev (geologist and President of Academy of Sciences, birth centenary) and book; 20t. Sambaev and Academy of Sciences. VERT: 3, 9, 30t. Dish aerial and "Intelsat" satellite.

1999. New Year. Year of the Rabbit.
250 **87** 40t. green, black and yellow 50 30

88 Steam Locomotive and Railway Route Map

89 Satellite

1999. Railway Locomotives. Multicoloured.
251 40t. Type **88** 50 30
252 50t. Electric locomotive . . . 60 55
253 60t. Diesel railcar 75 50
254 80t. Electric locomotive (different) . . . . 1·00 90

1999. Cosmonautics Day. Multicoloured.
255 50t. Type **89** 60 40
256 90t. Astronaut on Moon (30th anniv of first manned Moon landing) (horiz) . . 1·00 70

90 "Pseudoeremostachys severzowii"

91 Scene from *Turksib* (1929)

1999. Flowers. Multicoloured.
257 20t. Type **90** 25 20
258 30t. "Rhaphidophyton regelii" 35 25
259 90t. "Niedzwedzkia semiretschenskia" . . . . 1·00 70

1999. 70th Anniv of Kazak Cinema. Multicoloured.
260 15t. Type **91** 15 10
261 20t. M. Berkovich (director) and scenes from *Jambul's Youth* (1997) and *Wolf Cub among People* (1998) . . . 20 15
262 30t. Scenes from *The Devil Paths* (1935), *Our Dear Doctor* (1957) and *Amangeldy* (1938) 30 20
263 35t. Scenes from *Zama-ay* (1997), *Biography of a Young Accordionist* (1994) and *Who are you Rider?* (1989) 35 25
264 50t. Alfred Hitchcock (director) and scene from *The Birds* 50 35
265 60t. Sergei Eisenstein (director) 60 40

92 Red Fox

93 Magnifying Glass and Stamps

1999. Endangered Species. Foxes. Multicoloured.
266 20t. Type **92** 20 15
267 30t. Dhole 30 20
268 90t. Corsac fox 90 60

1999. 125th Anniv of Universal Postal Union.
269 **93** 10t. violet 10 10

95 Flower

96 T. Musabayev

1999. Endangered Flora (1st series).
271 **95** 4t. mauve 10 10
272 30t. green 30 20
See also Nos. 296/8 and 310/11.

1999. Cosmonauts. Multicoloured.
273 40t. Type **96** 40 25
274 50t. T. Aubakirov (first Kazakhstan cosmonaut) (vert) 50 35

97 Ice Hockey Match

1999. Sports. Multicoloured.
275 20t. Type **97** 20 15
276 30t. Ice hockey team 30 20
277 40t. G. Kosanov (athlete) . . 40 25

99 Oil Rig

2000. Centenary of Oil Extraction in Kazakhstan.
279 **99** 7t. red 10 10

100 Yurt, Horse racing and Artifacts

101 Millennium Emblem

2000. Navruz Bayram Festival. Imperf.
280 **100** 20t. multicoloured 15 10

2000. New Millennium.
281 **101** 30t. blue, deep blue and orange 25 15

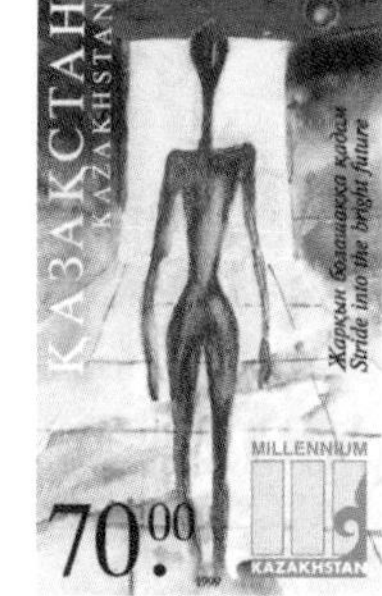

102 28th Guardsman-Panfilovs Memorial and Eternal Flame, Alma-Ata

103 "Stride into the Bright Future" (painting, Kostya Balakirev)

2000. 55th Anniv of End of Second World War.
282 **102** 3t. brown and red 10 10

2000. International Children's Day. New Millennium. Sheet 127 × 106 mm.
MS283 **103** 70t. multicoloured . . 60 60

104 Koumiss (fermented mare's milk) Flask

2000. Joint issue with People's Republic of China. Pots. Multicoloured.
284 15t. Type **104** 10 10
285 50t. He-pot (Chinese wine vessel) 40 25

105 Mukanov

106 Dulati

2000. Birth Centenary of Sabit Mukanov (writer).
286 **105** 1t. green 10 10

2000. 500th Birth Anniv of Mukhammed Khaidar Dulti (historian) (1999).
287 **106** 8t. blue 10 10

107 Canoeing

108 "Echo" Telecommunications Satellite

2000. Olympics Games, Sydney. Multicoloured.
288 35t. Type **107** 30 20
289 40t. Gymnastics 35 20
290 40t. Taekwondo 35 20
291 50t. Triathlon 40 25

2000.
292 **108** 5t. orange 10 10
293 15t. blue 10 10
294 20t. blue 15 10

109 Arystan Bab's Mausoleum

2000. 1500th Anniv of Turkestan (town). Sheet 160 × 140 mm containing T **109** and similar horiz designs. Multicoloured.
MS295 50t. Type **109**; 50t. Rabiy Sultan Begim's and Karashash Ana's mausolea; 70t. Kozhah Akhmet Yassauy's mausoleum 1·40 1·40
Stamps of a similar design were issued by Turkey.

110 Flower

111 Momysh-Uly and Gold Star of Hero of Soviet Union Medal

2000. Endangered Flora (2nd series).
296 **110** 1t. green 10 10
297 2t. blue 10 10
298 50t. blue 20 15

2000. 90th Birth Anniv of Baurdzhan Momyush-Uly (Soviet military leader).
299 **111** 4t. brown and black . . . 10 10

2001. Nos. 57/9 surch **2001 10.00**.
300 10t. on 1t. +30ty. multicoloured 10 10
301 10t. on 1t. +30ty. multicoloured 10 10
302 10t. on 1t. +30ty. multicoloured 10 10

113 Snail and Lunar Cycle

2001. New Year. Year of the Snail.
303 **113** 40t. black, blue and yellow 35 20

114 Rocket, Yuri Gagarin and Dogs

2001. Cosmonautics Day (2000). Multicoloured.
304 40t. Type **114** (40th anniv of space flight by Belka and Strelka (dogs)) 35 20
305 70t. Rocket launch (45th anniv of Baikonur cosmodrome) (vert) 60 30

115 Snake and Lunar Cycle

2001. New Year. Year of the Snake.
306 **115** 40t. black, brown and green 35 20

116 Dove, Globe and Transport

2001. 10th Anniv of Ministry of Transportation and Communication. Sheet 100 × 70 mm.
MS307 **116** 100t. multicoloured 85 85

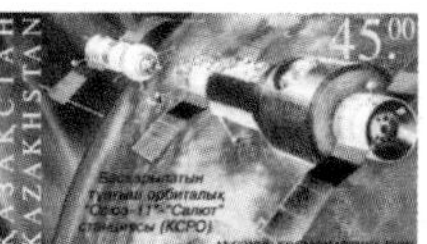

117 "Soyuz-II" Spacecraft and "Salyut" Space Station

118 *Aquilegia karatavica*

2001. Cosmonautics Day. Multicoloured.
308 45t. Type **117** 35 20
309 70t. Yuri Gagarin and earth (40th anniv of first manned space flight) 60 30

2001. Endangered Flora (3rd series).
310 **118** 3t. green 10 10
311 10t. green 10 10

119 Abulkhair-Khan (1693–1748) **120** Roborovski Hamster (*Phodopus roborovskii*)

2001. Khans (feudal rulers). Multicoloured.

312		50t. Type **119**	40	25
313		60t. Abylai-Khan (1711–1781)	50	30

2001. Fauna (1st series).

314	**120**	8t. orange	10	10
315		15t. blue	10	10
316		20t. blue	15	10
317		50t. brown	40	25

121 Northern Eagle Owl (*Bubo bubo*)

2001. Owls. Multicoloured.

318		30t. Type **121**	25	15
319		40t. Long-eared owl (*Asio otis*)	35	20
320		50t. Hawk owl (*Surnia ulula*)	40	25

122 Winged Lion and Fibre Optic Cable

2001. National Development Plan. Communications.

321	**122**	40t. multicoloured	35	20

KEDAH Pt. 1

A state of the Federation of Malaya, incorporated in Malaysia in 1963.

100 cents = 1 dollar (Straits or Malayan).

1 Sheaf of Rice **2** Malay ploughing

1912.

1	**1**	1c. black and green	60	25
26		1c. brown	70	20
52		1c. black	70	10
27		2c. green	1·50	20
2		3c. black and red	4·00	30
19		3c. purple	65	80
53		3c. green	2·00	90
3		4c. red and grey	10·00	25
20		4c. red	3·50	20
54		4c. violet	1·00	10
4		5c. green and brown	2·25	3·00
55		5c. yellow	1·50	10
56		6c. red	1·75	65
5		8c. black and blue	3·50	3·50
57		8c. black	11·00	10
6	**2**	10c. blue and brown	2·00	90
58		12c. black and blue	3·50	4·00
31		20c. black and green	4·00	2·00
32		21c. mauve and purple	2·00	13·00
33		25c. blue and purple	2·25	8·00
34		30c. black and pink	3·00	9·00
59		35c. purple	6·50	27·00
9		40c. black and purple	3·50	14·00
36		50c. brown and blue	2·50	13·00
37w	–	$1 black and red on yellow	6·50	8·50
38	–	$2 green and brown	13·00	95·00
39	–	$3 black and blue on blue	65·00	95·00
40	–	$5 black and red	75·00	£150

DESIGN—As Type **2**: $1 to $5, Council Chamber.

1919. Surch in words.

24		50c. on $2 green and brown	65·00	75·00
25		$1 on $3 black and blue on blue	20·00	90·00

1922. Optd **MALAYA-BORNEO EXHIBITION**.

45	**1**	1c. brown	3·00	16·00
41		2c. green	3·50	23·00
46		3c. purple	3·00	40·00
47		4c. red	3·00	25·00
48	**2**	10c. blue and sepia	4·50	42·00
42		21c. purple	26·00	80·00
43		25c. blue and purple	26·00	80·00
44		50c. brown and blue	26·00	95·00

6 Sultan Abdul Hamid Halimshah

1937.

60	**6**	10c. blue and brown	4·00	1·00
61		12c. black and violet	35·00	9·00
62		25c. blue and purple	7·50	4·50
63		30c. green and red	8·00	10·00
64		40c. black and purple	4·00	16·00
65		50c. brown and blue	6·00	4·50
66		$1 black and green	4·00	10·00
67		$2 green and brown	£120	75·00
68		$5 black and red	32·00	£150

1948. Silver Wedding. As T **4b/c** of Pitcairn Islands.

70		10c. violet	20	20
71		$5 red	26·00	32·00

1949. U.P.U. As T **4d/g** of Pitcairn Islands.

72		10c. purple	25	50
73		15c. blue	1·75	1·50
74		25c. orange	65	1·50
75		50c. black	1·00	2·50

7 Sheaf of Rice **8** Sultan Badlishah

1950.

76	**7**	1c. black	50	30
77		2c. orange	50	15
78		3c. green	2·00	1·00
79		4c. brown	75	10
79ab		5c. purple	1·50	1·00
80		6c. grey	70	15
81		8c. red	1·75	2·50
81a		8c. green	1·00	1·75
82		10c. mauve	70	10
82a		12c. red	85	2·50
83		15c. blue	1·25	35
84		20c. black and green	1·25	2·50
84a		20c. blue	1·00	10
85	**8**	25c. purple and orange	1·50	30
85a		30c. red and purple	2·25	1·25
85b		35c. red and purple	1·00	1·50
86		40c. red and purple	2·75	6·00
87		50c. black and blue	2·25	35
88		$1 blue and purple	3·00	4·00
89		$2 green and red	20·00	23·00
90		$5 green and brown	42·00	40·00

1953. Coronation. As T **4h** of Pitcairn Islands.

91		10c. black and purple	1·25	50

15 Fishing Craft **20** Sultan Abdul Halim Mu' Adzam Shah

1957. Inset portrait of Sultan Badlishah.

92	–	1c. black	10	60
93	–	2c. red	10	1·50
94	–	4c. sepia	10	75
95	–	5c. lake	10	65
96	–	8c. green	2·00	7·50
97	–	10c. sepia	50	30
98	**15**	20c. blue	2·50	2·25
99	–	50c. black and blue	2·00	3·25
100	–	$1 blue and purple	4·75	11·00
101	–	$2 green and red	23·00	30·00
102	–	$5 brown and green	38·00	35·00

DESIGNS—HORIZ: 1c. Copra; 2c. Pineapples; 4c. Ricefield; 5c. Masjid Alwi Mosque, Kangar; 8c. East Coast Railway "Golden Blowpipe" Express; $1 Govt Offices; $2 Bersilat (form of wrestling); $5 Weaving. VERT: 10c. Tiger; 50c. Aborigines with blowpipe.

1959. Installation of Sultan.

103	**20**	10c. yellow, brown and blue	10	10

21 Sultan Abdul Halim Shah

1959. As Nos. 92/102 but with inset portrait of Sultan Abdul Halim Shah as in T **21**.

104		1c. black	10	60
105		2c. red	10	1·50
106		4c. sepia	10	60
107		5c. lake	10	10
108		8c. green	3·50	3·25
109		10c. sepia	75	10
109a		10c. purple	4·50	30
110		20c. blue	60	75
111a		50c. black and blue	30	50
112		$1 blue and purple	1·75	2·25
113		$2 green and red	13·00	17·00
114a		$5 brown and green	22·00	15·00

22 "Vanda hookeriana"

1965. Flowers. Multicoloured.

115		1c. Type **22**	10	1·00
116		2c. "Arundina graminifolia"	10	1·50
117		5c. "Paphiopedilum niveum"	10	10
118		6c. "Spathoglottis plicata"	15	50
119		10c. "Arachnis flos-aeris"	30	10
120		15c. "Rhyncostylis retusa"	1·50	10
121		20c. "Phalaenopsis violacea"	1·75	75

The higher values used in Kedah were Nos. 20/7 of Malaysia.

23 "Danaus melanippus"

1971. Butterflies. Multicoloured.

124		1c. "Delias ninus"	30	1·50
125		2c. Type **23**	40	1·50
126		5c. "Parthenos sylvia"	1·00	30
127		6c. "Papilio demoleus"	1·00	1·75
128		10c. "Hebomoia glaucippe"	1·00	10
129		15c. "Precis orithya"	1·00	10
130		20c. "Valeria valeria"	1·25	60

The higher values in use with this issue were Nos. 64/71 of Malaysia.

24 "Pterocarpus indicus"

1979. Flowers. Multicoloured.

135		1c. "Rafflesia hasseltii"	10	70
136		2c. Type **24**	10	70
137		5c. "Lagerstroemia speciosa"	10	50
138		10c. "Durio zibethinus"	15	10
139		15c. "Hibiscus rosa-sinensis"	15	10
140		20c. "Rhododendron scortechinii"	20	10
141		25c. "Etlingera elatior" (inscr "Phaeomeria speciosa")	40	10

25 Sultan Abdul Halim Shah **26** Cocoa

1983. Silver Jubilee of Sultan's Installation. Multicoloured.

142		20c. Type **25**	70	30
143		40c. Paddy fields (horiz)	1·75	1·50
144		60c. Paddy fields and Mount Jerai (horiz)	2·50	4·50

1986. Agricultural Products of Malaysia. Mult.

152		1c. Coffee	10	10
153		2c. Coconuts	10	10
154		5c. Type **26**	10	10
155		10c. Black pepper	10	10
156		15c. Rubber	10	10
157		20c. Oil palm	10	10
158		30c. Rice	10	10

KELANTAN Pt. 1

A state in the Federation of Malaya, incorporated in Malaysia in 1963.

100 cents = 1 dollar (Straits or Malayan).

1 **3** Sultan Ismail

1911.

1a	**1**	1c. green	4·25	30
15		1c. black	75	50
16		2c. brown	6·50	3·75
16a		2c. green	3·25	40
2		3c. red	4·25	15
16b		3c. brown	4·25	1·00
17		4c. black and red	2·00	10
18		5c. green and red on yellow	1·25	10
19		6c. purple	3·25	1·50
19a		6c. red	4·00	5·50
5		8c. blue	5·50	1·00
20		10c. black and mauve	2·75	10
21		30c. purple and red	4·00	5·50
8		50c. black and orange	8·00	2·50
9		$1 green	45·00	48·00
9a		$1 green and brown	45·00	2·00
10		$2 green and red	1·50	4·00
11		$5 green and blue	4·00	7·50
12		$25 green and orange	42·00	80·00

1922. Optd **MALAYA BORNEO EXHIBITION**.

37	**1**	1c. green	3·00	45·00
30		4c. black and red	4·50	45·00
31		5c. green and red on yellow	5·50	45·00
38		10c. black and mauve	5·50	60·00
32		30c. purple and red	5·50	65·00
33		50c. black and orange	8·00	70·00
34		$1 green and brown	26·00	90·00
35		$2 green and red	60·00	£170
36		$5 green and blue	£160	£350

1928.

40	**3**	1c. olive and yellow	50	55
41		2c. green	3·75	20
42		4c. red	5·50	1·00
43		5c. brown	4·75	10
44		6c. red	11·00	7·50
45		8c. olive	4·75	10
46		10c. purple	22·00	2·75
47		12c. blue	3·50	5·50
48		25c. red and purple	5·00	3·50
49		30c. violet and red	40·00	19·00
50		40c. orange and green	8·50	25·00
51		50c. olive and orange	65·00	5·00
39		$1 blue	12·00	75·00
52		$1 violet and green	48·00	12·00
53		$2 red	£200	£180
54		$5 red	£350	£475

All except No. 39 are larger than T **3**.

1948. Silver Wedding. As T **4b/c** of Pitcairn Islands.

55		10c. violet	60	2·50
56		$5 red	25·00	48·00

1949. U.P.U. As T **4d/g** of Pitcairn Islands.

57		10c. purple	25	30
58		15c. blue	1·75	90
59		25c. orange	40	2·50
40		50c. black	60	2·25

5 Sultan Ibrahim **6** Sultan Yahya Petra and Crest of Kelantan

1951.

61	**5**	1c. black	50	30
62		2c. orange	1·25	35
63		3c. green	4·00	1·25
64		4c. brown	75	15
65		5c. purple	1·00	50
66		6c. grey	75	20
67		8c. red	2·00	3·50
68		8c. green	1·00	1·75
69		10c. mauve	50	10
70		12c. red	2·00	2·25
71		15c. blue	4·25	60
72		20c. black and green	70	6·00
73		20c. blue	80	25
74		25c. purple and orange	1·50	55
75		30c. red and purple	1·25	1·75
76		35c. red and purple	1·00	1·50
77		40c. red and purple	8·00	13·00
78		50c. black and blue	3·50	40
79		$1 blue and purple	7·50	4·50
80		$2 green and red	25·00	25·00
81		$5 green and brown	48·00	40·00

1953. Coronation. As T **4h** of Pitcairn Islands.

82		10c. black and purple	1·00	1·25

1957. As Nos. 92/102 of Kedah but inset portrait of Sultan Ibrahim.

83		1c. black	10	30
84		2c. red	60	1·25
85		4c. sepia	30	10
86		5c. lake	30	10
87		8c. green	1·00	2·75
88		10c. sepia	2·00	10
89		10c. purple	7·00	6·50
90		20c. blue	2·00	30
91		50c. black and blue	50	50
92		$1 blue and purple	6·00	1·50

93 $2 green and red 11·00 6·00
94 $5 brown and green 15·00 12·00

1961. Coronation of the Sultan.
95 **6** 10c. multicoloured 50 50

7 Sultan Yahya Petra

8 "Vanda hookeriana"

1961. As Nos. 83, etc, but with inset portrait of Sultan Yahya Petra as in T **7**.
96 1c. black 10 1·75
97 2c. red 10 1·75
98 4c. sepia 80 1·00
99 5c. lake 60 20
100 8c. green 7·50 9·50
101 10c. purple 1·50 25
102 20c. blue 4·50 1·25

1965. As Nos. 115/21 of Kedah but with inset portrait of Sultan Yahya Petra as in T **8**.
103 **8** 1c. multicoloured 10 80
104 – 2c. multicoloured 10 1·50
105 – 5c. multicoloured 15 30
106 – 6c. multicoloured 70 2·00
107 – 10c. multicoloured 30 25
108 – 15c. multicoloured 1·50 25
109 – 20c. multicoloured 1·50 1·50
The higher values used in Kelantan were Nos. 20/7 of Malaysia (National Issues).

9 "Parthenos sylvia"

1971. Butterflies. As Nos. 124/30 of Kedah but with portrait of Sultan Yahya Petra as in T **9**.
112 – 1c. multicoloured 30 2·00
113 – 2c. multicoloured 40 2·00
114 **9** 5c. multicoloured 1·25 50
115 – 6c. multicoloured 1·25 2·25
116 – 10c. multicoloured 1·25 30
117 – 15c. multicoloured 1·25 10
118 – 20c. multicoloured 1·75 1·50
The higher values in use with this series were Nos. 64/71 of Malaysia (National Issues).

10 "Lagerstroemia speciosa"

1979. Flowers. As Nos. 135/41 of Kedah but with portrait of Sultan Yahya Petra as in T **10**.
123 1c. "Rafflesia hasseltii" 10 85
124 2c. "Pterocarpus indicus" 10 85
125 5c. Type **10** 10 70
126 10c. "Durio zibethinus" 15 10
127 15c. "Hibiscus rosa-sinensis" 15 10
128 20c. "Rhododendron scortechinii" 20 10
129 25c. "Etlingera elatior" (inscr "Phaeomeria speciosa") 40 70

11 Sultan Tengku Ismail Petra

12 Black Pepper

1980. Coronation of Sultan Tengku Ismail Petra.
130 **11** 10c. multicoloured 40 1·25
131 15c. multicoloured 40 25
132 50c. multicoloured 90 2·75

1986. Agricultural Products of Malaysia. Mult.
140 1c. Coffee 10 10
141 2c. Coconuts 10 10
142 5c. Cocoa 10 10
143 10c. Type **12** 10 10
144 15c. Rubber 10 10
145 20c. Oil palm 10 10
146 30c. Rice 10 10

KENYA Pt. 1

Formerly part of Kenya, Uganda and Tanganyika (q.v.). Became independent in 1963 and a Republic in 1964.

100 cents = 1 shilling.

1 Cattle Ranching

4 Cockerel

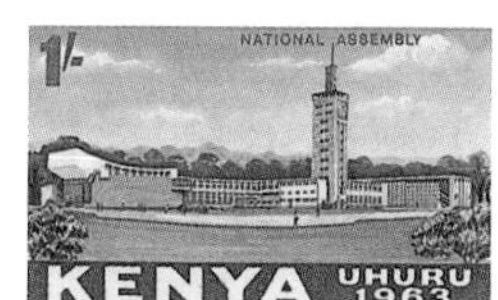

3 National Assembly

1963. Independence.
1 **1** 5c. multicoloured 10 55
2 – 10c. brown 10 10
3 – 15c. mauve 1·00 10
4 – 20c. black and green 15 10
5 – 30c. black and yellow 15 10
6 – 40c. brown and blue 15 30
7 – 50c. red, black and green 15 10
8 – 65c. turquoise and yellow 55 65
9 **3** 1s. multicoloured 20 10
10 – 1s.30 brown, black & green 4·25 30
11 – 2s. multicoloured 1·25 40
12 – 5s. brown, blue and green 1·25 40
13 – 10s. brown and blue 8·50 2·50
14 – 20s. black and red 4·00 8·00
DESIGNS—As Type **1**: 10c. Wood-carving; 15c. Heavy industry; 20c. Timber industry; 30c. Jomo Kenyatta facing Mt. Kenya; 40c. Fishing industry; 50c. Kenya flag, 65c. Pyrethrum industry. As Type **3**: 1s.30, Tourism (Treetops hotel); 2s. Coffee industry; 5s. Tea industry; 10s. Mombasa Port; 20s. Royal College, Nairobi.

1964. Inauguration of Republic. Multicoloured.
15 15c. Type **4** 15 15
16 30c. Pres. Kenyatta 15 10
17 50c. African lion 15 10
18 1s.30 Hartlaub's turaco 3·00 50
19 2s.50 Nandi flame 40 3·75

5 Thomson's Gazelle

7 Greater Kudu

1966.
20 **5** 5c. orange, black and sepia 20 20
21 – 10c. black and green 10 10
22 – 15c. black and orange 10 10
23 – 20c. ochre, black and blue 10 15
24 – 30c. indigo, blue and black 20 10
25 – 40c. black and brown 60 30
26 – 50c. black and orange 60 10
27 – 65c. black and green 1·25 2·00
28 – 70c. black and red 5·00 1·25
29 **7** 1s. brown, black and blue 30 10
30 – 1s.30 blue, green and black 4·00 20
31 – 1s.50 black, brown and green 3·00 2·00
32 – 2s.50 yellow, black & brown 3·25 1·25
33 – 5s. yellow, black and green 75 70
34 – 10s. ochre, black and brown 1·75 3·25
35 – 20s. multicoloured 5·50 13·00
DESIGNS—As Type **5**: 10c. Sable antelope; 15c. Aardvark ("Ant Bear"); 20c. Lesser bushbaby; 30c. Warthog; 40c. Common zebra; 50c. African buffalo; 65c. Black rhinoceros; 70c. Ostrich. As Type **7**: 1s.30, African elephant; 1s.50, Bat-eared fox; 2s.50, Cheetah; 5s. Savanna monkey ("Vervet Monkey"); 10s. Giant ground pangolin; 20s. Lion.

8 Perna Tellin

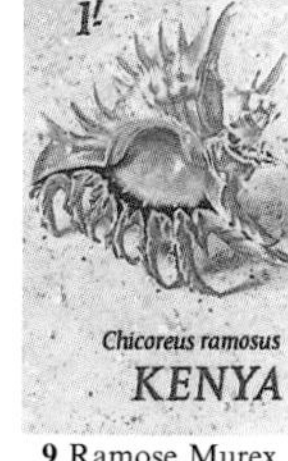

9 Ramose Murex

1971. Sea Shells. Multicoloured.
36 5c. Type **8** 10 30
37 10c. Episcopal mitre 15 10
38 15c. Purplish clanculus 15 20
39 20c. Humpback cowrie 15 20
40 30c. Variable abalone 20 10
41 40c. Flame top shell 20 10
42 50c. Common purple janthina 30 20
43 50c. Common purple janthina 11·00 2·75
44 60c. Bullmouth helmet 30 1·25
45 70c. Chambered or pearly nautilus 45 1·50
46 70c. Chambered or pearly nautilus 10·00 5·00
47a 1s. Type **9** 20 10
48 1s.50 Trumpet triton 1·00 10
49 2s.50 Trapezium horse conch 1·00 10
50a 5s. Great green turban 1·00 10
51 10s. Textile or cloth of gold cone 1·50 15
52a 20s. Scorpion conch 1·50 25
INSCRIPTIONS: No. 42, "Janthina globosa"; 43, "Janthina janthina"; 45, "Nautilus pompileus"; 46, "Nautilus pompilius".
Nos. 47/52 are larger, as Type **9**.

1975. Nos. 48/9 and 52a surch.
53 2s. on 1s.50 Trumpet triton 6·00 5·00
54 3s. on 2s.50 Trapezium horse conch 9·50 19·00
55 40s. on 20s. Scorpion conch 6·00 14·00

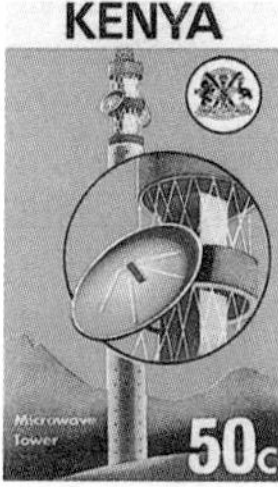

11 Microwave Tower

1976. Telecommunications Development. Mult.
56 50c. Type **11** 10 10
57 1s. Cordless switchboard (horiz) 10 10
58 2s. Telephones 20 30
59 3s. Message switching centre (horiz) 25 45
MS60 120 × 120 mm. Nos. 56/9. Imperf 1·10 2·50

12 Akii Bua, Ugandan Hurdler

1976. Olympic Games, Montreal. Multicoloured.
61 50c. Type **12** 10 10
62 1s. Filbert Bayi, Tanzanian runner 15 10
63 2s. Steve Muchoki, Kenyan boxer 45 35
64 3s. Olympic flame and East African flags 60 50
MS65 129 × 154 mm. Nos. 61/4 6·00 7·50

13 Diesel-hydraulic Train, Tanzania–Zambia Railway

1976. Railway Transport. Multicoloured.
66 50c. Type **13** 35 10
67 1s. Nile Bridge, Uganda 60 15
68 2s. Nakuru Station, Kenya 1·50 1·00
69 3s. Uganda Railway Class A steam locomotive, 1896 1·50 1·50
MS70 154 × 103 mm. Nos. 66/9 8·00 8·00

14 Nile Perch

1977. Game Fish of East Africa. Multicoloured.
71 50c. Type **14** 25 10
72 1s. Nile mouthbrooder ("Tilapia") 35 10
73 3s. Sailfish 75 60
74 5s. Black marlin 90 80
MS75 153 × 129 mm. Nos. 71/4 7·50 4·00

15 Maasai Manyatta (village), Kenya

1977. 2nd World Black and African Festival of Arts and Culture, Nigeria. Multicoloured.
76 50c. Type **15** 15 10
77 1s. "Heartbeat of Africa" (Ugandan dancers) 20 10
78 2s. Makonde sculpture, Tanzania 75 1·25
79 3s. "Early man and technology" (skinning hippopotamus) 1·00 2·00
MS80 132 × 109 mm. Nos. 76/9 4·00 5·50

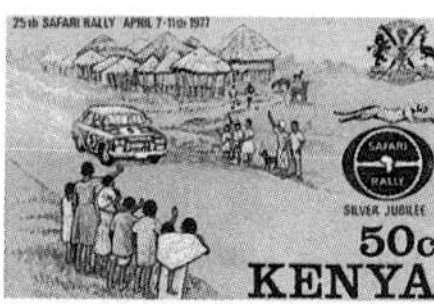

16 Rally Car and Villagers

1977. 25th Anniv of Safari Rally. Multicoloured.
81 50c. Type **16** 15 10
82 1s. Pres. Kenyatta starting rally 15 10
83 2s. Car fording river 50 60
84 5s. Car and elephants 1·40 1·50
MS85 126 × 93 mm. Nos. 81/4 3·75 6·50

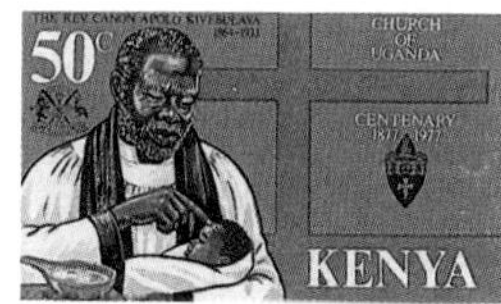

17 Canon Kivebulaya

1977. Centenary of Ugandan Church. Multicoloured.
86 50c. Type **17** 10 10
87 1s. Modern Namirembe Cathedral 10 10
88 2s. The first Cathedral 30 55
89 5s. Early congregation, Kigezi 50 1·00
MS90 126 × 94 mm. Nos. 86/9 1·40 2·50

18 Sagana Royal Lodge, Nyeri, 1952

1977. Silver Jubilee. Multicoloured.
91 2s. Type **18** 15 15
92 5s. Treetops Hotel (vert) 20 35
93 10s. Queen Elizabeth and Pres. Kenyatta 30 60
94 15s. Royal visit, 1972 45 1·00
MS95 Two sheets. (a) 140 × 60 mm. No. 94. (b) 152 × 127 mm. 50s. Queen and Prince Philip in Treetops Hotel Set of 2 sheets 2·00 1·40

19 Pancake Tortoise

1977. Endangered Species. Multicoloured.
96 50c. Type **19** 30 10
97 1s. Nile crocodile 40 10
98 2s. Hunter's hartebeest 1·60 40
99 3s. Red colobus monkey 1·75 50
100 5s. Dugong 2·00 75
MS101 127 × 101 mm. Nos. 97/100 7·00 8·50

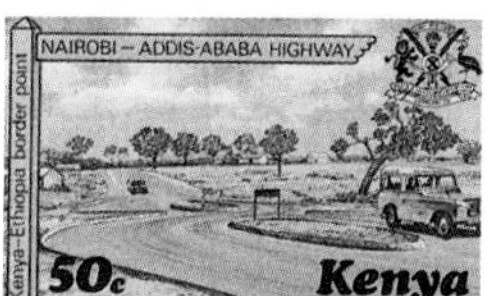

20 Kenya-Ethiopia Border Point

1977. Nairobi–Addis Ababa Highway. Mult.
102 50c. Type **20** 15 10
103 1s. Archer's Post 15 10
104 2s. Thika Flyover 30 25
105 5s. Marsabit Game Lodge 50 75
MS106 144 × 91 mm. Nos. 102/5 2·25 3·50

21 Gypsum

22 Amethyst

1977. Minerals. Multicoloured.

107	10c. Type **21**	1·25	20
108	20c. Trona	2·00	20
109	30c. Kyanite	2·00	20
110	40c. Amazonite	1·40	10
111	50c. Galena	1·40	10
112	70c. Silicified wood	7·50	60
113	80c. Fluorite	7·50	60
114	1s. Type **22**	1·40	10
115	1s.50 Agate	1·50	30
116	2s. Tourmaline	1·50	20
117	3s. Aquamarine	1·75	55
118	5s. Rhodolite garnet	1·75	1·40
119	10s. Sapphire	1·75	2·00
120	20s. Ruby	4·50	3·00
121	40s. Green grossular garnet	18·00	19·00

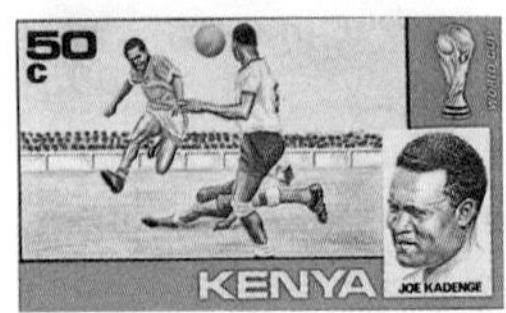

23 Joe Kadenge (Kenya) and Forwards

1978. World Cup Football Championship, Argentina. Multicoloured.

122	50c. Type **23**	10	10
123	1s. Mohamed Chuma (Tanzania) and cup presentation	10	10
124	2s. Omari Kidevu (Zanzibar) and goalmouth scene	30	70
125	3s. Polly Ouma (Uganda) and three forwards	40	95
MS126	136 × 81 mm. Nos. 122/5	3·75	3·50

24 Boxing

1978. Commonwealth Games, Edmonton. Mult.

127	50c. Type **24**	15	10
128	1s. Welcoming the Olympic Games Team, 1968	20	10
129	3s. Javelin throwing	60	1·00
130	5s. Pres. Kenyatta admiring boxer's trophy	75	1·60

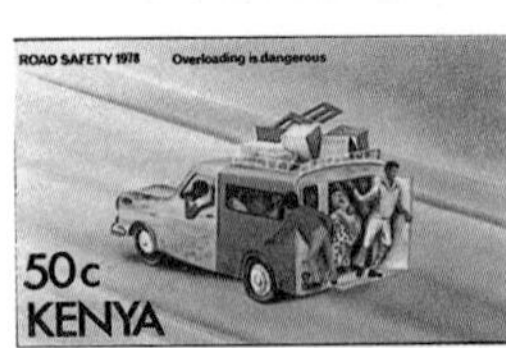

25 "Overloading is Dangerous"

1978. Road Safety. Multicoloured.

131	50c. Type **25**	50	10
132	1s. "Speed does not pay"	70	20
133	1s.50 "Ignoring Traffic Signs may cause death"	85	55
134	2s. "Slow down at School Crossing"	1·25	1·00
135	3s. "Never cross a continuous line"	1·40	2·50
136	5s. "Approach Railway Level Crossing with extreme caution"	2·00	3·50

26 Pres. Kenyatta at Mass Rally, 1963

1978. Kenyatta Day. Multicoloured.

137	50c. "Harambee Water Project"	15	10
138	1s. Handing over of Independence Instruments, 1963	15	10
139	2s. Type **26**	30	35
140	3s. "Harambee, 15 Great Years"	60	1·00
141	5s. "Struggle for Independence, 1952"	80	2·00

27 Freedom Fighters, Namibia

1978. International Anti-Apartheid Year.

142	**27**	50c. multicoloured	15	10
143	–	1s. black and blue	15	10
144	–	2s. multicoloured	30	30
145	–	3s. multicoloured	50	65
146	–	5s. multicoloured	55	1·00

DESIGNS: 1s. International seminar on apartheid; 2s. Steve Biko's tombstone; 3s. Nelson Mandela; 5s. Bishop Lamont.

28 Children Playing

1979. International Year of the Child. Multicoloured.

147	50c. Type **28**	20	10
148	2s. Boy fishing	60	60
149	3s. Children singing and dancing	80	1·10
150	5s. Children with camels	1·00	2·00

29 "The Lion and the Jewel"

1979. Kenya National Theatre. Multicoloured.

151	50c. Type **29**	15	10
152	1s. "Utisi"	15	10
153	2s. Theatre programmes	25	30
154	3s. Kenya National Theatre	35	45
155	5s. "Genesis"	50	75

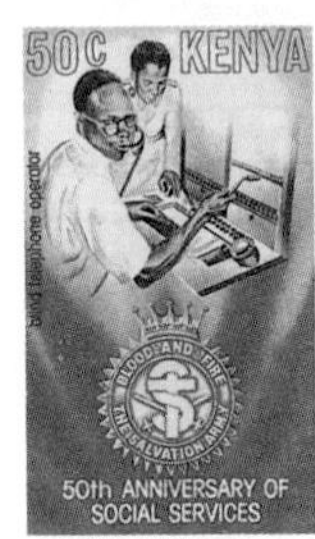

30 Blind Telephone Operator

31 "Father of the Nation" (Kenyatta's funeral procession)

1979. 50th Anniv of Salvation Army Social Services.

156	50c. Type **30**	30	10
157	1s. Care for the aged	30	10
158	3s. Village polytechnic (horiz)	60	1·50
159	5s. Vocational training (horiz)	1·00	2·50

1979. 1st Death Anniv of President Kenyatta. Multicoloured.

160	50c. Type **31**	10	10
161	1s. "First President of Kenya" (Kenyatta receiving independence)	10	10
162	3s. "Kenyatta the politician" (speaking at rally)	30	50
163	5s. "A true son of Kenya" (Kenyatta as a boy carpenter)	40	95

32 British East Africa Company 1890 1a. Stamp

1979. Death Centenary of Sir Rowland Hill.

164	**32**	50c. multicoloured	15	10
165	–	1s. multicoloured	15	10
166	–	2s. black, red and brown	20	40
167	–	5s. multicoloured	35	1·00

DESIGNS: 1s. Kenya, Uganda and Tanganyika 1935 1s. stamp; 2s. Penny Black; 5s. 1964 2s.50 Inauguration of Republic commemorative.

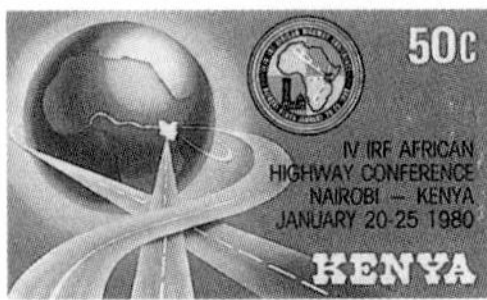

33 Roads, Globe and Conference Emblem

1980. International Road Federation. African Highway Conference, Nairobi. Multicoloured.

168	50c. Type **33**	15	10
169	1s. New weighbridge, Athi River	15	10
170	3s. New Nyali Bridge, Mombasa	40	85
171	5s. Highway to Jomo Kenyatta International Airport	50	2·00

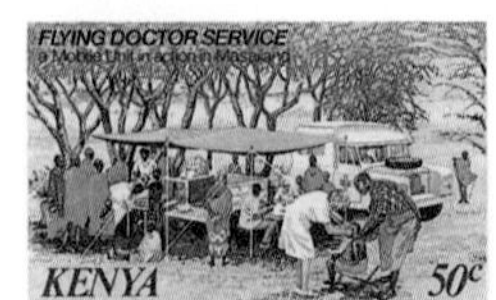

34 Mobile Unit in action in Masailand

1980. Flying Doctor Service. Multicoloured.

172	50c. Type **34**	10	10
173	1s. Donkey transport to Turkana airstrip (vert)	20	10
174	3s. Surgical team in action at outstation (vert)	65	1·00
175	5s. Emergency airlift from North Eastern Province	90	1·60
MS176	146 × 133 mm. Nos. 172/5	1·60	2·50

35 Statue of Sir Rowland Hill

37 Blue-spotted Stingray

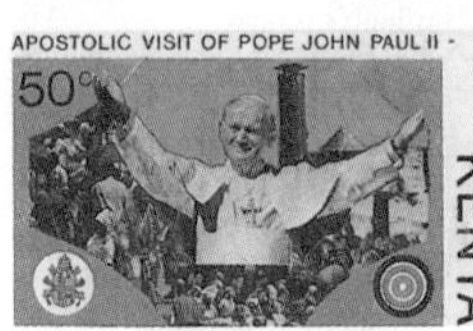

36 Pope John Paul II

1980. "London 1980" International Stamp Exhibition.

177	**35**	25s. multicoloured	1·00	2·50
MS178		114 × 101 mm. No. 177	1·00	2·75

1980. Papal Visit. Multicoloured.

179	50c. Type **36**	40	10
180	1s. Pope, arms and cathedral (vert)	40	10
181	5s. Pope, flags and dove (vert)	75	75
182	10s. Pope, President Moi and map of Africa	1·25	1·60

1980. Marine Life. Multicoloured.

183	50c. Type **37**	30	10
184	2s. Allard's anemonefish	1·00	80
185	3s. Four-coloured nudibranch	1·25	1·75
186	5s. "Eretmochelys imbricata"	1·75	2·75

38 National Archives

1980. Historic Buildings. Multicoloured.

187	50c. Type **38**	10	10
188	1s. Provincial Commissioner's Office, Nairobi	15	10
189	1s.50 Nairobi House	20	20
190	2s. Norfolk Hotel	25	50
191	3s. McMillan Library	35	85
192	5s. Kipande House	55	1·40

39 "Disabled enjoys Affection"

1981. Int Year for Disabled Persons. Mult.

193	50c. Type **39**	15	10
194	1s. President Moi presenting flag to Disabled Olympic Games team captain	15	10
195	3s. Blind people climbing Mount Kenya, 1975	55	65
196	5s. Disabled artist at work	70	1·00

40 Longonot Complex

1981. Satellite Communications. Multicoloured.

197	50c. Type **40**	15	10
198	2s. "Intelsat V"	40	35
199	3s. "Longonot I"	45	55
200	5s. "Longonot II"	60	85

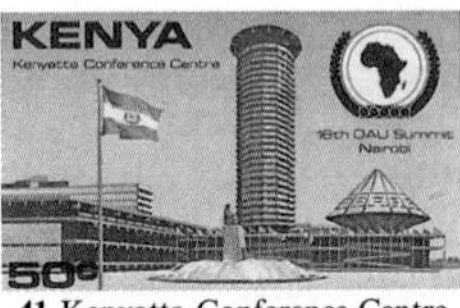

41 Kenyatta Conference Centre

1981. O.A.U. (Organization of African Unity) Summit Conference, Nairobi.

201	**41**	50c. multicoloured	15	10
202	–	1s. black, yellow and blue	15	10
203	–	3s. multicoloured	40	40
204	–	5s. multicoloured	70	65
205	–	10s. multicoloured	80	1·00
MS206		110 × 110 mm. No. 205	1·10	1·50

DESIGNS: 1s. "Panaftel" earth stations; 3s. Parliament Building; 5s. Jomo Kenyatta International Airport; 10s. O.A.U. flag.

42 St. Paul's Cathedral

43 Giraffe

1981. Royal Wedding. Multicoloured.

207	50c. Prince Charles and President Daniel Arap Moi	10	10
208	3s. Type **42**	15	20
209	5s. Royal Yacht "Britannia"	25	30
210	10s. Prince Charles on safari in Kenya	40	55
MS211	85 × 102 mm. 25s. Prince Charles and Lady Diana Spencer	75	80

1981. Rare Animals. Multicoloured.

212	50c. Type **43**	15	10
213	2s. Bongo	25	25
214	5s. Roan antelope	40	1·00
215	10s. Agile mangabey	60	2·25

44 "Technical Development"

45 Kamba

1981. World Food Day. Multicoloured.

216	50c. Type **44**	10	10
217	1s. "Mwea rice projects"	15	10
218	2s. "Irrigation schemes"	30	55
219	5s. "Breeding livestock"	60	1·75

1981. Ceremonial Costumes (1st series). Mult.

220	50c. Type **45**	40	10
221	1s. Turkana	45	10
222	2s. Giriama	1·25	85
223	3s. Masai	1·60	2·25
224	5s. Luo	1·75	3·50

See also Nos. 329/33, 413/17 and 515/19.

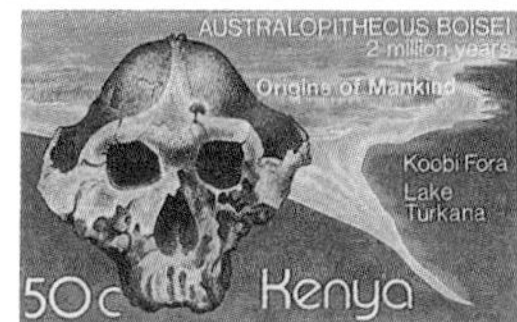

46 "Australopithecus boisei"

1982. "Origins of Mankind". Skulls. Multicoloured.
225 50c. Type **46** . . . . 1·75 30
226 2s. "Homo erectus" . . . . 3·25 1·50
227 3s. "Homo habilis" . . . . . 3·25 3·75
228 5s. "Proconsul africanus" . . 3·75 5·00

47 Tree-planting

1982. 75th Anniv of Boy Scout Movement (Nos. 229, 231, 233 and 235) and 60th Anniv of Girl Guide Movement (Nos. 230, 232, 234 and 236). Multicoloured.
229 70c. Type **47** 50 80
230 70c. Paying homage 50 80
231 3s.50 "Be Prepared" . . . . 1·25 2·00
232 3s.50 "International Friendship" . . . . 1·25 2·00
233 5s. Helping disabled . . . . 1·75 2·50
234 5s. Community service . . . 1·75 2·50
235 6s.50 Paxtu Cottage (Lord Baden-Powell's home) . . 2·00 2·75
236 6s.50 Lady Baden-Powell . . 2·00 2·75
MS237 112 × 112 mm. Nos. 229, 231, 233 and 235 . . . . 3·75 3·00

48 Footballer displaying Shooting Skill

1982. World Cup Football Championship, Spain. Footballers silhouetted against Map of World. Multicoloured.
238 70c. Type **48** . . . . 1·50 65
239 3s.50 Heading . . . . 2·75 2·75
240 5s. Goalkeeping . . . . . . 3·75 4·25
241 10s. Dribbling . . . . 5·50 8·00
MS242 101 × 76 mm. 20s. Tackling 5·50 4·00

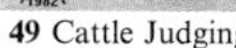

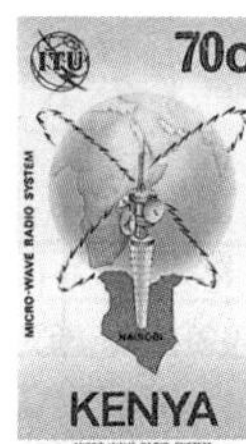

49 Cattle Judging
50 Micro-wave Radio System

1982. 80th Anniv of Agricultural Society of Kenya. Multicoloured.
243 70c. Type **49** 50 10
244 2s.50 Farm machinery . . . 1·25 1·25
245 3s.50 Musical ride . . . . . 1·50 2·50
246 6s.50 Agricultural Society emblem . . . . 2·00 4·25

1982. I.T.U. Plenipotentiary Conference, Nairobi. Multicoloured.
247 70c. Type **50** 50 10
248 3s.50 Sea-to-shore service link 1·75 1·75
249 5s. Rural telecommunications system . . . . 2·25 3·75
250 6s.50 I.T.U. emblem . . . . 2·50 4·50

1982. No. 113 surch **70c**.
251 70c. on 80c. Fluorite . . . . 1·00 1·25

52 Container Cranes

1983. 5th Anniv of Kenya Ports Authority. Mult.
252 70c. Type **52** 85 10
253 2s. Port by night . . . . . . 1·75 1·90
254 3s.50 Container cranes (different) . . . . 2·50 3·50
255 5s. Map of Mombasa Port . . 3·25 4·50
MS256 125 × 85 mm. Nos. 252/5 7·50 9·00

53 Shada Zambarau
54 Waridi Kikuba

1983. Flowers. Multicoloured.
257 10c. Type **53** 40 40
258 20c. Kilua Kingulima . . . 55 40
259 30c. Mwalika Mwiya . . . 55 40
260 40c. Ziyungi Buluu 55 40
261 50c. Kilua Habashia 55 30
262 70c. Chanuo Kato 60 20
262a 80c. As 40c. . . . . 4·00 4·00
262b 1s. Waridi Kikuba . . . . 4·00 80
263 1s. Type **54** 65 20
264 1s.50 Mshomoro Mtambazi 1·75 60
265 2s. Papatuo Boti . . . . . 1·75 60
266 2s.50 Tumba Mboni . . . . 1·75 60
266a 3s. Mkuku Mrembo . . . . 12·00 8·00
267 3s.50 Mtongo Mbeja . . . 1·50 1·50
267b 4s. Mnukia Muuma . . . . 4·75 6·50
268 5s. Nyungu Chepuo . . . . 1·50 1·50
268a 7s. Mlua Miba . . . . . . 6·50 10·00
269 10s. Muafunili . . . . . . 1·50 1·50
270 20s. Mbake Nyanza . . . . 1·50 2·50
271 40s. Njuga Pagwa . . . . . 2·25 8·00
The 1s.50 to 40s. are in the same format as T **54**.

55 Coffee Plucking
56 Examining Parcels

1983. Commonwealth Day. Multicoloured.
272 70c. Type **55** 10 10
273 2s. President Daniel Arap Moi 15 20
274 5s. Satellite view of Earth (horiz) 35 45
275 10s. Masai dance (horiz) . . 65 1·00

1983. 30th Anniv of Customs Co-operation Council. Multicoloured.
276 70c. Type **56** 25 10
277 2s.50 Customs Headquarters, Mombasa 65 30
278 3s.50 Customs Council Headquarters, Brussels . . 75 40
279 10s. Customs patrol boat . . 2·40 2·50

57 Communications via Satellite

1983. World Communications Year. Multicoloured.
280 70c. Type **57** 60 10
281 2s.50 "Telephone and Postal Services" . . . . 1·50 1·75
282 3s.50 Communications by sea and air (horiz) . . . . . . 2·00 3·00
283 5s. Road and rail communications (horiz) . . 2·50 4·00

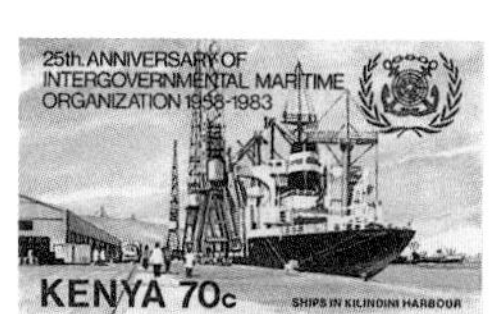

58 "Craftsman" (freighter) in Kilindini Harbour

1983. 25th Anniv of Intergovernmental Maritime Organization. Multicoloured.
284 70c. Type **58** 95 10
285 2s.50 Life-saving devices . . 2·00 1·75
286 3s.50 Mombasa container terminal . . . . 2·50 3·00
287 10s. Marine park . . . . . . 3·50 7·00

59 President Moi signing Visitors' Book

1983. 29th Commonwealth Parliamentary Conference. Multicoloured.
288 70c. Type **59** 25 10
289 2s.50 Parliament building, Nairobi (vert) . . . . . . 90 1·25
290 5s. State opening of Parliament (vert) . . . . . 1·60 3·00
MS291 122 × 141 mm. Nos. 288/90 2·50 5·00

60 Kenyan and British Flags

1983. Royal Visit. Multicoloured.
292 70c. Type **60** 50 10
293 3s.50 Sagana State Lodge . . 2·00 1·50
294 5s. Treetops Hotel . . . . . 2·25 2·75
295 10s. Queen Elizabeth II and President Moi . . . . . . 3·50 7·00
MS296 126 × 100 mm. 25s. Designs as Nos. 292/5, but without face values. Imperf . . . . 4·50 7·50

61 President Moi

1983. 20th Anniv of Independence. Mult.
297 70c. Type **61** 10 10
298 2s. President Moi planting tree 15 20
299 3s.50 Kenyan flag and emblem 25 35
300 5s. School milk scheme . . . 40 50
301 10s. People of Kenya . . . . 75 1·10
MS302 126 × 93 mm. 25s. Designs as Nos. 297 and 299/301, but without face values. Imperf . . . . . . 1·50 2·75

62 White-backed Night Heron
63 Radar Tower

1984. Rare Birds of Kenya. Multicoloured.
303 70c. Type **62** . . . . 1·75 30
304 2s.50 Quail plover . . . . . 3·00 2·50
305 3s.50 Taita olive thrush . . . 3·75 3·75
306 5s. Mufumbiri shrike . . . . 4·25 4·25
307 10s. White-winged apalis . . 5·50 7·00

1984. 40th Anniv of International Civil Aviation Organization. Multicoloured.
308 70c. Type **63** 15 10
309 2s.50 Kenya School of Aviation (horiz) 45 60
310 3s.50 Boeing 707 taking off from Moi airport (horiz) 65 1·25
311 5s. Air traffic control centre 95 1·60

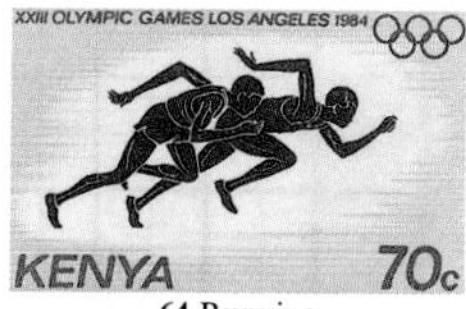

64 Running

1984. Olympic Games, Los Angeles.
312 **64** 70c. black, green & dp green 30 10
313 – 2s.50 black, purple & violet 60 70
314 – 5s. black, blue & deep blue 1·50 2·50
315 – 10s. black, yellow & brown 3·50 6·00
MS316 130 × 121 mm. 25s. Designs as Nos. 312/15, but without face values. Imperf . . . . 3·25 3·25
DESIGNS: 2s.50, Hurdling; 5s. Boxing; 10s. Hockey.

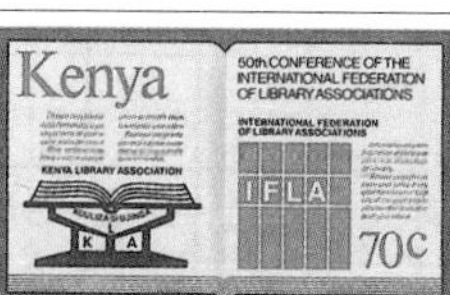

65 Conference and Kenya Library Association Logos

1984. 50th Conference of the International Federation of Library Associations. Multicoloured.
317 70c. Type **65** 10 10
318 3s.50 Mobile library 50 60
319 5s. Adult library . . . . . . 65 1·25
320 10s. Children's library . . . 1·00 3·00

66 Doves and Cross
67 Export Year Logo

1984. 4th World Conference on Religion and Peace. As T **66**, each design showing a different central symbol. Multicoloured.
321 70c. Type **66** 30 10
322 2s.50 Arabic inscription . . . 1·25 1·50
323 3s.50 Peace emblem . . . . 1·60 2·50
324 6s.50 Star and Crescent . . . 2·00 4·00

1984. Kenya Export Year. Multicoloured.
325 70c. Type **67** 30 10
326 3s.50 Forklift truck with air cargo (horiz) . . . . . . 1·75 2·00
327 5s. Loading ship's cargo . . 2·50 3·00
328 10s. Kenyan products (horiz) 3·75 6·50

1984. Ceremonial Costumes (2nd series). As T **45**. Multicoloured.
329 70c. Luhya 80 15
330 2s. Kikuyu . . . . 2·00 1·75
331 3s.50 Pokomo . . . . 2·50 2·25
332 5s. Nandi . . . . 3·00 3·00
333 10s. Rendile . . . . 4·00 6·50

68 Staunton Knight and Nyayo National Stadium

1984. 60th Anniv of International Chess Federation. Multicoloured.
334 70c. Type **68** . . . . 2·00 40
335 2s.50 Staunton rook and Fort Jesus . . . . 3·00 1·75
336 3s.50 Staunton bishop and National Monument . . . 3·50 2·00
337 5s. Staunton queen and Parliament Building . . . 3·75 3·75
338 10s. Staunton king and Nyayo Fountain . . . . . 5·50 8·00

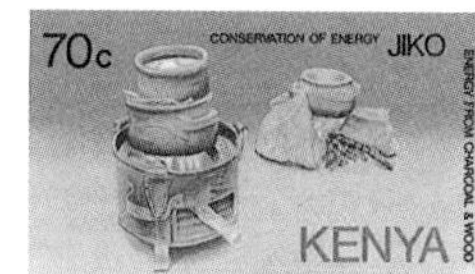

69 Cooking with Wood-burning Stove and Charcoal Fire

1985. Energy Conservation. Multicoloured.
339 70c. Type **69** 20 10
340 2s. Solar energy panel on roof 65 75
341 3s.50 Production of gas from cow dung . . . . 75 1·25
342 10s. Ploughing with oxen . . 2·25 6·00
MS343 110 × 85 mm. 20s. Designs as Nos. 339/42, but without face values . . . . 2·50 2·50

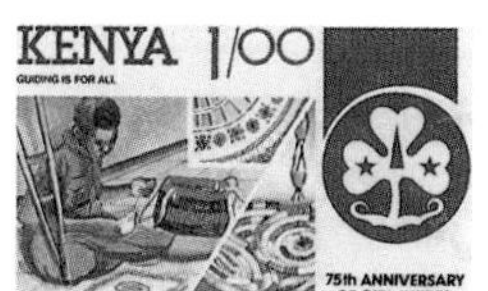

70 Crippled Girl Guide making Table-mat

1985. 75th Anniv of Girl Guide Movement. Multicoloured.
344 1s. Type **70** 75 15
345 3s. Girl Guides doing community service . . . . 1·75 1·50
346 5s. Lady Olave Baden-Powell (founder) . . . . 2·50 3·00
347 7s. Girl Guides gardening . . 4·00 6·50

71 Stylized Figures and Globe

1985. World Red Cross Day.
348 **71** 1s. black and red 80 15
349 – 4s. multicoloured . . . . . 3·00 3·00
350 – 5s. multicoloured . . . . . 3·25 3·50
351 – 7s. multicoloured . . . . . 4·50 6·50
DESIGNS: 4s. First Aid Team; 5s. Hearts containing crosses ("Blood Donation"); 7s. Cornucopia ("Famine Relief").

72 Man with Malaria **73** Repairing Water Pipes

1985. 7th International Congress of Protozoology, Nairobi. Multicoloured.
352 1s. Type **72** . . . . 1·50 20
353 3s. Child with Leishmaniasis 3·50 2·75
354 5s. Cow with Trypanosomiasis . . . . . 4·00 4·25
355 7s. Dog with Babesiosis . . . 6·50 7·50

1985. United Nations Women's Decade Conference. Multicoloured.
356 1s. Type **73** 20 10
357 3s. Traditional food preparation 60 70
358 5s. Basket-weaving . . . . . 75 1·25
359 7s. Dressmaking . . . . . . 1·00 3·00

74 The Last Supper

1985. 43rd International Eucharistic Congress, Nairobi. Multicoloured.
360 1s. Type **74** 50 10
361 3s. Village family ("The Eucharist and the Christian Family") . . . . 2·25 2·00
362 5s. Congress altar, Uhuru Park . . . . 2·50 3·00
363 7s. St. Peter Claver's Church, Nairobi . . . . 3·00 5·00
MS364 117 × 80 mm. 25s. Pope John Paul II . . . . 6·50 6·50

75 Black Rhinoceros

1985. Endangered Animals. Multicoloured.
365 1s. Type **75** . . . . 2·00 40
366 3s. Cheetah . . . . 3·25 2·75
367 5s. De Brazza's monkey . . . 3·50 4·00
368 10s. Grevy's zebra . . . . . 6·00 8·00
MS369 129 × 122 mm. 25s. Endangered species (122 × 114 mm). Imperf . . . . 8·50 4·50

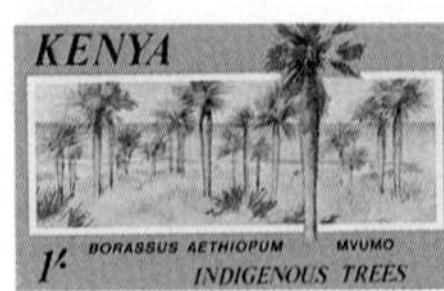

76 "Borassus aethiopum"

1986. Indigenous Trees. Multicoloured.
370 1s. Type **76** 65 15
371 3s. "Acacia xanthophloea" 2·50 2·50
372 5s. "Ficus natalensis" . . . . 3·50 4·00
373 7s. "Spathodea nilotica" . . 4·50 7·00
MS374 117 × 96 mm. 25s. Landscape with trees (109 × 90 mm). Imperf 3·25 4·00

77 Dove and U.N. Logo (from poster) **78** Dribbling the Ball

1986. International Peace Year. Multicoloured.
375 1s. Type **77** 30 10
376 3s. U.N. General Assembly (horiz) . . . . 1·00 75
377 7s. Nuclear explosion . . . . 2·50 3·50
378 10s. Quotation from Wall of Isaiah, U.N. Building, New York (horiz) . . . . 4·50 5·00

1986. World Cup Football Championship, Mexico. Multicoloured.
379 1s. Type **78** . . . . 1·25 20
380 3s. Scoring from a penalty . . 2·75 1·25
381 5s. Tackling . . . . 3·50 2·25
382 7s. Cup winners . . . . . . 4·25 3·75
383 10s. Heading the ball . . . . 5·50 4·75
MS384 110 × 86 mm. 30s. Harambee Stars football team (102 × 78 mm). Imperf . . . . 4·25 3·75

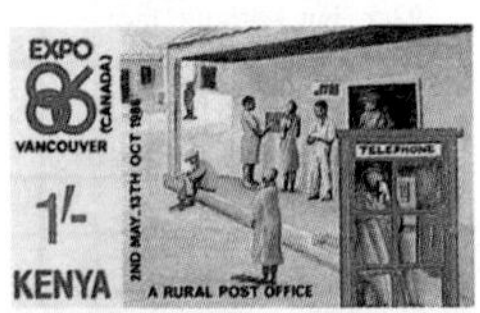

79 Rural Post Office and Telephone

1986. "Expo '86" World Fair, Vancouver. Mult.
385 1s. Type **79** 50 15
386 3s. Container depot, Embakasi . . . . 2·50 1·75
387 5s. Piper Twin Commanche airplane landing at game park airstrip . . . . 4·75 3·00
388 7s. Container ship . . . . . 5·00 6·00
389 10s. Transporting produce to market . . . . 5·50 7·00

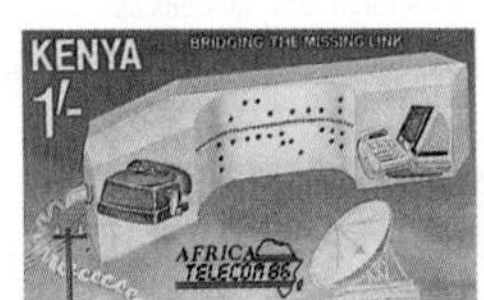

80 Telephone, Computer and Dish Aerial

1986. African Telecommunications. Multicoloured.
390 1s. Type **80** 35 10
391 3s. Telephones of 1876, 1936 and 1986 . . . . 1·00 85
392 5s. Dish aerial, satellite, telephones and map of Africa . . . . 1·25 1·25
393 7s. Kenyan manufacture of telecommunications equipment . . . . 1·75 2·25

81 Mashua

1986. Dhows of Kenya. Multicoloured.
394 1s. Type **81** 65 20
395 3s. Mtepe . . . . 1·75 1·50
396 5s. Dau La Mwao . . . . . 2·25 2·75
397 10s. Jahazi . . . . 3·75 5·50
MS398 118 × 80 mm. 25s. Lamu dhow and map of Indian Ocean 5·00 5·00

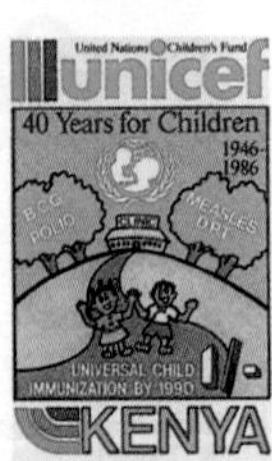

82 Nativity **83** Immunization

1986. Christmas. Multicoloured.
399 1s. Type **82** 30 10
400 3s. Shepherd and sheep . . . 1·00 55
401 5s. Angel and slogan "LOVE PEACE UNITY" (horiz) 1·60 1·40
402 7s. The Magi riding camels (horiz) . . . . 1·90 2·75

1987. 40th Anniv of U.N.I.C.E.F. Multicoloured.
403 1s. Type **83** 45 10
404 3s. Food and nutrition . . . 1·00 70
405 4s. Oral rehydration therapy 1·75 1·50
406 5s. Family planning . . . . 1·75 1·50
407 10s. Female literacy . . . . 2·50 4·00

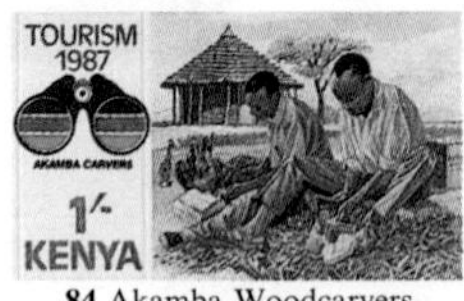

84 Akamba Woodcarvers

1987. Tourism. Multicoloured.
408 1s. Type **84** 30 10
409 3s. Tourism on beach . . . . 2·50 1·75
410 5s. Tourist and guide at view point . . . . 3·25 3·75
411 7s. Pride of lions . . . . . . 4·75 6·50
MS412 118 × 81 mm. 30s. Geysers 8·50 8·50

1987. Ceremonial Costumes (3rd series). As T **45**. Multicoloured.
413 1s. Embu 80 10
414 3s. Kisii . . . . 2·25 70
415 5s. Samburu . . . . 2·50 1·75
416 7s. Taita . . . . 3·25 3·50
417 10s. Boran . . . . 3·25 4·00

85 Telecommunications by Satellite

1987. 10th Anniv of Kenya Posts and Telecommunications Corporation. Multicoloured.
418 1s. Type **85** 60 30
419 3s. Rural post office, Kajiado 1·50 1·50
420 4s. Awarding trophy, Welfare Sports . . . . 1·60 1·75
421 5s. Village and telephone box 1·75 2·00
422 7s. Speedpost labels and outline map of Kenya . . 2·50 3·50
MS423 110 × 80 mm. 25s. Corporation flag . . . . 2·25 2·50

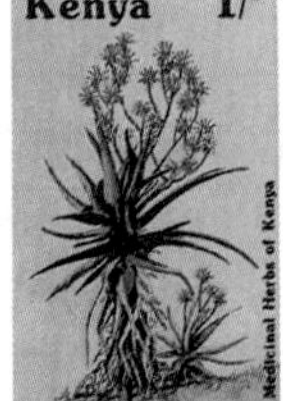

86 Volleyball **87** "Aloe volkensii"

1987. 4th All-Africa Games, Nairobi. Mult.
424 1s. Type **86** 20 10
425 3s. Cycling 70 30
426 4s. Boxing 35 55
427 5s. Swimming 40 60
428 7s. Steeplechasing . . . . . 50 1·10
MS429 117 × 80 mm. 30s. Kasarani Sports Complex (horiz) . . . . 2·50 2·75

1987. Medicinal Herbs. Multicoloured.
430 1s. Type **87** 60 10
431 3s. "Cassia didymobotrya" 1·50 1·00
432 5s. "Erythrina abyssinica" . . 2·25 2·00
433 7s. "Adenium obesum" . . . 2·75 3·25
434 10s. Herbalist's clinic . . . . 3·00 3·50

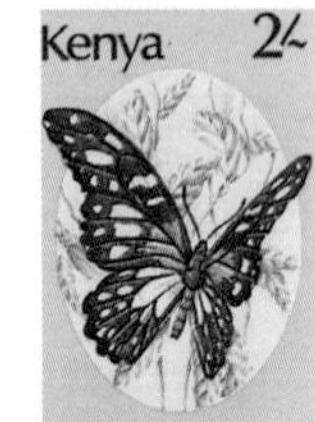

88 "Epamera sidus" **89** "Papilio rex"

1988. Butterflies. Multicoloured.
434a 10c. "Cyrestis camillus" . . 1·50 2·00
435 20c. Type **88** 35 70
436 40c. "Cynthia cardui" . . . 50 70
437 50c. "Colotis evippe" . . . 50 70
438 70c. "Precis westermanni" 50 70
439 80c. "Colias electo" 50 70
440 1s. "Eronia leda" 50 30
440a 1s.50 "Papilio dardanus" . . 4·75 30
441 2s. Type **89** 70 40
442 2s.50 "Colotis phisadia" . . 75 90
443 3s. "Papilio desmondi" . . . 80 90
444 3s.50 "Papilio demodocus" 80 60
445 4s. "Papilio phorcas" . . . 85 60
446 5s. "Charaxes druceanus" 90 70
447 7s. "Cymothoe teita" . . . 1·00 1·75
448 10s. "Charaxes zoolina" . . 1·00 1·75
449 20s. "Papilio dardanus" . . 1·25 3·00
450 40s. "Charaxes cithaeron" 2·00 5·50
The 10c. to 1s.50 are in the same format as T **88**.

90 Samburu Lodge and Crocodiles

1988. Kenyan Game Lodges. Multicoloured.
451 1s. Type **90** 50 10
452 3s. Naro Moru River Lodge and rock climbing . . . . 1·00 60
453 4s. Mara Serena Lodge and zebra with foal . . . . . . 1·00 1·25
454 5s. Voi Safari Lodge and buffalo . . . . 1·10 1·25
455 7s. Kilimanjaro Buffalo Lodge and giraffes . . . . 2·00 2·50
456 10s. Meru Mulika Lodge and rhinoceroses . . . . 2·50 3·00

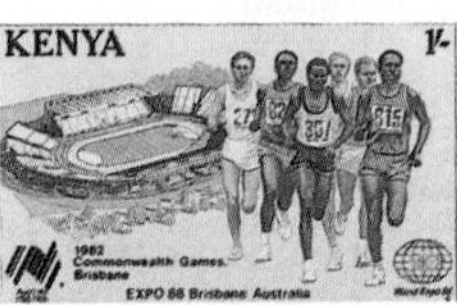

91 Athletes and Stadium, Commonwealth Games, Brisbane, 1982

1988. "Expo '88" World Fair, Brisbane, and Bicent of Australian Settlement. Multicoloured.
457 1s. Type **91** 40 10
458 3s. Flying Doctor Service De Havilland Drover 3 and Piper Twin Commanche aircraft . . . . 2·25 1·25
459 4s. H.M.S. "Sirius" (frigate), 1788 . . . . 2·50 2·25
460 5s. Ostrich and emu . . . . 2·75 2·25
461 7s. Queen Elizabeth II, Pres. Arap Moi of Kenya and Prime Minister Hawke of Australia . . . . 2·50 3·50
MS462 117 × 80 mm. 30s. Entrance to Kenya Pavilion . . . . . . 1·90 2·00

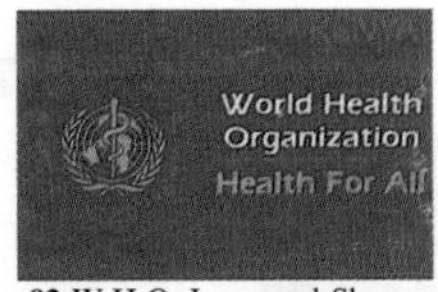

92 W.H.O. Logo and Slogan

1988. 40th Anniv of W.H.O.
463 **92** 1s. blue, gold and deep blue 25 10
464 – 3s. multicoloured 85 70
465 – 5s. multicoloured . . . . . 1·25 1·25
466 – 7s. multicoloured . . . . . 1·75 2·25
DESIGNS: 3s. Mother with young son and nutritious food; 5s. Giving oral vaccine to baby; 7s. Village women drawing clean water from pump.

93 Handball **94** Calabashes

1988. Olympic Games, Seoul. Multicoloured.
467 1s. Type **93** 40 10
468 3s. Judo 65 55
469 5s. Weightlifting 85 90
470 7s. Javelin . . . . 1·00 1·40
471 10s. Relay racing . . . . . . 1·40 2·00
MS472 110 × 78 mm. 30s. Tennis 2·25 2·50

1988. Kenyan Material Culture (1st issue). Mult.
473 1s. Type **94** 30 10
474 3s. Milk gourds 75 55
475 5s. Cooking pots (horiz) . . 85 85
476 7s. Winnowing trays (horiz) 1·25 1·60
477 10s. Reed baskets (horiz) . . 1·60 2·25
MS478 118 × 80 mm. 25s. Gourds, calabash and horn (horiz) . . . 1·50 1·60
See also Nos. 646/50.

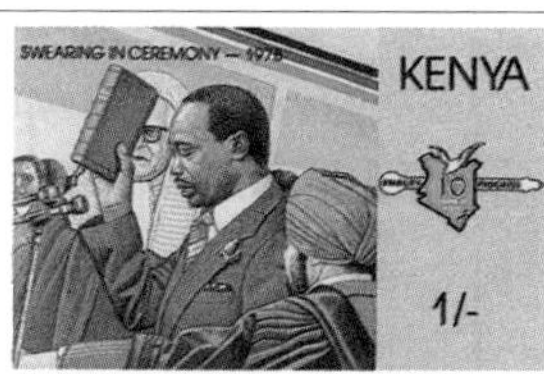

95 Pres. Arap Moi taking Oath, 1978

1988. 10th Anniv of "Nyayo" Era. Mult.
479 1s. Type **95** 30 10
480 3s. Building soil conservation barrier . . . . 1·00 70
481 3s.50 Passengers boarding bus . . . . 2·50 1·40
482 4s. Metalwork shop . . . . 1·25 1·50
483 5s. Moi University, Eldoret 1·25 1·50
484 7s. Aerial view of hospital . . 3·00 3·50
485 10s. Pres. Arap Moi and Mrs. Thatcher at Kapsabet Telephone Exchange . . . 6·50 6·00

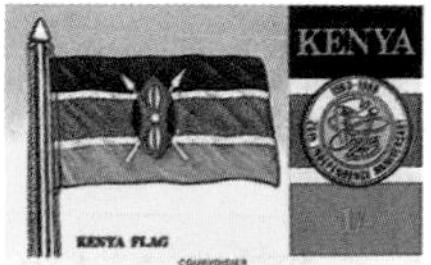

96 Kenya Flag

1988. 25th Anniv of Independence. Mult.
486 1s. Type **96** 60 10
487 3s. Coffee picking 70 50
488 5s. Proposed Kenya Posts and Telecommunications Headquarters building . . 1·00 1·10
489 7s. Kenya Airways Airbus Industrie A310-300 "Harambee Star" . . . . 4·50 2·75
490 10s. New diesel locomotive No. 9401 . . . . 6·50 4·50

97 Gedi Ruins, Malindi

1989. Historic Monuments. Multicoloured.
491 1s.20 Type **97** 50 10
492 3s.40 Vasco Da Gama Pillar, Malindi (vert) . . . . . . 1·25 1·10
493 4s.40 Ishiakani Monument, Kiunga . . . . 1·40 1·50
494 5s.50 Fort Jesus, Mombasa 1·60 1·75
495 7s.50 She Burnan Omwe, Lamu (vert) . . . . 2·50 3·25

98 125th Anniversary and Kenya Red Cross Logos

1989. 125th Anniv of International Red Cross. Multicoloured.
496 1s.20 Type **98** 50 10
497 3s.40 Red Cross workers with car crash victim . . . . . 1·25 90
498 4s.40 Disaster relief team distributing blankets . . . 1·40 1·40
499 5s.50 Henri Dunant (founder) 1·50 1·75
500 7s.70 Blood donor . . . . . 1·75 3·00

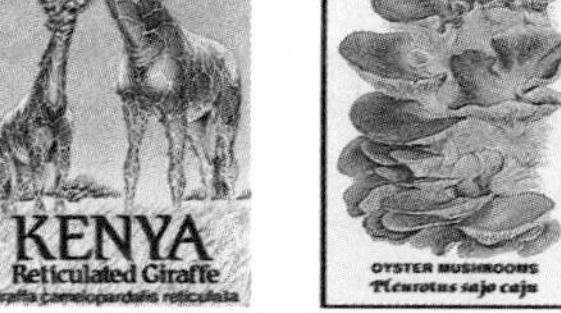

99 Female Giraffe and Calf

100 "Lentinus sajor-caju"

1989. Reticulated Giraffe. Multicoloured.
501 1s.20 Type **99** . . . . 1·75 30
502 3s.40 Giraffe drinking . . . 3·25 3·00
503 4s.40 Two giraffes . . . . . 3·75 4·00
504 5s.50 Giraffe feeding . . . . 4·50 5·50
MS505 80 × 110 mm. 30s. Designs as Nos. 501/4, but without face values . . . . 5·50 7·00
Designs from No. **MS**505 are without the Worldwide Fund for Nature logo.

1989. Mushrooms. Multicoloured.
506 1s.20 Type **100** . . . . . . 1·50 30
507 3s.40 "Agaricus bisporus" . . 2·50 2·00
508 4s.40 "Agaricus bisporus" (different) . . . . 2·75 2·50
509 5s.50 "Termitomyces schimperi" . . . . 3·50 3·50
510 7s.70 "Lentinus edodes" . . 4·25 5·50

101 Independence Monuments

1989. Birth Centenary of Jawaharlal Nehru (Indian statesman). Multicoloured.
511 1s.20 Type **101** . . . . . . 1·00 30
512 3s.40 Nehru with graduates and open book . . . . . 3·00 1·75
513 5s.50 Jawaharlal Nehru . . . 4·00 4·00
514 7s.70 Industrial complex and cogwheels . . . . 4·25 6·50

1989. Ceremonial Costumes (4th series). As T **45**. Multicoloured.
515 1s.20 Kipsigis . . . . 1·25 20
516 3s.40 Rabai . . . . 2·25 1·60
517 5s.50 Duruma . . . . 2·75 2·75
518 7s.70 Kuria . . . . 3·75 4·25
519 10s. Bajuni . . . . 4·00 6·00

102 EMS Speedpost Letters and Parcel

1990. 10th Anniv of Pan African Postal Union. Multicoloured.
520 1s.20 Type **102** 15 10
521 3s.40 Mail runner 35 35
522 5s.50 Mandera Post Office . . 55 70
523 7s.70 EMS Speedpost letters and globe (vert) . . . . . 80 1·60
524 10s. P.A.P.U. logo (vert) . . 90 1·60

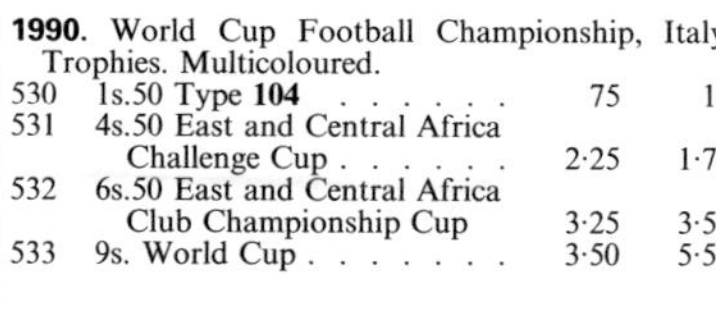
103 "Stamp King" with Tweezers and Magnifying Glass

104 Moi Golden Cup

1990. "Stamp World London '90" International Stamp Exhibition.
525 **103** 1s.50 multicoloured . . . 35 10
526 – 4s.50 multicoloured . . . 1·25 1·25
527 – 6s.50 black, red and blue 1·40 1·60
528 – 9s. multicoloured . . . 1·75 2·75
MS529 113 × 77 mm. Nos. 525/8 4·50 5·50
DESIGNS: 4s.50, Penny Black and Kenya Stamp Bureau postmark; 6s.50, Early British cancel-lations; 9s. Ronald Ngala Street Post Office, Nairobi.

1990. World Cup Football Championship, Italy. Trophies. Multicoloured.
530 1s.50 Type **104** 75 10
531 4s.50 East and Central Africa Challenge Cup . . . . . . 2·25 1·75
532 6s.50 East and Central Africa Club Championship Cup 3·25 3·50
533 9s. World Cup . . . . 3·50 5·50

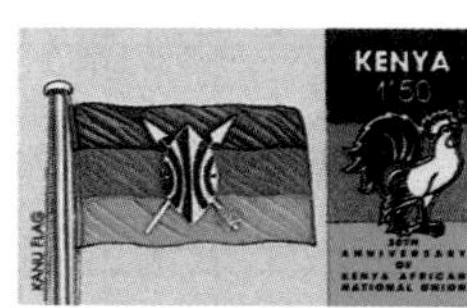

105 K.A.N.U. Flag

1990. 30th Anniv of Kenya African National Union. Multicoloured.
534 1s.50 Type **105** 15 10
535 2s.50 Nyayo Monument . . . 15 15
536 4s.50 Party Headquarters . . 35 35
537 5s. Jomo Kenyatta (Party founder) 40 40
538 6s.50 President Arap Moi . . 50 85
539 9s. President Moi addressing rally . . . . 70 1·60
540 10s. Queue of voters . . . . 80 1·60

106 Desktop Computer

1990. 125th Anniv of I.T.U. Multicoloured.
541 1s.50 Type **106** 15 10
542 4s.50 Telephone switchboard assembly, Gilgil 35 50
543 6s.50 "125 YEARS" . . . . 45 1·00
544 9s. Urban and rural telecommunications . . . . 70 2·25

107 Queen Mother at British Museum, 1988

108 Queen Elizabeth at Hospital Garden Party, 1947

1990. 90th Birthday of Queen Elizabeth the Queen Mother.
545 **107** 10s. multicoloured . . . . 1·50 1·75
546 **108** 40s. black and green . . . 3·25 5·00

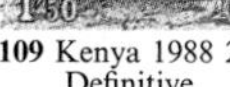
109 Kenya 1988 2s. Definitive

110 Adult Literacy Class

1990. Cent of Postage Stamps in Kenya. Mult.
547 1s.50 Type **109** . . . . . . 1·00 10
548 4s.50 East Africa and Uganda 1903 1a. . . . . . 2·25 90
549 6s.50 British East Africa Co 1890 ½a. optd on G.B. 1d. 2·75 2·00
550 9s. Kenya and Uganda 1922 20c. . . . . 3·25 3·25
551 20s. Kenya, Uganda, Tanzania 1971 2s.50 railway commemorative . . 5·50 8·50

1990. International Literacy Year. Multicoloured.
552 1s.50 Type **110** 30 10
553 4s.50 Teaching by radio . . . 1·00 1·10
554 6s.50 Technical training . . . 1·25 1·75
555 9s. International Literacy Year logo . . . . 2·00 3·50

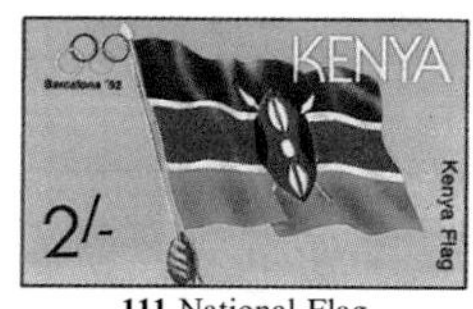

111 National Flag

1991. Olympic Games, Barcelona (1992) (1st issue). Multicoloured.
556 2s. Type **111** 85 10
557 6s. Basketball . . . . 2·50 1·25
558 7s. Hockey . . . . 2·50 2·00
559 8s.50 Table tennis . . . . . 2·25 3·25
560 11s. Boxing . . . . 2·25 3·75
See also Nos. 580/4.

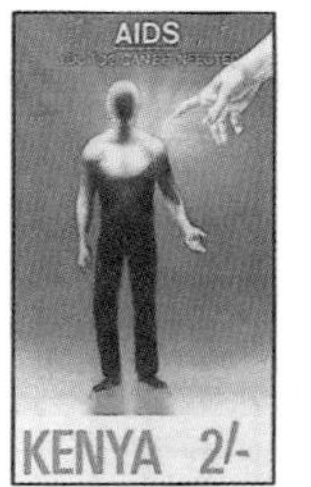

112 Symbolic Man and Pointing Finger

114 Leopard

113 Queen and Prince Philip with Pres. Moi

1992. AIDS Day. Multicoloured.
561 2s. Type **112** 90 15
562 6s. Victim and drugs . . . . 2·25 1·25
563 8s.50 Male and female symbols . . . . 2·75 3·25
564 11s. Symbolic figure and hypodermic syringe . . . . 3·75 4·75

1992. 40th Anniv of Queen Elizabeth II's Accession.
565 3s. Type **113** 50 10
566 8s. Marabou storks in tree 2·00 85
567 11s. Treetops Hotel . . . . . 1·25 1·00
568 14s. Three portraits of Queen Elizabeth . . . . 1·25 1·25
569 40s. Queen Elizabeth II . . . 2·50 4·50

1992. Kenya Wildlife. Multicoloured.
570 3s. Type **114** . . . . 1·50 30
571 8s. Lion . . . . 2·25 1·50
572 10s. Elephant . . . . 3·75 3·25
573 11s. Buffalo . . . . 2·25 3·25
574 14s. Black rhinoceros . . . . 5·00 5·50

115 International Harvester Safari Truck, 1926

1992. Vintage Cars. Multicoloured.
575 3s. Type **115** . . . . 1·25 20
576 8s. Fiat "509", 1924 . . . . 2·50 1·50
577 10s. Hupmobile, 1923 . . . . 2·75 2·50
578 11s. Chevrolet "Box Body", 1928 . . . . 2·75 2·75
579 14s. Bentley/Parkward, 1934 3·25 4·00

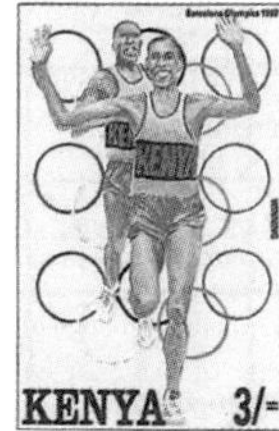

116 Kenyan Athlete winning Race

1992. Olympic Games, Barcelona (2nd issue). Mult.
580 3s. Type **116** 85 10
581 8s. Men's judo . . . . 1·75 1·25
582 10s. Kenyan women's volleyball players . . . . . 2·25 2·25
583 11s. Kenyan men's 4 × 100 m relay runners . . 2·25 2·50
584 14s. Men's 10,000 m . . . . 2·50 4·00

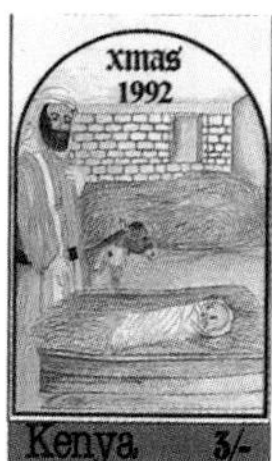

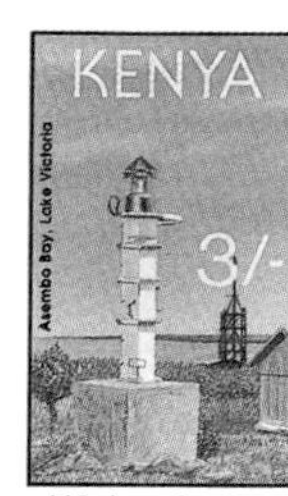

117 Holy Child, Joseph and Animals

118 Asembo Bay Lighthouse, Lake Victoria

1992. Christmas. Multicoloured.
585 3s. Type **117** 30 10
586 8s. Mary with Holy Child . . 75 50
587 11s. Christmas tree . . . . . 1·00 80
588 14s. Adoration of the Magi 1·25 2·00

1993. Lighthouses. Multicoloured.
589 3s. Type **118** . . . . 1·50 40
590 8s. Old Ras Serani lighthouse, Mombasa . . . 2·50 1·50
591 11s. New Ras Serani lighthouse, Mombasa . . . 2·75 2·50
592 14s. Gingira, Lake Victoria 3·50 4·25

119 Superb Starling

120 Yellow-billed Hornbill

1993. Birds. Multicoloured. (a) As T **119**.
593 50c. Type **119** 10 50
594 1s. Red and yellow barbet 15 40
594a 1s.50 Lady Ross's turaco . . 50 50
595 3s. Black-throated honeyguide ("Greater honeyguide") 30 10

595a 5s. African fish eagle . . . 60 60
595b 6s. Vulturine guineafowl . . 1·00 40
596 7s. Malachite kingfisher . . 50 30
597 8s. Speckled pigeon 50 20
598 10s. Cinnamon-chested bee eater 55 20
599 11s. Scarlet-chested sunbird 55 25
600 14s. Bagalafecht weaver ("Reichenow's weaver") 60 30

(b) As T 120.

601 50s. Type **120** . . . . 1·25 1·50
602 80s. Lesser flamingo . . . . 1·60 2·00
603 100s. Hadada ibis . . . . . 1·90 2·50

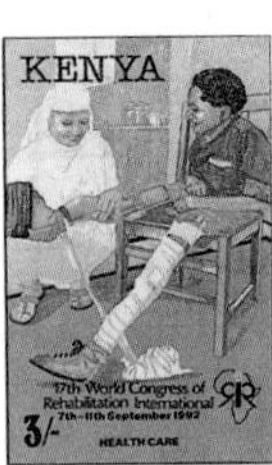
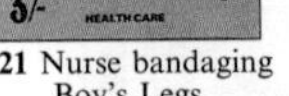

121 Nurse bandaging Boy's Legs

123 "Ansellia africana"

122 Maendeleo House, Nairobi

1993. 17th World Congress of Rehabilitation International.
611 **121** 3s. multicoloured 70 10
612 – 8s. multicoloured . . . . 1·10 70
613 – 10s. multicoloured . . . . 1·25 1·40
614 – 11s. multicoloured . . . . 1·25 1·60
615 – 14s. black, blue and orange . . . . 1·50 2·25
DESIGNS—HORIZ: 8s. Singing group on crutches; 10s. Vocational training; 11s. Wheelchair race. VERT: 14s. Congress emblem.

1994. 40th Anniv of Maendeleo Ya Wanawake Organization. Multicoloured.
616 3s.50 Type **122** 65 20
617 9s. Planting saplings 85 60
618 11s. Rural family planning clinic (vert) . . . . 1·00 1·00
619 12s.50 Women carrying water 1·25 1·75
620 15s.50 Improved wood-burning cooking stove (vert) . . . . 1·50 2·25

1994. Orchids. Multicoloured.
621 3s.50 Type **123** . . . . . . 1·50 30
622 9s. "Aerangis luteoalba var rhodosticta" . . . . 2·00 85
623 12s.50 "Polystachya bella" 2·25 2·00
624 15s.50 "Brachycorythis kalbreyeri" . . . . 2·50 2·75
625 20s. "Eulophia guineensis" 3·00 3·50

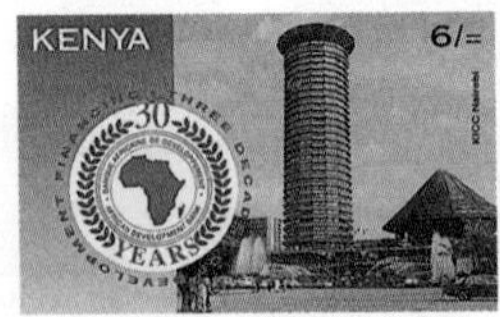

124 Emblem and K.I.C.C. Building, Nairobi

1994. 30th Anniv of African Development Bank. Multicoloured.
626 6s. Type **124** 60 25
627 25s. Isinya-Kajiado project 2·50 3·25

125 Kenyan Family

126 Paul Harris (founder of Rotary)

1994. International Year of the Family. Mult.
628 6s. Type **125** 50 10
629 14s.50 Nurse with mother and baby . . . . 2·00 1·40
630 20s. Schoolchildren and teacher (horiz) . . . . . 2·25 2·50
631 25s. Emblem (horiz) . . . . 2·50 3·00

1994. 50th Anniv of Rotary Club of Mombasa. Multicoloured.
632 6s. Type **126** 25 10
633 14s.50 Anniversary logo . . . 70 70
634 17s.50 Administering polio vaccine . . . . 1·00 1·40
635 20s. Women at stand pipe . . 1·00 1·50
636 25s. Rotary emblem . . . . 1·10 1·75

127 Donkey

128 Male Golfer in Bunker

1995. Kenya Society for Prevention of Cruelty to Animals. Multicoloured.
637 6s. Type **127** 30 10
638 14s.50 Cow 45 45
639 17s.50 Sheep 55 75
640 20s. Dog . . . . 1·50 2·00
641 25s. Cat . . . . 1·50 2·00

1995. Golf. Multicoloured.
642 6s. Type **128** 85 15
643 17s.50 Female golfer on fairway . . . . 1·75 1·50
644 20s. Male golfer teeing-off . . 1·75 2·25
645 25s. Head of golf club . . . 2·00 2·50

129 Perfume Containers

1995. Kenyan Material Culture (2nd issue). Mult.
646 6s. Type **129** 30 10
647 14s.50 Basketry 75 75
648 17s.50 Preserving pots . . . 85 1·25
649 20s. Gourds . . . . 1·10 1·60
650 25s. Wooden containers . . . 1·25 1·90

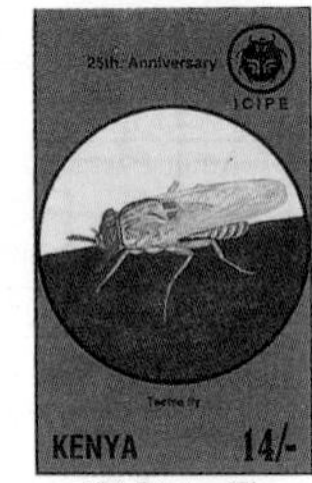

130 Tsetse Fly

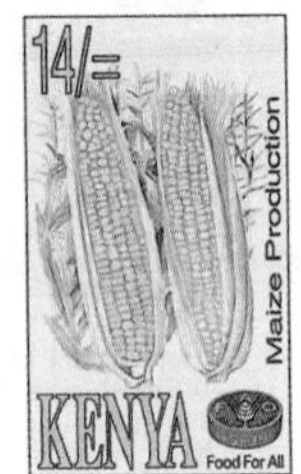

131 Maize

1995. 25th Anniv of I.C.I.P.E. Insect Pests. Multicoloured.
651 14s. Type **130** 50 30
652 26s. Tick 80 80
653 32s. Wild silkmoth . . . . 95 1·10
654 33s. Maize borer . . . . . . 1·00 1·75
655 40s. Locust . . . . 1·60 2·50

1995. 50th Anniv of F.A.O. Multicoloured.
656 14s. Type **131** 70 30
657 28s. Cattle . . . . 1·10 80
658 32s. Chickens . . . . 1·60 1·60
659 33s. Fisherman with catch . . 1·90 2·50
660 40s. Fruit . . . . 2·25 3·00

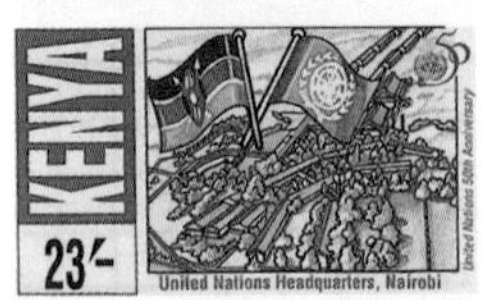

132 Kenyan and United Nations Flags over Headquarters, Nairobi

1995. 50th Anniv of United Nations.
661 **132** 23s. multicoloured 70 70
662 – 26s. multicoloured 80 90
663 – 32s. multicoloured . . . . 95 1·10
664 – 40s. blue, red and black 1·40 2·00
DESIGNS: 26s. Multi-racial group with emblem; 32s. United Nations helmet; 40s. 50th anniversary emblem.

133 Swimming

1996. Olympic Games, Atlanta (1st issue). Events and Gold Medal Winners. Multicoloured.
665 14s. Type **133** . . . . 1·00 1·10
666 20s. Archery . . . . 1·00 1·10
667 20s. Weightlifting . . . . . 1·00 1·10
668 20s. Pole vault (vert) . . . . 1·00 1·10
669 20s. Equestrian (vert) . . . . 1·00 1·10
670 20s. Diving (vert) . . . . . 1·00 1·10
671 20s. Sprinting (vert) . . . . 1·00 1·10
672 20s. Athlete carrying Olympic Torch (vert) . . . . 1·00 1·10
673 20s. Hurdling (vert) . . . . 1·00 1·10
674 20s. Kayak (vert) . . . . . 1·00 1·10
675 20s. Boxing (vert) . . . . . 1·00 1·10
676 20s. Gymnastics (vert) . . . 1·00 1·10
677 25s. Greg Louganis (U.S.A.) (diving, 1984 and 1988) (vert) . . . . 1·00 1·10
678 25s. Cassius Clay (U.S.A.) (boxing, 1960) (vert) . . . 1·00 1·10
679 25s. Nadia Comaneci (Rumania) (gymnastics, 1980) (vert) . . . . 1·00 1·10
680 25s. Daley Thompson (Great Britain) (decathlon, 1980 and 1984) (vert) . . . . . 1·00 1·10
681 25s. Kipchoge Keino (Kenya) (running, 1968) (vert) . . . 1·00 1·10
682 25s. Kornelia Enders (Germany) (swimming, 1976) (vert) . . . . 1·00 1·10
683 25s. Jackie Joyner-Kersee (U.S.A.) (long jump, 1988) (vert) . . . . 1·00 1·10
684 25s. Michael Jordan (U.S.A.) (basketball, 1984) (vert) . . 1·00 1·10
685 25s. Shun Fujimoto (Japan) (gymnastics, 1972) (vert) 1·00 1·10
686 32s. Javelin . . . . 1·00 1·10
687 40s. Fencing . . . . 1·10 1·25
688 50s. Discus . . . . 1·40 1·60
MS689 Two sheets, each 79 × 109 mm. (a) 100s. Athlete with medal (vert). (b) 100s. Athlete carrying Olympic Torch (different) (vert) Set of 2 sheets . . . . . 7·00 9·00
Nos. 665/7 with 686/8, 668/76 and 677/85 respectively were printed together, se-tenant, forming composite designs.
See also Nos. 702/6.

134 Lions

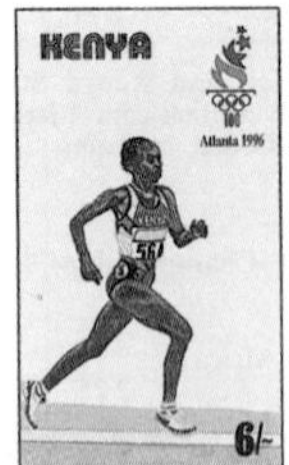

136 Women's 10,000 Metres

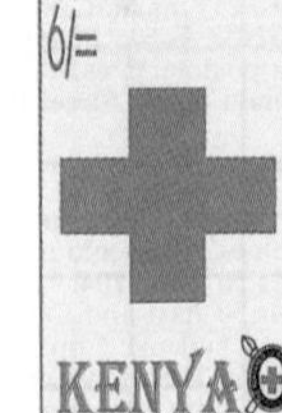

137 Red Cross Emblem

135 Water Buck

1996. Tourism. Multicoloured. (a) Designs as T **134**.
690 6s. Type **134** 30 10
691 14s. Mt. Kenya 35 30
692 20s. Sail boards 55 70
693 25s. Hippopotami . . . . . 1·25 1·40
694 40s. Couple in traditional dress . . . . 1·25 2·25
MS695 100 × 80 mm. 50s. Female giraffe and calf (vert) . . . . . 2·00 2·75

(b) Horiz designs as T **135**.

696 20s. Type **135** . . . . 95 1·25
697 20s. Pair of rhinoceroses . . 95 1·25
698 20s. Cheetah . . . . 95 1·25
699 20s. Group of oryx . . . . . 95 1·25
700 20s. Pair of giraffes . . . . . 95 1·25
701 20s. Monkey and bongo . . 95 1·25

1996. Olympic Games, Atlanta (2nd issue). Multicoloured.
702 6s. Type **136** 25 10
703 14s. Steeple-chasing 45 30
704 20s. Victorious athletes with flag 70 80
705 25s. Boxing . . . . 70 1·00
706 40s. Men's 1500 m . . . . . 1·25 2·00

1996. Kenya Red Cross Society.
707 **137** 6s. red and black 25 10
708 – 14s. multicoloured 45 35
709 – 20s. multicoloured 70 80
710 – 25s. multicoloured 80 95
711 – 40s. multicoloured . . . . 1·40 2·00
DESIGNS: 14s. Giving blood; 20s. Immunization; 25s. Refugee child with food; 40s. Cleaning the environment.

138 Impala

139 Kenya Lions Club Logo

1996. East African Wildlife Society. Multicoloured.
712 6s. Type **138** 20 10
713 20s. Colobus monkey 60 60
714 25s. African elephant . . . 1·40 1·40
715 40s. Black rhinoceros . . . . 2·00 2·75

1996. Work of Lions Club International in Kenya. Multicoloured.
716 6s. Type **139** 15 10
717 14s. Eye operation 55 45
718 20s. Two disabled children in wheelchair . . . . 70 1·00
719 25s. Modern ambulance . . . 1·00 1·40

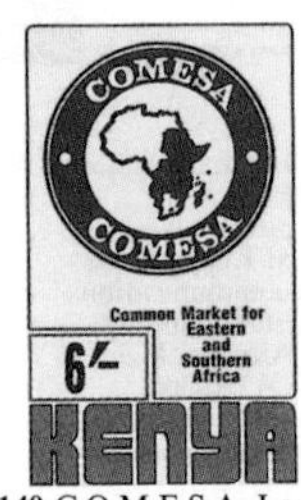

140 C.O.M.E.S.A. Logo

1997. Inauguration of Common Market for Eastern and Southern Africa. Multicoloured.
720 6s. Type **140** 15 15
721 20s. Kenyan flag and logo . . 85 1·10

141 "Haplochromis cinctus"

1997. Endangered Species. Lake Victoria Cichlid Fishes. Multicoloured.
722 25s. Type **141** . . . . 75 1·00
723 25s. "Haplochromis" "Orange Rock Hunter" . . 75 1·00
724 25s. "Haplochromis chilotes" 75 1·00
725 25s. "Haplochromis nigricans" . . . . 75 1·00

142 Class 94 Diesel-electric Locomotive No. 9401, 1981

1997. Kenya Railway Locomotives. Multicoloured.
726 6s. Type **142** 55 15
727 14s. Class 87 diesel-electric No. 8721, 1964 . . . . . 80 40
728 20s. Class 59 Garratt steam No. 5905, 1955 . . . . . 90 65
729 25s. Class 57 Garratt steam No. 5701, 1939 . . . . . 1·00 1·00
730 30s. Class 23 steam No. 2305, 1923 . . . . 1·10 1·40
731 40s. Class 10 steam No. 1001, 1914 . . . . 1·40 2·00

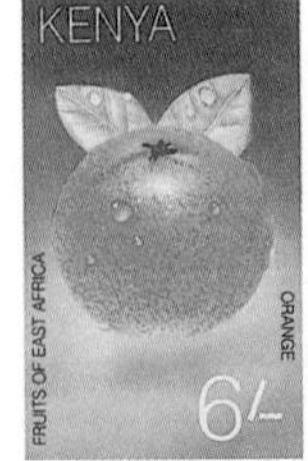

143 Orange

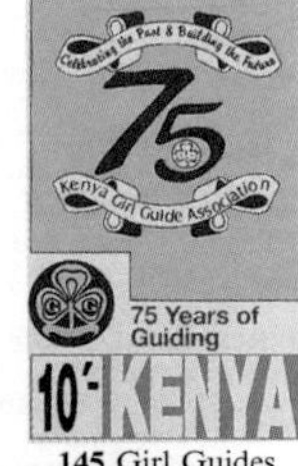

145 Girl Guides Anniversary Logo

144 Crocodile

1997. Fruits of East Africa. Multicoloured.
732 6s. Type **143** 45 15
733 14s. Pineapple 85 45
734 20s. Mango . . . . 1·40 1·40
735 25s. Pawpaw . . . . 1·60 2·00

1997. Local Tourist Attractions. Multicoloured.
736 10s. Type **144** 75 25
737 27s. Lake Bogoria hot springs 1·40 1·00
738 30s. Warthogs . . . . 1·40 1·40
739 33s. Windsurfing . . . . . . 1·40 1·75
740 42s. Traditional huts . . . . 1·60 2·50

1997. 75th Anniv of Kenyan Girl Guides Anniversary. Multicoloured.
741 10s. Type **145** 40 70
742 10s. Lord Baden-Powell . . . 40 70
743 27s. Girl guides hiking . . . 75 1·10
744 27s. Rangers in camp . . . . 75 1·10
745 33s. Girl guides planting seedlings . . . . 85 1·25
746 33s. Boy scouts giving first aid . . . . 85 1·25
747 42s. Boy scouts in camp . . . 90 1·25
748 42s. Brownies entertaining the elderly . . . . 90 1·25

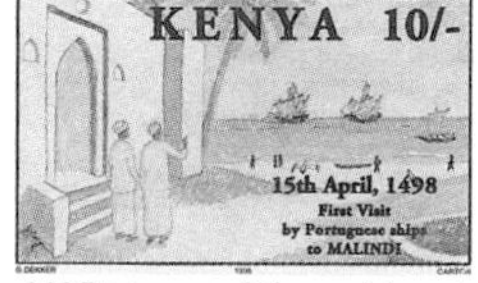

146 Portuguese Ships arriving at Malindi

1998. 500th Anniv of Vasco da Gama's Arrival at Malindi. Multicoloured.
749 10s. Type **146** 45 25
750 24s. Portuguese ships 90 70
751 33s. Map of Africa . . . . . 1·10 1·50
752 42s. Vasco da Gama Pillar and harbour . . . . 1·25 1·90

147 Lion

1998. 18th Anniv of Pan African Postal Union. Wildlife. Multicoloured.
753 10s. Type **147** 70 25
754 24s. Buffalo . . . . 1·10 70
755 33s. Grant's gazelle . . . . . 1·40 1·75
756 42s. Cheetah . . . . 2·50 3·00
MS757 94 × 76 mm. 50s. Hirola gazelle . . . . 2·00 2·50

148 Pres. Arap Moi taking Oath, 1998

1998. Daniel Arap Moi's 5th Presidential Term.
758 **148** 14s. multicoloured 80 60

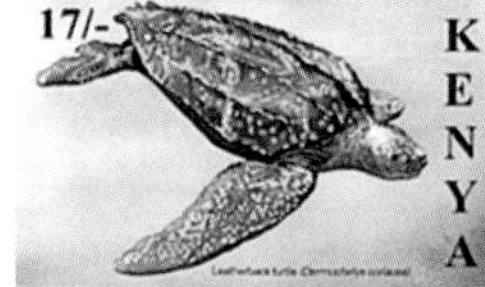

149 Leatherback Turtle

2000. Turtles. Multicoloured.
759 17s. Type **149** 65 35
760 20s. Green sea turtle 70 40
761 30s. Hawksbill turtle 90 80
762 47s. Olive Ridley turtle . . . 1·40 1·60
763 59s. Loggerhead turtle . . . 1·75 2·00

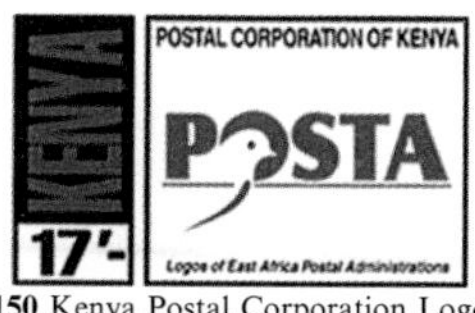

150 Kenya Postal Corporation Logo

2000. East Africa Postal Administrations' Co-operation. Multicoloured (except 17s.).
764 17s. Type **150** (red, blue and black) 45 35
765 35s. Uganda Post Ltd logo 75 80
766 50s. Tanzania Posts Corporation logo . . . . 1·00 1·40
MS767 100 × 80 mm. 70s. As 50s. 1·50 1·75

151 Cotton

152 Tea

2001. Crops. Multicoloured. (a) Vert designs as T **151**.
768 2s. Type **151** 10 10
769 4s. Bananas 10 10
770 5s. Avocado 10 10
771 6s. Cassava 10 10
772 8s. Arrowroot 15 20
773 10s. Pawpaw 15 20
774 19s. Orange 30 35
775 20s. Pyrethrum 30 35
776 30s. Groundnuts 50 55
777 35s. Coconut 55 60
778 40s. Sisal 65 70
779 50s. Cashew nuts 80 85

(b) Vert designs as T **152**.
780 60s. Type **152** . . . . 95 1·00
781 80s. Maize . . . . 1·25 1·40
782 100s. Coffee . . . . 1·60 1·75
783 200s. Finger millet . . . . . 3·25 3·50
784 400s. Sorghum . . . . 6·50 6·75
785 500s. Sugar cane . . . . . . 8·00 8·25

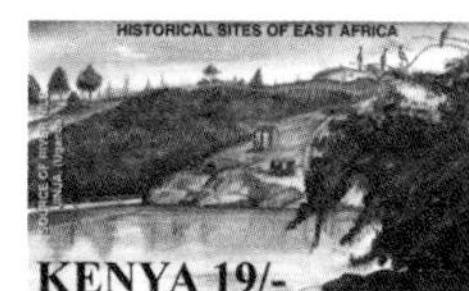

153 Source of the Nile, Jinja, Uganda

2002. Historical Sites of East Africa. Multicoloured.
786 19s. Type **153** 30 35
787 35s. Kamu Fort, Kenya (35 × 35 mm) 55 60
788 40s. Olduvai Gorge, Tanzania 65 70
789 50s. Thimlich Ohinga (ancient settlement), Kenya (35 × 35 mm) 80 85

OFFICIAL STAMPS

Intended for use on official correspondence of the Kenya Government only, but there is no evidence that they were so used.

1964. Stamps of 1963 optd **OFFICIAL**.
O21 **46** 5c. multicoloured 10
O22 – 10c. brown 10
O23 – 15c. mauve . . . . 1·25
O24 – 20c. black and green . . . 20
O25 – 30c. black and yellow . . 30
O26 – 50c. red, black and green 2·75

POSTAGE DUE STAMPS

D 3

1967.
D13 **D 3** 5c. red . . . . 15 2·75
D41 10c. green . . . . 40 1·50
D42 20c. blue . . . . 40 1·50
D44 30c. brown 15 75
D45 40c. purple 15 75
D49 50c. green 10 10
D46 80c. red 20 90
D50 1s. orange 10 10
D51 2s. violet 10 10
D52 3s. blue 10 10
D53 5s. red 10 10

KENYA, UGANDA AND TANGANYIKA (TANZANIA) Pt. 1

From 1903 joint issues were made for British East Africa (later Kenya) and Uganda. In 1933 the postal administrations of Kenya, Uganda and Tanganyika were combined.

On independence of the constituent territories in the 1960s the postal administration became the East African Posts and Telecommunications Corporation. As well as separate issues for each state (q.v.), joint commemorative issues (which however were not valid in Zanzibar) were made until the dissolution of the Corporation in 1977.

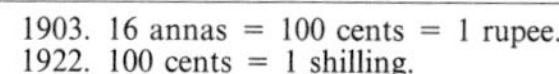

1903. 16 annas = 100 cents = 1 rupee.
1922. 100 cents = 1 shilling.

1

2

1903.
17a **1** ½a. green . . . . 7·00 3·25
2 1a. grey and red . . . . . 1·75 1·00
19a 2a. purple . . . . 2·50 2·75
21 2½a. blue . . . . 7·50 17·00
22a 3a. purple and green . . . . 3·75 28·00
23 4a. green and black . . . . 7·50 18·00
24 5a. grey and brown . . . . 8·00 15·00
25 8a. grey and blue . . . . . 7·00 8·50
9 **2** 1r. green . . . . 16·00 55·00
27 2r. purple . . . . 38·00 55·00
28 3r. green and black . . . . 55·00 £100
29 4r. grey and green . . . . . 75·00 £140
30 5r. grey and red . . . . . . 80·00 £110
31 10r. grey and blue £150 £180
15 20r. grey and stone £500 £1000
16 50r. grey and brown £1400 £2500

1907.
34 **1** 1c. brown . . . . 2·50 15
35 3c. green . . . . 10·00 70
36 6c. red . . . . 2·75 10
37 10c. lilac and olive . . . . . 9·00 8·50
38 12c. purple . . . . 10·00 2·75
39 15c. blue . . . . 18·00 8·50
40 25c. green and black . . . . 8·00 7·00
41 50c. green and brown . . . . 12·00 12·00
42 75c. grey and blue . . . . . 4·50 32·00

1912. As T **1/2** but portraits of King George V.
44 1c. black . . . . 30 1·75
45 3c. green . . . . 2·00 60
46 6c. red 70 60
47 10c. orange . . . . 2·00 50
48 12c. grey . . . . 2·75 50
49 15c. blue . . . . 2·75 80
50 25c. black and red on yellow 50 1·25
51 50c. black and lilac . . . . . 1·50 1·25
52b 75c. black and green . . . . 6·00 7·50
53 1r. black and green . . . . . 1·75 4·25
54 2r. red and black on blue . . 20·00 38·00
55 3r. violet and green . . . . . 20·00 80·00
56 4r. red and green on yellow 45·00 £100
57 5r. blue and purple . . . . . 48·00 £140
58 10r. red and green on green £100 £170
59 20r. black and purple on red £300 £300
60 20r. purple and blue on blue £325 £350
61 50r. red and green £550 £600
62 100r. purple and black on red £4250 £2250
63 500r. green and red on green £15000

1919. No. 46 surch **4 cents**.
64 4c. on 6c. red . . . . 1·25 15

6

7

1922.
76 **6** 1c. brown . . . . 1·00 3·00
77 5c. violet . . . . 3·25 75
78 5c. green . . . . 2·00 50
79 10c. green . . . . 1·50 30
80 10c. black . . . . 4·00 20
81a 12c. black . . . . 4·25 26·00
82 15c. red . . . . 1·25 10
83 20c. orange . . . . 3·25 10
84 30c. blue . . . . 2·00 50
85 50c. grey . . . . 2·50 10
86 75c. olive . . . . 4·25 9·00
87 **7** 1s. green . . . . 4·00 2·50
88 2s. purple . . . . 8·00 9·00
89 2s.50 brown . . . . 18·00 70·00
90 3s. grey . . . . 17·00 6·50
91 4s. grey . . . . 21·00 80·00
92 5s. red . . . . 22·00 22·00
93 7s.50 orange . . . . 70·00 £150
94 10s. blue . . . . 48·00 48·00
95 £1 black and orange . . . £150 £225
96 £2 green and purple . . . £600 £950
97 £3 purple and yellow . . . £800
98 £4 black and mauve . . . £1600
99 £5 black and blue £1700
100 £10 black and green . . . £7500
101 £20 red and green £15000
102 £25 black and red £18000
103 £50 black and brown . . . £25000
104 £75 purple and grey . . . £60000
105 £100 red and black £60000

8 South African Crowned Cranes

9 Dhow on Lake Victoria

1935. King George V.
110 **8** 1c. black and brown . . . . 1·00 1·50
111 **9** 5c. black and green . . . . 1·75 60
112 – 10c. black and yellow . . . 3·50 60
113 – 15c. black and red . . . . 1·75 10
114 **8** 20c. black and orange . . . 2·50 20
115 – 30c. black and blue . . . . 2·00 1·00
116 **9** 50c. purple and black . . . 1·75 10
117 – 65c. black and brown . . . 2·75 2·00
118 – 1s. black and green . . . . 1·50 75
119 – 2s. red and purple . . . . 4·75 4·00
120 – 3s. blue and black . . . . . 6·50 15·00
121 – 5s. black and red . . . . . 17·00 27·00
122 **8** 10s. purple and blue . . . . 60·00 85·00
123 – £1 black and red £140 £170

DESIGNS—VERT: 10c., £1 Lion; 30c., 5s. Nile Railway Bridge, Ripon Falls. HORIZ: 15c., 2s. Kilimanjaro; 65c. Mt. Kenya; 1s., 3s. Lake Naivasha.

14a Windsor Castle

1935. Silver Jubilee.
124 **14a** 20c. blue and olive . . . 60 10
125 30c. brown and blue . . . 2·50 3·50
126 65c. green and blue . . . 1·75 2·75
127 1s. grey and purple . . . 2·00 2·50

14b King George VI and Queen Elizabeth

1937. Coronation.
128 **14b** 5c. green 20 10
129 20c. orange 40 30
130 30c. blue . . . . 60 1·25

15 Dhow on Lake Victoria

1938. As 1935 (except 10c.) but with portrait of King George VI as in T **15**.
131a **8** 1c. black and brown . . 30 50
132 **15** 5c. black and green . . . 3·00 50
133 5c. brown and orange . . 50 3·00
134 – 10c. brown and orange 1·75 10
135 – 10c. black and green . . 30 85
136 – 10c. brown and grey . . 1·00 55
137a – 15c. black and red . . . 4·25 3·75
138 – 15c. black and green . . 2·00 3·75
139b **8** 20c. black and orange . . 6·50 10
140 **15** 25c. black and red . . . 1·25 2·25
141b – 30c. black and blue . . . 2·75 10
142 – 30c. purple and brown 1·50 40
143 **8** 40c. black and blue . . . 1·75 3·25
144e **15** 50c. purple and black . . 7·00 55
145a – 1s. black and brown . . 11·00 30
146b – 2s. red and purple . . . 17·00 30
147ac – 3s. blue and black . . . 24·00 2·50
148b – 5s. black and red . . . 24·00 1·25
149b **8** 10s. purple and blue . . 38·00 3·50
150a – £1 black and red . . . . 21·00 15·00

DESIGN—HORIZ: 10c. Lake Naivasha.

1941. Stamps of South Africa surch **KENYA TANGANYIKA UGANDA** and value. Alternate stamps inscr in English or Afrikaans.
151 **7** 5c. on 1d. black and red 85 15
152 **22a** 10c. on 3d. blue . . . . . 1·75 30
153 **8** 20c. on 6d. green and red 1·75 20
154 – 70c. on 1s. brown and blue (No. 120) . . . . 12·00 40

Prices for Nos. 151/4 are for unused pairs and used singles.

1946. Victory. As T **4a** of Pitcairn Islands.
155 20c. orange 30 10
156 30c. blue 30 50

1948. Silver Wedding. As T **4b/c** of Pitcairn Islands.
157 20c. orange 15 10
158 £1 red . . . . 35·00 50·00

1949. U.P.U. As T **4d/g** of Pitcairn Islands.
159 20c. orange 15 10
160 30c. blue . . . . 1·50 1·25
161 50c. grey 40 20
162 1s. brown 40 40

1952. Visit of Queen Elizabeth II (as Princess) and Duke of Edinburgh. As Nos. 135 and 145ba but inscr "ROYAL VISIT 1952".
163 10c. black and green . . . . 10 1·50
164 1s. black and brown . . . . 20 1·75

1953. Coronation. As T **4h** of Pitcairn Islands.
165 20c. black and orange . . . 15 10

1954. Royal Visit. As No. 171 but inscr "ROYAL VISIT 1954".
166 **18** 30c. black and blue 40 15

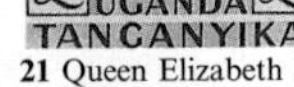

18 Owen Falls Dam **21** Queen Elizabeth II

20 Royal Lodge, Sagana

1954.

167 **18** 5c. black and brown . . . 50 50
168 – 10c. red 75 10
169a – 15c. black and blue . . . 55 1·25
170 – 20c. black and orange . . 80 10
171 **18** 30c. black and blue . . . 80 10
172 – 40c. brown . . . . 1·25 75
173 – 50c. purple . . . . 1·50 10
174 – 65c. green and purple . . . 2·75 1·50
175 – 1s. black and purple . . . 1·25 10
176 – 1s.30 lilac and orange . . 8·50 10
177 – 2s. black and green . . . 6·00 80
178 – 5s. black and orange . . . 16·00 1·75
179 **20** 10s. black and blue . . . 23·00 2·50
180 **21** £1 red and black . . . . 16·00 11·00

DESIGNS—VERT (Size as Type **18**): 10, 50c. Giraffe; 20, 40c., 1s. Lion. HORIZ: 15c., 1s.30, 5s. Elephants; 65c., 2s. Mt. Kilimanjaro.

25 Map of E. Africa showing Lakes

1958. Centenary of Discovery of Lakes Tanganyika and Victoria by Burton and Speke.

181 **25** 40c. blue and green 30 40
182 1s.30 green and purple . . 30 1·40

26 Sisal **29** Queen Elizabeth II

28 Mt. Kenya and Giant Plants

1960.

183 **26** 5c. blue 10 15
184 – 10c. green 10 10
185 – 15c. purple 30 10
186 – 20c. mauve 20 10
187 – 25c. green . . . . 3·25 1·25
188 – 30c. red 15 10
189 – 40c. blue 15 20
190 – 50c. violet 15 10
191 – 65c. olive . . . . 30 1·00
192 **28** 1s. violet and purple . . . 80 10
193 – 1s.30 brown and red . . . 2·50 15
194 – 2s. indigo and blue . . . . 2·75 40
195 – 2s.50 olive and turquoise . 4·25 2·75
196 – 5s. red and purple . . . . 3·75 60
197 – 10s. myrtle and green . . . 8·00 6·50
198 **29** 20s. blue and lake . . . . 16·00 20·00

DESIGNS—As Type **26**: 10c. Cotton; 15c. Coffee; 20c. Blue wildebeest; 25c. Ostrich; 30c. Thomson's gazelle; 40c. Manta; 50c. Common zebra; 65c. Cheetah. As Type **28**: 1s.30, Murchison Falls and hippopotamus; 2s. Mt. Kilimanjaro and giraffe; 2s.50, Candelabra tree and black rhinoceros; 5s. Crater Lake and Mountains of the Moon; 10s. Ngorongoro Crater and African buffalo.

30 Land Tillage

1963. Freedom from Hunger.

199 **30** 15c. blue and olive 10 10
200 – 30c. brown and yellow . . 20 10
201 **30** 50c. blue and orange . . . 30 10
202 – 1s.30 brown and blue . . . 55 1·75

DESIGN: 30c., 1s.30, African with corncob.

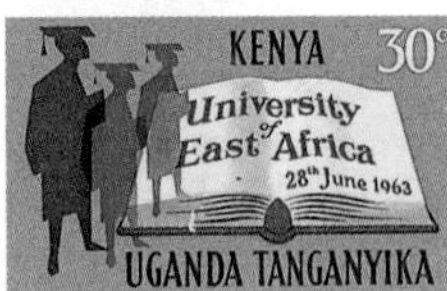

31 Scholars and Open Book

1963. Founding of East African University.

203 **31** 30c. multicoloured 10 10
204 1s.30 multicoloured 20 20

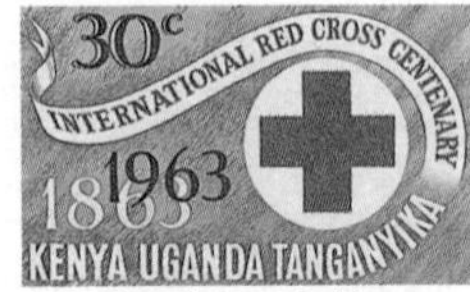

32 Red Cross Emblem

1963. Centenary of Red Cross.

205 **32** 30c. red and blue . . . . 1·00 10
206 50c. red and brown . . . . 1·25 55

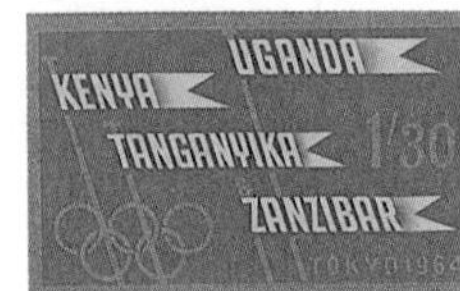

35 East African "Flags"

1964. Olympic Games, Tokyo.

207 – 30c. yellow and purple . . 10 10
208 – 50c. purple and yellow . . 15 10
209 **35** 1s.30 yellow, green and blue 40 10
210 2s.50 mauve, violet & blue 45 1·40

DESIGN—VERT: 30, 50c. Chrysanthemum emblem.

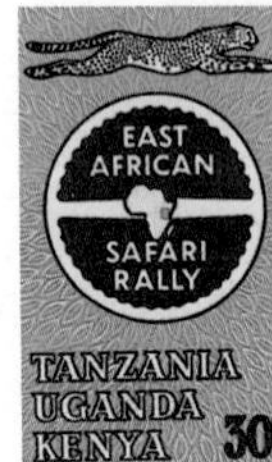

36 Rally Badge

1965. 13th East African Safari Rally.

211 **36** 30c. black, yellow & turq 10 10
212 50c. black, yellow & brown 10 10
213 – 1s.30 green, ochre and blue 25 10
214 – 2s.50 green, red and blue 40 1·50

DESIGN: 1s.30, 2s.50, Cars en route.

38 I.T.U. Emblem and Symbols

1965. Centenary of I.T.U. "I.T.U." and symbols in gold.

215 **38** 30c. brown and mauve . . 20 10
216 50c. brown and grey . . . 20 10
217 1s.30 brown and blue . . . 55 10
218 2s.50 brown and turquoise 1·00 2·25

39 I.C.Y. Emblem

1965. International Co-operation Year.

219 **39** 30c. green and gold 10 10
220 50c. black and gold 15 10
221 1s.30 blue and gold 30 10
222 2s.50 red and gold . . . . 75 2·50

40 Game Park Lodge, Tanzania

1966. Tourism. Multicoloured.

223 30c. Type **40** 15 10
224 50c. Murchison Falls, Uganda 50 10
225 1s.30 Lesser flamingoes, Lake Nakuru, Kenya . . . . . 2·75 30
226 2s.50 Deep sea fishing, Tanzania . . . . 2·00 2·25

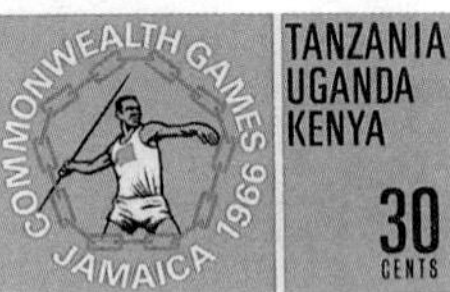

41 Games Emblem

1966. 8th British Empire and Commonwealth Games, Jamaica.

227 **41** 30c. multicoloured 10 10
228 50c. multicoloured 15 10
229 1s.30 multicoloured 20 10
230 2s.50 multicoloured . . . . 35 1·50

42 U.N.E.S.C.O. Emblem

1966. 20th Anniv of U.N.E.S.C.O.

231 **42** 30c. black, green and red 30 10
232 50c. black, green and brown 35 10
233 1s.30 black, green and grey 1·00 15
234 2s.50 black, green & yellow 1·75 3·50

43 De Havilland Dragon Rapide

1967. 21st Anniv of East African Airways.

235 **43** 30c. violet, blue and green 30 10
236 – 50c. multicoloured 40 10
237 – 1s.30 multicoloured 85 30
238 – 2s.50 multicoloured . . . . 1·25 2·50

DESIGNS: 50c. Vickers Super VC-10; 1s.30, Hawker Siddeley Comet 4B; 2s.50, Fokker Friendship.

44 Pillar Tomb

1967. Archaeological Relics.

239 **44** 30c. ochre, black and purple 15 10
240 – 50c. red, black and brown 65 10
241 – 1s.30 black, yellow & green 85 15
242 – 2s.50 black, ochre and red 1·40 2·50

DESIGNS: 50c. Rock painting; 1s.30, Clay head; 2s.50, Proconsul skull.

48 Unified Symbols of Kenya, Tanzania and Uganda

1967. Foundation of East African Community.

243 **48** 5s. gold, black and grey . . 40 1·25

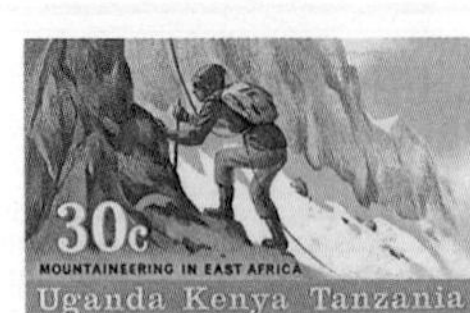

49 Mountaineering

1968. Mountains of East Africa. Multicoloured.

244 30c. Type **49** 15 10
245 50c. Mt. Kenya 30 10
246 1s.30 Mt. Kilimanjaro . . . 60 10
247 2s.50 Ruwenzori Mountains 90 2·25

50 Family and Rural Hospital

1968. World Health Organization.

248 **50** 30c. green, lilac and brown 10 10
249 – 50c. slate, lilac and black 15 10
250 – 1s.30 brown, lilac & lt brown 20 15
251 – 2s.50 grey, black and lilac 30 1·90

DESIGNS: 50c. Family and nurse; 1s.30, Family and microscope; 2s.50, Family and hypodermic syringe.

51 Olympic Stadium, Mexico City

1968. Olympic Games, Mexico.

252 **51** 30c. green and black . . . 10 10
253 – 50c. green and black . . . 15 10
254 – 1s.30 red, black and grey 25 15
255 – 2s.50 sepia and brown . . 35 1·50

DESIGNS—HORIZ: 50c. High-diving boards; 1s.30, Running tracks. VERT: 2s.50, Boxing ring.

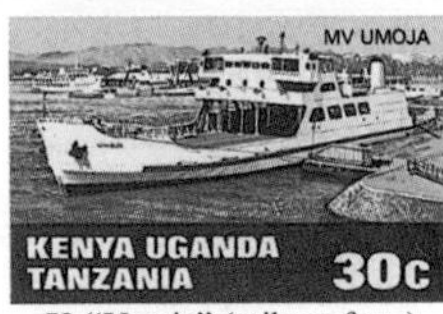

52 "Umoja" (railway ferry)

1969. Water Transport.

256 **52** 30c. blue and grey 40 10
257 – 50c. multicoloured 45 10
258 – 1s.30 green and blue . . . 85 20
259 – 2s.50 orange and blue . . . 1·40 3·25

DESIGNS: 50c. S.S. "Harambee"; 1s.30, M.V. "Victoria"; 2s.50, "St. Michael".

53 I.L.O. Emblem and Agriculture

1969. 50th Anniv of Int Labour Organization.

260 **53** 30c. black, green and yellow 10 10
261 – 50c. multicoloured 10 10
262 – 1s.30 black, brown and orange 10 10
263 – 2s.50 black, blue & turq . . 20 90

DESIGNS—I.L.O. emblem and: 50c. Building-work; 1s.30, Factory-workers; 2s.50, Shipping.

54 Pope Paul VI and Ruwenzori Mountains **55** Euphorbia Tree shaped as Africa, and Emblem

1969. Visit of Pope Paul VI to Uganda.

264 **54** 30c. black, gold and blue 15 10
265 70c. black, gold and red . . 20 10
266 1s.50 black, gold and blue 25 20
267 2s.50 black, gold and violet 30 1·40

1969. 5th Anniv of African Development Bank.

268 **55** 30c. green and gold 10 10
269 70c. green, gold and violet 15 10
270 1s.50 green, gold and blue 30 10
271 2s.50 green, gold & brown 35 1·00

56 Marimba

1970. Musical Instruments.

272 **56** 30c. buff and brown . . . 15 10
273 – 70c. green, brown & yellow 25 10
274 – 1s.50 brown and yellow . . 50 10
275 – 2s.50 orange, yellow and brown . . . . 75 2·50

DESIGNS: 70c. Amadinda; 1s.50, Nzomari; 2s.50, Adeudeu.

57 Satellite Earth Station

1970. Inauguration of Satellite Earth Station.
276 **57** 30c. multicoloured 10 10
277 – 70c. multicoloured 15 10
278 – 1s.50 black, violet & orge 25 10
279 – 2s.50 multicoloured . . . 55 2·25
DESIGNS: 70c. Transmitter—daytime; 1s.50, Transmitter—night; 2s. 50, Earth and satellite.

58 Athlete

1970. 9th Commonwealth Games.
280 **58** 30c. brown and black . . . 10 10
281 70c. green, brown and black 10 10
282 1s.50 lilac, brown and black 15 10
283 2s.50 blue, brown and black . . . . 20 1·25

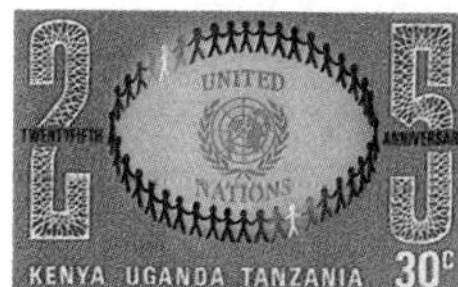

59 "25" and U.N. Emblem

1970. 25th Anniv of United Nations.
284 **59** 30c. multicoloured 10 10
285 70c. multicoloured 10 10
286 1s.50 multicoloured 20 10
287 2s.50 multicoloured . . . . 45 2·00

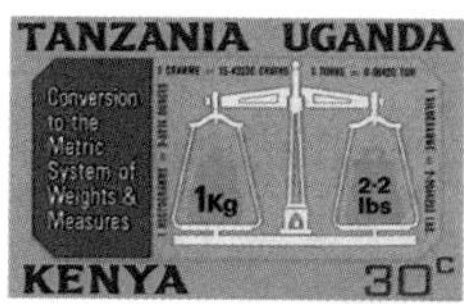

60 Balance and Weight Equivalents

1970. Conversion to Metric System. Multicoloured.
288 30c. Type **60** 10 10
289 70c. Fahrenheit and Centigrade thermometers 10 10
290 1s.50 Petrol pump and liquid capacities 15 10
291 2s.50 Surveyors and land measures . . . . 35 2·00

61 Class 11 Tank Locomotive

1971. Railway Transport. Multicoloured.
292 30c. Type **61** 35 10
293 70c. Class 90 diesel-electric locomotive 40 10
294 1s.50 Class 59 steam locomotive 60 20
295 2s.50 Class 30 steam locomotive . . . . 1·00 2·25
MS296 120 × 88 mm. Nos. 292/5 6·50 10·00

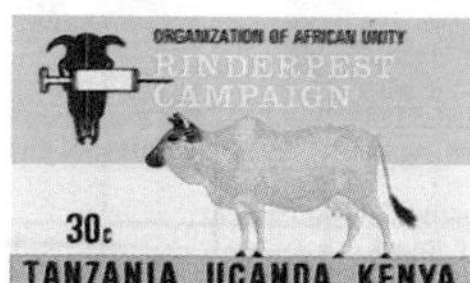

62 Syringe and Cow

1971. O.A.U. Rinderpest Campaign.
297 **62** 30c. black, brown and green 10 10
298 – 70c. black, blue and brown 10 10
299 **62** 1s.50 black, purple & brn 15 10
300 – 2s.50 black, red and brown 25 70
DESIGN: 70c., 2s.50, as Type **62** but with bull facing right.

63 Livingstone meets Stanley

1971. Centenary of Livingstone and Stanley meeting at Ujiji.
301 **63** 5s. multicoloured 30 75

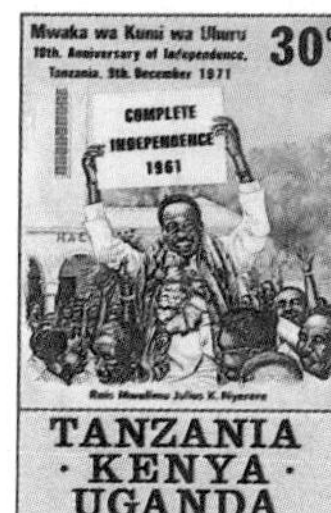

64 Pres. Nyerere and Supporters

1971. 10th Anniv of Tanzanian Independence. Multicoloured.
302 30c. Type **64** 10 10
303 70c. Ujamaa village 15 10
304 1s.50 Dar-es-Salaam University 30 25
305 2s.50 Kilimanjaro International Airport . . . 1·00 3·25

65 Flags and Trade Fair Emblem

1972. All-Africa Trade Fair.
306 **65** 30c. multicoloured 10 10
307 70c. multicoloured 10 10
308 1s.50 multicoloured 10 10
309 2s.50 multicoloured 25 80

66 Child with Cup

1972. 25th Anniv of U.N.I.C.E.F. Multicoloured.
310 30c. Type **66** 10 10
311 70c. Children with ball . . . 10 10
312 1s.50 Child at blackboard . . 10 10
313 2s.50 Child and tractor . . . 25 80

67 Hurdling

1972. Olympic Games, Munich. Multicoloured.
314 40c. Type **67** 10 10
315 70c. Running 10 10
316 1s.50 Boxing 20 15
317 2s.50 Hockey . . . . 30 1·75
MS318 131 × 98 mm. Nos. 314/17 4·50 7·00

68 Ugandan Kobs

1972. 10th Anniv of Ugandan Independence. Multicoloured.
319 40c. Type **68** 30 10
320 70c. Conference Centre . . . 30 10
321 1s.50 Makerere University . . 65 30
322 2s.50 Coat of arms . . . . . 1·00 3·50
MS323 132 × 120 mm. Nos. 319/22 3·50 3·50

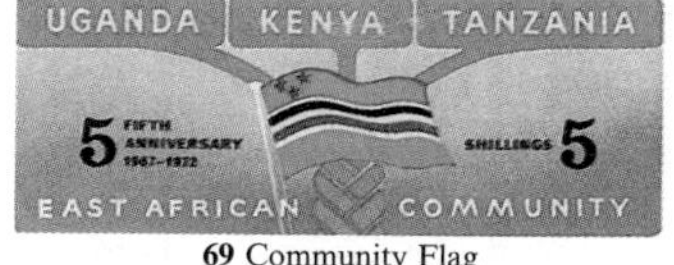

69 Community Flag

1972. 5th Anniv of East African Community.
324 **69** 5s. multicoloured . . . . . 55 1·90

70 Run-of-the-wind Anemometer

1972. Centenary of IMO/WMO. Multicoloured.
325 40c. Type **70** 10 10
326 70c. Weather balloon (vert) 20 10
327 1s.50 Meteorological rocket 30 15
328 2s.50 Satellite receiving aerial 55 2·25

71 "Learning by Serving"

73 Police Dog-handler

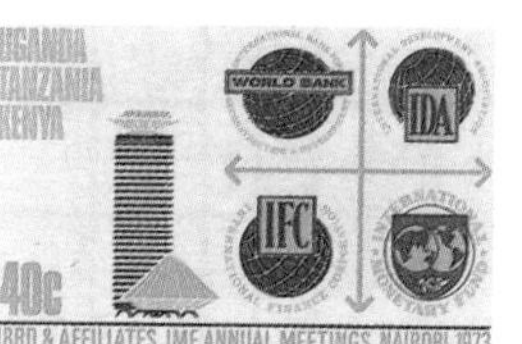

72 Kenyatta Conference Centre

1973. 24th World Scouting Conference, Nairobi.
329 **71** 40c. multicoloured 15 10
330 – 70c. red, violet and black 20 10
331 – 1s.50 blue, violet and black 45 30
332 – 2s.50 multicoloured . . . 1·00 2·25
DESIGNS: 70c. Baden-Powell's grave, Nyeri; 1s.50, World Scout emblem; 2s.50, Lord Baden-Powell.

1973. I.M.F./World Bank Conference.
333 **72** 40c. green, grey and black 10 10
334 – 70c. brown, grey and black 10 10
335 – 1s.50 multicoloured 25 35
336 – 2s.50 orange, grey & black 35 1·75
MS337 166 × 141 mm. Nos. 333/6. Imperf . . . . 1·40 3·75
DESIGNS: Nos. 334/6 show different arrangements of Bank emblems and the Conference Centre, the 1s.50 being vertical.

1973. 50th Anniv of Interpol.
338 **73** 40c. yellow, blue and black 55 15
339 – 70c. green, yellow and black 90 15
340 – 1s.50 violet, yellow & black 1·50 90
341 – 2s.50 green, orange & black . . . . 3·75 6·00
342 – 2s.50 green, orange & black . . . . 3·75 6·00
DESIGNS: 70c. East African policemen; 1s.50, Interpol emblem; 2s.50 (2), Interpol H.Q.
No. 341 is inscribed "St. Clans" and 342 "St. Cloud".

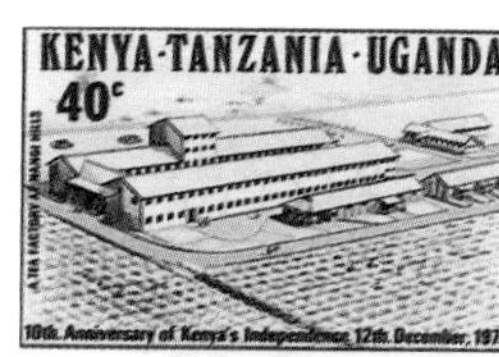

74 Tea Factory

1973. 10th Anniv of Kenya's Independence. Mult.
343 40c. Type **74** 10 10
344 70c. Kenyatta Hospital . . . 15 10
345 1s.50 Nairobi Airport 50 20
346 2s.50 Kindaruma hydro-electric scheme . . . . . . 65 1·75

75 Party H.Q.

1973. 10th Anniv of Zanzibar's Revolution. Mult.
347 40c. Type **75** 10 10
348 70c. Housing scheme 15 10
349 1s.50 Colour T.V. 35 30
350 2s.50 Amaan Stadium . . . 70 2·75

76 "Symbol of Union"

1974. 10th Anniv of Tanganyika–Zanzibar Union. Multicoloured.
351 40c. Type **76** 10 10
352 70c. Handclasp and map . . 15 10
353 1s.50 "Communications" . . 35 30
354 2s.50 Flags of Tanu, Tanzania and Afro-Shirazi Party . . . . 70 2·50

77 East African Family ("Stability of the Home")

1974. 17th Social Welfare Conference, Nairobi.
355 **77** 40c. yellow, brown & black 10 10
356 – 70c. multicoloured 10 10
357 – 1s.50 yellow, green & black 20 30
358 – 2s.50 red, violet and black 1·00 2·00
DESIGNS: 70c. Dawn and drummer (U.N. Second Development Plan); 1s.50, Agricultural scene (Rural Development Plan); 2s.50, Transport and telephone ("Communications").

78 New Postal H.Q., Kampala

1974. Centenary of U.P.U. Multicoloured.
359 40c. Type **78** 10 10
360 70c. Mail-train and post-van 20 10
361 1s.50 U.P.U. Building, Berne 15 20
362 2s.50 Loading mail into Vickers Super VC-10 . . . 55 1·50

79 Family-planning Clinic

1974. World Population Year.
363 **79** 40c. multicoloured 10 10
364 – 70c. mauve and red 10 10
365 – 1s.50 multicoloured 15 20
366 – 2s.50 blue, emerald and green . . . . 30 1·90
DESIGNS: 70c. "Tug of War"; 1s.50, "Population scales"; 2s.50, W.P.Y. emblem.

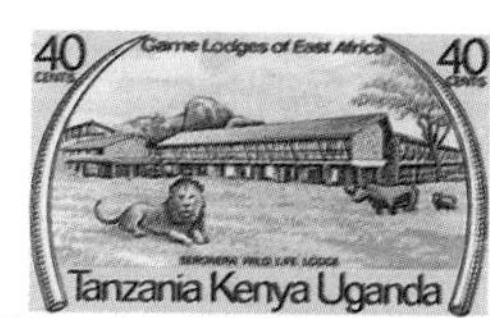

80 Seronera Wildlife Lodge, Tanzania

1975. East African Game Lodges. Multicoloured.
367 40c. Type **80** 15 10
368 70c. Mweya Safari Lodge, Uganda 20 10
369 1s.50 "Ark"—Aberdare Forest Lodge, Kenya . . . 25 30
370 2s.50 Paraa Safari Lodge, Uganda . . . . 60 2·25

81 Kitana (wooden comb), Bajun of Kenya

83 Ahmed ("Presidential" Elephant)

82 International Airport, Entebbe

1975. African Arts. Multicoloured.

371		50c. Type **81**	10	10
372		1s. Earring, Chaga of Tanzania	15	10
373		2s. Okoco (armlet), Acholi of Uganda	35	70
374		3s. Kitete, Kamba gourd, Kenya	65	1·40

1975. O.A.U. Summit Conf, Kampala. Mult.

375		50c. Type **82**	30	10
376		1s. Map of Africa and flag (vert)	30	10
377		2s. Nile Hotel, Kampala	30	85
378		3s. Martyrs' Shrine, Namugongo (vert)	40	1·60

1975. Rare Animals. Multicoloured.

379		50c. Type **83**	50	10
380		1s. Albino buffalo	50	10
381		2s. Ahmed in grounds of National Museum	1·10	1·50
382		3s. Abbott's duiker	1·25	3·00

84 Maasai Manyatta (village), Kenya

1975. 2nd World Black and African Festival of Arts and Culture, Nigeria (1977). Multicoloured.

383		50c. Type **84**	15	10
384		1s. "Heartbeat of Africa" (Ugandan Dancers)	15	10
385		2s. Makonde sculpture, Tanzania	50	85
386		3s. "Early Man and Technology" (skinning animal)	75	1·40

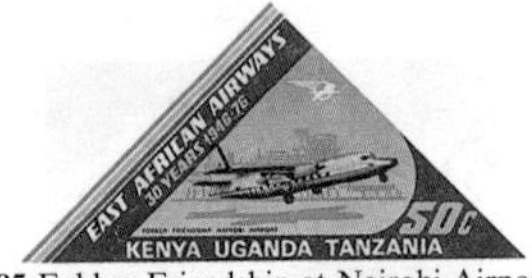

85 Fokker Friendship at Nairobi Airport

1975. 30th Anniv of East African Airways. Multicoloured.

387		50c. Type **85**	1·00	40
388		1s. Douglas DC-9 at Kilimanjaro Airport	1·10	40
389		2s. Vickers Super VC-10 at Entebbe Airport	3·50	3·25
390		3s. East African Airways crest	3·75	3·75

Further commemorative sets were released during 1976–78 using common designs, but each inscribed for one republic only. See Kenya, Tanzania and Uganda.

Co-operation between the postal services of the three member countries virtually ceased after 30 June 1977. The postal services of Kenya, Tanzania and Uganda then operated independently.

OFFICIAL STAMPS

For use on official correspondence of the Tanganyika Government only.

1959. Stamps of 1954 optd **OFFICIAL**.

O 1	**18**	5c. black and brown	10	75
O 2	–	10c. red	15	75
O 3	–	15c. black and blue	30	85
O 4	–	20c. black and orange	20	20
O 5	**18**	30c. black and blue	15	65
O 6	–	50c. purple	20	20
O 7	–	1s. black and red	20	65
O 8	–	1s.30 orange and lilac	2·25	1·50
O 9	–	2s. black and green	1·25	1·00
O10	–	5s. black and orange	3·00	2·25
O11	**20**	10s. black and blue	2·00	2·75
O12	**21**	£1 red and black	6·50	13·00

1960. Stamps of 1960 optd **OFFICIAL**.

O13	**26**	5c. blue	10	85
O14	–	10c. green	10	85
O15	–	15c. purple	10	85
O16	–	20c. mauve	10	10
O17	–	30c. red	10	10
O18	–	50c. violet	30	50
O19	**28**	1s. violet and purple	30	10
O20	–	5s. red and purple	10·00	65

POSTAGE DUE STAMPS

D 1

D 2

1923.

D1	**D 1**	5c. violet	2·50	50
D2		10c. red	2·50	15
D3		20c. green	2·50	3·00
D4		30c. brown	17·00	14·00
D5		40c. blue	6·50	14·00
D6		1s. green	65·00	£120

1935.

D 7	**D 2**	5c. violet	2·75	1·75
D 8		10c. red	30	50
D 9		20c. green	40	50
D10		30c. brown	1·25	50
D11		40c. blue	1·50	3·00
D12		1s. grey	19·00	19·00

KHMER REPUBLIC Pt. 21

Cambodia was renamed Khmer Republic on 9 October 1970.

Following the fall of the Khmer Republic, the People's Republic of Kampuchea was proclaimed on 10 January 1979.

100 cents = 1 riel.

78 "Attack"

1971. Defence of Khmer Territory.

285	**78**	1r. multicoloured	10	10
286		3r. multicoloured	20	10
287		10r. multicoloured	50	20

79 "World Races" and U.N. Emblem

1971. Racial Equality Year.

288	**79**	3r. multicoloured	10	10
289		7r. multicoloured	35	15
290		8r. multicoloured	55	25

80 General Post Office, Phnom Penh

1971.

291	**80**	3r. multicoloured	20	15
292		9r. multicoloured	40	20
293		10r. multicoloured	50	30

81 Global Emblem

1971. World Telecommunications Day.

294	**81**	3r. multicoloured	10	10
295		4r. multicoloured	20	10
296	–	7r. multicoloured	30	15
297	–	8r. red, black and orange	40	20

DESIGN: 7, 8r. I.T.U. emblem.

82 Indian Coral Bean

1971. Wild Flowers. Multicoloured.

298		2r. Type **82**	25	20
299		3r. Orchid tree	35	25
300		6r. Flame-of-the-forest	70	30
301		10r. Malayan crape myrtle (vert)	90	50

83 Arms of the Republic

84 Monument and Flag

1971. 1st Anniv of Republic.

302	**83**	3r. bistre and green	15	10
303	**84**	3r. multicoloured	10	10
304		4r. multicoloured	20	10
305	**83**	8r. bistre and orange	25	15
306		10r. bistre and brown	50	20
307	**84**	10r. multicoloured	50	25

85 U.N.I.C.E.F. Emblem

86 Book Year Emblem

1971. 25th Anniv of U.N.I.C.E.F.

309	**85**	3r. purple	20	10
310		5r. blue	25	15
311		9r. red and violet	45	30

1972. International Book Year.

312	**86**	3r. green, purple and blue	15	10
313		8r. blue, green and purple	25	15
314		9r. bistre, blue and green	45	20

87 Lion of St. Mark's

1972. U.N.E.S.C.O. "Save Venice" Campaign.

316	**87**	3r. brown, buff and purple	20	10
317	–	5r. brown, buff and green	35	20
318	–	10r. brown, blue and green	65	20

DESIGNS—HORIZ: 5r. St. Mark's Basilica. VERT: 10r. Bridge of Sighs.

88 U.N. Emblem

89 Dancing Apsaras (relief), Angkor

1972. 25th Anniv of Economic Commission for Asia and the Far East (C.E.A.E.O.).

320	**88**	3r. red	15	10
321		6r. blue	20	15
322		9r. red	35	20

1972.

324	**89**	1r. brown	10	10
325		3r. violet	15	10
326		7r. purple	25	15
327		8r. brown	30	15
328		9r. green	40	20
329		10r. blue	55	20
330		12r. purple	70	25
331		14r. blue	85	40

90 "UIT" on T.V. Screen

91 Conference Emblem

1972. World Telecommunications Day.

332	**90**	3r. black, blue and yellow	15	10
333		9r. black, blue and mauve	35	15
334		14r. black, blue and brown	55	25

1972. United Nations Environmental Conservation Conference, Stockholm.

335	**91**	3r. green, brown and violet	15	10
336		12r. violet and green	40	20
337		15r. green and violet	55	35

92 Javan Rhinoceros

94 Hoisting Flag

1972. Wild Animals.

339	**92**	3r. black, red and violet	25	10
340	–	4r. violet, bistre and purple	35	10
341	–	6r. brown, green and blue	60	20
342	–	7r. ochre, green and brown	60	20
343	–	8r. black, green and blue	85	20
344	–	10r. black, blue and green	1·25	30

DESIGNS: 4r. Mainland serow; 6r. Thamin; 7r. Banteng; 8r. Water buffalo; 10r. Gaur.

1972. Olympic Games, Munich. Nos. 164 of Cambodia and 302, 306 and 336/7 of Khmer Republic optd **XXe JEUX OLYMPIQUES MUNICH 1972**, Olympic rings and emblem.

345	**83**	3r. bistre and green	25	20
346		10r. bistre and brown	60	50
347	–	12r. green and brown	75	65
348	**91**	12r. violet and green	70	50
349		15r. green and violet	75	50

1972. 2nd Anniv of Republic.

350	**94**	3r. multicoloured	10	10
351		5r. multicoloured	15	10
352		9r. multicoloured	35	20

1972. Red Cross Aid for War Victims. No. 164 of Cambodia and 302, 306 and 336/7 of Khmer Republic surch **SECOURS AUX VICTIMES DE GUERRE**, red cross and value.

353	**83**	3r.+2r. bistre and green	20	20
354		10r.+6r. bistre and brown	45	45
355	–	12r.+7r. green and brown	95	95
356	**91**	12r.+7r. violet and green	55	55
357		15r.+8r. green and violet	1·00	1·00

96 Garuda

97 Crest and Temple

1973. Air.

358	**96**	3r. red	10	15
359		30r. blue	1·40	70
360		50r. lilac	2·50	1·40
361		100r. green	4·00	2·25

1973. New Constitution.

362	**97**	3r. multicoloured	10	10
363		12r. multicoloured	15	15
364		14r. multicoloured	35	20

98 Apsara

99 Interpol Emblem

1973. Angkor Sculptures.

366	**98**	3r. black	10	10
367	–	8r. blue	15	10
368	–	10r. brown	35	20

DESIGNS: 8r. Devata (12th century); 10f. Devata (10th century).

1973. 50th Anniv of International Criminal Police Organization (Interpol).

370	**99**	3r. green and turquoise	10	10
371		7r. green and red	20	15
372		10r. green and brown	30	20

100 Marshal Lon Nol

1973. Honouring Marshal Lon Nol, 1st President of Republic.
374 **100** 3r. black, brown and green 10 10
375 8r. black, brown and green 20 15
376 14r. black, brown and agate 20 15

102 Copernicus and Space Rocket

1974. 500th Birth Anniv of Nicolas Copernicus (astronomer). Multicoloured.
382 1r. Type **102** (postage) . . . 10 10
383 5r. Copernicus and "Mariner II" 10 10
384 10r. Copernicus and "Apollo" 25 15
385 25r. Copernicus and "Telstar" 70 35
386 50r. Copernicus and space-walker . . . . 1·25 70
387 100r. Copernicus and spaceship landing on Moon 3·00 1·50
388 150r. Copernicus and Moon-landing craft leaving "Apollo" . . . . 4·25 2·75
389 200r. Copernicus and "Skylab III" (air) . . . . 5·25 2·75
390 250r. Copernicus and Concorde . . . . 7·50 3·75

1974. 4th Anniv of Republic. Various stamps optd **4E ANNIVERSAIRE DE LA REPUBLIQUE**.
391 **78** 10r. multicoloured 70 50
392 **77** 50r. on 3r. multicoloured 1·75 1·40
393 **94** 100r. on 5r. multicoloured 3·75 3·25

No. 392 is additionally optd **REPUBLIQUE KHMERE** in French and Cambodian.

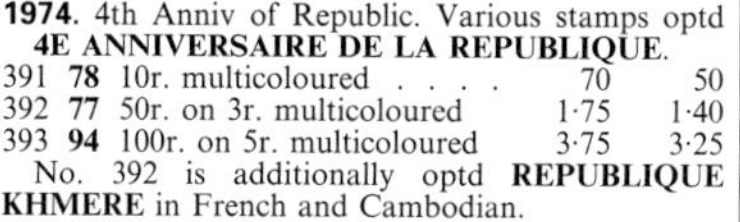

104 Xylophone

1975. Unissued stamps of Cambodia showing musical instruments, surch **REPUBLIQUE KHMERE** in French and Cambodian and new value. Multicoloured.
394 5r. on 8r. Type **104** . . . . .
395 20r. on 1r. So (two-stringed violin) . . . .
396 160r. on 7r. Khoung vong (bronze gongs) . . . . . .
397 180r. on 14r. Two drums . .
398 235r. on 12r. Barrel-shaped drum . . . .
399 500r. on 9r. Xylophone (different) . . . .
400 1000r. on 10r. Boat-shaped xylophone . . . .
401 2000r. on 3r. Twenty-stringed guitar on legs . . . . . .
Set of 8 . . . . £130

POSTAGE DUE STAMPS

D 101 Frieze, Angkor Vat

1974.
D378 **D 101** 2r. brown 15 15
D379 6r. green 25 25
D380 8r. red 30 30
D381 10r. blue 35 35

APPENDIX

The following stamps have either been issued in excess of postal needs or have not been available to the public in reasonable quantities at face value. Such stamps may later be given full listing if there is evidence of regular postal use.

1972.

Moon Landing of "Apollo 16". Embossed on gold foil. Air 900r. × 2.

Visit of Pres. Nixon to China. Embossed on gold foil. Air 900r. × 2.

Olympic Games, Munich. Embossed on gold foil. Air 900r. × 2.

1973.

Gold Medal Winners, Munich Olympics. Embossed on gold foil. Air 900r. × 2.

World Cup Football Championship, West Germany (1974). Embossed on gold foil. Air 900r. × 4.

1974.

Pres. Kennedy and "Apollo 11". Embossed on gold foil. Air 1100r. × 2.

500th Birth Anniv of Nicolas Copernicus (astronomer). Embossed on gold foil. Air 1200r.

Centenary of U.P.U. (1st issue). Postage 10, 60r.; Air 700; 1200r. embossed on gold foil.

1975.

Olympic Games, Montreal (1976). Postage 5, 10, 15, 25 r.; Air 50, 100, 150, 200, 250 r.; 1200 r. embossed on gold foil.

World Cup Football Championship, West Germany (1974). Postage 1, 5, 10, 25 r.; Air 50, 100, 150, 200, 250, 1200r. embossed on gold foil.

Centenary of U.P.U. (2nd issue). Postage 15, 20, 70, 160, 180, 235r.; Air 500, 1000, 2000, 2000r. embossed on gold foil.

KHOR FAKKAN Pt. 19

From 1965 various issues were produced for this dependency, some being overprinted on, or in the same designs as, issues for Sharjah.

APPENDIX

The following stamps have either been issued in excess of postal needs or have not been available to the public in reasonable quantities at face value. Such stamps may later be given full listing if there is evidence of regular postal use.

1965.

Views. Nos. 75/80 of Sharjah optd. Air 10, 20, 30, 40, 75, 100n.p.

Boy and Girl Scouts. Nos. 74 and 89 of Sharjah optd. 2, 2r.

Birds. Nos. 101/6 of Sharjah optd. Air 30, 40, 75, 150n.p., 2, 3r.

Olympic Games, Tokyo 1964. Nos. 95/7 of Sharjah optd. 40, 50n.p., 2r.

New York World's Fair. Nos. 81/3 of Sharjah optd. Air 20, 40n.p., 1r.

Pres. Kennedy Commem. Nos. 98/100 of Sharjah optd. Air 40, 60, 100n.p.

Centenary of I.T.U. Postage 1, 2, 3, 4, 5, 50n.p., 1r., 120n.p.

Pan-Arab Games, Cairo. 50p. × 5.

1966.

International Co-operation Year. 50n.p. × 8.

Churchill Commemoration. 2, 3, 4, 5r.

Roses. 20, 35, 60, 80n.p., 1r., 125n.p.

Fish. 1, 2, 3, 4, 5, 15, 20, 30, 40, 50, 75n.p., 1, 2, 3, 4, 5, 10r.

Int Stamp Exhibition, Washington D.C. (SIPEX). 80, 120n.p., 2r.

New Currency Surcharges in Rials and Piastres.

(a) 1965 I.T.U. Centenary issue. 10p. on 50n.p., 16p. on 120n.p., 1r. on 1r.

(b) Churchill issue. 1r. on 2r., 2r. on 3r., 3r. on 4r., 4r. on 5r.

(c) Roses issue. 1p. on 20n.p., 2p. on 35n.p., 4p. on 60n.p., 6p. on 80n.p., 10p. on 125n.p., 12p. on 1r.

New Currency Surcharges in Dirhams and Riyals.

(a) 1965 Pan-Arab Games issue. 20d. on 50p. × 5.

(b) Fish issue. 1d. on 1n.p., 2d. on 2n.p., 3d. on 3n.p., 4d. on 4n.p., 5d. on 5n.p., 15d. on 15n.p., 20d. on 20n.p., 30d. on 30n.p., 40d. on 40n.p., 50d. on 50n.p., 75d. on 75n.p., 1r. on 1r., 2r. on 2r., 3r. on 3r., 4r. on 4r., 5r. on 5r., 10r. on 10r.

3rd Death Anniv of Pres. J. Kennedy. Optd on Int Stamp Exhibition, Washington issue. 80d. on 80n.p., 120d. on 120n.p., 2r. on 2r.

World Football Cup Championship, England. ½r. × 7.

1967.

4th Death Anniv of Pres. J. Kennedy. Optd on 1966 Int Stamp Exhibition issue. 80d. on 80n.p., 120d. on 120n.p., 2r. on 2r.

1968.

Famous Paintings. Optd on Sharjah. Postage 1, 2, 3, 4, 5, 30, 40, 60, 75d.; Air 1, 2, 3, 4, 5r.

Winter Olympic Games, Grenoble. Optd on Sharjah. Postage 1, 2, 3, 4, 5d.; Air 1, 2, 3r.

Previous Olympic Games. Optd on Sharjah. Air 25, 50, 75d., 1r.50, 3, 4r.

Olympic Games, Mexico. Optd on Sharjah. 10, 20, 30d., 2, 2r.40, 5r.

1969.

12th World Jamboree. Optd on 1968 issue of Sharjah. Postage 1, 2, 3, 4, 5, 10d.; Air 30, 50, 60d., 1r.50.

Martyrs of Liberty. Optd on 1968 issue of Sharjah. Air 35d. × 4, 60d. × 4, 1r. × 4

Sportsmen and Women. Optd on 1968 issue of Sharjah. Postage 20, 30, 40, 60d., 1r.50, 2r.50; Air 35, 50d., 1, 2, 3r.25, 4, 4r.

A number of issues on gold or silver foil also exist, but it is understood that these were mainly for presentation purposes, although valid for postage.

In common with the other states of the United Arab Emirates the Khor Fakkan stamp contract was terminated on 1 August 1972, and any further new issues released after that date were unauthorised.

KIAUTSCHOU (KIAOCHOW) Pt. 7

A port in Shantung, China, leased by Germany from China in 1898. It was occupied by Japan in 1914, but reverted to China in 1922.

1900. 100 pfennige = 1 mark.
1905. 100 cents = 1 dollar (Chinese).

1900. No. 9 of German Post Offices in China surch **5 Pfg.**
3 5pf. on 10pf. red . . . . 40·00 45·00

1901. "Yacht" key-types inscr "KIAUTSCHOU".
11 N 3pf. brown . . . . 2·00 2·40
12 5pf. green 80 60
13 10pf. red . . . . 2·75 1·40
14 20pf. blue . . . . 7·50 8·00
15 25pf. black & red on yellow 15·00 15·00
16 30pf. black & orge on buff 15·00 15·00
17 40pf. black and red . . . . 15·00 15·00
18 50pf. black & purple on buff 15·00 19·00
19 80pf. black and red on pink 29·00 40·00
20 O 1m. red . . . . 55·00 65·00
21 2m. blue . . . . 75·00 80·00
22 3m. black . . . . 80·00 £150
23 5m. red and black £200 £600

1905. Chinese currency. "Yacht" key-types inscr "KIAUTSCHOU".
34 N 1c. brown 50 80
35 2c. green . . . . 1·25 50
36 4c. red 80 60
37 10c. blue . . . . 1·10 2·40
38 20c. black and red . . . . . 1·90 12·00
39 40c. black and red on pink 3·75 42·00
40 O ½d. red . . . . 6·75 48·00
41 1d. blue . . . . 5·75 48·00
42 1½d. black . . . . 7·00 £120
43 2½d. red and black . . . . . 16·00 £350

KING EDWARD VII LAND Pt. 1

Stamp issued in connection with the Shackleton Antarctic Expedition in 1908. The expedition landed at Cape Royds in Victoria Land, instead of King Edward VII Land, the intended destination.

1908. Stamp of New Zealand optd **KING EDWARD VII LAND.**
A1 **42** 1d. red . . . . £400 35·00

KIONGA Pt. 9

Part of German E. Africa, occupied by the Portuguese during the 1914/18 war, and now incorporated in Mozambique.

1916. "King Carlos" key-type of Lourenco Marques optd **REPUBLICA** and surch **KIONGA** and new value.
1 S ½c. on 100r. blue on blue . . . 5·50 5·00
2 1c. on 100r. blue on blue . . . 5·50 5·00
3 2½c. on 100r. blue on blue . . 5·50 5·00
4 5c. on 100r. blue on blue . . . 5·50 5·00

KIRIBATI Pt. 1

This group of islands in the Pacific, formerly known as the Gilbert Islands, achieved independence on 12 July 1979 and was renamed Kiribati.

100 cents = 1 dollar.

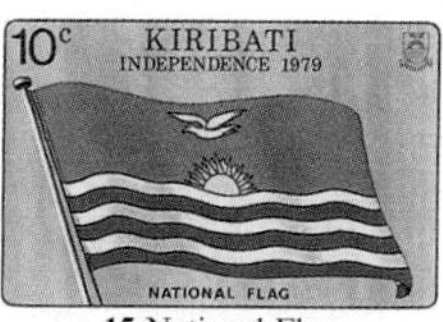

15 National Flag

1979. Independence. Multicoloured.
84 10c. Type **15** 10 35
85 45c. Houses of Parliament and Maneaba ni Maungatabu (House of Assembly) . . . 20 65

16 "Teraaka" (training ship)

1979. Multicoloured.
86 1c. Type **16** 10 90
122 3c. "Tautunu" (inter-island freighter) 15 30
123 5c. Hibiscus 10 15
124 7c. Catholic Cathedral, Tarawa 10 15
125 10c. Maneaba, Bikenibeu . . 10 15
91 12c. Betio Harbour 15 20
92 15c. Reef heron 35 25
93 20c. Flamboyant tree 20 25

129 25c. Moorish idol (fish) . . . 30 30
95 30c. Frangipani 25 30
96 35c. G.I.P.C. Chapel, Tangintebu 25 30
97 50c. "Hypolimnas bolina" (butterfly) 75 55
133 $1 "Tabakea" (Tarawa Lagoon ferry) 50 75
134 $2 Evening scene 50 75
135 $5 National flag . . . . . . 1·00 2·00

17 Gilbert and Ellice Islands 1911 ½d. Stamp

18 Boy with Giant Clam Shell

1979. Death Cent of Sir Rowland Hill. Mult.
100 10c. Type **17** 10 10
101 20c. Gilbert & Ellice Islands 1956 2s.6d. definitive . . . 15 20
102 25c. G.B. Edward VII 2s.6d. 15 20
103 45c. Gilbert and Ellice Islands 1924 10s. 25 35
MS104 113 × 110 mm. Nos. 100/3 70 1·00

1979. International Year of the Child. Mult.
105 10c. Type **18** 10 10
106 20c. Child climbing coconut palm (horiz) 10 10
107 45c. Girl reading 15 20
108 $1 Child in traditional costume 30 50

19 Downrange Station, Christmas Island

1980. Satellite Tracking. Multicoloured.
109 25c. Type **19** 10 10
110 45c. Map showing satellite trajectory 15 15
111 $1 Rocket launch, Tanegashima, Japan (vert) 30 35

20 T.S. "Teraaka"

1980. "London 1980" Int Stamp Exhibition. Mult.
112 12c. Type **20** 15 10
113 25c. Loading Air Tungaru Britten Norman Islander, Bonriki Airport 15 10
114 30c. Radio operator 15 10
115 $1 Bairiki Post Office 20 35
MS116 139 × 116 mm. Nos. 112/15 60 85

21 "Achaea janata"

1980. Moths. Multicoloured.
117 12c. Type **21** 10 10
118 25c. "Ethmia nigroapicella" 15 15
119 30c. "Utetheisa pulchelloides" 15 15
120 50c. "Anua coronata" . . . 25 25

22 Captain Cook Hotel

1980. Development. Multicoloured.
136 10c. Type **22** 10 10
137 20c. Sports stadium 10 10
138 25c. International Airport, Bonriki 15 10
139 35c. National Library and Archives, Bairiki 15 10
140 $1 Otintai Hotel, Bikenibeu 20 40

23 "Acalypha godseffiana"

1981. Flowers. Multicoloured.
141 12c. Type **23** 10 10
142 30c. "Hibiscus schizopetalus" 15 15
143 35c. "Calotropis gigantea" 15 15
144 50c. "Euphorbia pulcherrima" 20 20

25 Maps of Abaiang and Marakei, and String Figures

1981. Islands (1st series). Multicoloured.
145 12c. Type **25** 15 10
146 30c. Maps of Little Makin and Butaritari, and village house 20 10
147 35c. Map of Maiana and coral road 25 15
148 $1 Map of Christmas Island, and Captain Cook's H.M.S. "Resolution" . . . 70 75
See also Nos. 201/4, 215/18, 237/40, 256/60 and 270/3.

26 "Katherine"

27 Prince Charles and Lady Diana Spencer (½-size illustration)

1981. Royal Wedding. Royal Yachts. Multicoloured.
149 12c. Type **26** 10 15
150 12c. Type **27** 20 30
151 50c. "Osborne" 25 40
152 50c. Type **27** 50 75
153 $2 "Britannia" 35 80
154 $2 Type **27** . . . . 1·50 2·50
MS155 120 × 109 mm. $1.20 Type **27** 75 1·00

28 Tuna Bait Breeding Centre, Bonriki Fish Farm

1981. Tuna Fishing Industry. Multicoloured.
158 12c. Type **28** 15 10
159 30c. Tuna fishing 20 20
160 35c. Cold storage, Betio . . . 20 25
161 50c. Government Tuna Fishing Vessel "Nei Manganibuka" 30 50
MS162 134 × 99 mm. Nos. 158/61 1·00 1·40

29 Pomarine Skua

1982. Birds. Multicoloured.
163 1c. Type **29** 15 15
164 2c. Mallard 15 15
165 4c. Collared petrel 20 20
166 5c. Blue-faced booby . . . 20 20
167 7c. Friendly quail dove . . 20 20
168 8c. Common shoveler ("Shoveler") 20 20
169 12c. Polynesian reed warbler 20 20
170 15c. Pacific golden plover ("Pacific Plover") 25 25
171 20c. Reef heron 30 30
171a 25c. Common noddy ("Brown Noddy") . . . . 2·25 1·50
172 30c. Brown booby 30 30
173 35c. Audubon's shearwater 60 35
174 40c. White-throated storm petrel (vert) 35 40
175 50c. Bristle-thighed curlew (vert) 40 45
175a 55c. White tern ("Fairy Tern") (vert) . . . . . . 11·00 16·00
176 $1 Kuhl's lory ("Scarlet-breasted Lorikeet") (vert) 1·25 40
177 $2 Long-tailed koel ("Long-tailed Cuckoo") (vert) . . 1·25 55
178 $5 Great frigate bird (vert) 1·75 1·25

30 Riley Turbo Skyliner

1982. Air. Inaug of Tungaru Airline. Mult.
179 12c. Type **30** 15 10
180 30c. Britten Norman "short nose" Trislander 20 20
181 35c. Casa-212 Aviocar . . . 20 25
182 50c. Boeing 727-200 . . . . 30 35
No. 179 is inscr "De Havilland DH114 Heron" in error.

31 Mary of Teck, Princess of Wales, 1893

1982. 21st Birthday of Princess of Wales. Mult.
183 12c. Type **31** 10 10
184 50c. Coat of arms of Mary of Teck 20 20
185 $1 Diana, Princess of Wales 30 35

1982. Birth of Prince William of Wales. Nos. 183/5 optd **ROYAL BABY**.
186 12c. Type **31** 10 15
187 50c. Coat of arms of Mary of Teck 25 40
188 $1 Diana, Princess of Wales 40 60

32 First Aid Practice

1982. 75th Anniv of Boy Scout Movement. Mult.
189 12c. Type **32** 20 15
190 25c. Boat repairs 20 30
191 30c. On parade 25 35
192 40c. Gilbert Islands 1977 8c. Scouting stamp and "75" 25 60

33 Queen and Duke of Edinburgh with Local Dancer

1982. Royal Visit. Multicoloured.
193 12c. Type **33** 15 15
194 25c. Queen, Duke of Edinburgh and outrigger canoe 20 20
195 35c. New Philatelic Bureau building 30 30
MS196 88 × 76 mm. 50c. Queen Elizabeth II 60 60
On No. **MS**196 the captions on the map for the islands of Teraina and Tabuaeran have been transposed.

34 "Obaia, The Feathered" (Kiribati legend)

1983. Commonwealth Day. Multicoloured.
197 12c. Type **34** 10 10
198 30c. Robert Louis Stevenson Hotel, Abemama 15 10
199 50c. Container ship off Betio 15 25
200 $1 Map of Kiribati 20 50

1983. Island Maps (2nd series). As T **25**. Mult.
201 12c. Beru, Nikunau and canoe 20 15
202 25c. Abemama, Aranuka, Kuria and fish 20 20
203 35c. Nonouti and reef fishing (vert) 25 35
204 50c. Tarawa and House of Assembly (vert) 30 50

35 Collecting Coconuts

1983. Copra Industry. Multicoloured.
205 12c. Type **35** 20 15
206 25c. Selecting coconuts for copra 35 25
207 30c. Removing husks 35 30
208 35c. Drying copra 35 35
209 50c. Loading copra at Betio 40 45

36 War Memorials

1983. 40th Anniv of Battle of Tarawa. Multicoloured.
210 12c. Type **36** 15 15
211 30c. Maps of Tarawa and Pacific Ocean 20 30
212 35c. Gun emplacement . . . 20 35
213 50c. Modern and war-time landscapes 25 55
214 $1 Aircraft carrier U.S.S. "Tarawa" 40 75

1983. Island Maps (3rd series). As T **25**. Mult.
215 12c. Teraina and Captain Fanning's ship "Betsey", 1798 . . . . 25 15
216 30c. Nikumaroro and hawksbill turtle 30 35
217 35c. Kanton and local postmark 35 40
218 50c. Banaba and flying fish 40 55

37 Tug "Riki"

1984. Kiribati Shipping Corporation. Mult.
219 12c. Type **37** 50 15
220 35c. Ferry "Nei Nimanoa" 90 35
221 50c. Ferry "Nei Tebaa" . . . 1·25 60
222 $1 Cargo ship "Nei Momi" 1·50 1·10
MS223 115 × 98 mm. Nos. 219/22 3·25 5·50

38 Water and Sewage Schemes

1984. "Ausipex" International Stamp Exhibition, Melbourne. Multicoloured.
224 12c. Type **38** 15 15
225 30c. "Nouamake" (game fishing boat) 20 30
226 35c. Overseas training schemes 20 40
227 50c. International communications link . . . 25 55

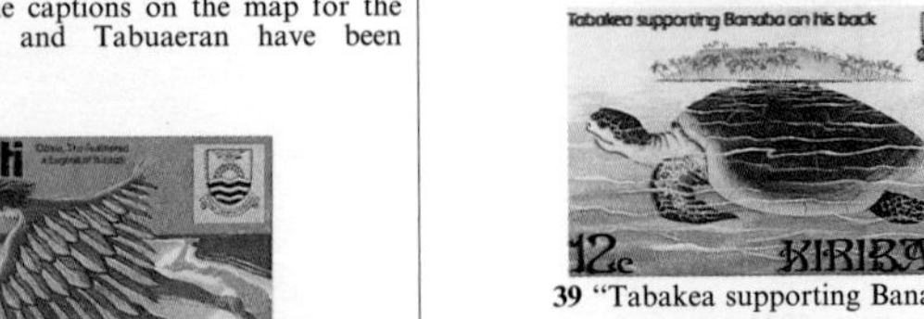

39 "Tabakea supporting Banaba"

1984. Kiribati Legends (1st series). Multicoloured.
228 12c. Type **39** 15 20
229 30c. "Nakaa, Judge of the Dead" 15 35

230 35c. "Naareau and Dragonfly" 15 45
231 50c. "Whistling Ghosts" . . 20 55
See also Nos. 245/8.

40 Sail-finned Tang

1985. Reef Fishes. Multicoloured.
232 12c. Type **40** 60 25
233 25c. Picasso triggerfish . . . 1·00 65
234 35c. Clown surgeonfish . . . 1·25 85
235 80c. Red squirrelfish . . . . 2·00 2·50
MS236 140 × 107 mm. Nos. 232/5 6·00 4·75

1985. Island Maps (4th series). As T **25**. Mult.
237 12c. Tabuaeran and great frigate bird ("Frigate Bird") . . . . 1·50 25
238 35c. Rawaki and germinating coconuts . . . . 2·00 40
239 50c. Arorae and xanthid crab 2·25 65
240 $1 Tamana and fish hook . . 2·75 1·50

41 Youths playing Football on Beach

1985. International Youth Year. Multicoloured.
241 15c. Type **41** 70 70
242 35c. Logos of I.Y.Y. and Kiribati Youth Year . . . 1·10 1·40
243 40c. Girl preparing food (vert) . . . . 1·25 1·60
244 55c. Map illustrating Kiribati's youth exchange links . . . . 1·40 2·25

1985. Kiribati Legends (2nd series). As T **39**. Mult.
245 15c. "Nang Kineia and the Tickling Ghosts" 50 30
246 35c. "Auriaria and Tituabine" 85 85
247 40c. "The first coming of Babai at Arorae" . . . . 1·00 1·25
248 55c. "Riiki and the Milky Way" . . . . 1·25 1·75

42 Map showing Telecommunications Satellite Link

1985. Transport and Telecommunications Decade (1st issue). Multicoloured.
249 15c. Type **42** . . . . 1·50 1·00
250 40c. M. V. "Moanaraoi" (Tarawa–Suva service) . . 2·75 3·00
See also Nos. 268/9, 293/4 and 314/15.

1986. 60th Birthday of Queen Elizabeth II. As T **246a** of Papua New Guinea. Multicoloured.
251 15c. Princess Elizabeth in Girl Guide uniform, Windsor Castle, 1938 . . . 15 15
252 35c. At Trooping the Colour, 1980 . . . . 20 30
253 40c. With Duke of Edinburgh in Kiribati, 1982 . . . . . 20 35
254 55c. At banquet, Austrian Embassy, London, 1966 . . 25 50
255 $1 At Crown Agents Head Office, London, 1983 . . . 45 1·25

1986. Island Maps (5th series). As T **25**. Mult.
256 15c. Manra and coconut crab 2·50 1·25
257 30c. Birnie and McKean Islands and cowrie shells 3·25 2·50
258 35c. Orona and red-footed booby . . . . 4·00 2·75
259 40c. Malden Island and whaling ship, 1844 . . . . 4·00 3·50
260 55c. Vostok, Flint and Caroline Islands and Bellingshausen's "Vostok", 1820 . . . . 4·00 4·00

43 "Lepidodactylus lugubris"

1986. Geckos. Multicoloured.
261 15c. Type **43** . . . . 1·50 70
262 35c. "Gehyra mutilata" . . . 1·75 1·50
263 40c. "Hemidactylus frenatus" 1·90 1·75
264 55c. "Gehyra oceanica" . . . 2·25 2·50
See also Nos. 274/7.

44 Maps of Australia and Kiribati

46 Henri Dunant (founder)

45 Freighter "Moamoa"

1986. America's Cup Yachting Championship. Multicoloured.
265 15c. Type **44** 20 65
266 55c. America's Cup and map of course . . . . 50 1·25
267 $1.50 "Australia II" (1983 winner) . . . . 1·00 1·50

1987. Transport and Telecommunications Decade (2nd issue). Multicoloured.
268 30c. Type **45** . . . . . . 2·75 2·50
269 55c. Telephone switchboard and automatic exchange . . 3·75 3·50

1987. Island Maps (6th series). As T **25**. Multicoloured.
270 15c. Starbuck and red-tailed tropic bird ("Red-tailed Tropicbird"!) 60 80
271 30c. Enderbury and white tern 70 85
272 55c. Tabiteuea and pandanus tree 70 90
273 $1 Onotoa and okai (house) 80 2·50

1987. Skinks. As T **43**. Multicoloured.
274 15c. "Emoia nigra" 30 45
275 35c. "Cryptoblepharus sp." 30 50
276 40c. "Emoia cyanura" . . . 30 55
277 $1 "Lipinia noctua" . . . . 45 1·50
MS278 130 × 114 mm. Nos. 274/7 1·10 3·25

1987. Royal Ruby Wedding. Nos. 251/5 optd **40TH WEDDING ANNIVERSARY**.
279 15c. Princess Elizabeth in Girl Guide uniform, Windsor Castle, 1938 . . . 15 25
280 35c. At Trooping the Colour, 1980 . . . . 20 30
281 40c. With Duke of Edinburgh in Kiribati, 1982 . . . . . 25 35
282 55c. At banquet, Austrian Embassy, London, 1966 . . 30 45
283 $1 At Crown Agents Head Office, London, 1983 . . . 50 1·25

1988. 125th Anniv of Int Red Cross. Mult.
284 15c. Type **46** 80 65
285 35c. Red Cross workers in Independence parade, 1979 1·25 1·50
286 40c. Red Cross workers with patient . . . . 1·25 1·60
287 55c. Gilbert & Ellice Islands 1970 British Red Cross Centenary 10c. stamp . . . 1·60 1·75

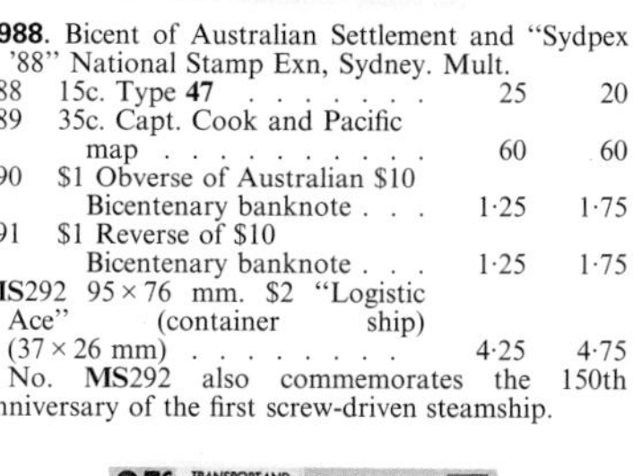
47 Causeway built by Australia

1988. Bicent of Australian Settlement and "Sydpex '88" National Stamp Exn, Sydney. Mult.
288 15c. Type **47** 25 20
289 35c. Capt. Cook and Pacific map 60 60
290 $1 Obverse of Australian $10 Bicentenary banknote . . . 1·25 1·75
291 $1 Reverse of $10 Bicentenary banknote . . . 1·25 1·75
MS292 95 × 76 mm. $2 "Logistic Ace" (container ship) (37 × 26 mm) . . . . 4·25 4·75
No. **MS**292 also commemorates the 150th anniversary of the first screw-driven steamship.

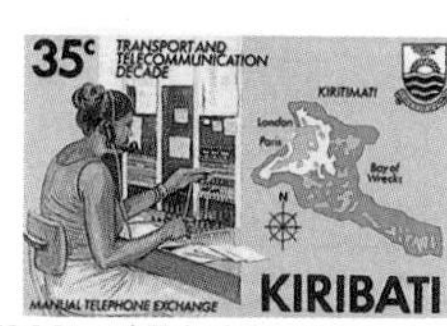
48 Manual Telephone Exchange and Map of Kiritimati

1988. Transport and Telecommunications Decade (3rd issue). Multicoloured.
293 35c. Type **48** 75 75
294 45c. Betio-Bairiki Causeway 1·00 1·00

49 "Hound" (brigantine), 1835

1989. Nautical History (1st series). Multicoloured.
295 15c. Type **49** 90 55
296 30c. "Phantom" (brig), 1854 1·50 1·10
297 40c. H.M.S. "Alacrity" (schooner), 1873 . . . . . 1·60 1·60
298 $1 "Charles W. Morgan" (whaling ship), 1851 . . . 3·00 3·75
See also Nos. 343/7 and 523/6.

50 Reef Heron ("Eastern Reef Heron")

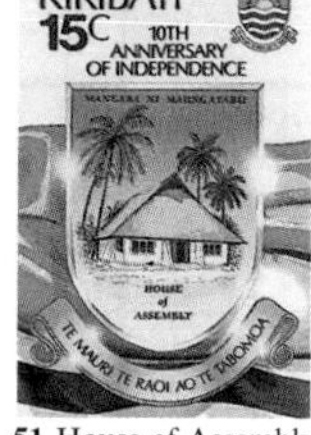
51 House of Assembly

1989. Birds with Young. Multicoloured.
299 15c. Type **50** . . . . 1·25 1·50
300 15c. Reef heron ("Eastern Reef Heron") chicks in nest . . . . 1·25 1·50
301 $1 White-tailed tropic bird 2·50 3·25
302 $1 Young white-tailed tropic bird . . . . 2·50 3·25
Nos. 299/300 and 301/2 were each printed together, se-tenant, each pair forming a composite design

1989. 10th Anniv of Independence. Mult.
303 15c. Type **51** 25 25
304 $1 Constitution . . . . . . 1·25 1·75

51a "Apollo 10" on Launch Gantry

1989. 20th Anniv of First Manned Landing on Moon. Multicoloured.
305 20c. Type **51a** 30 30
306 50c. Crew of "Apollo 10" (30 × 30 mm) 70 90
307 60c. "Apollo 10" emblem (30 × 30 mm) . . . . . . 80 1·00
308 75c. "Apollo 10" splashdown, Hawaii . . . . 95 1·25
MS309 82 × 100 mm. $2.50 "Apollo 11" command module in lunar orbit . . . . 6·50 7·50

51b Gilbert and Ellice Islands, 1949 75th Anniv of U.P.U. 3d. Stamp

51c Examining Fragment of Statue

1989. "Philexfrance 89" International Stamp Exhibition, Paris, and "World Stamp Expo '89", Washington (1st issue). Sheet 104 × 86 mm.
MS310 **51b** $2 multicoloured . . 3·50 5·00

1989. "Philexfrance 89" International Stamp Exhibition, Paris, and "World Stamp Expo '89", Washington (2nd issue). Designs showing Statue of Liberty. Multicoloured.
311 35c. Type **51c** . . . . 1·10 1·40
312 35c. Workman drilling Statue 1·10 1·40
313 35c. Surveyor with drawing 1·10 1·40

52 Telecommunications Centre

1989. Transport and Telecommunications Decade (4th issue). Multicoloured.
314 30c. Type **52** . . . . 1·50 1·25
315 75c. "Mataburo" (inter-island freighter) . . . . 3·50 4·00

1989. "Melbourne Stampshow '89". Nos. 301/2 optd with Exhibition emblem showing tram.
316 $1 White-tailed tropic bird 3·00 3·50
317 $1 Young white-tailed tropic bird . . . . 3·00 3·50

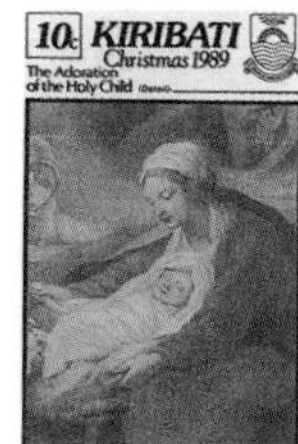
54 Virgin and Child (detail, "The Adoration of the Holy Child" (Denys Calvert))

1989. Christmas. Paintings. Multicoloured.
318 10c. Type **54** . . . . 1·00 55
319 15c. "The Adoration of the Holy Child" (Denys Calvert) . . . . 1·25 70
320 55c. "The Holy Family and St. Elizabeth" (Rubens) . . 3·00 1·25
321 $1 "Madonna with Child and Maria Magdalena" (School of Correggio) . . . . . . 4·50 7·00

55 Gilbert and Ellice Islands 1912 1d. and G.B. Twopence Blue Stamps

1990. 150th Anniv of the Penny Black and "Stamp World London 90" International Stamp Exhibition. Multicoloured.
322 15c. Type **55** . . . . 1·00 1·00
323 50c. Gilbert and Ellice Islands 1911 ½d. and G.B. Penny Black . . . . 2·50 2·75
324 60c. Kiribati 1982 1c. bird and G.B. 1870 ½d. . . . . 2·50 2·75
325 $1 Gilbert Islands 1976 1c. ship and G.B. 1841 1d. brown . . . . 2·75 3·50

56 Blue-barred Orange Parrotfish

1990. Fishes. Multicoloured.
326 1c. Type **56** 30 75
327 5c. Honeycomb grouper . . . 45 75
328 10c. Blue-finned trevally . . . 55 85
329 15c. Hump-backed snapper 70 50
330 20c. Variegated emperor . . 75 70
356 23c. Bennett's pufferfish . . . 1·25 1·50
331 25c. Rainbow runner 80 65
332 30c. Black-saddled coral grouper 90 65
333 35c. Great barracuda . . . . 1·00 75
334 40c. Convict tang . . . . . 1·00 80
335 50c. Violet squirrelfish . . . . 1·25 90
336 60c. Stocky hawkfish . . . . 1·75 1·40
337 75c. Pennant coralfish . . . 1·90 1·60
338 $1 Common blue-striped snapper ("Yellow and blue sea perch") . . . . 2·25 1·90
339 $2 Sailfish . . . . 3·25 4·75
340 $5 White-tipped reef shark 6·50 9·50

1990. 90th Birthday of Queen Elizabeth the Queen Mother. As T **107** (75c.) or **108** ($2) of Kenya.
341 75c. multicoloured . . . . . 1·25 1·50
342 $2 black and green . . . . . 2·75 3·50
DESIGNS—21 × 36 mm: 75c. Queen Elizabeth the Queen Mother. 29 × 37 mm: $2 King George VI and Queen Elizabeth with air raid victim, London, 1940.

1990. Nautical History (2nd series). As T **49**. Multicoloured.
343 15c. "Herald" (whaling ship), 1851 . . . . 75 55
344 50c. "Belle" (barque), 1849 1·50 1·50

345 60c. "Supply" (schooner), 1851 . . . . 1·75 2·25
346 75c. "Triton" (whaling ship), 1848 . . . . 1·75 2·25
MS347 95 × 75 mm. $2 "Charlotte" (convict transport), 1789 . . . 7·50 8·50

57 Manta

1991. Endangered Species. Fishes. Multicoloured.
348 15c. Type **57** . . . . 1·10 55
349 20c. Manta (different) . . . . 1·25 90
350 30c. Whale shark . . . . . . 1·75 2·00
351 35c. Whale shark (different) 2·00 2·25

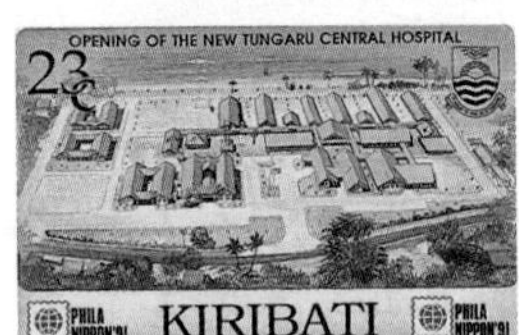

58 Queen Elizabeth II

1991. 65th Birthday of Queen Elizabeth II and 70th Birthday of Prince Philip. Multicoloured.
366 65c. Type **58** . . . . 1·25 1·50
367 70c. Prince Philip in R.A.F. uniform . . . . 1·25 1·50

59 Aerial View of Hospital

1991. "Phila Nippon '91" International Stamp Exhibition, Tokyo, and Opening of Tungaru Central Hospital. Multicoloured.
368 23c. Type **59** 40 30
369 50c. Traditional dancers . . . 75 85
370 60c. Hospital entrance . . . 85 1·10
371 75c. Foundation stone and plaques . . . . 1·25 1·60
MS372 125 × 83 mm. $5 Casualty on trolley and ambulance . . . . 7·00 8·00

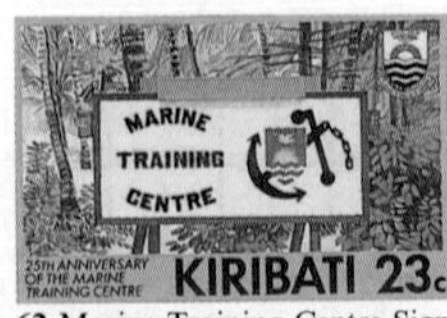

60 Mother and Child

1991. Christmas. Multicoloured.
373 23c. Type **60** 60 40
374 50c. The Holy Family in Pacific setting . . . . . . 1·10 90
375 60c. The Holy Family in traditional setting . . . . 1·25 1·50
376 75c. Adoration of the Shepherds . . . . 1·50 2·00

1992. 40th Anniv of Queen Elizabeth II's Accession. As T **214** of Lesotho. Multicoloured.
377 23c. Kiribati village 30 30
378 30c. Lagoon at sunset 40 45
379 50c. Tarawa waterfront . . . 60 70
380 60c. Three portraits of Queen Elizabeth 70 90
381 75c. Queen Elizabeth II . . . 90 1·10

1992. "EXPO '92" World's Fair, Seville. Nos. 356, 336/7 and 339 optd **EXPO'92 SEVILLA**.
382 23c. Bennett's pufferfish . . . 55 40
383 60c. Stocky hawkfish . . . . 1·25 1·50
384 75c. Pennant coralfish . . . 1·40 1·60
385 $2 Sailfish . . . . 3·00 4·00

62 Marine Training Centre Sign

1992. 25th Anniv of Marine Training Centre. Multicoloured.
386 23c. Type **62** 45 40
387 50c. Cadets on parade . . . 80 1·00
388 60c. Fire school . . . . . . 80 1·00
389 75c. Lifeboat training . . . . 1·10 1·40

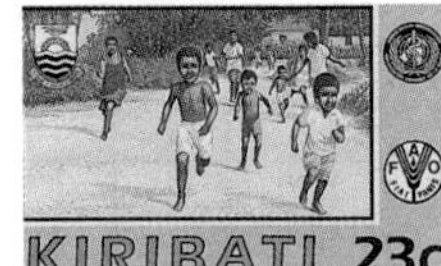

63 Healthy Children

1992. United Nations World Health and Food and Agriculture Organizations. Multicoloured.
390 23c. Type **63** 55 50
391 50c. Fishing at night . . . . 1·00 1·00
392 60c. Fruit . . . . 1·25 1·50
393 75c. "Papuan Chief" (container ship) . . . . . 2·50 2·50

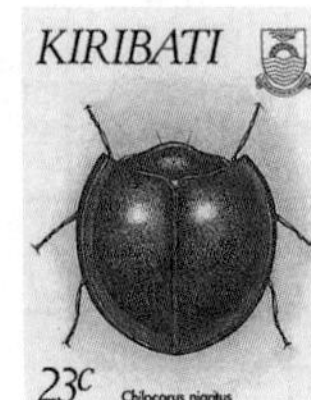

64 Phoenix Petrel **65** "Chilocorus nigritus"

1993. Birds. Multicoloured.
394 23c. Type **64** 40 70
395 23c. Cook's petrel 40 70
396 60c. Pintail ("Northern Pintail") . . . . 90 1·25
397 60c. European wigeon ("Eurasian Wigeon") . . . 90 1·25
398 75c. Spectacled tern . . . . 1·00 1·25
399 75c. Black-naped tern . . . . 1·00 1·25
400 $1 Australian stilt ("Stilt Wader") . . . . 1·25 1·40
401 $1 Wandering tattler . . . . 1·25 1·40

1993. Insects. Multicoloured.
402 23c. Type **65** . . . . 1·00 55
403 60c. "Rodolia pumila" (ladybird) . . . . 2·00 2·00
404 75c. "Rodolia cardinalis" (ladybird) . . . . 2·25 2·50
405 $1 "Cryptolaemus montrouzieri" . . . . . . 2·50 3·00

66 U.S. Air Reconnaissance Consolidated B-24 Liberator

1993. 50th Anniv of Battle of Tarawa. Multicoloured.
406 23c. Type **66** 60 65
407 23c. U.S.S. "Nautilus" (submarine) 60 65
408 23c. U.S.S. "Indianapolis" (cruiser) 60 65
409 23c. U.S.S. "Pursuit" (destroyer) 60 65
410 23c. Vought Sikorsky Kingfisher spotter seaplane 60 65
411 23c. U.S.S. "Ringgold" and "Dashiell" (destroyers) . . 60 65
412 23c. Sherman tank on seabed 60 65
413 23c. Grumman Hellcat fighter aircraft in lagoon 60 65
414 23c. Naval wreck on seabed 60 65
415 23c. First U.S. aircraft to land on Betio 60 65
416 75c. Landing craft leaving transports . . . . 1·00 1·10
417 75c. Marines landing on Betio . . . . 1·00 1·10
418 75c. Landing craft approaching beach . . . . 1·00 1·10
419 75c. Marines pinned down in surf . . . . 1·00 1·10
420 75c. U.S.S. "Maryland" (battleship) . . . . 1·00 1·10
421 75c. Aerial view of Betio Island . . . . 1·00 1·10
422 75c. U.S. Navy memorial . . 1·00 1·10
423 75c. Memorial to expatriates 1·00 1·10
424 75c. Japanese memorial . . . 1·00 1·10
425 75c. Plan of Betio Island . . 1·00 1·10

67 Shepherds and Angels

1993. Christmas. Pacific Nativity Scenes. Mult.
426 23c. Type **67** 40 30
427 40c. Three Kings 65 70
428 60c. Holy Family . . . . . . 85 1·25
429 75c. Virgin and Child . . . . 1·10 1·50
MS430 100 × 81 mm. $3 Virgin and Child (different) . . . . 3·75 5·50

68 Group of Dogs

1994. "Hong Kong '94" International Stamp Exhibition. Chinese New Year ("Year of the Dog"). Sheet 120 × 90 mm.
MS431 **68** $3 multicoloured . . . 4·00 5·50

69 Bryde's Whale and Calf

1994. Whales. Multicoloured.
432 23c. Type **69** . . . . 1·00 1·25
433 23c. Bryde's whale with two calves . . . . 1·00 1·25
434 40c. Blue whale and calf (face value at left) . . . . 1·25 1·40
435 40c. Blue whales and calf (face value at right) . . . . 1·25 1·40
436 60c. Humpback whale and calf (face value at left) . . 1·90 2·25
437 60c. Humpback whale and calf (face value at right) . . 1·90 2·25
438 75c. Killer whale and calf . . 1·90 2·25
439 75c. Killer whale and two calves . . . . 1·90 2·25

70 Family silhouetted on Beach

1994. 15th Anniv of Independence. Protecting the Environment. Multicoloured.
440 40c. Type **70** 60 60
441 60c. Fish and coral . . . . . 1·00 1·25
442 75c. Great frigate birds in flight . . . . 1·25 1·50

71 "Diaphania indica" **72** "Nerium oleander"

1994. Butterflies and Moths. Multicoloured.
443 1c. Type **71** 10 15
444 5c. "Herpetogramma licarsisalis" 15 20
445 10c. "Parotis suralis" 25 20
446 12c. "Sufetula sunidesalis" . . 25 20
447 20c. "Aedia sericea" 35 25
448 23c. "Anomis vitiensis" . . . 35 25
449 30c. "Anticarsia irrorata" . . 45 30
450 35c. "Spodoptera litura" . . 55 40
451 40c. "Mocis frugalis" 65 50
452 45c. "Agrius convolvuli" . . . 70 50
453 50c. "Cephonodes picus" . . 75 55
454 55c. "Gnathothlibus erotus" 80 60
455 60c. "Macroglossum hirundo" 80 60
456 75c. "Badamia exclamationis" 1·00 75
457 $1 "Precis villida" . . . . . 1·40 1·40
458 $2 "Danaus plexippus" . . . 2·25 2·50
459 $3 "Hypolimnas bolina" (male) . . . . 2·75 3·25
460 $5 "Hypolimnas bolina" (female) . . . . 3·75 4·50
See also No. **MS**527.

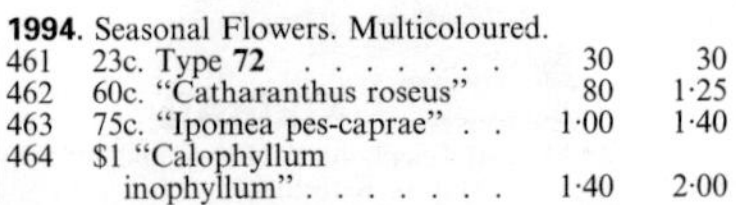

1994. Seasonal Flowers. Multicoloured.
461 23c. Type **72** 30 30
462 60c. "Catharanthus roseus" 80 1·25
463 75c. "Ipomea pes-caprae" . . 1·00 1·40
464 $1 "Calophyllum inophyllum" . . . . 1·40 2·00

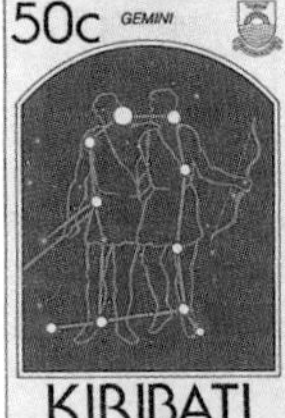

73 Gemini (The Twins) **74** Church and Traditional Meeting Hut

1995. Night Sky over Kiribati. Multicoloured.
465 50c. Type **73** 75 75
466 60c. Cancer (The Crab) . . . 85 1·00
467 75c. Cassiopeia (The Queen of Ethiopia) . . . . 1·00 1·40
468 $1 Southern Cross . . . . . 1·25 1·75

1995. Tourism. Multicoloured.
469 30c. Type **74** 85 95
470 30c. Fishermen and outrigger canoes 85 95
471 30c. Gun emplacement and map 85 95
472 30c. Children with marine creatures 85 95
473 30c. Sports 85 95
474 40c. Local girls in traditional costume 85 95
475 40c. Windsurfing 85 95
476 40c. Fishermen and wood carver 85 95
477 40c. Underwater sport . . . 85 95
478 40c. Women weaving 85 95

75 Grumman TBF Avenger

1995. 50th Anniv of End of Second World War. American Aircraft. Multicoloured.
489 23c. Type **75** 60 45
490 40c. Curtiss SOC.3-1 Seagull seaplane 80 70
491 50c. Consolidated B-24 Liberator bomber 90 90
492 60c. Grumman G-21 Goose amphibian . . . . 1·10 1·10
493 75c. Martin B-26 Marauder bomber . . . . 1·40 1·50
494 $1 Northrop P-61 Black Widow bomber . . . . . 1·60 1·75
MS495 75 × 85 mm. $2 Reverse of 1939–45 War Medal (vert) . . 2·50 3·00

76 Eclectus Parrots, Great Frigate Bird and Coconut Crabs

1995. Protecting the Environment. Multicoloured.
496 60c. Type **76** . . . . 85 1·10
497 60c. Red-tailed tropic birds, common dolphin and pantropical spotted dolphin 85 1·10
498 60c. Blue-striped snapper ("Yellow and blue sea perch"), blue-barred orange parrotfish and green turtle 85 1·10
499 60c. Red-breasted wrasse, pennant coralfish and violet squirrelfish . . . . 85 1·10

1995. "Jakarta '95" Stamp Exhibition, Indonesia. Nos. 496/9 optd **JAKARTA 95** within emblem.
500 60c. Type **76** . . . . 1·60 1·75
501 60c. Red-tailed tropic birds, common dolphin and pantropical spotted dolphin 1·60 1·75
502 60c. Blue-striped snapper, blue-barred orange parrotfish and green turtle 1·60 1·75
503 60c. Red-breasted wrasse, pennant coralfish and violet squirrelfish . . . . 1·60 1·75

78 Sow feeding Piglets

1995. "Singapore '95" International Stamp Exhibition and Beijing International Coin and Stamp Expo '95. Two sheets, each 113 × 85 mm, containing T **78**.
MS504 $2 multicoloured ("Singapore '95") . . . . . . 2·50 3·25
MS505 $2 multicoloured ("Beijing '95") . . . . 3·00 3·75
Nos. **MS**504/5 show the exhibition logos on the sheet margins.

79 "Teanoai" (police patrol boat)

1995. Police Maritime Unit. Multicoloured.
506 75c. Type **79** . . . . 1·40 1·75
507 75c. "Teanoai" at sea . . . . 1·40 1·75

80 Pantropical Spotted Dolphins

1996. Dolphins. Multicoloured.
508 23c. Type **80** . . . . 1·00 55
509 60c. Spinner dolphins . . . . 1·75 1·25
510 75c. Fraser's dolphins . . . . 1·90 1·75
511 $1 Rough-toothed dolphins 2·00 2·25

81 Tap and Top Left Segment of U.N.I.C.E.F. Emblem

1996. 50th Anniv of U.N.I.C.E.F. Multicoloured.
512 30c. Type **81** 50 70
513 30c. Documents and top right segment 50 70
514 30c. Syringe and bottom left segment 50 70
515 30c. Open book and bottom right segment 50 70
Nos. 512/15 were printed together, se-tenant, with each block of 4 showing the complete emblem.

82 Chinese Dragon

1996. "CHINA '96" 9th Asian International Stamp Exhibition, Peking. Sheet 110 × 86 mm.
MS516 **82** 50c. multicoloured . . 1·00 1·50

83 L.M.S. No. 5609 "Gilbert and Ellice Islands" Locomotive

1996. "CAPEX '96" International Stamp Exhibition, Toronto. Sheet 111 × 80 mm.
MS517 **83** $2 multicoloured . . . 2·40 3·00

84 Rathbun Red Crab

1996. Sea Crabs. Multicoloured.
518 23c. Type **84** 40 40
519 60c. Red and white painted crab 80 80
520 75c. Red-spotted crab . . . . 95 1·10
521 $1 Red-spotted white crab . . 1·40 2·25

85 Kiribati Canoe

1996. "Taipei '96" International Stamp Exhibition, Taiwan. Sheet 110 × 86 mm.
MS522 **85** $1.50 multicoloured 3·00 3·50

1996. Nautical History (3rd series). As T **49**. Multicoloured.
523 23c. "Potomac" (whaling ship), 1843 . . . . 50 40
524 50c. "Southern Cross IV" (missionary ship), 1891 . . 80 90
525 60c. "John Williams III" (missionary sailing ship), 1890 . . . . 95 1·10
526 $1 H.M.S. "Dolphin" (frigate), 1765 . . . . . . 1·40 1·75

1997. "HONG KONG '97" International Stamp Exhibition. Sheet 130 × 90 mm, containing No. 457. Multicoloured.
MS527 $1 "Precis villida" . . . 1·10 1·60

1997. "Pacific '97" International Stamp Exhibition, San Francisco. Nos. 489/94 optd **PACIFIC 97 World Philatelic Exhibition San Francisco, California 29 May - 8 June**.
528 23c. Type **75** 40 35
529 40c. Curtiss SOC.3-1 Seagull seaplane 60 55
530 50c. Consolidated B-24 Liberator bomber 70 70
531 60c. Grumman G-21 Goose amphibian 80 90
532 75c. Martin B-26 Marauder bomber . . . . 90 1·10
533 $1 Northrop P-61 Black Widow bomber . . . . . 1·10 1·40
MS534 75 × 85 mm. $2 Reverse of 1939–45 War Medal (vert) . . 2·10 2·75

87 Queen Elizabeth II in 1996 **88** Young Rock Dove

1997. Golden Wedding of Queen Elizabeth and Prince Philip. Multicoloured.
535 50c. Type **87** . . . . 1·25 1·50
536 50c. Prince Philip carriage-driving at Windsor Horse Show . . . . 1·25 1·50
537 60c. Queen in phaeton at Trooping the Colour . . . 1·25 1·50
538 60c. Prince Philip on Montserrat, 1993 . . . . . 1·25 1·50
539 75c. Queen Elizabeth and Prince Philip, 1989 . . . . 1·25 1·50
540 75c. Prince Edward on horseback . . . . 1·25 1·50
MS541 110 × 70 mm. $2 Queen Elizabeth and Prince Philip in Landau (horiz) . . . . 3·50 4·25
Nos. 535/6, 537/8 and 539/40 respectively were printed together, se-tenant, with the backgrounds forming composite designs.

1997. Birds. Multicoloured.
542 50c. Type **88** . . . . 90 1·10
543 50c. Adult rock dove . . . . 90 1·10
544 60c. Adult Pacific pigeon . . 90 1·10
545 60c. Young Pacific pigeon . . 90 1·10
546 75c. Adult Micronesian pigeon . . . . 90 1·10
547 75c. Young Micronesian pigeon . . . . 90 1·10

1997. "ASIA '97" Stamp Exhibition, Bangkok. Nos. 542/3 and 546/7 optd **ASIA '97 KIRIBATI 5 - 14 OCTOBER** and elephant.
548 50c. Type **88** . . . . 75 1·00
549 50c. Adult rock dove . . . . 75 1·00
550 75c. Adult Micronesian pigeon . . . . 90 1·25
551 75c. Young Micronesian pigeon . . . . 90 1·25

90 Spiny Lobster

1998. Endangered Species. Spiny Lobster. Multicoloured.
552 25c. Type **90** 30 45
553 25c. Facing right 30 45
554 25c. With coral in foreground 30 45
555 25c. On sponge 30 45
MS556 69 × 49 mm. $1.50 Spiny Lobster . . . . 1·60 2·00
No. **MS**556 does not show the W.W.F. panda emblem.

91 Diana, Princess of Wales, 1992

1998. Diana, Princess of Wales Commemoration.
557 **91** 25c. multicoloured 30 40
MS558 145 × 70 mm. 25c. Type **91**; 50c. Wearing black evening dress, 1981; 60c. With scarf over head, 1992; 75c. Wearing brown jacket, 1993 (sold at $2.10 + 50c. charity premium) . . . . 2·50 3·00

92 Children and Smiling Sun

1998. "Towards the Millennium" (1st issue). Sheet 102 × 69 mm.
MS559 **92** $1 multicoloured . . . 1·00 1·50
See also Nos. 580/4 and 594/8.

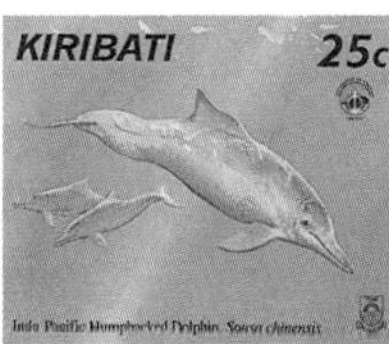

93 Indo-Pacific Humpbacked Dolphin

1998. Whales and Dolphins. Multicoloured.
560 25c. Type **93** 45 65
561 25c. Bottlenose dolphin . . . 45 65
562 60c. Short-snouted spinner dolphin . . . . 80 1·00
563 60c. Risso's dolphin . . . . 80 1·00
564 75c. Striped dolphin . . . . 90 1·00
565 75c. Sei whale . . . . 90 1·00
566 $1 Fin whale . . . . 1·00 1·25
567 $1 Minke whale . . . . . . 1·00 1·25

94 Reuben K. Uatioa Stadium, Kiribati

1998. "Italia '98" International Stamp Exhibition, Milan. Sheet 110 × 85 mm.
MS568 **94** $2 multicoloured . . . 1·75 2·25

95 Pollutants and Harmful Emissions

1998. The Greenhouse Effect. Multicoloured.
569 25c. Type **95** 20 30
570 50c. Diagram of greenhouse effect 40 50
571 60c. Diagram of rising sea levels on Tarawa 45 60
572 75c. Diagram of rising sea levels on Kiritimati 55 65
MS573 103 × 69 mm. $1.50 Outrigger canoe . . . . 2·50 2·50

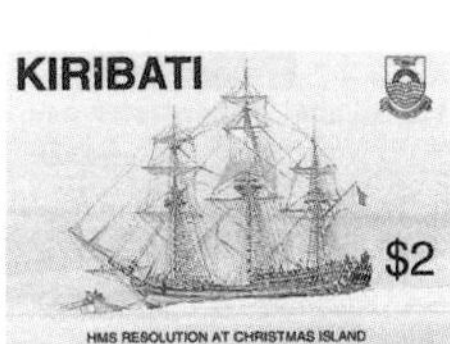

96 H.M.S. "Resolution" (Cook) at Christmas Island, 1777

1999. "Australia '99" World Stamp Exhibition, Melbourne. Sheet 136 × 56 mm.
MS574 **96** $2 multicoloured . . . 1·75 2·25

97 Northern Shoveler (male)

1999. "iBRA '99" International Stamp Exhibition, Nuremberg. Ducks. Multicoloured.
575 25c. Type **97** 50 50
576 50c. Northern Shoveler (female) and ducklings . . 65 65
577 60c. Green-winged teal (male) 70 70
578 75c. Green-winged teal (female) and ducklings . . 80 80
MS579 100 × 70 mm. $3 Green-winged teal (male) and duckling 2·75 3·25

98 Map of Millennium Island

1999. "Towards the Millennium" (2nd issue). 20th Anniv of Independence. Multicoloured.
580 25c. Type **98** 70 70
581 60c. Map of Kiribati . . . . 1·10 1·10
582 75c. Map of Nikumaroro . . 1·10 1·10
583 $1 Amelia Earhart (aviator) 1·50 1·50
MS584 100 × 80 mm. Nos. 582/3 2·75 3·25
No. 581 shows Tarawa as "TAROWA" in error.
See also Nos. 594/8.

98a Buzz Aldrin (astronaut)

1999. 30th Anniv of First Manned Landing on Moon. Multicoloured.
585 25c. Type **98a** 35 35
586 60c. Service module docking with lunar module 65 75
587 75c. "Apollo 11" on Moon's surface 75 85
588 $1 Command module separating from service section . . . . 95 1·10
MS589 90 × 80 mm. $2 Kiribati as seen from Moon (circular, 40 mm diam) . . . . 1·90 2·25

99 Santa Claus in Sailing Canoe

1999. Christmas and 125th Anniv of Universal Postal Union. Multicoloured.
590 25c. Type **99** 30 25
591 60c. Santa and unloading freighter 55 65
592 75c. Santa in sleigh passing aircraft 70 80
593 $1 Santa using computer . . 90 1·10

100 Open Hands around Globe ("FAITH")

2000. "Towards the Millennium" (3rd issue). "A Region of Peace". Multicoloured.
594 25c. Type **100** 30 35
595 40c. Solar eclipse ("HARMONY") 45 55
596 60c. Stars and Sun over Earth ("HOPE") 60 75
597 75c. Sun over Earth ("ENLIGHTENMENT") 75 90
598 $1 Dove over Earth ("PEACE") . . . . 90 1·10

101 Bert feeding Pigeons

2000. "Sesame Street" (children's T.V. programme). Multicoloured.
599 20c. Type **101** 20 30
600 20c. Little Bear flying kite . . 20 30
601 20c. Grover calling 20 30
602 20c. Elmo and Cookie Monster 20 30
603 20c. Telly leaning out of window 20 30
604 20c. Zoe painting house . . . 20 30
605 20c. Ernie with bird 20 30
606 20c. Big Bird and Rosita reading 20 30
607 20c. Oscar the Grouch and Slimey in dustbin 20 30
MS608 139 × 86 mm. $1.50 Grover as postman . . . . 1·40 1·60
Nos. 599/607 were printed together, se-tenant, with the backgrounds forming a composite design.

102 Queen Elizabeth II in Kiribati, 1982

2000. "The Stamp Show 2000" International Stamp Exhibition, London. Sheet 80 × 70 mm.
MS609 **102** $5 multicoloured . . 4·25 4·75

2000. "EXPO 2000" World's Fair, Hanover. Nos. 444/5, 447, 457 and 459 optd **KIRIBATI AT EXPO 2000 1.06-31.10.2000**.
610 5c. *Herpetogramma licarsisalis* 15 25
611 10c. *Parotis suralis* 15 25
612 20c. *Aedia sericea* 25 30
613 $1 *Precis villida* . . . . . . 1·00 1·25
614 $3 *Hypolimnas bolina* (male) 2·75 3·00

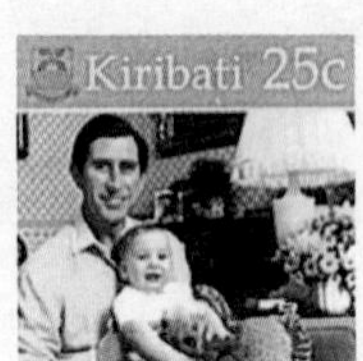

104 Prince William as a Baby with Prince Charles

2000. 18th Birthday of Prince William. Each showing Prince William with Prince Charles. Multicoloured.
615 25c. Type **104** 40 35
616 60c. In Italy, 1985 . . . . . 75 75
617 75c. At Sandringham, Christmas, 1992 . . . . . 85 85
618 $1 At Balmoral, 1997 . . . . 1·10 1·25

105 Wandering Whistling Duck

2001. Ducks. Multicoloured.
619 25c. Type **105** 35 40
620 25c. Green-winged teal . . . 35 40
621 25c. Mallard 35 40
622 25c. Northern shoveler . . . 35 40
623 25c. Pacific black duck . . . 35 40
624 25c. Mountain duck ("Blue Duck") 35 40
MS625 85 × 75 mm. $1 Grey teal 1·50 1·75

106 Man with Tap (Tiare Hongkai)

2001. Water Conservation. Children's Drawings. Multicoloured.
626 25c. Type **106** 35 30
627 50c. Cooking pot on fire and house in rain (Gilbert Tluanga) 50 45
628 60c. Map in raindrop and cup (Mantokataake Tebaiuea) (vert) 55 50
629 75c. Hand holding drop (Tokaman Karanebo) (vert) 70 70
630 $2 Water management system (Taom Simon) . . . . . . 1·60 1·90

107 Betio Port

2001. "Philanippon '01" International Stamp Exhibition, Tokyo. Development Projects. Multicoloured.
631 75c. Type **107** 75 65
632 $2 New Parliament House complex . . . . 1·75 2·00

108 Norwegian Cruise Liner and Map of Route

2001. Tourism. Fanning Island. Multicoloured.
633 75c. Type **108** 55 60
634 $3 *Betsey* (full-rigged sealer) and map of Fanning Island 2·10 2·25

109 *Paracanthrus hepatus*

2002. Tropical Fish. Multicoloured.
635 5c. Type **109** 10 10
636 10c. *Centropyge flavissimus* 10 10
637 15c. *Anthias squamipinnis* . . 10 15
638 20c. *Centropyge loriculus* . . 15 20
639 25c. *Acanthurus lineatus* . . . 20 25
640 30c. *Oxycirrhites typus* . . . 20 25
641 40c. *Dascyllus trimaculatus* 30 35
642 50c. *Acanthurus achilles* . . . 35 40
643 60c. *Pomacentrus caeruleus* 45 50
644 75c. *Acanthurus glaucopareius* 55 60
645 80c. *Thalassoma lunare* . . . 60 65
646 90c. *Arothron meleagris* . . . 65 70
647 $1 *Odonus niger* 70 75
648 $2 *Cephalopholis miniatus* . . 1·40 1·50
649 $5 *Pomacanthus imperator* . . 3·50 3·75
650 $10 *Balistoides conspicillum* 7·25 7·50
The 60c. is inscribed "coeruleus" in error.

110 Admiral Bellinghausen and *Vostok*, 1820

2002. Pacific Explorers. Multicoloured.
651 25c. Type **110** 20 25
652 40c. Captain Wilkes and the U.S.S. *Vincennes* (sail frigate), 1838–42 . . . . . 30 35
653 60c. Captain Fanning and *Betsey* (full-rigged sealer), 1798 . . . . 45 50
654 75c. Captain Coffin and *Transit* (full-rigged ship), 1823 . . . . 55 60
655 $1 Commodore Byron and H.M.S. *Dolphin* (frigate), 1765 . . . . 70 75
656 $3 Captain Broughton and H.M.S. *Providence* (sloop), 1795 . . . . 2·10 2·25
MS657 92 × 63 mm. $5 Captain Cook (vert) . . . . 3·50 3·75

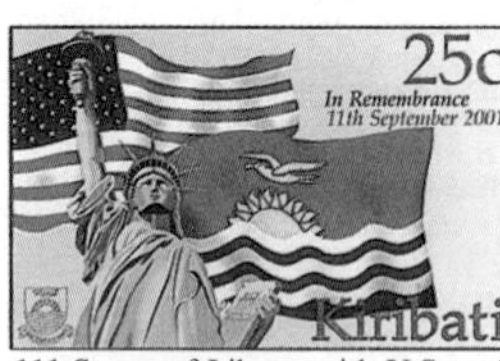

111 Statue of Liberty with U.S. and Kiribati Flags

2002. In Remembrance. Victims of Terrorist Attacks on U.S.A. (11 September 2001).
658 **111** 25c. multicoloured 20 25
659 $2 multicoloured . . . . 1·40 1·50

112 Queen Elizabeth in 1953

113 Woven "Parcel"

2002. Golden Jubilee. Featuring photographs by Dorothy Wilding. Multicoloured.
660 25c. Type **112** 20 25
MS661 135 × 110 mm. $2 Queen Elizabeth wearing Garter sash; $2 Queen Elizabeth in evening dress 3·00 3·25

2002. Christmas.
662 **113** 25c. multicoloured 20 25
663 – 60c. multicoloured 45 50
664 – 75c. multicoloured 55 60
665 – $1 multicoloured 70 75
666 – $2.50 multicoloured . . . 1·75 2·00
DESIGNS: 60c. to $2.50 show different weave patterns.

OFFICIAL STAMPS

1981. Nos. 86/135 optd **O.K.G.S.**
O11 1c. Type **16** 10 50
O12 3c. M.V. "Tautunu" (inter-island freighter) 10 30
O13 5c. Hibiscus 10 20
O14 7c. Catholic Cathedral, Tarawa 10 20
O15 10c. Maneaba, Bikenibeu . . 10 20
O16 12c. Betio Harbour 30 30
O17 15c. Reef heron . . . . . . 1·50 30
O18 20c. Flamboyant tree 20 30
O19 25c. Moorish idol (fish) . . . 30 30
O20 30c. Frangipani 30 35
O21 35c. G.I.P.C. Chapel, Tangintebu 35 40
O22 50c. "Hypolimnas bolina" (butterfly) . . . . 1·00 55
O23 $1 "Tabakea" (Tarawa Lagoon ferry) 65 50
O24 $2 Evening scene 70 70
O25 $5 National flag . . . . . . 1·25 1·75

1983. Nos. 169, 172/3, 175 and 177 optd **O.K.G.S.**
O36 12c. Polynesian reed warbler 40 30
O37 30c. Brown booby 70 50
O38 35c. Audubon's shearwater 80 60
O39 50c. Bristle-thighed curlew 1·00 80
O40 $2 Long-tailed koel . . . . 3·00 2·75

POSTAGE DUE STAMPS

D 1 Kiribati Coat of Arms

1981.
D1 **D 1** 1c. black and mauve . . . 10 10
D2 2c. black and blue 10 10
D3 5c. black and green . . . 10 10
D4 10c. black and brown . . . 10 15
D5 20c. black and blue . . . 15 25
D6 30c. black and brown . . . 15 35
D7 40c. black and purple . . 20 45
D8 50c. black and green . . . 20 50
D9 $1 black and red 30 75

KISHANGARH Pt. 1

A state of Rajasthan, India. Now uses Indian stamps.

12 pies = 1 anna; 16 annas = 1 rupee.

1

1899. Imperf or perf.
1 **1** 1a. green . . . . 22·00 55·00
3 1a. blue £400

2 (¼a.)

5 (2a.) Maharaja Sardul Singh

1899. Various arms designs. Perf or imperf.
21 **2** ¼a. green £200 £375
22a ¼a. red 25 40
25 ½a. green . . . . 13·00 16·00
8 ½a. red £2000 £1100
26a ½a. blue 85 50
7 ½a. lilac £120 £200
27 1a. grey . . . . 4·75 3·25
29 1a. mauve . . . . 75 1·00
12b 1a. pink . . . . 60·00 £170
15 **5** 2a. orange . . . . 4·50 4·50
31 **2** 4a. brown . . . . 2·00 5·50
32 1r. green . . . . 10·00 15·00
17 1r. lilac . . . . 20·00 25·00
33 1r. yellow £650
34 2r. red . . . . 32·00 48·00
35 5r. mauve . . . . 32·00 48·00

11 (¼a.)

12 Maharaja Sardul Singh

1903. Imperf or perf.
39 **11** ¼a. pink . . . . 10·00 3·00
40 **12** 2a. orange . . . . 3·00 6·00
41 **2** 8a. grey . . . . 5·00 7·50

13 Maharaja Madan Singh

14 Maharaja Madan Singh

1904.
42 **13** ¼a. red 45 65
43a ½a. brown 75 30
44a 1a. blue . . . . 1·75 1·75
45 2a. orange . . . . 15·00 7·00
46a 4a. brown . . . . 14·00 16·00
47 8a. violet . . . . 8·00 20·00
48 1r. green . . . . 24·00 35·00
49 2r. yellow . . . . 25·00 £130
50 5r. brown . . . . 23·00 £160

1912.
63 **14** ¼a. blue 20 45
64 ½a. green . . . . 20 1·00
65 1a. red . . . . 1·00 2·50
54 2a. purple . . . . 2·50 5·00
67 4a. blue . . . . 6·00 8·00
68 8a. brown . . . . 7·00 38·00
69 1r. mauve . . . . 16·00 £110
70 2r. green . . . . 85·00 £250
71 5r. brown . . . . 45·00 £375

15

16 Maharaja Yagyanarayan Singh

1913.

59	**15**	¼a. blue	30	90
60		2a. purple	7·00	18·00

1928.

72	**16**	¼a. blue	80	2·00
73		½a. green	2·75	1·75
74	–	1a. red	75	1·50
75	–	2a. purple	3·00	8·50
76	**16**	4a. brown	1·50	1·75
77		8a. violet	3·50	26·00
78		1r. green	15·00	50·00
79		2r. yellow	28·00	£170
80		5r. red	35·00	£190

Nos. 74/5 are larger.

OFFICIAL STAMPS

1918. Optd **ON K S D.**

O 5	**2**	¼a. green	—	£120
O 6		¼a. pink	2·25	60
O 7		½a. blue	£150	38·00
O 9		1a. mauve	38·00	1·50
O10	**5**	2a. orange	—	£120
O11	**2**	4a. brown	48·00	16·00
O16		8a. grey	70·00	22·00
O12		1r. green	£150	80·00
O13		2r. brown	—	£750
O14		5r. mauve	—	£1500

1918. Optd **ON K S D.**

O15	**12**	2a. orange	65·00	5·00

1918. Optd **ON K S D.**

O17	**13**	¼a. red	—	£275
O18		½a. brown	75	35
O19		1a. blue	7·50	4·00
O20		2a. orange	—	£800
O21		4a. brown	55·00	18·00
O22		8a. violet	£300	£180
O23		1r. green	£600	£550
O24		5r. brown		

1918. Optd **ON K S D.**

O28	**14**	¼a. blue	60	50
O29		½a. green	90	75
O30a		1a. red	1·00	1·00
O31		2a. purple	6·00	4·00
O32		4a. blue	21·00	15·00
O33		8a. brown	£110	40·00
O34		1r. mauve	£325	£325
O35		2r. green		
O36		5r. brown	£1400	

1918. Optd **ON K S D.**

O25	**15**	¼a. blue	6·00	
O27		2a. purple	£425	£450

For later issues see **RAJASTHAN.**

KOREA Pt. 18

A peninsula to the S. of Manchuria in E. Asia. Formerly an empire under Chinese suzerainty, it was annexed by Japan in 1910 and used Japanese stamps. After the defeat of Japan in 1945, Russian and United States Military administrations were set up in Korea to the north and south of the 38th Parallel respectively; in 1948 South Korea and North Korea became independent republics.

KOREAN EMPIRE

1884. 100 mon = 1 tempo.
1895. 5 poon = 1 cheun.
1900. 10 re (or rin) = 1 cheun; 100 cheun = 1 weun.

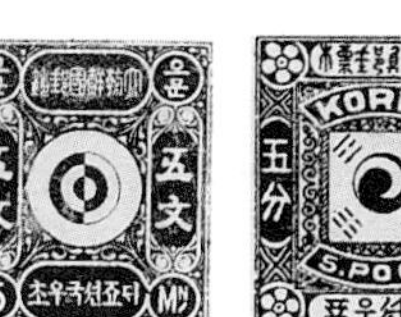

1 3 Korean Flag (4)

1894.

1	**1**	5m. pink	34·00	£4000
2	–	10m. blue	7·50	£2500

DESIGN: 10m. Central motif as in Type **1** but different frame and inscribed "CORGAN POST".

1895.

7	**3**	5p. green	14·00	12·00
8		10p. blue	18·00	10·00
9		25p. red	14·00	16·00
10a		50p. lilac	12·00	6·50

1897. Optd with T **4**.

12	**3**	5p. green	20·00	15·00
13		10p. blue	24·00	20·00
14		25p. red	30·00	24·00
16		50p. lilac	30·00	20·00

1899. Surch in Korean characters.

17	**3**	1(p.) on 5p. green (No. 7)	£1200	£750
20		1(p.) on 5p. green (No. 12)	£250	£200
18		1(p.) on 25p. red (No. 9)	£150	75·00
21		1(p.) on 25p. red (No. 14)	50·00	32·00

6 7 National Emblems 8

1900. T **6**, **7** (2ch.), **8** (2ch.) and similar designs.

22a	2r. grey	75	1·50
23	1ch. green	5·50	4·00
24	2ch. blue (T **7**)	35·00	38·00
25	2ch. blue (T **8**)	8·00	7·00
26	3ch. orange	7·50	7·50
27	4ch. red	10·00	9·00
28	5ch. pink	10·00	10·00
29	6ch. blue	12·00	11·00
30	10ch. purple	18·00	16·00
31a	15ch. purple	30·00	25·00
32	20ch. red	50·00	38·00
33	50ch. green and pink	£200	£140
34	1wn. multicoloured	£300	£200
35	2wn. green and purple	£500	£250

9 Imperial Crown

17 Falcon, Sceptre and Orb

1902. 40th Anniv of Emperor's Accession as King.

36	**9**	3ch. orange	32·00	25·00

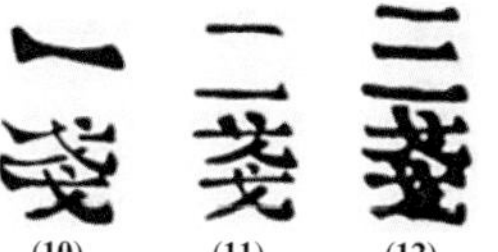

(10) (11) (12) (16)

Types **10** to **12** are in two parts, the horizontal strokes (one, two or three) representing the value figures and the bottom part being the character for "cheun".

Some variation can be found in these woodblock overprints.

1902. (a) Surch as Types **10** to **12**.

37	**3**	1ch. on 25p. red (No. 9)	8·50	6·50
38		1ch. on 25p. red (No. 14)	45·00	45·00
39		2ch. on 25p. red (No. 9)	8·50	7·00
40		2ch. on 25p. red (No. 14)	42·00	40·00
42		2ch. on 50p. lilac (No 10a)	–	£350
43		3ch. on 25p. red (No. 9)	42·00	90·00
44		3ch. on 25p. red (No. 14)		
46		3ch. on 50p. lilac (No. 10a)	8·00	10·00
47		3ch. on 50p. lilac (No. 16)	12·00	12·00

(b) Surch as T **16** (Japanese "sen" character) and strokes.

49	**3**	3ch. on 50p. lilac	£650	£500

1903.

50	**17**	2r. grey	50	75
51		1ch. purple	4·50	4·50
52		2ch. green	4·50	4·50
53		3ch. orange	5·50	5·50
54		4ch. pink	6·50	6·00
55		5ch. brown	9·00	8·00
56		6ch. lilac	9·00	8·50
57		10ch. blue	12·00	10·00
58		15ch. red on yellow	22·00	22·00
59		20ch. purple on yellow	30·00	32·00
60		50ch. red on green	90·00	95·00
61		1wn. lilac on lilac	£150	£160
62		2wn. purple on orange	£250	£250

SOUTH KOREA

1946. 100 cheun = 1 weun.
1953. 100 weun = 1 hwan.
1962. 100 chon = 1 won.

A. UNITED STATES MILITARY GOVERNMENT

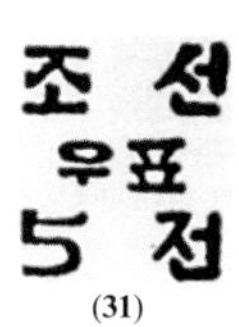

(31)

33 National Emblem

1946. Stamps of Japan surch as T **31**.

69	5ch. on 5s. purple (No. 396)	7·00	7·00
70	5ch. on 14s. red & brn (No. 324)	1·50	1·75
71	10ch. on 40s. purple (No. 407)	1·50	1·50
72	20ch. on 6s. blue (No. 397)	1·50	1·25
73	30ch. on 27s. red (No. 404)	1·50	1·25
74	5w. on 17s. violet (No. 402)	6·50	5·50

1946. Liberation from Japanese Rule.

75	–	3ch. orange	75	65
76	–	5ch. green	75	55
77	–	10ch. red	75	45
78	–	20ch. blue	75	45
79	**33**	50ch. purple	1·10	80
80		1w. brown	1·40	70

DESIGN: 3ch. to 20ch. Family and flag.

34 Dove of Peace and Map of Korea

1946. 1st Anniv of Liberation.

81	**34**	50ch. violet	5·00	2·75

35 U.S. and Korean Flags

36 Kyongju Observatory

39 Golden Crown of Silla

40 Admiral Li Sun Sin

1946. Resumption of Postal Service between Korea and U.S.A.

82	**35**	10w. red	6·00	4·00

1946.

83	**36**	50ch. blue	75	45
84	–	1w. brown	1·25	60
85	–	2w. blue	1·50	40
86	**39**	5w. mauve	14·00	6·00
87	**40**	10w. green	14·00	7·00

DESIGNS—As Type **36**: 1w. Hibiscus; 2w. Map of Korea.

41 Korean Alphabet

42 Li Jun, patriot

44 16th-century "Turtle" Ship 45 Letters Surrounding Globe

1946. 500th Anniv of Creation of Korean Alphabet.

88	**41**	50ch. blue	3·50	2·00

1947.

89	**42**	5w. green	8·50	3·00
90	–	10w. blue	8·50	3·00
91	–	20w. red	3·00	65
92	**44**	50w. brown	40·00	10·00

DESIGNS: 10w. Admiral Li Sun Sin; 20w. Independence Arch, Seoul.

1947. Resumption of Int Postal Service.

93	**45**	10w. blue	12·00	5·00

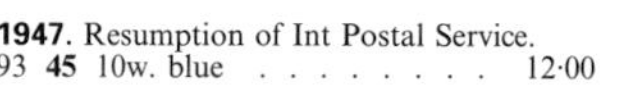

46 Douglas DC-4 Airliner

1947. Air. Inauguration of Air Mail Service.

94	**46**	50w. red	6·00	2·50
126		150w. blue	1·00	90
127		150w. green	8·50	4·00

47 Hand and Ballot Slip

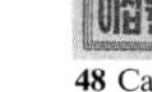

48 Casting Votes

1948. South Korea Election.

95	**47**	2w. orange	10·00	7·00
96		5w. mauve	10·00	6·00
97		10w. violet	20·00	8·00
98	**48**	20w. red	30·00	16·00
99		50w. blue	28·00	17·00

49 Korean Flag and Laurel Wreath

1948. Olympic Games.

100	**49**	5w. green	65·00	35·00
101	–	10w. violet	25·00	14·00

DESIGN—VERT: 10w. Runner with torch.

50 Capitol and Ears of Rice

1948. Meeting of First National Assembly.

102	**50**	4w. brown	16·00	8·00

51 Korean Family

1948. Promulgation of Constitution.

103	**51**	4w. green	45·00	16·00
104	–	10w. brown	32·00	10·00

DESIGN—HORIZ: 10w. Flag of Korea.

52 Dr. Syngman Rhee (First President)

53 Hibiscus

1948. Election of First President.

105	**52**	5w. blue	60·00	25·00

B. REPUBLIC OF KOREA

1948. Proclamation of Republic.

106	–	4w. blue	30·00	18·00
107	**53**	5w. mauve	26·00	16·00

DESIGN: 4w. Dove and olive branch.

54 Li Jun

55 Kyongju Observatory

1948.

108	**54**	4w. red	40	20
109	**55**	14w. blue	40	25

56 Doves and U.N. Emblem

57 Citizen and Date

1949. Arrival of U.N. Commission.
110 **56** 10w. blue . . . . 30·00 14·00

1949. National Census.
111 **57** 15w. violet . . . . 30·00 14·00

58 Children and Plant

1949. 20th Anniv of Children's Day.
112 **58** 15w. violet . . . . 15·00 7·00

59 Hibiscus

61 Dove and Globe

60 Map of Korea and Black-billed Magpies

62 Admiral Li Sun Sin

1949.
113 – 1w. red . . . . 3·00 1·50
114 – 2w. grey . . . . 1·50 60
115 – 5w. green . . . . 7·50 2·25
116 – 10w. green . . . . 2·75 1·40
117 **59** 15w. red 45 20
118 – 20w. brown 45 20
119 – 30w. green 50 20
120 – 50w. blue 45 20
121 **60** 65w. blue . . . . 2·10 1·40
122 – 100w. green 50 20
123 **61** 200w. green 60 35
124 – 400w. brown 60 40
125 **62** 500w. blue 60 45
DESIGNS—As Type **59**: 1w. Postman; 2w. Worker and factory; 5w. Harvesting rice; 10w. Manchurian cranes; 20w. Diamond Mountains; 30w. Ginseng plant; 50w. South Gate, Seoul; 100w. Tabo Pogoda, Kyongju. As Type **61**: 400w. Diamond Mountains.

63 Symbol and Phoenix

65 Korean Flag

64 Steam Train

1949. 1st Anniv of Independence.
128 **63** 15w. blue . . . . 18·00 7·50

1949. 50th Anniv of Korean Railways.
129 **64** 15w. blue . . . . 65·00 35·00

1949. 75th Anniv of U.P.U.
130 **65** 15w. multicoloured . . . . 12·00 8·00

66 Post-horse Warrant

67 Douglas DC-2 Airplane and Globe

1950. 50th Anniv of Membership of U.P.U.
131 **66** 15w. green . . . . 15·00 6·00
132 65w. brown . . . . 10·00 3·50

1950. Air. Opening of Internal Air Mail Service.
133 **67** 60w. blue . . . . 10·00 3·50

68 Demonstrators

69 Capitol, Seoul

1950. 31st Anniv of Abortive Proclamation of Independence.
134 **68** 15w. green . . . . 14·00 6·00
135 65w. violet . . . . 6·00 2·50

1950. 2nd South Korean Election.
136 **69** 30w. multicoloured . . . . 8·00 3·00

70 Dr. Syngman Rhee

71 Flag and Mountains

1950. Unification of Korea.
137 **70** 100w. blue . . . . 2·50 1·00
138 **71** 100w. green . . . . 3·50 1·00
139 – 200w. green . . . . 2·00 75
DESIGN—35 × 24 mm: 200w. Map of Korea and flags of U.N. and Korea.

73 Manchurian Crane

76 Post-horse Warrant

77 Fairy (8th cent painting)

1951. Perf or roul.
140 **73** 5w. brown . . . . 2·40 1·40
181 – 20w. violet . . . . 1·00 30
187 – 50w. green . . . . 2·00 30
183 **76** 100w. blue . . . . 1·25 25
193 **77** 1000w. green . . . . . . 2·25 40
DESIGNS—HORIZ: 20w. Astrological Tiger (ancient painting); 50w. Dove and Korean flag.

1951. Surch with new value.
145 **54** 100w. on 4w. red . . . . . 2·75 75
146 **59** 200w. on 15w. red . . . . 4·50 2·00
147 **54** 300w. on 4w. red . . . . . 1·50 1·00
156 – 300w. on 10w. green (116) 13·00 4·00
149 **55** 300w. on 14w. blue . . . . 2·25 75
150 **59** 300w. on 15w. red . . . . 1·75 75
151 – 300w. on 20w. brown (118) 2·50 85
152 – 300w. on 30w. green (119) 2·00 75
153 – 300w. on 50w. blue (120) 2·00 80
154 **60** 300w. on 65w. blue . . . . 5·75 3·50
155 – 300w. on 100w. green (122) 2·25 75

80 Statue of Liberty and Flags

1951. Participation in Korean War. Flags in national colours. A. As Type **80** in green. B. As Type **80** but showing U.N. Emblem and doves in blue.
158A 500w. Australia . . . . . 6·00 6·00
159A 500w. Belgium . . . . . 6·00 6·00
160A 500w. Britain . . . . . . 6·00 6·00
161A 500w. Canada . . . . . . 6·00 6·00
162A 500w. Colombia . . . . . 6·00 6·00
163A 500w. Denmark . . . . . 12·00 12·00
164A 500w. Ethiopia . . . . . . 6·00 6·00
165A 500w. France . . . . . . 6·00 6·00
166A 500w. Greece . . . . . . 6·00 6·00
167A 500w. India . . . . 10·00 10·00
168A 500w. Italy (with crown) . . 15·00 15·00
169A 500w. Italy (without crown) 7·00 7·00
170A 500w. Luxembourg . . . . 10·00 10·00
171A 500w. Netherlands . . . . 6·00 6·00
172A 500w. New Zealand . . . . 6·00 6·00
173A 500w. Norway . . . . . . 10·00 10·00
174A 500w. Philippines . . . . . 6·00 6·00
175A 500w. Sweden . . . . . . 6·00 6·00
176A 500w. Thailand . . . . . . 6·00 6·00
177A 500w. Turkey . . . . . . 6·00 6·00
178A 500w. Union of South Africa . . . . 6·00 6·00
179A 500w. U.S.A. . . . . . . 5·00 5·00
158B 500w. Australia . . . . . 6·00 6·00
159B 500w. Belgium . . . . . 6·00 6·00
160B 500w. Britain . . . . . . 6·00 6·00
161B 500w. Canada . . . . . . 6·00 6·00
162B 500w. Colombia . . . . . 6·00 6·00
163B 500w. Denmark . . . . . 15·00 15·00
164B 500w. Ethiopia . . . . . . 6·00 6·00
165B 500w. France . . . . . . 6·00 6·00
166B 500w. Greece . . . . . . 6·00 6·00
167B 500w. India . . . . 10·00 10·00
168B 500w. Italy (with crown) . . 15·00 15·00
169B 500w. Italy (without crown) 7·00 7·00
170B 500w. Luxembourg . . . . 10·00 10·00
171B 500w. Netherlands . . . . 6·00 6·00
172B 500w. New Zealand . . . . 6·00 6·00
173B 500w. Norway . . . . . . 10·00 10·00
174B 500w. Philippines . . . . . 6·00 6·00
175B 500w. Sweden . . . . . . 6·00 6·00
176B 500w. Thailand . . . . . . 6·00 6·00
177B 500w. Turkey . . . . . . 6·00 6·00
178B 500w. Union of South Africa . . . . 6·00 6·00
179B 500w. U.S.A. . . . . . . 5·00 5·00

1951. Air. No. **126** surch **500 WON**.
180 **46** 500w. on 150w. blue . . . 2·50 75

82 Buddha of Sokkuram

83 Pulguksa Temple, Kyongju

84 Monument to King Muryol, Kyongju

85 Shrine of Admiral Li Sun Sin, Tongyong

1952. Inscr "KOREA".
184 **82** 200w. red . . . . 1·00 25
185 **83** 300w. green 80 25
191 **84** 500w. red . . . . 2·00 40
192 500w. blue . . . . 10·00 50·00
194 **85** 2000w. blue . . . . 1·50 40
See also Nos. 200/1 and 205.

86 President Syngman Rhee

1952. President's Election to 2nd Term of Office.
195 **86** 1000w. green . . . . . . 2·00 70

87 Douglas DC-3 over Freighter

1952. Air.
196 **87** 1200w. brown . . . . . . 1·10 40
197 1800w. blue . . . . 1·25 40
198 4200w. violet . . . . . . 1·50 50
For stamps in new currency, see Nos. 210/12.

88 Tree-planting

89 Monument to King Muryol, Kyongju

91 Pagoda Park, Seoul

92 Sika Deer

93 Sika Deer

1953. New currency. With character "hwan" after figure of value.
244 **88** 1h. blue 25 10
200 **84** 2h. blue 50 10
201 5h. green 60 10
202 **89** 5h. green 50 10
203 **88** 10h. green . . . . 1·00 10
204 – 10h. brown . . . . 2·50 10
205 **85** 20h. brown . . . . 3·25 10
206 **91** 30h. blue . . . . 1·00 10
242 **92** 100h. brown . . . . 7·50 30
243 **91** 200h. violet . . . . 3·50 25
208 **93** 500h. orange . . . . . . 28·00 1·60
209 1000h. brown . . . . . . 60·00 3·00
DESIGN: No. 204, "Metopta rectifasciata" (moth) and Korean flag.
For designs without character after figure of value, see 1955 issue (No. 273 etc).

1953. Air. Colours changed and new Currency.
210 **87** 12h. blue . . . . 1·25 35
211 18h. violet . . . . 1·50 40
212 42h. green . . . . 2·00 70

94 Field Hospital

1953. Red Cross Fund. Crosses in red.
213 **94** 10h.+5h. green . . . . . . 5·00 1·50
214 – 10h.+5h. blue . . . . . . 5·00 1·50
DESIGN—VERT: No. 214, Nurses supporting wounded soldier.

95 Y.M.C.A. Badge and Map

96 Douglas DC-6 over East Gate, Seoul

1953. 50th Anniv of Korean Young Men's Christian Association.
215 **95** 10h. red and black . . . . 2·00 70

1954. Air.
216 **96** 25h. brown . . . . 2·00 80
217 35h. purple . . . . 2·75 1·00
218 38h. green . . . . 2·75 1·10
219 58h. blue . . . . 2·50 1·25
258 70h. green . . . . 4·75 2·00
220 71h. blue . . . . 6·50 1·50
259 110h. brown . . . . 4·75 2·00
260 205h. mauve . . . . 7·00 2·00

98 Tokto Island

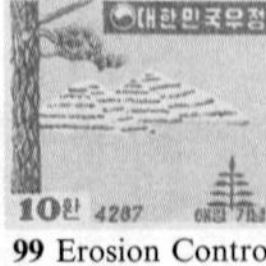

99 Erosion Control

1954.
221 – 2h. purple . . . . 1·00 15
222 – 5h. blue 80 15
223 **98** 10h. green . . . . 1·25 15
DESIGN: 2, 5h. Rocks off Tokto Island.

1954. 4th World Forestry Congress, Dehru Dun.
224 **99** 10h. light green and green 1·00 15
225 19h. light green and green 1·00 15

100 Presidents Syngman Rhee and Eisenhower

101 "Rebirth of Industry"

1954. Korea–United States Mutual Defence Treaty.
226 **100** 10h. blue . . . . 1·75 40
227 19h. brown . . . . 1·25 40
228 71h. green . . . . 2·50 85

1955. Reconstruction.
229 **101** 10h. brown . . . . 2·50 15
230 15h. violet . . . . 2·25 15

231 20h. blue . . . . 2·25 15
232 50h. mauve . . . . 3·00 25
269 50h. red . . . . 5·00 15

102 Rotary Emblem **103** Pres. Syngman Rhee

1955. 50th Anniv of Rotary International.
236 **102** 20h. violet . . . . 2·50 85
237 25h. green . . . . 1·25 45
238 71h. purple . . . . 1·50 50

1955. 80th Birthday of President.
239 **103** 20h. blue . . . . 3·25 1·00

104 Independence Arch, Seoul

1955. 10th Anniv of Liberation.
240 **104** 40h. green . . . . 2·00 70
241 100h. brown . . . . . . 2·00 1·00

105 Hibiscus **106** King Sejong **107** Kyongju Observatory

1955. Without character after figure of value.
273 **88** 2h. blue 25 10
309 **89** 4h. blue 60 10
310 5h. green 60 10
247 **105** 10h. mauve . . . . 1·00 10
277 – 10h. green 75 10
248 **106** 20h. purple . . . . 2·50 10
279 **105** 20h. mauve 60 15
280 – 30h. violet 75 15
281 **106** 40h. purple 85 15
249 **107** 50h. violet . . . . 2·75 10
315 – 55h. purple . . . . 2·00 10
250 **92** 100h. purple . . . . . . 12·00 10
284 **107** 100h. violet . . . . . . 2·75 15
285 **92** 200h. purple . . . . . . 3·25 15
286 **91** 400h. violet . . . . . . 32·00 35
251 **93** 500h. brown . . . . . . 28·00 40
288 1000h. brown . . . . . . 50·00 2·25
DESIGNS—HORIZ: No. 277, South Gate, Seoul; 280, Tiger. VERT: No. 315, Haegumgang (cliff face).

108 Runners and Torch **109** U.N. Emblem

1955. 36th National Athletic Meeting.
252 **108** 20h. purple . . . . 3·00 1·00
253 55h. green . . . . 3·00 1·00

1955. 10th Anniv of U.N.
254 **109** 20h. green . . . . 2·25 60
255 55h. blue . . . . 2·25 60

110 Admiral Li Sun Sin and 16th-century "Turtle" Ship

1955. 10th Anniv of Korean Navy.
256 **110** 20h. blue . . . . 3·00 1·50

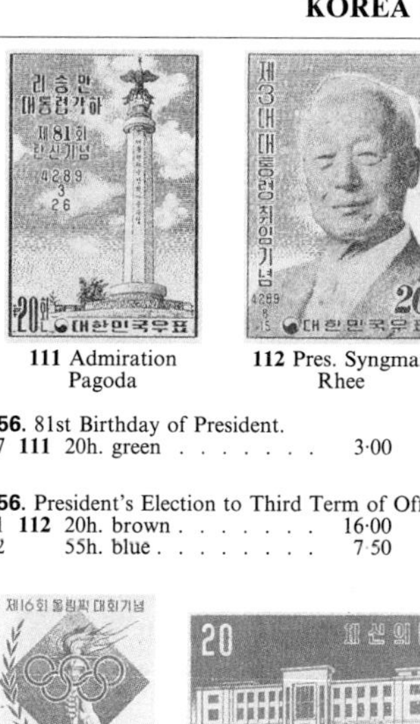

111 Admiration Pagoda **112** Pres. Syngman Rhee

1956. 81st Birthday of President.
257 **111** 20h. green . . . . 3·00 1·00

1956. President's Election to Third Term of Office.
261 **112** 20h. brown . . . . 16·00 5·00
262 55h. blue . . . . 7·50 3·00

113 Torch and Olympic Rings **114** Central P.O., Seoul

1956. Olympic Games.
263 **113** 20h. brown . . . . 3·00 80
264 55h. green . . . . 3·00 80

1956. Stamp Day. Inscr "4289.12.4".
265 **114** 20h. turquoise . . . . . 3·00 55
266 – 50h. red . . . . 3·75 1·00
267 – 55h. green . . . . 1·50 55
DESIGNS—VERT: 50h. Stamp of 1884. HORIZ: 55h. Man leading post-pony.

119 I.T.U. Emblem and Radio Mast

1957. 5th Anniv of Korea's Admission to I.T.U.
290 **119** 40h. blue . . . . 1·50 60
291 55h. green . . . . 1·50 60

120 Korean Scout and Badge

1957. 50th Anniv of Boy Scout Movement.
293 **120** 40h. purple . . . . 1·75 60
294 55h. purple . . . . 1·75 60

1957. Flood Relief Fund. As No. 281 but Korean inscr and premium added and colour changed.
299 40h.+10h. green . . . . . . 2·50 50

123 Mercury, Flags and Freighters **124** Star of Bethlehem and Pine Cone

1957. Korean–American Friendship Treaty.
301 **123** 40h. orange . . . . . . 1·25 60
302 205h. green . . . . 1·60 80

1957. Christmas and New Year Issue.
304 **124** 15h. brown, green & orange . . . . 2·50 50
305 – 25h. green, red and yellow 2·50 30
306 – 30h. blue, green and yellow . . . . 4·25 1·25
DESIGNS: 25h. Christmas tree and tassels; 30h. Christmas tree and dog by window.

125 Winged Letter **126** Korean Children regarding future

1958. Postal Week.
321 **125** 40h. blue and red 80 25

1958. 10th Anniv of Republic of Korea.
323 **126** 20h. grey 80 25
324 – 40h. red . . . . 1·25 25
DESIGN—HORIZ: 40h. Hibiscus flowers forming figure "10".

127 U.N.E.S.C.O. Headquarters, Paris **128** Children flying Kites

1958. Inaug of U.N.E.S.C.O. Building, Paris.
326 **127** 40h. orange and green . . 1·00 25

1958. Christmas and New Year.
330 **128** 15h. green . . . . 1·00 30
331 – 25h. red, yellow and blue 1·00 30
332 – 30h. red, blue and yellow 2·00 50
DESIGNS—VERT: 25h. Christmas tree, tassels and wicker basket (cooking sieve); 30h. Children in traditional festive costume.

129 Rejoicing Crowds in Pagoda Park, Flag and Torch

1959. 40th Anniv of Abortive Proclamation of Independence.
334 **129** 40h. purple and brown . . 1·00 25

130 Marines going Ashore from Landing-craft

1959. 10th Anniv of Korean Marine Corps.
336 **130** 40h. green . . . . 1·00 25

131

1959. 10th Anniv of Korea's Admission to W.H.O.
339 **131** 40h. purple and pink . . 1·00 25

132 Diesel Train

1959. 60th Anniv of Korean Railways.
341 **132** 40h. sepia and brown . . 1·90 1·00

133 Runners in Relay Race

1959. 40th Korean National Games.
343 **133** 40h. brown and blue . . . 1·00 25

134 Red Cross and Korea

1959. Red Cross. Inscr "1959 4292".
345 **134** 40h. red and green . . . 1·00 25
346 – 55h. red and mauve . . . 1·00 25
DESIGN: 55h. Red Cross on Globe.

135 Korean Postal Flags Old and New **136** Mice in Korean Costume and New Year Emblem

1959. 75th Anniv of Korean Postal Service.
348 **135** 40h. red and blue . . . . 1·00 25

1959. Christmas and New Year.
350 **136** 15h. pink, blue and grey 1·00 15
351 – 25h. red, green and blue 80 15
352 – 30h. red, black and mauve 1·40 15
DESIGNS: 25h. Carol singers; 30h. Crane.

137 U.P.U. Monument **138** Honey Bee and Clover

1960. 60th Anniv of Admission of Korea to U.P.U.
354 **137** 40h. brown and blue . . . 1·60 75

1960. Children's Savings Campaign.
356 **138** 10h. yellow, brown and green 75 10
357 – 20h. brown, blue and pink 1·25 10
DESIGN: 20h. Snail and Korean money-bag.
For these stamps in new currency, see Nos. 452 etc.

139 "Uprooted Tree" **140** Pres. Eisenhower

1960. World Refugee Year.
358 **139** 40h. red, blue and green 80 10

1960. Visit of President Eisenhower of United States.
360 **140** 40h. blue, red and green 3·00 80

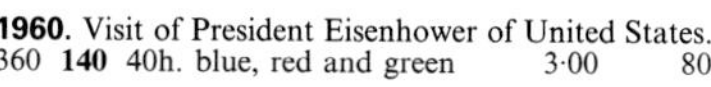

141 Schoolchildren

1960. 75th Anniv of Educational System.
362 **141** 40h. purple, brown & green . . . . 1·00 25

142 Assembly **143** "Liberation"

1960. Inauguration of House of Councillors.
364 **142** 40h. blue . . . . 1·00 25

1960. 15th Anniv of Liberation.
366 **143** 40h. red, blue and brown 1·00 25

144 Weightlifting **145** Barn Swallow and Insulators

1960. Olympic Games.
368 **144** 20h. brown, flesh & turq 1·00 35
369 – 40h. brown, blue & turq 1·00 35
DESIGN: 40h. South Gate, Seoul.

1960. 75th Anniv of Korean Telegraph Service.
371 **145** 40h. violet, grey and blue 1·50 65

146 "Rebirth of Republic"   147 "Torch of Culture"

1960. Establishment of New Government.
373 **146** 40h. green, blue and orange . . . . 1·00 25

1960. Cultural Month.
376 **147** 40h. yellow, lt blue & blue 1·00 25

148 U.N. Flag   149 U.N. Emblem and Gravestones

1960. 15th Anniv of U.N.
378 **148** 40h. blue, green and mauve . . . . 1·00 25

1960. Establishment of U.N. Memorial Cemetery.
380 **149** 40h. brown and orange 1·00 25

150 "National Stocktaking"   151 Festival Stocking

1960. Census of Population and Resources.
382 **150** 40h. red, drab and blue 1·00 25

1960. Christmas and New Year Issue.
384 – 15h. brown, yellow & grey 50 15
385 **151** 25h. red, green and blue 40 10
386 – 30h. red, yellow and blue 75 15
DESIGNS: 15h. Ox's head; 30h. Girl bowing in New Year's greeting.

152 Wind-sock and Ancient Rain-gauge

1961. World Meteorological Day.
388 **152** 40h. ultramarine and blue 1·00 25

153 Family, Sun and Globe

1961. World Health Day.
390 **153** 40h. brown and orange 1·00 25

154 Students' Demonstration

1961. 1st Anniv of April Revolution (Overthrow of Pres. Syngman Rhee).
392 **154** 40h. green, red and blue 1·00 30

155 Workers and Conference Emblem   157 Soldier's Grave

156 Girl Guide, Camp and Badge

1961. Int Community Development Conf, Seoul.
394 **155** 40h. green 80 25

1961. 15th Anniv of Korean Girl Guide Movement.
396 **156** 40h. green . . . . 1·00 25

1961. Memorial Day.
398 **157** 40h. black and drab . . . 1·00 30

158 Soldier with Torch   159 "Three Liberations"

1961. Revolution of 16 May (Seizure of Power by Gen. Pak Chung Hi).
400 **158** 40h. brown and yellow . . 1·00 30

1961. Liberation Day.
402 **159** 40h. multicoloured . . . 1·00 30

160 Korean Forces, Flag and Destroyer

1961. Armed Forces Day.
404 **160** 40h. multicoloured . . . 1·25 30

161 "Korean Art" (Kyongbok Palace Art Gallery)

1961. 10th Korean Art Exhibition.
406 **161** 40h. chocolate and brown 1·00 25

162 Birthday Candle

1961. 15th Anniv of U.N.E.S.C.O.
408 **162** 40h. blue and green . . . 25 25

163 Mobile X-Ray Unit

1961. Tuberculosis Vaccination Week.
410 **163** 40h. brown, black & lt brn 75 25

164 Ginseng   165 King Sejong

166 White-bellied Black Woodpecker   167 Rice Harvester

168 Korean Drum   169 Douglas DC-8 Jetliner over Pagoda

1961.

412 **164** 20h. red 80 10
413 **165** 30h. purple 80 10
414 **166** 40h. blue and red . . . . 4·00 65
415 **167** 40h. green . . . . 1·10 10
416 **168** 100h. brown . . . . . . 1·75 10

See also 1962 issue (No. 537 etc), and for stamps inscribed "REPUBLIC OF KOREA", see Nos. 641 etc and 785/95.

1961. Air.
417 **169** 50h. violet and blue . . . 10·00 3·50
418 – 100h. brown and blue . . 15·00 12·00
419 – 200h. brown and blue . . 20·00 6·00
420 – 400h. green and blue . . 20·00 6·50
DESIGNS—Plane over: 100h. West Gate, Suwon; 200h. Gateway and wall of Toksu Palace, Seoul; 400h. Pavilion, Kyongbok Palace, Seoul.
See also Nos. 454 etc.

170 I.T.U. Emblem as Satellite

1962. 10th Anniv of Admission to I.T.U.
421 **170** 40h. red and blue . . . . 1·25 40

171 Triga Mark II Reactor

1962. 1st Korean Atomic Reactor.
423 **171** 40h. green, drab and blue 1·00 25

172 Mosquito and Emblem

1962. Malaria Eradication.
424 **172** 40h. red and green . . . 50 25

173 Girl and Y.W.C.A. Emblem

1962. 40th Anniv of Korean Young Women's Christian Association.
426 **173** 40h. blue and orange . . 1·00 30

174 Emblem of Asian Film Producers' Federation   175 Soldiers crossing Han River Bridge

1962. 9th Asian Film Festival, Seoul.
427 **174** 40h. violet, red & turquoise . . . . 1·25 25

1962. 1st Anniv of 16th May Revolution.
428 – 30h. green and brown . . 1·50 50
429 **175** 40h. brown, green & turq 1·50 50
430 – 200h. yellow, red and blue 11·00 3·00
DESIGNS—HORIZ: 30h. "Industrial Progress" (men moving cogwheel up slope); 200h. "Egg" containing Korean badge and industrial skyline.

176 20-oared "Turtle" Ship

1962. 370th Anniv of Hansan Naval Victory over Japanese.
433 **176** 2w. blue and light blue . . 1·50 70
434 – 4w. black, violet & turq 2·75 1·00
DESIGN: 4w. 16-oared "turtle" ship.

177 Chindo Dog   178 "Hanabusaya asiatica"

179 Statue of Goddess Mikuk Besal   213 Longhorn Beetle

180 Farmers' Dance   181 12th-century Wine-jug

214 Factory, Fishes and Corn   182 Mison

183 13th-century Printing-block and Impression used for "Tripitaka Koreana"   191 Sika Deer

192 Bell of King Kyongdok   215 Boddhisatva, Sokkuram Shrine

216 Tile, Silla Dynasty **217** "Azure Dragon", Koguryo period

1962. New Currency.
537 **177** 20ch. brown 25 10
436 **178** 40ch. blue 30 10
785 – 40ch. green 40 10
539 **179** 50ch. brown 30 10
540 **213** 60ch. brown 40 10
541 **180** 1w. blue . . . . 1·00 10
542 **179** 1w.50 grey 30 10
543 **164** 2w. red . . . . 1·25 10
472 **165** 3w. purple . . . . 2·25 10
545 **167** 4w. green 30 10
442 **181** 5w. blue . . . . 4·25 10
547 **214** 7w. mauve . . . . 1·10 10
548 **168** 10w. brown . . . . . . 2·00 10
549 **182** 20w. mauve . . . . . . 3·00 10
550 **183** 40w. purple . . . . . . 4·50 10
551 **191** 50w. brown . . . . . . 6·00 15
552 **192** 100w. green . . . . . . 15·00 20
553 **215** 200w. deep green and green . . . . 5·00 10
554 **216** 300w. green and brown 10·00 10
555 **217** 500w. blue and light blue 7·00 10
DESIGN—18 × 72 mm: No. 785, motif as Type **178** but inscriptions differently arranged.
See also Nos. 607, 609 and 641/9.

184 Scout Badge and Korean Flag **185** Chub Mackerel, Trawler and Nets

1962. 40th Anniv of Korean Scout Movement.
446 **184** 4w. brown, red and blue 80 25
447 4w. green, red and blue 80 25

1962. 10th Indo-Pacific Fishery Council Meeting, Seoul.
449 **185** 4w. ultramarine and blue 1·40 30

186 I.C.A.O. Emblem

1962. 10th Anniv of Korea's Entry into I.C.A.O.
450 **186** 4w. blue and brown . . . 1·25 25

1962. Children's Savings Campaign. As Nos. 356/7 but new currency.
452 1w. yellow, brown and green 3·25 10
453 2w. brown, blue and pink . . 8·25 65

1962. Air. New Currency.
454 **169** 5w. blue and violet . . . 12·50 2·40
512 – 10w. brown and green (As No. 418) . . . . 2·75 30
513 – 20w. brown and green (As No. 419) . . . . 3·50 35
563 **169** 39w. drab and blue . . . 4·75 35
514 – 40w. green and blue (As No. 420) . . . . 4·00 50
564 – 64w. green and blue (As No. 418) . . . . 2·10 25
565 – 78w. blue and green (As No. 419) . . . . 3·00 30
566 – 112w. green and blue (As No. 420) . . . . 3·00 30

187 Electric Power Plant

1962. Inauguration of 1st Korean Economic Five Year Plan.
458 **187** 4w. violet and orange . . 1·25 40
459 – 4w. ultramarine and blue 1·25 40
DESIGN: No. 459, Irrigation Dam.
See also Nos. 482/3, 528/9, 593/4 and 634/5.

188 Campaign Emblem

1963. Freedom from Hunger.
460 **188** 4w. green, buff and blue 75 25

189 Globe and Letters

1963. 1st Anniv of Asian-Oceanic Postal Union.
462 **189** 4w. purple, green and blue 90 25

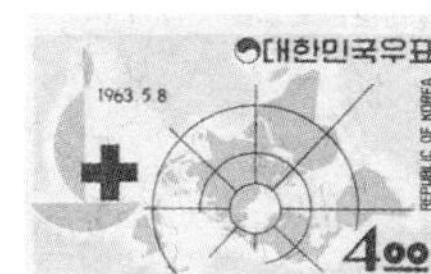
190 Centenary Emblem and Map

1963. Centenary of Red Cross.
464 **190** 4w. red, grey and blue . . 90 25
465 4w. red, grey and orange 90 25

1963. Flood Relief. As No. 545, but new colour and inscr with premium.
479 4w.+1w. blue . . . . 1·50 45

193 "15" and Hibiscus

1963. 15th Anniv of Republic.
480 **193** 4w. red, violet and blue 1·40 30

194 Nurse and Emblem

1963. 15th Anniv of Korean Army Nursing Corps.
481 **194** 4w. black, turquoise & grn . . . . 1·00 25

1963. Five Year Plan. Dated "1963". As T **187**.
482 4w. violet and blue 90 25
483 4w. chocolate and brown . . 4·25 85
DESIGNS: No. 482, Cement Factory, Mun'gyong, and bag of cement; 483, Miner and coal train, Samch'ok region.

195/6 Rock Temples of Abu Simbel

1963. Nubian Monuments Preservation.
484 **195** 3w. green and drab . . . 2·25 40
485 **196** 4w. green and drab . . . 2·25 40
Nos. 484/5 were issued together, se-tenant, forming the composite design illustrated.

197 Rugby Football and Athlete

1963. 44th National Games.
487 **197** 4w. green, brown and blue . . . . 1·00 25

198 Nurse and Motor Clinic

1963. 10th Anniv of Korean Tuberculosis Prevention Society.
488 **198** 4w. blue and red . . . . 1·00 25

199 Eleanor Roosevelt **200** U.N. Headquarters

1963. 15th Anniv of Declaration of Human Rights.
489 **199** 3w. brown and blue . . . 80 25
490 – 4w. blue, green and buff 80 25
DESIGN: 4w. Freedom torch and globe.

1963. 15th Anniv of U.N. Recognition of Korea.
492 **200** 4w. green, blue and black 1·00 25

201 Pres. Pak Chong Hi and Capitol

1963. Inaug of President Pak Chong Hi.
494 **201** 4w. blue, turquoise & black . . . . 11·00 3·50

202 "Tai-Keum" (Bamboo Flute) **204** "U.N.E.S.C.O."

203 Symbols of Metric System

1963. Musical Instruments and Players. As T **202**.
495 4w. green, brown and drab 2·25 60
496 4w. black, blue and light blue 2·25 60
497 4w. green, mauve and pink 2·25 60
498 4w. brown, violet and grey 2·25 60
499 4w. blue, brown and pink . . 2·25 60
500 4w. turquoise, black and blue 2·25 60
501 4w. violet, bistre and yellow 2·25 60
502 4w. blue, brown and mauve 2·25 60
503 4w. black, blue and purple 2·25 60
504 4w. black, brown and pink 2·25 60
MUSICAL INSTRUMENTS (and players)—VERT: No. 495, Type **202**; 496, "Wul-keum" (banjo); 497, "Tang-piri" (flageolet); 498, "Na-bal" (trumpet); 499, "Hyang-pipa" (lute); 500, "Pyenkyeng" jade chimes; 501, "Taipyeng-so" (clarinet); 502, "Chang-ko" (double-ended drum). HORIZ: No. 503, "Wa-kong-hu" (harp); 504, "Kaya-ko" (zither).

1964. Introduction of Metric System in Korea.
505 **203** 4w. multicoloured 90 25

1964. 10th Anniv of Korean U.N.E.S.C.O. Committee.
506 **204** 4w. ultramarine, red & blue 90 25

205 Symbols of Industry and Census

1964. National Industrial Census (1963).
507 **205** 4w. brown, black and grey . . . . 1·25 60

206 Y.M.C.A. Emblem and Profile of Young Man

1964. 50th Anniv of Korean Young Men's Christian Association.
508 **206** 4w. red, blue and green 75 25

207 Fair Emblem, Ginseng Root and Freighter

1964. New York World's Fair.
509 **207** 40w. brown, green & yellow . . . . 2·00 40
510 – 100w. ultramarine, brown and blue . . . . 9·00 1·50
DESIGN: 100w. Korean pavilion at Fair.

208 Secret Garden

1964. Background in light blue.
517 **208** 1w. green 60 20
518 – 2w. green . . . . 1·00 25
519 – 3w. green . . . . 1·00 25
520 – 4w. green . . . . 1·50 30
521 – 5w. violet . . . . 2·00 30
522 – 6w. blue . . . . 2·00 40
523 – 7w. brown . . . . 2·40 40
524 – 8w. brown . . . . 2·50 40
525 – 9w. violet . . . . 2·50 40
526 – 10w. green . . . . 2·75 45
DESIGNS: 2w. Whahong Gate; 3w. Uisang Pavilion; 4w. Mt. Songni; 5w. Paekma River; 6w. Anab Pond; 7w. Choksok Pavilion; 8w. Kwanghan Pavilion; 9w. Whaom Temple; 10w. Chonjeyon Falls.

1964. Five Year Plan. Dated "1964". As T **187**.
528 4w. black and blue . . . . . 1·50 30
529 4w. blue and yellow . . . . 1·00 30
DESIGNS: No. 528, Trawlers and fish; 529, Oil refinery and barrels.

209 Wheel and Globe

1964. Colombo Plan Day.
530 **209** 4w. lt brown, brown & grn 70 25

210 "Helping Hand"

1964. 15th Anniv of Korea's Admission to W.H.O.
532 **210** 4w. black, green and light green 50 25

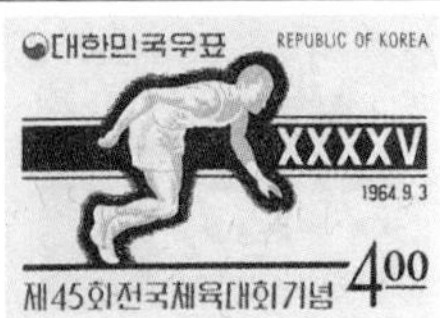
211 Running

1964. 45th National Games, Inchon.
534 **211** 4w. pink, green and purple . . . . 1·00 25

212 U.P.U. Monument, Berne, and Ribbons

1964. 90th Anniv of U.P.U.
535 **212** 4w. brown, blue and pink 75 25

218 Federation Emblem

219 Olympic "V" Emblem

1964. 5th Meeting of Int Federation of Asian and Western Pacific Contractors' Assns.
556 **218** 4w. green, light green and brown 75 25

1964. Olympic Games, Tokyo.
557 **219** 4w. blue, turquoise & brn 1·50 60
558 – 4w. mauve, blue and green . . . . 1·50 60
559 – 4w. brown, ultram & blue 1·50 60
560 – 4w. red, brown and blue 1·50 60
561 – 4w. brown, purple and blue . . . . 1·50 60
DESIGNS—HORIZ: No. 558, Running; 559, Rowing; 560, Horse-jumping; 561, Gymnastics.

220 Unissued 1884 100m. Stamp

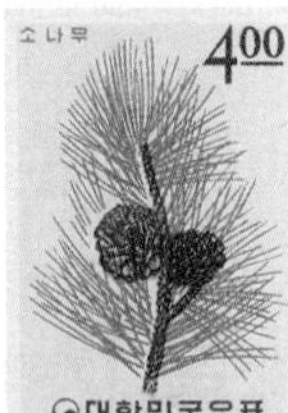
221 Pine Cone

1964. 80th Anniv of Korean Postal Services.
567 **220** 3w. blue, violet and mauve . . . . 1·00 40
568 – 4w. black, violet and green . . . . 1·60 60
DESIGN: 4w. Hong Yong Sik, 1st Korean Postmaster-general.

1965. Korean Plants. Plants multicoloured, background colours given.
571 **221** 4w. green . . . . 1·25 40
572 – 4w. brown (Plum blossom) . . . . 1·25 40
573 – 4w. blue (Forsythia) . . . 1·25 40
574 – 4w. green (Azalea) . . . 1·25 40
575 – 4w. pink (Lilac) . . . . . 1·25 40
576 – 4w. grey (Wild rose) . . . 1·25 40
577 – 4w. green (Balsam) . . . 1·25 40
578 – 4w. grey (Hibiscus) . . . 1·25 40
579 – 4w. flesh (Crepe myrtle) 1·25 40
580 – 4w. blue (Ullung chrysanthemum) . . . 1·25 40
581 – 4w. buff (Paulownia, tree) 1·25 40
582 – 4w. blue (Bamboo) . . . 1·25 40

222 Folk Dancing

1965. Pacific Area Travel Assn Conf, Seoul.
584 **222** 4w. violet, brown & green 1·00 25

223 Flag and Doves

1965. Military Aid for Vietnam.
586 **223** 4w. brown, blue and yellow 60 50

224 "Food Production"

1965. Agricultural Seven Year Plan.
588 **224** 4w. brown, green and black 50 25

225 "Family Scales"

1965. Family Planning Month.
589 **225** 4w. green, drab & lt green 65 25

226 I.T.U. Emblem and Symbols

1965. Centenary of I.T.U.
591 **226** 4w. black, red and blue 65 20

1965. Five Year Plan. Dated "1965". As T **187**.
593 4w. blue and pink . . . . . 1·00 25
594 4w. sepia and brown 80 25
DESIGNS: No. 593, "Korea" (freighter) at quayside and crates; 594, Fertilizer plant and wheat.

227 Flags of Australia, Belgium, Great Britain, Canada and Colombia

1965. 15th Anniv of Outbreak of Korean War.
595 **227** 4w. multicoloured . . . . 1·00 40
596 – 4w. multicoloured . . . . 1·00 40
597 – 4w. multicoloured . . . . 1·00 40
598 – 4w. multicoloured . . . . 1·00 40
599 – 10w. multicoloured . . . 2·50 60
DESIGNS—U.N. Emblem and flags of: No. 596, Denmark, Ethiopia, France, Greece and India; 597, Italy, Luxembourg, Netherlands, New Zealand and Norway; 598, Philippines, Sweden, Thailand, Turkey and South Africa; 599, General MacArthur and flags of Korea, U.N. and U.S.A.

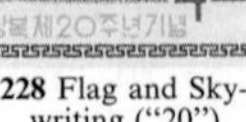
228 Flag and Sky-writing ("20")

229 Ants and Leaf

1965. 20th Anniv of Liberation.
601 **228** 4w. red, violet and blue 65 25
602 – 10w. red, blue and violet 1·10 40
DESIGN: 10w. South Gate and fireworks.

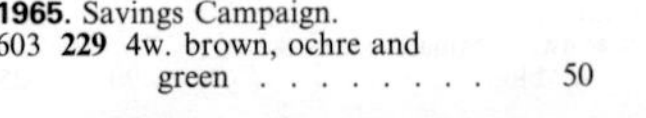
1965. Savings Campaign.
603 **229** 4w. brown, ochre and green 50 25

230 Hoisting Flag

231 Radio Aerial

1965. 15th Anniv of Recapture of Seoul.
604 **230** 3w. green, blue and orange . . . . 1·10 35

1965. 80th Anniv of Korean Telecommunications.
605 **231** 3w. green, black and blue 60 25
606 – 10w. black, blue and yellow . . . . 1·00 35
DESIGN: 10w. Telegraphist of 1885.

1965. Flood Relief. As No. 545 (1962 issue), but colour changed and inscr with premium.
607 4w.+2w. blue . . . . 1·00 30

232 Pole Vaulting

1965. National Athletic Meeting, Kwangju.
608 **232** 3w. multicoloured . . . . 1·00 40

1965. Aid for Children. As No. 545 (1962 issue), but colour changed and inscr with premium.
609 4w.+2w. purple . . . . . . 1·10 30

233 I.C.Y. Emblem

1965. International Co-operation Year and 20th Anniv of United Nations.
610 **233** 3w. red, green & dp green 50 25
611 – 10w. ultramarine, grn & bl . . . . 1·10 25
DESIGN—VERT: 10w. U.N. flag and headquarters, New York.

234 Child posting Letter

235 Children with Toboggan

1965. 10th Communications Day.
613 **234** 3w. multicoloured . . . . 1·00 25
614 – 10w. red, blue and green 1·60 30
DESIGN: 10w. Airmail envelope and telephone receiver.

1965. Christmas and New Year.
615 **235** 3w. blue, red and green 60 25
616 – 4w. blue, red and green 75 25
DESIGN: 4w. Boy and girl in traditional costume.

236 Freedom House

1966. Opening of Freedom House, Panmunjom.
618 **236** 7w. black, emerald & grn 1·00 40
619 39w. black, lilac and green . . . . 4·25 60

237 Mandarins

1966. Korean Birds. Multicoloured.
621 3w. Type **237** . . . . 2·40 1·25
622 5w. Manchurian crane . . . 2·50 1·25
623 7w. Common pheasant . . . 3·75 1·25

238 Pine Forest

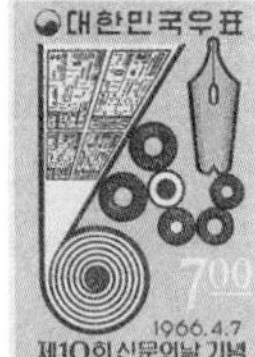
239 Printing Press and Pen

1966. Reafforestation Campaign.
625 **238** 7w. brown, green and light green 70 15

1966. 10th Newspaper Day.
626 **239** 7w. purple, yellow & green 60 15

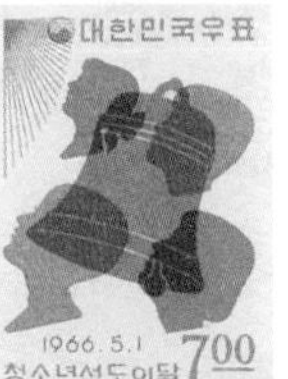
240 Curfew Bell and Young Koreans

241 W.H.O. Building

1966. Youth Guidance Month.
627 **240** 7w. orange, green and blue 60 15

1966. Inauguration of W.H.O. Headquarters, Geneva.
628 **241** 7w. black, blue and yellow . . . . 1·00 40
629 39w. red, grey and yellow 4·00 1·00

242 Pres. Pak, Handclasp and Flags

1966. Pres. Pak Chung Hi's State Tour of South-East Asia.
631 **242** 7w. multicoloured . . . . 3·00 1·00

243 Girl Scout and Flag

1966. 20th Anniv of Korean Girl Scouts.
632 **243** 7w. black, green and yellow . . . . 1·00 20

244 Student and Ehwa Women's University

1966. 80th Anniv of Korean Women's Education.
633 **244** 7w. multicoloured 65 20

1966. 5-Year Plan. Dated "1966". As T **187**.
634 7w. ultramarine and blue . . 1·75 60
635 7w. black and yellow . . . . 1·00 30
DESIGNS: No. 634, Map and transport; 635, Radar aerials and telephone.

246 Wall-eyed Pollack

1966. Korean Fishes. Multicoloured.
637 3w. Type **246** . . . . 1·00 45
638 5w. Lenok . . . . 1·60 45
639 7w. Manchurian croaker . . 1·75 45

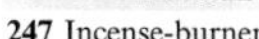
247 Incense-burner

249 Buddha, Kwanchok Temple

1966. As previous issues (some redrawn) and new designs, all inscr "REPUBLIC OF KOREA".
641 **213** 60ch. green 20 10
642 **180** 1w. green . . . . 1·10 10
643 **164** 2w. green 15 10
644 **165** 3w. brown 15 10
645 **181** 5w. blue . . . . 2·00 10
646 **214** 7w. blue . . . . 1·75 10
789 **168** 10w. blue (22 × 18 mm) 3·50 10
647 **247** 13w. blue . . . . 1·90 10
709 **182** 20w. green and light green 6·00 10
710 **183** 40w. green and olive . . . 7·00 10
793 40w. blue and pink (18 × 22 mm) . . . . . 6·50 10
711 **191** 50w. brown and bistre . . 5·75 10
648 – 60w. green . . . . 2·25 10
649 **249** 80w. green . . . . 2·25 10
DESIGN—As Type **247**: 60w. 12th-century porcelain vessel.

250 Children and Hemispheres

1966. 15th Assembly of World Conf of Teaching Profession (WCOTP), Seoul.
650 **250** 7w. violet, brown and blue 45 15

251 Factory within Pouch

1966. Savings Campaign.
652 **251** 7w. multicoloured 45 15

252 People on Map of Korea

1966. National Census.
653 **252** 7w. multicoloured 45 15

253 "Lucida lateralis"

1966. Insects. Multicoloured.
654 3w. Type **253** 90 50
655 5w. "Hexacentrus japonicus" (grasshopper) 90 50
656 7w. "Sericinus montela" (butterfly) . . . . 1·00 50

254 C.I.S.M. Emblem and "Round Table" Meeting

1966. 21st General Assembly of International Military Sports Council (C.I.S.M.), Seoul.
658 **254** 7w. multicoloured 50 15

255 Soldiers and Flags

1966. 1st Anniv of Korean Troops in Vietnam.
660 **255** 7w. multicoloured . . . . 3·00 90

256 Wrestling

1966. 47th Athletic Meeting, Seoul.
661 **256** 7w. multicoloured . . . . 2·00 45

257 Lions Emblem and Map

1966. 5th Orient and South-East Asian Lions Convention, Seoul.
662 **257** 7w. multicoloured 50 15

258 University Emblem, "20" and Shields

1966. 20th Anniv of Seoul University.
664 **258** 7w. multicoloured 40 15

259 A.P.A.C.L. Emblem

1966. 12th Conference of Asian People's Anti-Communist League (A.P.A.C.L.), Seoul.
665 **259** 7w. multicoloured 50 25

260 Presidents Pak and Johnson

261 U.N.E.S.C.O. Symbols and Emblem

1966. President Johnson's Visit to Korea.
667 **260** 7w. multicoloured . . . . 1·00 25
668 83w. multicoloured . . . 5·00 70

1966. 20th Anniv of U.N.E.S.C.O.
670 **261** 7w. multicoloured 55 20

1966. Hurricane Relief. As No. 646 but colour changed and premium added.
672 **214** 7w.+2w. red . . . . . . 1·10 15

262 "Lucky Bag"

263 Eurasian Badger

1966. Christmas and New Year. Multicoloured.
673 5w. Type **262** 45 15
674 7w. Sheep (vert) 45 15

1966. Korean Fauna. Multicoloured.
676 3w. Type **263** . . . . 1·25 25
677 5w. Asiatic black bear . . . 1·25 25
678 7w. Tiger . . . . 1·50 25

264 "Syncom" Satellite

265 Presidents Pak and Lubke

1967. 15th Anniv of Korea's Admission to I.T.U.
680 **264** 7w. multicoloured 70 30

1967. Visit of Pres. Lubke of West Germany to Korea.
682 **265** 7w. multicoloured . . . . 2·00 80

266 Coin, Factories and Houses

267 Okwangdae Mask

1967. 1st Anniv of Korean Revenue Office.
684 **266** 7w. sepia and green . . . 50 25

1967. Folklore. Multicoloured.
685 4w. Type **267** . . . . 1·00 25
686 5w. Sandi mask (horiz) . . . 1·00 25
687 7w. Mafoe mask . . . . . . 1·00 25

268 J.C.I. Emblem and Pavilion

269 Map Emblem

1967. International Junior Chamber of Commerce Conference, Seoul.
689 **268** 7w. multicoloured 50 25

1967. 5th Asian Pacific Dental Congress, Seoul.
691 **269** 7w. multicoloured 55 25

270 Korean Pavilion

271 Worker and Soldier

1967. World Fair, Montreal.
693 **270** 7w. black, red and yellow 1·00 35
694 83w. black, red and blue 6·50 70

1967. Veterans' Day.
696 **271** 7w. multicoloured 50 25

272 Railway Wheel and Rail

1967. 2nd Five Year Plan. Dated "1967".
697 **272** 7w. black, yellow & brown . . . . 2·40 1·10
698 – 7w. orange, brown & black . . . . 1·00 30
DESIGN: No. 698, Nut and bolt.
See also Nos. 773/4, 833/4, 895/6 and 981/2.

273 Sword Dance

1967. Folklore. Multicoloured.
699 4w. Type **273** 85 25
700 5w. Peace dance (vert) . . . 85 25
701 7w. Buddhist dance (vert) . . 1·10 25

274 Soldier and Family

275 President Pak and Phoenix

1967. Fund for Korean Troops Serving in Vietnam.
703 **274** 7w.+3w. black & purple 1·00 15

1967. Inaug of President Pak for 2nd Term.
704 **275** 7w. multicoloured . . . . 4·00 1·00

276 Scout, Badge and Camp

1967. 3rd Korean Scout Jamboree. Multicoloured.
706 7w. Type **276** . . . . 1·00 30
707 20w. Scout badge, bridge and tent . . . . 2·50 50

280 Girls on Swing

1967. Folklore. Multicoloured.
712 4w. Type **280** . . . . 1·00 25
713 5w. Girls on seesaw (vert) . . 1·00 25
714 7w. Girls dancing (vert) . . . 1·40 25

281 Freedom Centre

282 Boxing

1967. 1st World Anti-Communist League Conference, Taipei. Multicoloured.
716 5w. Type **281** 50 25
717 7w. Hand grasping chain (vert) 50 25

1967. National Athletic Meeting, Seoul. Mult.
719 5w. Type **282** . . . . 1·10 25
720 7w. Basketball . . . . 1·10 25

283 Students' Memorial, Kwangjoo

284 Decade Emblem

1967. Students' Day.
721 **283** 7w. multicoloured 50 25

1967. International Hydrological Decade.
722 **284** 7w. multicoloured 50 25

285 Children spinning Top

286 Playing Shuttlecock

1967. Christmas and New Year.
723 **285** 5w. blue, red and pink . . 50 15
724 – 7w. brown, blue and bistre 50 15
DESIGN: 7w. Monkey and Signs of the Zodiac.

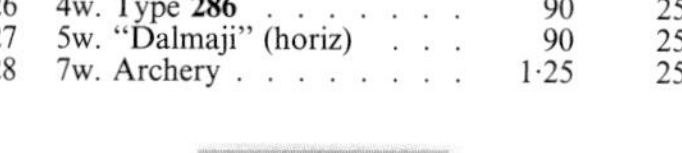
1967. Folklore. Multicoloured.
726 4w. Type **286** 90 25
727 5w. "Dalmaji" (horiz) . . . 90 25
728 7w. Archery . . . . 1·25 25

287 Microwave Transmitter

1967. Inaug of Microwave Telecommunications Service.
730 **287** 7w. black, green and blue 50 25

288 Carving, King Songdok's Bell **289** 5th–6th century Earrings **290** Korean Flag

1968.

732	**288**	1w. brown and yellow	25	10
733	**289**	5w. yellow and green	1·25	10
734	**290**	7w. red and blue	70	10
787		7w. blue	45	10
788		7w. blue*	30	10
790		10w. blue*	60	10

*Nos. 788 and 790 have their face values shown as "7" or "10" only, omitting the noughts shown on Nos. 734 and 787.

For designs similar to Type **290** see Nos. 771, 780 and 827.

291 W.H.O. Emblem **292** E.A.T.A. Emblem and Korean Motif

1968. 20th Anniv of W.H.O.
735 **291** 7w. multicoloured 55 25

1968. 2nd East Asia Travel Association Conference, Seoul.
737 **292** 7w. multicoloured 50 25

293 C.A.C.C.I. Emblem, Korean Doorknocker and Factories

1968. 2nd Conference of Confederation of Asian Chambers of Commerce and Industry (C.A.C.C.I.), Seoul.
739 **293** 7w. multicoloured 50 25

294 Pres. Pak and Emperor Haile Selassie

1968. Visit of Emperor of Ethiopia.
741 **294** 7w. multicoloured 2·00 75

295 Post-bag

1968. Postman's Day. Multicoloured.
743 5w. Type **295** 1·25 50
744 7w. Postman 50 25

296 Atomic and Development Symbols

1968. Promotion of Science and Technology.
745 **296** 7w. blue, green and red 50 25

297 Kyung Hi University and Conference Emblem

1968. 2nd Conf of Int Assn of University Presidents.
746 **297** 7w. multicoloured 50 25

298 "Liberation" **299** Reservist

1968. Liberation of Suppressed Peoples' Campaign.
748 **298** 7w. multicoloured 50 25

1968. Army Reservists' Fund.
749 **299** 7w.+3w. black & green 1·50 30

300 Stylized Peacock **301** Fair Entrance

1968. 20th Anniv of Republic.
750 **300** 7w. multicoloured 60 25

1968. 1st Korean Trade Fair, Seoul.
751 **301** 7w. multicoloured 50 25

302 Assembly Emblem **303** Scout Badge

1968. 3rd General Assembly of Asian Pharmaceutical Association Federation.
752 **302** 7w. multicoloured 50 25

1968. 6th Far East Scout Conference, Seoul.
753 **303** 7w. multicoloured 1·25 25

304 Soldier and Battle Scene **305** Colombo Plan Emblem and Globe

1968. 20th Anniv of Korean Armed Forces.

754	**304**	7w. orange and green	2·00	40
755	–	7w. blue and light blue	2·00	40
756	–	7w. blue and orange	2·00	40
757	–	7w. light blue and blue	2·00	40
758	–	7w. green and orange	2·00	40

DESIGNS: No. 755, Sailor and naval guns; 756, Servicemen and flags; 757, Airman and jet fighters; 758, Marine and landings.

1968. 19th Meeting of Colombo Plan Consultative Committee, Seoul.
759 **305** 7w. multicoloured 50 15

306 (I) Olympic Emblems **307** (II) Olympic Emblems

1968. Olympic Games, Mexico. Multicoloured.

760	7w. Type **306**	2·00	60
761	7w. Type **307**	2·00	60
762	7w. Cycling (I)	2·00	60
763	7w. Cycling (II)	2·00	60
764	7w. Boxing (I)	2·00	60
765	7w. Boxing (II)	2·00	60
766	7w. Wrestling (I)	2·00	60
767	7w. Wrestling (II)	2·00	60

The two types of each design may be identified by the position of the country name at the foot of the design—ranged right in types I, and left in types II. On three of the designs (excluding "Cycling") the figures of value are on left and right respectively. Types I and II of each design were issued together horizontally se-tenant within the sheets of 50 stamps.

308 Statue of Woman **309** Coin and Symbols

1968. 60th Anniv of Women's Secondary Education.
769 **308** 7w. multicoloured 50 20

1968. National Wealth Survey.
770 **309** 7w. multicoloured 50 20

1968. Disaster Relief Fund. As No. 734, but with additional inscr and premium added.
771 **290** 7w.+3w. red and blue 5·00 50

The face value on No. 771 is expressed as "7 00+3 00", see also Nos. 780 and 827.

310 Shin Eui Ju Memorial **311** Demonstrators

1968. Anniv of Student Uprising, Shin Eui Ju (1945).
772 **310** 7w. multicoloured 50 20

1968. 2nd Five Year Plan. As T **272**. Dated "1968". Multicoloured.
773 7w. Express motorway 60 25
774 7w. "Clover-leaf" road junction 60 25

1968. Human Rights Year.
775 **311** 7w. multicoloured 50 20

312 Christmas Lanterns **314** Korean House and U.N. Emblems

1968. Christmas and New Year. Multicoloured.
776 5w. Type **312** 75 10
777 7w. Cockerel 75 10

1968. 20th Anniv of South Korea's Admission to U.N.
779 **314** 7w. multicoloured 50 20

1969. Military Helicopter Fund. As No. 734 but colours changed and inscr with premium added.
780 **290** 7w.+3w. red, blue & grn 1·25 40

315 Torch and Monument, Pagoda Park, Seoul **316** Hyun Choong Sa and "Turtle" Ships

1969. 50th Anniv of Samil (Independence) Movement.
781 **315** 7w. multicoloured 60 25

1969. Dedication of Rebuilt Hyun Choong Sa (Shrine of Admiral Li Sun Sin).
782 **316** 7w. multicoloured 80 25

317 President Pak and Yang di-Pertuan Agong **318** Stone Temple Lamp

1969. Visit of Yang di-Pertuan Agong (Malaysian Head-of-State).
783 **317** 7w. multicoloured 2·00 75

1969.

786	**318**	5w. purple	50	10
791	–	20w. green	1·50	10
792	–	30w. green	2·25	10
794	–	40w. mauve and blue	1·75	10
795	–	100w. brown and purple	28·00	10

DESIGNS—As Type **318**. VERT: 20w. Wine jug; 40w. Porcelain Jar, Yi Dynasty; 100w. Seated Buddha (bronze). HORIZ: 30w. "Duck" vase.

323 "Red Cross" between Faces **324** "Building the Nation's Economy"

1969. 50th Anniv of League of Red Cross Societies.
796 **323** 7w. multicoloured 85 20

1969. "Second Economy Drive".
798 **324** 7w. multicoloured 40 15

325 Presidents Pak and Nguyen van Thieu

1969. Visit of President Nguyen van Thieu of South Vietnam.
799 **325** 7w. multicoloured 2·00 65

326 Reafforestation and Flooded Fields **327** Ignition of Second-stage Rocket

1969. Flood and Drought Damage Prevention Campaign. Multicoloured.
801 7w. Type **326** 60 25
802 7w. Withered and flourishing plants 60 25

1969. First Man on the Moon.

803	**327**	10w. blue, black and red	1·50	50
804	–	10w. blue, black and red	1·50	50
805	–	20w. multicoloured	1·50	50
806	–	20w. multicoloured	1·50	50
807	–	40w. blue, red and black	1·50	50

DESIGNS: No. 804, Separation of modules from rocket; 805, Diagram of lunar orbit; 806, Astronauts on Moon; 807, Splashdown of "Apollo 11".

328 Stepmother admonishing Kongji **332** Steam Locomotive of 1899

1969. Korean Fairy Tales (1st series). "Kongji and Patji". Multicoloured.

809	5w. Type **328**	65	25
810	7w. Kongji and sparrows	75	25
811	10w. Kongji and ox	1·10	40
812	20w. Kongji in sedan-chair	1·25	40

See also Nos. 828/31, 839/42, 844/7 and 853/6.

1969. 70th Anniv of Korean Railways. Multicoloured.
814 7w. Type **332** 1·50 50
815 7w. Early steam and modern diesel locomotives 1·50 50

333 Northrop F-5A Freedom Jet Fighters

1969. 20th Anniv of Korean Air Force. Multicoloured.
816 10w. Type **333** 1·25 25
817 10w. McDonnell-Douglas F-4D Phantom II jet fighter 1·25 25

334 Game of Cha-jun

1969. 10th Korean Traditional Arts Contest, Taegu.
818 **334** 7w. multicoloured 60 15

335 Molecule and Institute Building

1969. Completion of Korean Institute of Science and Technology.
819 **335** 7w. multicoloured 60 15

336 Presidents Pak and Hamani

1969. Visit of President Hamani of Niger Republic.
820 **336** 7w. multicoloured . . . . 1·25 40

337 Football **342** Students ringing "Education"

1969. 50th Anniv of National Athletic Meeting. Multicoloured.
822 10w. Type **337** . . . . 1·10 40
823 10w. Volleyball . . . . . . 1·10 40
824 10w. Korean wrestling (horiz) 1·10 40
825 10w. Fencing (horiz) . . . . 1·10 40
826 10w. Taekwondo (karate) (horiz) . . . . 1·10 40

1969. Searchlight Fund. As T **290** but with additional inscr and premium. Face value expressed as "7+3".
827 7w.+3w. red and blue 80 25

1969. Korean Fairy Tales (2nd series). "The Hare's Liver". As T **328**. Multicoloured.
828 5w. Princess and Doctors . . 65 30
829 7w. Hare arriving at Palace 70 30
830 10w. Preparing to remove the Hare's liver . . . . 1·10 40
831 20w. Escape of the Hare . . 1·25 40

1969. 2nd Five-year Plan. As T **272**. Dated "1969". Multicoloured.
833 7w. "Agriculture and Fisheries" 75 40
834 7w. Industrial emblems . . . 50 15

1969. 1st Anniv of National Education Charter.
835 **342** 7w. multicoloured 50 15

343 Toy Dogs **344** Woman with Letter and U.P.U. Monument, Berne

1969. Lunar New Year ("Year of the Dog"). Multicoloured.
836 5w. Type **343** 60 25
837 7w. Candle and lattice doorway 60 25

1970. 70th Anniv of Korea's Admission to U.P.U.
838 **344** 10w. multicoloured . . . 3·00 70

1970. Korean Fairy Tales (3rd series). "The Sun and the Moon". As T **328**. Multicoloured.
839 5w. Mother meets the tiger 65 25
840 7w. Tiger in disguise 70 25
841 10w. Children chased up a tree . . . . 1·10 40
842 20w. Children escape to Heaven . . . . 1·25 40

1970. Korean Fairy Tales (4th series). "The Woodcutter and the Fairy". As T **328**. Mult.
844 10w. Woodcutter hiding Fairy's dress . . . . 1·10 40
845 10w. Fairy as Woodcutter's Wife . . . . 1·10 40
846 10w. Fairy and children fly to Heaven . . . . 1·10 40
847 10w. Happy reunion . . . . 1·10 40

353 I.E.Y. Emblem on Open Book **354** Seated Buddha and Korean Pavilion

1970. International Education Year.
849 **353** 10w. multicoloured . . . 3·00 70

1970. "EXPO 70" World Fair, Osaka, Japan.
850 **354** 10w. multicoloured . . . 2·25 60

355 "4-11" Club Emblem **356** Bank Emblem and Cash

1970. 15th "4-11" Club (young farmers' organization) Central Contest, Suwon.
851 **355** 10w. multicoloured . . . 80 30

1970. 3rd General Meeting of Asian Development Bank, Seoul.
852 **356** 10w. multicoloured . . . 80 30

1970. Korean Fairy Tales (5th series). "Heungbu and Nolbu". As T **328**. Multicoloured.
853 10w. Heungbu tending swallow . . . . 1·00 25
854 10w. Heungbu finds treasure in pumpkin . . . . 1·00 25
855 10w. Nolbu with pumpkin . . 1·00 25
856 10w. Nolbu chased by devil 1·00 25

361 Royal Palanquin (Yi dynasty) **362** New Headquarters Building

1970. Early Korean Transport.
858 **361** 10w. multicoloured . . . 1·00 25
859 – 10w. multicoloured . . . 2·25 85
860 – 10w. multicoloured . . . 1·00 25
861 – 10w. black, stone and blue . . . . 1·25 25
DESIGNS—HORIZ: No. 859, Tramcar, 1899; 860, Emperor Sunjong's cadillac, 1903; 861, An Chang Nam's Nieuport 28 biplane, 1922.

1970. Opening of New U.P.U. Headquarters Building, Berne.
862 **362** 10w. multicoloured . . . 70 30

363 Dish Aerial and Hemispheres

1970. Inauguration of Satellite Communications Station, Kum San.
863 **363** 10w. multicoloured . . . 1·10 30

364 "PEN" and Quill Pen **366** Postal Code Symbol

365 Section of Motorway

1970. 37th International P.E.N. (literary organization) Congress, Seoul.
864 **364** 10w. multicoloured . . . 70 25

1970. Opening of Seoul–Pusan Motorway.
865 **365** 10w. multicoloured . . . 1·25 30

1970. Introduction of Postal Codes.
866 **366** 10w. multicoloured . . . 60 25

367 Parcel Sorting Area **368** Children's Hall and Boy

1970. Inauguration of Postal Mechanization.
867 **367** 10w. multicoloured . . . 60 25

1970. Opening of Children's Hall, Seoul.
869 **368** 10w. multicoloured . . . 60 30

369 "Mountain and River" (Yi In Moon)

1970. Korean Paintings of Yi Dynasty (1st series). Multicoloured.
870 10w. Type **369** . . . . . . 1·25 30
871 10w. "Jongyangsa Temple" (Chong Son) . . . . . . 1·25 30
872 10w. "Mountain and River by Moonlight" (Kim Doo Ryang) (vert) . . . . . . 1·25 30
See also Nos. 887/89, 897/899, 947/52, 956/8 and 961/5.

370 P.T.T.I. Emblem **371** WAC and Corps Badge

1970. Councillors' Meeting, Asian Chapter of Postal, Telegraph and Telephone International (Post Office Trade Union Federation).
874 **370** 10w. multicoloured . . . 55 25

1970. 20th Anniv of Korean Women's Army Corps.
875 **371** 10w. multicoloured . . . 60 25

372 Pres. Pak and Flag

1970.
876 **372** 10w. multicoloured . . . 3·75 55
877 – 10w. black, green and blue . . . . 2·75 50
DESIGN—VERT: No. 877, Pres. Pak and industrial complex.

373 Presidents Pak and Sanchez Hernandez

1970. Visit of Pres. Sanchez Hernandez of El Salvador.
878 **373** 10w. multicoloured . . . 2·00 60

374 "People and Houses"

1970. National Census.
880 **374** 10w. multicoloured . . . 90 25

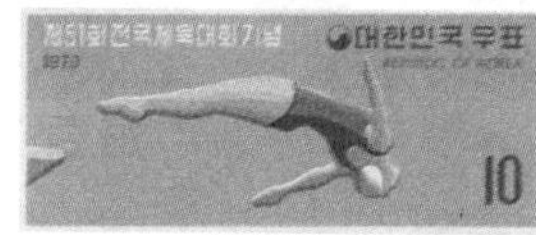

375 Diving

1970. 51st National Athletic Games, Seoul.
881 10w. Type **375** . . . . 1·40 50
882 10w. Hockey . . . . 1·40 50
883 10w. Baseball . . . . 1·40 50

376 Police Badge and Activities **377** Bell and Globe

1970. National Police Day.
885 **376** 10w. multicoloured . . . 1·00 30

1970. 25th Anniv of United Nations.
886 **377** 10w. multicoloured . . . 75 30

1970. Korean Paintings of the Yi Dynasty (2nd series). Vert designs at T **369**, showing animals. Multicoloured.
887 30w. "Fierce Tiger" (Shim Sa Yung) . . . . 2·50 75
888 30w. "Cats and Sparrows" (Pyun Sang Byuk) . . . . 2·50 75
889 30w. "Dog with Puppies" (Yi Am) . . . . 2·50 75

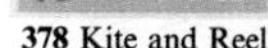

378 Kite and Reel **380** Fields ("Food Production")

379 Quotation and Emblems on Globe

1970. Lunar New Year ("Year of the Pig"). Multicoloured.
891 10w. Type **378** 65 20
892 10w. Toy pig 65 20

1970. 15th Communications Day.
894 **379** 10w. multicoloured . . . 65 30

1970. 2nd Five Year Plan. At T **272**. Dated "1970". Multicoloured.
895 10w. "Port Development" . . 50 20
896 10w. "House Construction" 50 20

1970. Korean Paintings of the Yi Dynasty (3rd series). Vert designs as T **369**. Multicoloured.
897 10w. "Chokpyokdo" (river cliff) (Kim Hong Do) . . . 1·75 30
898 10w. "Hen and Chicks" (Pyn Sang Byuk) . . . . 1·75 30
899 10w. "The Flute-player" (Shin Yun Bok) . . . . . 1·75 30

1971. Economic Development (1st series). Mult.
901 10w. Type **380** 65 30
902 10w. Dam ("Electric Power") (horiz) 65 30
903 10w. Map on crate ("Exports") (horiz) 65 30
See also Nos. 905/7 and 910/12.

381 Coal-mining **382** Globe, Torch and Spider

1971. Economic Development (2nd series). Mult.
905 10w. Type **381** . . . . 1·10 40
906 10w. Cement works (vert) . . 60 20
907 10w. Fertilizer plant 60 20

1971. Anti-espionage Month.
909 **382** 10w. multicoloured . . . 70 20

383 Motorway Junction **384** Reservist and Badge

1971. Economic Develepment (3rd series). Mult.
910 10w. Type **383** 60 20
911 10w. Scales ("Gross National Income") (horiz) 60 20
912 10w. Bee and coins ("Increased Savings") (horiz) 60 20

1971. 3rd Home Reserve Forces Day.
914 **384** 10w. multicoloured . . . 1·00 30

385 W.H.O. Emblem, Stethoscope and Microscope **386** Underground Train

1971. 20th World Health Day.
915 **385** 10w. multicoloured . . . 50 30

1971. Construction of Seoul Underground Railway System.
916 **386** 10w. multicoloured . . . 1·10 20

387 Footballer **388** Veteran and Association Flag

1971. 1st Asian Soccer Games, Seoul.
917 **387** 10w. multicoloured . . . 1·40 40

1971. 20th Korean Veterans' Day.
918 **388** 10w. multicoloured . . . 50 20

389 Girl Scouts **390** Torch and Economic Symbols

1971. 25th Anniv of Korean Girl Scouts Federation.
919 **389** 10w. multicoloured . . . 55 20

1971. 10th Anniv of May 16th Revolution.
920 **390** 10w. multicoloured . . . 50 20

391 "Tele-communications" **392** F.A.O. Emblem

1971. 3rd World Telecommunications Day.
921 **391** 10w. multicoloured . . . 50 20

1971. "The Work of the United Nations Organization".
922 – 10w. mauve, black & green . . . . 1·50 50
923 **392** 10w. blue, black and mauve . . . . 1·50 50
924 – 10w. multicoloured . . . 1·50 50
925 – 10w. blue, black and mauve . . . . 1·50 50
926 – 10w. mauve, black & green . . . . 1·50 50
927 – 10w. blue, black and mauve . . . . 1·50 50
928 – 10w. mauve, black and blue . . . . 1·50 50
929 – 10w. black, green & mauve . . . . 1·50 50
930 – 10w. mauve, black and blue . . . . 1·50 50
931 – 10w. blue, black and mauve . . . . 1·50 50
932 – 10w. mauve, black and blue . . . . 1·50 50
933 – 10w. black, mauve & green . . . . 1·50 50
934 – 10w. mauve, blue and black . . . . 1·50 50
935 – 10w. black, mauve & green . . . . 1·50 50
936 – 10w. mauve, black and blue . . . . 1·50 50
937 – 10w. blue, black and mauve . . . . 1·50 50
938 – 10w. mauve, black and blue . . . . 1·50 50
939 – 10w. black, mauve & green . . . . 1·50 50
940 – 10w. mauve, black and blue . . . . 1·50 50
941 – 10w. blue, black and mauve . . . . 1·50 50
942 – 10w. mauve, black & green . . . . 1·50 50
943 – 10w. black, blue and mauve . . . . 1·50 50
944 – 10w. multicoloured . . . 1·50 50
945 – 10w. black, blue and mauve . . . . 1·50 50
946 – 10w. black, mauve & green . . . . 1·50 50

EMBLEMS: No. 992, I.L.O.; 924, General Assembly and New York Headquarters; 925, U.N.E.S.C.O.; 926, W.H.O.; 927, World Bank; 928, International Development Association; 929, Security Council; 930, International Finance Corporation; 931, International Monetary Fund; 932, International Civil Aviation Organization; 933, Economic and Social Council; 934, South Korean flag; 935, Trusteeship Council; 936, U.P.U.; 937, I.T.U.; 938, World Meteorological Organization; 939, Int Court of Justice; 940, I.M.C.O.; 941, U.N.I.C.E.F.; 942, International Atomic Energy Agency; 943, United Nations Industrial Development Organization; 944, United Nations Commission for the Unification and Rehabilitation of Korea; 945, United Nations Development Programme; 946, United Nations Conference on Trade and Development.

393 "Boating" (Shin Yun Bok)

1971. Korean Paintings of the Yi Dynasty (4th series). Multicoloured.
947 10w. Type **393** . . . . 2·75 75
948 10w. "Greeting Travellers" 2·75 75
949 10w. "Tea Ceremony" . . . 2·75 75
950 10w. "Lady and Servants on Country Road" . . . . . 2·75 75
951 10w. "Couple Walking" . . . 2·75 75
952 10w. "Fairy and Boy beneath Pine Tree" (Li Chae Kwan) (vert) . . . . 2·75 75
Nos. 947/51 show "Folk Customs" paintings by Shin Yun Bok.

394 Pres. Pak, Emblem and Motorway **395** Campfire and Badge

1971. Re-election of Pres. Pak for 3rd Term.
954 **394** 10w. multicoloured . . . 2·00 1·00

1971. Korean Paintings of the Yi Dynasty (5th series). As T **393**. Multicoloured.
956 10w. "Chasing the Cat" (Kim Deuk Shin) . . . . 2·00 50
957 10w. "Valley Family" (Li Chae Kwan) (vert) . . . . 2·00 50
958 10w. "Man Reading" (Li Chae Kwan) (vert) . . . . 2·00 50

1971. 13th World Scout Jamboree, Asagiri, Japan.
960 **395** 10w. multicoloured . . . 55 20

1971. Korean Paintings of the Yi Dynasty (6th series). As T **393** but vert. Multicoloured.
961 10w. "Classroom" . . . . . 2·50 85
962 10w. "Wrestling Match" . . 2·50 85
963 10w. "Dancer with Musicians" . . . . 2·50 85
964 10w. "Weavers" . . . . . . 2·50 85
965 10w. "Drawing Water at the Well" . . . . 2·50 85
Nos. 961/5 depict genre paintings by Kim Hong Do.

396 Cogwheel and Asian Map

1971. 3rd Asian Labour Minister's Conference, Seoul.
967 **396** 10w. multicoloured . . . 50 20

397 Judo

1971. 52nd National Athletic Meeting, Seoul. Multicoloured.
969 10w. Type **397** . . . . 1·25 40
970 10w. Archery . . . . 1·25 40

398 Korean Symbol on Palette

1971. 20th National Fine Art Exhibition.
972 **398** 10w. multicoloured . . . 50 20

399 Doctor and Globe **400** Emblems and "Vocational Skills"

1971. 7th Congress of Medical Associations from Asia and Oceania.
973 **399** 10w. multicoloured . . . 55 20

1971. 2nd National Vocational Skill Contest for High School Students.
974 **400** 10w. multicoloured . . . 50 20

401 Callipers and "K" Emblem

1971. 10th Anniv of Industrial Standardisation.
976 **401** 10w. multicoloured . . . 50 20

402 Fairy Tale Rats **403** Emblem and Hangul Alphabet

1971. Lunar New Year ("Year of the Rat"). Multicoloured.
977 10w. Type **402** . . . . 1·00 50
978 10w. Flying crane . . . . . 1·00 50

1971. 50th Anniv of Hangul Hakhoe (Korean Language Research Society).
980 **403** 10w. multicoloured . . . 50 20

1971. 2nd Five Year Plan. As T **272**. Dated "1971". Multicoloured.
981 10w. Atomic power plant . . 60 20
982 10w. Hydro-electric power project 65 20

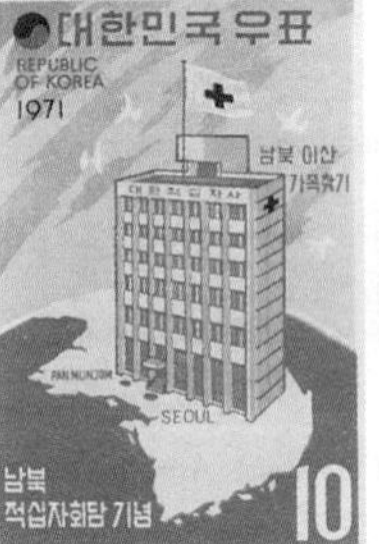

404 Korean Red Cross Building on Map **405** Globe and Open Book

1971. South–North Korean Red Cross Conference, Panmunjom.
983 **404** 10w. multicoloured . . . 1·00 30

1971. International Book Year.
985 **405** 10w. multicoloured . . . 60 20

406 "Intelsat 4" and Korean Earth Station **407** Speed Skating

1971. 20th Anniv of Korea's Membership of I.T.U.
987 **406** 10w. multicoloured . . . 50 20

1972. Winter Olympic Games, Sapporo, Japan. Multicoloured.
988 10w. Type **407** . . . . 1·00 30
989 10w. Figure-skating . . . . 1·00 30

408 Forestry Map **410** E.C.A.F.E. Emblem and Industrial Symbols

409 Scarab Beetles and Emblem

1972. "Trees for Unity" Campaign.
991 **408** 10w. multicoloured . . . 50 20

1972. 20th Anniv of Korean Junior Chamber of Commerce.
992 **409** 10w. multicoloured . . . 70 20

1972. 25th Anniv of U.N. Economic Commission for Asia and the Far East.
993 **410** 10w. multicoloured . . . 55 20

411 Flags of Member Countries

412 Reserve Forces' Flag

1972. 10th Anniv of Asian and Oceanic Postal Union.
994 **411** 10w. multicoloured . . . 50 20

1972. Home Reserve Forces Day.
995 **412** 10w. multicoloured . . . 1·00 30

413 Emblem and "Terias harina"

414 Rural Activities

1972. 50th Anniv of Korean Young Women's Christian Association.
996 **413** 10w. multicoloured . . . 1·75 50

1972. "New Community" (rural development) Movement.
997 **414** 10w. multicoloured . . . 50 20

415 "Anti-Espionage" and Korean Flag

416 Children with Balloons

1972. Anti-Espionage Month.
998 **415** 10w. multicoloured . . . 50 20

1972. 50th Children's Day.
999 **416** 10w. multicoloured . . . 50 20

417 Leaf Ornament from Gold Crown

418 Lake Paengnokdam, Mt. Halla Park

419 Kalkot, Koje Island, Hanryo Straits Park

1972. Treasures from King Munyong's Tomb. Multicoloured.
1000 10w. Type **417** 60 20
1001 10w. Gold earrings (horiz) 65 20

1972. National Parks (1st series).
1002 **418** 10w. multicoloured . . . 75 40
1003 **419** 10w. multicoloured . . . 75 40
See also Nos. 1018/19 and 1026/7.

420 Marguerite and Conference Emblem

421 Gwanghwa Gate and National Flags

1972. U.N. Environmental Conservation Conference, Stockholm.
1004 **420** 10w. multicoloured . . . 45 20

1972. 7th Asian and Pacific Council (ASPAC) Ministerial Meeting, Seoul.
1006 **421** 10w. multicoloured . . . 60 25

422 Pasture ("Development of Rural Economy")

423 "Love Pin"

1972. 3rd Five Year Plan. Dated "1972". Multicoloured.
1007 10w. Type **422** 60 25
1008 10w. Foundry ladle ("Heavy Industries") 60 25
1009 10w. Crate and Globe ("Increased Exports") . . 60 25

1972. Disaster Relief Fund.
1010 **423** 10w.+5w. red and blue 75 20

424 Judo

425 Family Reunion through Red Cross

1972. Olympic Games, Munich. Multicoloured.
1011 20w. Type **424** 75 20
1012 20w. Weightlifting 75 20
1013 20w. Wrestling 75 20
1014 20w. Boxing 75 20

1972. 1st Plenary Meeting of South–North Korean Red Cross Conference, Pyongyang.
1016 **425** 10w. multicoloured . . . 1·25 35

426 Bulkuk Temple, Kyongju Park

428 Conference Emblem within "5"

427 Statue and Bopju Temple, Mt. Sokri Park

1972. National Parks (2nd series).
1018 **426** 10w. multicoloured . . . 75 40
1019 **427** 10w. multicoloured . . . 75 40

1972. 5th Asian Judicial Conference, Seoul.
1020 **428** 10w. multicoloured . . . 55 20

429 Lions Badge between Korean Emblems

1972. 11th Orient and South-East Asian Lions Convention, Seoul.
1021 **429** 10w. multicoloured . . . 50 20

430 Scout taking Oath

431 Dolls and Ox's Head

1972. 50th Anniv of Korean Boy Scouts Movement.
1022 **430** 10w. multicoloured . . . 1·00 25

1972. Lunar New Year ("Year of the Ox"). Multicoloured.
1023 10w. Type **431** 60 20
1024 10w. Revellers in balloon . . 60 20

432 Temple, Mt. Naejang Park

433 Madeungryong Pass, Mt. Sorak Park

1972. National Parks (3rd series).
1026 **432** 10w. multicoloured . . . 75 40
1027 **433** 10w. multicoloured . . . 75 40

434 President Pak, Flag and "Development"

1972. Re-election of President Pak.
1028 **434** 10w. multicoloured . . . 2·00 65

435 National Central Museum, Kyongbok Palace

437 Korean Family

436 Temple, Mt. Sorak

1973. Korean Tourist Attractions (1st series).
1030 **435** 10w. multicoloured . . . 75 15
1031 **436** 10w. multicoloured . . . 75 15
See also Nos. 1042/3, 1048/9, 1057/8 and 1075/6.

1973. Korean Unification Campaign.
1032 **437** 10w. multicoloured . . . 50 15

438 "V" Sign and Flags

439 Construction Workers and Cogwheel

1973. Return of Korean Forces from South Vietnam.
1033 **438** 10w. multicoloured . . . 60 20

1973. 10th Workers' Day.
1034 **439** 10w. multicoloured . . . 50 15

440 W.M.O. Emblem and Satellite

442 Wonsam Costume (woman's ceremonial)

1973. Centenary of World Meteorological Organization.
1035 **440** 10w. multicoloured . . . 50 15

1973. Korean Court Costumes of the Yi Dynasty (1st series). Multicoloured. Background colours given.
1037 – 10w. orange . . . . . . 1·10 30
1038 **442** 10w. orange . . . . . . 1·10 30
DESIGN: No. 1037, Kujangbok (king's ceremonial costume).
See also Nos. 1045/6, 1053/4, 1060/1 and 1078/9.

443 Nurse with Lamp

444 Reservists and Flag

1973. 50th Anniv of Korean Nurses' Association.
1040 **443** 10w. multicoloured . . . 65 15

1973. Home Reserve Forces Day.
1041 **444** 10w. multicoloured . . . 75 30

445 Palmi Island

446 Sain-am Rock, Mt. Dokjol

1973. Korean Tourist Attractions (2nd series).
1042 **445** 10w. multicoloured . . . 75 25
1043 **446** 10w. multicoloured . . . 75 25

447 Table Tennis Player

1973. Victory of South Korean Women's Team in World Table Tennis Championships, Sarajevo.
1044 **447** 10w. multicoloured . . . 1·25 30

1973. Korean Court Costumes of the Yi Dynasty (2nd series). As T **442**. Mult. Background colours given.
1045 10w. purple 80 15
1046 10w. green 80 15
DESIGNS: No. 1045, Konryongpo (king's costume); 1046, Jokui (queen's ceremonial costume).

450 Admiral Li Sun Sin's Shrine, Asan

451 Limestone Cavern, Kusan-ni

1973. Korean Tourist Attractions (3rd series).
1048 **450** 10w. multicoloured . . . 80 25
1049 **451** 10w. multicoloured . . . 80 25

452 Children's Choir

1973. 20th Anniv of World Vision Int.
1050 **452** 10w. multicoloured . . . 75 25

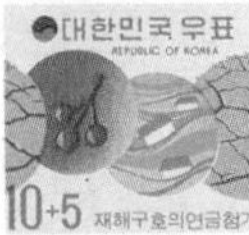
453 Love Pin and "Disasters"

1973. Disaster Relief Fund.
1051 **453** 10w.+5w. mult 45 15

454 Steel Converter

457 Table Tennis Bat and Ball

1973. Inauguration of Pohang Steel Works.
1052 **454** 10w. multicoloured . . . 50 15

1973. Korean Court Costumes of the Yi Dynasty (3rd series). As T **442**. Mult. Background colours given.
1053 10w. blue . . . . 1·25 15
1054 10w. pink . . . . 1·25 15
DESIGNS: No. 1053, Kangsapo (crown prince's) costume; 1054, Tangui (princess's) costume.

1973. Table Tennis Gymnasium Construction Fund.
1056 **457** 10w.+5w. mauve & grn 75 20

458 Namhae Suspension Bridge

459 Hongdo Island

1973. Korean Tourist Attractions (4th series).
1057 **458** 10w. multicoloured . . . 55 10
1058 **459** 10w. multicoloured . . . 55 10

460 Interpol and Korean Police Emblems

1973. 50th Anniv of International Criminal Police Organization (Interpol).
1059 **460** 10w. multicoloured . . . 65 10

1973. Korean Court Costumes of the Yi Dynasty (4th series). As T **442**. Mult. Background colours given.
1060 10w. yellow 75 10
1061 10w. blue 75 10
DESIGNS: No. 1060, Kumkwanchobok (court official's) costume; 1061, Hwalot (queen's wedding) costume.

465 Manchurian Cranes

466 Sommal Lily

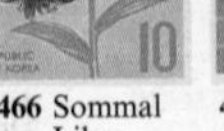
467 Motorway and Farm

1973.
1063 – 1w. brown 40 10
1063a – 3w. black and blue . . 25 10
1064 – 5w. brown 10 10
1064a – 6w. turquoise and green 30 10
1065 **465** 10w. ultramarine & blue 80 10
1066 **466** 10w. red, black & green 75 10
1067 **467** 10w. green and red . . 50 10
1068 – 30w. brown and yellow 65 10
1068a – 50w. green and brown 50 10
1068b – 60w. brown and yellow 50 10
1068c – 80w. black and brown 75 10
1069 – 100w. yellow and brown . . . . 15·00 40
1069a – 100w. red . . . . . . 1·00 15
1069b – 200w. brown and pink 1·40 20
1069c – 300w. red and lilac . . 2·00 25
1069d – 500w. multicoloured . . 10·00 30
1069e – 500w. purple and brown . . . . 4·00 25
1069f – 1000w. green . . . . . 5·00 60
DESIGNS—VERT: 1w. Mask of old man; 5w. Siberian chipmunk; 6w. Lily; 30w. Honey bee; 50w. Pot with lid; 60w. Jar; 100w. (No. 1069) Gold Crown, Silla dynasty; 100w. (No. 1069a) Admiral Yi Soon Shin; 300w. Pobjusa Temple; 500w. (No. 1069d) Gold Crown; 500w. (No. 1069e) Carved dragon (tile Backje Dynasty). LARGER 24 × 33 mm: 100w. Flying deities (relief from bronze bell, Sangweon Temple). HORIZ: 3w. Black-billed magpie; 80w. Ceramic horseman; 200w. Muryangsujeon Hall, Busok Temple.
For designs similar to Type **465** but with frame, see Type **703**.

470 Tennis

1973. 54th National Athletic Meeting, Pusan. Multicoloured.
1070 10w. Type **470** 65 15
1071 10w. Hurdling 65 15

471 Children with Stamp Albums

1973. Philatelic Week.
1072 **471** 10w. multicoloured . . . 40 10

472 Soyang River Dam

1973. Inauguration of Soyang River Dam.
1074 **472** 10w. multicoloured . . . 40 10

473 Mt. Mai, Chinan

474 Tangerine Grove, Cheju Island

1973. Korean Tourist Attractions (5th series).
1075 **473** 10w. multicoloured . . . 50 10
1076 **474** 10w. multicoloured . . . 50 10

475 Match, Cigarette and Flames

478 Tiger and Candles

1973. 10th Fire Prevention Day.
1077 **475** 10w. multicoloured . . . 40 10

1973. Korean Court Costumes of the Yi Dynasty (5th series). As T **442**. Mult. Background colours given.
1078 10w. orange 75 10
1079 10w. pink 75 10
DESIGNS: No. 1078, Pyongsangbok (official's wife) costume; 1079, Kokunbok (military officer's) costume.

1973. Lunar New Year ("Year of the Tiger"). Multicoloured.
1081 10w. Type **478** 75 10
1082 10w. Decorated top 75 10

479 Korean Girl and Flame Emblem

1973. 25th Anniv of Declaration of Human Rights.
1084 **479** 10w. multicoloured . . . 40 10

480 Boeing 747-200 Jetliner and Polar Zone

1973. Air.
1085 **480** 110w. blue and pink . . 3·00 30
1086 – 135w. red and green . . 3·00 30
1087 – 145w. red and blue . . . 3·00 30
1088 – 180w. yellow and lilac 3·00 30
DESIGNS—Boeing 747-200 jetliner and postal zones on map: 135w. South-east Asia; 145w. India, Australasia and North America; 180w. Europe, Africa and South America.

481 "Komunko" (zither)

1974. Traditional Musical Instruments (1st series). Multicoloured. Background colours given.
1089 **481** 10w. blue . . . . 1·00 10
1090 – 30w. orange . . . . . . 1·00 40
DESIGN: 30w. "Nagak" (trumpet triton).
See also Nos. 1098/9, 1108/9, 1117/18 and 1132/3.

483 Apricots

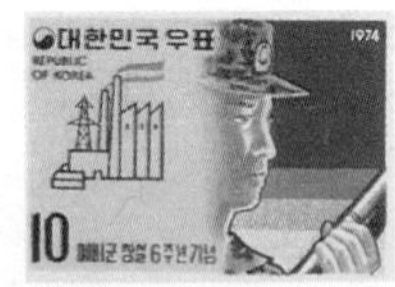
485 Reservist and Factory

1974. Fruits (1st series). Multicoloured.
1092 10w. Type **483** 30 10
1093 30w. Strawberries 60 15
See also Nos. 1104/5, 1111/2, 1120/1 and 1143/4.

1974. Home Reserve Forces Day.
1095 **485** 10w. multicoloured . . . 30 10

486 W.P.Y. Emblem

489 Diesel Mail Train and Communications Emblem

1974. World Population Year.
1096 **486** 10w. multicoloured . . . 25 10

1974. Traditional Musical Instruments (2nd series). As T **481**. Multicoloured. Background colours given.
1098 10w. blue 75 10
1099 30w. green . . . . 1·50 15
DESIGNS: 10w. "Tchouk"; 30w. "Eu".

1974. Communications Day.
1101 **489** 10w. multicoloured . . . 75 15

490 C.A.F.E.A.-I.C.C. Emblem on Globe

491 Port Installations

1974. 22nd Session of International Chamber of Commerce's Commission on Asian and Far Eastern Affairs, Seoul.
1102 **490** 10w. multicoloured . . . 30 10

1974. Inaug of New Port Facilities, Inchon.
1103 **491** 10w. multicoloured . . . 40 10

1974. Fruits (2nd series). As T **483**. Mult.
1104 10w. Peaches 40 10
1105 30w. Grapes 60 15

494 U.N.E.S.C.O. Emblem and Extended Fan

499 Cross and Emblems

1974. 20th Anniv of South Korean U.N.E.S.C.O. Commission.
1107 **494** 10w. multicoloured . . . 30 10

1974. Traditional Musical Instruments (3rd series). As T **481**. Multicoloured. Background colours given.
1108 10w. orange 65 10
1109 30w. pink . . . . 1·25 15
DESIGNS: 10w. "A-chaing" (stringed instrument); 30w. "Kyobang-ko" (drum).

1974. Fruits (3rd series). As T **483**. Multicoloured.
1111 10w. Pears 40 10
1112 30w. Apples 60 15

1974. "Explo 74" 2nd International Training Congress on Evangelism. Multicoloured.
1114 10w. Type **499** 30 10
1115 10w. Emblem and Korean map on Globe 30 10

501 Underground Train

1974. Opening of Seoul Underground Railway.
1116 **501** 10w. multicoloured . . . 85 10

1974. Traditional Musical Instruments (4th series). As T **481**. Multicoloured. Background colours given.
1117 10w. blue 65 10
1118 30w. pink . . . . 1·10 15
DESIGNS: No. 1117, So ("Pan pipes"); 1118, Haikem (Two-stringed fiddle).

1974. Fruits (4th series). As T **483**. Multicoloured.
1120 10w. Cherries 40 10
1121 30w. Persimmons 60 10

506 Rifle Shooting

1974. 55th National Athletic Meeting, Seoul. Multicoloured.
1123 10w. Type **506** 30 10
1124 30w. Rowing 80 10

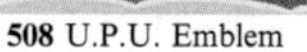

508 U.P.U. Emblem

509 Symbols of Member Countries

1974. Centenary of U.P.U.
1125 **508** 10w. multicoloured (postage) 30 10
1126 110w. multicoloured (air) 1·25 50

1974. 1st World Conference of People to People International.
1128 **509** 10w. multicoloured . . . 30 10

510 Korean Stamps of 1884

1974. Philatelic Week and 90th Anniv of First Korean Stamps.
1129 **510** 10w. multicoloured . . . 50 10

511 Taekwondo Contestants

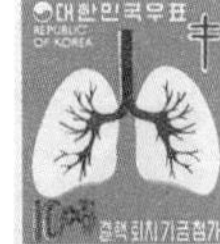

514 Lungs

1974. 1st Asian Taekwondo Championships, Seoul.
1131 **511** 10w. multicoloured . . . 50 10

1974. Traditional Musical Instruments (5th series). As T **481**. Multicoloured. Background colours given.
1132 10w. pink 50 10
1133 30w. ochre 75 15
DESIGNS: 10w. Pak (clappers); 30w. Pyenchong (chimes).

1974. Tuberculosis Control Fund.
1135 **514** 10w.+5w. red & green 40 10

515 Presidents Pak and Ford

516 Yook Young Soo (wife of Pres. Pak)

1974. State Visit of President Ford of United States.
1136 **515** 10w. multicoloured . . . 55 20

1974. Yook Young Soo Memorial Issue.
1138 **516** 10w. green 50 15
1139 10w. orange 50 15
1140 10w. violet 50 15
1141 10w. blue 50 15

1974. Fruits (5th series). As T **483**. Multicoloured.
1143 10w. Tangerines 40 10
1144 30w. Chestnuts 50 15

519 "Good Luck" Purse

521 U.P.U. Emblem and "75"

1974. Lunar New Year ("Year of the Rabbit"). Multicoloured.
1146 10w. Type **519** 40 10
1147 10w. Toy rabbits 40 10

1975. 75th Anniv of Korea's Membership of U.P.U. Multicoloured.
1149 10w. Type **521** 30 10
1150 10w. U.P.U. emblem and paper dart 30 10

523 Dove with "Good Luck" Card

1975. Inauguration of National Welfare Insurance System.
1151 **523** 10w. multicoloured . . . 20 10

524 Dr. Schweitzer, Map and Syringe

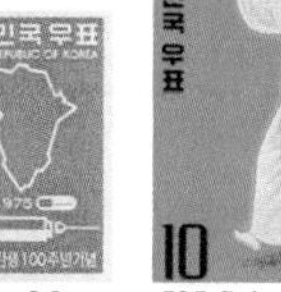

525 Salpuli Dancer

1975. Birth Centenary of Dr. Albert Schweitzer.
1152 **524** 10w. bistre 50 15
1153 10w. mauve 50 15
1154 10w. orange 50 15
1155 10w. green 50 15

1975. Korean Folk Dances (1st series). Multicoloured. Background colour given.
1156 **525** 10w. green 40 10
1157 – 10w. blue 40 10
DESIGN: No. 1157, Exorcism in dance.
See also Nos. 1168/9, 1175/6, 1193/4 and 1208/9.

527 Globe and Rotary Emblem

1975. 70th Anniv of Rotary International.
1159 **527** 10w. multicoloured . . . 25 10

528 Women and I.W.Y. Emblem

1975. International Women's Year.
1160 **528** 10w. multicoloured . . . 25 10

529 Violets

531 Saemaeul Township

1975. Flowers (1st series). Multicoloured.
1161 10w. Type **529** 40 10
1162 10w. Anemones 40 10
See also Nos. 1171/2, 1184/5, 1199/1200 and 1213/4.

1975. National Afforestation Campaign. Mult.
1163 10w. Type **531** 50 10
1164 10w. Lake and trees 50 10
1165 10w. "Green" forest 50 10
1166 10w. Felling timber 50 10
Nos. 1163/6 were issued together, se-tenant, forming a composite design.

535 H.R.F. Emblem on Map of Korea

536 Butterfly Dance

1975. Homeland Reserve Forces Day.
1167 **535** 10w. multicoloured . . . 40 10

1975. Folk Dances (2nd series). Multicoloured. Background colour given.
1168 **536** 10w. green 45 10
1169 – 10w. yellow 45 10
DESIGN: No. 1169, Victory dance.

538 Rhododendron

540 Metric Symbols

1975. Flowers (2nd series). Multicoloured.
1171 10w. Type **538** 40 10
1172 10w. Clematis 40 10

1975. Centenary of Metric Convention.
1173 **540** 10w. multicoloured . . . 25 10

541 Soldier and Incense Pot

542 Mokjoong Dance

1975. 20th Memorial Day.
1174 **541** 10w. multicoloured . . . 25 10

1975. Folk Dances (3rd series). Multicoloured.
1175 **542** 10w. blue 45 10
1176 – 10w. pink 45 10
DESIGN: No. 1176, Malttungi dancer.

544 Flags of South Korea, U.N. and U.S.

1975. 25th Anniv of Korean War. Multicoloured.
1178 10w. Type **544** 45 10
1179 10w. Flags of Ethiopia, France, Greece, Canada and South Africa 45 10
1180 10w. Flags of Luxembourg, Australia, U.K., Colombia and Turkey 45 10
1181 10w. Flags of Netherlands, Belgium, Philippines, New Zealand and Thailand . . 45 10

548 Presidents Pak and Bongo

549 Iris

1975. State Visit of President Bongo of Gabon.
1182 **548** 10w. multicoloured . . . 40 10

1975. Flowers (3rd series). Multicoloured.
1184 10w. Type **549** 40 10
1185 10w. Thistle 40 10

551 Scout Scarf

552 Freedom Flame

1975. "Nordjamb 75" World Scout Jamboree, Norway. Multicoloured.
1186 10w. Type **551** 40 10
1187 10w. Scout oath 40 10
1188 10w. Scout camp 40 10
1189 10w. Axe and rope 40 10
1190 10w. Camp fire 40 10

1975. 30th Anniv of Liberation. Multicoloured.
1191 20w. Type **552** 45 10
1192 20w. Balloon emblems . . . 45 10

554 Drum Dance

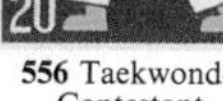

556 Taekwondo Contestant

1975. Folk Dances (4th series). Multicoloured. Background colour given.
1193 **554** 20w. yellow 60 10
1194 – 20w. orange 60 10
DESIGN: No. 1194, Bara dance.

1975. 2nd World Taekwondo Championships, Seoul.
1196 **556** 20w. multicoloured . . . 30 10

557 Assembly Hall

1975. Completion of National Assembly Hall.
1197 **557** 20w. multicoloured . . . 30 10

558 Dumper Truck and Emblem

559 Broad-bell Flower

1975. Contractors' Association Convention, Seoul.
1198 **558** 20w. multicoloured . . . 40 10

1975. Flowers (4th series). Multicoloured.
1199 20w. Type **559** 45 10
1200 20w. Bush clover 45 10

561 Morse Key and Dish Aerial

1975. 90th Anniv of Korean Telecommunications.
1201 **561** 20w. black, orange & pur 35 10

562 Yeongweol Caves

564 Flag and Missiles

1975. International Tourism Day. Multicoloured.
1202 20w. Type **562** 30 10
1203 20w. Mount Sorak 30 10

1975. Korean Armed Forces Day.
1204 **564** 20w. multicoloured . . . 30 10

565 "Gymnastics"

567 "Kangaroo" Collector

1975. 56th National Athletic Meeting. Multicoloured.
1205 20w. Type **565** 25 10
1206 20w. "Handball" 25 10

1975. Philatelic Week.
1207 **567** 20w. multicoloured . . . 30 10

568 Sogo Dance

570 U.N. Emblem and Handclasps

1975. Folk Dances (5th series). Multicoloured. Background colour given.
1208 **568** 20w. blue 45 10
1209 – 20w. yellow 55 10
DESIGN: No. 1209, Bupo Nori dance.

1975. 30th Anniv of United Nations.
1211 **570** 20w. multicoloured . . . 25 10

571 Red Cross and Emblems

572 Camellia

1975. 70th Anniv of Korean Red Cross.
1212 **571** 20w. multicoloured . . . 35 10

1975. Flowers (5th series). Multicoloured.
1213 20w. Type **572** 50 10
1214 20w. Gentian 50 10

574 Union Emblem

575 Children Playing

1975. 10th Anniv of Asian Parliamentary Union.
1215 **574** 20w. multicoloured . . . 30 10

1975. Lunar New Year. Multicoloured.
1216 20w. Type **575** 30 10
1217 20w. Dragon ("Year of the Dragon") 30 10

577 Electric Train

1975. Opening of Cross-country Electric Railway.
1219 **577** 20w. multicoloured . . . 50 10

578 "Dilipa fenestra"

1976. Butterflies (1st series). Multicoloured, background colour given.
1220 **578** 20w. red . . . . 1·00 10
1221 – 20w. blue . . . . 1·00 10
DESIGN: No. 1221, "Luehdorfia puziloi".
See also Nos. 1226/7, 1246/7, 1254/5 and 1264/5.

580 Institute Emblem and Science Emblems

581 Japanese White-naped Crane

1976. 10th Anniv of Korean Institute of Science and Technology.
1222 **580** 20w. multicoloured . . . 25 10

1976. Birds (1st series). Multicoloured.
1223 20w. Type **581** . . . . . . 1·00 30
1224 20w. Great bustard . . . . 1·00 30
See also Nos. 1243/4, 1251/2, 1257/8 and 1266/7.

583 Globe and Telephones

1976. Telephone Centenary.
1225 **583** 20w. multicoloured . . . 20 10

584 "Papilio xuthus"

1976. Butterflies (2nd series). Multicoloured, background colour given.
1226 **584** 20w. yellow . . . . . . 1·00 10
1227 – 20w. green . . . . . . 1·00 10
DESIGN: No. 1227, "Parnassius bremeri".

586 "National Development"

587 Eye and People

1976. Homeland Reserve Forces Day.
1228 **586** 20w. multicoloured . . . 30 10

1976. World Health Day. Prevention of Blindness.
1229 **587** 20w. multicoloured . . . 30 10

588 Pres. Pak and Flag

589 Ruins of Moenjodaro

1976. 6th Anniv of Saemaul Movement (community self-help programme). Multicoloured.
1230 20w. Type **588** 45 15
1231 20w. People ("Intellectual edification") 45 15
1232 20w. Village ("Welfare") . . 45 15
1233 20w. Produce and fields ("Production") 45 15
1234 20w. Produce and factory ("Increase of Income") . . 45 15

1976. Moenjodaro (Pakistan) Preservation Campaign.
1235 **589** 20w. multicoloured . . . 40 10

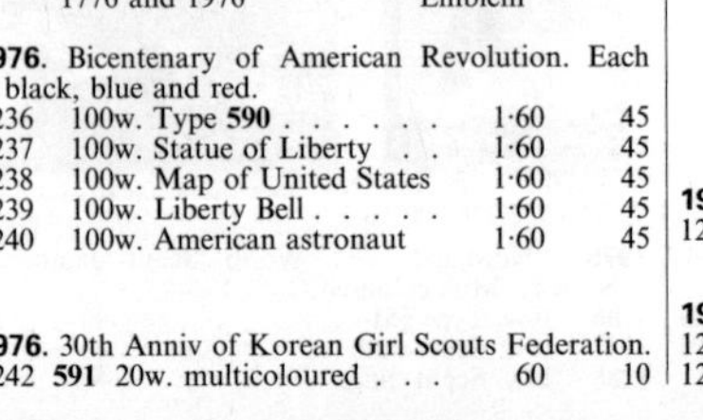

590 U.S. Flags of 1776 and 1976

591 Camp Scene on Emblem

1976. Bicentenary of American Revolution. Each black, blue and red.
1236 100w. Type **590** . . . . . 1·60 45
1237 100w. Statue of Liberty . . 1·60 45
1238 100w. Map of United States 1·60 45
1239 100w. Liberty Bell . . . . . 1·60 45
1240 100w. American astronaut 1·60 45

1976. 30th Anniv of Korean Girl Scouts Federation.
1242 **591** 20w. multicoloured . . . 60 10

592 Blue-winged Pitta

594 Buddha and Temple

1976. Birds (2nd series). Multicoloured.
1243 20w. Type **592** . . . . . . 1·00 35
1244 20w. White-bellied black woodpecker . . . . . . 1·00 35

1976. U.N.E.S.C.O. Campaign for Preservation of Borobudur Temple (in Indonesia).
1245 **594** 20w. multicoloured . . . 25 10

595 Eastern Pale Clouded Yellow

1976. Butterflies (3rd series). Multicoloured, background colour given.
1246 **595** 20w. olive 75 10
1247 – 20w. violet 75 10
DESIGN: No. 1247, Chinese windmill.

597 Protected Family

598 Volleyball

1976. National Life Insurance.
1248 **597** 20w. multicoloured . . . 30 10

1976. Olympic Games, Montreal. Multicoloured.
1249 20w. Type **598** 35 10
1250 20w. Boxing 35 10

600 Black Wood Pigeon

602 Children and Books

1976. Birds (3rd series). Multicoloured.
1251 20w. Type **600** . . . . . . 1·00 35
1252 20w. Oystercatcher . . . . 1·00 35

1976. Books for Children.
1253 **602** 20w. multicoloured . . . 25 10

603 "Hestina assimilis"

1976. Butterflies (4th series). Multicoloured, background colour given.
1254 **603** 20w. brown 75 10
1255 – 20w. drab 75 10
DESIGN: No. 1255, Blue triangle.

604a Corps Members and Flag

605 Black-faced Spoonbill

1976. 1st Anniv of Korean Civil Defence Corps.
1256 **604a** 20w. multicoloured . . 30 10

1976. Birds (4th series). Multicoloured.
1257 20w. Type **605** . . . . . . 1·00 35
1258 20w. Black stork . . . . . 1·00 35

607 Chamsungdan, Mani Mountain

1976. International Tourism Day. Multicoloured.
1259 20w. Type **607** 40 10
1260 20w. Ilchumun Gate, Tongdosa 40 10

609 Cadet and Parade

610 "Musa basjoo" (flower arrangement, Cheong Jo the Great)

1976. 30th Anniv of Korean Military Academy.
1261 **609** 20w. multicoloured . . . 25 10

1976. Philatelic Week.
1262 **610** 20w. black, red and drab 25 10

611 Yellow-legged Tortoiseshell

613 Cinereous Vulture

1976. Butterflies (5th series). Multicoloured, background colour given.
1264 **611** 20w. light green 75 10
1265 – 20w. purple 75 10
DESIGN: No. 1265, "Fabriciana nerippe".

1976. Birds (5th series). Multicoloured.
1266 20w. Type **613** . . . . . . 3·75 1·25
1267 20w. Tundra swan . . . . 3·75 1·25

615 Snake (bas-relief, Kim Yu Shin's tomb)

619 Dish Aerial

617 "Training Technicians"

1976. Lunar New Year (Year of the Snake). Multicoloured.
1268 20w. Type **615** 50 10
1269 20w. Door knocker with Manchurian cranes . . . 40 20

1977. 4th Five Year Economic Development Plan. Multicoloured.
1271 20w. Type **617** 40 10
1272 20w. Tanker ("Heavy Industries") 50 10

1977. 25th Anniv of Korea's I.T.U. Membership.
1273 **619** 20w. multicoloured . . . 30 10

620 Korean Broadcasting Centre

621 Jar with Grape Design

1977. 50th Anniv of Broadcasting in Korea.
1274 **620** 20w. multicoloured . . . 35 10

1977. Korean Ceramics (1st series). Multicoloured, background colours given.
1275 20w. Type **621** (brown) 75 10
1276 20w. Celadon vase (grey) 75 10
See also Nos. 1285/6, 1287/8, 1290/1 and 1300/1.

623 "Two-children" Family
624 Reserve Soldier

1977. Family Planning.
1277 **623** 20w. green, turq & orge 30 10

1977. 9th Homeland Reserve Forces Day.
1278 **624** 20w. multicoloured 35 10

625 Diagram of Brain
626 Medical Book and Equipment

1977. 10th Anniv of Science Day.
1279 **625** 20w. multicoloured 25 10

1977. 35th International Military Medicine Meeting.
1280 **626** 20w. multicoloured 45 10

627 Child with Flowers
628 Veterans' Flag and Emblem

1977. 20th Anniv of Children's Charter.
1281 **627** 20w. multicoloured 25 10

1977. 25th Anniv of Korean Veterans' Day.
1282 **628** 20w. multicoloured 40 10

629 Statue of Buddha, Sokkulam Grotto
630 Celadon Jar

1977. 2600th Birth Anniv of Buddha.
1283 **629** 20w. green and brown 40 10

1977. Korean Ceramics (2nd series). Multicoloured, background colours given.
1285 20w. Type **630** (pink) 45 10
1286 20w. Porcelain vase (blue) (vert) 45 10

632 "Buddha" Celadon Wine Jar

1977. Korean Ceramics (3rd series). Multicoloured, background colours given.
1287 20w. Type **632** (mauve) 45 10
1288 20w. Celadon vase (pale blue) 45 10

수해구제
+10
(634)

635 Celadon Vase, Black Koryo Ware

1977. Flood Relief. No. 791 surch with T **634**.
1289 20w.+10w. green 1·25 40

1977. Korean Ceramics (4th series). Multicoloured, background colours given.
1290 20w. Type **635** (stone) 45 10
1291 20w. White porcelain bowl (green) (horiz) 45 10

637 Ulleung-do Island
639 Servicemen

1977. World Tourism Day. Multicoloured.
1292 20w. Type **637** 30 10
1293 20w. Haeundae Beach 30 10

1977. Armed Forces Day.
1294 **639** 20w. multicoloured 20 10

640/1 "Mount Inwang Clearing-up after the Rain" (detail from drawing by Chung Seon)

1977. Philatelic Week.
1295 **640** 20w. multicoloured 40 10
1296 **641** 20w. multicoloured 40 10
Nos. 1294/5 were issued together, se-tenant, forming the composite design illustrated.

642 Rotary Emblem and Koryo Dynasty Bronze Bell
643 South Korean Flag over Everest

1977. 50th Anniv of Korean Rotary Club.
1298 **642** 20w. multicoloured 50 10

1977. South Korean Conquest of Mount Everest.
1299 **643** 20w. multicoloured 50 10

644 Punch'ong Bottle
646 Hands preserving Nature

1977. Korean Ceramics (5th series). Multicoloured, background colours given.
1300 20w. Type **644** (brown) 50 10
1301 20w. Celadon cylindrical bottle (pale brown) 50 10

1977. Nature Conservation.
1302 **646** 20w. blue, green & brown 30 10

647 Children with Kites
649 Clay Pigeon Shooting

1977. Lunar New Year ("Year of the Horse"). Multicoloured.
1303 20w. Type **647** 30 10
1304 20w. Horse (bas-relief, Kim Yu Shin's tomb) 30 10

1977. 42nd World Shooting Championships, Seoul. Multicoloured.
1306 20w. Type **649** 35 10
1307 20w. Air pistol shooting 35 10
1308 20w. Air rifle shooting 35 10

652 Korean Airlines Boeing 747-200

1977. 25th Anniv of Korean Membership of I.C.A.O.
1310 **652** 20w. multicoloured 45 10

653 "Exports"

1977. Korean Exports.
1311 **653** 20w. multicoloured 35 10

654 Ships and World Map

1978. National Maritime Day.
1312 **654** 20w. multicoloured 30 10

655 Three-storey Pagoda, Hwaom Temple
656 Seven-storey Pagoda, T'app'yong-ri

1978. Stone Pagodas (1st series).
1313 **655** 20w. multicoloured 35 10
1314 **656** 20w. multicoloured 35 10
See also Nos. 1319/20, 1322/5 and 1340/1.

657 Ants with Coins
658 Seoul Sejong Cultural Centre, Hahoe Mask and Violin

1978. Savings Encouragement.
1315 **657** 20w. multicoloured 30 10

1978. Opening of Seoul Sejong Cultural Centre.
1316 **658** 20w. multicoloured 60 10

659 Standard Bearer
660 Pigeon and Young

1978. 10th Homeland Reserve Forces Day.
1317 **659** 20w. multicoloured 25 10

1978. Family Planning.
1318 **660** 20w. black and green 35 10

661 Pagoda, Punhwang Temple

662 Pagoda, Miruk Temple

1978. Stone Pagodas (2nd series).
1319 **661** 20w. multicoloured 35 10
1320 **662** 20w. multicoloured 35 10

663 National Assembly

1978. 30th Anniv of National Assembly.
1321 **663** 20w. multicoloured 25 10

664 Tabo Pagoda, Pulguk Temple
665 Three-storey Pagoda, Pulguk Temple

1978. Stone Pagodas (3rd series).
1322 **664** 20w. multicoloured 35 10
1323 **665** 20w. multicoloured 35 10

666 Ten-storey Pagoda, Kyongch'on Temple
667 Nine-storey Octagonal Pagoda, Wolchong Temple

1978. Stone Pagodas (4th series).
1324 **666** 20w. multicoloured 45 10
1325 **667** 20w. multicoloured 45 10

668 Emblem and Hands with Tools
669 Crater Lake, Mt. Baeguda and Bell of Joy

1978. 24th International Youth Skill Olympics, Pusan.
1326 **668** 20w. multicoloured . . . 25 10

1978. 30th Anniv of Republic of Korea.
1328 **669** 20w. multicoloured . . . 25 10

670 Army Nursing Officer

671 Sobaeksan Observatory and Telescope

1978. 30th Anniv of Army Nursing Corps.
1329 **670** 20w. multicoloured . . . 25 10

1978. Opening of Sobaeksan Observatory.
1330 **671** 20w. multicoloured . . . 40 10

672 Kyonghoeru Pavilion, Kyonbok Palace

673 Baeg-do Island

1978. World Tourism Day.
1331 **672** 20w. multicoloured . . . 30 10
1332 **673** 20w. multicoloured . . . 30 10

674 Customs Officers and Flag

1978. Centenary of Custom House.
1333 **674** 20w. multicoloured . . . 25 10

675 Armed Forces

676 Earthenware Figures, Silla Dynasty

1978. 30th Anniv of Korean Armed Forces.
1334 **675** 20w. multicoloured . . . 40 10

1978. Culture Month.
1335 **676** 20w. black and green . . 25 10

677 Painting of a Lady (Shin Yoon-bok)

678 Young Men and Y.M.C.A. Emblem

1978. Philatelic Week.
1336 **677** 20w. multicoloured . . . 35 10

1978. 75th Anniv of Korean Y.M.C.A.
1338 **678** 20w. multicoloured . . . 25 10

679 Hand smothering Fire

1978. Fire Prevention Campaign.
1339 **679** 20w. multicoloured . . . 25 10

680 Thirteen-storey Pagoda, Jeonghye Temple

681 Three-storey Pagoda, Jinjeon Temple

1978. Stone Pagodas (5th series).
1340 **680** 20w. multicoloured . . . 30 10
1341 **681** 20w. multicoloured . . . 30 10

682 Snow Scene

684 People within Hibiscus

1978. Lunar New Year ("Year of the Sheep"). Multicoloured.
1342 20w. Type **682** 30 10
1343 20w. Sheep (bas-relief, Kim Yu Shin's tomb) 30 10

1978. 10th Anniv of National Education Charter.
1345 **684** 20w. multicoloured . . . 25 10

685 President Pak

1978. Re-election of President Pak.
1346 **685** 20w. multicoloured . . . 40 10

686 Golden Mandarinfish

687 Lace Bark Pine

1979. Nature Conservation.
1348 **686** 20w. multicoloured . . . 35 10
1349 **687** 20w. multicoloured . . . 35 10

688 Samil Monument

689 Worker and Bulldozer

1979. 60th Anniv of Samil Independence Movement.
1350 **688** 20w. multicoloured . . . 25 10

1979. Labour Day.
1351 **689** 20w. multicoloured . . . 25 10

690 Tabo Pagoda, Pulgak Temple

695 Hand holding Symbols of Security

1979. Korean Art. Multicoloured.
1352 20w. Type **690** 25 10
1353 20w. Gilt-bronze Maitreya 25 10
1354 20w. Gold crown of Silla . . 25 10
1355 20w. Celadon vase 25 10
1356 60w. "Tano Day Activities" (silk screen) (50 × 33 mm) 45 10

1979. Strengthening National Security.
1358 **695** 20w. multicoloured . . . 25 10

696 Pulguk Temple and P.A.T.A. Emblem

1979. 28th Pacific Area Travel Association Conference, Seoul.
1359 **696** 20w. multicoloured . . . 25 10

697 Presidents Pak and Senghor

1979. Visit of President Senghor of Senegal.
1360 **697** 20w. multicoloured . . . 25 10

698 Basketball

699 Children playing

1979. 8th World Women's Basketball Championships, Seoul.
1362 **698** 20w. multicoloured . . . 40 10

1979. International Year of the Child.
1363 **699** 20w. multicoloured . . . 30 10

700 Children on Swing

1979. Family Planning.
1364 **700** 20w. multicoloured . . . 30 10

701 Mandarins

702 "Neofinettia falcata" (orchid)

1979. Nature Conservation.
1365 **701** 20w. multicoloured . . . 1·00 20
1366 **702** 20w. multicoloured . . . 40 10

703 Manchurian Cranes

1979.
1367 **703** 10w. black and green 65 15
1368 – 15w. deep green & green 15 10
1369 – 20w. bistre, black & blue 20 10
1370 – 30w. multicoloured . . 25 10
1371 – 40w. multicoloured . . 30 10
1372 – 50w. brown, red & orge 20 10
1373 – 60w. grey, purple & mve 30 10
1374 – 70w. multicoloured . . 50 10
1375 – 80w. yellow, black & red 60 10
1376 – 90w. buff, green and orange 75 10
1377 – 100w. purple and mauve 45 10
1377a – 100w. black 45 10
1378 – 150w. black, bistre and blue 50 10
1379 – 200w. brown and green 1·10 10
1380 – 300w. blue . . . . . . 2·00 20
1381 – 400w. green, brown and deep green . . . . . 2·25 20
1381a – 400w. blue, ochre, brown and grey . . . 3·00 30
1382 – 450w. brown . . . . . 1·60 40
1383 – 500w. dp green & green 2·00 40
1383a – 550w. black . . . . . 2·00 50
1384 – 600w. multicoloured . . 2·25 1·00
1385 – 700w. multicoloured . . 3·25 40
1386 – 800w. multicoloured . . 2·40 50
1387 – 1000w. lt brown & brn 3·25 40
1388 – 1000w. lt brown & brn 3·25 40
1389 – 5000w. multicoloured 18·00 4·00

DESIGNS—As T **703**: HORIZ: 15w. Mt. Sorak; 50w. Earthenware model of wagon; 90w. Paikryung Island; 1000w. Duck earthenware vessels (1387 facing right; 1388 facing left). VERT: 20w. Tolharubang (stone grandfather); 30w. National flag; 40w. "Hibiscus syriacus"; 60w. Porcelain jar, Yi Dynasty; 70w. Kyongju Observatory; 80w. Mounted warrior (pottery vessel); 100w. (1377) Ryu Kwan Soon; 100w. (1377a) Chung Yak Yong (writer); 150w. Porcelain jar, Chosun Dynasty; 200w. Ahn Joong Geun; 300w. Ahn Chang Ho; 400w. Koryo celadon incense burner; 450, 550w. Kim Ku (organizer of Korean Independence Party); 500w. Brick with mountain landscape; 600w. Hong Yung Sik (postal reformer); 700w. Duck (lid of incense burner). 29 × 41 mm: 800w. Dragon's head flagpole finial; 5000w. Tiger.

See also No. 1065.

725 People suffering from Traffic Pollution

1979. Environmental Protection.
1390 **725** 20w. brown and green 30 10

726 Common Goral

727 "Convallaria leiskei" Miquel

1979. Nature Conservation.
1391 **726** 20w. multicoloured . . . 40 10
1392 **727** 20w. multicoloured . . . 40 10

728 Presidents Pak and Carter

1979. Visit of President Carter of United States.
1393 **728** 20w. multicoloured . . . 20 10

729 Exhibition Building and Emblem

1979. Opening of Korea Exhibition Centre.
1395 **729** 20w. multicoloured . . . 20 10

730 Boeing 747-200 Jetliner and Globe

1979. 10th Anniv of Korean Air Lines.
1396 **730** 20w. multicoloured . . . 30 10

731 "The Courtesans' Sword Dance" (Shin Yun-bok)

1979. United States "5000 Years of Korean Art" Exhibition (1st issue).
1397 **731** 60w. multicoloured . . . 75 15
See also Nos. 1402/3, 1406/7, 1420/1, 1426/7, 1433/4, 1441/2 and 1457/8.

732 Mount Mai, North Cholla Province
733 Dragon's Head Rock, Cheju Island

1979. World Tourism Day.
1399 **732** 20w. multicoloured . . . 25 10
1400 **733** 20w. multicoloured . . . 25 10

734 Heart, Donors and Blood Drop

1979. Blood Donors.
1401 **734** 20w. red and green . . . 50 10

735 White Porcelain Jar with Grape Design
736 Mounted Warrior (pottery vessel)

1979. "5000 Years of Korean Art" Exhibition (2nd issue).
1402 **735** 20w. multicoloured . . . 40 10
1403 **736** 20w. multicoloured . . . 40 10

737 "Moon Travel" (Park Chung Jae)

1979. Philatelic Week.
1404 **737** 20w. multicoloured . . . 20 10

738 Hahoe Mask
739 Golden Amitabha with Halo

1979. "5000 Years of Korean Art" Exhibition (3rd issue).
1406 **738** 20w. multicoloured . . . 40 10
1407 **739** 20w. multicoloured . . . 40 10

740 Rain Frog
741 Asian Polypody

1979. Nature Conservation.
1408 **740** 20w. multicoloured . . . 45 10
1409 **741** 20w. multicoloured . . . 45 10

742 Monkey (bas-relief, Kim Yun Shin's tomb)
743 Children playing Yut

1979. Lunar New Year ("Year of the Monkey").
1410 **742** 20w. multicoloured . . . 20 10
1411 **743** 20w. multicoloured . . . 20 10

744 President Choi Kyu Hah

1979. Presidential Inauguration.
1413 **744** 20w. multicoloured . . . 30 10

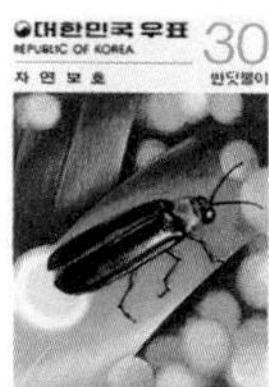

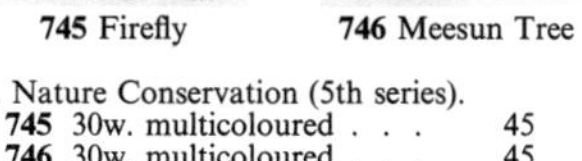
745 Firefly
746 Meesun Tree

1980. Nature Conservation (5th series).
1415 **745** 30w. multicoloured . . . 45 10
1416 **746** 30w. multicoloured . . . 45 10

747 President Pak
748 Earthenware Kettle

749 "Landscape" (Kim Hong Do)

1980. President Pak Commemoration.
1417 **747** 30w. red 25 10
1418 30w. purple 25 10

1980. "5000 Years of Korean Art" Exhibition (4th issue).
1420 **748** 30w. multicoloured . . . 40 10
1421 **749** 60w. multicoloured . . . 55 10

750 "Lotus"
751 "Magpie and Tiger"

1980. Folk Paintings (1st series).
1423 **750** 30w. multicoloured . . . 50 20
1424 **751** 60w. multicoloured . . . 1·25 40
See also Nos. 1429/31, 1437/40 and 1453/6.

752 Merchant Ships

1980. Korean Merchant Navy.
1425 **752** 30w. multicoloured . . . 30 10

753 "Heavenly Horse" (tomb painting)
754 Banner Staff with Dragonhead Finial

1980. "5000 Years of Korean Art" Exhibition (5th series).
1426 **753** 30w. multicoloured . . . 40 10
1427 **754** 30w. multicoloured . . . 40 10

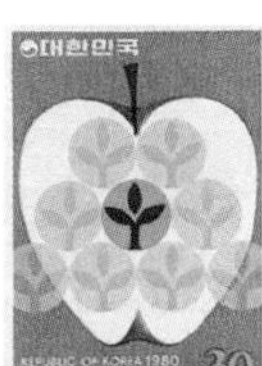
755 "Fruition"

1980. 10th Anniv of Saemaul Movement (community self-help programme).
1428 **755** 30w. multicoloured . . . 25 10

756 "Red Phoenix"

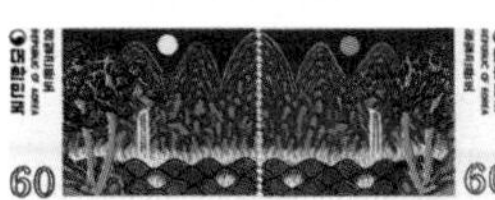
757/8 "Sun and Moon over Mt. Konryun" (½-size illustration)

1980. Folk Paintings (2nd series).
1429 **756** 30w. multicoloured . . . 30 10
1430 **757** 60w. multicoloured . . . 50 40
1431 **758** 60w. multicoloured . . . 50 40
Nos. 1430/1 were issued together, se-tenant, forming a composite design.

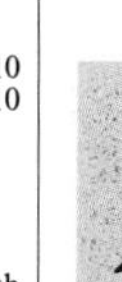

759 "Man on a Horse" (mural, Koguryo period)
760 "Tiger" (granite sculpture)

1980. "5000 Years of Korean Art" Exhibition (6th issue).
1433 **759** 30w. multicoloured . . . 40 10
1434 **760** 30w. multicoloured . . . 40 10

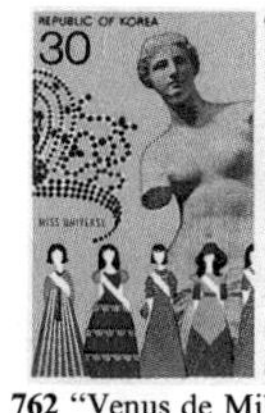
761 U.N. Flag and Rifle
762 "Venus de Milo" and Contestants

1980. 30th Anniv of Intervention of U.N. Forces in Korean War.
1435 **761** 30w. multicoloured . . . 30 10

1980. "Miss Universe" Beauty Contest, Seoul.
1436 **762** 30w. multicoloured . . . 30 10

763 "Rabbits pounding Grain in a Mortar"
764 "Dragon in Cloud"

1980. Folk Paintings (3rd series).
1437 **763** 30w. multicoloured . . . 40 10
1438 **764** 30w. multicoloured . . . 40 10

765 "Pine Tree"
766 "Flowers and Manchurian Cranes" (detail, folding screen)

1980. Folk Paintings (4th series).
1439 **765** 30w. multicoloured . . . 40 10
1440 **766** 30w. multicoloured . . . 75 20

767 Human faced Roof Tile
768 "White Tiger" (mural)

1980. "5000 Years of Korean Art" Exhibition (7th issue).
1441 **767** 30w. multicoloured . . . 30 10
1442 **768** 30w. multicoloured . . . 30 10

769 Football
770 President Chun Doo Hwan

1980. 10th President's Cup Football Tournament.
1443 **769** 30w. multicoloured . . . 30 10

1980. Presidential Inauguration.
1444 **770** 30w. multicoloured . . . 25 10

771 Woman Soldier and Emblem

1980. 30th Anniv of Women's Army Corps.
1446 **771** 30w. multicoloured . . . 25 10

772 River Baegma

773 Three Peaks of Dodam

1980. World Tourism Day.
1447 **772** 30w. pink and purple . . 30 10
1448 **773** 30w. yellow, green & blue 30 10

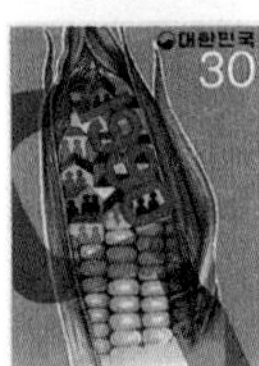
774 Corn-cob and Micrometer

775 Tree

1980. Population and Housing Census.
1449 **774** 30w. multicoloured . . . 30 10

1980. 75th Anniv of Korean Red Cross.
1450 **775** 30w. multicoloured . . . 35 10

776 "Angels delivering Mail" (Kim Ki Chul)

1980. Philatelic Week.
1451 **776** 30w. multicoloured . . . 25 10

777 "Ten Long-life Symbols"

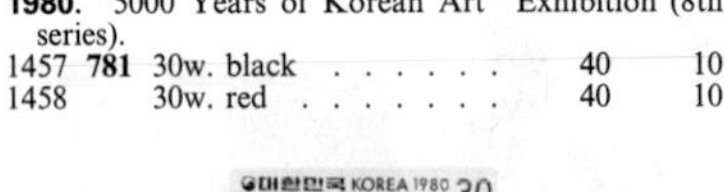
781 Deva King (sculpture)

1980. Folk Paintings (5th series). Multicoloured.
1453 30w. Type **777** . . . . . . 1·40 25
1454 30w. "Herb of eternal youth" and deer 30 10
1455 30w. Pine and deer eating herb 30 10
1456 30w. Pine, water and rock 30 10
Nos. 1453/6 were issued together, se-tenant, forming a composite design.

1980. "5000 Years of Korean Art" Exhibition (8th series).
1457 **781** 30w. black 40 10
1458 30w. red 40 10

782 "Cable Enterprise" (cable ship) and Cross-section of Cable

1980. Inauguration of Korea–Japan Submarine Cable.
1459 **782** 30w. multicoloured . . . 35 10

783 Cock (bas-relief, Kim Yu Shin's tomb)

784 Cranes

1980. Lunar New Year ("Year of the Cock").
1460 **783** 30w. multicoloured . . . 30 10
1461 **784** 30w. multicoloured . . . 30 10

785 President Chun Doo Hwan and Factory within "Hibiscus syriacus"

1981. Presidential Inauguration.
1463 **785** 30w. multicoloured . . . 25 10

786 "Korea Sun" (tanker)

787 "Asia Yukho" (freighter)

1981. Ships (1st series).
1465 **786** 30w. multicoloured . . . 55 15
1466 **787** 90w. multicoloured . . . 85 25
See also Nos. 1470/1, 1482/5 and 1501/2.

788 National Assembly Building

1981. Inaugural Session of 11th National Assembly.
1467 **788** 30w. brown and gold . . 30 10

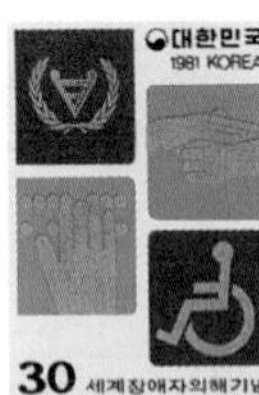
789 Symbols of Disability and I.Y.D.P. Emblem

790 Disabled Person in Wheelchair at Foot of Steps

1981. International Year of Disabled Persons.
1468 **789** 30w. multicoloured . . . 30 10
1469 **790** 90w. multicoloured . . . 60 35

791 "Saturn" (bulk-carrier)

792 "Hanjin Seoul" (container ship)

1981. Ships (2nd series).
1470 **791** 30w. deep purple, purple and blue 55 15
1471 **792** 90w. grey, blue and red 85 25

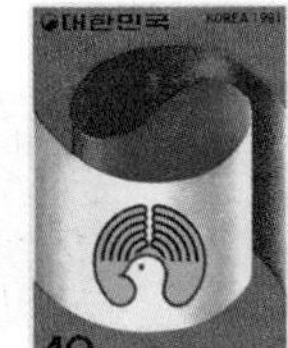
793 Council Emblem on Ribbon

1981. Advisory Council on Peaceful Unification Policy.
1472 **793** 40w. multicoloured . . . 30 10

794 "Clean Rivers and Air"

795 White Storks visiting Breeding Grounds

1981. World Environment Day.
1473 **794** 30w. multicoloured . . . 30 10
1474 **795** 90w. multicoloured . . . 65 20

796 Presidents Chun and Suharto of Indonesia

1981. Presidential Visit to A.S.E.A.N. Countries. Multicoloured.
1475 40w. Type **796** 50 10
1476 40w. Pres. Chun and Sultan of Malaysia 50 10
1477 40w. Handshake and flags of South Korea and Singapore 50 10
1478 40w. Pres. Chun and King of Thailand 50 10
1479 40w. Presidents Chun and Marcos of Philippines . . 50 10
1480 40w. Pres. Chun and flags of Korea, Singapore, Malaysia and Philippines (39 × 43 mm) 50 10

802 "Chung Ryong No. 3" (tug)

803 "Soo Gong No. 71" (trawler)

1981. Ships (3rd series).
1482 **802** 40w. multicoloured . . . 65 15
1483 **803** 100w. multicoloured . . 95 25

804 "Aldebaran" (log carrier)

805 "Hyundai No. 1" (car carrier)

1981. Ships (4th series).
1484 **804** 40w. multicoloured . . . 65 15
1485 **805** 100w. multicoloured . . 95 25

806 Korean with Flag and Dates on Graph

812 W.H.O. Emblem and Citizens

807 Glider

1981. 36th Anniv of Liberation.
1486 **806** 40w. multicoloured . . . 30 10

1981. 3rd Model Aeronautic Competition. Mult.
1487 10w. Type **807** 40 10
1488 20w. Elastic-powered airplane 40 10
1489 40w. Line-controlled airplane 40 15
1490 50w. Radio-controlled airplane 60 20
1491 80w. Radio-controlled helicopter 75 30

1981. 32nd Session of W.H.O. Regional Committee for the Western Pacific, Seoul.
1492 **812** 40w. multicoloured . . . 30 10

813 Seoul Communications Tower

814 Ulreung Island

1981. World Tourism Day.
1493 **813** 40w. multicoloured . . . 30 10
1494 **814** 40w. multicoloured . . . 30 10

815 Cycling

816 Swimming

1981. 62nd National Sports Meeting, Seoul.
1495 **815** 40w. multicoloured . . . 35 10
1496 **816** 40w. multicoloured . . . 35 10

817 Presidents Chun and Carazo Odio

818 Hand holding Plate with F.A.O. Emblem

1981. Visit of President Carazo Odio of Costa Rica.
1497 **817** 40w. multicoloured . . . 30 10

1981. World Food Day.
1498 **818** 40w. multicoloured . . . 30 10

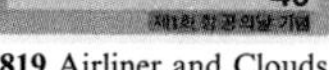

819 Airliner and Clouds **820** South Gate of Seoul and Olympic Rings

1981. National Aviation Day.
1499 **819** 40w. orange, brown and silver 40 10

1981. Choice of Seoul as 1988 Olympic Host City.
1500 **820** 40w. multicoloured . . . 30 10

821 "Stolt Hawk" (chemical carrier)

822 Passenger Ferry

1981. Ships (5th series).
1501 **821** 40w. black 65 15
1502 **822** 100w. blue 95 25

823 "Hang-gliding" (Kim Kyung Jun)

1981. Philatelic Week.
1503 **823** 40w. multicoloured . . . 30 10

824 Camellia and Dog **825** Children flying Kite

1981. Lunar New Year ("Year of the Dog").
1505 **824** 40w. multicoloured . . . 30 10
1506 **825** 40w. multicoloured . . . 30 10

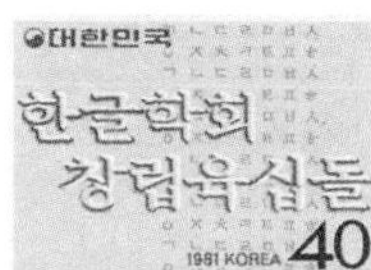

826 "Hangul Hakhoe"

1981. 60th Anniv of Hangul Hakhoe (Korean Language Society).
1508 **826** 40w. multicoloured . . . 35 10

827 Telephone and Dish Aerial **828** Scout Emblem and Logs forming "75"

1982. Inauguration of Korea Telecommunication Authority.
1509 **827** 60w. multicoloured . . . 40 10

1982. 75th Anniv of Boy Scout Movement.
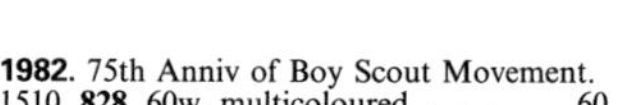
1510 **828** 60w. multicoloured . . . 60 10

829 Young Woman **830** Dividers and World Map

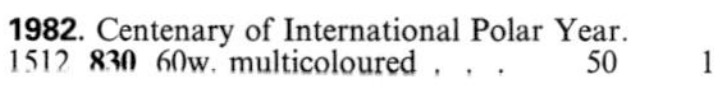

1982. 60th Anniv of Korean Young Women's Christian Association.
1511 **829** 60w. multicoloured . . . 35 10

1982. Centenary of International Polar Year.
1512 **830** 60w. multicoloured . . . 50 10

831 Music and "Hibiscus syriacus"

1982. Children's Day.
1513 **831** 60w. multicoloured . . . 40 10

832 President Chun and Samuel Doe

1982. Visit of Samuel Doe (Liberian Head of State).
1514 **832** 60w. multicoloured . . . 35 10

833 Centenary Emblem

1982. Centenary of Korea–United States Friendship Treaty.
1516 **833** 60w. multicoloured . . . 30 10
1517 – 60w. multicoloured . . . 30 10
DESIGN: No. 1517, Statue of Liberty and Seoul South Gate.

835 Presidents Chun and Mobutu

1982. Visit of President Mobutu of Zaire.
1519 **835** 60w. multicoloured . . . 30 10

836 "Territorial Expansion by Kwanggaeto the Great" (Lee Chong Sang)

837 "General Euljimunduck's Great Victory at Salsoo" (Park Kak Soon)

1982. Documentary Paintings (1st series).
1521 **836** 60w. multicoloured . . . 40 10
1522 **837** 60w. multicoloured . . . 40 10
See also Nos. 1523/4, 1537/8 and 1548/9.

838 "Shilla's Repulse of Invading Tang Army" (Oh Seung Woo)

839 "General Kang Kam Chan's Great Victory at Kyiju" (Lee Yong Hwan)

1982. Documentary Paintings (2nd series).
1523 **838** 60w. multicoloured . . . 40 10
1524 **839** 60w. multicoloured . . . 40 10

840 Convention Emblem and Globe **841** Presidents Chun and Moi of Kenya

1982. 55th International Y's Men's Club Convention, Seoul.
1525 **840** 60w. multicoloured . . . 20 10

1982. Presidential Visits to Africa and Canada. Multicoloured.
1526 60w. Type **841** 35 10
1527 60w. Presidents Chun and Shagari of Nigeria 35 10
1528 60w. Presidents Chun and Bongo of Gabon 35 10
1529 60w. Presidents Chun and Diouf of Senegal 35 10
1530 60w. Flags of South Korea and Canada 35 10

846 National Flag

1982. Centenary of National Flag.
1532 **846** 60w. multicoloured . . . 40 10

847 Emblem and Player

1982. 2nd Seoul Table Tennis Championships.
1534 **847** 60w. multicoloured . . . 40 10

848 Baseball Player

1982. 27th World Baseball Championship Series, Seoul.
1535 **848** 60w. brown 40 10

849 Exhibition Centre

1982. Seoul International Trade Fair.
1536 **849** 60w. multicoloured . . . 30 10

850 "Admiral Yi Sun Sin's Great Victory at Hansan" (Kim Hyung Ku)

851 "General Kim Chwa Jin's Chungsanri Battle" (Sohn Soo Kwang)

1982. Documentary Paintings (3rd series).
1537 **850** 60w. multicoloured . . . 60 15
1538 **851** 60w. multicoloured . . . 35 10

852 "Miners reading Consolatory Letters" (Um Soon Keun)

1982. Philatelic Week.
1539 **852** 60w. multicoloured . . . 45 10

853 Presidents Chung and Suharto

1982. Visit of President Suharto of Indonesia.
1541 **853** 60w. multicoloured . . . 30 10

854 J.C.I. Emblem over World Map **855** "Intelsat 5" and "4-A" orbiting Globe

1982. 37th Junior Chamber International World Congress, Seoul.
1543 **854** 60w. multicoloured . . . 30 10

1982. Second U.N. Conference on the Exploration and Peaceful Uses of Outer Space, Vienna.
1544 **855** 60w. multicoloured . . . 30 10

856 Pig (bas-relief, Kim Yu Shin's tomb)

1982. Lunar New Year ("Year of the Pig").
1545 60w. Type **856** 35 10
1546 60w. Black-billed magpies and Korean moneybag . . 40 10

858 "General Kwon Yul's Great Victory at Haengju" (Oh Seung Woo)

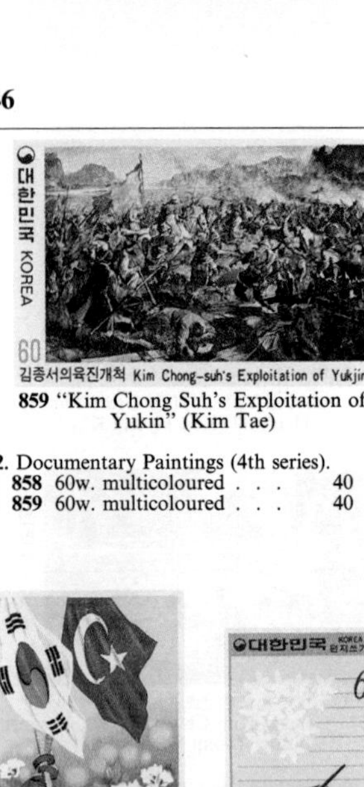

859 "Kim Chong Suh's Exploitation of Yukin" (Kim Tae)

1982. Documentary Paintings (4th series).
1548 **858** 60w. multicoloured . . . 40 10
1549 **859** 60w. multicoloured . . . 40 10

860 Flags of South Korea and Turkey

861 Hand writing Letter

1982. Visit of President Evran of Turkey.
1550 **860** 60w. multicoloured . . . 35 10

1982. Letter Writing Campaign.
1552 **861** 60w. multicoloured . . . 30 10

862 Emblem, Airliner, Container Ship and Cranes

1983. International Customs Day.
1553 **862** 60w. multicoloured . . . 50 15

863 Hyundai "Pony 2"

1983. Korean-made Vehicles (1st series). Multicoloured.
1554 60w. Type **863** 50 10
1555 60w. Keohwa Jeep 50 10
See also Nos. 1558/9, 1564/5, 1572/3 and 1576/7.

865 President Chun and Sultan of Malaysia

1983. Visit of King of Malaysia.
1556 **865** 60w. multicoloured . . . 30 10

866 Daewoo "Maepsy"

867 Kia "Bongo" Minibus

1983. Korean-made Vehicles (2nd series).
1558 **866** 60w. multicoloured . . . 50 10
1559 **867** 60w. multicoloured . . . 50 10

868 Former General Bureau of Postal Administration

869 Central Post Office, Seoul

1983. "Philakorea 84" International Stamp Exhibition, Seoul. Centenary of Korean Postal Service (1st series).
1560 **868** 60w. multicoloured . . . 30 10
1561 **869** 60w. multicoloured . . . 30 10
See also Nos. 1566/7, 1574/5 and 1603/6.

870 Old Village Schoolroom

1983. Teachers' Day.
1562 **870** 60w. multicoloured . . . 35 10

871 Asia Motor Co. Bus

872 Kia "Super Titan" Truck

1983. Korean-made Vehicles (3rd series).
1564 **871** 60w. multicoloured . . . 45 10
1565 **872** 60w. multicoloured . . . 45 10

873 Early Postman

1983. "Philakorea 84" International Stamp Exhibition, Seoul. Centenary of Korean Postal Service (2nd series).
1566 **873** 70w. multicoloured . . . 40 10
1567 – 70w. multicoloured . . . 40 10
DESIGN: No. 1567, Modern postman on motor-cycle.

875 "Communications in Outer Space" (Chun Ja Eun)

1983. World Communications Year.
1568 **875** 70w. multicoloured . . . 35 10

876 Whooper Swans at Sunrise

1983. Inaug of Communications Insurance.
1570 **876** 70w. multicoloured . . . 50 15

877 Emblems of Science and Engineering

1983. Korean Symposium on Science and Technology, Seoul.
1571 **877** 70w. multicoloured . . . 35 10

878 Daewoo Dump Truck

879 Hyundai Cargo Lorry

1983. Korean-made Vehicles (4th series).
1572 **878** 70w. multicoloured . . . 45 10
1573 **879** 70w. multicoloured . . . 45 10

880 Mail carried by Horse

1983. "Philakorea 84" International Stamp Exhibition, Seoul. Centenary of Korean Postal Service (3rd series). Multicoloured.
1574 70w. Type **880** 35 10
1575 70w. Mail truck and Douglas DC-8-60 Super Sixty jetliner 40 10

882 Dong-A Concrete Mixer Truck

883 Dong-A Tanker

1983. Korean-made Vehicles (5th series).
1576 **882** 70w. multicoloured . . . 50 10
1577 **883** 70w. multicoloured . . . 50 10

884 President Chun and King Hussein

1983. Visit of King Hussein of Jordan.
1578 **884** 70w. multicoloured . . . 35 10

885 Woman with Fan

886 I.P.U. Emblem and Flags

1983. 53rd American Society of Travel Agents World Congress, Seoul.
1580 **885** 70w. multicoloured . . . 35 10

1983. 70th Inter-Parliamentary Union Conference, Seoul.
1581 **886** 70w. multicoloured . . . 35 10

887 Gymnastics

888 Football

1983. 64th National Sports Meeting, Inchon.
1583 **887** 70w. multicoloured . . . 40 10
1584 **888** 70w. multicoloured . . . 40 10

889 Presidents Chun and U San Yu of Burma

894 Rain Drops containing Symbols of Industry, Light and Food

1983. Presidential Visits. Multicoloured.
1585 70w. Type **889** 60 50
1586 70w. Presidents Chun and Giani Zail Singh of India 60 50
1587 70w. Presidents Chun and Jayewardene of Sri Lanka 60 50
1588 70w. Flags of South Korea and Australia 60 50
1589 70w. Flags of South Korea and New Zealand 60 50

1983. Development of Water Resources and 10th Anniv of Soyang-gang Dam.
1591 **894** 70w. multicoloured . . . 35 10

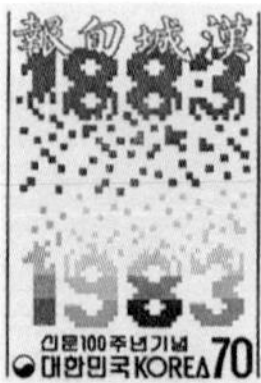

895 Centenary Dates

896 Tree with Lungs and Cross of Lorraine

1983. Centenary of 1st Korean Newspaper "Hansong Sunbo".
1592 **895** 70w. multicoloured . . . 35 10

1983. 30th Anniv of Korean National Tuberculosis Association.
1593 **896** 70w. multicoloured . . . 35 10

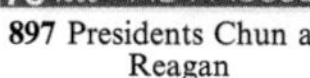

897 Presidents Chun and Reagan

898 Child collecting Stamps

1983. Visit of President Reagan of United States of America.
1594 **897** 70w. multicoloured . . . 35 10

1983. Philatelic Week.
1596 **898** 70w. multicoloured . . . 35 10

899 Rat (bas-relief, Kim Yu Shin's tomb)

1983. Lunar New Year ("Year of the Rat"). Multicoloured.
1598 70w. Type **899** 35 10
1599 70w. Manchurian cranes and pine 40 10

901 Bicentenary Emblem

902 5m. and 10m. Stamps, 1884

1984. Bicentenary of Catholic Church in Korea.
1601 **901** 70w. red, violet and silver 35 10

1984. "Philakorea 84" International Stamp Exhibition, Seoul. Centenary of Korean Postal Service (4th series). Multicoloured.
1603 70w. Type **902** 40 10
1604 70w. 5000w. stamp, 1983 . . 40 10

904 Old Postal Emblem and Post Box

1984. "Philakorea 84" International Stamp Exhibition, Seoul. Centenary of Korean Postal Service (5th series). Multicoloured.
1605 70w. Type **904** 40 10
1606 70w. Modern postal emblem and post box 40 10

906 President Chun and Sultan

1984. Visit of Sultan of Brunei.
1607 **906** 70w. multicoloured . . . 40 10

907 President Chun and Sheikh Khalifa

1984. Visit of Sheikh Khalifa of Qatar.
1609 **907** 70w. multicoloured . . . 35 10

908 Child posting Letter

1984. Centenary of Korean Postal Administration. Multicoloured.
1611 70w. Type **908** 35 10
1612 70w. Postman in city . . . 35 10

910 Pope John Paul II

911 Cogwheel, Worker's Tools and Flowers

1984. Visit of Pope John Paul II.
1614 **910** 70w. black 35 10
1615 70w. multicoloured . . . 35 10

1984. Labour Festival.
1617 **911** 70w. multicoloured . . . 30 10

912 Globe, Jetliner, Container Ship and Emblem

913 Map and Flags of S. Korea and Sri Lanka

1984. 63rd/64th Sessions of Customs Co-operation Council, Seoul.
1618 **912** 70w. multicoloured . . . 65 15

1984. Visit of President Jayewardene of Sri Lanka.
1619 **913** 70w. multicoloured . . . 35 10

914 Symbols and Punctuation Marks

915 Expressway

1984. 14th Asian Advertising Congress, Seoul.
1621 **914** 70w. multicoloured . . . 35 10

1984. Opening of 88 Olympic Expressway.
1622 **915** 70w. multicoloured . . . 35 10

916 Laurel, "Victory" and Olympic Rings

917 A.B.U. Emblem and Microphone

1984. 90th Anniv of International Olympic Committee.
1623 **916** 70w. multicoloured . . . 35 10

1984. 20th Anniv of Asia-Pacific Broadcasting Union.
1624 **917** 70w. multicoloured . . . 35 10

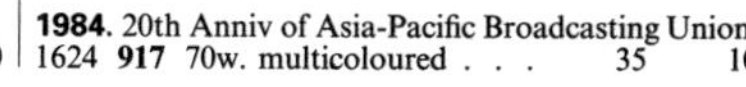

918 Flags of S. Korea and Senegal

1984. Visit of President Abdou Diouf of Senegal.
1625 **918** 70w. multicoloured . . . 35 10

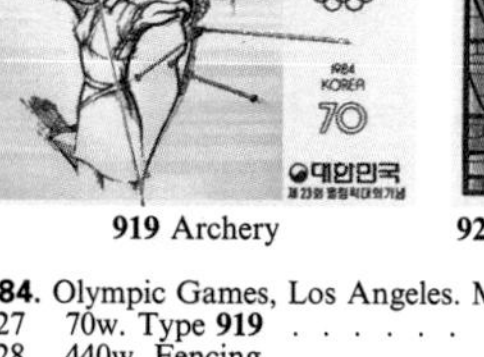

919 Archery

921 Crucifixion

1984. Olympic Games, Los Angeles. Multicoloured.
1627 70w. Type **919** 40 10
1628 440w. Fencing . . . . . . 1·60 35

1984. Centenary of Korean Protestant Church. Multicoloured.
1629 70w. Type **921** 40 10
1630 70w. Cross, vine and dove 40 10

923 Man carrying Silk-covered Lantern

1984. Folk Customs (1st series). "Wedding" (Kim Kyo Man). Multicoloured.
1632 70w. Type **923** 40 10
1633 70w. Bridegroom on horse 40 10
1634 70w. Man playing clarinet 40 10
1635 70w. Bride in sedan chair (51 × 35 mm) 40 10

See also Nos. 1657/8, 1683/4, 1734/8, 1808/11, 1840/3, 1858/61 and 1915/18.

927 Pres. Chun and Mt. Fuji

1984. Pres. Chun's Visit to Japan.
1637 **927** 70w. multicoloured . . . 40 10

928 Flags of S. Korea and Gambia

1984. Visit of President Sir Dawada Kairaba Jawara of Gambia.
1639 **928** 70w. multicoloured . . . 40 10

929 Symbols of International Trade

930 Namsan Tower and National Flags

1984. "Sitra '84" International Trade Fair, Seoul.
1641 **929** 70w. multicoloured . . . 40 10

1984. Visit of President El Hadj Omar Bongo of Gabon.
1642 **930** 70w. multicoloured . . . 40 10

931 Badminton

932 Magnifying Glass and Exhibition Emblem

1984. 65th National Sports Meeting, Taegu. Multicoloured.
1644 70w. Type **931** 40 10
1645 70w. Wrestling 40 10

1984. "Philakorea 1984" International Stamp Exhibition, Seoul. Multicoloured.
1646 70w. Type **932** 40 10
1647 70w. South Gate, Seoul, and stamps (horiz) 40 10

934 Presidents Chun and Gayoom

1984. Visit of President Maumoon Abdul Gayoom of the Maldives.
1650 **934** 70w. multicoloured . . . 40 10

935 "100" and Industrial Symbols

1984. Centenary of Korean Chamber of Commerce and Industry.
1652 **935** 70w. multicoloured . . . 40 10

936 Children playing Jaegi-chagi

937 Ox (bas-relief, Kim Yu Shin's tomb)

1984. Lunar New Year ("Year of the Ox").
1653 **936** 70w. multicoloured . . . 40 10
1654 **937** 70w. multicoloured . . . 40 10

938 I.Y.Y. Emblem

1985. International Youth Year.
1656 **938** 70w. multicoloured . . . 40 10

939 Pounding Rice for New Year Rice Cake

940 Welcoming Year's First Full Moon

1985. Folk Customs (2nd series).
1657 **939** 70w. multicoloured . . . 40 10
1658 **940** 70w. multicoloured . . . 40 10

941 Seoul Olympic Emblem

1985. Olympic Games, Seoul (1988) (1st issue). Multicoloured.
1659 70w.+30w. Type **941** 45 20
1660 70w.+30w. Hodori (mascot) 45 20
See also Nos. 1673/4, 1678/8, 1694/5, 1703/10, 1747/50, 1752/5, 1784/7, 1814/17, 1826/7, 1835/6 and 1844/7.

943 "Still Life with Doll" (Lee Chong Woo)

944 "Rocky Mountain in Early Spring Morning" (Ahn Jung Shik)

1985. Modern Art (1st series).
1662 **943** 70w. multicoloured . . . 40 10
1663 **944** 70w. multicoloured . . . 40 10
See also Nos. 1680/1, 1757/60, 1791/4 and 1875/8.

945 Flags, Statue of Liberty and President Chun

946 Flags, Seoul South Gate and National Flower

1985. Presidential Visit to United States.
1664 **945** 70w. multicoloured . . . 40 10

1985. Visit of President Mohammed Zia-ul-Haq of Pakistan.
1666 **946** 70w. multicoloured . . . 40 10

947 Underwood Hall

1985. Centenary of Yonsei University.
1668 **947** 70w. black, buff and green 40 10

948 Flags and Map

1985. Visit of President Luis Alberto Monge of Costa Rica.
1669 **948** 70w. multicoloured . . . 40 10

949 Rasbora

950 Sailfish

1985. Fishes (1st series).
1671 **949** 70w. multicoloured . . . 75 15
1672 **950** 70w. multicoloured . . . 75 15
See also Nos. 1730/3, 1797/1800, 1881/4, 1903/6 and 1951/4.

951 Rowing

952 National Flags

1985. Olympic Games, Seoul (1988) (2nd issue). Multicoloured.
1673 70w.+30w. Type **951** 45 30
1674 70w.+30w. Hurdling 45 30

1985. Visit of President Hussain Muhammed Ershad of Bangladesh.
1676 **952** 70w. multicoloured . . . 40 10

953 National Flags

1985. Visit of President Joao Bernardo Vieira of Guinea-Bissau.
1678 **953** 70w. multicoloured . . . 40 10

954 "Spring Day on the Farm" (Huh Paik Ryun)

955 "The Exorcist" (Kim Chung Hyun)

1985. Modern Art (2nd issue).
1680 **954** 70w. multicoloured . . . 40 10
1681 **955** 70w. multicoloured . . . 40 10

956 Heavenly Lake, Paekdu and National Flower

1985. 40th Anniv of Liberation.
1682 **956** 70w. multicoloured . . . 40 10

957 Wrestling

958 Janggi

1985. Folk Customs (3rd series).
1683 **957** 70w. multicoloured . . . 40 10
1684 **958** 70w. multicoloured . . . 40 10

959 "The Spring of My Home" (Lee Won Su and Hong Nan Pa)

960 "A Leaf Boat" (Park Hong Keun and Yun Yong Ha)

1985. Korean Music (1st series).
1685 **959** 70w. multicoloured . . . 45 10
1686 **960** 70w. multicoloured . . . 45 10
See also Nos. 1728/9, 1776/7, 1854/5, 1862/3, 1893/4, 1935/6, 1996/7 and 2064/5.

1985. Olympic Games, Seoul (1988) (3rd issue). As T **951**. Multicoloured.
1687 70w.+30w. Basketball . . . 45 20
1688 70w.+30w. Boxing 45 20

961 Satellite, "100" and Dish Aerial

962 Meetings Emblem

1985. Centenary of First Korean Telegraph Service.
1690 **961** 70w. multicoloured . . . 40 10

1985. World Bank and International Monetary Fund Meetings, Seoul.
1691 **962** 70w. multicoloured . . . 40 10

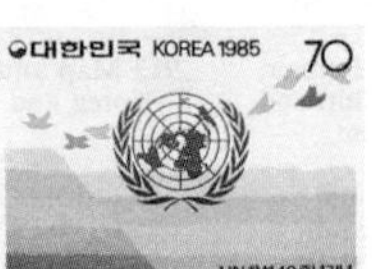

963 U.N. Emblem and Doves

1985. 40th Anniv of U.N.O.
1692 **963** 70w. multicoloured . . . 40 10

964 Red Cross and Hands (detail "Creation of Adam", Michelangelo)

1985. 80th Anniv of Korea Red Cross.
1693 **964** 70w. black, red and blue 45 10

1985. Olympic Games, Seoul (1988) (4th issue). As T **951**. Multicoloured.
1694 70w.+30w. Cycling 40 20
1695 70w.+30w. Canoeing . . . 40 20

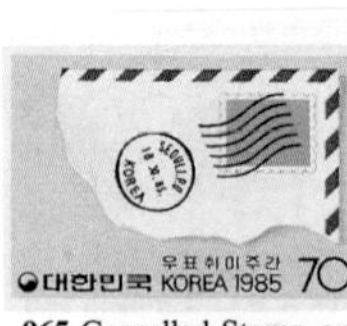

965 Cancelled Stamp on Envelope

966 Tiger (bas-relief, Kim Yu Shin's tomb)

1985. Philatelic Week.
1697 **965** 70w. multicoloured . . . 40 10

1985. Lunar New Year ("Year of the Tiger").
1698 **966** 70w. multicoloured . . . 40 10

967 Mount Fuji and Boeing 747 Jetliner

1985. 20th Anniv of Korea–Japan Treaty on Basic Relations.
1699 **967** 70w. mult (postage) . . 45 10
1700 370w. multicoloured (air) 1·50 50

968 Doves and Globe

970 Pres. Chun, Big Ben and Korean and British Flags

1986. International Peace Year.
1701 **968** 70w. multicoloured . . . 35 10
1702 400w. multicoloured . . 1·75 40

1986. Olympic Games, Seoul (1988) (5th series). As T **951**. Multicoloured.
1703 70w.+30w. Show jumping (postage) 40 20
1704 70w.+30w. Fencing 40 20
1705 70w.+30w. Football 40 20
1706 70w.+30w. Gymnastics . . . 40 20
1707 370w.+100w. As No. 1703 (air) . . . . 1·60 70
1708 400w.+100w. As No. 1704 1·75 70
1709 440w.+100w. As No. 1705 1·90 70
1710 470w.+100w. As No. 1706 2·00 70

1986. Presidential Visit to Europe. Multicoloured.
1711 70w. Type **970** 40 10
1712 70w. Pres. Chun, Eiffel Tower and Korean and French flags 40 10
1713 70w. Pres. Chun, Belgian Parliament and Korean and Belgian flags 40 10
1714 70w. Pres. Chun, Cologne Cathedral and Korean and West German flags 40 10

974/5 Kyongju and Kwanchon Observatories

1986. Science (1st series). Appearance of Halley's Comet.
1716 **974** 70w. multicoloured . . . 30 10
1717 **975** 70w. multicoloured . . . 30 10
See also Nos. 1781/2, 1833/4, 1864/5 and 1898/9.

976 General Assembly Emblem

977 Swallowtail and Flowers

1986. 5th Association of National Olympic Committees General Assembly, Seoul.
1718 **976** 70w. multicoloured . . . 45 10

1986. "Ameripex '86" International Stamp Exhibition, Chicago. Multicoloured.
1719 70w. Type **977** . . . . . . 2·00 75
1720 370w. "Papilio bianor" . . 2·00 75
1721 400w. Swallowtails . . . . 2·00 75
1722 440w. Swallowtail and frog 2·00 75
1723 450w. Swallowtail . . . . . 2·00 75
1724 470w. "Papilio bianor" . . 2·00 75
Nos. 1719/24 were printed together, se-tenant, forming a composite design.

983 Male and Female Symbols in Balance

1986. Centenary of Korean Women's Education.
1725 **983** 70w. multicoloured . . . 35 10

984 National Flags

1986. Visit of President Andre Kolingba of Central African Republic.
1726 **984** 70w. multicoloured . . . 35 10

985 "Half Moon" (Yun Keuk Young)

986 "Let's Go and Pick the Moon" (Yun Seok Jung and Park Tae Hyun)

1986. Korean Music (2nd series).
1728 **985** 70w. multicoloured . . . 35 10
1729 **986** 70w. multicoloured . . . 35 10

987 Cyprinid Fish

988 Ayu

989 Black-spotted Sardine

990 Hammerheads

1986. Fishes (2nd series).
1730 **987** 70w. multicoloured . . . 85 20
1731 **988** 70w. multicoloured . . . 85 20
1732 **989** 70w. multicoloured . . . 85 20
1733 **990** 70w. multicoloured . . . 85 20

991 Flag Carrier and Gong Player

996 Child

1986. Folk Customs (4th series). Farm Music. Multicoloured.
1734 70w. Type **991** 30 10
1735 70w. Drummer and piper 30 10
1736 70w. Drummer and gong player 30 10
1737 70w. Men with ribbons . . 30 10
1738 70w. Man and woman with child 30 10

Nos. 1734/8 were printed together, se-tenant, forming a composite design.

1986. Family Planning.
1739 **996** 80w. multicoloured . . . 40 10

997 Bridge and "63" Building, Seoul

1986. Completion of Han River Development. Multicoloured.
1740 30w. Type **997** 85 25
1741 60w. Buildings and excursion boat 60 25
1742 80w. Rowing boat and Seoul Tower 40 10

Nos. 1740/2 were printed together, se-tenant, forming a composite design.

1000 Emblem

1004 Boy fishing for Stamp

1002 "5", Delegates and Juan Antonio Samaranch (President of International Olympic Committee)

1986. 10th Asian Games, Seoul. Multicoloured.
1743 80w. Type **1000** 40 10
1744 80w. Firework display . . . 40 10

1986. 5th Anniv of Choice of Seoul as 1988 Olympic Games Host City.
1746 **1002** 80w. multicoloured . . 45 10

1986. Olympic Games, Seoul (1988) (6th issue). As T **951**. Multicoloured.
1747 80w.+50w. Weightlifting (postage) . . . . 1·25 60
1748 80w.+50w. Handball . . . . 1·25 60
1749 370w.+100w. As No. 1747 (air) . . . . 1·75 75
1750 400w.+100w. As No. 1748 1·90 75

1986. Olympic Games, Seoul (1988) (7th issue). As T **951**. Multicoloured.
1752 80w.+50w. Judo (postage) 1·10 60
1753 80w.+50w. Hockey . . . . 1·10 60
1754 440w.+100w. As No. 1752 (air) . . . . 1·75 70
1755 470w.+100w. As No. 1753 1·90 70

1986. Philatelic Week.
1756 **1004** 80w. multicoloured . . 40 10

1005 "Chunhyang-do" (Kim Un Ho)

1006 "Flowers" (Lee Sang Bum)

1007 "Portrait of a Friend" (Ku Bon Wung)

1008 "Woman in a Ski Suit" (Son Ung Seng)

1986. Modern Art (3rd series).
1757 **1005** 80w. multicoloured . . 40 10
1758 **1006** 80w. multicoloured . . 40 10
1759 **1007** 80w. multicoloured . . 40 10
1760 **1008** 80w. multicoloured . . 40 10

1009 Rabbit

1010 Eastern Broad-billed Roller ("Roller")

1986. Lunar New Year ("Year of the Rabbit").
1761 **1009** 80w. multicoloured . . 35 10

1986. Birds. Multicoloured.
1762 80w. Type **1010** . . . . . . 1·00 10
1763 80w. Japanese waxwing ("Waxwing") . . . . . . 1·00 10
1764 80w. Black-naped oriole ("Oriole") . . . . 1·00 10
1765 80w. Black-capped kingfisher ("Kingfisher") 1·00 10
1766 80w. Hoopoe . . . . 1·00 10

1011 Siberian Tiger

1012 Bleeding Heart ("Dicentra spectabilis")

1987. Endangered Animals. Multicoloured.
1767 80w. Type **1011** . . . . . . 1·00 30
1768 80w. Leopard cat . . . . . 1·00 30
1769 80w. Red fox . . . . 1·00 30
1770 80w. Wild boar . . . . . . 1·00 30

1987. Flowers. Multicoloured.
1771 550w. Type **1012** . . . . . 1·50 25
1772 550w. Diamond bluebell ("Hanabusaya asiatica") 1·50 25
1773 550w. "Erythronium japonicum" . . . . . . 1·50 25
1774 550w. Pinks ("Dianthus chinensis") . . . . 1·50 25
1775 550w. "Chrysanthemum zawadskii" . . . . 1·50 25

1013 "Barley Field" (Park Wha Mok and Yun Yong Ha)

1014 "Magnolia" (Cho Young Shik and Kim Dong Jin)

1987. Korean Music (3rd series).
1776 **1013** 80w. multicoloured . . 40 10
1777 **1014** 80w. multicoloured . . 40 10

1015 National Flags and Korean National Flower

1987. Visit of President Ahmed Abdallah Abderemane of Comoros.
1778 **1015** 80w. multicoloured . . 35 10

1016 "100", Light Bulb and Hyang Woen Jeong

1987. Centenary of Electric Light in Korea.
1780 **1016** 80w. multicoloured . . 35 10

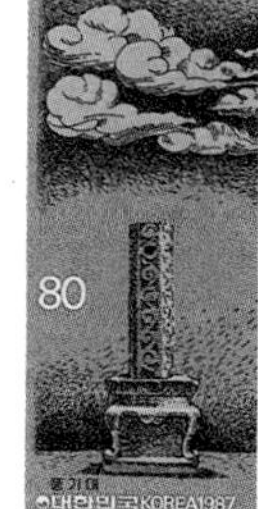

1017 Punggi Wind Observatory

1019 Globes, Crane and Ship

1987. Science (2nd series).
1781 **1017** 80w. dp brown & brown 40 10
1782 – 80w. brown & dp brown 40 10
DESIGN: No. 1782, Rain gauge.

1987. 15th International Association of Ports and Harbours General Session, Seoul.
1783 **1019** 80w. multicoloured . . 40 10

1987. Olympic Games, Seoul (1988) (8th issue). As T **951**. Multicoloured.
1784 80w.+50w. Wrestling . . . 80 25
1785 80w.+50w. Tennis 80 25
1786 80w.+50w. Diving 80 25
1787 80w.+50w. Show jumping 80 25

1020 Flags and Doves

1987. Visit of President U San Yu of Burma.
1789 **1020** 80w. multicoloured . . 40 10

1021 "Valley of Peach Blossoms" (Pyen Kwan Sik)

1022 "Rural Landscape" (Lee Yong Wu)

1023 "Man" (Lee Ma Dong)

1024 "Woman with Water Jar on Head" (sculpture, Yun Hyo Chung)

1987. Modern Art (4th series).
1791 **1021** 80w. multicoloured . . 35 10
1792 **1022** 80w. multicoloured . . 35 10
1793 **1023** 80w. multicoloured . . 35 10
1794 **1024** 80w. multicoloured . . 35 10

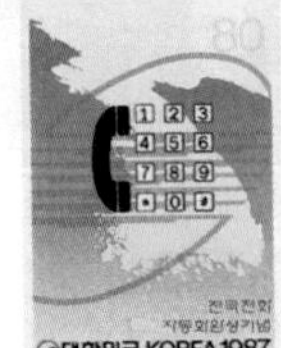
1025 Map and Digital Key Pad

1987. Completion of Automatic Telephone Network (1795) and Communications for Information Year (1796).
1795 80w. Type **1025** 35 10
1796 80w. Emblem 35 10

1027 Cyprinid Fishes

1028 Russell's Oarfish

1029 Cyprinid Fish

1030 Spine-tailed Mobula

1987. Fishes (3rd series).
1797 **1027** 80w. multicoloured . . 85 20
1798 **1028** 80w. multicoloured . . 85 20
1799 **1029** 80w. multicoloured . . 85 20
1800 **1030** 80w. multicoloured . . 85 20

1031 Statue of Indomitable Koreans (detail) and Flags

1033 Map and Pen within Profile

1987. Opening of Independence Hall. Mult.
1801 80w. Type **1031** 35 10
1802 80w. Monument of the Nation and aerial view of Hall 35 10

1987. 16th Pacific Science Congress, Seoul.
1804 **1033** 80w. multicoloured . . 35 10

1034 Flags and Seoul South Gate

1987. Visit of President Virgilio Barco of Colombia.
1806 **1034** 80w. multicoloured . . 40 10

1035/1038 Festivities (½-size illustration)

1987. Folk Customs (5th series). Harvest Moon Day.
1808 **1035** 80w. multicoloured . . 35 10
1809 **1036** 80w. multicoloured . . 35 10
1810 **1037** 80w. multicoloured . . 35 10
1811 **1038** 80w. multicoloured . . 35 10
Nos. 1808/11 were issued together, se-tenant, forming a composite design.

1039 Telephone Dials forming Number

1040 Service Flags and Servicemen

1987. Installation of over 10,000,000 Telephone Lines.
1812 **1039** 80w. multicoloured . . 40 10

1987. Armed Forces Day.
1813 **1040** 80w. multicoloured . . 40 10

1987. Olympic Games, Seoul (1988) (9th issue). As T **951**. Multicoloured.
1814 80w.+50w. Table tennis . . 70 20
1815 80w.+50w. Shooting 70 20
1816 80w.+50w. Archery 70 20
1817 80w.+50w. Volleyball . . . 70 20

1041 Stamps around Child playing Trumpet

1042 Korean Scientist and Map

1987. Philatelic Week.
1819 **1041** 80w. multicoloured . . 35 10

1987. 1st Anniv of South Korea's Signing of Antarctic Treaty.
1820 **1042** 80w. multicoloured . . 80 30

1043 Dragon

1044 Scattered Sections of Apple

1987. Lunar New Year ("Year of the Dragon").
1821 **1043** 80w. multicoloured . . 35 10

1988. Compulsory Pension Programme.
1822 **1044** 80w. multicoloured . . 30 10

1045 Base and Gentoo Penguins

1046 Flag, Olympic Stadium and President Roh Tae Woo

1988. Completion of Antarctic Base.
1823 **1045** 80w. multicoloured . . 70 25

1988. Presidential Inauguration.
1824 **1046** 80w. multicoloured . . 30 10

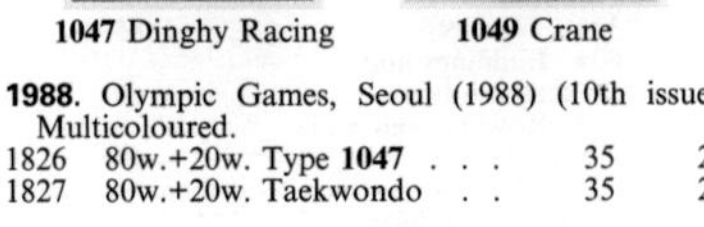
1047 Dinghy Racing

1049 Crane

1988. Olympic Games, Seoul (1988) (10th issue). Multicoloured.
1826 80w.+20w. Type **1047** . . . 35 20
1827 80w.+20w. Taekwondo . . 35 20

1988. Japanese White-naped Crane. Mult.
1829 80w. Type **1049** . . . . . . 1·25 60
1830 80w. Crane taking off . . . 1·25 60
1831 80w. Crane with wings spread . . . . 1·25 60
1832 80w. Two cranes in flight . . 1·25 60

1053 Water Clock

1055 Torch Carrier

1988. Science (3rd series). Multicoloured.
1833 80w. Type **1053** 30 10
1834 80w. Sundial 30 10
Nos. 1833/4 were issued together, se-tenant, forming a composite design.

1988. Olympic Games, Seoul (1988) (11th issue). Multicoloured.
1835 80w.+20w. Type **1055** . . . 35 20
1836 80w.+20w. Stadium 35 20

1057 Globe and Red Cross as Candle

1058 Computer Terminal

1988. 125th Anniv of International Red Cross.
1838 **1057** 80w. multicoloured . . 30 10

1988. 1st Anniv of National Use of Telepress.
1839 **1058** 80w. multicoloured . . 30 10

1059 Woman sitting by Pool and Woman on Swing

1063 Olympic Flag and Pierre de Coubertin (founder of modern Games)

1988. Folk Customs (6th series). Tano Day. Multicoloured.
1840 80w. Type **1059** 65 35
1841 80w. Women dressing their hair 65 35
1842 80w. Woman on swing and boy smelling flowers . . . 65 35
1843 80w. Boys wrestling 65 35
Nos. 1840/3 were issued together, se-tenant, forming a composite design.

1988. Olympic Games, Seoul (1988) (12th issue). Multicoloured.
1844 80w. Type **1063** 30 10
1845 80w. Olympic monument . . 30 10
1846 80w. View of Seoul (vert) 30 10
1847 80w. Women in Korean costume (vert) 30 10

1067 Stamps forming Torch Flame

1068 Pouring Molten Metal from Crucible

1988. "Olymphilex '88" Olympic Stamps Exhibition, Seoul.
1849 **1067** 80w. multicoloured . . 30 10

1988. 22nd International Iron and Steel Institute Conference, Seoul.
1851 **1068** 80w. multicoloured . . 30 10

1069 Gomdoori (mascot)

1988. Paralympic Games, Seoul.
1852 80w. Type **1069** . . . . . . 1·00 50
1853 80w. Archery 50 10

1071 "Homesick" (Lee Eun Sang and Kim Dong Jin)

1072 "The Pioneer" (Yoon Hae Young and Cho Doo Nam)

1988. Korean Music (4th series).
1854 **1071** 80w. multicoloured . . 35 10
1855 **1072** 80w. multicoloured . . 35 10

1073 Girls on See-saw

1075 Dancers

1988. Lunar New Year ("Year of the Snake").
1856 **1073** 80w. multicoloured . . 25 10

1989. Folk Customs (7th series). Mask Dance. Multicoloured.
1858 80w. Type **1075** 25 10
1859 80w. Dancer with fans . . . 25 10
1860 80w. Dancer holding branch 25 10
1861 80w. Dancer with "Lion" 25 10
Nos. 1858/61 were issued together, se-tenant, forming a composite design.

1079 "Arirang"

1080 "Doraji-taryong"

1989. Korean Music (5th series).
1862 **1079** 80w. multicoloured . . 25 10
1863 **1080** 80w. multicoloured . . 25 10

1081/2 Wooden and metal Type Printing

1989. Science (4th series).
1864 **1081** 80w. brown, bis & stone 25 10
1865 **1082** 80w. brown, bis & stone 25 10
Nos. 1864/5 were issued together, se-tenant, forming a composite design.

1083 Teeth, Globe, Pencil and Book

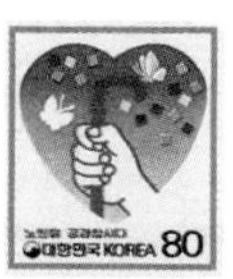
1084 Hand with Stick in Heart

1989. 14th Asian–Pacific Dental Congress.
1866 **1083** 80w. multicoloured . . 25 10

1989. Respect for the Elderly.
1867 **1084** 80w. multicoloured . . 25 10

1085 Emblem

1086 Profiles within Heart

1989. Rotary Int Convention, Seoul.
1868 **1085** 80w. multicoloured . . 25 10

1989. 19th International Council of Nurses Congress, Seoul.
1869 **1086** 80w. multicoloured . . 25 10

1087 "Communication"

1088 "Longevity"

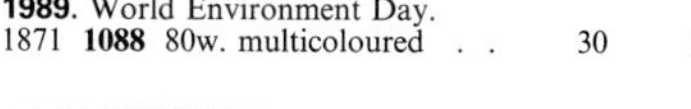
1989. National Information Technology Month.
1870 **1087** 80w. multicoloured . . 25 10

1989. World Environment Day.
1871 **1088** 80w. multicoloured . . 30 10

1089 Satellite, Globe and Dish Aerial

1090 "Liberty guiding the People" (detail, Eugene Delacroix)

1989. 10th Anniv of Asia–Pacific Telecommunity.
1872 **1089** 80w. multicoloured . . 25 10

1989. Bicentenary of French Revolution.
1873 **1090** 80w. multicoloured . . 25 10

1091 Apple and Flask

1989. 5th Asian and Oceanic Biochemists Federation Congress, Seoul.
1874 **1091** 80w. multicoloured . . 25 10

1092 "White Ox" (Lee Joong Sub)

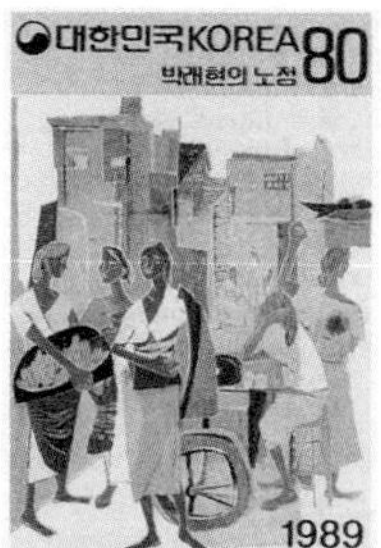
1093 "Street Stall" (Park Lae Hyun)

1094 "Little Girl" (Lee Bong Sang)

1095 "Autumn Scene" (Oh Ji Ho)

1989. Modern Art (5th series).
1875 **1092** 80w. multicoloured . . 30 10
1876 **1093** 80w. multicoloured . . 30 10
1877 **1094** 80w. multicoloured . . 30 10
1878 **1095** 80w. multicoloured . . 30 10

1096 Hunting Scene

1097 Goddess of Law and Ancient Law Code

1989. Seoul Olympics Commemorative Festival and World Sports Festival for Ethnic Koreans.
1879 **1096** 80w. multicoloured . . 25 10

1989. 1st Anniv of Constitutional Court.
1880 **1097** 80w. multicoloured . . 25 10

1098 Banded Knifejaw

1099 Banded Loach

1100 Torrent Catfish

1101 Japanese Pinecone Fish

1989. Fishes (4th series).
1881 **1098** 80w. multicoloured . . 85 20
1882 **1099** 80w. multicoloured . . 85 20
1883 **1100** 80w. multicoloured . . 85 20
1884 **1101** 80w. multicoloured . . 85 20

1102 Emblem

1989. 44th International Eucharistic Congress, Seoul.
1885 **1102** 80w. multicoloured . . 25 10

1103 Control Tower and Boeing 747 Jetliner

1989. 29th International Civil Airports Association World Congress, Seoul.
1886 **1103** 80w. multicoloured . . 35 10

1104 Scissors cutting Burning Banner

1105 Lantern

1989. Fire Precautions Month.
1887 **1104** 80w. multicoloured . . 25 10

1989. Philatelic Week.
1888 **1105** 80w. multicoloured . . 25 10

1106 Cranes

1107 New Year Custom

1989. Lunar New Year ("Year of the Horse").
1890 **1106** 80w. multicoloured . . 25 10
1891 **1107** 80w. multicoloured . . 25 10

1108 "Pakyon Fall"

1109 "Chonan Samgori"

1990. Korean Music (6th series).
1893 **1108** 80w. multicoloured . . 25 10
1894 **1109** 80w. multicoloured . . 25 10

1110 Clouds, Umbrella and Satellite

1111 Child with Rose

1990. World Meteorological Day.
1895 **1110** 80w. multicoloured . . 40 10

1990. 40th Anniv of U.N.I.C.E.F. Work in Korea.
1896 **1111** 80w. multicoloured . . 25 10

1112 Cable, Fish and Route Map

1990. Completion of Cheju Island–Kohung Optical Submarine Cable.
1897 **1112** 80w. multicoloured . . 40 10

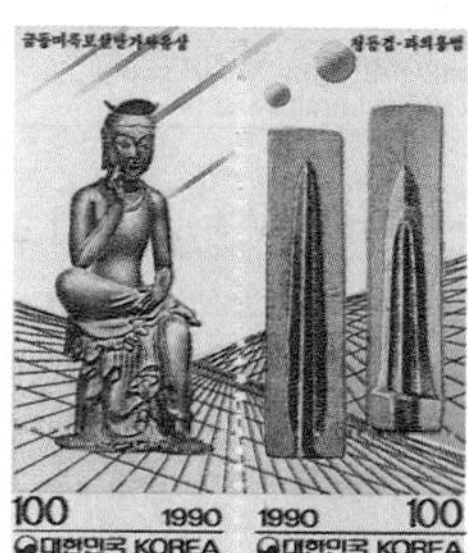
1113/4 Gilt-bronze Maitreya, Spear and Dagger Moulds

1990. Science (5th series). Metallurgy.
1898 **1113** 100w. multicoloured . . 30 15
1899 **1114** 100w. multicoloured . . 30 15
Nos. 1898/9 were issued together, se-tenant, forming the composite design illustrated.

1115 Housing and "20"

1990. 20th Anniv of Saemaul Movement (community self-help programme).
1900 **1115** 100w. multicoloured . . 30 15

1116 Youths

1117 Butterfly Net catching Pollution

1990. Youth Month.
1901 **1116** 100w. multicoloured . . 30 15

1990. World Environmental Day.
1902 **1117** 100w. multicoloured . . 30 15

1118 Belted Bearded Grunt

1119 Kusa Pufferfish

1120 Cherry Salmon

1121 Rosy Bitterling

1990. Fishes (5th series).
1903 **1118** 100w. multicoloured . . 75 20
1904 **1119** 100w. multicoloured . . 75 20
1905 **1120** 100w. multicoloured . . 75 20
1906 **1121** 100w. multicoloured . . 75 20

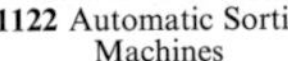

1122 Automatic Sorting Machines
1123 Bandaged Teddy Bear in Hospital Bed

1990. Opening of Seoul Mail Centre.
1907 **1122** 100w. multicoloured . . 30 15

1990. Road Safety Campaign.
1909 **1123** 100w. multicoloured . . 75 30

1124 Campfire
1125 Lily

1990. 8th Korean Boy Scouts Jamboree, Kosong.
1910 **1124** 100w. multicoloured . . 30 15

1990. Wild Flowers (1st series). Multicoloured.
1911 370w. Type **1125** . . . . . 1·25 60
1912 400w. Asters . . . . . 1·40 60
1913 440w. Pheasant's eye . . . 1·25 60
1914 470w. Scabious . . . . . 1·90 60
See also Nos. 1956/9, 1992/5, 2082/5, 2133/6, 2162/5, 2191/4 and 2244/7.

1129 Washing Wool
1133 Church

1990. Folk Customs (8th series). Hand Weaving.
1915 **1129** 100w. red, yellow & blk 30 15
1916 – 100w. multicoloured . . 30 15
1917 – 100w. multicoloured . . 30 15
1918 – 100w. multicoloured . . 30 15
DESIGNS: No. 1916, Spinning; 1917, Dyeing spun yarn; 1918, Weaving.

1990. Centenary of Anglican Church in Korea.
1919 **1133** 100w. multicoloured . . 30 15

1134 Top of Tower
1135 Peas in Pod

1990. 10th Anniv of Seoul Communications Tower.
1920 **1134** 100w. black, blue & red 30 15

1990. Census.
1921 **1135** 100w. multicoloured . . 30 15

1136 "40" and U.N. Emblem
1137 Inlaid Case with Mirror

1990. 40th Anniv of U.N. Development Programme.
1922 **1136** 100w. multicoloured . . 30 15

1990. Philatelic Week.
1923 **1137** 100w. multicoloured . . 30 15

1138 Children feeding Ram
1140 Mascot

1990. Lunar New Year ("Year of the Sheep"). Multicoloured.
1925 100w. Type **1138** 30 15
1926 100w. Crane flying above mountains 30 15

1990. "Expo '93" World's Fair, Taejon (1st issue). Multicoloured.
1928 100w. Type **1140** 30 20
1929 440w. Yin and Yang (exhibition emblem) . . . 1·25 60
See also Nos. 1932/3, 2000/1 and 2058/61.

1142 Books and Emblem
1143 Earth

1991. 30th Anniv of Saemaul Minilibrary.
1931 **1142** 100w. multicoloured . . 30 15

1991. "Expo '93" World's Fair, Taejon (2nd issue). Multicoloured.
1932 100w. Type **1143** 30 15
1933 100w. Expo Tower 30 15

1145 "In a Flower Garden" (Uh Hyo Sun and Kwon Kil Sang)
1146 "Way to the Orchard" (Park Hwa Mok and Kim Kong Sun)

1991. Korean Music (7th series).
1935 **1145** 100w. multicoloured . . 30 15
1936 **1146** 100w. multicoloured . . 30 15

1147 Moth
1148 Beetle

1149 Butterfly
1150 Beetle

1151 Cicada
1152 Water Beetle

1153 Hornet
1154 Ladybirds

1155 Dragonfly
1156 Grasshopper

1991. Insects.
1937 **1147** 100w. multicoloured . . 40 15
1938 **1148** 100w. multicoloured . . 40 15
1939 **1149** 100w. multicoloured . . 40 15
1940 **1150** 100w. multicoloured . . 40 15
1941 **1151** 100w. multicoloured . . 40 15
1942 **1152** 100w. multicoloured . . 40 15
1943 **1153** 100w. multicoloured . . 40 15
1944 **1154** 100w. multicoloured . . 40 15
1945 **1155** 100w. multicoloured . . 40 15
1946 **1156** 100w. multicoloured . . 40 15

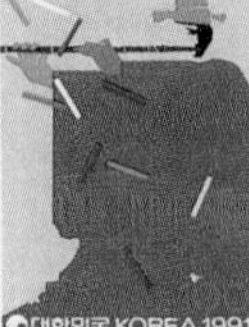

1157 Flautist and Centre
1158 Flag and Provisional Government Building

1991. 40th Anniv of Korean Traditional Performing Arts Centre.
1947 **1157** 100w. multicoloured . . 30 15

1991. 72nd Anniv of Establishment of Korean Provisional Government in Shanghai.
1948 **1158** 100w. multicoloured . . 30 15

1159 Urban Landscape and Emblem

1991. Employment for Disabled People.
1949 **1159** 100w. multicoloured . . 30 15

1160 Bouquet

1991. Teachers' Day.
1950 **1160** 100w. multicoloured . . 30 15

1161 Asian Minnow

1162 Majime Minnows

1163 Blotched Grunter

1164 Ijima's Left-eyed Flounder

1991. Fishes (6th series).
1951 **1161** 100w. multicoloured . . 65 25
1952 **1162** 100w. multicoloured . . 65 25
1953 **1163** 100w. multicoloured . . 65 25
1954 **1164** 100w. multicoloured . . 65 25

1165 Animals waiting to Board Bus
1166 "Aerides japonicum"

1991. "Waiting One's Turn" Campaign.
1955 **1165** 100w. multicoloured . . 30 15

1991. Wild Flowers (2nd series). Mult.
1956 100w. Type **1166** 35 15
1957 100w. "Heloniopsis orientalis" 35 15
1958 370w. "Aquilegia buergeriana" 90 40
1959 440w. "Gentiana zollingeri" 1·25 40

1167 Scout with Semaphore Flags
1168 "Y.M.C.A."

1991. 17th World Scout Jamboree.
1960 **1167** 100w. multicoloured . . 30 10

1991. Young Men's Christian Association World Assembly, Seoul.
1962 **1168** 100w. multicoloured . . 25 10

1169 Derelict Steam Locomotive and Family Members Reunited
1170 Globe, Rainbow, Dove and U.N. Emblem

1991. "North–South Reunification".
1963 **1169** 100w. multicoloured . . 90 20

1991. Admission of South Korea to United Nations Organization.
1964 **1170** 100w. multicoloured . . 25 10

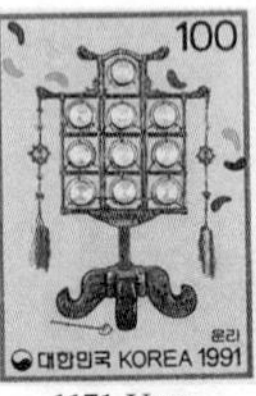

1171 Unra
1172 Jing

1173 Galgo
1174 Saeng-hwang

1991. Traditional Musical Instruments (1st series).
1965 **1171** 100w. multicoloured . . 40 20
1966 **1172** 100w. multicoloured . . 40 20
1967 **1173** 100w. multicoloured . . 40 20
1968 **1174** 100w. multicoloured . . 40 20
See also Nos. 1981/4.

1175 Film and Theatrical Masks

1176 Globe and Satellite

1991. Culture Month.
1969 **1175** 100w. multicoloured . . 25 10

1991. "Telecom 91" Int Telecommunications Exhibition, Geneva.
1970 **1176** 100w. multicoloured . . 25 10

1177 Hexagonals

1178 Bamboo

1179 Geometric

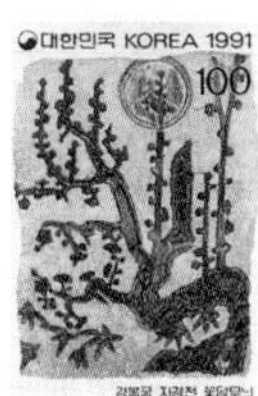
1180 Tree

1991. Korean Beauty (1st series). Kottams (patterns on walls) from Jakyung Hall, Kyungbok Palace.
1971 **1177** 100w. multicoloured . . 55 25
1972 **1178** 100w. multicoloured . . 55 25
1973 **1179** 100w. multicoloured . . 55 25
1974 **1180** 100w. multicoloured . . 55 25
See also Nos. 2006/9, 2068/71, 2103/6, 2157/60, 2219/22, 2257/60, 2308/15, 2350/6 and 2437/40.

1181 Light Bulb turning off Switch

1182 "Longevity"

1991. Energy Saving Campaign.
1975 **1181** 100w. multicoloured . . 25 10

1991. Lunar New Year ("Year of the Monkey"). Multicoloured.
1976 100w. Type **1182** 40 10
1977 100w. Flying kites 55 10

1184 Stamps

1991. Philatelic Week.
1979 **1184** 100w. multicoloured . . 25 10

1185 Yonggo

1186 Chwago

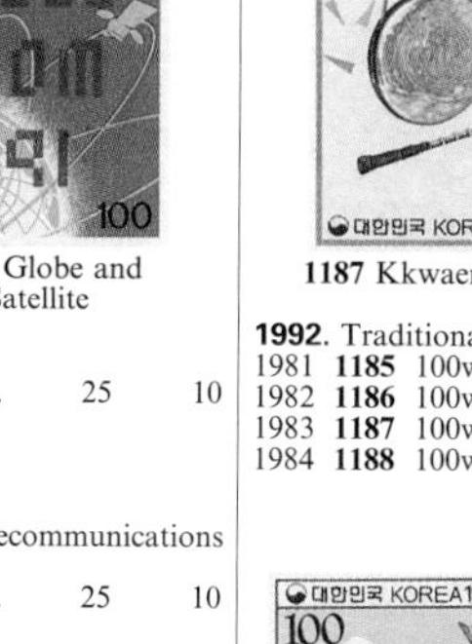
1187 Kkwaenggwari

1188 T'ukchong

1992. Traditional Musical Instruments (2nd series).
1981 **1185** 100w. multicoloured . . 40 15
1982 **1186** 100w. multicoloured . . 40 15
1983 **1187** 100w. multicoloured . . 40 15
1984 **1188** 100w. multicoloured . . 40 15

1189 White Hibiscus

1191 Satellite

1992. "Hibiscus syriacus" (national flower). Multicoloured.
1985 100w. Type **1189** 45 25
1986 100w. Pink hibiscus 45 25

1992. Science Day.
1987 **1191** 100w. multicoloured . . 25 10

1192 Yoon Pong Gil

1193 Children and Heart

1992. 60th Death Anniv of Yoon Pong Gil (independence fighter).
1988 **1192** 100w. multicoloured . . 25 10

1992. Child Protection.
1989 **1193** 100w. multicoloured . . 30 10

1194 Japanese Warship attacking Korean Settlement

1195 Farmer

1992. 400th Anniv of Start of Im-Jin War.
1990 **1194** 100w. multicoloured . . 35 10

1992. 60th International Fertilizer Industry Association Conference, Seoul.
1991 **1195** 100w. multicoloured . . 25 10

1992. Wild Flowers (3rd series). As T **1166**. Multicoloured.
1992 100w. "Lychnis wilfordii" 30 10
1993 100w. "Lycoris radiata" . . 30 10
1994 370w. "Commelina communis" . . . . 1·00 45
1995 440w. "Calanthe striata" . . 1·00 45

1196 "Longing for Mt. Keumkang" (Han Sang Ok and Choi Young Shurp)

1197 "The Swing" (Kim Mal Bong and Geum Su Hyeon)

1992. Korean Music (8th series).
1996 **1196** 100w. multicoloured . . 30 10
1997 **1197** 100w. multicoloured . . 30 10

1198 Gymnastics

1199 Stylized View of Exhibition

1992. Olympic Games, Barcelona. Multicoloured.
1998 100w. Type **1198** 30 10
1999 100w. Pole vaulting 30 10

1992. "Expo '93" World's Fair, Taejon (3rd issue). Multicoloured.
2000 100w. Type **1199** 25 10
2001 100w. "Expo 93" 25 10

1201 Korea Exhibition Centre and South Gate, Seoul

1992. 21st Universal Postal Union Congress, Seoul (1st issue). Multicoloured.
2003 100w. Type **1201** 25 10
2004 100w. Tolharubang (stone grandfather), Cheju . . . 25 10
See also Nos. 2075/6, 2088 and 2112/15.

1203 Woven Pattern

1204 Fruit and Flower Decorations

1205 Carved Decorations

1206 Coral, Butterfly and Pine Resin Decorations

1992. Korean Beauty (2nd series). Maedeups (tassels).
2006 **1203** 100w. multicoloured . . 40 15
2007 **1204** 100w. multicoloured . . 40 15
2008 **1205** 100w. multicoloured . . 40 15
2009 **1206** 100w. multicoloured . . 40 15

1207 Lee Pong Chang

1208 Hwang Young Jo (Barcelona, 1992)

1992. 60th Death Anniv of Lee Pong Chang (independence fighter).
2010 **1207** 100w. brown and orange 30 10

1992. Korean Winners of Olympic Marathon. Multicoloured.
2011 100w. Type **1208** 60 15
2012 100w. Shon Kee Chung (Berlin, 1936) 60 15

1209 Sails on Map of Americas

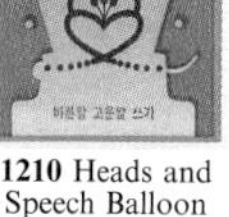

1210 Heads and Speech Balloon

1992. 500th Anniv of Discovery of America by Columbus.
2014 **1209** 100w. multicoloured . . 70 10

1992. Campaign for Purification of Language.
2015 **1210** 100w. multicoloured . . 70 10

1211 Flowers and Stamps

1212 Cockerels in Snow-covered Yard

1992. Philatelic Week.
2016 **1211** 100w. multicoloured . . 70 10

1992. Lunar New Year ("Year of the Cock"). Mult.
2018 100w. Type **1212** 60 10
2019 100w. Flying kites 60 10

1214 Emblem, Globe and Woman holding Bowl

1992. International Nutrition Conference, Rome.
2021 **1214** 100w. multicoloured . . 85 10

1215 View of Centre and Logo

1993. Inauguration of Seoul Arts Centre's Opera House.
2022 **1215** 110w. multicoloured . . 85 15

1216 Pres. Kim Young Sam, Flag and Mt. Paekdu Lake

1217 National Flag

1993. Inauguration of 14th President.
2023 **1216** 110w. multicoloured . . 85 15

1993. No. 2036a orange, black and pink, others multicoloured.
2025 10w. Type **1217** 10 10
2026 20w. White stork 40 10
2026a 20w. Black-crowned night heron 10 10
2027 30w. White magnolia . . . 10 10
2028 40w. Korean white pine . . 10 10
2028a 40w. "Purpuricenus lituralus" (beetle) . . . 10 10
2028b 50w. Water cock 10 10
2029 60w. Squirrel 10 10
2030 70w. Chinese lanterns (plant) 10 10
2030a 80w. Japanese white eye on japonica branch 10 10
2031 90w. Oriental scops owl . . 15 10
2031a 100w. Dishcloth gourd . . 35 10
2032 110w. "Hibiscus syriacus" (plant) 25 10
2033 120w. As 110w. 15 10
2034 130w. Narcissi 20 10
2034c 140w. As 130w. 15 10
2035 150w. Painted porcelain jar 25 10
2036 160w. Pine tree (horiz) . . 30 10
2036a 170w. Crayfish 20 10
2036c 170w. Far eastern curlew 20 10
2037 180w. Little tern (horiz) . . 50 15
2037a 190w. As 110w. 20 10
2038 200w. Turtle (horiz) . . . 30 10
2038a 200w. Snow crab (horiz) 30 10
2038b 210w. As 180w. 35 10
2038c 260w. As 180w. 25 10
2039 300w. Eurasian skylark (horiz) 45 15
2040 370w. Drum and drum dance (horiz) 65 15
2041 400w. Celadon cockerel water dropper (horiz) . . 65 15
2042 420w. As 370w. 65 15
2043 440w. Haho'i mask and Ssirum wrestlers (horiz) 80 15
2044 480w. As 440w. 75 15
2045 500w. Celadon pomegranate water dropper 80 15
2045a 600w. Hong Yong-sik (first Postmaster General) . . 90 15
2046 700w. Gilt-bronze Bongnae-san incense burner (23 × 34 mm) . . 1·10 25

2046a 700w. Cloud and crane jade ornament, Koryo Dynasty . . . . 1·10 25
2046b 710w. King Sejong and alphabet . . . . 1·25 25
2046c 800w. Cheju ponies . . . . 1·25 20
2047 900w. Gilt-bronze buddha triad (23 × 34 mm) . . . 1·60 30
2048 910w. As 710w. . . . . . 1·60 30
2049 930w. Celadon pitcher (blue background) (23 × 31 mm) . . . . . 1·50 25
2049a 930w. As No. 2049 (brown background) . . . . . . 1·60 25
2049b 1000w. Stone guardian animal (from tomb of King Muryong) (32 × 21 mm) . . . . . 1·60 35
2050 1050w. As 930w. . . . . . 1·60 40
2050a 1170w. Bronze incense burner . . . . 2·25 25
2050b 1190w. As 930w. . . . . . 2·75 30
2050c 2000w. Crown from tomb of Shinch'on-ni . . . . 3·00 35

1243 Student and Computer

1244 Emblem and Map

1993. Korean Student Inventions Exhibition.
2051 **1243** 110w. mauve and silver 85 10

1993. International Human Rights Conference, Vienna, Austria.
2052 **1244** 110w. multicoloured . . 85 10

1245 Hand scooping Globe from Water

1246 Matsu-take Mushroom ("Tricholoma matsutake")

1993. "Water is Life".
2053 **1245** 110w. multicoloured . . 85 10

1993. Fungi (1st series). Multicoloured.
2054 110w. Type **1246** 60 10
2055 110w. "Ganoderma lucidum" 60 10
2056 110w. "Lentinula edodes" . . 60 10
2057 110w. Oyster fungus ("Pleurotus ostreatus") . . 60 10
See also Nos. 2095/8, 2146/9, 2207/10, 2249/52 and 2293/6.

1247 Government Pavilion

1248 International Pavilion and Mascot

1249 Recycling Art Pavilion

1250 Telecom Pavilion

1993. "Expo '93" World's Fair, Taejon (4th issue).
2058 **1247** 110w. multicoloured . . 50 10
2059 **1248** 110w. multicoloured . . 50 10
2060 **1249** 110w. multicoloured . . 50 10
2061 **1250** 110w. multicoloured . . 50 10

1251 Emblems

1993. 19th Congress of International Society of Orthopaedic and Trauma Surgery.
2063 **1251** 110w. multicoloured . . 85 10

1252 "O Dol Ddo Gi" (Cheju Island folk song)

1253 "Ong He Ya" (barley threshing song)

1993. Korean Music (9th series).
2064 **1252** 110w. multicoloured . . 60 10
2065 **1253** 110w. multicoloured . . 60 10

1254 Janggu Drum Dance

1255 Emblem

1993. "Visit Korea" Year (1994) (1st issue).
2066 **1254** 110w. multicoloured . . 50 10
2067 **1255** 110w. multicoloured . . 50 10
See also Nos. 2086/7.

1256 "Twin Tigers" (military officials, 1st to 3rd rank)

1260 Campaign Emblem

1993. Korean Beauty (3rd series). Hyoongbae (embroidered insignia of the Chosun dynasty). Multicoloured.
2068 110w. Type **1256** 50 10
2069 110w. "Single Crane" (civil officials, 4th to 9th rank) 50 10
2070 110w. "Twin Cranes" (civil officials, 1st to 3rd rank) 50 10
2071 110w. "Dragon" (King) . . 50 10

1993. Anti-litter Campaign.
2072 **1260** 110w. multicoloured . . 50 10

1261 "Eggplant and Oriental Long-nosed Locust" (Shin Saim Dang)

1262 "Weaving"

1993. Philatelic Week.
2073 **1261** 110w. multicoloured . . 50 10

1993. 21st U.P.U. Congress, Seoul (2nd issue). Paintings by Kim Hong Do. Multicoloured.
2075 110w. Type **1262** 50 10
2076 110w. "Musicians and a Dancer" (vert) 50 10

1263 Ribbon and Globe as "30", Freighter and Ilyushin Il-86 Airliner

1993. 30th Trade Day.
2078 **1263** 110w. multicoloured . . 60 10

1264 Sapsaree and Kite

1993. Lunar New Year ("Year of the Dog"). Multicoloured.
2079 110w. Type **1264** 50 10
2080 110w. Puppy with New Year's Greetings bow . . 50 10

1993. Wild Flowers (4th series). As T **1166**.
2082 110w. "Weigela hortensis" 75 10
2083 110w. "Iris ruthenica" . . . 75 10
2084 110w. "Aceriphyllum rosii" 75 10
2085 110w. Marsh marigold ("Caltha palustris") . . . 75 10

1266 Flautist on Cloud

1267 T'alch'um Mask Dance

1994. "Visit Korea" Year (2nd issue).
2086 **1266** 110w. multicoloured . . 50 10
2087 **1267** 110w. multicoloured . . 50 10

1268 Map'ae, Horse, Envelope and Emblem

1269 Monument

1994. 21st U.P.U. Congress, Seoul (3rd issue).
2088 **1268** 300w. multicoloured . . 1·25 15
The map'ae was a token which gave authority to impress post horses.

1994. 75th Anniv of Samil (Independence) Movement.
2090 **1269** 110w. multicoloured . . 65 10

1270 Great Purple ("Sasakia charonda")

1994. Protection of Wildlife and Plants (1st series). Multicoloured.
2091 110w. Type **1270** (butterfly) 60 10
2092 110w. "Allomyrina dichotoma" (beetle) . . . 60 10
See also Nos. 2143/4, 2186/7, 2241/2, 2275/8, 2326/9, 2383/6 and 2481/4.

1271 Family of Mandarins

1994. International Year of the Family.
2094 **1271** 110w. multicoloured . . 65 10

1994. Fungi (2nd series). As T **1246**. Multicoloured.
2095 110w. Common morel ("Morchella esculenta") 50 10
2096 110w. "Gomphus floccosus" 50 10
2097 110w. "Cortinarius purpurascens" 50 10
2098 110w. "Oudemansiella platyphylla" 50 10

1272 Museum

1994. Inauguration of War Memorial Museum, Yongsan (Seoul).
2100 **1272** 110w. multicoloured . . 65 10

1273 Text and Dove

1994. "Philakorea 1994" International Stamp Exhibition, Seoul (1st issue).
2101 **1273** 910w. multicoloured . . 2·00 40
See also Nos. 2107/9.

1274 Taeguk (Yin-Yang) Fan

1275 Crane Fan

1276 Pearl Fan

1277 Wheel Fan

1994. Korean Beauty (4th series). Fans.
2103 **1274** 110w. multicoloured . . 50 10
2104 **1275** 110w. multicoloured . . 50 10
2105 **1276** 110w. multicoloured . . 50 10
2106 **1277** 110w. multicoloured . . 50 10

1278 "Wintry Days" (Kim Chong Hui)

1282 "Sword Dance" (Sin Yun Bok)

1994. "Philakorea 1994" International Stamp Exhibition, Seoul (2nd issue). Multicoloured.
2107 130w. Type **1278** 50 10
2108 130w. "Grape" (Choe Sok Hwan) 50 10
2109 130w. "Riverside Scene" (Kim Duk Sin) 50 10

1994. 21st U.P.U. Congress, Seoul (4th issue). Multicoloured.
2112 130w. Type **1282** 50 10
2113 130w. "Book Shelves" (detail of folk painting showing stamps) 50 10
2114 130w. Congress emblem . . 50 10
2115 130w. Hong Yung Sik (postal reformer) and Heinrich von Stephan (founder of U.P.U.) (horiz) 75 10

1283 Old Map

1284 Mail Van

1994. 600th Anniv of Adoption of Seoul as Capital of Korea (1st issue).
2118 **1283** 130w. multicoloured . . 60 10
See also No. 2139.

1994. Transport. Multicoloured.
2121 300w. Type **1284** 60 15
2122 330w. Airplane 80 15
2122a 340w. Airplane facing left 70 10
2122b 380w. As 340w. 60 10
2123 390w. Airplane (different) 1·10 15
2124 400w. As 330w. . . . . . 1·25 15
2126 540w. Streamlined diesel train . . . . 2·10 15
2127 560w. As 330w. . . . . . 2·25 15
2130 1190w. River cruiser . . . 3·75 25
2131 1300w. As 330w. . . . . . 4·00 40
2132 1340w. As 340w. . . . . . 4·25 35
2132a 1380w. As 340w. . . . . . 4·50 35

1994. Wild Flowers (5th series). As T **1166**. Multicoloured.
2133 130w. "Gentiana jamesii" . . . 45 10
2134 130w. "Geranium eriostemon var. megalanthum" 45 10
2135 130w. "Leontopodium japonicum" 45 10
2136 130w. "Lycoris aurea" . . . 45 10

1285 "Water Melon and Field Mice" (detail of folding screen, Shin Saimdang)

1286 "600"

1994. Philatelic Week.
2137 **1285** 130w. multicoloured . . 65 10

1994. 600th Anniv of Seoul as Capital (2nd issue).
2139 **1286** 130w. multicoloured . . 65 10

1287 Pigs travelling in Snow

1994. Lunar New Year ("Year of the Pig"). Multicoloured.
2140 130w. Type **1287** 60 10
2141 130w. Family in forest . . . 60 10

1995. Protection of Wildlife and Plants (2nd series). Multicoloured.
2143 130w. Plancy's green pond frog ("Rana plancyi") . . 60 10
2144 130w. Common toad ("Bufo bufo") 60 10

1995. Fungi (3rd series). As T **1246**. Multicoloured.
2146 130w. Shaggy ink caps ("Coprinus comatus") . . 45 10
2147 130w. Chicken mushroom ("Laetiporus sulphureus") 45 10
2148 130w. "Lentinus lepideus" 45 10
2149 130w. Cracked green russula ("Russula virescens") . . 45 10

1290 Spheres around Reactor

1291 Scales of Justice

1995. Completion of Hanaro Research Reactor.
2151 **1290** 130w. multicoloured . . 65 10

1995. Centenary of Judicial System.
2152 **1291** 130w. multicoloured . . 65 10

1292 Tiger

1995. Centenary of Law Education.
2153 **1292** 130w. multicoloured . . 65 10

1293 Dooly the Little Dinosaur (Kim Soo Jeung)

1294 Kochuboo (Kim Yong Hwan)

1995. Cartoons (1st series). Multicoloured.
2154 **1293** 130w. multicoloured . . 70 10
2155 **1294** 440w. multicoloured . . 1·25 15
See also Nos. 2196/7, 2234/5, 2280/1, 2322/4 and 2498/500.

1295 Gate of Eternal Youth, Changdokkung Palace

1296 Fish Water Gate, Chuhamru Pavilion, Changdokkung Palace

1297 Pomosa Temple Gate, Pusan City

1298 Yangban Residence Gate, Hahoe Village

1995. Korean Beauty (5th series). Gates.
2157 **1295** 130w. multicoloured . . 50 10
2158 **1296** 130w. multicoloured . . 50 10
2159 **1297** 130w. multicoloured . . 50 10
2160 **1298** 130w. multicoloured . . 50 10

1299 Lion and Emblem

1995. 78th Convention of Lions Clubs International.
2161 **1299** 130w. multicoloured . . 65 10

1995. Wild Flowers (6th series). As T **1166**. Multicoloured.
2162 130w. "Halenia corniculata" 50 10
2163 130w. "Erythronium japonicum" 50 10
2164 130w. "Iris odaesanensis" 50 10
2165 130w. "Leontice microrrhyncha" 50 10

1300 National Flag

1301 Telescope

1995. 50th Anniv of Liberation. Multicoloured.
2166 130w. Type **1300** 60 10
2167 440w. Anniversary emblem (96 × 19 mm) . . . . . . 1·40 15

1995. Inauguration of Mt. Bohyun Optical Astronomy Observatory.
2169 **1301** 130w. multicoloured . . 65 10

1302 Turtle's Back Song

1303 Song from "Standards of Musical Science"

1995. Literature (1st series).
2170 **1302** 130w. multicoloured . . 60 10
2171 **1303** 130w. multicoloured . . 60 10
See also Nos. 2212/13, 2269/70, 2301/2 and 2344/7.

1304 "50 Th" incorporating Man with Wheat

1995. 50th Anniv of F.A.O.
2172 **1304** 150w. black and violet 70 10

1305 Open Bible

1306 Families in Houses

1995. Centenary of Korean Bible Society.
2174 **1305** 150w. multicoloured . . 70 10

1995. Population and Housing Census.
2175 **1306** 150w. multicoloured . . 70 10

1307 Dove of Flags

1995. 50th Anniv of United Nations Organization.
2176 **1307** 150w. multicoloured . . 70 10

1308 Rontgen

1309 "Water Pepper and Mantis" (detail of folding screen, Shin Saim Dang)

1995. Centenary of Discovery of X-Rays by Wilhelm Rontgen.
2177 **1308** 150w. multicoloured . . 70 10

1995. Philatelic Week.
2178 **1309** 150w. multicoloured . . 70 10

1310 Rat and Snowman

1312 Miroku Bosatsu, Koryu Temple, Kyoto

1995. Lunar New Year ("Year of the Rat"). Multicoloured.
2180 150w. Type **1310** 60 10
2181 150w. Cranes and pine trees (horiz) 60 10

1995. 30th Anniv of Resumption of Korea–Japan Diplomatic Relations.
2183 **1312** 420w. multicoloured . . 1·40 15

1313 Cable Route

1314 "30" and Molecule

1996. Inauguration of Korea–China Submarine Cable.
2184 **1313** 420w. multicoloured . . 70 15

1996. 30th Anniv of Korea Institute of Science and Technology.
2185 **1314** 150w. multicoloured . . 70 10

1996. Protection of Wildlife and Plants (3rd series). As T **1270**. Multicoloured.
2186 150w. Black pond turtle ("Geoclemys reevesii") . . 60 10
2187 150w. Ground skink ("Scincella laterale") . . . 60 10

1315 Satellite and Launching Pad

1996. Launch of "Mugunghwa 2" Telecommunications Satellite.
2189 **1315** 150w. multicoloured . . 70 10

1316 So Chae P'il (founder) and Leader from First Issue

1996. Centenary of "Tongnip Shinmun" (first independent newspaper).
2190 **1316** 150w. multicoloured . . 70 10

1996. Wild Flowers (7th series). As T **1166**. Multicoloured.
2191 150w. "Cypripedium macranthum" 55 10
2192 150w. "Trilium tschonoskii" 55 10
2193 150w. "Viola variegata" . . 55 10
2194 150w. "Hypericum ascyron" 55 10

1317 Anniversary Emblem and Cadets

1996. 50th Anniv of Korean Military Academy.
2195 **1317** 150w. multicoloured . . 70 10

1318 Gobau (Kim Song Hwan)

1319 Battle between Kkach'i and Caesarius (Lee Hyun Se) (from film "Armageddon")

1996. Cartoons (2nd series).
2196 **1318** 150w. multicoloured . . 60 10
2197 **1319** 150w. multicoloured . . 60 10

1320 Anniversary Emblem

1321 Globe and Congress Emblem

1996. 50th Anniv of Korean Girl Scouts.
2199 **1320** 150w. multicoloured . . 70 10

1996. 35th World Congress of International Advertising Association, Seoul.
2200 **1321** 150w. multicoloured . . 70 10

1322 Syringes and Drugs

1996. International Anti-drug Day.
2201 **1322** 150w. multicoloured . . 70 10

1323 Skater

1324 Torch Bearer

1996. World University Students' Games, Muju and Chonju (1st issue). Multicoloured.
2202 150w. Type **1323** 90 10
2203 150w. Games emblem (vert) 90 10
See also Nos. 2228/9.

1996. Olympic Games, Atlanta. Multicoloured.
2204 150w. Type **1324** 65 10
2205 150w. Games emblem . . . 65 10

1996. Fungi (4th series). As T **1246**. Multicoloured.
2207 150w. "Amanita inaurata" 70 10
2208 150w. "Paxillus atrotomentosus" 70 10
2209 150w. "Rhodophyllus crassipes" 70 10
2210 150w. "Sarcodon imbricatum" 70 10

1327 Requiem for a Deceased Sister

1328 Ode to Knight Kip'a

1996. Literature (2nd series).
2212 **1327** 150w. multicoloured . . 75 10
2213 **1328** 150w. multicoloured . . 75 10

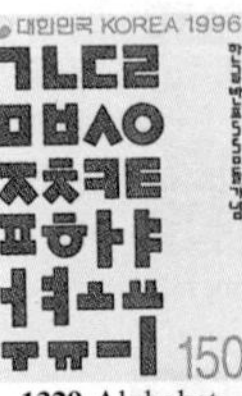
1329 Alphabet

1330 Castle

1996. 550th Anniv of Han-Gul (Korean alphabet created by King Sejong).
2215 **1329** 150w. black and grey 70 10

1996. Bicentenary of Suwon Castle.
2217 **1330** 400w. multicoloured . . 1·90 15

1331 Front Gate, University Flag and Emblem

1996. 50th Anniv of Seoul National University.
2218 **1331** 150w. multicoloured . . 70 10

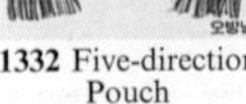
1332 Five-direction Pouch

1333 Chinese Phoenix Pouch (Queen's Court Pouch)

1334 Princess Pokon's Wedding Pouch

1335 Queen Yunbi's Pearl Pouch

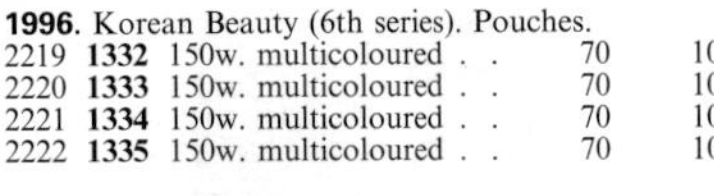
1996. Korean Beauty (6th series). Pouches.
2219 **1332** 150w. multicoloured . . 70 10
2220 **1333** 150w. multicoloured . . 70 10
2221 **1334** 150w. multicoloured . . 70 10
2222 **1335** 150w. multicoloured . . 70 10

1336 "Poppy and Lizard" (detail of folding screen, Shin Saimdang)

1337 Children riding Ox

1996. Philatelic Week.
2223 **1336** 150w. multicoloured . . 70 10

1996. Lunar New Year ("Year of the Ox"). Multicoloured.
2225 150w. Type **1337** 95 10
2226 150w. Boy piper and resting ox 95 10

1339 Figure Skating

1340 Coins forming "100"

1997. World University Students' Games, Muju and Chonju (2nd issue). Multicoloured.
2228 150w. Type **1339** 95 10
2229 150w. Skiing 95 10

1997. Centenary of Foundation of Hansong Bank (first commercial bank in Korea).
2231 **1340** 150w. multicoloured . . 70 10

1341 "Auspicious Turtles" (painting)

1342 Globe, Pen and open Book (Jeon Chong Kwan)

1997. Interparliamentary Union Conference, Seoul.
2232 **1341** 150w. multicoloured . . 70 10

1997. World Book and Copyright Day.
2233 **1342** 150w. multicoloured . . 70 10

1343 A Long, Long Journey in Search of Mummy (Kim Chong Nae)

1344 Run, Run, Hannie (Lee Chin Ju)

1997. Cartoons (3rd series).
2234 **1343** 150w. multicoloured . . 70 10
2235 **1344** 150w. multicoloured . . 70 10

1345 Torch Bearer

1997. 2nd East Asian Games, Pusan.
2237 **1345** 150w. multicoloured . . 70 10

1346 Jules Rimet (founder)

1347 "Chukkuk" (Lee Chul Joo)

1997. World Cup Football Championship (2002), South Korea and Japan (1st issue).
2238 **1346** 150w. multicoloured . . 60 10
2239 **1347** 150w. multicoloured . . 60 10
See also Nos. 2284/7.

1997. Protection of Wildlife and Plants (4th series). As T **1270**. Multicoloured.
2241 150w. Chinese nine-spined sticklebacks ("Pungitius sinensis") 70 10
2242 150w. Spot-eared brook perch ("Coreoperca kawamebari") 70 10

1997. Wild Flowers (8th series). As T **1166**. Multicoloured.
2244 150w. "Belamcanda chinensis" 75 10
2245 150w. "Belamcanda chinensis" 75 10
2246 150w. "Campanula takesimana" 75 10
2247 150w. "Magnolia sieboldii" 75 10

1348 Emblem and "97" forming Face

1349 Seoul South Gate and Emblem

1997. 2nd Art Biennale, Kwangju.
2248 **1348** 150w. multicoloured . . 70 10

1997. Fungi (5th series). As T **1246**. Multicoloured.
2249 150w. "Inocybe fastigiata" 75 10
2250 150w. "Panaeolus papilionaceus" 75 10
2251 150w. "Ramaria flava" . . 75 10
2252 150w. Fly agaric ("Amanita muscaria") 75 10

1997. 85th World Dental Congress, Seoul.
2254 **1349** 170w. multicoloured . . 20 10

1350 Harbour and Score

1997. Centenary of Mokpo Port.
2255 **1350** 170w. multicoloured . . 70 10

1351 Main Building, Pyongyang

1997. Centenary of Founding of Soongsil Academy in Pyongyang (now situated in Seoul).
2256 **1351** 170w. multicoloured . . 70 10

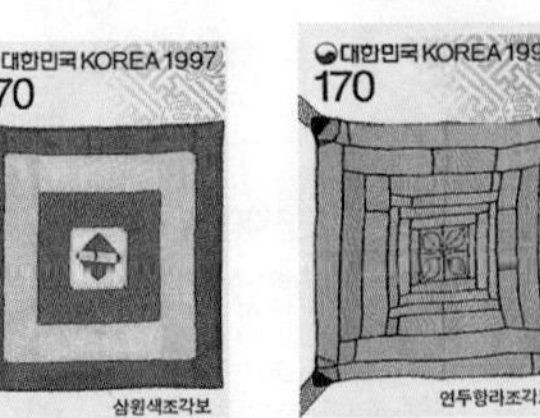
1352 Concentric Squares

1353 Green Silk

1354 Pattern of Squares

1355 Pattern of Squares and Triangles

1997. Korean Beauty (7th series). Patchwork Pojagi (wrapping cloths).
2257 **1352** 170w. multicoloured . . 65 10
2258 **1353** 170w. multicoloured . . 65 10
2259 **1354** 170w. multicoloured . . 65 10
2260 **1355** 170w. multicoloured . . 65 10

1356 "Hollyhock and Frog" (detail of folding screen, Shin Saimdang)

1357 Tiger's Head

1997. Philatelic Week.
2261 **1356** 170w. multicoloured . . 70 10

1997. Lunar New Year ("Year of the Tiger"). Multicoloured.
2263 170w. Type **1357** 70 10
2264 170w. "Magpie and Tiger" (folk painting) 70 10

1359 Buddha, Sokkuram Shrine

1360 Pulguk Temple

1997. World Heritage Sites (1st series).
2266 **1359** 170w. multicoloured . . 20 10
2267 **1360** 380w. multicoloured . . 40 10
See also Nos. 2317/18, 2365/6 and 2457/8.

1361 "Poem to Sui General Yu Zhong Wen" (Ulchi Mundok)

1362 "Record of Travel to Five Indian Kingdoms" (Hye Ch'o)

1997. Literature (3rd series).
2269 **1361** 170w. multicoloured . . 70 10
2270 **1362** 170w. multicoloured . . 70 10

1363 Neon Lights on Globe and Nuclear Power Plant

1998. Centenary of Introduction of Electricity to Korea.
2272 **1363** 170w. multicoloured . . 70 10

1364 Pres. Kim Dae Jung and Flag

1998. Inauguration of 15th President of South Korea.
2273 **1364** 170w. multicoloured . . 60 10

1998. Protection of Wildlife and Plants (5th series). Vert designs as T **1270**. Multicoloured.
2275 340w. Korean leopard ("Panthera pardus orientalis") . . . . 1·25 75
2276 340w. Asiatic black bears ("Selenarctos thibetanus") 1·25 75
2277 340w. European otters ("Lutra lutra") . . . . . 1·25 75
2278 340w. Siberian musk deers ("Moschus moschiferus") 1·25 75

1365 Aktong-i (Lee Hi Jae)

1366 Challenger (Park Ki Jong)

1998. Cartoons (4th series).
2280 **1365** 170w. multicoloured . . 40 10
2281 **1366** 340w. multicoloured . . 70 10

1367 Assembly Building and Firework Display

1368 Player with Ball

1998. 50th Anniv of National Assembly.
2283 **1367** 170w. multicoloured . . 60 10

1998. World Cup Football Championship (2002), Korea and Japan (2nd issue). Multicoloured.
2284 170w. Type **1368** 50 10
2285 170w. Two players chasing ball 50 10
2286 170w. Players heading ball 50 10
2287 170w. Player kicking ball over head 50 10

1369 Writing on Stone Tablets

1998. Information Technology. Multicoloured.
2289 170w. Type **1369** 50 10
2290 170w. Pony Express 50 10
2291 170w. Man using telephone and post box 50 10
2292 170w. Old and modern forms of communication (68 × 22 mm) 50 10

1998. Fungi (6th series). As T **1246**. Multicoloured.
2293 170w. "Pseudocolus schellenbergiae" 50 10
2294 170w. "Cyptotrama asprata" 50 10
2295 170w. "Laccaria vinaceoavellanea" 50 10
2296 170w. "Phallus rugulosus" 50 10

1373 Flag and Runners

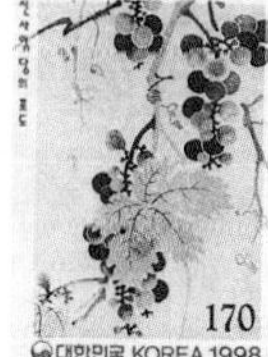
1374 "Grapes" (Lady Shin Saimdang)

1998. 50th Anniv of Proclamation of Republic.
2298 **1373** 170w. multicoloured . . 60 10

1998. Philatelic Week.
2299 **1374** 170w. multicoloured . . 60 10

1375 Thinking of Mother

1376 Would You Leave Me Now?

1998. Literature (4th series). Sogyo Songs.
2301 **1375** 170w. multicoloured . . 60 10
2302 **1376** 170w. multicoloured . . 60 10

1377 Film Strips and Masks

1998. 3rd Pusan International Film Festival.
2304 **1377** 170w. multicoloured . . 20 10

1378 Myungnyundang Hall

1998. 600th Anniv of Sungkyunkwan University.
2305 **1378** 170w. multicoloured . . 20 10

1379 National Constabulary, Badge and Lake Ch'onji

1380 Hot-air Balloon

1998. 50th Anniv of Korean Armed Forces.
2306 **1379** 170w. multicoloured . . 20 10

1998. World Stamp Day.
2307 **1380** 170w. multicoloured . . 20 10

1381 Peach

1382 Double Crane

1383 Carp

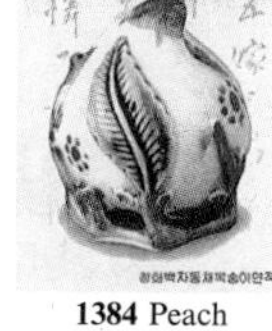
1384 Peach

1385 Toad

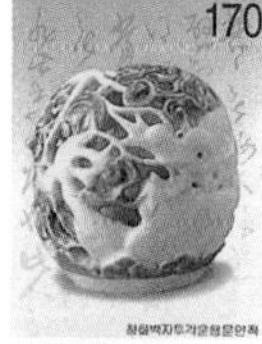
1386 Dragon and Cloud

1387 Monkey

1388 House

1998. Korean Beauty (8th series). Porcelain Water Droppers.
2308 **1381** 170w. multicoloured . . 20 10
2309 **1382** 170w. multicoloured . . 20 10
2310 **1383** 170w. multicoloured . . 20 10
2311 **1384** 170w. multicoloured . . 20 10
2312 **1385** 170w. multicoloured . . 20 10
2313 **1386** 170w. multicoloured . . 20 10
2314 **1387** 170w. multicoloured . . 20 10
2315 **1388** 170w. multicoloured . . 20 10

1389 Rabbits

1390 Tripitaka Koreana (scriptures engraved on wooden blocks)

1391 Changgyong P'anjon (woodblock repository)

1998. Lunar New Year ("Year of the Rabbit").
2316 **1389** 170w. multicoloured . . 20 10

1998. World Heritage Sites (2nd series). Haein Temple.
2317 **1390** 170w. multicoloured . . 20 10
2318 **1391** 380w. multicoloured . . 40 10

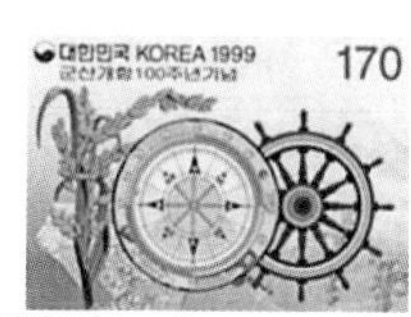
1392 Maize, Compass and Ship's Wheel

1999. Centenary of Kunsan Port.
2320 **1392** 170w. multicoloured . . 20 10

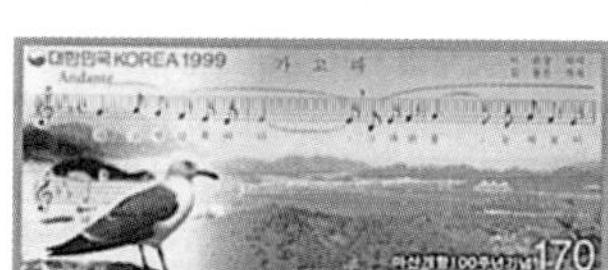
1393 Masan and Score of "I Want to Go" by Lee Eun Sang

1999. Centenary of Masan Port.
2321 **1393** 170w. multicoloured . . 20 10

1394 Rai-Fi (Kim San Ho)

1395 Tokgo T'ak (Lee Sang Mu)

1396 Im Kkuk Jung (Lee Du Ho)

1999. Cartoons (5th series).
2322 **1394** 170w. multicoloured . . 20 10
2323 **1395** 170w. multicoloured . . 20 10
2324 **1396** 170w. multicoloured . . 20 10

1999. Protection of Wildlife and Plants (6th series). Vert designs as T **1270**.
2326 170w. Peregrine falcon ("Falco peregrinus") . . . 20 10
2327 170w. Grey frog hawk ("Accipiter soloensis") . . 20 10
2328 340w. Steller's sea eagle ("Haliaeetus pelagicus") 35 10
2329 340w. Northern eagle owl ("Bubo bubo") 35 10

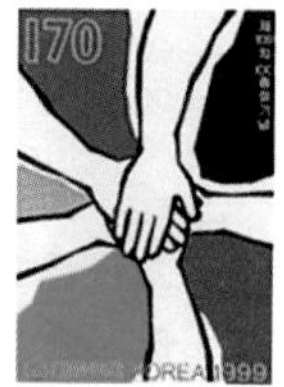
1397 Five clasped Hands

1398 Goethe (after Joseph Stieler)

1999. 109th International Olympic Committee Congress, Seoul.
2331 **1397** 170w. multicoloured . . 20 10

1999. 250th Birth Anniv of Johann Wolfgang von Goethe (poet and playwright).
2332 **1398** 170w. multicoloured . . 20 10

1399 "Kumgang Mountain" (Kyomjae Chong Son)

1999. Philatelic Week.
2334 **1399** 170w. multicoloured . . 20 10

1400 Mogul Tank Locomotive No. 101 (first locomotive in Korea)

1999. Centenary of Railway in Korea.
2336 **1400** 170w. multicoloured . . 20 10

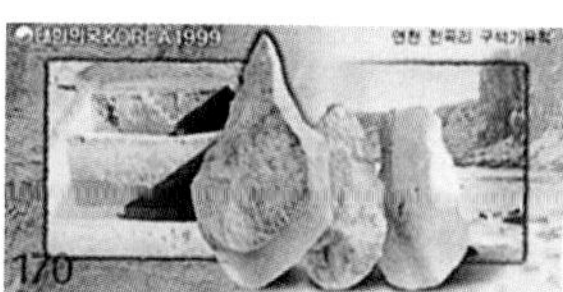
1401 Flint Tools and Paleolithic Ruins, Chungok-ri, Yonch'on

1999. New Millennium (1st series). Multicoloured.
2337 170w. Type **1401** 20 10
2338 170w. Comb-patterned pottery, burnt-out and reconstructed Neolithic dwellings, Amsa-dong, Seoul 20 10
2339 170w. Shell bracelets, bone spear heads and Neolithic shell mounds, Tongsam-dong, Pusan 20 10
2340 170w. Dolmen, Pukon-ri, Kanghwa-do Island . . . 20 10
2341 170w. Bronze and stone daggers and Bronze-age earthenware, Son-gguk-ri, Puyo 20 10
2342 170w. Rock carvings, Pan'gudae 20 10
See also Nos. 2357/62, 2374/8, 2388/92, 2397/2401, 2406/10, 2420/5, 2431/6, 2460/5, 2487/91 and 2511/15.

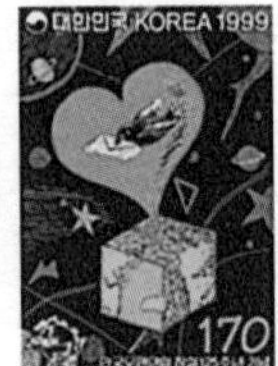

1402 Bird carrying Letter

1999. 125th Anniv of Universal Postal Union.
2343 **1402** 170w. multicoloured . . 20 10

1403 Little Odes on the Kwandong Area (Chong Ch'ol)

1404 Alas! How foolish I am! (Hwang Jin-i)

1405 Story of Hong Kil-dong (Ho Kyun)

1406 Story of Ch'unhyang

1999. Literature (5th series).
2344 **1403** 170w. multicoloured . . 20 10
2345 **1404** 170w. multicoloured . . 20 10
2346 **1405** 170w. multicoloured . . 20 10
2347 **1406** 170w. multicoloured . . 20 10

1407 Chrysanthemum, Bird and Duck

1408 Birds in Tree and Snake on Korean Character

1409 Pot Plant with Butterfly on Korean Character

1410 Fish on Korean Character

1411 Plant behind Tub of Fishes

1412 Crab on Korean Character

1413 Bird on Korean Character

1414 Chest and Plant behind Deer

1999. Korean Beauty (9th series).
2349 **1407** 340w. multicoloured . . 40 10
2350 **1408** 340w. multicoloured . . 40 10
2351 **1409** 340w. multicoloured . . 40 10
2352 **1410** 340w. multicoloured . . 40 10
2353 **1411** 340w. multicoloured . . 40 10
2354 **1412** 340w. multicoloured . . 40 10
2355 **1413** 340w. multicoloured . . 40 10
2356 **1414** 340w. multicoloured . . 40 10

1415 Ornament and Bird-shaped Vase

1416 Crown and Bowl

1417 Man on Horseback and Cave Paintings

1418 Gold Ornament and Jade Jewellery

1419 Stone Crafts

1420 Carved Stone Face

1999. New Millennium (2nd series).
2357 **1415** 170w. multicoloured . . 20 10
2358 **1416** 170w. multicoloured . . 20 10
2359 **1417** 170w. multicoloured . . 20 10
2360 **1418** 170w. multicoloured . . 20 10
2361 **1419** 170w. multicoloured . . 20 10
2362 **1420** 170w. multicoloured . . 20 10

1421 Dragon

1999. Lunar New Year "Year of the Dragon".
2363 **1421** 170w. multicoloured . . 20 10

1422 Building

1423 Man and Musicians

1999. World Heritage Sites (3rd series).
2365 **1422** 170w. multicoloured . . 20 10
2366 **1423** 340w. multicoloured . . 40 10

1424 Player

1426 Sunset, Altar and Tablet

1425 Emblem

1999. World Cup Football Championship, Japan and Korea (2002). Multicoloured.
2368 170w. Type **1424** 20 10
2369 170w. Players tackling . . . 20 10
2370 170w. Player receiving ball 20 10
2371 170w. Goalkeeper catching ball 20 10
Nos. 2368/71 were issued together, se-tenant, forming a composite design.

2000. Centenary of South Korea's Membership of Universal Postal Union.
2373 **1425** 170w. multicoloured . . 20 10

2000. New Millennium (3rd series). Multicoloured.
2374 170w. Type **1426** 20 10
2375 170w. Cave painting of wrestlers 20 10
2376 170w. Inscribed bronze disc and warrior 20 10
2377 170w. Silhouettes of archers and inscribed standing stone 20 10
2378 170w. Junk and warrior . . 20 10

1427 Pashi Steam Locomotive

1428 Teho Steam Locomotive

1429 Mika Steam Locomotive

1430 Hyouki Steam Locomotive

2000. Railways (1st series).
2379 **1427** 170w. black, violet and mauve 20 10
2380 **1428** 170w. black, violet and mauve 20 10
2381 **1429** 170w. black, violet and grey 20 10
2382 **1430** 170w. black, violet and bistre 20 10
See also Nos. 2477/80.

2000. Protection of Wildlife and Plants (7th series). As T **1270**. Multicoloured.
2383 170w. *Lilium cernum* 20 10
2384 170w. *Sedirea japonica* . . . 20 10
2385 170w. *Hibiscus hamabo* . . . 20 10
2386 170w. *Cypripedium japonicum* 20 10
Nos. 2383/6 are impregnated with the scent of flowers.

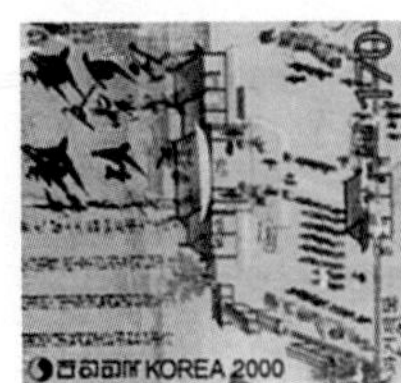

1431 State Civil Service Examination and Text

2000. New Millennium (4th series). Multicoloured.
2388 170w. Type **1431** 20 10
2389 170w. Man carving wood blocks 20 10
2390 170w. Pieces of metal type 20 10
2391 170w. An-Hyang (scholar) and Korean script 20 10
2392 170w. Mun Ik-jom (scholar), spinning wheel and cotton plant 20 10

1432 Children playing and House (Kim Chin Sook)

1433 Globe and Satellite

2000. World Water Day. Winning Design in Children's Painting Competition.
2393 **1432** 170w. multicoloured . . 20 10

2000. 50th Anniv of World Meteorological Organization.
2394 **1433** 170w. multicoloured . . 20 10

1434 Hand holding Rose

2000. "Share Love" (good neighbour campaign).
2395 **1434** 170w. multicoloured . . 20 10
No. 2395 is impregnated with the scent of roses.

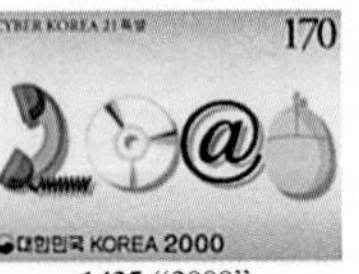

1435 "2000"

2000. "CYBER KOREA 21".
2396 **1435** 170w. multicoloured . . 20 10

1436 King Sejong and Korean Script

2000. New Millennium (5th series). Multicoloured.
2397 170w. Type **1436** 20 10
2398 170w. Lady Shin Saimdang (caligrapher poet and painter) and detail of "Ch'ochung-do" (painting) . . . 20 10
2399 170w. Yi Hwang and Yi I (founders of Confucian Academy) 20 10
2400 170w. Admiral Yi Sun-shin and model of "turle" ship 20 10
2401 170w. Sandae-nori (mask-dance drama) 20 10

1437 Park Soo Dong **1438** Bae Gum Taek

2000. Cartoons (6th series).
2402 **1437** 170w. multicoloured . . 20 10
2403 **1438** 170w. multicoloured . . 20 10

1439 Seedling on Map of Korean Peninsula

2000. Pyongyang, Korean Summit.
2405 **1439** 170w. multicoloured . . 20 10

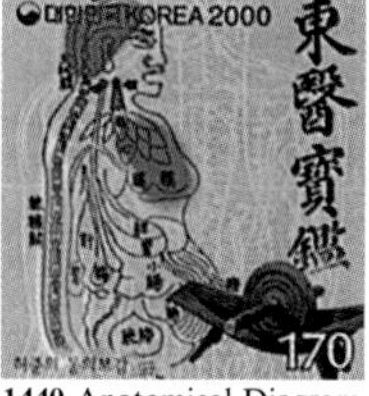

1440 Anatomical Diagram from *Tonui Pogam* (medical treatise by Huh Joan) **1441** Numbers and Mathematical Symbols

2000. Millennium (6th series). Multicoloured.
2406 170w. Type **1440** 20 10
2407 170w. "Dancer with Musicians" (illustration by Kim Hong Do) 20 10
2408 170w. "Plum Blossoms and Bird" (painting, Chong Yak Yong) and house in Kangjin where he served his exile 20 10
2409 170w. Map of Korea by Kim Chong Ho and wheel chart 20 10
2410 170w. Chon Bong Joan (revolutionary) and Tonghak Peasant Uprising monument . . . 20 10

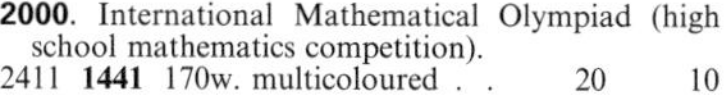

2000. International Mathematical Olympiad (high school mathematics competition).
2411 **1441** 170w. multicoloured . . 20 10

1442 *Yolha Diary* (Park Ji Won) **1443** *Fisherman's Calender*

1444 *The Nine-Cloud Dream*

1445 *Tears of Blood*

1446 *From the Sea to a Child*

2000. Literature (6th series).
2412 **1442** 170w. multicoloured . . 20 10
2413 **1443** 170w. multicoloured . . 20 10
2414 **1444** 170w. multicoloured . . 20 10
2415 **1445** 170w. multicoloured . . 20 10
2416 **1446** 170w. multicoloured . . 20 10

1447 Mountain

2000. Philately Week.
2418 **1447** 340w. multicoloured . . 40 10

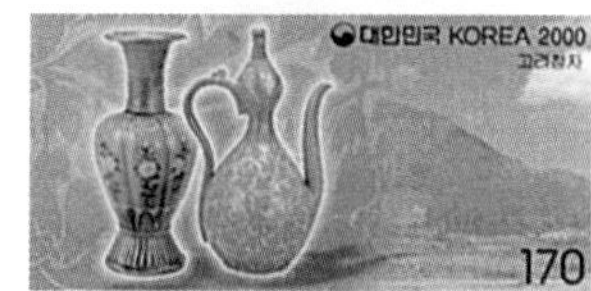

1448 Porcelain

2000. Millennium (7th series). Multicoloured.
2420 170w. Type **1448** 20 10
2421 170w. "Bongjongsa" Temple (Paradise Pavilion) . . . 20 10
2422 170w. Hahoe Tal masks . . 20 10
2423 170w. Royal Palace 20 10
2424 170w. Landscape painting 20 10
2425 170w. Water clock 20 10

1454 Taekwondo

2000. Olympic Games, Sydney.
2426 **1454** 170w. multicoloured . . 20 10

1455 Former Kyunngi High School Building, Hwadong

2000. Centenary of Public Secondary Schools.
2427 **1455** 170w. multicoloured . . 10 10

1456 "Returning to the Retirement House" (illustration from "Album of the Gathering of Old Statesmen")

2000. 3rd Asia-Europe Meeting, Seoul.
2428 **1456** 170w. multicoloured . . 10 10

1457 Emblem

2000. Icograde Millennium Congress, Seoul.
2429 **1457** 170w. black and yellow 10 10

1458 Mr. Gobau

2000. 50th Anniv of Mr. Gobau (cartoon character).
2430 **1458** 170w. multicoloured . . 10 10

1459 18th-Century Painting (Sin Yun Bok)

2000. Millennium (8th series). Multicoloured.
2431 170w. Type **1459** 10 10
2432 170w. Calligraphy by Kim Jeong Hui 10 10
2433 170w. Bongdon-Chiseong Hwaseong Fortress, Suwon 10 10
2434 170w. Myeongdong Cathedral 10 10
2435 170w. Wongaska theatre actors 10 10
2436 170w. The KITSat-satellite 10 10

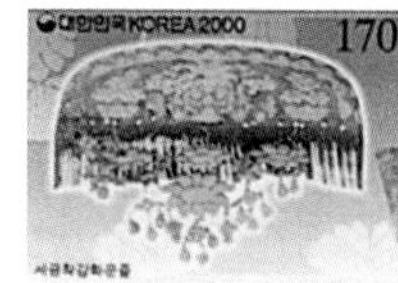

1460 Decorated Comb

2000. Korean Beauty (10th series). Multicoloured.
2437 170w. Type **1460** 10 10
2438 170w. Woman's ceremonial headdress 10 10
2439 170w. Butterfly-shaped hairpin 10 10
2440 170w. Hairpin with dragon decoration and jade hairpin with Chinese phoenix decoration . . . 10 10

1461 Seoul World Cup Stadium

1462 Busan Sports Complex Main Stadium

1463 Daegu Sports Complex Stadium

1464 Incheon Munhak Stadium

1465 Gwangu World Cup Stadium

1466 Daejeon World Cup Stadium

1467 Ulsan Munsu Football Stadium

1468 Suwon World Cup Stadium

1469 Jeonju World Cup Stadium

1470 Jeju World Cup Stadium

2000. World Cup Football Championship (2002), South Korea and Japan.
2441 **1461** 170w. multicoloured . . 10 10
2442 **1462** 170w. multicoloured . . 10 10
2443 **1463** 170w. multicoloured . . 10 10
2444 **1464** 170w. multicoloured . . 10 10
2445 **1465** 170w. multicoloured . . 10 10
2446 **1466** 170w. multicoloured . . 10 10
2447 **1467** 170w. multicoloured . . 10 10
2448 **1468** 170w. multicoloured . . 10 10
2449 **1469** 170w. multicoloured . . 10 10
2450 **1470** 170w. multicoloured . . 10 10

1471 Snake

2000. Lunar New Year "Year of the Snake". Ordinary or self-adhesive gum.
2452 **1471** 170w. multicoloured . . 10 10

1472 President Kim Dae Jung and Children

2000. Award of Nobel Peace Prize to President Kim Dae Jung.
2455 **1472** 170w. multicoloured . . 10 10

1473 Repository, Jeongjok Mountain and Taejo Sillok (script)

2000. World Heritage Sites (4th series). Multicoloured.

2457 340w. Type **1473** 35 10
2458 340w. King Sejong and script 35 10

1474 Bicycle with coloured wheels (reunification of Korea)

2001. Millennium (9th series). Multicoloured.

2460 170w. Type **1474** 10 10
2461 170w. Rainbow (environmental protection) 10 10
2462 170w. Human D.N.A. and figure (eradication of incurable diseases) 10 10
2463 170w. Satellite and mobile telephone (communications technology) 10 10
2464 170w. Space (space travel) 10 10
2465 170w. Solar panels, solar-powered car and windmills (alternative energy sources) 10 10

1475 "Oksunn Peaks" (Kim Hong Do)

2001. Visit Korea Year 2001.

2466 **1475** 170w. multicoloured . . 10 10

1476 Plough

2001. Agricultural Implements. Multicoloured.

2467 170w. Type **1476** 10 10
2468 170w. Harrow 10 10
2469 170w. Sowing basket and namtae 10 10
2470 170w. Short-handled hoes 10 10
2471 170w. Manure barrel and fertilizer ash container . . 10 10
2472 170w. Water dipper 10 10
2473 170w. Winnower and thresher 10 10
2474 170w. Square straw drying mat and wicker tray . . . 10 10
2475 170w. Pestle, mortar and grinding stones 10 10
2476 170w. Rice basket and carrier 10 10

1486 2000 Series Diesel-electric Locomotive

1487 7000 Series Diesel-electric Locomotive

1488 Diesel Urban Commuter Train

1489 Diesel Saemaul Train

2001. Railways (2nd series).

2477 **1486** 170w. multicoloured . . 10 10
2478 **1487** 170w. multicoloured . . 10 10
2479 **1488** 170w. multicoloured . . 10 10
2480 **1489** 170w. multicoloured . . 10 10

2001. Protection of Wildlife and Plants (8th series). Vert designs as T **1270**. Multicoloured.

2481 170w. *Jeffersonia dubia* . . . 10 10
2482 170w. *Diapensia lapponica* 10 10
2483 170w. *Rhododendron aureum* 10 10
2484 170w. *Sedum orbiculatum* . . 10 10

Nos. 2481/4 are impregnated with the scent of the Ume tree.

1490 Incheon Airport and Emblem

2001. Inauguration of Incheon Airport.

2486 **1490** 170w. multicoloured . . 10 10

1491 Kim Ku (leader of Independence Movement)

2001. Millennium (10th series). Multicoloured.

2487 170w. Type **1491** 10 10
2488 170w. Statue commemorating the March 1st Independence Movement 10 10
2489 170w. Interim Korean Government Headquarters, Shanghai and Members 10 10
2490 170w. Ahn Ik Tae (composer) and music score 10 10
2491 170w. Yun Dong Ju (poet) and *Seosi* (poem) 10 10

1492 Emblem

2001. International Olympic Fair, Seoul.

2492 **1492** 170w. multicoloured . . 10 10
MS2493 105 × 70 mm. No. 2492 × 2 15 15

1493 Bears hugging

2001. Greetings Stamps. Multicoloured.

2494 170w. Type **1493** 10 10
2495 170w. Flower 10 10
2496 170w. Trumpets (Congratulations) 10 10
2497 170w. Cake 10 10

1494 Iljimae (Ko Woo Young) **1495** Kkeobeongi (Kil Chang Duk)

2001. Cartoons (7th series).

2498 **1494** 170w. multicoloured . . 10 10
2499 **1495** 170w. multicoloured . . 10 10
MS2500 Two sheets, each 90 × 60 mm. (a) No. 2498. (b) No. 2499 Price for 2 sheets . . 15 15

1496 Players and Mountains (Switzerland, 1954)

2001. World Cup Football Championship, Japan and South Korea. Multicoloured.

2501 170w. Type **1496** 10 10
2502 170w. Players and Ancient settlement (Mexico, 1986) 10 10
2503 170w. Players and Coliseum (Italy, 1990) 10 10
2504 170w. Players and buildings (United States of America, 1994) 10 10
2505 170w. Players and Eiffel Tower (France, 1998) . . 10 10
MS2506 Five sheets, each 60 × 90 mm. (a) No. 2501 × 2. (b) No. 2502 × 2. (c) No. 2503 × 2. (d) No. 2504 × 2. (e) No. 2505 × 2 Price for 5 sheets 90 90

1497 Baechu Kimchi (Chinese Cabbage)

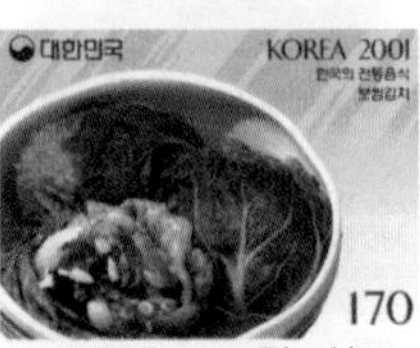

1498 Bossam Kimchi

1499 Dongchimi

1500 Klakdugi

2001. Korean Foods (1st series).

2507 **1497** 170w. multicoloured . . 10 10
2508 **1498** 170w. multicoloured . . 10 10
2509 **1499** 170w. multicoloured . . 10 10
2510 **1500** 170w. multicoloured . . 10 10

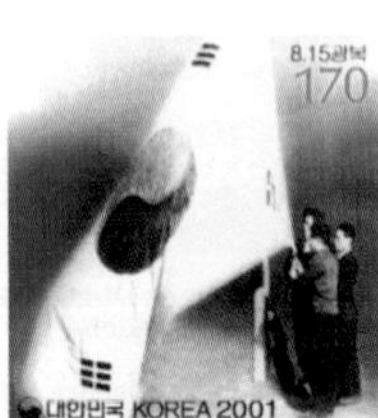

1501 Raising Flag (Liberation, 1945)

2001. Millennium (11th series). Multicoloured.

2511 170w. Type **1501** 10 10
2512 170w. Soldiers embracing (statue) (Korean War) . . 10 10
2513 170w. Seoul–Busan Expressway 10 10
2514 170w. Working in fields (Saemaul Undong movement) 10 10
2515 170w. Athletes forming emblem (Olympic Games, Seoul, 1988) 10 10

1502 Red Queen

1503 Pink Lady

2001. "Philakorea 2002" International Stamp Exhibition, Seoul. Roses.

2516 **1502** 170w. multicoloured . . 10 10
2517 **1503** 170w. multicoloured . . 10 10
MS2518 Two sheets, each 115 × 73 mm. (a) No. 2516 × 2. (b) No. 2517 × 2 Price for 2 sheets 35 35

C. NORTH KOREAN OCCUPATION.

(**1** "Democratic People's Republic of Korea")

1950. Nos. 116 and 118/19 optd with Type **1**.

1 10w. green . . . . 45·00
2 20w. brown . . . . 12·50
3 30w. green . . . . 15·00

NORTH KOREA

100 cheun = 1 won.

GUM. All stamps of North Korea up to No. N1506 are without gum, except where otherwise stated.

A. RUSSIAN OCCUPATION

1 Hibiscus **2** Diamond Mountains

1946. Perf, roul or imperf.

N1 **1** 20ch. red . . . . 55·00 38·00
N2 **2** 50ch. green . . . . 17·00 15·00
N4b 50ch. red . . . . 10·00 10·00
N5b 50ch. violet . . . . 10·00 12·00

4 Gen. Kim Il Sung and Flag **5** Peasants

1946. 1st Anniv of Liberation from Japan.

N6 **4** 50ch. brown £190 £190

1947. Perf, roul or imperf.

N 7 **5** 1wn. green . . . . 5·00 4·00
N 8 1wn. violet . . . . 15·00 10·00
N 9 1wn. blue on buff . . . . 5·50 4·50
N10 1wn. blue . . . . 3·25 2·50

6 **7**

1948. 2nd Anniv of Labour Law.
N11 **6** 50ch. blue £225 £180

1948. 3rd Anniv of Liberation from Japan.
N12 **7** 50ch. red . . . . — £325

8

1948. Promulgation of Constitution.
N13 **8** 50ch. blue and red . . . . £160 40·00

B. KOREAN PEOPLE'S DEMOCRATIC REPUBLIC

9 North Korean Flag
10

1948. Establishment of People's Republic. Roul.
N16 **9** 25ch. violet . . . . 3·50 3·50
N17 50ch. blue . . . . 6·00 6·00

1949. Roul or perf.
N18 **10** 6wn. red and blue . . . . 2·00 2·00

11 Kim Il Sung University, Pyongyang
12 North Korean Flags

11a Kim Il Sung University, Pyongyang

1949. Roul.
N19 **11** 1wn. violet . . . . . . 45·00 20·00
N20 **11a** 1wn. blue . . . . 45·00 20·00

1949. 4th Anniv of Liberation from Japan. Roul or perf.
N22 **12** 1wn. red, green and blue 35·00 14·00

13 Order of the National Flag
14 Liberation Monument, Pyongyang

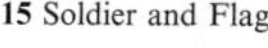

15 Soldier and Flags
16 Peasant and Worker

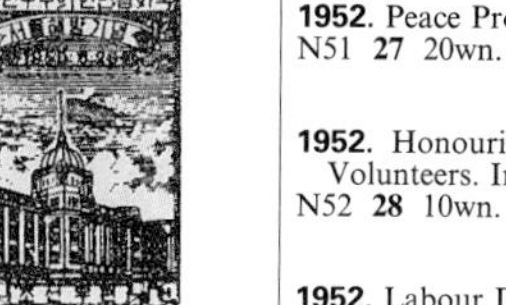

17 Tractor
18 Capitol, Seoul

1950. Perf, roul or imperf. Various sizes.
N24 **13** 1wn. green (A) . . . . . 4·00 1·00
N25 1wn. orange (A) . . . . . — 25·00
N26 1wn. orange (B) . . . . . 17·00 12·00
N27 1wn. green (C) . . . . . 4·00 1·25
N28 1wn. olive (D) . . . . . 7·00 4·50
SIZES: (A) 23¼ × 37¼ mm. (B) 20 × 32½ mm. (C) 22 × 35½ mm. (D) 22½ × 36½ mm.

1950. 5th Anniv of Liberation from Japan. Roul, perf or imperf. Various sizes.
N29 **14** 1wn. red, indigo and blue 1·25 90
N30 1wn. orange . . . . . . 7·00 5·00
N31 **15** 2wn. black, blue and red 1·25 90
N32 **16** 6wn. green (A) . . . . . 1·75 1·25
N36 6wn. red (B) . . . . . . 12·50 11·00
N33 **17** 10wn. brown (C) . . . . 2·50 2·00
N37 10wn. brown (D) . . . . 18·00 13·50
SIZES: (A) 20 × 30 mm. (B) 22 × 33 mm. (C) 20 × 28 mm. (D) 22 × 30 mm.

1950. Capture of Seoul by North Korean Forces. Roul.
N38 **18** 1wn. red, blue and green 40·00 32·00

19
20 Kim Gi Ok and Aeroplane

1951. Order of Admiral Li Sun Sin. Imperf or perf.
N39 **19** 6wn. orange . . . . . . 6·50 5·00

1951. Air Force Hero Kim Gi Ok. Imperf.
N40 **20** 1wn. blue . . . . 8·00 3·00

21 Russian and North Korean Flags
22 Kim Ki U (hero)
23 N. Korean and Chinese Soldiers

1951. 6th Anniv of Liberation from Japan. Roul or perf.
N41 **21** 1wn. blue . . . . 3·50 2·50
N42 1wn. red . . . . 3·50 2·50
N43 **22** 1wn. blue . . . . 3·50 2·50
N44 1wn. red . . . . 3·75 2·50
N45 **23** 2wn. blue . . . . 6·50 5·00
N46 2wn. red . . . . 10·00 7·50
All values exist on buff and on white paper.

24 Order of Soldier's Honour
25
26 Woman Partisan, Li Su Dok

1951. Imperf or perf.
N47 **24** 40wn. red . . . . 9·00 4·50

1951. Co-operation of Chinese People's Volunteers. Imperf or perf.
N49 **25** 10wn. blue . . . . 5·00 3·25

1952. Partisan Heroes. Imperf or perf.
N50 **26** 70wn. brown . . . . . . 4·00 1·00

27
28 Gen. P'eng Teh-huai
29 Munition Worker

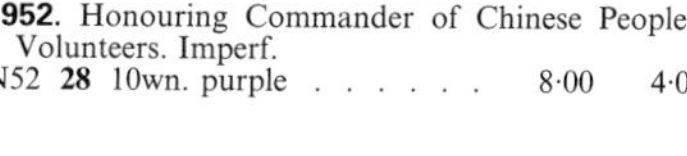

1952. Peace Propaganda. Imperf or perf.
N51 **27** 20wn. blue, green and red 6·00 2·00

1952. Honouring Commander of Chinese People's Volunteers. Imperf.
N52 **28** 10wn. purple . . . . . . 8·00 4·00

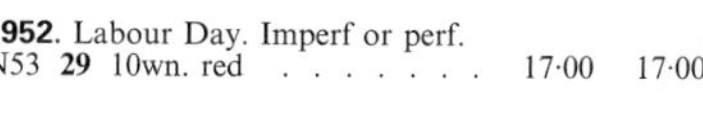

1952. Labour Day. Imperf or perf.
N53 **29** 10wn. red . . . . 17·00 17·00

30 **31** **32**

1952. 6th Anniv of Labour Law. Imperf or perf.
N54a **30** 10wn. blue . . . . . . 11·00 11·00

1952. Anti-U.S. Imperialism Day. Imperf or perf.
N55 **31** 10wn. red . . . . 13·00 13·00

1952. North Korean and Chinese Friendship. Imperf or perf.
N56b **32** 20wn. deep blue . . . . 9·00 9·00

33 **34**

1952. 7th Anniv of Liberation from Japan. Imperf or perf.
N57 **33** 10wn. red . . . . 10·00 10·00
N58 **34** 10wn. red . . . . 12·00 12·00

35

1952. Int Youth Day. With gum. Imperf or perf.
N59 **35** 10wn. green . . . . . . 8·00 8·00

36 **37**

1953. 5th Anniv of People's Army. Imperf or perf.
N60 **36** 10wn. red . . . . 12·50 12·50
N61 **37** 40wn. purple . . . . . 12·50 12·50

38 **39**

1953. Int Women's Day. With gum. Imperf or perf.
N62 **38** 10wn. red . . . . 10·00 8·00
N63 **39** 40wn. green . . . . . . 10·00 8·00

40 **41**

1953. Labour Day. Imperf or perf.
N64 **40** 10wn. green . . . . . . 7·50 7·50
N65 **41** 40wn. orange . . . . . 7·50 7·50

42 **43**

1953. Anti-U.S. Imperialism Day. With gum. Imperf or perf.
N66 **42** 10wn. turquoise . . . . 15·00 13·00
N67 **43** 40wn. red . . . . 15·00 13·00

44 **45**

1953. 4th World Youth Festival, Bucharest. With gum. Imperf or perf.
N68 **44** 10wn. blue and green . . 4·00 3·25
N69 **45** 20wn. green and pink . . 4·00 3·25

46 **47**

1953. Armistice and Victory Issue. With gum. Imperf or perf.
N70a **46** 10wn. brown and yellow 38·00 32·00

1953. 8th Anniv of Liberation from Japan. Imperf.
N71 **47** 10wn. red . . . . £120 90·00

48
49 Liberation Monument, Pyongyang

1953. 5th Anniv of People's Republic. Imperf or perf.
N72 **48** 10wn. blue and red . . . 11·00 11·00

1953. With gum. Imperf or perf.
N73 **49** 10wn. slate . . . . 3·75 3·50

(50) **(51)**

1954. No. N18 optd "Fee Collected" in Korean characters, T **50**.
N74 **10** 6wn. red and blue £150 £150

1954. Nos. N18 and N39 surch with T **51**.
N75 **10** 5wn. on 6wn. red and blue 12·00 12·00
N76 **19** 5wn. on 6wn. orange . . . 55·00 45·00

52 **53**

1954. Post-war Economic Reconstruction. With gum. Imperf or perf.
N77 **52** 10wn. blue . . . . 15·00 9·00

1954. 6th Anniv of People's Army. With gum. Imperf or perf.
N78 **53** 10wn. red . . . . 13·00 10·00

54 **55**

1954. Int Women's Day. With gum. Imperf or perf.
N79 **54** 10wn. red . . . . 5·50 5·50

1954. Labour Day. With gum. Imperf or perf.
N80 **55** 10wn. red . . . . 6·00 6·00

56

57 Taedong Gate, Pyongyang

1954. Anti-U.S. Imperialism Day. With gum. Imperf or perf.
N81 **56** 10wn. red . . . . 17·00 15·00

1954. Imperf or perf.
N82 **57** 5wn. lake . . . . 2·00 75
N83 5wn. brown . . . . 2·00 75

58

59 Soldier

1954. National Young Activists' Conference With gum. Imperf or perf.
N84 **58** 10wn. red, blue and slate 3·00 3·00

1954. 9th Anniv of Liberation from Japan. With gum. Imperf or perf.
N85 **59** 10wn. red . . . . 6·00 6·00

60 North Korean Flag

61 Hwanghae Iron Works

62 Hwanghae Iron Works and Workers

1954. 6th Anniv of People's Republic. With gum. Imperf or perf.
N86 **60** 10wn. blue and red . . . 5·00 5·00

1954. Economic Reconstruction. Imperf or perf.
N87 **61** 10wn. blue . . . . 4·50 50
N88 **62** 10wn. brown . . . . . . 4·50 50

63

64

1955. 7th Anniv of People's Army. With gum. Imperf or perf.
N89 **63** 10wn. red . . . . 4·50 3·50

1955. Int Women's Day. With gum. Imperf or perf.
N90 **64** 10wn. deep blue . . . . . 5·00 3·50

65

66

1955. Labour Day. With gum. Imperf or perf.
N91 **65** 10wn. green . . . . . . 3·25 3·25
N92 **66** 10wn. red . . . . 3·25 3·25

67 Admiral Li Sun Sin

68

1955. Imperf or perf.
N93 **67** 1wn. blue on green . . . 1·25 20
N94 2wn. red on buff . . . . 1·75 25
N95 2wn. red . . . . 3·00 50

1955. 9th Anniv of Labour Law. With gum. Imperf or perf.
N96 **68** 10wn. red . . . . 3·50 2·50

69 Liberation Monument and Flags

1955. 10th Anniv of Liberation from Japan. Imperf or perf.
N97 **69** 10wn. green . . . . . . 2·00 1·50
N98 10wn. red, blue and brown (29½ × 42½ mm) . . . . 1·25 1·00

70

71

1955. Soviet Union Friendship Month. Imperf or perf.
N 99 **70** 10wn. red . . . . 1·50 1·00
N100 10wn. red and blue . . . 2·25 1·50
N101 **71** 20wn. red and slate . . . 3·25 2·50
N102 20wn. red and blue . . . 1·50 1·25
SIZES: No. N99, 22 × 32½ mm; N100, 29½ × 43 mm; N101, 18½ × 32 mm; N102, 25 × 43 mm.

72 Son Rock

73

1956. Haegumgang Maritime Park. Imperf or perf.
N103 **72** 10wn. blue on blue . . . 3·00 1·75

1956. 8th Anniv of People's Army. Imperf or perf.
N104 **73** 10wn. red on green . . . 5·50 5·50

74

1956. Labour Day. Imperf or perf.
N105 **74** 10wn. blue . . . . . . 4·50 2·75

75 Machinist

76 Taedong Gate, Pyongyang

77 Woman Harvester

78 Moranbong Theatre, Pyongyang

1956. Imperf or perf.
N106 **75** 1wn. brown . . . . . . 1·25 60
N107 **76** 2wn. blue 90 60
N108 **77** 10wn. red 90 60
N109 **78** 40wn. green . . . . . . 8·00 3·50

79 Miner

80 Boy Bugler and Girl Drummer

1956. 10th Anniv of Labour Law. Imperf or perf.
N110 **79** 10wn. brown . . . . . . 2·50 1·00

1956. 10th Anniv of Children's Union. Imperf or perf.
N111 **80** 10wn. brown . . . . . . 4·00 2·75

81 Workers

82 Industrial Plant

1956. 10th Anniv of Sex Equality Law. Imperf or perf.
N112 **81** 10wn. brown . . . . . . 2·00 1·40

1956. 10th Anniv of Nationalization of Industry. Imperf or perf.
N113 **82** 10wn. brown . . . . . . 45·00 16·00

83 Liberation Tower

84 Kim Il Sung University

1956. 11th Anniv of Liberation from Japan. Imperf or perf.
N114 **83** 10wn. red . . . . 3·00 1·25

1956. 10th Anniv of Kim Il Sung University. Imperf or perf.
N115 **84** 10wn. brown . . . . . . 2·50 1·75

85 Boy and Girl

86 Pak Ji Won

1956. 4th Democratic Youth League Congress. Imperf or perf.
N116 **85** 10wn. brown . . . . . . 2·50 1·50

1957. 220th Birth Anniv of Pak Ji Won "Yonam", (statesman). Imperf or perf.
N117 **86** 10wn. blue . . . . . . 1·50 90

87 Tabo Pagoda, Pulguksa

88 Ulmil Pavilion, Pyongyang

89 Furnaceman

1957. Imperf, perf or roul.
N118 **87** 5wn. blue . . . . 1·00 75
N119 **88** 40wn. green . . . . . . 2·00 1·25

1957. Production and Economy Campaign. With or without gum. Imperf or perf.
N121 **89** 10wn. blue . . . . . . 2·50 1·25

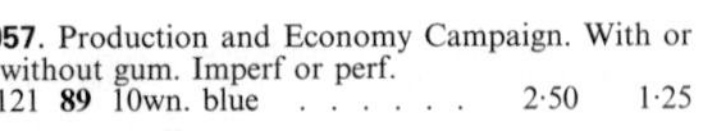

90 Furnaceman

91 Voters and Polling Booth

1957. 2nd General Election. Imperf or perf.
N122 **90** 1wn. orange 75 30
N123 2wn. brown 75 30
N124 **91** 10wn. red . . . . 3·75 1·25

92 Ryongwangjong, Pyongyang

93 Lenin and Flags

94 Kim Il Sung at Pochonbo

95 Lenin

96 Pouring Steel

1957. 1530th Anniv of Pyongyang. Imperf or perf.
N125 **92** 10wn. green . . . . . . 1·00 25

1957. 40th Anniv of Russian Revolution. Imperf or perf.
N126 **93** 10wn. green 75 40
N127 **94** 10wn. red 75 40
N128 **95** 10wn. blue 75 40
N129 **96** 10wn. orange . . . . . 2·00 40
No. N126 exists with gum.

97 Congress Emblem

98 Liberation Monument, Spassky Tower and Flags

1957. 4th World Trade Unions Federation Congress. Leipzig. Imperf (with or without gum) or perf.
N130 **97** 10wn. blue and green . . 1·25 50

1957. Russian Friendship Month. Imperf or perf.
N131 **98** 10wn. green . . . . . . 1·75 50

99 Weighing a Baby

100 Bandaging a Hand

1957. Red Cross. Imperf, perf or roul.
N132 **99** 1wn. red . . . . 6·00 1·00
N133 2wn. red . . . . 6·00 1·00
N134 **100** 10wn. red . . . . . . 15·00 2·75
No. N133 exists with or without gum.

101 Koryo Celadon Jug (12th century)

102 Koryo Incense-burner (12th century)

1958. Korean Antiquities. Imperf (with or without gum) or perf.
N135 **101** 10wn. blue . . . . . . 4·50 75
N136 **102** 10wn. green . . . . . 4·50 75

103 Woljong Temple Pagoda

104 Soldier

1958. With gum (5wn.), without gum (10wn.). Imperf or perf.
N137 **103** 5wn. green . . . . . . 1·00 50
N138 10wn. blue . . . . . . 1·50 75

1958. 10th Anniv of People's Army. No gum (No. N139) with or without gum (No. N140). Imperf or perf.
N139 **104** 10wn. blue . . . . . . 1·75 50
N140 – 10wn. red . . . . . . 4·50 65
DESIGN—HORIZ ($37\frac{1}{2}\times26$ mm): No. N140, Soldier, flag and Hwanghae Iron Works.

106 Lisunov Li-2 Airliner over Pyongyang

1958. Air. Imperf or perf.
N141 **106** 20wn. blue . . . . . . 5·50 1·00

107 Sputniks

108 Sputnik encircling Globe

1958. I.G.Y. Inscr "1957–1958". Imperf or perf.
N142 **107** 10wn. slate 45 10
N143 **108** 20wn. slate 45 10
N144 – 40wn. slate . . . . . . 1·75 30
N145 **107** 70wn. slate 50 20
DESIGN—HORIZ: 40wn. Sputnik over Pyongyang Observatory.
Nos. N142/4 exist with or without gum.

109 Furnaceman

110 Hwanghae Iron Works

1958. Young Socialist Constructors' Congress, Pyongyang. Imperf or perf.
N146 **109** 10wn. blue . . . . . . 2·75 50

1958. Opening of Hwanghae Iron Works. Imperf or perf.
N147 **110** 10wn. blue . . . . . . 4·25 65

111 Commemorative Badge

112 Federation Emblem

1958. Farewell to Chinese People's Volunteers (1st issue). Imperf or perf.
N148 **111** 10wn. purple and blue 1·50 40
See also No. N158.

1958. 4th International Women's Federation Democratic Congress. Imperf or perf.
N149 **112** 10wn. blue . . . . . . 1·00 35

113 Conference Emblem

1958. 1st World Young Workers' Trade Union Federation Conference, Prague. Imperf or perf.
N150 **113** 10wn. brown and green 1·75 35

114 Flats, East Ward, Pyongyang

115 Workers' Flats, Pyongyang

1958. Rehousing Progress. Imperf or perf.
N151 **114** 10wn. blue . . . . . . 2·00 50
N152 **115** 10wn. green . . . . . 2·00 50

117 Pyongyang Railway Station

119 Textile Worker

1958. 10th Anniv of Korean People's Republic. Imperf or perf.
N153 – 10wn. green . . . . . 3·00 50
N154 **117** 10wn. green . . . . . 11·00 1·50
N155 – 10wn. brown and buff 1·50 50
N156 **119** 10wn. brown . . . . . 7·50 1·75
N157 – 10wn. brown . . . . . 6·50 1·00
DESIGNS—HORIZ: No. N153, Hungnam Fertiliser Plant; N157, Yongp'ung Dam, Pyongyang. VERT: No. N155, Arms of People's Republic.

121 Volunteer and Steam Troop Train

122 Transplanting Rice

1958. Farewell to Chinese People's Volunteers (2nd issue). Imperf or perf.
N158 **121** 10wn. sepia . . . . . . 24·00 8·00

1958. Imperf or perf.
N159 **122** 10wn. sepia 75 15

123 Winged Horse of Chollima

124 N. Korean and Chinese Flags

1958. National Production Executives' Meeting, Pyongyang. With or without gum. Imperf or perf.
N160 **123** 10wn. red . . . . . . 1·60 30

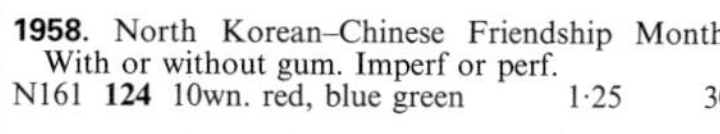
1958. North Korean–Chinese Friendship Month. With or without gum. Imperf or perf.
N161 **124** 10wn. red, blue green 1·25 30

125 Farm Workers

126 Gen. Ulji Mun Dok

1959. National Co-operative Farming Congress, Pyongyang. With or without gum. Imperf or perf.
N162 **125** 10wn. blue 90 25

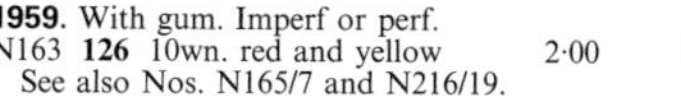
1959. With gum. Imperf or perf.
N163 **126** 10wn. red and yellow 2·00 50
See also Nos. N165/7 and N216/19.

127 Women with Banner

128 Rocket and Moon

1959. National Conference of Women Socialist Constructors, Pyongyang. With or without gum.
N164 **127** 10ch. brown and red . . 75 30

1959. Revalued currency. Portraits as T **126**. Imperf (with or without gum) or perf (with gum).
N165 – 2ch. blue on green . . . 60 10
N166 – 5ch. purple on buff . . 70 10
N167 **126** 10ch. red on cream . . 85 10
PORTRAITS: 2ch. General Kang Gam Chan; 5ch. General Chon Bong Jun.

1959. Launch of Soviet Moon Rocket. With or without gum. Imperf or perf.
N168 **128** 2ch. purple on buff . . 1·25 25
N169 10ch. blue on green . . 1·50 35

129 "Irrigation"

130 Inscribed Tree at Partisan H.Q., Chongbong

131 Kim Il Sung Statue

132 Mt. Paekdu

1959. Land Irrigation Project. Imperf or perf.
N170 **129** 10ch. multicoloured . . 3·75 65

1959. Partisan Successes against Japanese, 1937–39. With gum (No. N172) or no gum (others). Perf (N172) or imperf or perf (others).
N171 **130** 5ch. multicoloured . . . 2·75 45
N172 **131** 10ch. blue and turquoise 1·00 10
N173 **132** 10ch. violet . . . . . . 2·25 40

133 "Flying Horse" Tractor

1959. "Great Perspectives" (1st issue: Development of Industrial Mechanization). With or without gum. Perf, roul or imperf.
N174 **133** 1ch. red, olive and green 65 10
N175 – 2ch. multicoloured . . . 3·25 75
N176 – 2ch. red, pink and violet 60 10
N177 – 5ch. orange, brown and ochre 60 15
N178 – 10ch. blue, green & brn 70 15
N179 – 10ch. grn, lt grn & brn 1·50 25
DESIGNS: No. N175, Electric mine locomotive; N176, "Red Star 58" bulldozer; N177, "Flying Horse" excavator; N178, "SU-50" universal lathe; N179, "Victory 58" lorry.
See also Nos. N189a/200 and N275/79.

134 Armistice Building, Panmunjom

135 Protest Meeting

136 "Hoisting link between N. and S. Korea"

1959. Campaign for Withdrawal of U.S. Forces from S. Korea. With gum. Perf (20ch.) or imperf or perf (others).
N180 **134** 10ch. blue & ultramarine 55 20
N181 **135** 20ch. deep blue and blue 75 30
N182 **136** 70ch. brown, cream and purple . . . . 13·00 6·00

137 Emigration "Pickets"

1959. Campaign Against Emigration of South Koreans. With gum.
N183 **137** 20ch. brown and sepia 3·50 1·00

138 Korean Type of "1234"

139 Books breaking Chains

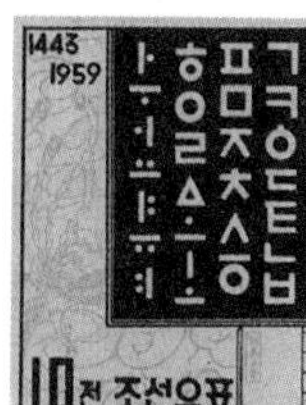
141 Korean Alphabet of 1443

140 Emblems of Peace, Labour and Letters

1959. International Book Exibition, Leipzig. With gum (No. N184, N186) or no gum (others).
N184 **138** 5ch. sepia . . . . . . 15·00 5·00
N185 **139** 5ch. red and green . . . 4·50 1·50
N186 **140** 10ch. blue . . . . . . 4·50 1·50
N187 **141** 10ch. violet and blue . . 7·00 2·50

142 Pig Farm

1959. Animal Husbandry. With gum (5ch.) or no gum (2ch.).
N188 – 2ch. brown, green & buff 75 15
N189 **142** 5ch. cream, blue & brn 1·00 20
DESIGN—HORIZ: 2ch. Cow-girl with Cattle.

143 Rotary Cement Kiln

1959. "Great Perspectives" (2nd issue: Production Targets). With gum (Nos. N190 and N192) or no gum (others). Perf (N197/8 and N200), perf or imperf (others)

N189a	**143** 1ch. cinnamon, brn & bl	40	10
N190	– 2ch. multicoloured	60	10
N191	– 5ch. multicoloured	1·00	25
N192	– 10ch. multicoloured	1·25	35
N193	– 10ch. purple, yell & bl	60	10
N194	– 10ch. yellow, grn & red	90	10
N195	– 10ch. multicoloured	60	10
N196	– 10ch. blue, light blue and green	75	10
N197	– 10ch. multicoloured	60	10
N198	– 10ch. green, buff and brown	90	10
N199	– 10ch. brown and orange	60	10
N200	– 10ch. multicoloured	1·10	15

DESIGNS—VERT: No. N190, Electric power lines and dam; N191, Loading fertilizers into goods wagon. HORIZ: No. N192, Factory, electric power lines and dam; N163, Harvesting; N194, Sugar-beet, factory and pieces of sugar; N195, Steel furnace; N196, Trawlers; N197, Pig-iron workers; N198, Coal miners; N199, Girl picking apples; N200, Textile worker.

144 Sika Deer

145 Congress Emblem

1959. Game Preservation. No gum (5ch.), with gum (10ch.).

N201	– 5ch. multicoloured	1·75	20
N202	– 5ch. yellow, brown & bl	1·75	10
N203	– 5ch. sepia, green & brn	1·75	10
N204	– 5ch. brown, black & blue	1·75	10
N205	**144** 10ch. multicoloured	1·75	25
N206	– 10ch. red, brown and green on cream	12·00	1·75

DESIGNS—HORIZ: No. N201, Chinese water deer; N202, Siberian weasel; N203, Steppe polecat; N204, European otter; N206, Common pheasant.

1960. 3rd Korean Trade Unions Federation Congress. With gum.

N207	**145** 5ch. multicoloured	45	20

146 "Chungnyon-ho" (freighter)

1959. Transport. With gum.

N208	– 5ch. purple	6·75	75
N209	**146** 10ch. green	2·50	60

DESIGN: 5ch. Electric train.

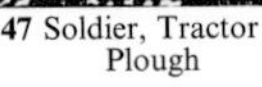
147 Soldier, Tractor and Plough

148 Knife Dance

1960. 12th Anniv of Korean People's Army. With gum.

N210	**147** 5ch. violet and blue	35·00	28·00

1960. Korean National Dances. Multicoloured.

N211	5ch. Type **148**	3·50	20
N212	5ch. Drum dance	3·50	20
N213	10ch. Farmers' dance	3·50	25

149 Women of Three Races

150 Kim Jong Ho (geographer)

1960. 50th Anniv of Int Women's Day. With gum.

N214	**149** 5ch. mauve and blue	90	15
N215	– 10ch. green and orange	90	25

DESIGN—VERT: 10ch. Woman operating lathe.

1960. Korean Celebrities. With gum.

N216	**150** 1ch. grey and green	75	10
N217	– 2ch. blue and yellow	90	10
N218	– 5ch. blue and yellow	3·00	20
N219	– 10ch. brown and ochre	85	10

PORTRAITS: 2ch. Kim Hong Do (painter); 5ch. Pak Yon (musician); 10ch. Chong Da San (scholar).

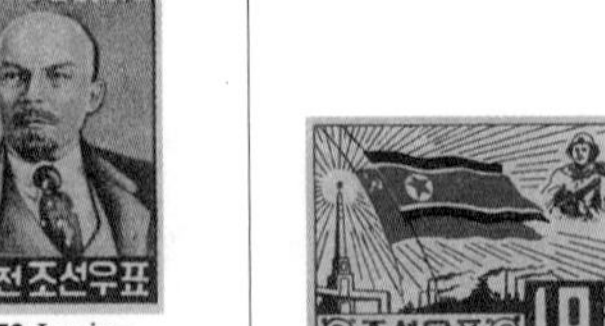
151 Grapes

152 Lenin

1960. Wild Fruits. Fruits in natural colours. With or without gum (N221/2), with gum (others).

N220	5ch. olive and turquoise	80	15
N221	5ch. drab and blue	80	15
N222	5ch. olive and blue	80	15
N223	10ch. olive and orange	1·25	20
N224	10ch. green and pink	1·25	20

FRUITS: No. N220, T **151**; N221, Fruit of "Actinidia arguta planch"; N222, Pine-cone; N223, Hawthorn berries; N224, Horse-chestnut.

1960. 90th Birth Anniv of Lenin. With gum.

N225	**152** 10ch. purple	55	15

153 Koreans and American Soldier (caricature)

154 Arch of Triumph Square, Pyongyang

1960. Campaign Day for Withdrawal of U.S. Forces from South Korea. With gum.

N226	**153** 10ch. blue	3·25	40

1960. Views of Pyongyang.

N227	**154** 10ch. green	75	20
N228	– 20ch. slate	1·00	30
N229	– 40ch. green	2·25	50
N230	– 70ch. green	3·00	60
N231	– 1wn. blue	4·50	90

VIEWS OF PYONGYANG: 20ch. River Taedong promenade; 40ch. Youth Street; 70ch. People's Army Street; 1wn. Sungri Street.

155 Russian Flag on Moon (14.9.59)

156 "Mirror Rock"

1960. Russian Cosmic Rocket Flights. With gum (5ch.) or no gum (10ch.).

N232	– 5ch. turquoise	2·00	1·10
N233	**155** 10ch. multicoloured	2·00	75

DESIGN: 5ch. "Lunik 3" approaching Moon (4.10.59).

1960. Diamond Mountains Scenery (1st issue). Multicoloured.

N234	5ch. Type **156**	1·00	10
N235	5ch. Devil-faced Rock	1·00	10
N236	10ch. Dancing Dragon Bridge (horiz)	3·00	25
N237	10ch. Nine Dragon Falls	3·50	25
N238	10ch. Mt. Diamond on the Sea (horiz)	90	10

See also Nos. N569/72, N599/601 and N1180/4.

157 Lily

158 Guerrillas in the Snow

1960. Flowers. Multicoloured. With gum (N242), with or without gum (others).

N239	5ch. Type **157**	90	15
N240	5ch. Rhododendron	90	15
N241	10ch. Hibiscus	1·75	20
N242	10ch. Blue campanula	1·75	20
N243	10ch. Mauve campanula	1·75	20

1960. Revolutionary Leadership of Kim Il Sung.

N244	**158** 5ch. red	45	10
N245	– 10ch. blue	70	10
N246	– 10ch. red	70	10
N247	– 10ch. blue	70	10
N248	– 10ch. red	70	10

DESIGNS: No. N245, Kim Il Sung talks to guerrillas; N246, Kim Il Sung at Pochonbo; N247, Kim Il Sung on bank of Amnok River; N248, Kim Il Sung returns to Pyongyang.

159 Korean and Soviet Flags

160 "North Korean–Soviet Friendship"

1960. 15th Anniv of Liberation from Japan.

N249	**159** 10ch. red, blue & brown	60	15

1960. North Korean–Soviet Friendship Month.

N250	**160** 10ch. lake on cream	35	15

161 Okryu Bridge, Pyongyang

1960. Pyongyang Buildings.

N251	**161** 10ch. blue	2·25	20
N252	– 10ch. violet	1·50	15
N253	– 10ch. green	75	10

DESIGNS: No. N252, Grand Theatre, Pyongyang; N253, Okryu Restaurant.

162 Tokro River Dam

1960. Inauguration of Tokro River Hydro-electric Power Station. With gum.

N254	**162** 5ch. blue	70	10

163

164 Quayside Welcome

1960. 15th Anniv of World Federation of Trade Unions.

N255	**163** 10ch. lt blue, ultram & bl	25	10

1960. Repatriation of Korean Nationals from Japan.

N256	**164** 10ch. purple	2·50	35

165 Lenin and Workers

166 Football

1960. Korea–Soviet Friendship. With gum.

N257	**165** 10ch. brown and flesh	35	15

1960. Liberation Day Sports Meeting, Pyongyang. Multicoloured.

N258	5ch. Running (vert)	60	10
N259	5ch. Weightlifting (vert)	60	10
N260	5ch. Cycling (vert)	2·25	15
N261	5ch. Gymnastics (vert)	60	10
N262	5ch. Type **166**	1·10	15
N263	10ch. Swimming	60	10
N264	10ch. Moranbong Stadium, Pyongyang	60	10

167 Friendship Monument, Pyongyang

168 Federation Emblem

1960. 10th Anniv of Entry of Chinese Volunteers into Korean War. With gum.

N265	– 5ch. mauve	30	10
N266	**167** 10ch. blue	30	10

DESIGN—HORIZ: 5ch. Chinese and Korean soldiers celebrating.

1960. 15th Anniv of World Democratic Youth Federation.

N267	**168** 10ch. multicoloured	30	10

169 White-backed Woodpecker

170 Korean Wrestling

1960. Birds.

N268	**169** 2ch. multicoloured	9·00	15
N268a	– 5ch. multicoloured	12·50	35
N269	– 5ch. brown, yellow & bl	17·00	70
N270	– 10ch. yellow, brn & grn	11·00	55

DESIGNS—HORIZ: 5ch. (N268a), Mandarins; 10ch. Black-naped oriole. VERT: 5ch. (N269), Oriental scops owl.

1960. Sports and Games. Multicoloured.

N271	5ch. Type **170**	60	10
N272	5ch. Riding on swing (vert)	60	10
N273	5ch. Archery	2·25	30
N274	10ch. Jumping on see-saw (vert)	60	10

171 Cogwheel and Textiles

172 Wild Ginseng (perennial herb)

1961. "Great Perspectives" (3rd issue: Targets of Seven-Year Plan, 1961–67. Inscr "1961"). Mult.

N275	5ch. Type **171**	60	10
N276	5ch. Cogwheel and Corn ("Mechanization of Rural Economy")	1·10	10
N277	10ch. Hammer, sickle and torch on flag (vert)	30	10
N278	10ch. Cogwheels around power station	60	10
N279	10ch. Cogwheel and molten steel	45	10

1961. Multicoloured.

N280	5ch. Type **172**	1·50	10
N281	10ch. Cultivated ginseng	1·50	10

173 Aldehyde Shop

1961. Construction of Vinalon Factory. With gum.

N282	**173** 5ch. red and yellow	60	10
N283	– 10ch. green and yellow	1·10	10
N284	– 10ch. blue and yellow	1·10	10
N285	– 20ch. purple and yellow	1·25	15

DESIGNS: No. N283, Glacial acetic acid shop; N284, Polymerization and saponification shop; N285, Spinning shop.

See also Nos. N338/41.

174 Construction Work

175 Museum Building

1961. Construction of Children's Palace, Pyongyang. With gum.
N286 **174** 2ch. red on yellow . . . 35 15

1961. Completion of Museum of Revolution, Pyongyang. With gum.
N287 **175** 10ch. red 25 10

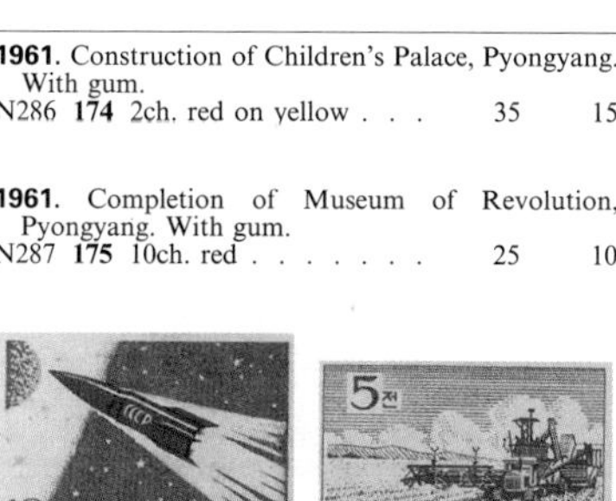
176 Cosmic Rocket

177 Wheat Harvester

1961. Launching of Soviet Venus Rocket.
N288 **176** 10ch. red, yellow & blue 60 15

1961. Agricultural Mechanization. With gum.
N289 – 5ch. violet 50 10
N290 – 5ch. green 50 10
N291 **177** 5ch. green 50 10
N292 – 10ch. blue 60 10
N293 – 10ch. purple 60 10
DESIGNS: No. N289, Tractor-plough; N290, Disc-harrow; N292, Maize-harvester; N293, Tractors.

178

179 Agriculture

1961. Opening of Training Institute.
N294 **178** 10ch. brown on buff . . 25 10

1961. 15th Anniv of Land Reform Law. With gum.
N295 **179** 10ch. green on yellow 45 15

180

182 Tractor-crane

181 Chub Mackerel

1961. 15th Anniv of National Programme. With gum.
N296 **180** 10ch. purple and yellow 20 10

1961. Marine Life.
N297 **181** 5ch. multicoloured . . . 1·25 10
N298 – 5ch. black and blue . . 2·00 25
N299 – 10ch. blue, black & lt bl 2·50 25
N300 – 10ch. multicoloured . . 1·25 10
N301 – 10ch. brown, yell & grn 1·25 10
DESIGNS: No. N298, Common dolphin; N299, Whale sp; N300, Yellow-finned tuna; N301, Pacific cod.

1961. With gum.
N302 **182** 1ch. brown 65 10
N303 – 2ch. brown 65 10
N304 – 5ch. green 90 10
N305 – 10ch. violet 90 20
DESIGNS—HORIZ: 2ch. Heavy-duty lorry; 5ch. Eight-metres turning lathe. VERT: 10ch. 3000-ton press.
See also Nos. N378/9c.

183 Tree-planting

184 "Peaceful Unification" Banner

1961. Re-afforestation Campaign. With gum.
N306 **183** 10ch. green . . . . . . 1·00 25

1961. Propaganda for Peaceful Reunification of Korea.
N307 **184** 10ch. multicoloured . . 6·50 1·50

185 Pioneers visiting Battlefield

1961. 15th Anniv of Children's Union. Mult.
N308 5ch. Pioneers bathing . . . 40 10
N309 10ch. Pioneer bugler . . . 1·25 20
N310 10ch. Type **185** 40 10

186 "Labour Law"

1961. 15th Anniv of Labour Law. With gum.
N311 **186** 10ch. blue on yellow . . 45 20

187 Apples

1961. Fruit. Multicoloured.
N312 5ch. Peaches 75 10
N313 5ch. Plums 75 10
N314 5ch. Type **187** 75 10
N315 10ch. Persimmons 75 10
N316 10ch. Pears 75 10

188 Yuri Gagarin and "Vostok 1"

1961. World's First Manned Space Flight.
N317 **188** 10ch. ultramarine & blue 35 10
N318 10ch. violet and blue . . 35 10

189 Power Station

1961. 15th Anniv of Nationalization of Industries Law. With gum.
N319 **189** 10ch. brown . . . . . 4·50 60

190 Women at Work

191 Children planting Tree

1961. 15th Anniv of Sex Equality Law. With gum.
N320 **190** 10ch. red 35 10

1961. Children. Multicoloured.
N321 5ch. Type **191** 60 10
N322 5ch. Reading book 30 10
N323 10ch. Playing with ball . . 30 10
N324 10ch. Building a house . . 30 10
N325 10ch. Waving flag 30 10

192 Poultry and Stock-breeding

193 Soldiers on March (statue)

1961. Improvement in Living Standards. Mult.
N326 5ch. Type **192** 60 10
N327 10ch. Fabrics and textile factory . . . . 1·10 10
N328 10ch. Trawler and fish (horiz) . . . . 1·50 20
N329 10ch. Grain-harvesting (horiz) 50 10

1961. 25th Anniv of Fatherland Restoration Association. With gum.
N330 – 10ch. violet 40 10
N331 – 10ch. violet 25 10
N332 **193** 10ch. blue and buff . . 25 10
DESIGNS—Marshal Kim Il Sung: No. N330, Seated under tree; N331, Working at desk.

194 Party Emblem and Members

195 Miner

1961. 4th Korean Workers' Party Congress, Pyongyang. With gum.
N333 **194** 10ch. green 20 10
N334 – 10ch. purple 20 10
N335 – 10ch. red 20 10
DESIGNS—VERT: No. N334, "Chollima" statue, Pyongyang. HORIZ: No. N335, Marshal Kim Il Sung.

1961. Miners' Day. With gum.
N336 **195** 10ch. brown . . . . . 1·75 60

196 Pak in Ro

197 Aldehyde Shop

1961. 400th Birth Anniv of Pak in Ro (poet).
N337 **196** 10ch. indigo on blue . . 45 15

1961. Completion of Vinalon Factory. With gum.
N338 **197** 5ch. red and yellow . . 60 10
N339 – 10ch. brown and yellow 90 10
N340 – 10ch. blue and yellow 90 10
N341 – 20ch. purple and yellow 1·40 20
DESIGNS: No. N339, Glacial-acetic shop; N340, Polymerization and saponification shop; N341, Spinning shop.

198 Korean and Chinese Flags

199 Basketball

1961. North Korean Friendship Treaties with China and the U.S.S.R.
N342 – 10ch. multicoloured . . 40 10
N343 **198** 10ch. red, blue & yellow 40 10
DESIGN: No. N342, Korean and Soviet flags.

1961. Physical Culture Day. With gum.
N344 – 2ch. grey 75 10
N345 – 5ch. blue 90 10
N346 **199** 10ch. blue 90 10
N347 – 10ch. blue 90 10
N348 – 10ch. purple 90 10
N349 – 20ch. purple 75 10
DESIGNS: 2ch. Table tennis; 5ch. Flying model glider; 10ch. (N347) Rowing; 10ch. (N348) High jumping; 20ch. Sports emblem.

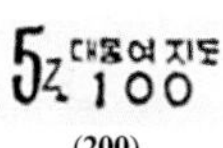
(200)

1961. Centenary of Publication of Map "Taidong Yu Jido" by Kim Jung Ho. No. N216 surch with T **200**.
N350 **150** 5ch. on 1ch. grey & grn 38·00 24·00

201 General Rock

202 "Agriculture and Industry"

1961. Mt. Chilbo Scenery. With gum.
N351 **201** 5ch. blue 75 10
N352 – 5ch. brown 75 10
N353 – 10ch. violet . . . . . 1·40 20
N354 – 10ch. blue . . . . . . 1·40 20
N355 – 10ch. blue . . . . . . 1·40 20
DESIGNS—HORIZ: No. N352, Chonbul Peak; N354, Tiled House Rock; N355, Rainbow Rock. VERT: No. N353, Mansa Peak.

1961. With gum.
N356 **202** 10ch. green 35 10

203 Winged Horse and Congress Emblem

1961. 5th World Federation of Trade Unions Congress, Moscow. With gum.
N357 **203** 10ch. blue, purple & vio 25 10

204 Class "Red Banner" Electric Locomotive

1961. Railway Electrification. With gum.
N358 **204** 10ch. violet and yellow 4·00 1·60

205 Ice Hockey

1961. Winter Sports. With gum.
N359 – 10ch. brown and green 75 10
N360 – 10ch. brown and green 75 10
N361 **205** 10ch. brown and blue 75 10
N362 – 10ch. brown and blue 75 10
DESIGNS: No. N359, Figure skating; N360, Speed skating; N362, Skiing.

206 Grain Harvest

207 Tiger

1962. "Six Heights" of Production Targets (1st series). Inscr "1962". With gum.
N363 – 5ch. red, violet and grey 30 10
N364 – 5ch. brown and grey . . 1·75 30
N365 **206** 10ch. yellow, black & bl 30 10
N366 – 10ch. red, yellow & blue 90 10
N367 – 10ch. black and blue . . 1·10 15
N368 – 10ch. yellow, brown & bl 30 10
DESIGNS: No. N363, Ladle and molten steel; N364, Electric mine train; N366, Fabrics and mill; N367, Trawler and catch; N368, Construction of flats.
See also Nos. N440/5.

1962. Animals.
N369 **207** 2ch. multicoloured . . . 2·00 15
N370 – 2ch. brown and green 1·50 10
N371 – 5ch. yellow and green 1·50 10
N372 – 10ch. brown and green 1·75 15
ANIMALS—HORIZ: 2ch. (N370), Racoon-dog; 5ch. Chinese ferret-badger; 10ch. Asiatic black bear.

208 Kayagum Player

209 "Leuhdorfia puziloi"

1962. Musical Instruments and Players (1st series). Multicoloured.

N373 10ch. Type **208** . . . . . . 1·75 20
N374 10ch. Man playing haegum (two-stringed bowed instrument) . . . . . . 1·75 20
N375 10ch. Woman playing wolgum (banjo) . . . . 1·75 20
N376 10ch. Man playing chotdae (flute) . . . . 1·75 20
N377 10ch. Woman playing wagonghu (harp) . . . . 1·75 20

See also Nos. N473/7.

1962. As T **182**. Inscr "1962". With gum (Nos. N379 and 379b), no gum (others).

N378 5ch. green 50 10
N379 10ch. blue 75 15
N379a 10ch. brown . . . . . . – 3·75
N379b 5wn. brown . . . . 9·50 3·00
N379c 10wn. purple . . . . . . 11·50 6·00

DESIGNS—VERT: 5ch. Hydraulic press; 10ch. (2), Three-ton hammer; 10wn. Tunnel drill. HORIZ: 5wn. Hobbing machine.

See also Nos. N415/22, N513/15 and N573.

1962. Butterflies. Multicoloured.

N380 5ch. Type **209** . . . . . . 2·50 15
N381 10ch. "Sericinus telamon" (purple background) . . 2·50 15
N382 10ch. Keeled apollo (lilac background) . . . . . . 2·50 15
N383 10ch. Peacock (green background) . . . . . . 2·50 15

210 G. S. Titov and "Vostok 2"

1962. 2nd Soviet Manned Space Flight.

N384 **210** 10ch. multicoloured . . 45 15

211 Marshal Kim Il Sung and (inset) addressing Workers

1962. Marshal Kim Il Sung's 50th Birthday. With gum.

N385 **211** 10ch. red 45 15
N386 – 10ch. green 45 15
N387 – 10ch. blue 45 10

DESIGN: No. 387, Kim Il Sung in fur hat and (inset) inspecting battle-front.

212 Kim Chaek

214 Black-faced Spoonbill

213 Mother with Children

1962. Korean Revolutionaries (1st series). With gum.

N388 **212** 10ch. sepia 35 10
N389 – 10ch. blue 35 10
N390 – 10ch. red 35 10
N391 – 10ch. purple 35 10
N392 – 10ch. green 35 10
N393 – 10ch. blue 35 10
N394 – 10ch. brown 35 10

PORTRAITS: No. N389, Kang Gon; N390, An Gil; N391, Ryu Gyong Su; N392/3, Kim Jong Suk; N394, Choe Chun Guk.

See also Nos. N478/82 and N733/5.

1962. National Mothers' Meeting, Pyongyang.

N395 **213** 10ch. multicoloured . . 30 10

1962. Birds. Inscr "1962". Multicoloured.

N396 5ch. Type **214** . . . . . . 1·75 20
N397 5ch. Brown hawk owl . . . 7·50 20
N398 10ch. Eastern broad-billed roller . . . . 4·25 50
N399 10ch. Black paradise flycatcher . . . . 4·25 50
N400 20ch. Tundra swan . . . . 6·50 90

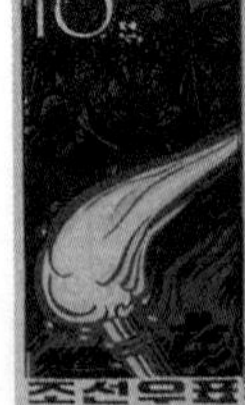
215 Victory Flame

216 Japanese Croaker

1962. 25th Anniv of Battle of Pochonbo.

N401 **215** 10ch. multicoloured . . 55 10

1962. Fishes. Multicoloured.

N402 5ch. Type **216** . . . . . . 1·50 10
N403 5ch. Hairtail . . . . 1·50 10
N404 10ch. Dotted gizzard shad (head pointing to right) 1·75 20
N405 10ch. Japanese spotted seabass (blue background) . . . . . . 1·75 20
N406 10ch. Japanese croaker (green background) . . . 1·75 20

217 Waterdropper

218 Radial Drill

1962. Antiques. With gum.

N407 – 4ch. black and blue . . 1·00 10
N408 **217** 5ch. black and ochre . . 1·00 10
N409 A 10ch. black and green 1·25 10
N410 B 10ch. black and orange 1·25 10
N411 C 10ch. black and purple 1·25 10
N412 D 10ch. black and brown 1·25 10
N413 E 10ch. black and yellow 1·25 10
N414 – 40ch. black and grey . . 3·50 35

DESIGNS—VERT: 4ch. Brush pot; 40ch. Porcelain decanter. HORIZ: A, Inkstand; B, Brushstand; C, Turtle paperweight; D, Inkstone; E, Document case.

1962. Double frame-line. With gum.

N415 – 2ch. green 40 10
N415a – 2ch. brown . . . . . — 4·00
N416 – 4ch. blue . . . . . . 1·75 10
N417 **218** 5ch. blue 40 10
N418 – 5ch. purple 40 10
N419 – 10ch. purple 50 10
N420 – 40ch. blue . . . . . . 3·75 20
N421 – 90ch. blue . . . . . . 1·60 30
N422 – 1wn. brown . . . . . 4·75 50

DESIGNS—VERT: 2ch. Vertical milling machine; 5ch. (N418), Hydraulic hammer; 1wn. Spindle drill. HORIZ: 4ch. "Victory April 15" motor-car; 10ch. All-purpose excavator; 40ch. Trolley-bus; 90ch. Planing machine.

See also Nos. N513/15 and N573.

219 Chong Da San

220 Voter

1962. Birth Bicentenary of Chong Da San (philosopher).

N423 **219** 10ch. purple 35 10

1962. Election of Deputies to National Assembly. Multicoloured.

N424 10ch. Type **220** 80 10
N425 10ch. Family going to poll 80 10

221 Pyongyang

1962. 1535th Anniv of Pyongyang. With gum.

N426 **221** 10ch. black and blue . . 65 10

222 Globe and "Vostok 3" and "4"

223 Spiraea

1962. 1st "Team" Manned Space Flight.

N427 **222** 10ch. indigo, blue & red 60 20

1962. Korean Plants. Plants in natural colours; frame and inscr colours given.

N428 **223** 5ch. light green & green 1·25 10
N429 – 10ch. green and red . . 1·25 10
N430 – 10ch. blue and purple 1·25 10
N431 – 10ch. green and olive 1·25 10

PLANTS: No. N429, Ginseng; N430, Campanula; N431, "Rheumcoreanum makai (Polyonaceae)".

224 "Uibang Ryuchui"

225 Science Academy

1962. 485th Anniv of Publication of "Uibang Ryuchui" (medical encyclopaedia).

N432 **224** 10ch. multicoloured . . 3·50 30

1962. 10th Anniv of Korean Science Academy.

N433 **225** 10ch. blue and turquoise 1·00 10

226 Fisherwomen

227 European Mink

1962.

N434 **226** 10ch. blue . . . . . . 1·00 10

1962. Animals.

N435 **227** 4ch. brown and green 70 10
N436 – 5ch. blue, drab and green 70 10
N437 – 10ch. blue and yellow 90 10
N438 – 10ch. sepia and turquoise 90 10
N439 – 20ch. brown and blue 1·50 15

ANIMALS—HORIZ: No. N436, Chinese hare. VERT: No. N437, Eurasian red squirrel; N438, Common goral; N439, Siberian chipmunk.

228 Harvesting

1963. "Six Heights" of Production Targets (2nd issue). Inscr "1963". Multicoloured.

N440 5ch. Miner . . . . 1·00 20
N441 10ch. Type **228** 40 10
N442 10ch. Furnaceman 30 10
N443 10ch. Construction worker 30 10
N444 10ch. Textiles loom operator 65 10
N445 40ch. Fisherman and trawler . . . . 2·25 40

229 Soldier

230 Peony

1963. 15th Anniv of Korean People's Army. With gum.

N446 – 5ch. brown 50 10
N447 **229** 10ch. red 60 10
N448 – 10ch. blue 85 10

DESIGNS: 5ch. Airman; 10ch. Sailor.

1963. Korean Flowers. Multicoloured.

N449 5ch. Type **230** 60 10
N450 10ch. Rugosa rose 90 10
N451 10ch. Azalea 90 10
N452 20ch. Campion 90 10
N453 40ch. Orchid . . . . 2·50 35

231 "Sadang-ch'um" (Korean folk dance)

1963. International Music and Dancing Contest, Pyongyang. Multicoloured.

N454 10ch. Type **231** . . . . . . 1·75 15
N455 10ch. Dancer with fan . . . 1·75 15

232 Revolutionaries

1963. 3rd Anniv of South Korean Rising of April, 1960.

N456 **232** 10ch. multicoloured . . 40 15

233 Karl Marx

234 Children in Chemistry Class

1963. 145th Birth Anniv of Karl Marx. With gum.

N457 **233** 10ch. blue 30 10

1963. Child Care and Amenities. Multicoloured.

N458 2ch. Type **234** 80 20
N459 5ch. Children running . . . 70 15
N460 10ch. Boy conducting choir 1·75 20
N461 10ch. Girl chasing butterfly 3·50 25

235 Armed Koreans and American Soldier (caricature)

1963. Campaign Month for Withdrawal of U.S. Forces from South Korea.

N462 **235** 10ch. multicoloured . . 45 10

236 "Cyrtoclytus capra"

237 Soldier with Flag

1963. Korean Beetles. Multicoloured designs. Colours of beetles given.

N463 5ch. Type **236** 75 10
N464 10ch. multicoloured . . . . 1·10 10
N465 10ch. red and blue . . . . 1·10 10
N466 10ch. indigo, blue and purple . . . . 1·10 10

BEETLES: No. N464, "Cicindela chinensis" (tiger beetle); N465, "Purpuricenus lituratus"; N466, "Agapanthia pilicornis".

1963. 10th Anniv of Victory in Korean War.

N467 **237** 10ch. multicoloured . . 50 10

238 North Korean Flag

239 Namdae Gate, Kaesong

1963. 15th Anniv of People's Republic. Mult.
N468 10ch. Type **238** 30 10
N469 10ch. North Korean Badge 30 10

1963. Ancient Korean Buildings (1st series). With gum.
N470 **239** 5ch. black 20 10
N471 – 10ch. blue 40 10
N472 – 10ch. brown 40 10
BUILDINGS: No. N471, Taedong Gate, Pyongyang; N472, Potong Gate, Pyongyang.
See also Nos. N537/8.

240 Ajaeng (bowed zither)

241 Nurse with Children

1963. Musical Instruments and Players (2nd series). Multicoloured. Nos. N473 and N476 with gum.
N473 3ch. Type **240** . . . . . . 1·25 15
N474 5ch. Pyongyon (jade chimes) . . . . 1·25 15
N475 10ch. Saenap (brass bowl) 1·50 15
N476 10ch. Rogo (drums in frame) . . . . 1·50 15
N477 10ch. Piri ("wooden pipe") 1·50 15

1963. Korean Revolutionaries (2nd issue). As T **212**. With gum.
N478 5ch. brown 40 10
N479 5ch. purple 40 10
N480 10ch. rose 50 10
N481 10ch. slate 50 10
N482 10ch. dull purple 50 10
PORTRAITS: No. N478, Kwon Yong Byok; N479, Ma Dong Hui; N480, Li Je Sun; N481, Pak Dal; N482, Kim Yong Bom.

1963. Child Welfare. Multicoloured.
N483 10ch. Type **241** 50 10
N484 10ch. Children in playground 50 10

242 Hwajang Hall

243 Furnaceman

1963. Mount Myohyang Resort. Multicoloured.
N485 5ch. Type **242** 35 10
N486 10c. Mountain stream and chalet 75 10
N487 10ch. Kwanum Pavilion and stone pagoda (horiz) 65 10
N488 10ch. Rope bridge across river (horiz) . . . . . . 1·75 15

1963. Seven Year Plan. With gum.
N489 **243** 5ch. red 20 10
N490 – 10ch. grey . . . . . . 1·50 20
N491 – 10ch. red . . . . . . 1·50 20
N492 – 10ch. lilac 85 10
DESIGNS—VERT: No. N490, Construction workers. HORIZ: No. N491, Power technicians; N492, Miners.

244 Children hoeing

1963. "Hung Bo" (fairytale). Multicoloured.
N493 5ch. Type **244** 30 10
N494 10ch. Tying up broken leg of swallow 90 10
N495 10ch. Barn swallow dropping gourd seed . . 90 15
N496 10ch. Sawing through giant gourd 50 10
N497 10ch. Treasure inside gourd 50 10

245 Marksman

1963. Marksmanship. Multicoloured.
N498 5ch. Type **245** 30 10
N499 10ch. Marksman with small-bore rifle 55 10
N500 10ch. Marksman with standard rifle 55 10

246 Sinuiju Chemical Fibre Factory

1964. Chemical Fibres Factories. With gum.
N501 **246** 10ch. slate 75 10
N502 – 10ch. purple 75 10
DESIGN: No. N502, Chongjin Chemical Fibre Factory.

247 Strikers

1964. 35th Anniv of Wonsan General Strike. With gum.
N503 **247** 10ch. brown 60 10

248 Korean Alphabet

1964. 520th Anniv of Korean Alphabet.
N504 **248** 10ch. green, buff & brn 60 20

249 Lenin

250 Whale-catcher

1964. 40th Death Anniv of Lenin. With gum.
N505 **249** 10ch. red 30 10

1964. Fishing Industry. Multicoloured.
N506 5ch. Type **250** 50 10
N507 5ch. Trawler No. 051 . . . 50 10
N508 10ch. Trawler No. 397 . . 1·00 20
N509 10ch. Trawler No. 738 . . 1·00 20

251 Insurgents

1964. 45th Anniv of Rising of 1st March. With gum.
N510 **251** 10ch. purple 30 10

252 Warring Peasants

1964. 70th Anniv of Kabo Peasants' War. With gum.
N511 **252** 10ch. purple 30 10

253 Students' Palace, Pyongyang

254 "Changbaek" Excavator

1964. With gum.
N512 **253** 10ch. green 30 10

1964. Single frame-line. Dated "1964" or "1965" (No. N573). With gum.
N513 – 5ch. violet 60 10
N514 **254** 10ch. green 90 10
N515 – 10ch. blue 90 10
N573 – 10ch. violet 75 20
DESIGNS—VERT: 5ch. 200 metre drill; 10ch. (N573) "Horning 500" machine. HORIZ: 10ch. (N515) 400 h.p. Diesel engine.

255 "On the March"

1964. 5th Korean Democratic Youth League Congress, Pyongyang.
N516 **255** 10ch. multicoloured . . 30 10

256 Electric Train

1964. Inauguration of Pyongyang–Sinuiju Electric Railway.
N517 **256** 10ch. multicoloured . . 2·50 20

257 Rejoicing in Chongsan-ri Village

1964. Popular Movement at Chongsan-ri. With gum.
N517a **257** 5ch. brown . . . . .

258 Drum Dance

259 "For the Sake of the Fatherland"

1964. Korean Dances.
N518 **258** 2ch. mauve, buff & black . . . . 1·50 15
N519 – 5ch. red, black & yellow 1·75 15
N520 – 10ch. multicoloured . . 2·00 15
DESIGNS: 5ch. "Ecstasy" (solo); 10ch. Tabor.

1964. Li Su Bok Commemorative. With gum.
N521 **259** 5ch. red 20 10

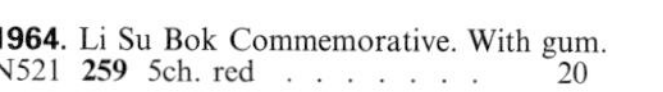

260 Nampo Smelting Works

1964. With gum.
N522 **260** 5ch. green . . . . . . 2·50 10
N523 – 10ch. slate . . . . . . 2·75 20
DESIGN: 10ch. Hwanghae iron works.

261 Torch, Chollima Statue and Cogwheel

1964. Asian Economic Seminar, Pyongyang. Multicoloured.
N524 5ch. Type **261** 25 10
N525 10ch. Flags, statue and cogwheel 30 10

262 Korean People and Statue of Kang Ho Yong (war hero)

1964. Struggle for Reunification of Korea.
N526 **262** 10ch. multicoloured . . 45 10

263 Hawk Fowl

1964. Domestic Poultry. Multicoloured.
N527 2ch. Type **263** 35 10
N528 4ch. White fowl 35 10
N529 5ch. Ryongyon fowl . . . 55 10
N530 5ch. Black fowl 55 10
N531 40ch. Helmet guineafowl . . 4·00 1·40

264 Skiing

1964. Winter Olympic Games, Innsbruck.
N532 **264** 5ch. red, blue and buff 50 10
N533 – 10ch. blue, green & buff 75 10
N534 – 10ch. blue, red and buff 75 10
DESIGNS: No. N533, Ice skating; N534, Skiing (slalom).

265 "Tobolsk" (passenger ship) and Flags

266 Tonggun Pavilion Uiju

1964. 5th Anniv of Agreement for Repatriation of Koreans in Japan.
N535 **265** 10ch. red, blue & lt blue 1·40 30
N536 – 30ch. multicoloured . . 1·10 15
DESIGN: 30ch. Return of repatriates.

1964. Ancient Korean Buildings (2nd series). With gum.
N537 **266** 5ch. purple 20 10
N538 – 10ch. green 30 10
DESIGN: 10ch. Inpang Pavilion, Kanggye City.

267 Cycling

268 Burning of the "General Sherman"

1964. Olympic Games, Tokyo.
N539 – 2ch. brown and blue . . 25 10
N540 **267** 5ch. brown and green 75 10
N541 – 10ch. orange and blue 35 10
N542 – 10ch. orange and green 35 10
N543 – 40ch. brown and blue 60 35
DESIGNS—HORIZ: 2ch. Rifle-shooting; 10ch. blue, Running. VERT: 10ch. green, Wrestling; 40ch. Volleyball.

1964. The "General Sherman" Incident, 1866. With gum.
N544 **268** 30ch. brown . . . . . 2·00 30

269 Organizing Guerrillas

1964. Guerrilla Operations in the 1930s against the Japanese. With gum.
N545 **269** 2ch. violet 25 10
N546 – 5ch. blue 35 10
N547 – 10ch. black 45 10
DESIGNS: 5ch. Kim Il Sung addressing guerillas; 10ch. Battle scene at Xiaowangqing.

270 Students attacking **271** Weightlifting

1964. Kwangju Students Rising, 1929. With gum.
N548 **270** 10ch. violet . . . . . . 1·60 15

1964. "GANEFO" Athletic Games, Djakarta, Indonesia (1963). Multicoloured.
N549 2ch. Type **271** 40 10
N550 5ch. Athlete breasting tape 40 10
N551 5ch. Boxing (horiz) 40 10
N552 10ch. Football (horiz) . . . 1·00 15
N553 10ch. Globe emblem (horiz) 40 15

272 Lynx

1964. Animals. With gum.
N554 2ch. sepia (Type **272**) . . . 75 10
N555 5ch. sepia (Leopard cat) . . 1·75 10
N556 10ch. brown (Leopard) . . 2·25 10
N557 10ch. sepia (Yellow-throated marten) . . . . 2·25 10

273 Vietnamese Attack

1964. Support for People of Vietnam.
N558 **273** 10ch. multicoloured . . 30 10

274 Prof. Kim Bong Han and Emblems

1964. Kyongrak Biological Systems.
N559 **274** 2ch. purple and olive . . 65 10
N560 – 5ch. green, orange & bl 90 10
N561 – 10ch. red, yellow & blue 1·25 10
DESIGNS—33 × 23½ mm: 5ch. "Bonghan" duct; 10ch. "Bonghan" corpuscle. Each include emblems as in Type **274**.

275 Farmers, Tractor and Lorry

1964. Agrarian Programme. Multicoloured.
N562 5ch. Type **275** 20 10
N563 10ch. Peasants with scroll and book 30 10
N564 10ch. Peasants, one writing in book 30 10

276 Chung Jin gets a Pistol

1964. The Struggle to capture Japanese Arms. With gum.
N565 **276** 4ch. brown 25 10

277 Girl with Korean Products **278** Three Fairies Rock

1964. Economic 7 Year Plan. Multicoloured. With gum (5ch.) or no gum (others).
N566 5ch. Type **277** 40 10
N567 10ch. Farm girl 40 10
N568 10ch. Couple on winged horse (23½ × 23½ mm) . . 25 10

1964. Diamond Mountains Scenery (2nd issue). Inscr "1964". Multicoloured. Without gum (2, 4ch.) or with gum (others).
N569 2ch. Type **278** 75 10
N570 4ch. Ryonju Falls . . . . 2·75 10
N571 10ch. The Ten Thousand Rocks, Manmulsang . . 75 10
N572 10ch. Chinju Falls . . . . 2·75 10

280 Soldiers Advancing, Fusong

1965. Guerrilla Operations against the Japanese, 1934–40. With gum.
N574 **280** 10ch. violet 50 10
N575 – 10ch. violet 50 10
N576 – 10ch. green 50 10
DESIGNS: No. N575, Soldiers descending hill, Hongqihe; N576, Soldiers attacking hill post, Luozigou.

281 Tuman River

1965. Korean Rivers. Multicoloured.
N577 2ch. Type **281** 60 10
N578 5ch. Taedong (vert) . . . . 1·75 15
N579 10ch. Amnok 75 10

282 Union Badge

1965. 1st Congress of Landworkers' Union, Pyongyang. With gum.
N580 **282** 10ch. multicoloured . . 30 10

283 Furnacemen and Workers

1965. 10 Major Tasks of 7 Year Plan. With gum.
N581 **283** 10ch. multicoloured . . 30 10

284 Miners' Strike, Sinhung Colliery

1965. 35th Anniv of Strikes and Peasants' Revolt. With gum.
N582 **284** 10ch. olive . . . . . . 1·25 15
N583 – 10ch. brown . . . . . 1·50 15
N584 – 40ch. purple . . . . . 1·00 15
DESIGNS: 10ch. Strikers at Pyongyang Rubber Factory; 40ch. Revolt of Tanchon peasants.

285 Embankment Construction

1965. Sunhwa River Works. With gum.
N585 **285** 10ch. multicoloured . . 30 10

286 Hand holding Torch

1965. 5th Anniv of South Korean Rising of April 19th. Multicoloured. With gum.
N586 10ch. Type **286** 20 10
N587 40ch. Student-hero, Kim Chio 45 20

287 Power Station under Construction

1965. Construction of Thermal Power Station, Pyongyang. With gum.
N588 **287** 5ch. brown and blue . . 25 10

288 African and Asian

1965. 10th Anniv of 1st Afro-Asian Conference, Bandung. With gum.
N589 **288** 10ch. multicoloured . . 30 10

289 Rejoicing of Koreans

1965. 10th Anniv of General Assn of Koreans in Japan. With gum.
N590 **289** 10ch. blue and red . . . 25 10
N591 – 40ch. indigo, blue & red 45 15
DESIGN: 40ch. Patriot and flag.

290 Workers in Battle **291** "Victory 64" 10-ton Lorry

1965. 2nd Afro-Asian Conf, Algiers. With gum.
N592 **290** 10ch. black, yellow red 75 10
N593 – 40ch. black, yellow red 1·25 25
DESIGN: 40ch. Korean and African soldiers.
The Algiers Conference did not take place.

1965. With gum.
N594 **291** 10ch. green . . . . . . 1·25 20

292 Kim Chang Gol

1965. War Heroes (1st series). With gum.
N595 **292** 10ch. green 30 10
N596 – 10ch. brown 30 10
N597 – 40ch. purple 75 20
PORTRAITS: No. N596, Cho Gun Sil and machine-gun; N597, An Hak Ryong and machine-gun.
See also Nos. N781/3 and N842/3.

293 Marx and Lenin

1965. Postal Ministers' Congress, Peking. With gum.
N598 **293** 10ch. black, yellow red 1·50 15

294 Lake Samil

1965. Diamond Mountains Scenery (3rd issue). Multicoloured. With gum.
N599 2ch. Type **294** 60 10
N600 5ch. Chipson Peak . . . . 1·00 10
N601 10ch. Kwanum Falls . . . 2·75 25

295 Amnok River, Kusimuldong

1965. Scenes of Japanese War. With gum.
N602 **295** 5ch. green and blue . . 35 10
N603 – 10ch. turquoise and blue 60 10
DESIGN: 10ch. Lake Samji.

296 Footballer and Games' Emblem **297** Workers and Map

1965. "GANEFO" Football Games, Pyongyang. Multicoloured. With gum.
N604 10ch. Type **296** . . . . . . 1·25 10
N605 10ch. Games emblem and Moranbong Stadium . . 1·25 10

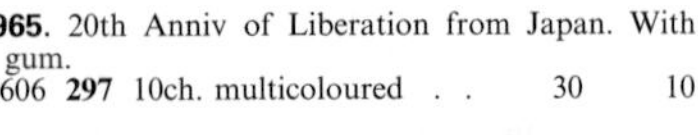

1965. 20th Anniv of Liberation from Japan. With gum.
N606 **297** 10ch. multicoloured . . 30 10

298 Engels **299** Pole Vaulting

1965. 145th Birth Anniv of Engels. With gum.
N607 **298** 10ch. brown 30 10

1965. Sports. Multicoloured. With gum.
N608 2ch. Type **299** 50 10
N609 4ch. Throwing the javelin 1·75 20
N610 10ch. Throwing the discus 50 10

N611 10ch. High jumping (horiz) . . 50 10
N612 10ch. Putting the shot (horiz) 50 10

301 Korean Fighters

1965. 20th Anniv of Korean Workers' Party. Each black, yellow and red. With gum.
N613 10ch. Type **301** 45 10
N614 10ch. Party emblem 45 10
N615 10ch. Lenin and Marx . . 45 10
N616 10ch. Workers marching . . 45 10
N617 10ch. Fighters 45 10
N618 40ch. Workers 45 10
Nos. N613/8 each have a red banner in the background and were issued together in blocks of 6 (3 × 2), forming a composite design, within the sheet.

302 Kim Chaek Iron Works

303 Grass Carp

1965. With gum.
N620 **302** 10ch. purple . . . . . 3·50 10
N621 – 10ch. brown . . . . . . 3·50 10
DESIGN: No. 621, Chongjin Steel Works.

1965. Freshwater Fish. Multicoloured. With gum.
N622 2ch. Rainbow trout 70 10
N623 4ch. Dolly Varden charr . . 90 10
N624 10ch. Brown trout (surfacing water) . . . . 2·25 15
N625 10ch. Common carp diving (date at left) . . . . . . 2·25 15
N626 10ch. Type **303** . . . . . . 2·25 15
N627 40ch. Crucian carp . . . . 3·25 55

304 Building House

305 Children in Workshop

1965. Kim Hong Do's Drawings. With gum.
N628 2ch. green (Type **304**) . . . 45 10
N629 4ch. purple (Weaving) . . . 90 10
N630 10ch. brown (Wrestling) . . 80 10
N631 10ch. blue (School class) . . 80 10
N632 10ch. red (Dancing) . . . . 1·25 10
N633 10ch. violet (Blacksmiths) 1·10 10

1965. Life at Pyongyang Children's and Students' Palace. Multicoloured. With gum.
N634 2ch. Type **305** 20 10
N635 4ch. Boxing 20 10
N636 10ch. Chemistry 75 10
N637 10ch. Playing violin and accordion 75 10

306 Whale-catcher

1965. Korean Fishing Boats. With gum.
N638 **306** 10ch. blue . . . . . . 1·40 25
N639 – 10ch. green . . . . . . 1·40 25
DESIGN: No. N639, Fishing fleet service vessel.

307 Great Tit

308 Silkworm Moth ("Bombyx mori") and Cocoon

1965. Korean Birds. Inscr "1965". Multicoloured. With gum.
N640 4ch. Black-capped kingfisher (vert) . . . . 2·40 50
N641 10ch. Type **307** . . . . . . 3·50 1·25
N642 10ch. Pied wagtail (facing left) . . . . 3·50 1·25
N643 10ch. Azure-winged magpie (facing right) . . . . . . 3·50 1·25
N644 40ch. Black-tailed hawfinch 8·00 4·50

1965. Korean Sericulture. With gum.
N645 **308** 2ch. green . . . . . . 5·00 20
N646 – 10ch. brown . . . . . 5·00 30
N647 – 10ch. purple . . . . . 5·00 30
MOTHS AND COCOONS: No. N646, Ailathus silk moth ("Samia cynthia"); N647, Chinese oak silk moth ("Antheraea pernyi").

309 Hooded Crane

310 Japanese Common Squid

1965. Wading Birds. With gum.
N648 **309** 2ch. brown . . . . . . 4·25 15
N649 – 10ch. blue . . . . . . 4·50 45
N650 – 10ch. purple . . . . . 4·50 45
N651 – 40ch. green . . . . . . 8·75 90
BIRDS: No. N649, Japanese white-naped crane; N650, Manchurian crane; N651, Grey heron.

1965. Korean Molluscs. Multicoloured. With gum.
N652 5ch. Type **310** . . . . . . 1·25 10
N653 10ch. Giant Pacific octopus 1·75 10

311 Spotbill Duck

1965. Korean Ducks. Multicoloured. With gum.
N654 2ch. Type **311** . . . . . . 2·75 15
N655 4ch. Ruddy shelduck . . . 2·75 25
N656 10ch. Mallard . . . . . . 4·25 55
N657 40ch. Baikal teal . . . . . 6·25 1·25

312 Circus Theatre, Pyongyang

313 "Marvel of Peru" ("Mirabilis jalapa")

1965. Korean Circus. With gum except No. N661.
N658 **312** 2ch. blue, black & brown 75 10
N659 – 10ch. blue, red and black . . . . 1·50 10
N660 – 10ch. red, black & green 1·50 10
N661 – 10ch. orange, sepia & grn . . . . 1·50 10
N662 – 10ch. red, yellow & turq 1·50 10
DESIGNS—VERT: No. N659, Trapeze artistes; N660, Performer with hoops on seesaw; N661, Tightrope dancers; N662, Performer with revolving cap on stick.

1965. Korean Flowers. Multicoloured. With gum except No. N663.
N663 4ch. Type **313** . . . . . . 1·10 10
N664 10ch. Peony . . . . 1·50 10
N665 10ch. Moss rose . . . . . 1·50 10
N666 10ch. Magnolia . . . . . 1·50 10

314 "Finn" Class Dinghy

315 Cuban, Korean and African

1965. Yachts. Multicoloured. With gum.
N667 2ch. Type **314** 70 20
N668 10ch. "5.5m" class yacht 1·00 30
N669 10ch. "Dragon" class yacht 1·00 30
N670 40ch. "Star" class yacht . . 2·00 60

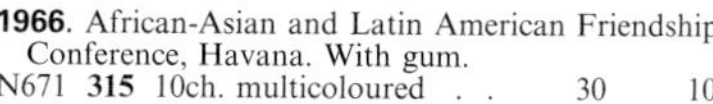

1966. African-Asian and Latin American Friendship Conference, Havana. With gum.
N671 **315** 10ch. multicoloured . . 30 10

316 Hosta

1966. Wild Flowers. Mult. With gum. (a) 1st series.
N672 2ch. Type **316** 50 10
N673 4ch. Dandelion 50 10
N674 10ch. Pink convolvulus . . 75 10
N675 10ch. Lily-of-the-valley . . 75 10
N676 40ch. Catalpa blossom . . 2·00 20

(b) 2nd series.
N677 2ch. Polyanthus 50 10
N678 4ch. Lychnis 50 10
N679 10ch. Adonis 75 10
N680 10ch. Orange lily 75 10
N681 90ch. Rhododendron . . . 3·00 30
Nos. N672/6 exist imperf and without gum.

317 Farmer and Wife

1966. 20th Anniv of Land Reform Law. With gum.
N682 **317** 10ch. multicoloured . . 20 10

318 Troops advancing, Dashahe

319 Silla Bowl

1966. Paintings of Guerrilla Battles, 1937–39. With gum, except No. N684.
N683 **318** 10ch. red 30 10
N684 – 10ch. turquoise 30 10
N685 – 10ch. purple 30 10
DESIGNS AND BATTLES: No. N684, Troops firing from trees, Taehongdan; N685, Troops on hillside, Jiansanfeng.

1966. Art Treasures of Silla Dynasty. With gum.
N686 **319** 2ch. ochre . . . . . . 1·25 10
N687 – 5ch. black . . . . . . 1·25 10
N688 – 10ch. violet . . . . . . 1·25 10
DESIGNS: 5ch. Earthenware jug. 10ch. Censer.

320 Hands holding Torch, Rifle and Hammer

321 Torch and Patriots

1966. 80th Anniv of Labour Day. With gum.
N689 **320** 10ch. multicoloured . . 30 10

1966. 30th Anniv of Association for Restoration of Fatherland.
N690 **321** 10ch. red and yellow . . 30 10

322 Harvester

1966. Aid for Agriculture. Multicoloured.
N691 5ch. Type **322** 25 10
N692 10ch. Labourer 35 10

323 Young Pioneers

1966. 20th Anniv of Korean Children's Union. Without gum.
N693 **323** 10ch. multicoloured . . 50 10

324 Kangson Steel Works

1966. Korean Industries. With gum.
N694 **324** 10ch. grey . . . . . . 3·50 15
N695 – 10ch. red (Pongung Chemical Works) . . 3·50 15

325 Pacific Saury

1966. Korean Fishes. With gum, except Nos. N699/700.
N696 **325** 2ch. blue, green & purple 80 10
N697 – 5ch. purple, green & brn 1·00 10
N698 – 10ch. blue, buff & green 1·50 15
N699 – 10ch. purple and & green . . . . 1·50 15
N700 – 40ch. green, buff & blue 3·50 60
FISHES: 5ch. Pacific cod; 10ch. (N698), Chum salmon, (N699), Yellowfish; 40ch. Pink salmon.

326 Professor Kim Bong Han

1966. Kyungrak Biological System. With gum.
N701 **326** 2ch. blue, green & yellow 60 10
N702 – 4ch. multicoloured . . . 60 10
N703 – 5ch. multicoloured . . . 60 10
N704 – 10ch. multicoloured . . 60 10
N705 – 10ch. multicoloured . . 60 10
N706 – 10ch. multicoloured . . 60 10
N707 – 15ch. multicoloured . . 60 10
N708 – 40ch. multicoloured . . 60 10
DESIGNS: No. N704, Kyongrak Institute; N708, Figure of Man; N702/3, 705/7, Diagram of system.
Nos. N701/8 were issued together, se-tenant, forming a composite design.

327 Leonov in Space ("Voskhod 2")

1966. Cosmonauts Day. Multicoloured.
N710 5ch. Type **327** 20 10
N711 10ch. "Luna 9" 55 10
N712 40ch. "Luna 10" . . . . . 1·10 20

328 Footballers

1966. World Cup Football Championship. Mult.
N713 10ch. Type **328** . . . . . . 1·25 25
N714 10ch. Jules Rimet Cup, football and boots . . . 1·25 25
N715 10ch. Goalkeeper saving goal (vert) . . . . 1·25 25

329 Defence of Seoul

1966. Korean War of 1950–53. With gum.
N716 **329** 10ch. green 35 10
N717 – 10ch. purple 35 10
N718 – 10ch. purple 35 10
DESIGNS: No. N717, Battle on Mt. Napal; N718, Battle for Height 1211.

330 Women in Industry

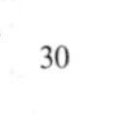

1966. 20th Anniv of Sex Equality Law.
N719 **330** 10ch. multicoloured . . 30 10

331 Industrial Workers

332 Water-jar Dance

1966. 20th Anniv of Industrial Nationalization.
N720 **331** 10ch. multicoloured . . 90 10

1966. Korean Dances. Multicoloured. 5, 40ch. with or without gum; others without.
N721 5ch. Type **332** . . . . . . 1·00 10
N722 10ch. Bell dance . . . . . 1·75 15
N723 10ch. "Dancer in a Mural Painting" . . . . 1·75 15
N724 15ch. Sword dance . . . . 1·75 20
N725 40ch. Gold Cymbal dance 3·25 30

333 Korean attacking U.S. Soldier

334 Yakovlev Yak-12M Crop-spraying

1966. Korean Reunification Campaign. With gum.
N726 **333** 10ch. green 60 10
N727 – 10ch. purple 60 10
N728 – 10ch. lilac . . . . . . 3·75 45
DESIGNS: No. N727, Korean with young child; N728, Korean with shovel, industrial scene and electric train.

1966. Industrial Uses of Aircraft. With gum except 2 and 5ch.
N729 **334** 2ch. green and purple 50 10
N730 – 5ch. brown and green 6·00 20
N731 – 10ch. brown and blue 1·50 10
N732 – 40ch. brown and blue 1·50 10
DESIGNS: 5ch. Yakovlev Yak-18U (forest-fire observation); 10ch. Lisunov Li-2 (geological survey); 40ch. Lisunov Li-2 (detection of fish shoals).

1966. Korean Revolutionaries (3rd issue). As T **212**. With gum.
N733 10ch. violet (O Jung Hub)
N734 10ch. green (Kim Gyong Sok) . . . .
N735 10ch. blue (Li Dong Gol)

335 Kim Il Sung University

1966. 20th Anniv of Kim Il Sung University. With gum.
N736 **335** 10ch. violet 50 10

336 Judo

1966. Ganefo Games, Phnom Penh.
N737 **336** 5ch. black, green & blue 60 10
N738 – 10ch. blk, grn & dp grn 60 10
N739 – 10ch. black and red . . 60 10
DESIGNS: No. N738, Basketball; N739, Table tennis.

337 Hoopoe

1966. Korean Birds. Multicoloured. Inscr "1966".
N740 2ch. Common rosefinch (horiz) . . . . 2·00 15
N741 5ch. Type **337** . . . . . . 2·40 20
N742 10ch. Black-breasted thrush (blue background) (horiz) 2·75 35
N743 10ch. Crested lark (green background) (horiz) . . . 2·75 35
N744 40ch. White-bellied black woodpecker . . . . . . 6·00 90

338 Building Construction

1966. "Increased Production with Economy". Multicoloured. Without gum (40ch.) or with gum (others).
N745 5ch. Type **338** 25 10
N746 10ch. Furnaceman and graph 45 10
N747 10ch. Machine-tool production 45 10
N748 40ch. Miners and pit-head 1·40 15

339 Parachuting

1966. National Defence Sports. With gum.
N749 **339** 2ch. brown 75 10
N750 – 5ch. red 55 10
N751 – 10ch. blue . . . . . . 2·75 30
N752 – 40ch. green . . . . . . 1·60 20
DESIGNS: 5ch. Show jumping; 10ch. Motor cycle racing; 40ch. Radio receiving and transmitting competition.

340 "Samil Wolgan" (Association Magazine)

1966. 30th Anniv of "Samil Wolgan" Magazine.
N753 **340** 10ch. multicoloured . . 90 15

341 Red Deer

342 Blueberries

1966. Korean Deer. Multicoloured.
N754 2ch. Type **341** 30 10
N755 5ch. Sika deer 50 10
N756 10ch. Indian muntjac (erect) 90 10
N757 10ch. Reindeer (grazing) . . 90 10
N758 70ch. Fallow deer . . . . 2·25 25

1966. Wild Fruit. Multicoloured.
N759 2ch. Type **342** 50 10
N760 5ch. Wild pears 70 10
N761 10ch. Wild raspberries . . . 90 10
N762 10ch. Schizandra 90 10
N763 10ch. Wild plums 90 10
N764 40ch. Jujube . . . . 2·25 15

343 Onpo Rest Home

1966. Korean Rest Homes. With gum.
N765 **343** 2ch. violet 25 10
N766 – 5ch. turquoise 35 10
N767 – 10ch. green 50 10
N768 – 40ch. black 80 20
REST HOMES: 5ch. Mt. Myohyang; 10ch. Songdowon; 40ch. Hongwon

344 Soldier

1967. 19th Anniv of Army Day. Without gum.
N769 **344** 10ch. green, yellow & red 25 10

345 Sow

1967. Domestic Animals. Multicoloured. Without gum. 40ch. also with gum.
N770 5ch. Type **345** 40 10
N771 10ch. Goat 50 10
N772 40ch. Ox . . . . 1·00 25

346 Battle Scene

1967. 30th Anniv of Battle of Pochonbo. With gum.
N773 **346** 10ch. orange, red & grn 50 10

347 Students

1967. Compulsory Technical Education for Nine Years.
N774 **347** 10ch. multicoloured . . 25 10

348 Table Tennis Player

1967. 29th Int Table Tennis Championships, Pyongyang. Designs showing players in action. 5ch. with or without gum.
N775 **348** 5ch. multicoloured . . . 40 10
N776 – 10ch. multicoloured . . 70 10
N777 – 40ch. multicoloured . . 1·10 15

349 Anti-aircraft Defences

1967. Paintings of Guerrilla War against the Japanese. With gum.
N778 **349** 10ch. blue 35 10
N779 – 10ch. purple . . . . . 3·00 25
N780 – 10ch. violet 35 10
PAINTINGS: No. N779, Blowing-up railway bridge; N780, People helping guerrillas in Wangyugou.

1967. War Heroes (2nd series). As T **292**. Designs showing portraits and combat scenes. With gum.
N781 10ch. slate 40 10
N782 10ch. violet 40 10
N783 10ch. blue 75 10
PORTRAITS: No. N781, Li Dae Hun and grenade-throwing; N782, Choe Jong Un and soldiers charging; N783, Kim Hwa Ryong and air dog-fighter aircraft.

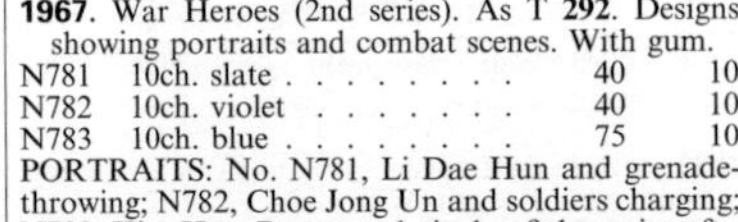

350 Workers

1967. Labour Day.
N784 **350** 10ch. multicoloured . . 25 10

351 Card Game

1967. Korean Children. Multicoloured.
N785 5ch. Type **351** . . . . . . 1·00 10
N786 10ch. Children modelling tractor 60 10
N787 40ch. Children playing with ball . . . . 1·10 20

352 Victory Monument

1967. Unveiling of Battle of Ponchonbo Monument.
N788 **352** 10ch. multicoloured . . 30 10

353 Attacking Tank

354 "Polygonatum japonicum"

1967. Monuments to War of 1950–53. 2ch. with or without gum.
N789 **353** 2ch. green and turquoise 20 10
N790 – 5ch. sepia and green . . 85 10
N791 – 10ch. brown and buff 30 10
N792 – 40ch. brown and blue 60 15
MONUMENTS: 5ch. Soldier-musicians; 10ch. Soldier; 40ch. Soldier with children.

1967. Medicinal Plants. Mult; background colour of 10ch. values given to aid identification. Nos. 793/5 and 797 with or without gum.
N793 2ch. Type **354** . . . . . . 1·00 10
N794 5ch. "Hibiscus manihot" 1·00 10
N795 10ch. "Scutellaria baicalensis" (turquoise) 1·25 10
N796 10ch. "Pulsatilla koreana" (blue) . . . . 1·25 10
N797 10ch. "Rehmannian glutinosa" (yellow) . . . 1·25 10
N798 40ch. "Tanacetum boreale" 3·25 35

355 Servicemen

1967. People's Army. Multicoloured. 5ch. with or without gum.
N799 5ch. Type **355** 20 10
N800 10ch. Soldier and farmer 25 10
N801 10ch. Officer decorating soldier 25 10

356 Freighter "Chollima"

1967. With gum.
N802 **356** 10ch. green . . . . . . 1·10 10

357 "Reclamation of Tideland"

1967. "Heroic Struggle of the Chollima Riders". Paintings. Without gum (5ch.) or with gum (others).
N803 – 5ch. brown 40 10
N804 **357** 10ch. grey 55 10
N805 – 10ch. green 85 10
DESIGNS—VERT: 5ch. "Drilling Rock Precipice"; 10ch. (N805), "Felling Trees".

358 "Erimaculus isenbeckii"

1967. Crabs. Multicoloured.
N806 2ch. Type **358** 90 15
N807 5ch. "Neptunus trituberculatus" . . . . 1·10 15
N808 10ch. "Paralithodes camtschatica" . . . . . 1·60 15
N809 40ch. "Chionoecetes opilio" 2·50 40

359 Electric Train and Hand switching Points

1967. Propaganda for Reunification of Korea.
N810 **359** 10ch. multicoloured . . 2·25 40

360 Tongrim Waterfall

361 Chollima Flying Horse and Banners

1967. Korean Waterfalls. 2ch. with or without gum. Multicoloured.
N811 2ch. Type **360** . . . . . . 2·75 15
N812 10ch. Sanju waterfall, Mt. Myohyang . . . . 3·25 20
N813 40ch. Sambang waterfall, Mt. Chonak . . . . . . 5·00 45

1967. "The Revolutionary Surge Upwards". Various designs incorporating the Chollima Flying Horse.
N814 – 5ch. blue . . . . 1·40 20
N815 – 10ch. red 25 10
N816 – 10ch. green 25 10
N817 – 10ch. lilac 25 10
N817 **361** 10ch. red 20 10
DESIGNS—HORIZ: 5ch. Ship, electric train and lorry (Transport); N815, Bulldozers (Building construction); N816, Tractors (Rural development); N817, Heavy presses (Machine-building industry).

362 Lenin

1967. 50th Anniv of Russian October Revolution.
N819 **362** 10ch. brown, yell & red 25 10

363 Voters and Banner

1967. Korean Elections. Multicoloured.
N820 10ch. Type **363** 35 10
N821 10ch. Woman casting vote (vert) 35 10

364 Cinereous Black Vulture

1967. Birds of Prey. Multicoloured. With gum.
N822 2ch. Type **364** . . . . . . 3·00 45
N823 10ch. Booted eagle (horiz) 5·75 75
N824 40ch. White-bellied sea eagle . . . . 7·25 1·10

365 Chongjin

1967. North Korean Cities. With gum.
N825 **365** 5ch. green 70 10
N826 – 10ch. lilac 70 10
N827 – 10ch. violet 70 10
DESIGNS: No. N826, Humhung; N827, Sinuiju.

366 Soldier brandishing Red Book

1967. "Let us carry out the Decisions of the Workers' Party Conference!". Multicoloured.
N828 10ch. Type **366** 25 10
N829 10ch. Militiaman holding bayonet 25 10
N830 10ch. Foundryman and bayonet 25 10

367 Whaler firing Harpoon

1967. With gum.
N831 **367** 10ch. blue . . . . . . 2·00 25

368 Airman, Soldier and Sailor

1968. 20th Anniv of People's Army. Mult. With gum.
N832 10ch. Type **368** 30 10
N833 10ch. Soldier below attack in snow 30 10
N834 10ch. Soldier below massed ranks 30 10
N835 10ch. Soldier holding flag 30 10
N836 10ch. Soldier holding book 30 10
N837 10ch. Soldiers and armed workers with flag 30 10
N838 10ch. Furnaceman and soldier 30 10
N839 10ch. Soldier saluting . . . 30 10
N840 10ch. Charging soldiers . . 30 10
N841 10ch. Soldier, sailor and airman below flag . . . 30 10

1968. War Heroes (3rd series). As T **292**. With gum.
N842 10ch. violet 25 10
N843 10ch. purple 25 10
PORTRAITS: No. N842, Han Gye Ryol firing Bren gun; N843, Li Su Bok charging up hill.

369 Dredger "September 2"

370 Ten-storey Flats, East Pyongyang

371 Palace of Students and Children, Kaesong

1968. With gum.
N844 **369** 5ch. green 75 10
N845 **370** 10ch. blue 30 10
N846 **371** 10ch. blue 30 10

372 Marshal Kim Il Sung

1968. Marshal Kim Il Sung's 56th Birthday. With gum.
N847 **372** 40ch. multicoloured . . 65 40

373 Kim Il Sung with Mother

1968. Childhood of Kim Il Sung. Multicoloured.
N848 10ch. Type **373** 35 10
N849 10ch. Kim Il Sung with his father 35 10
N850 10ch. Setting out from home, aged 13 . . . . . 35 10
N851 10ch. Birthplace at Mangyongdae 35 10
N852 10ch. Mangyong Hill . . . 35 10

374 Matsu-take Mushroom

1968. Mushrooms. With gum.
N853 **374** 5ch. brown and green 4·25 50
N854 – 10ch. ochre, brn & grn 6·00 75
N855 – 10ch. brown and green 6·00 75
DESIGNS: No. N854, Black mushroom; N855, Cultivated mushroom.

375 Leaping Horseman

1968. 20th Anniv of Korean People's Democratic Republic. Multicoloured. With gum.
N856 10ch. Type **375** . . . . . . 1·25 10
N857 10ch. Four servicemen . . 1·25 10
N858 10ch. Soldier with bayonet 1·25 10
N859 10ch. Advancing with banners . . . . 1·25 10
N860 10ch. Statue . . . . 1·25 10
N861 10ch. Korean flag . . . . 1·25 10
N862 10ch. Soldier and peasant with flag . . . . 1·25 10
N863 10ch. Machine-gunner with flag . . . . 1·25 10

376 Domestic Products

377 Proclaiming the Ten Points

1968. Development of Light Industries. Multicoloured. With gum.
N864 2ch. Type **376** 25 10
N865 5ch. Textiles . . . . 1·00 10
N866 10ch. Tinned produce . . . 40 10

1968. Kim Il Sung's Ten Point Political Programme. Multicoloured.
N867 2ch. Type **377** 15 10
N868 5ch. Soldier and artisan (horiz) 20 10

378 Livestock

1968. Development of Agriculture. Mult. With gum.
N869 5ch. Type **378** 25 10
N870 10ch. Fruit-growing 25 10
N871 10ch. Wheat-harvesting . . 25 10

379 Yesso Scallop

1968. Shellfish. Multicoloured. With gum.
N872 5ch. Type **379** . . . . . . 1·10 10
N873 5ch. Meretrix chione (venus clam) . . . . 1·10 10
N874 10ch. "Modiolus hanleyi" (mussel) . . . . 1·75 20

380 Kim Il Sung at Head of Columns

1968. Battle of Pochonbo Monument. Detail of Monument. Multicoloured.
N875 10ch. Type **380** 25 10
N876 10ch. Head of right-hand column 25 10
N877 10ch. Tail of right-hand column 25 10
N878 10ch. Head of left-hand column 25 10
N879 10ch. Tail of left-hand column 25 10
N880 10ch. Centre of right-hand column 25 10
N881 10ch. Centre of left-hand column 25 10
SIZES—HORIZ: Nos. N876/8, 43 × 28 mm. 880/1, 56 × 28 mm.
The centrepiece of the Monument is flanked by two columns of soldiers, headed by Kim Il Sung.

381 Museum of the Revolution, Pochonbo

382 Grand Theatre, Pyongyang

1968.
N883 **381** 2ch. green 20 10
N884 **382** 10ch. brown 65 10

383 Irrigation

1969. Rural Development. Multicoloured.
N885 3ch. Type **383** 20 10
N886 5ch. Agricultural mechanization 20 10
N887 10ch. Electrification 40 10
N888 40ch. Applying fertilizers and spraying trees . . . 60 10

384 Grey Rabbits

1969. Rabbits. Mult. With or without gum.
N889 2ch. Type **384** 45 10
N890 10ch. Black rabbits 45 10
N891 10ch. Brown rabbits . . . 45 10
N892 10ch. White rabbits 45 10
N893 40ch. Doe and young . . . 1·40 15

385 "Age and Youth"

1969. Public Health Service.
N894 **385** 2ch. brown and blue . . 35 10
N895 – 10ch. blue and red . . . 75 10
N896 – 40ch. green and yellow 1·50 20
DESIGNS: 10ch. Nurse with syringe; 40ch. Auscultation by woman doctor.

386 Sowing Rice Seed

1969. Agricultural Mechanization.
N897 **386** 10ch. green 75 10
N898 – 10ch. orange 75 10
N899 – 10ch. black 75 10
N900 – 10ch. brown 75 10
DESIGNS: No. N898, Rice harvester; N899, Weed-spraying machine; N900, Threshing machine.

387 Ponghwa

1969. Revolutionary Historical Sites. Multicoloured.
N901 10ch. Type **387** 25 10
N902 10ch. Mangyongdae, birthplace of Kim Il Sung 25 10

388 Kim crosses into Manchuria, 1926, aged 13

1969. Kim Il Sung in Manchuria. Multicoloured. No. N907 with gum.
N903 10ch. Type **388** 40 10
N904 10ch. Leading strike of Yuwen Middle School boys, 1927 . . . . 40 10
N905 10ch. Leading anti-Japanese demonstration in Kirin, 1928 . . . . 40 10
N906 10ch. Presiding at meeting of Young Communist League, 1930 . . . . . 40 10
N907 10ch. Meeting of young revolutionaries 40 10

389 Birthplace at Chilgol

1969. Commemoration of Mrs. Kang Ban Sok, mother of Kim Il Sung. Multicoloured.
N908 10ch. Type **389** 30 10
N909 10ch. With members of Women's Association . . 30 10
N910 10ch. Resisting Japanese police . . . . 2·50 40

390 Pegaebong Bivouac

1969. Bivouac Sites in the Guerrilla War against the Japanese. Multicoloured.
N911 5ch. Type **390** 20 10
N912 10ch. Mupo site (horiz) . . . 30 10
N913 10ch. Chongbong site . . . 30 10
N914 40ch. Konchang site (horiz) 1·00 20

391 Chollima Statue

392 Museum of the Revolution, Pyongyang

1969.
N915 **391** 10ch. blue 25 10
N916 **392** 10ch. green 25 10

393 Mangyong Chickens

395 Statue of Marshal Kim Il Sung

394 Marshal Kim Il Sung and Children

1969. Korean Poultry.
N917 **393** 10ch. blue 45 10
N918 – 10ch. violet . . . . . . 1·25 15
DESIGN: No. N918, Kwangpo ducks.

1969. Kim Il Sung's Educational System. Mult.
N919 2ch. Type **394** 25 10
N920 10ch. Worker with books 25 10
N921 40ch. Students with books 50 20

1969. Memorials on Pochonbo Battlefield. Inscr "1937.6.4". Multicoloured.
N922 5ch. Machine-gun post . . 25 10
N923 10ch. Type **395** 25 10
N924 10ch. "Aspen-tree" monument 25 10
N925 10ch. Glade Konjang Hill 25 10

396 Teaching at Myongsin School

1969. Commemoration of Kim Hyong Jik, father of Kim Il Sung. Multicoloured.
N926 10ch. Type **396** 30 10
N927 10ch. Secret meeting with Korean National Association members . . 30 10

397 Relay Runner

1969. 20th Anniv of Sports Day.
N928 **397** 10ch. multicoloured . . 35 10

398 President Nixon attacked by Pens

1969. Anti-U.S. Imperialism Journalists' Conference, Pyongyang.
N929 **398** 10ch. multicoloured . . 35 10

399 Fighters and Battle

1969. Implementation of Ten-Point Programme of Kim Il Sung. Multicoloured.
N930 5ch. Type **399** (Reunification of Korea) 30 10
N931 10ch. Workers upholding slogan (vert) 30 10

400 Bayonet Attack over U.S. Flag

1969. Anti-American Campaign.
N932 **400** 10ch. multicoloured . . 35 10

401 Armed Workers

1969. Struggle for the Reunification of Korea. Multicoloured.
N933 10ch. Workers stabbing U.S. soldier (vert) . . . 20 10
N934 10ch. Kim Il Sung and crowd with flags (vert) 20 10
N935 50ch. Type **401** 50 20

402 Buri

1969. Korean Fishes. Multicoloured.
N936 5ch. Type **402** . . . . . . 1·00 10
N937 10ch. Eastern dace . . . . 1·75 10
N938 40ch. Flat-headed grey mullet . . . . 3·00 40

403 Freighter "Taesungsan"

1969.
N939 **403** 10ch. purple 75 10

405 Dahwangwai (1935)

407 Vietnamese Soldier and Furnaceman

406 Lake Chon

1970. Guerrilla Conference Places.
N940 **405** 2ch. blue and green . . 25 10
N941 – 5ch. brown and green 25 10
N942 – 10ch. lt green & green 25 10
DESIGNS: 5ch. Yaoyinggou (barn) (1935); 10ch. Xiaohaerbaling (tent) (1940).

1970. Mt. Paekdu, Home of Revolution (1st issue). Inscr "1970".
N943 **406** 10ch. black, brown & grn 60 10
N944 – 10ch. black, green & yell 60 10
N945 – 10ch. purple, blue & yell 60 10
N946 – 10ch. black, blue and pink 60 10
DESIGNS: No. N944, Piryu Peak; N945, Pyongsa (Soldier) Peak; N946, Changgun (General) Peak.
See also Nos. N979/81.

1970. Help for the Vietnamese People.
N947 **407** 10ch. green, brown & red 20 10

408 Receiving his Father's Revolvers from his Mother

1970. Revolutionary Career of Kim Il Sung. Multicoloured.
N948 10ch. Type **408** 65 20
N949 10ch. Receiving smuggled weapons from his mother 65 20

N950 10ch. Talking to farm workers 65 20
N951 10ch. At Kalun meeting, 1930 . . . . 65 20

409 Lenin

410 March of Koreans

1970. Birth Centenary of Lenin.
N952 **409** 10ch. brown & cinnamon 30 10
N953 – 10ch. brown and green 30 10
DESIGN: No. N953, Lenin making a speech.

1970. 15th Anniv of Association of Koreans in Japan.
N954 **410** 10ch. red 20 10
N955 10ch. purple 20 10

411 Uniformed Factory Worker

413 "Electricity Flows"

412 Students and Newspapers

1970. Workers' Militia.
N956 **411** 10ch. green, brn & mve 20 10
N957 – 10ch. green, brown & bl 20 10
DESIGN—HORIZ: No. N957, Militiaman saluting.

1970. Peasant Education. Multicoloured.
N958 2ch. Type **412** 35 10
N959 5ch. Peasant with book . . 20 10
N960 10ch. Students in class . . 20 10

1970. Commemoration of Army Electrical Engineers.
N961 **413** 10ch. brown 40 10

414 Soldier with Rifle

1970. Campaign Month for Withdrawal of U.S. Troops from South Korea.
N962 **414** 5ch. violet 15 10
N963 – 10ch. purple 30 10
DESIGN: 10ch. Soldier and partisan.

415 Rebel wielding Weapons

1970. Struggle in South Korea against U.S. Imperialism.
N964 **415** 10ch. violet 20 10

416 Labourer ("Fertilizers")

1970. Encouragement of Increased Productivity.
N965 **416** 10ch. green, pink & brn 40 10
N966 – 10ch. green, red & brn 70 10
N967 – 10ch. blue, green & brn 40 10
N968 – 10ch. bistre, brn & grn 40 10
N969 – 10ch. violet, green & brn 50 10
DESIGNS: No. N966, Furnaceman ("Steel"); N967, Operative ("Machines"); N968, Labourer ("Building Construction"); N969, Miner ("Mining").

417 Railway Guard

1970. "Speed the Transport System".
N970 **417** 10ch. blue, orange & grn . . . . 1·25 15

418 Agriculture

421 Emblem of League

419 Chollima Statue and Workers' Party Banner

1970. Executive Decisions of the Workers' Party Congress. Designs embodying book.
N971 **418** 5ch. red 20 10
N972 – 10ch. green . . . . . . 1·10 15
N973 – 40ch. green . . . . . . 1·10 15
DESIGNS: 10ch. Industry; 40ch. The Armed Forces.

1970. 25th Anniv of Korean Workers' Party.
N974 **419** 10ch. red, brown & buff 20 10

1971. 25th Anniv of League of Socialist Working Youth.
N976 **421** 10ch. red, brown & blue 20 10

422 Log Cabin, Nanhutou

1971. 35th Anniv of Nanhutou Guerrilla Conference.
N977 **422** 10ch. multicoloured . . 20 10

423 Tractor Driver

1971. 25th Anniv of Land Reform Law.
N978 **423** 2ch. red, green and black 20 10

1971. Mt. Paekdu, Home of Revolution (2nd issue). As T **406** but inscr "1971".
N979 2ch. black, olive and green 35 10
N980 5ch. pink, black and slate 2·25 15
N981 10ch. black, red and grey 60 10
DESIGNS—HORIZ: 2ch. General view; 10ch. Western peak. VERT: 5ch. Waterfall.

424 Popyong Museum

1971. Museum of the Revolution.
N982 **424** 10ch. brown and yellow 20 10
N983 – 10ch. blue and orange 20 10
N984 – 10ch. green and orange 20 10
DESIGNS: No. N983, Mangyongdae Museum; N984, Chunggang Museum.

425 Miner

1971. Six Year Plan for Coal Industry.
N985 **425** 10ch. multicoloured . . 40 10

426 Kim Il Sung

1971. Founding of Anti-Japanese Guerrilla Army. Multicoloured.
N986 10ch. Type **426** 35 10
N987 10ch. Kim Il Sung founding Anti-Japanese Guerrilla Army (horiz) 35 10
N988 10ch. Kim Il Sung addressing the people (horiz) 35 10
N989 10ch. Kim Il Sung and members of Children's Corps (horiz) 35 10

428 Hands holding Hammer and Rifle

1971. 85th Anniv of Labour Day.
N990 **428** 1wn. red, brown and buff . . . . 2·25 40

429 Soldiers and Map

430 Monument

1971. 35th Anniv of Association for Restoration of Fatherland.
N991 **429** 10ch. red, buff and black 35 10

1971. Battlefields in Musan Area, May 1939. Multicoloured.
N992 5ch. Type **430** 15 10
N993 10ch. Machine guns in perspex cases (horiz) . . 20 10
N994 40ch. Huts among birch trees (horiz) 55 15

431 Koreans Marching

432 Flame Emblem

1971. Solidarity of Koreans in Japan.
N995 **431** 10ch. brown 20 10

1971. 25th Anniv of Korean Childrens' Union.
N996 **432** 10ch. red, yellow and blue 20 10

433 Marchers and Banners

434 Foundryman

1971. 6th Congress of League of Socialist Working Youth.
N997 **433** 5ch. red, buff and black 10 10
N998 – 10ch. red, green & black 20 10
DESIGN: 10c. Marchers and banner under globe.

1971. 25th Anniv of Labour Law.
N999 **434** 5ch. black, purple & buff 20 10

435 Young Women

1971. 25th Anniv of Sex Equality Law.
N1000 **435** 5ch. multicoloured . . 20 10

436 Schoolchildren

1971. 15th Anniv of Compulsory Primary Education.
N1001 **436** 10ch. multicoloured . . 50 10

437 Choe Yong Do and Combat Scene

1971. Heroes of the Revolutionary Struggle in South Korea.
N1002 **437** 5ch. black and green 25 10
N1003 – 10ch. red and brown 25 10
N1004 – 10ch. black and red . . 25 10
DESIGNS: No. N1003, Revolutionary with book; N1004, Kim Jong Tae and scene of triumph.

438 Two Foundrymen

1971. 25th Anniv of Nationalization of Industry Law.
N1005 **438** 5ch. black, green & brn . . . . 1·50 10

439 Struggle in Korea

1971. The Anti-Imperialist and Anti-U.S. Imperialist Struggles.
N1006 **439** 10ch. red, black and brown 25 10
N1007 – 10ch. brown, black and blue 35 10
N1008 – 10ch. red, black and pink 50 10
N1009 – 10ch. black, olive and green 25 10
N1010 – 10ch. orange, black and red 50 10
N1011 – 40ch. green, black and pink 50 15
DESIGNS: No. N1007, Struggle in Vietnam; N1008, Soldier with rifle and airplane marked "EC"; N1009, Struggle in Africa; N1010, Cuban soldier and Central America; N1011, Bayoneting U.S. soldier.

440 Kim Il Sung University

1971. 25th Anniv of Kim Il Sung University.
N1012 **440** 10ch. grey, red & yellow 20 10

441 Iron-ore Ladle (Mining)

1971. Tasks of Six Year Plan. Multicoloured.
N1013 10ch. Type **441** . . . . . 2·75 15
N1014 10ch. Workers and text . . 30 10
N1015 10ch. Electric train and track (Transport) . . . 2·75 15
N1016 10ch. Hand and wrench (Industry) 30 10
N1017 10ch. Mechanical scoop (Construction) . . . . 2·75 15
N1018 10ch. Manufactured goods (Trade) 30 10
N1019 10ch. Crate on hoists (Exports) 25 10
N1020 10ch. Lathe (Heavy Industries) . . . . . . 2·75 15
N1021 10ch. Freighter (Shipping) 60 10
N1022 10ch. Household equipment (Light Industries) 25 10
N1023 10ch. Corncob and wheat (Agriculture) 40 10

442 Technicians

1971. Cultural Revolution. Multicoloured.
N1024 2ch. Type **442** 20 10
N1025 5ch. Mechanic 25 10
N1026 10ch. Schoolchildren . . . 30 10
N1027 10ch. Chemist 50 10
N1028 10ch. Composer at piano 85 15

443 Workers with Red Books

1971. Ideological Revolution. Multicoloured.
N1029 10ch. Type **443** 20 10
N1030 10ch. Workers reading book 20 10
N1031 10ch. Workers' lecture . . 20 10
N1032 10ch. Worker and pneumatic drill 20 10

444 Korean Family

1971. Improvement in Living Standards.
N1033 **444** 10ch. multicoloured . . 15 10

445 Furnaceman

1971. Implementation of Decisions of Fifth Workers' Party Conference.
N1034 **445** 10ch. multicoloured . . 1·00 10

446

447 6000-ton Press

1971. Solidarity with South Korean Revolutionaries.
N1036 **446** 10ch. brown, bl & blk 30 10
N1037 – 10ch. brn, flesh & red 30 10
N1038 – 10ch. multicoloured . . 30 10
N1039 – 10ch. multicoloured . . 30 10
DESIGNS—VERT: No. N1037, U.S. soldier attacked by poster boards; N1038, Hands holding rifles aloft. HORIZ: No. N1039, Men advancing with rifles.

1971.
N1040 **447** 2ch. brown 70 10
N1041 – 5ch. blue 90 15
N1042 – 10ch. green . . . . . 1·10 10
N1043 – 10ch. green . . . . . 1·10 10
DESIGNS: No. N1041, Refrigerated freighter "Ponghwasan"; N1042, 300 h.p. bulldozer; N1043, "Sungrisan" lorry.

448 Title-page and Militants

1971. 35th Anniv of "Samil Wolgan" Magazine.
N1044 **448** 10ch. red, green & black 45 10

452 Poultry Chicks

1972. Poultry Breeding.
N1051 **452** 5ch. yellow, black and brown 25 10
N1052 – 10ch. orange, bistre and brown 35 10
N1053 – 40ch. blue, orange and deep blue 55 15
DESIGNS: 10ch. Chickens and battery egg house; 40ch. Eggs and fowls suspended from hooks.

453 Scene from "Village Shrine"

1972. Films of Guerrilla War.
N1054 **453** 10ch. grey and green 60 10
N1055 – 10ch. blue, pur & orge 60 10
N1056 – 10ch. purple, blue & yell 60 10
DESIGNS: No. N1055, Patriot with pistol ("A Sea of Blood"); N1056, Guerrilla using bayonet ("The Lot of a Self-Defence Corps Member").

454 Kim Il Sung acknowledging Greetings

1972. Kim Il Sung's 60th Birthday. Scenes in the life of Kim Il Sung, dated "1912–1972". Mult.
N1057 5ch. Type **454** 20 10
N1058 5ch. In campaign H.Q. . . 20 10
N1059 5ch. Military conference (horiz) 20 10
N1060 10ch. In wheatfield (horiz) 30 10
N1061 10ch. Directing construction (horiz) . . 2·00 40
N1062 10ch. Talking to foundry workers (horiz) 20 10
N1063 10ch. Aboard whaler (horiz) 55 10
N1064 10ch. Visiting a hospital (horiz) 75 10
N1065 10ch. Viewing orchard (horiz) 20 10
N1066 10ch. With survey party on Haeju–Hasong railway line (horiz) . . . 2·00 40
N1067 10ch. Meeting female workers at silk factory (horiz) . . . . 1·00 15
N1068 10ch. Village conference (horiz) 20 10
N1069 10ch. Touring chicken factory (horiz) 35 10
N1070 40ch. Relaxing with children 45 20
N1071 1wn. Giant portrait and marchers 70 40

455 Bugler sounding "Charge"

1972. 40th Anniv of Guerrilla Army.
N1073 **455** 10ch. multicoloured . . 45 10

456 Pavilion of Ryongpo

1972. Historic Sites of the 1950–53 War. Mult.
N1074 2ch. Type **456** 15 10
N1075 5ch. Houses at Onjong . . 15 10
N1076 10ch. Headquarters, Kosanjin 15 10
N1077 40ch. Victory Museum, Chonsung-dong 30 10

457 Volleyball

1972. Olympic Games, Munich. Multicoloured.
N1078 2ch. Type **457** 35 10
N1079 5ch. Boxing (horiz) . . . 50 10
N1080 10ch. Judo 50 10
N1081 10ch. Wrestling (horiz) . . 50 10
N1082 40ch. Rifle-shooting . . . 1·10 20

458 Chollima Street, Pyongyang

1971. Chollima Street, Pyongyang.
N1083 – 5ch. orange and black 1·60 15
N1084 **458** 10ch. yellow and black 60 15
N1085 – 10ch. green and black 60 15
DESIGNS: No. N1083, Bridge and skyscraper blocks; N1085, Another view looking up street.

459 Dredger

1972. Development of Natural Resources. Multicoloured.
N1086 5ch. Type **459** 35 10
N1087 10ch. Forestry 50 10
N1088 40ch. Reclaiming land from the sea 60 15

460 Ferrous Industry

1972. Tasks of the Six-Year Plan. The Metallurgical Industry. Inscr "1971–1976". Multicoloured.
N1089 10ch. Type **460** . . . . . 1·40 10
N1090 10ch. Non-ferrous Industry 40 10

461 Iron Ore Industry

1972. Tasks of the Six-Year Plan. The Mining Industry. Inscr "1971–1976". Multicoloured.
N1091 10ch. Type **461** 40 10
N1092 10ch. Coal mining industry . . . . 1·50 15

462 Electronic and Automation Industry

1972. Tasks of the Six-Year Plan. The Engineering Industry. Inscr "1971–1976". Multicoloured.
N1093 10ch. Type **462** 60 10
N1094 10ch. Single-purpose machines 40 10
N1095 10ch. Machine tools . . . 40 10

463 Clearing Virgin Soil

1972. Tasks of the Six-Year Plan. Rural Economy. Multicoloured.
N1096 10ch. Type **463** 45 10
N1097 10ch. Irrigation 45 10
N1098 10ch. Harvesting 45 10

464 Automation

1972. Tasks of the Six-Year Plan. Inscr "1971–1976". Multicoloured.
N1099 10ch. Type **464** . . . . . 1·60 10
N1100 10ch. Agricultural mechanization 50 10
N1101 10ch. Lightening of household chores . . . 50 10

465 Chemical Fibres and Materials

1972. Tasks of the Six-Year Plan. The Chemical Industry. Inscr "1971–1976". Multicoloured.
N1102 10ch. Type **465** 60 10
N1103 10ch. Fertilizers, insecticides and weed killers 60 10

466 Textiles

1972. Tasks of the Six-Year Plan. Consumer Goods. Inscr "1971–1976". Multicoloured.
N1104 10ch. Type **466** 65 10
N1105 10ch. Kitchen ware and overalls 45 10
N1106 10ch. Household goods . . 45 10

467 Fish, Fruit and Vegetables

1972. Tasks of the Six-Year Plan. The Food Industry. Multicoloured.
N1107 10ch. Type **467** 90 10
N1108 10ch. Tinned foods . . . 65 10
N1109 10ch. Food packaging . . 65 10

468 Electrifying Railway Lines

1972. Tasks of the Six-Year Plan. Transport. Inscr "1971–1976". Multicoloured.

N1110 10ch. Type **468** 45 10
N1111 10ch. Laying new railway track 45 10
N1112 10ch. Freighters 55 10

469 Soldier with Shell

1972. North Korean Armed Forces. Multicoloured.

N1113 10ch. Type **469** 35 10
N1114 10ch. Marine 35 10
N1115 10ch. Air Force pilot . . . 35 10

470 "Revolution of 19 April 1960"

1972. The Struggle for Reunification of Korea. Multicoloured.

N1116 10ch. Type **470** 15 10
N1117 10ch. Marchers with banner 15 10
N1118 10ch. Insurgents with red banner 15 10
N1119 10ch. Attacking U.S. and South Korean soldiers 15 10
N1120 10ch. Workers with posters 15 10
N1121 10ch. Workers acclaiming revolution . . . . . . 3·50 40
N1122 10ch. Workers and manifesto 15 10

471 Single-spindle Automatic Lathe

1972. Machine Tools.

N1123 **471** 5ch. green and purple 25 10
N1124 – 10ch. blue and green 35 10
N1125 – 40ch. green and brown 80 15

DESIGNS—HORIZ: 10ch. "Kusong-3" lathe; VERT: 40ch. 2,000 ton crank press.

472 Casting Vote

1972. National Elections. Multicoloured.

N1126 10ch. Type **472** 25 10
N1127 10ch. Election campaigner 25 10

475 Soldier

1973. 25th Anniv of Founding of Korean People's Army. Multicoloured.

N1130 5ch. Type **475** 20 10
N1131 10ch. Sailor 30 10
N1132 40ch. Airman 70 25

476 Wrestling Site

1973. Scenes of Kim Il Sung's Childhood, Mangyongdae. Multicoloured.

N1133 2ch. Type **476** 15 10
N1134 5ch. Warship rock 15 10
N1135 10ch. Swinging site (vert) 20 10
N1136 10ch. Sliding rock 20 10
N1137 40ch. Fishing site 60 15

477 Monument to Socialist Revolution and Construction, Mansu Hill

1973. Museum of the Korean Revolution.

N1138 **477** 10ch. multicoloured . . 25 10
N1139 – 10ch. multicoloured . . 25 10
N1140 – 40ch. multicoloured . . 50 15
N1141 – 3wn. green and yellow 2·50 60

DESIGNS—As Type **477**: 10ch. (N1139) Similar monument but men in military clothes; 40ch. Statue of Kim Il Sung. HORIZ—60 × 29 mm: 3wn. Museum building.

478 Karajibong Camp

1973. Secret Camps by Tuman-Gang in Guerrilla War, 1932. Multicoloured.

N1142 10ch. Type **478** 15 10
N1143 10ch. Soksaegol Camp . . 15 10

479

1973. Menace of Japanese Influence in South Korea.

N1144 **479** 10ch. multicoloured . . 20 10

480 Wrecked U.S. Tanks

1973. Five-point Programme for Reunification of Korea. Multicoloured.

N1145 2ch. Type **480** 40 10
N1146 5ch. Electric train and crane lifting tractor . . 2·50 20
N1147 10ch. Leaflets falling on crowd 20 10
N1148 10ch. Hand holding leaflet and map of Korea . . . 40 10
N1149 40ch. Banner and globe 60 20

481 Lorries **482** Volleyball

1973. Lorries and Tractors. Multicoloured.

N1150 10ch. Type **481** 50 10
N1151 10ch. Tractors and earth-moving machine 50 10

1973. Socialist Countries' Junior Women's Volleyball Games, Pyongyang.

N1152 **482** 10ch. multicoloured . . 50 10

483 Battlefield

1973. 20th Anniv of Victory in Korean War.

N1153 **483** 10ch. green, pur & blk 20 10
N1154 – 10ch. brown, bl & blk 20 10

DESIGN: 10ch. Urban fighting.

484 "The Snow Falls"

1973. Mansudae Art Troupe. Dances. Multicoloured.

N1155 10ch. Type **484** 60 10
N1156 25ch. "A Bumper Harvest of Apples" . . . . . . 1·50 25
N1157 40ch. "Azalea of the Fatherland" . . . . . 1·75 30

485 Schoolchildren

1973. Ten Years Compulsory Secondary Education.

N1158 **485** 10ch. multicoloured . . 25 10

486 "Fervour in the Revolution"

1973. The Works of Kim Il Sung (1st series).

N1159 **486** 10ch. brown, red and yellow 15 10
N1160 – 10ch. brown, green and yellow 15 10
N1161 – 10ch. lake, brown and yellow 15 10

DESIGNS: No. N1160, Selected works; N1161, "Strengthen the Socialist System".

See also Nos. N1217/18.

487 Celebrating Republic

1973. 25th Anniv of People's Republic. Multicoloured.

N1162 5ch. Type **487** 10 10
N1163 10ch. Fighting in Korean War 10 10
N1164 40ch. Peace and reconstruction . . . . . 1·60 40

488 Pobwang Peak

1973. Mt. Myohyang. Multicoloured.

N1165 2ch. Type **488** 25 10
N1166 5ch. Inhodae Pavilion . . 35 10
N1167 10ch. Taeha Falls (vert) 1·75 30
N1168 40ch. Rongyon Falls (vert) 2·50 30

489 Party Memorial Building

1973. Party Memorial Building.

N1169 **489** 1wn. brn, grey & buff 1·25 30

490 Football and Handball

1973. National People's Sports Meeting. Mult.

N1170 2ch. Type **490** 60 10
N1171 5ch. High jumper and woman sprinter 40 10
N1172 10ch. Skaters and skiers 50 10
N1173 10ch. Wrestling and swinging 40 10
N1174 40ch. Parachutist and motor cyclists . . . . . 3·00 25

491 Weightlifting **492** Chongryu Cliff

1973. Junior Weightlifting Championships of Socialist Countries.

N1175 **491** 10ch. blue, brn & grn 50 10

1973. Scenery of Moran Hill, Pyongyang. Multicoloured.

N1176 2ch. Type **492** 70 15
N1177 5ch. Moran Waterfall . . 2·75 40
N1178 10ch. Pubyok Pavilion . . 75 10
N1179 40ch. Ulmil Pavilion . . . 90 15

493 Rainbow Bridge **494** Magnolia Flower

1973. Diamond Mountains Scenery (4th issue). Multicoloured.

N1180 2ch. Type **493** . . . . . . 1·50 15
N1181 5ch. Suspension footbridge, Okryudong (horiz) . . . . 1·50 15
N1182 10ch. Chonnyo Peak . . 75 10
N1183 10ch. Chilchung Rock and Sonji Peak (horiz) . . . 75 10
N1184 40ch. Sujong and Pari Peaks (horiz) 85 15

1973.

N1185 **494** 10ch. multicoloured . . 60 10

495 S. Korean Revolutionaries

1973. South Korean Revolution. Multicoloured
N1186 10ch. Type **495** 30 10
N1187 10ch. Marching revolutionaries 30 10

496 Cock sees Butterflies

1973. Scenes from "Cock Chasing Butterflies". Fairy Tale. Multicoloured.
N1188 2ch. Type **496** . . . . . . 1·50 10
N1189 5ch. Butterflies discuss how to repel cock . . . 1·50 10
N1190 10ch. Cock chasing butterflies with basket 2·00 15
N1191 10ch. Cock chasing butterfly up cliff . . . . 2·00 20
N1192 40ch. Cock chasing butterflies over cliff . . 2·25 25
N1193 90ch. Cock falls into sea and butterflies escape 2·75 30

497 Yonpung

1973. Historical Sites of War and Revolution (40ch.). Multicoloured.
N1196 2ch. Type **497** 10 10
N1197 5ch. Hyangha 10 10
N1198 10ch. Changgol 15 10
N1199 40ch. Paeksong 55 10

498 Science Library, Kim Il Sung University

1973. New Buildings in Pyongyang.
N1200 **498** 2ch. violet 50 10
N1201 – 5ch. green 15 10
N1202 – 10ch. brown 25 10
N1203 – 40ch. brown and buff 55 15
N1204 – 90ch. buff 95 30
DESIGNS—HORIZ: 10ch. Victory Museum; 40ch. People's Palace of Culture; 90ch. Indoor stadium. VERT: 5ch. Building No. 2, Kim Il Sung University.

499 Red Book

1973. Socialist Constitution of North Korea. Multicoloured.
N1205 10ch. Type **499** 15 10
N1206 10ch. Marchers with red book and banners . . . 15 10
N1207 10ch. Marchers with red book and emblem . . . 15 10

500 Oriental Great Reed Warbler

1973. Korean Songbirds. Multicoloured.
N1208 5ch. Type **500** . . . . . . 2·40 40
N1209 10ch. Grey starling (facing right) . . . . 3·50 70
N1210 10ch. Daurian starling (facing left) . . . . . . 3·50 70

503 Chollima Statue

1974. The Works of Kim Il Sung (2nd series). Multicoloured.
N1217 10ch. Type **503** 65 10
N1218 10ch. Bayonets threatening U.S. soldier 15 10

504 Train in Station

1974. Opening of Pyongyang Metro. Multicoloured.
N1219 10ch. Type **504** 45 10
N1220 10ch. Escalators 45 10
N1221 10ch. Station hall 45 10

505 Capital Construction Front

1974. Five Fronts of Socialist Construction. Multicoloured.
N1222 10ch. Type **505** 15 10
N1223 10ch. Agricultural front 25 10
N1224 10ch. Transport front . . 1·25 15
N1225 10ch. Fisheries front . . . 90 15
N1226 10ch. Industrial front (vert) 25 10

506 Marchers with Banners

1974. 10th Anniv of Publication of "Theses on the Socialist Rural Question in Our Country". Multicoloured.
N1227 10ch. Type **506** 15 10
N1228 10ch. Book and rejoicing crowd 15 10
N1229 10ch. Tractor and banners 15 10
Nos. N1227/9 were issued together, se-tenant, forming a composite design.

507 Manure Spreader

1974. Farm Machinery.
N1230 **507** 2ch. green, black & red 60 10
N1231 – 5ch. red, black and blue 60 10
N1232 – 10ch. red, black and green 60 10
DESIGNS: 5ch. "Progress" tractor; 10ch. "Mount Taedoksan" tractor.

508 Archery (Grenoble)

1974. North Korean Victories at International Sports Meetings. Multicoloured.
N1233 2ch. Type **508** . . . . . . 1·00 15
N1234 5ch. Gymnastics (Varna) 25 10
N1235 10ch. Boxing (Bucharest) 40 10
N1236 20ch. Volleyball (Pyongyang) 25 10
N1237 30ch. Rifle shooting (Sofia) 60 10
N1238 40ch. Judo (Tbilisi) . . . 80 15
N1239 60ch. Model aircraft flying (Vienna) (horiz) . . . . 1·25 20
N1240 1wn. 50 Table tennis (Peking) (horiz) . . . . 2·25 30

509 Book and Rejoicing Crowd

1974. The First Country with No Taxes.
N1241 **509** 10ch. multicoloured . . 20 10

510 Drawing up Programme in Woods

1974. Kim Il Sung during the Anti-Japanese Struggle. Multicoloured.
N1242 10ch. Type **510** 25 10
N1243 10ch. Giving directions to Pak Dal 25 10
N1244 10ch. Presiding over Nanhutou Conference 25 10
N1245 10ch. Supervising creation of strongpoint 25 10

511 Sun Hui loses her Sight

1974. Scenes from "The Flower Girl" (revolutionary opera). Multicoloured.
N1246 2ch. Type **511** 65 10
N1247 5ch. Death of Ggot Bun's mother 65 10
N1248 10ch. Ggot Bun throws boiling water at landlord . . . . 1·40 10
N1249 40ch. Ggot Bun joins revolutionaries . . . . 1·75 15

512 Leopard Cat

1974. 15th Anniv of Pyongyang Zoo. Multicoloured.
N1251 2ch. Type **512** 60 10
N1252 5ch. Lynx 60 10
N1253 10ch. Red fox 60 10
N1254 10ch. Wild boar 60 10
N1255 20ch. Dhole 60 15
N1256 40ch. Brown bear 75 25
N1257 60ch. Leopard . . . . . 1·25 25
N1258 70ch. Tiger . . . . 1·75 30
N1259 90ch. Lion . . . . 2·00 35

513 "Rosa acucularis lindly"

1974. Roses. Multicoloured.
N1261 2ch. Type **513** 40 10
N1262 5ch. Yellow sweet briar . . 45 10
N1263 10ch. Pink aromatic rose 55 10
N1264 10ch. Aronia sweet briar (yellow centres) 55 10
N1265 40ch. Multi-petal sweet briar . . . . 1·40 10

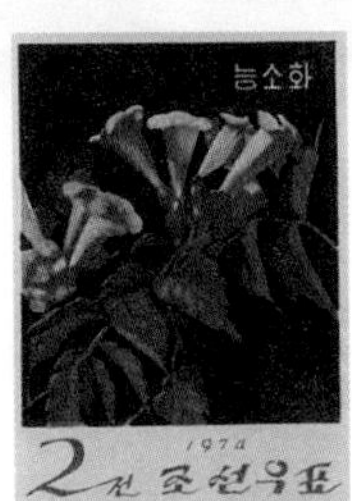

515 Weigela

1974. Flowering Plants of Mt. Paekdu. Mult.
N1267 2ch. Type **515** 50 10
N1268 5ch. Amaryllis 50 10
N1269 10ch. Red lily 50 10
N1270 20ch. Orange lily 65 10
N1271 40ch. Azalea 90 10
N1272 60ch. Yellow lily . . . . 1·50 10

516 Postwoman and Construction Site

1974. Centenary of U.P.U. and Admission of North Korea to Union. Multicoloured.
N1273 10ch. Type **516** . . . . . 1·50 15
N1274 25ch. Chollima monument 25 10
N1275 40ch. Globe and Antonov An-12 transport planes 1·00 15

517 Common Pond Frog

1974. Amphibians. Multicoloured.
N1276 2ch. Type **517** . . . . . . 1·00 10
N1277 5ch. Oriental fire-bellied toad . . . . 1·25 10
N1278 10ch. Bullfrog . . . . . . 1·50 15
N1279 40ch. Common toad . . . 2·00 25

518 "Women of Namgang Village"

1974. Korean Paintings. Multicoloured.
N1281 2ch. Type **518** 60 10
N1282 5ch. "An Old Man on the Rakdong River" (60 × 49 mm) 75 10
N1283 10ch. "Morning in the Nae-kumgang" (bridge) 1·50 10
N1284 20ch. "Mt. Kumgang" (60 × 49 mm) . . . . . 1·25 15

519 "Elektron 1" and "Elektron 2", 1964

1974. Cosmonauts Day. Multicoloured.

N1286	10ch. Type **519**	15	10
N1287	20ch. "Proton 1", 1965	25	10
N1288	30ch. "Venera 3", 1966	40	10
N1289	40ch. "Venera 5" and "Venera 6", 1969	50	10

521 Antonov An-2 Biplane

1974. Civil Aviation. Multicoloured

N1292	2ch. Type **521**	65	10
N1293	5ch. Lisunov Li-2	65	10
N1294	10ch. Ilyushin Il-14P	90	10
N1295	40ch. Antonov An-24	1·25	35
N1296	60ch. Ilyushin Il-18	2·00	50

522 "Rhododendron redowskianum"

1974. Plants of Mt. Paekdu. Multicoloured.

N1298	2ch. Type **522**	45	10
N1299	5ch. "Dryas octopetala"	45	10
N1300	10ch. "Potentilla fruticosa"	50	10
N1301	20ch. "Papaver somniferum"	65	10
N1302	40ch. "Phyllodoce caerulea"	90	20
N1303	60ch. "Oxytropis anertii"	1·50	40

523 "Sobaek River in the Morning"

1974. Modern Korean Paintings (1st series). Multicoloured.

N1304	10ch. Type **523**	60	10
N1305	20ch. "Combatants of Mt. Laohei" (60 × 40 mm)	65	10
N1306	30ch. "Spring in the Fields"	75	15
N1307	40ch. "Tideland Night"	5·25	60
N1308	60ch. "Daughter" (60 × 54 mm)	1·10	40

See also Nos. N1361/5, N1386/96 and N1485/9.

525 Log Cabin, Unha Village

1974. Historic Sites of the Revolution. Multicoloured.

N1310	5ch. Munmyong	25	10
N1311	10ch. Type **525**	25	10

526 Sesame

1974. Oil-producing Plants. Multicoloured.

N1312	2ch. Type **526**	75	10
N1313	5ch. "Perilla frutescens"	80	10
N1314	10ch. Sunflower	90	10
N1315	40ch. Castor bean	1·25	40

527 Kim Il Sung as Guerrilla Leader

1974. Kim Il Sung. Multicoloured.

N1316	10ch. Type **527**	20	10
N1317	10ch. Commander of the People's Army (52 × 35 mm)	20	10
N1318	10ch. "The commander is also a son of the people" (52 × 35 mm)	20	10
N1319	10ch. Negotiating with the Chinese anti-Japanese unit (52 × 35 mm)	20	10

528

1974. Grand Monument on Mansu Hill. Mult.

N1320	10ch. Type **528**	15	10
N1321	10ch. As T **528** but men in civilian clothes	15	10
N1322	10ch. As T **528** but men facing left	15	10
N1323	10ch. As No. N1322 but men in civilian clothes	15	10

529 Factory Ship "Chilbosan"

1974. Deep-sea Fishing. Multicoloured.

N1324	2ch. Type **529**	70	25
N1325	5ch. Trawler support ship "Paekdusan"	70	25
N1326	10ch. Freighter "Moranbong"	70	25
N1327	20ch. Whale-catcher	70	25
N1328	30ch. Trawler	70	25
N1329	40ch. Stern trawler	70	25

539 Kim Il Sung crossing River Agrok

1975. 50th Anniv of Kim Il Sung's crossing of River Agrok.

N1349	**539**	10ch. multicoloured	25	10

540 Pak Yong Sun "World Table Tennis Queen"

1975. Pak Yong Sun, Winner of 33rd World Table Tennis Championships, Calcutta.

N1350	**540**	10ch. multicoloured	1·00	10

541 Common Zebra

1975. Pyongyang Zoo. Multicoloured.

N1352	10ch. Type **541**	30	10
N1353	10ch. African buffalo	30	10
N1354	20ch. Giant panda (horiz)	80	10
N1355	25ch. Bactrian camel	70	15
N1356	30ch. Indian elephant	1·25	20

542 "Blue Dragon"

1975. 7th-century Mural Paintings from Koguryo Tombs, Kangso.

N1357	10ch. Type **542**	75	10
N1358	15ch. "White Tiger"	1·00	10
N1359	25ch. "Red Phoenix" (vert)	1·25	10
N1360	40ch. "Snake-turtle"	1·75	25

543 "Spring in the Guerrilla Base" (1968)

1975. Modern Korean Paintings (2nd series). Anti-Japanese struggle. Multicoloured.

N1361	10ch. Type **543**	35	10
N1362	10ch. "Revolutionary Army landing at Unggi" (1969)	35	10
N1363	15ch. "Sewing Team Members" (1961)	55	10
N1364	20ch. "Girl Watering Horse" (1969)	1·00	15
N1365	30ch. "Kim Jong Suk giving Guidance to Children's Corps" (1970)	80	20

544 Cosmonaut

1975. Cosmonauts' Day. Multicoloured.

N1366	10ch. Type **544**	15	10
N1367	30ch. "Lunokhod" moon vehicle (horiz)	40	10
N1368	40ch. "Soyuz" spacecraft and "Salyut" space laboratory (horiz)	55	15

546 The Beacon lit at Pochonbo, 1937

1975. Kim Il Sung during the Guerrilla War against the Japanese. Multicoloured.

N1370	10ch. Type **546**	25	10
N1371	10ch. "A Bowl of Parched-rice Powder", 1938	25	10
N1372	10ch. Guiding the Nanpaizi meeting, November, 1938	25	10
N1373	10ch. Welcoming helper	25	10
N1374	10ch. Lecturing the guerrillas	25	10
N1375	15ch. Advancing into the homeland, May 1939	35	10
N1376	25ch. By Lake Samji, May 1939	45	10
N1377	30ch. At Sinsadong, May 1939	55	10
N1378	40ch. Xiaohaerbaling meeting, 1940	65	15

547 Vase of Flowers and Kim Il Sung's Birthplace

1975. Kim Il Sung's 63rd Birthday. Multicoloured.

N1379	10ch. Type **547**	10	10
N1379a	40ch. Kim Il Sung's birthplace, Mangyongdae	35	10

548 South Korean Insurgent

1975. 15th Anniv of April 19th Rising.

N1380	**548**	10ch. multicoloured	15	10

549 "Kingfisher at a Lotus Pond"

1975. Paintings of Li Dynasty. Multicoloured.

N1381	5ch. Type **549**	1·50	10
N1382	10ch. "Crabs"	1·00	10
N1383	15ch. "Rose of Sharon"	1·75	20
N1384	25ch. "Lotus and Water Cock"	2·50	45
N1385	30ch. "Tree Peony and Red Junglefowl"	4·25	45

1975. Modern Korean Paintings (3rd series). Fatherland Liberation War. Dated designs as T **543**. Multicoloured.

N1386	5ch. "On the Advance Southward" (1966) (vert)	30	10
N1387	10ch. "The Assigned Post" (girl sentry) (1968) (vert)	40	10
N1388	15ch. "The Heroism of Li Su Bok" (1965)	40	10

N1389	25ch. "Retaliation" (woman machine-gunner) (1970)	65	20
N1390	30ch. "The awaited Troops" (1970)	80	20

1975. Modern Korean Paintings (4th series). Socialist Construction. As T **543**. Multicoloured.

N1391	10ch. "Pine Tree" (1966) (vert)	90	10
N1392	10ch. "The Blue Signal Lamp" (1960) (vert)	2·75	10
N1393	15ch. "A Night of Snowfall" (1963)	90	10
N1394	20ch. "Smelters" (1968)	1·00	15
N1395	25ch. "Tideland Reclamation" (1961)	1·00	15
N1396	30ch. "Mount Paekgum" (1966)	1·00	20

550 Flag and Building

552 "Feet first" entry (man)

1975. 20th Anniv of "Chongryon" Association of Koreans in Japan.

N1397 **550**	10ch. multicoloured	15	10
N1398	3wn. multicoloured	2·50	55

1975. Diving. Multicoloured.

N1400	10ch. Type **552**	25	10
N1401	25ch. Piked somersault (man)	50	10
N1402	40ch. "Head first" entry (woman)	1·00	15

553

1975. Campaign against U.S. Imperialism.

N1403 **553**	10ch. multicoloured	30	10

554 Silver Carp

1975. Fresh-water Fish. Multicoloured.

N1404	10ch. Type **554**	70	10
N1405	10ch. Elongate ilisha (swimming to right)	70	10
N1406	15ch. Banded minnow	1·00	15
N1407	25ch. Bare-headed bagrid	1·60	20
N1408	30ch. Amur catfish (swimming to right)	2·00	30
N1409	30ch. Chevron snakehead (swimming to left)	2·00	30

555

1975. 10th Socialist Countries' Football Tournament, Pyongyang.

N1410 **555**	5ch. multicoloured	35	10
N1411 –	10ch. multicoloured	35	10
N1412 –	15ch. multicoloured	40	10
N1413 –	20ch. multicoloured	50	15
N1414 –	50ch. multicoloured	90	35

DESIGNS: 10ch. to 50ch. Various footballers.

556 Blue and Yellow Macaw

557 Flats

1975. Birds. Multicoloured.

N1416	10ch. Type **556**	1·50	20
N1417	15ch. Sulphur-crested cockatoo	1·75	25
N1418	20ch. Blyth's parakeet	2·25	40
N1419	25ch. Rainbow lory	2·75	45
N1420	30ch. Budgerigar	3·25	60

1975. New Buildings in Pyongyang. Multicoloured.

N1421	90ch. Saesallim (formerly Sarguson) Street	1·50	40
N1422	1wn. Type **557**	1·75	45
N1423	2wn. Potonggang Hotel	2·75	60

558 White Peach Blossom

559 Sejongbong

1975. Blossoms of Flowering Trees. Multicoloured.

N1424	10ch. Type **558**	40	10
N1425	15ch. Red peach blossom	40	10
N1426	20ch. Red plum blossom	60	15
N1427	25ch. Apricot blossom	75	15
N1428	30ch. Cherry blossom	1·00	20

1975. Landscapes in the Diamond Mountains. Multicoloured.

N1429	5ch. Type **559**	40	10
N1430	10ch. Chonsondae	65	10
N1431	15ch. Pisamun	85	10
N1432	25ch. Manmulsang	1·10	20
N1433	30ch. Chaehabong	1·25	20

560 Azalea

1975. Flowers of the Azalea Family. Multicoloured.

N1434	5ch. Type **560**	50	10
N1435	10ch. White azalea	50	10
N1436	15ch. Wild rhododendron	60	10
N1437	20ch. White rhododendron	60	15
N1438	25ch. Rhododendron	80	15
N1439	30ch. Yellow rhododendron	1·10	20

561 Gliders

1975. Training for National Defence. Mult.

N1440	5ch. Type **561**	60	10
N1441	5ch. Radio-controlled model airplane	60	10
N1442	10ch. "Free fall parachutist" (vert)	75	10
N1443	10ch. Parachutist landing on target (vert)	75	10
N1444	20ch. Parachutist with bouquet of flowers (vert)	1·10	15

562 Wild Apple

1975. Fruit Tree Blossom. Multicoloured.

N1446	10ch. Type **562**	40	10
N1447	15ch. Wild pear	40	10
N1448	20ch. Hawthorn	50	15
N1449	25ch. Chinese quince	70	20
N1450	30ch. Flowering quince	80	20

563 Torch of Juche

1975. 30th Anniv of Korean Workers' Party. Multicoloured.

N1451	2ch. "Victory" and American graves	10	10
N1452	2ch. Sunrise over Mt. Paekdu-san	10	10
N1453	5ch. Type **563**	10	10
N1454	5ch. Chollima Statue and sunset over Pyongyang	10	10
N1455	10ch. Korean with Red Book	10	10
N1456	10ch. Chollima Statue	10	10
N1457	25ch. Crowds and burning building	35	10
N1458	70ch. Flowers and map of Korea	95	15

564 Welcoming Crowd

1975. 30th Anniv of Kim Il Sung's Return to Pyongyang.

N1460 **564**	20ch. multicoloured	25	15

565 Workers holding "Juche" Torch

1975. 30th Anniv of "Rodong Simmun" (Journal of the Central Committee of the Worker's Party.)

N1461 **565**	10ch. multicoloured	50	10

566 Hyonmu Gate

1975. Ancient Wall-Gates of Pyongyang. Mult.

N1463	10ch. Type **566**	10	10
N1464	10ch. Taedong Gate	10	10
N1465	15ch. Potong Gate	20	10
N1466	20ch. Chongum Gate	35	15
N1467	30ch. Chilsong Gate (vert)	45	25

567

1975. Views of Mt. Chilbo.

N1468 **567**	10ch. multicoloured	40	10
N1469 –	10ch. multicoloured	40	10
N1470 –	15ch. multicoloured	65	10
N1471 –	20ch. multicoloured	75	15
N1472 –	30ch. multicoloured	85	20

DESIGNS: Nos. N1468/72, Various views.

568 Right-hand Section of Monument

1975. Historic Site of Revolution in Wangjaesan. Multicoloured.

N1473	10ch. Type **568**	10	10
N1474	15ch. Left-hand section of monument	20	10
N1475	25ch. Centre section of monument (38 × 60mm)	30	15
N1476	30ch. Centre section, close up (60 × 38mm)	40	20

569 Marchers with Flags

1976. 30th Anniv of Korean League of Socialist Working Youth. Multicoloured.

N1477	2ch. Flags and Emblem	15	10
N1478	70ch. Type **569**	90	40

570 Geese

1976. Ducks and Geese. Multicoloured.

N1479	10ch. Type **570**	40	10
N1480	20ch. "Perennial" duck	90	10
N1481	40ch. Kwangpo duck	1·60	20

571 "Oath"

1976. Korean Peoples Army (sculptural works). Multicoloured.

N1482	5ch. Type **571**	10	10
N1483	10ch. "Union of Officers with Men" (horiz)	15	10
N1484	10ch. "This Flag to the Height"	15	10

572 "Rural Road at Evening"

1976. Modern Korean Paintings (5th series). Social Welfare. Multicoloured.

N1485	10ch. Type **572**	60	10
N1486	15ch. "Passing on Technique" (1970)	70	10
N1487	25ch. "Mother (and Child)" (1965)	85	15
N1488	30ch. "Medical Examination at School" (1970) (horiz)	1·50	15
N1489	40ch. "Lady Doctor of Village" (1970) (horiz)	1·75	20

573 Worker holding Text of Law

1976. 30th Anniv of Agrarian Reform Law.

N1490	**573**	10ch. multicoloured	20	10

574 Telephones and Satellite

1976. Centenary of First Telephone Call. Multicoloured. With or without gum.

N1491	2ch. Type **574**	40	10
N1492	5ch. Satellite and antenna	40	10
N1493	10ch. Satellite and telecommunications systems	40	10
N1494	15ch. Telephone and linesman	1·10	10
N1495	25ch. Satellite and map of receiving stations	1·50	15
N1496	40ch. Satellite and cable-laying barge	1·75	20

575 Cosmos

1976. Flowers. Multicoloured.

N1498	5ch. Type **575**	25	10
N1499	10ch. Dahlia	25	10
N1500	20ch. Zinnia	45	15
N1501	40ch. China aster	70	25

576 Fruit and Products

1976. Pukchong Meeting of Korean Workers' Party Presidium. Multicoloured.

N1502	5ch. Type **576**	75	10
N1503	10ch. Fruit and orchard scene	75	10

577 "Pulgungi" Electric Locomotive

1976. Railway Locomotives. Multicoloured.

N1504	5ch. Type **577**	40	10
N1505	10ch. "Chaju" underground train	75	10
N1506	15ch. "Saebyol" diesel locomotive	95	15

GUM. All the following stamps were issued with gum, except where otherwise stated.

578 Satellite

1976. Space Flight. With or without gum.

N1507	**578**	2ch. multicoloured	15	10
N1508	–	5ch. multicoloured	15	10
N1509	–	10ch. multicoloured	20	10
N1510	–	15ch. multicoloured	30	10
N1511	–	25ch. multicoloured	45	15
N1512	–	40ch. multicoloured	70	20

DESIGNS: 5ch. to 40ch. Various satellites and space craft.

579 Kim Il Sung beside Car

1976. Kim Il Sung's 64th Birthday.

N1514	**579**	10ch. multicoloured	40	10

580 Bat and Ribbon

1976. 3rd Asian Table Tennis Championships. Multicoloured. Without gum.

N1516	5ch. Type **580**	40	10
N1517	10ch. Three women players with flowers	40	10
N1518	20ch. Player defending	65	10
N1519	25ch. Player making attacking shot	1·00	15

581 Kim Il Sung announcing Establishment of Association

1976. 40th Anniv of Association for the Restoration of the Fatherland. Without gum.

N1521	**581**	10ch. multicoloured	10	10

582 Golden Pheasant

1976. Pheasants. Multicoloured. With or without gum.

N1522	2ch. Type **582**	1·00	15
N1523	5ch. Lady Amherst's pheasant	1·10	15
N1524	10ch. Silver pheasant	1·40	25
N1525	15ch. Reeves's pheasant	1·50	35
N1526	25ch. Temminck's tragopan	2·00	60
N1527	40ch. Common pheasant (albino)	2·40	1·00

583 Monument and Map of River

584 Running

1976. Potong River Monument. Without gum.

N1529	**583**	10ch. brown and green	20	10

1976. Olympic Games, Montreal. Multicoloured.

N1530	2ch. Type **584**	30	10
N1531	5ch. Diving	30	10
N1532	10ch. Judo	30	10
N1533	15ch. Gymnastics	40	10
N1534	25ch. Gymnastics	80	15
N1535	40ch. Fencing	3·00	20

585 Bronze Medal (Hockey, Pakistan)

1976. Olympic Medal Winners (1st issue). Multicoloured.

N1537	2ch. Type **585**	75	10
N1538	5ch. Bronze medal (shooting, Rudolf Dollinger)	25	10
N1539	10ch. Silver medal (boxing, Li Byong Uk)	25	15
N1540	15ch. Silver medal (cycling, Daniel Morelon)	2·00	15
N1541	25ch. Gold medal (marathon, Waldemar Cierpinski)	90	20
N1542	40ch. Gold medal (boxing, Ku Yong Jo)	1·10	25

586 Boxing (Ku Yong Jo)

1976. Olympic Medal Winners (2nd issue). Multicoloured.

N1544	2ch. Type **586**	25	10
N1545	5ch. Gymnastics (Nadia Comaneci)	25	10
N1546	10ch. Pole vaulting (Tadeusz Slusarki)	25	10
N1547	15ch. Hurdling (Guy Drut)	30	10
N1548	20ch. Cycling (Bernt Johansson)	2·50	15
N1549	40ch. Football (East Germany)	1·50	20

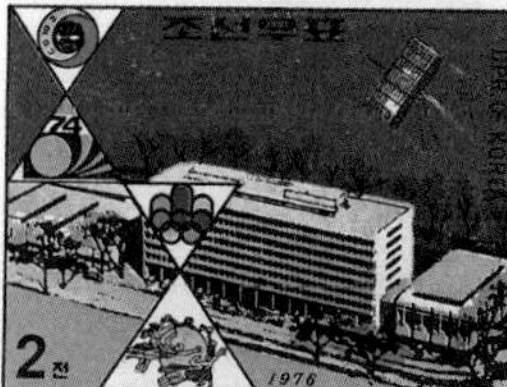

587 U.P.U. Headquarters, Berne

1976. International Festivities. Multicoloured.

N1551	2ch. Type **587**	40	10
N1552	5ch. Footballers (World Cup)	40	10
N1553	10ch. Olympic Stadium	40	10
N1554	15ch. Olympic Village	40	10
N1555	25ch. Junk and satellite	70	20
N1556	40ch. Satellites	75	20

588 Azure-winged Magpies

1976. Embroidery. Multicoloured. With or without gum.

N1558	2ch. Type **588**	1·75	20
N1559	5ch. White magpie	90	15
N1560	10ch. Roe deer	30	10
N1561	15ch. Black-naped oriole and magnolias	2·10	20
N1562	25ch. Fairy with flute (horiz)	70	15
N1563	40ch. Tiger	1·60	40

589 Roman "5" and Flame

1976. 5th Non-aligned States' Summit Conference, Colombo. Without gum.

N1565	**589**	10ch. multicoloured	10	10

590 Trophy and Certificate

1976. World Model Plane Championships (1975). Multicoloured. Without gum.

N1566	5ch. Type **590**	20	10
N1567	10ch. Trophy and medals	30	10
N1568	20ch. Model airplane and emblem	45	10
N1569	40ch. Model glider and medals	75	15

591 "Pulgungi" Diesel Shunting Locomotive

1976. Locomotives. Multicoloured.

N1570	2ch. Type **591**	40	10
N1571	5ch. "Saebyol" diesel locomotive	55	10
N1572	10ch. "Saebyol" diesel shunting locomotive	65	10
N1573	15ch. Electric locomotive	75	10

N1574 25ch. "Kumsong" diesel locomotive 95 15
N1575 40ch. "Pulgungi" electric locomotive . . . . . . 1·10 20

592 House of Culture

1976. House of Culture. Without gum.
N1577 **592** 10ch. brown and black 15 10

593 Kim Il Sung visiting Tosongrang

1976. Revolutionary Activities of Kim Il Sung. Multicoloured.
N1578 2ch. Type **593** 20 10
N1579 5ch. Kim Il Sung visits pheasants 20 10
N1580 10ch. Kim Il Sung on hilltop 25 10
N1581 15ch. Kim Il Sung giving house to farmhand . . 30 10
N1582 25ch. Kim Il Sung near front line 70 10
N1583 40ch. Kim Il Sung walking in rain 70 15

594 Kim Il Sung with Union Members

1976. 50th Anniv of Down-with-Imperialism Union. Without gum.
N1585 **594** 20ch. multicoloured . . 35 15

604 Searchlights and Kim Il Sung's Birthplace

605 Spring Costume

1977. New Year. Without gum.
N1589 **604** 10ch. multicoloured . . 10 10

1977. National Costumes of Li Dynasty. Mult.
N1590 10ch. Type **605** (postage) 45 10
N1591 15ch. Summer costume . . 60 10
N1592 20ch. Autumn costume . . 70 15
N1593 40ch. Winter costume (air) 1·10 20

606 Two Deva Kings (Koguryo Dynasty)

1977. Korean Cultural Relics. Multicoloured.
N1594 2ch. Type **606** (postage) 40 10
N1595 5ch. Gold-copper decoration, Koguryo Dynasty 40 10
N1596 10ch. Copper Buddha, Koryo Dynasty 60 10
N1597 15ch. Gold-copper Buddha, Paekje Dynasty 70 10
N1598 25ch. Gold crown, Koguryo Dynasty . . . 85 15
N1599 40ch. Gold-copper sun decoration, Koguryo Dynasty (horiz) . . . . 1·00 20
N1600 50ch. Gold crown, Silla Dynasty (air) . . . . . 1·10 35

607 Worker with Five-point Programme

1977. Five-point Programme for Remaking Nature. Without gum.
N1601 **607** 10ch. multicoloured . . 20 10

608 Pine Branch and Map of Korea

1977. 60th Anniv of Korean National Association. Without gum.
N1602 **608** 10ch. multicoloured . . 35 10

609 Championship Emblem and Trophy

1977. 34th World Table Tennis Championships. Multicoloured. Without gum.
N1603 10ch. Type **609** (postage) 30 10
N1604 15ch. Pak Yong Sun . . . 40 10
N1605 20ch. Pak Yong Sun with trophy 70 15
N1606 40ch. Pak Yong Ok and Yang Ying (air) . . . . 1·10 20

610 Kim Il Sung founds Guerrilla Army at Mingyuegou

1977. Kim Il Sung's 65th Birthday. Multicoloured.
N1607 2ch. Type **610** 10 10
N1608 5ch. In command of army 10 10
N1609 10ch. Visiting steel workers in Kangson . . 25 10
N1610 15ch. Before battle 20 10
N1611 25ch. In schoolroom . . . 25 10
N1612 40ch. Viewing bumper harvest 35 10

611 "Chollima 72" Trolleybus

1977. Trolleybuses. Without gum.
N1614 **611** 5ch. blue, lilac and black . . . . 1·00 10
N1615 – 10ch. red, green & black . . . . 1·00 10
DESIGN: 10ch. "Chollima 74" trolleybus.

612 Red Flag and Hand holding Rifle

1977. 45th Anniv of Korean People's Revolutionary Army. Without gum.
N1616 **612** 40ch. red, yellow & blk 50 20

613 Proclamation and Watchtower

1977. 40th Anniv of Pochonbo Battle. Without gum.
N1617 **613** 10ch. multicoloured . . 10 10

614 Koryo White Ware Teapot

1977. Korean Porcelain. Multicoloured.
N1618 10ch. Type **614** (postage) 70 10
N1619 15ch. White vase, Li Dynasty 85 10
N1620 20ch. Celadon vase, Koryo Dynasty . . . . 1·00 10
N1621 40ch. Celadon vase with lotus decoration, Koryo Dynasty (air) . . . . . 1·50 15

615 Postal Transport

1977. Postal Services. Multicoloured. Without gum.
N1623 2ch. Type **615** . . . . . . 1·00 15
N1624 10ch. Postwoman delivering letter 40 10
N1625 30ch. Mil Mi-8 helicopter 1·00 30
N1626 40ch. Ilyushin Il-18 airliner and world map 1·10 30

616 "Rapala arata"

1977. Butterflies and Dragonflies. Multicoloured.
N1627 2ch. Type **616** (postage) 60 10
N1628 5ch. "Colias aurora" . . . 80 10
N1629 10ch. Poplar admiral . . . 1·00 10
N1630 15ch. "Anax parthenope" (dragonfly) . . . . . . 1·50 10
N1631 25ch. "Sympetrum pedemontanum" (dragonfly) . . . . . . 1·75 10
N1632 50ch. "Papilio maackii" (air) . . . . 2·25 20

617 Grey Cat

618

1977. Cats. Multicoloured.
N1634 2ch. Type **617** . . . . . . 1·25 10
N1635 10ch. Black and white cat 1·60 15
N1636 25ch. Ginger cat . . . . . 2·75 20

1977. Dogs. Multicoloured.
N1638 5ch. Type **618** (postage) 1·00 10
N1639 15ch. Chow . . . . 1·25 10
N1640 50ch. Pungsang dog (air) 1·75 15

619 Kim Il Sung and President Tito

1977. Visit of President Tito.
N1642 **619** 10ch. multicoloured . . 10 10
N1643 15ch. multicoloured . . 15 10
N1644 20ch. multicoloured . . 20 10
N1645 40vh. multicoloured . . 25 10

620 Girl and Symbols of Education

1977. 5th Anniv of 11-year Compulsory Education. Without gum.
N1646 **620** 10ch. multicoloured . . 10 10

621 Chinese Mactra and Cobia

622 Students and "Theses"

1977. Shellfish and Fish. Multicoloured.
N1647 2ch. Type **621** (postage) 45 10
N1648 5ch. Bladder moon . . . 65 10
N1649 10ch. "Arca inflata" and pomfret 95 15
N1650 25ch. Thomas's rapa whelk and grouper . . . 1·40 40
N1651 50ch. Thomas's rapa whelk and globefish (air) 2·10 75

1977. Kim Il Sung's "Theses on Socialist Education". Multicoloured. Without gum.
N1653 10ch. Type **622** 20 10
N1654 20ch. Students, crowd and text 30 10

623 "Juche" Torch **624** Jubilant Crowd

1977. Seminar on the Juche Idea. Multicoloured. Without gum.

N1655	2ch. Type **623**	10	10
N1656	5ch. Crowd and red book	10	10
N1657	10ch. Chollima Statue and flags	10	10
N1658	15ch. Handclasp and red flag on world map	10	10
N1659	25ch. Map of Korea and anti-U.S. slogans	15	10
N1660	40ch. Crowd and Mt. Paekdu-san	20	10

1977. Election of Deputies to Supreme People's Assembly. Without gum.

N1662 **624**	10ch. multicoloured	10	10

625 Footballers

1977. World Cup Football Championship, Argentina. Without gum.

N1663 **625**	10ch. multicoloured	90	15
N1664 –	15ch. multicoloured	1·25	20
N1665 –	40ch. multicoloured	2·00	25

DESIGNS: 15, 40ch. Different football scenes.

626 Kim Il Sung with Rejoicing Crowds

1977. Re-election of Kim Il Sung. Without gum.

N1667 **626**	10ch. multicoloured	20	10

627 Chollima Statue and Symbols of Communication

1977. 20th Anniv of Socialist Countries' Communication Organization. Without gum.

N1668 **627**	10ch. multicoloured	20	10

638 Chollima Statue and City Skyline

1978. New Year. Without gum.

N1687 **638**	10ch. multicoloured	20	10

639 Skater in 19th-century Costume

1978. Winter Olympic Games, Sapporo and Innsbruck. Multicoloured.

N1688	2ch. Type **639** (postage)	50	10
N1699	5ch. Skier	50	10
N1690	10ch. Woman skater	50	10
N1691	15ch. Hunter on skis	60	10
N1692	20ch. Woman (in 19th-century costume) on skis	60	10
N1693	25ch. Viking with longbow	2·75	15
N1694	40ch. Skier (air)	1·50	15

640 Post-rider and "Horse-ticket"

1978. Postal Progress. Multicoloured.

N1696	2ch. Type **640** (postage)	40	10
N1697	5ch. Postman on motor cycle	1·75	10
N1698	10ch. Electric train and post-van	1·75	15
N1699	15ch. Mail steamer and Mil Mi-8 helicopter	1·00	15
N1700	25ch. Tupolev Tu-154 jetliner and satellite	90	15
N1701	40ch. Dove and U.P.U. headquarters (air)	60	15

641 Self-portrait

1978. 400th Birth Anniv of Rubens.

N1703 **641**	2ch. multicoloured	25	10
N1704	5ch. multicoloured	25	10
N1705	40ch. multicoloured	1·50	20

642 "Chungsong" Tractor

1978. Farm Machines. Without gum.

N1707 **642**	10ch. red and black	45	10
N1708 –	10ch. brown and black	45	10

DESIGN: No. N1708, Sprayer.

643 Show Jumping

1978. Olympic Games, Moscow (1980). Equestrian Events. Multicoloured.

N1709	2ch. Type **643**	25	10
N1710	5ch. Jumping bar	35	10
N1711	10ch. Cross-country	45	10
N1712	15ch. Dressage	50	10
N1713	25ch. Water splash	75	15
N1714	40ch. Dressage (different)	1·25	15

644 Soldier

1978. Korean People's Army Day. Multicoloured. Without gum.

N1716	5ch. Type **644**	10	10
N1717	10ch. Servicemen saluting	10	10

645 "Mangyongbong" (Freighter)

1978. Korean Ships. Multicoloured.

N1718	2ch. Type **645** (postage)	1·75	45
N1719	5ch. "Hyoksin" (freighter)	35	15
N1720	10ch. "Chongchongang" (gas carrier)	35	15
N1721	30ch. "Sonbong" (tanker)	60	20
N1722	50ch. "Taedonggang" (freighter) (air)	1·10	40

646 Uruguayan Footballer

1978. World Cup Football Championship Winners. Multicoloured.

N1724	5ch. Type **646** (postage)	50	10
N1725	10ch. Italian player	50	10
N1726	15ch. West German player	50	10
N1727	25ch. Brazilian player	50	10
N1728	40ch. English player	1·00	10
N1729	50ch. Hands holding World Cup (vert) (air)	1·50	15

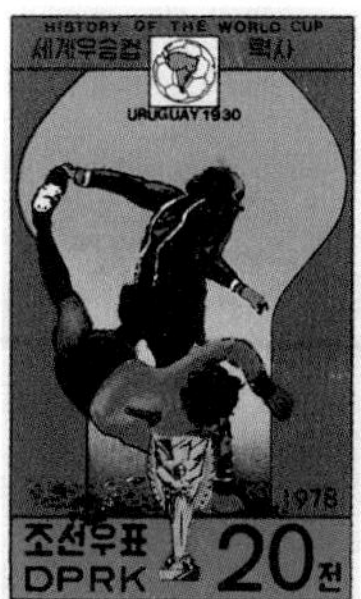

647 Footballers (1930 Winners, Uruguay)

1978. History of World Cup Football Championship. Multicoloured.

N1731	20ch. Type **647** (postage)	85	15
N1732	20ch. Italy, 1934	85	15
N1733	20ch. France, 1938	85	15
N1734	20ch. Brazil, 1950	85	15
N1735	20ch. Switzerland, 1954	85	15
N1736	20ch. Sweden, 1958	85	15
N1737	20ch. Chile, 1962	85	15
N1738	20ch. England, 1966	85	15
N1739	20ch. Mexico, 1970	85	15
N1740	20ch. West Germany, 1974	85	15
N1741	20ch. Argentina, 1978	85	15
N1742	50ch. Footballers and emblem (air)	85	15

648 "Sea of Blood" (opera)

1978. Art from the Period of Anti-Japanese Struggle. Multicoloured.

N1744	10ch. Type **648**	40	10
N1745	15ch. Floral kerchief embroidered with map of Korea	50	10
N1746	20ch. "Tansimjul" (maypole dance)	75	15

649 Red Flag and "7", Electricity and Coal

1978. Second 7 Year Plan. Multicoloured. Without gum.

N1748	5ch. Type **649**	25	10
N1749	10ch. Steel and non-ferrous metal	30	10
N1750	15ch. Engineering and chemical fertilizer	35	10
N1751	30ch. Cement and fishing	70	10
N1752	50ch. Grain and tideland reclamation	75	10

650 Gymnastics (Alfred Flatow)

1978. Olympic Games History and Medal-winners. Multicoloured.

N1753	20ch. Type **650**	75	15
N1754	20ch. Runners (Michel Theato)	75	15
N1755	20ch. Runners (Wyndham Halswelle)	75	15
N1756	20ch. Rowing (William Kinnear)	75	15
N1757	20ch. Fencing (Paul Anspach)	1·50	25
N1758	20ch. Runners (Ugo Frigerio)	75	15
N1759	20ch. Runners (Ahmed El Quafi)	75	15
N1760	20ch. Cycling (Robert Charpentier)	1·75	35
N1761	20ch. Gymnastics (Josep Stalder)	75	15
N1762	20ch. Boxing (Lazio Papp)	1·00	20
N1763	20ch. Runners (Ronald Delany)	75	15
N1764	20ch. High jump (Jolanda Balas)	75	15
N1765	20ch. High jump (Valery Brumel)	75	15
N1766	20ch. Gymnastics (Vera Caslavska)	75	15
N1767	20ch. Rifle shooting (Li Ho Jun)	75	15

651 Douglas DC-8-63 and Comte Gentleman

1978. Airplanes. Multicoloured.

N1769	2ch. Type **651**	70	10
N1770	10ch. Ilyushin Il-62M and Avia BH-25	80	10

N1771	15ch. Douglas DC-8-63 and Savoia Marchetti S-71	90	10
N1772	20ch. Tupolev Tu-144 and Kalinin K-5	1·10	10
N1773	25ch. Tupolev Tu-154 and Antonov An-2 biplane	1·10	10
N1774	30ch. Ilyushin Il-18	1·10	10
N1775	40ch. Concorde and Wibault 283 trimotor	2·25	40

652 White-bellied Black Woodpecker and Map

1978. White-bellied Black Woodpecker Preservation. Multicoloured.

N1777	5ch. Type **652**	1·50	15
N1778	10ch. Woodpecker and eggs	1·75	20
N1779	15ch. Woodpecker feeding young	2·25	30
N1780	25ch. Woodpecker feeding young (different)	2·75	60
N1781	50ch. Adult woodpecker on tree trunk	5·00	1·25

653 Demonstrators and Korean Map

1978. 30th Anniv of Democratic People's Republic of Korea. Multicoloured. Without gum.

N1783	10ch. Type **653**	10	10
N1784	10ch. Flag and soldiers	10	10
N1785	10ch. Flag and "Juche"	10	10
N1786	10ch. Red Flag	10	10
N1787	10ch. Chollima Statue and city skyline	10	10
N1788	10ch. "Juche" torch and men of three races	10	10

654 Cat and Pup

668 Red Flag and Pine Branch

655 Footballers

1978. Animal Paintings by Li Am. Multicoloured.

N1789	10ch. Type **654**	2·50	30
N1790	15ch. Cat up a tree	2·50	30
N1791	40ch. Wild geese	2·50	30

1978. Argentina's Victory in World Cup Football Championship. Without gum.

N1792 **655**	10ch. multicoloured	75	10
N1793 –	15ch. multicoloured	85	15
N1794 –	25ch. multicoloured	1·10	20

DESIGNS: 15, 25ch. Different football scenes.

1979. New Year. Without gum.

N1812 **668**	10ch. multicoloured	15	10

669 Kim Il Sung with Children's Corps Members, Maanshan

1979. International Year of the Child (1st issue). Multicoloured. (a) Paintings of Kim Il Sung and children.

N1813	5ch. Type **669**	15	10
N1814	10ch. Kim Il Sung and Children's Corps members in classroom	25	10
N1815	15ch. New Year gathering	30	10
N1816	20ch. Kim Il Sung and children in snow	45	10
N1817	30ch. Kim Il Sung examines children's schoolbooks (vert)	50	10

(b) Designs showing children

N1818	10ch. Tug-of-war	15	10
N1819	15ch. Dance "Growing up Fast"	40	15
N1820	20ch. Children of many races and globe	40	10
N1821	25ch. Children singing	65	15
N1822	30ch. Children in toy spaceships	40	10

See also Nos. N1907/17.

670 Rose

1979. Roses. Multicoloured.

N1824	1wn. Red rose
N1825	3wn. White rose
N1826	5wn. Type **670**
N1827	10wn. Deep pink rose

See also Nos. N1837/42.

671 Warriors on Horseback

1979. "The Story of Two Generals". Multicoloured. Without gum.

N1828	5ch. Type **671**	20	10
N1829	10ch. Farm labourer blowing feather	30	10
N1830	10ch. Generals fighting on foot	30	10
N1831	10ch. Generals on horseback	30	10

672 Red Guard and Industrial Skyline

1979. 20th Anniv of Worker-Peasant Red Guards. Without gum.

N1832 **672**	10ch. multicoloured	15	10

673 Clement-Bayard Airship "Fleurus"

1979. Airships. Multicoloured. Without gum.

N1833	10ch. Type **673**	1·25	15
N1834	20ch. N.1 "Norge"	1·25	15

674 Crowd of Demonstrators

1979. 60th Anniv of 1st March Popular Uprising. Without gum.

N1836 **674**	10ch. blue and red	15	10

1979. Roses. As Nos. N1824/7. Multicoloured.

N1837	5ch. Type **670** (postage)	40	10
N1838	10ch. As No. N1827	45	10
N1839	15ch. As No. N1824	50	10
N1840	20ch. Yellow rose	60	10
N1841	30ch. As No. 1825	70	10
N1842	50ch. Deep pink rose (different) (air)	90	15

675 Table Tennis Trophy

1979. 35th World Table Tennis Championship, Pyongyang. Multicoloured. With or without gum.

N1843	5ch. Type **675**	20	10
N1844	10ch. Women's doubles	20	10
N1845	15ch. Women's singles	40	10
N1846	20ch. Men's doubles	60	10
N1847	30ch. Men's singles	80	10

676 Marchers with Red Flag

1979. Socialist Construction under Banner of Juche Idea. Multicoloured. Without gum.

N1849	5ch. Type **676**	10	10
N1850	10ch. Map of Korea	10	10
N1851	10ch. Juche torch	10	10

677 Badge

678 Emblem, Satellite orbiting Globe and Aerials

1979. Order of Honour of the Three Revolutions. Without gum.

N1852 **677**	10ch. blue	10	10

1979. World Telecommunications Day. Without gum.

N1853 **678**	10ch. multicoloured	25	10

679 Advancing Soldiers and Monument

1979. 40th Anniv of Battle in Musan Area. Without gum.

N1854 **679**	10ch. mauve, light blue and blue	20	10

680 Exhibition Entrance

1979. Int Friendship Exhibition. Without gum.

N1855 **680**	10ch. multicoloured	10	10

681 "Peonies"

1979. 450th Death Anniv (1978) of Albrecht Durer (artist) (1st issue). Multicoloured.

N1856	15ch. Type **681**	75	20
N1857	20ch. "Columbines"	1·25	20
N1858	25ch. "A Great Tuft of Grass"	1·25	20
N1859	30ch. "Wing of a Bird"	2·10	55

See also No. N2012.

682 Fencing

1979. Olympic Games, Moscow (2nd issue). Multicoloured. With gum (10, 40ch. only).

N1861	5ch. Type **682**	1·50	10
N1862	10ch. Gymnastics	40	10
N1863	20ch. Yachting	75	15
N1864	30ch. Athletics	60	15
N1865	40ch. Weightlifting	60	15

683 Hunting

1979. Horse-riding (people of Koguryo Dynasty). Multicoloured.

N1867	5ch. Type **683**	65	10
N1868	10ch. Archery contest	65	10
N1869	15ch. Man beating drum on horseback	25	10
N1870	20ch. Man blowing horn	25	10
N1871	30ch. Man and horse, armoured with chainmail	25	10
N1872	50ch. Hawking (air)	2·00	15

684 Judo

685 Warrior's Costume

1979. Olympic Games, Moscow (3rd issue). Multicoloured. With gum (5, 15, 20, 30ch. only).

N1873	5ch. Type **684**	40	10
N1874	10ch. Volleyball	40	10
N1875	15ch. Cycling	1·50	25
N1876	20ch. Basketball	60	15
N1877	25ch. Canoeing	60	15
N1878	30ch. Boxing	90	25
N1879	40ch. Shooting	85	20

1979. Warrior Costumes of Li Dynasty.

N1881 **685**	5ch. multicoloured	20	10
N1882 –	10ch. multicoloured	20	10
N1883 –	15ch. multicoloured	30	10
N1884 –	20ch. multicoloured	45	10

N1885 – 30ch. multicoloured . . 60 10
N1886 – 50ch. multicoloured (air) 90 15
DESIGNS: 10ch. to 50ch. Different costumes.

686 Wrestling
687 Monument

1979. Olympic Games, Moscow (4th issue). Multicoloured.
N1887 10ch. Type **686** 25 10
N1888 15ch. Handball 30 10
N1889 20ch. Archery . . . . . . 1·60 25
N1890 25ch. Hockey . . . . . . 1·60 45
N1891 30ch. Rowing 75 15
N1892 40ch. Football . . . . . 1·50 25

1979. Chongbong Monument. Without gum.
N1894 **687** 10ch. multicoloured . . 20 10

688 Bottle-feeding Fawn

1979. Sika Deer. Multicoloured.
N1895 5ch. Type **688** (postage) 20 10
N1896 10ch. Doe and fawn . . . 20 10
N1897 15ch. Stag drinking from stream 20 15
N1898 20ch. Stag 25 15
N1899 30ch. Stag and doe . . . 35 25
N1900 50ch. Antlers and deer (air) 50 35

689 Moscovy Ducks

1979. Central Zoo, Pyongyang. Multicoloured.
N1901 5ch. Type **689** (postage) 40 10
N1902 10ch. Ostrich 85 10
N1903 15ch. Common turkey . . 1·10 10
N1904 20ch. Dalmatian pelican 1·25 10
N1905 30ch. Vulturine guineafowl 1·75 15
N1906 50ch. Mandarins (air) . . 2·75 20

690 Girl with Model Viking Ship

1979. International Year of the Child (2nd issue). Multicoloured.
N1907 20ch. Type **690** . . . . . 1·00 20
N1908 20ch. Boys with model steam railway locomotive . . . . . . 2·50 85
N1909 20ch. Boy with model biplane . . . . 1·25 20
N1910 20ch. Boy with model spaceman 80 20
N1911 30ch. Boy with model speedboat . . . . . . 1·50 30
N1912 30ch. Boy sitting astride toy electric train . . . . 2·50 85
N1913 30ch. Boy and model airplane . . . . 1·60 30
N1914 30ch. Boy and flying spaceman . . . . 1·00 30

691 Footballers

1979. International Year of the Child (3rd issue). Multicoloured.
N1916 20ch. Type **691** . . . . . 1·25 20
N1917 30ch. Footballers (different) . . . . . . 1·75 30

692 Japanese Stonefish

1979. Marine Life. Multicoloured.
N1919 20ch. Type **692** . . . . . 1·25 10
N1920 30ch. Schlegel's redfish . . 1·40 20
N1921 50ch. Northern sealion . . 1·75 30

693 Cross-country Skiing (Sergei Saveliev)

1979. Winter Olympic Games, Lake Placid. Mult.
N1922 10ch. Figure skating (Irina Rodnina and Aleksandr Zaitsev) (horiz) 40 15
N1923 20ch. Ice hockey (Russian team) (horiz) 65 20
N1924 30ch. Women's 5 km relay (horiz) . . . . 1·10 25
N1925 40ch. Type **693** . . . . . 1·25 30
N1926 50ch. Women's speed skating (Tatiana Averina) . . . . 1·50 35

694 The Honey Bee collecting Nectar

1979. The Honey Bee. Multicoloured.
N1928 20ch. Type **694** . . . . . 1·40 10
N1929 30ch. Bee and flowers . . 1·75 15
N1930 50ch. Bee hovering over flower . . . . 2·00 25

695 Kim Jong Suk's Birthplace, Heoryong

1979. Historic Revolutionary Sites.
N1931 **695** 10ch. multicoloured . . 15 10
N1932 – 10ch. brown, blue & blk 15 10
DESIGN: No. N1932, Sinpa Revolutionary Museum.

696 Mt. Paekdu

1980. New Year.
N1933 **696** 10ch. multicoloured . . 55 10

697 Student and Books

1980. Studying.
N1934 **697** 10ch. multicoloured . . 25 10

698 Conveyor Belt

1980. Unryul Mine Conveyor Belt.
N1935 **698** 10ch. multicoloured . . 55 10

699 Children of Three Races

1980. International Day of the Child. Multicoloured.
N1936 10ch. Type **699** 30 10
N1937 10ch. Girl dancing to accordion 50 10
N1938 10ch. Children in fairground airplane . . 40 10
N1939 10ch. Children as astronauts 30 10
N1940 10ch. Children on tricycles 1·25 30
N1941 10ch. Children with toy diesel train . . . . . . 1·75 45
N1942 10ch. "His loving care for the children, future of the fatherland" ($59\frac{1}{2}\times38$ mm) 30 10

700 Monument

1980. Chongsan-ri Historic Site. Multicoloured.
N1944 5ch. Type **700** 10 10
N1945 10ch. Meeting place of the General Membership . . 15 10

701 Monument

1980. Monument marking Kim Jong Suk's Return.
N1946 **701** 10ch. multicoloured . . 15 10

702 Vasco Nunez de Balboa

1980. Conquerors of the Earth. Multicoloured.
N1947 10ch. Type **702** 50 10
N1948 20ch. Francisco de Orellana 75 20
N1949 30ch. Haroun Tazieff . . 1·00 35
N1950 40ch. Edmund Hillary and Sherpa Tenzing . . . . 1·50 45

703 Museum

1980. Ryongpo Revolutionary Museum.
N1952 **703** 10ch. blue and black 20 10

704 Rowland Hill and Stamps

1980. Death Centenary (1979) of Sir Rowland Hill. Multicoloured.
N1953 30ch. Type **704** . . . . . 3·50 75
N1954 50ch. Rowland Hill and stamps (different) . . . 3·50 75

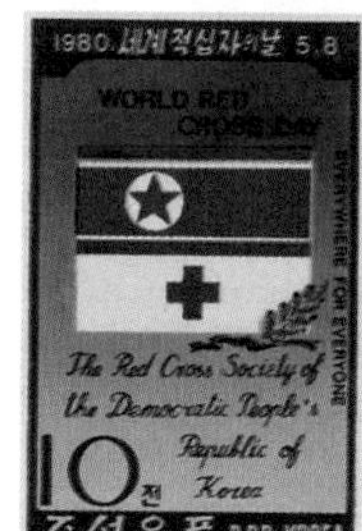

705 North Korean Red Cross Flag

1980. World Red Cross Day. Multicoloured.
N1955 10ch. Type **705** 70 20
N1956 10ch. Henri Dunant (founder) 70 20
N1957 10ch. Nurse and child . . 70 20
N1958 10ch. Polikarpov Po-2 biplane and ship . . . . 1·00 25
N1959 10ch. Mil Mi-4 helicopter 1·00 25
N1960 10ch. Children playing at nurses 70 20
N1961 10ch. Red Cross map over Korea and forms of transport . . . . 3·50 60

706 Fernando Magellan

1980. Conquerors of the Sea. Multicoloured.
N1963 10ch. Type **706** . . . . . 1·75 25
N1964 20ch. Fridtjof Nansen . . 1·75 25
N1965 30ch. Auguste and Jacques Piccard . . . . 2·25 25
N1966 40ch. Jacques-Yves Cousteau . . . . 3·00 55

707 Korean Stamps and Penny Black

1980. "London 1980" International Stamp Exhibition. Multicoloured.
N1968 10ch. Type **707** (postage) 2·00 40
N1969 20ch. Korean cover and British Guiana 1c. black and red . . . . 3·00 40
N1970 30ch. Early Korean stamp and modern cover . . . 2·00 40
N1971 50ch. Korean stamps . . . 2·50 35
N1972 40ch. Korean stamp and miniature sheet (air) . . 1·60 35

708 Wright Brothers

1980. Conquerors of Sky and Space. Multicoloured.

N1974	10ch. Type **708**	75	15
N1975	20ch. Louis Bleriot	1·00	25
N1976	30ch. Anthony Fokker	1·50	40
N1977	40ch. Secondo Campini and Sir Frank Whittle	2·00	45

709 Space Station on Planet　**710** Flag and Banners

1980. Conquerors of the Universe. Multicoloured.

N1979	10ch. Orbiting space station	20	10
N1980	20ch. Type **709**	25	20
N1981	30ch. Prehistoric animals and spaceships	90	35
N1982	40ch. Prehistoric animals and birds and spaceship	1·10	45

1980. 25th Anniv of General Association of Korean Residents in Japan (Chongryon).

N1984	**710** 10ch. multicoloured	20	10

711 Hospital

1980. Pyongyang Maternity Hospital.

N1985	**711** 10ch. blue, purple & blk	45	15

712 Health Centre

1980. Changgangwon Health Centre, Pyongyang.

N1986	**712** 2ch. black and blue	25	10

713 Hand holding Rifle　**714** Workers' Hostel, Samjiyon

1980. 50th Anniv of Revolutionary Army.

N1987	**713** 10ch. multicoloured	25	10

1980.

N1988	**714** 10ch. brown, blue & blk	30	10
N1989	– 10ch. black and green	50	20
N1990	– 10ch. black and red	50	20
N1991	– 10ch. black and yellow	50	20
N1992	– 10ch. multicoloured	30	10
N1993	– 10ch. multicoloured	30	10
N1994	– 10ch. multicoloured	1·00	35
N1995	– 10ch. green and black	75	25
N1996	– 10ch. grey, blue & black	3·50	60
N1997	– 10ch. multicoloured	6·00	85

DESIGNS: No. N1989, "Taedonggang" rice transplanter; N1990, "Chongsan-ri" rice harvester; N1991, Maize harvester; N1992, Revolutionary building, Songmun-ri; N1993, Revolutionary building, Samhwa; N1994, Sundial of 1438; N1995, 16th-century "turtle" ship; N1996, Pungsan dog; N1997, Japanese quail.

715 Party Emblem

1980. 6th Korean Workers' Party Congress. Multicoloured.

N1998	10ch. Type **715**	15	10
N1999	10ch. Students and Laurel leaf on globe	15	10
N2000	10ch. Group with accordion	45	15
N2001	10ch. Group with banner, microscope, book and trophy	25	10
N2002	10ch. Worker with book and flag	75	25
N2003	10ch. Worker with spanner and flag	75	25
N2004	10ch. Marchers with torch and flags	15	10
N2005	10ch. Emblem, marchers and map	20	10

716 Dribbling Ball

1980. World Cup Football Championship, 1978–82. Multicoloured.

N2007	20ch. Type **716**	2·50	60
N2008	30ch. Tackle	3·00	80

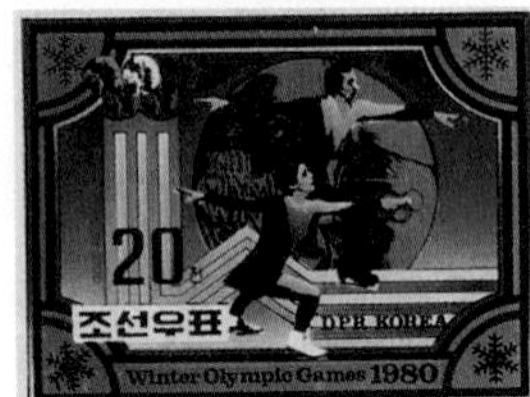

717 Irina Rodnina and Aleksandr Zaitsev

1980. Winter Olympic Gold Medal Winners.

N2010	**717** 20ch. multicoloured	4·00	1·75

718 "Soldier with Horse"　**719** Kepler, Astrolabe and Satellites

1980. 450th Death Anniv (1978) of Albrecht Durer (artist) (2nd issue).

N2012	**718** 20ch. multicoloured	5·00	1·50

1980. 350th Death Anniv of Johannes Kepler (astronomer).

N2014	**719** 20ch. multicoloured	2·50	90

720 German 1m. and Russian 30k. Zeppelin Stamps

1980. 3rd International Stamp Fair, Essen. Mult.

N2016	10ch. Type **720**	85	25
N2017	20ch. German 2m. and Russian 35k. Zeppelin stamps	1·75	45
N2018	30ch. German 4m. and Russian 1r. Zeppelin stamps	2·50	65

721 Shooting (Aleksandr Melentev)

1980. Olympic Medal Winners. Multicoloured.

N2020	10ch. Type **721**	30	15
N2021	20ch. Cycling (Robert Dill-Bundi)	3·25	75
N2022	25ch. Gymnastics (Stoyan Deltchev)	50	25
N2023	30ch. Wrestling (Chang Se Hong and Li Ho Pyong)	50	25
N2024	35ch. Weightlifting (Ho Bong Chol)	50	25
N2025	40ch. Running (Marita Koch)	50	30
N2026	50ch. Modern Pentathlon (Anatoli Starostin)	70	35

722 Tito

1980. President Tito of Yugoslavia Commemoration.

N2028	**722** 20ch. multicoloured	30	10

723 Convair CV 340 Airliner

1980. 25th Anniv of First Post-War Flight of Lufthansa.

N2029	**723** 20ch. multicoloured	4·75	1·75

724 Early Steam Locomotive

1980. 150th Anniv of Liverpool–Manchester Railway.

N2031	**724** 20ch. multicoloured	5·00	1·75

725 Steam and Electric Locomotives

1980. Centenary of First Electric Train.

N2033	**725** 20ch. multicoloured	5·00	1·75

726 Hammarskjold

1980. 75th Birth Anniv of Dag Hammarskjold (Former Secretary General of United Nations).

N2035	**726** 20ch. multicoloured	2·50	1·25

727 Bobby Fischer and Boris Spassky

1980. World Chess Championship, Merano.

N2037	**727** 20ch. multicoloured	5·50	1·75

728 Stolz

1980. Birth Centenary of Robert Stolz (composer).

N2039	**728** 20ch. multicoloured	2·50	75

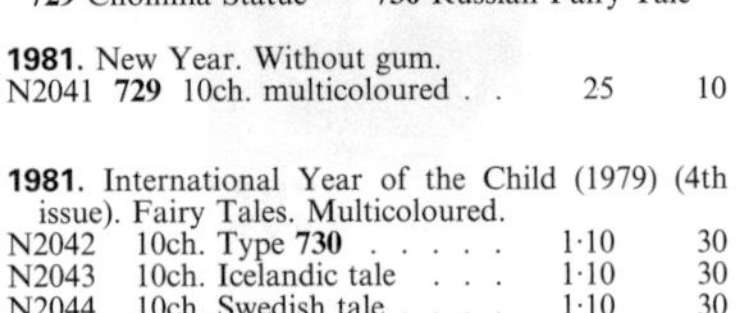

729 Chollima Statue　**730** Russian Fairy Tale

1981. New Year. Without gum.

N2041	**729** 10ch. multicoloured	25	10

1981. International Year of the Child (1979) (4th issue). Fairy Tales. Multicoloured.

N2042	10ch. Type **730**	1·10	30
N2043	10ch. Icelandic tale	1·10	30
N2044	10ch. Swedish tale	1·10	30
N2045	10ch. Irish tale	1·40	30
N2046	10ch. Italian tale	1·10	30
N2047	10ch. Japanese tale	1·10	30
N2048	10ch. German tale	1·10	30

731 Changgwang Street

1981. Changgwang Street, Pyongyang.

N2050	**731** 10ch. multicoloured	35	10

732 Footballers

1981. World Cup Football Championship, Spain (1982) (1st issue). Multicoloured.

N2051	10ch. Type **732**	2·25	45
N2052	20ch. Hitting ball past defender	2·25	45
N2053	30ch. Disputing possession of ball	2·25	45

See also Nos. N2055/9 and N2201/6.

733 Map, Emblem and World Cup

1981. World Cup Football Championship, Spain (1982) (2nd issue). Multicoloured.

N2055 10ch. Type **733** . . . . . 1·50 30
N2056 15ch. Footballers . . . . 1·50 30
N2057 20ch. Heading ball . . . . 1·50 30
N2058 25ch. Footballers (different) . . . . . . 1·50 30
N2059 30ch. Footballers (different) . . . . . . 1·50 30

734 Workers with Book and Marchers with Banner

1981. Implementation of Decision of the 6th Koreans' Party Congress. Multicoloured.

N2061 2ch. Type **734** 10 10
N2062 10ch. Worker with book 10 10
N2063 10ch. Workers and industrial plant 25 10
N2064 10ch. Electricity and coal (horiz) . . . . 1·25 25
N2065 10ch. Steel and non-ferrous metals (horiz) 25 10
N2066 10ch. Cement and fertilizers (horiz) 25 10
N2067 30ch. Fishing and fabrics (horiz) 35 10
N2068 40ch. Grain and harbour (horiz) 25 10
N2069 70ch. Clasped hands . . . 20 10
N2070 1wn. Hand holding torch 30 15

735 Footballers

1981. Gold Cup Football Championship, Uruguay.

N2071 **735** 20ch. multicoloured . . 2·50 75

736 Dornier Do-X Flying Boat

1981. "Naposta '81" International Stamp Exhibition, Stuttgart. Multicoloured.

N2073 10ch. Type **736** . . . . . 2·75 50
N2074 20ch. Airship LZ-120 "Bodensee" . . . . . . 2·75 50
N2075 30ch. "Gotz von Berlichingen" . . . . . 1·50 40

737 Telecommunications Equipment

1981. World Telecommunications Day.

N2077 **737** 10ch. multicoloured . . 1·75 20

738 "Iris pseudacorus"

1981. Flowers. Multicoloured.

N2078 10ch. Type **738** . . . . . 1·00 15
N2079 20ch. "Iris pallasii" . . . 1·25 20
N2080 30ch. "Gladiolus gandavensis" . . . . . 1·60 30

739 Austrian "WIPA 1981" and Rudolf Kirchschlager Stamps

1981. "WIPA 1981" International Stamp Exhibition, Vienna. Multicoloured.

N2081 20ch. Type **739** . . . . . 1·90 60
N2082 30ch. Austrian Maria Theresa and Franz Joseph stamps . . . . 2·50 80

740 Rings Exercise

741 Armed Workers

1981. Centenary of International Gymnastic Federation. Multicoloured.

N2084 10ch. Type **740** 50 20
N2085 15ch. Horse exercise . . . 60 20
N2086 20ch. Backwards somersault 80 20
N2087 25ch. Floor exercise . . . 90 25
N2088 30ch. Exercise with hoop 1·10 25

1981. 50th Anniv of Mingyuehgou Meeting.

N2090 **741** 10ch. multicoloured . . 20 10

742 Farm Building, Sukchon

1981. 20th Anniv of Agricultural Guidance System and Taean Work System.

N2091 **742** 10ch. green, black and gold 20 10
N2092 – 10ch. blue, black and gold 20 10

DESIGN: No. N2092, Taean Revolutionary Museum.

743 Woman and Banner

1981. 55th Anniv of Formation of Women's Anti-Japanese Association.

N2093 **743** 5wn. multicoloured . . 2·75 75

743a Scene from Opera

1981. 10th Anniv of "Sea of Blood" (opera).

N2094 **743a** 10wn. multicoloured.

744 Joan of Arc

1981. 550th Death Anniv of Joan of Arc. Multicoloured.

N2095 10ch. Type **744** . . . . . 2·00 50
N2096 10ch. Archangel Michael 2·25 50
N2097 70ch. Joan of Arc in armour . . . . 2·25 50

745 Torch, Mountains and Flag

1981. 55th Anniv of Down with Imperialism Union.

N2099 **745** 1wn.50 multicoloured 40 20

746 "Young Girl by the Window"

1981. 375th Birth Anniv of Rembrandt (artist). Multicoloured.

N2100 10ch. Type **746** 70 25
N2101 20ch. "Rembrandt's Mother" . . . . 1·50 45
N2102 30ch. "Saskia van Uylenburgh" . . . . . 2·00 70
N2103 40ch. "Pallas Athene" . . 2·50 90

747 Emblem and Banners over Pyongyang

1981. Symposium of Non-Aligned Countries on Food Self-Sufficiency, Pyongyang. Multicoloured.

N2105 10ch. Type **747** 20 10
N2106 50ch. Harvesting 50 10
N2107 90ch. Factories, tractors and marchers with banner 70 15

748 St. Paul's Cathedral

1981. Wedding of Prince of Wales (1st issue). Multicoloured.

N2108 10ch. Type **748** . . . . . 1·40 35
N2109 20ch. Great Britain Prince of Wales Investiture stamp . . . . 1·40 35
N2110 30ch. Lady Diana Spencer 1·40 35
N2111 40ch. Prince Charles in military uniform . . . . 1·40 35

See also Nos. N2120/3.

749 "Four Philosophers" (detail)

1981. Paintings by Rubens. Multicoloured.

N2113 10ch. Type **749** 40 20
N2114 15ch. "Portrait of Helena Fourment" 60 25
N2115 20ch. "Portrait of Isabella Brandt" 90 25
N2116 25ch. "Education of Maria de Medici" . . . . . . 1·10 30
N2117 30ch. "Helena Fourment and her Child" . . . . 1·40 35
N2118 40ch. "Helena Fourment in her Wedding Dress" 1·75 40

750 Royal Couple

1981. Wedding of Prince of Wales (2nd issue). Multicoloured.

N2120 10ch. Type **750** . . . . . 1·75 45
N2121 20ch. Couple on balcony after wedding . . . . . 1·75 45
N2122 30ch. Couple outside St. Paul's Cathedral . . 1·75 45
N2123 70ch. Full-length wedding portrait of couple . . . 1·75 45

751 Rowland Hill and Stamps

1981. "Philatokyo '81" International Stamp Exhibition. Multicoloured.

N2125 10ch. Korean 2ch. Seminar on Juche Idea stamp (41 × 29 mm) . . 75 20
N2126 10ch. Korean and 70ch. stamps (41 × 29 mm) 2·00 75
N2127 10ch. Type **751** . . . . . 2·00 75
N2128 20ch. Korean Fairy Tale stamps . . . . 1·75 40
N 2129 30ch. Japanese stamps . . 3·00 90

752 League Members and Flag

1981. Seventh League of Socialist Working Youth Congress, Pyongyang.

N2131 **752** 10ch. multicoloured . . 20 10
N2132 80ch. multicoloured . . 60 10

753 Government Palace, Sofia, Bulgarian Arms and Khan Asparuch

1981. 1300th Anniv of Bulgarian State.
N2133 **753** 10ch. multicoloured . . 25 10

754 Dimitrov

1981. Birth Centenary of Georgi Dimitrov (Bulgarian statesman).
N2134 **754** 10ch. multicoloured . . 25 10

755 Emblem, Boeing 747-200, City Hall and Mercedes "500"

1981. "Philatelia '81" International Stamp Fair, Frankfurt-am-Main.
N2135 **755** 20ch. multicoloured . . 2·50 35

756 Concorde, Airship "Graf Zeppelin" and Count Ferdinand von Zeppelin

1981. "Philexfrance 82" International Stamp Exhibition, Paris. Multicoloured. (a) As T **756**.
N2136 10ch. Type **756** . . . . . 2·75 40
N2137 20ch. Concorde, Breguet Provence airliner and Santos-Dumont's biplane "14 bis" . . . . 3·25 75
N2138 30ch. "Mona Lisa" (Leonardo da Vinci) and stamps . . . . . . 1·75 30

(b) Size 32 × 53 mm.
N2140 10ch. Hotel des Invalides, Paris . . . . 1·00 45
N2141 20ch. President Mitterrand of France . . . . . . 1·00 45
N2142 30ch. International Friendship Exhibition building . . . . 1·00 45
N2143 70ch. Kim Il Sung . . . . 1·00 45

757 Rising Sun **758** Emblem and Flags

1982. New Year.
N2144 **757** 10ch. multicoloured . . 30 10

1982. "Prospering Korea". Multicoloured.
N2145 2ch. Type **758** 15 10
N2146 10ch. Industry 25 10
N2147 10ch. Agriculture 25 10
N2148 10ch. Mining 45 10
N2149 10ch. Arts 25 10
N2150 10ch. Al Islet lighthouse, Uam-ri . . . . 2·50 40
N2151 40ch. Buildings 50 15

759 "The Hair-do"

1982. Birth Centenary of Pablo Picasso (artist). Multicoloured.
N2152 10ch. Type **759** 75 20
N2153 10ch. "Paulo on a donkey" . . . . 1·75 35
N2154 20ch. "Woman leaning on Arm" 90 25
N2155 20ch. "Harlequin" . . . . 1·75 35
N2156 25ch. "Child with Pigeon" 1·90 50
N2157 25ch. "Reading a Letter" 1·75 35
N2158 35ch. "Portrait of Gertrude Stein" . . . . 1·50 30
N2159 35ch. "Harlequin" (different) . . . . . . 1·75 35
N2160 80ch. "Minotaur" . . . . 1·75 35
N2161 90ch. "Mother with Child" . . . . 1·75 35

760 Fireworks over Pyongyang

1982. Kim Il Sung's 70th Birthday. Multicoloured.
N2163 10ch. Kim Il Sung's birthplace, Mangyongdae 20 10
N2164 10ch. Type **760** 20 10
N2165 10ch. "The Day will dawn on downtrodden Korea" (horiz) 20 10
N2166 10ch. Signalling start of Pochonbo Battle (horiz) 20 10
N2167 10ch. Kim Il Sung starting Potong River project (horiz) 20 10
N2168 10ch. Embracing bereaved children (horiz) 20 10
N2169 10ch. Kim Il Sung as Supreme Commander (horiz) 20 10
N2170 10ch. "On the Road of Advance" (horiz) . . . 20 10
N2171 10ch. Kim Il Sung kindling flame of Chollima Movement, Kansong Steel Plant (horiz) 75 25
N2172 10ch. Kim Il Sung talking to peasants (horiz) . . . 20 10
N2173 10ch. Kim Il Sung fixing site of reservoir (horiz) 30 10
N2174 20ch. Kim Il Sung visiting Komdok Valley (horiz) 75 25
N2175 20ch. Kim Il Sung visiting Red Flag Company (horiz) 20 10
N2176 20ch. Kim Il Sung teaching Juche farming methods (horiz) 20 10
N2177 20ch. Kim Il Sung visiting iron works (horiz) . . . 35 10
N2178 20ch. Kim Il Sung talking with smelters (horiz) . . 35 10
N2179 20ch. Kim Il Sung at chemical plant (horiz) 45 10
N2180 20ch. Kim Il Sung with fishermen (horiz) . . . 40 10

761 Soldier saluting

1982. 50th Anniv of People's Army.
N2182 **761** 10ch. multicoloured . . 25 10

762 "The Bagpiper" (Durer) **763** Surveyors

1982. 4th Essen International Stamp Fair.
N2183 **762** 30ch. multicoloured . . 3·75 40

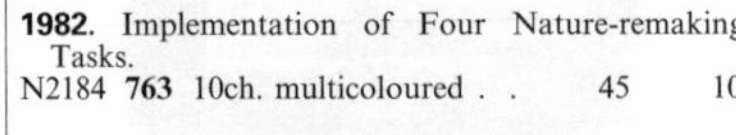
1982. Implementation of Four Nature-remaking Tasks.
N2184 **763** 10ch. multicoloured . . 45 10

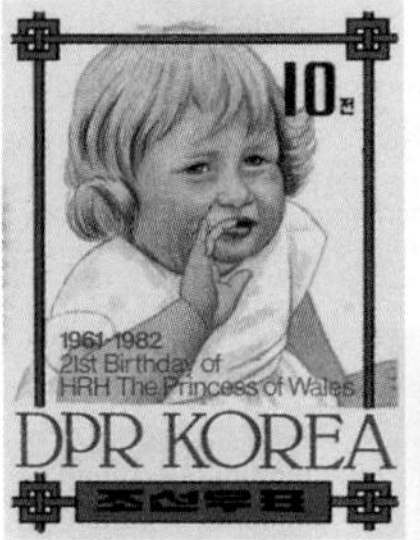

764 Princess as Baby **765** Tower of the Juche Idea, Pyongyang

1982. 21st Birthday of Princess of Wales.
N2185 **764** 10ch. multicoloured . . 30 20
N2186 – 20ch. multicoloured . . 65 35
N2187 – 30ch. multicoloured . . 75 45
N2188 – 50ch. multicoloured . . 1·00 40
N2189 – 60ch. multicoloured . . 1·00 40
N2190 – 70ch. multicoloured . . 1·00 40
N2191 – 80ch. multicoloured . . 1·00 40
DESIGNS: 20 to 80ch. Princess at various ages.

1982.
2193 **765** 2wn. multicoloured . . . 1·25 30
2194 – 3wn. orange and black 1·75 40
DESIGN (26 × 38 mm): 3wn. Arch of Triumph.

766 Tiger

1982. Tigers.
N2195 **766** 20ch. multicoloured . . 1·25 35
N2196 – 30ch. multicoloured . . 1·90 35
N2197 – 30ch. mult (horiz) . . 2·75 45
N2198 – 40ch. mult (horiz) . . 2·75 45
N2199 – 80ch. mult (horiz) . . 2·75 45
DESIGNS: 30 to 80ch. Tigers.

767 Group 1 Countries

1982. World Cup Football Championship, Spain (3rd issue). Multicoloured.
N2201 10ch. Type **767** 45 20
N2202 20ch. Group 2 countries 1·00 25
N2203 30ch. Group 3 countries 1·40 30
N2204 40ch. Group 4 countries 1·75 40
N2205 50ch. Group 5 countries 2·00 50
N2206 60ch. Group 6 countries 2·25 50

768 Rocket Launch **769** Charlotte von Stein

1982. The Universe. Multicoloured.
N2208 10ch. Type **768** . . . . . 1·25 40
N2209 20ch. Spaceship over globe 1·25 40
N2210 80ch. Spaceship between globe and moon . . . . 1·50 40

1982. 150th Death Anniv of Johann von Goethe (writer). Multicoloured.
N2212 10ch. Type **769** 50 25
N2213 10ch. Goethe's mother . . 1·50 45
N2214 20ch. Goethe's sister . . . 75 30
N2215 20ch. Angelika Kauffmann 1·50 45
N2216 25ch. Charlotte Buff . . . 90 35
N2217 25ch. Anna Amalia . . . . 1·50 45
N2218 35ch. Lili Schonemann . . 1·25 40
N2219 35ch. Charlotte von Lengefeld . . . . 1·50 45
N2220 80ch. Goethe . . . . . . 1·60 45

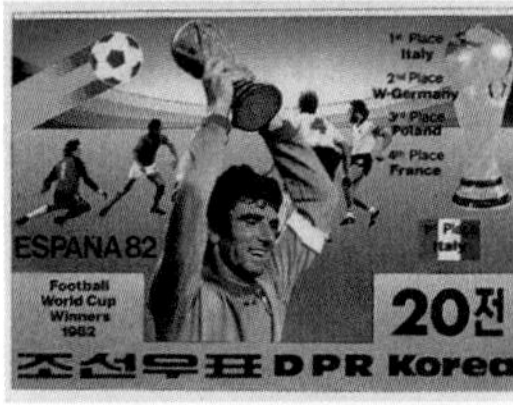

770 Player holding aloft World Cup

1982. World Cup Football Championship Results. Multicoloured.
N2222 20ch. Type **770** . . . . . 1·25 30
N2223 30ch. Group of players with World Cup . . . . 1·75 50
N2224 30ch. Type **770** . . . . . 2·50 65
N2225 40ch. As No. N2203 . . . 2·50 65
N2226 80ch. King Juan Carlos of Spain and two players with World Cup . . . . 2·50 65

771 Princess and Prince William of Wales

1982. 1st Wedding Anniv of Prince and Princess of Wales.
N2228 **771** 30ch. multicoloured . . 2·75 90

772 Royal Couple with Prince William

1982. Birth of Prince William of Wales. Mult.
N2230 10ch. Couple with Prince William (different) . . . 75 25
N2231 10ch. Princess of Wales holding bouquet . . . . 1·50 75
N2232 20ch. Couple with Prince William (different) . . . 90 30
N2233 20ch. Prince Charles carrying baby, and Princess of Wales . . . 1·50 75
N2234 30ch. Type **772** . . . . . 1·00 40
N2235 30ch. Prince Charles carrying baby, and Princess of Wales (different) . . . . . . 1·50 75
N2236 40ch. Princess with baby 1·40 45
N2237 40ch. Prince and Princess of Wales (horiz) . . . . 2·40 95

N2238 50ch. Princess with baby (different) 1·75 50
N2239 50ch. Prince and Princess of Wales in evening dress (horiz) 2·40 95
N2240 80ch. Couple with Prince William (different) 1·50 75
N2241 80ch. Prince Charles holding baby, and Princess of Wales (horiz) 2·40 95

773 Airship "Nulli Secundus II", 1908

1982. Bicentenary of Manned Flight (1st issue). Multicoloured.
N2243 10ch. Type **773** 1·25 40
N2244 10ch. Pauley and Durs Egg's dirigible balloon "The Dolphin", 1818 2·50 60
N2245 20ch. Tissandier Brothers' airship, 1883 1·50 50
N2246 20ch. Guyton de Morveau's balloon with oars, 1784 2·50 60
N2247 30ch. Parseval airship PL-VII, 1912 2·00 60
N2248 30ch. Sir George Cayley's airship design, 1837 2·50 60
N2249 40ch. Count de Lennox's balloon "Eagle", 1834 2·25 60
N2250 40ch. Camille Vert's balloon "Poisson Volant", 1859 2·50 60
N2251 80ch. Dupuy de Lome's airship, 1872 2·50 60

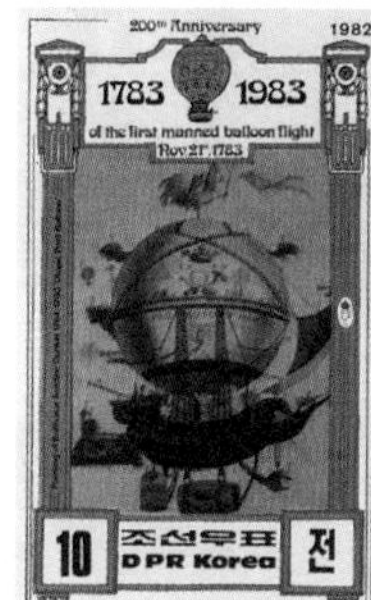

774 "Utopic Balloon Post" (Balthasar Antoine Dunker)

1982. Bicentenary of Manned Flight (2nd issue). Multicoloured.
N2253 10ch. Type **774** 1·50 40
N2254 10ch. Montgolfier balloon at Versailles, 1783 3·00 60
N2255 20ch. "... and they fly into heaven and have no wings ..." 2·00 50
N2256 20ch. Montgolfier Brothers' balloon, 1783 3·00 60
N2257 30ch. Pierre Testu-Brissy's balloon ascent on horseback, 1798 2·50 60
N2258 30ch. Charles's hydrogen balloon landing at Nesle, 1783 3·00 60
N2259 40ch. Gaston Tissandier's test flight of "Zenith", 1875 3·00 60
N2260 40ch. Blanchard and Jeffries' balloon flight over English Channel, 1785 3·00 60
N2261 80ch. Henri Giffard's balloon "Le Grand Ballon Captif" at World Fair, 1878 3·00 60

775 Turtle with Scroll

1982. Tale of the Hare. Multicoloured.
N2263 10ch. Type **775** 1·00 15
N2264 20ch. Hare riding on turtle 1·50 20
N2265 30ch. Hare and turtle before Dragon King 1·75 30
N2266 40ch. Hare back on land 2·25 40

776 Flag, Red Book and City

777 Tower of Juche Idea

1982. 10th Anniv of Socialist Constitution.
N2267 **776** 10ch. multicoloured 25 10

1983. New Year.
N2268 **777** 10ch. multicoloured 15 10

778 Children reading "Saenal"

1983. 55th Anniv of "Saenal" Newspaper.
N2269 **778** 10ch. multicoloured 50 10

779 "Man in Oriental Costume"

1983. Paintings by Rembrandt. Multicoloured.
N2270 10ch. Type **779** 60 20
N2271 10ch. "Child with dead Peacocks" (detail) 2·00 40
N2272 20ch. "The Noble Slav" 1·25 30
N2273 20ch. "Old Man in Fur Hat" 2·00 40
N2274 30ch. "Dr. Tulp's Anatomy Lesson" (detail) 3·25 50
N2275 30ch. "Portrait of a fashionable Couple" 2·00 40
N2276 40ch. "Two Scholars disputing" 1·50 35
N2277 40ch. "Woman with Child" 2·00 40
N2278 80ch. "Woman holding an Ostrich Feather Fan" 2·00 40

780 Airships "Gross Basenach II" and "Graf Zepplin" over Cologne

1983. "Luposta" International Air Mail Exhibition, Cologne. Multicoloured.
N2280 30ch. Type **780** 3·00 90
N2281 40ch. Parsevel airship PL-II over Cologne 3·00 90

781 Banner and Monument

1983. 50th Anniv of Wangjaesan Meeting.
N2283 **781** 10ch. multicoloured 20 10

782 Karl Marx

1983. Death Centenary of Karl Marx.
N2284 **782** 10ch. multicoloured 50 25

783 Scholar, Marchers and Map of Journey

1983. 60th Anniv of Thousand-ri Journey for Learning.
N2285 **783** 10ch. multicoloured 1·00 10

784 "Madonna of the Goldfinch"

1983. 500th Birth Anniv of Raphael. Multicoloured.
N2286 10ch. Type **784** 1·75 50
N2287 20ch. "The School of Athens" (detail) 1·50 40
N2288 30ch. "Madonna of the Grand Duke" 1·75 45
N2289 50ch. "Madonna of the Chair" 1·90 45
N2290 50ch. "Madonna of the Lamb" 1·50 50
N2291 80ch. "The Beautiful Gardener" 1·50 50

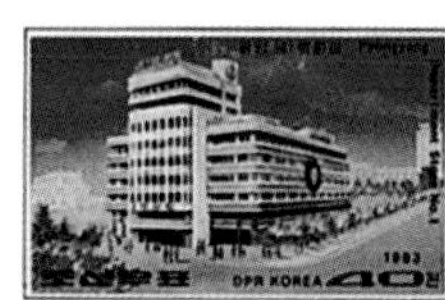

785 Department Store No. 1

1983. Pyongyang Buildings. Multicoloured.
N2293 2ch. Chongryu Restaurant 20 10
N2294 10ch. Part of Munsu Street 30 10
N2295 10ch. Ice Rink 40 10
N2296 40ch. Type **785** 60 15
N2297 70ch. Grand People's Study House 75 25

786 Emblem and Crowd

788 Satellite, Masts and Dish Aerial

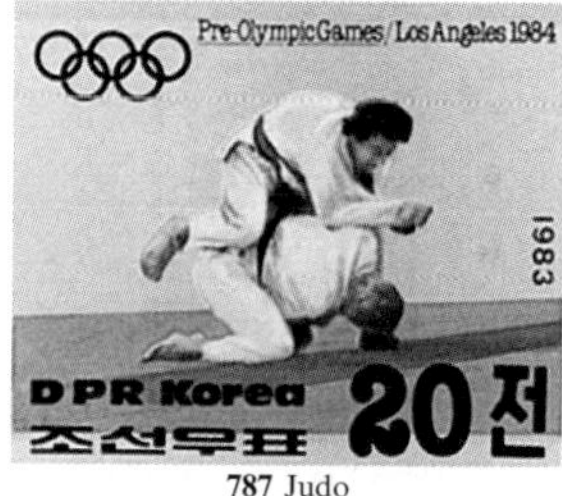

787 Judo

1983. 5th Anniv of International Institute of Juche Idea.
N2298 **786** 10ch. multicoloured 15 10

1983. Olympic Games, Los Angeles (1st issue). Multicoloured.
N2299 20ch. Type **787** 65 40
N2300 20ch. Wrestling 1·25 40
N2301 30ch. Judo (different) (value in gold) 65 40
N2302 30ch. Judo (different) (value in black) 1·25 40
N2303 40ch. Boxing 65 40
N2304 40ch. Li Ho Jun (1972 shooting gold medalist) 1·25 40
N2305 50ch. Weightlifting 65 40
N2306 50ch. Wrestling (different) 1·25 40
N2307 80ch. Boxing (different) 1·25 40
See also Nos. N2359/64.

1983. World Communications Year (1st issue).
N2309 **788** 10ch. multicoloured 1·50 20
See also Nos. N2349/53.

789 Emblem, Giant Panda and Stamp

1983. "Tembal 83" International Thematic Stamp Exhibition, Basel. Multicoloured.
N2310 20ch. Type **789** 1·75 35
N2311 30ch. Emblem, flag and Basel Town Post stamp 1·90 35

790 "Colourful Cow" (kogge), 1402

1983. Old Ships. Multicoloured.
N2312 20ch. Type **790** 1·10 45
N2313 20ch. "Kwi-Sun" ("turtle" ship), 1592 2·50 75
N2314 35ch. "Great Harry" (warship), 1555 1·50 55
N2315 35ch. Admiral Li Sun Sin and "turtle" ship 2·50 75
N2316 50ch. "Eagle of Lubeck" (galleon), 1567 2·10 70
N2317 50ch. "Merkur" (full-rigged sailing ship), 1847 2·50 75
N2318 80ch. "Herzogin Elisabeth" (cadet ship) 2·50 75

791 "Locomotion", 1825, Great Britain

1983. Railway Locomotives. Multicoloured.
N2320 20ch. Type **791** 1·50 60
N2321 20ch. "Drache", 1848, Germany 4·75 1·00
N2322 35ch. "Adler", 1835, Germany 2·00 80
N2323 35ch. Korean steam locomotive 4·50 1·00
N2324 50ch. "Austria", 1837, Austria 3·25 80
N2325 50ch. Bristol and Exeter Railway steam locomotive, 1853 4·75 1·00
N2326 80ch. Caledonian Railway locomotive, 1859 4·75 1·00

792 Map, Hand and Weapons

1983. 10th Anniv of Publication of Five-point Policy for Korea's Reunification.
N2328 **792** 10ch. multicoloured . . 25 10

793 Emblem, Tower of Juche Idea and Fireworks

1983. World Conference on Journalists against Imperialism and for Friendship and Peace, Pyongyang. Multicoloured.
N2329 10ch. Type **793** 20 10
N2330 40ch. Emblem and rainbow and clasped hands 40 15
N2331 70ch. Emblem, map and hand with raised forefinger 50 20

794 Worker and Banners

1983. "Let's Create the Speed of the 80s".
N2332 **794** 10ch. multicoloured . . 25 10

795 Soldier and Rejoicing Crowd

1983. 30th Anniv of Victory in Liberation War.
N2333 **795** 10ch. multicoloured . . 25 10

796 "Gorch Fock" (cadet barque) and Korean 1978 2ch. Stamp

1983. "Bangkok 1983" International Stamp Exhibition.
N2334 **796** 40ch. multicoloured . . 3·00 1·25

797 Skiing

1983. Winter Olympic Games, Sarajevo (1984). Multicoloured.
N2336 10ch. Type **797** 55 25
N2337 20ch. Figure skating (vert) 2·00 45
N2338 30ch. Skating (pair) . . . 1·60 55
N2339 50ch. Ski jumping . . . . 1·60 55
N2340 50ch. Ice hockey (vert) . . 2·00 45
N2341 80ch. Speed skating (vert) 2·00 45

798 Workers and Soldier with Books

1983. 35th Anniv of Korean People's Democratic Republic.
N2343 **798** 10ch. multicoloured . . 35 10

799 Archery

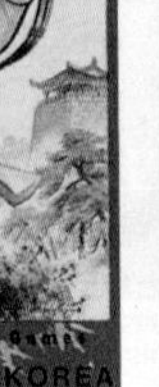

800 Girls holding Hands

1983. Folk Games. Multicoloured.
N2344 10ch. Type **799** . . . . . 2·50 40
N2345 10ch. Flying kites 65 20
N2346 40ch. See-sawing 65 20
N2347 40ch. Swinging 65 20

1983. Korean–Chinese Friendship.
N2348 **800** 10ch. multicoloured . . 50 10

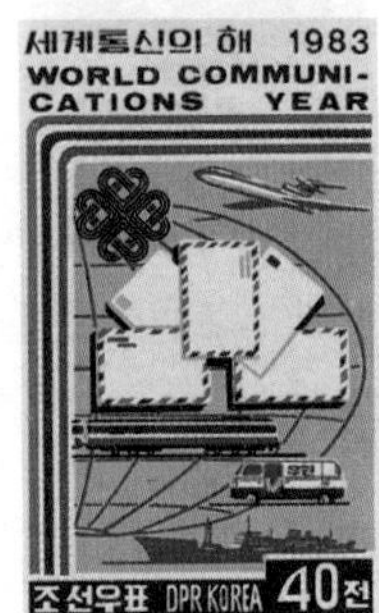

801 Envelopes and Forms of Transport

1983. World Communications Year (2nd issue). Multicoloured.
N2349 30ch. Mail van, motorcyclist and hand holding magazines . . . 4·75 90
N2350 30ch. Satellite, globe and dish aerial . . . . . . 1·25 40
N2351 40ch. Type **801** . . . . . 4·75 1·10
N2352 40ch. Television cameraman . . . . 1·25 40
N2353 80ch. Telephone and aerial 1·25 40

802 Portrait

1983. Paintings by Rubens. Multicoloured.
N2355 40ch. Type **802** . . . . . 1·40 60
N2356 40ch. Portrait (different) (horiz) . . . . 1·75 75
N2357 80ch. "The Sentencing of Midas" (horiz) . . . . 1·75 75

803 Sprinting

1983. Olympic Games, Los Angeles (2nd issue). Multicoloured.
N2359 10ch. Type **803** 75 20
N2360 20ch. Show jumping . . . 1·75 45
N2361 30ch. Cycling . . . . . . 3·00 55
N2362 50ch. Handball . . . . . 2·00 60
N2363 50ch. Fencing . . . . . . 1·75 45
N2364 80ch. Gymnastics . . . . 1·75 45

804 "St. Catherine"

805 Kimilsungflower

804a Cat

1983. 450th Death Anniv (1984) of Antonio Correggio (artist). Multicoloured.
N2366 20ch. Type **804** . . . . . 1·75 60
N2367 20ch. "Morning" (detail) 2·50 75
N2368 35ch. "Madonna" . . . . 1·75 60
N2369 35ch. "Morning" (different) . . . . . . 2·50 75
N2370 50ch. "Madonna with St. John" . . . . 1·75 60
N2371 50ch. "St. Catherine" (different) . . . . . . 2·50 75
N2372 80ch. "Madonna and Child" . . . . 2·50 75

1983. Cats. Multicoloured, frame colour given.
N2373a **804a** 10ch. green . . . . 1·25 10
N2373b – 10ch. gold . . . . . 1·25 10
N2373c – 10ch. blue . . . . . 1·25 10
N2373d – 10ch. red . . . . . 1·25 10
N2373e – 10ch. silver . . . . 1·25 10
DESIGNS: Different cats' heads.

1983. New Year.
N2374 **805** 10ch. multicoloured . . 85 10

806 Worker and Workers' Party Flag

1984. "Under the Leadership of the Workers' Party". Multicoloured.
N2375 10ch. Type **806** 25 10
N2376 10ch. Ore-dressing plant No. 3, Komdok General Mining Enterprise, and Party Flag 40 10

807 Farm Worker, Rice and Maize

1984. 20th Anniv of Publication of "Theses of the Socialist Rural Question in Our Country".
N2377 **807** 10ch. multicoloured . . 25 10

808 Changdok School, Chilgol

1984. Kim Il Sung's 72nd Birthday.
N2378 **808** 5ch. green, black & blue 25 10
N2379 – 10ch. multicoloured . . 25 10
DESIGN: 10ch. Birthplace, Mangyongdae, and rejoicing crowd.

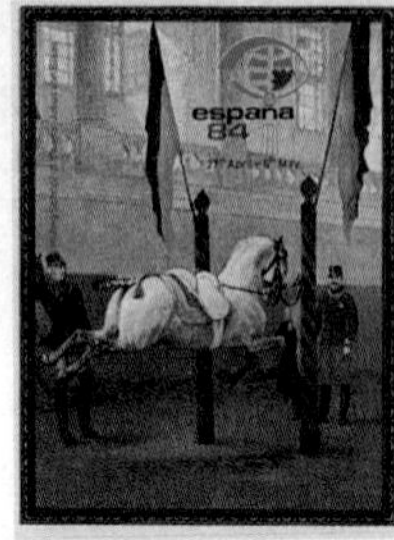

809 "Spanish Riding School" (Julius von Blaas)

1984. "Espana 84" International Stamp Exhibition, Madrid. Multicoloured.
N2380 10ch. Type **809** . . . . . 1·75 50
N2381 20ch. "Ferdinand of Austria" (Rubens) . . . 1·75 50

810 "La Donna Velata"

812 Construction Site

811 Map and Second Stage Pumping Station

1984. 500th Birth Anniv (1983) of Raphael (artist). Multicoloured.
N2383 10ch. "Portrait of Agnolo Doni" . . . . 1·50 50
N2384 20ch. Type **810** . . . . . 1·50 50
N2385 30ch. "Portrait of Jeanne d'Aragon" . . . . . . 1·50 50

1984. 25th Anniv of Kiyang Irrigation System.
N2387 **811** 10ch. multicoloured . . 50 10

1984. Construction on Five District Fronts.
N2388 **812** 10ch. red, black & yell 50 10

813 Bobsleighing (East Germany)

1984. Winter Olympic Games Medal Winners. Multicoloured.
N2389 10ch. Ski jumping (Matti Nykaenen) . . . . . . 1·75 50
N2390 20ch. Speed skating (Karin Enke) . . . . 1·50 40
N2391 20ch. Slalom (Max Julen) 1·75 50
N2392 30ch. Type **813** . . . . . 1·50 40
N2393 30ch. Downhill skiing (Maria Walliser) . . . 1·75 50
N2394 40ch. Cross-country skiing (Thomas Wassberg) . . 2·75 60
N2395 80ch. Cross-country skiing (Marja-Liisa Hamalainen) . . . . . 2·75 60

814 Steam Locomotive, 1919

1984. Essen International Stamp Fair. Mult.
N2397 20ch. Streamlined steam locomotive, 1939 . . . 4·00 65
N2398 30ch. Type **814** . . . . . 4·00 65

815 "Mlle. Fiocre in the Ballet 'La Source' "

1984. 150th Birth Anniv of Edgar Degas (artist). Multicoloured.
N2400 10ch. Type **815** . . . . . 1·50 25
N2401 20ch. "The Dance Foyer at the Rue le Peletier Opera" . . . . 2·50 25
N2402 30ch. "Race Meeting" . . 3·75 40

816 Map of Pyongnam Irrigation System and Reservoir

1984. Irrigation Experts Meeting, Pyongyang.
N2404 **816** 2ch. multicoloured . . 40 10

817 Korean Stamp and Building

818 Crowd and Banners

1984. U.P.U. Congress Stamp Exn, Hamburg.
N2405 **817** 20ch. multicoloured . . 3·00 40

1984. Proposal for Tripartite Talks.
N2407 **818** 10ch. multicoloured . . 40 10

819 Nobel experimenting

1984. 150th Birth Anniv (1983) of Alfred Bernhard Nobel (inventor). Multicoloured.
N2408 20ch. Type **819** . . . . . 3·00 45
N2409 30ch. Portrait of Nobel . . 3·00 45

820 Drinks, Tinned Food, Clothes and Flats

1984. Improvements of Living Standards.
N2411 **820** 10ch. multicoloured . . 55 10

821 Sunhwa School, Mangyongdae

1984. School of Kim Hyong Jik (Kim Il Sung's Father).
N2412 **821** 10ch. multicoloured . . 40 10

822 Armed Crowd with Banners

1984. 65th Anniv of Kuandian Conference.
N2413 **822** 10ch. multicoloured . . 40 10

823 "Thunia bracteata"

1984. Flowers. Multicoloured.
N2414 10ch. "Cattleya loddigesii" 1·00 10
N2415 20ch. Type **823** . . . . . 1·25 25
N2416 30ch. "Phalaenopsis amabilis" . . . . 1·75 40

824 Swordfish and Trawler

1984. Fishing Industry. Multicoloured.
N2418 5ch. Type **824** . . . . . . 1·25 15
N2419 10ch. Blue marlin and trawler . . . . 1·75 25
N2420 40ch. Sailfish and game fishing launch . . . . . 4·50 1·25

825 Revolutionary Museum, Chilgol

1984.
N2421 **825** 10ch. multicoloured . . 40 10

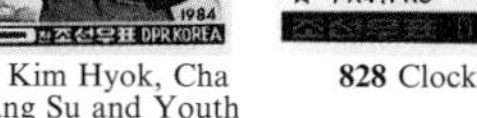
826 Kim Hyok, Cha Gwang Su and Youth

828 Clock Face

827 Inauguration of a French Railway Line, 1860

1984. "Let's All become the Kim Hyoks and Cha Gwang Sus of the '80s".
N2422 **826** 10ch. multicoloured . . 60 10

1984. Centenary (1983) of "Orient Express". Multicoloured.
N2423 10ch. Type **827** . . . . . 1·40 25
N2424 20ch. Opening of a British railway line, "1821" . . 2·50 50
N2425 30ch. Inauguration of Paris–Rouen line, 1843 3·00 90

1984. Centenary of Greenwich Meridian.
N2427 **828** 10ch. multicoloured . . 2·50 1·00

829 Grand Theatre, Hamburg

830 Turning on Machinery

1984.
N2429 **829** 10ch. blue 40 10

1984. Automation of Industry.
N2430 **830** 40ch. multicoloured . . 60 30

831 "Dragon Angler"

1984. Paintings. Multicoloured.
N2431 10ch. Type **831** . . . . . 1·00 10
N2432 20ch. "Ox Driver" (Kim Du Ryang) (47 × 35 mm) . . . . . 1·25 25
N2433 30ch. "Bamboo" (Kim Jin U) (47 × 35 mm) . . . . 1·75 40

832 Tsiolkovsky

1984. K. E. Tsiolkovsky (space scientist). Mult.
N2435 20ch. Type **832** 90 25
N2436 30ch. "Sputnik" orbiting Earth . . . . 1·25 40

833 "Pongdaesan"

1984. Container Ships. Multicoloured.
N2438 10ch. Type **833** 95 10
N2439 20ch. "Ryongnamsan" . . 1·10 35
N2440 30ch. "Rungrado" . . . . 1·50 55

834 Caracal

1984. Animals. Multicoloured.
N2442 10ch. Spotted hyenas . . . 60 10
N2443 20ch. Type **834** 90 25
N2444 30ch. Black-backed jackals 1·25 40
N2445 40ch. Foxes . . . . 1·60 60

835 Marie Curie

836 Chestnut-eared Aracari ("Toucan")

1984. 50th Anniv of Marie Curie (physicist).
N2447 **835** 10ch. multicoloured . . 2·00 25

1984. Birds. Multicoloured.
N2449 10ch. Hoopoe . . . . . . 1·40 20
N2450 20ch. South African crowned cranes ("Crowned Crane") . . 1·75 50
N2451 30ch. Saddle-bill stork ("Stork") . . . . 2·50 70
N2452 40ch. Type **836** . . . . . 3·50 90

837 Cosmonaut

1984. Space Exploration. Multicoloured.
N2454 10ch. Type **837** 50 10
N2455 20ch. Cosmonaut on space-walk 75 25
N2456 30ch. Cosmonaut (different) . . . . . . 1·00 40

838 "Arktika"

1984. Russian Ice-breakers. Multicoloured.
N2458 20ch. Type **838** . . . . . 1·25 35
N2459 30ch. "Ermak" . . . . . 1·75 50

839 Mendeleev

1984. 150th Birth Anniv of Dmitri Mendeleev (chemist).
N2461 **839** 10ch. multicoloured . . 95 10

840 Kim Il Sung in U.S.S.R.

1984. Kim Il Sung's Visits to Eastern Europe. Multicoloured.
N2463 10ch. Type **840** 60 10
N2464 10ch. In Poland 60 10
N2465 10ch. In German Democratic Republic . . 60 10
N2466 10ch. In Czechoslovakia 60 10
N2467 10ch. In Hungary 60 10
N2468 10ch. In Bulgaria 60 10
N2469 10ch. In Rumania 60 10

841 Freesia

1985. New Year.
N2471 **841** 10ch. multicoloured . . 75 10

842 Journey Route, Steam Locomotive and Memorials

1985. 60th Anniv of 1000 ri Journey by Kim Il Sung. Multicoloured.
N2472 5ch. Type **842** . . . . . . 1·25 10
N2473 10ch. Boy trumpeter and schoolchildren following route 50 10
Nos. N2472/3 were issued together, se-tenant, forming a composite design.

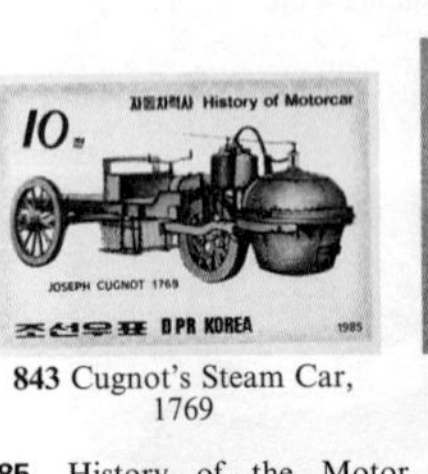
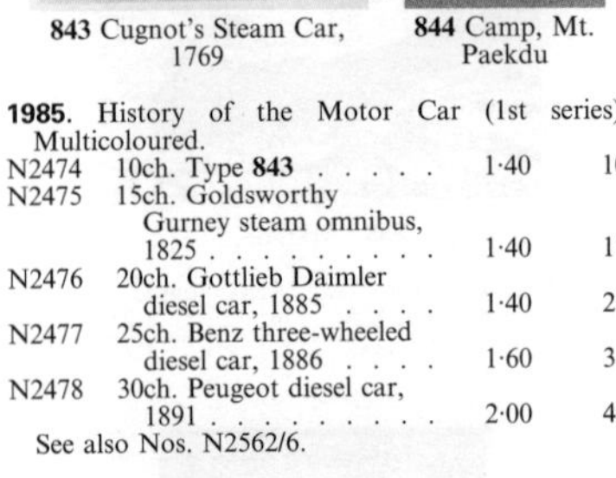

843 Cugnot's Steam Car, 1769 **844** Camp, Mt. Paekdu

1985. History of the Motor Car (1st series). Multicoloured.
N2474 10ch. Type **843** . . . . . 1·40 10
N2475 15ch. Goldsworthy Gurney steam omnibus, 1825 . . . . 1·40 15
N2476 20ch. Gottlieb Daimler diesel car, 1885 . . . . 1·40 25
N2477 25ch. Benz three-wheeled diesel car, 1886 . . . . 1·60 35
N2478 30ch. Peugeot diesel car, 1891 . . . . 2·00 40
See also Nos. N2562/6.

1985. Korean Revolution Headquarters.
N2480 **844** 10ch. multicoloured . . 40 20

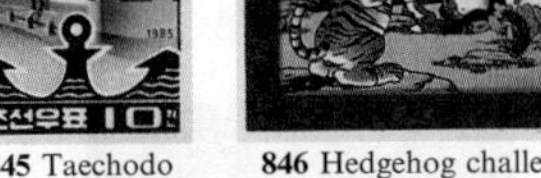

845 Taechodo Lighthouse **846** Hedgehog challenges Tiger

1985. Lighthouses. Multicoloured.
N2481 10ch. Type **845** . . . . . 1·75 10
N2482 20ch. Sodo . . . . 1·90 30
N2483 30ch. Pido . . . . 2·25 45
N2484 40ch. Suundo . . . . . . 2·75 70

1985. "The Hedgehog defeats the Tiger" (fable). Multicoloured.
N2485 10ch. Type **846** 60 10
N2486 20ch. Tiger goes to stamp on rolled-up hedgehog 90 25
N2487 30ch. Hedgehog clings to tiger's nose . . . . . . 1·25 40
N2488 35ch. Tiger flees . . . . . 1·40 50
N2489 40ch. Tiger crawls before hedgehog . . . . 1·60 60

847 "Pleurotus cornucopiae" **848** West Germany v. Hungary, 1954

1985. Fungi. Multicoloured.
N2490 10ch. Type **847** . . . . . 1·10 10
N2491 20ch. Oyster fungus . . . 1·40 25
N2492 30ch. "Catathelasma ventricosum" . . . . . 1·90 40

1985. World Cup Football Championship Finals.
N2493 **848** 10ch. black, buff & brn 60 10
N2494 – 10ch. multicoloured . . 60 10
N2495 – 20ch. black, buff & brn 90 25
N2496 – 20ch. multicoloured . . 90 25
N2497 – 30ch. black, buff & brn 1·25 40
N2498 – 30ch. multicoloured . . 1·25 40
N2499 – 40ch. black, buff & brn 1·60 60
N2500 – 40ch. multicoloured . . 1·60 60
DESIGNS—VERT: No. N2496 West Germany v. Netherlands, 1974; N2499, England v. West Germany, 1966. HORIZ: No. N2494, Brazil v. Italy, 1970; N2495, Brazil v. Sweden, 1958; N2497, Brazil v. Czechoslovakia, 1962; N2498, Argentina v. Netherlands, 1968; N2500, Italy v. West Germany, 1982.

849 Date and Kim Il Sung's Birthplace **850** Horn Player

1985. 73rd Birthday of Kim Il Sung.
N2502 **849** 10ch. multicoloured . . 40 10

1985. 4th-century Musical Instruments. Mult.
N2503 10ch. Type **850** . . . . . 1·40 10
N2504 20ch. So (pipes) player . . 1·40 25

851 Chongryon Hall, Tokyo **852** Common Marmoset

1985. 30th Anniv of Chongryon (General Association of Korean Residents in Japan).
N2505 **851** 10ch. brown 40 10

1985. Mammals. Multicoloured.
N2506 5ch. Type **852** 85 10
N2507 10ch. Ring-tailed lemur . . 85 10

854 Buenos Aires and Argentina 1982 Stamp **855** Dancer and Gymnast

1985. "Argentina '85" International Stamp Exhibition, Buenos Aires. Multicoloured.
N2509 10ch. Type **854** 75 10
N2510 20ch. Iguacu Falls and Argentina 1984 and North Korea 1978 stamps (horiz) . . . . . 2·50 25

1985. 12th World Youth and Students' Festival, Moscow. Multicoloured.
N2512 10ch. Type **855** 60 10
N2513 20ch. Spassky Tower, Moscow, and Festival emblem 90 25
N2514 40ch. Youths of different races . . . . 1·60 60

856 Peace Pavilion, Youth Park **857** Liberation Celebrations

1985. Pyongyang Buildings.
N2515 **856** 2ch. black and green 20 10
N2516 – 40ch. brown & lt brn 45 20
DESIGN: 40ch. Multi-storey flats, Chollima Street.

1985. 40th Anniv of Liberation.
N2517 – 5ch. red, black and blue 20 10
N2518 – 10ch. multicoloured . . 40 10
N2519 – 10ch. brown, blk & grn 40 10
N2520 – 10ch. multicoloured . . 40 10
N2521 **857** 10ch. yellow, blk & red 40 10
N2522 – 10ch. red, orange & blk 40 10
N2523 – 40ch. multicoloured . . 60 20
DESIGNS—HORIZ: No. N2517, Soldiers with rifles and flag; N2518, Crowd with banners and Flame of Juche; N2519, Korean and Soviet soldiers raising arms; N2520, Japanese soldiers laying down weapons; N2523, Students bearing banners. VERT: No. N2522, Liberation Tower, Moran Hill, Pyongyang.

858 Halley and Comet

1985. Appearance of Halley's Comet. Multicoloured.
N2525 10ch. Type **858** 90 10
N2526 20ch. Diagram of comet's flight and space probe 1·25 25

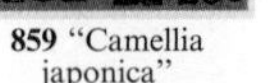

859 "Camellia japonica" **861** Party Founding Museum

860 "Hunting"

1985. Flowers. Multicoloured.
N2528 10ch. "Hippeastrum hybridum" 90 10
N2529 20ch. Type **859** . . . . . 1·25 25
N2530 30ch. "Cyclamen persicum" . . . . . . 1·75 40

1985. Koguryo Culture.
N2531 10ch. "Hero" (vert) . . . 60 10
N2532 15ch. "Heroine" (vert) . . 75 15
N2533 20ch. "Flying Fairy" . . . 90 25
N2534 25ch. Type **860** . . . . . 1·10 35

1985. 40th Anniv of Korean Workers' Party. Multicoloured.
N2536 5ch. Type **861** 20 10
N2537 10ch. Soldier with gun and workers 40 10
N2538 10ch. Soldiers and flag . . 40 10
N2539 40ch. Statue of worker, peasant and intellectual holding aloft party emblem 60 20

862 Arch of Triumph, Pyongyang **863** Colosseum, Rome, and N. Korea 1975 10ch. Stamp

1985. 40th Anniv of Kim Il Sung's Return.
N2541 **862** 10ch. brown and green 40 10

1985. "Italia '85" International Stamp Exhibition, Rome. Multicoloured.
N2542 10ch. Type **863** 60 10
N2543 20ch. "The Holy Family" (Raphael) (vert) 90 25
N2544 30ch. Head of "David" (statue, Michelangelo) (vert) . . . . 1·25 40

864 Mercedes Benz Type "300"

1985. South-West German Stamp Fair, Sindelfingen. Multicoloured.
N2546 10ch. Type **864** . . . . . 1·00 10
N2547 15ch. Mercedes Benz Type "770" . . . . . . 1·40 15
N2548 20ch. Mercedes Benz "W 150" . . . . 1·75 25
N2549 30ch. Mercedes Type "600" . . . . . . 2·00 40

865 Tackle

1985. World Cup Football Championship, Mexico (1st issue). Multicoloured.
N2551 20ch. Type **865** . . . . . 1·10 25
N2552 30ch. Three players . . . 1·40 40
See also Nos. N2558/9 and N2577/82.

866 Dancers

1985. International Youth Year. Multicoloured.
N2554 10ch. Type **866** 60 10
N2555 20ch. Sports activities . . 90 25
N2556 30ch. Technology . . . . 1·25 40

867 Players

1985. World Cup Football Championship, Mexico (2nd issue). Multicoloured.
N2558 20ch. Type **867** . . . . . 1·25 25
N2559 30ch. Goalkeeper and players . . . . 1·60 40

868 Juche Torch **869** Amedee Bollee and Limousine, 1901

1986. New Year.
N2561 **868** 10ch. multicoloured . . 40 10

1986. History of the Motor Car (2nd series). Multicoloured.
N2562 10ch. Type **869** 75 10
N2563 20ch. Stewart Rolls, Henry Royce and "Silver Ghost", 1906 . . . . . 1·25 25

N2564 25ch. Giovanni Agnelli and Fiat car, 1912 . . . 1·40 35

N2565 30ch. Ettore Bugatti and "Royal" coupe, 1928 . . 1·60 40

N2566 40ch. Louis Renault and fiacre, 1906 . . . . . . 2·25 60

870 Gary Kasparov

872 Tongdu Rock, Songgan

871 Cemetery Gate

1986. World Chess Championship, Moscow.
N2568 **870** 20ch. multicoloured . . 2·25 25

1986. Revolutionary Martyrs' Cemetery, Pyongyang. Multicoloured.
N2570 5ch. Type **871** 20 10
N2571 10ch. Bronze sculpture (detail) 55 10

1986. 37th Anniv of Pres. Kim Il Sung's Visit to Songgan Revolutionary Site.
N2572 **872** 10ch. multicoloured . . 40 10

873 Buddhist Scriptures Museum

1986. Mt. Myohyang Buildings.
N2573 **873** 10ch. brown and green 40 10
N2574 – 20ch. violet and red . . 50 10
DESIGN: 20ch. Taeung Hall.

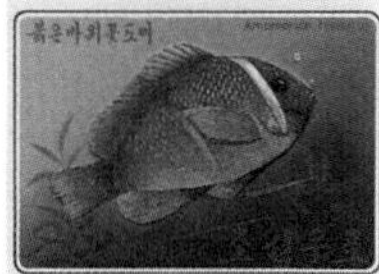

874 Tomato Anemonefish

1986. Fishes. Multicoloured.
N2575 10ch. Pennant coralfish . . 1·50 20
N2576 20ch. Type **874** . . . . . 2·25 45

875 Footballers and Flags of Italy, Bulgaria and Argentina

1986. World Cup Football Championship, Mexico (3rd issue). Designs showing footballers and flags of participating countries. Multicoloured.
N2577 10ch. Type **875** 60 10
N2578 20ch. Mexico, Belgium, Paraguay and Iraq . . . 90 25
N2579 25ch. France, Canada, U.S.S.R. and Hungary 1·10 35
N2580 30ch. Brazil, Spain, Algeria and Northern Ireland . . . . 1·25 40
N2581 35ch. West Germany, Uruguay, Scotland and Denmark . . . . 1·40 50
N2582 40ch. Poland, Portugal, Morocco and England 1·60 60

876 Singer, Pianist and Emblem

1986. 4th Spring Friendship Art Festival, Pyongyang.
N2584 **876** 1wn. multicoloured . . 1·25 55

877 Daimler "Motorwagen", 1886

878 Mangyong Hill

1986. 60th Anniv of Mercedes-Benz (car manufacturers). Multicoloured.
N2585 10ch. Type **877** 75 10
N2586 10ch. Benz "velo", 1894 75 10
N2587 20ch. Mercedes car, 1901 1·00 25
N2588 20ch. Benz limousine, 1909 1·00 25
N2589 30ch. Mercedes "tourenwagen", 1914 . . 1·40 40
N2590 30ch. Mercedes-Benz "170" 6-cylinder, 1931 1·40 40
N2591 40ch. Mercedes-Benz "380", 1933 . . . . . 1·75 60
N2592 40ch. Mercedes-Benz "540 K", 1936 . . . . 1·75 60

1986. 74th Birthday of Kim Il Sung.
N2594 **878** 10ch. multicoloured . . 30 10

879 Crowd

1968. 50th Anniv of Association for the Restoration of the Fatherland.
N2595 **879** 10ch. multicoloured . . 30 10

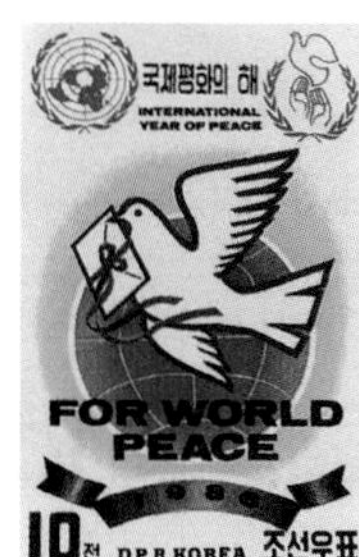

880 Dove carrying Letter

1986. International Peace Year. Multicoloured.
N2596 10ch. Type **880** 50 10
N2597 20ch. U.N. Headquarters, New York 80 25
N2598 30ch. Dove, globe and broken missiles . . . . 1·10 40

881 "Mona Lisa" (Leonardo da Vinci)

1986.
N2600 **881** 20ch. multicoloured . . 90 25

882 Pink Iris

883 Kim Un Suk

1986. Irises. Multicoloured.
N2601 20ch. Type **882** . . . . . 1·25 25
N2602 30ch. Violet iris . . . . . 1·75 40

1986. Tennis Players. Multicoloured.
N2604 10ch. Type **883** (postage) 2·00 35
N2605 20ch. Ivan Lendl . . . . 2·00 35
N2606 30ch. Steffi Graf . . . . . 2·00 35
N2607 50ch. Boris Becker (air) 2·00 35

884 Sulphur-crested Cockatoo ("Cockatoo")

1986. "Stampex '86" Stamp Exhibition, Adelaide, Australia.
N2608 **884** 10ch. multicoloured . . 1·60 20

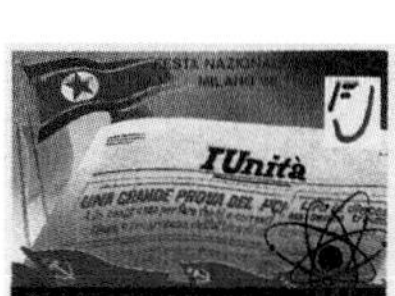

885 First Issue of "L'Unita"

886 "Express II" (icebreaker) and Sweden 1872 20 ore Stamp

1986. National "L'Unita" (Italian Communist Party newspaper) Festival, Milan. Multicoloured.
N2610 10ch. Type **885** 60 10
N2611 20ch. Milan Cathedral . . 90 25
N2612 30ch. "Pieta" (Michelangelo) (vert) . . 1·25 40

1986. "Stockholmia 86" International Stamp Exhibition, Stockholm.
N2614 **886** 10ch. multicoloured . . 2·00 10

887 Reprint of First Stamp

1986. 40th Anniv of First North Korean Stamps (1st issue). Multicoloured.
N2616 10ch. Type **887** (postage) 75 10
N2617 15ch. Imperforate reprint of first stamp 50 35
N2618 50ch. 1946 50ch. violet stamp (air) . . . . . . 2·00 75
See also Nos. N2619/21.

888 Postal Emblems and 1962 and 1985 Stamps

1986. 40th Anniv of First North Korean Stamps (2nd issue). Multicoloured.
N2619 10ch. Type **888** (postage) 2·00 25
N2620 15ch. General Post Office and 1976 and 1978 stamps . . . . 2·00 35
N2621 50ch. Kim Il Sung, first stamp and reprint (vert) (air) . . . . 1·60 45

1986. World Cup Football Championship Results. Nos. N2577/82 optd **1st: ARG 2nd: FRG 3rd: FRA 4th: BEL**.
N2622 10ch. multicoloured . . . 80 10
N2623 20ch. multicoloured . . . 1·10 25
N2624 25ch. multicoloured . . . 1·40 35
N2625 30ch. multicoloured . . . 1·50 40
N2626 35ch. multicoloured . . . 1·60 50
N2627 40ch. multicoloured . . . 1·90 60

890 Flag and Man with raised Fist

892 Schoolchildren

891 Gift Animals House

1986. 60th Anniv of Down-with-Imperialism Union.
N2629 **890** 10ch. multicoloured . . 30 10

1986. 1st Anniv of Gift Animals House, Central Zoo, Pyongyang.
N2630 **891** 2wn. multicoloured . . 3·00 1·10

1986. 40th Anniv of U.N.E.S.C.O. Multicoloured.
N2631 10ch. Type **892** 60 10
N2632 50ch. Anniversary emblem, Grand People's Study House and telecommunications (horiz) . . . . 1·50 75

893 Communications Satellite

1986. 15th Anniv of Intersputnik.
N2633 **893** 5wn. multicoloured . . 7·00 3·00

894 Oil tanker leaving Lock

1986. West Sea Barrage.
N2634 **894** 10ch. multicoloured . . 50 10
N2635 – 40ch. grn, blk & gold 1·25 20
N2636 – 1wn. 20 multicoloured 2·75 60
DESIGNS: 20ch. Aerial view of dam; 1wn.20, Aerial view of lock.

895 Common Morel

1986. Minerals and Fungi. Multicoloured.
N2637 10ch. Lengenbachite (postage) . . . . 2·00 25
N2638 10ch. Common funnel cap 2·00 25
N2639 15ch. Rhodochrosite . . . 2·00 25
N2640 15ch. Type **895** . . . . . 2·00 25
N2641 50ch. Annabergite (air) . . 2·00 25
N2642 50ch. Blue russula . . . . 2·00 25

896 Machu Picchu, Peru, and N. Korea Taedong Gate Stamp

1986. North Korean Three-dimensional Photographs and Stamps Exhibition, Lima, Peru.
N2643 **896** 10ch. multicoloured . . 1·25 20

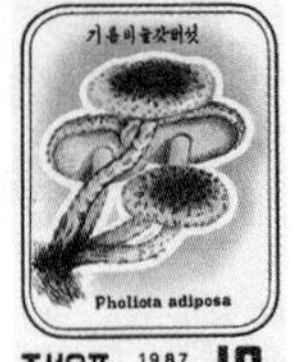

897 Pine Tree **898** "Pholiota adiposa"

1987. New Year. Multicoloured.

N2645	10ch. Type **897**	75	15
N2646	40ch. Hare	90	25

1987. Fungi. Multicoloured.

N2647	10ch. Type **898**	1·50	20
N2648	20ch. Chanterelle	1·75	20
N2649	30ch. "Boletus impolitus"	2·00	30

899 Kim Ok Song (composer) **901** East Pyongyang Grand Theatre

1987. Musicians' Death Anniversaries. Mult.

N2651	10ch. Maurice Ravel (composer, 50th anniv)	1·50	20
N2652	10ch. Type **899** (22nd anniv)	1·50	20
N2653	20ch. Giovanni Lully (composer, 300th anniv)	1·50	20
N2654	30ch. Franz Liszt (composer, centenary (1986))	1·50	20
N2655	40ch. Violins (250th anniv of Antonio Stradivari (violin maker))	1·50	20
N2656	40ch. Christoph Gluck (composer, bicent)	1·50	20

1987. Buildings.

N2658 **901**	5ch. green	35	10
N2659 –	10ch. brown	45	10
N2660 –	3wn. blue	3·00	90

DESIGNS—VERT: 10ch. Pyongyang Koryo Hotel. HORIZ: 3wn. Rungnado Stadium.

902 "Gorch Fock" (German cadet barque)

1987. Sailing Ships. Multicoloured.

N2661	20ch. Type **902** (postage)	70	20
N2662	30ch. "Tovarishch" (Russian cadet barque) (vert)	1·00	30
N2663	50ch. "Belle Poule" (cadet schooner) (vert) (air)	1·50	50
N2664	50ch. "Sagres II" (Portuguese cadet barque) (vert)	1·50	50
N2665	1wn. Koryo period merchantman	3·00	1·00
N2666	1wn. "Dar Mlodziezy" (Polish cadet full-rigged ship) (vert)	3·00	1·00

903 Road Signs

1987. Road Safety.

N2667 **903**	10ch. blue, red and black (postage)	1·00	10
N2668 –	10ch. red and black	1·00	10
N2669 –	20ch. blue, red & black	1·25	20
N2670 –	50ch. red and black (air)	1·50	50

DESIGNS: Nos. N2668/70, Different road signs.

904 Fire Engine

1987. Fire Engines.

N2671 **904**	10ch. mult (postage)	1·75	25
N2672 –	20ch. multicoloured	1·90	25
N2673 –	30ch. multicoloured	2·50	30
N2674 –	50ch. multicoloured (air)	3·25	50

DESIGNS: N2672/4, 20ch. to 50ch. Different machines.

905 "Apatura ilia" and Spiraea

1987. Butterflies and Flowers. Multicoloured.

N2675	10ch. Type **905**	70	10
N2676	10ch. "Ypthima argus" and fuchsia	70	10
N2677	20ch. "Neptis philyra" and aquilegia	1·00	20
N2678	20ch. "Papilio protenor" and chrysanthemum	1·00	20
N2679	40ch. "Parantica sita" and celosia	1·60	40
N2680	40ch. "Vanessa indica" and hibiscus	1·60	40

906 Association Monument, Pyongyang **907** Doves, Emblem and Tree

1987. 70th Anniv of Korean National Association (independence movement).

N2681 **906**	10ch. red, silver & black	25	10

1987. 5th Spring Friendship Art Festival, Pyongyang.

N2682 **907**	10ch. multicoloured	25	10

908 Mangyong Hill **909** Bay

1987. 75th Birthday of Kim Il Sung. Mult.

N2683	10ch. Type **908**	25	10
N2684	10ch. Kim Il Sung's birthplace, Mangyongdae (horiz)	25	10
N2685	10ch. "A Bumper Crop of Pumpkins" (62 × 41 mm)	25	10
N2686	10ch. "Profound Affection for the Working Class"	25	10

1987. Horses. Multicoloured.

N2687	10ch. Type **909**	40	10
N2688	10ch. Bay (different)	40	10
N2689	40ch. Grey rearing	1·25	40
N2690	40ch. Grey on beach	1·25	40

910 "Sputnik 1" (first artificial satellite)

1987. Transport. Multicoloured.

N2691	10ch. "Juche" high speed train (horiz)	40	10
N2692	10ch. Electric locomotive "Mangyongdae" (horiz)	40	10
N2693	10ch. Type **910** (30th anniv of flight)	40	10
N2694	20ch. Laika (30th anniv of first animal in space)	70	20
N2695	20ch. Tupolev Tu-144 supersonic airliner (horiz)	70	20
N2696	20ch. Concorde (11th anniv of first commercial flight) (horiz)	70	20
N2697	30ch. Count Ferdinand von Zeppelin (70th death anniv) and airship LZ-4 (horiz)	1·00	30
N2698	80ch. Zeppelin and diagrams and drawings of airships (horiz)	3·00	1·00

911 Musk Ox

1987. "Capex '87" International Stamp Exhibition, Toronto. Multicoloured.

N2699	10ch. Type **911**	65	10
N2700	40ch. Jacques Cartier, his ship "Grande Hermine" and "Terry Fox" (ice-breaker) (horiz)	1·75	40
N2701	60ch. Ice hockey (Winter Olympics, Calgary, 1988) (horiz)	1·75	60

912 Trapeze Artistes

1987. International Circus Festival, Monaco. Multicoloured.

N2702	10ch. Type **912**	40	10
N2703	10ch. "Brave Sailors" (North Korean acrobatic act) (vert)	40	10
N2704	20ch. Clown and elephant (vert)	70	20
N2705	20ch. North Korean artiste receiving "Golden Clown" award	70	20
N2706	40ch. Performing horses and cat act	2·10	40
N2707	50ch. Prince Rainier and his children applauding	1·50	50

913 Attack on Watch Tower

1987. 50th Anniv of Battle of Pochonbo.

N2708 **913**	10ch. brown, black and ochre	25	10

914 Sports

1987. Angol Sports Village.

N2709 **914**	5ch. brown and gold	15	10
N2710 –	10ch. blue and gold	25	10
N2711 –	40ch. brown and gold	75	25
N2712 –	70ch. blue and gold	1·25	40
N2713 –	1wn. red and gold	1·90	60
N2714 –	1wn.20 violet	2·25	70

DESIGNS: Exteriors of—10ch. Indoor swimming pool; 40ch. Weightlifting gymnasium; 70ch. Table tennis gymnasium; 1wn. Football stadium; 1wn.20, Handball gymnasium.

915 Mandarins

1987. Mandarins. Multicoloured.

N2715	20ch. Type **915**	1·50	40
N2716	20ch. Mandarins on shore	1·50	40
N2717	20ch. Mandarins on branch	1·50	40
N2718	40ch. Mandarins in water	2·25	60

916 Exhibition Site and 1987 3wn. Stamp

1987. "Olymphilex '87" Olympic Stamps Exhibition, Rome.

N2719 **916**	10ch. multicoloured	90	10

917 Underground Station and Guard

1987. Railway Uniforms. Multicoloured.

N2721	10ch. Type **917**	40	10
N2722	10ch. Underground train and station supervisor	40	10
N2723	20ch. Guard and electric train	60	15
N2724	30ch. Guard with flag and electric train	85	20
N2725	40ch. "Orient Express" guard and steam locomotive	1·10	25
N2726	40ch. German ticket controller and diesel train	1·10	25

918 White Stork **920** Victory Column

919 Ice Skating

1987. "Hafnia 87" International Stamp Exhibition, Copenhagen. Multicoloured.
N2727 40ch. Type **918** . . . . . 2·40 50
N2728 60ch. "Danmark" (cadet full-rigged ship) and "Little Mermaid", Copenhagen . . . . . 1·75 40

1987. Winter Olympic Games, Calgary (1988). Multicoloured.
N2729 40ch. Type **919** . . . . . 1·00 30
N2730 40ch. Ski jumping . . . . 1·00 30
N2731 40ch. Skiing (value on left) (horiz) . . . . 1·00 30
N2732 40ch. Skiing (value on right) (horiz) . . . . . 1·00 30

1987. 750th Anniv of Berlin and "Philatelia '87" International Stamp Exhibition, Cologne. Mult.
N2734 10ch. Type **920** 40 10
N2735 20ch. Reichstag (horiz) . . 70 20
N2736 30ch. Pfaueninsel Castle 1·00 30
N2737 40ch. Charlottenburg Castle (horiz) . . . . . 1·25 40

921 Garros and Bleriot XI

1987. Birth Centenary of Roland Garros (aviator) and Tennis as an Olympic Sport. Multicoloured.
N2739 20ch. Type **921** . . . . . 1·50 20
N2740 20ch. Ivan Lendl (tennis player) . . . . 2·25 20
N2741 40ch. Steffi Graf (tennis player) . . . . 3·00 40

923 Pyongyang Buildings

1988. New Year. Multicoloured.
N2744 10ch. Type **923** 20 10
N2745 40ch. Dragon 75 25

924 Banner and Newspaper

925 Birthplace, Mt. Paekdu

1988. 60th Anniv of "Saenal" Newspaper.
N2746 **924** 10ch. multicoloured . . 45 10

1988. Kim Jong Il's Birthday.
N2747 **925** 10ch. multicoloured . . 20 10

926 Henry Dunant (founder)

1988. 125th Anniv of International Red Cross. Multicoloured.
N2749 10ch. Type **926** 75 10
N2750 20ch. North Korean Red Cross emblem and map 1·00 15
N2751 20ch. International Committee headquarters, Geneva 1·10 15
N2752 40ch. Pyongyang Maternity Hospital, doctor and baby . . . . 1·25 25

927 "Santa Maria"

1988. 500th Anniv (1992) of Discovery of America by Christopher Columbus. Multicoloured.
N2754 10ch. Type **927** . . . . . 1·25 10
N2755 20ch. "Pinta" . . . . . . 1·25 20
N2756 30ch. "Nina" . . . . . . 1·25 30
Nos. N2754/6 were issued together, se-tenant, forming a composite design of Columbus's ships leaving Palos.

928 Montgolfier Balloon and Modern Hot-air Balloons

929 Dancers

1988. "Juvalux '88" International Youth Stamp Exhibition, Luxembourg. Multicoloured.
N2758 40ch. Type **928** 90 25
N2759 60ch. Steam locomotive and railway map of Luxembourg, 1900 . . . 1·60 35

1988. 6th Spring Friendship Art Festival, Pyongyang. Multicoloured.
N2760 10ch. Singer (poster) . . . 20 10
N2761 1wn.20 Type **929** . . . . 1·90 75

930 Inaugural Congress Emblem

931 Birthplace, Mangyongdae

1988. 10th Anniv of International Institute of the Juche Idea.
N2762 **930** 10ch. multicoloured . . 20 10

1988. 76th Birthday of Kim Il Sung.
N2763 **931** 10ch. multicoloured . . 20 10

932 "Urho" (ice-breaker)

1988. "Finlandia 88" International Stamp Exhibition, Helsinki. Multicoloured.
N2765 40ch. Type **932** . . . . . 1·40 25
N2766 60ch. Matti Nykaenen (Olympic Games ski-jumping medallist) . . . 1·10 35

933 Postcard for 1934 Championship

934 Emblem

1988. World Cup Football Championship, Italy (1st issue). Multicoloured.
N2767 10ch. Football match . . 50 10
N2768 20ch. Type **933** 85 15
N2769 30ch. Player tackling (horiz) . . . . 1·25 20
See also Nos. N2924/7.

1988. 13th World Youth and Students' Festival, Pyongyang (1st issue). Multicoloured.
N2771 5ch. Type **934** 10 10
N2772 10ch. Dancer 40 10
N2773 10ch. Gymnast and gymnasium, Angol Sports Village 20 10
N2774 10ch. Map of Korea, globe and doves 30 10
N2775 10ch. Finger pointing at shattered nuclear rockets 75 10
N2776 1wn.20 Three differently coloured hands and dove . . . . 2·10 75
See also Nos. N2860/3 and N2879/80.

935 Fairy

936 Mallards

1988. "Eight Fairies of Mt. Kumgang" (tale). Multicoloured.
N2777 10ch. Type **935** 20 10
N2778 15ch. Fairy at pool and fairies on rainbow . . . 30 10
N2779 20ch. Fairy and woodman husband 40 15
N2780 25ch. Couple with baby 70 20
N2781 30ch. Couple with son and daughter 55 20
N2782 35ch. Family on rainbow 1·00 35

1988. "Praga '88" International Stamp Exhibition, Prague. Multicoloured.
N2783 20ch. Type **936** . . . . . 1·90 25
N2784 40ch. Vladimir Remek (Czechoslovak cosmonaut) 75 25

937 Red Crossbill

1988. Birds. Multicoloured.
N2785 10ch. Type **937** 70 20
N2786 15ch. Common stonechat 1·00 30
N2787 20ch. Eurasian nuthatch 1·40 35
N2788 25ch. Great spotted woodpecker . . . . . . 1·60 45
N2789 30ch. River kingfisher . . 2·00 50
N2790 35ch. Bohemian waxwing 2·10 65

938 Fair Emblem

1988. 40th International Stamp Fair, Riccione.
N2791 **938** 20ch. multicoloured . . 40 15

939 Emu

1988. Bicentenary of Australian Settlement. Mult.
N2793 10ch. Type **939** 60 15
N2794 15ch. Satin bowerbirds . . 85 20
N2795 25ch. Laughing kookaburra (vert) . . . 1·40 35

940 Floating Crane "5-28"

1988. Ships. Multicoloured.
N2797 10ch. Type **940** 40 15
N2798 20ch. Freighter "Hwanggumsan" . . . 60 20
N2799 30ch. Freighter "Changjasan Chongnyon-ho" 75 25
N2800 40ch. Liner "Samjiyon" 1·00 30

941 "Hansa"

1988. 150th Birth Anniv of Count Ferdinand von Zeppelin (airship pioneer). Multicoloured.
N2801 10ch. Type **941** 40 10
N2802 20ch. "Schwaben" 75 15
N2803 30ch. "Viktoria Luise" . . 90 20
N2804 40ch. LZ-3 . . . . 1·25 25

942 Kim Il Sung and Jambyn Batmunkh

1988. Kim Il Sung's Visit to Mongolia.
N2806 **942** 10ch. multicoloured . . 20 10

943 Hero and Labour Hero of the D.P.R.K. Medals

1988. National Heroes Congress.
N2807 **943** 10ch. multicoloured . . 20 10

944 Tower of Juche Idea

1988. 40th Anniv of Democratic Republic. Multicoloured.
N2808 5ch. Type **944** 10 10
N2809 10ch. Smelter and industrial buildings . . 20 10
N2810 10ch. Soldier and Mt. Paekdu 20 10
N2811 10ch. Map of Korea and globe 20 10
N2812 10ch. Hand holding banner, globe and doves 20 10

945 "Sunflowers" (Vincent van Gogh) **946** Emblem

1988. "Filacept 88" Stamp Exhibition, The Hague. Multicoloured.
N2814 40ch. Type **945** . . . . . 1·50 25
N2815 60ch. "The Chess Game" (Lucas van Leyden) (horiz) . . . . 2·50 35

1988. 16th Session of Socialist Countries' Post and Telecommunications Conference, Pyongyang.
N2816 **946** 10ch. multicoloured . . 20 10

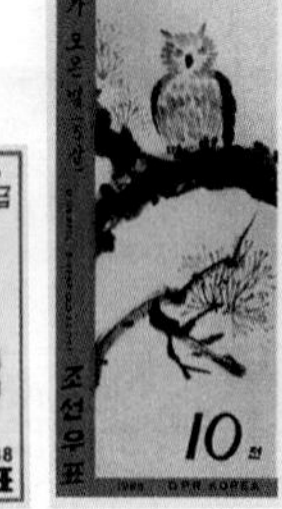

947 Chaju "82" 10-ton Truck **948** "Owl"

1988. Tipper Trucks. Multicoloured.
N2817 20ch. Type **947** 40 15
N2818 40ch. Kumsusan-ho 40-ton truck 75 25

1988. Paintings by O Un Byol. Multicoloured.
N2819 10ch. Type **948** . . . . . 2·25 25
N2820 15ch. "Dawn" (red junglefowl) . . . . . . 1·00 25
N2821 20ch. "Beautiful Rose received by Kim Il Sung" 60 15
N2822 25ch. "Sun and Bamboo" 75 15
N2823 30ch. "Autumn" (fruit tree) . . . . 1·10 35

949 "Chunggi" Steam Locomotive No. 35

1988. Railway Locomotives. Multicoloured.
N2824 10ch. Type **949** 70 10
N2825 20ch. "Chunggi" steam locomotive No. 22 . . . 95 15
N2826 30ch. "Chongiha" electric locomotive No. 3 . . . 1·10 20
N2827 40ch. "Chunggi" steam locomotive No. 307 . . 1·40 25

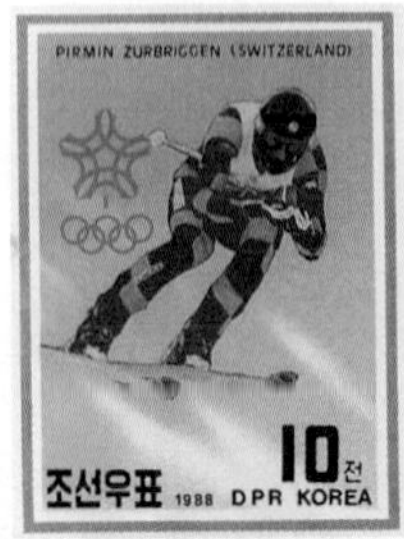

950 Pirmen Zurbriggen (downhill skiing)

1988. Winter Olympic Games, Calgary, Medal Winners. Multicoloured.
N2828 10ch. Type **950** 20 10
N2829 20ch. Yvonne van Gennip (speed skating) 40 15
N2830 30ch. Marjo Matikainen (cross-country skiing) 55 20
N2831 40ch. U.S.S.R. (ice hockey) (horiz) 75 25

951 Yuri Gagarin

1988. 1st Man and Woman in Space. Mult.
N2833 20ch. Type **951** 40 15
N2834 40ch. Valentina Tereshkova 75 25

952 Nehru **953** Chollima Statue

1988. Birth Centenary of Jawaharlal Nehru (Indian statesman) and "India 89" International Stamp Exhibition, New Delhi.
N2835 **952** 20ch. purple, black and gold 60 15

1989. New Year. Multicoloured.
N2837 10ch. Type **953** 20 10
N2838 20ch. "The Dragon Angler" (17th-century painting) 60 15
N2839 40ch. "Tortoise and Serpent" (Kangso tomb painting) (horiz) 90 25

954 Archery

1989. National Defence Training. Multicoloured.
N2840 10ch. Type **954** 90 10
N2841 15ch. Rifle shooting . . . 30 10
N2842 20ch. Pistol shooting . . . 40 15
N2843 25ch. Parachuting 50 15
N2844 30ch. Launching model glider 55 20

955 Dobermann Pinscher **957** Agriculture

1989. Animals presented to Kim Il Sung. Mult.
N2845 10ch. Type **955** 50 10
N2846 20ch. Labrador 70 15
N2847 25ch. German shepherd 1·00 15
N2848 30ch. Rough collies (horiz) 1·00 20
N2849 35ch. Serval (horiz) 1·25 20

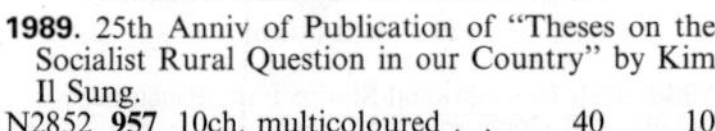

1989. 25th Anniv of Publication of "Theses on the Socialist Rural Question in our Country" by Kim Il Sung.
N2852 **957** 10ch. multicoloured . . 40 10

958 The Gypsy and Grapes **959** Korean Girl

1989. Fungi and Fruits. Multicoloured.
N2853 10ch. Type **958** 50 10
N2854 20ch. Caesar's mushroom and magnolia vine . . . 80 15
N2855 25ch. "Lactarius hygrophoides" and "Eleagnus crispa" . . . 1·10 15
N2856 30ch. "Agaricus placomyces" and Chinese gooseberries . . 1·25 20
N2857 35ch. Horse mushroom and "Lycium chinense" 1·50 20
N2858 40ch. Elegant boletus and "Juglans cordiformis" 1·75 25

1989. 13th World Youth and Students' Festival, Pyongyang (2nd issue). Multicoloured.
N2860 10ch. Type **959** 20 10
N2861 20ch. Children of different races 40 15
N2862 30ch. Fairy and rainbow 55 20
N2863 40ch. Young peoples and Tower of Juche Idea . . 45 25

960 "Parnassius eversmanni"

1969. Insects. Multicoloured.
N2864 10ch. Type **960** 50 15
N2865 15ch. "Colias heos" . . . 60 15
N2866 20ch. "Dilipa fenestra" . . 70 15
N2867 25ch. "Buthus martensis" 80 15
N2868 30ch. "Trichogramma ostriniae" 95 15
N2869 40ch. "Damaster constricticollis" . . . . 1·00 15

961 Dancers (poster) **962** Birthplace, Mangyongdae

1989. Spring Friendship Art Festival, Pyongyang.
N2871 **961** 10ch. multicoloured . . 45 10

1989. 77th Birthday of Kim Il Sung.
N2872 **962** 10ch. multicoloured . . 20 10

963 Battle Plan and Monument to the Victory

1989. 50th Anniv of Battle of the Musan Area.
N2873 **963** 10ch. blue, flesh and red 60 10

964 Modern Dance

1989. Chamo System of Dance Notation. Multicoloured.
N2874 10ch. Type **964** 55 10
N2875 20ch. Ballet 70 15
N2876 25ch. Modern dance (different) 85 15
N2877 30ch. Traditional dance 1·00 20

965 Hands supporting Torch **966** Victorious Badger

1989. 13th World Youth and Students' Festival, Pyongyang (3rd issue).
N2879 **965** 5ch. blue 10 10
N2880 – 10ch. brown 20 10
DESIGN: 10ch. Youth making speech.

1989. "Badger measures the Height" (cartoon film). Multicoloured.
N2881 10ch. Cat, bear and badger race to flag pole 80 10
N2882 40ch. Cat and bear climb pole while badger measures shadow . . . 1·25 25
N2883 50ch. Type **966** . . . . . 1·50 30

967 Kyongju Observatory and Star Chart **969** Pele (footballer) and 1978 25ch. Stamp

1989. Astronomy.
N2884 **967** 20ch. multicoloured . . 1·00 15

1989. "Brasiliana 89" International Stamp Exhibition, Rio de Janeiro.
N2887 **969** 40ch. multicoloured . . 1·25 25

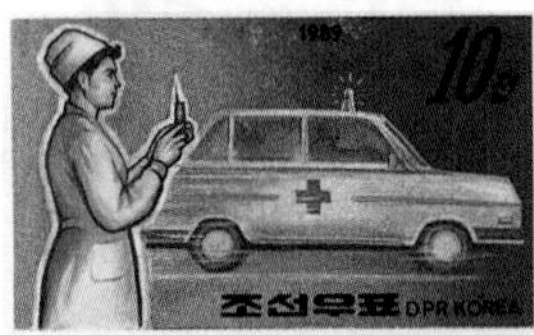

970 Nurse and Ambulance

1989. Emergency Services. Multicoloured.
N2888 10ch. Type **970** 20 10
N2889 20ch. Surgeon and ambulance 30 15
N2890 30ch. Fireman and fire engine . . . . 2·25 20
N2891 40ch. Fireman and engine (different) . . . . . . 2·25 25

971 Kaffir Lily **972** Air Mail Letter and Postal Transport

1989. Plants presented to Kim Il Sung. Mult.
N2892 10ch. Type **971** 40 10
N2893 15ch. Tulips 50 10
N2894 20ch. Flamingo lily . . . 75 15
N2895 25ch. "Rhododendron obtusum" 90 15
N2896 30ch. Daffodils . . . . . 1·00 20

1989. 150th Anniv of the Penny Black and "Stamp World London 90" International Stamp Exhibition (1st issue). Multicoloured.
N2898 5ch. Type **972** 40 10
N2899 10ch. Post box and letters 55 10
N2900 20ch. Stamps, tweezers and magnifying glass . . 60 15
N2901 30ch. First North Korean stamps 75 20
N2902 40ch. Universal Postal Union emblem and headquarters, Berne . . 1·00 25
N2903 50ch. Sir Rowland Hill and Penny Black . . . 1·25 30
See also No. N2956.

973 "Bistorta incana"

1989. Alpine Flowers. Multicoloured.
N2904 10ch. "Iris setosa" 50 10
N2905 15ch. "Aquilegia japonica" 60 10
N2906 20ch. Type **973** 75 15
N2907 25ch. "Rodiola elongata" 90 15
N2908 30ch. "Sanguisorba sitchensis" 95 20

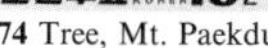

974 Tree, Mt. Paekdu **975** Skipping

1989. Slogan-bearing Trees (1st series). Mult.
N2910 10ch. Type **974** 20 10
N2911 3wn. Tree, Oun-dong, Pyongyang . . . . . . 5·50 1·75
N2912 5wn. Tree, Mt. Kanbaek 9·50 3·25
See also No. N2931.

1989. Children's Games. Multicoloured.
N2913 10ch. Type **975** 20 10
N2914 20ch. Windmill . . . . . 1·25 15
N2915 30ch. Kite 55 20
N2916 40ch. Whip and top . . . 75 25

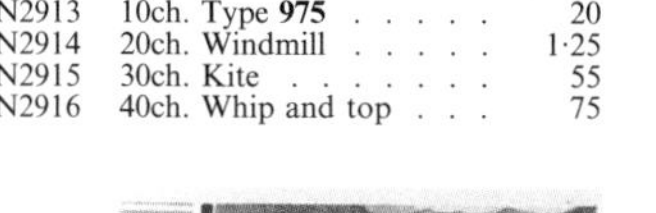

977 Diesel Train and Sinpa Youth Station

1989. Railway Locomotives. Multicoloured.
N2918 10ch. Type **977** 40 10
N2919 20ch. "Pulgungi" electric locomotive 60 15
N2920 25ch. Diesel goods train 70 15
N2921 30ch. Diesel train 85 20
N2922 40ch. Steam locomotive 1·00 25
N2923 50ch. Steam locomotive (different) . . . . . . 1·10 30

978 Players and Map of Italy

1989. World Cup Football Championship, Italy (2nd issue). Multicoloured.
N2924 10ch. Type **978** . . . . . 1·00 10
N2925 20ch. Free kick 50 15
N2926 30ch. Goal mouth scrimmage 75 20
N2927 40ch. Goalkeeper diving for ball 95 25

979 Magellan (navigator) and his Ship "Vitoria"

1989. "Descobrex '89" International Stamp Exhibition, Portugal.
N2928 **979** 30ch. multicoloured . . 1·25 20

980 Mangyong Hill and Pine Branches **981** Ryukwoli

1990. New Year. Multicoloured.
N2929 10ch. Type **980** 20 10
N2930 20ch. Koguryo mounted archers 90 15

1990. Slogan-bearing Trees (2nd series). As T **974**. Multicoloured.
N2931 5ch. Tree, Mt. Paekdu . . 25 10

1990. Dogs. Multicoloured.
N2932 20ch. Type **981** . . . . . 1·25 20
N2933 30ch. Palryuki . . . . . . 1·25 20
N2934 40ch. Komdungi . . . . 1·25 20
N2935 50ch. Oulruki . . . . . . 1·25 20

982 Birthplace, Mt. Paekdu **983** Stone Instruments and Primitive Man

1990. Birthday of Kim Jong Il.
N2936 **982** 10ch. brown 20 10

1990. Evolution of Man. Multicoloured.
N2937 10ch. Type **983** 45 10
N2938 40ch. Palaeolithic and Neolithic man 90 25

984 Rungna Bridge, Pyongyang

1990. Bridges. Multicoloured.
N2939 10ch. Type **984** 45 10
N2940 20ch. Potong bridge, Pyongyang 60 15
N2941 30ch. Sinuiji-Ryucho Island Bridge 85 20
N2942 40ch. Chungsongui Bridge, Pyongyang . . . . . . 1·10 25

985 Infantryman **987** Dancers

986 "Atergatis subdentatus"

1990. Warriors' Costumes. Multicoloured.
N2943 20ch. Type **985** 40 15
N2944 30ch. Archer 55 20
N2945 50ch. Military commander in armour 95 30
N2946 70ch. Officer's costume, 10th–14th centuries . . 1·25 40
Nos. N2943/5 depict costumes from the 3rd century B.C. to the 7th century A.D.

1990. Crabs. Multicoloured.
N2947 20ch. Type **986** 60 15
N2948 30ch. "Platylambrus validus" 75 20
N2949 50ch. "Uca arcuata" . . . 1·10 30

1990. Spring Friendship Art Festival, Pyongyang.
N2950 **987** 10ch. multicoloured . . 30 10

988 Monument at Road Folk, Mangyongdae **989** "Gymnocalycium sp."

1990. 78th Birthday of Kim Il Sung.
N2951 **988** 10ch. green and gold 20 10

1990. Cacti. Multicoloured.
N2953 10ch. Type **989** 50 10
N2954 30ch. "Pyllocactus hybridus" 90 20
N2955 50ch. "Epiphyllum truncatum" . . . . . . 1·50 30

990 Exhibition Emblem **991** Congo Peafowl

1990. "Stamp World London 90" International Stamp Exhibition (2nd issue).
N2956 **990** 20ch. red and black . . 40 15

1990. Peafowl. Multicoloured.
N2958 10ch. Type **991** 75 25
N2959 20ch. Common peafowl 2·00 60

992 Dolphin and Submarine

1990. Bio-engineering. Multicoloured.
N2961 10ch. Type **992** . . . . . 1·10 25
N2962 20ch. Bat and dish aerial 1·10 25
N2963 30ch. Owl and Tupolev Tu-154 jetliner . . . . 1·25 35
N2964 40ch. Squid, "Soyuz" rocket and Concorde supersonic jetliner . . . 1·10 25

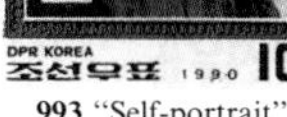

993 "Self-portrait" (Rembrandt) **994** K. H. Rummenigge (footballer)

1990. "Belgica 90" International Stamp Exhibition, Brussels. Multicoloured.
N2965 10ch. Type **993** 30 10
N2966 20ch. "Self-portrait" (Raphael) 60 15
N2967 30ch. "Self-portrait" (Rubens) 75 20

1990. "Dusseldorf '90" International Youth Stamp Exhibition. Multicoloured.
N2968 20ch. Steffi Graf (tennis player) 85 15
N2969 30ch. Exhibition emblem 55 20
N2970 70ch. Type **994** . . . . . 1·25 40

995 Workers' Stadium, Peking, and Games Mascot

1990. 11th Asian Games, Peking (Nos. N2971/2) and 3rd Asian Winter Games, Samjiyon (N2973). Multicoloured.
N2971 10ch. Type **995** 30 10
N2972 30ch. Chollima Statue and sportsmen 75 20
N2973 40ch. Sportsmen and Games emblem . . . . 1·00 25

996 Ball

1990. West Germany, Winners of World Cup Football Championship. Multicoloured.
N2974 15ch. Emblem of F.I.F.A. (International Federation of Football Associations) 40 10
N2975 20ch. Jules Rimet 50 15
N2976 25ch. Type **996** 60 15
N2977 30ch. Olympic Stadium, Rome (venue of final) 65 20
N2978 35ch. Goalkeeper 75 20
N2979 40ch. Emblem of West German Football Association 90 25

997 Kakapo and Map of New Zealand

1990. "New Zealand 1990" International Stamp Exhibition, Auckland.
N2981 **997** 30ch. multicoloured . . 1·60 50

999 Head of Procession

1990. Koguryo Wedding Procession. Mult.
N2983 10ch. Type **999** . . . . . 1·00 20
N2984 30ch. Bridegroom . . . . . 1·00 20
N2985 50ch. Bride in carriage . . 1·00 20
N2986 1wn. Drummer on horse 1·00 20
Nos. N2983/6 were issued together, se-tenant, forming a composite design.

1000 Marchers descending Mt. Paekdu

1990. Rally for Peace and Reunification of Korea.
N2987 **1000** 10ch. multicoloured 20 10

1001 Praying Mantis

1990. Insects. Multicoloured.
N2989 20ch. Type **1001** 40 15
N2990 30ch. Ladybird 55 20
N2991 40ch. "Pheropsophus jessoensis" 75 25
N2992 70ch. "Phyllium siccifolium" . . . . . . 1·25 40

1002 Footballers

1990. North–South Reunification Football Match, Pyongyang. Multicoloured.

N2993 10ch. Type **1002** 75 10
N2994 20ch. Footballers (different) 75 15

1003 Concert Emblem

1004 Ox

1990. National Reunification Concert.

N2996 **1003** 10ch. multicoloured 20 10

1990. Farm Animals.

N2997 **1004** 10ch. brown and green 20 10
N2998 – 20ch. lilac and yellow 40 15
N2999 – 30ch. grey and red . . 55 20
N3000 – 40ch. green and yellow 75 25
N3001 – 50ch. brown and blue 95 30

DESIGNS: 20ch. Pig; 30ch. Goat; 40ch. Sheep; 50ch. Horse.

1005 Chinese and North Korean Soldiers

1990. 40th Anniv of Participation of Chinese Volunteers in Korean War. Multicoloured.

N3002 10ch. Type **1005** 20 10
N3003 20ch. Populace welcoming volunteers (horiz) . . . 40 15
N3004 30ch. Rejoicing soldiers and battle scene (horiz) 50 20
N3005 40ch. Post-war reconstruction (horiz) 60 25

1006 Anniversary Emblem

1990. 40th Anniv of United Nations Development Programme.

N3007 **1006** 1wn. blue, silver & blk . . . . 1·90 65

1007 Mikado Sturgeon

1008 Sheep

1990. Fishes.

N3008 **1007** 10ch. brown and green 25 10
N3009 – 20ch. green and blue 55 15
N3010 – 30ch. blue and purple 75 25
N3011 – 40ch. brown and blue 1·00 30
N3012 – 50ch. violet and green 1·25 35

DESIGNS: 20ch. Large-headed sea bream; 30ch. Agoo flyingfish, 40ch. Fat greenling, 50ch. Toblj-el eagle ray.

1990. New Year.

N3013 **1008** 40ch. multicoloured 75 25

1009 Moorhen

1010 Giant Panda

1990. Birds.

N3014 **1009** 10ch. blue, green & blk 55 15
N3015 – 20ch. brown, bistre and black 90 30
N3016 – 30ch. green, grey and black . . . . . . 1·10 50
N3017 – 40ch. brown, orange and black . . . . 1·75 60
N3018 – 50ch. ochre, brown and black . . . . 2·25 70

DESIGNS: 20ch. Jay; 30ch. Three-toed woodpecker; 40ch. Whimbrel; 50ch. Water rail.

1991. "Phila Nippon '91" International Stamp Exhibition, Tokyo. Multicoloured.

N3019 10ch. Type **1010** 30 10
N3020 20ch. Two giant pandas feeding 50 15
N3021 30ch. Giant panda clambering onto branch 70 20
N3022 40ch. Giant panda on rock 90 25
N3023 50ch. Two giant pandas 1·10 30
N3024 60ch. Giant panda in tree fork . . . . 1·25 35

1011 Changsan

1991. Revolutionary Sites.

N3026 5ch. Type **1011** 10 10
N3027 10ch. Oun 20 10

1012 Black-faced Spoonbills

1014 Hedgehog Fungus

1013 "Clossiana angarensis"

1991. Endangered Birds. Multicoloured.

N3028 10ch. Type **1012** 30 10
N3029 20ch. Grey herons 60 15
N3030 30ch. Great egrets 85 25
N3031 40ch. Manchurian cranes 1·10 30
N3032 50ch. Japanese white-naped cranes . . . . . 1·75 35
N3033 70ch. White storks . . . . 2·25 50

1991. Alpine Butterflies. Multicoloured.

N3034 10ch. Type **1013** 25 10
N3035 20ch. "Erebia embla" . . 40 15
N3036 30ch. Camberwell beauty 60 20
N3037 40ch. Comma 75 30
N3038 50ch. Eastern pale clouded yellow 90 35
N3039 60ch. "Theela betulae" . . 1·10 45

1991. Fungi. Multicoloured.

N3040 10ch. Type **1014** 25 10
N3041 20ch. "Phylloporus rhodoxanthus" 45 15
N3042 30ch. "Calvatia craniiformis" 60 20
N3043 40ch. Cauliflower clavaria 80 30
N3044 50ch. "Russula integra" 1·00 35

1015 Kumchon

1991. Revolutionary Sites. Multicoloured.

N3045 10ch. Type **1015** 15 10
N3046 40ch. Samdung 60 30

1016 Dr. Kye Ung Sang (researcher)

1017 Emblem and Venue

1991. Silkworm Research. Multicoloured.

N3047 10ch. Type **1016** 15 10
N3048 20ch. Chinese oak silk moth 30 15
N3049 30ch. "Attacus ricini" . . 45 20
N3050 40ch. "Antheraea yamamai" 60 30
N3051 50ch. Silkworm moth . . 75 35
N3052 60ch. "Aetias artemis" . . 90 45

1991. 9th Spring Friendship Art Festival, Pyongyang.

N3053 **1017** 10ch. multicoloured 10 10

1018 Emperor Penguins

1020 Map and Kim Jong Ho

1019 People's Palace of Culture (venue)

1991. Antarctic Exploration. Multicoloured.

N3054 10ch. Type **1018** 35 20
N3055 20ch. Research station . . 40 15
N3056 30ch. Elephant seals . . . 75 20
N3057 40ch. Research ship . . . 90 40
N3058 50ch. Southern black-backed gulls . . . . . 1·60 40

1991. 85th Interparliamentary Union Conference, Pyongyang.

N3060 **1019** 10ch. dp green, grn & sil 15 10
N3061 – 1wn.50 multicoloured 2·25 1·10

DESIGN: 1wn.50, Conference emblem and azalea.

1991. 130th Anniv of Publication of Kim Jong Ho's Map "Taidong Yu Jido".

N3062 **1020** 90ch. black, brn & sil 1·40 70

1021 Cynognathus

1991. Dinosaurs. Multicoloured.

N3063 10ch. Type **1021** 25 10
N3064 20ch. Brontosaurus . . . 40 15
N3065 30ch. Stegosaurus and allosaurus 55 20
N3066 40ch. Pterosauria 70 30
N3067 50ch. Ichthyosaurus . . . 85 35

1022 Sprinting

1991. Olympic Games, Barcelona (1992 (1st issue). Multicoloured.

N3068 10ch. Type **1022** 15 10
N3069 10ch. Hurdling 15 10
N3070 20ch. Long jumping 30 15
N3071 20ch. Throwing the discus 30 15
N3072 30ch. Putting the shot . . 45 20
N3073 30ch. Pole vaulting . . . 45 20
N3074 40ch. High jumping . . . 60 30
N3075 40ch. Throwing the javelin 60 30

See also Nos. N3142/7.

1023 Cats and Eurasian Tree Sparrows

1991. Cats. Multicoloured.

N3077 10ch. Type **1023** 50 35
N3078 20ch. Cat and rat 40 15
N3079 30ch. Cat and butterfly . . 55 20
N3080 40ch. Cats with ball . . . 75 30
N3081 50ch. Cat and frog . . . 90 35

1025 Wild Horse

1991. Horses. Multicoloured.

N3083 10ch. Type **1025** 25 10
N3084 20ch. Hybrid of wild ass and wild horse 40 15
N3085 30ch. Przewalski's horse 60 20
N3086 40ch. Wild ass 75 30
N3087 50ch. Wild horse (different) 90 35

1026 Pennant Coralfish

1991. Fishes. Multicoloured.

N3088 10ch. Type **1026** (postage) 40 10
N3089 20ch. Clown triggerfish . . 75 25
N3090 30ch. Tomato anemonefish 1·00 30
N3091 40ch. Palette surgeonfish 1·40 45
N3092 50ch. Freshwater angelfish (air) . . . . 1·60 55

1027 Rhododendrons

1991. Flowers. Multicoloured.

N3094 10ch. Begonia 25 10
N3095 20ch. Gerbera 40 15
N3096 30ch. Type **1027** 55 20
N3097 40ch. Phalaenopsis 70 30
N3098 50ch. "Impatiens sultanii" 85 35
N3099 60ch. Streptocarpus . . . 1·00 45

Nos. N3097/9 commemorate "CANADA '92" international youth stamp exhibition, Montreal.

1028 Panmunjom

1991.
N3100 **1028** 10ch. multicoloured 15 10

1029 Magnolia 1030 Players

1991. National Flower.
N3101 **1029** 10ch. multicoloured 40 10

1991. Women's World Football Championship, China. Multicoloured.
N3102 10ch. Type **1030** 25 10
N3103 20ch. Dribbling the ball 40 15
N3104 30ch. Heading the ball . . 55 20
N3105 40ch. Overhead kick . . . 70 30
N3106 50ch. Tackling 85 35
N3107 60ch. Goalkeeper . . . . 1·10 45

1031 Squirrel Monkeys

1992. Monkeys. Multicoloured.
N3108 10ch. Type **1031** 25 10
N3109 20ch. Pygmy marmosets 40 15
N3110 30ch. Red-handed tamarins 60 20

1032 Eagle Owl

1992. Birds of Prey. Multicoloured.
N3112 10ch. Type **1032** 25 20
N3113 20ch. Common buzzard 55 30
N3114 30ch. African fish eagle . . 2·00 60
N3115 40ch. Steller's sea eagle . . 1·25 65
N3116 50ch. Golden eagle . . . 1·40 75

1033 Birthplace, Mt. Paekdu

1992. Birthday of Kim Jong Il. Mt. Paekdu. Multicoloured.
N3118 10ch. Type **1033** 15 10
N3119 20ch. Mountain summit 30 15
N3120 30ch. Lake Chon (crater lake) 45 20
N3121 40ch. Lake Sarryi 60 30

1034 Service Bus

1992. Transport.
N3123 **1034** 10ch. multicoloured 25 10
N3124 – 20ch. multicoloured 40 15
N3125 – 30ch. multicoloured 60 20
N3126 – 40ch. multicoloured 75 30
N3127 – 50ch. multicoloured 90 35
N3128 – 60ch. multicoloured 1·10 45
DESIGNS: 20ch. to 60ch. Different buses and electric trams.

1035 Dancers and Emblem

1992. Spring Friendship Art Festival, Pyongyang.
N3129 **1035** 10ch. multicoloured 30 10

1036 Birthplace, Mangyongdae

1992. 80th Birthday of Kim Il Sung. Revolutionary Sites. Multicoloured.
N3130 10ch. Type **1036** (postage) 15 10
N3131 10ch. Party emblem and Turubong monument 15 10
N3132 10ch. Map and Ssuksom 15 10
N3133 10ch. Statue of soldier and Tongchang 15 10
N3134 40ch. Cogwheels and Taean 60 30
N3135 40ch. Chollima Statue and Kangson 60 30
N3136 1wn.20 Monument and West Sea Barrage (air) 1·75 85

1038 Soldiers on Parade

1992. 60th Anniv of People's Army. Multicoloured.
N3139 10ch. Type **1038** 15 10
N3140 10ch. Couple greeting soldier 15 10
N3141 10ch. Army, air force and navy personnel 15 10

1039 Hurdling

1992. Olympic Games, Barcelona (2nd issue). Multicoloured.
N3142 10ch. Type **1039** 25 10
N3143 20ch. High jumping . . . 40 15
N3144 30ch. Putting the shot . . 60 20
N3145 40ch. Sprinting 75 30
N3146 50ch. Long jumping . . . 90 35
N3147 60ch. Throwing the javelin 1·10 45

1040 Planting Crops

1992. Evolution of Man. Designs showing life in the New Stone Age (10, 20ch.) and the Bronze Age (others). Multicoloured.
N3149 10ch. Type **1040** (postage) 15 10
N3150 20ch. Family around cooking pot 30 15
N3151 30ch. Ploughing fields . . 45 20
N3152 40ch. Performing domestic chores 60 30
N3153 50ch. Building a dolmen (air) 75 35

1041 White-bellied Black Woodpecker 1042 Map and Hands holding Text

1992. Birds. Multicoloured.
N3154 10ch. Type **1041** 20 15
N3155 20ch. Common pheasant 40 25
N3156 30ch. White stork 60 35
N3157 40ch. Blue-winged pitta . . 85 55
N3158 50ch. Pallas's sandgrouse 1·10 60
N3159 60ch. Black grouse . . . . 1·25 80

1992. 20th Anniv of Publication of North–South Korea Joint Agreement.
N3161 **1042** 1wn.50 multicoloured 90 30

1043 "Bougainvillea spectabilis" 1044 Venus, Earth, Mars and Satellite

1992. Flowers. Multicoloured.
N3163 10ch. Type **1043** 25 10
N3164 20ch. "Ixora chinensis" . . 40 15
N3165 30ch. "Dendrobium taysuwie" 60 20
N3166 40ch. "Columnea gloriosa" 75 30
N3167 50ch. "Crinum" 90 35
N3168 60ch. "Ranunculus asiaticus" . . . . 1·10 45

1992. The Solar System. Multicoloured.
N3169 50ch. Type **1044** 90 35
N3170 50ch. Jupiter 90 35
N3171 50ch. Saturn 90 35
N3172 50ch. Uranus 90 35
N3173 50ch. Neptune and Pluto 90 35
Nos. N3169/73 were issued together, se-tenant, forming a composite design.

1045 "470" Dinghy 1046 Moreno Mannini (defender)

1992. "Riccione '92" Stamp Fair. Multicoloured.
N3175 10ch. Type **1045** 15 10
N3176 20ch. Sailboard 30 15
N3177 30ch. Sailing dinghy . . . 45 20
N3178 40ch. "Finn" dinghy . . . 60 30
N3179 50ch. "420" dinghy . . . 75 35
N3180 60ch. Fair emblem 90 45

1992. Sampdoria, Italian Football Champion, 1991. Multicoloured.
N3181 20ch. Type **1046** 30 15
N3182 30ch. Gianluca Vialli (forward) 45 30
N3183 40ch. Pietro Vierchowod (defender) 60 30
N3184 50ch. Fausto Pari (defender) 75 35
N3185 60ch. Roberto Mancini (forward) 90 45
N3186 1wn. Paolo Mantovani (club president) . . . . 1·50 75

1047 Black-belts warming up

1992. 8th World Taekwondo Championship, Pyongyang. Multicoloured.
N3188 10ch. Type **1047** 15 10
N3189 30ch. "Roundhouse" kick 45 30
N3190 50ch. High kick 75 35
N3191 70ch. Flying kick . . . . 1·00 50
N3192 90ch. Black-belt breaking tiles with fist . . . . . 1·40 70

1048 Common Toad ("Bufo bufo")

1992. Frogs and Toads. Multicoloured.
N3194 40ch. Type **1048** (postage) 75 30
N3195 40ch. Moor frog ("Rana arvalis") 75 30
N3196 40ch. "Rana chosenica" 75 30
N3197 70ch. Common pond frog ("Rana nigromaculata") 1·25 50
N3198 70ch. Japanese tree toad ("Hyla japonica") . . . 1·25 50
N3199 70ch. "Rana coreana" (air) . . . . 1·25 50

1049 "Rhododendron mucronulatum"

1992. World Environment Day. Multicoloured.
N3200 10ch. Type **1049** (postage) 15 10
N3201 30ch. Barn swallow . . . 55 35
N3202 40ch. "Stewartia koreana" (flower) 60 30
N3203 50ch. "Dictyoptera aurora" (beetle) 75 35
N3204 70ch. "Metasequoia glyptostroboides" (tree) 1·00 50
N3205 90ch. Chinese salamander 1·40 70
N3206 1wn. 20 "Ginkgo biloba" (tree) (air) . . . . . . 1·75 85
N3207 1wn. 40 Alpine bullhead 3·00 1·25

1050 Fin Whale ("Balaenoptera physalus")

1992. Whales and Dolphins. Multicoloured.
N3208 50ch. Type **1050** (postage) 1·00 35
N3209 50ch. Common dolphin ("Delphinus delphis") 1·00 35
N3210 50ch. Killer Whale ("Orcinus orca") . . . 1·00 35
N3211 50ch. Hump-backed whale ("Megaptera nodosa") 1·00 35
N3212 50ch. Bottle-nosed whale ("Berardius bairdii") . . 1·00 35
N3213 50ch. Sperm whale ("Physeter catadon") (air) . . . . 1·00 35

1051 Mother and Chicks

1992. New Year. Roosters in various costumes. Multicoloured.
N3214 10ch. Type **1051** 15 10
N3215 20ch. Lady 30 15
N3216 30ch. Warrior 45 20
N3217 40ch. Courtier 60 30
N3218 50ch. Queen 75 35
N3219 60ch. King 90 45

1052 Choe Chol Su (boxing)

1992. Gold Medal Winners at Barcelona Olympics. Multicoloured.
N3221 10ch. Type **1052** 15 10
N3222 20ch. Pae Kil Su (gymnastics) 30 15
N3223 50ch. Ri Hak Son (freestyle wrestling) . . 75 35
N3224 60ch. Kim Il (freestyle wrestling) 90 45

1053 Golden Mushroom 1055 League Members and Flag

1054 "Keumkangsania asiatica"

1993. Fungi. Multicoloured.

N3227	10ch. Type **1053**	15	10
N3228	20ch. Shaggy caps	30	15
N3229	30ch. "Ganoderma lucidum"	45	20
N3230	40ch. Brown mushroom	60	30
N3231	50ch. "Volvaria bombycina"	75	35
N3232	60ch. "Sarcodon aspratus"	90	45

1993. Plants. Multicoloured.

N3234	10ch. Type **1054**	25	10
N3235	20ch. "Echinosophora koreensis"	80	15
N3236	30ch. "Abies koreana"	55	20
N3237	40ch. "Benzoin angustifolium"	75	30
N3238	50ch. "Abeliophyllum distichum"	85	35
N3239	60ch. "Abelia mosanensis"	1·00	45

1993. 8th League of Socialist Working Youth Congress. Multicoloured.

N3241	10ch. Type **1055**	15	10
N3242	40ch. Flame, League emblem and text	60	30

1056 Phophyong Revolutionary Site Tower and March Corps Emblem

1057 Tower of Juche Idea and Grand Monument, Mt. Wangjae

1993. 70th Anniv of 1000-ri Journey for Learning.

N3243	**1056** 10ch. multicoloured	15	10

1993. 60th Anniv of Wangjaesan Meeting.

N3244	**1057** 5ch. multicoloured	10	10

1058 "Kimjomgil" (begonia)

1993. 51st Birthday of Kim Jong Il.

N3245	**1058** 10ch. multicoloured	40	10

1059 Pilot Fish

1993. Fishes. Multicoloured.

N3247	10ch. Type **1059**	25	10
N3248	20ch. Japanese stingray	55	20
N3249	30ch. Opah	80	30
N3250	40ch. Coelacanth	1·10	45
N3251	50ch. Moara grouper	1·25	50

1060/1064 "Spring on the Hill" (⅓-size illustration)

1993. 18th-century Korean Painting.

N3253	**1060** 40ch. multicoloured	60	30
N3254	**1061** 40ch. multicoloured	60	30
N3255	**1062** 40ch. multicoloured	60	30
N3256	**1063** 40ch. multicoloured	60	30
N3257	**1064** 40ch. multicoloured	60	30

Nos. N3253/7 were issued together, se-tenant, forming the composite design illustrated.

1065 Violinist, Dancers and Emblem

1993. Spring Friendship Art Festival, Pyongyang.

N3258	**1065** 10ch. multicoloured	15	10

1066 Books

1993. 81st Birthday of Kim Il Sung and Publication of his Reminiscences "With the Century".

N3259	**1066** 10ch. multicoloured	15	10

1067 Kwangbok Street

1993. Pyongyang. Multicoloured.

N3261	10ch. Type **1067**	15	10
N3262	20ch. Chollima Street	30	15
N3263	30ch. Munsu Street	45	20
N3264	40ch. Moranbong Street	60	30
N3265	50ch. Thongil Street	75	35

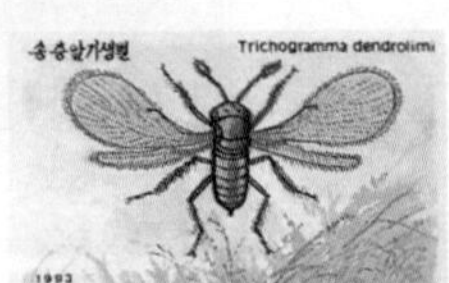

1068 "Trichogramma dendrolimi" (fly)

1993. Insects. Multicoloured.

N3267	10ch. Type **1068**	15	10
N3268	20ch. "Brachymeria obscurata" (fly)	30	15
N3269	30ch. "Metrioptera brachyptera" (cricket)	45	20
N3270	50ch. European field cricket	75	35
N3271	70ch. "Geocoris pallidipennis" (beetle)	1·00	50
N3272	90ch. "Cyphonony x dorsalis" (wasp) fighting spider	1·40	70

1069 Ri In Mo

1071 Grey-headed Woodpecker

1070 Footballers

1993. Return from Imprisonment of Ri In Mo (war correspondent).

N3273	**1069** 10ch. multicoloured	15	10

1993. World Cup Football Championship, U.S.A.

N3275	**1070** 10ch. multicoloured	25	10
N3276	– 20ch. multicoloured	40	15
N3277	– 30ch. multicoloured	60	20
N3278	– 50ch. multicoloured	90	35
N3279	– 70ch. multicoloured	1·25	50
N3280	– 90ch. multicoloured	1·75	70

DESIGNS: 20ch. to 90ch. Various footballing scenes.

1993. Birds. Multicoloured.

N3281	10ch. Type **1071**	20	15
N3282	20ch. King bird of paradise	40	20
N3283	30ch. Lesser bird of paradise	45	35
N3284	40ch. Paradise whydah	80	55
N3285	50ch. Magnificent bird of paradise	1·00	60
N3286	60ch. Greater bird of paradise	1·25	80

Nos. N3283/4 also commemorate "Indopex '93" international stamp exhibition, Surabaya.

1072 Korean Peninsula and Flag (½-size illustration)

1993. Self-adhesive. Roul.

N3287	**1072** 1wn.50 multicoloured	2·00	30

No. N3287 is for any one of the six stamps which together make up the design illustrated. They are peeled from a card backing.

1073 Kim Myong Nam (weightlifting, 1990)

1993. World Champions. Multicoloured.

N3293	10ch. Type **1073**	15	10
N3294	20ch. Kim Kwang Suk (gymnastics, 1991)	30	15
N3295	30ch. Pak Yong Sun (table tennis, 1975, 1977)	45	20
N3296	50ch. Kim Yong Ok (radio direction-finding, 1990)	75	35
N3297	70ch. Han Yun Ok (taekwondo, 1987, 1988, 1990)	1·00	50
N3298	90ch. Kim Yong Sik (free-style wrestling, 1986, 1989)	1·40	70

1074 Cabbage and Chilli Peppers

1075 State Arms

1993. Fruits and Vegetables. Multicoloured.

N3299	10ch. Type **1074**	15	10
N3300	20ch. Squirrels and horse chestnuts	30	15
N3301	30ch. Grapes and peach	45	20
N3302	40ch. Birds and persimmon	60	30
N3303	50ch. Tomatoes, aubergine and cherries	75	35
N3304	60ch. Radish, onion and garlic	90	45

1993.

N3305	**1075** 10ch. red	15	10

1076 Soldiers and Civilians

1993. 40th Anniv of Victory in Liberation War. Multicoloured.

N3306	10ch. Type **1076**	15	10
N3307	10ch. Officer and soldier	15	10
N3308	10ch. Guided missiles on low-loaders on parade	15	10
N3309	10ch. Anti-aircraft missiles on lorries on parade	15	10
N3310	10ch. Self-propelled missile launchers (tracked vehicles) on parade	15	10
N3311	10ch. Machine gun emplacement (30 × 48 mm)	15	10
N3312	10ch. Soldier holding flag (bronze statue) (30 × 48 mm)	15	10
N3314	10ch. Kim Il Sung at strategic policy meeting	15	10
N3315	10ch. Kim Il Sung directing battle for Height 1211	15	10
N3316	10ch. Kim Il Sung at munitions factory	15	10
N3317	10ch. Kim Il Sung with tank commanders	15	10
N3318	10ch. Kim Il Sung with triumphant soldiers	15	10
N3319	20ch. Kim Il Sung with artillery unit	30	15
N3320	20ch. Kim Il Sung encouraging machine gun crew	30	15
N3321	20ch. Kim Il Sung studying map of Second Front	30	15
N3322	20ch. Kim Il Sung with airmen	30	15
N3323	20ch. Musicians ("Alive is art of Korea")	30	15
N3313	40ch. Soldiers and flags ("Let us become Kim Jims and Ri Su Boks of the 90s") (30 × 48 mm)	60	30

1077 Choe Yong Do

1078 "Robinia sp."

1993. National Reunification Prize Winners. Multicoloured.

N3325	10ch. Type **1077**	15	10
N3326	20ch. Kim Ku	30	15
N3327	30ch. Hong Myong Hui	45	20
N3328	40ch. Ryo Un Hyong	60	30
N3329	50ch. Kim Jong Thae	75	35
N3330	60ch. Kim Chaek	90	45

1993. "Taipei '93" International Stamp Exhibition, Taipeh. Multicoloured.

N3331	20ch. Type **1078**	40	15
N3332	30ch. "Hippeastrum"	60	20

1079 Newton

1080 King Tongmyong shooting Bow

1993. 350th Birth Anniv (1992) of Sir Isaac Newton (mathematician and scientist). Multicoloured.

N3334	10ch. Type **1079**	25	10
N3335	20ch. Apple tree and formula of law of gravitation	40	15
N3336	30ch. Satellite, reflecting telescope, dish aerial, globe and rocket	60	20
N3337	50ch. Formula of binomial theorem	90	35
N3338	70ch. Newton's works and statue	1·10	50

1993. Restoration of King Tongmyong of Koguryo's Tomb. Multicoloured.

N3339	10ch. Type **1080**	15	10
N3340	20ch. King Tongmyong saluting crowd	30	15
N3341	30ch. Restoration monument	45	20
N3342	40ch. Temple of the Tomb of King Tongmyong (horiz)	60	30
N3343	50ch. Tomb (horiz)	75	35

1082 "Cyrtopodium andresoni"

1084 Mao Tse-tung at Yanan, 1944

1993. Orchids. Multicoloured.

N3346	10ch. Type **1082**	25	10
N3347	20ch. "Cattleya"	40	15
N3348	30ch. "Cattleya intermedia" "Oculata"	60	20

N3349 40ch. Potinaria "Maysedo godensia" 75 30
N3350 50ch. Kim Il Sung flower 1·00 35

1993. Birth Centenary of Mao Tse-tung. Multicoloured.
N3352 10ch. Type **1084** 15 10
N3353 20ch. Seated portrait (Peking, 1960) 30 15
N3354 30ch. Casting a vote, 1953 45 20
N3355 40ch. With pupils at Shaoshan Secondary School, 1959 . . . . . 60 30

1085 Phungsan

1086 Purple Hyosong Flower

1994. New Year. Dogs. Multicoloured.
N3358 10ch. Type **1085** 15 10
N3359 20ch. Yorkshire terriers 30 15
N3360 30ch. Gordon setter . . . 45 20
N3361 40ch. Pomeranian 60 30
N3362 50ch. Spaniel with pups 75 35

1994. 52nd Birthday of Kim Jong Il. Multicoloured.
N3364 10ch. Type **1086** 25 10
N3365 40ch. Yellow hyosong flower 80 30

1087 Red and Black Dragon-eyed

1994. Goldfishes. Multicoloured.
N3367 10ch. Type **1087** 20 10
N3368 30ch. Red and white bubble-eyed 70 30
N3369 50ch. Red and white veil-tailed wenyu . . . . . 1·10 50
N3370 70ch. Red and white fringe-tailed . . . . . . 1·60 75

1088 Crowd with Banners

1089 Wheat, Banner and Woman writing

1994. 20th Anniv of Publication of "Programme for Modelling the Whole Society on the Juche Idea" by Kim Jong Il.
N3371 **1088** 20ch. multicoloured 30 15

1994. 30th Anniv of Publication of "Theses on the Socialist Rural Question in Our Country" by Kim Il Sung. Multicoloured.
N3373 10ch. Type **1089** 15 10
N3374 10ch. Electricity generating systems and pylon . . . 15 10
N3375 10ch. Lush fields, grain and tractor 15 10
N3376 40ch. Modern housing, books, food crops and laboratory technician . . 60 30
N3377 40ch. Revellers 60 30

1090 "Mangyongbong-92" (ferry)

1091 National Flag

1994. Ships. Multicoloured.
N3379 20ch. Type **1090** 30 15
N3380 30ch. "Osandok" (freighter) 45 20
N3381 40ch. "Ryongaksan" (stern trawler) 60 30
N3382 50ch. Stern trawler 75 35

1994.
N3384 **1091** 10ch. red and blue . . 15 10

1092 Birthplace and Magnolia (national flower)

1093 "Chrysosplenium sphaerospermum"

1994. 82nd Birthday of Kim Il Sung. Multicoloured.
N3385 10ch. Type **1092** 15 10
N3386 40ch. Birthplace, Manyongdae, and Kim Il Sung flower 60 30

1994. Alpine Plants on Mt. Paekdu. Multicoloured.
N3388 10ch. Type **1093** 25 10
N3389 20ch. "Campanula cephalotes" 40 15
N3390 40ch. "Trollius macropetalus" 75 30
N3391 40ch. "Gentiana algida" 75 30
N3392 50ch. "Sedum kamtschaticum" 90 35

1094 National Olympic Committee Emblem

1095 Red Cross Launch ("Relief on the Sea")

1994. Centenary of International Olympic Committee. Multicoloured.
N3394 10ch. Type **1094** 15 10
N3395 20ch. Pierre de Coubertin (founder) 30 15
N3396 30ch. Olympic flag and flame 45 20
N3397 50ch. Emblem of Centennial Olympic Congress, Paris 75 35

1994. 75th Anniv of International Red Cross and Red Crescent Federation. Multicoloured.
N3399 10ch. Electric tram, pedestrians on footbridge and traffic lights ("Prevention of Traffic Accident") . . . 45 10
N3400 20ch. Type **1095** 30 15
N3401 30ch. Planting tree ("Protection of Environment") 45 20
N3402 40ch. Dam ("Prevention of Drought Damage") 60 30

1994. No. N3287 surch **160** in circle.
N3403 **1072** 1wn.60 on 1wn.50 multicoloured . . . 2·10 1·00

1097 Northern Fur Seal

1994. Marine Mammals. Multicoloured.
N3404 10ch. Type **1097** 25 10
N3405 40ch. Southern elephant seal 75 30
N3406 60ch. Southern sealion . . 1·10 45

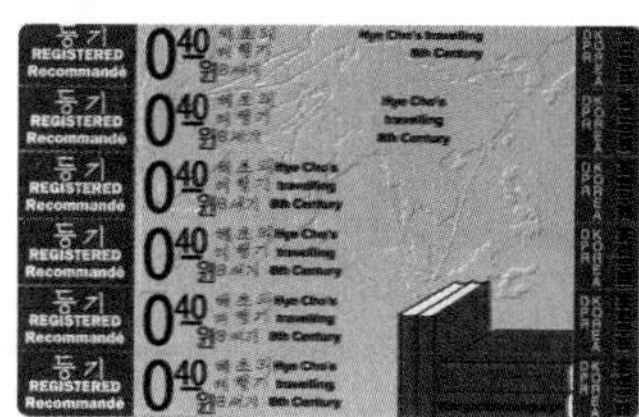
1098 Map of Asia and Books (½-size illustration)

1994. 8th-century Travels of Hye Cho. Self-adhesive. Roul.
N3408 **1098** 40ch. multicoloured 55 25
No. N3408 is for any one of the six stamps which together make up the design illustrated. They are peeled from a card backing.

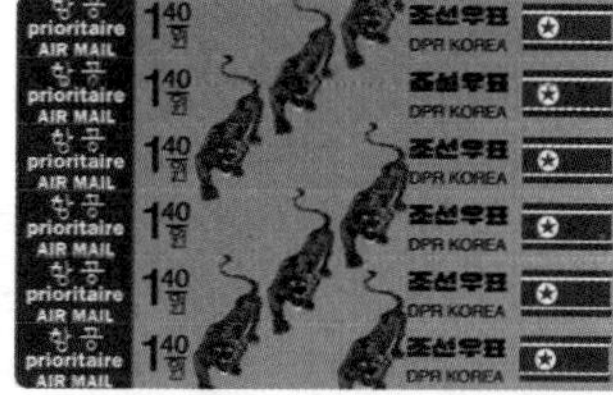
1099 Tigers (½-size illustration)

1994. Self-adhesive. Roul.
N3409 **1099** 1wn.40 multicoloured 1·90 95
No. N3409 is for any one of the six stamps which together make up the design illustrated. They are peeled from a card backing.

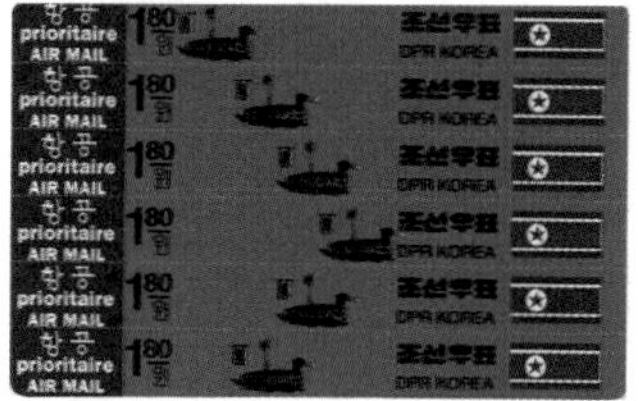
1101 "Turtle" Ships (½-size illustration)

1994. Self-adhesive. Roul.
N3411 **1101** 1wn.80 multicoloured 2·40 1·10
No. N3411 is for any one of the six stamps which together make up the design illustrated. They are peeled from a card backing.

1102 Striped Bonnet

1994. Molluscs. Multicoloured.
N3412 30ch. Type **1102** 60 20
N3413 40ch. Equilateral venus . . 1·00 30

1103 Trapeze

1994. Circus Acrobatics. Multicoloured.
N3416 10ch. Type **1103** 15 10
N3417 20ch. Reino (Swedish acrobat) performing rope dance 30 15
N3418 30ch. Seesaw performer 45 20
N3419 40ch. Unicycle juggler . . 60 30

1104 Korean Script and "100"

1994. Birth Centenary of Kim Hyong Jik (father of Kim Il Sung). Multicoloured.
N3420 **1104** 10ch. multicoloured 10 10

1105 Jon Pong Jun and Battle Scene

1994. Centenary of Kabo Peasant War.
N3422 **1105** 10ch. multicoloured 15 10

1107 Workers and Banner

1109 "Acorus calamus"

1108 Onsong Fish

1994. Revolutionary Economic Strategy.
N3424 **1107** 10ch. multicoloured 15 10

1994. Fossils. Multicoloured.
N3425 40ch. Type **1108** 90 30
N3426 40ch. Metasequoia 75 30
N3427 40ch. Mammoth teeth . . 75 30
N3428 80ch. Archaeopteryx . . . 1·60 2·50

1994. Medicinal Plants. Multicoloured.
N3429 20ch. Type **1109** 30 15
N3430 30ch. "Arctium lappa" . . 45 20

1110 Ribbon Exercise

1111 Chou En-lai at Tianjun, 1919

1994. Callisthenics. Multicoloured.
N3432 10ch. Type **1110** 15 10
N3433 20ch. Ball exercise 30 15
N3434 30ch. Hoop exercise . . . 45 20
N3435 40ch. Ribbon exercise (different) 60 30
N3436 50ch. Club exercise . . . 75 35

1994. 96th Birth Anniv of Chou En-lai (Chinese statesman). Multicoloured.
N3437 10ch. Type **1111** 15 10
N3438 20ch. Arrival in Northern Shanxi from Long March 30 15
N3439 30ch. At Conference of Asian and African Countries, Bandung, Indonesia, 1955 . . . . 45 20
N3440 40ch. Surrounded by children in Wulumuqi, Xinjiang Province . . . 60 30

1113 Kim Il Sung as Youth, 1927

1994. Kim Il Sung Commemoration (1st issue).
(a) As T **1113**. Each red, gold and black.
N3444 40ch. Type **1113** 60 30
N3445 40ch. Kim Il Sung and Kim Jong Suk 60 30
N3446 40ch. Kim Il Sung as young man 60 30
(b) Horiz designs as T **1115**. Each purple, gold and black.
N3447 40ch. Kim Il Sung making speech, Pyongyang, 1945 . . . . 60 30
N3448 40ch. Kim Il Sung sitting at desk 60 30
N3449 40ch. Kim Il Sung at microphone 60 30
See also Nos. N3459/63.

1114 Player No. 4

1994. World Cup Football Championship, U.S.A. Multicoloured.

N3451	10ch. Type **1114**	15	10
N3452	20ch. Player No. 5	30	15
N3453	30ch. Player No. 6	45	20
N3454	40ch. Player No. 7	60	30
N3455	1wn. Player No. 8	1·50	75
N3456	1wn.50 Player No. 9	2·25	1·10

1115 Kim Il Sung making Radio Broadcast, 1950

1994. Kim Il Sung Commemoration (2nd issue).

(a) Each green, gold and black.

N3458	40ch. Type **1115**	60	30
N3459	40ch. Kim Il Sung with four soldiers, 1951	60	30
N3460	40ch. Kim Il Sung and crowd of soldiers, 1953	60	30

(b) Multicoloured (N3463) or lilac, gold and black (others).

N3461	40ch. Kim Il Sung with workers at Chongjin Steel Plant, 1959	60	30
N3462	40ch. Kim Il Sung on Onchon Plain	60	30
N3463	40ch. Kim Il Sung at desk using telephone	60	30

1116 National Flags and Flowers

1117 Ri Myon Sang and Score of "Snow Falls"

1994. Korean–Chinese Friendship.

N3465	**1116** 40ch. multicoloured	60	30

1994. Composers. Multicoloured.

N3467	50ch. Type **1117**	1·00	35
N3468	50ch. Pak Han Kyu and score of "Nobody Knows"	1·00	35
N3469	50ch. Ludwig van Beethoven and score of piano sonata No. 14	1·00	35
N3470	50ch. Wolfgang Amadeus Mozart and score of symphony No. 39	1·00	35

1118 National Emblem

1994.

N3471	**1118** 1wn. green	1·50	75
N3472	3wn. brown	4·00	2·00

1119 P. Wiberg (Alpine combined skiing)

1994. Winter Olympic Games, Lillehammer, Gold Medal Winners. Multicoloured.

N3473	10ch. Type **1119**	15	10
N3474	20ch. D. Compagnoni (slalom)	30	15
N3475	30ch. O. Baiul (figure skating)	45	20
N3476	40ch. D. Jansen (speed skating)	60	30
N3477	1wn. L. Yegorova (cross-country sking)	1·50	75
N3478	1wn.50 B. Blair (speed skating)	2·25	1·10

1120 Pig Couple

1121 Pison Waterfalls, Mt. Myohyang

1995. New Year. Year of the Pig. Multicoloured.

N3480	20ch. Type **1120**	45	15
N3481	40ch. Pigs carrying bucket and spade	80	30

1995. 20th Anniv of World Tourism Organization. Multicoloured.

N3483	30ch. Tower of Juche Idea, Pyongyang	45	20
N3484	30ch. Type **1121**	45	20
N3485	30ch. Myogilsang (cliff-face carving of Buddha), Mt. Kumgang	45	20

1122 Mangyongdae, Badaogou and Badge

1123 Monument bearing 50th Birthday Ode, Mt. Paekdu

1995. 70th Anniv of 1000-ri (250 mile) Journey by Kim Il Sung to Restore Fatherland.

N3486	**1122** 40ch. multicoloured	60	30

1995. 53rd Birthday of Kim Jong Il.

N3487	**1123** 10ch. multicoloured	15	10

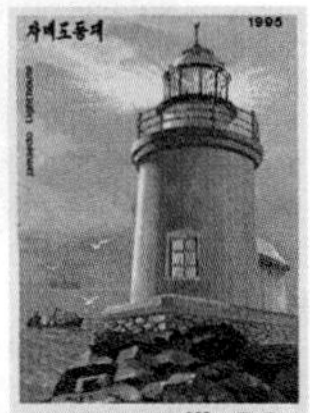
1124 Reconstruction Monument

1125 Jamaedo Lighthouse

1995. Completion of Reconstruction of King Tangun's Tomb. Multicoloured.

N3489	10ch. Type **1124**	15	10
N3490	30ch. Bronze dagger on plinth	45	20
N3491	50ch. Monument inscribed with exploits of King Tangun	75	15
N3492	70ch. Gateway (horiz)	1·00	50

1995. Lighthouses. Multicoloured.

N3494	20ch. Type **1125**	30	15
N3495	1wn. Phido Lighthouse, West Sea Barrage	1·75	85

1126 Cracked Green Russula

1127 Couple planting Tree

1995. Fungi. Multicoloured.

N3496	20ch. Type **1126**	50	15
N3497	30ch. "Russula atropurpurea"	75	20

1995. Tree Planting Day.

N3499	**1127** 10ch. multicoloured	30	10

1128 Birthplace, Mangyongdae

1995. 83rd Birth Anniv of Kim Il Sung. Multicoloured.

N3500	10ch. Type **1128**	15	10
N3501	40ch. Tower of Juche Idea and Kim Il Sung flower (vert)	60	30

1129 Deng Xiaoping waving

1995. 20th Anniv of Kim Il Sung's Visit to China. Multicoloured.

N3503	10ch. Type **1129**	15	10
N3504	20ch. Deng Xiaoping of China sitting in armchair (vert)	30	15

1130 Venue

1995. 40th Anniv of Asian–African Conference, Bandung.

N3506	**1130** 10ch. black, buff and red	15	10
N3507	– 50ch. brown, gold and black	75	35

DESIGN: 50ch. Kim Il Sung receiving honorary Doctorate at Indonesia University.

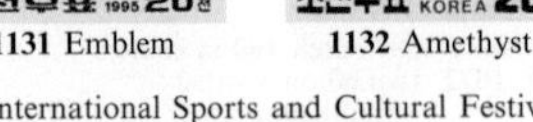
1131 Emblem

1132 Amethyst

1995. International Sports and Cultural Festival for Peace, Pyongyang. Multicoloured.

N3509	20ch. Type **1131**	30	15
N3510	40ch. Dancer	60	30
N3511	40ch. Inoki Kanji (leader of Sports Peace Party of Japan)	60	30

1995. Minerals.

N3513	**1132** 20ch. multicoloured	50	15

1133 Eurasian Tree Sparrow

1134 Ostrea

1995. White Animals. Multicoloured.

N3514	40ch. Type **1133**	60	30
N3515	40ch. "Stichopus japonicus" (sea slug)	60	30

1995. Fossils. Multicoloured.

N3516	50ch. Type **1134**	1·00	35
N3517	1wn. Cladophlebis (fern)	1·50	75

1135 Chess

1136 National Flag and Korean Hall, Tokyo

1995. Traditional Games. Multicoloured.

N3518	30ch. Type **1135**	50	20
N3519	60ch. Taekwondo	1·00	45
N3520	70ch. Yut	1·25	50

1995. 40th Anniv of Association of Koreans in Japan.

N3521	**1136** 1wn. multicoloured	1·50	75

1137 Weightlifting

1138 "Russula citrina"

1995. Olympic Games, Atlanta (1996). Multicoloured.

N3522	50ch. Type **1137**	90	35
N3523	50ch. Boxing	90	35

1995. Fungi. Multicoloured.

N3525	40ch. Type **1138**	75	30
N3526	60ch. Black trumpets	1·00	45
N3527	80ch. Shaggy caps	1·40	60

1140 Mt. Paekdu and Revolutionaries

1141 Markswoman

1995. 50th Anniv of Liberation. Multicoloured.

N3529	10ch. Type **1140**	15	10
N3530	30ch. Map of Korea and family	45	20
N3531	60ch. Medal	90	45

1995. 1st Military World Games, Rome.

N3534	**1141** 40ch. multicoloured	60	30

1143 Emblem and Banner

1144 Arch of Triumph, Pyongyang

1995. 50th Anniv of Korean Workers' Party. Multicoloured.

N3536	10ch. Type **1143**	15	10
N3537	20ch. Statue of worker, peasant and intellectual	30	15
N3538	30ch. Party monument	45	20

1995. 50th Anniv of Kim Il Sung's Return to Homeland.

N3540	**1144** 10ch. multicoloured	15	10

1145 Tuna

1147 Guinea Pig

1995. Designs as T **1145**. Each brown and black.

(a) Fishes.

N3541	40ch. Type **1145**	70	30
N3542	50ch. Pennant coralfish (with two bands)	90	35
N3543	50ch. Needlefish	90	35

N3544 60ch. Seascorpion . . . . 1·00 45
N3545 5wn. Emperor angelfish 6·50 3·25

(b) Buildings on Kwangbok Street, Pyongyang.
N3546 60ch. Circus 90 45
N3547 70ch. Flats . . . . 1·00 50
N3548 80ch. Ryanggang Hotel . . 1·25 60
N3549 90ch. Tower apartment block (vert) . . . . . . 1·40 70
N3550 1wn. Sosan Hotel (vert) 1·50 75

(c) Machines.
N3551 10ch. Kamsusan tipper truck 15 10
N3552 20ch. Bulldozer 30 15
N3553 30ch. Excavator 45 20
N3554 40ch. Earth mover (vert) 60 30
N3555 10wn. "Chollima 80" tractor (vert) . . . . . 13·00 6·50

(d) Animals.
N3556 30ch. Giraffe (vert) . . . 45 20
N3557 40ch. Ostrich (vert) . . . 60 30
N3558 60ch. Bluebuck (vert) . . 90 45
N3559 70ch. Bactrian camel . . . 1·00 50
N3560 3wn. Indian rhinoceros . . 4·25 2·00

(e) Sculptures of Children.
N3561 30ch. Boy holding bird (vert) 45 20
N3562 40ch. Boy with goose (vert) 60 30
N3563 60ch. Girl with geese (vert) 90 45
N3564 70ch. Boy and girl with football (vert) . . . . . 1·00 50
N3565 2wn. Boy and girl arguing over football (vert) . . . 3·00 1·50

1996. Rodents. Multicoloured.
N3567 20ch. Type **1147** 50 15
N3568 20ch. Squirrel 50 15
N3569 30ch. White mouse . . . 70 20

1148 Emblem, Badge and Flag
1149 Restoration Mounument

1996. 50th Anniv of League of Socialist Working Youth.
N3570 **1148** 10ch. multicoloured 15 10

1996. Reconstruction of Tomb of King Wanggon. Multicoloured.
N3571 30ch. Type **1149** 60 20
N3572 40ch. Entrance gate . . . 75 30
N3573 50ch. Tomb 90 35

1152 Jong Il Peak and Kim Jong Il Flower
1153 Pairs Skating

1996. 54th Birthday of Kim Jong Il.
N3576 **1152** 10ch. multicoloured 40 10

1996. 5th Paektusan Prize Figure Skating Championships. Multicoloured.
N3578 10ch. Type **1153** 25 10
N3579 20ch. Pairs skating (different) 40 15
N3580 30ch. Pairs skating (different) 60 20
N3581 50ch. Women's individual skating 90 35

1155 Farm Worker

1156 1946 20ch. Stamp and Tower of Juche Idea

1996. 50th Anniv of Agrarian Reform Law.
N3584 **1155** 10ch. multicoloured 15 10

1996. 50th Anniv of First North Korean Stamps.
N3585 **1156** 1wn. multicoloured 1·40 70

1158 Birthplace, Mangyongdae

1996. 84th Birth Anniv of Kim Il Sung.
N3587 **1158** 10ch. multicoloured 15 10

1159 Gateway

1996. "China '96" Asian International Stamp Exhibition, Peking. Landmarks in Zhejiang. Multicoloured.
N3589 10ch. Type **1159** 25 10
N3590 10ch. Haiyin Pool 25 10

1160 Hopscotch
1161 Association Pamphlets

1996. Children's Games. Multicoloured.
N3592 20ch. Type **1160** 40 15
N3593 40ch. Shuttlecock 75 30
N3594 50ch. Sledging 90 35

1996. 60th Anniv of Association for Restoration of the Fatherland.
N3595 **1161** 10ch. multicoloured 15 10

1163 Arctic Fox

1164 Boy Saluting

1996. Polar Animals. Multicoloured.
N3597 50ch. Type **1163** 75 35
N3598 50ch. Polar bear 75 35
N3599 50ch. Emperor penguins 75 35
N3600 50ch. Leopard seals . . . 75 35

1996. 50th Anniv of Korean Children's Union.
N3601 **1164** 10ch. multicoloured 40 10

1165 Steam Locomotive

1167 Open Book and Characters

1996. Railway Locomotives. Multicoloured.
N3603 50ch. Type **1165** 75 35
N3604 50ch. Electric locomotive (green livery) 75 35
N3605 50ch. Steam locomotive (facing right) 75 35
N3606 50ch. Diesel locomotive (red and yellow livery) 75 35

1996. 760th Anniv of Publication of "Complete Collection of Buddhist Scriptures printed from 80,000 Wooden Blocks".
N3608 **1167** 40ch. multicoloured 60 30

1168 Worker using Microphone

1996. 50th Anniv of Labour Law.
N3609 **1168** 50ch. multicoloured 75 35

1171 Kumsusan Memorial Palace

1996. 2nd Death Anniv of Kim Il Sung.
N3612 **1171** 10ch. multicoloured 15 10

1172 Kim Il Sung meeting Jiang Zemin of China, 1991

1173 Football and Ancient Greek Athletes

1996. 35th Anniv of Korean–Chinese Treaty for Friendship, Co-operation and Mutual Assistance.
N3614 **1172** 10ch. brown, gold and black 15 10
N3615 – 10ch. green, gold and black 15 10
DESIGN: 10ch. Kim Il Sung meeting Pres. Mao Tse-tung of China, 1954.

1996. Centenary of Modern Olympic Games and Olympic Games, Atlanta. Multicoloured.
N3617 50ch. Type **1173** 85 35
N3618 50ch. Tennis, Olympic Anthem and 1896 5l. Greek stamp 85 35
N3619 50ch. Throwing the hammer and advertisement poster for first modern olympics 85 35
N3620 50ch. Baseball and Olympic stadium, Atlanta 85 35

1174 Couple

1175 State Arms and Symbols of Industry and Communications

1996. 50th Anniv of Sex Equality Law.
N3621 **1174** 50ch. multicoloured 70 35

1996. 50th Anniv of Nationalization of Industries.
N3623 **1175** 50ch. bistre and brown 65 30

1176 Boy with Ball

1178 University Buildings, Pyongyang

1996. 50th Anniv of U.N.I.C.E.F. Multicoloured.
N3624 10ch. Type **1176** 25 10
N3625 20ch. Boy with building blocks 35 15
N3626 50ch. Boy eating melon . . 75 30
N3627 60ch. Girl playing accordion 90 40

1996. 50th Anniv of Kim Il Sung University.
N3629 **1178** 10ch. multicoloured 15 10

1179 Tiger

1180 Red Flag and Tower of Juche Idea

1996. World Conservation Union Congress, Montreal, Canada. Multicoloured.
N3630 50ch. Type **1179** 75 30
N3631 50ch. Royal spoonbill . . 75 30

1996. 70th Anniv of Down-with-Imperialism Union.
N3633 **1180** 10ch. multicoloured 30 10

1183 Japanese Eel

1996. Freshwater Fishes. Multicoloured.
N3636 20ch. Type **1183** 70 15
N3637 20ch. Menada grey mullet ("Liza haematocheila") 70 15

1184 Soldiers and Supreme Commander's Flag

1996. 5th Anniv of Appointment of Kim Jong Il as Supreme Commander of the People's Army.
N3639 **1184** 20ch. multicoloured 50 15

1185 "Ox Driver" (Kim Tu Ryang)

1997. New Year. Year of the Ox. Multicoloured.
N3640 70ch. Type **1185** . . . . . 2·25 45
N3641 70ch. Bronze ritual plate of two bulls and a tiger 2·25 45
N3642 70ch. Boy with bull (ceramic) . . . . 2·25 45
N3643 70ch. Boy flautist sitting on bull (sculpture) . . . 2·25 45

1186 Left-hand Detail
1187 Kitten with Dogs in Basket

1997. "Flowers and Butterflies" by Nam Kye U. Multicoloured.
N3645 50ch. Type **1186** . . . . . 1·25 30
N3646 50ch. Centre detail . . . . 1·25 30
N3647 50ch. Right-hand detail . . 1·25 30
Nos. N3645/7 were issued together, se-tenant, forming a composite design of the painting.

1997. Paintings of Cats and Dogs. Multicoloured.
N3648 50ch. Type **1187** . . . . . 1·25 30
N3649 50ch. Pup in vine-wreathed basket, kitten and pumpkin . . . . . 1·50 30

1189 Birthplace, Mt. Paekdu

1997. 55th Birthday of Kim Jong Il.
N3652 **1189** 10ch. multicoloured 40 10

1190 Pair

1997. 6th Paektusan Prize International Figure Skating Championships, Pyongyang. Multicoloured.
N3654 50ch. Type **1190** . . . . . 1·50 30
N3655 50ch. Pair (mauve) . . . . 1·50 30
N3656 50ch. Pair (green) . . . . 1·50 30

1193 "Prunus ansu"

1194 Foundation Monument

1997. Apricots. Multicoloured.
N3659 50ch. Type **1193** . . . . . 1·40 30
N3660 50ch. "Prunus mandshurica" . . . . . 1·40 30
N3661 50ch. Hoeryong white apricot ("Prunus armeniaca") . . . . . 1·40 30
N3662 50ch. Puksan apricot ("Prunus sibirica") . . . 1·40 30

1997. 80th Anniv of Foundation of Korean National Association.
N3663 **1194** 10ch. brown and green 50 10

1195 Sapling

1196 Birthplace, Mangyongdae

1997. 50th Anniv of Reforestation Day.
N3664 **1195** 10ch. multicoloured

1997. 85th Birth Anniv of Kim Il Sung. Multicoloured.
N3666 10ch. Type **1196** 50 10
N3667 20ch. Sliding Rock (horiz) 1·00 10
N3668 40ch. Warship Rock (horiz) . . . . 1·25 25

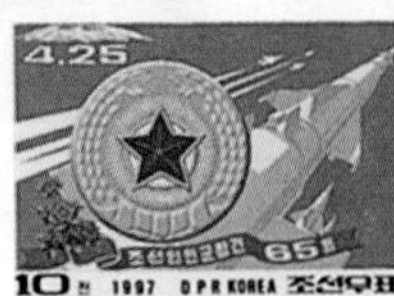
1197 Cap Badge and Modern Weapons

1997. 65th Anniv of People's Army.
N3670 **1197** 10ch. multicoloured 10 10

1198 Map of Korea

1199 Tower of Juche Idea, People and Flag

1997. 25th Anniv of Publication of North–South Korea Joint Agreement.
N3672 **1198** 10ch. multicoloured 10 10

1997. Posters reflecting Joint New Year Newspaper Editorials. Multicoloured.
N3674 10ch. Type **1199** 10 10
N3675 10ch. Man with flag . . . 10 10
N3676 10ch. Soldier, miner, farmer, intellectual and bugler 10 10

1201 Memorial Post and Blazing Fortress

1204 "Redlichia chinensis"

1997. 60th Anniv of Battle of Pochonbo.
N3678 **1201** 40ch. multicoloured 35 15

1997. Fossils. Multicoloured.
N3681 50ch. Type **1204** 45 20
N3682 1wn. "Ptychoparia coreanica" 90 45

1205 Kim Il Sung at Kim Chaek Ironworks, June 1985

1207 Spring

1206 Blindman's Buff

1997. 3rd Death Anniv of Kim Il Sung. Multicoloured.
N3683 50ch. Kim Il Sung at microphones (party conference, October 1985) 45 20
N3684 50ch. Type **1205** 45 20
N3685 50ch. Kim Il Sung and farmers holding wheat (Songsin Co-operative Farm, Sadong District, 1993) 45 20
N3686 50ch. Performing artists applauding Kim Il Sung, 1986 . . . . . . 45 20
N3687 50ch. Kim Il Sung at Jonchon Factory, Jagang Province, 1991 45 20
N3688 50ch. Kim Il Sung receiving flowers at People's Army Conference, 1989 . . . 45 20

1997. Children's Games. Multicoloured.
N3689 30ch. Type **1206** 30 15
N3690 60ch. Five stones 55 25
N3691 70ch. Arm wrestling . . . 65 30

1997. Women's National Costumes. Multicoloured.
N3692 10ch. Type **1207** 10 10
N3693 40ch. Summer 35 15
N3694 50ch. Autumn 45 20
N3695 60ch. Winter 55 25

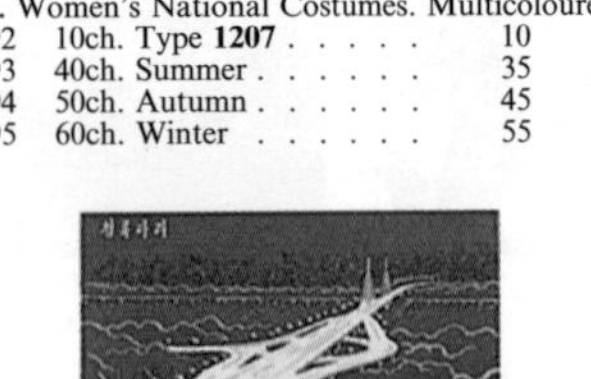
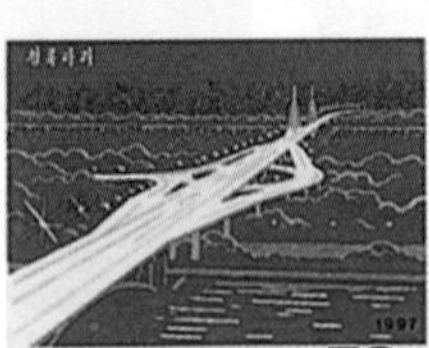
1208 Aerial View

1997. Chongryu Bridge, Pyongyang. Multicoloured.
N3696 50ch. Type **1208** 45 20
N3697 50ch. Chongryu Bridge and birds 45 20

1209 Sun, Magnolias and Balloons

1997. 85th Anniv of Juche Era and Sun Day.
N3698 **1209** 10ch. multicoloured 10 10

1210 Korean Text and Kim Il Sung University

1997. 20th Anniv of Publication of Theses on Socialist Education.
N3700 **1210** 10ch. multicoloured 10 10

1212 Chonbul Peak

1997. 10th Anniv of Korean Membership of World Tourism Organization. Mt Chilbo. Multicoloured.
N3702 50ch. Type **1212** 45 20
N3703 50ch. Sea-Chilbo (coast) 45 20
N3704 50ch. Rojok Peak 45 20

1213 Podok Hermitage

1997. Kumgang Mountains. Multicoloured.
N3705 50ch. Type **1213** 45 20
N3706 50ch. Kumgang Gate . . 45 20

1214 School, Pupil and Mt. Paekdu

1997. 50th Anniv of Mangyongdae Revolutionary School.
N3707 **1214** 40ch. multicoloured 35 15

1215 Lion

1217 Ten-pin Bowling

1997. Animals presented as Gifts to Kim Il Sung. Multicoloured.
N3708 20ch. Type **1215** (Ethiopia, 1987) 15 10
N3709 30ch. Jaguar (Japan, 1992) 30 15
N3710 50ch. Barbary sheep (Czechoslovakia, 1992) 45 20
N3711 80ch. Scarlet macaw (Austria, 1979) 70 35

1997. Sports. Multicoloured.
N3713 50ch. Type **1217** 45 20
N3714 50ch. Golf 45 20
N3715 50ch. Fencing 45 20

1218 Snails

1220 "Juche 87" and Temple

1997. Snails. Multicoloured.
N3716 50ch. Type **1218** 45 20
N3717 50ch. Two snails on leaf 45 20
N3718 50ch. Snail laying eggs . . 45 20

1997. New Year. Year of the Tiger. Multicoloured.
N3720 10ch. Type **1220** 10 10
N3721 50ch. Tiger in rocket (24 × 34 mm) 45 20
N3722 50ch. Tiger steering ship (24 × 34 mm) 45 20

1221 Birthplace, Hoeryong

1997. 80th Birth Anniv of Kim Jong Suk (revolutionary).
N3724 **1221** 10ch. multicoloured 10 10

1222 Skiing

1223 Birthdate and Celebration Ribbon

1998. Winter Olympic Ganes, Nagano, Japan. Multicoloured.
N3726 20ch. Type **1222** 15 10
N3727 40ch. Speed skating . . . 35 15

1998. 56th Birth Anniv of Kim Jong Il.
N3728 **1223** 10ch. multicoloured 10 10

1224 Korean Tigers

1998. Wildlife Paintings. Multicoloured.
N3730 50ch. Type **1224** 45 20
N3731 50ch. Manchurian cranes 45 20

1225 Route Map, Birthplace at Mangyongdae and Trail Followers

1998. 75th Anniv of 1000-ri (250 mile) Journey by Kim Il Sung.
N3733 **1225** 10ch. multicoloured 10 10

1226 Soldiers and Balloons

1998. 5th Anniv of Appointment of Kim Jong Il as Chairman of National Defence Commission.
N3734 **1226** 10ch. multicoloured 10 10

1227 Flags and Birthplace, Mangyongdae

1229 United Front Tower and Moranbong Theatre

1998. 86th Birth Anniv of Kim Il Sung.
N3735 **1227** 10ch. multicoloured 10 10

1998. 50th Anniv of North–South Conference, Pyongyang.
N3737 **1229** 10ch. brown, blue and black 10 10

1230 Players and Championship Emblem

1231 Cabbages

1998. World Cup Football Championship, France. Multicoloured.
N3738 30ch. Type **1230** 30 15
N3739 50ch. Player winning ball and emblem 45 20

1998. Vegetables. Multicoloured.
N3741 10ch. Type **1231** 10 10
N3742 40ch. Radishes 35 15
N3743 50ch. Spring onions . . . 45 20
N3744 60ch. Cucumbers 55 25
N3745 70ch. Pumpkins 65 30
N3746 80ch. Carrots 70 35
N3747 90ch. Garlic 80 40
N3748 1wn. Peppers 90 45

1232 "Countryside in May" (Jong Jong Yo)

1998. Paintings. Multicoloured.
N3749 60ch. Type **1232** 55 25
N3750 1wn.40 "Dance" (Kim Yong Jun) . . . . . . 1·25 65

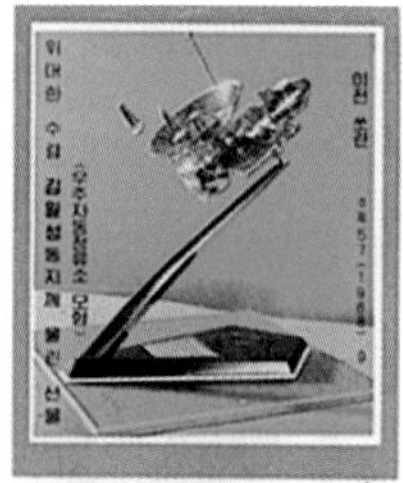
1233 Model of Automatic Space Station (from U.S.S.R.)

1998. International Friendship Exhibition, Myohyang Mountains (2nd series). Multicoloured.
N3752 1wn. Type **1233** 90 45
N3753 1wn. Ceramic flower vase (from Egypt) 90 45
N3754 1wn. "Crane" (statuette, from Billy Graham (evangelist)) 90 45

1234 Research Ship, Buoy and Dolphins in Globe and Hydro-meteorological Headquarters

1235 Stone Age Implement

1998. International Year of the Ocean. Multicoloured.
N3756 10ch. Type **1234** 10 10
N3757 80ch. Sailing dinghies and mother with child . . . 70 35

1998. Korean Central History Museum, Pyongyang. Multicoloured.
N3759 10ch. Type **1235** 10 10
N3760 2wn.50 Fossil skull of monkey . . . . 2·25 1·10

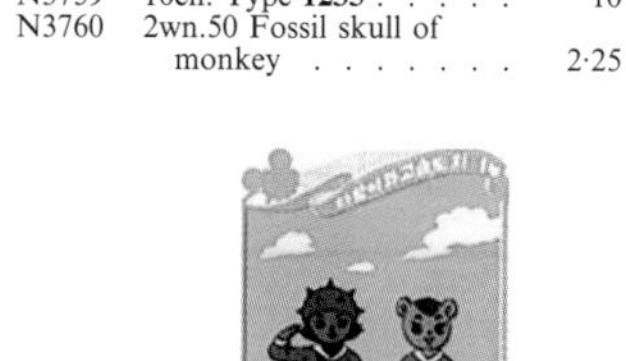
1236 Commander of Hedgehog Unit and Squirrel

1998. "Squirrels and Hedgehogs" (cartoon film). Multicoloured.
N3762 20ch. Type **1236** 15 10
N3763 30ch. Commander of hedgehog unit receiving invitation to banquet . . 30 15
N3764 60ch. Weasel ordering mouse to poison bear 55 25
N3765 1wn.20 Squirrel with poisoned bear . . . . . 1·10 55
N3766 2wn. Weasel and mice invade Flower Village 1·75 90
N3767 2wn.50 Hedgehog scout rescues squirrel . . . . 2·25 1·10

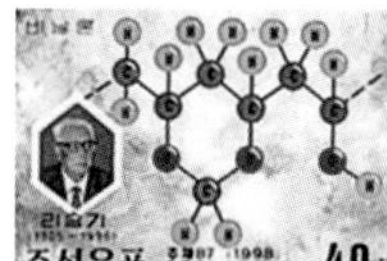
1237 Ri Sung Gi and Molecular Model

1998. 2nd Death Anniv of Ri Sung Gi (inventor of vinalon material).
N3768 **1237** 40ch. multicoloured 35 20

1238 Tiger Cub

1239 "Victory" (Liberation War Monument, Pyongyang) and Medal

1998. Young Mammals. Multicoloured.
N3770 10ch. Type **1238** 10 10
N3771 50ch. Donkey foal 45 20
N3772 1wn.60 Elephant . . . . 1·50 75
N3773 2wn. Two lion cubs . . . 1·75 90

1998. 45th Anniv of Victory in Liberation War.
N3774 **1239** 45ch. brown and pink 40 20

1240 "White Herons in Forest"

1241 Pouch

1998. Embroidery. Multicoloured.
N3776 10ch. Type **1240** 10 10
N3777 40ch. "Carp" 35 20
N3778 1wn.20 "Hollyhock" . . . 1·10 55
N3779 1wn.50 "Cockscomb" . . 1·40 70

1998. Traditional Costume Adornments. Multicoloured.
N3781 10ch. Type **1241** 10 10
N3782 50ch. Tassels 45 25
N3783 1wn.50 Hairpin . . . . . 1·40 70
N3784 1wn.90 Silver knife . . . 1·75 90

1242 Rocket and State Flag

1243 Kim Jong Il Flower

1998. Launch of First Korean Artificial Satellite "Kwangmyongsong 1".
N3785 **1242** 40ch. multicoloured 35 20

1998. Re-election of Kim Jong Il as Chairman of National Defence Commission.
N3787 **1243** 10ch. multicoloured 10 10

1244 Tower of Juche Idea, State Arms and Flag

1998. 50th Anniv of Democratic Republic (1st issue). Multicoloured.
N3789 10ch. Type **1244** 10 10
N3790 1wn. Painting "The Founding of the Democratic People's Republic of Korea, Our Glorious Fatherland" (Kim Il Sung waving from balcony) (48 × 30 mm) 90 45
N3791 1wn. Painting "Square of Victory" (Kim Il Sung and crowd with banners) (48 × 30 mm) 90 45
N3792 1wn. Poster "The Sacred Marks of the Great Leader Kim Il Sung will shine on this Land of Socialism" (Kim Il Sung with produce against panoramic background of Korea) (48 × 30 mm) 90 45

1245 "Let Us Push Ahead with the Forced March for Final Victory"

1247 Cycling

1998.
N3793 **1245** 10ch. multicoloured 10 10

1998. Olympic Games, Sydney, Australia (2000). Multicoloured.
N3795 20ch. Type **1247** 15 10
N3796 50ch. Football 45 25
N3797 80ch. Show jumping . . . 70 35
N3798 1wn.50 Throwing the javelin . . . . 1·40 70

1248 "Cyclamen persicum"

1249 Oral Vaccination

1998. Plants presented as Gifts to Kim Jong Il. Multicoloured.
N3800 20ch. Type **1248** (France, 1994) 15 10
N3801 2wn. "Dianthus chinensis" var. "laciniatus" (Japan, 1994) . . . . 1·75 90

1998. National Vaccination Day.
N3802 **1249** 40ch. multicoloured 35 20

1250 Leopard

1998. The Leopard. Multicoloured.
N3803 1wn. Type **1250** 90 45
N3804 1wn. Leopard in snow . . 90 45
N3805 1wn. Leopard looking to left 90 45
N3806 1wn. Leopard's face . . . 90 45

1251 Canal

1998. Land and Environment Conservation Day. Multicoloured.
N3807 10ch. Type **1251** 10 10
N3808 40ch. Motorway, tower blocks and lorry 35 20

1254 Liu Shaoqi

1255 Victory in Yonsong Monument, Yonan Fortress and Banners

1998. Birth Centenary of Liu Shaoqi (Chairman of Chinese People's Republic, 1959–68). Multicoloured.
N3812 10ch. Type **1254** 10 10
N3813 20ch. Liu Shaoqi and Mao Tse-tung 15 10
N3814 30ch. Liu Shaoqi and his daughter, Xiao Xiao . . 30 15
N3815 40ch. Liu Shaoqi and his wife, Wang Guangmei 35 15

1998. 400th Anniv of Victory in Korean–Japanese War. Multicoloured.
N3817 10ch. Type **1255** 10 10
N3818 30ch. Naval Victory in Myongryang Monument, General Ri Sun Sin and "turtle" ship 30 15
N3819 1wn.60 Monument to Hyujong in Kwangwon province, Hyujong (Buddhist priest), sword and helmet 90 45

1256 Dish Aerial, Artificial Satellite, Globe and Relay Tower

1257 Goat

1998. 15th Anniv of North Korean Membership of Intersputnik.
N3821 **1256** 1wn. dp grn & grn . . 90 45

1998.
N3822 **1257** 10ch. black and green 10 10
N3823 1wn. black and red 90 45

1258 "A Floral Carriage of Happiness" (sculpture) and Palace

1259 Emblem

1998. Mangyongdae Schoolchildren's Palace.
N3824 **1258** 40ch. multicoloured 35 15

1998. 50th Anniv of Universal Declaration of Human Rights.
N3826 **1259** 20ch. multicoloured 15 10

1260 Reeves's Turtle

1261 Thajong Rock

1998. Reptiles and Amphibians. Multicoloured.
N3827 10ch. Type **1260** 10 10
N3828 40ch. Skink 35 15
N3829 60ch. Loggerhead turtle 55 25
N3830 1wn.20 Leatherback turtle 1·10 55
Nos. N3827/30 were issued together, se-tenant, forming a composite design.

1998. Mt. Chilbo. Multicoloured.
N3831 30ch. Type **1261** 30 15
N3832 50ch. Peasant Rock . . . 45 20
N3833 1wn.70 Couple Rock . . . 1·50 75

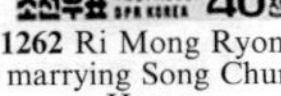

1262 Ri Mong Ryong marrying Song Chun Hyang **1263** Chollima Statue

1998. Tale of Chun Hyang. Multicoloured.
N3834 40ch. Type **1262** 35 15
N3835 1wn.60 Pyon Hak Do watching Chun Hyang 1·50 75
N3836 2wn.50 Ri Mong Ryong and Chun Hyang . . . 2·40 1·10

1998. Pyongyang Monuments.
N3838 **1263** 10ch. red 10 10
N3839 A 10ch. red 10 10
N3840 B 10ch. red 10 10
N3841 A 20ch. orange 15 10
N3842 **1263** 30ch. orange 30 15
N3843 A 40ch. yellow 35 15
N3844 B 40ch. yellow 35 15
N3845 **1263** 70ch. green 65 30
N3846 B 70ch. green 65 30
N3847 1wn.20 green . . . . 1·00 50
N3848 **1263** 1wn.50 green . . . . 1·40 70
N3849 A 2wn. blue . . . . . 1·75 85
N3850 B 3wn. blue . . . . . 2·75 1·40
N3851 **1263** 5wn. blue . . . . . 4·50 2·25
N3852 A 10wn. violet . . . . 9·00 4·50
DESIGNS: A, Arch of Triumph; B, Tower of Juche Idea.

1264 Rabbit meeting Lion **1265** Automatic Rifle and Star

1999. New Year. Year of the Rabbit. Multicoloured.
N3853 10ch. Type **1264** 10 10
N3854 1wn. Rabbit with mirror and lion . . . . 1·40 70
N3855 1wn.50 Lion in trap . . . 2·00 1·00
N3856 2wn.50 Rabbit . . . . . 3·50 1·75

1999. 40th Anniv of Worker-Peasant Red Guards.
N3858 **1265** 10ch. multicoloured 10 10

1266 Log Cabin (birthplace, Mt. Paekdu) **1267** Cranes, Rice Sheaf and "35"

1999. 57th Birth Anniv of Kim Jong Il.
N3859 **1266** 40ch. multicoloured 30 15

1999. 35th Anniv of Publication of *Theses on the Socialist Rural Question in Our Country* by Kim Il Sung.
N3860 **1267** 10ch. multicoloured 10 10

1268 Korean Script and Crowd **1270** Birthplace, Mangyondae

1269 16th-century "Turtle" Ship

1999. 80th Anniv of 1 March Uprising.
N3861 **1268** 10ch. black and brown 10 10

1999. "Australia '99" International Stamp Exhibition, Melbourne.
N3862 **1269** 2wn. multicoloured 1·40 70

1999. 87th Birth Anniv of Kim Il Sung.
N3864 **1270** 10ch. brown, flesh and grey 10 10

1271 Player

1999. 45th Table Tennis Championship, Belgrade, Yugoslavia.
N3866 **1271** 1wn.50 multicoloured 1·10 55

1272 Korean Sports Stamps and Emblem

1999. "iBRA'99" International Stamp Exhibition, Nuremberg, Germany.
N3867 **1272** 1wn. multicoloured 80 40

1273 *Benzoin obtus* **1274** Chimpanzee and Rhinoceros

1999. 40th Anniv of Central Botanical Garden, Mt. Taesong, Pyongyang. Multicoloured.
N3868 10ch. Type **1273** 10 10
N3869 30ch. *Styrax obassia* . . . 20 10
N3870 70ch. *Petunia hybrida* . . 45 20
N3871 90ch. *Impatiens hybrida* . . 60 30

1999. 40th Anniv of Central Zoo, Mt. Taesong, Pyongyang. Multicoloured.
N3873 50ch. Type **1274** 35 15
N3874 60ch. Manchurian crane and deer 45 20
N3875 70ch. Common zebra and kangaroo 50 25

1275 Light Industry Hall

1999. Three Revolutions Museum, Ryonmotdong, Pyongyang. Multicoloured.
N3877 60ch. Type **1275** 45 20
N3878 80ch. Heavy Industry Hall 60 30

1276 Methods of Communication, Satellite and Globe

1999. 20th Anniv of Asia–Pacific Telecommunications Union.
N3876 **1276** 1wn. multicoloured 75 35

1277 Monument

1999. 60th Anniv of Victory in Battle of Musan.
N3880 **1277** 10ch. multicoloured 10 10

1278 Seagulls **1279** "Princess Margarita in a White Dress"

1999. 190th Birth Anniv of Charles Darwin (naturalist). Multicoloured.
N3881 30ch. Type **1278** 15 10
N3882 50ch. Bats 35 15
N3883 1wn. Dolphins 75 35
N3884 1wn.20 Man on horseback 1·00 50
N3885 1wn.50 Dancer . . . . . 1·10 55

1999. 400th Birth Anniv of Diego Velazquez (artist). Multicoloured.
N3887 50ch. Type **1279** 35 15
N3888 50ch. "Men drawing Water from a Well" . . 35 15
N3889 3wn.50 "Self-portrait" . . 3·75 2·00

1280 Rimyongsu Power Station

1999. Hydro-electric Power Stations. Multicoloured.
N3891 50ch. Type **1280** 35 15
N3892 1wn. Jangjasan Power Station 75 35

1281 Players tackling

1999. 3rd Women's World Football Championship, U.S.A. Multicoloured.
N3893 1wn. Type **1281** 75 35
N3894 1wn.50 Player No. 3 and player wearing blue and white strip tackling . . 1·10 55
N3895 1wn.50 Player and goalkeeper . . . . . . 1·10 55
N3896 2wn. Player No. 7 and player wearing blue strip 1·50 75

1283 Man with Candlesticks

1999. *The Nation and Destiny* (Korean film). Scenes from the film. Multicoloured.
N3898 1wn. Type **1283** 80 40
N3899 1wn. Woman holding gun and man in white suit 80 40
N3900 1wn. Man behind bars . . 80 40
N3901 1wn. Man with protective goggles on head 80 40

1284 Samil Lagoon

1999. Mt. Kumgang. Multicoloured.
N3902 20ch. Type **1284** 15 10
N3903 40ch. Samson Rocks (vert) 30 15
N3904 60ch. Rock, Kumgang Sea 45 20
N3905 80ch. Kuryong Waterfall (vert) 60 30
N3906 1wn. Kwimyon Rock (vert) . . . . 1·10 55

1287 Mercedes Motor Car

1999. 5th Death Anniv of Kim Il Sung. Multicoloured.
N3909 1wn. Type **1287** 70 35
N3910 1wn. Railway carriage . . 70 35

1288 Chinese Characters and Mangyong Hill

1999. 105th Birth Anniv of Kim Hyong Jik (revolutionary).
N3911 **1288** 10ch. multicoloured 10 10

1289 Patterned Vessel

1999. Ceramics. Multicoloured.
N3912 70ch. Type **1289** 50 25
N3913 80ch. Wit and Beauty jar 60 50
N3914 1wn. Patterned vase . . . 80 40
N3915 1wn.50 Celadon kettle . . 1·10 55
N3916 2wn.50 White china vase 1·75 85

1290 Silver Carp

1999. Fish Breeding. Multicoloured.
N3917 50ch. Type **1290** 35 15
N3918 1wn. Common carp . . . 80 40
N3919 1wn.50 Spotted silver carp 1·10 55

1291 Map and Crowd

1999. Year of National Independence and Solidarity.
N3920 **1291** 40ch. multicoloured 35 15

1292 Samjiyon with Maps of Japan and Korea

1999. 40th Anniv of Repatriation of Korean Nationals in Japan.
N3921 **1292** 1wn.50 multicoloured 1·10 55

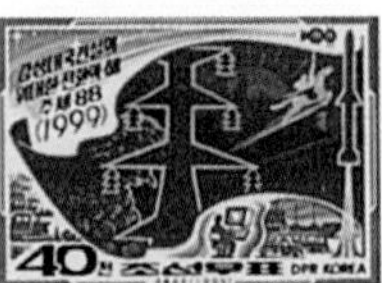

1293 Symbols of Prosperity

1999.
N3922 **1293** 40ch. multicoloured 55 25

1294 100 m Race **1295** *Acalypha hispida*

1999. World Athletics Championships, Seville, Spain. Multicoloured.
N3923 30ch. Type **1294** 40 20
N3924 40ch. Hurdles 55 25
N3925 80ch. Discus . . . . . . 1·10 55

1999. Plants presented to Kim Il Sung. Multicoloured.
N3926 40ch. Type **1295** 55 25
N3927 40ch. *Allamanda neriifolia* 55 25
N3928 40ch. *Begonia x hiemalis* 55 25
N3929 40ch. *Fatsia japonica* . . . 55 25
N3930 40ch. *Streptocarpus hybrida* 55 25
N3931 40ch. *Streptocarpus rexii* 55 25
Nos. N3926/31 were issued together, se-tenant, forming a composite design.

1297 *Grifola frondosa*

1999. Mushrooms. Multicoloured.
N3933 40ch. Type **1297** 55 25
N3934 60ch. *Lactarius volemus* . . 80 40
N3935 1wn. *Coriolus versicolor* 1·40 70

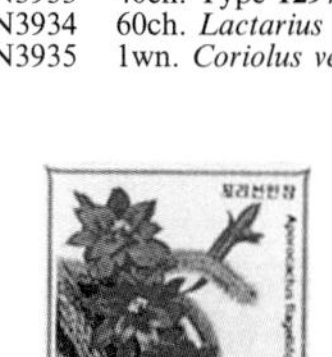

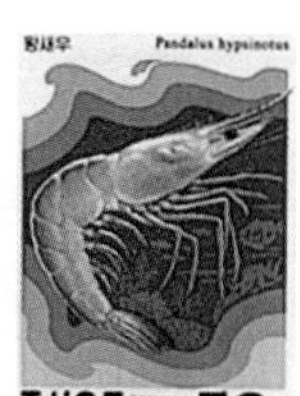

1298 *Aporocactus flagelliformis* **1300** Shrimp

1999. Cacti. Multicoloured.
N3936 40ch. Type **1298** 55 25
N3937 50ch. *Astrophytum ornatum* 70 35
N3938 60ch. *Gymnocalycium michano vichii* 80 40

1999. Crustacea. Multicoloured.
N3943 50ch. Type **1300** 70 35
N3944 70ch. Shrimp 95 45
N3945 80ch. Lobster . . . . . . 1·10 55

1301 Jong Song Ok (marathon runner)

1999. Victory of Jong Song Ok at World Athletics Championship, Seville.
N3946 **1301** 40ch. multicoloured 55 25

1302 Mt. Kumgang, North Korea

1999. 50th Anniv of North Korean–China Diplomatic Relations. Multicoloured.
N3948 40ch. Type **1302** 30 15
N3949 60ch. Mt. Lushan, China 40 20

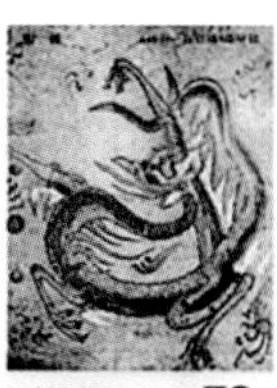

1304 Steel Worker holding Torch **1305** Yellow Dragon

2000. New Year. 40th Anniv of 19 April Rising.
N3952 **1304** 10ch. multicoloured 10 10

2000. Koguryo Era Tomb Murals, Jian.
N3953 **1035** 70ch. multicoloured 50 25

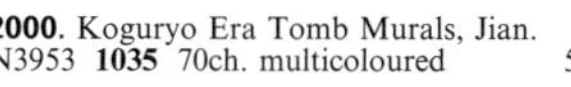

1306 Weeding

2000. "Rural Life" (anon). Showing details from the painting. Multicoloured.
N3955 40ch. Type **1306** 30 10
N3956 40ch. Hemp cloth weaving 30 10
N3957 40ch. Threshing 30 10
N3958 40ch. Riverside market . . 30 10

1307 Views across Lake Chou

2000. Mt. Paektu. Multicoloured.
N3959 20ch. Type **1307** 15 10
N3960 20ch. Eagle-shaped rock formation 15 10
N3961 20ch. Owl-shaped rock formation 15 10

1308 Chuibari Mask Dance **1309** Cat

2000. Pongsan Mask Dance. Depicting masks and characters from component dances. Multicoloured.
N3962 50ch. Type **1308** 35 15
N3963 80ch. Ryangban Mask Dance 55 25
N3964 1wn. Malttugi Mask Dance 70 35

2000. Cats. Multicoloured.
N3965 50ch. Type **1309** 35 15
N3966 50ch. Three kittens . . . 35 15
N3967 50ch. Mother and kittens 35 15

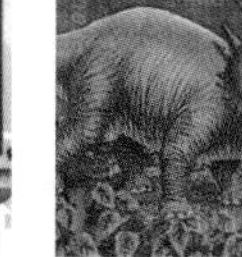
1310 Singapura Cat **1312** Styracosaurus

1311 Log Cabin (birthplace, Mt. Paekdu)

2000. Fauna. Multicoloured.
N3968 2wn. Type **1310** . . . . . 1·10 25
N3969 2wn. Blue Abyssinian cat 1·10 25
N3970 2wn. Oriental cat . . . . 1·10 25
N3971 2wn. Scottish fold tabby cat . . . . 1·10 25
N3972 2wn. Shiba inu . . . . . . 1·10 25
N3973 2wn. Yorkshire terrier . . 1·10 25
N3974 2wn. Japanese chin . . . 1·10 25
N3975 2wn. Afghan hound . . . 1·10 25
N3976 2wn. Przewalski's horse 1·10 25
N3977 2wn. Grey cob . . . . . 1·10 25
N3978 2wn. White horse rearing 1·10 25
N3979 2wn. Donkeys . . . . . . 1·10 25
N3980 2wn. Panda in tree . . . . 1·10 25
N3981 2wn. Panda eating . . . . 1·10 25
N3982 2wn. Panda scratching against tree . . . . . 1·10 25
N3983 2wn. Mother and cub . . 1·10 25
N3984 2wn. Two polar bears (*Ursus maritimus*) . . . 1·10 25
N3985 2wn. Mother and cub . . 1·10 25
N3986 2wn. Standing bear . . . 1·10 25
N3987 2wn. Bear lying down . . 1·10 25
N3988 2wn. Mexican lance-headed rattlesnake (*Crotalus polystictus*) . . 1·10 25
N3989 2wn. Scarlet king snake (*Lampropeltis triangulum elapsoides*) . . . . . . 1·10 25
N3990 2wn. Green tree python (*Chondropython viridis*) 1·10 25
N3991 2wn. Blood python (*Python curtus*) . . . . 1·10 25
N3992 2wn. Corythosaurus . . . 1·10 25
N3993 2wn. Psittacosaurus . . . 1·10 25
N3994 2wn. Megalosaurus . . . 1·10 25
N3995 2wn. Muttaburrasaurus . . 1·10 25
N3996 2wn. Burmeister's porpoise (*Phocoena spinipinnis*) 1·10 25
N3997 2wn. Finless porpoise (*Neophocaena phocaenoides*) . . . . . 1·10 25
N3998 2wn. Bottle-nosed dolphin (*Tursiops truncatus*) . . 1·10 25
N3999 2wn. Curvier's beaked whale (*Ziphius cavirostris*) . . . . . . 1·10 25
N4000 2wn. Port Jackson shark (*Heterodontus portusjacksoni*) . . . . 1·10 25
N4001 2wn. Great hammerhead shark (*Sphyrna mokarran*) (inscr "mokkarran") . . . . . 1·10 25
N4002 2wn. Zebra shark (*Stegostoma fasciatum*) 1·10 25
N4003 2wn. Ornate wobbegong (*Orectolobus ornatus*) . . 1·10 25
N4004 2wn. Ruddy shelduck (*Tadorna ferruginea*) . . 1·10 25
N4005 2wn. European widgeon (*Anas penelope*) . . . . 1·10 25
N4006 2wn. Mandarin drake (*Aix galericulata*) . . . . . 1·10 25
N4007 2wn. Hottentot teal (*Anas hottentota*) . . . . . . 1·10 25
N4008 2wn. Little owl (*Athene noctua*) . . . . 1·10 25
N4009 2wn. Ural owl (*Strix uralensis*) . . . . 1·10 25
N4010 2wn. Great horned owl (*Bubo virginianus*) . . . 1·10 25
N4011 2wn. Snowy owl (*Nyctea scandiaca*) . . . . . . 1·10 25
N4012 2wn. Slaty-headed parakeet (*Psittacula himalayana*) . . . . . . 1·10 25
N4013 2wn. Male eclectus parrot (*Eclectus roratus*) . . . 1·10 25
N4014 2wn. Major Mitchell's cockatoo (*Cacatua leadbeateri*) . . . . . . 1·10 25
N4015 2wn. Female eclectus parrot (*Eclectus roratus*) 1·10 25
N4016 2wn. Indian leaf butterfly (*Kallima paralekta*) . . 1·10 25
N4017 2wn. Spanish festoon (*Zerynthia rumina*) . . . 1·10 25
N4018 2wn. Male and female emerald swallowtails (*Papilio palinurus*) . . . 1·10 25
N4019 2wn. *Bhutanitis lidderdalii* 1·10 25
N4020 2wn. Bumble bee . . . . 1·10 25
N4021 2wn. Bumble bee on flower . . . . 1·10 25
N4022 2wn. Honey bee (*Apis mellifera*) . . . . 1·10 25
N4023 2wn. Honey bee attacking spider . . . . 1·10 25
N4024 2wn. *Micrommata virescens* (spider) . . . 1·10 25
N4025 2wn. *Araneus quadratus* (spider) . . . . 1·10 25
N4026 2wn. *Dolomedes fimbriatus* (spider) . . . . 1·10 25
N4027 2wn. *Aculepeira ceropegia* (spider) . . . . 1·10 25
Nos. N3980/3 are wrongly inscr "Aculepeira ceropegia".

2000. 58th Birth Anniv of Kim Jong Il.
N4028 **1311** 40ch. multicoloured 20 10

2000. Dinosaurs. Sheet 120 × 80 mm, containing T **1312** and similar multicoloured designs.
MSN4029 1wn. Type **1312**; 1wn. Saltasaurus (29 × 41 mm); 1wn. Tyrannosaurus . . . 1·75 40

1313 Peacock (*Inachis io*)

2000. Butterflies. Multicoloured.
N4030 40ch. Type **1313** 20 10
N4031 60ch. Swallowtail (*Papilio machaon*) 35 10
N4032 80ch. Mimic (*Hypolimnas misippus*) 45 10
N4034 1wn.20 *Papilio bianor Cramer* 70 15

1314 Patas Monkey (*Erythrocebus patas*) **1315** Red Flag, Top of Chollima Statue and Emblem

2000. Primates. Multicoloured.
N4035 50ch. Type **1314** . . . 30 10
N4036 50ch. Western tarsier (*Tarsius spectrm*) . . 30 10
MSN4037 Sheet 75 × 65 mm. 2wn. Mona monkey (*Cercopithecus mona*) 1·10 25

2000. 55th Anniv of Korean Worker's Party (1st issue).
N4038 **1315** 10ch. multicoloured 10 10
See also Nos. N4083/**MSN**4084.

1316 Demonstrators

2000. 40th Anniv of 19 April Uprising, South Korea.
N4039 **1316** 40ch. multicoloured 20 10

1317 Kim Il Sun Flower

2000. 88th Birth Anniv of Kim Il Sung.
N4040 **1317** 40ch. multicoloured 20 10

1318 Mun Ik Hwan **1319** Symbols of Technology, Globe, Flag and Chollima Statue

2000. 6th Death Anniv of Mun Ik Hwan (National Reunification Prize winner).
N4041 **1318** 50ch. multicoloured 30 10

2000. New Millennium. 55th Anniv of Korean Worker's Party. Multicoloured.
N4042 40ch. Type **1319** 20 10
N4043 1wn.20 Dove with envelope, globe and satellites 70 15

1320 *Cattleya intermedia*

2000. Orchids. Multicoloured.
N4044 20ch. Type **1320** . . . 10 10
N4045 50ch. *Dendrobium moschatum* 30 10
N4046 70ch. *Brassolaeliocattleya* 40 10
MSN4047 85 × 60 mm. 2wn. *Laeliocattleya* . . . 1·10 25

1321 Okryu Bridge (River Taedong)

2000. Bridges.
N4048 20ch. Type **1321** 10 10
N4049 30ch. Ansan Bridge (River Pothong) 15 10
N4050 1wn. Rungna Bridge (River Taedong) 60 15

1322 Okryugum and Jaengggang Dancers

1323 Half Moon (Yun Kuk Yong)

2000. Air. "WIPA 2000" International Stamp Exhibition, Vienna. Traditional Instruments and Folk Dances. Sheet 150 × 84 mm, containing T **1322** and similar vert designs. Multicoloured.
MSN4051 1wn. Type **1322**; 1wn.50 Oungum and Full Moon Viewing; 1wn.50 Janggo (drum) and Trio . . 1·75 40

The 1wn. stamp does not carry an airmail inscription.

2000. Children's Songs. Multicoloured.
N4052 40ch. Type **1323** . . . 20 10
N4053 60ch. Kangnam Nostalgia (Kim Sok Song and An Ki Yong) 35 10
MSN4054 95 × 80 mm. 2wn. Spring in Home Village (Ri Won Su and Hong Ran Pha) 1·10 25

1324 Pearly Nautilus (*Nautilus pompilius*)

1325 Drake and Duck

2000. Cephalopods. Multicoloured.
N4055 40ch. Type **1324** . . . 20 10
N4056 60ch. Common octopus (*Octopus vulgaris*) 35 10
N4057 1w.50 Squid (*Ommastrephes sloanei pacificus*) . . 85 20
MSN4058 60 × 70 mm. 1wn.50 No. N4057 . . . . 85 20

2000. Mandarin Ducks. Multicoloured.
N4059 50ch. Type **1325** . . . 30 10
N4060 50ch. Drake with duck and couple on bridge 30 10
MSN4061 92 × 75 mm. 1wn. Duck, drake and ducklings 60 15

1326 Table Tennis

2000. "World Expo 2000" International Stamp Exhibition, Anaheim, California. Sport. Multicoloured.
N4062 80ch. Type **1326** 45 10
N4063 1wn. Basketball 60 15
N4064 1wn.20 Baseball 70 15

1327 Sungri-61 NA

2000. Trucks. Multicoloured.
N4065 40ch. Type **1327** 20 10
N4066 70ch. Tipper truck 40 10
N4067 1wn.50 Konsol 25 ton dump truck 85 20

1328 Ri Tae Hun (artillery company commander) and 76 mm Field Gun

2000. Weaponry. Multicoloured.
N4068 60ch. Type **1328** 35 10
N4069 80ch. Ko Hyon Bin (tank commander) and T-34 tank 45 10
N4070 1wn. Squadron leader Paek Ki Rak and Yakovlev Yak-9P pursuit plane 60 15

1329 Fluorite

2000. Minerals. Multicoloured.
N4071 30ch. Type **1329** . . . 15 10
N4072 60ch. Graphite 35 10
N4073 1w.60 Magnesite . . . 90 20
MSN4074 74 × 74 mm. 1w.60 No. N4073 . . . . 90 20

2000. "Indonesia 2000" International Stamp Exhibition, Jakarta. Nos. N4059/**MSN**4061 optd **WORLD PHILATELIC EXHIBITION JAKARTA 15-21 AUGUST 2000** and emblem, No. **MSN**4061 optd in the margin.
N4075 50ch. multicoloured . . 30 10
N4076 50ch. multicoloured . . 30 10
MSN4077 1wn. multicoloured . . 60 15

1331 Swimming

2000. Olympic Games, Sydney. Triathlon. Sheet 78 × 110 mm, containing T **1331** and similar horiz designs. Multicoloured.
MSN4078 80ch. Type **1331**; 1w.20 Cycling; 2w. Running . . . . . 2·00 50

1332 Sanju Falls

2000. Myohyang Mountain. Multicoloured.
N4079 40ch. Type **1332** 20 10
N4080 40ch. Inho rock 20 10
N4081 1w.20 Sangwon valley . . 70 15

2000. "Espana 2000" International Stamp Exhibition, Madrid. No. **MSN**4029 optd **Exposioion Mundial de Filatolia 2000. 0.6 - 14.** in the margin.
MSN4082 120 × 80 mm. 1w. Type **1312**; 1w. Saltasaurus; 1w. Tyrannosaurus . . . 1·10 25

1334 Anniversary Emblem and Party Museum

2000. 55th Anniv of Korean Worker's Party (2nd issue). Multicoloured.
N4083 40ch. Type **1334** . . . 20 10
MSN4084 120 × 83 mm. 30ch. Kim Il Sung (35 × 56 mm); 50ch. Kim Jong Il (35 × 56 mm); 50ch. Kim Jong Suk (35 × 56 mm) 80 20

1335 Flag, Bulldozer and Fields

2000. Land Re-organization.
N4085 **1335** 10ch. multicoloured 10 10

1336 Potatoes, Pigs, Fields and Scientist

2000. Taehongdan (potato production centre). Multicoloured.
N4086 40ch. Type **1336** . . . 20 10
MSN4087 110 × 92 mm. 2w. Kim Il Sung with farmers in potato field (42 × 34 mm) . . . . 1·10 25

1337 Kim Jong Il and Pres. Jiang Zemin

2000. Visit of Kim Jong Il to People's Republic of China. Sheet 110 × 80 mm.
MSN4088 **1337** 1w.20 multicoloured 70 15

1338 Kim Jong Il and Pres. Kim Dae Jung

2000. North Korea–South Korea Summit Meeting, Pyongyang. Sheet 85 × 110 mm.
MSN4089 **1338** 2w. multicoloured 1·10 25

1339 Kim Jong Il and Pres. Putin

2000. Visit of Pres. Vladimir Putin of Russian Federation. Sheet 94 × 108 mm.
MSN4090 **1339** 1w.50 multicoloured 85 20

1340 Soldiers crossing River Amnok

2000. 50th Anniv of Chinese People's Volunteers Participation in Korean War (1st issue). Sheet 139 × 164 mm, containing T **1340** and similar horiz designs. Multicoloured.
MSN4091 10ch. Type **1340**; 10ch. Battle; 50ch. Chinese and Korean soldiers; 50ch. Mao Tse-tung and Chinese leaders; 80ch. Soldiers and gun emplacement . . 1·10 25

1341 Chinese and Korean Soldiers

1342 *Aquilegia oxysepala*

2000. 50th Anniv of Chinese People's Volunteers Participation in Korean War (2nd issue).
N4092 **1341** 30ch. multicoloured 15 10

2000. Alpine Flowers. Multicoloured.
N4093 30ch. Type **1342** 15 10
N4094 50ch. Brilliant campion (*Lychnis fulgens*) 25 10
N4095 70ch. Self-heal (*Prunela vulgaris*) 40 10

1343 Women presenting Prisoners with Flowers (½-size illustration)

2000. Repatriation of Long-term Prisoners of War. Sheets containing horiz designs as T **1343**. Multicoloured.
MSN4096 Two sheets. (a) 139 × 87 mm. 80ch. Type **1343**. (b) 165 × 120 mm. 1w.20 Prisoners and crowd Price for 2 sheets . . 1·10 25

1344 Flag, Factories and Trees

2001. New Year (1st issue).
N4097 **1344** 10ch. multicoloured 10 10

1345 White Snake meeting Xu Xian

2001. New Year (2nd issue). Tale of the White Snake. Multicoloured.
N4098 10ch. Type **1345** . . . 10 10
N4099 40ch. Stealing the Immortal Grass . . 20 10
N4100 50ch. White and Green snakes and Xu Xian 25 10
N4101 80ch. Flooding of Jinshan Hill 45 10
MSN4102 105 × 80 mm. 1wn.20 White snake and Green snake (32 × 52 mm) 70 15

1346 E. Lasker and J-R. Capablanca

2001. World Chess Champions. 165th Birth Anniv of Wilhelm Steinitz (19th-century champion) (**MSN**4109). Multicoloured.
N4103 10ch. Type **1346** . . . 10 10
N4104 20ch. A. Alekhine and M. Euwe 10 10

N4105	30ch. M. Botvinnik and V. Smylov	15	10
N4106	40ch. T. Petrosian and M. Tal	20	10
N4107	50ch. B. Spassky and R. Fisher	25	10
N4108	1wn. A. Karpov and G. Kasparov	50	10
MSN4109	105 × 80 mm. 2wn.50 Wilhelm Steinitz (32 × 52 mm)	1·40	30

1347 White Suit and Black Hat

2001. Ri-Dynasty Men's Costumes. Multicoloured.

N4110	10ch. Type **1347**	10	10
N4111	40ch. White suit with blue waistcoat	20	10
N4112	50ch. White trousers, brown jacket and pagoda-shaped hat	25	10
N4113	70ch. Knee-length pale blue coat, black hat and stick	40	10
MSN4114	110 × 80 mm. 1wn.50 Blue knee-length coat with ornamental cummerbund and black boots	85	20

1348 Small Appliance (fire)

2001. Fire Engines. Designs showing engines and fire hazards. Multicoloured.

N4115	20ch. Type **1348**	10	10
N4116	30ch. Large engine with hydraulic ladder (oil can)	15	10
N4117	40ch. Small engine with two-door cab and closed back (match)	20	10
N4118	60ch. Small engine with ladder, spotlight and external hose reel (gas canister)	30	10
N4119	2wn. Older-style engine (cigarette)	80	20
MSN4120	95 × 90 mm. 2wn. As No. N4119 (32 × 52 mm)	1·10	25

1349 Black-naped Oriole (*Oriolus chinensis*)

2001. "HONG KONG 2001" International Stamp Exhibition. Sheet 72 × 80 mm.

MSN4121 **1349**	1wn.40 multicoloured	80	20

1350 Jjong Il Peak and Flower

2001. 59th Birth Anniv of Kim Jong Il.

N4122 **1350**	10ch. multicoloured	10	10

1351 Flag and Symbols of Industry and Agriculture

2001. New Millennium. Rodong Sinmun, Josoninmingun and Chongnyonjonwi Newspapers Joint Editorial.

N4123 **1351**	10ch. multicoloured	10	10

1352 Log Cabin (revolutionary headquarters, Mt. Paekdu)

2001.

N4124 **1352**	40ch. multicoloured	20	10

APPENDIX

The following stamps have either been issued in excess of postal needs or have not been available to the public in reasonable quantities at face value. Such stamps may later be given full listing if there is evidence of regular postal use.

1976.

Olympic Games, Montreal. Three-dimensional stamps showing Olympic events. 5, 10, 15, 20, 25, 40ch.

1977.

Olympic Games, Montreal. Three-dimensional stamps showing medals. 5, 10, 15, 20, 25, 40ch.

Olympic Games, Montreal. 1976 Olympic Games issue optd with winners' names. 5, 10, 15, 20, 25, 40ch.

1979.

XIII Winter Olympic Games, 1980. Nos. N1688/94 optd. 2, 5, 10, 15, 20, 25, 40ch.

1981.

Nobel Prizes for Medicine. Nos. N1955/61 optd. 7 × 10ch.

World Cup Football Championship, Spain (1982). Nos. N1731/41 optd. 12 × 20ch.

World Cup Football Championship, Spain (1982). Three-dimensional stamps. Air 20, 30ch.

1982.

21st Birthday of Princess of Wales. Nos. N2108/11 and N2120/3 optd. 10, 20, 30, 40ch.; 10, 20, 30, 70ch.

Birth of Prince William of Wales. Nos. N2185/91 optd. 10, 20, 30, 50, 60, 70, 80ch.

World Cup Football Championship, Spain, Results. Nos. N2201/6 optd. 10, 20, 30, 40, 50, 60ch.

Birth of Prince William of Wales. Three-dimensional stamps. 3 × 30ch.

1983.

XXIII Olympic Games, Los Angeles, 1984. Nos. N2084/8 optd. 10, 15, 20, 25, 30ch.

1984.

European Royal History. 81 × 10ch.

KOUANG TCHEOU (KWANGCHOW) Pt. 17

An area and port of S. China, leased by France from China in April 1898. It was returned to China in February 1943.

1906. 100 centimes = 1 franc.
1919. 100 cents = 1 piastre.

Unless otherwise stated the following are optd or surch on stamps of Indo-China.

1906. Surch **Kouang Tcheou-Wan** and value in Chinese.

1 **8**	1c. green	4·25	4·25
2	2c. red on yellow	4·00	4·00
3	4c. mauve on blue	4·00	4·25
4	5c. green	4·50	5·00
5	10c. red	4·50	4·50
6	15c. brown on blue	10·50	10·50
7	20c. red on green	5·00	4·75
8	25c. blue	4·50	4·75
9	30c. brown on cream	5·75	6·25
10	35c. black on yellow	8·25	8·25
11	40c. black on grey	5·75	5·50
12	50c. brown on cream	25·00	25·00
13 D	75c. brown on orange	32·00	32·00
14 **8**	1f. green	32·00	35·00
15	2f. brown on yellow	32·00	35·00
16 D	5f. mauve on lilac	£160	£160
17 **8**	10f. red on green	£180	£200

1908. Native types surch **KOUANG-TCHEOU** and value in Chinese.

18 **10**	1c. black and brown	85	65
19	2c. black and brown	45	1·60
20	4c. black and blue	1·25	1·75
21	5c. black and green	1·75	1·25
22	10c. black and red	1·75	1·90
23	15c. black and violet	3·00	3·50
24 **11**	20c. black and violet	3·75	5·00
25	25c. black and blue	6·00	6·25
26	30c. black and brown	8·25	11·00
27	35c. black and green	14·00	15·00
28	40c. black and brown	12·50	15·00
29	50c. black and red	16·00	16·00
30 **12**	75c. black and orange	16·00	16·00
31 –	1f. black and red	19·00	19·00
32 –	2f. black and green	35·00	38·00
33 –	5f. black and blue	65·00	70·00
34 –	10f. black and violet	65·00	£110

1919. Nos. 18/34 surch in figures and words.

35 **10**	⅖ on 1c. black and brown	60	2·50
36	⅘c. on 2c. black and brown	35	2·75
37	1⅗c. on 4c. black and blue	1·10	2·25
38	2c. on 5c. black and green	3·00	3·25
39	4c. on 10c. black and red	4·00	2·50
40	6c. on 15c. black and violet	2·75	3·00
41 **11**	8c. on 20c. black and violet	5·00	4·75
42	10c. on 25c. black and blue	13·50	12·50
43	12c. on 30c. black & brown	3·75	3·75
44	14c. on 35c. black and green	4·00	3·50
45	16c. on 40c. black & brown	3·25	3·25
46	20c. on 50c. black and red	3·50	3·25
47 **12**	30c. on 75c. black & orange	7·75	8·75
48 –	40c. on 1f. black and red	11·00	9·50
49 –	80c. on 2f. black and green	11·50	10·00
50 –	2p. on 5f. black and blue	£130	£120
51 –	4p. on 10f. black and violet	21·00	25·00

1923. Native types optd **KOUANG-TCHEOU** only. (Value in cents and piastres).

52 **10**	⅒c. red and grey	15	2·75
53	⅕c. black and blue	15	3·00
54	⅖c. black and brown	15	2·50
55	⅘c. black and red	15	3·00
56	1c. black and brown	30	2·75
57	2c. black and green	55	3·25
58	3c. black and violet	45	3·25
59	4c. black and orange	55	3·00
60	5c. black and red	1·25	2·50
61 **11**	6c. black and red	55	3·50
62	7c. black and green	40	3·00
63	8c. black on lilac	1·75	3·25
64	9c. black and yellow on green	2·50	3·25
65	10c. black and blue	1·75	3·25
66	11c. black and violet	2·75	3·25
67	12c. black and brown	3·00	3·25
68	15c. black and orange	3·50	4·00
69	20c. black and blue on buff	3·00	3·75
70	40c. black and red	4·25	4·75
71	1p. black and green on green	9·25	13·00
72	2p. black and purple on pink	15·00	20·00

1927. Pictorial types optd **KOUANG-TCHEOU**.

73 **22**	⅒c. green	15	2·75
74	⅕c. yellow	20	2·50
75	⅖c. blue	25	3·00
76	⅘c. brown	20	2·25
77	1c. orange	85	3·00
78	2c. green	35	3·00
79	3c. blue	95	3·25
80	4c. pink	55	3·00
81	5c. violet	80	3·25
82 **23**	6c. red	55	2·25
83	7c. brown	1·10	3·25
84	8c. green	1·60	3·00
85	9c. purple	1·50	3·00
86	10c. blue	1·90	3·00
87	11c. orange	3·00	3·50
88	12c. grey	1·75	3·00
89 **24**	15c. brown and red	3·50	4·00
90	20c. grey and violet	3·75	4·00
91 –	25c. mauve and brown	3·50	4·00
92 –	30c. olive and blue	3·50	3·50
93 –	40c. blue and red	3·25	3·25
94 –	50c. grey and green	3·50	3·50
95 –	1p. black, yellow and blue	4·75	6·25
96 –	2p. blue, orange and red	6·25	7·00

1937. 1931 issue optd **KOUANG-TCHEOU**.

98 **33**	⅒c. blue	15	2·75
99	⅕c. lake	15	3·00
100	⅖c. red	15	3·00
101	½c. brown	15	2·75
102	⅘c. violet	30	2·75
103 **33**	1c. brown	15	2·75
104	2c. green	15	2·50
126 –	3c. brown	50	30
105 –	3c. green	75	3·00
106 –	4c. blue	2·50	3·25
127 –	4c. green	50	30
128 –	4c. yellow	1·75	1·00
107 –	5c. purple	2·50	3·00
129 –	5c. green	50	35
108 –	6c. red	20	3·00
130 –	7c. black	50	45
131 –	8c. lake	50	45
132 –	9c. black on yellow	50	45
109 –	10c. blue	2·50	3·00
133 –	10c. blue on pink	75	55
110 –	15c. blue	70	3·00
134 –	18c. blue	30	30
111 –	20c. red	20	3·00
112 –	21c. green	20	3·00
135 –	22c. green	50	35
113 –	25c. purple	2·00	1·60
136 –	25c. blue	70	45
114 –	30c. brown	3·50	4·75
115 **36**	50c. brown	1·40	3·00
116	60c. purple	35	3·25
137	70c. blue	40	3·25
117	1p. green	2·00	3·25
118	2p. red	2·75	3·75

1939. New York World's Fair. As T **28** of Mauritania.

119	13c. red	75	3·25
120	23c. deep blue and blue	1·40	3·25

1939. 150th Anniv of French Revolution. As T **29** of Mauritania.

121	6c.+2c. green	6·00	9·25
122	7c.+3c. brown	6·00	9·25
123	9c.+4c. orange	7·25	9·25
124	13c.+10c. red	5·50	9·25
125	23c.+20c. blue	6·75	9·25

KUWAIT Pt. 1, Pt. 19

An independent Arab Shaikhdom on the N.W. coast of the Persian Gulf with Indian and later British postal administration. On 1 February 1959 the Kuwait Government assumed responsibility for running its own postal service. In special treaty relations with Great Britain until 19 June 1961 when Kuwait became completely independent.

1923. 12 pies = 1 anna; 16 annas = 1 rupee.
1957. 100 naye paise = 1 rupee.
1961. 1000 fils = 1 dinar.

Stamps of India optd **KUWAIT**.

1923. King George V.

16 **56**	½a. green	3·25	1·40
16b **79**	½a. green	4·50	1·40
2 **57**	1a. brown	2·75	3·25
17b **81**	1a. brown	5·50	1·25
3 **58**	1½a. brown (No. 163)	2·25	4·25
4 **59**	2a. lilac	3·75	3·75
19c	2a. red	4·50	2·50
18 **70**	2a. lilac	3·25	1·25
19	2a. red	20·00	85·00
5 **61**	2a.6p. blue	2·75	8·00
6 **62**	3a. orange	4·25	20·00
20	3a. blue	2·75	1·75
21	3a. red	5·50	4·25
22 **71**	4a. green	25·00	80·00
22a **63**	4a. green	6·50	14·00
9 **64**	6a. bistre	8·50	13·00
23 **65**	8a. mauve	19·00	13·00
11 **66**	12a. red	14·00	42·00
12 **67**	1r. brown and green	21·00	30·00
26	2r. red and orange	10·00	65·00
27	5r. blue and violet	80·00	£200
28	10r. green and red	£170	£375
29	15r. blue and olive	£500	£750

1933. Air.

31 **72**	2a. green	14·00	27·00
32	3a. blue	3·00	2·50
33	4a. olive	85·00	£170
34	6a. bistre	3·25	4·50

1939. King George VI.

36 **91**	½a. brown	7·00	1·75
38	1a. red	7·00	1·50
39 **92**	2a. red	7·00	2·50
41 –	3a. green	7·00	2·00
43 –	4a. brown	38·00	16·00
44 –	6a. green	25·00	8·00
45 –	8a. violet	28·00	32·00
46 –	12a. red	20·00	55·00
47 **93**	1r. slate and brown	10·00	3·00
48	2r. purple and brown	3·75	15·00
49	5r. green and blue	12·00	18·00
50	10r. purple and red	60·00	75·00
51	15r. brown and green	£140	£200

1942. King George VI stamps of 1940.

52 **100a**	3p. slate	2·00	3·25
53	½a. purple	1·75	3·00
54	9p. green	3·75	9·00
55	1a. red	1·50	2·25
56 **101**	1½a. violet	4·00	8·50
57	2a. red	4·25	3·00
58	3a. violet	4·75	4·75
59	3½a. blue	4·25	8·50
60 **102**	4a. brown	4·75	3·00
60a	6a. green	14·00	8·50
61	8a. violet	7·00	3·75
62	12a. purple	8·00	4·00
63 –	14a. purple (No. 277)	15·00	17·00

From 1948 onwards, for stamps with similar surcharges, but without name of country, see British Postal Agencies in Eastern Arabia.

Stamps of Great Britain surch **KUWAIT** and new values in Indian currency.

1948. King George VI.

64 **128**	½a. on ½d. green	1·50	1·75
84	½a. on ½d. orange	2·50	1·50
65	1a. on 1d. red	1·50	1·75
85	1a. on 1d. blue	2·00	1·60
66	1½a. on 1½d. brown	2·00	1·00
86	1½a. on 1½d. green	2·00	2·25
67	2a. on 2d. orange	1·50	1·00
87	2a. on 2d. brown	2·00	1·50
68	2½a. on 2½d. blue	2·00	1·00
88	2½a. on 2½d. red	2·00	2·75
69	3a. on 3d. violet	1·50	60

89 **129** 4a. on 4d. blue . . . . . 1·75 1·50
70 6a. on 6d. purple . . . . 1·50 75
71 **130** 1r. on 1s. brown . . . . 3·50 1·50
72 **131** 2r. on 2s.6d. green . . . 3·75 4·50
73 5r. on 5s. red . . . . . 5·50 4·50
73a – 10r. on 10s. blue (No. 478a) . . . . . . 38·00 6·00

1948. Silver Wedding.
74 **137** 2½a. on 2½d. blue . . . . 1·75 1·75
75 **138** 15r. on £1 blue . . . . . 30·00 30·00

1948. Olympic Games.
76 **139** 2½a. on 2½d. blue . . . . 1·00 2·00
77 **140** 3a. on 3d. violet . . . . . 1·00 2·00
78 – 6a. on 5d. purple . . . . . 1·25 2·00
79 – 1r. on 1s. brown . . . . . 1·25 2·00

1949. U.P.U.
80 **143** 2½a. on 2½d. blue . . . . 90 2·00
81 **144** 3a. on 3d. violet . . . . . 1·00 2·75
82 – 6a. on 6d. purple . . . . . 1·00 2·75
83 – 1r. on 1s. brown . . . . . 1·00 1·25

1951. Pictorial high values.
90 **147** 2r. on 2s.6d. green . . . . 15·00 4·75
91 – 5r. on 5s. red (No. 510) . . 22·00 5·00
92 – 10r. on 10s. blue (No. 511) 30·00 8·00

1952. Queen Elizabeth II.
93 **154** ½a. on ½d. orange . . . . 20 1·25
94 1a. on 1d. blue 20 10
95 1½a. on 1½d. green . . . 15 75
96 2a. on 2d. brown 35 10
97 **155** 2½a. on 2½d. red 15 75
98 3a. on 3d. lilac 40 10
99 4a. on 4d. blue . . . . . 1·25 75
100 **157** 6a. on 6d. purple . . . . 1·25 10
101 **160** 12a. on 1s.3d. green . . . 5·00 2·50
102 1r. on 1s.6d. blue . . . . 4·50 10

1953. Coronation.
103 **161** 2½a. on 2½d. red . . . . 3·50 3·00
104 – 4a. on 4d. blue . . . . . 3·50 3·00
105 **163** 12a. on 1s.3d. green . . . 5·00 4·75
106 – 1r. on 1s.6d. blue . . . . 4·00 1·00

1955. Pictorials.
107 **166** 2r. on 2s.6d. brown . . . 7·50 2·25
108 – 5r. on 5s. red . . . . . . 8·00 6·00
109 – 10r. on 10s. blue . . . . 8·00 4·75

1957. Queen Elizabeth II.
120 **157** 1n.p. on 5d. brown . . . 10 70
121 **154** 3n.p. on ½d. orange . . . 60 3·00
122 6n.p. on 1d. blue . . . . 60 1·25
123 9n.p. on 1½d. green . . . 60 2·25
124 12n.p. on 2d. brown . . . 60 3·00
125 **155** 15n.p. on 2½d. red . . . . 60 2·50
126 20n.p. on 3d. lilac 60 30
127 25n.p. on 4d. blue . . . . 2·25 3·25
128 **157** 40n.p. on 6d. purple . . . 1·00 30
129 **158** 50n.p. on 9d. olive . . . . 5·50 4·00
130 **160** 75n.p. on 1s.3d. green . . 5·50 4·50

20 Shaikh Abdullah

21 Dhow

1958.
131 **20** 5n.p. green 50 10
132a 10n.p. red 20 10
133 15n.p. brown 20 15
134 20n.p. violet 20 10
135 25n.p. orange 35 10
136 40n.p. purple . . . . . . 1·50 55
137 **21** 40n.p. blue 45 20
138 – 50n.p. red 40 20
139 – 75n.p. green 45 30
140 – 1r. purple 50 35
141 – 2r. blue and brown . . . 2·50 70
142 – 5r. green . . . . 4·00 1·50
143 – 10r. lilac . . . . 13·00 4·50
DESIGNS—HORIZ: As Type **21**: 50n.p. Oil pipelines; 75n.p. Shuwaikh Power Station. 36 × 20 mm: 1r. Oil rig; 2r. Single-masted dhow; 5r. Kuwait Mosque; 10r. Main Square, Kuwait Town.

22 Shaikh Abdullah and Flag

1960. 10th Anniv of Shaikh's Accession.
144 **22** 40n.p. red and green . . . 35 10
145 60n.p. red and blue . . . 45 20

1961. As 1958 issue but currency changed and new designs.
146 **20** 1f. green 15 10
147 2f. red 15 10
148 4f. brown 15 10
149 5f. violet 15 10
150 8f. red 20 10
151 15f. purple 25 10
152 – 20f. green (as No. 142) . . 50 10
153 – 25f. blue 90 10
154 – 30f. blue and brown (as No. 141) . . . . 1·25 10
155 – 35f. black and red 75 40
156 **21** 40f. blue (32 × 22 mm) . . 1·25 15
157 – 45f. brown 50 10
158 – 75f. brown & grn (as No. 141) . . . . 2·50 60
159 – 90f. brown and blue . . . 1·75 35
160 – 100f. red . . . . 3·25 10
161 **21** 250f. green (32 × 22 mm) 8·00 1·50
162 – 1d. orange . . . . 10·00 1·50
163 – 3d. red (as No. 142) . . . 25·00 18·00
NEW DESIGNS—37 × 20 mm: 25, 100f. Vickers Viscount 700 airliner over South Pier, Mina al Ahmadi; 35, 90f. Shuwaikh Secondary School; 45f., 1d. Wara Hill.

23 Telegraph Pole

1962. 4th Arab Telecommunications Union Conference.
164 **23** 8f. blue and black 15 10
165 20f. red and black 35 20

1962. Arab League Week. As T **76** of Libya.
166 20f. purple 20 10
167 45f. brown 50 20

25 Mubarakiya School, Shaikh Abdullah and Shaikh Mubarak

1962. Golden Jubilee of Mubarakiya School.
168 **25** 8f. multicoloured 20 10
169 20f. multicoloured 50 20

26 National Flag and Crest

27 Campaign Emblem

1962. National Day.
170 **26** 8f. multicoloured 10 10
171 20f. multicoloured 35 20
172 45f. multicoloured 80 30
173 90f. multicoloured . . . . 1·25 1·25

1962. Malaria Eradication.
174 **27** 4f. green and turquoise . . 15 10
175 25f. grey and green 55 25

28 "Industry and Progress"

1962. Bicentenary of Sabah Dynasty.
176 **28** 8f. multicoloured 10 10
177 20f. multicoloured 35 15
178 45f. multicoloured 75 15
179 75f. multicoloured . . . . 1·25 50

29 Mother and Child

31 "Education from Oil"

30 Campaign Emblem, Palm and Domestic Animals

1963. Mothers' Day. Centres black and green; value black; country name red.
180 **29** 8f. yellow 10 10
181 20f. blue 20 15
182 45f. olive 50 25
183 75f. grey 80 40

1963. Freedom from Hunger. Design in brown and green. Background colours given.
184 **30** 4f. blue 10 10
185 8f. yellow 25 15
186 20f. lilac 50 25
187 45f. pink . . . . 1·10 70

1963. Education Day.
188 **31** 4f. brown, blue and yellow 10 10
189 20f. green, blue and yellow 50 15
190 45f. purple, blue and yellow 90 35

32 Shaikh Abdullah and Flags

1963. 2nd Anniv of National Day. Flags in green, black and red; values in black.
191 **32** 4f. blue 40 30
192 5f. ochre 60 55
193 20f. violet . . . . 3·25 2·25
194 50f. brown . . . . 6·50 3·75

33 Human Lungs, and Emblems of W.H.O. and Kuwait

1963. W.H.O. "Tuberculosis Control" Campaign. Emblem yellow; arms black, green and red.
195 **33** 2f. black and stone 10 10
196 4f. black and green 20 10
197 8f. black and blue 25 10
198 20f. black and red . . . . 1·00 35

34 Municipal Hall and Scroll

1963. New Constitution. Centres dull purple; Amir red.
199 **34** 4f. red 15 10
200 8f. green 20 10
201 20f. purple 35 10
202 45f. brown 60 15
203 75f. violet . . . . 1·25 50
204 90f. blue . . . . 1·40 75

35 Football

36 Scales of Justice and Globe

1963. Arab Schools Games. Multicoloured.
205 1f. Type **35** 10 10
206 4f. Basketball 10 10
207 5f. Swimming (horiz) 10 10
208 8f. Running 15 10
209 15f. Throwing the javelin (horiz) 30 15
210 20f. Pole vaulting (horiz) . . 40 20
211 35f. Gymnastics (horiz) . . . 90 35
212 45f. Gymnastics . . . . . . 1·25 75

1963. 15th Anniv of Declaration of Human Rights.
213 **36** 8f. black, green and violet 10 10
214 20f. black, yellow and grey 40 20
215 25f. black, brown and blue 60 30

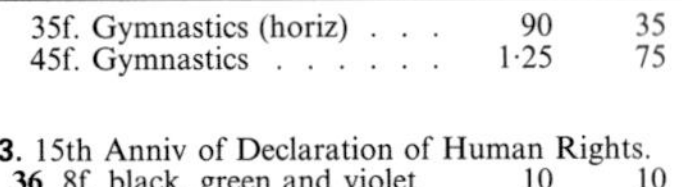

37 Shaikh Abdullah

38 Rameses II in War Chariot

1964. Multicoloured, frame colours given.
216 **37** 1f. grey 10 10
217 2f. blue 10 10
218 4f. brown 15 10
219 5f. brown 15 10
220 8f. brown 25 10
221 10f. green 25 10
222 15f. green 35 35
223 20f. blue 35 10
224 25f. green 40 10
225 30f. green 50 10
226 40f. violet 70 15
227 45f. violet 85 15
228 50f. yellow 90 20
229 70f. purple . . . . 1·10 25
230 75f. red . . . . 1·25 35
231 90f. blue . . . . 1·60 35
232 100f. lilac . . . . 1·75 40
233 250f. brown (25 × 30 mm) 5·00 90
234 1d. purple (25 × 30 mm) . . 14·00 3·75

1964. Nubian Monuments Preservation.
235 **38** 8f. purple, blue and buff 15 10
236 20f. violet, blue & light blue 40 20
237 30f. violet, blue & turquoise 55 35

39 Mother and Child

1964. Mother's Day.
238 **39** 8f. blue, green and grey . . 10 10
239 20f. blue, green and red . . 25 10
240 30f. blue, green and bistre 40 20
241 45f. indigo, green and blue 65 30

40 Nurse giving B.C.G. Vaccine to Patient, and Bones of Chest

41 Dhow and Microscope

1964. World Health Day.
242 **40** 8f. green and brown . . . 30 10
243 20f. red and green 85 25

1964. Education Day.
244 **41** 8f. multicoloured 15 10
245 15f. multicoloured 30 10
246 20f. multicoloured 35 15
247 30f. multicoloured 60 25

42 Dhow and Doves

1964. 3rd Anniv of National Day. Badge in blue, brown, black, red and green.
248 **42** 8f. black and brown . . . 25 15
249 20f. black and green . . . 40 25
250 30f. black and grey . . . 60 35
251 45f. black and blue 85 55

43 A.P.U. Emblem

44 Hawker Siddeley Comet 4C and Douglas DC-3 Airliners

1964. 10th Anniv of Arab Postal Union's Permanent Office, Cairo.
252 **43** 8f. brown and blue . . . 25 10
253 20f. blue and yellow . . . 45 20
254 45f. brown and green . . . 85 50

1964. Air. 10th Anniv of Kuwait Airways. Sky in blue; aircraft blue, red and black.
255 **44** 20f. black and bistre . . . 45 25
256 25f. black and brown . . . 60 30
257 30f. black and green . . . 70 30
258 45f. black and brown . . . 1·00 40

45 Conference Emblem

46 Dhow, Doves and Oil-drilling Rig

1965. 1st Arab Journalists' Conference, Kuwait.
259 **45** 8f. multicoloured 30 10
260 20f. multicoloured 55 20

1965. 4th Anniv of National Day.
261 **46** 10f. multicoloured 15 10
262 15f. multicoloured 35 15
263 20f. multicoloured 75 20

47 I.C.Y. Emblem

48 Mother and Children

1965. International Co-operation Year.
264 **47** 8f. black and red 25 10
265 20f. black and blue 55 25
266 30f. black and green . . . 1·00 40
The stamps are inscribed "CO-OPERATIVE".

1965. Mothers' Day.
267 **48** 8f. multicoloured 20 10
268 15f. multicoloured 40 20
269 20f. multicoloured 65 25

49 Weather Kite

1965. World Meteorological Day.
270 **49** 4f. blue and yellow 25 10
271 5f. blue and orange 25 10
272 20f. blue and green . . . . 1·10 25

50 Census Graph

1965. Population Census.
273 **50** 8f. black, brown and blue 20 10
274 20f. black, pink and green 60 25
275 50f. black, green and red 1·40 60

50a Dagger on Deir Yassin, Palestine

51 Atomic Symbol and Tower of Shuwaikh Secondary School

1965. Deir Yassin Massacre.
276 **50a** 4f. red and blue 40 20
277 45f. red and green . . . . 1·90 65

1965. Education Day.
278 **51** 4f. multicoloured 15 10
279 20f. multicoloured 45 15
280 45f. multicoloured 80 30

52 I.T.U. Emblem and Symbols

53 Saker Falcon

52a Lamp and Burning Library

1965. I.T.U. Centenary.
281 **52** 8f. red and blue 40 25
282 20f. red and green 80 40
283 45f. blue and red . . . . . 1·50 70

1965. Reconstitution of Burnt Algiers Library.
284 **52a** 8f. green, red and black 40 15
285 15f. red, green and black 1·00 20

1965. Centre in brown.
286 **53** 8f. purple . . . . 1·60 25
287 15f. green . . . . 1·40 25
288 20f. blue . . . . 2·25 40
289 25f. red . . . . 2·50 60
290 30f. green . . . . 3·00 70
291 45f. blue . . . . 5·25 1·00
292 50f. purple . . . . 6·50 1·25
293 90f. red . . . . 10·50 2·40

54 Open Book

55 Shaikh Sabah

1966. Education Day.
294 **54** 8f. multicoloured 20 10
295 20f. multicoloured 45 10
296 30f. multicoloured 85 25

1966.
297 **55** 4f. multicoloured 15 10
298 5f. multicoloured 15 10
299 20f. multicoloured 40 15
300 30f. multicoloured 55 25
301 40f. multicoloured 70 35
302 45f. multicoloured 75 40
303 70f. multicoloured . . . . 1·75 60
304 90f. multicoloured . . . . 2·00 80

56 Pomfrets and Ears of Wheat

1966. Freedom from Hunger.
305 **56** 20f. multicoloured . . . . 1·00 50
306 45f. multicoloured . . . . 2·25 95

57 Eagle and Scales of Justice

1966. 5th Anniv of National Day.
307 **57** 20f. multicoloured 80 30
308 25f. multicoloured 90 30
309 45f. multicoloured . . . . 1·60 60

58 Cogwheel and Map of Arab States

1966. Arab Countries Industrial Development Conference, Kuwait.
310 **58** 20f. green, black and blue 50 15
311 50f. green, black and brown . . . . 1·00 45

59 Mother and Children

60 Red Crescent and Emblem of Medicine

1966. Mothers' Day.
312 **59** 20f. multicoloured 50 15
313 45f. multicoloured . . . . 1·00 30

1966. 5th Arab Medical Conference, Kuwait.
314 **60** 15f. red and blue 35 15
315 30f. red, blue and pink . . 80 40

61 "Man and his Cities"

62 W.H.O. Building

1966. World Health Day.
316 **61** 8f. multicoloured 50 15
317 10f. multicoloured 75 20

1966. Inaug of W.H.O. Headquarters, Geneva.
318 **62** 5f. green, blue and red . . 50 10
319 10f. green, blue & turquoise 90 15

62a Traffic Signals

63 Symbol of Blood Donation

1966. Traffic Day.
320 **62a** 10f. red, emerald and green 50 10
321 20f. emerald, red and green 75 25

1966. Blood Bank Day.
322 **63** 4f. multicoloured 40 10
323 8f. multicoloured 85 25

64 Shaikh Ahmad and "British Fusilier" (tanker)

1966. 20th Anniv of 1st Crude Oil Shipment.
324 **64** 20f. multicoloured 60 25
325 45f. multicoloured . . . . 1·40 55

65 Ministry Building

1966. Inauguration of Ministry of Guidance and Information Building.
326 **65** 4f. red and brown 20 10
327 5f. brown and green . . . 20 10
328 8f. green and violet . . . 30 10
329 20f. orange and blue . . . 65 20

66 Dhow, Lobster, Fish and Crab

67 U.N. Flag

1966. F.A.O. Near East Countries Fisheries Conference, Kuwait.
330 **66** 4f. multicoloured 85 25
331 20f. multicoloured . . . . 1·10 50

1966. U.N. Day.
332 **67** 20f. multicoloured 75 25
333 45f. multicoloured . . . . 1·10 50

68 UNESCO Emblem

1966. 20th Anniv of UNESCO.
334 **68** 20f. multicoloured 75 60
335 45f. multicoloured . . . . 1·50 1·25

69 Ruler and University Shield

1966. Opening of Kuwait University.
336 **69** 8f. multicoloured 25 10
337 10f. multicoloured 25 15
338 20f. multicoloured 75 25
339 45f. multicoloured . . . . 1·50 75

70 Ruler and Heir-Apparent

1966. Appointment of Heir-Apparent.
340 **70** 8f. multicoloured 25 10
341 20f. multicoloured 60 30
342 45f. multicoloured . . . . 1·25 70

71 Scout Badge

72 Symbols of Learning

1966. 30th Anniv of Kuwait Scouts.
343 **71** 4f. brown and green . . . 50 15
344 20f. green and brown . . . 1·75 50

1967. Education Day.
345 **72** 10f. multicoloured 30 15
346 45f. multicoloured 80 35

73 Fertiliser Plant

1967. Inauguration of Chemical Fertiliser Plant.
347 **73** 8f. multicoloured 40 15
348 20f. multicoloured . . . . 1·00 30

74 Ruler, Dove and Olive-branch

76 Arab Family

75 Map and Municipality Building

1967. 6th Anniv of National Day.
349 **74** 8f. multicoloured 30 10
350 20f. multicoloured 80 30

1967. 1st Arab Cities Organization Conf, Kuwait.
351 **75** 20f. multicoloured . . . . 1·00 25
352 30f. multicoloured . . . . 1·40 60

1967. Family's Day.
353 **76** 20f. multicoloured 80 25
354 45f. multicoloured . . . . 1·60 60

77 Arab League Emblem

78 Sabah Hospital

1967. Arab Cause Week.
355 **77** 8f. blue and grey 30 10
356 10f. green and yellow . . . 60 15

1967. World Health Day.
357 **78** 8f. multicoloured 85 15
358 20f. multicoloured . . . . 1·00 40

79 Nubian Statues

1967. Arab Week for Nubian Monuments Preservation.
359 **79** 15f. green, brown and yellow 60 20
360 20f. green, purple and blue 90 25

80 Traffic Policeman

1967. Traffic Day.
361 **80** 8f. multicoloured 80 25
362 20f. multicoloured . . . . 1·75 65

81 I.T.Y. Emblem

1967. International Tourist Year.
363 **81** 20f. black, blue & turquoise 65 40
364 45f. black, blue and mauve 1·25 85

82 "Reaching for Knowledge"

83 Map of Palestine

1967. "Eliminate Illiteracy" Campaign.
365 **82** 8f. multicoloured 75 10
366 20f. multicoloured . . . . 1·50 35

1967. U.N. Day.
367 **83** 20f. red and blue 50 20
368 45f. red and orange . . . 1·10 50

84 Factory and Cogwheels

1967. 3rd Arab Labour Ministers' Conference.
369 **84** 20f. yellow and red 60 20
370 45f. yellow and grey . . . 1·40 50

85 Open Book and Kuwaiti Flag

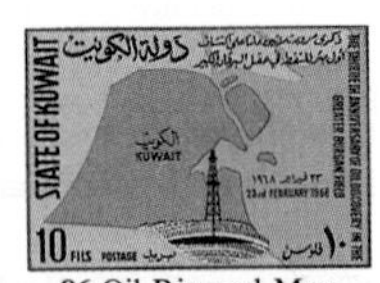

86 Oil Rig and Map

1968. Education Day.
371 **85** 20f. multicoloured 50 30
372 45f. multicoloured . . . . 1·25 60

1968. 30th Anniv of Oil Discovery in Greater Burgan Field.
373 **86** 10f. multicoloured 75 40
374 20f. multicoloured . . . . 1·25 70

87 Ruler and Sun's Rays

88 Book, Eagle and Sun

1968. 7th Anniv of National Day.
375 **87** 8f. multicoloured 25 10
376 10f. multicoloured 25 20
377 15f. multicoloured 45 25
378 20f. multicoloured 60 35

1968. Teachers' Day.
379 **88** 8f. multicoloured 30 10
380 20f. multicoloured 40 15
381 45f. multicoloured 75 40

89 Family Picnicking

1968. Family Day.
382 **89** 8f. multicoloured 20 10
383 10f. multicoloured 20 10
384 15f. multicoloured 30 10
385 20f. multicoloured 45 20

90 Ruler, W.H.O. and State Emblems

1968. World Health Day and 20th Anniv of W.H.O.
386 **90** 20f. multicoloured 60 50
387 45f. multicoloured . . . . 1·50 1·10

91 Dagger on Deir Yassin, and Scroll

1968. 20th Anniv of Deir Yassin Massacre.
388 **91** 20f. red and blue 80 25
389 45f. red and violet . . . . 2·75 50

92 Pedestrians on Road Crossing

93 Torch and Map

1968. Traffic Day.
390 **92** 10f. multicoloured 75 60
391 15f. multicoloured . . . . 1·25 85
392 20f. multicoloured . . . . 1·75 1·00

1968. Palestine Day.
393 **93** 10f. multicoloured 70 10
394 20f. multicoloured . . . . 1·25 25
395 45f. multicoloured . . . . 2·50 50

94 Palestine Refugees

1968. Human Rights Year.
396 **94** 20f. multicoloured 25 15
397 30f. multicoloured 35 15
398 45f. multicoloured 65 15
399 90f. multicoloured . . . . 1·25 45

95 National Museum

96 Man reading Book

1968.
400 **95** 1f. green and brown . . . 10 10
401 2f. green and purple . . . 10 10
402 5f. red and black 15 10
403 8f. green and brown . . . 20 10
404 10f. purple and blue . . . 20 10
405 20f. blue and brown . . . 45 10
406 25f. orange and blue . . . 55 10
407 30f. green and blue 70 20
408 45f. deep purple and purple 1·10 20
409 50f. red and green . . . . 1·60 45

1968. International Literacy Day.
410 **96** 15f. multicoloured 30 10
411 20f. multicoloured 70 15

97 Refugee Children and U.N. Headquarters

1968. United Nations Day.
412 **97** 20f. multicoloured 30 10
413 30f. multicoloured 40 20
414 45f. multicoloured 70 25

98 Chamber of Commerce Building

1968. Inauguration of Kuwait Chamber of Commerce and Industry Building.
415 **98** 10f. purple and orange . . 25 10
416 15f. blue and mauve . . . 30 15
417 20f. green and brown . . . 45 15

99 Conference Emblem

1968. 14th Arab Chambers of Commerce, Industry and Agriculture Conference.
418 **99** 10f. multicoloured 25 10
419 15f. multicoloured 30 10
420 20f. multicoloured 40 15
421 30f. multicoloured 70 30

100 Refinery Plant

101 Holy Koran, Scales and People

1968. Inauguration of Shuaiba Refinery.
422 **100** 10f. multicoloured 30 15
423 20f. multicoloured 60 20
424 30f. multicoloured 95 35
425 45f. multicoloured . . . . 1·75 45

1968. 1,400th Anniv of the Holy Koran.
426 **101** 8f. multicoloured 30 15
427 20f. multicoloured 75 40
428 30f. multicoloured . . . . 1·25 60
429 45f. multicoloured . . . . 1·60 85

102 Boeing 707 Airliner

1969. Inauguration of Boeing 707 Aircraft by Kuwait Airways.
430 **102** 10f. multicoloured 35 20
431 20f. multicoloured 75 35
432 25f. multicoloured . . . . 1·10 45
433 45f. multicoloured . . . . 2·00 65

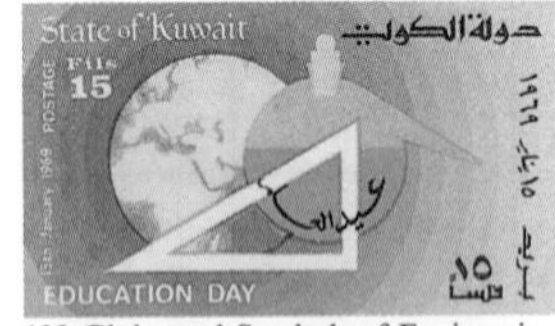

103 Globe and Symbols of Engineering and Science

1969. Education Day.
434 **103** 15f. multicoloured 35 25
435 20f. multicoloured 65 30

104 Hilton Hotel

105 Family and Teachers' Society Emblem

1969. Inauguration of Kuwait Hilton Hotel.
436 **104** 10f. multicoloured 35 15
437 20f. multicoloured 65 15

1969. Education Week.
438 **105** 10f. multicoloured 35 15
439 20f. multicoloured 65 15

106 Flags and Laurel

107 Emblem, Teacher and Class

1969. 8th Anniv of National Day.

440 **106** 15f. multicoloured 25 15
441 20f. multicoloured 40 20
442 30f. multicoloured 60 40

1969. Teachers' Day.

443 **107** 10f. multicoloured 30 15
444 20f. multicoloured 55 15

108 Kuwaiti Family

1969. Family Day.

445 **108** 10f. multicoloured 30 15
446 20f. multicoloured 55 20

109 Ibn Sina, Nurse with Patient and W.H.O. Emblem
110 Motor-cycle Police

1969. World Health Day.

447 **109** 15f. multicoloured 70 15
448 20f. multicoloured 80 20

1969. Traffic Day.

449 **110** 10f. multicoloured 75 15
450 20f. multicoloured . . . . 2·00 25

111 I.L.O. Emblem

1969. 50th Anniv of I.L.O.

451 **111** 10f. gold, black and red 30 10
452 20f. gold, black and green 50 15

112 Tanker "Al Sabahiah"

1969. 4th Anniv of Kuwait Shipping Company.

453 **112** 20f. multicoloured 90 35
454 45f. multicoloured . . . . 1·90 90

113 Woman writing Letter

1969. International Literacy Day.

455 **113** 10f. multicoloured 25 10
456 20f. multicoloured 55 20

114 Amir Shaikh Sabah
115 "Appeal to World Conscience"

1969. Portraits mult; background colours given.

457 **114** 8f. blue 25 10
458 10f. pink 25 10
459 15f. grey 35 15
460 20f. yellow 40 15
461 25f. lilac 50 20
462 30f. orange 70 25
463 45f. grey 95 35
464 50f. green . . . . 1·10 40
465 70f. blue . . . . 1·25 50
466 75f. blue . . . . 1·40 55
467 90f. brown . . . . 1·40 70
468 250f. purple . . . . . . 5·50 2·00
469 500f. green . . . . . . 10·50 6·50
470 1d. purple . . . . 17·00 11·00

1969. United Nations Day.

471 **115** 10f. blue, black and green 30 10
472 20f. blue, black and stone 60 15
473 45f. blue, black and red 1·00 30

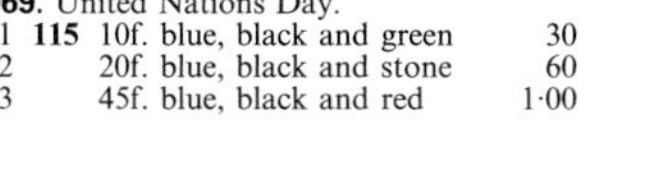

116 Earth Station

1969. Inauguration of Kuwait Satellite Communications Station. Multicoloured.

474 20 Type **116** 90 20
475 45f. Dish aerial on Globe (vert) . . . . 1·90 50

117 Refugee Family
118 Globe, Symbols and I.E.Y. Emblem

1969. Palestinian Refugee Week.

476 **117** 20f. multicoloured . . . . 1·40 40
477 45f. multicoloured . . . . 3·00 1·25

1970. International Education Year.

478 **118** 20f. multicoloured 40 25
479 45f. multicoloured . . . . 1·00 60

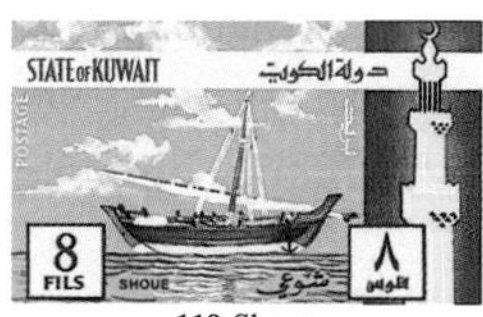

119 Shoue

1970. Kuwait Sailing Dhows. Multicoloured.

480 8f. Type **119** 40 10
481 10f. Sambuk 40 10
482 15f. Baggala 60 20
483 20f. Battela 75 15
484 25f. Bum 90 25
485 45f. Baggala . . . . 1·75 55
486 50f. Dhow-building . . . . . 2·00 55

120 Kuwaiti Flag

1970. 9th Anniv of National Day.

487 **120** 15f. multicoloured 65 15
488 20f. multicoloured 75 15

121 Young Commando and Dome of the Rock, Jerusalem

1970. Support for Palestinian Commandos. Multicoloured.

489 10f. Type **121** 50 20
490 20f. Commando in battle-dress . . . . 1·00 40
491 45f. Woman commando . . . 2·50 90

122 Parents with "Children"

1970. Family Day.

492 **122** 20f. multicoloured 40 15
493 30f. multicoloured 60 25

123 Arab League Flag, Emblem and Map

1970. 25th Anniv of Arab League.

494 **123** 20f. brown, green and blue 50 10
495 45f. violet, green and orange 75 30

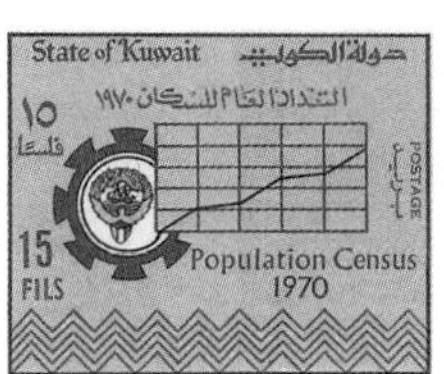

124 Census Emblem and Graph

1970. Population Census.

496 **124** 15f. multicoloured 20 10
497 20f. multicoloured 50 10
498 30f. multicoloured 70 20

125 Cancer the Crab in "Pincers"
126 Traffic Lights and Road Signs

1970. World Health Day.

499 **125** 20f. multicoloured 45 10
500 30f. multicoloured 65 20

1970. Traffic Day.

501 **126** 20f. multicoloured . . . . 1·00 45
502 30f. multicoloured . . . . 1·50 70

127 Red Crescent

1970. International Red Cross and Crescent Day.

503 **127** 10f. multicoloured 40 15
504 15f. multicoloured 60 20
505 30f. multicoloured . . . . 1·50 50

128 New Headquarters Building

1970. Opening of New U.P.U. Headquarters Building, Berne.

506 **128** 20f. multicoloured 60 20
507 30f. multicoloured 90 35

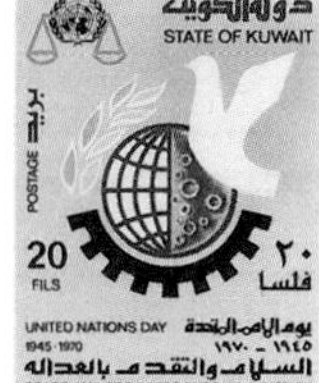

129 Amir Shaikh Sabah
130 U.N. Symbols

1970.

508 **129** 20f. multicoloured 65 20
509 45f. multicoloured . . . . 1·60 75

1970. 25th Anniv of United Nations.

511 **130** 20f. multicoloured 40 15
512 45f. multicoloured 70 30

131 "Medora" (tanker) at Sea Island Jetty

1970. Oil Shipment Facilities, Kuwait.

513 **131** 20f. multicoloured 90 30
514 45f. multicoloured . . . . 2·10 65

132 Kuwaiti and U.N. Emblems and Hand writing

1970. International Literacy Day.

515 **132** 10f. multicoloured 70 15
516 15f. multicoloured 90 15

133 Guards and Badge

1970. First Graduation of National Guards.

517 **133** 10f. multicoloured 55 15
518 20f. multicoloured . . . . 1·10 20

134 Symbols and Flag
136 Map of Palestine on Globe

135 Dr. C. Best and Sir F. Banting (discoverers of insulin) and Syringe

1971. 10th Anniv of National Day.

519 **134** 20f. multicoloured 70 30
520 30f. multicoloured 95 45

1971. World Health Day, and 50th Anniv of Discovery of Insulin.

521 **135** 20f. multicoloured 50 15
522 45f. multicoloured . . . . 1·10 40

1971. Palestine Week.

523 **136** 20f. multicoloured . . . . 1·00 75
524 45f. multicoloured . . . . 2·25 1·50

137 I.T.U. Emblem

1971. World Telecommunications Day.
525 **137** 20f. black, brown and silver 70 20
526 45f. black, brown and gold . . . . 1·60 60

138 "Three Races"

1971. Racial Equality Year.
527 **138** 15f. multicoloured 35 20
528 30f. multicoloured 65 50

139 A.P.U. Emblem

1971. 25th Anniv of Founding of Arab Postal Union at Sofar Conference.
529 **139** 20f. multicoloured 50 25
530 45f. multicoloured . . . . 1·00 40

140 Book, Pupils, Globes and Pen

1971. International Literacy Day.
531 **140** 25f. multicoloured 60 20
532 60f. multicoloured . . . . 1·50 60

141 Footballers

1971. Regional Sports Tournament, Kuwait. Multicoloured.
533 20f. Type **141** 95 35
534 30f. Footballer blocking attack . . . . 1·40 50

142 Emblems of UNICEF and Kuwait

1971. 25th Anniv of UNICEF.
535 **142** 25f. multicoloured 40 25
536 60f. multicoloured 90 50

143 Book Year Emblem

1972. International Book Year.
537 **143** 20f. black and brown . . 50 30
538 45f. black and green . . . 1·10 60

144 Crest and Laurel

1972. 11th Anniv of National Day.
539 **144** 20f. multicoloured 85 50
540 45f. multicoloured . . . . 1·40 85

145 Telecommunications Centre

1972. Inauguration of Telecommunications Centre, Kuwait.
541 **145** 20f. multicoloured . . . . 1·00 40
542 45f. multicoloured . . . . 2·50 1·00

146 Human Heart **147** Nurse and Child

1972. World Health Day and World Heart Month.
543 **146** 20f. multicoloured . . . . 1·25 25
544 45f. multicoloured . . . . 2·75 50

1972. International Red Cross and Crescent Day.
545 **147** 8f. multicoloured 75 10
546 40f. multicoloured . . . . 2·40 75

148 Football

1972. Olympic Games, Munich. Multicoloured.
547 2f. Type **148** 10 10
548 4f. Running 15 10
549 5f. Swimming 20 10
550 8f. Gymnastics 30 10
551 10f. Throwing the discus . . 35 10
552 15f. Show jumping 45 15
553 20f. Basketball 50 20
554 25f. Volleyball 65 30

149 Produce and Fishing Boat **151** Ancient Capitals

1972. 11th F.A.O. Near East Regional Conference, Kuwait.
555 **149** 5f. multicoloured 40 30
556 10f. multicoloured . . . . 1·25 75
557 20f. multicoloured . . . . 2·50 1·40

1972. 20th Anniv of National Bank of Kuwait.
558 **150** 10f. multicoloured 30 15
559 35f. multicoloured . . . . 1·00 70

1972. Archaeological Excavations on Failaka Island. Multicoloured.
560 2f. Type **151** 10 15
561 5f. View of excavations . . . 25 10
562 10f. "Leaf" capital 45 10
563 15f. Excavated building . . . 95 20

150 Bank Emblem

152 Floral Emblem **153** Interpol Emblem

1973. 12th Anniv of National Day.
564 **152** 10f. multicoloured 30 15
565 20f. multicoloured 65 45
566 30f. multicoloured 95 65

1973. 50th Anniv of International Criminal Police Organization (Interpol).
567 **153** 10f. multicoloured 50 45
568 15f. multicoloured . . . . 1·00 65
569 20f. multicoloured . . . . 1·50 95

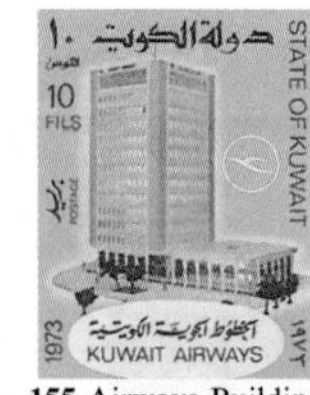

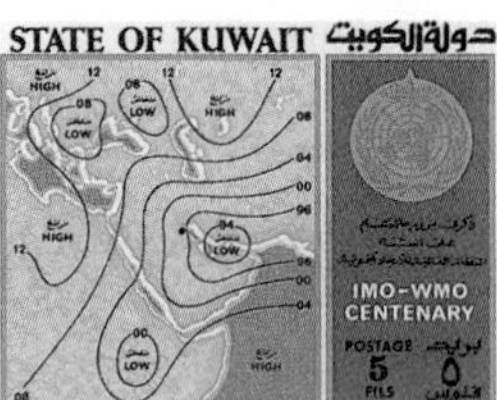

154 C.I.S.M. Badge and Flags **155** Airways Building

1973. 25th Anniv of International Military Sports Council (C.I.S.M.).
570 **154** 30f. multicoloured 65 40
571 40f. multicoloured . . . . 1·00 50

1973. Opening of Kuwait Airways H.Q. Building.
572 **155** 10f. multicoloured 35 15
573 15f. multicoloured 55 25
574 20f. multicoloured 70 30

156 Weather Map of Middle East

1973. Centenary of World Meteorological Organization.
575 **156** 5f. multicoloured 30 10
576 10f. multicoloured 50 15
577 15f. multicoloured 85 25

157 Shaikhs Ahmed and Sabah

1973. 50th Anniv of 1st Kuwait Stamp Issue (overprints on India of 1923).
578 **157** 10f. multicoloured 40 15
579 20f. multicoloured 75 25
580 70f. multicoloured . . . . 2·50 1·10

158 Mourning Dove

1973. Birds and Hunting Equipment. Multicoloured.

(a) Size 32 × 32 mm.
581 5f. Type **158** 65 15
582 5f. Hoopoe ("Upupa epops") 65 15
583 5f. Feral rock pigeon ("Columba livia") 65 15
584 5f. Stone-curlew ("Burhinus oedicnemus") 65 15
585 8f. Great grey shrike ("Lanius excubitor") . . . 85 15
586 8f. Red-backed shrike ("Lanius collurio") 85 15
587 8f. Black-headed shrike ("Lanius schach") 85 15
588 8f. Golden oriole ("Oriolus chinensis") 85 15
589 10f. Willow warbler ("Phylloscopus trochilus") 85 15
590 10f. Great reed warbler ("Acrocephalus arundinaceus") 85 15
591 10f. Blackcap ("Sylvia atricapilla") 85 15
592 10f. Barn swallow ("Hirundo rustica") 85 15
593 15f. Rock thrush ("Monticola solitarius") . . . . 1·25 35
594 15f. Common redstart ("Phoenicurus phoenicurus") . . . . . . 1·25 35
595 15f. Northern wheatear ("Oenanthe oenanthe") . . 1·25 35
596 15f. Bluethroat ("Luscinia svecica") . . . . 1·25 35
597 20f. Houbara bustard ("Chlamydotis undulata") 1·75 35
598 20f. Pin-tailed sandgrouse ("Pterocles alchata") . . . 1·75 35
599 20f. Greater wood rail ("Aramides ypecaha") . . 1·75 35
600 20f. Spotted crake ("Porzana porzana") . . . . 1·75 35

(b) Size 38 × 38 mm.
601 25f. American kestrel ("Falco sparverius") . . . . 2·50 50
602 25f. Great black-backed gull ("Larus marinus") . . . . 2·50 50
603 25f. Purple heron ("Ardea purpurea") . . . . 2·50 50
604 25f. Wryneck ("Jynx torquilla") . . . . 2·50 50
605 30f. European bee eater ("Merops apiaster") . . . 2·75 65
606 30f. Saker falcon ("Accipiter") . . . . 2·75 65
607 30f. Grey wagtail ("Motacilla cinerea") . . . . 2·75 65
608 30f. Pied wagtail ("Motacilla alba") . . . . 2·75 65
609 45f. Bird traps . . . . 4·00 1·25
610 45f. Driving great grey shrikes into net . . . . . 4·00 1·25
611 45f. Stalking Feral rock pigeon with hand net . . . 4·00 1·25
612 45f. Great grey shrike and disguised lure . . . . . . 4·00 1·25

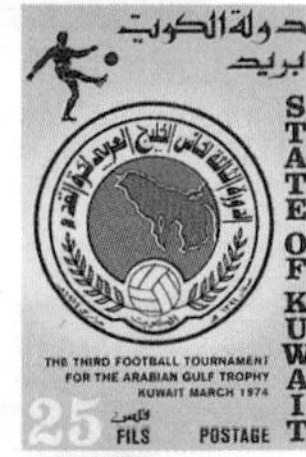

159 Flame Emblem **160** Congress Emblem

1973. 25th Anniv of Declaration of Human Rights.
613 **159** 10f. multicoloured 40 10
614 40f. multicoloured . . . . 1·10 35
615 75f. multicoloured . . . . 1·75 60

1974. 4th Congress of Arab Veterinary Union, Kuwait.
616 **160** 30f. multicoloured 60 20
617 40f. multicoloured 85 35

161 Flag and Wheat Ear Symbol **163** Tournament Emblem

162 A.M.U. Emblem

1974. 13th Anniv of National Day.
618 **161** 20f. multicoloured 30 10
619 30f. multicoloured 50 25
620 70f. multicoloured . . . . 1·40 1·00

1974. 12th Conference of Arab Medical Union and 1st Conference of Kuwait Medical Society.
621 **162** 30f. multicoloured . . . . 1·25 30
622 40f. multicoloured . . . . 1·75 80

1974. 3rd Arabian Gulf Trophy Football Tournament, Kuwait.
623 **163** 25f. multicoloured 80 15
624 45f. multicoloured . . . . 1·75 70

164 Institute Buildings

1974. Inauguration of Kuwait Institute for Scientific Research.
625 **164** 15f. multicoloured 70 25
626 20f. multicoloured . . . . 1·40 30

165 Emblems of Kuwait, Arab Postal Union and U.P.U.

1974. Centenary of U.P.U.
627 **165** 20f. multicoloured 25 15
628 30f. multicoloured 30 30
629 60f. multicoloured 50 45

166 Symbolic Telephone Dial

167 Council Emblem and Flags of Member States

1974. World Telecommunications Day.
630 **166** 10f. multicoloured 60 20
631 30f. multicoloured . . . . 1·90 75
632 40f. multicoloured . . . . 3·00 1·00

1974. 17th Anniv of Signing Arab Economic Unity Agreement.
633 **167** 20f. green, black and red 60 25
634 30f. red, black and green 70 40

168 "Population Growth"

1974. World Population Year.
635 **168** 30f. multicoloured 75 30
636 70f. multicoloured . . . . 1·75 70

169 Fund Building

1974. Kuwait Fund for Arab Economic Development.
637 **169** 10f. multicoloured 45 10
638 20f. multicoloured 75 25

170 Shuaiba Emblem

1974. 10th Anniv of Shuaiba Industrial Area.
639 **170** 10f. multicoloured 40 15
640 20f. multicoloured . . . . 1·00 30
641 30f. multicoloured . . . . 1·40 55

171 Arms of Kuwait and "14"

1975. 14th Anniv of National Day.
642 **171** 20f. multicoloured 40 20
643 70f. multicoloured . . . . 1·25 60
644 75f. multicoloured . . . . 1·60 70

172 Census Symbols

1975. Population Census.
645 **172** 8f. multicoloured 15 10
646 20f. multicoloured 35 10
647 30f. multicoloured 50 25
648 70f. multicoloured . . . . 1·40 75
649 100f. multicoloured . . . 1·75 1·10

173 I.W.Y. and Kuwait Women's Union Emblems

1975. International Women's Year.
650 **173** 15f. multicoloured 50 15
651 20f. multicoloured 60 30
652 30f. multicoloured 85 45

174 Classroom within Open Book

1975. International Literacy Day.
653 **174** 20f. multicoloured 50 15
654 30f. multicoloured 85 45

175 I.S.O. Emblem

176 U.N. Flag, Rifle and Olive-branch

1975. World Standards Day.
655 **175** 10f. multicoloured 30 15
656 20f. multicoloured 55 25

1975. 30th Anniv of U.N.O.
657 **176** 20f. multicoloured 50 15
658 45f. multicoloured . . . . 1·10 50

177 Shaikh Sabah

1975.
659 **177** 8f. multicoloured 35 15
660 20f. multicoloured 60 20
661 30f. multicoloured 70 30
662 50f. multicoloured . . . . 1·25 50
663 90f. multicoloured . . . . 2·40 85
664 100f. multicoloured . . . 3·00 1·10

178 Kuwait "Skyline"

1976. 15th Anniv of National Day.
665 **178** 10f. multicoloured 50 15
666 20f. multicoloured 90 15

178a Emblem, Microscope and Operation

179 Early and Modern Telephones

1976. 2nd Annual Conference of Kuwait Medical Association.
667 **178a** 5f. multicoloured 30 15
668 10f. multicoloured . . . 60 20
669 30f. multicoloured . . . 1·90 55

1976. Telephone Centenary.
670 **179** 5f. black and orange . . . 20 15
671 15f. black and blue . . . 65 15

180 Eye

1976. World Health Day.
672 **180** 10f. multicoloured 40 15
673 20f. multicoloured 75 15
674 30f. multicoloured . . . . 1·25 35

181 Red Crescent Emblem

1976. 10th Anniv of Kuwait Red Crescent Society.
675 **181** 20f. multicoloured 40 15
676 30f. multicoloured 70 30
677 45f. multicoloured . . . . 1·25 55
678 75f. multicoloured . . . . 2·00 1·40

182 Suburb of Manama

183 Basketball

1976. U.N. Human Settlements Conference.
679 **182** 10f. multicoloured 35 15
680 20f. multicoloured 65 15

1976. Olympic Games, Montreal. Multicoloured.
681 4f. Type **183** 10 10
682 8f. Running 15 10
683 10f. Judo 20 10
684 15f. Handball 30 10
685 20f. Figure-skating 35 10
686 30f. Volleyball 55 25
687 45f. Football 70 35
688 70f. Swimming . . . . 1·10 85

184 Ethnic Heads and Map of Sri Lanka

1976. Non-Aligned Countries' Congress, Colombo.
689 **184** 20f. multicoloured 35 10
690 30f. multicoloured 50 30
691 45f. multicoloured 85 45

185 Torch, UNESCO. Emblem and Kuwaiti Arms

1976. 30th Anniv of UNESCO.
692 **185** 20f. multicoloured 45 10
693 45f. multicoloured . . . . 1·00 50

186 Pot-throwing

187 Diseased Knee

1977. Popular Games. Multicoloured.
694 5f. Type **186** 20 10
695 5f. Kite-flying 20 10
696 5f. Balancing sticks 20 10
697 5f. Spinning tops 20 10
698 10f. Blind-man's-buff (horiz) 25 15
699 10f. Rowing (horiz) 25 15
700 10f. Rolling hoops (horiz) . . 25 15
701 10f. Rope game (horiz) . . . 25 15
702 15f. Skipping 50 25
703 15f. Marbles 50 25
704 15f. Carting 50 25
705 15f. Teetotum (tops) 50 25
706 20f. Halma (horiz) 80 40
707 20f. Model boating (horiz) . . 80 40
708 20f. Pot and candle (horiz) 80 40
709 20f. Hide-and-seek (horiz) . . 80 40
710 30f. Knucklebones 90 50
711 30f. Hiding the stone 90 50
712 30f. Hopscotch 90 50
713 30f. Catch-as-catch-can . . . 90 50
714 40f. Bowls (horiz) . . . . . 1·60 70
715 40f. Hockey (horiz) . . . . . 1·60 70
716 40f. Guessing which hand (horiz) . . . . 1·60 70
717 40f. Jacks (horiz) . . . . . 1·60 70
718 60f. Hiding the cake (horiz) 2·00 1·25
719 60f. Chess (horiz) . . . . . 2·00 1·25
720 60f. Story-telling (horiz) . . . 2·00 1·25
721 60f. Treasure hunt (horiz) . . 2·00 1·25
722 70f. Hobby horses (horiz) . . 2·25 1·40
723 70f. Hide-and-seek (horiz) . . 2·25 1·40
724 70f. Catch shadow (horiz) . . 2·25 1·40
725 70f. Throwing game (horiz) 2·25 1·40

1977. World Rheumatism Year.
726 **187** 20f. multicoloured 40 15
727 30f. multicoloured 60 30
728 45f. multicoloured 90 45
729 75f. multicoloured . . . . 1·25 85

188 Shaikh Sabah

1977. 16th National Day.
730 **188** 10f. multicoloured 15 10
731 15f. multicoloured 30 15
732 30f. multicoloured 65 20
733 80f. multicoloured . . . . 1·40 55

189 Kuwait Tower

190 A.P.U. Emblem and Flags

1977. Inauguration of Kuwait Tower.
734 **189** 30f. multicoloured 75 15
735 80f. multicoloured . . . . 2·00 55

1977. 25th Anniv of Arab Postal Union.
736 **190** 5f. multicoloured 20 10
737 15f. multicoloured 20 10
738 30f. multicoloured 40 20
739 80f. multicoloured . . . . 1·10 60

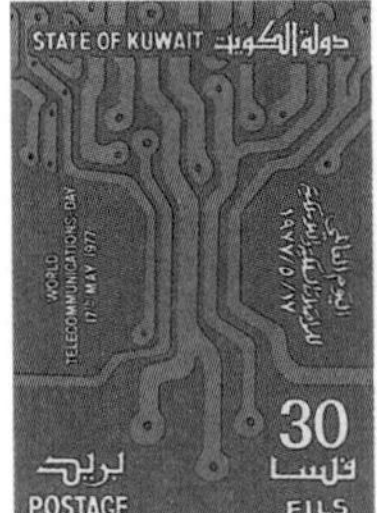

191 Printed Circuit

192 Shaikh Sabah

1977. World Telecommunications Day.
740 **191** 30f. orange and brown . . 60 30
741 80f. orange and green . . 1·50 70

1977.
742 **192** 15f. brown, black and blue 80 35
743 25f. brown, black & yellow . . . . 1·40 35
744 30f. brown, black and red 1·75 50
745 80f. brown, black and lilac . . . . 4·00 1·25
746 100f. brown, black & orge 5·00 1·40
747 150f. brown, black & blue 9·00 2·25
748 200f. brown, black & green . . . . 10·00 3·25

192a Aerogramme stamp

193 Championship Emblem

1977. Aerogramme stamp. Imperf.
748a **192a** 55f. red and blue . . .

No. 748a was applied before sale to aerogrammes to uprate the imprinted 25f. stamp. It was not available separately.

1977. 4th Asian Youth Basketball Championships.
749 **193** 30f. multicoloured 50 50
750 80f. multicoloured . . . . 1·50 1·00

194 "Popular Dancing" (O. Al-Nakeeb)

1977. Children's Paintings. Multicoloured.
751 15f. Type **194** 35 20
752 15f. "Al Deirah" (A. M. al-Onizi) 35 20
753 30f. "Fishing" (M. al-Jasem) 60 45
754 30f. "Dugg al-Harees" (B. al-Sa'adooni) (vert) 60 45
755 80f. "Fraisa Dancing" (M. al-Mojaibel) (vert) . . . . . 1·50 1·25
756 80f. "Kuwaiti Girl" (K. Ghazi) (vert) . . . . . 1·50 1·25

195 Dome of the Rock and Palestinian Freedom Fighters

1978. Palestinian Freedom Fighters.
757 **195** 30f. multicoloured . . . . 1·25 70
758 80f. multicoloured . . . . 2·40 1·50

196 Dentist treating Patient

1978. 10th Arab Dental Union Congress.
759 **196** 30f. multicoloured 70 55
760 80f. multicoloured . . . . 1·75 1·10

197 Carrying Water from Dhows

1978. Water Resources. Multicoloured.
761 5f. Type **197** 25 10
762 5f. Camel 25 10
763 5f. Water carrier 25 10
764 5f. Pushing water in cart . . 25 10
765 10f. Irrigation with donkey 35 10
766 10f. Water troughs in desert 35 10
767 10f. Pool by a town 35 10
768 10f. Watering crops 35 10
769 15f. Bedouin watering sheep 50 10
770 15f. Bedouin women by pool 50 10
771 15f. Camels watered by pipeline 50 10
772 15f. Water skins in Bedouin tent 50 10
773 20f. Oasis with wells 55 10
774 20f. Washing and drinking at home 55 10
775 20f. Water urn 55 10
776 20f. Filling vessels from taps 55 10
777 25f. Desalination plant . . . 65 15
778 25f. Water tanker 65 15
779 25f. Filling water tankers . . 65 15
780 25f. Modern water tanks . . 65 15
781 30f. Catching water during storm (vert) 85 15
782 30f. Water tank (vert) 85 15
783 30f. Sheet to catch rain (vert) 85 15
784 30f. Trees by water tanks (vert) 85 15
785 80f. Carrying water on donkey (vert) . . . . . . 2·00 60
786 80f. Woman carrying water-can (vert) . . . . 2·00 60
787 80f. Woman with water-skins (vert) . . . . 2·00 60
788 80f. Tanker delivering water to house (vert) . . . . . 2·00 60
789 100f. Tanker delivering to courtyard tank (vert) . . . 2·75 90
790 100f. Household cistern (vert) 2·75 90
791 100f. Filling cistern (vert) . . 2·75 90
792 100f. Drawing water from well (vert) . . . . 2·75 90

198 Symbols of Development

1978. 17th National Day.
793 **198** 30f. multicoloured 35 25
794 80f. multicoloured . . . . 1·00 70

199 Face of Smallpox Victim

1978. Global Eradication of Smallpox.
795 **199** 30f. multicoloured 40 30
796 80f. multicoloured . . . . 1·10 70

200 Microwave Antenna

201 Shaikh Jabir

1978. 10th World Telecommunications Day.
797 **200** 30f. multicoloured 35 25
798 80f. multicoloured . . . . 1·10 70

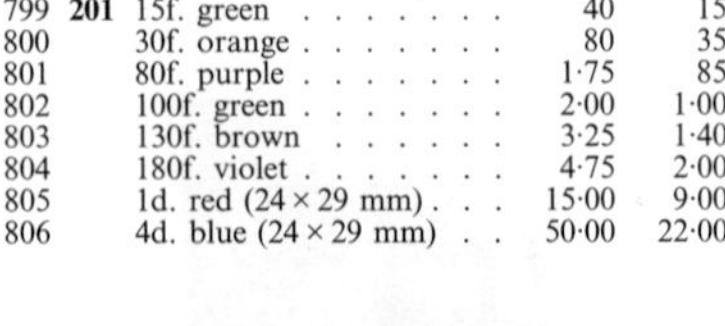

1978. Portrait in brown; background colour given.
799 **201** 15f. green 40 15
800 30f. orange 80 35
801 80f. purple . . . . 1·75 85
802 100f. green . . . . 2·00 1·00
803 130f. brown . . . . . . 3·25 1·40
804 180f. violet . . . . 4·75 2·00
805 1d. red (24 × 29 mm) . . . 15·00 9·00
806 4d. blue (24 × 29 mm) . . 50·00 22·00

202 Mount Arafat, Pilgrims and Kaaba

1978. Pilgrimage to Mecca.
807 **202** 30f. multicoloured 50 40
808 80f. multicoloured . . . . 1·40 1·00

203 U.N. and Anti-Apartheid Emblems

1978. International Anti-Apartheid Year.
809 **203** 30f. multicoloured 40 25
810 80f. multicoloured . . . . 1·00 70
811 180f. multicoloured . . . 2·10 1·50

204 Refugees

1978. 30th Anniv of Declaration of Human Rights.
812 **204** 30f. multicoloured 40 30
813 80f. multicoloured . . . . 1·25 75
814 100f. multicoloured . . . 1·75 1·00

205 Information Centre

1978. Kuwait Information Centre.
815 **205** 5f. multicoloured 10 10
816 15f. multicoloured 20 10
817 30f. multicoloured 35 20
818 80f. multicoloured 90 60

206 Kindergarten

207 Kuwaiti Flag and Doves

1979. International Year of the Child.
819 **206** 30f. multicoloured 40 35
820 80f. multicoloured . . . . 1·00 85

1979. 18th National Day.
821 **207** 30f. multicoloured 40 30
822 80f. multicoloured 95 75

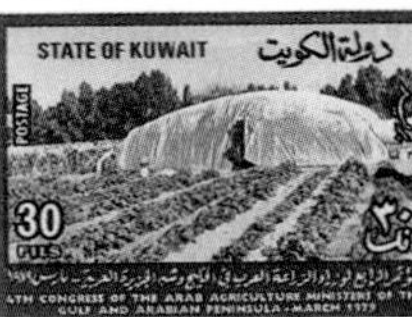

208 Crops and Greenhouse

1979. 4th Arab Agriculture Ministers' Congress.
823 **208** 30f. multicoloured 40 25
824 80f. multicoloured 95 75

209 World Map, Koran and Symbols of Arab Achievements

1979. The Arabs.
825 **209** 30f. multicoloured 40 30
826 80f. multicoloured 95 75

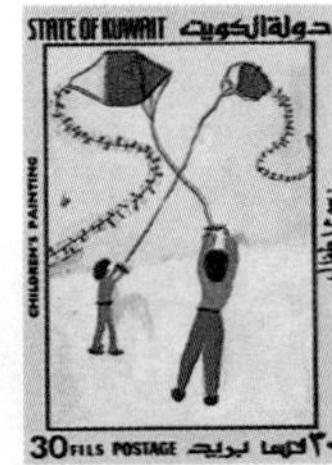

210 Children flying Kites

1979. Children's Paintings. Multicoloured.
827 30f. Type **210** 40 35
828 30f. Girl and doves 40 35
829 30f. Crowd and balloons . . 40 35
830 80f. Boys smiling (horiz) . . 1·00 90
831 80f. Children in landscape (horiz) . . . . 1·00 90
832 80f. Tug-of-war (horiz) . . . 1·00 90

211 Wave Pattern and Television Screen

212 International Military Sports Council Emblem

1979. World Telecommunications Day.
833 **211** 30f. multicoloured 35 30
834 80f. multicoloured 95 85

1979. 29th International Military Football Championship.
835 **212** 30f. multicoloured 45 25
836 80f. multicoloured . . . . 1·25 85

213 Child and Industrial Landscape

1979. World Environment Day.
837 **213** 30f. multicoloured 50 40
838 80f. multicoloured . . . . 1·40 1·10

214 Children supporting Globe

215 Children with Television

1979. 50th Anniv of Int Bureau of Education.
839 **214** 30f. multicoloured 35 25
840 80f. multicoloured 85 75
841 130f. multicoloured . . . 1·40 1·25

1979. 25th Anniv of Kuwaiti Kindergartens. Children's Drawings. Multicoloured.
842 30f. Type **215** 40 25
843 80f. Children with flags . . . 1·00 75

216 The Kaaba, Mecca

1979. Pilgrimage to Mecca.
844 **216** 30f. multicoloured 40 30
845 80f. multicoloured . . . . 1·50 85

217 Figure, with Dove and Torch, clothed in Palestinian Flag

1979. Int Day of Solidarity with Palestinians.
846 **217** 30f. multicoloured . . . . 1·50 65
847 80f. multicoloured . . . . 3·00 1·25

218 Boeing 747 and Douglas DC-3 Airliners

1979. 25th Anniv of Kuwait Airways.
848 **218** 30f. multicoloured 55 40
849 80f. multicoloured . . . . 1·50 1·25

219 "Pinctada" Shell bearing Map of Kuwait

1980. 19th National Day.
850 **219** 30f. multicoloured 40 30
851 80f. multicoloured . . . . 1·10 75

220 Graph with Human Figures

1980. Population Census.
852 **220** 30f. black, silver and blue 50 25
853 80f. black, gold and orange . . . . 1·10 60

221 Campaign Emblem

1980. World Health Day. Anti-smoking Campaign.
854 **221** 30f. multicoloured 60 35
855 80f. multicoloured . . . . 1·75 1·10

222 Municipality Building

1980. 50th Anniv of Kuwait Municipality.
856 **222** 15f. multicoloured 20 10
857 30f. multicoloured 40 30
858 80f. multicoloured . . . . 1·25 75

223 "The Future"

1980. Children's Imagination of Future Kuwait. Multicoloured.
859 30f. Type **223** 50 30
860 80f. Motorways . . . . . . 1·50 95

224 Hand blotting out Factory

1980. World Environment Day.
861 **224** 30f. multicoloured 55 30
862 80f. multicoloured . . . . 1·50 60

225 Volleyball

226 O.P.E.C. Emblem and Globe

1980. Olympic Games, Moscow. Multicoloured.
863 15f. Type **225** 20 20
864 15f. Tennis 20 20
865 30f. Swimming 35 25
866 30f. Weightlifting 35 25
867 30f. Basketball 35 25
868 30f. Judo 35 25
869 80f. Gymnastics 95 60
870 80f. Badminton 95 60
871 80f. Fencing 95 60
872 80f. Football 95 60

1980. 20th Anniv of Organization of Petroleum Exporting Countries.
873 **226** 30f. multicoloured 50 35
874 80f. multicoloured . . . . 1·50 55

227 Mosque and Kaaba, Mecca

1980. 1400th Anniv of Hegira.
875 **227** 15f. multicoloured 25 15
876 30f. multicoloured 50 30
877 80f. multicoloured . . . . 1·40 85

228 Dome of the Rock

1980. International Day of Solidarity with Palestinian People.
878 **228** 30f. multicoloured . . . . 1·00 40
879 80f. multicoloured . . . . 2·50 1·25

229 Ibn Sina (Avicenna)

1980. Birth Millenary of Ibn Sina (philosopher and physician).
880 **229** 30f. multicoloured 60 25
881 80f. multicoloured . . . . 1·25 85

230 Islamic Symbols

231 Person in Wheelchair playing Snooker

1981. 1st Islamic Medicine Conference, Kuwait.
882 **230** 30f. multicoloured 50 30
883 80f. multicoloured . . . . 1·50 85

1981. International Year of Disabled Persons. Multicoloured.
884 30f. Type **231** 50 30
885 80f. Girl in wheelchair . . . 1·50 85

232 Symbols of Development and Progress

1981. 20th National Day.
886 **232** 30f. multicoloured 50 30
887 80f. multicoloured . . . . 1·50 85

233 Emblem of Kuwait Dental Association

234 "Lamp"

1981. 1st Kuwait Dental Association Conference.
888 **233** 30f. multicoloured . . . . 1·00 55
889 80f. multicoloured . . . . 2·50 1·50

1981. World Red Cross and Red Crescent Day.
890 **234** 30f. multicoloured 90 55
891 80f. multicoloured . . . . 2·50 1·50

235 Emblems of I.T.U. and W.H.O. and Ribbons forming Caduceus

236 Tanker polluting Sea and Car polluting Atmosphere

1981. World Telecommunications Day.
892 **235** 30f. multicoloured 70 50
893 80f. multicoloured . . . . 2·25 1·40

1981. World Environment Day.
894 **236** 30f. multicoloured 75 50
895 80f. multicoloured . . . . 2·40 1·25

237 Sief Palace

1981.
896 **237** 5f. multicoloured 10 10
897 10f. multicoloured 10 10
898 15f. multicoloured 10 10
899 25f. multicoloured 15 15
900 30f. multicoloured 20 15
901 40f. multicoloured 25 15
902 60f. multicoloured 40 20
903 80f. multicoloured 50 30
904 100f. multicoloured . . . 65 45
905 115f. multicoloured . . . 70 50
906 130f. multicoloured . . . 80 70
907 150f. multicoloured . . . 1·10 70
908 180f. multicoloured . . . 1·25 75
909 250f. multicoloured . . . 1·50 80
910 500f. multicoloured . . . 3·25 1·10
911 1d. multicoloured . . . . 6·25 1·50
912 2d. multicoloured . . . . 12·00 2·25
913 3d. multicoloured . . . . 16·00 6·75
914 4d. multicoloured . . . . 25·00 8·50
Nos. 911/14 are larger, 33×28 mm and have a different border.

238 Pilgrims

1981. Pilgrimage to Mecca.
915 **238** 30f. multicoloured 60 50
916 80f. multicoloured . . . . 2·25 1·25

239 Palm Trees, Sheep, Camel, Goat and F.A.O. Emblem

1981. World Food Day.
917 **239** 30f. multicoloured 65 45
918 80f. multicoloured . . . . 2·00 1·25

240 Television Emblem

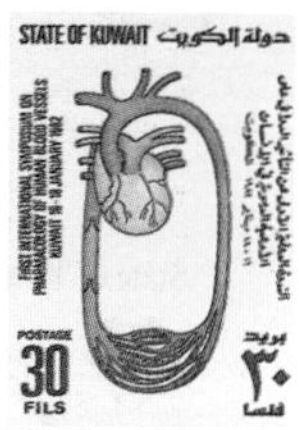

241 Blood Circulation Diagram

1981. 20th Anniv of Kuwait Television.
919 **240** 30f. multicoloured 70 45
920 80f. multicoloured . . . . 2·00 1·25

1982. 1st International Symposium on Pharmacology of Human Blood Vessels.
921 **241** 30f. multicoloured . . . . 1·00 80
922 80f. multicoloured . . . . 2·25 1·10

242 Symbols of Development, Progress and Peace

1982. 21st National Day.
923 **242** 30f. multicoloured 50 30
924 80f. multicoloured . . . . 1·40 85

243 Emblem of Kuwait Boy Scouts Association on Globe

1982. 75th Anniv of Boy Scout Movement.
925 **243** 30f. multicoloured 60 40
926 80f. multicoloured . . . . 1·75 1·00

244 Emblem of Arab Pharmacists Union

1982. Arab Pharmacists Day.
927 **244** 30f. multicoloured 85 60
928 80f. multicoloured . . . . 2·75 1·75

245 Red Crescent, Arab and W.H.O. Emblem

246 A.P.U. Emblem

1982. World Health Day.
929 **245** 30f. multicoloured . . . . 1·00 65
930 80f. multicoloured . . . . 3·00 1·75

1982. 30th Anniv of Arab Postal Union.
931 **246** 30f. black, orange and green 85 60
932 80f. black, green and orange . . . . 2·75 1·50

247 Lungs and Microscope

249 Museum Exhibits

248 Crest and Emblems of Kuwait Football Association and Olympic Committee

1982. Centenary of Discovery of Tubercle Bacillus.
933 **247** 30f. multicoloured . . . . 1·00 60
934 80f. multicoloured . . . . 2·75 1·60

1982. World Cup Football Championship, Spain.
935 **248** 30f. multicoloured 75 40
936 80f. multicoloured . . . . 2·00 1·25

1982. 10th Anniv of Science and Natural History Museum.
937 **249** 30f. multicoloured . . . . 1·50 1·00
938 80f. multicoloured . . . . 4·50 3·00

250 "Al-Wattyah" (container ship)

1982. 6th Anniv of United Arab Shipping Company. Multicoloured.
939 30f. Type **250** 75 35
940 80f. "Al-Salimiah" (freighter) 1·75 90

251 Palm Trees

253 Desert Flower

252 Pilgrims

1982. Arab Palm Tree Day.
941 **251** 30f. multicoloured 50 30
942 80f. multicoloured . . . . 1·50 90

1982. Pilgrimage to Mecca.
943 **252** 15f. multicoloured 30 20
944 30f. multicoloured 70 45
945 80f. multicoloured . . . . 1·90 1·25

1983. Desert Plants. As T **253**. Multicoloured; background colours given. (a) Vert designs.
946 10f. green 10 10
947 10f. violet 10 10
948 10f. salmon 10 10
949 10f. pink (blue flowers) . . . 10 10
950 10f. bistre 10 10
951 10f. green 10 10
952 10f. light orange 10 10
953 10f. red (poppy) 10 10
954 10f. brown 10 10
955 10f. blue 10 10
956 15f. green 15 15
957 15f. purple 15 15
958 15f. blue 15 15
959 15f. blue (iris) 15 15
960 15f. olive 15 15
961 15f. red 15 15
962 15f. brown 15 15
963 15f. blue (bellflowers) 15 15
964 15f. mauve 15 15
965 15f. pink 15 15
966 30f. brown 40 25
967 30f. mauve 40 25
968 30f. blue 40 25
969 30f. green 40 25
970 30f. pink 40 25
971 30f. blue 40 25
972 30f. green 40 25
973 30f. mauve 40 25
974 30f. bistre 40 25
975 30f. yellow 40 25

(b) Horiz designs.
976 40f. red (fungi) 75 35
977 40f. green (fungi) 75 35
978 40f. violet 50 35
979 40f. blue 50 35
980 40f. grey 50 35
981 40f. green 50 35
982 40f. mauve 50 35
983 40f. brown 50 35
984 40f. blue 50 35
985 40f. green (daisies) 50 35
986 80f. violet 90 70
987 80f. green 90 70
988 80f. yellow (yellow flowers) 90 70
989 80f. brown (green leaves) . . 90 70
990 80f. blue 90 70
991 80f. yellow 90 70
992 80f. green 90 70
993 80f. violet (red berries) . . . 90 70
994 80f. brown (yellow flowers) 90 70
995 80f. yellow (red and blue flowers) 90 70

DESIGNS: Various plants.

254 Peace Dove on Map of Kuwait

1983. 22nd National Day.
996 **254** 30f. multicoloured 60 35
997 80f. multicoloured . . . . 1·50 95

255 I.M.O. Emblem

1983. 25th Anniv of International Maritime Organization.
998 **255** 30f. multicoloured 35 20
999 80f. multicoloured . . . . 1·00 60

256 Virus and Map of Africa

1983. 3rd International Conference on Impact of Viral Diseases on Development of Middle East and African Countries.
1000 **256** 15f. multicoloured . . . 30 15
1001 30f. multicoloured . . . 60 35
1002 80f. multicoloured . . . 1·50 95

257 Stylized Figures exercising

1983. World Health Day.
1003 **257** 15f. multicoloured . . . 30 20
1004 30f. multicoloured . . . 65 45
1005 80f. multicoloured . . . 1·90 1·25

258 U.P.U., W.C.Y. and I.T.U. Emblems

1983. World Communications Year.
1006 **258** 15f. multicoloured . . . 35 20
1007 30f. multicoloured . . . 65 45
1008 80f. multicoloured . . . 1·60 1·25

259 Map of Kuwait and Dhow

1983. World Environment Day.
1009 **259** 15f. multicoloured . . . 45 20
1010 30f. multicoloured . . . 85 45
1011 80f. multicoloured . . . 2·00 1·25

260 Walls of Jerusalem

1983. World Heritage Convention.
1012 **260** 15f. multicoloured . . . 35 20
1013 30f. multicoloured . . . 65 45
1014 80f. multicoloured . . . 1·60 1·25

261 Pilgrims in Mozdalipha

1983. Pilgrimage to Mecca.
1015 **261** 15f. multicoloured . . . 35 20
1016 30f. multicoloured . . . 65 45
1017 80f. multicoloured . . . 1·60 1·25

262 Arab within Dove

1983. International Day of Solidarity with Palestinian People.
1018 **262** 15f. multicoloured . . . 35 20
1019 30f. multicoloured . . . 65 45
1020 80f. multicoloured . . . 1·60 1·25

263 Kuwait Medical Association and Congress Emblems

1984. 21st Pan-Arab Medical Congress.
1021 **263** 15f. multicoloured . . . 35 20
1022 30f. multicoloured . . . 65 45
1023 80f. multicoloured . . . 1·60 1·25

264 State Arms within Key

1984. Inauguration of New Health Establishments.
1024 **264** 15f. multicoloured . . . 35 20
1025 30f. multicoloured . . . 65 45
1026 80f. multicoloured . . . 1·60 1·25

265 Dove and Globe

266 Symbols of Medicine within Head

1984. 23rd National Day.
1027 **265** 15f. multicoloured . . . 35 20
1028 30f. multicoloured . . . 65 45
1029 80f. multicoloured . . . 1·60 1·25

1984. 2nd International Medical Science Conference.
1030 **266** 15f. multicoloured . . . 35 20
1031 30f. multicoloured . . . 65 45
1032 80f. multicoloured . . . 1·60 1·25

267 Douglas DC-3 Airliner

1984. 30th Anniv of Kuwait Airways Corporation.
1033 **267** 30f. blue, dp blue & yell 75 60
1034 80f. blue, dp blue & mve 2·00 1·10

268 Magazine Covers

269 Family and Emblems

1984. 25th Anniv of "Al-Arabi" (magazine).
1035 **268** 15f. multicoloured . . . 30 20
1036 30f. multicoloured . . . 60 35
1037 80f. multicoloured . . . 1·50 1·00

1984. World Health Day.
1038 **269** 15f. multicoloured . . . 30 20
1039 30f. multicoloured . . . 70 40
1040 80f. multicoloured . . . 1·90 1·10

270 Sudanese Orphan and Village

1984. Hanan Kuwaiti Village, Sudan.

1041	270	15f. multicoloured	35	20
1042		30f. multicoloured	75	40
1043		80f. multicoloured	1·90	1·10

271 I.C.A.O., Kuwait Airport and Kuwait Airways Emblems

1984. 40th Anniv of I.C.A.O.

1044	271	15f. multicoloured	35	20
1045		30f. multicoloured	75	40
1046		80f. multicoloured	1·90	1·10

272 Map of Arab Countries and Youths

1984. Arab Youth Day.

1047	272	30f. multicoloured	70	40
1048		80f. multicoloured	1·90	1·10

273 Swimming

1984. Olympic Games, Los Angeles. Multicoloured.

1049	30f. Type **273**	40	25
1050	30f. Hurdling	40	25
1051	80f. Judo	75	60
1052	80f. Equestrian	75	60

274 Anniversary Emblem, Camera, Airplane, Al-Aujairy Observatory and Wind Tower

1984. 10th Anniv of Science Club.

1053	274	15f. multicoloured	35	15
1054		30f. multicoloured	85	40
1055		80f. multicoloured	2·10	1·10

275 Stoning the Devil

1984. Pilgrimage to Mecca.

1056	275	30f. multicoloured	80	40
1057		80f. multicoloured	1·75	1·10

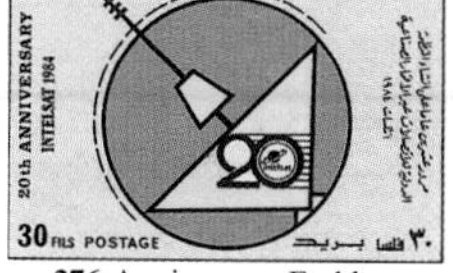

276 Anniversary Emblem

1984. 20th Anniv of International Telecommunications Satellite Consortium (Intelsat).

1058	276	30f. multicoloured	80	40
1059		80f. multicoloured	1·75	1·10

277 Council Emblem

278 Hands breaking Star

1984. 5th Supreme Council Session of Gulf Co-operation Council.

1060	277	30f. multicoloured	70	40
1061		80f. multicoloured	1·75	1·10

1984. International Day of Solidarity with Palestinian People.

1062	278	30f. multicoloured	70	40
1063		80f. multicoloured	1·75	1·10

279 Company Emblem as Satellite

280 I.Y.Y. Emblem

1984. 50th Anniv of Kuwait Oil Company.

1064	279	30f. multicoloured	70	40
1065		80f. multicoloured	1·75	1·10

1985. International Youth Year.

1066	280	30f. multicoloured	40	20
1067		80f. multicoloured	1·25	75

281 "24", Hand holding Flame and Dove

282 Programme Emblem

1985. 24th National Day.

1068	281	30f. multicoloured	60	30
1069		80f. multicoloured	1·75	1·10

1985. International Programme for Communications Development.

1070	282	30f. multicoloured	70	40
1071		80f. multicoloured	1·75	1·10

283 Emblem

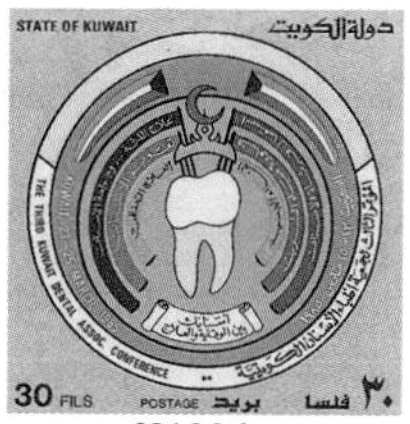

284 Molar

1985. 1st Arab Gulf Social Work Week.

1072	283	30f. multicoloured	70	40
1073		80f. multicoloured	1·75	1·10

1985. 3rd Kuwait Dental Association Conference.

1074	284	30f. multicoloured	70	40
1075		80f. multicoloured	1·75	1·10

285 Emblem

286 Globe and Figures

1985. Population Census.

1076	285	30f. multicoloured	85	40
1077		80f. multicoloured	1·75	1·10

1985. World Health Day.

1078	286	30f. multicoloured	85	40
1079		80f. multicoloured	1·75	1·10

287 Arabic Script

No. 1080

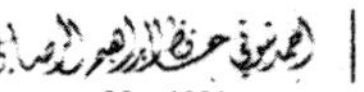

No. 1081

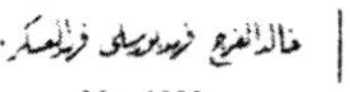

No. 1082

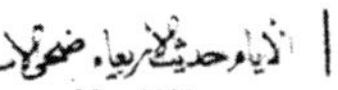

No. 1083

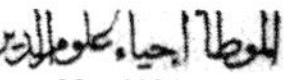

No. 1084

No. 1085

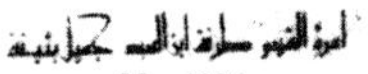

No. 1086

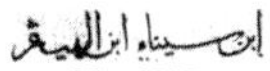

No. 1087

1985. 50th Anniv of Central Library. Designs showing titles of books and names of authors in Arabic script (first line of text illustrated above).

1080	30f. gold	1·00	45
1081	30f. gold	1·00	45
1082	30f. gold	1·00	45
1083	30f. gold	1·00	45
1084	80f. black and gold	2·50	1·00
1085	80f. black and gold	2·50	1·00
1086	80f. black and gold	2·50	1·00
1087	80f. black and gold	2·50	1·00

288 Seascape

1985. World Environment Day.

1088	288	30f. multicoloured	1·50	40
1089		80f. multicoloured	3·00	1·10

289 Anniversary Emblem

1985. 25th Anniv of Organization of Petroleum Exporting Countries.

1090	289	30f. ultramarine, bl & mve	85	40
1091		80f. ultramarine, bl & brn	1·90	1·10

290 Emblem and Heads

1985. Introduction of Civilian Identity Cards.

1092	290	30f. multicoloured	85	40
1093		80f. multicoloured	1·90	1·10

291 Flag on Globe within Symbolic Design

1985. International Day of Solidarity with Palestinian People.

1094	291	15f. multicoloured	75	30
1095		30f. multicoloured	1·40	60
1096		80f. multicoloured	2·50	1·50

292 Birds

1986. 25th National Day.

1097	292	15f. multicoloured	20	15
1098		30f. multicoloured	75	35
1099		80f. multicoloured	2·00	90

293 Emblem

294 W.H.O. Emblem as Flower

1986. 20th Anniv of Kuwait Red Crescent.

1100	293	20f. multicoloured	60	45
1101		25f. multicoloured	85	70
1102		70f. multicoloured	2·50	1·90

1986. World Health Day.

1103	294	20f. multicoloured	60	45
1104		25f. multicoloured	85	70
1105		70f. multicoloured	2·50	1·90

295 I.P.Y. Emblem

1986. International Peace Year.

1106	295	20f. green, blue and black	50	45
1107		25f. blue, yellow and black	75	50
1108		70f. blue, mauve and black	2·25	1·40

296 "Al Mirqab"

1986. 10th Anniv of United Arab Shipping Company. Container Ships. Multicoloured.

1109	20f. Type **296**	1·00	45
1110	70f. "Al Mubarakiah"	3·50	1·90

297 Bank Emblem on Map

1986. 25th Anniv of Gulf Bank.

1111	297	20f. multicoloured	50	30
1112		25f. multicoloured	75	40
1113		70f. multicoloured	2·25	1·50

298 Zig-zags and Diamonds

1986. Sadu Art. Multicoloured.
1114 20f. Type **298** 50 25
1115 70f. Triangles and symbols 1·60 95
1116 200f. Stripes and triangles 3·75 2·75

299 Dove on Manacled Hand pointing to Map

1986. International Day of Solidarity with Palestinian People.
1117 **299** 20f. multicoloured . . . 75 50
1118 25f. multicoloured . . . 1·00 70
1119 70f. multicoloured . . . 3·00 2·00

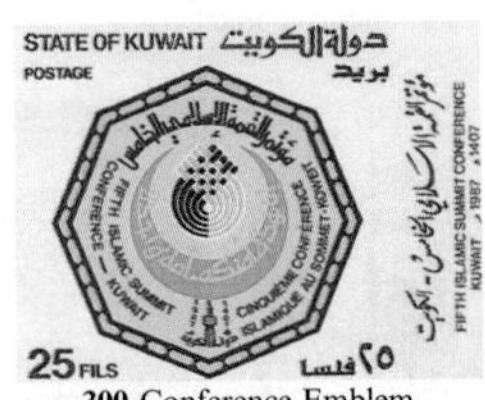

300 Conference Emblem

1987. 5th Islamic Summit Conference.
1120 **300** 25f. multicoloured . . . 60 30
1121 50f. multicoloured . . . 1·25 70
1122 150f. multicoloured . . . 3·25 2·00

301 Map in National Colours and Symbols of Development

1987. 26th National Day.
1123 **301** 50f. multicoloured . . . 1·25 50
1124 150f. multicoloured . . . 3·00 1·50

302 Health Science Centre

1987. 3rd Kuwait International Medical Sciences Conference: Infectious Diseases in Developing Countries.
1125 **302** 25f. multicoloured . . . 75 25
1126 150f. multicoloured . . . 3·00 1·50

303 Campaign Emblem

1987. World Health Day. Child Immunization Campaign.
1127 **303** 25f. multicoloured . . . 60 25
1128 50f. multicoloured . . . 1·00 50
1129 150f. multicoloured . . . 2·40 1·50

304 Jerusalem

1987. "Jerusalem is an Arab City".
1130 **304** 25f. multicoloured . . . 60 15
1131 50f. multicoloured . . . 1·00 40
1132 150f. multicoloured . . . 2·40 1·25

305 Pilgrims in Miqat Wadi Mihrim

1987. Pilgrimage to Mecca.
1133 **305** 25f. multicoloured . . . 50 15
1134 50f. multicoloured . . . 75 40
1135 150f. multicoloured . . . 2·25 1·00

306 Emblem

308 Project Monument and Site Plan

307 Buoy and Container Ship

1987. Arab Telecommunications Day.
1136 **306** 25f. multicoloured . . . 50 15
1137 50f. multicoloured . . . 75 40
1138 150f. multicoloured . . . 2·25 1·00

1987. World Maritime Day.
1139 **307** 25f. multicoloured . . . 50 20
1140 50f. multicoloured . . . 75 40
1141 150f. multicoloured . . . 2·25 1·00

1987. Al-Qurain Housing Project.
1142 **308** 25f. multicoloured . . . 50 15
1143 50f. multicoloured . . . 75 40
1144 150f. multicoloured . . . 2·25 1·00

309 Unloading Container Ship

1987. 10th Anniv of Ports Public Authority.
1145 **309** 25f. multicoloured . . . 20 10
1146 50f. multicoloured . . . 55 25
1147 150f. multicoloured . . . 2·00 85

310 Symbolic Design

311 Emblem

1987. International Day of Solidarity with Palestinian People.
1148 **310** 25f. multicoloured . . . 20 10
1149 50f. multicoloured . . . 60 25
1150 150f. multicoloured . . . 2·00 85

1988. 25th Anniv of Women's Cultural and Social Society.
1151 **311** 25f. multicoloured . . . 20 10
1152 50f. multicoloured . . . 60 25
1153 150f. multicoloured . . . 2·00 85

312 Emblem

313 Hands holding W.H.O. Emblem

1988. 27th National Day.
1154 **312** 25f. multicoloured . . . 20 10
1155 50f. multicoloured . . . 60 25
1156 150f. multicoloured . . . 2·00 85

1988. World Health Day. 40th Anniv of W.H.O.
1157 **313** 25f. multicoloured . . . 20 10
1158 50f. multicoloured . . . 60 25
1159 150f. multicoloured . . . 2·00 85

314 Regional Maritime Protection Organization Symbol

315 Society Emblem

1988. 10th Anniv of Kuwait Regional Convention for Protection of Marine Environment.
1160 **314** 35f. ultram, blue & brn 25 15
1161 50f. ultram, blue & grn 60 25
1162 150f. ultram, blue & pur 2·00 85

1988. 25th Anniv of Kuwait Teachers' Society.
1163 **315** 25f. multicoloured . . . 20 10
1164 50f. multicoloured . . . 60 25
1165 150f. multicoloured . . . 2·00 75

316 Pilgrims at al-Sail al-Kabir Miqat

1988. Pilgrimage to Mecca.
1166 **316** 25f. multicoloured . . . 20 10
1167 50f. multicoloured . . . 60 25
1168 150f. multicoloured . . . 2·00 75

317 Gang of Youths lying in wait for Soldiers

318 Ring of Dwellings around Key

1988. Palestinian "Intifida" Movement.
1169 **317** 50f. multicoloured . . . 75 40
1170 150f. multicoloured . . . 3·00 1·50

1988. Arab Housing Day.
1171 **318** 50f. multicoloured . . . 50 30
1172 100f. multicoloured . . . 1·00 60
1173 150f. multicoloured . . . 2·00 75

319 Map of Palestine highlighted on Globe

320 Volunteers embracing Globe

1988. International Day of Solidarity with Palestinian People.
1174 **319** 50f. multicoloured . . . 40 25
1175 100f. multicoloured . . . 1·00 60
1176 150f. multicoloured . . . 2·00 75

1988. International Volunteer Day.
1177 **320** 50f. multicoloured . . . 50 30
1178 100f. multicoloured . . . 1·00 60
1179 150f. multicoloured . . . 2·00 75

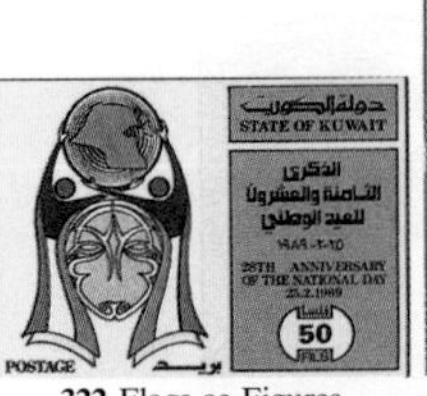

321 Conference, Kuwait Society of Engineers and Arab Engineers Union Emblems

1989. 18th Arab Engineering Conference.
1180 **321** 50f. multicoloured . . . 50 30
1181 100f. multicoloured . . . 1·00 60
1182 150f. multicoloured . . . 2·00 75

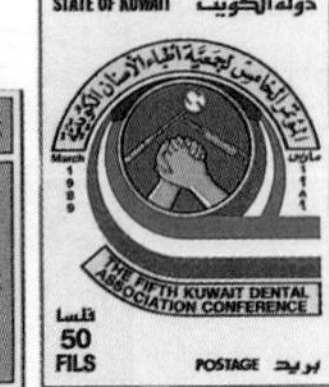

322 Flags as Figures supporting Map

323 Conference Emblem

1989. 28th National Day.
1183 **322** 50f. multicoloured . . . 50 30
1184 100f. multicoloured . . . 1·00 60
1185 150f. multicoloured . . . 2·00 75

1989. 5th Kuwait Dental Association Conference.
1186 **323** 50f. multicoloured . . . 50 30
1187 150f. multicoloured . . . 1·00 70
1188 250f. multicoloured . . . 1·75 1·10

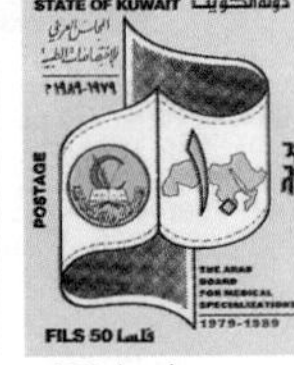

324 Emblems

325 Anniversary Emblem

1989. World Health Day.
1189 **324** 50f. multicoloured . . . 50 30
1190 150f. multicoloured . . . 1·00 70
1191 250f. multicoloured . . . 1·75 1·10

1989. 10th Anniv of Arab Board for Medical Specializations.
1192 **325** 50f. multicoloured . . . 50 20
1193 150f. multicoloured . . . 1·00 55
1194 250f. multicoloured . . . 1·75 85

326 Torch, Pen and Flag

1989. 25th Anniv of Kuwait Journalists' Association.
1195 **326** 50f. multicoloured . . . 40 35
1196 200f. multicoloured . . . 1·50 1·00
1197 250f. multicoloured . . . 2·00 1·40

327 Attan'eem Miqat, Mecca

1989. Pilgrimage to Mecca.
1198 **327** 50f. multicoloured . . . 85 55
1199 150f. multicoloured . . . 2·75 1·75
1200 200f. multicoloured . . . 3·50 2·25

328 Al-Qurain Housing Project

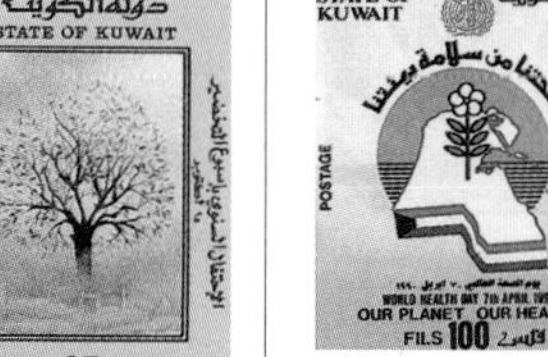

329 Tree

1989. Arab Housing Day.

1201	**328**	25f. multicoloured	45	30
1202		50f. multicoloured	85	55
1203		150f. multicoloured	2·75	1·75

1989. Greenery Week.

1204	**329**	25f. multicoloured	45	30
1205		50f. multicoloured	85	55
1206		150f. multicoloured	2·75	1·75

330 Dhow

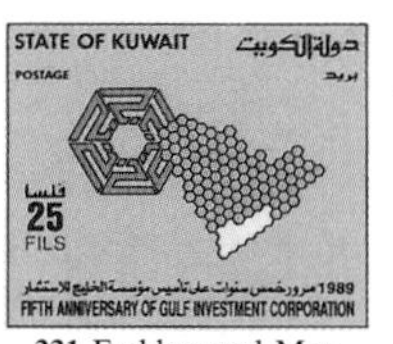

331 Emblem and Map

1989. Coil Stamps.

1207	**330**	50f. gold and green	1·25	85
1208		100f. gold and blue	2·50	1·75
1209		200f. gold and red	5·00	3·50

1989. 5th Anniv of Gulf Investment Corporation.

1210	**331**	25f. multicoloured	45	30
1211		50f. multicoloured	85	55
1212		150f. multicoloured	2·75	1·75

332 Emblem

333 Zakat House

1989. 1st Anniv of "Declaration of Palestine State".

1213	**332**	50f. multicoloured	85	55
1214		150f. multicoloured	2·75	1·75
1215		200f. multicoloured	3·50	2·25

1989. Orphanage Sponsorship Project.

1216	**333**	25f. multicoloured	45	30
1217		50f. multicoloured	85	55
1218		150f. multicoloured	2·75	1·75

334 Shaikh Sabah al-Salem as-Sabah (former Chief) and Officers

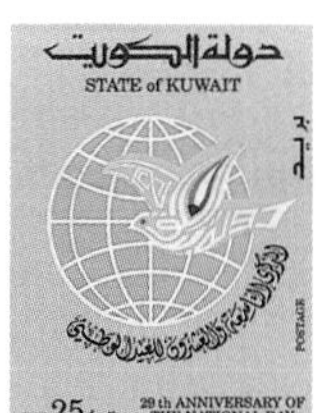

335 Globe and Dove

1989. 50th Anniv (1988) of Kuwait Police.

1219	**334**	25f. multicoloured	45	30
1220		50f. multicoloured	85	55
1221		150f. multicoloured	2·75	1·75

1990. 29th National Day.

1222	**335**	25f. multicoloured	45	30
1223		50f. multicoloured	85	55
1224		150f. multicoloured	2·75	1·75

336 Earth, Clouds and Weather Balloon

1990. World Meteorological Day.

1225	**336**	50f. multicoloured	85	55
1226		100f. multicoloured	1·75	1·10
1227		150f. multicoloured	2·75	1·75

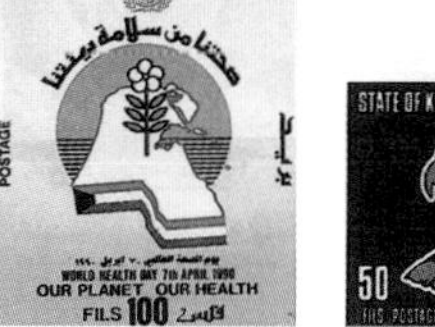

337 Map bordered by National Flag

338 Lanner Falcon

1990. World Health Day.

1228	**337**	50f. multicoloured	85	55
1229		100f. multicoloured	1·75	1·10
1230		150f. multicoloured	2·75	1·75

1990.

1231	**338**	50f. gold and blue	5·50	5·50
1232		100f. gold and red	10 50	10 50
1233		150f. gold and green	17·00	17·00

339 Soldiers carrying Kuwait Flag

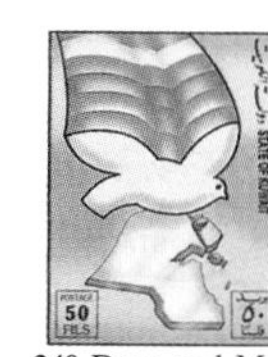

340 Dove and Map

1991. Liberation (1st issue).

1234	**339**	25f. multicoloured	40	25
1235		50f. multicoloured	80	50
1236		150f. multicoloured	2·40	1·60

See also Nos. 1243/84.

1991. Peace.

1237	**340**	50f. multicoloured	80	50
1238		100f. multicoloured	1·60	1·00
1239		150f. multicoloured	2·40	1·60

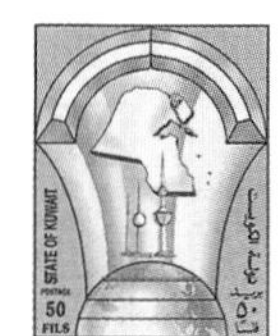

341 Flag, Map, Kuwait Towers and Globe

1991. Reconstruction.

1240	**341**	50f. multicoloured	80	50
1241		150f. multicoloured	2·40	1·60
1242		200f. multicoloured	3·00	1·90

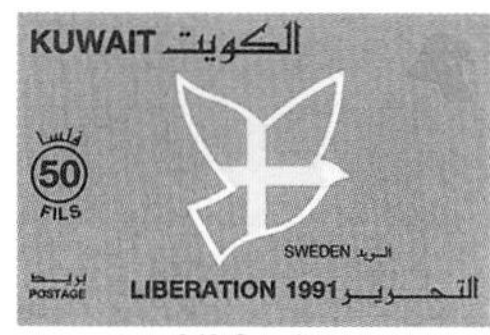

342 Sweden

1991. Liberation (2nd issue). Each showing a dove coloured with the flag of one of the assisting nations. Multicoloured.

1243	50f. Type **342**	45	30
1244	50f. Soviet Union	45	30
1245	50f. United States of America	45	30
1246	50f. Kuwait	45	30
1247	50f. Saudi Arabia	45	30
1248	50f. United Nations	45	30
1249	50f. Singapore	45	30
1250	50f. France	45	30
1251	50f. Italy	45	30
1252	50f. Egypt	45	30
1253	50f. Morocco	45	30
1254	50f. United Kingdom	45	30
1255	50f. Philippines	45	30
1256	50f. United Arab Emirates	45	30
1257	50f. Syria	45	30
1258	50f. Poland	45	30
1259	50f. Australia	45	30
1260	50f. Japan	45	30
1261	50f. Hungary	45	30
1262	50f. Netherlands	45	30
1263	50f. Denmark	45	30
1264	50f. New Zealand	45	30
1265	50f. Czechoslovakia	45	30
1266	50f. Bahrain	45	30
1267	50f. Honduras	45	30
1268	50f. Turkey	45	30
1269	50f. Greece	45	30
1270	50f. Oman	45	30
1271	50f. Qatar	45	30
1272	50f. Belgium	45	30
1273	50f. Sierra Leone	45	30
1274	50f. Argentina	45	30
1275	50f. Norway	45	30
1276	50f. Canada	45	30
1277	50f. Germany	45	30
1278	50f. South Korea	45	30
1279	50f. Bangladesh	45	30
1280	50f. Bulgaria	45	30
1281	50f. Senegal	45	30
1282	50f. Spain	45	30
1283	50f. Niger	45	30
1284	50f. Pakistan	45	30

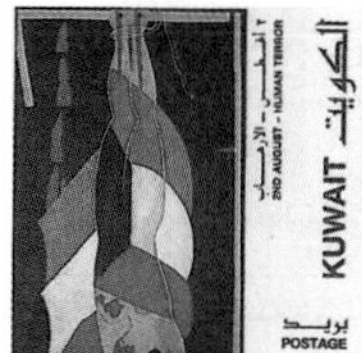

343 "Human Terror"

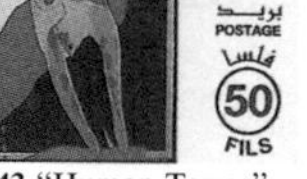

344 Emblem

1991. 1st Anniv of Iraqi Invasion. Multicoloured.

1286	50f. Type **343**	80	50
1287	100f. "Invasion of Kuwait"	1·60	1·00
1288	150f. "Environmental Terrorism" (horiz)	2·40	1·60

1991. 30th Anniv (1990) of Organization of Petroleum Exporting Countries.

1290	**344**	25f. multicoloured	45	30
1291		50f. multicoloured	80	50
1292		150f. multicoloured	2·40	1·60

345 National Flag, Arabic Script and Broken Chains

1991. Campaign to Free Kuwaiti Prisoners of War. Each black and yellow.

1293	50f. Type **345**	70	45
1294	150f. Prison bars, "Don't Forget Our P.O.W.'s" and broken chains	2·00	1·25

346 Names of Member Countries forming Tree

1991. 12th Gulf Co-operation Council Summit Conference, Kuwait. Multicoloured.

1296	25f. Type **346**	35	25
1297	150f. National flags as leaves of plant	2·00	1·25

347 I.L.Y. Emblem

1992. International Literacy Year (1990).

1299	**347**	50f. blue and brown	70	45
1300		100f. blue and yellow	1·40	90
1301		150f. blue and mauve	2·00	1·25

348 Doves and National Flag

1992. 31st National Day (1302) and 1st Anniv of Liberation (1303).

1302	**348**	50f. black, green and red	40	25
1303	–	150f. multicoloured	1·25	80

DESIGN: 150f. Assisting nations' flags.

349 Dromedaries

1992.

1305	**349**	25f. multicoloured	15	10
1306		50f. multicoloured	30	20
1307		150f. multicoloured	95	60
1308		200f. multicoloured	1·25	80
1309		350f. multicoloured	2·10	1·25

350 Paddle, La Giralda Tower and Kuwaiti Pavilion

1992. "Expo '92" World's Fair, Seville. Multicoloured.

1310	50f. Type **350**	30	20
1311	50f. Dhows	30	20
1312	50f. Dhow	30	20
1313	50f. Kuwaiti Pavilion and dhow	30	20
1314	150f. Kuwaiti Pavilion on Spanish flag	90	60
1315	150f. Paddle and La Giralda Tower on hoist of Kuwaiti flag	90	60
1316	150f. Paddle, La Giralda Tower and dhow on Spanish flag	90	60
1317	150f. Kuwaiti Pavilion and dhow on fly of Kuwaiti flag	90	60

351 Snake around Top of Palm Tree

1992. 2nd U.N. Conference on Environment and Development, Rio de Janeiro, Brazil. Mult.

1319	150f. Type **351**	1·25	80
1320	150f. Snakes, Kuwait colours on map and palm tree	1·25	80
1321	150f. Skull, snake around tree trunk and dead fish	1·25	80
1322	150f. Snake around camel's neck and bird	1·25	80

Nos. 1319/22 were issued together, se-tenant, forming a composite design of the painting "Environmental Terrorism".

352 Palace of Justice

1992.

1324	**352**	25f. multicoloured	20	10
1325		50f. multicoloured	40	25
1326		100f. multicoloured	80	50
1327		150f. multicoloured	1·25	80
1328		250f. multicoloured	2·00	1·25

353 Running and Handball

1992. Olympic Games, Barcelona. Multicoloured.
1329 50f. Swimming and football . . . 65 40
1330 100f. Type **353** . . . . . . 1·25 80
1331 150f. Judo and show jumping . . . . 1·90 1·25

Each value also portrays the Olympic flag and Prince Fahed al-Ahmad al-Sabah, President of several sports organizations, who was killed in the Iraqi invasion.

354 Tanks, Demonstrators with Placards and Executed Civilians

1992. 2nd Anniv of Iraqi Invasion. Children's Drawings. Multicoloured.
1332 50f. Type **354** 30 20
1333 50f. Soldiers rounding up civilians 30 20
1334 50f. Military vehicles and Kuwait Towers 30 20
1335 50f. Battle scene 30 20
1336 150f. Tanks, bleeding eye and soldiers 95 60
1337 150f. Battle scene around fortifications 95 60
1338 150f. Liberation 95 60
1339 150f. Soldiers and military vehicles 95 60

355 Burning Well

1992. 1st Anniv of Extinguishing of Oil Well Fires. Multicoloured.
1341 25f. Type **355** 15 10
1342 50f. Spraying dampener on fire 30 20
1343 150f. Close-up of spraying 95 60
1344 250f. Extinguished well (horiz) . . . . 1·60 1·00

356 Kuwait Towers

357 Laying Bricks to form "32"

1993.
1345 **356** 25f. multicoloured . . . 15 10
1346 100f. multicoloured . . . 70 45
1347 150f. multicoloured . . . 95 60

1993. 32nd National Day.
1348 **357** 25f. multicoloured . . . 15 10
1349 50f. multicoloured . . . 30 20
1350 150f. multicoloured . . . 95 60

358 Symbols of Oppression and Freedom

359 Hands Signing

1993. 2nd Anniv of Liberation.
1351 **358** 25f. multicoloured . . . 15 10
1352 50f. multicoloured . . . 30 20
1353 150f. multicoloured . . . 95 60

1993. Deaf Child Week.
1354 **359** 25f. multicoloured . . . 15 10
1355 50f. multicoloured . . . 30 20
1356 150f. multicoloured . . . 95 60
1357 350f. multicoloured . . . 2·10 1·40

360 Chained Prisoner

361 Hand scratching Map

1993. Campaign to Free Kuwaiti Prisoners of War. Multicoloured.
1358 50f. Type **360** 35 20
1359 150f. Chained hand, hoopoe and barred window (horiz) . . . . 1·10 70
1360 200f. Screaming face on wall of empty cell . . . . . 1·50 1·00

1993. 3rd Anniv of Iraqi Invasion.
1361 **361** 50f. multicoloured . . . 30 20
1362 150f. multicoloured . . . 85 55

362 Emblem

1993. 40th Anniv of Kuwait Air Force.
1363 **362** 50f. multicoloured . . . 40 25
1364 150f. multicoloured . . . 1·10 70

363 Flower and Dove

364 Anniversary Emblem

1994. 33rd National Day.
1365 **363** 25f. multicoloured . . . 15 10
1366 50f. multicoloured . . . 30 20
1367 150f. multicoloured . . . 90 60

1994. 3rd Anniv of Liberation.
1368 **364** 25f. multicoloured . . . 15 10
1369 50f. multicoloured . . . 30 20
1370 150f. multicoloured . . . 90 60

365 Anniversary Emblem

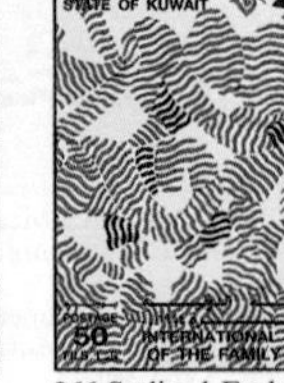

366 Stylized Emblems

1994. 25th Anniv of Central Bank of Kuwait.
1371 **365** 25f. multicoloured . . . 15 10
1372 50f. multicoloured . . . 30 20
1373 150f. multicoloured . . . 90 60

1994. Int Year of the Family. Mult.
1374 50f. Type **366** 30 20
1375 150f. Three I.Y.F. emblems 90 60
1376 200f. Globe, emblem and spheres (horiz) . . . . . 1·00 65

367 Emblem on Sky

368 Fingerprint in Water

1994. 20th Anniv of Industrial Bank of Kuwait.
1377 **367** 50f. multicoloured . . . 25 10
1378 100f. gold, blue and black 55 35
1379 150f. multicoloured . . . 80 50

1994. Martyrs' Day. Multicoloured.
1380 50f. Type **368** 30 10
1381 100f. Fingerprint in sand . . 60 40
1382 150f. Fingerprint in national colours 90 60
1383 250f. Fingerprint in clouds over Kuwait Towers . . . 1·50 1·00

369 Anniversary Emblem

370 Free and Imprisoned Doves

1994. 75th Anniv of I.L.O.
1385 **369** 50f. multicoloured . . . 25 10
1386 150f. multicoloured . . . 80 50
1387 350f. gold, blue and black . . . . 1·75 1·10

1994. 4th Anniv of Iraqi Invasion.
1388 **370** 50f. multicoloured . . . 25 10
1389 150f. multicoloured . . . 80 50
1390 350f. multicoloured . . . 1·75 1·10

371 Emblem

372 Anniversary Emblem

1994. Kuwait Ports Authority.
1391 **371** 50f. multicoloured . . . 25 10
1392 150f. multicoloured . . . 80 50
1393 350f. multicoloured . . . 1·75 1·10

1994. 20th Anniv of Kuwait Science Club.
1394 **372** 50f. multicoloured . . . 25 10
1395 100f. multicoloured . . . 55 35
1396 150f. multicoloured . . . 75 50

373 Map and Building

374 I.C.A.O. and Kuwait International Airport Emblems

1994. Inauguration of Arab Towns Organization Permanent Headquarters. Multicoloured.
1397 50f. Type **373** 25 10
1398 100f. Close-up of arched facade 55 35
1399 150f. Door 75 50

1994. 50th Anniv of I.C.A.O. Mult.
1400 100f. Type **374** 55 35
1401 150f. Emblems and control tower 85 55
1402 350f. Airplane and "50 years" . . . . 1·90 1·25

375 Anniversary Emblem

376 Family

1994. 40th Anniv of Kuwait Airways.
1403 **375** 50f. multicoloured . . . 20 10
1404 100f. multicoloured . . . 50 35
1405 150f. multicoloured . . . 75 50

1995. Population Census.
1406 **376** 50f. multicoloured . . . 25 10
1407 100f. multicoloured . . . 45 30
1408 150f. multicoloured . . . 70 45

377 Children waving Flags

378 Falcon dragging Kuwaiti Flag from Snake's Grip

1995. 34th National Day.
1409 **377** 25f. multicoloured . . . 10 10
1410 50f. multicoloured . . . 25 10
1411 150f. multicoloured . . . 70 45

1995. 4th Anniv of Liberation.
1412 **378** 25f. multicoloured . . . 10 10
1413 50f. multicoloured . . . 25 10
1414 150f. multicoloured . . . 70 45

379 Conference Venue

1995. International Medical Conference. Mult.
1415 50f. Type **379** 25 10
1416 100f. Lecture 45 30
1417 150f. Emblem on map of Kuwait in national colours 70 45

380 Anniversary Emblem and Flags

381 Emblem

1995. 50th Anniv of Arab League. Multicoloured.
1418 50f. Type **380** 25 10
1419 100f. Kuwaiti and League flags and League emblem (horiz) 45 30
1420 150f. Handshake and League emblem 70 45

1995. World Health Day. "A World without Polio".
1421 **381** 50f. multicoloured . . . 30 20
1422 150f. multicoloured . . . 1·00 90
1423 200f. multicoloured . . . 1·40 1·40

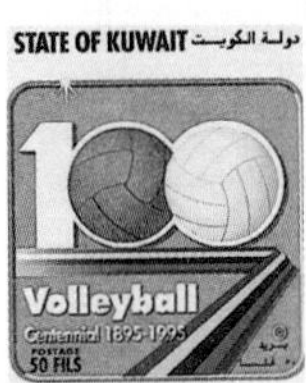

382 "100"

383 Olive Branch falling from Wounded Dove's Beak

1995. Centenary of Volleyball.
1424 **382** 50f. multicoloured . . . 25 10
1425 100f. multicoloured . . . 45 30
1426 150f. multicoloured . . . 70 45

1995. 5th Anniv of Iraqi Invasion.
1427 **383** 50f. multicoloured . . . 20 10
1428 100f. multicoloured . . . 40 25
1429 150f. multicoloured . . . 60 40

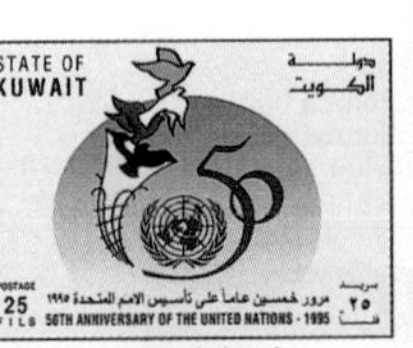

384 Doves and Anniversary Emblem

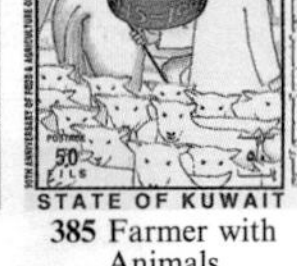

385 Farmer with Animals

1995. 50th Anniv of U.N.O.
1430 **384** 25f. multicoloured . . . 10 10
1431 50f. multicoloured . . . 20 10
1432 150f. multicoloured . . . 60 40

1995. 50th Anniv of F.A.O. Multicoloured.
1433 50f. Type **385** 20 10
1434 100f. Fish market 40 25
1435 150f. Agriculture 60 40

386 Emblems within Ruler

387 "Onobrychis ptolemaica"

1995. World Standards Day. Multicoloured.
1437 50f. Type **386** 20 10
1438 100f. Emblems and aspects of industry (48 × 27 mm) 40 25
1439 150f. As No. 1438 . . . . . 60 40

1995. Flowers. Multicoloured.
1440 5f. Type **387** 10 10
1441 15f. "Convolvulus oxyphyllus" 10 10
1442 25f. Corn poppy 10 10
1443 50f. "Moltkiopsis ciliata" . . 20 10
1444 150f. "Senecio desfontainei" 60 40

388 Coins forming Map of Kuwait

389 Boy Scout in Watchtower

1996. Money Show.
1445 **388** 25f. multicoloured . . . 10 10
1446 100f. multicoloured . . . 40 25
1447 150f. multicoloured . . . 60 40

1996. 60th Anniv of Scout Movement in Kuwait. Multicoloured.
1448 50f. Type **389** 20 10
1449 100f. Scout drawing water from well 40 25
1450 150f. Scouts planting sapling 60 40

390 Hands supporting Ear of Wheat

391 Saker Falcon trailing National Colours, Falcon and City

1996.
1451 **390** 50f. multicoloured . . . 20 10
1452 100f. multicoloured . . . 40 25
1453 150f. multicoloured . . . 60 40

1996. 35th National Day.
1454 **391** 25f. multicoloured . . . 10 10
1455 50f. multicoloured . . . 20 10
1456 150f. multicoloured . . . 60 40

392 Horses

393 View through Gateway

1996. 5th Anniv of Liberation.
1457 **392** 25f. multicoloured . . . 10 10
1458 50f. multicoloured . . . 20 10
1459 150f. multicoloured . . . 60 40

1996. Arab City Day.
1460 **393** 50f. multicoloured . . . 20 10
1461 100f. multicoloured . . . 40 25
1462 150f. multicoloured . . . 60 40

394 Emblem

395 Figures holding Open Book within Bird

1996. 7th Kuwait Dental Association Conference.
1463 **394** 25f. multicoloured . . . 10 10
1464 50f. multicoloured . . . 20 10
1465 150f. multicoloured . . . 60 40

1996. 50th Anniv of UNESCO.
1466 **395** 25f. multicoloured . . . 10 10
1467 100f. multicoloured . . . 40 25
1468 150f. multicoloured . . . 60 40

396 Flags, Anniversary Emblem and Tanker

397 Shaikh Mubarak al-Sabah

1996. 50th Anniv of First Oil Shipment from Kuwait.
1469 **396** 25f. multicoloured . . . 10 10
1470 100f. multicoloured . . . 40 25
1471 150f. multicoloured . . . 60 40

1996. Centenary of Accession as Emir of Shaikh Mubarak al-Sabah. Multicoloured.
1472 25f. Type **397** 10 10
1473 50f. Shaikh Mubarak al-Sabah and ribbons . . . 20 10
1474 150f. Type **397** 60 40

398 Rifle Shooting

399 Festival Emblem

1996. Olympic Games, Atlanta. Multicoloured.
1475 25f. Type **398** 10 10
1476 50f. Running 20 10
1477 100f. Weightlifting 40 25
1478 150f. Fencing 60 40

1996. National Council for Culture, Art and Letters. First Children's Cultural Festival.
1479 **399** 25f. multicoloured . . . 10 10
1480 100f. multicoloured . . . 40 25
1481 150f. multicoloured . . . 60 40

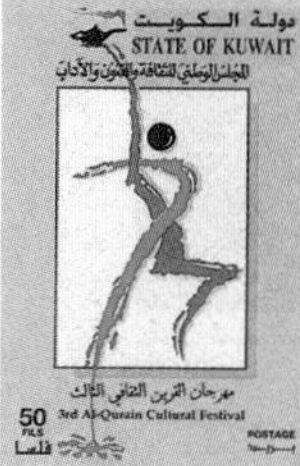
400 Emblem

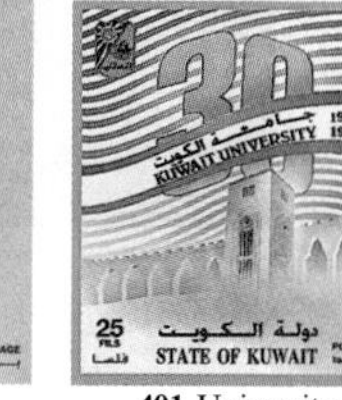
401 University

1996. 3rd Al-Qurain Cultural Festival
1482 **400** 50f. multicoloured . . . 20 10
1483 100f. multicoloured . . . 40 25
1484 150f. multicoloured . . . 60 40

1996. 30th Anniv of Kuwait University.
1485 **401** 25f. multicoloured . . . 10 10
1486 100f. multicoloured . . . 40 25
1487 150f. multicoloured . . . 60 40

402 Liberation Tower

403 Sehel's Grey Mullet

1996.
1488 **402** 5f. multicoloured 10 10
1489 10f. multicoloured . . . 10 10
1490 15f. multicoloured . . . 10 10
1491 25f. multicoloured . . . 10 10
1492 50f. multicoloured . . . 20 10
1493 100f. multicoloured . . . 40 25
1494 150f. multicoloured . . . 60 40
1495 200f. multicoloured . . . 80 50
1496 250f. multicoloured . . . 1·00 65
1497 350f. multicoloured . . . 1·40 90

1997. Marine Life. Multicoloured. (a) Fishes.
1498 25f. Type **403** 10 10
1499 50f. Yellow-finned seabream 20 10
1500 100f. Greasy grouper . . . 40 25
1501 150f. Silver-backed seabream 60 40
1502 200f. Silver grunt 80 50
1503 350f. Silver pomfret . . . . 1·40 90

(b) Shrimps.
1504 25f. Tail and body segments of shrimps 10 10
1505 25f. Head and body segments of shrimps . . . 10 10
1506 25f. Underside of fish and body and legs of shrimp 10 10
1507 25f. Head of shrimp, fish and body and legs of shrimp 10 10
1508 50f. Tail and body segments of two shrimps 20 10
1509 50f. Legs and body segments of shrimp 20 10
1510 50f. Body segments of shrimp and fish 20 10
1511 50f. Head of shrimp, seaweed and body and legs of shrimp 20 10
1512 100f. Tail and body segments of two shrimps 40 25
1513 100f. Head, legs and body segments of shrimps . . . 40 25
1514 100f. Body of shrimp . . . 40 25
1515 100f. Part of head, legs, tail and body of three shrimps 40 25
1516 150f. Body segments of two shrimps and upper half of fish 60 40
1517 150f. Front part of bodies of two shrimps and tail of fish 60 40
1518 150f. Heads of two shrimps, complete shrimp and fish 60 40
1519 150f. Body segments of two shrimps and front part of shrimps head 60 40

Nos. 1504/19 were issued together, se-tenant, forming a composite design of shrimps in a marine environment.

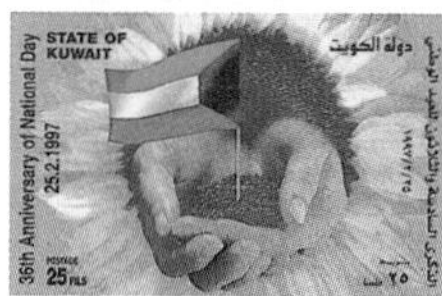
404 Flag, Cupped Hands and Sunflower

1997. 36th National Day.
1520 **404** 25f. multicoloured . . . 10 10
1521 50f. multicoloured . . . 20 10
1522 150f. multicoloured . . . 60 40

405 Flag, rejoicing Crowd and Shaikh Jabir

1997. 6th Anniv of Liberation.
1523 **405** 25f. multicoloured . . . 10 10
1524 50f. multicoloured . . . 20 10
1525 150f. multicoloured . . . 60 40

406 Emblem

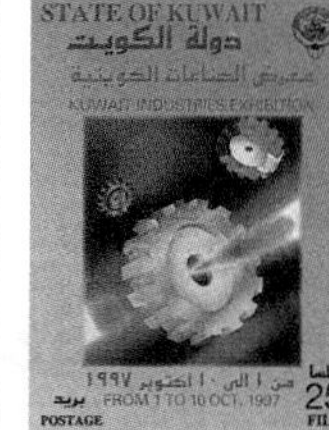
407 Emblem

1997. 10th Anniv of Montreal Protocol (on reduction of use of chlorofluorocarbons).
1526 **406** 25f. multicoloured . . . 10 10
1527 50f. multicoloured . . . 20 10
1528 150f. multicoloured . . . 60 40

1997. Kuwait Industries Exhibition.
1529 **407** 25f. multicoloured . . . 10 10
1530 50f. multicoloured . . . 20 10
1531 150f. multicoloured . . . 60 40

408 Signs of Zodiac and Whale

1997. 25th Anniv of Educational Science Museum.
1532 25f. Type **408** 10 10
1533 50f. Space shuttle orbiting Earth, whale, astronaut and dinosaur (horiz) . . . 20 10
1534 150f. Symbols of past, present and future around whale 60 40

409 National Council for Culture, Arts and Letters Emblem

1997. 22nd Kuwait Arabic Book Exhbition.
1536 **409** 25f. multicoloured . . . 10 10
1537 50f. multicoloured . . . 20 10
1538 150f. multicoloured . . . 60 40

410 Ink-well and Book (first book fair, 1975)

1997. Kuwait Cultural History.
1539 25f. Type **410** 10 10
1540 25f. Front page of "Kuwait Magazine" (1928) 10 10
1541 25f. Front page "A'lam al-Fikr" (periodical) (1970) 10 10
1542 25f. Pyramids and dhow ("Al'Bitha" magazine, 1946) 10 10
1543 25f. Rising sun over open book and quill ("Al'am al Ma'rifa" (periodical), 1978) 10 10
1544 25f. Book with dhow on front cover ("Dalil Almohtar Fi Alaam Al-Bihar", 1923) 10 10
1545 25f. Arabic script and "brick" design ("Al-Arabi" magazine, 1958) 10 10
1546 25f. Open book (inauguration of first public library, 1923) . . . 10 10
1547 25f. Two covers showing Arabic script in boxes and cosmic explosion ("Al Thaqafa Al-Alamiya" (periodical), 1981) 10 10
1548 25f. Actors and curtain ("The World Theatre" (periodical), 1969) 10 10
1549 50f. Entrance to Qibliya Girls' School (1937) . . . 20 10
1550 50f. Scissors cutting ribbon (first Fine Arts Exhibition, 1959) 20 10
1551 50f. Mubarakiya School (1912) 20 10
1552 50f. Family entering Kuwait National Museum (1958) 20 10
1553 50f. Shuwaikh Secondary School (1953) 20 10
1554 50f. Door and three windows (Al-Marsam Al-Hor, 1959) 20 10
1555 50f. Decorated screen (Alma'had Aldini, 1947) 20 10
1556 50f. Courtyard of Folklore Centre (1956) 20 10
1557 50f. Three columns of Arabic script (Al Ma'arif printing press, 1947) . . . 20 10
1558 50f. Class photograph (Literary Club, 1924) . . 20 10
1559 150f. Heads and curtains (Folk Theatre Group, 1956) 60 40
1560 150f. Musical instruments and notes (Academy of Music, 1972) 60 40
1561 150f. Film frames, audience and camera (opening of Al-Sharqiya cinema, 1955) 60 40
1562 150f. Curtains around couple at oasis (Theatrical Academy, 1967) 60 40
1563 150f. Marine views in film frame ("Bas Ya Bahar" (first Kuwaiti feature film), 1970) 60 40

411 Doves flying over Members' Flags

1997. 18th Gulf Co-operation Council Summit, Kuwait. Multicoloured.
1564 25f. Type **411** 10 10
1565 50f. Members' flags forming doves wheeling over map (horiz) 20 10
1566 150f. Doves perched atop wall of members' flags . . 60 40

412 State Flag

1998. 37th National Day.
1567 **412** 25f. multicoloured . . . 10 10
1568 50f. multicoloured . . . 20 10
1569 150f. multicoloured . . . 60 40

413 Flag, Map and Dove

1998. 7th Anniv of Liberation.
1570 **413** 25f. multicoloured . . . 10 10
1571 50f. multicoloured . . . 20 10
1572 150f. multicoloured . . . 60 40

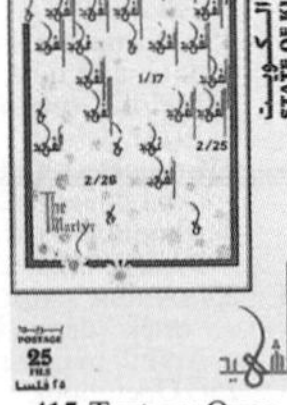

414 Emblem **415** Text on Open Page with Flowers

1998. Anti-drugs Campaign.
1573 **414** 25f. multicoloured . . . 10 10
1574 50f. multicoloured . . . 20 10
1575 150f. multicoloured . . . 60 40

1998. Martyrs' Day. Multicoloured.
1576 25f. Type **415** 10 10
1577 50f. Tree 20 10
1578 150f. Calligraphy 60 40

416 Woman selling Cooked Vegetables **417** Child's Face

1998. Life in Pre-Oil Kuwait (1st series). Mult.
1580 25f. Type **416** 10 10
1581 50f. Ship-building 20 10
1582 100f. Sailor strapping his box 40 25
1583 150f. Pearl divers wading out to boat 60 40
1584 250f. Delivering fresh water 1·00 65
1585 350f. Pigeon trainer . . . . 1·40 90
See also Nos. 1599/604.

1998. 12th Anniv of Chernobyl Nuclear Disaster.
1586 **417** 25f. multicoloured . . . 10 10
1587 50f. multicoloured . . . 20 10
1588 150f. multicoloured . . . 60 40

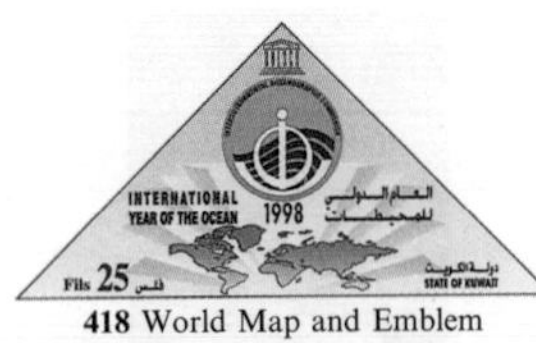

418 World Map and Emblem

1998. International Year of the Ocean. Multicoloured.
1589 25f. Type **418** 10 10
1590 50f. Motifs as in Type **418** but differently arranged in rectangle (27 × 37 mm) . . 20 10
1591 150f. Type **418** 60 40

419 Emblem

1998. 25th Anniv of Union of Consumer Co-operative Societies. Multicoloured.
1592 **419** 25f. multicoloured . . . 10 10
1593 50f. multicoloured . . . 20 10
1594 150f. multicoloured . . . 60 40

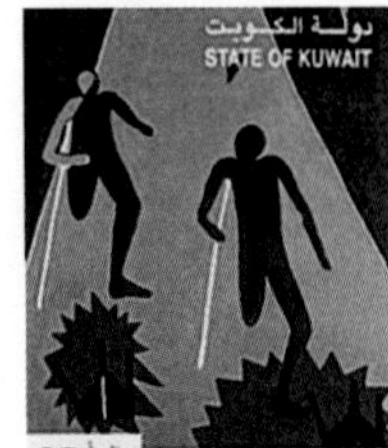

420 Men on Crutches

1998. Anti-landmine Campaign. Details from painting by Jafar Islah. Multicoloured.
1595 25f. Type **420** 10 10
1596 50f. Man on crutch 20 10
1597 150f. Man on crutches and woman helping child . . 60 40

1998. Life in Pre-Oil Kuwait (2nd series). As T **416**. Multicoloured.
1599 25f. Hairdresser 10 10
1600 50f. Hand-grinding 20 10
1601 100f. Tailor 40 25
1602 150f. Artist 60 40
1603 250f. Potter . . . . 1·00 65
1604 350f. Hand-spinning . . . . 1·40 90

421 New Postal Emblem

1998.
1605 **421** 25f. multicoloured . . . 10 10
1606 50f. multicoloured . . . 20 10
1607 100f. multicoloured . . . 40 25
1608 150f. multicoloured . . . 60 40
1609 250f. multicoloured . . . 1·00 65

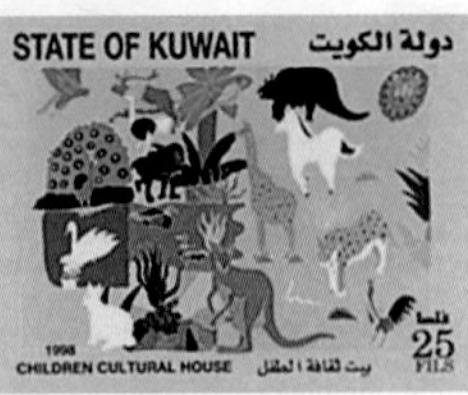

422 Child's Painting

1998. Children's Cultural House.
1610 **422** 25f. multicoloured . . . 10 10
1611 50f. multicoloured . . . 20 10
1612 150f. multicoloured . . . 60 40

423 Collage **424** Falcon

1998. 50th Anniv of Universal Declaration of Human Rights.
1613 **423** 25f. multicoloured . . . 10 10
1614 50f. multicoloured . . . 20 15
1615 150f. multicoloured . . . 60 40

1998.
1616 25f. Type **424** 10 10
1617 50f. Young camels 20 10
1618 150f. Dhow 65 40

425 Emblem

1998. 25th Anniv of Public Authority for Applied Education and Training.
1619 **425** 25f. multicoloured . . . 10 10
1620 50f. multicoloured . . . 20 10
1621 150f. multicoloured . . . 65 40

426 Entrance and Palm Trees

1999. Seif Palace. Different views of the Palace. Mult.
1622 25f. Type **426** 10 10
1623 50f. Palace buildings 20 10
1624 100f. Tower 45 30
1625 150f. Type **426** 65 40
1626 250f. As No. 1623 . . . . . 1·10 70
1627 350f. As No. 1624 . . . . . 1·60 1·00

427 "38"

1999. 38th National Day.
1628 **427** 50f. multicoloured . . . 20 10
1629 150f. multicoloured . . . 65 40

428 Building, Dove and "8"

1999. 8th Anniv of Liberation.
1630 **428** 50f. multicoloured . . . 20 10
1631 150f. multicoloured . . . 65 40

429 Liver and Kuwait Flag

1999. 20th Anniv of Organ Transplantation in Kuwait. Multicoloured.
1632 50f. Type **429** 20 10
1633 150f. Heart and Kuwait flag 65 40

430 Emblem and Kuwait Flag **432** "2000" and Emblem

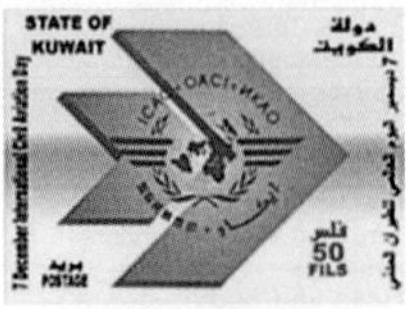

431 Emblem

1999. 40th Anniv of *Al-Arabi* (magazine).
1634 **430** 50f. multicoloured . . . 20 10
1635 150f. multicoloured . . . 65 40

2000. International Civil Aviation Day.
1636 **431** 50f. multicoloured . . . 20 10
1637 150f. multicoloured . . . 65 40
1638 250f. multicoloured . . . 1·10 70

2000. Kuwait International Airport.
1639 **432** 50f. multicoloured . . . 20 10
1640 150f. multicoloured . . . 65 40
1641 250f. multicoloured . . . 1·10 70

433 Children, Globe and Jigsaw Pieces

2000. International Conference on Autism and Communication Deficiencies, Kuwait. Children's paintings. Multicoloured.
1642 25f. Type **433** 10 10
1643 50f. Globe and children . . 20 10
1644 150f. Children holding hands 65 40

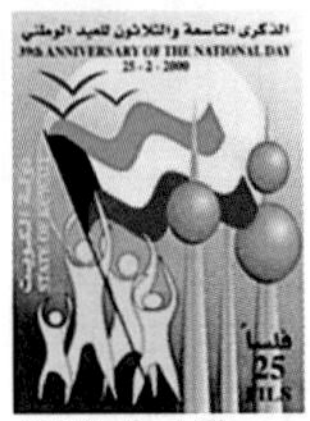

434 Stylized Figures and Flag **435** State Flag

2000. 39th National Day.
1645 **434** 25f. multicoloured . . . 10 10
1646 50f. multicoloured . . . 20 10
1647 150f. multicoloured . . . 65 40

2000. 9th Anniv of Liberation.
1648 **435** 25f. multicoloured . . . 10 10
1649 50f. multicoloured . . . 20 10
1650 150f. multicoloured . . . 65 40

436 Emblem

2000. 25th Anniv (1999) of Kuwait Science Club.
1651 **436** 50f. multicoloured . . . 20 10
1652 150f. multicoloured . . . 65 40
1653 350f. multicoloured . . . 1·60 1·00

437 Emblem

2000. International Investment Forum, Kuwait.
1654 **437** 25f. multicoloured . . . 10 10
1655 50f. multicoloured . . . 25 15
1656 150f. multicoloured . . . 70 30

438 View over City **439** Emblem and Hand holding Scroll

2000. Kuwait City.
1657 **438** 50f. multicoloured . . . 25 15
1658 150f. multicoloured . . . 70 30
1659 350f. multicoloured . . . 1·60 1·00

2000. 3rd Private Education Week.
1660 **439** 50f. multicoloured . . . 25 15
1661 150f. multicoloured . . . 70 30
1662 350f. multicoloured . . . 1·60 1·00

440 Emblem and Stamps Encircling Globe

2000. 125th Anniv of Universal Postal Union.
1663 **440** 50f. multicoloured . . . 25 15
1664 150f. multicoloured . . . 70 30
1665 350f. multicoloured . . . 1·60 1·00

441 Hands and Emblem

2000. World Environment Day.
1667 **441** 50f. multicoloured . . . 25 15
1668 150f. multicoloured . . . 70 30
1669 350f. multicoloured . . . 1·60 1·00

442 Galleon and Emblem

2000. Cent of General Customs' Administration.
1670 **442** 50f. multicoloured . . . 25 15
1671 150f. multicoloured . . . 70 30
1672 350f. multicoloured . . . 1·60 1·50

443 Emblem

2000. 10th Anniv of Committee for Missing and Prisoners of War Affairs. Multicoloured.
1674 25f. Type **443** 10 10
1675 50f. Emblem and chains . . 20 10
1676 150f. Emblem forming "10" 60 35

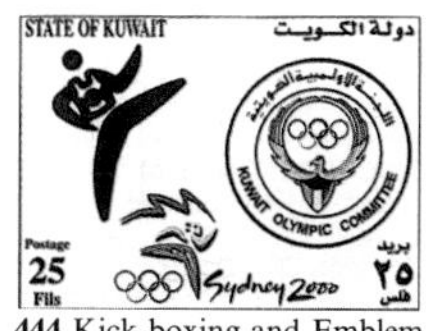
444 Kick-boxing and Emblem

2000. Olympic Games, Sydney. Multicoloured.
1677 25f. Type **444** 10 10
1678 50f. Shooting 20 10
1679 150f. Swimming 60 35
1680 200f. Weight-lifting 80 45
1681 250f. Running . . . . . . 1·00 60
1682 350f. Football . . . . . . 1·40 80

A 1d. imperforate miniature sheet, the design consisting of the emblem and pictograms as depicted on the stamps, exists in a cover inscribed "With the Compliments of Ministry of Communications - Post Sector".

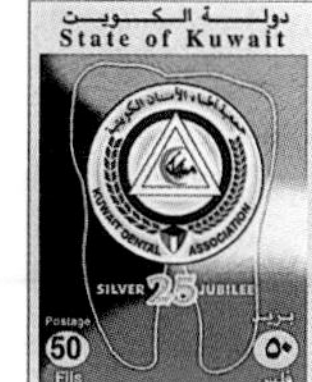
445 Emblem and Outline of Tooth

2000. 25th Anniv of Kuwait Dental Association.
1683 **445** 50f. multicoloured . . . 20 10
1684 150f. multicoloured . . . 60 35
1685 350f. multicoloured . . . 1·40 80

446 Emblem

2000. 6th Gulf Cooperation Council (G.C.C.) Joint Stamp Exhibition, Kuwait.
1686 **446** 25f. multicoloured . . . 10 10
1687 50f. multicoloured . . . 20 10
1688 150f. multicoloured . . . 60 35
MS1689 146 × 111 mm. 1d. Emblems of current and previous exhibitions. Imperf 40 20

447 Building and "15" in Laurel Wreath

2000. 15th Anniv of Gulf Investment Corporation and Inauguration of New Headquarters Building. Multicoloured.
1690 25f. Type **447** 10 10
1691 50f. Building in centre with "15" at left 20 10
1692 150f. Building at right with "15" in centre 60 35

OFFICIAL STAMPS

1923. Stamps of India (King George V) optd **KUWAIT SERVICE**.
O 1 **56** ½a. green . . . . 2·00 25·00
O 2 **57** 1a. brown . . . . 3·00 14·00
O 3 **58** 1½a. brown (No. 163) . . 3·50 35·00
O 4 **59** 2a. lilac . . . . 4·75 26·00
O17 **70** 2a. lilac . . . . 55·00 £170
O 5 **61** 2a.6p. blue . . . . 4·50 60·00
O 6 **62** 3a. orange . . . . 3·50 65·00
O19 3a. blue . . . . 4·50 40·00
O 8 **63** 4a. green . . . . 3·50 60·00
O20 **71** 4a. green . . . . 4·25 70·00
O 9 **65** 8a. mauve . . . . 6·00 85·00
O22 **66** 12a. red . . . . 26·00 £170
O10 **67** 1r. brown and green . . . 22·00 £150
O11 2r. red and orange . . . . 18·00 £200
O12 5r. blue and violet . . . . 75·00 £400
O13 10r. green and red £120 £350
O14 15r. blue £180 £475

POSTAGE DUE STAMPS

D 34

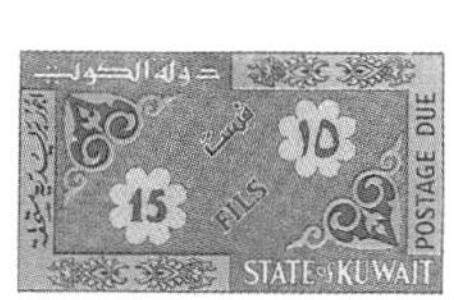
D 51

1963.
D199 **D 34** 1f. brown and black 10 20
D200 2f. lilac and black . . 15 25
D201 5f. blue and black . . 25 20
D202 8f. green and black . . 50 35
D203 10f. yellow and black 70 65
D204 25f. red and black . . 1·60 2·00

The above stamps were not sold to the public unused until 1 July 1964.

1965.
D276 **D 51** 4f. pink and yellow . . 15 20
D277 15f. red and blue . . . 50 35
D278 40f. blue and green . . 1·00 75
D279 50f. green and mauve 1·40 1·00
D280 100f. blue and yellow 2·50 2·00

KYRGYZSTAN Pt. 10

Formerly Kirghizia, a constituent republic of the Soviet Union, Kyrgyzstan became independent in 1991. Its capital Frunze reverted to its previous name of Bishkek.

1992. 100 kopeks = 1 rouble.
1993. 100 tyin = 1 som.

1 Sary-C'helek Nature Reserve

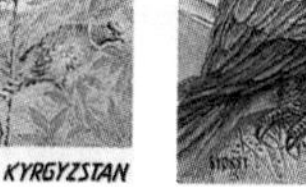
2 Golden Eagle

1992.
1 **1** 15k. multicoloured 15 15

1992.
2 **2** 50k. multicoloured 25 20

3 "Cattle at Issyk-Kule" (G. A. Aitiev)

1992.
3 **3** 1r. multicoloured 25 15

4 Carpet and Samovar

1992.
4 **4** 1r.50 multicoloured 25 15

5 Cave Paintings

1993. National Monuments. Multicoloured.
5 10k. Type **5** 10 10
6 50k. 11th-century tower, Burana (vert) 10 10
7 1r.+25k. Mausoleum of Manas, Talas (vert) 10 10
8 2r.+50k. Mausoleum, Uzgen 15 10
9 3r. Yurt 20 15
10 5r.+50k. Statue of Manas, Bishkek 35 25
11 9r. Cultural complex, Bishkek 55 35

The premium on Nos. 7/8 and 10 were used for the financing of a Manas museum.

1000 КЫРГЫЗСТАН (6)

20 т. КЫРГЫЗСТАН (7)

1993. Nos. 5940, 6073 and 4671 of Russia surch as T **6**.
13 10k. on 1k. brown 15 10
14 20k. on 2k. brown 40 20
15 30k. on 3k. red 60 40

1993. Nos. 4672/3 of Russia surch as T **7**.
16 20t. on 4k. red 20 10
17 30t. on 6k. blue 40 30

8 Map

1993. 2nd Anniv of Independence (18) and 1st Anniv of Admission to United Nations (19). Multicoloured.
18 50t. Type **8** 35 25
19 60t. U.N. emblem, national flag and Government Palace, Bishkek (vert) 45 30

9 Komuz

1993. Music.
20 **9** 30t. multicoloured 25 15

10 Dog

12 Mauve Flowers

11 Adult and Cub

1994. New Year. Year of the Dog.
22 **10** 60t. multicoloured 20 15

1994. The Snow Leopard. Multicoloured.
23 10t. Type **11** 15 10
24 20t. Lying curled-up 35 20
25 30t. Sitting 45 30
26 40t. Head 60 40

1994. Flowers. Multicoloured.
27 1t. Type **12** 10 10
28 3t. Daisies (horiz) 10 10
29 10t. Tulip 10 10
30 16t. Narcissi 10 10
31 20t. Deep pink flower 15 10
32 30t. White flower 20 15
33 40t. Yellow flower 30 25

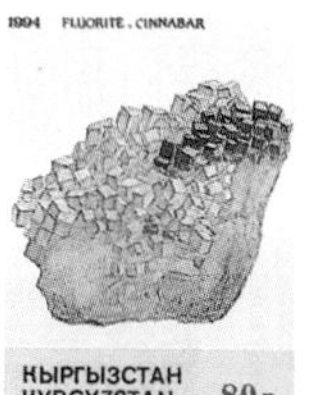
13 Fluorite

15 Woman with Rug

14 Turkestan Catfish

1994. Minerals. Multicoloured.
36 80t. Type **13** 20 15
37 90t. Calcite 20 15
38 100t. Getchellite 20 15
39 110t. Barite 25 20
40 120t. Auripigment 25 20
41 140t. Antimonite 30 20

1994. Fishes. Multicoloured.
43 110t. Type **14** 30 20
44 120t. Schmidt's dace 40 30
45 130t. Scaleless osman 50 40
46 140t. Spotted stone loach . . . 60 45

1995. Traditional Costumes. Multicoloured.
48 50t. Type **15** 10 10
49 50t. Musician 10 10
50 100t. Falconer 25 15
51 100t. Woman with long plaits 25 15

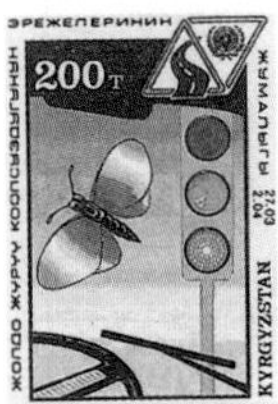

16 Butterfly, Traffic Lights and Emblem

17 Brown Bear

1995. Road Safety Week.
52 **16** 200t. multicoloured 30 20

1995. Animals. Multicoloured.
53 110t. Type **17** 10 10
54 120t. Snow leopard (horiz) . . 15 10
55 130t. Golden eagle 30 15
56 140t. Menzbier's marmot (horiz) 25 15
57 150t. Short-toed eagle (horiz) 35 15
58 160t. Golden eagle (different) 40 20
59 190t. Red fox (horiz) 35 20

19 Aitschurek (wife of Manas)

20 Osprey

1995. Millenary of "Manas" (epic poem). Each blue and gold.
62 10t.+5t. Type **19** 10 10
63 20t.+10t. Hoopoe on youth's wrist 10 10
64 30t.+10t. Birth of Semetey, son of Manas 10 10
65 30t.+10t. Woman carrying spear and leading horse . . 10 10
66 40t.+15t. Warrior astride dead dragon 15 10
67 50t.+15t. Jakyp, father of Manas 20 15
68 50t.+15t. Manas on horseback 20 15
69 50t.+15t. Seytek, grandson of Manas 20 15

1995. Birds. Multicoloured.
71 10t. Type **20** 10 10
72 50t. Tawny eagle 10 10
73 100t. Lammergeier 20 15
74 140t. Saker falcon 25 15
75 150t. Short-toed eagle 25 15
76 200t. Lammergeier 35 25
77 300t. Golden eagle 50 30

21 Envelopes on Map and U.P.U. Emblem

22 State Arms

1995. Postage Stamp Week.
79 **21** 200t. multicoloured 30 20

1995.
80 **22** 20t. violet 10 10
81 50t. blue 10 10
82 100t. brown 15 10
83 500t. green 65 50

23 Mare and Foal Galloping

1995. Horses. Multicoloured.
89 10t. Type **23** 10 10
90 50t. Palamino mare and foal (vert) 10 10
91 100t. Brown mare and foal (vert) 20 15
92 140t. Chestnut mare and foal (vert) 25 15
93 150t. Chestnut mare and foal 25 15
94 200t. Grey mare and foal . . . 35 25
95 300t. Pair of foals 50 30

25 River Nile, Egypt

1995. Natural Wonders of the World. Multicoloured.
98 10t. Type **25** 10 10
99 50t. Mt. Kilimanjaro, Tanzania 10 10
100 100t. Sahara Desert, Algeria 15 10
101 140t. Amazon River, Brazil (vert) 20 15
102 150t. Grand Canyon, U.S.A. (vert) 20 15
103 200t. Victoria Falls, Zimbabwe (vert) 25 20
104 350t. Mt. Everest, Nepal . . 50 35
105 400t. Niagara Falls, Canada 55 40
No. 98 is wrongly inscribed "Egipt".

26 Steppe Ribbon Snake

1996. Reptiles. Multicoloured.
107 20t. Type **26** 10 10
108 50t. Fat-tailed panther gecko 10 10
109 50t. Tessellated water snake 10 10
110 100t. Central Asian viper . . 15 10
111 150t. Arguta 25 20
112 200t. Dione snake 35 25
113 250t. "Asyblepharus sp." (wrongly inscr "Asymblepharus") 40 30

28 Show Jumping and Traditional Horse Race

1996. Olympic Games, Atlanta, U.S.A. Multicoloured.
116 100t.+20t. Type **28** 25 15
117 140t.+30t. Boxing and traditional wrestling match 35 25
118 150t.+30t. Archer and mounted archer shooting at eagle 50 40
119 300t.+50t. Judo competitor, ballooning, yachting and water-skiing 85 65

29 Golden Eagle

1997. Animals.
120 600t. Type **29** 85 60
121 600t. Markhor ("Capra falconeri") 85 60
122 600t. Argali ("Ovis ammon") 85 60
123 600t. Himalayan griffon ("Gyps himalayensis") . . 85 60
124 600t. Asiatic wild ass ("Equus hemionus") 85 60
125 600t. Wolf ("Canis lupus") 85 60
126 600t. Brown bear ("Ursus arctos") (wrongly inscr "arctor") 85 60
127 600t. Saiga ("Saiga tatarica") 85 60

30 Tiger

1998. New Year. Year of the Tiger.
128 **30** 600t. multicoloured 65 45

31 "Parnassius actius"

1998. Butterflies. Multicoloured.
129 600t. Type **31** (wrongly inscr "Parnasius") 65 45
130 600t. "Colias christophi" . . 65 45
131 600t. Swallowtail ("Papilio machaon") 65 45
132 600t. "Colias thisoa" 65 45
133 600t. "Parnassius delphius" 65 45
134 600t. "Parnassius tianschanicus" 65 45

32 Roe Deer

1998. Animals. Multicoloured.
135 600t. Type **32** 60 45
136 600t. Osprey ("Pandion haliaetus") 60 45
137 600t. Hoopoe ("Upupa epops") 60 45
138 600t. White stork ("Ciconia ciconia") 60 45
139 1000t. Golden oriole ("Oriolus oriolus") 60 45
140 1000t. Snow leopard 60 45
141 1000t. River kingfisher ("Alcedo althis") 60 45
142 1000t. Common kestrel ("Falco tinnunculus") . . . 60 45

33 Andrei Dimitriyevich Sakharov (physicist)

1998. 50th Anniv of Universal Declaration of Human Rights. Multicoloured.
143 10s. Type **33** 80 45
144 10s. Crowd cheering 80 45
145 10s. Martin Luther King (civil rights leader) 80 45
146 10s. Mahatma Ghandi (Indian leader) 80 45
147 10s. Eleanor Roosevelt (humanitarian) 80 45

34 Tyrannosaurus

1998. Prehistoric Animals. Multicoloured.
148 10s. Type **34** 80 45
149 10s. Saurolophus 80 45
150 10s. Gallimimus (horiz) . . . 80 45
151 10s. Euoplocephalus (horiz) 80 45
152 10s. Protoceratops (horiz) . . 80 45
153 10s. Velociraptor (horiz) . . 80 45

35 Fish

1998. Fauna. Multicoloured.
154 600t. Type **35** 50 30
155 600t. Fish (with orange tail and fins) 50 30
156 1000t. Bar-headed goose . . 80 45
157 1000t. Chukar partridge . . . 80 45
158 1000t. Goosander by water 80 45
159 1000t. Common shelduck swimming 80 45
160 1000t. Rodent 80 45
161 1000t. Himalayan snowcock standing on one leg 80 45

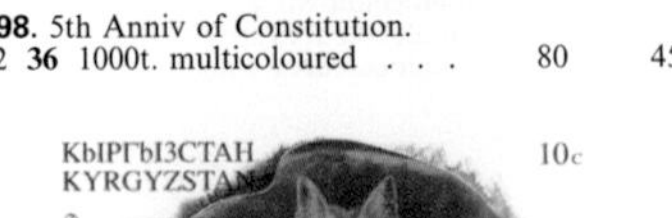

36 Map of Kyrgyzstan

1998. 5th Anniv of Constitution.
162 **36** 1000t. multicoloured . . . 80 45

37 Fox

1999. "iBRA" International Stamp Exhibition, Nuremberg, Germany. The Corsac Fox (*Vulpes corsac*). Multicoloured.
163 10s. Type **37** 85 50
164 10s. Fox sleeping 85 50
165 30s. Two foxes standing . . . 2·50 1·50
166 50s. Mother and cubs . . . . 4·25 2·50

38 Fox

1999. The Corsac Fox (*Vulpes corsac*). Multicoloured.
167 10s. Type **38** 85 50
168 10s. Fox sleeping 85 50
169 30s. Two foxes standing . . . 2·50 1·50
170 50s. Mother and cubs . . . . 4·25 2·50

39 "The Fisherman and the Golden Fish" (poem)

40 State Arms

1999. Birth Bicentenary of Alexander Sergeevich Pushkin. Multicoloured.
171 36t. "Ruslan and Lyudmila" (poem) 10 10
172 6s. Type **39** 50 30
173 10s. "Tsar Saltan" (poem) . . 85 50
174 10s. "The Golden Cockerel" (fairy tale) 85 50
MS175 74 × 99 mm. 20s. Pushkin 1·70 1·70

1999.
176 **40** 20t. blue 10 10

41 Giant Panda (*Ailuropoda melanoleuca*)

1999. "China '99" International Stamp Exhibition, Beijing, China. Sheet 90 × 90 mm containing T **41** and similar horiz design. Multicoloured.
MS180 10s. Type **41**; 15s. Brown wood owl (*Strix leptogrammica*) 2·20 2·20

42 State Flag and Emblem

1999. World Kick Boxing Championships, Bishkek. Multicoloured.
181 3s. Type **42** 20 15
182 3s. Emblem on blue background with Cyrillic championship title in red 20 15

183		3s. "WORLD" in green across globe and emblem	20	15
MS184		121 × 62 mm 6s. "WORLD" in blue across globe and emblem (different); 6s. "KICKBOXING" and emblem on yellow rectangle	1·00	1·00

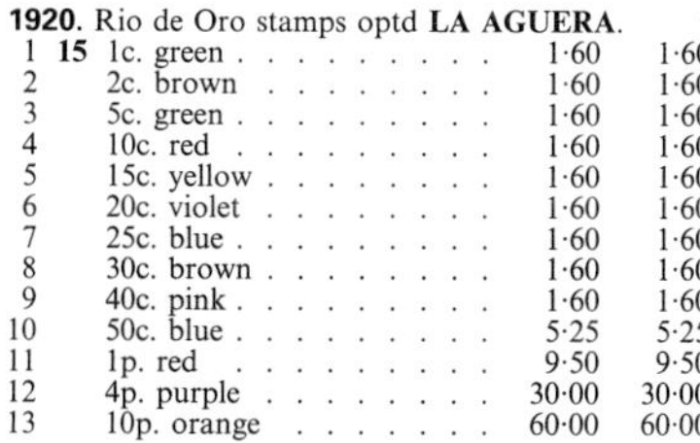

43 Envelopes and Emblem

1999. 125th Anniv of Universal Postal Union. Multicoloured.

185		3s. Type **43**	25	15
186		6s. Airplane, envelopes, horseman and emblem	50	30

44 Anniversary Emblem

2000. 3000th Anniv of Osh. Sheet 139 × 109 mm containing Multicoloured.

MS187		6s.+25t. Type **44**; 6s.+25t. Ravat Abdullakhan Mosque; 6s.+25t. Tahti Suleiman Mosque; 6s.+25t. Asaf ibn Burhia tower	2·20	2·20

45 Taigan

2000. Asian Dogs. Multicoloured.

188		3s. Type **45**	25	15
189		6s. Tasy	50	30
190		6s. Afghan hound	50	30
191		10s. Saluki	85	50
192		15s. Mid-Asian shepherd	1·25	75
193		15s. Akbash	1·25	75
194		20s. Chow Chow	1·70	1·00
195		25s. Akita-inu	2·00	1·30

46 Minjilkiev

2000. 60th Birth Anniv of Bulat Minzhilkiev (opera singer).

196	46	5s. multicoloured	40	25

No. 196 is wrongly inscribed "1940–1998" instead of "1940–1997".

47 Private Cholponbai Tuleberdiev and Medal

2000. 55th Anniv of End of Second World War. Showing recipients of Gold Star of Hero of Soviet Union Medal. Multicoloured.

197		6s. Type **47**	50	30
198		6s. Major-General Ivan Vasilievich Panfilov (vert)	50	30
199		6s. Private Duishenkul Shopokov	50	30

LA AGUERA Pt. 9

An administrative district of Spanish Sahara, whose stamps it later used.

1920. Rio de Oro stamps optd **LA AGUERA**.

1	15	1c. green	1·60	1·60
2		2c. brown	1·60	1·60
3		5c. green	1·60	1·60
4		10c. red	1·60	1·60
5		15c. yellow	1·60	1·60
6		20c. violet	1·60	1·60
7		25c. blue	1·60	1·60
8		30c. brown	1·60	1·60
9		40c. pink	1·60	1·60
10		50c. blue	5·25	5·25
11		1p. red	9·50	9·50
12		4p. purple	30·00	30·00
13		10p. orange	60·00	60·00

2

1923.

14	2	1c. blue	70	70
15		2c. green	70	70
16		5c. green	70	70
17		10c. red	70	70
18		15c. brown	70	70
19		20c. yellow	70	70
20		25c. blue	70	70
21		30c. brown	70	70
22		40c. red	90	90
23		50c. purple	3·25	3·25
24		1p. mauve	6·25	6·25
25		4p. violet	16·00	16·00
26		10p. orange	25·00	25·00

LABUAN Pt. 1

An Island off the N. coast of Borneo, ceded to Great Britain in 1846, and a Crown Colony from 1902. Incorporated with Straits Settlements in 1906, it used Straits stamps till it became part of N. Borneo in 1946.

100 cents = 1 dollar.

1

18

1879.

17	1	2c. green	17·00	26·00
39		2c. red	4·00	3·50
6		6c. orange	95·00	£100
40		6c. green	8·00	4·50
7		8c. red	95·00	95·00
41		8c. violet	3·50	8·50
43		10c. brown	10·00	8·00
9		12c. red	£225	£300
45		12c. blue	5·00	6·50
4		16c. blue	55·00	£110
46		16c. grey	5·50	9·00
47		40c. orange	20·00	32·00

1880. (a) Surch **8**.

11	1	8 on 12c. red	£1100	£700

(b) Surch **6 6** or **8 8**.

12	1	6 on 16c. blue	£1900	£800
13		8 on 12c. red	£1300	£900

1881. Surch **EIGHT CENTS**.

14	1	8c. on 12c. red	£300	£350

1881. Surch **Eight Cents**.

15	1	8c. on 12c. red	£110	£120

1883. Manuscript surch **one Dollar A.S.H.**

22	1	$1 on 16c. blue	£3000	

1885. Surch **2 CENTS** horiz.

23	1	2c. on 8c. red	£190	£400
24		2c. on 16c. blue	£950	£850

1885. Surch **2 Cents** horiz.

25	1	2c. on 16c. blue	£110	£160

1885. Surch with large **2 Cents** diag.

26	1	2c. on 8c. red	65·00	£100

1891. Surch **6 Cents**.

35	1	6c. on 8c. violet	8·00	7·50
37		6c. on 16c. blue	£1900	£1700
38		6c. on 40c. orange	£7500	£4000

1892. Surch as **Two CENTS** or **Six CENTS**.

49	1	2c. on 40c. orange	£160	90·00
50		6c. on 16c. grey	£325	£150

Most issues from 1894 exist cancelled-to-order with black bars. Our prices are for stamps postally used, cancelled-to-order examples being worth considerably less.

1894. Types of North Borneo (different colours) optd **LABUAN**.

62	24	1c. black and mauve	1·50	8·00
63	25	2c. black and blue	2·50	7·50
64a	26	3c. black and yellow	8·00	9·00
65a	27	5c. black and green	38·00	13·00
67	28	6c. black and red	2·50	14·00
69	29	8c. black and pink	7·00	23·00
70	30	12c. black and orange	23·00	48·00
71	31	18c. black and brown	22·00	55·00
74a	32	24c. blue and mauve	13·00	45·00
80	10	25c. green	24·00	28·00
81	–	50c. purple (as No. 82)	24·00	28·00
82	–	$1 blue (as No. 83)	60·00	55·00

1895. No. 83 of North Borneo surch **LABUAN** and value in cents.

75		4c. on $1 red	1·00	2·00
76		10c. on $1 red	3·50	1·40
77		20c. on $1 red	27·00	10·00
78		30c. on $1 red	30·00	38·00
79		40c. on $1 red	27·00	28·00

1896. Jubilee of Cession of Labuan to Gt. Britain. Nos. 62/8 optd **1846 JUBILEE 1896**.

83	24	1c. black and mauve	18·00	21·00
84d	25	2c. black and blue	38·00	14·00
85	26	3c. black and yellow	35·00	22·00
86	27	5c. black and green	55·00	16·00
87	28	6c. black and red	26·00	20·00
88b	29	8c. black and pink	40·00	11·00

1897. Stamps of North Borneo, Nos. 92 to 106 (different colours), optd **LABUAN**. Opt at top of stamp.

89		1c. black and purple	4·00	4·75
90		2c. black and blue	13·00	4·25
91b		3c. black and yellow	8·50	6·50
92a		5c. black and green	45·00	55·00
93b		6c. black and red	6·00	21·00
94a		8c. black and pink	18·00	12·00
95a		12c. black and orange	38·00	48·00

Overprint at foot of stamp.

98a	–	12c. black and orange (as No. 106)	42·00	50·00

Opt at foot. Inscr "POSTAL REVENUE".

96b	–	18c. black and bistre (as No. 108)	16·00	45·00

Opt at foot. Inscr "POSTAGE AND REVENUE".

99a	–	18c. black and bistre (as No. 110)	80·00	60·00

Opt at top. Inscr "POSTAGE AND REVENUE".

101b	–	18c. black and bistre (as No. 110)	35·00	55·00

Opt at top. "POSTAGE AND REVENUE" omitted.

97a	–	24c. blue and lilac (as No. 109)	13·00	48·00

Opt at top. Inscr "POSTAGE AND REVENUE".

100	–	24c. blue and mauve (No. 111)	28·00	55·00

1899. Stamps of Labuan surch **4 CENTS**.

102		4c. on 5c. black & grn (92a)	35·00	26·00
103		4c. on 6c. black & red (93b)	22·00	19·00
104a		4c. on 8c. black and pink (94a)	28·00	32·00
105		4c. on 12c. black and orange (98a)	38·00	35·00
106		4c. on 18c. black and olive (101b)	26·00	18·00
107a		4c. on 24c. blue and mauve (100)	19·00	25·00
108		4c. on 25c. green (80)	6·00	7·50
109		4c. on 50c. purple (81)	6·50	7·50
110		4c. on $1 blue (82)	6·50	7·50

1900. Stamps of North Borneo, as Nos. 95 to 107, optd **LABUAN**.

111		2c. black and green	3·75	2·50
112		4c. black and brown	8·00	40·00
113a		4c. black and red	6·50	9·00
114		5c. black and blue	29·00	18·00
115		10c. brown and grey	50·00	80·00
116		16c. green and brown	50·00	£110

1902.

117	18	1c. black and purple	3·75	7·00
118		2c. black and green	3·50	4·50
119		3c. black and brown	3·25	11·00
120		4c. black and red	3·25	3·50
121		8c. black and orange	9·00	9·00
122		10c. brown and blue	3·25	11·00
123		12c. black and yellow	5·00	13·00
124		16c. green and brown	4·75	17·00
125		18c. black and brown	3·25	21·00
126		25c. green and blue	7·00	18·00
127		50c. purple and lilac	10·00	42·00
128		$1 red and orange	8·50	50·00

1904. Surch **4 cents**.

129	–	4c. on 5c. black and green (92a)	40·00	40·00
130	–	4c. on 6c. black and red (93b)	12·00	38·00
131	–	4c. on 8c. black and pink (94a)	25·00	42·00
132	–	4c. on 12c. black and orange (98a)	19·00	42·00
133	–	4c. on 18c. black and olive (101b)	23·00	45·00
134a	–	4c. on 24c. blue and mauve (100)	26·00	38·00
135	10	4c. on 25c. green (80)	8·50	24·00
136		4c. on 50c. purple (81)	8·50	24·00
137		4c. on $1 blue (82)	8·50	24·00

POSTAGE DUE STAMPS

1901. Optd **POSTAGE DUE**.

D1		2c. black and green (111)	14·00	22·00
D2		3c. black and yellow (91)	17·00	75·00
D3b		4c. black and red (113)	30·00	75·00
D4		5c. black and blue (114)	48·00	90·00
D5		6c. black and red (93b)	25·00	85·00
D6		8c. black and pink (94a)	50·00	80·00
D7b		12c. black and orange (98a)	75·00	95·00
D8		18c. black and olive (101b)	20·00	90·00
D9c		24c. blue and mauve (100)	40·00	75·00

LAGOS Pt. 1

A British colony on the southern coast of Nigeria. United with Southern Nigeria in 1906 to form the Colony and Protectorate of Southern Nigeria.

12 pence = 1 shilling;
20 shillings = 1 pound.

1

3

1874.

21	1	½d. green	2·00	80
17		1d. mauve	19·00	10·00
22		1d. red	2·00	80
11		2d. blue	40·00	13·00
23		2d. grey	60·00	5·50
19		3d. brown	15·00	5·00
5		4d. red	80·00	40·00
24		4d. lilac	£100	8·50
25		6d. green	8·00	38·00
26		1s. orange	7·00	20·00
27		2s.6d. black	£275	£250
28		5s. blue	£500	£425
29		10s. brown	£1300	£950

1887.

30	1	2d. mauve and blue	3·00	2·00
31		2½d. blue	3·50	1·75
32		3d. mauve and brown	2·50	3·25
33		4d. mauve and black	2·25	1·75
34		5d. mauve and green	2·00	11·00
35		6d. mauve	4·75	3·00
35a		6d. mauve and red	5·00	12·00
36		7½d. mauve and red	2·00	28·00
37		10d. mauve and yellow	3·25	13·00
38		1s. green and black	5·50	24·00
39		2s.6d. green and red	23·00	80·00
40		5s. green and blue	40·00	£150
41		10s. green and brown	75·00	£200

1893. Surch **HALF PENNY** and bars.

42	1	½d. on 4d. mauve and black	4·00	2·50

1904.

44	3	½d. green	1·50	5·50
45		1d. purple and black on red	1·00	15
56		2d. purple and blue	2·25	2·00
47		2½d. purple and blue on blue	1·00	1·50
48		3d. purple and brown	2·25	1·75
59a		6d. purple and mauve	4·25	1·50
60a		1s. green and black	23·00	2·25
61		2s.6d. green and red	16·00	55·00
62		5s. green and blue	22·00	95·00
63		10s. green and brown	60·00	£200

LAOS Pt. 21

Previously part of French Indo-China, the Kingdom of Laos was proclaimed in 1947. In 1949 it became an Associated State within the French Union and in 1953 it became fully independent within the Union.

Laos left the French Union in 1956. In 1976 it became a Republic.

1951. 100 cents = 1 piastre.
1955. 100 cents = 1 kip.

1 River Mekong

2 King Sisavang Vong

1951.
1 **1** 10c. green and turquoise 20 20
2 20c. red and purple 20 30
3 30c. blue and indigo 1·00 85
4 – 50c. brown and deep brown 50 35
5 – 60c. orange and red 45 50
6 – 70c. turquoise and blue 45 50
7 – 1p. violet and deep violet 45 50
8 **2** 1p.50 purple and brown 85 65
9 – 2p. green and turquoise 16·00 4·00
10 – 3p. red and purple 90 75
11 – 5p. blue and indigo 1·25 80
12 – 10p. purple and brown 2·75 1·25
DESIGNS—As Type **1**: 50c. to 70c. Luang Prabang; 1p. and 2p. to 10p. Vientiane.

3 Laotian Woman

4 Laotian Woman Weaving

1952.
13 **3** 30c. violet and blue (postage) 40 35
14 80c. turquoise and green 40 35
15 1p.10 red and crimson 90 35
16 1p.90 blue and indigo 1·40 80
17 3p. deep brown and brown 1·40 80
18 – 3p.30 violet and deep violet (air) 85 60
19 **4** 10p. green and blue 1·90 1·25
20 20p. red and crimson 3·25 2·00
21 30p. brown and black 4·75 3·50
DESIGN—As Type **4**: 3p.30, Vat Pra Keo shrine.

5 King Sisavang Vong and U.P.U. Monument

1952. 1st Anniv of Admission to U.P.U.
22 **5** 80c. violet, bl & ind (postage) 75 85
23 1p. brown, red and lake 75 75
24 1p.20 blue and violet 75 85
25 1p.50 brown, emerald & grn 75 85
26 1p.90 turquoise and sepia 1·10 1·25
27 25p. indigo and blue (air) 4·25 4·75
28 50p. sepia, purple and brown 5·00 5·50

6 Girl carrying her Brother

7 Court of Love

1953. Red Cross Fund. Cross in red.
29 **6** 1p.50+1p. purple and blue 2·75 2·75
30 3p.+1p.50 red and green 2·50 2·75
31 3p.90+2p.50 purple & brn 2·50 2·75

1953.
32 **7** 4p.50 turquoise and blue 1·00 85
33 6p. brown and slate 1·10 85

8 Buddha

1953. Air. Statues of Buddha.
34 – 4p. green 95 85
35 – 6p.50 green 1·40 1·10
36 – 9p. green 2·00 1·50
37 **8** 11p.50 orange, brown and red 2·75 2·50
38 – 40p. purple 6·50 2·50
39 – 100p. green 13·50 10·50
DESIGNS—HORIZ: 4p. Reclining. VERT: 6p.50, Seated; 9p. Standing (full-face); 40p. Standing (facing right); 100p. Buddha and temple dancer.

9 Vientiane

1954. Golden Jubilee of King Sisavang Vong.
40 **9** 2p. violet and blue (postage) 50·00 35·00
41 3p. red and brown 45·00 38·00
42 50p. turquoise and blue (air) £140 £160

10 Ravana

1955. Air. "Ramayana" (dramatic poem).
43 **10** 2k. blue, emerald and green 1·00 90
44 – 4k. red and brown 1·25 1·25
45 – 5k. green, brown and red 2·50 1·75
46 – 10k. black, orange and brown 4·50 3·00
47 – 20k. olive, green and violet 5·50 4·25
48 – 30k. black, brown and blue 7·50 5·50
DESIGNS—HORIZ: 4k. Hanuman, the white monkey; 5k. Ninh Laphath, the black monkey. VERT: 10k. Sita and Rama; 20k. Luci and Ravana's friend; 30k. Rama.

11 Buddha and Worshippers

1956. 2500th Anniv of Buddhist Era.
49 **11** 2k. brown (postage) 3·50 2·25
50 3k. black 3·50 2·25
51 5k. sepia 5·50 3·50
52 20k. carmine and red (air) 35·00 30·00
53 30k. green and bistre 35·00 32·00
Nos. 49/53 were wrongly inscribed as commemorating the birth anniversary of Buddha.

12 U.N. Emblem

13 U.N. Emblem

1956. 1st Anniv of Admission to U.N.
54 **12** 1k. black (postage) 50 45
55 2k. blue 65 50
56 4k. red 90 70
57 6k. violet 1·10 90
58 **13** 15k. blue (air) 4·00 4·00
59 30k. red 5·50 5·50

14 Flute Player

1957. Native Musicians.
60 **14** 2k. multicoloured (postage) 1·25 80
61 – 4k. multicoloured 1·25 80
62 – 8k. blue, brown and orange 2·10 95
63 – 12k. multicoloured (air) 1·90 1·90
64 – 14k. multicoloured 2·25 2·25
65 – 20k. multicoloured 2·50 2·50
DESIGNS—VERT: 4k. Piper; 14k. Violinist; 20k. Drummer. HORIZ: 8k. Xylophonist; 12k. Bells player.

15 Harvesting Rice

1957. Rice Cultivation.
66 **15** 3k. multicoloured 70 40
67 – 5k. brown, red and green 70 50
68 – 16k. violet, olive and blue 1·50 90
69 – 26k. chocolate, brown & grn 1·90 1·50
DESIGNS—VERT: 5k. Drying rice; 16k. Winnowing rice. HORIZ: 26k. Polishing rice.

16 "The Offertory"

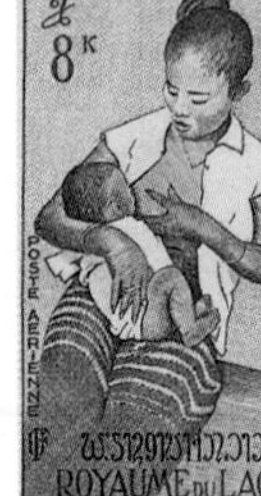
18 Mother and Child

17 Carrier Elephants

1957. Air. Buddhism.
70 **16** 10k. multicoloured 60 60
71 – 15k. brown, yellow & choc 90 90
72 – 18k. yellow and green 1·25 1·25
73 – 24k. red, black and yellow 2·40 2·40
DESIGNS—As T **16**: HORIZ: 15k. "Meditation" (children on river craft). 48 × 36½ mm: 24k. "The Great Renunciation" (dancers with horse). VERT: 18k. "Serenity" (head of Buddhist).

1958. Laotian Elephants. Multicoloured.
74 10c. Type **17** 45 20
75 20c. Elephant's head with head-dress 45 20
76 30c. Elephant with howdah (vert) 45 20
77 2k. Elephant hauling log 65 35
78 5k. Elephant walking with calf (vert) 1·90 75
79 10k. Caparisoned elephant (vert) 2·25 90
80 13k. Elephant bearing throne (vert) 3·75 1·50

1958. Air. 3rd Anniv of Laotian Red Cross. Cross in red.
81 **18** 8k. black and grey 90 90
82 12k. olive and brown 90 90
83 15k. turquoise and green 1·10 1·10
84 20k. violet and bistre 1·25 1·25

19

1958. Inauguration of UNESCO Headquarters Building, Paris.
85 **19** 50c. blue, orange and red 25 20
86 – 60c. violet, brown and green 25 20
87 – 70c. blue, brown and red 25 20
88 – 1k. red, blue and bistre 45 25
DESIGNS—VERT: 60c. Woman, children and part of exterior of UNESCO building; 70c. Woman and children hailing UNESCO building superimposed on globe. HORIZ: 1k. General view of UNESCO building and Eiffel Tower.

20 King Sisavang Vong

1959.
89 **20** 4k. lake 30 30
90 6k.50 red 30 30
91 9k. mauve 30 30
92 13k. green 30 30

21 Stage Performance

22 Portal of Vat Phou Temple, Pakse

1959. Education and Fine Arts.
93 **21** 1k. multicoloured 20 15
94 – 2k. lake, violet and black 25 15
95 – 3k. black, green and purple 30 20
96 – 5k. green, yellow and violet 45 35
DESIGNS—VERT: 2k. Student and "Lamp of Learning"; 5k. Stage performers and Buddhist temple. HORIZ: 3k. Teacher and children with "Key to Education".

1959. Laotian Monuments. Multicoloured.
97 50c. Type **22** 15 15
98 1k.50 That Ing Hang, Savannakhet (horiz) 15 15
99 2k.50 Vat Phou Temple, Pakse (horiz) 20 20
100 7k. That Luang, Vientiane 30 30
101 11k. As 7k., but different view (horiz) 30 30
102 12k.50 Phou-Si Temple, Luang Prabang 45 45

1960. World Refugee Year. Nos. 89 and 79 surch **ANNEE MONDIALE DU REFUGIE 1959–1960** and premium.
103 4k.+1k. red 50 70
104 10k.+1k. multicoloured 50 70

24 Plain of Jars, Xieng Khouang

25 Funeral Urn

1960. Air. Tourism.
105 **24** 9k.50 red, bistre and blue 25 25
106 – 12k. brown, violet and green 35 30
107 – 15k. red, green and brown 50 45
108 – 19k. brown, orange and green 60 50
DESIGNS—HORIZ: 12k. Phapheng Falls, Champassak; 15k. Pair of bullocks with cart. VERT: 19k. Buddhist monk and village.

1961. Funeral of King Sisavang Vong.
109 **25** 4k. bistre, black and red 30 30
110 – 6k.50 brown and black 30 30
111 – 9k. brown and black 30 30
112 – 25k. black 70 70
DESIGNS: 6k.50, Urn under canopy; 9k. Catafalque on dragon carriage; 25k. King Sisavang Vong.

26 Temples and Statues ("Pou Gneu Nha Gneu")

27 King Savang Vatthana

1962. Air. Festival of Makha Bousa.
113 **26** 11k. brown, red and green 30 30
114 – 14k. blue and orange 30 30

115 – 20k. green, yellow and mauve 50 50
116 – 25k. red, blue and green 60 60
DESIGNS—As T 26: 14k. Bird ("Garuda"); 20k. Flying deities ("Hanuman"). 36×48 mm: 25k. Warriors ("Nang Teng One").

1962.
117 27 1k. brown, red and blue . . 10 10
118 2k. brown, red and mauve 15 15
119 5k. brown, red and blue . . 25 15
120 10k. brown, red and bistre 40 25

28 Laotian Boy **29** Royal Courier

1962. Malaria Eradication.
121 28 4k. olive, black and green 20 10
122 – 9k. brown, black & turq 20 20
123 – 10k. red, yellow and green 40 25
DESIGNS: 9k. Laotian girl; 10k. Campaign emblem.

1962. Philatelic Exhibition, Vientiane, and Stamp Day.
124 – 50c. multicoloured . . . . 1·00 1·00
125 – 70c. multicoloured 20 20
126 – 1k. black, green and red 35 35
127 29 1k.50 multicoloured . . . 35 35
DESIGNS—HORIZ: 50c. Modern mail transport; 70c. Dancer and globe. VERT: 1k. Royal courtier on elephant.

30 Fisherman

1963. Freedom from Hunger.
128 30 1k. bistre, violet and green 20 15
129 – 4k. blue, brown and green 20 20
130 – 5k. blue, bistre and green 25 25
131 – 9k. blue, green and brown 40 40
DESIGNS—VERT: 4k. Threshing rice; 9k. Harvesting rice. HORIZ: 5k. Ploughing paddy field.

31 Queen of Laos

1963. Red Cross Centenary.
132 31 4k. red, blue and brown . . 20 20
133 6k. multicoloured 25 25
134 10k. red, blue and brown 30 30

32 Laotian supporting U.N. Emblem

1963. 15th Anniv of Declaration of Human Rights.
135 32 4k. purple, blue and red . . 50 30

33 Temple, Map and Rameses II

1964. Nubian Monuments Preservation.
136 33 4k. multicoloured 20 20
137 6k. multicoloured 30 30
138 10k. multicoloured 35 35

34 Offertory Vase and Horn

1964. "Constitutional Monarchy". Multicoloured.
139 10k. Type **34** 20 15
140 15k. Seated Buddha of Vat Pra Keo 30 20
141 20k. Laotians walking across map 35 30
142 40k. Royal Palace, Luang Prabang 70 55

35 Phra Vet and Wife **36** Meo Warrior

1964. Folklore. Phra Vet Legend. Multicoloured.
143 10k. Type **35** 25 25
144 32k. "Benediction" 35 35
145 45k. Phame and wife 40 40
146 55k. Arrest of Phame 70 70

1964. "People of Laos".
147 – 25k. black, brown and green (postage) 60 60
148 36 5k. multicoloured (air) . . 25 15
149 – 10k. pink, grey and purple 35 20
150 – 50k. brown, drab and lilac 1·40 85
DESIGNS: 10k. Kha hunter; 25k. Girls of three races; 50k. Thai woman.

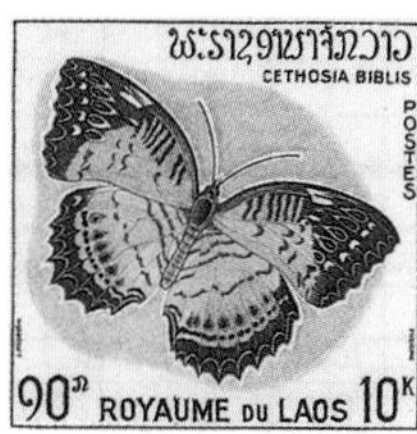

37 Red Lacewing

1965. Butterflies and Moths.
151 37 10k. chestnut, brown and green (postage) 75 40
152 – 25k. blue, black and yellow 1·10 60
153 – 40k. yellow, brown & green 1·90 90
154 – 20k. red and yellow (air) 1·10 60
BUTTERFLIES—As Type 37: 25k. Yellow pansy. 48×27 mm: 20k. Atlas moth; 40k. "Dysphania militaris" (moth).

38 Wattay Airport ("French Aid")

1965. Foreign Aid.
155 38 25k. mauve, brown & turq 30 20
156 – 45k. brown and green . . . 35 30
157 – 55k. brown and blue . . . 50 40
158 – 75k. multicoloured 60 50
DESIGNS—VERT: 45k. Mother bathing child (water resources: "Japanese Aid"); 75k. School and plants (education and cultivation: "American Aid"). HORIZ: 55k. Studio of radio station ("British Aid").

39 Hophabang

1965.
159 39 10k. multicoloured 20 15

40 Teleprinter Operator, Globe and Map

1965. I.T.U. Centenary.
160 40 5k. brown, violet and purple 20 15
161 – 30k. brown, blue and green 30 30
162 – 50k. multicoloured 50 35
DESIGNS: 30k. Globe, map, telephonist and radio operator; 50k. Globe, radio receiver and mast.

1965. Nos. 89/90 surch.
163 20 1k. on 4k. lake 20 15
164 5k. on 6k.50 brown . . . 25 20

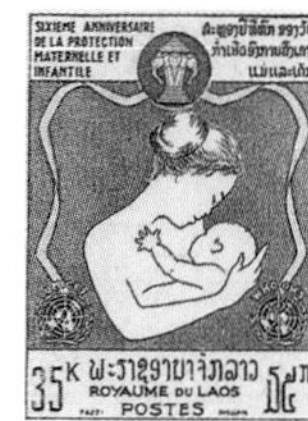

42 Mother and Baby **43** Leopard Cat

1965. 6th Anniv of U.N. "Protection of Mother and Child".
165 42 35k. blue and red 70 30

1965. Air. Laotian Fauna.
166 43 25k. yellow, brown & green 30 25
167 – 55k. brown, sepia and blue 40 30
168 – 75k. brown and green . . . 65 40
169 – 100k. brown, black & yell 90 60
170 – 200k. black and red . . . 1·90 1·40
DESIGNS: 55k. Phayre's flying squirrel; 75k. Javan mongoose; 100k. Chinese porcupine; 200k. Binturong.

44 U.N. Emblem on Map **45** Bulls in Combat

1965. 20th Anniv of U.N.
171 44 5k. blue, grey and green . . 20 15
172 25k. blue, grey and mauve 25 20
173 40k. blue, grey and turquoise 35 35

1965. Laotian Pastimes.
174 45 10k. brown, black and orange 25 20
175 – 20k. blue, red and green 30 20
176 – 25k. red, blue and green 45 30
177 – 50k. multicoloured 50 40
DESIGNS: 20k. Tikhy (form of hockey); 25k. Pirogue race; 50k. Rocket festival.

46 Slaty-headed Parakeet

1966. Birds.
178 46 5k. green, brown and red 90 30
179 – 15k. brown, black & turq 1·10 55
180 – 20k. sepia, ochre and blue 1·50 85
181 – 45k. blue, sepia and violet 4·75 3·00
BIRDS: 15k. White-crested laughing thrush; 20k. Osprey; 45k. Indian roller (or "blue jay").

47 W.H.O. Building

1966. Inaug of W.H.O. Headquarters, Geneva.
182 47 10k. blue and turquoise . . 20 20
183 25k. green and red 25 20
184 50k. black and blue . . . 45 45

48 Ordination of Priests

1966. Laotian Ceremonies. Multicoloured.
186 10k. Type **48** 25 15
187 25k. Sand-hills ceremony . . 25 20
188 30k. "Wax pagoda" procession (vert) 35 30
189 40k. "Sou-Khouan" ceremony (vert) 40 35

49 UNESCO Emblem

1966. 20th Anniv of UNESCO.
190 49 20k. orange and black . . 15 15
191 30k. blue and black . . . 25 20
192 40k. green and black . . . 30 25
193 60k. red and black 45 40

50 Letter, Carrier Pigeon and Emblem

1966. International Correspondence Week.
195 50 5k. blue, brown and red . . 20 15
196 20k. purple, black and green 30 20
197 40k. brown, red and blue 40 25
198 45k. black, green and purple 45 30

51 Flooded Village **52** Carving, Siprapouthbat Pagoda

1967. Mekong Delta Flood Relief. Multicoloured.
200 20k.+5k. Type **51** 25 25
201 40k.+10k. Flooded market-place 40 40
202 60k.+15k. Flooded airport . . 1·10 1·10

1967. Buddhist Art.
204 52 5k. green and brown . . . 15 15
205 – 20k. blue and sepia 25 20
206 – 50k. purple and sepia . . . 35 35
207 – 70k. grey and brown . . . 45 35
DESIGNS (carvings in temple pagodas, Luang Prabang): 30k. Visoun; 50k. Xiengthong; 70k. Visoun (different).

53 General Post Office

1967. Opening of New G.P.O. Building, Vientiane.
208 53 25k. brown, green & purple 20 20
209 50k. blue, green and slate 30 25
210 70k. red, green and brown 50 35

54 Giant Snakehead **55** "Cassia fistula"

1967. Fishes.
211 **54** 20k. black, bistre and blue 35 30
212 – 35k. slate, bistre and blue 45 30
213 – 45k. sepia, ochre and green 75 35
214 – 60k. black, bistre and green 95 45
DESIGNS: 35k. Giant catfish; 45k. Tire-track spiny eel; 60k. Bronze knifefish.

1967. Flowers.
215 **55** 30k. yellow, green and mauve 25 25
216 – 55k. red, green and orange 35 30
217 – 75k. red, green and blue 50 40
218 – 80k. yellow, mauve and green 60 45
DESIGNS: 55k. "Cucuma singulario"; 75k. "Poinciana regia"; 80k. "Plumeria acutifolia".

56 Harvesting

1967. 10th Anniv of Laotian Red Cross.
219 **56** 20k.+5k. multicoloured . . 25 25
220 50k.+10k. multicoloured 85 35
221 60k.+15k. multicoloured 55 55

57 Banded Krait

1967. Reptiles.
223 **57** 5k. blue, yellow and green 20 15
224 – 40k. brown, bistre and green 25 20
225 – 100k. chocolate, brown and green 75 50
226 – 200k. black, brown and green . . . . 1·60 1·25
DESIGNS: 40k. Marsh crocodile; 100k. Pit viper; 200k. Water monitor.

58 Human Rights Emblem

1968. Human Rights Year. Emblem in red and green.
227 **58** 20k. green 20 20
228 30k. brown 25 20
229 50k. blue 50 35

59 Military Parade

1968. Army Day. Multicoloured.
231 15k. Type **59** (postage) . . . 20 15
232 20k. Soldiers and tank in battle 30 15
233 60k. Soldiers and Laotian flag 50 25
234 200k. Parade of colours before National Assembly building (air) 75 55
235 300k. As No. 234 . . . . . 1·25 70

60 W.H.O. Emblem

1968. 20th Anniv of W.H.O.
237 **60** 15k. brown, red and purple 25 20
238 30k. brown, green and blue 30 20
239 70k. brown, purple and red 50 30
240 110k. light brown, purple and brown 70 45
241 250k. brown, blue and green . . . . 1·75 1·00

61 "Chrysochroa mnizechi"

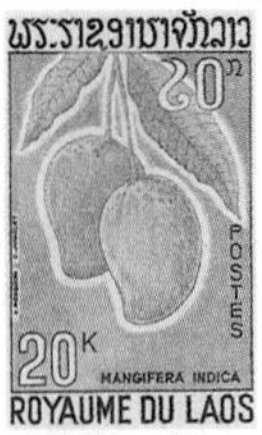

62 "Mangifera indica"

1968. Beetles.
243 **61** 30k. blue, yellow and green (postage) 40 25
244 – 50k. black, orange & purple 55 35
245 – 90k. blue, orange and ochre . . . . 1·10 55
246 – 120k. black and orange (air) . . . . 1·10 55
247 – 160k. multicoloured . . . 1·40 75
INSECTS—VERT: 50k. "Aristobia approximator"; 90k. "Eutaenia corbetti". HORIZ: 120k. "Dorysthenes walkeri"; 160k. "Megaloxantha bicolor".

1968. Laotian Fruits.
248 **62** 20k. green, blue and black 15 15
249 – 50k. green, red and blue 30 25
250 – 180k. green, brown & orge 80 70
251 – 250k. green, brown & yell 1·25 90
DESIGNS—VERT: 50k. "Tamarindus indica". HORIZ: 180k. "Artocarpus intregrifolia"; 250k. "Citrullus vulgaris".

63 Hurdling

1968. Olympic Games, Mexico.
252 **63** 15k. green, blue & brown 20 15
253 – 80k. brown, turquoise & blue 40 30
254 – 100k. blue, brown and green 55 30
255 – 110k. brown, red and blue 65 40
DESIGNS: 80k. Tennis; 100k. Football; 110k. High jumping.

64 Oriental Door, Wat Ongtu (detail)

1969. Wat Ongtu Temple.
256 **64** 150k. gold, black and red 1·10 60
257 – 200k. gold, black and red 1·75 90
DESIGN: 200k. Central door, Wat Ongtu.

65 "Pharak praying to the Gods"

1969. Laotian "Ballet Royal". Designs showing dance characters. Multicoloured.
258 10k. Type **65** (postage) . . . 25 15
259 15k. "Soukhib ordered to attack" 35 20
260 20k. "Thotsakan reviewing troops" 40 30
261 30k. "Nang Sida awaiting punishment" 60 35
262 40k. "Pharam inspecting his troops" 75 35
263 60k. "Hanuman about to rescue Nang Sida" . . . . 1·25 50
264 110k. "Soudagnou battling with Thotsakan" (air) . . . 1·75 1·25
265 300k. "Pharam dancing with Thotsakkan" . . . . . . 3·75 2·25

66 Handicrafts Workshop, Vientiane

1969. 10th Anniv of I.L.O.
267 **66** 30k. violet & purple (postage) 25 20
268 60k. brown and green . . . 60 30
269 – 300k. black & brown (air) 2·25 1·40
DESIGN: 300k. Elephants moving logs.

67 Chinese Pangolin

1969. "Wild Animals" (1st series). Multicoloured.
270 15k. Type **67** (postage) . . . 30 20
271 30k. Type **67** 30 25
272 70k. Sun bear (air) 35 30
273 120k. Common gibbon (vert) 75 50
274 150k. Tiger 80 60
See also Nos. 300/3 and 331/5.

68 Royal Mausoleum, Luang Prabang

1969. 10th Death Anniv of King Sisavang Vong.
275 **68** 50k. ochre, blue and green 60 40
276 – 70k. ochre and lake . . . 70 40
DESIGN: 70k. King Sisavang Vong (medallion).

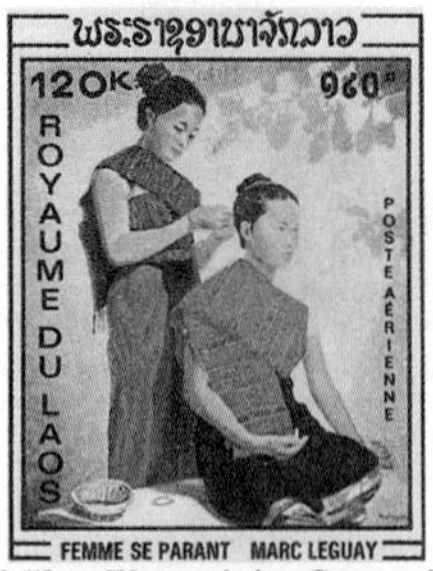

69 "Lao Woman being Groomed" (Leguay)

1969. Air. Paintings by Marc Leguay (1st series). Multicoloured.
277 10k. Type **69** . . . . 1·25 70
278 150k. "Village Market" (horiz) . . . . 1·75 90
See also Nos. 285, 307/9 and 357/61.

70 Carved Capital, Wat Xiengthong

1970. Laotian Pagodas. Multicoloured.
279 70k. Type **70** (postage) . . . 60 50
280 100k. Library, Wat Sisaket (air) 90 40
281 120k. Wat Xiengthong (horiz) 1·50 70

71 "Noon" Drum

1970. Laotian Drums.
282 **71** 30k. mult (postage) 65 50
283 – 55k. black, green and brown . . . . 1·00 65
284 – 125k. brown, yellow and flesh (air) . . . . 1·75 1·00
DESIGNS—HORIZ: 55k. Bronze drum. VERT: 125k. Wooden drum.

1970. Air. Paintings by Marc Leguay (2nd series). As T **69**. Multicoloured.
285 150k. "Banks of the Mekong" (horiz) . . . . . 1·75 90

72 Franklin D. Roosevelt

1970. Air. 25th Death Anniv of Franklin D. Roosevelt (American statesman).
286 **72** 120k. slate and green . . . 1·00 70

73 "Lenin explaining Electrification Plan" (L. Shmatko)

1970. Birth Centenary of Lenin.
287 **73** 30k. multicoloured 35 25
288 70k. multicoloured 45 40

1970. "Support for War Victims". Nos. 258/65 ("Ballet Royal") surch **Soutien aux Victimes de la Guerre** and premium.
289 10k.+5k. mult (postage) . . . 40 40
290 15k.+5k. multicoloured . . . 40 40
291 20k.+5k. multicoloured . . . 40 40
292 30k.+5k. multicoloured . . . 40 40
293 40k.+5k. multicoloured . . . 70 70
294 60k.+5k. multicoloured . . . 90 90
295 110k.+5k. mult (air) . . . . 1·75 1·75
296 300k.+5k. multicoloured . . 2·75 2·75

75 Weaving Silk

1970. "EXPO 70" World Fair, Osaka, Japan. Laotian Silk Industry.
297 **75** 30k. bl, brn & red (postage) 40 25
298 – 70k. multicoloured 70 45
299 – 125k. multicoloured (air) 85 70
DESIGNS: 70k. Silk-spinning; 125k. Winding skeins.

76 Wild Boar

77 Buddha, U.N. Emblem and New York H.Q.

1970. Wild Animals (2nd series).
300 **76** 20k. brown & grn (postage) 45 25
301 – 60k. brown and olive . . . 75 40
302 – 210k. brown, red and yellow (air) . . . . . . 2·00 1·25
303 – 500k. green, brown & orge 4·00 2·40
ANIMALS: 210k. Leopard; 500k. Gaur.

1970. 25th Anniv of U.N.O.
304 **77** 30k. brown, mauve and blue (postage) 40 30
305 70k. brown, blue and green 60 50
306 – 125k. multicoloured (air) 1·25 85
DESIGN—26 × 36 mm: 125k. Nang Thorani ("Goddess of the Earth") and New York Headquarters.

1970. Air. Paintings by Marc Leguay (3rd series). As T **69**. Multicoloured.
307 100k. "Village Track" . . . 50 40
308 120k. "Paddy-field in the Rainy Season" (horiz) . . 70 50
309 150k. "Village Elder" 80 60

78 "Nakhanet"

1971. Laotian Mythology (1st series). Frescoes from Triumphal Arch, Vientiane. Multicoloured.
310 **78** 70k. orange, brown and red (postage) 50 35
311 – 85k. green, yellow and blue 60 45
312 – 125k. multicoloured (air) 1·25 65
DESIGNS: As T **78**: 85k. "Rahu". 49 × 36 mm: 125k. "Underwater duel between Nang Matsa and Hanuman".
See also Nos. 352/4 and 385/7.

79 Silversmiths

1971. Laotian Traditional Crafts. Multicoloured.
313 30k. Type **79** 20 20
314 50k. Potters 40 20
315 70k. Pirogue-builder (49 × 36 mm) 50 30

80 Laotian and African Children

1971. Racial Equality Year.
316 **80** 30k. blue, red and green 25 15
317 – 60k. violet, red and yellow 45 30
DESIGN: 60k. Laotian dancers and musicians.

81 Buddhist Monk at That Luang

1971. 50th Anniv of Vientiane Rotary Club.
318 **81** 30k. violet, brown and blue 35 20
319 – 70k. grey, red and blue . . 50 35
DESIGN—VERT: 70k. Laotian girl on "Dragon" staircase.

82 "Dendrobium agregatum" **83** Dancers from France and Laos

1971. Laotian Orchids. Multicoloured.
320 30k. Type **82** (postage) . . . 45 25
321 40k. "Rynchostylis giganterum" 65 40
322 50k. "Ascocentrum miniatur" (horiz) 70 40
323 60k. "Paphiopedilum exul" 90 50
324 70k. "Trichoglottis fasciata" (horiz) 95 65
325 80k. Cattleya (horiz) . . . . 1·10 65
326 125k. Brazilian cattleya (horiz) (air) . . . . 1·75 80
327 150k. "Vanda teres" (horiz) 1·90 1·10
Nos. 321, 323 and 325 are smaller, 22 × 36 or 36 × 22 mm. Nos. 326/7 are larger, 48 × 27 mm.

1971. Air. "Twin Cities" of St. Astier (France) and Keng-Kok (Laos).
328 **83** 30k. brown and light brown 20 15
329 70k. purple and plum . . . 30 20
330 100k. green and deep green 55 35

84 Common Palm Civet

1971. Wild Animals (3rd series).
331 **84** 25k. black, violet and blue (postage) 20 20
332 40k. black, green and olive 30 30
333 – 50k. orange and green . . 45 40
334 – 85k. brown, green & emerald 70 60
335 – 300k. brown and green (air) . . . . 1·40 1·00
DESIGNS: 50k. Lesser Malay chevrotain; 85k. Sambar; 300k. Javan rhinoceros.

85 Laotian Woman (design from 1952 issue)

1971. 20th Anniv of Laotian Stamps.
336 **85** 30k. chocolate, brown and violet (postage) 20 20
337 – 40k. multicoloured 20 20
338 – 50k. black, flesh and blue 35 25
339 – 125k. violet, brn & grn (air) 70 50
DESIGNS—36 × 48 mm: 40k. Violinist (As No. 64); 50k. Rama (As No. 48); 125k. "The Offertory" (As Type **16**).

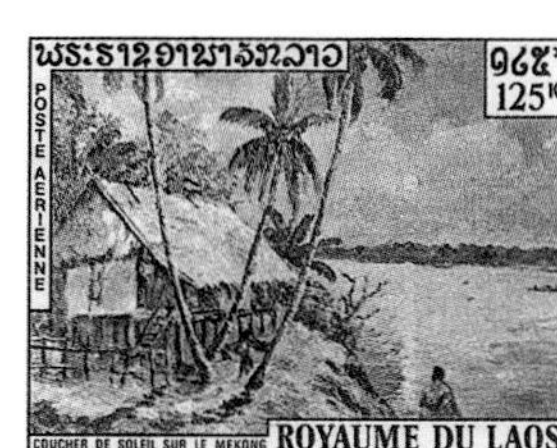

86 "Sunset on the Mekong"

1971. Air. Paintings by Chamnane Prisayane. Mult.
341 125k. Type **86** 55 45
342 150k. "Quiet Morning at Ban Tane Pieo" 75 65

87 Children reading Book

1972. International Book Year.
343 **87** 30k. green (postage) . . . 20 15
344 – 70k. brown 30 25
345 – 125k. violet (air) 70 45
DESIGNS—36 × 22 mm: 70k. Laotian illustrating manuscript. 48 × 27 mm: 125k. Father showing manuscripts to children.

88 Nam Ngum Dam and Obelisk

1972. 25th Anniv of U.N. Economic Commission for Asia and the Far East (E.C.A.F.E.). Multicoloured.
346 40k. Type **88** (postage) . . . 20 20
347 80k. Type **88** 30 25
348 145k. Lake and spill-way, Nam Ngum Dam (air) . . 80 50

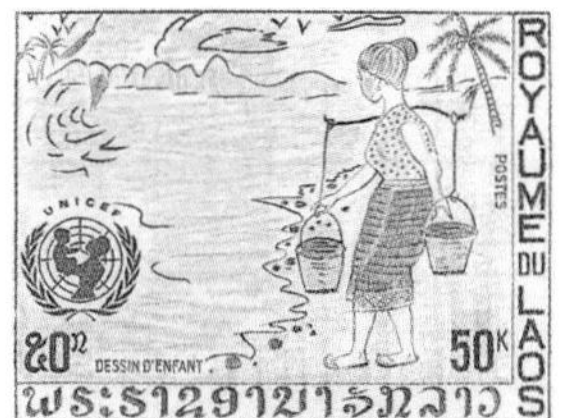

89 "The Water-carrier"

1972. 25th Anniv of UNICEF Drawings by Lao Schoolchildren. Multicoloured.
349 50k. Type **89** (postage) . . . 25 20
350 80k. "Teaching Bamboo-weaving" 30 25
351 120k. "Riding a Water-buffalo" (air) 70 45

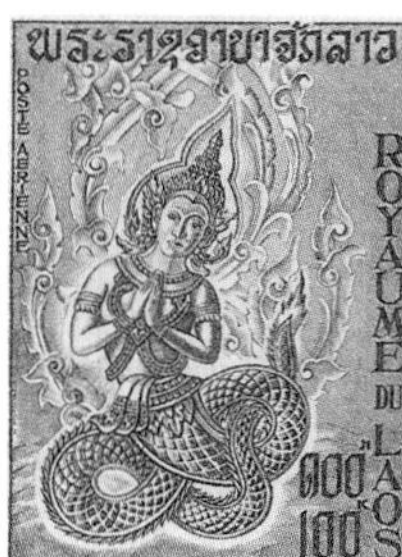

90 "Nakharath"

1972. Air. Laotian Mythology (2nd series).
352 **90** 100k. turquoise 40 30
353 – 120k. lilac 70 45
354 – 150k. brown 80 55
DESIGNS: 120k. "Nang Kinnali"; 150k. "Norasing".

91 Festival Offerings

1972. Air. That Luang Religious Festival.
355 **91** 110k. brown 45 35
356 – 125k. purple 65 50
DESIGN: 125k. Festival procession.

1972. Air. Paintings by Marc Leguay (4th series). As T **69**. Multicoloured.
357 50k. "In the Paddy Field" (detail) 25 20
358 50k. "In the Paddy Field" (different detail) 25 20
359 70k. "Village in the Rainy Season" (detail) 35 25
360 70k. "Village in the Rainy Season" (different detail) 35 25
361 120k. "Laotian Mother" . . 70 45
Nos. 357/8 and 359/60 when placed together form the complete painting in each case.

92 Attopeu Religious Costume **93** "Lion" Guardian, That Luang

1973. Regional Costumes.
362 **92** 40k. yellow, mauve & brown (postage) 40 20
363 – 90k. black, red and brown 70 30
364 – 120k. brown, sepia and mauve (air) 70 35
365 – 150k. ochre, red and brown 90 45
DESIGNS: 90k. Phongsaly festival costume; 120k. Luang Prabang wedding costume; 150k. Vientiane evening dress.

1973. 55th Anniv of Lions International.
366 **93** 40k. red, pur & bl (postage) 35 20
367 80k. red, yellow and blue 55 35
368 – 150k. multicoloured (air) 1·00 70
DESIGN—48 × 27 mm: 150k. Lions emblems and statue of King Saysetthathirath, Vientiane.

94 Satellite passing Rahu

1973. Traditional and Modern Aspects of Space. Multicoloured.
369 80k. Type **94** 35 20
370 150k. Landing module and Laotian festival rocket . . 80 40

95 Dr. Gerhard Hansen and Map of Laos

1973. Centenary of Identification of Leprosy Bacillus by Hansen.
371 **95** 40k. purple, dp pur & orge 45 30
372 80k. purple, brown & yell 70 40

96 "Benediction" **97** "Nang Mekhala". (Goddess of the Sea)

1973. 25th Anniv of Laotian Boy Scouts Association.
373 **96** 70k. yellow & brn (postage) 55 35
374 – 110k. violet and orange (air) 55 20
375 – 150k. blue, drab and brown 75 35
DESIGNS—48 × 27 mm: 110k. Campfire entertainment; 150k. Scouts helping flood victims, Vientiane, 1966.

1973. Air. Centenary of World Meteorological Organization.
376 **97** 90k. lilac, red and brown 55 30
377 – 150k. brown, red & lt brn 1·00 50
DESIGN—HORIZ: 150k. "Chariot of the Sun".

99 Interpol H.Q., Paris

1973. 50th Anniv of Int Criminal Police Organization (Interpol).

382	**99**	40k. blue (postage)	30	20
383		80k. brown and light brown	35	20
384	–	150k. violet, red and green (air)	80	35

DESIGN—48 × 27 mm: 150k. Woman in opium poppy field.

100 "Phra Sratsvady"

1974. Air. Laotian Mythology (3rd series).

385	**100**	100k. red, brown and lilac	70	30
386	–	110k. brown, lilac and red	85	40
387	–	150k. violet, brown and light brown	1·25	60

DESIGNS: 110k. "Phra Indra"; 150k. "Phra Phrom".

101 Boy and Postbox

102 "Eranthemum nervosum"

1974. Centenary of U.P.U.

388	**101**	70k. brown, green and blue (postage)	40	25
389		80k. brown, blue and green	50	30
390	–	200k. brown and red (air)	1·75	1·00

DESIGN—48 × 36 mm: 200k. Laotian girls with letters, and U.P.U. Monument, Berne (Type **105**).

1974. Laotian Flora.

391	**102**	30k. violet & grn (postage)	35	25
392	–	50k. multicoloured	50	30
393	–	80k. red, green and brown	80	40
394	–	500k. green & brown (air)	3·50	1·90

DESIGNS—As T **102**: HORIZ: 50k. Water lily; 80k. Red silk-cotton. 36 × 36 mm: 500k. Pitcher plant.

103 Mekong Ferry carrying Bus

1974. Laotian Transport.

395	**103**	25k. brown & orge (postage)	45	20
396	–	90k. brown and bistre	1·10	70
397	–	250k. brown & green (air)	2·00	1·25

DESIGNS—VERT: 90k. Bicycle rickshaw. HORIZ: 250k. Mekong house boat.

104 Marconi, and Laotians with Transistor Radio

1974. Birth Centenary of Guglielmo Marconi (radio pioneer).

398	**104**	60k. grey, green and brown (postage)	30	20
399		90k. grey, brown and green	45	30
400	–	200k. blue and brown (air)	1·50	60

DESIGN: 200k. Communications methods.

105 U.P.U. Monument and Laotian Girls

1974. Air. Centenary of U.P.U.

401	**105**	500k. lilac and red	2·25	1·75

106 "Diastocera wallichi"

1974. Beetles.

403	**106**	50k. brown, black and green (postage)	55	45
404	–	90k. black, turquoise & grn	1·10	60
405	–	100k. black, orange & brn	1·25	85
406	–	110k. violet, red & grn (air)	1·25	55

DESIGNS: 90k. "Macrochenus isabellunus"; 100k. "Purpuricenus malaccensis"; 110k. "Sternocera multipunctata".

107 Pagoda and Sapphire

1974. "Mineral Riches".

407	**107**	100k. brown, green & blue	40	30
408	–	110k. brown, blue & yellow	50	30

DESIGN: 110k. Gold-panning and necklace.

108 King Savang Vatthana, Prince Souvanna Phouma and Prince Souvanouvong

1975. 1st Anniv (1974) of Laotian Peace Treaty.

409	**108**	80k. brown, ochre & green	30	25
410		300k. brown, ochre & pur	70	50
411		420k. brown, ochre and turquoise	80	60

109 Fortune-teller's Chart

1975. Chinese New Year ("Year of the Rabbit").

413	**109**	40k. brown and green	35	20
414	–	200k. black, brown and green	1·10	50
415	–	350k. brown, green and blue	2·00	90

DESIGNS—HORIZ: 200k. Fortune-teller. VERT: 350k. Woman riding hare.

110 U.N. Emblem and Frieze

112

1975. International Women's Year.

416	**110**	100k. blue and turquoise	40	25
417	–	200k. orange and green	70	35

DESIGN: 200k. I.W.Y. Emblem.

1975. "Pravet Sandone" Religious Festival.

420	**112**	80k. multicoloured	35	20
421	–	110k. multicoloured	45	25
422	–	120k. multicoloured	55	45
423	–	130k. multicoloured	90	50

DESIGNS: 110k. to 130k. Various legends.

113 Buddha and Stupas

1975. UNESCO Campaign for Preservation of Borobudur Temple (in Indonesia).

424	**113**	100k. green, blue & brown	30	25
425	–	200k. ochre, green & brown	55	30

DESIGN: 200k. Temple sculptures.

114 Laotian Arms

115 Thathiang, Vien-Tran

1976. Multicoloured, background colour given.

427	**114**	1k. blue	10	10
428		2k. mauve	10	10
429		5k. green	15	10
430		10k. violet	20	20
431		200k. orange	1·00	1·00

1976. Pagodas. Multicoloured.

433	1k. Type **115**	10	10
434	2k. Phonsi, Luang Prabang	10	10
435	30k. Type **115**	10	10
436	80k. As 2k.	40	30
437	100k. As 2k.	50	45
438	300k. Type **115**	1·50	90

116 Silversmith

1977. Laotian Crafts. Multicoloured.

440	1k. Type **116**	10	10
441	2k. Weaver	10	10
442	20k. Potter	25	25
443	50k. Basket-weaver (vert)	30	25

117 Gubarev, Grechko and "Salyut" Space Station

1977. 60th Anniv of Russian Revolution. Mult.

445	5k. Type **117**	10	10
446	20k. Lenin	10	10
447	50k. As 20k.	20	20
448	60k. Type **117**	35	25
449	100k. Government Palace, Vientiane, and Kremlin, Moscow (horiz)	70	50
450	250k. As 100k.	1·60	1·25

118 Laotian Arms

119 Soldiers with Flag

1978.

452	**118**	5k. yellow and black	10	10
453		10k. sepia and black	10	10
454		50k. purple and black	15	10
455		100k. green and black	50	25
456		250k. violet and black	1·25	70

1978. Army Day. Multicoloured.

457	20k. Type **119**	10	10
458	40k. Soldiers attacking village (horiz)	15	15
459	300k. Anti-aircraft guns	1·60	75

120 Marchers with Banner

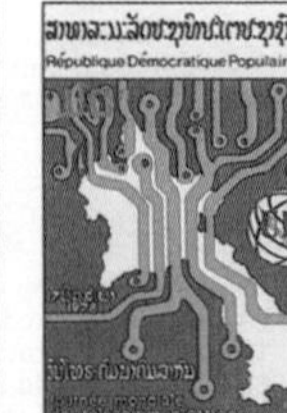

121 Printed Circuit and Map of Laos

1978. National Day. Multicoloured.

460	20k. Type **120**	10	10
461	50k. Women with flag	25	15
462	400k. Dancer	1·75	75

1979. World Telecommunications Day.

464	**121**	30k. orange, brown & sil	10	10
465	–	250k. multicoloured	70	50

DESIGN: 250k. Printed circuit, map of Laos and transmitter tower.

122 Woman posting Letter

1979. 15th Anniv of Asian-Oceanic Postal Union. Multicoloured.

466	5k. Type **122**	10	10
467	10k. Post Office counter	10	10
468	80k. As 10k.	40	25
469	100k. Type **122**	50	30

123 Children playing Ball

1979. International Year of the Child (1st issue). Multicoloured. Without gum.

470	20k. Type **123**	10	10
471	50k. Children at school (horiz)	25	15
472	200k. Mother feeding child	1·50	45
473	500k. Nurse immunising child	4·25	1·10

124 Elephant, Buffalo and Pirogues

1979. Transport. Multicoloured.

475	5k. Type **124**	15	10
476	10k. Buffalo carts	15	10
477	70k. As No. 476	50	15
478	500k. Type **124**	2·25	1·25

125 Dancing Child

1979. International Year of the Child (2nd issue). Multicoloured. Without gum.

479	100k. Children playing musical instruments (horiz)	40	25
480	200k. Child releasing dove	65	40
481	600k. Type **125**	2·25	1·25

126 Forest and Paddy Field

1980. 5th Anniv of Republic (1st issue) and 25th Anniv of People's Front. Mult. Without gum.

No.	Description		
483	30c. Type **126**	15	10
484	50c. Classroom and doctor examining baby (horiz)	20	10
485	1k. Three women	50	20
486	2k. Dam and electricity pylons (horiz)	1·10	65

127 Lenin Reading

1980. 110th Birth Anniv of Lenin. Multicoloured.

No.	Description		
488	1k. Type **127**	15	10
489	2k. Lenin writing	35	15
490	3k. Lenin and Red Flag (vert)	55	20
491	4k. Lenin making speech (vert)	90	30

128 Workers in Field

1980. 5th Anniv of Republic (2nd issue). Multicoloured. Without gum.

No.	Description		
493	50c. Type **128**	10	10
494	1k.60 Loading logs on lorry and elephant hauling logs	30	15
495	4k.60 Veterinary workers tending animals	70	35
496	5k.40 Workers in paddy field	1·00	45

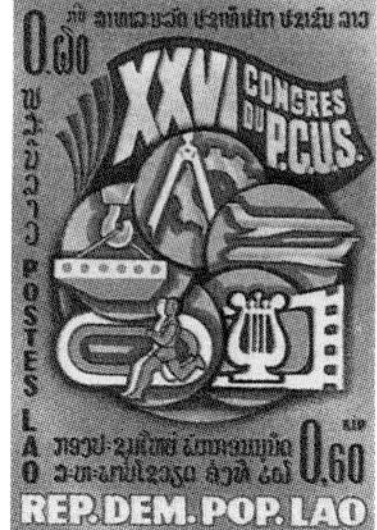

129 Emblems of Industry, Technology, Transport, Sport and Art

1981. 26th P.C.U.S. (Communist Party) Congress. Multicoloured.

No.	Description		
498	60c. Type **129**	15	10
499	4k.60 Communist star breaking manacles and globe	80	30
500	5k. Laurel branch and broken bomb	1·00	35

131 Player heading Ball

132 Disabled Person on Telephone

1981. World Cup Football Championship, Spain (1982) (1st issue). Multicoloured.

No.	Description		
503	1k. Type **131**	20	10
504	2k. Receiving ball	35	10
505	3k. Passing ball	55	20
506	4k. Goalkeeper diving for ball (horiz)	80	25
507	5k. Dribbling	1·10	40
508	6k. Kicking ball	1·50	50

See also Nos. 545/50.

1981. International Year of Disabled Persons. Multicoloured.

No.	Description		
509	3k. Type **132**	50	20
510	5k. Disabled teacher	1·10	40
511	12k. Person in wheelchair mending net	3·00	60

133 Wild Cat

1981. Wild Cats. Multicoloured.

No.	Description		
512	10c. Type **133**	10	10
513	20c. Fishing cat	10	10
514	30c. Caracal	10	10
515	40c. Clouded leopard	15	10
516	50c. Flat-headed cat	15	10
517	9k. Jungle cat	3·00	70

134 Dish Aerial and Flag

1981. 6th National Day Festival. Multicoloured.

No.	Description		
518	3k. Type **134**	50	30
519	4k. Soldier and flag	65	40
520	5k. Girls presenting flowers to soldier, flag and map of Laos	95	50

135 Indian Elephant

1982. Indian Elephant. Multicoloured.

No.	Description		
521	1k. Type **135**	20	10
522	2k. Elephant carrying log	45	15
523	3k. Elephant with passengers	70	25
524	4k. Elephant in trap	90	35
525	5k. Elephant and young	1·25	35
526	5k.50 Herd of elephants	1·60	50

136 Laotian Wrestling

1982. Wrestling.

No.	Description		
527 **136**	50c. multicoloured	10	10
528 –	1k.20 multicoloured	20	10
529 –	2k. multicoloured	35	20
530 –	2k.50 multicoloured	55	30
531 –	4k. multicoloured	80	35
532 –	5k. multicoloured	1·40	45

DESIGNS: 1k.20 to 5k. Various wrestling scenes.

137 "Nymphaea zanzibariensis"

1982. Water Lilies. Multicoloured.

No.	Description		
533	30c. Type **137**	10	10
534	40c. "Nelumbo nucifera" "Gaertn Rose"	10	10
535	60c. "Nymphaea rosea"	10	10
536	3k. "Nymphaea nouchali"	60	35
537	4k. "Nymphaea" White	95	40
538	7k. "Nelumbo nucifera" "Gaertn White"	1·90	50

138 Barn Swallow

1982. Birds. Multicoloured.

No.	Description		
539	50c. Type **138**	25	10
540	1k. Hoopoe	45	10
541	2k. River kingfisher	1·75	15
542	3k. Black-naped blue monarch	1·40	15
543	4k. Grey wagtail (horiz)	1·50	65
544	10k. Long-tailed tailor bird (horiz)	5·00	85

139 Football

1982. World Cup Football Championship, Spain (2nd issue).

No.	Description		
545 **139**	1k. multicoloured	20	10
546 –	2k. multicoloured	40	10
547 –	3k. multicoloured	55	20
548 –	4k. multicoloured	70	25
549 **139**	5k. multicoloured	1·10	40
550 –	6k. multicoloured	1·40	45

DESIGNS: 2, 3, 4, 6k. Various football scenes.

140 "Herona marathus"

1982. Butterflies. Multicoloured.

No.	Description		
552	1k. Type **140**	20	10
553	2k. "Neptis paraka"	40	20
554	3k. "Euripus halitherses"	70	30
555	4k. "Lebadea martha"	1·10	40
556	5k. "Iton semamora" (42 × 26 mm)	1·75	75
557	6k. Common palm fly (59 × 41 mm)	2·00	1·00

142 River Raft

1982. River Craft. Multicoloured.

No.	Description		
559	50c. Type **142**	10	10
560	60c. River sampan	15	10
561	1k. River house boat	25	10
562	2k. River passenger steamer	50	25
563	3k. River ferry	70	30
564	8k. Self-propelled barge	1·90	70

143 Vat Chanh

1982. Pagodas. Multicoloured.

No.	Description		
565	50c. Type **143**	10	10
566	60c. Vat Inpeng	15	10
567	1k. Vat Dong Mieng	25	10
568	2k. Ho Tay	50	20
569	3k. Vat Ho Pha Keo	70	25
570	8k. Vat Sisaket	1·90	60

1982. Various stamps optd **1982**.

No.	Description		
571 **114**	1k. multicoloured		
572 **116**	1k. multicoloured		
573 –	2k. multicoloured (441)		
574 **117**	5k. multicoloured		
575 **118**	5k. yellow and black		
576 **122**	5k. multicoloured		
577 **124**	5k. multicoloured		
578 –	10k. multicoloured (467)		
579 –	10k. multicoloured (476)		
580 –	20k. multicoloured (446)		
581 **119**	20k. multicoloured		
582 **121**	30k. orange, brown & sil		
583 –	40k. multicoloured (458)		
584 –	50k. multicoloured (443)		
585 –	70k. multicoloured (477)		
586 –	80k. multicoloured (468)		
587 **122**	100k. multicoloured		
588 **114**	200k. multicoloured		
589 **121**	250k. multicoloured		

145 Poodle

1982. Dogs. Multicoloured.

No.	Description		
591	50c. Type **145**	10	10
592	60c. Samoyed	10	10
593	1k. Boston terrier	25	10
594	2k. Cairn terrier	65	20
595	3k. Chihuahua	90	25
596	8k. Bulldog	2·50	60

146 Woman watering Crops

1982. World Food Day. Multicoloured.

No.	Description		
597	7k. Type **146**	1·40	45
598	8k. Woman transplanting rice	1·75	55

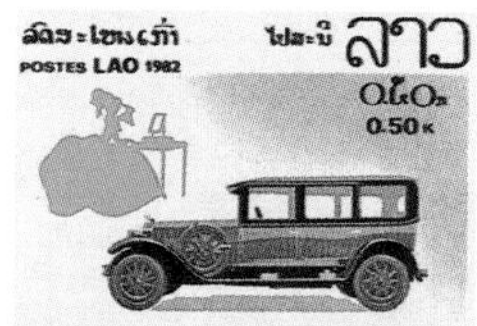

147 Fiat, 1925

1982. Cars. Multicoloured.

No.	Description		
599	50c. Type **147**	10	10
600	60c. Peugeot, 1925	10	10
601	1k. Berliet, 1925	25	10
602	2k. Ballot, 1925	65	20
603	3k. Renault, 1926	90	25
604	8k. Ford, 1925	2·50	60

148 President Souphanouvong

1982. 7th Anniv of Republic. Multicoloured.

No.	Description		
605	50c. Type **148**	10	10
606	1k. Tractors (horiz)	25	10
607	2k. Cow (horiz)	35	20
608	3k. Lorry passing dish aerial (horiz)	50	35
609	4k. Nurse examining child	75	35
610	5k. Classroom (horiz)	95	45
611	6k. Dancer	1·40	50

149 Dimitrov, Flag and Arms of Bulgaria

1982. Birth Centenary of Georgi Dimitrov (Bulgarian statesman).

No.	Description		
612 **149**	10k. multicoloured	1·90	1·25

150 Kremlin and Arms of U.S.S.R.

151 Hurdling

1982. 60th Anniv of U.S.S.R. Multicoloured.

613 3k. Type **150** 60 40
614 4k. Doves and maps of U.S.S.R. and Laos 90 70

1983. Olympic Games, Los Angeles (1984) (1st issue). Multicoloured.

616 50c. Type **151** 10 10
617 1k. Javelin 20 10
618 2k. Basketball 40 15
619 3k. Diving 60 25
620 4k. Gymnastics 80 40
621 10k. Weightlifting . . . . . 2·25 60

See also Nos. 708/14.

152 Bucking Horse

1983. Horses. Multicoloured.

623 50c. Type **152** 10 10
624 1k. Rearing black horse . . . 20 10
625 2k. Trotting brown horse . . 40 15
626 3k. Dappled grey horse . . . 65 25
627 4k. Wild horse crossing snow 90 40
628 10k. Horse in paddock . . . 2·50 60

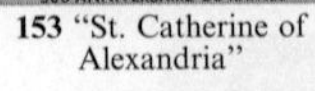

153 "St. Catherine of Alexandria"

154 A. Gubarev (Soviet) and V. Remek (Czechoslovak)

1983. 500th Birth Anniv of Raphael (artist). Multicoloured.

629 50c. Type **153** 10 10
630 1k. "Adoration of the Kings" 20 10
631 2k. "Madonna of the Grand Duke" 40 15
632 3k. "St. George and the Dragon" 65 25
633 4k. "The Vision of Ezekiel" 90 35
634 10k. "Adoration of the Kings" (different) . . . . 2·50 60

1983. Cosmonauts. Multicoloured.

636 50c. Type **154** 10 10
637 50c. P. Klimuk (Soviet) and Miroslaw Hermaszewski (Polish) 10 10
638 1k. V. Bykovsky (Soviet) and Sigmund Jahn (East German) 20 10
639 1k. Nikolai Rukavishnikov (Soviet) and Georgi Ivanov (Bulgarian) 20 10
640 2k. V. Kubasov (Soviet) and Bertalan Farkas (Hungarian) 40 15
641 3k. V. Dzhanibekov (Soviet) and Gurragchaa (Mongolian) 65 25
642 4k. L. Popov (Soviet) and D. Prunariu (Rumanian) 80 35
643 6k. Soviet cosmonaut and Arnaldo Tamayo (Cuban) 1·25 40
644 10k. Soviet and French cosmonauts . . . . 2·40 60

155 Jacques Charles's Hydrogen Balloon, 1783

1983. Bicentenary of Manned Flight. Mult.

646 50c. Type **155** 10 10
647 1k. Blanchard and Jeffries' balloon, 1785 . . . . . . 20 10
648 2k. Vincenzo Lunardi's balloon (London–Ware flight), 1784 . . . . 40 15
649 3k. Modern hot-air balloon over city 75 25
650 4k. Massed balloon ascent, 1890 . . . . 80 30
651 10k. Auguste Piccard's stratosphere balloon "F.N.R.S.", 1931 . . . . 2·50 60

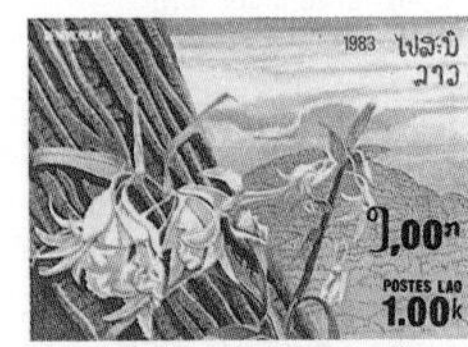

157 "Dendrobium sp."

1983. Flowers. Multicoloured.

654 1k. Type **157** 20 10
655 2k. "Aerides odoratum" . . 40 15
656 3k. "Dendrobium aggregatum" 70 25
657 4k. "Dendrobium" 80 30
658 5k. "Moschatum" . . . . . 1·00 40
659 6k. "Dendrobium sp." (different) . . . . 1·25 45

158 Downhill Skiing

1983. Winter Olympic Games, Sarajevo (1984) (1st issue). Multicoloured.

660 50c. Type **158** 10 10
661 1k. Slalom 25 10
662 2k. Ice hockey 50 15
663 3k. Speed skating 75 25
664 4k. Ski jumping . . . . . . 1·00 30
665 10k. Luge . . . . 2·40 80

See also Nos. 696/702.

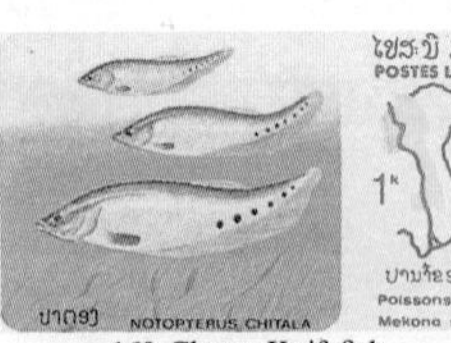

160 Clown Knifefish

1983. Fishes of Mekong River. Multicoloured.

668 1k. Type **160** 30 15
669 2k. Common carp 65 25
670 3k. Lesser Mekong catfish . . 1·00 45
671 4k. Giant barb . . . . 1·10 50
672 5k. Black shark . . . . . . 1·50 70
673 6k. Nile mouthbrooder . . . 2·00 75

161 Magellan and "Vitoria"

1983. Explorers and their Ships. Multicoloured.

674 1k. Type **161** 50 20
675 2k. Jacques Cartier and "Grande Hermine" 90 30
676 3k. Columbus and "Santa Maria" . . . . 1·40 50
677 4k. Pedro Alvares Cabral and "El Ray" . . . . 1·50 60
678 5k. Cook and H.M.S. "Resolution" . . . . . . 2·10 80
679 6k. Charcot and "Pourquoi-pas?" . . . . 2·40 90

No. 679 is wrongly inscribed "Cabot".

162 Tabby Cat

1983. Domestic Cats. Multicoloured.

680 1k. Type **162** 20 10
681 2k. Long-haired Persian . . . 40 15
682 3k. Siamese 65 25
683 4k. Burmese 75 30
684 5k. Persian . . . . 1·00 40
685 6k. Tortoiseshell . . . . . . 1·25 45

1983. Nos. 430 and 466 optd **1983**.

685a **122** 5k. multicoloured . . .
685b **114** 10k. multicoloured . . .

163 Marx, Book, Sun and Signature

1983. Death Centenary of Karl Marx. Mult.

686 1k. Marx, dove, globe and flags 30 10
687 4k. Type **163** 90 35
688 6k. Marx and flags . . . . . 1·60 65

164 Elephant dragging Log

1983. 8th Anniv of Republic. Multicoloured.

689 1k. Type **164** 30 10
690 4k. Cattle and pig (horiz) . . 90 35
691 6k. Crops . . . . 1·60 65

165 Carrier Pigeon and Telex Machine

1983. World Communications Year. Multicoloured.

692 50c. Type **165** 10 10
693 1k. Early telephone, handset and receiver 25 10
694 4k. Television tube and aerial 80 35
695 6k. Satellite and dish aerial 1·50 55

166 Ice Skating

167 Tiger

1984. Winter Olympic Games, Sarajevo (2nd issue). Multicoloured.

696 50c. Type **166** 10 10
697 1k. Speed skating 30 10
698 2k. Biathlon 40 15
699 3k. Luge (horiz) 80 30
700 4k. Downhill skiing (horiz) 95 35
701 5k. Ski jumping . . . . . . 1·40 45
702 6k. Slalom . . . . 1·60 55

1984. Endangered Animals. The Tiger. Mult.

704 25c. Type **167** 10 10
705 25c. Tigers (horiz) 10 10
706 3k. Tiger and cubs (horiz) . . 90 30
707 4k. Tiger cubs . . . . 1·10 40

168 Diving

1984. Olympic Games, Los Angeles (2nd issue). Multicoloured.

708 50c. Type **168** 10 10
709 1k. Volleyball 25 10
710 2k. Running 40 15
711 4k. Basketball 85 25
712 5k. Judo . . . . 1·10 35
713 6k. Football . . . . 1·50 40
714 7k. Gymnastics . . . . . . 1·75 50

169 Tuned Drums

1984. Musical Instruments. Multicoloured.

716 1k. Type **169** 20 10
717 2k. Xylophone 35 15
718 3k. Pair of drums 70 25
719 4k. Hand drum 90 25
720 5k. Barrel drum . . . . . . 1·10 35
721 6k. Pipes and string instrument . . . . 1·75 55

170 National Flag

171 Chess Game

1984. National Day. Multicoloured.

722 60c. Type **170** 15 10
723 1k. National arms 35 10
724 2k. As No. 723 . . . . 50 20

1984. 60th Anniv of World Chess Federation. Multicoloured.

725 50c. Type **171** 10 10
726 1k. Renaissance game from "The Three Ages of Man" (miniature attr. to Estienne Porchier) 25 10
727 2k. Woman teaching girls . . 40 15
728 2k. Margrave Otto IV of Brandenburg playing chess with his wife 40 15
729 3k. Four men at chessboard 75 30
730 4k. Two women playing . . . 1·00 35
731 8k. Two men playing . . . . 2·25 55

Nos. 725, 727 and 729/31 show illustrations from King Alfonso X's "Book of Chess, Dice and Tablings".

172 "Cardinal Nino de Guevara" (El Greco)

173 "Adonis aestivalis"

1984. "Espana 84" International Stamp Exhibition, Madrid. Multicoloured.

733 50c. Type **172** 10 10
734 1k. "Gaspar de Guzman, Duke of Olivares, on Horseback" (Velazquez) . . 25 10
735 2k. "The Annunciation" (Murillo) 40 15
736 2k. "Portrait of a Lady" (Zurbaran) 40 15
737 3k. "The Family of Charles IV" (Goya) 75 30

738	4k. "Two Harlequins" (Picasso)	1·00	35
739	8k. "Abstract" (Miro)	2·25	55

1984. Woodland Flowers. Multicoloured.

741	50c. Type **173**	10	10
742	1k. "Alpinia speciosa"	25	10
743	2k. "Cassia lechenaultiana"	40	15
744	2k. "Aeschynanthus speciosus"	40	15
745	3k. "Datura meteloides"	75	30
746	4k. "Quamoclit pennata"	95	35
747	8k. "Commelina benghalensis"	2·25	55

174 Nazzaro

1984. 19th Universal Postal Union Congress Philatelic Salon, Hamburg. Cars. Multicoloured.

748	50c. Type **174**	10	10
749	1k. Daimler	25	10
750	2k. Delage	40	15
751	2k. Fiat "S 57/14B"	40	15
752	3k. Bugatti	75	30
753	4k. Itala	1·10	35
754	8k. Blitzen Benz	2·25	55

175 "Madonna and Child"

1984. 450th Death Anniv of Correggio (artist). Multicoloured.

756	50c. Type **175**	10	10
757	1k. Detail showing horsemen resting	25	10
758	2k. "Madonna and Child" (different)	40	15
759	2k. "Mystical Marriage of St. Catherine"	40	15
760	3k. "Four Saints"	75	30
761	4k. "Noli me Tangere"	95	35
762	8k. "Christ bids Farewell to the Virgin Mary"	1·90	55

176 "Luna 1"

1984. Space Exploration. Multicoloured.

764	50c. Type **176**	10	10
765	1k. "Luna 2"	25	10
766	2k. "Luna 3"	40	15
767	2k. Kepler and "Sputnik 2"	40	15
768	3k. Newton and Lunokhod 2	75	30
769	4k. Jules Verne and "Luna 13"	1·00	35
770	8k. Copernicus and space station	2·10	60

177 Malaclemys Terrapin

1984. Reptiles. Multicoloured.

771	50c. Type **177**	10	10
772	1k. Banded krait	25	10
773	2k. Indian python (vert)	40	15
774	2k. Reticulated python	40	15
775	3k. Tokay gecko	80	30
776	4k. "Natrix subminiata" (snake)	1·10	40
777	8k. Dappled ground gecko	2·40	65

178 Greater Glider

1984. "Ausipex 84" International Stamp Exhibition, Melbourne. Marsupials. Mult.

778	50c. Type **178**	10	10
779	1k. Platypus	25	10
780	2k. Southern hairy-nosed wombat ("Lasiorhinus latifrons")	40	15
781	2k. Tasmanian devil ("Sarcophilus harrisii")	40	15
782	3k. Thylacine	75	30
783	4k. Tiger cat	1·00	35
784	8k. Wallaby	2·10	60

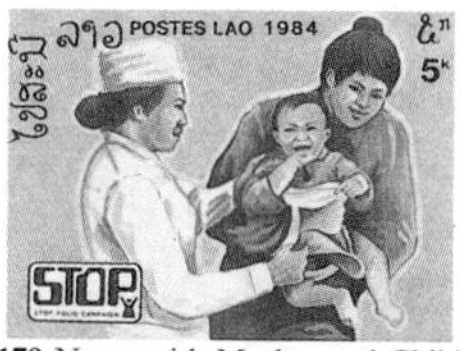

179 Nurse with Mother and Child

1984. Anti-poliomyelitis Campaign. Multicoloured.

786	5k. Type **179**	1·10	50
787	6k. Doctor inoculating child	1·40	55

180 Dragon Stair-rail

1984. Laotian Art. Multicoloured.

788	50c. Type **180**	10	10
789	1k. Capital of column	25	10
790	2k. Decorative panel depicting god	40	15
791	2k. Decorative panel depicting leaves	40	15
792	3k. Stylized leaves (horiz)	70	30
793	4k. Triangular flower decoration (horiz)	1·00	35
794	8k. Circular lotus flower decoration	1·90	60

181 River House Boats

1984. 9th Anniv of Republic. Multicoloured.

795	1k. Type **181**	45	15
796	2k. Passengers boarding Fokker Friendship airliner	50	20
797	4k. Building a bridge	1·10	45
798	10k. Building a road	2·50	1·00

182 Players with Ball

1985. World Cup Football Championship, Mexico (1986) (1st issue). Multicoloured.

799	50c. Type **182**	10	10
800	1k. Heading the ball	25	10
801	2k. Defending the ball	45	15
802	3k. Running with ball	70	20
803	4k. Taking possession of ball	1·10	35
804	5k. Heading the ball (different)	1·40	45
805	6k. Saving a goal	1·75	55

See also Nos. 868/74.

183 Motor Cycle

1985. Centenary of Motor Cycle. Multicoloured.

807	50c. Type **183**	10	10
808	1k. Gnome Rhone, 1920	25	10
809	2k. F.N. "M67C", 1928	45	15
810	3k. Indian "Chief", 1930	70	20
811	4k. Rudge Multi, 1914	1·10	35
812	5k. Honda "Benly J", 1953	1·40	45
813	6k. CZ, 1938	1·75	55

1985. Various stamps optd **1985**.

813a	– 40k. multicoloured (458)		
813b	– 50k. multicoloured (443)		
813c	– 50k. multicoloured (447)		
813d	– 70k. multicoloured (477)		
813e	– 80k. multicoloured (468)		
813f	– 100k. multicoloured (449)		
813g	**122** 100k. multicoloured		
813h	**114** 200k. multicoloured		
813i	– 250k. multicoloured (450)		
813j	**118** 250k. violet and black		
813k	**121** 250k. multicoloured		
813m	– 300k. multicoloured (459)		

184 Fly Agaric

1985. Fungi. Multicoloured.

814	50c. Type **184**	15	10
815	1k. Cep	30	10
816	2k. Shaggy ink cap ("Coprinus comatus")	70	20
817	2k. The blusher ("Amanita rubescens")	70	20
818	3k. Downy boletus	1·25	30
819	4k. Parasol mushroom	2·10	45
820	8k. Brown roll-rim	3·25	90

184a Battle Plan, Kursk, and Tanks

1985. 40th Anniv of End of Second World War. Multicoloured.

820a	1k. Type **184a**	30	15
820b	2k. Monument and military parade, Red Square, Moscow	60	25
820c	4k. Street battle and battle plan, Stalingrad	1·25	40
820d	5k. Battle plan and Reichstag, Berlin	1·50	50
820e	6k. Soviet Memorial, Berlin-Treptow, and military parade at Brandenburg Gate	1·75	60

185 Lenin reading "Pravda"

1985. 115th Birth Anniv of Lenin. Multicoloured.

821	1k. Type **185**	25	10
822	2k. Lenin (vert)	45	30
823	10k. Lenin addressing meeting (vert)	2·40	1·50

186 "Cattleya percivaliana"

1985. "Argentina '85" International Stamp Exhibition, Buenos Aires. Orchids. Multicoloured.

824	50c. Type **186**	10	10
825	1k. "Odontoglossum luteo-purpureum"	25	10
826	2k. "Cattleya lueddemanniana"	45	15
827	2k. "Maxillaria sanderiana"	45	15
828	3k. "Miltonia vexillaria"	70	25
829	4k. "Oncidium varicosum"	1·10	35
830	8k. "Cattleya dowiana"	2·50	70

187 Rhesus Macaque

188 "Saturn" Rocket on Launch Pad

1985. Mammals. Multicoloured.

832	2k. Type **187**	45	15
833	3k. Kouprey	70	25
834	4k. Porcupine (horiz)	1·10	35
835	5k. Asiatic black bear (horiz)	1·40	45
836	10k. Chinese pangolin	2·75	90

1985. 10th Anniv of "Apollo"–"Soyuz" Space Link. Multicoloured.

837	50c. Type **188**	10	10
838	1k. Soviet rocket on launch pad	25	10
839	2k. "Apollo" approaching "Soyuz 19" (horiz)	50	15
840	2k. "Soyuz 19" approaching "Apollo" (horiz)	50	15
841	3k. "Apollo" and crew T. Stafford, V. Brand and D. Stayton (horiz)	80	25
842	4k. "Soyuz 19" and crew A. Leonov and V. Kubasov (horiz)	1·10	35
843	8k. "Apollo" and "Soyuz 19" docked (horiz)	2·25	70

189 Fiat Biplane

1985. "Italia '85" International Stamp Exhibition, Rome. Multicoloured. (a) Aircraft. As T **189**.

844	50c. Type **189**	15	10
845	1k. Cant Z.501 Gabbiano flying boat	30	10
846	2k. Marina Fiat MF.5 flying boat	60	15
847	3k. Macchi Castoldi MC-100 flying boat	90	25
848	4k. Anzani biplane	1·25	35
849	5k. Ambrosini biplane	1·50	45
850	6k. Piaggio P-148	1·90	55

(b) Columbus and his Ships. Size 40 × 29 mm.

852	1k. "Pinta"	45	10
853	2k. "Nina"	60	10
854	3k. "Santa Maria"	90	25
855	4k. Christopher Columbus	1·25	35
856	5k. Map of Columbus's first voyage	1·50	45

190 U.N. and National Flags on Globe

191 Woman feeding Child

1985. 40th Anniv of U.N.O. Multicoloured.

857	2k. Type **190**	65	40
858	3k. U.N. emblem and Laotian arms on globe	95	55
859	10k. Map on globe	3·25	1·75

1985. Lao Health Services. Multicoloured.

860	1k. Type **191**	25	15
861	3k. Red Cross nurse injecting child (horiz)	90	40
862	4k. Red Cross nurse tending patient (horiz)	1·10	70
863	10k. Mother breast-feeding baby	2·50	1·50

192 Soldier, Workers and Symbols of Industry and Agriculture

1985. 10th Anniv of Republic. Multicoloured.

864	3k. Type **192**	80	50
865	10k. Soldier, workers and symbols of transport and communications	2·75	1·75

193 Soldier with Flag and Workers

1985. 30th Anniv of Lao People's Revolutionary Party. Multicoloured.

866	2k. Type **193**	70	40
867	8k. Soldier with flag and workers (different)	2·40	1·40

194 Footballers

194a Cosmonaut, "Mir" Space Complex and Earth

1986. World Cup Football Championship, Mexico (2nd issue).

868 **194**	50c. multicoloured	10	10
869 –	1k. multicoloured	25	10
870 –	2k. multicoloured	50	15
871 –	3k. multicoloured	75	25
872 –	4k. multicoloured	90	30
873 –	5k. multicoloured	1·10	40
874 –	6k. multicoloured	1·40	55

DESIGNS: 1k. to 6k. Various football scenes.

1986. 17th Soviet Communist Party Congress. Multicoloured.

875a	4k. Type **194a**	90	35
875b	20k. Lenin and Red Flag	4·50	95

195 "Pelargonium grandiflorum"

196 "Aporia hippia"

1986. Flowers. Multicoloured.

876	50c. Type **195**	10	10
877	1k. Columbine	25	10
878	2k. "Fuchsia globosa"	50	15
879	3k. "Crocus aureus"	75	25
880	4k. Hollyhock	90	30
881	5k. "Gladiolus purpureo"	1·10	45
882	6k. "Hyacinthus orientalis"	1·75	65

1986. Butterflies. Multicoloured.

883	50c. Type **196**	10	10
884	1k. "Euthalia irrubescens"	25	10
885	2k. "Japonica lutea"	50	15
886	3k. "Pratapa ctesia"	75	25
887	4k. Leaf butterfly	90	30
888	5k. Yellow orange-tip	1·10	45
889	6k. Chestnut tiger	1·75	65

197 Rocket launch at Baikanur Space Centre

198 Giraffe

1986. 25th Anniv of First Man in Space. Mult.

890	50c. Type **197**	10	10
891	1k. "Molniya" communications satellite	20	10
892	2k. "Salyut" space station (horiz)	50	20
893	3k. Yuri Gagarin, "Sputnik 1" and rocket debris (horiz)	70	30
894	4k. "Luna 3" and Moon	95	40
895	5k. Vladimir Komarov on first space walk	1·40	50
896	6k. "Luna 16" lifting off from Moon	1·60	90

1986. Animals. Multicoloured.

898	50c. Type **198**	10	10
899	1k. Lion	20	10
900	2k. African elephant	40	20
901	3k. Red kangaroo	60	30
902	4k. Koala	80	40
903	5k. Greater flamingo	1·40	40
904	6k. Giant panda	1·75	90

199 Boeing 747-100

1986. Air. Aircraft. Multicoloured.

906	20k. Type **199**	2·50	1·90
907	50k. Ilyushin Il-86	7·00	5·25

200 Great Argus Pheasant (½-size illustration)

1986. Pheasants. Multicoloured.

908	50c. Type **200**	10	10
909	1k. Silver pheasant	25	10
910	2k. Common pheasant	50	15
911	3k. Lady Amherst's pheasant	75	20
912	4k. Reeves's pheasant	90	30
913	5k. Golden pheasant	1·10	40
914	6k. Copper pheasant	1·75	65

201 Scarlet King Snake

1986. Snakes. Multicoloured.

915	50c. Corn snake	10	10
916	1k. Type **201**	25	10
917	1k. Richard's blind snake (vert)	25	10
918	2k. Western ring-necked snake	50	25
919	4k. Mangrove snake	90	40
920	5k. Indian python	1·10	50
921	6k. Common cobra (vert)	1·75	90

202 Bayeux Tapestry (detail) and Comet Head

1986. Appearance of Halley's Comet. Multicoloured.

922	50c. Comet over Athens (65×21 mm)	10	10
923	1k. Type **202**	30	10
924	2k. Edmond Halley (astronomer) and comet tail (20×21 mm)	60	20
925	3k. "Vega" space probe and comet head	90	30
926	4k. Galileo and comet tail (20×21 mm)	1·10	40
927	5k. Comet head (20×21 mm)	1·40	50
928	6k. "Giotto" space probe and comet tail	1·75	90

Nos. 923/4, 925/6 and 927/8 resepctively were issued together, se-tenant, each pair forming a composite design.

203 Keeshond

204 "Mammillaria matudae"

1986. "Stockholmia 86" International Stamp Exhibition. Dogs. Multicoloured.

930	50c. Type **203**	10	10
931	1k. Elkhound (horiz)	20	10
932	2k. Bernese (horiz)	45	25
933	3k. Pointing griffon (horiz)	70	35
934	4k. Collie (horiz)	90	45
935	5k. Irish water spaniel (horiz)	1·10	55
936	6k. Briard (horiz)	1·60	80

1986. Cacti. Multicoloured.

938	50c. Type **204**	10	10
939	1k. "Mammillaria theresae"	25	10
940	2k. "Ariocarpus trigonus"	45	20
941	3k. "Notocactus crassigibbus"	65	30
942	4k. "Astrophytum asterias" hybrid	80	40
943	5k. "Melocactus manzanus"	1·00	50
944	6k. "Astrophytum ornatum" hybrid	1·25	60

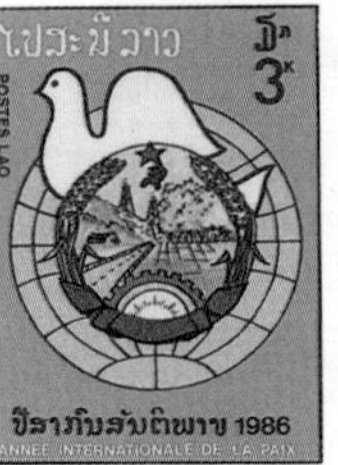

205 Arms and Dove on Globe

206 Vat Phu Champasak

1986. International Peace Year.

945 **205**	3k. multicoloured	85	40
946 –	5k. black, blue and red	1·25	60
947 –	10k. multicoloured	2·50	1·25

DESIGNS: 5k. Dove on smashed bomb; 10k. People supporting I.P.Y. emblem.

1987. 40th Anniv of UNESCO. Multicoloured.

948	3k. Type **206**	75	30
949	4k. Dish aerial and map of Laos on globe	1·00	40
950	9k. People reading books (horiz)	2·00	80

207 Speed Skating

1987. Winter Olympic Games, Calgary (1988) (1st issue). Multicoloured.

951	50c. Type **207**	10	10
952	1k. Biathlon	25	10
953	2k. Figure skating (pairs)	50	25
954	3k. Luge (horiz)	70	35
955	4k. Four-man bobsleigh (horiz)	90	45
956	5k. Ice hockey (horiz)	1·10	55
957	6k. Ski jumping (horiz)	1·40	70

See also Nos. 1046/51.

208 Gymnast and Urn

1987. Olympic Games, Seoul (1988) (1st issue). Sports and Greek Pottery. Multicoloured.

959	50c. Type **208**	10	10
960	1k. Throwing the discus and vase (horiz)	25	10
961	2k. Running and urn	50	25
962	3k. Show jumping and bowl (horiz)	70	35
963	4k. Throwing the javelin and plate	90	45
964	5k. High jumping and bowl with handles (horiz)	1·10	55
965	6k. Wrestling and urn	1·40	70

See also Nos. 1053/9.

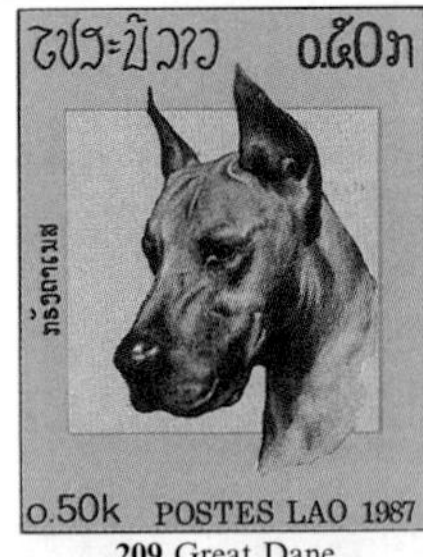

209 Great Dane

1987. Dogs. Multicoloured.

967	50c. Type **209**	10	10
968	1k. Black labrador	25	10
969	2k. St. Bernard	50	15
970	3k. Tervuren shepherd dog	70	25
971	4k. German shepherd	90	30
972	5k. Beagle	1·10	45
973	6k. Golden retriever	1·50	50

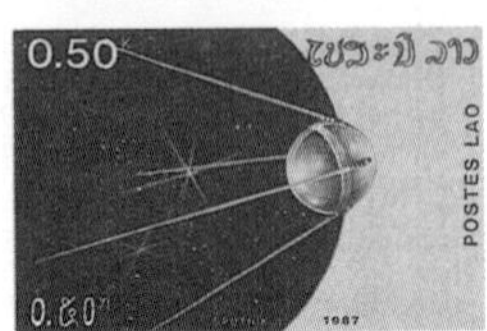

210 "Sputnik 1"

1987. 30th Anniv of Launch of First Artificial Satellite. Multicoloured.

974	50c. Type **210**	10	10
975	1k. "Sputnik 2"	20	10
976	2k. "Cosmos 97"	40	20
977	3k. "Cosmos"	60	30
978	4k. "Mars"	75	35
979	5k. "Luna 1"	95	45
980	9k. "Luna 3" (vert)	1·50	75

211 "MONTREAL" Handstamp on Letter to Quebec and Schooner

1987. "Capex 87" International Stamp Exhibition, Toronto. Ships and Covers. Multicoloured.

981	50c. Type **211**	25	10
982	1k. "PAID MONTREAL" on letter and schooner	35	10
983	2k. Letter from Montreal to London and "William D. Lawrence" (full-rigged ship)	55	20
984	3k. 1840 letter to Williamsburgh and "Neptune" (steamer)	75	30
985	4k. 1844 letter to London and "Athabasca" (screw-steamer)	95	40
986	5k. 1848 letter and "Chicora" (paddle-steamer)	1·10	50
987	6k. 1861 letter and "Passport" (river paddle-steamer)	1·40	60

212 Horse

1987. Horses. Multicoloured.

989	50c. Type **212**	10	10
990	1k. Chestnut (vert)	25	15
991	2k. Black horse with sheepskin noseband (vert)	50	30
992	3k. Dark chestnut (vert)	75	45
993	4k. Black horse (vert)	1·00	60
994	5k. Chestnut with plaited mane (vert)	1·40	85
995	6k. Grey (vert)	1·75	1·00

213 Volvo "480"

1987. Motor Cars. Multicoloured.

996	50c. Type **213**	10	10
997	1k. Alfa Romeo "33"	20	10
998	2k. Ford "Fiesta"	40	20
999	3k. Ford "Fiesta" (different)	65	30

1000 4k. Ford "Granada" . . . 80 40
1001 5k. Citroen "AX" . . . . 1·25 60
1002 6k. Renault "21" . . . . 1·40 70

214 "Vanda teres"

1987. Orchids. Multicoloured.
1004 3k. Type **214** 10 10
1005 7k. "Laeliocattleya" sp. . . 15 10
1006 10k. "Paphiopedilum" hybrid 25 10
1007 39k. "Sobralia" sp. 85 40
1008 44k. "Paphiopedilum" hybrid (different) 95 45
1009 47k. "Paphiopedilum" hybrid (different) . . . . 1·10 50
1010 50k. "Cattleya trianaei" . . 1·25 60

215 Elephants

1987. "Hafnia 87" International Stamp Exhibition, Copenhagen. Elephants. Multicoloured.
1012 50c. Type **215** 10 10
1013 1k. Three elephants 20 10
1014 2k. Elephant feeding 40 20
1015 3k. Elephant grazing on grass 60 30
1016 4k. Adult with calf 80 40
1017 5k. Elephant walking . . . 1·10 60
1018 6k. Elephant (vert) . . . . 1·40 70

216 Building Bamboo House

1987. International Year of Shelter for the Homeless. Multicoloured.
1020 1k. Type **216** 10 10
1021 27k. Building wooden house 60 30
1022 46k. House on stilts . . . . 1·25 60
1023 70k. Street of houses on stilts . . . . 1·75 90

217 Clown Loach

1987. Fishes. Multicoloured.
1024 3k. Type **217** 15 10
1025 7k. Harlequin filefish . . . 25 10
1026 10k. Silver-spotted squirrelfish 40 15
1027 39k. Mandarin fish . . . . 1·40 55
1028 44k. Coral hind . . . . . 1·60 65
1029 47k. Zebra lionfish . . . . 1·90 70
1030 50k. Semicircle angelfish . . 2·10 85

218 Watering Seedlings

1987. World Food Day. Multicoloured.
1031 1k. Type **218** 10 10
1032 3k. Harvesting maize (vert) 10 10
1033 5k. Harvesting rice 15 10
1034 63k. Children with fish (vert) 2·00 70
1035 142k. Tending pigs and poultry . . . . 3·50 1·50

219 Wounded Soldiers on Battlefield

1987. 70th Anniv of Russian Revolution. Multicoloured.
1036 1k. Type **219** 20 10
1037 2k. Mother and baby . . . 40 20
1038 4k. Storming the Winter Palace 80 40
1039 8k. Lenin amongst soldiers and sailors . . . . 1·50 70
1040 10k. Lenin labouring in Red Square . . . . 1·90 90

220 Hoeing

1987. Rice Culture in Mountain Regions. Mult.
1041 64k. Type **220** . . . . . . 1·40 70
1042 100k. Working in paddy fields . . . . 2·25 1·10

221 Laotheung Costume

1987. Ethnic Costumes. Multicoloured.
1043 7k. Type **221** 25 10
1044 38k. Laoloum costume . . . 90 40
1045 144k. Laosoun costume . . 3·00 1·40

222 Two-man Bobsleigh

1988. Winter Olympic Games, Calgary (2nd issue). Multicoloured.
1046 1k. Type **222** 10 10
1047 4k. Biathlon (shooting) . . . 15 10
1048 20k. Cross-country skiing 50 25
1049 42k. Ice hockey . . . . . . 1·00 50
1050 63k. Speed skating . . . . 1·50 75
1051 70k. Slalom . . . . 1·75 90

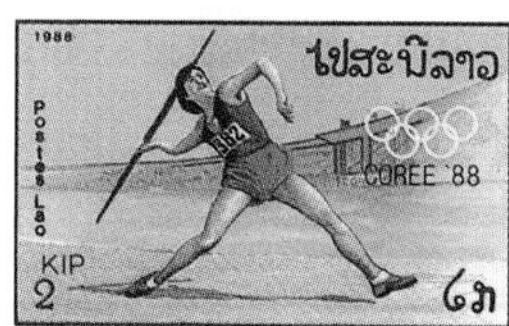
223 Throwing the Javelin

1988. Olympic Games, Seoul (2nd issue). Mult.
1053 2k. Type **223** 10 10
1054 5k. Triple jumping 15 10
1055 10k. Men's gymnastics . . . 25 15
1056 12k. Pirogue racing 30 15
1057 38k. Women's gymnastics 90 45
1058 46k. Fencing . . . . 1·10 50
1059 100k. Wrestling . . . . . . 2·50 1·25

224 Tyrannosaurus

1988. "Juvalux 88" Youth Philately Exhibition, Luxembourg. Prehistoric Animals. Multicoloured.
1061 3k. Type **224** (wrongly inscr "Trachodon") 10 10
1062 7k. "Ceratosaurus nasicornis" (vert) 15 10
1063 39k. "Iguanodon bernissartensis" (vert) . . 80 35
1064 44k. Scolosaurus (vert) . . . 1·25 60
1065 47k. "Phororhacus" sp. (vert) . . . . 1·60 35
1066 50k. Anatosaurus (wrongly inscr "Tyrannosaurus") 1·40 65

225 Adults in Hygiene Class

1988. 40th Anniv of W.H.O. Multicoloured.
1068 5k. Type **225** 10 10
1069 27k. Fumigating houses . . 55 25
1070 164k. Woman pumping fresh water (vert) . . . . 3·50 1·40

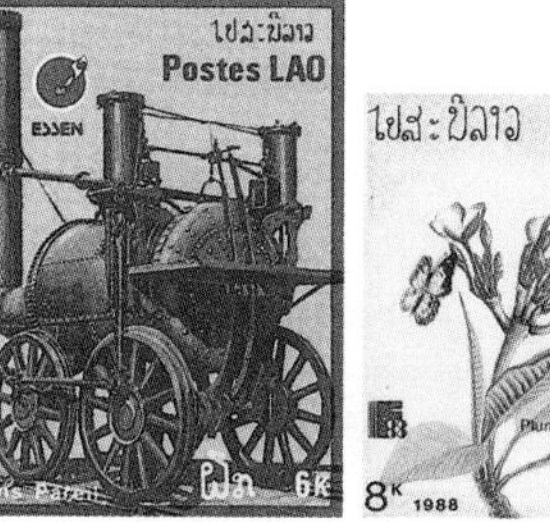
226 "Sans Pareil", 1829 227 Red Frangipani

1988. "Essen 88" International Stamp Fair. Early Railway Locomotives. Multicoloured.
1071 6k. Type **226** 15 10
1072 15k. "Rocket", 1829 . . . . 40 15
1073 20k. "Royal George", 1827 (horiz) 60 20
1074 25k. Trevithick's locomotive, 1803 (horiz) 75 25
1075 30k. "Novelty", 1829 (horiz) 1·00 30
1076 100k. "Tom Thumb", 1829 (horiz) . . . . 3·50 1·10

1988. "Finlandia 88" International Stamp Exhibition, Helsinki. Flowers. Multicoloured.
1078 8k. Type **227** 20 10
1079 9k. Hollyhock 25 10
1080 15k. Flame-of-the-forest . . 35 15
1081 33k. Golden shower 75 35
1082 64k. "Dahlia coccinea" (red) 1·50 70
1083 69k. "Dahlia coccinea" (yellow) . . . . 1·75 90

228 Sash Pattern

1988. Decorative Stencil Patterns.
1085 **228** 1k. multicoloured . . . 10 10
1086 – 2k. yellow, red and black 10 10
1087 – 3k. multicoloured . . . 10 10
1088 – 25k. multicoloured . . . 50 25
1089 – 163k. multicoloured . . 3·50 1·25
DESIGNS (stencils for)—VERT: 2k. Pagoda doors; 3k. Pagoda walls. HORIZ: 25k. Pagoda pillars; 163k. Skirts.

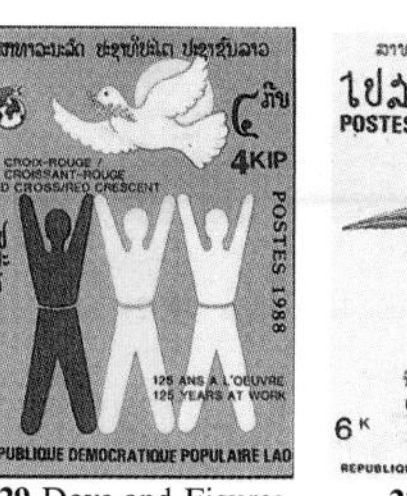
229 Dove and Figures

230 Stork-billed Kingfisher

1988. 125th Anniv of Red Cross Movement. Multicoloured.
1090 4k. Type **229** 10 10
1091 52k. Red Cross workers with handicapped people 1·00 50
1092 144k. Red Cross worker vaccinating baby (horiz) 3·50 1·10

1988. Birds. Multicoloured.
1093 6k. Type **230** 25 10
1094 10k. Japanese quail 30 10
1095 13k. Blossom-headed parakeet 45 15
1096 44k. Orange-breasted green pigeon . . . . 1·00 40
1097 63k. Black-crested bulbul . . 1·75 70
1098 64k. Mountain imperial pigeon . . . . 2·00 80

231 Red Cross Workers loading Supplies into Pirogue

1988. Completion of 1st Five Year Plan. Multicoloured.
1099 20k. Type **231** 50 10
1100 40k. Library 90 45
1101 50k. Irrigating fields . . . . 1·25 60
1102 100k. Improvement in communications . . . . . 2·50 1·40

232 Ruy Lopez Segura

1988. Chess Masters. Multicoloured.
1103 1k. Type **232** 10 10
1104 2k. Karl Anderssen 10 10
1105 3k. Paul Morphy (wrongly inscr "Murphy") 15 10
1106 6k. Wilhelm Steinitz 25 10
1107 7k. Emanuel Lasker 30 15
1108 12k. Jose Raul Capablanca 50 20
1109 172k. Aleksandr Alekhine 4·25 1·75

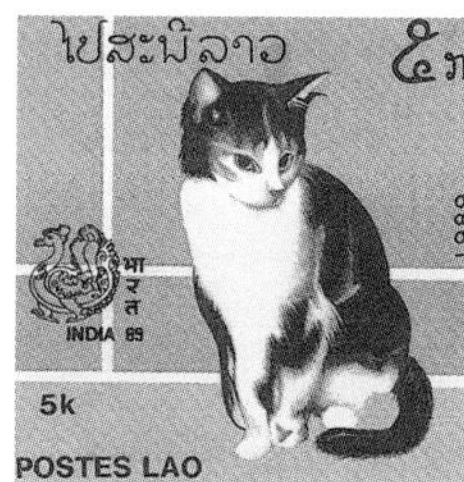

233 Tortoiseshell and White

1989. "India 89" International Stamp Exhibition, New Delhi. Cats. Multicoloured.
1110 5k. Type **233** 10 10
1111 6k. Brown tabby 15 10
1112 10k. Black and white . . . 25 10
1113 20k. Red tabby 50 15
1114 50k. Black . . . . 1·00 35
1115 172k. Silver tabby and white 3·50 1·25

234 Gunboat, Tank, Soldiers and Flags

1989. 40th Anniv of People's Army. Multicoloured.
1117 1k. Type **234** 10 10
1118 2k. Soldier teaching mathematics (vert) 10 10
1119 3k. Army medics vaccinating civilians 15 10
1120 250k. Peasant, revolutionary, worker and soldiers . . . . 5·50 1·00

235 Footballers

1989. World Cup Football Championship, Italy (1990) (1st issue). Multicoloured.
1121 10k. Type **235** 15 10
1122 15k. Footballer looking to pass ball 25 10
1123 20k. Ball hitting player on chest 40 15
1124 25k. Tackle 55 20
1125 45k. Dribbling ball 90 35
1126 105k. Kicking ball . . . . . 2·25 90
See also Nos. 1168/73.

236 Couple planting Sapling

1989. Preserve Forests Campaign. Multicoloured.
1128 4k. Type **236** 10 10
1129 10k. Burning and fallen trees 20 10
1130 12k. Man felling tree (vert) 25 15
1131 200k. Trees on map (vert) 4·00 2·50

237 Camilo Cienfuegos, Fidel Castro and Flag
238 Skaters

1989. 30th Anniv of Cuban Revolution. Multicoloured.
1132 45k. Type **237** . . . . . . 1·25 35
1133 50d. Cuban and Laotian flags . . . . 1·25 35

1989. Winter Olympic Games, Albertville (1992) (1st issue). Figure Skating. Multicoloured.
1134 9k. Type **238** 20 10
1135 10k. Pair (horiz) 20 10
1136 15k. Ice dancing 35 15
1137 24k. Female skater 50 25
1138 29k. Pair 55 25
1139 114k. Male skater . . . . . 2·50 1·00
See also Nos. 1196/1201, 1237/41 and 1276/80.

239 High Jumping
241 Sapodillas

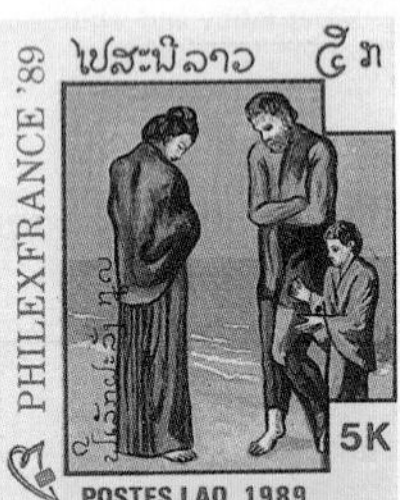

240 "Poor on Seashore"

1989. Olympic Games, Barcelona (1992) (1st issue). Multicoloured.
1141 5k. Type **239** 15 10
1142 15k. Gymnastics 45 25
1143 20k. Cycling (horiz) 60 30
1144 25k. Boxing (horiz) 75 40
1145 70k. Archery . . . . 1·90 1·00
1146 120k. Swimming . . . . . 3·75 2·10
See also Nos. 1179/84, 1231/5 and 1282/6.

1989. "Philexfrance '89" International Stamp Exhibition, Paris. Paintings by Picasso. Mult.
1148 5k. Type **240** 10 10
1149 7k. "Motherhood" 15 10
1150 8k. "Portrait of Jaime S. le Bock" 20 15
1151 9k. "Harlequins" 25 15
1152 105k. "Boy with Dog" . . . 2·25 1·00
1153 114k. "Girl on Ball" . . . . 2·25 1·00

1989. Fruits. Multicoloured.
1155 5k. Type **241** 10 10
1156 20k. Sugar-apples 45 20
1157 20k. Guavas 45 20
1158 30k. Durians 70 30
1159 50k. Pomegranates . . . . 1·10 50
1160 172k. "Moridica charautia" 3·75 1·75

242 Sikhotabong Temple, Khammouane
243 Nehru and Woman

1989. Temples. Multicoloured.
1161 5k. Type **242** 10 10
1162 15k. Dam Temple, Vientiane 35 20
1163 61k. Ing Hang Temple, Savannakhet . . . . . . 1·10 65
1164 161k. Ho Vay Phra Luang Temple, Vientiane . . . . 3·75 2·10

1989. Birth Centenary of Jawaharlal Nehru (Indian statesman). Multicoloured.
1165 1k. Type **243** 10 10
1166 60k. Nehru and group of children (horiz) . . . . . 1·25 35
1167 200k. Boy garlanding Nehru 4·25 1·25

244 Footballer

1990. World Cup Football Championship, Italy (2nd issue).
1168 **244** 10k. multicoloured . . . 25 10
1169 – 15k. multicoloured . . . 35 15
1170 – 20k. multicoloured . . . 50 25
1171 – 25k. multicoloured . . . 60 30
1172 – 45k. multicoloured . . . 1·10 55
1173 – 105k. multicoloured . . 2·75 1·25
DESIGNS: 15 to 105k. Different footballing scenes.

245 Teacher and Adult Class

1990. International Literacy Year. Multicoloured.
1175 10k. Type **245** 25 10
1176 50k. Woman teaching child (vert) . . . . 1·40 70
1177 60k. Monk teaching adults 1·50 75
1178 150k. Group reading and writing under tree . . . . 3·75 1·75

246 Basketball

1990. Olympic Games, Barcelona (1992) (2nd issue). Multicoloured.
1179 10k. Type **246** 20 10
1180 30k. Hurdling 60 25
1181 45k. High jumping 95 40
1182 50k. Cycling . . . . 1·10 45
1183 60k. Throwing the javelin 1·25 50
1184 90k. Tennis . . . . 2·00 80

247 Great Britain 1840 Penny Black and Mail Coach

1990. "Stamp World London 90" International Stamp Exhibition. Multicoloured.
1186 15k. Type **247** 35 15
1187 20k. U.S 1847 5c. stamp and early steam locomotive . . . . 1·50 25
1188 40k. France 1849 20c. stamp and mail balloons, Paris, 1870 . . . . 90 35
1189 50k. Sardinia 1851 5c. stamp and post rider . . . . . 1·10 45
1190 60k. Indo-China 1892 1c. stamp and elephant . . . 1·40 50
1191 100k. Spain 1850 6c. stamp and Spanish galleon . . . 2·25 90

248 Ho Chi Minh addressing Crowd

1990. Birth Centenary of Ho Chi Minh. Mult.
1193 40k. Type **248** 85 35
1194 60k. Ho Chi Minh and Laotian President . . . . 1·25 50
1195 160k. Ho Chi Minh and Vietnamese flag (vert) . . 3·50 1·40

249 Speed Skating

1990. Winter Olympic Games, Albertville (1992) (2nd issue). Multicoloured.
1196 10k. Type **249** 20 10
1197 25k. Cross-country skiing (vert) 55 20
1198 30k. Downhill skiing . . . 65 25
1199 35k. Tobogganing 75 30
1200 80k. Figure skating (pairs) (vert) . . . . 1·75 70
1201 90k. Biathlon . . . . 2·00 80

250 That Luang, 1990

1990. 430th Anniv of That Luang. Multicoloured.
1203 60k. That Luang, 1867 (horiz) . . . . 1·40 55
1204 70k. That Luang, 1930 (horiz) . . . . 1·50 60
1205 130k. Type **250** . . . . . . 2·75 1·10

251 Parson Bird

1990. "New Zealand 1990" International Stamp Exhibition, Auckland. Multicoloured.
1206 10k. Type **251** 25 10
1207 15k. Eurasian sky lark . . . 35 10
1208 20k. Oystercatcher 45 20
1209 50k. Variable cormorant . . 1·10 45
1210 60k. Great Reef heron . . . 1·40 55
1211 100k. Brown kiwi . . . . . 3·00 1·10

252 Brown-antlered Deer

1990. Mammals. Multicoloured.
1213 10k. Type **252** 25 10
1214 20k. Gaur 50 20
1215 40k. Wild water buffalo . . 1·00 40
1216 45k. Kouprey . . . . 1·00 40
1217 120k. Javan rhinoceros . . . 3·00 1·25

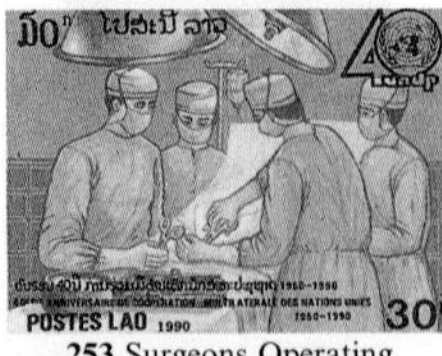

253 Surgeons Operating

1990. 40th Anniv of United Nations Development Programme. Multicoloured.
1218 30k. Type **253** 60 25
1219 45k. Fishermen inspecting catch . . . . 1·50 55
1220 80k. Air-traffic controller (vert) . . . . 1·60 65
1221 90k. Electricity plant workers . . . . 1·75 70

254 Rice Ceremony

1990. New Year. Multicoloured.
1222 5k. Type **254** 10 10
1223 10k. Elephant in carnival parade 25 10
1224 50k. Making offerings at temple . . . . 1·25 50
1225 150k. Family ceremony . . 3·75 1·50

255 Memorial, Wreath and Eternal Flame

1990. 15th National Day Festival. Multicoloured.
1226 15k. Type **255** 40 15
1227 20k. Celebration parade . . 50 20
1228 80k. Hospital visit . . . . . 2·00 80
1229 120k. Girls parading with banner . . . . 2·75 1·10

257 Two-man Kayak

1991. Olympic Games, Barcelona (1992) (3rd issue). Multicoloured.
1231 22k. Type **257** 10 10
1232 32k. Canoeing 10 10
1233 285k. Diving (vert) 95 40
1234 330k. Racing dinghies (vert) 1·10 45
1235 1000k. Swimming . . . . . 3·25 1·25

258 Bobsleighing

1991. Winter Olympic Games, Albertville (1992) (3rd issue). Multicoloured.
1237 32k. Type **258** 10 10
1238 135k. Cross-country skiing (horiz) 45 20
1239 250k. Ski jumping (horiz) 85 35
1240 275k. Biathlon (horiz) . . . 95 40
1241 900k. Speed skating (horiz) 3·00 1·25

259 Pha Pheng Falls, Champassak

1991. Tourism. Multicoloured.

1243	155k. Type **259**	45	15
1244	220k. Pha Tang mountains, Vangvieng	65	25
1245	235k. Tat Set waterfall, Saravane (vert)	75	30
1246	1000k. Plain of Jars, Xieng Khouang (vert)	2·75	1·10

260 Match Scene

1991. World Cup Football Championship, U.S.A. (1994) (1st issue). Multicoloured.

1247	32k. Type **260**	10	10
1248	330k. Goalkeeper catching ball	1·10	45
1249	340k. Player controlling ball (vert)	1·25	50
1250	400k. Player dribbling ball	1·50	60
1251	500k. Tackle	1·90	75

See also Nos. 1292/6, 1370/4 and 1386/90.

261 Planting Saplings

1991. National Tree Planting Day. Multicoloured.

1253	350k. Type **261**	70	25
1254	700k. Planting saplings (different)	2·00	80
1255	800k. Removing saplings from store	2·40	95

262 "Mallard", 1938, Great Britain

1991. "Espamer '91" Spain–Latin America Stamp Exhibition, Buenos Aires. Railway Locomotives. Multicoloured.

1256	25k. Type **262**	10	10
1257	32k. Class 4500 steam locomotive, France (inscr "Pacific 231")	15	10
1258	285k. Streamlined steam locomotive, U.S.A.	1·40	45
1259	650k. Canadian Pacific Class T1b steam locomotive, 1938	3·00	1·00
1260	750k. East African Railways Class 59 steam locomotive, 1955	3·75	1·25

263 Spindle Festival

1991. Traditional Music. Multicoloured.

1262	20k. Type **263**	10	10
1263	220k. Mong player (vert)	60	25
1264	275k. Siphandone singer (vert)	70	25
1265	545k. Khap ngum singer	1·60	60
1266	690k. Phouthaydam dance	2·00	80

264 Great Purple

1991. "Phila Nippon '91" International Stamp Exhibition, Tokyo. Butterflies. Multicoloured.

1267	55k. Type **264**	20	10
1268	90k. "Luehdorfia puziloi" (wrongly inscr "Luendorfia")	30	10
1269	255k. "Papilio bianor"	75	30
1270	285k. Swallowtail	85	35
1271	900k. Mikado swallowtail	2·75	1·10

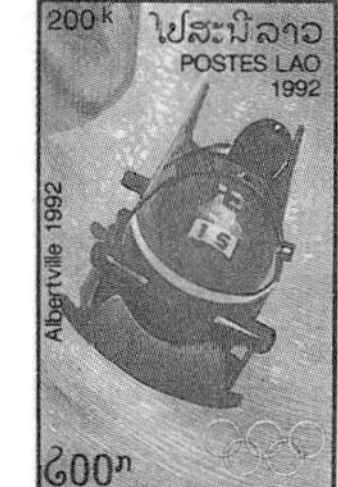

265 Emblem and Pattern **266** Bobsleighing

1991. International Decade for Cultural Development (1988–97). Multicoloured.

1273	285k. Type **265**	45	20
1274	330k. Emblem and drum	55	20
1275	1000k. Emblem and pipes	1·60	65

1992. Winter Olympic Games, Albertville (4th issue). Multicoloured.

1276	200k. Type **266**	60	25
1277	220k. Slalom skiing	65	25
1278	250k. Downhill skiing (horiz)	75	30
1279	500k. One-man luge	1·50	60
1280	600k. Figure skating	1·75	70

267 Running **269** Argentinian and Italian Players and Flags

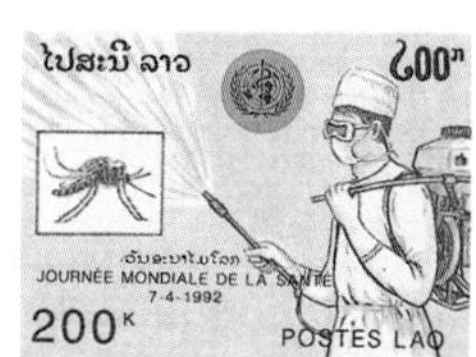

268 Pest Control

1992. Olympic Games, Barcelona (4th issue). Multicoloured.

1282	32k. Type **267**	10	10
1283	245k. Baseball	75	30
1284	275k. Tennis	80	30
1285	285k. Basketball	85	35
1286	900k. Boxing (horiz)	2·75	1·10

1992. World Health Day. Multicoloured.

1288	200k. Type **268**	60	25
1289	255k. Anti-smoking campaign	75	30
1290	330k. Donating blood	1·00	40
1291	1000k. Vaccinating child (vert)	3·25	1·25

1992. World Cup Football Championship, U.S.A. (1994) (2nd issue). Multicoloured.

1292	260k. Type **269**	60	25
1293	305k. German and English players and flags	85	35
1294	310k. United States flag, ball and trophy	90	35
1295	350k. Italian and English players and flags	1·10	45
1296	800k. German and Argentinian players and flags	2·50	1·00

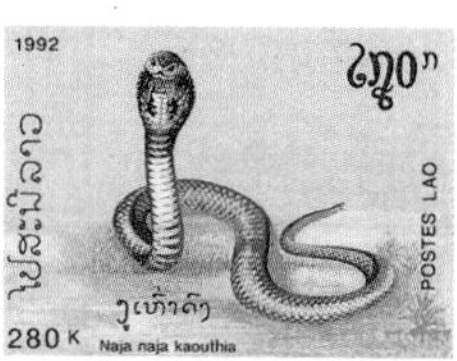

270 Common Cobra

1992. Snakes. Multicoloured.

1298	280k. Type **270**	75	30
1299	295k. Common cobra	80	30
1300	420k. Wagler's pit viper	1·10	45
1301	700k. King cobra (vert)	2·25	90

271 Doorway and Ruins

1992. Restoration of Wat Phou. Multicoloured.

1302	185k. Type **271**	50	20
1303	220k. Doorway (different)	60	25
1304	1200k. Doorway with collapsed porch (horiz)	3·50	1·40

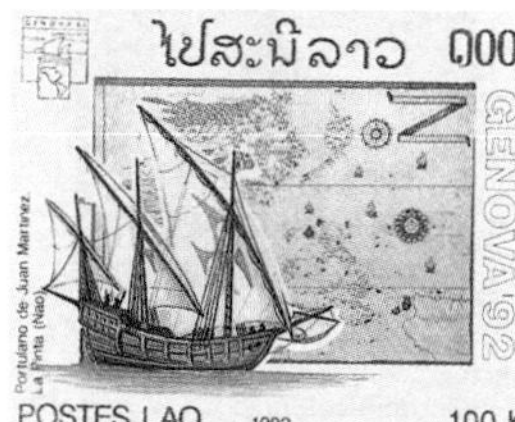

272 "Pinta" and Juan Martinez's Map

1992. "Genova '92" International Thematic Stamp Exhibition. Multicoloured.

1305	100k. Type **272**	30	10
1306	300k. Piri Reis's letter and caravelle (vert)	90	35
1307	350k. Magellan's ship and Paolo del Pozo Toscanelli's world map	1·10	45
1308	400k. Gabriel de Vallesca's map and Vasco da Gama's flagship "Sao Gabriel"	1·25	50
1309	455k. Juan Martinez's map and Portuguese four-masted caravel	1·40	55

273 Woman in Traditional Costume **274** Boy Drumming

1992. Traditional Costumes of Laotian Mountain Villages.

1311	**273** 25k. multicoloured	10	10
1312	– 55k. multicoloured	15	10
1313	– 400k. multicoloured	1·10	45
1314	– 1200k. multicoloured	3·75	1·25

DESIGNS: 55 to 1200k. Different costumes.

1992. International Children's Day. Children at Play. Multicoloured.

1315	220k. Type **274**	75	30
1316	285k. Girls skipping (horiz)	1·00	40
1317	330k. Boys racing on stilts	1·10	45
1318	400k. Girls playing "escape" game (horiz)	1·40	55

275 Praying before Buddha **276** Crested Gibbon

1992. National Customs. Multicoloured.

1319	100k. Type **275**	30	10
1320	140k. Wedding (horiz)	40	15
1321	160k. Religious procession (horiz)	50	20
1322	1500k. Monks receiving alms (horiz)	4·75	1·90

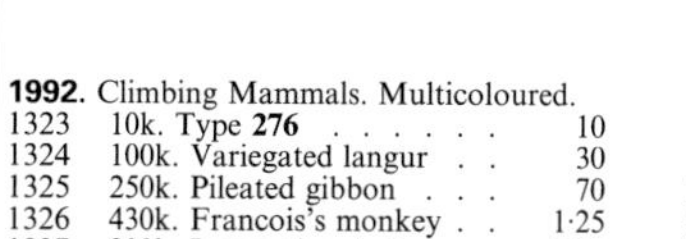

1992. Climbing Mammals. Multicoloured.

1323	10k. Type **276**	10	10
1324	100k. Variegated langur	30	10
1325	250k. Pileated gibbon	70	30
1326	430k. Francois's monkey	1·25	50
1327	800k. Lesser slow loris	2·25	90

277 New York

1993. 130th Anniv of Underground Railway Systems. Multicoloured.

1328	15k. Type **277**	15	10
1329	50k. West Berlin	25	10
1330	100k. Paris	50	15
1331	200k. London	1·00	30
1332	900k. Moscow	4·75	1·40

278 Malayan Bullfrog

1993. Amphibians. Multicoloured.

1334	55k. Type **278**	20	10
1335	90k. Muller's clawed frog	30	10
1336	100k. Glass frog (vert)	35	15
1337	185k. Giant toad	70	30
1338	1200k. Common tree frog (vert)	4·25	1·75

279 Common Tree-shrew **280** Noble Scallop

1993. Mammals. Multicoloured.

1339	45k. Type **279**	15	10
1340	60k. Philippine flying lemur	20	10
1341	120k. Loris	35	15
1342	500k. Eastern tarsier	1·50	60
1343	600k. Giant gibbon	1·75	70

1993. Molluscs. Multicoloured.

1344	20k. Type **280**	10	10
1345	30k. Precious wentletrap	10	10
1346	70k. Spider conch	25	10
1347	500k. Aulicus cone	1·75	70
1348	1000k. Milleped spider conch	3·50	1·40

281 Drugs and Skull smoking

1993. Anti-drugs Campaign. Multicoloured.

1349	200k. Type **281**	70	30
1350	430k. Burning seized drugs	1·50	60
1351	900k. Instructing on dangers of drugs	3·00	1·25

282 House **283** Greater Spotted Eagle

1993. Traditional Houses. Multicoloured.

1352	32k. Type **282**	10	10
1353	200k. Thatched house with gable end (horiz)	70	30
1354	650k. Thatched house (horiz)	2·25	90
1355	750k. House with tiled roof (horiz)	2·50	1·00

1993. Birds of Prey. Multicoloured.

1356	10k. Type **283**	15	15
1357	100k. Spotted little owl	45	25
1358	330k. Pied harrier (horiz)	1·50	70
1359	1000k. Short-toed eagle	4·50	2·50

284 Fighting Forest Fire

1993. Environmental Protection. Multicoloured.

1360	32k. Type **284**	10	10
1361	40k. Wildlife on banks of River Mekong	15	10
1362	260k. Paddy fields	85	35
1363	1100k. Oxen in river	1·40	55

285 "Narathura atosia"

1993. "Bangkok 1993" International Stamp Exhibition. Butterflies. Multicoloured.

1364	35k. Type **285**	10	10
1365	80k. "Parides philoxenus"	25	10
1366	150k. "Euploea harrisi"	50	20
1367	220k. Yellow orange-tip	75	30
1368	500k. Female common palm fly	1·75	70

286 Footballer

1993. World Cup Football Championship, U.S.A. (3rd issue). Multicoloured.

1370	10k. Type **286**	10	10
1371	20k. Brazil player	10	10
1372	285k. Uruguay player	90	35
1373	400k. Germany player	1·25	50
1374	800k. Forward challenging goalkeeper	2·50	1·00

287 Hesperornis

1994. Prehistoric Birds. Multicoloured.

1376	10k. Type **287**	15	10
1377	20k. Mauritius dodo	15	15
1378	150k. Archaeopteryx	65	25
1379	600k. Phororhachos	2·25	90
1380	700k. Giant moa	2·75	1·10

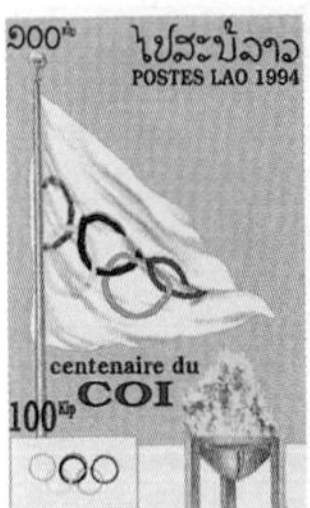

288 Olympic Flag and Flame

289 Bridge and National Flags

1994. Centenary of International Olympic Committee. Multicoloured.

1382	100k. Type **288**	35	10
1383	250k. Ancient Greek athletes (horiz)	90	30
1384	1000k. Pierre de Coubertin (founder) and modern athlete	3·50	1·10

1994. Opening of Friendship Bridge between Laos and Thailand.

1385 **289**	500k. multicoloured	70	25

290 World Map and Players

1994. World Cup Football Championship, U.S.A. (4th issue).

1386 **290**	40k. multicoloured	10	10
1387 –	50k. multicoloured	10	10
1388 –	60k. multicoloured	10	10
1389 –	320k. multicoloured	45	15
1390 –	900k. multicoloured	1·25	45

DESIGNS: 50 to 900k. Different players on world map.

291 Pagoda

1994. Pagodas.

1392 **291**	30k. multicoloured	10	10
1393 –	150k. multicoloured	20	10
1394 –	380k. multicoloured	55	20
1395 –	1100k. multicoloured	1·60	55

DESIGNS: 150 to 1100k. Different gabled roofs.

292 Bear eating

1994. The Malay Bear. Multicoloured.

1396	50k. Type **292**	10	10
1397	90k. Bear's head	15	10
1398	200k. Adult and cub	30	10
1399	220k. Bear	30	10

293 Grass Snake

1994. Amphibians and Reptiles. Multicoloured.

1400	70k. Type **293**	10	10
1401	80k. Tessellated snake	10	10
1402	90k. Fire salamander	15	10
1403	600k. Alpine newt	85	30
1404	800k. Green lizard (vert)	1·10	40

294 Phra Xayavoraman 7

295 Family supporting Healthy Globe

1994. Buddhas. Multicoloured.

1406	15k. Type **294**	10	10
1407	280k. Phra Thong Souk	40	15
1408	390k. Phra Manolom	55	20
1409	800k. Phra Ongtu	1·10	40

1994. International Year of the Family. Multicoloured.

1410	200k. Type **295**	30	10
1411	500k. Mother taking child to school (horiz)	70	25
1412	700k. Mother and children	1·00	35

296 Kong Hang

1994. Traditional Laotian Drums. Multicoloured.

1414	370k. Type **296**	50	20
1415	440k. Kong Leng (portable drum)	60	20
1416	450k. Kong Toum (drum on stand)	65	25
1417	600k. Kong Phene (hanging drum)	85	30

297 Elephant in Procession

1994. Ceremonial Elephants. Multicoloured.

1418	140k. Type **297**	20	10
1419	400k. Elephant in pavilion	55	20
1420	890k. Elephant in street procession (vert)	1·25	45

298 Theropodes

1994. Prehistoric Animals. Multicoloured.

1421	50k. Type **298**	10	10
1422	380k. Iguanodontides	55	20
1423	420k. Sauropodes	60	20

299 Playing Musical Instruments

1995. 20th Anniv of World Tourism Organization. Multicoloured.

1424	60k. Type **299**	10	10
1425	250k. Women dancing	35	15
1426	400k. Giving alms to monks	55	20
1427	650k. Waterfall (vert)	90	30

300 Trachodon

302 Children and Emblem

1995. Prehistoric Animals. Multicoloured.

1429	50k. Type **300**	10	10
1430	70k. Protoceratops	10	10
1431	300k. Brontosaurus	40	15
1432	400k. Stegosaurus	55	20
1433	600k. Tyrannosaurus	85	30

301 Indian Jungle Mynah

1995. Birds. Multicoloured.

1434	50k. Type **301**	10	10
1435	150k. Jerdon's starling	20	10
1436	300k. Common mynah	40	15
1437	700k. Southern grackle	1·00	35

1995. 25th Anniv of Francophonie. Multicoloured.

1438	50k. Type **302**	10	10
1439	380k. Golden roof decorations	55	20
1440	420k. Map	60	20

303 Pole Vaulting

304 Chalice

1995. Olympic Games, Atlanta, U.S.A. (1st issue). Multicoloured.

1441	60k. Type **303**	10	10
1442	80k. Throwing the javelin	10	10
1443	200k. Throwing the hammer	25	10
1444	350k. Long jumping	45	15
1445	700k. High jumping	95	35

See also Nos. 1484/9.

1995. Antique Vessels. Multicoloured.

1447	70k. Type **304**	10	10
1448	200k. Resin and silver bowl (horiz)	25	10
1449	450k. Geometrically decorated bowl (horiz)	60	20
1450	600k. Religious chalice (horiz)	80	30

305 Procession

1995. Rocket Festival. Multicoloured.

1451	80k. Launching rocket (vert)	10	10
1452	160k. Type **305**	20	10
1453	500k. Musicians in procession	70	25
1454	700k. Crowds and rockets	95	35

306 Red Tabby Longhair

1995. Cats. Multicoloured.

1455	40k. Type **306**	10	10
1456	50k. Siamese sealpoint	10	10
1457	250k. Red tabby longhair (different)	35	15
1458	400k. Tortoiseshell shorthair	55	20
1459	650k. Head of tortoiseshell shorthair (vert)	90	30

307 "Nepenthes villosa"

1995. Insectivorous Plants. Multicoloured.

1461	90k. Type **307**	10	10
1462	100k. "Dionaea muscipula"	15	10
1463	350k. "Sarracenia flava"	45	15
1464	450k. "Sarracenia purpurea"	60	20
1465	500k. "Nepenthes ampullaria"	70	25

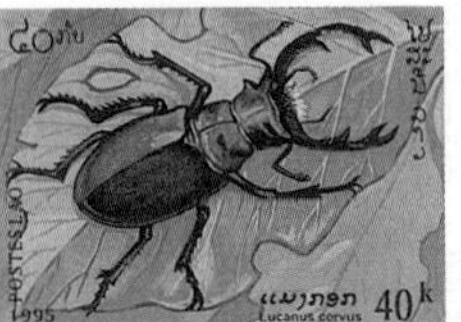

308 Stag Beetle

1995. Insects. Multicoloured.

1467	40k. Type **308**	10	10
1468	50k. May beetle	10	10
1469	500k. Blue carpenter beetle	70	25
1470	800k. Great green grasshopper	1·10	40

309 Cattle grazing

1995. 50th Anniv of F.A.O. Multicoloured.
1471 80k. Type **309** 10 10
1472 300k. Working paddy-field 40 15
1473 1000k. Agriculture . . . . 1·40 50

310 At Meeting

1995. 50th Anniv of U.N.O. Peoples of Different Races. Multicoloured.
1474 290k. Type **310** 40 15
1475 310k. Playing draughts . . . 40 15
1476 440k. Children playing . . . 60 20

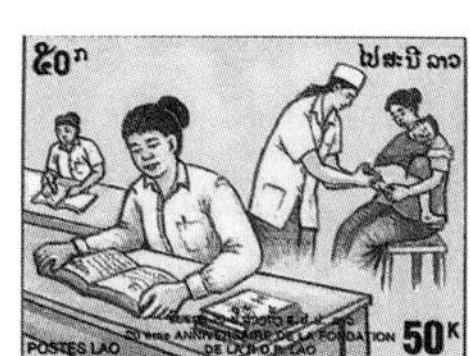

311 Students and Nurse vaccinating Child

1995. 20th Anniv of Republic. Multicoloured.
1477 50k. Type **311** 10 10
1478 280k. Agricultural land . . 40 15
1479 600k. Bridge 80 30

312 Mong

1996. Traditional New Year Customs. Multicoloured.
1480 50k. Type **312** 10 10
1481 280k. Phouthai 40 15
1482 380k. Ten Xe 55 20
1483 420k. Lao Loum 60 20

313 Cycling

1996. Olympic Games, Atlanta, U.S.A. (2nd issue). Multicoloured.
1484 30k. Type **313** 10 10
1485 150k. Football 20 10
1486 200k. Basketball (vert) . . . 30 10
1487 300k. Running (vert) . . . 40 15
1488 500k. Shooting 70 25

314 Sun Bear

1996. Animals. Multicoloured.
1490 40k. Type **314** 10 10
1491 60k. Grey pelican 10 10
1492 200k. Leopard 30 10
1493 250k. Swallowtail 35 15
1494 700k. Indian python . . . . 1·00 35

315 Weaving

1996. International Women's Year. Multicoloured.
1495 20k. Type **315** 10 10
1496 290k. Physical training instructress 40 15
1497 1000k. Woman feeding child (vert) . . . . 1·40 50

316 Rat

317 Players

1996. New Year. Year of the Rat.
1498 **316** 50k. multicoloured . . . 10 10
1499 – 340k. multicoloured . . 50 20
1500 – 350k. multicoloured . . 50 20
1501 – 370k. multicoloured . . 50 20
DESIGNS: 340k. to 370k. Different rats.

1996. World Cup Football Championship, France (1998) (1st issue).
1502 **317** 20k. multicoloured . . . 10 10
1503 – 50k. multicoloured . . . 10 10
1504 – 300k. multicoloured . . 40 15
1505 – 400k. multicoloured . . 55 20
1506 – 500k. multicoloured . . 70 25
DESIGNS: 50k. to 500k. Different footballing scenes.
See also Nos. 1589/94.

318 Village Women grinding Rice

1996. Children's Drawings. Multicoloured.
1508 180k. Type **318** 25 10
1509 230k. Women picking fruit 30 10
1510 310k. Village women preparing food 45 15
1511 370k. Women tending vegetable crops 50 20

319 Morane Monoplane

1996. "Capex'96" International Stamp Exhibition, Toronto, Canada. Aircraft. Multicoloured.
1512 25k. Type **319** 10 10
1513 60k. Sopwith Camel biplane 10 10
1514 150k. De Havilland D.H.4 biplane 20 10
1515 250k. Albatros biplane . . . 35 15
1516 800k. Caudron biplane . . . 1·10 40

320 Front View

1996. Ox-carts. Multicoloured.
1517 50k. Type **320** 10 10
1518 100k. Side view 15 10
1519 440k. Oxen pulling cart . . 60 20

321 "Dendrobium secundum"

322 White Horse

1996. Orchids. Multicoloured.
1520 50k. Type **321** 10 10
1521 200k. "Ascocentrum miniatum" 30 10
1522 500k. "Aerides multiflorum" 70 25
1523 520k. "Dendrobium aggregatum" 75 25

1996. Saddle Horses. Multicoloured.
1524 50k. Type **322** 10 10
1525 80k. Horse with red and black bridle 10 10
1526 200k. Bay horse with white bridle and reins 30 10
1527 400k. Horse with red and yellow cords braided into mane 55 20
1528 600k. Chestnut horse with white blaze 85 30

323 Pupils displaying Slates to Teacher

1996. 50th Anniv of UNICEF. Multicoloured.
1530 200k. Type **323** 30 10
1531 500k. Mother breastfeeding (vert) 70 25
1532 600k. Woman drawing water at public well . . . 85 30

324 Leatherback Turtle

1996. 25th Anniv of Greenpeace (environmental organization). Turtles. Multicoloured.
1533 150k. Type **324** 20 10
1534 250k. Leatherback turtle at water's edge 35 15
1535 400k. Hawksbill turtle . . . 55 20
1536 450k. "Chelonia agassizi" 65 20

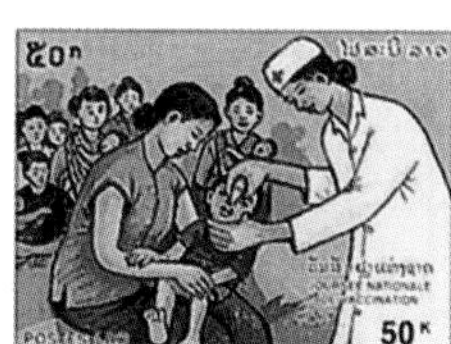

325 Oral Vaccination

1997. National Vaccination Day. Multicoloured.
1537 50k. Type **325** 10 10
1538 340k. Nurse injecting child's leg 45 15
1539 370k. Nurse pushing child in wheelchair 50 15

326 George Stephenson and "Pioneer", 1836

1997. Steam Railway Locomotives. Multicoloured.
1540 100k. "Kinnaird", 1846 (44 × 27 mm) 10 10
1541 200k. Type **326** 30 10
1542 300k. Robert Stephenson and long-boiler express locomotive, 1848 . . . . 40 15
1543 400k. Stephenson locomotive "Adler", 1835, Germany 55 20
1544 500k. "Lord of the Isles", 1851–84 . . . . 70 25
1545 600k. "The Columbine", 1845 . . . . 80 25
The 200 and 300k. are wrongly inscr "Stepheson".

327 Pseudoryx lying down

1997. Pseudoryx (Saola). Multicoloured.
1547 350k. Type **327** 50 15
1548 380k. Grazing (vert) 50 15
1549 420k. Scratching with hind leg 60 20

328 Masked Lovebirds ("Agapornis personata")

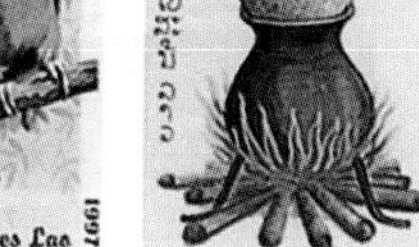

330 Steaming Rice

329 Signs of the Chinese Zodiac

1997. Lovebirds. Multicoloured.
1550 50k. Type **328** 10 10
1551 150k. Grey-headed lovebird ("Agapornis cana") . . . 10 10
1552 200k. Nyasa lovebirds ("Agapornis lilianae") . . 30 10
1553 400k. Fischer's lovebirds ("Agapornis fischeri") . . 55 20
1554 500k. Black-cheeked lovebirds ("Agapornis nigregenis") 70 25
1555 800k. Peach-faced lovebird ("Agapornis roseicollis") 1·10 35

1997. New Year. Year of the Ox. Multicoloured.
1557 50k. Type **329** 10 10
1558 300k. Woman riding ox (vert) 40 15
1559 440k. Ox on float in procession 60 20

1997. Food Preparation. Multicoloured.
1560 50k. Type **330** 10 10
1561 340k. Water containers (horiz) 45 15
1562 370k. Table laid with meal (horiz) 50 15

331 "Vanda roeblingiana"

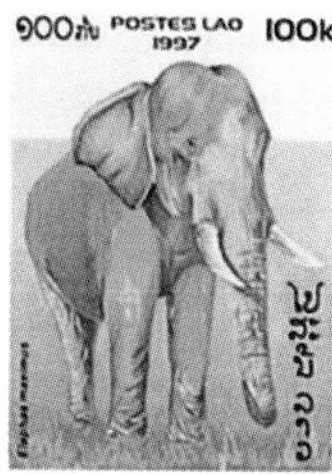

332 Indian Elephant ("Elephas maximus")

1997. Orchids. Multicoloured.
1563 50k. Type **331** 10 10
1564 100k. "Dendrobium findleyanum" 10 10
1565 150k. "Dendrobium crepidatum" 10 10
1566 250k. "Sarcanthus birmanicus" 35 10
1567 400k. "Cymbidium lowianum" 55 20
1568 1000k. "Dendrobium gratiosissimum" . . . . . 1·40 45

1997. Elephants. Multicoloured.
1570 100k. Type **332** 10 10
1571 250k. Indian elephant carrying log (horiz) . . . 35 10
1572 300k. Indian elephant with young (horiz) 40 15
1573 350k. African elephant ("Loxodonta africana") (horiz) 50 15
1574 450k. African elephant in water (horiz) 60 20
1575 550k. African elephant with ears flapping 75 25

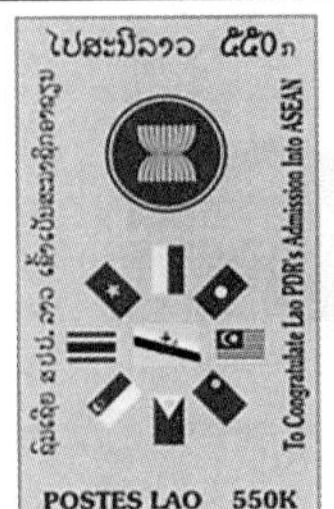
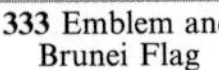

333 Emblem and Brunei Flag **336** Players

335 Headquarters, Djakarta, Indonesia

1997. Admission of Laos into Association of South East Asian Nations. Members' flags, centre flag given.

1577	550k. Type **333**	75	25
1578	550k. Indonesia (red and white bands)	75	25
1579	550k. Laos (red, blue with white circle, red bands)	75	25
1580	550k. Malaysia (crescent and star on blue quarter, red and white stripes)	75	25
1581	550k. Myanmar (flower and stars on blue quarter, red)	75	25
1582	550k. Philippines (sun and stars on white triangle, blue and red bands)	75	25
1583	550k. Singapore (crescent and five stars on red band, white band)	75	25
1584	550k. Thailand (red, white, blue, red bands)	75	25
1585	550k. Vietnam (yellow star on red)	75	25

1997. 30th Anniv of Association of South East Asian Nations. Multicoloured.

1587	150k. Type **335**	10	10
1588	600k. Map of Laos and state flag	80	25

1997. World Cup Football Championship, France (1998) (2nd issue).

1589	**336**	100k. multicoloured	10	10
1590	–	200k. multicoloured	30	10
1591	–	250k. multicoloured	35	10
1592	–	300k. multicoloured	40	15
1593	–	350k. multicoloured	50	15
1594	–	700k. multicoloured	1·00	35

DESIGNS: 200k. to 700k. Various football scenes.

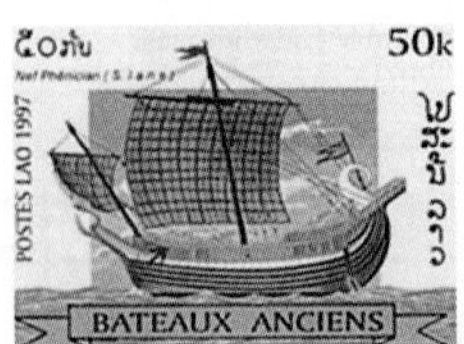

337 Phoenician Nef

1997. Sailing Ships. Multicoloured.

1596	50k. Type **337**	10	10
1597	100k. 13th-century nef	10	10
1598	150k. 15th-century nef	10	10
1599	200k. 16th-century Portuguese caravel	30	10
1600	400k. 17th-century Dutch ship	55	20
1601	900k. H.M.S. "Victory" (Nelson's flagship)	1·25	40

338 Headdress

1997. Headdresses and Masks. Multicoloured.

1603	50k. Type **338**	10	10
1604	100k. Headdress with flower at left	10	10
1605	150k. Mask with curved tusks (horiz)	10	10
1606	200k. Mask tipped with headdress decorated with two faces	30	10
1607	350k. Mask with green face	50	15

339 Two Pirogues

1997. Pirogue Race. Multicoloured.

1608	50k. Type **339**	10	10
1609	100k. Crowd cheering competitors from land	10	10
1610	300k. Side view of two competing pirogues	40	15
1611	500k. People cheering on spectator boat	70	25

340 Sunken Net

1998. Traditional Fishing Methods. Multicoloured.

1612	50k. Type **340**	15	10
1613	100k. Fisherman throwing net (horiz)	30	10
1614	450k. Funnel net	1·10	35
1615	650k. Lobster pots (horiz)	1·50	50

341 Man riding Tiger

1998. New Year. Year of the Tiger.

1616	**341**	150k. multicoloured	35	10
1617		350k. multicoloured	80	25
1618		400k. multicoloured	95	35

342 Wat Sisaket Shrine **344** Buddha, Luang Phabang Temple

343 Boat and Pole

1998. Temples. Multicoloured.

1619	10000k. Type **342**	90	30
1620	25000k. Wat Phou temple, Pakse (horiz)	1·75	55
1621	45000k. That Luang (royal mausoleum) (horiz)	2·75	85

1998. Water Transport. Multicoloured.

1622	1100k. Type **343**	1·25	40
1623	1200k. Covered canoe	1·40	45
1624	2500k. Motorized canoe	2·60	80

1998.

1625	**344**	3000k. multicoloured	3·00	90

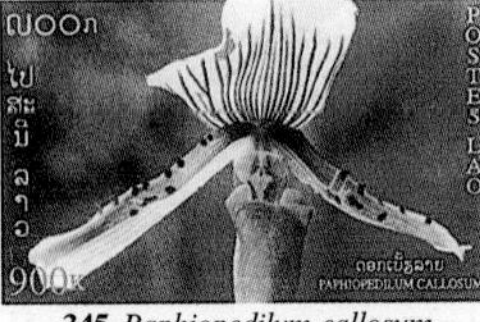

345 *Paphiopedilum callosum*

1998. Orchids. Multicoloured.

1626	900k. Type **345**	1·50	45
1627	950k. *Paphiopedilum concolor*	1·60	50
1628	1000k. *Dendrobium thyrsiflorum* (vert)	1·75	55
1629	1050k. *Dendrobium lindleyi* (vert)	1·75	55

346 Children in Classroom

1998. 50th Anniv of Universal Declaration of Human Rights. Multicoloured.

1630	300k. Type **346**	45	15
1631	1700k. Woman posting vote into ballot box	2·25	70

347 Gaeng

1998. Wind Instruments. Multicoloured.

1632	900k. Type **347**	1·50	45
1633	1200k. Khuoy (flute)	1·90	60
1634	1500k. Khaen (bamboo pipes of various lengths)	2·25	70

348 Military Personnel and Flag

1999. 50th Anniv of People's Army. Multicoloured.

1635	1300k. Type **348**	1·25	40
1636	1500k. Soldier with upraised arm and jungle fighters (vert)	1·60	50

349 Inscribed Monument (world heritage)

1999. UNESCO World Heritage Site. Luang Prabang. Multicoloured.

1637	400k. Type **349**	45	15
1638	1150k. House with veranda and dovecote (horiz)	1·10	35
1639	1250k. Wat Xiengthong (horiz)	2·25	70

350 Yao Children celebrating New Year, Muong Sing

1999. Tourism Year (1st issue). Multicoloured.

1640	200k. Type **350**	20	10
1641	500k. Phadeang, Vangvieng district	45	15
1642	1050k. Wat That Makmo, Luang Prabang	80	25
1643	1300k. Patuxay (victory monument), Vientiane (vert)	2·25	70

See also No. **MS**1653.

351 Rabbit and Chinese Zodiac Animals **353** Collared Owlet (*Glaucidium brodiei*)

352 Iron Plough

1999. New Year. Year of the Rabbit. Multicoloured.

1644	1500k. Type **351**	80	20
1645	1600k. White rabbit (horiz)	1·75	55

1999. Traditional Farming Implements. Multicoloured.

1646	1500k. Type **352**	1·25	40
1647	2000k. Harrow	1·60	50
1648	3200k. Wooden plough	2·50	75

1999. Owls and Bat. Multicoloured.

1649	900k. Type **353**	85	25
1650	1600k. Collared scops owl (*Otus lempiji*)	1·60	50
1651	2100k. Barn owl (*Tyto alba*)	2·40	75
1652	2800k. Black capped fruit bat (*Chironax melanocephalus*)	3·25	1·00

354 Patuxay (victory monument), Vientiane

1999. Tourism (2nd issue). Sheet 135 × 100 mm containing T **354** and similar horiz designs.

MS1653	2500k. Type **354**; 4000k. Ho Phra Keo, Vientiane; 5500k. Wat Xieng Thong, Luang Prabang; 8000k. Pha That Luang, Vientiane	10·00	3·00

355 Envelope and Globe

1999. 125th Anniv of Universal Postal Union. Multicoloured.

1654	2600k. Type **355**	1·90	60
1655	3400k. Postman delivering letter	2·75	85

356 Carved Tree Stump

1999. International Horticultural Exposition, Kunming, China. Exposition buildings. Multicoloured.

1656	300k. Type **356**	30	10
1657	900k. China Hall	95	30
1658	2300k. Science and Technology Hall	1·75	55
1659	2500k. Traditional Laotian house	2·00	60

357 Javan Rhino (*Rhinoceros sondaicus*)

1999. Animals. Multicoloured.

1660	700k. Type **357**	65	20
1661	900k. Water buffalo (*Bubalus bubalis*) (vert)	75	25

1662 1700k. Spotted linsang (*Prionodon pardicolor*) . . 1·40 45
1663 1800k. Sambar deer (*Cervus unicolor*) . . . . 1·50 50
1664 1900k. Lion (*Panthera leo*) (vert) . . . . 1·60 55

POSTAGE DUE STAMPS

D 5 Vat Sisaket Shrine D 6 Sampans D 98 Serpent

1952.

D22 **D 5** 10c. brown 20 35
D23 20c. violet 20 35
D24 50c. red 20 30
D25 1p. green 25 35
D26 2p. blue 25 35
D27 5p. purple 70 80
D28 **D 6** 10p. blue . . . . 1·10 1·25

1973.

D378 **D 98** 10k. black, brn & yell 10 10
D379 15k. black, yell & grn 10 10
D380 20k. black, green & bl 15 15
D381 50k. black, blue & red 30 30

APPENDIX

The following stamps have either been issued in excess of postal needs or have not been available to the public in reasonable quantities at face value. Such stamps may later be given full listing if there is evidence of regular postal use.

1975.

Centenary of U.P.U. Postage 10, 15, 30, 40k.; Air 1000, 1500k. On gold foil 2500, 3000k.

"Apollo–Soyuz" Space Link. Postage 125, 150, 200, 300k.; Air 450, 700k.

Bicentenary of American Revolution. Postage 10, 15, 40, 50, 100, 125, 150, 200k.; Air 1000, 1500k.

LAS BELA Pt. 1

A state of Baluchistan. Now part of Pakistan.

12 pies = 1 anna; 16 annas = 1 rupee.

1

1897.

1 **1** ½a. black on white . . . . . 21·00 14·00
11 ½a. black on blue . . . . . 11·00 6·50
3 ½a. black on grey . . . . . 12·00 7·00
12 ½a. black on green . . . . . 11·00 6·50
8 – 1a. black on orange . . . . 16·00 18·00

The 1a. has the English inscription in a circle with the native inscription across the centre.

LATAKIA Pt. 19

The former state of the Alaouites which changed its name to Latakia in 1930.

Latakia was merged with Syria in 1936.

100 centimes = 1 piastre.

1931. As 1930 stamps of Syria (T **26/7**) optd **LATTAQUIE** in French and Arabic.

65 0p.10 mauve . . . . 1·50 1·90
66 0p.20 blue . . . . 30 2·25
67 0p.20 red . . . . 1·75 3·50
68 0p.25 green . . . . 1·00 2·75
69 0p.25 violet . . . . 2·00 3·25
70 0p.50 violet . . . . 2·00 3·00
71 0p.75 red . . . . 2·75 3·00
72 1p. green . . . . 1·50 1·75
73 1p.50 brown . . . . 3·75 4·00
74 1p.50 green . . . . 4·25 4·25
75 2p. violet . . . . 2·75 1·90
76 3p. green . . . . 5·75 5·25
77 4p. orange . . . . 3·50 2·25
78 4p.50 red . . . . 4·75 5·25
79 6p. green . . . . 5·00 5·00
80 7p.50 blue . . . . 5·50 4·75
81 10p. brown . . . . 7·25 7·00
82 15p. green . . . . 10·50 10·50
83 25p. purple . . . . 24·00 24·00
84 50p. brown . . . . 21·00 22·00
85 100p. red . . . . 55·00 70·00

1931. Air. As 1931 air stamps of Syria optd **LATTAQUIE** in French and Arabic.

86 0p.50 yellow . . . . 1·40 2·25
87 0p.50 brown . . . . 1·50 2·75
88 1p. brown . . . . 2·50 2·50
89 2p. blue . . . . 3·50 3·25
90 3p. green . . . . 3·25 3·25
91 5p. purple . . . . 7·25 7·25
92 10p. blue . . . . 9·00 9·00
93 15p. red . . . . 10·50 10·50
94 25p. orange . . . . 24·00 24·00
95 50p. black . . . . 30·00 35·00
96 100p. mauve . . . . 29·00 34·00

POSTAGE DUE STAMPS

1931. Nos. D197/8 of Syria optd **LATTAQUIE** in French and Arabic.

D86 8p. black on blue . . . . . 22·00 24·00
D87 15p. black on pink . . . . . 11·50 17·00

LATVIA Pt. 10

A country on the Baltic Sea. Previously part of the Russian Empire, Latvia was independent from 1918 to 1940 when it became part of the U.S.S.R.

Following the dissolution of the U.S.S.R. in 1991, Latvia once again became an independent republic.

1918. 100 kapeikas = 1 rublis.
1923. 100 santimu = 1 lats.
1991. 100 kopeks = 1 (Russian) rouble.
1992. 100 kopeks = 1 Latvian rouble.
1993. 100 santimu = 1 lats.

1 4 5 Rising Sun

1918. Printed on back of German war maps. Imperf or perf.

15 **1** 3k. lilac 10 10
16 5k. red 10 10
17 10k. blue 10 10
18 15k. green 10 10
41 20k. orange 10 10
20 25k. grey 50 35
21 35k. brown 20 20
42 40k. purple 30 10
22 50k. violet 20 20
44 75k. green 25 15
29 3r. red and blue . . . . . 1·25 75
30 5r. red and brown . . . . . 1·25 60

1919. Liberation of Riga. Imperf.

24 **4** 5k. red 20 20
25 15k. green 20 20
26 35k. brown 35 45

For stamps of Types **1** and **4** optd with a cross, with or without Russian letters "Z A", see under North-West Russia Nos. 21/42.

1919. Imperf or perf.

27 **5** 10k. blue 50 35

6 7

1919. 1st Anniv of Independence. (a) Size 33 × 45 mm.

32 **6** 10k. red and brown 35 35

(b) Size 28 × 38 mm.

33 **6** 10k. red and brown 20 20
34 35k. green and blue 20 20
35 1r. red and green 75 75

1919. Liberation of Courland.

36 **7** 10k. red and brown 10 10
37 25k. green and blue 20 20
38 35k. blue and black 30 30
39 1r. brown and green 55 55

8

1920. Red Cross stamps. (a) On backs of blue Bolshevist notes. Perf.

46 **8** 20-30k. red and brown . . . 50 1·50
47 40-55k. red and blue . . . . 50 1·50
48 50-70k. red and green . . . . 50 1·75
49 1r.-1r.30 red and grey . . . . 75 2·00

(b) On backs of green Western Army notes. Perf.

50 **8** 20-30k. red and brown . . . 40 90
51 40-55k. red and blue 40 90
52 50-70k. red and green 60 90
53 1r.-1r.30 red and grey . . . . 75 1·75

(c) On backs of red, green and brown Bolshevist notes. Imperf.

54 **8** 20-30k. red and brown . . . 1·00 2·75
55 40-55k. red and blue . . . . 1·00 2·75
56 50-70k. red and green . . . . 1·00 2·75
57 1r.-1r.30 red and grey . . . . 2·00 4·00

CHARITY PREMIUMS. In the above and later issues where two values are expressed, the lower value represents the franking value and the higher the price charged, the difference being the charity premium.

9 10

1920. Liberation of Latgale.

58 **9** 50k. pink and green 20 30
59 1r. brown and green 30 40

1920. 1st Constituent Assembly.

60 **10** 50k. red 50 20
61 1r. blue 50 15
62 3r. green and brown 90 70
63 5r. purple and grey . . . . 1·00 80

1920. Surch in white figures on black oval.

64 **6** 10r. on 1r. red and green . . 2·00 1·10
65 20r. on 1r. red and green . . 3·50 2·50
66 30r. on 1r. red and green . . 4·50 4·00

1920. Surch **2 DIWI RUBLI**. Perf.

67 **1** 2r. on 10k. blue . . . . . . 2·00 1·25
68 **4** 2r. on 35k. brown 50 30

1920. (a) Surch **WEENS** or **DIVI**, value and **RUBLI**.

69 **7** 1 (WEENS) r. on 35k. blue and black 30 30
70 2 (DIVI) r. on 10k. red and brown 45 40
71 2 (DIVI) r. on 25k. green and blue 70 30

(b) Surch **DIWI RUBLI 2.**

72 **6** 2r. on 35k. green and blue 90 70

(c) Surch **DIVI 2 RUB. 2.**

73 **10** 2r. on 50k. red 25 40

(d) Surch **Desmit rubli.**

74 **6** 10r. on 10r. on 1r. red and green (No. 64) . . . . . 1·00 65

1921. Red Cross. Nos. 51/3 surch **RUB 2 RUB.**

75 **8** 2r. on 20-30k. red and brown 2·50 4·50
76 2r. on 40-55k. red and blue 2·50 4·50
77 2r. on 50-70k. red and green 2·50 4·50
78 2r. on 1r.-1r.30k. red and grey . . . . 2·50 4·50

1921. Surch in figures and words over thick bar of crossed lines.

79 **9** 10r. on 50k. pink and green 90 70
80 20r. on 50k. pink and green 4·25 3·25
81 30r. on 50k. pink and green 4·00 3·00
82 50r. on 50k. pink and green 7·00 6·50
83 100r. on 50k. pink and green 18·00 15·00

19 Bleriot XI

1921. Air. Value in "RUBLU". Imperf or perf.

84 **19** 10r. green . . . . 5·00 3·00
85 20r. blue . . . . 5·00 1·50

See also Nos. 155/7.

21 Latvian Coat of Arms 22 Great Seal of Latvia

1921. Value in "Kopeks" or "Roubles".

86 **21** 50k. violet 25 10
87b 1r. yellow 25 25
88 2r. green 20 10
89 3r. green 30 25
90 5r. red 80 10
91 6r. red . . . . 1·25 75
92 9r. orange 90 25
93 10r. blue . . . . 1·10 10
94 15r. blue . . . . 4·50 1·00
95c 20r. lilac . . . . 11·00 1·50
96 **22** 50r. brown . . . . 20·00 5·00
97 100r. blue . . . . 24·00 4·25

1923. Value in "Santimi" or "Lats".

127 **21** 1s. mauve 15 10
129 2s. yellow 15 10
130 3s. red 15 10
100 4s. green 45 10
132 5s. green 30 10
133 6s. green and yellow . . . 10 10
134 7s. green 30 15
103 10s. red 85 10
136d 10s. green and yellow . . 7·00 10
104 12s. mauve 25 20
105c 15s. purple and orange . . 2·75 10
107 20s. blue . . . . 1·50 10
139 20s. pink . . . . 3·00 20
108 25s. blue 20 10
109 30s. pink . . . . 4·00 15
140 30s. blue . . . . 1·25 10
141 35s. blue . . . . 1·50 10
110 40s. purple . . . . 1·50 15
143 50s. grey . . . . 3·00 15
144 **22** 1l. brown and bistre . . . 6·00 15
116 2l. blue and light blue . . 14·00 90
117 5l. green and light green 48·00 3·75
118 10l. red and light red . . 6·00 15·00

1923. Charity. War Invalids. Surch **KARA INVALIDIEM S.10S.** and cross.

112 **21** 1s.+10s. mauve . . . . . 50 1·00
113 2s.+10s. yellow . . . . . 50 1·00
114 4s.+10s. green . . . . . 50 1·00

24 Town Hall 28 Pres. J. Cakste

1925. 300th Anniv of City of Libau.

119 – 6-12s. blue and red . . . . 1·75 4·50
120 **24** 15-25s. brown and blue . . 90 3·50
121 – 25-35s. green and violet . . 1·75 3·50
122 – 30-40s. lake and blue . . . 4·00 14·00
123 – 50-60s. violet and green . . 5·00 16·00

DESIGNS—HORIZ: 6-12s. Harbour and lighthouse; 25-35s. Spa health pavilion. VERT: 30-40s. St. Anna's Church; 50-60s. Arms of Libau.

1927. Surch.

124 **1** 15s. on 40k. purple 50 40
125 15s. on 50k. violet . . . . 1·10 1·25
126 **10** 1l. on 3r. green and brown 7·50 12·00

1928. Death of President Cakste and Memorial Fund.

150 **28** 2-12s. orange . . . . . . 2·50 4·00
151 6-16s. green . . . . . . 2·50 4·00
152 15-25s. lake . . . . . . 2·50 4·00
153 25-35s. blue . . . . . . 2·50 4·00
154 30-40s. red . . . . 2·50 4·00

1928. Air. Value in "SANTIMU" or "SANTIMI".

193 **19** 10s. green . . . . 1·50 75
156 15s. red . . . . 2·00 1·00
157 25s. blue . . . . 3·50 1·75

29 Ruins at Rezekne 30 Venta

1928. 10th Anniv of Independence. Views.

158 **29** 6s. purple and green . . . 50 15
159 – 15s. green and brown . . . 40 15
160 – 20s. green and red 90 50
161 – 30s. brown and blue . . . 1·10 20
162 – 50s. pink and grey . . . . 2·50 2·50
163 – 1l. sepia and brown . . . . 3·00 1·75

DESIGNS: 15s. Jelgava (Mitau); 20s. Cesis (Wenden); 30s. Liepaja (Libau); 50s. Riga; 1l. National Theatre, Riga.

1928. Liberty Memorial Fund. Imperf or perf.

164 **30** 6-16s. green . . . . . . 2·25 2·25
165 – 10-20s. red . . . . 2·25 2·25
166 – 15-25s. brown . . . . . . 2·25 2·25
167 – 30-40s. blue . . . . . . 2·25 2·25
168 – 50-60s. black . . . . . . 2·25 2·25
169 – 1l.-1l.10s. purple . . . . 3·50 3·50

DESIGNS: 10-20s. "Latvia" (Woman); 15-25s. Mitau; 30-40s. National Theatre, Riga; 50-60s. Wenden; 1l.-1l.10s. Trenches, Riga Bridge.

32 Z. A. Meierovics 33 J. Rainis

1929. 3rd Death Anniv of Meierovics (Foreign Minister). Imperf or perf.
170 **32** 2-4s. yellow . . . . 3·00 3·00
171 6-12s. green . . . . 3·00 3·00
172 15-25s. purple . . . . . . 3·00 3·00
173 25-35s. blue . . . . 3·00 3·00
174 30-40s. blue . . . . 3·00 3·00

1930. Memorial Fund for J. Rainis (writer and politician). Imperf or perf.
175 **33** 1-2s. purple . . . . 75 1·75
176 2-4s. orange . . . . 75 1·75
177 4-8s. green . . . . 75 1·75
178 6-12s. brown and green . . 75 1·75
179 10-20s. red . . . . 15·00 32·00
180 15-30s. green and brown 15·00 32·00

34 Klemm KI-20 over Durbe Castle

1930. Air. J. Rainis Memorial Fund. Imperf or perf.
181 **34** 10-20s. green and red . . . 10·00 11·50
182 15-30s. red and green . . . 10·00 11·50

35 36

1930. Anti-T.B. Fund.
183 – 1-2s. red and purple . . . 50 50
184 – 2-4s. red and orange . . . 50 50
185 **35** 4-8s. red and green . . . 65 80
186 – 5-10s. brown and green . . 75 1·10
187 – 6-12s. yellow and green . . 75 1·10
188 – 10-20s. black and red . . . 1·00 1·60
189 – 15-30s. green and brown 1·50 1·50
190 – 20-40s. blue and red . . . 1·50 1·75
191 – 25-50s. lilac, blue and red 2·00 2·50
192 **36** 30-60s. lilac, green and blue . . . . 2·75 3·00
DESIGNS—VERT: As Type **35**: 1-2s., 2-4s. The Crusaders' Cross; 5-10s. G. Zemgalis; 6-12s. Tower; 10-20s. J. Cakste; 15-30s. Floral design; 20-40s. A. Kviesis. HORIZ: As Type **36**: 25-50s. Sanatorium.

1931. Nos. 183/92 surch.
196 9 on 6-12s. yellow and green 65 1·00
197 16 on 1-2s. red and purple 10·00 20·00
198 17s. on 2-4s. red and orange 1·25 2·25
199 19 on 4-8s. red and green . . 3·00 7·00
200 20 on 5-10s. brown and green 2·00 8·00
201 23 on 15-30s. green and brown . . . . 75 1·00
202 25 on 10-20s. black and red 2·00 3·75
203 35 on 20-40s. blue and red 3·75 4·50
204 45 on 25-50s. lilac, blue and red . . . . 12·00 16·00
205 55 on 30-60s. lilac, green & bl 13·00 17·00

1931. Air. Charity. Nos. 155/7 surch **LATVIJAS AIZSARGI** and value. Imperf or perf.
206 **19** 50 on 10s. green . . . . . 13·00 18·00
207 1l. on 15s. red . . . . . . 13·00 18·00
208 1l.50 on 2s. blue . . . . . 13·00 18·00

38 Foreign Invasion

1932. Militia Maintenance Fund. Imperf or perf.
209 – 1-11s. blue and purple . . 1·90 2·10
210 **38** 2-17s. orange and olive . . 1·90 2·10
211 – 3-23s. red and brown . . . 1·90 2·10
212 – 4-34s. green . . . . 1·90 2·10
213 – 5-45s. green . . . . 1·90 2·10
DESIGNS: 1-11s. The Holy Oak and Kriva telling stories; 3-23s. Lacplesis, the deliverer; 4-34s. The Black Knight (enemy) slaughtered; 5-45s. Laimdota, the spirit of Latvia, freed.

39 Infantry Manoeuvres

1932. Militia Maintenance Fund. Imperf or perf.
214 – 6-25s. purple and brown 4·00 4·50
215 **39** 7-35s. blue and green . . . 4·00 4·50
216 – 10-45s. sepia and green . . 4·00 4·50
217 – 12-55s. green and red . . . 4·00 4·50
218 – 15-75s. violet and red . . . 4·00 4·50
DESIGNS—HORIZ: 6-25s. Troops on march. VERT: 10-45s. First aid to soldier; 12-55s. Army kitchen; 15-75s. Gen. J. Balodis.

41

1932. Air. Charity. Imperf or perf.
219 **41** 10-20s. black and green . . 12·00 18·00
220 15-30s. red and grey . . . 12·00 18·00
221 25-50s. blue and grey . . . 12·00 18·00

1932. Riga Exn of Lettish Products. Optd **Latvijas razojumu izstade Riga. 1932.g.10.-18.IX.**
222 **21** 3s. red 50 40
223 10s. green on yellow . . . 1·50 80
224 20s. pink . . . . 1·50 70
225 35s. blue . . . . 2·40 1·60

43 Leonardo da Vinci 44 "Mourning Mother" Memorial, Riga

1932. Air. Charity. Pioneers of Aviation. Imperf or perf.
226 – 5-25s. green and brown . . 10·00 15·00
227 **43** 10-50s. green and brown 10·00 15·00
228 – 15-75s. green and red . . . 13·50 17·00
229 – 20-100s. mauve and green 13·50 17·00
230 – 25-125s. blue and brown 13·50 17·00
DESIGNS—VERT: 5s. Icarus; 15s. Jacques Charles's hydrogen balloon, 1783 (inscr "Charliers"). HORIZ: 20s. Wright Type A biplane; 25s. Bleriot XI monoplane.

1933. Air. Wounded Latvian Airmen Fund. Imperf or perf.
231 – 2-52s. brown and black . . 6·00 14·00
232 **44** 3-53s. red and black . . . 6·00 14·00
233 – 10-60s. green and black . . 6·00 14·00
234 – 20-70s. red and black . . . 6·00 14·00
DESIGNS: 2s. Fall of Icarus; 10s., 20s. Proposed tombs for airmen.

1933. Air. Charity. Riga–Bathurst Flight. Nos. 155/7 optd **LATVIJA-AFRIKA 1933** or surch also.
235 10s. green . . . . 15·00 50·00
236 15s. red . . . . 15·00 50·00
237 25s. blue . . . . 18·00 50·00
238 50s. on 15s. red £120 £325
239 100s. on 25s. blue £120 £325
In the event the aircraft crashed at Neustettin, Germany, and the mail was forwarded by ordinary post.

46 Biplane under Fire at Riga

1933. Air. Charity. Wounded Latvian Airmen Fund. Imperf or perf.
240 – 3-53s. blue and orange . . 20·00 24·00
241 **46** 7-57s. brown and blue . . 20·00 24·00
242 – 35-135s. black and blue . . 20·00 24·00
DESIGNS: 3s. Monoplane taking off; 35s. Map and aircraft.

47 Glanville Brothers' Gee Bee Super Sportster

1933. Air. Charity. Wounded Latvian Airmen Fund. Imperf or perf.
243 **47** 8-68s. grey and brown . . 30·00 50·00
244 – 12-112s. green and purple 30·00 50·00
245 – 30-130s. grey and blue . . 30·00 50·00
246 – 40-190s. blue and purple 30·00 50·00
DESIGNS: 12s. Supermarine S6B seaplane; 30s. Airship "Graf Zeppelin" over Riga; 40s. Dornier Do-X flying boat.

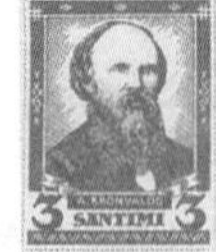

48 President's Palace 50 A. Kronvalds 51

1934. 15th Anniv of New Constitution.
247 **48** 3s. red 10 15
248 – 5s. green 15 10
249 – 10s. green . . . . 1·75 10
250 – 20s. red . . . . 1·75 10
251 – 35s. blue 10 15
252 **48** 40s. brown 20 15
DESIGNS: 5, 10s. Arms and shield; 20s. Allegory of Latvia; 35s. Government Building.

1936. Lettish Intellectuals.
253 **50** 3s. red . . . . 1·10 4·00
254 – 10s. green . . . . 1·10 4·00
255 – 20s. mauve . . . . 1·10 5·00
256 – 35s. blue . . . . 1·10 5·00
PORTRAITS: 10s. A. Pumpurs; 20s. J. Maters; 35s. Auseklis.

1936. White Cross Fund. Designs incorporating Cross and Stars device as in T **51**.
257 **51** 3s. red . . . . 1·50 4·00
258 – 10s. green . . . . 1·50 4·00
259 – 20s. mauve . . . . 1·50 5·00
260 – 35s. blue . . . . 1·50 5·00
DESIGNS: 10s. Oak leaves; 20s. Doctors and patient; 35s. Woman holding shield.

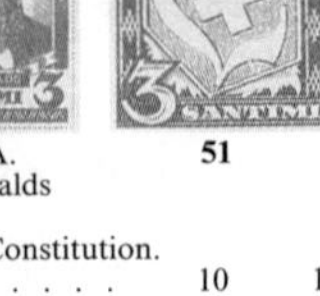

53 Independence Monument, Rauna (Ronneburg) 54 President Ulmanis

1937. Monuments.
261 **53** 3s. red . . . . 35 1·40
262 – 5s. green 35 60
263 – 10s. green 35 35
264 – 20s. red . . . . 85 1·00
265 – 30s. blue . . . . 90 1·25
266 – 35s. blue . . . . 1·40 1·50
267 – 40s. brown . . . . 2·25 2·50
DESIGNS—VERT: 10s. Independence Monument, Jelgava (Mitau); 20s. War Memorial, Valka (Walk); 30s. Independence Monument, Iecava (Eckau); 35s. Independence Monument, Riga; 40s. Col. Kalpak's Grave, Visagalas Cemetery. HORIZ: 5s. Cemetery Gate, Riga.

1937. President Ulmanis's 60th Birthday.
268 **54** 3s. red and orange 15 10
269 5s. light green and green 15 15
270 10s. deep green and green 25 35
271 20s. purple and red 55 35
272 25s. grey and blue 85 70
273 30s. deep blue and blue . . 85 60
274 35s. indigo and blue . . . 75 50
275 40s. light brown and brown 85 75
276 50s. green and black . . . 90 80

56 Gaizinkalns, Livonia 57 General J. Balodis

1938. 20th Anniv of Independence.
278 **56** 3s. red 10 10
279 – 5s. green 10 10
280 **57** 10s. green 30 10
281 – 20s. mauve 20 10
282 – 30s. blue 60 20
283 – 35s. slate 90 10
284 – 40s. mauve 80 15
DESIGNS: As Type **56**: 5s. Latgale landscape; 30s. City of Riga; 35s. Rumba waterfall, Courland; 40s. Zemgale landscape. As Type **57**: 20s. President Ulmanis.

58 Elementary School, Riga

1939. 5th Anniv of Authoritarian Government.
285 **58** 3s. brown 30 60
286 – 5s. green 30 60
287 – 10s. green 95 60
288 – 20s. red 95 65
289 – 30s. blue . . . . 1·40 1·00
290 – 35s. blue . . . . 1·40 1·50
291 – 40s. purple . . . . 1·75 1·00
292 – 50s. black . . . . 2·00 1·25
DESIGNS: 5s. Jelgava Castle; 10s. Riga Castle; 20s. Independence Memorial; 30s. Eagle and National Flag; 35s. Town Hall, Daugavpils; 40s. War Museum and Powder-magazine, Riga; 50s. Pres. Ulmanis.

59 Reaping 60 Arms of Courland, Livonia and Latgale 61 Arms of Latvian Soviet Socialist Republic

1939. Harvest Festival. Dated "8 X 1939".
294 **59** 10s. green 40 40
295 – 20s. red (Apples) 70 30

1940.
296 **60** 1s. violet 25 50
297 2s. yellow 30 50
298 3s. red 10 15
299 5s. brown 10 10
300 7s. green 10 60
301 10s. green 75 15
302 20s. red 75 10
303 30s. brown 90 40
304 35s. blue 10 85
305 50s. green . . . . 1·00 50
306 1l. olive . . . . 2·00 60

1940. Incorporation of Latvia in U.S.S.R.
307 **61** 1s. violet 15 20
308 2s. yellow 15 15
309 3s. red 10 10
310 5s. olive 10 10
311 7s. green 10 45
312 10s. green 30 10
313 20s. red 65 10
314 30s. blue 80 30
315 35s. blue 10 55
316 40s. brown 60 20
317 50s. grey 90 25
318 1l. brown . . . . 2·00 35
319 5l. green . . . . 11·00 5·50

64 Latvian Arms 65 Latvian Arms

1991.
320 **64** 5k. silver, brown & lt brn 35 20
321 10k. silver, brown & drab 15 10
322 15k. silver, sepia & brown 15 10
323 20k. silver, blue & lt blue 60 20
324 40k. silver, green and light green . . . . 1·25 40
325 50k. silver, brown and lilac 1·40 45
326 **65** 100k. multicoloured . . . 2·75 80
327 200k. multicoloured . . . 5·00 1·40

1991. Nos. 6073 and 6077a of Russia surch **LATVIJA** and new value.
332 100k. on 7k. blue 10 10
333 300k. on 2k. brown 35 25
334 500k. on 2k. brown 60 40
335 1000k. on 2k. brown . . . . 1·25 70

67 Main Statue, Liberty Monument, Riga 68 Olympic Committee Symbol

1991.
336 **67** 10k. multicoloured 10 10
337 15k. multicoloured 10 10
338 20k. multicoloured 15 10
339 30k. multicoloured 25 15
340 50k. multicoloured 40 20
341 100k. multicoloured . . . 80 45

1992. Recognition of Latvian Olympic Committee.
342 **68** 50k.+25k. red, silver and drab 40 20
343 – 50k.+25k. red, silver and grey 40 20
344 **68** 100k.+50k. red, gold and bistre 80 45
DESIGN: No. 343, as T **68** but symbols smaller and inscribed "BERLIN 18.09.91." at left.

69 Vaidelotis

72 Children in Fancy Dress around Christmas Tree

1992. Statues from the base of the Liberty Monument, Riga.
345 – 10k. black and brown 10 10
346 **69** 20k. brown and grey 15 10
347 – 30k. deep lilac and lilac 25 15
348 **69** 30k. deep brown and brown 25 15
349 – 40k. blue and grey 35 20
350 **69** 50k. green and grey 40 25
351 – 50k. black and grey 40 25
352 – 100k. purple and mauve 85 45
353 – 200k. deep blue and blue 1·60 80
DESIGNS: Nos. 345, 347, 353, Kurzeme (warrior with shield); 349, 351/2, Lachplesis (two figures).

1992. Nos. 4672, 6073 and 6077a of Russia surch **LATVIJA** and new value.
354a 1r. on 7k. blue 10 10
355 3r. on 2k. brown 10 10
356 5r. on 2k. brown 20 10
357 10r. on 2k. brown 40 20
358 25r. on 4k. red 95 45

1992. Birds of the Baltic. As Nos. 506/9 of Lithuania.
359 5r. black and red 50 45
360 5r. brown, black and red 50 45
361 5r. sepia, brown and red 50 45
362 5r. brown, black and red 50 45
DESIGNS: Nos 359, Osprey ("Pandion haliaetus"); 360, Black-tailed godwit ("Limosa limosa"); 361, Goosander ("Mergus merganser"); 362, Common shelducks ("Tadorna tadorna").

1992. Christmas. Multicoloured.
363 2r. Type **72** 20 10
364 3r. Angel choir 30 15
365 10r. Type **72** 50 20
366 15r. Adoration of the Kings 65 30

1993. Nos. 4855, 5296 and 5295 of Russia surch **LATVIJA** and new value.
367 50r. on 6k. multicoloured 75 35
368 100r. on 6k. multicoloured 1·50 75
369 300r. on 6k. multicoloured 3·25 1·60

74 Kuldiga Couple

75 Emblem

1993. Traditional Costumes. Multicoloured.
370 5s. Type **74** 15 10
371 10s. Alsunga 30 20
372 20s. Lielvarde 55 35
373 50s. Rucava 1·40 1·00
374 100s. Zemgale 3·00 2·00
375 500s. Ziemellatgale 13·50 9·00
See also Nos. 428, 442, 467 and 491.

1993. National Song Festival.
377 **75** 3s. black, gold and brown 15 10
378 5s. black, gold and lilac 30 15
379 – 15s. multicoloured 1·00 50
DESIGN: 15s. Abstract.

76 Pope John Paul II

77 Flags

1993. Papal Visit.
380 **76** 15s. multicoloured 50 35

1993. 75th Anniv of First Republic.
381 **77** 5s. multicoloured 15 10
382 15s. multicoloured 45 35

78 Valters

79 Biathlon

1994. 100th Birthday of Evalds Valters (actor).
383 **78** 15s. brown, light brown and gold 50 35

1994. Winter Olympic Games, Lillehammer, Norway. Multicoloured.
384 5s. Type **79** 15 10
385 10s. Two-man bobsleigh 25 15
386 15s. One-man luge 50 35
387 100s. Figure skating 2·75 1·50

80 Reed Hut

1994. 70th Anniv of Latvian Ethnological Open-air Museum, Bergi.
389 **80** 5s. multicoloured 25 10

81 Streetball

82 Kurzeme

1994. Basketball Festival, Riga.
390 **81** 15s. black, grey and orange 50 35

1994. Arms (1st series). (a) Size 18 × 21 mm.
391 **82** 1s. red, black and silver 10 10
392 – 2s. multicoloured 10 10
393 – 3s. silver, black and blue 10 10
394 – 5s. silver, black and red 10 10
395 – 8s. silver, black and blue 20 10
396 – 10s. silver, black and blue 25 10
396a – 10s. multicoloured 20 10
397 – 13s. black, gold and silver 30 15
397a – 16s. multicoloured 35 15
398 – 20s. silver, black and grey 50 25
398a – 20s. multicoloured 45 20
399 – 24s. green, black and silver 55 25
399a – 28s. multicoloured 60 30
400 – 30s. multicoloured 65 30
401 – 36s. silver, black and red 75 35
402 – 50s. multicoloured 1·10 55

(b) Size 29 × 23½ mm.
403 – 100s. multicoloured 2·10 1·00
404 – 200s. multicoloured 4·25 1·10
DESIGNS: 2s. Auce; 3s. Zemgale; 5s. Vidzeme; 8s. Livani; 10s. (396) Latgale; 10s. (396a) Valmiera; 13s. Preila; 16s. Ainazi; 20s. (398) Grobina; 20s. (398a) Rezekne; 24s. Tukums; 28s. Madona; 30, 100s. Riga; 36s. Priekule; 50, 200s. State arms.
See also Nos. 501/6.

83 Emblem

84 Coins in Scales

1994. 75th Anniv of Latvia University.
405 **83** 5s. gold, blue and green 10 10

1994. Europa. Multicoloured.
406 10s. Type **84** 25 20
407 50s. Money chest and notes in scales 1·25 60

85 Eating Cherries

86 Angel

1994. The Fat Dormouse. Multicoloured.
408 5s. Type **85** 15 10
409 10s. Eating strawberries 30 15
410 10s. On leafy branch 30 15
411 15s. On branch of apple tree 60 30

1994. Christmas. Multicoloured.
412 3s. Type **86** 10 10
413 8s. Angels playing violin and flute 30 15
414 13s. Angels singing 50 25
415 100s. Wreath of candles 2·75 1·40

87 Gnome with Candle

88 Emblem

1994. 80th Birthday of Margarita Staraste (children's writer and illustrator). Multicoloured.
416 5s. Type **87** 15 10
417 10s. Bear 30 15
418 10s. Child on sledge 30 15

1994. Road Safety Year.
419 **88** 10s. multicoloured 35 10

89 Emblem

90 Bauska Castle (Latvia)

1995. 50th Anniv of U.N.O.
420 **89** 15s. blue, red and silver 50 25

1995. Via Baltica Motorway Project. Multicoloured.
421 **90** 8s. multicoloured 30 15

91 White-backed Woodpecker

92 Vaivods

1995. European Nature Conservation Year. Birds. Multicoloured.
423 8s. Type **91** 30 15
424 20s. Corncrake 75 40
425 24s. White-winged black tern 95 50

1995. Birth Centenary of Cardinal Julijans Vaivods.
426 **92** 8s. multicoloured 20 10

93 Sun and Open Book

1995. 60th Anniv of Karlis Ulmaris Schools Appeal.
427 **93** 8s. multicoloured 20 10

1995. Traditional Costumes. As T **74**. Multicoloured.
428 8s. Nica 30 15

94 National Opera House

95 Lacplesis, the Bear Slayer

1995. 800th Anniv of Riga (1st issue). Multicoloured.
430 8s. Type **94** 25 10
431 16s. National Theatre 45 20
432 24s. Art School (44 × 26 mm) 70 35
433 36s. Art Museum (44 × 26 mm) 95 45
See also Nos. 456/9, 479/82, 493/6, 522/5, 540/3 and 560/3.

1995. European Peace and Freedom. Multicoloured.
434 16s. Type **95** 50 25
435 50s. Spidola 1·60 80

96 Christmas Tree at Night

97 Stradins

1995. Christmas. Multicoloured.
436 6s. Type **96** 20 10
437 6s. Elf flying with candle 20 10
438 15s. Cottage at night 40 20
439 24s. Elf with dog and cat 75 35

1996. Birth Centenary of Pauls Stradins (surgeon).
440 **97** 8s. multicoloured 20 10

98 Zenta Maurina (writer)

100 Cycling

1996. Europa. Famous Women.
441 **98** 36s. multicoloured 1·10 50

1996. Traditional Costumes. As T **74**. Multicoloured.
442 8s. Barta 25 15

1996. Olympic Games, Atlanta. Multicoloured.
445 8s. Type **100** 20 10
446 16s. Basketball 40 20
447 24s. Walking 65 30
448 36s. Canoeing (horiz) 1·00 50

101 Swallowtail

1996. Butterflies. Multicoloured.
450 8s. Type **101** 25 10
451 24s. Clifden's nonpareil 75 40
452 80s. Large tiger moth 2·00 1·00

102 1912 Russo-Balt Fire Engine

103 Apartment Block (E. Laube)

1996. Latvian Car Production. Multicoloured.
453 8s. Type **102** 25 10
454 24s. 1899 Leutner-Russia carriage 70 35
455 36s. 1939 Ford-Vairogs motor car 1·00 50

1996. 800th Anniv of Riga (2nd issue). Multicoloured.
456 8s. Type **103** 25 10
457 16s. Stained glass window (F. Sefels) (30 × 26 mm) 45 20
458 24s. Turreted buildings (E. Laube) (38 × 26 mm) 75 35
459 30s. Couple welcoming charioteer (mural, J. Rozentals) (38 × 26 mm) 1·00 50

104 Elves and Presents

1996. Christmas. Multicoloured.
460 6s. Type **104** 15 10
461 14s. Children with dog and Father Christmas on skis 35 20
462 20s. Child at tree and Father Christmas in armchair . . 50 25

105 European Nightjar **106** Symbols of Independence

1997. 75th Anniv of Birdlife International (conservation organization). Multicoloured.
463 10s. Type **105** 30 15
464 20s. Greater spotted eagle . . 75 35
465 30s. Aquatic warbler . . . . 1·10 55

1997. 6th Anniv of Independence.
466 **106** 10s. multicoloured 30 15

1997. Traditional Costumes. As T **74**. Multicoloured.
467 10s. Rietumvidzeme 20 10

107 Turaidas Roze **108** "Wappen der Herzogin von Kurland" (galleon)

1997. Europa. Tales and Legends.
469 **107** 32s. multicoloured 90 45

1997. Baltic Sailing Ships.
470 **108** 10s. multicoloured 30 15

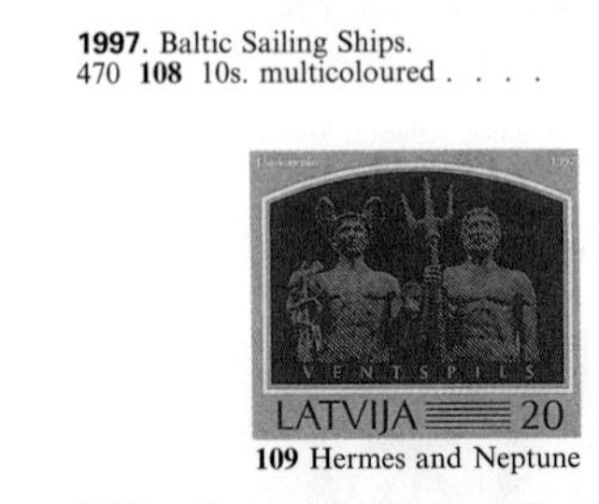
109 Hermes and Neptune

1997. Centenary of Ventspils International Commercial Port.
472 **109** 20s. blue, silver and yellow 60 30

110 Stamp Collecting

1997. Children's Leisure Pursuits. Multicoloured.
473 10s. Type **110** 25 10
474 12s. Motor cycle trials (vert) 40 20
475 20s. Ice hockey and skiing (vert) 60 30
476 30s. Tennis, football and basketball . . . . 1·00 50

111 Moricsala

1997. Nature Reserves. Multicoloured.
477 10s. Type **111** 25 10
478 30s. Slītere 75 35

112 Woman, Wooden Building and Jewellery (12th century)

1997. 800th Anniv of Riga (3rd issue). 12th–16th Centuries. Multicoloured.
479 10s. Type **112** 25 10
480 20s. 13th-century Cathedral cloister, statue (K. Bernevics) and seal of Bishop Albert, rosary beads and writing implement 55 25
481 30s. Livonian Order's castle, statue of V. von Plettenberg (Order Master) and weapons 80 40
482 32s. "Three Brothers" terrace, statue of St. John and seal (27 × 27 mm) 90 45

113 Man and Bear

1997. Christmas. Mummers. Multicoloured.
483 8s. Type **113** 20 10
484 18s. Witches 50 25
485 28s. Horse 70 35

114 Flames **115** Sculpture of Character

1998. Winter Olympic Games, Nagano, Japan.
486 **114** 20s. multicoloured 55 25

1998. Spridisi Memorial (to Anna Brigadere (writer)) Museum, Tervete.
487 **115** 10s. multicoloured 25 10

116 Song Festival

1998. Europa. National Festivals.
488 **116** 30s. multicoloured 65 30

117 Grini

1998. Nature Reserves. Multicoloured.
489 10s. Type **117** 20 10
490 30s. Teici 65 30

1998. Traditional Costumes. As T **74**. Multicoloured.
491 10s. Krustpils 20 10

118 Dannenstern House, Wooden Sculpture and Polish and Swedish Coins

1998. 800th Anniv of Riga (4th issue). 16th–20th Centuries. Multicoloured.
493 10s. Type **118** 20 10
494 20s. Library, medallion and monument to G. Herder (poet and philosopher) . . 45 20
495 30s. Arsenal, Victory column, octant and compass . . . 65 30
496 40s. Entrance gate to Warrior's Cemetery, "Mother Latvia" (statue) and 5l. coin 85 40

1998. Arms (2nd series). As T **82**.
497 5s. multicoloured 10 10
499 10s. multicoloured 20 10
500 15s. multicoloured 30 15
501 15s. black, blue and silver . . 30 15
502 15s. multicoloured 30 15
503 15s. multicoloured 30 15
504 15s. black, silver and red . . 30 15
505 30s. multicoloured 65 30
506 40s. multicoloured 75 35

DESIGNS: No. 497, Smiltene; 499, Valmiera; 500, Bauska; 501, Ogre; 502, Daugavpils; 503, Jurmala; 504 Kuldiga; 505, Liepaja; 506, Jelgava.

119 1918 5k. Stamp **120** Dome Church, Riga

1998. 70th Anniv of First Latvian Stamp.
510 **119** 30s. red, cream and grey 65 30

1998. Churches.
511 **120** 10s. multicoloured 20 10

121 Janis Cakste (1922–27) **122** State Flag

1998. Presidents.
512 **121** 10s. multicoloured 20 10

1998. 80th Anniv of Declaration of Independence. Multicoloured.
513 10s. Type **122** 20 10
514 30s. State arms and flags . . 65 30

123 Elves building Snowman

1998. Christmas. Multicoloured.
515 10s. Type **123** 20 10
516 20s. Elves decorating tree . . 40 20
517 30s. Elves sledging 65 30

124 Krustkalnu Nature Reserve **125** Playing Cards and Edgars (from novel "Purva Bridejs")

1999. Europa. Parks and Gardens.
518 30s. Type **124** 65 30
519 60s. Gauja National Nature Park . . . . 1·25 60

1999. Latvian Literature. Rudolfs Blaumanis.
520 **125** 110s. multicoloured . . . 2·25 1·10

126 Council Emblem

1999. 50th Anniv of Council of Europe.
521 **126** 30s. multicoloured 65 30

127 "Widwud" (schooner)

1999. 800th Anniv of Riga (5th issue). Transport. Multicoloured.
522 10s. Electric tramcar No. 258 (30 × 26½ mm) 20 10
523 30s. Type **127** 65 30
524 40s. Biplane 75 35
525 70s. Steam locomotive No. Tk-236 . . . . 1·50 75

128 Aglona Basilica **129** Family and State Flag

1999. Churches.
526 **128** 15s. multicoloured 30 15

1999. 10th Anniv of Baltic Chain (human chain uniting capitals of Latvia, Lithuania and Estonia).
527 **129** 15s. multicoloured 30 15

130 Rundale Palace

1999. Palaces.
529 **130** 20s. multicoloured 40 20

131 "Perse"

1999. 90th Death Anniv of Julijs Feders (painter).
530 **131** 15s. multicoloured 30 15

132 Gustavs Zemgals (1927–30) **133** Harbour, Letters and Emblem

1999. Presidents.
531 **132** 15s. multicoloured 35 15

1999. 125th Anniv of Universal Postal Union.
532 **133** 40s. multicoloured 90 45

134 Father Christmas and Candle **135** "Artist's Model" (J. Rosentals)

1999. Christmas. Multicoloured.
533 12s. Type **134** 25 10
534 15s. Children watching television 35 15
535 40s. Father Christmas placing toys under tree 90 45

2000.
536 **135** 40s. multicoloured 90 45

136 Scene from *The Wagon Driver* (poem) **137** "Building Europe"

2000. 50th Death Anniv of Aleksandrs Caks (poet).
537 **136** 40s. multicoloured 90 45

2000. Europa.
538 **137** 60s. multicoloured . . . . 1·40 70

138 Ice Hockey Players

2000. Ice Hockey.
539 **138** 70s. multicoloured . . . . 1·50 75

140 Central Market

2000. 800th Anniv of Riga (6th issue). Tourist Sights. Multicoloured.
540 20s. Type **140** 45 20
541 40s. Dome Church organ (25 × 30 mm) 90 45
542 40s. Zoo (44 × 26 mm) . . . 90 45
543 70s. The Powder Tower (25 × 30 mm) . . . . . . 1·50 75

141 Jelgava Palace

2000. Palaces.
544 **141** 40s. multicoloured 45 20

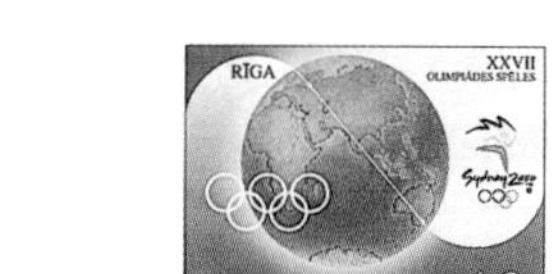

142 Globe and Olympic Rings

2000. Olympic Games, Sydney.
545 **142** 40s. multicoloured 45 20
546 70s. multicoloured . . . . 1·60 80

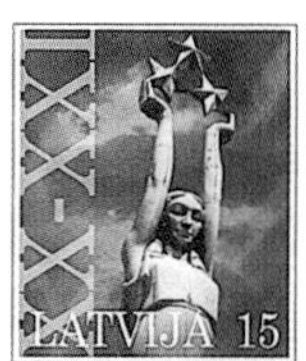
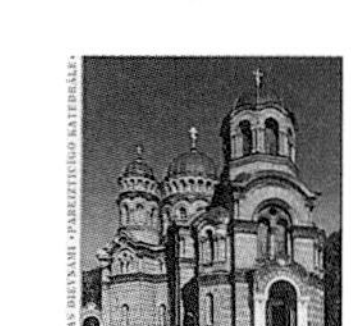
143 Main Statue, Liberty Monument, Riga (Karlis Zale)

144 Alberts Kviesis (1930–36)

2000. New Millennium. Multicoloured.
547 15s. Type **143** 30 15
548 50s. Brotherhood of Blackheads meeting house, Riga . . . . 1·10 55

2000. Presidents.
549 **144** 15s. multicoloured 30 15

145 Orthodox Church, Riga

146 Nurses tending to Elderly Lady

2000. Churches.
550 **145** 40s. multicoloured 45 20

2000. Latvian Red Cross.
551 **146** 15s. multicoloured 30 15

147 Elf and Sleigh

148 People around Bonfire

2000. Christmas. Multicoloured.
552 12s. Type **147** 25 10
553 15s. Cherubs 30 15
554 15s. Mary and baby Jesus . . 30 15

2001. Sovereignty.
555 **148** 40s. multicoloured 45 20

149 "When Silava's Forest Wakes" (V. Purvitis)

2001.
556 **149** 40s. multicoloured 45 20

150 Karlis Ulmanis (1936–40)

152 Ventas Rumba (waterfall), Kuldiga

151 ML Series Steam Locomotive

2001. Presidents.
557 **150** 15s. multicoloured 30 15

2001. Narrow-gauge Railway.
558 **151** 40s. multicoloured 45 20

2001. Europa. Water Resources.
559 **152** 60s. multicoloured . . . . 1·40 70

153 Modern View of Riga

2001. 800th Anniv of Riga (7th issue). Multicoloured.
560 15s. Type **153** 30 15
561 15s. Modern View of Riga with three spires 30 15
562 60s. 16th-century view of Riga . . . . 1·40 70
563 70s. 17th-century view of Riga . . . . 1·50 75
Nos. 560/1 were issued together, se-tenant, forming a composite design.

154 Cat with Pipe ("Pussy's Water Mill" (fairytale))

2001. Literature. Karlis Skalbe (writer) Commemoration.
564 **154** 40s. multicoloured 45 20

155 Tals

2001. 10th Death Anniv of Mikhail Nekhemevich Tal (World Chess Champion, 1960–1961). Sheet 98 × 68 mm.
MS565 **155** 100s. multicoloured 2·25 2·25

156 Beach, Vidzeme, Latvia

2001. Baltic Sea Coast. Multicoloured.
566 15s. Type **156** 30 15
MS567 125 × 60 mm. 30s. As Type **156**; 30 s. Sand dunes, Palanga, Lithuania; 30s. Rocky coastline, Lahemaa, Estonia . . 2·00 2·00
Stamps in similar designs were issued by Estonia and Lithuania.

157 Cesvaines Palace

2001. Palaces.
568 **157** 40s. multicoloured 45 20

158 Synagogue, Riga

160 White Rabbits

159 Krisjanis Valdemars (½-size illustration)

2001.
569 **158** 70s. multicoloured . . . . 1·50 75

2001. Ship Building, Trade and Discovery. Multicoloured.
570 15s. Type **159** (founder of Naval College and ship builder) 30 15
571 70s. Hercogs Jekabs, Duke of Courland (ship builder) . . 1·50 75

2001. Christmas. Multicoloured.
572 12s. Type **160** 25 10
573 15s. Dog and rabbit 30 15
574 15s. Sheep 30 15

LEBANON Pt. 19

A territory north of the Holy Land, formerly part of the Turkish Empire, Greater Lebanon was given a separate status under French Mandate in 1920. Until September 1923, the French occupation stamps of Syria were used and these were followed by the joint issue of 1923, Nos. 97 etc, of Syria. Independence was proclaimed in 1941, but the country was not evacuated by French troops until 1946.

100 centimes = 1 piastre;
100 piastres = 1 Lebanese pound.

1924. Stamps of France surch **GRAND LIBAN** and value. (a) Definitive stamps.
1 **11** 10c. on 2c. purple . . . . . 55 1·75
2 **18** 25c. on 5c. orange 95 90
3 50c. on 10c. green . . . . . 1·50 1·00
4 **15** 75c. on 15c. green . . . . . 1·40 3·00
5 **18** 1p. on 20c. brown . . . . . 2·25 1·10
6 1,25p. on 25c. blue . . . . 2·75 2·50
7 1,50p. on 30c. orange . . . 2·00 3·25
8 1,50p. on 30c. red . . . . . 1·75 3·25
9 **15** 2,50p. on 50c. blue . . . . 1·75 95
10 **13** 2p. on 40c. red and blue . . 1·25 1·40
11 3p. on 60c. violet and blue 5·75 5·50
12 5p. on 1f. red and yellow . . 7·50 8·00
13 10p. on 2f. orange and green . . . . 13·00 9·25
14 25p. on 5f. blue and buff . . 20·00 28·00

(b) Pasteur issue.
15 **30** 50c. on 10c. green . . . . . 95 2·50
16 1,50p. on 30c. red . . . . . 2·50 3·75
17 2,50p. on 50c. blue . . . . 85 3·00

(c) Olympic Games issue.
18 **31** 50c. on 10c. green and light green . . . . 28·00 65·00
19 – 1,25p. on 25c. deep red and red . . . . 16·00 65·00
20 – 1,50p. on 30c. red and black 19·00 48·00
21 – 2,50p. on 50c. blue . . . . 15·00 48·00

1924. Air. Stamps of France surch **Poste par Avion GRAND LIBAN** and value.
22 **13** 2p. on 40c. red and blue . . 13·50 15·00
23 3p. on 60c. violet and blue 11·00 16·00
24 5p. on 1f. red and yellow . . 11·00 11·00
25 10p. on 2f. orange and green . . . . 10·00 13·50

1924. Stamps of France surch **Grand Liban** (T **13**) or **Gd Liban** (others) and value in French and Arabic. (a) Definitive stamps.
26 **11** 0p.10 on 2c. purple 30 95
27 **18** 0p.25 on 5c. orange . . . . 75 1·00
28 0p.50 on 10c. green . . . . 2·25 2·25
29 **15** 0p.75 on 15c. green . . . . 1·10 3·00
30 **18** 1p. on 20c. brown . . . . . 1·00 3·00
31 1p.25 on 25c. blue . . . . . 2·25 2·50
32 1p.50 on 30c. red . . . . . 1·90 2·25
33 1p.50 on 30c. orange . . . 48·00 48·00
34 2p. on 35c. violet . . . . . 2·00 3·50
35 **13** 2p. on 40c. red and blue . . 1·75 50
36 2p. on 45c. green and blue 16·00 18·00
37 3p. on 60c. violet and blue 2·25 2·25
38 **15** 3p. on 60c. violet . . . . . 3·00 4·00
39 4p. on 85c. red . . . . . . 75 2·50
40 **13** 5p. on 1f. red and yellow . . 2·25 2·50
41 10p. on 2f. orange and green . . . . 6·00 13·00
42 25p. on 5f. blue and buff . . 8·50 14·50

(b) Pasteur issue.
43 **30** 0p.50 on 10c. green 65 25
44 0p.75 on 15c. green . . . . 2·75 3·25
45 1p.50 on 30c. red . . . . . 2·25 80
46 2p. on 45c. red . . . . . . 3·25 4·00
47 2p.50 on 50c. blue 75 40
48 4p. on 75c. blue . . . . . . 1·50 2·75

(c) Olympic Games issue.
49 **31** 0p.50 on 10c. green and light green . . . . 16·00 42·00
50 – 1p.25 on 25c. deep red and red . . . . 19·00 42·00
51 – 1p.50 on 30c. red and black 13·50 40·00
52 – 2p.50 on 50c. ultramarine and blue . . . . 21·00 40·00

(d) Ronsard issue.
53 **35** 4p. on 75c. blue on bluish 65 4·25

1924. Air. Stamps of France surch **Gd Liban Avion** and value in French and Arabic.
54 **13** 2p. on 40c. red and blue . . 7·25 13·50
55 3p. on 60c. violet and blue 5·50 13·50
56 5p. on 1f. red and yellow . . 5·25 13·50
57 10p. on 2f. orange and green . . . . 6·50 14·50

5 Cedar of Lebanon

7 Tripoli

6 Beirut

1925. Views.
58 **5** 0p.10c. violet . . . . 25 1·25
59 **6** 0p.25c. black . . . . 40 1·25
60 – 0p.50c. green (Tripoli) . . . 90 1·25
61 – 0p.75c. red (Beit ed-Din) . . 95 2·50
62 – 1p. purple (Baalbek ruins) . . 1·25 55
63 – 1p.25 green (Mouktara) . . . 1·90 2·25
64 – 1p.50 pink (Tyre) . . . . . 1·00 50
65 – 2p. brown (Zahle) . . . . . 1·75 35
66 – 2p.50 blue (Baalbek) 45 50
67 – 3p. brown (Deir el-Kamar) 1·00 1·00
68 – 5p. violet (Sidon) . . . . . . 6·75 6·75
69 **7** 10p. purple . . . . 6·50 6·00
70 – 25p. blue (Beirut) . . . . . 12·00 29·00

1925. Air. Nos. 65 and 67/9 optd **AVION** in French and Arabic.
71 – 2p. brown . . . . 4·00 6·00
72 – 3p. brown . . . . 4·25 5·75
73 – 5p. violet . . . . 4·00 5·75
74 **7** 10p. purple . . . . 4·00 5·75

1926. Air. Nos. 65 and 67/9 optd with Bleriot XI airplane.
75 – 2p. brown . . . . 3·00 5·75
76 – 3p. brown . . . . 3·00 5·75
77 – 5p. violet . . . . 3·25 6·00
78 **7** 10p. purple . . . . 2·50 6·00

1926. War Refugee Charity. Various stamps surch **Secours aux Refugies Afft** and premium in French and Arabic. (a) Postage. Stamps of 1925.
79 **6** 0p.25+0p.25 black . . . . . 2·00 3·75
80 – 0p.50+0p.25 green . . . . . 2·50 5·25
81 – 0p.75+0p.25 red . . . . . . 1·50 4·75
82 – 1p.+0p.50 purple . . . . . . 2·25 4·75
83 – 1p.25+0p.50 green . . . . . 2·00 6·50
84 – 1p.50+0p.50 pink . . . . . 4·00 5·50
85 – 2p.+0p.75 brown . . . . . . 3·50 5·00
86 – 2p.50+0p.75 blue . . . . . . 2·50 7·50
87 – 3p.+1p. brown . . . . 3·00 7·25
88 – 5p.+1p. violet . . . . 5·50 8·50

89 7 10p.+2p. purple . . . . . . 6·50 11·00
90 – 25p.+5p. blue . . . . 6·50 13·00

(b) Air. Nos. 75/78 surch.

91 – 2p.+1p. brown . . . . 4·75 13·00
92 – 3p.+2p. brown . . . . 4·75 13·00
93 – 5p.+3p. violet . . . . 4·75 13·00
94 7 10p.+5p. purple . . . . . . 4·75 13·50

1926. Stamps of 1925 surch in English and Arabic.
95 – 3p.50 on 0p.75 red . . . . 3·00 3·00
96 6 4p. on 0p.25 black . . . . 3·50 3·50
98 – 4p.50 on 0p.75 red . . . . 3·25 3·25
99 – 6p. on 2p.50 blue . . . . . 3·50 3·50
100 – 7p.50 on 2p.50 blue . . . . 3·25 1·25
101 – 12p. on 1p.25 green . . . . 2·50 3·75
102 – 15p. on 25p. blue . . . . . 4·50 2·25
103 – 20p. on 1p.25 green . . . . 7·25 7·25

1927. Stamps of 1925 and provisional stamps of Lebanon optd **Republique Libanaise**.
104 5 0p.10 violet . . . . 65 1·60
105 – 0p.50 green . . . . 75 1·00
106 – 1p. purple 35 15
107 – 1p.50 pink . . . . 1·60 2·00
108 – 2p. brown . . . . 2·00 1·75
109 – 3p. brown . . . . 1·25 75
110 6 4p. on 0p.25 black (No. 96) 1·10 85
111 – 4p.50 on 0p.75 red (No. 98) 1·00 40
112 – 5p. violet . . . . 3·25 3·75
113 – 7p.50 on 2p.50 bl (No. 100) 2·00 1·10
114 7 10p. purple . . . . 4·00 5·00
115 – 15p. on 25p. blue (No. 102) 11·00 9·00
117 – 25p. blue . . . . 12·00 24·00

1927. Air. Nos. 75/78 optd **Republique Libanaise**.
118 – 2p. brown . . . . 4·25 6·00
119 – 3p. brown . . . . 3·25 5·75
120 – 5p. violet . . . . 4·50 5·75
121 7 10p. purple . . . . 4·00 5·75

الجمهورية اللبنانية

(10)

1928. Nos. 104/117 optd with T 10 or surch also.
145 5 05 on 0p.10 violet . . . . 15 1·00
124 0p.10 violet 65 25
125 – 0p.50 green . . . . 2·50 2·50
146 – 0p.50 on 0p.75 red 35 40
126 – 1p. purple 95 50
127 – 1p.50 pink . . . . 2·75 3·50
128 – 2p. brown . . . . 4·25 4·50
147 – 2p. on 1p.25 green . . . . 1·40 35
129 – 3p. brown . . . . 2·25 1·00
148 6 4p. on 0p.25 black . . . . 2·50 15
131 – 4p.50 on 0p.75 red . . . . 2·50 2·25
132a – 5p. violet . . . . 2·00 3·75
149 – 7p.50 on 2p.50 blue . . . 1·00 45
134 7 10p. purple . . . . 8·50 9·00
123 – 15p. on 25p. blue . . . . 10·00 15·00
136 – 25p. blue . . . . 10·00 18·00

1928. Air. Optd or surch with airplane, **Republique Libanaise** and line of Arabic as T 10.
151 – 0p.50 green . . . . 95 3·00
152 – 0p.50 on 0p.75 red (No. 146) . . . . 1·25 2·25
153 – 1p. purple . . . . 1·90 3·50
141 – 2p. brown . . . . 3·50 4·75
154 – 2p. on 1p.25 grn (No. 147) 2·25 3·00
142 – 3p. brown . . . . 2·50 3·25
143 – 5p. violet . . . . 3·50 4·50
144 7 10p. purple . . . . 3·75 4·25
155 – 15p. on 25p. blue (No. 123) £180 £200
156 – 25p. blue £120 £120

14 Silkworm Larva, Cocoon and Moth

1930. Silk Congress.
157 14 4p. sepia . . . . 17·00 18·00
158 4½p. red . . . . 16·00 21·00
159 7½p. blue . . . . 14·50 14·50
160 10p. violet . . . . 17·00 21·00
161 15p. green . . . . 19·00 14·50
162 25p. purple . . . . 16·00 17·00

15 Cedars of Lebanon **16a** Baalbek

1930. Views.
163b – 0p.10 orange (Beirut) . . 55 35
164 15 0p.20 brown . . . . 75 1·40
165a – 0p.25 blue (Baalbek) . . 70 25
166 – 0p.50 brown (Bickfaya) 95 65
166b – 0p.75 brown (Baalbek) 3·50 2·50
167 – 1p. green (Saida) . . . . 4·75 55
167a – 1p. purple (Saida) . . . 5·75 65
168 – 1p.50 purple (Beit ed-Din) . . . . 4·00 1·25
168a – 1p.50 green (Beit ed-Din) 8·50 55
169 – 2p. blue (Tripoli) . . . . 6·00 1·10
170 – 3p. sepia (Baalbek) . . . 7·00 1·10
171 – 4p. brown (Nahr-el-Kalb) . . . . 7·00 70
172 – 4p.50 red (Beaufort) . . 6·00 85
173 – 5p. green (Beit ed-Din) 3·00 75
251 – 5p. blue (Nahr el-Kalb) 1·75 15
174 – 6p. purple (Tyre) . . . . 8·00 1·10
175 16a 7p.50 blue . . . . . . 6·00 75
176 – 10p. green (Hasbaya) . . 9·00 1·10
177 – 15p. purple (Afka Falls) 10·50 1·10
178 – 25p. green (Beirut) . . . 11·50 1·40
179 – 50p. green (Deir el-Kamar) . . . . 60·00 15·00
180 – 100p. black (Baalbek) . . 60·00 20·00

17 Jebeil (Byblos)

1930. Air. Potez 29-4 biplane and views as T 17.
181 0p.50 purple (Rachaya) . . . 1·25 2·00
182 1p. green (Broumana) 30 90
183 2p. orange (Baalbek) . . . . 1·10 75
184 3p. red (Hasroun) . . . . . 1·75 1·75
185 5p. green (Byblos) . . . . . 1·75 1·60
186 10p. red (Kadisha) . . . . . 2·00 1·75
187 15p. brown (Beirut) . . . . 1·75 1·40
188 25p. violet (Tripoli) . . . . 2·25 1·75
189 50p. lake (Kabelais) . . . . 6·00 4·75
190 100p. brown (Zahle) . . . . 7·25 9·00

18 Skiing

1936. Air. Tourist Propaganda.
191 18 0p.50 green . . . . 2·75 2·50
192 – 1p. orange . . . . 3·25 3·25
193 18 2p. violet . . . . 1·75 2·75
194 – 3p. green . . . . 2·50 2·75
195 18 5p. red . . . . 4·00 4·00
196 – 10p. brown . . . . . . 3·75 4·25
197 – 15p. red . . . . 38·00 35·00
198 18 25p. green £100 £100
DESIGN: 1, 3, 10, 15p. Jounieh Bay.

20 Cedar of Lebanon **21** President Edde

22 Lebanese Landscape

1937.
199 20 0p.10 red 15 15
200 0p.20 blue . . . . 25 2·40
201 0p.25 lilac . . . . 35 2·40
202 0p.50 mauve 20 20
203 0p.75 brown . . . . . . 35 1·25
207 21 3p. violet . . . . 3·00 1·40
208 4p. brown 95 25
209 4p.50 red . . . . 1·90 20
211 22 10p. red . . . . 2·75 25
212 12½p. blue . . . . 1·25 20
213 15p. green . . . . 2·75 25
214 20p. brown . . . . 3·25 25
215 25p. red . . . . 4·25 50
216 50p. violet . . . . 8·50 2·00
217 100p. sepia . . . . 9·00 2·75

23 Exhibition Pavilion, Paris

1937. Air. Paris International Exhibition.
218 23 0p.50 black . . . . 1·25 1·75
219 1p. green . . . . 80 3·00
220 2p. brown . . . . 1·50 3·00
221 3p. green . . . . 1·10 3·00
222 5p. green . . . . 1·25 3·25
223 10p. red . . . . 9·75 13·50
224 15p. purple . . . . 6·00 13·50
225 25p. brown . . . . 17·00 20·00

25 Ruins of Baalbek

1937. Air.
226 – 0p.50 blue 10 35
227 – 1p. red . . . . 1·00 1·60
228 – 2p. sepia . . . . 1·75 1·75
229 – 3p. red . . . . 3·25 2·50
230 – 5p. green . . . . 1·50 40
231 25 10p. violet 70 40
232 – 15p. blue . . . . 1·50 2·25
233 – 25p. violet . . . . 4·25 2·75
234 – 50p. green . . . . 8·75 2·25
235 – 100p. brown . . . . . . 4·25 3·50
DESIGN: 0p.50 to 5p. Beit ed-Din.

1938. Nos. 207/8 surch in English and Arabic figures.
236 21 2p. on 3p. violet 75 20
237 2½p. on 4p. brown . . . . 1·10 25

27 Medical College, Beirut **32** Emir Bechir Chehab

28 Maurice Nogues and Liore et Olivier LeO H.24-3 Flying Boat over Beirut

1938. Air. Medical Congress.
238 27 2p. green . . . . 2·75 3·50
239 3p. orange . . . . 3·00 4·00
240 5p. violet . . . . 3·75 5·50
241 10p. red . . . . 9·50 14·50

1938. Air. 10th Anniv of 1st Air Service between France and Lebanon.
242 28 10p. purple . . . . 4·25 6·00

1938. Surch.
243 16a 6p. on 7p.50 blue . . . . 2·50 95
244 – 7p.50 on 50p. grn (No. 179) . . . . . . 2·75 1·75
245 – 7p.50 on 100p. blk (No. 180) . . . . . . 1·90 2·50
246 22 12p.50 on 7p.50 blue . . 3·00 2·00
247 12½p. on 7p.50 blue . . . 1·00 30

1939. As T 16a, but with differing figures and Arabic inscriptions in side panels, and imprint at foot "IMP. CATHOLIQUE-BEYROUTH-LIBAN" instead of "HELIO VAUGIRARD".
248 1p. green . . . . 1·10 75
249 1p.50 purple . . . . 1·50 45
250 7p.50 red . . . . 3·00 40
DESIGN: 1p. to 7p.50, Beit ed-Din.

1942. 1st Anniv of Proclamation of Independence.
252 32 0p.50 green (postage) . . . 2·00 2·00
253 1p.50 purple . . . . . . 2·00 2·00
254 6p. red . . . . 2·00 2·00
255 15p. blue . . . . 2·00 2·00
256 – 10p. purple (air) . . . . . 3·75 3·75
257 – 50p. green . . . . 3·75 3·75
DESIGN: 10, 50p. Airplane over mountains.

1943. Surch in English and Arabic and with old values cancelled with ornaments.
258 21 2p. on 4p. brown . . . . 4·25 3·75
261 – 2p. on 5p. blue (No. 251) 55 40
262 – 3p. on 5p. blue (No. 251) 55 40
259 – 6p. on 7p.50 red (No. 250) 85 55
263 22 6p. on 12½p. blue 75 55
264 7½p. on 12½p. blue . . . . 1·25 1·25
260 10p. on 12½p. blue 95 65

37 Parliament House

38 Bechamoun

1944. 2nd Anniv of Proclamation of Independence.
265 37 25p. red (postage) . . . . 7·50 7·50
266 – 50p. blue . . . . 7·50 7·50
267 37 150p. blue . . . . 7·50 7·50
268 – 200p. purple . . . . . . 7·50 7·50
DESIGN: 50p., 200p. Government House.

269 38 25p. green (air) . . . . . 2·25 2·00
270 50p. orange . . . . 3·25 2·50
271 – 100p. brown . . . . . . 3·50 2·25
272 – 200p. violet . . . . . . 4·75 3·75
273 – 300p. green . . . . . . 15·00 12·00
274 – 500p. brown . . . . . . 35·00 25·00
DESIGNS: 100p., 200p. Rachaya Citadel; 300p., 500p. Beirut.

38a Beirut Isolation Hospital (**39**)

1944. 6th Medical Congress. Optd with T 39.
275 38a 10p. red (postage) . . . . 5·00 5·00
276 20p. blue . . . . 5·00 5·00
277 – 20p. orange (air) . . . . 2·25 2·25
278 – 50p. blue . . . . 2·25 2·25
279 – 100p. purple . . . . . . 3·75 3·75
DESIGN: Nos. 277/9, Bhannes Sanatorium.

(**40** Trans "Nov. 23, 1943")

1944. 1st Anniv of President's Return to Office. Nos. 265/74 optd with T 40.
280 37 25p. red (postage) . . . . 10·00 10·00
281 – 50p. blue . . . . 10·00 10·00
282 37 150p. blue . . . . 10·00 10·00
283 – 200p. purple . . . . . . 10·00 10·00
284 38 25p. green (air) . . . . . 3·75 3·75
285 – 50p. orange . . . . 6·75 6·75
286 – 100p. brown . . . . 8·75 8·75
287 – 200p. violet . . . . 16·00 16·00
288 – 300p. green . . . . 21·00 21·00
289 – 500p. brown . . . . 40·00 40·00

41 Crusader Castle, Byblos **42** Falls of R. Litani

1945.
397 41 7p.50 red (postage) . . . . 2·40 20
398 10p. purple . . . . 3·75 25
399 12p.50 blue . . . . 8·75 30
290 15p. brown . . . . 2·50 2·25
291 20p. green . . . . 2·50 2·25
292 – 25p. blue . . . . 2·50 2·25
400 41 25p. violet . . . . 16·00 65
293 – 50p. red . . . . 4·75 2·50
401 41 50p. green . . . . 38·00 4·25
294 42 25p. brown (air) . . . . . 1·90 1·25
295 50p. purple . . . . 2·50 1·90
296 – 200p. violet . . . . . . 8·75 3·25
297 – 300p. black . . . . . . 18·00 6·25
DESIGNS—HORIZ: Nos. 292/3, Crusader Castle, Tripoli; 296/7, Cedar of Lebanon and skier.

43 V(ictory) and National Flag

44 V(ictory) and Lebanese Soldiers at Bir-Hakeim

1946. Victory. "V" in design. (a) Postage.
298 43 7p.50 brown, red and pink 70 10
299 10p. purple, pink and red 1·00 10
300 12p.50 purple, blue and red 1·25 15
301 15p. green, emerald and red . . . . 1·25 25
302 20p. myrtle, green and red 2·00 25
303 25p. blue, light blue and red . . . . 3·00 45
304 50p. blue, violet and red 5·75 1·50
305 100p. black, blue and red 9·50 3·50

(b) Air.

306 44 15p. blue, yellow and red 50 20
307 20p. red and blue 50 35
308 25p. blue, yellow and red 60 35
309 50p. black, violet and red 1·00 40
310 100p. violet and red . . . 3·25 90
311 150p. brown and red . . . 4·00 1·75

1946. As T 43 but without "V" sign.
312 7p.50 lake, red and mauve . . 70 10
313 10p. violet, mauve and red 1·00 10
314 12p.50 brown, green and red 1·25 20
315 15p. brown, pink and red . . 2·25 25
316 20p. blue, orange and red . . 1·90 25
317 25p. myrtle, green and red . . 3·25 40
318 50p. blue, light blue and red 7·00 1·50
319 100p. black, blue and red . . 11·50 3·50

45 Grey Herons

1946.

No.	Type	Description	Unused	Used
320	45	12p.50 red (postage) . . .	18·00	70
321		10p. orange (air)	4·50	95
322		25p. blue	6·50	45
323		50p. green	15·50	1·40
324		100p. purple	27·00	6·50

46 Cedar of Lebanon

47

1946.

No.	Type	Description	Unused	Used
325	46	0p.50 brown	25	20
326		1p. purple	35	20
327		2p.50 violet	1·25	20
328		5p. red	1·90	20
329		6p. grey	2·50	20

1946. Air. Arab Postal Congress.

No.	Type	Description	Unused	Used
330	47	25p. blue	75	50
331		50p. green	1·10	75
332		75p. red	1·90	1·25
333		150p. violet	4·50	2·25

48 Cedar of Lebanon

49 President, Bridge and Tablet

1947.

No.	Type	Description	Unused	Used
333a	48	0p.50 brown	1·00	10
333b		2p.50 green	1·50	10
333c		5p. red	2·50	20

1947. Air. Evacuation of Foreign Troops from Lebanon.

No.	Type	Description	Unused	Used
334	49	25p. blue	75	65
335		50p. red	1·10	95
336		75p. black	2·50	1·25
337		150p. green	4·50	2·50

50 Crusader Castle, Tripoli

51 Jounieh Bay

1947.

No.	Type	Description	Unused	Used
338	50	12p.50 red (postage) . . .	6·25	30
339		25p. blue	7·75	40
340		50p. green	25·00	75
341		100p. violet	32·00	5·50
342	51	5p. green (air)	30	10
343		10p. mauve	40	10
344		15p. red	60	10
403		15p. green	7·50	1·00
345		20p. orange	95	10
345a		20p. red	1·25	20
346		25p. blue	1·25	10
347		50p. red	3·00	25
348		100p. purple	6·25	25
349	–	150p. purple	12·50	1·10
350	–	200p. slate	19·00	5·00
351	–	300p. black	30·00	11·50

DESIGN: 150p. to 300p. Grand Serail Palace.

54 Phoenician Galley

1947. Air. 12th Congress of U.P.U., Paris.

No.	Type	Description	Unused	Used
352	–	10p. blue	75	35
353	–	15p. red	1·10	50
354	–	25p. blue	1·50	85
355	54	50p. green	3·50	1·00
356	–	75p. violet	4·50	1·40
357	–	100p. brown	6·25	3·00

DESIGN—VERT: 10p. to 25p. Posthorn.

55 Faraya Bridge and Statue

1947. Air. Red Cross Fund. Cross in red.

No.	Type	Description	Unused	Used
358	55	12p.50+25p. green	6·25	5·00
359		25p.+50p. blue	7·00	5·75
360	–	50p.+100p. brown	9·50	7·00
361	–	75p.+150p. violet	20·00	14·00
362	–	100p.+200p. grey	35·00	25·00

DESIGN: 50p. to 100p. Djounie Bay and statue.

56 Cedar of Lebanon

58 Lebanese Landscape

1948.

No.	Type	Description	Unused	Used
363	56	0p.50 blue (postage) . . .	15	10
364		1p. brown	65	10
395		1p. orange	30	10
365		2p.50 mauve	60	10
366		3p. green	1·40	10
367		5p. red	2·00	10
368	–	7p.50 red	5·00	20
369	–	10p. purple	3·25	20
370	–	12p.50 blue	8·25	25
371	–	25p. blue	11·00	65
372	–	50p. green	25·00	5·00
373	58	5p. red (air)	50	10
374		10p. mauve	1·10	10
375		15p. brown	2·75	10
376		20p. slate	4·50	20
377		25p. blue	8·25	90
378		50p. black	14·50	1·75

DESIGN—As T **58**: Nos. 368/72, Zebaide Aqueduct.

59 Europa on Bull

61 Apollo on Sun Chariot

1948. 3rd Meeting of UNESCO, Beirut.

No.	Type	Description	Unused	Used
379	59	10p. orange and red (postage)	1·90	1·25
380		12p.50 mauve and violet	2·50	1·90
381		25p. green and light green	3·00	1·90
382	–	30p. buff and brown . . .	3·75	2·25
383	–	40p. green and turquoise	5·75	2·25

DESIGN—VERT: 30, 40p. Avicenna (philosopher and scientist).

No.	Type	Description	Unused	Used
384	61	7p.50 blue & lt blue (air)	1·60	1·25
385		15p. black and grey . . .	1·90	1·25
386		20p. brown and pink . . .	3·25	1·90
387	–	35p. red	5·25	2·50
388	–	75p. green	10·50	5·50

DESIGN—HORIZ: 35, 75p. Symbolical figure.

63 Camel

64 Sikorsky S-51 Helicopter

1949. 75th Anniv of U.P.U.

No.	Type	Description	Unused	Used
389	63	5p. violet (postage)	1·00	75
390		7p.50 red	1·50	1·25
391		12p.50 blue	2·25	1·60
392	64	25p. blue (air)	5·00	2·50
393		50p. green	7·50	3·75

65 Cedar of Lebanon

66 Nahr el-Kalb Bridge

1950.

No.	Type	Description	Unused	Used
407	65	0p.50 red	25	10
408		1p. red	65	10
409		2p.50 violet	1·00	10
410		5p. purple	1·90	10
411	66	7p.50 red	2·25	10
412		10p. lilac	2·75	10
413		12p.50 blue	4·50	20
414		25p. blue	8·75	95
415		50p. green	25·00	5·00

67 Congressional Flags

1950. Lebanese Emigrants' Congress. Inscr "MOIS DES EMIGRES–ETE 1950".

No.	Type	Description	Unused	Used
416	67	7p.50 green (postage) . . .	65	20
417		12p. mauve	65	20
418	–	5p. blue (air)	2·25	60
419	–	15p. violet	3·00	85
420	–	25p. brown	1·25	75
421	–	35p. green	2·50	1·25

DESIGNS: 5, 15p. House martins; 25, 35p. Pres. Bishara al-Khoury and building.

70 Crusader Castle, Sidon

1950. Air.

No.	Type	Description	Unused	Used
422	70	10p. brown	50	20
423		15p. green	1·00	15
424		20p. red	2·25	30
425		25p. blue	5·00	1·25
426		50p. grey	7·50	2·50

1950. Surch with figures and bars.

No.	Type	Description	Unused	Used
427	56	1p. on 3p. green	50	20
428	46	2p.50 on 6p. grey	75	20

73 Cedar of Lebanon

74 Nahr el-Kalb Bridge

75 Crusader Castle, Sidon

1951.

No.	Type	Description	Unused	Used
429	73	0p.50 red (postage)	25	10
430		1p. brown	50	10
431		2p.50 grey	2·50	10
432		5p. purple	2·75	10
433	74	7p.50 red	3·00	30
434		10p. purple	3·75	20
435		12p.50 turquoise	7·50	35
436		25p. blue	11·50	1·25
437		50p. green	25·00	6·75
438	75	10p. turquoise (air)	80	10
439		15p. brown	1·75	10
440		20p. red	1·75	20
441		25p. blue	2·00	20
442		35p. mauve	5·00	2·50
443		50p. blue	9·00	2·00

Type **74** is similar to Type **66** but left value tablets differ.

For design as Type **74** but inscr "LIBAN", see Nos. 561/3.

76 Cedar of Lebanon

77 Baalbek

1952.

No.	Type	Description	Unused	Used
444	76	0p.50 green (postage) . . .	60	10
445		1p. brown	60	10
446		2p.50 blue	90	20
447		5p. red	1·60	25
448	77	7p.50 red	1·90	45
449		10p. violet	4·50	50
450		12p.50 blue	4·50	50
451		25p. blue	5·75	1·25
452	–	50p. green	17·00	2·25
453	–	100p. brown	35·00	7·00
454	–	5p. red (air)	30	10
455	–	10p. grey	45	10
456	–	15p. mauve	80	10
457	–	20p. orange	1·25	30
458	–	25p. blue	1·25	40
459	–	35p. blue	2·10	45
460	–	50p. green	7·00	50
461	–	100p. blue	48·00	2·10
462	–	200p. green	28·00	4·00
463	–	300p. sepia	38·00	8·75

DESIGNS—As Type **77**: Nos. 452/3, Beaufort Castle; 454/9, Beirut Airport; 460/3, Amphitheatre, Byblos.

78 Cedar of Lebanon

79 General Post Office

80 Douglas DC-4

1953.

No.	Type	Description	Unused	Used
559	78	0p.50 blue (postage) . . .	20	10
465		1p. red	70	10
466		2p.50 violet	90	20
560		2p.50 purple	60	10
467		5p. green	1·60	25
468	79	7p.50 red	2·50	35
469		10p. green	3·00	50
470		12p.50 turquoise	4·25	55
471		25p. blue	6·25	1·10
472		50p. brown	11·50	2·50
473	80	5p. green (air)	30	10
474		10p. red	55	10
475		15p. red	80	10
476		20p. turquoise	1·25	10
477		25p. blue	3·25	10
478		35p. brown	4·50	20
479		50p. blue	6·50	45
480		100p. sepia	12·00	4·25

For 20p. green as Type **79** see No. 636.

81 Cedar of Lebanon

82 Beit ed-Din Palace

83 Baalbek

1954.

No.	Type	Description	Unused	Used
481	81	0p.50 blue (postage) . . .	20	10
482		1p. orange	35	10
483		2p.50 violet	60	20
484		5p. green	1·10	20
485	82	7p.50 red	1·90	45
486		10p. green	2·75	45
487		12p.50 blue	4·50	60
488		25p. deep blue	6·25	2·25
489		50p. turquoise	11·00	3·75
490		100p. sepia	25·00	7·50
491	83	5p. green (air)	40	10
492		10p. lilac	70	10
493		15p. red	80	10
494		20p. brown	1·10	10
495		25p. blue	1·25	20
496		35p. sepia	1·75	25
497	–	50p. green	5·50	40
498	–	100p. red	9·00	60
499	–	200p. sepia	20·00	1·90
500	–	300p. blue	32·00	3·75

DESIGN—As T **83**: 50p. to 300p. Litani Irrigation Canal.

For other values as Nos. 497/500, see Nos. 564/7.

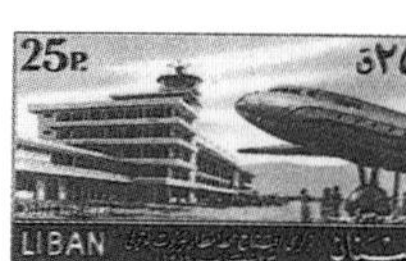
84 Khalde Airport, Beirut

1954. Air. Opening of Beirut International Airport.

No.	Type	Description	Unused	Used
501	84	10p. red and pink	45	25
502		25p. blue and ultramarine	1·25	40
503		35p. brown and sepia . . .	1·75	65
504		65p. green and turquoise	4·25	2·50

84a

1955. Arab Postal Union.

No.	Type	Description	Unused	Used
505	84a	12p.50 green (postage) . .	50	35
506		25p. violet	75	35
507		2p.50 brown (air)	40	30

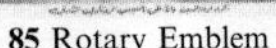

85 Rotary Emblem

86 Cedar of Lebanon

87 Jeita Grotto

88 Skiers

1955. Air. 50th Anniv of Rotary International.
508 **85** 35p. green 90 65
509 65p. blue . . . . 1·60 95

1955.
510 **86** 0p.50 blue (postage) . . . 20 10
511 1p. red 25 10
512 2p.50 violet 45 10
552 2p.50 blue . . . . 6·25 25
513 5p. green 70 10
514 **87** 7p.50 orange 95 10
515 10p. green . . . . 1·60 10
516 12p.50 blue . . . . 1·60 10
517 25p. blue . . . . 4·00 25
518 50p. green . . . . 5·75 75
519 **88** 5p. turquoise (air) 50 35
520 15p. red 85 20
521 20p. violet . . . . 1·50 20
522 25p. blue . . . . 2·75 30
523 35p. brown . . . . 4·50 50
524 50p. brown . . . . 7·50 70
525 65p. blue . . . . 14·00 2·25

The face value on No. 510 reads "0.50 PIASTRE"; on No. 512 the "2" and "50" are different sizes and the 1 and 5p. have no dash under "P".

For other colours and new values as Type **88** see Nos. 568/70 and for redrawn Type **86** see Nos. 582/5, 686 and 695/7.

89 Visitor from Abroad

90 Cedar of Lebanon

91 Globe and Columns

92 Oranges

1955. Air. Tourist Propaganda.
526 **89** 2p.50 slate and purple . . 10 10
527 12p.50 blue & ultramarine 30 20
528 25p. blue and indigo . . . 80 35
529 35p. blue and green . . . 1·25 50

1955.
530 **90** 0.50p. blue (postage) . . . 20 10
531 1p. orange 20 10
532 2p.50 violet 25 10
533 5p. green 50 10
534 **91** 7p.50 red and orange . . . 65 10
535 10p. green and brown . . . 75 10
536 12p.50 blue and green . . 95 10
537 25p. blue and mauve . . . 1·90 20
538 50p. green and blue . . . 2·75 35
539 100p. brown and orange 4·50 1·10
540 **92** 5p. yellow and green (air) 25 10
541 10p. orange and green . . 60 10
542 15p. orange and green . . 60 10
543 20p. orange and brown . . 1·00 10
544 – 25p. violet and blue . . . 1·25 10
545 – 35p. purple and green . . 2·50 25
546 – 50p. yellow and black . . 2·50 25
547 – 65p. yellow and green . . 5·00 35
548 – 100p. orange and green . 8·25 1·00
549 – 200p. red and green . . . 15·00 4·50

DESIGNS—VERT: 25p. to 50p. Grapes. HORIZ: 4p. to 200p. Quinces.

93 U.N. Emblem

1956. Air. 10th Anniv of U.N.
550 **93** 35p. blue . . . . 4·00 3·25
551 65p. green . . . . 5·25 3·75

94 Masks, Columns and Gargoyle

1956. Air. Baalbek International Drama Festival. Inscr "FESTIVAL INTERNATIONAL DE BAALBECK".
553 **94** 2p.50 sepia 30 15
554 10p. green 45 25
555 – 12p.50 blue 45 35
556 – 25p. violet . . . . . . 1·00 45
557 – 35p. purple . . . . . . 1·90 65
558 – 65p. slate . . . . 3·00 1·90

DESIGNS—HORIZ: 12p.50, 25p. Temple ruins at Baalbek. VERT: 35p., 65p. Double bass, masks and columns.

1957. As earlier designs but redrawn. (a) Postage. As T **74** but inscr "LIBAN".
561 7p.50 red . . . . 1·10 10
562 10p. brown . . . . 1·60 10
563 12p.50 blue . . . . 1·90 10

(b) Air. Arabic inscription changed. New values and colours.
564 – 10p. violet 25 10
565 – 15p. orange 40 10
566 – 20p. green 50 10
567 – 25p. blue 60 10
568 **88** 35p. green . . . . 2·10 20
569 65p. purple . . . . 3·75 55
570 100p. brown . . . . 6·25 1·25

DESIGN: 10p. to 25p. As Nos. 497/500.

95 Pres. Chamoun and King Faisal II of Iraq

1957. Air. Arab Leaders' Conference, Beirut.
571 **95** 15p. orange 65 40
572 – 15p. blue 65 40
573 – 15p. maroon 65 40
574 – 15p. purple 65 40
575 – 15p. green 65 40
576 – 25p. turquoise 65 40
577 – 100p. brown . . . . 4·50 2·25

DESIGNS—As T **95**: 15p. values show Pres. Chamoun and: King Hussein of Jordan (No. 572), Abdallah Khalil of Sudan (No. 573), Pres. Shukri Bey al-Quwatli of Syria (No. 574) and King Saud of Saudi Arabia (No. 575); 25p. Map and Pres. Chamoun. 44 × 44 mm (Diamond shape): 100p. The six Arab Leaders.

97 Runners

98 Miners

1957. 2nd Pan-Arabian Games, Beirut.
578 **97** 2p.50 sepia (postage) . . . 65 40
579 – 12p.50 blue 95 50
580 – 35p. purple (air) . . . . . 2·50 1·00
581 – 50p. green . . . . 3·00 1·50

DESIGNS—VERT: 12p.50, Footballers. HORIZ: 35p. Fencers; 50p. Stadium.

1957.
582 **86** 0p.50 blue (16½ × 20½ mm) (postage) 15 10
582a 0p.50 violet (17 × 21¼ mm) 25 10
583 1p. brown (16½ × 20½ mm) 20 10
583a 1p. purple (17 × 21¼ mm) 25 10
584 2p.50 violet (16½ × 20½ mm) 35 10
584a 2p.50 blue (17 × 21¼ mm) 40 10
585 5p. green (16½ × 20½ mm) 50 10
586 **98** 7½p. pink 75 10
587 10p. brown . . . . 1·00 10
588 12½p. blue . . . . 1·40 10
589 25p. blue . . . . 1·40 10
590 – 50p. green . . . . 2·50 30
591 – 100p. brown . . . . 4·50 90
592 – 5p. green (air) 20 10
593 – 10p. orange 25 10
594 – 15p. brown 25 10
595 – 20p. purple 40 10
596 – 25p. blue 50 15
597 – 35p. purple 80 30
598 – 50p. green . . . . 1·50 45
599 – 65p. brown . . . . 2·50 45
600 – 100p. grey . . . . 3·25 1·25

DESIGNS: POSTAGE—As Type **86**: 50c. inscr "0 P.50", 2p.50, Figures in uniform size; 1p., 5p. Short dash under "P". As Type **98**: VERT: 25p. to 100p. Potter. AIR—As Type **98**: HORIZ: 5p. to 25p. Cedar of Lebanon with signs of the Zodiac, bird and ship; 35 to 100p. Chamoun Electric Power Station.

99 Cedar of Lebanon

100 Soldier and Flag

101 Douglas DC-6B at Khalde Airport

1959.
601 **99** 0p.50 blue (postage) . . . 15 10
602 1p. orange 25 10
603 2p.50 violet 35 10
604 5p. green 50 10
605 **100** 12p.50 blue . . . . 1·00 10
606 25p. blue . . . . 1·10 10
607 50p. brown . . . . 1·90 25
608 100p. sepia . . . . 3·50 45
609 **101** 5p. green (air) 55 10
610 10p. purple 55 10
611 15p. violet 80 10
612 20p. red . . . . 1·10 15
613 25p. violet . . . . 1·50 25
614 – 35p. myrtle . . . . 1·10 25
615 – 50p. turquoise . . . . . 1·40 25
616 – 65p. sepia . . . . 2·75 45
617 – 100p. blue . . . . 3·25 75

DESIGN—HORIZ: Nos. 614/17, Factory, cogwheel and telegraph pylons.

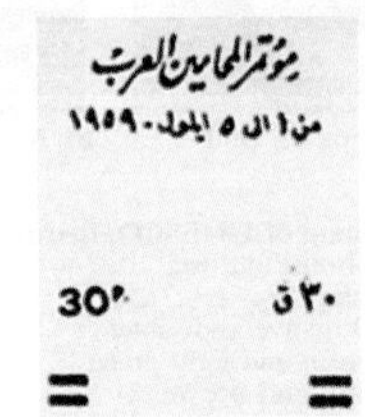

(102)

1959. Lawyers' Conference. Nos. 538 and 546 surch as T **102**.
618 30p. on 50p. myrtle and blue (postage) . . . . 1·10 65
619 40p. on 50p. yellow & blk (air) . . . . 1·00 65

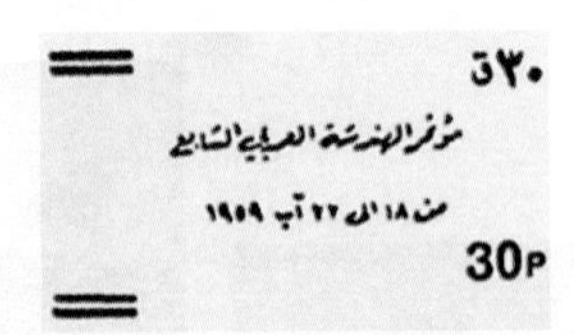

(103)

1959. Air. Engineers' Conference. Nos. 614 and 616 surch as T **103**.
620 30p. on 35p. myrtle 65 50
621 40p. on 65p. sepia . . . . . 1·25 75

(104) 105 Discus Thrower

1959. Emigrants' Conference. No. 590 surch as T **104**.
622 30p. on 50p. green 75 30
623 40p. on 50p. green . . . . . 1·10 60

1959. Air. 3rd Mediterranean Games, Beirut.
624 **105** 15p. green 50 25
625 – 30p. brown 75 40
626 – 40p. blue . . . . 1·60 65

DESIGNS—VERT: 30p. Weightlifting. HORIZ: 40p. Games emblem.

106 Soldiers with Standard

108 Planting Tree

1959. Air. 16th Anniv of Independence.
627 **106** 40p. red and black . . . 95 65
628 60p. red and green . . . 1·25 90

1959. Surch.
629 **100** 7p.50 on 12p.50 blue . . 50 10
630 10p. on 12p.50 blue . . . 65 10
631 15p. on 25p. blue 75 10
632 – 40p. on 50p. green (No. 590) . . . . . . 1·25 90
633 **88** 40p. on 65p. purple (No. 569) (air) . . . . 2·50 60

1960. Air. 25th Anniv of Friends of the Tree Society.
634 **108** 20p. purple and green . . 75 50
635 40p. sepia and green . . . 1·10 75

1960. Air. As T **79** but colours of name and value tablets reversed.
636 20p. green 70 45

109 Pres. Chehab

111 "Uprooted Tree"

110 Arab League Centre

1960. Air.
637 **109** 5p. green 10 10
638 10p. blue 10 10
639 15p. brown 10 10
640 20p. sepia 15 10
641 30p. olive 20 10
642 40p. red 45 15
643 50p. blue 60 20
644 70p. purple . . . . 1·10 25
645 100p. green . . . . 2·25 65

1960. Inaug of Arab League Centre, Cairo.
646 **110** 15p. turquoise 50 40

1960. Air. World Refugee Year. (a) Size 20¼ × 36½ mm.
647 **111** 25p. brown 75 50
648 40p. green . . . . 1·10 75

(b) Size 19½ × 35½ mm.
648b **111** 25p. brown . . . . 1·00 1·00
648c 40p. green . . . . 1·25 1·25

112 Martyrs' Monument

1960. Air. Martyrs' Commemoration.
649 **112** 20p. purple and green . . 50 30
650 40p. blue and green . . . 75 50
651 – 70p. olive and black . . 1·60 75

DESIGN—VERT: 70p. Detail of statues on monument.

113 Pres. Chehab and King Mohammed V

114 Pres. Chehab

1960. Air. Visit of King Mohammed V of Morocco.
652 **113** 30p. chocolate and brown . . 75 50
653 70p. brown and black . . 1·50 75

1960.
654 **114** 50c. green 10 10
655 2p.50 olive 10 10
656 5p. green 15 10
657 7p.50 red 30 10
658 15p. blue 50 25
659 50p. purple . . . . 1·25 30
660 100p. brown . . . . . . 2·50 50

115 Child

116 Dove, Map and Flags

1960. Air. Mother and Child Days.
661 **115** 20p. red and yellow . . . 50 25
662 20p.+10p. red and yellow 75 40
663 – 60p. blue and light blue 1·25 85
664 – 60p.+15p. blue & lt bl . . 1·90 1·00
DESIGN: Nos. 663/4, Mother and child.

1960. Air. World Lebanese Union Meeting, Beirut. Multicoloured.
665 20p. Type **116** 25 20
666 40p. Cedar of Lebanon and homing pigeons 75 40
667 70p. Globes and Cedar of Lebanon (horiz) 90 50

(**117**)

1960. Arabian Oil Congress, Beirut. Optd with T **117**.
668 **86** 5p. green (No. 585) . . . 30 10
669 **110** 15p. turquoise 65 40

1960. Air. World Refugee Year. Nos. 648b/c surch in English and Arabic.
669a **111** 20p.+10p. on 40p. grn 7·00 7·00
669b 30p.+15p. on 25p. brn 10·00 10·00

119 Boxing

1961. Olympic Games.
670 **119** 2p.50+2p.50 brown and blue (postage) 20 20
671 – 5p.+5p. brown & orge . . 30 25
672 – 7p.50+7p.50 brn & vio . . 50 40
673 – 15p.+15p. brown & red (air) . . . . 2·50 2·25
674 – 25p.+25p. brown & grn 2·50 2·25
675 – 35p.+35p. brown & bl . . 2·50 2·25
DESIGNS: 5p. Wrestling; 7p.50, Putting the shot; 15p. Fencing; 25p. Cycling; 35p. Swimming.

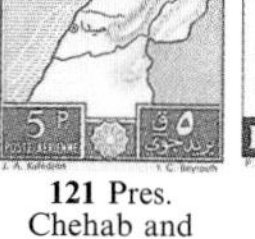
120 Pres. Chehab

121 Pres. Chehab and Map of Lebanon

122 U.N. Emblem and Map

1961.
676 **120** 2p.50 ultramarine and blue (postage) 20 10
677 7p.50 violet and mauve 25 10
678 10p. brown and yellow . . 50 10
679 **121** 5p. green & lt green (air) 15 10
680 10p. brown and ochre . . 45 10
681 70p. violet and mauve . . 1·90 60
682 – 200p. blue and bistre . . 4·25 2·50
DESIGN—HORIZ: 200p. Casino, Maameltein.

1961. Air. 15th Anniv of U.N.O.
683 **122** 20p. purple and blue . . . 50 25
684 – 30p. green and brown . . 75 40
685 – 50p. blue and ultramarine 1·25 60
DESIGNS—VERT: 30p. U.N. emblem and Baalbek ruins. HORIZ: 50p. View of U.N. Headquarters and Manhattan.

123 Cedar of Lebanon

124 Bay of Maameltein

1961. Redrawn version of T **86** (different arrangement at foot). Shaded background.
686 **123** 2p.50 myrtle 50 10
See also Nos. 695/7.

1961. Air.
687 **124** 15p. lake 40 20
688 30p. blue 65 30
689 40p. sepia 90 45

125 Weaving

1961. Air. Labour Day.
690 – 30p. red . . . . 1·25 60
691 **125** 70p. blue . . . . 2·50 1·25
DESIGN: 30p. Pottery.

126 Water-skiers

1961. Air. Tourist Month.
692 – 15p. violet and blue . . . 60 35
693 **126** 40p. blue and flesh . . . 1·25 50
694 – 70p. olive and flesh . . . 1·90 1·00
DESIGNS—VERT: 15p. Firework display. HORIZ: 70p. Tourists in punt.

1961. As T **123** but plain background.
695 2p.50 yellow 30 10
696 5p. lake 40 15
697 10p. black 65 25

127 G.P.O., Beirut

1961.
698 **127** 2p.50 mauve (postage) . . 30 10
699 5p. green 50 20
700 15p. blue . . . . 1·00 35
701 – 35p. green (air) 60 45
702 – 50p. brown 90 55
703 – 100p. black . . . . 1·25 90
DESIGN: 35p. to 100p. Motor highway, Dora.

128 Cedars of Lebanon

129 Tyre Waterfront

1961.
704 **128** 0p.50 green (postage) . . 10 10
705 1p. brown 10 10
706 2p.50 blue 10 10
707 5p. red 25 10
708 7p.50 violet 35 10
709 – 10p. purple 80 10
710 – 15p. blue . . . . 1·10 20
711 – 50p. green . . . . 1·25 75
712 – 100p. black . . . . 3·00 1·10
713 **129** 5p. red (air) 20 10
714 10p. violet 25 10
715 15p. blue 45 10
716 20p. orange 45 10
717 30p. green 50 15
718 – 40p. purple 75 25
719 – 50p. blue 90 40
720 – 70p. green . . . . 1·25 60
721 – 100p. sepia . . . . 2·25 95
DESIGNS—HORIZ: Nos. 709/12, Zahle. VERT: Nos. 718/21, Afka Falls.
See also Nos. 729/34.

130 UNESCO Building, Beirut

1961. Air. 15th Anniv of UNESCO. Mult.
722 20p. Type **130** 35 25
723 30p. UNESCO emblem and cedar (vert) 65 40
724 50p. UNESCO Building, Paris . . . . 1·00 60

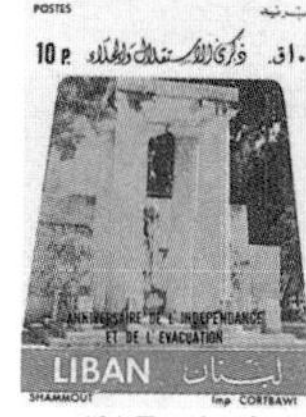
131 Tomb of Unknown Soldier

132 Scout Bugler

1961. Independence and Evacuation of Foreign Troops Commemoration. Multicoloured.
725 10p. Type **131** (postage) . . . 35 10
726 15p. Soldier and flag 50 10
727 25p. Cedar emblem (horiz) (air) 45 25
728 50p. Emirs Bashir and Fakhreddine (horiz) . . . 65 50

1962. As Nos. 704/21 but with larger figures of value.
729 **128** 50c. green (postage) . . . 20 10
730 1p. brown 20 10
731 2p.50 blue 25 10
732 – 15p. blue . . . . 3·00 25
733 **129** 5p. red (air) 35 10
734 – 40p. purple . . . . 5·50 75

1962. Lebanese Scout Movement Commemorative.
735 ½p. black, yell & grn (postage) 10 10
736 1p. multicoloured 10 10
737 2½p. green, black and red . . 10 10
738 6p. multicoloured 35 10
739 10p. yellow, black and blue 65 10
740 15p. multicoloured (air) . . . 65 25
741 20p. yellow, black and violet 75 35
742 25p. multicoloured . . . . . 1·25 65
DESIGNS—VERT: ½p. Type **132**; 6p. Lord Baden-Powell; 20p. Saluting hand. HORIZ: 1p. Scout with flag, cedar and badge; 2½p. Stretcher party, badge and laurel; 10p. Scouts at campfire; 15p. Cedar and Guide badge; 25p. Cedar and Scout badge.

133 Arab League Centre, Cairo, and Emblem

134 Blacksmith

1962. Air. Arab League Week.
743 **133** 20p. ultramarine and blue 40 25
744 30p. lake and pink . . . 45 40
745 50p. green and turquoise 75 65
See also Nos. 792/5.

1962. Air. Labour Day.
746 **134** 5p. green and blue . . . 20 10
747 10p. blue and pink . . . 30 10
748 – 25p. violet and pink . . . 50 20
749 – 35p. mauve and blue . . 65 40
DESIGN—HORIZ: 25, 35p. Tractor.

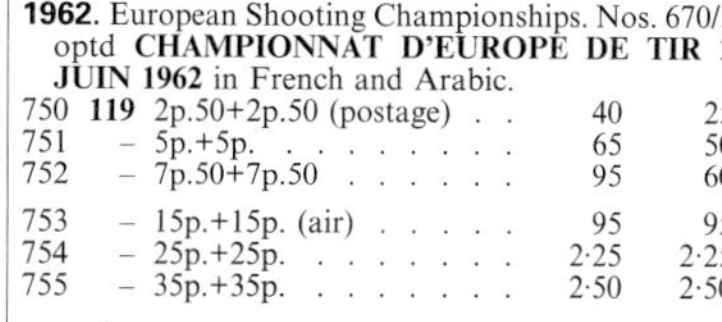

1962. European Shooting Championships. Nos. 670/5 optd **CHAMPIONNAT D'EUROPE DE TIR 2 JUIN 1962** in French and Arabic.
750 **119** 2p.50+2p.50 (postage) . . 40 25
751 – 5p.+5p. 65 50
752 – 7p.50+7p.50 . . . . . . 95 60
753 – 15p.+15p. (air) 95 95
754 – 25p.+25p. . . . . 2·25 2·25
755 – 35p.+35p. . . . . 2·50 2·50

136 Hand grasping Emblem

137 Rock Temples of Abu Simbel

1962. Air. Malaria Eradication.
756 **136** 30p. brown & light brown 75 50
757 – 70p. violet and lilac . . . 1·25 75
DESIGN: 70p. Campaign emblem.

1962. Nubian Monuments.
758 **137** 5p. bl & ultram (postage) 50 20
759 15p. lake and brown . . . 75 25
760 – 30p. yellow and green (air) . . . . 1·25 60
761 – 50p. olive and grey . . . 2·50 1·25
DESIGNS: 30, 50p. Bas-relief.

138 Playing-card Symbols

139 Schoolboy

1962. Air. European Bridge Championships.
762 **138** 25p. multicoloured . . . 3·00 1·90
763 40p. multicoloured . . . 3·25 1·90

1962. Schoolchildren's Day.
764 **139** 30p. mult (postage) . . . 50 25
765 – 45p. multicoloured (air) 75 40
DESIGN: 45p. Teacher.

140

141 Cherries

1962. Air. 19th Anniv of Independence.
766 **140** 25p. green, red & turq . . 75 35
767 25p. violet, red & turq . . 75 35
768 25p. blue, red & turquoise 75 35

1962. Fruits. Multicoloured.
769 0p.50 Type **141** (postage) . . 25 10
770 1p. Figs 25 10
771 2p.50 Type **141** 40 10
772 5p. Figs 50 10
773 7p.50 Type **141** 25 10
774 10p. Grapes 35 10
775 17p.50 Grapes 75 10
776 30p. Grapes . . . . 1·25 25
777 50p. Oranges . . . . 2·25 65
778 100p. Pomegranates . . . . 5·00 1·40
779 5p. Apricots (air) 20 10
780 10p. Plums 25 10
781 20p. Apples 55 10
782 30p. Plums 75 25
783 40p. Apples 90 25
784 50p. Pears . . . . 1·10 40
785 70p. Medlars . . . . 1·90 50
786 100p. Lemons . . . . 3·25 1·10

142 Reaping

143 Nurse tending Baby

1963. Air. Freedom from Hunger.
787 **142** 2p.50 yellow and blue . . 15 10
788 5p. yellow and green . . . 15 10
789 7p.50 yellow and purple 20 10
790 – 15p. green and red . . . 50 25
791 – 20p. green and red . . . 65 40
DESIGN—HORIZ: 15, 20p. Three ears of wheat within hand.

1963. Air. Arab League Week. As T **133** but inscr "1963".
792 5p. violet and blue 10 10
793 10p. green and blue 20 20
794 15p. brown and blue 30 25
795 20p. grey and blue 65 45

1963. Air. Red Cross Centenary.
796 – 5p. green and red 10 10
797 – 20p. blue and red 30 10
798 **143** 35p. red and black . . . 55 25
799 40p. violet and red . . . 90 45
DESIGN—HORIZ: 5, 20p. Blood transfusion.

144 Allegory of Music

145 Flag and rising Sun

1963. Air. Baalbek Festival.
800 **144** 35p. orange and blue . . 95 50

1963. Air. 20th Anniv of Independence. Flag and sun in red and yellow.
801 **145** 5p. turquoise 15 10
802 10p. green 25 25
803 25p. blue 50 40
804 40p. drab 75 65

146 Cycling

147 Hyacinth

1964. 4th Mediterranean Games, Naples (1963).
805 **146** 2p.50 brown and purple (postage) 20 10
806 – 5p. orange and blue . . . 25 10
807 – 10p. brown and violet . . 40 10
808 – 15p. orange and green (air) 40 25
809 – 17p.50 brown and blue . . 50 30
810 – 30p. brown and turquoise 75 50
DESIGNS—VERT: 5p. Basketball; 10p. Running; 15p. Tennis. HORIZ: 17p.50, Swimming; 30p. Skiing.

1964. Flowers. Multicoloured.
811 0p.50 Type **147** (postage) . . 10 10
812 1p. Type **147** 10 10
813 2p.50 Type **147** 10 10
814 5p. Cyclamen 10 10
815 7p.50 Cyclamen 15 10
816 10p. Poinsettia (vert) . . . 25 10
817 17p.50 Anemone (vert) . . . 50 10
818 30p. Iris (vert) . . . . . . 1·10 40
819 50p. Poppy (vert) . . . . . 2·50 65
820 5p. Lily (vert) (air) 25 20
821 10p. Ranunculus (vert) . . . 45 20
822 20p. Anemone (vert) 60 20
823 40p. Tuberose (vert) . . . . 1·00 40
824 45p. Rhododendron (vert) . . 1·10 40
825 50p. Jasmine (vert) . . . . . 1·25 40
826 70p. Yellow broom (vert) . . 1·90 65
Nos. 816/26 are size 26½ × 37 mm.

148 Cedar of Lebanon

149 Cedar of Lebanon

1964.
827 **148** 0p.50 green 25 10
828 **149** 0p.50 green 15 10
829 2p.50 blue 15 10
830 5p. mauve 20 10
831 7p.50 orange 40 10
832 17p.50 purple 70 10

150 Child on Rocking-horse

152 "Flame of Freedom"

151 League Session

1964. Air. Children's Day.
833 – 5p. red, orange and green 15 10
834 – 10p. red, orange and brown 25 15
835 **150** 20p. orange, blue and ultramarine 50 35
836 40p. yellow, blue and purple 90 65
DESIGN—HORIZ: 5, 10p. Girls skipping.

1964. Air. Arab League Meeting.
837 **151** 5p. buff, brown and black 25 20
838 10p. black 35 25
839 15p. turquoise 65 40
840 20p. mauve, brn & sepia 1·00 45

1964. Air. 15th Anniv of Declaration of Human Rights.
841 **152** 20p. red, pink and brown 25 25
842 – 40p. orange, blue and light blue 50 35
DESIGN: 40p. Flame on pedestal bearing U.N. emblem.

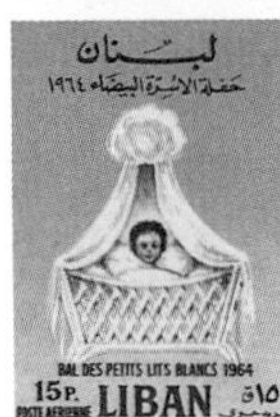

153 Sick Child

154 Clasped Wrists

1964. Air. "Bal des Petits Lits Blancs" (Ball for children's charity).
843 **153** 2p.50 multicoloured . . . 15 10
844 5p. multicoloured 15 10
845 15p. multicoloured . . . 25 10
846 – 17p.50 multicoloured . . 40 25
847 – 20p. multicoloured . . . 50 25
848 – 40p. multicoloured . . . 80 40
DESIGN—55 × 25½ mm: 17p.50 to 40p. Children in front of palace (venue of ball).

1964. Air. World Lebanese Union Congress, Beirut.
849 **154** 20p. black, yellow & green 50 25
850 40p. black, yellow & pur 90 50

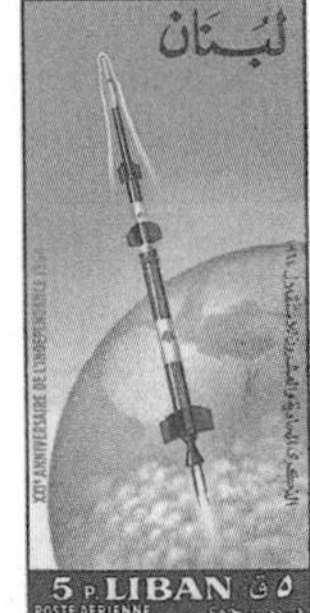

155 Rocket in Flight

1964. Air. 21st Anniv of Independence.
851 **155** 5p. multicoloured 25 20
852 10p. multicoloured 25 20
853 – 40p. blue and black . . . 95 45
854 – 70p. purple and black . . 1·40 1·10
DESIGNS—HORIZ: 40p. to 70p. "Struggle for Independence" (battle scene).

156 Temple Columns

1965. Baalbek Festival.
855 **156** 2p.50 black and orange (postage) 25 20
856 – 7p.50 black and blue . . 50 35
857 – 10p. multicoloured (air) 10 10
858 – 15p. multicoloured . . . 25 10
859 – 25p. multicoloured . . . 50 40
860 – 40p. multicoloured . . . 1·00 50
DESIGNS—28 × 55 mm: 10, 15p. Man in costume; 25, 40p. Woman in costume.

157 Swimming

1965. Olympic Games, Tokyo.
861 **157** 2p.50 black, blue and mauve (postage) . . . 20 10
862 – 7p.50 purple, green & brn 75 50
863 – 10p. grey, brown & green 95 60
864 – 15p. black and green (air) 25 10
865 – 25p. green and purple . . 50 25
866 – 40p. brown and blue . . . 80 40
DESIGNS—HORIZ: 7p.50, Fencing; 15p. Horse-jumping; 40p. Gymnastics. VERT: 10p. Basketball; 25p. Rifle-shooting.

158 Red Admiral

1965. (a) Postage. Birds.
867 – 5p. multicoloured 45 10
868 – 10p. multicoloured 60 10
869 – 15p. chocolate, orange & brn . . . . 1·10 15
870 – 17p.50 purple, red and blue 1·60 20
871 – 20p. black, yellow and green 1·75 20
872 – 32p.50 yellow, brown & grn 4·50 75

(b) Air. Butterflies.
873 – 30p. yellow, brown and red 75 10
874 – 35p. blue, red and bistre 1·10 20
875 **158** 40p. brown, red and green 1·40 20
876 – 45p. brown, yellow & blue 1·75 40
877 – 70p. multicoloured . . . 2·75 50
878 – 85p. black, orange & green . . . . 3·00 65
879 – 100p. blue and plum . . . 4·50 75
880 – 200p. brown, blue & pur 8·00 90
881 – 300p. sepia, yellow & green . . . . 12·00 2·50
882 – 500p. brown, blue and light blue . . . . . . 20·00 5·00
DESIGNS—As T **158**. BIRDS: 5p. Northern bullfinch; 10p. Eurasian goldfinch; 15p. Hoopoe; 17p.50, Red-legged partridge; 20p. Golden oriole; 32p.50, European bee eater. BUTTERFLIES: 30p. Large tiger moth; 35p. Small postman; 45p. Common grayling; 70p. Swallowtail; 85p. Orange-tip; 100p. Blue morpho; 200p. "Erasmia sanguiflua"; 300p. "Papilio crassus". 35½ × 25 mm: 500p. Amelia's charakes.

159 Pope Paul and Pres. Helou

1965. Air. Pope Paul's Visit to Lebanon.
883 **159** 45p. violet and gold . . . 3·25 1·90

160 Sheep

1965.
884 – 50c. multicoloured 50 10
885 – 1p. grey, black and mauve 65 10
886 **160** 2p.50 yellow, sepia & grn 75 10
DESIGNS: 50c. Cow and calf; 1p. Rabbit.

161 "Cedars of Friendship"

162 "Silk Manufacture"

1965. Air.
887 **161** 40p. multicoloured . . . 1·25 25

1965. Air. World Silk Congress, Beirut. Mult.
888 2p.50 Type **162** 20 10
889 5p. Type **162** 20 10
890 7p.50 Type **162** 25 10
891 15p. Weaver and loom . . . 25 10
892 30p. As 15p. 65 25
893 40p. As 15p. . . . . 1·00 40
894 50p. As 15p. . . . . 1·25 50

163 Parliament Building

1965. Air. Centenary of Lebanese Parliament.
895 **163** 35p. brown, ochre and red 40 25
896 40p. brown, ochre & green 65 40

164 U.N. Emblem and Headquarters

165 Playing-card "King"

1965. Air. 20th Anniv of U.N.O.
897 **164** 2p.50 blue 10 10
898 10p. red 10 10
899 17p.50 violet 10 10
900 30p. green 40 25
901 40p. brown 50 40

1965. Air. World Bridge Championships, Beirut.
902 **165** 2p.50 multicoloured . . . 20 10
903 15p. multicoloured . . . 45 10
904 17p.50 multicoloured . . 65 25
905 40p. multicoloured . . . 1·25 50

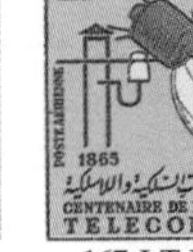

166 Dagger on Deir Yassin, Palestine

167 I.T.U. Emblem and Symbols

1965. Air. Deir Yassin Massacre.
906 **166** 50p. multicoloured . . . 2·25 50

1966. Air. Centenary (1965) of I.T.U.
907 **167** 2p.50 multicoloured . . . 20 10
908 15p. multicoloured . . . 20 10
909 17p.50 multicoloured . . 45 15
910 25p. multicoloured . . . 75 30
911 40p. multicoloured . . . 1·00 40

168 Stage Performance

1966. Air. Baalbek Festival. Multicoloured.
912 2p.50 Type **168** 20 10
913 5p. Type **168** 20 10
914 7p.50 Ballet performance (vert) 20 10
915 15p. Ballet performance (vert) 30 10
916 30p. Concert 65 25
917 40p. Concert . . . . 1·00 40

169 Tabarja

1966. Tourism. Multicoloured.
918 50c. Hippodrome, Beirut (postage) 10 10
919 1p. Pigeon Grotto, Beirut . . 10 10
920 2p.50 Type **169** 10 10
921 5p. Ruins, Beit-Mery 10 10
922 7p.50 Ruins, Anjar 10 10
923 10p. Djezzine Falls (air) . . . 10 10
924 15p. Sidon Castle 15 10
925 20p. Amphitheatre, Byblos 25 10
926 30p. Sun Temple, Baalbek . . 40 10
927 50p. Palace, Beit ed-Din . . . 65 10
928 60p. Nahr-el Kalb . . . . . 1·50 45
929 70p. Tripoli . . . . 1·25 40

170 W.H.O. Building

1966. Air. Inauguration of W.H.O. Headquarters, Geneva.
930 **170** 7p.50 green 25 10
931 17p.50 red 35 25
932 25p. blue 65 35

171 Skiing

1966. Air. International Cedars Festival.
933 **171** 2p.50 brown, red & green 25 10
934 – 5p. multicoloured 25 10
935 – 17p.50 multicoloured 35 20
936 – 25p. red, brown and green 1·00 40
DESIGNS: 5p. Toboganning; 17p.50, Cedar in snow; 25p. Ski-lift.

172 Inscribed Sarcophagus

1966. Air. Phoenician Invention of the Alphabet.
937 **172** 10p. brown, black & green 10 10
938 – 15p. brown, ochre & mve 25 10
939 – 20p. sepia, blue and ochre 40 25
940 – 30p. brown, orange & yell 65 40
DESIGNS: 15p. Phoenician sailing ship; 20p. Mediterranean route map showing spread of Phoenician alphabet; 30p. Kadmus with alphabet tablet.

173 Child in Bath **174** Decade Emblem

1966. Air. Int Children's Day. Multicoloured.
941 2p. Type **173** 10 10
942 5p. Boy and doll in rowing boat 15 10
943 7p.50 Girl skiing 25 10
944 15p. Girl giving food to bird 40 25
945 20p. Boy doing homework 65 40

1966. Air. International Hydrological Decade.
947 **174** 5p. ultramarine, bl & orge 20 10
948 10p. red, blue and orange 20 10
949 – 15p. sepia, green & orange 25 15
950 – 20p. blue, green & orange 40 25
DESIGN: 15p., 20p. Similar "wave" pattern.

175 Rev. Daniel Bliss (founder) **176** I.T.Y. Emblem

177 Beit ed-Din Palace

1966. Air. Centenary of American University, Beirut.
951 **175** 20p. brown, yellow & grn 35 15
952 – 30p. green, brown and blue 45 30
DESIGN: 30p. University Chapel.

1967. International Tourist Year (1st issue).
(a) Postage.
954 **176** 50c. multicoloured 10 10
955 1p. multicoloured 10 10
956 2p.50 multicoloured 10 10
957 5p. multicoloured 15 10
958 7p.50 multicoloured 25 10

(b) Air. Multicoloured.
959 10p. Tabarja 20 10
960 15p. Pigeon Rock, Beirut 25 10
961 17p.50 Type **177** 30 10
962 20p. Sidon 30 10
963 25p. Tripoli 35 10
964 30p. Byblos 45 10
965 35p. Ruins, Tyre 55 10
966 40p. Temple, Baalbek 75 10
See also Nos. 977/80.

178 Signing Pact, and Flags

1967. Air. 22nd Anniv of Arab League Pact.
967 **178** 5p. multicoloured 10 10
968 10p. multicoloured 15 10
969 15p. multicoloured 25 20
970 20p. multicoloured 35 30

179 Veterans War Memorial Building, San Francisco

1967. Air. San Francisco Pact of 1945. Mult.
971 2p.50 Type **179** 1·00 30
972 5p. Type **179** 1·00 30
973 7p.50 Type **179** 1·00 30
974 10p. Scroll and flags of U.N. and Lebanon 20 20
975 20p. As 10p. 25 20
976 30p. As 10p. 50 20

180 Temple Ruins, Baalbek

1967. Air. International Tourist Year (2nd issue). Multicoloured.
977 5p. Type **180** 10 10
978 10p. Ruins, Anjar 15 10
979 15p. Ancient bridge, Nahr-Ibrahim 25 10
980 20p. Grotto, Jeita 40 15

181

1967. Air. India Day.
981 **181** 2p.50 red 10 10
982 5p. purple 10 10
983 7p.50 brown 10 10
984 10p. blue 20 10
985 15p. green 45 15

182

1967. Air. 22nd Anniv of Lebanon's Admission to U.N.O.
986 **182** 2p.50 red 10 10
987 5p. blue 10 10
988 7p.50 green 10 10
989 – 10p. red 10 10
990 – 20p. blue 25 10
991 – 30p. green 45 25
DESIGN: 10, 20, 30p. U.N. Emblem.

183 Goat and Kid

1967. Animals and Fishes. Multicoloured.
992 50c. Type **183** (postage) 20 10
993 1p. Cattle 20 10
994 2p.50 Sheep 20 10
995 5p. Dromedaries 20 10
996 10p. Donkey 25 10
997 15p. Horses 55 10
998 20p. Basking shark (air) 80 10
999 30p. Garfish 80 10
1000 40p. Pollack 1·25 10
1001 50p. Cuckoo wrasse 1·40 20
1002 70p. Striped red mullet 3·00 25
1003 100p. Rainbow trout 4·50 25

184 Ski Jumping

1968. Air. International Ski Congress, Beirut.
1004 **184** 2p.50 multicoloured 10 10
1005 – 5p. multicoloured 20 10
1006 – 7p.50 multicoloured 20 10
1007 – 10p. multicoloured 25 20
1008 – 25p. multicoloured 50 25
DESIGNS: 5p. to 10p. Skiing (all different); 25p. Congress emblem of Cedar and skis.

185 Princess Khaskiah

1968. Air. Emir Fakhreddine II Commem. Mult.
1009 2p.50 Type **185** 10 10
1010 5p. Emir Fakhreddine II 10 10
1011 10p. Sidon Citadel (horiz) 10 10
1012 15p. Chekif Citadel (horiz) 25 10
1013 17p.50 Beirut Citadel (horiz) 40 15

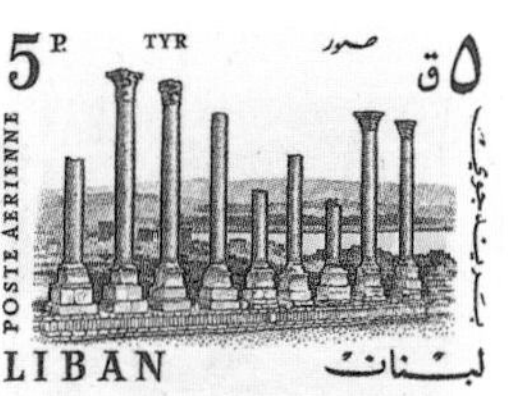

186 Colonnade

1968. Air. Tyre Antiquities.
1014 – 2p.50 brn, cream & pink 20 10
1015 **186** 5p. brown, blue & yellow 20 10
1016 – 7p.50 brown, buff & grn 25 20
1017 – 10p. brown, blue & orange 25 20
DESIGNS—VERT: 2p.50, Roman bust; 10p. Bas-relief. HORIZ: 7p.50, Arch.

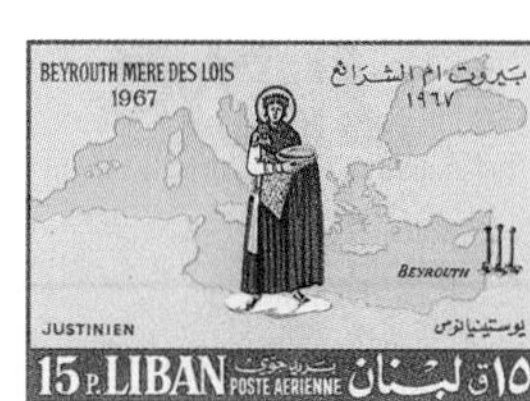

187 Justinian and Mediterranean Map

1968. Air. 1st Anniv of Faculty of Law, Beirut.
1019 5p. Justinian (vert) 10 10
1020 10p. Justinian (vert) 10 10
1021 15p. Type **187** 20 10
1022 20p. Type **187** 25 15

188 Arab League Emblem

1968. Air. Arab Appeal Week.
1023 **188** 5p. multicoloured 10 10
1024 10p. multicoloured 10 10
1025 15p. multicoloured 25 15
1026 20p. multicoloured 40 15

189 Cedar on Globe

1968. Air. 3rd World Lebanese Union Congress, Beirut.
1027 **189** 2p.50 multicoloured 10 10
1028 5p. multicoloured 10 10
1029 7p.50 multicoloured 20 10
1030 10p. multicoloured 20 15

190 Jupiter's Temple Ruins, Baalbek

1968. Air. Baalbek Festival. Multicoloured.
1031 5p. Type **190** 10 10
1032 10p. Bacchus's Temple 10 10
1033 15p. Corniche, Jupiter's Temple 25 15
1034 20p. Portal, Bacchus's Temple 40 20
1035 25p. Columns, Bacchus's Temple 50 30

191 Long Jumping and Atlantes

1968. Air. Olympic Games, Mexico.
1036 **191** 5p. black, yellow and blue 10 10
1037 – 10p. black, blue & purple 10 10
1038 – 15p. multicoloured 25 10
1039 – 20p. multicoloured 40 20
1040 – 25p. brown 65 40
DESIGNS (each incorporating Aztec relic): 10p. High jumping; 15p. Fencing; 20p. Weightlifting; 25p. "Sailing boat" with oars.

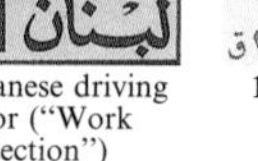
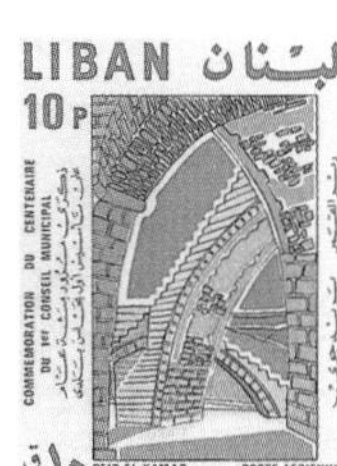

192 Lebanese driving Tractor ("Work protection") **193** Minshiya Stairs

1968. Air. Human Rights Year. Multicoloured.
1041 10p. Type **192** 10 10
1042 15p. Citizens ("Social Security") 20 10
1043 25p. Young men of three races ("Unity") 25 20

1968. Air. Centenary of 1st Municipal Council (Deir el-Kamar). Multicoloured.
1044 10p. Type **193** 10 10
1045 15p. Serai kiosk 20 10
1046 25p. Ancient highway . . . 25 20

194 Nurse and Child

1969. Air. UNICEF. Multicoloured.
1047 **194** 5p. black, brown and blue 10 10
1048 – 10p. black, green & yell 10 10
1049 – 15p. black, red and purple 10 10
1050 – 20p. black, blue & yellow 25 20
1051 – 25p. black, ochre & mve 40 20
DESIGNS: 10p. Produce; 15p. Mother and child; 20p. Child with book; 25p. Children with flowers.

195 Ancient Coin

1969. Air. 20th Anniv of International Museums Council (I.C.O.M.). Exhibits in National Museum, Beirut. Multicoloured.
1052 2p.50 Type **195** 10 10
1053 5p. Gold dagger, Byblos . . 20 10
1054 7p.50 Detail of Ahiram's Sarcophagus 20 10
1055 30p. Jewelled pectoral . . . 40 25
1056 40p. Khalde "bird" vase . . 50 40

196 Water-skiing

1969. Air. Water Sports. Multicoloured.
1057 2p.50 Type **196** 10 10
1058 5p. Water-skiing (group) . . 10 10
1059 7p.50 Paraskiing (vert) . . . 35 10
1060 30p. Racing dinghies (vert) 50 35
1061 40p. Racing dinghies . . . 75 60

197 Frontier Guard

1969. Air. 25th Anniv of Independence. The Lebanese Army.
1062 2p. Type **197** 10 10
1063 5p. Unknown Soldier's Tomb 10 10
1064 7p.50 Army Foresters . . . 20 10
1065 15p. Road-making 20 15
1066 30p. Military ambulance and Sud Aviation Alouette III helicopter 40 35
1067 40p. Skiing patrol 60 50

198 Concentric Red Crosses

1971. Air. 25th Anniv of Lebanese Red Cross.
1068 **198** 15p. red and black . . . 40 25
1069 – 85p. red and black . . . 1·50 1·00
DESIGN: 85p. Red Cross in shape of cedar of Lebanon.

199 Foil and Flags of Arab States

1971. Air. 10th International Fencing Championships. Multicoloured.
1070 10p. Type **199** 10 10
1071 15p. Foil and flags of foreign nations 10 10
1072 35p. Contest with foils . . . 50 40
1073 40p. Epee contest 65 40
1074 50p. Contest with sabres . . 80 50

200 "Farmers at Work" (12th-century Arab painting)

1971. Air. 50th Anniv (1969) of I.L.O.
1075 **200** 10p. multicoloured . . . 20 10
1076 40p. multicoloured . . . 65 40

201 U.P.U. Monument and New H.Q. Building, Berne

1971. Air. New U.P.U. Headquarters Building, Berne.
1077 **201** 15p. red, black and yellow 20 10
1078 35p. yellow, black and orange 65 40

202 "Ravens setting fire to Owls" (14th-century painting)

1971. Air. Children's Day. Multicoloured.
1079 15p. Type **202** 35 20
1080 85p. "The Lion and the Jackal" (13th-century painting) (39 × 29 mm) . . 1·60 75

203 Arab League Flag and Map

1971. Air. 25th Anniv of Arab League.
1081 **203** 30p. multicoloured . . . 40 15
1082 70p. multicoloured . . . 75 50

204 Jamhour Electricity Sub-station

1971. Air. Multicoloured.
1083 5p. Type **204** 10 10
1084 10p. Maameltein Bridge . . 10 10
1085 15p. Hoteliers' School . . . 10 10
1086 20p. Litani Dam 20 10
1087 25p. Interior of T.V. set . . 25 10
1088 35p. Bziza Temple 40 10
1089 40p. Jounieh Harbour . . . 40 15
1090 45p. Radar scanner, Beirut Airport 55 20
1091 50p. Hibiscus 75 20
1092 70p. School of Sciences Building . . . . 1·00 25
1093 85p. Oranges . . . . 1·25 40
1094 100p. Satellite Communications Station, Arbanieh . . . . 1·50 65

205 Insignia of Imam al Ouzai (theologian)

1971. Air. Lebanese Celebrities.
1095 **205** 25p. brown, gold & green 35 20
1096 – 25p. brown, gold & yell 35 20
1097 – 25p. brown, gold & yell 35 20
1098 – 25p. brown, gold & green 35 20
PORTRAITS: No. 1096, Bechara el Khoury (poet and writer); 1097, Hassan Kamel el Sabbah (scientist); 1098, Gibran Khalil Gibran (writer).

206 I.E.Y. Emblem and Computer Card

1971. Air. International Education Year.
1099 **206** 10p. black, blue and violet 10 10
1100 40p. black, yellow and red 40 25

207 Dahr-el-Basheq Sanatorium

208 "Solar Wheel" Emblem

1971. Air. Tuberculosis Relief Campaign.
1101 **207** 50p. multicoloured . . . 75 40
1102 – 100p. multicoloured . . 1·10 65
DESIGN: 100p. Different view of Sanatorium.

1971. Air. 16th Baalbek Festival.
1103 **208** 15p. orange and blue . . 20 10
1104 – 85p. black, blue & orange 80 55
DESIGN: 85p. Corinthian capital.

209 Field-gun

1971. Air. Army Day. Multicoloured.
1105 15p. Type **209** 25 20
1106 25p. Dassault Mirage IIICJ jet fighters 80 30
1107 40p. Army Command H.Q. 75 50
1108 70p. "Tarablous" (naval patrol boat) . . . . . . 1·50 90

210 Interior Decoration

212 U.N. Emblem

211 Lenin

1971. Air. 2nd Anniv of Burning of Al-Aqsa Mosque, Jerusalem.
1109 **210** 15p. brown and deep brown 50 20
1110 35p. brown and deep brown . . . . 1·00 65

1971. Air. Birth Centenary of Lenin. Mult.
1111 30p. Type **211** 50 25
1112 70p. Lenin in profile . . . . 1·10 65

1971. Air. 25th Anniv of United Nations.
1113 **212** 15p. multicoloured . . . 20 10
1114 85p. multicoloured . . . 95 50

213 "Europa" Mosaic, Byblos

1971. Air. World Lebanese Union.
1115 **213** 10p. multicoloured . . . 25 10
1116 40p. multicoloured . . . 1·00 40

1972. Various stamps surch.
1117 5p. on 7p.50 (No. 922) (postage) 10 10
1118 5p. on 7p.50 (No. 958) . . 10 10
1119 25p. on 32p.50 (No. 872) . . 90 10
1120 5p. on 7p.50 (No. 1016) (air) 10 10
1121 100p. on 300p. (No. 881) . . 3·25 90
1122 100p. on 500p. (No. 882) . . 3·25 90
1123 200p. on 300p. (No. 881) . . 4·50 1·75

217 Morning Glory

218 Ornate Arches

1973. Air. Multicoloured.
1124 2p.50 Type **217** 10 10
1125 5p. Roses 20 10
1126 15p. Tulips 25 10
1127 25p. Lilies 40 10
1128 40p. Carnations 50 20
1129 50p. Iris 75 10
1130 70p. Apples . . . . 1·25 20
1131 75p. Grapes . . . . 1·25 20
1132 100p. Peaches . . . . . . 2·00 60
1133 200p. Pears . . . . 3·25 45
1134 300p. Cherries . . . . . . 4·50 85
1135 500p. Oranges . . . . . . 6·25 1·50

1973. Air. Lebanese Domestic Architecture.
1136 – 35p. multicoloured . . . 50 25
1137 **218** 50p. multicoloured . . . 75 35
1138 – 85p. multicoloured . . . 1·25 45
1139 – 100p. multicoloured . . 1·40 60
DESIGNS: Nos. 1136 and 1138/39, Various Lebanese dwellings.

219 Girl with Lute

1973. Air. Ancient Costumes. Multicoloured.
1140 5p. Woman with rose . . . 15 10
1141 10p. Shepherd 25 10
1142 20p. Horseman 25 20
1143 25p. Type **219** 40 20

220 Swimming

1973. Air. 5th Pan-Arab Schools' Games, Beirut. Multicoloured.
1144 5p. Type **220** 10 10
1145 10p. Running 15 10
1146 15p. Gymnastics 25 10

1147 20p. Volleyball 40 10
1148 25p. Basketball 40 20
1149 50p. Table-tennis 75 35
1150 75p. Handball . . . . . . 1·00 45
1151 100p. Football . . . . . . 2·00 1·10

221 Brasilia

1973. Air. 150th Anniv of Brazil's Independence. Multicoloured.
1153 5p. Type **221** 10 10
1154 20p. Salvador (Bahia) in 1823 . . . . 25 10
1155 25p. Map and Phoenician galley 40 20
1156 50p. Emperor Pedro I and Emir Fakhreddine II . . 85 40

222 Marquetry

223 Cedar of Lebanon

1973. Air. Lebanese Handicrafts. Multicoloured.
1157 10p. Type **222** 15 10
1158 20p. Weaving 25 10
1159 35p. Glass-blowing 40 15
1160 40p. Pottery 65 20
1161 50p. Metal-working 75 20
1162 70p. Cutlery-making . . . . 1·00 25
1163 85p. Lace-making . . . . . 1·40 40
1164 100p. Handicrafts Museum 1·75 50

1974.
1165 **223** 50c. green, brown & orge 20 10

224 Camp Site and Emblems

1974. Air. 11th Arab Scout Jamboree, Smar-Jubeil, Lebanon. Multicoloured.
1166 2p.50 Type **224** 10 10
1167 5p. Scout badge and map 10 10
1168 7p.50 Map of Arab countries 20 10
1169 10p. Lord Baden-Powell and Baalbek 20 10
1170 15p. Guide and camp . . . 20 10
1171 20p. Lebanese Guide and Scout badge 30 10
1172 25p. Scouts around campfire 45 10
1173 30p. Globe and Scout badge 50 20
1174 35p. Flags of participating countries 70 20
1175 50p. Scout chopping wood for old man . . . . . . 1·00 35

225 Mail Train

1974. Centenary of U.P.U. Multicoloured.
1176 5p.50 Type **225** 75 45
1177 20p. Container ship 45 10
1178 25p. Congress building, Lausanne, and U.P.U. H.Q., Berne 45 10
1179 50p. Mail plane 75 45

226 Congress Building, Sofar

227 "Mountain Road" (O. Onsi)

1974. Air. 25th Anniv of Arab Postal Union. Multicoloured.
1180 5p. Type **226** 10 10
1181 20p. View of Sofar 20 10
1182 25p. A.P.U. H.Q., Cairo . . 25 10
1183 50p. Ministry of Posts, Beirut . . . . 1·00 55

1974. Air. Lebanese Paintings. Multicoloured.
1184 50p. Type **227** 65 30
1185 50p. "Clouds" (M. Farroukh) 65 30
1186 50p. "Woman" (G. K. Gebran) 65 30
1187 50p. "Embrace" (C. Gemayel) 65 30
1188 50p. "Self-portrait" (H. Serour) 65 30
1189 50p. "Portrait" (D. Corm) 65 30

228 Hunter killing Lion

1974. Air. Hermel Excavations. Multicoloured.
1190 5p. Type **228** 10 10
1191 10p. Astarte 15 10
1192 25p. Dogs hunting boar . . 40 20
1193 35p. Greco-Roman tomb . . 65 40

229 Book Year Emblem

1974. Air. International Book Year (1972).
1194 **229** 5p. multicoloured . . . 10 10
1195 10p. multicoloured . . . 15 10
1196 25p. multicoloured . . . 40 15
1197 35p. multicoloured . . . 50 60

230 Magnifying Glass

231 Georgina Rizk in Lebanese Costume

1974. Air. Stamp Day. Multicoloured.
1198 5p. Type **230** 10 10
1199 10p. Linked posthorns . . . 10 10
1200 15p. Stamp-printing 20 10
1201 20p. "Stamp" in mount . . 35 20

1974. Air. Miss Universe 1971 (Georgina Rizk). Multicoloured.
1202 5p. Type **231** 10 10
1203 20p. Head-and-shoulders portrait 15 10
1204 25p. Type **231** 25 15
1205 50p. As 20p. 65 40

232 Winds

234 Discus-throwing

233 UNICEF Emblem and Sikorsky S-55 Helicopter

1974. Air. U.N. Conference on Human Environment, Stockholm, 1972. Multicoloured.
1207 5p. Type **232** 10 10
1208 25p. Mountains and plain 40 10
1209 30p. Trees and flowers . . . 40 20
1210 40p. Sea 50 40

1974. Air. 25th Anniv of UNICEF. Multicoloured.
1212 20p. Type **233** 45 10
1213 25p. Emblem and child welfare clinic 25 10
1214 35p. Emblem and kindergarten class 45 20
1215 70p. Emblem and schoolgirls in laboratory 85 25

1974. Air. Olympic Games, Munich (1972). Mult.
1217 5p. Type **234** 10 10
1218 10p. Putting the shot . . . 10 10
1219 15p. Weight-lifting 15 10
1220 35p. Running 50 25
1221 50p. Wrestling 65 25
1222 85p. Javelin-throwing . . . 1·25 40

235 Symbols of Archaeology

1975. Air. Beirut—"University City". Mult.
1224 20p. Type **235** 25 10
1225 25p. Science and medicine 25 10
1226 35p. Justice and commerce 45 35
1227 70p. Industry and commerce 90 50

(236)

1978. Air. Various stamps optd with different patterns as T **236**. (a) Tourist Views. Nos. 1090, 1092/3.
1228 45p. Radar scanner, Beirut Airport 45 20
1229 70p. School of Sciences Building 90 25
1230 85p. Oranges . . . . 1·00 35

(b) Flowers and Fruits. Nos. 1124/35.
1231 2p.50 Type **217** 10 10
1232 5p. Roses 10 10
1233 15p. Tulips 25 10
1234 25p. Lilies 45 10
1235 40p. Carnations 45 15
1236 50p. Iris 65 15
1237 70p. Apples 90 25
1238 75p. Grapes . . . . 1·25 25
1239 100p. Peaches . . . . 1·25 40
1240 200p. Pears . . . . 2·50 1·40
1241 300p. Cherries . . . . . . 3·75 2·50
1242 500p. Oranges . . . . . . 6·25 3·75

(c) Lebanese Domestic Architecture. Nos. 1136/9.
1243 – 35p. multicoloured . . . 55 10
1244 **218** 50p. multicoloured . . . 65 15
1245 – 85p. multicoloured . . . 1·00 35
1246 – 100p. multicoloured . . 1·25 40

(d) Ancient Costumes. Nos. 1140/3.
1247 5p. Woman with rose . . . 10 10
1248 10p. Shepherd 15 10
1249 20p. Horseman 30 10
1250 25p. Type **219** 45 10

(e) Lebanese Handicrafts. Nos. 1157/8, 1160/4.
1251 10p. Type **222** 15 10
1252 20p. Weaving 30 10
1253 40p. Pottery 45 15
1254 50p. Metal-working 75 15
1255 70p. Cutlery-making 90 25
1256 85p. Lace-making . . . . . 1·00 35
1257 100p. Handicraft Museum 1·25 40

237 Mikhail Naimy (poet) and View of al-Chakroub Baskinta

1978. Air. Mikhail Naimy Festival Week. Mult.
1258 25p. Mikhail Naimy and Sannine mountains . . . 25 10
1259 50p. Type **237** 50 25
1260 75p. Mikhail Naimy (vert) 80 40

238 Heart and Arrow

239 Army Badge

1978. Air. World Health Day. "Down with Blood Pressure".
1261 **238** 50p. blue, red and black 75 40

1980. Army Day. Multicoloured.
1262 25p. Type **239** (postage) . . 40 20
1263 50p. Statue of Emir Fakhr el Dine on horseback (air) 65 25
1264 75p. Soldiers with flag (horiz) 95 25

240 13th-century European King

1980. Air. 50th Anniv (1974) of International Chess Federation. Multicoloured.
1265 50p. Rook, knight and Jubilee emblem (horiz) . . 75 25
1266 75p. Type **240** . . . . . . 1·25 40
1267 100p. Rook and Lebanon Chess Federation emblem 1·90 65
1268 150p. 18th-century French rook, king and knight . . 2·50 1·00
1269 200p. Painted faience rook, queen and bishop . . . . 3·25 1·50

241 Congress, U.P.U. and Lebanon Post Emblems

1981. Air. 18th U.P.U. Congress, Rio de Janeiro (1979).
1270 **241** 25p. blue, brown and black 40 15
1271 50p. pink, brown & black 65 25
1272 75p. green, brown and black . . . . 1·00 40

242 Children on Raft

1981. Air. International Year of the Child (1979).
1273 **242** 100p. multicoloured . . 1·25 65

243 President Sarkis

1981. 5th Anniv of Election of President Sarkis.
1274 **243** 125p. multicoloured . . 95 50
1275 300p. multicoloured . . 2·75 1·10
1276 500p. multicoloured . . 4·50 1·60

244 Society Emblem and Children

1981. Air. Centenary (1978) of Al-Makassed Islamic Welfare Society. Multicoloured.
1277 50p. Type **244** 50 15
1278 75p. Institute building . . . 75 20
1279 100p. Al-Makassed (founder) 95 35

245 Stork carrying Food

1982. World Food Day (1981). Multicoloured.
1280 50p. Type **245** 50 25
1281 75p. Ear of wheat and globe 75 40
1282 100p. Fruit, fish and grain 1·50 65

246 W.C.Y. Emblem **247** Phoenician Galley flying Scout Flag

1983. World Communications Year.
1283 **246** 300p. multicoloured . . 2·50 1·25

1983. 75th Anniv of Boy Scout Movement. Multicoloured.
1284 200p. Type **247** . . . . . . 1·90 95
1285 300p. Scouts lowering flag and signalling by semaphore . . . . 2·50 1·25
1286 500p. Camp . . . . 4·50 1·90

248 "The Soul is Back"

1983. Birth Centenary of Gibran (poet and painter). Multicoloured.
1287 200p. Type **248** . . . . . 1·90 95
1288 300p. "The Family" . . . . 2·50 1·25
1289 500p. "Gibran" . . . . . . 4·50 1·90
1290 1000p. "The Prophet" . . . 8·75 4·75

249 Cedar of Lebanon **250** Iris

1984.
1292 **249** 5p. multicoloured . . . 20 10

1984. Flowers. Multicoloured.
1293 10p. Type **250** 25 10
1294 25p. Periwinkle 40 25
1295 50p. Barberry 95 40

251 Dove with Laurel over Buildings

1984. Lebanese Army. Multicoloured.
1296 75p. Type **251** 70 40
1297 150p. Cedar and soldier holding rifle . . . . . . 1·50 90
1298 300p. Broken chain, hand holding laurel wreath and cedar . . . . 3·25 1·90

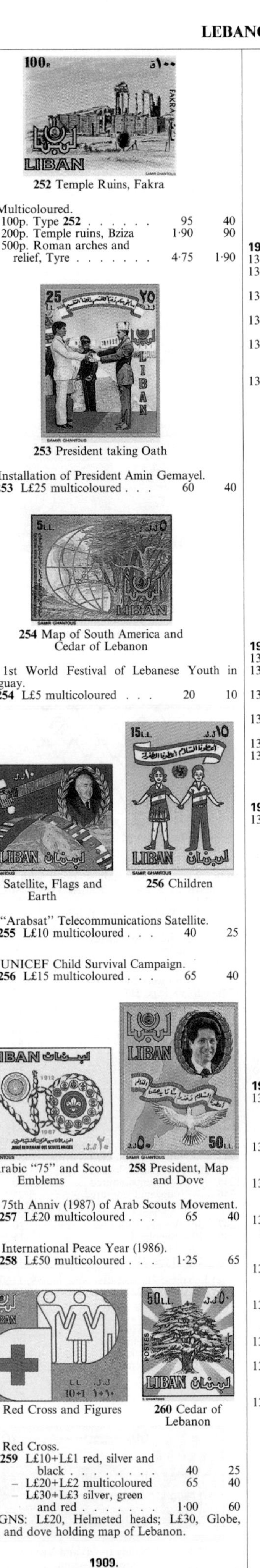

252 Temple Ruins, Fakra

1984. Multicoloured.
1299 100p. Type **252** 95 40
1300 200p. Temple ruins, Bziza 1·90 90
1301 500p. Roman arches and relief, Tyre . . . . 4·75 1·90

253 President taking Oath

1988. Installation of President Amin Gemayel.
1302 **253** L£25 multicoloured . . . 60 40

254 Map of South America and Cedar of Lebanon

1988. 1st World Festival of Lebanese Youth in Uruguay.
1303 **254** L£5 multicoloured . . . 20 10

255 Satellite, Flags and Earth **256** Children

1988. "Arabsat" Telecommunications Satellite.
1304 **255** L£10 multicoloured . . . 40 25

1988. UNICEF Child Survival Campaign.
1305 **256** L£15 multicoloured . . . 65 40

257 Arabic "75" and Scout Emblems **258** President, Map and Dove

1988. 75th Anniv (1987) of Arab Scouts Movement.
1306 **257** L£20 multicoloured . . . 65 40

1988. International Peace Year (1986).
1307 **258** L£50 multicoloured . . . 1·25 65

259 Red Cross and Figures **260** Cedar of Lebanon

1988. Red Cross.
1308 **259** L£10+L£1 red, silver and black 40 25
1309 – L£20+L£2 multicoloured 65 40
1310 – L£30+L£3 silver, green and red . . . . 1·00 60
DESIGNS: L£20, Helmeted heads; L£30, Globe, flame, and dove holding map of Lebanon.

1989.
1311 **260** L£50 green and mauve 25 15
1312 L£70 green and brown 40 20
1313 L£100 green and yellow 65 30
1314 L£200 green and blue . . 1·25 65
1315 L£500 deep green & green . . . . 3·25 1·60

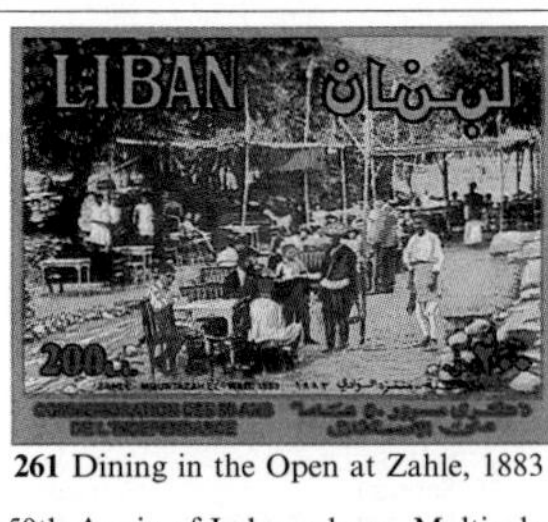

261 Dining in the Open at Zahle, 1883

1993. 50th Anniv of Independence. Multicoloured.
1316 L£200 Type **261** 40 25
1317 L£300 Castle ruins, Saida (vert) 55 40
1318 L£500 Presidential Palace, Baabda 95 65
1319 L£1000 Sword ceremony (vert) . . . . 1·90 1·25
1320 L£3000 Model for the rebuilding of central Beirut . . . . 5·50 3·00
1321 L£5000 President Elias Hrawi and state flag (vert) 10·00 6·75

262 Protection of Plants **263** Martyrs' Monument, Beirut

1994. Environmental Protection. Multicoloured.
1323 L£100 Type **262** 15 10
1324 L£200 Protection against forest fires 30 20
1325 L£500 Reforesting with cedars 75 50
1326 L£1000 Creation of urban green zones . . . . 1·50 1·00
1327 L£2000 Trees . . . . 2·50 1·60
1328 L£5000 Green tree in town 8·00 5·25

1995. Martyrs' Day.
1329 **263** L£1500 multicoloured . . 1·75 1·10

264 Arabic Script under Magnifying Glass and Headquarters

1996. Anniversaries and Events. Multicoloured.
1330 L£100 Type **264** (inauguration of Postal Museum, Arab League Headquarters, Cairo) . . 10 10
1331 L£500 Anniversary emblem (50th anniv of UNICEF) (horiz) 40 25
1332 L£500 Ears of wheat and anniversary emblem (50th anniv (1995) of F.A.O.) 40 25
1333 L£1000 U.N. Building (New York) and anniversary emblem (50th anniv (1995) of U.N.O.) 80 55
1334 L£1000 Emblem (International Year of the Family (1994)) (horiz) . . 80 55
1335 L£2000 Anniversary emblem (75th anniv (1994) of I.L.O.) (horiz) . . . . . 1·60 1·10
1336 L£2000 Emblem (50th anniv of Arab League) . . . . 1·60 1·10
1337 L£3000 Emblem (75th anniv (1994) of Lebanese Law Society) . . . . 2·40 1·60
1338 L£3000 Rene Moawad (former President, 70th birth anniv (1995)) . . . 2·40 1·60

265 Commemorative Medallion

1997. 1st Anniv of Shelling of Cana Refugee Camp.
1339 **265** L£1100 multicoloured . . 90 60

266 Pope John Paul II and President Hrawi

1998. Papal Visit.
1340 **266** L£10000 multicoloured 8·00 5·25

POSTAGE DUE STAMPS

1924. Postage Due stamps of France surch **GRAND LIBAN** and value in "CENTIEMES" or "PIASTRES".
D26 **D 11** 50c. on 10c. brown . . 1·90 3·25
D27 1p. on 20c. green . . . 3·50 7·00
D28 2p. on 30c. red . . . . 1·90 5·25
D29 3p. on 50c. purple . . . 2·25 5·25
D30 5p. on 1f. purple on yellow . . . . 1·75 3·75

1924. Postage Due stamps of France surch **Gd Liban** and value in French and Arabic.
D58 **D 11** 0p.50 on 10c. brown . . 1·00 3·75
D59 1p. on 20c. green . . . 1·25 3·75
D60 2p. on 30c. red . . . . 1·25 3·00
D61 3p. on 50c. purple . . . 1·25 3·75
D62 5p. on 1f. purple on yell 75 4·00

D 7 Nahr el-Kalb

1925.
D75 **D 7** 0p.50 brown on yellow 95 1·75
D76 – 1p. red on pink . . . . 75 3·00
D77 – 2p. black on blue . . . 1·75 3·25
D78 – 3p. brown on orange . . 1·90 4·50
D79 – 5p. black on green . . . 1·75 5·00
DESIGNS—HORIZ: 1p. Pine Forest, Beirut; 2p. Pigeon Grotto, Beirut; 3p. Beaufort Castle; 5p. Baalbeck.

1927. Optd **Republique Libanaise**.
D122 **D 7** 0p.50 brown on yellow 40 2·00
D123 – 1p. red on pink . . . . 70 3·00
D124 – 2p. black on blue . . . 1·90 3·75
D125 – 3p. brown on orange 2·00 3·00
D126 – 5p. black on green . . 3·25 6·75

1928. Nos. D122/6 optd with T **10**.
D145 **D 7** 0p.50 brown on yellow 1·50 3·75
D146 – 1p. red on pink . . . . 1·60 3·25
D147 – 2p. black on blue . . . 1·75 3·50
D148 – 3p. brown on orange 2·25 6·00
D149 – 5p. black on green . . 2·75 8·25

D 18

D 19 Bas-relief from Sarcophagus of King Ahiram at Byblos

D 32

1931.
D191 **D 18** 0p.50 black on pink 80 1·60
D192 – 1p. black on blue . . 1·50 1·00
D193 – 2p. black on yellow . . 2·25 1·75
D194 – 3p. black on green . . 3·25 2·25
D195 **D 32** 5p. black on orange 8·25 9·75
D196 **D 19** 8p. black on pink . . 4·75 5·25
D252 **D 32** 10p. green . . . . . . 8·25 7·25
D197 – 15p. black . . . . . . 3·50 3·50
DESIGNS: 1p. Bas-relief of Phoenician galley; 2p. Arabesque; 3p. Garland; 15p. Statuettes.

D 43 National Museum

1945.

D298	D 43	2p. black on lemon . .	2·75	2·75
D299		5p. blue on pink . . .	3·25	3·25
D300		25p. blue on green . .	4·75	4·75
D301		50p. purple on blue . .	5·00	5·00

D 53

1947.

D352	D 53	5p. black on green . .	3·75	1·25
D353		25p. black on yellow	38·00	3·25
D354		50p. black on blue . .	22·00	8·25

D 59 Monument at Hermel

1948.

D379	D 59	2p. black on yellow . .	2·50	65
D380		3p. black on pink . .	5·75	2·50
D381		10p. black on blue . .	14·00	5·00

D 67

1950.

D416	D 67	1p. red	95	20
D417		5p. blue	2·75	75
D418		10p. green	5·00	1·60

D 78

1952.

D464	D 78	1p. mauve	20	10
D465		2p. violet	30	20
D466		3p. green	45	20
D467		5p. blue	65	25
D468		10p. brown	1·25	50
D469		25p. black	9·75	1·25

D 81 D 93

1953.

D481	D 81	1p. red	15	10
D482		2p. green	15	10
D483		3p. orange	15	10
D484		5p. purple	25	20
D485		10p. brown	65	20
D486		15p. blue	1·25	65

1955.

D550	D 93	1p. brown	10	10
D551		2p. green	10	10
D552		3p. turquoise	10	10
D553		5p. purple	10	10
D554		10p. green	30	20
D555		15p. blue	30	20
D556		25p. purple	75	50

D 178

D 184 Emir Fakhreddine II

1967.

D967	D 178	1p. green	10	10
D968		5p. mauve	10	10
D969		15p. blue	30	30

1968.

D1004	D 184	1p. slate and grey	10	10
D1005		2p. turquoise & green	10	10
D1006		3p. orange & yellow	10	10
D1007		5p. purple and red	10	10
D1008		10p. olive and yellow	10	10
D1009		15p. blue and violet	35	35
D1010		25p. blue & lt blue	60	60

POSTAL TAX STAMPS

These were issued between 1945 and 1962 for compulsory use on inland mail (and sometimes on mail to Arab countries) to provide funds for various purposes.

T 41

(T 42)

1945. Lebanese Army. Fiscal stamp as Type T **41** surch with Type T **42**.

T289	T 41	5p. on 30c. brown . .	£425	1·75

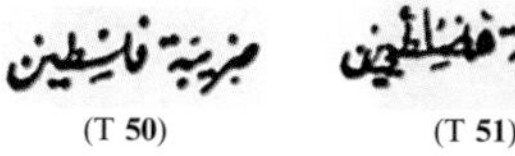
(T **50**) (T **51**)

(T **52**) (T **56** "Palestine stamp")

1947. Aid to War in Palestine. Surch as Type T **42**.

(a) With top line Type T **50**.

T338	T 41	5p. on 25c. green . . .	13·00	1·40
T339		5p. on 30c. brown . .	18·00	2·75
T340		5p. on 60c. blue . . .	27·00	2·00
T341		5p. on 3p. pink	13·50	2·50
T342		5p. on 15p. blue . . .	13·50	1·00

(b) With top line Type T **51**.

T343	T 41	5p. on 10p. red	60·00	3·00

(c) With top line Type T **52**.

T344	T 41	5p. on 3p. pink	13·50	1·75

(d) As No. T344 but with figure "5" at left instead of "0" and without inscr between figures.

T345	T 41	5p. on 3p. pink	£300	22·00

1948. Palestine Aid. No. T289 optd with Type T **56**.

T363	T 41	5p. on 30c. brown . .	18·00	2·40

T **95** Family and Ruined House

1956. Earthquake Victims.

T559	T 95	2p.50 brown	2·00	20

T **99** Rebuilding

T **100** Rebuilding

1957. Earthquake Victims.

T601	T 99	2p.50 brown	2·00	20
T602		2p.50 green	1·25	20
T603	T 100	2p.50 brown	1·25	10

T **132** Rebuilding

T **133** Rebuilding

1961. Earthquake Victims.

T729	T 132	2p.50 brown	1·25	10
T730	T 133	2p.50 blue	1·00	10

LEEWARD ISLANDS — Pt.1

A group of islands in the Br. W. Indies, including Antigua, Barbuda, British Virgin Islands, Dominica (till end of 1939), Montserrat, Nevis and St. Christopher (St. Kitts). Stamps of Leeward Islands were used concurrent with the issues for the respective islands until they were withdrawn on the 1 July 1956.

1890. 12 pence = 1 shilling;
20 shillings = 1 pound.
1951. 100 cents = 1 West Indian dollar.

1 (3)

1890.
1 1 ½d. mauve and green 3·50 1·25
2 1d. mauve and red 3·75 20
3 2½d. mauve and blue 4·50 20
4 4d. mauve and orange 4·50 7·50
5 6d. mauve and brown 11·00 12·00
6 7d. mauve and grey 4·00 11·00
7 1s. green and red 18·00 48·00
8 5s. green and blue £120 £250

1897. Diamond Jubilee. Optd with T 3.
9 1 ½d. mauve and green 3·75 12·00
10 1d. mauve and red 4·25 12·00
11 2½d. mauve and blue 4·50 12·00
12 4d. mauve and orange 35·00 70·00
13 6d. mauve and brown 48·00 90·00
14 7d. mauve and grey 48·00 90·00
15 1s. green and red £120 £190
16 5s. green and blue £450 £750

1902. Surch **One Penny**.
17 1 1d. on 4d. mauve and orange 2·50 4·75
18 1d. on 6d. mauve and brown 3·50 11·00
19 1d. on 7d. mauve and grey 3·00 6·00

1902. As T 1, but portrait of King Edward VII.
29 ½d. purple and green 3·50 2·00
21 1d. purple and red 7·00 20
22 2d. purple and brown 2·75 4·25
23 2½d. purple and blue 5·50 2·25
24 3d. purple and black 4·25 7·50
25 6d. purple and brown 2·50 8·00
26 1s. green and red 3·50 19·00
27 2s.6d. green and black 27·00 70·00
28 5s. green and blue 48·00 75·00

1907. As last, but colours changed.
36 ¼d. brown 2·75 1·75
37 ½d. green 3·50 1·25
38 1d. red 10·00 80
39 2d. grey 3·50 7·50
40 2½d. blue 7·00 4·25
41 3d. purple and yellow 3·50 7·50
42 6d. purple 8·50 7·00
43 1s. black on green 5·00 21·00
44 2s.6d. black and red on blue 40·00 48·00
45 5s. green and red on yellow 42·00 65·00

10 King George V

14 King George VI

1912.
46 10 ¼d. brown 1·75 1·00
59 ½d. green 1·00 75
60 1d. red 2·25 55
61 1d. violet 2·25 1·00
63 1½d. red 3·25 2·00
64 1½d. brown 1·25 10
65 2d. grey 2·00 80
67 2½d. blue 3·50 1·25
66 2½d. yellow 6·50 50·00
69 3d. purple on yellow 1·50 6·50
68 3d. blue 4·25 26·00
70 4d. black and red on yellow 3·00 21·00
71 5d. purple and green 2·50 4·25
53 6d. purple 3·00 8·00
54 1s. black on green 3·00 8·00
74a 2s. purple and blue on blue 7·50 48·00
75 2s.6d. black and red on blue 6·50 23·00
76 3s. green and violet 12·00 25·00
77 4s. black and red 12·00 42·00
57b 5s. green and red on yellow 24·00 65·00

Larger type, as T **15** of Malta.
79 13 10s. green and red on green 55·00 80·00
80 £1 purple and black on red £225 £250

1935. Silver Jubilee. As T **14a** of Kenya, Uganda and Tanganyika.
88 1d. blue and red 1·60 1·50
89 1½d. blue and grey 2·25 70
90 2½d. brown and blue 2·25 3·50
91 1s. grey and purple 8·00 16·00

1937. Coronation. As T **14b** of Kenya, Uganda and Tanganyika.
92 1d. red 50 15
93 1½d. brown 60 35
94 2½d. blue 60 70

1938.
95a 14 ¼d. brown 30 1·75
96 ½d. green 70 70
97 ½d. grey 60 1·50
99 1d. red 2·25 1·75
100 1d. green 55 15
101 1½d. brown 1·00 50
102 1½d. orange and black 85 40
103 2d. grey 3·00 1·00
104 2d. red 1·40 1·25
105a 2½d. blue 80 1·25
106 2½d. black and purple 55 15
107a 3d. orange 50 85
108 3d. blue 65 15
109a 6d. purple 6·50 2·25
110b 1s. black on green 4·25 1·00
111a 2s. purple and blue on blue 10·00 2·00
112b 5s. green and red on yellow 32·00 14·00
113c – 10s. green and red on green £120 75·00
114b – £1 purple and black on red 35·00 24·00

The 10s. and £1 are as Type **15** of Bermuda but with portrait of King George VI.

1946. Victory. As T **4a** of Pitcairn Islands.
115 1½d. brown 15 40
116 3d. orange 15 40

1949. Silver Wedding. As T **4b/c** of Pitcairn Islands.
117 2½d. blue 10 10
118 5s. green 4·00 3·00

1949. U.P.U. As T **4d/g** of Pitcairn Islands.
119 2½d. black 15 1·50
120 3d. blue 1·50 1·50
121 6d. mauve 15 1·50
122 1s. turquoise 15 1·50

15a Arms of University

15b Princess Alice

1951. Inauguration of B.W.I. University College.
123 15a 3c. orange and black 30 90
124 15b 12c. red and violet 70 90

1953. Coronation. As T **4h** of Pitcairn Islands.
125 3c. black and green 50 2·25

1954. As T **14** but portrait of Queen Elizabeth II facing left.
126 ½c. brown 10 60
127 1c. grey 1·00 1·00
128 2c. green 1·00 10
129 3c. yellow and black 2·00 1·00
130 4c. red 1·50 10
131 5c. black and purple 2·00 1·00
132 6c. yellow 2·00 60
133 8c. blue 2·50 10
134 12c. purple 1·75 10
135 24c. black and green 1·75 20
136 48c. purple and blue 6·00 2·75
137 60c. brown and green 6·00 2·25
138 $1.20 green and red 5·00 3·25

Larger type as T **15** of Malta, but portrait of Queen Elizabeth II facing left.
139 $2.40 green and red 6·50 5·50
140 $4.80 purple and black 6·50 7·00

LESOTHO — Pt. 1

Formerly Basutoland, attained independence on 4 October 1966 and changed its name to Lesotho.

1966. 100 cents = 1 rand.
1979. 100 lisente = 1 (ma)loti.

33 Moshoeshoe I and Moshoeshoe II

1966. Independence.
106 33 2½c. brown, black and red 10 10
107 5c. brown, black and blue 10 10
108 10c. brown, black and green 15 10
109 20c. brown, black and purple 20 15

1966. Nos. 69 etc. of Basutoland optd **LESOTHO**.
110A 8 ½c. black and sepia 10 10
111A – 1c. black and green 10 10
112A – 2c. blue and orange 60 10
113B 26 2½c. sage and red 50 10
114A – 3½c. indigo and blue 30 10
115A – 5c. brown and green 10 10
116A – 10c. bronze and purple 10 10
117B – 12½c. brown and turquoise 30 20
118A – 25c. blue and red 30 20
119B – 50c. black and red 60 50
120B 9 1r. black and purple 65 75

35 "Education, Culture and Science"

36 Maize

1966. 20th Anniv of UNESCO.
121 35 2½c. yellow and green 10 10
122 5c. green and olive 15 10
123 12½c. blue and red 35 15
124 25c. orange and blue 60 75

1967.
125 36 ½c. green and violet 10 10
126 – 1c. sepia and red 10 10
149 – 2c. yellow and green 10 10
128 – 2½c. black and ochre 10 10
151 – 3c. chocolate, green & brn 15 15
152 – 3½c. blue and yellow 15 10
130 – 5c. bistre and blue 20 10
131 – 10c. brown and grey 10 10
132 – 12½c. black and orange 20 10
133 – 25c. black and blue 55 20
134 – 50c. black, blue & turquoise 4·50 1·25
135 – 1r. multicoloured 65 75
136 – 2r. black, gold and purple 1·00 1·75

DESIGNS—HORIZ: 1c. Cattle; 2c. Aloes; 2½c. Basotho hat; 3c. Sorghum; 3½c. Merino sheep ("Wool"); 5c. Basotho pony; 10c. Wheat; 12½c. Angora goat ("Mohair"); 25c. Maletsunyane Falls; 50c. Diamonds; 1r. Arms of Lesotho. VERT: 2r. Moshoeshoe II.
See also Nos. 191/203.

46 Students and University

1967. 1st Conferment of University Degrees.
137 46 1c. sepia, blue and orange 10 10
138 2½c. sepia, ultramarine & bl 10 10
139 12½c. sepia, blue and red 10 10
140 25c. sepia, blue and violet 15 15

47 Statue of Moshoeshoe I

1967. 1st Anniv of Independence.
141 47 2½c. black and green 10 10
142 – 12½c. multicoloured 25 15
143 – 25c. black, green and ochre 35 25

DESIGNS: 12½c. National flag; 25c. Crocodile (national emblem).

50 Lord Baden-Powell and Scout Saluting

1967. 60th Anniv of Scout Movement.
144 50 15c. multicoloured 20 10

51 W.H.O. Emblem and World Map

1968. 20th Anniv of World Health Organization.
145 51 2½c. blue, gold and red 15 10
146 – 25c. multicoloured 45 60

DESIGN: 25c. Nurse and child.

55 Running Hunters

1968. Rock Paintings.
160 55 3c. brown, turquoise & grn 25 10
161 – 3½c. yellow, olive and sepia 30 10
162 – 5c. red, ochre and brown 35 10
163 – 10c. yellow, red and purple 45 10
164 – 15c. buff, yellow and brown 75 30
165 – 20c. green, yellow & brown 90 55
166 – 25c. yellow, brown & black 1·00 75

DESIGNS—HORIZ: 3½c. Baboons; 10c. Archers; 20c. Eland; 25c. Hunting scene. VERT: 5c. Javelin thrower; 15c. Blue cranes.

62 Queen Elizabeth II Hospital

1969. Centenary of Maseru (capital). Mult.
167 2½c. Type **62** 10 10
168 10c. Lesotho Radio Station 10 10
169 12½c. Leabua Jonathan Airport 35 10
170 25c. Royal Palace 25 15

66 Rally Car passing Basuto Tribesman

1969. "Roof of Africa" Car Rally.
171 66 2½c. yellow, mauve & plum 15 10
172 – 12½c. blue, yellow and grey 20 10
173 – 15c. blue, black and mauve 20 10
174 – 20c. black, red and yellow 20 10

DESIGNS: 12½c. Rally car on mountain road; 15c. Chequered flags and "Roof of Africa" Plateau; 20c. Map of rally route and Independence Trophy.

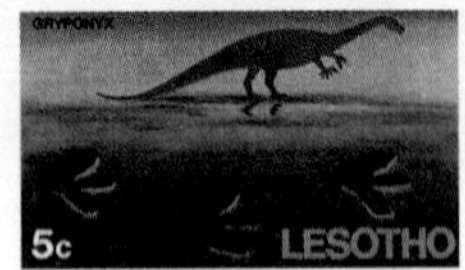

71 Gryponyx and Footprints

1970. Prehistoric Footprints (1st series).
175 – 3c. brown and sepia 80 70
176 71 5c. purple, pink and sepia 1·00 30
177 – 10c. yellow, black and sepia 1·25 35
178 – 15c. yellow, black and sepia 1·75 2·25
179 – 25c. blue and black 2·75 2·25

DESIGNS: 3c. Dinosaur footprints at Moyeni; 10c. Plateosauravus and footprints; 15c. Tritylodon and footprints; 25c. Massospondylus and footprints.
No. 175 is larger, 60 × 23 mm.
See also Nos. 596/8.

75 Moshoeshoe I as a Young Man

1970. Death Centenary of Chief Moshoeshoe I.
180 75 2½c. green and mauve 10 10
181 – 25c. blue and brown 20 20

DESIGN: 25c. Moshoeshoe I as an old man.

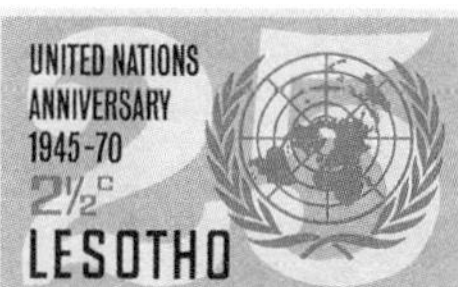

77 U.N. Emblem and "25"

1970. 25th Anniv of United Nations.
182 **77** 2½c. pink, blue and purple . . . 10 10
183 – 10c. multicoloured 10 10
184 – 12½c. red, blue and drab . . . 10 25
185 – 25c. multicoloured 15 65
DESIGNS: 10c. U.N. Building; 12½c. "People of the World"; 25c. Symbolic dove.

78 Gift Shop, Maseru

1970. Tourism. Multicoloured.
186 2½c. Type **78** 10 10
187 5c. Trout fishing 20 10
188 10c. Pony trekking 25 10
189 12½c. Skiing, Maluti Mountains 50 10
190 20c. Holiday Inn, Maseru . . 40 50

79 Maize **80** Lammergeier

1971. As Nos. 147/58 but in new format omitting portrait, as in T **79**. New designs for 4c., 2r.
191 **79** ½c. green and violet . . . 10 10
192 – 1c. brown and red 10 10
193 – 2c. yellow and green . . . 10 10
194 – 2½c. black, green & yellow 10 10
195 – 3c. brown, green & yellow 10 10
196 – 3½c. blue and yellow . . . 10 10
196a – 4c. multicoloured 20 10
197 – 5c. brown and blue . . . 15 10
198 – 10c. brown and grey . . . 15 10
199 – 12½c. brown and orange . 25 30
200 – 25c. slate and blue . . . 60 40
201 – 50c. black, blue and green 6·00 4·50
202 – 1r. multicoloured . . . . 1·25 1·75
401 – 2r. brown and blue . . . 70 2·25
DESIGNS—HORIZ: 4c. National flag. VERT: 2r. Statue of Moshoeshoe I.

1971. Birds. Multicoloured.
204 2½c. Type **80** . . . . . . 2·50 20
205 5c. Bald ibis . . . . 3·50 2·50
206 10c. Orange-breasted rockjumper . . . . . . 3·50 2·00
207 12½c. Blue bustard ("Blue korhaan") . . . . . . 3·75 3·50
208 15c. Painted-snipe . . . . 4·25 4·50
209 20c. Golden-breasted bunting 4·25 4·50
210 25c. Ground woodpecker . . 4·75 4·50

81 Lionel Collett Dam

1971. Soil Conservation. Multicoloured.
211 4c. Type **81** 10 10
212 10c. Contour ridges 10 10
213 15c. Earth dams 25 10
214 25c. Beaver dams 35 35

82 Diamond Mining

1971. Development. Multicoloured.
215 4c. Type **82** 75 40
216 10c. Pottery 30 10
217 15c. Weaving 45 60
218 20c. Construction . . . . . 55 1·50

83 Mail Cart

1972. Centenary of Post Office.
219 **83** 5c. brown and pink 15 20
220 – 10c. multicoloured 15 10
221 – 15c. blue, black and brown 20 15
222 – 20c. multicoloured 30 90
DESIGNS—HORIZ: 10c. Postal bus; 20c. Maseru Post Office. VERT: 15c. 4d. Cape of Good Hope stamp of 1876.

84 Sprinting

1972. Olympic Games, Munich. Multicoloured.
223 4c. Type **84** 15 10
224 10c. Shot putting 20 10
225 15c. Hurdling 30 10
226 25c. Long-jumping 35 55

85 "Adoration of the Shepherds" (Matthias Stomer)

1972. Christmas.
227 **85** 4c. multicoloured 10 10
228 10c. multicoloured 10 10
229 25c. multicoloured 15 20

86 W.H.O. Emblem

1973. 25th Anniv of W.H.O.
230 **86** 20c. yellow and blue . . . 30 30

1973. O.A.U. 10th Anniv. Nos. 194 and 196a/8 optd **O.A.U. 10th Anniversary Freedom in Unity.**
231 2½c. black, green and brown 10 10
232 4c. multicoloured 10 10
233 5c. brown and blue 10 10
234 10c. brown and blue 15 15

88 Basotho Hat and W.F.P. Emblem

1973. 10th Anniv of World Food Programme. Multicoloured.
235 4c. Type **88** 10 10
236 15c. School feeding 20 15
237 20c. Infant feeding 20 20
238 25c. "Food for work" . . . 25 25

89 "Aeropetes tulbaghia"

1973. Butterflies. Multicoloured.
239 4c. Type **89** 75 10
240 5c. "Papilio demodocus" . . 85 50
241 10c. "Cynthia cardui" . . . 1·25 50
242 15c. "Precis hierta" . . . . 2·25 1·75
243 20c. "Precis oenone" . . . . 2·25 1·75
244 25c. "Danaus chrysippus" . . 2·50 2·75
245 30c. "Colotis evenina" . . . 2·50 3·75

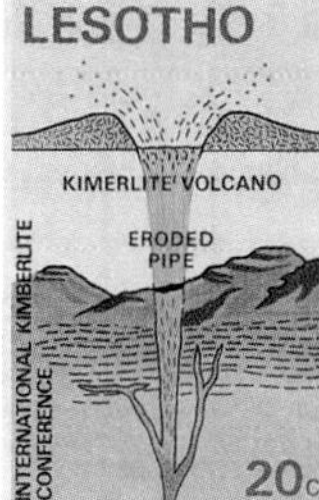

90 Kimberlite Volcano **92** Open Book and Wreath

91 "Health"

1973. International Kimberlite Conference. Mult.
246 10c. Map of diamond mines (horiz) . . . . 2·00 50
247 15c. Kimberlite-diamond rock (horiz) . . . . 2·25 2·25
248 20c. Type **90** . . . . 2·25 2·50
249 30c. Diamond prospecting . . 3·75 7·00

1974. Youth and Development. Multicoloured.
250 4c. Type **91** 10 10
251 10c. "Education" 15 10
252 20c. "Agriculture" 20 10
253 25c. "Industry" 30 20
254 30c. "Service" 30 25

1974. 10th Anniv of U.B.L.S. Multicoloured.
255 10c. Type **92** 15 10
256 15c. Flags, mortar-board and scroll 20 20
257 20c. Map of Africa 25 25
258 25c. King Moshoeshoe II capping a graduate 25 65

93 Senqunyane River Bridge, Marakabei

1974. Rivers and Bridges. Multicoloured.
259 4c. Type **93** 10 10
260 5c. Tsoelike River and bridge 10 10
261 10c. Makhaleng River Bridge 20 10
262 15c. Seaka Bridge, Orange/ Senqu River 35 35
263 20c. Masianokeng Bridge, Phuthiatsana River 40 40
264 25c. Mahobong Bridge, Hlotse River 45 45

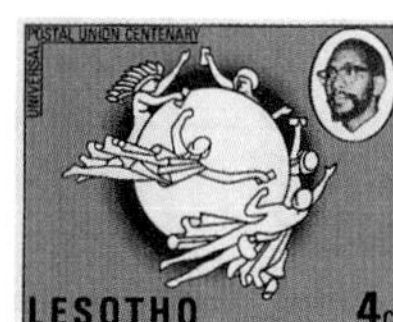

94 U.P.U. Emblem

1974. Centenary of U.P.U.
265 **94** 4c. green and black 10 10
266 – 10c. orange, yellow & black 15 10
267 – 15c. multicoloured 20 60
268 – 20c. multicoloured 45 85
DESIGNS: 10c. Map of airmail routes; 15c. Post Office H.Q., Maseru; 20c. Horseman taking rural mail.

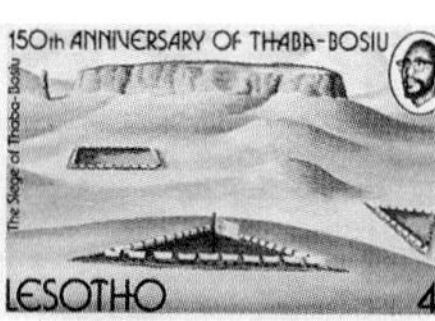

95 Siege of Thaba-Bosiu

1974. 150th Anniv of Siege of Thaba-Bosiu. Multicoloured.
269 4c. Type **95** 10 10
270 5c. The wreath-laying 10 10
271 10c. Moshoeshoe I (vert) . . 25 10
272 20c. Makoanyane, the warrior (vert) 90 55

96 Mamokhorong

1974. Basotho Musical Instruments. Multicoloured.
273 4c. Type **96** 10 10
274 10c. Lesiba 10 10
275 15c. Setolotolo 15 20
276 20c. Meropa 15 20
MS277 108 × 92 mm. Nos. 273/6 1·00 2·00

97 Horseman in Rock Archway

1975. Sehlabathebe National Park. Mult.
278 4c. Type **97** 30 10
279 5c. Mountain view through arch 30 10
280 15c. Antelope by stream . . 50 45
281 20c. Mountains and lake . . 50 50
282 25c. Tourists by frozen waterfall 65 75

98 Morena Moshoeshoe I **99** Mokhibo Dance

1975. Leaders of Lesotho.
283 **98** 3c. black and blue 10 10
284 – 4c. black and mauve . . . 10 10
285 – 5c. black and pink 10 10
286 – 6c. black and brown . . . 10 10
287 – 10c. black and red 10 10
288 – 15c. black and red 20 20
289 – 20c. black and green . . . 25 30
290 – 25c. black and blue 25 40
DESIGNS: 4c. King Moshoeshoe II; 5c. Morena Letsie I; 6c. Morena Lerotholi; 10c. Morena Letsie II; 15c. Morena Griffith; 20c. Morena Seeiso Griffith Lerotholi; 25c. Mofumahali Mantsebo Seeiso, O.B.E.
The 25c. also commemorates International Women's Year.

1975. Traditional Dances. Multicoloured.
291 4c. Type **99** 15 10
292 10c. Ndlamo 20 10
293 15c. Baleseli 35 75
294 20c. Mohobelo . . . . 40 1·25
MS295 111 × 100 mm. Nos. 291/4 3·75 3·50

100 Enrolment

1976. 25th Anniv of Lesotho Red Cross. Mult.
296 4c. Type **100** 50 10
297 10c. Medical aid 70 10
298 15c. Rural service . . . . . 1·00 1·25
299 25c. Relief supplies . . . . . 1·40 2·50

101 Tapestry

1976. Multicoloured.
300 2c. Type **101** 10 35
301 3c. Mosotho horseman . . . 20 30
302 4c. Map of Lesotho . . . . 1·25 10
303 5c. Lesotho Brown diamond 75 1·00
304 10c. Lesotho Bank 30 10
305 15c. Lesotho and O.A.U. flags . . . . 1·75 1·00
306 25c. Sehlabathebe National Park 60 35
307 40c. Pottery . . . . 60 1·00
308 50c. Prehistoric rock art . . . 2·50 2·00
309 1r. King Moshoeshoe II (vert) . . . . 60 1·75

102 Football **103** "Rising Sun"

1976. Olympic Games, Montreal. Mult.
310 4c. Type **102** 15 10
311 10c. Weightlifting 15 10
312 15c. Boxing 35 35
313 25c. Throwing the discus . . 50 80

1976. 10th Anniv of Independence. Multicoloured.
314 4c. Type **103** 10 10
315 10c. Open gates 10 10
316 15c. Broken chains 40 20
317 25c. Britten Norman Islander aircraft over hotel 50 35

104 Telephones, 1876 and 1976

1976. Centenary of Telephone. Multicoloured.
318 4c. Type **104** 10 10
319 10c. Early handset and telephone-user, 1976 . . . 15 10
320 15c. Wall telephone and telephone exchange 25 20
321 25c. Stick telephone and Alexander Graham Bell . . 45 50

105 "Aloe striatula" **106** Large-toothed Rock Hyrax

1977. Aloes and Succulents. Multicoloured.
322 3c. Type **105** 25 10
323 4c. "Aloe aristata" 25 10
324 5c. "Kniphofia caulescens" . 25 10
325 10c. "Euphorbia pulvinata" . 35 10
326 15c. "Aloe saponaria" . . . 1·00 30
327 20c. "Caralluma lutea" . . . 1·00 50
328 25c. "Aloe polyphylla" . . . 1·25 70
See also Nos. 347/54.

1977. Animals. Multicoloured.
329 4c. Type **106** . . . . 3·50 30
330 5c. Cape porcupine . . . . . 3·50 75
331 10c. Zorilla (polecat) . . . . 3·50 30
332 15c. Klipspringer . . . . . . 11·00 2·50
333 25c. Chacma baboon . . . . 12·00 3·75

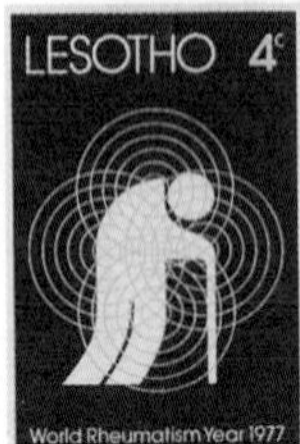

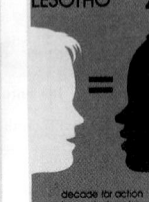

107 "Rheumatic Man" **110** Black and White Heads

108 Small-mouthed Yellowfish

1977. World Rheumatism Year.
334 **107** 4c. yellow and red 10 10
335 – 10c. blue and deep blue 15 10
336 – 15c. yellow and blue . . . 30 10
337 – 25c. red and black 40 45
DESIGNS—Each show the "Rheumatic Man" as Type **107**: 10c. Surrounded by "pain"; 15c. Surrounded by "chain"; 25c. Supporting globe.

1977. Fish. Multicoloured.
338 4c. Type **108** 30 10
339 10c. Mudfish 45 10
340 15c. Rainbow trout . . . . . 1·00 35
341 25c. Barnard's mudfish . . . 1·10 60

1977. No. 198 surch **3**.
342 3c. on 10c. brown and blue 1·00 1·00

1977. Decade for Action to Combat Racism.
343 **110** 4c. black and mauve . . . 10 10
344 – 10c. black and blue . . . 10 10
345 – 15c. black and orange . . 15 15
346 – 25c. black and green . . . 25 25
DESIGNS: 10c. Jigsaw pieces; 15c. Cogwheels; 25c. Handshake.

1978. Flowers. As T **105**. Multicoloured.
347 2c. "Papaver aculeatum" . . 10 50
348 3c. "Diascia integerrima" . . 10 50
349 4c. "Helichrysum trilineatum" 10 10
350 5c. "Zaluzianskya maritima" 10 10
351 10c. "Gladiolus natalensis" 15 10
352 15c. "Chironia krebsii" . . . 20 40
353 25c. "Wahlenbergia undulata" . . . . 35 1·00
354 40c. "Brunsvigia radulosa" 65 2·00

111 Edward Jenner vaccinating Child **112** Tsoloane Falls

1978. Global Eradication of Smallpox. Mult.
355 5c. Type **111** 25 35
356 25c. Head of child and W.H.O. emblem 75 90

1978. Waterfalls. Multicoloured.
357 4c. Type **112** 15 10
358 10c. Qiloane Falls 25 10
359 15c. Tsoelikana Falls 35 60
360 25c. Maletsunyane Falls . . . 55 1·50

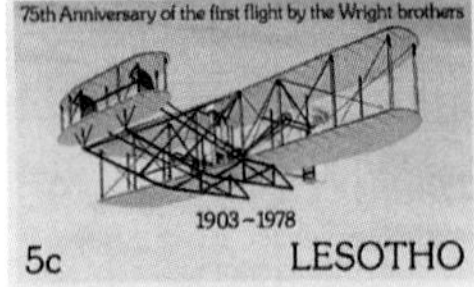

113 Wright Flyer III, 1903

1978. 75th Anniv of First Powered Flight. Mult.
361 5c. Type **113** 15 30
362 25c. Wilbur and Orville Wright 40 60

114 "Orthetrum farinosum" **115** Oudehout Branch in Flower

1978. Insects. Multicoloured.
363 4c. Type **114** 10 10
364 10c. "Phymateus viridipes" 20 10
365 15c. "Belonogaster lateritis" 30 50
366 25c. "Sphodromantis gastrica" 50 90

1979. Trees. Multicoloured.
367 4c. Type **115** 15 10
368 10c. Wild olive 20 10
369 15c. Blinkblaar 35 80
370 25c. Cape holly . . . . 70 1·50

116 Mampharoane

1979. Reptiles. Multicoloured.
371A 4s. Type **116** 10 10
372A 10s. Qoaane 20 10
373A 15s. Leupa 30 70
374A 25s. Masumu . . . . 60 1·40

117 Basutoland 1933 1d. Stamp **118** Detail of painting "Children's Games" by Brueghel

1979. Death Centenary of Sir Rowland Hill.
375 **117** 4s. multicoloured 10 10
376 – 15s. multicoloured 30 20
377 – 25s. black, orange & bistre 40 30
MS378 118 × 95 mm. 50s. multicoloured 60 80
DESIGNS: 15s. Basutoland 1962 ½c. new currency definitive; 25s. Penny Black; 50s. 1972 15c. Post Office Centenary commemorative.

1979. International Year of the Child.
379 **118** 4s. multicoloured 10 10
380 – 10s. multicoloured 10 10
381 – 15s. multicoloured 15 15
MS382 113 × 88 mm. 25s. multicoloured (horiz) 55 45
DESIGNS: 10, 15s, 25s. Different details taken from Brueghel's "Children's Games".

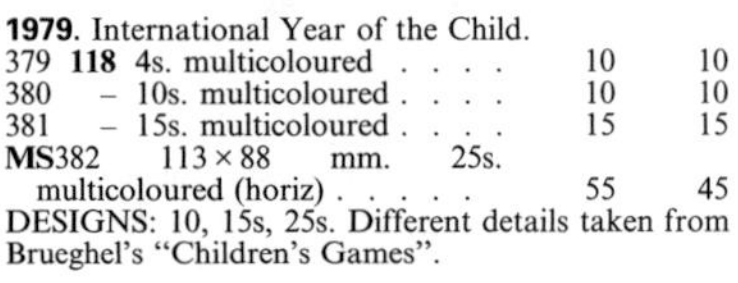

119 Beer Strainer, Broom and Mat

1980. Grasswork. Multicoloured.
383 4s. Type **119** 10 10
384 10s. Winnowing basket . . . 10 10
385 15s. Basotho hat 20 25
386 25s. Grain storage 35 40

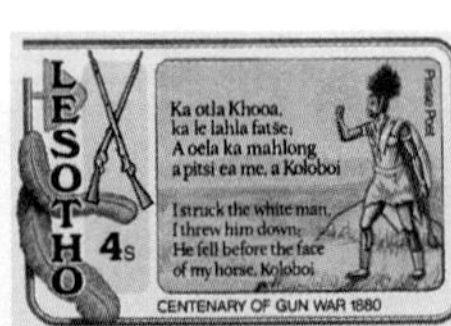

120 Praise Poet

1980. Centenary of Gun War. Multicoloured.
387 4s. Type **120** 15 10
388 5s. Lerotholi, Commander of Basotho Army 15 10
389 10s. Ambush at Qalabane . . 20 10
390 15s. Snider and Martini-Henry rifles 60 45
391 25s. Map showing main areas of action 70 55

121 Olympic Flame, Flags and Kremlin

1980. Olympic Games, Moscow. Multicoloured.
392 25s. Type **121** 25 25
393 25s. Doves, flame and flags 25 25
394 25s. Football 25 25
395 25s. Running 25 25
396 25s. Opening ceremony . . . 25 25
MS397 110 × 85 mm. 1m.40 Ancient and modern athletes carrying Olympic torch . . . . 1·10 1·25

1980. Nos. 203 and 300/9 surch **s** or new value.
402A 2s. on 2c. Type **101** 10 10
403A 3s. on 3c. Mosotho horseman 20 10
410A 5s. on 5c. Lesotho Brown diamond . . . . 1·25 10
404B 6s. on 4c. Map of Lesotho 50 10
411B 10s. on 10c. Lesotho Bank 10 10
412A 25s. on 25c. Sehlabathebe National Park 25 30
406A 40s. on 40c. Pottery 45 50
414A 50s. on 50c. Prehistoric rock art . . . . 1·75 55
415B 75s. on 15c. Lesotho and O.A.U. flags . . . . . . 1·00 75
409A 1m. on 1r. King Moshoeshoe II . . . . . 80 1·00
417A 2m. on 2r. Statue of King Moshoeshoe I . . . . . 80 1·40

123 Beer Mug **124** Queen Elizabeth the Queen Mother with Prince Charles

1980. Pottery. Multicoloured.
418 4s. Type **123** 10 10
419 10s. Beer brewing pot 10 10
420 15s. Water pot 15 15
421 25s. Pot shapes 25 30
MS422 150 × 110 mm. 40s. × 4 Wedgwood plaques of Prince Philip; Queen Elizabeth II; Prince Charles; Princess Anne (each 22 × 35 mm) 50 90
No. **MS**422 was issued to commemorate the 250th birth anniversary of Josiah Wedgwood.

1980. 80th Birthday of The Queen Mother. Mult.
423 5s. Type **124** 25 25
424 10s. The Queen Mother . . . 25 25
425 1m. 1947 Basutoland Royal Visit 2d. stamp (54 × 43 mm) 90 90

125 Lesotho Evangelical Church, Morija

1980. Christmas. Multicoloured.
426 4s. Type **125** 10 10
427 15s. St. Agnes' Anglican Church, Teyateyaneng . . 10 10
428 25s. Cathedral of Our Lady of Victories, Maseru . . . 15 10
429 75s. University Chapel, Roma 45 50
MS430 110 × 85 mm. 1m.50 Nativity scene (43 × 29 mm) 50 80

126 "Voyager" Satellite and Jupiter

1981. Space Exploration. Multicoloured.
431 25c. Type **126** 30 25
432 25c. "Voyager" and Saturn 30 25
433 25c. "Voyager" passing Saturn 30 25
434 25c. "Space Shuttle" releasing satellite 30 25
435 25c. "Space Shuttle" launching into space . . . 30 25
MS436 111 × 85 mm. 1m.40 Saturn 1·75 1·00

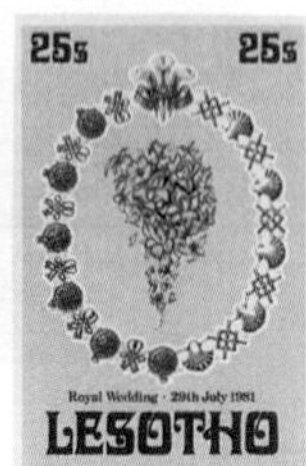

127 Greater Kestrel **128** Wedding Bouquet from Lesotho

1981. Birds. Multicoloured.
437 1s. Type **127** 15 40
438 2s. Speckled pigeon ("Rock Pigeon") (horiz) 15 40
439 3s. South African crowned crane ("Crowned Crane") 20 40
440 5s. Bokmakierie shrike ("Bokmakierie") 20 40
504 6s. Cape robin chat ("Cape Robin") 30 10
505 7s. Yellow canary 30 10
506 10s. Red-billed pintail ("Red-billed Teal") (horiz) . . . 30 10
507 25s. Malachite kingfisher . . 80 30
508 40s. Yellow-tufted malachite sunbird ("Malachite Sunbird") (horiz) . . . . . 1·00 45
509 60s. Cape longclaw ("Orange-throated Longclaw") (horiz) . . . . 1·25 90

510 75s. Hoopoe ("African Hoppoe") (horiz) . . . . . 1·50 90
448 1m. Red bishop (horiz) . . . 1·00 75
449 2m. Egyptian goose (horiz) 1·25 1·50
450 5m. Lilac-breasted roller (horiz) . . . . 1·75 4·00

1981. Royal Wedding (1st issue). Multicoloured.
451 25s. Type **128** 10 10
452 50s. Prince Charles riding . . 20 25
453 75s. Prince Charles and Lady Diana Spencer 30 50

129 Prince Charles and Lady Diana Spencer (½ - size illustration)

1981. Royal Wedding (2nd issue). Sheet 115 × 90 mm.
MS454 **129** 1m.50, multicoloured 1·00 1·25

130 "Santa planning his Annual Visit"

1981. Christmas. Paintings by Norman Rockwell. Multicoloured.
455 6s. Type **130** 15 10
456 10s. "Santa reading his Mail" 25 10
457 15s. "The Little Spooners" 30 20
458 20s. "Raleigh Rockwell Travels" 30 25
459 25s. "Ride 'em Cowboy" . . 30 30
460 60s. "The Discovery" . . . . 50 1·00
MS461 111 × 85 mm. 1m.25 "Mystic Nativity" (48 × 31 mm) . . . . 1·10 1·10

131 Duke of Edinburgh, Award Scheme Emblem and Flags

1981. 25th Anniv of Duke of Edinburgh Award Scheme. Multicoloured.
462 6s. Type **131** 10 10
463 7s. Tree planting 10 10
464 25s. Gardening 25 20
465 40s. Mountain climbing . . . 40 40
466 75s. Award Scheme emblem 70 75
MS467 111 × 85 mm. 1m.40 Duke of Edinburgh (45 × 30 mm) . . . 1·25 1·25

132 Wild Cat

1981. Wildlife. Multicoloured.
468 6s. Type **132** . . . . 1·25 30
469 20s. Chacma baboon (44 × 31 mm) . . . . . . 2·00 70
470 25s. Cape eland . . . . . 2·50 75
471 40s. Porcupine . . . . . . 3·25 1·75
472 50s. Oribi (44 × 31 mm) . . . 3·25 1·75
MS473 111 × 85 mm. 1m.50 Black-backed Jackal (47 × 31 mm) . . 2·75 1·90

133 Scout Bugler

1982. 75th Anniv of Boy Scout Movement. Multicoloured.
474 6s. Type **133** 40 25
475 30s. Scouts hiking 45 50
476 40s. Scout sketching 50 60
477 50s. Scout with flag 50 65
478 75s. Scouts saluting 55 80
MS479 117 × 92 mm. 1m.50 Lord Baden-Powell . . . . 1·50 2·00

134 Jules Rimet Trophy with Footballers and Flags of 1930 Finalists (Argentina and Uruguay)

1982. World Cup Football Championship, Spain. Each showing Trophy with Players and Flags from Past Finals. Multicoloured.
480 15s. Type **134** 25 25
481 15s. Czechoslovakia and Italy, 1934 . . . . 25 25
482 15s. Hungary and Italy, 1938 25 25
483 15s. Brazil and Uruguay, 1950 . . . . 25 25
484 15s. Hungary and W. Germany, 1954 . . . 25 25
485 15s. Sweden and Brazil, 1958 25 25
486 15s. Czechoslovakia and Brazil, 1962 . . . . . . 25 25
487 15s. W. Germany and England, 1966 . . . . . . 25 25
488 15s. Italy and Brazil, 1970 . . 25 25
489 15s. Holland and W. Germany, 1974 . . . . 25 25
490 15s. Holland and Argentina, 1978 . . . . 25 25
491 15s. Map of World on footballs 25 25
MS492 118 × 93 mm. 1m.25 Bernabeu Stadium, Madrid (47 × 35 mm) . . . . 1·10 1·25
Nos. 480/8 show the Jules Rimet Trophy and Nos. 489/91 the World Cup Trophy.

135 Portrait of George Washington

1982. 250th Birth Anniv of George Washington. Multicoloured.
493 6s. Type **135** 10 10
494 7s. Washington with step-children and dog 10 10
495 10s. Washington with Indian chief 15 10
496 25s. Washington with troops 30 30
497 40s. Washington arriving in New York 40 40
498 1m. Washington on parade 1·00 1·10
MS499 117 × 92 mm. 1m.25 Washington crossing the Delaware 1·00 1·00

136 Lady Diana Spencer in Tetbury, May 1981

137 Mosotho reading Sesotho Bible

1982. 21st Birthday of Princess of Wales. Mult.
514a 30s. Lesotho coat of arms 40 40
515 50s. Type **136** 60 60
516 75s. Wedding picture at Buckingham Palace . . . 80 1·00
517 1m. Formal portrait . . . . 1·25 1·40

1982. Centenary of Sesotho Bible. Multicoloured.
518 6s. Type **137** 15 20
519 15s. Sesotho bible and Virgin Mary holding infant Jesus 20 25
520 1m. Sesotho bible and Cathedral (62 × 42 mm) . . 50 75

138 Birthday Greetings

1982. Birth of Prince William of Wales. Mult.
521 6s. Type **138** . . . . 2·25 2·75
522 60s. Princess Diana and Prince William . . . . . . 1·00 1·00

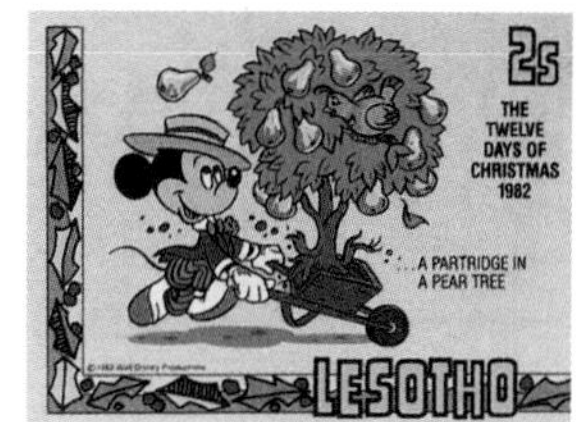

139 "A Partridge in a Pear Tree"

1982. Christmas. "The Twelve Days of Christmas". Walt Disney cartoon characters. Multicoloured.
523 2s. Type **139** 10 10
524 2s. "Two turtle doves" . . . 10 10
525 3s. "Three French hens" . . 10 10
526 3s. "Four calling birds" . . . 10 10
527 4s. "Five golden rings" . . . 10 10
528 4s. "Six geese a-laying" . . . 10 10
529 75s. "Seven swans a-swimming" . . . . 1·40 1·75
530 75s. "Eight maids a-milking" 1·40 1·75
MS531 126 × 101 mm. 1m.50, "Nine ladies dancing, ten lords a-leaping, eleven pipers piping, twelve drummers drumming" . . . . 2·40 2·75

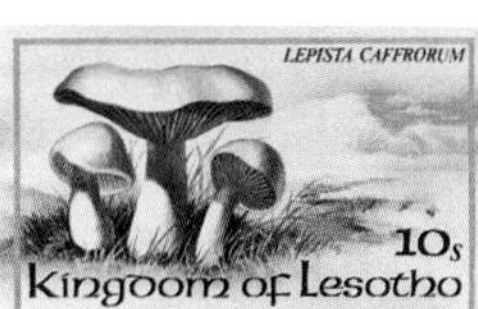

140 "Lepista caffrorum"

1983. Fungi. Multicoloured.
532 10s. Type **140** 15 10
533 30s. "Broomeia congregata" 30 40
534 50s. "Afroboletus luteolus" 60 90
535 75s. "Lentinus tuber-regium" 90 1·40

141 Ba-Leseli Dance

1983. Commonwealth Day. Multicoloured.
536 5s. Type **141** 10 10
537 30s. Tapestry weaving . . . 20 30
538 60s. Queen Elizabeth II (vert) 35 65
539 75s. King Moshoeshoe II (vert) 40 80

142 "Dancers in a Trance" (rock painting from Ntloana Tsoana)

1983. Rock Paintings. Multicoloured.
540 6s. Type **142** 20 10
541 25s. "Baboons", Sehonghong 55 35
542 60s. "Hunters attacking Mountain Reedbuck", Makhetha . . . . 60 1·10
543 75s. "Eland", Lehaha la Likhomo . . . . 65 1·60
MS544 166 × 84 mm. Nos. 540/3 and 10s. "Cattle herding", Sehonghong (52 × 52 mm) . . 1·25 3·50

143 Montgolfier Balloon, 1783

1983. Bicentenary of Manned Flight. Mult.
545 7s. Type **143** 15 10
546 30s. Wright brothers and Flyer I 30 40
547 60s. First airmail flight . . . 50 1·25
548 1m. Concorde . . . . 2·25 2·50
MS549 180 × 92 mm. Nos. 545/8 and 6s. Dornier Do-28D Skyservant of Lesotho Airways (60 × 60 mm) 2·75 2·75

144 Rev. Eugene Casalis

1983. 150th Anniv of Arrival of the French Missionaries. Multicoloured.
550 6s. Type **144** 10 10
551 25s. The founding of Morija 10 10
552 40s. Baptism of Libe 10 15
553 75s. Map of Lesotho 20 25

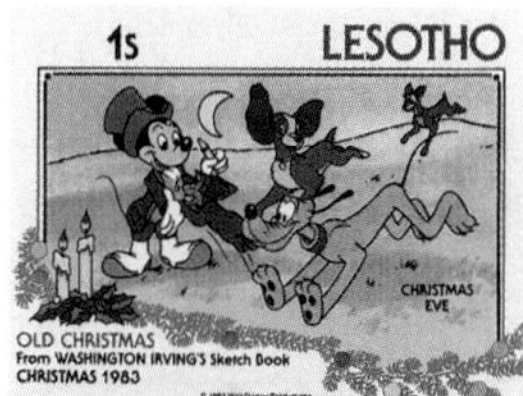

145 Mickey Mouse and Pluto greeted by Friends

1983. Christmas. Walt Disney Characters in scenes from "Old Christmas" (Washington Irving's sketchbook). Multicoloured.
554 1s. Type **145** 10 10
555 2s. Donald Duck and Pluto 10 10
556 3s. Donald Duck with Huey, Dewey and Louie . . . 10 10
557 4s. Goofy, Donald Duck and Mickey Mouse 10 10
558 5s. Goofy holding turkey, Donald Duck and Mickey Mouse 10 10
559 6s. Goofy and Mickey Mouse 10 10
560 7s. Donald and Daisy Duck 2·00 2·40
561 1m. Goofy and Clarabell . . 2·50 2·75
MS562 132 × 113 mm. 1m.75 Scrooge McDuck, Pluto and Donald Duck . . . . 3·25 4·50

146 "Danaus chrysippus"

1984. Butterflies. Multicoloured.
563 1s. Type **146** 30 40
564 2s. "Aeropetes tulbaghia" . . 30 40
565 3s. "Colotis evenina" 35 40
566 4s. "Precis oenone" 35 40
567 5s. "Precis hierta" 35 40
568 6s. "Catopsilia florella" . . . 35 10
569 7s. "Phalanta phalantha" . . 35 10
570 10s. "Acraea stenobea" . . . 40 10
571 15s. "Cynthia cardui" . . . 75 10
572 20s. "Colotis subfasciatus" . 75 10
573 30s. "Charaxes jasius" . . . 85 30
574 50s. "Terias brigitta" . . . 1·00 40
575 60s. "Pontia helice" . . . . 1·00 50
576 75s. "Colotis regina" . . . . 1·00 50
577 1m. "Hypolimnas misippus" 1·00 1·50
578 5m. "Papilio demodocus" . . 1·75 7·50

147 "Thou shalt not have Strange Gods before Me"

1984. Easter. The Ten Commandments. Mult.
579 20s. Type **147** 30 30
580 20s. "Thou shalt not take the name of the Lord thy God in vain" 30 30
581 20s. "Remember thou keep holy the Lord's Day" . . . 30 30
582 20s. "Honour thy father and mother" 30 30
583 20s. "Thou shalt not kill" . . 30 30
584 20s. "Thou shalt not commit adultery" 30 30
585 20s. "Thou shalt not steal" 30 30
586 20s. "Thou shalt not bear false witness against thy neighbour" 30 30
587 20s. "Thou shalt not covet thy neighbour's wife" . . . 30 30
588 20s. "Thou shalt not covet thy neighbour's goods" . . 30 30
MS589 102 × 73 mm. 1m.50 Moses with Tablets (45 × 28 mm) . . 1·00 2·25

148 Torch Bearer

1984. Olympic Games, Los Angeles. Multicoloured.
590 10s. Type **148** 10 10
591 30s. Horse-riding 10 10
592 50s. Swimming 15 20
593 75s. Basketball 20 25
594 1m. Running 25 30
MS595 101 × 72mm. 1m.50 Olympic Flame and flags . . . . 1·25 2·50

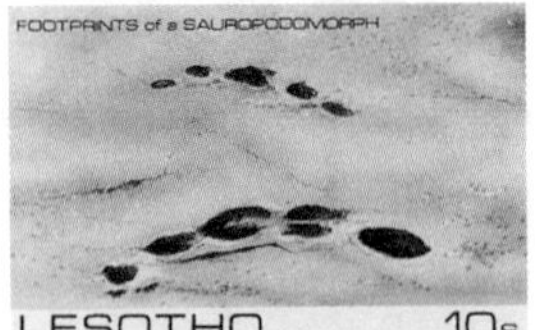

149 Sauropodomorph Footprints

1984. Prehistoric Footprints (2nd series). Mult.
596 10s. Type **149** 50 30
597 30s. Lesothosaurus footprints 60 1·25
598 50s. Footprint of carnivorous dinosaur . . . . 70 2·00

150 Wells Fargo Coach, 1852

1984. "Ausipex" Int Stamp Exhibition, Melbourne. Bicent of First Mail Coach Run. Mult.
599 6s. Type **150** 10 10
600 7s. Basotho mail cart, circa 1900 . . . . 10 10
601 10s. Bath mail coach, 1784 10 10
602 30s. Cobb coach, 1853 . . . 15 15
603 50s. Exhibition logo and Royal Exhibition Buildings, Melbourne (82 × 25 mm) 50 80
MS604 147 × 98 mm. 1m.75 G.B. Penny Black, Basutoland 1934 "OFFICIAL" optd 6d. and Western Australia 1854 4d. with frame inverted (82 × 25 mm) . . 2·25 3·75

151 "The Orient Express" (1900)

1984. Railways of the World. Multicoloured.
605 6s. Type **151** 30 15
606 15s. Class 05 streamlined steam locomotive No. 001, Germany (1935) 30 30
607 30s. Caledonian Railway steam locomotive "Cardean" (1906) 35 60
608 60s. Atchison, Topeka & Santa Fe "Super Chief" express (1940) . . . . . . 40 1·75
609 1m. L.N.E.R. "Flying Scotsman" (1934) . . . . 40 2·00
MS610 108 × 82mm. 2m. South African Railways "The Blue Train" (1972) . . . . 1·00 2·50

152 Eland Calf

1984. Baby Animals. Multicoloured.
611 15s. Type **152** 35 20
612 20s. Young chacma baboons 35 25
613 30s. Oribi calf 35 40
614 75s. Young Natal red hares 50 1·60
615 1m. Black-backed jackal pups (46 × 27 mm) . . . . . . 50 2·00

153 Crown of Lesotho **154** Christ condemned to Death

1985. Silver Jubilee of King Moshoeshoe II. Mult.
616 6s. Type **153** 10 10
617 30s. King Moshoeshoe in 1960 . . . . 20 30
618 75s. King Moshoeshoe in traditional dress, 1985 . . 50 75
619 1m. King Moshoeshoe in uniform, 1985 . . . . . . 70 1·10

1985. Easter. The Stations of the Cross. Mult.
620 20s. Type **154** 25 35
621 20s. Christ carrying the Cross 25 35
622 20s. Falling for the first time 25 35
623 20s. Christ meets Mary . . . 25 35
624 20s. Simon of Cyrene helping to carry the Cross 25 35
625 20s. Veronica wiping the face of Christ 25 35
626 20s. Christ falling a second time 25 35
627 20s. Consoling the women of Jerusalem 25 35
628 20s. Falling for the third time 25 35
629 20s. Christ being stripped . . 25 35
630 20s. Christ nailed to the Cross 25 35
631 20s. Dying on the Cross . . . 25 35
632 20s. Christ taken down from the Cross 25 35
633 20s. Christ being laid in the sepulchre 25 35
MS634 138 × 98 mm. 2m. "The Crucifixion" (Mathias Grunewald) 1·50 3·50

155 Duchess of York with Princess Elizabeth, 1931

1985. Life and Times of Queen Elizabeth the Queen Mother. Multicoloured.
635 10s. Type **155** 35 10
636 30s. The Queen Mother in 1975 . . . . 70 50
637 60s. Queen Mother with Queen Elizabeth and Princess Margaret, 1980 . . 80 90
638 2m. Four generations of Royal Family at Prince Harry's christening, 1984 1·25 2·50
MS639 139 × 98 mm. 2m. Queen Elizabeth with the Princess of Wales and her children at Prince Harry's christening (37 × 50 mm) 2·25 2·75

156 B.M.W. "732i"

1985. Century of Motoring. Multicoloured.
640 6s. Type **156** 25 15
641 10s. Ford "Crown Victoria" 35 15
642 30s. Mercedes-Benz "500SE" 75 50
643 90s. Cadillac "Eldorado Biarritz" . . . . 1·50 2·50
644 2m. Rolls-Royce "Silver Spirit" . . . . 2·00 4·00
MS645 139 × 98 mm. 2m. Rolls-Royce "Silver Ghost Tourer", 1907 (37 × 50 mm) . . . . . . 4·00 6·00

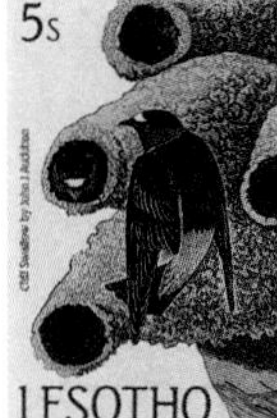

157 American Cliff Swallow **158** Two Youths Rock-climbing

1985. Birth Bicentenary of John J. Audubon (ornithologist). Designs showing original paintings. Multicoloured.
646 5s. Type **157** 40 30
647 6s. Great crested grebe (horiz) 40 30
648 10s. Vesper sparrow ("Vester Sparrow") (horiz) 55 30
649 30s. Common greenshank ("Greenshank") (horiz) . . 1·25 75
650 60s. Stilt sandpiper (horiz) . . 1·75 2·75
651 2m. Glossy ibis (horiz) . . . 2·50 6·00

1985. International Youth Year and 75th Anniv of Girl Guide Movement. Multicoloured.
652 10s. Type **158** 20 10
653 30s. Young technician in hospital laboratory 50 40
654 75s. Three guides on parade 1·00 1·25
655 2m. Guide saluting . . . . . 1·75 3·00
MS656 138 × 98 mm. 2m. "Olave, Lady Baden-Powell" (Grace Wheatley) (37 × 50 mm) . . . 2·40 2·75

159 U.N. (New York) 1951 1c. Definitive and U.N. Flag **160** Cosmos

1985. 40th Anniversary of U.N.O.
657 **159** 10s. multicoloured 25 10
658 – 30s. multicoloured 60 35
659 – 50s. multicoloured 95 85
660 – 2m. black and green . . . 5·00 6·50
DESIGNS—VERT: 30s. Ha Sofonia Earth Satellite Station; 2m. Maimonides (physician, philosopher and scholar). HORIZ: 50s. Lesotho Airways Fokker F.27 Friendship at Maseru Airport.

1985. Wild Flowers. Multicoloured.
661 6s. Type **160** 40 15
662 10s. Small agapanthus . . . 55 15
663 30s. Pink witchweed . . . . 1·10 70
664 60s. Small iris . . . . 1·50 2·00
665 90s. Wild geranium or cranesbill . . . . 1·75 3·00
666 1m. Large spotted orchid . . 3·00 5·00

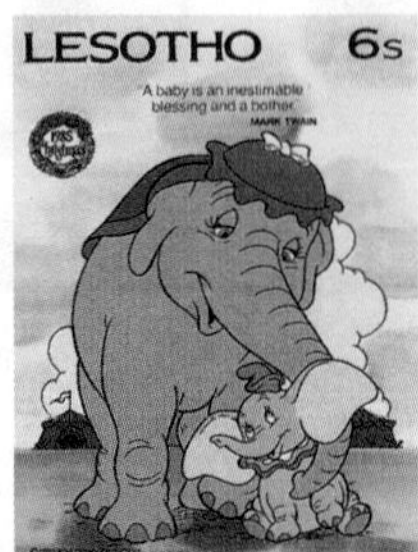

160a Mrs Jumbo and Baby Dumbo

1985. 150th Birth Anniv of Mark Twain. Walt Disney cartoon characters illustrating various Mark Twain quotations. Multicoloured.
667 6s. Type **160a** 40 15
668 50s. Uncle Scrooge and Goofy reading newspaper 1·25 1·00
669 90s. Winnie the Pooh, Tigger, Piglet and Owl . . . . . 1·75 2·00
670 1m.50 Goofy at ship's wheel 2·75 3·00
MS671 127 × 102 mm. 1m.25 Mickey Mouse as astronaut . . . . . 4·75 3·75

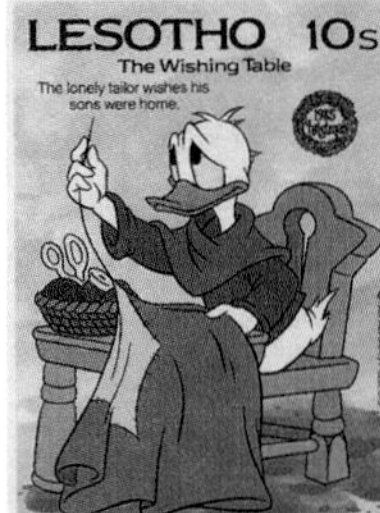

160b Donald Duck as the Tailor

1985. Birth Bicentenaries of Grimm Brothers (folklorists). Walt Disney cartoon characters in scenes from "The Wishing Table". Mult.
672 10s. Type **160b** 50 20
673 60s. The second son (Dewey) with magic donkey and gold coins . . . . 1·50 1·50
674 75s. The eldest son (Huey) with wishing table laden with food . . . . 1·75 1·75
675 1m. The innkeeper stealing the third son's (Louie) magic cudgel . . . . . . 2·00 2·75
MS676 127 × 102 mm. 1m.50 The tailor and eldest son with wishing table . . . . 4·75 5·50

161 Male Lammergeier on Watch **162** Two Players chasing Ball

1986. Flora and Fauna of Lesotho. Multicoloured.
677 7s. Type **161** . . . . 1·75 65
678 9s. Prickly pear 70 20
679 12s. Stapelia 70 20
680 15s. Pair of lammergeiers . . 2·50 60
681 35s. Pig's ears . . . . 1·10 60
682 50s. Male lammergeier in flight . . . . 3·75 2·75
683 1m. Adult and juvenile lammergeiers . . . . . . 3·75 4·75
684 2m. Columnar cereus . . . . 3·75 6·50
MS685 125 × 106 mm. 2m. Verreaux's eagle ("Black Eagle") 8·00 11·00

1986. World Cup Football Championship, Mexico. Multicoloured.
686 35s. Type **162** . . . . 1·25 50
687 50s. Goalkeeper saving goal 1·75 1·25
688 1m. Three players chasing ball . . . . 3·00 2·75
689 2m. Two players competing for ball . . . . 5·00 5·00
MS690 104 × 74 mm. 3m. Player heading ball . . . . 9·00 8·50

162a Galileo and 200 inch Hale Telescope at Mount Palomar Observatory, California

1986. Appearance of Halley's Comet. Multicoloured.
691 9s. Type **162a** 50 15
692 15s. Halley's Comet and "Pioneer Venus 2" spacecraft 75 20
693 70s. Halley's Comet of 684 A.D. (from "Nuremberg Chronicle", 1493) . . . . 1·60 1·40
694 3m. Comet and landing of William the Conqueror, 1066 . . . . 4·00 5·50
MS695 101 × 70 mm. 4m. Halley's Comet over Lesotho . . . . . 6·50 7·00

163 International Year of the Child Gold Coin

1986. 1st Anniv of New Currency (1980). Mult.
696 30s. Type **163** . . . . 4·00 6·50
697 30s. Five maloti banknote . . 4·00 6·50
698 30s. Fifty lisente coin . . . . 4·00 6·50
699 30s. Ten maloti banknote . . 4·00 6·50
700 30s. One sente coin . . . . . 4·00 6·50
These stamps were prepared in 1980, but were not issued at that time.

163a Princess Elizabeth in Pantomime

1986. 60th Birthday of Queen Elizabeth II.
701 **163a** 90s. black and yellow . . 50 60
702 – 1m. multicoloured . . . 55 65
703 – 2m. multicoloured . . . 90 1·40
MS704 119 × 85 mm. 4m. black and grey-brown . . . . 1·75 3·25
DESIGNS: 1m. Queen at Windsor Horse Show, 1971; 2m. At Royal Festival Hall, 1971; 4m. Princess Elizabeth in 1934.

163b Statue of Liberty and Bela Bartok (composer)

1986. Centenary of Statue of Liberty. Immigrants to the U.S.A. Multicoloured.
705 15s. Type **163b** 85 30
706 35s. Felix Adler (philosopher) 85 30
707 1m. Victor Herbert (composer) . . . . 3·00 2·00
708 3m. David Niven (actor) . . 4·25 4·25
MS709 103 × 74 mm. 3m. Statue of Liberty (vert) . . . . 3·50 5·00

163c Mickey Mouse and Goofy as Japanese Mail Runners

1986. "Ameripex" International Stamp Exhibition, Chicago. Walt Disney cartoon characters delivering mail. Multicoloured.
710 15s. Type **163c** 80 20
711 35s. Mickey Mouse and Pluto with mail sledge . . . . . 1·10 30
712 1m. Goofy as postman riding Harley-Davidson motorcycle . . . . 2·25 2·75
713 2m. Donald Duck operating railway mailbag apparatus 2·50 4·00
MS714 127 × 101 mm. 4m. Goofy driving mail to aircraft . . . . 6·50 7·00

1986. Various stamps surch. (a) On Nos. 437 etc (Birds)
729 9s. on 5s. Bokmakierie shrike 75 20
715 9s. on 10s. Red-billed pintail (horiz) . . . . 3·50 1·25
716 15s. on 1s. Type **127** . . . . 7·00 3·00
717 15s. on 2s. Speckled pigeon (horiz) . . . . 4·00 4·50
718 15s. on 5s. Bokmakierie shrike . . . . 2·25 35
719 15s. on 60s. Cape longclaw (horiz) 20 10
730 16s. on 25s. Malachite kingfisher . . . . 2·75 1·00
731 35s. on 25s. Malachite kingfisher . . . . 1·50 60
721 35s. on 75s. Hoopoe . . . . 23·00 18·00

(b) On Nos. 563 etc (Butterflies).
722 9s. on 30s. "Charaxes jasius" 15 10
723 9s. on 60s. "Pontia helice" 4·00 4·00
724 15s. on 1s. Type **146** . . . . 2·75 2·75
725 15s. on 2s. "Aeropetes tulbaghia" 20 20
726 15s. on 3s. "Colotis evenina" 20 20
727 15s. on 5s. "Precis hierta" . . 20 20
732 20s. on 4s. "Precis oenone" 10 10
728 35s. on 75s. "Colotis regina" 35 35
733 40s. on 7s. "Phalanta phalantha" 15 20

(c) No. 722 further surch.
734 3s. on 9s. on 30s. "Charaxes jasius" . . . . 1·00 1·00
735 7s. on 9s. on 30s. "Charaxes jasius" . . . . 1·25 1·00

170a Prince Andrew and Miss Sarah Ferguson

1986. Royal Wedding. Multicoloured.
736 50s. Type **170a** 40 40
737 1m. Prince Andrew 70 80
738 3m. Prince Andrew piloting helicopter . . . . 2·75 2·25
MS739 88 × 88 mm. 4m. Prince Andrew and Miss Sarah Ferguson (different) . . . . 3·50 4·50

171 Basotho Pony and Rider

1986. 20th Anniv of Independence. Multicoloured.
740 9s. Type **171** 40 10
741 15s. Basotho woman spinning mohair 40 15
742 35s. Crossing river by rowing boat 50 30
743 3m. Thaba Tseka Post Office 1·00 3·00
MS744 109 × 78 mm. 4m. King Moshoeshoe I . . . . 4·75 8·00

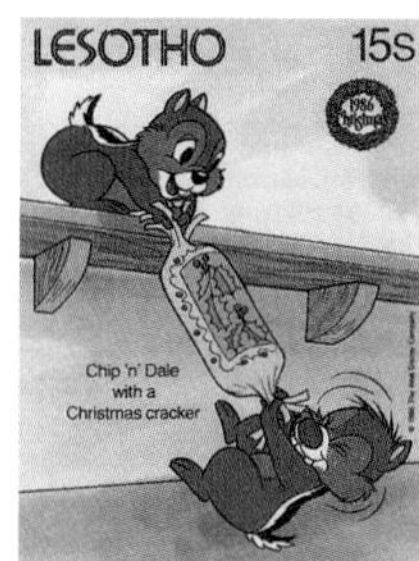

171a Chip'n' Dale pulling Christmas Cracker

1986. Christmas. Walt Disney cartoon characters. Multicoloured.
745 15s. Type **171a** 80 20
746 35s. Mickey and Minnie Mouse . . . . 1·10 30
747 1m. Pluto pulling Christmas taffy . . . . 1·90 2·75
748 2m. Aunt Matilda baking . . 2·25 4·00
MS749 126 × 102 mm. 5m. Huey and Dewey with gingerbread house 5·50 7·00

172 Rally Car

173 Lawn Tennis

1987. Roof of Africa Motor Rally. Multicoloured.
750 9s. Type **172** 30 10
751 15s. Motorcyclist 35 15
752 35s. Motorcyclist (different) 55 35
753 4m. Rally car (different) . . . 3·00 5·00

1987. Olympic Games, Seoul (1988) (1st issue). Multicoloured.
754 9s. Type **173** 60 10
755 15s. Judo 60 15
756 20s. Athletics 65 20
757 35s. Boxing 75 30
758 1m. Diving . . . . 1·00 1·75
759 3m. Ten-pin bowling . . . . 2·50 5·00
MS760 Two sheets, each 75 × 105 mm. (a) 2m. Lawn tennis (different). (b) 4m. Football. Set of 2 sheets . . . . 5·00 5·00
See also Nos. 838/41.

174 Isaac Newton and Reflecting Telescope

1987. Great Scientific Discoveries. Multicoloured.
761 5s. Type **174** 30 10
762 9s. Alexander Graham Bell and first telephone 30 15
763 75s. Robert Goddard and liquid fuel rocket 80 75
764 4m. Chuck Yeager and Bell XS-1 rocket plane . . . . 2·75 4·50
MS765 98 × 68 mm. 4m. "Mariner 10" spacecraft . . . . 2·75 3·00

175 Grey Rhebuck

1987. Flora and Fauna. Multicoloured.
766 5s. Type **175** 40 15
767 9s. Cape clawless otter . . . 40 15
768 15s. Cape grey mongoose . . 55 20
769 20s. Free State daisy (vert) 60 20
770 35s. River bells (vert) 75 30
771 1m. Turkey flower (vert) . . 1·75 2·50
772 2m. Sweet briar (vert) . . . . 2·25 3·75
773 3m. Mountain reedbuck . . . 2·75 5·00
MS774 Two sheets, each 114 × 98 mm. (a) 2m. Pig-Lily (vert). (b) 4m. Cape Wildebeest. Set of 2 sheets . . . . 4·75 8·00

176 Scouts hiking

178 "Madonna and Child" (detail)

177 Spotted Trunkfish and Columbus's Fleet

1987. World Scout Jamboree, Australia. Mult.
775 9s. Type **176** 60 20
776 15s. Scouts playing football 65 20
777 35s. Kangaroos 80 50
778 75s. Scout saluting . . . . . 1·75 1·25
779 4m. Australian scout windsurfing . . . . 3·75 6·50
MS780 96 × 66 mm. 4m. Outline map and flag of Australia . . . 3·25 4·00

1987. 500th Anniv (1992) of Discovery of America by Columbus. Multicoloured.
781 9s. Type **177** 65 20
782 15s. Green turtle and ships 80 20
783 35s. Columbus watching common dolphins from ship . . . . 1·00 40
784 5m. White-tailed tropic bird and fleet at sea . . . . . 5·00 6·50
MS785 105 × 76 mm. 4m. "Santa Maria" and Cuban Amazon in flight . . . . 4·50 4·00
No. 782 is inscribed "Carribbean" in error.

1987. Christmas. Paintings by Raphael. Mult.
786 9s. Type **178** 30 10
787 15s. "Marriage of the Virgin" 45 15
788 35s. "Coronation of the Virgin" (detail) 90 40
789 90s. "Madonna of the Chair" 2·00 3·50
MS790 75 × 100 mm. 3m. "Madonna and Child enthroned with Five Saints" (detail) . . . . 3·00 3·00

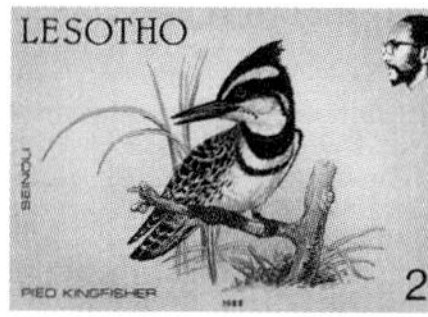

179 Lesser Pied Kingfisher

1988. Birds. Multicoloured.
791 2s. Type **179** 20 30
792 3s. Three-banded plover . . . 20 30
793 5s. Spur-winged goose . . . 20 30
794 10s. Clapper lark 20 20
795 12s. Red-eyed bulbul 30 10
796 16s. Cape weaver 30 10
797 20s. Paradise sparrow ("Red-headed Finch") 30 10
798 30s. Mountain wheater ("Mountain Chat") 35 20
799 40s. Common stonechat ("Stone Chate") 40 20
800 55s. Pied barbet 50 25
801 60s. Red-shouldered glossy starling 55 50
802 75s. Cape sparrow 65 60
803 1m. Cattle egret 75 80
804 3m. Giant kingfisher . . . . 1·25 2·50
805 10m. Helmeted guineafowl 2·75 7·00

1988. Royal Ruby Wedding. Nos. 701/3 optd **40TH WEDDING ANNIVERSARY H.M. QUEEN ELIZABETH II H.R.H. THE DUKE OF EDINBURGH.**
806 90s. black and yellow 70 65
807 1m. multicoloured 80 80
808 2m. multicoloured . . . . . 1·40 1·40
MS809 119 × 85 mm. 4m. black and grey-brown . . . . 2·75 2·75

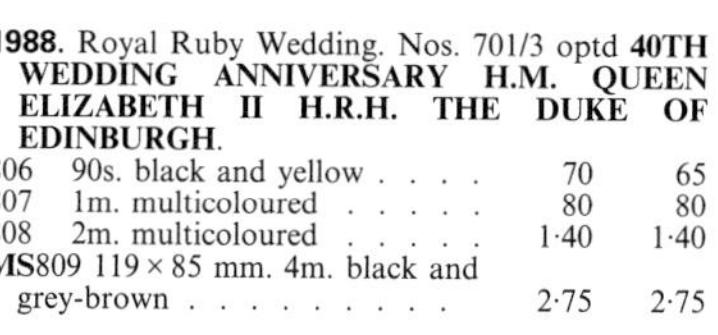

181 Mickey Mouse and Goofy outside Presidential Palace, Helsinki

1988. "Finlandia '88" International Stamp Exhibition, Helsinki. Designs showing Walt Disney cartoon characters in Finland. Mult.
810 1s. Type **181** 10 10
811 2s. Goofy and Mickey Mouse in sauna 10 10
812 3s. Goofy and Mickey Mouse fishing in lake 10 10
813 4s. Mickey and Minnie Mouse and Finlandia Hall, Helsinki 10 10
814 5s. Mickey Mouse photographing Goofy at Sibelius Monument, Helsinki 10 10
815 10s. Mickey Mouse and Goofy pony trekking . . . 10 10
816 3m. Goofy, Mickey and Minnie Mouse at Helsinki Olympic Stadium . . . . . 3·75 3·00
817 5m. Mickey Mouse and Goofy meeting Santa at Arctic Circle . . . . 4·75 4·00
MS818 Two sheets, each 127 × 102 mm. (a) 4m. Mickey Mouse and nephew as Lapps. (b) 4m. Daisy Duck, Goofy, Mickey and Minnie Mouse by fountain, Helsinki. Set of 2 sheets . . . 5·50 7·00

182 Pope John Paul II giving Communion

183 Large-toothed Rock Hyrax

1988. Visit of Pope John Paul II. Mult.
819 55s. Type **182** 40 25
820 2m. Pope leading procession 1·25 1·50
821 3m. Pope at airport . . . . 1·75 2·00
822 4m. Pope John Paul II . . . 2·25 2·75
MS823 98 × 79 mm. 5m. Archbishop Morapeli (horiz) . . . . 5·00 4·50

1988. Small Mammals of Lesotho. Mult.
824 16s. Type **183** 55 15
825 40s. Ratel and black-throated honey guide (bird) . . . 1·75 55
826 75s. Small-spotted genet . . . 1·50 85
827 3m. Yellow mongoose . . . 3·25 5·50
MS828 110 × 78 mm. 4m. Meerkat 3·25 4·00

184 "Birth of Venus" (detail) (Botticelli)

1988. Famous Paintings. Multicoloured.

829 15s. Type **184** 30 15
830 25s. "View of Toledo" (El Greco) 35 20
831 40s. "Maids of Honour" (detail) (Velasquez) 45 25
832 50s. "The Fifer" (Manet) . . 55 30
833 55s. "Starry Night" (detail) (Van Gogh) 55 30
834 75s. "Prima Ballerina" (Degas) 70 70
835 2m. "Bridge over Water Lilies" (Monet) . . . . . 1·75 2·25
836 3m. "Guernica" (detail) (Picasso) . . . . 1·75 2·75
MS837 Two sheets, each 110 × 95 mm. (a) 4m. "The Presentation of the Virgin in the Temple" (Titian). (b) 4m. "The Miracle of the Newborn Infant" (Titian). Set of 2 sheets . . . . 4·00 4·50

185 Wrestling

1988. Olympic Games, Seoul (2nd series). Mult.

838 12s. Type **185** 10 10
839 16s. Show jumping (vert) . . 10 10
840 55s. Shooting 20 30
841 3m.50 As 16s. (vert) . . . . 1·40 2·00
MS842 108 × 77 mm. 4m. Olympic flame (vert) . . . . 2·75 3·50

186 Yannick Noah and Eiffel Tower, Paris

1988. 75th Anniv of Int Tennis Federation. Mult.

843 12s. Type **186** 50 25
844 20s. Rod Laver and Sydney Harbour Bridge and Opera House 70 30
845 30s. Ivan Lendl and Prague 55 25
846 65s. Jimmy Connors and Tokyo (vert) 70 40
847 1m. Arthur Ashe and Barcelona (vert) . . . . . 1·00 60
848 1m.55 Althea Gibson and New York (vert) . . . . . 1·00 90
849 2m. Chris Evert and Vienna (vert) . . . . 1·50 1·25
850 2m.40 Boris Becker and Houses of Parliament, London (vert) . . . . . . 1·75 1·75
851 3m. Martina Navratilova and Golden Gate Bridge, San Francisco . . . . 1·75 2·00
MS852 98 × 72 mm. 4m. Steffi Graf and Berlin . . . . 3·00 3·75

No. 844 is inscribed "SIDNEY" in error.

186a "The Averoldi Polyptych" (detail)

1988. Christmas. 500th Birth Anniv of Titian (artist). Multicoloured.

853 12s. Type **186a** 20 10
854 20s. "Christ and the Adulteress" (detail) 20 10
855 35s. "Christ and the Adulteress" (different detail) 30 20
856 45s. "Angel of the Annunciation" 40 30
857 65s. "Saint Dominic" 55 50
858 1m. "The Vendramin Family" (detail) 75 80
859 2m. "Mary Magdalen" . . . 1·25 1·75
860 3m. "The Tribute Money" 1·75 2·50
MS861 (a) 94 × 110 mm. 5m. "Mater Dolorosa". (b) 110 × 94 mm. 5m. "Christ and the Woman taken in Adultery" (horiz). Set of 2 sheets 6·00 8·00

187 Pilatus PC-6 Turbo Porter

1989. 125th Anniv of International Red Cross. Aircraft. Multicoloured.

862 12s. Type **187** 50 10
863 20s. Unloading medical supplies from Cessna Caravan I 60 20
864 55s. De Havilland D.H.C.6 Twin Otter 200/300 . . . . 90 50
865 3m. Douglas DC-3 . . . . . 2·75 3·50
MS866 109 × 80 mm. 4m. Red Cross logo and Douglas DC-3 (vert) 5·00 3·75

187a "Dawn Mist at Mishima"

1989. Japanese Art. Paintings by Hiroshige. Mult.

867 12s. Type **187a** 30 10
868 16s. "Night Snow at Kambara" 35 10
869 20s. "Wayside Inn at Mariko Station" 35 10
870 35s. "Shower at Shono" . . 55 10
871 55s. "Snowfall on the Kisokaido near Oi" . . . 65 40
872 1m. "Autumn Moon at Seba" 85 85
873 3m.20 "Evening Moon at Ryogoku Bridge" . . . . 2·25 3·00
874 5m. "Cherry Blossoms at Arashiyama" . . . . . . 2·75 3·75
MS875 Two sheets, each 102 × 76 mm. (a) 4m. "Listening to the Singing Insects at Dokanyama". (b) 4m. "Moonlight, Nagakubo". Set of 2 sheets . . . . 6·00 7·00

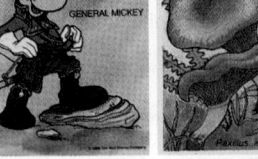

188 Mickey Mouse as General

189 "Paxillus involutus"

1989. "Philexfrance 89" International Stamp Exhibition, Paris. Designs showing Walt Disney cartoon characters in French military uniforms of the Revolutionary period. Multicoloured.

876 1s. Type **188** 10 10
877 2s. Ludwig von Drake as infantryman 10 10
878 3s. Goofy as grenadier . . . 10 10
879 4s. Horace Horsecollar as cavalryman 10 10
880 5s. Pete as hussar 10 10
881 10s. Donald Duck as marine 10 10
882 3m. Gyro Gearloose as National Guard . . . . . 3·25 3·25
883 5m. Scrooge McDuck as admiral . . . . 4·00 4·25
MS884 Two sheets, each 127 × 102 mm. (a) 4m. Mickey and Minnie Mouse as King Louis XVI and Marie Antoinette with Goofy as a National Guard (horiz). (b) 4m. Mickey Mouse as drummer. Set of 2 sheets . . . . 7·50 9·00

No. 879 is inscribed "CALVARYMAN" in error.

1989. Fungi. Multicoloured.

900 12s. Type **189** 20 10
901 16s. "Ganoderma applanatum" 20 15
902 55s. "Suillus granulatus" . . 45 35
903 5m. "Stereum hirsutum" . . 3·25 4·50
MS904 96 × 69 mm. 4m. "Scleroderma cepa" ("flavidum") 5·00 5·50

190 Sesotho Huts

192 Launch of "Apollo 11"

191 Marsh Sandpiper

1989. Maloti Mountains. Multicoloured.

905 1m. Type **190** . . . . 70 1·00
906 1m. American aloe and mountains . . . . 70 1·00
907 1m. River valley with waterfall . . . . 70 1·00
908 1m. Sesotho tribesman on ledge . . . . 70 1·00
MS909 86 × 117 mm. 4m. Spiral Aloe . . . . 3·00 4·00

Nos. 905/8 were printed together, se-tenant, forming a composite design.

1989. Migrant Birds. Multicoloured.

910 12s. Type **191** 80 30
911 65s. Little stint . . . . 1·50 70
912 1m. Ringed plover . . . . . 2·00 1·50
913 4m. Curlew sandpiper . . . 3·50 5·50
MS914 97 × 69 mm. 5m. Ruff (vert) 8·50 9·00

1989. 20th Anniv of First Manned Landing on Moon. Multicoloured.

915 12s. Type **192** 25 10
916 16s. Lunar module "Eagle" landing on Moon (horiz) 25 15
917 40s. Neil Armstrong leaving "Eagle" 45 25
918 55s. Edwin Aldrin on Moon (horiz) 50 30
919 1m. Aldrin performing scientific experiment (horiz) 85 85
920 2m. "Eagle" leaving Moon (horiz) . . . . 1·50 1·75
921 3m. Command module "Columbia" in Moon orbit (horiz) . . . . 2·00 2·25
922 4m. Command module on parachutes . . . . 2·50 2·75
MS923 81 × 111 mm. 5m. Astronaut on Moon . . . . 4·50 5·50

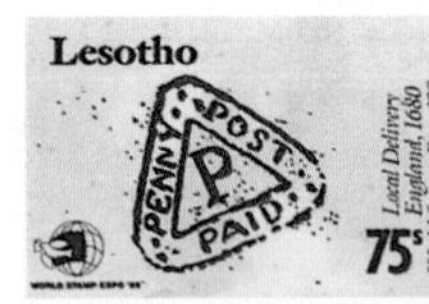

193 English Penny Post Paid Mark, 1680

1989. "World Stamp Expo '89" International Stamp Exhibition, Washington (1st issue). Stamps and Postmarks.

924 **193** 75s. red, black and stone 60 70
925 – 75s. black, grey and red 60 70
926 – 75s. violet, black & brown 60 70
927 – 75s. brown, black & lt brn 60 70
928 – 75s. black and yellow . . 60 70
929 – 75s. multicoloured 60 70
930 – 75s. black and lilac . . . 60 70
931 – 75s. black, red and brown 60 70
932 – 75s. red, black and yellow 60 70

DESIGNS: No. 925, German postal seal and feather, 1807; 926, British Post Office in Crete 1898 20pa. stamp; 927, Bermuda 1848 Perot 1d. provisional; 928, U.S.A. Pony Express cancellation, 1860; 929, Finland 1856 5k. stamp; 930, Fiji 1870 "Fiji Times" 1d. stamp, 1870; 931, Sweden newspaper wrapper handstamp, 1823; 932, Bhor 1879 ½a. stamp.

193a Cathedral Church of St. Peter and St. Paul, Washington

1989. "World Stamp Expo '89" International Stamp Exhibition, Washington (2nd issue). Sheet 78 × 61 mm.

MS933 **193a** 4m. multicoloured 2·50 3·00

193b "The Immaculate Conception"

1989. Christmas. Paintings by Velazquez. Mult.

934 12s. Type **193b** 10 10
935 20s. "St. Anthony Abbot and St. Paul the Hermit" . . . 15 10
936 35s. "St. Thomas the Apostle" 25 25
937 55s. "Christ in the House of Martha and Mary" 35 35
938 1m. "St. John writing The Apocalypse on Patmos" . . 60 75
939 3m. "The Virgin presenting the Chasuble to St. Ildephonsus" . . . . . 1·60 2·25
940 4m. "The Adoration of the Magi" . . . . 2·00 2·75
MS941 71 × 96 mm. 5m. "The Coronation of the Virgin" . . 6·50 7·50

194 Scene from 1966 World Cup Final, England

1989. World Cup Football Championship, Italy. Scenes from past finals. Multicoloured.

942 12s. Type **194** 50 10
943 16s. 1970 final, Mexico . . . 50 15
944 55s. 1974 final, West Germany . . . . 1·00 40
945 5m. 1982 final, Spain . . . . 3·75 5·50
MS946 106 × 85 mm. 4m. Player's legs and symbolic football . . 5·50 6·50

1990. No. 889 and 798/9 surch **16 s**.

948 16s. on 12s. Red-eyed bulbul 1·50 20
948e 16s. on 30s. Common wheater 60 15
948f 16s. on 40s. Common stonechat 60 15

197 "Byblia anvatara"

198a Lady Elizabeth Bowes-Lyon and Brother in Fancy Dress

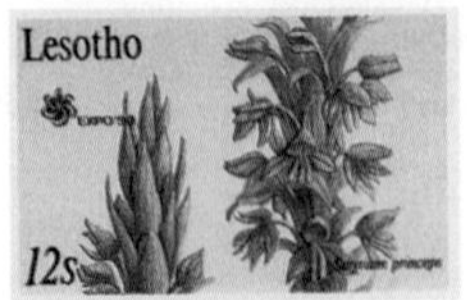

198 "Satyrium princeps"

1990. Butterflies. Multicoloured.

949 12s. Type **197** 60 15
950 16s. "Cynthia cardui" . . . 75 15
951 55s. "Precis oenone" . . . . 1·00 40
952 65s. "Pseudacraea boisduvali" 1·10 65
953 1m. "Precis orithya" . . . . 1·75 1·25
954 2m. "Precis sophia" . . . . 2·75 2·50
955 3m. "Danaus chrysippus" . . 3·50 3·75
956 4m. "Druryia antimachus" 4·50 6·00
MS957 105 × 70 mm. 5m. "Papilio demodocus" . . . . 7·50 9·00

1990. "EXPO 90" International Garden and Greenery Exhibition, Osaka. Local Orchids. Multicoloured.

958 12s. Type **198** 55 15
959 16s. "Huttonaea pulchra" . . 60 15
960 55s. "Herschelia graminifolia" . . . . 1·25 30
961 1m. "Ancellia gigantea" . . . 1·75 75
962 1m.55 "Polystachya pubescens" . . . . 2·00 1·75
963 2m.40 "Penthea filicornis" . . 2·00 2·25
964 3m. "Disperis capensis" . . . 2·25 3·25
965 4m. "Disa uniflora" . . . . 3·00 4·00
MS966 95 × 68 mm. 5m. "Stenoglottis longifolia" . . . 7·50 9·00

1990. 90th Birthday of Queen Elizabeth the Queen Mother.

967 **198a** 1m.50 black and mauve 1·25 1·25
968 – 1m.50 black and mauve 1·25 1·25

969 – 1m.50 black and mauve 1·25 1·25
MS970 90 × 75 mm. 5m. brown, black and mauve 3·75 3·75
DESIGNS: No. 968, Lady Elizabeth Bowes-Lyon in evening dress; 969, Lady Elizabeth Bowes-Lyon wearing hat; MS970, Lady Elizabeth Bowes-Lyon as a child.

199 King Moshoeshoe II and Prince Mohato wearing Seana-Marena Blankets
200 Filling Truck at No. 1 Quarry

1990. Traditional Blankets. Multicoloured.
971 12s. Type **199** 10 10
972 16s. Prince Mohato wearing Seana-Marena blanket 10 10
973 1m. Pope John Paul II wearing Seana-Marena blanket 1·75 1·10
974 3m. Basotho horsemen wearing Matlama blankets 2·00 3·00
MS975 85 × 104 mm. 5m. Pope John Paul II wearing hat and Seana-Marena blanket (horiz) 4·50 4·75

1990. Lesotho Highlands Water Project. Mult.
976 16s. Type **200** 65 10
977 20s. Tanker lorry on Pitseng–Malibamatso road 70 10
978 55s. Piers for Malibamatso Bridge 80 30
979 2m. Excavating Mphosong section of Pitseng–Malibamatso road 2·75 3·75
MS980 104 × 85 mm. 5m. Sinking blasting borcholes on Pitseng–Malibamatso road 5·50 6·50

201 Mother breastfeeding Baby
202 Men's Triple Jump

1990. UNICEF Child Survival Campaign. Multicoloured.
981 12s. Type **201** 60 10
982 55s. Baby receiving oral rehydration therapy 1·10 45
983 1m. Weight monitoring 1·75 2·75

1990. Olympic Games, Barcelona (1992). Mult.
984 16s. Type **202** 55 10
985 55s. Men's 200 m race 70 25
986 1m. Men's 5000 m race 1·10 1·25
987 4m. Show jumping 3·50 5·00
MS988 100 × 70 mm. 5m. Olympic flame (horiz) 5·50 6·50

203 "Virgin and Child" (detail, Rubens)

1990. Christmas. Paintings by Rubens. Mult.
989 12s. Type **203** 20 10
990 16s. "Adoration of the Magi" (detail) 20 10
991 55s. "Head of One of the Three Kings" 45 25
992 80s. "Adoration of the Magi" (different detail) 60 60
993 1m. "Virgin and Child" (different detail) 70 70
994 2m. "Adoration of the Magi" (different detail) 1·25 1·75
995 3m. "Virgin and Child" (different detail) 2·00 2·50
996 4m. "Adoration of the Magi" (different detail) 2·25 3·25
MS997 71 × 100 mm. 5m. "Assumption of the Virgin" (detail) 4·00 5·50

204 Mickey Mouse at Nagasaki Peace Park

1991. "Phila Nippon '91" International Stamp Exhibition, Tokyo. Walt Disney cartoon characters in Japan. Multicoloured.
998 20s. Type **204** 65 15
999 30s. Mickey Mouse on Kamakura Beach 70 20
1000 40s. Mickey and Donald Duck with Bunraku puppet 80 25
1001 50s. Mickey and Donald eating soba 90 35
1002 75s. Mickey and Minnie Mouse at tea house 1·10 70
1003 1m. Mickey running after "Hikari" express train 1·10 1·00
1004 3m. Mickey Mouse with deer at Todaiji Temple, Nara 2·75 3·50
1005 4m. Mickey and Minnie outside Imperial Palace 2·75 4·00
MS1006 Two sheets, each 127 × 112 mm. (a) 5m. Mickey Mouse skiing. (b) 5m. Mickey and Minnie having a picnic. Set of 2 sheets 7·00 8·00

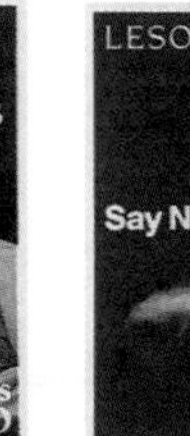

205 Stewart Granger ("King Solomon's Mines")
207 Victim of Drug Abuse

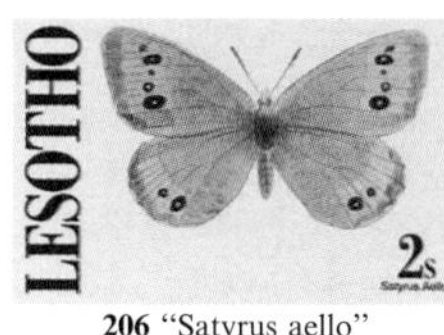

206 "Satyrus aello"

1991. Famous Films with African Themes. Mult.
1007 12s. Type **205** 35 20
1008 16s. Johnny Weissmuller ("Tarzan the Ape Man") 35 20
1009 30s. Clark Gable and Grace Kelly ("Mogambo") 50 35
1010 55s. Sigourney Weaver and gorilla ("Gorillas in the Mist") 75 55
1011 70s. Humphrey Bogart and Katharine Hepburn ("The African Queen") 90 80
1012 1m. John Wayne and capture of rhinoceros ("Hatari!") 1·25 1·00
1013 2m. Meryl Streep and De Havilland Gipsy Moth light aircraft ("Out of Africa") 2·00 2·25
1014 4m. Arsenio Hall and Eddie Murphy ("Coming to America") 2·75 3·50
MS1015 108 × 77 mm. 5m. Elsa the Lioness ("Born Free") 3·75 4·50

1991. Butterflies. Multicoloured.
1016B 2s. Type **206** 10 30
1017B 3s. "Erebia medusa" 10 30
1018A 5s. "Melanargia galathea" 10 30
1019B 10s. "Erebia aethiops" 15 30
1020A 20s. "Coenonympha pamphilus" 20 10
1021B 25s. "Pyrameis atalanta" 20 10
1022B 30s. "Charaxes jasius" 25 10
1023B 40s. "Colias palaeno" 25 10
1024B 50s. "Colias cliopatra" 30 10
1025B 60s. "Colias philodice" 30 10
1026B 70s. "Rhumni gonepterix" 30 10
1027B 1m. "Colias caesonia" 50 25
1028B 2m. "Pyrameis cardui" 90 75
1029cA 3m. "Danaus chrysippus" 1·40 1·75
1030B 10m. "Apatura iris" 4·00 4·50

1991. "Say No To Drugs" Campaign.
1031 **207** 16s. multicoloured 1·50 60

208 Wattled Cranes

1991. Southern Africa Development Co-ordination Conference Tourism Promotion. Multicoloured.
1032 12s. Type **208** 1·25 1·00
1033 16s. Butterfly on flowers 1·25 1·00
1034 25s. Zebra and tourist bus at Mukorob (rock formation), Namibia 1·50 60
MS1035 75 × 117 mm. 3m. Basotho women in ceremonial dress 3·25 4·00

209 De Gaulle in 1939
211 "St. Anne with Mary and the Child Jesus"

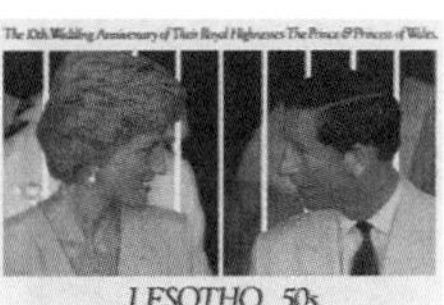

210 Prince and Princess of Wales

1991. Birth Centenary of Charles de Gaulle (French statesman).
1036 **209** 20s. black and brown 70 15
1037 – 40s. black and purple 1·00 25
1038 – 50s. black and green 1·00 40
1039 – 60s. black and blue 1·00 70
1040 – 4m. black and red 3·00 5·00
DESIGNS: 40s. General De Gaulle as Free French leader; 50s. De Gaulle as provisional President of France, 1944–46; 60s. Charles de Gaulle in 1958; 4m. Pres. De Gaulle.

1991. 10th Wedding Anniv of Prince and Princess of Wales. Multicoloured.
1041 50s. Type **210** 1·25 25
1042 70s. Prince Charles at polo and Princess Diana holding Prince Harry 1·25 45
1043 1m. Prince Charles with Prince Harry and Princess Diana in evening dress 1·40 70
1044 3m. Prince William and Prince Harry in school uniform 2·00 3·00
MS1045 68 × 91 mm. 4m. Portraits of Prince with Princess and sons 4·75 4·25

1991. Christmas. Drawings by Albrecht Durer.
1046 **211** 20s. black and mauve 50 10
1047 – 30s. black and blue 65 20
1048 – 50s. black and green 80 25
1049 – 60s. black and red 85 30
1050 – 70s. black and yellow 95 60
1051 – 1m. black and orange 1·10 1·10
1052 – 2m. black and purple 2·25 2·75
1053 – 4m. black and blue 3·00 5·00
MS1054 Two sheets, each 102 × 127 mm. (a) 5m. black and red. (b) 5m. black and blue. Set of 2 sheets 5·50 7·50
DESIGNS: 30s. "Mary on Grass Bench"; 50s. "Mary with Crown of Stars"; 60s. "Mary with Child beside Tree"; 70s. "Mary with Child beside Wall"; 1m. "Mary in Halo on Crescent Moon"; 2m. "Mary breastfeeding Child"; 4m. "Mary with Infant in Swaddling Clothes".

212 Mickey Mouse and Pluto pinning the Tail on the Donkey

1991. Children's Games. Walt Disney cartoon characters. Multicoloured.
1055 20s. Type **212** 60 15
1056 30s. Mickey playing mancala 65 20
1057 40s. Mickey rolling hoop 75 20
1058 50s. Minnie Mouse hula-hooping 80 25
1059 70s. Mickey and Pluto throwing a frisbee 1·10 75
1060 1m. Donald Duck with a diabolo 1·40 1·40
1061 2m. Donald's nephews playing marbles 2·25 3·00
1062 3m. Donald with Rubik's cube 2·75 4·00
MS1063 Two sheets, each 127 × 112 mm. (a) 5m. Donald's and Mickey's nephews playing tug-of-war. (b) 5m. Mickey and Donald mock fighting. Set of 2 sheets 7·00 8·00

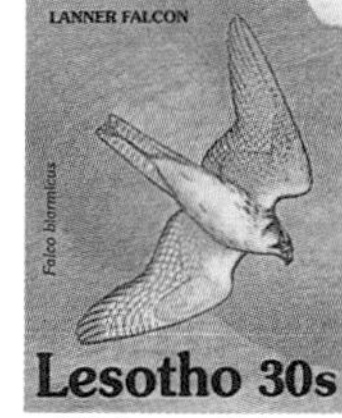

213 Lanner Falcon

1992. Birds. Multicoloured.
1064 30s. Type **213** 60 55
1065 30s. Bateleur 60 55
1066 30s. Paradise sparrow (inscr "Red-headed Finch") 60 55
1067 30s. Lesser striped swallow 60 55
1068 30s. Alpine swift 60 55
1069 30s. Didric cuckoo ("Diederik Cuckoo") 60 55
1070 30s. Yellow-tufted malachite sunbird ("Malachite Sunbird") 60 55
1071 30s. Burchell's gonolek ("Crimson-breasted Shrike") 60 55
1072 30s. Pin-tailed whydah 60 55
1073 30s. Lilac-breasted roller 60 55
1074 30s. Black bustard ("Korhaan") 60 55
1075 30s. Black-collared barbet 60 55
1076 30s. Secretary bird 60 55
1077 30s. Red-billed quelea 60 55
1078 30s. Red bishop 60 55
1079 30s. Ring-necked dove 60 55
1080 30s. Yellow canary 60 55
1081 30s. Cape longclaw ("Orange-throated Longclaw") 60 55
1082 30s. Cordon-bleu (inscr "Blue Waxbill") 60 55
1083 30s. Golden bishop 60 55
Nos. 1064/83 were printed together, se-tenant, forming a composite design.

214 Queen Elizabeth and Cooking at a Mountain Homestead

1992. 40th Anniv of Queen Elizabeth II's Accession. Multicoloured.
1084 20s. Type **214** 30 15
1085 30s. View from mountains 30 20
1086 1m. Cacti and mountain 85 65
1087 4m. Thaba-Bosiu 2·75 3·50
MS1088 75 × 97 mm. 5m. Mountains at sunset 3·75 4·00

215 Minnie Mouse as Spanish Lady, 1540–1660

1992. International Stamp Exhibitions. Walt Disney cartoon characters. Multicoloured. (a) "Granada '92", Spain. Traditional Spanish Costumes.
1089 20s. Type **215** 70 20
1090 50s. Mickey Mouse as Don Juan at Lepanto, 1571 85 40
1091 70s. Donald in Galician costume, 1880 1·00 70
1092 2m. Daisy Duck in Aragonese costume, 1880 2·25 3·25
MS1093 127 × 112 mm. 5m. Goofy the bullfighter 4·50 5·00

(b) "World Columbian Stamp Expo '92". Red Indian Life.
1094 30s. Donald Duck making arrowheads 40 30
1095 40s. Goofy playing lacrosse 50 40

1096 1m. Mickey Mouse and Donald Duck planting corn . . . . 90 1·10
1097 3m. Minnie Mouse doing bead work . . . . 2·25 3·25
MS1098 127 × 112 mm. 5m. Mickey paddling canoe . . . . 4·50 5·00

216 Stegosaurus

1992. Prehistoric Animals. Multicoloured.
1099 20s. Type **216** 85 30
1100 30s. Ceratosaurus 95 35
1101 40s. Procompsognathus . . 1·10 45
1102 50s. Lesothosaurus . . . . 1·40 55
1103 70s. Plateosaurus . . . . . 1·40 70
1104 1m. Gasosaurus . . . . . . 1·50 1·25
1105 2m. Massospondylus . . . 2·00 2·75
1106 3m. Archaeopteryx . . . . . 2·25 3·50
MS1107 Two sheets, each 105 × 77 mm. (a) 5m. As 50s. (b) 5m. As 3m. Set of 2 sheets . . 9·50 9·00

217 Men's Discus **218** "Virgin and Child" (Sassetta)

1992. Olympic Games, Albertville and Barcelona. Multicoloured.
1108 20s. Type **217** 20 15
1109 30s. Men's long jump . . . 25 15
1110 40s. Women's 4 × 100 m relay 30 25
1111 70s. Women's 100 m 50 50
1112 1m. Men's parallel bars . . 70 70
1113 2m. Men's double luge (horiz) . . . . 1·40 1·75
1114 3m. Women's 30k cross-country skiing (horiz) . . 1·75 2·50
1115 4m. Men's biathlon . . . . 2·00 2·75
MS1116 Two sheets, each 100 × 70 mm. (a) 5m. Women's figure skating. (b) 5m. Ice hockey (horiz). Set of 2 sheets . . . . 6·75 7·50

1992. Christmas. Religious Paintings. Mult.
1117 20s. Type **218** 40 15
1118 30s. "Coronation of the Virgin" (Master of Bonastre) 50 20
1119 40s. "Virgin and Child" (Master of SS. Cosmas and Damian) 60 25
1120 70s. "The Virgin of Great Panagia" (detail) (12th-century Russian school) 95 55
1121 1m. "Madonna and Child" (Vincenzo Foppa) . . . . 1·40 1·10
1122 2m. "Madonna and Child" (School of Lippo Memmi) 2·00 2·50
1123 3m. "Virgin and Child" (Barnaba da Modena) . . 2·50 3·25
1124 4m. "Virgin and Child with Saints" (triptych) (Simone dei Crocifissi) . . . . . . 2·75 3·50
MS1125 Two sheets, each 76 × 102 mm. (a) 5m. "Virgin and Child with Saints" (different detail) (Simone dei Crocifissi). (b) 5m. "Virgin and Child enthroned and surrounded by Angels" (Cimabue). Set of 2 sheets . . 8·00 10·00

219 World Trade Centre, New York

1992. Postage Stamp Mega Event, New York. Sheet 100 × 70 mm.
MS1126 5m. multicoloured . . . 5·00 5·50

220 Baby Harp Seal (Earth Summit '92, Rio)

1993. Anniversaries and Events. Multicoloured.
1127 20s. Type **220** 70 40
1128 30s. Giant panda (Earth Summit '92, Rio) 90 40
1129 40s. Airship "Graf Zeppelin" over globe (75th death anniv of Count Ferdinand von Zeppelin) 90 40
1130 70s. Woman grinding maize (International Conference on Nutrition, Rome) . . . 60 45
1131 4m. Lt. Robinson's Royal Aircraft Factory B.E.2C shooting down Schutte Lanz SL-11 airship (75th death anniv of Count Ferdinand von Zeppelin) 3·25 4·00
1132 5m. Valentina Tereshkova and "Vostok 6" (30th anniv of first woman in space) . . . . 3·25 4·00
MS1133 Two sheets, each 100 × 70 mm. (a) 5m. Dr. Ronald McNair ("Challenger" astronaut) (International Space Year). (b) 5m. South African crowned crane (Earth Summit '92, Rio). Set of 2 sheets . . . . 8·00 8·00

221 "Orpheus and Eurydice" (detail)

1993. Bicentenary of the Louvre, Paris. Paintings by Poussin. Multicoloured.
1134 70s. Type **221** 80 80
1135 70s. "Rape of the Sabine Women" (left detail) . . . 80 80
1136 70s. "Rape of the Sabine Women" (right detail) . . 80 80
1137 70s. "The Death of Sapphira" (left detail) . . 80 80
1138 70s. "The Death of Sapphira" (right detail) 80 80
1139 70s. "Echo and Narcissus" (left detail) 80 80
1140 70s. "Echo and Narcissus" (right detail) 80 80
1141 70s. "Self-portrait" 80 80
MS1142 70 × 100 mm. 5m. "The Money Lender and his Wife" (57 × 89 mm) (Metsys) . . . . 4·75 5·00

222 Aloe

1993. Flowers. Multicoloured.
1143 20s. Type **222** 35 10
1144 30s. Calla lily 40 15
1145 40s. Bird of paradise plant 40 15
1146 70s. Amaryllis 65 40
1147 1m. Agapanthus 85 60
1148 2m. Crinum . . . . 2·50 2·00
1149 4m. Watsonia . . . . 2·25 3·00
1150 5m. Gazania . . . . 2·25 3·25
MS1151 Two sheets, each 98 × 67 mm. (a) 7m. Plumbago. (b) 7m. Desert Rose. Set of 2 sheets 7·50 8·50

223 "Precis westermanni"

1993. Butterflies. Multicoloured.
1152 20s. Type **223** 40 15
1153 40s. "Precis sophia" 50 20
1154 70s. "Precis terea" 65 45
1155 1m. "Byblia acheloia" . . . 75 75
1156 2m. "Papilio antimachus" 1·25 1·50
1157 5m. "Pseudacraea boisduvali" . . . . 1·75 3·00
MS1158 Two sheets, each 96 × 62 mm. (a) 7m. "Precis oenone". (b) 7m. "Precis octavia". Set of 2 sheets . . . . 7·00 7·00
No. 1157 is inscribed "Pesudacraea boisduvali" in error.

224 Queen Elizabeth II at Coronation (photograph by Cecil Beaton)

1993. 40th Anniv of Coronation.
1159 **224** 20s. multicoloured . . . 80 85
1160 – 40s. multicoloured . . . 1·00 1·10
1161 – 1m. black and green . . 1·40 1·50
1162 – 5m. multicoloured . . . 3·25 3·50
MS1163 70 × 100 mm. 7m. multicoloured (42½ × 28½ mm) 5·50 6·00
DESIGNS—VERT: 40s. St. Edward's Crown and Sceptre; 1m. Queen Elizabeth the Queen Mother; 5m. Queen Elizabeth II and family. HORIZ: 7m. "Conversation Piece at Royal Lodge, Windsor" (detail) (Sir James Gunn).

225 East African Railways Vulcan Steam Locomotive, 1929

1993. African Railways. Multicoloured.
1164 20s. Type **225** 75 25
1165 30s. Beyer-Garratt Class 15A steam locomotive, Zimbabwe Railways, 1952 85 30
1166 40s. Class 25 steam locomotive, South African Railways, 1953 . . . . . 90 30
1167 70s. Class A 58 steam locomotive, East African Railways . . . . 1·25 60
1168 1m. Class 9E electric locomotives, South African Railways . . . . 1·40 85
1169 2m. Class 87 diesel-electric locomotive, East African Railways, 1971 . . . . . 1·75 1·60
1170 3m. Class 92 diesel locomotive, East African Railways, 1971 . . . . . 2·00 2·25
1171 5m. Class 26 steam locomotive No. 3450, South African Railways, 1982 . . . . 2·50 3·50
MS1172 Two sheets, each 104 × 82 mm. (a) 7m. Class 6E electric locomotive, South African Railways, 1969. (b) 7m. Class 231-132BT steam locomotive, Algerian Railways, 1937. Set of 2 sheets . . . . 9·00 9·00

226 Court-house

1993. Traditional Houses. Multicoloured.
1173 20s. Type **226** 50 10
1174 30s. House with reed fence 55 15
1175 70s. Unmarried girls' house 1·00 40
1176 4m. Hut made from branches . . . . 3·50 5·00
MS1177 81 × 69 mm. 4m. Decorated houses . . . . 3·00 4·00

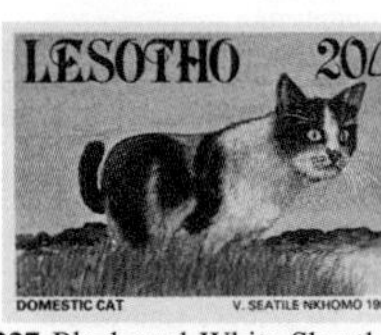

227 Black and White Shorthair

1993. Domestic Cats. Multicoloured.
1178 20s. Type **227** 60 25
1179 30s. Shorthair tabby lying down 60 25
1180 70s. Head of shorthair tabby 80 40
1181 5m. Black and white shorthair with shorthair tabby . . . . 2·75 4·00
MS1182 113 × 89mm. 5m. Shorthair Tabby with rat (vert) . . . . . 3·00 3·50

228 Pluto in Chung Cheng Park, Keelung

1993. "Taipei '93" Asian International Stamp Exhibition, Taiwan. Walt Disney cartoon characters in Taiwan. Multicoloured.
1183 20s. Type **228** 60 10
1184 30s. Donald Duck at Chiao-Tienkung Temple Festival 70 15
1185 40s. Goofy with lantern figures 80 20
1186 70s. Minnie Mouse shopping at temple festival . . . . 1·00 40
1187 1m. Daisy Duck at Queen's Head Rock, Yehliu (vert) 1·25 70
1188 1m.20 Mickey and Minnie at National Concert Hall (vert) . . . . 1·40 1·60
1189 2m. Donald at Chiang Kai-shek Memorial Hall (vert) 1·60 2·00
1190 2m.50 Donald and Daisy at the Grand Hotel, Taipei 1·90 2·75
MS1191 Two sheets, each 128 × 102 mm. (a) 5m. Goofy over National Palace Museum, Taipei. (b) 6m. Mickey and Minnie at Presidential Palace Museum, Taipei (vert). Set of 2 sheets . . 8·50 8·50

229 Tseliso "Frisco" Khomari (Lesotho) **230** King Letsie III signing Oath of Office

1994. World Cup Football Championship, U.S.A. Multicoloured.
1192 20s. Type **229** 50 10
1193 30s. Thato "American Spoon" Mohale (Lesotho) 55 15
1194 40s. Jozic Davor (Yugoslavia) and Freddy Rincorn (Colombia) . . . 65 20
1195 50s. Lefika "Mzee" Lekhotla (Lesotho) . . . 70 25
1196 70s. Litsiso "House-on-fire" Khali (Lesotho) 85 55
1197 1m. Roger Milla (Cameroun) . . . . . . 1·00 85
1198 1m.20 David Platt (England) 1·50 2·00
1199 2m. Karl Heinz Rummenigge (Germany) and Soren Lerby (Denmark) . . . . 1·75 2·50
MS1200 Two sheets, each 100 × 70 mm. (a) 6m. Klaus Lindenberger (Czechoslovakia). (b) 6m. Franco Baresi (Italy) and Ivan Hasek (Czechoslovakia) (horiz). Set of 2 sheets . . . . 8·50 8·50

1994. 1st Anniv of Restoration of Democracy. Multicoloured.
1201 20s. Type **230** 20 15
1202 30s. Parliament building (horiz) 25 15
1203 50s. Swearing-in of Dr. Ntsu Mokhehle as Prime Minister (horiz) 40 20
1204 70s. Maj-Gen P. Ramaema handing Instruments of Government to Dr. Ntsu Mokhehle (horiz) 70 40

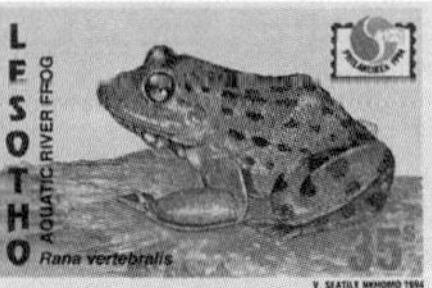

231 Aquatic River Frog

1994. "Philakorea '94" International Stamp Exhibition, Seoul. Frogs and Toads. Mult.
1205 35s. Type **231** 20 10
1206 50s. Bubbling kassina . . . 25 15

1207 1m. Guttural toad 50 50
1208 1m.50 Common river frog 70 90
MS1209 Two sheets, each 102 × 72 mm. (a) 5m. Jade frog (sculpture). (b) 5m. Black Spotted frog and oriental white-eye (bird) (vert). Set of 2 sheets . . . . . 7·50 7·50

232 De Havilland D.H.C.6 Twin Otter and Emblem

1994. 50th Anniv of I.C.A.O. Multicoloured.
1210 35s. Type **232** 30 15
1211 50s. Fokker F.27 Friendship on runway 40 20
1212 1m. Fokker F.27 Friendship over Moshoeshoe I International Airport . . 70 55
1213 1m.50 Cessna light aircraft over mountains . . . . . 1·00 1·25

1995. No. 1022 surch **20s**.
1214a 20s. on 30s. "Charaxes jasius" . . . . 1·00 65

234 "Tagetes minuta"
235 Pius XII College, 1962

1995. Medicinal Plants. Multicoloured.
1215 35s. Type **234** 15 10
1216 50s. "Plantago lanceolata" 20 15
1217 1m. "Amaranthus spinosus" 35 35
1218 1m.50 "Taraxacum officinale" 65 85
MS1219 120 × 91 mm. 5m. "Dativa stramonium" . . . . 1·75 1·90

1995. 50th Anniv of University Studies in Lesotho. Multicoloured.
1220 35s. Type **235** 15 10
1221 50s. Campus, University of Basutoland, Bechuanaland and Swaziland, 1966 . . . 20 15
1222 70s. Campus, University of Botswana, Lesotho and Swaziland, 1970 . . . . . 30 15
1223 1m. Administration Block, University of Botswana, Lesotho and Swaziland, 1975 . . . . 45 40
1224 1m.50 Administration Block, National University of Lesotho, 1988 . . . . . 65 75
1225 2m. Procession of Vice-Chancellors, National University of Lesotho, 1995 . . . . 80 1·10

236 Qiloane Pinnacle, Thaba-Bosiu
237 "Peace"

1995. 20th Anniv of World Tourism Organization. Multicoloured.
1226 35s. Type **236** 25 10
1227 50s. Ha Mohalenyane rock formation 30 15
1228 1m. Botsoela Falls (vert) . . 55 40
1229 1m.50 Backpackers in Makhaleng River Gorge 80 1·00
MS1230 143 × 88 mm. 4m. Red Hot Pokers (38 × 57 mm) . . . . . 1·75 1·90
No. **MS**1230 is inscribed "RED HOT PORKERS" in error.

1995. 50th Anniv of United Nations. Multicoloured.
1231 35s. Type **237** 20 10
1232 50s. "Justice" (scales) . . . 25 15
1233 1m.50 "Reconciliation" (clasped hands) (horiz) . . 70 90

238 "Sutter's Gold Rose"
240 Adding Iodized Salt to Cooking Pot

239 Part of 1911 Map showing Lephaqhoa

1995. Christmas. Roses. Multicoloured.
1234 5s. Type **238** 10 20
1235 50s. "Michele Meilland" . . 25 10
1236 1m. "J. Otto Thilow" . . . 45 40
1237 2m. "Papa Meilland" . . . 80 1·10

1996. Completion of New Standard Map of Lesotho (1994). Map Sections of Malibamatso Valley. Multicoloured. (a) 1911 Map.
1238 35s. Type **239** 20 20
1239 35s. Boritsa Tsuene 20 20
1240 35s. Molapo 20 20
1241 35s. Nkeu 20 20
1242 35s. Three rivers flowing east 20 20
1243 35s. Tibedi and Rafanyane 20 20
1244 35s. Two rivers flowing east 20 20
1245 35s. Madibatmatso River . . 20 20
1246 35s. Bokung River 20 20
1247 35s. Semena River 20 20

(b) 1978 Map.
1248 35s. Mountains and river valley 20 20
1249 35s. Pelaneng and Lepaqoa 20 20
1250 35s. Mamohau 20 20
1251 35s. Ha Lejone 20 20
1252 35s. Ha Thoora 20 20
1253 35s. Ha Mikia 20 20
1254 35s. Ha Kosetabole 20 20
1255 35s. Ha Seshote 20 20
1256 35s. Ha Rapooane 20 20
1257 35s. Bokong Ha Kennan . . 20 20

(c) 1994 Map.
1258 35s. Mafika-Lisiu Pass . . . 20 20
1259 35s. Ha Lesaoana 20 20
1260 35s. Ha Masaballa 20 20
1261 35s. Ha Nkisi 20 20
1262 35s. Ha Rafanyane 20 20
1263 35s. Laitsoka Pass 20 20
1264 35s. "Katse Reservoir" . . . 20 20
1265 35s. Seshote 20 20
1266 35s. Sephareng 20 20
1267 35s. Katse Dam 20 20
Nos. 1238/47, 1248/57 and 1258/67 respectively were printed together, se-tenant, forming composite designs.

1996. 50th Anniv of UNICEF. Multicoloured.
1268 35s. Type **240** 20 10
1269 50s. Herdboys with livestock (horiz) 25 15
1270 70s. Children in class (horiz) 35 15
1271 1m.50 Boys performing traditional dance (horiz) 75 1·00

241 U.S.A. Basketball Team, 1936

1996. Olympic Games, Atlanta. Previous Gold Medal Winners. Multicoloured.
1272 1m. Type **241** 40 20
1273 1m.50 Brandenburg Gate and stadium, Berlin, 1936 40 30
1274 1m.50 Glen Morris (U.S.A.) (decathlon, 1936) (vert) 40 40
1275 1m.50 Saidi Aouita (Morocco) (5000 m running, 1984) (vert) 40 40
1276 1m.50 Arnie Robinson (U.S.A.) (long jump, 1976) (vert) 40 40
1277 1m.50 Hans Woellke (Germany) (shot put, 1936) (vert) 40 40
1278 1m.50 Renate Stecher (Germany) (100 m running, 1972) (vert) 40 40
1279 1m.50 Evelyn Ashford (U.S.A.) (100 m running, 1984) (vert) 40 40
1280 1m.50 Willie Davenport (U.S.A.) (110 m hurdles, 1968) (vert) 40 40
1281 1m.50 Bob Beamon (U.S.A.) (long jump, 1968) (vert) 40 40
1282 1m.50 Heidi Rosendhal (Germany) (long jump, 1972) (vert) 40 40
1283 2m. Jesse Owens (U.S.A.) (track and field, 1936) (vert) 50 55
1284 3m. Speed boat racing . . . 70 85
MS1285 Two sheets, each 110 × 80 mm. (a) 8m. Michael Gross (Germany) (swimming, 1984) (vert). (b) 8m. Kornelia Ender (Germany) (swimming, 1976) (vert). Set of 2 sheets . . 6·00 6·50
No. 1273 is inscribed "BRANDEBOURG GATE" in error. No. 1274 incorrectly identifies Glen Morris as the gold medal winner in the 1936 long jump.
Nos. 1274/82 were printed together, se-tenant, with the backgrounds forming a composite design.

242 Class WP Steam Locomotive (India)

1996. Trains of the World. Multicoloured.
1286 1m.50 Type **242** 65 65
1287 1m.50 Canadian Pacific steam locomotive No. 2471 (Canada) . . . 65 65
1288 1m.50 The "Caledonian" (Great Britain) 65 65
1289 1m.50 Steam locomotive "William Mason" (U.S.A.) 65 65
1290 1m.50 "Trans-Siberian Express" (Russia) 65 65
1291 1m.50 Steam train (Switzerland) 65 65
1292 1m.50 ETR 450 high speed train (Italy) 65 65
1293 1m.50 TGV express train (France) 65 65
1294 1m.50 XPT high speed train (Australia) 65 65
1295 1m.50 "Blue Train" (South Africa) 65 65
1296 1m.50 Intercity 225 express train (Great Britain) . . . 65 65
1297 1m.50 "Hikari" express train (Japan) 65 65
MS1298 Two sheets, each 98 × 68 mm. (a) 8m. Class 52 steam locomotive (Germany) (57 × 43 mm). (b) 8m. ICE high speed train (Germany) (57 × 43 mm). Set of 2 sheets 6·50 7·00

243 Mothers' Union Member, Methodist Church

1996. Christmas. Mothers' Unions. Multicoloured.
1299 35s. Type **243** 20 10
1300 50s. Roman Catholic Church 25 10
1301 1m. Lesotho Evangelical Church 45 30
1302 1m.50 Anglican Church . . 70 90
No. 1302 is inscribed "Anglian" in error.

244 Hand Clasp (Co-operation for Development)
245 Land Reclamation

1997. 10th Anniv of Lesotho Highland Water Project (1996). Multicoloured.
1303 35s. Type **244** 20 10
1304 50s. Lammergeier and rock painting (Nature and Heritage) 35 20
1305 1m. Malibamatso Bridge (Engineering) 45 35
1306 1m.50 Katse Valley in 1986 and 1996 (75 × 28 mm) . . 70 95
No. 1305 is inscribed "Developement" in error.

1997. Environment Protection. Multicoloured.
1307 35s. Type **245** 20 10
1308 50s. Throwing rubbish into bin 25 15
1309 1m. Hands holding globe and tree 45 30
1310 1m.20 Recycling symbol and rubbish 55 55
1311 1m.50 Collecting rain water 65 75

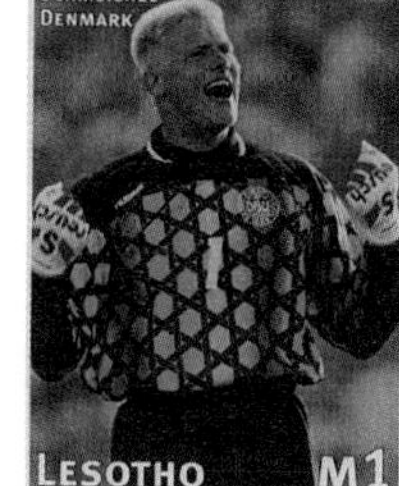

246 Schmeichel, Denmark

1997. World Cup Football Championship, France (1998). Multicoloured.
1312 1m. Type **246** 30 20
1313 1m.50 Bergkamp, Netherlands 45 45
1314 1m.50 Argentine players celebrating 45 45
1315 1m.50 Argentine and Dutch players competing for ball 45 45
1316 1m.50 Players heading ball 45 45
1317 1m.50 Goalkeeper deflecting ball 45 45
1318 1m.50 Goal-mouth melee . . 45 45
1319 1m.50 Argentine player kicking ball 45 45
1320 2m. Southgate, England . . 60 60
1321 2m.50 Asprilla, Colombia 70 75
1322 3m. Gascoigne, England . . 80 85
1323 4m. Giggs, Wales . . . . . 90 1·10
MS1324 Two sheets, each 127 × 102 mm. (a) 8m. Littbarski, West Germany (horiz). (b) 8m. Shearer, England. Set of 2 sheets 6·50 7·00

247 "Spialia spio"

1997. Butterflies. Multicoloured.
1325 1m.50 Type **247** 60 60
1326 1m.50 "Leptotes pirithous" 60 60
1327 1m.50 "Acratea satis" . . . 60 60
1328 1m.50 "Belenois aurota aurota" 60 60
1329 1m.50 "Spindasis natalensis" 60 60
1330 1m.50 "Torynesis orangica" 60 60
1331 1m.50 "Lepidochysops variabilis" 60 60
1332 1m.50 "Pinacopteryx eriphia" 60 60
1333 1m.50 "Anthene butleri livida" 60 60
MS1334 Two sheets, each 106 × 76 mm. (a) 8m. "Bematistes aganice". (b) 8m. "Papilio demodocus". Set of 2 sheets . . 6·50 6·50
Nos. 1325/33 were printed together, se-tenant, with the backgrounds forming a composite design.
No. 1326 is inscribed "Cyclyrius pirithous", No. 1332 "Pinacopteryx eriphea" and No. **MS**1334(b) "Papalio demodocus", all in error.

248 Rock Paintings and Boy
249 Diana, Princess of Wales

1998. 40th Anniv of Morija Museum and Archives. Multicoloured.
1335 35s. Type **248** 10 10
1336 45s. Hippopotamus and lower jaw bone (horiz) . . 10 10
1337 50s. Woman and cowhide skirt 10 10
1338 1m. Drum and "thomo" (musical bow) 15 20
1339 1m.50 Warrior with "khau" (gorget awarded for valour) 25 30
1340 2m. Herders with ox (horiz) 30 35

1998. Diana, Princess of Wales Commemoration. Multicoloured.
1341 3m. Type **249** . . . . . . 1·10 1·25
1342 3m. Wearing grey jacket . . 1·10 1·25
1343 3m. Wearing white polo-necked jumper . . . . . 1·10 1·25
1344 3m. Wearing pearl necklace 1·10 1·25
1345 3m. Wearing white evening dress . . . . 1·10 1·25
1346 3m. Wearing pale blue jacket . . . . 1·10 1·25
MS1347 70 × 100 mm. 9m. Accepting bouquet . . . . . . 6·50 6·50

250 Atitlan Grebe

1998. Fauna of the World. Multicoloured. (a) Vert designs as T **250**.
1348 1m. Type **250** 15 20
1349 1m. Cabot's tragopan 15 20
1350 1m. Spider monkey 15 20
1351 1m. Dibatag 15 20
1352 1m. Right whale 15 20
1353 1m. Imperial amazon ("Imperial Parrot") 15 20
1354 1m. Cheetah 15 20
1355 1m. Brown-eared pheasant 15 20
1356 1m. Leatherback turtle 15 20
1357 1m. Imperial woodpecker 15 20
1358 1m. Andean condor 15 20
1359 1m. Barbary deer 15 20
1360 1m. Grey gentle lemur 15 20
1361 1m. Cuban amazon ("Cuban Parrot") 15 20
1362 1m. Numbat 15 20
1363 1m. Short-tailed albatross 15 20
1364 1m. Green turtle 15 20
1365 1m. White rhinoceros 15 20
1366 1m. Diademed sifaka 15 20
1367 1m. Galapagos penguin 15 20

(b) Horiz designs, each 48 × 31 mm.
1368 1m.50 Impala 25 30
1369 1m.50 Black bear 25 30
1370 1m.50 American buffalo 25 30
1371 1m.50 African elephant 25 30
1372 1m.50 Kangaroo 25 30
1373 1m.50 Lion 25 30
1374 1m.50 Giant panda 25 30
1375 1m.50 Tiger 25 30
1376 1m.50 Zebra 25 30
MS1377 Four sheets, each 98 × 68 mm. (a) 8m. White-bellied sunbird. (b) 8m. Golden-shouldered parrot. (c) 8m. Snail darter. (d) 8m. Monkey (47 × 31 mm). Set of 4 sheets 4·75 5·00

251 Cape Vulture

1998. Endangered Species. Cape Vulture. Mult.
1378 1m. Type **251** 15 20
1379 1m. Looking towards ground 15 20
1380 1m. Looking over shoulder 15 20
1381 1m. Facing right 15 20

252 Siamese

1998. Cats of the World. Multicoloured.
1382 70s. Type **252** 10 10
1383 1m. Chartreux 15 20
1384 2m. Korat 30 35
1385 2m. Japanese bobtail 30 35
1386 2m. British white 30 35
1387 2m. Bengal 30 35
1388 2m. Abyssinian 30 35
1389 2m. Snowshoe 30 35
1390 2m. Scottish fold 30 35
1391 2m. Maine coon 30 35
1392 2m. Balinese 30 35
1393 2m. Persian 30 35
1394 2m. Javanese 30 35
1395 2m. Turkish angora 30 35
1396 2m. Tiffany 30 35
1397 3m. Egyptian mau 45 50
1398 4m. Bombay 60 65
1399 5m. Burmese 75 80
MS1400 Two sheets, each 98 × 69 mm. (a) 8m. Tonkinese. (b) 8m. Singapura. Set of 2 sheets 2·40 2·50
Nos. 1385/90 and 1391/6 respectively were printed together, se-tenant, with the backgrounds forming composite designs.

253 "Laccaria laccata"

1998. Fungi of the World. Multicoloured.
1401 70s. Type **253** 10 10
1402 1m. "Mutinus caninus" 15 20
1403 1m. "Hygrophorus psittacinus" 15 20
1404 1m. "Cortinarius obtusus" 15 20
1405 1m. "Volvariella bombycina" 15 20
1406 1m. "Cortinarius caerylescens" 15 20
1407 1m. "Laccaria amethystina" 15 20
1408 1m. "Tricholoma aurantium" 15 20
1409 1m. "Amanita excelsa (spissa)" 15 20
1410 1m. "Clavaria helvola" 15 20
1411 1m. Unidentified species (inscr "Cortinarius caerylescens") 15 20
1412 1m. "Russula queletii" 15 20
1413 1m. "Amanita phalloides" 15 20
1414 1m. "Lactarius deliciosus" 15 20
1415 1m.50 "Tricholoma lascivum" 25 30
1416 2m. "Clitocybe geotropa" 30 35
1417 3m. "Amanita excelsa" 45 50
1418 4m. Red-capped bolete 60 65
MS1419 Two sheets, each 98 × 68 mm. (a) 8m. "Amanita pantherina". (b) 8m. "Boletus satanas". Set of 2 sheets 2·40 2·50
Nos. 1406, 1407, 1414, 1416 and **MS**1419b are inscribed "Continarius caerylescens", "Laccaria amethystea", "Lactarius delicious", "Clitocybe geotrapa" and "Boletys satanus", all in error.

254 "Simba"

1998. World Cinema. Multicoloured. (a) Films about Africa.
1420 2m. Type **254** 30 35
1421 2m. "Call to Freedom" 30 35
1422 2m. "Cry the Beloved Country" 30 35
1423 2m. "King Solomon's Mines" 30 35
1424 2m. "Flame and the Fire" 30 35
1425 2m. "Cry Freedom" 30 35
1426 2m. "Bopha!" 30 35
1427 2m. "Zulu" 30 35

(b) Japanese Film Stars.
1428 2m. Takamine Hideko 30 35
1429 2m. James Shigeta 30 35
1430 2m. Miyoshi Umeki 30 35
1431 2m. May Ishimara 30 35
1432 2m. Sessue Hayakawa 30 35
1433 2m. Miiko Taka 30 35
1434 2m. Mori Masayuki 30 35
1435 2m. Hara Setsuko 30 35
1436 2m. Kyo Machiko 30 35
MS1437 Two sheets. (a) 68 × 98 mm. 10m. Lion cubs from "Born Free" (horiz). (b) 70 × 100 mm. 10m. Toshiro Mifune. Set of 2 sheets 3·00 3·25
Nos. 1420/7 and 1428/36 respectively were printed together, se-tenant, with the backgrounds forming composite designs.
No. 1423 is inscribed "KING SOLOMAN'S MINES" in error.

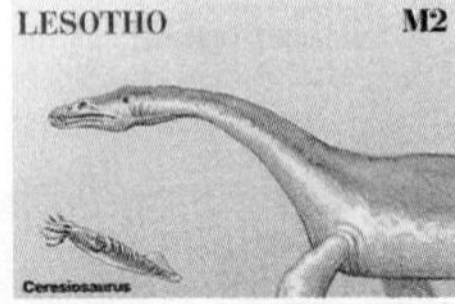

255 Ceresiosaurus

1998. Prehistoric Animals. Multicoloured.
1438 2m. Type **255** 30 35
1439 2m. Rhomaleosaurus 30 35
1440 2m. Anomalocaris 30 35
1441 2m. Mixosaurus 30 35
1442 2m. Stethacanthus 30 35
1443 2m. Dunklosteus 30 35
1444 2m. Tommotia 30 35
1445 2m. Sanctacaris 30 35
1446 2m. Ammonites 30 35
1447 2m. Rhamphorhynchus 30 35
1448 2m. Brachiosaurus 30 35
1449 2m. Mamenchisaurus hochuanensis 30 35
1450 2m. Ceratosaurus nasicornis 30 35
1451 2m. Archaeopteryx 30 35
1452 2m. Leaellynasaura amicagraphica 30 35
1453 2m. Chasmosaurus belli 30 35
1454 2m. Deinonychus and Pachyrhinosaurus 30 35
1455 2m. Deinonychus 30 35
1456 2m. Nyctosaurus 30 35
1457 2m. Volcanoes 30 35
1458 2m. Eudimorphodon 30 35
1459 2m. Apatosaurus 30 35
1460 2m. Peteinosaurus 30 35
1461 2m. Tropeognathus 30 35
1462 2m. Pteranodon ingens 30 35
1463 2m. Ornithodesmus 30 35
1464 2m. Wuerhosaurus 30 35
MS1465 Three sheets, each 100 × 70 mm. (a) 10m. Coelophysis (vert). (b) 10m. Tyrannosaurus (vert). (c) 10m. Woolly Rhinoceros. Set of 3 sheets 3·00 3·25
Nos. 1438/46, 1447/55 and 1456/64 respectively were printed together, se-tenant, with the backgrounds forming composite designs.

256 Treefish

1998. Year of the Ocean. Fishes. Multicoloured.
1466 1m. Type **256** 15 20
1467 1m. Tigerbarb 15 20
1468 1m. Bandtail puffer 15 20
1469 1m. Cod 15 20
1470 1m.50 Clown loach 25 30
1471 1m.50 Christy's lyretail 25 30
1472 1m.50 Filefish 25 30
1473 1m.50 Sicklefin killie 25 30
1474 2m. Brook trout 30 35
1475 2m. Emerald betta 30 35
1476 2m. Pacific electric ray 30 35
1477 2m. Bighead searobin 30 35
1478 2m. Weakfish 30 35
1479 2m. Red drum 30 35
1480 2m. Blue marlin 30 35
1481 2m. Yellowfin tuna 30 35
1482 2m. Barracuda 30 35
1483 2m. Striped bass 30 35
1484 2m. White shark 30 35
1485 2m. Permit 30 35
1486 2m. Purple firefish 30 35
1487 2m. Harlequin sweetlips 30 35
1488 2m. Clown wrasse 30 35
1489 2m. Bicolour angelfish 30 35
1490 2m. False cleanerfish 30 35
1491 2m. Mandarinfish 30 35
1492 2m. Regal tang 30 35
1493 2m. Clownfish 30 35
1494 2m. Bluegill 30 35
1495 2m. Grayling 30 35
1496 2m. Walleye 30 35
1497 2m. Brown trout 30 35
1498 2m. Atlantic salmon 30 35
1499 2m. Northern pike 30 35
1500 2m. Large-mouth bass 30 35
1501 2m. Rainbow trout 30 35
1502 2m. Platy variatus 30 35
1503 2m. Archerfish 30 35
1504 2m. Clown knifefish 30 35
1505 2m. Angelicus 30 35
1506 2m. Black arowana 30 35
1507 2m. Spotted scat 30 35
1508 2m. Kribensis 30 35
1509 2m. Golden pheasant 30 35
1510 3m. Harlequin tuskfish 45 50
1511 4m. Half-moon angelfish 60 65
1512 5m. Spotted trunkfish 75 80
1513 6m. Wolf eel 90 95
1514 7m. Cherubfish 1·25 1·40
MS1515 Four sheets, each 98 × 73 mm. (a) 12m. Common Carp. (b) 12m. Sockeye Salmon. (c) 12m. Winter Flounder. (d) 12m. Horn Shark. Set of 4 sheets 7·25 7·50
Nos. 1470/3 show the face value as "M1.5".

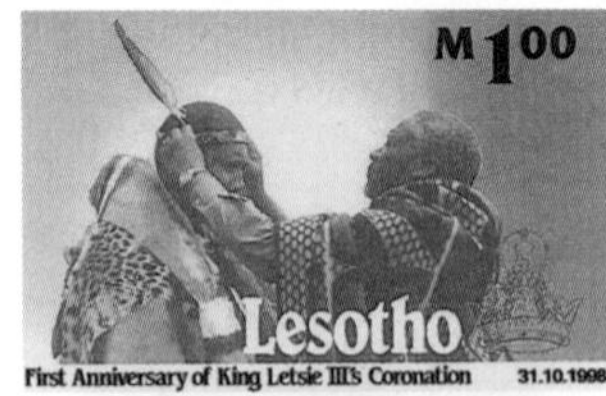

257 Crowning of King Letsie III

1998. 1st Anniv of Coronation of King Letsie III. Multicoloured.
1516 1m. Type **257** 15 20
1517 1m. King saluting Basotho nation 15 20
1518 1m. King Letsie in profile 15 20

258 "Pelargonium sidoides"

1998. Flowers. Multicoloured.
1519 10s. Type **258** 10 10
1520 15s. "Aponogeton ranunculiflorus" 10 10
1521 20s. "Sebaea leiostyla" 10 10
1522 40s. "Sebaea grandis" 10 10
1523 50s. "Satyrium neglectum" 10 10
1524 60s. "Massonia jasminiflora" 10 10
1525 70s. "Ajuga ophrydis" 10 10
1526 80s. "Nemesia fruticans" 10 10
1527 1m. "Aloe broomii" 15 20
1528 2m. "Wahlenbergia androsacea" 30 35
1529 2m.50 "Phygelius capensis" 40 45
1530 3m. "Dianthus basuticus" 45 50
1531 4m.50 "Rhodohypoxis baurii" 70 75
1532 5m. "Turbina oblongata" 75 80
1533 6m. "Hibiscus microcarpus" 90 95
1534 10m. "Lobelia erinus" ("Moraea stricta") 1·50 1·60

259 Japanese Akita

1999. Dogs. Multicoloured.
1535 70s. Type **259** 10 10
1536 1m. Canaan dog 15 20
1537 2m. Husky ("ESKIMO DOG") 30 35
1538 2m. Cirneco dell'Etna 30 35
1539 2m. Afghan hound 30 35
1540 2m. Finnish spitz 30 35
1541 2m. Dalmatian 30 35
1542 2m. Basset hound 30 35
1543 2m. Shar-pei 30 35
1544 2m. Boxer 30 35
1545 2m. Catalan sheepdog 30 35
1546 2m. English toy spaniel 30 35
1547 2m. Greyhound 30 35
1548 2m. Keeshond 30 35
1549 2m. Bearded collie 30 35
1550 4m.50 Norwegian elkhound 70 75
MS1551 Two sheets, each 98 × 69 mm. (a) 8m. Rough Collie. (b) 8m. Borzoi. Set of 2 sheets 2·40 2·50
Nos. 1538/43 and 1544/9 were printed together, se-tenant, with the backgrounds forming composite designs.

260 Belted Kingfisher

1999. Birds. Multicoloured.
1552 70s. Type **260** 10 10
1553 1m.50 Palm cockatoo (vert) 25 30
1554 2m. Red-tailed hawk 30 35
1555 2m. Evening grosbeak 30 35
1556 2m. Blue-winged pitta ("Lesser Blue-winged Pitta") 30 35
1557 2m. Lichtenstein's oriole ("Atlamira Oriole") 30 35
1558 2m. Rose-breasted grosbeak 30 35
1559 2m. Yellow warbler 30 35
1560 2m. Akiapolaau 30 35
1561 2m. American goldfinch 30 35
1562 2m. Common flicker ("Northern Flicker") 30 35
1563 2m. Western tanager 30 35
1564 2m. Blue jay (vert) 30 35
1565 2m. Common cardinal ("Northern Cardinal") (vert) 30 35
1566 2m. Yellow-headed blackbird (vert) 30 35
1567 2m. Red crossbill (vert) 30 35
1568 2m. Cedar waxwing (vert) 30 35
1569 2m. Vermilion flycatcher (vert) 30 35
1570 2m. Pileated woodpecker (vert) 30 35
1571 2m. Western meadowlark (vert) 30 35
1572 2m. Belted kingfisher ("Kingfisher") (vert) 30 35
1573 3m. Tufted puffin 45 50
1574 4m. Reddish egret 60 65
1575 5m. Hoatzin (vert) 75 80
MS1576 Two sheets. (a) 76 × 106 mm. 8m. Great egret. (b) 106 × 76 mm. 8m. Chestnut-flanked white-eye "Zosterops erythropleura". Set of 2 sheets 2·40 2·50
No. 1553 shows the face value as "M1.5".
Nos. 1555/63 and 1564/72 were printed together, se-tenant, with the backgrounds forming composite designs.

261 "Cattleya dowiana"

1999. Orchids of the World. Multicoloured.
1577 1m.50 Type **261** 25 30
1578 2m. "Cochleanthes discolor" 30 35
1579 2m. "Cischweinfia dasyandra" 30 35
1580 2m. "Ceratostylis retisquama" 30 35
1581 2m. "Comparettia speciosa" 30 35
1582 2m. "Cryptostylis subulata" 30 35
1583 2m. "Cycnoches ventricosum" 30 35

1584 2m. "Dactylorhiza maculata" 30 35
1585 2m. "Cypripedium calceolus" 30 35
1586 2m. "Cymbidium finlaysonianum" 30 35
1587 2m. "Apasia epidendroides" 30 35
1588 2m. "Barkaria lindleyana" 30 35
1589 2m. "Bifrenaria tetragona" 30 35
1590 2m. "Bulbophyllum graveolens" 30 35
1591 2m. "Brassavola flagellaris" 30 35
1592 2m. "Bollea lawrenceana" 30 35
1593 2m. "Caladenia carnea" . . 30 35
1594 2m. "Catasetum macrocarpum" 30 35
1595 2m. "Cattleya aurantiaca" 30 35
1596 2m. "Dendrobium bellatulum" 30 35
1597 2m. "Dendrobium trigonopus" 30 35
1598 2m. "Dimerandra emarginata" 30 35
1599 2m. "Dressleria eburnea" . . 30 35
1600 2m. "Dracula tubeana" . . 30 35
1601 2m. "Disa kirstenbosch" . . 30 35
1602 2m. "Encyclia alata" . . . 30 35
1603 2m. "Epidendrum pseudepidendrum" . . . 30 35
1604 2m. "Eriopsis biloba" . . . 30 35
1605 3m. "Diurus behrii" 45 50
1606 4m. "Ancistrochilus rothchildianus" 60 65
1607 5m. "Aerangis curnowiana" 75 80
1608 7m. "Arachnis flos-aeris" . . 1·10 1·25
1609 8m. "Aspasia principissa" 1·25 1·40
MS1610 Four sheets, each 110×82 mm. (a) 10m. "Paphiopedilum tonsum". (b) 10m. "Ansellia africana". (c) 10m. "Laelia rubescens". (d) 10m. "Ophrys apifera". Set of 4 sheets 6·00 6·25

No. 1583 was inscribed "Cycnoches ventricsum" in error.

262 "Austerity" Type Series 52 Steam Locomotive, Frankfurt, 1939

1999. "iBRA '99" International Stamp Exhibition, Nuremburg. Railway Locomotives. Multicoloured.
1611 7m. Type **262** . . . . 1·10 1·25
1612 8m. "Adler" and Brandenburg Gate, Berlin, 1835 . . . . 1·25 1·40

263 "View of Sumida River in Snow"

1999. 150th Death Anniv of Katsushika Hokusai (Japanese artist). Multicoloured.
1613 3m. Type **263** 45 50
1614 3m. "Two Carp" 45 50
1615 3m. "The Blind" (woman with eyes closed) 45 50
1616 3m. "The Blind" (woman with one eye open) . . . 45 50
1617 3m. "Fishing by Torchlight" 45 50
1618 3m. "Whaling off the Goto Islands" 45 50
1619 3m. "Makamaro watching the Moon from a Hill" 45 50
1620 3m. "Peonies and Butterfly" 45 50
1621 3m. "The Blind" (old man with open eyes) 45 50
1622 3m. "The Blind" (old man with one eye open) . . . 45 50
1623 3m. "People crossing an Arched Bridge" (four people on bridge) 45 50
1624 3m. "People crossing an Arched Bridge" (two people on bridge) 45 50
MS1625 Two sheets, each 102×72 mm. (a) 10m. "Bell-flower and Dragonfly" (vert). (b) 10m. "Moon above Yodo River and Osaka Castle" (vert). Set of 2 sheets . . . . 3·00 3·25

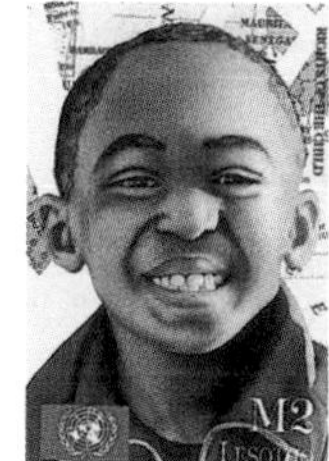

264 African Boy

1999. 10th Anniv of United Nations Rights of the Child Convention. Multicoloured.
1626 2m. Type **264** 30 35
1627 2m. Asian girl 30 35
1628 2m. European boy 30 35

Nos. 1626/8 were printed together, se-tenant, the backgrounds forming a composite design.

265 Mephistopheles appearing as Dog in Faust's Study

1999. 250th Birth Anniv of Johann von Goethe (German writer).
1629 **265** 6m. multicoloured . . . 90 95
1630 – 6m. blue, lilac and black 90 95
1631 – 6m. multicoloured . . . 90 95
MS1632 76×106 mm. 12m. red, violet and black . . . . 1·75 1·90

DESIGNS—HORIZ: No. 1630, Goethe and Schiller; 1631, Mephistopheles disguised as a dog scorching the Earth. VERT: No. MS1632, Mephistopheles.

No. 1629, in addition to the normal country name, shows "GUYANA" twice in violet across the centre of the design.

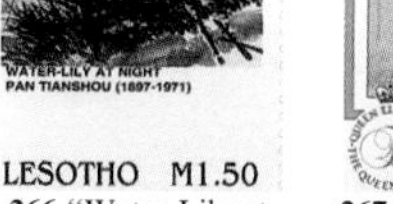

266 "Water Lily at Night" (Pan Tianshou)
267 Queen Elizabeth, 1938

1999. "China '99" International Stamp Exhibition, Beijing. Paintings of Pan Tianshou (Chinese artist). Multicoloured.
1633 1m.50 Type **266** 25 30
1634 1m.50 "Hen and Chicks" . . 25 30
1635 1m.50 "Plum Blossom and Orchid" 25 30
1636 1m.50 "Plum Blossom and Banana Tree" 25 30
1637 1m.50 "Crane and Pine" . . 25 30
1638 1m.50 "Swallows" 25 30
1639 1m.50 "Eagle on the Pine" (bird looking up) 25 30
1640 1m.50 "Palm Tree" 25 30
1641 1m.50 "Eagle on the Pine" (bird looking down) . . . 25 30
1642 1m.50 "Orchids" 25 30
MS1643 138×105 mm. 6m. "Sponge Gourd" (51×39 mm); 6m. "Dragonfly" (51×39 mm) . . 1·75 1·90

1999. "Queen Elizabeth the Queen Mother's Century".
1644 **267** 5m. black and gold . . . 75 80
1645 – 5m. multicoloured . . . 75 80
1646 – 5m. black and gold . . . 75 80
1647 – 5m. multicoloured . . . 75 80
MS1648 153×152 mm. 15m. multicoloured . . . . 2·25 2·40

DESIGNS: No. 1645, King George VI and Queen Elizabeth, 1948; 1646, Queen Mother wearing tiara, 1963; 1647, Queen Mother wearing blue hat, Canada, 1989. 37×50 mm.—No. MS1648, Queen Mother outside Clarence House.

No. MS1648 also shows the Royal Arms embossed in gold.

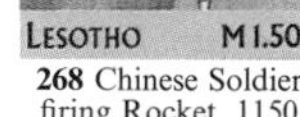

268 Chinese Soldier firing Rocket, 1150
270 King Letsie III and Miss Karabo Anne Motsoeneng

269 U.S.S. "New Jersey" (battleship)

1999. New Millennium. People and Events of Twelfth Century (1150–99). Multicoloured.
1649 1m.50 Type **268** 25 30
1650 1m.50 Burmese temple guardian, 1150 . . . . 25 30
1651 1m.50 Troubadour serenading Lady, 1150 . . 25 30
1652 1m.50 Abbot Suger (advisor to French Kings), 1150 25 30
1653 1m.50 Pope Adrian IV, 1154 25 30
1654 1m.50 Henry II of England, 1154 . . . . 25 30
1655 1m.50 Bust of Frederick Barbarossa, King of Germany, and Holy Roman Emperor, 1155 . . 25 30
1656 1m.50 Shogun Yoritomo of Japan, 1156 . . . . . 25 30
1657 1m.50 Count and Countess of Vaudemont (Crusader monument), 1165 . . . 25 30
1658 1m.50 Ibn Rushd (Arab translator), 1169 . . . 25 30
1659 1m.50 Archbishop Thomas a Becket, 1170 . . . . 25 30
1660 1m.50 Leaning Tower of Pisa, 1174 . . . . . . 25 30
1661 1m.50 Pivot windmill, 1180 25 30
1662 1m.50 Saladin (Saracen general), 1187 . . . . 25 30
1663 1m.50 King Richard the Lionheart of England, 1189 . . . . 25 30
1664 1m.50 Moai (statues), Easter Island, 1150 (59×39 mm) 25 30
1665 1m.50 Crusader, 1189 . . . 25 30

1999. Maritime Developments 1700–2000. Mult.
1666 4m. Type **269** 60 65
1667 4m. "Aquila" (Italian aircraft carrier) 60 65
1668 4m. "De Zeven Provincien" (Dutch cruiser) 60 65
1669 4m. H.M.S. "Formidable" (aircraft carrier) 60 65
1670 4m. "Vittorio Veneto" (Italian cruiser) 60 65
1671 4m. H.M.S. "Hampshire" (destroyer) 60 65
1672 4m. "France" (French liner) 60 65
1673 4m. "Queen Elizabeth 2" (liner) 60 65
1674 4m. "United States" (American liner) . . . 60 65
1675 4m. "Queen Elizabeth" (liner) 60 65
1676 4m. "Michelangelo" (Italian liner) 60 65
1677 4m. "Mauretania" (British liner) 60 65
1678 4m. "Shearwater" (British hydrofoil ferry) 60 65
1679 4m. British Class M submarine 60 65
1680 4m. SRN 130 hovercraft . . 60 65
1681 4m. Italian Second World War submarine 60 65
1682 4m. SRN 3 hovercraft . . 60 65
1683 4m. "Soucoupe Plongeante" (oceanographic submersible) 60 65
1684 4m. "James Watt" (early steamship) 60 65
1685 4m. "Savannah" (steam/sail ship), 1819 . . . . . . 60 65
1686 4m. "Amistad" (slave schooner) 60 65
1687 4m. American Navy brig . . 60 65
1688 4m. "Great Britain" (liner) 60 65
1689 4m. "Sirius" (paddle steamer) 60 65
MS1690 Four sheets, each 106×76 mm. (a) 15m. U.S.S. "Enterprise" (aircraft carrier) (vert). (b) 15m. "Titanic" (liner). (c) 15m. German U-boat. (d) 15m. "E. W. Morrison" (Great Lakes schooner) (vert). Set of 4 sheets 9·00 9·25

Nos. 1686 and 1687 both have their names wrongly inscribed as "ARMISTAD" and "BRICK" on the sheet margin.

2000. Wedding of King Letsie III. Multicoloured.
1691 1m. Type **270** 15 20
1692 1m. Miss Karabo Anne Motsoeneng 15 20
1693 1m. King Letsie III 15 20
1694 1m. King Letsie III and Miss Karabo Motsoeneng in traditional dress . . . 15 20

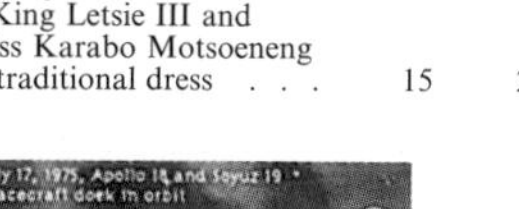

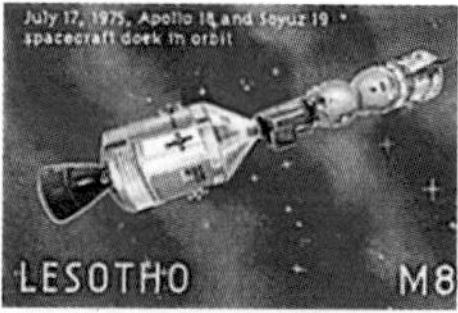

271 "Apollo 18" and "Soyuz 19" docked in Orbit

2000. 25th Anniv of "Apollo–Soyuz" Joint Project. Multicoloured.
1695 8m. Type **271** . . . . . . 1·25 1·40
1696 8m. "Apollo 18" and docking module . . . . . 1·25 1·40
1697 8m. "Soyuz 19" . . . . . . 1·25 1·40
MS1698 106×76mm. 15m. Docking module and "Soyuz 19" . . . 2·25 2·40

272 Gena Rowlands (actress), 1978
274 Johann Sebastian Bach

273 George Stephenson

2000. 50th Anniv of Berlin Film Festival. Showing actors, directors and film scenes with awards. Multicoloured.
1699 6m. Type **272** 90 95
1700 6m. Vlastimil Brodsky (actor), 1975 . . . . . 90 95
1701 6m. Carlos Saura (director), 1966 . . . . 90 95
1702 6m. Scene from *La Collectionneuse*, 1967 . . 90 95
1703 6m. Scene from *Le Depart*, 1967 . . . . 90 95
1704 6m. Scene from *Le Diable Probablement*, 1977 . . . 90 95
MS1705 97×103 mm. 15m. Scene from *Stammeheim*, 1986 . . . 2·25 2·40

No. 1704 is inscribed "LE DIIABLE PROBABLEMENT" in error.

2000. 175th Anniv of Stockton and Darlington Line (first public railway). Multicoloured.
1706 8m. Type **273** . . . . 1·25 1·40
1707 8m. Stephenson's Patent locomotive . . . . 1·25 1·40
1708 8m. Robert Stephenson's Britannia Tubular Bridge, Menai Straits . . . . . . 1·25 1·40

2000. 250th Death Anniv of Johann Sebastian Bach (German composer). Sheet 105×101 mm.
MS1709 **274** 15m. multicoloured 2·25 2·40

275 Albert Einstein

2000. Election of Albert Einstein (mathematical physicist) as *Time Magazine* "Man of the Century". Sheet 117×91 mm.
MS1710 **275** 15m. multicoloured 2·25 2·40

276 Ferdinand Zeppelin and LZ-127 *Graf Zeppelin*, 1928

2000. Centenary of First Zeppelin Flight. Mult.
1711 8m. Type **276** . . . . 1·25 1·40
1712 8m. LZ-130 *Graf Zeppelin II*, 1938 . . . . 1·25 1·40
1713 8m. LZ-10 *Schwaben*, 1911 1·25 1·40
MS1714 83 × 119 mm. 15m. LZ-130 *Graf Zeppelin II*, 1938 (50 × 37 mm) . . . . 2·25 2·40

277 Nedo Nadi (Italian fencer), 1920

2000. Olympic Games, Sydney. Multicoloured.
1715 6m. Type **277** 90 95
1716 6m. Swimming (butterfly stroke) 90 95
1717 6m. Aztec Stadium, Mexico City, 1968 . . . . 90 95
1718 6m. Ancient Greek boxing 90 95

278 Prince William in Evening Dress

279 Spotted-leaved Arum

2000. 18th Birthday of Prince William. Multicoloured.
1719 4m. Type **278** 60 65
1720 4m. Wearing coat and scarf 60 65
1721 4m. Wearing striped shirt and tie 60 65
1722 4m. Getting out of car . . . 60 65
MS1723 100 × 80 mm. 15m. Prince William (37 × 50 mm) . . . . 2·25 2·40

2000. African Flowers. Multicoloured.
1724 3m. Type **279** 45 50
1725 3m. Christmas bells 45 50
1726 3m. Lady Monson 45 50
1727 3m. Wild pomegranate . . . 45 50
1728 3m. Blushing bride 45 50
1729 3m. Bot River protea . . . 45 50
1730 3m. Drooping agapanthus 45 50
1731 3m. Yellow marsh Afrikander 45 50
1732 3m. Weak-stemmed painted lady 45 50
1733 3m. Impala lily 45 50
1734 3m. Beatrice Watsonia . . . 45 50
1735 3m. Pink arum 45 50
1736 3m. Starry gardenia 45 50
1737 3m. Pink hibiscus 45 50
1738 3m. Dwarf poker 45 50
1739 3m. Coast kaffirboom . . . 45 50
1740 3m. Rose cockade 45 50
1741 3m. Pride of Table Mountain 45 50
1742 4m. Moore's crinum 60 65
1743 5m. Flame lily 75 80
1744 6m. Cape clivia 90 95
1745 8m. True sugarbush . . . . 1·25 1·40
MS1746 Two sheets, each 107 × 77 mm. (a) 15m. Red Hairy Erika (horiz). (b) 15m. Green Arum. Set of 2 sheets . . . . 4·50 4·75

Nos. 1724/9, 1730/5 and 1736/41 were each printed together, se-tenant, with the backgrounds forming composite designs.

No. 1733 is inscribed "LIly", No. 1736 "Gardenia thunbengii" and No. 1741 "Disa unoflora", all in error.

280 Black Rhinoceros

2000. "The Stamp Show 2000", International Stamp Exhibition, London. Endangered Wildlife. Multicoloured.
1747 4m. Type **280** 60 65
1748 4m. Leopard 60 65
1749 4m. Roseate tern 60 65
1750 4m. Mountain gorilla . . . 60 65
1751 4m. Mountain zebra 60 65
1752 4m. Zanzibar red colobus monkey 60 65
1753 4m. Cholo alethe 60 65
1754 4m. Temminck's pangolin 60 65
1755 4m. Cheetah 60 65
1756 4m. African elephant . . . 60 65
1757 4m. Chimpanzee 60 65
1758 4m. Northern white rhinoceros 60 65
1759 5m. Blue wildebeest 75 80
1760 5m. Tree hyrax 75 80
1761 5m. Red lechwe 75 80
1762 5m. Eland 75 80
MS1763 Two sheets, each 65 × 118 mm. (a) 15m. Dugong (vert). (b) 15m. West African Manatee (vert). Set of 2 sheets 4·50 4·75

Nos. 1747/52, 1753/8 and 1759/62 were each printed together, se-tenant, with the backgrounds forming composite designs.

281 Cadillac Eldorado Seville (1960)

2000. Classic Cars. Multicoloured.
1764 3m. Type **281** 45 50
1765 3m. Citroen DS (1955–75) 45 50
1766 3m. Ford Zephyr Zodiac MK II (1961) 45 50
1767 3m. MG TF (1945–55) . . . 45 50
1768 3m. Porsche 356 (1949–65) 45 50
1769 3m. Ford Thunderbird (1955) 45 50
1770 3m. Cisitalia 202 Coupe (1948–52) 45 50
1771 3m. Dodge Viper (1990s) . . 45 50
1772 3m. TVR Vixen SI (1968–69) 45 50
1773 3m. Lotus 7 (1957–70) . . . 45 50
1774 3m. Ferrari 275 GTB/4 (1964–68) 45 50
1775 3m. Pegasus - Touring Spider (1951–58) 45 50
1776 4m. Fiat Type O (1913) . . 60 65
1777 4m. Stutz Bearcat (1914) . . 60 65
1778 4m. French Leyat (1924) . . 60 65
1779 4m. Benz gasoline-driven Motorwagon (1886) . . . 60 65
1780 4m. Isotta Fraschini Type 8A (1925) 60 65
1781 4m. Markus Motor Carriage (1887) 60 65
1782 4m. Morris Minor (1951) . . 60 65
1783 4m. Hispano-Suiza Type 68 (1935) 60 65
1784 4m. MG TC (1949) 60 65
1785 4m. Morgan 4/4 (1955) . . 60 65
1786 4m. Jaguar XK120 (1950) 60 65
1787 4m. Triumph 1800/2000 Roadster (1946–49) . . . 60 65
MS1788 Four sheets. (a) 110 × 85 mm. 15m. AC ACE (1953–63). (b) 110 × 85 mm. 15m. Morris Minor 1000 (1948–71). (c) 85 × 110 mm. 15m. Ferrari F 40 (vert). (d) 110 × 85 mm. 15m. Bersey Electric Cab (1896). Set of 4 sheets . . . . 9·00 9·25

282 Basotho Warrior fighting "AIDS"

2001. Fight Against Aids. Multicoloured.
1789 70c. Type **282** 10 15
1790 1m. "Speed Kills So Does Aids" 15 20
1791 1m.50 "People with Aids need friends not rejection" 25 30
1792 2m.10 "Even when you're off duty protect the nation" 30 35

283 Great Orange Tip

2001. Butterflies. Multicoloured.
1793 70s. Type **283** 10 15
1794 1m. Red-banded pereute . . 15 20
1795 1m.50 Sword grass brown 25 30
1796 2m. Striped blue crow . . . 30 35
1797 2m. Orange-banded sulphur 30 35
1798 2m. Large wood nymph . . 30 35
1799 2m. The postman 30 35
1800 2m. Palmfly 30 35
1801 2m. Gulf fritillary 30 35
1802 2m. Cairns birdwing 30 35
1803 2m. Common morpho . . . 30 35
1804 2m. Common dotted border 30 35
1805 2m. African migrant 30 35
1806 2m. Large oak blue 30 35
1807 2m. The wanderer 30 35
1808 2m. Tiger swallowtail . . . 30 35
1809 2m. Union jack 30 35
1810 2m. Saturn 30 35
1811 2m. Broad-bordered grass yellow 30 35
1812 2m. Hewitson's uraneis . . 30 35
1813 3m. Bertoni's antwren bird 45 50
1814 3m. Clorinde 45 50
1815 3m. Iolas blue 45 50
1816 3m. Mocker swallowtail . . 45 50
1817 3m. Common Indian crow 45 50
1818 3m. Grecian shoemaker . . 45 50
1819 3m. Small flambeau 45 50
1820 3m. Orchid swallowtail . . . 45 50
1821 3m. Alfalfa butterfly 45 50
1822 4m. Doris butterfly 60 65
MS1823 Two sheets, each 70 × 100 mm. (a) 15m. Forest Queen. (b) 15m. Crimson Tip. Set of 2 sheets . . . . . . 4·50 4·75

Nos. 1797/1804, 1805/12 and 1813/20 were each printed together, se-tenant, with the backgrounds forming composite designs.

284 Roman General and Soldiers from "Battle of Lepanto and Map of the World" (anon)

2001. "Philanippon 01" International Stamp Exhibition, Tokyo. Paintings from Momoyama Era. Multicoloured.
1824 1m.50 Type **284** 25 30
1825 2m. Pikemen and musketeers from "Battle of Lepanto and Map of the World" 30 35
1826 3m. Manchurian crane from "Birds and Flowers of the Four Seasons" (Kano Eitoku) 45 50
1827 4m. Travellers in the mountains from "Birds and Flowers of the Four Seasons" 60 65
1828 5m. "Portrait of a Lady" (24½ × 81½ mm) 75 80
1829 5m. "Honda Tadakatsu" (24½ × 81½ mm) 75 80
1830 5m. "Wife of Goto Tokujo" (24½ × 81½ mm) 75 80
1831 5m. "Emperor Go-Yozei" (Kano Takanobu) (24½ × 81½ mm) 75 80
1832 5m. "Tenzuiin Hideyoshi's Mother, Hoshuku Sochin" (24½ × 81½ mm) 75 80
1833 6m. "Hosokawa Yusai" (Ishin Suden) (24½ × 81½ mm) 90 95
1834 6m. "Sen No Rikyu" (attr Hasegawa Tohaku) (24½ × 81½ mm) 90 95
1835 6m. "Oichi No Kata" (24½ × 81½ mm) 90 95
1836 6m. "Inaba Ittetsu" (attr Hasegawa Tohaku) (24½ × 81½ mm) 90 95
1837 6m. "Oda Nobunaga" (Kokei Sochin) (24½ × 81½ mm) 90 95
1838 7m. "Viewing the Maples at Mount Takao" . . . . . 1·10 1·25
1839 8m. "The Four Accomplishments" (Kaiho Yusho) . . . . 1·25 1·40
MS1840 Two sheets. (a) 98 × 131 mm. 15m. "Tokugawa Ieyasu". (b) 114 × 134 mm. 15m. "Toyotomi Hideyoshi". Set of 2 sheets . . . . 4·50 4·75

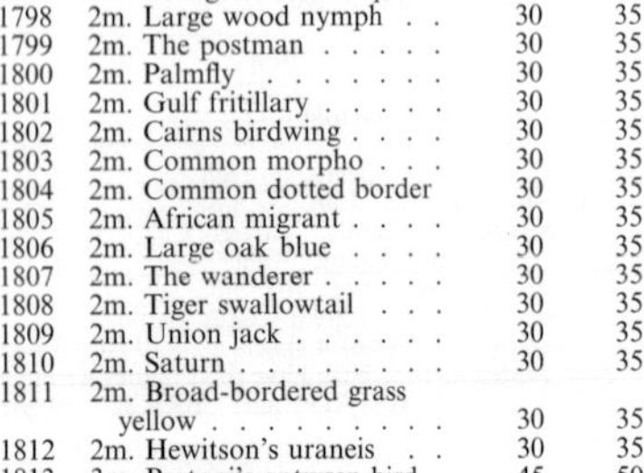

285 *Cortinarius violaceus*

287 Black Kite

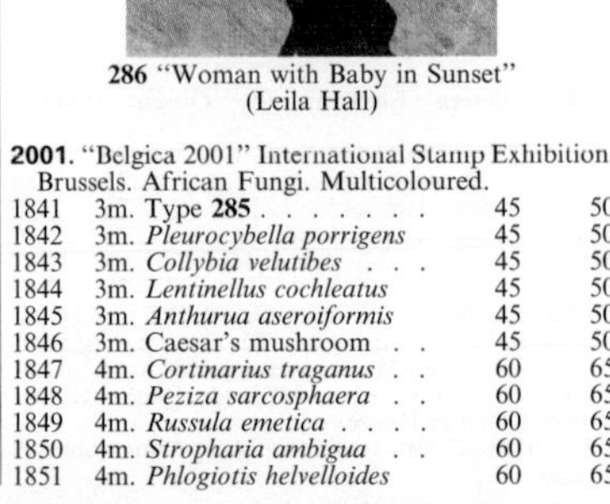

286 "Woman with Baby in Sunset" (Leila Hall)

2001. "Belgica 2001" International Stamp Exhibition, Brussels. African Fungi. Multicoloured.
1841 3m. Type **285** 45 50
1842 3m. *Pleurocybella porrigens* 45 50
1843 3m. *Collybia velutibes* . . . 45 50
1844 3m. *Lentinellus cochleatus* 45 50
1845 3m. *Anthurua aseroiformis* 45 50
1846 3m. Caesar's mushroom . . . 45 50
1847 4m. *Cortinarius traganus* . . 60 65
1848 4m. *Peziza sarcosphaera* . . 60 65
1849 4m. *Russula emetica* 60 65
1850 4m. *Stropharia ambigua* . . 60 65
1851 4m. *Phlogiotis helvelloides* 60 65
1852 4m. *Clitocybe odora* 60 65
1853 5m. Golden false pholiota 75 80
1854 5m. *Coprinus micaceus* . . . 75 80
1855 5m. *Hygrophorus camarophyllus* 75 80
1856 5m. *Panaeolus campanulatus* 75 80
MS1857 Two sheets, each 75 × 55 mm. (a) 15m. *Boletus parasiticus* (horiz). (b) 15m. *Hygrophorus hygrocybe conicus* (horiz). Set of 2 sheets . . . . 4·50 4·75

No. 1841 is inscribed "violaceys", 1842 "Pleyrocybella", 1844 "Cochleathus", 1852 "Clitoeybe" and 1856 "Panaelus companulatus", all in error.

2001. Winners of United Nations Children's Art Competition. Multicoloured.
1858 70s. Type **286** 10 15
1859 1m. "Herdboy with Lamb" (Chambeli Ramathe) . . . 15 20
1860 1m.50 "Girl with A.I.D.S. Ribbon" (Chambeli Ramathe) (vert) 25 30
1861 2m.10 "Satellite Dish and Map seen through Keyhole" (Mika Sejake) (vert) 30 35

2001. Birds of Prey. Multicoloured.
1862 70s. Type **287** 10 15
1863 1m. Martial eagle 15 20
1864 1m.50 Bateleur 25 30
1865 2m.10 African goshawk . . 30 35
1866 2m.50 Lammergeier ("Bearded Vulture") . . . 40 45
1867 3m. Jackal buzzard 45 50

No. 1865 is inscribed "GASHAWK" in error.

288 Grass Owl

2001. Wildlife of Southern Africa. Multicoloured.
1868 1m. Type **288** 15 20
1869 2m.10 Klipspringer 30 35
1870 3m. Saddle-backed jackal . . 45 50
1871 4m. Aardvark 60 65
1872 4m. Common kestrel ("Rock Kestrel") 60 65
1873 4m. Black-footed cat 60 65
1874 4m. Springhare 60 65
1875 4m. Aardwolf 60 65
1876 4m. Rock hyrax 60 65
1877 4m. Damara zebra 60 65
1878 4m. Bontebok 60 65
1879 4m. Eland 60 65
1880 4m. Lion 60 65
1881 4m. Saddle-backed jackal . . 60 65
1882 4m. Black kite ("Yellow-billed Kite") 60 65
1883 5m. Black wildebeest . . . 75 80
MS1884 Two sheets, each 90 × 64 mm. (a) 15m. Black-shouldered kite. (b) 15m. Caracal (vert). Set of 2 sheets . . . . . 4·50 4·75

Nos. 1871/6 and 1877/82 were each printed together, se-tenant, with the backgrounds forming composite designs.

289 Queen Elizabeth wearing Purple Coat

2002. Golden Jubilee. Multicoloured.
1885 8m. Type **289** . . . . 1·25 1·40
1886 8m. Queen Elizabeth with Duke of Edinburgh on launch . . . . 1·25 1·40
1887 8m. Queen Elizabeth with mayor . . . . 1·25 1·40
1888 8m. Duke of Edinburgh wearing sunglasses . . . 1·25 1·40
MS1889 76 × 108 mm. 20m. Queen Elizabeth inspecting R.A.F. guard of honour . . . . 3·00 3·25

290 Homer Wood (Rotary pioneer)

2002. 25th Anniv of Rotary International in Lesotho. Multicoloured.
1890 8m. Type **290** . . . . 1·25 1·40
1891 10m. Paul Harris (founder of Rotary International) 1·50 1·60
MS1892 Two sheets. (a) 60 × 75 mm. 25m. Coloured globe and Rotary logo. (b) 75 × 60 mm. 25m. Golden Gate Bridge, San Francisco, and Rotary logo (horiz) . . . . . 7·75 8·00
No. 1890 is inscribed "HORNER" in error.

291 Machache

2002. International Year of Mountains. Showing Lesotho mountains (except No. **MS**1897). Multicoloured.
1893 8m. Type **291** . . . . 1·25 1·40
1894 8m. Thabana-li-Mele . . . 1·25 1·40
1895 8m. Qiloane . . . . 1·25 1·40
1896 8m. Thaba-Bosiu . . . . . 1·25 1·40
MS1897 64 × 83 mm. 25m. The Matterhorn, Switzerland (vert) 3·75 4·00
No. MS1897 is inscribed "Mount Rainer" in error.

292 Boys with Calf, Lithabaneng

2002. S.O.S. Children's Villages (Kinderdorf International).
1898 **292** 10m. multicoloured . . . 1·50 1·60

293 Spiral Aloe

2002. U.N. Year of Eco Tourism. Multicoloured.
1899 6m. Type **293** 90 95
1900 6m. Athrixia gerradii (flower) 90 95
1901 6m. Horseman and packhorse 90 95
1902 6m. Lion 90 95
1903 6m. Frog 90 95
1904 6m. Thatched building . . . 90 95
MS1905 77 × 83 mm. 20m. European bee eater (vert) . . . . 3·00 3·25

294 U.S. Flag as Statue of Liberty with Lesotho Flag

2002. "United We Stand". Support for Victims of 11 September 2001 Terrorist Attacks.
1906 **294** 7m. multicoloured . . . 1·10 1·25

295 Sheet Bend Knot

2002. 20th World Scout Jamboree, Thailand. Multicoloured.
1907 9m. Type **295** . . . . 1·40 1·50
1908 9m. Pup and forester tents 1·40 1·50
1909 9m. Scouts in canoe . . . . 1·40 1·50
1910 9m. Life-saving . . . . . . 1·40 1·50
MS1911 75 × 59 mm. 25m. Scouts asleep in tent . . . . 3·75 4·00

POSTAGE DUE STAMPS

1966. Nos. D9/10 of Basutoland optd **LESOTHO**.
D11 D **2** 1c. red 30 75
D12 5c. violet 30 90

D 1

D 2

1967.
D13 D **1** 1c. blue . . . . 15 3·00
D14 2c. red . . . . 15 3·50
D15 5c. green . . . . 20 3·50

1986.
D19 D **2** 2s. green . . . . 20 1·25
D20 5s. blue . . . . 20 1·25
D21 35s. violet . . . . 60 1·50

APPENDIX

The following stamps have either been issued in excess of postal needs, or have not been available to the public in reasonable quantities at face value.

1981.

15th Anniv of Independence. Classic Stamps of the World. 10m. × 40, each embossed on gold foil.

LIBERIA Pt. 13

A republic on the W. coast of Africa, founded as a home for freed slaves.

100 cents = 1 dollar.

1

2

1860.
7 **1** 6c. red . . . . 23·00 32·00
8 12c. blue . . . . 20·00 32·00
9 24c. green . . . . 23·00 32·00

1880.
13 **1** 1c. blue . . . . 3·25 4·75
14 2c. red . . . . 2·25 3·25
15 6c. mauve . . . . 4·25 5·50
16 12c. yellow . . . . 4·25 6·00
17 24c. red . . . . 5·00 6·75

1881.
18 **2** 3c. black . . . . 4·25 4·00

3

4

5 "Alligator" (first settlers' ship)

1882.
47 **3** 8c. blue . . . . 3·25 3·25
20 16c. red . . . . 4·25 3·25

1886.
49 **3** 1c. red 95 95
50 2c. green . . . . 95 1·00
23 3c. mauve . . . . 1·00 1·00
52 4c. brown . . . . 1·10 1·00
27 6c. grey . . . . 1·50 1·50
54 **4** 8c. grey . . . . 2·75 2·75
55 16c. yellow . . . . 4·25 4·25
29 **5** 32c. blue . . . . 17·00 17·00

7 Liberian Star

8 African Elephant

9 Oil Palm

10 Pres. H. R. W. Johnson

11 Vai Woman

12 Seal

13 Star

15 Hippopotamus **17** President Johnson

1892.
75 **7** 1c. red 30 30
76 2c. blue 30 30
77 **8** 4c. black and green . . . . 2·10 1·60
78 **9** 6c. green 85 75
79 **10** 8c. black and brown 60 75
80 **11** 12c. red 60 85
81 **12** 16c. lilac . . . . 2·10 1·60
82 **13** 24c. green on yellow . . . 1·50 1·25
83 **12** 32c. blue . . . . 3·00 2·50
84 **15** $1 black and blue . . . . 10·00 5·75
85 **13** $2 brown on buff . . . . 4·25 3·75
86 **17** $5 black and red . . . . 5·50 5·50

1893. Surch **5 5 Five Cents**.
103 **9** 5c. on 6c. green . . . . . . 1·50 1·50

24

1894. Imperf or roul.
117 **24** 5c. black and red . . . . 6·25 6·25

35

36

1897.
144 **9** 1c. purple 70 35
145 1c. green 85 50
146 **15** 2c. black and bistre . . . . 1·50 1·10
147 2c. black and red . . . . 1·60 1·40
148 **8** 5c. black and lake . . . . 1·60 1·10
149 5c. black and blue . . . . 3·00 2·00
150 **10** 10c. blue and yellow . . . 60 50
151 **11** 15c. black 60 65
152 **12** 20c. red . . . . 1·90 1·25
153 **13** 25c. green . . . . 1·25 85
154 **12** 30c. blue . . . . 4·25 3·00
155 **35** 50c. black and brown . . . 2·10 2·75

1897.
156 **36** 3c. red and green 25 40

1901. Official stamps of 1892–98 optd **ORDINARY**.
175 **9** 1c. purple (No. O157) . . 50·00 35·00
176 1c. green (O158) . . . . . 28·00 32·00
177 **7** 2c. blue (O120) . . . . . 75·00 80·00
178 **15** 2c. black and brown (O159) . . . . £100 45·00
179 2c. black and red (O160) 28·00 32·00
180 **24** 5c. green and lilac (O130) £225 £225
181 **8** 5c. black and red (O161) £150 £150
182 5c. black and blue (O162) 22·00 28·00
183 **10** 8c. black and brown (O122) . . . . 75·00
184 10c. blue and yellow (O163) . . . . 28·00 32·00
169 **11** 12c. red (O92) £100 £100
185 15c. black (O164) . . . . 28·00 32·00
170 **12** 16c. lilac (O93) . . . . .
186 16c. lilac (O124) £325 £325
187 20c. red (O165) . . . . . 32·00 38·00
171 **13** 24c. green and yellow (O94) £300 £300
188 24c. green on yellow (O125) . . . . 32·00 38·00
189 25c. green (O166) . . . . 32·00 38·00
190 **12** 30c. blue (O167) . . . . . 28·00 32·00
191 **13** 32c. blue (O126) £150 £150
192 **35** 50c. black & brown (O168) 38·00 42·00
172 **15** $1 black and blue (O96) . . £1300 £1300
193 $1 black and blue (O127) £225 £250
194 **13** $2 brown on buff (O128) £1300 £1300
174 **17** $5 black and red (O98) . . £3000 £3000
196 $5 black and red (O129) £1400 £1400

1902. Surch **75c.** and bar.
206 **15** 75c. on $1 black and blue 8·25 7·75

40 Liberty

1903.
209 **40** 3c. black 25 15

1903. Surch in words.
216 **12** 10c. on 16c. lilac . . . . . 2·50 4·50
217 **13** 15c. on 24c. green on yell 3·00 5·00
218 **12** 20c. on 32c. blue . . . . . 4·25 5·25

1904. Surch.
219 **9** 1c. on 5c. on 6c. green (No. 103) 60 80
220 **8** 2c. on 4c. black and green (No. O89) . . . . 2·50 3·25
221 **12** 2c. on 30c. blue (No. 154) 6·25 9·25

50 African Elephant

51 Head of Mercury

52 Mandingo Tribesmen

53 Pres. Barclay and Executive Mansion

1906.
224 **50** 1c. black and green . . . . 1·00 50
225 **51** 2c. black and red 15 15
226 – 5c. black and blue . . . . 2·00 75
227 – 10c. black and red . . . . 3·00 90
228 – 15c. green and violet . . . 7·00 2·75
229 – 20c. black and orange . . 7·25 2·50
230 – 25c. grey and blue 75 20
231 – 30c. violet 70 15
232 – 50c. black and green . . . 75 20
233 – 75c. black and brown . . . 7·00 2·10
234 – $1 black and pink . . . . 1·90 25
235 **52** $2 black and green . . . . 3·00 35
236 **53** $5 grey and red . . . . . 5·75 50
DESIGNS—As Type **50**: 5c. Chimpanzee; 15c. Agama lizard; 75c. Pygmy hippopotamus. As Type **51**: 10c. Great blue turaco; 20c. Great egret; 25c. Head of Liberty on coin; 30c. Figures "30"; 50c. Liberian flag. As Type **53**: $1 Head of Liberty.

55 Coffee Plantation

56 Gunboat "Lark"

57 Commerce

1909†. The 10c. is perf or roul.
250 **55** 1c. black and green 25 15
251 – 2c. black and red 25 15
252 **56** 5c. black and blue . . . . 1·75 35
254 **57** 10c. black and purple . . . 25 20
255 – 15c. black and blue . . . . 1·25 35
256 – 20c. green and red . . . . 2·50 50
257 – 25c. black and brown . . . 1·75 35
258 – 30c. brown . . . . 1·75 35
259 – 50c. black and green . . . 2·75 60
260 – 75c. black and brown . . . 2·25 45
DESIGNS—As Type **55**: 2c. Pres. Barclay; 15c. Vai woman spinning cotton; 20c. Pepper plant; 25c. Village hut; 30c. Pres. Barclay (in picture frame). As Type **56**: 50c. Canoeing; 75c. Village (design shaped like a book).

1909. No. 227 surch **Inland 3 Cents**.
261 3c. on 10c. black and red . . 4·75 5·25

1910†. Surcharged **3 CENTS INLAND POSTAGE**. Perf or rouletted.
274 **57** 3c. on 10c. black and purple 35 25

1913. Various types surch with new value and bars or ornaments.
322 – 1c. on 2c. black and red (No. 251) . . . . 2·25 3·00
290 **57** + 2c. on 3c. on 10c. black and purple . . . . . . 60 2·00
323 **56** 2c. on 5c. black and blue 2·25 3·00

292	–	2c. on 15c. black and blue (No. 255)	1·25	1·25
279	–	2c. on 25c. grey & blue (A) (No. 230)	7·50	3·75
281	–	2c. on 25c. black and brown (A) (No. 257)	7·50	3·75
295	–	2c. on 25c. black and brown (B) (No. 257)	6·25	6·25
296	–	5c. on 20c. green and red (No. 256)	85	4·50
280	–	5c. on 30c. violet (C) (No. 231)	7·50	3·75
282	–	5c. on 30c. brown (C) (No. 258)	7·50	3·75
297	–	5c. on 30c. brown (D) (No. 258)	3·75	3·75
278	**36**	8c. on 3c. red and green	60	30
283	–	10c. on 50c. black and green (E) (No. 259)	9·25	5·75
299	–	10c. on 50c. black and green (F) (No. 259)	6·75	6·75
303	–	20c. on 75c. black and brown (No. 260)	3·25	6·25
304	**53**	25c. on $1 black and pink	32·00	32·00
305	–	50c. on $2 black and green (No. 235)	9·25	9·25
308	–	$1 on $5 grey and red (No. 236)	42·00	42·00

Descriptions of surcharges. (A) **1914 2 CENTS**. (B) **2** over ornaments. (C) **1914 5 CENTS**. (D) **5** over ornaments. (E) **1914 10 CENTS**. (F) **10** and ornaments.

64 House on Providence Is

65 Monrovia Harbour, Providence Is

1915.

288	**64**	2c. red	20	10
289	**65**	3c. violet	20	10

1916. Liberian Frontier Force. Surch **LFF 1 C**.

332	**9**	1c. on 1c. green	£120	£120
333	**50**	1c. on 1c. black and green	£375	£375
334	**55**	1c. on 1c. black and green	2·75	4·25
335	–	1c. on 2c. black and red (No. 251)	2·75	4·25

1916. Surch **1916** over new value.

339	**1**	3c. on 6c. mauve	32·00	32·00
340		5c. on 12c. yellow	4·00	4·00
341		10c. on 24c. red	3·25	3·75

1917. Surch **1917** and value in words.

342	**13**	4c. on 25c. green	8·25	9·25
343	**52**	5c. on 30c. violet (No. 231)	60·00	65·00

1918. Surch **3 CENTS**.

345	**57**	3c. on 10c. black & purple	2·40	3·75

91 Bongo **93**

92 African Palm Civet

94 Traveller's Tree

1918.

349	**91**	1c. black and green	65	25
350	**92**	2c. black and red	65	25
351	–	5c. black and blue	15	10
352	**93**	10c. green	20	10
353	–	15c. green and black	2·50	20
354	–	20c. black and red	50	15
355	**94**	25c. green	3·25	25
356	–	30c. black and mauve	11·00	95
357	–	50c. black and blue	13·00	1·10
358	–	75c. black and olive	1·00	25
359	–	$1 blue and brown	4·25	25
360	–	$2 black and violet	6·00	30
361	–	$5 brown	6·00	40

DESIGNS—As Type **91**: 5c. Coat of Arms; 15c. Oil palm; 20c. Statue of Mercury; 75c. Heads of Mandingos; $5 "Liberia" seated. As Type **92**: 50c. West African mudskipper; $1 Coast view; $2 Liberia College. As Type **93**: 30c. Palm-nut Vulture.

1918. Geneva Red Cross Fund. Surch **TWO CENTS** and red cross.

375	**91**	1c.+2c. black and green	75	75
376	**92**	2c.+2c. black and red	75	75
377	–	5c.+2c. black and blue	25	1·00
378	**93**	10c.+2c. green	50	1·00
379	–	15c.+2c. green and black	2·40	1·75
380	–	20c.+2c. black and red	1·50	3·00
381	**94**	25c.+2c. green	3·25	3·25
382	–	30c.+2c. black and mauve	10·50	5·75
383	–	50c.+2c. black and blue	7·00	5·75
384	–	75c.+2c. black and olive	2·10	5·25
385	–	$1+2c. blue and brown	4·25	7·00
386	–	$2+2c. black and violet	5·75	11·50
387	–	$5+2c. brown	14·00	23·00

1920. Surch **1920** and value and two bars.

393	**91**	3c. on 1c. black & green	1·50	2·75
394	**92**	4c. on 2c. black and red	1·50	3·00
395	**R 42**	5c. on 10c. black & blue	3·75	4·25
396		5c. on 10c. black and red	3·75	4·25
397		5c. on 10c. black & grn	3·75	4·25
398		5c. on 10c. black & vio	3·75	4·25
399		5c. on 10c. black and red	3·75	4·25

100 Cape Mesurado

101 Pres. D. E. Howard

1921.

402	**100**	1c. green	20	10
403	**101**	5c. black and blue	25	10
404	–	10c. blue and red	80	10
405	–	15c. green and purple	3·00	50
406	–	20c. green and red	1·50	25
407	–	25c. black and yellow	2·75	50
408	–	30c. purple and green	1·00	15
409	–	50c. blue and yellow	1·00	25
410	–	75c. sepia and red	1·00	40
411	–	$1 black and red	17·00	1·00
412	–	$2 violet and yellow	24·00	1·40
413	–	$5 red and purple	22·00	1·50

DESIGNS—VERT: 10c. Arms. HORIZ: 15c. Crocodile; 20c. Pepper plant; 25c. Leopard; 30c. Village; 50c. "Kru" boatman; 75c. St. Paul's River; $1 Bongo (antelope); $2 Great Indian hornbill; $5 African elephant.

1921. Optd **1921**.

414	**100**	1c. green	9·25	50
415	**64**	2c. red	9·25	50
416	**65**	3c. violet	12·50	50
417	**101**	5c. black and blue	2·75	50
418	–	10c. blue and red	20·00	50
419	–	15c. green and purple	11·50	1·00
420	–	20c. green and red	5·25	60
421	–	25c. black and yellow	11·50	1·00
422	–	30c. purple and green	3·00	50
423	–	50c. blue and yellow	3·00	70
424	–	75c. sepia and red	3·75	50
425	–	$1 black and red	30·00	1·50
426	–	$2 violet and yellow	28·00	1·60
427	–	$5 red and purple	32·00	5·25

107 Arrival of First Settlers in "Alligator"

1923. Centennial issue.

466	**107**	1c. black and blue	14·00	70
467		2c. brown and red	17·00	70
468		5c. blue and olive	17·00	70
469		10c. mauve and green	4·75	70
470		$1 brown and red	7·00	70

108 J. J. Roberts Memorial

109 House of Representatives, Monrovia

110 Rubber Plantation

1923.

471	**108**	1c. green	3·75	10
472	**109**	2c. brown and red	3·75	10
473	–	3c. black and lilac	25	10
474	–	5c. black and blue	42·00	15
475	–	10c. brown and grey	25	10
476	–	15c. blue and bistre	18·00	50
477	–	20c. mauve and green	2·00	50
478	–	25c. brown and red	65·00	50
479	–	30c. mauve and brown	50	20
480	–	50c. orange and purple	1·00	40
481	–	75c. blue and grey	1·50	65
482	**110**	$1 violet and red	3·75	1·00
483	–	$2 blue and orange	4·00	65
484	–	$5 brown and green	10·00	65

DESIGNS—As Type **108**: 3c. Star; 5, 10c. Pres. King; 50c. Pineapple. As Type **109**: 15c. Hippopotamus; 20c. Kob (antelope); 25c. African buffalo; 30c. Natives making palm oil; 75c. Carrying elephant tusk. As Type **110**: $2 Stockton lagoon; $5 Styles of huts.

1926. Surch **Two Cents** and thick bar or wavy lines or ornamental scroll.

504	**91**	2c. on 1c. black and green	3·00	3·25

116 Palm Trees

117 Map of Africa

118 President King

1928.

511	**116**	1c. green	40	15
512		2c. violet	20	20
513		3c. brown	35	20
514	**117**	5c. blue	55	35
515	**118**	10c. grey	70	35
516	**117**	15c. purple	3·75	1·40
517		$1 brown	42·00	15·00

1936. Nos. O518 and 512/13 surch **AIR MAIL SIX CENTS**.

525	**116**	6c. on 1c. green	£170	90·00
526		6c. on 2c. violet	£170	90·00
527		6c. on 3c. brown	£170	90·00

122 Ford "Tin Goose"

1936. Air. 1st Air Mail Service of 28th February.

530	**122**	1c. black and green	25	10
531		2c. black and red	25	10
532		3c. black and violet	40	10
533		4c. black and orange	40	15
534		5c. black and blue	45	15
535		6c. black and green	45	20

1936. Nos. 350/61 surch **1936** and new values in figures.

536	1c. on 2c. black and red	30	50
537	3c. on 5c. black and blue	30	45
538	4c. on 10c. green	25	40
539	6c. on 15c. green and black	30	55
540	8c. on 20c. black and red	20	60
541	12c. on 30c. black and mauve	1·25	1·40
542	14c. on 50c. black and blue	1·50	1·75
543	16c. on 75c. black and olive	50	60
544	18c. on $1 blue and brown	60	80
545	22c. on $2 black and violet	60	95
546	24c. on $5 brown	75	1·25

1936. Nos. O363/74 optd with star and **1936** or surch also in figures and words.

547	1c. on 2c. black and red	30	50
548	3c. on 5c. black and blue	25	50
549	4c. on 10c. green	20	45
550	6c. on 15c. green and brown	25	60
551	8c. on 20c. black and lilac	30	60
552	12c. on 30c. black and violet	95	1·25
553	14c. on 50c. black and brown	1·00	1·50
554	16c. on 75c. black and brown	45	60
555	18c. on $1 blue and olive	50	65
556	22c. on $2 black and olive	60	90
557	24c. on $5 green	75	95
558	25c. green and brown	75	1·25

126 Hippopotamus

1937.

559	–	1c. black and green	1·25	60
560	–	2c. black and red	1·00	30
561	–	3c. black and purple	1·00	35
562	**126**	4c. black and orange	1·50	60
563	–	5c. black and blue	1·75	85
564	–	6c. black and green	45	20

DESIGNS: 1c. Black and white casqued hornbill; 2c. Bushbuck; 3c. African buffalo; 5c. Western reef heron; 6c. Pres. Barclay.

127 Tawny Eagle in Flight

128 Three-engine Flying Boat

129 Little Egrets

1938. Air.

565	**127**	1c. green	25	20
566	**128**	2c. red	15	10
567	–	3c. olive	35	20
568	**129**	4c. orange	50	10
569	–	5c. green	65	20
570	**128**	10c. violet	25	10
571	–	20c. mauve	30	15
572	–	30c. grey	1·25	20
573	**127**	50c. brown	1·75	20
574	–	$1 blue	1·40	25

DESIGNS—VERT: 20c., $1 Sikorsky S-43 amphibian. HORIZ: 3, 30c. Lesser black-backed gull in flight.

130 Immigrant Ships nearing Liberian Coast

1940. Centenary of Founding of Liberian Commonwealth.

575	**130**	3c. blue	50	15
576	–	5c. brown	20	10
577	–	10c. green	25	15

DESIGNS: 5c. Seal of Liberia and Flags of original Settlements; 10c. Thos. Buchanan's house and portrait.

1941. Centenary of First Postage Stamps. Nos. 575/7 optd **POSTAGE STAMP CENTENNIAL 1840–1940** and portrait of Rowland Hill.

578	**130**	3c. blue (postage)	1·75	1·75
579	–	5c. brown	1·75	1·75
580	–	10c. green	1·75	1·75
581	**130**	3c. blue (air)	1·40	1·40
582	–	5c. brown	1·40	1·40
583	–	10c. green	1·40	1·40

Nos. 581/3 are additionally optd with airplane and **AIR MAIL**.

1941. Red Cross Fund. Nos. 575/7 surch **RED CROSS** plus Red Cross and **TWO CENTS**.

584	**130**	+ 2c. on 3c. bl (postage)	1·40	1·40
585	–	+ 2c. on 5c. brown	1·40	1·40
586	–	+ 2c. on 10c. green	1·40	1·40
587	**130**	+ 2c. on 3c. blue (air)	1·40	1·40
588	–	+ 2c. on 5c. brown	1·40	1·40
589	–	+ 2c. on 10c. green	1·40	1·40

Nos. 587/9 are additionally optd with airplane and **AIR MAIL**.

1941. Air. 1st Flight to U.S.A. Nos. 565/74 surch **First Flight LIBERIA - U.S. 1941 50c** and bar.

594	**127**	50c. on 1c.	£2500	£225
595	**128**	50c. on 2c.	£150	75·00
596	–	50c. on 3c.	£180	90·00
597	**129**	50c. on 4c.	60·00	38·00

598 50c. on 5c. . . . . . . 60·00 38·00
599 **128** 50c. on 10c. . . . . . . 45·00 38·00
600 – 50c. on 20c. £1500 £150
601 – 50c. on 30c. . . . . . . 60·00 24·00
602 **127** 50c. brown . . . . 60·00 24·00
603 – $1 blue . . . . 45·00 30·00

The first flight was cancelled and covers were sent by ordinary mail. The flight took place in 1942 and the stamps were reissued but with the date obliterated.

1942. As Nos. 594/601 but with date "1941" obliterated by two bars.
604 **127** 50c. on 1c. green . . . . 7·00 7·00
605 **128** 50c. on 2c. red . . . . 6·00 6·75
606 – 50c. on 3c. green . . . . 5·50 4·75
607 **129** 50c. on 4c. orange . . . . 4·00 6·25
608 50c. on 5c. green . . . . 2·40 2·40
609 **128** 50c. on 10c. violet . . . . 5·25 6·25
610 – 50c. on 20c. mauve . . . . 5·25 6·25
611 – 50c. on 30c. grey . . . . 4·00 4·00
612 **127** 50c. brown . . . . 4·00 4·00
613 – $1 blue . . . . 6·25 7·50

138 Miami–Monrovia Air Route

1942. Air.
614 **138** 10c. red 20 10
615 – 12c. blue 30 10
616 – 24c. green 35 10
617 **138** 30c. green 35 10
618 35c. lilac 40 15
619 50c. purple 50 15
620 70c. olive 55 30
621 $1.40 red 75 50

DESIGN: 12, 24c. Boeing 247 airliner over Liberian Agricultural and Industrial Fair.

139 Bushbuck

1942.
622 – 1c. brown and violet . . . 80 20
623 – 2c. brown and blue . . . 80 20
624 – 3c. brown and green . . . 1·25 45
625 **139** 4c. red and black . . . . 2·00 70
626 – 5c. brown and olive . . . 1·75 70
627 – 10c. black and red . . . . 3·75 1·10

DESIGNS—HORIZ: 1c. Royal antelope; 2c. Water chevrotain; 3c. Jentink's duiker; 5c. Banded duiker. VERT: 10c. Diana monkey.

1944. Stamps of 1928 and 1937 surch.
628 **116** 1c. on 2c. violet . . . . . 7·50 7·50
634 **126** 1c. on 4c. black & orange 48·00 40·00
629 **118** 1c. on 10c. grey . . . . . 10·00 6·25
635 – 2c. on 3c. black and purple (No. 561) . . . 50·00 40·00
630 **117** 2c. on 5c. blue . . . . . 3·25 3·25
632 **116** 3c. on 2c. violet . . . . . 27·00 30·00
636 – 4c. on 5c. black and blue (No. 563) . . . . . . 18·00 18·00
633 **118** 4c. on 10c. grey . . . . . 3·25 3·25
637 – 5c. on 1c. black and green (No. 559) . . . . . . 85·00 45·00
638 – 6c. on 2c. black and red (No. 560) . . . . . . 12·50 12·50
639 – 10c. on 6c. black and green (No. 564) . . . . 14·00 12·50

1944. Air stamps of 1936 and 1938 surch.
643 **128** 10c. on 2c. red . . . . . 27·00 30·00
644 **129** 10c. on 5c. green . . . . 9·50 9·50
640 **122** 30c. on 1c. black & green 80·00 50·00
645 30c. on 3c. olive (No. 567) £120 55·00
646 **129** 30c. on 4c. orange . . . . . 9·50 9·50
641 **122** 50c. on 3c. black & violet 20·00 23·00
642 70c. on 2c. black and red 50·00 50·00
647 – $1 on 3c. olive (No. 567) 25·00 25·00
648 **127** $1 on 50c. brown . . . . 35·00 25·00

150 Pres. Roosevelt reviewing Troops

1945. Pres. Roosevelt Memorial.
650 **150** 3c. black & pur (postage) 15 15
651 5c. black and blue 30 25
652 70c. black and brown (air) 1·00 1·00

151 Opening Monrovia Harbour Project

1946. Opening of Monrovia Harbour Project by Pres. Tubman.
653 **151** 5c. blue (postage) 25 15
654 24c. green (air) . . . . . 1·90 2·10

1947. As T **151**, but without inscr at top.
655 5c. violet (postage) 15 15
656 25c. red (air) . . . . 1·00 1·10

152 1st Postage Stamps of United States and Liberia

1947. U.S. Postage Stamps Centenary and 87th Anniv of Liberian Postal Issues.
657 **152** 5c. red (postage) 30 15
658 12c. green (air) 40 15
659 22c. violet 50 20
660 50c. blue 60 25

153 Matilda Newport Firing Canon

1947. 125th Anniv of Defence of Monrovia.
662 **153** 1c. black & green (postage) 15 10
663 3c. black and violet . . . 20 10
664 5c. black and blue 20 15
665 10c. black and yellow . . 1·50 45
666 25c. black and red (air) 1·40 35

154 Liberty

156 Douglas DC-3

1947. Centenary of National Independence.
667 – 1c. green (postage) . . . 20 10
668 **154** 2c. purple 20 10
669 – 3c. purple 30 15
670 – 5c. blue 40 15
671 – 12c. orange (air) 60 20
672 – 25c. red 75 35
673 – 50c. brown 90 70

DESIGNS—VERT: 1c. Liberian star; 3c. Arms of Liberia; 4c. Map of Liberia; 12c. J. J. Roberts Monument; 25c. Liberian Flag; 50c. (26½ × 33 mm) Centenary Monument.

1948. Air. 1st Liberian International Airways Flight (Monrovia–Dakar).
674 **156** 25c. red . . . . 1·50 1·00
675 50c. blue . . . . 2·40 1·50

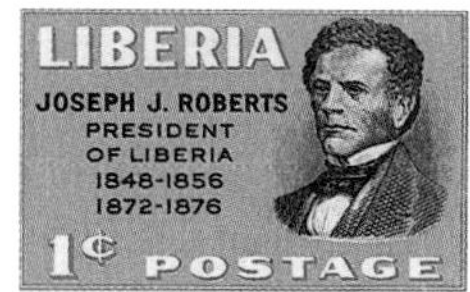

157 Joseph J. Roberts

1949. Liberian Presidents. Portrait and name in black. (a) Postage.
676 – 1c. green (Roberts) . . . 1·60 3·25
677 **157** 1c. green 15 10
678 – 1c. pink (Roberts) 25 15
679 – 2c. pink (Benson) 35 35
680 – 2c. yellow (Benson) . . . 35 15
681 – 3c. mauve (Warner) . . . 35 35
682 – 4c. olive (Payne) 35 55
683 – 5c. blue (Mansion) . . . 45 55
684 – 6c. orange (Roye) 55 95
685 – 7c. green (Gardner and Russell) . . . . 70 1·25
686 – 8c. red (Johnson) . . . . 70 1·40
687 – 9c. purple (Cheeseman) 1·10 1·10
688 – 10c. yellow (Coleman) . . 75 35
689 – 10c. grey (Coleman) . . . 40 20
690 – 15c. orange (Gibson) . . 85 40
691 – 15c. blue (Gibson) 25 15
692 – 20c. grey (A. Barclay) . . 1·25 70
693 – 20c. red (A. Barclay) . . . 50 45
694 – 25c. red (Howard) . . . . 1·60 1·10
695 – 25c. blue (Howard) . . . 50 45
696 – 50c. turquoise (King) . . 3·25 95
697 – 50c. purple (King) 70 60
698 – $1 mauve (E. Barclay) . . 5·75 70
699 – $1 brown (E. Barclay) . . 4·00 55

(b) Air.
700 – 25c. blue (Tubman) . . . . 1·00 55
701 – 25c. green (Tubman) 75 35

Nos. 676 and 678 have a different portrait of Roberts wearing a moustache.

158 Colonists and Map

1949. Multicoloured.
702 1c. Settlers approaching village (postage) 50 75
703 2c. Rubber tapping and planting 50 75
704 3c. Landing of first colonists in 1822 . . . . 1·00 1·50
705 5c. Jehudi Ashmun and Matilda Newport defending stockade 50 75
706 25c. Type **158** (air) . . . . . 1·25 1·50
707 50c. Africans and coat of arms . . . . 2·75 3·25

159 Hand holding Book

1950. National Literacy Campaign.
708 **159** 5c. blue (postage) 20 15
709 – 25c. red (air) 70 70

DESIGN—VERT: 25c. Open book and rising sun.

160 U.P.U. Monument, Berne

1950. 75th Anniv of U.P.U.
711 **160** 5c. black and green (post) 20 15
712 – 10c. black and mauve . . 30 30
713 – 25c. purple & orange (air) 3·25 3·25

DESIGNS—HORIZ: 10c. Standehaus, Berne. VERT: 25c. U.P.U. Monument, Berne.

161 Carey, Ashmun and Careysburg

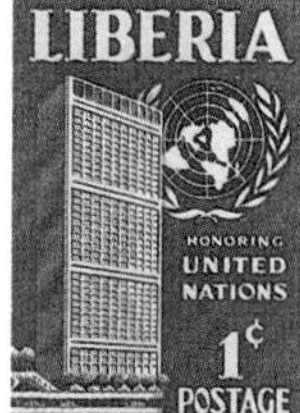

162 U.N. Headquarters

163 Flags and U.N. Emblem

1952. Designs all show portrait of Ashmun.
715 – 1c. green (postage) . . . 10 10
716 **161** 2c. blue and red 10 10
717 – 3c. green and purple . . . 10 10
718 – 4c. green and brown . . . 15 10
719 – 5c. red and blue 20 15
720 – 10c. blue and red 25 20
721 – 25c. black and purple (air) 35 35
722 – 50c. red and blue . . . 1·00 45

DESIGNS—VERT: 1c. Seal of Liberia; 3c. Harper and Harper City; 5c. Buchanan and Upper Buchanan. HORIZ: 4c. Marshall and Marshall City; 10c. Roberts and Robertsport; 25c. Monroe and Monrovia; 50c. Tubman and map.

1952. U.N. Commemoration.
724 **162** 1c. blue (postage) 10 10
725 – 4c. blue and pink 15 10
726 – 10c. brown and yellow . . 25 20
727 **163** 25c. red and blue (air) . . 55 45

DESIGNS—HORIZ: 4c. Liberian and U.N. flags and scroll; 10c. Liberian and U.N. emblems.

164 Modern Road-building

1953. Air. Transport.
729 **164** 12c. brown 15 15
730 – 25c. purple 75 30
731 – 35c. violet . . . . 1·60 30
732 – 50c. orange 65 25
733 – 70c. green . . . . 1·25 40
734 – $1 blue . . . . 1·40 55

DESIGNS: 25c. "African Glen" (freighter) in Monrovia Harbour; 35c. Diesel locomotive; 50c. Free Port of Monrovia; 70c. Roberts Field Airport; $1 Tubman Bridge.

165 Garden Bulbul ("Pepper Bird")

166 Blue-throated Roller ("Roller")

1953. Imperf or perf.
735 **165** 1c. red and blue . . . . 1·00 20
736 **166** 3c. blue and salmon . . . 1·00 25
737 – 4c. brown and yellow . . 1·50 30
738 – 5c. turquoise and mauve 1·75 35
739 – 10c. mauve and green . . 1·75 35
740 – 12c. orange and brown . . 2·75 50

BIRDS: As Type **165**: 4c. Yellow-casqued hornbill ("Hornbill"); 5c. Giant kingfisher ("Kingfisher"). As Type **166**: 10c. African jacana ("Jacana"); 12c. Broad-tailed paradise whydah ("Weaver").

167 Hospital

1954. Liberian Govt. Hospital Fund.
741 – 5c.+5c. black and purple (postage) 20 15
742 – 10c.+5c. black and red (air) 15 20
743 **167** 20c.+5c. black & green . . 25 25
744 – 25c.+5c. black, red and blue 30 20

DESIGNS—As Type **167**: 5c. Medical research workers; 10c. Nurses. 46 × 35 mm: 25c. Doctor examining patient.

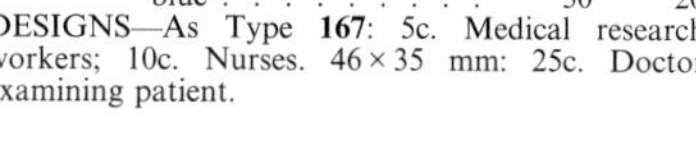

168 Children of the World

1954. Air. UNICEF.
745 **168** $5 ultramarine, red and blue . . . . 27·00 23·00

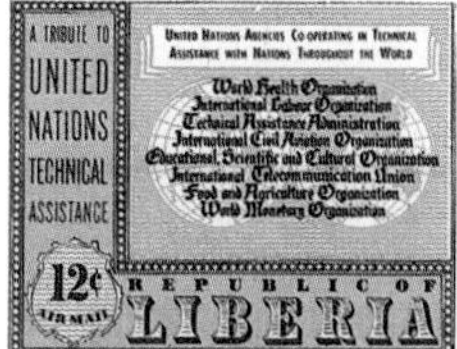

169 U.N. Organizations

1954. Air. U.N. Technical Assistance.
746 **169** 12c. black and blue . . . 25 15
747 – 15c. brown and yellow . . 25 15

748 – 20c. black and green . . . 30 20
749 – 25c. blue and red 35 25
DESIGNS: 15c. Printers; 20c. Mechanic; 25c. Teacher and students.

1954. Air. Visit of President Tubman to U.S.A. As Nos. 729/34 but colours changed and inscr "COMMEMORATING PRESIDENTIAL VISIT U.S.A.—1954".
750 12c. orange 20 20
751 25c. blue 80 25
752 35c. red . . . . 4·00 1·50
753 50c. mauve 80 30
754 70c. brown . . . . 1·10 50
755 $1 green . . . . 1·60 3·25

170 Football

171 "Callichilia stenosepala"

1955. Sports.
756 – 3c. red and green (postage) 15 10
757 **170** 5c. black and orange . . 15 10
758 – 25c. violet and yellow . . 25 20
759 – 10c. blue and mauve (air) 20 15
760 – 12c. brown and blue . . . 15 15
761 – 25c. red and green 20 20
DESIGNS—VERT: 3c. Tennis; 25c. Boxing (No. 758). HORIZ: 10c. Baseball; 12c. Swimming; 25c. Running (No. 761).

1955. Flowers.
763 **171** 6c. yellow, salmon and green (postage) 15 10
764 – 7c. red, yellow and green 15 10
765 – 8c. buff, blue and green 20 10
766 – 9c. green and orange . . 25 15
767 – 20c. yellow, green and violet (air) 15 15
768 – 25c. yellow, green and red 20 20
FLOWERS—VERT: 7c. "Gomphia subcordata"; 8c. "Listrostachys chudata"; 9c. "Mussaenda isertiana". HORIZ: 20s. "Costus"; 25c. "Barteria nigritiana".

172 U.N. General Assembly

173 Tapping Rubber and Rotary Emblem

1955. Air. 10th Anniv of U.N.
769 – 10c. blue and red 20 10
770 **172** 15c. black and violet . . . 25 15
771 – 25c. brown and green . . . 35 15
772 – 50c. green and red . . . . 1·00 20
DESIGNS—VERT: 10c. U.N. emblem; 25c. Liberian Secretary of State signing U.N. Charter. HORIZ: 50c. Page from U.N. Charter.

1955. 50th Anniv of Rotary International.
773 **173** 5c. green & yell (postage) 25 15
774 – 10c. blue and red (air) . . 15 50
775 – 15c. brown, yellow and red 20 65
DESIGNS: 10c. Rotary International H.Q., Evanston; 15c. View of Monrovia.

174 Coliseum, New York

1956. 5th Int Philatelic Exhibition, New York.
777 – 3c. brown and green (postage) 15 10
778 **174** 4c. brown and green . . . 10 25
779 – 6c. purple and black . . . 20 10
780 **174** 10c. blue and red (air) . . 25 15
781 – 12c. violet and orange . . 20 15
782 – 15c. purple and turquoise 25 20
DESIGNS—VERT: 3c., 15c. Statue of Liberty. HORIZ: 6c., 12c. The Globe.

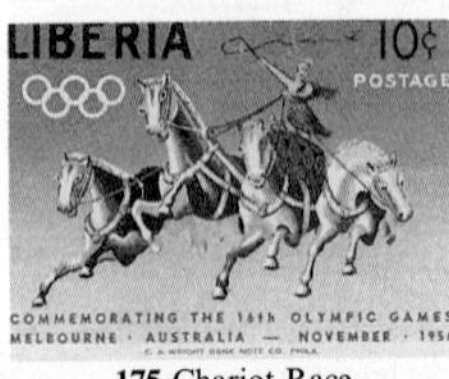

175 Chariot Race

1956. Olympic Games.
784 – 4c. brown & olive (postage) 10 10
785 – 6c. black and green . . . 15 10
786 – 8c. brown and blue . . . 20 10
787 **175** 10c. black and red 25 10
788 – 12c. purple and green (air) 20 15
789 – 20c. multicoloured 30 20
DESIGNS—HORIZ: 4c. Olympic rings, eastern grey kangaroo and emu; 8c. Goddess of Victory; 12c., 20c. Olympic torch superimposed on map of Austrialia. VERT: 6c. Discus thrower.

176 Douglas DC-6B "John Alden" at Idlewild Airport

1957. 1st Anniv of Inauguration of Liberia–U.S. Direct Air Service.
791 **176** 3c. blue & orange (postage) 15 15
792 – 5c. black and mauve . . . 20 20
793 **176** 12c. blue and green (air) 30 25
794 – 15c. black and brown . . 30 25
795 **176** 25c. blue and red 45 25
796 – 50c. black and blue . . . 85 30
DESIGN: 5, 15, 50c. President Tubman and "John Alden" at Roberts Field, Liberia.

177 Children's Playground

1957. Inauguration of Antoinette Tubman Child Welfare Foundation. Inscr as in T **177**.
797 **177** 4c. green and red (postage) 10 10
798 – 5c. brown and turquoise 15 10
799 – 6c. violet and bistre . . . 15 10
800 – 10c. blue and red 20 15
801 – 15c. brown and blue (air) 20 15
802 – 35c. purple and grey . . . 35 25
DESIGNS: 5c. Teacher with pupil; 6c. National anthem with choristers; 10c. Children viewing welfare home; 15c. Nurse inoculating youth; 35c. Kamara triplets.

178 German Flag and Brandenburg Gate

1958. Pres. Tubman's European Tour. Flags in national colours.
804 **178** 5c. blue (postage) 15 10
805 – 5c. brown 15 10
806 – 5c. red 15 10
807 – 10c. black (air) 25 15
808 – 15c. green 25 20
809 – 15c. blue 25 20
810 – 15c. violet 25 20
DESIGNS: Flags of: Netherlands and windmill (No. 805); Sweden and Royal Palace, Stockholm (No. 806); Italy and Colosseum (No. 807); France and Arc de Triomphe (No. 808); Switzerland and Alpine chalet (No. 809); Vatican City and St. Peter's Basilica (No. 810).

179 Map of the World

180 Africans and Map

1958. 10th Anniv of Declaration of Human Rights.
811 **179** 3c. blue and black 25 15
812 – 5c. brown and blue . . . 20 20
813 – 10c. orange and black . . 30 75
814 – 12c. black and red 40 35
DESIGNS: 5c. U.N. Emblem and H.Q. building; 10c. U.N. Emblem; 12c. U.N. Emblem and initials of U.N. agencies.

1959. Africa Freedom Day.
816 **180** 20c. orge & brn (postage) 30 30
817 – 25c. brown and blue (air) 35 20
DESIGN: 25c. Two Africans looking at Pres. Tubman's declaration of Africa Freedom Day.

181

182 Abraham Lincoln

1959. Inaug of UNESCO Building, Paris.
818 **181** 25c. purple & grn (postage) 35 40
819 – 25c. red and blue (air) . . 35 30
DESIGN—HORIZ: No. 819 UNESCO Headquarters, Paris.

1959. 150th Birth Anniv of Abraham Lincoln.
821 **182** 10c. black & blue (postage) 25 30
822 15c. black and orange . . 30 30
823 25c. black and green (air) 55 50

183 Presidents Toure, Tubman and Nkrumah at Conference Table

184 "Care of Refugees"

1960. "Big Three" Conf, Saniquellie, Liberia.
825 **183** 25c. black & red (postage) 35 25
826 – 25c. black, bl & buff (air) 35 25
DESIGN: No. 826, Medallion portraits of Presidents Toure (Guinea), Tubman (Liberia) and Nkrumah (Ghana).

1960. World Refugee Year.
827 **184** 25c. green & blk (postage) 35 30
828 25c. blue and black (air) 55 40

185

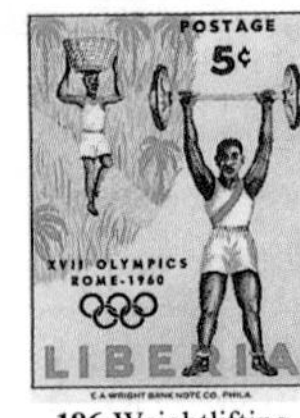

186 Weightlifting

1960. 10th Anniv of African Technical Co-operation Commission (C.C.T.A.).
830 **185** 25c. green & blk (postage) 35 50
831 – 25c. brown and blue (air) 45 35
DESIGN: No. 831, Map of Africa with symbols showing fields of assistance.

1960. Olympic Games, Rome.
832 **186** 5c. brown & grn (postage) 20 15
833 – 10c. brown and purple . . 40 75
834 – 15c. brown and orange . . 35 30
835 – 25c. brown and blue (air) 70 80
DESIGNS—HORIZ: 10c. Rowing; 25c. Javelin-throwing. VERT: 15c. Walking.

187 Stamps of 1860 and Map

188 "Guardians of Peace"

1960. Liberian Stamp Centenary. Stamps, etc., in green, red and blue. Colours of map and inscriptions given.
837 **187** 5c. black (postage) . . . 25 15
838 20c. brown 40 40
839 25c. blue (air) 50 40

1961. Membership of U.N. Security Council.
841 **188** 25c. blue and red (postage) 45 35
842 – 25c. blue and red (air) . . 45 25
DESIGN—HORIZ: No. 842, Dove of Peace, Globe and U.N. Emblem.

189 Anatomy Class, University of Liberia

190 President Roberts

1961. 15th Anniv of UNESCO.
845 **189** 25c. brown & grn (postage) 35 35
846 – 25c. brown and violet (air) 35 25
DESIGN: No. 846, Science class, University of Liberia.

1961. 150th Birth Anniv of Joseph J. Roberts (first President of Liberia).
848 **190** 5c. sepia & orge (postage) 20 15
849 – 10c. sepia and blue . . . 35 15
850 – 25c. sepia and green (air) 45 35
DESIGNS—HORIZ: 10c. Pres. Roberts and old and new presidential mansions; 25c. Pres. Roberts and Providence Is.

191 Scout and Sports

1961. Liberian Boy Scout Movement.
852 **191** 5c. sepia & violet (postage) 25 20
853 – 10c. ochre and blue . . . 30 20
854 – 25c. sepia and green (air) 40 30
DESIGNS—HORIZ: 10c. Scout badge and scouts in camp. VERT: 25c. Scout and badge.

192 Hammarskjold and U.N. Emblem

193 Campaign Emblem

1962. Dag Hammarskjold Commem.
856 **192** 20c. black & blue (postage) 30 20
857 25c. black and purple (air) 35 25

1962. Malaria Eradication.
859 **193** 25c. green & red (postage) 35 25
860 – 25c. orange and violet (air) 35 25
DESIGN—HORIZ: No. 860, Campaign emblem and slogan.

194 Pres. Tubman and New York Skyline

1962. Air. President's Visit to U.S.A.
862 **194** 12c. multicoloured 25 15
863 25c. multicoloured 35 30
864 50c. multicoloured 70 55

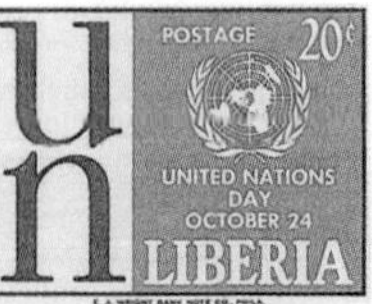

195 U.N. Emblem

1962. U.N. Day.
865 **195** 20c. bistre & grn (postage) 35 30
866 – 25c. blue & deep blue (air) 45 30
DESIGN: 25c. U.N. emblem and flags.

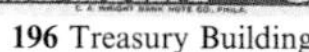
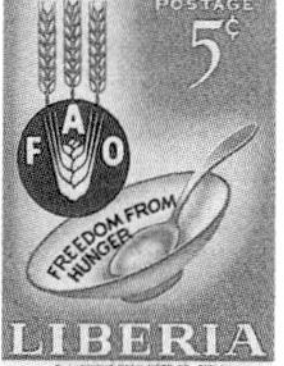

196 Treasury Building **197** F.A.O. Emblem, Bowl and Spoon

1962. Liberian Government Buildings.
868 – 1c. orange & blue (postage) 10 15
869 **196** 5c. violet and blue 15 10
870 – 10c. brown and buff . . . 20 15
871 – 15c. blue and salmon . . 25 20
872 – 80c. yellow and brown . . 1·60 1·00
873 – 12c. red and green (air) 25 15
874 – 50c. blue and orange . . 1·00 90
875 – 70c. blue and mauve . . . 1·40 1·00
876 **196** $1 black and orange . . . 2·00 1·10
BUILDINGS: 1, 80c. Executive; 10, 50c. Information; 12, 15, 70c. Capitol.

1963. Freedom from Hunger.
877 **197** 5c. purple & turq (postage) 15 10
878 – 25c. yellow and green (air) 35 20
DESIGN: 25c. F.A.O. emblem and Globe.

198 Rocket

1963. Space Exploration.
880 **198** 10c. yellow & bl (postage) 20 15
881 – 15c. brown and blue . . . 35 40
882 – 25c. green and orange (air) 45 30
DESIGNS—HORIZ: 15c. Space capsule. VERT: 25c. "Telstar" TV satellite.

199 Red Cross **200** "Unity" Scroll

1963. Red Cross Centenary.
884 **199** 5c. green and red (postage) 15 15
885 – 10c. grey and red 20 20
886 – 25c. violet and red (air) 35 30
887 – 50c. blue and red . . . . 1·00 85
DESIGNS—VERT: 10c. Emblem and torch. HORIZ: 25c. Red Cross and Globe; 50c. Emblem and Globe.

1963. Conference of African Heads of State, Addis Ababa.
888 **200** 20c. brn & grn (postage) 40 35
889 – 25c. red and green (air) 45 30
DESIGN: 25c. Map of Africa (inscr "AFRICAN SUMMIT CONFERENCE").

201 Ski-jumping **202** President Kennedy

1963. Winter Olympic Games, Innsbruck. (1964).
890 **201** 5c. blue and red (postage) 20 20
891 – 10c. red and blue (air) . . 25 25
892 – 25c. orange and green . . 35 35
DESIGNS—VERT: 10c. Olympic flame. HORIZ: 25c. Olympic rings. All have mountain scenery as backgrounds.

1964. President Kennedy Memorial Issue.
894 **202** 20c. black & blue (postage) 35 20
895 – 25c. black and purple (air) 45 25
DESIGN—VERT: 25c. Pres. Kennedy, full face portrait.

203 "Relay I" Satellite **204** Mt. Fuji

1964. Space Communications.
897 – 10c. orange and green . . 20 15
898 **203** 15c. blue and mauve . . . 25 20
899 – 25c. yellow, black and blue 45 25
SATELLITES—HORIZ: 10c. "Syncom"; 25c. "Mariner II".

1964. Olympic Games, Tokyo.
901 **204** 10c. green and yellow . . 15 10
902 – 15c. purple and red . . . 20 15
903 – 25c. red and buff 45 20
DESIGNS: 15c. Japanese arch and Olympic Flame; 25c. Cherry blossom and stadium.

205 Scout Bugle **206** "The Great Emancipator" (statue)

1965. Liberian Boy Scouts.
905 – 5c. brown and blue (postage) 25 15
906 **205** 10c. ochre and green . . . 40 25
907 – 25c. blue and red (air) . . 50 35
DESIGNS—VERT: 5c. Scout badge and saluting hand; 25c. Liberian flag within scout badge.

1965. Death Centenary of Abraham Lincoln.
909 **206** 5c. brown and sepia . . . 20 25
910 – 20c. green and light brown 35 30
911 – 25c. blue and purple . . . 40 40
DESIGNS—HORIZ: 20c. Bust of Lincoln, and Pres. Kennedy. VERT: 25c. Lincoln statue, Chicago (after St. Gaudens).

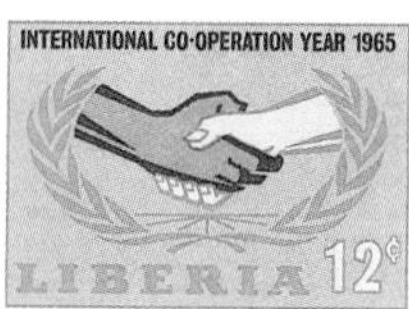

207 I.C.Y. Emblem

1965. International Co-operation Year.
913 **207** 12c. brown and orange . . 70 25
914 25c. brown and blue . . . 40 25
915 50c. brown and green . . 80 70

208 I.T.U. Emblem and Symbols

1965. Centenary of I.T.U.
917 **208** 25c. brn & grn (postage) 40 50
918 35c. mauve and black . . 60 50
919 50c. blue and red (air) . . 80 45

209 Pres. Tubman and Flag **210** Sir Winston Churchill

1965. Pres. Tubman's 70th Birthday. Multicoloured.
921 25c. Type **209** (postage) . . . 35 30
922 25c. President and Liberian arms (air) 35 25

1966. Churchill Commemoration.
924 **210** 15c. black & orge (postage) 30 30
925 – 20c. black and green . . . 35 25
926 – 25c. black and blue (air) 40 30
DESIGNS—HORIZ: 20c. Churchill in uniform of Trinity House Elder Brother; 25c. Churchill and Houses of Parliament.

211 Pres. Roberts **212** Footballers and Hemispheres

1966. Liberian Presidents.
928 **211** 1c. black & pink (postage) 10 10
929 – 2c. black and yellow . . . 10 10
930 – 3c. black and violet . . . 10 10
931 – 4c. black and yellow . . . 75 50
932 – 5c. black and orange . . 10 10
933 – 10c. black and green . . . 15 10
934 – 25c. black and blue . . . 35 20
935 – 50c. black and mauve . . 70 65
936 – 80c. black and red . . . . 1·25 95
937 – $1 black and brown . . . 1·40 15
938 – $2 black and purple . . . 3·25 2·75
939 – 25c. black and green (air) 35 25
PRESIDENTS: 2c. Benson; 3c. Warner; 4c. Payne; 5c. Roye; 10c. Coleman; 25c. (postage) Howard; 25c. (air) Tubman; 50c. King; 80c. Johnson; $1 Barclay; $2 Cheesman.

1966. World Cup Football Championships.
940 **212** 10c. brown and turquoise 15 15
941 – 25c. brown and mauve . . 35 30
942 – 35c. brown and orange . . 50 45
DESIGNS—VERT: 25c. Presentation cup, football and boots; 35c. Footballer.

213 Pres. Kennedy taking Oath

1966. 3rd Death Anniv of Pres. Kennedy.
944 **213** 15c. black & red (postage) 25 15
945 – 20c. purple and blue . . . 35 20
946 – 25c. blue, black and ochre (air) 45 30
947 – 35c. blue and pink . . . 85 45
DESIGNS: 20c. Kennedy stamps of 1964; 25c. U.N. General Assembly and Pres. Kennedy; 35c. Pres. Kennedy and rocket on launching pad.

214 Children on See-saw

1966. 20th Anniv of UNICEF.
949 **214** 5c. blue and red 20 20
950 – 80c. brown and green . . 1·50 1·50
DESIGN: 80c. Child playing "Doctors".

215 Giraffe **216** Scout Emblem and Various Sports

1966. Wild Animals. Multicoloured.
951 2c. Type **215** 10 10
952 3c. Lion 20 15
953 5c. Crocodile (horiz) 15 10
954 10c. Chimpanzees 40 20
955 15c. Leopard (horiz) 50 25
956 20c. Black rhinoceros (horiz) 60 40
957 25c. African elephant 70 50

1967. World Scout Jamboree, Idaho.
958 – 10c. purple and green . . 20 15
959 **216** 25c. red and blue 35 50
960 – 40c. brown and green . . 85 60
DESIGNS—VERT: 10c. Jamboree emblem. HORIZ: 40c. Scout by campfire, and Moon landing.

217 Pre-Hispanic Sculpture **218** W.H.O. Building, Brazzaville

1967. Publicity for Olympic Games, Mexico (1968).
962 **217** 10c. violet and orange . . 75 85
963 – 25c. orange, black and blue 35 40
964 – 40c. red and green 60 65
DESIGNS—VERT: 25c. Aztec calendar. HORIZ: 40c. Mexican sombrero, guitar and ceramics.

1967. Inauguration of W.H.O.'s Regional Office, Brazzaville.
966 **218** 5c. yellow and blue . . . 20 20
967 – 80c. green and yellow . . 1·25 1·25
DESIGN—VERT: 80c. As Type **218** but in vertical format.

219 Boy with Rattle **220** Ice-hockey

1967. Musicians and Instruments. Multicoloured.
968 2c. Type **219** 15 15
969 3c. Tomtom and soko violin (horiz) 20 20
970 5c. Mang harp (horiz) . . . 25 25
971 10c. Alimilim 30 30
972 15c. Xylophone drums . . . 35 35
973 25c. Tomtoms 50 40
974 35c. Oral harp 75 60

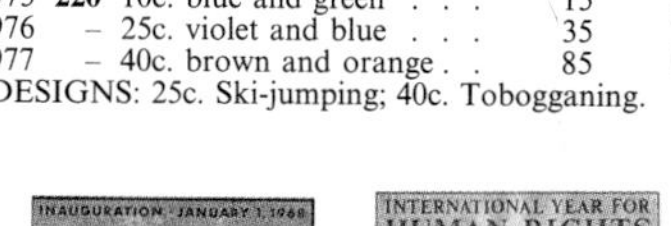

1967. Publicity for Winter Olympic Games, Grenoble (1968).
975 **220** 10c. blue and green . . . 15 20
976 – 25c. violet and blue . . . 35 30
977 – 40c. brown and orange . . 85 50
DESIGNS: 25c. Ski-jumping; 40c. Tobogganing.

221 Pres. Tubman **222** Human Rights Emblem

1967. Re-election of Pres. Tubman for 6th Term.
979 **221** 25c. brown and blue . . . 35 25

1968. Human Rights Year.
981 **222** 3c. blue and red 10 10
982 80c. green and brown . . 1·60 1·60

223 Dr. King and Hearse **224** Throwing the Javelin and Statue of Diana

1968. Martin Luther King Commemoration.
984 **223** 15c. brown and blue . . . 25 20
985 – 25c. brown and blue . . . 40 30
986 – 35c. black and olive . . . 60 65
DESIGNS—VERT: 25c. Dr. Martin Luther King. HORIZ: Dr. King and Lincoln Monument.

1968. Olympic Games, Mexico.
988 **224** 15c. violet and brown . . 25 15
989 – 25c. blue and red 35 15
990 – 35c. brown and green . . 50 30
DESIGNS: 25c. Throwing the discus and Quetzalcoatl sculpture; 35c. High-diving and Xochilcalco bas-relief.

225 President Tubman

1968. 25th Anniv of Pres. Tubman's Administration.
992 **225** 25c. black, brown & silver . . . 1·10 50

226 I.L.O. Symbol

1969. 50th Anniv of I.L.O.
994 **226** 25c. blue & gold (postage) . . . 35 35
995 – 80c. green and gold (air) . . . 1·50 1·40
DESIGN: 80c. As Type **226** but vert.

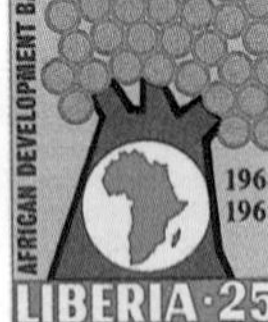

227 "Prince Balthasar Carlos" (Velasquez)
228 Bank Emblem on "Tree"

1969. Paintings (1st series). Multicoloured.
996 3c. Type **227** . . . 10 10
997 5c. "Red Roofs" (Pissarro) (horiz) . . . 20 10
998 10c. "David and Goliath" (Caravaggio) (horiz) . . . 30 15
999 12c. "Still Life" (Chardin) (horiz) . . . 30 15
1000 15c. "The Last Supper" (Leonardo da Vinci) (horiz) . . . 35 15
1001 20c. "Regatta at Argenteuil" (Monet) (horiz) . . . 50 20
1002 25c. "Judgement of Solomon" (Giorgione) . . . 45 25
1003 35c. "The Sistine Madonna" (Raphael) . . . 85 30
See also Nos. 1010/1017.

1969. 5th Anniv of African Development Bank.
1004 **228** 25c. brown and blue . . . 45 40
1005 80c. red and green . . . 1·50 1·10

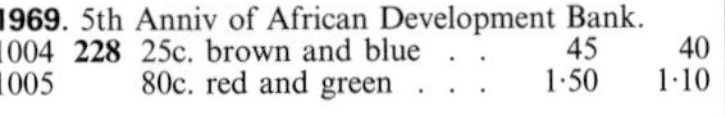
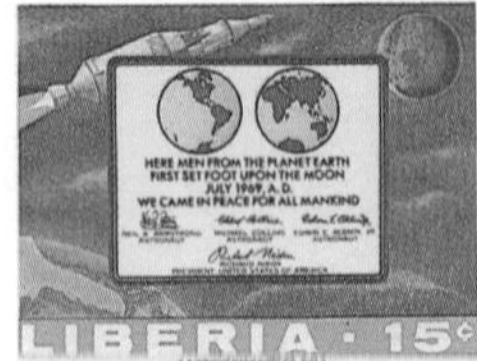

229 Memorial Plaque

1969. 1st Man on the Moon.
1006 **229** 15c. blue and ochre . . . 25 15
1007 – 25c. blue and orange . . . 70 20
1008 – 35c. red and slate . . . 1·00 25
DESIGNS—VERT: 25c. Moon landing and Liberian; 35c. "Kennedy" stamp of 1966; 35c. Module lifting off from Moon.

1969. Paintings (2nd series). As T **227**. Multicoloured.
1010 3c. "The Gleaners" (Millet) (horiz) . . . 15 10
1011 5c. "View of Toledo" (El Greco) . . . 20 15
1012 10c. "Heads of Negroes" (Rubens) (horiz) . . . 30 15
1013 12c. "The Last Supper" (El Greco) (horiz) . . . 30 20
1014 15c. "Peasants Dancing" (Brueghel) (horiz) . . . 35 20
1015 20c. "Hunters in the Snow" (Brueghel) (horiz) . . . 40 25
1016 25c. "Descent from the Cross" (detail, Weyden) . . . 45 30
1017 35c. "The Conception" (Murillo) . . . 60 40

230 Peace Dove and Emblems

1970. 25th Anniv of United Nations.
1018 **230** 5c. green & sil (postage) . . . 15 25
1019 – $1 blue and silver (air) . . . 1·25 1·00
DESIGN: $1, U.N. emblem and olive branch.

231 World Cup "Football" Emblem

1970. World Cup Football Championship, Mexico.
1020 **231** 5c. brown and blue . . . 20 15
1021 – 10c. brown and green . . . 25 20
1022 – 25c. gold and purple . . . 45 30
1023 – 35c. red and blue . . . 60 45
DESIGN—VERT: 10c. Tialoc, Mexican Rain God; 25c. Jules Rimet Cup. HORIZ: 35c. Football in sombrero.

232 Japanese Singer and Festival Plaza

1970. Expo 70. Multicoloured.
1025 2c. Type **232** . . . 10 10
1026 3c. Japanese singer and Expo hall . . . 15 10
1027 5c. Aerial view of "EXPO 70" . . . 30 10
1028 7c. "Tanabata" Festival . . . 30 10
1029 8c. "Awa" Dance Festival . . . 30 15
1030 25c. "Sado-Okesa" Dance Festival . . . 1·10 25

233 New H.Q. Building

1970. Inauguration of New U.P.U. Headquarters Building, Berne.
1032 **233** 25c. brown and blue . . . 35 35
1033 – 80c. brown and chestnut . . . 1·50 1·50
DESIGN—VERT: 80c. Similar to Type **233** but with larger U.P.U. monument.

234 "The First Consul" (Vien)

1970. Birth Bicentenary of Napoleon Bonaparte. Multicoloured.
1034 3c. Type **234** . . . 20 10
1035 5c. "Napoleon visiting school" (unknown artist) . . . 30 15
1036 10c. "Napoleon Bonaparte" (detail, Isabey) . . . 35 15
1037 12c. "The French Campaign" (Meissonier) . . . 40 20
1038 20c. "The Abdication" (Bouchot) . . . 80 30
1039 25c. "Meeting of Napoleon and Pope Pius VII" (Demarne) . . . 1·50 35
Design of 10c. is incorrectly attributed to Gerard on the stamp.

235 Pres. Tubman

1970. Pres. Tubman's 75th Birthday.
1041 **235** 25c. multicoloured . . . 75 25

236 "Adoration of the Magi" (Van der Weyden)

1970. Christmas. "The Adoration of the Magi" by artists as below. Multicoloured.
1043 3c. Type **236** . . . 10 10
1044 5c. H. Memling . . . 15 10
1045 10c. S. Lochner . . . 25 15
1046 12c. A. Altdorfer (vert) . . . 30 15
1047 20c. H. van der Goes . . . 35 15
1048 25c. H. Bosch (vert) . . . 40 30

237 Bapende Mask
239 Pres. Tubman and Women at Ballot Box

238 Astronauts on Moon

1971. African Ceremonial Masks. Masks from different tribes. Multicoloured.
1050 2c. Type **237** . . . 10 10
1051 3c. Dogon . . . 15 10
1052 5c. Baoule . . . 15 15
1053 6c. Dedougou . . . 20 15
1054 9c. Dan . . . 25 15
1055 15c. Bamileke . . . 30 20
1056 20c. Bapende (different) . . . 40 30
1057 25c. Bamileke costume . . . 60 30

1971. "Apollo 14" Moon Mission. Multicoloured.
1058 3c. Type **238** . . . 15 10
1059 5c. Astronaut and Moon vehicle . . . 15 10
1060 10c. Erecting U.S. flag on Moon . . . 20 10
1061 12c. Splashdown . . . 40 15
1062 20c. Astronauts leaving capsule . . . 45 15
1063 25c. "Apollo 14" crew . . . 60 20

1971. 25th Anniv of Liberian Women's Suffrage.
1065 **239** 3c. blue and brown . . . 15 30
1066 – 80c. brown and green . . . 1·50 1·50
DESIGN—HORIZ: 80c. Pres. Tubman, women and map.

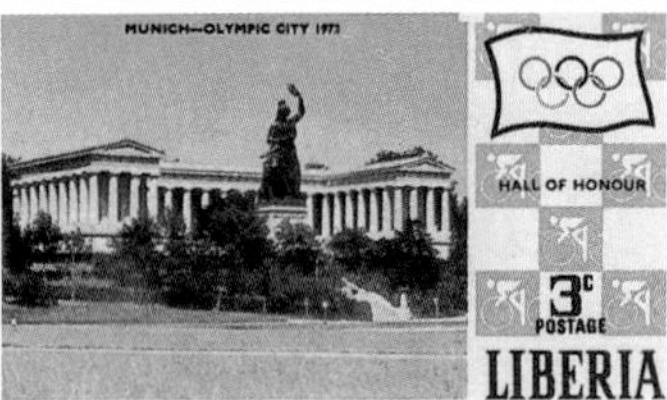

240 Hall of Honour, Munich

1971. Olympic Games, Munich (1972) (1st issue). Views of Munich. Multicoloured.
1067 3c. Type **240** . . . 15 10
1068 5c. View of central Munich . . . 15 10
1069 10c. National Museum . . . 20 10
1070 12c. Max Joseph's Square . . . 25 10
1071 20c. Propylaen, King's Square . . . 40 15
1072 25c. Liesel-Karistadt Fountain . . . 60 20

241 American Scout
242 Pres. William Tubman

1971. World Scout Jamboree, Asagiri, Japan. Scouts in national uniforms. Multicoloured.
1074 3c. Type **241** . . . 15 10
1075 5c. West Germany . . . 15 10
1076 10c. Australia . . . 20 15
1077 12c. Great Britain . . . 25 15
1078 20c. Japan . . . 40 20
1079 25c. Liberia . . . 60 30

1971. Pres. Tubman Memorial Issue.
1081 **242** 3c. brown, blue and black . . . 10 10
1082 25c. brown, purple & blk . . . 35 35

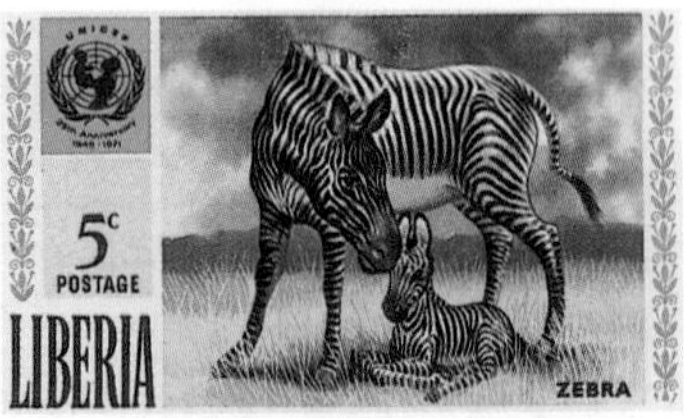

243 Common Zebra and Foal

1971. 25th Anniv of UNICEF. Animals with young. Multicoloured.
1083 5c. Type **243** . . . 20 10
1084 7c. Koalas . . . 30 15
1085 8c. Guanaco . . . 35 15
1086 10c. Red fox and cubs . . . 45 15
1087 20c. Savanna monkeys . . . 65 25
1088 25c. Brown bears . . . 90 35

244 Cross-country Skiing and Sika Deer

1971. Winter Olympic Games, Sapporo, Japan. Sports and Hokkaido Animals. Multicoloured.
1090 2c. Type **244** . . . 10 10
1091 3c. Tobogganing and black woodpecker . . . 70 20
1092 5c. Ski-jumping and brown bear . . . 15 10
1093 10c. Bobsleighing and common guillemots . . . 1·00 20
1094 15c. Figure-skating and northern pika . . . 30 20
1095 25c. Slalom skiing and Manchurian cranes . . . 2·00 50

245 A.P.U. Emblem, Dove and Letter

1971. 10th Anniv of African Postal Union.
1097 **245** 25c. orange and blue . . . 35 50
1098 80c. brown and grey . . . 1·10 1·00

246 "Elizabeth" (emigrant ship) at Providence Island

1972. 150th Anniv of Liberia.
1099 **246** 3c. green and blue . . . 70 50
1100 – 20c. blue and orange . . 35 20
1101 **246** 25c. purple and orange 2·00 55
1102 – 35c. purple and green . . 1·10 75
DESIGNS—VERT: 20, 35c. Arms and Founding Fathers Monument, Monrovia.

247 Pres. Tolbert and Map

1972. Inaug of Pres. Wm. R. Tolbert Jnr.
1104 **247** 25c. brown and green . . 35 25
1105 – 80c. brown and blue . . 1·60 80
DESIGN—VERT: 80c. Pres. Tolbert standing by desk.

248 Football

1972. Olympic Games, Munich (2nd issue). Multicoloured.
1106 3c. Type **248** 10 10
1107 5c. Swimming 15 10
1108 10c. Show-jumping 25 10
1109 12c. Cycling 30 15
1110 20c. Long-jumping 45 20
1111 25c. Running 60 25

249 Globe and Emblem

251 Emperor Haile Selassie

250 Astronaut and Moon Rover

1972. 50th Anniv of Int Y's Men's Clubs.
1113 **249** 15c. violet and gold . . 40 15
1114 – 90c. green and blue . . . 1·75 1·75
DESIGN: 90c. Club emblem on World Map.

1972. Moon Mission of "Apollo 16". Mult.
1115 3c. Type **250** 10 10
1116 5c. Reflection on visor . . . 10 10
1117 10c. Astronauts with cameras 15 10
1118 12c. Setting up equipment 50 15
1119 20c. "Apollo 16" emblem 65 20
1120 25c. Astronauts in Moon Rover 90 50

1972. Emperor Haile Selassie of Ethiopia's 80th Birthday.
1122 **251** 20c. green and yellow . . 40 30
1123 25c. purple and yellow 45 40
1124 35c. brown and yellow 85 85

252 H.M.S. "Ajax" (ship of the line), 1809

1972. Famous Ships of the British Royal Navy. Multicoloured.
1125 3c. Type **252** 35 25
1126 5c. HMS "Hogue" (screw ship of the line), 1848 . . 65 25
1127 7c. HMS "Ariadne" (frigate), 1816 . . . . . 85 30
1128 15c. HMS "Royal Adelaide" (ship of the line), 1828 . . 1·00 55
1129 20c. HMS "Rinaldo" (screw sloop), 1860 . . . . . . 1·40 70
1130 25c. HMS "Nymphe" (screw sloop), 1888 . . . . . . 1·90 1·00

253 Pres. Tolbert taking Oath

1972. 1st Year of President Tolbert Presidency.
1132 **253** 15c. multicoloured . . . 65 55
1133 25c. multicoloured . . . 95 95

254 Klaus Dibiasi and Italian Flag

1973. Olympic Games, Munich. Gold-medal Winners. Multicoloured.
1135 5c. Type **254** 10 10
1136 8c. Borzov and Soviet flag 15 10
1137 10c. Yanagida and Japanese flag 15 10
1138 12c. Spitz and U.S. flag . . 20 15
1139 15c. Keino and Kenyan flag 25 15
1140 25c. Meade and Union Jack 35 25

255 Astronaut on Moon

1973. Moon Flight of "Apollo 17". Multicoloured.
1142 2c. Type **255** 10 10
1143 3c. Testing lunar rover at Cape Kennedy 10 10
1144 10c. Collecting Moon rocks 15 10
1145 15c. Lunar rover on Moon 20 15
1146 20c. "Apollo 17" crew at Cape Kennedy 30 20
1147 25c. Astronauts on Moon 35 25

256 Steam Locomotive, Great Britain

1973. Historical Railways. Steam locomotives of 1895–1905 Multicoloured.
1149 2c. Type **256** 25 10
1150 3c. Netherlands 35 10
1151 10c. France 65 15
1152 15c. No. 1800, U.S.A. . . . 95 20
1153 20c. Class 150 No. 1, Japan 2·00 25
1154 25c. Germany . . . . . . 3·00 30

257 O.A.U. Emblem

1973. 10th Anniv of Organization of African Unity.
1156 **257** 3c. multicoloured 10 10
1157 5c. multicoloured 10 10
1158 10c. multicoloured . . . 15 10
1159 15c. multicoloured . . . 20 15
1160 25c. multicoloured . . . 35 25
1161 50c. multicoloured . . . 1·00 1·00

258 Edward Jenner and Roses

1973. 25th Anniv of W.H.O. Multicoloured.
1162 1c. Type **258** 15 10
1163 4c. Sigmund Freud and violets 15 10
1164 10c. Jonas Salk and chrysanthemums 25 10
1165 15c. Louis Pasteur and scabious 40 15
1166 20c. Emil von Behring and mallow 45 20
1167 25c. Sir Alexander Fleming and rhododendrons . . . 85 25

259 Stanley Steamer, 1910

1973. Vintage Cars. Multicoloured.
1169 2c. Type **259** 10 10
1170 3c. Cadillac Model A, 1903 10 10
1171 10c. Clement-Baynard, 1904 15 10
1172 15c. Rolls-Royce Silver Ghost tourer, 1907 . . . 25 15
1173 20c. Maxwell gentleman's speedster, 1905 . . . . 35 20
1174 25c. Chadwick, 1907 . . . . 50 25

260 Copernicus, Armillary Sphere and Satellite Communications System

1973. 500th Birth Anniv of Copernicus. Mult.
1176 1c. Type **260** 10 10
1177 4c. Eudoxus solar system . . 10 10
1178 10c. Aristotle, Ptolemy and Copernicus 15 10
1179 15c. "Saturn" and "Apollo" spacecraft 25 15
1180 20c. Astronomical observatory satellite . . . 35 20
1181 25c. Satellite tracking-station 50 25

261 Radio Mast and Map of Africa

1974. 20th Anniv of "Eternal Love Winning Africa". Radio Station. Multicoloured.
1183 13c. Type **261** 25 25
1184 15c. Radio mast and map of Liberia 35 25
1185 17c. Type **261** 35 50
1186 25c. As 15c. 50 40

262 "Thomas Coutts" (full-rigged sailing ship) and "Aureol" (liner)

1974. Cent of U.P.U. Multicoloured.
1187 2c. Type **262** 20 10
1188 3c. Boeing 707 airliner and "Brasil" (liner), satellite and Monrovia Post Office 30 10
1189 10c. U.S. and Soviet Telecommunications satellites 15 10
1190 15c. Postal runner and Boeing 707 airliner . . . 25 20

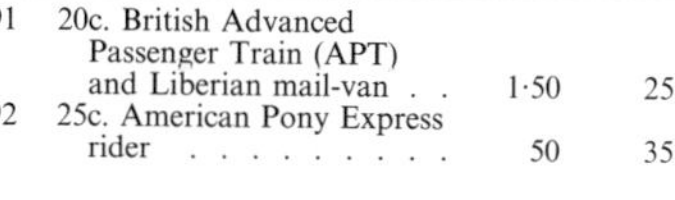
1191 20c. British Advanced Passenger Train (APT) and Liberian mail-van . . 1·50 25
1192 25c. American Pony Express rider 50 35

263 Fox Terrier

1974. Dogs. Multicoloured.
1194 5c. Type **263** 15 10
1195 10c. Boxer 20 10
1196 16c. Chihuahua 30 15
1197 19c. Beagle 35 20
1198 25c. Golden retriever . . . 40 25
1199 50c. Collie . . . . 1·10 50

264 West Germany v. Chile Match

1974. World Cup Football Championship, West Germany. Scenes from semi-final matches. Multicoloured.
1201 1c. Type **264** 10 10
1202 2c. Australia v. East Germany 10 10
1203 5c. Brazil v. Yugoslavia . . 15 10
1204 10c. Zaire v. Scotland . . . 20 10
1205 12c. Netherlands v. Uruguay 25 15
1206 15c. Sweden v. Bulgaria . . 30 15
1207 20c. Italy v. Haiti 40 20
1208 25c. Poland v. Argentina . . 60 25

265 "Chrysiridia madagascariensis"

1974. Tropical Butterflies. Multicoloured.
1210 1c. Type **265** 10 10
1211 2c. "Catagramma sorana" 10 10
1212 5c. "Erasmia pulchella" . . 20 10
1213 17c. "Morpho cypris" . . . 50 25
1214 25c. "Agrias amydon" . . . 70 35
1215 40c. "Vanessa cardui" . . . 1·40 45

266 Pres. Tolbert and Gold Medallion

1974. "Family of Man" Award to President Tolbert. Multicoloured.
1217 3c. Type **266** 10 25
1218 $1 Pres. Tolbert, medallion and flag . . . . 1·40 1·40

267 Churchill with Troops

1975. Birth Centenary of Sir Winston Churchill. Multicoloured.
1219 3c. Type **267** 10 10
1220 10c. Churchill and aerial combat 30 10
1221 15c. Churchill aboard "Liberty" ship in Channel 55 15
1222 17c. Churchill reviewing troops in desert 30 15
1223 20c. Churchill crossing Rhine 40 20
1224 25c. Churchill with Roosevelt 50 25

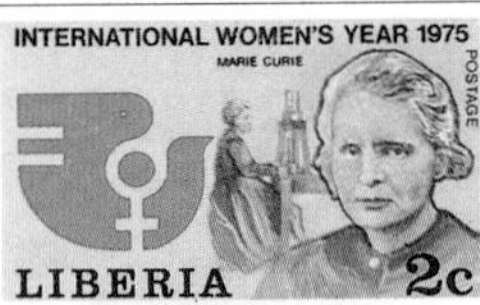

268 Marie Curie

1975. International Women's Year. Multicoloured.

1226	2c. Type **268**	10	10
1227	3c. Mahalia Jackson	10	10
1228	5c. Joan of Arc	10	10
1229	10c. Eleanor Roosevelt	15	10
1230	25c. Matilda Newport	50	25
1231	50c. Valentina Tereshkova	70	55

269 Old State House, Boston, and U.S. 2c. "Liberty Bell" Stamp of 1926

1975. Bicentenary of American Independence.

1233	5c. Type **269**	15	10
1234	10c. George Washington and 1928 "Valley Forge" stamp	30	10
1235	15c. Philadelphia and 1937 "Constitution" stamp	45	15
1236	20c. Benjamin Franklin and 1938 "Ratification" stamp	50	15
1237	25c. Paul Revere's Ride and 1925 "Lexington-Concord" stamp	70	20
1238	50c. "Santa Maria" and 1893 "Columbus' Landing" stamp	2·25	55

270 Dr. Schweitzer, Yellow Baboon and Lambarene Hospital

1975. Birth Centenary of Dr Albert Schweitzer. Multicoloured.

1240	1c. Type **270**	10	10
1241	3c. Schweitzer, African elephant and canoe	15	10
1242	5c. Schweitzer, African buffalo and canoe	25	20
1243	6c. Schweitzer, kob and dancer	30	10
1244	25c. Schweitzer, lioness and village woman	75	25
1245	50c. Schweitzer, common zebras and clinic scene	1·40	65

271 "Apollo" Spacecraft

1975. "Apollo–Soyuz" Space Link. Multicoloured.

1247	5c. Type **271**	10	10
1248	10c. "Soyuz" spacecraft	15	10
1249	15c. American–Russian handclasp	20	15
1250	20c. Flags and maps of America and Russia	25	15
1251	25c. Leonov and Kubasov	35	20
1252	50c. Slayton, Brand and Stafford	95	50

272 Presidents Tolbert and Stevens, and Signing Ceremony

1975. Liberia–Sierra Leone Mano River Union Agreement.

1254 **272**	2c. multicoloured	10	10
1255	3c. multicoloured	10	10
1256	5c. multicoloured	10	10
1257	10c. multicoloured	15	10
1258	25c. multicoloured	35	25
1259	50c. multicoloured	70	70

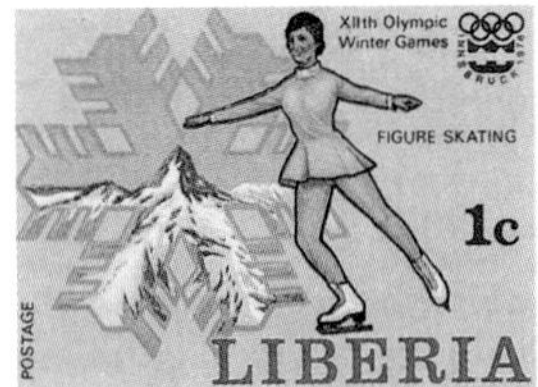

273 Figure Skating

1976. Winter Olympic Games, Innsbruck. Multicoloured.

1260	1c. Type **273**	10	10
1261	4c. Ski jumping	20	20
1262	10c. Skiing (slalom)	30	20
1263	25c. Ice hockey	60	30
1264	35c. Speed skating	90	40
1265	50c. Two-man bobsledding	1·25	65

274 Pres. Tolbert taking Oath

1976. Inauguration of President William R. Tolbert, Jr. Multicoloured.

1267	3c. Type **274**	10	10
1268	25c. Pres. Tolbert in Presidential Chair (vert)	35	25
1269	$1 Liberian crest, flag and commemorative gold coin	1·90	1·40

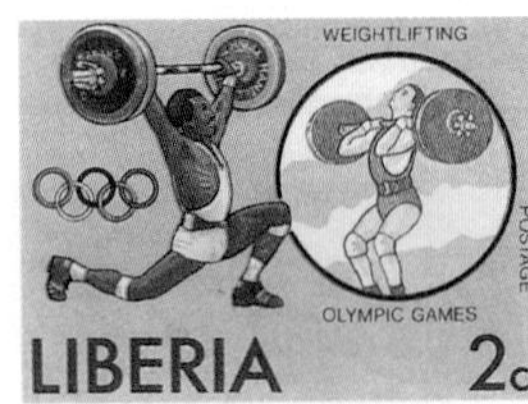

275 Weightlifting

1976. Olympic Games, Montreal. Multicoloured.

1270	2c. Type **275**	10	10
1271	3c. Pole-vaulting	10	10
1272	10c. Hammer and shot-put	30	15
1273	25c. "Tempest" dinghies	65	35
1274	35c. Gymnastics	90	60
1275	50c. Hurdling	1·25	65

276 Bell's Telephone and Receiver

1976. Telephone Centenary. Multicoloured.

1277	1c. Type **276**	10	10
1278	4c. Mail-coach	10	10
1279	5c. "Intelsat 4" satellite	15	10
1280	25c. Cable-ship "Dominia", 1926	1·25	30
1281	40c. British Advanced Passenger Train (APT)	1·60	50
1282	50c. Wright Flyer I, airship "Graf Zeppelin" and Concorde	1·75	60

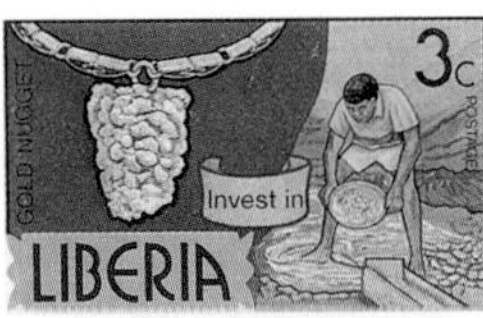

277 Gold Nugget Pendant

1976. Liberian Products (1st series). Multicoloured.

1284	1c. Mano River Bridge	10	10
1285	3c. Type **277**	10	10
1286	5c. "V" ring	10	10
1286a	7c. As No. 1286	15	25
1287	10c. Rubber tree and tyre	15	10
1287a	15c. Combine harvester	20	10
1287b	17c. As No. 1289	45	10
1287c	20c. Hydro-electric plant	60	45
1288	25c. Mesurado shrimp	75	25
1288a	27c. Dress and woman tie-dying cloth	80	60
1289	55c. Great barracuda	1·40	35
1289a	$1 Train carrying iron ore	4·50	60

For designs as T **277** but in a smaller size, see Nos. 1505/8.

278 Black Rhinoceros

1976. Animals. Multicoloured.

1290	2c. Type **278**	10	10
1291	3c. Bongo	10	10
1292	5c. Chimpanzee (vert)	15	10
1293	15c. Pygmy hippopotamus	40	15
1294	25c. Leopard	80	40
1295	$1 Gorilla	3·00	90

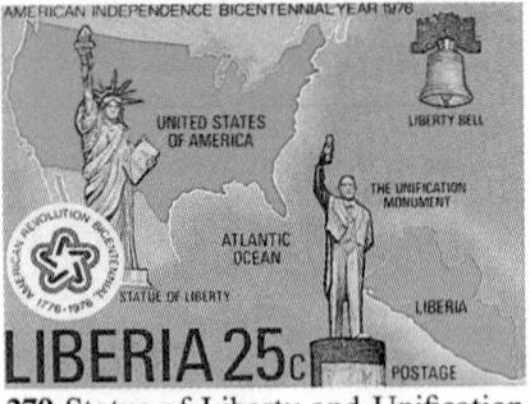

279 Statue of Liberty and Unification Monument on Maps of U.S.A. and Liberia

1976. Bicentenary of American Revolution. Multicoloured.

1297	25c. Type **279**	35	25
1298	$1 Presidents Washington and Ford (U.S.A.), Roberts and Tolbert (Liberia)	1·75	65

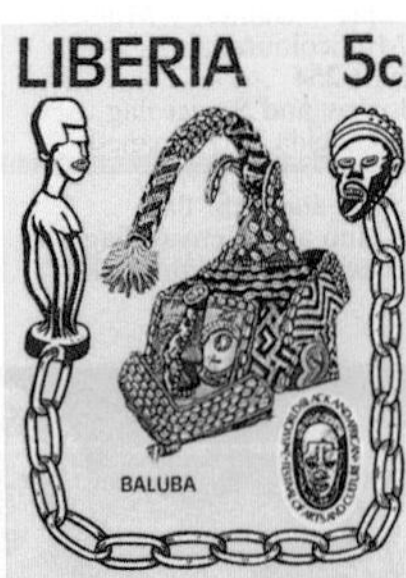

280 Baluba Masks

1977. Second World Black and African Festival of Arts and Culture, Lagos (Nigeria). Tribal Masks. Multicoloured.

1300	5c. Type **280**	10	10
1301	10c. Bateke	15	10
1302	15c. Basshilele	20	15
1303	20c. Igungun	30	15
1304	25c. Maisi	60	20
1305	50c. Kifwebe	1·10	45

281 Latham's Francolin

1977. Liberian Wild Birds. Multicoloured.

1307	5c. Type **281**	50	10
1308	10c. Narina's trogon ("Narina Trogon")	80	15
1309	15c. Rufous-crowned roller	80	20
1310	20c. Brown-cheeked hornbill	85	25
1311	25c. Garden bulbul ("Pepper Bird")	1·00	35
1312	50c. African fish eagle ("Fish Eagle")	1·10	85

282 Alwin Schockemohle (individual jumping)

1977. Olympic Games, Montreal. Equestrian Gold-medal Winners. Multicoloured.

1314	5c. Edmund Coffin (military dressage) (postage)	15	10
1315	15c. Type **282**	40	20
1316	20c. Christine Stuckelberger (dressage)	50	30
1317	25c. "Nations Prize" (French team)	70	35
1318	55c. Military dressage (U.S.A. team) (air)	1·25	70

283 Queen Elizabeth II

1977. Silver Jubilee of Queen Elizabeth II. Multicoloured.

1320	15c. Type **283**	35	15
1321	25c. Queen Elizabeth and Prince Philip with President and Mrs. Tubman of Liberia	55	25
1322	80c. Queen Elizabeth, Prince Philip and Royal Arms	2·40	70

284 "Blessing the Children"

1977. Christmas. Multicoloured.

1324	20c. Type **284**	50	25
1325	25c. "The Good Shepherd"	70	35
1326	$1 "Jesus and the Woman of Samaria at the Well"	2·00	1·00

285 Dornier Do-X Flying Boat

1978. "Progress in Aviation". Multicoloured.

1327	2c. Type **285**	10	10
1328	3c. Space shuttle "Enterprise" on Boeing 747	10	10
1329	5c. Edward Rickenbacker and Douglas DC-3	10	10
1330	25c. Charles Lindbergh and "Spirit of St. Louis"	45	20
1331	35c. Louis Bleriot and Bleriot XI monoplane	65	35
1332	50c. Wright Brothers and Flyer I	90	55

286 Santos-Dumont's Airship "Ballon No. 9 La Badaleuse", 1903

1978. 75th Anniv of First Zeppelin Flight. Multicoloured.

1334	2c. Type **286**	10	10
1335	3c. Thomas Baldwin's airship "U.S. Military No. 1", 1908	10	10
1336	5c. Tissandier brothers' airship, 1883	10	10
1337	25c. Parseval airship PL-VII, 1912	40	20
1338	40c. Airship "Nulli Secundus II", 1908	75	35
1339	50c. Beardmore airship R-34, 1919	85	55

287 Tackling

1978. World Cup Football Championship, Argentina.

1341	**287**	2c. multicoloured	10	10
1342	–	3c. multicoloured (horiz)	10	10
1343	–	10c. multicoloured (horiz)	15	10
1344	–	25c. multicoloured (horiz)	60	20
1345	–	35c. multicoloured	80	25
1346	–	50c. multicoloured (horiz)	1·25	50

DESIGNS: Nos. 1342/6, Different match scenes.

288 Coronation Chair

1978. 25th Anniv of Coronation. Multicoloured.

1348	5c. Type **288**	10	25
1349	25c. Imperial State Crown	35	25
1350	$1 Buckingham Palace (horiz)	1·75	1·00

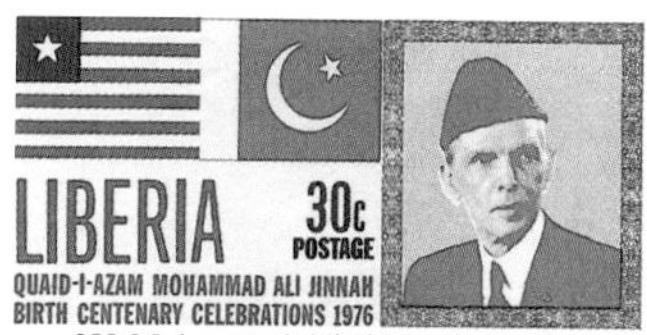

289 Mohammed Ali Jinnah and Flags

1978. Birth Centenary of Mohammed Ali Jinnah (first Governor-General of Pakistan).

1352	**289**	30c. multicoloured	1·50	1·50

290 Carter and Tolbert Families

1978. Visit of President Carter of U.S.A. Mult.

1353	5c. Type **290**	10	10
1354	25c. Presidents Carter and Tolbert with Mrs. Carter at microphones	50	45
1355	$1 Presidents Carter and Tolbert in open car	2·00	2·00

291 Italy v. France

292 Timber Truck

1978. Argentina's Victory in World Cup Football Championship. Multicoloured.

1356	1c. Brazil v. Spain (horiz)	10	10
1357	2c. Type **291**	10	10
1358	10c. Poland v. West Germany (horiz)	15	10
1359	27c. Peru v. Scotland	65	25
1360	35c. Austria v. West Germany	80	55
1361	50c. Argentinian players with Cup	1·25	80

1978. 8th World Forestry Congress, Djakarta. Multicoloured.

1363	5c. Chopping up log (horiz)	10	10
1364	10c. Type **292**	15	10
1365	25c. Felling trees (horiz)	60	20
1366	50c. Loggers (horiz)	1·10	70

293 Presidents Gardner and Tolbert with Monrovia Post Office

1979. Centenary of U.P.U. Membership. Mult.

1367	5c. Type **293**	10	10
1368	35c. Presidents Gardner and Tolbert with U.P.U. emblem	90	90

294 "25" and Radio Waves

1979. 25th Anniv of Radio ELWA. Multicoloured.

1369	35c. Type **294**	75	75
1370	$1 Radio tower	2·10	2·10

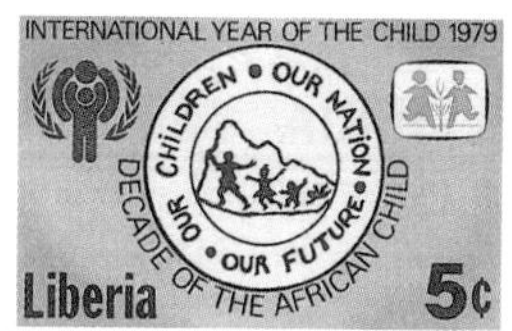

295 I.Y.C., Decade of the African Child and S.O.S. Villages Emblems

1979. International Year of the Child. Multicoloured.

1371	5c. Type **295**	10	10
1372	25c. As Type **295** but with UNICEF instead of S.O.S. Villages emblem	25	20
1373	35c. Type **295**	50	25
1374	$1 As No. 1372	1·40	1·40

296 Clasped Arms and Torches

1979. Organization for African Unity Summit Conference, Monrovia. Multicoloured.

1375	5c. Type **296**	10	10
1376	27c. Masks	40	25
1377	35c. African animals	50	50
1378	50c. Thatched huts and garden bulbuls	1·50	65

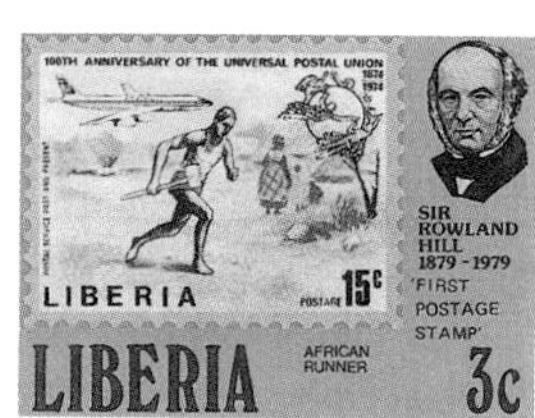

297 Sir Rowland Hill and Liberian 15c. Stamp, 1974

1979. Death Centenary of Sir Rowland Hill. Multicoloured.

1379	3c. Type **297**	10	10
1380	10c. Pony Express rider	15	10
1381	15c. British mail coach	20	35
1382	25c. "John Penn" (paddle-steamer)	75	55
1383	27c. Class "Coronation" streamlined steam locomotive No. 6235, Great Britain	1·10	25
1384	50c. Concorde	1·50	90

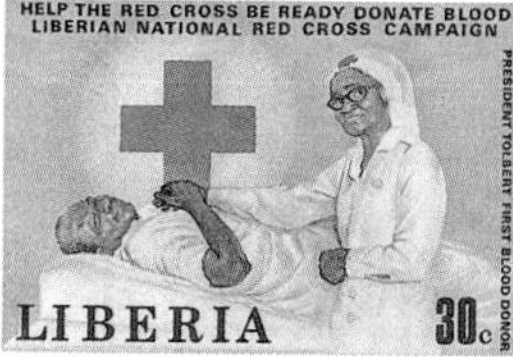

298 President Tolbert giving Blood

1979. National Red Cross Blood Donation Campaign. Multicoloured.

1386	30c. Type **298**	45	25
1387	50c. President Tolbert and Red Cross	1·00	1·00

299 "World Peace" (tanker)

1979. 2nd World Maritime Day and 30th Anniv of Liberia Maritime Programme. Multicoloured.

1388	5c. Type **299**	30	15
1389	$1 "World Peace" (different)	2·25	2·00

300 "A Good Turn"

1979. Scout Paintings by Norman Rockwell. Multicoloured.

1390	5c. Scout giving first aid to pup ("A Good Scout")	20	15
1391	5c. Type **300**	20	15
1392	5c. "Good Friends"	20	15
1393	5c. "Spirit of America"	20	15
1394	5c. "Scout Memories"	20	15
1395	5c. "The Adventure Trail"	20	15
1396	5c. "On My Honour"	20	15
1397	5c. "A Scout is Reverent"	20	15
1398	5c. "The Right Way"	20	15
1399	5c. "The Scoutmaster"	20	15
1400	10c. "A Scout is Loyal"	40	25
1401	10c. "An Army of Friendship"	35	20
1402	10c. "Carry on"	35	20
1403	10c. "A Good Scout"	35	20
1404	10c. "The Campfire Story"	35	20
1405	10c. "High Adventure"	35	20
1406	10c. "Mighty Proud"	35	20
1407	10c. "Tomorrow's Leader"	35	20
1408	10c. "Ever Onward"	35	20
1409	10c. "Homecoming"	35	20
1410	15c. "Scouts of Many Trails"	40	25
1411	15c. "America builds for Tomorrow"	40	25
1412	15c. "The Scouting Trail"	40	25
1413	15c. "A Scout is Reverent"	40	25
1414	15c. "A Scout is Helpful"	40	25
1415	15c. "Pointing the Way"	40	25
1416	15c. "A Good Sign All Over the World"	40	25
1417	15c. "To Keep Myself Physically Strong"	40	25
1418	15c. "A Great Moment"	40	25
1419	15c. "Growth of a Leader"	40	25
1420	25c. "A Scout is Loyal"	60	35
1421	25c. "A Scout is Friendly"	60	35
1422	25c. "We Too, Have a Job to Do"	60	35
1423	25c. "I Will do my Best"	60	35
1424	25c. "A Guiding Hand"	60	35
1425	25c. "Breakthrough for Freedom"	1·25	40
1426	25c. "Scouting is Outing"	60	35
1427	25c. "Beyond the Easel"	60	35
1428	25c. "Come and Get It"	60	35
1429	25c. "America's Manpower begins with Boypower"	60	35
1430	35c. "All Together"	80	45
1431	35c. "Men of Tomorrow"	80	45
1432	35c. "Friend in Need"	80	45
1433	35c. "Our Heritage"	80	45
1434	35c. "Forward America"	80	45
1435	35c. "Can't Wait"	80	45
1436	35c. "From Concord to Tranquility"	80	45
1437	35c. "We Thank Thee"	80	45
1438	35c. "So Much Concern"	80	45
1439	35c. "Spirit of '76"	80	45

301 Mrs. Tolbert and Children

1979. S.O.S. Children's Village, Monrovia. Multicoloured.

1440	25c. Mrs. Tolbert and children (different) (horiz)	35	50
1441	40c. Type **301**	90	90

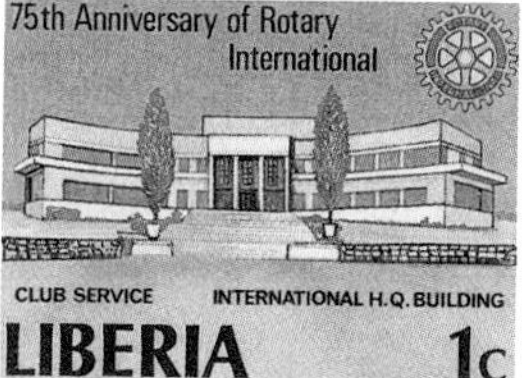

302 International Headquarters, Evanston, Illinois

1979. 75th Anniv of Rotary International. Multicoloured.

1442	1c. Type **302**	10	10
1443	5c. Vocational services	10	10
1444	17c. Wheelchair patient and nurse (community service) (vert)	20	35
1445	27c. Flags (international service)	40	50
1446	35c. Different races holding hands around globe (health, hunger and humanity)	50	50
1447	50c. President Tolbert and map of Africa (17th anniv of Monrovia Rotary Club) (vert)	1·00	1·00

303 Ski Jumping

1980. Winter Olympic Games, Lake Placid. Multicoloured.

1449	1c. Type **303**	10	10
1450	5c. Pairs figure skating	10	10
1451	17c. Bobsleigh	20	35
1452	27c. Cross-country skiing	75	75
1453	35c. Speed skating	75	75
1454	50c. Ice hockey	1·00	1·00

304 Presidents Tolbert of Liberia and Stevens of Sierra Leone and View of Mano River

1980. 5th Anniv of Mano River Union and 1st Anniv (1979) of Postal Union.

1456	**304**	8c. multicoloured	15	10
1457		27c. multicoloured	45	50
1458		35c. multicoloured	80	75
1459		80c. multicoloured	1·75	1·75

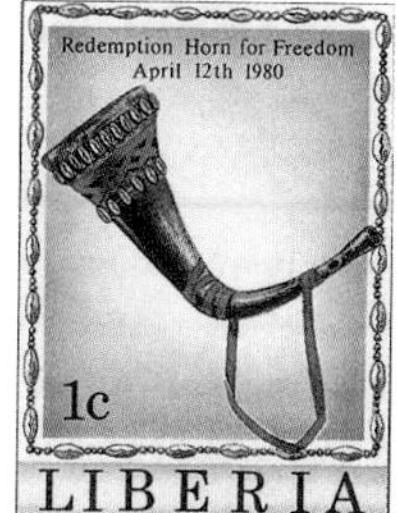

305 Redemption Horn

1981. People's Redemption Council (1st series). Multicoloured.
1460 1c. Type **305** 10 10
1461 10c. M/Sgt. Doe and allegory of redemption (horiz) 10 10
1462 14c. Map, soldier and citizens (horiz) 15 15
1463 $2 M/Sgt. Samuel Doe (chairman of Council) . . 3·75 3·75
See also Nos. 1475/8.

306 Players and Flags of Argentine, Uruguay, Italy and Czechoslovakia

1981. World Cup Football Championship, Spain (1982). Multicoloured.
1464 3c. Type **306** 10 10
1465 5c. Players and flags of Hungary, Italy, Germany, Brazil and Sweden . . . 10 10
1466 20c. Players and flags of Italy, Germany, Brazil and Sweden 20 20
1467 27c. Players and flags of Czechoslovakia, Brazil, Great Britain and Germany 25 25
1468 40c. Players and flags of Italy, Brazil, Germany and Netherlands 60 60
1469 55c. Players and flags of Netherlands and Uruguay 1·10 1·10

307 M/Sgt. Doe and Crowd

1981. 1st Anniv of People's Redemption Council. Multicoloured.
1471 22c. Type **307** 20 20
1472 27c. M/Sgt. Doe and national flag 25 25
1473 30c. Hands clasping arms, sunrise and map 45 45
1474 $1 M/Sgt. Doe, "Justice" and soldiers . . . . . . 1·75 1·75

1981. People's Redemption Council (2nd series).
1475 6c. Type **305** 10 10
1476 23c. As No. 1461 . . . . . 20 20
1477 31c. As No. 1462 . . . . . 45 45
1478 41c. As No. 1463 . . . . . 60 60

308 John Adams

1981. Presidents of the United States (1st series). Multicoloured.
1479 4c. Type **308** 10 10
1480 5c. William Henry Harrison 10 10
1481 10c. Martin Van Buren . . 15 15
1482 17c. James Monroe 20 20
1483 20c. John Quincy Adams . . 25 25
1484 22c. James Madison 25 25
1485 27c. Thomas Jefferson . . . 35 30
1486 30c. Andrew Jackson . . . 55 50
1487 40c. John Tyler 80 70
1488 80c. George Washington . . 1·50 1·50
See also Nos. 1494/1503, 1519/27 and 1533/42.

309 Prince Charles and Lady Diana Spencer

1981. British Royal Wedding. Multicoloured.
1490 31c. Type **309** 30 30
1491 41c. Intertwined initials . . 40 40
1492 62c. St. Paul's Cathedral . . 1·10 1·10

1981. Presidents of the United States (2nd series). As T **308**. Multicoloured.
1494 6c. Rutherford B. Hayes . . 10 10
1495 12c. Ulysses S. Grant . . . 15 15
1496 14c. Millard Fillmore . . . 20 15
1497 15c. Zachary Taylor 20 15
1498 20c. Abraham Lincoln . . . 25 20
1499 27c. Andrew Johnson . . . 30 25
1500 31c. James Buchanan . . . 50 45
1501 41c. James A. Garfield . . . 70 60
1502 50c. James K. Polk 80 70
1503 55c. Franklin Pierce . . . . 1·00 85

1981. Liberian Products (2nd series). As T **277**, but smaller, 33 × 20 mm. Multicoloured.
1504a 1c. Mano River Bridge . . 10 10
1505 3c. Type **277** 10 10
1506 6c. Rubber tree and tyre 10 10
1506a 15c. Combine harvester . . 20 15
1507 25c. Mesurado shrimp . . 35 35
1508 31c. Hydro-electric plant 70 70
1509 41c. Dress and woman tie-dying cloth 60 55
1509a 80c. Great barracuda . . . 2·50 1·50
1510 $1 Diesel train carrying iron ore . . . . 5·75 1·60

310 Disabled Children

312 Lady Diana Spencer

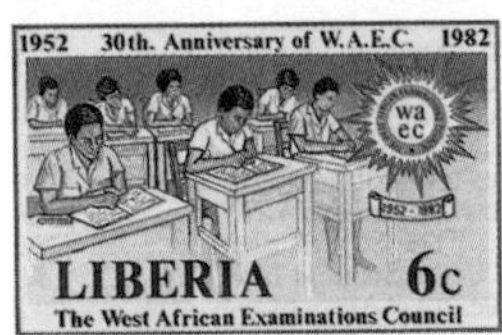

311 Examination Room

1982. International Year of Disabled People (1981). Multicoloured.
1515 23c. Type **310** 35 35
1516 62c. Child leading blind woman . . . . 1·25 95

1982. 30th Anniv of West African Examination Council.
1517 **311** 6c. multicoloured 10 10
1518 31c. multicoloured . . . 45 45

1982. Presidents of the United States (3rd series). As T **308**. Multicoloured.
1519 4c. William Taft 10 25
1520 5c. Calvin Coolidge 10 10
1521 6c. Benjamin Harrison . . . 15 15
1522 10c. Warren Harding . . . 20 25
1523 22c. Grover Cleveland . . . 45 45
1524 27c. Chester Arthur 50 70
1525 31c. Woodrow Wilson . . . 60 60
1526 41c. William McKinley . . 70 80
1527 80c. Theodore Roosevelt . . 1·50 1·60

1982. Princess of Wales. 21st Birthday. Mult.
1529 31c. Type **312** 70 70
1530 41c. Lady Diana Spencer (different) 85 85
1531 62c. Lady Diana accepting flower . . . . 1·25 1·25

1982. Presidents of the United States (4th series). As T **308**. Multicoloured.
1533 4c. Jimmy Carter 10 10
1534 6c. Gerald Ford 15 15
1535 14c. Harry Truman 25 25
1536 17c. Franklin D. Roosevelt 30 30
1537 23c. Lyndon B. Johnson . . 40 40
1538 27c. Richard Nixon 45 50
1539 31c. John F. Kennedy . . . 50 60
1540 35c. Ronald Reagan 60 80
1541 50c. Herbert Hoover 80 90
1542 55c. Dwight D. Eisenhower 1·00 1·00

1982. Birth of Prince William of Wales. Nos. 1529/31 optd **ROYAL BABY 21-6-82 PRINCE WILLIAM**.
1544 31c. Type **312** 45 45
1545 41c. Lady Diana Spencer (different) 60 60
1546 62c. Lady Diana accepting flower 95 95

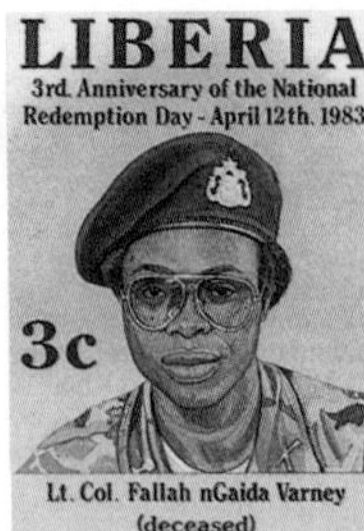

314 Lt. Col. Fallah nGaida Varney

1983. 3rd Anniv of National Redemption Day. Multicoloured.
1548 3c. Type **314** 10 10
1549 6c. Commander-in-Chief Samuel Doe 10 10
1550 10c. Major-General Jlatoh Nicholas Podier 15 15
1551 15c. Brigadier-General Jeffery Sei Gbatu 20 15
1552 31c. Brigadier-General Thomas Gunkama Quiwonkpa 50 45
1553 41c. Colonel Abraham Doward Kollie 60 80

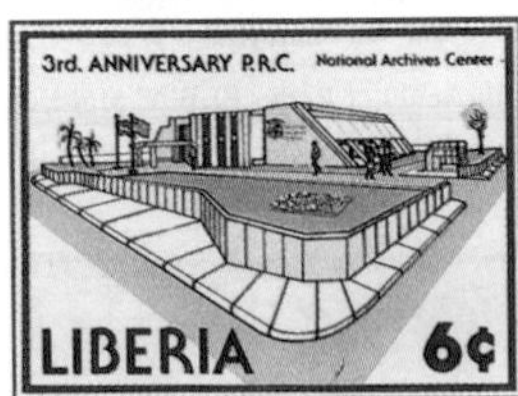

315 National Archives Centre

1983. Opening of National Archives Centre. Multicoloured.
1555 6c. Type **315** 10 10
1556 31c. National Archives Centre 50 45

316 "Circumcision of Christ"

1983. Christmas. 500th Birth Anniv of Raphael. Multicoloured.
1557 6c. Type **316** 10 10
1558 15c. "Adoration of the Magi" (detail) 20 15
1559 25c. "The Annunciation" (detail) 40 35
1560 31c. "Madonna of the Baldachino" 50 45
1561 41c. "Holy Family" (detail) 60 55
1562 62c. "Madonna and Child with Five Saints" (detail) 90 85

317 Graduates of M.U.R. Training Programmes

1984. 10th Anniv (1983) of Mano River Union. Multicoloured.
1564 6c. Type **317** 10 10
1565 25c. Map of Africa 40 35
1566 31c. Presidents and map of member states 50 45
1567 41c. President of Guinea signing Accession Agreement 70 85

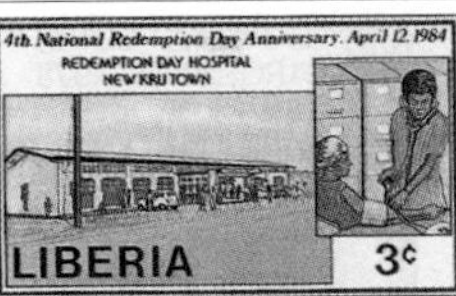

318 Redemption Day Hospital, New Kru Town

1984. 4th Anniv of National Redemption Day. Multicoloured.
1569 3c. Type **318** 10 10
1570 10c. Ganta–Harpa Highway project 15 15
1571 20c. Opening of Constitution Assembly . . 35 30
1572 31c. Commander-in-Chief Doe launching Ganta–Harper Highway project 50 45
1573 41c. Presentation of Draft Constitution 70 85

319 "Adoration of the Magi"

1984. Rubens Paintings (1st series). Multicoloured.
1574 6c. Type **319** 10 10
1575 15c. "Coronation of Catherine" 25 20
1576 25c. "Adoration of the Magi" 70 70
1577 31c. "Madonna and Child with Halo" 85 85
1578 41c. "Adoration of the Shepherds" . . . . 1·10 1·10
1579 62c. "Madonna and Child with Saints" . . . . . . 1·75 1·75
See also Nos. 1612/17.

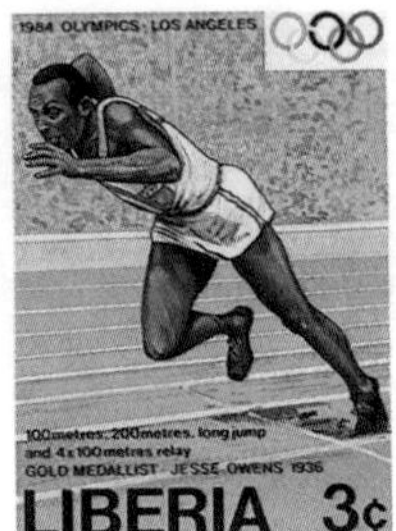

320 Jesse Owens

1984. Olympic Games, Los Angeles. Multicoloured.
1581 3c. Type **320** 10 10
1582 4c. Rafer Johnson 10 10
1583 25c. Miruts Yifter 65 65
1584 41c. Kipchoge Keino . . . 1·10 1·10
1585 62c. Muhammad Ali . . . . 1·75 1·75

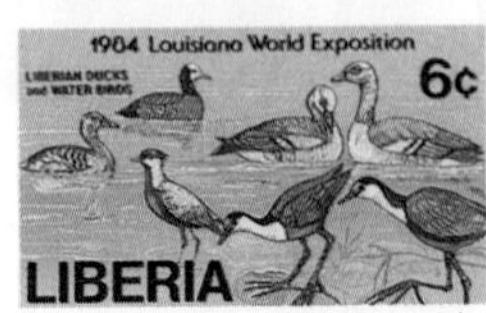

321 Liberian Ducks and Water Birds

1984. Louisiana World Exposition. Multicoloured.
1587 6c. Type **321** 20 20
1588 31c. Bulk carrier loading ore at Buchanan Harbour . . 1·60 75
1589 41c. Peters' mormyrid, electric catfish, Nile perch, krib and jewel cichlid . . 1·50 1·10
1590 62c. Diesel train carrying iron ore . . . . 1·75 90

322 Mother and Calf

1984. Pygmy Hippopotami. Multicoloured.
1591 6c. Type **322** 20 10
1592 10c. Pair of hippopotami . . 80 80
1593 20c. Close-up of hippopotamus . . . . . 1·40 1·40
1594 31c. Hippopotamus and map . . . . 2·10 2·10

323 Mrs. Doe and Children

1984. Indigent Children's Home, Bensonville. Multicoloured.
1595 6c. Type **323** 10 10
1596 31c. Mrs. Doe and children (different) 50 50

324 New Soldiers' Barracks

1985. 5th Anniv of National Redemption Day. Multicoloured.
1597 6c. Type **324** 10 10
1598 31c. Pan-African Plaza . . . 50 50

325 Bohemian Waxwing

1985. Birth Bicentenary of John J. Audubon (ornithologist). Multicoloured.
1599 1c. Type **325** 15 10
1600 3c. Bay-breasted warbler . . 30 10
1601 6c. White-winged crossbill 35 15
1602 31c. Grey phalarope ("Red Phalarope") . . . . . . 2·00 1·00
1603 41c. Eastern bluebird . . . 2·50 1·50
1604 62c. Common cardinal ("Northern Cardinal") . . 3·50 2·40

326 Germany v. Morocco, 1970

1985. World Cup Football Championship, Mexico (1986). Multicoloured.
1605 6c. Type **326** 10 10
1606 15c. Zaire v. Brazil, 1974 . . 20 15
1607 25c. Tunisia v. Germany, 1978 . . . . 60 60
1608 31c. Cameroun v. Peru, 1982 (vert) 75 75
1609 41c. Algeria v. Germany, 1982 . . . . 95 95
1610 62c. Senegal team . . . . . 1·40 1·40

327 "Mirror of Venus" (detail)
328 Women transplanting Rice

1985. Rubens Paintings (2nd series). Mult.
1612 6c. Type **327** 10 10
1613 15c. "Adam and Eve in Paradise" (detail) 20 15
1614 25c. "Andromeda" (detail) 60 60
1615 31c. "The Three Graces" (detail) 75 75
1616 41c. "Venus and Adonis" (detail) 95 95
1617 62c. "The Daughters of Leucippus" (detail) . . . 1·40 1·40

1985. World Food Day.
1619 **328** 25c. multicoloured . . . 1·25 85
1620 31c. multicoloured . . . 1·50 1·10

329 Queen Mother in Garter Robes
330 Alamo, San Antonio, Texas

1985. 85th Birthday of Queen Elizabeth the Queen Mother. Multicoloured.
1621 31c. Type **329** 35 30
1622 41c. At the races 80 75
1623 62c. Waving to the crowds 1·10 1·10

1986. "Ameripex '86" International Stamp Exhibition, Chicago. Multicoloured.
1625 25c. Type **330** 60 60
1626 31c. Liberty Bell, Philadelphia 75 75
1627 80c. Magnifying glass, emblem and Liberian stamps . . . . 3·00 2·25

331 Unveiling Ceremony, 1886 (after E. Moran)
333 Royal Theatre, Gendarmenmarkt

332 Max Julen (Men's Giant Slalom)

1986. Centenary of Statue of Liberty. Multicoloured.
1628 20c. Type **331** 30 50
1629 31c. Frederic-Auguste Bartholdi (sculptor) and statue 75 75
1630 $1 Head of statue . . . . . 2·40 2·40

1987. Winter Olympic Games, Calgary (1988). 1984 Games Gold Medallists. Multicoloured.
1631 3c. Type **332** 10 10
1632 6c. Debbi Armstrong (women's giant slalom) . . 10 10
1633 31c. Peter Angerer (biathlon) 35 55
1634 60c. Bill Johnson (men's downhill) . . . . 1·10 1·10
1635 80c. East German team (four-man bobsleigh) . . 1·40 1·40

1987. Liberian–German Friendship. 750th Anniv of Berlin. Multicoloured.
1637 6c. Type **333** 10 10
1638 31c. Kaiser Friedrich Museum, River Spree . . 35 55
1639 60c. Charlottenburg Palace 1·10 1·10
1640 80c. Kaiser Wilhelm Memorial Church . . . . 1·40 1·40

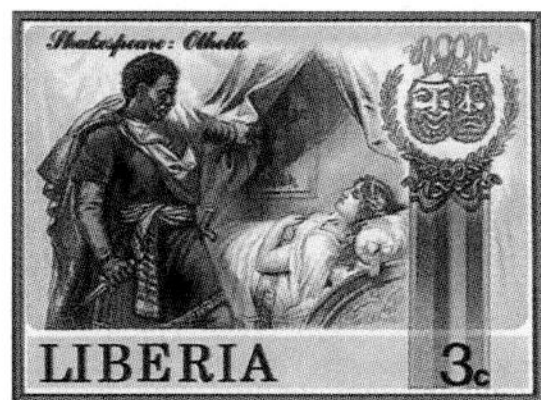

334 Othello and Desdemona ("Othello")

1987. William Shakespeare. Multicoloured.
1642 3c. Type **334** 10 10
1643 6c. Romeo and Juliet ("Romeo and Juliet") . . 10 10
1644 10c. Falstaff ("The Merry Wives of Windsor") . . . 15 10
1645 15c. Falstaff, Doll Tearsheet and Prince Hal ("Henry IV", Part 2) 20 15
1646 31c. Hamlet holding Yorick's skull ("Hamlet") 60 50
1647 60c. Macbeth and the three witches ("Macbeth") . . . 1·25 1·25
1648 80c. Lear and companions in the storm ("King Lear") . . . . 1·75 1·75
1649 $2 William Shakespeare and Globe Theatre, Southwark 4·00 4·00

335 Emblem

1987. Amateur Radio Week. 25th Anniv of Liberia Radio Amateur Association. Multicoloured.
1650 10c. Type **335** 15 10
1651 10c. Amateur radio enthusiasts 15 10
1652 35c. Certificate awarded to participants in anniversary "On the Air" activity . . 80 70
1653 35c. Globe, flags and banner 80 70

336 Illuminated Torch Flame

1987. Centenary of Statue of Liberty. Multicoloured.
1654 6c. Type **336** 10 10
1655 6c. Scaffolding around statue's head 10 10
1656 6c. Men working on head 10 10
1657 6c. Men working on crown 10 10
1658 6c. Statue's toes 10 10
1659 15c. Statue behind "Sir Winston Churchill" (cadet schooner) 45 20
1660 15c. "Bay Queen" (harbour ferry) 45 20
1661 15c. Posters on buildings and crowd 20 15
1662 15c. Tug and schooner in bay 45 20
1663 15c. Decorated statues around building 20 15
1664 31c. Fireworks display around statue 60 50
1665 31c. Statue floodlit 60 50
1666 31c. Statue's head 60 50
1667 31c. Fireworks display around statue (different) 60 50
1668 31c. Statue (half-length) . . 60 50
1669 60c. Wall poster on building (vert) . . . . 1·10 1·00
1670 60c. Yachts and cabin cruisers on river (vert) . . 1·50 1·00
1671 60c. Measuring statue's nose (vert) . . . . 1·10 1·00
1672 60c. Plastering nose (vert) 1·10 1·00
1673 60c. Finishing off repaired nose (vert) . . . . 1·10 1·00

337 Dr. Doe (President), Dr. Moniba (Vice-President), Flags and Hands

1988. 2nd Anniv of Second Republic.
1674 **337** 10c. multicoloured . . . 15 10
1675 35c. multicoloured . . . 65 55

338 Breast-feeding

1988. UNICEF Child Survival and Development Campaign. Multicoloured.
1676 3c. Type **338** 10 10
1677 6c. Oral rehydration therapy (vert) 10 10
1678 31c. Immunization 60 50
1679 $1 Growth monitoring (vert) 2·00 2·00

339 Chief Justice Emmanuel N. Gbalazeh swearing-in Dr. Samuel Kanyon Doe

1988. Inauguration of Second Republic.
1680 **339** 6c. multicoloured 10 10

340 Footballer and Stadium

1988. 2nd Anniv of Opening of Samuel Kanyon Doe Sports Complex.
1681 **340** 31c. multicoloured . . . 60 50

341 Child and Volunteer reading

1988. 25th Anniv of U.S. Peace Corps in Liberia.
1682 **341** 10c. multicoloured . . . 10 10
1683 35c. multicoloured . . . 70 60

342 Pres. Doe, Farm Workers and Produce

1988. Green Revolution.
1684 **342** 10c. multicoloured . . . 25 10
1685 35c. multicoloured . . . 85 35

344 Emblem
345 Type GP10 Diesel Locomotive, Nimba

1988. 25th Anniv of Organization of African Unity.
1687 **344** 10c. multicoloured . . . 10 10
1688 35c. multicoloured . . . 70 60
1689 $1 multicoloured . . . . 2·00 2·00

1988. Locomotives. Multicoloured.
1690 10c. Type **345** 25 15
1691 35c. Triple-headed diesel iron ore train 85 50

346 Helping Boy to Walk
347 Baseball

1988. 25th Anniv of St. Joseph's Catholic Hospital. Multicoloured.
1693 10c. Type **346** 10 10
1694 10c. Medical staff and hospital 10 10
1695 35c. Monk, child, candle and hospital 65 65
1696 $1 Map behind doctor with nurse holding baby . . . 1·90 1·90

1988. Olympic Games, Seoul. Multicoloured.
1697 10c. Type **347** 10 10
1698 35c. Hurdling 65 65
1699 45c. Fencing 80 80
1700 80c. Synchronized swimming 1·40 1·40
1701 $1 Yachting . . . . 1·75 1·75

348 Monkey Bridge
349 Tending Crops

1988.
1703 10c. Type **348** 10 10
1704 35c. Sasa players (horiz) 40 60
1705 45c. Snake dancers 70 75

1988. 10th Anniv of International Fund for Agricultural Development. Multicoloured.
1706 10c. Type **349** 10 10
1707 35c. Farmers tending livestock and spraying crops 70 60

350 Destruction of Royal Exchange, 1838

1988. 300th Anniv of Lloyd's of London. Multicoloured.
1708 10c. Type **350** 10 10
1709 35c. Britten Norman Islander airplane (horiz) 60 60
1710 45c. "Chevron Antwerp" (tanker) (horiz) 70 75
1711 $1 "Lakonia" (liner) ablaze, 1963 2·00 2·00

351 Honouring Head of Operational Smile Team

1989. 3rd Anniv of Second Republic.
1712 **351** 10c. black and blue 10 10
1713 35c. black and red 80 85
1714 – 50c. black and mauve 1·25 1·25
DESIGN: 50c. Pres. Samuel Doe at John F. Kennedy Memorial Hospital.

1989. Presidents of United States (5th series). As T **308**. Multicoloured.
1715 $1 George Bush 2·50 2·50

352 "Harmony"

353 Union Glass Factory, Gardersville, Monrovia

1989. Liberia–Japan Friendship. 50th Anniv of Rissho Kosei-Kai (lay Buddhist association). Multicoloured.
1716 10c. Type **352** 10 10
1717 10c. Nikkyo Niwano (founder and president of association) 10 10
1718 10c. Rissho Kosei-Kai headquarters, Tokyo 10 10
1719 50c. Eternal Buddha, Great Sacred Hall 1·40 1·40

1989. 15th Anniv of Mano River Union. Mult.
1721 10c. Type **353** 15 10
1722 35c. Presidents of Guinea, Sierra Leone and Liberia 70 60
1723 45c. Monrovia–Freetown highway 85 80
1724 50c. Flags, map and mail van 85 85
1725 $1 Presidents at 1988 Summit 2·00 1·90

354 Symbols of International Co-operation

357 Helicopter Carrier U.S.S. "Okinawa"

1989. World Telecommunications Day.
1726 **354** 50c. multicoloured 85 85

1989. 20th Anniv of First Manned Landing on Moon. Multicoloured.
1728 10c. Type **357** 60 15
1729 35c. Edwin Aldrin, Neil Armstrong and Michael Collins (crew) (28 × 28 mm) 70 60
1730 45c. "Apollo 11" flight emblem (28 × 28 mm) 1·00 1·00
1731 $1 Aldrin descending to Moon's surface 2·00 2·00

358 Renovation of Statue of Liberty

360 Nehru and Flag

1989. "Philexfrance '89" International Stamp Exhibition, Paris, and "World Stamp Expo '89" International Stamp Exhibition, Washington D.C. Multicoloured.
1733 25c. Type **358** 55 45
1734 25c. French contingent at statue centenary celebrations 55 45
1735 25c. Statue, officials and commemorative plaque 55 45

1989. Birth Centenary of Jawaharlal Nehru (Indian statesman). Multicoloured.
1737 45c. Type **360** 85 70
1738 50c. Nehru 95 80

361 Close View of Station

1990. New Standard A Earth Satellite Station. Multicoloured.
1739 10c. Type **361** 15 10
1740 35c. Distant view of station 85 85

362 Emblem

1990. 25th Anniv of United States Educational and Cultural Foundation in Liberia. Multicoloured.
1741 10c. Type **362** 15 10
1742 45c. Similar to Type **362** but differently arranged 85 70

363 Flags, Arms, Map and Union Emblem

364 Bomi County

1990. 10th Anniv of Pan-African Postal Union.
1743 **363** 35c. multicoloured 70 55

1990. County Flags. Multicoloured.
1744 10c. Type **364** 10 10
1745 10c. Bong 10 10
1746 10c. Grand Bassa 10 10
1747 10c. Grand Cape Mount 10 10
1748 10c. Grand Gedeh 10 10
1749 10c. Grand Kru 10 10
1750 10c. Lofa 10 10
1751 10c. Margibi 10 10
1752 10c. Maryland 10 10
1753 10c. Montserrado 10 10
1754 10c. Nimba 10 10
1755 10c. Rivercress 10 10
1756 10c. Sinoe 10 10
1757 35c. Type **364** 65 55
1758 35c. Bong 65 55
1759 35c. Grand Bassa 65 55
1760 35c. Grand Cape Mount 65 55
1761 35c. Grand Gedeh 65 55
1762 35c. Grand Kru 65 55
1763 35c. Lofa 65 55
1764 35c. Margibi 65 55
1765 35c. Maryland 65 55
1766 35c. Montserrado 65 55
1767 35c. Nimba 65 55
1768 35c. Rivercress 65 55
1769 35c. Sinoe 65 55
1770 45c. Type **364** 85 70
1771 45c. Bong 85 70
1772 45c. Grand Bassa 85 70
1773 45c. Grand Cape Mount 85 70
1774 45c. Grand Gedeh 85 70
1775 45c. Grand Kru 85 70
1776 45c. Lofa 85 70
1777 45c. Margibi 85 70
1778 45c. Maryland 85 70
1779 45c. Montserrado 85 70
1780 45c. Nimba 85 70
1781 45c. Rivercress 85 70
1782 45c. Sinoe 85 70
1783 50c. Type **364** 1·10 1·10
1784 50c. Bong 1·10 1·10
1785 50c. Grand Bassa 1·10 1·10
1786 50c. Grand Cape Mount 1·10 1·10
1787 50c. Grand Gedeh 1·10 1·10
1788 50c. Grand Kru 1·10 1·10
1789 50c. Lofa 1·10 1·10
1790 50c. Margibi 1·10 1·10
1791 50c. Maryland 1·10 1·10
1792 50c. Montserrado 1·10 1·10
1793 50c. Nimba 1·10 1·10
1794 50c. Rivercress 1·10 1·10
1795 50c. Sinoe 1·10 1·10
1796 $1 Type **364** 2·00 2·00
1797 $1 Bong 2·00 2·00
1798 $1 Grand Bassa 2·00 2·00
1799 $1 Grand Cape Mount 2·00 2·00
1800 $1 Grand Gedeh 2·00 2·00
1801 $1 Grand Kru 2·00 2·00
1802 $1 Lofa 2·00 2·00
1803 $1 Margibi 2·00 2·00
1804 $1 Maryland 2·00 2·00
1805 $1 Montserrado 2·00 2·00
1806 $1 Nimba 2·00 2·00
1807 $1 Rivercress 2·00 2·00
1808 $1 Sinoe 2·00 2·00

365 Lady Elizabeth Bowes-Lyon as Girl

368 Boxing

367 Clasped Hands and Map

1991. 90th Birthday (1990) of Queen Elizabeth the Queen Mother. Multicoloured.
1809 10c. Type **365** 15 10
1810 $2 As Duchess of York (29 × 36½ mm) 4·00 4·00

1991. National Unity. Multicoloured.
1812 35c. Type **367** 65 50
1813 45c. National flag and map of Africa (ECOMOG (West African States Economic Community peace-keeping forces)) 85 65
1814 50c. Brewer, Konneh and Michael Francis (co-chairmen) and national flag (All-Liberia Conference) 95 75

1992. Olympic Games, Barcelona. Multicoloured.
1815 45c. Type **368** 85 65
1816 50c. Football 95 75
1817 $1 Weightlifting 1·90 1·75
1818 $2 Water polo 3·75 3·50

369 "Disarm Today"

1993. Peace and Redevelopment. Multicoloured.
1820 50c. Type **369** 95 70
1821 $1 "Join your Parents and build Liberia" 1·90 1·40
1822 $2 "Peace must prevail in Liberia" 3·75 2·75

OFFICIAL STAMPS

1892. Stamps of 1892 optd **OFFICIAL**.
O 87 **7** 1c. red 30 40
O 88 2c. blue 30 50
O 89 **8** 4c. black and green 50 50
O104 **9** 5c. on 6c. green (No. 89) 80 80
O 90 6c. green 60 50
O 91 **10** 8c. black and brown 45 45
O 92 **11** 12c. red 1·10 1·10
O 93 **12** 16c. lilac 1·10 1·10
O 94 **13** 24c. green on yellow 1·10 1·10
O 95 **12** 32c. blue 1·10 1·10
O 96 **15** $1 black and blue 22·00 8·75
O 97 **13** $2 brown on buff 9·00 6·25
O 98 **17** $5 black and red 13·50 5·75

1894. Stamps of 1892 optd **O S**.
O119 **7** 1c. red 30 20
O120 2c. blue 60 25
O121 **8** 4c. black and green 95 35
O122 **10** 8c. black and brown 80 35
O123 **11** 12c. red 1·10 40
O124 **12** 16c. lilac 1·10 40
O125 **13** 24c. green on yellow 1·10 45
O126 **12** 32c. blue 1·60 55
O127 $1 black and blue 13·50 13·50
O128 $2 brown on buff 13·50 13·50
O129 $5 black and red 80·00 55·00

1894. Stamp of 1894 in different colours optd **O S**. Imperf or roul.
O130 **24** 5c. green and lilac 1·75 2·00

1898. Stamps of 1897 optd **O S**.
O157 **9** 1c. purple 35 35
O158 1c. green 35 35
O159 **15** 2c. black and bistre 1·00 30
O160 2c. black and red 1·50 70
O161 **8** 5c. black and lake 1·50 70
O162 5c. black and blue 1·90 70
O163 **10** 10c. blue and yellow 85 80
O164 **11** 15c. black 85 80
O165 **12** 20c. red 1·40 95
O166 **13** 25c. green 85 80
O167 **12** 30c. blue 2·40 1·40
O168 **35** 50c. black and brown 2·10 1·40

1903†. Stamp of 1903, but different colour, optd **O S**.
O210 **40** 3c. green 20 15

1904. Nos. O104 and 167 surch **ONE O.S.** and bars or **OS 2** and bars.
O222 **9** 1c. on 5c. on 6c. green 1·10 1·10
O223 **12** 2c. on 30c. blue 7·75 7·50

1906†. Stamps of 1906, but different colours, optd **OS**.
O237 **50** 1c. black and green 50 50
O238 **51** 2c. black and red 15 15
O239 – 5c. black and blue 55 35
O240 – 10c. black and violet 2·50 60
O241 – 15c. black and brown 2·00 40
O242 – 20c. black and green 2·50 50
O243 – 25c. grey and purple 30 15
O244 – 30c. brown 50 15
O245 – 50c. green and brown 50 20
O246 – 75c. black and blue 1·10 75
O247 – $1 black and green 55 25
O248 **52** $2 black and purple 1·50 25
O249 **53** $5 black and orange 3·75 30

1909†. Stamps of 1909, but different colours, optd **OS**. 10c. perf or roul.
O262 **55** 1c. black and green 15 10
O263 – 2c. brown and red 15 10
O264 **56** 5c. black and blue 1·00 15
O266 **57** 10c. blue and black 50 25
O267 – 15c. black and purple 50 25
O268 – 20c. green and bistre 75 45
O269 – 25c. green and blue 70 50
O270 – 30c. blue 60 40
O271 – 50c. green and brown 2·25 40
O272 – 75c. black and violet 1·10 40

1910. No. O266 surch **3 CENTS INLAND POSTAGE**. Perf or roul.
O276 **57** 3c. on 10c. blue and black 55 45

1914. Official stamps surch: (A) **1914 2 CENTS**. (B) **+2c**. (C) **5**. (D) **CENTS 20 OFFICIAL**.
O291 **57** +2c. on 3c. on 10c. blue and black (B) (No. O275) 60 1·60
O284 – 2c. on 25c. grey and purple (A) (No. O243) 15·00 6·25
O285 – 5c. on 30c. blue (C) (No. O270) 5·25 3·00
O286 – 20c. on 75c. black and violet (D) (No. O272) 7·00 3·00

1914. No. 233 surch **CENTS 20 OFFICIAL**.
O287 20c. on 75c. black and brown 5·25 3·00

1915. Official stamps of 1906 and 1909 surch in different ways.
O325 – 1c. on 2c. brown and red (No. O263) 2·25 2·50
O326 **56** 2c. on 5c. black and blue (No. O264) 2·50 3·00
O310 – 2c. on 15c. black and purple (No. O267) 65 45
O311 – 2c. on 25c. green and blue (No. O269) 3·75 3·75
O312 – 5c. on 20c. green and bistre (No. O268) 65 50
O313 – 5c. on 30c. green and brown (No. O270) 5·75 5·75
O314 – 10c. on 50c. green and brown (No. O271) 6·50 7·50
O316 – 20c. on 75c. black and violet (No. O272) 2·00 2·00
O317 – 25c. on $1 black and green (No. O247) 13·50 13·50

O318 **52** 50c. on $2 black and purple (No. O248) . . 15·00 15·00
O320 **53** $1 on $5 black and orange (No. O249) . . 15·00 15·00

1915. No. O168 surch **10 10** and ornaments and bars.
O321 **35** 10c. on 50c. black & brn 9·75 9·75

1915. Military Field Post. Official stamps surch **L E F 1 c.**
O336 **50** 1c. on 1c. black and green (No. O237) . . . £325 £325
O337 **55** 1c. on 1c. black and green (No. O262) . . . 3·00 3·50
O338 – 1c. on 2c. brown and red (No. O263) . . . . . 2·40 2·50

1917. No. O244 surch **FIVE CENTS 1917** and bars.
O344 5c. on 30c. brown . . . . 15·00 15·00

1918. No. O266 surch **3 CENTS.**
O348 **57** 3c. on 10c. blue and black . . . . 1·40 1·50

1918†. Stamps of 1918, but in different colours, optd **O S.**
O362 **91** 1c. brown and green . . 50 15
O363 **92** 2c. black and red 50 15
O364 – 5c. black and blue . . . 75 10
O365 **93** 10c. blue 35 10
O366 – 15c. green and brown . . 1·75 40
O367 – 20c. black and lilac . . . 55 10
O368 **94** 25c. green and brown . . 3·25 45
O369 – 30c. black and violet . . 4·75 50
O370 – 50c. black and brown . . 5·00 50
O371 – 75c. black and brown . . 2·00 15
O372 – $1 blue and olive . . . . 3·75 30
O373 – $2 black and olive . . . 6·25 20
O374 – $5 green . . . . 8·25 20

1920. Nos. O362/3 surch **1920** and value and two bars.
O400 **91** 3c. on 1c. brown & green 95 50
O401 **92** 4c. on 2c. black and red 60 50

1921†. Stamps of 1915 and 1921, in different colours, optd **O S** or **OFFICIAL.**
O428 **100** 1c. green 70 10
O429 **64** 2c. red . . . . 4·50 10
O430 **65** 3c. brown 70 10
O431 **101** 5c. brown and blue . . 70 10
O432 – 10c. black and purple 35 15
O433 – 15c. green and black . . 2·75 50
O434 – 20c. blue and brown . . 1·10 25
O435 – 25c. green and orange 3·75 50
O436 – 30c. red and brown . . 75 15
O437 – 50c. green and black . . 75 25
O438 – 75c. purple and blue . . 1·90 25
O439 – $1 black and blue . . . 12·50 55
O440 – $2 green and orange . . 16·00 1·00
O441 – $5 blue and green . . . 17·00 1·75

1921†. Nos. O400/41 optd **1921.**
O442 **100** 1c. green . . . . 4·00 20
O443 **64** 2c. red . . . . 4·00 20
O444 **65** 3c. brown . . . . 4·00 25
O445 **101** 5c. brown and blue . . 2·40 25
O446 – 10c. black and purple 4·00 25
O447 – 15c. green and black . . 4·25 15
O448 – 20c. blue and brown . . 4·25 35
O449 – 25c. green and orange 5·00 40
O450 – 30c. red and brown . . 4·00 30
O451 – 50c. green and black . . 4·75 15
O452 – 75c. purple and blue . . 2·75 15
O453 – $1 black and blue . . . 8·75 1·10
O454 – $2 green and orange . . 15·00 1·75
O455 – $5 blue and green . . . 16·00 3·00

1923†. Stamps of 1923, but different colours, optd **O S.**
O485 **108** 1c. black and green . . 5·25 10
O486 **109** 2c. brown and red . . . 5·25 10
O487 – 3c. black and blue . . . 5·25 10
O488 – 5c. green and orange . . 5·25 10
O489 – 10c. purple and olive . . 5·25 10
O490 – 15c. blue and green . . 75 40
O491 – 20c. blue and lilac . . . 75 40
O492 – 25c. brown . . . . . . 16·00 40
O493 – 30c. brown and blue . . 70 20
O494 – 50c. brown and bistre 70 30
O495 – 75c. green and grey . . 70 25
O496 **110** $1 green and red . . . 1·50 40
O497 – $2 red and purple . . . 2·00 50
O498 – $5 brown and blue . . . 3·75 50

1926. No. O362 surch **Two Cents** and either thick bar, wavy lines, ornamental scroll or two bars.
O506 **91** 2c. on 1c. brown & green 90 80

1928. Stamps of 1928 optd **OFFICIAL SERVICE.**
O518 **116** 1c. green 70 35
O519 2c. violet . . . . 1·40 50
O520 3c. brown . . . . 1·40 15
O521 **117** 5c. blue 80 15
O522 **118** 10c. grey . . . . 2·40 1·00
O523 **117** 15c. lilac . . . . 1·40 60
O524 $1 brown . . . . 40·00 16·00

1944. No. O522 surch.
O649 **118** 4c. on 10c. grey . . . . 8·00 8·00

POSTAGE DUE STAMPS

1892. Stamps of 1886 surch **POSTAGE DUE** and value in frame.
D 99 **4** 3c. on 3c. mauve . . . . 1·25 1·25
D100 6c. on 6c. grey . . . . . 6·25 6·25

D 23

1894.
D110 **D 23** 2c. black and orange on yellow 95 55
D111 4c. black & red on rose 95 55
D112 6c. black & brn on buff 95 75
D113 8c. black & blue on bl 1·00 75
D114 10c. black and green on mauve . . . . . 1·25 95
D115 20c. black and violet on grey . . . . . . 1·25 95
D116 40c. black and brown on green . . . . . 2·50 1·75

REGISTRATION STAMPS

R 22

1893.
R105 **R 22** (10c.) black (Buchanan) £275 £350
R106 (10c.) blk ("Grenville") £1000 £1250
R107 (10c.) black (Harper) £1000 £1250
R108 (10c.) black (Monrovia) . . . . 40·00 £175
R109 (10c.) blk (Robertsport) . . . £500 £575

1894. Surch **10 CENTS 10** twice.
R140 **R 22** 10c. blue on pink (Buchanan) . . . . 3·75 3·75
R141 10c. green on buff (Harper) . . . . . 3·75 3·75
R142 10c. red on yellow (Monrovia) . . . . 3·75 3·75
R143 10c. red on blue (Robertsport) . . . 3·75 3·75

R 42 Pres. Gibson

1904†.
R211 **R 42** 10c. black and blue (Buchanan) . . . . 1·50 25
R212 10c. black and red ("Grenville") . . . 1·50 25
R213 10c. black and green (Harper) . . . . . 1·50 25
R214 10c. black and violet (Monrovia) . . . . 1·50 25
R215 10c. black and purple (Robertsport) . . . 1·50 25

R 96 Patrol Boat "Quail"

1919. Roul or perf.
R388 **R 96** 10c. blue and black (Buchanan) . . . . 90 5·75
R389 10c. black and brown ("Grenville") . . . 90 7·50
R390 10c. black and green (Harper) . . . . . 90 5·25
R391 10c. blue and violet (Monrovia) . . . . 90 5·75
R392 10c. black and red (Robertsport) . . . 90 7·50

R 106 Gabon Viper

1921†.
R456 **R 106** 10c. black and red (Buchanan) . . . . 23·00 2·50
R457 10c. black and red (Greenville) . . . . 14·00 2·50
R458 10c. black and blue (Harper) . . . . . 18·00 2·50
R459 10c. black and orange (Monrovia) . . . . 14·00 2·50
R460 10c. black and green (Robertsport) . . . 14·00 2·50

1921†. Optd **1921.**
R461 **R 106** 10c. black and lake 20·00 4·25
R462 10c. black and red . . 20·00 4·25
R463 10c. black and blue 20·00 4·25
R464 10c. black and orange 20·00 4·25
R465 10c. black and green 20·00 4·25

R 111 Sailing Skiff (Buchanan)

1923†. Various sea views.
R499 **R 111** 10c. red and black . . 8·50 55
R500 – 10c. green and black 8·50 55
R501 – 10c. orange and black 8·50 55
R502 – 10c. blue and black 8·50 55
R503 – 10c. violet and black 8·50 55

DESIGNS: No. R500, Lighter (Greenville); R501, Full-rigged sailing ship (Harper); R502, "George Washington" (liner) (Monrovia); R503, Canoe (Robertsport).

1941. No. 576 surch **REGISTERED 10 CENTS 10.**
R592 10c. on 5c. brown (postage) 1·40 1·40
R593 10c. on 5c. brown (air) . . 1·40 1·40

No. R593 is additionally optd with airplane and **AIR MAIL.**

SPECIAL DELIVERY STAMPS

1941. No. 576 surch with postman and **SPECIAL DELIVERY 10 CENTS 10.**
S590 10c. on 5c. brown (postage) 1·40 1·40
S591 10c. on 5c. brown (air) . . . 1·40 1·40

No. S591 is additionally optd with airplane and **AIR MAIL.**

LIBYA Pt. 8; Pt. 13

A former Italian colony in N. Africa, comprising the governorates of Cyrenaica and Tripolitania. From the end of 1951 an independent kingdom including the Fezzan also. Following a revolution in 1969 the country became the Libyan Arab Republic.

1912. 100 centesimi = 1 lira.
1952. 1000 milliemes = 1 Libyan pound.
1972. 1000 dirhams = 1 dinar.

A. ITALIAN COLONY

1912. Stamps of Italy optd **LIBIA** (No. 5) or **Libia** (others).
1 **30** 1c. brown 85 85
2 **31** 2c. brown 85 50
3 **37** 5c. green 85 35
4 10c. red 85 35
5 **41** 15c. grey . . . . £100 1·70
6 **37** 15c. grey . . . . 3·50 3·50
7 **33** 20c. orange . . . . 2·40 35
8 **41** 20c. orange . . . . 2·75 3·50
9 **39** 25c. blue . . . . 2·75 35
10 40c. brown . . . . 5·25 1·00
11 **33** 45c. green . . . . 22·00 17·00
12 **39** 50c. violet . . . . 17·00 1·40
13 60c. red . . . . 12·00 13·50
14 **34** 1l. brown and green . . . . 50·00 1·70
15 5l. blue and red £275 £200
16 10l. green and pink . . . . 24·00 80·00

1915. Red Cross stamps of Italy optd **LIBIA.**
17 **53** 10c.+5c. red . . . . 2·10 8·50
18 **54** 15c.+5c. grey . . . . 11·00 19·00
19 20c. on 15c.+5c. grey . . . 11·00 19·00
20 20c.+5c. orange . . . . . . 3·50 19·00

1916. No. 100 of Italy optd **LIBIA.**
21 **41** 20c. on 15c. grey . . . . . 27·00 5·25

4 Roman Legionary 5 Goddess of Plenty

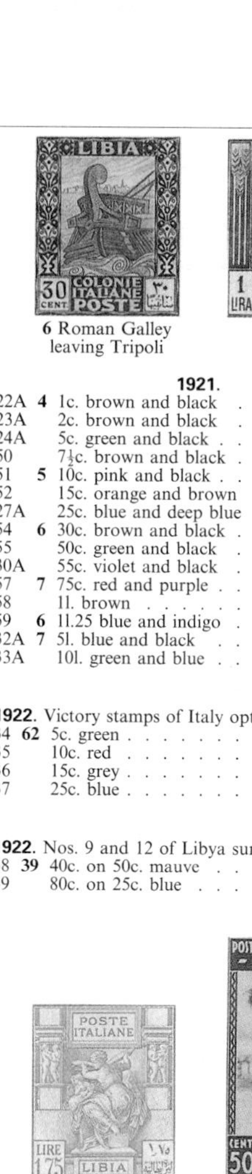
6 Roman Galley leaving Tripoli

7 Victory

1921.
22A **4** 1c. brown and black . . . 35 2·50
23A 2c. brown and black . . . 35 2·50
24A 5c. green and black 50 45
50 $7\frac{1}{2}$c. brown and black . . . 35 4·00
51 **5** 10c. pink and black 35 25
52 15c. orange and brown . . 4·25 1·00
27A 25c. blue and deep blue . . 50 15
54 **6** 30c. brown and black . . . 25 50
55 50c. green and black . . . 25 50
30A 55c. violet and black . . . 3·50 7·50
57 **7** 75c. red and purple . . . . 1·90 10
58 1l. brown . . . . 6·00 35
59 **6** 1l.25 blue and indigo . . . 25 10
32A **7** 5l. blue and black . . . . 21·00 13·50
33A 10l. green and blue . . . . £150 75·00

1922. Victory stamps of Italy optd **LIBIA.**
34 **62** 5c. green . . . . 1·20 5·25
35 10c. red . . . . 1·20 5·25
36 15c. grey . . . . 1·20 6·75
37 25c. blue . . . . 1·20 6·75

1922. Nos. 9 and 12 of Libya surch.
38 **39** 40c. on 50c. mauve . . . . 2·20 1·70
39 80c. on 25c. blue . . . . . 2·20 5·25

9 "Libyan Sibyl" by Michelangelo

10 Bedouin Woman

1924.
41 **9** 20c. green 70 10
42 40c. brown . . . . 1·70 50
43 60c. blue 70 10
44 1l.75 orange 25 10
45 2l. red . . . . 2·10 85
46 2l.55 violet . . . . 4·00 5·75

1928. Air. Air stamps of Italy optd **Libia.**
63 **88** 50c. pink . . . . 6·75 8·50
64 80c. brown and purple . . . 21·00 33·00

1928. Types of Italy optd **LIBIA** (No. 67) or Libia (others).
65 **92** $7\frac{1}{2}$c. brown . . . . 5·25 26·00
66 **34** 1l.25 blue . . . . 38·00 13·50
67 **91** 1l.75 brown . . . . 43·00 1·70

1936. 10th Tripoli Trade Fair.
68 **10** 50c. violet . . . . 1·20 2·40
69 1l.25 blue . . . . 1·40 6·25

1936. Air. Nos. 96 and 99 of Cyrenaica optd **LIBIA.**
70 – 50c. violet . . . . 1·70 35
71 **17** 1l. black . . . . 3·50 17·00

1937. Air. Stamps of Tripolitania optd **LIBIA.**
72 **18** 50c. red 10 10
73 60c. red 60
74 75c. blue . . . . 60 17·00
75 80c. purple . . . . 60 31·00
76 **19** 1l. blue . . . . 1·50 85
77 1l.20 brown . . . . 60 38·00
78 1l.50 orange 60
79 5l. green 60

11 Triumphal Arch

12 Roman Theatre, Sabrata

1937. Inauguration of Coastal Highway.
80 **11** 50c. red (postage) . . . . . 2·20 3·50
81 1l.25 blue . . . . 2·20 7·75
82 **12** 50c. purple (air) . . . . . . 2·20 4·25
83 1l. black . . . . 2·20 4·25

1937. 11th Tripoli Trade Fair. Optd **XI FIERA DI TRIPOLI.**
84 **11** 50c. red (postage) . . . . . 10·50 24·00
85 1l.25 blue . . . . 10·50 24·00
86 **12** 50c. purple (air) . . . . . . 10·50 24·00
87 1l. black . . . . 10·50 24·00

14 Benghazi Waterfront

1938. 12th Tripoli Trade Fair.
88 **14** 5c. brown (postage) 10 1·00
89 – 10c. brown 10 70
90 **14** 25c. green 45 1·20
91 – 50c. violet 50 50
92 **14** 75c. red 85 1·70
93 – 1l.25 blue 95 3·50
DESIGN: 10c., 50c., 1l.25, Fair Buildings.

94 50c. brown (air) 1·00 1·90
95 1l. blue 1·00 4·00
DESIGN—VERT: View of Tripoli.

16 Statue of Augustus
17 Eagle and Serpent

1938. Birth Bimillenary of Augustus the Great.
96 **16** 5c. green (postage) 10 1·00
97 – 10c. red 10 1·00
98 **16** 25c. green 50 60
99 – 50c. mauve 50 45
100 **16** 75c. red 1·50 3·25
101 – 1l.25 blue 1·50 2·20
102 **17** 50c. brown (air) 35 1·40
103 1l. mauve 50 3·00
DESIGN: 10, 50c., 1l.25, Statue of Goddess of Plenty.

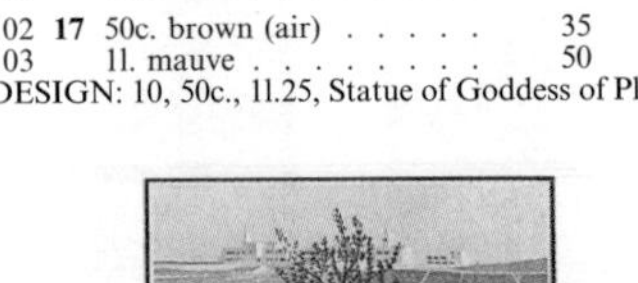

18 Agricultural Landscape

1939. 13th Tripoli Trade Fair. Inscr "XIII FIERA CAMPIONARIA DE TRIPOLI" etc.
104 **18** 5c. green (postage) 25 85
105 – 20c. red 50 85
106 **18** 50c. mauve 55 85
107 – 75c. red 55 1·70
108 **18** 1l.25 blue 55 2·50
DESIGN: 20, 75c. View of Ghadames.

109 – 25c. green (air) 25 1·30
110 – 50c. green 35 1·30
111 – 1l. mauve 45 1·70
DESIGNS—Fiat G18V airplane over: 25c., 1l. Arab and camel in desert; 50c. Fair entrance.

19 Buildings

1940. Naples Exhibition.
112 **19** 5c. brown (postage) 1·50 1·00
113 – 10c. orange 1·00 70
114 – 25c. green 60 1·00
115 **19** 50c. violet 60 70
116 – 75c. red 70 2·20
117 – 1l.25 blue 85 3·75
118 – 2l.+75c. red 85 13·00
DESIGNS—HORIZ: 10, 75c., 2l. Oxen and plough. VERT: 25c., 1l.25, Mosque.

119 – 50c. black (air) 50 85
120 – 1l. brown 50 1·70
121 – 2l.+75c. blue 85 5·25
122 – 5l.+2l.50 brown 85 7·75
DESIGNS—HORIZ: 50c., 2l. Savoia Marchetti S.M.75 airplane over city; 1, 5l. Savoia Marchetti S-73 airplane over oasis.

19a Hitler and Mussolini

1941. Rome–Berlin Axis Commemoration.
123 **19a** 5c. orange (postage) 10 2·75
124 10c. brown 10 2·75
125 20c. purple 85 2·75
126 25c. green 85 2·75
127 50c. violet 85 2·75
128 75c. red 85 8·50
129 1l.25 blue 85 8·50
130 50c. green (air) 85 12·00

B. INDEPENDENT

ليبيا — LIBYA (20)
-- ليبيا -- ٤ ليرة ع. — 4 MAL. LIBYA (21)
-- ليبيا -- ٨ فرنك — 8 FRANCS LIBYA (22)

1951. Stamps of Cyrenaica optd. (a) For use in Cyrenaica, optd as T **20**.
131 **24** 1m. brown 15 15
132 2m. red 20 20
133 3m. yellow 25 25
134 4m. green 28·00 19·00
135 5m. brown 35 35
136 8m. orange 40 40
137 10m. violet 60 60
138 12m. red 1·10 1·10
139 20m. blue 1·50 1·50
140 **25** 50m. blue and brown 8·75 8·75
141 100m. red and black 14·50 14·50
142 200m. violet and blue 45·00 40·00
143 500m. yellow and green £150 £130

(b) For use in Tripolitania. Surch as T **21** in Military Authority lire.
151 **24** 1mal. on 2m. red 25 25
152 2mal. on 4m. green 25 25
153 4mal. on 8m. orange 25 25
154 5mal. on 10m. violet 35 35
155 6mal. on 12m. red 35 35
156 10mal. on 20m. blue 65 65
157 **25** 24 mal. on 50m. blue and brown 3·00 3·00
158 48mal. on 100m. red 11·00 11·00
159 96mal. on 200m. violet and blue 27·00 27·00
160 240mal. on 500m. yellow and green 70·00 70·00

(c) For use in Fezzan. Surch as T **22**.
166 **24** 2f. on 2m. red 20 20
167 4f. on 4m. green 30 30
168 8f. on 8m. orange 35 40
169 10f. on 10m. violet 50 50
170 12f. on 12m. red 75 75
171 20f. on 20m. blue 2·00 2·00
172 **25** 48f. on 50m. blue & brown 38·00 35·00
173 96f. on 100m. red and black 40·00 35·00
174 192f. on 200m. violet and blue £110 80·00
175 480f. on 500m. yellow and green £190 £190

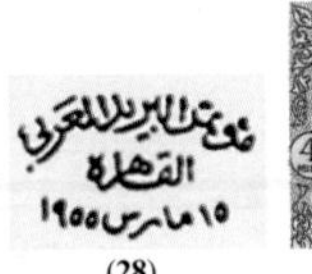

23 King Idris (**28**) **30**

1952.
176 **23** 2m. brown 10 10
177 4m. grey 10 10
178 5m. green 12·50 35
179 8m. red 40 25
180 10m. violet 12·50 15
181 12m. red 75 15
182 20m. blue 13·50 45
183 25m. brown 13·50 45
184 – 50m. blue and brown 1·75 65
185 – 100m. red and black 3·75 1·90
186 – 200m. violet and blue 6·00 3·50
187 – 500m. orange and green 25·00 17·00
Nos. 184/7 are larger.

1955. Arab Postal Union. As T **84a** of Lebanon but inscr "LIBYE" at top.
200 5m. brown 1·25 60
201 10m. green 1·90 90
202 30m. violet 4·25 2·00

1955. 2nd Arab Postal Congress, Cairo. Nos. 200/2 optd with T **28**.
203 5m. brown 40 30
204 10m. green 95 50
205 30m. violet 2·25 1·25

1955. No. 177 surch.
206 **23** 5m. on 4m. grey 1·25 45

1955.
207 **30** 1m. black on yellow 10 10
208 2m. bistre 1·40 50
209 2m. brown 10 10
210 3m. blue 10 10
211 4m. black 1·50 50
212 4m. lake 20 15
213 5m. green 40 20
214 10m. lilac 65 25
215 18m. red 15 10
216 20m. orange 25 15
217 30m. blue 50 20
218 35m. brown 65 25
219 40m. lake 1·10 40
220 50m. olive 85 25
221 – 100m. purple and slate 1·75 50
222 – 200m. lake and blue 9·25 1·40
223 – 500m. orange and green 15·00 7·25
224 – £L1 green, brown and sepia on yellow 21·00 11·50
Nos. 221/4 are larger, 27 × 32 mm.
See also Nos. 242/57.

33 Immam's Tomb at Djaghboub

1956. Death Centenary of Imam Essayed Mohamed Aly el Senussi.
225 **33** 5m. green 20 20
226 10m. lilac 35 20
227 15m. red 95 75
228 30m. blue 1·60 1·25

34 Map of Libya **35**

1956. 1st Anniv of Admission to U.N.
229 **34** 15m. buff and blue 30 15
230 35m. buff, purple and blue 1·00 30

1957. Arab Postal Congress, Tripoli.
231 **35** 15m. blue 1·75 90
232 500m. brown 12·50 6·50

36 **39**

37 F.A.O. Emblem and Date Palms

1958. 10th Anniv of Declaration of Human Rights.
233 **36** 10m. violet 20 15
234 15m. green 25 20
235 30m. blue 95 50

1959. 1st Int Dates Conf, Tripoli.
236 **37** 10m. black and violet 20 15
237 15m. black and green 50 20
238 45m. black and blue 1·00 50

1960. Inauguration of Arab League Centre, Cairo. As T **110** of Lebanon, but with Arms of Libya and inscr "LIBYA".
239 10m. black and green 50 20

1960. World Refugee Year.
240 **39** 10m. black and violet 25 15
241 45m. black and blue 1·25 75

1960. As Nos. 207 etc. On coloured paper.
242 **30** 1m. black on grey 10 10
243 2m. brown on buff 10 10
244 3m. indigo on blue 10 10
245 4m. lake on red 10 10
246 5m. green on green 10 10
247 10m. lilac on violet 10 10
248 15m. sepia on buff 10 10
249 20m. orange on orange 20 10
250 30m. red on pink 20 15
251 40m. lake on red 30 20
252 45m. blue on blue 35 20
253 50m. olive on bistre 35 20
254 – 100m. purple & slate on blue 1·25 35
255 – 200m. lake and blue on blue 3·25 1·40
256 – 500m. orange and green on green 23·00 5·50
257 – £L1 green, brown and sepia 23·00 11·00

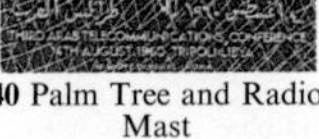

40 Palm Tree and Radio Mast **41** Military Watchtower (medallion)

1960. 3rd Arab Telecommunications Conf, Tripoli.
258 **40** 10m. violet 15 10
259 15m. turquoise 20 10
260 45m. lake 1·40 65

1961. Army Day.
261 **41** 5m. brown and green 20 10
262 15m. brown and blue 60 15

42 Zelten Field and Marsa Brega Port

1961. Inaug of First Libyan Petrol Pipeline.
263 **42** 15m. green and buff 25 10
264 50m. brown and lavender 75 40
265 100m. blue and light blue 2·25 90

43 Broken Chain and Agricultural Scenes

1961. 10th Anniv of Independence.
266 **43** 15m. sepia, turquoise and green 15 10
267 – 50m. sepia, brown and buff 45 25
268 – 100m. sepia, blue & salmon 2·10 80
DESIGNS—(embodying broken chain): 50m. Modern highway and buildings; 100m. Industrial machinery.

44 Tuareg Camel Riders

1962. International Fair, Tripoli.
269 **44** 10m. chestnut and brown 60 10
270 – 15m. green and purple 75 25
271 – 50m. blue and green 2·00 1·60
DESIGNS: 15m. Well; 50m. Oil derrick.

45 Campaign Emblem **46** Ahmed Rafik

1962. Malaria Eradication.
273 **45** 15m. multicoloured 25 20
274 50m. multicoloured 1·10 90

1962. 1st Death Anniv of Ahmed Rafik el Mehdawi (poet).
276 **46** 15m. green 15 10
277 20m. brown 55 20

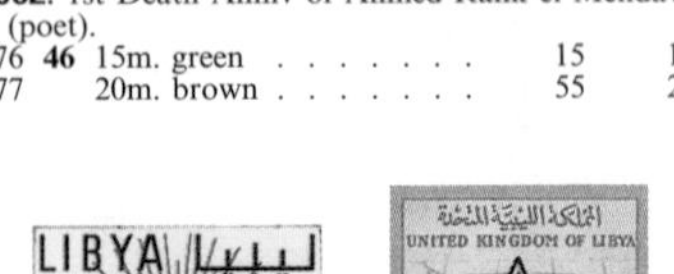

47 Scout Badge and Handclasp **48** City within Oildrop

1962. 3rd Boy Scouts' Meeting, Tripoli.
278 **47** 5m. sepia, red and yellow 10 10
279 – 10m. sepia, yellow and blue 20 10
280 – 15m. sepia, yellow and grey 25 20
DESIGNS: 10m. Scouts and badge; 15m. Badge and camp.

1962. Inauguration of Essider Terminal, Sidrah Oil Pipeline.
282 **48** 15m. purple and green 45 15
283 50m. olive and brown 1·10 45

49 Red Crescent encircling Globe

1963. International Red Cross Centenary.
284 **49** 10m. multicoloured 20 15
285 15m. multicoloured 25 20
286 20m. multicoloured 90 60

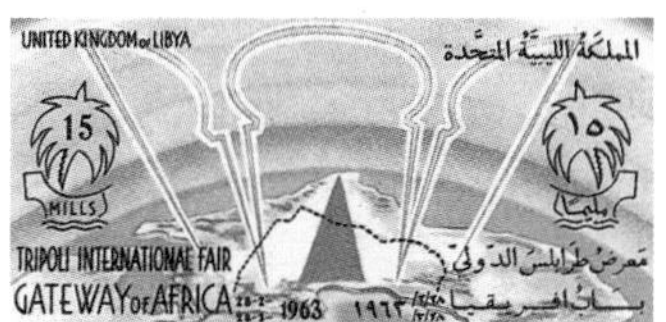

50 Rainbow over Map of Tripoli

1963. International Trade Fair, Tripoli.
287 **50** 15m. multicoloured 25 20
288 30m. multicoloured 70 20
289 50m. multicoloured . . . . 1·40 60

51 Palm and Well

1963. Freedom from Hunger.
290 **51** 10m. green, brown and blue 20 10
291 – 15m. ochre, purple & green 25 20
292 – 45m. sepia, blue and salmon . . . . 1·10 75
DESIGNS: 15m. Camel and sheep; 45m. Farmer sowing and tractor.

52 "Emancipation"

1963. 15th Anniv of Declaration of Human Rights.
293 **52** 5m. brown and blue . . . 10 10
294 15m. purple and blue . . . 20 10
295 50m. green and blue . . . 45 30

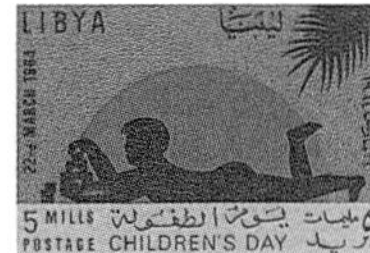

54 Map and Fair Entrance **55** Child playing in Sun

1964. International Fair, Tripoli.
300 **54** 10m. green, brown and red 75 15
301 15m. green, brown & purple . . . . 1·00 50
302 30m. green, brown and blue . . . . 1·40 75

1964. Children's Day. Sun gold.
303 **55** 5m. violet, red and pink . . 10 10
304 – 15m. brown, bistre and buff 20 15
305 **55** 45m. violet, blue & lt blue 1·25 65
DESIGN: 15m. Child in bird's nest.

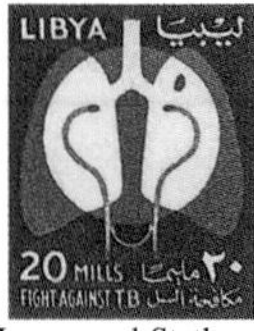

56 Lungs and Stethoscope

1964. Anti-tuberculosis Campaign.
307 **56** 20m. violet 90 25

57 Crown and Map **58** Libyan Woman, Silk Moth and Cocoon

1964. 1st Anniv of Libyan Union.
308 **57** 5m. orange and green . . . 15 10
309 50m. yellow and blue . . . 1·00 50

1964. Emancipation of Libyan Women.
310 **58** 10m. blue and green . . . 15 10
311 20m. blue and yellow . . . 55 35
312 35m. blue and pink 85 80

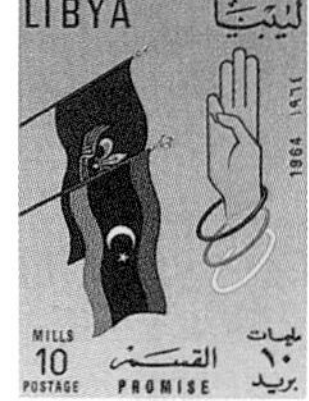

59 Flags and Scout Salute **60** Bayonet

1964. Libyan Scouts. Multicoloured.
314 10m. Type **59** 65 20
315 20m. Scout badge and saluting hands . . . . . . 1·25 60

1964. Foundation of the Senussi Army.
317 **60** 10m. brown and green . . 15 10
318 20m. black and orange . . 65 40

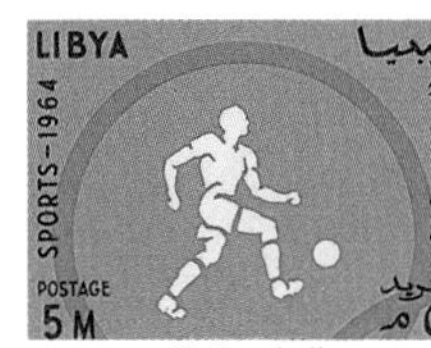

61 Ahmed Bahloul (poet) **62** Football

1964. Ahmed Bahloul El-Sharef Commem.
319 **61** 15m. purple 20 10
320 20m. blue 65 20

1964. Olympic Games, Tokyo. Rings in Gold.
321 5m. black and blue (Type **62**) 25 20
322 10m. black & purple (Cycling) 25 20
323 20m. black and red (Boxing) 50 20
324 30m. black and buff (Runner) 65 50
325 35m. black and olive (High-diving) 65 50
326 50m. black & green (Hurdling) 65 50
Nos. 321/6 were arranged together se-tenant in the sheets, each block of six being superimposed with the Olympic "rings" symbol.

63 A.P.U. Emblem **64** I.C.Y. Emblem

1964. 10th Anniv of Arab Postal Union.
328 **63** 10m. blue and yellow . . . 10 10
329 15m. brown and lilac . . . 20 10
330 30m. brown and green . . 95 65

1965. International Co-operation Year.
331 **64** 5m. gold and blue (postage) 25 10
332 15m. gold and red 90 25
333 50m. gold and violet (air) 1·50 35

65 European Bee Eater

1965. Birds. Multicoloured.
335 5m. Long-legged buzzard (vert) . . . . 1·10 30
336 10m. Type **65** . . . . 1·50 30
337 15m. Black-bellied sandgrouse . . . . 2·25 30
338 20m. Houbara bustard . . . 2·75 55
339 30m. Spotted sandgrouse . . 3·50 90
340 40m. Barbary partridge (vert) 4·25 1·25

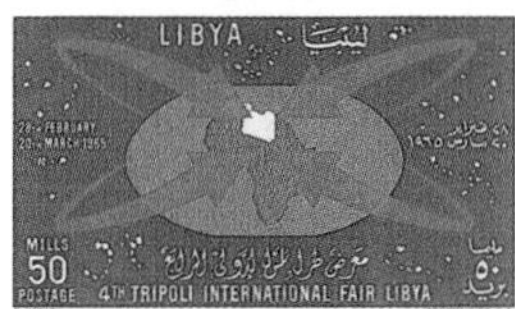

66 Fair Emblem

1965. International Trade Fair, Tripoli.
341 **66** 50m. multicoloured 75 50

67 Compass, Rocket and Balloons

1965. World Meteorological Day.
342 **67** 10m. multicoloured 10 10
343 15m. multicoloured 20 15
344 50m. multicoloured . . . . 1·00 70

68 I.T.U. Emblem and Symbols

1965. Centenary of I.T.U.
345 **68** 10m. brown 10 10
346 20m. purple 15 10
347 50m. mauve 90 65

69 Lamp and Burning Library **70** Rose

1965. Reconstitution of Burnt Algiers Library.
348 **69** 15m. multicoloured 20 10
349 50m. multicoloured 90 25

1965. Flowers. Multicoloured.
351 1m. Type **70** 10 10
352 2m. Iris 10 10
353 3m. Cactus flower 10 10
354 4m. Sunflower 50 10

71 Sud Aviation Super Caravelle over Globe **72** Forum, Cyrene

1965. Inaug of Kingdom of Libya Airlines.
355 **71** 5m. multicoloured 10 10
356 10m. multicoloured 20 10
357 15m. multicoloured 70 10

1965.
358 **72** 50m. olive and blue . . . 70 25
359 – 100m. brown and blue . . 1·25 45
360 – 200m. blue and purple . . 3·00 95
361 – 500m. green and red . . . 6·50 2·75
362 – £L1 brown and green . . . 14·00 6·50
DESIGNS–VERT: 100m. Trajan's Arch, Leptis Magna; 200m. Apollo's Temple, Cyrene. HORIZ: 500m. Antonine Temple, Sabratha; £L1 Theatre, Sabratha.

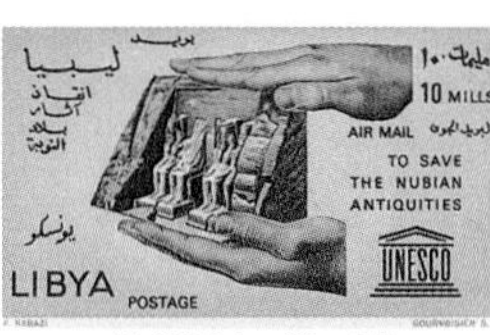

73 "Helping Hands"

1966. Air. Nubian Monuments Preservation.
363 **73** 10m. brown and bistre . . 20 10
364 15m. brown and green . . 25 10
365 40m. brown and chestnut 1·10 50

74 Germa Mausoleum

1966.
367 **74** 70m. violet and brown . . 1·40 75
See also No. E368.

75 Globe and Satellites

1966. International Trade Fair, Tripoli.
369 **75** 15m. black, gold and green 20 10
370 45m. black, gold and blue 70 20
371 55m. black, gold and purple 95 60

76 League Centre, Cairo, and Emblem **77** W.H.O. Building

1966. Arab League Week.
372 **76** 20m. red, green and black 10 10
373 55m. blue, red and black 65 50

1966. Air. Inaug of W.H.O. Headquarters, Geneva.
374 **77** 20m. black, yellow and blue 20 10
375 50m. black, green and red 65 25
376 65m. black, salmon and lake 95 70

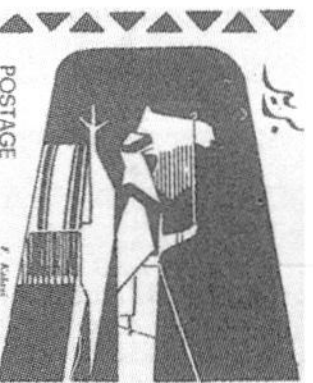

78 Tuareg with Camel **80** Leaping Deer

1966. Tuaregs.
378 **78** 10m. red 95 65
379 – 20m. blue . . . . 2·25 1·25
380 – 50m. multicoloured . . . . 4·50 3·25
DESIGNS—VERT: 20m. As Type **78** but positions of Tuareg and camel reversed. 62 × 39 mm: 50m. Tuareg with camel (different).

1966. 1st Arab Girl Scouts Camp (5m.) and 7th Arab Boy Scouts Camp (25 and 65m.). Multicoloured.
382 5m. Type **80** 10 10
383 25m. Boy scouts Camp emblem (vert) 20 10
384 65m. As 25m. . . . . 1·00 50

81 Airline Emblem

1966. Air. 1st Anniv of Kingdom of Libya Airlines.
385 **81** 25m. multicoloured 20 15
386 60m. multicoloured . . . . 1·00 75
387 85m. multicoloured . . . . 1·40 1·00

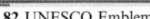

82 UNESCO Emblem **83** Castle of Columns, Tolemaide

1967. 20th Anniv of UNESCO.
388 **82** 15m. multicoloured 20 10
389 25m. multicoloured 90 20

1967. Tourism.
390 **83** 25m. black, brown & violet 20 10
391 – 55m. brown, violet & black 90 50
DESIGN—HORIZ: 55m. Sebba Fort.

84 "British Confidence" (tanker) at Oil Terminal

1967. Inaug of Marsa al Hariga Oil Terminal.
392 **84** 60m. multicoloured . . . . 1·75 65

85 Fair Emblem **86** I.T.Y. Emblem

1967. International Fair, Tripoli.
393 **85** 15m. multicoloured 50 10
394 55m. multicoloured 75 50

1967. International Tourist Year.
395 **86** 5m. black and blue 10 10
396 10m. blue and black . . . 10 10
397 45m. black, blue and pink 60 15

87 Running **88** Open Book and Arab League Emblem

1967. Mediterranean Games, Tunisia. Designs showing action "close-ups".
398 **87** 5m. black, orange and blue 10 10
399 – 10m. black, brown and blue 10 10
400 – 15m. black, violet and blue 10 10
401 – 45m. black, red and blue 30 25
402 – 75m. black, green and blue 75 30
DESIGNS: 10m. Throwing the javelin; 15m. Cycling; 45m. Football; 75m. Boxing.

1967. Literacy Campaign.
403 **88** 5m. orange and violet . . . 10 10
404 10m. green and violet . . . 10 10
405 15m. purple and violet . . 15 10
406 25m. blue and violet . . . 20 15

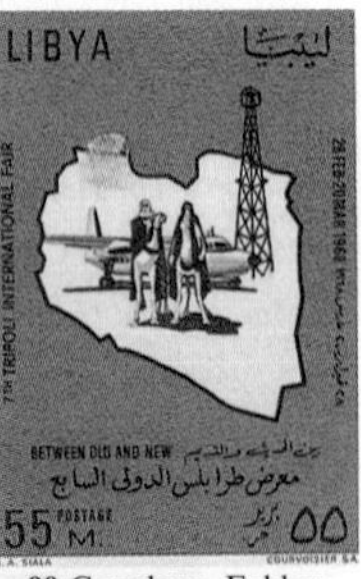

89 Human Rights Emblem **90** Cameleers, Fokker Friendship, Oil Rig and Map

1968. Human Rights Year.
407 **89** 15m. red and green 15 10
408 60m. blue and orange . . . 65 25

1968. International Fair, Tripoli.
409 **90** 55m. multicoloured 95 30

91 Arab League Emblem

1968. Arab League Week.
410 **91** 10m. red and blue 10 10
411 45m. green and orange . . 65 50

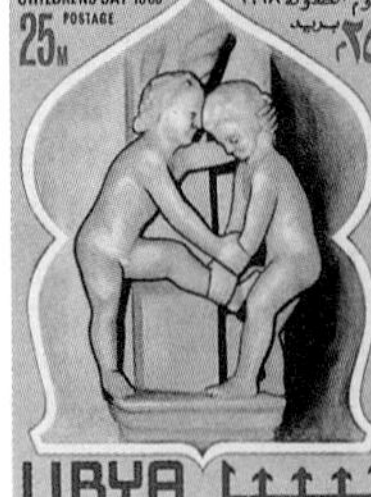

92 Children "Wrestling" (statue) **93** W.H.O. Emblem and Reaching Hands

1968. Children's Day. Multicoloured.
412 25m. Type **92** 45 15
413 55m. Libyan mother and children 80 55

1968. 20th Anniv of W.H.O.
414 **93** 25m. blue and purple . . . 25 15
415 55m. brown and blue . . . 40 25

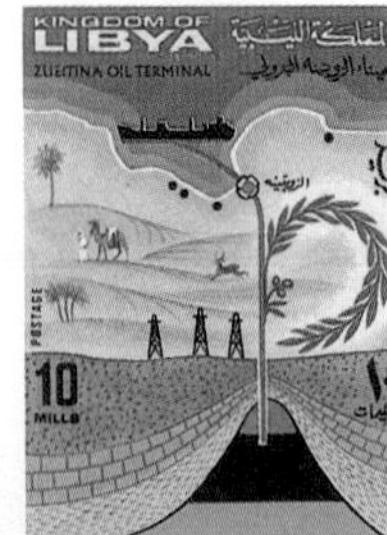

94 Oil Pipeline Map

1968. Inauguration of Zueitina Oil Terminal.
416 **94** 10m. multicoloured 20 10
417 60m. multicoloured . . . . 1·10 65

95 "Teaching the People"

1968. "Eliminate Illiteracy".
418 **95** 5m. mauve 10 10
419 10m. orange 10 10
420 15m. blue 10 10
421 20m. green 20 20

96 Conference Emblem

1968. 4th Session of Arab Labour Ministries Conference, Tripoli.
422 **96** 10m. multicoloured 10 10
423 15m. multicoloured 20 10

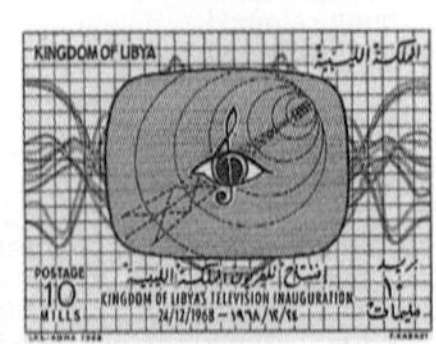

97 Treble Clef, Eye and T.V. Screen

1968. Inauguration of Libyan Television Service.
424 **97** 10m. multicoloured 10 10
425 30m. multicoloured 65 20

98 Bridge, Callipers and Road Sign

1968. Opening of Wadi El Kuf Bridge.
426 **98** 25m. multicoloured 15 15
427 60m. multicoloured 70 25

99 Melons **100** Fair Emblem

1969. Fruits. Multicoloured.
428 5m. Type **99** 10 10
429 10m. Dates 10 10
430 15m. Lemons 10 10
431 20m. Oranges 15 10
432 25m. Peaches 50 15
433 35m. Pears 90 50

1969. 8th International Trade Fair, Tripoli.
434 **100** 25m. multicoloured . . . 15 10
435 35m. multicoloured . . . 25 15
436 40m. multicoloured . . . 60 20

101 Hoisting Weather Balloon

1969. World Meteorological Day.
437 **101** 60m. multicoloured . . . 1·10 65

102 Family on Staircase within Cogwheel **103** I.L.O. Emblem

1969. 10th Anniv of Libyan Social Insurance.
438 **102** 15m. multicoloured . . . 15 10
439 55m. multicoloured . . . 30 25

1969. 50th Anniv of I.L.O.
440 **103** 10m. green, black & turq 10 10
441 60m. green, black and red 70 50

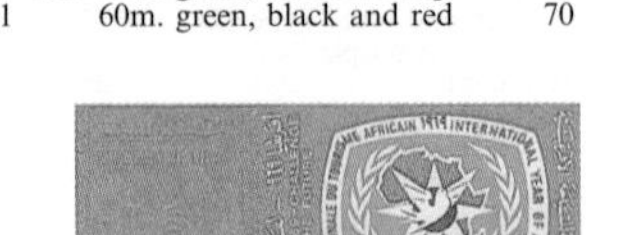

104 Emblem and Desert Scene

1969. African Tourist Year.
442 **104** 15m. multicoloured . . . 15 10
443 30m. multicoloured . . . 65 50

105 Members of the Armed Forces and Olive Branch **106** Dish Aerial and Flags

1969. Revolution of 1st September.
444 **105** 5m. multicoloured 25 10
445 10m. multicoloured . . . 35 20
446 15m. multicoloured . . . 55 25
447 25m. multicoloured . . . 85 40
448 45m. multicoloured . . . 1·00 60
449 60m. multicoloured . . . 2·10 1·00
On Nos. 444/9 the value is in white and the designer's name appears at the foot of design.

1970. 5th Anniv of Arab Satellite Communications Co-operation Agreement.
450 **106** 15m. multicoloured . . . 50 15
451 20m. multicoloured . . . 75 20
452 25m. multicoloured . . . 1·00 25
453 40m. multicoloured . . . 1·50 75

107 Arab League Flag, Arms and Map

1970. Silver Jubilee of Arab League.
454 **107** 10m. sepia, green and blue 10 10
455 15m. brown, green & orge 15 15
456 20m. purple, green & olive 50 25

1970. Revolution of 1 September. Designs as T **105**, but without imprint "M. A. Siala" at foot, and figures of value differently inscr.
457 **87** 5m. multicoloured 25 10
458 10m. multicoloured 35 20
459 15m. multicoloured 55 25
460 25m. multicoloured 85 40
461 45m. multicoloured . . . . 1·00 60
462 60m. multicoloured . . . . 2·10 1·00

108 New Headquarters Building **109** Arms and Soldiers

1970. New U.P.U. Headquarters Building, Berne.
463 **108** 10m. multicoloured . . . 15 10
464 25m. multicoloured . . . 20 20
465 60m. multicoloured . . . 95 60

1970. Nos. 358 and 360/2 with "KINGDOM OF LIBYA" inscriptions obliterated.
465a **72** 50m. olive and blue . . .
466 – 200m. blue and purple . .
467 – 500m. green and pink . .
468 – £L1 brown and green . .
These stamps were sold only for use on parcel post items. Other values may exist so overprinted, but were unauthorized.
See also Nos. 518/23.

1970. Evacuation of Foreign Military Bases in Libya.
469 **109** 15m. black and red . . . 15 15
470 25m. yellow, blue and red 45 20
471 45m. yellow, red and green . . . . 1·25 30

110 Soldiers and Libyan Flag **111** U.N. Emblem, Dove and Scales

1970. 1st Anniv of Libyan Arab Republic.
472 **110** 20m. multicoloured . . . 55 15
473 25m. multicoloured . . . 70 15
474 30m. multicoloured . . . 1·25 75

1970. 25th Anniv of United Nations.
475 **111** 5m. brown, red and green 25 10
476 10m. green, red & emerald 65 15
477 60m. green, red and blue 1·75 75

112 Map and Flags **113** Dove, U.N. Emblem and Globe

1970. Signing of Tripoli Charter of Co-operation.
478 **112** 15m. green, black and red 5·00 1·50

1971. 10th Anniv of U.N. De-colonisation Declaration.
479 **113** 15m. multicoloured . . . 50 15
480 20m. multicoloured . . . 75 20
481 60m. multicoloured . . . 1·90 75

114 Education Year Emblem

115 Palestinian Guerrilla

1971. International Education Year.
482 **114** 5m. brown, red and black . . . 15 10
483 10m. green, red and black . . . 50 10
484 20m. blue, red and black . . . 1·10 15

1971. "Al-Fatah" Movement for the Liberation of Palestine.
485 **115** 5m. multicoloured 15 10
486 10m. multicoloured . . . 50 15
487 100m. multicoloured . . . 1·75 1·00

116 Fair Emblem

117 O.P.E.C. Emblem

1971. 9th International Trade Fair, Tripoli.
488 **116** 15m. multicoloured . . . 15 10
489 30m. multicoloured . . . 65 20

1971. Organization of Petroleum Exporting Countries (O.P.E.C.).
490 **117** 10m. brown and yellow . . . 15 10
491 70m. violet and pink . . . 1·25 65

118 Global Symbol

1971. World Telecommunications Day (Nos. 494/5) and Pan-African Telecommunications Network.
492 – 5m. multicoloured 10 10
493 – 15m. multicoloured . . . 10 10
494 **118** 25m. multicoloured . . . 20 15
495 35m. multicoloured . . . 50 25
DESIGN: 5m., 15m. Telecommunications map of Africa.

119 Soldier, Torch and Flag

120 Ramadan Suehli

1971. 1st Anniv of Evacuation of Foreign Troops.
496 **119** 5m. multicoloured 10 10
497 10m. multicoloured . . . 15 10
498 15m. multicoloured . . . 20 15

1971. Ramadan Suehli (patriot). Commem.
499 **120** 15m. multicoloured . . . 15 10
500 55m. multicoloured . . . 75 35
For similar portraits see Nos. 503/4, 507/8, 526/7 and 553/4.

121 Palm and Dates

122 Pres. Gamal Nasser

1971. 2nd Anniv of 1 September Revolution.
501 **121** 5m. multicoloured 20 10
502 15m. multicoloured . . . 1·00 15

1971. 40th Death Anniv of Omar el Mukhtar (patriot). As T **120**.
503 5m. multicoloured 10 10
504 100m. multicoloured . . . . 1·75 90

1971. 1st Death Anniv of Pres. Nasser of Egypt.
505 **122** 5m. black, green & purple 10 10
506 15m. black, purple & green 95 10

1971. 21st Death Anniv of Ibrahim Usta Omar (poet). As T **120**.
507 25m. multicoloured 25 15
508 30m. multicoloured 80 20

123 Racial Equality Year Emblem

124 A.P.U. Emblem

1971. Racial Equality Year.
509 **123** 25m. multicoloured . . . 25 15
510 35m. multicoloured . . . 70 15

1971. 25th Anniv of Founding of Arab Postal Union at Sofar Conference.
511 **124** 5m. multicoloured 10 10
512 10m. multicoloured . . . 20 10
513 15m. multicoloured . . . 15 10

125 Arab Postal Union Emblem and Envelopes

126 Book Year Emblem

1971. 10th Anniv of African Postal Union. Mult.
514 10m. Type **125** 10 10
515 15m. Type **125** 15 10
516 25m. A.P.U. Emblem and dove with letter 25 15
517 55m. As 25m. 95 35

1971. Nos. 423/33 with "KINGDOM OF LIBYA" inscriptions obliterated.
518 5m. Type **99** . . . .
519 10m. Dates . . . .
520 15m. Lemons . . . .
521 20m. Oranges . . . .
522 25m. Peaches . . . .
523 35m. Pears . . . .

1972. International Book Year.
524 **126** 15m. multicoloured . . . 15 10
525 20m. multicoloured . . . 25 20

1972. Ahmed Gnaba (poet) Commem. As T **120**.
526 20m. multicoloured 25 10
527 35m. multicoloured 65 20

127 Libyan Arms

128 Tombs, Ghirza

1972. Values in Milliemes.
528 **127** 5m. multicoloured 10 10
529 10m. multicoloured . . . 10 10
530 25m. multicoloured . . . 15 10
531 30m. multicoloured . . . 20 10
532 35m. multicoloured . . . 25 10
533 40m. multicoloured . . . 50 15
534 45m. multicoloured . . . 60 15
535 55m. multicoloured . . . 85 20
536 60m. multicoloured . . . 1·00 35
537 90m. multicoloured . . . 1·60 90
For values in dirhams and dinars see Nos. 555/62.

1972. Libyan Antiquities. Multicoloured.
538 5m. Type **128** 10 10
539 10m. Cufic inscription, Ajdabiya 10 10
540 15m. Marcus Aurelius' Arch, Tripoli (horiz) 15 10
541 25m. Exchanging Weapons (cave painting, Wadi Zigza) 65 15
542 55m. Garamantian chariot (wall drawing, Wadi Zigza) 1·40 65
543 70m. "Libya crowning Cyrene" (Roman relief, Cyrene) . . . . 2·50 90

129 Fair Emblem

130 Heart and Skeletal Arm

1972. 10th International Trade Fair, Tripoli.
544 **129** 25m. multicoloured . . . 20 15
545 35m. multicoloured . . . 25 20
546 50m. multicoloured . . . 95 25
547 70m. multicoloured . . . 1·40 35

1972. World Health Day.
548 **130** 15m. multicoloured . . . 1·10 25
549 25m. multicoloured . . . 2·25 75

131 "Unity" Symbol on Map

132

1972. 1st Anniv of Libyan–Egyptian Federation Agreement.
550 **131** 15m. yellow, blue and black 10 10
551 20m. yellow, green & emer 20 10
552 25m. yellow, red and black 80 20

1972. Birth Centenary (1970) of Suleiman el Baruni (writer). As T **120**.
553 10m. multicoloured 95 15
554 70m. multicoloured . . . . . 1·25 75

1972. New Currency (Dirhams and Dinars). As T **127**. (a) Size 19 × 24 mm.
555 **127** 15dh. multicoloured . . . 10 10
556 65dh. multicoloured . . . 75 50
557 70dh. multicoloured . . . 90 65
558 80dh. multicoloured . . . 1·25 65

(b) Size 27 × 32 mm.
559 **127** 100dh. multicoloured . . 1·75 2·00
560 200dh. multicoloured . . 3·25 1·60
561 500dh. multicoloured . . 7·50 5·00
562 1D. multicoloured . . . . 13·50 10·00

1972.
563 **132** 5m. multicoloured . . . . 1·90 50
564 20m. multicoloured . . . 7·50 1·40
565 50m. multicoloured . . . 18·00 3·75
Nos. 563/5 were also issued with the Arabic face values expressed in the new currency.
See also Nos. 657/9.

133 Environmental Emblem

134 Olympic Emblems

1972. U.N. Environmental Conservation Conference, Stockholm.
566 **133** 15dh. multicoloured . . . 50 10
567 55dh. multicoloured . . . 1·10 35

1972. Olympic Games, Munich.
568 **134** 25dh. multicoloured . . . 1·50 35
569 35dh. multicoloured . . . 2·25 90

135 Symbolic Tree and "Fruit"

136 Dome of the Rock

1972. 3rd Anniv of 1 September Revolution.
570 **135** 15dh. multicoloured . . . 15 10
571 25dh. multicoloured . . . 70 15

1973. Dome of the Rock, Jerusalem.
572 **136** 10dh. multicoloured . . . 10 10
573 25dh. multicoloured . . . 50 15

137 Nicolas Copernicus

138 Libyan Eagle and Fair

1973. 500th Birth Anniv of Copernicus. Mult.
574 15dh. Type **137** 15 10
575 25dh. "Copernicus in his Observatory" (horiz) . . . 50 15

1973. 11th International Trade Fair, Tripoli.
576 **138** 5dh. multicoloured . . . 15 10
577 10dh. multicoloured . . . 50 10
578 15dh. multicoloured . . . 90 15

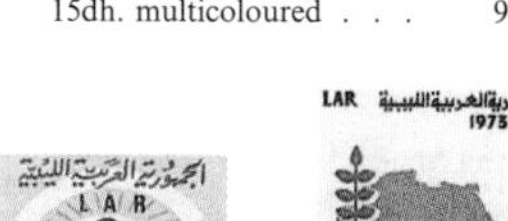
139 Blind Persons and Occupations

140 Map and Laurel

1973. Role of the Blind in Society.
579 **139** 20dh. multicoloured . . . 5·50 1·25
580 25dh. multicoloured . . . 10·00 2·50

1973. 10th Anniv of Organization of African Unity.
584 **140** 15dh. multicoloured . . . 20 10
585 25dh. multicoloured . . . 65 45

141 Interpol H.Q., Paris

1973. 50th Anniv of International Criminal Police Organization (Interpol).
586 **141** 10dh. multicoloured . . . 10 10
587 15dh. multicoloured . . . 15 10
588 25dh. multicoloured . . . 60 20

142 Map and Emblems

143 W.M.O. Emblem

1973. Census.
589 **142** 10dh. blue, black and red 3·00 65
590 25dh. green, black and blue . . . . 4·25 1·25
591 35dh. orange, black and grn . . . . 8·00 2·50

1973. W.M.O. Centenary.
592 **143** 5dh. blue, black and red 10 10
593 10dh. blue, black and green 15 10

144 Footballers

1973. 2nd Palestine Cup Football Championship.
594 **144** 5dh. brown and green . . 45 20
595 25dh. brown and red . . 80 15

145 Revolutionary Torch

146 "Writing Ability"

1973. 4th Anniv of 1 September Revolution.
596 **145** 15dh. multicoloured . . . 20 10
597 25dh. multicoloured . . . 85 10

1973. Literacy Campaign.
598 **146** 25dh. multicoloured . . . 50 15

147 Doorway of Old City Hall

148 Militiamen and Flag

1973. Cent of Tripoli Municipality. Mult.
599 10dh. Type **147** 20 10
600 25dh. Khondok fountain . . 50 10
601 35dh. Clock tower 75 40

1973. Libyan Militia.
602 **148** 15dh. multicoloured . . . 15 10
603 25dh. multicoloured . . . 55 10

149 Arabic Quotation from Speech of 15 April 1973

1973. Declaration of Cultural Revolution by Col. Gaddafi. Multicoloured.
604 25dh. Type **149** 20 10
605 70dh. As Type **149** but text in English 60 30

150 Ploughing with Camel

151 Human Rights Emblem

1973. 10th Anniv of World Food Programme.
606 **150** 10dh. multicoloured . . . 10 10
607 25dh. multicoloured . . . 20 10
608 35dh. multicoloured . . . 55 15

1973. 25th Anniv of Declaration of Human Rights.
609 **151** 25dh. red, purple and blue 20 10
610 70dh. red, green and blue 1·10 30

152 Flat-headed Grey Mullet

154 Emblem formed with National Flags

153 Lookout Post and Scout Salute

1973. Fishes. Multicoloured.
611 5dh. Type **152** 15 10
612 10dh. Zebra seabream . . . 70 10
613 15dh. Grouper . . . . 1·00 15
614 20dh. Painted comber . . . . 1·50 20
615 25dh. Yellow-finned tunny . . 2·75 30

1974. 20th Anniv of Scouting in Libya.
616 **153** 5dh. multicoloured . . . 95 10
617 20dh. multicoloured . . . 2·50 50
618 25dh. multicoloured . . . 4·00 1·25

1974. 12th International Trade Fair, Tripoli.
619 **154** 10dh. multicoloured . . . 50 10
620 25dh. multicoloured . . . 75 15
621 35dh. multicoloured . . . 1·25 35

155 Family within Protective Hands

156 Minaret within Star

1974. World Health Day.
622 **155** 5dh. multicoloured . . . 15 10
623 25dh. multicoloured . . . 50 20

1974. Inauguration of Benghazi University.
624 **156** 10dh. multicoloured . . . 20 10
625 25dh. multicoloured . . . 75 15
626 35dh. multicoloured . . . 1·10 25

157 U.P.U. Emblem within Star

158 Traffic Lights and Signs

1974. Centenary of U.P.U.
627 **157** 25dh. multicoloured . . . 5·50 75
628 70dh. multicoloured . . . 10·00 1·50

1974. Motoring and Touring Club of Libya.
629 **158** 5dh. multicoloured . . . 10 10
630 10dh. multicoloured . . . 15 10
631 25dh. multicoloured . . . 15 10

159 Tank, Refinery and Pipeline

160 W.P.Y. Emblem and People

1974. 5th Anniv of 1 September Revolution.
632 **159** 5dh. multicoloured . . . 10 10
633 20dh. multicoloured . . . 15 10
634 25dh. multicoloured . . . 15 10
635 35dh. multicoloured . . . 20 15

1974. World Population Year.
637 **160** 25dh. multicoloured . . . 20 10
638 35dh. multicoloured . . . 50 20

161

162 Congress Emblem

1975. 13th International Trade Fair, Tripoli. Libyan Costumes.
639 **161** 5dh. multicoloured . . . 10 10
640 – 10dh. multicoloured . . . 10 10
641 – 15dh. multicoloured . . . 10 10
642 – 20dh. multicoloured . . . 20 10
643 – 25dh. multicoloured . . . 75 10
644 – 50dh. multicoloured . . . 1·10 20
DESIGNS: 10dh. to 50dh. Various costumes.

1975. Arab Workers' Congress.
645 **162** 10dh. multicoloured . . . 10 10
646 25dh. multicoloured . . . 15 15
647 35dh. multicoloured . . . 50 15

163 Teacher at Blackboard

1975. Teachers' Day.
648 **163** 10dh. multicoloured . . . 10 10
649 25dh. multicoloured . . . 20 10

164 Human Figures, Text and Globe

1975. World Health Day.
650 **164** 20dh. multicoloured . . . 15 10
651 25dh. multicoloured . . . 20 10

165 Readers and Bookshelves

166 Festival Emblem

1975. Arab Book Exhibition.
652 **165** 10dh. multicoloured . . . 10 10
653 20dh. multicoloured . . . 20 10
654 25dh. multicoloured . . . 50 15

1975. 2nd Arab Youth Festival.
655 **166** 20dh. multicoloured . . . 15 10
656 25dh. multicoloured . . . 20 15

1975. As Nos. 563/5 but without "L.A.R.".
657 **132** 5dh. black, orange & blue 35 10
658 20dh. black, yellow & blue 75 10
659 50dh. black, green and blue . . . . 1·40 15

167 Games Emblem

168 Dove of Peace

1975. 7th Mediterranean Games, Algiers.
660 **167** 10dh. multicoloured . . . 10 10
661 25dh. multicoloured . . . 45 10
662 50dh. multicoloured . . . 85 20

1975. 6th Anniv of 1 September Revolution. Multicoloured.
663 25dh. Type **168** 20 10
664 70dh. Peace dove with different background . . . 95 25

169 Khalil Basha Mosque

170 Arms and Crowds

1975. Mosques. Multicoloured.
666 5dh. Type **169** 10 10
667 10dh. Sidi Abdulla El Shaab 10 10
668 15dh. Sidi Ali El Fergani . . 10 10
669 20dh. Al Kharruba (vert) . . 15 10
670 25dh. Katiktha (vert) 20 10
671 30dh. Murad Agha (vert) . . 45 15
672 35dh. Maulai Mohamed (vert) 55 15

1976. National People's Congress.
673 **170** 35dh. multicoloured . . . 20 10
674 40dh. multicoloured . . . 25 10

171 Dialogue Emblem

172 Woman blowing Bugle

1976. Islamic–Christian Dialogue Seminar.
675 **171** 40dh. multicoloured . . . 50 15
676 115dh. multicoloured . . 1·40 60

1976. International Trade Fair, Tripoli. Mult.
677 10dh. Type **172** 10 10
678 20dh. Lancer 15 10
679 30dh. Drummer 65 10
680 40dh. Bagpiper 75 20
681 100dh. Woman with jug on head . . . . 1·90 35

173 Early and Modern Telephones

1976. Telephone Centenary. Multicoloured.
682 40dh. Type **173** . . . . . . 1·60 15
683 70dh. Alexander Graham Bell 2·75 50

174 Mother and Child

175 Hands supporting Eye

1976. International Children's Day.
685 **174** 85dh. multicoloured . . . 75 30
686 110dh. multicoloured . . 1·10 40

1976. World Health Day.
687 **175** 30dh. multicoloured . . . 20 10
688 35dh. multicoloured . . . 20 10
689 40dh. multicoloured . . . 50 15

176 Great Grey Shrike

1976. Libyan Birds. Multicoloured.
690 5dh. Little bittern 75 25
691 10dh. Type **176** . . . . . . 1·40 40
692 15dh. Fulvous babbler . . . 2·00 50
693 20dh. European bee eater (vert) . . . . 2·75 70
694 25dh. Hoopoe . . . . 3·00 95

177 Barabekh Plant

178 Cycling

1976. Natural History Museum. Multicoloured.
695 10dh. Type **177** 10 10
696 15dh. Fin whale (horiz) . . . 15 10
697 30dh. Lizard (horiz) 20 10
698 40dh. Elephant's skull (horiz) 70 15
699 70dh. Bonnelli's eagle . . . 4·50 55
700 115dh. Barbary sheep . . . . 2·00 40

1976. Olympic Games, Montreal. Multicoloured.
701 15dh. Type **178** 10 10
702 25dh. Boxing 20 10
703 70dh. Football 95 20

179 Global "Tree"

180 Agricultural and Industrial Symbols

1976. Non-Aligned Countries' Colombo Conference.
705 **179** 115dh. multicoloured . . 95 35

1976. 7th Anniv of Revolution.
706 **180** 30dh. multicoloured . . . 15 10
707 40dh. multicoloured . . . 45 15
708 100dh. multicoloured . . 90 55

181 Various Sports

182 Chessboard and Pieces

1976. 5th Arab Games, Damascus.
710 **181** 15dh. multicoloured . . . 10 10
711 30dh. multicoloured . . . 15 10
712 100dh. multicoloured . . 1·00 55

1976. Arab Chess Olympiad, Tripoli.
714 **182** 15dh. multicoloured . . . 95 15
715 30dh. multicoloured . . . 1·60 60
716 100dh. multicoloured . . 5·00 95

183 Ratima

186 Kaaba, Mecca

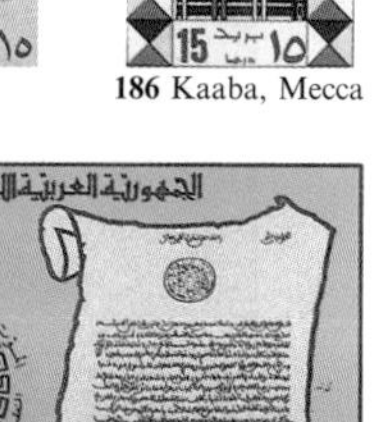
184 Emblem and Text

1976. Libyan Flora. Multicoloured.
717 15dh. Type **183** 15 10
718 20dh. "Sword of Crow" . . . 15 10
719 35dh. "Lasef" 50 10
720 40dh. "Yadid" 80 15
721 70dh. Esparto grass . . . . 1·90 25

1976. International Archives Council.
722 **184** 15dh. multicoloured . . . 10 10
723 35dh. multicoloured . . . 15 10
724 70dh. multicoloured . . . 55 20

1976. Pilgrimage to Mecca.
729 **186** 15dh. multicoloured . . . 10 10
730 30dh. multicoloured . . . 15 10
731 70dh. multicoloured . . . 30 20
732 100dh. multicoloured . . 75 30

187

188 Basket

1977. Coil Stamps.
733 **187** 5dh. multicoloured . . . 10 10
734 20dh. multicoloured . . . 10 10
735 50dh. multicoloured . . . 55 40

1977. 15th International Trade Fair, Tripoli. Mult.
736 10dh. Type **188** 10 10
737 20dh. Leather bag 10 10
738 30dh. Vase 15 10
739 40dh. Slippers 45 15
740 50dh. Saddle 60 15

189 Girl with Flowers

1977. Children's Day. Multicoloured.
742 10dh. Type **189** 10 10
743 30dh. Clothes shop 15 10
744 40dh. Orchard 20 15

190 Fighters and Machine-gun

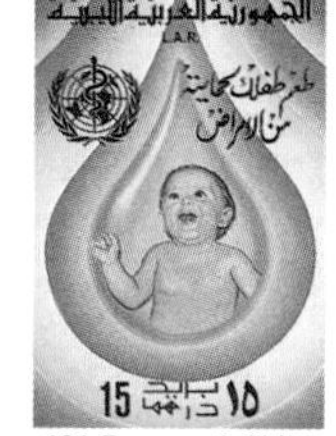
191 Protected Child

1977. 9th Anniv of Battle of Al-Karamah.
745 **190** 15dh. multicoloured . . . 10 10
746 25dh. multicoloured . . . 15 10
747 70dh. multicoloured . . . 80 25

1977. World Health Day.
748 **191** 15dh. multicoloured . . . 10 10
749 30dh. multicoloured . . . 15 10

192 A.P.U. Emblem

1977. 25th Anniv of Arab Postal Union.
750 **192** 15dh. multicoloured . . . 10 10
751 20dh. multicoloured . . . 15 10
752 40dh. multicoloured . . . 20 15

193 Maps of Libya and Africa

194 Heart on Map of Libya

1977. Organization of African Unity Conference, Tripoli.
753 **193** 40dh. multicoloured . . . 1·00 20
754 70dh. multicoloured . . . 1·50 30

1977. Red Crescent Commemoration.
755 **194** 5dh. multicoloured . . . 10 10
756 10dh. multicoloured . . . 15 10
757 30dh. multicoloured . . . 65 15

195 Messenger and Jet Fighter

1977. Communications Progress. Multicoloured.
758 20dh. Type **195** 15 10
759 25dh. Arab rider and Concorde 30 15
760 60dh. Satellite and aerial . . 55 20
761 115dh. Television relay via satellite . . . . 1·10 65
762 150dh. Camel rider and Boeing 727 airliner loading 1·75 90
763 200dh. "Apollo–Soyuz" link 2·25 1·10

196 Mosque

197 Archbishop Capucci

1977. Libyan Mosques.
765 **196** 40dh. multicoloured . . . 20 15
766 – 50dh. multicoloured (vert) 50 15
767 – 70dh. multicoloured . . . 70 20
768 – 90dh. multicoloured . . . 85 30
769 – 100dh. multicoloured (vert) . . . . 1·00 35
770 – 115dh. multicoloured . . 1·25 75
DESIGNS: 50dh. to 115dh. Various mosques.

1977. 3rd Anniv of Archbishop Capucci's Imprisonment.
771 **197** 30dh. multicoloured . . . 15 10
772 40dh. multicoloured . . . 20 15
773 115dh. multicoloured . . 1·25 60

198 Clasped Hands and Emblems

199 Swimming

1977. 8th Anniv of Revolution.
774 **198** 15dh. multicoloured . . . 10 10
775 30dh. multicoloured . . . 15 10
776 85dh. multicoloured . . . 80 25

1977. Arab School Sports. Multicoloured.
778 5dh. Type **199** 10 10
779 10dh. Handball (horiz) . . . 10 10
780 15dh. Football 15 10
781 25dh. Table tennis (horiz) . . 50 20
782 40dh. Basketball . . . . . . 1·10 65

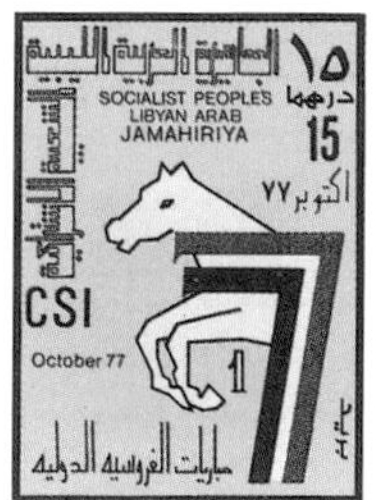
200 Championship Emblem

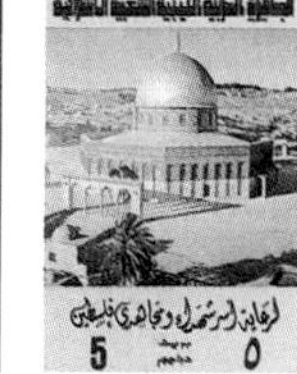
201 Dome of the Rock

1977. 1st International Turf Championships, Tripoli. Multicoloured.
783 5dh. Horse jumping fence (facing left) 10 10
784 10dh. Arab horseman 10 10
785 15dh. Type **200** 15 10
786 45dh. Horse jumping fence (facing right) 55 15
787 115dh. Arab horseman racing 1·40 80

1977. Palestine Welfare.
789 **201** 5dh. multicoloured . . . 10 10
790 10dh. multicoloured . . . 10 10

202 Fort, and Hands writing Arabic Script in Book

203 Emblem

1977. "The Green Book". Multicoloured.
791 35dh. Type **202** 15 10
792 40dh. Type **202** (text in English) 20 15
793 115dh. Dove with "Green Book" and map . . . . . 1·25 70

1977. World Standards Day.
794 **203** 5dh. multicoloured . . . 10 10
795 15dh. multicoloured . . . 10 10
796 30dh. multicoloured . . . 15 10

204 Giraffe

1978. Rock Drawings from Wadi Mathendous. Multicoloured.
797 10dh. Crocodiles (horiz) . . . 10 10
798 15dh. Elephant hunt (horiz) 10 10
799 20dh. Type **204** 15 10
800 30dh. Antelope (horiz) . . . 45 15
801 40dh. Elephant (horiz) . . . 65 20

205 Silver Pendant

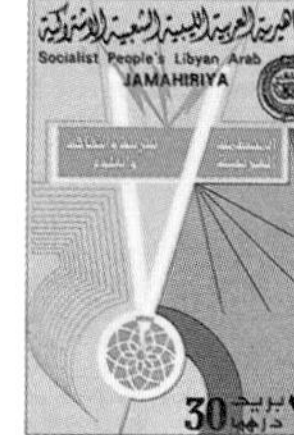
206 Compass and Lightning Flash

1978. 16th Tripoli International Fair.
802 **205** 5dh. silver, black and red 10 10
803 – 10dh. silver, black & violet 10 10
804 – 20dh. silver, black & green 10 10
805 – 25dh. silver, black and blue 15 10
806 – 115dh. silver, black & blue . . . . 1·10 70
DESIGNS: 10dh. Silver ornamental plate; 20dh. Necklace with three pendants; 25dh. Crescent-shaped silver brooch; 115dh. Silver armband.

1978. Arab Cultural Education Organization.
807 **206** 30dh. multicoloured . . . 20 15
808 115dh. multicoloured . . 1·40 65

207 Dancing a Round

1978. Children's Day. Children's Paintings. Multicoloured.
809 40dh. Type **207** 20 15
810 40dh. Children with placards 20 15
811 40dh. Shopping street 20 15
812 40dh. Playground 20 15
813 40dh. Wedding ceremony . . 20 15

208 Brickwork Clenched Fist

1978. The Arabs.
814 **208** 30dh. multicoloured . . . 20 15
815 115dh. multicoloured . . 1·10 35

209 Blood Pressure Meter

211 Games Emblem

210 Microwave Antenna

1978. World Hypertension Month.

816	209	30dh. multicoloured	15	15
817		115dh. multicoloured	1·25	35

1978. World Telecommunications Day.

818	210	30dh. multicoloured	15	15
819		115dh. multicoloured	1·00	35

1978. 3rd African Games, Algiers.

820	211	15dh. copper, violet & blk	10	10
821		30dh. silver, lilac and black	15	10
822		115dh. gold, purple & blk	1·10	35

212 Aerial View of Airport

1978. Inauguration of Tripoli International Airport. Multicoloured.

823	40dh. Type **212**	30	10
824	115dh. Terminal building	1·25	65

213 Ankara

1978. Turkish–Libyan Friendship.

825	213	30dh. multicoloured	15	10
826		35dh. multicoloured	15	10
827		115dh. multicoloured	1·10	35

214 "Armed Forces" **215** Crater

1978. 9th Anniv of 1 September Revolution. Multicoloured.

828	30dh. Type **214**	60	15
829	35dh. Tower, Green Book and symbols of progress	15	10
830	115dh. "Industry"	95	70

1978. 2nd Symposium on Geology of Libya. Multicoloured.

832	30dh. Type **215**	15	10
833	40dh. Oasis	20	15
834	115dh. Crater (different)	1·10	60

216 "Green Book" and Different Races

1978. International Anti-Apartheid Year.

835	216	30dh. multicoloured	15	10
836		40dh. multicoloured	20	15
837		115dh. multicoloured	85	35

217 Pilgrims, Minarets and Kaaba **218** Clasped Hands and Globe

1978. Pilgrimage to Mecca.

838	217	5dh. multicoloured	10	10
839		10dh. multicoloured	10	10
840		15dh. multicoloured	10	10
841		20dh. multicoloured	15	10

1978. U.N. Conference for Technical Co-operation between Developing Countries.

842	218	30dh. multicoloured	15	10
843		40dh. multicoloured	20	15
844		115dh. multicoloured	85	35

219 Workers, Rifles, Torch and Flag **220** Human Figure and Scales

1978. Arab Countries Summit Conference. Multicoloured.

845	30dh. Type **219**	15	10
846	40dh. Map of Middle East, eagle and crowd (horiz)	20	15
847	115dh. As	40	
848	145dh. Type **219**	1·00	45

1978. 30th Anniv of Declaration of Human Rights.

849	220	15dh. multicoloured	10	10
850		30dh. multicoloured	20	15
851		115dh. multicoloured	50	35

221 Horse Racing and Fort **222** Lilienthal's Biplane Glider

1978. Libyan Study Centre.

852	221	20dh. multicoloured	15	10
853		40dh. multicoloured	20	15
854		115dh. multicoloured	95	60

1978. 75th Anniv of First Powered Flight. Mult.

855	20dh. Type **222**	10	10
856	25dh. Lindbergh's "Spirit of St. Louis"	10	10
857	30dh. Admiral Richard Byrd's Trimotor "Floyd Bennett"	80	25
858	50dh. Bleriot 5190 Santos Dumont flying boat and airship "Graf Zeppelin"	95	35
859	115dh. Wright brothers and Wright Type A	1·10	75

223 Libyans, Torch and Laurel Wreath **224** Mounted Dorcas Gazelle Head

1979.

861	223	5dh. multicoloured	10	10
862		10dh. multicoloured	10	10
863		15dh. multicoloured	10	10
864		30dh. multicoloured	20	10
865		50dh. multicoloured	20	10
866		60dh. multicoloured	25	15
867		70dh. multicoloured	30	15
868		100dh. multicoloured	75	25
869		115dh. multicoloured	85	30
870		200dh. multicoloured	1·10	45
871		250dh. multicoloured	1·90	65
871		500dh. multicoloured	3·50	65
872		1000dh. multicoloured	6·75	3·50
872a		1500dh. multicoloured	12·50	4·25
872b		2500dh. multicoloured	23·00	7·50

Nos. 861/9 measure 18 × 23 mm and Nos. 870/2b 26 × 32 mm.

1979. Coil Stamps.

873	224	5dh. multicoloured	15	10
874		20dh. multicoloured	25	10
875		50dh. multicoloured	80	25

225 Tortoise

1979. Libyan Animals. Multicoloured.

876	5dh. Type **225**	10	10
877	10dh. Addax (vert)	10	10
878	15dh. Algerian hedgehog	20	10
879	20dh. North African crested porcupine	20	10
880	30dh. Dromedaries	30	15
881	35dh. Wild cat (vert)	40	15
882	45dh. Dorcas gazelle (vert)	95	25
883	115dh. Cheetah	1·90	75

226 Carpet

1979. 17th Tripoli International Trade Fair.

884	226	10dh. multicoloured	10	10
885	–	15dh. multicoloured	10	10
886	–	30dh. multicoloured	15	10
887	–	45dh. multicoloured	15	10
888	–	115dh. multicoloured	85	35

DESIGNS: 15dh. to 115dh. Different carpets

227 Aircraft and People

1979. International Year of the Child. Children's Paintings (1st series). Multicoloured.

889	20dh. Type **227**	10	10
890	20dh. Shepherd with flock	10	10
891	20dh. Open air cafe	10	10
892	20dh. Boat in storm	10	10
893	20dh. Policeman on traffic duty	10	10

See also Nos. 975/9.

228 World Map, Koran and Symbols of Arab Achievements **229** Radar Tower and Map

1979. The Arabs.

894	228	45dh. multicoloured	20	15
895		70dh. multicoloured	55	20

1979. World Meteorological Day.

896	229	15dh. multicoloured	10	10
897		30dh. multicoloured	15	10
898		50dh. multicoloured	20	15

230 Medical Care

1979. World Health Day.

899	230	40dh. multicoloured	20	15

231 "Carpobrotus acinaciformis"

1979. Libyan Flowers. Multicoloured.

900	10dh. Type **231**	10	10
901	15dh. "Caralluma europaea"	10	10
902	20dh. "Arum cirenaicum"	10	10
903	35dh. "Lavatera arborea"	50	15
904	40dh. "Capparis spinosa"	50	15
905	50dh. "Ranunculus asiaticus"	60	15

232 Farmer and Sheep

1979. 10th Anniv of Revolution. Mult.

906	15dh. Type **232**	10	10
907	15dh. Crowd with Green Book	10	10
908	15dh. Oil field	10	10
909	15dh. Refinery	10	10
910	30dh. Dish aerial	15	10
911	30dh. Hospital	15	10
912	30dh. Doctor examining patient	15	10
913	30dh. Surgeon	15	10
914	40dh. Street, Tripoli	20	15
915	40dh. Steel mill	20	15
916	40dh. Tanks	20	15
917	40dh. Tuareg horsemen	20	15
918	70dh. Revolutionaries and Green Book	70	20
919	70dh. Crowd within map of Libya	70	20
920	70dh. Mullah	70	20
921	70dh. Student	70	20

233 Volleyball **234** Emblem

1979. "Universiada '79" World University Games, Mexico City. Multicoloured.

923	45dh. Type **233**	20	15
924	115dh. Football	1·10	30

1979. 3rd World Telecommunications Exhibition, Geneva.

925	234	45dh. multicoloured	20	15
926		115dh. multicoloured	1·25	30

235 Seminar Emblem and Crowd

1979. International Seminar on the "Green Book". Multicoloured.

927	10dh. Type **235**	10	10
928	35dh. Seminar in progress (horiz) (70 × 43 mm)	45	15
929	100dh. Colonel Gaddafi with "Green Book"	1·00	30

236 Horsemen in Town

1979. Evacuation of Foreign Forces. Multicoloured.

931	30dh. Type **236**	15	10
932	40dh. Tuareg horsemen	20	15

237 Football Match

1979. Mediterranean Games, Split.
934 **237** 15dh. multicoloured . . . 10 10
935 30dh. multicoloured . . . 50 10
936 70dh. multicoloured . . . 1·25 20

238 Cyclist and Emblem

1979. Junior Cycling Championships, Tripoli. Multicoloured.
937 15dh. Type **238** 10 10
938 30dh. Cyclists and emblem 15 10

239 Horse-jumping

1979. Pre-Olympics. Multicoloured.
939 45dh. Type **239** 20 15
940 60dh. Javelin 55 15
941 115dh. Hurdles . . . . . . 1·10 55
942 160dh. Football . . . . . . 1·40 65
Nos. 939/42 exist from sheets on which an overall Moscow Olympics emblem in silver was superimposed on the stamps.

240 Figure clothed in Palestinian Flag

1979. Solidarity with Palestinian People.
944 **240** 30dh. multicoloured . . . 15 10
945 115dh. multicoloured . . 1·10 30

241 Ploughing

1980. World Olive Oil Year.
946 **241** 15dh. multicoloured . . . 10 10
947 30dh. multicoloured . . . 15 10
948 45dh. multicoloured . . . 20 15

242 Hockey (left) **243** Pipes

1980. National Sports. Multicoloured.
949 10dh. Type **242** 10 10
950 10dh. Hockey (right) 10 10
951 10dh. Leap-frog (left) . . . 10 10
952 10dh. Leap-frog (right) . . . 10 10
953 15dh. Long jump (left) . . . 10 10
954 15dh. Long jump (right) . . 10 10
955 15dh. Ball catching (left) . . 10 10
956 15dh. Ball catching (right) . . 10 10
957 20dh. Wrestling (left) 10 10
958 20dh. Wrestling (right) . . . 10 10
959 20dh. Stone throwing (left) 10 10
960 20dh. Stone throwing (right) 10 10
961 30dh. Tug-of-war (left) . . . 15 10
962 30dh. Tug-of-war (right) . . 15 10
963 30dh. Jumping (left) 15 10
964 30dh. Jumping (right) 15 10
965 45dh. Horsemen (left) 45 15
966 45dh. Horsemen (right) . . . 45 15
967 45dh. Horsemen with whips (left) 45 15
968 45dh. Horsemen with whips (right) 45 15

Nos. 949/68 were issued together, divided into se-tenant blocks of four within the sheet, each horizontal pair forming a composite design.

1980. 18th Tripoli International Fair. Multicoloured.
969 5dh. Drum (horiz) 10 10
970 10dh. Drum (different) (horiz) 10 10
971 15dh. Type **243** 10 10
972 20dh. Bagpipes (horiz) . . . 10 10
973 25dh. Stringed instrument and bow (horiz) 15 10

1980. International Year of the Child (1979) (2nd issue). As T **227**. Multicoloured.
975 20dh. "Horse Riding" . . . 10 10
976 20dh. "Beach scene" 10 10
977 20dh. "Fish" 10 10
978 20dh. "Birthday party" . . . 10 10
979 20dh. "Sheep Festival" . . . 10 10

244 Mosque and Kaaba

1980. 400th Anniv of Hejira.
980 **244** 50dh. multicoloured . . . 25 15
981 115dh. multicoloured . . 1·10 55

245 Surgical Operation and Hospital

1980. World Health Day.
982 **245** 20dh. multicoloured . . . 10 10
983 50dh. multicoloured . . . 50 15

246 Battle of Shoghab "Shahat", 1913

1980. Battles (1st series). Multicoloured.
984 20dh. Gardabia, 1915 . . . . 20 15
986 20dh. Type **246** 10 10
988 20dh. Fundugh al-Shibani "Garian" 10 10
990 20dh. Yefren 10 10
992 20dh. Ghira "Brak" 20 15
994 20dh. El Hani (Shiat) 35 15
996 20dh. Sebah 20 15
998 20dh. Sirt 10 10
985 35dh. Gardabia 10 10
987 35dh. Shoghab "Shahat" . . 20 15
989 35dh. Fundagh al-Shibani "Garian" 20 15
991 35dh. Yefren 20 15
993 35dh. Ghira "Brak" 20 15
995 35dh. El Hani (Shiat) 60 25
997 35dh. Sebah 20 15
999 35dh. Sirt 10 10
The two values commemorating each battle were issued in se-tenant pairs, each pair forming a composite design.
See also Nos. 1027/50, 1140/63 and 1257/80.

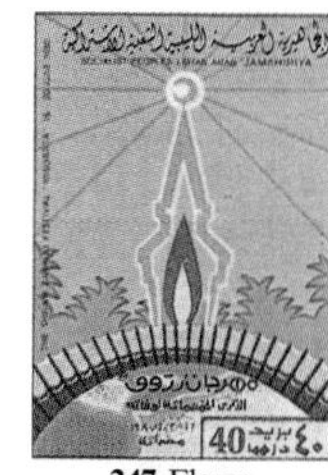
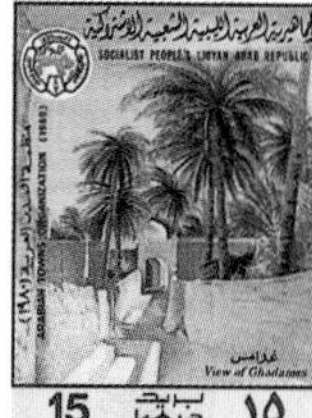
247 Flame **248** Ghadames

1980. Sheikh Zarruq Festival.
1000 **247** 40dh. multicoloured . . 20 15
1001 115dh. multicoloured . . 1·00 65

1980. Arabian Towns Organization. Mult.
1003 15dh. Type **248** 10 10
1004 30dh. Derna 15 10
1005 50dh. Ahmad Pasha Mosque, Tripoli 50 15

249 Guides on Hike

1980. 14th Pan-Arab Scout Jamboree. Multicoloured.
1006 15dh. Type **249** 10 10
1007 30dh. Guides cooking . . . 15 10
1008 50dh. Cub Scouts cooking 25 15
1009 115dh. Scouts map-reading 1·10 60

250 Oil Refinery

1980. 11th Anniv of Revolution. Multicoloured.
1011 5dh. Type **250** 10 10
1012 10dh. Recreation and youth 10 10
1013 15dh. Agriculture 10 10
1014 25dh. Boeing 727-200 airplane and liner 60 15
1015 40dh. Education 20 15
1016 115dh. Housing 95 30

251 Camels, Map of Libya and Conference Emblem

1980. World Tourism Conference, Manila. Mult.
1018 45dh. Type **251** 20 15
1019 115dh. Emblem, map and camel riders 95 30

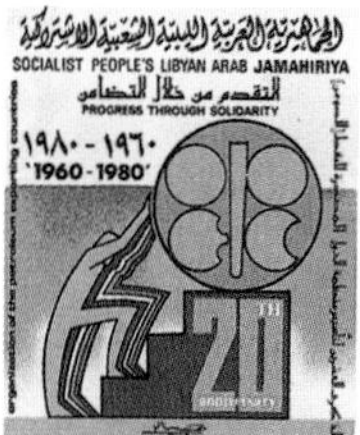
252 Figures supporting O.P.E.C. Emblem

1980. 20th Anniv of Organization of Petroleum Exporting Countries. Multicoloured.
1020 45dh. O.P.E.C. emblem and globe 20 15
1021 115dh. Type **252** 95 30

253 Death of Omar el Mukhtar

1980. 49th Death Anniv of Omar el Mukhtar (patriot).
1022 **253** 20dh. multicoloured . . 10 10
1023 35dh. multicoloured . . 20 15

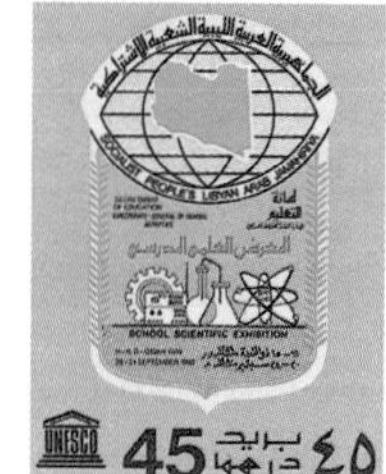
253a Map of Libya and Science Symbols

1980. Birth Millenary of Avicenna (philosopher) and School Scientific Exhibition. Multicoloured.
1025 45dh. Type **253a** 20 15
1026 115d. Avicenna and Exhibition Emblem . . . 1·10 30

1981. Battles (2nd series). As T **246**. Mult.
1027 20dh. Zuara 10 10
1029 20dh. Tawargha 10 10
1031 20dh. Dernah 10 10
1033 20dh. Bir Tagreft 10 10
1035 20dh. Funduk El Jamel "Misurata" 10 10
1037 20dh. Sidi El Khemri "Gusbat" 10 10
1039 20dh. El Khoms 10 10
1041 20dh. Roghdalin "Menshia" 10 10
1043 20dh. Ain Zara "Tripoli" 10 10
1045 20dh. Rughbat el Naga "Benina" 10 10
1047 20dh. Tobruk 10 10
1049 20dh. Ikshadia "Werfella" 10 10
1028 35dh. Zuara 15 15
1030 35dh. Tawargha 15 15
1032 35dh. Dernah 15 15
1034 35dh. Bir Tagreft 15 15
1036 35dh. Funduk El Jamel "Misurata" 15 15
1038 35dh. Sidi El Khemri "Gusbat" 15 15
1040 35dh. El Khoms 15 15
1042 35dh. Roghdalin "Menshia" 15 15
1044 35dh. Ain Zara "Tripoli" 15 15
1046 35dh. Rughbat el Naga "Benina" 15 15
1048 35dh. Tobruk 15 15
1050 35dh. Ikshadia "Werfella" 15 15
The two values commemorating each battle were issued in se-tenant pairs, each pair forming a composite design.

254 Tent, Trees and Sun

1981. Children's Day. Children's Paintings. Multicoloured.
1051 20dh. Type **254** 10 10
1052 20dh. Women 10 10
1053 20dh. Picnic 10 10
1054 20dh. Aeroplane and playing children 10 10
1055 20dh. Mosque and man with camel 10 10

255 Central Bank **257** Crowd and "Green Book" Stamp of 1977

256 Pots

1981. 25th Anniv of Central Bank of Libya.
1056 **255** 45dh. multicoloured . . 15 15
1057 115dh. multicoloured . . 95 35

1981. Tripoli International Fair. Multicoloured.
1059 5dh. Type **256** 10 10
1060 10dh. Silver coffee pot (vert) 10 10
1061 15dh. Long-necked vase (vert) 10 10
1062 45dh. Round-bellied vase . . 45 15
1063 115dh. Jug . . . . 1·10 35

1981. People's Authority Declaration.
1064 **257** 50dh. multicoloured . . 15 15
1065 115dh. multicoloured . . 95 35

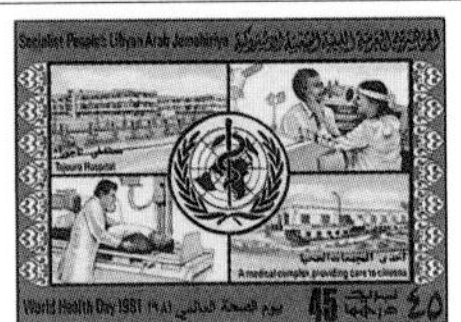

258 Tajoura Hospital, Medical Complex, Patients receiving Treatment and W.H.O. Emblem

1981. World Health Day.
1066 **258** 45dh. multicoloured . . 15 15
1067 115dh. multicoloured . . 95 35

259 Eye and Man on Crutches

1981. International Year of Disabled People.
1068 **259** 20dh. green, blue & black 10 10
1069 – 45dh. green, black & blue 15 15
1070 – 115dh. blue and green 1·00 35
DESIGNS: 45dh. Globe and I.Y.D.P. emblem; 115dh. Hands holding shield with I.Y.D.P. emblem, eye and man on crutch.

260 Horse

1981. Libyan Mosaics. Multicoloured.
1071 10dh. Type **260** 10 10
1072 20dh. Ship 10 10
1073 30dh. Birds, fish and flowers 10 10
1074 40dh. Leopard 40 15
1075 50dh. Man playing musical instrument 50 15
1076 115dh. Fishes . . . . 1·10 35

261 Racial Discrimination Emblem

262 Jet Fighters and Sud Aviation Alouette III Helicopter (left-hand stamp)

1981. Int Year Against Racial Discrimination.
1077 **261** 45dh. multicoloured . . 25 25
1078 50dh. multicoloured . . 55 30

1981. 12th Anniv of Revolution.
1079 **262** 5dh. blue and light blue 15 10
1080 – 5dh. blue and light blue 15 10
1081 – 5dh. blue and light blue 10 10
1082 – 5dh. blue and light blue 10 10
1083 – 10dh. black and blue . . 10 10
1084 – 10dh. black and blue . . 10 10
1085 – 10dh. black and blue . . 10 10
1086 – 10dh. black and blue . . 10 10
1087 – 15dh. brown & lt brown 10 10
1088 – 15dh. brown & lt brown 10 10
1089 – 15dh. brown & lt brown 10 10
1090 – 15dh. brown & lt brown 10 10
1091 – 20dh. blue and green . . 15 15
1092 – 20dh. blue and green . . 15 15
1093 – 20dh. blue and green . . 15 15
1094 – 20dh. blue and green . . 15 15
1095 – 25dh. brown and yellow 15 15
1096 – 25dh. brown and yellow 15 15
1097 – 25dh. brown and yellow 15 15
1098 – 25dh. brown and yellow 15 15
DESIGNS—VERT: No. 1080, Jet fighter (right-hand stamp); 1081/2, Parachutists; 1083/4, Tank parade; 1085/6, Marching frogmen; 1087/8, Anti-aircraft rocket trucks; 1089/90, Missile trucks. HORIZ: 1091/2, Marching sailors; 1093/4, Jeeps and anti-aircraft rocket trucks; 1095/6, Armoured vehicles and landrovers; 1097/8, Tank parade.

Each pair forms a horizontal composite design, the first number being the left-hand stamp in each instance.

263 Wheat and Plough

1981. World Food Day.
1100 **263** 45dh. multicoloured . . 25 25
1101 200dh. multicoloured . . 1·75 95

264 "Pseudotergumia fidia"

1981. Butterflies. Multicoloured.
1102 5dh. Type **264** 15 10
1103 5dh. "Chazara prieuri" (sun in background) 15 10
1104 5dh. "Polygonia c-album" (trees in background) . . 15 10
1105 5dh. "Colias crocea" (mosque in background) 15 10
1106 10dh. "Anthocharis bellia" (face value bottom right) 15 10
1107 10dh. "Pandoriana pandora" (face value bottom left) 15 10
1108 10dh. "Melanargia ines" (face value top right) . . 15 10
1109 10dh. "Charaxes jasius" (face value top left) . . . 15 10
1110 15dh. "Nymphales antiopa" (face value bottom right) 30 30
1111 15dh. "Eurodryas desfontainii" (face value bottom left) 30 30
1112 15dh. "Iphiclides podalirius" (face value top right) . . 30 30
1113 15dh. "Glaucopsyche melanops" (face value top left) 30 30
1114 25dh. "Spialia sertorius" (face value bottom right) 50 45
1115 25dh. "Pieris brassicae" (face value bottom left) 50 45
1116 25dh. "Lysandra albicans" (face value top right) . . 50 45
1117 25dh. "Celastrina argiolus" (face value top left) . . . 50 45
The four designs of each value were issued together in small sheets of four, showing composite background designs.

265 Grapes

266 I.Y.D.P. Emblem and Globe

1981. Fruit. Multicoloured.
1119 5dh. Type **265** 10 10
1120 10dh. Dates 10 10
1121 15dh. Lemons 10 10
1122 20dh. Oranges 15 15
1123 35dh. Barbary figs 20 20
1124 55dh. Pomegranate 65 30

1981. International Year of Disabled Persons.
1125 **266** 45dh. multicoloured . . 25 25
1126 115dh. multicoloured . . 90 55

267 Animals (looking right)

1982. Libyan Mosaics. Multicoloured.
1127 45dh. Type **267** 50 25
1128 45dh. Orpheus 50 25
1129 45dh. Animals (looking left) 50 25
1130 45dh. Fishes 50 25
1131 45dh. Fishermen 50 25
1132 45dh. Fishes and ducks . . 50 25
1133 45dh. Farm 50 25
1134 45dh. Birds and fruit . . . 50 25
1135 45dh. Milking 50 25

268 Koran Texts leading to Ka'aba

269 Grinding Flour

1982. 3rd Koran Reading Contest. Multicoloured.
1136 10dh. Type **268** 10 10
1137 35dh. Koran and formation of the World 20 20
1138 115dh. Reading the Koran 95 55

1982. Battles (3rd series). As T **246**. Multicoloured.
1140 20dh. Hun "Gioffra" . . . 15 15
1142 20dh. Gedabia 15 15
1144 20dh. El Asaba "Gianduba" 15 15
1146 20dh. El Habela 15 15
1148 20dh. Suk El Ahad "Tarhuna" 15 15
1150 20dh. El Tangi 15 15
1152 20dh. Sokna 15 15
1154 20dh. Wadi Smalus "Jabel El Akdar" 15 15
1156 20dh. Sidi Abuagela "Agelat" 15 15
1158 20dh. Sidi Surur "Zeliten" 15 15
1160 20dh. Kuefia 15 15
1162 20dh. Abunjeim 15 15
1141 35dh. Hun "Gioffra" . . . 20 20
1143 35dh. Gedabia 20 20
1145 35dh. El Asaba "Gianduba" 20 20
1147 35dh. El Habela 20 20
1149 35dh. Suk El Ahad "Tarhuna" 20 20
1151 35dh. El Tangi 20 20
1153 35dh. Sokna 20 20
1155 35dh. Wadi Smalus "Jabel El Akdar" 20 20
1157 35dh. Sidi Abuagela "Agelat" 20 20
1159 35dh. Sidi Surur "Zeliten" 20 20
1161 35dh. Kuefia 20 20
1163 35dh. Abunjeim 20 20
The two values commemorating each battle were issued in se-tenant pairs, each pair forming a composite design.

1982. Tripoli International Fair. Multicoloured.
1164 5dh. Type **269** 10 10
1165 10dh. Ploughing 10 10
1166 25dh. Stacking hay 15 15
1167 35dh. Weaving 20 20
1168 45dh. Cooking 50 25
1169 100dh. Harvesting 95 50

270 "ALFATAH" forming Farm Vehicle

1982. People's Authority Declaration. Multicoloured.
1170 100dh. Type **270** 75 50
1171 200dh. Colonel Gaddafi, old man, "Green Book" and guns . . . . 1·75 95
1172 300dh. Rejoicing crowd . . 2·50 1·40

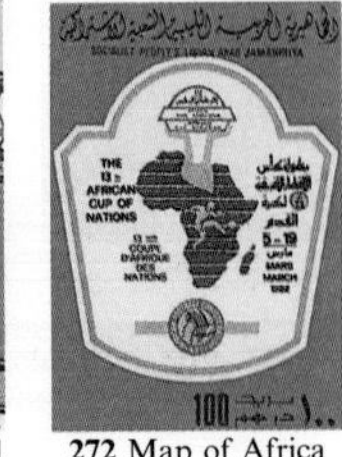

271 Scout flying Model Airship

272 Map of Africa and A.F.C. Emblem

1982. 75th Anniv of Boy Scout Movement. Mult.
1173 100dh. Type **271** 75 50
1174 200dh. Scouts helping injured dog . . . . 1·75 95
1175 300dh. Scout reading to old man . . . . 1·75 1·40
1176 400dh. Scout with model rocket . . . . 3·75 2·25

1982. African Football Cup Competition.
1178 **272** 100dh. multicoloured . . 95 50
1179 200dh. multicoloured . . 1·90 95

273 Footballer

1982. World Cup Football Championship, Spain. Multicoloured.
1180 45dh. Type **273** 25 25
1181 100dh. Footballer (different) 75 50
1182 200dh. As No. 1173 . . . . 1·60 95
1183 300dh. Footballer and goalkeeper . . . . 2·25 1·40

274 Palestinian Children

1982. Palestinian Children's Day. Multicoloured.
1185 20dh. Type **274** 15 15
1186 20dh. Girl with dish 15 15
1187 20dh. Child with turban . . 15 15
1188 20dh. Young child 15 15
1189 20dh. Young boy 15 15

275 Lanner Falcon

277 Map of Libya and A.P.U. Emblem

276 Nurses' Class, Operating Theatre and Doctor examining Child

1982. Birds. Multicoloured.
1190 15dh. Type **275** 35 25
1191 15dh. Eurasian swift 35 25
1192 15dh. Peregrine falcon . . . 35 25
1193 15dh. Greater flamingo . . 35 25
1194 25dh. Whitethroat 60 35
1195 25dh. Turtle dove 60 35
1196 25dh. Black-bellied sandgrouse 60 35
1197 25dh. Egyptian vulture . . . 60 35
1198 45dh. Golden oriole . . . . 1·00 60
1199 45dh. European bee eater 1·00 60
1200 45dh. River kingfisher . . . 1·00 60
1201 45dh. European roller . . . 1·00 60
1202 95dh. Barbary partridge . . 2·00 1·25
1203 95dh. Barn owl . . . . . . 2·00 1·25
1204 95dh. Cream-coloured courser . . . . 2·00 1·25
1205 95dh. Hoopoe . . . . . . 2·00 1·25
The four designs of each value were printed together in se-tenant blocks of four, forming a composite design.

1982. Teaching Hospitals.
1207 **276** 95dh. multicoloured . . 85 50
1208 100dh. multicoloured . . 85 50
1209 205dh. multicoloured . . 2·00 1·10

1982. 30th Anniv of Arab Postal Union.
1210 **277** 100dh. multicoloured . . 95 50
1211 200dh. multicoloured . . 1·90 95

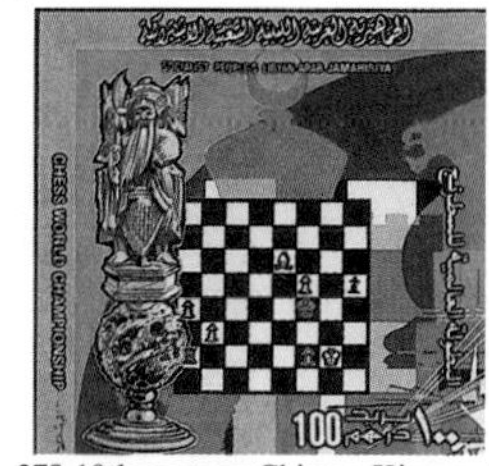

278 19th-century Chinese King and Diagram of Fischer v Spassky, 1972

1982. World Chess Championship, Moscow. Mult.

1212 100dh. Type **278** . . . . . 1·25 50
1213 100dh. African king and diagram of Karpov v Korchnoi, 1978 . . . . . 1·25 50
1214 100dh. Modern bishop and diagram of Smyslov v Karpov, 1971 . . . . . . 1·25 50
1215 100dh. 19th-century European rook and diagram of Tal v Vadasz, 1977 . . . . 1·25 50

Nos. 1212/15 were printed together, se-tenant, forming a composite design.

279 Hexagonal Pattern

1982. World Telecommunications Day.

1217 **279** 100dh. multicoloured . . 75 50
1218 200dh. multicoloured . . 1·50 95

280 Map of Libya and "Green Book"

1982. 51st Anniv of International Philatelic Federation (F.I.P.).

1219 **280** 200dh. multicoloured . . 1·75 95

281 Family and Flag

283 Palm Tree and Red Crescent

282 Pres. Gaddafi and Jet Aircraft

1982. Organization of African Unity Summit. Multicoloured.

1221 50dh. Type **281** 30 30
1222 100dh. Map, dove and symbols of industry and agriculture 75 50
1223 200dh. Pres. Gaddafi and crowd with "Green Book" (65 × 36 mm.) . . . . . . 1·90 95

1982. 13th Anniv of Revolution. Multicoloured.

1225 15dh. Type **282** 15 10
1226 20dh. Gaddafi, soldiers and rockets 15 10
1227 30dh. Gaddafi, sailors and naval vessels 50 25
1228 45dh. Gaddafi, soldiers and tanks 25 25

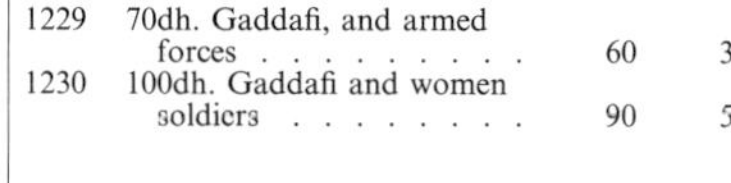

1229 70dh. Gaddafi, and armed forces 60 35
1230 100dh. Gaddafi and women soldiers 90 50

1982. 25th Anniv of Libyan Red Crescent. Multicoloured.

1232 100dh. Type **283** 95 50
1233 200dh. "25" within crescents 1·90 95

284 Globe, Dove and Rifle

286 Philadelphus

285 Gaddafi, Crowd, "Green Book" and Emblems

1982. Solidarity with Palestinian People.

1234 **284** 100dh. black, mauve and green 95 40
1235 200dh. black, blue and green . . . . 1·90 80

1982. Al Fateh University Symposium on the "Green Book". Multicoloured.

1236 100dh. Type **285** 95 45
1237 200dh. Gaddafi, "Green Book", map and emblems 1·90 95

1983. Flowers. Multicoloured.

1238 25dh. Type **286** 15 10
1239 25dh. Hypericum 15 10
1240 25dh. Antirrhinum 15 10
1241 25dh. Lily 15 10
1242 25dh. Capparis 15 10
1243 25dh. Tropaeolum 15 10
1244 25dh. Roses 15 10
1245 25dh. Chrysanthemum . . . 15 10
1246 25dh. "Nigella damascena" 15 10
1247 25dh. "Guilladia lanceolata" 15 10
1248 25dh. Dahlia 15 10
1249 25dh. "Dianthus caryophyllus" 15 10
1250 25dh. "Notobasis syriaca" 15 10
1251 25dh. "Nerium oleander" 15 10
1252 25dh. "Iris histroides" . . . 15 10
1253 25dh. "Scolymus hispanicus" 15 10

287 Customs Council Building, Brussels, and Warrior on Horseback

288 Camel

1983. 30th Anniv of Customs Co-operation Council. Multicoloured.

1254 25dh. Type **287** 15 10
1255 50dh. Customs building . . 25 20
1256 100dh. Customs building and warrior with sword 50 45

1983. Battles (4th series). As T **246**. (a) Battle of Ghaser Ahmed.

1257 50dh. multicoloured 25 20
1258 50dh. multicoloured 25 20

(b) Battle of Sidi Abuarghub.

1259 50dh. multicoloured 25 20
1260 50dh. multicoloured 25 20

(c) Battle of Ghar Yunes.

1261 50dh. multicoloured 25 20
1262 50dh. multicoloured 25 20

(d) Battle of Bir Otman.

1263 50dh. multicoloured 25 20
1264 50dh. multicoloured 25 20

(e) Battle of Sidi Sajeh.

1265 50dh. multicoloured 25 20
1266 50dh. multicoloured 25 20

(f) Battle of Ras el-Hamam.

1267 50dh. multicoloured 25 20
1268 50dh. multicoloured 25 20

(g) Battle of Zawiet Ishghefa.

1269 50dh. multicoloured 25 20
1270 50dh. multicoloured 25 20

(h) Battle of Wadi Essania.

1271 50dh. multicoloured 25 20
1272 50dh. multicoloured 25 20

(i) Battle of El-Meshiashta.

1273 50dh. multicoloured 25 20
1274 50dh. multicoloured 25 20

(j) Battle of Gharara.

1275 50dh. multicoloured 25 20
1276 50dh. multicoloured 25 20

(k) Battle of Abughelan.

1277 50dh. multicoloured 20 20
1278 50dh. multicoloured 20 20

(l) Battle of Mahruka.

1279 50dh. multicoloured 20 20
1280 50dh. multicoloured 20 20

The two values for each battle were printed together in se-tenant pairs, forming composite designs.

1983. Farm Animals. Multicoloured.

1281 25dh. Type **288** 15 10
1282 25dh. Cow 15 10
1283 25dh. Horse 15 10
1284 25dh. Bull 15 10
1285 25dh. Goat 15 10
1286 25dh. Sheep dog 15 10
1287 25dh. Ewe 15 10
1288 25dh. Ram 15 10
1289 25dh. Greylag goose 35 25
1290 25dh. Helmeted guineafowl 35 25
1291 25dh. Rabbit 15 10
1292 25dh. Wood pigeon 35 25
1293 25dh. Common turkey . . . 35 25
1294 25dh. Cockerel 15 10
1295 25dh. Hen 15 10
1296 25dh. Goose 15 10

289 Musician with Twin-horned Pipe

1983. Tripoli International Fair. Multicoloured.

1297 40dh. Type **289** 20 15
1298 45dh. Bagpipes (horiz) . . . 25 20
1299 50dh. Horn 25 20
1300 55dh. Flute (horiz) 30 25
1301 75dh. Pipe 65 35
1302 100dh. Man and woman at well 90 45

290 Phoenician Galley

1983. 25th Anniv of International Maritime Organization. Multicoloured.

1303 100dh. Type **290** . . . . . 1·25 55
1304 100dh. Ancient Greek galley 1·25 55
1305 100dh. Ancient Egyptian ship . . . . 1·25 55
1306 100dh. Roman sailing ship 1·25 55
1307 100dh. Viking longship . . 1·25 55
1308 100dh. Libyan xebec . . . . 1·25 55

291 Motorist

1983. Children's Day. Multicoloured.

1309 20dh. Type **291** 10 10
1310 20dh. Tractor and trailer . . 10 10
1311 20dh. Child with dove and globe 10 10
1312 20dh. Scout camp 10 10
1313 20dh. Dinosaur 10 10

292 Pres. Gaddafi with Children

1983. World Health Day. Multicoloured.

1314 25dh. Type **292** 15 10
1315 50dh. Gaddafi and old man in wheelchair 25 20
1316 100dh. Gaddafi visiting sick girl (horiz) 80 45

293 Gaddafi, Map and "Green Book"

294 Economic Emblems on Map of Africa

1983. 1st World "Green Book" Symposium. Mult.

1317 50dh. Type **293** 25 20
1318 70dh. Syposium in session and emblem (56 × 37 mm) 60 30
1319 80dh. Gaddafi, "Green Book", emblem and "Jamahiriya" 65 35

1983. 25th Anniv of African Economic Committee.

1321 **294** 50dh. multicoloured . . 25 20
1322 100dh. multicoloured . . 90 45
1323 250dh. multicoloured . . 1·90 1·10

296 Cuckoo Wrasse ("Labrus bimaculatus")

1983. Fishes. Multicoloured.

1325 25dh. Type **296** 30 15
1326 25dh. Streaked gurnard ("Trigoporus lastoviza") 30 15
1327 25dh. Peacock wrasse ("Thalassoma pavo") . . 30 15
1328 25dh. Mediterranean cardinal-fish ("Apogon imberbis") 30 15
1329 25dh. Atlantic mackerel ("Scomber scombrus") . . 30 15
1330 25dh. Black seabream ("Spondyliosoma cantharus") 30 15
1331 25dh. Greater weaver ("Trachinus draco") . . . 30 15
1332 25dh. Peacock blenny ("Blennius pavo") 30 15
1333 25dh. Lesser red scorpionfish ("Scorpaena notata") 30 15
1334 25dh. Painted comber ("Serranus scriba") . . . 30 15
1335 25dh. Angler ("Lophius piscatorius") 30 15
1336 25dh. Stargazer ("Uranoscopus scaber") 30 15
1337 25dh. Frigate mackerel ("Auxis thazard") 30 15
1338 25dh. John dory ("Zeus faber") 30 15
1339 25dh. Flying gurnard ("Dactylopterus volitans") 30 15
1340 25dh. Corb ("Umbrina cirrosa") 30 15

297 "Still-life" (Gauguin)

1983. Paintings. Multicoloured.

1341	50dh. Type **297**	25	20
1342	50dh. Abstract	25	20
1343	50dh. "The Conquest of Tunis by Charles V" (Rubens)	25	20
1344	50dh. "Arab Band in Horse-drawn Carriage"	25	20
1345	50dh. "Apotheosis of Gaddafi" (vert)	25	20
1346	50dh. Horses (detail of Raphael's "The Triumph of David over the Assyrians") (vert)	25	20
1347	50dh. "Workers" (vert)	25	20
1348	50dh. "Sunflowers" (Van Gogh) (vert)	25	20

298 Basketball

1983. Olympic Games, Los Angeles. Mult.

1349	10dh. Type **298**	10	10
1350	15dh. High jumping	10	10
1351	25dh. Running	15	10
1352	50dh. Gymnastics	25	20
1353	100dh. Windsurfing	80	45
1354	200dh. Shot-putting	1·50	95

299 I.T.U. Building, Antenna and W.C.Y. Emblem

1983. World Communications Year.

1356	**299**	10dh. multicoloured	10	10
1357		50dh. multicoloured	25	20
1358		100dh. multicoloured	75	45

300 "The House is to be served by its Residents"

1983. Extracts from the Green Book. Mult.

1359	10dh. Type **300**	10	10
1360	15dh. "Power, wealth and arms are in the hands of the people"	10	10
1361	20dh. "Masters in their own castles" (vert)	10	10
1362	35dh. "No democracy without popular congresses"	20	15
1363	100dh. "The authority of the people" (vert)	50	45
1364	140dh. "The Green Book is the guide of humanity for final release"	1·10	70

301 Handball

1983. 2nd African Youth Festival. Multicoloured.

1366	100dh. Type **301**	85	45
1367	100dh. Basketball	85	45
1368	100dh. High jumping	85	45
1369	100dh. Running	85	45
1370	100dh. Football	85	45

302 Marching Soldiers

1983. 14th Anniv of September Revolution. Mult.

1371	65dh. Type **302**	35	30
1372	75dh. Weapons and communications training	40	35
1373	90dh. Women with machine-guns and bazookas	70	40
1374	100dh. Machine-gun training	75	45
1375	150dh. Bazooka training	1·10	70
1376	250dh. Rifle training	2·00	1·10

303 Saluting Scouts

1983. Scout Jamborees. Multicoloured.

1378	50dh. Type **303**	25	20
1379	100dh. Scouts around camp fire	90	45

EVENTS. 50dh. Second Islamic Scout Jamboree; 100dh. 15th Pan Arab Scout Jamboree.

304 Traffic Cadets

305 Saadun

1983. Traffic Day. Multicoloured.

1381	30dh. Type **304**	40	15
1382	70dh. Traffic policeman	70	30
1383	200dh. Police motorcyclists	1·90	1·25

1983. 90th Birth Anniv of Saadun (patriot soldier).

1384	**305**	100dh. multicoloured	90	45

306 Walter Wellman's airship "America", 1910

1983. Bicentenary of Manned Flight. Mult.

1385	100dh. Type **306**	1·00	55
1386	100dh. Airship "Nulli Secundus", 1907	1·00	55
1387	100dh. Jean-Baptiste Meusnier's balloon design, 1784	1·00	55
1388	100dh. Blanchard and Jeffries' Channel crossing, 1785 (vert)	1·00	55
1389	100dh. Pilatre de Rozier's hydrogen/hot-air balloon flight, 1784 (vert)	1·00	55
1390	100dh. First Montgolfier balloon, 1783 (vert)	1·00	55

307 Globe and Dove

1983. Solidarity with Palestinian People.

1393	**307**	200dh. green, blue & blk	1·60	95

308 Gladiators fighting

1983. Mosaics. Multicoloured.

1394	50dh. Type **308**	50	20
1395	50dh. Gladiators fighting (different)	50	20
1396	50dh. Gladiators and slave	50	20
1397	50dh. Two musicians	50	20
1398	50dh. Three musicians	50	20
1399	50dh. Two gladiators	50	20
1400	50dh. Two Romans and bound victim	50	20
1401	50dh. Leopard and man hunting deer	50	20
1402	50dh. Deer and man with boar	50	20

309 Traditional Architecture

1983. Achievements of the Revolution. Mult.

1403	10dh. Type **309**	10	10
1404	15dh. Camels drinking and mechanization of farming	10	10
1405	20dh. Computer operator and industrial scene	10	10
1406	35dh. Modern architecture	15	10
1407	100dh. Surgeons and nurses treating patients and hospital	90	40
1408	140dh. Airport and airplane	1·25	75

310 Flooding a River Bed

311 Mahmud Burkis

1983. Colonel Gaddafi—River Builder. Multicoloured.

1410	50dh. Type **310**	20	15
1411	50dh. Irrigation pipe and agricultural produce	20	15
1412	100dh. Colonel Gaddafi, irrigation pipe and farmland (62 × 44 mm)	1·00	40
1413	100dh. Colonel Gaddafi and map (68 × 32 mm)	1·00	40
1414	150dh. Colonel Gaddafi explaining irrigation project (35 × 32 mm)	1·40	65

Nos. 1410/12 were printed together in se-tenant strips of three forming a composite design.

1984. Personalities. Multicoloured.

1416	100dh. Type **311**	1·00	40
1417	100dh. Ahmed el-Bakbak	1·00	40
1418	100dh. Mohamed el-Misurati	1·00	40
1419	100dh. Mahmud Ben Musa	1·00	40
1420	100dh. Abdulhamid el-Sherif	1·00	40
1421	100dh. Mehdi el-Sherif	1·00	40
1422	100dh. Mahmud Mustafa Dreza	1·00	40
1423	100dh. Hosni Fauzi el-Amir	1·00	40
1424	100dh. Ali Haidar el-Saati	1·00	40
1425	200dh. Ahmed el-Feghi Hasan	1·50	80
1426	200dh. Bashir el-Jawab	1·50	80
1427	200dh. Ali el-Gariani	1·50	80
1428	200dh. Muktar Shakshuki	1·50	80
1429	200dh. Abdurrahman el-Busayri	1·50	80
1430	200dh. Ibbrahim Bakir	1·50	80
1431	200dh. Mahmud el-Janzuri	1·50	80

312 Windsurfing

313 Col. Gaddafi with Schoolchildren

1984. Water Sports. Multicoloured.

1432	25dh. Type **312**	30	10
1433	25dh. Dinghy sailing (orange and red sails)	30	10
1434	25dh. Dinghy sailing (mauve sails)	30	10
1435	25dh. Hang-gliding on water skis	20	10
1436	25dh. Water-skiing	20	10
1437	25dh. Angling from boat	30	10
1438	25dh. Men in speed boat	30	10
1439	25dh. Water-skiing (different)	20	10
1440	25dh. Fishing	30	10
1441	25dh. Canoeing	20	10
1442	25dh. Surfing	20	10
1443	25dh. Water-skiing (different)	20	10
1444	25dh. Scuba diving	30	10
1445	25dh. Diving	30	10
1446	25dh. Swimming in snorkel and flippers	30	10
1447	25dh. Scuba diving for fish	30	10

1984. African Children's Day. Multicoloured.

1448	50dh. Type **313**	50	15
1449	50dh. Colonel Gaddafi and children in national dress	50	15
1450	100dh. Colonel Gaddafi on map and children at various activities (62 × 43 mm)	1·90	60

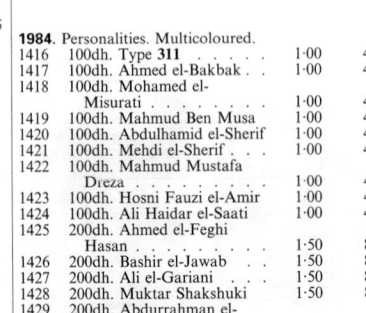

314 Women in National, Casual and Military Dress

1984. Libyan Women's Emancipation. Multicoloured.

1451	55dh. Type **314**	50	20
1452	70dh. Women in traditional, casual and military dress (vert)	75	25
1453	100dh. Colonel Gaddafi and women in military dress	95	40

315 Theatre, Sabratha

1984. Roman Ruins of Cyrenaica. Multicoloured.

1454	50dh. Type **315**	20	15
1455	60dh. Temple, Cyrene	50	20
1456	70dh. Monument, Sabratha (vert)	60	25
1457	100dh. Amphitheatre, Leptis Magna	90	40
1458	150dh. Temple, Cyrene (different)	1·40	65
1459	200dh. Basilica, Leptis Magna	1·90	80

316 Silver Dirham, 115h.

318 Muktar Shiaker Murabet

317 Men at Tea Ceremony

1984. Arabic Islamic Coins (1st series).

No.	Type	Description	Mint	Used
1460	**316**	200dh. silver, yellow and black	1·90	85
1461	–	200dh. silver, mauve and black	1·90	85
1462	–	200dh. silver, green and black	1·90	85
1463	–	200dh. silver, orange and black	1·90	85
1464	–	200dh. silver, blue and black	1·90	85

DESIGNS: No. 1461, Silver dirham, 93h; 1462, Silver dirham, 121h; 1463, Silver dirham, 49h; 1464, Silver dirham, 135h.

See also Nos. 1643/5.

1984. International Trade Fair, Tripoli. Mult.

No.	Description	Mint	Used
1465	25dh. Type **317**	15	10
1466	35dh. Woman making tea	15	15
1467	45dh. Men taking tea	20	15
1468	55dh. Family taking tea	50	20
1469	75dh. Veiled women pouring tea	70	30
1470	100dh. Robed men taking tea	1·00	40

1984. Musicians. Multicoloured.

No.	Description	Mint	Used
1471	100dh. Type **318**	1·25	65
1472	100dh. El-Aref el-Jamal	1·25	65
1473	100dh. Ali Shiaalia	1·25	65
1474	100dh. Bashir Fehmi	1·25	65

319 Playing among Trees

1984. Children's Day. Designs showing children's paintings. Multicoloured.

No.	Description	Mint	Used
1475	20dh. Type **319**	10	10
1476	20dh. A rainy day	10	10
1477	20dh. Weapons of war	10	10
1478	20dh. Playing on the swing	10	10
1479	20dh. Playing in the park	10	10

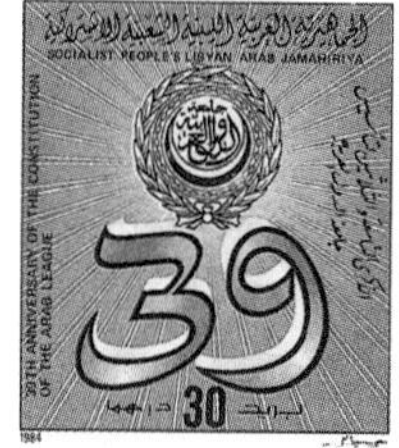
320 Crest and "39"

1984. 39th Anniv of Arab League.

No.	Type	Description	Mint	Used
1480	**320**	30dh. multicoloured	15	15
1481		40dh. multicoloured	20	15
1482		50dh. multicoloured	55	20

321 Red Four-seater Car

1984. Motor Cars and Steam Locomotives. Mult.

No.	Description	Mint	Used
1483	100dh. Type **321**	1·25	65
1484	100dh. Red three-seater car	1·25	65
1485	100dh. Yellow two-seater car with three lamps	1·25	65
1486	100dh. Covered red four-seater car	1·25	65
1487	100dh. Yellow two-seater car with two lamps	1·25	65
1488	100dh. Cream car with spare wheel at side	1·25	65
1489	100dh. Green car with spare wheel at side	1·25	65
1490	100dh. Cream four-seater car with spare wheel at back	1·25	65
1491	100dh. Locomotive pulling wagon and coach	1·40	45
1492	100dh. Purple and blue locomotive	1·40	45
1493	100dh. Cream locomotive	1·40	45
1494	100dh. Lilac and brown locomotive	1·40	45
1495	100dh. Lilac and black locomotive with red wheels	1·40	45
1496	100dh. Cream and red locomotive	1·40	45
1497	100dh. Purple and black locomotive with red wheels	1·40	45
1498	100dh. Green and orange locomotive	1·40	45

322 Stylized People and Campaign Emblem

1984. World Health Day. Anti-Polio Campaign. Multicoloured.

No.	Description	Mint	Used
1499	20dh. Type **322**	10	10
1500	30dh. Stylized people and 1981 20dh. stamp	15	15
1501	40dh. Stylized people and Arabic emblem	50	15

323 Man making Slippers

1984. Handicrafts. Multicoloured.

No.	Description	Mint	Used
1502	150dh. Type **323**	1·60	65
1503	150dh. Man making decorative harness	1·60	65
1504	150dh. Women forming cotton into skeins	1·60	65
1505	150dh. Woman spinning by hand	1·60	65
1506	150dh. Man weaving	1·60	65
1507	150dh. Women weaving	1·60	65

324 Telephones, Dial and Mail

1984. Postal and Telecommunications Union Congress. Multicoloured.

No.	Description	Mint	Used
1508	50dh. Type **324**	50	20
1509	50dh. Woman working at computer console, dial and man working on computer	50	20
1510	100dh. Satellite, map, laurel branches and telephone handset	1·00	40

325 Armed Soldiers and Civilians

326 Children behind Barbed Wire

1984. Abrogation of 17 May Treaty. Multicoloured.

No.	Description	Mint	Used
1511	50dh. Type **325**	65	20
1512	50dh. Map, dove and burning banner	65	20
1513	50dh. Soldiers shaking hands and crowd with banners (30 × 40 mm)	65	20
1514	100dh. Hands tearing treaty, Gaddafi and crowd (62 × 40 mm)	1·25	40
1515	100dh. Gaddafi addressing crowd	1·25	40

Nos. 1512/14 were printed together in se-tenant strips of three, forming a composite design.

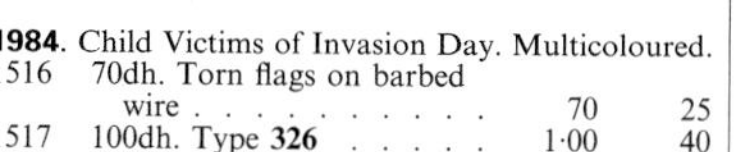

1984. Child Victims of Invasion Day. Multicoloured.

No.	Description	Mint	Used
1516	70dh. Torn flags on barbed wire	70	25
1517	100dh. Type **326**	1·00	40

327 "The Party System Aborts Democracy"

328 Man in Brown Robes

1984. Quotations from "The Green Book". Multicoloured.

No.	Description	Mint	Used
1518	100dh. Type **327**	95	40
1519	100dh. Colonel Gaddafi	95	40
1520	100dh. "Partners not wage-workers"	95	40
1521	100dh. "No representation in lieu of the people. Representation is falsification"	95	40
1522	100dh. The Green Book	95	40
1523	100dh. "Committees everywhere"	95	40
1524	100dh. "Forming parties splits societies"	95	40
1525	100dh. Skyscraper and earthmover	95	40
1526	100dh. "No democracy without popular congresses"	95	40

1984. Costumes. Multicoloured.

No.	Description	Mint	Used
1527	100dh. Type **328**	1·25	65
1528	100dh. Woman in green dress and red shawl	1·25	65
1529	100dh. Man in ornate costume and turban	1·25	65
1530	100dh. Man in short trousers and plain shirt	1·25	65
1531	100dh. Woman in shift and trousers with white shawl	1·25	65
1532	100dh. Man in long white robe and red shawl	1·25	65

329 Footballer tackling

1984. World Cup Football Championship. Mult.

No.	Description	Mint	Used
1533	70dh. Type **329**	70	25
1534	70dh. Footballers in magenta and green shirts	70	25
1535	70dh. Footballers in orange and lemon shirts	70	25
1536	70dh. Goalkeeper failing to save ball	70	25
1537	70dh. Footballers in yellow and brown shirts	70	25
1538	70dh. Top of Trophy and footballer in green striped shirt	70	25
1539	70dh. Top of Trophy and footballers in blue and pink shirts	70	25
1540	70dh. Footballers in black and white striped and green and red striped shirts	70	25
1541	70dh. Footballers in green and red striped shirts	70	25
1542	70dh. Foot of Trophy and footballers in orange striped and blue shirts	70	25
1543	70dh. Foot of trophy and goalkeeper	70	25
1544	70dh. Goalkeeper saving headed ball	70	25
1545	70dh. Referee and footballers	70	25
1546	70dh. Footballers in white with red striped sleeves and orange shirts	70	25
1547	70dh. Footballers in white and green striped and orange shirts	70	25
1548	70dh. Footballer in pink shirt	70	25

Nos. 1533/48 were printed in sheetlets of 16 stamps, the backgrounds to the stamps forming an overall design of a stadium.

330 Football

331 Palm Trees

1984. Olympic Games, Los Angeles. Mult.

No.	Description	Mint	Used
1549	100dh. Type **330**	1·25	65
1550	100dh. Swimming	1·25	65
1551	100dh. Throwing the discus	1·25	65
1552	100dh. Windsurfing	1·25	65
1553	100dh. Basketball	1·25	65
1554	100dh. Running	1·25	65

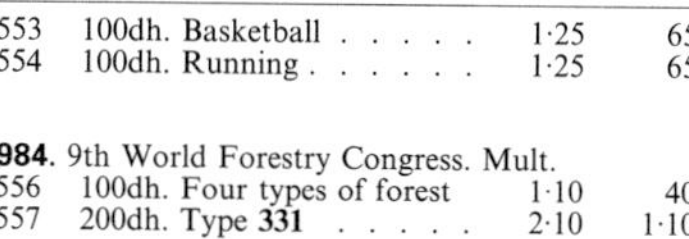

1984. 9th World Forestry Congress. Mult.

No.	Description	Mint	Used
1556	100dh. Four types of forest	1·10	40
1557	200dh. Type **331**	2·10	1·10

332 Modern Building

1984. 15th Anniv of Revolution. Multicoloured.

No.	Description	Mint	Used
1558	25dh. Type **332**	15	10
1559	25dh. Front of building	15	10
1560	25dh. Building by pool	15	10
1561	25dh. Col. Gaddafi (three-quarter portrait)	15	10
1562	25dh. High-rise block	15	10
1563	25dh. Crane and mosque	15	10
1564	25dh. Motorway interchange	15	10
1565	25dh. House and garden	15	10
1566	25dh. Shepherd and flock	15	10
1567	25dh. Combine harvester	15	10
1568	25dh. Tractors	15	10
1569	25dh. Scientific equipment	15	10
1570	25dh. Col. Gaddafi (full face)	15	10
1571	25dh. Water pipeline	15	10
1572	25dh. Lighthouse	15	10
1573	25dh. Liner at quay	45	10

333 Armed Man

334 Soldier flogging Civilian

1984. Evacuation of Foreign Forces. Mult.

(a) As T **333**.

No.	Description	Mint	Used
1574	50dh. Type **333**	50	20
1575	50dh. Armed man (different)	50	20
1576	100dh. Men on horseback charging (62 × 40 mm)	1·00	40

(b) As T **334**.

No.	Description	Mint	Used
1577	100dh. Type **334**	1·00	40
1578	100dh. Girl on horse charging soldiers	1·00	40
1579	100dh. Mounted soldiers and wounded being tended by women	1·00	40

335 Woman riding Skewbald Showjumper

1984. Equestrian Events. Multicoloured.

No.	Description	Mint	Used
1580	25dh. Type **335**	15	10
1581	25dh. Man riding black showjumper (stands in background)	15	10
1582	25dh. Jockey riding chestnut horse (stands in background)	15	10
1583	25dh. Man on chestnut horse jumping in cross-country event	15	10
1584	25dh. Man riding bay horse in showjumping competition	15	10

1585 25dh. Woman on black horse in dressage competition 15 10
1586 25dh. Man on black horse in dressage competition 15 10
1587 25dh. Woman riding chestnut horse in cross-country event 15 10
1588 25dh. Jockey riding bay horse 15 10
1589 25dh. Woman on bay horse in dressage competition 15 10
1590 25dh. Man on grey horse in dressage competition . . . 15 10
1591 25dh. Jockey riding grey steeplechaser 15 10
1592 25dh. Woman riding grey showjumper 15 10
1593 25dh. Woman riding through water in cross-country competition . . . 15 10
1594 25dh. Woman on chestnut horse in cross-country competition 15 10
1595 25dh. Man riding dun showjumper 15 10

Nos. 1580/95 were printed together in sheetlets of 16 stamps, the backgrounds of the stamps forming an overall design of an equestrian ring.

336 Man cleaning Corn **337** Map and Pharmaceutical Equipment

1984. Traditional Agriculture. Multicoloured.
1596 100dh. Type **336** . . . . . 1·25 65
1597 100dh. Man using oxen to draw water from well . . 1·25 65
1598 100dh. Man making straw goods . . . . 1·25 65
1599 100dh. Shepherd with sheep 1·25 65
1600 100dh. Man treating animal skin . . . . 1·25 65
1601 100dh. Man climbing coconut tree . . . . . . 1·25 65

1984. 9th Conference of Arab Pharmacists Union.
1602 **337** 100dh. multicoloured . . 1·25 40
1603 200dh. multicoloured . . 2·50 1·10

338 Crowd with Banner showing Map of North Africa

1984. Arab–African Unity. Multicoloured.
1604 100dh. Type **338** . . . . . 1·25 65
1605 100dh. Crowd and men holding flags . . . . . . 1·25 65

339 1982 and 1983 Solidarity Stamps and Map of Palestine

1984. Solidarity with Palestinian People.
1606 **339** 100dh. multicoloured . . 1·25 40
1607 150dh. multicoloured . . 1·90 1·00

340 Boeing 747SP, 1975

1984. 40th Anniv of International Civil Aviation Organization. Multicoloured.
1608 70dh. Type **340** 95 30
1609 70dh. Concorde, 1969 . . . 95 30
1610 70dh. Lockheed TriStar 500, 1978 . . . . 95 30
1611 70dh. Airbus Industrie A310, 1982 . . . . 95 30
1612 70dh. Tupolev Tu-134A, 1962 . . . . 95 30
1613 70dh. Shorts 360, 1981 . . . 95 30
1614 70dh. Boeing 727-100, 1963 95 30
1615 70dh. Sud Aviation Caravelle 10R, 1965 . . . 95 30
1616 70dh. Fokker Friendship, 1955 . . . . 95 30
1617 70dh. Lockheed Constellation, 1946 . . . 95 30
1618 70dh. Martin M-130 flying boat, 1955 . . . . 95 30
1619 70dh. Douglas DC-3, 1936 95 50
1620 70dh. Junkers Ju-52/3m, 1932 . . . . 95 30
1621 70dh. Lindbergh's "Spirit of St. Louis", 1927 . . . . 95 30
1622 70dh. De Havilland Moth, 1925 . . . . 95 30
1623 70dh. Wright Flyer I, 1903 95 30

Nos. 1608/23 were printed together in sheetlets of 16 stamps, the backgrounds of the stamps forming an overall design of a runway.

341 Coin **342** Mother and Son

1984. 20th Anniv of African Development Bank. Multicoloured.
1624 50dh. Type **341** 55 20
1625 70dh. Map of Africa and "20" . . . . 1·00 25
1626 100dh. "20" and symbols of industry and agriculture 1·25 65

1985. UNICEF Child Survival Campaign. Multicoloured.
1627 70dh. Type **342** . . . . . . 1·00 50
1628 70dh. Couple and children 1·00 50
1629 70dh. Col. Gaddafi and children . . . . 1·00 50
1630 70dh. Boys in uniform . . . 1·00 50

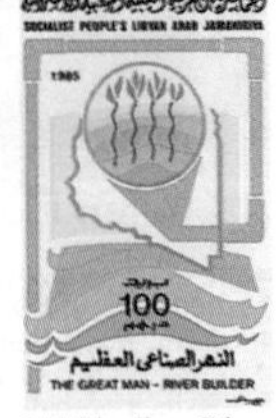
343 Mohamed Hamdi **344** Pipeline, River, Plants and Map

1985. Musicians and Instruments. Multicoloured.
1631 100dh. Kamel el-Ghadi . . 1·25 65
1632 100dh. Fiddle rebab . . . . 1·25 65
1633 100dh. Ahmed el-Khogia . . 1·25 65
1634 100dh. Violin . . . . 1·25 65
1635 100dh. Mustafa el-Fallah . . 1·25 65
1636 100dh. Zither . . . . 1·25 65
1637 100dh. Type **343** . . . . . 1·25 65
1638 100dh. Mask . . . . 1·25 65

1985. Col. Gaddafi—River Builder. Multicoloured.
1639 100dh. Type **344** . . . . . 1·25 65
1640 100dh. Water droplet, river and flowers . . . . 1·25 65
1641 100dh. Dead tree with branch thriving in water droplet . . . . 1·25 65

345 Gold Dinar, 105h.

1985. Arabic Islamic Coins (2nd series). Mult.
1643 200dh. Type **345** . . . . . 2·50 1·25
1644 200dh. Gold dinar, 91h. . . 2·50 1·25
1645 200dh. Gold dinar, 77h. . . 2·50 1·25

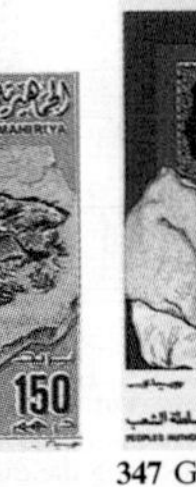
346 Fish **347** Gaddafi in Robes and Hat

1985. Fossils. Multicoloured.
1647 150dh. Type **346** . . . . . 3·00 90
1648 150dh. Frog . . . . 1·90 55
1649 150dh. Mammal . . . . . . 1·90 55

1985. People's Authority Declaration. Mult.
1650 100dh. Type **347** . . . . . 1·25 65
1651 100dh. Gaddafi in black robe holding book . . . 1·25 65
1652 100dh. Gaddafi in dress uniform without cap . . . 1·25 65
1653 100dh. Gaddafi in black dress uniform with cap . . 1·25 65
1654 100dh. Gaddafi in white dress uniform . . . . . . 1·25 65

348 Cymbal Player

1985. International Trade Fair, Tripoli. Mult.
1655 100dh. Type **348** . . . . . 1·25 65
1656 100dh. Piper and drummer 1·25 65
1657 100dh. Drummer and bagpipes player . . . . . 1·25 65
1658 100dh. Drummer . . . . . 1·25 65
1659 100dh. Tambour player . . 1·25 65

349 Goalkeeper catching Ball **350** Emblem, Radio Transmitter and Satellite

1985. Children's Day. Multicoloured.
1660 20dh. Type **349** 10 10
1661 20dh. Child on touchline with ball 10 10
1662 20dh. Letters of alphabet as players 10 10
1663 20dh. Goalkeeper saving ball 10 10
1664 20dh. Player heading ball 10 10

1985. International Communications Development Programme.
1665 **350** 30dh. multicoloured . . 15 10
1666 70dh. multicoloured . . 75 25
1667 100dh. multicoloured . . 1·10 65

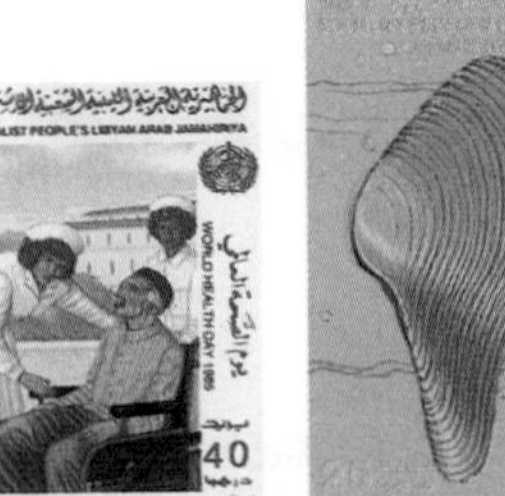
351 Nurses and Man in Wheelchair **352** "Mytilidae"

1985. World Health Day. Multicoloured.
1668 40dh. Type **351** 50 10
1669 60dh. Nurses and doctors 75 15
1670 100dh. Nurse and child . . 1·25 65

1985. Sea Shells. Multicoloured.
1671 25dh. Type **352** 40 15
1672 25dh. Purple dye murex ("Muricidae") 40 15
1673 25dh. Tuberculate cockle ("Cardiidae") 40 15
1674 25dh. "Corallophilidae" . . 40 15
1675 25dh. Trunculus murex ("Muricidae") 40 15
1676 25dh. "Muricacea" 40 15
1677 25dh. "Turridae" 40 15
1678 25dh. Nodose paper nautilus ("Argonautidae") 40 15
1679 25dh. Giant tun ("Tonnidae") 40 15
1680 25dh. Common pelican's-foot ("Aporrhaidae") . . 40 15
1681 25dh. "Trochidae" 40 15
1682 25dh. "Cancellariidae" . . . 40 15
1683 25dh. "Epitoniidae" 40 15
1684 25dh. "Turbinidae" 40 15
1685 25dh. Zoned mitre ("Mitridae") 40 15
1686 25dh. Cat's-paw scallop ("Pectinidae") 40 15

Nos. 1671/86 were printed se-tenant, the backgrounds forming an overall design of the sea bed.

353 Books and Emblem **354** Girls Skipping

1985. International Book Fair, Tripoli.
1687 **353** 100dh. multicoloured . . 1·25 60
1688 200dh. multicoloured . . 2·25 1·25

1985. International Youth Year. Multicoloured.
1689 20dh. Type **354** 10 10
1690 20dh. Boys playing with stones 10 10
1691 20dh. Girls playing hopscotch 10 10
1692 20dh. Boys playing with sticks 10 10
1693 20dh. Boys playing with spinning top 10 10

355 Abdussalam Lasmar Mosque **356** Jamila Zemerli

1985. Minarets. Multicoloured.
1695 50dh. Type **355** 50 15
1696 50dh. Zaoviat Kadria Mosque 50 15
1697 50dh. Zaoviat Amura Mosque 50 15
1698 50dh. Gurgi Mosque . . . 50 15
1699 50dh. Mizran Mosque . . . 50 15
1700 50dh. Salem Mosque . . . 50 15
1701 50dh. Ghat Mosque 50 15
1702 50dh. Ahmed Karamanli Mosque 50 15
1703 50dh. Atya Mosque 50 15
1704 50dh. El Kettani Mosque 50 15
1705 50dh. Benghazi Mosque . . 50 15
1706 50dh. Derna Mosque . . . 50 15
1707 50dh. El Derug Mosque . . 50 15
1708 50dh. Ben Moussa Mosque 50 15
1709 50dh. Ghadames Mosque 50 15
1710 50dh. Abdulwahab Mosque 50 15

1985. Teachers' Day. Multicoloured.
1711 100dh. Type **356** . . . . . 1·25 65
1712 100dh. Hamida El-Anezi . . 1·25 65

357 "Philadelphia" exploding **358** Gaddafi and Followers

1985. Battle of the "Philadelphia". Multicoloured.
1713 50dh. Type **357** 60 20
1714 50dh. Men with swords . . 60 20
1715 100dh. Men fighting and ship's rigging (59 × 45 mm) . . . . . . 1·25 45

Nos. 1713/15 were printed together, se-tenant, forming a composite design.

1986. Colonel Gaddafi's Islamic Pilgrimage. Multicoloured.
1716 200dh. Gaddafi writing . . 2·50 1·25
1717 200dh. Gaddafi praying . . 2·50 1·25
1718 200dh. Gaddafi, crowds and Kaaba . . . . 2·50 1·25
1719 200dh. Gaddafi and mirror 2·50 1·25
1720 200dh. Type **358** . . . . . 2·50 1·25

359 "Leucopaxillus lepistoides"

1985. Mushrooms. Multicoloured.
1722 50dh. Type **359** 1·10 25
1723 50dh. "Amanita caesarea" 1·10 25
1724 50dh. "Coriolus hirsutus" 1·10 25
1725 50dh. "Cortinarius subfulgens" 1·10 25
1726 50dh. "Dermocybe pratensis" 1·10 25
1727 50dh. "Macrolepiota excoriata" 1·10 25
1728 50dh. "Amanita curtipes" 1·10 25
1729 50dh. "Trametes ljubarskyi" 1·10 25
1730 50dh. "Pholiota aurivella" 1·10 25
1731 50dh. "Boletus edulis" 1·10 25
1732 50dh. "Geastrum sessile" 1·10 25
1733 50dh. "Russula sanguinea" 1·10 25
1734 50dh. "Cortinarius herculeus" 1·10 25
1735 50dh. "Pholiota lenta" 1·10 25
1736 50dh. "Amanita rubescens" 1·10 25
1737 50dh. "Seleroderma polyrhizum" 1·10 25

Nos. 1722/37 were printed together, se-tenant, the backgrounds of the stamps forming an overall design of map of Mediterranean.

360 Woman in Purple Striped Dress

361 "In Need Freedom is Latent"

1985. Traditional Women's Costumes. Multicoloured.
1738 100dh. Type **360** 1·25 65
1739 100dh. Woman in robes covering her face 1·25 65
1740 100dh. Woman in colourful robes with heavy jewellery 1·25 65
1741 100dh. Woman in long blue striped dress 1·25 65
1742 100dh. Woman in red dress and trousers 1·25 65

1985. Quotations from "The Green Book".
1743 **361** 100dh. lt green, grn & blk 45 35
1744 – 100dh. multicoloured 45 35
1745 – 100dh. lt green, grn & blk 45 35
1746 – 100dh. lt green, grn & blk 45 35
1747 – 100dh. multicoloured 45 35
1748 – 100dh. lt green, grn & blk 45 35
1749 – 100dh. lt green, grn & blk 45 35
1750 – 100dh. multicoloured 45 35
1751 – 100dh. lt green, grn & blk 45 35

DESIGNS: No. 1744, Gaddafi in uniform reading; 1745, "To make a party you split society"; 1746, "Public sport is for all the masses"; 1747, "Green Books" and doves; 1748, "Wage-workers are a type of slave, however improved their wages may be"; 1749, "People are only harmonious with their own arts and heritages"; 1750, Gaddafi addressing crowd; 1751, "Democracy means popular rule not popular expression".

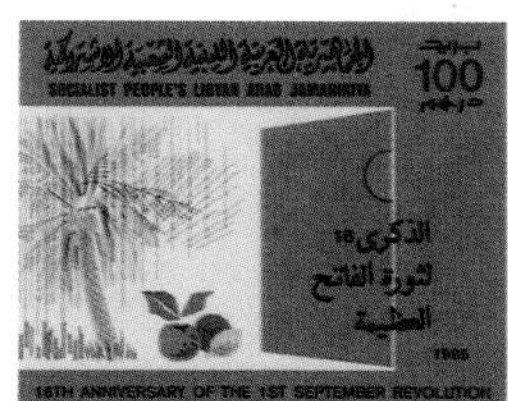
362 Tree and Citrus Fruits

1985. 16th Anniv of Revolution. Multicoloured.
1752 100dh. Type **362** 1·25 65
1753 100dh. Oil pipeline and tanks 1·25 65
1754 100dh. Capital and olive branch 1·25 65
1755 100dh. Mosque and modern buildings 1·25 65
1756 100dh. Flag and mountains 1·25 65
1757 100dh. Telecommunications 1·25 65

363 Zauiet Amoura, Janzour

364 Players in Red No. 5 and Green Shirts

1985. Mosque Gateways. Multicoloured.
1759 100dh. Type **363** 1·25 65
1760 100dh. Shiaieb El-Ain, Tripoli 1·25 65
1761 100dh. Zauiet Abdussalam El-Asmar, Zliten 1·25 65
1762 100dh. Karamanli, Tripoli 1·25 65
1763 100dh. Gurgi, Tripoli 1·25 65

1985. Basketball. Multicoloured.
1764 25dh. Type **364** 15 10
1765 25dh. Players in green number 7 and red shirts 15 10
1766 25dh. Players in green number 8 and red shirts 15 10
1767 25dh. Players in red number 6 and green shirts 15 10
1768 25dh. Players in red number 4 and green number 7 shirts 15 10
1769 25dh. Players in green numbers 6 and 5 and red number 9 shirts 15 10
1770 25dh. Basket and one player in red and two in green shirts 15 10
1771 25dh. Players in red number 8 and green number 7 shirts 15 10
1772 25dh. Two players in green shirts and two in red shirts, one number 4 15 10
1773 25dh. Players in red numbers 4 and 7 and green shirts 15 10
1774 25dh. Players in red numbers 4 and 9 and green numbers 7 and 4 shirts 15 10
1775 25dh. Players in red number 6 and green shirts 15 10
1776 25dh. Players in red number 9 and green number 8 shirts 15 10
1777 25dh. Players in red number 8 and green number 5 shirts 15 10
1778 25dh. Players in red number 4 and green shirts 15 10
1779 25dh. Players in red number 5 and green number 10 shirts 15 10

Nos. 1764/79 were printed together se-tenant, the backgrounds of the stamps forming an overall design of basketball court and basket.

365 People in Light Ray

1985. Evacuation of Foreign Forces. Multicoloured.
1780 100dh. Man on crutches in web and light shining on tree 1·25 65
1781 100dh. Hands pulling web away from man 1·25 65
1782 100dh. Type **365** 1·25 65

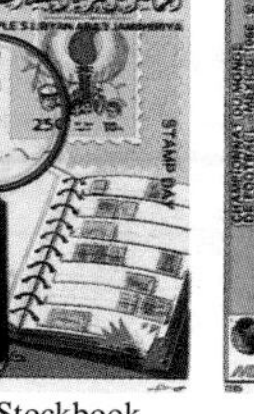
366 Stockbook, Magnifying Glass and Stamps

367 Players

1985. Stamp Day. "Italia '85" International Stamp Exhibition, Rome. Multicoloured.
1783 50dh. Man and desk on flying stamp above globe 65 15
1784 50dh. Type **366** 65 15
1785 50dh. Stamps escaping from wallet 65 15

1986. World Cup Football Championship, Mexico (1st issue). Multicoloured.
1786 100dh. Type **367** 1·25 65
1787 100dh. Players in red and white number 10 and yellow shirts 1·25 65
1788 100dh. Goalkeeper and player defending goal against attack 1·25 65
1789 100dh. Goalkeeper diving to make save 1·25 65
1790 100dh. Goalkeeper jumping to make save 1·25 65
1791 100dh. Player in red and white shirt tackling player in lime shirt 1·25 65

See also Nos. 1824/9.

368 Hands releasing Dove

1985. Solidarity with Palestinian People.
1793 **368** 100dh. multicoloured 95 35
1794 150dh. multicoloured 1·60 75

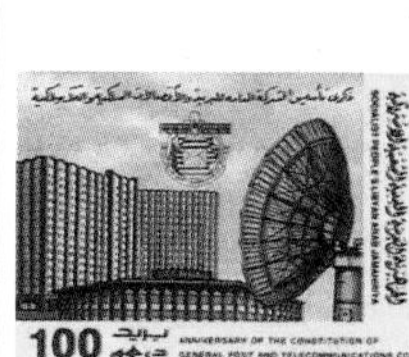
370 Headquarters and Dish Aerial

371 Paper and Quill in Hand

1986. 1st Anniv of General Posts and Telecommunications Corporation.
1807 **370** 100dh. multicoloured 1·00 30
1808 150dh. multicoloured 1·50 75

1986. Peoples' Authority Declaration. Multicoloured.
1809 50dh. Type **371** 65 40
1810 50dh. Paper and globe in hand 65 40
1811 100dh. "Green Books" and dove (53 × 37 mm) 1·25 65

372 Flute

1986. International Trade Fair, Tripoli. Mult.
1812 100dh. Type **372** 1·25 65
1813 100dh. Drums 1·25 65
1814 100dh. Double pipes 1·25 65
1815 100dh. Tambourines 1·25 65
1816 100dh. Drum hung from shoulder 1·25 65

373 Boy Scout with Fish on Hook

1986. Children's Day. Multicoloured.
1817 50dh. Type **373** 1·10 25
1818 50dh. Boy on camel 65 15
1819 50dh. Boy catching butterflies 65 15
1820 50dh. Boy playing drum 65 15
1821 50dh. Boy and giant goalkeeper on football pitch 65 15

374 Emblem, Man and Skull in Blood Droplet

1986. World Health Day. Multicoloured, background colours given.
1822 **374** 250dh. silver 2·50 1·25
1823 250dh. gold 2·50 1·25

375 Footballers

1986. World Cup Football Championship, Mexico (2nd issue). Multicoloured.
1824 50dh. Type **375** 65 15
1825 50dh. Player jumping over player on ground 65 15
1826 50dh. Referee and players 65 15
1827 50dh. Goalkeeper trying to save ball 65 15
1828 50dh. Player about to tackle 65 15
1829 50dh. Player jumping over ball 65 15

376 Peas

377 Health Programmes

1986. Vegetables. Multicoloured.
1831 50dh. Type **376** 45 15
1832 50dh. Marrow 45 15
1833 50dh. Beans 45 15
1834 50dh. Aubergine 45 15
1835 50dh. Corn on the cob 45 15
1836 50dh. Tomato 45 15
1837 50dh. Red pepper 45 15
1838 50dh. Zucchini 45 15
1839 50dh. Garlic 45 15
1840 50dh. Cabbage 45 15
1841 50dh. Cauliflower 45 15
1842 50dh. Celery 45 15
1843 50dh. Onions 45 15
1844 50dh. Carrots 45 15
1845 50dh. Potato 45 15
1846 50dh. Radishes 45 15

Nos. 1831/46 were printed together in sheetlets of 16 stamps, the backgrounds of the stamps forming an overall design of a garden.

1986. Jamahiriya Thought. Multicoloured.
1847 50dh. Type **377** 50 15
1848 50dh. Education programmes 50 15
1849 100dh. "Green Book", agricultural scenes and produce (agriculture programmes) (62 × 41 mm) 1·75 45

378 Gaddafi studying Plan

1986. Colonel Gaddafi, "Great man-made River Builder". Multicoloured.
1850 100dh. Type **378** 95 30
1851 100dh. Gaddafi showing planned route on map 95 30
1852 100dh. Gaddafi and old well 95 30
1853 100dh. Gaddafi in desert 95 30
1854 100dh. Gaddafi and pipe 95 30
1855 100dh. Gaddafi at pumping station 95 30
1856 100dh. Gaddafi and storage tank 95 30
1857 100dh. Workers' hut 95 30

1858 100dh. Water in cupped hands and irrigation equipment 95 30
1859 100dh. Gaddafi turning wheel at opening ceremony 95 30
1860 100dh. Laying pipes 95 30
1861 100dh. Pipe sections on lorries 95 30
1862 100dh. Gaddafi in robes holding "Green Book" . . 95 30
1863 100dh. Boy giving Gaddafi bowl of fruit 95 30
1864 100dh. Boy drinking from tap 95 30
1865 100dh. Gaddafi praying . . 95 30

379 Gaddafi with Children

1986. Colonel Gaddafi, "Man of Peace". Mult.
1866 100dh. Type **379** . . . . . 1·10 30
1867 100dh. Reading book in tent 1·10 30
1868 100dh. With his mother . . 1·10 30
1869 100dh. Praying in tent with his sons . . . . 1·10 30
1870 100dh. Talking to hospital patient . . . . 1·10 30
1871 100dh. Driving tractor . . . 1·10 30

380 General Dynamics F-111 Exploding above Man with injured Child

381 Gaddafi, Ruined buildings and Stretcher-bearers

1986. Battle of the U.S.S. "Philadelphia" and American Attack on Libya. Multicoloured.
(a) As T **380**.
1872 50dh. Type **380** 40 25
1873 50dh. American aircraft carrier and escaping family 60 25
1874 100dh. "Philadelphia" exploding (59 × 38 mm) 1·25 50

(b) As T **381**.
1875 70dh. Type **381** 80 20
1876 70dh. Burning wreckage of car and man and boy in rubble 80 20
1877 70dh. Woman and child by burning ruin 80 20
1878 70dh. Men running from bomb strike 80 20
1879 70dh. Covered body and rescue workers searching ruins 80 20
1880 70dh. Libyans and General Dynamics F-111 airplane tail and wing 80 25
1881 70dh. Libyans waving fists 80 20
1882 70dh. Rescue workers lifting child from rubble 80 20
1883 70dh. Weeping women and soldier carrying baby . . 80 20
1884 70dh. Libyans and glare of explosion 80 20
1885 70dh. Libyans and General Dynamics F-111 airplane wing and nose 80 25
1886 70dh. Man carrying girl . . 80 20
1887 70dh. Coffins held aloft by crowd 80 20
1888 70dh. Crowd carrying pictures of Gaddafi . . . 80 20
1889 70dh. Wounded being tended 80 20
1890 70dh. Hands tending wounded baby 80 20

(c) Size 89 × 32 mm.
1891 100dh. General Dynamics F-111 bombers, Gaddafi and anti-aircraft rockets 1·25 35

Nos. 1872/4 were printed together in se-tenant strips of three within the sheet, each strip forming a composite design.

382 "The House must be served by its own Tenant"

1986. Quotations from the "Green Book".
1892 **382** 100dh. lt green, grn & blk . . . . 1·00 30
1893 – 100dh. multicoloured . . 1·00 30
1894 – 100dh. lt green, grn & blk . . . . 1·00 30
1895 – 100dh. lt green, grn & blk . . . . 1·00 30
1896 – 100dh. multicoloured . . 1·00 30
1897 – 100dh. lt green, grn & blk . . . . 1·00 30
1898 – 100dh. lt green, grn & blk . . . . 1·00 30
1899 – 100dh. multicoloured . . 1·00 30
1900 – 100dh. lt green, grn & blk . . . . 1·00 30

DESIGNS: No. 1893, Gaddafi; 1894, "The Child is raised by his mother"; 1895, "Democracy is the Supervision of the People by the People"; 1896, "Green Books"; 1897, "Representation is a Falsification of Democracy"; 1898, "The Recognition of Profit is an Acknowledgement of Exploitation"; 1899, Vase of roses, iris, lilies and jasmine; 1900, "Knowledge is a Natural Right of every Human Being which Nobody has the Right to deprive him of under any Pretext".

383 Map, Chrysanthemum and Health Services

1986. 17th Anniv of Revolution. Multicoloured.
1901 200dh. Type **383** . . . . . 2·50 95
1902 200dh. Map, sunflower and agriculture programme . . 2·50 95
1903 200dh. "Sunflowers" (Van Gogh) . . . . 2·50 95
1904 200dh. Map, rose and defence programme . . . 2·50 95
1905 200dh. Map, campanula and oil exploration programme . . . . 2·50 95

384 Moroccan and Libyan Women

1986. Arab–African Union. Multicoloured.
1906 250dh. Type **384** . . . . . 2·50 80
1907 250dh. Libyan and Moroccan horsemen . . . 2·50 80

385 Libyan Horseman

1986. Evacuation of Foreign Forces. Multicoloured.
1908 50dh. Type **385** 50 15
1909 100dh. Libyan horsemen trampling Italian soldiers 1·10 30
1910 150dh. Italian soldiers charging . . . . 1·50 50

386 Globe and Rose

1986. International Peace Year. Multicoloured, background colours given.
1911 **386** 200dh. green . . . . . 1·90 70
1912 200dh. blue . . . . . . 1·90 70

387 Brick "Fists" and Maps within Laurel Wreath

1986. Solidarity with Palestinian People. Multicoloured, background colours given.
1913 **387** 250dh. blue . . . . . . 2·50 80
1914 250dh. red . . . . . . 2·50 80

388 Drummer

1986. Folk Music. Multicoloured.
1915 70dh. Type **388** 95 20
1916 70dh. Masked stick dancer 95 20
1917 70dh. Woman dancer with pot headdress 95 20
1918 70dh. Bagpipe player . . . 95 20
1919 70dh. Tambour player . . . 95 20

389 Gazelles

1987. Endangered Animals. Sand Gazelle. Multicoloured.
1920 100dh. Type **389** . . . . . 1·25 30
1921 100dh. Mother and calf . . 1·25 30
1922 100dh. Gazelle drinking . . 1·25 30
1923 100dh. Gazelle lying down 1·25 30

390 Oil Derricks and Crowd **391** Sheep and Shepherd

1987. People's Authority Declaration. Multicoloured.
1924 500dh. Type **390** . . . . . 4·00 1·75
1925 500dh. Buildings and crowd 4·00 1·75
1926 1000dh. Gaddafi addressing crowd and globe (40 × 38 mm) . . . . . . 8·00 3·25

1987. 18th Anniv of Revolution. Multicoloured.
1927 150dh. Type **391** . . . . . 1·50 50
1928 150dh. Col. Gaddafi in robes . . . . 1·50 50
1929 150dh. Mosque . . . . . . 1·50 50
1930 150dh. Water flowing from irrigation pipe . . . . . 1·50 50
1931 150dh. Combine harvester 1·50 50
1932 150dh. Col. Gaddafi in army uniform with microphone 1·50 50
1933 150dh. Harvesting crop . . 1·50 50
1934 150dh. Irrigation . . . . . 1·50 50
1935 150dh. Soldier with rifle . . 1·50 50
1936 150dh. Buildings behind Libyan with rifle . . . . 1·50 50
1937 150dh. Fountain . . . . . . 1·50 50
1938 150dh. Buildings and beach 1·50 50
1939 150dh. Fort and girls . . . 1·50 50
1940 150dh. Children and hand on rifle butt . . . . . . 1·50 50
1941 150dh. Theatre . . . . . . 1·50 50
1942 150dh. Couple . . . . . . 1·50 50

392 Omar Abed Anabi al Mansusri

1988. Personalities. Multicoloured.
1943 100dh. Type **392** 75 30
1944 200dh. Ahmed Ali al Emrayd . . . . 1·50 70
1945 300dh. Khalifa Said Ben Asker . . . . 2·50 1·00
1946 400dh. Mohamed Ben Farhat Azawi . . . . . . 3·00 1·10
1947 500dh. Mohamed Souf al Lafi al Marmori . . . . 3·75 1·50

393 Gaddafi and Crowd with Raised Fists around Earthmover Bucket

1988. Freedom Festival Day.
1948 **393** 100dh. multicoloured . . 95 30
1949 150dh. multicoloured . . 1·60 75
1950 250dh. multicoloured . . 2·50 1·25

394 Woman and Children running

1988. 2nd Anniv of American Attack on Libya. Multicoloured.
1951 150dh. Type **394** . . . . . 1·40 50
1952 150dh. Gaddafi playing chess with boy . . . . . 1·40 50
1953 150dh. Gaddafi and children 1·40 50
1954 150dh. Gaddafi in robes . . 1·40 50
1955 150dh. Gaddafi and boys praying . . . . 1·40 50
1956 150dh. Gaddafi and injured girl . . . . 1·40 50
1957 150dh. Gaddafi in robes with children (horiz) . . . 1·40 50
1958 150dh. Gaddafi making speech (horiz) . . . . . 1·40 50
1959 150dh. Gaddafi and family (horiz) . . . . 1·40 50

395 Roses

1988. 19th Anniv of Revolution.
1961 **395** 100dh. multicoloured . . 75 30
1962 250dh. multicoloured . . 2·00 80
1963 300dh. multicoloured . . 2·25 1·00
1964 500dh. multicoloured . . 4·25 1·50

396 Relay **397** Dates

1988. Olympic Games, Seoul. Multicoloured.
1965 150dh. Type **396** . . . . . 1·25 50
1966 150dh. Cycling . . . . . . 1·25 50
1967 150dh. Football . . . . . . 1·25 50
1968 150dh. Tennis . . . . . . 1·25 50
1969 150dh. Running . . . . . . 1·25 50
1970 150dh. Showjumping . . . 1·25 50

1988. The Palm Tree. Multicoloured.
1972 500dh. Type **397** . . . . . 4·25 1·50
1973 1000dh. Tree . . . . 8·00 3·75

398 Petrol Bomb, Sling and Map

399 Globe, Declaration and Dove

1988. Palestinian "Intifada" Movement. Mult.

1974	100dh. Type **398**	95	30
1975	200dh. Boy holding stones (45 × 38 mm)	1·60	70
1976	300dh. Map and flag	2·50	1·00

1989. People's Authority Declaration.

1977 **399**	260dh. multicoloured	1·10	65
1978	500dh. multicoloured	2·00	1·25

400 Crowd and Green Books (½-size illustration)

1989. 20th Anniv of Revolution. Multicoloured.

1979	150dh. Type **400**	1·25	40
1980	150dh. Soldiers, Colonel Gaddafi and water pipeline	1·25	40
1981	150dh. Military hardware, Gaddafi in uniform, education, communications and medicine	1·25	40
1982	150dh. Armed horsemen	1·25	40
1983	150dh. U.S.S. "Philadelphia" exploding	1·25	55

401 Execution Victims, Soldiers and Colonel Gaddafi

1989. 78th Anniv of Deportation of Libyans to Italy. Multicoloured.

1985	100dh. Type **401**	40	25
1986	100dh. Colonel Gaddafi and Libyans	40	25
1987	100dh. Soliders, deportees and Gaddafi	40	25
1988	100dh. Deportees on jetty and in boats	55	25
1989	100dh. Gaddafi and corpses	40	25

402 Demoliton of Wall

403 Emblem of Committee for supporting "Intifida"

1989. "Demolition of Borders".

1991 **402**	150dh. multicoloured	1·60	1·60
1992	200dh. multicoloured	2·10	2·10

1989. Palestinian "Intifada" Movement. Mult.

1993	100dh. Type **403**	1·10	1·10
1994	300dh. Crowd of youths	3·00	3·00
1995	500dh. Emblem (1st anniv of declaration of state of Palestine)	4·75	4·75

404 Circulation Diagram and Annafis

1989. Ibn Annafis (physician) Commemoration.

1996 **404**	100dh. multicoloured	1·25	1·25
1997	150dh. multicoloured	1·90	1·90

405 Green Books and Fort

406 Libyan People and Soldier

1990. People's Authority Declaration.

1998 **405**	300dh. multicoloured	2·75	2·75
1999	500dh. multicoloured	5·00	5·00

1990. 20th Anniv of American Forces Evacuation.

2000 **406**	100dh. multicoloured	1·00	1·00
2001	400dh. multicoloured	4·00	4·00

407 Eagle

408 Anniversary Emblem

1990. 21st Anniv of Revolution.

2002 **407**	100dh. multicoloured	1·00	1·00
2003	400dh. multicoloured	4·00	4·00
2004	1000dh. multicoloured	10·50	10·50

1990. 30th Anniv of Organization of Petroleum Exporting Countries.

2006 **408**	100dh. multicoloured	1·00	1·00
2007	400dh. multicoloured	4·00	4·00

409 I.L.Y. Emblem and Figures

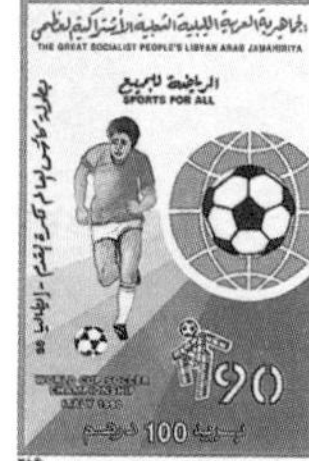

410 Player, Globe and Ball

1990. International Literacy Year.

2008 **409**	100dh. multicoloured	1·10	1·10
2009	300dh. multicoloured	3·00	3·00

1990. World Cup Football Championship, Italy.

2010 **410**	100dh. multicoloured	1·00	1·00
2011	400dh. multicoloured	4·00	4·00
2012	500dh. multicoloured	5·00	5·00

411 Hand holding Ears of Wheat

412 Members' Flags

1990. World Food Day. Multicoloured.

2014	500dh. Type **411**	5·00	5·00
2015	2000dh. Ploughing	20·00	20·00

1991. 2nd Anniv of Union of Arab Maghreb.

2016 **412**	100dh. multicoloured	1·10	1·10
2017	300dh. multicoloured	3·00	3·00

413 Flame, Scroll and Koran

1991. People's Authority Declaration.

2018 **413**	300dh. multicoloured	2·75	2·75
2019	400dh. multicoloured	3·75	3·75

414 Girl and International Year of the Child Emblem

415 World Health Organization Emblem

1991. Children's Day. Multicoloured.

2020	100dh. Type **414**	95	95
2021	400dh. Boy and Day of the African Child emblem	3·75	3·75

1991. World Health Day. Multicoloured.

2022	100dh. Type **415**	95	95
2023	200dh. As Type **415** but with emblem additionally inscr "WHO OMS"	1·90	1·90

416 Wadi el Hayat

1991. Scenes from Libya. Multicoloured.

2024	100dh. Type **416**	95	95
2025	250dh. Mourzuk (horiz)	2·50	2·50
2026	500dh. Ghadames (horiz)	5·00	5·00

417 Digging Riverbed and laying Pipes

1991. Great Man-made River. Multicoloured.

2027	50dh. Type **417**	25	15
2028	50dh. Col. Gaddafi, agricultural projects and livestock (59 × 37 mm)	25	15
2029	50dh. Produce	25	15

Nos. 2027/9 were printed together, se-tenant, forming a composite design.

418 "22", Roses and Broken Chain

1991. 22nd Anniv of Revolution. Multicoloured.

2030	300dh. Type **418**	2·75	2·75
2031	400dh. "22" within wheat/cogwheel wreath and broken chain	3·75	3·75

419 Emblem and Globe

1991. "Telecom 91" International Telecommunications Exhibition, Geneva. Multicoloured.

2033	100dh. Type **419**	95	95
2034	500dh. Buldings and dish aerial (horiz)	4·50	4·50

420 Monument and Soldier

1991. 80th Anniv of Deportation of Libyans to Italy. Multicoloured.

2035	100dh. Type **420**	95	95
2036	400dh. Naval transport, Libyans and soldiers	3·75	3·75

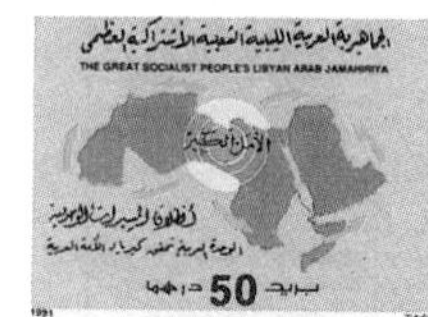
421 Map

1991. Arab Unity.

2038 **421**	50dh. multicoloured	20	10
2039	100dh. multicoloured	40	20

422 Lorry

424 State Arms

423 Gaddafi and Camels

1991. Paris–Dakar Trans-Sahara Rally. Mult.

2040	50dh. Type **422**	20	10
2041	50dh. Blue lorry	20	10
2042	50dh. African Product lorry	20	10
2043	50dh. Tomel lorry	20	10
2044	50dh. All-terrain vehicle No. 173	20	10
2045	50dh. Mitsusuki all-terrain vehicle	20	10
2046	50dh. Michedop all-terrain vehicle	20	10
2047	50dh. All-terrain vehicle No. 401	20	10
2048	50dh. Motor cycle No. 100	20	10
2049	50dh. Rider pushing red motor cycle	20	10
2050	50dh. Rider pushing white motor cycle	20	10
2051	50dh. Motor cycle No. 98	20	10
2052	50dh. Motor cycle No. 101	20	10
2053	50dh. Motor cycle No. 80	20	10
2054	50dh. Motor cycle No. 12	20	10
2055	50dh. Motor cycle No. 45	20	10

1992. "Gaddafi, Man of Peace 1992". Multicoloured, colour of frame given.

2056 **423**	100dh. green	40	20
2057	100dh. grey	40	20
2058	100dh. red	40	20
2059	100dh. ochre	40	20

1992.

2061 **424**	100dh. green, brn & yell	40	20
2062	150dh. green, brn & grey	60	30
2063	200dh. green, brown & bl	85	45
2064	250dh. green, brn & orge	1·10	55
2065	300dh. green, brn & vio	1·25	65
2066	400dh. green, brn & mve	1·75	90
2067	450dh. emerald, brn & grn	1·90	95

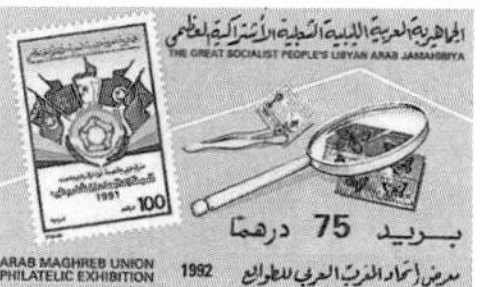

425 1991 100dh. Stamp, Tweezers, Magnifying Glass and Stamps

1992. 3rd Anniv of Union of Arab Maghreb.

2068 **425**	75dh. multicoloured	30	15
2069	80dh. multicoloured	35	20

426 Horse-drawn Carriage

1992. International Trade Fair, Tripoli. Mult.
2070 50dh. Type **426** 20 10
2071 100dh. Horse-drawn cart . . 40 20

427 Emblem

1992. People's Authority Declaration.
2072 **427** 100dh. multicoloured . . 40 20
2073 150dh. multicoloured . . 60 30

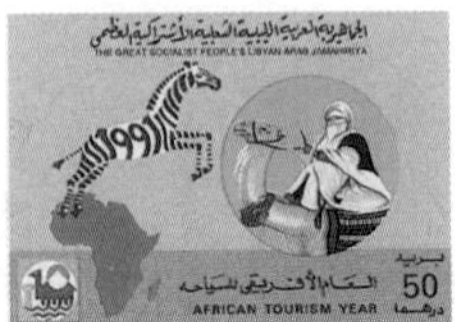

428 Emblem and Camel Rider

1992. African Tourism Year.
2074 **428** 50dh. multicoloured . . 20 10
2075 100dh. multicoloured . . 40 20

429 Big-eyed Tuna

1992. Fishes. Multicoloured.
2076 100dh. Type **429** 75 30
2077 100dh. Mackerel scad . . . 75 30
2078 100dh. Little tuna (seven spines on back) 75 30
2079 100dh. Seabream (continuous dorsal fin) . . 75 30
2080 100dh. Spanish mackerel (four spines on back) . . 75 30
2081 100dh. Striped red mullet (with whiskers) 75 30

430 Horsewoman with Rifle

1992. Horse Riders. Multicoloured.
2082 100dh. Type **430** 40 20
2083 100dh. Man on rearing white horse 40 20
2084 100dh. Man on brown horse with ornate bridle 40 20
2085 100dh. Roman soldier on brown horse 40 20
2086 100dh. Man in blue coat on brown horse 40 20
2087 100dh. Arab on white horse 40 20

431 Long Jumping

1992. Olympic Games, Barcelona. Multicoloured.
2089 50dh. Type **431** 20 10
2090 50dh. Throwing the discus 20 10
2091 50dh. Tennis 20 10

432 Palm Trees

1992. Achievements of the Revolution. Mult.
2093 100dh. Type **432** 40 20
2094 150dh. Ingots and foundry 60 30
2095 250dh. Container ship . . . 1·10 55
2096 300dh. Airplane . . . . . . 1·25 65
2097 400dh. Assembly hall . . . 1·75 90
2098 500dh. Water pipes and Gaddafi . . . . 2·10 1·10

433 Gaddafi

434 Laurel Wreath, Torch and "23"

1992. Multicoloured, background colours given.
2099 **433** 500dh. green . . . . . 2·50 1·10
2100 1000dh. pink . . . . . 5·00 2·50
2101 2000dh. blue . . . . . 10·00 5·00
2102 5000dh. violet . . . . . 25·00 12·50
2103 6000dh. orange . . . . 32·00 16·00

1992. 23rd Anniv of Revolution. Multicoloured.
2104 50dh. Type **434** 20 10
2105 100dh. Laurel wreath, flag, sun and "23" 40 20

435 Antelope drinking **436** Horse and Broken Chain

1992. Oases. Multicoloured.
2107 100dh. Type **435** 40 20
2108 200dh. Sun setting behind camel train (vert) 85 45
2109 300dh. Camel rider . . . . 1·25 65

1992. Evacuation of Foreign Forces. Multicoloured.
2110 75dh. Type **436** 30 15
2111 80dh. Flag and broken chain 35 20

437 Monument and Dates

1992. 81st Anniv of Deportation of Libyans to Italy.
2112 **437** 100dh. multicoloured . . 40 20
2113 250dh. multicoloured . . 1·10 55

438 Dome of the Rock and Palestinian

1992. Palestinian "Intifada" Movement. Mult.
2114 100dh. Type **438** 40 20
2115 300dh. Map, Dome of the Rock, flag and fist (vert) 1·25 65

439 Red and White Striped Costume **440** Mohamed Ali Imsek

1992. Women's Costumes. Multicoloured.
2116 50dh. Type **439** 20 10
2117 50dh. Large red hat with silver decorations, white tunic and red wrap . . . 20 10
2118 50dh. Brown and orange striped costume with small gold necklace and horseshoe brooch 20 10
2119 50dh. Purple and white costume 20 10
2120 50dh. Orange striped costume 20 10

1993. Physicians
2121 **440** 40dh. black, yellow and silver 15 10
2122 – 60dh. black, green and gold 20 15
DESIGN: 60dh. Aref Adhani Arif.

441 Globe, Crops and Spoon-feeding Man

1993. International Nutrition Conference, Rome.
2123 **441** 70dh. multicoloured . . 35 25
2124 80dh. multicoloured . . 40 30

442 Gaddafi, Eagle and Oil Refinery

1993. People's Authority Declaration.
2125 **442** 60dh. multicoloured . . 20 15
2126 65dh. multicoloured . . 25 15
2127 75dh. multicoloured . . 25 15

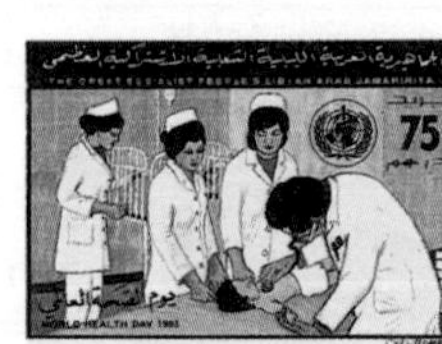

443 Crowd with Tambours **445** Girl

444 Examining Baby

1993. International Trade Fair, Tripoli. Mult.
2128 60dh. Type **443** 20 15
2129 60dh. Crowd with camel . . 20 15
2130 60dh. Dance of veiled men (horiz) 20 15
2131 60dh. Women preparing food (horiz) 20 15

1993. World Health Day. Multicoloured.
2133 75dh. Type **444** 25 15
2134 85dh. Medical staff attending patient 30 20

1993. Children's Day. Multicoloured.
2135 75dh. Type **445** 25 15
2136 75dh. Girl wearing blue and white veil and gold cuff 25 15
2137 75dh. Girl with white fluted collar and silver veil . . 25 15
2138 75dh. Girl with hands clasped 25 15
2139 75dh. Girl wearing blue scallop-edged veil . . . 25 15

446 Phoenician Ship

1993. Ships. Multicoloured
2140 50dh. Type **446** 20 15
2141 50dh. Arab galley 20 15
2142 50dh. Pharaonic ship . . . 20 15
2143 50dh. Roman bireme . . . 20 15
2144 50dh. Carvel 20 15
2145 50dh. Yacht (globe showing Italy) 20 15
2146 50dh. Yacht (globe showing Greece) 20 15
2147 50dh. Galeasse 20 15
2148 50dh. Nau 20 15
2149 50dh. Yacht (globe showing left half of Libya) 20 15
2150 50dh. Yacht (globe showing right half of Libya) 20 15
2151 50dh. "Santa Maria" . . . 20 15
2152 50dh. "France" (liner) . . . 20 15
2153 50dh. Schooner 20 15
2154 50dh. Sail/steam warship . . 20 15
2155 50dh. Modern liner 20 15

Nos. 2140/55 were issued together, se-tenant, the centre four stamps forming a composite design.

447 Combine Harvesters **448** Woman tending Youth

1993. 24th Anniv of Revolution. Multicoloured.
2156 50dh. Type **447** 20 15
2157 50dh. Col. Gaddafi 20 15
2158 50dh. Cattle behind men filling sack with grain . . 20 15
2159 50dh. Chickens behind shepherd with flock . . . 20 15
2160 50dh. Oil rig 20 15
2161 50dh. Eagle and camel . . . 20 15
2162 50dh. Industrial plant . . . 20 15
2163 50dh. Water pipeline . . . 20 15
2164 50dh. Man harvesting dates 20 15
2165 50dh. Man in field and boxes of produce 20 15
2166 50dh. Pile of produce . . . 20 15
2167 50dh. Man picking courgettes 20 15
2168 50dh. Children reading . . . 20 15
2169 50dh. Typist and laboratory worker 20 15
2170 50dh. Hand-picking crop and ploughing with tractor 20 15
2171 50dh. Tractor towing circular harrow 20 15

Nos. 2156/71 were issued together, se-tenant, forming several composite designs.

1993. 82nd Anniv of Deportation of Libyans to Italy. Multicoloured.
2172 50dh. Type **448** 20 15
2173 50dh. Soldiers and Libyan family 20 15
2174 50dh. Col. Gaddafi (in turban) 20 15
2175 50dh. Libyans in food queue 20 15
2176 50dh. Man being flogged . . 20 15
2177 50dh. Horseman charging between soldiers and Libyans 20 15
2178 50dh. Soldier with manacled Libyan before court . . . 20 15
2179 50dh. Libyans gazing at hanged man 20 15
2180 50dh. Crowd of Libyans and two soldiers 20 15
2181 50dh. Soldiers guarding procession of Libyans . . 20 15

2182 50dh. Soldiers and manacled Libyans on quayside 20 15
2183 50dh. Deportees in boat 20 15
2184 50dh. Col. Gaddafi (bare-headed) 20 15
2185 50dh. Two Libyan families and branch of palm tree 20 15
2186 50dh. Soldiers in disarray (ruins in background) 20 15
2187 50dh. Libyan horsemen 20 15

Nos. 2172/87 were issued together, se-tenant, forming several composite designs.

449 Brooch **451** Player and Trophy

450 Gaddafi, Soldiers and Jet Fighters

1994. Silver Jewellery. Multicoloured.

2188 55dh. Type **449** 20 15
2189 55dh. Armlet 20 15
2190 55dh. Pendant 20 15
2191 55dh. Pendants hanging from oblong 20 15
2192 55dh. Necklace 20 15
2193 55dh. Slippers 20 15

1994. 25th Anniv of Revolution. Multicoloured.

2194 100dh. Type **450** 35 25
2195 100dh. Libyan tribesmen and Gaddafi in uniform (59 × 38 mm) 35 25
2196 100dh. Peaceful pursuits and elderly couple 35 25

Nos. 2194/6 were issued together, se-tenant, forming a composite design.

1994. World Cup Football Championship, U.S.A. Multicoloured.

2198 100dh. Type **451**
2199 100dh. Kicking ball with inside of foot 35 25
2200 100dh. Kicking ball in air 35 25
2201 100dh. Goalkeeper 35 25
2202 100dh. Running with ball 35 25
2203 100dh. Player taking ball on chest 35 25

452 Gaddafi

1994. 83rd Anniv of Deportation of Libyans to Italy. Multicoloured.

2205 95dh. Type **452** 35 25
2206 95dh. Light plane over rifleman 35 25
2207 95dh. Couple running from biplane 35 25
2208 95dh. Biplane flying over men and boy 35 25
2209 95dh. Man trapped beneath fallen horse 35 25
2210 95dh. Soldiers and Libyans fighting (camel's head and neck in foreground) 35 25
2211 95dh. Soldiers surrounding fallen Libyan 35 25
2212 95dh. Man carrying boy 35 25
2213 95dh. Soldier with whip raised 35 25
2214 95dh. Robed man shouting 35 25
2215 95dh. Tank and battle scene 35 25
2216 95dh. Women fleeing mounted soliers 35 25
2217 95dh. Man being flogged and woman cradling head of fallen Libyan 35 25
2218 95dh. Soldiers and Libyans fighting (camels in background) 35 25
2219 95dh. Women and soldiers on quayside 35 25
2220 95dh. Deportees in two boats 35 25

Nos. 2205/20 were issued together, se-tenant, forming several composite designs.

453 Darghut **454** Armed Forces

1994. Mosques. Multicoloured.

2221 70dh. Type **453** 25 15
2222 70dh. Benghazi 25 15
2223 70dh. Kabao 25 15
2224 70dh. Gouzgu 25 15
2225 70dh. Siala 25 15
2226 70dh. El Kettani 25 15

1994. People's Authority Declaration. Multicoloured.

2227 80dh. Type **454** 30 20
2228 80dh. Truck, hand holding Green Book and ears of wheat 30 20
2229 80dh. Pipes on trailers, water pipeline and family 30 20
2230 80dh. Crowd with Green Books 30 20
2231 80dh. Col. Gaddafi 30 20
2232 80dh. Youths and produce 30 20

Nos. 2227/32 were issued together, se-tenant, forming a composite design.

455 Sun over Cemetery, National Flag, Dove and Footprints **457** Declaration and Flowers

456 Men with Weapons and Troops in Background

1994. Evacuation of Foreign Forces.

2233 **455** 65dh. multicoloured 25 15
2234 95dh. multicoloured 35 20

1994. Gaddafi Prize for Human Rights. Multicoloured.

2235 95dh. Type **456** 35 20
2236 95dh. Men with weapons 35 20
2237 95dh. President Nelson Mandela of South Africa 35 20
2238 95dh. President Gaddafi 35 20
2239 95dh. Amerindian meditating 35 20
2240 95dh. Warriors on horseback 35 20
2241 95dh. Amerindian chief 35 20
2242 95dh. Amerindian 35 20
2243 95dh. Riflemen and aircraft 35 20
2244 95dh. Bomber, women, fire and left page of book 35 20
2245 95dh. Right page of book and surgeon operating 35 20
2246 95dh. Surgeons operating 35 20
2247 95dh. Masked revolutionaries with flag 35 20
2248 95dh. Revolutionaries raising arms with flag 35 20
2249 95dh. Young boys with stones 35 20
2250 95dh. Revolutionaries, fire and troops 35 20

Nos. 2235/50 were issued together, se-tenant, forming a composite design.

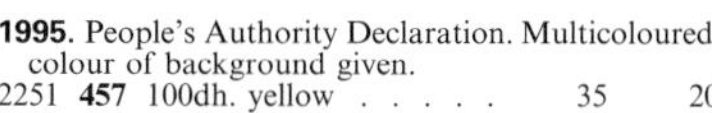

1995. People's Authority Declaration. Multicoloured, colour of background given.

2251 **457** 100dh. yellow 35 20
2252 100dh. blue 35 20
2253 100dh. green 35 20

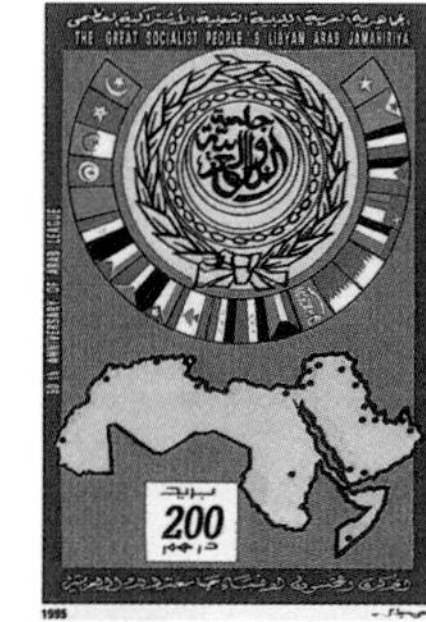

458 Emblem, Members' Flags and Map showing Member Countries

1995. 50th Anniv of Arab League. Multicoloured, frame colour given.

2254 **458** 200f. blue 70 45
2255 200f. green 70 45

459 Messaud Zentuti

1995. 60th Anniv of National Football Team. Designs showing players. Multicoloured.

2257 100dh. Type **459** 35 20
2258 100dh. Salem Shermit 35 20
2259 100dh. Ottoman Marfua 35 20
2260 100dh. Ghaleb Siala 35 20
2261 100dh. Team, 1935 35 20
2262 100dh. Senussi Mresila 35 20

Nos. 2257/62 were issued together, se-tenant, forming a composite design.

460 Dromedary **461** Grapefruit

1995. Libyan Zoo. Multicoloured.

2263 100dh. Type **460** 35 20
2264 100dh. Secretary bird 35 20
2265 100dh. African wild dog 35 20
2266 100dh. Oryx 35 20
2267 100dh. Baboon 35 20
2268 100dh. Golden jackal 35 20
2269 100dh. Crowned eagle 35 20
2270 100dh. Desert eagle owl ("Eagle Owl") 35 20
2271 100dh. Desert hedgehog 35 20
2272 100dh. Sand gerbil 35 20
2273 100dh. Addax 35 20
2274 100dh. Fennec fox 35 20
2275 100dh. Lanner falcon 35 20
2276 100dh. Desert wheatear 35 20
2277 100dh. Pin-tailed sandgrouse 35 20
2278 100dh. Jerboa 35 20

Nos. 2263/78 were issued together, se-tenant, the backgrounds forming a composite design.

1995. Fruit. Multicoloured.

2279 100dh. Type **461** 35 20
2280 100dh. Wild cherry 35 20
2281 100dh. Mulberry 35 20
2282 100dh. Strawberry 35 20
2283 100dh. Plum 35 20
2284 100dh. Pear 35 20
2285 100dh. Apricot 35 20
2286 100dh. Almond 35 20
2287 100dh. Prickly pear 35 20
2288 100dh. Lemon 35 20
2289 100dh. Peach 35 20
2290 100dh. Dates 35 20
2291 100dh. Olive 35 20
2292 100dh. Orange 35 20
2293 100dh. Fig 35 20
2294 100dh. Grape 35 20

Nos. 2279/94 were issued together, se-tenant, the backgrounds forming a composite design.

462 Students

1995. 26th Anniv of Revolution. Multicoloured.

2295 100dh. Type **462** 35 20
2296 100dh. Mosque, teacher and students 35 20
2297 100dh. President Gaddafi 35 20
2298 100dh. Laboratory workers 35 20
2299 100dh. Hospital patient, doctor examining child, and nurse 35 20
2300 100dh. Surgeons operating 35 20
2301 100dh. Cobblers and keyboard operator 35 20
2302 100dh. Sound engineers and musician 35 20
2303 100dh. Crane and apartment block 35 20
2304 100dh. Silos 35 20
2305 100dh. Oil rig platform 35 20
2306 100dh. Airplane and ships 35 20
2307 100dh. Animals grazing and farmer 35 20
2308 100dh. Pipeline 35 20
2309 100dh. Camels at trough and crops 35 20
2310 100dh. Crops and farm vehicle 35 20

Nos. 2295/2310 were issued together, se-tenant, forming a composite design.

463 Scout Badge and Wildlife

1995. Scouting. Multicoloured.

2311 250dh. Type **463** 85 55
2312 250dh. Badge, butterflies and scouts with animals (59 × 39 mm) 85 55
2313 250dh. Badge and scouts 85 55

Nos. 2311/13 were issued together, se-tenant, forming a composite design.

464 Warships and Rocket

1995. 9th Anniv of American Attack on Libya. Multicoloured.

2314 100dh. Type **464** 35 20
2315 100dh. Bombers, helicopters, warships and Libyans (59 × 49 mm) 35 20
2316 100dh. Bomber and woman holding baby 35 20

Nos. 2314/16 were issued together, se-tenant, forming a composite design.

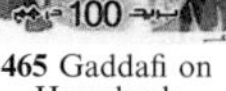

465 Gaddafi on Horseback **466** Dromedary and Woman with Water Jars

1995. International Trade Fair, Tripoli. Multicoloured.

2317 100dh. Type **465** 35 20
2318 100dh. Horseman 35 20

2319 100dh. Horseman (horse galloping to right) 35 20
2320 100dh. Horsemen with whips (horiz) 35 20
2321 100dh. Horseman holding rifle (horiz) 35 20
2322 100dh. Horsewoman brandishing rifle in air (horiz) 35 20

1995. City of Ghadames. Multicoloured.
2324 100dh. Type **466** 35 20
2325 100dh. Making cheeses . . . 35 20
2326 100dh. Woman holding jar 35 20
2327 100dh. Feeding chickens . . 35 20
2328 100dh. Spinning wool . . . 35 20
2329 100dh. Woman in traditional costume . . . 35 20
2330 100dh. Drying grain 35 20
2331 100dh. Milking goat 35 20
2332 100dh. Making shoes . . . 35 20
2333 100dh. Weaving 35 20
2334 100dh. Engraving brass tabletops 35 20
2335 100dh. Harvesting dates . . 35 20
2336 100dh. Reading scriptures 35 20
2337 100dh. Potter 35 20
2338 100dh. Washing clothes in well 35 20
2339 100dh. Picking fruit 35 20

467 Family with Torch and National Flag

1995. Evacuation of Foreign Forces.
2340 **467** 50dh. multicoloured . . 20 10
2341 100dh. multicoloured . . 35 20
2342 200dh. multicoloured . . 70 45

468 Honeycomb and Bees on Flowers

1995. Arab Beekeepers' Association. Multicoloured, colour of border given.
2343 **468** 100dh. mauve 35 20
2344 100dh. lilac 35 20
2345 100dh. green 35 20

469 Stubbing out Cigarette and holding Rose

470 Dr. Mohamed Feituri

1995. World Health Day. Multicoloured, colour of central band given.
2346 **469** 100dh. yellow 35 20
2347 100dh. orange 35 20

1995.
2348 **470** 200dh. multicoloured . . 70 45

471 Gaddafi and Horsemen

1995. 84th Anniv of Deportation of Libyans to Italy. Multicoloured.
2349 100dh. Type **471** 35 20
2350 100dh. Horsemen 35 20
2351 100dh. Battle scene 35 20
2352 100dh. Bomber over battle scene 35 20
2353 100dh. Libyans with rifles 35 20
2354 100dh. Soldiers fighting with Libyans 35 20
2355 100dh. Soldiers with weapons and man on ground 35 20
2356 100dh. Soldiers with rifles and building in background 35 20
2357 100dh. Libyans 35 20
2358 100dh. Soldiers charging men on ground 35 20
2359 100dh. Soldiers shooting at horseman 35 20
2360 100dh. Soldiers pushing Libyan to ground 35 20
2361 100dh. Horsemen charging 35 20
2362 100dh. Horses falling to ground 35 20
2363 100dh. Children 35 20
2364 100dh. Deportees in boats 35 20
Nos. 2349/64 were issued together, se-tenant, forming a composite design.

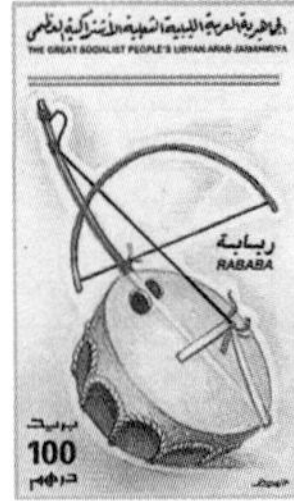

472 Rababa

473 Blue Door

1995. Musical Instruments. Multicoloured.
2365 100dh. Type **472** 35 20
2366 100dh. Nouba 35 20
2367 100dh. Clarinet 35 20
2368 100dh. Drums 35 20
2369 100dh. Magruna 35 20
2370 100dh. Zukra 35 20
2371 100dh. Zil 35 20
2372 100dh. Kaman 35 20
2373 100dh. Guitar 35 20
2374 100dh. Trumpet 35 20
2375 100dh. Tapla 35 20
2376 100dh. Gonga 35 20
2377 100dh. Saxophone 35 20
2378 100dh. Piano 35 20
2379 100dh. Ganoon 35 20
2380 100dh. Ood 35 20

1995. Doors from Mizda. Multicoloured.
2381 100dh. Type **473** 35 20
2382 100dh. Door with arch detail 35 20
2383 100dh. Door made of logs 35 20
2384 100dh. Arched door 35 20
2385 100dh. Wide door with bolts 35 20

474 Sports within Olympic Rings

1995. Centenary of International Olympic Committee. Multicoloured, colour of face value given.
2386 **474** 100dh. black 35 20
2387 100dh. red 35 20

475 Baryonyx

1995. Prehistoric Animals. Multicoloured.
2388 100dh. Type **475** 35 20
2389 100dh. Oviraptor 35 20
2390 100dh. Stenonychosaurus . . 35 20
2391 100dh. Tenontosaurus . . . 35 20
2392 100dh. Yangchuanosaurus 35 20
2393 100dh. Stegotetrabelodon (facing right) 35 20
2394 100dh. Stegotetrabelodon (facing left) 35 20
2395 100dh. Psittacosaurus . . . 35 20
2396 100dh. Heterodontosaurus 35 20
2397 100dh. "Loxodonta atlantica" 35 20
2398 100dh. "Mammuthus africanavus" 35 20
2399 100dh. Erlikosaurus 35 20
2400 100dh. Cynognathus 35 20
2401 100dh. Plateosaurus 35 20
2402 100dh. Staurikosaurus . . . 35 20
2403 100dh. Lystrosaurus 35 20
Nos. 2388/2403 were issued together, se-tenant, the backgrounds forming a composite design.

476 Child and Dinosaur walking with Stick

1995. Children's Day. Multicoloured.
2405 100dh. Type **476** 35 20
2406 100dh. Child on mammoth's back 35 20
2407 100dh. Child on way to school and tortoise under mushroom 35 20
2408 100dh. Dinosaur playing football 35 20
2409 100dh. Child pointing rifle at pteranodon 35 20

477 Helicopter, Soldier and Stone-thrower

1995. Palestinian "Intifada" Movement. Mult.
2410 100dh. Type **477** 35 20
2411 100dh. Dome of the Rock and Palestinian with flag 35 20
2412 100dh. Women with flag . . 35 20
Nos. 2410/12 were issued together, se-tenant, forming a composite design.

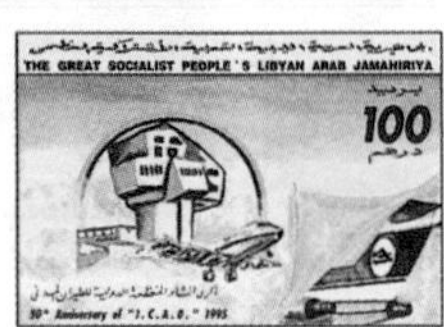

478 Airplane, Control Tower and Tailfin

1995. 50th Anniv of I.C.A.O. Multicoloured, colour of face value given.
2413 **478** 100dh. blue 35 20
2414 100dh. black 35 20

479 Headquarters, New York

480 "Iris germanica"

1995. 50th Anniv of U.N.O. Multicoloured, colour of background given.
2415 **479** 100dh. pink 35 20
2416 100dh. lilac 35 20

1995. Flowers. Multicoloured.
2417 200dh. Type **480** 35 20
2418 200dh. "Canna edulis" . . . 35 20
2419 200dh. "Nerium oleander" 35 20
2420 200dh. Corn poppy ("Papaver rhoeas") . . . 35 20
2421 200dh. Bird of Paradise flower ("Strelitzia reginae") 35 20
2422 200dh. "Amygdalus communis" 35 20

481 Open Hand

483 Man holding Fruit

482 Football

1996. People's Authority Declaration. Multicoloured.
2423 **481** 100dh. multicoloured . . 35 20
2424 150dh. multicoloured . . 50 30
2425 200dh. multicoloured . . 65 40

1996. Olympic Games, Atlanta, U.S.A. Multicoloured.
2426 100dh. Type **482** 35 20
2427 100dh. Long jumping . . . 35 20
2428 100dh. Tennis 35 20
2429 100dh. Cycling 35 20
2430 100dh. Boxing 35 20
2431 100dh. Equestrian show jumping 35 20
Nos. 2426/31 were issued together, se-tenant, the background forming a composite design of the Games emblem.

1996. 27th Anniv of Revolution. Multicoloured.
2433 100dh. Type **483** 35 20
2434 100dh. Water flowing along chute and out of pipe . . 35 20
2435 100dh. Tractor, water and women with flowers . . . 35 20
2436 100dh. Man working on pipe by water 35 20
2437 100dh. Man sewing 35 20
2438 100dh. Woman textile worker 35 20
2439 100dh. President Gaddafi in white shirt and red cape 35 20
2440 100dh. Women laboratory workers 35 20
2441 100dh. Anatomy instruction and man using microscope 35 20
2442 100dh. Child holding hand to face 35 20
2443 100dh. Woman praying before open Koran . . . 35 20
2444 100dh. Man weaving . . . 35 20
2445 100dh. Two aircraft 35 20
2446 100dh. Man on camel, liner and dish aerial 35 20
2447 100dh. Stern of liner and television camera 35 20
2448 100dh. Woman using microphone and woman being filmed 35 20
Nos. 2433/48 were issued together, se-tenant, forming a composite design.

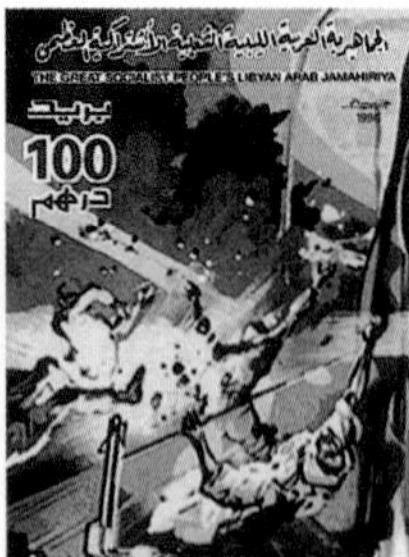

484 Bomb Exploding

1996. 10th Anniv of American Attack on Libya. Multicoloured.
2449 100dh. Type **484** 35 20
2450 100dh. Man with raised arms 35 20
2451 100dh. Woman carrying child 35 20
2452 100dh. Injured man on ground and fighter plane 35 20
2453 100dh. Fireman hosing down burning car 35 20
2454 100dh. Exploding plane . . 35 20
2455 100dh. Head of President Gaddafi 35 20
2456 100dh. Airplane bombing tented camp 35 20
2457 100dh. Rescuers helping two women 35 20
2458 100dh. Man with bandaged head and hand 35 20
2459 100dh. Woman with hankerchief to mouth . . 35 20
2460 100dh. Stretcher bearers . . 35 20
2461 100dh. Explosion and man being carried away . . . 35 20
2462 100dh. Explosion and man with injured hand 35 20
2463 100dh. Rescuers helping injured mother with baby 35 20
2464 100dh. Burning car and helpers tending injured boy 35 20
Nos. 2449/64 were issued together, se-tenant, forming a composite design.

485 "Necora puber" (crab)

1996. Crustaceans. Multicoloured.
2465 100dh. Type **485** 35 20
2466 100dh. "Lissa chiragra" (crab) 35 20
2467 100dh. Rock lobster ("Palinurus elephas") 35 20
2468 100dh. "Scyllarus arctus" 35 20
2469 100dh. Green crab ("Carcinus maenas") 35 20
2470 100dh. Helmet crab ("Calappa granulata") 35 20
2471 100dh. "Parapenaeus longirostris" (prawn) 35 20
2472 100dh. Norway lobster ("Nephrops norvegicus") 35 20
2473 100dh. "Eriphia verrucosa" (crab) 35 20
2474 100dh. Edible crab ("Cancer pagurus") 35 20
2475 100dh. "Penaeus kerathurus" (prawn) 35 20
2476 100dh. Mantis shrimp ("Squilla mantis") 35 20
2477 100dh. Spider crab ("Maja squinado") 35 20
2478 100dh. "Pilumnus hirtellus" (crab) 35 20
2479 100dh. "Pagurus alatus" (crab) 35 20
2480 100dh. "Macropodia tenuirostris" 35 20
Nos. 2465/80 were issued together, se-tenant, the backgrounds forming a composite design.

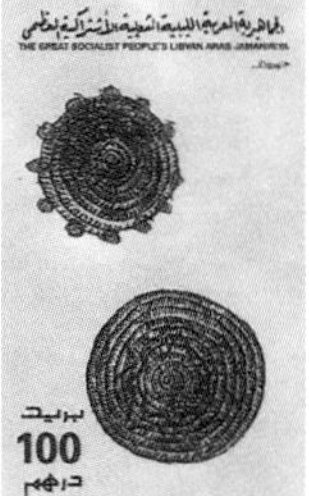

486 Mats

487 Woman kneeling over Boy

1996. Maghreb Handicrafts Day. Basketwork. Multicoloured.
2481 100dh. Type **486** 35 20
2482 100dh. Lidded storage vessel 35 20
2483 100dh. Bowl 35 20
2484 100dh. Mug and teapot 35 20
2485 100dh. Box with open lid 35 20
2486 100dh. Bird's-eye view of dish 35 20
2487 100dh. Pot with wide base and mouth and narrower neck 35 20
2488 100dh. Lidded pot with carrying handle 35 20
2489 100dh. Bulbous bottle-shaped carrier 35 20
2490 100dh. Large dish 35 20
2491 100dh. Oval dish with well in centre 35 20
2492 100dh. Straight-sided bottle-shaped carrier 35 20
2493 100dh. Vessel with double carrying handles and open lid 35 20
2494 100dh. Dish on stand 35 20
2495 100dh. Pot with wide base and narrow mouth 35 20
2496 100dh. Bag with lid 35 20

1996. 85th Anniv of Deportation of Libyans to Italy. Multicoloured.
2497 100dh. Type **487** 35 20
2498 100dh. Horseman leading prisoner 35 20
2499 100dh. President Gaddafi wearing turban 35 20
2500 100dh. Old man holding stick in camp 35 20
2501 100dh. Man being flogged 35 20
2502 100dh. Horseman, soldiers and crowd wearing fezzes 35 20
2503 100dh. Prisoner, advocate and man in tricolour sash 35 20
2504 100dh. Family and soldier 35 20
2505 100dh. Soldiers guarding prisoners (boy at front) 35 20
2506 100dh. Soldiers escorting woman on camel and man on donkey 35 20
2507 100dh. Prisoners being escorted through street 35 20
2508 100dh. Prisoners in boat 35 20
2509 100dh. President Gaddafi in white embroided shirt with open hand 35 20
2510 100dh. Group of prisoners including man with raised arm 35 20
2511 100dh. Horsemen charging and soldiers 35 20
2512 100dh. Horseman with rifle 35 20
Nos. 2497/2512 were issued together, se-tenant, forming several composite designs.

488 Bay

1996. Horses. Multicoloured.
2513 100dh. Type **488** 35 20
2514 100dh. Light brown horse under tree (branches at right of stamp) 35 20
2515 100dh. Light brown horse by lake under tree (branch at left) 35 20
2516 100dh. Dark brown horse (edge of lake at left) 35 20
2517 100dh. Black horse with hoof raised 35 20
2518 100dh. Chestnut horse 35 20
2519 100dh. Grey horse running 35 20
2520 100dh. Piebald 35 20
2521 100dh. Head of grey and tail of black horses 35 20
2522 100dh. Head of black and tail of chestnut horses 35 20
2523 100dh. Head and rump of chestnut horses 35 20
2524 100dh. Head of chestnut horse with white mane 35 20
2525 100dh. Head of black horse and parts of three other horses 35 20
2526 100dh. Head of chestnut horse with blond mane and parts of three other horses 35 20
2527 100dh. Head of dark brown horse and parts of three other horses 35 20
2528 100dh. Head of dark brown and part of chestnut horses 35 20
Nos. 2513/28 were issued together, se-tenant, forming a composite design.

489 Camel

490 Photographer, Newspapers and Computer

1996. Camels. Multicoloured.
2529 200dh. Type **489** 65 40
2530 200dh. Head of camel 65 40
2531 200dh. Dark brown dromedary 65 40
2532 200dh. Long-haired Bactrian camel 65 40
2533 200dh. Light brown Bactrian camel 65 40
2534 200dh. Brown Bactrian camel with white stripe and tail 65 40
Nos. 2529/34 were issued together, se-tenant, forming a composite design.

1996. The Press and Information. Multicoloured.
2535 100dh. Type **490** 35 20
2536 200dh. Television, control desk, musicians, computer and dish aerial 65 40

491 "Mene rhombea" **492** Palestinian Flag and Hands holding up Stones

1996. Fossils. Multicoloured.
2537 200dh. Type **491** 65 40
2538 200dh. "Mesodon macrocephalus" 65 40
2539 200dh. "Eyron arctiformis" 65 40
2540 200dh. Stegosaurus 65 40
2541 200dh. Pteranodon 65 40
2542 200dh. Allosaurus 65 40

1996. Palestinian "Intifada" Movement.
2543 **492** 100dh. multicoloured 35 20
2544 150dh. multicoloured 50 30
2545 200dh. multicoloured 65 40

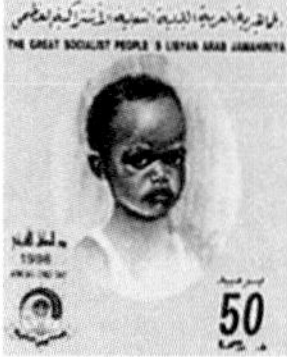

493 Child

494 Cat

1996. African Child Day. Multicoloured.
2546 50dh. Type **493** 10 10
2547 150dh. Type **493** 40 25
2548 200dh. Mother and child 50 35

1996. Children's Day. Cats. Multicoloured.
2549 100dh. Type **494** 25 15
2550 100dh. Tabby (back view with head turned) 25 15
2551 100dh. Colourpoint (black and white) 25 15
2552 100dh. Tabby adult and kitten 25 15
2553 100dh. Tortoiseshell white (sitting) 25 15

495 Family and Tower Block

1996. World Family Day. Multicoloured.
2554 150dh. Type **495** 40 25
2555 150dh. Family and car parked by palm trees 40 25
2556 200dh. Family, symbolic globe and flowers (45 × 26 mm) 50 35
Nos. 2554/6 were issued together, se-tenant, forming a composite design.

496 Mohamed Kamel el-Hammali

1996. Libyan Teachers. Multicoloured.
2557 100dh. Type **496** 25 15
2558 100dh. Mustafa Abdalla ben-Amer 25 15
2559 100dh. Mohamed Messaud Fesheka 25 15
2560 100dh. Kairi Mustafa Serraj 25 15
2561 100dh. Muftah el-Majri 25 15
2562 100dh. Mohamed Hadi Arafa 25 15

497 Mohamed Salim

1996. Libyan Singers. Multicoloured.
2563 100dh. Type **497** 25 15
2564 100dh. Mohamed M. Sayed Bumedyen 25 15
2565 100dh. Otman Najim 25 15
2566 100dh. Mahmud Sherif 25 15
2567 100dh. Mohamed Ferjani Marghani 25 15
2568 100dh. Mohamed Kabazi 25 15

498 Snake

1996. Reptiles. Multicoloured.
2569 100dh. Type **498** 25 15
2570 100dh. Diamond-back snake beside river 25 15
2571 100dh. Turtle on water (segmented shell and large flippers) 25 15
2572 100dh. Snake wrapped around tree branch 25 15
2573 100dh. Brown lizard on tree trunk 25 15
2574 100dh. Coiled snake with head raised and mouth open 25 15
2575 100dh. Snake with head raised beside water 25 15
2576 100dh. Turtle on water (flat shell, pointed snout and small flippers) 25 15
2577 100dh. Green lizard on tree trunk 25 15
2578 100dh. Snake with wavy pattern on ground 25 15
2579 100dh. Snake with horns 25 15
2580 100dh. Chameleon 25 15
2581 100dh. Tortoise on ground (facing right) 25 15
2582 100dh. Snake on rock with head raised 25 15
2583 100dh. Tortoise on ground (facing left) 25 15
2584 100dh. Grey lizard on rock 25 15
Nos. 2569/84 were issued together, se-tenant, forming a composite design.

499 Mirror and Clothes Brush

1996. International Trade Fair, Tripoli. Each silver, pink and black.
2585 100dh. Type **499** 25 15
2586 100dh. Decanter on tray 25 15
2587 100dh. Two round-bottomed flasks 25 15
2588 100dh. Two long-necked flasks 25 15
2589 100dh. Covered bowl 25 15
2590 100dh. Backs of hairbrush and mirror 25 15

500 Gaddafi and Symbolic Scenes

501 Scouts and Stamp Album

1997. People's Authority Declaration.
2591 **500** 100dh. multicoloured 25 15
2592 200dh. multicoloured 25 15
2593 300dh. multicoloured 25 15

1997. Postal Savings Bank. Multicoloured.
2594 50dh. Type **501** 10 10
2595 50dh. Two Girl Guides and albums 10 10
2596 100dh. Bank books and butterflies 25 15
Nos. 2594/6 were issued together, se-tenant, forming a composite design.

502 Scientist with Test Tubes

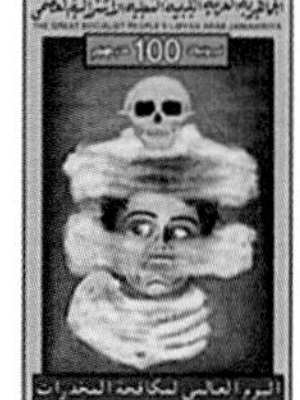

503 Death enveloping Man's Head

1997. World Health Day. Multicoloured.
2597 50dh. Type **502** 10 10
2598 50dh. Scientist at microscope 10 10
2599 100dh. Doctor and nurse examining baby 25 15
Nos. 2597/9 were issued together, se-tenant, forming a composite design.

1997. Anti-drugs Campaign.
2600 **503** 100dh. multicoloured . . 25 15
2601 150dh. multicoloured . . 40 25
2602 200dh. multicoloured . . 50 35

504 Library

1997. Arab National Central Library.
2603 **504** 100dh. multicoloured . . 25 15
2604 200dh. multicoloured . . 50 35

505 Dancer and Local Crafts

1997. Arab Tourism Year.
2606 **505** 100dh. multicoloured . . 25 15
2607 200dh. multicoloured . . 50 25
2608 250dh. multicoloured . . 65 45

CONCESSIONAL LETTER POST

1929. No. CL227 of Italy optd **LIBIA**.
CL68 CL **93** 10c. blue . . . . . . 22·00 17·00

1941. No. CL267 of Italy optd **LIBIA**.
CL123 CL **109** 10c. brown . . . . 8·50 8·50

EXPRESS LETTER STAMPS
A. ITALIAN ISSUES

1915. Express Letter stamps of Italy optd **Libia**.
E17 E **35** 25c. pink . . . . 19·00 8·50
E18 E **41** 30c. blue and pink . . . 5·25 22·00

E 8

1921.
E34 E **8** 30c. red and blue . . . . 1·70 5·25
E35 50c. brown and red . . . 2·50 6·75
E42 60c. brown and red . . . 5·25 10·50
E43 2l. red and blue . . . . 8·50 21·00
Nos. E34 and E43 are inscribed "EXPRES".

1922. Nos. E17/18 surch.
E40 E **35** 60c. on 25c. pink . . . 9·50 11·00
E41 E **41** 1l.60 on 30c. blue and pink . . . . 11·00 23·00

1926. Nos. E42/3 surch.
E62 E **8** 70 on 60c. brown and red 5·25 10·50
E64 1l.25 on 60c. brown and red . . . . 4·25 1·50
E63 2.50 on 2l. red and blue 8·50 21·00

B. INDEPENDENT ISSUES

1966. Design similar to T **74** inscr "EXPRES".
E368 90m. red and green . . . . 2·30 1·30
DESIGN—HORIZ: 90m. Saracen Castle, Zuela.

OFFICIAL STAMPS

1952. Optd **Official** in English and Arabic.
O192 **23** 2m. brown 40 35
O193 4m. grey 65 50
O194 5m. green . . . . 4·50 1·60
O195 8m. red . . . . 2·50 75
O196 10m. violet . . . . . . 3·75 1·25
O197 12m. red . . . . 6·75 2·50
O198 20m. blue . . . . 13·50 5·25
O199 25m. brown . . . . . . 17·00 6·75

PARCEL POST STAMPS
Unused prices are for complete pairs, used prices for a half.

1915. Parcel Post stamps of Italy optd **LIBIA** on each half of the stamp.
P17 P **53** 5c. brown . . . . 85 3·50
P18 10c. blue . . . . 85 3·50
P19 20c. black . . . . 1·00 3·50
P20 25c. red . . . . 1·00 3·50
P21 50c. orange . . . . . . 1·90 3·50
P22 1l. violet . . . . 1·90 5·25
P23 2l. green . . . . 2·75 5·25
P24 3l. yellow . . . . 3·50 5·25
P25 4l. grey . . . . 3·50 5·25
P26 10l. purple . . . . . . 43·00 39·00
P27 12l. brown . . . . . . 85·00 £110
P28 15l. green . . . . 85·00 £140
P29 20l. purple £110 £150

1927. Parcel Post stamps of Italy optd **LIBIA** on each half of the stamp.
P62 P **92** 5c. brown £9000
P63 10c. blue . . . . 2·10 3·50
P64 25c. red . . . . 2·10 3·50
P65 30c. blue . . . . 35 1·70
P66 50c. orange . . . . . . 48·00 £100
P67 60c. red . . . . 35 1·70
P68 1l. violet . . . . 19·00 50·00
P69 2l. green . . . . 22·00 50·00
P70 3l. bistre . . . . 1·00 4·25
P71 4l. black . . . . 1·00 7·75
P72 10l. mauve £180 £200
P73 20l. purple £180 £250

POSTAGE DUE STAMPS
A. ITALIAN ISSUES

1915. Postage Due stamps of Italy optd **Libia**.
D17 D **12** 5c. mauve and orange 1·40 4·25
D18 10c. mauve and orange 1·50 2·50
D19 20c. mauve and orange 2·10 3·50
D20 30c. mauve and orange 2·50 4·25
D21 40c. mauve and orange 3·75 6·00
D22 50c. mauve and orange 2·50 3·50
D23 60c. mauve and orange 4·00 7·75
D24 60c. brown and orange 60·00 85·00
D25 1l. mauve and blue . . 2·50 7·75
D26 2l. mauve and blue . . 38·00 50·00
D27 5l. mauve and blue . . 50·00 75·00

1934. Postage Due stamps of Italy optd **LIBIA**.
D68 D **141** 5c. brown . . . . . . 10 2·10
D69 10c. blue . . . . . . 10 2·10
D70 20c. red . . . . 1·00 1·20
D71 25c. green . . . . . . 1·00 1·20
D72 30c. red . . . . 1·00 4·25
D73 40c. brown . . . . . 1·00 3·00
D74 50c. violet . . . . . . 1·20 35
D75 60c. blue . . . . . . 1·50 10·50
D76 D **142** 1l. orange . . . . . . 1·40 35
D77 2l. green . . . . . . 38·00 10·50
D78 5l. violet . . . . . . 60·00 21·00
D79 10l. blue . . . . . . 10·50 31·00
D80 20l. red . . . . 10·50 41·00

B. INDEPENDENT ISSUES

1951. Postage Due stamps of Cyrenaica optd. (a) For use in Cyrenaica. Optd as T **20**.
D144 D **26** 2m. brown . . . . . 5·00 5·00
D145 4m. green . . . . . 5·00 5·00
D146 8m. red . . . . 6·75 6·25
D147 10m. orange . . . . . 7·50 6·25
D148 20m. yellow . . . . 11·00 10·00
D149 40m. blue . . . . . 30·00 20·00
D150 100m. black . . . . 40·00 23·00

(b) For use in Tripolitania. Surch as T **21**.
D161 D **26** 1mal. on 2m. brown 5·50 5·00
D162 2mal. on 4m. green . . 7·50 5·50
D163 4mal. on 8m. red . . . 12·50 10·00
D164 10mal. on 20m. yellow 27·00 20·00
D165 20mal. on 40m. blue 45·00 35·00

D 25

D 53 Government Building, Tripoli 1952.

1951.
D188 D **25** 2m. brown 65 25
D189 5m. green 95 50
D190 10m. red . . . . . . 2·25 95
D191 50m. blue . . . . . . 7·50 2·25

1964.
D296 D **53** 2m. brown 10 10
D297 6m. green 20 10
D298 10m. red 70 45
D299 50m. blue . . . . . . 1·25 85

D **185** Men in Boat

1976. Ancient Mosaics. Multicoloured.
D725 5dh. Type D **185** 10 10
D726 10dh. Head of Medusa . . 10 10
D727 20dh. Peacock 10 10
D728 50dh. Fish 80 25

LIECHTENSTEIN Pt. 8

A small independent principality lying between Austria and Switzerland.

1912. 100 heller = 1 krone.
1921. 100 rappen = 1 franc (Swiss).

1 Prince John II

1912.
4 **1** 5h. green . . . . 8·75 6·00
2 10h. red . . . . 40·00 6·00
3 25h. blue . . . . 40·00 20·00

2 **3**

1917.
7 **2** 3h. violet 75 55
8 5h. green 75 55
9 **3** 10h. purple 95 85
10 15h. brown 95 75
11 20h. green 95 85
12 25h. blue 95 75

1918. 60th Anniv of Prince John's Accession. As T **3** but dated "1858–1918" in upper corners.
13 **3** 20h. green . . . . 60 1·00

1920. Optd with a scroll pattern.
14 **2** 5h. green . . . . 1·60 4·50
15 **3** 10h. purple . . . . 1·60 4·50
16 25h. blue . . . . 1·60 4·50

1920. Surch.
17 **2** 40h. on 3h. violet . . . . . 1·60 4·50
18 **3** 1k. on 15h. brown . . . . 1·60 4·50
19 2½k. on 20h. green . . . . 1·60 4·50

7 **8** Castle of Vaduz

1920. Imperf.
20 **7** 5h. bistre . . . . 15 2·40
21 10h. orange . . . . 15 2·40
22 15h. blue . . . . 15 2·40
23 20h. brown . . . . 15 2·40
24 25h. green . . . . 15 2·40
25 30h. grey . . . . 15 2·40
26 40h. red . . . . 15 2·40
27 **8** 1k. blue . . . . 15 2·40

9 Prince John I **10** Arms

1920. Perf.
28 **7** 5h. bistre 10 35
29 10h. orange 10 35
30 15h. blue 10 35
31 20h. brown 10 35
32 – 25h. green 10 35
33 **7** 30h. grey 10 35
34 – 40h. purple 10 35
35 – 50h. green 10 35
36 – 60h. brown 10 35
37 – 80h. pink 10 35
38 **8** 1k. lilac 20 55
39 – 2k. blue 25 60
40 **9** 5k. black 40 70
41 – 7½k. grey 55 90
42 **10** 10k. brown . . . . 60 1·00
DESIGNS—As Type **8**: 25h. St. Mamertus Chapel; 40h. Gutenberg Castle; 50h. Courtyard, Vaduz Castle; 60h. Red House, Vaduz; 80h. Church Tower, Schaan; 2k. Bendern. As Type **9**: 7½k. Prince John II.

11 Madonna

14 Arms

15 St. Mamertus Chapel

16 Vaduz

1920. Prince John's 80th Birthday. Imperf or perf.
43 **11** 50h. green . . . . 50 1·80
44 80h. red . . . . 50 1·80
45 2k. blue . . . . 50 1·80

1921. Surch **2 Rp.** and bars.
47 **7** 2r. on 10h. orange (No. 21) 40 13·50

1921.
47a **14** 2r. yellow . . . . 65 6·00
48 2½r. brown . . . . 55 6·00
49 3r. orange . . . . 65 5·00
50 5r. green . . . . 6·50 85
51 7½r. blue . . . . 7·25 20·00
65 10r. green . . . . 14·00 3·00
53 13r. brown . . . . 5·00 43·00
54 15r. violet . . . . 10·50 11·50
55 **15** 20r. black and violet . . 30·00 85
56 – 25r. black and red . . . . 1·90 3·00
57 – 30r. black and green . . . 38·00 5·75
66 – 30r. black and blue . . . . 9·75 90
58 – 35r. black and brown . . . 2·75 6·25
59 – 40r. black and blue . . . . 4·75 2·50
60 – 50r. black and green . . . 5·75 3·25
61 – 80r. black and grey . . . . 16·00 38·00
62 **16** 1f. black and red . . . . . 31·00 23·00
DESIGNS—As Type **15**: 25r. Vaduz Castle; 30r. Bendern; 35r. Prince John II; 40r. Church Tower at Schaan; 50r. Gutenberg Castle; 80r. Red House, Vaduz.

1924. Surch.
63 **14** 5 on 7½r. blue . . . . . . 75 1·10
64 10 on 13r. brown . . . . . 55 1·60

19 Vine-dresser

21 Government Bldg. and Church, Vaduz

1924.
67 **19** 2½r. mauve and green . . . 85 3·50
68 5r. blue and brown . . . . 1·20 55
69 7½r. brown and green . . . 90 4·00
70 – 10r. green . . . . 8·50 50
71 **19** 15r. green and purple . . . 4·75 17·00
72 – 20r. red . . . . 20·00 60
73 **21** 1½f. blue . . . . 60·00 50·00
DESIGN—As Type **19**: 10, 20r. Castle of Vaduz.

22 Prince John II

23

1925. 85th Birthday of Prince John.
74 **22** 10+5r. green . . . . 21·00 9·25
75 20+5r. red . . . . 15·00 9·25
76 30+5r. blue . . . . 4·75 2·00

1927. 87th Birthday of Prince. Arms multicoloured.
77 **23** 10+5r. green . . . . 5·75 13·50
78 20+5r. purple . . . . 5·75 13·50
79 30+5r. blue . . . . 5·50 12·50

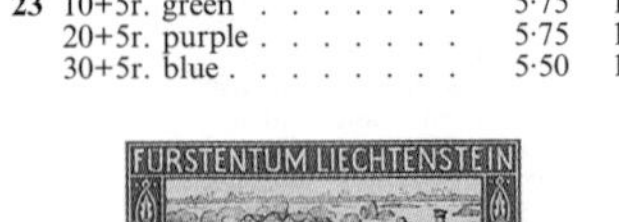

24 Salvage Work by Austrian soldiers

1928. Flood Relief.
80 – 5r.+5r. brown and purple 13·50 18·00
81 – 10r.+10r. brown and green 13·00 16·00
82 **24** 20r.+10r. brown and red . . 13·00 16·00
83 – 30r.+10r. brown and blue 8·75 16·00
DESIGNS: 5r. Railway bridge between Buchs and Schaan; 10r. Village of Ruggell; 30r. Salvage work by Swiss soldiers.

26 Prince John II, 1858–1928

1928. 70th Anniv of Accession of Prince John II.
84 – 10r. green and brown . . . 2·10 2·30
85 – 20r. green and red . . . . . 4·75 5·75
86 – 30r. green and blue . . . 11·00 13·00
87 – 60r. green and mauve . . . 35·00 65·00
88 **26** 1f.20 blue . . . . 36·00 65·00
89 1f.50 brown . . . . 65·00 £160
90 2f. red . . . . 65·00 £160
91 5f. green . . . . 65·00 £200
DESIGN—VERT: 10r. to 60r. Prince John II.

28 Prince Francis I **31** Girl Vintager

32 Prince Francis I and Princess Elsa **34** Monoplane over Vaduz Castle and Rhine Valley

1929. Accession of Prince Francis I.
92 – 10r. green . . . . 50 1·60
93 **28** 20r. red . . . . 75 2·10
94 – 30r. blue . . . . 1·10 12·00
95 – 70r. brown . . . . 10·50 60·00
PORTRAITS: 10r. Prince Francis I as a boy; 30r. Princess Elsa; 70r. Prince Francis and Princess Elsa.

1930.
96 **31** 3r. red 45 65
97 – 5r. green . . . . 1·00 75
98 – 10r. lilac . . . . 1·00 50
99 – 20r. red . . . . 21·00 80
100 – 25r. green . . . . 5·00 18·00
101 – 30r. blue . . . . 5·00 1·10
102 – 35r. green . . . . 6·25 10·50
103 – 40r. brown . . . . 6·25 3·50
104 – 50r. black . . . . 60·00 9·50
105 – 60r. green . . . . 60·00 18·00
106 – 90r. purple . . . . 60·00 £100
107 – 1f.20 brown . . . . 80·00 £160
108 – 1f.50 blue . . . . 34·00 42·00
109 **32** 2f. brown and green . . . 48·00 75·00
DESIGNS—VERT: 5r. Mt. Three Sisters–Edelweiss; 10r. Alpine cattle-alpine roses; 20r. Courtyard of Vaduz Castle; 25r. Mt. Naafkopf; 30r. Valley of Samina; 35r. Rofenberg Chapel; 40r. St. Mamertus' Chapel; 50r. Kurhaus at Malbun; 60r. Gutenberg Castle; 90r. Schellenberg Monastery; 1f.20, Vaduz Castle; 1f.50, Pfaelzer club hut.

1930. Air.
110 – 15r. brown . . . . 4·50 6·00
111 – 20r. green . . . . 11·50 12·00
112 – 25r. brown . . . . 5·75 19·00
113 – 35r. blue . . . . 9·00 13·00
114 **34** 45r. green . . . . 25·00 44·00
115 1f. purple . . . . 40·00 30·00
DESIGNS—VERT: 15, 20r. Biplane over snowy mountain peak. HORIZ: 25, 35r. Biplane over Vaduz Castle.

35 Airship "Graf Zeppelin" over Alps

1931. Air.
116 **35** 1f. green . . . . 28·00 24·00
117 – 2f. blue . . . . 80·00 £225
DESIGN: 2f. Airship "Graf Zeppelin" (different).

37 Princess Elsa **38** Mt. Naafkopf **39** Prince Francis I

1932. Youth Charities.
118 – 10r.+5r. green . . . . . 14·50 22·00
119 **37** 20r.+5r. red . . . . . 15·00 23·00
120 – 30r.+10r. blue . . . . . 17·00 27·00
DESIGNS—22 × 29 mm: 10r. Arms of Liechtenstein. As Type **37**: 30r. Prince Francis.

1933.
121 **38** 25r. orange . . . . £190 60·00
122 – 90r. green . . . . 6·50 48·00
123 – 1f.20 brown . . . . . . 48·00 £180
DESIGNS: 90r. Gutenberg Castle; 1f.20, Vaduz Castle.

1933. Prince Francis's 80th Birthday.
124 **39** 10r. violet . . . . 13·00 33·00
125 20r. red . . . . 13·00 33·00
126 30r. blue . . . . 13·00 33·00

40 **41** "Three Sisters"

42 Vaduz Castle **44** Prince Francis I

45 Arms of Liechtenstein **46** Golden Eagle

1933.
127 **40** 3r. red 20 45
128 **41** 5r. green . . . . 2·50 45
129 – 10r. violet 65 35
130 – 15r. orange 25 85
131 – 20r. red 60 45
132 – 25r. brown . . . . 15·00 40·00
133 – 30r. blue . . . . 3·25 85
134 – 35r. green . . . . 85 3·50
135 – 40r. brown . . . . 95 2·40
136 **42** 50r. brown . . . . 17·00 11·00
137 – 60r. purple . . . . 1·70 4·00
138 – 90r. green . . . . 5·25 13·50
139 – 1f.20 blue . . . . 1·90 12·50
140 – 1f.50 brown . . . . 2·30 16·00
141 – 2f. brown . . . . 42·00 £130
142 **44** 3f. blue . . . . 55·00 £130
143 **45** 5f. purple £300 £650
DESIGNS—As Type **41**: 10r. Schaan Church; 15r. Bendern am Rhein; 20r. Town Hall, Vaduz; 25r. Saminatal. As Type **44**: 2f. Princess Elsa. As Type **42**: 30r. Saminatal (different); 35r. Schellenberg ruins; 40r. Government Building, Vaduz; 60r. Vaduz Castle (different); 90r. Gutenberg Castle; 1f.20, Pfalzer Hut, Bettlerjoch; 1f.50, Valuna.
See also Nos. 174, 225/6 and 258.

1934. Air.
145 **46** 10r. violet . . . . 5·25 13·50
146 – 15r. orange . . . . 13·00 30·00
147 – 20r. red . . . . 14·00 30·00
148 – 30r. blue . . . . 14·00 30·00
149 – 50r. green . . . . 20·00 25·00
DESIGNS: 10r. to 20r. Golden eagles in flight; 30r. Ospreys in nest; 50r. Golden eagle on rock.

1935. Air. No. 115 surch **60 Rp.**
150 **34** 60r. on 1f. purple . . . . 21·00 32·00

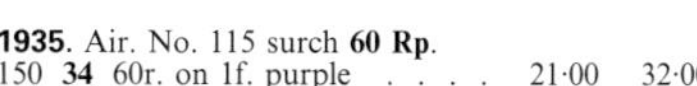

49 "Hindenburg" and Schaan Church

1936. Air.
151 **49** 1f. red . . . . 26·00 55·00
152 – 2f. violet . . . . 22·00 55·00
DESIGN: 2f. "Graf Zeppelin" over Schaan Airport.

51 Masescha am Triesenberg **52** Schellenberg Castle

1937.
154 – 3r. brown . . . . 20 13·50
155 **51** 5r. green and buff 15 20
156 – 10r. violet and buff 15 15
157 – 15r. black and buff 40 50
158 – 20r. red and buff 25 30
159 – 25r. brown and buff . . . 60 2·20
160 – 30r. blue and buff . . . . 1·40 55
161 **52** 40r. green and buff . . . . 1·40 1·20
162 – 50c. brown and buff . . . 95 1·80
163 – 60r. purple and buff . . . 1·40 1·70
164 – 90r. violet and buff . . . 7·50 8·75
165 – 1f. purple and buff . . . 1·30 8·25
166 – 1f.20 brown and buff . . . 6·00 11·50
167 – 1f.50 grey and buff . . . . 3·00 12·00
DESIGNS—As Type **51**: 3r. Schalun ruins; 10r. Knight and Vaduz Castle; 15r. Upper Saminatal; 20r. Church and Bridge at Bendern; 25r. Steg Chapel and girl. As Type **52**: 30r. Farmer and orchard, Triesenberg; 50r. Knight and Gutenberg Castle; 60r. Baron von Brandis and Vaduz Castle; 90r. "Three Sisters" mountain; 1f. Boundary-stone on Luziensteig; 1f.20, Minstrel and Gutenberg Castle; 1f.50, Lawena (Schwarzhorn).

53 Roadmakers at Triesenberg

1937. Workers' Issue.
168 – 10r. mauve 80 45
169 **53** 20r. red . . . . 1·10 75
170 – 30r. blue . . . . 1·50 1·60
171 – 50r. brown . . . . 95 2·10
DESIGNS: 10r. Bridge at Malbun; 30r. Binnen Canal Junction; 50r. Francis Bridge, near Planken.

1938. Death of Prince Francis I.
174 **44** 3f. black on yellow . . . . 6·25 49·00

54 Josef Rheinberger **55** Black-headed Gulls

1939. Birth Centenary of Rheinberger (composer).
175 **54** 50r. grey . . . . 55 2·75

1939. Air.
176 – 10r. violet (Barn swallows) 25 50
177 **55** 15r. orange . . . . 40 1·40
178 – 20r. red (Herring gull) . . 80 45
179 – 30r. blue (Common buzzard) . . . . 80 1·10
180 – 50r. green (Northern goshawk) . . . . 2·75 1·70
181 – 1f. red (Lammergeier) . . . 2·20 11·00
182 – 2f. violet Lammergeier . . 1·90 11·50

56 Offering Homage to First Prince

1939. Homage to Francis Joseph II.
183 **56** 20r. red . . . . 75 1·20
184 30r. blue . . . . 75 1·20
185 50r. green . . . . 75 1·30

57 Francis Joseph II

1939.
186 – 2f. green on cream . . . . 5·00 25·00
187 – 3f. violet on cream . . . . 4·50 25·00
188 **57** 5f. brown on cream . . . 10·50 21·00
DESIGNS: 2f. Cantonal Arms; 3f. Arms of Principality.

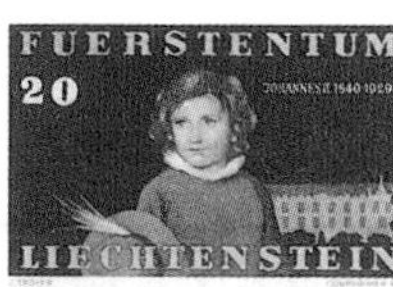
58 Prince John when a Child

1940. Birth Centenary of Prince John II.
189 **58** 20r. red . . . . 50 1·40
190 – 30r. blue . . . . 70 2·20
191 – 50r. green . . . . 1·10 5·75
192 – 1f. violet . . . . 6·50 43·00
193 – 1f.50 black . . . . 5·25 42·00
194 – 3f. brown . . . . 3·50 12·00
DESIGNS—As Type **58**: Portraits of Prince John in early manhood (30r.), in middle age (50r.) and in later life (1f.), and Memorial tablet (1f.50). As Type **44**: 3f. Framed portrait of Prince John II.

60 Wine Press

1941. Agricultural Propaganda.
195 – 10r. brown 45 40
196 **60** 20r. purple 65 75
197 – 30r. blue . . . . 75 1·40
198 – 50r. green . . . . 2·30 10·50
199 – 90r. violet . . . . 2·30 11·50
DESIGNS: 10r. Harvesting maize; 30r. Sharpen-ing scythe; 50r. Milkmaid and cow; 90r. Girl wearing traditional headdress.

61 Madonna and Child **62** Prince Hans Adam

1941.
200 **61** 10f. purple on stone . . . 33·00 70·00

1941. Princes (1st issue).
201 **62** 20r. red . . . . 35 1·20
202 – 30r. blue (Wenzel) . . . . 65 1·90
203 – 1f. grey (Anton Florian) 1·90 11·00
204 – 1f.50 green (Joseph) . . . 1·90 11·50
See also Nos. 210/13 and 217/20.

63 St. Lucius preaching

1942. 600th Anniv of Separation from Estate of Montfort.
205 **63** 20r. red on pink 75 65
206 – 30r. blue on pink . . . . 70 1·40
207 – 50r. green on pink . . . . 1·60 5·00
208 – 1f. brown on pink . . . . 2·00 9·75
209 – 2f. violet on pink . . . . 2·30 9·75
DESIGNS: 30r. Count of Montfort replanning Vaduz; 50r. Counts of Montfort-Werdenberg and Sargans signing treaty; 1f. Battle of Gutenberg; 2f. Homage to Prince of Liechtenstein.

64 Prince John Charles **65** Princess Georgina

1942. Princes (2nd issue).
210 **64** 20r. pink 25 75
211 – 30r. blue (Francis Joseph I) 45 1·40
212 – 1f. purple (Alois I) . . . . 1·40 9·50
213 – 1f.50 brown (John I) . . . 1·40 9·50

1943. Marriage of Prince Francis Joseph II and Countess Georgina von Wildczek.
214 – 10r. purple 50 70
215 **65** 20r. red . . . . 50 1·10
216 – 30r. blue . . . . 50 1·10
PORTRAITS—VERT: 10r. Prince Francis Joseph II. HORIZ (44 × 25 mm): 30r. Prince and Princess.

66 Alois II **67** Marsh Land

1943. Princes (3rd issue).
217 **66** 20r. brown 50 50
218 – 30r. blue 80 95
219 – 1f. brown . . . . 1·30 5·50
220 – 1f.50 green . . . . 1·30 5·50
PORTRAITS: 30r. John II; 1f. Francis I; 1f.50, Francis Joseph II.

1943. Completion of Irrigation Canal.
221 **67** 10r. violet 20 35
222 – 30r. blue . . . . 35 1·70
223 – 50r. green . . . . 65 6·25
224 – 2f. brown . . . . 1·60 9·75
DESIGNS: 30r. Draining the canal; 50r. Ploughing reclaimed land; 2f. Harvesting crops.

1943. Castles. As T **41**.
225 10r. grey (Vaduz) 40 55
226 20r. brown (Gutenberg) . . . 35 70

69 Planken **70** Prince Francis Joseph II

1944. Various designs. Buff backgrounds.
227 **69** 3r. brown 20 20
228 – 5r. green (Bendern) . . . 20 15
228a – 5r. brown (Bendern) . . . 10·00 45
229 – 10r. grey (Triesen) . . . . 12·00 45
230 – 15r. grey (Ruggell) . . . 40 55
231 – 20r. red (Vaduz) 40 35
232 – 25r. brown (Triesenberg) 45 55
233 – 30r. blue (Schaan) 50 40
234 – 40r. brown (Balzers) . . . 65 1·10
235 – 50r. blue (Mauren) . . . 1·50 1·70
236 – 60r. green (Schellenberg) 4·25 3·25
237 – 90r. green (Eschen) . . . 4·25 3·50
238 – 1f. purple (Vaduz Castle) 3·00 3·75
239 – 1f.20 brown (Valunatal) 3·25 4·00
240 – 1f.50 blue (Lawena) . . . 3·25 3·75

1944.
241 **70** 2f. brown and buff . . . . 4·00 10·00
242 – 3f. green and buff . . . . 3·50 8·00
DESIGN: 3f. Princess Georgina.
See also Nos. 302/3.

72 **73**

1945. Birth of Crown Prince Johann Adam Pius (known as Prince Hans Adam).
243 **72** 20r. red, yellow and gold 65 40
244 30r. blue, yellow and gold 80 1·00
245 100r. grey, yellow and gold 2·10 4·00

1945.
246 **73** 5f. blue on buff . . . . . 16·00 18·00
247 5f. brown on buff . . . . 17·00 27·00

74 First Aid **75** St. Lucius

1945. Red Cross. Cross in red.
248 – 10r.+10r. purple and buff 1·40 1·40
249 **74** 20r.+20r. purple and buff 1·40 2·00
250 – 1f.+1f.40 blue and buff . . 6·25 18·00
DESIGNS: 10r. Mother and children; 1f. Nurse and invalid.

1946.
251 **75** 10f. grey on buff . . . . . 24·00 22·00

76 Red Deer Stag **79** Wilbur Wright

1946. Wild Life.
252 **76** 20r. red . . . . 1·20 1·30
255 – 20r. red (Chamois) . . . . 2·00 2·10
283 – 20r. red (Roebuck) . . . . 7·75 2·30
253 – 30r. blue (Arctic hare) . . 1·60 2·10
256 – 30r. blue (Alpine marmot) 3·00 2·75
284 – 30r. green (Black grouse) 13·50 7·75
285 – 80r. brown (Eurasian badger) . . . . 27·00 30·00
254 – 1f.50 green (Western capercaillie) . . . . . . 5·75 8·50
257 – 1f.50 brown (Golden eagle) 6·75 12·00

1947. Death of Princess Elsa. As No. 141.
258 – 2f. black on yellow . . . . 2·20 9·25

1948. Air. Pioneers of Flight.
259 – 10r. green 65 20
260 – 15r. violet . . . . 65 1·00
261 – 20r. brown 80 25
262 – 25r. red . . . . 1·10 1·25
263 – 40r. blue . . . . 1·30 1·60
264 – 50r. blue . . . . 1·70 1·60
265 – 1f. purple . . . . 3·50 2·40
266 – 2f. purple . . . . 4·00 3·75
267 **79** 5f. green . . . . 5·25 4·75
268 – 10f. black . . . . 28·00 14·00
PORTRAITS: 10r. Leoardo da Vinci; 15r. Joseph Montgolfier; 20r. Jakob Degen; 25r. Wilhelm Kress; 40r. Etienne Robertson; 50r. William Henson; 1f. Otto Lilienthal; 2f. Salomon Andree; 10f. Icarus

80 "Ginevra de Benci" (Da Vinci)

1949. Paintings.
269 **80** 10r. green 45 25
270 – 20r. red 95 50
271 – 30r. brown . . . . 2·50 1·20
272 – 40r. blue . . . . 5·25 60
273 – 50r. violet . . . . 4·50 5·25
274 – 60r. grey . . . . 9·25 4·75
275 – 80r. brown . . . . 2·30 3·25
276 – 90r. green . . . . 9·25 4·00
277 – 120r. mauve . . . . 2·30 4·00
DESIGNS: 20r. "Portrait of a Young Girl" (Rubens); 30r. Self-portrait of Rembrandt in plumed hat; 40r. "Stephan Gardiner, Bishop of Winchester" (Quentin Massys); 50r. "Madonna and Child" (Hans Memling); 60r. "Franz Meister in 1456" (Jehan Fouquet); 80r. "Lute Player" (Orazio Gentileschi); 90r. "Portrait of a Man" (Bernhardin Strigel); 120r. "Portrait of a Man (Duke of Urbino)" (Raphael).

1949. No. 227 surch **5 Rp.** and bars.
278 **69** 5r. on 3r. brown and buff 50 35

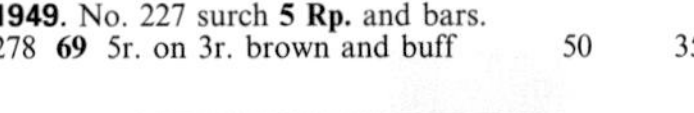

82 Posthorn and Map of World

1949. 75th Anniv of U.P.U.
279 **82** 40r. blue . . . . 2·75 3·25

83 Rossauer Castle **86** Boy cutting Loaf

1949. 250th Anniv of Acquisition of Domain of Schellenberg.
280 **83** 20r. purple . . . . 1·50 1·40
281 – 40r. blue . . . . 5·25 6·00
282 – 1f.50 red . . . . 8·00 7·50
DESIGN—HORIZ: 40r. Bendern Church. VERT: 1f.50, Prince Johann Adam I.

1950. Surch **100 100**.
286 **82** 100r. on 40r. blue . . . . 19·00 31·00

1951. Agricultural scenes.
287 **86** 5r. mauve 25 10
288 – 10r. green 50 10
289 – 15r. brown . . . . 4·25 4·75
290 – 20r. brown 95 20
291 – 25r. purple . . . . 4·25 4·75
292 – 30r. green . . . . 2·50 50
293 – 40r. blue . . . . 7·50 4·25
294 – 50r. purple . . . . 6·50 3·00
295 – 60r. brown . . . . 6·25 3·00
296 – 80r. brown . . . . 6·25 6·75
297 – 90r. green . . . . 13·00 4·50
298 – 1f. blue . . . . 42·00 5·50
DESIGNS: 10r. Man whetting scythe; 15r. Mowing; 20r. Girl and sweet corn; 25r. Haywain; 30r. Gathering grapes; 40r. Man with scythe; 50r. Herdsman with cows; 60r. Ploughing; 80r. Girl carrying basket of fruit; 90r. Woman gleaning; 1f. Tractor hauling corn.

87 "Lock on the Canal" (Aelbert Cuyp) **88** "Willem von Heythuysen, Burgomaster of Haarlem" (Frans Hals)

1951. Paintings.
299 **87** 10r.+10r. green . . . . . 7·50 5·25
300 **88** 20r.+10r. brown . . . . . 8·00 10·50
301 – 40r.+10r. blue . . . . . . 6·75 7·00
DESIGN—As Type **87**: 40r. "Landscape" (Jacob van Ruysdael).

90 Vaduz Castle **96** Lord Baden-Powell

1951.
302 **70** 2f. blue . . . . 12·50 22·00
303 – 3f. brown . . . . £110 75·00
304 **90** 5f. green £130 £110
DESIGN: 3f. Princess Georgina.

1952. No. 281 surch **1.20**
308 1f.20 on 40r. blue . . . . . 17·00 37·00

1952. Paintings from Prince's Collection. (a) As T **80** but size 25 × 30 mm.
309 10r. green . . . . 1·00 65
305 20r. purple . . . . 25·00 2·20
307 40r. blue . . . . 9·00 3·75
312 40r. blue . . . . 24·00 34·00
PAINTINGS: No. 309, "Portrait of a Young Man" (A. G.); 305, "Portrait" (Giovanni Salvoldo); 307, "St. John" (Andrea del Sarto); 312, "Leonhard, Count of Hag" (Hans von Kulmbach).

(b) As T **88** (22½ × 24 mm).
310 20r. brown . . . . 11·00 1·70
306 30r. green . . . . 17·00 5·75
311 30r. brown . . . . 22·00 5·25
PAINTINGS: No. 310, "St. Nicholas" (Bartholomaus Zeitblom); 306, "Madonna and Child" (Sandro Botticelli); 311, "St. Christopher" (Lucas Cranach the elder).

1953. 14th International Scout Conference.
313 **96** 10r. green . . . . 1·40 90
314 20r. brown . . . . 9·50 1·50
315 25r. red . . . . 9·00 15·00
316 40r. blue . . . . 8·75 3·25

97 Alemannic Ornamental Disc, (c. A.D. 600) **98** Prehistoric Walled Settlement, Borscht

1953. Opening of National Museum, Vaduz.
317 **97** 10r. brown . . . . 7·00 8·25
318 **98** 20r. green . . . . 7·00 8·00
319 – 1f.20 blue . . . . 36·00 24·00
DESIGN—VERT: 1f.20, Rossen jug (3000 B.C.).

99 Footballers **100** Madonna and Child

1954. Football.
320 **99** 10r. brown and red . . . . 1·60 75
321 – 20r. deep green and green 5·75 2·00
322 – 25r. deep brown and brown . . . . 13·00 21·00
323 – 40r. violet and grey . . . . 11·50 7·25
DESIGNS: 20r. Footballer kicking ball; 25r. Goalkeeper; 40r. Two footballers.
For stamps in similar designs see Nos. 332/5, 340/3, 351/4 and 363/6.

1954. Nos. 299/301 surch in figures.
324 **87** 35r. on 10r.+10r. green . . 3·00 1·60
325 **88** 60r. on 20r.+10r. brown 11·00 8·25
326 – 65r. on 40r.+10r. blue . . 6·50 5·75

1954. Termination of Marian Year.
327 **100** 20r. brown . . . . 2·50 2·75
328 40r. black . . . . 13·00 14·00
329 1f. brown . . . . 14·00 13·50

101 Princess Georgina **102** Crown Prince John Adam Pius

1955.
330 – 2f. brown . . . . 55·00 31·00
331 **101** 3f. green . . . . 55·00 31·00
PORTRAIT: 2f. Prince Francis Joseph II.

1955. Mountain Sports. As T **99**.
332 10r. purple and blue . . . . 1·70 75
333 20r. green and bistre . . . . 4·00 75
334 25r. brown and blue . . . . 13·00 12·50
335 40r. green and red . . . . . 11·50 3·50
DESIGNS: 10r. Slalom racer; 20r. Mountaineer hammering in piton; 25r. Skier; 40r. Mountaineer resting on summit.

1955. 10th Anniv of Liechtenstein Red Cross. Cross in red.
336 **102** 10r. violet . . . . 1·30 40
337 – 20r. green . . . . 3·00 1·20
338 – 40r. brown . . . . 5·00 5·25
339 – 60r. red . . . . 5·00 3·50
PORTRAITS: 20r. Prince Philip; 40r. Prince Nicholas; 60r. Princess Nora.
See also No. 350.

1956. Athletics. As T **99**.
340 10r. green and brown 90 50
341 20r. purple and green . . . . 2·50 75
342 40r. brown and blue . . . . 3·75 4·25
343 1f. brown and red . . . . . 7·50 8·75
DESIGNS: 10r. Throwing the javelin; 20r. Hurdling; 40r. Pole vaulting; 1f. Running.

103 **104** Prince Francis Joseph II

1956. 150th Anniv of Sovereignty of Liechtenstein.
344 **103** 10r. purple and gold . . . 2·00 60
345 1f.20 blue and gold . . . 8·50 3·25

1956. 50th Birthday of Prince Francis Joseph II.
346 **104** 10r. green . . . . 1·30 35
347 15r. blue . . . . 2·10 2·10
348 25r. purple . . . . 2·10 2·10
349 60r. brown . . . . 6·00 2·10

1956. 6th Philatelic Exhibition, Vaduz. As T **102** but inscr "6. BRIEFMARKEN-AUSSTELLUNG".
350 20r. green . . . . 2·30 40

1956. Gymnastics. As T **99**.
351 10r. green and pink . . . . 2·00 70
352 15r. purple and green . . . . 4·25 4·75
353 25r. green and drab . . . . 5·00 6·25
354 1f.50 brown and yellow . . . 13·00 11·00
DESIGNS: 10r. Somersaulting; 15r. Vaulting; 25r. Exercising with rings; 1f.50, Somersaulting on parallel bars.

105 Norway Spruce **106** Lord Baden-Powell

1957. Liechtenstein Trees and Bushes.
355 **105** 10r. purple . . . . 2·75 1·40
356 – 20r. red . . . . 3·00 50
357 – 1f. green . . . . 5·00 5·00
DESIGNS: 20r. Wild rose bush; 1f. Silver birch.
See also Nos. 369/71, 375/7 and 401/3.

1957. 50th Anniv of Boy Scout Movement and Birth Centenary of Lord Baden-Powell (founder).
358 – 10r. blue . . . . 1·00 1·00
359 **106** 20r. brown . . . . 1·00 1·00
DESIGN: 10r. Torchlight procession.

107 St. Mamertus Chapel **108** Relief Map of Liechtenstein

1957. Christmas.
360 **107** 10r. brown 70 20
361 – 40r. blue . . . . 2·20 5·00
362 – 1f.50 purple . . . . . . 7·75 8·00
DESIGNS—(from St. Mamertus Chapel): 40r. Altar shrine; 1f.50, "Pieta" (sculpture).
See also Nos. 372/4 and 392/4.

1958. Sports. As T **99**.
363 15r. violet and blue . . . . . 90 1·00
364 30r. green and purple . . . . 3·00 5·25

365 40r. green and orange . . . . 5·00 5·50
366 90r. brown and green . . . . 2·75 3·50
DESIGNS: 15r. Swimmer; 30r. Fencers; 40r. Tennis player; 90r. Racing cyclists.

1958. Brussels International Exhibition.
367 **108** 25r. violet, stone and red 50 50
368 40r. purple, blue and red 65 55

1958. Liechtenstein Trees and Bushes. As T **105**.
369 20r. brown (Sycamore) . . . 2·30 50
370 50r. green (Holly) . . . . . 9·00 3·75
371 90r. violet (Yew) . . . . . . 2·30 2·50

1958. Christmas. As T **107**.
372 20r. green . . . . 2·20 1·90
373 35r. violet . . . . 2·20 2·50
374 80r. brown . . . . 2·50 2·10
DESIGNS: 20r. "St. Maurice and St. Agatha"; 35r. "St. Peter"; 80r. St. Peter's Chapel, Mals-Balzers.

1959. Liechtenstein Trees and Bushes. As T **105**.
375 20r. lilac (Red-berried larch) 3·75 1·90
376 50r. red (Red-berried elder) 3·50 2·10
377 90r. green (Linden) . . . . . 3·00 2·50

109 **111** Harvester

110 Flags of Vaduz Castle and Rhine Valley

1959. Pope Pius XII Mourning.
378 **109** 30r. purple and gold . . . 60 60

1959. Views.
379 – 5r. brown 10 10
380 **110** 10r. purple 10 10
381 – 20r. mauve 25 10
382 – 30r. red 35 25
383 – 40r. green 70 40
384 – 50r. blue 50 40
385 – 60r. blue 65 50
386 **111** 75r. brown . . . . . . 95 1·10
387 – 80r. green 85 65
388 – 90r. purple . . . . . . 1·00 95
389 – 1f. brown . . . . . . 1·00 80
390 – 1f.20 red . . . . . . 1·30 1·20
390a – 1f.30 green . . . . . . 1·30 1·40
391 – 1f.50 blue . . . . . . 1·50 1·50
DESIGNS—HORIZ: 5r. Bendern Church; 20r. Rhine Dam; 30r. Gutenberg Castle; 40r. View from Schellenberg; 50r. Vaduz Castle; 60r. Naafkopf-Falknis Mountains (view from the Bettlerjoch); 1f.20, Harvesting apples; 1f.30, Farmer and wife; 1f.50, Saying grace at table. VERT: 80r. Alpine haymaker; 90r. Girl in vineyard; 1f. Mother in kitchen.

1959. Christmas. As T **107**.
392 5r. green 50 20
393 60r. brown . . . . 5·00 3·75
394 1f. purple . . . . 3·00 2·00
DESIGNS: 5r. Bendern Church belfry; 60r. Relief on bell of St. Theodul's Church; 1f. Sculpture on tower of St. Lucius's Church.

112 Bell 47J Ranger Helicopter

1960. Air. 30th Anniv of 1st Liechtenstein Air Stamps.
395 **112** 30r. red . . . . 1·80 1·90
396 – 40r. blue . . . . 4·00 1·90
397 – 50r. purple . . . . 6·00 3·75
398 – 75r. green . . . . 2·00 2·00
DESIGNS: 40r. Boeing 707 jetliner; 50r. Convair Coronado jetliner; 75r. Douglas DC-8 jetliner.

1960. World Refugee Year. Nos. 367/8 surch **WELTFLUCHTLINGSJAHR 1960**, uprooted tree and new value.
399 **108** 30+10r. on 40r. purple, blue and red 80 80
400 50+10r. on 25r. violet, stone and red . . . . . 1·20 1·20

1960. Liechtenstein Trees and Bushes. As T **105**.
401 20r. brown (Beech) . . . . . 5·50 5·25
402 30r. purple (Juniper) . . . . 6·25 8·00
403 50r. turquoise (Mountain pines) . . . . 18·00 10·00

114 Europa "Honeycomb" **115** Princess Gina

1960. Europa.
404 **114** 50r. multicoloured . . . . 65·00 44·00

1960.
404a – 1f.70 violet . . . . . . 1·40 1·00
405 **115** 2f. blue . . . . 1·90 1·60
406 – 3f. brown . . . . 2·40 1·60
PORTRAITS: 1f.70, Crown Prince Hans Adam; 3f. Prince Francis Joseph II.

116 Heinrich von Frauenberg **117** "Power Transmission"

1961. Minnesingers (1st issue). Multicoloured. Reproduction from the Manessian Manuscript of Songs.
407 15r. Type **116** 30 30
408 25r. Ulrich von Liechtenstein 50 45
409 35r. Ulrich von Gutenberg 70 60
410 1f. Konrad von Altstatten . . 1·10 1·00
411 1f.50 Walther von der Vogelweide . . . . 4·75 7·25
See also Nos. 415/18 and 428/31.

1961. Europa.
412 **117** 50r. multicoloured 30 30

118 Clasped Hands **119** Campaign Emblem

1962. Europa.
413 **118** 50r. red and blue 40 40

1962. Malaria Eradication.
414 **119** 50r. blue 35 35

1962. Minnesingers (2nd issue). As T **116**. Mult.
415 20r. King Konradin 25 25
416 30r. Kraft von Toggenburg 65 70
417 40r. Heinrich von Veldig . . 65 70
418 2f. Tannhauser . . . . . . 1·90 2·00

120 Pieta **121** Prince Francis Joseph II

1962. Christmas.
419 **120** 30r. mauve 40 45
420 – 50r. red 55 55
421 – 1f.20 blue . . . . . . 1·20 1·20
DESIGNS: 50r. Fresco with angel; 1f.20, View of Mauren.
See also Nos. 438/40.

1963. 25th Anniv of Reign of Prince Francis Joseph II.
422 **121** 5f. green . . . . 3·50 2·50

122 Milk and Bread

1963. Freedom from Hunger.
423 **122** 50r. brown, purple and red 35 40

123 "Angel of Annunciation" **124** "Europa"

1963. Red Cross Cent. Cross in red; background grey.
424 **123** 20r. yellow and green . . 25 25
425 – 80r. violet and mauve . . 40 55
426 – 1f. blue and ultramarine 95 75
DESIGNS: 80r. "The Epiphany"; 1f. "Family".

1963. Europa.
427 **124** 50r. multicoloured 60 50

1963. Minnesingers (3rd issue). As T **116**. Mult.
428 25r. Heinrich von Sax . . . 20 20
429 30r. Kristan von Hamle . . . 35 35
430 75r. Werner von Teufen . . . 60 60
431 1f.70 Hartmann von Aue . . 1·40 1·40

125 Olympic Rings and Flags **126** Arms of Counts of Werdenberg, Vaduz

1964. Olympic Games, Tokyo.
432 **125** 50r. red, black and blue 35 40

1964. Arms (1st issue). Multicoloured.
433 20f. Type **126** 20 20
434 30f. Barons of Brandis . . . 25 25
435 80r. Counts of Sulz 70 70
436 1f.50 Counts of Hohenems 90 95
See also Nos. 443/6.

127 Roman Castle, Schaan **128** P. Kaiser

1964. Europa.
437 **127** 50f. multicoloured 65 45

1964. Christmas. As T **120**.
438 10r. purple 10 10
439 40r. blue 20 20
440 1f.30 purple 85 85
DESIGNS: 10r. Masescha Chapel; 40r. "Mary Magdalene" (altar painting); 1f.30, "St. Sebastian, Madonna and Child, and St. Rochus" (altar painting).

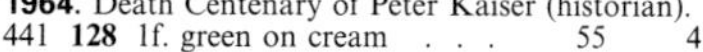

1964. Death Centenary of Peter Kaiser (historian).
441 **128** 1f. green on cream . . . 55 45

129 "Madonna" (wood sculpture, c. 1700) **130** Europa "Links" (ancient belt-buckle)

1965.
442 **129** 10f. red . . . . 7·25 3·00

1965. Arms (2nd issue). As T **126**. Multicoloured.
443 20r. Von Schellenberg . . . 20 20
444 30r. Von Gutenberg 30 20
445 80r. Von Frauenberg 80 70
446 1f. Von Ramschwag 80 70

1965. Europa.
447 **130** 50r. brown, grey and blue 45 35

131 "Jesus in the Temple"

1965. Birth Centenary of Ferdinand Nigg (painter).
448 – 10r. deep green and green 15 15
449 – 30r. brown and orange . . 20 20
450 **131** 1f.20 green and blue . . . 85 85
DESIGNS—VERT: 10r. "The Annunciation"; 30r. "The Magi".

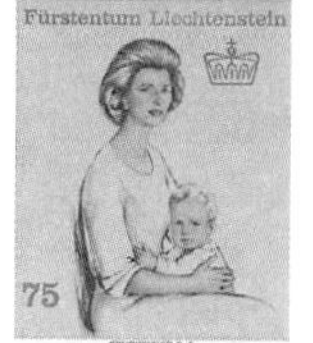
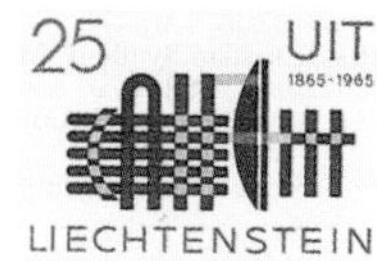

132 Princess Gina and Prince Franz (after painting by Pedro Leitao) **133** Telecommunications Symbols

1965. Special Issue.
451 **132** 75r. multicoloured 45 45
See also No. 457.

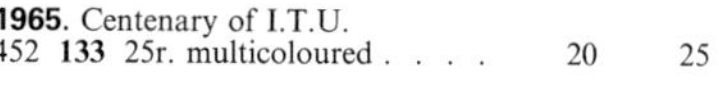

1965. Centenary of I.T.U.
452 **133** 25r. multicoloured 20 25

134 Tree ("Wholesome Earth")

1966. Nature Protection.
453 **134** 10r. green and yellow . . 10 10
454 – 20r. blue and light blue 10 10
455 – 30r. blue and green . . . 10 10
456 – 1f.50 red and yellow . . . 55 55
DESIGNS: 20r. Bird ("Pure Air"); 30r. Fish ("Clean Water"); 1f.50, Sun ("Protection of Nature").

1966. Prince Franz Joseph II's 60th Birthday. As T **132**, but with portrait of Prince Franz and inscr "1906–1966".
457 1f. multicoloured 45 45

135 Arms of Herren von Richenstein **136** Europa "Ship"

1966. Arms of Triesen Families. Multicoloured.
458 20r. Type **135** 10 10
459 30r. Jinker Vaistli 15 15
460 60r. Edle von Trisun 40 40
461 1f.20 Die von Schiel 55 55

1966. Europa.
462 **136** 50r. multicoloured 35 35

137 Vaduz Parish Church **138** Cogwheels

1966. Restoration of Vaduz Parish Church.
463 **137** 5r. green and red 10 10
464 – 20r. purple and bistre . . 10 10
465 – 30r. blue and red 10 15
466 – 1f.70 brown and green . . 65 70
DESIGNS: 20r. St. Florin; 30r. Madonna; 1f.70, God the Father.

1967. Europa.
467 **138** 50r. multicoloured 35 35

139 "The Man from Malanser"

141 "Alpha and Omega"

1967. Liechtenstein Sagas (1st series). Multicoloured.
468 20r. Type **139** 10 15
469 30r. "The Treasure of Gutenberg" 25 25
470 1f.20 "The Giant of Guflina" 70 60
See also Nos. 492/4 and 516/18.

1967. Christian Symbols. Multicoloured.
472 20r. Type **141** 10 10
473 30r. "Tropaion" (Cross as victory symbol) 10 10
474 70r. Christ's monogram . . . 75 55

142 Father J. B. Buchel (educator, historian and poet)

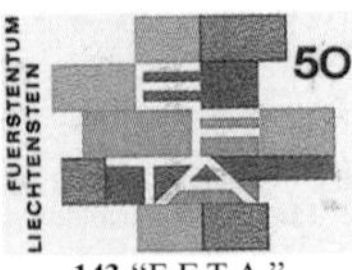
143 "E.F.T.A."

1967. Buchel Commemoration.
475 **142** 1f. red and green 60 50

1967. European Free Trade Association.
476 **143** 50r. multicoloured 35 30

144 "Peter and Paul", Mauren

145 Campaign Emblem

1967. "Patrons of the Church". Multicoloured.
477 5r. "St. Joseph", Planken . . 10 10
478 10r. "St. Lawrence", Schaan 10 10
479 20r. Type **144** 20 10
480 30r. "St. Nicholas", Balzers 25 15
480a 40r. "St. Sebastian", Nendeln 50 25
481 50r. "St. George", Schellenberg 60 30
482 60r. "St. Martin", Eschen 60 35
483 70r. "St. Fridolin", Ruggell 60 45
484 80r. "St. Gallus", Triesen 75 55
485 1f. "St. Theodolus", Triesenberg 85 55
486 1f.20 "St. Anna", Vaduz Castle . . . . 1·20 80
487 1f.50 "St. Marie", Bendern-Camprin . . . . 1·70 1·10
488 2f. "St. Lucius", (patron saint of Liechtenstein) . . 1·90 1·30

1967. "Technical Assistance".
489 **145** 50r.+20r. multicoloured 50 35

146 Europa "Key"

1968. Europa.
490 **146** 50r. multicoloured 35 35

147 Arms of Liechtenstein and Wilczek

148 Sir Rowland Hill

1968. Silver Wedding Anniv of Prince Francis Joseph II and Princess Gina.
491 **147** 75r. multicoloured 50 55

1968. Liechtenstein Sagas (2nd series). As T **139**. Multicoloured.
492 30r. "The Treasure of St. Mamerten" 10 10
493 50r. "The Hobgoblin in the Bergerwald" 25 25
494 80r. "The Three Sisters" . . 70 60

1968. "Pioneers of Philately" (1st series).
495 **148** 20r. green 10 10
496 – 30r. brown 10 10
497 – 1f. black 85 70
PORTRAITS: 30r. Philippe de Ferrary; 1f. Maurice Burrus.
See also Nos. 504/5 and 554/6.

150 Arms of Liechtenstein

151 Colonnade

1969.
498 **150** 3f.50 brown . . . . . . 2·50 1·20

1969. Europa.
499 **151** 50r. multicoloured 60 40

152 "Biology"

1969. 250th Anniv of Liechtenstein. Multicoloured.
500 10r. Type **152** 10 10
501 30r. "Physics" 10 15
502 50r. "Astronomy" 35 30
503 80r. "Art" 60 60

1969. "Pioneers of Philately" (2nd series). As T **148**.
504 80r. brown 50 50
505 1f.20 blue . . . . 1·10 85
PORTRAITS: 80r. Carl Lindenberg; 1f.20, Theodore Champion.

153 Arms of St. Luzi Monastery

154 Symbolic "T"

1969. Arms of Church Patrons. Multicoloured.
506 20r. St. Johann's Abbey . . . 20 25
507 30r. Type **153** 30 25
508 30r. Ladies' Priory, Schanis 25 20
509 30r. Knights Hospitallers, Feldkirch 35 25
510 50r. Pfafers Abbey 30 40
511 50r. Weingarten Abbey . . . 40 45
512 75r. St. Gallen Abbey 55 65
513 1f.20 Ottobeuren Abbey . . . 1·40 1·00
514 1f.50 Chur Episcopate . . . 1·30 1·20

1969. Centenary of Liechtenstein Telegraph System.
515 **154** 30r. multicoloured 25 25

1969. Liechtenstein Sagas (3rd series). As T **139**. Multicoloured.
516 20r. "The Cheated Devil" . . 10 10
517 50r. "The Fiery Red Goat" 40 35
518 60r. "The Grafenberg Treasure" 60 50

155 Orange Lily

156 "Flaming Sun"

1970. Nature Conservation Year. Multicoloured.
519 20r. Type **155** 20 10
520 30r. Wild orchid 25 20
521 50r. Ranunculus 40 35
522 1f.20 Bog bean 85 85
See also Nos. 532/5 and 548/51.

1970. Europa.
523 **156** 50r. yellow, blue and green 45 35

157 Prince Wenzel

158 Prince Francis Joseph II

1970. 25th Anniv of Liechtenstein Red Cross.
524 **157** 1f. multicoloured 85 70

1970.
526 – 1f.70 green . . . . . . 2·00 1·50
526a – 2f.50 blue . . . . 2·10 1·70
527 **158** 3f. black . . . . 2·50 1·80
DESIGNS: 1f.70, Prince Hans Adam; 2f.50, Princess Gina.

159 "Mother and Child" (R. Schadler)

160 Bronze Boar (La Tene period)

1970. Christmas.
528 **159** 30r. multicoloured 30 20

1971. National Museum Inauguration.
529 **160** 25r. black, blue & ultram 20 20
530 – 30r. green and brown . . 25 20
531 – 75r. multicoloured 55 50
DESIGNS: 30r. Ornamental peacock (Roman, 2nd-century); 75r. Engraved bowl (13th-century).

1971. Liechtenstein Flowers (2nd series). As T **155**. Multicoloured.
532 10r. Cyclamen 20 10
533 20r. Moonwort 20 20
534 50r. Superb pink 40 35
535 1f.50 Alpine columbine . . . 1·30 1·00

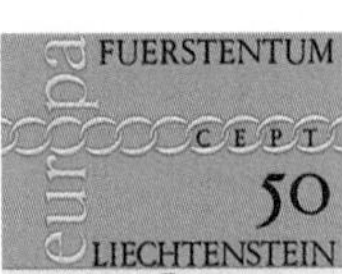
161 Europa Chain

1971. Europa.
536 **161** 50r. yellow, blue & black 40 40

162 Part of Text

163 Cross-country Skiing

1971. 50th Anniv of 1921 Constitution. Mult.
537 70r. Type **162** 65 55
538 80r. Princely crown 70 60

1971. Winter Olympic Games, Sapporo, Japan (1972). Multicoloured.
539 15r. Type **163** 20 10
540 40r. Ice hockey 35 30
541 65r. Downhill skiing 60 35
542 1f.50 Figure skating . . . . 1·60 1·10

164 "Madonna and Child" (sculpture, Andrea della Robbia)

165 Gymnastics

1971. Christmas.
543 **164** 30r. multicoloured 30 20

1972. Olympic Games, Munich. Multicoloured.
544 10r. Type **165** 10 10
545 20r. High jumping 15 10
546 40r. Running 30 25
547 60r. Throwing the discus . . 45 35

1972. Liechtenstein Flowers (3rd series). As T **155**. Multicoloured.
548 20r. Sulphur anemone . . . 15 10
549 30r. Turk's-cap lily 25 15
550 60r. Alpine centaury 50 40
551 1f.20 Reed-mace 95 75

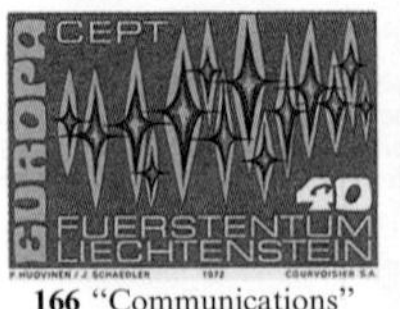
166 "Communications"

168 "Faun"

1972. Europa.
552 **166** 40r. multicoloured 30 30

1972. "Pioneers of Philately" (3rd series). As T **148**.
554 30r. green 25 25
555 40r. purple 30 30
556 1f.30 blue . . . . 1·10 85
PORTRAITS: 30r. Emilio Diena; 40r. Andre de Cock; 1f.30, Theodore E. Steinway.

1972. "Natural Art". Motifs fashioned from roots and branches. Multicoloured.
557 20r. Type **168** 10 10
558 30r. "Dancer" 20 20
559 1f.10 "Owl" 85 80

169 "Madonna with Angels" (F. Nigg)

170 Lawena Springs

1972. Christmas.
560 **169** 30r. multicoloured 30 20

1972. Landscapes.
561 – 5r. purple and yellow . . 15 10
562 **170** 10r. green and light green 10 10
563 – 15r. brown and green . . 10 10
564 – 25r. purple and blue . . . 30 20
565 – 30r. purple and brown . . 35 30
566 – 40r. purple and brown . . 45 30
567 – 50r. blue and lilac 40 35
568 – 60r. green and yellow . . 60 50
569 – 70r. blue and cobalt . . . 70 60
570 – 80r. green and light green 80 60
571 – 1f. brown and green . . . 1·00 75
572 – 1f.30 blue and green . . . 1·10 1·00
573 – 1f.50 brown and blue . . 1·40 1·20
574 – 1f.80 brown & lt brown 1·70 1·50
575 – 2f. brown and blue . . . 2·20 1·50
DESIGNS: 5r. Silum; 15r. Ruggeller Reed; 25r. Steg Kirchlispitz; 30r. Feld Schellenberg; 40r. Rennhof Mauren; 50r. Tidrufe; 60r. Eschner Riet; 70r. Mittagspitz; 80r. Schaan Forest; 1f. St. Peter's Chapel, Mals; 1f.30, Frommenhaus; 1f.50, Ochsenkopf; 1f.80, Hehlawangspitz; 2f. Saminaschlucht.

171 Europa "Posthorn"

1973. Europa.
576 **171** 30r. multicoloured 35 20
577 40r. multicoloured 40 30

172 Chambered Nautilus Goblet

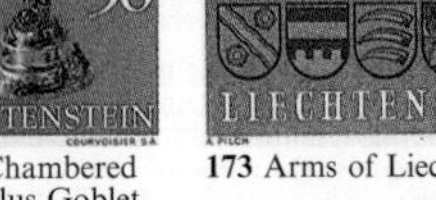
173 Arms of Liechtenstein

1973. Treasures from Prince's Collection (1st issue). Drinking Vessels. Multicoloured.

578	30r. Type **172**	25	20
579	70r. Ivory tankard	60	45
580	1f.10 Silver cup	85	70

See also Nos. 589/92.

1973.

581 **173** 5f. multicoloured . . . . 4·75 3·00

174 False Ringlet

175 "Madonna" (Bartolomeo di Tommaso da Foligno)

1973. Small Fauna of Liechtenstein (1st series). Multicoloured.

582	30r. Type **174**	20	20
583	40r. Curlew	90	35
584	60r. Edible frog	35	40
585	80r. Grass snake	70	55

See also Nos. 596/9.

1973. Christmas.

586 **175** 30r. multicoloured 30 25

176 "Shouting Horseman" (sculpture, Andrea Riccio)

177 Footballers

1974. Europa. Multicoloured.

587	30r. Type **176**	30	20
588	40r. "Squatting Aphrodite" (sculpture, Antonio Susini)	45	35

1974. Treasures from Prince's Collection (2nd issue). Porcelain. As T **172**. Multicoloured.

589	30r. Vase, 19th century	20	20
590	50r. Vase, 1740	40	25
591	60r. Vase, 1830	45	35
592	1f. Vase, c. 1700	75	65

1974. World Cup Football Championship, West Germany.

593 **177** 80f. multicoloured 75 50

178 Posthorn and U.P.U. Emblem

179 Bishop Marxer

1974. Centenary of Universal Postal Union.

594 **178**	40r. black, green and gold	35	25
595	60r. black, red and gold	45	35

1974. Small Fauna of Liechtenstein (2nd series). As T **174**. Multicoloured.

596	15r. Mountain newt	10	10
597	25r. Adder	10	10
598	70r. Cynthia's fritillary (butterfly)	80	55
599	1f.10 Three-toed woodpecker	1·20	80

1974. Death Centenary of Bishop Franz Marxer.

600 **179** 1f. multicoloured 75 50

180 Prince Francis Joseph II and Princess Gina

1974.

601 **180** 10f. brown and gold . . . 9·25 6·25

181 "St. Florian"

182 Prince Constantin

1974. Christmas. Glass Paintings. Multicoloured.

602	30r. Type **181**	25	15
603	50r. "St. Wendelin"	50	30
604	60r. "St. Mary, Anna and Joachim"	65	35
605	70r. "Jesus in Manger"	85	55

1975. Liechtenstein Princes.

606 **182**	70r. green and gold	55	50
607 –	80r. purple and gold	70	70
608 –	1f.20 blue and gold	1·00	90

PORTRAITS: 80r. Prince Maximilian; 1f.20, Prince Alois.

183 "Cold Sun" (M. Frommelt)

184 Imperial Cross

1975. Europa. Paintings. Multicoloured.

609	30r. Type **183**	25	20
610	60r. "Village" (L. Jager)	70	55

1975. Imperial Insignia (1st series). Multicoloured.

611	30r. Type **184**	30	20
612	60r. Imperial sword	45	35
613	1f. Imperial orb	90	65
614	1f.30 Imperial robe (50 × 32 mm)	6·25	4·75
615	2f. Imperial crown	2·75	1·90

See also Nos. 670/3.

185 "Red Cross Activities"

186 St. Mamerten, Triesen

1975. 30th Anniv of Liechtenstein Red Cross.

616 **185** 60r. multicoloured 75 45

1975. European Architectural Heritage Year. Multicoloured.

617	40r. Type **186**	30	25
618	50r. Red House, Vaduz	35	30
619	70r. Prebendary buildings, Eschen	60	55
620	1f. Gutenberg Castle, Balzers	90	80

187 Speed Skating

188 "Daniel in the Lions' Den"

1975. Winter Olympic Games, Innsbruck (1976). Multicoloured.

621	20r. Type **187**	20	10
622	25r. Ice hockey	25	20
623	70r. Downhill skiing	65	55
624	1f.20 Slalom	1·10	90

1975. Christmas and Holy Year. Capitals in Chur Cathedral.

625 **188**	30r. violet and gold	25	20
626 –	60r. green and gold	50	35
627 –	90r. red and gold	70	85

DESIGNS: 60r. "Madonna"; 90r. "St. Peter".

189 Mouflon

190 Crayfish

1976. Europa. Ceramics by Prince Hans von Liechtenstein. Multicoloured.

628	40r. Type **189**	50	30
629	80r. "Ring-necked Pheasant and Brood"	75	70

1976. World Wildlife Fund. Multicoloured.

630	25r. Type **190**	30	30
631	40r. Turtle	60	30
632	70r. European otter	85	70
633	80r. Northern lapwing	1·70	90

191 Roman Fibula

193 Judo

1976. 75th Anniv of National Historical Society.

634 **191** 90r. multicoloured 85 60

1976. Olympic Games, Montreal. Multicoloured.

636	35r. Type **193**	30	25
637	50r. Volleyball	35	40
638	80r. Relay	60	50
639	1f.10 Long jumping	85	75

194 "Singing Angels"

195 "Pisces"

1976. 400th Birth Anniv (1977) of Peter Paul Rubens (painter). Multicoloured.

640	50r. Type **194**	60	65
641	70r. "Sons of the Artist"	90	85
642	1f. "Daughters of Cecrops" (49 × 39 mm)	3·50	3·50

1976. Signs of the Zodiac (1st series). Multicoloured.

643	20r. Type **195**	20	20
644	40r. "Aries"	30	25
645	80r. "Taurus"	60	55
646	90r. "Gemini"	85	70

See also Nos. 666/9 and 710/13.

196 "Child Jesus of Prague"

197 Sarcophagus Statue, Chur Cathedral

1976. Christmas. Monastic Wax Sculptures. Mult.

647	20r. Type **196**	20	10
648	50r. "The Flight into Egypt" (vert)	60	35
649	80r. "Holy Trinity" (vert)	90	55
650	1f.50 "Holy Family"	1·40	1·00

1976. Bishop Ortlieb von Brandis of Chur Commemoration.

651 **197** 1f.10 brown and gold . . 1·00 70

199 Map of Liechtenstein, 1721 (J. Heber)

200 Coin of Emperor Constantine II

1977. Europa. Multicoloured.

664	40r. Type **199**	25	25
665	80r. "View of Vaduz, 1815" (F. Bachmann)	60	60

1977. Signs of the Zodiac (2nd series). As T **195**. Multicoloured.

666	40r. "Cancer"	30	25
667	70r. "Leo"	60	55
668	80r. "Virgo"	75	70
669	1f.10 "Libra"	85	90

1977. Imperial Insignia (2nd series). As T **184**. Multicoloured.

670	40r. Holy Lance and Reliquary with Particle of the Cross	30	25
671	50r. "St. Matthew" (Imperial Book of Gospels)	35	50
672	80r. St. Stephen's Purse	50	50
673	90r. Tabard of Imperial Herald	70	75

1977. Coins (1st series). Multicoloured.

674	35r. Type **200**	30	30
675	70r. Lindau Brakteat	55	55
676	80r. Coin of Ortlieb von Brandis	65	55

See also Nos. 707/9.

201 Frauenthal Castle, Styria

202 Children in Costume

1977. Castles.

677 **201**	20r. green and gold	25	20
678 –	50r. red and gold	50	40
679 –	80r. lilac and gold	75	60
680 –	90r. blue and gold	80	70

DESIGNS: 50r. Gross-Ullersdorf, Moravia; 80r. Liechtenstein Castle, near Modling, Austria; 90r. Palais Liechtenstein, Alserbachstrasse, Vienna.

1977. National Costumes. Multicoloured.

681	40r. Type **202**	30	25
682	70r. Two girls in traditional costume	45	45
683	1f. Woman in festive costume	65	65

203 Princess Tatjana

1977. Princess Tatjana.

684 **203** 1f.10 lt brn, brn & gold 95 95

204 "Angel"

205 Palais Liechtenstein, Bankgasse, Vienna

1977. Christmas. Sculptures by Erasmus Kern. Multicoloured.

685	20r. Type **204**	15	15
686	50r. "St. Rochus"	40	35
687	80r. "Madonna"	65	60
688	1f.50 "God the Father"	1·00	1·00

1978. Europa.

689 **205**	40r. blue and gold	35	30
690 –	80r. red and gold	80	60

DESIGN: 80r. Feldsberg Castle.

206 Farmhouse, Triesen

207 Vaduz Castle

1978. Buildings. Multicoloured.

691	10r. Type **206**	10	10
692	20r. Upper village of Triesen	15	15
693	35r. Barns at Balzers	30	30
694	40r. Monastery building, Bendern	30	25
695	50r. Rectory tower, Balzers-Mals	40	40

696 70r. Rectory, Mauren 55 55
697 80r. Farmhouse, Schellenberg 65 65
698 90r. Rectory, Balzers 75 85
699 1f. Rheinberger House, Vaduz 80 80
700 1f.10 Vaduz Mitteldorf . . . 85 90
701 1f.50 Town Hall, Triesenberg 1·20 1·20
702 2f. National Museum and Administrator's residence, Vaduz . . . . 1·70 1·60

1978. 40th Anniv of Prince Francis Joseph II's Accession. Royal Residence. Multicoloured.
703 40r. Type **207** 35 35
704 50r. Courtyard 35 35
705 70r. Hall 65 55
706 80r. High Altar, Castle Chapel 70 60

208 Coin of Prince Charles

209 "Portrait of a Piebald" (J. G. von Hamilton and A. Faistenberger)

1978. Coins (2nd series). Multicoloured.
707 40r. Type **208** 30 30
708 50r. Coin of Prince John Adam 40 35
709 80r. Coin of Prince Joseph Wenzel 65 60

1978. Signs of the Zodiac (3rd series). As T **195**. Multicoloured.
710 40r. "Scorpio" 30 25
711 50r. "Sagittarius" 40 35
712 80r. "Capricorn" 65 55
713 1f.50 "Aquarius" . . . . . . 1·10 1·00

1978. Paintings. Multicoloured.
714 70r. Type **209** 60 60
715 80r. "Portrait of a Blackish-brown Stallion" (J. G. von Hamilton) 80 80
716 1f.10 "Golden Carriage of Prince Joseph Wenzel" (Martin von Meytens) (48½ × 38 mm) . . . . . . 1·00 1·00

210 "Adoration of the Shepherds"

211 Comte AC-8 Mail Plane "St. Gallen" over Schaan

1978. Christmas. Church Windows, Triesenberg. Multicoloured.
717 20r. Type **210** 15 15
718 50r. "Enthroned Madonna with St. Joseph" 40 40
719 80r. "Adoration of the Magi" 70 75

1979. Europa. Multicoloured.
720 40r. Type **211** 55 50
721 80r. Airship "Graf Zeppelin" over Vaduz Castle 95 75

212 Child Drinking

213 Ordered Wave-field

1979. International Year of the Child. Multicoloured.
722 80r. Type **212** 50 60
723 90r. Child eating 55 70
724 1f.10 Child reading . . . . . 1·00 85

1979. 50th Anniv of International Radio Consultative Committee (CCIR).
725 **213** 50r. blue and black . . . 40 35

214 Abstract Composition

215 Sun rising over Continents

1979. Liechtenstein's Entry into Council of Europe.
726 **214** 80r. multicoloured 70 60

1979. Development Aid.
727 **215** 1f. multicoloured 85 75

216 Arms of Carl Ludwig von Sulz

1979. Heraldic Windows in the Liechtenstein National Museum. Multicoloured.
728 40r. Type **216** 35 30
729 70r. Arms of Barbara von Sulz 70 60
730 1f.10 Arms of Ulrich von Ramschwag and Barbara von Hallwil 90 80

217 Sts. Lucius and Florian (fresco, Waltensberg-Vuorz Church)

1979. Patron Saints.
731 **217** 20f. multicoloured . . . . 16·00 11·00

218 Base of Ski Slope, Valuna

1979. Winter Olympic Games, Lake Placid (1980). Multicoloured.
732 40r. Type **218** 30 25
733 70r. Malbun and Ochsenkopf 65 60
734 1f.50 Ski-lift, Sareis . . . . . 1·20 1·00

219 "The Annunciation"

1979. Christmas. Embroideries by Ferdinand Nigg. Multicoloured.
735 20r. Type **219** 20 40
736 50r. "Christmas" 40 35
737 80r. "Blessed are the Peacemakers" 60 75

220 Maria Leopoldine von Esterhazy (bust by Canova)

221 Arms of Andreas Buchel, 1690

1980. Europa.
738 **220** 40r. green, turq & gold 50 50
739 – 80r. brown, red and gold 80 75
DESIGN: 80r. Maria Theresia von Liechtenstein (after Martin von Meytens).

1980. Arms of Bailiffs (1st series). Multicoloured.
740 40r. Type **221** 30 25
741 70r. Georg Marxer, 1745 . . 60 55
742 80r. Luzius Frick, 1503 . . . 70 85
743 1f.10 Adam Oehri, 1634 . . . 85 75
See also Nos. 763/6, and 788/91.

222 3r. Stamp of 1930

223 Milking Pail

1980. 50th Anniv of Postal Museum.
744 **222** 80r. red, green and grey 70 65

1980. Alpine Dairy Farming Implements. Mult.
745 20r. Type **223** 20 10
746 50r. Wooden heart dairy herd descent marker 40 35
747 80r. Butter churn 65 60

224 Crossbow

1980. Hunting Weapons.
748 **224** 80r. brown and lilac . . . 65 60
749 – 90r. black and green . . . 75 65
750 – 1f.10 black and stone . . 90 80
DESIGNS: 90r. Spear and knife; 1f.10, Rifle and powder-horn.

225 Triesenberg Costumes

1980. Costumes. Multicoloured.
751 40r. Type **225** 30 30
752 70r. Dancers, Schellenberg . . 65 60
753 80r. Brass band, Mauren . . 75 70

226 Beech Trees, Matrula (spring)

227 Angel bringing Shepherds Good Tidings

1980. The Forest in the Four Seasons. Multicoloured.
754 40r. Type **226** 30 30
755 50r. Firs in the Valorsch (summer) 40 35
756 80r. Beech tree, Schaan (autumn) 65 55
757 1f.50 Edge of forest at Oberplanken (winter) . . . 1·10 1·20

1980. Christmas. Multicoloured.
758 20r. Type **227** 20 45
759 50r. Crib 40 35
760 80r. Epiphany 60 60

228 National Day Procession

230 Scout Emblems

1981. Europa. Multicoloured.
761 40r. Fireworks at Vaduz Castle 35 25
762 80r. Type **228** 80 70

1981. Arms of Bailiffs (2nd series). As T **221**. Multicoloured.
763 40r. Anton Meier, 1748 . . . 25 25
764 70r. Kaspar Kindle, 1534 . . 55 45
765 80r. Hans Adam Negele, 1600 . . . . 65 55
766 1f.10 Peter Matt, 1693 . . . 80 75

1981. 50th Anniv of Liechtenstein Boy Scout and Girl Guide Movements.
768 **230** 20r. multicoloured 45 35

231 Symbols of Disability

232 St. Theodul (sculpture)

1981. International Year of Disabled Persons.
769 **231** 40r. multicoloured 35 35

1981. 1600th Birth Anniv of St. Theodul.
770 **232** 80r. multicoloured 65 60

233 "Xanthoria parietina"

1981. Mosses and Lichens. Multicoloured.
771 40r. Type **233** 25 25
772 50r. "Parmelia physodes" . . 50 40
773 70r. "Sphagnum palustre" . . 65 60
774 80r. "Amblystegium serpens" 75 70

234 Gutenberg Castle

1981. Gutenberg Castle. Multicoloured.
775 20r. Type **234** 20 20
776 40r. Courtyard 25 30
777 50r. Parlour 45 35
778 1f.10 Great Hall . . . . . . 1·00 90

235 Cardinal Karl Borromaus von Mailand

236 St. Nicholas blessing Children

1981. Famous Visitors to Liechtenstein (1st series). Multicoloured.
779 40r. Type **235** 30 30
780 70r. Johann Wolfgang von Goethe (writer) 70 75
781 89r. Alexander Dumas the younger (writer) 75 65
782 1f. Hermann Hesse (writer) 85 75
See also Nos. 804/7 and 832/5.

1981. Christmas. Multicoloured.
783 20r. Type **236** 20 20
784 50r. Adoration of the Kings 40 40
785 80r. Holy Family 75 65

237 Peasant Revolt, 1525

1982. Europa. Multicoloured.
786 40r. Type **237** 35 35
787 80r. King Wenceslaus with Counts (Imperial direct rule, 1396) 75 70

1982. Arms of Bailiffs (3rd series). As T **221**. Multicoloured.
788 40r. Johann Kaiser, 1664 . . 35 25
789 70r. Joseph Anton Kaufmann, 1748 . . . . . 65 50
790 80r. Christoph Walser, 1690 75 60
791 1f.10 Stephan Banzer, 1658 1·00 95

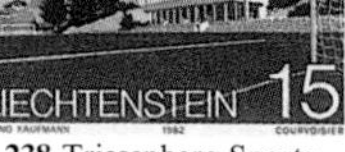

238 Triesenberg Sports Ground

239 Crown Prince Hans Adam

1982. World Cup Football Championship, Spain. Multicoloured.
792 15r. Type **238** 15 60
793 25r. Eschen/Mauren playing fields 25 25
794 1f.80 Rheinau playing fields, Balzers . . . . 1·50 1·40

1982. "Liba 82" Stamp Exhibition. Multicoloured.
795 1f. Type **239** 85 85
796 1f. Princess Marie Aglae . . 85 85

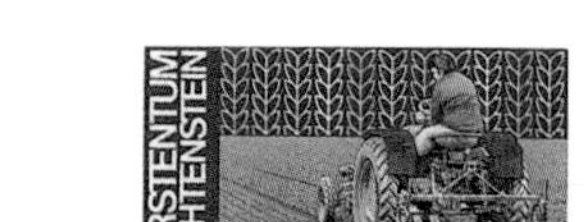

240 Tractor (agriculture)

1982. Rural Industries. Multicoloured.
797 30r. Type **240** 25 20
798 50r. Cutting flowers (horticulture) 45 35
799 70r. Workers with logs (forestry) 60 55
800 150r. Worker and milk (dairy farming) . . . . 1·30 1·20

241 "Neu Schellenberg"

1982. 150th Birth Anniv of Mortiz Menzinger (artist). Multicoloured.
801 40r. Type **241** 30 30
802 50r. "Vaduz" 60 45
803 100r. "Bendern" 95 90

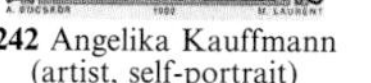

242 Angelika Kauffmann (artist, self-portrait)

243 Angel playing Lute

1982. Famous Visitors to Liechtenstein (2nd series). Multicoloured.
804 40r. Emperor Maximilian I (after Benhard Strigel) . . 25 25
805 70f. Georg Jenatsch (liberator of Grisons) 55 50
806 80r. Type **242** 65 55
807 1f. St. Fidelis of Sigmaringen 85 80

1982. Christmas. Details from High Altar by Jakob Russ, Chur Cathedral. Multicoloured.
808 20r. Type **243** 15 15
809 50r. Madonna and child . . 45 35
810 80r. Angel playing organ . . 70 65

244 Notker Balbulus of St. Gall

245 Shrove Thursday

1983. Europa. Multicoloured.
811 40r. Type **244** 30 25
812 80r. Hildegard of Bingen . . 80 55

1983. Shrovetide and Lent Customs. Mult.
813 40r. Type **245** 30 25
814 70r. Shrovetide carnival . . . 70 50
815 1f.80 Lent Sunday bonfire . . 1·70 1·40

246 River Bank

247 "Schaan"

1983. Anniversaries and Events. Multicoloured.
816 20r. Type **246** 35 20
817 40r. Montgolfier Brothers' balloon 50 35
818 50r. Airmail envelope 55 45
819 80r. Plant and hands holding spade 75 65

EVENTS: 20r. Council of Europe river and coasts protection campaign; 40r. Bicentenary of manned flight; 50r. World Communications Year; 80r. Overseas aid.

1983. Landscape Paintings by Anton Ender. Mult.
820 40r. Type **247** 35 25
821 50r. "Gutenberg Castle" . . 60 45
822 200r. "Steg Reservoir" . . . 2·50 1·90

248 Princess Gina

249 Pope John Paul II

1983. Multicoloured.
823 2f.50 Type **248** . . . . . . 2·75 2·50
824 3f. Prince Francis Joseph II 3·25 3·00

1983. Holy Year.
825 **249** 80r. multicoloured . . . . 1·20 80

250 Snowflakes and Stripes

251 Seeking Shelter

1983. Winter Olympic Games, Sarajevo. Mult.
826 40r. Type **250** 30 25
827 80r. Snowflake 85 75
828 1f.80 Snowflake and rays . . 1·70 1·70

1983. Christmas. Multicoloured.
829 20r. Type **251** 15 20
830 50r. Infant Jesus 55 35
831 80r. Three Kings 80 70

252 Aleksandr Vassilievich Suvorov (Russian general)

253 Bridge

1984. Famous Visitors to Liechtenstein (3rd series). Multicoloured.
832 40r. Type **252** 40 30
833 70r. Karl Rudolf von Buol-Schauenstein, Bishop of Chur 70 60
834 80r. Carl Zuckmayer (dramatist) 80 65
835 1f. Curt Goetz (actor) 95 90

1984. Europa. 25th Anniv of E.P.T. Conf.
836 **253** 50r. blue and deep blue 55 40
837 80r. pink and brown . . . 80 80

254 The Warning Messenger

255 Pole Vaulting

1984. Liechtenstein Legends. The Destruction of Trisona. Each brown, grey and blue.
838 35r. Type **254** 25 25
839 50r. The buried town 55 40
840 80r. The spared family . . . 80 70

1984. Olympic Games, Los Angeles. Mult.
841 70r. Type **255** 65 65
842 80r. Throwing the discus . . 80 80
843 1f. Putting the shot . . . . . 1·00 1·00

256 Currency (trade and banking)

1984. Occupations. Multicoloured.
844 5r. Type **256** 10 10
845 10r. Plumber adjusting pipe (building trade) 10 10
846 20r. Operating machinery (industry—production) . . 25 25
847 35r. Draughtswoman (building trade—planning) 35 35
848 45r. Office worker and world map (industry—sales) . . . 50 50
849 50r. Cook (tourism) 50 25
850 60r. Carpenter (building trade—interior decoration) 60 50
851 70r. Doctor injecting patient (medical services) 70 70
852 80r. Scientist (industrial research) 80 75
853 100r. Bricklayer (building trade) . . . . 1·00 85
854 120r. Flow chart (industry—administration) . . . . . 1·20 1·40
855 150r. Handstamping covers (post and communications) 1·90 1·40

257 Princess Marie

258 Annunciation

1984. Multicoloured.
856 1f.70 Type **257** . . . . . . 1·40 1·40
857 2f. Crown Prince Hans Adam 1·40 1·70

1984. Christmas. Multicoloured.
858 35r. Type **258** 40 30
859 50r. Holy Family 35 40
860 80r. The Three Kings 65 70

259 Apollo and the Muses playing Music (detail from 18th-century harpsichord lid)

1985. Europa. Music Year. Multicoloured.
861 50r. Type **259** 60 50
862 80r. Apollo and the Muses playing music (different) 85 75

260 St. Elisabeth Convent, Schaan

1985. Monasteries. Multicoloured.
863 50r. Type **260** 60 45
864 1f. Schellenberg Convent . . 1·10 1·00
865 1f.70 Gutenberg Mission, Balzers . . . . 1·50 1·50

261 Princess Gina and handing out of Rations

1985. 40th Anniv of Liechtenstein Red Cross. Multicoloured.
866 20r. Type **261** 30 25
867 50r. Princess Gina and Red Cross ambulance 55 60
868 120r. Princess Gina with refugee children . . . . . 95 1·20

262 Justice

264 "Portrait of a Canon" (Quentin Massys)

1985. Cardinal Virtues. Multicoloured.
869 35r. Type **262** 35 30
870 50r. Temperance 55 50
871 70r. Prudence 70 65
872 1f. Fortitude 75 85

1985. Paintings in Metropolitan Museum, New York. Multicoloured.
874 50r. Type **264** 70 60
875 1f. "Clara Serena Rubens" (Rubens) . . . . 1·10 1·10
876 1f.20 "Duke of Urbino" (Raphael) . . . . 70 1·20

265 Halberd used by Charles I's Bodyguard

1985. Guards' Weapons and Armour. Mult.
877 35r. Type **265** 45 35
878 50r. Morion used by Charles I's bodyguard 55 50
879 80r. Halberd used by Carl Eusebius's bodyguard . . . 75 70

266 Frankincense

267 Puppets performing Tragedy

1985. Christmas. Multicoloured.
880 35r. Type **266** 40 30
881 50r. Gold 65 60
882 80r. Myrrh 65 75

1985. Theatre. Multicoloured.
883 50r. Type **267** 65 65
884 80r. Puppets performing comedy 85 80
885 1f.50 Opera . . . . 1·30 1·20

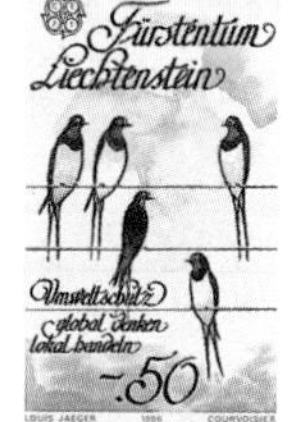

268 Courtyard

269 Barn Swallows

1986. Vaduz Castle. Multicoloured.
886 20r. Type **268** 25 20
887 25r. Keep 40 35
888 50r. Castle 60 55
889 90r. Inner gate 90 75
890 1f.10 Castle from gardens . . 1·20 1·00
891 1f.40 Courtyard (different) . . 1·50 1·30

1986. Europa. Birds. Multicoloured.
892 50r. Type **269** 60 55
893 90r. European robin 95 85

270 "Offerings"

271 Palm Sunday

1986. Lenten Fast.
894 **270** 1f.40 multicoloured . . . 1·40 1·40

1986. Religious Festivals. Multicoloured.
895 35r. Type **271** 45 30
896 50r. Wedding 55 35
897 70r. Rogation Day procession 80 55

272 Karl Freiherr Haus von Hausen

273 Francis Joseph II

1986. 125th Anniv of Liechtenstein Land Bank.
898 **272** 50r. brown, ochre and buff 55 55

1986. 80th Birthday of Prince Francis Joseph II.
899 **273** 3f.50 multicoloured . . . 3·25 3·00

274 Roebuck in Ruggeller Riet

275 Cabbage and Beetroot

1986. Hunting. Multicoloured.
900 35r. Type **274** 45 45
901 50r. Chamois at Rappenstein 70 70
902 1f.70 Stag in Lawena . . . . 1·50 1·50

1986. Field Crops. Multicoloured.
903 50r. Type **275** 50 50
904 80r. Red cabbages 85 85
905 90r. Potatoes, onions and garlic 95 95

276 Archangel Michael

277 Silver Fir

1986. Christmas. Multicoloured.
906 35r. Type **276** 30 30
907 50r. Archangel Gabriel . . . 65 65
908 90r. Archangel Raphael . . . 90 90

1986. Tree Bark. Multicoloured.
909 35r. Type **277** 30 30
910 90r. Norway spruce 95 95
911 1f.40 Pedunculate oak . . . 1·50 1·50

278 Gamprin Primary School

280 Niklaus von Flue

1987. Europa. Multicoloured.
912 50r. Type **278** 60 55
913 90r. Schellenberg parish church 95 90

1987. 500th Death Anniv of Niklaus von Flue (martyr).
914 **280** 1f.10 multicoloured . . . 1·20 1·20

281 Bullhead

282 Prince Alois (frame as in first stamps)

1987. Fishes (1st series). Multicoloured.
915 50r. Type **281** 55 55
916 90r. Brown trout 85 85
917 1f.10 European grayling . . . 1·40 1·40
See also Nos. 959/61.

1987. 75th Anniv of First Liechtenstein Stamps.
918 **282** 2f. multicoloured . . . . 2·20 2·20

283 Staircase

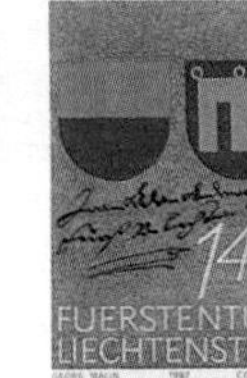

284 Arms

1987. Liechtenstein City Palace, Vienna. Multicoloured.
919 35r. Type **283** 35 35
920 50r. Minoritenplatz doorway 75 70
921 90r. Staircase (different) . . . 1·00 1·00

1987. 275th Anniv of Transfer of County of Vaduz to House of Liechtenstein.
922 **284** 1f.40 multicoloured . . . 1·50 1·50

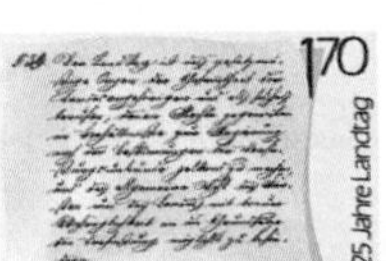

285 Constitution Charter, 1862

286 St. Matthew

1987. 125th Anniv of Liechtenstein Parliament.
923 **285** 1f.70 multicoloured . . . 1·80 1·80

1987. Christmas. Illuminations from Golden Book of Pfafers Abbey. Multicoloured.
924 35r. Type **286** 40 35
925 50r. St. Mark 60 60
926 60r. St. Luke 65 65
927 90r. St. John . . . . 1·20 1·20

287 "The Toil of the Cross-country Skier"

288 Dish Aerial

1987. Winter Olympic Games, Calgary (1988). Multicoloured.
928 25r. Type **287** 35 35
929 90r. "The Courageous Pioneers of Skiing" . . . . 1·00 1·00
930 1f.10 "As our Grandfathers used to ride on a Bobsled" 1·40 1·40

1988. Europa. Transport and Communications. Mult.
931 50r. Type **288** 40 40
932 90r. Maglev monorail . . . . 1·10 1·00

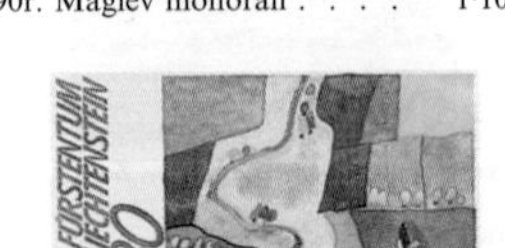

289 Agriculture

1988. European Campaign for Rural Areas. Multicoloured.
933 80r. Type **289** 80 80
934 90r. Village centre . . . . . 1·20 1·20
935 1f.70 Road . . . . 1·90 1·90

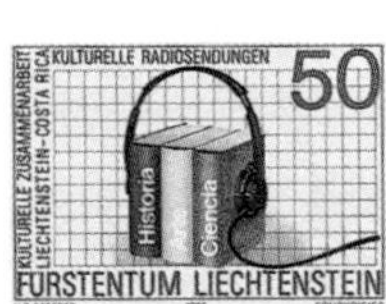

290 Headphones on Books (Radio Broadcasts)

292 St. Barbara's Shrine, Balzers

1988. Costa Rica–Liechtenstein Cultural Co-operation.
936 **290** 50r. multicoloured 60 60
937 – 1f.40 red, brown and green . . . . 1·50 1·50
DESIGN: 1f.40, Man with pen and radio (Adult education).

1988. Wayside Shrines. Multicoloured.
939 25r. Type **292** 35 35
940 35r. Shrine containing statues of Christ, St. Peter and St. Paul at Oberdorf, Vaduz 40 40
941 50r. St. Anthony of Egypt's shrine, Fallagass, Ruggel 50 50

293 Cycling

294 Joseph and Mary

1988. Olympic Games, Seoul. Multicoloured.
942 50r. Type **293** 45 45
943 80r. Gymnastics 80 85
944 90r. Running . . . . 1·00 1·10
945 1f.40 Equestrian event . . . 1·80 1·90

1988. Christmas. Multicoloured.
946 35r. Type **294** 35 30
947 50r. Baby Jesus 65 70
948 90r. Wise Men presenting gifts to Jesus . . . . . . 1·10 1·10

295 Letter beside Footstool (detail)

296 "Cat and Mouse"

1988. "The Letter" (portrait of Marie-Theresa, Princesse de Lamballe by Anton Hickel). Multicoloured.
949 50r. Type **295** 65 75
950 90r. Desk and writing materials (detail) . . . . 1·00 1·10
951 2f. "The Letter" (complete painting) . . . . 2·10 2·40

1989. Europa. Children's Games. Multicoloured.
952 50r. Type **296** 65 65
953 90r. "Hide and Seek" . . . . 1·20 1·20

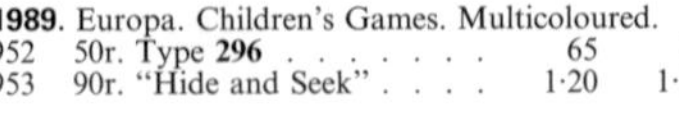

298 Rheinberger and Score

299 Little Ringed Plover

1989. 150th Birth Anniv of Josef Gabriel Rheinberger (composer).
954 **298** 2f.90 black, blue & purple 3·50 3·75

1989. Endangered Animals. Multicoloured.
955 25r. Type **299** 65 30
956 35r. Green tree frog 45 45
957 50r. "Libelloides coccajus" (lace-wing) 65 60
958 90r. Polecat . . . . 1·30 1·20

300 Northern Pike

1989. Fishes (2nd series). Multicoloured.
959 50r. Type **300** 50 55
960 1f.10 Brown trout . . . . . 1·20 1·30
961 1f.40 Stone loach . . . . . 1·70 1·90

301 Return of Cattle from Alpine Pastures

302 Falknis

1989. Autumn Customs. Multicoloured.
962 35r. Type **301** 40 45
963 50r. Peeling corn cobs . . . 70 75
964 80r. Cattle market 80 80

1989. Mountains. Watercolours by Josef Schadler.
965 – 5r. multicoloured 10 10
966 – 10r. multicoloured 10 10
967 – 35r. multicoloured 30 35
968 – 40r. multicoloured 40 50
969 – 45r. multicoloured 45 55
970 **302** 50r. multicoloured 45 55
971 – 60r. multicoloured 55 60
972 – 70r. multicoloured 65 75
973 – 75r. multicoloured 70 80
974 – 80r. violet, brown & black 75 85
975 – 1f. multicoloured . . . . 90 1·10
976 – 1f.20 multicoloured . . . 1·10 1·20
977 – 1f.50 multicoloured . . . 1·50 1·40
978 – 1f.60 multicoloured . . . 1·90 1·70
979 – 2f. multicoloured . . . . 1·60 1·75
DESIGNS: 5r. Augstenberg; 10r. Hahnenspiel; 35r. Nospitz; 40r. Ochsenkopf; 45r. Three Sisters; 60r. Kuhgrat; 70r. Galinakopf; 75r. Plassteikopf; 80pf. Naafkopf; 1f. Schonberg; 1f.20, Bleikaturm; 1f.50, Garselliturm; 1f.60, Schwarzhorn; 2f. Scheienkopf.

303 "Melchior and Balthasar"

304 Mace Quartz

1989. Christmas. Details of triptych by Hugo van der Goes. Multicoloured.
981 35r. Type **303** 55 45
982 50r. "Kaspar and Holy Family" (27 × 34 mm) . . 55 65
983 90r. "St. Stephen" 90 90

1989. Minerals. Multicoloured.
984 50r. Type **304** 60 60
985 1f.10 Globe pyrite . . . . . 1·50 1·50
986 1f.50 Calcite . . . . 1·90 1·90

305 Nendeln Forwarding Agency, 1864

306 Penny Black

1990. Europa. Post Office Buildings. Mult.
987 50r. Type **305** 65 65
988 90r. Vaduz post office, 1976 1·00 1·00

1990. 150th Anniv of the Penny Black.
989 **306** 1f.50 multicoloured . . . 1·90 1·80

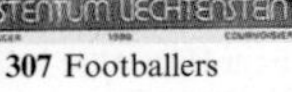

307 Footballers

308 Tureen, Oranges and Grapes

1990. World Cup Football Championship, Italy.
990 **307** 2f. multicoloured . . . . 2·30 2·20

1990. 9th Death Anniv of Benjamin Steck (painter). Multicoloured.
991 50r. Type **308** 75 75
992 80r. Apples and pewter bowl 1·00 1·00
993 1f.50 Basket, apples, cherries and pewter jug . . . . . . 1·50 1·50

309 Princess Gina **310** Common Pheasant

1990. Prince Francis Joseph II and Princess Gina Commemoration. Multicoloured.
994 2f. Type **309** . . . . 2·10 2·10
995 3f. Prince Francis Joseph II 3·25 3·25

1990. Game Birds. Multicoloured.
996 25r. Type **310** 35 35
997 50r. Black grouse 65 65
998 2f. Mallard . . . . 2·40 2·40

311 Annunciation **312** St. Nicholas

1990. Christmas. Paintings. Multicoloured.
999 35r. Type **311** 45 45
1000 50r. Nativity 55 60
1001 90r. Adoration of the Magi 1·00 1·00

1990. Winter Customs. Multicoloured.
1002 35r. Type **312** 45 45
1003 50r. Awakening on New Year's Eve 55 55
1004 1f.50 Giving New Year greetings . . . . 1·60 1·60

313 Mounted Courier **314** "Olympus 1" Satellite

1990. 500th Anniv of Regular European Postal Services.
1005 **313** 90r. multicoloured . . . 1·00 1·00

1991. Europa. Europe in Space. Multicoloured.
1006 50r. Type **314** 60 60
1007 90r. "Meteosat" satellite . . 1·00 1·00

315 St. Ignatius de Loyola (founder of Society of Jesus) **316** U.N. Emblem and Dove

1991. Anniversaries. Multicoloured.
1008 80r. Type **315** (500th birth anniv) 95 90
1009 90r. Wolfgang Amadeus Mozart (composer, death bicentenary) . . . . . . 1·00 1·00

1991. Admission to U.N. Membership (1990).
1010 **316** 2f.50 multicoloured . . . 2·75 2·75

317 Non-Commissioned Officer and Private **318** "Near Maloja" (Giovanni Giacometti)

1991. 125th Anniv of Last Mobilization of Liechtenstein's Military Contingent (to the Tyrol). Multicoloured.
1011 50r. Type **317** 55 60
1012 70r. Tunic, chest and portrait 75 70
1013 1f. Officer and private . . . 1·20 1·20

1991. 700th Anniv of Swiss Confederation. Paintings by Swiss artists. Multicoloured.
1014 50r. Type **318** 55 55
1015 80r. "Rhine Valley" (Ferdinand Gehr) 90 85
1016 90r. "Bergell" (Augusto Giacometti) 95 95
1017 1f.10 "Hoher Kasten" (Hedwig Scherrer) . . . . 1·20 1·20

319 Stampless and Modern Covers **320** Princess Marie

1991. "Liba 92" National Stamp Exhibition, Vaduz.
1018 **319** 90r. multicoloured . . . 1·00 1·00

1991. Multicoloured.
1019 3f. Type **320** . . . . 3·25 3·25
1020 3f.40 Prince Hans Adam II 3·50 3·50

321 Virgin of the Annunciation (exterior of left wing) **322** Cross-country Skiers and Testing for Drug Abuse

1991. Christmas. Details of the altar from St. Mamertus Chapel, Triesen. Multicoloured.
1021 50r. Type **321** 55 55
1022 80r. Madonna and Child (wood-carving attr. Jorg Syrlin, inner shrine) . . . 85 85
1023 90r. Angel Gabriel (exterior of right wing) 95 90

1991. Winter Olympic Games, Albertville. Mult.
1024 70r. Type **322** 80 80
1025 80r. Ice hockey player tackling opponent and helping him after fall . . 85 85
1026 1f.60 Downhill skier and fallen skier caught in safety net . . . . 1·90 1·80

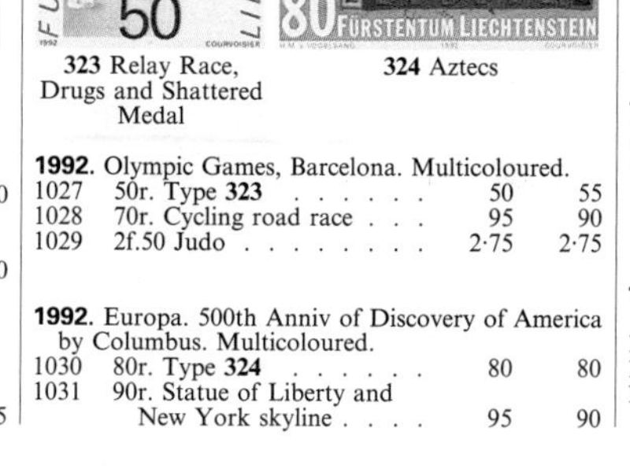

323 Relay Race, Drugs and Shattered Medal **324** Aztecs

1992. Olympic Games, Barcelona. Multicoloured.
1027 50r. Type **323** 50 55
1028 70r. Cycling road race . . . 95 90
1029 2f.50 Judo . . . . 2·75 2·75

1992. Europa. 500th Anniv of Discovery of America by Columbus. Multicoloured.
1030 80r. Type **324** 80 80
1031 90r. Statue of Liberty and New York skyline 95 90

325 Clown in Envelope ("Good Luck") **327** "Blechnum spicant"

1992. Greetings Stamps. Multicoloured.
1032 50r. Type **325** 50 50
1033 50r. Wedding rings in envelope and harlequin violinist 50 50
1034 50r. Postman blowing horn (31 × 21 mm) 50 50
1035 50r. Flying postman carrying letter sealed with heart (31 × 21 mm) . . . 50 50

1992. Ferns. Multicoloured.
1037 40r. Type **327** 40 40
1038 50r. Maidenhair spleenwort 55 50
1039 70r. Hart's-tongue 75 70
1040 2f.50 "Asplenium ruta-muraria" . . . . 2·40 2·50

328 Reading Edict **329** Chapel of St. Mamertus, Triesen

1992. 650th Anniv of County of Vaduz.
1041 **328** 1f.60 multicoloured . . . 1·70 1·70

1992. Christmas. Multicoloured.
1042 50r. Type **329** 55 50
1043 90r. Crib, St. Gallus's Church, Triesen 95 95
1044 1f.60 St. Mary's Chapel, Triesen . . . . 1·70 1·70

330 Crown Prince Alois **331** "Nafkopf and Huts, Steg"

1992.
1045 **330** 2f.50 multicoloured . . . 2·50 2·40

1993. 1400th Birth Anniv of Hans Gantner (painter). Multicoloured.
1046 50r. Type **331** 40 40
1047 60r. "Hunting Lodge, Sass" 70 70
1048 1f.80 "Red House, Vaduz" 2·20 2·20

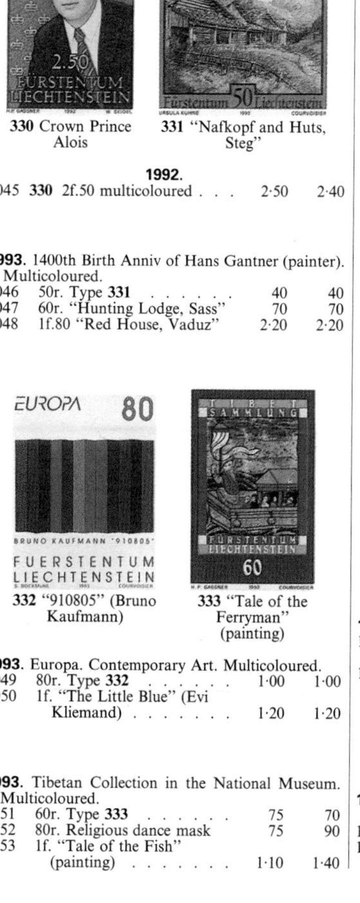
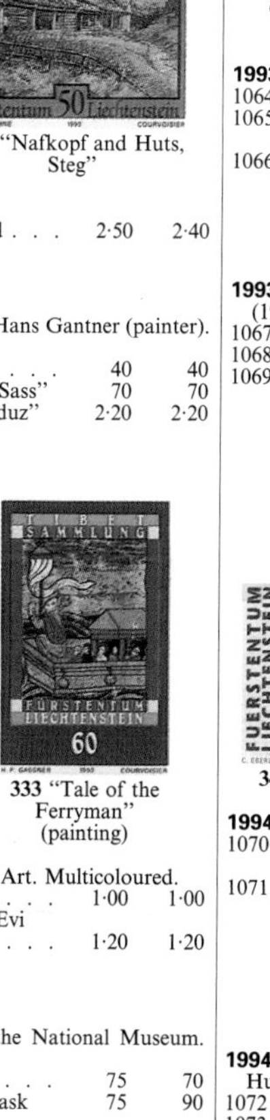

332 "910805" (Bruno Kaufmann) **333** "Tale of the Ferryman" (painting)

1993. Europa. Contemporary Art. Multicoloured.
1049 80r. Type **332** . . . . . . 1·00 1·00
1050 1f. "The Little Blue" (Evi Kliemand) . . . . 1·20 1·20

1993. Tibetan Collection in the National Museum. Multicoloured.
1051 60r. Type **333** 75 70
1052 80r. Religious dance mask 75 90
1053 1f. "Tale of the Fish" (painting) . . . . 1·10 1·40

334 "Tree of Life" **335** "The Black Hatter"

1993. Missionary Work.
1054 **334** 1f.80 multicoloured . . . 2·20 2·00

1993. Homage to Liechtenstein.
1055 **335** 2f.80 multicoloured . . . 3·75 3·75

337 Origanum **338** Eurasian Badger

1993. Flowers. Illustrations from "Hortus Botanicus Liechtensteinsis". Multicoloured.
1057 50r. Type **337** 75 65
1058 60r. Meadow sage 85 70
1059 1f. "Seseli annuum" . . . . 1·40 1·10
1060 2f.50 Large self-heal . . . . 2·20 2·75

1993. Animals. Multicoloured.
1061 60r. Type **338** 70 75
1062 80r. Beech marten . . . . . 1·00 1·00
1063 1f. Red fox . . . . 1·30 1·30

339 "Now that the Quiet Days are Coming ..." (Rainer Maria Rilke) **340** Ski Jump

1993. Christmas. Multicoloured.
1064 60r. Type **339** 70 70
1065 80r. "Can You See the Light ..." (Th. Friedrich) 1·00 1·00
1066 1f. "Christmas, Christmas ..." (R. A. Schroder) . . . 1·10 1·10

1993. Winter Olympic Games, Lillehammer, Norway (1994). Multicoloured.
1067 60r. Type **340** 90 90
1068 80r. Slalom . . . . 1·10 1·10
1069 2f.40 Bobsleighing . . . . . 2·50 2·50

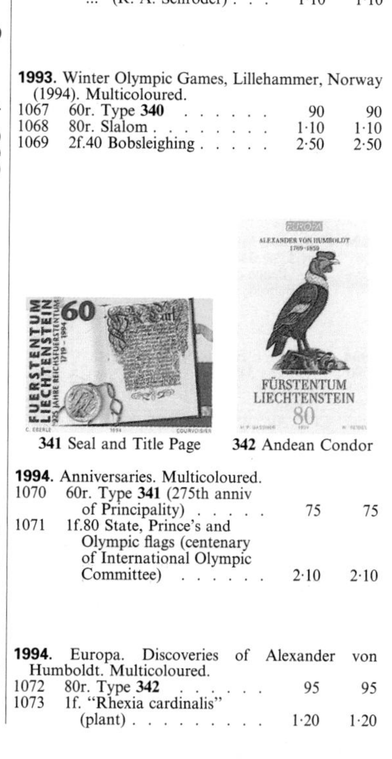

341 Seal and Title Page **342** Andean Condor

1994. Anniversaries. Multicoloured.
1070 60r. Type **341** (275th anniv of Principality) 75 75
1071 1f.80 State, Prince's and Olympic flags (centenary of International Olympic Committee) . . . . . . 2·10 2·10

1994. Europa. Discoveries of Alexander von Humboldt. Multicoloured.
1072 80r. Type **342** 95 95
1073 1f. "Rhexia cardinalis" (plant) . . . . 1·20 1·20

343 Football Pitch and Hopi Indians playing Kickball

344 Elephant with Letter

1994. World Cup Football Championship, U.S.A.
1074 **343** 2f.80 multicoloured . . . 3·25 3·25

1994. Greetings Stamps. Multicoloured.
1075 60r. Type **344** 75 75
1076 60r. Cherub with flower and hearts 75 75
1077 60r. Pig with four-leaf clover 75 75
1078 60r. Dog holding bunch of tulips 75 75

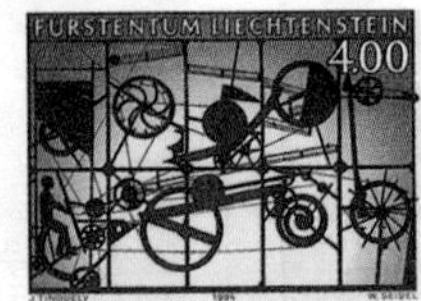

345 "Eulogy of Madness" (mobile, Jean Tinguely)

1994. Homage to Liechtenstein.
1079 **345** 4f. black, pink and violet 5·00 5·00

346 Spring

1994. Seasons of the Vine. Multicoloured.
1080 60r. Type **346** 75 75
1081 60r. Vine leaves (Summer) 75 75
1082 60r. Trunk in snowy landscape (Winter) . . . 75 75
1083 60r. Grapes (Autumn) . . . 75 75
Nos. 1080/3 were issued together, se-tenant, forming a composite design.

347 Strontium

1994. Minerals. Multicoloured.
1084 60r. Type **347** 85 90
1085 80r. Quartz . . . . 1·10 1·10
1086 3f.50 Iron dolomite . . . . 4·00 3·75

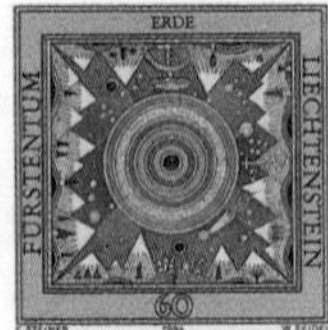

348 "The True Light"

349 Earth

1994. Christmas. Multicoloured.
1087 60r. Type **348** 70 70
1088 80r. "Peace on Earth" . . . 95 95
1089 1f. "Behold, the House of God" . . . . 1·20 1·20

1994. The Four Elements. Multicoloured.
1090 60r. Type **349** 75 75
1091 80r. Water 95 95
1092 1f. Fire . . . . 1·20 1·20
1093 2f.50 Air . . . . 2·75 2·75

350 "The Theme of all our Affairs must be Peace"

351 U.N. Flag and Bouquet of Flowers

1995. Europa. Peace and Freedom. Quotations of Franz Josef II. Multicoloured.
1094 80r. Type **350** 95 95
1095 1f. "Through Unity comes Strength and the Bearing of Sorrows" . . . . . . 1·30 1·30

1995. Anniversaries and Event. Multicoloured.
1096 60r. Princess Marie with children (50th anniv of Liechtenstein Red Cross) (horiz) 75 75
1097 1f.80 Type **351** (50th anniv of U.N.O.) . . . . 2·20 2·20
1098 3f.50 Alps (European Nature Conservation Year) . . . . 4·25 4·25

352 "Falknis Mountains"

353 "One Heart and One Soul"

1995. Birth Centenary of Anton Frommelt (painter). Multicoloured.
1099 60r. Type **352** 75 75
1100 80r. "Three Oaks" . . . . 1·00 1·00
1101 4f.10 "The Rhine" . . . . 4·75 4·75

1995. Greetings Stamps. Multicoloured.
1102 60r. Type **353** 75 75
1103 60r. Bandage round sunflower ("Get Well") 75 75
1104 60r. Baby arriving over rainbow ("Hurrah! Here I am") 75 75
1105 60r. Delivering letter by hot-air balloon ("Write again") 75 75

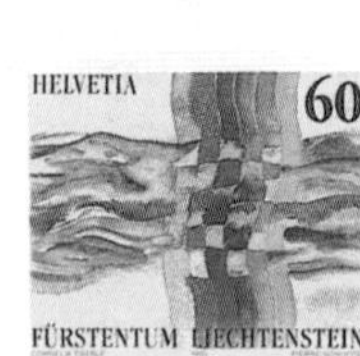

354 Coloured Ribbons woven through River

355 Arnica

1995. Liechtenstein–Switzerland Co-operation.
1106 **354** 60r. multicoloured . . . 75 75
No. 1106 was valid for use in both Liechtenstein and Switzerland (see No. 1308 of Switzerland).

1995. Medicinal Plants. Multicoloured.
1107 60r. Type **355** 70 75
1108 80r. Giant nettle 95 75
1109 1f.80 Common valerian . . 2·20 2·20
1110 3f.50 Fig-wort . . . . . . 3·50 3·75

356 Angel (detail of painting)

357 "Lady with Lap-dog" (Paul Wunderlich)

1995. Christmas. Painting by Lorenzo Monaco. Multicoloured.
1111 60r. Type **356** 70 70
1112 80r. "Virgin Mary with Infant and Two Angels" 95 95
1113 1f. Angel facing left (detail of painting) . . . . . . 1·20 1·20

1995. Homage to Liechtenstein.
1114 **357** 4f. multicoloured . . . . 4·75 4·75

358 Eschen

359 Crucible

1996. Scenes. Multicoloured.
1115 10r. Type **358** 10 10
1116 20r. Planken 25 25
1117 50r. Ruggell 55 55
1117a 60r. Balzers 60 60
1117b 70r. Schellenberg 75 75
1118 80r. Ruggell 85 85
1120 1f. Nendeln . . . . 1·10 1·10
1120a 1f.10 Eschen . . . . . . 1·20 1·20
1122 1f.20 Triesen . . . . . . 1·30 1·30
1123 1f.30 Triesen . . . . . . 1·40 1·40
1124 1f.40 Mauren . . . . . . 1·50 1·50
1125 1f.70 Schaanwald . . . . 1·80 1·80
1125a 1f.80 Malbun . . . . . . 1·90 1·90
1125b 1f.90 Schaan . . . . . . 2·10 2·10
1126 2f. Gamprin . . . . 2·10 2·10
1126a 2f.20 Balzers . . . . . . 2·30 2·30
1127 4f. Triesenberg . . . . . . 4·25 4·25
1127a 4f.50 Bendern . . . . . . 4·75 4·75
1128 5f. Vaduz Castle . . . . . 5·25 5·25

1996. Bronze Age in Europe.
1130 **359** 90r. multicoloured . . . 1·10 1·10

360 Kinsky and Diary Extract, 7 March 1917

1996. Europa. Famous Women. Nora, Countess Kinsky (mother of Princess Gina of Liechtenstein)
1131 **360** 90r. grey, purple and blue . . . . 1·00 1·00
1132 – 1f.10 grey, blue and purple . . . . 1·20 1·20
DESIGN: 1f.10, Kinsky and diary extract for 28 February 1917.

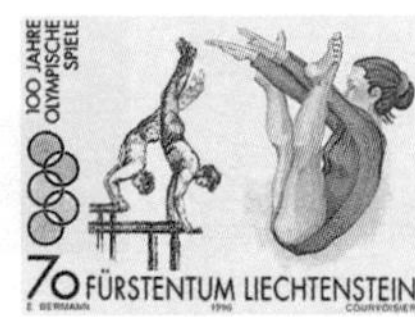

361 Gymnastics

1996. Centenary of Modern Olympic Games. Multicoloured.
1133 70r. Type **361** 75 75
1134 90r. Hurdling 95 95
1135 1f.10 Cycling . . . . 1·30 1·30

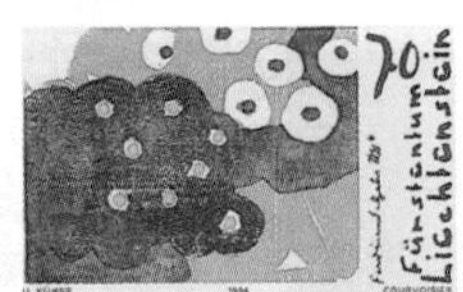

362 "Primroses"

1996. Birth Centenary of Ferdinand Gehr (painter). Multicoloured.
1136 70r. Type **362** 80 80
1137 90r. "Daisies" . . . . . . 1·00 1·00
1138 1f.10 "Poppy" . . . . . . 1·20 1·20
1139 1f.80 "Buttercups" (33 × 23 mm) . . . . . . 2·00 2·00

363 State Arms

1996.
1140 **363** 10f. multicoloured . . . 10·50 10·50

364 Veldkirch, 1550

1996. Millenary of Austria.
1141 **364** 90r. multicoloured . . . 1·10 1·10

1996. 43rd Death Anniv of Eugen Zotow (painter). Multicoloured.
1142 70r. Type **365** 75 75
1143 1f.10 "Three Bathers in a Berlin Park" 75 75
1144 1f.40 "Vaduz" . . . . . . 1·00 1·00

1996. Christmas. Illustrations from Illuminated Manuscript "Liber Viventium Fabariensis". Multicoloured.
1145 70r. Type **366** 80 75
1146 90r. Emblems of St. Mark 1·00 95
1147 1f.10 Emblems of St. Luke 1·20 1·20
1148 1f.80 Emblems of St. John 2·00 2·00

365 "Poltava"

366 St. Matthew

367 Schubert

368 The Wild Gnomes

1997. Birth Bicent of Franz Schubert (composer).
1149 **367** 70r. multicoloured . . . 85 85

1997. Europa. Tales and Legends. Multicoloured.
1150 90r. Type **368** 90 90
1151 1f.10 Man, pumpkin and rabbit (The Foal of Planken) . . . . 1·20 1·20

369 "Madonna and Child with St. Lucius and St. Florinus" (Gabriel Dreher)

1997. National Patron Saints.
1152 **369** 20f. multicoloured . . . 17·00 17·00

370 "Phaeolepiota aurea"

1997. Fungi (1st series). Multicoloured.
1153 70r. Type **370** 70 70
1154 90r. "Helvella silvicola" . . 90 90
1155 1f.10 Orange peel fungus . . 1·20 1·20
See also Nos. 1238/40.

371 Steam Train, Schaanwald Halt

372 "Girl with Flower" (Enrico Baj)

1997. 125th Anniv of Liechtenstein Railways. Mult.
1156 70r. Type **371** 75 75
1157 90r. Diesel-electric train, Nendeln station 95 95
1158 1f.80 Electric train, Schaan-Vaduz station . . . . . . 1·90 1·90

1997. Homage to Liechtenstein.
1159 **372** 70r. multicoloured . . . 75 75

373 Basket of Roses

374 Cross-country skiing

1997. Christmas. Glass Tree Decorations. Multicoloured.
1160 70r. Type **373** 70 70
1161 90r. Bell 90 90
1162 1f.10 Bauble . . . . 1·10 1·10

1997. Winter Olympic Games, Nagano, Japan (1998). Skiing. Multicoloured.
1163 70r. Type **374** 70 70
1164 90r. Slalom 95 95
1165 1f.80 Downhill . . . . . . 1·90 1·90

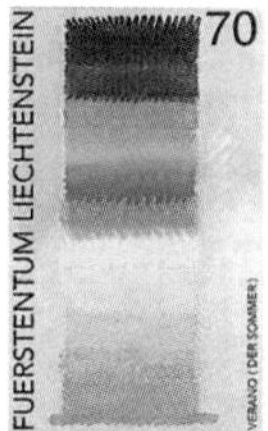

375 "Verano (The Summer)"

1998. Homage to Liechtenstein. Paintings by Heinz Mack. Multicoloured.
1166 70r. Type **375** 70 70
1167 70r. "Homage to Liechtenstein" 70 70
1168 70r. "Between Day and Dream" 70 70
1169 70r. "Salute Cirico!" 70 70

376 Prince's Festival Procession, Vaduz

1998. Europa. National Festivals. Multicoloured.
1170 90r. Type **376** 95 95
1171 1f.10 Music Societies Festival, Gutenberg Castle, Balzers . . . . . 1·20 1·20

377 National Flags on Bridge

1998. 75th Anniv of Liechtenstein–Switzerland Customs Treaty.
1172 **377** 1f.70 multicoloured . . . 1·80 1·80

378 Goalkeeper

1998. World Cup Football Championship, France.
1173 **378** 1f.80 multicoloured . . . 1·90 1·90

379 Clown with Queen of Hearts

380 Wooden Milk Vat

1998. Greeting Stamps. Clowns. Multicoloured.
1174 70r. Type **379** 70 70
1175 70r. Clown holding four-leaf clovers 70 70
1176 70r. Clown raising hat . . . 70 70
1177 70r. Clown holding heart . . 70 70

1998. Traditional Crafts (1st series). Multicoloured.
1178 90r. Type **380** 90 90
1179 2f.20 Clog . . . . 2·20 2·20
1180 3f.50 Wheel . . . . 3·50 3·50
See also Nos. 1257/9.

381 Expelling Johann Langer from Liechtenstein

1998. 150th Anniv of 1848 Revolutions in Europe.
1181 **381** 1f.80 multicoloured . . . 1·90 1·90

382 Virgin Mary

1998. Christmas. Multicoloured.
1182 70r. Type **382** 75 75
1183 90r. "The Nativity" (35 × 26 mm) 90 90
1184 1f.10 Joseph . . . . 1·20 1·20
Nos. 1182 and 1184 show details of the complete relief depicted on No. 1183.

383 Zum Lowen Guest House **384** Automatic and Manual Switchboards

1998. Preservation of Historical Environment. Hinterschellenberg. Multicoloured.
1185 90r. Type **383** 90 95
1186 1f.70 St. George's Chapel (vert) . . . . 1·90 1·90
1187 1f.80 Houses . . . . 1·90 1·90

1998. Centenary of Telephone in Liechtenstein.
1188 **384** 2f.80 multicoloured . . . 3·00 3·00

386 Smooth Snake and Schwabbrunnen-Aescher Nature Park

387 Council Anniversary Emblem and Silhouettes

1999. Europa. Parks and Gardens. Multicoloured.
1190 90r. Type **386** . . . . . . 1·00 1·00
1191 1f.10 Corn crake and Ruggell marsh . . . . . 1·10 1·10

1999. Anniversaries and Event. Multicoloured.
1192 70r. Type **387** (50th anniv of Council of Europe and European Convention on Human Rights) 75 75
1193 70r. Bird with envelope in beak (125th anniv of U.P.U.) 75 75
1194 70r. Heart in hand (75th anniv of Caritas Liechtenstein (welfare organization)) 75 75

388 Judo

1999. 8th European Small States Games, Liechtenstein. Multicoloured.
1195 70r. Type **388** 70 70
1196 70r. Swimming 70 70
1197 70r. Throwing the javelin . . 70 70
1198 90r. Cycling 95 95
1199 90r. Shooting 95 95
1200 90r. Tennis 95 95
1201 90r. Squash 95 95
1202 90r. Table tennis 95 95
1203 90r. Volleyball 95 95

389 "Herrengasse"

1999. Paintings by Eugen Verling. Multicoloured.
1204 70r. Type **389** 85 85
1205 2f. "Old Vaduz with Castle" 1·20 1·20
1206 4f. "House in Furst-Franz-Josef Street, Vaduz" . . . 5·00 5·00

390 Scene from "Faust", Act I

1999. 250th Birth Anniv of Johann Wolfgang Goethe (poet and playwright). Multicoloured.
1207 1f.40 Type **390** . . . . . . 1·50 1·50
1208 1f.70 Faust and the Devil sealing wager . . . . . . 1·80 1·80

391 "The Annunciation"

392 Identification Mark on Door, Ubersaxen

1999. Christmas. Paintings by Joseph Walser from Chapel of Our Lady of Comfort, Dux. Mult.
1209 70r. Type **391** 75 75
1210 90r. "Nativity" 95 95
1211 1f.10 "Adoration" . . . . . 1·20 1·20

1999. Walser Identification Marks. Multicoloured.
1212 70r. Type **392** 75 75
1213 90r. Mark on mural 95 95
1214 1f.80 Mark on axe . . . . 1·90 1·90

393 Gutenberg

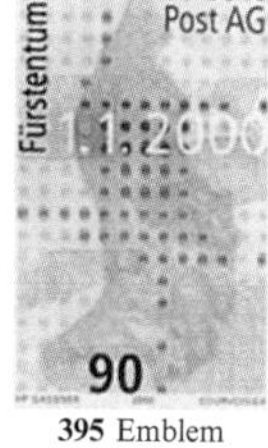

395 Emblem

1999. 600th Birth Anniv of Johannes Gutenberg (inventor of printing press).
1215 **393** 3f.60 multicoloured . . . 2·75 2·75

2000. Provision of Postal Services by Liechtenstein Post in Partnership with Swiss Post.
1217 **395** 90r. multicoloured . . . 95 95

396 "Mars and Rhea Silvia" (Peter Paul Rubens)

2000. Paintings. Multicoloured.
1218 70r. Type **396** 75 75
1219 1f.80 "Cupid with Soap-Bubble" (Rembrandt) . . 1·90 1·90

397 "Fragrance of Humus"

398 "Building Europe"

2000. "EXPO 2000" World's Fair, Hanover, Germany. Paintings by Friedensreich Hundertwasser. Multicoloured.
1220 70r. Type **397** 75 75
1221 90r. "Do Not Wait Houses-Move" . . . . 1·00 1·00
1222 1f.10 "The Car: a Drive Towards Nature and Creation" . . . . 1·20 1·20

2000. Europa.
1223 **398** 1f.10 multicoloured . . . 1·10 1·10

399 "Dove of Peace" (Antonio Martini)

2000. "Peace 2000". Paintings by members of Association of Mouth and Foot Painting Artists. Mult.
1224 1f.40 Type **399** . . . . . . 1·50 1·50
1225 1f.70 "World Peace" (Alberto Alvarez) . . . . 1·80 1·80
1226 2f.20 "Rainbow" (Eiichi Minami) . . . . 2·30 2·30

400 Koalas on Rings (Gymnastics)

2000. Olympic Games, Sydney. Multicoloured.
1227 80r. Type **400** 80 80
1228 1f. Joey leaping over crossbar (High jump) . . 95 95
1229 1f.30 Emus approaching finish line (Athletics) . . . 1·40 1·40
1230 1f.80 Duckbill platypuses in swimming race . . . . . 1·90 1·90

401 "The Dreaming Bee" (Joan Miro)

2000. Inauguration of Art Museum. Multicoloured.
1231 80r. Type **401** 85 85
1232 1f.20 "Cube" (Sol LeWitt) 1·30 1·30
1233 2f. "Bouquet of Flowers" (Raelant Savery) (31 × 46 mm) . . . . . . 2·00 2·00

402 "Peace Doves"

2000. 25th Anniv of Organization for Security and Co-operation in Europe.
1234 **402** 1f.30 multicoloured . . . 1·40 1·40

403 Root Crib

2000. Christmas. Cribs. Multicoloured.
1235 80r. Type **403** 80 80
1236 1f.30 Oriental crib . . . . . 1·40 1·40
1237 1f.80 Crib with cloth figures 1·90 1·90

2000. Fungi (2nd series). As T **370**. Multicoloured.
1238 90r. Mycena adonis 90 90
1239 1f.10 Chalciporus amarellus 1·20 1·20
1240 2f. Pink waxcap . . . . . . 2·10 2·10

404 Postman delivering Parcel

2001. Greetings Stamps. Multicoloured.
1241 70r. Type **404** 75 75
1242 70r. Postman delivering flowers 75 75
Nos. 1241/2 are for the stamps with the parcel (1241) and flowers (1242) intact. The parcel and flowers can be scratched away to reveal a greetings message.

405 Silver Easter Egg

406 Mountain Spring

2001. Decorated Easter Eggs. Multicoloured.
1243 1f.20 Type **405** . . . . . . 1·30 1·30
1244 1f.80 Cloissonne egg . . . . 2·00 2·00
1245 2f. Porcelain egg . . . . . 2·00 2·00

2001. Europa. Water Resources.
1246 **406** 1f.30 multicoloured . . . 1·40 1·40

407 Emblem

2001. Liechtenstein Presidency of Council of Europe.
1247 **407** 1f.80 multicoloured . . . 1·90 1·90

408 Carolingian Cruciform Fibula

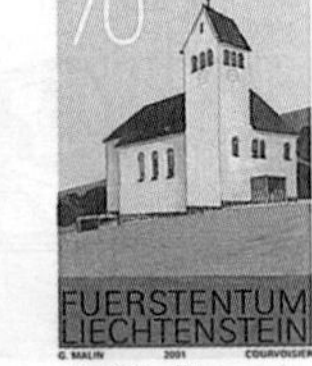

409 St. Theresa's Chapel, Schaanwald

2001. Centenary of Historical Association. Multicoloured.
1248 70r. Type **408** 75 75
1249 70r. "Mars of Gutenberg" (statue) 75 75

2001. Preservation of Historical Environment (2nd series). Multicoloured.
1250 70r. Type **409** 75 75
1251 90r. St. Johann's Torkel (wine press), Mauren . . 1·00 1·00
1252 1f.10 Pirsch Transformer Station, Schaanwald . . . 1·10 1·10
See also Nos. 1274/5.

410 Mary and kneeling Votant (Chapel of Our Lady, Dux, Schann)

2001. Votive Paintings. Multicoloured.
1253 70r. Type **410** 70 70
1254 1f.20 Mary and Jesus, St. George among other Saints, and text of vow (St. George's Chapel, Schellenberg) . . . . . . 1·20 1·20
1255 1f.30 Mary, St. Joseph of Arimathea, St. Christopher, Johann Christoph Walser (votant) and text of vow (Chapel of Our Lady, Dux, Schann) . . . . 1·50 1·50

411 Rheinberger and Scene from *Zauberwort* (song cycle)

412 "Annunciation"

2001. Death Centenary of Josef Gabriel Rheinberger (composer).
1256 **411** 3f.50 multicoloured . . . 3·75 3·75

2001. Traditional Crafts (2nd series). As T **380**. Multicoloured.
1257 70r. Agricultural implements and horseshoe 75 75
1258 90r. Rake . . . . 1·00 1·00
1259 1f.20 Harness . . . . 1·30 1·30

2001. Christmas. Medallions from The Joyful, Sorrowful and Glorious Rosary Cycle. Multicoloured.
1260 70r. Type **412** 70 70
1261 90r. Nativity 90 90
1262 1f.30 Presentation of Jesus at the Temple . . . . . . 1·50 1·50

413 Square

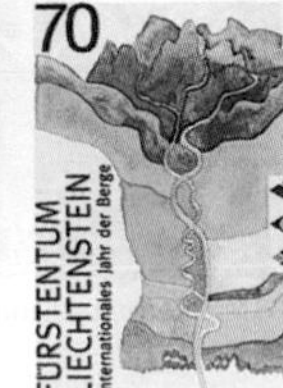

414 Mountains and River

2001. Paintings by Gottfried Honeggar. Mult.
1263 1f.80 Type **413** . . . . . . 2·00 2·00
1264 2f.20 Circle . . . . 2·20 2·20

2002. International Year of Mountains and 50th Anniv of the International Commission of Alpine Protection. Multicoloured.
1265 70r. Type **414** 65 65
1266 1f.20 Stylized mountains . . 1·10 1·10

415 "Schellenberg"

2002. 30th Death Anniv of Friedrich Kaufmann (artist). Multicoloured.
1267 70r. Type **415** 65 65
1268 1f.30 "Schaan" . . . . . . 1·20 1·20
1269 1f.80 "Steg" . . . . 3·50 3·50

416 Space Shuttle and Bee

2002. Liechtenstein's participation in N.A.S.A. Space Technology and Research Students Project.
1270 **416** 90r. multicoloured . . . 85 85
The project submitted by the Liechtenstein Gymnasium concerned the study of the effects of space on carpenter bees.

417 Man on Tightrope

2002. Europa. Circus. Multicoloured.
1271 90r. Type **417** 85 85
1272 1f.30 Juggler . . . . 1·20 1·20

418 Emblem

2002. "Liba '02" National Stamp Exhibition, Vaduz (1st issue).
1273 **418** 1f.20 multicoloured . . . 1·10 1·10
See also Nos. 1282/3.

419 Houses, Popers

2002. Preservation of Historical Environment (2nd series). Multicoloured.
1274 70r. Type **419** 65 65
1275 1f.20 House, Weiherring . . 1·10 1·10

420 Footballers

2002. World Cup Football Championship, Japan and South Korea.
1276 **420** 1f.80 multicoloured . . . 1·70 1·70

421 Princess Marie

2002. The Royal Couple. Multicoloured.
1277 3f. Type **421** . . . . 2·75 2·75
1278 3f.50 Prince Hans-Adam II . 3·25 3·25

422 Ghost Orchid (*Epipogium aphyllum*)

423 Stamps and Emblem

2002. Orchids. Multicoloured.
1279 70r. Type **422** 65 65
1280 1f.20 Fly orchid (*Ophrys insectifera*) . . . . 1·10 1·10
1281 1f.30 Black vanilla orchid (*Nigritella nigra*) . . . . 1·20 1·20

2002. "Liba 02" National Stamp Exhibition, Vaduz (2nd issue). 90th Anniv of First Liechtenstein Stamps. Multicoloured.
1282 90r. Type **423** 85 85
1283 1f.30 Stamps showing royal family . . . . 1·20 1·20

424 Princess Sophie

2002. Prince Alois and Princess Sophie. Multicoloured.
1284 2f. Type **424** . . . . 1·90 1·90
1285 2f.50 Prince Alois . . . . . 2·30 2·30

425 Mary and Joseph

2002. Christmas. Batik. Multicoloured.
1286 70r. Type **425** 65 65
1287 1f.20 Nativity . . . . 1·10 1·10
1288 1f.80 Flight into Egypt . . . 1·70 1·70

426 The Eagle, Vaduz

2002. Inn Signs. Multicoloured.
1289 1f.20 Type **426** . . . . . . 1·10 1·10
1290 1f.80 The Angel, Balzers . . 1·70 1·70
1291 3f. The Eagle, Bendern . . . 2·75 2·75

OFFICIAL STAMPS

1932. Stamps of 1930 optd **REGIERUNGS DIENSTSACHE** under crown.
O118 5r. green . . . . 8·00 6·25
O119 10r. lilac . . . . 40·00 6·25
O120 20r. red . . . . 40·00 6·25
O121 30r. blue . . . . 8·75 8·00
O122 35r. green . . . . 6·25 16·00
O123 50r. black . . . . 36·00 10·00
O124 60r. green . . . . 7·50 21·00
O125 1f.20 brown . . . . 90·00 £225

1933. Nos. 121 and 123 optd **REGIERUNGS DIENSTSACHE** in circle round crown.
O126 **38** 25r. orange . . . . . . 25·00 25·00
O127 – 1f.20 brown . . . . . . 55·00 £170

1934. Nos. 128 etc. optd **REGIERUNGS DIENSTSACHE** in circle round crown.
O150 **41** 5r. green . . . . 1·00 1·20
O151 – 10r. violet . . . . 2·50 95
O152 – 15r. orange . . . . . . 30 1·50
O153 – 20r. red 35 95
O155 – 25r. brown . . . . . . 1·90 9·25
O156 – 30r. blue . . . . 2·50 5·00
O157 **42** 50r. brown . . . . . . 1·00 1·90
O158 – 90r. green . . . . . . 5·50 25·00
O159 – 1f.50 brown . . . . . . 32·00 £110

1937. Stamps of 1937 optd **REGIERUNGS DIENSTSACHE** in circle round crown.
O174 **51** 5r. green and buff . . . 20 20
O175 – 10r. violet and buff . . . 35 60
O176 – 20r. red and buff . . . . 95 1·10
O177 – 25r. brown and buff . . 55 1·40
O178 – 30r. blue and buff . . . 1·10 1·40
O179 – 50r. brown and buff . . 60 1·10
O180 – 1f. purple and buff . . . 75 5·50
O181 – 1f.50 grey and buff . . . 2·20 8·00

1947. Stamps of 1944 optd **DIENSTMARKE** and crown.
O255 5r. green . . . . 1·10 75
O256 10r. violet . . . . 1·10 95
O257 20r. red . . . . 1·60 1·00
O258 30r. blue . . . . 1·70 1·40
O259 50r. grey . . . . 1·70 2·75
O260 1f. red . . . . 7·50 9·25
O261 1f.50 blue . . . . 7·50 9·25

O 86

O 198 Government Building, Vaduz

1950. Buff paper.
O287 **O 86** 5r. purple and grey . . 10 10
O288 10r. green and mauve 10 10
O289 20r. brown and blue 25 25
O290 30r. purple and red . . 35 35
O291 40r. blue and brown 50 50
O292 55r. green and red . . 85 1·00
O293 60r. grey and mauve 1·40 1·10
O294 80r. orange and grey 95 95
O295 90r. brown and blue 1·00 1·00
O296 1f.20 turquoise and orange . . . . . . 1·40 1·40

1968. White paper.
O495 **O 86** 5r. brown and orange 10 10
O496 10r. violet and red . . 10 10
O497 20r. red and green . . 25 25
O498 30r. green and red . . 35 35
O499 50r. blue and red . . . 60 60
O500 60r. orange and blue 60 60
O501 70r. purple and green 75 75
O502 80r. green and red . . 75 75
O503 95r. green and red . . 1·20 1·20
O504 1f. purple & turquoise 1·00 1·00
O505 1f.20 brown & turq . . 1·20 1·20
O506 2f. brown and orange 2·50 2·50

1976.
O652 **O 198** 10r. brown and violet 10 10
O653 20r. red and blue . . 10 25
O654 35r. blue and red . . 20 60
O655 40r. violet and green 30 30
O656 50r. green and mauve 35 30
O657 70r. purple and green 45 50
O658 80r. green and purple 50 60
O659 90r. violet and blue 55 60
O660 1f. grey and purple 60 50
O661 1f.10 brown and blue 75 1·20
O662 1f.50 green and red 95 75
O663 2f. orange and blue 1·20 60
O664 5f. purple and orange 8·75 7·50

POSTAGE DUE STAMPS

D 11

D 25

D 30

1920.
D43 **D 11** 5h. red 20 35
D44 10h. red 20 35
D45 15h. red 20 35
D46 20h. red 20 35
D47 25h. red 20 35

D48 30h. red 20 35
D49 40h. red 20 35
D50 50h. red 20 35
D51 80h. red 20 35
D52 1k. blue 20 35
D53 2k. blue 20 35
D54 5k. blue 20 35

1928.
D84 D 25 5r. red and violet 60 1·90
D85 10r. red and violet 1·20 1·70
D86 15r. red and violet 2·50 10·00
D87 20r. red and violet 2·10 1·90
D88 25r. red and violet 2·10 7·50
D89 30r. red and violet 5·00 9·25
D90 40r. red and violet 6·75 10·50
D91 50r. red and violet 6·75 15·00

1940.
D189 D 58 5r. red and blue 1·20 2·50
D190 10r. red and blue 50 1·00
D191 15r. red and blue 60 5·00
D192 20r. red and blue 75 1·20
D193 25r. red and blue 1·40 2·75
D194 30r. red and blue 2·75 5·00
D195 40r. red and blue 2·75 4·25
D196 50r. red and blue 3·00 5·00

LITHUANIA Pt. 10

A country on the Baltic Sea, under Russian rule until occupied by the Germans in the first World War (see German Eastern Command). It was an independent republic from 1918 to 1940, when it was incorporated into the U.S.S.R.

Lithuania declared its independence in 1990, and the U.S.S.R. formally recognized the republic in 1991.

1918. 100 skatiku = 1 auksinas.
1922. 100 centu = 1 litas.
1990. 100 kopeks = 1 rouble.
1992. Talons.
1993. 100 centu = 1 litas.

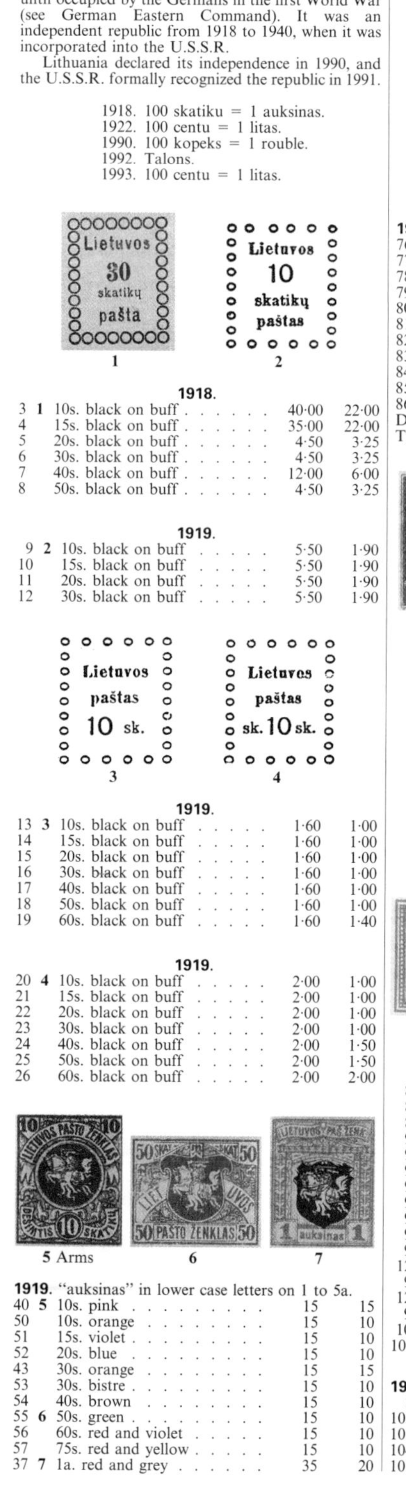

1 2

1918.
3 1 10s. black on buff 40·00 22·00
4 15s. black on buff 35·00 22·00
5 20s. black on buff 4·50 3·25
6 30s. black on buff 4·50 3·25
7 40s. black on buff 12·00 6·00
8 50s. black on buff 4·50 3·25

1919.
9 2 10s. black on buff 5·50 1·90
10 15s. black on buff 5·50 1·90
11 20s. black on buff 5·50 1·90
12 30s. black on buff 5·50 1·90

3 4

1919.
13 3 10s. black on buff 1·60 1·00
14 15s. black on buff 1·60 1·00
15 20s. black on buff 1·60 1·00
16 30s. black on buff 1·60 1·00
17 40s. black on buff 1·60 1·00
18 50s. black on buff 1·60 1·00
19 60s. black on buff 1·60 1·40

1919.
20 4 10s. black on buff 2·00 1·00
21 15s. black on buff 2·00 1·00
22 20s. black on buff 2·00 1·00
23 30s. black on buff 2·00 1·00
24 40s. black on buff 2·00 1·50
25 50s. black on buff 2·00 1·50
26 60s. black on buff 2·00 2·00

5 Arms 6 7

1919. "auksinas" in lower case letters on 1 to 5a.
40 5 10s. pink 15 15
50 10s. orange 15 10
51 15s. violet 15 10
52 20s. blue 15 10
43 30s. orange 15 15
53 30s. bistre 15 10
54 40s. brown 15 10
55 6 50s. green 15 10
56 60s. red and violet 15 10
57 75s. red and yellow 15 10
37 7 1a. red and grey 35 20
38 3a. red and brown 35 20
39 5a. red and green 40 30

1921. As T 7, but "AUKSINAS" or "AUKSINAI" in capital letters.
58 7 1a. red and grey 15 10
59 3a. red and brown 25 15
60 5a. red and green 40 25

11 Lithuania receiving Independence
12 Lithuania arises

1920. 2nd Anniv of Independence.
65 11 10s. lake 1·50 2·00
66 15s. lilac 1·50 2·00
67 20s. blue 1·50 2·00
68 12 30s. brown 1·50 2·00
69 – 40s. green and brown 1·50 2·00
70 12 50s. red 1·50 2·00
71 60s. lilac 1·50 2·00
72 – 80s. red and violet 1·50 2·00
73 – 1a. red and green 1·50 2·00
74 – 3a. red and brown 1·60 2·00
75 – 5a. red and green 1·60 2·00
DESIGNS—VERT: 40s., 80s., 1a. Lithuania with chains broken; 3, 5a. (25 × 25 mm) Arms.

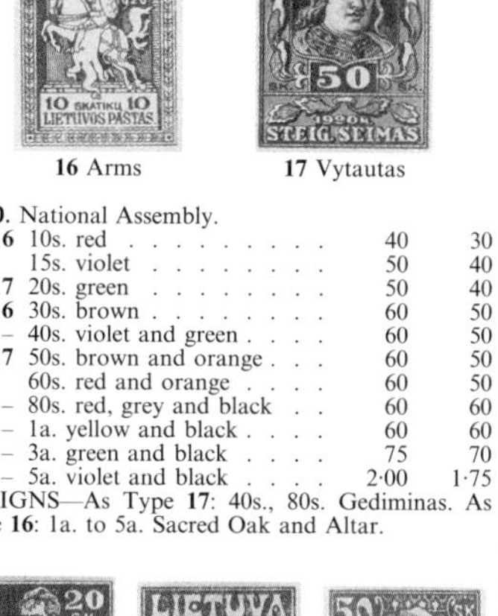

16 Arms
17 Vytautas

1920. National Assembly.
76 16 10s. red 40 30
77 15s. violet 50 40
78 17 20s. green 50 40
79 16 30s. brown 60 50
80 – 40s. violet and green 60 50
81 17 50s. brown and orange 60 50
82 60s. red and orange 60 50
83 – 80s. red, grey and black 60 60
84 – 1a. yellow and black 60 60
85 – 3a. green and black 75 70
86 – 5a. violet and black 2·00 1·75
DESIGNS—As Type 17: 40s., 80s. Gediminas. As Type 16: 1a. to 5a. Sacred Oak and Altar.

20 Sower
21 Kestutis
22 Reaper

23

28 Allegory of Flight

24 Flying Posthorn

25 Junkers F-13 over River Niemen

1921.
87 20 10s. red 30 1·75
88 15s. mauve 15 1·00
89 20s. blue 10 10
90 22 30s. brown 50 4·25
91 21 40s. red 15 10
92 22 50s. olive 10 10
93 60s. mauve and green 40 5·00
94 21 80s. red and orange 20 15
95 1a. green and brown 15 10
96 2a. red and blue 15 10
97 23 3a. blue and brown 50 2·00
124 20 4a. blue and yellow 30 75
98 23 5a. red and grey 60 3·25
125 20 8a black and green 35 1·00
99 23 10a. mauve and red 75 35
100 25a. green and brown 1·40 1·25
101 100a. grey and red 6·00 6·00

1921. Air. Inauguration of Kaunas–Konigsberg Air Service.
102 24 20s. blue 65 55
103 40s. orange 65 55
104 60s. green 75 65
105 80s. red 75 65
106 25 1a. green and red 2·00 1·25
107 – 2a. brown and blue 2·00 1·50
108 – 5a. grey and yellow 2·75 2·75
DESIGNS—As Type 25: 2a. Three Junkers F-13 monoplanes; 5a. Junkers F-13 over Gediminas Castle.

1921. Air. Inauguration of Air Mail Service.
109 28 20s. lilac and orange 90 1·50
110 40s. red and blue 90 1·50
111 60s. olive and blue 1·00 1·60
112 80s. green and yellow 1·00 1·60
113 1a. blue and green 90 1·60
114 2a. red and grey 1·50 1·75
115 5a. green and purple 1·50 1·75

1922. Surch 4 **AUKSINAI** with or without frame.
116 6 4a. on 75s. red and yellow 40 40

30 Junkers F-13

1922. Air.
118 30 1a. red and brown 1·40 2·00
119 3a. green and violet 1·40 2·00
120 5a. yellow and blue 1·90 2·75

31 Junkers F-13 over Gediminas Castle

33 Pte. Luksis

1922. Air.
121 31 2a. red and blue 1·25 1·00
122 4a. red and brown 1·25 1·00
123 10a. blue and black 2·00 1·50

1922. "De jure" Recognition of Lithuania by League of Nations. Inscr "LIETUVA DE JURE".
126 33 20s. red and black 50 50
127 – 40s. violet and green 40 40
128 – 50s. blue and purple 40 40
129 – 60s. orange and violet 40 40
130 – 1a. blue and red 40 40
131 – 2a. brown and blue 50 50
132 – 3a. blue and brown 50 50
133 – 4a. purple and green 50 50
134 – 5a. red and brown 50 50
135 – 6a. blue 60 50
136 – 8a. yellow and blue 60 50
137 – 10a. green and violet 90 75
DESIGNS—VERT: 40s. Lt. Juozapavicius; 50s. Dr. Basanavicius; 60s. Mrs. Petkevicaite; 1a. Prof. Voldemaras; 2a. Dovidaitis; 3a. Dr. Slezevicius; 4a. Dr. Galvanauskas; 5a. Dr. Grinius; 6a. Dr. Stulginskis; 8a. Pres. Smetona. HORIZ: (39 × 27 mm): 10a. Stauguitis, Pres. Smetona and Silingas.

1922. Surch.
138 5 1c. on 10s. orange (postage) 50 5·00
139 1c. on 15s. violet 50 5·00
143 1c. on 20s. blue 50 4·00
144 1c. on 30s. orange 40·00 £100
145 1c. on 30s. bistre 20 40
146 1c. on 40s. brown 50 4·00
148 22 1c. on 50s. olive 10 15
149 6 2c. on 50s. green 75 4·00
150 2c. on 60s. red and violet 10 10
151 2c. on 75s. red and yellow 50 5·00
152 20 3c. on 10s. red 1·10 6·00
153 3c. on 15s. mauve 15 15
154 3c. on 20s. blue 20 3·00
155 22 3c. on 30s. brown 90 8·50
156 21 3c. on 40s. red 15 15
157 7 3c. on 1a. (No. 37) 75·00 £120
158 3c. on 1a. (No. 58) 25 1·25
159 3c. on 3a. (No. 38) 60·00 £100
160 3c. on 3a. (No. 59) 10 65
161 3c. on 5a. (No. 39) 32·00 55·00
162 3c. on 5a. (No. 60) 20 80
163 22 5c. on 50s. olive 10 10
164 5c. on 60s. mauve & green 2·75 16·00
165 21 5c. on 80s. red and orange 20 40
166 6 5c. on 4a. on 75s. red and yellow 50 11·00
168 21 10c. on 1a. green & brown 25 10
169 10c. on 2a. red and blue 10 10
170 20 15c. on 4a. blue and yellow 20 10
171 23 25c. on 3a. blue and green 5·00 24·00
172 25c. on 5a. red and grey 3·00 8·50
173 25c. on 10a. mauve and red 75 1·60
174 20 30c. on 8a. black and green 25 25
175 23 50c. on 25a. green & brown 1·10 3·00
176 1l. on 100 a grey and red 2·00 3·25
177 24 10c. on 20s. blue (air) 1·00 3·50
178 10c. on 40s. orange 1·25 5·00
179 10c. on 60s. green 1·00 5·00
180 10c. on 80s. red 1·25 5·00
181 25 20c. on 1a. green and red 4·75 12·50
182 – 20c. on 2a. (No. 107) 8·00 18·00
183 31 25c. on 2a. red and blue 1·00 85
184 30c. on 4a. red and brown 1·00 80
185 – 50c. on 5a. (No. 108) 1·40 1·25
186 31 50c. on 10a. blue and black 65 1·25
187 30 1l. on 5a. yellow and blue 12·50 27·00

38 Wayside Cross

39 Ruins of Kaunas Castle

40 Seminary Church

1923.
201 38 2c. brown 60 30
202 3c. bistre 85 25
203 5c. green 85 10
204 10c. violet 1·50 10
189 15c. red 1·00 10
190 20c. green 1·00 15
191 25c. blue 1·00 10
206 36c. brown 7·50 65
192 39 50c. green 1·00 10
193 60c. red 1·10 15
194 40 1l. orange and green 5·50 10
195 3l. red and grey 5·50 55
196 5l. brown and blue 7·00 90

43 Arms of Memel

44 Ruins of Trakai

1923. Union of Memel with Lithuania.
210 43 1c. red and green 80 1·25
211 – 2c. mauve 80 1·25
212 – 3c. yellow 80 1·25
213 43 5c. buff and blue 80 1·25
214 – 10c. red 1·50 1·50
215 – 15c. green 1·50 1·50
216 44 25c. violet 2·00 1·75
217 – 30c. red 2·00 2·50
218 – 60c. green 4·50 4·75
219 – 1l. green 3·00 3·00
220 – 2l. red 5·00 6·00
221 44 3l. blue 5·50 7·00
222 – 5l. blue 13·50 14·50
DESIGNS—As Type 43: 3c., 2l. Chapel of Biruta; 10c., 15c. War Memorial Kaunas; As Type 44: 2, 30c. Arms of Lithuania; 60c., 5l. Memel Lighthouse; 1l. Memel Harbour.

45 Biplane

46 Biplane

1924. Air.
223 45 20c. yellow 1·40 70
224 40c. green 1·40 70
225 60c. red 1·50 75
226 46 1l. brown 3·25 65

1924. Charity. War Orphans Fund. Surch **KARO NASLAICIAMS** and premium.
227 38 2c.+2c. bistre (postage) 1·00 1·50
228 3c.+3c. bistre 1·00 1·50
229 5c.+5c. green 1·00 1·50
231 10c.+10c. violet 1·00 2·50
232 15c.+15c. red 1·00 2·50
233 20c.+20c. olive 2·00 3·00
235 25c.+25c. blue 4·00 7·00
236 36c.+34c. brown 6·00 9·00
237 39 50c.+50c. green 6·00 9·00
238 60c.+60c. red 7·50 12·00
239 40 1l.+1l. orange and green 7·50 12·00
240 3l.+2l. red and grey 12·00 16·00
241 5l.+3l. brown and blue 18·00 25·00
242 45 20c.+20c. yellow (air) 8·00 10·00
243 40c.+40c. green 8·00 10·00
244 60c.+60c. red 8·00 10·00
245 46 1l.+1l. brown 12·00 14·00

49 Barn Swallow carrying Letter

56

57

1926. Air.
246 **49** 20c. red . . . . 1·25 55
247 40c. orange and mauve . . 1·25 55
248 60c. black and blue . . . . 2·75 65

1926. Charity. War Invalids. Nos. 227/39 surch with new values and small ornaments.
249 **38** 1c.+1c. on 2c.+2c. . . . . 1·00 1·25
250 2c.+2c. on 3c.+3c. . . . . 1·00 1·25
251 2c.+2c. on 5c.+5c. . . . . 1·00 1·25
253 5c.+5c. on 10c.+10c. . . . 1·75 2·00
254 5c.+5c. on 15c.+15c. . . . 1·75 2·00
255 10c.+10c. on 20c.+20c. . . 1·75 2·00
257 10c.+10c. on 25c.+25c. . . 4·00 5·00
258 14c.+14c. on 36c.+34c. . . 6·00 7·00
259 **39** 20c.+20c. on 50c.+50c. . . 4·00 5·00
260 25c.+25c. on 60c.+60c. . . 6·00 9·00
261 **40** 30c.+30c. on 1l.+1l. . . . 10·00 15·00

1926. Charity. War Orphans. Nos. 227/39 surch **V.P.** and new values in circular ornament.
262 **38** 1c.+1c. on 2c.+2c. . . . . 1·00 1·25
263 2c.+2c. on 3c.+3c. . . . . 1·00 1·25
264 2c.+2c. on 5c.+5c. . . . . 1·00 1·25
266 5c.+5c. on 10c.+10c. . . . 2·00 2·50
267 10c.+10c. on 15c.+15c. . . 2·00 2·50
268 15c.+15c. on 20c.+20c. . . 2·50 2·50
270 15c.+15c. on 25c.+25c. . . 5·00 5·00
271 19c.+19c. on 36c.+34c. . . 5·00 6·00
272 **39** 25c.+25c. on 50c.+50c. . . 6·00 7·50
273 30c.+30c. on 60c.+60c. . . 9·00 12·00
274 **40** 50c.+50c. on 1l.+1l. . . . 12·00 18·00

1927.
275 **56** 2c. orange 75 10
276 3c. brown 75 10
277 5c. green . . . . 1·00 10
278 10c. violet . . . . 2·00 10
279 15c. red . . . . 1·75 10
280 25c. blue . . . . 1·75 10
283 30c. blue . . . . 12·00 1·00

1927. Dr. Basanavicius Mourning Issue.
285 **57** 15c. red . . . . 90 1·00
286 25c. blue . . . . 90 1·00
287 50c. green . . . . 1·10 1·00
288 60c. violet . . . . 2·00 2·75

58 "Vytis" of the Lithuanian Arms

1927.
289 **58** 1l. green and grey . . . . 1·25 50
290 3l. violet and green . . . . 3·25 50
291 5l. brown and grey . . . . 5·00 1·25

59 President Antanas Smetona

60 Lithuania liberated

1928. 10th Anniv of Independence.
292 **59** 5c. green and brown . . . 25 10
293 10c. black and violet . . . 25 10
294 15c. brown and orange . . 30 10
295 25c. slate and blue 65 10
296 **60** 50c. purple and blue . . . 85 20
297 60c. black and red . . . . 1·10 45
298 – 1l. brown . . . . 1·75 90
DESIGN—HORIZ: 1l. Lithuania's resurrection (angel and soldiers). Dated "1918-1928".

62

63

64 J. Tubelis

66 Railway Station, Kaunas

1930. 500th Death Anniv of Grand Duke Vytautas.
299 **62** 2c. brown (postage) . . . 25 10
300 3c. violet and brown . . . 25 10
301 5c. red and green 25 10
302 10c. green and violet . . . 25 10
303 15c. violet and red 25 10
304 30c. purple and blue . . . 25 10
305 36c. olive and purple . . . 35 15
306 50c. blue and green . . . 35 20
307 60c. red and blue 60 10
308 **63** 1l. purple, grey and green 1·50 40
309 3l. violet, pink and mauve 3·25 1·25
310 5l. red, grey and brown . . 4·00 1·75
311 10l. black and blue . . . . 13·00 18·00
312 25l. green and brown . . . 35·00 48·00

313 **64** 5c. brown, yellow and black (air) 35 35
314 10c. black, drab and blue 40 40
315 15c. blue, grey and purple 40 40
316 – 20c. red, orange and brown 1·00 55
317 – 40c. violet, light blue & blue . . . . 1·40 80
318 – 60c. black, lilac and green 1·60 1·40
319 – 1l. black, lilac and red . . 3·00 1·50
DESIGNS—HORIZ: 20c., 40c. Vytautas and Kaunas; 60c., 1l. Vytautas and Smetona.

1932. Orphans' Fund. Imperf or perf.
320 **66** 5c. blue and brown . . . . 1·00 1·00
321 10c. purple and brown . . 1·00 1·00
322 – 15c. brown and green . . . 30 30
323 – 25c. blue and green 45 50
324 – 50c. grey and olive . . . . 70 1·25
325 – 60c. grey and mauve . . . 1·00 4·25
326 – 1l. blue and grey . . . . . 2·50 3·25
327 – 3l. purple and green . . . 4·50 5·00
DESIGNS—As Type **66**: 15, 25c. "The Two Pines" (painting); 50c. G.P.O. VERT: 60c., 1, 3l. Vilnius Cathedral.

68 Map of Lithuania, Memel and Vilna

1932. Air. Orphans' Fund. Imperf or perf.
328 **68** 5c. red and green 25 25
329 10c. purple and brown . . 25 25
330 – 15c. blue and buff 40 40
331 – 20c. black and brown . . . 2·40 2·00
332 – 40c. purple and yellow . . 2·00 2·50
333 – 60c. blue and buff . . . . 3·00 5·50
334 – 1l. purple and green . . . 3·50 5·50
335 – 2l. blue and green . . . . 3·75 5·50
DESIGNS: 15, 20c. Airplane over R. Niemen; 40, 60c. Town Hall, Kaunas; 1, 2l. Vytautas Church, Kaunas.

69 Vytautas escapes from Prison

71 Coronation of Mindaugas

1932. 15th Anniv of Independence. Imperf or perf.
336 **69** 5c. purple and red (postage) 50 50
337 10c. brown and grey . . . 50 50
338 – 15c. green and red 50 50
339 – 25c. brown and purple . . 75 1·25
340 – 50c. brown and green . . . 1·00 1·25
341 – 60c. red and green . . . . 2·50 5·00
342 – 1l. black and blue . . . . 3·25 3·25
343 – 3l. green and purple . . . 3·50 5·50

344 – 5c. lilac and green (air) . . 15 20
345 – 10c. red and green 15 25
346 **71** 15c. brown and violet . . . 20 30
347 – 20c. black and red 45 45
348 – 40c. black and purple . . . 65 1·25
349 – 60c. black and orange . . . 1·90 6·00
350 – 1l. green and violet . . . . 3·00 3·50
351 – 2l. brown and blue . . . . 3·25 6·00
DESIGNS—POSTAGE. As Type **69**: 15, 25c. Vytautas and Jagello preaching the gospel; 50, 60c. Battle of Grunewald; 1, 3l. Proclamation of Independence. AIR. As Type **71**: 5, 10c. Battle of Saules; 40c. Gediminas in Council; 60c. Founding of Vilnius; 1l. Russians surrendering to Gediminas; 2l. Algirdas before Moscow.

72 A. Visteliauskas

1933. 50th Anniv of Publication of "Ausra".
352 **72** 5c. red and green 20 25
353 10c. red and blue 20 25
354 – 15c. red and orange . . . 20 25
355 – 25c. brown and blue . . . 55 75
356 – 50c. blue and green . . . . 65 1·00
357 – 60c. deep brown & lt brown . . . . 2·00 5·00
358 – 1l. purple and red . . . . 2·50 3·75
359 – 3l. purple and blue . . . . 3·50 6·00
PORTRAITS: 15, 25c. P. Vileisis; 50, 60c. J. Sliupas; 1, 3l. J. Basanavicius.

73 Trakai Castle

1933. Air. 550th Death Anniv of Grand Duke Kestutis.
360 **73** 5c. blue and green 20 35
361 10c. brown and violet . . . 20 35
362 – 15c. violet and blue 20 35
363 – 20c. purple and brown . . 55 80
364 – 40c. purple and blue . . . 90 1·60
365 – 60c. blue and red . . . . 2·25 7·00
366 – 1l. blue and green . . . . 3·00 4·50
367 – 2l. green and violet . . . . 3·75 9·00
DESIGNS: 15, 20c. Kestutis encounters Birute; 40, 60c. Birute; 1, 2l. Kestutis and Algirdas.

74 Mother and Child

75 J. Tumas Vaizgantas

1933. Child Welfare. (a) Postage.
373 **74** 5c. brown and green . . . 15 20
374 10c. blue and red 15 20
375 – 15c. purple and green . . . 20 25
376 – 25c. black and orange . . 40 75
377 – 50c. red and green . . . . 55 1·00
378 – 60c. orange and black . . 1·90 4·50
379 – 1l. blue and brown . . . . 2·50 3·50
380 – 3l. green and purple . . . 3·50 6·00
DESIGNS—VERT: 15, 25c. Boy reading a book; 50, 60c. Boy with building bricks; 1, 3l. Mother and child weaving.

(b) Air. Various medallion portraits in triangular frames.
381 – 5c. blue and red 15 15
382 – 10c. green and violet . . . 15 15
383 **75** 15c. brown and green . . . 15 15
384 20c. blue and red 25 35
385 – 40c. green and lake . . . 85 1·25
386 – 60c. brown and blue . . . 1·75 3·25
387 – 1l. blue and yellow . . . . 1·90 2·75
388 – 2l. lake and green . . . . 3·25 4·00
DESIGNS: 5, 10c. Maironis; 40, 60c. Vincas Kudirka; 1, 2l. Zemaite.

76 Captains S. Darius and S. Girenas

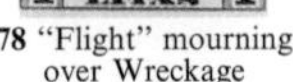

78 "Flight" mourning over Wreckage

81 President A. Smetona

1934. Air. Death of Darius and Girenas (trans-Atlantic airmen).
389 **76** 20c. red and black 10 10
390 – 40c. blue and red 10 10
391 **76** 60c. violet and black . . . 10 10
392 **78** 1l. black and red 35 15
393 – 3l. orange and green . . . 1·00 2·00
394 – 5l. blue and brown . . . . 4·00 4·25
DESIGNS—HORIZ: 40c. Bellanca monoplane "Lituanica" over Atlantic. VERT: 3l. "Lituanica" and globe; 5l. "Lituanica" and Vytis.

1934. President's 60th Birthday.
395 **81** 15c. red . . . . 3·00 10
396 30c. green . . . . 5·00 15
397 60c. blue . . . . 10·00 30

82

83

84 Gleaner

85

1934.
398 **82** 2c. red and orange 25 10
399 5c. green 30 10
400 **83** 10c. brown 75 10
401 **84** 25c. brown and green . . . 2·00 10
402 **83** 35c. red . . . . 2·00 10
403 **84** 50c. blue . . . . 3·50 10
404 **85** 1l. purple and red . . . . 18·00 10
405 3l. green 20 10
406 – 5l. purple and blue 20 20
407 – 10l. brown and yellow . . 1·25 1·25
DESIGNS—HORIZ: as Type **85**: 5l., 10l. Knight.
For design as Type **82** but smaller, see Nos. 411/12.

1935. Air. Honouring Atlantic Flyer Vaitkus. No. 390 optd **F. VAITKUS nugalejo Atlanta 21-22-IX-1935.**
407a 40c. blue and red £190 £300

87 Vaitkus and Air Route

88 President Smetona

1936. Air. Felix Vaitkus's New York–Ireland Flight.
408 **87** 15c. purple . . . . 1·40 45
409 30c. green . . . . 1·60 1·10
410 60c. blue . . . . 2·50 1·10

1936. As T **82** but smaller (18 × 23 mm).
411 **82** 2c. orange 10 10
412 5c. green 10 10

1936.
413 **88** 15c. red . . . . 4·00 10
414 30c. green . . . . 9·00 10
415 60c. blue . . . . 7·50 10

89

90 Archer

1937.
416 **89** 10c. green . . . . 1·10 10
417 25c. mauve 10 10
418 35c. red 60 10
419 50c. brown 30 10
419a 1l. blue 15 30

1938. 1st National Olympiad Fund.
420 **90** 5c.+5c. green . . . . . . 7·00 9·00
421 – 15c.+5c. red . . . . 9·00 10·00
422 – 30c.+10c. blue . . . . . . 12·00 14·00
423 – 60c.+15c. brown . . . . . 18·00 20·00
DESIGNS: 15c. Throwing the javelin; 30c. Diving; 60c. Relay runner breasting tape.

1938. Scouts' and Guides' National Camp Fund. Nos. 420/3 optd **TAUTINE SKAUCIU** (or **SKAUTU**) **STOVYKLA** and badge.
424 **90** 5c.+5c. green . . . . . . 7·00 8·50
425 – 15c.+5c. red . . . . 9·00 9·50
426 – 30c.+10c. blue . . . . . . 12·00 14·00
427 – 60c.+15c. brown . . . . . 17·00 19·00

92 President Smetona

93 Scoring a Goal

1939. 20th Anniv of Independence.
428 – 15c. red 30 10
429 **92** 30c. green 30 10
430 – 35c. mauve 55 25
431 **92** 60c. blue 60 25
DESIGN: 15, 35c. Dr. Basanvicius proclaiming Lithuanian independence.

1939. 3rd European Basketball Championship and Physical Culture Fund.
432 – 15c.+10c. brown . . . . . 7·50 7·50
433 **93** 30c.+15c. green . . . . . 7·50 7·50
434 – 60c.+40c. violet . . . . . 15·00 17·00
DESIGNS—VERT: 15c. Scoring a goal. HORIZ: (40½ × 36 mm); 60c. International flags and ball.

1939. Recovery of Vilnius. Nos. 428/31 optd **VILNIUS 1939-X-10** and trident.
435 – 15c. red 75 30
436 **92** 30c. green 75 40
437 – 35c. mauve . . . . 1·00 55
438 **92** 60c. blue . . . . 1·40 85

95 Vytis **96** Vilnius

1940. "Liberty" Issue.
439 **95** 5c. brown 10 10
440 – 10c. green 40 30
441 – 15c. orange 10 10
442 – 25c. brown 10 30
443 – 30c. green 15 10
444 – 35c. orange 20 45
DESIGNS: 10c. Angel; 15c. Woman releasing a dove; 25c. Mother and children; 30c. "Liberty Bell"; 35c. Mythical animal.

1940. Recovery of Vilnius.
445 **96** 15c. brown 30 15
446 – 30c. green 55 25
447 – 60c. blue . . . . 1·10 90
DESIGNS—VERT: 30c. Portrait of Gediminas. HORIZ: 60c. Ruins of Trakai Castle.

1940. Incorporation of Lithuania in U.S.S.R. Optd **LTSR 1940 VII 21.**
448 **82** 2c. red and orange 15 40
449 **95** 5c. brown 15 40
450 – 10c. green (No. 440) . . . 3·25 5·00
451 – 15c. orange (No. 441) . . . 15 50
452 – 25c. brown (No. 442) . . . 20 75
453 – 30c. green (No. 443) . . . 25 80
454 – 35c. orange (No. 444) . . . 25 1·50
455 **89** 50c. brown . . . . 25 1·40

From 1940 to 1990 Lithuania used stamps of Russia.

99 Angel and Map

1990. No gum. Imperf.
456 **99** 5k. green 10 10
457 10k. lilac 10 10
458 20k. blue 20 10
459 50k. red 75 40

1990. No gum. Imperf (simulated perfs).
460 **99** 5k. green and brown . . . 10 10
461 10k. purple and brown . . 10 10
462 20k. blue and brown . . . 30 20
463 50k. red and brown . . . 90 45

100 Vytis **101** Hill of Crosses, Siauliai

1991.
464 **100** 10k. black, gold and brown 10 10
465 15k. black, gold and green 10 10
466 20k. black, gold and blue 10 10
467 30k. black, gold and red 15 10
468 40k. black and gold . . . 10 10
469 50k. black, gold and violet 10 10
470 **101** 50k. brown, chestnut & blk 10 10
471 **100** 100k. black, gold & green 10 10
472 – 200k. brown, chest & blk 80 40
473 **100** 500k. black, gold and blue 40 20
DESIGN: As T **101**—200k. Lithuanian Liberty Bell.
See also Nos. 482 and 488/9.

102 Liberty Statue, Kaunas

103 Angel with Trumpet

1991. National Day.
480 **102** 20k. mauve, silver & black 15 10

1991. 1st Anniv of Declaration of Independence from U.S.S.R.
481 **103** 20k. deep green and green 15 10

1991. No gum. Imperf (simulated perfs).
482 **100** 15k. green and black . . 10 10

104 Wayside Crosses

1991.
483 **104** 40k. green and silver . . . 15 10
484 – 70k. brown, buff and gold 30 15
485 – 100k. brown, yellow & sil 45 20
DESIGNS: 70k. "Madonna" (icon from Pointed Gate Chapel, Vilnius); 100k. Towers of St. Anne's Church, Vilnius.

105 Candle

1991. 50th Anniv of Resistance to Soviet and German Occupations.
486 **105** 20k. yellow, black & bistre 10 10
487 – 50k. rose, black and red 25 10
488 – 70k. multicoloured . . . 35 15
DESIGNS: 50k. Shield pierced by swords; 70k. Sword and wreath.

1991. No gum. Imperf.
489 **100** 25k. black and brown . . 10 10
490 30k. black and purple . . 15 10

106 World Map and Games Emblem **107** National Flag in Ice-axe and Mt. Everest

1991. 4th International Lithuanians' Games.
491 **106** 20k. green, black & yellow 20 10
492 – 50k.+25k. green, black and yellow 55 25
DESIGN: 50k. Symbolic female athlete.

1991. Lithuanian Expedition to Mt. Everest.
493 **107** 20k. multicoloured . . . 20 10
494 70k. multicoloured . . . 55 25

108 Trakai Castle

109 Black Storks

1991. 650th Death Anniv of Grand Duke Gediminas. Each brown, ochre and green.
495 30k. Type **108** 15 10
496 50k. Gediminas 25 15
497 70k. Vilnius in 14th century 40 20

1991. Birds in the Red Book. Multicoloured.
498 30k.+15k. Type **109** . . . . 1·10 75
499 50k. Common cranes . . . . 1·40 90

110 U.N. and National Emblems and National Flag **111** National Team Emblem and Colours

1992. Admission to U.N.O.
500 **110** 100k. multicoloured . . . 15 10

1992. Winter Olympic Games, Albertville, and Summer Games, Barcelona. Multicoloured.
501 50k.+25k. Type **111** 15 10
502 130k. Winter Games emblem 30 15
503 280k. Summer Games emblem 55 25

112 Slipper Orchid **113** Goosander ("Mergus merganser")

1992. Plants in the Red Book. Multicoloured.
504 200k. Type **112** 30 15
505 300k. Sea holly 50 25

1992. Birds of the Baltic. No value expressed.
506 **113** B (15t.) black and green 70 45
507 – B (15t.) brown, blk & grn 70 45
508 – B (15t.) sepia, brown & grn 70 45
509 – B (15t.) brown, blk & grn 70 45
DESIGNS: No. 506, Osprey ("Pandion haliaetus"); 507, Black-tailed godwit ("Limosa limosa"); 509, Common shelduck ("Tadorna tadorna").

114 Kedainiai

115 Couple

1992. Arms. Multicoloured.
510 2t. Type **114** 10 10
511 3t. Vilnius 10 10
512 10t. State arms 30 15
See also Nos. 531/3, 569/71, 594/5, 628/30, 663/5, 682/4, 712/14, 742/4, 769/71 and 781/3.

1992. Costumes of Suvalkija.
513 **115** 2t. multicoloured 15 10
514 – 5t. multicoloured 30 15
515 – 7t. multicoloured 45 20
DESIGNS: 5, 7t. Different costumes.

116 Zapyskis Church

1993. Churches.
516 **116** 3t. black and stone . . . 10 10
517 – 10t. black and blue . . . 25 10
518 – 15t. black and grey . . . 40 20
DESIGNS: 10t. Church of St. Peter and St. Paul, Vilnius; 15t. Church of the Resurrection, Kaunas.

1993. Nos. 467, 490 and 468 surch.
519 **100** 1t. on 30k. blk, gold & red 10 10
520 1t. on 30k. black & purple 10 10
521 3t. on 40k. black and gold 15 10

118 Jonas Basanavicius (statesman)

1993. National Day. No value expressed.
522 **118** A (3t.) red, cinn & brn . . 10 10
523 – B (15t.) grn, stone & brn 55 25
DESIGN: No. 523, Jonas Vileisis (politician).

119 Vytautas

120 Simonas Daukantas (historian)

1993. 600th Anniv (1987) of Accession of Grand Duke Vytautas.
524 – 5t. gold, red and black . . 10 10
525 **119** 10t. green, black and red 25 10
526 – 15t. black, yellow and red 40 20
DESIGNS: 5t. Seal; 15t. "Battle of Grunwald" (Jan Matejka).

1993. Birth Anniversaries. Each brown and yellow.
528 10t. Type **120** (bicent) 15 10
529 20t. Vydunas (125th anniv) 35 20
530 45t. Vincas Mykolaitis-Putinas (philosopher, centenary) 80 40

1993. Town Arms. As T **114**. Multicoloured.
531 5c. Skuodas 10 10
532 30c. Telsiai 20 10
533 50c. Klaipeda 35 15

121 "Watchtower" (M. K. Ciurlionis)

122 State Arms

1993. World Unity Day (5c.) and Transatlantic Flight (80c.). Multicoloured.
534 5c. Type **121** 10 10
535 80c. Steponas Dariaus and Stasys Gireno 50 25

1993. No value expressed.
536 **122** A, green, brown and red 10 10
537 B, red, green and bistre 35 20

123 Pope John Paul II and View of Siluva

124 Couple

1993. Papal Visit. Multicoloured.
538 60c. Type **123** 35 20
539 60c. Pope and Hill of Crosses 35 20
540 80c. Pope and Kaunas . . . 50 25
541 80c. Pope and Ausra Gates, Vilnius 50 25

1993. Costumes of Dzukai.
542 **124** 60c. multicoloured 25 10
543 – 80c. multicoloured 40 20
544 – 1l. multicoloured 55 25
DESIGNS: 80c. to 1l. Different costumes.

125 Klaipeda Post Office

1993. 75th Anniv of First Lithuanian Postage Stamps.
545 **125** 60c. multicoloured 35 15
546 – 60c. multicoloured 30 15
547 – 80c. multicoloured 50 25
548 – 1l. black, brown and green 60 30
DESIGNS: No. 546, Kaunas post office; 547, Ministry for Post and Information, Vilnius; 548, First Lithuanian stamp.

126 "The Ladle Carver" (A. Gudaitis) 127 European Pond Turtle

1993. Europa. Contemporary Art.
549 **126** 80c. multicoloured 45 25

1993. Pond Life. Multicoloured.
550 80c. Type **127** 40 20
551 1l. Running toad 45 25

128 Games Emblem and Team Colours **130** Kristijonas Donelaitis

129 Antanas Smetona (President 1919–22 and 1926–40)

1994. Winter Olympic Games, Lillehammer, Norway.
552 **128** 1l.10 multicoloured . . . 45 20

1994. National Day.
553 **129** 1l. red and black 30 15
554 – 1l. brown and black . . . 30 15
DESIGN: No. 554, Aleksandras Stulginskis (President 1922–26).

1994. Writers. Each cream, brown and orange.
555 60c. Type **130** 25 10
556 80c. Vincas Kudirka 35 15
557 1l. Jonas Maciulis Maironis 45 20

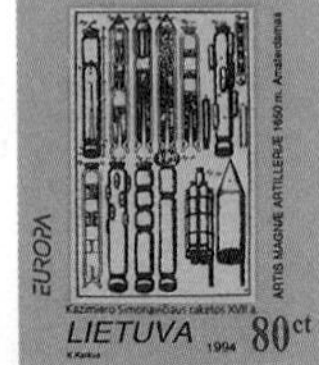
131 State Arms **132** Rockets by Kazimieras Simonavicius (illus from "Artis Magnae Artilleriae")

1994.
558 **131** 5c. brown 10 10
559 10c. lilac 10 10
560 20c. green 10 10
612 40c. purple 15 10
613 50c. blue 20 10

1994. Europa. Inventions and Discoveries.
561 **132** 80c. multicoloured 45 20

133 Couple **134** Music Note, Globe and Flag

1994. 19th-century Costumes of Zemaiciai (Lowlands).
563 **133** 5c. multicoloured 10 10
564 – 80c. multicoloured 35 15
565 1l. multicoloured 45 20
DESIGNS: 80c., 1l., Different costumes from Zemaiciai.

1994. Lithuanians of the World Song Festival.
566 **134** 10c. multicoloured 10 10

135 State Arms **136** Common Bat

1994.
567 **135** 2l. multicoloured 80 40
568 3l. multicoloured . . . . 1·25 60

1994. Town Arms. As T **114** but size 25×32 mm. Multicoloured.
569 10c. Punia 10 10
570 60c. Alytus 25 10
571 80c. Perloja 35 15

1994. Mammals. Multicoloured.
572 20c. Type **136** 15 10
573 20c. Fat dormouse 15 10

137 Kaunas Town Hall

1994. Town Halls.
574 **137** 10c. black and mauve . . 10 10
575 – 60c. black and blue . . . 25 10
576 – 80c. black and green . . . 35 15
DESIGNS: 60c. Kedainiai; 80c. Vilnius.

138 Madonna and Child

1994. Christmas.
577 **138** 20c. multicoloured 15 10

139 Steponas Kairys

1995. National Day. Signatories to 1918 Declaration of Independence.
578 **139** 20c. lilac, grey and black 10 10
579 – 20c. blue, grey and black 10 10
DESIGN: No. 579, Pranas Dovydaitis (Head of Government, March–April 1919).

140 Kaunas (Lithuania) **141** "Lithuanian School, 1864–1904" (P. Rimsa)

1995. Via Baltica Motorway Project.
581 **140** 20c. multicoloured 10 10

1995. Europa. Peace and Freedom.
583 **141** 1l. multicoloured 40 20

142 Couple **143** Motiejus Valancius (120th death)

1995. Costumes of the Highlands.
584 – 20c. multicoloured 10 10
585 – 70c. multicoloured 25 15
586 **142** 1l. multicoloured 40 20
DESIGNS: 70c. to 1l. Different 19th-century costumes.

1995. Anniversaries.
587 **143** 30c. cream, pur & yell . . 10 10
588 – 40c. cream, grn & orge . . 20 10
589 – 70c. cream, dp bl & pink 30 15
DESIGNS: 40c. Zemaite (150th birth); 70c. Kipras Petrauskas (110th birth).

144 Pieta **145** Torch-bearer

1995. Day of Mourning and Hope.
590 **144** 20c. multicoloured 10 10

1995. 5th World Lithuanians Games.
591 **145** 30c. multicoloured 15 10

146 "Baptria tibiale" **147** "Valerija Mesalina"

1995. Butterflies and Moths in "The Red Book". Multicoloured.
592 30c. Type **146** 20 10
593 30c. Cream-spot tiger moth ("Arctia villica") 20 10

1995. Town Arms. As T **114**. Multicoloured.
594 40c. Virbalis 20 10
595 1l. Kudirkos Naumiestis (horiz) 40 20

1995. 250th Birth Anniv of Pranciskus Smuglevicius (painter).
596 **147** 40c. multicoloured 20 10

148 Trakai Island Castle

1995. Castles.
597 – 40c. multicoloured 15 10
598 **148** 70c. blue, dp blue & black 30 15
599 – 1l. multicoloured 35 20
DESIGNS: 40c. Vilnius Upper Castle; 1l. Birzai Castle.

149 Star over Winter Scene **150** Bison

1995. Christmas. Multicoloured.
600 40c. Type **149** 20 10
601 1l. Churchgoers with lanterns 40 20

1996. The European Bison. Multicoloured.
602 30c. Type **150** 10 10
603 40c. Pair of bison 15 10
604 70c. Adult and calf 25 10
605 1l. Parents and calf 30 15

151 Kazys Grinius (130th)

1996. Birth Anniversaries.
606 **151** 40c. cream, brown & blue 15 10
607 – 1l. cream, bistre & yellow 40 20
608 – 1l. cream, blue and red 40 20
DESIGNS: No. 607, Antanas Zmuidzinavicius (120th); 608, Balys Sruoga (centenary).

152 Vladas Mironas

1996. National Day. Signatories to 1918 Declaration of Independence.
609 **152** 40c. cream, grey and black 15 10
610 – 40c. bistre, brown and black 15 10
DESIGN: No. 610, Jurgis Saulys.

153 Barbora Radvilaite **154** Couple

1996. Europa. Famous Women
611 **153** 1l. multicoloured 30 15

1996. Costumes of Klaipeda. 19th-century costumes. Multicoloured.
618 40c. Type **154** 15 10
619 1l. Woman in red skirt and man in frock-coat 45 20
620 1l. Woman in black skirt and man in blue waistcoat . . 45 20

155 Angel **156** "The Discus Thrower"

1996. Day of Mourning and Hope.
621 **155** 40c. blue, red and black 20 10
622 – 40c. green, red and black 20 10
DESIGN: No. 622, Head of crucifix.

1996. Olympic Games, Atlanta. Multicoloured.
623 1l. Type **156** 35 15
624 1l. Basketball 35 15

157 "Sacrifice" **159** Angels heralding

1996. 85th Death Anniv of Mikolajus Ciurlionis (artist). Multicoloured.
625 40c. Type **157** 15 10
626 40c. "Cemetery" 15 10

1996. Town Arms. As T **114** but size 25×32 mm.
628 50c. multicoloured 20 10
629 90c. red, black and yellow . . 40 20
630 1l.20 multicoloured 50 25
DESIGN: 50c. Seduva; 90c. Panevezys; 1l.20, Zarasai.

1996. Christmas. Multicoloured.
632 50c. Type **159** 20 10
633 1l.20 Elf riding on "Pegasus" 40 20

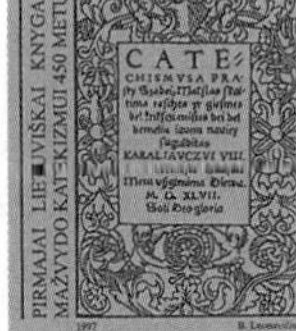
160 Ieva Simonaityte (writer, birth centenary) **161** Title Page

1997. Anniversaries.
634 **160** 50c. stone, brown and green 15 10
635 – 90c. stone, grey and yellow 35 20
636 – 1l.20 stone, grn & orge . . 40 20
DESIGNS: 90c. Jonas Sliupas (physician, 53rd death); 1l.20, Vladas Jurgutis (financier, 31st death).

1997. 450th Anniv of Publication of "Catechism of Mazvydas" (first Lithuanian book).
637 **161** 50c. brown and grey . . . 20 10

162 Mykolas Birziska

1997. National Day. Signatories to 1918 Declaration of Independence.
639 **162** 50c. green, lt grn & blk 20 10
640 – 50c. purple, stone and black 20 10
DESIGN: No. 640, Kazimieras Saulys.

164 "Little Witch" (Jovita Jankeviciute)

165 Lecture

1997. Europa. Tales and Legends. Multicoloured.
642 1l.20 Type **164** 45 20
643 1l.20 "Rainbow" (Ieva Staseviciute) (horiz) 45 20

1997. 600th Anniv of First Lithuanian School.
644 **165** 50c. multicoloured 20 10

166 Kurshes Ship

1997. Baltic Sailing Ships.
645 **166** 50c. multicoloured 20 10

167 Park

1997. Centenary of Palanga Botanical Park.
647 **167** 50c. yellow, black and brown 20 10

168 Ship of Flags

169 Elk's-horn Staff, 3000 B.C.

1997. 2nd Baltic Sea Games, Lithuania.
648 **168** 90c. multicoloured 35 15

1997. Museum Exhibits. Multicoloured.
649 90c. Type **169** 35 15
650 1l.20 Silver coins of Grand Duke Kazimierz IV, 15th century A.D. 45 20

170 Vytis's Cross

171 Black Morel

1997.
651 **170** 5c. yellow & light yellow 10 10
652 10c. yellow and cream . . 10 10
653 20c. green and brown . . 10 10
654 35c. purple and lilac . . . 10 10
655 50c. brown and cinnamon 15 10
656 70c. yellow and cream . . 20 10

1997. Fungi in the Red Book. Multicoloured.
660 1l.20 Type **171** 50 25
661 1l.20 Bronze boletus 50 25

172 Letter and Seal

173 Cherub holding Lantern above Town

1997. 674th Anniv of Letters of Invitation for Migrants sent by Grand Duke Gediminas to European Cities.
662 **172** 50c. multicoloured 20 10

1997. Town Arms. As T **114** but size 25 × 33 mm.
663 50c. Neringa 15 10
664 90c. Vilkaviskis 30 15
665 1l.20 Pasvalys 40 20

1997. Christmas. Multicoloured.
666 50c. Type **173** 15 10
667 1l.20 Snow-covered trees . . 40 20

174 Figure Skaters

1998. Winter Olympic Games, Nagano, Japan.
668 **174** 1l.20 ultramarine and blue 35 15

175 Alfonsas Petrulis (priest)

1998. National Day. Signatories to 1918 Declaration of Independence.
669 **175** 50c. green, grey and black 15 10
670 – 90c. brown, lt brn & blk 30 15
DESIGN: No. 670, Jokubas Sernas (lawyer and politician).

178 Gustaitis and ANBO-41 (reconnaissance plane)

1998. Birth Centenary of Antanas Gustaitis (pilot and aircraft constructor). Multicoloured.
673 2l. Type **178** 60 30
674 3l. ANBO-VIII (light bomber) and diagrams . . 90 45

179 National Song Festival

180 Tadas Ivanauskas (zoologist, 27th death anniv)

1998. Europa. National Festivals.
675 **179** 1l.20 multicoloured . . . 35 15

1998. Anniversaries.
676 **180** 50c. green, lt yell & yell 15 10
677 – 90c. red, yellow & orge 30 15
678 – 90c. green, yellow & orge 30 15
DESIGNS—45 × 25 mm: No. 677, Stasys Lozoraitis (diplomat, birth centenary) and Stasys Lozoraitis (diplomat, 10th death anniv); No. 678, Jurgis Baltrusaitis (writer and diplomat, 125th birth anniv) and Jurgis Baltrusaitis (art historian, 4th death anniv).

181 Long Jumping

1998. 6th World Lithuanian Games and Second National Games.
679 **181** 1l.35 multicoloured . . . 40 20

182 Atlantic Salmon

1998. Fishes in the Red Book. Multicoloured.
680 1l.40 Type **182** 45 20
681 1l.40 Whitefish ("Coregonus lavaretus") 45 20

1998. Town Arms. As T **114** but size 25 × 33 mm. Multicoloured.
682 70c. Kernave 20 10
683 70c. Trakai 20 10
684 1l.35 Kaunas 40 20

183 Vilnius–Cracow Postal Service, 1562

1998. Postal History.
685 **183** 70c. multicoloured 20 10

184 "All Night Long" (Antanas Zmuidzinavicius)

1998. Paintings. Multicoloured.
687 70c. Type **184** 20 10
688 1l.35 "Vilnius: Bernardines' Garden" (Juozapas Marsevskis) 40 20

185 Girl holding Church

1998. Christmas. Multicoloured.
689 70c. Type **185** 20 10
690 1l.35 Couple going into tree house 40 20

186 Mickiewicz (statue, G. Jokuonis)

1998. Birth Bicentenary of Adam Mickiewicz (poet).
691 **186** 70c. multicoloured 20 10

188 Petras Klimas (historian and diplomat)

1999. National Day. Signatories to 1918 Declaration of Independence.
693 **188** 70c. red and black 20 10
694 – 70c. blue and black . . . 20 10
DESIGN: No. 694, Donatas Malinauskas (diplomat).

189 Augustinas Gricius (dramatist)

190 Emblem and State Flag

1999. Birth Centenaries.
695 **189** 70c. black, cream & orge 20 10
696 – 70c. brown, cream & pink 20 10
697 – 1l.35 green, cream and orange 40 20
DESIGNS: No. 696, Juozas Matulis (chemist); 697, Pranas Skardzius (philologian).

1999. 50th Anniv of North Atlantic Treaty Organization.
698 **190** 70c. multicoloured 20 10

191 Aukstaitija National Park

1999. Europa. Parks and Gardens. Multicoloured.
699 1l.35 Type **191** 40 20
700 1l.35 Curonian Spit National Park 40 20

192 Council Flag

193 Boarded Clay Windmill, Melniai

1999. 50th Anniv of Council of Europe.
701 **192** 70c. multicoloured 20 10

1999. Windmills. Multicoloured.
702 70c. Type **193** 20 10
703 70c. Red-brick windmill, Pumpenai 20 10

194 "Dasypoda argentata"

195 Sculpture of U.P.U. Emblem, Berne

1999. Bumble Bees. Multicoloured.
704 70c. Type **194** 20 10
705 2l. "Bombus pomorum" . . 60 30

1999. 125th Anniv of Universal Postal Union.
706 **195** 70c. multicoloured 20 10

196 1918 and 1990 Stamps and Society Emblems

1999. 75th Anniv of Lithuanian Philatelic Society.
707 **196** 1l. multicoloured 30 15

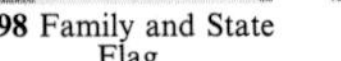

198 Family and State Flag

199 Emblem

1999. 10th Anniv of the Baltic Chain (human chain uniting the capitals of Lithuania, Estonia and Latvia).
709 **198** 1l. multicoloured 30 15

1999. 50th Anniv of Establishment of Lithuanian Freedom Fight Movement.
711 **199** 70c. multicoloured 20 10

1999. Town Arms. Designs as T **114** but size 25 × 33 mm. Multicoloured.
712 70c. Marijampole 20 10
713 1l. Siauliai 30 15
714 1l.40 Rokiskis 40 20

200 Sword of General S. Zukauskas, 1927

201 "Horse and Bear" (fable)

1999. Exhibits in Vytautas Magnus War Museum. Multicoloured.
715 70c. Type **200** 20 10
716 3l. 17th-century Hussar's armour 90 45

1999. Birth Bicentenary of Simonas Stanevicius (writer).
717 **201** 70c. multicoloured 20 10

202 "Winter Symphony"

203 Top of Monument

1999. Christmas. Multicoloured.
718 70c. Type **202** 20 10
719 1l.35 Cathedral, candles and bell 40 20

2000. Ironwork.
720 **203** 10c. blue and brown . . . 10 10
721 – 20c. blue and stone . . . 10 10
722 – 1l. blue and pink 30 15
723 – 1l.30 blue and green . . . 40 20
724 – 1l.70 blue and light blue 50 25
DESIGNS: 20c. to 1l.70, Different examples of ornamental ironwork.

204 Jonas Vailokaitis

2000. National Day. Signatories to 1918 Declaration of Independence.
725 **204** 1l.30 orange, stone & blk 40 25
726 – 1l.70 brown, stone & blk 50 25
DESIGN: 1l.70, Jonas Smilgevicius.

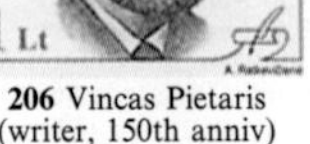

206 Vincas Pietaris (writer, 150th anniv)

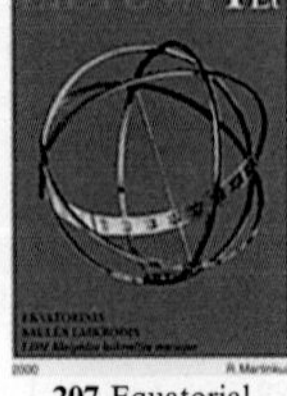

207 Equatorial Sundial

2000. Birth Anniversaries.
728 **206** 1l. green, black and purple 30 15
729 – 1l.30 blue, black & brown 40 20
730 – 1l.70 brown, black & bl 50 25
DESIGNS:1l.30, Kanutas Ruseckas (painter, bicentenary); 1l.70, Povilas Visinskis (literary critic, 125th anniv).
See also Nos. 753/5.

2000. Exhibits in Klaipeda Clock Museum. Mult.
731 1l. Type **207** 35 15
732 2l. Renaissance-style clock case 70 35

208 "Building Europe"

209 Osprey

2000. Europa.
733 **208** 1l.70 multicoloured . . . 60 30

2000. Birds of Prey. Multicoloured.
734 1l. Type **209** 35 15
735 2l. Black kite 70 35

210 Grey Seal

2000. Lithuanian Marine Museum, Kopgalis. Mult.
736 1l. Type **210** 35 15
737 1l. Magellanic penguin (*Spheniscus magellanicus*) 35 15

211 Cycling

2000. Olympic Games, Sydney. Multicoloured.
738 1l. Type **211** 35 15
739 3l. Swimming . . . . 1·00 50

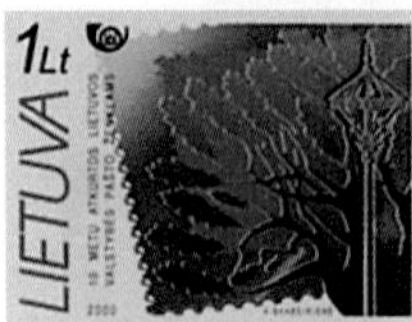

213 Tree and Emblem

2000. 10th Anniv of Lithuanian Postal Service.
741 **213** 1l. multicoloured 35 15

2000. Town Arms. As T **114** but size 25 × 33 mm. Multicoloured.
742 1l. Raseiniai 35 15
743 1l. Taurage 35 15
744 1l.30 Utena 45 20

214 Snow-covered Village

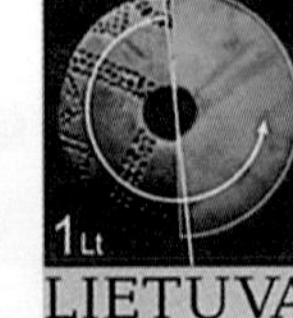

216 Neolithic Amber Artefact

2000. Christmas. Multicoloured.
745 1l. Type **214** 35 15
746 1l.70 Snow-covered church 60 30

2000. New Millennium.
748 **216** 1l. multicoloured 35 15

218 Vilnius Television Tower and Flag

220 Lake Galve

219 Saliamonas Banaitis

2001. 10th Anniv of Soviet Action in Vilnius.
750 **218** 1l. multicoloured 35 15

2001. National Day. Signatories to 1918 Declaration of Independence.
751 **219** 1l. brown, grey and black 35 15
752 – 2l. lilac, grey and black 70 35
DESIGN: 2l. Justinas Staugaitis.

2001. Anniversaries. As T **206**.
753 1l. blue, red and black . . . 35 15
754 1l. green, red and black . . . 35 15
755 1l.70 brown, violet and black 60 30
DESIGNS: No. 753, Juozas MikEnas (artist, birth centenary); 754, Pranas Vaicaitis (poet, death centenary); 755, Petras Vileisis (civil engineer, 150th birth anniv).

2001. Europa. Water Resources. Multicoloured.
756 1l.70 Type **220** 60 30
757 1l.70 River Nemunas 60 30

221 Floating Bogbean (*Nymphoides peltata*)

2001. Plants in the Red Book. Multicoloured.
758 2l. Type **221** 70 35
759 3l. Crossleaf heather (*Erica tetralix*) . . . . 1·10 55

222 Paplauja Bridge, Vilnius

2001. Bridges. Multicoloured.
760 1l. Type **222** 35 15
761 1l.30 Pakruojis, Kruoja . . . 50 25

224 Sand Dunes, Palanga, Lithuania

2001. Baltic Sea Coast.
763 **224** 1l. multicoloured 35 15

225 19th-century Cottage, Kirdeikiai, Utena District

2001. 35th Anniv of Open Air Museum, Rumsiskes. Multicoloured.
765 1l. Type **225** 35 15
766 2l. Farmer's house, Darlenai, Kretinga district 70 35

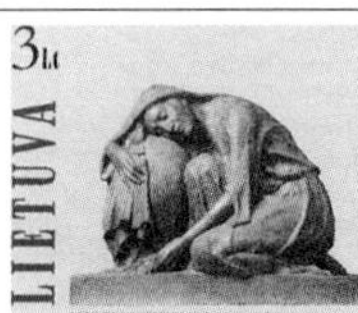

226 "Sadness" (sculpture)

2001. 120th Birth Anniv of Juozas Zikaras (artist).
767 **226** 3l. multicoloured . . . . 1·10 55

227 Charter and King Stephan I Batory of Poland

2001. 418th Anniv of Introduction of Postal Rates based on Weight.
768 **227** 1l. multicoloured 35 15

2001. Town Arms. As T **114** but size 25 × 33 mm. Multicoloured.
769 1l. Lazdijai 35 15
770 1l.30 Birzai 50 25
771 1l.70 Veliuona 60 30

228 Birds on Straw and Pine Pyramid ("Winter troubles")

2001. Christmas and New Year. Multicoloured.
772 1l. Type **228** 40 20
773 1l.70 Birds and crib ("Jesus' cradle") 70 35

229 Basanavicius

230 Skier

2001. 150th Birth Anniv of Jonas Basanavicius (politician and signatory to 1918 Declaration of Independence). Sheet 82 × 60 mm.
MS774 **229** 5l. multicoloured . . 2·10 2·10

2002. Winter Olympic Games, Salt Lake City, U.S.A.
775 **230** 1l. 70 multicoloured . . . 70 35

231 Kazys Bizauskas

2002. National Day. Signatories to 1918 Declaration of Independence.
776 **231** 1l. sepia, brown and black 40 20
777 — 1l. violet, brown and black 40 20
DESIGN: No. 777 Stanislovas Narutavicius (politician).

232 Antanas Salys

2002. Birth Anniversaries. Multicoloured.
778 1l. Type **232** (linguist, centenary) 40 20
779 1l. 30 Satrijos Ragana (writer, 125th anniv) . . . 55 25
780 1l. 70 Oskaras Milasius (poet, 125th anniv) 70 35

2002. Town Arms. As T **114** but size 25 × 33 mm. Multicoloured.
781 1l. Birstonas 40 20
782 1l. Anyksciai 40 20
783 1l. 70 Prienai 70 35

LOMBARDY AND VENETIA Pt. 2

Formerly known as Austrian Italy. Although these provinces used a different currency the following issues were valid throughout Austria. Lombardy was annexed by Sardinia in 1859 and Venetia by Italy in 1866.

1850. 100 centesimi = 1 lira.
1858. 100 soldi = 1 florin.
100 kreuzer = 1 gulden.

1 Arms of Austria

1850. Imperf.
1c 1 5c. orange £1000 75·00
2c 10c. black £1900 70·00
7 15c. red £475 2·75
4a 30c. brown £1700 5·50
5e 45c. blue £4500 13·50

1859. As T **4** and **5** of Austria (Emperor Francis Joseph I) but value in soldi. Perf.
16 5 2s. yellow £350 70·00
17 4 3s. black £1600 £190
18 3s. green £225 50·00
19 5 5s. red £150 3·00
20 10s. brown £250 38·00
21 15s. blue £1100 13·50

3 Emperor Francis Joseph I

4 Arms of Austria

1861.
25 3 5s. red £1000 1·70
26 10s. brown £1600 17·00

1863.
27 4 2s. yellow 65·00 £120
33 3s. green 6·25 12·50
34 5s. red 2·10 1·00
35 10s. blue 12·50 3·75
36 15s. brown 45·00 37·00

JOURNAL STAMPS

J 5

1858. Imperf.
J22 J 5 1k. black £1100 £3000
J23 2k. red £170 60·00
J24 4k. red £2750

LOURENCO MARQUES Pt. 9

A Portuguese colony in E. Africa, now part of Mozambique, whose stamps it uses.

1895. 1000 reis = 1 milreis.
1913. 100 centavos = 1 escudo.

1895. "Figures" key-type inscr "LOURENCO MARQUES".
1 R 5r. yellow 20 15
2 10r. mauve 25 15
3 15r. brown 40 35
4 20r. lilac 40 35
10 25r. green 30 15
12 50r. blue 35 15
18 75r. pink 80 40
14 80r. green 1·10 75
7 100r. brown on yellow 85 50
16 150r. red on pink 90 75
8 200r. blue on blue 1·50 90
9 300r. blue on brown 1·50 90

1895. 700th Death Anniv of St. Anthony. Optd **L. MARQUES CENTENARIO DE S. ANTONIO MDCCCXCV** on (a) "Embossed" key-type inscr "PROVINCIA DE MOCAMBIQUE".
19 Q 5r. black 4·50 4·00
20 10r. green 7·00 4·50
21 20r. red 8·00 5·50
22 25r. purple 10·00 7·25
23 40r. brown 8·00 6·75
27a 50r. blue 5·50 4·50
25 100r. brown 15·00 11·00
26 200r. violet 12·00 11·00
27 300r. orange 18·00 16·00

(b) "Figures" key-type inscr "MOCAMBIQUE"
28 R 5r. orange 5·25 3·75
29 10r. mauve 8·50 7·50
30 50r. blue 13·00 7·50
35 75r. pink 14·00 9·50
32 80r. green 23·00 17·00
33 100r. brown on yellow 25·00 23·00
35a 150r. red on pink 16·00 13·00

1897. No. 9 surch **50 reis**.
36 R 50r. on 300r. blue on brown 70·00 50·00

1898. "King Carlos" key-type inscr "LOURENCO MARQUES". Name and value in black.
37 S 2½r. grey 15 15
38 5r. orange 15 15
39 10r. green 15 15
40 15r. brown 50 45
83 15r. green 20 15
41 20r. lilac 30 15
42 25r. green 35 15
84 25r. red 20 15
43 50r. blue 50 25
85 50r. brown 45 35
86 65r. blue 2·25 2·00
44 75r. pink 1·00 80
87 75r. purple 65 60
45 80r. mauve 95 65
46 100r. blue on blue 50 25
88 115r. brown on pink 2·50 2·00
89 130r. brown on yellow 2·50 2·00
47 150r. brown on yellow 85 75
48 200r. purple on pink 1·50 75
49 300r. blue on pink 1·00 80
90 400r. blue on yellow 2·50 2·00
50 500r. black on blue 2·10 1·25
51 700r. mauve on yellow 3·75 2·75

1899. Green and brown fiscal stamps of Mozambique, as T **9** of Macao, bisected and each half surch **Correio de Lourenco Marques** and value. Imperf.
55 – 5r. on half of 10r. 60 30
56 – 25r. on half of 10r. 60 30
57 – 50r. on half of 30r. 60 30
58 – 50r. on half of 800r. 90 50

1899. No. 44 surch **50 Reis**.
59 S 50r. on 75r. pink 1·50 1·10

1902. "Figures" and "Newspaper" key-types surch.
60 V 65r. on 2½r. brown 1·25 1·10
62 R 65r. on 5r. yellow 1·25 1·10
63 65r. on 15r. brown 1·25 1·10
64 65r. on 20r. lilac 1·25 1·10
66 115r. on 10r. mauve 1·25 1·10
67 115r. on 200r. blue on blue 1·25 1·10
68 115r. on 300r. blue on brn 1·25 1·10
70 130r. on 25r. green 1·25 1·10
72 130r. on 80r. green 1·25 1·10
73 130r. on 150r. red on pink 1·25 1·10
74 400r. on 50r. blue 4·25 1·90
76 400r. on 75r. pink 3·25 2·10
78 400r. on 100r. brown on yellow 2·10 1·40

1902. "King Carlos" key-type inscr "LOURENCO MARQUES" optd **PROVISORIO**.
79 S 15r. brown 75 50
80 25r. green 65 40
81 50r. blue 80 60
82 75r. pink 1·25 75

1905. No. 86 surch **50 REIS**.
91 S 50r. on 65r. blue 1·00 95

1911. "King Carlos" key-type inscr "LOURENCO MARQUES" optd **REPUBLICA**.
92 S 2½r. grey 10 10
93 5r. orange 10 10
94 10r. green 15 15
95 15r. green 15 15
96 20r. lilac 30 20
97 25r. red 20 15
98 50r. brown 35 25
99 75r. purple 35 25
100 100r. blue on blue 35 25
178 115r. brown on pink 35 35
102 130r. brown on yellow 30 25
103 200r. purple on pink 30 25
104 400r. blue on yellow 50 35
105 500r. black on blue 60 50
106 700r. mauve on yellow 80 50

1913. Surch **REPUBLICA LOURENCO MARQUES** and value on "Vasco da Gama" issues of (a) Portuguese Colonies.
107 ¼c. on 2½r. green 50 45
108 ½c. on 5r. red 50 45
109 1c. on 10r. purple 50 45
110 2½c. on 25r. green 50 45
111 5c. on 50r. blue 50 45
112 7½c. on 75r. brown 1·25 85
113 10c. on 100r. brown 65 45
114 15c. on 150r. brown 65 45

(b) Macao.
115 ¼c. on ½a. green 60 45
116 ½c. on 1a. red 60 45
117 1c. on 2a. purple 60 45
118 2½c. on 4a. green 60 45
119 5c. on 8a. blue 60 45
120 7½c. on 12a. brown 1·00 85
121 10c. on 16a. brown 75 45
122 15c. on 24a. brown 75 45

(c) Timor.
123 ¼c. on ½a. green 60 45
124 ½c. on 1a. red 60 45
125 1c. on 2a. purple 60 45
126 2½c. on 4a. green 60 45
127 5c. on 8a. blue 60 45
128 7½c. on 12a. brown 1·00 90
129 10c. on 16a. brown 80 45
130 15c. on 24a. brown 80 45

1914. "Ceres" key-type inscr "LOURENCO MARQUES".
147 U ¼c. green 10 10
148 ½c. black 10 10
149 1c. green 10 10
150 1½c. brown 15 15
151 2c. red 15 15
152 2½c. violet 15 15
153 5c. blue 15 15
154 7½c. brown 15 15
155 8c. grey 15 15
140 10c. red 80 40
157 15c. purple 35 35
142 20c. green 45 35
143 30c. brown on green 70 50
144 40c. brown on pink 2·50 2·00
145 50c. orange on orange 1·00 90
146 1e. green on blue 1·10 90

1914. Provisionals of 1902 overprinted **REPUBLICA**.
166 R 115r. on 10r. mauve 30 30
167 115r. on 200r. blue on blue 35 30
168 115r. on 300r. blue on brn 30 30
161 130r. on 25r. green 50 40
164 130r. on 80r. green 50 40
169 130r. on 150r. red on pink 30 30
184 400r. on 50r. blue 80 45
185 400r. on 75r. pink 80 25

1915. Nos. 93 and 148 perf diagonally and each half surch ¼.
170 S ¼ on half of 5r. orange 1·40 1·10
171 U ¼ on half of ½c. black 1·40 1·10
Prices for Nos. 170/1 are for whole stamps.

1915. Surch **Dois centavos**.
172 S 2c. on 15r. (No. 83) 45 35
173 2c. on 15c. (No. 95) 45 35

1918. Red Cross Fund. "Ceres" key-type inscr "LOURENCO MARQUES", optd **9-3-18** and Red Cross or surch with value in figures and bars also.
188 U ¼c. green 85 85
189 ½c. black 85 85
190 1c. green 85 85
191 2½c. violet 85 85
192a 5c. blue 85 85
193 10c. red 1·75 85
194 20c. on 1½c. brown 1·75 85
195 30c. brown on green 1·75 1·50
196 40c. on 2c. red 1·75 1·50
197 50c. on 7½c. brown 1·75 1·50
198 70c. on 8c. grey 1·75 1·50
199 1e. on 15c. purple 1·75 1·50

1920. No. 166 surch **Um quarto de centavo**.
200 R ¼c. on 115r. on 10

1920. No. 152 surch in figures or words.
201 U 1c. on 2½c. violet 20 15
202 1½c. on 2½c. violet 20 15
203 4c. on 2½c. violet 20 15

For other surcharges on "Ceres" key-type of Lourenco Marques, see Mozambique Nos. 309/10 and Nos. D44 and 46.

NEWSPAPER STAMPS

1893. "Newspaper" key-type inscr "LOURENCO MARQUES".
N1 V 2½r. brown 15 15

1895. 700th Death Anniv of St. Anthony. "Newspaper" key-type inscr "MOCAMBIQUE" optd **L. MARQUES CENTENARIO DE S. ANTONIO MDCCCXCV**.
N36 V 2½r. brown 2·25 1·90

LUBECK Pt. 7

Formerly one of the free cities of the Hanseatic League. In 1868 joined the North German Confederation.

16 schilling = 1 mark.

1

3

1859. Imperf.
9 1 ½s. lilac 12·50 £1400
10 1s. orange 24·00 £1400
3 2s. brown 18·00 £225
4 2½s. red 36·00 £700
6 4s. green 18·00 £550

1863. Rouletted.
11 3 ½s. green 36·00 60·00
13 1s. orange £120 £140
14 2s. red 22·00 55·00
16 2½s. blue 90·00 £350
17 4s. bistre 38·00 95·00

4

5

1864. Imperf.
19 4 1¼s. brown 22·00 60·00

1865. Roul.
21 5 1½s. mauve 22·00 75·00

LUXEMBOURG Pt. 4

An independent Grand Duchy lying between Belgium and the Saar District. Under German Occupation from 1940 to 1944.

1852. 12½ centimes = 1 silver groschen.
100 centimes = 1 franc.
1940. 100 pfennig = 1 reichsmark.
1944. 100 centimes = 1 franc (Belgian).
2002. 100 cents = 1 euro.

1 Grand Duke William III

3

4

1852. Imperf.
2 1 10c. black £1900 32·00
3a 1s. red £1200 £100

1859. Imperf or roul.
23 3 1c. brown 30·00 7·25
21 1c. orange 25·00 5·75
17 2c. black 14·00 10·50
8 4c. yellow £160 £150
20 4c. green 30·00 21·00
10 4 10c. blue £160 13·50
24 10c. purple £100 1·60
25 10c. lilac £110 2·50
28 12½c. red £140 4·50
30 20c. brown £120 10·50
12 25c. brown £325 £225
32 25c. blue £1000 9·00
13 30c. purple £220 £190
14 37½c. green £275 £140
35 37½c. bistre £650 £225
39 40c. orange 42·00 75·00

1872. Surch **UN FRANC**. Roul.
37 4 1f. on 37½c. bistre £900 55·00

1874. Perf.
57a 3 1c. brown 6·50 6·00
58a 2c. black 6·00 1·25
42 4c. green 1·00 9·00
43 5c. yellow £150 12·00
60a 4 10c. lilac £150 75
61 12½c. red £160 £160
62a 20c. brown 14·00 13·50
63a 25c. blue £225 3·75
64 30c. red 2·75 15·00
55 40c. orange 85 5·00

1879. Surch **Un Franc**. Perf.
56 4 1f. on 37½c. bistre 6·25 42·00

7 Agriculture and Trade

8 Grand Duke Adolf

9

1882.
81a 7 1c. grey 20 50
82c 2c. brown 10 25
83c 4c. bistre 30 1·50
84c 5c. green 55 25
85a 10c. red 4·50 75
86a 12½c. blue 1·00 21·00
87c 20c. orange 2·00 1·75
88a 25c. blue £130 1·50
89a 30c. green 13·00 11·00
90c 50c. brown 1·00 6·25
91a 1f. lilac 60 23·00
92a 5f. orange 28·00 £150

1891.
125a 8 10c. red 15 25
126b 12½c. green 45 50
128 20c. orange 11·00 65
129c 25c. blue 85 40
130b 30c. green 1·00 85
131b 37½c. green 2·40 2·75
132b 50c. brown 6·00 3·25
133a 1f. purple 11·00 11·50
134 2½f. black 1·50 19·00
135 5f. lake 32·00 60·00

1895.
152 9 1c. grey 1·40 30
153 2c. brown 15 15
154 4c. bistre 20 70
155 5c. green 1·40 15
156 10c. red 6·50 15

10

11 Grand Duke William IV

13 Grand Duchess Adelaide

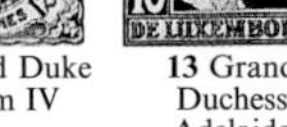

1906.

157	**10**	1c. grey	10	15
158		2c. brown	10	15
159		4c. bistre	15	20
160		5c. green	25	15
231		5c. mauve	10	15
161		6c. lilac	20	30
161a		7½c. orange	15	2·10
162	**11**	10c. red	1·50	10
163		12½ slate	1·50	30
164		15c. brown	1·50	50
165		20c. orange	3·00	45
166		25c. blue	45·00	30
166a		30c. olive	70	50
167		37½c. green	75	55
168		50c. brown	4·25	70
169		87½c. blue	1·75	6·25
170		1f. purple	4·75	1·25
171		2½f. red	50·00	60·00
172		5f. purple	7·00	42·00

1912. Surch **62½ cts.**

173	**11**	62½c. on 87½c. blue	1·25	1·75
173a		62½c. on 2½f. red	1·40	3·00
173b		62½c. on 5f. purple	55	1·90

1914.

174	**13**	10c. purple	10	10
175		12½c. green	10	10
176		15c. brown	10	10
176a		17½c. brown	10	30
177		25c. blue	10	10
178		30c. brown	10	40
179		35c. blue	10	30
180		37½c. brown	10	30
181		40c. red	15	30
182		50c. grey	25	40
183		62½c. green	35	1·90
183a		87½c. orange	35	1·90
184		1f. brown	2·00	60
185		2½f. red	45	1·90
186		5f. violet	7·00	32·00

1916. Surch in figures and bars.

187	**10**	2½ on 5c. green	10	10
188		3 on 2c. brown	10	10
212		5 on 1c. grey	10	15
213		5 on 4c. bistre	10	20
214		5 on 7½c. orange	10	15
215		6 on 2c. brown	25	25
189	**13**	7½ on 10c. red	10	10
190		17½ on 30c. brown	10	35
191		20 on 17½c. brown	10	20
216		25 on 37½c. sepia	10	20
217		75 on 62½c. green	10	20
218		80 on 87½c. orange	10	20
192		87½ on 1f. brown	55	6·25

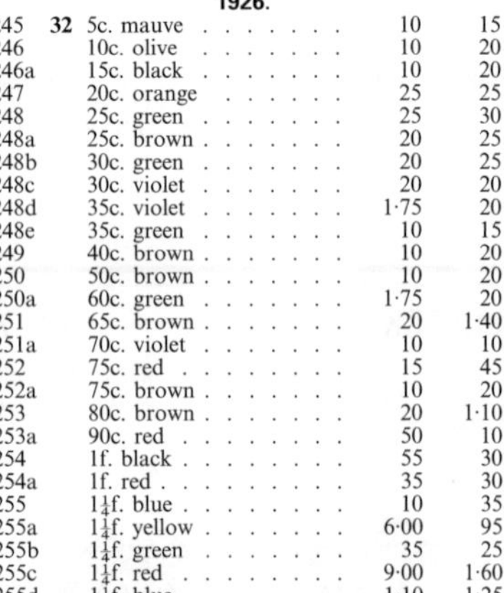
17 Grand Duchess Charlotte

18 Vianden Castle

1921. Perf.

194	**17**	2c. brown	10	15
195		3c. green	10	15
196		6c. purple	10	15
197		10c. green	10	15
193a		15c. red*	10	15
198		15c. green	10	15
234		15c. orange	10	30
199		20c. orange	15	30
235		20c. green	10	30
200		25c. green	15	15
201		30c. red	15	15
202		40c. orange	15	15
203		50c. blue	15	35
236		50c. red	10	25
204		75c. red	15	1·25
237		75c. blue	10	25
205		80c. black	15	65
206a	**18**	1f. red	20	35
238		1f. blue	25	40
207	–	2f. blue	40	55
239	–	2f. brown	2·40	1·40
208	–	5f. violet	12·00	6·00

DESIGNS—As Type **18**: 2f. Factories at Esch; 5f. Railway viaduct over River Alzette.

*No. 193a was originally issued on the occasion of the birth of Crown Prince Jean.

See also Nos. 219/20.

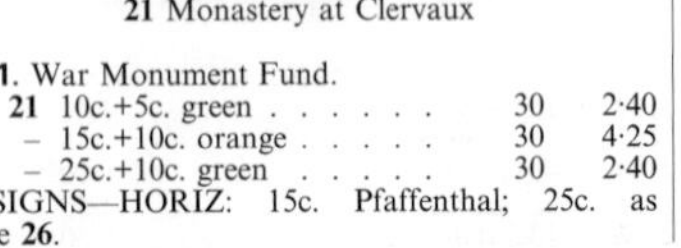
21 Monastery at Clervaux

1921. War Monument Fund.

209	**21**	10c.+5c. green	30	2·40
210	–	15c.+10c. orange	30	4·25
211	–	25c.+10c. green	30	2·40

DESIGNS—HORIZ: 15c. Pfaffenthal; 25c. as Type **26**.

1922. Philatelic Exhibition. Imperf.

219	**17**	25c. green	1·75	4·50
220		30c. red	1·75	4·50

26 Luxembourg

28 Echternach

1923.

222a	**26**	10f. black	4·00	8·75

1923. Unveiling of War Memorial by Prince Leopold of Belgium. Nos. 209/11 surch **27 mai 1923** and additional values.

223	**21**	10+5+25c. green	1·40	14·00
224	–	15+10+25c. orange	1·40	19·00
225	–	25+10+25c. green	1·40	14·00

1923.

226a	**28**	3f. blue	75	55

1924. Charity. Death of Grand Duchess Marie Adelaide. Surch **CARITAS** and new value.

227	**13**	12½c.+7½c. green	15	1·75
228		35c.+10c. blue	15	1·75
229		2½f.+1f. red	75	19·00
230		5f.+2f. violet	60	13·50

1925. Surch 5.

240	**17**	5 on 10c. green	10	15

31

32 Grand Duchess Charlotte

1925. Anti-T.B. Fund.

241	**31**	5c.+5c. violet	25	50
242		30c.+5c. orange	25	2·25
243		50c.+5c. brown	25	4·25
244		1f.+10c. blue	65	10·50

1926.

245	**32**	5c. mauve	10	15
246		10c. olive	10	20
246a		15c. black	10	20
247		20c. orange	25	25
248		25c. green	25	30
248a		25c. brown	20	25
248b		30c. green	20	25
248c		30c. violet	20	20
248d		35c. violet	1·75	20
248e		35c. green	10	15
249		40c. brown	10	20
250		50c. brown	10	20
250a		60c. green	1·75	20
251		65c. brown	20	1·40
251a		70c. violet	10	10
252		75c. red	15	45
252a		75c. brown	10	20
253		80c. brown	20	1·10
253a		90c. red	50	10
254		1f. black	55	30
254a		1f. red	35	30
255		1¼f. blue	10	35
255a		1¼f. yellow	6·00	95
255b		1¼f. green	35	25
255c		1¼f. red	9·00	1·60
255d		1½f. blue	1·10	1·25
255e		1¾f. blue	75	30

33 Prince Jean

34 Grand Duchess and Prince Felix

1926. Child Welfare.

256	**33**	5c.+5c. black and mauve	15	35
257		40c.+10c. black & green	15	75
258		50c.+15c. black & yellow	15	75
259		75c.+20c. black and red	30	8·00
260		1f.50+30c. black & bl	3·00	8·50

1927. International Philatelic Exhibition.

261	**34**	25c. purple	1·25	11·00
262		50c. green	1·75	15·00
263		75c. red	1·25	11·00
264		1f. black	1·25	11·00
265		1½f. blue	1·25	11·00

35 Princess Elisabeth

37 Clervaux

1927. Child Welfare.

266	**35**	10c.+5c. black and blue	15	40
267		50c.+10 black and brown	15	75
268		75c.+20c. black & orange	15	1·10
269		1f.+30c. black and red	30	8·00
270		1½f.+50c. black and blue	30	8·00

1927. Stamps of 1921 and 1926 surch.

270a	**32**	10 on 30c. green	35	30
271	**17**	15 on 20c. green	10	20
272	**32**	15 on 25c. green	15	50
273	**17**	35 on 40c. orange	15	15
274	**32**	60 on 65c. brown	15	35
275	**17**	60 on 75c. blue	15	25
276	**32**	60 on 75c. red	15	35
277	**17**	60 on 80c. black	15	35
278	**32**	60 on 80c. brown	15	45
278a		70 on 75c. brown	4·50	30
278b		75 on 90c. red	1·40	55
278c		1¾ on 1½f. blue	3·25	1·25

1928. Perf.

279a	**37**	2f. black	85	60

See also No. 339.

38 Princess Marie Adelaide

39 Princess Marie Gabrielle

1928. Child Welfare.

280	**38**	10c.+5c. purple & green	20	85
281		60c.+10c. olive & brown	30	2·25
282		75c.+15c. green and red	50	5·00
283		1f.+25c. brown & green	1·25	16·00
284		1½f.+50c. blue & yellow	1·25	16·00

1928. Child Welfare.

285	**39**	10c.+10c. green & brown	20	55
286		35c.+15c. brown & green	85	4·75
287		75c.+30c. black and red	85	6·50
288		1¼f.+50c. green and red	2·00	17·00
289		1¾f.+75c. black and blue	2·50	22·00

40 Prince Charles

41 Arms of Luxembourg

1930. Child Welfare.

290	**40**	10c.+5c. brown & green	20	90
291		75c.+10c. green & brown	1·40	4·75
292		1f.+25c. violet and red	3·00	17·00
293		1¼f.+75c. black & yellow	4·25	24·00
294		1¾f.+1f.50 brown & blue	5·00	24·00

1930.

295	**41**	5c. red	35	35
296		10c. green	45	20

42 Biplane over River Alzette

43 Luxembourg, Lower Town

1931. Air.

296a	**42**	50c. green	60	1·10
297		75c. brown	60	1·25
298		1f. red	60	1·40
299		1¼f. purple	60	1·40
300		1¾f. blue	60	1·40
300a		3f. black	90	5·00

1931.

301	**43**	20f. green	3·25	19·00

44 Princess Alix

45 Countess Ermesinde

46 Emperor Henry VII

1931. Child Welfare.

302	**44**	10c.+5c. grey and brown	20	85
303		75c.+10c. green and red	3·50	11·00
304		1f.+25c. grey and green	6·00	23·00
305		1¼f.+75c. green and violet	6·00	23·00
306		1¾f.+1f.50 grey and blue	10·50	45·00

1932. Child Welfare.

307	**45**	10c.+5c. brown	35	90
308		75c.+10c. violet	2·10	13·50
309		1f.+25c. red	9·25	38·00
310		1¼f.+75c. lake	9·25	38·00
311		1¾f.+1f.50 blue	9·25	38·00

1933. Child Welfare.

312	**46**	10c.+5c. brown	35	80
313		75c.+10c. purple	4·25	13·00
314		1f.+25c. red	12·00	32·00
315		1¼f.+75c. brown	14·50	40·00
316		1¾f.+1f.50 blue	14·50	60·00

47 Gateway of the Three Towers

48 Arms of John the Blind

1934.

317	**47**	5f. green	1·00	7·25

1934. Child Welfare.

318	**48**	10c.+5c. violet	10	85
319		35c.+10c. green	2·75	9·25
320		75c.+15c. red	2·75	9·25
321		1f.+25c. red	14·50	40·00
322		1¼f.+75c. orange	16·00	50·00
323		1¾f.+1½f. blue	15·00	50·00

50 Surgeon

1935. International Relief Fund for Intellectuals.

324	–	5c. violet	20	1·00
325	–	10c. red	40	1·00
326	–	15c. olive	35	1·75
327	–	20c. orange	55	3·00
328	–	35c. green	80	4·00
329	–	50c. black	95	5·50
330	–	70c. green	2·00	6·00
331	**50**	1f. red	2·00	6·00
332	–	1f.25 turquoise	8·00	50·00
333	–	1f.75 blue	10·00	50·00
334	–	2f. brown	30·00	£110
335	–	3f. brown	42·00	£150
336	–	5f. blue	70·00	£275
337	–	10f. purple	£180	£476
338	**50**	20f. green	£200	£575

DESIGNS—HORIZ: 5c., 10f. Schoolteacher; 15c., 3f. Journalist; 20c., 1f.75, Engineer; 35c., 1f.25, Chemist. VERT: 10c., 2f. "The Arts"; 50c., 5f. Barrister; 70c. University.

This set was sold at the P.O. at double face value.

1935. Esch Philatelic Exhibition. Imperf.

339	**37**	2f.(+50c.) black	6·00	16·00

52 Vianden

1935.

340	**52**	10f. green	1·40	9·00

53 Charles I

54 Town Hall

1935. Child Welfare.

341	**53**	10c.+5c. violet	10	40
342		35c.+10c. green	35	60
343		70c.+20c. brown	85	1·50
344		1f.+25c. red	12·50	38·00
345		1f.25+75c. brown	12·50	38·00
346		1f.75+1f.50 blue	12·50	48·00

1936. 11th Int Philatelic Federation Congress.

347	**54**	10c. brown	35	40
348		35c. green	45	75
349		70c. orange	55	1·10
350		1f. red	1·60	6·50
351		1f.25 violet	2·75	8·50
352		1f.75 blue	1·60	7·25

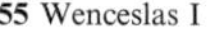

55 Wenceslas I

56 Wenceslas II

1936. Child Welfare.

353	**55**	10c.+5c. brown	10	25
354		35c.+10c. green	15	45
355		70c.+20c. slate	35	60
356		1f.+25c. red	2·10	10·00
357		1f.25+75c. violet	4·00	23·00
358		1f.75+1f.50 blue	4·00	14·50

1937. Child Welfare.

360	**56**	10c.+5c. black and red	10	20
361		35c.+10c. green & purple	25	35
362		70c.+20c. red and blue	25	35
363		1f.+25c. red and green	1·25	11·00
364		1f.25+75c. purple & brn	1·60	11·50
365		1f.75+1f.50 blue & blk	1·75	13·00

57 St. Willibrord

61 Sigismond of Luxembourg

1938. Echternach Abbey Restoration Fund (1st issue). 1200th Death Anniv of St. Willibrord.

366	**57**	35c.+10c. green	35	45
367	–	70c.+10c. black	85	55
368	–	1f.25+25c. red	1·40	2·25
369	–	1f.75+50c. blue	2·40	2·40
370	–	3f.+2f. red	6·25	7·50
371	–	5f.+5f. violet	7·00	7·25

DESIGNS—As Type **57**: 70c. Town Hall, Echternach; 1f.25, Pavilion, Echternach Municipal Park. 31 × 51 mm: 1f.75, St. Willibrord (from miniature). 42 × 38 mm: 3f. Echternach Basilica; 5f. Whitsuntide dancing procession.

See also Nos. 492/7 and 569/70.

1938. Child Welfare.

372	**61**	10c.+5c. black & mauve	10	35
373		35c.+10c. black & green	25	40
374		70c.+20c. black & brown	35	40
375		1f.+25c. black and red	2·00	11·50
376		1f.25+75c. black & grey	2·00	11·50
377		1f.75+1f.50 black & bl	2·75	17·00

62 Arms of Luxembourg

63 William I

1939. Centenary of Independence.

378	**62**	35c. green	15	20
379	**63**	50c. orange	20	20
380	–	70c. green	10	20
381	–	75c. olive	45	75
382	–	1f. red	1·00	1·50
383	–	1f.25 violet	15	30
384	–	1f.75 blue	15	30
385	–	3f. brown	30	45
386	–	5f. black	30	3·00
387	–	10f. red	85	7·00

PORTRAITS—As Type **63**: 70c. William II; 75c. William III; 1f. Prince Henry; 1f.25 Grand Duke Adolphe; 1f.75 William IV; 3f. Marie-Anne, wife of William IV; 5f. Grand Duchess Marie Adelaide; 10f. Grand Duchess Charlotte.

1939. Surch in figures.

388	**32**	30c. on 60c. green	15	1·60

65 Allegory of Medicinal Spring

66 Prince Jean

1939. Mondorf-les-Bains Propaganda.

389	**65**	2f. red	40	2·50

1939. 20th Anniv of Reign and of Royal Wedding.

390	**66**	10c.+5c. brn on cream	10	40
391	–	35c.+10c. green on cream	25	1·25
392	–	70c.+20c. black on cream	95	1·60
393	**66**	1f.+25c. red on cream	4·00	35·00
394	–	1f.25+75c. violet on cream	5·00	48·00
395	–	1f.75+1f.50 blue on cream	6·00	65·00

PORTRAITS: 35c., 1f.25, Prince Felix; 70c., 1f.75, Grand Duchess Charlotte.

1940. Anti-T.B. Fund. Surch with Cross of Lorraine and premium.

396	**65**	2f.+50c. grey	1·25	13·00

1940–44. GERMAN OCCUPATION.

1940. T **94** of Germany optd **Luxemburg**.

397	**94**	3pf. brown	10	35
398		4pf. blue	10	40
399		5pf. green	10	40
400		6pf. green	10	35
401		8pf. red	10	35
402		10pf. brown	10	40
403		12pf. red	10	30
404		15pf. purple	20	65
405		20pf. blue	20	1·10
406		25pf. blue	45	1·25
407		30pf. green	45	1·00
408		40pf. mauve	45	1·25
409		50pf. black and green	45	1·60
410		60pf. black and purple	1·75	3·25
411		80pf. black and blue	2·40	12·00
412		100pf. black and yellow	90	4·25

1940. Types of Luxembourg surch.

413	**32**	3 Rpf. on 15c. black	10	50
414		4 Rpf. on 20c. orange	10	50
415		5 Rpf. on 35c. green	10	50
416		6 Rpf. on 10c. green	10	50
417		8 Rpf. on 25c. brown	10	50
418		10 Rpf. on 40c. brown	10	50
419		12 Rpf. on 60c. green	10	50
420		15 Rpf. on 1f. red	10	3·50
421		20 Rpf. on 50c. brown	10	85
422		25 Rpf. on 5c. mauve	30	2·75
423		30 Rpf. on 70c. violet	10	85
424		40 Rpf. on 75c. brown	10	1·10
425		50 Rpf. on 1¼f. green	10	85
426	**65**	60 Rpf. on 2f. red	1·25	18·00
427	**47**	80 Rpf. on 5f. green	20	3·25
428	**52**	100 Rpf. on 10f. green	20	3·25

1941. Nos. 739/47 of Germany optd **Luxemburg**.

429		3pf.+2pf. brown	20	75
430		4pf.+3pf. blue	20	75
431		5pf.+3pf. green	20	75
432		6pf.+4pf. green	20	75
433		8pf.+4pf. orange	20	75
434		12pf.+6pf. red	20	75
435		15pf.+10pf. purple	1·40	5·50
436		25pf.+15pf. blue	1·40	6·00
437		40pf.+35pf. purple	1·40	6·00

1944. INDEPENDENCE REGAINED.

70 Grand Duchess Charlotte

71 "Britannia"

1944.

438	**70**	5c. brown	10	15
439		10c. slate	10	15
440		20c. orange	30	15
441		25c. brown	10	15
442		30c. red	40	35
443		35c. green	15	30
444		40c. blue	40	35
445		50c. violet	15	15
445a		60c. orange	2·25	15
446		70c. red	15	20
447		70c. green	75	1·10
448		75c. brown	40	20
449		1f. olive	10	15
450		1¼f. orange	20	55
451		1½f. orange	40	20
452		1¾f. blue	10	45
453		2f. red	3·50	30
454		2½f. mauve	8·00	5·50
455		3f. green	75	60
456		3½f. blue	90	75
457		5f. green	10	40
458		10f. red	15	1·10
459		20f. blue	50	19·00

1945. Liberation.

460	–	60c.+1f.40 green	20	25
461	–	1f.20+1f.80 red	20	25
462	**71**	2f.50+3f.50 blue	20	25
463	–	4f.20+4f.80 violet	20	25

DESIGNS: 60c. Ship symbol of Paris between Cross of Lorraine and Arms of Luxembourg; 1f.20, Man killing snake between Arms of Russia and Luxembourg; 4f.20, Eagle between Arms of U.S.A. and Luxembourg.

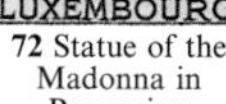

72 Statue of the Madonna in Procession

74 Lion of Luxembourg

73 Altar and Shrine of the Madonna

1945. Our Lady of Luxembourg.

464	**72**	60c.+40c. green	30	1·00
465	–	1f.20+80c. red	30	1·00
466	–	2f.50+2f.50 blue	40	5·50
467	–	5f.50+6f.50 violet	1·25	65·00
468	**73**	20f.+20f. brown	1·25	65·00

DESIGNS: As Type **72**: 1f.20, The Madonna; 2f.50, The Madonna and Luxembourg; 5f.50, Portal of Notre Dame Cathedral.

1945.

469	**74**	20c. black	20	20
470		30c. green	20	20
470a		60c. violet	20	25
471		75c. brown	20	20
472		1f.20 red	20	20
473		1f.50 violet	20	15
474		2f.50 blue	30	30

75 Members of the Maquis

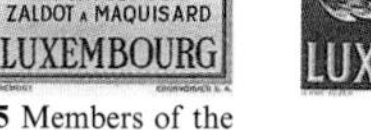

76

1945. National War Victims Fund.

475	**75**	20c.+30c. green and buff	20	1·00
476	–	1f.50+1f. red and buff	20	1·00
477	–	3f.50+3f.50 blue & buff	40	9·25
478	–	5f.+10f. brown and buff	35	9·25

DESIGNS: 1f.50, Mother and children; 3f.50, Political prisoner; 5f. Executed civilian.

1946. Air.

479	–	1f. green and blue	35	20
480	**76**	2f. brown and yellow	20	35
481	–	3f. brown and yellow	35	20
482	–	4f. violet and grey	50	30
483	**76**	5f. purple and yellow	45	30
484	–	6f. purple and blue	50	35
485	–	10f. brown and yellow	1·75	50
486	**76**	20f. blue and grey	2·10	1·25
487	–	50f. green and light green	4·00	1·50

DESIGNS: 1, 4, 10f. Airplane wheel; 3, 6, 50f. Airplane engine and castle.

77 John the Blind, King of Bohemia

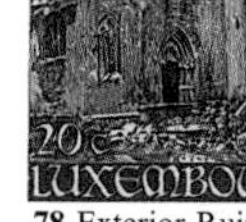

78 Exterior Ruins of St. Willibrord Basilica

79 St. Willibrord

1946. 600th Death Anniv of John the Blind.

488	**77**	60c.+40c. green and grey	30	1·60
489		1f.50+50c. red and buff	35	2·10
490		3f.50+3f.50 blue & grey	1·75	23·00
491		5f.+10f. brown and grey	1·00	19·00

1947. Echternach Abbey Restoration (2nd issue). Inscr "ECHTERNACH".

492	**78**	20c.+10c. black	35	30
493	–	60c.+10c. green	55	60
494	–	75c.+25c. red	85	75
495	–	1f.50c.+50c. brown	1·00	70
496	–	3f.50c.+ 2f.50 blue	5·00	4·50
497	**79**	25f.+25f. purple	27·00	21·00

DESIGNS—As Type **78**: 60c. Statue of Abbot Bertels; 75c. Echternach Abbey emblem; 1f.50, Ruined interior of Basilica; 3f.50, St. Irmine and Pepin II carrying model of Abbey.

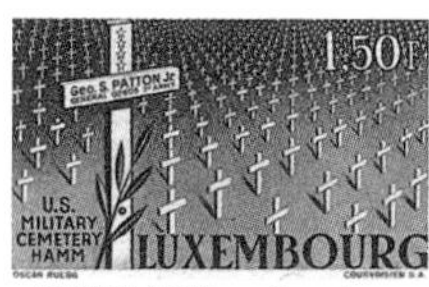

80 U.S. Military Cemetery, Hamm

82 Michel Lentz (national poet)

1947. Honouring Gen. George S. Patton.

498	**80**	1f.50 red and buff	40	20
499	–	3f.50 blue and buff	2·25	2·25
500	**80**	5f. green and grey	2·25	2·25
501	–	10f. purple and grey	9·25	35·00

PORTRAIT: 3f.50, 10f. Gen. G. S. Patton.

1947. National Welfare Fund.

502	**82**	60c.+40c. brown & buff	65	75
503		1f.50+50c. pur & buff	75	75
504		3f.50+3f.50 blue & grey	6·00	17·00
505		10f.+5f. green and grey	6·50	17·00

83 L'Oesling

85 "Dicks" (Edmund de la Fontaine)

1948. Tourist Propaganda.

505a	–	2f.50 brown and chocolate	1·75	35
505b	–	3f. violet	5·00	95
505c	–	4f. blue	3·75	95
506	**83**	7f. brown	15·00	65
507	–	10f. green	1·90	20
508	–	15f. red	1·90	35
509	–	20f. blue	1·90	35

DESIGNS—HORIZ: 2f.50, Television transmitter, Dudelange; 3f. Radio Luxembourg; 4f. Victor Hugo's house, Vianden; 10f. River Moselle; 15f. Mining district. VERT: 20f. Luxembourg.

1948. National Welfare Fund.

510	**85**	60c.+40c. brown & bistre	45	75
511		1f.50+50c. red and pink	70	85
512		3f.50+3f.50 blue & grey	9·25	18·00
513		10f.+5f. green and grey	11·50	18·00

86 Grand Duchess Charlotte

87 Date-stamp and Map

1948.

513a	**86**	5c. orange	10	20
513b		10c. blue	10	25
514		15c. olive	10	20
514a		20c. purple	20	20
515		25c. grey	10	20
515a		30c. olive	20	20
515b		40c. red	40	40
515c		50c. orange	40	20
516		60c. bistre	30	25
517		80c. green	30	20
518		1f. red	85	20
518a		1f.20 black	85	30
518b		1f.25 brown	85	35

519 1f.50 turquoise 85 15
520 1f.60 grey 1·25 1·25
521 2f. purple 85 15
521a 2f.50 red 1·40 30
521b 3f. blue 10·00 40
521c 3f.50 red 3·25 45
522 4f. blue 3·25 45
522a 5f. violet 8·00 40
523 6f. purple 6·00 55
524 8f. green 4·50 1·00

1949. 75th Anniv of U.P.U.
525 **87** 80c. green, lt green & black 60 55
526 2f.50 red, pink and black 2·75 1·60
527 4f. ultramarine, blue & black 5·00 5·25
528 8f. brown, buff and black 16·00 26·00

88 Michel Rodange — 89 Young Girl

1949. National Welfare Fund.
529 **88** 60c.+40c. green and grey 55 45
530 2f.+1f. purple and claret 5·50 4·50
531 4f.+2f. blue and grey 9·00 9·00
532 10f.+5f. brown and buff 9·00 17·00

1950. War Orphans Relief Fund.
533 – 60c.+15c. turquoise 1·75 75
534 **89** 1f.+20c. red 4·50 1·10
535 – 2f.+30c. brown 2·10 1·10
536 **89** 4f.+75c. blue 12·00 14·00
537 – 8f.+3f. black 32·00 38·00
538 **89** 10f.+5f. purple 32·00 38·00
DESIGN: 60c., 2f., 8f. Mother and boy.

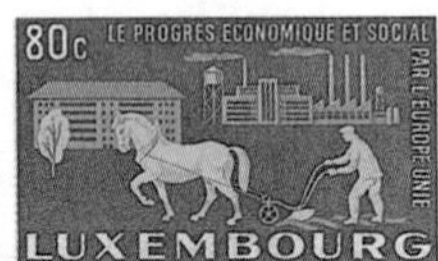

90 J. A. Zinnen (composer) — 91 Ploughman and Factories

1950. National Welfare Week.
539 **90** 60c.+10c. violet and grey 55 25
540 2f.+15c. red and buff 70 35
541 4f.+15c. blue and grey 5·50 6·00
542 8f.+5f. brown and buff 19·00 23·00

1951. To Promote United Europe.
543 **91** 80c. green and light green 10·05 8·25
544 – 1f. violet and light violet 4·50 50
545 – 2f. brown and grey 21·00 50
546 **91** 2f.50 red and orange 21·00 17·00
547 – 3f. brown and yellow 35·00 26·00
548 – 4f. blue and light blue 50·00 35·00
DESIGNS: 1, 3f. Map, people and "Rights of Man" Charter; 2, 4f. Scales balancing "United Europe" and "Peace".

92 L. Menager (composer)

1951. National Welfare Fund.
549 **92** 60c.+10c. black and grey 40 35
550 2f.+15c. green and grey 40 35
551 4f.+15c. blue and grey 4·50 3·00
552 8f.+5f. purple and grey 24·00 27·00

92a T 1 and 86

92b T 1

1952. National Philatelic Exhibition ("CENTILUX") and Stamp Centenary.
552a **92a** 80c. black, pur & grn (air) 50 55
552b 2f.50 black, purple & red 1·25 1·40
552c 4f. black, purple and blue 3·25 3·25
552d 8f. black, purple and red 40·00 50·00
552e 10f. black, purple & brn 35·00 42·00
552f **92b** 2f. blk & grn (postage) 26·00 35·00
552g 4f. red and green 26·00 35·00

93 Hurdling

1952. 15th Olympic Games, Helsinki.
553 **93** 1f. black and green 55 40
554 – 2f. blk & lt brn (Football) 2·25 40
555 – 2f.50 blk & pink (Boxing) 3·50 1·25
556 – 3f. blk & drab (Water polo) 4·50 1·40
557 – 4f. black and blue (Cycling) 21·00 6·75
558 – 8f. black and lilac (Fencing) 13·50 4·00

94 J. B. Fresez (painter) — 95 Prince Jean and Princess Josephine Charlotte

1952. National Welfare Fund.
559 **94** 60c.+15c. green and blue 40 40
560 2f.+25c. brown & orange 40 40
561 4f.+25c. violet and grey 3·50 3·50
562 8f.+4f.75 purple & lt pur 25·00 32·00

1953. Royal Wedding.
563 **95** 80c. violet and deep mauve 45 35
564 1f.20 deep brown & brown 45 35
565 2f. deep green and green 1·40 35
566 3f. deep purple and purple 1·40 55
567 4f. deep blue and blue 6·00 1·00
568 9f. brown and red 6·00 1·00

96 Echternach Basilica — 97 Pierre D'Aspelt

1953. Echternach Abbey Restoration (3rd issue).
569 **96** 2f. red 3·50 35
570 – 2f.50 olive 5·00 5·25
DESIGN: 2f.50, Interior of Basilica.

1953. 7th Birth Centenary of Pierre D'Aspelt.
571 **97** 4f. black 8·25 4·50

98 "Candlemas Singing" — 99 Foils, Mask and Gauntlet

1953. National Welfare Fund.
572 **98** 25c.+15c. carmine and red 40 40
573 – 80c.+20c. blue and brown 40 40
574 – 1f.20+30c. green & turq 95 75
575 **98** 2f.+25c. brown and red 50 40
576 – 4f.+50c. blue & turquoise 6·75 6·50
577 – 7f.+3f.35 lilac and violet 19·00 18·00
DESIGNS: 80c., 4f. "The Rattles"; 1f.20, 7f. "The Easter-eggs".

1954. World Fencing Championships.
578 **99** 2f. deep brown and brown on cream 4·25 60

100 Fair Emblem — 101 Earthenware Whistle

1954. Luxembourg International Fair.
579 **100** 4f. multicoloured 10·00 4·00

1954. National Welfare Fund.
580 **101** 25c.+5c. red and orange 50 45
581 – 80c.+20c. grey & black 50 45
582 – 1f.20+30c. green and cream 1·75 1·40
583 **101** 2f.+25c. brown and buff 70 55
584 – 4f.+50c. dp blue & blue 6·50 6·25
585 – 7f.+3f.45 violet & mve 26·00 22·00
DESIGNS: 80c., 4f. Sheep and drum; 1f.20, 7f. Merry-go-round horses.

102 Tulips — 103

1955. Mondorf-les-Bains Flower Show.
586 **102** 80c. red, green and brown 25 25
587 – 2f. yellow, green and red 35 25
588 – 3f. purple, green & emer 2·75 4·50
589 – 4f. orange, green and blue 4·50 4·50
FLOWERS: 2f. Daffodils; 3f. Hyacinths; 4f. Parrot tulips.

1955. 1st National Crafts Exhibition.
590 **103** 2f. black and grey 1·50 35

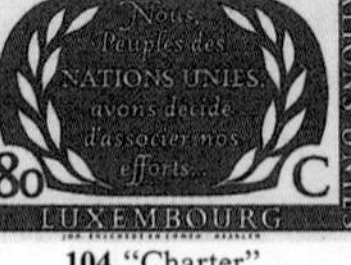

104 "Charter" — 105 "Christmas Day"

1955. 10th Anniv of U.N.
591 **104** 80c. blue and black 65 55
592 – 2f. brown and red 5·00 30
593 – 4f. red and blue 3·75 3·00
594 – 9f. green and brown 1·60 85
SYMBOLIC DESIGNS: 2f. "Security"; 4f. "Justice"; 9f. "Assistance".

1955. National Welfare Fund.
595 – 25c.+5c. red and pink 35 30
596 **105** 80c.+20c. black and grey 35 30
597 – 1f.20+30c. deep green and green 60 80
598 – 2f.+25c. deep brown and brown 70 30
599 **105** 4f.+50c. blue & lt blue 6·50 9·50
600 – 7f.+3f.45 purple & mve 13·00 13·50
ALLEGORICAL DESIGNS: 25c., 2f. "St. Nicholas's Day"; 1f.20, 7f. "Twelfth Night".

1956. Mondorf-les-Bains Flower Show. As T **102** but inscription at top in one line. Multicoloured.
601 2f. Anemones 75 25
602 3f. Crocuses 3·00 1·60

1956. Roses. As T **102** but inscr at top "LUXEMBOURG-VILLE DES ROSES". Multicoloured.
603 2f.50 Yellow roses 5·00 4·00
604 4f. Red roses 2·50 2·25

108 Steel Plant and Girder — 109 Blast Furnaces and Map

1956. 50th Anniv of Esch-sur-Alzette.
605 **108** 2f. red, black & turquoise 2·75 45

1956. European Coal and Steel Community. Inscr as in T **109**.
606 **109** 2f. red 26·00 50
607 – 3f. blue 26·00 20·00
608 – 4f. green 5·00 4·25
DESIGNS—VERT: 3f. Girder supporting City of Luxembourg. HORIZ: 4f. Chain and miner's lamp.

110 — 111 Luxembourg Central Station

1956. Europa.
609 **110** 2f. black and brown £250 35
610 3f. red and orange 42·00 35·00
611 4f. deep blue and blue 2·50 2·50

1956. Electrification of Luxembourg Railways.
612 **111** 2f. sepia and black 2·00 45

112 I. de la Fontaine — 113 Arms of Echternach

1956. Council of State Centenary. Inscr as in T **112**.
613 **112** 2f. sepia 1·40 35
614 – 7f. purple 2·75 75
DESIGN: 7f. Grand Duchess Charlotte.

1956. National Welfare Fund. Inscr "CARITAS 1956". Arms. Multicoloured.
615 25c.+5c. Type **113** 30 35
616 80c.+20c. Esch-sur-Alzette 30 35
617 1f.20+30c. Grevenmacher 45 70
618 2f.+25c. Type **113** 35 35
619 4f.+50c. Esch-sur-Alzette 3·50 4·00
620 7f.+3f.45 Grevenmacher 7·50 11·50

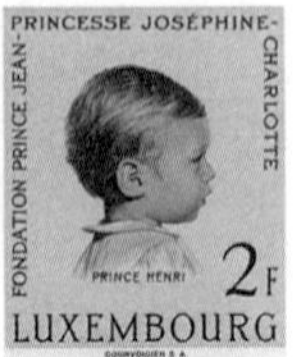

114 Lord Baden-Powell and Scout Emblems — 115 Prince Henri

1957. Birth Centenary of Lord Baden-Powell, and 50th Anniv of Scouting Movement.
621 **114** 2f. brown and green 1·00 25
622 – 2f.50 red and violet 2·50 2·40
DESIGN: 2f.50, as Type **114** but showing Girl Guide emblems.

1957. "Prince Jean and Princess Josephine-Charlotte Foundation" Child Welfare Clinic.
623 **115** 2f. deep brown and brown 1·00 25
624 – 3f. deep green and green 3·50 3·00
625 – 4f. deep blue and blue 2·50 2·50
DESIGNS—HORIZ: 3f. Children's Clinic Project. VERT: 4f. Princess Marie-Astrid.

116 "Peace" — 117 Fair Entrance and Flags

1957. Europa.
626 **116** 2f. brown . . . . 2·40 25
627 3f. red . . . . 38·00 15·00
628 4f. purple . . . . 32·00 15·00

1957. National Welfare Fund. Arms as T **113** inscr "CARITAS 1957". Multicoloured.
629 25c.+5c. Luxembourg 35 40
630 80c.+20c. Mersch 35 40
631 1f.20+30c. Vianden 45 60
632 2f.+25c. Luxembourg 30 35
633 4f.+50c. Mersch . . . . . 3·50 4·50
634 7f.+3f.45 Vianden . . . . . 5·50 7·00

1958. 10th Anniv of Luxembourg Int Fair.
635 **117** 2f. multicoloured 30 25

118 Luxembourg Pavilion

119 St. Willibrord holding Child (after Puseel)

1958. Brussels Exhibition.
636 **118** 2f.50 blue and red 30 25

1958. 1300th Birth Anniv of St. Willibrord.
637 – 1f. red 30 30
638 **119** 2f.50 sepia 35 20
639 – 5f. blue 90 85
DESIGNS: 1f. St. Willibrord and St. Irmina holding inscribed plaque; 5f. St. Willibrord and suppliant. (Miracle of the wine-cask).

119a Europa

120 Open-air Theatre at Wiltz

1958. Europa.
640 **119a** 2f.50 blue and red . . . 15 15
641 3f.50 brown and green 2·50 25
642 5f. red and blue 65 65

1958. Wiltz Open-air Theatre Commemoration.
643 **120** 2f.50 sepia and grey . . . 55 15

121 Vineyard

122 Grand Duchess Charlotte

1958. Bimillenary of Moselle Wine Industry.
644 **121** 2f.50 brown and green . . 55 15

1958. National Welfare Fund. Arms as T **113** inscr "CARITAS 1958". Multicoloured.
645 30c.+10c. Capellen 35 30
646 1f.+25c. Diekirch 35 30
647 1f.50+25c. Redange 55 45
648 2f.50+50c. Capellen 35 30
649 5f.+50c. Diekirch . . . . . . 3·25 4·00
650 8f.50+4f.60 Redange . . . . 5·00 6·75

1959. 40th Anniv of Accession of Grand Duchess Charlotte.
651 **122** 1f.50 deep green & green 70 35
652 2f.50 brown & lt brown 70 35
653 5f. lt blue and ultramarine 1·40 1·10

123 N.A.T.O. Emblem

123a Europa

1959. 10th Anniv of N.A.T.O.
654 **123** 2f.50 blue and olive . . . 20 15
655 8f.50 blue and brown . . 55 40

1959. Mondorf-les-Bains Flower Show. As T **102** but inscr "1959".
656 1f. violet, yellow and turquoise 30 30
657 2f.50 red, green and blue . . 40 25
658 3f. blue, green and purple . . 65 60
FLOWERS: 1f. Iris; 2f.50, Peony; 3f. Hortensia.

1959. Europa.
659 **123a** 2f.50 green 45 20
660 5f. blue 75 85

124 Steam Locomotive and First Bars of Hymn "De Feierwon"

1959. Railways Centenary.
661 **124** 2f.50 blue and red . . . . 1·90 40

1959. National Welfare Fund. Arms as T **113** inscr "CARITAS 1959". Multicoloured.
662 30c.+10c. Clervaux 35 30
663 1f.+25c. Remich 35 30
664 1f.50+25c. Wiltz 60 45
665 2f.50+50c. Clervaux 35 30
666 5f.+50c. Remich . . . . . . 1·50 1·90
667 8f.50+4f.60 Wiltz . . . . . . 6·50 9·50

125 Refugees seeking Shelter

126 Steel Worker

1960. World Refugee Year.
668 **125** 2f.50 blue and salmon . . 20 15
669 – 5f. blue and violet 35 40
DESIGN—HORIZ: 5f. "The Flight into Egypt" (Biblical scene).

1960. 10th Anniv of Schuman Plan.
670 **126** 2f.50 lake 30 25

127 European School, Luxembourg

128 Grand Duchess Charlotte

1960. European School Commemoration.
671 **127** 5f. black and blue 95 95

1960.
672 **128** 10c. red 10 25
673 20c. red 10 25
673a 25c. orange 20 25
674 30c. drab 10 15
675 50c. green 50 15
676 1f. violet 50 15
677 1f.50 mauve 50 15
678 2f. turquoise 55 25
679 2f.50 purple 85 25
680 3f. dull purple . . . . . 2·40 15
680a 3f.50 turquoise . . . . . 2·50 1·75
681 5f. brown . . . . 1·25 25
681a 6f. turquoise . . . . . . 2·40 25

129 Heraldic Lion, and Tools

1960. 2nd National Crafts Exhibition.
682 **129** 2f.50 multicoloured . . . 1·40 35

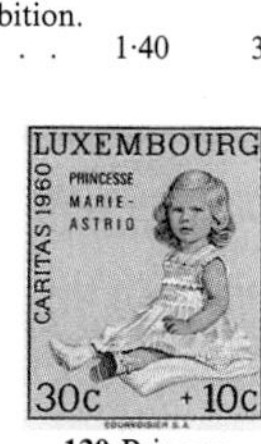

129a Conference Emblem

130 Princess Marie-Astrid

1960. Europa.
683 **129a** 2f.50 green and black . . 40 15
684 5f. black and red 65 35

1960. National Welfare Fund. Inscr "CARITAS 1960". Centres and inscr in sepia.
685 **130** 30c.+10c. blue 20 25
686 – 1f.+25c. pink 20 25
687 – 1f.50+25c. turquoise . . . 50 60
688 **130** 2f.50+50c. yellow 40 35
689 – 5f.+50c. lilac . . . . . . 85 2·40
690 – 8f.50+4f.60 sage . . . . 3·25 12·00
DESIGNS: Princess Marie-Astrid standing (1, 5f.), sitting with book on lap (1f.50, 8f.50).

131 Great Spotted Woodpecker

132 Patton Monument, Ettelbruck

1961. Animal Protection Campaign. Inscr "PROTECTION DES ANIMAUX".
691 **131** 1f. multicoloured 20 25
692 – 1f.50 buff, blue and black 25 25
693 – 3f. brown, buff and violet 40 40
694 – 8f.50 multicoloured . . . 60 70
DESIGNS—VERT: 8f.50, Dachshund. HORIZ: 1f.50, Cat; 3f. Horse.

1961. Tourist Publicity.
695 **132** 2f.50 blue and black . . . 50 25
696 – 2f.50 green 50 25
DESIGN—VERT: No. 696, Clervaux.

133 Doves

134 Prince Henri

1961. Europa.
697 **133** 2f.50 red 15 15
698 5f. blue 25 25

1961. National Welfare Fund. Inscr "CARITAS 1961". Centres and inscr in sepia.
699 **134** 30c.+10c. mauve 35 35
700 – 1f.+25c. lavender 35 35
701 – 1f.50+25c. salmon 45 50
702 **134** 2f.50+50c. green 45 35
703 – 5f.+50c. yellow . . . . . 2·40 2·40
704 – 8f.50+4f.60 grey . . . . 4·00 6·50
DESIGNS: Prince Henri when young boy (1, 5f.); youth in formal dress (1f.50, 8f.50).

135 Cyclist carrying Cycle

136 Europa "Tree"

1962. World Cross-country Cycling Championships, Esch-sur-Alzette.
705 **135** 2f.50 multicoloured . . . 30 25
706 – 5f. multicoloured (Emblem) 30 40

1962. Europa.
707 **136** 2f.50 multicoloured . . . 25 15
708 5f. brown, green & purple 35 30

137 St. Laurent's Church, Diekirch

138 Prince Jean and Princess Margaretha as Babies

1962.
709 **137** 2f.50 black and brown . . 45 25

1962. National Welfare Fund. inscr "CARITAS 1962". Centres and inscr in sepia.
710 **138** 30c.+10c. buff 30 25
711 – 1f.+25c. blue 30 25
712 – 1f.50+25c. olive 35 40
713 – 2f.50+50c. pink 35 25
714 – 5f.+50c. green . . . . . 1·40 2·40
715 – 8f.50+4f.60 violet . . . . 3·25 4·50

PORTRAITS—VERT: 1f., 2f.50, Prince Jean and: 2f.50, 5f. Princess Margaretha, at various stages of childhood. HORIZ: 8f.50, The Royal Children.

139 Blackboard

140 Benedictine Abbey, Munster

1963. 10th Anniv of European Schools.
716 **139** 2f.50 green, red and grey 20 15

1963. Millenary of City of Luxembourg and International Philatelic Exhibition. (a) Horiz views.
717 – 1f. blue 20 25
718 **140** 1f.50 red 20 25
719 – 2f.50 green 20 25
720 – 3f. brown 20 25
721 – 5f. violet 45 60
722 – 11f. blue . . . . 1·40 1·75
VIEWS: 1f. Bock Rock; 2f.50, Rham Towers; 3f. Grand Ducal Palace; 5f. Castle Bridge; 11f. Millenary Buildings.

(b) Vert multicoloured designs.
723 1f. "Three Towers" Gate 20 25
724 1f.50 Great Seal 20 30
725 2f.50 "The Black Virgin" (statue), St. John's Church 20 30
726 3f. Citadel 35 30
727 5f. Town Hall 20 45

141 Colpach Castle

1963. Red Cross Centenary.
728 **141** 2f.50 red and slate 30 25

142 "Human Rights"

1963. 10th Anniv of European "Human Rights" Convention.
729 **142** 2f.50 blue on gold 20 25

143 "Co-operation"

144 Brown trout snapping Bait

1963. Europa.
730 **143** 3f. green, orange & turq 20 15
731 6f. orange, red and brown 35 35

1963. World Fishing Championships, Wormeldange.
732 **144** 3f. slate 25 15

145 Telephone Dial

146 St. Roch (patron saint of bakers)

1963. Inauguration of Automatic Telephone System.
733 **145** 3f. green, black and blue 25 15

1963. National Welfare Fund. Patron Saints of Crafts and Guilds. Inscr "CARITAS 1963". Multicoloured.
734 50c.+10c. Type **146** 20 25
735 1f.+25c. St. Anne (tailors) . . 20 25
736 2f.+25c. St. Eloi (smiths) . . 20 35

737 3f.+50c. St. Michel (haberdashers) 20 25
738 6f.+50c. St. Barthelemy (butchers) 1·00 1·90
739 10f.+5f.90 St. Thibaut (seven crafts) 1·75 3·25

147 Power House

148 Barge entering Canal

1964. Inauguration of Vianden Reservoir.
740 **147** 2f. blue, brown and red 20 15
741 – 3f. blue, turq & red 20 15
742 – 6f. brown, blue and green 30 30
DESIGNS—HORIZ: 3f. Upper reservoir. VERT: 6f. Lohmuhle Dam.

1964. Inauguration of Moselle Canal.
743 **148** 3f. indigo and blue 30 15

149 Europa "Flower"

150 Students thronging "New Athenaeum"

1964. Europa.
744 **149** 3f. blue, brown and cream 20 15
745 6f. sepia, green and yellow 30 25

1964. Opening of "New Athenaeum" (education centre).
746 **150** 3f. black and green 20 25

150a King Baudouin, Queen Juliana and Grand Duchess Charlotte

1964. 20th Anniv of "BENELUX".
747 **150a** 3f. brown, yellow & blue 20 25

151 Grand Duke Jean and Princess Josephine-Charlotte

152 Three Towers

1964. Accession of Grand Duke Jean.
748 **151** 3f. deep blue and light blue 30 15
749 6f. sepia and light brown 35 30

1964. National Welfare Fund. Inscr "CARITAS 1964". Multicoloured.
750 50c.+10c. Type **152** 20 25
751 1f.+25c. Grand Duke Adolphe Bridge 20 25
752 2f.+25c. Lower Town 20 25
753 3f.+50c. Type **152** 20 25
754 6f.+50c. Grand Duke Adolphe Bridge 85 1·75
755 10f.+5f.90 Lower Town 1·40 2·50

153 Rotary Emblem and Cogwheels

154 Grand Duke Jean

1965. 60th Anniv of Rotary International.
756 **153** 3f. multicoloured 20 15

1965.
757 **154** 25c. brown 20 10
758 50c. red 20 10
759 1f. blue 20 10
760 1f.50 purple 10 10
761a 2f. red 35 10
762 2f.50 orange 35 30
763a 3f. green 45 10
763b 3f.50 brown 45 45
764a 4f. purple 50 10
764ba 5f. green 45 10
765a 6f. lilac 55 10
765b 7f. orange 50 20
765c 8f. blue 70 25
766 9f. green 70 25
766a 10f. black 50 10
767 12f. red 1·00 25
767a 14f. blue 70 40
767b 16f. green 1·00 30
767c 18f. green 35 45
767d 20f. blue 85 25
767e 22f. brown 1·25 85

155 I.T.U. Emblem and Symbols

1965. Centenary of I.T.U.
768 **155** 3f. blue, lake and violet 30 25

156 Europa "Sprig"

157 "The Roman Lady of the Titelberg"

1965. Europa.
769 **156** 3f. turquoise, red and black 20 25
770 6f. brown, blue and green 30 30

1965. National Welfare Fund. Fairy Tales. Inscr "CARITAS 1965". Multicoloured.
771 50c.+10c. Type **157** 15 25
772 1f.+25c. "Schappchen, the Huntsman" 15 25
773 2f.+25c. "The Witch of Koerich" 20 25
774 3f.+50c. "The Goblins of Schoendels" 20 25
775 6f.+50c. "Tollchen, Watchman of Hesperange" 35 1·10
776 10f.+5f.90 "The Old Spinster of Heispelt" 1·10 3·00

158 "Flag" and Torch

159 W.H.O. Building

1966. 50th Anniv of Luxembourg Workers' Union.
777 **158** 3f. red and grey 20 15

1966. Inaug of W.H.O. Headquarters, Geneva.
778 **159** 3f. green 20 15

160 Golden Key

161 Europa "Ship"

1966. Tercentenary of Solemn Promise to Our Lady of Luxembourg.
779 **160** 1f.50 green 10 15
780 – 2f. red 10 15
781 – 3f. blue 15 15
782 – 6f. brown 30 30
DESIGNS: 2f. Interior of Luxembourg Cathedral (after painting by J. Martin); 3f. Our Lady of Luxembourg (after engraving by R. Collin); 6f. Gallery pillar, Luxembourg Cathedral (after sculpture by D. Muller).

1966. Europa.
783 **161** 3f. blue and grey 20 25
784 6f. green and brown 35 30

162 Class 1800 Diesel-electric Locomotive

1966. Luxembourg Railwaymen's Philatelic Exhibition. Multicoloured.
785 1f.50 Type **162** 50 25
786 3f. Class 3600 electric locomotive 50 30

163 Grand Duchess Charlotte Bridge

164 Kirchberg Building and Railway Viaduct

1966. Tourism.
787 **163** 3f. lake 20 15
See also Nos. 807/8, 828 and 844/5.

1966. "Luxembourg-European Centre".
788 **164** 1f.50 green 20 25
789 – 13f. blue (Robert Schuman monument) 50 35

165 "Mary, Veiled Matron of Wormeldange"

166 City of Luxembourg, 1850 (after engraving by N. Liez)

1966. National Welfare Fund. Luxembourg Fairy Tales. Multicoloured.
790 50c.+10c. Type **165** 15 25
791 1f.50+25c. "Jekel Warden of the Wark" 15 25
792 2f.+25c. "The Black Gentleman of Vianden" 15 30
793 3f.+50c. "The Gracious Fairy of Rosport" 20 25
794 6f.+1f. "The Friendly Shepherd of Donkolz" 45 85
795 13f.+6f.90 "The Little Sisters of Trois-Vierges" 60 2·50

1967. Centenary of Treaty of London.
796 **166** 3f. brown, blue and green 20 25
797 – 6f. red, brown and blue 30 30
DESIGN—VERT: 6f. Plan of Luxembourg fortress c. 1850 (after T. de Cederstolpe).

167 Cogwheels

168 Lion on Globe

1967. Europa.
798 **167** 3f. purple, grey and buff 35 25
799 6f. sepia, purple and blue 40 35

1967. 50th Anniv of Lions International.
800 **168** 3f. yellow, purple & black 20 25

169 European Institutions Building, Luxembourg

170 Hikers and Hostel

1967. N.A.T.O. Council Meeting, Luxembourg.
801 **169** 3f. turquoise and green 20 25
802 6f. red and pink 35 40

1967. Luxembourg Youth Hostels.
803 **170** 1f.50 multicoloured 15 25

171 Shaving-dish (after Degrotte)

172 "Gardener"

1967. "200 Years of Luxembourg Pottery".
804 **171** 1f.50 multicoloured 20 25
805 – 3f. multicoloured 20 25
DESIGN—VERT: 3f. Vase, c. 1820.

1967. "Family Gardens" Congress, Luxembourg.
806 **172** 1f.50 orange and green 15 25

1967. Tourism. As T **163**.
807 3f. indigo and blue 30 25
808 3f. purple, green and blue 45 25
DESIGNS—HORIZ: No. 807, Moselle River and quayside, Mertert. VERT: No. 808, Moselle, Church and vines, Wormeldange.

173 Prince Guillaume

174 Football

1967. National Welfare Fund. Royal Children and Residence.
809 **173** 50c.+10c. brown & buff 20 25
810 – 1f.50+25c. brown & bl 20 25
811 – 2f.+25c. brown and red 20 25
812 – 3f.+50c. brown & yell 65 25
813 – 6f.+1f. brown & lav 45 1·00
814 – 13f.+6f.90 brn, grn & bl 60 3·25
DESIGNS: 1f.50, Princess Margaretha; 2f. Prince Jean; 3f. Prince Henri; 6f. Princess Marie-Astrid; 13f. Berg Castle.

1968. Olympic Games, Mexico.
815 – 50c. light blue and blue 20 15
816 **174** 1f.50 green and emerald 20 15
817 – 2f. yellow and green 25 15
818 – 3f. light orange and orange 20 15
819 – 6f. green and blue 25 25
820 – 13f. red and crimson 45 35
DESIGNS: 50c. Diving; 2f. Cycling; 3f. Running; 6f. Walking; 13f. Fencing.

175 Europa "Key"

1968. Europa.
821 **175** 3f. brown, black and green 35 15
822 6f. green, black and orange 40 35

176 Thermal Bath Pavilion, Mondorf-les-Bains

1968. Mondorf-les-Bains Thermal Baths.
823 **176** 3f. multicoloured 25 15

177 Fair Emblem

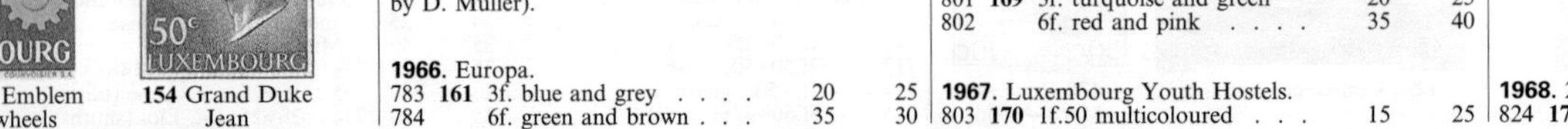

1968. 20th Anniv of Luxembourg Int Fair.
824 **177** 3f. multicoloured 25 25

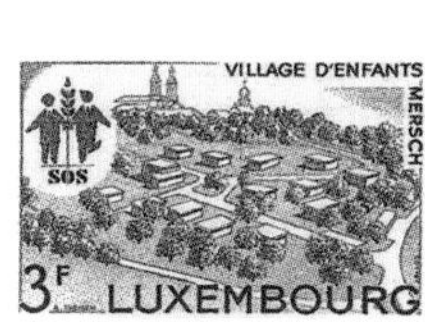

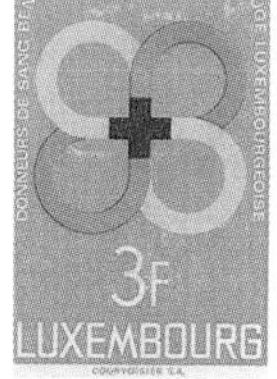

178 Village Project **179** "Blood Transfusion"

1968. Luxembourg SOS Children's Village.
825 **178** 3f. purple and green . . . 30 15
826 – 6f. black, blue and purple 35 30
DESIGN—VERT: 6f. Orphan with foster-mother.

1968. Blood Donors of Luxembourg Red Cross.
827 **179** 3f. red and blue 40 25

180 Fokker Friendship over Luxembourg **181** Cap Institute

1968. Tourism.
828 **180** 50f. dp blue, brown & blue . . . . 2·50 25

1968. National Welfare Fund. Luxembourg Handicapped Children.
829 **181** 50c.+10c. brown and blue 20 25
830 – 1f.50+25c. brn & grn . . 20 25
831 – 2f.+25c. brown & yell . . 30 35
832 – 3f.+50c. brown and blue 30 25
833 – 6f.+1f. brown and buff . . 50 90
834 – 13f.+6f.90 brown and pink . . . . 1·25 3·00
DESIGNS: 1f.50, Deaf and dumb child; 2f. Blind child; 3f. Nurse supporting handicapped child; 6f. and 13f. Mentally handicapped children (different).

183 Colonnade

1969. Europa.
836 **183** 3f. multicoloured 35 15
837 6f. multicoloured 40 35

184 "The Wooden Horse" (Kutter)

1969. 75th Birth Anniv of Joseph Kutter (painter). Multicoloured.
838 3f. Type **184** 50 25
839 6f. "Luxembourg" (Kutter) 50 40

185 ILO Emblem **186** National Colours

1969. 50th Anniv of Int Labour Organization.
840 **185** 3f. gold, violet and green 30 15

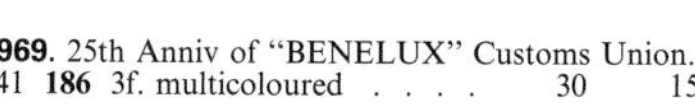
1969. 25th Anniv of "BENELUX" Customs Union.
841 **186** 3f. multicoloured 30 15

187 N.A.T.O. Emblem **188** Ear of Wheat and Agrocentre, Mersch

1969. 20th Anniv of N.A.T.O.
842 **187** 3f. orange and brown . . 35 15

1969. "Modern Agriculture".
843 **188** 3f. grey and green 20 15

189 Echternach **190** Vianden Castle

1969. Tourism.
844 **189** 3f. indigo and blue . . . 30 25
845 – 3f. blue and green 30 25
DESIGN: No. 845, Wiltz.

1969. National Welfare Fund. Castles (1st series). Multicoloured.
846 50c.+10c. Type **190** 15 25
847 1f.50+25c. Lucilinburhuc . . 15 25
848 2f.+25c. Bourglinster 20 25
849 3f.+50c. Hollenfels 20 25
850 6f.+1f. Ansembourg . . . . 50 1·40
851 13f.+6f.90 Beaufort . . . . . 85 3·25
See also Nos. 862/7.

191 Pasque Flower **192** Firecrest

1970. Nature Conservation Year. Multicoloured.
852 3f. Type **191** 20 25
853 6f. West European hedgehogs 35 40

1970. 50 Years of Bird Protection.
854 **192** 1f.50 green, black & orge 20 20

193 "Flaming Sun"

1970. Europa.
855 **193** 3f. multicoloured 35 15
856 6f. multicoloured 40 40

194 Road Safety Assoc. Emblem and Traffic

1970. Road Safety.
857 **194** 3f. black, red and lake . . 20 15

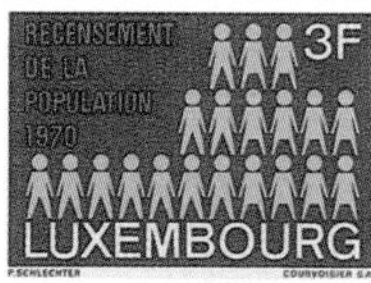

195 "Empress Kunegonde and Emperor Henry II" (stained-glass windows, Luxembourg Cathedral)

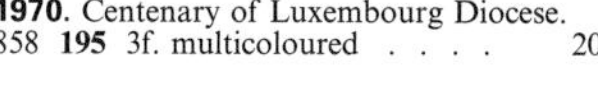
1970. Centenary of Luxembourg Diocese.
858 **195** 3f. multicoloured 20 25

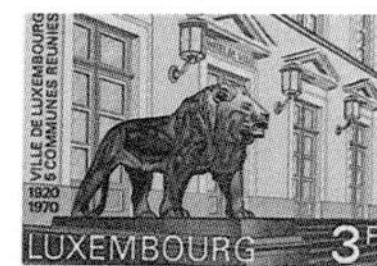

196 Population Pictograph

1970. Population Census.
859 **196** 3f. red, blue and green . . 20 15

197 Facade of Town Hall, Luxembourg

1970. 50th Anniv of Union of Four Suburbs with Luxembourg City.
860 **197** 3f. brown, ochre and blue 20 15

198 U.N. Emblem **199** Monks in the Scriptorium

1970. 25th Anniv of United Nations.
861 **198** 1f.50 violet and blue . . . 10 15

1970. National Welfare Fund. Castles (2nd series). Designs as T **190**.
862 50c.+10c. Clervaux 15 25
863 1f.50+25c. Septfontaines . . 15 25
864 2f.+25c. Bourscheid 20 25
865 3f.+50c. Esch-sur-Sure . . . 20 25
866 6f.+1f. Larochette . . . . . 50 1·40
867 13f.+6f.90 Brandenbourg . . 80 3·25

1971. Medieval Miniatures produced at Echternach. Multicoloured.
868 1f.50 Type **199** 20 25
869 3f. Vine-growers going to work 20 15
870 6f. Vine-growers at work and returning home 20 25
871 13f. Workers with spades and hoe 50 55

200 Europa Chain

1971.
872 **200** 3f. black, brown and red 35 15
873 6f. black, brown and green 50 55

201 Olympic Rings and Arms of Luxembourg **202** "50" and Emblem

1971. Int Olympic Committee Meeting, Luxembourg.
874 **201** 3f. red, gold and blue . . 20 25

1971. 50th Anniv of Luxembourg's Christian Workers' Union (L.C.G.B.).
875 **202** 3f. purple, orange & yell 20 15

203 Artificial Lake, Upper Sure Valley **204** Child with Coin

1971. Man-made Landscapes.
876 **203** 3f. blue, grey and brown 35 15
877 – 3f. brown, green and blue 35 25
878 – 15f. black, blue and brown 65 15
DESIGNS: No. 877, Water-processing plant, Esch-sur-Sure; No. 878, ARBED (United Steelworks) Headquarters Building, Luxembourg.

1971. Schoolchildren's Saving Campaign.
879 **204** 3f. multicoloured 25 25

205 "Bethlehem Children" **206** Coins of Belgium and Luxembourg

1971. National Welfare Fund. "The Nativity"–wood-carvings in Beaufort Church. Multicoloured.
880 1f.+25c. Type **205** 30 25
881 1f.50+25c. "Shepherds" . . . 30 25
882 3f.+50c. "Virgin, Child Jesus and St. Joseph" 30 25
883 8f.+1f. "Herdsmen" . . . . 85 2·40
884 18f.+6f.50 "One of the Magi" 1·60 5·25

1972. 50th Anniv of Belgium–Luxembourg Economic Union.
885 **206** 1f.50 silver, black & green 20 25

207 Bronze Mask (1st cent) **208** "Communications"

1972. Gallo-Roman Exhibits from Luxembourg State Museum. Multicoloured.
886 1f. Samian bowl (2nd century) (horiz) 20 15
887 3f. Type **207** 35 15
888 8f. Limestone head (2nd/3rd century) 65 75
889 15f. Glass "head" flagon (4th century) 60 65

1972. Europa.
890 **208** 3f. multicoloured 35 15
891 8f. multicoloured 85 85

209 Archer

210 R. Schuman (after bronze by R. Zilli)

1972. 3rd European Archery Championships, Luxembourg.
892 **209** 3f. multicoloured 35 15

1972. 20th Anniv of Establishment of European Coal and Steel Community in Luxembourg.
893 **210** 3f. green and grey 45 15

211 National Monument **212** "Renert"

1972. Monuments and Buildings.
894 **211** 3f. brown, green and violet 35 25
895 – 3f. brown, green and blue 55 25
DESIGN: No. 895, European Communities' Court of Justice.

1972. Cent of Publication of Michel Rodange's "Renert" (satirical poem).
896 **212** 3f. multicoloured 30 25

213 "Angel" **214** "Epona on Horseback"

1972. National Welfare Fund. Stained Glass Windows in Luxembourg Cathedral. Multicoloured.
897 1f.+25c. Type **213** 20 25
898 1f.50+25c. "St. Joseph" . . . 20 25
899 3f.+50c. "Holy Virgin with Child Jesus" 20 25
900 8f.+1f. "People of Bethlehem" . . . . 85 2·40
901 18f.+6f.50 "Angel" (facing left) . . . . 2·50 6·00

1973. Archaeological Relics. Multicoloured.
902 1f. Type **214** 20 15
903 4f. "Panther attacking swan" (horiz) 30 25
904 8f. Celtic gold coin 85 85
905 15f. Bronze boar (horiz) . . . 70 60

215 Europa "Posthorn" **216** Bee on Honeycomb

1973. Europa.
906 **215** 4f. orange, blue and violet 35 25
907 8f. green, yellow & purple 1·00 90

1973. Bee-keeping.
908 **216** 4f. multicoloured 45 15

217 Nurse and Child **218** Capital, Vianden Castle

1973. Day Nurseries in Luxembourg.
909 **217** 4f. multicoloured 35 15

1973. Romanesque Architecture in Luxembourg.
910 **218** 4f. purple and green . . . 30 15
911 – 8f. blue and brown . . . 70 75
DESIGN: 8f. Detail of altar, St. Irmina's Chapel, Rosport.

219 Labour Emblem **220** J. de Busleyden

1973. 50th Anniv of Luxembourg Board of Labour.
912 **219** 3f. multicoloured 25 15

1973. 500th Anniv of Great Council of Malines.
913 **220** 4f. purple and brown . . 30 15

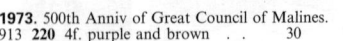

221 Monument, Wiltz **222** Joachim and St. Anne

1973. National Strike Monument.
914 **221** 4f. green, brown and grey 35 15

1973. National Welfare Fund. "The Nativity". Details from 16th-century reredos, Hachiville Hermitage. Multicoloured.
915 1f.+25c. Type **222** 20 25
916 3f.+25c. "Mary meets Elizabeth" 20 25
917 4f.+50c. "Magus presenting gift" 25 25
918 8f.+1f. "Shepherds at the manger" . . . . 85 2·25
919 15f.+7f. "St. Joseph with Candle" . . . . 2·50 6·75

223 Princess Marie-Astrid, Association President **224** Flame Emblem

1974. Luxembourg Red Cross Youth Association.
920 **223** 4f. multicoloured . . . . 1·40 30

1974. 50th Anniv of Luxembourg Mutual Insurance Federation.
921 **224** 4f. multicoloured 45 30

225 Seal of Henry VII, King of the Romans **226** "Hind" (A. Tremont)

1974. Seals in Luxembourg State Archives.
922 **225** 1f. brown, yellow & purple 20 15
923 – 3f. brown, yellow & green 30 30
924 – 4f. dk brown, yellow & brn 35 25
925 – 19f. brown, yellow & blue 85 75
DESIGNS: 3f. Equestrian seal of John the Blind, King of Bohemia; 4f. Municipal seal of Diekirch; 19f. Seal of Marienthal Convent.

1974. Europa. Sculptures. Multicoloured.
926 4f. Type **226** 80 25
927 8f. "Abstract" (L. Wercollier) 1·90 1·50

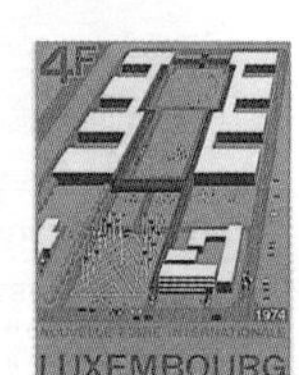

227 Churchill Memorial, Luxembourg **228** Diagram of Fair

1974. Birth Centenary of Sir Winston Churchill.
928 **227** 4f. multicoloured 35 15

1974. New International Fair, Luxembourg-Kirchberg.
929 **228** 4f. multicoloured 35 15

229 "Theis the Blind" (artist unknown) **230** "Crowning of St. Cecily and St. Valerien" (Hollenfels Church)

1974. 150th Death Anniv of "Theis the Blind" (Mathias Schou, folk singer).
930 **229** 3f. multicoloured 35 40

1974. Gothic Architecture.
931 **230** 4f. brown, green and violet 30 15
932 – 4f. black, brown and blue 30 15
DESIGN: No. 932, Interior of Septfontaines Church.

231 U.P.U. Emblem on "100"

1974. Centenary of Universal Postal Union.
933 **231** 4f. multicoloured 25 25
934 8f. multicoloured 35 75

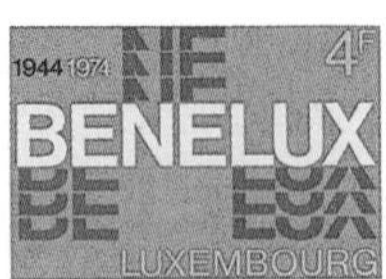

232 "Benelux"

1974. 30th Anniv of Benelux (Customs Union).
935 **232** 4f. turquoise, green & blue 85 25

233 Differdange

1974. Tourism.
936 **233** 4f. purple 85 15

234 "Annunciation" **236** The Fish Market, Luxembourg

1974. National Welfare Fund. Illustrations from "Codex Aureus Epternacensis". Multicoloured.
937 1f.+25c. Type **234** 20 25
938 3f.+25c. "Visitation" 20 25
939 4f.+50c. "Nativity" 25 25
940 8f.+1f. "Adoration of the Magi" . . . . 1·00 2·40
941 15f.+7f. "Presentation at the Temple" . . . . 1·90 5·25

1975. European Architectural Heritage Year.
943 **236** 1f. green 35 25
944 – 3f. brown 85 35
945 – 4f. lilac . . . . 1·00 25
946 – 19f. red . . . . 1·00 90
DESIGNS—HORIZ: 3f. Bourglinster Castle; 4f. Market Square, Echternach. VERT: 19f. St. Michael's Square, Mersch.

237 "Joseph Kutter" (self-portrait) **238** Dr. Albert Schweitzer

1975. Luxembourg Culture, and Europa. Paintings. Multicoloured.
947 1f. Type **237** 30 25
948 4f. "Remich Bridge" (N. Klopp) (horiz) . . . . 1·00 30
949 8f. "Still Life" (J. Kutter) (horiz) . . . . 2·00 1·75
950 20f. "The Dam" (D. Lang) 1·25 50

1975. Birth Centenary of Dr. Albert Schweitzer (medical missionary).
951 **238** 4f. blue 55 25

239 Robert Schuman, G. Martino and P.-H. Spaak **240** Civil Defence Emblem

1975. 25th Anniv of Robert Schuman Declaration for European Unity.
952 **239** 4f. black, gold and green 55 25

1975. 15th Anniv of Civil Defence Reorganization.
953 **240** 4f. multicoloured 50 25

241 Ice Skating **242** Fly Orchid

1975. Sports. Multicoloured.
954 **241** 3f. purple, blue and green 35 30
955 – 4f. brown, green & dp brn 50 15
956 – 15f. blue, brown and green . . . . 1·00 70
DESIGNS—HORIZ: 4f. Water-skiing. VERT: 15f. Rock-climbing.

1975. National Welfare Fund. Protected Plants (1st series). Multicoloured.
957 1f.+25c. Type **242** 20 25
958 3f.+25c. Pyramid orchid . . . 40 30
959 4f.+50c. Marsh helleborine 50 15
960 8f.+1f. Pasque flower . . . . 1·10 1·75
961 15f.+7f. Bee orchid . . . . . 2·50 5·00
See also Nos. 976/80 and 997/1001.

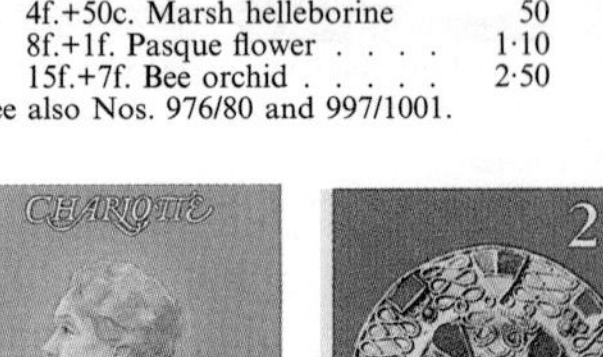

243 Grand Duchess Charlotte (80th) **244** 7th-century Disc-shaped Brooch

1976. Royal Birthdays. Multicoloured.
962 6f. Type **243** . . . . 1·25 35
963 6f. Prince Henri (21st) . . . 1·25 35

1976. Luxembourg Culture. Ancient Treasures from Merovingian Tombs. Multicoloured.
964 2f. Type **244** 20 15
965 5f. 5th-6th century glass beaker (horiz) 30 30
966 6f. Ancient pot (horiz) . . . 30 25
967 12f. 7th century gold coin . . 90 90

245 Soup Tureen

1976. Europa. 19th-century Pottery. Multicoloured.
968 6f. Type **245** 65 25
969 12f. Bowl . . . . 1·50 1·40

246 Independence Hall, Philadelphia **247** Symbol representing "Strength and Impetus"

1976. Bicentenary of American Revolution.
970 **246** 6f. multicoloured 35 30

1976. Olympic Games, Montreal.
971 **247** 6f. gold, magenta and mauve 35 30

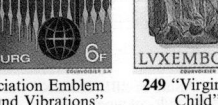

248 Association Emblem and "Sound Vibrations" **249** "Virgin and Child"

1976. 30th Anniv of "Jeunesses Musicales" (Youth Music Association).
972 **248** 6f. multicoloured 35 30

1976. Renaissance Art. Multicoloured.
973 6f. Type **249** 35 25
974 12f. Bernard de Velbruck, Lord of Beaufort (funeral monument) 85 85

250 Alexander Graham Bell

1976. Telephone Centenary.
975 **250** 6f. green 35 25

1976. National Welfare Fund. Protected Plants (2nd series). As T **242**. Multicoloured.
976 2f.+25c. Gentian 20 25
977 5f.+25c. Wild daffodil . . . 20 25
978 6f.+50c. Red helleborine (orchid) 30 25
979 12f.+1f. Late spider orchid 85 2·00
980 20f.+8f. Twin leaved squill 2·50 5·00

251 Johann von Goethe (poet)
252 Fish Market, Luxembourg

1977. Luxembourg Culture. Famous Visitors to Luxembourg.
981 **251** 2f. purple 20 15
982 – 5f. violet 30 30
983 – 6f. black 50 25
984 – 12f. violet 65 70
DESIGNS: 5f. Joseph Mallard William Turner (painter); 6f. Victor Hugo (writer); 12f. Franz Liszt (musician).

1977. Europa. Multicoloured.
985 6f. Type **252** 45 30
986 12f. Grand Duke Adolphe railway bridge and European Investment Bank 1·40 1·25

253 Esch-sur-Sure
254 Marguerite de Busbach (founder)

1977. Tourism.
987 **253** 5f. blue 45 25
988 – 6f. brown 35 25
DESIGNS 6f. Ehnen.

1977. Anniversaries. Multicoloured.
989 6f. Type **254** 40 25
990 6f. Louis Braille (after Filippi) 40 25
ANNIVERSARIES: No. 989, 350th anniv of foundation of Notre Dame Congregation; No. 990, 125th death anniv.

256 St. Gregory the Great
257 Head of Medusa

1977. Baroque Art. Sculpture from Feulen Parish Church pulpit attributed to J.-G. Scholtus.
992 **256** 6f. purple 40 25
993 – 12f. grey 70 80
DESIGN: 12f. St. Augustine.

1977. Roman Mosaic at Diekirch.
994 **257** 6f. multicoloured 70 25

258 Scene from "Orpheus and Eurydice" (Gluck)

1977. 25th Wiltz International Festival.
995 **258** 6f. multicoloured 65 25

259 Map of E.E.C. and "Europa" (R. Zilli)

1977. 20th Anniv of Rome Treaties.
996 **259** 6f. multicoloured 55 25

1977. National Welfare Fund. Protected Plants (3rd series). As T **242**. Multicoloured.
997 2f.+25c. Lily of the valley 20 25
998 5f.+25c. Columbine 30 30
999 6f.+50c. Mezereon 50 30
1000 12f.+1f. Early spider orchid 1·40 2·40
1001 20f.+8f. Spotted orchid . . 2·40 5·00

262 Charles IV

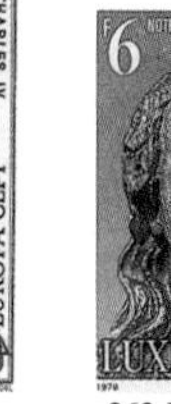

263 Head of Our Lady of Luxembourg

1978. Europa.
1004 **262** 6f. lilac 35 25
1005 – 12f. red . . . . 1·00 1·10
DESIGN: 12f. Pierre d'Aspelt (funeral monument, Mainz Cathedral).

1978. Anniversaries. Multicoloured.
1006 6f. Type **263** (300th anniv of election as patron saint) 35 30
1007 6f. Trumpeters (135th anniv of Grand Ducal Military Band) 35 30

264 Emile Mayrisch (after T. van Rysselberghe)

265 Child with Ear of Millet

1978. 50th Death Anniv of Emile Mayrisch (iron and steel magnate).
1008 **264** 6f. multicoloured 85 25

1978. "Solidarity 1978". Multicoloured.
1009 2f. Type **265** (Terre des Hommes) 20 15
1010 5f. Flower and lungs (70th anniv of Luxembourg Anti-tuberculosis League) 20 25
1011 6f. Open cell (Amnesty International and 30th anniv of Declaration of Human Rights) 30 25

266 Perfect Ashlar

267 "St. Matthew"

1978. 175th Anniv of Luxembourg Grand Lodge.
1012 **266** 6f. blue 35 30

1978. National Welfare Fund. Glass Paintings (1st series). Multicoloured.
1013 2f.+25c. Type **267** 15 25
1014 5f.+25c. "St. Mark" 30 30
1015 6f.+50c. "Nativity" 40 30
1016 12f.+1f. "St. Luke" . . . . 1·40 65
1017 20f.+8f. "St. John" . . . . 1·75 4·50
See also Nos. 1035/9 and 1055/8.

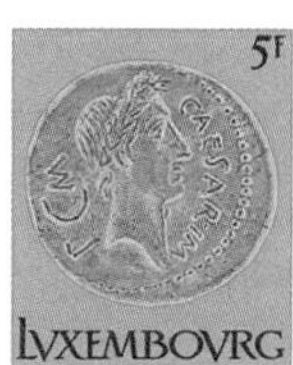

268 Denarius of Gaius Julius Caesar

269 Mondorf-les-Bains

1979. Luxembourg Culture. Roman Coins in the State Museum. Multicoloured.
1018 5f. Type **268** 30 25
1019 6f. Sestertius of Faustina I 50 25
1020 9f. Follis of Helena 70 45
1021 26f. Solidus of Valens . . . 1·40 1·25
See also Nos. 1040/3 and 1060/3.

1979. Tourism.
1022 **269** 5f. green, brown and blue 50 15
1023 – 6f. red 85 15
DESIGN: 6f. Luxembourg Central Station.

270 Stage Coach

271 Antoine Meyer (poet)

1979. Europa. Multicoloured.
1024 6f. Type **270** . . . . 2·40 25
1025 12f. Old wall telephone (vert) . . . . 2·40 1·50

1979. Anniversaries.
1026 – 2f. purple 45 25
1027 **271** 5f. red 35 25
1028 – 6f. turquoise 35 25
1029 – 9f. grey-black 35 35
DESIGNS—36 × 36 mm: 2f. Michel Pintz on trial (after L. Piedboeuf) and monument to rebels (180th anniv of peasant uprising against French). 22 × 36 mm: 5f. Type **271** (150th anniv of first publication in Luxembourg dialect); 6f. S. G. Thomas (cent of purchase of Thomas patent for steel production); 9f. "Abundance crowning Work and Saving" (ceiling painting by August Vinet) (50th anniv of Stock Exchange).

272 "European Assembly"

273 Blindfolded Cherub with Chalice

1979. First Direct Elections to European Assembly.
1030 **272** 6f. multicoloured . . . . 1·10 60

1979. Rococo Art. Details from altar of St. Michael's Church by Barthelemy Namur. Multicoloured.
1031 6f. Type **273** 35 30
1032 12f. Cherub with anchor . . 50 75

274 Child with Traffic Symbol Balloons jumping over Traffic

1979. International Year of the Child.
1033 **274** 2f. blue, brown and red 20 15

275 Radio Waves, "RTL" and Dates

1979. 50th Anniv of Broadcasting in Luxembourg.
1034 **275** 6f. blue and red 45 25

1979. National Welfare Fund. Glass Paintings (2nd series). As T **267**. Multicoloured.
1035 2f.+25c. "Spring" 15 20
1036 5f.+25c. "Summer" 30 30
1037 6f.+50c. "Charity" 40 30
1038 12f.+1f. "Autumn" 70 15
1039 20f.+8f. "Winter" . . . . . 1·25 4·50

1980. Luxembourg Culture. Medieval Coins in the State Museum. As T **268**. Multicoloured.
1040 2f. Grosso of Emperor Henry VII 15 15
1041 5f. Grosso of John the Blind of Bohemia 20 25
1042 6f. "Mouton d'or" of Wenceslas I and Jeanne, Duke and Duchess of Brabant 65 25
1043 20f. Grosso of Wenceslas II, Duke of Luxembourg . . 1·60 75

276 State Archives Building

277 Jean Monnet (statesman)

1980. Tourism.
1044 **276** 6f. purple, ultram & bl 50 15
1045 – 6f. red and brown . . . 60 15
DESIGN—VERT: No. 1045, Ettelbruck Town Hall.

1980. Europa.
1046 **277** 6f. black 50 25
1047 – 12f. olive . . . . 1·00 90
DESIGN: 12f. St. Benedict of Nursia (founder of Benedictine Order) (statue in Echternach Abbey).

278 Sports Equipment

279 Gloved Hand protecting Worker from Machinery

1980. "Sports for All".
1048 **278** 6f. black, orange & green 1·40 30

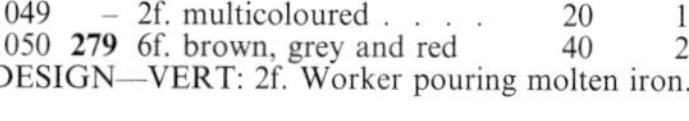

1980. 9th World Congress on the Prevention of Accidents at Work and Occupational Diseases, Amsterdam.
1049 – 2f. multicoloured 20 15
1050 **279** 6f. brown, grey and red 40 25
DESIGN—VERT: 2f. Worker pouring molten iron.

280 "Mercury" (Jean Mich)

281 Postcoded Letter

1980. Art Nouveau Sculpture. Statues beside entrance to State Savings Bank.
1051 **280** 8f. lilac 45 30
1052 – 12f. blue 65 60
DESIGN: 12f. "Ceres" (Jean Mich).

1980. Postcode Publicity.
1053 **281** 4f. brown, ochre and red 50 15

282 Policemen and Patrol Car

1980. 50th Anniv of National Police Force.
1054 **282** 8f. multicoloured 55 25

1980. National Welfare Fund. Glass Paintings (3rd series). As T **267**. Multicoloured.
1055 4f.+50c. "St. Martin" . . . 30 25
1056 6f.+50c. "St. Nicholas" . . 30 25
1057 8f.+1f. "Virgin and child" 40 1·00
1058 30f.+10f. "St. George" . . . 2·25 4·50

1981. Luxembourg Culture. Coins in the State Museum. As T **268**.
1060 4f. Patagon of Philip IV of Spain, 1635 . . . . . . 20 25
1061 6f. 12 sols coin of Maria Theresa, 1775 . . . . . . 30 30
1062 8f. 12 sols coin of Emperor Joseph II, 1789 . . . . . 30 30
1063 30f. Siege crown of Emperor Francis II, 1795 . . . . . 1·00 1·00

284 European Parliament Building, Luxembourg

285 Cock-shaped Whistle sold at Easter Monday Market

1981. Tourism.
1064 **284** 8f. brown and blue . . . 35 25
1065 – 8f. red and blue 35 25
DESIGN: No. 1065, National Library.

1981. Europa. Multicoloured.
1066 8f. Procession of beribboned sheep and town band to local fair 45 25
1067 12f. Type **285** 70 65

286 Staunton Knight on Chessboard

287 Prince Henri and Princess Maria Teresa

1981. Anniversaries.
1068 **286** 4f. multicoloured 30 25
1069 – 8f. ochre, brown & silver 40 30
1070 – 8f. multicoloured 40 30
DESIGNS—VERT: 4f. Type **286** (50th anniv of Luxembourg Chess Federation); 8f. (1070), Pass-book and State Savings Bank (125th anniv of State Savings Bank). HORIZ: 8f. (1069), First Luxembourg banknote (125th anniv of International Bank of Luxembourg's issuing rights).

1981. Royal Wedding.
1071 **287** 8f. multicoloured 55 50

288 Gliders over Useldange

289 Flame

1981. Aviation. Multicoloured.
1072 8f. Type **288** 45 30
1073 16f. Cessna 172F Skyhawk and 182H Skylane sports planes 70 65
1074 35f. Boeing 747-200F 182H over Luxembourg-Findel airport terminal . . . . . 1·40 90

1981. Energy Conservation.
1075 **289** 8f. multicoloured 50 20

290 Arms of Petange

291 "Apple Trees in Blossom" (Frantz Seimetz)

1981. National Welfare Fund. Arms of Local Authorities (1st series). Multicoloured.
1076 4f.+50c. Type **290** 20 25
1077 6f.+50c. Larochette 25 25
1078 8f.+1f. "Adoration of the Magi" (School of Rubens) 40 35
1079 16f.+2f. Stadtbredimus . . . 70 1·75
1080 35f.+12f. Weiswampach . . . 2·50 4·50
See also Nos. 1097/1101 and 1119/23.

1982. Luxembourg Culture. Landscapes through the Four Seasons. Multicoloured.
1081 4f. Type **291** 30 30
1082 6f. "Landscape" (Pierre Blanc) 40 40
1083 8f. "The Larger Hallerbach" (Guido Oppenheim) . . . 45 30
1084 16f. "Winter Evening" (Eugene Mousset) 85 80

292 Cross of Hinzert and Statue "Political Prisoner" (Lucien Wercollier)

293 Treaty of London, 1867, and Luxembourg Fortress

1982. National Monument of the Resistance and Deportation, Notre-Dame Cemetery.
1085 **292** 8f. multicoloured 40 20

1982. Europa. Multicoloured.
1086 8f. Type **293** 50 30
1087 16f. Treaty of Paris, 1951, and European Coal and Steel Community Building, Luxembourg . . 85 80

294 St. Theresa of Avila (wood statue, Carmel Monastery)

295 State Museum

1982. Anniversaries. Multicoloured.
1088 4f. Type **294** (400th death anniv) 20 15
1089 8f. Raoul Follereau (social worker for lepers, 5th death anniv) 35 25

1982. Tourism.
1090 **295** 8f. brown, blue and black 40 20
1091 – 8f. buff, black and blue 40 20
DESIGN: No. 1091, Luxembourg Synagogue.

296 Bourscheid Castle

297 Key in Lock

1982. Classified Monuments (1st series).
1092 **296** 6f. blue 30 20
1093 – 8f. red 45 20
DESIGN—HORIZ: 8f. Vianden Castle.
See also Nos. 1142/3 and 1165/6.

1982. Anniversaries. Multicoloured.
1094 4f. Type **297** (50th anniv of International Youth Hostel Federation) . . . 45 30
1095 8f. Scouts holding hands around globe (75th anniv of Scouting Movement) (vert) 70 30

298 Monument to Civilian and Military Deportation

1982. Civilian and Military Deportation Monument, Hollerich Station.
1096 **298** 8f. multicoloured 40 30

1982. National Welfare Fund. Arms of Local Authorities (2nd series) and Stained Glass Window (8f.). As T **290**. Multicoloured.
1097 4f.+50c. Bettembourg . . . 25 25
1098 6f.+50c. Frisange 30 25
1099 8f.+1f. "Adoration of the Shepherds" (Gustav Zanter, Hoscheid parish church) 45 80
1100 16f.+2f. Mamer . . . . . . 85 1·75
1101 35f.+12f. Heinerscheid . . . 2·40 4·75

299 Modern Fire Engine

300 "Mercury" (Auguste Tremont)

1983. Centenary of National Federation of Fire Brigades. Multicoloured.
1102 8f. Type **299** 45 30
1103 16f. Hand fire-pump (18th century) 70 75

1983. Anniversaries and Events.
1104 **300** 4f. multicoloured 30 30
1105 – 6f. multicoloured 30 30
1106 – 8f. brown, black and blue 40 30
1107 – 8f. deep blue and blue 40 30
DESIGNS: No. 1104, Type **300** (25th Congress of International Association of Foreign Exchange Dealers); 1105, N.A.T.O. emblem surrounded by flags of member countries (25th anniv of N.A.T.O.); 1106, Echternach Cross of Justice (30th Congress of International Union of Barristers); 1107, Globe and customs emblem (30th anniv of Customs Co-operation Council).

301 Robbers attacking Traveller

1983. Europa. Miniatures from "Codex Aureus Escorialensis", illustrating Parable of the Good Samaritan. Multicoloured.
1108 8f. Type **301** . . . . 1·25 40
1109 16f. Good Samaritan helping traveller . . . . . 2·75 1·25

302 Initial "H" from "Book of Baruch"

303 Despatch Rider and Postcode

1983. Luxembourg Culture. Echternach Abbey Giant Bible. Multicoloured.
1110 8f. Type **302** 45 35
1111 35f. Initial "B" from letter of St. Jerome to Pope Damasius I . . . . 1·40 1·10

1983. World Communications Year. Mult.
1112 8f. Type **303** 85 20
1113 8f. Europan Communications Satellite (horiz) . . . . 1·75 30

304 St. Lawrence's Church, Diekirch

305 Basketball

1983. Tourism.
1114 **304** 7f. orange, brown and blue 35 20
1115 – 10f. orange, brown & bl 55 20
DESIGN—HORIZ: 10f. Dudelange Town Hall.

1983. Anniversaries and Events. Multicoloured.
1116 7f. Type **305** (50th anniv of Luxembourg basketball Federation) 45 35
1117 10f. Sheepdog (European Working Dog Championships) 65 35
1118 10f. City of Luxembourg ("The Green Heart of Europe") . . . . 1·10 35

1983. National Welfare Fund. Arms of Local Authorities (3rd series) and Painting. As T **290**. Multicoloured.
1119 4f.+1f. Winseler 30 30
1120 7f.+1f. Beckerich 40 35
1121 10f.+1f. "Adoration of the Shepherds" (Lucas Bosch) 45 50
1122 16f.+2f. Feulen . . . . . . 85 1·75
1123 40f.+13f. Mertert . . . . . 2·40 4·25

306 Lion and First Luxembourg Stamp

307 Pedestrian Precinct

1984. Anniversaries. Each black, red and blue.
1124 10f. Type **306** 70 35
1125 10f. Lion and ministry buildings 70 35
1126 10f. Lion and postman's bag 70 35
1127 10f. Lion and diesel locomotive 70 35
ANNIVERSARIES: No. 1124, 50th anniv of Federation of Luxembourg Philatelic Societies; 1125, 75th anniv of Civil Service Trade Union Movement; 1126, 75th anniv of Luxembourg Postmen's Trade Union; 1127, 125th anniv of Luxembourg Railways.

1984. Environmental Protection. Multicoloured.
1128 7f. Type **307** 45 35
1129 10f. City of Luxembourg sewage treatment plant . . 45 35

308 Hands supporting European Parliament Emblem

309 Bridge

1984. 2nd Direct Elections to European Parliament.
1130 **308** 10f. multicoloured . . . 70 40

1984. Europa. 25th Anniv of European Post and Telecommunications Conference.
1131 **309** 10f. green, dp green & blk . . . . 1·60 35
1132 16f. orange, brown & blk 3·25 1·40

310 "The Smoker" (David Teniers the Younger)

311 "The Race" (Jean Jacoby)

1984. Paintings. Multicoloured.
1133 4f. Type **310** 50 30
1134 7f. "Young Turk caressing his Horse" (Eugene Delacroix) (horiz) 65 35
1135 10f. "Ephiphany" (Jan Steen) (horiz) 85 35
1136 50f. "The Lacemaker" (Pieter van Slingelandt) 3·50 2·50

1984. Olympic Games, Los Angeles.
1137 **311** 10f. orange, black & blue 65 30

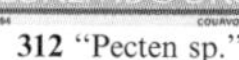

312 "Pecten sp."

313 "American Soldier" (statue by Michel Heitz at Clervaux)

1984. Luxembourg Culture. Fossils in the Natural History Museum. Multicoloured.
1138 4f. Type **312** 45 20
1139 7f. Devil's toe-nail 50 35
1140 10f. "Coeloceras raquinianum" (ammonite) 85 35
1141 16f. Dapedium (fish) . . . . 1·00 85

1984. Classified Monuments (2nd series). As T **296**.
1142 7f. turquoise 35 35
1143 10f. brown 45 30
DESIGNS: 7f. Hollenfels Castle; 10f. Larochette Castle.

1984. 40th Anniv of Liberation.
1144 **313** 10f. black, red and blue 1·40 30

314 Infant astounded by Surroundings

315 Jean Bertels (abbot of Echternach Abbey)

1984. National Welfare Fund. The Child. Mult.
1145 4f.+1f. Type **314** 35 35
1146 7f.+1f. Child dreaming . . . 50 50
1147 10f.+1f. "Nativity (crib, Steinsel church) 85 55
1148 16f.+2f. Child sulking . . . 2·40 2·50
1149 40f.+13f. Girl admiring flower . . . . 6·00 6·75

1985. Luxembourg Culture. Portrait Medals in State Museum (1st series). Multicoloured.
1150 4f. Type **315** (steatite medal, 1595) 25 30
1151 7f. Emperor Charles V (bronze medal, 1537) . . 35 35
1152 10f. King Philip II of Spain (silver medal, 1555) . . . 45 35
1153 30f. Maurice of Orange-Nassau (silver medal, 1615) . . . . 1·40 1·00
See also Nos. 1173/6.

316 Fencing

317 Papal Arms

1985. Anniversaries. Multicoloured.
1154 10f. Type **316** (50th anniv of Luxembourg Fencing Federation) 60 30
1155 10f. Benz "Velo" (centenary of automobile) 60 30
1156 10f. Telephone within concentric circles (centenary of Luxembourg telephone service) 60 30

1985. Visit of Pope John Paul II.
1157 **317** 10f. multicoloured . . . 45 30

318 Treble Clef within Map of National Anthem

320 Little Owl

1965. Europa. Music Year. Multicoloured.
1158 10f. Type **318** (Grand Duke Adolphe Union of choral, instrumental and folklore societies) . . . . 1·50 35
1159 16f. Neck of violin, music school and score of Beethoven's Violin Concerto opus 61 . . . . 3·00 1·60

1985. Endangered Animals. Multicoloured.
1161 4f. Type **320** 85 35
1162 7f. European wildcat (horiz) 1·75 50
1163 10f. Red admiral (horiz) . . 2·50 40
1164 50f. European tree frog . . 3·50 2·40

1985. Classified Monuments (3rd series). As T **296**.
1165 7f. red 35 30
1166 10f. green 35 30
DESIGNS—HORIZ: 7f. Echternach orangery. VERT: 10f. Mohr de Waldt house.

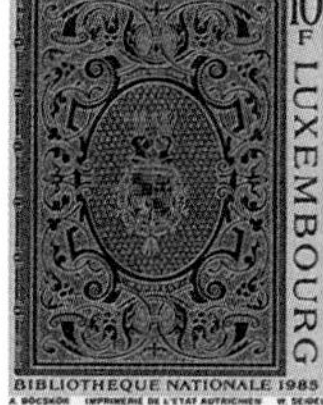
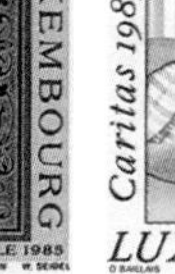

321 Mansfeld Arms (book binding)

322 Application

1985. Luxembourg Culture.
1167 **321** 10f. multicoloured . . . 50 35

1985. National Welfare Fund. Multicoloured.
1168 4f.+1f. Type **322** 40 30
1169 7f.+1f. Friendship 55 45
1170 10f.+1f. "Adoration of the Magi" (16th century alabaster sculpture) . . . 85 45
1171 16f.+2f. Child identifying with his favourite characters . . . . 2·50 2·50
1172 40f.+13f. Shame . . . . . 6·25 8·25

1986. Luxembourg Culture. Portrait Medals in State Museum (2nd series). As T **315**.
1173 10f. multicoloured 45 35
1174 12f. multicoloured 50 30
1175 18f. black, grey and blue . . 70 60
1176 20f. multicoloured . . . . . 1·00 75
DESIGNS: 10f. Count of Monterey (silver medal, 1675); 12f. Louis XIV of France (silver medal, 1684); 18f. Pierre de Weyms (president of Provincial Council) (pewter medal, 1700); 20f. Duke of Marlborough (silver medal, 1706).

323 Bee on Flower

324 Forest and City

1986. Anniversaries. Multicoloured.
1177 12f. Type **323** (centenary of Federation of Luxembourg Beekeeper's Associations) 70 30
1178 12f. Table tennis player (50th anniv of Luxembourg Table Tennis Federation) 70 30
1179 11f. Mosaic of woman with water jar (centenary of Mondorf State Spa) . . . 70 30

1986. Europa. Multicoloured.
1180 12f. Type **324** . . . . . . 1·00 35
1181 20f. Mankind, industry and countryside . . . . 1·60 1·10

325 Fort Thungen

326 Schuman

1986 Luxembourg Town Fortifications. Mult.
1182 15f. Type **325** . . . . . . 1·25 50
1183 18f. Invalids' Gate (vert) . . 1·25 50
1184 50f. Malakoff Tower (vert) 2·00 65

1986. Birth Centenary of Robert Schuman (politician).
1185 **326** 2f. black and red 15 15
1186 10f. black and blue . . . 40 35

327 Road through Red Triangle on Map

328 Ascent to Chapel of the Cross, Grevenmacher

1986. European Road Safety Year.
1187 **327** 10f. multicoloured . . . 50 30

1986. Tourism.
1188 **328** 12f. multicoloured . . . 65 30
1189 – 12f. brown, stone and red 65 30
DESIGN: No. 1189, Relief from Town Hall facade, Esch-sur-Alzette.

329 Presentation of Letter of Freedom to Echternach (after P. H. Witkamp)

330 Annunciation

1986. 800th Birth Anniv of Countess Ermesinde of Luxembourg.
1190 **329** 12f. brown and stone . . 55 35
1191 – 30f. buff, black and grey 1·60 1·00
DESIGN: 30f. Seal, 1238.

1986. National Welfare Fund. Illustrations from 15th-century "Book of Hours". Multicoloured.
1192 6f.+1f. Type **330** 85 35
1193 10f.+1f. Angel appearing to shepherds 45 35
1194 12f.+2f. Nativity 85 45
1195 18f.+2f. Adoration of the Magi . . . . 2·50 3·00
1196 20f.+8f. Flight into Egypt 4·25 5·50

331 Garden Dormouse

332 Network Emblem

1987. Endangered Animals. Multicoloured.
1197 6f. Type **331** 65 65
1198 10f. Banded agrion (vert) . . 1·00 40
1199 12f. White-throated dipper (vert) . . . . 1·50 40
1200 25f. Salamander . . . . . . 2·40 1·25

1987. 50th Anniversaries. Multicoloured.
1201 12f. Type **332** (Amateur Short Wave Network) . . 45 40
1202 12f. Anniversary Emblem (International Fair) . . . 45 30

333 "St. Bernard of Siena and St. John the Baptist"

334 National Swimming Centre (Roger Taillibert)

1987. Paintings by Giovanni Ambrogio Bevilacqua in State Museum. Multicoloured.
1203 10f. Type **333** 45 40
1204 18f. "St. Jerome and St. Francis of Assisi" . . 70 80

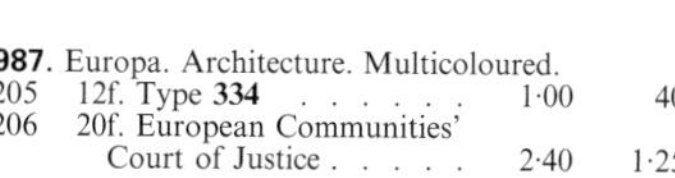

1987. Europa. Architecture. Multicoloured.
1205 12f. Type **334** . . . . . . 1·00 40
1206 20f. European Communities' Court of Justice . . . . . 2·40 1·25

335 "Consecration" (stained glass window by Gustav Zanter)

336 Charles Metz (first President) (after Jean-Baptiste Fresez)

1987. Millenary of St. Michael's Church. Multicoloured.
1207 12f. Type **335** 45 30
1208 20f. Baroque organ-chest . . 85 80

1987. Chamber of Deputies.
1209 **336** 6f. brown 30 30
1210 – 12f. blue 55 50
DESIGN: 12f. Chamber of Deputies building.

337 Hennesbau, Niederfeulen

338 Annunciation

1987. Rural Architecture. Each ochre, brown and blue.
1211 10f. Type **337** 50 35
1212 12f. 18th-century dwelling house converted to health centre, Mersch 50 20
1213 100f. 18th-century house converted to Post Office, Bertrange . . . . 3·25 1·10

1987. National Welfare Fund. Illustrations from 15th-century Paris "Book of Hours". Multicoloured.
1214 6f.+1f. Type **338** 60 55
1215 10f.+1f. Visitation . . . . . 95 1·00
1216 12f.+2f. Adoration of the Magi . . . . 1·25 1·00
1217 18f.+2f. Presentation in the Temple . . . . 2·40 2·40
1218 20f.+8f. Flight into Egypt 5·00 5·00

339 Lilies and Water-lily

340 Rail, Road and Water Transport

1988. Luxembourg Culture. Flower Illustrations by Pierre-Joseph Redoute. Multicoloured.
1219 6f. Type **339** 60 35
1220 10f. Primulas and double narcissus 60 40
1221 12f. Tulips and chrysanthemums . . . . 1·00 45
1222 50f. Irises and gorterias . . 3·25 2·10

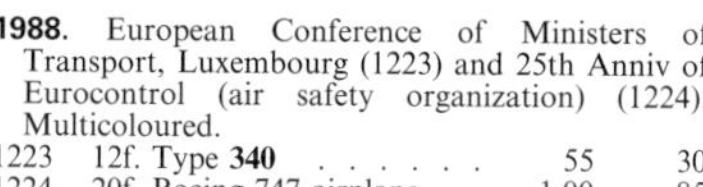
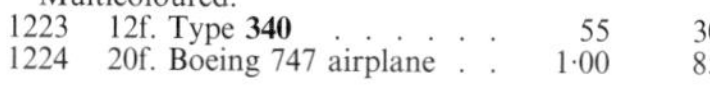

1988. European Conference of Ministers of Transport, Luxembourg (1223) and 25th Anniv of Eurocontrol (air safety organization) (1224). Multicoloured.
1223 12f. Type **340** 55 30
1224 20f. Boeing 747 airplane . . 1·00 85

342 Wiltz Town Hall and Cross of Justice

1988. Tourism. Multicoloured.
1226 10f. Type **342** 60 40
1227 12f. Differdange Castle (vert) 60 40
See also Nos. 1254/5 and 1275/6.

343 Athletes

1988. 50th Anniv of League of Luxembourg Student Sports Associations.
1228 **343** 12f. multicoloured . . . 70 45

344 Automated Mail Sorting

1988. Europa. Transport and Communications. Multicoloured.
1229 12f. Type **344** . . . . . . 2·40 35
1230 20f. Electronic communications . . . . . 2·50 1·75

345 Jean Monnet (statesman, birth centenary) 346 Emblem and Flame

1988. European Anniversaries.
1231 **345** 12f. pink, brn & lt brn 50 35
1232 – 12f. brown and green . . 85 35
DESIGN: No. 1232, European Investment Bank headquarters, Kirchberg (30th anniv).

1988. Olympic Games, Seoul.
1233 **346** 12f. multicoloured . . . 50 35

347 Septfontaines Castle 348 Annunciation to Shepherds

1988. Doorways.
1234 **347** 12f. black and brown . . 60 30
1235 – 25f. black and green . . 1·25 90
1236 – 50f. black and brown . . 2·25 1·40
DESIGNS: 25f. National Library; 50f. Holy Trinity Church.

1988. National Welfare Fund. Illustrations from 16th-century "Book of Hours". Multicoloured.
1237 9f.+1f. Type **348** 45 45
1238 12f.+2f. Adoration of the Magi 50 50
1239 18f.+3f. Madonna and Child 2·40 2·40
1240 20f.+8f. Pentecost . . . . . 1·50 2·50

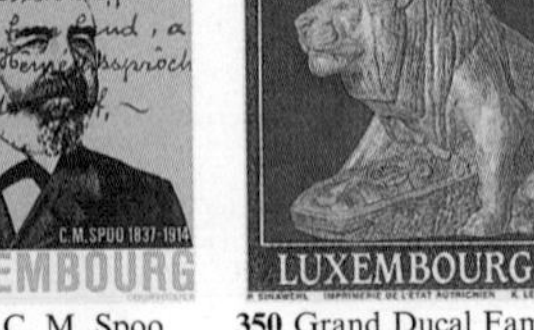

349 C. M. Spoo (promoter of Luxembourgish) 350 Grand Ducal Family Vault Bronze (Auguste Tremont)

1989. Anniversaries.
1241 **349** 12f. black, red and brown 50 45
1242 – 18f. multicoloured . . . 85 60·00
1243 – 20f. red, black and grey 1·25 1·00
DESIGNS: 12f. Type **349** (75th death anniv); 18f. Stylized inking pad (125th anniv of Book Workers' Federation); 20f. Henri Dunant (founder of International Red Cross) (75th anniv of Luxembourg Red Cross).

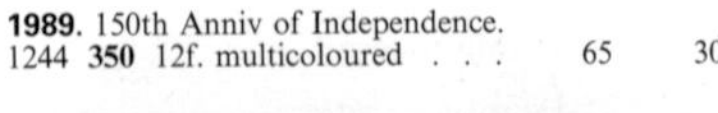

1989. 150th Anniv of Independence.
1244 **350** 12f. multicoloured . . . 65 30

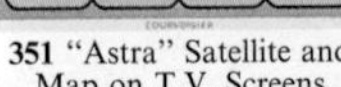

351 "Astra" Satellite and Map on T.V. Screens 352 Cyclist

1989. Launch of 16-channel T.V. Satellite.
1245 **351** 12f. multicoloured . . . 60 40

1989. Start in Luxembourg of Tour de France Cycling Race.
1246 **352** 9f. multicoloured 65 40

353 Assembly and Flag 354 Emblem

1989. 40th Anniv of Council of Europe.
1247 **353** 12f. multicoloured . . . 65 30

1989. Centenary of Interparliamentary Union.
1248 **354** 12f. yellow, blue & indigo 70 30

355 Hands 356 "Three Children in a Park" (anon)

1989. 3rd Direct Elections to European Parliament.
1249 **355** 12f. multicoloured . . . 65 30

1989. Europa. Children's Games and Toys. Multicoloured.
1250 12f. Type **356** 65 35
1251 20f. "Child with Drum" (anon) . . . . 1·40 1·00

357 Grand Duke Jean 358 Charles IV

1989. 25th Anniv of Accession of Grand Duke Jean.
1252 **357** 3f. black and orange . . 1·00 75
1253 9f. black and green . . . 1·00 95

1989. Tourism. As T **342**. Multicoloured.
1254 12f. Clervaux Castle 50 30
1255 18f. 1st-century bronze wild boar, Titelberg 85 70

1989. Luxembourg History. Stained Glass Windows by Joseph Oterberger, Luxembourg Cathedral. Multicoloured.
1256 12f. Type **358** 60 40
1257 20f. John the Blind 85 90
1258 25f. Wenceslas II . . . . . 1·00 1·10

359 St. Lambert and St. Blase, Fennange 360 Funfair (650th anniv of Schueberfouer)

1989. National Welfare Fund. Restored Chapels (1st series). Multicoloured.
1259 9f.+1f. Type **359** 50 50
1260 12f.+2f. St. Quirinus, Luxembourg (horiz) . . . 60 65
1261 18f.+3f. St. Anthony the Hermit, Reisdorf (horiz) 2·00 2·00
1262 25f.+8f. The Hermitage, Hachiville . . . . 3·00 3·00
See also Nos. 1280/3 and 1304/7.

1990. Anniversaries.
1263 **360** 9f. multicoloured 65 35
1264 – 12f. brown, pink & black 50 35
1265 – 18f. multicoloured . . . 80 75
DESIGNS: 12f. Batty Weber (writer, 50th death anniv); 18f. Dish aerial (125th anniv of International Telecommunications Union).

361 Troops at Fortress

1990. Luxembourg Culture. Etchings of the Fortress by Christoph Wilhelm Selig. Multicoloured.
1266 9f. Type **361** 45 40
1267 12f. Soldiers by weir 50 40
1268 20f. Distant view of fortress 1·25 90
1269 25f. Walls . . . . 1·60 1·10

362 Paul Eyschen (75th anniv) 363 "Psallus pseudoplatini" (male and female) on Maple

1990. Statesmen's Death Anniversaries.
1270 **362** 9f. brown and blue . . . 45 40
1271 – 12f. blue and brown . . 55 35
DESIGN: 12f. Emmanuel Servais (centenary).

1990. Centenary of Luxembourg Naturalists' Society.
1272 **363** 12f. multicoloured . . . 60 35

364 General Post Office, Luxembourg City 365 Hammelsmarsch Fountain (Will Lofy)

1990. Europa. Post Office Buildings.
1273 **364** 12f. black and brown . . 1·50 35
1274 – 20f. black and blue . . . 2·10 1·25
DESIGN—VERT: 20f. Esch-sur-Alzette Post Office.

1990. Tourism. As T **342**. Multicoloured.
1275 12f. Mondercange administrative offices . . 60 30
1276 12f. Schifflange town hall and church 60 30

1990. Fountains. Multicoloured.
1277 12f. Type **365** 50 35
1278 25f. Doves Fountain . . . . 1·00 90
1279 50f. Maus Ketty Fountain, Mondorf-les-Bains (Will Lofy) . . . . 2·00 2·40

366 Congregation of the Blessed Virgin Mary, Vianden 368 "Geastrum varians"

1990. National Welfare Fund. Restored Chapels (2nd series). Multicoloured.
1280 9f.+1f. Type **366** 60 60
1281 12f.+2f. Notre Dame, Echternach (horiz) 85 70
1282 18f.+3f. Consoler of the Afflicted, Grentzingen (horiz) . . . . 1·75 1·75
1283 25f.+8f. St. Pirmin, Kaundorf . . . . 3·00 2·75

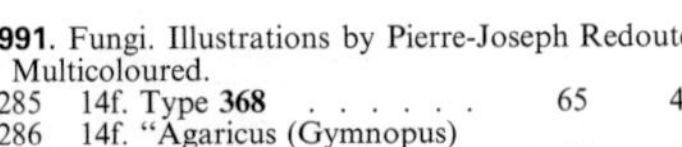

1991. Fungi. Illustrations by Pierre-Joseph Redoute. Multicoloured.
1285 14f. Type **368** 65 40
1286 14f. "Agaricus (Gymnopus) thiebautii" 65 50
1287 18f. "Agaricus (Lepiota) lepidocephalus" 85 95
1288 25f. "Morchella favosa" . . 1·40 1·25

369 "View from the Trier Road"

1991. Luxembourg Culture. 50th Death Anniv of Sosthene Weis (painter). Multicoloured.
1289 14f. Type **369** 60 40
1290 18f. "Vauban Street and the Viaduct" 70 75
1291 25f. "St. Ulric Street" (vert) 1·25 1·10

370 Dicks (after Jean Goedert)

1991. Death Centenary of Edmond de la Fontaine (pen-name Dicks) (poet).
1292 **370** 14f. multicoloured . . . 70 45

371 Claw grasping Piece of Metal (after Emile Kirscht) 372 National Miners' Monument, Kayl

1991. 75th Anniv of Trade Union Movement in Luxembourg.
1293 **371** 14f. multicoloured . . . 70 45

1991. Tourism. Multicoloured.
1294 14f. Type **372** 70 40
1295 14f. Magistrates' Court, Redange-sur-Attert (horiz) 70 40

373 Earth and Orbit of "Astra 1A" and "1B" Satellites 374 Telephone

1991. Europa. Europe in Space. Multicoloured.
1296 14f. Type **373** . . . . . . 1·10 45
1297 18f. Betzdorf Earth Station 1·75 1·00

1991. Posts and Telecommunications.
1298 **374** 4f. brown . . . . 2·00 1·40
1299 – 14f. blue 55 55
DESIGN: 14f. Postbox.

375 1936 International Philatelic Federation Congress Stamp 376 Girl's Head

1991. 50th Stamp Day.
1300 **375** 14f. multicoloured . . . 70 40
The stamp illustrated on No. 1300 incorrectly shows a face value of 10f.

1991. Mascarons (stone faces on buildings) (1st series).
1301 **376** 14f. black, buff & brown 60 40
1302 – 25f. black, buff and pink 1·10 90
1303 – 50f. black, buff and blue 1·90 1·75
DESIGNS: 25f. Woman's head; 50f. Man's head.
See also Nos. 1320/22.

377 Chapel of St. Donatus, Arsdorf

378 Jean-Pierre Pescatore Foundation

1991. National Welfare Fund. Restored Chapels (3rd series). Multicoloured.
1304 14f.+2f. Type **377** 85 70
1305 14f.+2f. Chapel of Our Lady of Sorrows, Brandenbourg (horiz) 85 90
1306 18f.+3f. Chapel of Our Lady, Luxembourg (horiz) 1·75 1·25
1307 22f.+7f. Chapel of the Hermitage, Wolwelange 2·50 2·75

1992. Buildings. Multicoloured.
1308 14f. Type **378** 70 50
1309 14f. Higher Technology Institute, Kirchberg . . . 70 50
1310 14f. New Fairs and Congress Centre, Kirchberg 70 50

379 Inner Courtyard, Bettembourg Castle

1992. Tourism. Multicoloured.
1311 18f. Type **379** 70 65
1312 25f. Walferdange railway station . . . . 1·00 95

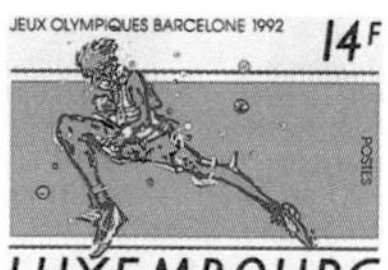

380 Athlete (detail of mural, Armand Strainchamps)

1992. Olympic Games, Barcelona.
1313 **380** 14f. multicoloured . . . 1·25 35

381 Luxembourg Pavilion

382 Lions Emblem

1992. "Expo '92" World's Fair, Seville.
1314 **381** 14f. multicoloured . . . 65 40

1992. 75th Anniv of Lions International.
1315 **382** 14f. multicoloured . . . 60 40

383 Memorial Tablet (Lucien Wercollier)

384 Nicholas Gonner (editor)

1992. 50th anniv of General Strike.
1316 **383** 18f. brown, grey and red 70 70

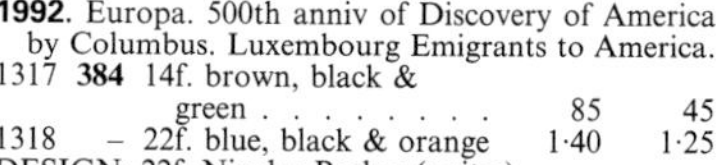

1992. Europa. 500th anniv of Discovery of America by Columbus. Luxembourg Emigrants to America.
1317 **384** 14f. brown, black & green 85 45
1318 – 22f. blue, black & orange 1·40 1·25
DESIGN: 22f. Nicolas Becker (writer).

385 Star and European Community Emblem

386 Posthorn and Letters

1992. Single European Market.
1319 **385** 14f. multicoloured . . . 65 40

1992. Mascarons (2nd series). As T **376**.
1320 14f. black, buff and green 55 40
1321 22f. black, buff and blue . . 1·10 1·00
1322 50f. black, buff and purple 1·75 1·60
DESIGNS: 14f. Ram's head; 22f. Lion's head; 50f. Goat's head.

1992. 150th Anniv of Post and Telecommunications Office. Designs showing stained glass windows by Auguste Tremont. Mult.
1323 14f. Type **386** 50 45
1324 22f. Post rider . . . . . . 1·40 1·25
1325 50f. Telecommunications . . 1·60 1·60

387 Hazel Grouse

388 Grand Duke Jean

1992. National Welfare Fund. Birds (1st series). Multicoloured.
1326 14f.+2f. Type **387** 85 95
1327 14f.+2f. Golden oriole (vert) 85 95
1328 18f.+3f. Black stork . . . . 2·40 2·10
1329 22f.+7f. Red kite (vert) . . . 3·00 3·00
See also Nos. 1364/7 and 1383/6.

1993.
1330 **388** 1f. black and yellow . . 10 10
1331 2f. black and green . . . 10 10
1332 5f. black and yellow . . 20 20
1333 7f. black and brown . . 30 20
1334 8f. black and green . . . 30 25
1335 9f. black and mauve . . 35 35
1336 10f. black and blue . . . 45 30
1337 14f. black and purple . . 1·40 30
1338 15f. black and green . . 50 45
1339 16f. black and orange . . 50 45
1340 18f. black and yellow . . 70 40
1341 20f. black and red . . . 70 55
1342 22f. black and green . . 90 55
1343 25f. black and blue . . . 85 70
1344 100f. black and brown 3·00 2·00

389 Old Ironworks Cultural Centre, Steinfort

1993. Tourism. Multicoloured.
1350 14f. Type **389** 65 35
1351 14f. "Children with Grapes" Fountain, Schwebsingen 65 35

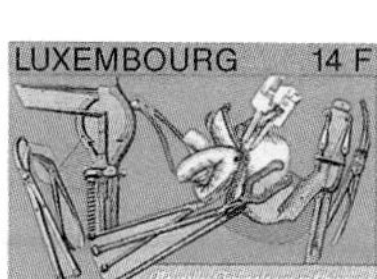

390 Collage by Maurice Esteve

1993. New Surgical Techniques.
1352 **390** 14f. multicoloured . . . 60 40

391 Hotel de Bourgogne (Prime Minister's offices)

1993. Historic Houses. Multicoloured.
1353 14f. Type **391** 55 40
1354 20f. Simons House (now Ministry of Agriculture) 85 70
1355 50f. Cassal House . . . . . 2·40 1·75

392 "Rezlop" (Fernand Roda)

1993. Europa. Contemporary Art. Multicoloured.
1356 14f. Type **392** 70 45
1357 22f. "So Close" (Sonja Roef) . . . . 1·40 1·00

393 Monument (detail, D. Donzelli), Tetange Cemetery

394 Emblem

1993. 75th Death Anniv of Jean Schortgen (first worker elected to parliament).
1358 **393** 14f. multicoloured . . . 60 40

1993. Centenary of Artistic Circle of Luxembourg.
1359 **394** 14f. mauve and violet . . 60 40

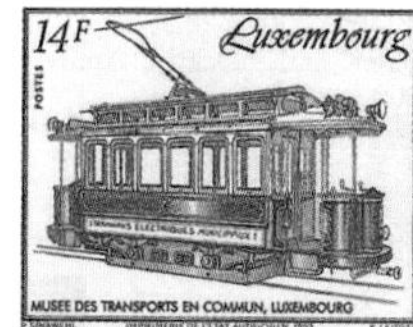

395 European Community Ecological Label

396 Tram No. 1 (Transport Museum, Luxembourg)

1993. Protection of Environment.
1360 **395** 14f. blue, green & emerald 60 40

1993. Museum Exhibits (1st series). Multicoloured.
1361 14f. Type **396** 70 40
1362 22f. Iron ore tipper wagon (National Mining Museum, Rumelange) . . 1·00 1·00
1363 60f. Horse-drawn carriage (Arts and Ancient Crafts Museum, Wiltz) . . . . . 2·40 4·75
See also Nos. 1404/6 and 1483/4.

1993. National Welfare Fund. Birds (2nd series). As T **387**. Multicoloured.
1364 14f.+2f. Common snipe ("Becassine") 70 70
1365 14f.+2f. River kingfisher ("Martin-Pecheur") (vert) 70 70
1366 18f.+3f. Little ringed plover ("Petit Gravelot") . . . . 1·40 1·40
1367 22f.+7f. Sand martin ("Hirondelle de Rivage") (vert) . . . . 2·50 2·50

397 "Snow-covered Landscape" (Joseph Kutter)

1994. Artists' Birth Centenaries. Multicoloured.
1368 14f. Type **397** 60 40
1369 14f. "The Moselle" (Nico Klopp) 60 40

398 Members' Flags

399 17th-century Herald's Tabard

1994. 4th Direct Elections to European Parliament.
1370 **398** 14f. multicoloured . . . 60 40

1994. Congresses. Multicoloured.
1371 14f. Type **399** (21st International Genealogy and Heraldry Congress) 60 40
1372 18f. International Police Association emblem on map (14th World Congress) 70 40

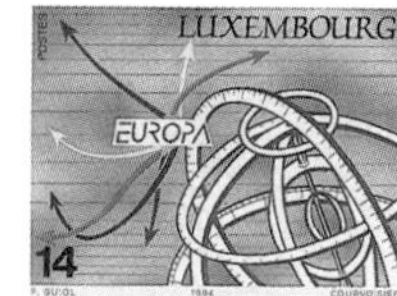

400 Arrows and Terrestrial Globe

1994. Europa. Discoveries. Multicoloured.
1373 14f. Type **400** 85 45
1374 22f. Chart, compass rose and sails . . . . 1·40 1·25

401 "Family" (Laura Lammar)

1994. International Year of the Family.
1375 **401** 25f. multicoloured . . . 1·00 95

402 Crowds cheering American Soldiers

1994. 50th Anniv of Liberation.
1376 **402** 14f. multicoloured . . . 60 50

403 Western European Union Emblem (40th anniv)

1994. Anniversaries and Campaign.
1377 **403** 14f. blue, lilac and ultramarine 70 50
1378 – 14f. multicoloured . . . 70 45
1379 – 14f. multicoloured . . . 2·40 70
DESIGNS—No. 1378, Emblem (25th anniv in Luxembourg of European Communities' Office for Official Publications); 1379, 10th-century B.C. ceramic bowl from cremation tomb, Bigelbach (European Bronze Age Campaign).

404 Munster Abbey (General Finance Inspectorate)

1994. Former Refuges now housing Government Offices. Multicoloured.
1380 15f. Type **404** 70 65
1381 25f. Holy Spirit Convent (Ministry of Finance) . . 85 1·00
1382 60f. St. Maximine Abbey of Trier (Ministry of Foreign Affairs) . . . . 2·00 2·75

1994. National Welfare Fund. Birds (3rd series). As T **387**. Multicoloured.
1383 14f.+2f. Common stonechat ("Traquet Patre") (vert) 70 85
1384 14f.+2f. Grey partridge ("Perdix Grise") 70 85
1385 18f.+3f. Yellow wagtail ("Bergeronnette Printaniere") . . . . . . 1·40 1·40
1386 22f.+7f. Great grey shrike ("Pie-Grieche Grise") (vert) . . . . 2·50 2·50

405 "King of the Antipodes"

406/409 Panoramic View of City (⅓-size illustration)

1995. Luxembourg, European City of Culture.

1387 **405** 16f. multicoloured . . . 1·00 65
1388 – 16f. multicoloured . . . 1·00 65
1389 – 16f. multicoloured . . . 1·00 65
1390 **406** 16f. multicoloured . . . 70 60
1391 **407** 16f. multicoloured . . . 70 60
1392 **408** 16f. multicoloured . . . 70 60
1393 **409** 16f. multicoloured . . . 70 60
1394 – 16f. multicoloured . . . 70 60

DESIGNS—As T **405**: No. 1388, "House with Arcades and Yellow Tower"; 1389, "Small Path" (maze). 35 × 26 mm: No. 1394, Emblem.

Nos. 1390/3 were issued together, se-tenant, forming the composite design illustrated.

410 Landscape and Slogan

411 Colour Spectrum and Barbed Wire

1995. European Nature Conservation Year.

1395 **410** 16f. multicoloured . . . 70 40

1995. Europa. Peace and Freedom. 50th Anniv of Liberation of Concentration Camps. Mult.

1396 16f. Type **411** 70 65
1397 25f. Wire barbs breaking through symbolic sky and earth . . . . 1·10 1·10

412 Emblem

1995. Anniversaries and Event. Multicoloured.

1398 16f. Type **412** (6th Small European States Games, Luxembourg) 60 60
1399 32f. Diagram of section through Earth (27th anniv of underground Geodynamics Laboratory, Walferdange) (33 × 34 mm) . . . . . . 1·25 1·25
1400 80f. Anniversary emblem (50th anniv of U.N.O.) 2·75 2·75

413 Boeing 757

1995. 40th Anniv of Luxembourg–Iceland Air Link.

1401 **413** 16f. multicoloured . . . 60 60

414 Erpeldange Castle

415 Stained Glass Window from Alzingen Church

1995. Tourism. Multicoloured.

1402 16f. Type **414** 60 65
1403 16f. Schengen Castle 60 65

1995. Museum Exhibits (2nd series). Vert designs as T **396**. Multicoloured.

1404 16f. Churn (Country Art Museum, Vianden) . . . 70 70
1405 32f. Wine-press (Wine Museum, Ehnen) . . . . 1·25 1·50
1406 80f. Sculpture of potter (Leon Nosbusch) (Pottery Museum, Nospelt) . . . . 3·25 3·00

1995. Christmas.

1407 **415** 16f.+2f. multicoloured 1·00 1·25

416 Broad-leaved Linden ("Tilia platyphyllos")

417 Mayrisch (after Theo van Rysselberghe)

1995. National Welfare Fund. Trees (1st series). Multicoloured.

1408 16f.+2f. Type **416** 70 95
1409 16f.+2f. Horse chestnut ("Aesculus hippocastanum") (horiz) 70 95
1410 20f.+3f. Pedunculate oak (horiz) . . . . 1·25 1·40
1411 32f.+7f. Silver birch . . . . 2·25 2·40

See also Nos. 1432/5 and 1458/61.

1996. 68th Death Anniv of Emile Mayrisch (engineer).

1412 **417** A (16f.) multicoloured 70 65

418 Mounument, Place Clairefontaine (Jean Cardot)

420 "Marie Munchen"

419 Electric Railcar

1996. Birth Centenary of Grand Duchess Charlotte.

1413 **418** 16f. multicoloured . . . 85 60

1996. 50th Anniv of Luxembourg National Railway Company. Multicoloured.

1414 16f. Type **419** 70 70
1415 16f. Linked cars 70 70
1416 16f. Train (right-hand detail) 70 70

Nos. 1414/16 were issued together, se-tenant, forming a composite design of a Series 2000 electric railcar set.

1996. 96th Death Anniv of Mihaly Munkacsy (painter). Multicoloured.

1417 16f. Type **420** 70 80
1418 16f. Munkacsy (after Edouard Charlemont) (horiz) 70 80

421 Workers and Emblem

422 Marie de Bourgogne

1996. Anniversaries.

1419 **421** 16f. green, orge & blk 60 65
1420 – 20f. multicoloured . . . 70 90
1421 – 25f. multicoloured . . . 1·00 1·25
1422 – 32f. multicoloured . . . 1·25 1·40

DESIGNS—HORIZ: 16f. Type **421** (75th anniv of Luxembourg Confederation of Christian Trade Unions); 32f. Film negative (centenary of motion pictures). VERT: 20f. Transmitter and radio waves (centenary of Guglielmo Marconi's patented wireless telegraph); 25f. Olympic flame and rings (centenary of modern Olympic Games).

1996. Europa. Famous Women. Duchesses of Luxembourg. Multicoloured.

1423 16f. Type **422** 60 65
1424 25f. Maria-Theresa of Austria . . . . 1·00 1·25

423 Handstamp

1996. Bicentenary (1995) of Registration and Property Administration.

1425 **423** 16f. multicoloured . . . 60 65

424 Children of different Cultures (Michele Dockendorf)

1996. "Let us Live Together". Multicoloured.

1426 16f. Type **424** 65 65
1427 16f. "L'Abbraccio" (statue, Marie-Josee Kerschen) (vert) 65 65

425 Eurasian Badger

1996. Mammals. Multicoloured.

1428 16f. Type **425** 65 65
1429 20f. Polecat 65 70
1430 80f. European otter . . . . 3·00 3·25

426 "The Birth of Christ" (icon, Eva Mathes)

427 John the Blind

1996. Christmas.

1431 **426** 16f.+2f. multicoloured 1·40 1·40

1996. National Welfare Fund. Trees (2nd series). As T **416**. Multicoloured.

1432 16f.+2f. Willow ("Salix sp.") (horiz) 65 85
1433 16f.+2f. Ash ("Fraxinus excelsior") 65 85
1434 20f.+3f. Mountain ash (horiz) . . . . 1·25 1·60
1435 32f.+7f. Common beech . . 2·40 2·75

1996. 700th Birth Anniv of John the Blind (King of Bohemia and Count of Luxembourg).

1436 **427** 32f. multicoloured . . . 1·25 1·40

428 Koerich Church

1997. Tourism. Multicoloured.

1437 16f. Type **428** 70 50
1438 16f. Servais House, Mersch (horiz) 70 50

429 Birthplace of Robert Schuman (politician), Luxembourg-Clausen

1997. Anniversaries. Multicoloured.

1439 16f. Type **429** (40th anniv of Treaties of Rome establishing European Economic Community and European Atomic Energy Community) . . . 70 50
1440 20f. National colours forming wing of Mercury (75th anniv of Belgium–Luxembourg Economic Union) 85 75

430 "Grand Duchess Charlotte"

1997. 11th World Federation of Rose Societies Congress, Belgium, Mondorf (Luxembourg) and the Netherlands. Roses. Multicoloured.

1441 16f. Type **430** 70 70
1442 20f. "The Beautiful Sultana" (33 × 26 mm) 70 80
1443 80f. "In Memory of Jean Soupert" (33 × 26 mm) . . 2·75 2·50

431 Badge, Luxembourg Fortress, Shako and Sword

432 The Beautiful Melusina

1997. Anniversaries.

1444 **431** 16f. multicoloured . . . 60 60
1445 – 16f. black, blue and red 60 60
1446 – 16f. brown, green and pink 60 60

DESIGNS—As T **431**: No. 1444, Type **431** (bicentenary of Grand Ducal Gendarmerie Corps); 1445, Cock and rabbit (75th anniv of Luxembourg Union of Small Domestic Animals Farming Societies). 33 × 33 mm: No. 1446, Bather and attendant, early 1900s (150th anniv of Mondorf spa).

1997. Europa. Tales and Legends. Multicoloured.

1447 16f. Type **432** 70 65
1448 25f. The Hunter of Hollenfels . . . . 1·00 1·25

433 Face on Globe

1997. "Juvalux 98" Youth Stamp Exhibition (1st issue). Multicoloured.

1449 16f. Type **433** 70 65
1450 80f. Postmen (painting, Michel Engels) . . . . . 2·75 2·75

See also Nos. 1475/8.

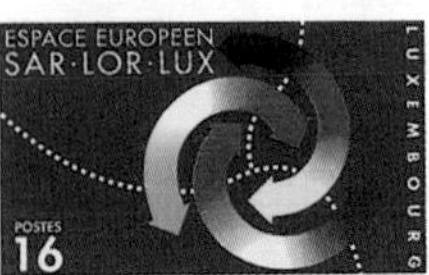

434 Emblem

1997. Sar–Lor–Lux (Saarland–Lorraine–Luxembourg) European Region.

1451 **434** 16f. multicoloured . . . 70 65

Stamps in similar designs were issued by France and Germany.

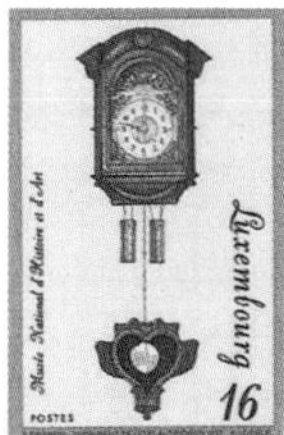

435 Wall Clock by Dominique Nauens, 1816

436 "Kalborn Mill" (Jean-Pierre Gleis)

1997. Clocks. Multicoloured.
1452 16f. Type **435** 70 65
1453 32f. Astronomical clock by J. Lebrun, 1850 (26 × 44 mm) . . . . . . 1·10 1·40
1454 80f. Wall clock by Mathias Hebeler, 1815 . . . . . . 2·75 2·50

1997. Water Mills. Multicoloured.
1455 16f. Type **436** 70 65
1456 50f. Interior of Ramelli mill, 1588 (from book "The Water Wheel" by Wilhelm Wolfel) (vert) . . . . . . 1·75 2·10

437 Holy Family

438 Count Henri V

1997. Christmas.
1457 **437** 16f.+2f. multicoloured 1·25 1·25

1997. National Welfare Fund. Trees (3rd series). As T **416**. Multicoloured.
1458 16f.+2f. Wych elm ("Ulmus glabra") 70 85
1459 16f.+2f. Norway maple ("Acer platanoides") . . . 70 85
1460 20f.+3f. Wild cherry . . . . 1·00 1·00
1461 32f.+7f. Walnut (horiz) . . 1·75 1·75

1997. 750th Anniv of Accession of Henri V, Count of Luxembourg.
1462 **438** 32f. multicoloured . . . 1·25 1·00

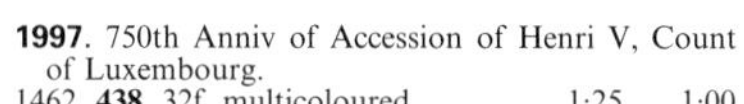

439 Rodange Church

440 Cog and "50"

1998. Tourism. Multicoloured.
1463 16f. Type **439** 70 65
1464 16f. Back of local authority building, Hesperange (horiz) 70 65

1998. Anniversaries.
1465 **440** 16f. multicoloured . . . 70 65
1466 – 16f. multicoloured . . . 70 65
1467 – 20f. multicoloured . . . 70 90
1468 – 50f. black, red and stone 1·75 2·10
DESIGNS: No. 1465, Type **440** (50th anniv of Independent Luxembourg Trade Union); 1466, Festival poster (Rene Wismer) (50th anniv of Broom Festival, Wiltz); 1467, Memorial (death centenary of Jean Antoine Zinnen (composer of national anthem)); 1468, Typewriter keys and page from first issue of "Luxemburger Wort" (150th anniv of abolition of censorship).

441 Brown Trout

1998. Freshwater Fishes. Multicoloured.
1469 16f. Type **441** 70 65
1470 25f. Bullhead . . . . 1·00 1·25
1471 50f. Riffle minnow . . . . 2·00 2·10

442 Henri VII and Flags outside Fair Venue, Kirchberg

1998. 700th Anniv of Granting to Count Henri VII of Right to Hold a Fair. Value indicated by letter.
1472 **442** A (16f.) multicoloured 70 70

443 Fireworks over Adolphe Bridge (National Day)

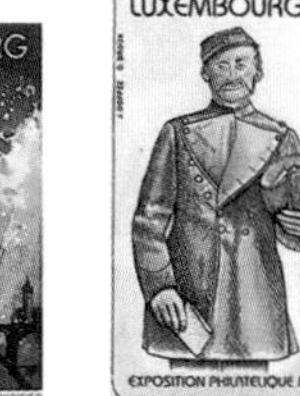

444 Town Postman, 1880

1998. Europa. National Festivals. Multicoloured.
1473 16f. Type **443** 85 70
1474 25f. Stained-glass window and flame (National Remembrance Day) . . . 1·00 1·25

1998. "Juvalux '98" Youth Stamp Exhibition (2nd issue). Multicoloured.
1475 16f. Type **444** 70 65
1476 25f. Letter, 1590 (horiz) . . 80 1·25
1477 50f. Rural postman, 1880 1·75 2·10

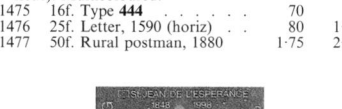

445 Masonic Symbols (Paul Moutschen)

1998. 150th Anniv of St. John of Hope Freemason Lodge.
1479 **445** 16f. multicoloured . . . 60 65

446 Echternach

1998. 1300th Anniv of Echternach Abbey. Multicoloured.
1480 16f. Type **446** 60 65
1481 48f. Buildings in Echternach 2·40 2·10
1482 60f. Echternach Abbey . . . 2·00 2·25

447 Spanish Morion (late 16th century)

1998. Museum Exhibits (3rd series). City of Luxembourg History Museum. Multicoloured.
1483 16f. Type **447** 70 65
1484 80f. Wayside Cross from Hollerich (1718) . . . . . 2·75 3·00

448 "Nativity" (altarpiece by Georges Saget, St. Mauritius Abbey, Clervaux)

1998. Christmas.
1485 **448** 16f.+2f. multicoloured 1·40 1·10

449 "Bech"

1998. National Welfare Fund (1st series). Villages. 16th-century drawings by Jean Bertels. Multicoloured.
1486 16f.+2f. Type **449** 70 85
1487 16f.+2f. "Ermes Turf" (now Ermsdorf) 70 85
1488 20f.+3f. "Itsich" (now Itzig) 1·00 1·25
1489 32f.+7f. "Stein Hem" (now Steinheim) . . . . 1·75 1·90
See also Nos. 1510/13 and 1550/3.

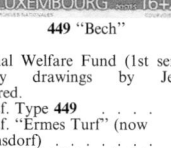

450 Globe and Jigsaw

1998. 40th Anniv of North Atlantic Maintenance and Supply Agency.
1490 **450** 36f. multicoloured . . . 1·40 1·50

451 Council Building and Emblem

1999. 50th Anniv of Council of Europe.
1491 **451** 16f. multicoloured . . . 70 70

452 Euro Coin and Map

1999. Introduction of the Euro (European currency). Value expressed by letter.
1492 **452** A (16f.) multicoloured 1·00 65

453 Tawny Owl

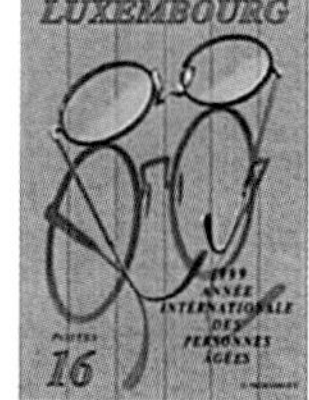

455 Spectacles

454 Globe and Emblem

1999. Owls. Multicoloured.
1493 A (16f.) Type **453** 70 65
1494 32f. Eagle owl (horiz) . . . 1·25 1·25
1495 60f. Barn owl (horiz) . . . 2·50 3·00

1999. 50th Anniv of N.A.T.O.
1496 **454** 80f. multicoloured . . . 3·00 3·50

1999. International Year of the Elderly.
1497 **455** 16f. multicoloured . . . 70 65

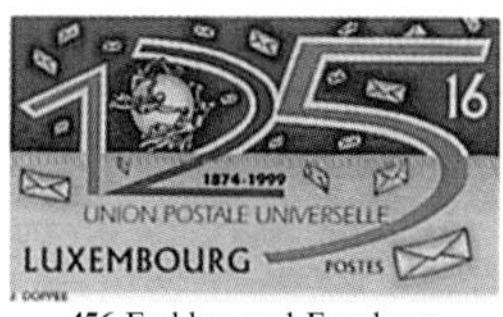

456 Emblem and Envelopes

1999. 125th Anniv of Universal Postal Union.
1498 **456** 16f. multicoloured . . . 70 65

457 Haute-Sure National Park

1999. Europa. Parks and Gardens. Multicoloured.
1499 16f. Type **457** 70 70
1500 25f. Ardennes-Eifel National Park . . . . 1·00 1·25

458 Emblem

1999. Anniversaries. Multicoloured.
1501 16f. Type **458** (75th anniv of National Federation of Mutual Socieites) 70 65
1502 32f. Camera and roll of film (50th anniv of Luxembourg Federation of Amateur Photographers) . . . . . 1·40 1·40
1503 80f. Gymnasts (centenary of Luxembourg Gymnastics Federation) . . . . 3·50 3·50

459 Prince Guillaume

461 A. Mayrisch de Saint-Hubert

460 Cars on Motorway

1999. 18th Birthday of Prince Guillaume.
1504 **459** 16f. multicoloured . . . 70 70

1999. Communications of the Future. Mult.
1505 16f. Type **460** 60 70
1506 20f. Earth and satellite . . . 70 85
1507 80f. Planets and spacecraft 3·00 3·00

1999. 125th Birth Anniv of Aline Mayrisch de Saint-Hubert (President of Luxembourg Red Cross).
1508 **461** 20f. multicoloured . . . 70 80

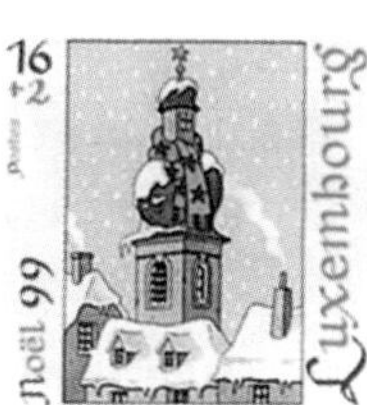

462 Decorated Church Tower

1999. Christmas
1509 **462** 16f.+2f. multicoloured 1·00 90

1999. National Welfare Fund. Villages (2nd series). As T **449**, showing 6th-century drawings by Jean Bertels. Multicoloured.
1510 16f.+2f. "Oswiler" (now Osweiler) 70 80
1511 16f.+2f. "Bettem Burch" (now Bettembourg) . . . 70 80
1512 20f.+3f. "Cruchte auf der Alset" (now Cruchten) . . 80 1·00
1513 32f.+7f. "Berchem" . . . . 2·00 2·10

463 "Gateway" (sketch by Goethe)

1999. 250th Birth Anniv of Johann Wolfgang von Goethe (poet and playwright).
1514 **463** 20f. chestnut, cream & brn 70 80

464 "2000"

2000. New Millennium. Value expressed by letter. Multicoloured. Self-adhesive.
1515 A (16f.) Type **464** (blue streaks emanating from bottom right) 70 65
1516 A (16f.) Blue streaks emanating from bottom left 70 65
1517 A (16f.) Blue streaks emanating from top right 70 65
1518 A (16f.) Blue streaks emanating from top left 70 65

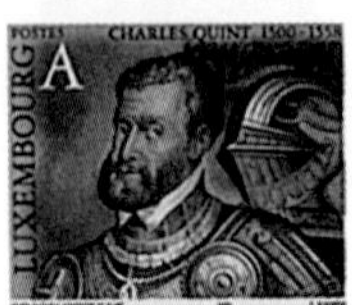

465 Charles V

2000. 500th Birth Anniv of Emperor Charles V. Value expressed by letter.
1519 **465** A (16f.) multicoloured 70 60

466 Walferdange Castle

2000. Tourism. Value expressed by letter. Multicoloured.
1520 A (16f.) Type **466** 70 60
1521 A (16f.) Local government offices, Wasserbillig (vert) 70 60

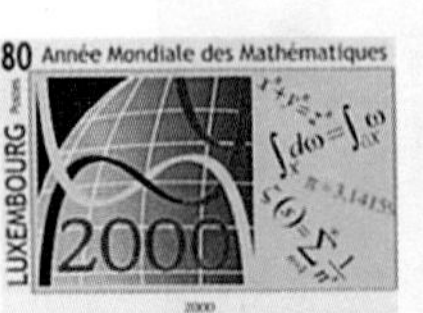

467 "2000" and Formulae

468 French Horn

2000. World Mathematics Year.
1522 **467** 80f. multicoloured . . . 2·75 3·00

2000. Musical Instruments.
1523 **468** 3f. black and violet . . . 20 10
1524 – 9f. black and green . . . 40 35
1525 – 12f. black and yellow . . . 45 40
1526 – 21f. black and pink . . . 75 75
1527 – 24f. black and blue . . . 80 55
1528 – 30f. black and pink . . . 85 65
DESIGNS: 9f. Electric guitar; 12f. Saxophone; 21f. Violin; 24f. Accordion; 30f. Grand piano.

469 Production and Storage Facilities, 1930s (Harry Rabinger)

2000. Centenary (1999) of Esch-sur-Alzette Gas Works.
1535 **469** 18f. multicoloured . . . 70 75

470 Mallard

471 "Building Europe"

2000. Ducks. Multicoloured.
1536 18f. Type **470** 70 75
1537 24f. Common pochard (vert) 80 80
1538 30f. Tufted duck (vert) . . . 1·00 85

2000. Europa.
1539 **471** 21f. multicoloured . . . 85 70

472 Jean Monnet and Robert Schuman

2000. 50th Anniv of Schuman Plan (proposal for European Coal and Steel Community).
1540 **472** 21f. black, blue & yellow 85 70

473 Blast Furnace

2000. 20th Anniv of Blast Furnace "B", Esch-Belval.
1541 **473** A (18f.) multicoloured 55 35

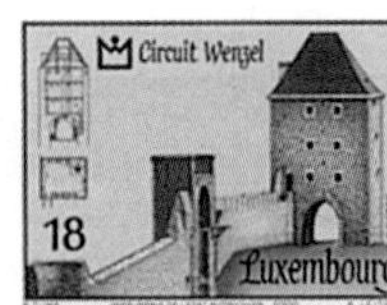

474 Castle Walls and Tower (Wenzel Walk)

2000. Circular City Walks. Multicoloured.
1542 18f. Type **474** 55 35
1543 42f. Bridge and tower (Vauban walk) . . . . . 1·25 75

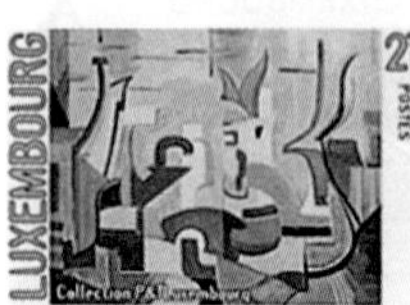

475 Will Kesseler

2000. Modern Art (1st series). Showing paintings by artist named. Multicoloured.
1544 21f. Type **475** 55 35
1545 24f. Joseph Probst (vert) . . 85 85
1546 36f. Mett Hoffmann 65 40
See also Nos. 1612/14.

476 Prince Henri in Uniform and Princess Maria

2000. Swearing in of Prince Henri as Head of State of the Grand Duchy of Luxembourg.
1547 **476** 18f. multicoloured . . . 70 45

477 Child before Christmas Tree

2000. Christmas.
1549 **477** 18f.+2f. multicoloured 85 85

2000. National Welfare Fund. Villages (3rd series). As T **449** showing 16th-century drawings by Jean Bertels. Multicoloured.
1550 18f.+2f. "Lorentzwiller" (now dorentzweiler) . . . 70 70
1551 21f.+3f. "Coosturf" (now Consdorf) 95 95
1552 24f.+3f. "Elfingen" (now Elvange) 95 95
1553 36f.+7f. "Sprenckigen" (now Sprinkange) . . . . . . 1·75 1·75

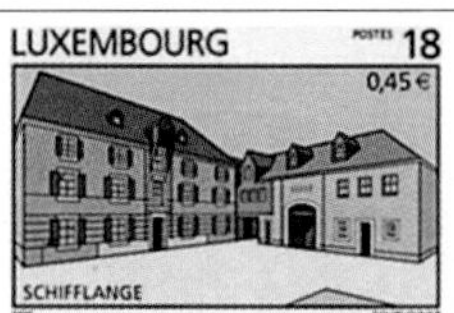

478 Bestgensmillen Mill, Schifflange

2001. Tourism. Multicoloured.
1554 18f. Type **478** 70 50
1555 18f. Vineyard, Wormeldange (vert) 70 50

479 Nik Welter

2001. Writers' Death Anniversaries. Multicoloured.
1556 18f. Type **479** (50th anniv) 70 50
1557 24f. Andre Gide (50th anniv) . . . . 1·00 65
1558 30f. Michel Rodange (125th anniv) . . . . 1·40 1·00

480 Signatures and Seal

2001. 50th Anniv of Treaty of Paris.
1559 **480** 21f. multicoloured . . . 85 65

481 Citroen 2CV Mini-Van

482 Stream, Mullerthal

2001. Postal Vehicles. Mult. Self-adhesive.
1560 3f. Type **481** 20 15
1561 18f. Volkswagen Beetle . . . 65 50

2001. Europa. Water Resources. Multicoloured. Value expressed by letter (No. 1562) or with face value (No. 1563).
1562 A (18f.) Type **482** 70 70
1563 21f. Pond and Kaltreis water tower (vert) . . . . 1·00 70

483 "Mother and Child" (Ger Maas)

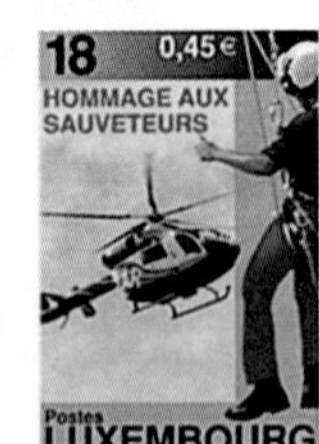

484 Helicopter and Rescuer

2001. Humanitarian Projects. Multicoloured.
1564 18f. Type **483** (humanitarian aid) 65 50
1565 24f. International Organization for Migration emblem 85 65

2001. Rescue Services. Multicoloured.
1566 18f. Type **484** 65 50
1567 30f. Divers and rubber dinghy . . . . 1·00 85
1568 45f. Fire engine and fireman wearing protective clothing . . . . 1·75 1·40

DENOMINATION. From No. 1569 Luxembourg stamps are denominated in euros only.

485 Five Cent Coin

486 Grand Duke Henri

2001. Euro Currency. Coins. Multicoloured.
1569 5c. Type **485** 20 20
1570 10c. Ten cent coin 20 20
1571 20c. Twenty cent coin . . . 35 35
1572 50c. Fifty cent coin 65 65
1573 €1 One euro coin . . . . 1·40 1·40
1574 €2 Two euro coin . . . . 2·75 2·75

2001. Grand Duke Henri.
1575 **486** 7c. dp blue, blue & red 10 10
1583 22c. sepia, brown & red 35 30
1585 30c. dp green, grn & red 40 35
1588 45c. dp violet, vio & red 60 40
1589 52c. brown, buff and red 65 40
1590 59c. deep blue, blue and red 75 45
1591 74c. brown, stone and red 95 55
1592 89c. mauve, brown and red . . . . 1·10 80

487 Emblem

2001. European Year of Languages. Value expressed by letter.
1596 **487** A (45c.) multicoloured 60 50

488 Sun, Wind-powered Generators and Houses (renewable energy)

2001. Environment and Medicine of the Future. Multicoloured.
1597 45c. Type **488** 65 55
1598 59c. Tyre, tins, bottle and carton (recycling) 85 65
1599 74c. Microscope and test-tubes (biological research) 1·00 1·00

489 St. Nicholas

2001. Christmas.
1600 **489** 45c.+5c. multicoloured 60 45

490 Squirrel

2001. National Welfare Fund. Animals (1st issue). Multicoloured.
1601 45c.+5c. Type **490** 60 45
1602 52c.+8c. Wild boar 75 55
1603 59c.+11c. Hare (vert) . . . 90 65
1604 89c.+21c. Wood pigeon (vert) . . . . 1·40 1·40
See also Nos. 1632/5.

491 Emblem

2001. Kiwanis International (community organization).
1605 **491** 52c. dp blue, bl & gold 65 40

New Currency. 100 cents = 1 euro.

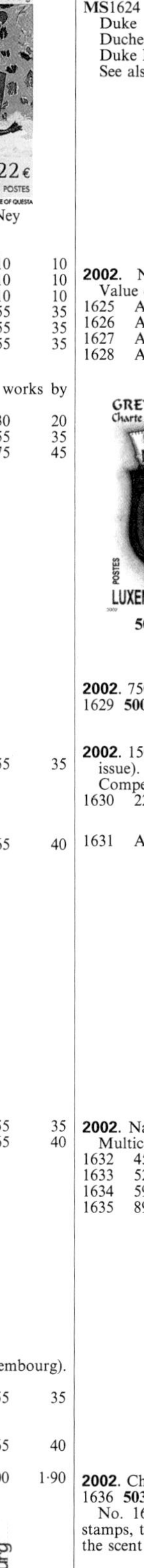

492 Snowboarding
493 Mortiz Ney

2002. Sports. Self-adhesive. Multicoloured.
1606 7c. Type **492** 10 10
1607 7c. Skateboarding 10 10
1608 7c. Inline skating 10 10
1609 45c. BMX biking 55 35
1610 45c. Beach volleyball . . . 55 35
1611 45c. Street basketball . . . 55 35

2002. Modern Art (2nd series). Showing works by artist named. Multicoloured.
1612 22c. Type **493** 30 20
1613 45c. Dany Prum (horiz) . . 55 35
1614 59c. Christiane Schmit . . . 75 45

494 Map of Europe and "1977"

2002. Anniversaries. Multicoloured.
1615 45c. Type **494** (25th anniv of European Court of Auditors) 55 35
1616 52c. Scales of Justice and map of Europe (50th anniv of European Communities Court of Justice) 65 40

495 Tightrope Walker

2002. Europa. The Circus. Multicoloured.
1617 45c. Type **495** 55 35
1618 52c. Clown juggling 65 40

496 Emblem

2002. 2002 Tour de France (starting in Luxembourg). Multicoloured.
1619 45c. Type **496** 55 35
1620 52c. Francois Faber (winner of 1909 Tour de France) (vert) 65 40
1621 €2.45 "The Champion" (Joseph Kutter) (vert) . . 3·00 1·90

497 Orchestra on Stage (50th Anniv of Festival of Wiltz)

2002. Cultural Anniversaries. Value expressed by letter (No. 1622) or face value (No. 1623). Multicoloured.
1622 A (45c.) Type **497** 55 35
1623 €1.12 Victor Hugo and signature (birth bicentenary) . . . . . . 1·40 85

498 Grand Duke William III of Netherlands

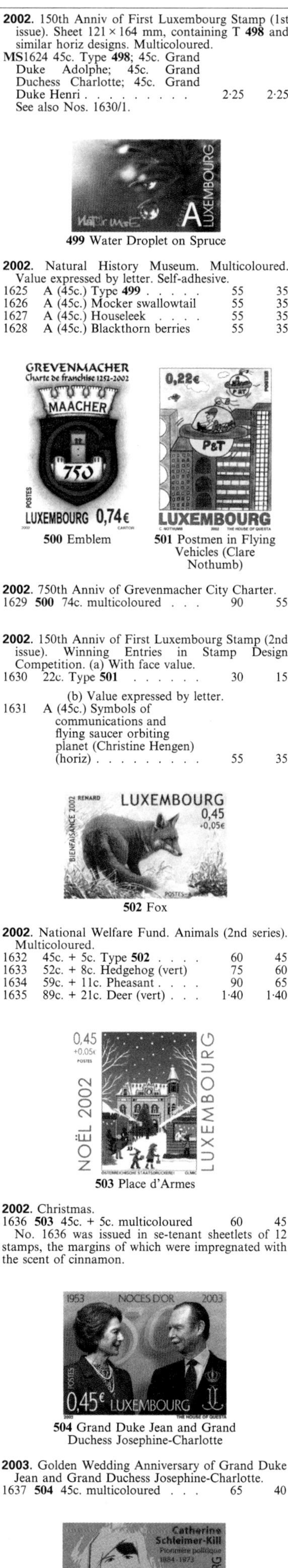

2002. 150th Anniv of First Luxembourg Stamp (1st issue). Sheet 121 × 164 mm, containing T **498** and similar horiz designs. Multicoloured.
MS1624 45c. Type **498**; 45c. Grand Duke Adolphe; 45c. Grand Duchess Charlotte; 45c. Grand Duke Henri . . . . 2·25 2·25
See also Nos. 1630/1.

499 Water Droplet on Spruce

2002. Natural History Museum. Multicoloured. Value expressed by letter. Self-adhesive.
1625 A (45c.) Type **499** 55 35
1626 A (45c.) Mocker swallowtail 55 35
1627 A (45c.) Houseleek 55 35
1628 A (45c.) Blackthorn berries 55 35

500 Emblem
501 Postmen in Flying Vehicles (Clare Nothumb)

2002. 750th Anniv of Grevenmacher City Charter.
1629 **500** 74c. multicoloured . . . 90 55

2002. 150th Anniv of First Luxembourg Stamp (2nd issue). Winning Entries in Stamp Design Competition. (a) With face value.
1630 22c. Type **501** 30 15

(b) Value expressed by letter.
1631 A (45c.) Symbols of communications and flying saucer orbiting planet (Christine Hengen) (horiz) 55 35

502 Fox

2002. National Welfare Fund. Animals (2nd series). Multicoloured.
1632 45c. + 5c. Type **502** 60 45
1633 52c. + 8c. Hedgehog (vert) 75 60
1634 59c. + 11c. Pheasant 90 65
1635 89c. + 21c. Deer (vert) . . . 1·40 1·40

503 Place d'Armes

2002. Christmas.
1636 **503** 45c. + 5c. multicoloured 60 45
No. 1636 was issued in se-tenant sheetlets of 12 stamps, the margins of which were impregnated with the scent of cinnamon.

504 Grand Duke Jean and Grand Duchess Josephine-Charlotte

2003. Golden Wedding Anniversary of Grand Duke Jean and Grand Duchess Josephine-Charlotte.
1637 **504** 45c. multicoloured . . . 65 40

505 Catherine Schleimer-Kill

2003. 30th Death Anniversaries. Multicoloured.
1638 45c. Type **505** (political pioneer) 65 40
1639 45c. Lou Koster (composer) 65 40

506 Citeaux Abbey, Differdange

2003. Tourism. Multicoloured.
1640 50c. Type **506** 70 40
1641 €1 Mamer Castle . . . . . 1·40 85
1642 €2.50 St. Joseph Church, Esch-sur-Alzette (vert) . . 3·50 2·10

507 Pamphlets and Compact Discs

2003. 50th Anniv of Official Journal of European Communities (daily publication of official reports).
1643 **507** 52c. multicoloured . . . 75 45

OFFICIAL STAMPS

1875. Stamps of 1859–72 optd **OFFICIEL**. Roul.
O79 **3** 1c. brown . . . . 26·00 35·00
O80 2c. black . . . . 26·00 35·00
O81 **4** 10c. lilac £1900 £1900
O82 12½c. red £425 £450
O83 20c. brown . . . . . . 35·00 55·00
O84 25c. blue £225 £150
O85 30c. purple . . . . . . 29·00 70·00
O88b 40c. orange £250 £250
O87 1f. on 37½c. bistre (No. 37) . . . . £100 23·00

1875. Stamps of 1874–79 optd **OFFICIEL**. Perf.
O 89 **3** 1c. brown . . . . 8·00 32·00
O 90 2c. black . . . . 10·00 32·00
O 91 4c. green . . . . 85·00 £130
O 92 5c. yellow . . . . . . 48·00 70·00
O 93a **4** 10c. lilac . . . . . . 75·00 80·00
O111 12½c. red . . . . . . 60·00 £100
O 99a 25c. blue . . . . . . 3·00 2·50
O 96 1f. on 37½c. bistre (No. 56) . . . . 29·00 40·00

1881. Stamp of 1859 optd **S. P.** Roul.
O116 **3** 40c. orange . . . . 32·00 60·00

1881. Stamps of 1874–79 optd **S. P.** Perf.
O121 **3** 1c. brown . . . . 23·00 50·00
O122 2c. black . . . . 23·00 50·00
O118 4c. green £140 £170
O123 5c. yellow . . . . . . 70·00 85·00
O124 **4** 10c. lilac . . . . 95·00 £140
O125 12½c. red £110 £140
O126 20c. brown . . . . . . 60·00 £100
O127 25c. blue . . . . 60·00 £100
O128 30c. red . . . . 70·00 £100
O120 1f. on 37½c. bistre (No. 56) 30·00 42·00

1882. Stamps of 1882 optd **S. P.**
O141 **7** 1c. grey 30 40
O142 2c. brown 30 40
O143 4c. olive 35 50
O144 5c. green 35 55
O145 10c. red . . . . 16·00 15·00
O146 12½c. blue . . . . . . 2·50 4·00
O147 20c. orange . . . . . . 2·50 4·00
O148 25c. blue . . . . 17·00 23·00
O149 30c. olive . . . . . . 5·25 8·50
O150 50c. brown . . . . . . 1·00 2·25
O151 1f. lilac . . . . 1·00 2·75
O152 5f. orange . . . . . . 16·00 30·00

1891. Stamps of 1891 optd **S. P.**
O188 **8** 10c. red 30 45
O189 12½c. green . . . . . . 6·00 6·00
O190 20c. orange . . . . . . 9·50 7·00
O191a 25c. blue 30 40
O192 30c. green . . . . . . 6·50 6·75
O193a 37½c. green . . . . . 6·00 7·50
O194 50c. brown . . . . . . 5·00 8·25
O195a 1f. purple . . . . . . 5·00 10·00
O196 2½f. black . . . . . . 38·00 60·00
O197 5f. lake . . . . 29·00 55·00

1898. Stamps of 1895 optd **S. P.**
O213 **9** 1c. grey . . . . 1·90 1·75
O214 2c. brown . . . . . . 1·40 1·50
O215 4c. bistre . . . . . . 1·40 1·50
O216 5c. green . . . . 3·25 4·00
O217 10c. red . . . . 40·00 32·00

1908. Stamps of 1906 optd **Officiel**.
O218 **10** 1c. grey 10 30
O219 2c. brown 10 30
O220 4c. bistre 10 30
O221 5c. green 10 30
O271 5c. mauve 10 30
O222 6c. lilac 10 30
O223 7½c. yellow 25 30
O224 10c. red 30 45
O225 12½c. slate 30 50
O226 15c. brown 40 65
O227 20c. orange 40 65
O228 25c. blue 40 60
O229 30c. olive . . . . . . 4·50 4·50
O230 37½c. green 70 75
O231 50c. brown . . . . . . 1·10 1·40
O232 87½c. blue . . . . . . 1·75 3·25
O233 1f. purple . . . . . . 2·50 3·50
O234 2½f. red . . . . 70·00 65·00
O235 5f. purple . . . . . . 65·00 40·00

1915. Stamps of 1914 optd **Officiel**.
O236 **13** 10c. purple 20 60
O237 12½c. green 20 60
O238 15c. brown 20 60
O239 17½c. brown 20 60
O240 25c. blue 20 60
O241 30c. brown . . . . . . 1·40 3·75
O242 35c. blue 25 25
O243 37½c. brown . . . . . . 25 1·00
O244 40c. red 35 95
O245 50c. grey 35 85
O246 62½c. green . . . . . . 35 1·25
O247 87½c. orange . . . . . . 35 1·40
O248 1f. brown . . . . 35 1·25
O249 2½f. red . . . . 40 2·50
O250 5f. violet . . . . 40 3·25

1922. Stamps of 1921 optd **Officiel**.
O251 **17** 2c. brown 15 20
O252 3c. green 15 15
O253 6c. purple 15 30
O272 10c. green 10 30
O273 15c. green 10 30
O274 15c. orange 10 30
O256 20c. orange 25 40
O275 20c. green 10 30
O257 25c. green 25 40
O258 30c. red 25 40
O259 40c. orange 25 40
O260 50c. blue 30 55
O276 50c. red 15 35
O261 75c. red 30 55
O277 75c. blue 20 45
O266 80c. black 25 50
O263 **18** 1f. red . . . . 50 1·50
O278 1f. blue . . . . 40 1·25
O267 – 2f. blue . . . . 40 1·75
O279 – 2f. brown . . . . . . 1·50 4·75
O269 – 5f. violet . . . . . . 5·00 8·50

1922. Stamps of 1923 optd **Officiel**.
O268b **28** 3f. blue . . . . 40 1·40
O270 **26** 10f. black . . . . . . 9·50 25·00

1926. Stamps of 1926 optd **Officiel**.
O280 **32** 5c. mauve 10 20
O281 10c. green 10 20
O298 15c. black 30 95
O282 20c. orange 10 20
O283 25c. green 10 20
O300 25c. brown 35 70
O301 30c. green . . . . . . 30 1·25
O302 30c. violet . . . . . . 40 1·00
O303 35c. violet 40 35
O304 35c. green 40 95
O286 40c. brown 15 25
O287 50c. brown 15 25
O307 60c. green 40 75
O288 65c. brown 15 40
O308 70c. violet . . . . . . 1·90 6·00
O289 75c. red 15 40
O309 75c. brown 40 75
O291 80c. brown 25 45
O292 90c. red 35 65
O293 1f. black 30 50
O312 1f. red . . . . 45 1·50
O294 1¼f. blue 15 15
O313 1¼f. yellow . . . . . . 1·40 4·00
O314 1¼f. green . . . . . . 2·50 4·75
O315 1½f. blue . . . . 40 1·25
O316 1¾f. blue . . . . 45 1·25

1928. Stamp of 1928 optd **Officiel**.
O317 **37** 2f. black . . . . 55 1·40

1931. Stamp of 1931 optd **Officiel**.
O318 **43** 20f. green . . . . 2·40 6·50

1934. Stamp of 1934 optd **Officiel**.
O319 **47** 5f. green . . . . 1·75 5·00

1935. No. 340 optd **Officiel**.
O341 **52** 10f. green . . . . 1·60 6·75

POSTAGE DUE STAMPS

D 12 Arms of Luxembourg
D 77

1907.
D173 **D 12** 5c. black and green . . 10 20
D174 10c. black and green 85 20
D175 12½c. black and green 30 85
D176 20c. black and green 55 60
D177 25c. black and green 17·00 1·10
D178 50c. black and green 45 3·00
D179 1f. black and green . . 30 3·25

1920. Surch.
D193 **D 12** 15 on 12½c. blk & grn 2·00 5·25
D194 30 on 25c. black & grn 2·50 7·50

1922.
D221 **D 12** 5c. red and green . . . 10 30
D222 10c. red and green . . 10 30
D223 20c. red and green . . 25 30
D224 25c. red and green . . 30 45

D225 30c. red and green . . 30 50
D226 35c. red and green . . 40 65
D227 50c. red and green . . 40 65
D228 60c. red and green . . 40 60
D229 70c. red and green . . 4·50 4·50
D230 75c. red and green . . 70 75
D231 1f. red and green . . . 1·10 1·40
D232 2f. red and green . . . 1·75 3·25
D233 3f. red and green . . . 2·50 3·50

1946.

D488 D 77 5c. green 35 65
D489 10c. green 35 45
D490 20c. green 35 45
D491 30c. green 35 45
D492 50c. green 35 35
D493 70c. green 45 70
D494 75c. green . . . . . . 1·40 30
D495 1f. red 35 30
D496 1f.50 red 35 30
D497 2f. red 45 30
D498 3f. red 70 30
D499 5f. red . . . . . . 1·00 35
D500 10f. red . . . . . . 1·75 3·50
D501 20f. red . . . . . . 3·50 20·00

MACAO Pt. 9; Pt. 17

A former Portuguese territory in China at the mouth of the Canton River.

1884. 1000 reis = 1 milreis.
1894. 78 avos = 1 rupee.
1913. 100 avos = 1 pataca.

1884. "Crown" key-type inscr "MACAU".
10 P 5r. black . . . . 8·00 5·00
2 10r. orange . . . . 14·00 10·00
21 10r. green . . . . 15·00 10·00
12 20r. bistre . . . . 20·00 13·00
27 20r. red . . . . 20·00 15·00
13 25r. red . . . . 7·50 5·00
22 25r. lilac . . . . 15·00 10·00
14 40r. blue . . . . 40·00 35·00
23 40r. buff . . . . 25·00 15·00
15 50r. green . . . . 50·00 38·00
24 50r. blue . . . . 15·00 12·00
31 80r. grey . . . . 40·00 30·00
16 100r. lilac . . . . 22·00 16·00
17 200r. orange . . . . 24·00 16·00
9 300r. brown . . . . 25·00 18·00

1885. "Crown" key type of Macao surch **80 reis** in circle. No gum.
19 P 80r. on 100r. lilac . . . . . 60·00 38·00

1885. "Crown" key type of Macao surch in Reis. With gum (43, 44, 45), no gum (others).
32 P 5r. on 25r. pink . . . . . 15·00 10·00
43 5r. on 80r. grey . . . . . 7·50 6·00
46 5r. on 100r. lilac . . . . . 50·00 40·00
33 10r. on 25r. pink . . . . . 25·00 15·00
38 10r. on 50r. green . . . . . 85·00 70·00
44 10r. on 80r. grey . . . . . 20·00 15·00
47 10r. on 200r. orange . . . . 50·00 40·00
35 20r. on 50r. green . . . . . 18·00 12·00
45 20r. on 80r. grey . . . . . 38·00 20·00
40 40r. on 50r. green . . . . . 75·00 60·00

1885. "Crown" key-type of Macao surch with figure of value only and bar. No gum.
41 P 5 on 25r. red . . . . . . 40·00 25·00
42a 10 on 50r. green . . . . . 30·00 22·00

9

1887. Fiscal stamps as **T 9** surch **CORREIO** and new value. No gum.
50 5r. on 10r. green and brown £100 80·00
51 5r. on 20r. green and brown £100 80·00
52 5r. on 60r. green and brown £100 80·00
53 10r. on 10r. green and brown £120 90·00
54 10r. on 60r. green and brown £120 90·00
55 40r. on 20r. green and brown £200 £140

1888. "Embossed" key-type inscr "PROVINCIA DE MACAU".
56 Q 5r. black . . . . 7·50 5·00
57 10r. green . . . . 7·50 5·00
58 20r. red . . . . 12·50 7·50
59 25r. mauve . . . . 14·00 7·50
60 40r. brown . . . . 15·00 8·00
61 50r. blue . . . . 16·00 8·00
62 80r. grey . . . . 20·00 12·00
63 100r. brown . . . . 22·00 14·00
71 200r. lilac . . . . 35·00 12·00
72 300r. orange . . . . 32·00 12·00

1892. No. 71 surch **3030**.
73 Q 30 on 200r. lilac . . . . . . 40·00 30·00

1894. "Embossed" key-type of Macao surch **PROVISORIO**, value and Chinese characters. No gum.
75b Q 1a. on 5r. black . . . . . 10·00 5·00
76 3a. on 20r. red . . . . . . 12·00 5·00
77 4a. on 25r. violet . . . . . 15·00 8·00
89 5a. on 30 on 200r. lilac (No. 73) . . . . 75·00 60·00
78 6a. on 40r. brown . . . . 16·00 8·00
79 8a. on 50r. blue . . . . . 35·00 15·00
80 13a. on 80r. grey . . . . . 15·00 12·00
81 16a. on 100r. brown . . . 20·00 10·00
82 31a. on 200r. lilac . . . . 70·00 35·00
83 47a. on 300r. orange . . . 85·00 18·00

1894. "Figures" key-type inscr "MACAU".
91 R 5r. yellow . . . . 6·00 2·50
92 10r. mauve . . . . 6·00 2·50
93 15r. brown . . . . 8·00 5·00
94 20r. lilac . . . . 12·00 6·00
95 25r. green . . . . 20·00 12·00
96 50r. blue . . . . 24·00 12·00
97 75r. pink . . . . 48·00 32·00
98 80r. green . . . . 35·00 18·00
99 100r. brown on buff . . . 35·00 16·00
100 150r. red on pink . . . . 45·00 16·00
101 200r. blue on blue . . . . 60·00 20·00
102 300r. blue on brown . . . 75·00 22·00

1898. As Vasco da Gama types of Portugal but inscr "MACAU".
104 ½a. green . . . . 3·00 1·90
105 1a. red . . . . 3·00 1·90
106 2a. purple . . . . 3·00 1·90
107 4a. green . . . . 4·00 1·90
108 8a. blue . . . . 7·50 2·75
109 12a. brown . . . . 8·00 3·25
110 16a. brown . . . . 8·00 2·75
111 24a. brown . . . . 10·00 5·00

1898. "King Carlos" key-type inscr "MACAU". Name and value in black.
112 S ½a. grey . . . . 1·50 60
113 1a. yellow . . . . 1·50 60
114 2a. green . . . . 1·50 60
115 2½a. brown . . . . 2·50 1·50
116 3a. lilac . . . . 2·50 1·50
174 3a. grey . . . . 4·00 2·00
117 4a. green . . . . 5·00 2·75
175 4a. red . . . . 3·75 2·00
176 5a. brown . . . . 5·00 3·00
177 6a. brown . . . . 5·00 3·50
119 8a. blue . . . . 6·00 3·00
178 8a. brown . . . . 6·00 3·75
120 10a. blue . . . . 6·00 3·00
121 12a. pink . . . . 8·00 6·00
179 12a. purple . . . . 20·00 12·50
122 13a. mauve . . . . 10·00 7·00
180 13a. lilac . . . . 10·00 6·50
123 15a. green . . . . 20·00 12·00
124 16a. blue on blue . . . . 10·00 5·00
181 18a. brown on pink . . . . 18·00 15·00
125 20a. brown on cream . . . 11·00 6·00
126 24a. brown on yellow . . . 15·00 8·00
127 31a. purple . . . . 18·00 8·00
182 31a. purple on pink . . . 18·00 15·00
128 47a. blue on pink . . . . 28·00 11·00
183 47a. blue on yellow . . . 30·00 25·00
129 78a. black on blue . . . . 35·00 16·00

1900. "King Carlos" key-type of Macao surch **PROVISORIO** and new value.
132 S 5 on 13a. mauve . . . . . 6·00 3·50
133 10 on 16a. blue on blue . . 8·50 4·00
134 15 on 24a. brown on yellow 18·00 4·50
135 20 on 31a. purple . . . . . 24·00 5·00

1902. Various types of Macao surch.
138 Q 6a. on 5r. black . . . . . 5·00 2·50
142 R 6a. on 5r. yellow . . . . . 5·00 3·00
136 P 6a. on 10r. yellow . . . . 15·00 8·00
137 6a. on 10r. green . . . . 10·00 7·50
139 Q 6a. on 10r. green . . . . 5·00 3·00
143 R 6a. on 10r. mauve . . . . 10·00 6·00
144 6a. on 15r. brown . . . . 10·00 6·00
145 6a. on 25r. green . . . . 6·00 4·00
140 Q 6a. on 40r. brown . . . . 5·00 3·00
146 R 6a. on 80r. green . . . . . 6·00 3·50
148 6a. on 100r. brown on buff 15·00 4·50
149 6a. on 200r. blue on blue 5·00 3·00
151 V 18a. on 2½r. brown . . . . 6·50 5·00
153 Q 18a. on 20r. red . . . . . 16·00 4·00
162 R 18a. on 20r. lilac . . . . 15·00 6·00
154 Q 18a. on 25r. mauve . . . . 75·00 32·00
163 R 18a. on 50r. blue . . . . . 15·00 6·00
165 18a. on 75r. pink . . . . . 15·00 5·00
155 Q 18a. on 80r. grey . . . . . £100 50·00
156 18a. on 100r. brown . . . 12·00 7·50
166 R 18a. on 150r. red on pink 15·00 6·00
158 Q 18a. on 200r. lilac . . . . £100 50·00
160 18a. on 300r. orange . . . 18·00 6·75
167 R 18a. on 300r. blue on brn 15·00 7·50

1902. "King Carlos" type of Macao optd **PROVISORIO**.
168 S 2a. green . . . . 10·00 5·00
169 4a. green . . . . 10·00 5·00
170 8a. blue . . . . 10·00 5·00
171 10a. blue . . . . 10·00 6·00
172 12a. pink . . . . 18·00 7·50

1905. No. 179 surch **10 AVOS** and bar.
184 S 10a. on 12a. purple . . . . 18·00 10·00

1910. "Due" key-type of Macao, but with words "PORTEADO" and "RECEBER" cancelled.
185 W ½a. green . . . . 10·00 6·00
186 1a. green . . . . 10·00 6·00
187 2a. grey . . . . 10·00 6·00

1911. "King Carlos" key-type of Macao optd **REPUBLICA**.
188 S ½a. grey . . . . 1·00 75
189 1a. orange . . . . 1·00 75
190 2a. green . . . . 1·00 75
191 3a. grey . . . . 1·00 75
192 4a. red . . . . 3·00 2·50
193 5a. brown . . . . 3·00 2·00
194 6a. brown . . . . 3·00 2·00
195 8a. brown . . . . 3·00 2·00
196 10a. blue . . . . 3·00 2·00
197 13a. lilac . . . . 4·50 3·00
198 16a. blue on blue . . . . 4·50 3·00
199 18a. brown on pink . . . . 10·00 7·00
200 20a. brown on cream . . . 10·00 7·00
201 31a. purple on pink . . . . 10·00 7·00
202 47a. blue on yellow . . . . 15·00 10·00
203 78a. black on blue . . . . 25·00 15·00

30 32

1911. Fiscal stamp surch **POSTAL 1 AVO** and bar.
204 **30** 1a. on 5r. brown, yellow and black . . . . 10·00 5·00

1911. Stamps bisected and surch.
205 S 2a. on half of 4a. red (No. 175) . . . . 30·00 15·00
206 5a. on half of 10a. blue (No. 120) . . . . 75·00 60·00
207 5a. on half of 10a. blue (No. 171) . . . . 85·00 75·00

1911.

210 **32** 1a. black £350 £300
211 2a. black £400 £325

1913. Provisionals of 1902 surch in addition with new value and bars over old value and optd **REPUBLICA**.
212 R 2a. on 18a. on 20r. lilac (No. 162) . . . . . . 8·00 3·00
213 2a. on 18a. on 50r. blue (No. 163) . . . . . . 8·00 3·00
215 2a. on 18a. on 75r. pink (No. 165) . . . . . . 10·00 3·00
216 2a. on 18a. on 150r. red on pink (No. 166) . . . . . 10·00 3·00

1913. Provisionals of 1902 and 1905 optd **REPUBLICA**.
218 Q 6a. on 5r. (No. 138) . . . . 5·00 3·50
284 R 6a. on 5r. (No. 142) . . . . 3·00 2·00
217 P 6a. on 10r. (No. 137) . . . 15·00 10·00
285 Q 6a. on 10r. (No. 139) . . . 3·00 1·50
286 R 6a. on 10r. (No. 143) . . . 3·00 2·00
287 6a. on 15r. (No. 144) . . . 1·90 1·50
288 6a. on 25r. (No. 145) . . . 1·90 1·50
220 Q 6a. on 40r. (No. 140) . . . 6·00 5·00
289 R 6a. on 80r. (No. 146) . . . 1·90 1·50
291 6a. on 100r. (No. 148) . . . 4·00 2·50
292 6a. on 200r. (No. 149) . . . 4·00 2·50
281 S 8a. (No. 170) . . . . . . 2·50 1·50
282 10a. (No. 171) . . . . . . 2·50 1·50
283 10a. on 12a. (No. 184) . . 2·50 1·50
293 V 18a. on 2½r. (No. 151) . . . 2·00 2·25
229 Q 18a. on 20r. (No. 153) . . . 8·50 6·75
295 R 18a. on 20r. (No. 162) . . . 4·00 3·00
296 18a. on 50r. (No. 163) . . . 5·00 4·00
298 18a. on 75r. (No. 165) . . . 5·00 4·00
230 Q 18a. on 100r. (No. 156) . . 42·00 30·00
299 R 18a. on 150r. (No. 166) . . 5·00 4·00
233 Q 18a. on 300r. (No. 160) . . 20·00 10·00
300 R 18a. on 300r. (No. 167) . . 9·50 6·00

1913. Stamps of 1911 issue surch.
252 S ½a. on 5a. brown . . . . . 5·00 3·00
255 1a. on 13a. lilac . . . . . 6·50 4·00
253 4a. on 8a. brown . . . . . 6·00 4·50

1913. Vasco da Gama stamps of Macao optd **REPUBLICA**, and the 12a. surch **10 A.**
256 ½a. green . . . . 4·00 1·50
257 1a. red . . . . 6·00 1·50
258 2a. purple . . . . 6·00 1·50
259 4a. green . . . . 5·00 1·50
260 8a. blue . . . . 6·00 2·75
261 10a. on 12a. brown . . . . 12·00
262 16a. brown . . . . 7·50 3·25
263 24a. brown . . . . 10·00 4·00

1913. "Ceres" key-type inscr "MACAU".
264 U ½a. green . . . . 1·00 60
310 1a. black . . . . 1·75 75
311 1½a. green . . . . 1·10 60
280 2a. green . . . . 2·00 55
313 3a. orange . . . . 4·00 2·00
267 4a. red . . . . 2·25 1·25
315 4a. yellow . . . . 3·00 1·75
268 5a. brown . . . . 3·00 1·90
269 6a. violet . . . . 3·00 2·00
270 8a. brown . . . . 3·25 2·00
271 10a. blue . . . . 3·25 2·25
272 12a. brown . . . . 3·50 2·25
320 14a. mauve . . . . 10·00 7·50
321 16a. grey . . . . 6·00 3·25
274 20a. red . . . . 8·00 5·00
322 24a. green . . . . 8·50 5·00
323 32a. brown . . . . 12·00 9·00
275 40a. purple . . . . 9·00 6·00
324 56a. pink . . . . 20·00 15·00
276 58a. brown on green . . . 15·00 10·00
325 72a. brown . . . . 35·00 12·00
277 76a. brown on pink . . . . 16·00 11·00
278 1p. orange on orange . . . 18·00 14·00
326 1p. orange . . . . 50·00 25·00
279 3p. green on blue . . . . 75·00 50·00
327 3p. turquoise . . . . £120 75·00
328 5p. red £190 £100

1919. Surch.
301 U ½a. on 5a. brown (No. 268) 40·00 30·00
330 1a. on 24a. grn (No. 322) 3·00 1·60
302 R 2 on 6a. on 25r. green (No. 288) £200 £100
303 2 on 6a. on 80r. green (No. 289) . . . . 20·00 15·00
304 S 2a. on 6a. (No. 177) . . . 65·00 40·00
331 U 2a. on 32a. (No. 323) . . . 3·00 1·60
332 4a. on 12a. (No. 272) . . . 3·00 1·60
329 5a. on 6a. violet (No. 269) 4·50 2·50
334 7a. on 8a. brn (No. 270) . . 3·00 2·25
335 12a. on 14a. (No. 320) . . 3·00 2·25
336 15a. on 16a. (No. 321) . . 3·00 2·25
337 20a. on 56a. pink (No. 324) 40·00 25·00

50 "Portugal" and Galeasse

1934.

338 **50** ½a. brown 30 30
339 1a. brown 30 30
340 2a. green 75 40
341 3a. mauve 75 40
342 4a. black 80 50
343 5a. grey 80 50
344 6a. brown 80 50
345 7a. red . . . . 1·00 60
346 8a. blue . . . . 1·00 60
347 10a. red . . . . 1·50 1·00
348 12a. blue . . . . 1·50 1·00
349 14a. green . . . . 1·50 1·10
350 15a. purple . . . . 1·50 1·00
351 20a. orange . . . . 1·50 1·00
352 30a. green . . . . 4·00 1·90
353 40a. violet . . . . 4·00 1·90
354 50a. brown . . . . 7·50 6·00
355 1p. blue . . . . 20·00 10·00
356 2p. brown . . . . 30·00 16·00
357 3p. green . . . . 42·00 22·00
358 5p. mauve . . . . 65·00 35·00

1936. Air. Stamps of 1934 optd **Aviao** and with Greek characters or surch also.
359 **40** 2a. green . . . . 4·00 2·00
360 3a. mauve . . . . 4·00 2·00
361 5a. on 6a. brown . . . . . 4·00 2·00
362 7a. red . . . . 4·00 2·00
363 8a. blue . . . . 6·00 4·00
364 15a. purple . . . . 20·00 10·00

54 Vasco da Gama **56** Airplane over Globe

1938. Name and value in black.
365 **54** 1a. green (postage) . . . . 1·00 60
366 2a. brown . . . . 1·00 60
367 3a. violet . . . . 1·00 60
368 4a. green . . . . 1·00 60
369 – 5a. red . . . . 1·00 60
370 – 6a. grey . . . . 2·00 1·00
371 – 8a. purple . . . . 2·00 1·00
372 – 10a. mauve . . . . 2·50 1·10
373 – 12a. red . . . . 2·50 1·10
374 – 15a. orange . . . . 2·50 1·25
375 – 20a. blue . . . . 4·75 2·00
376 – 40a. black . . . . 8·00 3·00
377 – 50a. brown . . . . 8·00 3·00
378 – 1p. red . . . . 22·00 8·50
379 – 2p. green . . . . 40·00 12·50
380 – 3p. blue . . . . 65·00 16·00
381 – 5p. brown . . . . £110 20·00
382 **56** 1a. red (air) 35 35
383 2a. violet 45 35
384 3a. orange 45 35
385 5a. blue . . . . 1·00 60
386 10a. red . . . . 2·00 95
387 20a. green . . . . 3·25 1·50
388 50a. brown . . . . 6·00 2·25
389 70a. red . . . . 12·00 4·00
390 1p. mauve . . . . 25·00 5·50

DESIGNS: Nos. 369/71, Mousinho de Albuquerque; 372/4, Henry the Navigator; 375/7, Dam; 378/81, Afonso de Albuquerque.

1940. Surch.

391	50	1a. on 6a. brown (No. 344)	5·00	3·50
394		2a. on 6a. brown (No. 344)	2·00	1·60
395		3a. on 6a. brown (No. 344)	2·00	1·60
401	–	3a. on 6a. grey (No. 370)	60·00	45·00
396	50	5a. on 7a. red (No. 345)	2·00	1·60
397		5a. on 8a. blue (No. 346)	2·00	1·60
398		8a. on 30a. (No. 352)	7·50	4·50
399		8a. on 40a. (No. 353)	7·50	4·50
400		8a. on 50a. (No. 354)	7·50	4·50

61 Mountain Fort

62 Our Lady of Fatima

1948.

410	–	1a. brown and orange	2·00	50
427	–	1a. violet and pink	1·00	25
411	61	2a. purple	1·40	50
428		2a. brown and yellow	1·00	25
412	–	3a. purple	3·00	1·10
429	–	3a. orange	1·75	40
413	–	8a. red	4·00	1·75
430	–	8a. grey	40	70
414	–	10a. purple	4·25	1·75
431	–	10a. brown and orange	6·00	1·00
415	–	20a. blue	8·50	2·00
416	–	30a. grey	9·00	2·00
432	–	30a. blue	14·00	2·50
417	–	50a. brown and buff	12·50	2·25
433	–	50a. olive and green	30·00	4·00
418	–	1p. green	50·00	18·00
419	–	1p. blue	80·00	
434	–	1p. brown	60·00	7·50
420	–	2p. red	50·00	12·00
421	–	3p. green	70·00	15·00
422	–	5p. violet	85·00	20·00

DESIGNS—HORIZ: 1a. Macao house; 3a. Port of Macao; 8a. Praia Grande Bay; 10a. Leal Senado Sq; 20a. Sao Jerome Hill; 30a. Street scene, Macao; 50a. Relief of goddess of Ma (allegory); 5p. Forest road. VERT: 1p. Cerco Gateway; 2p. Barra Pagoda, Ma-Cok-Miu; 3p. Post Office.

1948. Honouring the Statue of Our Lady of Fatima.

423	62	8a. red	20·00	7·50

64 Globe and Letter

65 Bells and Dove

1949. 75th Anniv of U.P.U.

424	64	32a. purple	40·00	12·00

1950. Holy Year.

425	65	32a. black	12·00	5·00
426	–	50a. red	18·00	7·50

DESIGN: 50a. Angel holding candelabra.

66 Arms and Dragon

1950.

435	66	1a. yellow on cream	1·00	40
436		2a. green on green	1·00	40
437		10a. purple on green	4·00	85
438		10a. mauve on green	4·00	85

67 F. Mendes Pinto

68 Junk

1951.

439	67	1a. indigo and blue	60	20
440	–	2a. brown and green	1·25	20
441	–	3a. green and light green	2·00	25
442	–	6a. violet and blue	3·50	40
443	–	10a. brown and orange	6·50	85
444	67	20a. purple and light purple	14·00	1·40
445	–	30a. brown and green	22·00	2·10
446	–	50a. red and orange	35·00	3·25

DESIGNS: 2, 10a. St. Francis Xavier; 3, 50a. J. Alvaras; 6, 30a. L. de Camoens.

1951.

447	–	1p. ultramarine and blue	15·00	3·00
448	–	3p. black and blue	75·00	20·00
449	68	5p. brown and orange	£100	25·00

DESIGNS—HORIZ: 1p. Sampan. VERT: 3p. Junk.

69 Our Lady of Fatima

71 St. Raphael Hospital

1951. Termination of Holy Year.

450	69	60a. mauve and pink	32·00	8·00

1952. 1st Tropical Medicine Congress, Lisbon.

451	71	6a. lilac and black	5·00	1·00

72 St. Francis Xavier Statue

73 The Virgin

1952. 400th Death Anniv of St. Francis Xavier.

452	72	3a. black on cream	1·75	60
453	–	16a. brown on buff	5·00	2·00
454	–	40a. black on blue	10·00	3·00

DESIGNS: 16a. Miraculous Arm of St. Francis; 40a. Tomb of St. Francis.

1953. Missionary Art Exhibition.

455	73	8a. brown and drab	3·00	60
456		10a. blue and brown	7·50	2·00
457		50a. green and drab	18·00	3·00

74 Honeysuckle

75 Portuguese Stamp of 1853 and Arms of Portuguese Overseas Provinces

1953. Indigenous Flowers.

458	74	1a. yellow, green and red	50	10
459	–	3a. purple, green and yellow	50	10
460	–	5a. red, green and brown	50	10
461	–	10a. multicoloured	50	15
462	–	16a. yellow, green & brown	85	15
463	–	30a. pink, brown and green	2·00	50
464	–	39a. multicoloured	2·75	50
465	–	1p. yellow, green and purple	7·00	85
466	–	3p. red, brown and grey	20·00	3·00
467	–	5p. yellow, green and red	30·00	7·50

FLOWERS: 3a. Myosotis; 5a. Dragon claw; 10a. Nunflower; 16a. Narcissus; 30a. Peach blossom; 39a. Lotus blossom; 1p. Chrysanthemum; 3p. Plum blossom; 5p. Tangerine blossom.

1954. Portuguese Stamp Centenary.

468	75	10a. multicoloured	12·00	3·00

76 Father M. de Nobrega and View of Sao Paulo

77 Map of Macao

1954. 4th Centenary of Sao Paulo.

469	76	39a. multicoloured	9·00	3·50

1956. Map multicoloured. Values in red, inscr in brown. Colours given are of the backgrounds.

470	77	1a. drab	25	10
471		3a. slate	40	10
472		5a. brown	1·00	10
473		10a. buff	1·75	40
474		30a. blue	3·50	75
475		40a. green	4·00	2·00
476		90a. grey	10·00	2·50
477		1p.50 pink	18·00	4·00

78 Exhibition Emblem and Atomic Emblems

79 "Cinnamomum camphora"

1958. Brussels International Exhibition.

478	78	70a. multicoloured	7·50	2·00

1958. 6th International Congress of Tropical Medicine.

479	79	20a. multicoloured	8·00	2·00

80 Globe girdled by Signs of the Zodiac

81 Boeing 707 over Ermida da Penha

1960. 500th Death Anniv of Prince Henry the Navigator.

480	80	2p. multicoloured	12·00	2·00

1960. Air. Multicoloured.

481		50a. Praia Grande Bay	3·00	70
482		76a. Type **81**	5·00	1·25
483		3p. Macao	10·00	1·50
484		5p. Mong Ha	22·00	2·00
485		10p. Shore of Praia Grande Bay	30·00	4·00

82 Hockey

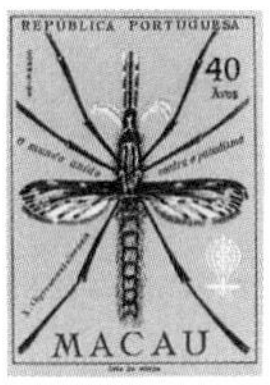

83 "Anopheles hycranus sinensis"

1962. Sports. Multicoloured.

486		10a. Type **82**	30	10
487		16a. Wrestling	75	10
488		20a. Table tennis	85	35
489		50a. Motor cycle racing	1·50	40
490		1p.20 Relay racing	12·00	2·50
491		2p.50 Badminton	32·00	6·50

1962. Malaria Eradication.

492	83	40a. multicoloured	8·00	2·00

84 Bank Building

85 I.T.U. Emblem and St. Gabriel

1964. Centenary of National Overseas Bank.

493	84	20a. multicoloured	12·00	3·00

1965. Centenary of I.T.U.

494	85	10a. multicoloured	6·00	1·50

86 Infante Dom Henrique Academy and Visconde de Sao Januario Hospital

87 Drummer, 1548

1966. 40th Anniv of Portuguese National Revolution.

495	86	10a. multicoloured	9·00	1·00

1966. Portuguese Military Uniforms. Mult.

496		10a. Type **87**	1·50	30
497		15a. Soldier, 1548	3·00	30
498		20a. Arquebusier, 1649	3·00	35
499		40a. Infantry officer, 1783	5·00	75
500		50a. Infantryman, 1783	5·00	1·00
501		60a. Infantryman, 1902	8·00	2·00
502		1p. Infantryman, 1903	11·00	3·00
503		3p. Infantryman, 1904	22·00	10·00

88 O. E. Carmo and Patrol Boat "Vega"

89 Arms of Pope Paul VI, and "Golden Rose"

1967. Centenary of Military Naval Assn. Mult.

504		10a. Type **88**	2·50	1·00
505		20a. Silva Junior and sail frigate "Don Fernando"	7·50	2·00

1967. 50th Anniv of Fatima Apparitions.

506	89	50a. multicoloured	6·50	1·50

90 Cabral Monument, Lisbon

91 Adm. Gago Coutinho with Sextant

1968. 500th Birth Anniv of Pedro Cabral (explorer). Multicoloured.

507		20a. Type **90**	5·00	1·00
508		70a. Cabral's statue, Belmonte	10·00	1·50

1969. Birth Centenary of Admiral Gago Coutinho.

509	91	20a. multicoloured	5·00	1·00

92 Church and Convent of Our Lady of the Reliquary, Vidigueira

93 L. A. Rebello da Silva

1969. 500th Birth Anniv of Vasco da Gama (explorer).

510	92	1p. multicoloured	14·00	2·00

1969. Centenary of Overseas Administrative Reforms.

511	93	90a. multicoloured	5·00	1·00

94 Bishop D. Belchoir Carneiro

95 Facade of Mother Church, Golega

1969. 400th Anniv of Misericordia Monastery, Macao.

512	94	50a. multicoloured	5·00	1·00

1969. 500th Birth Anniv of King Manoel I.

513	95	30a. multicoloured	9·00	1·00

96 Marshal Carmona

97 Dragon Mask

1970. Birth Centenary of Marshal Carmona.

514	96	5a. multicoloured	2·50	75

1971. Chinese Carnival Masks. Multicoloured.

515		5a. Type **97**	1·50	50
516		10a. Lion mask	3·00	75

98 Portuguese Traders at the Chinese Imperial Court

1972. 400th Anniv of Camoens' "The Lusiads" (epic poem).

517 **98** 20a. multicoloured . . . . 10·00 6·00

99 Hockey

1972. Olympic Games, Munich.

518 **99** 50a. multicoloured . . . . 3·50 1·00

100 Fairey IIID Seaplane "Santa Cruz" arriving at Rio de Janeiro

1972. 50th Anniv of First Flight from Lisbon to Rio de Janeiro.

519 **100** 5p. multicoloured . . . . 16·00 2·75

101 Lyre Emblem and Theatre Facade **102** W.M.O. Emblem

1972. Centenary of Pedro V Theatre, Macao.

520 **101** 2p. multicoloured . . . . 12·00 1·25

1973. Centenary of W.M.O.

521 **102** 20a. multicoloured . . . 4·50 1·00

103 Visconde de Sao Januario **104** Chinnery (self-portrait)

1974. Centenary of Visconde de Sao Januario Hospital. Multicoloured.

522 15a. Type **103** . . . . 1·50 50

523 60a. Hospital buildings of 1874 and 1974 . . . . . . 3·00 1·00

1974. Birth Bicent of George Chinnery (painter).

524 **104** 30a. multicoloured . . . 4·00 1·00

105 Macao–Taipa Bridge

1975. Inauguration of Macao–Taipa Bridge. Multicoloured.

525 20a. Type **105** . . . . 2·00 50

526 2p.20 View of Bridge from below . . . . 12·00 2·00

106 Man waving Banner

1975. 1st Anniv of Portuguese Revolution.

527 **106** 10a. multicoloured . . . 3·00 90

528 1p. multicoloured . . . . 12·00 3·00

107 Pou Chai Pagoda

1976. Pagodas. Multicoloured.

529 10p. Type **107** . . . . 12·00 1·00

530 20p. Tin Hau Pagoda . . . . 25·00 3·00

108 Symbolic Figure

1977. Legislative Assembly.

531 **108** 5a. blue, dp blue & black 3·00 1·00

532 2p. brown and black . . . 20·00 5·00

533 5p. yellow, green and black . . . . 30·00 6·00

1979. Nos. 462, 464, 469, 482, 523 and 526 surch.

536 – 10a. on 16a. yellow, green and brown . . . . . . 3·00 75

537 – 30a. on 39a. multicoloured 5·00 90

538 **76** 30a. on 39a. multicoloured 45·00 7·50

539 – 30a. on 60a. multicoloured 3·00 1·25

540 **81** 70a. on 76a. multicoloured 8·50 2·00

541 – 2p. on 2p.20 multicoloured 7·50 2·00

111 Camoes and Macao Harbour **113** Buddha and Macao Cathedral

1981. 400th Death Anniv (1980) of Camoes (Portuguese poet).

542 **111** 10a. multicoloured . . . 30 20

543 30a. multicoloured . . . 30 20

544 1p. multicoloured . . . . 1·50 1·00

545 3p. multicoloured . . . . 5·00 2·00

1981. Transcultural Psychiatry Symposium.

547 **113** 15a. multicoloured . . . 30 10

548 40a. multicoloured . . . 30 15

549 50a. multicoloured . . . 70 25

550 60a. multicoloured . . . 70 30

551 1p. multicoloured . . . . 1·75 50

552 2p.20 multicoloured . . . 3·00 1·50

115 Health Services Buildings

1982. Buildings.

554 – 10a. grey, blue and yellow 15 10

555 – 20a. black, green & lt grn 15 10

556 **115** 30a. green, grey and stone 25 10

557 – 40a. yellow, lt green & grn 25 10

558 – 60a. orange, chocolate and brown 25 15

559 – 80a. pink, green & brown 40 10

560 – 90a. purple, blue and red 30 15

561 – 1p. multicoloured 50 15

562 – 1p.50 yellow, brn & grey 60 15

563 – 2p. purple, ultramarine and blue . . . . 1·00 30

564 – 2p.50 ultramarine, pink and blue . . . . 1·00 30

565 – 3p. yellow, green and olive 85 30

566 – 7p.50 lilac, blue and red 2·00 1·00

567 – 10p. grey, lilac and mauve 7·00 1·75

568 – 15p. yellow, brown and red . . . . 3·00 1·00

DESIGNS: 10a. Social Welfare Institute; 20a. Holy House of Mercy; 40a. Guia lighthouse; 60a. St. Lawrence's Church; 80a. St. Joseph's Seminary; 90a. Pedro V Theatre; 1p. Cerco city gate; 1p.50, St. Domenico's Church; 2p. Luis de Camoes Museum; 2p.50, Ruins of St. Paul's Church; 3p. Palace of St. Sancha (Governor's residence); 7p.50, Senate House; 10p. Schools Welfare Service building; 15p. Barracks of the Moors (headquarters of Port Captaincy and Maritime Police).

116 Heng Ho (Moon goddess)

1982. Autumn Festival. Multicoloured.

569 40a. Type **116** 45 40

560 1p. Decorated gourds . . . . 1·40 60

561 2p. Paper lantern . . . . . . 2·00 85

562 5p. Warrior riding lion . . . 5·00 1·00

117 Aerial View of Macao, Taipa and Coloane Islands **118** "Switchboard Operators" (Lou Sok Man)

1982. Macao's Geographical Situation. Mult.

573 50a. Type **117** 25 15

574 3p. Map of South China . . 3·50 1·50

1983. World Communications Year. Children's Drawings. Multicoloured.

575 60a. Type **118** 30 10

576 3p. Postman and pillar box (Lai Sok Pek) . . . . . . 1·50 60

577 6p. Globe with methods of communication (Loi Chak Keong) . . . . 5·50 3·00

119 "Asclepias curassavica" **120** Galleon and Map of Macao (left)

1983. Medicinal Plants. Multicoloured.

578 20a. Type **119** 30 15

579 40a. "Acanthus ilicifolius" . . 60 25

580 60a. "Melastoma sanguineum" . . . . 1·25 30

581 70a. Indian lotus ("Nelumbo nucifera") . . . . 1·50 45

582 1p.50 "Bombax malabaricum" . . . . . . 3·00 1·00

583 2p.50 "Hibiscus mutabilis" 6·00 2·00

1983. 16th Century Portuguese Discoveries. Multicoloured.

585 4p. Type **120** . . . . 2·00 1·25

586 4p. Galleon, astrolabe and map of Macao (right) . . . 2·00 1·25

Nos. 585/6 were printed together, se-tenant, forming a composite design.

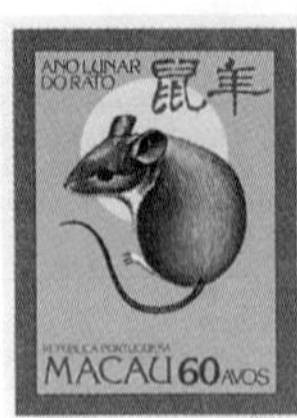

121 Rat **122** Detail of First Macao Stamp, 1884

1984. New Year. "Year of the Rat".

587 **121** 60a. multicoloured . . . 7·50 3·00

1984. Centenary of Macao Stamps.

588 **122** 40a. black and red . . . 1·00 30

589 3p. black and red . . . . 3·00 1·00

590 5p. black and brown . . . 4·00 2·00

123 Jay

1984. "Ausipex 84" International Stamp Exhibition, Melbourne. Birds. Multicoloured.

592 30a. White-throated and river kingfishers . . . . 1·00 40

593 40a. Type **123** . . . . 1·25 40

594 50a. Japanese white-eye . . . 1·50 60

595 70a. Hoopoe . . . . 2·00 75

596 2p.50 Pekin robin . . . . . 6·00 1·25

597 6p. Mallard . . . . 12·00 4·00

124 Hok Lou T'eng

1984. "Philakorea 84" International Stamp Exhibition, Seoul. Fishing Boats. Multicoloured.

598 20a. Type **124** 25 20

599 60a. Tai Tong 60 30

600 2p. Tai Mei Chai . . . . . 1·50 70

601 5p. Ch'at Pong T'o . . . . . 4·00 1·75

125 Ox and Moon **126** Open Hand with Stylized Doves

1985. New Year. Year of the Ox.

602 **125** 1p. multicoloured . . . . 3·00 1·00

1985. International Youth Year. Multicoloured.

603 2p.50 Type **126** . . . . . . 1·50 50

604 3p. Open hands and plants 2·00 75

127 Pres. Eanes

1985. Visit of President Ramalho Eanes of Portugal.

605 **127** 1p.50 multicoloured . . . 1·25 50

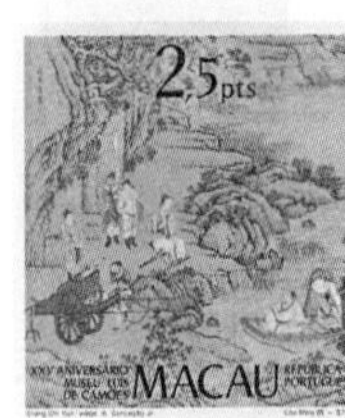

128 Riverside Scene **129** "Euploea midamus"

1985. 25th Anniv of Luis de Camoes Museum. Paintings by Cheng Chi Yun. Multicoloured.

606 2p.50 Type **128** . . . . . . 5·00 1·00

607 2p.50 Man on seat and boy filling jar from river . . . 5·00 1·00

608 2p.50 Playing harp in summerhouse . . . . . . 5·00 1·00

609 2p.50 Three men by river . . 5·00 1·00

1985. World Tourism Day. Butterflies. Mult.

610 30a. Type **129** 50 20

611 50a. Great orange-tip 50 30

612 70a. "Lethe confusa" 85 30

613 2p. Purple sapphire . . . . . 1·75 1·00

614 4p. "Euthalia phemius seitzi" 3·00 1·50

615 7p.50 Common birdwing . . 6·00 3·50

130 Tou (sailing barge) **131** Tiger and Moon

1985. "Italia '85" International Stamp Exhibition, Rome. Cargo Boats. Multicoloured.

617 50a. Type **130** 50 30

618 70a. "Veng Seng Lei" (motor junk) 70 30

619 1p. "Tong Heng Long No. 2" (motor junk) . . . 1·00 40

620 6p. "Fong Vong San" (container ship) . . . . . 5·00 3·00

1986. New Year. Year of the Tiger.

621 **131** 1p.50 multicoloured . . . 2·50 1·00

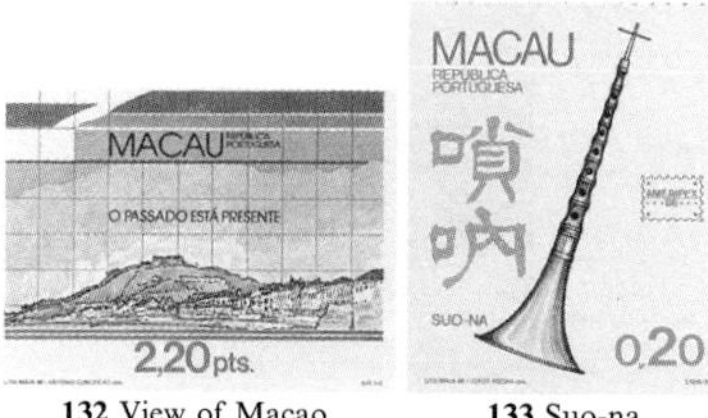
132 View of Macao **133** Suo-na

1986. Macao, "the Past is still Present".
622 **132** 2p.20 multicoloured . . . 2·00 75

1986. "Ameripex '86" International Stamp Exn, Chicago. Musical Instruments. Multicoloured.
623 20a. Type **133** 30 15
624 50a. Sheng (pipes) 35 25
625 60a. Er-hu (bowed instrument) 50 40
626 70a. Ruan (string instrument) 75 40
627 5p. Cheng (harp) . . . . . . 7·50 2·50
628 8p. Pi-pa (lute) . . . . 12·00 7·50

134 "Flying Albatros" (hydrofoil)

1986. "Stockholmia 86" International Stamp Exhibition. Passenger Ferries. Multicoloured.
630 10a. Type **134** 25 40
631 40a. "Tejo" (hovercraft) . . . 30 60
632 3p. "Tercera" (jetfoil) . . . . 1·25 2·00
633 7p.50 "Cheung Kong" (high speed ferry) . . . . 3·50 5·00

135 Taipa Fortress **136** Sun Yat-sen

1986. 10th Anniv of Security Forces. Fortresses. Multicoloured.
634 2p. Type **135** . . . . 2·50 1·60
635 2p. St. Paul on the Mount . . 2·50 1·60
636 2p. St. Francis . . . . 2·50 1·60
637 2p. Guia . . . . 2·50 1·60
Nos. 634/7 were printed together, se-tenant, forming a composite design.

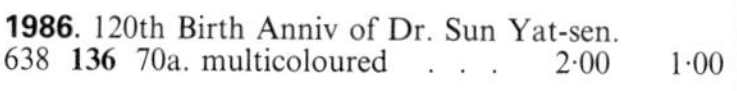

1986. 120th Birth Anniv of Dr. Sun Yat-sen.
638 **136** 70a. multicoloured . . . 2·00 1·00

137 Hare and Moon **138** Wa To (physician)

1987. New Year. Year of the Hare.
640 **137** 1p.50 multicoloured . . . 4·00 1·00

1987. Shek Wan Ceramics. Multicoloured.
641 2p.20 Type **138** . . . . . . 1·60 1·60
642 2p.20 Choi San, God of Fortune . . . . 1·60 1·60
643 2p.20 Yi, Sun God . . . . . 1·60 1·60
644 2p.20 Cung Kuei, Keeper of Demons . . . . 1·60 1·60

139 Boats

1987. Dragon Boat Festival. Multicoloured.
645 50a. Type **139** 50 10
646 5p. Dragon boat prow . . . 3·00 1·50

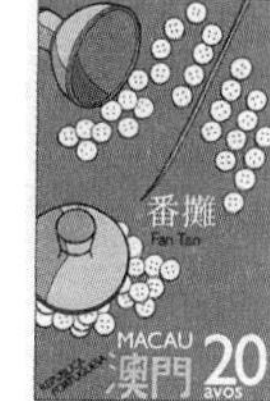
140 Circular Fan **141** Fantan

1987. Fans. Multicoloured.
647 30a. Type **140** 30 15
648 70a. Folding fan with tree design 60 25
649 1p. Square-shaped fan with peacock design . . . . . . 4·00 1·25
650 6p. Heart-shaped fan with painting of woman and tree . . . . 10·00 3·25

1987. Casino Games. Multicoloured.
652 20a. Type **141** 25 15
653 40a. Cussec 40 25
654 4p. Baccarat . . . . 2·50 85
655 7p. Roulette . . . . 8·00 2·10

142 Goods Hand-cart **143** Dragon and Moon

1987. Traditional Vehicles. Multicoloured.
656 10a. Type **142** 30 10
657 70a. Open sedan chair . . . 50 10
658 90a. Rickshaw . . . . 1·50 65
659 10p. Cycle rickshaw . . . . 7·25 1·60

1988. New Year. Year of the Dragon.
661 **143** 2p.50 multicoloured . . . 2·50 1·00

144 West European Hedgehog

1988. Protected Mammals. Multicoloured.
662 3p. Type **144** . . . . 3·00 1·00
663 3p. Eurasian badger . . . . 3·00 1·00
664 3p. European otter . . . . . 3·00 1·00
665 3p. Chinese pangolin . . . . 3·00 1·00

145 Breastfeeding

1988. 40th Anniv of W.H.O. Multicoloured.
666 60a. Type **145** 25 10
667 80a. Vaccinating child . . . 50 25
668 2p.40 Donating blood . . . 2·00 65

146 Bicycles

1988. Transport. Multicoloured.
669 20a. Type **146** 15 10
670 50a. Lambretta and Vespa . . 25 10
671 3p.30 Open-sided motor car 1·25 80
672 5p. Renault delivery truck, 1912 . . . . 2·50 1·50

147 Hurdling **148** Intelpost (electronic mail)

1988. Olympic Games, Seoul. Multicoloured.
674 40a. Type **147** 30 10
675 60a. Basketball 50 15
676 1p. Football . . . . 1·50 65
677 8p. Table tennis . . . . . . 4·50 1·60

1988. New Postal Services. Multicoloured.
679 13p.40 Type **148** . . . . . . 3·00 1·00
680 40p. Express Mail Service (EMS) . . . . 10·00 4·00

149 B.M.W. Saloon Car **150** Snake and Moon

1988. 35th Macao Grand Prix. Multicoloured.
681 80a. Type **149** 25 15
682 2p.80 Motor cycle . . . . . 1·25 65
683 7p. Formula 3 car . . . . . 4·00 1·60

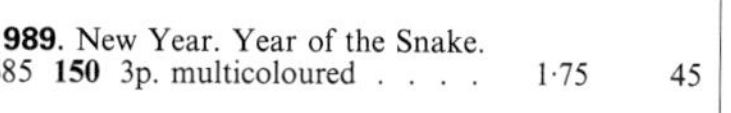

1989. New Year. Year of the Snake.
685 **150** 3p. multicoloured . . . . 1·75 45

151 Water Carrier **152** White Building

1989. Traditional Occupations (1st series). Multicoloured.
686 50a. Type **151** 25 10
687 1p. Tan-kya (boat) woman 40 15
688 4p. Tin-tin man (pedlar) . . 1·25 85
689 5p. Tao-fu-fa (soya bean cheese) vendor . . . . . . 2·50 1·00
See also Nos. 714/17 and 743/6.

1989. Paintings by George Vitalievich Smirnoff in Luis Camoes Museum. Multicoloured.
690 2p. Type **152** 40 40
691 2p. Building with railings . . 40 40
692 2p. Street scene 40 40
693 2p. White thatched cottage 40 40

153 Common Cobra **154** Talu

1989. "Philexfrance 89" International Stamp Exhibition, Paris. Snakes of Macao. Mult.
694 2p.50 Type **153** 90 30
695 2p.50 Banded krait ("Bungarus fasciatus") . . 90 30
696 2p.50 Bamboo pit viper ("Trimeresurus albolabris") 90 30
697 2p.50 Rat snake ("Elaphe radiata") 90 30

1989. Traditional Games. Multicoloured.
698 10a. Type **154** 15 10
699 60a. Triol (marbles) 35 10
700 3p.30 Chiquia (shuttlecock) 1·25 30
701 5p. Chinese chequers . . . . 2·25 1·10

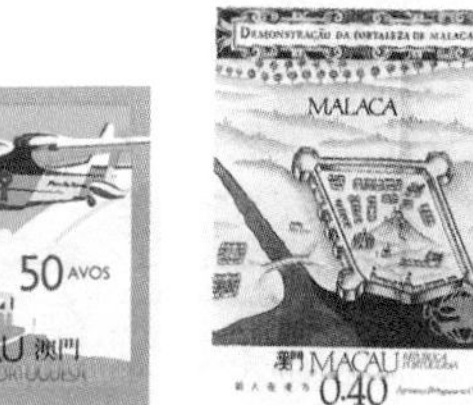
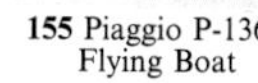
155 Piaggio P-136L Flying Boat **156** Malacca

1989. Aircraft. Multicoloured.
702 50a. Type **155** 40 25
703 70a. Martin M-130 flying boat 40 25
704 2p.80 Fairey 111D seaplane 75 40
705 4p. Hawker Osprey seaplane 2·00 1·25

1989. "World Stamp Expo '89" International Stamp Exhibition, Washington D.C. Portuguese Presence in Far East. Multicoloured.
707 40a. Type **156** 15 10
708 70a. Thailand 25 10
709 90a. India 40 10
710 2p.50 Japan 75 35
711 7p.50 China . . . . 2·00 1·50

157 Horse and Moon **159** Long-finned Grouper ("Epinephelus megachir")

1990. New Year. Year of the Horse.
713 **157** 4p. multicoloured . . . . 1·00 45

1990. Traditional Occupations (2nd series). As T **151**. Multicoloured.
714 30a. Long-chau singer . . . 15 10
715 70a. Cobbler 25 10
716 1p.50 Travelling penman . . 75 35
717 7p.50 Fisherman with wide nets . . . . 2·50 1·40

1990. Fishes. Multicoloured.
719 2p.40 Type **159** . . . . . . 1·10 45
720 2p.40 Malabar snapper ("Lutianus malabaricus") 1·10 45
721 2p.40 Spotted snakehead ("Ophiocepalus maculatus") . . . . 1·10 45
722 2p.40 Paradise fish ("Macropodus opercularis") . . . . . . 1·10 45

160 Porcelain

1990. "New Zealand 1990" International Stamp Exhibition, Auckland. Industrial Diversification. Multicoloured.
723 3p. Type **160** 30 30
724 3p. Furniture 30 30
725 3p. Toys . . . . 1·00 75
726 3p. Artificial flowers 30 30

161 Cycling **162** Rose by Lazaro Luis

1990. 11th Asian Games, Peking. Multicoloured.
728 80a. Type **161** 15 10
729 1p. Swimming 25 10
730 3p. Judo 75 30
731 4p.20 Shooting . . . . . . 1·75 1·00

1990. Compass Roses. Designs showing roses from ancient charts by cartographer named. Mult.
733 50a. Type **162** 15 10
734 1p. Diogo Homem 25 10
735 3p.50 Diogo Homem (different) 80 35
736 6p.50 Fernao Vaz Dourado 2·00 1·00

163 Cricket Fight **164** Goat and Moon

1990. Betting on Animals. Multicoloured.
738 20a. Type **163** 20 10
739 80a. Melodious laughing thrush fight 45 15

740 1p. Greyhound racing . . . 75 25
741 10p. Horse racing . . . . . 2·50 1·10

1991. New Year. Year of the Goat.
742 **164** 4p.50 multicoloured . . . 1·25 40

1991. Traditional Occupations (3rd series). As T **151**. Multicoloured.
743 80a. Knife-grinder 25 10
744 1p.70 Flour-puppets vendor 50 25
745 3p.50 Street barber . . . . . 1·00 50
746 4p.20 Fortune-teller . . . . 1·50 85

165 True Harp ("Harpa harpa")

1991. Sea Shells. Multicoloured.
747 3p. Type **165** . . . . 1·25 40
748 3p. Oil-lamp tun ("Tonna zonata") . . . . 1·25 40
749 3p. Bramble murex ("Murex pecten") . . . . 1·25 40
750 3p. Rose-branch murex ("Chicoreus rosarius") . . 1·25 40
The Latin names on Nos. 749/50 are incorrect.

166 Character and Backcloth

1991. Chinese Opera. Multicoloured.
751 **166** 60a. multicoloured . . . 40 35
752 – 80a. multicoloured . . . 40 35
753 – 1p. multicoloured 85 65
754 – 10p. multicoloured . . . 3·75 2·10
DESIGNS: Nos. 752/4, Different backcloths and costumes.

167 "Delonix regia" and Lou Lim Ioc Garden

1991. Flowers and Gardens (1st series). Mult.
755 1p.70 Type **167** 40 25
756 3p. "Ipomoea cairica" and Sao Francisco Garden . . 75 50
757 3p.50 "Jasminum mesyi" and Sun Yat Sen Park 90 60
758 4p.20 "Bauhinia variegata" and Seac Pai Van Park . . 1·00 65
See also Nos. 815/18.

168 Portuguese Traders unloading Boats **169** Firework Display

1991. Cultural Exchange. Nambam Paintings attr. Kano Domi. Multicoloured.
760 4p.20 Type **168** . . . . . . 1·00 55
761 4p.20 Portuguese traders displaying goods to buyers 1·00 40

1991. Christmas. Multicoloured.
763 1p.70 Type **169** 40 20
764 3p. Father Christmas 60 40
765 3p.50 Man dancing 75 45
766 4p.20 January 1st celebrations 1·00 55

170 Concertina Door

1992. Doors and Windows. Multicoloured.
767 1p.70 Type **170** 40 20
768 3p. Window with four shutters 60 40
769 3p.50 Window with two shutters 75 45
770 4p.20 Louvred door . . . . 1·00 55

171 Monkey and Moon **172** T'it Kuai Lei

1992. New Year. Year of the Monkey.
771 **171** 4p.50 multicoloured . . . 1·00 60

1992. Gods of Chinese Mythology (1st series). Multicoloured.
772 3p.50 (1) Type **172** . . . . . 1·25 1·00
773 3p.50 (2) Chong Lei Kun . . 1·25 1·00
774 3p.50 (3) Cheong Kuo Lou on donkey . . . . 1·25 1·00
775 3p.50 (4) Loi Tong Pan . . . 1·25 1·00
See also Nos. 796/9.

173 Lion Dance

1992. "World Columbian Stamp Expo '92", Chicago. Chinese Dances. Multicoloured.
776 1p. Type **173** 20 10
777 2p.70 Lion dance (different) 75 35
778 6p. Dragon dance . . . . . 1·60 85

174 High Jumping

1992. Olympic Games, Barcelona. Multicoloured.
779 80a. Type **174** 20 10
780 4p.20 Badminton 80 55
781 4p.70 Roller hockey . . . . 1·00 60
782 5p. Yachting . . . . 1·25 65

175 Na Cha Temple

1992. Temples (1st series). Multicoloured.
784 1p. Type **175** 20 10
785 1p.50 Kun Iam 40 25
786 1p.70 Hong Kon 50 30
787 6p.50 A Ma . . . . 2·00 1·10
See also Nos. 792/5 and 894/8.

176 Tung Sin Tong Services

1992. Centenary of Tung Sin Tong (medical and educational charity).
788 **176** 1p. multicoloured 35 20

177 Rooster and Dragon

1992. Portuguese–Chinese Friendship.
789 **177** 10p. multicoloured . . . 2·00 1·25

178 Red Junglefowl **179** Children carrying Banners

1992. New Year. Year of the Cock.
791 **178** 5p. multicoloured . . . . 1·10 65

1993. Temples (2nd series). As T **175**. Mult.
792 50a. T'am Kong 15 10
793 2p. T'in Hau 40 25
794 3p.50 Lin Fong 75 45
795 8p. Pau Kong . . . . 1·50 1·10

1993. Gods of Chinese Mythology (2nd series). As T **172**. Multicoloured.
796 3p.50 (1) Lam Ch'oi Wo flying on crane 75 45
797 3p.50 (2) Ho Sin Ku (goddess) on peach blossom 75 45
798 3p.50 (3) Hon Seong Chi crossing sea on basket of flowers 75 45
799 3p.50 (4) Ch'ou Kuok K'ao crossing river on plank . . 75 45

1993. Chinese Wedding. Multicoloured.
800 3p. Type **179** 50 40
801 3p. Bride 50 40
802 3p. Bridegroom 50 40
803 3p. Wedding guests 50 40
Nos. 800/3 were issued together, se-tenant, forming a composite design.

180 Bird perched on Hand **181** Eurasian Scops Owl

1993. Environmental Protection.
805 **180** 1p. multicoloured 75 20

1993. Birds of Prey. Multicoloured.
806 3p. Type **181** . . . . 2·25 40
807 3p. Barn owl ("Tyto alba") 2·25 40
808 3p. Peregrine falcon ("Falco peregrinus") . . . . . . 2·25 40
809 3p. Golden eagle ("Aquila obrysaetos") . . . . 2·25 40

182 Town Hall

1993. Union of Portuguese-speaking Capital Cities.
811 **182** 1p.50 green, blue and red 50 20

183 Portuguese Missionaries

1993. 450th Anniv of First Portuguese Visit to Japan. Multicoloured.
812 50a. Japanese man with musket 20 10
813 3p. Type **183** 60 40
814 3p.50 Traders carrying goods 75 45

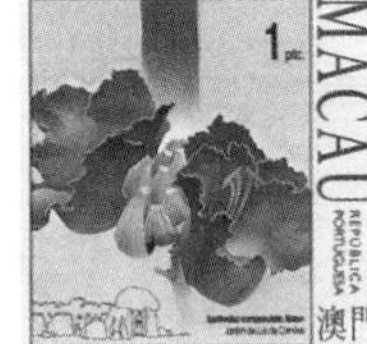

184 "Spathodea campanulata" and Luis de Camoes Garden

1993. Flowers and Gardens (2nd series). Multicoloured.
815 1p. Type **184** 25 10
816 2p. "Tithonia diversifolia" and Montanha Russa Garden 45 25
817 3p. "Rhodomyrtus tomentosa" and Cais Garden 75 40
818 8p. "Passiflora foetida" and Flora Garden . . . . . . 2·00 1·10

185 Caravel

1993. 16th-century Sailing Ships. Multicoloured.
820 1p. Type **185** 25 10
821 2p. Caravel (different) . . . 45 25
822 3p.50 Nau 75 45
823 4p.50 Galleon . . . . 1·00 60

186 Saloon Car

1993. 40th Anniv of Macao Grand Prix. Multicoloured.
825 1p.50 Type **186** 30 20
826 2p. Motor cycle 40 25
827 4p.50 Racing car 80 60

187 Chow-chow and Moon

1994. New Year. Year of the Dog.
828 **187** 5p. multicoloured . . . . 1·00 65

188 Map and Prince Henry (½-size illustration)

1994. 600th Birth Anniv of Prince Henry the Navigator.
829 **188** 3p. multicoloured 60 40

189 Lakeside Hut

1994. Birth Bicentenary of George Chinnery (artist). Multicoloured.
830 3p.50 Type **189** 60 45
831 3p.50 Fisherman on sea wall 60 45
832 3p.50 Harbour 60 45
833 3p.50 Sao Tiago Fortress . . 60 45

190 Lai Sis Exchange

1994. Spring Festival of Lunar New Year. Multicoloured.
835 1p. Type **190** 20 10
836 2p. Flower and tangerine tree decorations 40 25
837 3p.50 Preparing family meal 75 45
838 4p.50 Paper decorations bearing good wishes 1·00 60

191 "Longevity" **192** Footballer

1994. Legends and Myths (1st series). Chinese Gods. Multicoloured.
839 3p. Type **191** 50 40
840 3p. "Prosperity" 50 40
841 3p. "Happiness" 50 40
See also Nos. 884/7, 930/2, 994/7 and 1035/8.

1994. World Cup Football Championship, U.S.A. Multicoloured.
843 2p. Type **192** 40 25
844 3p. Tackling 60 40
845 3p.50 Heading ball 75 45
846 4p.50 Goalkeeper saving goal 95 60

193 Rice Shop **194** Astrolabe

1994. Traditional Chinese Shops. Multicoloured.
848 1p. Type **193** 20 10
849 1p.50 Medicinal tea shop 30 20
850 2p. Salt-fish shop 50 25
851 3p.50 Pharmacy 90 45

1994. Nautical Instruments. Multicoloured.
852 3p. Type **194** 60 40
853 3p.50 Quadrant 75 45
854 4p.50 Sextant 1·00 65

195 Fencing

1994. 12th Asian Games, Hiroshima, Japan. Multicoloured.
855 1p. Type **195** 20 10
856 2p. Gymnastics 45 25
857 3p. Water-polo 70 40
858 3p.50 Pole vaulting 80 45

196 Nobre de Carvalho Bridge

1994. Bridges. Multicoloured.
859 1p. Type **196** 20 10
860 8p. Friendship Bridge 1·75 1·10

197 Carp **199** Pig and Moon

198 Angel's Head (stained glass window, Macao Cathedral)

1994. Good Luck Signs. Multicoloured.
861 3p. Type **197** 70 40
862 3p.50 Peaches 75 45
863 4p.50 Water lily 1·00 60

1994. Religious Art. Multicoloured.
864 50a. Type **198** 15 10
865 1p. Holy Ghost (stained glass window, Macao Cathedral) 25 10
866 1p.50 Silver sacrarium 30 20
867 2p. Silver salver 50 25
868 3p. "Escape into Egypt" (ivory statuette) 75 40
869 3p.50 Gold and silver cup 85 45

1995. New Year. Year of the Pig.
870 **199** 5p.50 multicoloured 1·00 70

200 "Lou Lim Iok Garden"

1995. Paintings of Macao by Lio Man Cheong. Multicoloured.
871 50a. Type **200** 15 10
872 1p. "Guia Fortress and Lighthouse" 20 10
873 1p.50 "Barra Temple" 35 20
874 2p. "Avenida da Praia, Taipa" 45 25
875 2p.50 "Kun Iam Temple" 60 30
876 3p. "St. Paul's Seminary" 70 40
877 3p.50 "Penha Hill" 80 45
878 4p. "Gates of Understanding Monument" 90 50

201 Magnifying Glass over Goods

1995. World Consumer Day.
879 **201** 1p. multicoloured 25 10

202 Pangolin **203** Kun Sai Iam

1995. Protection of Chinese ("Asian") Pangolin. Multicoloured.
880 1p.50 In fork of tree 35 20
881 1p.50 Hanging from tree by tail 35 20
882 1p.50 On leafy branch 35 20
883 1p.50 Type **202** 35 20

1995. Legends and Myths (2nd series). Kun Sai Iam (Buddhist god). Multicoloured.
884 3p. Type **203** 50 40
885 3p. Holding baby 50 40
886 3p. Sitting behind water lily 50 40
887 3p. With water lily and dragonfish 70 40

204/7 Senado Square (½-size illustration)

1995. Senado Square.
889 **204** 2p. multicoloured 55 25
890 **205** 2p. multicoloured 55 25
891 **206** 2p. multicoloured 55 25
892 **207** 2p. multicoloured 55 25
Nos. 889/92 were issued together, se-tenant, forming the composite design illustrated.

1995. Temples (3rd series). As T **175**. Multicoloured.
894 50a. Kuan Tai 10 10
895 1p. Pak Tai 15 10
896 1p.50 Lin K'ai 25 20
897 3p. Se Kam Tong 50 40
898 3p.50 Fok Tak 60 45

208 Pekin Robin ("Leiothrix lutea")

1995. "Singapore'95" International Stamp Exhibition. Birds. Multicoloured.
899 2p.50 Type **208** 1·10 30
900 2p.50 Japanese white-eye ("Zosterops japonica") 1·10 30
901 2p.50 Island canary ("Serinus canarius canarius") 1·10 30
902 2p.50 Melodious laughing thrush ("Gurrulax canonus") 1·10 30

209 Pipa

1995. International Music Festival. Musical Instruments. Multicoloured.
904 1p. Type **209** 60 10
905 1p. Erhu (string instrument) 60 10
906 1p. Gong (hand-held drum) 60 10
907 1p. Sheng (string instrument) 60 10
908 1p. Xiao (flute) 60 10
909 1p. Tambor (drum) 60 10

210 Anniversary Emblem, World Map and U.N. Headquarters, New York

1995. 50th Anniv of United Nations Organization.
911 **210** 4p.50 multicoloured 75 60

211 Terminal Building

1995. Inauguration of Macao International Airport. Multicoloured.
912 1p. Type **211** 15 10
913 1p.50 Terminal (different) 25 20
914 2p. Loading airplane and cargo building 35 20
915 3p. Control tower 50 40

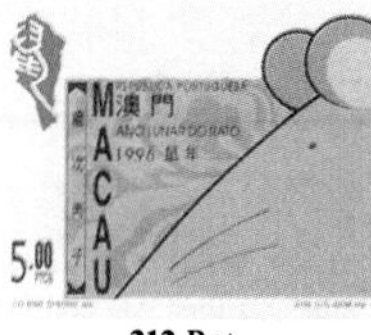

212 Rat

1996. New Year. Year of the Rat.
918 **212** 5p. multicoloured 85 65

213 Cage

1996. Traditional Chinese Cages.
920 **213** 1p. multicoloured 15 10
921 – 1p.50 multicoloured 25 20
922 – 3p. multicoloured 50 40
923 – 4p.50 multicoloured 75 60
DESIGNS: 1p.50 to 4p.50, Different cages.

214 Street **215** Tou Tei (God of Earth)

1996. Paintings of Macao by Herculano Estorninho. Multicoloured.
925 50a. Fishing boats (horiz) 10 10
926 1p.50 Town square 25 20
927 3p. Type **214** 50 40
928 5p. Townscape (horiz) 85 65

1996. Legends and Myths (3rd series). Multicoloured.
930 3p.50 Type **215** 60 45
931 3p.50 Choi San (God of Fortune) 60 45
932 3p.50 Chou Kuan (God of the Kitchen) 60 45

216 Customers

1996. Traditional Chinese Tea Houses. Mult.
934 2p. Type **216** 35 25
935 2p. Waiter with tray of steamed stuffed bread 35 25
936 2p. Newspaper vendor 35 25
937 2p. Waiter pouring tea at table 35 25
Nos. 934/7 were issued together, se-tenant, forming a composite design.

217 Get Well Soon

1996. Greetings stamps. Multicoloured.
939 50a. Type **217** 10 10
940 1p.50 Congratulations on new baby 25 20
941 3p. Happy birthday 50 40
942 4p. Wedding congratulations 65 50

218 Swimming

1996. Olympic Games, Atlanta, U.S.A. Mult.
943 2p. Type **218** 35 25
944 3p. Football 50 40
945 3p.50 Gymnastics 60 45
946 4p.50 Sailboarding 75 60

219 Crane (civil, 1st rank)

1996. Civil and Military Insignia of the Mandarins (1st series). Multicoloured.

948 2p.50 Type **219** 40 30
949 2p.50 Lion (military, 2nd rank) 40 30
950 2p.50 Golden pheasant (civil, 2nd rank) 40 30
951 2p.50 Leopard (military, 3rd rank) 40 30

See also Nos. 1061/4.

220 Trawler with Multiple Nets

1996. Nautical Sciences: Fishing Nets. Mult.

952 3p. Type **220** 50 40
953 3p. Modern trawler with net from stern 50 40
954 3p. Two sailing junks with common net 50 40
955 3p. Junk with two square nets at sides 50 40

Nos. 952/5 were issued together, se-tenant, forming a composite design.

221 National Flag and Statue (½-size illustration)

1996. 20th Anniv of Legislative Assembly.

956 **221** 2p.80 multicoloured 45 35

222 Dragonfly

1996. Paper Kites. Multicoloured.

958 3p.50 Type **222** 55 45
959 3p.50 Butterfly 55 45
960 3p.50 Owl 55 45
961 3p.50 Swallow 55 45

223 Doll

1996. Traditional Chinese Toys. Multicoloured.

963 50a. Type **223** 10 10
964 1p. Fish 20 10
965 3p. Painted doll 50 40
966 4p.50 Dragon 70 55

224 Ox

1997. New Year. Year of the Ox.

967 **224** 5p.50 multicoloured 85 65

225 Colourful and Gold Twos

1997. Lucky Numbers. Multicoloured.

969 2p. Type **225** 30 25
970 2p.80 Eights 45 35
971 3p. Threes 45 35
972 3p.90 Nines 65 50

226 "Sail Boats"  **227** Elderly Woman

1997. Paintings of Macao by Kwok Se. Multicoloured.

974 2p. Type **226** 30 25
975 3p. "Fortress on the Hill" 45 35
976 3p.50 "Asilum" 55 40
977 4p.50 "Portas do Cerco" 70 55

1997. Tan-Ka (boat) People. Multicoloured.

979 1p. Type **227** 15 10
980 1p.50 Elderly woman holding tiller 20 15
981 2p.50 Woman with child on back 35 25
982 5p.50 Man mending fishing nets 80 60

228 Entrance to Temple  **229** Dragon Dancers

1997. A-Ma Temple. Multicoloured.

983 3p.50 Type **228** 50 40
984 3p.50 Wall and terraces of Temple 50 40
985 3p.50 View of incense smoke through gateway 50 40
986 3p.50 Incense smoke emanating from pagoda 50 40

1997. Drunken Dragon Festival. Multicoloured.

988 2p. Type **229** 30 20
989 3p. Dragon dancer 45 35
990 5p. Dancer holding "tail" of dragon 75 60

230 Frois with Japanese Man

1997. 400th Death Anniv of Father Luis Frois (author of "The History of Japan"). Multicoloured.

992 2p.50 Type **230** 35 25
993 2p.50 Father Frois and church (vert) 35 25

231 Wat Lot

1997. Legends and Myths (4th series). Door Gods. Multicoloured.

994 2p.50 Type **231** 35 25
995 2p.50 San Su 35 25
996 2p.50 Chon Keng 35 25
997 2p.50 Wat Chi Kong 35 25

232 Globe and First Aid and Family Health School

1997. 77th Anniv of Macao Red Cross.

999 **232** 1p.50 multicoloured 20 15

233 Balconies

1997. Balconies.

1000 **233** 50a. multicoloured 10 10
1001 – 1p. multicoloured 15 10
1002 – 1p.50 multicoloured 20 15
1003 – 2p. multicoloured 30 20
1004 – 2p.50 multicoloured 35 25
1005 – 3p. multicoloured 45 35

DESIGNS: 1p. to 3p. Various balcony styles.

234 Plant Leaf Fan

1997. Fans. Multicoloured.

1007 50a. Type **234** 10 10
1008 1p. Paper fan 15 10
1009 3p.50 Silk fan 50 40
1010 4p. Feather fan 60 45

235 Wood  **236** Kung Fu

1997. Feng Shui. The Five Elements. Mult.

1012 50a. Type **235** 10 10
1013 1p. Fire 15 10
1014 1p.50 Earth 20 15
1015 2p. Metal 30 20
1016 2p.50 Water 35 25

1997. Martial Arts. Multicoloured.

1018 1p.50 Type **236** 20 15
1019 3p.50 Judo 50 40
1020 4p. Karate 60 45

237 Tiger

1998. New Year. Year of the Tiger.

1021 **237** 5p.50 multicoloured 80 65

238 Soup Stall

1998. Street Traders. Multicoloured.

1023 1p. Type **238** 15 10
1024 1p.50 Snack stall 25 20
1025 2p. Clothes stall 30 20
1026 2p.50 Balloon stall 40 30
1027 3p. Flower stall 45 35
1028 3p.50 Fruit stall 55 40

239 Beco da Se

1998. Gateways. Multicoloured.

1030 50a. Type **239** 10 10
1031 1p. Patio da Ilusao 15 10
1032 3p.50 Travessa das galinhas 55 40
1033 4p. Beco das Felicidades 60 45

240 Woman and Child

1998. Legends and Myths (5th series). Gods of Ma Chou. Multicoloured.

1035 4p. Type **240** 60 45
1036 4p. Woman and man's face in smoke 60 45
1037 4p. Woman with children playing instruments 60 45
1038 4p. Goddess and sailing barges 60 45

241 "Sao Gabriel" (flagship)

1998. 500th Anniv of Vasco da Gama's Voyage to India via Cape of Good Hope. Multicoloured.

(a) Wrongly dated "1598 1998".

1040 1p. Type **241** 15 10
1041 1p.50 Vasco da Gama 25 20
1042 2p. "Sao Gabriel" and map of India 30 20

(b) Correctly dated "1498 1998".

1044 1p. Type **241** 15 10
1045 1p.50 As No. 1041 25 20
1046 2p. As No. 1042 30 20

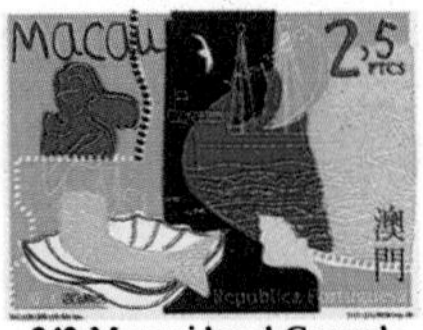

242 Mermaid and Caravel

1998. International Year of the Ocean. Mult.

1048 2p.50 Type **242** 40 30
1049 3p. Whale and oil-rig 45 35

243 Players

1998. World Cup Football Championship, France. Multicoloured.

1051 3p. Type **243** 45 35
1052 3p.50 Players competing for ball 55 40
1053 4p. Player kicking ball clear while being tackled 60 45
1054 4p.50 Player beating another to ball 70 55

244 Lio Seak Chong Mask

1998. Chinese Opera Masks. Multicoloured.

1056 1p.50 Type **244** 25 20
1057 2p. Wat Chi Kong 30 20
1058 3p. Kam Chin Pao 45 35
1059 5p. Lei Kwai 75 60

1998. Civil and Military Insignia of the Mandarins (2nd series). As T **219**. Multicoloured.

1061 50a. Lion (military, 2nd rank) 10 10
1062 1p. Bear (military, 5th rank) 15 10
1063 1p.50 Golden pheasant (civil, 2nd rank) 25 20
1064 2p. Silver pheasant (civil, 5th rank) 30 20

245 Smiling Buddha

1998. Kun Iam Temple. Multicoloured.
1066 3p.50 Type **245** 55 40
1067 3p.50 Pavilion and temple gardens 55 40
1068 3p.50 Temple gateway . . . 55 40
1069 3p.50 Pagoda, stream and gardens 55 40
Nos. 1066/9 were issued together, se-tenant, forming a composite design.

246 Carriage in Street

1998. Paintings of Macao by Didier Rafael Bayle. Multicoloured.
1071 2p. Type **246** 30 20
1072 3p. Street (horiz) 45 35
1073 3p.50 Building (horiz) . . . 55 40
1074 4p.50 Kiosk in square . . . 70 55

247 Dragon

1998. Tiles by Eduardo Nery (from panel at Departure Lounge of Macao Airport). Multicoloured.
1076 1p. Type **247** 15 10
1077 1p.50 Galleon 25 20
1078 2p.50 Junk 40 30
1079 5p.50 Phoenix 85 65

248 Rabbit

1999. New Year. Year of the Rabbit.
1081 **248** 5p.50 multicoloured . . 85 65

249 Jia Bao Yu

1999. Literature. Characters from "A Dream of Red Mansions" by Cao Xue Qin. Multicoloured.
1083 2p. Type **249** 30 25
1084 2p. Lin Dai Yu holding pole and cherry blossom . . . 30 25
1085 2p. Bao Chai holding fan 30 25
1086 2p. Wang Xi Feng sitting in chair 30 25
1087 2p. You San Jie holding sword 30 25
1088 2p. Qing Wen sewing "peacock" cloak 30 25

250 Sailing Ships

1999. "Australia'99" International Stamp Exhibition, Melbourne. Oceans and Maritime Heritage. Multicoloured.
1090 1p.50 Type **250** 25 20
1091 2p.50 Marine life 40 30

251 De Havilland D.H.9 Biplane

1999. 75th Anniv of Sarmento de Beires and Brito Pais's Portugal–Macao Flight. Multicoloured.
1093 3p. Breguet 16 Bn2 Patria 45 35
1094 3p. Type **251** 45 35

252 Carrying Containers on Yoke

1999. The Water Carrier. Multicoloured.
1096 1p. Type **252** 10 10
1097 1p.50 Filling containers from pump 10 10
1098 2p. Lowering bucket down well 30 25
1099 2p.50 Filling containers from tap 40 30

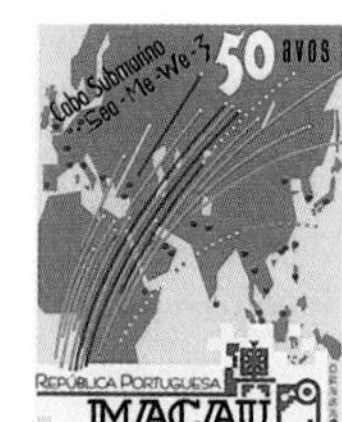
253 "Sea-Me-We-3" Undersea Fibre Optic Cable

1999. Telecommunications Services. Multicoloured.
1101 50a. Type **253** 10 10
1102 1p. Dish aerial at Satellite Earth Station 10 10
1103 3p.50 Analogue mobile phone 55 45
1104 4p. Televisions 60 50
1105 4p.50 Internet and e-mail . . 70 55

254 Macao Cultural Centre

1999. Modern Buildings. Multicoloured.
1107 1p. Type **254** 10 10
1108 1p.50 Museum of Macao . . 25 20
1109 2p. Macao Maritime Museum 30 25
1110 2p.50 Ferry Terminal . . . 40 30
1111 3p. Macao University . . . 45 35
1112 3p.50 Public Administration building (vert) 55 45
1113 4p.50 Macao World Trade Centre (vert) 70 55
1114 5p. Coloane kart-racing track (vert) 75 60
1115 8p. Bank of China (vert) . . 1·25 1·00
1116 12p. National Overseas Bank (vert) . . . . 1·90 1·50

255 Health Department

1999. Classified Buildings in Tap Seac District. Multicoloured.
1117 1p.50 Type **255** 25 20
1118 1p.50 Central Library (face value in salmon) 25 20
1119 1p.50 Centre of Modern Art of the Orient Foundation (face value in yellow) . . 25 20
1120 1p.50 Portuguese Institute of the Orient (face value in light blue) 25 20
Nos. 1117/20 were issued together, se-tenant, forming a composite design.

256 Teapot and Plate of Food

258 Chinese and Portuguese Ships, Christ's Cross and Yin Yang

257 "Portuguese Sailor and Chinese Woman" (Lagoa Henriques), Company of Jesus Square

1999. Dim Sum. Multicoloured.
1122 2p.50 Type **256** 40 30
1123 2p.50 Plates of food, chopsticks and left half of bowls 40 30
1124 2p.50 Plates of food, glass, cups and right half of bowls 40 30
1125 2p.50 Plates of food and large teapot 40 30
Nos. 1122/5 were issued together, se-tenant, forming a composite design.

1999. Contemporary Sculptures (1st series). Multicoloured.
1127 1p. Type **257** 10 10
1128 1p.50 "The Gate of Understanding" (Charters de Almeida), Praia Grande Bay (vert) 25 20
1129 2p.50 "Statue of the Goddess Kun Iam" (Cristina Leiria), Macao Cultural Centre (vert) . . 40 30
1130 3p.50 " Taipa Viewing Point" (Dorita Castel-Branco), Nobre de Carvalho Bridge, Taipa 55 45
See also Nos. 1186/9.

1999. Portuguese–Chinese Cultural Mix. Mult.
1132 1p. Type **258** 10 10
1133 1p.50 Ah Mah Temple and Portuguese and Macanese architecture 25 20
1134 2p. Bridge, steps and Chinese architecture . . . 30 25
1135 3p. Macanese architecture and Portuguese terrace . . 45 35
Nos. 1132/5 were issued together, se-tenant, forming a composite design.

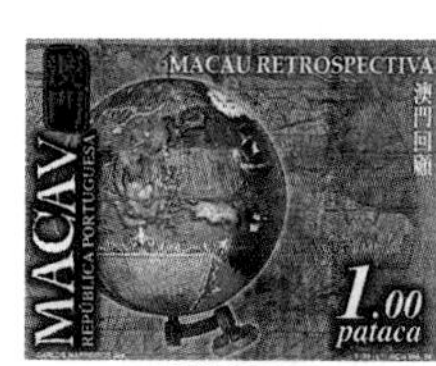
259 Globe

1999. Macao Retrospective. Multicoloured.
1137 1p. Type **259** 10 10
1138 1p.50 Roof terrace 25 20
1139 2p. Portuguese and Chinese people 30 25
1140 3p.50 Modern Macao . . . 55 45

260 Gateway

1999. Establishment of Macao as Special Administrative Region of People's Republic of China. Multicoloured.
1142 1p. Type **260** 20 10
1143 1p.50 Bridge and boat race 25 20
1144 2p. Wall of ruined church 35 25
1145 2p.50 Lighthouse and racing cars 40 30
1146 3p. Building facade 55 45
1147 3p.50 Stadium and orchestra 60 50

262 Dragon

2000. New Year. Year of the Dragon.
1150 **262** 5p.50 multicoloured . . 95 75

263 Buildings

2000. Classified Buildings in Almeida Ribeiro Avenue, Macao City. Multicoloured.
1152 1p. Type **263** 20 15
1153 1p.50 Yellow and pink buildings 25 20
1154 2p. Yellow building 35 25
1155 3p. Purple, green and pink buildings 55 45

SERIAL NUMBERS. In sets containing several stamps of the same denomination, the serial number is quoted in brackets to assist identification. This is the last figure in the bottom right corner of the stamp.

264 Zhong (Leong Pai Wan)

2000. Arts in Macao. Chinese Calligraphy. Showing Chinese characters by named calligraphy masters. Each black and red.
1157 3p. (1) Type **264** 55 45
1158 3p. (2) Guo (Lin Ka Sang) 55 45
1159 3p. (3) Shu (Lok Hong) . . 55 45
1160 3p. (4) Fa (Sou Su Fai) . . 55 45

265 Chinese Chess

2000. Board Games. Multicoloured.
1162 1p. Type **265** 20 15
1163 1p.50 Chess 25 20
1164 2p. Go 35 25
1165 2p.50 Flying chess 40 30

266 Group of Friends

2000. Tea. Multicoloured.
1167 2p. Type **266** 35 25
1168 3p. Family drinking tea . . 55 45
1169 3p.50 Women drinking tea 60 50
1170 4p.50 Men drinking tea . . 80 65

267 Tricycle Driver and Foreign Tourists

2000. Tricycle Drivers. Multicoloured.
1172 2p. (1) Type **267** 35 25
1173 2p. (2) With couple in carriage 35 25
1174 2p. (3) With empty carriage 35 25
1175 2p. (4) With feet resting on saddle 35 25
1176 2p. (5) Sitting in carriage . . 35 25
1177 2p. (6) Mending tyre 35 25

268 Monkey King standing on Tiger Skin

2000. Classical Literature. *Journey to the West* (Ming dynasty novel). Multicoloured.

1179	1p. Type **268**	20	15
1180	1p.50 Monkey King tasting the heavenly peaches	25	20
1181	2p. Monkey King, Prince Na Zha and flaming wheels	35	25
1182	2p.50 Erlang Deity with spear	40	30
1183	3p. Heavenly Father Lao Jun	55	45
1184	3p.50 Monkey King in Buddha's hand	60	55

269 "Wing of Good Winds" (Augusto Cid), Pac On Roundabout, Taipa

2000. Contemporary Sculptures (2nd series). Multicoloured.

1186	1p. Type **269**	15	10
1187	2p. "The Embrace" (Irene Vilar), Luis de Camoes Garden (vert)	35	25
1188	3p. Monument (Soares Branco), Guia's Tunnel, Outer Harbour (vert)	55	40
1189	4p. "The Arch of the Orient" (Zulmiro de Carvalho), Avienda Rodrigo Rodrigues Viaduct	70	55

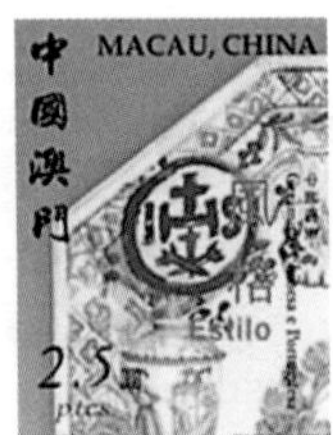

270 Decorated Pot

2000. Ceramics. Multicoloured.

1191	2p.50 (1) Type **270**	45	35
1192	2p.50 (2) Vase, dish and teapot	45	35
1193	2p.50 (3) Blue vase	45	35
1194	2p.50 (4) Cabbage-shaped pot and leaf-shaped dish	45	35
1195	2p.50 (5) Plate and fishes	45	35
1196	2p.50 (6) Blue and white vase	45	35

Nos. 1191/6 were issued together, se-tenant, with the backgrounds forming a composite design.

271 Phoenix crouching, Shang Dynasty

2000. Jade Ornaments. Multicoloured.

1198	1p.50 Type **271**	25	20
1199	2p. Archer's white jade ring, Warring States period	35	25
1200	2p.50 Dragon and phoenix, Six Dynasties	45	35
1201	3p. Pendant with dragon decoration, Western Han Dynasty	55	40

272 Dancers with National and Special Administrative Flags

2000. 1st Anniv of Macau as Special Administrative Region of People's Republic of China. Multicoloured.

1203	2p. Type **272**	35	25
1204	3p. Chinese dragons and lotus flower	55	40

Nos. 1203/4 were issued together, se-tenant, forming a composite design.

273 Snake

2001. New Year. Year of the Snake.

1206	**273** 5p.50 multicoloured	95	75

274 Man holding Bottle ("Nursing Vengeance despite Hardships")

2001. Ancient Proverbs. Multicoloured.

1208	2p. (1) Type **274**	35	25
1209	2p. (2) Man waiting for a rabbit ("Trusting to Chance and Windfalls")	35	25
1210	2p. (3) Fox and tiger ("Bullying Others by Flaunting One's Powerful Connections")	35	25
1211	2p. (4) Mother with child ("Selecting a Proper Surrounding to Bring up Children")	35	25

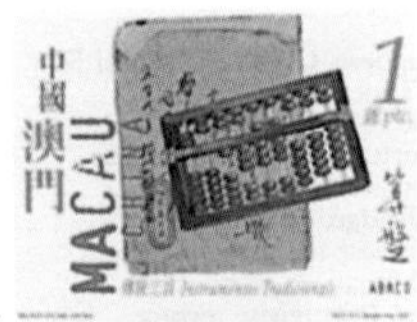

275 Abacus

2001. Traditional Tools. Multicoloured.

1213	1p. Type **275**	15	10
1214	2p. Plane	35	25
1215	3p. Iron	55	40
1216	4p. Scales	70	55

276 Buddha

2001. Religions. Multicoloured.

1218	1p. Type **276**	15	10
1219	1p.50 Worshippers	25	20
1220	2p. Man carrying Cross and religious procession	35	25
1221	2p.50 Procession	45	35

Nos. 1218/19 and 1220/1 respectively were issued together, se-tenant, forming a composite design.

277 Fireman and Platform Car

2001. Fire Brigade. Multicoloured.

1223	1p.50 Type **277**	25	20
1224	2p.50 Fireman wearing chemical protection suit using portable flammable gases detector and Pumping Tank vehicle	45	35
1225	3p. Foam car and fireman wearing asbestos suit using foam hose	55	40
1226	4p. Fire officers in dress uniforms and ambulance	70	55

278 Electronic Keys

2001. E-Commerce. Multicoloured.

1228	1p.50 Type **278**	25	20
1229	2p. Hands passing letter (e-mail)	35	25
1230	2p.50 Mobile phone	45	35
1231	3p. Palm hand-held computer	55	40

279 Emblem

2001. Choice of Beijing as 2008 Olympic Games Host City.

1233	**279** 1p. multicoloured	15	10

280 Praying

2001. Classical Literature. *Romance of the Three Kingdoms* (novel by Luo Guanzhong). Multicoloured.

1234	3p. (1) Type **280**	55	40
1235	3p. (2) Soldier and man fighting	55	40
1236	3p. (3) Men talking	55	40
1237	3p. (4) Man dreaming	55	40

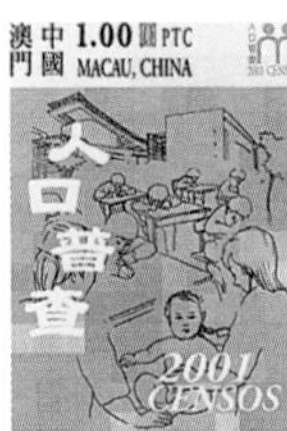

281 Baby, Doctor and Schoolchildren

283 DNA Helix containing Guanine Base

282 Municipal Market

2001. National Census. Multicoloured.

1239	1p. Type **281**	15	10
1240	1p.50 Street scene	25	20
1241	2p.50 Suspension bridge and crowd	45	35

2001. Macau Markets. Multicoloured.

1243	1p.50 Type **282**	25	20
1244	2p.50 Building and road-side stall	45	35
1245	3p.50 Covered market	60	45
1246	4p.50 Multi-storey building	80	60

2001. Science and Technology. Composition and Structure of DNA. Showing chemical bases of DNA. Multicoloured.

1248	1p. Type **283**	15	10
1249	2p. Helix containing cytosine base	35	25
1250	3p. Helix containing adenine base	55	40
1251	4p. Helix containing thymine base	70	55

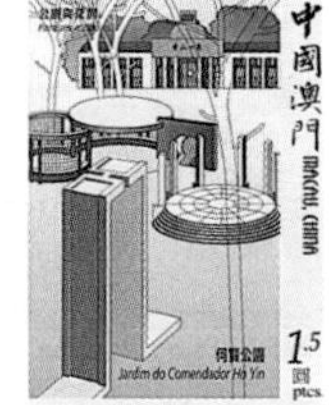

284 Commander Ho Yin's Garden

2001. Parks and Gardens. Multicoloured.

1253	1p.50 Type **284**	25	20
1254	2p.50 Mong Há Hill municipal park	45	35
1255	3p. City of Flowers Garden	55	40
1256	4p.50 Great Taipa Natural Park	80	60

285 Trigrams and Dragons

2001. Pa Kua (martial art). Multicoloured.

1258	2p. (1) Type **285**	35	25
1259	2p. (4) Trigrams, couple and deer	35	25
1260	2p. (7) Trigrams, fields and buffaloes	35	25
1261	2p. (3) Trigrams and volcano	35	25
1262	2p. (6) Trigrams and three men crawling	35	25
1263	2p. (2) Trigrams, man and donkey	35	25
1264	2p. (5) Trigrams, horse and carriage	35	25
1265	2p. (8) Trigrams, men with gifts and potentate	35	25

CHARITY TAX STAMPS

The notes under this heading in Portugal also apply here.

43

C 48 Our Lady of Charity (altarpiece, Macao Cathedral)

1919. Fiscal stamp optd **TAXA DE GUERRA**.

C305	**43** 2a. green	7·50	5·00
C306	11a. green	10·00	7·50

The above was for use in Timor as well as Macao.

1925. As Marquis de Pombal issue of Portugal but inscr "MACAU".

C329	**C 73** 2a. red	2·00	1·00
C330	– 2a. red	2·00	1·25
C331	**C 75** 2a. red	2·00	1·75

1930. No gum.

C332	**C 48** 5a. brown and buff	40·00	30·00

1945. As Type **C 48** but values in Arabic and Chinese numerals left and right, at bottom of design. No gum.

C486	1a. olive and green	1·00	25
C487	2a. purple and grey	1·00	25
C415	5a. brown and yellow	30·00	30·00
C416	5a. blue and light blue	42·00	38·00
C417	10a. green and light green	28·00	18·00
C488	10a. blue and green	1·75	25
C418	15a. orange and light orange	28·00	18·00
C419	20a. red and orange	42·00	35·00
C489	20a. brown and yellow	3·00	40
C420	50a. lilac and buff	42·00	35·00
C472	50a. red and pink	30·00	10·00

1981. No. C487 and similar higher (fiscal) values surch **20 avos** and Chinese characters.

C546	20a. on 2a. purple on grey	4·00	2·00
C534	20a. on 1p. green & lt green	4·00	1·25
C535	20a. on 3p. black and pink	4·00	1·25
C536	20a. on 5p. brown & yellow		

1981. No. C418 surch **10 avos** and Chinese characters.

C553	10a. on 15a. orange and light orange	4·00	2·50

NEWSPAPER STAMPS

1892. "Embossed" key-type of Macao surch **JORNAES** and value. No gum.
N73 Q 2½r. on 10r. green . . . . 15·00 5·00
N74 2½r. on 40r. brown . . . . 15·00 5·00
N75 2½r. on 80r. grey . . . . . 15·00 5·00

1893. "Newspaper" key-type inscr "Macau".
N80 V 2½r. brown . . . . 4·00 3·00

1894. "Newspaper" key-type of Macao surch ½ **avo PROVISORIO** and Chinese characters.
N82 V ½a. on 2½r. brown . . . . 8·00 6·00

POSTAGE DUE STAMPS

1904. "Due" key-type inscr "MACAU". No gum (12a. to 1p.), with or without gum (others).
D184 W ½a. green . . . . 1·25 1·00
D185 1a. green . . . . 1·25 1·00
D186 2a. grey . . . . 1·25 1·00
D187 4a. brown . . . . 1·25 1·00
D188 5a. orange . . . . 2·50 1·50
D189 8a. brown . . . . 2·50 1·50
D190 12a. brown . . . . . . 3·00 2·00
D191 20a. blue . . . . 7·50 5·00
D192 40a. red . . . . 8·00 5·50
D193 50a. orange . . . . . . 18·00 12·00
D194 1p. lilac . . . . 35·00 20·00

1911. "Due" key-types of Macao optd **REPUBLICA**.
D204 W ½a. green . . . . 1·00 90
D205 1a. green . . . . 1·00 90
D206 2a. grey . . . . 1·00 90
D207 4a. brown . . . . 1·00 90
D208 5a. orange . . . . 1·00 90
D209 8a. brown . . . . 1·00 90
D287 12a. brown . . . . . . 3·00 1·50
D211 20a. blue . . . . 5·00 2·50
D212 40a. red . . . . 10·00 5·00
D290 50a. orange . . . . . . 15·00 7·00
D291 1p. lilac . . . . 12·00 10·00

1925. Marquis de Pombal issue, as Nos. C329/31 optd **MULTA**.
D329 C 73 4a. red . . . . 2·00 1·50
D330 – 4a. red . . . . 2·00 1·50
D331 C 75 4a. red . . . . 2·00 1·50

1947. As Type D 1 of Portuguese Colonies, but inscr "MACAU".
D410 D 1 1a. black and purple . . 45 20
D411 2a. black and violet . . 45 20
D412 4a. black and blue . . . 80 45
D413 5a. black and brown . . 80 45
D414 8a. black and purple . . 1·25 80
D415 12a. black and brown 2·10 1·60
D416 20a. black and green . . 4·00 2·50
D417 40a. black and red . . 6·75 3·25
D418 50a. black and yellow 9·25 3·25
D419 1p. black and blue . . 18·00 3·25

1949. Postage stamps of 1934 surch **PORTEADO** and new value.
D424 50 1a. on 4a. black . . . . 2·00 85
D425 2a. on 6a. brown . . . . 2·00 85
D426 4a. on 8a. blue . . . . . 2·00 85
D427 5a. on 10a. red . . . . . 2·00 85
D428 8a. on 12a. blue . . . . 4·00 1·25
D429 12a. on 30a. green . . . 6·00 3·00
D430 20a. on 40a. violet . . . 10·00 5·75

1951. Optd **PORTEADO** or surch also.
D439 66 1a. yellow on cream . . 1·75 40
D440 2a. green on green . . . 1·75 85
D441 7a. on 10a. mauve on green . . . . 1·75 85

D 70

1952. Numerals in red. Name in black.
D451 D 70 1a. blue and green . . 40 15
D452 3a. brown and salmon 40 15
D453 5a. slate and blue . . 40 15
D454 10a. red and blue . . 85 85
D455 30a. blue and brown 1·60 1·25
D456 1p. brown and grey . . 3·25 1·60

MACEDONIA Pt. 3

Part of Austro-Hungarian Empire until 1918 when it became part of Yugoslavia. Separate stamps were issued during German Occupation in the Second World War.

In 1991 Macedonia became an independent republic.

A. GERMAN OCCUPATION

100 stotinki = 1 lev.

Македония
8. IX. 1944
1 лв.
(G 1)

1944. Stamps of Bulgaria, 1940–44. (a) Surch as Type G **1**.
G1 1l. on 10st. orange . . . . . 3·50 14·00
G2 3l. on 15st. blue . . . . . . 3·50 14·00

(b) Surch similar to Type G **1** but larger.
G3 6l. on 10st. blue . . . . . . 4·00 18·00
G4 9l. on 15st. green . . . . . . 4·00 18·00
G5 9l. on 15st. green . . . . . . 5·00 24·00
G6 15l. on 4l. black . . . . . . 12·00 50·00
G7 20l. on 7l. blue . . . . 12·00 50·00
G8 30l. on 14l. brown . . . . . 20·00 50·00

B. INDEPENDENT REPUBLIC

1991. 100 paras = 1 dinar.
1992. 100 deni (de.) = 1 denar (d.).

1 Trumpeters

2 Emblems and Inscriptions

1991. Obligatory Tax. Independence.
1 **1** 2d.50 black and orange . . . 35 35

1992. Obligatory Tax. Anti-cancer Week. (a) T **2** showing Red Cross symbol at bottom left.
2 **2** 5d. mauve, black and blue . . 55 55
3 – 5d. multicoloured 55 55
4 – 5d. multicoloured 55 55
5 – 5d. multicoloured 55 55
DESIGNS: No. 3, Flowers, columns and scanner; 4, Scanner and couch; 5, Computer cabinet.

(b) As T **2** but with right-hand inscr reading down instead of up and without Red Cross symbol.
6 5d. mauve, black & blue (as No. 2) 25 25
7 5d. multicoloured (as No. 3) . . 25 25
8 5d. multicoloured (as No. 4) . . 25 25
9 5d. multicoloured (as No. 5) . . 25 25

3 Red Cross Aircraft dropping Supplies

1992. Obligatory Tax. Red Cross Week. Multicoloured.
10 10d. Red Cross slogans (dated "08–15 MAJ 1992") 15 15
11 10d. Type **3** 15 15
12 10d. Treating road accident victim 15 15
13 10d. Evacuating casualties from ruined building . . . 15 15
The three pictorial designs are taken from children's paintings.

4 "Skopje Earthquake"

6 Nurse with Baby

5 "Wood-carvers Petar and Makarie" (icon), St. Joven Bigorsk Monastery, Debar

1992. Obligatory Tax. Solidarity Week.
14 **4** 20d. black and mauve . . . 15 15
15 – 20d. multicoloured 15 15
16 – 20d. multicoloured 15 15
17 – 20d. multicoloured 15 15
DESIGNS: No. 15, Red Cross nurse with child; 16, Mothers carrying toddlers at airport; 17, Family at airport.

1992. 1st Anniv of Independence.
18 **5** 30d. multicoloured 35 35
For 40d. in same design see No. 33.

1992. Obligatory Tax. Anti-tuberculosis Week. Multicoloured.
19 20d. Anti-tuberculosis slogans (dated "14–21.IX.1992") . . 10 10
20 20d. Type **6** 10 10
21 20d. Nurse giving oxygen . . 10 10
22 20d. Baby in cot 10 10

7 "The Nativity" (fresco, Slepce Monastery)

9 Radiography Equipment

8 Mixed Bouquet

1992. Christmas. Multicoloured.
23 100d. Type **7** 50 50
24 500d. "Madonna and Child" (fresco), Zrze Monastery . . 1·75 1·75

1993. Obligatory Tax. Red Cross Fund. Multicoloured.
25 20d. Red Cross slogans . . . 10 10
26 20d. Marguerites 10 10
27 20d. Carnations 10 10
28 20d. Type **8** 10 10

1993. Obligatory Tax. Anti-cancer Week. Multicoloured.
29 20d. Anti-cancer slogans (dated "1–8 MART 1993") 10 10
30 20d. Type **9** 10 10
31 20d. Overhead treatment unit 10 10
32 20d. Scanner 10 10

1993. As No. 18 but changed value.
33 **5** 40d. multicoloured 40 40

10 Macedonian Flag

1993.
34 **10** 10d. multicoloured 10 10
35 40d. multicoloured 45 45
36 50d. multicoloured 55 55

11 Macedonian Roach

1993. Fishes from Lake Ohrid. Multicoloured.
37 50d. Type **11** 15 15
38 100d. Lake Ohrid salmon . . 20 20
39 1000d. Type **11** . . . . . . 2·00 2·00
40 2000d. As No. 38 . . . . . . 3·00 3·00

12 Crucifix, St. George's Monastery

1993. Easter.
41 **12** 300d. multicoloured 70 70

13 Diagram of Telecommunications Cable and Map

1993. Opening of Trans-Balkan Telecommunications Line.
42 **13** 500d. multicoloured 70 70

14 Red Cross Worker with Baby

1993. Obligatory Tax. Red Cross Week. Multicoloured.
43 50d. Red Cross inscriptions (dated "08–15 MAJ 1993") 10 10
44 50d. Type **14** 10 10
45 50d. Physiotherapist and child in wheelchair 10 10
46 50d. Stretcher party 10 10
See also No. 73.

15 Unloading U.N.I.C.E.F. Supplies from Lorry

1993. Obligatory Tax. Solidarity Week.
47 – 50de. black, mauve and silver 10 10
48 **15** 50de. multicoloured 10 10
49 – 50de. multicoloured 10 10
50 – 50de. multicoloured 10 10
DESIGNS: No. 47, "Skopje Earthquake"; 49, Labelling parcels in warehouse; 50, Consignment of parcels on fork-lift truck.
See also No. 72.

16 U.N. Emblem and Rainbow

1993. Admission to United Nations Organization.
51 **16** 10d. multicoloured . . . . 1·00 1·00

17 "Insurrection" (detail), (B. Lazeski)

19 Tapestry

18 Children in Meadow

1993. 90th Anniv of Macedonian Insurrection.
52 **17** 10d. multicoloured . . . . 1·00 1·00

1993. Obligatory Tax. Anti-tuberculosis Week. Multicoloured.
54 50de. Anti-tuberculosis slogans (dated "14–21.09.1993") . . 10 10
55 50de. Type **18** 10 10
56 50de. Bee on flower 10 10
57 50de. Goat behind boulder . . 10 10
See also No. 71.

1993. Centenary of Founding of Inner Macedonia Revolutionary Organization.
58 **19** 4d. multicoloured 30 30

20 "The Nativity" (fresco from St. George's Monastery, Rajcica)

1993. Christmas. Multicoloured.
60 2d. Type **20** 25 25
61 20d. "The Three Kings" (fresco from Slepce Monastery) . . . . 1·00 1·00

21 Lily

1994. Obligatory Tax. Anti-cancer Week. Multicoloured.
62 1d. Red Cross and anti-cancer emblems 10 10
63 1d. Type **21** 10 10
64 1d. Caesar's mushroom . . . 20 20
65 1d. Mute swans on lake . . . 10 10

1994. Nos. 1, 18 and 34 surch.
66 **5** 2d. on 30d. multicoloured . . 15 15
67 **1** 8d. on 2d.50 black and orange 40 40
68 **6** 15d. on 10d. multicoloured 70 70

23 Decorated Eggs **24** Kosta Racin (writer)

1994. Easter.
69 **23** 2d. multicoloured 25 25

1994. Obligatory Tax. Red Cross Week. As previous designs but values, and date (70), changed. Multicoloured.
70 1d. Red Cross inscriptions (dated "8–15 MAJ 1994") 10 10
71 1d. Type **18** 10 10
72 1d. As No. 50 . . . . 10 10
73 1d. Type **14** 10 10

1994. Revolutionaries. Portraits by Dimitar Kondovski. Multicoloured.
74 8d. Type **24** 45 45
75 15d. Grigor Prlicev (writer) . . 1·00 1·00
76 20d. Nikola Vaptsarov (Bulgarian poet) . . . . . 1·75 1·75
77 50d. Goce Delcev (founder of Internal Macedonian–Odrin Revolutionary–Organization) . . . . 2·40 2·40

25 "Skopje Earthquake" **26** Tree and Family

1994. Obligatory Tax. Solidarity Week.
78 **25** 1d. black, red and silver . . 10 10

1994. Census.
79 **26** 2d. multicoloured 25 25

27 St. Prohor Pcinski Monastery (venue) **28** Swimmer

1994. 50th Anniv of Macedonian National Liberation Council.
80 **27** 5d. multicoloured 30 30

1994. Swimming Marathon, Ohrid.
82 **28** 8d. multicoloured 45 45

29 Turkish Cancellation and 1992 30d. Stamp on Cover

1994. 150th Anniv (1993) of Postal Service in Macedonia.
83 **29** 2d. multicoloured 20 20

30 Mastheads

1994. 50th Anniversaries of "Nova Makedonija", "Mlad Borec" and "Makedonka" (newspapers).
84 **30** 2d. multicoloured 25 25

31 Open Book

1994. 50th Anniv of St. Clement of Ohrid Library. Multicoloured.
85 2d. Type **31** 15 15
86 10d. Page of manuscript (vert) 50 50

32 Globe **33** Wireless and Gramophone Record

1994. Obligatory Tax. Anti-AIDS Week.
87 – 2d. red and black 10 10
88 **32** 2d. black, red and blue . . 10 10
89 – 2d. black, yellow and red . . 10 10
90 – 2d. black and red 10 10
DESIGNS: No. 87, Inscriptions in Cyrillic (dated "01-08.12.1994"); 89, Exclamation mark in warning triangle; 90, Safe sex campaign emblem.

1994. 50th Anniv of Macedonian Radio.
91 **33** 2d. multicoloured 20 20

34 Macedonian Pine

1994. Flora and Fauna. Multicoloured.
92 5d. Type **34** 35 35
93 10d. Lynx 80 80

1995. Nos. 35 and 33 surch.
94 **10** 2d. on 40d. multicoloured 35 35
96 **5** 5d. on 40d. multicoloured 35 35

36 Emblems and Inscriptions **38** Voluntary Workers

37 Fresco

1995. Obligatory Tax. Anti-cancer Week. Multicoloured.
97 1d. Type **36** 10 10
98 1d. White lilies 10 10
99 1d. Red lilies 10 10
100 1d. Red roses 10 10

1995. Easter.
101 **37** 4d. multicoloured 30 30

1995. Obligatory Tax. Red Cross. Multicoloured.
102 1d. Cross and inscriptions in Cyrillic (dated "8–15 MAJ 1995") 10 10
103 1d. Type **38** 10 10
104 1d. Volunteers in T-shirts . . 10 10
105 1d. Globe, red cross and red crescent 10 10

39 Troops on Battlefield

1995. 50th Anniv of End of Second World War.
106 **39** 2d. multicoloured 25 25

40 Anniversary Emblem

1995. 50th Anniv of Macedonian Red Cross.
107 **40** 2d. multicoloured 20 20

41 Rontgen and X-Ray Lamp

1995. Centenary of Discovery of X-Rays by Wilhelm Rontgen.
108 **41** 2d. multicoloured 20 20

42 "Skopje Earthquake"

1995. Obligatory Tax. Solidarity Week.
109 **42** 1d. black, red and gold . . 10 10

43 Cernodrinski (dramatist)

1995. 50th Anniv of Vojdan Cernodrinski Theatre Festival.
110 **43** 10d. multicoloured 50 50

44 Kraljevic (fresco, Markov Monastery, Skopje)

1995. 600th Death Anniv of Marko Kraljevic (Serbian Prince).
111 **44** 20d. multicoloured . . . . 1·00 1·00

45 Puleski

1995. Death Centenary of Gorgi Puleski (linguist and revolutionary).
112 **45** 2d. multicoloured 20 20

46 Manuscript, Bridge and Emblem

1995. Writers' Festival, Struga.
113 **46** 2d. multicoloured 25 25

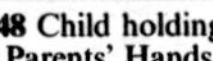

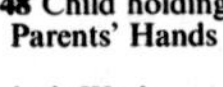

47 Robert Koch (discoverer of tubercule bacillus) **48** Child holding Parents' Hands

1995. Obligatory Tax. Anti-tuberculosis Week.
114 **47** 1d. brown, black and red 10 10

1995. Obligatory Tax. Childrens' Week. Self-adhesive. Imperf.
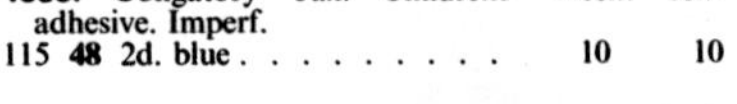
115 **48** 2d. blue 10 10

49 Maleshevija **50** Interior of Mosque

1995. Buildings. Multicoloured.
116 2d. Type **49** 15 15
117 20d. Krakornica . . . . . . 1·10 1·10

1995. Tetovo Mosque.
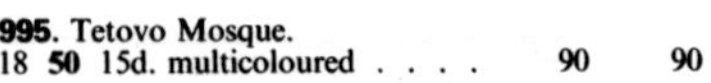
118 **50** 15d. multicoloured 90 90

51 Lumiere Brothers (inventors of cine-camera)

1995. Centenary of Motion Pictures. Multicoloured.
119 10d. Type **51** 55 55
120 10d. Milton and Janaki Manaki (Macedonian cinematographers) 55 55
Nos. 119/20 were issued together, se-tenant, forming a composite design.

52 Globe in Nest within Frame

1995. 50th Anniv of U.N.O. Multicoloured.
121 20d. Type **52** 80 80
122 50d. Sun within frame . . . 2·50 2·50

53 Male and Female Symbols

1995. Obligatory Tax. Anti-AIDS Week.
123 **53** 1d. multicoloured 10 10

54 Madonna and Child

1995. Christmas.
124 **54** 15d. multicoloured 75 75

55 Dalmatian Pelican

1995. Birds. Multicoloured.
125 15d. Type **55** 75 75
126 40d. Lammergeier . . . . . 2·00 2·00

56 Letters of Alphabet and Jigsaw Pieces

1995. 50th Anniv of Alphabet Reform.
127 **56** 5d. multicoloured 35 35

57 St. Clement of Ohrid (detail of fresco)

1995. 700th Anniv of Fresco, St. Bogorodica's Church, Ohrid.
128 **57** 8d. multicoloured 45 45

58 Postal Headquarters, Skopje

1995. 2nd Anniv of Membership of U.P.U.
130 **58** 10d. multicoloured 60 60

59 Zip joining Flags

1995. Entry to Council of Europe and Organization for Security and Co-operation in Europe.
131 **59** 20d. multicoloured . . . . 1·10 1·10

60 Hand holding out Apple **61** Inscriptions

1996. Obligatory Tax. Anti-cancer Week.
132 **60** 1d. multicoloured 10 10

1996. Obligatory Tax. Red Cross Week. Each red, black and yellow.
133 1d. Type **61** 10 10
134 1d. Red Cross principles in Macedonian 10 10
135 1d. Red Cross principles in English 10 10
136 1d. Red Cross principles in French 10 10
137 1d. Red Cross principles in Spanish 10 10

62 Canoeing

1996. Olympic Games, Atlanta. Designs showing statue of discus thrower and sport. Multicoloured.
138 2d. Type **62** 10 10
139 8d. Basketball (vert) 40 40
140 15d. Swimming 75 75
141 20d. Wrestling 95 95
142 40d. Boxing (vert) . . . . . 1·75 1·75
143 50d. Running (vert) . . . . 2·25 2·25

63 "Skopje Earthquake"

1996. Obligatory Tax. Solidarity Week.
144 **63** 1d. gold, red and black . . 10 10

64 Scarecrow Drug Addict **65** Boy

1996. United Nations Anti-drugs Decade.
145 **64** 20d. multicoloured 75 75

1996. Children's Week. Children's Drawings. Multicoloured.
146 2d. Type **65** 10 10
147 8d. Girl 35 35

66 Fragment from Tomb and Tsar Samuel (after Dimitar Kondovski)

1996. Millenary of Crowning of Tsar Samuel (ruler of Bulgaria and Macedonia).
148 **66** 40d. multicoloured . . . . 1·50 1·50

67 Petrov

1996. 75th Death Anniv of Gorce Petrov (revolutionary).
149 **67** 20d. multicoloured 75 75

68 Ohrid Seal, 1903, and State Flag

1996. 5th Anniv of Independence.
150 **68** 10d. multicoloured 40 40

69 Lungs on Globe **70** Vera Ciriviri-Trena (freedom fighter)

1996. Obligatory Tax. Anti-tuberculosis Week.
151 **69** 1d. red, blue and black . . 10 10

1996. Europa. Famous Women. Multicoloured.
152 20d. Type **70** 65 65
153 40d. Mother Teresa (Nobel Peace Prize winner and founder of Missionaries of Charity) . . . . 1·25 1·25

71 Hand holding Syringe

1996. Obligatory Tax. Anti-AIDS Week.
154 **71** 1d. black, red and yellow 10 10

72 Candle, Nuts and Fruit **73** "Daniel in the Lions' Den"

1996. Christmas. Multicoloured.
155 10d. Type **72** 35 35
156 10d. Tree and carol singers 35 35

1996. Early Christian Terracotta Reliefs. (a) Green backgrounds.
157 4d. Type **73** 15 15
158 8d. St. Christopher and St. George 25 25
159 20d. Joshua and Caleb . . . 60 60
160 50d. Unicorn . . . . 1·40 1·40

(b) Blue backgrounds.
161 4d. Type **73** 15 15
162 8d. As No. 158 . . . . . . 25 25
163 20d. As No. 159 . . . . . . 60 60
164 50d. As No. 160 . . . . . . 1·40 1·40

74 Nistrovo **76** U.N.I.C.E.F. Coach

75 "Pseudochazara cingovskii"

1996. Traditional Houses. Multicoloured.
165 2d. Type **74** 10 10
166 8d. Brodec 30 30
167 10d. Niviste 35 35

1996. Butterflies. Multicoloured.
168 4d. Type **75** 15 15
169 40d. Danube clouded yellow 1·25 1·25

1996. 50th Anniversaries. Multicoloured.
170 20d. Type **76** (U.N.I.C.E.F.) 65 65
171 40d. Church in Mtskheta, Georgia (U.N.E.S.C.O.) . . 1·40 1·40

77 Skier

1997. 50 Years of Ski Championships at Sar Planina.
172 **77** 20d. multicoloured 70 70

78 Bell

1997. 150th Birth Anniv of Alexander Graham Bell (telephone pioneer).
173 **78** 40d. multicoloured . . . . 1·40 1·40

79 Family and Healthy Foodstuffs **81** Red Cross on Globe

80 Hound

1997. Obligatory Tax. Anti-cancer Week.
174 **79** 1d. multicoloured 10 10

1997. Roman Mosaics from Heraklia. Mult.
175 2d. Type **80** 10 10
176 8d. Steer 25 25
177 20d. Lion 70 70
178 40d. Leopard with prey . . . 1·25 1·25

1997. Obligatory Tax. Red Cross Week.
180 **81** 1d. mult 10 10

82 Gold Plate

1997. 1100th Anniv of Cyrillic Alphabet. Mult.
181 10d. Type **82** 30 30
182 10d. Sts. Cyril and Methodius 30 30

83 School-children **84** Mountain Flowers

1997. Obligatory Tax. Solidarity Week.
183 **83** 1d. multicoloured 10 10

1997. 5th Anniv of Ecological Association.
184 **84** 15d. multicoloured 55 55

85 Itar Pejo **86** St. Naum and St. Naum's Church, Ohrid

1997. Europa. Tales and Legends. Multicoloured.
185 20d. Type **85** 70 70
186 40d. Stork-men . . . . . . 1·25 1·25

1997. 1100th Birth Anniv of St. Naum.
187 **86** 15d. multicoloured 55 55

87 Diseased Lungs **88** Stibnite

1997. Obligatory Tax. Anti-tuberculosis Week.
188 **87** 1d. multicoloured 10 10

1997. Minerals. Multicoloured.
189 27d. Type **88** 95 95
190 40d. Lorandite . . . . 1·40 1·40

89 Dove and Sun above Child in Open Hand

1997. International Children's Day.
191 **89** 27d. multicoloured 95 95

90 Chanterelle

1997. Fungi. Multicoloured.
192 2d. Type **90** 10 10
193 15d. Bronze boletus 50 50
194 27d. Caesar's mushroom . . 95 95
195 50d. "Morchella conica" . . 1·75 1·75

91 Group of Children **92** Gandhi

1998. Obligatory Tax. Anti-AIDS Week.
196 **91** 1d. multicoloured 10 10

1998. 50th Death Anniv of Mahatma Gandhi (Indian independence campaigner).
197 **92** 30d. multicoloured . . . . 1·00 1·00

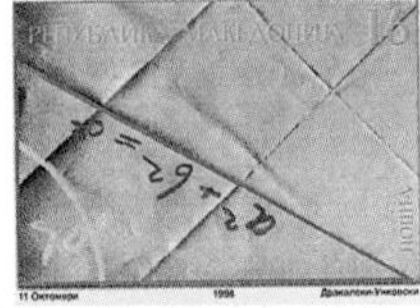

93 Formula of Pythagoras's Theory

1998. 2500th Death Anniv of Pythagoras (philosopher and mathematician).
198 **93** 16d. multicoloured 55 55

94 Alpine Skiing

1998. Winter Olympic Games, Nagano, Japan. Multicoloured.
199 4d. Type **94** 15 15
200 30d. Cross-country skiing . . 1·00 1·00

95 Novo Selo

1998. Traditional Houses. Multicoloured.
201 1d. Bogomila 10 10
201a 2d. Type **95** 10 10
202 4d. Jablanica 15 15
202a 4d. Svekani 10 10
202b 5d. Teovo 10 10
202c 6d. Zdunje 15 10
203 16d. Kiselica 35 35
204 20d. Konopnica 70 70
205 30d. Ambar . . . . 1·00 1·00
206 50d. Galicnik . . . . 1·75 1·75

96 "Exodus" (Kole Manev)

1998. 50th Anniv of Exodus of Children during Greek Civil War.
215 **96** 30d. multicoloured . . . . 1·00 1·00

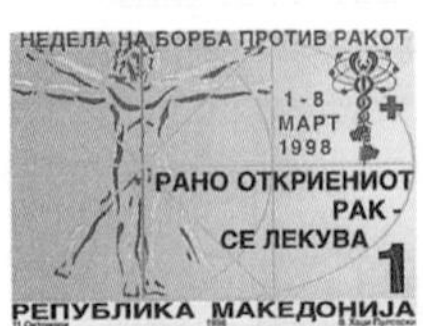

97 "Proportions of Man" (Leonardo da Vinci)

1998. Obligatory Tax. Anti-cancer Week.
216 **97** 1d. multicoloured 10 10

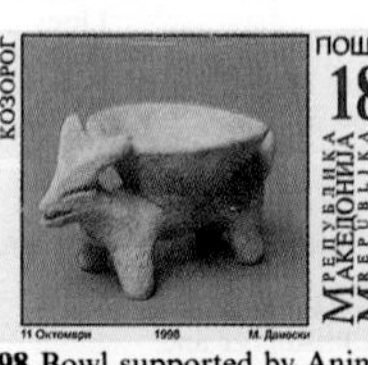

98 Bowl supported by Animal

1998. Archaeological Finds from Nedit. Mult.
217 4d. Carafes 15 15
218 18d. Type **98** 60 60
219 30d. Sacred female figurine 1·00 1·00
220 60d. Stemmed cup . . . . . 2·10 2·10

99 Football Pitch

1998. World Cup Football Championship, France. Multicoloured.
221 4d. Type **99** 15 15
222 30d. Globe and football pitch 1·00 1·00

100 Folk Dance

1998. Europa. National Festivals. Multicoloured.
223 30d. Type **100** . . . . 1·00 1·00
224 40d. Carnival . . . . 1·40 1·40

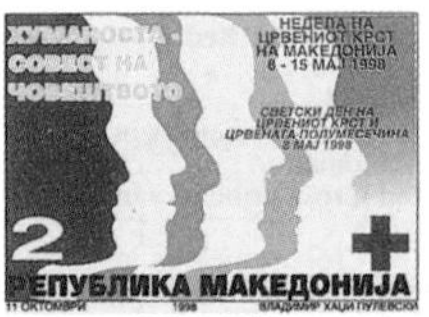

101 Profiles

1998. Obligatory Tax. Red Cross Week.
225 **101** 2d. multicoloured 10 10

102 Carnival Procession **103** Hands and Red Cross

1998. 18th Congress of Carnival Towns, Strumica.
226 **102** 30d. multicoloured . . . 1·00 1·00

1998. Obligatory Tax. Solidarity Week.
227 **103** 2d. multicoloured 10 10

104 Flower **105** Cupovski

1998. Environmental Protection. Multicoloured.
228 4d. Type **104** 15 15
229 30d. Polluting chimney uprooting tree . . . . . . 1·00 1·00

1998. 120th Birth Anniv of Dimitrija Cupovski.
230 **105** 16d. multicoloured . . . 55 55

106 Steam Locomotive and Station **107** Doctor and Patient

1997. 150th Anniv of Railways in Macedonia. Multicoloured.
231 30d. Type **106** . . . . 1·00 1·00
232 60d. Steam locomotive, 1873 (horiz) . . . . 2·10 2·10

1998. Obligatory Tax. Anti-tuberculosis Week.
233 **107** 2d. multicoloured 10 10

108 "Ursus spelaeus"

1998. Fossilized Skulls. Multicoloured.
234 4d. Type **108** 10 10
235 8d. "Mesopithecus pentelici" 15 15
236 18d. "Tragoceros" 40 40
237 30d. "Aceratherium incsivum" 65 65

109 Atanos Badev (composer) and Score

1998. Centenary of "Zlatoustova Liturgy".
238 **109** 25d. multicoloured . . . 50 50

110 Child with Kite

1998. Children's Day.
239 **110** 30d. multicoloured . . . 65 65

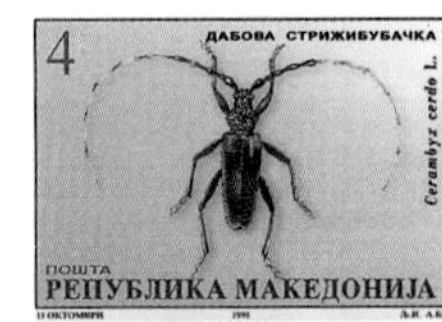

111 "Cerambyx cerdo" (longhorn beetle)

1998. Insects. Multicoloured.
240 4d. Type **111** 10 10
241 8d. Alpine longhorn beetle 15 15
242 20d. European rhinoceros beetle 40 40
243 40d. Stag beetle 85 85

112 Reindeer and Snowflakes

1998. Christmas and New Year. Multicoloured.
244 4d. Type **112** 10 10
245 30d. Bread and oak leaves . . 65 65

113 Ribbon and Gender Symbols

1998. Obligatory Tax. Anti-AIDS Week.
246 **113** 2d. multicoloured 10 10

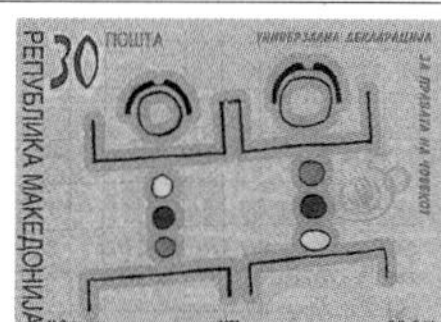

114 Stylized Couple

1998. 50th Anniv of Universal Declaration of Human Rights.
247 **114** 30d. multicoloured . . . 65 65

115 Sharplaninec

1999. Dogs.
248 **115** 15d. multicoloured . . . 30 30

116 Girl's Face
117 "The Annunciation" (Demir Hisar, Slepce Monastery)

1999. Obligatory Tax. Anti-cancer Week.
249 **116** 2d. multicoloured 10 10

1999. Icons. Multicoloured.
250 4d. Type **117** 10 10
251 8d. "Saints" (St. Nicholas's Church, Ohrid) 15 15
252 18d. "Madonna and Child" (Demir Hisar, Slepce Monastery) 40 40
253 30d. "Christ the Redeemer" (Zrze Monastery, Prilep) 65 65

118 Pandilov and "Hay Harvest"

1999. Birth Centenary of Dimitar Pandilov (painter).
255 **118** 4d. multicoloured 10 10

119 Telegraph Apparatus

1999. Centenary of the Telegraph in Macedonia.
256 **119** 4d. multicoloured 10 10

120 University and Sts. Cyril and Methodius

1999. 50th Anniv of Sts. Cyril and Methodius University.
257 **120** 8d. multicoloured 15 15

121 Anniversary Emblem and Map of Europe

1999. 50th Anniv of Council of Europe.
258 **121** 30d. multicoloured . . . 65 65

122 Pelister National Park

1999. Europa. Parks and Gardens. Multicoloured.
259 30d. Type **122** 65 65
260 40d. Mavrovo National Park 85 85

123 Figures linking Raised Arms

1999. Obligatory Tax. Red Cross Week.
261 **123** 2d. multicoloured 10 10

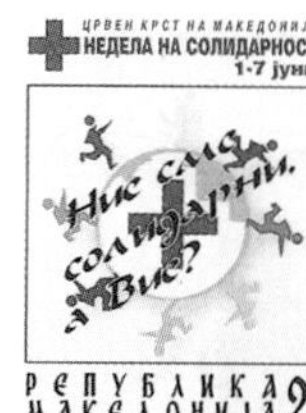

124 People running round Globe
125 Tree

1999. Obligatory Tax. Solidarity Week.
262 **124** 2d. multicoloured 10 10

1999. Environmental Protection.
263 **125** 30d. multicoloured . . . 65 65

126 Tsar Petur Delyan

1999. Medieval Rulers of Macedonia. Mult.
264 4d. Type **126** 10 10
265 8d. Prince Gjorgji Vojteh . . 15 15
266 18d. Prince Dobromir Hrs . . 40 40
267 30d. Prince Strez 65 65
Nos. 264/7 were issued together, se-tenant, forming a composite design.

127 Kuzman Shaikarev (author)

1999. 125th Anniv of First Macedonian Language Primer.
268 **127** 4d. multicoloured 10 10

128 Faces in Outline of Lungs
129 "Crocus scardicus"

1999. Obligatory Tax. Anti-tuberculosis Week.
269 **128** 2d. multicoloured 10 10

1999. Flowers. Multicoloured.
270 4d. Type **129** 10 10
271 8d. "Astragalus mayeri" . . 15 15
272 18d. "Campanula formanekiana" 40 40
273 30d. "Viola kosaninii" . . . 65 65

130 Child

1999. Children's Week.
274 **130** 30d. multicoloured . . . 60 60

131 Emblem

1999. 125th Anniv of Universal Postal Union. Mult.
275 5d. Type **131** 10 10
276 30d. Emblem (different) . . . 60 60

132 Men on Horseback
133 Misirkov

1999. 1400th Anniv of Slavs in Macedonia.
277 **132** 5d. multicoloured 10 10

1999. 125th Birth Anniv (2000) of Krste Petkov Misirkov (writer).
278 **133** 5d. multicoloured 10 10

134 Pine Needles

1999. Christmas. Multicoloured.
279 5d. Type **134** 10 10
280 30d. Traditional pastry (vert) 60 60

135 Stylized Figures supporting Globe

1999. Obligatory Tax. Anti-AIDS Week.
281 **135** 2d.50 multicoloured . . . 10 10

136 Altar Cross (19th-century), St. Nikita Monastery

2000. Bimillenary of Christianity. Multicoloured.
282 5d. Type **136** 10 10
283 10d. "Akathist of the Holy Mother of God" (14th-century fresco), Marko's Monastery (horiz) 20 20
284 15d. "St. Clement" (14th-century icon), Ohrid . . . 30 30
285 30d. "Paul the Apostle" (14th-century fresco), St. Andrew's Monastery . . 60 60

137 "2000"

2000. New Year. Multicoloured.
287 5d. Type **137** 30 30
288 30d. Religious symbols . . . 60 60

138 Globe Unravelling and Medical Symbols
139 Jewelled Brooch with Icon, Ohrid

2000. Obligatory Tax. Anti-cancer Week.
289 **138** 2d.50 multicoloured . . . 10 10

2000. Jewellery. Multicoloured.
290 5d. Type **139** 10 10
291 10d. Bracelet, Bitola 20 20
292 20d. Earrings, Ohrid 40 40
293 30d. Butterfly brooch, Bitola 60 60

140 Magnifying Glass and Perforation Gauge

2000. 50th Anniv of Philately in Macedonia.
294 **140** 5d. multicoloured 10 10

141 Globe and Emblem

2000. 50th Anniv of World Meteorological Organization.
295 **141** 30d. multicoloured . . . 60 60

142 Men with Easter Eggs
144 "Building Europe"

143 Stylized Figures

2000. Easter.
296 **142** 5d. multicoloured 10 10

2000. Obligatory Tax. Red Cross Week.
297 **143** 2d.50 multicoloured . . . 10 10

2000. Europa.
298 **144** 30d. multicoloured . . . 60 60

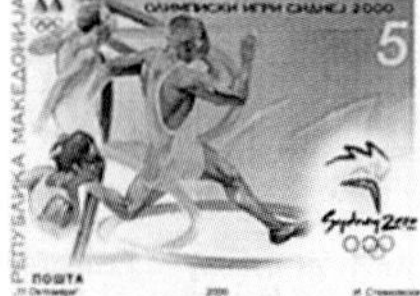

145 Running

2000. Olympic Games, Sydney. Multicoloured.
299 5d. Type **145** 10 10
300 30d. Wrestling 60 60

146 Cupped Hands
147 Flower and Globe

2000. Obligatory Tax. Solidarity Week.
301 **146** 2d.50 multicoloured . . . 10 10

2000. International Environmental Protection Day.
302 **147** 5d. multicoloured 10 10

148 Teodosija Sinaitski (printing pioneer)
150 Faces and Hands

149 Mother Teresa

2000. Printing. Multicoloured.
303 6d. Type **148** 10 10
304 30d. Johannes Gutenberg (inventor of printing press) 60 60

2000. 3rd Death Anniv of Mother Teresa (Order of Missionaries of Charity).
305 **149** 6d. multicoloured 10 10

2000. Obligatory Tax. Red Cross Week.
306 **150** 3d. multicoloured 10 10

151 Little Egret

2000. Birds. Multicoloured.
307 6d. Type **151** 10 10
308 10d. Grey heron 20 20
309 20d. Purple heron 40 40
310 30d. Glossy ibis 60 60

152 Children and Tree

2000. Children's Week.
311 **152** 6d. multicoloured 15 15

153 Dimov
154 Emblem

2000. 125th Birth Anniv of Dimo Hadzi Dimov (revolutionary).
312 **153** 6d. multicoloured 15 15

2000. 50th Anniv of Faculty of Economics, St. Cyril and St. Methodius University, Skopje.
313 **154** 6d. multicoloured 15 15

155 Church and Frontispiece

2000. 250th Birth Anniv of Joakim Krcovski (writer).
314 **155** 6d. multicoloured 15 15

156 Nativity

2000. Christmas.
315 **156** 30d. multicoloured . . . 70 70

157 Hand holding Condom

2000. Obligatory Tax. Anti-AIDS. Week.
316 **157** 3d. multicoloured 10 10

158 Handprints and Emblem

2001. 50th Anniv of United Nations Commissioner for Human Rights. Multicoloured.
317 6d. Type **158** 15 15
318 30d. Hands forming Globe (vert) 70 70

159 Imperial Eagle on Branch

2001. Endangered Species. The Imperial Eagle (*Aquila heliaca*). Multicoloured.
319 6d. Type **159** 15 15
320 8d. With chick 20 20
321 10d. Flying 25 25
322 30d. Head 70 70

160 Zografski

2001. 125th Death Anniv of Partenja Zografski (historian).
323 **160** 6d. multicoloured 15 15

161 Emblem
162 Woman in Costume

2001. Obligatory Tax. Anti-Cancer Week.
324 **161** 3d. multicoloured 10 10

2001. Regional Costumes. Multicoloured.
325 6d. Type **162** 15 15
326 12d. Couple in costume . . . 30 30
327 18d. Woman in costume . . . 45 45
328 30d. Couple in costume . . . 70 70
MS329 76 × 64 mm. 50d. Women working (30 × 30 mm). Imperf 1·25 1·25

163 Landscape

2001. Birth Centenary of Lazar Licenoski (artist).
330 **163** 6d. multicoloured 15 15

164 Text

2001. 50th Anniv of State Archives.
331 **164** 6d. multicoloured 15 15

165 Jesus and Sick Man

2001. Easter.
332 **165** 6d. multicoloured 15 15

166 Children

2001. Obligatory Tax. Red Cross Week.
333 **166** 3d. multicoloured 10 10

MADAGASCAR Pt. 6

A large island in the Indian Ocean off the east coast of Africa. French Post Offices operated there from 1885.

In 1896 the island was declared a French colony, absorbing Diego-Suarez and Ste. Marie de Madagascar in 1898 and Nossi-Be in 1901.

Madagascar became autonomous as the Malagasy Republic in 1958; it reverted to the name of Madagascar in 1992.

100 centimes = 1 franc.

A. FRENCH POST OFFICES

1889. Stamps of French Colonies "Commerce" type surch with value in figures.
1 J 05 on 10c. black on lilac . . . £525 £150
2 05 on 25c. black on red . . . £525 £140
4 05 on 40c. red on yellow . . . £130 80·00
5 5 on 10c. black on lilac . . . £170 90·00
6 5 on 25c. black on red . . . £170 £100
7 15 on 25c. black on red . . . £120 75·00
3 25 on 40c. red on yellow . . . £475 £130

5

1891. No gum. Imperf.
9 **5** 5c. black on green . . . . . £120 11·50
10 10c. black on blue . . . . . 90·00 25·00
11 15c. blue on blue . . . . . . 95·00 18·00
12 25c. brown on buff . . . . . 21·00 14·50
13 1f. black on yellow £900 £225
14 5f. black and lilac on lilac . . £1800 £900

1895. Stamps of France optd **POSTE FRANCAISE Madagascar**.
15 **10** 5c. green . . . . 6·00 6·50
16 10c. black on lilac . . . . . 45·00 32·00
17 15c. blue . . . . 50·00 12·00
18 25c. black on red . . . . . . 60·00 8·25
19 40c. red on yellow . . . . . 70·00 10·00
20 50c. red . . . . £110 12·50
21 75c. brown on orange . . . . £100 50·00
22 1f. olive . . . . £120 42·00
23 5f. mauve on lilac . . . . . £150 80·00

1896. Stamps of France surch with value in figures in oval.
29 **10** 5c. on 1c. black on blue . . £4250 £1600
30 15c. on 2c. brown on yellow £1700 £800
31 25c. on 3c. grey £2250 £800
32 25c. on 4c. red on grey . . £4750 £1500
33 25c. on 40c. red on yellow £1000 £600

B. FRENCH COLONY OF MADAGASCAR AND DEPENDENCIES

1896. "Tablet" key-type inscr "MADAGASCAR ET DEPENDANCES".
1 D 1c. black and red on blue 85 25
2 2c. brown and blue on buff 45 1·40
2a 2c. brown & blk on buff . . 6·75 7·00
3 4c. brown and blue on grey 95 1·25
17 5c. green and red . . . . . 3·00 15
6 10c. black and blue on lilac 11·00 1·25
18 10c. red and blue . . . . . 2·75 15
7 15c. blue and red . . . . . 9·00 1·00
19 15c. grey and red . . . . . 4·00 65
8 20c. red and blue on green 6·25 1·90
9 25c. black and red on pink 10·50 25
20 25c. blue and red . . . . . 23·00 35·00
10 30c. brown & bl on drab 8·50 2·25
21 35c. black and red on yellow . . . . 42·00 4·00
11 40c. red and blue on yellow 8·25 1·25
12 50c. red and blue on pink 15·00 1·40
22 50c. brown and red on blue 27·00 27·00
13 75c. violet & red on orge 2·75 3·25
14 1f. green and red . . . . . 17·00 2·50
15 1f. green and blue . . . . 27·00 16·00
16 5f. mauve and blue on lilac 42·00 30·00

1902. "Tablet" key-type stamps as above surch.
27 D 0,01 on 2c. brown and blue on buff . . . . 5·25 3·75
27a 0,01 on 2c. brown and black on buff . . . . . 3·75 9·00
29 0,05 on 30c. brown and blue on drab . . . . . . 3·75 5·25
23 05 on 50c. red and blue on pink . . . . 2·25 2·25
31 0,10 on 50c. red and blue on pink . . . . 3·25 5·00
24 10 on 5f. mauve and blue on lilac . . . . 18·00 13·50
32 0,15 on 75c. violet and red on orange . . . . 1·50 1·50
33 0,15 on 1f. green and red 3·50 3·75
25 15 on 1f. green and red . . 3·50 1·25

1902. Nos. 59 and 61 of Diego-Suarez surch.
34 D 0,05 on 30c. brown and blue on drab £110 £100
36 0,10 on 50c. red and blue on pink £3750 £3750

4 Zebu and Lemur
5 Transport in Madagascar

1903.
38 **4** 1c. purple 50 25
39 2c. brown 50 35
40 4c. brown . . . . 40 1·00
41 5c. green . . . . 6·75 35
42 10c. red . . . . 8·75 35
43 15c. red . . . . 9·00 30
44 20c. orange . . . . 2·75 1·50
45 25c. blue . . . . 30·00 1·40
46 30c. red . . . . 30·00 13·00
47 40c. lilac . . . . 38·00 4·00
48 50c. brown . . . . 60·00 28·00
49 75c. yellow . . . . 48·00 25·00
50 1f. green . . . . 50·00 35·00
51 2f. blue . . . . 55·00 32·00
52 5f. black . . . . 55·00 80·00

1908.
53a **5** 1c. green and violet 10 20
54 2c. green and red 10 20
55 4c. brown and green . . . 10 1·25
56 5c. olive and green . . . . 1·25 20
90 5c. red and black 30 15
57 10c. brown and pink . . . 1·60 20
91 10c. olive and green . . . 30 30
92 10c. purple and brown . . 45 30
58 15c. red and lilac 35 20
93 15c. green and olive . . . 45 2·75
94 15c. red and blue . . . . 65 3·75
59 20c. brown and orange . . 1·00 80
60 25c. black and blue . . . . 5·00 95
95 25c. black and violet . . . 25 25
61 30c. black and brown . . . 4·50 4·25
96 30c. brown and red . . . . 45 1·25
97 30c. purple and green . . . 35 20
98 30c. light green and green 2·25 3·00
62 35c. black and red . . . . 1·75 1·50
63 40c. black and brown . . . 90 70
64 45c. black and green . . . 1·50 2·75
99 45c. red and scarlet . . . . 60 2·75
100 45c. purple and lilac . . . 2·75 3·50
65 50c. black and violet . . . 1·00 1·10
101 50c. black and blue 65 30
102 50c. yellow and black . . . 20 40
103 60c. violet on pink . . . . 45 1·90
104 65c. blue and black . . . . 2·00 3·25
66 75c. black and red 90 40
105 85c. red and green . . . . 1·25 3·50
67 1f. green and brown . . . 30 40

106 1f. blue 35 1·40
107 1f. green and mauve 6·75 9·25
108 1f.10 green and brown 1·60 3·25
68 2f. green and blue 2·75 1·40
69 5f. brown and violet 16·00 8·25

1912. "Tablet" key-type surch.
70 D 05 on 15c. grey and red 25 75
71 05 on 20c. red and blue on green 80 1·75
72 05 on 30c. brown and blue on drab 50 3·00
73 10 on 75c. violet and red on orange 2·50 14·50
81 0.60 on 75c. violet and red on orange 9·75 11·00
82 1f. on 5f. mauve and blue on lilac 1·25 3·00

1912. Surch.
74 4 05 on 2c. brown 25 2·75
75 05 on 20c. orange 55 1·40
76 05 on 30c. red 45 3·00
77 10 on 40c. lilac 1·10 3·25
78 10 on 50c. brown 1·50 4·25
79 10 on 75c. brown 3·50 11·50
83 1f. on 5f. black 90·00 90·00

1915. Surch **5c** and red cross.
80 5 10c.+5c. brown and pink 50 1·60

1921. Surch **1 cent.**
84 5 1c. on 15c. red and lilac 20 1·60

1921. Type **5** (some colours changed) surch.
109 5 25c. on 15c. red and lilac 60 3·00
85 0,25 on 35c. black and red 6·50 7·00
86 0,25 on 40c. black and brown 4·50 5·75
87 0,25 on 45c. black and green 3·50 4·75
111 25c. on 2f. green and blue 40 1·90
112 25c. on 5f. brown and violet 40 3·00
88 0,30 on 40c. black and brown 85 2·25
113 50c. on 1f. green and brown 1·25 25
89 0,60 on 75c. black and red 2·75 3·25
114 60 on 75c. violet on pink 80 50
115 65c. on 75c. black and red 2·25 3·00
116 85c. on 45c. black and green 1·50 3·25
117 90c. on 75c. pink and red 80 2·25
118 1f.25 on 1f. blue 1·00 2·50
119 1f.50 on 1f. lt blue & blue 1·75 20
120 3f. on 5f. violet and green 2·25 2·75
121 10f. on 5f. mauve and red 8·00 7·50
122 20f. on 5f. blue and mauve 12·00 9·25

14 Sakalava Chief

15 Zebus

17 Betsileo Woman

18 General Gallieni

1930.
123 18 1c. blue 15 2·75
124 15 1c. green and blue 15 15
125 14 2c. brown and red 10 10
177 18 3c. blue 15 1·50
126a 14 4c. mauve and brown 25 25
127 15 5c. red and green 15 15
128 – 10c. green and red 10 10
129 17 15c. red 10 10
130 15 20c. blue and brown 10 15
131 – 25c. brown and lilac 20 10
132 17 30c. green 35 20
133 14 40c. red and green 55 30
134 17 45c. lilac 1·90 2·00
178 18 45c. green 1·25 1·75
179 50c. brown 25 10
180 60c. mauve 15 1·75
136 15 65c. mauve and brown 2·75 2·25
181 18 70c. red 1·50 2·50
137 17 75c. brown 2·25 20
138 15 90c. red 2·75 1·10
182 18 90c. brown 40 15
139 – 1f. blue and brown 3·25 2·50
140 – 1f. red and scarlet 1·25 1·25
140a – 1f.25 brown and blue 2·75 1·50
183 18 1f.40 orange 2·75 2·75
141 14 1f.50 ultramarine and blue 10·00 65
142 1f.50 red and brown 80 95
278 1f.50 brown and red 10 1·25
184 18 1f.60 violet 2·25 2·75
143 14 1f.75 red and brown 5·50 55
185 18 2f. red 40 20
186a 3f. green 60 1·50
146 14 5f. brown and mauve 8·75 2·75
147 18 10f. orange 1·90 1·40
148 14 20f. blue and brown 6·50 4·50
DESIGN—VERT: 10c., 25c., 1f., 1f.25, Hova girl.

1931. "Colonial Exhibition" key-types inscr "MADAGASCAR".
149 E 40c. black and green 2·50 3·00
150 F 50c. black and mauve 3·25 3·00
151 G 90c. black and red 2·75 3·00
152 H 1f.50 black and blue 3·75 3·00

19 Bloch 120 over Madagascar

20 J. Laborde and Tananarivo Palace

1935. Air.
153 19 50c. red and green 1·75 1·90
154 90c. red and green 30 2·75
155 1f.25 red and lake 1·50 2·25
156 1f.50 red and blue 1·50 2·25
157 1f.60 red and blue 55 2·25
158 1f.75 red and orange 9·00 5·75
159 2f. red and blue 1·60 2·00
160 3f. red and orange 70 2·25
161 3f.65 red and black 1·40 1·00
162 3f.90 red and green 40 2·50
163 4f. red and carmine 29·00 3·25
164 4f.50 red and black 16·00 60
165 5f.50 red and green 1·10 2·75
166 6f. red and mauve 85 2·50
167 6f.90 red and purple 60 2·50
168 8f. red and mauve 2·75 3·25
169 8f.50 red and green 3·00 3·25
170 9f. red and green 1·25 2·75
171 12f. red and brown 40 2·25
172 12f.50 red and violet 3·25 3·25
173 15f. red and orange 40 2·25
174 16f. red and green 3·00 4·00
175 20f. red and brown 4·00 3·75
176 50f. red and blue 5·50 7·00

1937. International Exhibition, Paris. As T **16** of Mauritania.
187 20c. violet 80 3·25
188 30c. green 1·75 3·25
189 40c. red 40 1·50
190 50c. brown and agate 35 75
191 90c. red 35 1·90
192 1f.50 blue 50 2·00

1938. 60th Death Anniv of Jean Laborde (explorer).
193 20 35c. green 75 40
194 55c. violet 55 65
195 65c. red 1·00 50
196 80c. purple 1·00 50
197 1f. red 65 50
198 1f.25 red 2·00 2·75
199 1f.75 blue 45 90
200 2f.15 brown 2·00 3·25
201 2f.25 blue 1·75 3·25
202 2f.50 brown 30 30
203 10f. green 40 80

1938. Int Anti-cancer Fund. As T **22** of Mauritania.
204 1f.75+50c. blue 4·50 13·50

1939. New York World's Fair. As T **28** of Mauritania.
205 1f.25 red 2·25 1·75
206 2f.25 blue 2·50 2·50

1939. 150th Anniv of French Revolution. As T **29** of Mauritania.
207 45c.+25c. green and black (postage) 5·75 13·50
208 70c.+30c. brown and black 7·25 13·50
209 90c.+35c. orange and black 5·25 13·50
210 1f.25+1f. red and black 5·75 13·50
211 2f.25+2f. blue and black 5·75 13·50
212 4f.50+4f. black and orange (air) 9·50 22·00

1942. Surch **50** and bars.
213 15 50 on 65c. mauve & brown 3·25 50

1942. Free French Administration. Optd **FRANCE LIBRE** or surch also.
214 14 2c. brown and red (postage) 2·75 3·25
215 18 3c. blue £120 £120
216 15 0,05 on 1c. green and blue 1·75 1·40
217 20 0,10 on 55c. violet 50 3·50
218 17 15c. red 15·00 14·50
219 20 0,30 on 65c. red 40 3·00
220 15 0f.50 on 0,05 on 1c. green and blue 2·25 3·25
221 50 on 65c. mauve & brown 1·25 10
222 18 50 on 90c. brown 2·00 10
223 15 65c. mauve and brown 3·25 3·25
224 18 70c. red 2·25 3·00
225 20 80c. purple 4·00 3·50
226 – 1,00 on 1f.25 brown and blue (No. 140a) 3·75 3·75
227 20 1,00 on 1f.25 red 9·75 8·50
228 18 1f.40 orange 2·75 2·75
229 5 1f.50 on 1f. blue 3·25 3·25
230 14 1f.50 ultramarine and blue 2·50 3·25
231 1f.50 red and brown 3·50 3·25
232 18 1,50 on 1f.60 violet 2·50 2·75
233 14 1,50 on 1f.75 red & brown 2·75 1·60
234 20 1,50 on 1f.75 blue 2·25 2·50
235 18 1f.60 violet 2·75 2·75
236 20 2,00 on 2f.15 brown 1·75 85
237 2f.25 blue 2·75 3·00
238 – 2f.25 blue (No. 206) 2·75 2·75
239 20 2f.50 brown 5·00 4·75
240 5 10f. on 5f. mauve and red 13·50 11·00
241 20 10f. green 5·25 5·00
242 5 20f. on 5f. blue and mauve 17·00 16·00
243 14 20f. blue and brown £700 £800
244 19 1,00 on 1f.25 red and lake (air) 7·00 7·00
245 1f.50 red and blue 8·25 9·25
246 1f.75 red and orange 90·00 £100
247 3,00 on 3f.65 red and black 2·75 15
248 8f. red and purple 3·25 3·25
249 8,00 on 8f.50 red and green 2·75 70
250 12f. red and brown 4·25 4·00
251 12f.50 red and violet 3·25 3·25
252 16f. red and green 7·25 7·25
253 50f. red and blue 6·00 6·00

24 Traveller's Tree

29 Gen. Gallieni

25a Legionaries by Lake Chad

1943. Free French Issue.
254 24 5c. brown 10 2·75
255 10c. mauve 10 10
256 25c. green 10 2·00
257 30c. orange 10 10
258 40c. blue 55 20
259 80c. purple 60 20
260 1f. blue 50 15
261 1f.50 red 60 15
262 2f. yellow 75 15
263 2f.50 blue 60 10
264 4f. blue and red 1·25 40
265 5f. green and black 60 10
266 10f. red and blue 85 15
267 20f. violet and brown 1·25 20

1943. Free French Administration. Air. As T **19a** of Oceanic Settlements, but inscr "MADAGASCAR".
268 1f. orange 30 1·50
269 1f.50 red 30 1·25
270 5f. purple 25 35
271 10f. black 1·00 1·60
272 25f. blue 90 2·50
273 50f. green 90 80
274 100f. red 1·10 35

1944. Mutual Aid and Red Cross Funds. As T **19b** of Oceanic Settlements.
275 5f.+20f. green 75 3·00

1944. Surch **1f.50.**
276 24 1f.50 on 5c. brown 20 60
277 1f.50 on 10c. mauve 70 3·00

1945. Eboue. As T **20a** of Oceanic Settlements.
279 2f. black 15 25
280 25f. green 70 3·50

1946. Air. Victory. As T **20b** of Oceanic Settlements.
281 8f. red 20 20

1945. Surch with new value.
282 24 50c. on 5c. brown 30 40
283 60c. on 5c. brown 40 2·50
284 70c. on 5c. brown 40 2·50
285 1f.20 on 5c. brown 25 2·25
286 2f.40 on 25c. green 45 60
287 3f. on 25c. green 45 30
288 4f.50 on 25c. green 1·50 2·00
289 15f. on 2f.50 blue 50 85

1946. Air. From Chad to the Rhine.
290 25a 5f. blue 55 3·00
291 – 10f. red 80 2·50
292 – 15f. green 1·00 3·25
293 – 20f. brown 90 3·00
294 – 25f. violet 85 3·25
295 – 50f. red 60 3·00
DESIGNS: 10f. Battle of Koufra; 15f. Tank Battle, Mareth; 20f. Normandy Landings; 25f. Liberation of Strasbourg.

1946.
296 – 10c. green (postage) 10 60
297 – 30c. orange 10 20
298 – 40c. olive 10 40
299 – 50c. purple 10 15
300 – 60c. blue 10 1·60
301 – 80c. green 10 1·60
302 – 1f. sepia 10 10
303 – 1f.20 green 20 1·40
304 29 1f.50 red 10 10
305 – 2f. black 10 10
306 – 3f. purple 25 10
307 – 3f.60 red 90 2·25
308 – 4f. blue 35 10
309 – 5f. orange 40 15
310 – 6f. blue 15 10
311 – 10f. lake 45 20
312 – 15f. brown 50 10
313 – 20f. blue 30 20
314 – 25f. brown 55 25
315 – 50f. blue and red (air) 1·10 1·25
316 – 100f. brown and red 85 45
317 – 200f. brown and green 2·25 2·50
DESIGNS—As T **29**. VERT: 10 to 50c. Native with spear; 6, 10f. Gen. Duchesne; 15, 20, 25f. Lt.-Col. Joffre. HORIZ: 60, 80c. Zebus; 1f., 1f.20, Sakalava man and woman; 3f.60, 4, 5f. Betsimisaraka mother and child. 49×28 mm: 50f. Aerial view of Port of Tamatave. 28×51 mm: 100f. Allegory of flight. 51×28 mm: Douglas DC-2 airplane and map of Madagascar.

36 Gen. Gallieni and View

1946. 50th Anniv of French Protectorate.
318 36 10f.+5f. purple 20 3·00

1948. Air. Discovery of Adelie Land, Antarctic. No. 316 optd **TERRE ADELIE DUMONT D'URVILLE 1840.**
319 100f. brown and red 26·00 55·00

1949. Air. 75th Anniv of U.P.U. As T **38** of New Caledonia.
320 25f. multicoloured 1·40 1·75

1950. Colonial Welfare Fund. As T **39** of New Caledonia.
321 10f.+2f. purple and green 3·50 9·25

38 Cacti and Succulents

39 Long-tailed Ground Roller

40 Woman and Forest Road

1952.
322 38 7f.50 green & blue (postage) 35 20
323 39 8f. lake 90 40
324 15f. blue and green 2·40 40
325 – 50f. green and blue (air) 2·50 30
326 – 100f. black, brown and blue 6·00 1·40
327 – 200f. brown and green 20·00 8·00
328 40 500f. brown, sepia & green 30·00 7·50
DESIGNS—As Type **40**: 50f. Palm trees; 100f. Antsirabe Viaduct; 200f. Ring-tailed lemurs.

1952. Military Medal Centenary As T **40** of New Caledonia.
329 15f. turquoise, yellow & green 1·10 1·50

1954. Air. 10th Anniv of Liberation. As T **42** of New Caledonia.
330 15f. purple and violet 2·25 1·25

41 Marshal Lyautey

1954. Birth Centenary of Marshal Lyautey.
331 41 10f. indigo, blue & ultram 45 10
332 40f. lake, grey and black 55 10

42 Gallieni School

43 Cassava

1956. Economic and Social Development Fund.
333 – 3f. brown and grey 25 10
334 **42** 5f. brown and chestnut . . 25 10
335 – 10f. blue and grey 30 10
336 – 15f. green and turquoise 40 10
DESIGNS: 3f. Tamatave and tractor; 10f. Dredging canal; 15f. Irrigation.

1956. Coffee. As T **44** of New Caledonia.
337 20f. sepia and brown 20 10

1957. Plants.
338 **43** 2f. green, brown and blue 25 10
339 – 4f. red, brown and green 15 10
340 – 12f. green, brown and violet 70 10
DESIGNS: 4f. Cloves; 12f. Vanilla.

Issues of 1958–92. For issues between these dates, see under MALAGASY REPUBLIC.

362 Children with Mascot

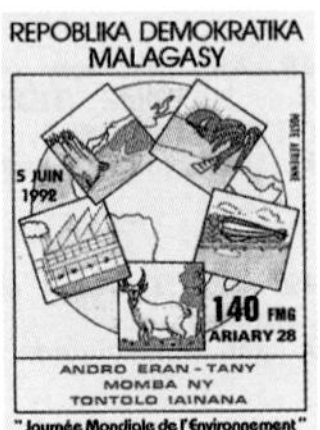

363 Environmental Projects

1992. School Sports Festival (1990).
910 **362** 140f. multicoloured . . . 35 10

1992. Air. World Environment Day.
911 **363** 140f. multicoloured . . . 10 10

364 Post Box and Globe

365 Basenji

1992. Air. World Post Day.
912 **364** 500f. multicoloured . . . 75 25

1992. Domestic Animals. Multicoloured.
913 140f. Type **365** 10 10
914 500f. Anglo-Arab horse . . . 90 25
915 640f. Tortoiseshell cat and kitten . . . . 1·10 30
916 1025f. Siamese and colourpoint (cats) . . . . 1·60 50
917 1140f. Holstein horse . . . . 2·25 60
918 5000f. German shepherd dogs 6·50 75

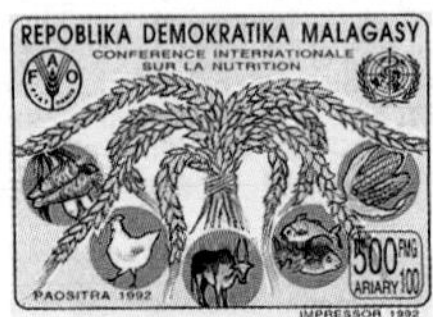

366 Foodstuffs

1992. International Nutrition Conference, Rome.
920 **366** 500f. multicoloured . . . 1·10 25

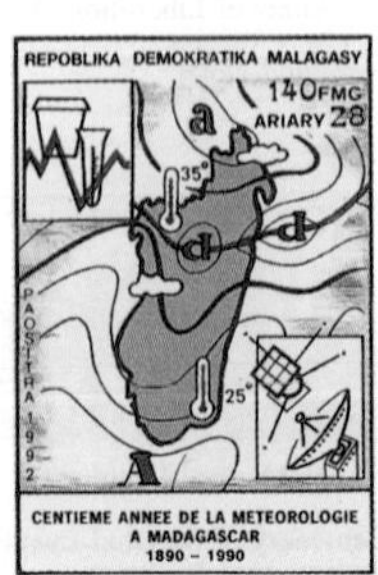

367 Weather Map

1992. Centenary of Meteorological Service.
921 **367** 140f. multicoloured . . . 35 10

368 "Eusemia bisma"

1992. Butterflies and Moths. Multicoloured.
922 15f. Type **368** 10 10
923 35f. Tailed comet moth (vert) 10 10
924 65f. "Alcides aurora" 10 10
925 140f. "Agarista agricola" . . 35 10
926 600f. "Trogonoptera croesus" 1·40 30
927 850f. "Trogonodtera priamus" . . . . 1·75 45
928 1300f. "Pereute leucodrosime" . . . . . . 2·25 70

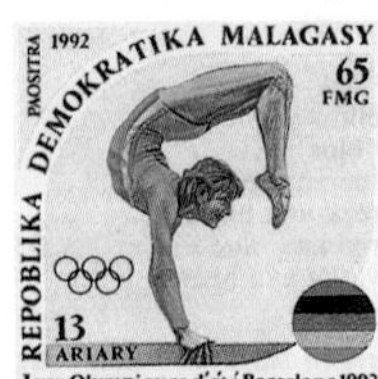

369 Barn Swallow

1992. Birds. Multicoloured.
930 40f. Type **369** 10 10
931 55f. Pied harrier (vert) . . . 10 10
932 60f. European cuckoo (vert) 10 10
933 140f. Sacred ibis 10 10
934 210f. Purple swamphen . . . 45 10
935 500f. Common roller . . . . 1·10 25
936 2000f. Golden oriole . . . . 4·00 1·10

370 Gymnastics

1992. Olympic Games, Barcelona. Multicoloured.
938 65f. Type **370** 10 10
939 70f. High jumping 10 10
940 120f. Archery 10 10
941 140f. Cycling 35 10
942 675f. Weightlifting . . . . . 1·10 30
943 720f. Boxing . . . . 1·40 35
944 1200f. Two-man kayak . . . 1·75 60

371 Pusher-tug, Pangalanes Canal

1993.
946 **371** 140f. multicoloured . . . 35 10

372 BMW 373 Hyacinth Macaw

1993. Motor Cars. Multicoloured.
947 20f. Type **372** 10 10
948 40f. Toyota "Carina" 10 10
949 60f. Cadillac 10 10
950 65f. Volvo 10 10
951 140f. Mercedes-Benz 10 10
952 640f. Ford "Sierra" . . . . 1·00 30
953 3000f. Honda "Concerto" . . 4·50 90

1993. Parrot Family. Multicoloured.
955 50f. Type **373** 10 10
956 60f. Cockatiel 10 10
957 140f. Budgerigar 10 10
958 500f. Jandaya conure 60 25
959 675f. Budgerigar (different) 1·10 35
960 800f. Red-fronted parakeet 1·40 45
961 1750f. Kea . . . . 2·75 65

375 Albert Einstein (physics, 1921) and Niels Bohr (physics, 1922)

1993. Nobel Prize Winners. Multicoloured.
964 500f. Type **375** 60 25
965 500f. Wolfgang Pauli (physics, 1945) and Max Born (physics, 1954) . . . 60 25
966 500f. Joseph Thomson (physics, 1906) and Johannes Stark (physics, 1919) 60 25
967 500f. Otto Hahn (physics, 1944) and Hideki Yukawa (physics, 1949) 60 25
968 500f. Owen Richardson (physics, 1928) and William Shockley (physics, 1956) . . 60 25
969 500f. Albert Michelson (physics, 1907) and Charles Townes (physics, 1964) . . 60 25
970 500f. Wilhelm Wien (physics, 1911) and Lev Landau (physics, 1962) 60 25
971 500f. Carl Braun (physics, 1909) and Sir Edward Appleton (physics, 1947) 60 25
972 500f. Percy Bridgman (physics, 1946) and Nikolai Semyonov (physics, 1956) 60 25
973 500f. Sir William Ramsay (chemistry, 1904) and Glenn Seaborg (chemistry, 1951) 60 25
974 500f. Otto Wallach (chemistry, 1910) and Hermann Staudinger (chemistry, 1953) 60 25
975 500f. Richard Synge (chemistry, 1952) and Axel Theorell (chemistry, 1955) 60 25
976 500f. Thomas Morgan (medicine, 1933) and Hermann Muller (medicine, 1946) 60 25
977 500f. Allvar Gullstrand (medicine, 1911) and Willem Einthoven (medicine, 1924) 60 25
978 500f. Sir Charles Sherrington (medicine, 1932) and Otto Loewi (medicine, 1936) . . 60 25
979 500f. Jules Bordet (medicine, 1936) and Sir Alexander Fleming (medicine, 1945) 60 25

376 1956 Bugatti

1993. Racing Cars and Railway Locomotives. Multicoloured.
980 20f. Type **376** 10 10
981 20f. 1968 Ferrari 10 10
982 20f. 1948 Class C62 steam locomotive, 1948, Japan . . 10 10
983 20f. Electric train, 1975, Russia 10 10
984 140f. 1962 Lotus Mk 25 . . . 10 10
985 140f. 1970 Matra 10 10
986 140f. Diesel locomotive, 1954, Norway 10 10
987 140f. Class 26 steam locomotive, 1982, South Africa 10 10
988 1250f. 1963 Porsche 90 65
989 1250f. 1980 Ligier JS 11 . . . 90 65
990 1250f. Metroliner electric train, 1967, U.S.A. 90 65
991 1250f. Diesel train, 1982, Canada 90 65
992 3000f. 1967 Honda . . . . . 2·10 1·50
993 3000f. 1992 Benetton B 192 2·10 1·50
994 3000f. Union Pacific Railroad diesel-electric locomotive, 1969, U.S.A. . . . . . . 2·10 2·10
995 3000f. TGV Atlantique express train, 1990, France 2·10 2·10

377 Pharaonic Ship

1993. Ships. Multicoloured.
996 5f. Type **377** 10 10
997 5f. Mediterranean carrack 10 10
998 5f. "Great Western" (sail paddle-steamer), 1837 . . 10 10
999 5f. "Mississippi" (paddle-steamer), 1850 . . . . . 10 10
1000 15f. Phoenician bireme . . . 10 10
1001 15f. Viking ship 10 10
1002 15f. "Clermont" (first commercial paddle-steamer), 1806 . . . . . 10 10
1003 15f. "Pourquoi Pas?" (Charcot's ship), 1936 . . 10 10
1004 140f. "Santa Maria" (Columbus's ship), 1492 10 10
1005 140f. H.M.S. "Victory" (ship of the line), 1765 . . 10 10
1006 140f. Motor yacht 10 10
1007 140f. "Bremen" (liner), 1950 10 10
1008 10000f. "Sovereign of the Seas" (galleon), 1637 . . 9·25 80
1009 10000f. "Cutty Sark" (clipper) . . . . 9·25 80
1010 10000f. "Savannah" (nuclear-powered freighter) . . . . 9·25 80
1011 10000f. "Condor" (hydrofoil) . . . . 9·25 80
No. 999 is wrongly inscribed "Mississipi".

378 Johannes Gutenberg and Printing Press

1993. Inventors. Multicoloured.
1012 500f. Type **378** 60 25
1013 500f. Sir Isaac Newton and telescope 60 25
1014 500f. John Dalton and atomic theory 60 25
1015 500f. Louis Jacques Daguerre and camera . . 60 25
1016 500f. Michael Faraday and electric motor 60 25
1017 500f. Wright brothers and "Flyer" 60 25
1018 500f. Alexander Bell and telephone 60 25
1019 500f. Thomas Edison and telegraph 60 25
1020 500f. Karl Benz and motor vehicle 60 25
1021 500f. Sir Charles Parsons and "Turbina" 60 25
1022 500f. Rudolf Diesel and diesel locomotive 60 35
1023 500f. Guglielmo Marconi and early radio 60 25
1024 500f. Lumiere brothers and cine-camera 60 35
1025 500f. Herman Oberth and space rocket 60 25
1026 500f. John Mauchly, J. Prosper Eckert and computer 60 25
1027 500f. Arthur Shawlow, compact disc and laser . . 60 25

379 Leonardo da Vinci and "Virgin of the Rocks"

1993. Painters. Multicoloured.
1028 50f. Type **379** 10 10
1029 50f. Titian and "Sacred and Profane Love" 10 10
1030 50f. Rembrandt and "Jeremiah crying" 10 10
1031 50f. J. M. W. Turner and "Ulysses" 10 10
1032 640f. Michelangelo and the Doni Tondo 70 30
1033 640f. Peter Paul Rubens and "Self-portrait" 70 30
1034 640f. Francisco Goya and "Don Manuel Osorio de Zuniga" 70 30
1035 640f. Eugene Delacroix and "Christ on Lake Gennesaret" 70 30
1036 1000f. Claude Monet and "Poppyfield" 95 50
1037 1000f. Paul Gauguin and "Two Tahitians" 95 50
1038 1000f. Henri Marie de Toulouse-Lautrec and "Woman with a Black Boa" 95 50
1039 1000f. Salvador Dali and "St. James of Compostela" 95 50
1040 2500f. Pierre Auguste Renoir and "Child carrying Flowers" . . . . 2·75 90
1041 2500f. Vincent Van Gogh and "Dr. Paul Gachet" 2·75 90
1042 2500f. Pablo Picasso and "Crying Woman" . . . . 2·75 90
1043 2500f. Andy Warhol and "Portrait of Elvis" . . . 2·75 90

380 Sunset Moth ("Chrysiridia madagascariensis")

1993. Butterflies, Moths and Birds. Multicoloured.
1044 45f. Type **380** 10 10
1045 45f. African monarch ("Hypolimnas misippus") 10 10
1046 45f. Southern crested Madagascar coucal ("Coua verreauxi") 10 10
1047 45f. African marsh owl ("Asio helvola") 10 10
1048 60f. "Charaxes antamboulou" 10 10
1049 60f. "Papilio antenor" 10 10
1050 60f. Crested Madagascar coucal ("Coua cristata") 10 10
1051 60f. Helmet bird ("Euryceros prevostii") 10 10
1052 140f. "Hypolimnas dexithea" 10 10
1053 140f. "Charaxes andronodorus" 10 10
1054 140f. Giant Madagascar coucal ("Couca gigas") 10 10
1055 140f. Madagascar red fody ("Foudia madagascarensis") 10 10
1056 3000f. "Euxanthe madagascarensis" 3·25 45
1057 3000f. "Papilio grosesmithi" 3·25 45
1058 3000f. Sicklebill ("Falculea palliata") 3·25 45
1059 3000f. Madagascar serpent eagle ("Eutriorchis astur") 3·25 45

Nos. 1044/59 were issued together, se-tenant, the butterfly and bird designs respectively forming composite designs.

381 Henri Dunant and Volunteers unloading Red Cross Lorry

1993. Anniversaries and Events. Multicoloured.
1060 500f. Type **381** (award of first Nobel Peace Prize, 1901) 35 25
1061 640f. Charles de Gaulle and battlefield (50th anniv of Battle of Bir-Hakeim (1992)) 45 30
1062 1025f. Crowd at Brandenburg Gate (bicentenary (1991) and fourth anniv of breach of Berlin Wall) 1·10 55
1063 1500f. Doctors giving health instruction to women (Rotary International and Lions International) 1·60 55
1064 3000f. Konrad Adenauer (German chancellor 1949–63, 24th death anniv (1991)) 3·25 60
1065 3500f. "LZ-4" (airship), 1908, and Count Ferdinand von Zeppelin (75th death anniv (1992)) 4·00 60

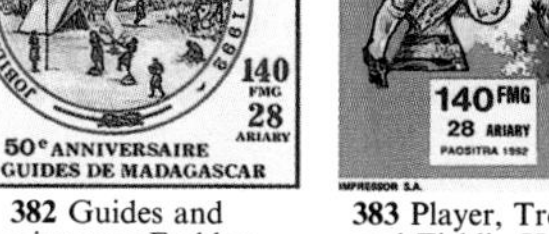

382 Guides and Anniversary Emblem

383 Player, Trophy and Ficklin Home, Macon

1993. Air. 50th Anniv of Madagascan Girl Guides.
1067 **382** 140f. multicoloured 10 10

1993. World Cup Football Championship, United States (1992). Multicoloured.
1068 140f. Type **383** 10 10
1069 640f. Player, trophy and Herndon Home, Atlanta 65 35
1070 1025f. Player, trophy and Cultural Centre, Augusta 1·40 55
1071 5000f. Player, trophy and Old Governor's Mansion, Milledgeville 6·00 1·00

1993. Various stamps optd with emblem and inscription. (a) Germany, World Cup Football Champion, 1990. Nos. 778/81 optd **VAINQEUR: ALLEMAGNE.**
1073 **328** 350f. multicoloured 25 15
1074 – 1000f. multicoloured 90 50
1075 – 1500f. multicoloured 1·50 80
1076 – 2500f. multicoloured 2·75 1·00

(b) Gold Medallists at Winter Olympic Games, Albertville (1992). Nos. 812/15 optd with Olympic rings, **"MEDAILLE D'OR"** and further inscr as below.
1077 350f. **BOB A QUATRE (AUT) INGO APPELT HARALD WINKLER GERHARD HAIDACHER THOMAS SCROLL** 25 15
1078 1000f. **1000 M. - OLAF ZINKE (GER)** 90 50
1079 1500f. **50 KM LIBRE BJOERN DAEHLIE (NOR)** 1·50 80
1080 2500f. **SUPER G MESSIEURS KJETIL-ANDRE AAMODT (NOR)** 2·75 1·25

(c) Anniversaries. Nos. 1060, 675 and 707 optd as listed below.
1082 500f. Red Cross and **130e ANNIVERSAIRE DE LA CREATION DE LA CROIX-ROUGE 1863–1993** 2·25 1·10
1083 550f. Lions emblem and **75eme ANNIVERSAIRE LIONS** 2·25 1·10
1084 1500f. Guitar and **THE ELVIS'S GUITAR 15TH ANNIVERSARY OF HIS DEATH 1977–1992** 1·75 80
1085 1500f. Guitar and **GUITARE ELVIS 15eme ANNIVERSAIRE DE SA MORT 1977–1992** 1·75 80

(d) 50th Death Anniv of Robert Baden-Powell (founder of Boy Scouts). Optd **50eme ANNIVERSAIRE DE LA MORT DE BADEN POWEL** and emblem. (i) On Nos. 870/5 with scout badge in wreath.
1086 **354** 140f. multicoloured 10 10
1087 – 500f. multicoloured 35 25
1088 – 640f. multicoloured 45 30
1089 – 1025f. multicoloured 1·10 30
1090 – 1140f. multicoloured 1·10 35
1091 – 3500f. multicoloured 3·25 1·10

(ii) On No. 676 with profile of Baden-Powell.
1093 1500f. multicoloured 1·75 80

(e) Bicentenary of French Republic. Nos. 761/5 optd **Republique Francaise** and emblem within oval and **BICENTENAIRE DE L'AN I DE LA REPUBLIQUE FRANCAISE.**
1094 250f. multicoloured 20 15
1095 350f. multicoloured 25 15
1096 1000f. multicoloured 1·10 50
1097 1500f. multicoloured 1·75 50
1098 2500f. multicoloured 2·75 90

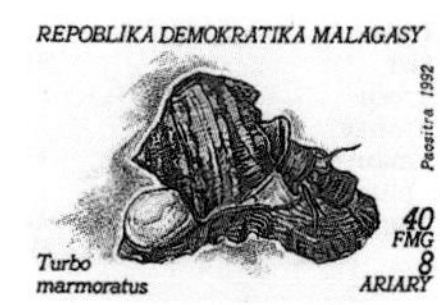

385 Great Green Turban

1993. Molluscs. Multicoloured.
1100 40f. Type **385** 10 10
1101 60f. Episcopal mitre 10 10
1102 65f. Common paper nautilis 10 10
1103 140f. Textile cone 10 10
1104 500f. European sea hare 90 25
1105 675f. "Harpa amouretta" 1·10 35
1106 2500f. Tiger cowrie 3·50 70

386 Tiger Shark

1993. Sharks. Multicoloured.
1108 10f. Type **386** 10 10
1109 45f. Japanese sawshark 10 10
1110 140f. Whale shark 15 10
1111 270f. Smooth hammerhead 30 20
1112 600f. Oceanic white-tipped shark 65 35
1113 1200f. Zebra shark 1·25 80
1114 1500f. Goblin shark 1·90 1·10

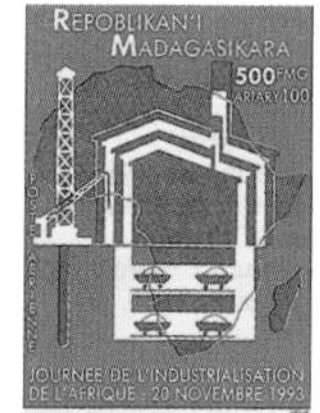

387 Map of Africa and Industry

1993. Air. African Industrialization Day.
1116 **387** 500f. red, yellow and blue 80 50

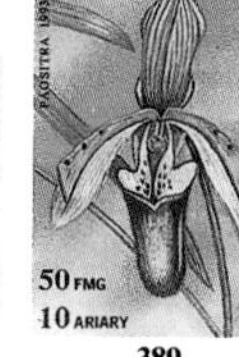

388 "Superviem Odoriko" Express Train

389 "Paphiopedilum siamense"

1993. Locomotives. Multicoloured.
1117 5f. Type **388** 10 10
1118 15f. Morrison Knudsen diesel locomotive No. 801 10 10
1119 140f. ER-200 diesel train, Russia 10 10
1120 265f. General Motors GP60 diesel-electric locomotive No. EKD-5, U.S.A. 20 15
1121 300f. New Jersey Transit diesel locomotive, U.S.A. 20 15
1122 575f. ICE high speed train, Germany 40 30
1123 2500f. X2000 high speed train, Sweden 1·75 1·25

1993. Orchids. Multicoloured.
1125 50f. Type **389** (wrongly inscr "Paphpiopedilum") 10 10
1126 65f. "Cypripedium calceolus" 10 10
1127 70f. "Ophrys oestrifera" 10 10
1128 140f. "Cephalanthera rubra" 10 10
1129 300f. "Cypripedium macranthon" 20 15
1130 640f. "Calanthe vestita" 80 30
1131 2500f. "Cypripedium guttatum" 3·25 90

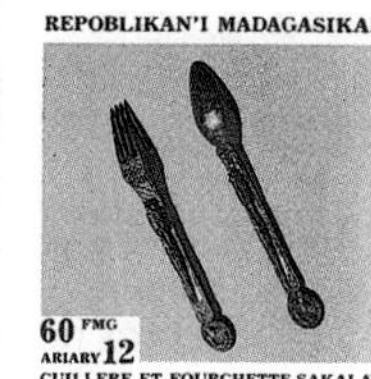

390 "Necrophorus tomentosus"

392 Fork and Spoon, Sakalava

391 Lufthansa Airliner, Germany

1994. Beetles. Multicoloured.
1133 20f. Type **390** 10 10
1134 60f. "Dynastes tityus" 10 10
1135 140f. "Megaloxanta bicolor" 10 10
1136 605f. Searcher 40 10
1137 720f. "Chrysochroa mirabilis" 50 15
1138 1000f. "Crioceris asparaqi" 70 25
1139 1500f. Rose chafer 1·10 35

1994. Aircraft. Multicoloured.
1141 10f. Type **391** 10 10
1142 10f. British Aerospace/Aerospatiale Concorde supersonic jetliner of Air France 10 10
1143 10f. Air Canada airliner 10 10
1144 10f. ANA airliner, Japan 10 10
1145 60f. Boeing 747 jetliner of British Airways 10 10
1146 60f. Dornier Do-X flying boat, Germany 10 10
1147 60f. Shinmeiwa flying boat, Japan 10 10
1148 60f. Royal Jordanian airliner 10 10
1149 640f. Alitalia airliner 45 15
1150 640f. French-European Development Project Hydro 2000 flying boat 45 15
1151 640f. Boeing 314 flying boat 45 15

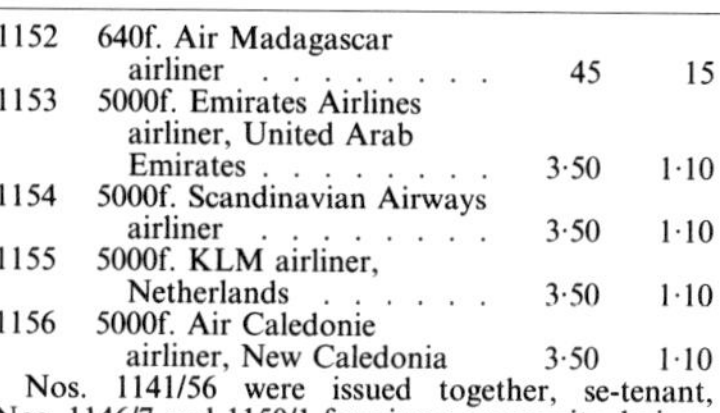

1152 640f. Air Madagascar airliner 45 15
1153 5000f. Emirates Airlines airliner, United Arab Emirates 3·50 1·10
1154 5000f. Scandinavian Airways airliner 3·50 1·10
1155 5000f. KLM airliner, Netherlands 3·50 1·10
1156 5000f. Air Caledonie airliner, New Caledonia 3·50 1·10

Nos. 1141/56 were issued together, se-tenant, Nos. 1146/7 and 1150/1 forming a composite design.

1994. Traditional Crafts. Multicoloured.
1157 30f. Silver jewellery, Mahafaly 10 10
1158 60f. Type **392** 10 10
1159 140f. Silver jewellery, Antandroy 10 10
1160 430f. Silver jewellery on table, Sakalava 30 10
1161 580f. Frames of decorated paper, Ambalavao 40 10
1162 1250f. Silver jewellery, Sakalava 90 30
1163 1500f. Marquetry table, Ambositra 1·10 35

393 "Chicoreus torrefactus" (shell)

1994. Marine Life. Multicoloured.
1165 15f. Type **393** 10 10
1166 15f. "Fasciolaria filamentosa" (shell) 10 10
1167 15f. Regal angelfish ("Pigopytes diacanthus") 10 10
1168 15f. Coelacanth ("Latimeria chalumnae") 10 10
1169 30f. "Stellaria solaris" (shell) 10 10
1170 30f. Ventral harp ("Harpa ventricosa") 10 10
1171 30f. Blue-tailed boxfish ("Ostracion cyanurus") 10 10
1172 30f. Clown wrasse ("Coris gaimardi") 10 10
1173 1250f. Lobster ("Panulirus sp.") 90 30
1174 1250f. "Stenopus hispidus" (crustacean) 90 30
1175 1250f. Undulate triggerfish ("Balistapus undulatus") 90 30
1176 1250f. Forceps butterflyfish ("Forcipiger longirostris") 90 30
1177 1500f. Hermit crab ("Pagure") 1·10 35
1178 1500f. Hermit crab ("Bernard l'Hermite") 1·10 35
1179 1500f. Diadem squirrelfish ("Adioryx diadema") 1·10 35
1180 1500f. Lunulate lionfish ("Pterois lunulata") 1·10 35

Nos. 1165/80 were issued together, se-tenant, the backgrounds forming a composite design.

394 Arms

395 Troops landing on Beach

1994. Air. Junior Economic Chamber Zone A (Africa, Middle East and Indian Ocean) Conference, Antananarivo. Multicoloured.
1181 140f. Type **394** 10 10
1182 500f. Arms as in Type **394** but with inscriptions differently arranged (vert) 70 20

1994. 50th Anniv of Allied Landings at Normandy. Multicoloured.
1183 1500f. Type **395** 1·10 35
1184 3000f. German troops defending ridge and allied troops (as T **397**) 2·25 75
1185 3000f. Airplanes over battle scene, trooper with U.S. flag and German officer (as T **397**) 2·25 75

Nos. 1183/5 were issued together, se-tenant, forming a composite design.

396 Emperor Angelfish

1994. Aquarium Fishes. Multicoloured.
1186 10f. Type **396** 10 10
1187 30f. Siamese fighting fish . . 10 10
1188 45f. Pearl gourami 10 10
1189 95f. Cuckoo-wrasse 10 10
1190 140f. Blotched upsidedown catfish ("Synodontis nigreventris") 10 10
1191 140f. Jack Dempsey ("Cichlasoma biocellatum") 10 10
1192 3500f. Mummichog . . . . 2·50 80

397 Notre Dame Cathedral, Armed Resistance Fighters and Rejoicing Crowd

1994. 50th Anniv of Liberation of Paris by Allied Forces. Multicoloured.
1194 1500f. Crowd and Arc de Triomphe (as T **395**) . . . 55 15
1195 3000f. Type **397** . . . . . . 1·10 35
1196 3000f. Eiffel Tower and tank convoy . . . . 1·10 35
Nos. 1194/6 were issued together, se-tenant, forming a composite design.

398 Emblem and "75"

1994. 75th Anniv of I.L.O.
1197 **398** 140f. multicoloured . . . 10 10

399 Biathlon

1994. Winter Olympic Games, Lillehammer, Norway. Multicoloured. (a) Without overprints.
1198 140f. Type **399** 10 10
1199 1250f. Ice hockey 45 15
1200 2000f. Figure skating . . . 75 25
1201 2500f. Skiing (downhill) . . . 95 30
(b) Gold Medal Winners. Nos. 1198/1201 optd.
1203 140f. Optd **M. BEDARD CANADA** 10 10
1204 1250f. Optd **MEDAILLE D'OR SUEDE** 45 15
1205 2000f. Optd **O. BAYUL UKRAINE** 75 25
1206 2500f. Optd **M. WASMEIER ALLEMAGNE** 95 30

401 Majestic performing Dressage Exercise and Windsor Hotel, 1892

1994. Olympic Games, Atlanta, U.S.A. Mult.
1208 640f. Type **401** 25 10
1209 1000f. Covington Courthouse, 1884, and putting the shot 35 10
1210 1500f. Table tennis and Carolton Community Activities Centre 55 15
1211 3000f. Newman Commercial Court Square, 1800, and footballer . . . . 1·10 35

402 Spider on Map of Madagascar

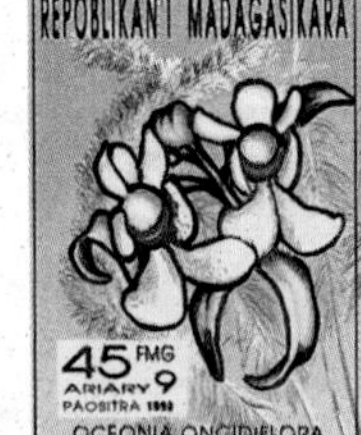

403 "Oceonia oncidiflora"

1994. "Archaea workmani" (spider).
1213 **402** 500f. multicoloured . . . 20 15

1994. Flowers, Fruit, Fungi and Vegetables. Multicoloured.
1214 45f. Type **403** 10 10
1215 45f. Breadfruit ("Artocarpus altilis") 10 10
1216 45f. "Russula annulata" . . 10 10
1217 45f. Sweet potato 10 10
1218 60f. "Cymbidella rhodochica" 10 10
1219 60f. "Eugenia malaceensis" 10 10
1220 60f. "Lactarius claricolor" 10 10
1221 60f. Yam 10 10
1222 140f. Vanilla orchid ("Vanilla planifolia") . . 10 10
1223 140f. "Jambosa domestica" 10 10
1224 140f. "Russula tuberculosa" 10 10
1225 140f. Avocado 10 10
1226 3000f. "Phaius humblotii" 1·10 35
1227 3000f. Papaya . . . . . . 1·10 35
1228 3000f. "Russula fistulosa" 1·10 35
1229 3000f. Manioc . . . . . . 1·10 35
Nos. 1214/29 were issued together, se-tenant, the backgrounds forming a composite design.

PARCEL POST STAMPS

1919. Receipt stamp of France surch **MADAGASCAR ET DEPENDANCES 0fr.10 COLIS POSTAUX.**
P81 0f.10 on 10c. grey . . . . . 5·50 4·75

1919. Fiscal stamp of Madagascar surch **COLIS POSTAUX 0f.10.**
P82 0f.10 on 1f. pink . . . . . . 70·00 42·00

1919. Fiscal stamps surch **Madagascar et Dependances** (in capitals on No. P83) **COLIS POSTAUX 0f.10.**
P83 0f.10 pink . . . . 12·00 6·75
P84 0f.10 red and green . . . . 3·50 3·75
P85 0f.10 black and green . . . . 3·50 3·25

POSTAGE DUE STAMPS

1896. Postage Due stamps of Fr. Colonies optd **Madagascar et DEPENDANCES.**
D17 U 5c. blue . . . . 5·50 9·00
D18 10c. brown . . . . . . 5·50 7·00
D19 20c. yellow . . . . . . 4·75 8·00
D20 30c. red . . . . 8·50 7·75
D21 40c. mauve . . . . . . 60·00 48·00
D22 50c. violet . . . . . . 5·00 5·00
D23 1f. green . . . . 90·00 60·00

D 6 Governor's Palace, Tananarive

D 37

1908.
D70 D 6 2c. red 10 10
D71 4c. violet 10 15
D72 5c. green 10 80
D73 10c. red 10 10
D74 20c. olive . . . . . . 10 1·90
D75 40c. brown on cream . . 15 2·50
D76 50c. brown on blue . . . 15 1·75
D77 60c. red . . . . 35 2·75
D78 1f. blue . . . . 30 1·50

1924. Surch in figures.
D123 D 6 60c. on 1f. red . . . . 55 3·75
D124 2f. on 1f. purple . . . 30 3·00
D125 3f. on 1f. blue . . . . 35 3·00

1942. Free French Administration. Optd **FRANCE LIBRE** or surch also.
D254 D 6 10c. red . . . . 1·40 3·25
D255 20c. green . . . . . . 35 3·25
D256 0,30 on 5c. green . . . 2·75 3·25
D257 40c. brown on cream . . 2·25 3·25
D258 50c. brown and blue . . 2·00 3·25
D259 60c. red . . . . 2·25 3·25
D260 1f. blue . . . . 30 3·00
D261 1f. on 2c. purple . . . 7·00 8·50
D262 2f. on 4c. violet . . . . 3·75 4·25
D263 2f. on 1f. mauve . . . 2·00 3·25
D264 3f. on 1f. blue . . . . 2·50 3·00

1947.
D319 D 37 10c. mauve . . . . . 10 2·25
D320 30c. brown . . . . . . 10 2·75
D321 50c. green . . . . . . 10 2·75
D322 1f. brown . . . . . . 10 2·00
D323 2f. red . . . . 90 1·60
D324 3f. brown . . . . . . 95 1·75
D325 4f. blue . . . . 90 2·50
D326 5f. red . . . . 1·40 2·75
D327 10f. green . . . . . . 1·10 45
D328 20f. blue . . . . . . 1·25 3·50

APPENDIX

The following stamps have either been issued in excess of postal needs or have not been available to the public in reasonable quantities at face value.

1992.

Olympic Games, Barcelona. 500f. (on gold foil).

1993.

Bicentenary of French Republic. 1989 "Philexfrance 89" issue optd. 5000f.

1994.

Elvis Presley (entertainer). 10000f. (on gold foil).

World Cup Football Championship, U.S.A. 10000f. (on gold foil).

Winter Olympic Games, Lillehammer, Norway. 10000f. (on gold foil).

Olympic Games, Atlanta, U.S.A. 5000f. (on gold foil).

MADEIRA Pt. 9

A Portuguese island in the Atlantic Ocean off the N.W. coast of Africa. From 1868 to 1929 and from 1980 separate issues were made.

1868. 1000 reis = 1 milreis.
1912. 100 centavos = 1 escudo.
2002. 100 cents = 1 euro.

Nos. 1/78b are stamps of Portugal optd **MADEIRA**.

1868. With curved value label. Imperf.
1 14 20r. bistre £180 £140
2 50r. green £180 £140
3 80r. orange £190 £140
4 100r. lilac £100 £140

1868. With curved value label. Perf.
10 14 5r. black . . . . 50·00 35·00
13 10r. yellow . . . . 85·00 75·00
14 20r. bistre £130 £100
15 25r. red . . . . 50·00 11·00
16 50r. green £160 £140
17 80r. orange £160 £140
19 100r. mauve £160 £140
20 120r. blue . . . . £100 80·00
21 240r. mauve £450 £400

1871. With straight value label.
30 15 5r. black . . . . 8·25 5·75
47 10r. yellow . . . . 26·00 20·00
72a 10r. green . . . . 60·00 50·00
48 15r. brown . . . . 18·00 11·00
49 20r. bistre . . . . 29·00 20·00
34 25r. pink . . . . 10·50 4·00
51 50r. green . . . . 60·00 27·00
71 50r. blue . . . . £110 55·00
36 80r. orange . . . . £100 75·00
53 100r. mauve . . . . 80·00 48·00
38 120r. blue . . . . £100 80·00
55 150r. blue £160 £130
74 150r. yellow £250 £225
39 240r. lilac £650 £500
67 300r. lilac . . . . 70·00 65·00

1880. Stamps of 1880.
79 16 5r. black . . . . 24·00 20·00
78 25r. grey . . . . 26·00 20·00
78b 25r. brown . . . . 26·00 20·00
77 17 25r. grey . . . . 26·00 20·00

1898. Vasco da Gama. As Nos. 378/85 of Portugal.
134 2½r. green . . . . 2·25 1·25
135 5r. red . . . . 2·25 1·25
136 10r. purple . . . . 3·00 1·50
137 25r. green . . . . 2·50 1·25
138 50r. blue . . . . 8·25 3·25
139 75r. brown . . . . 10·00 6·75
140 100r. brown . . . . 10·00 6·75
141 150r. brown . . . . 13·50 11·00
For Nos. 134/41 with **REPUBLICA** overprint, see Nos. 455/62 of Portugal.

6 Ceres

7 20r. Stamp, 1868

1929. Funchal Museum Fund. Value in black.
148 6 3c. violet 60 60
149 4c. yellow 60 60
150 5c. blue 60 60
151 6c. brown 75 75
152 10c. red 75 75
153 15c. green 75 75
154 16c. brown 75 75
155 25c. purple 80 80
156 32c. green 80 80
157 40c. brown 80 80
158 50c. grey 80 80
159 64c. blue 80 80
160 80c. brown 80 80
161 96c. red . . . . 3·25 3·25
162 1e. black 70 70
163 1e.20 pink 70 70
164 1e.60 blue 70 70
165 2e.40 yellow . . . . 1·00 1·00
166 3e.36 green . . . . 1·25 1·25
167 4e.50 red . . . . 1·25 1·25
168 7e. blue . . . . 2·50 2·50

1980. 112th Anniv of First Overprinted Madeira Stamps.
169 7 6e.50 black, bistre and green 20 10
170 – 19e.50 black, purple and red 90 55
DESIGN: 19e.50, 100r. stamp, 1868.

8 Ox Sledge

1980. World Tourism Conference, Manila, Philippines. Multicoloured.
172 50c. Type **8** 10 10
173 1e. Wine and grapes 10 10
174 5e. Map of Madeira 45 10
175 6e.50 Basketwork 55 10
176 8e. Orchid 85 35
177 30e. Fishing boat . . . . . . 1·70 60

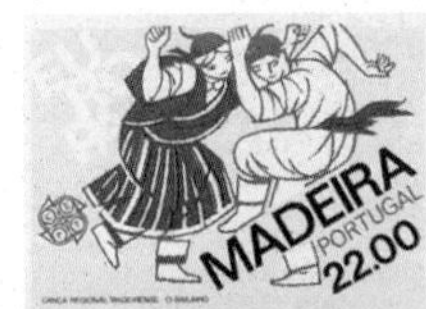

9 O Bailinho (folk dance)

1981. Europa.
178 9 22e. multicoloured . . . . . 1·30 70

10 Portuguese Caravel approaching Madeira

11 "Dactylorhiza foliosa"

1981. 560th Anniv (1980) of Discovery of Madeira. Multicoloured.
180 8e.50 Type **10** 45 10
181 33e.50 Prince Henry the Navigator and map of Atlantic Ocean . . . . . . 1·80 55

1981. Regional Flowers. Multicoloured.
182 7e. Type **11** 30 15
183 8e.50 "Geranium maderense" 40 15
184 9e. "Goodyera macrophylla" 40 10
185 10e. "Armeria maderensis" 45 10
186 12e.50 "Matthiola maderensis" 25 10
187 20e. "Isoplexis sceptrum" . . 70 40
188 27e. "Viola paradoxa" . . . 1·20 55
189 30e. "Erica maderensis" . . . 85 25
190 33e.50 "Scilla maderensis" . . 1·20 75
191 37e.50 "Cirsium latifolium" 90 55
192 50e. "Echium candicans" . . 1·60 80
193 100e. "Clethra arborea" . . . 2·20 85

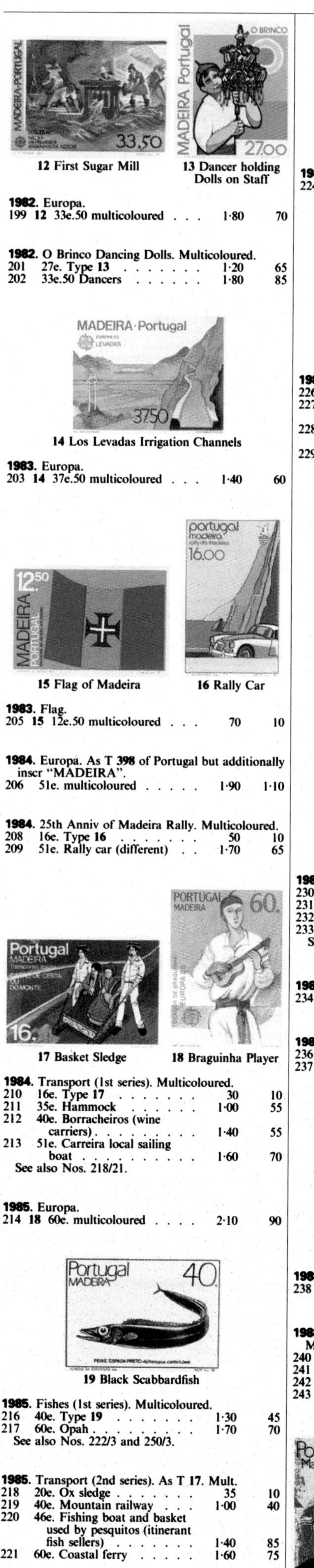

12 First Sugar Mill 13 Dancer holding Dolls on Staff

1982. Europa.
199 **12** 33e.50 multicoloured . . . 1·80 70

1982. O Brinco Dancing Dolls. Multicoloured.
201 27e. Type **13** . . . . 1·20 65
202 33e.50 Dancers . . . . . . 1·80 85

14 Los Levadas Irrigation Channels

1983. Europa.
203 **14** 37e.50 multicoloured . . . 1·40 60

15 Flag of Madeira 16 Rally Car

1983. Flag.
205 **15** 12e.50 multicoloured . . . 70 10

1984. Europa. As T **398** of Portugal but additionally inscr "MADEIRA".
206 51e. multicoloured . . . . . 1·90 1·10

1984. 25th Anniv of Madeira Rally. Multicoloured.
208 16e. Type **16** 50 10
209 51e. Rally car (different) . . 1·70 65

17 Basket Sledge 18 Braguinha Player

1984. Transport (1st series). Multicoloured.
210 16e. Type **17** 30 10
211 35e. Hammock . . . . . . 1·00 55
212 40e. Borracheiros (wine carriers) . . . . 1·40 55
213 51e. Carreira local sailing boat . . . . 1·60 70
See also Nos. 218/21.

1985. Europa.
214 **18** 60e. multicoloured . . . . 2·10 90

19 Black Scabbardfish

1985. Fishes (1st series). Multicoloured.
216 40e. Type **19** . . . . 1·30 45
217 60e. Opah . . . . 1·70 70
See also Nos. 222/3 and 250/3.

1985. Transport (2nd series). As T **17**. Mult.
218 20e. Ox sledge 35 10
219 40e. Mountain railway . . . 1·00 40
220 46e. Fishing boat and basket used by pesquitos (itinerant fish sellers) . . . . 1·40 85
221 60e. Coastal ferry . . . . . 1·60 75

1986. Fishes (2nd series). As T **19**. Multicoloured.
222 20e. Big-eyed tuna 60 10
223 75e. Alfonsino . . . . 2·75 80

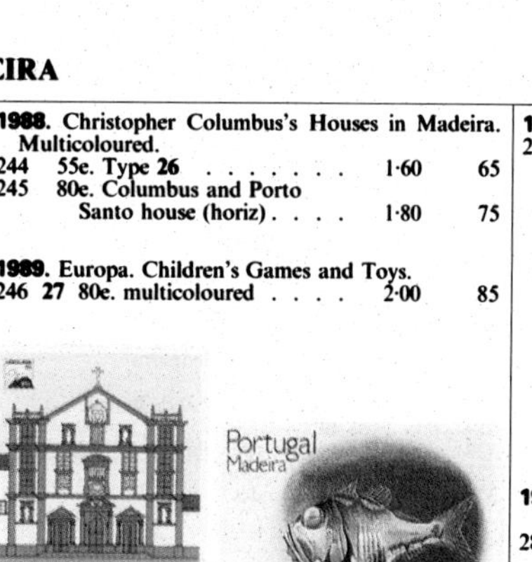

20 Cory's Shearwater and Tanker

1986. Europa.
224 **20** 68e.50 multicoloured . . . 2·30 95

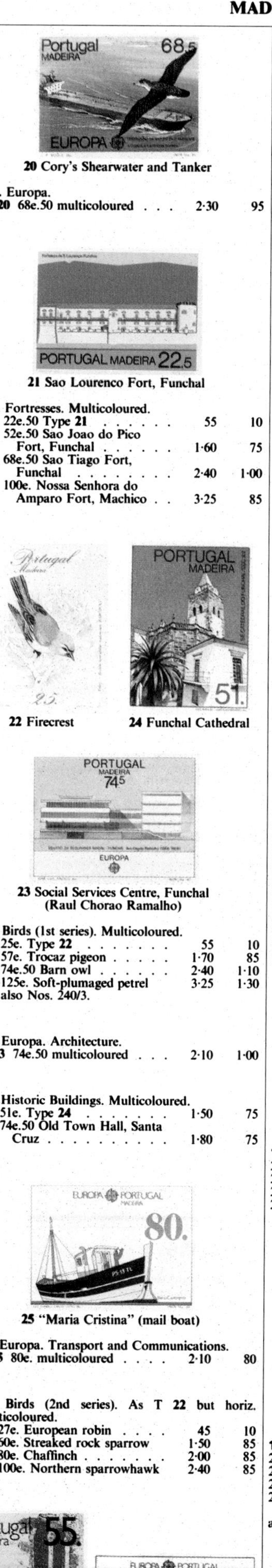

21 Sao Lourenco Fort, Funchal

1986. Fortresses. Multicoloured.
226 22e.50 Type **21** 55 10
227 52e.50 Sao Joao do Pico Fort, Funchal . . . . . . 1·60 75
228 68e.50 Sao Tiago Fort, Funchal . . . . 2·40 1·00
229 100e. Nossa Senhora do Amparo Fort, Machico . . 3·25 85

22 Firecrest 24 Funchal Cathedral

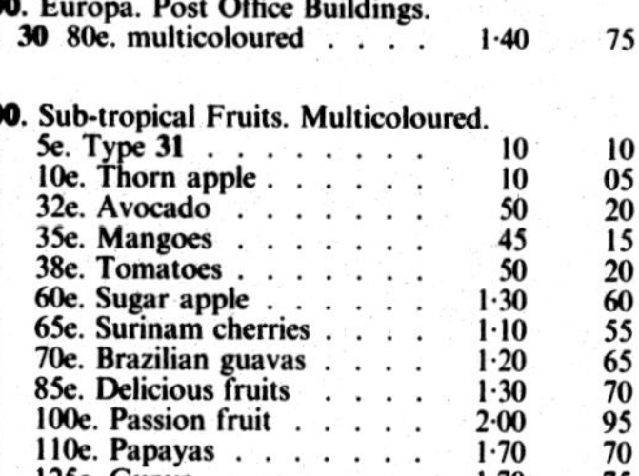

23 Social Services Centre, Funchal (Raul Chorao Ramalho)

1987. Birds (1st series). Multicoloured.
230 25e. Type **22** 55 10
231 57e. Trocaz pigeon . . . . . 1·70 85
232 74e.50 Barn owl . . . . . . 2·40 1·10
233 125e. Soft-plumaged petrel 3·25 1·30
See also Nos. 240/3.

1987. Europa. Architecture.
234 **23** 74e.50 multicoloured . . . 2·10 1·00

1987. Historic Buildings. Multicoloured.
236 51e. Type **24** . . . . 1·50 75
237 74e.50 Old Town Hall, Santa Cruz . . . . 1·80 75

25 "Maria Cristina" (mail boat)

1988. Europa. Transport and Communications.
238 **25** 80e. multicoloured . . . . 2·10 80

1988. Birds (2nd series). As T **22** but horiz. Multicoloured.
240 27e. European robin 45 10
241 60e. Streaked rock sparrow 1·50 85
242 80e. Chaffinch . . . . 2·00 85
243 100e. Northern sparrowhawk 2·40 85

26 Columbus and Funchal House 27 Child flying Kite

1988. Christopher Columbus's Houses in Madeira. Multicoloured.
244 55e. Type **26** . . . . 1·60 65
245 80e. Columbus and Porto Santo house (horiz) . . . . 1·80 75

1989. Europa. Children's Games and Toys.
246 **27** 80e. multicoloured . . . . 2·00 85

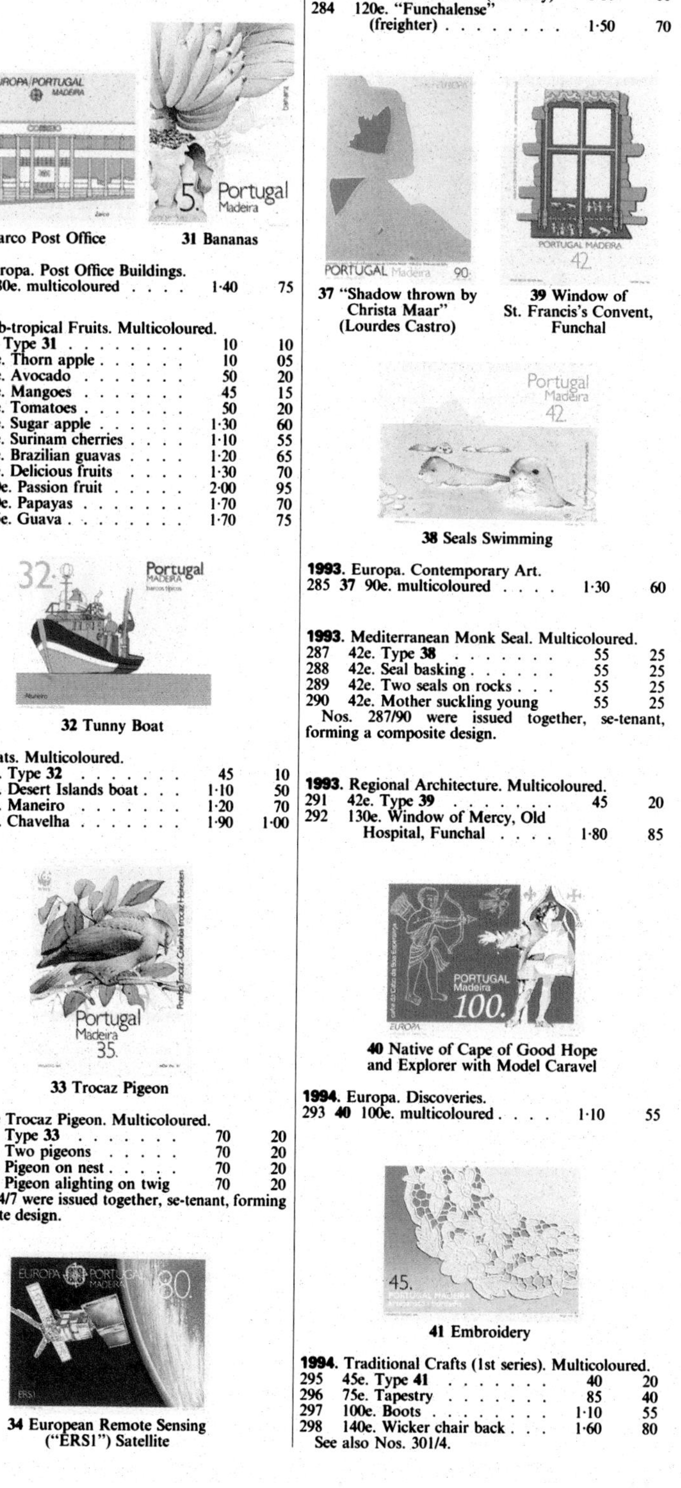

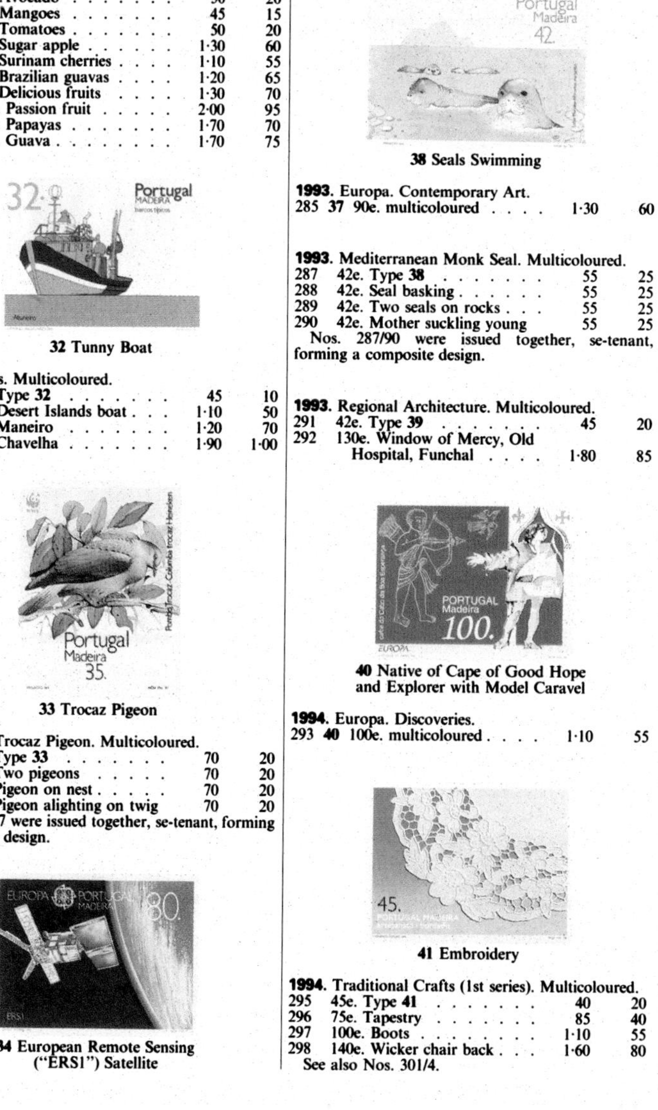

28 Church of St. John the Evangelist 29 Spiny Hatchetfish

1989. "Brasiliana 89" Stamp Exhibition, Rio de Janeiro. Madeiran Churches. Multicoloured.
248 29e. Type **28** 45 10
249 87e. St. Clara's Church and Convent . . . . 2·00 1·00

1989. Fishes (3rd series). Multicoloured.
250 29e. Type **29** 45 10
251 60e. Dog wrasse . . . . . . 1·30 70
252 87e. Rainbow wrasse . . . . 2·00 95
253 100e. Madeiran scorpionfish 2·00 1·30

30 Zarco Post Office 31 Bananas

1990. Europa. Post Office Buildings.
254 **30** 80e. multicoloured . . . . 1·40 75

1990. Sub-tropical Fruits. Multicoloured.
256 5e. Type **31** 10 10
257 10e. Thorn apple 10 05
258 32e. Avocado 50 20
259 35e. Mangoes 45 15
260 38e. Tomatoes 50 20
261 60e. Sugar apple . . . . . . 1·30 60
262 65e. Surinam cherries . . . . 1·10 55
263 70e. Brazilian guavas . . . . 1·20 65
264 85e. Delicious fruits . . . . 1·30 70
265 100e. Passion fruit . . . . . 2·00 95
266 110e. Papayas . . . . 1·70 70
267 125e. Guava . . . . 1·70 75

32 Tunny Boat

1990. Boats. Multicoloured.
270 32e. Type **32** 45 10
271 60e. Desert Islands boat . . . 1·10 50
272 70e. Maneiro . . . . 1·20 70
273 95e. Chavelha . . . . 1·90 1·00

33 Trocaz Pigeon

1991. The Trocaz Pigeon. Multicoloured.
274 35e. Type **33** 70 20
275 35e. Two pigeons 70 20
276 35e. Pigeon on nest 70 20
277 35e. Pigeon alighting on twig 70 20
Nos. 264/7 were issued together, se-tenant, forming a composite design.

34 European Remote Sensing ("ERS1") Satellite

1991. Europa. Europe in Space.
278 **34** 80e. multicoloured . . . . 1·40 85

35 Columbus and Funchal House

1992. Europa. 500th Anniv of Discovery of America by Columbus.
280 **35** 85e. multicoloured . . . . 1·10 60

36 "Gaviao" (ferry)

1992. Inter-island Ships. Multicoloured.
281 38e. Type **36** 45 15
282 65e. "Independencia" (catamaran ferry) 90 50
283 85e. "Madeirense" (car ferry) 1·10 60
284 120e. "Funchalense" (freighter) . . . . 1·50 70

37 "Shadow thrown by Christa Maar" (Lourdes Castro) 39 Window of St. Francis's Convent, Funchal

38 Seals Swimming

1993. Europa. Contemporary Art.
285 **37** 90e. multicoloured . . . . 1·30 60

1993. Mediterranean Monk Seal. Multicoloured.
287 42e. Type **38** 55 25
288 42e. Seal basking 55 25
289 42e. Two seals on rocks . . . 55 25
290 42e. Mother suckling young 55 25
Nos. 287/90 were issued together, se-tenant, forming a composite design.

1993. Regional Architecture. Multicoloured.
291 42e. Type **39** 45 20
292 130e. Window of Mercy, Old Hospital, Funchal . . . . 1·80 85

40 Native of Cape of Good Hope and Explorer with Model Caravel

1994. Europa. Discoveries.
293 **40** 100e. multicoloured . . . . 1·10 55

41 Embroidery

1994. Traditional Crafts (1st series). Multicoloured.
295 45e. Type **41** 40 20
296 75e. Tapestry 85 40
297 100e. Boots . . . . 1·10 55
298 140e. Wicker chair back . . . 1·60 80
See also Nos. 301/4.

42 Funchal

43 Bread Dough Figures

1994. District Arms. Multicoloured.
299 45e. Type **42** 40 20
300 140e. Porto Santo . . . . . 1·40 70

1995. Traditional Crafts (2nd series). Mult.
301 45e. Type **43** 40 25
302 80e. Inlaid wooden box . . . 85 40
303 95e. Bamboo cage 95 55
304 135e. Woollen bonnet . . . . 1·20 65

44 Guiomar Vilhena (entrepreneur)

1996. Europa. Famous Women.
305 **44** 98e. multicoloured 95 45

45 "Adoration of the Magi"

1996. Religious Paintings by Flemish Artists. Multicoloured.
307 47e. Type **45** 40 20
308 78e. "St. Mary Magdalene" 80 40
309 98e. "The Annunciation" (horiz) 95 50
310 140e. "Saints Peter, Paul and Andrew" (horiz) . . . . . 1·20 70

46 "Eumichtis albostigmata" (moth)

1997. Butterflies and Moths. Multicoloured.
311 49e. Type **46** 40 20
312 80e. Menophra maderae (moth) 75 30
313 100e. Painted lady 85 50
314 140e. Large white . . . . . 1·30 70

47 Robert Achim and Anne of Arfet (Legend of Machico)

1997. Europa. Tales and Legends.
315 **47** 100e. multicoloured . . . . 1·00 45

48 New Year's Eve Fireworks Display, Funchal

1998. Europa. National Festivals.
317 **48** 100e. multicoloured 85 45

49 "Gonepteryx cleopatra"

1998. Butterflies and Moths. Multicoloured.
319 50e. Type **49** 40 20
320 85e. "Xanthorhoe rupicola" 70 35
321 100e. "Noctua teixeirai" . . 85 40
322 140e. "Xenochlorodes nubigena" . . . . 1·20 65

50 Madeira Island Nature Park

1999. Europa. Parks and Gardens.
323 **50** 100e. multicoloured 85 40

51 Medieval Floor Tile

1999. Tiles from Frederico de Freitas Collection, Funchal. Multicoloured.
325 51e. Type **51** 40 20
326 80e. English art-nouveau tile (19th–20th century) 70 35
327 95e. Persian tile (14th century) 85 40
328 100e. Spanish Moor tile (13th century) 90 40
329 140e. Dutch Delft tile (18th century) . . . . 1·20 60
330 210e. Syrian tile (13th–14th century) . . . . 1·70 90

52 "Building Europe"

2000. Europa.
332 **52** 100e. multicoloured 85 40

53 Mountain Orchid

2000. Plants of Laurissilva Forest. Multicoloured.
334 52e. Type **53** 40 20
335 85e. White orchid 70 35
336 100e. Leafy plant 80 40
337 100e. Laurel 80 40
338 140e. Barbusano . . . . . . 1·10 55
339 350e. Visco . . . . 2·75 1·40

54 Marine Life

2001. Europa. Water Resources.
341 **54** 105e. multicoloured 85 40

55 Musicians

2001. Traditions of Madeira. Multicoloured.
343 53e. Type **55** 40 20
344 85e. Couple carrying produce 65 30
345 105e. Couple selling goods 80 40

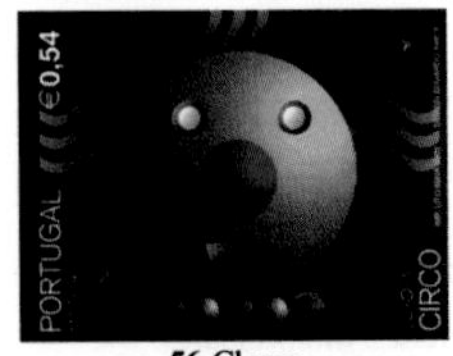
56 Clown

2002. Europa. Circus.
347 **56** 54c. multicoloured 75 45
MS348 140 × 110 mm. No. 347 × 3 2·30 2·30

57 Turtle Doves (*Streptopelia turtur*)

2002. Birds. Multicoloured.
349 28c. Type **57** 40 20
350 28c. Perching dove 40 20
351 28c. Dove with raised wings 40 20
352 28c. Dove with chicks . . . 40 20

CHARITY TAX STAMPS

The note under this heading in Portugal also applies here.

1925. As Marquis de Pombal stamps of Portugal but inscr "MADEIRA".
C142 **C 73** 15c. grey . . . . . . 1·25 1·25
C143 – 15c. grey . . . . . . 1·25 1·25
C144 **C 75** 15c. grey . . . . . . 1·25 1·25

NEWSPAPER STAMP

1876. Newspaper stamp of Portugal optd **MADEIRA.**
N69 **N 17** 2½r. green . . . . . . 8·00 3·25

POSTAGE DUE STAMPS

1925. Marquis de Pombal stamps as Nos. C1/3 optd **MULTA.**
D145 **C 73** 30c. grey . . . . . . 1·25 1·25
D146 – 30c. grey . . . . . . 1·25 1·25
D147 **C 75** 30c. grey . . . . . . 1·25 1·25

MAFEKING Pt. 1

A town in the Cape of Good Hope. Special stamps issued by British garrison during Boer War.

12 pence = 1 shilling;
20 shillings = 1 pound.

1900. Surch **MAFEKING, BESIEGED.** and value.
(a) On Cape of Good Hope stamps.
1 **6** 1d. on ½d. green . . . . . . £180 60·00
2 **17** 1d. on ½d. green . . . . . . £225 70·00
3 3d. on 1d. red . . . . £200 50·00
4 **6** 6d. on 3d. mauve £26000 £250
5 1s. on 4d. olive £6000 £325

(b) On stamps of Bechuanaland Protectorate (opts on Great Britain).
6 **71** 1d. on ½d. red (No. 59) . . £180 55·00
7 **57** 3d. on 1d. lilac (No. 61) . . £850 85·00
13 **73** 6d. on 2d. green and red (No. 62) . . . . £1100 70·00
9 **75** 6d. on 3d. purple on yellow (No. 63) £4250 £250
14 **79** 1s. on 6d. purple on red (No. 65) . . . . £4000 85·00

(c) On stamps of British Bechuanaland (opts on Great Britain).
10 **3** 6d. on 3d. lilac and black (No. 12) . . . . £350 60·00
11 **76** 1s. on 4d. green and brown (No. 35) . . . . £1200 75·00
15 **79** 1s. on 6d. purple on red (No. 36) £14000 £650
16 **82** 2s. on 1s. green (No. 37) . . £7500 £350

3 Cadet Sgt.-Major Goodyear

4 General Baden-Powell

1900.
17 **3** 1d. blue on blue £800 £275
20 **4** 3d. blue on blue £1200 £350

MAHRA SULTANATE OF QISHN AND SOCOTRA Pt. 1

The National Liberation Front took control on 1 October 1967, and full independence was granted by Great Britain on 30 November 1967. Subsequently part of Southern Yemen.

1000 fils = 1 dinar.

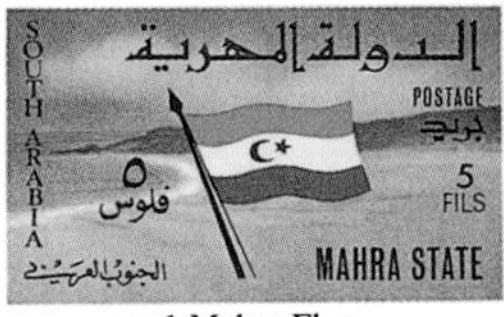
1 Mahra Flag

1967.
1 **1** 5f. multicoloured . . . . . . 1·50 40
2 10f. multicoloured . . . . . 1·50 40
3 15f. multicoloured . . . . . 1·50 40
4 20f. multicoloured . . . . . 1·50 40
5 25f. multicoloured . . . . . 1·50 40
6 35f. multicoloured . . . . . 1·50 40
7 50f. multicoloured . . . . . 1·50 40
8 65f. multicoloured . . . . . 1·50 40
9 100f. multicoloured . . . . . 1·50 40
10 250f. multicoloured . . . . . 1·50 45
11 500f. multicoloured . . . . . 1·50 60

APPENDIX

The following stamps have either been issued in excess of postal needs or have not been available to the public in reasonable quantities at face value.

1967.
Scout Jamboree, Idaho. 15, 75, 100, 150f.

President Kennedy Commemoration. Postage 10, 15, 25, 50, 75, 100, 150f.; Air 250, 500f.

Olympic Games, Mexico (1968). Postage 10, 25, 50f.; Air 250, 500f.

For later issues see **SOUTHERN YEMEN** and **YEMEN PEOPLE'S DEMOCRATIC REPUBLIC** in Volume 4.

MALACCA Pt. 1

A British Settlement on the Malay Peninsula which became a state of the Federation of Malaya, incorporated in Malaysia in 1963.

100 cents = 1 dollar (Malayan).

1948. Silver Wedding. As T **4b/c** of Pitcairn Islands.
1 10c. violet . . . . 30 1·75
2 $5 brown . . . . 28·00 38·00

1949. As T **58** of Straits Settlements.
3 1c. black 30 70
4 2c. orange 80 45
5 3c. green . . . . 30 1·75
6 4c. brown 30 10
6a 5c. purple . . . . 60 1·50
7 6c. grey 75 85
8 8c. red . . . . 75 5·50
8a 8c. green . . . . 1·00 4·50
9 10c. mauve 30 10
9a 12c. red . . . . 1·25 5·50
10 15c. blue . . . . 2·00 60
11 20c. black and green . . . . 50 6·00
11a 20c. blue . . . . 3·00 2·50
12 25c. purple and orange . . . 50 70
12a 35c. red and purple . . . . . 1·50 3·00
13 40c. red and purple . . . . . 1·25 11·00
14 50c. black and blue . . . . . 1·00 1·25
15 $1 blue and purple . . . . . 8·00 19·00
16 $2 green and red . . . . . . 20·00 21·00
17 $5 green and brown . . . . 42·00 35·00

1949. U.P.U. As T **4d/g** of Pitcairn Islands.
18 10c. purple 25 50
19 15c. blue . . . . 1·75 1·75
20 25c. orange . . . . 85 4·25
21 50c. black . . . . 60 4·25

1953. Coronation. As T **4h** of Pitcairn Islands.
22 10c. black and purple . . . . 75 1·25

1 Queen Elizabeth II

1954.

23 1 1c. black 10 60
24 2c. orange . . . . 30 1·00
25 4c. brown 40 10
26 5c. mauve . . . . 30 2·25
27 6c. grey 10 30
28 8c. green . . . . 40 2·50
29 10c. purple 80 10
30 12c. red . . . . 30 2·75
31 20c. blue . . . . 20 1·25
32 25c. purple and orange . . . 20 1·50
33 30c. red and purple 20 30
34 35c. red and purple . . . . 20 1·25
35 50c. black and blue . . . . 50 2·25
36 $1 blue and purple . . . . 6·00 7·50
37 $2 green and red . . . . . 22·00 32·00
38 $5 green and brown . . . . 23·00 40·00

1957. As Nos. 92/102 of Kedah but inset portrait of Queen Elizabeth II.
39 1c. black 10 40
40 2c. red 10 40
41 4c. sepia 30 10
42 5c. lake 20 10
43 8c. green . . . . 1·25 2·50
44 10c. sepia 30 10
45 20c. blue 30 50
46 50c. black and blue 30 75
47 $1 blue and purple . . . . 2·50 2·75
48 $2 green and red . . . . . 11·00 20·00
49 $5 brown and green . . . . 14·00 35·00

2 Copra

1960. As Nos. 39/49 but with inset picture of Melaka tree and Pelandok (mouse-deer) as in T 2.
50 1c. black 10 30
51 2c. red 10 50
52 4c. sepia 10 10
53 5c. lake 10 10
54 8c. green . . . . 2·75 2·75
55 10c. purple 30 10
56 20c. blue 75 70
57 50c. black and blue 60 70
58 $1 blue and purple . . . . 2·25 2·50
59 $2 green and red . . . . . 6·00 8·50
60 $5 brown and green . . . . 9·00 13·00

3 "Vanda hookeriana"

1965. As Nos. 115/21 of Kedah but with Arms of Malacca inset and inscr "MELAKA" as in T 3.
61 3 1c. multicoloured . . . . . . 10 1·25
62 – 2c. multicoloured . . . . . . 10 1·25
63 – 5c. multicoloured 10 30
64 – 6c. multicoloured 30 70
65 – 10c. multicoloured 20 10
66 – 15c. multicoloured . . . . . 1·75 40
67 – 20c. multicoloured . . . . . 2·25 1·00
The higher values used in Malacca were Nos. 20/7 of Malaysia.

4 "Papilio demoleus"

1971. Butterflies. As Nos. 124/30 of Kedah but with Arms of Malacca as in T 4. Inscr "melaka".
70 – 1c. multicoloured . . . . . . 50 2·00
71 – 2c. multicoloured . . . . . . 80 2·00
72 – 5c. multicoloured . . . . . . 1·25 80
73 4 6c. multicoloured . . . . . . 1·25 2·75
74 – 10c. multicoloured . . . . . 1·25 30
75 – 15c. multicoloured . . . . . 2·00 20
76 – 20c. multicoloured . . . . . 2·00 2·25
The higher values in use with this issue were Nos. 64/71 of Malaysia.

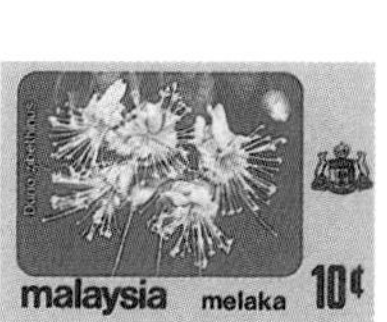

5 "Durio zibethinus"

6 Rubber

1979. Flowers. As Nos. 135/41 of Kedah but with Arms of Malacca and inscr "melaka" as in T 5.
82 1c. "Rafflesia hasseltii" . . . 10 1·00
83 2c. "Pterocarpus indicus" . . 10 1·00
84 5c. "Lagerstroemia speciosa" 15 85
85 10c. Type 5 . . . . 20 30
86 15c. "Hibiscus rosa-sinesis" . . 20 10
87 20c. "Rhododendron scortechinii" 25 10
88 25c. "Etlingera elatior" (inscr "Phaeomeria speciosa") . . 45 70

1986. As Nos. 152/8 of Kedah but with Arms of Malacca and inscr "MELAKA" as in T 6.
96 1c. Coffee 10 10
97 2c. Coconuts 10 10
98 5c. Cocoa 10 10
99 10c. Black pepper 10 10
100 15c. Type 6 . . . . 10 10
101 20c. Oil palm 10 10
102 30c. Rice 10 15

MALAGASY REPUBLIC

Pt. 6; Pt. 13

The former areas covered by Madagascar and Dependencies were renamed the Malagasy Republic within the French Community on 14 October 1958. It became independent on 26 June 1960. In 1992 it reverted to the name of Madagascar.

1958. 100 centimes = 1 franc.
1976. 5 francs = 1 ariary.

1958. 10th Anniv of Declaration of Human Rights. As T 48 of New Caledonia.
1 10f. brown and blue 65 45

1959. Tropical Flora. As T 47 of New Caledonia.
2 6f. green, brown and yellow . . 25 25
3 25f. multicoloured 75 35
DESIGNS—HORIZ: 6f. "Datura"; 25f. Poinsettia.

2a Malagasy Flag and Assembly Hall

1959. Proclamation of Malagasy Republic and "French Community" Commemorative (60f.).
4 2a 20f. red, green and purple . . 35 25
5 – 25f. red, green and grey . . . 45 25
6 – 60f. multicoloured . . . . . 1·10 55
DESIGNS—VERT: 25f. Malagasy flag on map of Madagascar; 60f. Natives holding French and Malagasy flags.

3 "Chionaema pauliani" (butterfly)

3a Reafforestation

1960.
7 – 30c. multicoloured (postage) 15 10
8 – 40c. brown, chocolate & green 15 10
9 – 50c. turquoise and purple . . 15 10
10 3 1f. red, purple and black . . 20 10
11 – 3f. black, red and olive . . . 20 10
12 – 5f. green, brown and red . . 20 20
13 – 6f. yellow and green 20 20
14 – 8f. black, green and red . . . 20 20
15 – 10f. green, brown & turquoise 40 20
16 – 15f. green and brown 50 20
17 – 30f. multicoloured (air) . . . 70 40
18 – 40f. brown and turquoise . . 1·25 30
19 – 50f. multicoloured . . . . . 2·50 50
20 – 100f. multicoloured . . . . 4·00 85
21 – 200f. yellow and violet . . . 5·50 1·50
22 – 500f. brown, blue and green 9·50 2·25
BUTTERFLIES—As Type 2: 30c. Purple-tip; 40c. "Acraea hova"; 50c. Clouded mother-of-pearl; 3f. "Hypolimnas dexithea". 48 × 27 mm: 50f. "Charaxes antamboulou"; 100f. Sunset moth. 27 × 48 mm: 200f. Tailed comet moth.
OTHER DESIGNS—As Type 2: HORIZ: 5f. Sisal; 8f. Pepper; 15f. Cotton. VERT: 6f. Ylang ylang (flower); 10f. Rice. 48½ × 27 mm: 30f. Sugar cane trucks; 40f. Tobacco plantation; 500f. Mandrare Bridge.

1960. Trees Festival.
23 3a 20f. brown, green and ochre 55 35

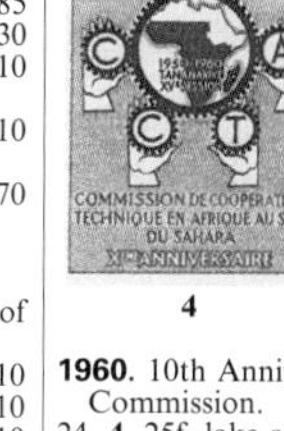

4

5 Pres. Philibert Tsiranana

1960. 10th Anniv of African Technical Co-operation Commission.
24 4 25f. lake and green 55 35

1960.
25 5 20f. brown and green 35 35

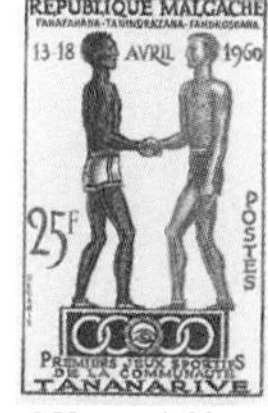

6 Young Athletes

7 Pres. Tsiranana

1960. 1st Youth Games, Tananarive.
26 6 25f. brown, chestnut and blue 65 35

1960.
27 7 20f. black, red and green . . 25 10

1960. Independence. Surch +10 F FETES DE L'INDEPENDANCE.
28 7 20f.+10f. black, red & grn . . 55 35

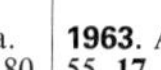
9 Ruffed Lemur

1961. Lemurs.
29 – 2f. purple & turq (postage) 15 15
30 9 4f. black, brown and myrtle 20 15
31 – 12f. brown and green 50 30
32 – 65f. brown, sepia and myrtle (air) . . . . 2·25 65
33 – 85f. black, sepia and green 2·25 1·00
34 – 250f. purple, black & turq . . 6·50 2·75
LEMURS—VERT: As Type 9: 2f. Grey gentle lemur; 12f. Mongoose-lemur. 48 × 27 mm: 65f. Diadem sifaka; 85f. Indris; 250f. Verreaux's sifaka.

10 Diesel Train

1962.
35 10 20f. myrtle . . . . 1·50 45
36 – 25f. blue 35 15
DESIGN: 25f. President Tsirianana Bridge.

11 U.N. and Malagasy Flags, and Govt. Building, Tananarive

1962. Admission into U.N.O.
37 11 25f. multicoloured 35 20
38 85f. multicoloured . . . . . 1·40 55

1962. Malaria Eradication. As T 43 of Mauritania.
39 25f.+5f. green 80 80

12 Ranomafana

1962. Tourist Publicity.
40 12 10f. purple, myrtle and blue (postage) 20 15
41 – 30f. purple, blue and myrtle 40 15
42 – 50f. blue, myrtle and purple 60 25
43 – 60f. myrtle, purple and blue 80 35
44 – 100f. brown, myrtle and blue (air) . . . . 1·75 95
DESIGNS—As Type 12: 30f. Tritriva Lake; 50f. Foulpointe; 60f. Fort Dauphin. 27 × 47½ mm: 100f. Boeing 707 airliner over Nossi-Be.

13 G.P.O., Tamatave

1962. Stamp Day.
45 13 25f.+5f. brn, myrtle & bl . . 35 40

14 Malagasy and U.N.E.S.C.O. Emblems

1962. U.N.E.S.C.O. Conference on Higher Education in Africa, Tananarive.
46 14 20f. black, green and red . . 35 25

1962. 1st Anniv of Union of African and Malagasy States. As T 45 of Mauritania.
47 30f. green 45 35

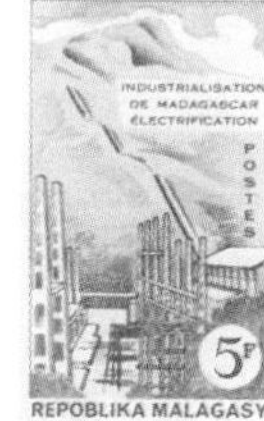

15 Hydro-electric Station

1962. Malagasy Industrialization.
48 15 5f. multicoloured 10 10
49 – 8f. multicoloured 15 10
50 – 10f. multicoloured 20 10
51 – 15f. brown, black and blue 35 15
52 – 20f. multicoloured 35 20
DESIGNS—HORIZ: 8f. Atomic plant; 15f. "Esso Gasikara" (tanker); 20f. Hertzian aerials at Tananarive-Fianarantsoa. VERT: 10f. Oilwell.

16 Globe and Factory

1963. International Fair, Tamatave.
53 16 25f. orange and black . . . 30 20

1963. Freedom from Hunger. As T 51 of Mauritania.
54 25f.+5f. lake, brown and red 60 60

17 Douglas DC-8 Airliner

1963. Air. Malagasy Commercial Aviation.
55 17 500f. blue, red and green . . 8·50 3·25

18 Central Post Office, Tananarive

19 Madagascar Blue Pigeon

1963. Stamp Day.
56 **18** 20f.+5f. brown & turq . . . 55 35

1963. Malagasy Birds and Orchids (8f. to 12f.). Multicoloured. (a) Postage as T **19**.
57 1f. Type **19** 70 35
58 2f. Blue Madagascar coucal 70 35
59 3f. Madagascar red fody . . . 70 35
60 6f. Madagascar pygmy kingfisher 70 35
61 8f. "Gastrorchis humblotii" . . 20 15
62 10f. "Eulophiella roempleriana" 65 25
63 12f. "Angraceum sesquipedale" 65 25

(b) Air. Horiz: 49½ × 28 mm.
64 40f. Helmet bird . . . . . . 2·75 60
65 100f. Pitta-like ground roller 6·50 1·25
66 200f. Crested wood ibis . . . 8·75 2·75

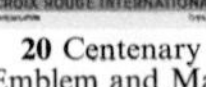
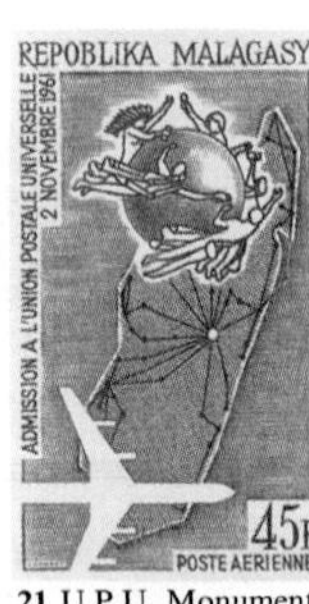

20 Centenary Emblem and Map

21 U.P.U. Monument, Berne, and Map of Malagasy

1963. Red Cross Centenary.
67 **20** 30f. multicoloured 80 60

1963. Air. African and Malagasy Posts and Telecommunications Union. As T **56** of Mauritania.
68 85f. multicoloured . . . . . . 1·40 90

1963. Air. 2nd Anniv of Malagasy's Admission to U.P.U.
69 **21** 45f. blue, red and turquoise 50 25
70 85f. blue, red and violet . . 90 50

22 Arms of Fianarantsoa

23 Flame, Globe and Hands

1963. Town Arms (1st series). Multicoloured.
71 1f.50 Antsirabe 10 10
72 5f. Antalaha 15 10
73 10f. Tulear 20 10
74 15f. Majunga 30 15
75 20f. Type **22** 40 15
75a 20f. Manajary 25 10
76 25f. Tananarive 45 15
76a 30f. Nossi Be 35 15
77 50f. Diego-Suarez 85 50
77a 90f. Antsohihy . . . . 1·40 55
See also Nos. 174/7 and 208/9.

1963. 15th Anniv of Declaration of Human Rights.
78 **23** 60f. ochre, bronze and mauve 55 45

24 Meteorological Station, Tananarive

1964. Air. World Meteorological Day.
79 **24** 90f. brown, blue and grey 1·50 1·25

25 Postal Cheques and Savings Bank Building, Tananarive

26 Scouts beside Campfire

1964. Stamp Day.
80 **25** 25f.+5f. brown, bl & grn . . 50 60

1964. 40th Anniv of Malagasy Scout Movement.
81 **26** 20f. multicoloured 55 25

27 Symbolic Bird and Globe within "Egg"

28 Statuette of Woman

1964. "Europafrique".
82 **27** 45f. brown and green . . . 45 35

1964. Malagasy Art.
83 **28** 6f. brown, blue and indigo (postage) 25 15
84 – 30f. brown, bistre & green 45 20
85 – 100f. brown, red & vio (air) 1·50 95
DESIGNS: 30f. Statuette of squatting vendor. 27 × 48½ mm: 100f. Statuary of peasant family, ox and calf.

1964. French, African and Malagasy Co-operation. As T **68** of Mauritania.
86 25f. brown, chestnut and black 40 25

29 Tree on Globe

30 Cithern

1964. University of Malagasy Republic.
87 **29** 65f. black, red and green . . 50 25

1965. Malagasy Musical Instruments.
88 – 3f. brown, blue and mauve (postage) 20 10
89 **30** 6f. sepia, purple and green 25 10
90 – 8f. brown, black and green 35 10
91 – 25f. multicoloured 90 50
92 – 200f. brown, orange and green (air) . . . . 4·00 2·25
DESIGNS—As Type **30**: 3f. Kabosa (lute); 8f. Hazolahy (sacred drum). LARGER—VERT: 35½ × 48 mm: 25f. "Valiha Player" (after E. Ralambo). 27 × 48 mm: 200f. Bara violin.

31 Foulpointe Post Office

1965. Stamp Day.
93 **31** 20f. brown, green and orange 20 15

32 I.T.U. Emblem

33 J.-J. Rabearivelo (poet)

1965. I.T.U. Centenary.
94 **32** 50f. green, blue and red . . 1·00 45

1965. Rabearivelo Commemorative.
95 **33** 40f. brown and orange . . . 40 25

34 Nurse weighing Baby

1965. Air. International Co-operation Year.
96 **34** 50f. black, bistre and blue 60 35
97 – 100f. purple, brown and blue . . . . 1·25 60
DESIGN: 100f. Boy and girl.

35 Pres. Tsiranana

36 Bearer

1965. Pres. Tsiranana's 55th Birthday.
98 **35** 20f. multicoloured 25 15
99 25f. multicoloured 30 20

1965. Postal Transport.
102 – 3f. violet, blue and brown 30 15
103 – 4f. blue, brown and green 25 15
104 **36** 10f. multicoloured 25 15
105 – 12f. multicoloured 30 20
106 – 20f. multicoloured 90 20
107 – 25f. multicoloured 80 20
108 – 30f. red, brown and blue 2·25 1·60
109 – 65f. brown, blue and violet 1·50 50
DESIGNS—HORIZ: 3f. Early car; 4f. Filanzane (litter); 12f. Pirogue; 20f. Horse-drawn mail-cart; 25f. Bullock cart; 30f. Early railway postal carriage; 65f. Hydrofoil, "Porthos", Betsiboka.

37 Diseased Hands

1966. World Leprosy Day.
110 **37** 20f. purple, red and green 35 20

38 Planting Trees

1966. Reafforestation Campaign.
111 **38** 20f. violet, brown & turq 35 20

39 "Cicindelidae chaetodera andriana"

1966. Malagasy Insects. Multicoloured.
112 1f. Type **39** 10 10
113 6f. "Mantodea tisma freiji" 20 10
114 12f. "Cerambycini mastododera nodicollis" . . 45 20
115 45f. "Trachelophoru giraffa" 85 30

40 Madagascar 1c. Stamp of 1903

41 Betsileo Dance

1966. Stamp Day.
116 **40** 25f. bistre and red 35 25

1966. Folk Dances. Multicoloured.
117 2f. Bilo Sakalava dance (vert) (postage) 15 10
118 5f. Type **41** 25 15
119 30f. Antandroy dance (vert) 55 20
120 200f. Southern Malagasy dancer (air) . . . . 3·50 1·50
121 250f. Sakalava Net Dance . . 4·00 2·25
Nos. 120/1 are size 27 × 48 mm.

43 "Tree" of Emblems

1966. O.C.A.M. Conference, Tananarive.
122 **43** 25f. multicoloured 30 15
The above was issued with "Janvier 1966" obliterated by bars, and optd **JUIN 1966**.

44 Singing Anthem

45 U.N.E.S.C.O. Emblem

1966. National Anthem.
123 **44** 20f. brown, mauve & green 25 10

1966. 20th Anniv of U.N.E.S.C.O.
124 **45** 30f. blue, bistre and red . . 35 20

46 Lions Emblem

47 Harvesting Rice

1967. 50th Anniv of Lions Int.
125 **46** 30f. multicoloured 40 20

1967. International Rice Year.
126 **47** 20f. multicoloured 30 15

48 Adventist Temple, Tanambao-Tamatave

1967. Religious Buildings (1st series).
127 **48** 3f. ochre, blue and green 10 10
128 – 5f. lilac, purple and green 10 10
129 – 10f. purple, blue and green 25 10
BUILDINGS—VERT: 5f. Catholic Cathedral, Tananarive. HORIZ: 10f. Mosque, Tamatave.
See also Nos. 148/50.

49 Raharisoa at Piano

1967. 4th Death Anniv of Norbert Raharisoa (composer).
130 **49** 40f. multicoloured 55 20

50 Jean Raoult's Bleriot XI, 1911

1967. "History of Malagasy Aviation".
131 **50** 5f. brown, blue and green (postage) 35 15
132 – 45f. black, blue and brown 90 35
133 – 500f. black, blue and ochre (air) . . . . 8·75 3·75
DESIGNS: 45f. Bernard Bougault and flying boat, 1926. 48 × 27 mm: 500f. Jean Dagnaux and Breguet 19A2 biplane, 1927.

51 Ministry of Communications, Tananarive

52 Church, Torch and Map

1967. Stamp Day.
134 **51** 20f. green, blue and orange 25 15

1967. Air. 5th Anniv of U.A.M.P.T. As T **101** of Mauritania.
135 100f. mauve, bistre and red 1·25 60

1967. Centenary of Malagasy Lutheran Church.
136 **52** 20f. multicoloured 30 15

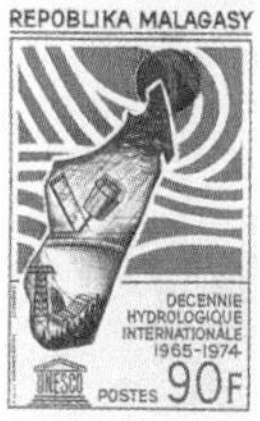

53 Map and Decade Emblem

54 Woman's Face and Scales of Justice

1967. Int Hydrological Decade.
137 **53** 90f. brown, red and blue 85 45

1967. Women's Rights Commission.
138 **54** 50f. blue, ochre and green 50 25

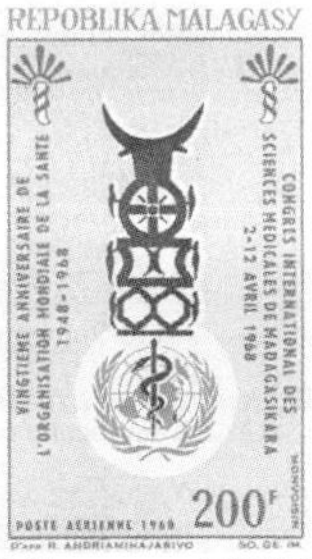

55 Human Rights Emblem

56 Congress and W.H.O. Emblems

1968. Human Rights Year.
139 **55** 50f. red, green and black 40 25

1968. Air. 20th Anniv of W.H.O. and Int Medical Sciences Congress, Tananarive.
140 **56** 200f. red, blue and ochre 2·40 1·25

57 International Airport, Tananarive-Ivato

1968. Air. Stamp Day.
141 **57** 500f. blue, green and brown . . . . 6·75 3·25

1968. Nos. 33 and 38 surch.
142 **11** 20f. on 85f. (postage) . . . 40 30
143 – 20f. on 85f. (No. 33) (air) 50 30

59 "Industry and Construction"

61 Isotry Protestant Church, Fitiavana, Tananarive

60 Church and Open Bible

1968. Five-year Plan (1st issue).
144 **59** 10f. plum, red and green 15 10
145 – 20f. black, red and green 20 15
146 – 40f. blue, brown & ultram 2·10 60
DESIGNS—VERT: 20f. "Agriculture". HORIZ: 40f. "Transport".
See also Nos. 156/7.

1968. 150th Anniv of Christianity in Madagascar.
147 **60** 20f. multicoloured 25 10

1968. Religious Buildings (2nd series).
148 **61** 4f. brown, green and red 10 10
149 – 12f. brown, blue and violet 20 10
150 – 50f. indigo, blue and green 45 25
DESIGNS: 12f. Catholic Cathedral, Fianarantsoa; 50f. Aga Khan Mosque, Tananarive.

62 President Tsiranana and Wife

63 Cornucopia, Coins and Map

1968. 10th Anniv of Republic.
151 **62** 20f. brown, red and yellow 20 10
152 30f. brown, red and blue 25 15

1968. 50th Anniv of Malagasy Savings Bank.
154 **63** 20f. multicoloured 25 10

64 "Dance of the Whirlwind"

1968. Air.
155 **64** 100f. multicoloured . . . . 1·50 65

65 Malagasy Family

1968. Five-year Plan (2nd issue).
156 **65** 15f. red, yellow and blue 15 10
157 – 45f. multicoloured 40 25
DESIGN—VERT: 45f. Allegory of "Achievement".

1968. Air. "Philexafrique" Stamp Exn, Abidjan (1969) (1st issue). As T **113a** of Mauritania.
158 100f. multicoloured . . . . . 2·75 80
DESIGN: 100f. "Young Woman sealing a Letter" (J. B. Santerre).

1969. Air. "Philexafrique" Stamp Exn, Abidjan, Ivory Coast (2nd issue). As T **114a** of Mauritania.
159 50f. red, green and drab . . . 1·60 90
DESIGN: 50f. Malagasy Arms, map and Madagascar stamp of 1946.

68 "Queen Adelaide receiving Malagasy Mission, London" (1836–37)

1969.
160 **68** 250f. multicoloured . . . . 4·50 3·25

69 Hand with Spanner, Cogwheels and I.L.O. Emblem

1969. 50th Anniv of I.L.O.
161 **69** 20f. multicoloured 25 15

70 Post and Telecommunications Building, Tananarive

1969. Stamp Day.
162 **70** 30f. multicoloured 35 20

71 Map, Steering Wheel and Vehicles

72 President Tsiranana making Speech

1969. 20th Anniv of Malagasy Motor Club.
163 **71** 65f. multicoloured 60 35

1969. 10th Anniv of President Tsiranana's Assumption of Office.
164 **72** 20f. multicoloured 20 10

73 Bananas

74 Start of Race and Olympic Flame

1969. Fruits.
165 **73** 5f. green, brown and blue 15 10
166 – 15f. red, myrtle and green 30 10
DESIGN: 15f. Lychees.

1969. Olympic Games, Mexico (1968).
167 **74** 15f. brown, red and green 25 20

75 "Malagasy Seashore, East Coast" (A. Razafinjohany)

1969. Air. Paintings by Malagasy Artists. Multicoloured.
168 100f. Type **75** . . . . 1·25 80
169 150f. "Sunset on the High Plateaux" (H. Ratovo) . . 2·50 1·40

76 Imerino House, High Plateaux

77 Ambalavao Arms

1969. Malagasy Traditional Dwellings (1st series).
170 – 20f. red, blue and green . . 20 10
171 – 20f. brown, red and blue 20 10
172 **76** 40f. red, blue and indigo 40 20
173 – 60f. purple, green and blue 60 25
HOUSES—HORIZ: 20f. (No. 170), Tsimihety hut, East Coast; 60f. Betsimisaraka dwellings, East Coast. VERT: 20f. (No. 171), Betsileo house, High Plateaux.
See also Nos. 205/6.

1970. Town Arms (2nd series). Multicoloured.
174 10f. Type **77** 20 10
175 25f. Morondava 35 15
176 25f. Ambatondrazaka 35 15
177 80f. Tamatave 90 35
See also Nos. 208/9.

78 Agate

80 U.N. Emblem and Symbols

1970. Semi-precious Stones. Multicoloured.
178 5f. Type **78** . . . . 1·60 55
179 20f. Ammonite . . . . 3·25 1·10

1970. New U.P.U. Headquarters Building, Berne. As T **81** of New Caledonia.
180 20f. blue, brown and mauve 30 20

1970. 25th Anniv of United Nations.
181 **80** 50f. black, blue and orange 65 25

81 Astronaut and Module on Moon

1970. Air. 1st Anniv of "Apollo 11" Moon-landing.
182 **81** 75f. green, slate and blue 1·10 40

82 Malagasy Fruits

1970.
183 **82** 20f. multicoloured 30 15

83 Delessert's Lyria

1970. Sea Shells (1st series). Multicoloured.
184 5f. Type **83** 50 15
185 10f. Bramble murex 65 25
186 20f. Thorny oyster . . . . . 1·40 50

84 Aye-aye

1970. International Nature Conservation Conference, Tananarive.
187 **84** 20f. multicoloured 40 30

85 Boeing 737 in Flight

1970. Air.
188 **85** 200f. red, green and blue 2·40 1·25

86 Pres. Tsiranana **87** Calcite

1970. Pres. Tsiranana's 60th Birthday.
189 **86** 30f. brown and green . . . 30 15

1971. Minerals. Multicoloured.
190 12f. Type **87** . . . . 1·60 45
191 15f. Quartz . . . . 2·25 65

88 Soap Works, Tananarive

1971. Malagasy Industries.
192 **88** 5f. multicoloured 15 10
193 – 15f. black, brown and blue 25 10
194 – 50f. multicoloured 55 15
DESIGNS: 15f. Chrome works, Comina-Andriamena; 50f. Textile complex, Sotema-Majunga.

89 Globe and Emblems

1971. Council Meeting of Common Market Countries with African and Malagasy Associated States, Tananarive.
195 **89** 5f. multicoloured 15 15

90 Rural Mobile Post Office

1971. Stamp Day.
196 **90** 25f. multicoloured 35 15

91 Gen. De Gaulle

1971. Death (1970) of Gen. Charles de Gaulle.
197 **91** 30f. black, red and blue . . 70 35

92 Palm Beach Hotel, Nossi-Be **93** Forestry Emblem

1971. Malagasy Hotels.
198 **92** 25f. multicoloured 30 20
199 – 65f. brown, blue and green 60 30
DESIGN: 65f. Hilton Hotel, Tananarive.

1971. Forest Preservation Campaign.
200 **93** 3f. multicoloured 15 10

94 Jean Ralaimongo

1971. Air. Malagasy Celebrities.
201 **94** 25f. brown, red and orange 30 15
202 – 65f. brown, myrtle & green 40 25
203 – 100f. brown, ultram & bl 90 40
CELEBRITIES: 65f. Albert Sylla; 100f. Joseph Ravoahangy Andrianavalona.

1971. Air. 10th Anniv of African and Malagasy Posts and Telecommunications Union. As T **139a** of Mauritania.
204 100f. U.A.M.P.T. H.Q., Brazzaville, and painting "Mpisikidy" (G. Rakotovao) . . . . . 1·00 60

96 Vezo Dwellings, South-east Coast

1971. Malagasy Traditional Dwellings (2nd series). Multicoloured.
205 5f. Type **96** 15 10
206 10f. Antandroy hut, South coast 20 10

97 "Children and Cattle in Meadow" (G. Rasoaharijaona)

1971. 25th Anniv of U.N.I.C.E.F.
207 **97** 50f. multicoloured 65 30

1972. Town Arms (3rd series). As T **77**. Mult.
208 1f. Maintirano Arms 10 10
209 25f. Fenerive-Est 35 20

99 Cable-laying train

1972. Co-axial Cable Link, Tananarive–Tamatave.
210 **99** 45f. brown, green and red 2·75 1·25

100 Telecommunications Station

1972. Inauguration of Philibert Tsiranana Satellite Communications Station.
211 **100** 85f. multicoloured 75 45

101 Pres. Tsiranana and Voters **102** "Moped" Postman

1972. Presidential Elections.
212 **101** 25f. multicoloured 40 35

1972. Stamp Day.
213 **102** 10f. multicoloured 40 20

1972. De Gaulle Memorial. No. 197 surch **MEMORIAL +20F.**
214 **91** 30f.+20f. black, red & bl 60 60

104 Exhibition Emblem and Stamps

1972. 2nd National Stamp Exn, Antanarive.
215 **104** 25f. multicoloured 35 30
216 40f. multicoloured 60 35
217 100f. multicoloured . . . 1·25 75

105 Road and Monument

1972. Opening of Andapa–Sambava Highway.
219 **105** 50f. multicoloured 35 25

106 Petroleum Refinery, Tamatave

1972. Malagasy Economic Development.
220 **106** 2f. blue, green and yellow 20 10
221 – 100f. multicoloured . . . 3·00 30
DESIGN: 100f. 3600 CV diesel locomotive.

107 R. Rakotobe

1972. Air. 1st Death Anniv of Rene Rakotobe (poet).
222 **107** 40f. brown, purple & orge 40 20

108 College Buildings

1972. 150th Anniv of Razafindrahety College, Tananarive.
223 **108** 10f. purple, brown & blue 15 10

109 Volleyball

1972. African Volleyball Championships.
224 **109** 12f. black, orange & brn 40 15

110 Runners breasting Tape

1972. Air. Olympic Games, Munich. Multicoloured.
225 100f. Type **110** . . . . 1·40 60
226 200f. Judo . . . . 2·25 90

111 Hospital Complex

1972. Inauguration of Ravoahangy Andrianavalona Hospital.
227 **111** 6f. multicoloured 20 15

112 Mohair Goat

1972. Air. Malagasy Wool Production.
228 **112** 250f. multicoloured . . . 3·75 2·25

113 Ploughing with Oxen

1972. Agricultural Expansion.
229 **113** 25f. multicoloured 25 15

114 "Virgin and Child" (15th-cent Florentine School)

1972. Air. Christmas. Religious Paintings. Mult.
230 85f. Type **114** 85 55
231 150f. "Adoration of the Magi" (A. Mantegna) (horiz) . . . . 2·00 85

115 Betsimisarka Women

1972. Traditional Costumes. Multicoloured.

232 10f. Type **115** 20 10

233 15f. Merina mother and child 30 20

116 Astronauts on Moon

1973. Air. Moon Flight of "Apollo 17".

234 **116** 300f. purple, brown & grey 3·25 1·75

117 "Natural Produce"

1973. 10th Anniv of Malagasy Freedom from Hunger Campaign Committee.

235 **117** 25f. multicoloured 30 15

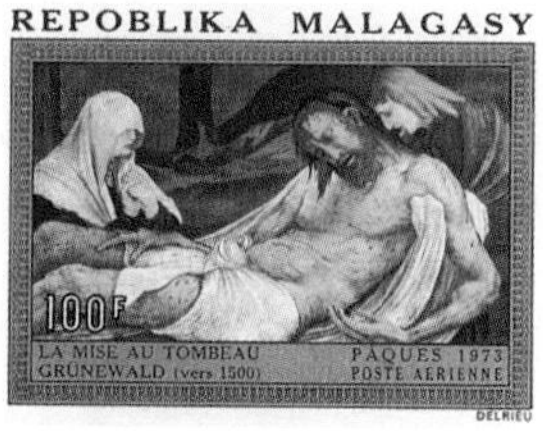

118 "The Entombment" (Grunewald)

1973. Air. Easter. Multicoloured.

236 100f. Type **118** 1·00 55

237 200f. "The Resurrection" (Grunewald) (vert) 2·25 1·10

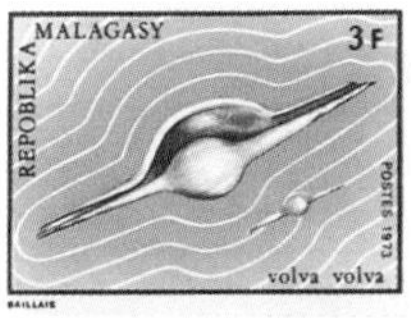

119 Shuttlecock Volva

1973. Sea Shells (2nd series). Multicoloured.

238 3f. Type **119** 15 10

239 10f. Arthritic spider conch 25 20

240 15f. Common harp 50 30

241 25f. Type **119** 70 45

242 40f. As 15f. 1·10 50

243 50f. As 10f. 2·25 60

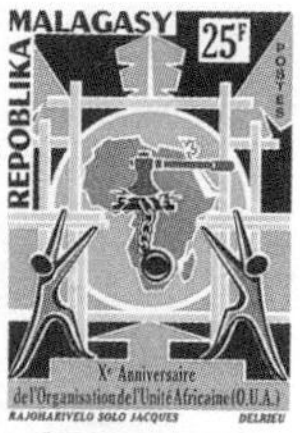

120 Postal Courier, Tsimandoa

121 "Africa" within Scaffolding

1973. Stamp Day.

244 **120** 50f. blue, green and brown 45 20

1973. 10th Anniv of Organization of African Unity.

245 **121** 25f. multicoloured 30 15

122 "Cameleon campani"

1973. Malagasy Chameleons. Multicoloured.

246 1f. Type **122** 10 10

247 5f. "Cameleon nasutus" (male) 10 10

248 10f. "Cameleon nasutus" (female) 15 10

249 40f. As 5f. 55 25

250 60f. Type **122** 85 35

251 85f. As 10f. 1·25 65

123 Excursion Carriage

1973. Air. Early Malagasy Railways. Multicoloured.

252 100f. Type **123** 1·75 85

253 150f. Mallet steam locomotive No. 24, 1907 2·50 1·40

124 "Cypripedium"

1973. Orchids. Multicoloured.

254 10f. Type **124** 30 15

255 25f. "Nepenthes pervillei" 50 20

256 40f. As 25f. 1·00 35

257 100f. Type **124** 2·25 85

1973. Pan African Drought Relief. No. 235 surch **SECHERESSE SOLIDARITE AFRICAINE** and value.

258 **117** 100f. on 25f. multicoloured 1·10 60

126 Dish Aerial and Meteorological Station

129 Pres. Kennedy

128 Greater Dwarf Lemur

1973. Air. W.M.O. Centenary.

259 **126** 100f. orange, blue & black 1·25 65

1973. 12th Anniv of African and Malagasy Posts and Telecommunications. As T **155a** of Mauritania.

260 100f. red, violet and green 90 45

1973. Malagasy Lemurs.

261 **128** 5f. brown, green and purple (postage) 55 15

262 – 25f. brown, sepia & green 1·10 65

263 – 150f. brn, grn & sepia (air) 2·75 1·25

264 **128** 200f. brown, turq & blue 4·00 1·75

DESIGN—VERT: 25f., 150f. Weasel-lemur.

1973. Air. 10th Death Anniv of Pres. John Kennedy.

265 **129** 300f. multicoloured 3·25 1·75

130 Footballers

1973. Air. World Cup Football Championship. West Germany.

266 **130** 500f. mauve, brown and light brown 5·50 2·50

CURRENCY. Issues from No. 267 to No. 389 have face values shown as "Fmg". This abbreviation denotes the Malagasy Franc which was introduced in 1966.

131 Copernicus, Satellite and Diagram

1974. Air. 500th Birth Anniv of Copernicus.

267 **131** 250f. blue, brown & green 3·25 1·50

1974. No. 76a surch.

268 25f. on 30f. multicoloured 25 15

133 Agricultural Training

135 Family and House

134 Male Player, and Hummingbird on Hibiscus

1974. 25th World Scouting Conference, Nairobi, Kenya.

269 **133** 4f. grey, blue and green (postage) 10 10

270 – 15f. purple, green and blue 20 15

271 – 100f. ochre, red & blue (air) 80 45

272 – 300f. brown, blue & black 3·50 1·75

DESIGNS—VERT: 15f. Building construction. HORIZ: 100f. First Aid training; 300f. Fishing.

1974. Air. Asia, Africa and Latin America Table-Tennis Championships, Peking.

273 **134** 50f. red, blue and brown 80 30

274 – 100f. red, blue and violet 1·60 70

DESIGN: 100f. Female player and stylized bird.

1974. World Population Year.

275 **135** 25f. red, orange and blue 25 10

136 Micheline Railcar

1974. Air. Malagasy Railway Locomotives.

276 **136** 50f. green, red and brown 75 25

277 – 85f. red, blue and green 1·25 30

278 – 200f. blue, lt blue & brown 3·25 80

DESIGNS: 85f. Track-inspection trolley; 200f. Garratt steam locomotive, 1926.

137 U.P.U. Emblem and Letters

1974. Air. Centenary of U.P.U.

279 **137** 250f. red, blue and violet 3·00 1·40

138 Rainibetsimisaraka

1974. Rainibetsimisaraka Commemoration.

280 **138** 25f. multicoloured 35 20

1974. Air. West Germany's Victory in World Cup Football Championship. No. 266 optd **R.F.A. 2 HOLLANDE 1**.

281 **130** 500f. mauve, brown and light brown 5·00 2·75

140 "Apollo" and "Soyuz" spacecraft

1974. Air. Soviet–U.S. Space Co-operation.

282 **140** 150f. orange, green & blue 1·10 60

283 – 250f. green, blue & brown 2·00 1·00

DESIGN: No. 283, As Type **140** but different view.

141 Marble Slabs

1974. Marble Industry. Multicoloured.

284 4f. Type **141** 55 15

285 25f. Quarrying 1·40 25

1974. Air. Universal Postal Union Centenary (2nd issue). No. 279 optd **100 ANS DE COLLABORATION INTERNATIONALE**.

286 **137** 250f. red, blue and violet 1·75 1·00

143 Faces and Maps

1974. Europafrique.

287 **143** 150f. brown, red & orange 1·40 70

144 "Food in Hand"

1974. "Freedom from Hunger".

288 **144** 80f. blue, brown and grey 65 35

145 "Coton"

146 Malagasy People

1974. Malagasy Dogs. Multicoloured.

289 50f. Type **145** 1·40 45

290 100f. Hunting dog 2·25 1·10

1974. Founding of "Fokonolona" Commune.

291 **146** 5f. multicoloured 15 10

292 10f. multicoloured 15 10

293 20f. multicoloured 20 10

294 60f. multicoloured 60 30

147 "Discovering Talent"

1974. National Development Council.

295 **147** 25f. multicoloured 20 10

296 35f. multicoloured 30 15

148 "Adoration of the Magi" (David)

1974. Air. Christmas. Multicoloured.
297 200f. Type **148** . . . . 2·25 95
298 300f. "Virgin of the Cherries and Child" (Metzys) . . . 3·25 1·25

149 Malagasy Girl and Rose

1975. International Women's Year.
299 **149** 100f. brown, orange & grn 85 40

150 Colonel Richard Ratsimandrava (Head of Government)

1975.
300 **150** 15f. brown, black & yellow 15 10
301 25f. brown, black and blue 20 15
302 100f. brown, black & green 80 35

151 Sofia Bridge

1975.
303 **151** 45f. multicoloured 50 20

152 U.N. Emblem and Part of Globe

1975. Air. 30th Anniv of U.N. Charter.
304 **152** 300f. multicoloured . . . 2·75 1·25

153 De Grasse (after Mauzaisse) and "Randolph"

1975. Bicentenary of American Revolution (1st issue). Multicoloured.
305 40f. Type **153** (postage) . . . 85 25
306 50f. Lafayette, "Lexington" and H.M.S. "Edward" . . 95 30
307 100f. D'Estaing and "Languedoc" (air) . . . . 1·75 50
308 200f. Paul Jones, "Bonhomme Richard" and H.M.S. "Serapis" . . . . 2·50 1·10
309 300f. Benjamin Franklin, "Millern" and "Montgomery" . . . . . 3·50 1·60

154 "Euphorbia viguieri"

1975. Malagasy Flora. Multicoloured.
311 15f. Type **154** (postage) . . . 25 15
312 25f. "Hibiscus rosesinensis" 40 20
313 30f. "Plumeria rubra acutitolia" 55 20
314 40f. "Pachypodium rosulatum" . . . . 1·00 30
315 85f. "Turraea sericea" (air) 1·75 1·00

1975. Air. "Apollo"–"Soyuz" Space Link. Nos. 282/3 optd **JONCTION 17 JUILLET 1975.**
316 **140** 150f. orange, green & blue 1·00 60
317 – 250f. green, blue & brown 2·25 1·00

156 Temple Frieze

1975. Air. "Save Borobudur Temple" (in Indonesia) Campaign.
318 **156** 50f. red, orange and blue 1·00 50

157 "Racial Unity"

1975. Namibia Day.
319 **157** 50f. multicoloured 45 20

158 Pryer's Woodpecker

1975. International Exposition, Okinawa. Fauna. Multicoloured.
320 25f. Type **158** (postage) . . . 50 25
321 40f. Ryukyu rabbit 50 20
322 50f. Toad 70 30
323 75f. Tortoise . . . . 1·40 40
324 125f. Sika deer (air) . . . . 1·50 55

159 Lily Waterfall

1975. Lily Waterfall. Multicoloured.
326 25f. Type **159** 40 15
327 40f. Lily Waterfall (distant view) 60 15

160 Hurdling

1975. Air. "Pre-Olympic Year". Olympic Games, Montreal (1976). Multicoloured.
328 75f. Type **160** 60 35
329 200f. Weightlifting (vert) . . 2·00 75

161 Bobsleigh "Fours"

1975. Winter Olympic Games, Innsbruck. Multicoloured.
330 75f. Type **161** (postage) . . . 50 25
331 100f. Ski-jumping 80 35
332 140f. Speed-skating . . . . . 1·25 50
333 200f. Cross-country skiing (air) . . . . 2·00 75
334 245f. Downhill skiing . . . . 2·25 90

162 Pirogue

1975. Malagasy Sailing-vessels. Multicoloured.
336 8f. Type **162** 55 15
337 45f. Malagasy schooner . . . 1·10 25

163 Canoeing

1976. Olympic Games, Montreal. Multicoloured.
338 40f. Type **163** (postage) . . . 25 15
339 50f. Sprinting and hurdling 35 20
340 100f. Putting the shot, and long-jumping (air) 90 35
341 200f. Gymnastics-horse and parallel bars . . . . . . 1·75 75
342 300f. Trampoline-jumping and high-diving . . . . . 2·40 1·00

164 "Apollo 14" Lunar Module and Flight Badge

1976. Air. 5th Anniv of "Apollo 14" Mission.
344 **164** 150f. blue, red and green 1·25 65

1976. Air. 5th Anniv of "Apollo 14" Mission. No. 344 optd **5e Anniversaire de la mission APOLLO XIV.**
345 **164** 150f. blue, red and green 1·25 75

166 "Graf Zeppelin" over Fujiyama

1976. 75th Anniv of Zeppelin. Multicoloured.
346 40f. Type **166** (postage) . . . 35 15
347 50f. "Graf Zeppelin" over Rio de Janeiro 40 15
348 75f. "Graf Zeppelin" over New York 80 25
349 100f. "Graf Zeppelin" over Sphinx and pyramids . . . 95 35
350 200f. "Graf Zeppelin" over Berlin (air) . . . . . . 2·25 75
351 300f. "Graf Zeppelin" over London . . . . 4·00 1·00

167 "Prevention of Blindness"

1976. World Health Day.
353 **167** 100f. multicoloured . . . 1·25 55

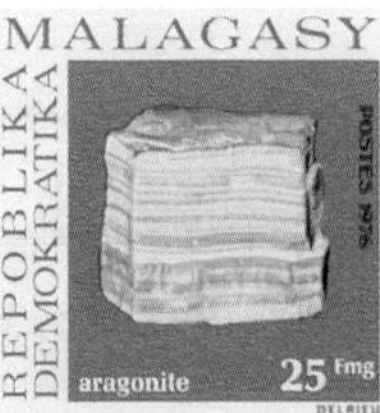
168 Aragonite

1976. Minerals and Fossils. Multicoloured.
354 25f. Type **168** 50 15
355 50f. Fossilized wood . . . . 1·10 55
356 150f. Celestyte . . . . 3·25 1·60

169 Alexander Graham Bell and Early Telephone

1976. Telephone Centenary. Multicoloured.
357 25f. Type **169** 15 10
358 50f. Cable maintenance, 1911 30 15
359 100f. Telephone operator and switchboard, 1895 . . . . 60 25
360 200f. "Emile Baudot" cable ship . . . . 2·25 90
361 300f. Man with radio-telephone . . . . 2·25 80

170 Children reading Book

1976. Children's Books Promotion. Multicoloured.
363 10f. Type **170** 15 10
364 25f. Children reading book (vert) 35 15

1976. Medal winners, Winter Olympic Games, Innsbruck. Nos. 330/4 optd **VAINQUEUR** and medal winner.
365 75f. Type **161** (postage) . . . 50 25
366 100f. Ski-jumping 80 40
367 140f. Skating . . . . 1·25 50
368 200f. Cross-country skiing (air) . . . . 1·40 75
369 245f. Downhill skiing . . . . 1·90 1·00

OPTS: 75f. **ALLEMAGNE FEDERALE**; 100f. **KARL SCHNABL, AUTRICHE**; 140f. **SHEILA YOUNG, ETATS-UNIS**; 200f. **IVAR FORMO, NORVEGE**; 245f. **ROSI MITTERMAIER, ALLEMAGNE DE L'OUEST.**

The subject depicted on No. 367 is speed-skating, an event in which the gold medal was won by J. E. Storholt, Norway.

1976. Bicentenary of American Revolution (2nd issue). Nos. 305/9 optd **4 JUILLET 1776–1976** in frame.
371 **153** 40f. multicoloured (postage) 35 25
372 – 50f. multicoloured 40 30
373 – 100f. multicoloured (air) 75 50
374 – 200f. multicoloured . . . 1·50 85
375 – 300f. multicoloured . . . 2·25 1·25

173 Descent Trajectory

1976. "Viking" Landing on Mars. Multicoloured.
377 75f. Type **173** 40 20
378 100f. "Viking" landing module separation 60 25
379 200f. "Viking" on Martian surface . . . . 1·25 55
380 300f. "Viking" orbiting Mars 2·00 80

174 Rainandriamampandry
175 Doves over Globe

1976. 30th Anniv of Treaties signed by Rainandriamampandry (Foreign Minister).
382 **174** 25f. multicoloured 30 20

1976. Indian Ocean—"Zone of Peace". Multicoloured.
383 60f. Type **175** 35 20
384 160f. Doves flying across Indian Ocean (horiz) . . . 1·10 55

1976. Olympic Games Medal Winners. Nos. 338/42 optd with names of two winners on each stamp.
385 **163** 40f. multicoloured (postage) 25 15
386 – 50f. multicoloured 35 25
387 – 100f. multicoloured (air) 70 40
388 – 200f. multicoloured . . . 1·40 65
389 – 300f. multicoloured . . . 2·00 1·00
OVERPRINTS: 40f. **V. DIBA, A. ROGOV**; 50f. **H. CRAWFORD, J. SCHALLER**; 100f. **U. BEYER, A. ROBINSON**; 200f. **N. COMANECI, N. ANDRIANOV**; 300f. **K. DIBIASI, E. VAYTSEKHOVSKAIA**.

177 Malagasy Arms

1976. 1st Anniv of Malagasy Democratic Republic.
391 **177** 25f. multicoloured 20 10

178 Rabezavana (Independence Movement Leader)

1977. National Heroes. Multicoloured.
392 25f. Type **178** 20 10
393 25f. Lt. Albert Randriamaromanana . . . 20 10
394 25f. Ny Avana Ramanantoanina (politician) 20 10
395 100f. Fasam-Pirenena National Mausoleum, Tananarive (horiz) 75 40

179 Family

1977. World Health Day.
396 **179** 5f. multicoloured 15 10

180 Medical School, Antananarivo

1977. 80th Anniv of Medical School, Antananarivo.
397 **180** 250f. multicoloured . . . 2·00 95

181 Rural Post Van

1977. Rural Mail.
398 **181** 35f. multicoloured 30 15

182 Morse Key and Man with Headphones

1977. 90th Anniv of Antananarivo–Tamatave Telegraph.
399 **182** 15f. multicoloured 15 10

183 Academy Emblem

1977. 75th Anniv of Malagasy Academy.
400 **183** 10f. multicoloured 15 10

184 Lenin and Russian Flag

1977. 60th Anniv of Russian Revolution.
401 **184** 25f. multicoloured . . . . 1·10 10

185 Raoul Follereau

1978. 25th Anniv of World Leprosy Day.
402 **185** 5f. multicoloured 90 10

186 Microwave Antenna
187 "Co-operation"

1978. World Telecommunications Day.
403 **186** 20f. multicoloured 15 10

1978. Anti-Apartheid Year.
404 **187** 60f. red, black and yellow 40 25

188 Children with Instruments of Revolution
189 Tractor, Factory and Labourers

1978. "Youth—Pillar of the Revolution".
405 **188** 25f. multicoloured 75 45

1978. Socialist Co-operatives.
406 **189** 25f. multicoloured 15 10

190 Women at Work
191 Children with Books, Instruments and Fruit

1979. "Women, Pillar of the Revolution".
407 **190** 40f. multicoloured 25 15

1979. International Year of the Child.
408 **191** 10f. multicoloured 20 10

192 Ring-tailed Lemur
193 J. V. S. Razakandraina

1979. Animals. Multicoloured.
409 25f. Type **192** (postage) . . . 25 15
410 125f. Black lemur . . . . . 1·40 30
411 1000f. Malagasy civet . . . . 8·50 2·25
412 20f. Tortoise (air) 20 20
413 95f. Black lemur (different) 1·00 40

1979. J. V. S. Razakandraina (poet) Commem.
414 **193** 25f. multicoloured 15 10

194 "Centella asiatica"

1979. Medicinal Plant.
415 **194** 25f. multicoloured 15 10

195 Map of Malagasy and Ste. Marie Telecommunications Station

1979. Telecommunications.
416 **195** 25f. multicoloured 20 10

196 Post Office, Antsirabe

1979. Stamp Day.
417 **196** 500f. multicoloured . . . 3·25 1·10

197 Palestinians with Flag

1979. Air. Palestinian Solidarity.
418 **197** 60f. multicoloured 50 20

198 Concorde and Map of Africa

1979. 20th Anniv of ASECNA (African Air Safety Organization).
419 **198** 50f. multicoloured 60 20

199 Lenin addressing Meeting

1980. 110th Birth Anniv of Lenin.
420 **199** 25f. multicoloured 45 10

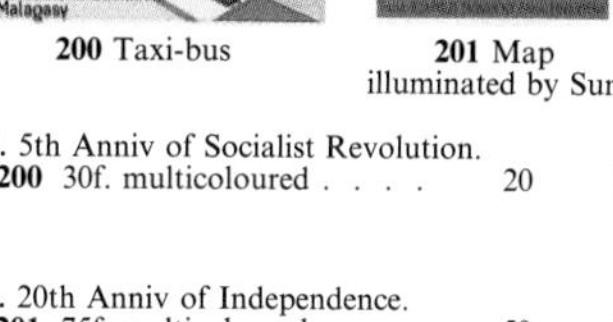

200 Taxi-bus
201 Map illuminated by Sun

1980. 5th Anniv of Socialist Revolution.
421 **200** 30f. multicoloured 20 10

1980. 20th Anniv of Independence.
422 **201** 75f. multicoloured 50 30

202 Military Parade

1980. 20th Anniv of Army.
423 **202** 50f. multicoloured 35 15

203 Joseph Raseta

1980. Dr. Joseph Raseta Commemoration.
424 **203** 30f. multicoloured 20 10

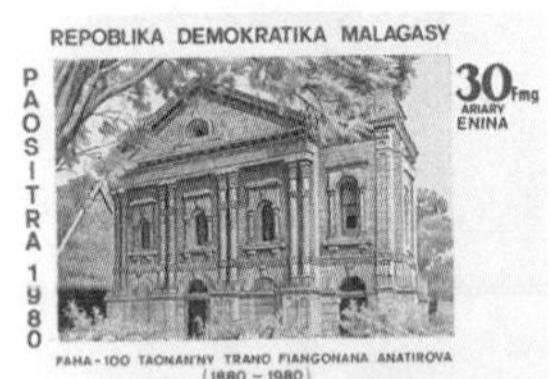

204 Anatirova Temple

1980. Anatirova Temple Centenary.
425 **204** 30f. multicoloured 20 10

205 Boxing

1980. Olympic Games, Moscow. Multicoloured.
426 30f. Hurdling 45 10
427 75f. Type **205** 90 25
428 250f. Judo . . . . 1·75 75
429 500f. Swimming . . . . . . 3·25 1·50

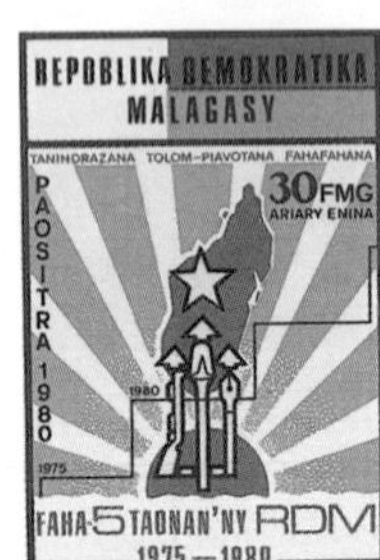

206 Emblem, Map and Sun

1980. 5th Anniv of Malagasy Democratic Republic.
430 **206** 30f. multicoloured 20 10

207 Skier

1981. Winter Olympic Games, Lake Placid (1980).
431 **207** 175f. multicoloured . . . 1·10 55

208 "Angraecum leonis" **209** Handicapped Student

1981. Flowers. Multicoloured.
432 5f. Type **208** 10 10
433 80f. "Angraecum famosum" 60 25
434 170f. "Angraecum sesquipedale" . . . . . . 1·25 55

1981. International Year of Disabled People. Mult.
435 25f. Type **209** 20 10
436 80f. Disabled carpenter . . . 55 25

210 Ribbons forming Caduceus, I.T.U. and W.H.O. Emblems

1981. World Telecommunications Day.
437 **210** 15f. blue, black and yellow 15 10
438 45f. multicoloured 35 15

211 Valentina Tereshkova (first woman in space)

1981. Space Achievements. Multicoloured.
439 30f. Type **211** 15 10
440 80f. Astronaut on Moon . . 55 25
441 90f. Yuri Gagarin (first man in space) 65 30

212 Raphael-Louis Rafiringa

1981. Raphael-Louis Rafiringa Commemoration.
442 **212** 30f. multicoloured 20 10

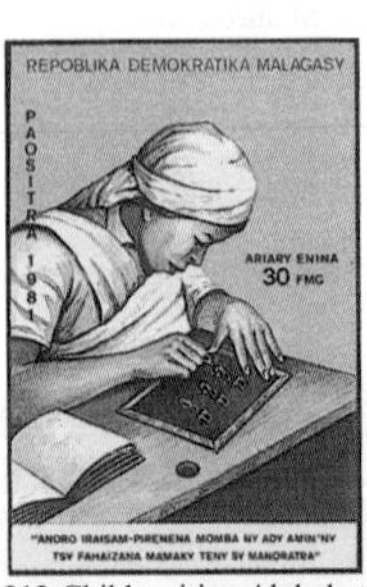

213 Child writing Alphabet

1981. World Literacy Day.
443 **213** 30f. multicoloured 20 10

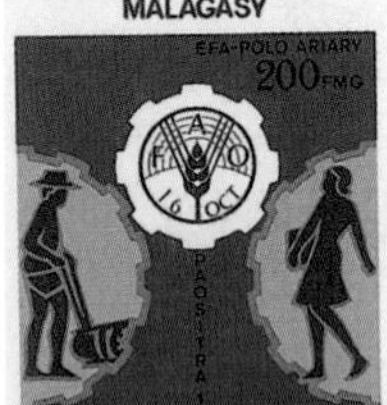

214 Ploughing and Sowing

1981. World Food Day.
444 **214** 200f. multicoloured . . . 1·25 60

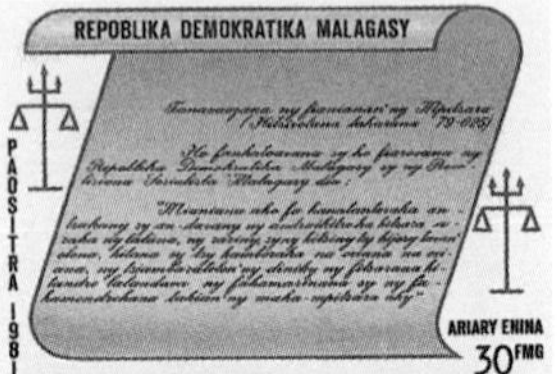

215 Magistrates' Oath

1981. Renewal of Magistrates' Oath.
445 **215** 30f. mauve and black . . 20 10

216 "Dove"

1981. Birth Centenary of Pablo Picasso.
446 **216** 80f. multicoloured 60 25

217 U.P.U. Emblem and Malagasy Stamps

1981. 20th Anniv of Admission to U.P.U.
447 **217** 5f. multicoloured 10 10
448 30f. multicoloured 20 10

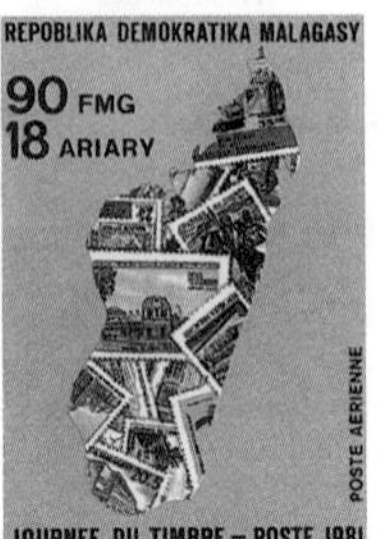

218 Stamps forming Map of Malagasy

1981. Stamp Day.
449 **218** 90f. multicoloured 65 30

219 Hook-billed Vanga

1982. Birds. Multicoloured.
450 25f. Type **219** 95 10
451 30f. Courol 95 10
452 200f. Madagascar fish eagle (vert) . . . . 7·25 85

220 Vaccination **221** Jeannette Mpihira

1982. Centenary of Discovery of Tubercule Bacillus.
453 **220** 30f. multicoloured 30 15

1982. Jeannette Mpihira Commemoration.
454 **221** 30f. multicoloured 20 10

222 Woman's Head formed from Map of Africa **223** Pierre Louis Boiteau

1982. Air. 20th Anniv of Pan-African Women's Organization.
455 **222** 80f. multicoloured 60 30

1982. Pierre Louis Boiteau Commemoration.
456 **223** 30f. multicoloured 20 15

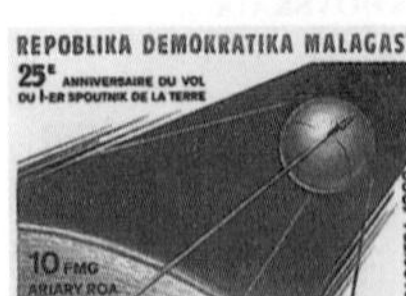

224 Andekaleka Dam

1982. Air. Andekaleka Hydro-electric Complex.
457 **224** 80f. multicoloured 60 30

225 "Sputnik I"

1982. 25th Anniv of First Artificial Satellite. Multicoloured.
458 10f. Type **225** 10 10
459 80f. Yuri Gagarin 60 30
460 100f. "Soyuz"–"Salyut" space station 75 35

226 Heading Ball

1982. World Cup Football Championship, Spain. Multicoloured.
461 30f. Type **226** 20 10
462 40f. Running with ball . . . 30 15
463 80f. Tackle 60 30

227 Ploughing, Sowing and F.A.O. Emblem

1982. World Food Day.
465 **227** 80f. multicoloured 50 30

228 Bar Scene

1982. 150th Anniv of Edouard Manet (artist). Multicoloured.
466 5f. Type **228** 45 15
467 30f. Woman in white 65 10
468 170f. Man with pipe . . . . 2·75 65

229 Emperor Snapper

1982. Fishes. Multicoloured.
470 5f. Type **229** 20 20
471 20f. Sailfish 30 20
472 30f. Lionfish 40 20
473 50f. Yellow-finned tuna . . . 65 20
474 200f. Black-tipped grouper 3·00 85

230 Fort Mahavelona

1982. Landscapes. Multicoloured.
476 10f. Type **230** (postage) . . . 10 10
477 30f. Ramena coast 20 10
478 400f. Jacarandas in flower (air) . . . . 2·75 1·50

231 Flags of Russia and Malagasy, Clasped Hands and Tractors

1982. 60th Anniv of U.S.S.R. Multicoloured.
479 10f. Type **231** 10 10
480 15f. Flags, clasped hands and radio antenna 10 10
481 30f. Map of Russia, Kremlin and Lenin 15 10
482 150f. Flags, clasped hands, statue and arms of Malagasy . . . . 1·00 45

232 Television, Drums, Envelope and Telephone

1983. World Communications Year. Multicoloured.
483 30f. Type **232** 15 10
484 80f. Stylized figures holding cogwheel . . . . 2·75 60

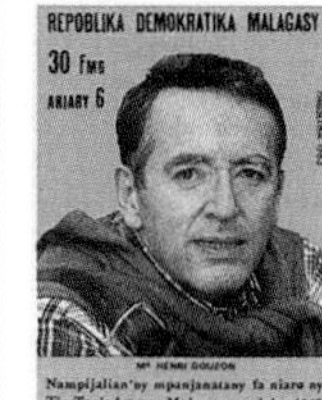

233 Axe breaking Chain on Map of Africa
234 Henri Douzon

1983. 20th Anniv of Organization of African Unity.
485 **233** 30f. multicoloured 20 10

1983. Henri Douzon (lawyer) Commemoration.
486 **234** 30f. multicoloured 20 10

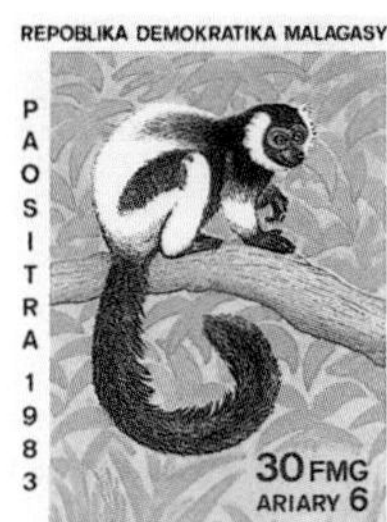

237 Ruffed Lemur

1984. Lemurs. Multicoloured.
489 30f. Type **237** 35 20
490 30f. Verreaux's sifaka 35 20
491 30f. Lesser mouse-lemur (horiz) 35 20
492 30f. Aye-aye (horiz) 35 20
493 200f. Indri (horiz) . . . . . 2·75 1·10

238 Ski Jumping

1984. Winter Olympic Games, Sarajevo. Mult.
495 20f. Type **238** 15 10
496 30f. Ice hockey 20 10
497 30f. Downhill skiing 20 10
498 30f. Speed skating 20 10
499 200f. Ice dancing . . . . . . 1·40 70

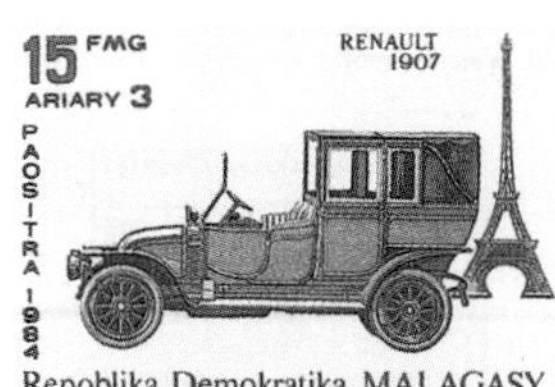

239 Renault, 1907

1984. Early Motor Cars. Multicoloured.
501 15f. Type **239** 20 10
502 30f. Benz, 1896 . . . . . . 30 15
503 30f. Baker, 1901 . . . . . . 30 15
504 30f. Blake, 1901 . . . . . . 30 15
505 200f. F.I.A.L., 1908 . . . . 2·00 75

240 Pastor Ravelojaona
241 "Noli me Tangere"

1984. Pastor Ravelojaona (encylopaedist) Commemoration.
507 **240** 30f. multicoloured 20 15

1984. 450th Death Anniv of Correggio. Paintings by Artist.
508 **241** 5f. multicoloured 10 10
509 – 20f. multicoloured 15 10
510 – 30f. multicoloured 25 15
511 – 80f. multicoloured 45 25
512 – 200f. multicoloured . . . 1·40 65

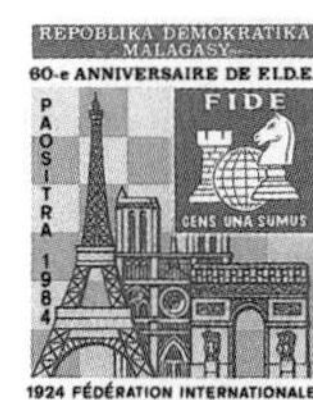

242 Paris Landmarks and Emblem
243 Football

1984. 60th Anniv of International Chess Federation. Multicoloured.
514 5f. Type **242** 15 15
515 20f. Wilhelm Steinitz and stylized king 20 15
516 30f. Vera Menchik and stylized queen 35 15
517 30f. Anatoly Karpov and trophy 35 15
518 215f. Nona Gaprindashvili and trophy . . . . 2·75 90

1984. Olympic Games, Los Angeles.
520 **243** 100f. multicoloured . . . 45 30

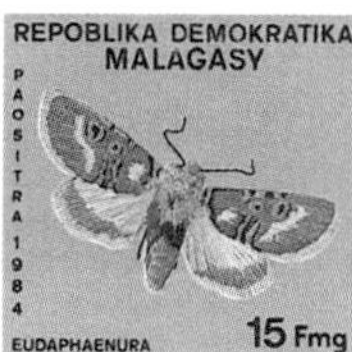

244 "Eudaphaenura splendens"
245 Ralaimongo

1984. Butterflies. Multicoloured.
521 15f. Type **244** 20 15
522 50f. "Acraea hova" 60 20
523 50f. "Othreis boesae" 60 20
524 50f. "Pharmocophagus antenor" 60 20
525 200f. "Epicausis smithii" . . 2·25 1·00

1984. Birth Centenary of Jean Ralaimongo (politician).
527 **245** 50f. multicoloured 30 15

246 Children in Brief-case
247 "Disa incarnata"

1984. 25th Anniv of Children's Rights Legislation.
528 **246** 50f. multicoloured 40 15

1984. Orchids. Multicoloured.
529 20f. Type **247** (postage) . . . 20 10
530 235f. "Eulophiella roempleriana" . . . . . . 2·25 85
531 50f. "Eulophiella roempleriana" (horiz) (air) 60 25
532 50f. "Grammangis ellisii" (horiz) 60 25
533 50f. "Grammangis spectabilis" 60 25

248 U.N. Emblem and Cotton Plant

1984. 20th Anniv of United Nations Conference on Commerce and Development.
535 **248** 100f. multicoloured . . . 60 30

249 "Sun Princess" (Sadio Diouf)

1984. 40th Anniv of International Civil Aviation Organization.
536 **249** 100f. multicoloured . . . 65 30

250 Bible, Map and Gothic Letters

1985. 150th Anniv of First Bible in Malagasy Language.
537 **250** 50f. brown, pink and black 30 15

251 Farming Scenes, Census-taker and Farmer
252 Lap-dog

1985. Agricultural Census.
538 **251** 50f. grey, black and mauve 30 15

1985. Cats and Dogs. Multicoloured.
539 20f. Type **252** 20 15
540 20f. Siamese cat 20 15
541 50f. Abyssinian cat (vert) . . 60 20
542 100f. Cocker spaniel (vert) . . 1·25 35
543 235f. Poodle . . . . 2·50 90

253 Russian Soldiers in Berlin

1985. 40th Anniv of Victory in Second World War.
545 20f. Type **253** 15 10
546 50f. Arms of French squadron and fighter planes 40 15
547 100f. Victory parade, Red Square, Moscow 75 30
548 100f. French troops entering Paris (vert) . . . . 1·25 30

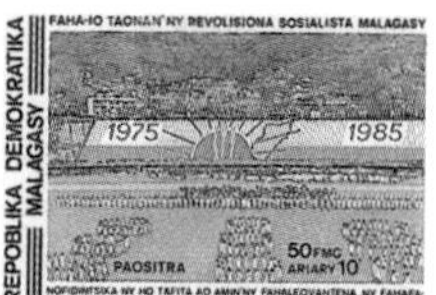

254 Parade in Stadium

1985. 10th Anniv of Malagasy Democratic Republic.
549 **254** 50f. multicoloured 40 15

255 Medal and Independence Obelisk
256 Peace Dove and Stylized People

1985. 25th Anniv of Independence.
550 **255** 50f. multicoloured 40 15

1985. 12th World Youth and Students' Festival, Moscow.
551 **256** 50f. multicoloured 40 15

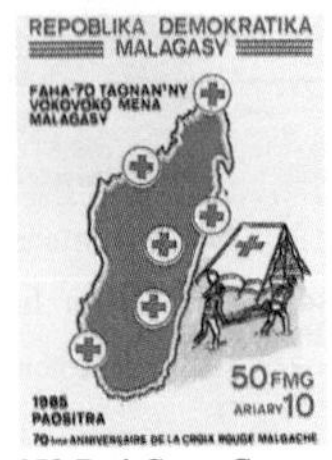

257 I.Y.Y. Emblem and Map of Madagascar
258 Red Cross Centres and First Aid Post

1985. International Youth Year.
552 **257** 100f. multicoloured . . . 60 25

1985. 70th Anniv of Malagasy Red Cross.
553 **258** 50f. multicoloured 60 25

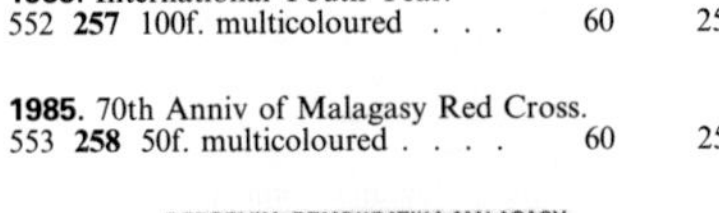

259 "View of Sea at Saintes-Maries" (Vincent van Gogh)

1985. Impressionist Paintings. Multicoloured.
554 20f. Type **259** 45 10
555 20f. "Rouen Cathedral in the Evening" (Claude Monet) (vert) 45 10
556 45f. "Young Girls in Black" (Pierre-Auguste Renoir) (vert) 80 20
557 50f. "Red Vineyard at Arles" (van Gogh) 80 20
558 100f. "Boulevard des Capucines, Paris" (Monet) 1·40 40

260 Indira Gandhi

1985. Indira Gandhi (Indian Prime Minister) Commemoration.
560 **260** 100f. multicoloured . . . 80 30

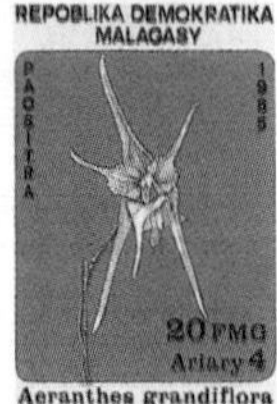

261 Figures and Dove on Globe and Flag
262 "Aeranthes grandiflora"

1985. 40th Anniv of U.N.O.
561 **261** 100f. multicoloured . . . 65 25

1985. Orchids. Multicoloured.
562 20f. Type **262** 20 10
563 45f. "Angraecum magdalenae" and "Nephele oenopion" (insect) (horiz) 35 15
564 50f. "Aerangis stylosa" . . . 35 15
565 100f. "Angraecum eburneum longicalcar" and "Hippotion batschi" (insect) 80 35
566 100f. "Angraecum sesquipedale" and "Xanthopan morganipredicta" (insect) 80 35

263 Russian and Czechoslovakian Cosmonauts

1985. Russian "Interkosmos" Space Programme. Multicoloured.
568 20f. Type **263** 15 10
569 20f. Russian and American flags and "Apollo"–"Soyuz" link 15 10
570 50f. Russian and Indian cosmonauts 30 15
571 100f. Russian and Cuban cosmonauts 50 25
572 200f. Russian and French cosmonauts . . . . 1·25 60

264 Emblem in "10"

1985. 10th Anniv of Malagasy Democratic Republic.
574 **264** 50f. multicoloured 30 15

265 Headquarters

1986. 10th Anniv of ARO (State insurance system).
575 **265** 50f. yellow and brown . . 30 15

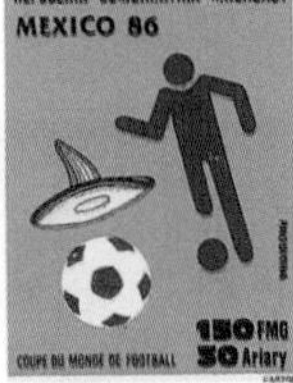

266 "David and Uriah" (Rembrandt)
268 Sombrero, Football and Player

267 Comet

1986. Foreign Paintings in Hermitage Museum, Leningrad. Multicoloured.
576 20f. Type **266** 20 10
577 50f. "Portrait of Old Man in Red" (Rembrandt) 50 30
578 50f. "Danae" (Rembrandt) (horiz) 50 30
579 50f. "Marriage of Earth and Water" (Rubens) 50 30
580 50f. "Portrait of Infanta Isabella's Maid" (Rubens) 50 30

1986. Air. Appearance of Halley's Comet.
582 **267** 150f. multicoloured . . . 1·00 50

1986. Russian Paintings in the Tretyakov Gallery, Moscow. As T **266**. Multicoloured.
583 20f. "Fruit and Flowers" (I. Khroutsky) (horiz) . . . 15 10
584 50f. "The Rooks have Returned" (A. Savrasov) 60 25
585 50f. "Unknown Woman" (I. Kramskoi) (horiz) . . . 30 20
586 50f. "Aleksandr Pushkin" (O. Kiprenski) 30 20
587 100f. "March, 1895" (I. Levitan) (horiz) 90 40

1986. World Cup Football Championship, Mexico.
589 **268** 150f. multicoloured . . . 1·10 30

269 Child Care
270 Jungle Cat

1986. U.N.I.C.E.F. Child Survival Campaign.
590 **269** 60f. multicoloured 40 15

1986. Wild Cats. Multicoloured.
591 10f. Type **270** 20 10
592 10f. Wild cat 20 10
593 60f. Caracal 45 20
594 60f. Leopard cat 45 20
595 60f. Serval 45 20

271 Dove above Hands holding Globe

1986. International Peace Year. Multicoloured.
597 60f. Type **271** 40 15
598 150f. Doves above emblem and map . . . . 1·00 45

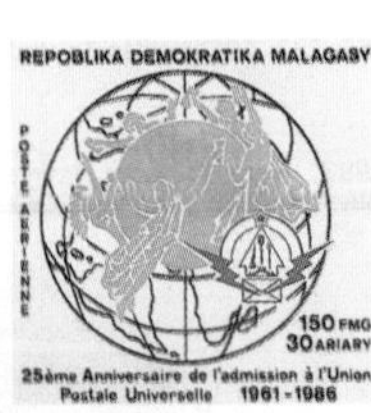

272 U.P.U. Emblem on Dove
273 U.P.U. Emblem on Globe

1986. World Post Day.
599 **272** 60f. multicoloured (postage) 40 15
600 150f. blue, black and red (air) . . . . 1·10 50

1986. Air. 25th Anniv of Admission to U.P.U.
601 **273** 150f. multicoloured . . . 1·10 50

274 Giant Madagascar Coucal

1986. Birds. Multicoloured.
602 60f. Type **274** . . . . 1·10 30
603 60f. Crested Madagascar coucal . . . . 1·10 30
604 60f. Rufous vangas (vert) . . 1·10 30
605 60f. Red-tailed vangas (vert) 1·10 30
606 60f. Sicklebill . . . . 1·10 30

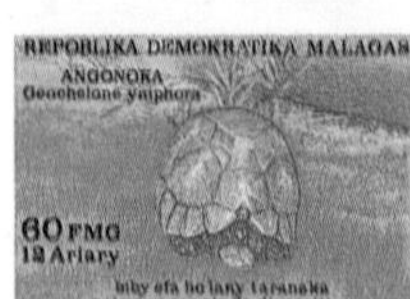

275 Tortoise

1987. Endangered Animals. Multicoloured.
608 60f. Type **275** 65 25
609 60f. Crocodile 65 25
610 60f. Crested wood ibis (vert) 65 25
611 60f. Vasa parrot 65 25

276 Crowd in "40"

1987. 40th Anniv of Anti-colonial Uprising.
613 **276** 60f. brown, red and yellow 35 15
614 – 60f. multicoloured 35 15
DESIGN: No. 614, Hands in broken manacles, map, rifleman and spearman.

277 Emblems, Map and Pictogram

1987. 1st Indian Ocean Towns Games.
615 **277** 60f. multicoloured 35 15
616 150f. multicoloured . . . 1·10 35

278 "Sarimanok"

1987. The "Sarimanok" (replica of early dhow). Multicoloured.
617 60f. Type **278** 50 20
618 150f. "Sarimanok" (different) 1·25 40

279 Coffee Plant
280 Rifle Shooting and Satellite

1987. 25th Anniv of African and Malagasy Coffee Producers Organization. Multicoloured.
619 60f. Type **279** 35 15
620 150f. Map showing member countries . . . . 1·10 35

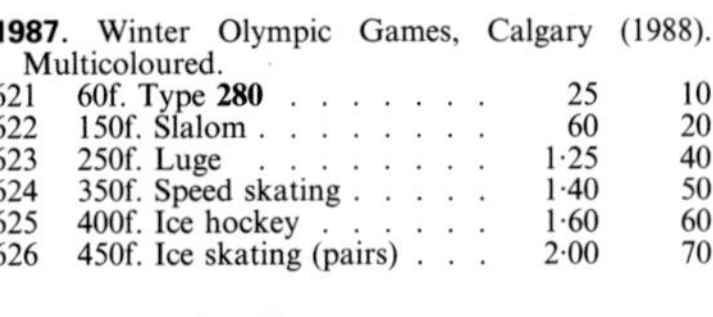

1987. Winter Olympic Games, Calgary (1988). Multicoloured.
621 60f. Type **280** 25 10
622 150f. Slalom 60 20
623 250f. Luge . . . . 1·25 40
624 350f. Speed skating . . . . . 1·40 50
625 400f. Ice hockey . . . . . . 1·60 60
626 450f. Ice skating (pairs) . . . 2·00 70

281 "Giotto" Space Probe

1987. Appearance of Halley's Comet (1986). Space Probes. Multicoloured.
628 60f. Type **281** 25 10
629 150f. "Vega 1" 60 20
630 250f. "Vega 2" . . . . . . 1·25 40
631 350f. "Planet A 1" . . . . . 1·40 50
632 400f. "Planet B 1" . . . . . 1·60 60
633 450f. "I.C.E." . . . . 2·00 70

282 Piper Aztec
283 Rabearivelo

1987. Air. 25th Anniv of Air Madagascar. Mult.
635 60f. Type **282** 40 20
636 60f. De Havilland Twin Otter 40 20
637 150f. Boeing 747-200 . . . . 1·00 40

1987. 50th Death Anniv of Jean-Joseph Rabearivelo (poet).
638 **283** 60f. multicoloured 30 15

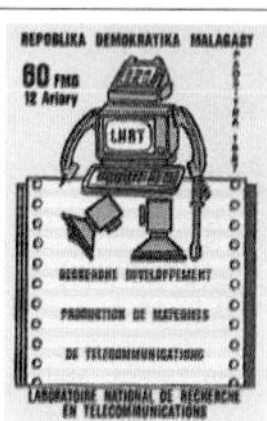

284 Communications Equipment Robot and Print-out Paper
285 Emblem

1987. National Telecommunications Research Laboratory.
639 **284** 60f. green, black and red 30 15

1987. 150th Anniv of Execution of Rafaravavy Rasalama (Christian martyr).
640 **285** 60f. black, deep blue and blue 30 15

286 Hand using Key and Telegraphist

1987. Cent of Antananarivo–Tamatave Telegraph.
641 **286** 60f. multicoloured 30 15

287 Bartholomeu Dias and Departure from Palos, 1492

1987. 500th Anniv (1992) of Discovery of America by Columbus. Multicoloured.
642 60f. Type **287** 30 20
643 150f. Route around Samana Cay and Henry the Navigator 60 25
644 250f. Columbus and crew disembarking, 1492, and A. de Marchena 75 30
645 350f. Building Fort Navidad and Paolo del Pozzo Toscanelli 1·10 40
646 400f. Columbus in Barcelona, 1493, and Queen Isabella of Spain 1·60 65
647 450f. Columbus and "Nina" 1·75 70

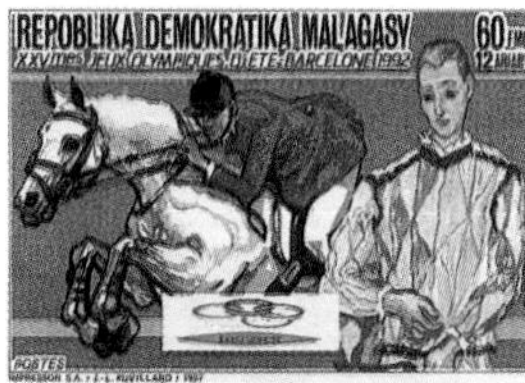
288 Showjumping and "Harlequin" (Picasso)

1987. Olympic Games, Barcelona (1992). Multicoloured.
649 60f. Type **288** (postage) 15 10
650 150f. Weightlifting and Barcelona Cathedral 40 20
651 250f. Hurdling and Canaletas Fountain 70 30
652 350f. High jumping and Parc d'Attractions 1·00 40
653 400f. Gymnast on bar and church (air) 1·40 50
654 450f. Gymnast with ribbon and Triumphal Arch 1·75 50

289 Anniversary Emblem, T.V. Tower and Interhotel "Berlin"
290 Musician and Dancers

1987. 750th Anniv of Berlin.
656 **289** 150f. multicoloured 25 15

1987. Schools Festival.
657 **290** 60f. multicoloured 15 10

291 Madagascar Pasteur Institute and Pasteur

1987. Centenary of Pasteur Institute, Paris.
658 **291** 250f. multicoloured 60 25

292 "After the Shipwreck" (Eugene Delacroix)

1987. Paintings in Pushkin Museum of Fine Arts, Moscow. Multicoloured.
659 10f. Type **292** 15 10
660 60f. "Jupiter and Callisto" (Francois Boucher) (vert) 15 10
661 60f. "Still Life with Swan" (Frans Snyders) 15 10
662 60f. "Chalet in the Mountains" (Gustave Courbet) 15 10
663 150f. "At the Market" (Joachim Bueckelaer) 40 15

293 Emblem
294 Family and House on Globe

1987. 10th Anniv of Pan-African Telecommunications Union.
665 **293** 250f. multicoloured 40 20

1988. International Year of Shelter for the Homeless (1987). Multicoloured.
666 80f. Type **294** 15 10
667 250f. Hands forming house protecting family from rain 35 20

295 Lenin addressing Crowd

1988. 70th Anniv of Russian Revolution. Mult.
668 60f. Type **295** 15 10
669 60f. Revolutionaries 15 10
670 150f. Lenin in crowd 25 15

296 Broad-nosed Gentle Lemur

1988. Endangered Species. Multicoloured.
671 60f. Type **296** 15 10
672 150f. Diadem sifaka 20 15
673 250f. Indri 35 15
674 350f. Ruffed lemur 60 25
675 550f. Purple herons (horiz) 1·60 50
676 1500f. Nossi-be chameleon (horiz) 2·40 1·25

297 Ice Skating

1988. Winter Olympic Games, Calgary. Mult.
678 20f. Type **297** 10 10
679 60f. Speed-skating 10 10
680 60f. Slalom 10 10
681 100f. Cross-country skiing 20 10
682 250f. Ice hockey 45 20

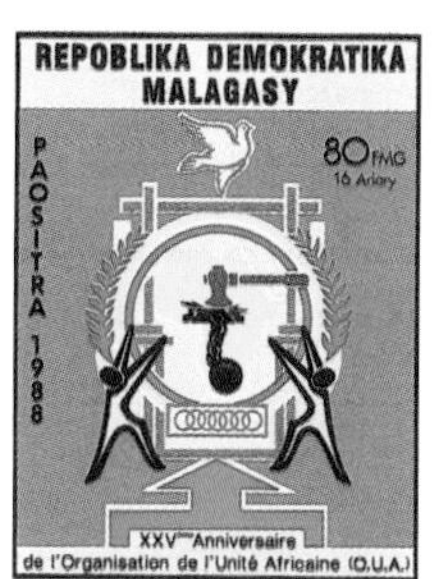
298 Dove, Axe breaking Chain and Map

1988. 25th Anniv of Organization of African Unity.
684 **298** 80f. multicoloured 15 10

299 Institute Building

1988. 20th Anniv of National Posts and Telecommunications Institute.
685 **299** 80f. multicoloured 15 10

300 College

1988. Centenary of St. Michael's College.
686 **300** 250f. multicoloured 30 20

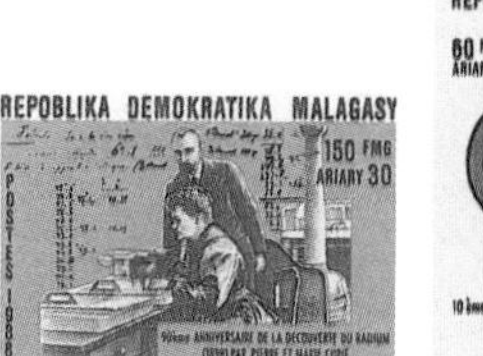
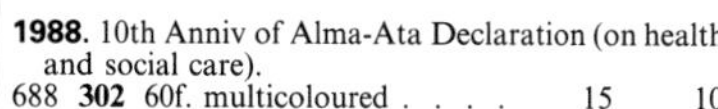
301 Pierre and Marie Curie in Laboratory
302 Emblem

1988. 90th Anniv of Discovery of Radium.
687 **301** 150f. brown and mauve 40 15

1988. 10th Anniv of Alma-Ata Declaration (on health and social care).
688 **302** 60f. multicoloured 15 10

303 Emblem
304 Ring-tailed Lemurs on Island

1988. 40th Anniv of W.H.O.
689 **303** 150f. brown, blue and black 20 15

1988. 50th Anniv of Tsimbazaza Botanical and Zoological Park. Multicoloured.
690 20f. Type **304** 15 10
691 80f. Ring-tailed lemur with young (25 × 37 mm) 20 10
692 250f. Palm tree and ring-tailed lemur within "Zoo" (47 × 32 mm) 40 20

305 Hoopoe and Blue Madagascar Coucal
306 Cattle grazing

1988. Scouts, Birds and Butterflies. Multicoloured.
694 80f. Type **305** 10 10
695 250f. "Chrysiridia croesus" (butterfly) 40 20
696 270f. Nelicourvi weaver and red forest fody 50 10
697 350f. "Papilio dardanus" (butterflies) 60 40
698 550f. Crested Madagascar coucal 1·00 25
699 1500f. "Argema mittrei" (butterfly) 2·50 2·00

1988. 10th Anniv of International Fund for Agricultural Development.
701 **306** 250f. multicoloured 30 20

307 Karl Bach and Clavier
308 Books

1988. Musicians' Anniversaries. Multicoloured.
702 80f. Type **307** (death bicentenary) 15 10
703 250f. Franz Schubert and piano (160th death) 40 15
704 270f. Georges Bizet and scene from "Carmen" (150th birth) 40 20
705 350f. Claude Debussy and scene from "Pelleas et Melisande" (70th death) 50 25
706 550f. George Gershwin at piano writing score of "Rhapsody in Blue" (90th birth) 75 45
707 1500f. Elvis Presley (10th death (1987)) 2·75 1·25

1988. "Ecole en Fete" Schools Festival.
709 **308** 80f. multicoloured 15 10

309 "Black Sea Fleet at Feodosiya" (Ivan Aivazovski)
310 "Tragocephala crassicornis"

1988. Paintings of Sailing Ships. Multicoloured.
710 20f. Type **309** 40 15
711 80f. "Lesnoie" (N. Semenov) 40 15
712 80f. "Seascape with Sailing Ships" (Simon de Vlieger) 40 15

713 100f. "Orel" (N. Golitsine) (horiz) 45 15
714 250f. "Naval Battle Exercises" (Adam Silo) . . 90 25

1988. Endangered Beetles. Multicoloured.
716 20f. Type **310** 15 10
717 80f. "Polybothris symptuosa-gema" 55 25
718 250f. "Euchroea auripigmenta" . . . . . . 1·25 60
719 350f. "Stellognata maculata" 1·60 80

311 Stretcher Bearers and Anniversary Emblem

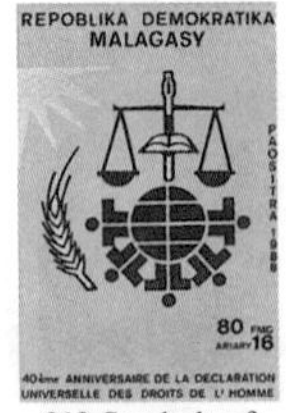

312 Symbols of Human Rights

1988. 125th Anniv of International Red Cross. Multicoloured.
720 80f. Type **311** 15 10
721 250f. Red Cross services, emblem and Henri Dunant (founder) 35 20

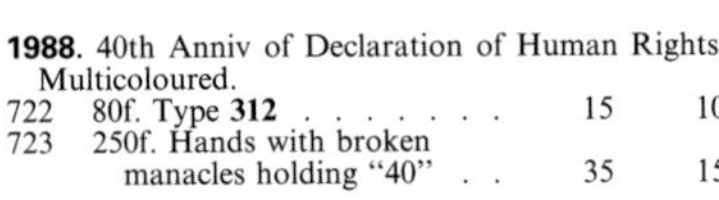

1988. 40th Anniv of Declaration of Human Rights. Multicoloured.
722 80f. Type **312** 15 10
723 250f. Hands with broken manacles holding "40" . . 35 15

313 Mercedes-Benz "Blitzen-Benz", 1909

1989. Cars and Trains. Multicoloured.
724 80f. Type **313** 15 10
725 250f. Micheline diesel railcar "Tsikirity", 1952, Tananarive–Moramanga line . . . . 1·50 15
726 270f. Bugatti coupe binder, "41" 40 20
727 350f. Class 1020 electric locomotive, Germany . . . 1·90 25
728 1500f. Souleze 701 diesel train, Malagasy . . . . . 4·75 1·25
729 2500f. Opel racing car, 1913 3·50 2·00

314 Tyrannosaurus

1989. Prehistoric Animals. Multicoloured.
731 20f. Type **314** 15 10
732 80f. Stegosaurus 20 10
733 250f. Arsinoitherium 40 15
734 450f. Triceratops 80 30

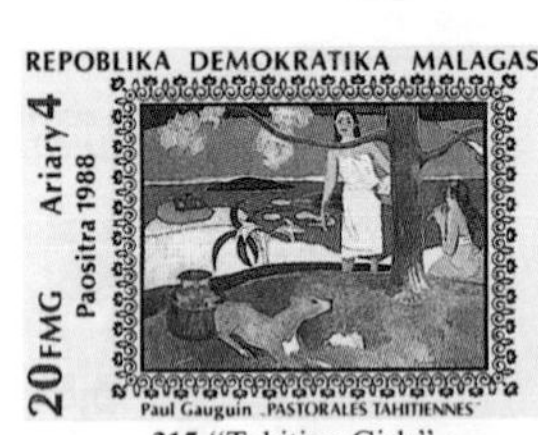

315 "Tahitian Girls"

1989. Woman in Art. Multicoloured.
736 20f. Type **315** 10 10
737 80f. "Portrait of a Girl" (Jean-Baptiste Greuze) . . 15 10
738 80f. "Portrait of a Young Woman" (Titian) 15 10
739 100f. "Woman in Black" (Auguste Renoir) 20 10
740 250f. "The Lace-maker" (Vasily Tropinine) 35 15

316 "Sobennikoffia robusta"

317 Nehru

1989. Orchids. Multicoloured.
742 5f. Type **316** 15 10
743 10f. "Grammangis fallax" (horiz) 15 10
744 80f. "Angraecum sororium" 20 10
745 80f. "Cymbidiella humblotii" 20 10
746 250f. "Oenia oncidiiflora" . . 60 20

1989. Birth Centenary of Jawaharlal Nehru (Indian statesman).
748 **317** 250f. multicoloured . . . 45 15

318 Mahamasina Sports Complex, Lake Anosy and Ampefiloha Quarter

1989. Antananarivo. Multicoloured.
749 5f. Type **318** 10 10
750 20f. Andravoahangy and Anjanahary Quarters . . . 10 10
751 80f. Zoma market and Faravohitra Quarter . . . 15 10
752 80f. Andohan' Analekely Quarter and 29 March Column 15 10
753 250f. Avenue de l'Independance and Jean Ralaimongo Column . . . 35 15
754 550f. Lake Anosy, Queen's Palace and Andohalo School 70 35

319 Rose Quartz

1989. Ornamental Minerals. Multicoloured.
755 80f. Type **319** 20 10
756 250f. Fossilized wood 60 20

320 Pope and Rasoamanarivo

321 Map and Runner with Torch

1989. Visit of Pope John Paul II and Beatification of Victoire Rasoamanarivo. Multicoloured.
757 80f. Type **320** 20 10
758 250f. Map and Pope 55 20

1989. Town Games.
759 **321** 80f.+20f. multicoloured 15 15

322 "Storming the Bastille"

1989. Bicentenary of French Revolution (1st issue).
760 **322** 250f. multicoloured . . . 35 15
See also Nos. 773/5.

323 Mirabeau and Gabriel Riqueti at Meeting of States General

1989. "Philexfrance 89" International Stamp Exhibition, Paris. Multicoloured.
761 250f. Type **323** 30 15
762 350f. Camille Desmoulins' call to arms 45 20
763 1000f. Lafayette and crowd demanding bread . . . . . 1·25 60
764 1500f. Trial of King Louis XVI . . . . 2·00 80
765 2500f. Assassination of Marat 3·25 1·25

324 "Mars 1"

1989. Space Probes. Multicoloured.
767 20f. Type **324** 10 10
768 80f. "Mars 3" 15 10
769 80f. "Zond 2" 15 10
770 250f. "Mariner 9" 35 15
771 270f. "Viking 2" 40 20

325 "Liberty guiding the People" (Eugene Delacroix)

1989. Bicentenary of French Revolution (2nd issue). Multicoloured.
773 5f. Type **325** (postage) . . . 10 10
774 80f. "La Marseillaise" (Francois Rude) 15 10
775 250f. "Oath of the Tennis Court" (Jacques Louis David) (air) 35 15

326 Rene Cassin (founder)

327 Mother and Young on Bamboo

1989. 25th Anniv of International Human Rights Institute for French Speaking Countries.
776 **326** 250f. multicoloured . . . 30 15

1989. Golden Gentle Lemur.
777 **327** 250f. multicoloured . . . 40 20

328 Footballer and Cavour Monument, Turin

330 Long Jumping

329 Pennant Coralfish

1989. World Cup Football Championship, Italy. Multicoloured.
778 350f. Type **328** 50 20
779 1000f. Footballer and Christopher Columbus monument, Genoa . . . . 1·40 50
780 1500f. Florentine footballer, 1530, and "David" (sculpture, Michelangelo) 2·00 75
781 2500f. Footballer and "Rape of Proserpina" (sculpture, Bernini), Rome . . . . . 3·25 1·40

1990. Fishes. Multicoloured.
783 5f. Type **329** 10 10
784 20f. Snub-nosed parasitic eel (vert) 20 10
785 80f. Manta ray (vert) 35 15
786 250f. Black-tipped grouper 90 30
787 320f. Smooth hammerhead 1·25 45

1990. Olympic Games, Barcelona (1992). Mult.
789 80f. Type **330** 10 10
790 250f. Pole vaulting 35 15
791 550f. Hurdling 65 25
792 1500f. Cycling . . . . 2·00 60
793 2000f. Baseball . . . . 2·50 80
794 2500f. Tennis . . . . 3·25 1·25

331 "Queen of the Isalo" (rock)

1990. Natural Features. Multicoloured.
796 70f. Type **331** 15 10
797 150f. Lonjy Island (as T **332**) 25 15

332 Pipe

1990. Sakalava Craft. Multicoloured.
798 70f. Type **332** 15 10
799 150f. Combs (as T **331**) . . . 25 15

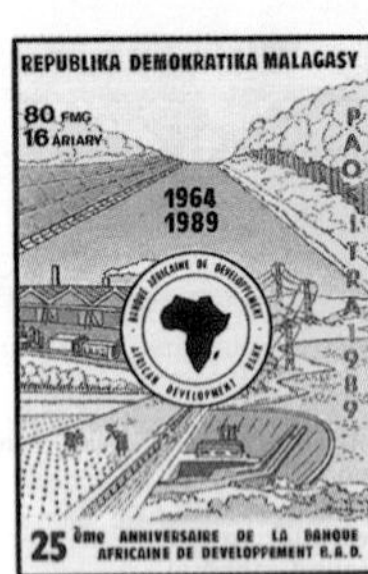

333 Emblem and Projects

1990. 25th Anniv of African Development Bank.
800 **333** 80f. multicoloured 15 10

334 "Voyager II" and Neptune

1990. 20th Anniv of First Manned Landing on Moon. Multicoloured.
801 80f. Type **334** 15 10
802 250f. Hughes Hercules flying boat, Boeing 747 airliner and flying boat "of the future" 40 15
803 550f. "Noah" satellite tracking elephants 70 25
804 1500f. Venus and "Magellan" space probe . . . . . . 1·25 55
805 2000f. Halley's Comet and Concorde . . . . 2·25 90
806 2500f. "Apollo 11" landing capsule and crew . . . . . 3·25 1·00

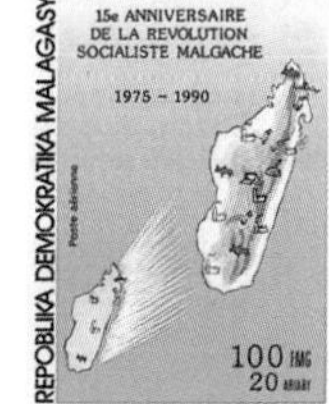

335 Liner on Globe

336 Maps showing Development between 1975 and 1990

1990. 30th Anniv of International Maritime Organization.
808 **335** 250f. ultramarine, bl & blk 55 15

1990. Air. 15th Anniv of Malagasy Socialist Revolution.
809 **336** 100f. multicoloured . . . 15 10
810 – 350f. black and grey . . . 45 25
DESIGN: 350f. Presidential Palaces, 1975 and 1990.

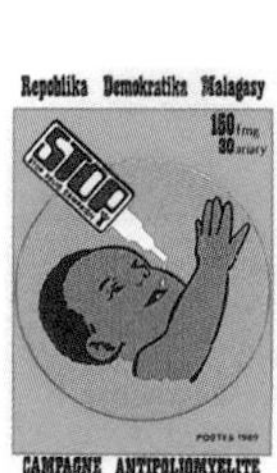

337 Oral Vaccination

338 Four-man Bobsleigh

1990. Anti-Polio Campaign.
811 **337** 150f. multicoloured . . . 30 15

1990. Winter Olympic Games, Albertville (1992) (1st issue). Multicoloured.
812 350f. Type **338** 40 20
813 1000f. Speed skating . . . . 1·25 40
814 1500f. Cross-country skiing 2·00 65
815 2500f. Super G . . . . . . 3·00 1·10
See also Nos. 862/8.

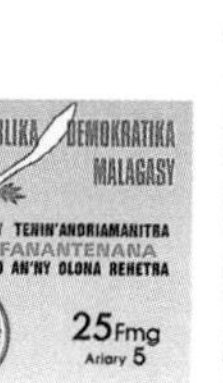

339 Society Emblem

340 Mascot

1990. Air. 25th Anniv of Malagasy Bible Society.
817 **339** 25f. multicoloured 10 10
818 – 100f. blue, black and green 15 10
DESIGN—VERT: 100f. Society emblem.

1990. 3rd Indian Ocean Island Games, Malagasy (1st issue).
819 **340** 100f.+20f. on 80f.+20f. multicoloured 15 15
820 350f.+20f. on 250f.+20f. multicoloured 75 40

The games were originally to be held in 1989 and the stamps were printed for release then. The issued stamps are handstamped with the correct date and new value.

See also Nos. 822/3.

341 Symbols of Agriculture and Industry

342 Torch

1990. 30th Anniv of Independence.
821 **341** 100f. multicoloured . . . 15 10

1990. 3rd Indian Ocean Island Games, Malagasy (2nd issue).
822 **342** 100f. multicoloured . . . 15 10
823 350f. multicoloured . . . 45 20

343 Envelopes forming Map and Mail Transportation

1990. Air. World Post Day.
824 **343** 350f. multicoloured . . . 2·00 55

344 Ho Chi Minh

345 "Avahi laniger"

1990. Birth Centenary of Ho Chi Minh (President of North Vietnam, 1945–69).
825 **344** 350f. multicoloured . . . 40 20

1990. Lemurs. Multicoloured.
826 10f. Type **345** 10 10
827 20f. "Lemur fulvus albifrons" 10 10
828 20f. "Lemur fulvus sanfordi" 10 10
829 100f. "Lemur fulvus collaris" 25 15
830 100f. "Lepulemur ruficaudatus" 25 15

346 Fluted Giant Clam

347 Letters in Book

1990. Shells. Multicoloured.
832 40f. Type **346** 25 15
833 50f. Dimidiate and subulate augers 35 15

1990. International Literacy Year. Multicoloured.
834 20f. Type **347** 10 10
835 100f. Open book and hand holding pen (horiz) 20 15

348 Cep

349 De Gaulle, Leclerc and Parod under Arc de Triomphe, 1944

1991. Fungi. Multicoloured.
836 25f. Type **348** 10 10
837 100f. Butter mushroom . . . 35 10
838 350f. Fly agaric 55 20
839 450f. Scarlet-stemmed boletus 75 25
840 680f. Flaky-stemmed witches' mushroom . . . . 1·10 40
841 800f. Brown birch bolete . . 1·25 45
842 900f. Orange birch bolete . . 1·40 55

1991. Multicoloured.
844 100f. Type **349** 10 10
845 350f. "Galileo" space probe near Jupiter 55 10
846 800f. Crew of "Apollo 11" on Moon . . . . 1·10 25
847 900f. De Gaulle and Free French emblem, 1942 . . . 1·40 30
848 1250f. Concorde aircraft and German ICE high speed train . . . . 3·25 80
849 2500f. Gen. Charles de Gaulle (French statesman) 3·25 95

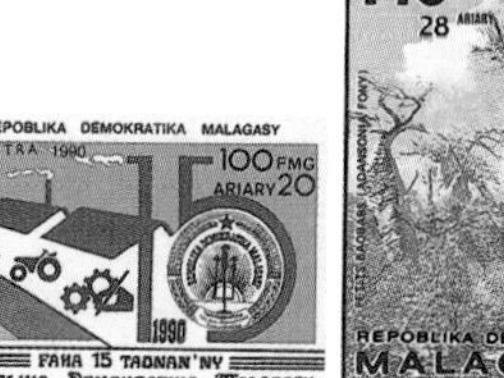

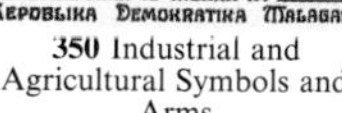

350 Industrial and Agricultural Symbols and Arms

351 Baobab Tree

1991. 15th Anniv (1990) of Republic.
851 **350** 100f. multicoloured . . . 10 10

1991. Trees. Multicoloured.
852 140f. Type **351** 55 10
853 500f. "Dideria madagascariensis" . . . . 1·10 45

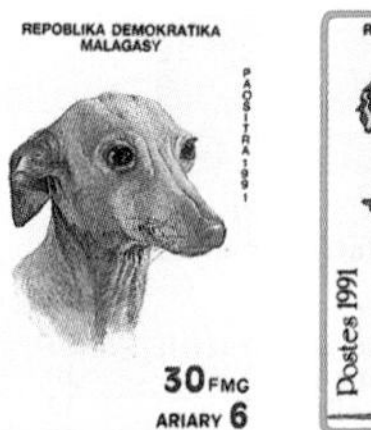

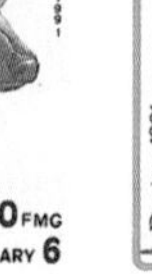

352 Whippet

353 Cross-country Skiing

1991. Dogs. Multicoloured.
854 30f. Type **352** 35 10
855 50f. Japanese spaniel 45 10
856 140f. Toy terrier 90 10
857 350f. Chow-chow 65 10
858 500f. Chihuahua 90 15
859 800f. Afghan hound . . . . 1·10 25
860 1140f. Papillon . . . . 1·75 65

1991. Winter Olympic Games, Albertville (2nd issue). Multicoloured.
862 5f. Type **353** 10 10
863 15f. Biathlon 10 10
864 60f. Ice hockey 35 10
865 140f. Skiing 45 10
866 640f. Ice skating 45 30
867 1000f. Ski jumping . . . . . 1·90 50
868 1140f. Speed skating . . . . 2·75 60

354 "Helictopleurus splendidicollis"

1992. Scouts, Insects and Fungi. Multicoloured.
870 140f. Type **354** 10 10
871 500f. "Russula radicans" (mushroom) 90 25
872 640f. "Cocles contemplator" (insect) . . . . 1·10 30
873 1025f. "Russula singeri" (mushroom) . . . . 1·60 50
874 1140f. "Euchroea oberthurii" (beetle) . . . . 1·75 60
875 3500f. "Lactariopsis pandani" (mushroom) . . . . 5·50 2·00

355 Former and Present Buildings

1992. 90th Anniv (1991) of Paul Minault College.
877 **355** 140f. multicoloured . . . 45 10

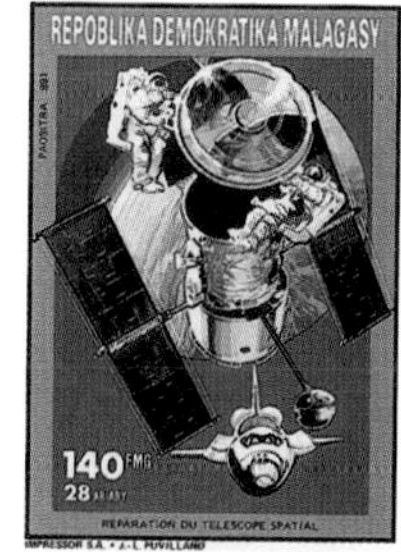

356 Repairing Space Telescope

1992. Space. Multicoloured.
878 140f. Type **356** 10 10
879 500f. "Soho" sun probe . . . 65 25
880 640f. "Topex-Poseidon" oceanic survey satellite . . 90 30
881 1025f. "Hipparcos" planetary survey satellite . . . . . . 1·25 50
882 1140f. "Voyager 2" Neptune probe . . . . 1·40 60
883 5000f. "ETS-VI" Japanese test communications satellite . . . . 6·75 1·25

357 Ryuichi Sakamoto

1992. Entertainers. Multicoloured.
885 100f. Type **357** 10 10
886 350f. John Lennon 55 15
887 800f. Bruce Lee . . . . . . 1·40 40
888 900f. Sammy Davis jun . . . 1·60 45
889 1250f. John Wayne . . . . . 1·60 60
890 2500f. James Dean . . . . . 3·25 1·25

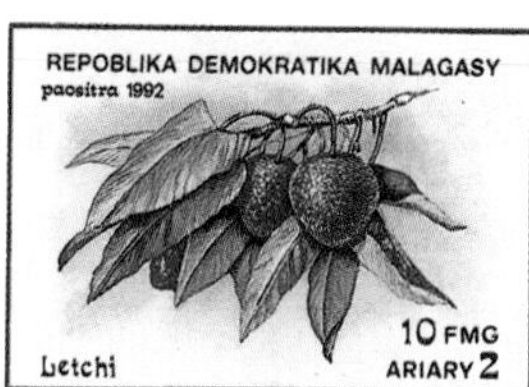

358 Lychees

1992. Fruits. Multicoloured.
892 10f. Type **358** 10 10
893 50f. Oranges 10 10
894 60f. Apples 10 10
895 140f. Peaches 35 10
896 555f. Bananas (vert) . . . . 1·10 30
897 800f. Avocados (vert) . . . . 1·40 40
898 1400f. Mangoes (vert) . . . . 2·40 75

359 9th-century Galley

360 Couple in Heart

1992. Sailing Ships. Multicoloured.
900 15f. Type **359** 10 10
901 65f. Full-rigged sailing ship, 1878 . . . . 10 10
902 140f. "Golden Hind" (Drake's flagship) 45 10
903 500f. 18th-century dhow . . 1·00 25
904 640f. "Ostrust" (galleon), 1721 (vert) . . . . 1·10 30
905 800f. Dutch caravel, 1599 (vert) . . . . 1·40 40
906 1025f. "Santa Maria" (Columbus's flagship), 1492 1·75 50

1992. Anti-AIDS Campaign.
908 **360** 140f. black and mauve . . 35 10

361 Tending Trees

1992. Reforestation.
909 **361** 140f. dp green, black & grn . . . 10 10

POSTAGE DUE STAMPS

D **13** Independence Obelisk

1962.

D45	**D 13**	1f. green	10	10
D46		2f. brown	10	10
D47		3f. violet	10	10
D48		4f. slate	10	10
D49		5f. red	10	10
D50		10f. green	15	15
D51		20f. purple	20	20
D52		40f. blue	50	45
D53		50f. red	75	70
D54		100f. black	1·40	1·25

APPENDIX

The following stamps have either been issued in excess of postal needs or have not been available to the public in reasonable quantities at face value.

1987.

Winter Olympic Games, Calgary (1988). 1500f. (on gold foil).

1989.

Scout and Butterfly. 5000f. (on gold foil).

"Philexfrance 89" Int Stamp Exhibition, Paris. 5000f. (on gold foil).

World Cup Football Championship, Italy. 5000f. (on gold foil).

1990.

Winter Olympic Games, Albertville (1992). 5000f. (on gold foil).

1991.

Birth Centenary of De Gaulle. 5000f. (on gold foil).

1992.

Olympic Games, Barcelona. 500f. (on gold foil).

1993.

Bicentenary of French Republic. 1989 "Philexfrance 89" issue optd. 5000f.

1994.

Elvis Presley (entertainer). 10000f. (on gold foil).

World Cup Football Championship, U.S.A. 10000f. (on gold foil).

Winter Olympic Games, Lillehammer, Norway. 10000f. (on gold foil).

Olympic Games, Atlanta, U.S.A. 5000f. (on gold foil).

For further issues see under **MADAGASCAR**.

MALAWI Pt. 1

Formerly Nyasaland, became an independent Republic within the Commonwealth on 6 July 1966.

1964. 12 pence = 1 shilling;
20 shillings = 1 pound.
1970. 100 tambalas = 1 kwacha.

44 Dr. H. Banda (Prime Minister) and Independence Monument

1964. Independence.

211	**44**	3d. olive and sepia	10	10
212	–	6d. multicoloured	10	10
213	–	1s.3d. multicoloured	35	10
214	–	2s.6d. multicoloured	45	1·25

DESIGNS—each with Dr. Hastings Banda: 6d. Rising sun; 1s.3d. National flag; 2s.6d. Coat of arms.

48 Tung Tree

1964. As Nos. 199/210 of Nyasaland but inscr "MALAWI" as in T **48**. The 9d., 1s.6d. and £2 are new values and designs.

252	½d. violet	10	10
216	1d. black and green	10	10
217	2d. brown	10	10
218	3d. brown, green and bistre	15	10
219	4d. blue and yellow	85	15
220	6d. purple, green and blue	75	10
221	9d. brown, green and yellow	30	15
258	1s. brown, blue and yellow	25	10
223	1s.3d. green and brown	50	60
259	1s.6d. brown and green	30	10
224	2s.6d. brown and blue	1·10	1·00
225	5s. multicoloured (I)	65	2·50
225a	5s. multicoloured (II)	6·50	90
226	10s. green, salmon and black	1·50	2·00
227	£1 brown and yellow	7·00	5·50
262	£2 multicoloured	25·00	24·00

DESIGNS (New): 1s.6d. Burley tobacco; £2 "Cyrestis camillus" (butterfly).

Two types of 5s. I, inscr "LAKE NYASA". II, inscr "LAKE MALAWI".

49 Christmas Star and Globe

1964. Christmas.

228	**49**	3d. green and gold	10	10
229		6d. mauve and gold	10	10
230		1s.3d. violet and gold	10	10
231		2s.6d. blue and gold	20	50
MS231a		83 × 126 mm. Nos. 228/31. Imperf	1·00	1·75

50 Coins

1964. Malawi's First Coinage. Coins in black and silver.

232	**50**	3d. green	10	10
233		9d. mauve	20	10
234		1s.6d. purple	25	10
235		3s. blue	35	70
MS235a		126 × 104 mm. Nos. 232/5. Imperf	1·40	1·10

1965. Nos. 223/4 surch.

236	1s.6d. on 1s.3d. green & brown	10	10
237	3s. on 2s.6d. brown and blue	20	20

52 Chilembwe leading Rebels

1965. 50th Anniv of 1915 Rising.

238	**52**	3d. violet and green	10	10
239		9d. olive and orange	10	10
240		1s.6d. brown and blue	15	10
241		3s. turquoise and blue	20	25
MS241a		127 × 83 mm. Nos. 238/41	5·00	6·00

53 "Learning and Scholarship"

1965. Opening of Malawi University.

242	**53**	3d. black and green	10	10
243		9d. black and mauve	10	10
244		1s.6d. black and violet	10	10
245		3s. black and blue	15	40
MS246		127 × 84 mm. Nos. 242/5	2·50	2·50

54 "Papilio ophidicephalus"

1966. Malawi Butterflies. Multicoloured.

247	4d. Type **54**	80	10
248	9d. "Papilio desmondi" (magdae)	1·25	10
249	1s.6d. "Epamera handmani"	1·75	30
250	3s. "Amauris crawshayi"	2·75	6·00
MS251	130 × 100 mm. Nos. 247/50	17·00	11·00

58 British Central Africa 6d. Stamp of 1891

59 President Banda

1966. 75th Anniv of Postal Services.

263	**58**	4d. blue and green	10	10
264		9d. blue and red	15	10
265		1s.6d. blue and lilac	20	10
266		3s. grey and blue	30	70
MS267		83 × 127 mm. Nos. 263/6	5·00	3·25

1966. Republic Day.

268	**59**	4d. brown, silver and green	10	10
269		9d. brown, silver and mauve	10	10
270		1s.6d. brown, silver & violet	15	10
271		3s. brown, silver and blue	25	15
MS272		83 × 127 mm. Nos. 268/71	2·00	3·00

60 Bethlehem

1966. Christmas.

273	**60**	4d. green and gold	10	10
274		9d. purple and gold	10	10
275		1s.6d. red and gold	15	10
276		3s. blue and gold	40	80

61 "Ilala I"

1967. Lake Malawi Steamers.

277	**61**	4d. black, yellow and green	40	10
278	–	9d. black, yellow and mauve	45	10
279	–	1s.6d. black, red and violet	65	20
280	–	3s. black, red and blue	1·25	1·75

DESIGNS: 9d. "Dove"; 1s.9d. "Chauncy Maples I" (wrongly inscr "Chauncey"); 3s. "Gwendolen".

62 Golden Mbuna (female)

1967. Lake Malawi Cichlids. Multicoloured.

281	4d. Type **62**	40	10
282	9d. Scraped-mouthed mbuna	55	10
283	1s.6d. Zebra mbuna	70	20
284	3s. Orange mbuna	1·75	1·75

63 Rising Sun and Gearwheel

1967. Industrial Development.

285	**63**	4d. black and green	10	10
286		9d. black and red	10	10
287		1s.6d. black and violet	10	10
288		3s. black and blue	15	30
MS289		134 × 108 mm. Nos. 285/8	75	1·40

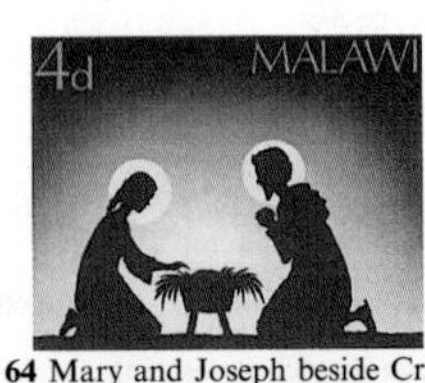

64 Mary and Joseph beside Crib

1967. Christmas.

290	**64**	4d. blue and green	10	10
291		9d. blue and red	10	10
292		1s.6d. blue and yellow	10	10
293		3s. deep blue and blue	15	30
MS294		114 × 100 mm. Nos. 290/3	1·00	2·75

65 "Calotropis procera"

1968. Wild Flowers. Multicoloured.

295	4d. Type **65**	15	10
296	9d. "Borreria dibrachiata"	15	10
297	1s.6d. "Hibiscus rhodanthus"	15	10
298	3s. "Bidens pinnatipartita"	20	95
MS299	135 × 91 mm. Nos. 295/8	1·25	3·00

66 Bagnall Steam Locomotive No. 1 "Thistle"

1968. Malawi Locomotives

300	**66**	4d. green, blue and red	30	10
301	–	9d. red, blue and green	40	15
302	–	1s.6d. multicoloured	55	30
303	–	3s. multicoloured	1·10	3·00
MS304		120 × 88 mm. Nos. 300/3	2·50	6·00

DESIGNS: 9d. Class G steam locomotive No. 49; 1s.6d. Class "Zambesi" diesel locomotive No. 202; 3s. Diesel railcar No. DR1.

67 "The Nativity" (Piero della Francesca)

1968. Christmas. Multicoloured.

305	4d. Type **67**	10	10
306	9d. "The Adoration of the Shepherds" (Murillo)	10	10
307	1s.6d. "The Adoration of the Shepherds" (Reni)	10	10
308	3s. "Nativity, with God the Father and Holy Ghost" (Pittoni)	15	15
MS309	115 × 101 mm. Nos. 305/8	35	1·60

69 Nyassa Lovebird

70 Carmine Bee Eater

1968. Birds (1st series). Multicoloured.

310	1d. Scarlet-chested sunbird (horiz)	15	10
311	2d. Violet starling (horiz)	20	10
312	3d. White-browed robin chat (horiz)	30	10
313	4d. Red-billed fire finch (horiz)	50	40
314	6d. Type **69**	80	15
315	9d. Yellow-rumped bishop	75	60
316	1s. Type **70**	80	15
317	1s.6d. Grey-headed bush shrike	5·00	8·00
318	2s. Paradise whydah	5·00	8·00
319	3s. African paradise flycatcher (vert)	6·00	4·25
320	5s. Bateleur (vert)	7·00	4·25
321	10s. Saddle-bill stork (vert)	5·50	7·50
322	£1 Purple heron (vert)	10·00	18·00
323	£2 Green turaco ("Livingstone's Loerie")	42·00	48·00

SIZES: 1d. to 9d. as Type **69**; 1s.6d. to £2 as Type **70**.

See also Nos. 473/85.

71 I.L.O. Emblem

1969. 50th Anniv of Int Labour Organization.

324	**71**	4d. gold and green	10	10
325		9d. gold and brown	10	10
326		1s.6d. gold and brown	10	10
327		3s. gold and blue	15	15
MS328		127 × 89 mm. Nos. 324/7	1·00	4·75

72 White-fringed Ground Orchid

1969. Orchids of Malawi. Multicoloured.
329 4d. Type **72** 15 10
330 9d. Red ground orchid . . . 20 10
331 1s.6d. Leopard tree orchid . . 30 20
332 3s. Blue ground orchid . . . 60 2·00
MS333 118 × 86 mm. Nos. 329/32 1·10 3·75

73 African Development Bank Emblem

74 Dove over Bethlehem

1969. 5th Anniv of African Development Bank.
334 **73** 4d. yellow, brown and ochre 10 10
335 9d. yellow, ochre and green 10 10
336 1s.6d. yellow, ochre & brn 10 10
337 3s. yellow, ochre and blue 15 15
MS338 102 × 137 mm. Nos. 334/7 50 90

1969. Christmas.
339 **74** 2d. black and yellow . . . 10 10
340 4d. black and turquoise . . 10 10
341 9d. black and red 10 10
342 1s.6d. black and violet . . 10 10
343 3s. black and blue 15 15
MS344 130 × 71 mm. Nos. 339/43 1·00 1·75

75 "Zonocerus elegans" (grasshopper)

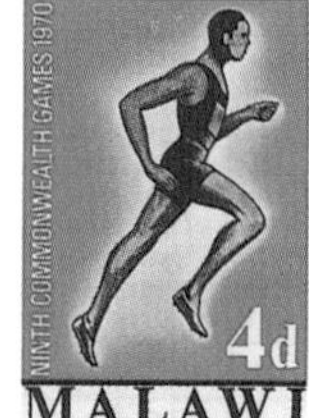

77 Runner

1970. Insects of Malawi. Multicoloured.
345 4d. Type **75** 15 10
346 9d. "Mylabris dicincta" (beetle) 15 10
347 1s.6d. "Henosepilachna elaterii" (ladybird) 20 10
348 3s. "Sphodromantis speculabunda" (mantid) . . 35 65
MS349 86 × 137 mm. Nos. 345/8 1·25 2·25

1970. Rand Easter Show. No. 317 optd **Rand Easter Show 1970**.
350 1s.6d. multicoloured . . . . 50 2·25

1970. 9th Commonwealth Games, Edinburgh.
351 **77** 4d. blue and green 10 10
352 9d. blue and red 10 10
353 1s.6d. blue and yellow . . 10 10
354 3s. deep blue and blue . . 15 15
MS355 146 × 96 mm. Nos. 351/4 55 90

1970. Decimal Currency. Nos. 316 and 318 surch.
356 10t. on 1s. multicoloured . . 2·25 25
357 20t. on 2s. multicoloured . . 2·75 3·25

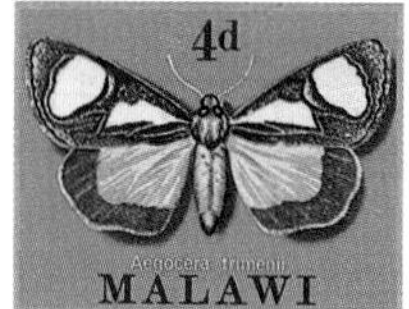

79 "Aegocera trimeni"

1970. Moths. Multicoloured.
358 4d. Type **79** 20 10
359 9d. "Faidherbia bauhiniae" 30 10
360 1s.6d. "Parasa karschi" . . 50 20
361 3s. "Teracotona euprepia" . . 1·25 3·50
MS362 112 × 92 mm. Nos. 358/61 4·00 5·50

80 Mother and Child

1970. Christmas.
363 **80** 2d. black and yellow . . . 10 10
364 4d. black and green . . . 10 10
365 9d. black and red 10 10
366 1s.6d. black and purple . . 10 10
367 3s. black and blue 15 15
MS368 166 × 100 mm. Nos. 363/7 1·00 2·25

1971. No. 319 surch **30t Special United Kingdom Delivery Service**.
369 30t. on 3s. multicoloured . . 50 2·00
No. 369 was issued for use on letters carried by an emergency airmail service from Malawi to Great Britain during the British postal strike. The fee of 30t. was to cover the charge for delivery by a private service, and ordinary stamps to pay the normal airmail postage had to be affixed as well. These stamps were in use from 8 February to 8 March.

82 Decimal Coinage and Cockerel

83 Greater Kudu

1971. Decimal Coinage.
370 **82** 3t. multicoloured 15 10
371 8t. multicoloured 20 10
372 15t. multicoloured 25 20
373 30t. multicoloured . . . . 35 1·50
MS374 140 × 101 mm. Nos. 370/3 1·00 1·75

1971. Decimal Currency. Antelopes. Mult.
375 1t. Type **83** 10 10
376 2t. Nyala 15 10
377 3t. Mountain reedbuck . . . 20 50
378 5t. Puku . . . . 40 1·25
379 8t. Impala . . . . 45 1·00
380 10t. Eland 60 10
381 15t. Klipspringer . . . . . . 1·00 20
382 20t. Suni . . . . 1·50 90
383 30t. Roan antelope . . . . . 9·50 1·00
384 50t. Waterbuck . . . . . . 1·00 65
385 1k. Bushbuck . . . . 1·50 85
386 2k. Red forest duiker . . . . 2·75 1·50
387 4k. Common duiker . . . . 20·00 19·00
Nos. 380/7 are larger, size 25 × 42 mm.
No. 387 is incorrectly inscr "Gray Duiker".

85 Christ on the Cross

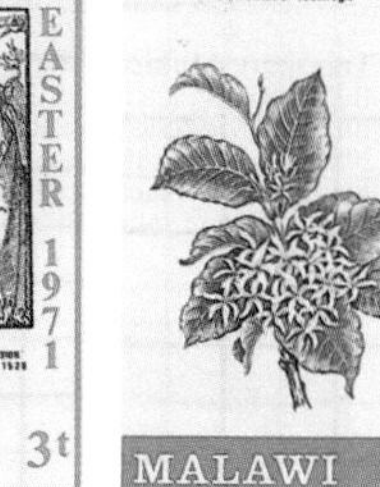

87 "Holarrhena febrifuga"

1971. Easter. Multicoloured.
388 **85** 3t. black and green 10 25
389 – 3t. black and green 10 25
390 **85** 8t. black and red 10 25
391 – 8t. black and red 10 25
392 **85** 15t. black and violet . . . 15 30
393 – 15t. black and violet . . . 15 30
394 **85** 30t. black and blue 20 45
395 – 30t. black and blue 20 45
MS396 Two sheets, each 95 × 145 mm. (a) Nos. 388, 390, 392 and 394. (b) Nos. 389, 391, 393 and 395 Set of 2 sheets . . 1·50 3·50
DESIGN: Nos. 389, 391, 393, 395, The Resurrection. Both designs from "The Small Passion" (Durer).

1971. Flowering Shrubs and Trees. Mult.
397 3t. Type **87** 10 10
398 8t. "Brachystegia spiciformis" 10 10
399 15t. "Securidaca longepedunculata" 15 10
400 30t. "Pterocarpus rotundifolius" 30 75
MS401 102 × 135 mm. Nos. 397/400 1·00 2·00

88 Drum Major

89 "Madonna and Child" (William Dyce)

1971. 50th Anniv of Malawi Police Force.
402 **88** 30t. multicoloured . . . . 65 1·25

1971. Christmas. Multicoloured.
403 3t. Type **89** 10 10
404 8t. "The Holy Family" (M. Schongauer) 15 10
405 15t. "The Holy Family with St. John" (Raphael) . . . 20 20
406 30t. "The Holy Family" (Bronzino) . . . . 50 1·40
MS407 101 × 139 mm. Nos. 403/6 1·10 2·50

90 Vickers Viscount 700

1972. Air. Malawi Aircraft. Multicoloured.
408 3t. Type **90** 30 10
409 8t. Hawker Siddeley H.S.748 50 10
410 15t. Britten Norman Islander 75 30
411 30t. B.A.C. One Eleven . . . 1·25 2·25
MS412 143 × 94 mm. Nos. 408/11 8·00 5·50

91 Figures (Chencherere Hill)

1972. Rock Paintings.
413 **91** 3t. green and black 25 10
414 – 8t. red, grey and black . . 30 10
415 – 15t. multicoloured 35 30
416 – 30t. multicoloured . . . . 45 1·00
MS417 121 × 97 mm. Nos. 413/16 2·75 2·75
DESIGNS: 8t. Lizard and cat (Chencherere Hill); 15t. Schematics (Diwa Hill); 30t. Sun through rain (Mikolongwe Hill).

92 Boxing

1972. Olympic Games, Munich.
418 **92** 3t. multicoloured 10 10
419 8t. multicoloured 15 10
420 15t. multicoloured 20 10
421 30t. multicoloured 35 45
MS422 110 × 92 mm. Nos. 418/21 1·25 1·75

93 Arms of Malawi

1972. Commonwealth Parliamentary Conf.
423 **93** 15t. multicoloured 30 35

94 "Adoration of the Kings" (Orcagna)

1972. Christmas. Multicoloured.
424 3t. Type **94** 10 10
425 8t. "Madonna and Child Enthroned" (Florentine School) 10 10
426 15t. "Virgin and Child" (Crivelli) 20 10
427 30t. "Virgin and Child with St. Anne" (Flemish School) 45 70
MS428 95 × 121 mm. Nos. 424/7 1·10 2·00

95 "Charaxes bohemani"

1973. Butterflies. Multicoloured.
429 3t. Type **95** 40 10
430 8t. "Uranothauma crawshayi" 65 10
431 15t. "Charaxes acuminatus" 85 30
432 30t. "Amauris ansorgei" (inscr in error "EUPHAEDRA ZADDACHI") . . . . . 3·75 8·00
433 30t. "Amauris ansorgei" (inscr corrected) . . . . . 3·50 8·00
MS434 145 × 95 mm. Nos. 429/32 7·00 11·50

96 Livingstone and Map

1973. Death Cent of David Livingstone (1st issue).
435 **96** 3t. multicoloured 10 10
436 8t. multicoloured 15 10
437 15t. multicoloured 20 10
438 30t. multicoloured 35 60
MS439 144 × 95 mm. Nos. 435/8 1·00 1·50
See also No. 450/**MS**451.

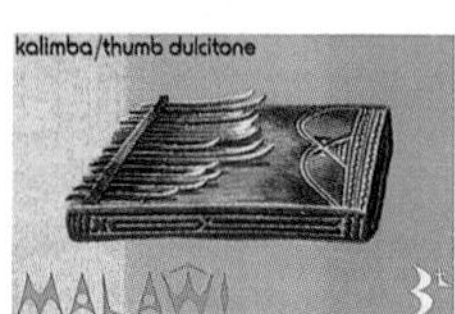

97 Thumb Dulcitone

1973. Musical Instruments. Multicoloured.
440 3t. Type **97** 10 10
441 8t. Hand zither (vert) 15 10
442 15t. Hand drum (vert) . . . 25 10
443 30t. One-stringed fiddle . . . 45 60
MS444 120 × 103 mm. Nos. 440/3 2·75 2·00

98 The Magi

1973. Christmas.
445 **98** 3t. blue, lilac & ultramarine 10 10
446 8t. red, lilac and brown . . 10 10
447 15t. mauve, blue & dp mve 15 10
448 30t. yellow, lilac and brown 30 70
MS449 165 × 114 mm. Nos. 445/8 75 1·40

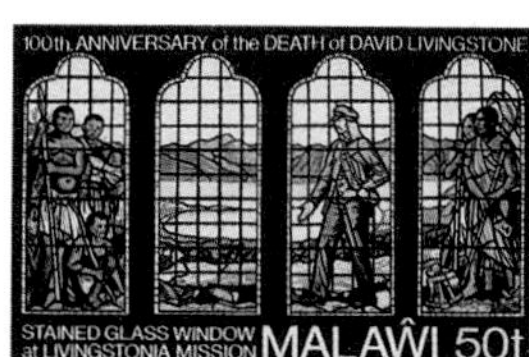

99 Stained-glass Window, Livingstonia Mission

1973. Death Cent of David Livingstone (2nd issue).
450 **99** 50t. multicoloured . . . . 45 1·00
MS451 71 × 77 mm. No. 450 . . 80 1·60

100 Large-mouthed Black Bass

1974. 35th Anniv of Malawi Angling Society. Multicoloured.
452 3t. Type **100** 25 10
453 8t. Rainbow trout 30 10
454 15t. Silver alestes ("Lake salmon") 55 20
455 30t. Tigerfish . . . . 85 1·75
MS456 169 × 93 mm. Nos. 452/5 2·50 2·25

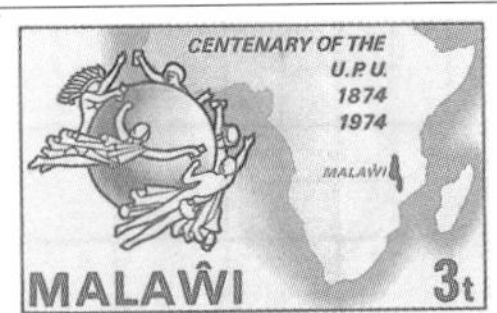

101 U.P.U. Monument and Map of Africa

1974. Centenary of U.P.U.
457 **101** 3t. green and brown . . . 10 10
458 8t. red and brown 10 10
459 15t. violet and brown . . 15 10
460 30t. blue and brown . . . 30 1·10
MS461 115 × 146 mm. Nos. 457/60 65 1·75

102 Capital Hill, Lilongwe

1974. 10th Anniv of Independence.
462 **102** 3t. multicoloured 10 10
463 8t. multicoloured 10 10
464 15t. multicoloured 10 10
465 30t. multicoloured 25 35
MS466 120 × 86 mm. Nos. 462/5 45 1·00

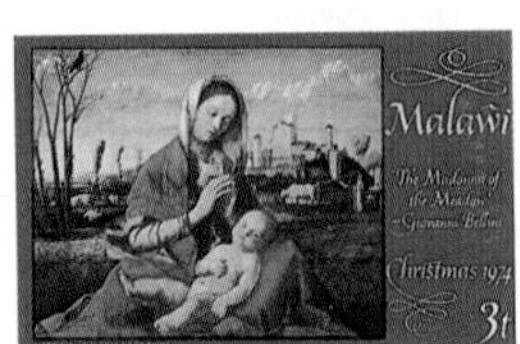

103 "Madonna of the Meadow" (Bellini)

1974. Christmas. Multicoloured.
467 3t. Type **103** 10 10
468 8t. "The Holy Family with Sts. John and Elizabeth" (Jordaens) 10 10
469 15t. "The Nativity" (Pieter de Grebber) 15 10
470 30t. "Adoration of the Shepherds" (Lorenzo di Credi) 30 50
MS471 163 × 107 mm. Nos. 467/70 60 1·25

104 Arms of Malawi

105 African Snipe

106 Spur-winged Goose ("Spurwing Goose")

1975.
472 **104** 1t. blue 20 40
472a 5t. red . . . . 65 1·60

1975. Birds (2nd series). Multicoloured. (a) As T **105**.
473 1t. Type **105** . . . . 1·25 1·75
474 2t. Double-banded sandgrouse (horiz) . . . . 1·25 1·75
475 3t. Indian blue quail ("Blue Quail") (horiz) . . . . 1·50 1·50
476 5t. Red-necked spurfowl ("Red-necked Francolin") . . . 3·50 1·25
477 8t. Harlequin quail (horiz) . . 4·75 1·00

(b) As T **106**.
502 10t. Type **106** . . . . . . 2·00 1·50
503 15t. Denham's bustard ("Stanley Bustard") . . . 2·00 2·00
480 20t. Comb duck ("Knob-billed Duck") . . . . . 1·00 2·25
481 30t. Helmeted guineafowl ("Crowned Guinea Fowl") 1·25 70
482 50t. African pygmy goose ("Pigmy Goose") (horiz) 2·00 1·60
483 1k. Garganey . . . . 3·00 8·50
504 2k. White-faced whistling duck ("White Face Tree Duck") . . . . 5·00 11·00
485 4k. African green pigeon ("Green Pigeon") . . . . 13·00 16·00

107 M.V. "Mpasa"

1975. Ships of Lake Malawi. Multicoloured.
486 3t. Type **107** 30 10
487 8t. M.V. "Ilala II" 40 10
488 15t. M.V. "Chauncy Maples II" 75 30
489 30t. M.V. "Nkwazi" . . . . 1·00 2·75
MS490 105 × 142 mm. Nos. 486/9 2·25 4·00

108 "Habenaria splendens"

109 Thick-tailed Bushbaby

1975. Malawi Orchids. Multicoloured.
491 3t. Type **108** 40 10
492 10t. "Eulophia cucullata" . . 50 10
493 20t. "Disa welwitschii" . . . 80 25
494 40t. "Angraecum conchiferum" . . . . . . 1·10 1·50
MS495 127 × 111 mm. Nos. 491/4 7·00 8·00

1976. Malawi Animals. Multicoloured.
496 3t. Type **109** 10 10
497 10t. Leopard 35 10
498 20t. Roan antelope 55 35
499 40t. Common zebra . . . . 1·00 2·75
MS500 88 × 130 mm. Nos. 496/9 2·50 3·00

1975. 10th Africa, Caribbean and Pacific Ministerial Conference. No. 482 optd **10th ACP Ministerial Conference 1975**.
514 50t. African pygmy goose . . 1·00 2·25

111 "A Castle with the Adoration of the Magi"

1975. Christmas. Religious Medallions. Mult.
515 3t. Type **111** 10 10
516 10t. "The Nativity" 15 10
517 20t. "Adoration of the Magi" (different) 20 10
518 40t. "Angel appearing to Shepherds" . . . . . . 50 2·25
MS519 98 × 168 mm. Nos. 515/18 1·50 3·00

112 Alexander Graham Bell

113 President Banda

1976. Centenary of Telephone.
520 **112** 3t. green and black . . . 10 10
521 10t. purple and black . . 10 10
522 20t. violet and black . . . 20 10
523 40t. blue and black . . . 50 1·40
MS524 137 × 114 mm. Nos. 520/3 1·10 1·75

1976. 10th Anniv of Republic. Multicoloured.
525 **113** 3t. green 10 10
526 10t. purple 10 10
527 20t. blue 20 10
528 40t. blue . . . . 50 1·40
MS529 102 × 112 mm. Nos. 524/8 1·00 2·25

114 Bagnall Diesel Shunter No. 100

1976. Malawi Locomotives. Multicoloured.
530 3t. Type **114** 40 15
531 10t. Class "Shire" diesel locomotive No. 503 . . . 70 15
532 20t. Nippon Sharyo diesel-hydraulic locomotive No. 301 . . . . 1·40 45
533 40t. Hunslet diesel-hydraulic locomotive No. 110 . . . 2·10 6·50
MS534 130 × 118 mm. Nos. 530/3 4·25 6·50

1976. Centenary of Blantyre Mission. Nos. 479 and 481 optd **Blantyre Mission Centenary 1876–1976**.
535 15t. Denham's bustard . . . 1·50 1·50
536 30t. Helmeted guineafowl . . 1·75 3·25

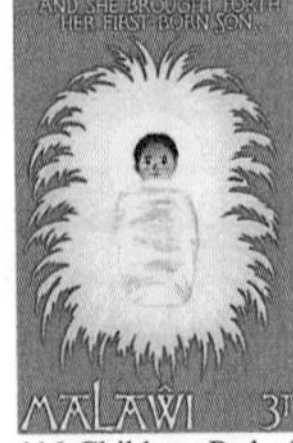

116 Child on Bed of Straw

117 Man and Woman

1976. Christmas.
537 **116** 3t. multicoloured 10 10
538 10t. multicoloured 10 10
539 20t. multicoloured 20 10
540 40t. multicoloured 40 60
MS541 135 × 95 mm. Nos. 537/40 1·40 1·75

1977. Handicrafts. Wood-carvings. Mult.
542 4t. Type **117** 10 10
543 10t. Elephant (horiz) 15 10
544 20t. Rhinoceros (horiz) . . . 20 10
545 40t. Antelope 50 70
MS546 153 × 112 mm. Nos. 542/5 1·50 2·50

118 Chileka Airport

1977. Transport. Multicoloured.
547 4t. Type **118** 40 10
548 10t. Blantyre–Lilongwe Road 40 10
549 20t. M.V. "Ilala II" . . . . 1·00 35
550 40t. Blantyre–Nacala rail line 1·50 4·75
MS551 127 × 83 mm. Nos. 547/50 3·00 4·50

119 Blue-grey Mbuna

1977. Fish of Lake Malawi. Multicoloured.
552B 4t. Type **119** 30 10
553B 10t. Livingston mbuna . . 50 20
554A 20t. Zebra mbuna . . . . 1·40 30
555B 40t. Malawi scale-eater . . 1·50 1·25
MS556A 147 × 99 mm. Nos. 552A/5B . . . . 3·00 4·50

120 "Madonna and Child with St. Catherine and the Blessed Stefano Maconi" (Borgognone)

121 "Entry of Christ into Jerusalem" (Giotto)

1977. Christmas.
557 **120** 4t. multicoloured 10 10
558 – 10t. multicoloured 10 10
559 – 20t. multicoloured 20 10
560 – 40t. multicoloured . . . . 50 1·00
MS561 150 × 116 mm. Nos. 557/60 2·50 3·00
DESIGNS: 10t. "Madonna and Child with the Eternal Father and Angels" (Borgognone); 20t. Bottigella altarpiece (detail, Foppa); 40t. "Madonna of the Fountain" (van Eyck).

1978. Easter. Paintings by Giotto. Multicoloured.
562 4t. Type **121** 10 10
563 10t. "The Crucifixion" . . . 15 10
564 20t. "Descent from the Cross" 30 10
565 40t. "Jesus appears before Mary" 50 55
MS566 150 × 99 mm. Nos. 562/5 1·90 2·40

122 Nyala

124 "Vanilla polylepis"

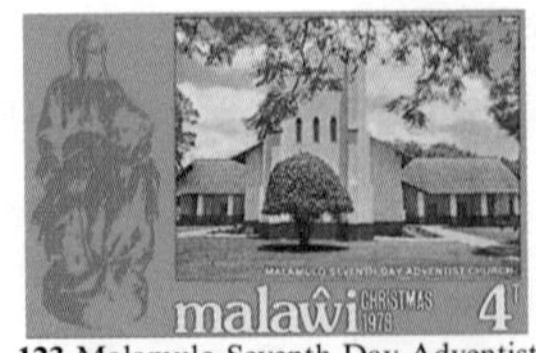

123 Malamulo Seventh Day Adventist Church

1978. Wildlife. Multicoloured.
567 4t. Type **122** . . . . 2·25 10
568 10t. Lion (horiz) . . . . . . 6·50 40
569 20t. Common zebra (horiz) . . 9·50 1·00
570 40t. Mountain reedbuck . . . 11·00 7·50
MS571 173 × 113 mm. Nos. 567/70 29·00 11·00

1978. Christmas. Multicoloured.
572 4t. Type **123** 10 10
573 10t. Likoma Cathedral . . . 10 10
574 20t. St. Michael's and All Angels', Blantyre 20 10
575 40t. Zomba Catholic Cathedral . . . . 40 1·50
MS576 190 × 105 mm. Nos. 572/5 70 1·50

1979. Orchids. Multicoloured.
577 1t. Type **124** 50 30
578 2t. "Cirrhopetalum umbellatum" 50 30
579 5t. "Calanthe natalensis" . . 50 10
580 7t. "Ansellia gigantea" . . . 50 50
581 8t. "Tridactyle bicaudata" . . 50 30
582 10t. "Acampe pachyglossa" . . 50 10
583 15t. "Eulophia quartiniana" . 50 15
584 20t. "Cyrtorchis arcuata" . . 50 50
585 30t. "Eulophia tricristata" . . 1·25 30
586 50t. "Disa hamatopetala" . . 85 50
587 75t. "Cynorchis glandulosa" . 2·00 6·00
588 1k. "Aerangis kotschyana" . . 1·60 1·75
589 1k.50 "Polystachya dendrobiiflora" . . . . 1·75 5·00
590 2k. "Disa ornithantha" . . . . 1·75 2·00
591 4k. "Cyrtorchis praetermissa" . 2·00 4·00

125 Tsamba

1979. National Tree Planting Day. Mult.
592 5t. Type **125** 20 10
593 10t. Mulanje cedar 25 10
594 20t. Mlombwa 40 20
595 40t. Mbawa . . . . 70 2·50
MS596 118 × 153 mm. Nos. 592/5 1·40 2·75

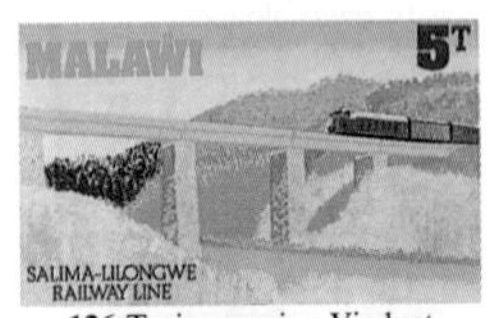

126 Train crossing Viaduct

1979. Opening of Salima–Lilongwe Railway Line. Multicoloured.
597 5t. Type **126** 25 15
598 10t. Diesel railcar at station 40 15
599 20t. Diesel train rounding bend 60 30
600 40t. Diesel train passing through cutting . . . . . 85 2·00
MS601 153 × 103 mm. Nos. 597/600 4·00 4·50

127 Young Child

1979. International Year of the Child. Designs showing young children. Multicoloured; background colours given.

602 **127** 5t. green 10 10
603 – 10t. red 10 10
604 – 20t. mauve 25 10
605 – 40t. blue . . . . 45 1·40

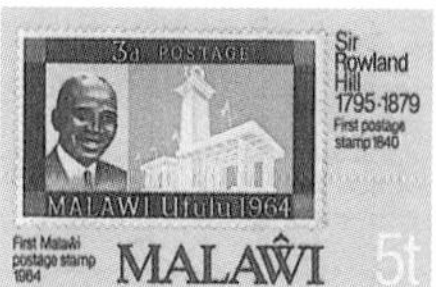

128 1964 3d. Independence Commemorative Stamp

1979. Death Centenary of Sir Rowland Hill. Designs showing 1964 Independence Commemorative Stamps. Multicoloured.

606 5t. Type **128** 10 10
607 10t. 6d. value 10 10
608 20t. 1s.3d. value 20 10
609 40t. 2s.6d. value 35 60
MS610 163 × 108 mm. Nos. 606/9 75 1·40

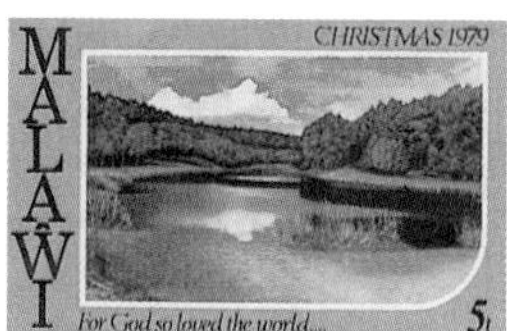

129 River Landscape

1979. Christmas. Multicoloured.

611 5t. Type **129** 10 10
612 10t. Sunset 10 10
613 20t. Forest and hill 25 15
614 40t. Plain and mountains . . 50 2·50

130 Limbe Rotary Club Emblem

132 Agate Nodule

131 Mangochi District Post Office

1980. 75th Anniv of Rotary International.

615 **130** 5t. multicoloured 10 10
616 – 10t. multicoloured 10 10
617 – 20t. blue, gold and red . . 30 15
618 – 40t. gold and blue . . . . 75 1·90
MS619 105 × 144 mm. Nos. 615/18 1·50 2·25

DESIGNS: 10t. Blantyre Rotary Club pennant; 20t. Lilongwe Rotary Club pennant; 40t. Rotary International emblem.

1980. "London 1980" International Stamp Exhibition.

620 **131** 5t. black and green . . . 10 10
621 – 10t. black and red . . . 10 10
622 – 20t. black and violet . . . 15 10
623 – 1k. black and blue . . . 65 1·10
MS624 114 × 89 mm. Nos. 620/3 1·25 2·25

DESIGNS: 10t. New Blantyre Sorting Office; 20t. Mail transfer hut, Walala; 1k. First Nyasaland Post Office, Chiromo.

1980. Gemstones. Multicoloured.

625 5t. Type **132** 60 10
626 10t. Sunstone 80 10
627 20t. Smoky quartz . . . . . 1·40 30
628 1k. Kyanite crystal . . . . . 3·50 6·00

133 Elephants

1980. Christmas. Children's Paintings. Mult.

629 5t. Type **133** 40 10
630 10t. Flowers 30 10
631 20t. Class "Shire" diesel train 75 20
632 1k. Malachite kingfisher . . . 1·60 2·00

134 Suni

1981. Wildlife. Multicoloured.

633 7t. Type **134** 15 10
634 10t. Blue duiker 20 10
635 20t. African buffalo 30 15
636 1k. Lichtenstein's hartebeest 1·25 1·60

135 "Kanjedza II" Standard "A" Earth Station

1981. International Communications. Mult.

637 7t. Type **135** 10 10
638 10t. Blantyre International Gateway Exchange 15 10
639 20t. "Kanjedza I" standard "B" earth station 25 15
640 1k. "Satellite communications" . . . . 1·50 1·90
MS641 101 × 151 mm. Nos. 637/40 1·75 3·00

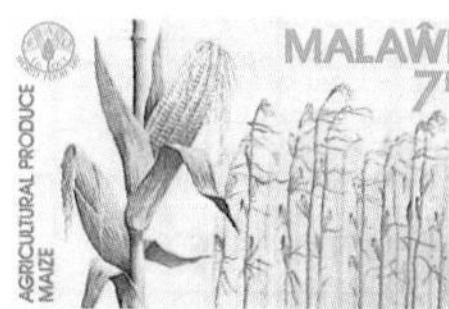

136 Maize

1981. World Food Day. Agricultural Produce. Multicoloured.

642 7t. Type **136** 15 10
643 10t. Rice 20 10
644 20t. Finger-millet 30 20
645 1k. Wheat . . . . 1·00 1·40

137 "The Adoration of the Shepherds" (Murillo)

138 Impala Herd

1981. Christmas. Paintings. Multicoloured.

646 7t. Type **137** 20 10
647 10t. "The Holy Family" (Lippi) (horiz) 25 10
648 20t. "The Adoration of the Shepherds" (Louis le Nain) (horiz) 45 15
649 1k. "The Virgin and Child, St. John the Baptist and an Angel" (Paolo Morando) 1·10 1·75

1982. National Parks. Wildlife. Multicoloured.

650 7t. Type **138** 20 10
651 10t. Lions 35 10
652 20t. Greater kudu 50 20
653 1k. Greater flamingoes . . . 2·25 5·00

139 Kamuzu Academy

1982. Kamuzu Academy.

654 **139** 7t. multicoloured 15 10
655 – 20t. multicoloured 20 10
656 – 30t. multicoloured 30 45
657 – 1k. multicoloured . . . . 1·00 3·50

DESIGNS: 20t. to 1k. Various views of the Academy.

140 Attacker challenging Goalkeeper

1982. World Cup Football Championship, Spain. Multicoloured.

658 7t. Type **140** 75 25
659 20t. FIFA World Cup trophy 1·60 1·25
660 30t. Football stadium . . . . 1·90 3·25
MS661 80 × 59 mm. 1k. Football 1·75 1·60

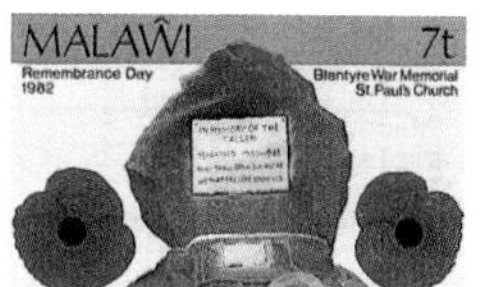

141 Blantyre War Memorial, St. Paul's Church

1982. Remembrance Day. Multicoloured.

662 7t. Type **141** 10 10
663 20t. Zomba war memorial . . 15 10
664 30t. Chichiri war memorial 20 30
665 1k. Lilongwe war memorial 65 4·00

142 Kwacha International Conference Centre

1983. Commonwealth Day. Multicoloured.

666 7t. Type **142** 10 10
667 20t. Tea-picking, Mulanje . . 20 10
668 30t. World map showing position of Malawi 25 30
669 1k. Pres. Dr. H. Kamuzu Banda . . . . 60 1·50

143 "Christ and St. Peter"

144 Pair by Lake

1983. 500th Birth Anniv of Raphael. Details from the cartoon for "The Miraculous Draught of Fishes" Tapestry. Multicoloured.

670 7t. Type **143** 35 10
671 20t. "Hauling in the Catch" 75 80
672 30t. "Fishing Village" (horiz) 90 2·50
MS673 110 × 90 mm. 1k. "Apostle" 1·60 1·60

1983. African Fish Eagle. Multicoloured.

674 30t. Type **144** . . . . 1·60 1·90
675 30t. Making gull-like call . . 1·60 1·90
676 30t. Diving on prey . . . . . 1·60 1·90
677 30t. Carrying fish . . . . . 1·60 1·90
678 30t. Feeding on catch . . . . 1·60 1·90

145 Kamuzu International Airport

1983. Bicentenary of Manned Flight. Mult.

679 7t. Type **145** 10 10
680 20t. Kamuzu International Airport (different) 25 15
681 30t. B.A.C. One Eleven . . . 40 45
682 1k. Short Empire "C" Class flying boat at Cape Maclear . . . . 1·10 2·50
MS683 100 × 121 mm. Nos. 679/82 2·00 4·00

146 "Clerodendrum myricoides"

147 Golden Mbuna

1983. Christmas. Flowers. Multicoloured.

684 7t. Type **146** 40 10
685 20t. "Gloriosa superba" . . . 90 15
686 30t. "Gladiolus laxiflorus" . . 1·00 60
687 1k. "Aframomum angustifolium" . . . . . . 2·25 7·00

1984. Fishes. Multicoloured.

688 1t. Type **147** 30 75
689 2t. Malawi eyebiter 30 75
690 5t. Blue mbuna 30 75
691 7t. Lombardo's mbuna . . . 30 10
692 8t. Golden zebra mbuna . . 30 10
693 10t. Fairy cichlid 30 10
694 15t. Crabro mbuna 30 10
695 20t. Marbled zebra mbuna 30 10
696 30t. Sky-blue mbuna 50 20
697 40t. Venustus cichlid 60 30
698 50t. Thumbi emperor cichlid 2·25 3·00
699 75t. Purple mbuna . . . . . 2·75 4·75
700 1k. Zebra mbuna . . . . . . 3·00 4·75
701 2k. Fairy cichlid (different) 4·00 6·50
702 4k. Mbenje emperor cichlid 5·00 10·00

Nos. 688 and 691/7 exist with different imprint dates at foot.

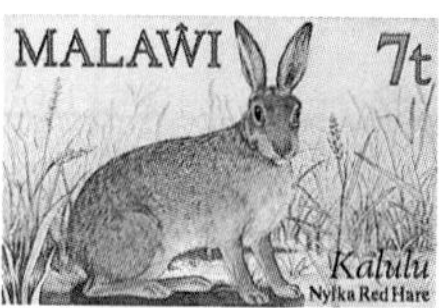

148 Smith's Red Hare

1984. Small Mammals. Multicoloured.

703 7t. Type **148** 30 10
704 20t. Gambian sun squirrel . . 45 50
705 30t. South African hedgehog 50 1·10
706 1k. Large-spotted genet . . . 70 5·50

149 Running

150 "Euphaedra neophron"

1984. Olympic Games, Los Angeles. Mult.

707 7t. Type **149** 15 10
708 20t. Boxing 35 20
709 30t. Cycling 75 70
710 1k. Long jumping . . . . . 1·40 3·75
MS711 90 × 128 mm. Nos. 707/10 2·40 5·00

1984. Butterflies.

712 **150** 7t. multicoloured 95 30
713 – 20t. yellow, brown and red . . . . 2·25 45
714 – 30t. multicoloured . . . . 2·50 1·10
715 – 1k. multicoloured . . . . 4·25 9·00

DESIGNS: 20t. "Papilio dardanus"; 30t. "Antanartia schaeneia"; 1k. "Spindasis nyassae".

151 "Virgin and Child" (Duccio)

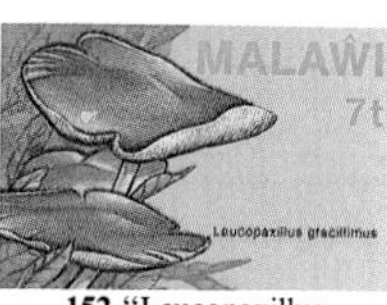

152 "Leucopaxillus gracillimus"

1984. Christmas. Religious Paintings. Mult.

716 7t. Type **151** 55 10
717 20t. "Madonna and Child" (Raphael) . . . . 1·40 20
718 30t. "Virgin and Child" (ascr to Lippi) . . . . 1·90 70
719 1k. "The Wilton Diptych" . . 3·50 8·00

1985. Fungi. Multicoloured.

720 7t. Type **152** . . . . 1·25 30
721 20t. "Limacella guttata" . . 2·50 45
722 30t. "Termitomyces eurrhizus" . . . . 3·00 1·25
723 1k. "Xerulina asprata" . . . 5·50 9·50

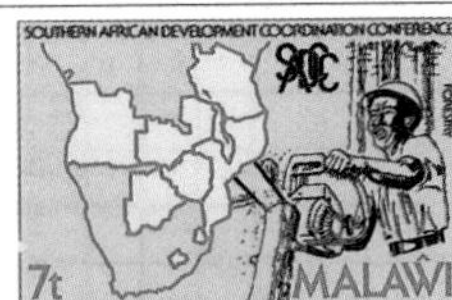

153 Map showing Member States and Lumberjack (Forestry)

1985. 5th Anniv of Southern African Development Co-ordination Conference. Designs showing map and aspects of development.

724 **153** 7t. black, green and light green 75 10
725 – 15t. black, red and pink 1·25 20
726 – 20t. black, violet and mauve 4·00 1·75
727 – 1k. black, blue and light blue 4·50 10·00

DESIGNS: 15t. Radio mast (Communications); 20t. Diesel locomotive (Transport); 1k. Trawler and net (Fishing).

154 M.V. "Ufulu"

1985. Ships of Lake Malawi (2nd series). Mult.

728 7t. Type **154** 90 10
729 15t. M.V. "Chauncy Maples II" 1·75 20
730 20t. M.V. "Mtendere" 2·25 65
731 1k. M.V. "Ilala II" 4·50 6·00
MS732 120 × 84 mm. Nos. 728/31 8·00 8·00

155 Stierling's Woodpecker

156 "The Virgin of Humility" (Jaime Serra)

1985. Birth Bicentenary of John J. Audubon (ornithologist). Multicoloured.

733 7t. Type **155** 1·25 30
734 15t. Lesser seedcracker 2·25 30
735 20t. East coast akelat ("Gunning's Akalat") 2·25 65
736 1k. Boehm's bee eater 4·25 6·00
MS737 130 × 90 mm. Nos. 733/6 10·00 10·00

1985. Christmas. Nativity Paintings. Mult.

738 7t. Type **156** 30 10
739 15t. "The Adoration of the Magi" (Stefano da Zevio) 75 15
740 20t. "Madonna and Child" (Gerard van Honthorst) 85 25
741 1k. "Virgin of Zbraslav" (Master of Vissy Brod) 2·25 5·50

157 Halley's Comet and Path of "Giotto" Spacecraft

1986. Appearance of Halley's Comet. Mult.

742 8t. Type **157** 60 10
743 15t. Halley's Comet above Earth 65 15
744 20t. Comet and dish aerial, Malawi 1·00 30
745 1k. "Giotto" spacecraft 2·00 5·50

158 Two Players competing for Ball

1986. World Cup Football Championship, Mexico. Multicoloured.

746 8t. Type **158** 70 10
747 15t. Goalkeeper saving goal 95 20
748 20t. Two players competing for ball (different) 1·10 35
749 1k. Player kicking ball 4·00 5·50
MS750 108 × 77 mm. Nos. 746/9 10·00 11·00

159 President Banda

160 "Virgin and Child" (Botticelli)

1986. 20th Anniv of Republic. Multicoloured.

751 8t. Type **159** 1·50 2·75
752 15t. National flag 80 15
753 20t. Malawi coat of arms 85 25
754 1k. Kamuzu International Airport and emblem of national airline 3·50 6·00

1986. Christmas. Multicoloured.

755 8t. Type **160** 45 10
756 15t. "Adoration of the Shepherds" (Guido Reni) 80 15
757 20t. "Madonna of the Veil" (Carlo Dolci) 1·25 35
758 1k. "Adoration of the Magi" (Jean Bourdichon) 3·75 9·00

161 Wattled Crane

1987. Wattled Crane. Multicoloured.

759 8t. Type **161** 1·50 40
760 15t. Two cranes 2·25 50
761 20t. Cranes at nest 2·25 80
762 75t. Crane in lake 4·50 12·00

162 Bagnall Steam Locomotive No. 2 "Shamrock"

1987. Steam Locomotives. Multicoloured.

767 10t. Type **162** 2·00 40
768 25t. Class D steam locomotive No. 8, 1914 2·75 50
769 30t. Bagnall steam locomotive No. 1 "Thistle" 3·00 85
770 1k. Kitson steam locomotive No. 6, 1903 6·00 12·00

163 Hippopotamus grazing

164 "Stathmostelma spectabile"

1987. Hippopotamus. Multicoloured.

771 10t. Type **163** 1·50 40
772 25t. Hippopotami in water 2·25 50
773 30t. Female and calf in water 2·25 75
774 1k. Hippopotami and cattle egret 6·00 12·00
MS775 78 × 101 mm. Nos. 771/4 11·00 12·00

1987. Christmas. Wild Flowers. Multicoloured.

776 10t. Type **164** 65 10
777 25t. "Pentanisia schweinfurthii" 1·50 25
778 30t. "Chironia krebsii" 1·75 55
779 1k. "Ochna macrocalyx" 3·00 9·00

165 African and Staunton Knights

166 High Jumping

1988. Chess. Local and Staunton chess pieces. Multicoloured.

780 15t. Type **165** 1·25 30
781 35t. Bishops 1·75 70
782 50t. Rooks 2·00 1·50
783 2k. Queens 6·00 12·00

1988. Olympic Games, Seoul. Multicoloured.

784 15t. Type **166** 30 10
785 35t. Javelin throwing 50 20
786 50t. Tennis 75 50
787 2k. Shot-putting 1·60 3·00
MS788 91 × 121 mm. Nos. 784/7 3·50 3·50

167 Evergreen Forest Warbler ("Eastern Forest Scrub Warbler")

167a Rebuilt Royal Exchange, 1844

1988. Birds. Multicoloured.

789 1t. Type **167** 20 60
790 2t. Yellow-throated woodland warbler ("Yellow-throated Warbler") 30 60
791 5t. Moustached green tinkerbird 50 60
792 7t. Waller's red-winged starling ("Waller's Chestnut-wing Starling") 50 60
793 8t. Oriole-finch 50 60
794 10t. White starred robin ("Starred Robin") 2·75 60
795 15t. Bar-tailed trogon 50 10
796 20t. Green-backed twin-spot ("Green Twinspot") 50 10
797 30t. African grey cuckoo shrike ("Grey Cuckoo Shrike") 50 10
798 40t. Black-fronted bush shrike 60 10
799 50t. White-tailed crested flycatcher 3·25 1·00
800 75t. Green barbet 70 50
801 1k. Lemon dove ("Cinnamon Dove") 70 50
802 2k. Silvery-cheeked hornbill 90 1·00
803 4k. Crowned eagle 1·25 1·75
804 10k. Anchieta's sunbird ("Red and Blue Sunbird") 9·00 9·50
804a 10k. As 10t. 1·50 2·00

1988. 300th Anniv of Lloyd's of London. Mult.

805 15t. Type **167a** 30 10
806 35t. Opening ceremony, Nkula Falls Hydro-electric Power Station (horiz) 60 20
807 50t. Air Malawi B.A.C. One Eleven airliner (horiz) 2·00 60
808 2k. "Seawise University" (formerly "Queen Elizabeth") on fire, Hong Kong, 1972 3·75 4·00

168 "Madonna in the Church" (Jan van Eyck)

1988. Christmas. Multicoloured.

809 15t. Type **168** 60 10
810 35t. "Virgin, Infant Jesus and St. Anna" (da Vinci) 90 25
811 50t. "Virgin and Angels" (Cimabue) 1·25 70
812 2k. "Virgin and Child" (Baldovinetti Apenio) 3·00 6·50

169 Robust Cichlid

1989. 50th Anniv of Malawi Angling Society. Multicoloured.

813 15t. Type **169** 60 20
814 35t. Small-scaled minnow ("Mpasa") 1·10 35
815 50t. Long-scaled yellowfish 1·50 1·40
816 2k. Tigerfish 4·00 9·50

170 Independence Arch, Blantyre

1989. 25th Anniv of Independence. Multicoloured.

817 15t. Type **170** 80 20
818 35t. Grain silos 1·50 35
819 50t. Capital Hill, Lilongwe 2·00 1·50
820 2k. Reserve Bank Headquarters 5·00 9·50

171 Blantyre Digital Telex Exchange

1989. 25th Anniv of African Development Bank. Multicoloured.

821 15t. Type **171** 80 20
822 40t. Dzalanyama steer 1·50 35
823 50t. Mikolongwe heifer 2·00 1·50
824 2k. Zebu bull 5·00 9·50

172 Rural House with Verandah

1989. 25th Anniv of Malawi–United Nations Co-operation. Multicoloured.

825 15t. Type **172** 80 20
826 40t. Rural house 1·50 35
827 50t. Traditional hut and modern houses 2·00 1·50
828 2k. Tea plantation 5·00 9·50

173 St. Michael and All Angels Church

1989. Christmas. Churches of Malawi. Mult.

829 15t. Type **173** 80 20
830 40t. Catholic Cathedral, Limbe 1·50 35
831 50t. C.C.A.P. Church, Nkhoma 2·00 1·50
832 2k. Cathedral, Likoma Island 5·00 9·50

174 Ford "Sedan", 1915

1990. Vintage Vehicles. Multicoloured.

833 15t. Type **174** 1·00 20
834 40t. Two-seater Ford, 1915 1·50 35
835 50t. Ford pick-up, 1915 2·00 1·50
836 1k. Chevrolet bus, 1930 5·00 9·50
MS837 120 × 85mm. Nos. 833/6 14·00 14·00

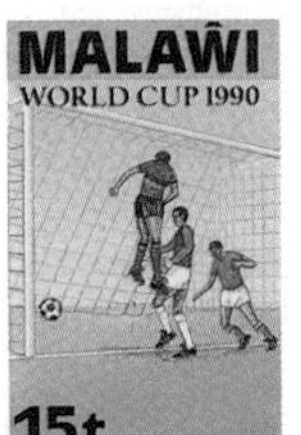

175 Player heading Ball into Net

1990. World Cup Football Championship, Italy. Multicoloured.

838 15t. Type **175** 1·00 20
839 40t. Player tackling 1·60 35
840 50t. Player scoring goal 2·00 1·50
841 2k. World Cup 5·50 10·00
MS842 88 × 118 mm. Nos. 838/41 9·50 11·00

176 Anniversary Emblem on Map

1990. 10th Anniv of Southern Africa Development Co-ordination Conference. Multicoloured.
843 15t. Type **176** . . . . 1·00 20
844 40t. Tilapia . . . . 1·00 40
845 50t. Cedar plantation . . . . 2·00 1·50
846 2k. Male nyala (antelope) . . 5·00 10·00
MS847 174 × 116 mm. Nos. 843/6 11·00 12·00

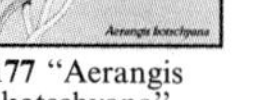

177 "Aerangis kotschyana" **178** "The Virgin and the Child Jesus" (Raphael)

1990. Orchids. Multicoloured.
848 15t. Type **177** . . . . 1·75 25
849 40t. "Angraecum eburneum" 2·75 80
850 50t. "Aerangis luteo-alba rhodostica" . . . . 2·75 1·60
851 2k. "Cyrtorchis arcuata whytei" . . . . 6·50 10·00
MS852 85 × 120 mm. Nos. 848/51 13·00 13·00

1990. Christmas. Paintings by Raphael. Mult.
853 15t. Type **178** . . . . . . 1·00 20
854 40t. "Transfiguration" (detail) 1·75 35
855 50t. "St. Catherine of Alexandrie" (detail) . . . 1·75 90
856 2k. "Transfiguration" . . . . 5·50 11·00
MS857 85 × 120 mm. Nos. 853/6 11·00 12·00

179 Buffalo

1991. Wildlife. Multicoloured.
858 20t. Type **179** . . . . 1·00 25
859 60t. Cheetah . . . . 2·25 1·00
860 75t. Greater kudu . . . . . 2·25 1·00
861 2k. Black rhinoceros . . . . 9·00 10·00
MS862 120 × 85 mm. Nos. 858/61 13·00 14·00

180 Chiromo Post Office, 1891

1991. Centenary of Postal Services. Mult.
863 20t. Type **180** . . . . 1·00 20
864 60t. Re-constructed mail exchange hut at Walala . . 1·75 85
865 75t. Mangochi post office . . 1·75 95
866 2k. Satellite Earth station . . 7·00 11·00
MS867 119 × 83 mm. Nos. 863/6 9·50 11·00

181 Red Locust **182** Child in a Manger

1991. Insects. Multicoloured.
868 20t. Type **181** . . . . 1·00 25
869 60t. Weevil . . . . 2·25 1·10
870 75t. Cotton stainer bug . . . 2·25 1·40
871 2k. Pollen beetle . . . . . . 6·50 10·00

1991. Christmas. Multicoloured.
872 20t. Type **182** 80 20
873 60t. Adoration of the Kings and Shepherds . . . . . 1·75 55
874 75t. Nativity . . . . 2·00 75
875 2k. Virgin and Child . . . . 4·75 11·00

183 Red Bishop

1992. Birds. Multicoloured.
876 75t. Type **183** . . . . 1·75 1·75
877 75t. Lesser striped swallow 1·75 1·75
878 75t. Long-crested eagle . . . 1·75 1·75
879 75t. Lilac-breasted roller . . 1·75 1·75
880 75t. African paradise flycatcher . . . . 1·75 1·75
881 75t. White-fronted bee eater 1·75 1·75
882 75t. White-winged black tern 1·75 1·75
883 75t. African fire finch ("Brown-backed Fire-finch") . . . . 1·75 1·75
884 75t. White-browed robin chat 1·75 1·75
885 75t. African fish eagle . . . . 1·75 1·75
886 75t. Malachite kingfisher . . 1·75 1·75
887 75t. Lesser masked weaver ("Cabani's Masked Weaver") . . . . 1·75 1·75
888 75t. Barn owl ("African Barn Owl") . . . . 1·75 1·75
889 75t. Variable sunbird ("Yellow-bellied Sunbird") 1·75 1·75
890 75t. Lesser flamingo . . . . 1·75 1·75
891 75t. South African crowned crane ("Crowned Crane!") 1·75 1·75
892 75t. African pitta . . . . . . 1·75 1·75
893 75t. African darter . . . . . 1·75 1·75
894 75t. White-faced whistling duck ("White-faced Tree-duck") . . . . 1·75 1·75
895 75t. African pied wagtail . . 1·75 1·75

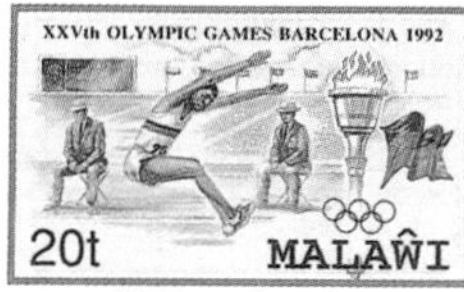

184 Long Jumping

1992. Olympic Games, Barcelona. Multicoloured.
896 20t. Type **184** 80 20
897 60t. High jumping . . . . . 1·25 60
898 75t. Javelin . . . . 1·50 90
899 2k. Running . . . . 3·50 6·50
MS900 110 × 100 mm. Nos. 896/9 6·50 7·50

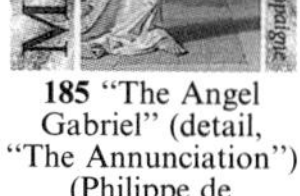
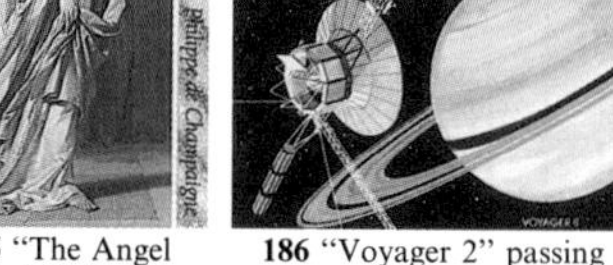

185 "The Angel Gabriel" (detail, "The Annunciation") (Philippe de Champaigne) **186** "Voyager 2" passing Saturn

1992. Christmas. Religious Paintings. Mult.
901 20t. Type **185** 70 20
902 75t. "Virgin and Child" (Bernandino Luini) . . . . 1·50 50
903 95t. "Virgin and Child" (Sassoferrato) . . . . . . 1·75 90
904 2k. "Virgin Mary" (detail, "The Annunciation") (De Champaigne) . . . . . . 4·50 8·50

1992. International Space Year. Multicoloured.
905 20t. Type **186** . . . . 1·00 30
906 75t. Centre of galaxy . . . . 2·00 90
907 95t. Kanjedza II Standard A Earth Station . . . . . . 2·00 1·00
908 2k. Communications satellite 4·50 7·50

187 "Strychnos spinosa" **188** "Apaturopsis cleocharis"

1993. World Forestry Day. Indigenous Fruit Trees. Multicoloured.
909 20t. Type **187** 70 20
910 75t. "Adansonia digitata" . . 1·50 80
911 95t. "Ximenia caffra" . . . . 1·60 1·00
912 2k. "Uapaca kirkiana" . . . 3·25 6·50

1993. Butterflies. Multicoloured.
913 20t. Type **188** 90 30
914 75t. "Euryphura achlys" . . 1·75 85
915 95t. "Cooksonia aliciae" . . 2·00 1·25
916 2k. "Charaxes protoclea azota" . . . . 3·00 5·50

189 The Holy Family **190** Kentrosaurus

1993. Christmas. Multicoloured.
917 20t. Type **189** 15 10
918 75t. Shepherds and star . . . 30 20
919 95t. Three Kings 30 30
920 2k. Adoration of the Kings 75 2·50

1993. Prehistoric Animals. Multicoloured.
921 20t. Type **190** 55 30
922 75t. Stegosaurus 90 90
923 95t. Sauropod . . . . 1·00 1·00
MS924 157 × 97 mm. 2k. Tyrannosaurus; 2k. Dilophosaurus; 2k. Brachiosaurus; 2k. Gallimimus; 2k. Triceratops; 2k. Velociraptor . . . . 11·00 12·00

191 Socolof's Mbuna

1994. Fishes. Multicoloured.
925 20t. Type **191** 20 10
926 75t. Golden mbuna 50 30
927 95t. Lombardo's mbuna . . . 55 35
928 1k. Scraper-mouthed mbuna 60 70
929 2k. Zebra mbuna . . . . . 1·25 2·00
930 4k. Elongate mbuna . . . . 2·00 3·75

192 "Ilala II" (lake vessel)

1994. Ships of Lake Malawi. Multicoloured.
931 20t. Type **192** 20 10
932 75t. "Ufulu" (tanker) 30 25
933 95t. "Pioneer" (steam launch) 35 30
934 2k. "Dove" (paddle-steamer) 60 1·75
MS935 85 × 51 mm. 5k. "Monteith" (lake vessel) . . . . 2·75 3·75

193 "Virgin and Child" (detail) (Durer) **194** Pres. Bakili Muluzi (C.O.M.E.S.A. chairman, 1994–95)

1994. Christmas. Religious Paintings. Mult.
936 20t. Type **193** 25 10
937 75t. "Wise Men present Gifts" (Franco-Flemish Book of Hours) 50 15
938 95t. "The Nativity" (detail) (Fra Filippo Lippi) (horiz) 55 15
939 2k. "Nativity Scene with Wise Men" (Rogier van der Weyden) (horiz) . . . 1·40 2·25

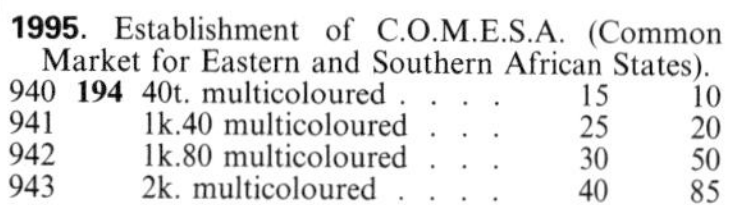

1995. Establishment of C.O.M.E.S.A. (Common Market for Eastern and Southern African States).
940 **194** 40t. multicoloured 15 10
941 1k.40 multicoloured . . . 25 20
942 1k.80 multicoloured . . . 30 50
943 2k. multicoloured 40 85

195 Telecommunications Training

1995. 50th Anniv of the United Nations. Mult.
944 40t. Type **195** 25 10
945 1k.40 Village women collecting water 50 25
946 1k.80 Mt. Mulanje 60 75
947 2k. Villagers in field 75 95
MS948 123 × 77 mm. Nos. 944/7 1·25 1·75

196 Teacher and Class

1995. Christmas. Multicoloured.
949 40t. Type **196** 15 10
950 1k.40 Dispensing medicine . . 40 25
951 1k.80 Crowd at water pump 45 60
952 2k. Refugees on ferries . . . 65 85

197 "Precis tugela"

1996. Butterflies. Multicoloured.
953 60t. Type **197** 20 10
954 3k. "Papilio pelodorus" . . . 45 35
955 4k. "Acrea acrita" 55 45
956 10k. "Melanitis leda" . . . . 1·00 2·00

198 Children's Party **199** Map of Malawi

1996. Christmas. Multicoloured.
957 10t. Type **198** 25 15
958 20t. Nativity play 40 15
959 30t. Children wearing party hats 50 20
960 60t. Mother and child . . . 85 1·00

1997. 50th Death Anniv of Paul Harris (founder of Rotary International). Multicoloured.
961 60t. Type **199** 30 10
962 3k. African fish eagle 65 50
963 4k.40 Leopard 75 85
964 5k. Rotary International emblem . . . . 75 1·00

200 Mother and Child **201** The Nativity

1997. 50th Anniv of U.N.I.C.E.F. Multicoloured.
965 60t. Type **200** 20 10
966 3k. Children in class 45 30
967 4k.40 Boy with fish 75 80
968 5k. Nurse inoculating child 90 1·10

1997. Christmas. Multicoloured.
969 60t. Type **201** 15 10
970 3k. The Nativity (different) 45 20
971 4k.40 Adoration of the Magi 60 70
972 5k. The Holy Family 65 95

1998. Diana, Princess of Wales Commemoration. As T **91** of Kiribati. Multicoloured.
973 60t. Wearing red dress . . . 15 10
974 6k. Wearing lilac jacket . . . 25 30
975 7k. With head scarf 35 60
976 8k. Wearing blue evening dress 35 70
MS977 145 × 70 mm. Nos. 973/6 1·00 1·25

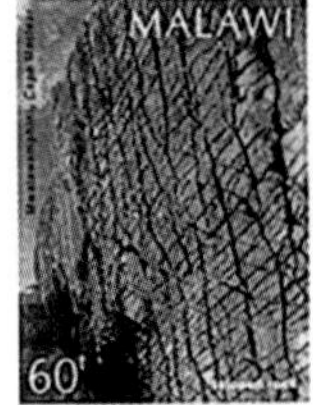

202 Tattooed Rock, Mwalawamphini, Cape Maclear

1998. Monuments. Multicoloured.
978 60t. Type **202** 10 10
979 6k. War Memorial Tower, Zomba 40 35
980 7k. Mtengatenga Postal Hut, Walala (horiz) 50 55
981 8k. P.I.M. Church, Chiradzulu (horiz) 65 75
No. 978 is inscribed "tatooed" and No. 979 "Memoral", both in error.

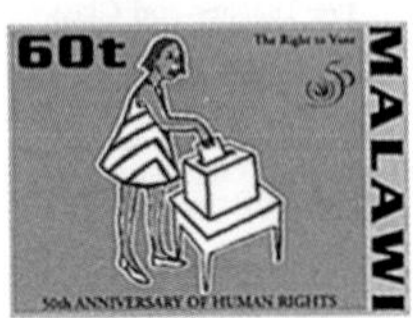

203 Woman voting

1998. 50th Anniv of Declaration of Human Rights. Multicoloured.
982 60t. Type **203** 10 10
983 6k. Books, pens and pencils ("Education") 40 35
984 7k. Man and woman on scales ("Justice") 50 55
985 8k. Person hugging house and land ("Property") 65 75

205 "Madonna and Child"

206 Ng'oma (hand drum)

1999. Christmas. Religious Paintings. Mult.
990 60t. Type **205** 10 10
991 6k. "The Nativity" 35 20
992 7k. "Adoration of the Magi" 40 35
993 8k. "Flight into Egypt" 50 60

2000. 50th Anniv of the Commonwealth. Musical Instruments. Multicoloured.
994 60t. Type **206** 10 10
995 6k. Kaligo (single stringed fiddle) 25 25
996 7k. Kalimba (thumb dulcitone) 35 35
997 8k. Chisekese (rattle) 40 55

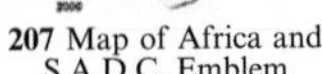
207 Map of Africa and S.A.D.C. Emblem

208 "Madonna and Child"

2000. South African Development Community. Mult.
998 60t. Type **207** 15 10
999 6k. Bottles of Malambe fruit juice 25 25
1000 7k. *Ndunduma* (fisheries research ship) (horiz) 45 45
1001 8k. Class "Shire" diesel locomotive and goods train (horiz) 55 70

2000. Christmas. Religious Paintings. Mult.
1002 5k. Type **208** 15 10
1003 18k. "Adoration of the Shepherds" 65 70
1004 20k. "Madonna and Child" 65 70

209 *Euxanthe wakefieldi*

2002. Butterflies. Multicoloured.
1005 1k. Type **209** 10 10
1006 2k. *Pseudacraea boisduvali* 10 10
1007 4k. *Catacroptera cloanthe* 10 10
1008 5k. *Myrina silenus ficedula* 10 10
1009 10k. *Cymothoe zombana* 15 20
1010 20k. *Charaxes castor* 30 35
1011 50k. *Charaxes pythoduras ventersi* 75 80
1012 100k. *Iolaus lalos* 1·50 1·60

POSTAGE DUE STAMPS

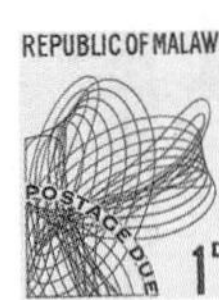

D 2

1967.
D 6 **D 2** 1d. red 15 3·75
D 7 2d. brown 20 3·75
D 8 4d. violet 25 4·00
D 9 6d. blue 25 4·25
D10 8d. green 35 4·75
D11 1s. black 45 5·00

1971. Values in tambalas. No accent over "W" of "MALAWI".
D12 **D 2** 2t. brown 30 4·50
D13 4t. mauve 50 3·00
D14 6t. blue 50 3·25
D15 8t. green 50 3·25
D16 10t. brown 60 3·25

1975. With circumflex over "W" of "MALAWI".
D27 **D 2** 2t. brown 1·75 2·50
D28 4t. purple 1·75 2·50
D29 6t. blue 1·75 2·50
D21 8t. green 1·50 3·25
D31 10t. black 2·00 2·50

MALAYA (BRITISH MILITARY ADMINISTRATION) Pt.1

The following stamps were for use throughout the Malayan States and in Singapore during the period of the British Military Administration and were gradually replaced by individual issues for each state.

100 cents = 1 dollar.

1945. Straits Settlements stamps optd **B M A MALAYA**.
1a **58** 1c. black 10 30
2a 2c. orange 20 10
4 3c. green 30 50
5 5c. brown 70 1·00
6a 6c. grey 30 20
7 8c. red 30 10
8a 10c. purple 50 10
10 12c. blue 1·75 5·00
12a 15c. blue 75 20
13a 25c. purple and red 1·40 30
14a 50c. black on green 75 10
15 $1 black and red 2·00 10
16 $2 green and red 2·75 75
17 $5 green and red on green 85·00 95·00
18 $5 purple and orange 3·75 3·00

For stamps inscribed "MALAYA" at top and with Arabic characters at foot see under Kelantan, Negri Sembilan, Pahang, Perak, Selangor or Trengganu.

MALAYA (JAPANESE OCCUPATION) Pt. 1

Japanese forces invaded Malaya on 8 December 1941 and the conquest of the Malay peninsula was completed by the capture of Singapore on 15 February.

The following stamps were used in Malaya until the defeat of Japan in 1945.

100 cents = 1 dollar.

(a) **JOHORE**

POSTAGE DUE STAMPS

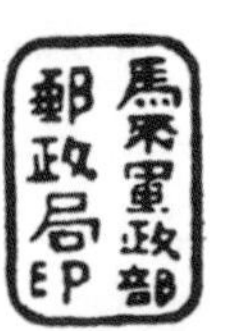
(1)

大日本郵便
(2)

1942. Nos. D1/5 of Johore optd with T **1**.
JD1a **D 1** 1c. red 20·00 70·00
JD2a 4c. green 65·00 80·00
JD3a 8c. orange 80·00 95·00
JD4a 10c. brown 16·00 50·00
JD5a 12c. purple 38·00 50·00

1943. Postage Due stamps of Johore optd with T **2**.
JD 6 **D 1** 1c. red 6·00 25·00
JD 7 4c. green 6·00 27·00
JD 8 8c. orange 7·50 27·00
JD 9 10c. brown 7·00 32·00
JD10 12c. purple 8·50 48·00

(b) **KEDAH**

1942. Stamps of Kedah optd **DAI NIPPON 2602**.
J 1 **1** 1c. black 4·75 8·00
J 2 2c. green 25·00 30·00
J 3 4c. violet 4·25 4·00
J 4 5c. yellow 4·25 4·25
J 5 6c. red 3·50 11·00
J 6 8c. black 3·50 2·25
J 7 **6** 10c. blue and brown 11·00 11·00
J 8 12c. black and violet 27·00 38·00
J 9 25c. blue and purple 8·50 12·00
J10 30c. green and red 70·00 80·00
J11 40c. black and purple 35·00 50·00
J12 50c. brown and blue 35·00 50·00
J13 $1 black and green £140 £150
J14 $2 green and brown £170 £170
J15 $5 black and red 65·00 90·00

(c) **KELANTAN**

(**5**) Sunagawa Seal

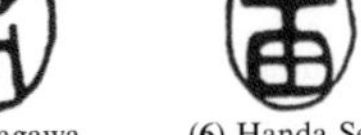
(**6**) Handa Seal

1942. Stamps of Kelantan surch. (a) With T **5**. (i) New value in **CENTS**.
J16 **4** 1c. on 50c. green and orange £225 £180
J17 2c. on 40c. orange and green £550 £300
J18 4c. on 30c. violet and red £1700 £1200
J19 5c. on 12c. blue £225 £190
J20 6c. on 25c. red and violet £300 £190
J21 8c. on 5c. brown £350 £140
J22 10c. on 6c. red 75·00 £120
J23 12c. on 8c. green 50·00 £110
J24 25c. on 10c. purple £1200 £1300
J25 30c. on 4c. red £1800 £2000
J26 40c. on 2c. green 60·00 85·00
J27 50c. on 1c. green and yellow £1400 £1300
J28 $1 on 4c. black and red 50·00 80·00
J29 $2 on 5c. green & red on yell 50·00 80·00
J30 $5 on 6c. red 50·00 80·00

(ii) New Value in **Cents**.
J32 **4** 1c. on 50c. green and orange £160 95·00
J33 2c. on 40c. orange and green £140 £100
J34 5c. on 12c. blue £140 £130
J35 8c. on 5c. brown £120 75·00
J36 10c. on 6c. red £325 £350

(b) With T **6** and new value.
J41 **4** 1c. on 50c. green and orange 95·00 £140
J42 2c. on 40c. orange and green £110 £150
J43 8c. on 5c. brown 65·00 £130
J44 10c. on 6c. red 85·00 £150
J31 12c. on 8c. green £170 £225

(d) **PENANG**

(**11**) Okugawa Seal

(**12**) Ochiburi Seal

1942. Straits Settlements stamps optd. (a) As T **11**.
J56 **58** 1c. black 9·50 11·00
J57 2c. orange 24·00 22·00
J58 3c. green 20·00 22·00
J59 5c. brown 24·00 25·00
J60 8c. grey 26·00 30·00
J61 10c. purple 50·00 50·00
J62 12c. blue 29·00 45·00
J63 15c. blue 48·00 50·00
J64 40c. red and purple 90·00 £110
J65 50c. black on green £200 £225
J66 $1 black and red on blue £200 £250
J67 $2 green and red £600 £600
J68 $5 green and red on green £1800 £1500

(b) With T **12**.
J69 **58** 1c. black £140 £110
J70 2c. orange £140 95·00
J71 3c. green 95·00 95·00
J72 5c. brown £1800 £1800
J73 8c. grey 80·00 90·00
J74 10c. purple £130 £140
J75 12c. blue 90·00 £110
J76 15c. blue £100 £110

1942. Stamps of Straits Settlements optd **DAI NIPPON 2602 PENANG**.
J77 **58** 1c. black 3·75 2·75
J78 2c. orange 4·25 4·00
J79 3c. green 4·50 3·50
J80 5c. brown 2·75 6·00
J81 8c. grey 2·25 1·40
J82 10c. purple 1·50 2·25
J83 12c. blue 3·50 13·00
J84 15c. blue 1·75 2·75
J85 40c. red and purple 4·50 13·00
J86 50c. black on green 3·75 23·00
J87 $1 black and red on blue 6·00 30·00
J88 $2 green and red 50·00 80·00
J89 $5 green and red on green £475 £550

(e) **SELANGOR**

1942. Agri-horticultural Exhibition. Stamps of Straits Settlements optd **SELANGOR EXHIBITION DAI NIPPON 2602 MALAYA**.
J90 **58** 2c. orange 12·00 24·00
J91 8c. grey 13·00 24·00

(f) **SINGAPORE**

(**15**) "Malay Military Government Division Postal Services Bureau Seal"

1942. Stamps of Straits Settlements optd with T **15**.
J92 **58** 1c. black 13·00 17·00
J93 2c. orange 13·00 13·00
J94 3c. green 50·00 70·00
J95 8c. grey 22·00 18·00
J96 15c. blue 15·00 15·00

(g) **TRENGGANU**

1942. Stamps of Trengganu optd with T **1**.
J 97 **4** 1c. black 95·00 90·00
J 98 2c. green £140 £140
J 99 2c. on 5c. pur & yell (No. 59) 40·00 40·00
J100 3c. brown 85·00 80·00
J101 4c. red £160 £140
J102 5c. purple on yellow 10·00 19·00
J103 6c. orange 9·00 25·00
J104 8c. grey 9·00 13·00
J105 8c. on 10c. blue (No. 60) 13·00 45·00
J106 10c. blue 21·00 35·00
J107 12c. blue 8·00 38·00
J108 20c. purple and orange 8·50 32·00
J109 25c. green and purple 7·50 40·00
J110 30c. purple and black 8·50 32·00
J111 35c. red on yellow 24·00 25·00
J112 50c. green and red 75·00 90·00
J113 $1 purple and blue on blue £3000 £3000
J114 $3 green and red on green 55·00 95·00
J115 – $5 green and red on yellow (No. 31) £150 £190
J116 – $25 purple and blue (No. 40) £1200
J117 – $50 green and yellow (No. 41) £10000
J118 – $100 green and red (No. 42) £1300

1942. Stamps of Trengganu optd **DAI NIPPON 2602 MALAYA**.
J119 **4** 1c. black 12·00 12·00
J120 2c. green £180 £200
J121 2c. on 5c. pur on yell (No. 59) 6·00 8·00
J122 3c. brown 12·00 22·00
J123 4c. red 11·00 11·00
J124 5c. purple on yellow 5·50 13·00
J125 6c. orange 5·00 13·00
J126 8c. grey 80·00 27·00
J127 8c. on 10c. blue (No. 60) 5·50 10·00
J128 12c. blue 5·00 24·00
J129 20c. purple and orange 13·00 14·00
J130 25c. green and purple 7·00 32·00
J131 30c. purple and black 7·50 28·00
J132 $3 green and red on green 75·00 £140

1942. Stamps of Trengganu optd with T **2**.
J133 **4** 1c. black 12·00 17·00
J134 2c. green 10·00 27·00
J135 2c. on 5c. pur on yell (No. 59) 7·00 19·00
J136 5c. purple on yellow 8·50 27·00
J137 6c. orange 9·50 30·00
J138 8c. grey 60·00 95·00
J139 8c. on 10c. blue (No. 60) 22·00 48·00
J140 10c. blue 85·00 £225
J141 12c. blue 14·00 42·00
J142 20c. purple and orange 19·00 42·00
J143 25c. green and purple 14·00 45·00
J144 30c. purple and black 20·00 48·00
J145 35c. red on yellow 20·00 50·00

POSTAGE DUE STAMPS

1942. Postage Due stamps of Trengganu optd with T **2**.
JD17 **D 1** 1c. red 50·00 85·00
JD18a 4c. green 50·00 90·00
JD19 8c. yellow 14·00 50·00
JD20 10c. brown 14·00 50·00

(h) **GENERAL ISSUES**

1942. Stamps of various states optd with T **1**. (a) Straits Settlements.
J146 **58** 1c. black 3·25 3·25
J147 2c. green £2500 £1800
J148 2c. orange 3·00 2·25
J149 3c. green 2·75 2·25
J150 5c. brown 22·00 28·00
J151 8c. grey 4·00 2·25
J152 10c. purple 45·00 45·00
J153 12c. blue 75·00 £120
J154 15c. blue 3·50 3·75
J155 30c. purple and orange £1800 £1800
J156 40c. red and purple 85·00 95·00
J157 50c. black and green 48·00 48·00

J158 $1 black and red on blue 75·00 75·00
J159 $2 green and red £130 £160
J160 $5 green and red on green £170 £190

There also exists a similar overprint with double-lined frame.

(b) Negri Sembilan.

J161b 6 1c. black . . . . 13·00 17·00
J162 2c. orange . . . . 25·00 17·00
J163 3c. green . . . . 32·00 20·00
J164c 5c. brown . . . . 15·00 11·00
J165 6c. grey £140 £120
J166 8c. red . . . . £100 90·00
J167 10c. purple £160 £160
J168 12c. blue £1200 £1200
J169 15c. blue . . . . 21·00 8·00
J170 25c. purple and red . . . 28·00 38·00
J171 30c. purple and orange . . £180 £160
J172a 40c. red and purple . . . £850 £800
J173 50c. black on green . . . £700 £700
J174a $1 black and red on blue £170 £190
J175 $5 green and red on green £500 £600

(c) Pahang.

J176 15 1c. black . . . . 50·00 42·00
J177a 3c. green £225 £275
J178 5c. brown . . . . 14·00 12·00
J179 8c. grey £700 £550
J180 8c. red . . . . 20·00 8·00
J181 10c. purple £250 £130
J182a 12c. blue £1200 £1200
J183 15c. blue £120 £110
J184 25c. purple and red . . . 21·00 29·00
J185 30c. purple and orange 12·00 28·00
J186 40c. red and purple . . . 20·00 32·00
J187 50c. black on green . . . £700 £700
J188 $1 black and red on blue £130 £150
J189 $5 green and red on green £650 £800

(d) Perak.

J190 51 1c. black . . . . 50·00 35·00
J191 2c. orange . . . . 29·00 20·00
J192 3c. green . . . . 26·00 28·00
J193 5c. brown . . . . 7·00 6·00
J194 8c. grey . . . . 70·00 48·00
J195 8c. red . . . . 35·00 40·00
J196 10c. purple . . . . 26·00 24·00
J197 12c. blue £225 £225
J198 15c. blue . . . . 24·00 32·00
J199 25c. purple and red . . . 14·00 25·00
J200 30c. purple and orange . . 17·00 32·00
J201 40c. red and purple . . . £350 £325
J202 50c. black on green . . . 38·00 50·00
J203 $1 black and red on blue £425 £400
J204 $2 green and red £2750 £2750
J205 $5 green and red on green £475

(e) Selangor.

J206 46 1c. black . . . . 12·00 24·00
J207 2c. green £1200 £1100
J208 2c. orange . . . . 85·00 60·00
J210a 3c. green . . . . 18·00 15·00
J211 5c. brown . . . . 6·00 5·50
J212a 6c. red £200 £250
J213 8c. grey . . . . 17·00 17·00
J214 10c. purple . . . . 13·00 21·00
J215 12c. blue . . . . 60·00 70·00
J216 15c. blue . . . . 16·00 22·00
J217a 25c. purple and red . . . 60·00 80·00
J218 30c. purple and orange 11·00 24·00
J219 40c. red and purple . . . £140 £140
J220a 50c. black on green . . . £130 £140
J221 48 $1 black and red on blue 30·00 45·00
J222 $2 green and red . . . . 35·00 60·00
J223 $5 green and red on green . . . . 65·00 90·00

1942. Various stamps optd **DAI NIPPON 2602 MALAYA**. (a) Stamps of Straits Settlements.

J224 58 2c. orange . . . . 1·60 50
J225 3c. green . . . . 50·00 65·00
J226 8c. grey . . . . 4·50 2·25
J227 15c. blue . . . . 12·00 8·00

(b) Stamps of Negri Sembilan.

J228 6 1c. black . . . . 2·00 60
J229 2c. orange . . . . 5·50 50
J230 3c. green . . . . 4·00 50
J231 5c. brown . . . . 1·25 2·25
J232 6c. grey . . . . 3·25 1·50
J233 8c. red . . . . 4·50 1·25
J234 10c. purple . . . . 3·00 2·50
J235 15c. blue . . . . 14·00 2·50
J236 25c. purple and red . . . 3·50 13·00
J237 30c. purple and orange . . 6·50 3·00
J238 $1 black and red on blue 80·00 95·00

(c) Stamps of Pahang.

J239 15 1c. black . . . . 2·25 2·50
J240 5c. brown . . . . 1·25 70
J241 8c. red . . . . 25·00 2·50
J242 10c. purple . . . . 9·50 6·50
J243 12c. blue . . . . 1·75 12·00
J244 25c. purple and red . . . 4·00 18·00
J245 30c. purple and orange . . 2·25 8·50

(d) Stamps of Perak.

J246 51 2c. orange . . . . 2·50 1·75
J247 3c. green . . . . 1·00 1·00
J248 8c. red 70 50
J249 10c. purple . . . . 13·00 6·00
J250 15c. blue . . . . 5·50 2·00
J251 50c. black on green . . . 2·50 3·75
J252 $1 black and red on blue £375 £425
J253 $5 green and red on green 35·00 70·00

(e) Stamps of Selangor.

J254 46 3c. green . . . . 1·25 2·75
J255 12c. blue . . . . 1·10 11·00
J256 15c. blue . . . . 4·75 1·50
J257 40c. red and purple . . . 2·00 3·75
J258 48 $2 green and red . . . . 10·00 38·00

1942. No. 108 of Perak surch **DAI NIPPON 2602 MALAYA 2 Cents**.

J259 88 2c. on 5c. brown . . . . 1·25 2·50

1942. Stamps of Perak optd **DAI NIPPON YUBIN** ("Japanese Postal Service") or surch also in figures and words.

J260 51 1c. black . . . . 4·25 9·00
J261 2c. on 5c. brown . . . . 2·00 6·50
J262 8c. red . . . . 4·25 2·25

1943. Various stamps optd vert or horiz with T 2 or surch in figures and words. (a) Stamps of Straits Settlements.

J263 58 8c. grey . . . . 1·40 50
J264 12c. blue . . . . 1·25 9·00
J265 40c. red and purple . . . 1·50 4·00

(b) Stamps of Negri Sembilan.

J266 6 1c. black . . . . 30 1·75
J267 2c. on 5c. brown 70 80
J268 6c. on 5c. brown . . . . 40 1·25
J269 25c. purple and red . . . 1·10 13·00

(c) Stamp of Pahang.

J270 7 6c. on 5c. brown 50 75

(d) Stamps of Perak.

J272 51 1c. black . . . . 1·00 70
J274 2c. on 5c. brown 60 50
J275 5c. brown 55 65
J276 8c. red . . . . 55 1·25
J277 10c. purple 60 50
J278 30c. purple and orange . . 3·25 4·75
J279 50c. black on green . . . 3·25 17·00
J280 $5 green and red on green 55·00 95·00

(e) Stamps of Selangor.

J288 46 1c. black 35 50
J289 2c. on 5c. brown 40 50
J282 3c. green 40 45
J290 3c. on 5c. brown . . . . 30 3·75
J291 5c. brown . . . . 1·25 3·75
J293 6c. on 5c. brown 30 70
J283 12c. blue . . . . 45 1·60
J284 15c. blue . . . . 3·50 3·25
J285 48 $1 black and red on blue 3·00 19·00
J295 46 $1 on 10c. purple . . . . 30 1·00
J296 $1.50 on 30c. purple and orange . . . . 30 1·00
J286 48 $2 green and red . . . . 10·00 45·00
J287 $5 green and red on green 22·00 80·00

25 Tapping Rubber

27 Japanese Shrine, Singapore

1943.

J297 25 1c. green 75 55
J298 – 2c. green 75 20
J299 25 3c. grey 30 20
J300 – 4c. red . . . . 1·75 20
J301 – 8c. blue 30 20
J302 – 10c. purple 30 20
J303 27 15c. violet . . . . 60 3·25
J304 – 30c. olive 90 35
J305 – 50c. blue . . . . 3·00 3·25
J306 – 70c. blue . . . . 16·00 10·00

DESIGNS—VERT: 2c. Fruit; 4c. Tin dredger; 8c. War Memorial, Bukit Batok, Singapore; 10c. Fishing village; 30c. Sago palms; 50c. Straits of Johore. HORIZ: 70c. Malay Mosque, Kuala Lumpur.

28 Ploughman

29 Rice-planting

1943. Savings Campaign.

J307 28 8c. violet . . . . 9·50 2·75
J308 15c. red . . . . 6·50 2·75

1944. "Re-birth of Malaya".

J309 29 8c. red . . . . 13·00 3·00
J310 15c. mauve . . . . 4·00 3·25

大日本
マライ郵便
50 セント
(30)

1944. Stamps intended for use on Red Cross letters. Surch with T **30**. (a) On Straits Settlements.

J311 58 50c. on 50c. black on grn 10·00 24·00
J312 $1 on $1 black & red on bl . . . . 18·00 35·00
J313 $1.50 on $2 green on red 28·00 70·00

(b) On Johore.

J314 24 50c. on 50c. purple & red 7·00 20·00
J315 $1.50 on $2 green and red 4·00 12·00

(c) On Selangor.

J316 48 $1 on $2 black & red on bl . . . . 3·50 14·00
J317 $1.50 on $2 green and red 5·00 20·00

POSTAGE DUE STAMPS

1942. Postage Due stamps of Malayan Postal Union optd with T **1**.

JD21 D 1 1c. violet . . . . 12·00 24·00
JD22 3c. green . . . . 60·00 65·00
JD23 4c. green . . . . 45·00 30·00
JD24 8c. red . . . . 80·00 70·00
JD25 10c. orange . . . . . . 24·00 40·00
JD26 12c. blue . . . . 24·00 50·00
JD27 50c. black . . . . . . 60·00 80·00

1942. Postage Due stamps of Malayan Postal Union optd **DAI NIPPON 2602 MALAYA**.

JD28 D 1 1c. violet . . . . 2·00 8·50
JD29 3c. green . . . . 13·00 19·00
JD30 4c. green . . . . 14·00 11·00
JD31 8c. red . . . . 18·00 16·00
JD32 10c. orange . . . . . . 1·75 13·00
JD33 12c. blue . . . . 1·75 27·00

1943. Postage Due stamps of Malayan Postal Union optd with T **2**.

JD34 D 1 1c. violet . . . . 1·50 3·50
JD35 3c. green . . . . 1·50 3·50
JD36 4c. green . . . . 50·00 40·00
JD37 5c. red . . . . 1·50 4·25
JD38 9c. orange . . . . . . 80 6·50
JD39 10c. orange . . . . . . 1·50 7·00
JD40 12c. blue . . . . 1·50 13·00
JD41 15c. blue . . . . 1·75 7·00

MALAYA (THAI OCCUPATION) Pt. 1

Stamps issued for use in the four Malay states of Kedah, Kelantan, Perlis and Trengganu ceded by Japan to Thailand on 19 October 1943 and restored to British rule on the defeat of the Japanese.

100 cents = 1 dollar.

TM 1 War Memorial

1943.

TM1 TM 1 1c. yellow . . . . . . 30·00 32·00
TM2 2c. brown . . . . . . 12·00 20·00
TM3 3c. green . . . . . . 20·00 38·00
TM4 4c. purple . . . . . . 14·00 28·00
TM5 8c. red . . . . 14·00 20·00
TM6 15c. blue . . . . . . 38·00 60·00

MALAYAN FEDERATION Pt. 1

An independent country within the British Commonwealth, comprising all the Malay States (except Singapore) and the Settlements of Malacca and Penang. The component units retained their individual stamps. In 1963 the Federation became part of Malaysia (q.v.).

100 cents (sen) = 1 Malayan dollar.

1 Tapping Rubber

1957.

1 1 6c. blue, red and yellow . . . 50 10
2 – 12c. multicoloured 85 75
3 – 25c. multicoloured . . . . . . 2·50 10
4 – 30c. red and lake . . . . . . 1·00 20

DESIGNS—HORIZ: 12c. Federation coat of arms; 25c. Tin dredge. VERT: 30c. Map of the Federation.

5 Prime Minister Tunku Abdul Rahman and Populace greeting Independence

1957. Independence Day.

5 5 10c. brown 10 10

6 United Nations Emblem

8 Merdeka Stadium, Kuala Lumpur

1958. U.N. Economic Commission for Asia and Far East Conference, Kuala Lumpur.

6 6 12c. red 30 75
7 – 30c. purple 40 75

DESIGN: 30c. As Type **6** but vert.

1958. 1st Anniv of Independence.

8 8 10c. multicoloured 15 10
9 – 30c. multicoloured 40 60

DESIGN—VERT: 30c. Portrait of the Yang di-Pertuan Agong (Tuanku Abdul Rahman).

11 Malayan with "Torch of Freedom"

12 Mace and Malayan Peoples

1958. 10th Anniv of Declaration of Human Rights.

10 – 10c. multicoloured 15 10
11 11 30c. green 45 50

DESIGN—VERT: 10c. "Human Rights".

1959. Inauguration of Parliament.

12 12 4c. red 10 10
13 10c. violet 10 10
14 25c. green 55 20

14

15 Seedling Rubber Tree and Map

1960. World Refugee Year.

15 – 12c. purple 10 50
16 14 30c. green 10 10

DESIGN: 12c. As Type **14** but horiz.

1960. Natural Rubber Research Conf and 15th Int Rubber Study Group Meeting, Kuala Lumpur.

17 15 6c. multicoloured . . . . . 20 1·00
18 30c. multicoloured 50 60

No. 18 is inscr "INTERNATIONAL RUBBER STUDY GROUP 15th MEETING KUALA LUMPUR" at foot.

16 The Yang di-Pertuan Agong (Tuanku Syed Putra)

1961. Installation of Yang di-Pertuan Agong, Tuanku Syed Putra.

19 16 10c. black and blue 10 10

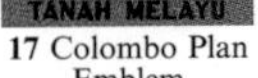

17 Colombo Plan Emblem

18 Malaria Eradication Emblem

1961. Colombo Plan Conf, Kuala Lumpur.
20 **17** 12c. black and mauve . . . 35 2·50
21 25c. black and green . . . . 80 2·00
22 30c. black and blue 70 75

1962. Malaria Eradication.
23 **18** 25c. brown 20 40
24 30c. lilac 20 15
25 50c. blue 40 70

19 Palmyra Palm Leaf

1962. National Language Month.
26 **19** 10c. brown and violet . . . 15 10
27 20c. brown and green . . . 40 1·00
28 50c. brown and mauve . . . 1·25 1·50

20 "Shadows of the Future"

1962. Introduction of Free Primary Education.
29 **20** 10c. purple 10 10
30 25c. ochre . . . . 50 1·00
31 30c. green . . . . 2·50 10

21 Harvester and Fisherman

1963. Freedom from Hunger.
32 **21** 25c. pink and green . . . . 2·00 2·75
33 30c. pink and lake . . . . 2·25 1·25
34 50c. pink and blue . . . . 2·25 2·75

22 Dam and Pylon

1963. Cameron Highlands Hydro-electric Scheme.
35 **22** 20c. green and violet 60 10
36 30c. turquoise and blue . . 90 1·25

MALAYAN POSTAL UNION Pt. 1

In 1936 postage due stamps were issued in Type D 1 for use in Negri Sembilan, Pahang, Perak, Selangor and Straits Settlements but later their use was extended to the whole of the Federation and Singapore, and from 1963 throughout Malaysia.

POSTAGE DUE STAMPS

D 1

1936.
D 7 **D 1** 1c. purple . . . . 3·25 2·00
D14 1c. violet . . . . 70 1·60
D15 2c. slate . . . . 1·25 2·25
D 8 3c. green . . . . 6·00 7·50
D 2 4c. green . . . . 17·00 1·00
D17 4c. sepia . . . . 70 7·00
D 9 5c. red . . . . 6·00 5·00
D 3 8c. red . . . . 9·00 3·50
D19 8c. orange . . . . 2·25 4·50
D11 9c. orange . . . . 50·00 48·00
D 4 10c. orange . . . . . . 12·00 30
D 5 12c. blue . . . . 13·00 14·00
D20 12c. mauve . . . . . . 1·25 6·00
D12 15c. blue . . . . £150 35·00
D21 20c. blue . . . . 6·00 6·50
D 6 50c. black . . . . 28·00 6·00

1965. Surch **10 cents**.
D29 **D 1** 10c. on 8c. orange . . . 50 2·50

MALAYSIA Pt. 1

Issues for use by the new Federation comprising the old Malayan Federation (Johore ("JOHOR"), Kedah, Kelantan, Malacca ("MELAKA"), Negri Sembilan ("NEGERI SEMBILAN"), Pahang, Penang ("PULAU PINANG"), Perak, Perlis, Selangor and Trengganu), Sabah (North Borneo), Sarawak and Singapore, until the latter became an independent state on 9 August 1965.

Stamps inscr "MALAYSIA" and state name are listed under the various states, as above.

100 cents (sen) = 1 Malaysian dollar.

A. NATIONAL SERIES

General issues for use throughout the Federation.

1 Federation Map

2 Bouquet of Orchids

1963. Inauguration of Federation.
1 **1** 10c. yellow and violet 40 10
2 12c. yellow and green . . . . 1·00 60
3 50c. yellow and brown . . . . 1·40 10

1963. 4th World Orchid Congress, Singapore.
4 **2** 6c. multicoloured . . . . . . 1·25 1·25
5 25c. multicoloured . . . . . . 1·25 25

4 Parliament House, Kuala Lumpur

1963. 9th Commonwealth Parliamentary Conf, Kuala Lumpur.
7 **4** 20c. mauve and gold . . . . 1·00 40
8 30c. green and gold . . . . . 1·00 15

5 "Flame of Freedom" and Emblems of Goodwill, Health and Charity

1964. Eleanor Roosevelt Commemoration.
9 **5** 25c. black, red and turquoise 20 10
10 30c. black, red and lilac . . . 20 15
11 50c. black, red and yellow . . 20 10

6 Microwave Tower and I.T.U. Emblem

1965. Centenary of I.T.U.
12 **6** 2c. multicoloured . . . . . . 15 1·00
13 25c. multicoloured . . . . . 1·25 60
14 50c. multicoloured . . . . . 1·75 10

7 National Mosque

1965. Opening of National Mosque, Kuala Lumpur.
15 **7** 6c. red 10 10
16 15c. brown 20 10
17 20c. green 20 15

8 Air Terminal

1965. Opening of Int Airport, Kuala Lumpur.
18 **8** 15c. black, green and blue . . 40 10
19 30c. black, green and mauve 60 20

9 Crested Wood Partridge

17 Sepak Raga (ball game) and Football

1965. Birds. Multicoloured.
20 25c. Type **9** 50 10
21 30c. Blue-backed fairy bluebird 60 10
22 50c. Black-naped oriole . . . 1·25 10
23 75c. Rhinoceros hornbill . . . 90 10
24 $1 Zebra dove . . . . 1·50 10
25 $2 Great argus pheasant . . . 4·25 30
26 $5 Asiatic paradise flycatcher 18·00 3·00
27 $10 Blue-tailed pitta . . . . . 48·00 13·00

For the lower values see the individual sets listed under each of the states which form Malaysia.

1965. 3rd South East Asian Peninsular Games.
28 **17** 25c. black and green . . . . 40 1·25
29 – 30c. black and purple . . . 40 20
30 – 50c. black and blue 70 30

DESIGNS: 30c. Running; 50c. Diving.

20 National Monument

21 The Yang di-Pertuan Agong (Tuanku Ismail Nasiruddin Shah)

1966. National Monument, Kuala Lumpur.
31 **20** 10c. multicoloured 30 10
32 20c. multicoloured 50 40

1966. Installation of Yang di-Pertuan Agong, Tuanku Ismail Nasiruddin Shah.
33 **21** 15c. black and yellow . . . 10 10
34 50c. black and blue 20 20

22 School Building

1966. 150th Anniv of Penang Free School.
35 **22** 20c. multicoloured 70 10
36 50c. multicoloured 90 10

23 "Agriculture"

1966. 1st Malaysia Plan. Multicoloured.
37 15c. Type **23** 20 10
38 15c. "Rural Health" 20 10
39 15c. "Communications" . . . 1·90 15
40 15c. "Education" 20 10
41 15c. "Irrigation" 20 10

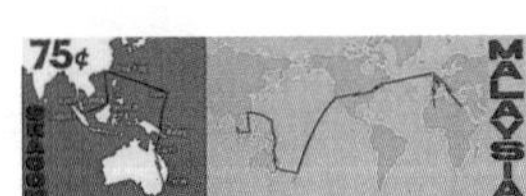

28 Cable Route Maps (½-size illustration)

1967. Completion of Malaysia–Hong Kong Link of SEACOM Telephone Cable.
42 **28** 30c. multicoloured 80 50
43 75c. multicoloured . . . . . 2·50 3·50

29 Hibiscus and Paramount Rulers

1967. 10th Anniv of Independence.
44 **29** 15c. multicoloured 20 10
45 50c. multicoloured . . . . . 1·25 80

30 Mace and Shield

1967. Centenary of Sarawak Council.
46 **30** 15c. multicoloured 10 10
47 50c. multicoloured 30 50

31 Straits Settlements 1867 8c. Stamp and Malaysian 1965 25c. Stamp

1967. Stamp Centenary.
48 **31** 25c. multicoloured . . . . . 1·40 3·00
49 – 30c. multicoloured . . . . . 1·40 2·50
50 – 50c. multicoloured . . . . . 2·25 3·25

DESIGNS: 30c. Straits Settlements 1867 24c. stamp and Malaysian 1965 30c. stamp; 50c. Straits Settlements 1867 32c. stamp and Malaysian 1965 50c. stamp.

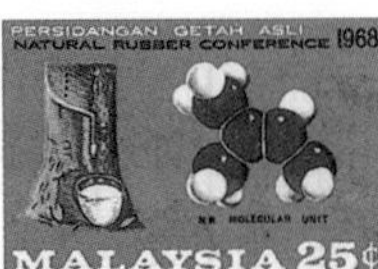

34 Tapping Rubber, and Molecular Unit

1968. Natural Rubber Conf, Kuala Lumpur. Mult.
51 25c. Type **34** 30 10
52 30c. Tapping rubber and export consignment 40 20
53 50c. Tapping rubber and aircraft tyres 40 10

37 Mexican Sombrero and Blanket with Olympic Rings

39 Tunku Abdul Rahman against background of Pandanus Weave

1968. Olympic Games, Mexico. Multicoloured.
54 30c. Type **37** 20 10
55 75c. Olympic Rings and Mexican embroidery 55 20

1969. Solidarity Week.
56 **39** 15c. multicoloured 15 10
57 – 20c. multicoloured . . . . . 45 1·50
58 – 50c. multicoloured 50 20

DESIGNS—VERT: 20c. As Type **39** (different). HORIZ: 50c. Tunku Abdul Rahman with pandanus pattern.

42 Peasant Girl with Sheaves of Paddy

1969. National Rice Year.
59 **42** 15c. multicoloured 15 10
60 75c. multicoloured . . . . . 55 1·25

43 Satellite-tracking Aerial

1970. Satellite Earth Station.
61 **43** 15c. drab, black and blue 1·00 15
62 – 30c. multicoloured 1·00 2·25
63 – 30c. multicoloured 1·00 2·25
DESIGN—40 × 27 mm: Nos. 62/3, "Intelstat III" in Orbit.
No. 62 has inscriptions and value in white and No. 63 has them in gold.

45 "Euploea leucostictus"
46 Emblem

1970. Butterflies. Multicoloured.
64 25c. Type **45** 1·00 10
65 30c. "Zeuxidia amethystus" 1·50 10
66 50c. "Polyura athamas" 2·00 10
67 75c. "Papilio memnon" 2·00 10
68 $1 "Appias nero" 2·50 10
69 $2 "Trogonoptera brookiana" 3·50 10
70 $5 "Narathura centaurus" 5·00 3·50
71 $10 "Terinos terpander" 17·00 5·00
Lower values were issued for use in the individual States.

1970. 50th Anniv of Int Labour Organization.
72 **46** 30c. grey and blue 10 20
73 75c. pink and blue 20 30

47 U.N. Emblem encircled by Doves
50 The Yang di-Pertuan Agong (Tuanku Abdul Halim Shah)

1970. 25th Anniv of United Nations.
74 **47** 25c. gold, black and brown 35 40
75 – 30c. multicoloured 35 35
76 – 50c. black and green 40 75
DESIGNS: 30c. Line of doves and U.N. emblem; 50c. Doves looping U.N. emblem.

1971. Installation of Yang di-Pertuan Agong (Paramount Ruler of Malaysia).
77 **50** 10c. black, gold and yellow 20 30
78 15c. black, gold and mauve 20 30
79 50c. black, gold and blue 70 1·60

51 Bank Negara Complex

1971. Opening of Bank Negara Building.
80 **51** 25c. black and silver 2·25 2·25
81 50c. black and gold 1·75 1·25

52 Aerial View of Parliament Buildings

1971. 17th Commonwealth Parliamentary Association Conference, Kuala Lumpur. Multicoloured.
82 25c. Type **52** 1·25 50
83 75c. Ground view of Parliament Buildings (horiz, 73 × 23½ mm) 2·75 1·75

53 **54** Malaysian Carnival **55**

1971. Visit ASEAN Year.
84 **53** 30c. multicoloured 1·60 55
85 **54** 30c. multicoloured 1·60 55
86 **55** 30c. multicoloured 1·60 55
ASEAN = Association of South East Asian Nations.
Nos. 84/6 form a composite design of a Malaysian Carnival, as illustrated.

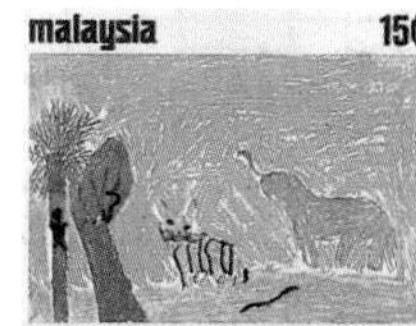

56 Trees, Elephant and Tiger

1971. 25th Anniv of U.N.I.C.E.F. Multicoloured.
87 15c. Type **56** 2·50 60
88 15c. Cat and kittens 2·50 60
89 15c. Sun, flower and bird (22 × 29 mm) 2·50 60
90 15c. Monkey, elephant and lion in jungle 2·50 60
91 15c. Spider and butterflies 2·50 60

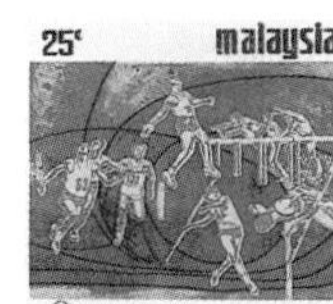

57 Athletics

1971. 6th S.E.A.P. Games, Kuala Lumpur. Mult.
92 25c. Type **57** 45 40
93 30c. Sepak Raga players 60 50
94 50c. Hockey 1·75 95
S.E.A.P. = South East Asian Peninsula.

58 **59** Map and Tourist Attractions **60**

1971. Pacific Area Tourist Association Conference.
95 **58** 30c. multicoloured 2·75 1·00
96 **59** 30c. multicoloured 2·75 1·00
97 **60** 30c. multicoloured 2·75 1·00
Nos. 95/7 form a composite design of a map showing tourist attractions, as illustrated.

BANDARAYA KUALA LUMPUR 1972
61 Kuala Lumpur City Hall

1972. City Status for Kuala Lumpur. Multicoloured.
98 25c. Type **61** 1·25 1·25
99 50c. City Hall in floodlights 2·00 1·25

62 SOCSO Emblem

64 Fireworks, National Flag and Flower

63 W.H.O. Emblem

1973. Social Security Organization.
100 **62** 10c. multicoloured 15 15
101 15c. multicoloured 15 10
102 50c. multicoloured 40 1·40

1973. 25th Anniv of W.H.O.
103 **63** 30c. multicoloured 50 25
104 – 75c. multicoloured 1·00 2·50
The 75c. is similar to Type **63**, but vertical.

1973. 10th Anniv of Malaysia.
105 **64** 10c. multicoloured 40 25
106 15c. multicoloured 55 15
107 50c. multicoloured 1·90 1·60

65 Emblems of Interpol and Royal Malaysian Police

1973. 50th Anniv of Interpol. Multicoloured.
108 25c. Type **65** 1·00 50
109 75c. Emblems within "50" 2·25 2·00

66 Boeing 737 and M.A.S. Emblem

1973. Foundation of Malaysian Airline System.
110 **66** 15c. multicoloured 35 10
111 30c. multicoloured 65 60
112 50c. multicoloured 95 1·60

67 Kuala Lumpur

1974. Establishment of Kuala Lumpur as Federal Territory.
113 **67** 25c. multicoloured 50 85
114 50c. multicoloured 1·00 1·75

68 Development Projects

1974. 7th Annual Meeting of Asian Development Bank's Board of Governors, Kuala Lumpur.
115 **68** 30c. multicoloured 25 50
116 75c. multicoloured 80 1·75

69 Scout Badge and Map

1974. Malaysian Scout Jamboree. Multicoloured.
117 10c. Type **69** 60 70
118 15c. Scouts saluting and flags (46 × 24 mm) 95 30
119 50c. Scout badge 1·75 2·75

70 Coat of Arms and Power Installations

1974. 25th Anniv of National Electricity Board. Multicoloured.
120 30c. Type **70** 30 50
121 75c. National Electricity Board building (37 × 27 mm) 1·00 2·50

71 U.P.U. and Post Office Emblems within "100"

1974. Centenary of U.P.U.
122 **71** 25c. green, yellow and red 20 35
123 30c. blue, yellow and red 25 35
124 75c. orange, yellow and red 65 1·75

72 Gravel Pump in Tin Mine

1974. 4th World Tin Conf, Kuala Lumpur. Mult.
125 15c. Type **72** 1·75 20
126 20c. Open-cast mine 2·00 2·00
127 50c. Dredger within "ingot" 3·75 5·00

73 Hockey-players, World Cup and Federation Emblem
74 Congress Emblem

1975. 3rd World Cup Hockey Championships.
128 **73** 30c. multicoloured 90 60
129 75c. multicoloured 2·10 2·25

1975. 25th Anniv of Malaysian Trade Union Congress.
130 **74** 20c. multicoloured 15 25
131 25c. multicoloured 20 30
132 30c. multicoloured 65 60

75 Emblem of M.K.P.W. (Malayan Women's Organization)
76 Ubudiah Mosque, Kuala Kangsar

1975. International Women's Year.
133 **75** 10c. multicoloured 15 25
134 15c. multicoloured 30 25
135 50c. multicoloured 1·25 2·25

1975. Koran Reading Competition. Multicoloured.
136 15c. Type **76** 1·75 60
137 15c. Zahir Mosque, Alor Star 1·75 60
138 15c. National Mosque, Kuala Lumpur 1·75 60
139 15c. Sultan Abu Bakar Mosque, Johore Bahru 1·75 60
140 15c. Kuching State Mosque, Sarawak 1·75 60

77 Plantation and Emblem

1975. 50th Anniv of Malaysian Rubber Research Institute. Multicoloured.
141 10c. Type **77** 40 15
142 30c. Latex cup and emblem 1·10 70
143 75c. Natural rubber in test-tubes 2·25 2·25

77a "Hebomoia glaucippe"

1976. Multicoloured.
144 10c. Type **77a** 2·50 6·50
145 15c. "Precis orithya" 2·50 6·50

78 Scrub Typhus

79 The Yang di-Pertuan Agong (Tuanku Yahya Petra)

1976. 75th Anniv of Institute of Medical Research. Multicoloured.
146 20c. Type **78** 25 15
147 25c. Malaria diagnosis . . . 40 20
148 $1 Beri-beri . . . . 1·60 2·50

1976. Installation of Yang di-Pertuan Agong.
149 **79** 10c. black, brown & yellow 25 10
150 15c. black, brown & mauve 40 10
151 50c. black, brown and blue 2·25 2·50

80 State Council Complex

1976. Opening of State Council Complex and Administrative Building, Sarawak.
152 **80** 15c. green and yellow . . . 35 10
153 20c. green and mauve . . . 45 40
154 50c. green and blue . . . . 1·00 1·40

81 E.P.F. Building

1976. 25th Anniv of Employees' Provident Fund. Multicoloured.
155 10c. Type **81** 15 10
156 25c. E.P.F. emblems (27 × 27 mm) 35 75
157 50c. E.P.F. Building at night 60 1·40

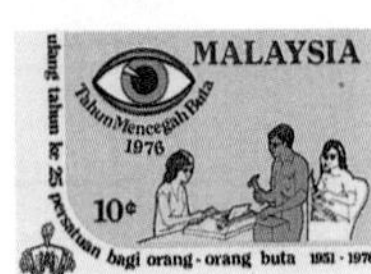

82 Blind People at Work

1976. 25th Anniv of Malayan Assn for the Blind. Multicoloured.
158 10c. Type **82** 15 15
159 75c. Blind man and shadow 1·25 2·75

83 Independence Celebrations, 1957

1977. 1st Death Anniv of Tun Abdul Razak (Prime Minister).
160 15c. Type **83** . . . . 1·50 60
161 15c. "Education" . . . . . . 1·50 60
162 15c. Tun Razak and map ("Development") . . . . . 1·50 60
163 15c. "Rukunegara" (National Philosophy) . . . . 1·50 60
164 15c. A.S.E.A.N. meeting . . 1·50 60

84 F.E.L.D.A. Village Scheme

1977. 21st Anniv of Federal Land Development Authority (F.E.L.D.A.). Multicoloured.
165 15c. Type **84** 30 10
166 30c. Oil palm settlement . . . 80 1·75

85 Figure "10"

86 Games Logos

1977. 10th Anniv of Association of South East Asian Nations (A.S.E.A.N.). Multicoloured.
167 10c. Type **85** 10 10
168 75c. Flags of members . . . 1·25 1·00

1977. 9th South East Asia Games, Kuala Lumpur. Multicoloured.
169 10c. Type **86** 15 15
170 20c. "Ball" 20 15
171 75c. Symbolic athletes . . . 75 1·75

87 Islamic Development Bank Emblem

1978. Islamic Development Bank Board of Governors' Meeting, Kuala Lumpur.
172 **87** 30c. multicoloured 25 15
173 75c. multicoloured 75 85

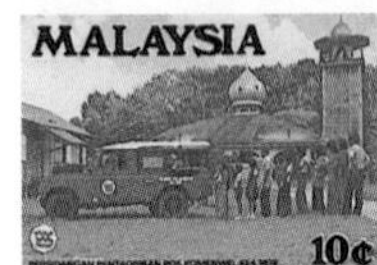

88 Mobile Post Office

1978. 4th Commonwealth Postal Administrations Conference, Kuala Lumpur. Multicoloured.
174 10c. Type **88** 30 10
175 25c. G.P.O., Kuala Lumpur 75 1·75
176 50c. Rural delivery by motorcycle . . . . 2·00 2·75

89 Boy Scout Emblem

1978. 4th Malaysian Scout Jamboree, Sarawak. Multicoloured.
177 15c. Type **89** 50 10
178 $1 Bees and honeycomb . . . 2·50 3·25

90 Dome of the Rock, Jerusalem

1978. Palestinian Welfare.
179 **90** 15c. multicoloured 60 25
180 30c. multicoloured . . . . 1·40 2·00

91 Globe and Emblems

1978. Global Eradication of Smallpox.
181 **91** 15c. black, red and blue . . 25 10
182 30c. black, red and green 40 30
183 50c. black, red and pink 70 95

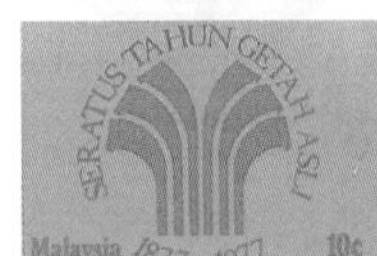

92 "Seratus Tahun Getah Asli" and Tapping Knives Symbol

1978. Centenary of Rubber Industry.
184 **92** 10c. gold and green 10 10
185 – 20c. blue, brown and green 10 10
186 – 75c. gold and green . . . . 45 1·00
DESIGNS: 20c. Rubber tree seedling and part of "maxi stump"; 75c. Graphic design of rubber tree, latex cup and globe arranged to form "100".

93 Sultan of Selangor's New Palace

1978. Inauguration of Shah Alam New Town as State Capital of Selangor. Multicoloured.
187 10c. Type **93** 10 10
188 30c. Aerial view of Shah Alam 20 15
189 75c. Shah Alam . . . . . . 55 2·00

94 Tiger

1979. Animals. Multicoloured.
190 30c. Type **94** . . . . 1·75 10
191 40c. Malayan flying lemur . . 80 10
192 50c. Lesser Malay chevrotain 1·75 10
193 75c. Leathery pangolin . . . 1·00 10
194 $1 Malayan turtle . . . . . 1·50 10
195 $2 Malayan tapir . . . . . 1·50 10
196 $5 Gaur . . . . 4·50 2·00
197 $10 Orang-utang (vert) . . . 7·00 3·50

96 View of Central Bank of Malaysia

97 I.Y.C. Emblem

1979. 20th Anniv of Central Bank of Malaysia. Multicoloured.
198 10c. Type **96** 10 10
199 75c. Central Bank (vert) . . . 40 1·25

1979. International Year of the Child.
200 **97** 10c. gold, blue and salmon 35 10
201 – 15c. multicoloured 60 10
202 – $1 multicoloured . . . . . 3·00 3·75
DESIGNS: 15c. Children holding hands in front of globe; $1 Children playing.

98 Dam and Power Station

1979. Opening of Hydro-electric Power Station, Temengor.
203 **98** 15c. multicoloured 20 15
204 – 25c. multicoloured 35 40
205 – 50c. multicoloured . . . . 55 1·40
DESIGNS: 25c., 50c. Different views of dam.

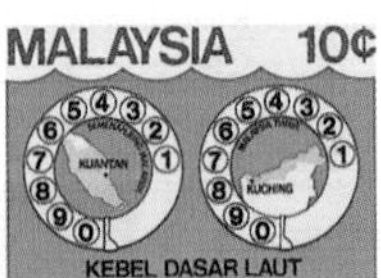

99 Exhibition Emblem

100 Tuanku Haji Ahmad Shah

1979. 3rd World Telecommunications Exhibition, Geneva.
206 **99** 10c. orange, blue and silver 10 40
207 – 15c. multicoloured 15 10
208 – 50c. multicoloured . . . . 40 2·00
DESIGNS—34 × 24 mm: 15c. Telephone receiver joining the one half of World to the other. 39 × 28 mm: 50c. Communications equipment.

1980. Installation of Tuanku Haji Ahmad Shah as Yang di-Pertuan Agong.
209 **100** 10c. black, gold and yellow 10 30
210 15c. black, gold and purple 15 10
211 50c. black, gold and blue 40 1·75

MALAYSIA 10¢
KEBEL DASAR LAUT

101 Pahang and Sarawak Maps within Telephone Dials

1980. Kuantan–Kuching Submarine Cable Project. Multicoloured.
212 10c. Type **101** 10 40
213 15c. Kuantan and Kuching views within telephone dials 15 10
214 50c. Pahang and Sarawak maps within telephone receiver . . . . 35 1·75

102 Bangi Campus

1980. 10th Anniv of National University of Malaysia. Multicoloured.
215 10c. Type **102** 15 20
216 15c. Jalan Pantai Baru campus 20 10
217 75c. Great Hall . . . . . . 75 2·75

103 Mecca

1980. Moslem Year 1400 A.H. Commemoration.
218 **103** 15c. multicoloured 10 10
219 50c. multicoloured . . . . 30 1·50
No. 219 is inscribed in Roman lettering.

104 Disabled Child learning to Walk

105 Industrial Scene

1981. International Year for Disabled Persons. Multicoloured.
220 10c. Type **104** 30 30
221 15c. Girl sewing 55 10
222 75c. Disabled athlete . . . . 1·50 3·50

1981. Expo "81" Industrial Training Exposition, Kuala Lumpur and Seminar, Genting Highlands. Multicoloured.
223 10c. Type **105** 10 10
224 15c. Worker and bulldozer 15 10
225 30c. Workers at shipbuilding plant 25 35
226 75c. Agriculture and fishing produce, workers and machinery . . . . 65 2·25

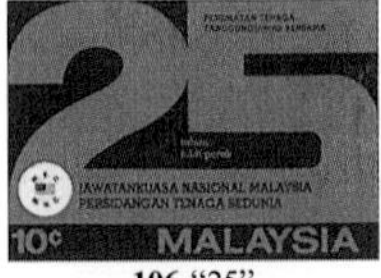

106 "25"

1981. 25th Anniv of Malaysian National Committee for World Energy Conferences. Multicoloured.
227 10c. Type **106** 20 20
228 15c. Drawings showing importance of energy sources in industry 45 10
229 75c. Symbols of various energy sources . . . . . . 2·00 3·25

107 Drawing showing development of Sabah from Village to Urbanized Area

1981. Centenary of Sabah. Multicoloured.
230 15c. Type **107** 50 15
231 80c. Drawing showing traditional and modern methods of agriculture . . 2·00 4·25

108 "Samanea saman"

1981. Trees. Multicoloured.
232 15c. Type **108** 55 10
233 50c. "Dyera costulata" (vert) 1·75 1·40
234 80c. "Dryobalanops aromatica" (vert) . . . . . 2·00 4·25

109 Jamboree Emblem

1982. 5th Malaysian/7th Asia–Pacific Boy Scout Jamboree. Multicoloured.
235 15c. Type **109** 35 10
236 50c. Malaysian flag and scout emblem 80 85
237 80c. Malaysian and Asia–Pacific scout emblem 1·25 4·25

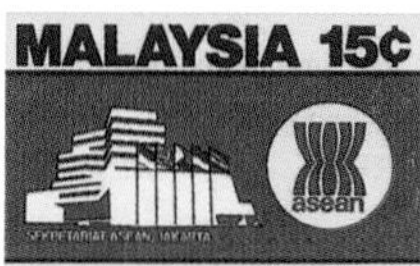

110 A.S.E.A.N. Building and Emblem

1982. 15th Anniv of Ministerial Meeting of A.S.E.A.N. (Association of South East Asian Nations). Multicoloured.
238 15c. Type **110** 15 10
239 $1 Flags of members 1·10 3·00

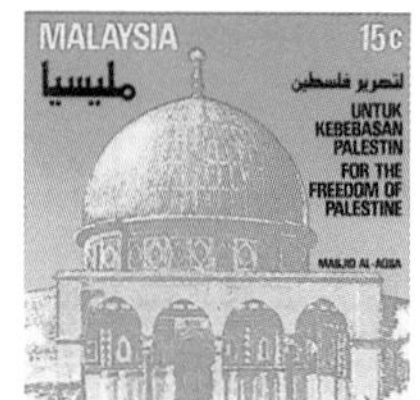

111 Dome of the Rock, Jerusalem

1982. "Freedom for Palestine".
240 **111** 15c. gold, green and black 75 15
241 $1 silver, green and black 3·25 4·50

112 Views of Kuala Lumpur in 1957 and 1982

1982. 25th Anniv of Independence. Multicoloured.
242 10c. Type **112** 10 10
243 15c. Malaysian industries 15 15
244 50c. Soldiers on parade 40 55
245 80c. Independence ceremony 70 2·75
MS246a 120 × 190 mm. Nos. 242/5 10·00 10·00

113 Shadow Play

1982. Traditional Games. Multicoloured.
247 10c. Type **113** 55 30
248 15c. Cross top 55 15
249 75c. Kite flying 2·25 4·50

114 Sabah Hats

1982. Malaysian Handicrafts. Multicoloured.
250 10c. Type **114** 25 30
251 15c. Gold-threaded cloth 25 20
252 75c. Sarawak pottery 1·25 3·50

115 Gas Exploitation Logo

1983. Export of Liquefied Natural Gas from Bintulu Field, Sarawak. Multicoloured.
253 15c. Type **115** 75 15
254 20c. "Tenaga Satu" (liquid gas tanker) 1·50 70
255 $1 Gas drilling equipment 3·50 6·00

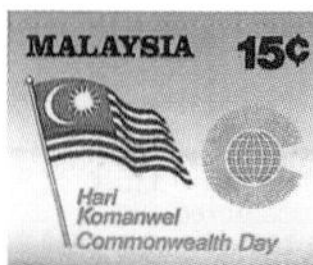

116 Flag of Malaysia

1983. Commonwealth Day. Multicoloured.
256 15c. Type **116** 10 10
257 20c. The King of Malaysia 15 20
258 40c. Oil palm tree and refinery 25 45
259 $1 Satellite view of Earth 60 2·50

117 Nile Mouthbrooder

1983. Freshwater Fishes. Multicoloured.
260 20c. Type **117** 1·50 2·00
261 20c. Common carp 1·50 2·00
262 40c. Lampan barb 2·25 2·75
263 40c. Grass carp 2·25 2·75

118 Lower Pergau River Bridge

1983. Opening of East–West Highway. Mult.
264 15c. Type **118** 80 15
265 20c. Perak river reservoir bridge 1·00 75
266 $1 Map showing East–West highway 3·75 6·50

119 Northrop Tiger II Fighter

1983. 50th Anniv of Malaysian Armed Forces. Multicoloured.
267 15c. Type **119** 1·25 15
268 20c. Missile boat 1·75 45
269 40c. Battle of Pasir Panjang 2·25 2·50
270 80c. Trooping the Colour 3·25 6·00
MS271 130 × 85 mm. Nos. 267/70 9·50 11·00

120 Helmeted Hornbill

122 Sky-scraper and Mosque, Kuala Lumpur

121 Bank Building, Ipoh

1983. Hornbills of Malaysia. Multicoloured.
280 15c. Type **120** 1·00 15
281 20c. Wrinkled hornbill 1·25 50
282 50c. Long-crested hornbill 2·00 2·00
283 $1 Rhinoceros hornbill 3·25 5·50

1984. 25th Anniv of Bank Negara. Multicoloured.
284 20c. Type **121** 40 30
285 $1 Bank building, Alor Setar 2·00 3·75

1984. 10th Anniv of Federal Territory of Kuala Lumpur. Multicoloured.
286 20c. Type **122** 80 20
287 40c. Aerial view 1·60 1·40
288 80c. Gardens and clock-tower (horiz) 2·50 6·50

123 Map showing Industries

124 Semenanjung Keris

1984. Formation of Labuan Federal Territory. Multicoloured.
289 20c. Type **123** 75 25
290 $1 Flag and map of Labuan 3·75 5·50

1984. Traditional Malay Weapons. Multicoloured.
291 40c. Type **124** 1·25 1·90
292 40c. Pekakak keris 1·25 1·90
293 40c. Jawa keris 1·25 1·90
294 40c. Lada tumbuk 1·25 1·90

125 Map of World and Transmitter

1984. 20th Anniv of Asia–Pacific Broadcasting Union. Multicoloured.
295 20c. Type **125** 40 25
296 $1 Clasped hands within "20" 2·00 4·50

126 Facsimile Service

127 Yang di-Pertuan Agong (Tuanku Mahmood)

1984. Opening of New General Post Office, Kuala Lumpur. Multicoloured.
297 15c. Type **126** 35 20
298 20c. New G.P.O. building 45 45
299 $1 Mailbag conveyor 2·00 4·50

1984. Installation of Yang di-Pertuan Agong (Tuanku Mahmood).
300 **127** 15c. multicoloured 60 20
301 20c. multicoloured 65 20
302 – 40c. multicoloured 1·25 1·00
303 – 80c. multicoloured 2·50 5·00
DESIGN—HORIZ: 40c., 80c. Yang di-Pertuan Agong and federal crest.

128 White Hibiscus

129 Parliament Building

1984. Hibiscus. Multicoloured.
304 10c. Type **128** 50 30
305 20c. Red hibiscus 1·00 20
306 40c. Pink hibiscus 1·75 2·00
307 $1 Orange hibiscus 2·75 5·75

1985. 25th Anniv of Federal Parliament. Mult.
308 20c. Type **129** 30 15
309 $1 Parliament Building (different) (horiz) 1·75 3·00

130 Banded Linsang

1985. Protected Animals of Malaysia (1st series). Multicoloured.
310 10c. Type **130** 60 10
311 40c. Slow loris (vert) 2·00 1·40
312 $1 Spotted giant flying squirrel (vert) 4·00 6·50
See also Nos. 383/6.

131 Stylized Figures

1985. International Youth Year. Multicoloured.
313 20c. Type **131** 40 15
314 $1 Young workers 3·50 5·00

132 Steam Locomotive No. 1, 1885

1985. Centenary of Malayan Railways.
315 **132** 15c. black, red and orange 1·40 50
316 – 20c. multicoloured 1·60 60
317 – $1 multicoloured 4·00 6·00
MS318 119 × 59 mm. 80c. multicoloured 7·00 8·00
DESIGNS—HORIZ: 20c. Class 20 diesel-electric locomotive, 1957; $1 Hitachi Class 23 diesel-electric locomotive, 1983. 48 × 31 mm: 80c. Class 56 steam locomotive No. 564.18, "Seletar", 1938.

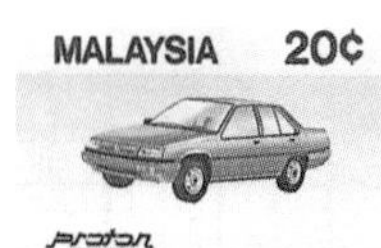

133 Blue Proton "Saga 1.3s" Car

1985. Production of Proton "Saga" (Malaysian national car). Multicoloured.
319 20c. Type **133** 80 15
320 40c. White Proton "Saga 1.3s" 1·40 1·00
321 $1 Red Proton "Saga 1.5s" 2·50 6·00

134 Penang Bridge **135** Offshore Oil Rig

1985. Opening of Penang Bridge. Multicoloured.
322 20c. Type **134** 90 15
323 40c. Penang Bridge and location map 1·75 90
324 $1 Symbolic bridge linking Penang to mainland (40 × 24 mm) 3·50 6·00

1985. Malaysian Petroleum Production. Mult.
325 15c. Type **135** 1·25 20
326 20c. Malaysia's first oil refinery (horiz) 1·40 50
327 $1 Map of Malaysian offshore oil and gas fields (horiz) 3·75 6·00

136 Sultan Azlan Shah and Perak Royal Crest

137 Crested Fireback Pheasant

1985. Installation of the Sultan of Perak.
328 **136** 15c. multicoloured 45 10
329 20c. multicoloured 50 25
330 $1 multicoloured 2·75 5·50

1986. Protected Birds of Malaysia (1st series). Multicoloured.
331 20c. Type **137** 2·50 3·25
332 20c. Malay peacock-pheasant 2·50 3·25
333b 40c. Bulwer's pheasant (horiz) 2·00 3·50
334b 40c. Great argus pheasant (horiz) 2·00 3·50
See also Nos. 394/7.

139 Two Kadazan Dancers, Sabah
140 Stylized Competitors

1986. Pacific Area Travel Association Conference, Malaysia. Multicoloured.
335 20c. Type **139** . . . . 85 1·25
336 20c. Dyak dancer and longhouse, Sarawak . . . 85 1·25
337 20c. Dancers and fortress, Malacca . . . . 85 1·25
338 40c. Malay dancer and Kuala Lumpur . . . . 1·25 1·50
339 40c. Chinese opera dancer and Penang Bridge . . . . 1·25 1·50
340 40c. Indian dancer and Batu Caves . . . . 1·25 1·50

1986. Malaysia Games. Multicoloured.
341 20c. Type **140** . . . . 1·25 20
342 40c. Games emblems (vert) 2·25 2·00
343 $1 National and state flags (vert) . . . . 7·00 7·75

141 Rambutan
142 Skull and Slogan "Drugs Can Kill"

1986. Fruits of Malaysia. Multicoloured.
344 40c. Type **141** 15 10
345 50c. Pineapple 15 10
346 80c. Durian 25 10
347 $1 Mangosteen 30 10
348 $2 Star fruit 65 10
349 $5 Banana . . . . 1·60 50
350 $10 Mango . . . . 3·25 1·25
351 $20 Papaya . . . . 6·50 3·25

1986. 10th Anniv of National Association for Prevention of Drug Addiction. Multicoloured.
352 20c. Type **142** . . . . 1·00 30
353 40c. Bird and slogan "Stay Free From Drugs" . . . . 1·40 1·10
354 $1 Addict and slogan "Drugs Can Destroy" (vert) . . . 2·25 5·00

143 MAS Logo and Map showing Routes
144 Building Construction

1986. Inaugural Flight of Malaysian Airlines Kuala Lumpur–Los Angeles Service. Multicoloured.
355 20c. Type **143** . . . . 1·75 20
356 40c. Logo, stylized aircraft and route diagram . . . . 2·50 80
357 $1 Logo and stylized aircraft 3·50 3·75

1986. 20th Anniv of National Productivity Council and 25th Anniv of Asian Productivity Organization (40c., $1). Multicoloured.
358 20c. Type **144** 85 25
359 40c. Planning and design (horiz) . . . . 1·40 1·25
360 $1 Computer-controlled car assembly line (horiz) . . . 3·75 6·50

145 Old Seri Menanti Palace, Negri Sembilan

1986. Historic Buildings of Malaysia (1st series). Multicoloured.
361 15c. Type **145** 85 20
362 20c. Old Kenangan Palace, Perak 95 20
363 40c. Old Town Hall, Malacca 1·75 80
364 $1 Astana, Kuching, Sarawak 3·00 4·50
See also Nos. 465/8.

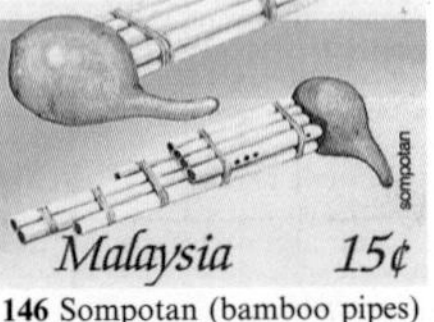

146 Sompotan (bamboo pipes)

1987. Malaysian Musical Instruments. Mult.
365 15c. Type **146** 85 10
366 20c. Sapih (four-stringed chordophone) 95 20
367 50c. Serunai (pipes) (vert) . . 2·00 40
368 80c. Rebab (three-stringed fiddle) (vert) . . . . 2·50 1·75

147 Modern Housing Estate

1987. International Year of Shelter for the Homeless. Multicoloured.
369 20c. Type **147** 75 15
370 $1 Stylized families and houses . . . . 2·25 1·25

148 Drug Addict and Family

1987. International Conference on Drug Abuse, Vienna. Multicoloured.
371 20c. Type **148** . . . . 1·50 1·25
372 20c. Hands holding drugs and damaged internal organs . . . . 1·50 1·25
373 40c. Healthy boy and broken drug capsule . . . . 2·25 1·40
374 40c. Drugs and healthy internal organs . . . . . . 2·25 1·40
Nos. 371/2 and 373/4 were printed together, se-tenant, forming composite designs.

149 Spillway and Power Station

1987. Opening of Sultan Mahmud Hydro-electric Scheme, Kenyir, Trengganu. Multicoloured.
375 20c. Type **149** 50 10
376 $1 Dam, spillway and reservoir . . . . 2·50 2·00

150 Crossed Maces and Parliament Building, Kuala Lumpur

1987. 33rd Commonwealth Parliamentary Conf. Multicoloured.
377 20c. Type **150** 25 10
378 $1 Parliament building and crossed mace emblem . . . 1·25 1·25

151 Dish Aerial, Satellite and Globe

1987. Asia/Pacific Transport and Communications Decade. Multicoloured.
379 15c. Type **151** 50 10
380 20c. Diesel train and car . . 1·50 75
381 40c. Container ships and lorry . . . . 1·75 1·40
382 $1 Malaysian Airlines Boeing 747, Kuala Lumpur Airport . . . . 3·50 6·00

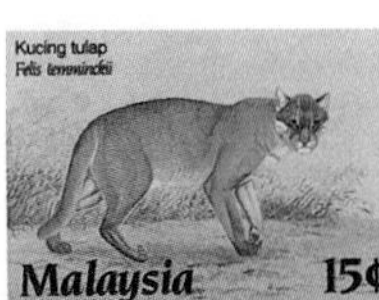

152 Temminck's Golden Cat

1987. Protected Animals of Malaysia (2nd series). Multicoloured.
383 15c. Type **152** . . . . 2·00 50
384 20c. Flatheaded cat . . . . . 2·00 50
385 40c. Marbled cat . . . . . . 3·25 1·75
386 $1 Clouded leopard . . . . 6·00 7·00

153 Flags of Member Nations and "20"

1987. 20th Anniv of Association of South East Asian Nations. Multicoloured.
387 20c. Type **153** 30 10
388 $1 Flags of member nations and globe . . . . 1·10 1·25

154 Mosque and Portico

1988. Opening of Sultan Salahuddin Abdul Aziz Shah Mosque. Multicoloured.
389 15c. Type **154** 20 10
390 20c. Dome, minarets and Sultan of Selangor 20 20
391 $1 Interior and dome (vert) 1·00 2·00

155 Aerial View

1988. Sultan Ismail Hydro-electric Power Station, Paka, Trengganu. Multicoloured.
392 20c. Type **155** 30 10
393 $1 Power-station and pylons 1·10 1·25

156 Black-naped Blue Monarch
157 Outline Map and Products of Sabah

1988. Protected Birds of Malaysia (2nd series). Multicoloured.
394 20c. Type **156** . . . . 1·75 2·25
395 20c. Scarlet-backed flowerpecker . . . . 1·75 2·25
396 50c. Yellow-backed sunbird 2·50 3·00
397 50c. Black and red broadbill 2·50 3·00

1988. 25th Anniv of Sabah and Sarawak as States of Malaysia. Multicoloured.
398 20c. Type **157** 65 80
399 20c. Outline map and products of Sarawak . . . 65 80
400 $1 Flags of Malaysia, Sabah and Sarawak (30 × 40 mm) 1·25 2·50

158 "Glossodoris atromarginata"
159 Sultan's Palace, Malacca

1988. Marine Life (1st series). Multicoloured.
401 20c. Type **158** . . . . 85 1·10
402 20c. Ocellate nudibranch . . 85 1·10
403 20c. "Chromodoris annae" 85 1·10
404 20c. "Flabellina macassarana" . . . . . . 85 1·10
405 20c. Ruppell's nudibranch . . 85 1·10
MS406 100 × 75 mm. $1 Blue-ringed angelfish (50 × 40 mm) . . . . 3·00 1·75
Nos. 401/5 were printed together, se-tenant, forming a composite background design.
See also Nos. 410/13, 450/3, 492/6 and 559/62.

1989. Declaration of Malacca as Historic City. Multicoloured.
407 20c. Type **159** 25 30
408 20c. Independence Memorial Building 25 30
409 $1 Porta De Santiago Fortress (vert) . . . . . . 1·25 2·00

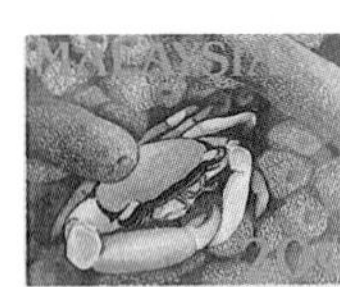

160 "Tetralia nigrolineata"
161 Map of Malaysia and Scout Badge

1989. Marine Life (2nd series). Crustaceans. Mult.
410 20c. Type **160** 45 90
411 20c. "Neopetrolisthes maculatus" (crab) 45 90
412 40c. "Periclimenes holthuisi" (shrimp) . . . . 55 1·10
413 40c. "Synalpheus neomeris" (shrimp) . . . . 55 1·10

1989. 7th National Scout Jamboree. Multicoloured.
414 10c. Type **161** 30 10
415 20c. Saluting national flag . . 60 25
416 80c. Scouts around camp fire (horiz) . . . . 1·40 2·75

162 Cycling
163 Sultan Azlan Shah

1989. 15th South East Asian Games, Kuala Lumpur. Multicoloured.
417 10c. Type **162** 75 40
418 20c. Athletics 40 20
419 50c. Swimming (vert) 75 85
420 $1 Torch bearer (vert) . . . 1·25 3·00

1989. Installation of Sultan Azlan Shah as Yang di-Pertuan Agong.
421 **163** 20c. multicoloured 20 15
422 40c. multicoloured 35 35
423 $1 multicoloured . . . . 1·00 2·50

164 Putra World Trade Centre and Pan-Pacific Hotel

1989. Commonwealth Heads of Government Meeting, Kuala Lumpur. Multicoloured.
424 20c. Type **164** 20 10
425 50c. Traditional dancers (vert) 65 75
426 $1 National flag and map showing Commonwealth countries . . . . 1·25 2·75

165 Clock Tower, Kuala Lumpur City Hall and Big Ben
166 Sloth and Map of Park

1989. Inaugural Malaysia Airlines "747" Non-stop Flight to London. Each showing Malaysia Airlines Boeing "747-400". Multicoloured.
427 20c. Type **165** . . . . 1·50 1·75
428 20c. Parliament Buildings, Kuala Lumpur, and Palace of Westminster . . . . . . 1·50 1·75
429 $1 World map showing route 4·00 4·50

1989. 50th Anniv of National Park. Multicoloured.
430 20c. Type **166** 75 30
431 $1 Pair of crested argus . . . 2·50 3·50

167 Outline Map of South-east Asia and Logo
168 "Dillenia suffruticosa"

1990. "Visit Malaysia Year". Multicoloured.
432 20c. Type **167** 65 15
433 50c. Traditional drums . . . 85 1·00
434 $1 Scuba diving, windsurfing and yachting . . . . . . 1·75 2·75

1990. Wildflowers (1st series). Multicoloured.
435 15c. Type **168** 25 15
436 20c. "Mimosa pudica" . . . 30 20
437 50c. "Ipmoea carnea" 60 80
438 $1 "Nymphaea pubescens" 80 2·50
See also Nos. 505/8.

169 Monument and Rainbow

171 Alor Setar

170 Seri Negara Building

1990. Kuala Lumpur, Garden City of Lights. Multicoloured.
439 20c. Type **169** 20 20
440 40c. Mosque and skyscrapers at night (horiz) 50 55
441 $1 Kuala Lumpur skyline (horiz) . . . . 1·25 2·75

1990. 1st Summit Meeting of South–South Consultation and Co-operation Group, Kuala Lumpur. Multicoloured.
442 20c. Type **170** 40 15
443 80c. Summit logo . . . . . 1·40 2·25

1990. 250th Anniv of Alor Setar. Multicoloured.
444 20c. Type **171** 40 20
445 40c. Musicians and monument (vert) 50 40
446 $1 Zahir Mosque (vert) . . . 1·25 3·00

172 Sign Language Letters

1990. International Literacy Year. Multicoloured.
447 20c. Type **172** 40 10
448 40c. People reading 60 40
449 $1 Symbolic person reading (vert) . . . . 1·50 3·00

173 Leatherback Turtle

1990. Marine Life (3rd series). Sea Turtles. Mult.
450 15c. Type **173** 60 10
451 20c. Common green turtle . . 60 15
452 40c. Olive Ridley turtle . . . 1·25 80
453 $1 Hawksbill turtle . . . . . 2·25 3·50

174 Safety Helmet, Dividers and Industrial Skyline

175 "Eustenogaster calyptodoma"

1991. 25th Anniv of MARA (Council of the Indigenous People). Multicoloured.
454 20c. Type **174** 15 10
455 40c. Documents and graph 30 35
456 $1 25th Anniversary logo . . 75 2·25

1991. Insects. Wasps. Multicoloured.
457 15c. Type **175** 25 30
458 20c. "Vespa affinis indonensis" 25 20
459 50c. "Sceliphorn javanum" 60 70
460 $1 "Ampulex compressa" . . 1·00 2·25
MS461 130 × 85 mm. Nos. 457/60 2·50 4·00

176 Tunku Abdul Rahman Putra and Independence Rally

1991. Former Prime Ministers of Malaysia. Multicoloured.
462 $1 Type **176** . . . . 70 1·25
463 $1 Tun Abdul Razak Hussein and jungle village . . . . 70 1·25
464 $1 Tun Hussein Onn and standard-bearers . . . . . 70 1·25

177 Maziah Palace, Trengganu

1991. Historic Buildings of Malaysia (2nd series). Multicoloured.
465 15c. Type **177** 20 10
466 20c. Grand Palace, Johore . . 20 15
467 40c. Town Palace, Kuala Langat, Selangor 45 50
468 $1 Jahar Palace, Kelantan . . 90 2·25

178 Museum Building in 1891, Brass Lamp and Fabric

179 Rural Postman on Cycle

1991. Centenary of Sarawak Museum. Mult.
469 30c. Type **178** 20 15
470 $1 Museum building in 1991, vase and fabric . . . . . 80 1·75

1992. Inauguration of Post Office Corporation. Multicoloured.
471 30c. Type **179** 60 85
472 30c. Urban postman on motorcycle 60 85
473 30c. Inner city post van . . . 60 85
474 30c. Industrial post van . . . 60 85
475 30c. Malaysian Airlines Boeing 747 and globe . . . 60 85

180 Hill Forest and Jelutong Tree

1992. Tropical Forests. Multicoloured.
476 20c. Type **180** 25 10
477 50c. Mangrove swamp and Bakau Minyak tree 55 50
478 $1 Lowland forest and Chengal tree . . . . 95 2·00

181 Tuanku Ja'afar and Coat of Arms

182 Badminton Players

1992. 25th Anniv of Installation of Tuanku Ja'afar as Yang di-Pertuan Besar of Negri Sembilan. Multicoloured.
479 30c. Type **181** 20 20
480 $1 Palace, Negri Sembilan . . 80 2·00

1992. Malaysian Victory in Thomas Cup Badminton Championship. Multicoloured.
481 $1 Type **182** . . . . 70 1·00
482 $1 Thomas Cup and Malaysian flag . . . . . . 70 1·00
MS483 105 × 80 mm. $2 Winning team (76 × 28 mm) . . . . . . 1·75 2·50

183 Women in National Costumes

1992. 25th Anniv of A.S.E.A.N. (Association of South East Asian Nations). Multicoloured.
484 30c. Type **183** 40 30
485 50c. Regional flowers 65 75
486 $1 Traditional architecture 1·25 2·75

184 Straits Settlements 1867 1½c. and Malaysian Federation 1957 10c. Stamps

1992. 125th Anniv of Postage Stamps and "Kuala Lumpur '92" Int Stamp Exn. Multicoloured.
487 30c. Type **184** 35 70
488 30c. Straits Settlements 1867 2c. and Malaysia 1963 Federation Inauguration 12c. 35 70
489 50c. Straits Settlements 1868 4c. and Malaysia 1990 Kuala Lumpur 40c. . . . 65 95
490 50c. Straits Settlements 1867 12c. and Malaysia "Kuala Lumpur '92" $2 . . . . . 65 95
MS491 120 × 92 mm. $2 "Kuala Lumpur '92" logo on Malaysian flag . . . . 1·75 2·75

185 "Acropora"

186 Girls smiling

1992. Marine Life (4th series). Corals. Mult.
492 30c. Type **185** 70 90
493 30c. "Dendronephthya" . . . 70 90
494 30c. "Dendrophyllia" 70 90
495 30c. "Sinularia" 70 90
496 30c. "Melithaea" 70 90
MS497 100 × 70 mm. $2 "Subergorgia" (38 × 28 mm) . . 2·25 3·50

1993. 16th Asian–Pacific Dental Congress. Mult.
498 30c. Type **186** 50 75
499 30c. Girls smiling with koala bear 50 75
500 50c. Dentists with Japanese, Malaysian and South Korean flags . . . . . . 80 1·00
501 $1 Dentists with New Zealand, Thai, Chinese and Indonesian flags . . . . . 1·00 1·75

187 View of Golf Course

188 "Alpinia rafflesiana"

1993. Cent of Royal Selangor Golf Club. Mult.
502 30c. Type **187** 60 20
503 50c. Old and new club houses 90 80
504 $1 Bunker on course (horiz) 1·75 3·25

1993. Wildflowers (2nd series). Gingers. Mult.
505 20c. Type **188** 40 10
506 30c. "Achasma megalocheilos" 50 20
507 50c. "Zingiber spectabile" . . 90 80
508 $1 "Costus speciosus" . . . 1·75 2·75

189 Forest under Magnifying Glass

190 White-throated Kingfisher

1993. 14th Commonwealth Forestry Conference, Kuala Lumpur. Multicoloured.
509 30c. Type **189** 40 20
510 50c. Hand holding forest . . 65 70
511 $1 Forest in glass dome (vert) 1·40 2·50

1993. Kingfishers. Multicoloured.
512 30c. Type **190** . . . . 1·00 1·40
513 30c. Pair of blue-eared kingfishers . . . . 1·00 1·40
514 50c. Chestnut-collared kingfisher . . . . 1·10 1·60
515 50c. Pair of three-toed kingfishers . . . . 1·10 1·60

191 SME MD3-160m Light Aircraft

1993. Langkawi International Maritime and Aerospace Exhibition '93. Multicoloured.
516 30c. Type **191** 35 20
517 50c. Eagle X-TS light aircraft 65 75
518 $1 "Kasturi" (frigate) . . . . 1·25 2·50
MS519 120 × 80 mm. $2 Map of Langkawi . . . . 1·60 2·50

192 Jeriau Waterfalls

1994. Visit Malaysia. Multicoloured.
520 20c. Type **192** 50 10
521 30c. Flowers 50 25
522 50c. Turtle and fishes 75 65
523 $1 Orang-utan and other wildlife . . . . 1·60 2·25

193 Planetarium and Planets

1994. National Planetarium, Kuala Lumpur. Mult.
524 30c. Type **193** 50 25
525 50c. Static displays 65 80
526 $1 Planetarium auditorium 1·50 2·50

194 "Spathoglottis aurea"

195 Decorative Bowl

1994. Orchids. Multicoloured.
527 20c. Type **194** 35 15
528 30c. "Paphiopedilum barbatum" 45 25
529 50c. "Bulbophyllum lobbii" 75 90
530 $1 "Aerides odorata" . . . . 1·25 2·50
MS531 120 × 82 mm. $2 "Grammato-phyllum speciosum" (horiz) . . . . 2·25 3·50
No. **MS**531 also commemorates the "Hong Kong '94" International Stamp Exhibition.

1994. World Islamic Civilisation Festival '94, Kuala Lumpur. Multicoloured.
532 20c. Type **195** 15 10
533 30c. Celestial globe 25 20
534 50c. Dinar coins 40 65
535 $1 Decorative tile . . . . . 75 1·75

196 Flock of Chickens and Vet examining Cat

197 Workers laying Electric Cable

1994. Centenary of Veterinary Services. Mult.
536 30c. Type **196** 50 25
537 50c. Vet in abattoir 70 55
538 $1 Herd of cows and veterinary equipment . . . 1·00 2·00

1994. Centenary of Electricity Supply. Mult.
539 30c. Type **197** 40 65
540 30c. Illuminated city 40 65
541 $1 City of the future . . . . 1·00 1·75

198 Expressway from the Air

199 Sultan Tuanku Ja'afar

1994. Opening of North–South Expressway. Mult.
542 30c. Type **198** 20 20
543 50c. Expressway junction . . 35 50
544 $1 Expressway bridge . . . . 80 1·75

1994. Installation of Sultan Tuanku Ja'afar as Yang di-Pertuan Agong.
545 **199** 30c. multicoloured 20 20
546 50c. multicoloured 40 50
547 $1 multicoloured . . . . 80 1·75

200 Map of Malaysia and Logo

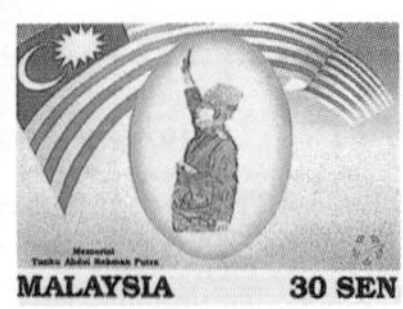

201 Tunku Abdul Rahman Putra and National Flag

1994. 16th Commonwealth Games, Kuala Lumpur (1998) (1st issue). Multicoloured.
548 $1 Type **200** . . . . 90 1·40
549 $1 Wira (games mascot) holding national flag . . . 90 1·40
See also Nos. 575/6, 627/30, 668/71, **MS**678, 693/708 and **MS**715/16.

1994. 5th Death Anniv of Tunku Abdul Rahman Putra (former Prime Minister). Multicoloured.
550 30c. Type **201** 25 20
551 $1 The Residency, Kuala Lumpur . . . . 75 1·50

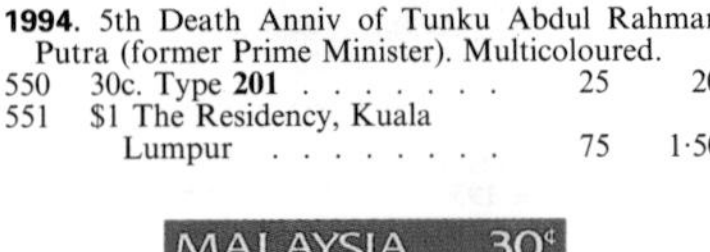

202 Library Building

1994. Opening of New National Library Building. Multicoloured.
552 30c. Type **202** 20 25
553 50c. Computer plan on screen 45 50
554 $1 Ancient Koran . . . . . 1·00 1·75

203 "Microporus xanthopus"

1995. Fungi. Mult.
555 20c. Type **203** 15 10
556 30c. "Cookeina tricholoma" 25 20
557 50c. "Phallus indusiatus" ("Dictyophora phalloidea") 45 55
558 $1 "Ramaria sp." . . . . . 90 2·00

204 Seafans

1995. Marine Life (5th series). Corals. Mult.
559 20c. Type **204** . . . . 85 1·10
560 20c. Feather stars . . . . . 85 1·10
561 30c. Cup coral . . . . 85 1·10
562 30c. Soft coral . . . . 85 1·10

205 Clouded Leopard on Branch

1995. Endangered Species. Clouded Leopard. Mult.
563 20c. Type **205** 45 25
564 30c. With cubs 50 30
565 50c. Crouched on branch . . 70 60
566 $1 Climbing tree . . . . . . 1·00 1·75

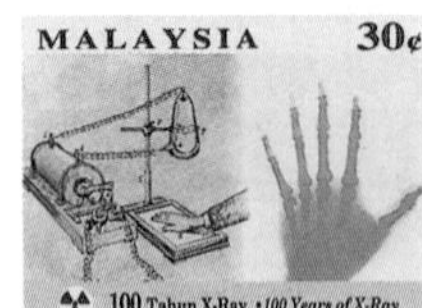

206 Early X-Ray Equipment and X-Ray of Hand

1995. Centenary of Discovery of X-Rays by Wilhelm Conrad Rontgen. Multicoloured.
567 30c. Type **206** 40 65
568 30c. Body scanner and brain scan 40 65
569 $1 Chest X-rays . . . . . . 1·00 1·60

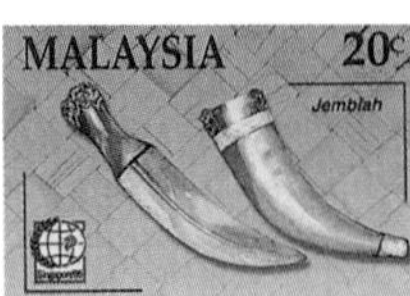

207 Jembiah (curved dagger)

1995. "Singapore '95" International Stamp Exhibition. Traditional Malay Weapons. Mult.
570 20c. Type **207** 15 10
571 30c. Keris panjang (sword) 25 20
572 50c. Kerambit (curved dagger) 40 50
573 $1 Keris sundang (sword) . . 80 1·75
MS574 100 × 70 mm. $2 Ladig terus (dagger) . . . . 2·25 2·75

208 Badminton, Cricket, Shooting, Tennis, Hurdling, Hockey and Weightlifting

1995. 16th Commonwealth Games, Kuala Lumpur (1998) (2nd issue). Multicoloured.
575 $1 Type **208** . . . . 1·75 2·00
576 $1 Cycling, bowls, boxing, basketball, rugby, gymnastics and swimming 1·75 2·00

209 Leatherback Turtle ("Dermochelys coriacea")

1995. Turtles. Multicoloured.
577 30c. Type **209** . . . . 1·25 1·25
578 30c. Green turtle ("Chelonia mydas") . . . . 1·25 1·25

210 Anniversary Emblem and Symbolic People around Globe

1995. 50th Anniv of United Nations. Multicoloured.
579 30c. Type **210** 15 20
580 $1 United Nations emblem 60 1·25

211 Boeing 747, Globe, Emblem and Malaysian Scenes

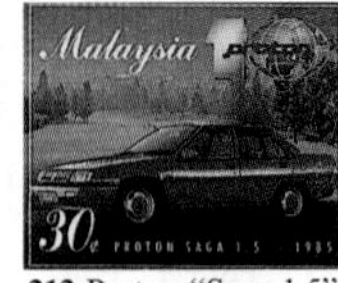

212 Proton "Saga 1.5" Saloon, 1985

1995. 50th Anniv of International Air Transport Association. Designs each showing Boeing 747 and Globe. Multicoloured.
581 30c. Type **211** 40 60
582 30c. Asian and Australasian scenes 40 60
583 50c. European and African scenes 60 80
584 50c. North and South American scenes 60 80

1995. 10th Anniv of Proton Cars. Multicoloured.
585 30c. Type **212** 50 75
586 30c. "Iswara 1.5" aeroback, 1992 . . . . 50 75
587 30c. "Iswara 1.5" saloon, 1992 . . . . 50 75
588 30c. "Wira 1.6" saloon, 1993 50 75
589 30c. "Wira 1.6" aeroback, 1993 . . . . 50 75
590 30c. Proton rally car, 1994 50 75
591 30c. "Satria 1.6" hatchback, 1994 . . . . 50 75
592 30c. "Perdana 2.0" saloon, 1995 . . . . 50 75
593 30c. "Wira 1.6" aeroback, 1995 . . . . 50 75
594 30c. "Wira 1.8" saloon, 1995 50 75

213 "Ariane 4" Launch Rocket

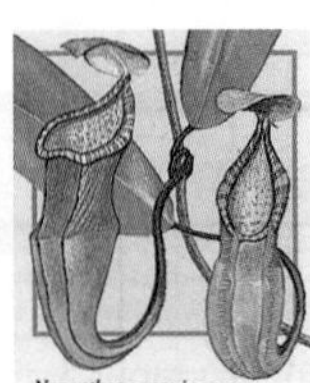

214 "Nepenthes sanguinea"

1996. Launch of MEASAT I (Malaysia East Asia Satellite). Multicoloured.
595 30c. Type **213** 25 20
596 50c. Satellite over Eastern Asia 40 45
597 $1 Satellite Earth station, Langkawi . . . . 90 1·75
MS598 100 × 70 mm. $5 Satellite orbiting Globe (hologram) (horiz) 4·25 4·75

1996. Pitcher Plants. Multicoloured.
599 30c. Type **214** 25 45
600 30c. "Nepenthes macfarlanei" 25 45
601 50c. "Nepenthes rajah" . . . 35 55
602 50c. "Nepenthes lowii" . . . 35 55

215 Brahminy Kite

1996. Birds of Prey. Multicoloured.
603 20c. Type **215** 20 15
604 30c. Crested serpent eagle . . 30 25
605 50c. White-bellied sea eagle 45 55
606 $1 Crested hawk eagle . . . 90 1·75
MS607 100 × 70 mm. $2 Blyth's Hawk Eagle (vert) . . . . . . 2·25 3·00
No. **MS**607 also includes the "CHINA '96" 9th Asian International Stamp Exhibition logo on the sheet margin.

216 Family, Globe and Burning Drugs

1996. International Day against Drug Abuse and Illicit Trafficking. Multicoloured.
608 30c. Type **216** 40 55
609 30c. Sporting activities . . . 40 55
610 $1 Family and rainbow . . . 75 1·25

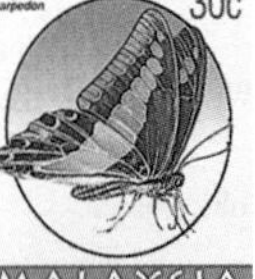

217 "Graphium sarpedon"

218 Kuala Lumpur Tower

1996. "ISTANBUL '96" International Stamp Exhibition. Butterflies. Multicoloured.
611 30c. Type **217** . . . . 1·25 1·25
612 30c. "Terinos terpander" . . 1·25 1·25
613 30c. "Melanocyma faunula" 1·25 1·25
614 30c. "Trogonoptera brookiana" . . . . 1·25 1·25
615 30c. "Delias hyparete" . . . 1·25 1·25

1996. Opening of Kuala Lumpur Telecommunications Tower. Multicoloured.
616 30c. Type **218** 20 20
617 50c. Diagram of top of tower 30 35
618 $1 Kuala Lumpur Tower at night . . . . 80 1·50
MS619 70 × 100 mm. $2 Top of Kuala Lumpur Tower (different) (vert) . . . . 1·25 2·00

219 C.A.P.A. Logo on Kite

1996. 14th Conference of the Confederation of Asian and Pacific Accountants. Multicoloured.
620 30c. Type **219** 25 20
621 $1 Globe and C.A.P.A. logo 75 1·10

1996. "TAIPEI '96" 10th Asian International Stamp Exhibition. As No. **MS**619, but with exhibition logo added to bottom right-hand corner of sheet.
MS622 70 × 100 mm. $2 Top of Kuala Lumpur Tower (vert) . . 1·25 1·75

220 Model of D.N.A. Molecule

1996. Opening of National Science Centre, Kuala Lumpur. Multicoloured.
623 30c. Type **220** 25 20
624 50c. Planetary model and Science Centre 40 40
625 $1 National Science Centre 90 1·25

221 Slow Loris

1996. Stamp Week. Wuildlife. Sheet 165 × 75 mm, containing T **221** and similar multicoloured designs.
MS626 20c. Type **221**; 30c. Prevost's squirrel; 50c. Atlas moth; $1 Rhinoceros hornbill (60 × 30 mm); $1 White-handed gibbon (30 × 60 mm); $2 Banded palm civet (60 × 30 mm) . . . . . . 2·75 3·50

222 Running

1996. 16th Commonwealth Games, Kuala Lumpur (1998) (3rd issue). Multicoloured.
627 30c. Type **222** 25 45
628 30c. Hurdling 25 45
629 50c. High jumping 30 55
630 50c. Javelin 30 55

223 Pygmy Blue Flycatcher

224 Transit Train leaving Station

1997. Highland Birds. Multicoloured.

631	20c. Type **223**	25	15
632	30c. Silver-eared mesia	30	20
633	50c. Black-sided flower-pecker	40	50
634	$1 Scarlet sunbird	70	1·25

1997. "HONG KONG '97" International Stamp Exhibition. As No. **MS**626, but with exhibition logo added to top sheet margin.

MS635 165 × 75 mm. 20c. Type **221**; 30c. Prevost's squirrel; 50c. Atlas moth; $1 Rhinoceros hornbill (60 × 30 mm); $1 White-handed gibbon (30 × 60 mm); $2 Banded palm civet (60 × 30 mm) . . . 4·00 4·75

1997. Opening of Kuala Lumpur Light Rail Transit System. Multicoloured.

636	30c. Type **224**	1·00	1·00
637	30c. Trains in central Kuala Lumpur	1·00	1·00

225 Bowler

1997. International Cricket Council Trophy, Kuala Lumpur. Multicoloured.

638	30c. Type **225**	30	15
639	50c. Batsman	45	40
640	$1 Wicket-keeper	80	1·25

226 Boeing 747-400 over World Map

1997. 50th Anniv of Aviation in Malaysia. Mult.

641	30c. Type **226**	65	15
642	50c. Boeing 747-400 over Kuala Lumpur	80	50
643	$1 Tail fins of four airliners	1·25	1·75

227 "Schima wallichii"

228 World Youth Football Championship Mascot

1997. Highland Flowers. Multicoloured.

644	30c. Type **227**	50	70
645	30c. "Aeschynanthus longicalyx"	50	70
646	30c. "Aeschynanthus speciosa"	50	70
647	30c. "Phyllagathis tuberculata"	50	70
648	30c. "Didymocarpus quinquevulnerus"	50	70

1997. 9th World Youth Football Championship, Malaysia. Multicoloured.

649	30c. Type **228**	15	10
650	50c. Football and players	30	35
651	$1 Map of Malaysia and football	65	1·40

229 Members of First Conference, 1897

1997. Centenary of Rulers' Conference. Mult.

652	30c. Type **229**	15	10
653	50c. State emblem	30	35
654	$1 Seal and press	65	1·40

230 A.S.E.A.N. Logo and Ribbons

1997. 30th Anniv of Association of South-east Asian Nations. Multicoloured.

655	30c. Type **230**	40	10
656	50c. "30" enclosing logo	60	40
657	$1 Chevrons and logo	1·10	1·50

231 "Tubastrea sp."

232 Women Athletes, Scientist and Politician

1997. International Year of the Coral Reefs. Multicoloured.

658	20c. Type **231**	15	10
659	30c. "Melithaea sp."	20	10
660	50c. "Aulostomus chinensis"	30	35
661	$1 "Symphillia sp."	45	1·25

MS662 70 × 100 mm. $2 Green Turtle (horiz) . . . 1·75 2·25

1997. 20th International Pan-Pacific and South-east Asia Women's Association Conference, Kuala Lumpur. Multicoloured.

663	30c. Type **232**	25	40
664	30c. Family and house	25	40

233 1867 12c. on 4 anna with Malacca Postmark

1997. "Malpex '97" Stamp Exhibition, Kuala Lumpur. 50th Anniv of Organised Philately. Sheet 120 × 70 mm, containing T **233** and similar diamond-shaped designs. Multicoloured.

MS665 20c. Type **233**; 30c. 1997 Highland Birds set; 50c. 1996 Wildlife miniature sheet seen through magnifying glass; $1 1867 cover to Amoy . . . 1·50 2·00

234 Group of 15 Emblem

1997. 7th Summit Conference of the Group of 15, Kuala Lumpur. Multicoloured.

666	30c. Type **234**	10	10
667	$1 Flags of member countries	70	90

235 Hockey

1997. 16th Commonwealth Games, Kuala Lumpur (1998) (4th issue). Multicoloured.

668	30c. Type **235**	40	45
669	30c. Netball	40	45
670	50c. Cricket	50	65
671	50c. Rugby	50	65

236 False Gharial

1997. Stamp Week '97. Endangered Wildlife. Sheet 165 × 75 mm, containing T **236** and similar multicoloured designs.

MS672 20c. Type **236**; 30c. Western tarsier (vert); 50c. Indian sambar (vert); $2 Crested wood partridge; $2 Malayan bony-tongue (fish) . . . 2·25 2·75

1997. "INDEPEX '97" International Stamp Exhibition, New Delhi. As No. **MS**665, but with exhibition logo added to the sheet margin, in gold, at bottom right.

MS673 120 × 70 mm. 20c. Type **233**; 30c. 1997 Highlands Bird set; 50c. 1996 Wildlife miniature sheet seen through magnifying glass; $1 1867 cover to Amoy . . . 1·00 1·50

237 Kundang

1998. Fruit. Multicoloured.

674	20c. Type **237**	10	10
675	30c. Sentul	15	10
676	50c. Pulasan	20	25
677	$1 Asam gelugur	65	1·40

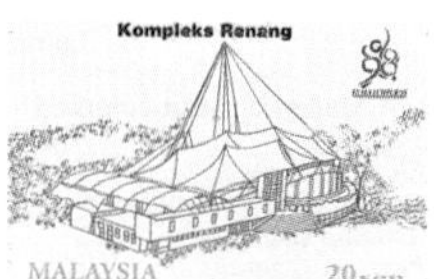

238 Swimming Complex

1998. 16th Commonwealth Games, Kuala Lumpur (5th issue). Venues. Sheet 120 × 80 mm, containing T **238** and similar horiz designs. Multicoloured.

MS678 20c. Type **238**; 30c. Hockey Stadium; 50c. Indoor Stadium; $1 Main Stadium . . . 1·00 1·50

239 Mas (coin) from Trengganu, 1793–1808

1998. Gold coins. Multicoloured.

679	20c. Type **239**	15	10
680	30c. Kupang from Kedah, 1661–1687	20	10
681	50c. Kupang from Johore, 1597–1615	35	35
682	$1 Kupang from Kelantan, 1400–1780	45	1·25

240 Red Crescent Ambulance Boat and Emblem

1998. 50th Anniv of Malaysian Red Crescent Society. Multicoloured.

683	30c. Type **240**	15	10
684	$1 Ambulance and casualty	60	1·10

241 Transit Train and Boeing 747-400 at Airport

1998. Opening of Kuala Lumpur International Airport. Designs showing control tower. Mult.

685	30c. Type **241**	30	10
686	50c. Airport Terminals	45	30
687	$1 Airliner in flight	1·00	1·50

MS688 119 × 70 mm. $2 Globe and control tower (22 × 32 mm) . . . 1·25 1·75

242 "Solanum torvum"

243 Weightlifting

1998. Medicinal Plants. Multicoloured.

689	20c. Type **242**	10	10
690	30c. "Tinospora crispa"	20	10
691	50c. "Jatropha podagrica"	30	30
692	$1 "Hibiscus rosa-sinensis"	50	1·00

1998. 16th Commonwealth Games, Kuala Lumpur, Malaysia (5th issue). Sports. Multicoloured.

693	20c. Type **243**	15	25
694	20c. Badminton	15	25
695	20c. Netball	15	25
696	20c. Shooting	15	25
697	30c. Men's hockey	25	35
698	30c. Women's hockey	25	35
699	30c. Cycling	25	35
700	30c. Bowls	25	35
701	50c. Gymnastics	25	40
702	50c. Cricket	25	40
703	50c. Rugby	25	40
704	50c. Running	25	40
705	$1 Swimming	30	50
706	$1 Squash	30	50
707	$1 Boxing	30	50
708	$1 Ten-pin bowling	30	50

244 L.R.T. "Putra" Type Train

1998. Modern Kuala Lumpur Rail Transport. Multicoloured.

709b	30c. Type **244**	50	15
710b	50c. L.R.T. "Star" type train	35	25
711	$1 K.T.M. commuter train	40	90

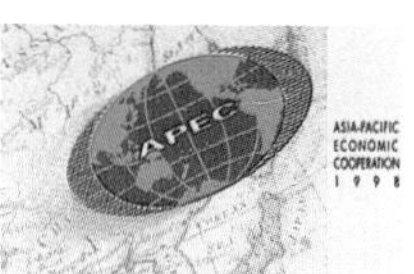

245 Globe and A.P.E.C. Logo

1998. Asia–Pacific Econmic Co-operation Conf. Multicoloured.

712b	30c. Type **245**	30	10
713	$1 Business meeting and computer office	40	90

246 "Xylotrupes gideon"

247 Nural Hudda (Women's Air Rifle Shooting)

1998. Stamp Week '98. Malaysian Insects. Sheet 165 × 75 mm, containing T **246** and similar multicoloured designs.

MS714 20c. Type **246**; 30c. "Pomponia imperatoria"; 50c. "Phyllium pulchrifolium"; $2 "Hymenopus coronatus" (43 × 27 mm); $2 "Macrolyristes corporalis" (43 × 27 mm) . . . 2·00 2·75

1998. 16th Commonwealth Games, Kuala Lumpur (7th issue). Malaysian Gold Medal Winners. Two miniature sheets, each 160 × 125 mm, containing multicoloured designs as T **247**.

MS715 $2 Malaysian badminton team celebrating (128 × 80 mm) . . . 2·50 2·75

MS716 30c. Type **247**; 30c. Sapok Biki (48kg Boxing); 30c. G. Saravanan (50km Walk); 30c. Muhamad Hidayat Hamidon (69kg Weightlifting); 50c. Kenny Ang and Ben Heng (Tenpin Bowling Men's Doubles); 50c. Kenny Ang (Tenpin Bowling Men's Singles); 50c. Choong Tan Fook and Lee Wan Wah (Badminton Men's Doubles); 50c. Wong Choon Hann (Badminton Men's Singles); $1 Women's Rhythmic Gymnastics team (63 × 26 mm) . . . 6·00 7·50

248 Profile of Elderly Couple, World Map and Emblem

1999. International Year of the Older Person. Multicoloured.
717 $1 Type **248** 40 80
718 $1 Four silhouettes of elderly people, world map and emblem 40 80

249 "Syzygium malaccense" **250** Kucing Malaysia Cat

1999. Rare Fruits of Malaysia. Multicoloured.
719 20c. Type **249** 15 15
720 30c. "Garcinia prainiana" . . 20 15
721 50c. "Mangifera caesia" 25 25
722 $1 "Salacca glabrescens" . . 50 90

1999. Malaysian Cats. Multicoloured.
727 30c. Type **250** 20 15
728 50c. Siamese 30 25
729 $1 Abyssinian . . . . 60 1·00
MS730 Two sheets, each 81 × 90 mm. (a) $1 British shorthair; $1 Scottish fold. (B) $1 Birman; $1 Persian Set of 2 sheets 1·50 2·00

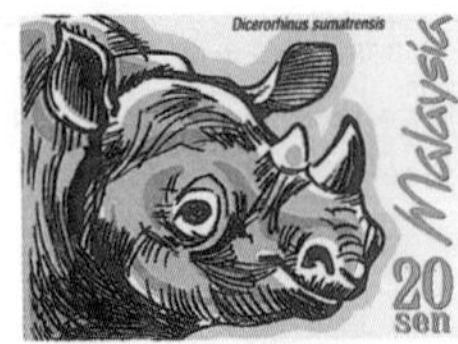

251 Sumatran Rhinoceros

1999. Protected Mammals of Malaysia (1st series). Multicoloured.
731 20c. Type **251** 15 15
732 30c. Panther 20 15
733 50c. Sun bear 25 25
734 $1 Indian elephant 50 75
739 $2 Orang-utan . . . . 1·00 1·25
MS740 119 × 80 mm. $2 No. 739 1·00 1·60
See also Nos. 923/31.

252 Hearts and AIDS Ribbons

1999. 5th International Conference on AIDS in Asia and the Pacific. Each red, blue and black.
741 30c. Type **252** 20 15
742 50c. Fragmenting and stylized AIDS ribbons 35 35
743 $1 Two AIDS ribbons . . . 55 90

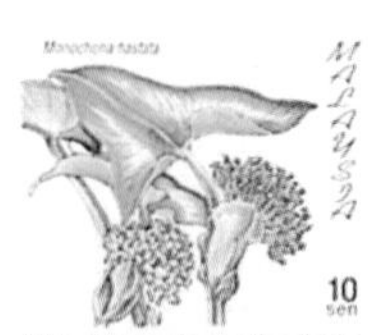

253 P. Ramlee in Traditional Dress **254** *Monochoria hastoria* (water plant)

1999. 70th Birth Anniv of P. Ramlee (actor and film director) Commemoration. (a) Multicoloured.
744 20c. Type **253** 30 15
745 30c. Receiving an award . . 35 15
746 50c. Playing part of soldier in film 45 30
747 $1 Using film camera . . . . 80 1·00
MS748a Two sheets, each 100 × 70 mm. (a) $1 Wearing check shirt. (b) $1 In traditional dress Set of 2 sheets . . . . . 10·00 10·00

(b) Each brown, light brown and black.
749 30c. In traditional dress . . . 40 45
750 30c. With hands raised . . . 40 45
751 30c. Singing into microphone 40 45
752 30c. Wearing army uniform 40 45

1999. Freshwater Fishes of Malaysia. Mult.
753 10c. Type **254** 20 30
754 10c. *Trichopsis vittatus* . . . 20 30
755 15c. *Limnocharis flava* (water plant) 25 35
756 15c. *Betta imbellis* 25 35
757 25c. *Nymphaea pubescens* (water plant) 30 40
758 25c. *Trichogaster trichopterus* 30 40
759 50c. *Eichhornia crassipes* (water plant) 40 50
760 50c. *Sphaerichthys osphromenoides* 40 50
761 50c. *Ipomea aquatica* (water plant) 40 50
762 50c. *Helostoma temmincki* . . 40 50
No. 760 is inscribed "Sphaerichthys osphronemodies" in error.

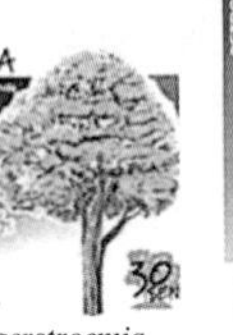

255 *Lagerstroemia floribunda* (tree) **256** Petronas Twin Towers, Kuala Lumpur

1999. Trees of Malaysia. Multicoloured.
763 30c. Type **255** 35 40
764 30c. *Elateriospermum tapos* 35 40
765 30c. *Dryobalanops aromatica* 35 40
766 30c. *Alstonia angustiloba* . . 35 40
767 30c. *Fagraea fragrans* 35 40

1999. Completion of Petronas Twin Towers Building, Kuala Lumpur. Multicoloured (except 50c.).
768 30c. Type **256** 25 15
769 50c. Construction sketches (blue, violet and black) . . 35 30
770 $1 Twin Towers at night . . 65 85
MS771 100 × 75 mm. $5 Hologram of Twin Towers (30 × 50 mm) 3·00 3·25

257 Peace Hotel and Rickshaw

1999. 125th Anniv of Taiping, Perak. Mult.
772 20c. Type **257** 15 15
773 30c. Town Hall and 1930s car 15 15
774 50c. Railway Station 30 25
775 $1 Airport 50 70
MS776 120 × 69 mm. $2 Perak Museum and horse-drawn carriage 3·25 3·50

258 Power Station at Night

1999. 50th Anniv of Tenaga Nasional Berhad (electricity generating company). Multicoloured.
777 30c. Type **258** 20 15
778 50c. Control room and pylon 30 25
779 $1 Kuala Lumpur skyline at night 60 80
MS780 Two sheets, each 69 × 99 mm. (a) $1 Electric cart. (b) $1 Pylon Set of 2 sheets . . 1·00 1·25

259 New National Theatre and Traditional Characters

1999. Opening of New National Theatre, Kuala Lumpur. Multicoloured.
781 30c. Type **259** 20 15
782 50c. New National Theatre and horseman 30 25
783 $1 New National Theatre and traditional musician . . . 60 80

260 New Yang di-Pertuan Agong and Malaysian Flag

1999. Installation of Sultan Salahuddin Abdul Aziz Shah of Selangor as Yang di-Pertuan Agong. (a) Horiz designs as T **260**. Multicoloured.
784 30c. Type **260** 20 15
785 50c. Yang di-Pertuan Agong and Palace 30 25
786 $1 Yang di-Pertuan Agong and Parliament Buildings 60 80

(b) Vert designs, 24 × 29 mm, showing portrait only.
787 (30c.) multicoloured (purple frame) 35 35
788 (30c.) multicoloured (yellow frame) 35 35
789 (30c.) multicoloured (blue frame) 35 35
Nos. 787/9 are inscribed "BAYARAN POS TEMPATAN HINGGA 20GM" and were valid on local mail weighing no more than 20 gm.

261 Motorway Junction outside Kuala Lumpur

1999. 21st World Road Congress, Kuala Lumpur. Mult.
790 30c. Type **261** 20 15
791 50c. Damansara Puchong Bridge at night 30 25
792 $1 Aerial view of motorway junction, Selatan 60 80

262 Driver's Helmet and Canopy Tower, Formula 1 Circuit, Sepang

1999. Malaysian Grand Prix, Sepang. Mult.
(a) Designs including driver's helmet.
793 20c. Type **262** 20 15
794 30c. Central Grandstand . . 20 15
795 50c. Formula 1 racing car . . 30 25
796 $1 Formula 1 racing car from Red Bull team 60 80

(b) Scenes from Sepang Formula 1 Circuit.
797 20c. Canopy Tower and Central Grandstand . . . 25 15
798 30c. Pit building 30 15
799 50c. Wheel-change in pits . . 40 30
800 $1 Race in progress 75 80

263 Sultan Haji Ahmad Shah and Flowers

1999. 25th Anniv of Installation of Sultan of Pahang. Multicoloured.
801 30c. Type **263** 25 30
802 30c. Butterfly and motorway 25 30
803 30c. Diver and beach 25 30
804 30c. Power station 25 30
805 30c. Mosque 25 30

264 World Cup

1999. World Cup Golf Championship, Mines Resort City. Multicoloured.
806 20c. Type **264** 20 10
807 30c. Emblem on golf ball . . 20 10
808 50c. Fairway 30 25
809 $1 First hole and club house 60 80

265 *Strelitzia augusta* **267** Fern, Pitcher Plant and Great Indian Hornbill

266 Letters and Computer Screen

1999. Stamp Week '99. Heliconias. Multicoloured.
814 30c. Type **265** 25 30
815 30c. *Heliconia rostrata* . . . 25 30
816 30c. *Heliconia psittacorum* (yellow) 25 30
817 30c. *Heliconia stricta* 25 30
818 30c. *Musa violascens* 25 30
819 30c. *Strelitzia reginae* 25 30
820 30c. *Heliconia colganta* . . . 25 30
821 30c. *Heliconia psittacorum* (white and pink) 25 30
822 30c. *Heliconia latispatha* . . . 25 30
823 30c. *Phaeomeria speciosa* . . 25 30
MS824 198 × 136 mm. Nos. 814/23 2·00 2·50

1999. 125th Anniv of Universal Postal Union. Mult.
825 20c. Type **266** 20 10
826 30c. Globe and Malaysian stamps 20 10
827 50c. World map and mail plane 30 25
828 $1 POS Malaysia emblem . . 60 80

1999. New Millennium (1st issue). Land and History. Multicoloured (except No. **MS**839).
829 30c. Type **267** 20 25
830 30c. Ceramic pots and Mt. Kinabalu 20 25
831 30c. Frog and tualang (tree) 20 25
832 30c. Rolling rubber and palm trees 20 25
833 30c. Angelfish and sailing barge 20 25
834 30c. Mousedeer and traditional Malay building 20 25
835 30c. Ruler on elephant and Straits of Malacca 20 25
836 30c. Malay kris (sword) and junks 20 25
837 30c. Clock Tower, Kuala Lumpur, and A Famosa ruins 20 25
838 30c. Sailing boat and palm trees 20 25
MS839 120 × 80 mm. $1 Traditional Malay sailing ship (horiz) (black and red) . . . . 1·00 1·10

2000. New Millennium (2nd issue). People and Achievements. As T **267**. Multicoloured.
840 30c. Iban playing sape and traditional costumes from East Malaysia 20 25
841 30c. Hurricane lamp, shell and couple from fishing village 20 25
842 30c. Doctor with patient and toddler with mother . . . 20 25
843 30c. Badminton player and young Malaysians 20 25
844 30c. Man with kite and traditional dancers 20 25
845 30c. Motor cycle, car and motorway 20 25
846 30c. Butterfly, Sepang motor racing circuit and airport 20 25
847 30c. High speed train and Kuala Lumpur skyline . . 20 25
848 30c. Computer operator and mosque 20 25
849 30c. Lorry and container port 20 25
MS850 120 × 80 mm. $1 Modern airliner (horiz) . . . . 1·00 1·10

268 Pottery Vase (New Stone Age)

2000. Chinese New Year ("Year of the Dragon"). Artefacts and Fish. Multicoloured.
851 30c. Type **268** 20 25
852 30c. Dragon eaves tile (Western Han Dynasty) . . 20 25
853 30c. Bronze knocker base (Tang Dynasty) 20 25
854 30c. Jade sword pommel (Western Han Dynasty) . . 20 25
855 30c. Dragon statue (Tang Dynasty) 20 25
856 30c. Arawana *(Osteoglossum bicirrhosum)* 20 25
857 30c. Spotted barramundi *(Scleropages leichardti)* . . 20 25
858 30c. Asian bonytongue (red) (Scleropages formosus) . . 20 25
859 30c. Black arawana *(Osteoglossum ferrerirai)* 20 25
860 30c. Asian bonytongue (gold) *(Scleropages formosus)* . . 20 25
MS861 Two sheets, each 120 × 65 mm. (a) $1 Dragon dance (square). (b) $1 Dragon boat (square) Set of 2 sheets . . . . 1·25 1·40

269 Table Tennis Bats and Globe

2000. World Table Tennis Championships, Bukit Jalil. Multicoloured.
862 30c. Type **269** 15 10
863 50c. Mascot and logo 30 25
864 $1 Table tennis bats and ball 60 80
MS865 100 × 70 mm. $1 Mascot and table tennis table; $1 Bats and table tennis table . . . . . . 1·00 1·25

270 Malaysian Climbers on Mt. Everest

2000. New Millennium (3rd issue). Malaysian Triumphs. Two sheets, each 120 × 80 mm, containing T **270** and similar vert designs. Multicoloured.
MS866 (a) 50c. Type **270**; 50c. Hikers; 50c. Arctic expedition and Proton car. (B) 50c. Solo yachtsman Set of 2 sheets . . . 1·50 1·75

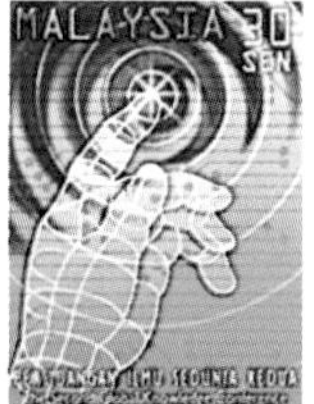

271 Outline Hand on Button

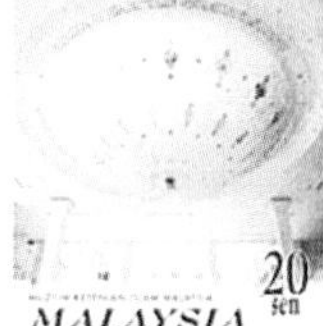

272 Internal Inverted Dome

2000. 2nd Global Knowledge Conference, Kuala Lumpur. Multicoloured.
867 30c. Type **271** 20 20
868 30c. Outline globe 20 20
869 50c. Woman's silhouette . . 30 35
870 50c. Man's silhouette 30 35

2000. Islamic Arts Museum, Kuala Lumpur. Mult.
871 20c. Type **272** 20 15
872 30c. Main dome of Museum 20 15
873 50c. Ottoman panel 30 30
874 $1 Ornate Mihrab 60 75

273 Buatan Barat Prahu

274 Unit Trust Emblem and Women with Flags

2000. Traditional Malaysian Prahus (canoes). Mult.
875 30c. Type **273** 20 25
876 30c. Payang prahu (red and blue hull) 20 25
877 30c. Payang prahu (red, white and green hull) 20 25
878 30c. Burung prahu 20 25

2000. Unit Trust Week. Multicoloured.
879 30c. Type **274** 20 10
880 50c. City skyline and Malaysians in traditional costume 30 25
881 $1 Map of South East Asia and Malaysians in traditional costume 65 75

275 Badminton Player and Cup Logo

2000. Thomas Cup Badminton Championships, Bukit Jalil. Multicoloured.
882 30c. Type **275** 20 25
883 30c. Thomas Cup and flags 20 25
884 30c. Championship logo and mascot 20 25
885 30c. Uber Cup and flags . . 20 25
886 30c. Badminton player and mascot 20 25
MS887 120 × 80 mm. $1 Thomas Cup (vert) . . . . 80 1·00

276 Children playing Ting Ting

2000. Children's Traditional Games (1st series). Multicoloured.
888 30c. Type **276** 60 60
889 30c. Tarik Upih 60 60
890 30c. Kite flying 60 60
891 30c. Marbles 60 60
892 30c. Bicycle rim racing . . . 60 60

277 Aspects of Computer Technology

2000. 27th Islamic Foreign Ministers' Conference, Kuala Lumpur. Multicoloured.
898 30c. Type **277** 20 25
899 30c. Traditonal Islamic scrollwork 20 25
900 30c. Conference logo 20 25
901 30c. Early coin 20 25
902 30c. Pens and satellite photograph 20 25

278 Malaysian Family on Map

2000. Population and Housing Census. Mult.
903 30c. Type **278** 20 25
904 30c. Symbolic house 20 25
905 30c. People on pie-chart . . . 20 25
906 30c. Diplomas and workers 20 25
907 30c. Male and female symbols 20 25

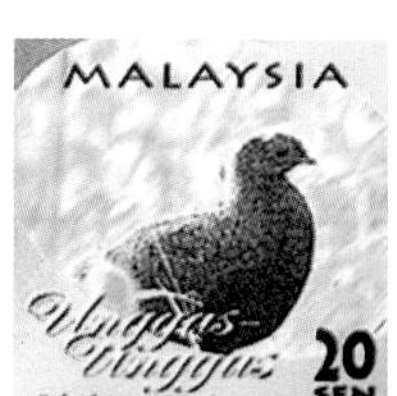

279 Rothchild's Peacock-pheasant

2000. Pheasants and Partridges. Multicoloured.
908 20c. Type **279** 20 10
909 30c. Crested argus (female) 20 10
910 50c. Great argus pheasant . . 35 30
911 $1 Crestless fireback pheasant 60 75
MS912 100 × 40 mm. $2 Crested argus (male) (31 × 26mm) . . . 1·00 1·25

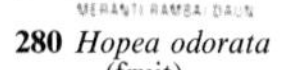

280 *Hopea odorata* (fruit)

282 Otter Civet

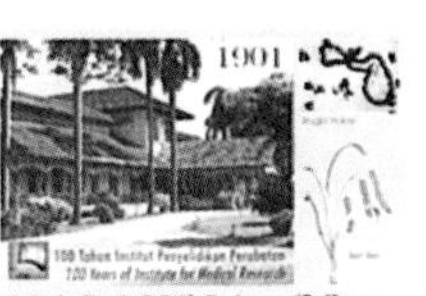

MALAYSIA 30sen

281 Institute in 1901, *Brugia malayi* and Beri-Beri

2000. International Union of Forestry Research Organisations Conference, Kuala Lumpur. Mult.
913 30c. Type **280** 50 50
914 30c. *Adenanthera pavonina* (seeds) 50 50
915 30c. *Shorea macrophylla* (seeds) 50 50
916 30c. *Dyera costulata* (fruits) 50 50
917 30c. *Alstonia angustiloba* (seeds) 50 50
MS918 Four sheets, each 92 × 71 mm. (a) Trees. 10c. *Fagraea fragrans*; 10c. *Dryobalanops aromatica*; 10c. *Terminalia catappa*; 10c. *Samanea saman*; 10c. *Dracontomelon dao*. (b) Leaves. 15c. *Heritiera javanica*; 15c. *Johannes-teijsmannia altifrons*; 15c. *Macaranga gigantea*; 15c. *Licuala grandis*; 15c. *Endospermum diadenum*. (c). Bark. 25c. *Pterocymbium javanicum*; 25c. *Dryobalanops aromatica*; 25c. *Dipterocarpus costulatus*; 25c. *Shorea leprosula*; 25c. *Ochanostachys amentacea*. (d) Forest fauna. 50c. Indian flycatcher; 50c. Slow loris; 50c. Marbled cat; 50c. Common carp; 50c. Pit viper Set of 4 sheets 3·00 3·50

No. **MS**918 contains four sheets each of five 18 × 22 mm designs, and a label showing the Conference logo.

2000. Centenary of Institute for Medical Research. Multicoloured.
919 30c. Type **281** 20 10
920 50c. Institute in 1953, bacteria and mosquito . . 35 30
921 $1 Institute in 1976, chromatogram and Eurycoma longifolia . . . 65 75
MS922 120 × 65 mm. $2 DNA molecule . . . . 1·25 1·25

2000. Protected Mammals of Malaysia (2nd series). Multicoloured.
923 20c. Type **282** 20 15
924 30c. Young otter civet . . . 20 20
927 30c. Hose's palm civet *(Hemigalus hosei)* 20 20
928 30c. Common palm civet *(Paradoxurus hermaphroditus)* 20 20
929 30c. Masked palm civet (Paguma larvata) 20 20
930 30c. Malay civet (Viverra tangalunga) 20 20
931 30c. Three-striped palm civet *(Arctogalidia trivirgata)* . . 20 20
925 50c. Binturong on bank . . . 35 30
926 $1 Head of binturong 65 75
MS932 140 × 80 mm. $1 Banded palm civet; $1 Banded linsang 1·50 1·50

283 Cogwheels

2000. 50th Anniv of RIDA-MARA (Rural and Industrial Development Authority – Council for Indigenous People). Multicoloured.
933 30c. Type **283** 20 10
934 50c. Compasses and stethoscope 35 30
935 $1 Computer disk, book and mouse 65 75

2000. Children's Traditional Games (2nd series). As T **276**. Multicoloured.
936 20c. Bailing tin 20 25
937 20c. Top-spinning 20 25
938 30c. Sepak Raga 25 30
939 30c. Letup-Letup 25 30

284 Cyclist and Pedestrians

285 *Rhododendron brookeanum*

2000. World Heart Day. Multicoloured.
940 30c. Type **284** 25 25
941 30c. Family at play 25 25
942 30c. Kite flying, football and no smoking sign 25 25
943 30c. Keep fit class 25 25
944 30c. Farmer, animals and food 25 25

Nos. 940/4 were printed together, se-tenant, with the backgrounds forming a composite design.

2000. Stamp Week 2000. Highland Flowers (2nd series). Multicoloured.
945 30c. Type **285** 20 25
946 30c. *Rhododendron jasminiflorum* 20 25
947 30c. *Rhododendron scortechinii* 20 25
948 30c. *Rhododendron pauciflorum* 20 25
949 30c. *Rhododendron crassifolium* 20 25
950 30c. *Rhododendron longiflorum* 20 25
951 30c. *Rhododendron javanicum* 20 25
952 30c. *Rhododendron variolosum* 20 25
953 30c. *Rhododendron acuminatum* 20 25
954 30c. *Rhododendron praetervisum* 20 25
955 30c. *Rhododendron himantodes* 20 25
956 30c. *Rhododendron maxwellii* 20 25
957 30c. *Rhododendron erocoides* 20 25
958 30c. *Rhododendron fallacinum* 20 25
MS959 55 × 90 mm. $1 *Rhododendron malayanum* . . . 70 80

No. 955 is inscribed "Rhodadendron", No. 957 "Ericoides", both in error.

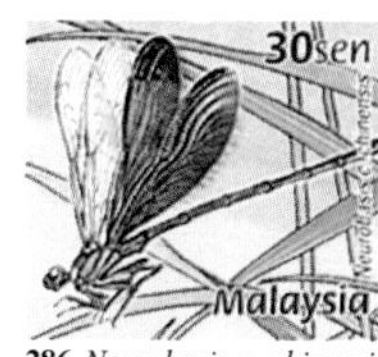

286 *Neurobasis c. chinensis*

2000. Dragonflies and Damselflies. Multicoloured.
960 30c. Type **286** 20 25
961 30c. *Aristocypha fenestrella* (blue markings on tail) . . 20 25
962 30c. *Vestalis gracilis* 20 25
963 30c. *Nannophya pymaea* . . . 20 25
964 30c. *Aristocypha fenestrella* (white markings on tail) . . 20 25
965 30c. *Rhyothemis p. phyllis* . . 20 25
966 30c. *Crocothemis s. servilia* 20 25
967 30c. *Euphaea ochracea* (male) 20 25
968 30c. *Euphaea ochracea* (female) 20 25
969 30c. *Ceriagrion cerinorubellum* 20 25
970 (30c.) *Vestalis gracilis* 20 25
971 (30c.) *Crocothemis s. servilia* (male) 20 25
972 (30c.) *Trithemis aurora* . . . 20 25
973 (30c.) *Pseudothemis jorina* . . 20 25
974 (30c.) *Diplacodes nebulosa* . . 20 25
975 (30c.) *Crocothemis s. servilia* (female) 20 25
976 (30c.) *Neurobasis c. chinensis* (male) 20 25
977 (30c.) *Burmagomphus divaricatus* 20 25
978 (30c.) *Ictinogomphus d. melaenops* 20 25
979 (30c.) *Orthetrum testaceum* 20 25
980 (30c.) *Trithemis festiva* . . . 20 25
981 (30c.) *Brachythemis contaminata* 20 25
982 (30c.) *Neurobasis c. chinensis* (female) 20 25
983 (30c.) *Neurothemis fluctuans* 20 25
984 (30c.) *Acisoma panorpoides* 20 25
985 (30c.) *Orthetrum s. sabina* . . 20 25
986 (30c.) *Rhyothemis p. phyllis* 20 25
987 (30c.) *Rhyothemis obsolescens* 20 25
988 (30c.) *Neurothemis t. tulia* . . 20 25
989 (30c.) *Lathrecista a. asiatica* 20 25
990 (30c.) *Aethriamanta gracilis* 20 25
991 (30c.) *Diplacodes trivialis* . . 20 25
992 (30c.) *Neurothemis fulvia* . . 20 25
993 (30c.) *Rhyothemis triangularis* 20 25
994 (30c.) *Orthetrum glaucum* . . 20 25

Nos. 960/9 were issued togetther, se-tenant, and show the backgrounds forming a composite design.

Nos. 970/94 are inscribed "Bayaran Pos Tempatan Hingga 20gm". They were valid at 30c. for local mail up to 20 g.

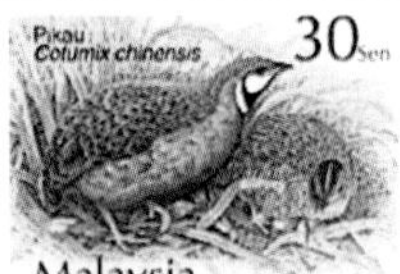

287 Indian Blue Quail

2001. Quails and Partridges. Multicoloured.
995 30c. Type **287** 25 10
996 50c. Sumatran hill partridge 35 30
997 $1 Bustard quail 65 75
MS998 100 × 170 mm. $2 Chestnut-breasted tree partridge; $2 Crimson-headed wood partridge 1·90 1·90

288 Federal Government Administrative Centre

2001. Formation of Putrajaya Federal Territory. Multicoloured.
999 30c. Type **288** 25 10
1000 $1 Government buildings and motorway bridge . . 75 90

289 Sabah and Sarawak Beadwork

2001. Sabah and Sarawak Beadwork. Mult, background colours given.
1001 **289** 30c. green 20 25
1002 – 30c. blue 20 25
1003 – 30c. buff 20 25
1004 – 30c. red 20 25
DESIGN: Nos 1001/4 Showing different styles of beadwork

290 *Cananga odorata*

291 Raja Tuanku Syed Sirajuddin

2001. Scented Flowers. Multicoloured.
1005 30c. Type **290** 20 10
1006 50c. *Mimusops elengi* . . . 35 30
1007 $1 *Mesua ferrea* 65 75
MS1008 70 × 100mm. $2 *Muchelia champaca* . . . . 1·00 1·10

2001. Installation of Tuanku Syed Sirajuddin as Raja of Perlis.
1009 **291** 30c. multicoloured . . . 15 15
1010 50c. multicoloured . . . 30 30
1011 $1 multicoloured 65 75
MS1012 100 × 70 mm. $2 Raja Tuanku Syed Sirajuddin and Tengku Fauziah (horiz). Multicoloured . . . . 1·00 1·10

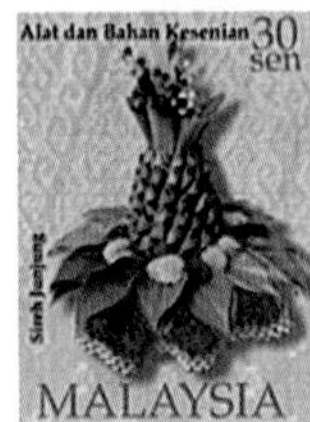

292 Beetlenut Leaf Arrangement

2001. Traditional Malaysian Artefacts. Mult.
1013 30c. Type **292** 20 20
1014 30c. Baby carrier 20 20
1015 50c. Quail trap 30 35
1016 50c. Ember container . . . 30 35

293 Perodua Kancil Car, 1995

2001. Malaysia-made Motor Vehicles. Mult.
1017 30c. Type **293** 20 25
1018 30c. Proton Tiara, 1995 . . 20 25
1019 30c. Perodua Rusa, 1995 . . 20 25
1020 30c. Proton Putra, 1997 . . 20 25
1021 30c. Inokom Permas, 1999 20 25
1022 30c. Perodua Kembara, 1999 . . . . 20 25
1023 30c. Proton GTI, 2000 . . . 20 25
1024 30c. TD 2000, 2000 . . . . 20 25
1025 30c. Perodua Kenari, 2000 20 25
1026 30c. Proton Waja, 2000 . . 20 25

294 Serama Bantam Cock **295** Diving

2001. Malaysian Bantams. Multicoloured.
1027 30c. Type **294** 20 15
1028 50c. Kapan bantam cock . . 30 30
1029 $1 Serama bantam hen . . . 60 70
MS1030 98 × 70 mm. $3 Red junglefowl hens and chicks (44 × 34 mm) . . . . 1·50 1·75

2001. 21st South East Asian Games, Kuala Lumpur. Mult.
1031 20c. Type **295** 15 10
1032 30c. Rhythmic gymnastics 20 15
1033 50c. Bowling 25 25
1034 $1 Weightlifting 45 50
1035 $2 Cycling . . . . 1·00 1·10
MS1036 110 × 90 mm. $5 Running 2·00 2·50

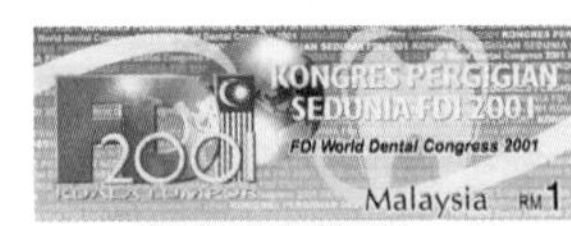

296 "F.D.I. 2001" Logo (½-size illustration)

2001. "F.D.I. 2001" World Dental Congress, Kuala Lumpur.
1037 **296** $1 multicoloured 60 65

297 K.W.S.P. Headquarters, Kuala Lumpur

2001. 50th Anniv of Employees' Provident Fund ("Kumpulan Wang Simpanan Pekerja"). Mult.
1038 30c. Type **297** 20 15
1039 50c. Column chart on coins and banknotes 30 30
1040 $1 Couple with K.W.S.P. logo 60 70

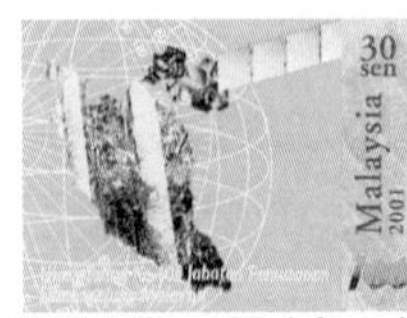

298 Satellite and Rainforest in Shape of Malaya Peninsula

2001. Centenary of Peninsular Malaysia Forestry Department. Multicoloured.
1041 30c. Type **298** 20 15
1042 50c. Cross-section through forest and soil 30 30
1043 $1 Newly-planted forest . . 60 70

299 *Tridacna gigas* (clam)

2001. Stamp Week. Endangered Marine Life. Multicoloured.
1044 20c. Type **299** 15 10
1045 30c. *Hippocampus sp.* (seahorse) 20 15
1046 50c. *Oreaster occidentalis* (starfish) 30 30
1047 $1 *Cassis cornu* (shell) . . . 60 70
MS1048 100 × 70 mm. $3 Dugong 1·50 1·75

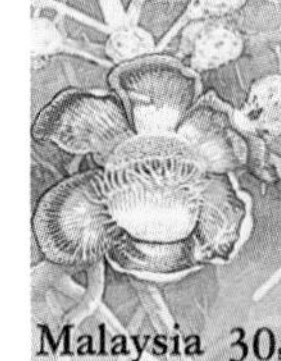

300 Hockey Player in Orange **301** *Couroupita guianensis*

2002. 10th Hockey World Cup, Kuala Lumpur. Multicoloured.
1049 30c. Type **300** 20 15
1050 50c. Goalkeeper 30 30
1051 $1 Hockey player in yellow 60 70
MS1052 100 × 70 mm. $3 Hockey player in blue (30 × 40 mm) . . 1·50 1·75

2002. Malaysia–China Joint Issue. Rare Flowers. Multicoloured.
1053 30c. Type **301** 10 10
1054 $1 *Couroupita guianensis* . . 15 20
1055 $1 *Camellia nitidissima* . . . 15 20
MS1056 108 × 79 mm. $2 *Schima brevifolia* buds (horiz); $2 *Schima brevifolia* blossom . . . . . . 1·25 1·40

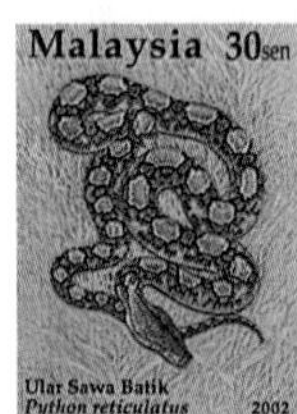

302 *Python reticulatus* **304** *Paraphalaenopsis labukensis*

303 Stesen Sentral Station, Kuala Lumpur

2002. Malaysian Snakes. Multicoloured.
1057 30c. Type **302** 10 10
1058 30c. *Gonyophis margaritatus* 10 10
1059 50c. *Bungarus candidus* . . . 15 20
1060 $1 *Maticora bivirgata* . . . 30 35
MS1061 108 × 78 mm. $2 *Ophiophagus hannah* (head of adult); $2 *Ophiophagus hannah* (juvenile) . . . . 1·25 1·40

2002. Express Rail Link from Central Kuala Lumpur to International Airport. Multicoloured.
1062 30c. Type **303** 10 10
1063 50c. Train and Central Station 15 20
1064 50c. Train and International Airport 15 20
MS1065 Two sheets, each 106 × 76 mm. (a) $1 KLIA Express and high speed train; $1 Express and local trains. (b) $2 KLIA Express Set of 2 sheets . . . . 1·25 1·40

2002. 17th World Orchid Conference. Multicoloured.
1066 30c. Type **304** 10 10
1067 30c. *Renanthera bella* . . . 10 10
1068 50c. *Paphiopedilum sanderianum* 15 20
1069 $1 *Coelogyne pandurata* . . 30 35
1070 $1 *Phalaenopsis amabilis* . . 30 35
MS1071 76 × 105 mm. $5 *Cleisocentron merillianum* (45 × 40 mm) . . . . 1·60 1·75

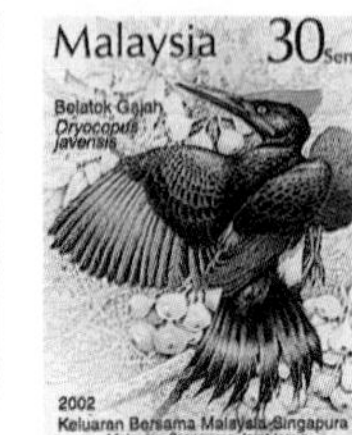

305 Raja Tuanku Syed Sirajuddin of Perlis **307** White-bellied Woodpecker (*Dryocopus javensis*)

306 *Cryptocoryne purpurea*

2002. Installation of Raja Tuanku Syed Sirajuddin as Yang di-Pertuan Agong.
1072 **305** 30c. multicoloured . . . 10 10
1073 50c. multicoloured . . . 15 20
1074 $1 multicoloured 30 35

2002. Aquatic Plants. Multicoloured.
1075 30c. Type **306** 10 10
1076 50c. *Barclaya kunstleri* . . . 15 20
1077 $1 *Neptunia oleracea* 30 35
1078 $1 *Monochoria hastata* . . . 30 35
MS1079 110 × 80 mm. $1 *Eichhornia crassipes* (vert); $2 *Nymphaea pubescens* . . . . 95 1·00

2002. Malaysia–Singapore Joint Issue. Birds. Multicoloured.
1080 30c. Type **307** 10 10
1081 30c. Black-naped oriole (*Oriolus chinensis*) 10 10
1082 $1 Red-throated sunbird (*Anthreptes rhodolaema*) 30 35
1083 $1 Asian fairy bluebird (*Irena puella*) 30 35
MS1084 99 × 70 mm. $5 Orange-bellied flowerpecker (*Dicaenum trigonostigma*) (60 × 40 mm) . . 1·60 1·75
Stamps with similar designs were issued by Singapore.

308 Sibu Island, Johore

2002. Tourist Beaches. Multicoloured.
1085 30c. Type **308** 10 10
1086 30c. Perhentian Islands, Trengganu 10 10
1087 50c. Manukan Island, Sabah 15 20
1088 50c. Tioman Island, Pahang 15 20
1089 $1 Singa Besar Island, Kedah 30 35
1090 $1 Pangkor Island, Perak 30 35
MS1091 110 × 80 mm. $1 Ferringhi Bay, Penang; $1 Port Dickson, Negri Sembilan 65 70

309 Ethnic Musicians and Dancers

2002. Malaysian Unity. Multicoloured.
1092 30c. Type **309** 10 10
1093 30c. Children playing mancala (game) 10 10
1094 50c. Children from different races (82 × 30 mm) . . . 15 20
MS1095 68 × 99 mm. $1 Children playing tug-of-war 30 35

310 Zainal Abidin bin Ahmad ("Za'ba") as a Student

2002. 30th Death Anniv of Zainal Abidin bin Ahmad ("Za'ba") (2003) (scholar). Multicoloured.
1096 30c. Type **310** 10 10
1097 50c. Za'ba with typewriter 15 20
1098 50c. Za'ba and traditional Malay building 15 20
MS1099 100 × 70 mm. $1 Za'ba at desk (vert) 30 35

311 Green Kebaya, Nyonya **313** Leopard Cat with Kittens

312 Suluh Budiman Building, Sultan Idris University of Education

2002. The Kebaya Nyonya (traditional Malay women's blouse). Multicoloured.
1100 30c. Type **311** 10 10
1101 30c. Red kebaya nyonya . . 10 10
1102 50c. Yellow kebaya nyonya 15 20
1103 50c. Pink kebaya nyonya . . 15 10
MS1104 70 × 100 mm. $2 Kebaya nyonya and sarong (34 × 69 mm) 65 70

2002. 80th Anniv of Sultan Idris University of Education. Multicoloured.
1105 30c. Type **312** 10 10
1106 50c. Tadahan Selatan Building 15 20
1107 50c. Chancellery Building 15 20
No. 1107 is inscribed "Chancellory" in error.

2002. Stamp Week. Wild and Domesticated Animals. Multicoloured.
1108 30c. Type **313** 10 10
1109 30c. Domestic cat and kittens 10 10
1110 $1 Lesser sulphur-crested cockatoo 30 35
1111 $1 Malay fish owl 30 35
MS1112 Two sheets, each 105 × 76 mm. (a) $1 Goldfish (horiz). $1 Porcupinefish (horiz); (b) $1 Giant squirrel; $1 Domestic rabbit with young Set of 2 sheets 1·25 1·40

314 Southern Serow

2003. Southern Serow. Multicoloured.
1113 30c. Type **314** 10 10
1114 50c. Southern serow lying down 15 20
1115 50c. Young southern serow 15 20

POSTAGE DUE STAMPS

Until 15 August 1966, the postage due stamps of Malaysian Postal Union were in use throughout Malaysia.

D 1

D 2

1966.
D 1 **D 1** 1c. red . . . . 20 3·25
D 2 2c. blue . . . . 25 2·75
D 3 4c. green . . . . 1·00 6·00
D18 8c. green . . . . 80 5·50
D19 10c. blue . . . . 80 2·75
D 6 12c. violet . . . . 60 4·50
D20 20c. brown . . . . 1·00 3·25
D21 50c. bistre . . . . 1·50 4·00

1986.
D22 **D 2** 5c. mauve and lilac . . . 10 20
D23 10c. black and grey . . . 15 25
D24 20c. red and brown . . . 20 30
D25 50c. green and blue . . . 30 40
D26 $1 blue and cobalt . . . 55 75

B. FEDERAL TERRITORY ISSUES

For use in the Federal Territories of Kuala Lumpur, Labuan (from 1984) and Putrajaya (from 2001).

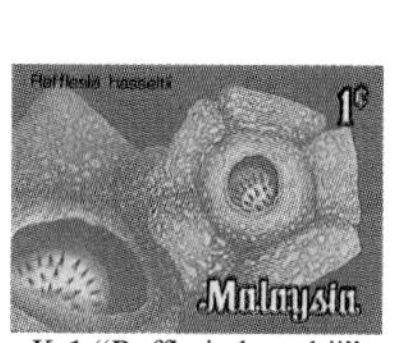

K **1** "Rafflesia hasseltii"

K **2** Coffee

1979. Flowers. Multicoloured.
K1 1c. Type **K 1** 10 40
K2 2c. "Pterocarpus indicus" . . 10 40
K3 5c. "Lagerstroemia speciosa" 15 40
K4 10c. "Durio zibethinus" . . . 15 10
K5 15c. "Hibiscus rosa-sinensis" 30 10
K6 20c. "Rhododendron scortechinii" 30 10
K7 25c. "Etlingera elatior" (inscr "Phaeomeria speciosa") . . 70 10

1986. Agricultural Products of Malaysia. Mult.
K15 1c. Type **K 2** 10 10
K16 2c. Coconuts 10 10
K17 5c. Cocoa 10 10
K18 10c. Black pepper 10 10
K19 15c. Rubber 10 10
K20 20c. Oil palm 10 10
K21 30c. Rice 10 15

MALDIVE ISLANDS Pt. 1

A group of islands W. of Ceylon. A republic from 1 January 1953, but reverted to a sultanate in 1954. Became independent on 26 July 1965 and left the British Commonwealth, but was re-admitted as an Associate Member on 9 July 1982.

1906. 100 cents = 1 rupee.
1951. 100 larees = 1 rupee.

1906. Nos. 268, 277/9 and 283/4 of Ceylon optd **MALDIVES**.
1 **44** 2c. brown . . . . 15·00 38·00
2 **48** 3c. green . . . . 18·00 38·00
3 4c. orange and blue . . . . 32·00 75·00
4 – 5c. purple . . . . 4·00 6·50
5 **48** 15c. blue . . . . 65·00 £130
6 25c. brown . . . . 75·00 £140

2 Minaret, Juma Mosque, Male

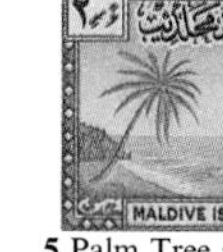

5 Palm Tree and Dhow

1909.
7a **2** 2c. brown . . . . 2·50 90
11A 2c. grey . . . . 2·75 2·00
8 3c. green 50 70
12A 3c. brown . . . . 70 2·75
9 5c. purple 50 35
15A 6c. red . . . . 1·50 5·50
10 10c. red . . . . 7·50 80
16A 10c. green 85 55
17A 15c. black . . . . 6·50 14·00
18A 25c. brown . . . . 6·50 14·00
19A 50c. purple . . . . 6·50 15·00
20B 1r. blue . . . . 13·00 3·25

1950.
21 **5** 2l. olive . . . . 2·00 1·00
22 3l. blue . . . . 9·50 50
23 5l. green . . . . 9·50 50
24 6l. brown 90 50
25 10l. red 90 50
26 15l. orange 90 50
27 25l. purple 90 60
28 50l. violet . . . . 90 1·50
29 1r. brown . . . . 9·50 28·00

8 Native Products

1952.
30 – 3l. blue (Fish) . . . . 1·75 50
31 **8** 5l. green . . . . 75 1·75

9 Male Harbour

10 Fort and Building

1956.
32 **9** 2l. purple 10 10
33 3l. slate 10 10
34 5l. brown 10 10
35 6l. violet 10 10
36 10l. green 10 10
37 15l. brown 10 85
38 25l. red 10 10
39 50l. orange 10 10
40 **10** 1r. green 15 10
41 5r. blue . . . . 1·00 30
42 10r. mauve . . . . 2·50 1·00

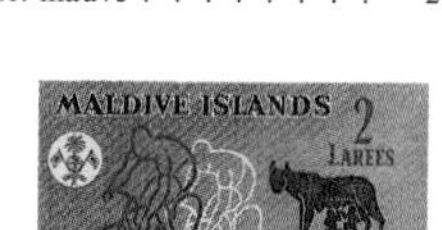

11 Cycling

1960. Olympic Games.
43 **11** 2l. purple and green 15 25
44 3l. slate and purple 15 25
45 5l. brown and blue 15 25
46 10l. green and brown . . . 15 25
47 15l. sepia and blue 15 25
48 – 25l. red and olive 15 25
49 – 50l. orange and violet . . . 20 40
50 – 1r. green and purple . . . . 40 1·25
DESIGN—VERT: 25l. to 1r. Basketball.

13 Tomb of Sultan

1960.
51 **13** 2l. purple 10 10
52 – 3l. green 10 10
53 – 5l. brown . . . . 3·25 3·25
54 – 6l. blue 10 10
55 – 10l. red 10 10
56 – 15l. sepia 10 10
57 – 25l. violet 10 10
58 – 50l. grey 10 10
59 – 1r. orange 15 10
60 – 5r. blue . . . . 4·25 60
61 – 10r. green . . . . 10·00 1·25
DESIGNS: 3l. Custom House; 5l. Cowrie shells; 6l. Old Royal Palace; 10l. Road to Juma Mosque, Male; 15l. Council House; 25l. New Government Secretariat; 50l. Prime Minister's Office; 1r. Old Ruler's Tomb; 5r. Old Ruler's Tomb (distant view); 10r. Maldivian port.

Higher values were also issued, intended mainly for fiscal use.

24 "Care of Refugees"

25 Coconuts

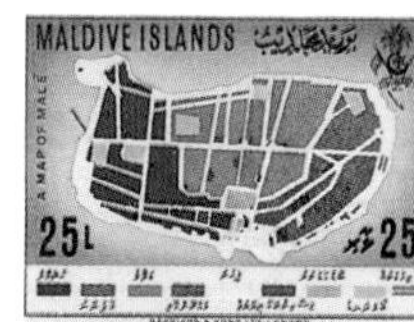

26 Map of Male

1960. World Refugee Year.
62 **24** 2l. violet, orange and green 10 10
63 3l. brown, green and red . . 10 10
64 5l. green, sepia and red . . 10 10
65 10l. green, violet and red . . 10 10
66 15l. violet, green and red . . 10 10
67 25l. blue, brown and green 10 10
68 50l. olive, red and blue . . . 10 10
69 1r. red, slate and violet . . 15 35

1961.
70 **25** 2l. brown and green 10 30
71 3l. brown and blue 10 30
72 5l. brown and mauve . . . 10 10
73 10l. brown and orange . . . 15 10
74 15l. brown and black . . . 20 15
75 **26** 25l. multicoloured 35 20
76 50l. multicoloured 35 40
77 1r. multicoloured 40 70

27 5c. Stamp of 1906

1961. 55th Anniv of First Maldivian Stamp.
78 **27** 2l. purple, blue and green 10 30
79 3l. purple, blue and green 10 30
80 5l. purple, blue and green 10 15
81 6l. purple, blue and green 10 50
82 – 10l. green, red and purple 10 15
83 – 15l. green, red and purple 15 15
84 – 20l. green, red and purple 15 20
85 – 25l. red, green and black . . 15 20
86 – 50l. red, green and black . . 25 80
87 – 1r. red, green and black . . 40 1·75
MS87a 114 × 88 mm. No. 87 (block of four). Imperf . . . . 1·50 4·50
DESIGNS: 10l. to 20l. Posthorn and 3c. stamp of 1906; 25l. to 1r. Olive sprig and 2c. stamp of 1906.

30 Malaria Eradication Emblem

31 Children of Europe and America

1962. Malaria Eradication.
88 **30** 2l. brown 10 40
89 3l. green 10 40
90 5l. turquoise 10 15
91 10l. red 10 15
92 – 15l. sepia 15 15
93 – 25l. blue 20 20
94 – 50l. myrtle 25 55
95 – 1r. purple 55 80
Nos. 92/5 are as Type **30**, but have English inscriptions at the side.

1962. 15th Anniv of U.N.I.C.E.F.
96 **31** 2l. multicoloured 10 50
97 6l. multicoloured 10 50
98 10l. multicoloured 10 10
99 15l. multicoloured 10 10
100 – 25l. multicoloured 15 10
101 – 50l. multicoloured 20 10
102 – 1r. multicoloured 25 20
103 – 5r. multicoloured . . . . . 1·00 3·75
DESIGN: Nos. 100/3, Children of Middle East and Far East.

33 Sultan Mohamed Farid Didi

39 Fishes in Net

34 Royal Angelfish

1962. 9th Anniv of Enthronement of Sultan.
104 **33** 3l. brown and green . . . 10 50
105 5l. brown and blue . . . 10 15
106 10l. brown and blue . . . 15 15
107 20l. brown and olive . . . 25 25
108 50l. brown and mauve . . 30 45
109 1r. brown and violet . . . 35 65

1963. Tropical Fish. Multicoloured.
110 2l. Type **34** 10 50
111 3l. Type **34** 10 50
112 5l. Type **34** 15 25
113 10l. Moorish idol (fish) . . . 25 25
114 25l. As 10l. 65 25
115 50l. Diadem soldierfish . . . 90 45
116 1r. Powder-blue surgeonfish 1·25 55
117 5r. Racoon butterflyfish . . . 6·25 10·00

1963. Freedom from Hunger.
118 **39** 2l. brown and green . . . 30 1·25
119 – 5l. brown and red 50 90
120 **39** 7l. brown and turquoise . . 70 90
121 – 10l. brown and blue . . . 85 90
122 **39** 25l. brown and red . . . . 3·00 3·50
123 – 50l. brown and violet . . . 4·75 8·00
124 **39** 1r. brown and mauve . . . 7·50 12·00
DESIGN—VERT: 5l., 10l., 50l. Handful of grain.

41 Centenary Emblem

42 Maldivian Scout Badge

1963. Centenary of Red Cross.
125 **41** 2l. red and purple . . . . 30 1·50
126 15l. red and green 65 80
127 50l. red and brown . . . . 1·25 1·75
128 1r. red and blue . . . . . 1·75 2·00
129 4r. red and olive . . . . . 4·00 21·00

1964. World Scout Jamboree, Marathon (1963).

130 **42** 2l. green and violet 10 50
131 3l. green and brown . . . 10 50
132 25l. green and blue 15 15
133 1r. green and red . . . . . 55 1·50

43 Mosque, Male

1964. "Maldives Embrace Islam".

134 **43** 2l. purple 10 50
135 3l. green 10 50
136 10l. red 10 10
137 40l. purple 30 25
138 60l. blue 50 30
139 85l. brown 60 45

44 Putting the Shot

1964. Olympic Games, Tokyo.

140 **44** 2l. purple and blue 10 55
141 3l. red and brown 10 55
142 5l. bronze and green . . . 15 15
143 10l. violet and purple . . . 20 15
144 – 15l. sepia and brown . . . 30 15
145 – 25l. indigo and blue . . . 50 15
146 – 50l. bronze and olive . . . 75 35
147 – 1r. purple and grey . . . . 1·25 75
MS147a 126 × 140 mm. Nos. 145/7. Imperf . . . . 2·25 3·50

DESIGN. 15l. to 1r. Running.

46 Telecommunications Satellite

1965. International Quiet Sun Years.

148 **46** 5l. blue 15 40
149 10l. brown 20 40
150 25l. green 40 40
151 1r. mauve 90 80

47 Isis (wall carving, Abu Simbel)

49 "XX" and U.N. Flag

48 Pres. Kennedy and Doves

1965. Nubian Monuments Preservation.

152 **47** 2l. green and purple . . . 10 20
153 – 3l. lake and green 10 20
154 **47** 5l. green and purple . . . 15 10
155 – 10l. blue and orange . . . 20 10
156 **47** 15l. brown and violet . . . 35 10
157 – 25l. purple and blue . . . 60 15
158 **47** 50l. green and sepia . . . 75 35
159 – 1r. ochre and green . . . . 1·10 55

DESIGN: 3, 10, 25l., 1r. Rameses II on throne (wall carving, Abu Simbel).

1965. 2nd Death Anniv of Pres. Kennedy.

160 **48** 2l. black and mauve . . . 10 40
161 5l. brown and mauve . . . 10 10
162 25l. blue and mauve . . . 10 10
163 – 1r. purple, yellow and green 25 25
164 – 2r. bronze, yellow and green 40 65
MS164a 150 × 130 mm. No. 164 in block of four. Imperf . . . . . 2·75 3·25

DESIGN: 1r., 2r. Pres. Kennedy and hands holding olive-branch.

1965. 20th Anniv of U.N.

165 **49** 3l. blue and brown 10 30
166 10l. blue and violet 20 10
167 1r. blue and green . . . . 1·10 35

50 I.C.Y. Emblem

1965. International Co-operation Year.

168 **50** 5l. brown and bistre . . . 15 20
169 15l. brown and lilac . . . 20 20
170 50l. brown and olive . . . 45 30
171 1r. brown and red . . . . 1·25 1·50
172 2r. brown and blue . . . . 1·75 3·50
MS173 101 × 126 mm. Nos. 170/2. Imperf . . . . 6·50 6·50

51 Princely Cone Shells

1966. Multicoloured.

174 2l. Type **51** . . . . 20 1·00
175 3l. Yellow flowers . . . . . 20 1·00
176 5l. Reticulate distorsio and leopard shells 30 15
177 7l. Camellias 30 15
178 10l. Type **51** . . . . 1·00 15
179 15l. Crab plover and seagull 3·75 30
180 20l. As 3l. 80 30
181 30l. Type **51** . . . . 2·75 35
182 50l. As 15l. . . . . 6·00 55
183 1r. Type **51** . . . . 4·00 55
184 1r. As 7l. . . . . 3·50 55
185 1r.50 As 3l. . . . . 3·75 3·00
186 2r. As 7l. . . . . 5·00 3·50
187 5r. As 15l. . . . . 23·00 13·00
188 10r. As 5l. . . . . 23·00 19·00

The 3l., 7l., 20l., 1r. (No. 184), 1r.50 and 2r. are DIAMOND (43½ × 43½ mm).

52 Maldivian Flag

1966. 1st Anniv of Independence.

189 **52** 10l. green, red and turquoise 75 30
190 1r. multicoloured . . . . . 2·75 70

53 "Luna 9" on Moon

1966. Space Rendezvous and Moon Landing.

191 **53** 10l. brown, indigo and blue 20 10
192 – 25l. green and red 30 10
193 **53** 50l. brown and green . . . 40 15
194 – 1r. turquoise and brown 70 35
195 – 2r. green and violet . . . . 1·50 65
196 – 5r. pink and turquoise . . 2·25 1·60
MS197 108 × 126 mm. Nos. 194/6. Imperf . . . . 3·50 4·50

DESIGNS: 25l., 1r., 5r. "Gemini 6" and "7" rendezvous in space; 2r. "Gemini" spaceship as seen from the other spaceship.

54 U.N.E.S.C.O. Emblem and Owl on Book

1966. 20th Anniv of U.N.E.S.C.O. Multicoloured.

198 2l. Type **54** 20 75
199 3l. U.N.E.S.C.O. emblem and globe and microscope . . . 20 75
200 5l. U.N.E.S.C.O. emblem and mask, violin and palette . . 50 20
201 50l. Type **54** . . . . 2·50 55
202 1r. Design as 3l. . . . . . . 3·50 90
203 5r. Design as 5l. . . . . . . 11·00 15·00

55 Sir Winston Churchill and Cortege

1966. Churchill Commem. Flag in red and blue.

204 **55** 2l. brown 15 80
205 – 10l. turquoise 85 10
206 **55** 15l. green . . . . 1·60 10
207 – 25l. violet . . . . 2·25 15
208 – 1r. brown . . . . 6·00 75
209 **55** 2r.50 red . . . . 12·00 10·00

DESIGN: 10l., 25l., 1r. Churchill and catafalque.

56 Footballers and Jules Rimet Cup

1967. England's Victory in World Cup Football Championship. Multicoloured.

210 2l. Type **56** 10 50
211 3l. Player in red shirt kicking ball 10 50
212 5l. Scoring goal 10 10
213 25l. As 3l. 60 10
214 50l. Making a tackle . . . . 1·00 20
215 1r. Type **56** . . . . 2·00 55
216 2r. Emblem on Union Jack 3·25 3·00
MS217 100 × 121 mm. Nos. 214/16. Imperf . . . . 8·50 6·50

57 Ornate Butterflyfish

1967. Tropical Fishes. Multicoloured.

218 2l. Type **57** 10 40
219 3l. Black-saddled pufferfish 15 40
220 5l. Blue boxfish 20 10
221 6l. Picasso triggerfish 20 20
222 50l. Semicircle angelfish . . . 3·25 30
223 1r. As 3l. . . . . 4·50 75
224 2r. As 50l. . . . . 8·50 8·00

58 Hawker Siddeley H.S.748 over Hulule Airport Building

1967. Inauguration of Hulule Airport.

225 **58** 2l. violet and olive 20 50
226 – 5l. green and lavender . . 25 10
227 **58** 10l. violet and green . . . 30 10
228 – 15l. green and ochre . . . 50 10
229 **58** 30l. ultramarine and blue 1·00 10
230 – 50l. brown and mauve . . 1·75 20
231 **58** 5r. blue and orange . . . . 5·50 5·50
232 – 10r. brown and blue . . . 7·50 9·00

DESIGN: 5, 15, 50l., 10r. Airport building and Hawker Siddeley H.S.748.

59 "Man and Music" Pavilion

1967. World Fair, Montreal. Multicoloured.

233 2l. Type **59** 10 40
234 5l. "Man and His Community" Pavilion . . . 10 10
235 10l. Type **59** 10 10
236 50l. As 5l. 40 30
237 1r. Type **59** 75 50
238 2r. As 5l. . . . . 1·75 1·75
MS239 102 × 137 mm. Nos. 237/8. Imperf . . . . 2·25 3·00

1968. International Tourist Year (1967). Nos. 225/32 optd **International Tourist Year 1967.**

240 **58** 2l. violet and olive 10 60
241 – 5l. green and lavender . . 15 15
242 **58** 10l. violet and green . . . 20 15
243 – 15l. green and ochre . . . 20 15
244 **58** 30l. ultramarine and blue 30 20
245 – 50l. brown and mauve . . 45 30
246 **58** 5r. blue and orange . . . . 3·50 4·00
247 – 10r. brown and blue . . . 5·00 6·50

61 Cub signalling and Lord Baden-Powell

63 Putting the Shot

62 French Satellite "A 1"

1968. Maldivian Scouts and Cubs.

248 **61** 2l. brown, green and yellow 10 50
249 – 3l. red, blue and light blue 10 50
250 **61** 25l. violet, lake and red . . 1·50 30
251 – 1r. green, brown and light green . . . . 3·50 1·60

DESIGN: 3l. and 1r. Scouts and Lord Baden-Powell.

1968. Space Martyrs.

252 **62** 2l. mauve and blue 10 40
253 – 3l. violet and brown . . . 10 40
254 – 7l. brown and lake 15 40
255 – 10l. blue, drab and black 15 15
256 – 25l. green and violet . . . 40 15
257 **62** 50l. blue and brown . . . 75 30
258 – 1r. purple and green . . . 1·10 50
259 – 2r. brown, blue and black 1·75 2·00
260 – 5r. mauve, drab and black 2·75 3·00
MS261 110 × 155 mm. Nos. 258/9. Imperf . . . . 3·75 4·00

DESIGNS: 3l., 25l. "Luna 10"; 7l., 1r. "Orbiter" and "Mariner"; 10l., 2r. Astronauts White, Grissom and Chaffee; 5r. Cosmonaut V. M. Komarov.

1968. Olympic Games, Mexico (1st Issue). Multicoloured.

262 2l. Type **63** 10 40
263 6l. Throwing the discus . . . 10 40
264 10l. Type **63** 15 10
265 25l. As 6l. 20 10
266 1r. Type **63** 60 35
267 2r.50 As 6l. . . . . 1·50 2·00

See also Nos. 294/7.

64 "Adriatic Seascape" (Bonington)

1968. Paintings. Multicoloured.

268 50l. Type **64** . . . . 1·50 30
269 1r. "Ulysses deriding Polyphemus" (Turner) . . 2·00 45
270 2r. "Sailing Boat at Argenteuil" (Monet) . . . 2·75 2·25
271 5r. "Fishing Boat at Les Saintes-Maries" (Van Gogh) . . . . 4·75 5·00

65 LZ-130 "Graf Zeppelin II" and Montgolfier's Balloon

1968. Development of Civil Aviation.

272 **65** 2l. brown, green and blue 15 50
273 – 3l. blue, violet and brown 15 50
274 – 5l. green, red and blue . . 15 15
275 – 7l. blue, purple and orange 90 60
276 **65** 10l. brown, blue and purple 35 15
277 – 50l. red, green and olive . . 1·50 20
278 – 1r. green, blue and red . . 2·25 50
279 – 2r. purple, bistre and blue 14·00 10·00

DESIGNS: 3l., 1r. Boeing 707-420 and Douglas DC-3; 5l., 50l. Wright Type A and Lilienthal's glider; 7l., 2r. Projected Boeing 733 and Concorde.

66 W.H.O. Building, Geneva

1968. 20th Anniv of World Health Organization.
280 **66** 10l. violet, turquoise & blue 60 10
281 25l. green, brown & yellow 1·00 15
282 1r. brown, emerald & green 3·25 90
283 2r. violet, purple and mauve . . . . 5·25 5·50

1968. 1st Anniv of Scout Jamboree, Idaho. Nos. 248/51 optd **International Boy Scout Jamboree, Farragut Park, Idaho, U.S.A. August 1–9, 1967**.
284 **61** 2l. brown, green and yellow 10 50
285 – 3l. red, blue and light blue 10 50
286 **61** 25l. violet, lake and red . . 1·50 40
287 – 1r. green, brown and light green . . . . 4·50 2·10

68 Curlew and Common Redshank

1968. Multicoloured.
288 2l. Type **68** 50 75
289 10l. Pacific grinning tun and Papal mitre shells . . . . 1·25 20
290 25l. Oriental angel wing and tapestry turban shells . . . 1·75 25
291 50l. Type **68** . . . . 7·00 1·10
292 1r. As 10l. . . . . 4·50 1·10
293 2r. As 25l. . . . . 5·00 4·75

69 Throwing the Discus

1968. Olympic Games, Mexico (2nd issue). Mult.
294 10l. Type **69** 10 10
295 50l. Running 20 10
296 1r. Cycling . . . . 3·25 60
297 2r. Basketball . . . . 4·00 2·00

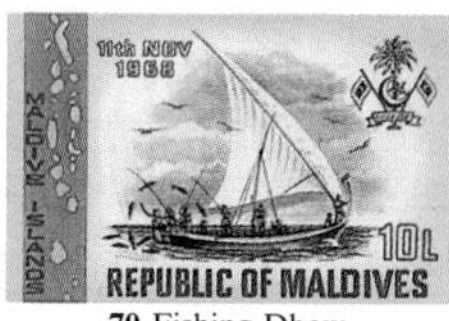

70 Fishing Dhow

1968. Republic Day.
298 **70** 10l. brown, blue and green 75 20
299 – 1r. green, red and blue . . 4·50 80
DESIGN: 1r. National flag, crest and map.

71 "The Thinker" (Rodin)

1969. U.N.E.S.C.O. "Human Rights". Designs showing sculptures by Rodin. Multicoloured.
300 6l. Type **71** 30 15
301 10l. "Hands" 30 15
302 1r.50 "Eve" . . . . 2·00 2·25
303 2r.50 "Adam" . . . . 2·50 3·00
MS304 112 × 130 mm. Nos. 302/3. Imperf . . . . 7·00 7·00

72 Module nearing Moon's Surface

1969. 1st Man on the Moon. Multicoloured.
305 6l. Type **72** 15 15
306 10l. Astronaut with hatchet 15 15
307 1r.50 Astronaut and module 2·25 1·40
308 2r.50 Astronaut using camera 2·50 2·00
MS309 101 × 130 mm. Nos. 305/8. Imperf . . . . 2·75 3·75

1969. Gold Medal Winner, Olympic Games, Mexico (1968). Nos. 295/6 optd **Gold Medal Winner Mohamed Gammoudi 5000m. run Tunisia REPUBLIC OF MALDIVES** or similar opt.
310 50l. multicoloured 60 60
311 1r. multicoloured . . . . . . 1·40 90
The overprint on No. 310 honours P. Trentin (cycling, France).

74 Racoon Butterflyfish

1970. Tropical Fishes. Mult.
312 2l. Type **74** 40 70
313 5l. Clown triggerfish 65 40
314 25l. Broad-barred lionfish . . 2·25 40
315 50l. Long-nosed butterflyfish 3·00 1·00
316 1r. Emperor angelfish . . . . 4·00 1·00
317 2r. Royal angelfish . . . . . 5·50 6·50

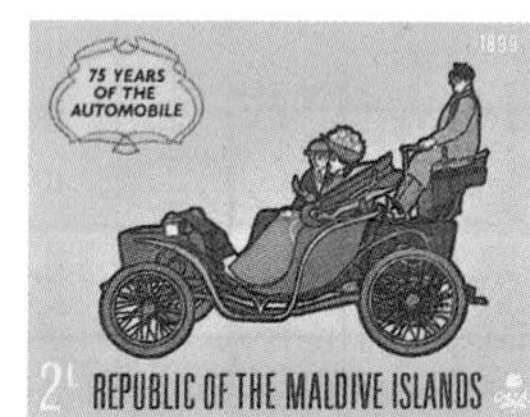

75 Columbia Dauman Victoria, 1899

1970. "75 Years of the Automobile". Mult.
318 2l. Type **75** 20 50
319 5l. Duryea phaeton, 1902 . . 25 30
320 7l. Packard S-24, 1906 . . . 30 30
321 10l. Autocar Runabout, 1907 35 30
322 25l. Type **75** . . . . 1·50 30
323 50l. As 5l. . . . . 2·75 55
324 1r. As 7l. . . . . 3·50 90
325 2r. As 10l. . . . . 4·50 5·50
MS326 95 × 143 mm. Nos. 324/5 5·00 7·50

76 U.N. Headquarters, New York

1970. 25th Anniv of United Nations. Mult.
327 2l. Type **76** 10 75
328 10l. Surgical operation (W.H.O.) . . . . 1·50 25
329 25l. Student, actress and musician (U.N.E.S.C.O.) 2·50 40
330 50l. Children at work and play (U.N.I.C.E.F.) . . . . 2·00 70
331 1r. Fish, corn and farm animals (F.A.O.) . . . . . 2·00 1·00
332 2r. Miner hewing coal (I.L.O.) . . . . 6·00 6·50

77 Ship and Light Buoy

78 "Guitar-player and Masqueraders" (A. Watteau)

1970. 10th Anniv of I.M.C.O. Multicoloured.
333 50l. Type **77** 50 40
334 1r. Ship and lighthouse . . . 4·25 85

1970. Famous Paintings showing the Guitar. Multicoloured.
335 3l. Type **78** 10 50
336 7l. "Spanish Guitarist" (Manet) 15 50
337 50l. "Costumed Player" (Watteau) 60 40
338 1r. "Mandolin-player" (Roberti) . . . . 1·00 55
339 2r.50 "Guitar-player and Lady" (Watteau) . . . . . 2·50 3·00
340 5r. "Mandolin-player" (Frans Hals) . . . . 4·50 5·00
MS341 132 × 80 mm. Nos. 339/40 6·50 7·50

79 Australian Pavilion

82 Footballers

80 Learning the Alphabet

1970. "EXPO 70" World Fair, Osaka, Japan. Multicoloured.
342 2l. Type **79** 10 65
343 3l. West German Pavilion . . 10 65
344 10l. U.S. Pavilion 40 10
345 25l. British Pavilion . . . . 1·00 15
346 50l. Soviet Pavilion . . . . . 1·60 45
347 1r. Japanese Pavilion . . . . 2·00 65

1970. Int Education Year. Multicoloured.
348 5l. Type **80** 25 30
349 10l. Training teachers 30 15
350 25l. Geography lesson . . . 1·00 20
351 50l. School inspector . . . . 1·25 45
352 1r. Education by television 1·75 75

1970. "Philympia 1970" Stamp Exn, London. Nos. 306/8 optd **Philympia London 1970**.
353 10l. multicoloured 10 10
354 1r.50 multicoloured 65 75
355 2r.50 multicoloured . . . . . 1·00 1·50
MS356 101 × 130 mm. Nos. 305/8 optd. Imperf . . . . 6·00 7·00

1970. World Cup Football Championship, Mexico.
357 **82** 3l. multicoloured 15 40
358 – 6l. multicoloured 20 40
359 – 7l. multicoloured 20 30
360 – 25l. multicoloured 90 20
361 – 1r. multicoloured . . . . . 2·50 90
DESIGNS: 6l. to 1r. Different designs showing footballers in action.

83 Little Boy and U.N.I.C.E.F. Flag

84 Astronauts Lovell, Haise and Swigert

1970. 25th Anniv of U.N.I.C.E.F. Multicoloured.
362 5l. Type **83** 10 15
363 10l. Little girl with U.N.I.C.E.F. "balloon" . . 10 15
364 1r. Type **83** . . . . 1·75 85
365 2r. As 10l. . . . . 2·75 3·00

1971. Safe Return of "Apollo 13". Multicoloured.
366 5l. Type **84** 25 25
367 20l. Explosion in Space . . . 55 15
368 1r. Splashdown . . . . . . 1·25 50

85 "Multiracial Flower"

86 "Mme. Charpentier and her Children" (Renoir)

1971. Racial Equality Year.
369 **85** 10l. multicoloured 10 15
370 25l. multicoloured 20 15

1971. Famous Paintings showing "Mother and Child". Multicoloured.
371 5l. Type **86** 25 20
372 7l. "Susanna van Collen and her Daughter" (Rembrandt) 30 20
373 10l. "Madonna nursing the Child" (Titian) 40 20
374 20l. "Baroness Belleli and her Children" (Degas) . . . . 1·00 20
375 25l. "The Cradle" (Morisot) 1·00 20
376 1r. "Helena Fourment and her Children" (Reubens) 3·00 85
377 3r. "On the Terrace" (Renoir) . . . . 5·50 6·50

87 Alan Shepard

1971. Moon Flight of "Apollo 14". Multicoloured.
378 6l. Type **87** 40 40
379 10l. Stuart Roosa 45 30
380 1r.50 Edgar Mitchell . . . . 5·50 3·50
381 5r. Mission insignia . . . . 11·00 11·00

88 "Ballerina" (Degas)

1971. Famous Paintings showing "Dancers". Mult.
382 5l. Type **88** 20 20
383 10l. "Dancing Couple" (Renoir) 25 20
384 2r. "Spanish Dancer" (Manet) . . . . 2·75 2·50
385 5r. "Ballerinas" (Degas) . . . 5·00 5·00
386 10r. "La Goulue at the Moulin Rouge" (Toulouse-Lautrec) . . . . 7·50 8·00

1972. Visit of Queen Elizabeth II and Prince Philip. Nos. 382/6 optd **ROYAL VISIT 1972**.
387 **88** 5l. multicoloured 15 10
388 – 10l. multicoloured 20 10
389 – 2r. multicoloured . . . . . 4·50 4·00
390 – 5r. multicoloured . . . . . 8·00 8·00
391 – 10r. multicoloured . . . . 9·50 10·00

90 Book Year Emblem

1972. International Book Year.
392 **90** 25l. multicoloured 15 10
393 5r. multicoloured . . . . . 1·60 2·00

91 Scottish Costume

1972. National Costumes of the World. Mult.
394 10l. Type **91** 70 10
395 15l. Netherlands 80 15
396 25l. Norway . . . . 1·50 15
397 50l. Hungary . . . . 2·25 55
398 1r. Austria . . . . 2·75 80
399 2r. Spain . . . . 4·00 3·25

92 Stegosaurus

1972. Prehistoric Animals. Multicoloured.
400 2l. Type **92** 75 75
401 7l. Dimetrodon (inscr "Edaphosaurus") . . . . . 1·50 60
402 25l. Diplodocus . . . . . . 2·25 50
403 50l. Triceratops . . . . . . 2·50 75
404 2r. Pteranodon . . . . . . 5·50 5·00
405 5r. Tyrannosaurus . . . . . 9·50 9·50

93 Cross-country Skiing

1972. Winter Olympic Games, Sapporo, Japan. Multicoloured.
406 3l. Type **93** 10 50
407 6l. Bobsleighing 10 50
408 15l. Speed skating 20 20
409 50l. Ski jumping . . . . . . 1·00 45
410 1r. Figure skating (pair) . . . 1·75 70
411 2r.50 Ice hockey . . . . . . 5·50 3·25

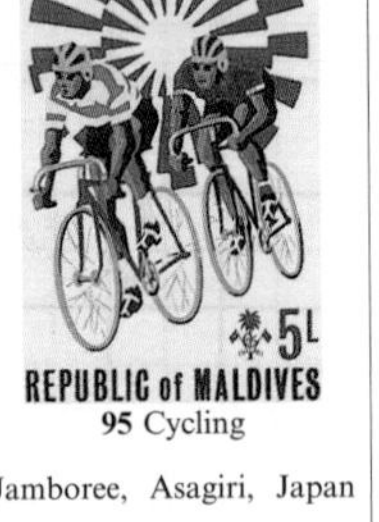

94 Scout Saluting **95** Cycling

1972. 13th Boy Scout Jamboree, Asagiri, Japan (1971). Multicoloured.
412 10l. Type **94** 75 20
413 15l. Scout signalling 95 20
414 50l. Scout blowing bugle . . 3·25 1·25
415 1r. Scout playing drum . . . 4·50 2·25

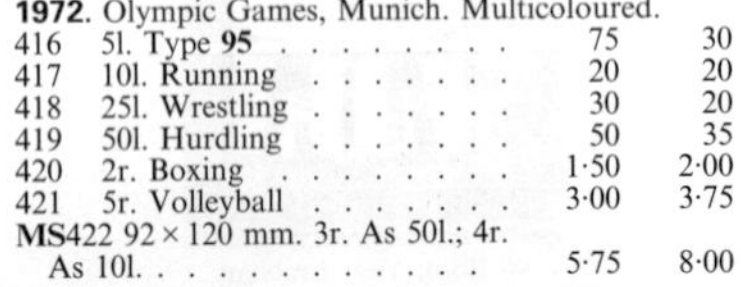

1972. Olympic Games, Munich. Multicoloured.
416 5l. Type **95** 75 30
417 10l. Running 20 20
418 25l. Wrestling 30 20
419 50l. Hurdling 50 35
420 2r. Boxing . . . . 1·50 2·00
421 5r. Volleyball . . . . 3·00 3·75
MS422 92 × 120 mm. 3r. As 50l.; 4r. As 10l. . . . . 5·75 8·00

96 Globe and Conference Emblem
97 "Flowers" (Van Gogh)

1972. U.N. Environmental Conservation Conference, Stockholm.
423 **96** 2l. multicoloured 10 40
424 3l. multicoloured 10 40
425 15l. multicoloured 30 15
426 50l. multicoloured 75 45
427 2r.50 multicoloured . . . . 3·25 4·25

1973. Floral Paintings. Multicoloured.
428 1l. Type **97** 10 60
429 2l. "Flowers in Jug" (Renoir) 10 60
430 3l. "Chrysanthemums" (Renoir) 10 60
431 50l. "Mixed Bouquet" (Bosschaert) . . . . 1·25 30
432 1r. As 3l. . . . . 1·75 40
433 5r. As 2l. . . . . 4·00 5·50
MS434 120 × 94 mm. 2r. As 50l.; 3r. Type **97** . . . . 7·00 8·50

1973. Gold-medal Winners, Munich Olympic Games. Nos. 420/1 optd as listed below.
435 2r. multicoloured . . . . . . 3·25 2·50
436 5r. multicoloured . . . . . . 4·25 2·75
MS437 92 × 120 mm. 3r. multicoloured; 4r. multicoloured 7·50 8·50
OVERPRINTS: 2r. **LEMECHEV MIDDLE-WEIGHT GOLD MEDALLIST**; 5r. **JAPAN GOLD MEDAL WINNERS**. Miniature sheet: 3r. **EHRHARDT 100 METER HURDLES GOLD MEDALLIST**; 4r. **SHORTER MARATHON GOLD MEDALLIST**.

99 Animal Care

1973. International Scouting Congress, Nairobi and Addis Ababa. Multicoloured.
438 1l. Type **99** 10 30
439 2l. Lifesaving 10 30
440 3l. Agricultural training . . . 10 30
441 4l. Carpentry 10 30
442 5l. Playing leapfrog 10 30
443 1r. As 2l. . . . . 2·75 75
444 2r. As 4l. . . . . 4·00 4·75
445 3r. Type **99** . . . . 4·50 7·00
MS446 101 × 79 mm. 5r. As 3l. 7·50 14·00

100 Blue Marlin

1973. Fishes. Multicoloured.
447 1l. Type **100** 10 40
448 2l. Skipjack tuna 10 40
449 3l. Blue-finned tuna 10 40
450 5l. Dolphin (fish) 10 40
451 60l. Humpbacked snapper . . 80 40
452 75l. As 60l. . . . . 1·00 40
453 1r.50 Yellow-edged lyretail . 1·75 2·00
454 2r.50 As 5l. . . . . 2·25 3·00
455 3r. Spotted coral grouper . . 2·25 3·25
456 10r. Spanish mackerel . . . 4·75 8·00
MS457 119 × 123 mm. 4r. As 2l. 5r. Type **100** . . . . 16·00 19·00
Nos. 451/2 are smaller, size 29 × 22 mm.

101 Golden-fronted Leafbird

1973. Fauna. Multicoloured.
458 1l. Type **101** 10 50
459 2l. Indian flying fox 10 50
460 3l. Land tortoise 10 50
461 4l. Butterfly ("Kallima inachus") 30 50
462 50l. As 3l. 60 40
463 2r. Type **101** . . . . 5·00 4·50
464 3r. As 2l. . . . . 3·50 4·50
MS465 66 × 74 mm. 5r. As 4l. . . 18·00 20·00

102 "Lantana camara"

1973. Flowers of the Maldive Islands. Mult.
466 1l. Type **102** 10 30
467 2l. "Nerium oleander" . . . 10 30
468 3l. "Rosa polyantha" 10 30
469 4l. "Hibiscus manihot" . . . 10 30
470 5l. "Bougainvillea glabra" . . 10 20
471 10l. "Plumera alba" 10 20
472 50l. "Poinsettia pulcherrima" 55 30
473 5r. "Ononis natrix" . . . . 3·25 5·00
MS474 110 × 100 mm. 2r. As 3l.; 3r. As 10l. . . . . 3·25 5·25

103 "Tiros" Weather Satellite

1974. Centenary of World Meteorological Organization. Multicoloured.
475 1l. Type **103** 10 20
476 2l. "Nimbus" satellite 10 20
477 3l. "Nomad" (weather ship) 10 20
478 4l. Scanner, A.P.T. Instant Weather Picture equipment 10 20
479 5l. Richard's wind-speed recorder 10 10
480 2r. Type **103** . . . . 3·25 3·50
481 3r. As 3l. . . . . 3·50 3·75
MS482 110 × 79 mm. 10r. As 2l. 8·50 14·00

104 "Apollo" Spacecraft and Pres. Kennedy

1974. American and Russian Space Exploration Projects. Multicoloured.
483 1l. Type **104** 10 25
484 2l. "Mercury" capsule and John Glenn 10 25
485 3l. "Vostok 1" and Yuri Gagarin 10 25
486 4l. "Vostok 6" and Valentina Tereshkova 10 25
487 5l. "Soyuz 11" and "Salyut" space-station 10 20
488 2r. "Skylab" space laboratory 3·50 3·50
489 3r. As 2l. . . . . 4·00 4·00
MS490 103 × 80 mm. 10r. Type **104** 11·00 13·00

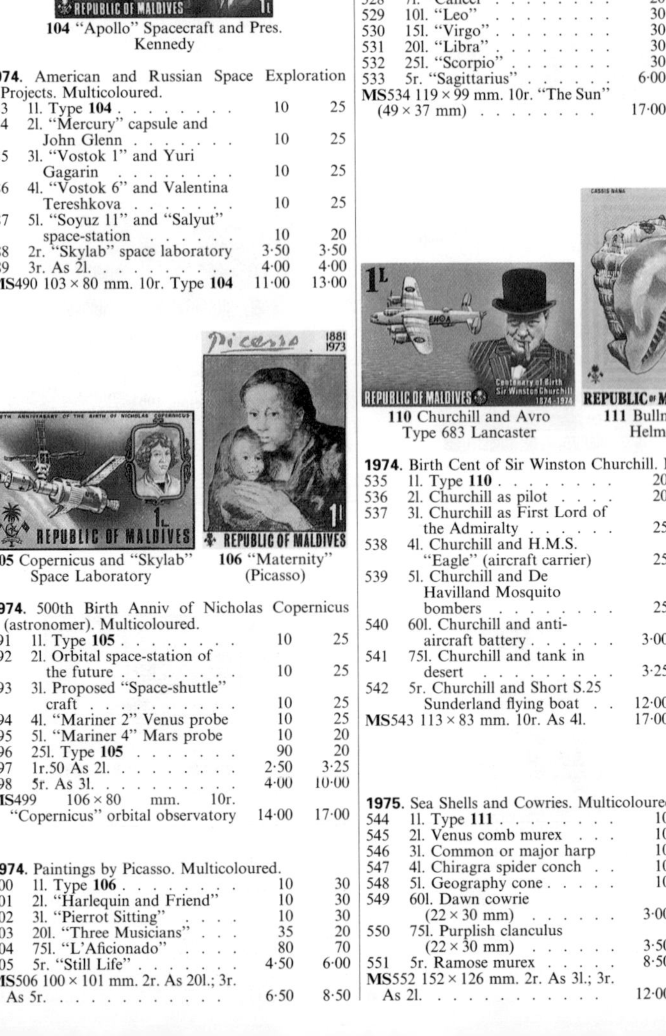

105 Copernicus and "Skylab" Space Laboratory
106 "Maternity" (Picasso)

1974. 500th Birth Anniv of Nicholas Copernicus (astronomer). Multicoloured.
491 1l. Type **105** 10 25
492 2l. Orbital space-station of the future 10 25
493 3l. Proposed "Space-shuttle" craft 10 25
494 4l. "Mariner 2" Venus probe 10 25
495 5l. "Mariner 4" Mars probe 10 20
496 25l. Type **105** 90 20
497 1r.50 As 2l. . . . . 2·50 3·25
498 5r. As 3l. . . . . 4·00 10·00
MS499 106 × 80 mm. 10r. "Copernicus" orbital observatory 14·00 17·00

1974. Paintings by Picasso. Multicoloured.
500 1l. Type **106** 10 30
501 2l. "Harlequin and Friend" . 10 30
502 3l. "Pierrot Sitting" 10 30
503 20l. "Three Musicians" . . . 35 20
504 75l. "L'Aficionado" 80 70
505 5r. "Still Life" . . . . 4·50 6·00
MS506 100 × 101 mm. 2r. As 20l.; 3r. As 5r. . . . . 6·50 8·50

107 U.P.U. Emblem, Steam and Diesel Locomotives

1974. Cent of Universal Postal Union. Mult.
507 1l. Type **107** 10 30
508 2l. Paddle-steamer and modern mailboat 10 30
509 3l. Airship "Graf Zeppelin" and Boeing 747 airliner . . 10 30
510 1r.50 Mailcoach and motor van . . . . 1·10 1·10
511 2r.50 As 2l. . . . . 1·40 1·75
512 5r. Type **107** . . . . 2·00 3·25
MS513 126 × 105 mm. 4r. Type **107** 5·50 7·00

108 Footballers **109** "Capricorn"

1974. World Cup Football Championship, West Germany.
514 **108** 1l. multicoloured 15 20
515 – 2l. multicoloured 15 20
516 – 3l. multicoloured 15 20
517 – 4l. multicoloured 15 20
518 – 75l. multicoloured . . . . 1·25 75
519 – 4r. multicoloured . . . . 2·50 4·00
520 – 5r. multicoloured . . . . 2·50 4·00
MS521 88 × 95 mm. 10r. multicoloured . . . . 10·00 12·00
DESIGNS: Nos. 515/**MS**521 show football scenes similar to Type **108**.

1974. Signs of the Zodiac. Multicoloured.
522 1l. Type **109** 20 40
523 2l. "Aquarius" 20 40
524 3l. "Pisces" 20 40
525 4l. "Aries" 20 40
526 5l. "Taurus" 20 40
527 6l. "Gemini" 20 40
528 7l. "Cancer" 20 40
529 10l. "Leo" 30 40
530 15l. "Virgo" 30 40
531 20l. "Libra" 30 40
532 25l. "Scorpio" 30 40
533 5r. "Sagittarius" . . . . . . 6·00 12·00
MS534 119 × 99 mm. 10r. "The Sun" (49 × 37 mm) . . . . 17·00 19·00

110 Churchill and Avro Type 683 Lancaster
111 Bullmouth Helmet

1974. Birth Cent of Sir Winston Churchill. Mult.
535 1l. Type **110** 20 50
536 2l. Churchill as pilot 20 50
537 3l. Churchill as First Lord of the Admiralty 25 50
538 4l. Churchill and H.M.S. "Eagle" (aircraft carrier) 25 50
539 5l. Churchill and De Havilland Mosquito bombers 25 30
540 60l. Churchill and anti-aircraft battery . . . . . 3·00 1·75
541 75l. Churchill and tank in desert . . . . 3·25 1·75
542 5r. Churchill and Short S.25 Sunderland flying boat . . 12·00 13·00
MS543 113 × 83 mm. 10r. As 4l. 17·00 20·00

1975. Sea Shells and Cowries. Multicoloured.
544 1l. Type **111** 10 30
545 2l. Venus comb murex . . . 10 30
546 3l. Common or major harp 10 30
547 4l. Chiragra spider conch . . 10 30
548 5l. Geography cone 10 30
549 60l. Dawn cowrie (22 × 30 mm) . . . . 3·00 2·00
550 75l. Purplish clanculus (22 × 30 mm) . . . . 3·50 2·00
551 5r. Ramose murex . . . . . 8·50 11·00
MS552 152 × 126 mm. 2r. As 3l.; 3r. As 2l. . . . . 12·00 15·00

112 Royal Throne **113** Guavas

1975. Historical Relics and Monuments. Mult.
553 1l. Type **112** 10 40
554 10l. Candlesticks 10 10
555 25l. Lamp-tree 15 10
556 60l. Royal umbrellas 30 30
557 75l. Eid-Miskith Mosque (horiz) 35 35
558 3r. Tomb of Al-Hafiz Abu-al Barakath-al Barubari (horiz) . . . . 1·60 2·75

1975. Exotic Fruits. Multicoloured.
559 2l. Type **113** 10 40
560 4l. Maldive mulberry 15 40
561 5l. Mountain apples 15 40
562 10l. Bananas 20 15
563 20l. Mangoes 40 25
564 50l. Papaya . . . . 1·00 60
565 1r. Pomegranates . . . . . . 1·75 70
566 5r. Coconut . . . . 5·50 11·00
MS567 136 × 102 mm. 2r. As 10l.; 3r. As 2l. . . . . 9·00 13·00

114 "Phyllangia"

1975. Marine Life. Corals, Urchins and Sea Stars. Multicoloured.
568 1l. Type **114** 10 30
569 2l. "Madrepora oculata" . . 10 30
570 3l. "Acropora gravida" . . . 10 30
571 4l. "Stylotella" 10 30
572 5l. "Acrophora cervicornis" 10 30
573 60l. "Strongylocentrotus purpuratus" 75 65
574 75l. "Pisaster ochraceus" . . 85 75
575 5r. "Marthasterias glacialis" 5·00 6·50
MS576 155 × 98 mm. 4r. As 1l. Imperf . . . . 11·00 14·00

115 Clock Tower and Customs Building within "10"

1975. 10th Anniv of Independence. Multicoloured.
577 4l. Type **115** 10 20
578 5l. Government offices . . . 10 15
579 7l. Waterfront 10 20
580 15l. Mosque and minaret . . 10 15
581 10r. Sultan Park and museum 2·25 6·00

1975. "Nordjamb 75" World Scout Jamboree, Norway. Nos. 443/5 and **MS**446 optd **14th Boy Scout Jamboree July 29–August 7, 1975**.
582 – 1r. multicoloured 85 60
583 – 2r. multicoloured . . . . . 1·25 80
584 **99** 3r. multicoloured . . . . . 1·75 1·60
MS585 101 × 79 mm. 5r. multicoloured . . . . 7·00 8·00

117 Madura Prau

1975. Ships. Multicoloured.
586 1l. Type **117** 10 20
587 2l. Ganges patela 10 20
588 3l. Indian palla (vert) 10 20
589 4l. Odhi (dhow) (vert) . . . 10 20
590 5l. Maldivian schooner . . . 10 20
591 25l. "Cutty Sark" (British tea clipper) 90 40
592 1r. Maldivian baggala (vert) 1·50 70
593 5r. "Maldive Courage" (freighter) . . . . 3·00 6·00
MS594 99 × 85 mm. 10r. As 1r. 10·00 14·00

118 "Brahmophthalma wallichi" (moth)

1975. Butterflies and Moth. Multicoloured.
595 1l. Type **118** 15 30
596 2l. "Teinopalpus imperialis" 15 30
597 3l. "Cethosia biblis" 15 30
598 4l. "Idea jasonia" 15 30
599 5l. "Apatura ilia" 15 30
600 25l. "Kallima horsfieldi" . . 1·25 35
601 1r.50 "Hebomoia leucippe" 3·50 3·75
602 5r. "Papilio memnon" . . . 8·00 10·00
MS603 134 × 97 mm. 10r. As 25l. 20·00 20·00

119 "The Dying Captive" **120** Beaker and Vase

1975. 500th Birth Anniv of Michelangelo. Mult.
604 1l. Type **119** 10 20
605 2l. Detail of "The Last Judgement" 10 20
606 3l. "Apollo" 10 20
607 4l. Detail of Sistine Chapel ceiling 10 20
608 5l. "Bacchus" 10 20
609 1r. Detail of "The Last Judgement" (different) . . 1·25 30
610 2r. "David" . . . . 1·50 2·00
611 5r. "Cumaean Sibyl" . . . . 2·25 5·00
MS612 123 × 113 mm. 10r. As 2r. 5·00 11·00

1975. Maldivian Lacquerware. Multicoloured.
613 2l. Type **120** 10 50
614 4l. Boxes 10 50
615 50l. Jar with lid 30 20
616 75l. Bowls with covers . . . 40 30
617 1r. Craftsman at work . . . 50 40

121 Map of Maldives

1975. Tourism. Multicoloured.
618 4l. Type **121** 30 40
619 5l. Motor launch and small craft 30 40
620 7l. Sailing-boats 30 40
621 15l. Underwater fishing . . . 30 30
622 3r. Hulule Airport . . . . . 4·50 3·00
623 10r. Motor cruisers . . . . . 6·50 7·50

122 Cross-country Skiing **123** "General Burgoyne" (Reynolds)

1976. Winter Olympic Games, Innsbruck. Mult.
624 1l. Type **122** 10 20
625 2l. Speed-skating (pairs) . . . 10 20
626 3l. Figure-skating (pairs) . . 10 20
627 4l. Four-man bobsleighing . . 10 20
628 5l. Ski-jumping 10 20
629 25l. Figure-skating (women's) 35 20
630 1r.15 Skiing (slalom) . . . . 90 1·25
631 4r. Ice-hockey . . . . 1·50 4·00
MS632 93 × 117 mm. 10r. Downhill Skiing . . . . 6·00 12·00

1976. Bicent of American Revolution. Mult.
633 1l. Type **123** 10 10
634 2l. "John Hancock" (Copley) 10 10
635 3l. "Death of Gen. Montgomery" (Trumbull) (horiz) 10 10
636 4l. "Paul Revere" (Copley) 10 10
637 5l. "Battle of Bunker Hill" (Trumbull) (horiz) 10 10
638 2r. "The Crossing of the Delaware" (Sully) (horiz) 2·00 2·50
639 3r. "Samuel Adams" (Copley) 2·50 3·00
640 5r. "Surrender of Cornwallis" (Trumbull) (horiz) . . . . 3·00 3·25
MS641 147 × 95 mm. 10r. "Washington at Dorchester Heights" (Stuart) . . . . . . 14·00 17·00

124 Thomas Edison

1976. Centenary of Telephone. Multicoloured.
642 1l. Type **124** 10 30
643 2l. Alexander Graham Bell 10 30
644 3l. Telephone of 1919, 1937 and 1972 . . . . 10 30
645 10l. Cable entrance into station 20 20
646 20l. Equalizer circuit assembly 30 20
647 1r. "Salernum" (cable ship) 1·75 55
648 10r. "Intelsat IV-A" and Earth Station . . . . . . 4·75 7·50
MS649 156 × 105 mm. 4r. Early telephones . . . . 7·50 9·00

1976. "Interphil 76" International Stamp Exhibition, Philadelphia. Nos. 638/**MS**641 optd **MAY 29TH–JUNE 6TH "INTERPHIL" 1976**.
650 2r. multicoloured . . . . . . 1·50 1·75
651 3r. multicoloured . . . . . . 2·00 2·25
652 5r. multicoloured . . . . . . 2·50 2·75
MS653 147 × 95 mm. 10r. multicoloured . . . . 10·00 12·00

126 Wrestling **127** "Dolichos lablab"

1976. Olympic Games, Montreal. Multicoloured.
654 1l. Type **126** 10 20
655 2l. Putting the shot 10 20
656 3l. Hurdling 10 20
657 4l. Hockey 10 20
658 5l. Running 10 20
659 6l. Javelin-throwing 10 20
660 1r.50 Discus-throwing . . . . 1·25 1·75
661 5r. Volleyball . . . . 2·75 5·25
MS662 135 × 106 mm. 10r. Throwing the hammer . . . . 8·50 12·00

1976. Vegetables. Multicoloured.
663 2l. Type **127** 10 40
664 4l. "Moringa pterygosperma" 10 40
665 10l. "Solanum melongena" 15 15
666 20l. "Moringa pterygosperma" . . . . . 2·00 2·00
667 50l. "Cucumis sativus" . . . 50 65
668 75l. "Trichosanthes anguina" 55 75
669 1r. "Momordica charantia" 65 85
670 2r. "Trichosanthes anguina" 3·50 7·00

128 "Viking" approaching Mars

1977. "Viking" Space Mission. Multicoloured.
671 5r. Type **128** . . . . . . 2·25 2·75
MS672 121 × 89 mm. 20r. Landing module on Mars . . . . 10·00 14·00

129 Coronation Ceremony

1977. Silver Jubilee of Queen Elizabeth II. Mult.
673 1l. Type **129** 10 30
674 2l. Queen and Prince Philip 10 30
675 3l. Royal couple with Princes Andrew and Edward . . . 10 30
676 1r.15 Queen with Archbishops 45 35
677 3r. State coach in procession 75 55
678 4r. Royal couple with Prince Charles and Princess Anne 75 90
MS679 120 × 77 mm. 10r. Queen and Prince Charles . . . . 4·50 3·25

130 Beethoven and Organ

1977. 150th Death Anniv of Ludwig van Beethoven. Multicoloured.
680 1l. Type **130** 20 30
681 2l. Portrait and manuscript of "Moonlight Sonata" . . . 20 30
682 3l. With Goethe at Teplitz . . 20 30
683 4l. Beethoven and string instruments 20 30
684 5l. Beethoven's home, Heiligenstadt 20 20
685 25l. Hands and gold medals 1·00 20
686 2r. Portrait and "Missa solemnis" . . . . 3·50 3·50
687 5r. Composer's hearing-aids 5·50 6·50
MS688 121 × 92 mm. 4r. Death mask and room where composer died 7·00 9·00

131 Printed Circuit and I.T.U. Emblem

1977. Inauguration of Satellite Earth Station. Mult.
689 10l. Type **131** 10 10
690 90l. Central Telegraph Office 45 45
691 10r. Satellite Earth Station 3·00 6·00
MS692 100 × 85 mm. 5r. "Intelsat IV-A" satellite over Maldives 4·50 5·50

132 "Miss Anne Ford" (Gainsborough) **133** Lesser Frigate Birds

1977. Artists' Birth Anniversaries. Multicoloured.
693 1l. Type **132** (250th anniv) . . 10 20
694 2l. Group painting by Rubens (400th anniv) . . . 10 20
695 3l. "Girl with Dog" (Titian) (500th Anniv) 10 20
696 4l. "Mrs. Thomas Graham" (Gainsborough) 10 20
697 5l. "Artist with Isabella Brant" (Rubens) 10 20
698 95l. Portrait by Titian . . . 1·00 30
699 1r. Portrait by Gainsborough 1·00 30
700 10r. "Isabella Brant" (Rubens) . . . . 3·75 7·00
MS701 152 × 116 mm. 5r. "Self-portrait" (Titian) . . . . . . 3·75 5·50

1977. Birds. Multicoloured.
702 1l. Type **133** 20 40
703 2l. Crab plover 20 40
704 3l. White-tailed tropic bird 20 40
705 4l. Wedge-tailed shearwater 20 40
706 5l. Grey heron 20 40
707 20l. White tern 90 30
708 95l. Cattle egret . . . . . . 2·25 1·60
709 1r.25 Black-naped tern . . . 2·50 2·50
710 5r. Pheasant coucal . . . . . 6·50 8·00
MS711 124 × 117 mm. 10r. Green-backed heron . . . . 25·00 25·00

134 Charles Lindbergh **136** Rheumatic Heart

135 Boat Building

1977. 50th Anniv of Lindbergh's Transatlantic Flight and 75th Anniv of First Navigable Airships. Multicoloured.

712 1l. Type **134** 20 30
713 2l. Lindbergh and "Spirit of St. Louis" 20 30
714 3l. Lindbergh's Miles Mohawk aircraft (horiz) . . 20 30
715 4l. Lebaudy-Juillot airship "Morning Post" (horiz) . . 20 30
716 5l. Airship "Graf Zeppelin" and portrait of Zeppelin 20 30
717 1r. Airship "Los Angeles" (horiz) . . . . 1·00 30
718 3r. Lindbergh and Henry Ford . . . . 1·75 2·00
719 10r. Vickers airship R-23 rigid airship . . . . . . 2·50 6·00
MS720 148 × 114 mm. 5r. Ryan NYP Special "Spirit of St. Louis", Statue of Liberty and Eiffel Tower; 7r.50, Airship L-31 over "Ostfriesland" (German battleship) . . . . 13·00 18·00

No. 715 is inscr "Lebaudy I built by H. Juillot 1902".

1977. Occupations. Multicoloured.

721 6l. Type **135** 45 30
722 15l. Fishing 75 20
723 20l. Cadjan weaving 80 20
724 90l. Mat-weaving . . . . . . 2·50 1·60
725 2r. Lace-making (vert) . . . 4·00 4·25

1977. World Rheumatism Year. Multicoloured.

726 1l. Type **136** 10 30
727 50l. Rheumatic shoulder . . 40 20
728 2r. Rheumatic hands . . . . 75 1·25
729 3r. Rheumatic knees . . . . 85 1·40

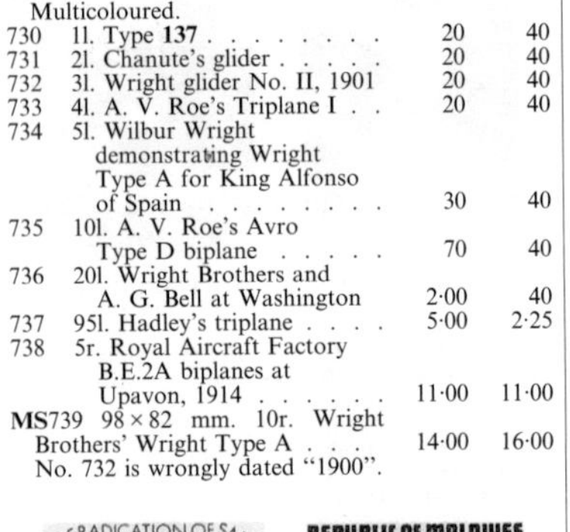

137 Lilienthal's Biplane Glider

1978. 75th Anniv of First Powered Aircraft. Multicoloured.

730 1l. Type **137** 20 40
731 2l. Chanute's glider 20 40
732 3l. Wright glider No. II, 1901 20 40
733 4l. A. V. Roe's Triplane I . . 20 40
734 5l. Wilbur Wright demonstrating Wright Type A for King Alfonso of Spain 30 40
735 10l. A. V. Roe's Avro Type D biplane 70 40
736 20l. Wright Brothers and A. G. Bell at Washington 2·00 40
737 95l. Hadley's triplane . . . . 5·00 2·25
738 5r. Royal Aircraft Factory B.E.2A biplanes at Upavon, 1914 . . . . . . 11·00 11·00
MS739 98 × 82 mm. 10r. Wright Brothers' Wright Type A . . . . 14·00 16·00

No. 732 is wrongly dated "1900".

138 Newgate Prison 139 Television Set

1978. World Eradication of Smallpox. Mult.

740 15l. Foundling Hospital, London (horiz) 50 30
741 50l. Type **138** . . . . 1·25 60
742 2r. Edward Jenner (discoverer of smallpox vaccine) . . . 2·25 4·00

1978. Inaug of Television in Maldive Islands. Mult.

743 15l. Type **139** 40 30
744 25l. Television aerials 55 30
745 1r.50 Control desk (horiz) . . 2·25 2·75

140 Mas Odi

1978. Ships. Multicoloured.

746 1l. Type **140** 10 25
747 2l. Battela 10 25
748 3l. Bandu odi (vert) 10 25
749 5l. "Maldive Trader" (freighter) 20 25
750 1r. "Fath-hul Baaree" (brigantine) 65 30
751 1r.25 Mas dhoni . . . . . . 85 1·00
752 3r. Baggala (vert) . . . . . 1·10 1·75
753 4r. As 1r.25 . . . . 1·10 1·75
MS754 152 × 138 mm. 1r. As No. 747; 4r. As No. 751 . . . 2·50 3·75

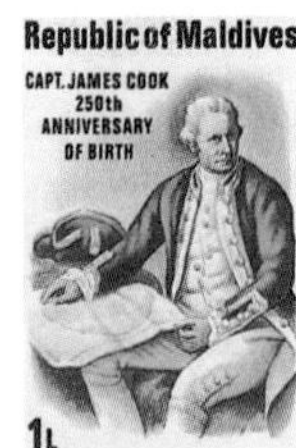

141 Ampulla 142 Capt. Cook

1978. 25th Anniv of Coronation. Multicoloured.

755 1l. Type **141** 10 20
756 2l. Sceptre with Dove 10 20
757 3l. Golden Orb 10 20
758 1r.15 St. Edward's Crown . . 25 20
759 2r. Sceptre with Cross . . . 35 35
760 5r. Queen Elizabeth II . . . 65 80
MS761 108 × 106 mm. 10r. Annointing spoon . . . . . . 1·50 2·00

1978. 250th Birth Anniv of Capt. James Cook and Bicent of Discovery of Hawaiian Islands. Mult.

762 1l. Type **142** 10 25
763 2l. Statue of Kamehameha I of Hawaii 10 25
764 3l. H.M.S. "Endeavour" . . 10 25
765 25l. Route of third voyage . . 45 45
766 75l. H.M.S. "Discovery", H.M.S. "Resolution" and map of Hawaiian Islands (horiz) . . . . 1·25 1·25
767 1r.50 Cook meeting Hawaiian islanders (horiz) . . . . . 2·00 2·25
768 10r. Death of Capt. Cook (horiz) . . . . 4·00 10·00
MS769 100 × 92 mm. 5r. H.M.S. "Endeavour" (different) . . . 15·00 20·00

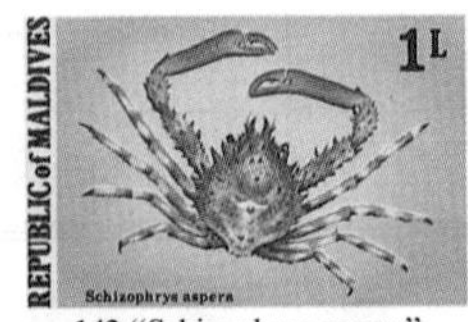

143 "Schizophrys aspera"

1978. Crustaceans. Multicoloured.

770 1l. Type **143** 10 25
771 2l. "Atergatis floridus" . . . 10 25
772 3l. "Perenon planissimum" . . 10 25
773 90l. "Portunus granulatus" . . 50 40
774 1r. "Carpilius maculatus" . . 50 40
775 2r. "Huenia proteus" . . . . 1·00 1·40
776 25r. "Etisus laevimanus" . . . 5·50 13·00
MS777 147 × 146 mm. 2r. "Panulirus longipes" (vert) . . . . 2·00 2·50

144 "Four Apostles" 145 T.V. Tower and Building

1978. 450th Death Anniv of Albrecht Durer (artist).

778 **144** 10l. multicoloured 10 10
779 – 20l. multicoloured 15 10
780 – 55l. multicoloured 20 20
781 – 1r. black, brown and buff 30 30
782 – 1r.80 multicoloured . . . 45 60
783 – 3r. multicoloured . . . . 70 1·25
MS784 141 × 122 mm. 10r. multicoloured . . . . 4·00 6·00

DESIGNS—VERT: 20l. "Self-portrait at 27"; 55l. "Madonna and Child with a Pear"; 1r.80, "Hare"; 3r. "Great Piece of Turf"; 10r. "Columbine". HORIZ: 1r. "Rhinoceros".

1978. 10th Anniv of Republic. Multicoloured.

785 1l. Fishing boat (horiz) . . . 10 40
786 5l. Montessori School (horiz) 10 20
787 10l. Type **145** 10 10
788 25l. Islet (horiz) 20 15
789 50l. Boeing 737 aircraft (horiz) 60 25
790 95l. Beach scene (horiz) . . . 60 30
791 1r.25 Dhow at night (horiz) 75 55
792 3r. President's residence (horiz) . . . . 80 1·25
793 5r. Masjidh Afeefuddin Mosque (horiz) . . . . . 1·00 2·75
MS794 119 × 88 mm. 3r. Fisherman casting net . . . . 2·25 4·00

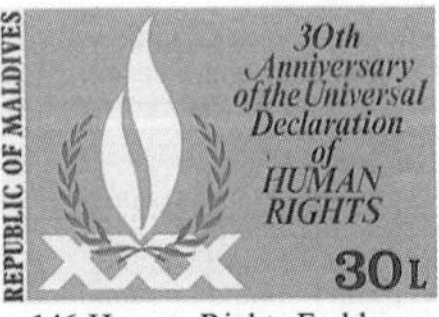

146 Human Rights Emblem

1978. 30th Anniv of Declaration of Human Rights.

795 **146** 30l. pink, lilac and green 15 15
796 90l. yellow, brown and green 40 60
797 1r.80 blue, deep blue and green . . . . 70 1·00

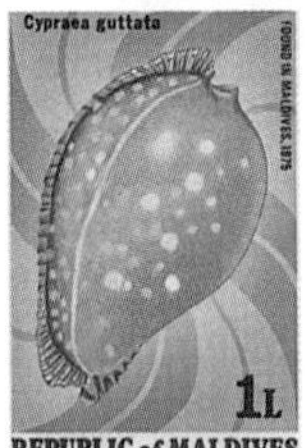

147 Great Spotted or Rare Spotted Cowrie 148 Delivery by Bellman

1979. Shells. Multicoloured.

798 1l. Type **147** 10 20
799 2l. Imperial cone 10 20
800 3l. Great green turban . . . 10 20
801 10l. Giant spider conch . . . 45 10
802 1r. White-toothed cowrie . . 2·00 40
803 1r.80 Fig cone . . . . 3·00 2·50
804 3r. Glory of the sea cone . . 4·50 3·75
MS805 141 × 110 mm. 5r. Common Pacific vase . . . . 11·00 10·50

1979. Death Cent of Sir Rowland Hill. Mult.

806 1l. Type **148** 10 20
807 2l. Mail coach, 1840 (horiz) 10 20
808 3l. First London letter box, 1855 . . . . 10 20
809 1r.55 Penny Black 40 50
810 5r. First Maldive Islands stamp . . . . 70 1·25
MS811 132 × 107 mm. 10r. Sir Rowland Hill . . . . 1·25 3·00

149 Girl with Teddy Bear 151 Sari with Overdress

150 "White Feathers"

1979. Int Year of the Child (1st issue). Mult.

812 5l. Type **149** 10 10
813 1r.25 Boy with sailing boat 40 50
814 2r. Boy with toy rocket . . . 45 55
815 3r. Boy with toy airship . . . 60 75
MS816 108 × 109 mm. 5r. Boy with toy train . . . . 1·25 2·00

See also Nos. 838/**MS**847.

1979. 25th Death Anniv of Henri Matisse (artist). Multicoloured.

817 20l. Type **150** 15 15
818 25l. "Joy of Life" 15 15
819 30l. "Eggplants" 15 15
820 1r.50 "Harmony in Red" . . 45 65
821 5r. "Still-life" . . . . 70 2·25
MS822 135 × 95 mm. 4r. "Water Pitcher" . . . . 3·50 4·00

1979. National Costumes. Multicoloured.

823 50l. Type **151** 20 15
824 75l. Sashed apron dress . . . 25 20
825 90l. Serape 30 25
826 95l. Ankle-length printed dress 35 30

152 "Gloriosa superba"

1979. Flowers. Multicoloured.

827 1l. Type **152** 10 10
828 3l. "Hibiscus tiliaceus" . . . 10 10
829 50l. "Barringtonia asiatica" 20 15
830 1r. "Abutilon indicum" . . . 40 25
831 5r. "Guettarda speciosa" . . 1·00 2·00
MS832 94 × 85 mm. 4r. "Pandanus odoratissimus" . . . . 1·75 2·75

153 Weaving

1979. Handicraft Exhibition. Multicoloured.

833 5l. Type **153** 10 10
834 10l. Lacquerwork 10 10
835 1r.30 Tortoiseshell jewellery 35 45
836 2r. Carved woodwork 50 80
MS837 125 × 85 mm. 5r. Gold and silver jewellery . . . . 1·25 2·25

154 Mickey Mouse attacked by Bird

1979. International Year of the Child (2nd issue). Disney Characters. Multicoloured.

838 1l. Goofy delivering parcel on motor-scooter (vert) . . . 10 10
839 2l. Type **154** 10 10
840 3l. Goofy half-covered with letters 10 10
841 4l. Pluto licking Minnie Mouse's envelopes 10 10
842 5l. Mickey Mouse delivering letters on roller skates (vert) 10 10
843 10l. Donald Duck placing letter in mail-box 10 10
844 15l. Chip and Dale carrying letter 10 10
845 1r.50 Donald Duck on monocycle (vert) 75 95
846 5r. Donald Duck with ostrich in crate (vert) . . . . . . 2·25 3·25
MS847 127 × 102 mm. 4r. Pluto putting parcel in mail-box . . 5·50 7·00

155 Post-Ramadan Dancing

1980. National Day. Multicoloured.

848 5l. Type **155** 10 10
849 15l. Musicians and dancer, Eeduu Festival 10 10
850 95l. Sultan's ceremonial band 35 30
851 2r. Dancer and drummers Circumcision Festival . . . 60 85
MS852 131 × 99 mm. 5r. Swordsmen 1·40 2·50

156 Leatherback Turtle

1980. Turtle Conservation Campaign. Mult.

853 1l. Type **156** 10 30
854 2l. Flatback turtle 10 30
855 5l. Hawksbill turtle 15 30
856 10l. Loggerhead turtle . . . 20 20
857 75l. Olive Ridley turtle . . . 80 45
858 10r. Atlantic Ridley turtle . . 3·00 4·25
MS859 85 × 107 mm. 4r. Green turtle 2·00 2·75

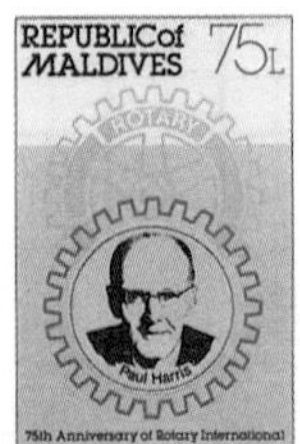

157 Paul Harris (founder)

1980. 75th Anniv of Rotary Int. Mult.

860 75l. Type **157** 35 10
861 90l. Humanity 40 20
862 1r. Hunger 40 25
863 10r. Health . . . . 2·75 4·50
MS864 109 × 85 mm. 5r. Globe 1·50 2·50

1980. "London 1980" International Stamp Exhibition. Nos. 809/**MS**811 optd **LONDON 1980**.

865 1r.55 Penny Black . . . . . 2·25 1·00
866 5r. First Maldives stamp . . 3·75 2·75
MS867 132 × 107 mm. 10r. Sir Rowland Hill . . . . 7·00 8·00

159 Swimming

1980. Olympic Games, Moscow. Multicoloured.
868 10l. Type **159** 10 10
869 50l. Running 20 20
870 3r. Putting the shot . . . . . 70 1·10
871 4r. High jumping . . . . . . 80 1·40
MS872 105 × 85 mm. 5r. Weightlifting . . . . 1·25 2·25

160 White-tailed Tropic Bird

1980. Birds. Multicoloured.
873 75l. Type **160** 25 15
874 95l. Sooty tern 35 30
875 1r. Common noddy 35 30
876 1r.55 Curlew 50 70
877 2r. Wilson's storm petrel ("Wilson's Petrel") 60 85
878 4r. Caspian tern . . . . . . 1·10 1·60
MS879 124 × 85 mm. 5r. Red-footed booby and brown booby . . . 7·00 8·00

161 Seal of Ibrahim II

1980. Seals of the Sultans.
880 **161** 1l. brown and black . . . 10 10
881 – 2l. brown and black . . . 10 10
882 – 5l. brown and black . . . 10 10
883 – 1r. brown and black . . . 30 30
884 – 2r. brown and black . . . 50 70
MS885 131 × 95 mm. 3r. brown and black . . . . 85 1·60
DESIGNS: 2l. Mohammed Imadudeen II; 5l. Bin Haji Ali; 1r. Kuda Mohammed Rasgefaanu; 2r. Ibrahim Iskander I; 3r. Ibrahim Iskander I (different).

162 Queen Elizabeth the Queen Mother

1980. 80th Birthday of the Queen Mother.
886 **162** 4r. multicoloured . . . . 1·00 1·25
MS887 85 × 110 mm. **162** 5r. multicoloured . . . . 1·90 2·25

163 Munnaru

1980. 1400th Anniv of Hegira. Multicoloured.
888 5l. Type **163** 15 10
889 10l. Hukuru Miskiiy mosque 20 10
890 30l. Medhuziyaaraiy (shrine of saint) 25 30
891 55l. Writing tablets with verses of Koran 35 35
892 90l. Mother teaching child Koran 55 70
MS893 124 × 101 mm. 2r. Map of Maldives and coat of arms . . 80 1·60

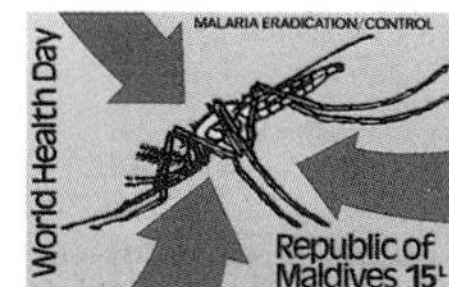

164 Malaria Eradication

1980. World Health Day.
894 **164** 15l. black, brown and red 10 10
895 – 25l. multicoloured 10 10
896 – 1r.50 brown, light brown and black . . . . . . 1·25 1·00
897 – 5r. multicoloured . . . . 2·50 2·75
MS898 68 × 85 mm. 4r. black, blue and light blue . . . . 1·25 2·50
DESIGNS: 25l. Nutrition; 1r.50, Dental health; 4, 5r. Clinics.

165 White Rabbit

1980. Walt Disney's "Alice in Wonderland". Multicoloured.
899 1l. Type **165** 10 10
900 2l. Alice falling into Wonderland 10 10
901 3l. Alice too big to go through door 10 10
902 4l. Alice with Tweedledum and Tweedledee 10 10
903 5l. Alice and caterpillar . . . 10 10
904 10l. The Cheshire cat 10 10
905 15l. Alice painting the roses 10 10
906 2r.50 Alice and the Queen of Hearts . . . . 2·00 2·25
907 4r. Alice on trial . . . . . . 2·25 2·50
MS908 126 × 101 mm. 5r. Alice at the Mad Hatter's tea-party . . 4·50 6·50

166 Indian Ocean Ridley Turtle

1980. Marine Animals. Multicoloured.
909 90l. Type **166** . . . . 2·25 60
910 1r.25 Pennant coralfish . . . 2·75 1·25
911 2r. Spiny lobster . . . . . . 3·25 1·75
MS912 140 × 94 mm. 4r. Oriental sweetlips and scarlet-finned squirrelfish . . . . 3·00 3·25

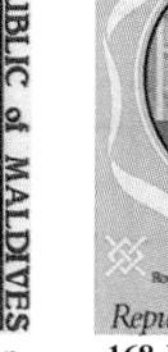

167 Pendant Lamp

168 Prince Charles and Lady Diana Spencer

1981. National Day. Multicoloured.
913 10l. Tomb of Ghaazee Muhammad Thakurufaan (horiz) 15 10
914 20l. Type **167** 20 10
915 30l. Chair used by Muhammad Thakurufaan 25 10
916 95l. Muhammad Thakurufaan's palace (horiz) 60 30
917 10r. Cushioned divan . . . . 2·50 4·25

1981. British Royal Wedding. Multicoloured.
918 1r. Type **168** 15 15
919 2r. Buckingham Palace . . . 25 25
920 5r. Prince Charles, polo player 40 50
MS921 95 × 83 mm. 10r. State coach 75 1·10

169 First Majlis Chamber

1981. 50th Anniv of Citizens' Majlis (grievance rights). Multicoloured.
922 95l. Type **169** 30 30
923 1r. Sultan Muhammed Shamsuddin III 35 35
MS924 137 × 94 mm. 4r. First written constitution (horiz) . . 1·75 3·75

170 "Self-portrait with a Palette"

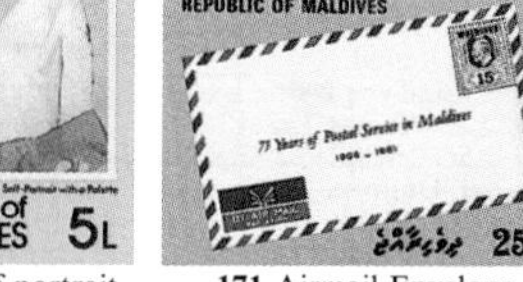

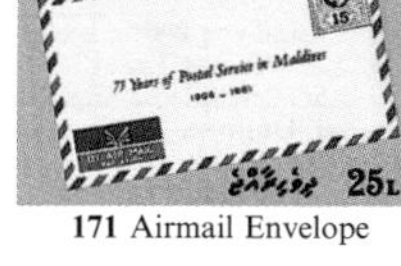

171 Airmail Envelope

1981. Birth Centenary of Pablo Picasso. Mult.
925 5l. Type **170** 15 10
926 10l. "Woman in Blue" . . . 20 10
927 25l. "Boy with Pipe" 30 10
928 30l. "Card Player" 30 10
929 90l. "Sailor" 50 40
930 3r. "Self-portrait" . . . . . 80 1·00
931 5r. "Harlequin" . . . . . . 1·00 1·25
MS932 106 × 130 mm. 10r. "Child holding a Dove". Imperf . . . 2·50 3·50

1981. 75th Anniv of Postal Service.
933 **171** 25l. multicoloured 15 10
934 75l. multicoloured 25 25
935 5r. multicoloured . . . . 70 1·25

172 Boeing 737 taking off

1981. Male International Airport. Multicoloured.
936 5l. Type **172** 20 20
937 20l. Passengers leaving Boeing 737 . . . . 40 20
938 1r.80 Refuelling . . . . . . 75 1·00
939 4r. Plan of airport . . . . . 1·00 2·00
MS940 106 × 79 mm. 5r. Aerial view of airport . . . . 2·00 2·75

173 Homer

174 Preparation of Maldive Fish

1981. International Year of Disabled People. Multicoloured.
941 2l. Type **173** 10 10
942 5l. Miguel Cervantes 10 10
943 1r. Beethoven . . . . 2·00 85
944 5r. Van Gogh . . . . 3·00 5·00
MS945 116 × 91 mm. 4r. Helen Keller and Anne Sullivan . . . 3·25 5·50

1981. Decade for Women. Multicoloured.
946 20l. Type **174** 10 10
947 90l. 16th-century Maldive women 25 25
948 1r. Farming 30 30
949 2r. Coir rope-making . . . . 55 1·10

175 Collecting Bait

1981. Fishermen's Day. Multicoloured.
950 5l. Type **175** 45 15
951 15l. Fishing boats 85 25
952 90l. Fisherman with catch . . 1·40 60
953 1r.30 Sorting fish . . . . . . 1·90 1·10
MS954 147 × 101 mm. 3r. Loading fish for export . . . . 1·50 2·50

176 Bread Fruit

1981. World Food Day. Multicoloured.
955 10l. Type **176** 35 10
956 25l. Hen with chicks 70 15
957 30l. Maize 70 20
958 75l. Skipjack tuna . . . . . 2·25 65
959 1r. Pumpkin . . . . 2·75 70
960 2r. Coconuts . . . . 3·00 3·25
MS961 110 × 85 mm. 5r. Eggplant 2·50 3·50

177 Pluto and Cat

1982. 50th Anniv of Pluto (Walt Disney Cartoon Character). Multicoloured.
962 4r. Type **177** . . . . 2·50 2·75
MS963 127 × 101 mm. 6r. Pluto (scene from "The Pointer") . . 3·25 4·00

178 Balmoral

180 Footballer

179 Scout saluting and Camp-site

1982. 21st Birthday of Princess of Wales. Mult.
964 95l. Type **178** 50 20
965 3r. Prince and Princess of Wales . . . . 1·00 65
966 5r. Princess on aircraft steps 1·75 95
MS967 103 × 75 mm. 8r. Princess of Wales . . . . 1·75 1·75

1983. 75th Anniv of Boy Scout Movement. Multicoloured.
968 1r.30 Type **179** 40 45
969 1r.80 Lighting a fire 50 60
970 4r. Life-saving . . . . 1·10 1·40
971 5r. Map-reading . . . . . . 1·40 1·75
MS972 128 × 66 mm. 10r. Scout emblem and flag of the Maldives 2·00 3·00

1982. World Cup Football Championship, Spain.
973 **180** 90l. multicoloured . . . . 1·50 60
974 – 1r.50 multicoloured . . . 2·00 1·10
975 – 3r. multicoloured . . . . 2·75 1·75
976 – 5r. multicoloured . . . . 3·25 2·50
MS977 94 × 63 mm. 10r. multicoloured . . . . 4·50 6·00
DESIGNS: 1r.50 to 10r. Various footballers.

1982. Birth of Prince William of Wales. Nos. 964/MS967 optd **ROYAL BABY 21.6.82.**
978 95l. Type **178** 20 20
979 3r. Prince and Princess of Wales 60 65
980 5r. Princess on aircraft steps 80 95
MS981 103 × 75 mm. 8r. Princess of Wales . . . . 3·00 2·50

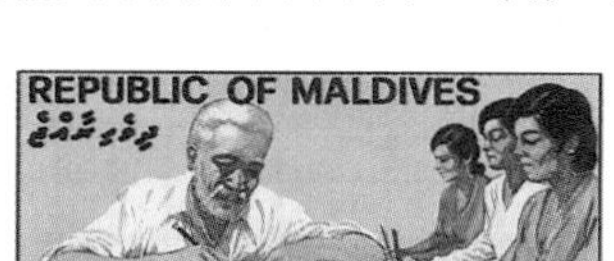

181 Basic Education Scheme

1983. National Education. Multicoloured.
982 90l. Type **181** 15 25
983 95l. Primary education . . . 15 25
984 1r.30 Teacher training . . . 20 30
985 2r.50 Printing educational material 40 60
MS986 100 × 70 mm. 6r. Thaana typewriter keyboard . . . . . 1·00 2·00

182 Koch isolates the Bacillus

183 Blohm and Voss Seaplane "Nordsee"

1983. Centenary of Robert Koch's Discovery of Tubercle Bacillus. Multicoloured.
987 5l. Type **182** 10 15
988 15l. Micro-organism and microscope 15 15
989 95l. Dr. Robert Koch in 1905 35 45
990 3r. Dr. Koch and plates from publication . . . . . . 85 1·50
MS991 77 × 61 mm. 5r. Koch in his laboratory (horiz) . . . . . . 1·00 2·00

1983. Bicentenary of Manned Flight. Mult.
992 90l. Type **183** . . . . 2·25 70
993 1r.45 Macchi Castoldi MC.72 seaplane . . . . 2·75 1·75
994 4r. Boeing F4B-3 biplane fighter . . . . 4·50 3·25
995 5r. Renard and Krebs airship "La France" . . . . . . 4·50 3·50
MS996 110 × 85 mm. 10r. Nadar's balloon "Le Geant" . . . . . 3·00 4·00

184 "Curved Dash" Oldsmobile, 1902

1983. Classic Motor Cars. Multicoloured.
997 5l. Type **184** 20 40
998 30l. Aston Martin "Tourer", 1932 . . . . 60 40
999 40l. Lamborghini "Muira", 1966 . . . . 60 45
1000 1r. Mercedes-Benz "300SL", 1945 . . . . 1·00 70
1001 1r.40 Stutz "Bearcat", 1913 1·25 2·00
1002 5r. Lotus "Elite", 1958 . . . 2·00 4·25
MS1003 132 × 103 mm. 10r. Grand Prix "Sunbeam", 1924 . . . . 6·00 10·00

185 Rough-toothed Dolphin

1983. Marine Mammals. Multicoloured.
1004 30l. Type **185** . . . . 1·60 60
1005 40l. Indo-Pacific hump-backed dolphin . . . . . 1·60 65
1006 4r. Finless porpoise . . . . 5·00 4·00
1007 6r. Pygmy sperm whale . . 10·00 7·00
MS1008 82 × 90 mm. 5r. Striped dolphin . . . . 6·00 5·50

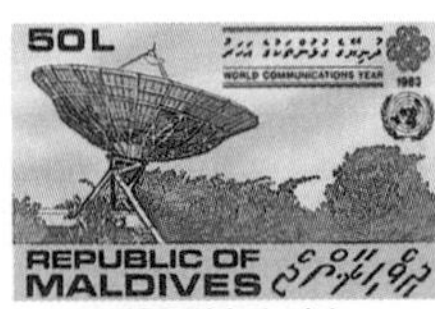

186 Dish Aerial

1983. World Communications Year. Multicoloured.
1009 50l. Type **186** 40 20
1010 1r. Land, sea and air communications . . . . . 1·25 60
1011 2r. Ship-to-shore communications . . . . . 1·75 1·50
1012 10r. Air traffic controller . . 4·00 7·00
MS1013 91 × 76 mm. 20r. Telecommunications . . . . . 3·75 4·75

187 "La Donna Gravida"

1983. 500th Birth Anniv of Raphael. Mult.
1014 90l. Type **187** 25 25
1015 3r. "Giovanna d'Aragona" (detail) . . . . 75 1·60
1016 4r. "Woman with Unicorn" 75 2·25
1017 6r. "La Muta" . . . . 1·00 2·75
MS1018 121 × 97 mm. 10r. "The Knight's Dream" (detail) . . . 3·00 5·50

188 Refugee Camp

1983. Solidarity with the Palestinian People. Multicoloured.
1019 4r. Type **188** . . . . 1·75 2·00
1020 5r. Refugee holding dead child . . . . 1·90 2·00
1021 6r. Child carrying food . . 2·00 2·50

189 Education Facilities

1983. National Development Programme. Mult.
1022 7l. Type **189** 20 10
1023 10l. Health service and education 50 10
1024 5r. Growing more food . . 1·50 1·25
1025 6r. Fisheries development 2·25 1·50
MS1026 134 × 93 mm. 10r. Air transport . . . . 2·25 2·75

190 Baseball

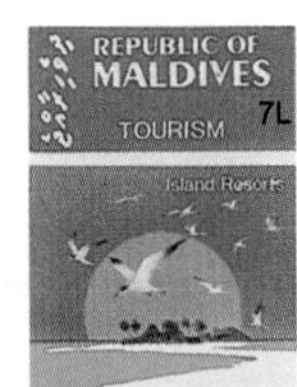

194 Island Resort and Common Terns

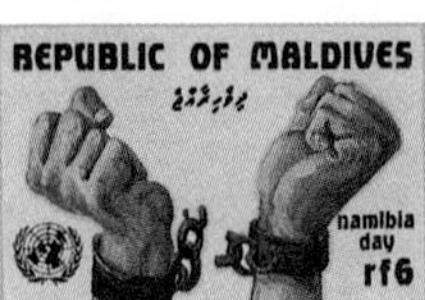

193 Hands breaking Manacles

1984. Olympic Games, Los Angeles. Multicoloured.
1027 50l. Type **190** 30 15
1028 1r.55 Backstroke swimming 65 40
1029 3r. Judo . . . . 1·40 90
1030 4r. Shot-putting . . . . . . 1·60 1·40
MS1031 85 × 105 mm. 10r. Team handball . . . . 2·40 2·75

1984. U.P.U. Congress, Hamburg. Nos. 994/**MS**996 optd **19th UPU CONGRESS HAMBURG**.
1032 4r. Boeing "F4B-3" . . . . 1·40 1·40
1033 5r. "La France" airship . . 1·60 1·60
MS1034 110 × 85 mm. 10r. Nadar's balloon "Le Geant" . . . . . 2·75 4·50

1984. Surch **Rf.1.45**. (a) Nos. 964/**MS**967.
1035 1r.45 on 95l. Type **178** . . . 2·00 1·50
1036 1r.45 on 3r. Prince and Princess of Wales . . . . 2·00 1·50
1037 1r.45 on 5r. Princess on aircraft steps . . . . . . 2·00 1·50
MS1038 103 × 75 mm. 1r.45 on 8r. Princess of Wales . . . . . . 2·00 3·75

(b) Nos. 978/**MS**981.
1039 1r.45 on 95l. Type **178** . . . 2·00 1·50
1040 1r.45 on 3r. Prince and Princess of Wales . . . . 2·00 1·50
1041 1r.45 on 5r. Princess on aircraft steps . . . . . . 2·00 1·50
MS1042 103 × 75 mm. 1r.45 on 8r. Princess of Wales . . . . . . 2·00 3·75

1984. Namibia Day. Multicoloured.
1043 6r. Type **193** . . . . 1·00 1·25
1044 8r. Namibian family . . . . 1·00 1·75
MS1045 129 × 104 mm. 10r. Map of Namibia . . . . 1·75 2·50

1984. Tourism. Multicoloured.
1046 7l. Type **194** 85 40
1047 15l. Dhow 60 15
1048 20l. Snorkelling 45 15
1049 2r. Wind-surfing . . . . . 1·50 50
1050 4r. Aqualung diving . . . . 2·00 1·10
1051 6r. Night fishing . . . . . 2·75 1·75
1052 8r. Game fishing . . . . . 3·00 2·00
1053 10r. Turtle on beach . . . . 3·25 2·25

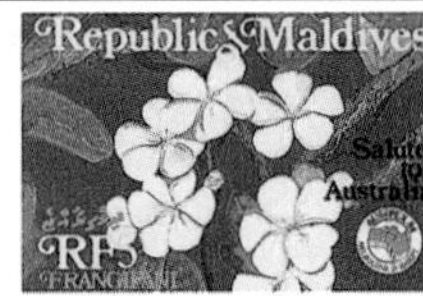

195 Frangipani

1984. "Ausipex" International Stamp Exhibition, Melbourne. Multicoloured.
1054 5r. Type **195** . . . . 2·25 1·75
1055 10r. Cooktown orchid . . . 4·75 3·75
MS1056 105 × 77 mm. 15r. Sun orchid . . . . 10·00 5·50

196 Facade of Male Mosque

1984. Opening of Islamic Centre. Multicoloured.
1057 2r. Type **196** 45 50
1058 5r. Male Mosque and minaret (vert) . . . . . . 1·10 1·25

197 Air Maldives Boeing 737

1984. 40th Anniv of I.C.A.O. Multicoloured.
1059 7l. Type **197** 50 15
1060 4r. Air Lanka Lockheed L-1011 TriStar . . . . . 2·50 1·25
1061 6r. Alitalia Douglas DC-10-30 . . . . 3·00 1·60
1062 8r. L.T.U. Lockheed L-1011 TriStar . . . . 3·25 2·25
MS1063 110 × 92 mm. 15r. Air Maldives Short S.7 Skyvan . . 3·75 4·00

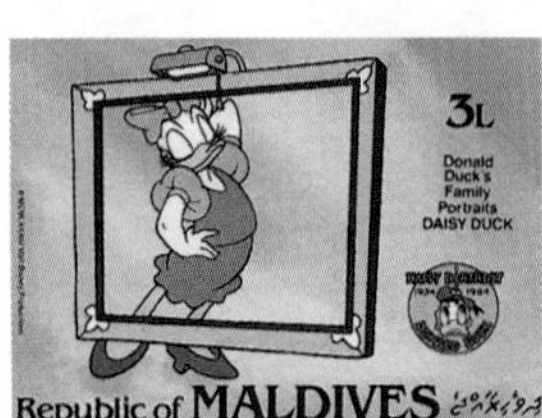

198 Daisy Duck

1984. 50th Birthday of Donald Duck. Walt Disney Cartoon Characters. Multicoloured.
1064 3l. Type **198** 10 10
1065 4l. Huey, Dewey and Louie 10 10
1066 5l. Ludwig von Drake . . . 10 10
1067 10l. Gyro Gearloose 10 10
1068 15l. Uncle Scrooge painting self-portrait 15 10
1069 25l. Donald Duck with camera 15 10
1070 5r. Donald Duck and Gus Goose . . . . 2·25 1·25
1071 8r. Gladstone Gander . . . 2·50 2·00
1072 10r. Grandma Duck . . . . 3·00 2·50
MS1073 102 × 126 mm. 15r. Uncle Scrooge and Donald Duck in front of camera . . . . 4·75 5·00
MS1074 126 × 102 mm. 15r. Uncle Scrooge . . . . 4·75 5·00

199 "The Day" (detail)

200 "Edmond Iduranty" (Degas)

1984. 450th Death Anniv of Correggio (artist). Multicoloured.
1075 5r. Type **199** . . . . 1·00 1·50
1076 10r. "The Night" (detail) . . 1·50 1·75
MS1077 60 × 80 mm. 15r. "Portrait of a Man" . . . . 3·50 3·25

1984. 150th Birth Anniv of Edgar Degas (artist). Multicoloured.
1078 75l. Type **200** 20 20
1079 2r. "James Tissot" 50 50
1080 5r. "Achille de Gas in Uniform" . . . . 1·00 1·00
1081 10r. "Lady with Chrysanthemums" . . . . 1·75 2·00
MS1082 100 × 70 mm. 15r. "Self-portrait" . . . . 3·25 3·75

201 Pale-footed Shearwater ("Flest-footed Shearwater")

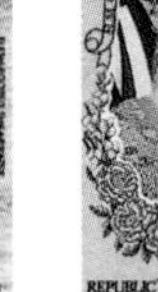

204 Queen Elizabeth the Queen Mother, 1981

202 Squad Drilling

1985. Birth Bicentenary of John J. Audubon (ornithologist) (1st issue). Designs showing original paintings. Multicoloured.
1083 3r. Type **201** . . . . 1·75 80
1084 3r.50 Little grebe (horiz) . . 2·00 90
1085 4r. Great cormorant . . . . 2·00 1·00
1086 4r.50 White-faced storm petrel (horiz) . . . . . . 2·00 1·10
MS1087 108 × 80 mm. 15r. Red-necked phalarope (horiz) . . . 3·50 3·50
See also Nos. 1192/200.

1985. National Security Service. Multicoloured.
1088 15l. Type **202** 50 10
1089 20l. Combat patrol 50 10
1090 1r. Fire fighting . . . . . . 2·00 40
1091 2r. Coastguard cutter . . . 2·50 1·00
1092 10r. Independence Day Parade (vert) . . . . . . 3·25 3·50
MS1093 128 × 85 mm. 10r. Cannon on saluting base and National Security Service badge . . . . 2·25 2·25

1985. Olympic Games Gold Medal Winners, Los Angeles. Nos. 1027/31 optd.
1094 50l. Type **190** (optd **JAPAN**) 30 10
1095 1r.55 Backstroke swimming (optd **GOLD MEDALIST THERESA ANDREWS USA**) 60 40
1096 3r. Judo (optd **GOLD MEDALIST FRANK WIENEKE USA**) . . . . 1·25 75
1097 4r. Shot-putting (optd **GOLD MEDALIST CLAUDIA LOCH WEST GERMANY**) . . . . . . 1·25 95
MS1098 85 × 105 mm. 10r. Team handball (optd **U.S.A.**) . . . . 1·90 2·00

1985. Life and Times of Queen Elizabeth the Queen Mother. Multicoloured.
1099 3r. Type **204** 45 60
1100 5r. Visiting the Middlesex Hospital (horiz) . . . . . 65 1·00
1101 7r. The Queen Mother . . . 85 1·25
MS1102 56 × 85 mm. 15r. With Prince Charles at Garter Ceremony . . . . 4·00 3·25
Stamps as Nos. 1099/1101 but with face values of 1r., 4r. and 10r. exist from additional sheetlets with changed background colours.

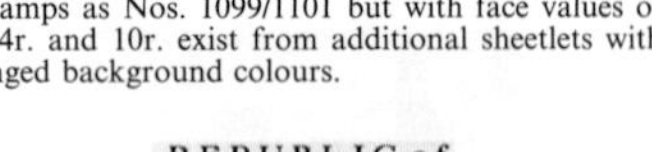

204a Lira da Braccio

1985. 300th Birth Anniversary of Johann Sebastian Bach (composer). Multicoloured (except No. **MS**1107).
1103 15l. Type **204a** 10 10
1104 2r. Tenor oboe 50 45
1105 4r. Serpent 90 85
1106 10r. Table organ . . . . . 1·90 2·25
MS1107 104 × 75 mm. 15r. Johann Sebastian Bach (black and orange) 3·00 3·50

205 Mas Odi (fishing boat)

1985. Maldives Ships and Boats. Multicoloured.
1108 3l. Type **205** 10 20
1109 5l. Battela (dhow) 10 20

1110 10l. Addu odi (dhow) . . . 10 20
1111 2r.60 Modern dhoni (fishing boat) . . . . 1·50 1·60
1112 2r.70 Mas dhoni (fishing boat) . . . . 1·50 1·60
1113 3r. Baththeli dhoni . . . . . 1·60 1·60
1114 5r. "Inter I" (inter-island vessel) . . . . 2·50 2·75
1115 10r. Dhoni-style yacht . . . 4·25 6·00

206 Windsurfing

207 United Nations Building, New York

1985. 10th Anniv of World Tourism Organization. Multicoloured.
1116 6r. Type **206** . . . . 2·25 1·75
1117 8r. Scuba diving . . . . . 2·50 2·00
MS1118 171 × 114 mm. 15r. Kuda Hithi Resort . . . . 2·75 3·00

1985. 40th Anniv of U.N.O. and International Peace Year. Multicoloured.
1119 15l. Type **207** 10 10
1120 2r. Hands releasing peace dove 40 45
1121 4r. U.N. Security Council meeting (horiz) 70 85
1122 10r. Lion and lamb . . . . 1·25 2·00
MS1123 76 × 92 mm. 15r. U.N. building and peace dove . . . 2·25 2·75

208 Maldivian Delegate voting in U.N. General Assembly

1985. 20th Anniv of United Nations Membership. Multicoloured.
1124 20l. Type **208** 10 10
1125 15r. U.N. and Maldivian flags, and U.N. Building, New York . . . . 2·00 3·00

209 Youths playing Drums

1985. International Youth Year. Multicoloured.
1126 90l. Type **209** 15 20
1127 6r. Tug-of-war . . . . . . 80 1·10
1128 10r. Community service (vert) . . . . 1·25 2·00
MS1129 85 × 84 mm. 15r. Raising the flag at youth camp (vert) 2·25 3·00

210 Quotation and Flags of Member Nations

1985. 1st Summit Meeting of South Asian Association for Regional Co-operation, Dhaka, Bangladesh.
1130 **210** 3r. multicoloured . . . . 1·50 1·25

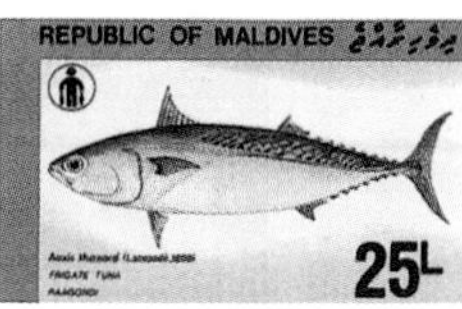

211 Mackerel Frigate

1985. Fishermen's Day. Species of Tuna. Mult.
1131 25l. Type **211** 35 10
1132 75l. Kawakawa ("Little tuna") 65 15
1133 3r. Dog-toothed tuna . . . 2·00 75
1134 5r. Yellow-finned tuna . . . 2·50 1·25
MS1135 130 × 90 mm. 15r. Skipjack tuna . . . . 3·50 3·50

1985. 150th Birth Anniv of Mark Twain. Designs as T **160a** of Lesotho, showing Walt Disney cartoon characters illustrating various Mark Twain quotations. Multicoloured.
1136 2l. Winnie the Pooh (vert) 10 10
1137 3l. Gepetto and Figaro the cat (vert) 10 10
1138 4l. Goofy and basket of broken eggs (vert) 10 10
1139 20l. Goofy as doctor scolding Donald Duck (vert) 25 10
1140 4r. Mowgli and King Louis (vert) . . . . 1·40 1·75
1141 13r. The wicked Queen and mirror (vert) . . . . . . 5·00 7·00
MS1142 126 × 101 mm. 15r. Mickey Mouse as Tom Sawyer on comet's tail . . . . 6·50 7·00

1985. Birth Bicentenaries of Grimm Brothers (folklorists). Designs as T **160b** of Lesotho, showing Walt Disney cartoon characters in scenes from "Dr. Knowall". Multicoloured.
1143 1l. Donald Duck as Crabb driving oxcart (horiz) . . 10 10
1144 5l. Donald Duck as Dr. Knowall (horiz) . . . 10 10
1145 10l. Dr. Knowall in surgery (horiz) 10 10
1146 15l. Dr. Knowall with Uncle Scrooge as a lord (horiz) 10 10
1147 3r. Dr. and Mrs. Knowall in pony and trap (horiz) . . 1·10 1·50
1148 15r. Dr. Knowall and thief (horiz) . . . . 5·50 7·00
MS1149 126 × 101 mm. 15r. Donald and Daisy Duck as Dr. and Mrs. Knowall . . . . 6·50 7·00

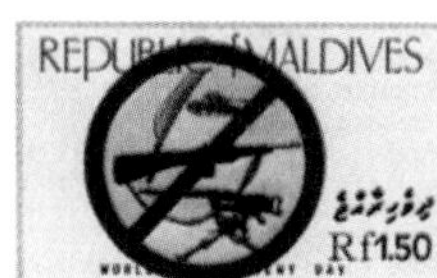

211a Weapons on Road Sign

1986. World Disarmament Day. Multicoloured.
1149a 1r.50 Type **211a** . . . . .
1149b 10r. Peace dove . . . . .

1986. Appearance of Halley's Comet (1st issue). As T **162a** of Lesotho. Multicoloured.
1150 20l. N.A.S.A. space telescope and Comet . . . 50 25
1151 1r.50 E.S.A. "Giotto" spacecraft and Comet . . 1·25 1·50
1152 2r. Japanese "Planet A" spacecraft and Comet . . 1·50 1·75
1153 4r. Edmond Halley and Stonehenge . . . . 2·25 2·75
1154 5r. Russian "Vega" spacecraft and Comet . . 2·25 2·75
MS1155 101 × 70 mm. 15r. Halley's Comet . . . . 8·00 9·50
See also Nos. 1206/11.

1986. Centenary of Statue of Liberty. Multicoloured. As T **163b** of Lesotho, showing the Statue of Liberty and immigrants to the U.S.A.
1156 50l. Walter Gropius (architect) 40 30
1157 70l. John Lennon (musician) 1·75 1·00
1158 1r. George Balanchine (choreographer) . . . . . 1·75 1·00
1159 10r. Franz Werfel (writer) 3·75 7·00
MS1160 100 × 72 mm. 15r. Statue of Liberty (vert) . . . . 6·00 7·00

1986. "Ameripex" International Stamp Exhibition, Chicago. As T **163c** of Lesotho, showing Walt Disney cartoon characters and U.S.A. stamps. Multicoloured.
1161 3l. Johnny Appleseed and 1966 Johnny Appleseed stamp 10 10
1162 4l. Paul Bunyan and 1958 Forest Conservation stamp 10 10
1163 5l. Casey and 1969 Professional Baseball Centenary stamp 10 10
1164 10l. Ichabod Crane and 1974 "Legend of Sleepy Hollow" stamp 10 10
1165 15l. John Henry and 1944 75th Anniv of completion of First Transcontinental Railroad stamp 15 15
1166 20l. Windwagon Smith and 1954 Kansas Territory Centenary stamp 15 15
1167 13r. Mike Fink and 1970 Great Northwest stamp 7·00 7·00
1168 14r. Casey Jones and 1950 Railroad Engineers stamp 8·00 8·00
MS1169 Two sheets, each 127 × 101 mm. (a) 15r. Davy Crockett and 1967 Davy Crockett stamp. (b) 15r. Daisy Duck as Pocahontas saving Captain John Smith (Donald Duck) Set of 2 sheets . . . . 12·00 15·00

1986. 60th Birthday of Queen Elizabeth II. As T **163** of Lesotho.
1170 1r. black and yellow 30 25
1171 2r. multicoloured 40 55
1172 12r. multicoloured . . . . . 1·50 2·50
MS1173 120 × 85 mm. 15r. black and brown . . . . 3·75 4·25
DESIGNS: 1r. Royal Family at Girl Guides Rally, 1938; 2r. Queen in Canada; 12r. At Sandringham, 1970; 15r. Princesses Elizabeth and Margaret at Royal Lodge, Windsor, 1940.

212 Player running with Ball

1986. World Cup Football Championship, Mexico. Multicoloured.
1174 15l. Type **212** 75 30
1175 2r. Player gaining control of ball . . . . 2·50 1·75
1176 4r. Two players competing for ball . . . . 4·00 3·50
1177 10r. Player bouncing ball on knee . . . . 7·50 8·00
MS1178 95 × 114 mm. 15r. Player kicking ball . . . . 5·00 6·00

1986. Royal Wedding. As T **170a** of Lesotho. Multicoloured.
1179 10l. Prince Andrew and Miss Sarah Ferguson . . 15 10
1180 2r. Prince Andrew 75 70
1181 12r. Prince Andrew in naval uniform . . . . 3·25 3·75
MS1182 88 × 88 mm. 15r. Prince Andrew and Miss Sarah Ferguson (different) . . . . 4·25 4·50

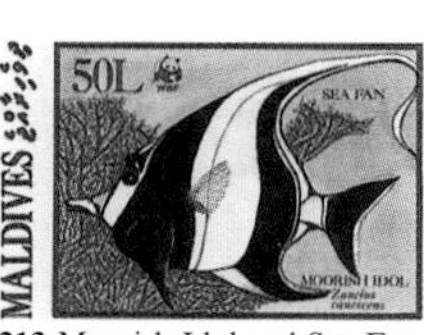

213 Moorish Idol and Sea Fan (213b)

1986. Marine Wildlife. Multicoloured.
1183 50l. Type **213** . . . . 1·50 40
1184 90l. Regal angelfish . . . . 2·00 55
1185 1r. Maldive anemonefish . . 2·00 55
1186 2r. Tiger cowrie and stinging coral . . . . 2·50 1·60
1187 3r. Emperor angelfish and staghorn coral . . . . . 2·50 2·00
1188 4r. Black-naped tern . . . . 3·00 3·00
1189 5r. Fiddler crab and staghorn coral . . . . . 2·50 3·00
1190 10r. Hawksbill turtle . . . . 3·00 5·00
MS1191 Two sheets, each 107 × 76 mm. (a) 15r. Long-nosed butterflyfish. (b) 15r. Oriental trumpetfish Set of 2 sheets . . 12·00 15·00

1986. Birth Bicentenary (1985) of John J. Audubon (ornithologist) (2nd issue). As T **201** showing original paintings. Multicoloured.
1192 3l. Little blue heron (horiz) 40 60
1193 4l. White-tailed kite 40 60
1194 5l. Greater shearwater (horiz) 40 60
1195 10l. Magnificent frigate bird 45 40
1196 15l. Black-necked grebe ("Eared Grebe") 85 40
1197 20l. Goosander ("Common Merganser") 90 40
1198 13r. Peregrine falcon ("Great Footed Hawk") (horiz) . . . . 7·00 7·50
1199 14r. Prairie chicken ("Greater Prairie Chicken") (horiz) . . . . 7·00 7·50
MS1200 Two sheets, each 74 × 104 mm. (a) 15r. Fulmar ("Northern Fulmar"). (b) 15r. White-fronted goose (horiz) Set of 2 sheets . . . . 22·00 21·00

1986. World Cup Football Championship Winners, Mexico. Nos. 1174/7 optd **WINNERS Argentina 3 W. Germany 2**.
1201 15l. Type **212** 40 30
1202 2r. Player gaining control of ball . . . . 1·25 1·10
1203 4r. Two players competing for ball . . . . 2·00 2·00
1204 10r. Player bouncing ball on knee . . . . 3·25 4·25
MS1205 95 × 114 mm. 15r. Player kicking ball . . . . 3·00 4·25

1986. Appearance of Halley's Comet (2nd issue). Nos. 1150/4 optd with T **213b**.
1206 20l. N.A.S.A. space telescope and Comet . . . 65 40
1207 1r.50 E.S.A. "Giotto" spacecraft and Comet . . 1·25 1·00
1208 2r. Japanese "Planet A" spacecraft and Comet . . 1·50 1·50
1209 4r. Edmond Halley and Stonehenge . . . . 2·00 2·25
1210 5r. Russia "Vega" spacecraft and Comet . . . . 2·00 2·25
MS1211 101 × 70 mm. 15r. Halley's Comet . . . . 5·00 5·50

214 Servicing Aircraft

216 Ixora

215 "Hypholoma fasciculare"

1986. 40th Anniv of U.N.E.S.C.O. Multicoloured.
1212 1r. Type **214** 70 30
1213 2r. Boat building . . . . . . 80 1·00
1214 3r. Children in classroom . . 90 1·40
1215 5r. Student in laboratory . . 1·00 2·50
MS1216 77 × 100 mm. 15r. Diving bell on sea bed . . . . 2·75 4·25

1986. Fungi of the Maldives. Multicoloured.
1217 15l. Type **215** 80 25
1218 50l. "Kuehneromyces mutabilis" (vert) . . . . 1·50 45
1219 1r. "Amanita muscaria" (vert) . . . . 1·75 60
1220 2r. "Agaricus campestris" 2·50 1·50
1221 3r. "Amanita pantherina" (vert) . . . . 2·50 1·75
1222 4r. "Coprinus comatus" (vert) . . . . 2·50 2·25
1223 5r. "Gymnopilus junonius" ("Pholiota spectabilis") 2·50 2·75
1224 10r. "Pluteus cervinus" . . 3·75 4·50
MS1225 Two sheets, each 100 × 70 mm. (a) 15r. "Armillaria mellea". (b) 15r. "Stropharia aeruginosa" (vert) Set of 2 sheets 15·00 14·00

1987. Flowers. Multicoloured.
1226 10l. Type **216** 10 10
1227 20l. Frangipani 10 10
1228 50l. Crinum . . . . 1·50 60
1229 2r. Pink rose 40 80
1230 4r. Flamboyant flower . . . 60 1·50
1231 10r. Ground orchid . . . . 4·75 7·00
MS1232 Two sheets, each 100 × 70 mm. (a) 15r. Gardenia. (b) 15r. Oleander Set of 2 sheets 4·75 6·50

217 Guides studying Wild Flowers

1987. 75th Anniv (1985) of Girl Guide Movement. Multicoloured.
1233 15l. Type **217** 30 20
1234 2r. Guides with pet rabbits 60 80
1235 4r. Guide observing white spoonbill . . . . 2·25 2·25
1236 12r. Lady Baden-Powell and Guide flag . . . . 2·50 6·00
MS1237 104 × 78 mm. 15r. Guides in sailing dinghy . . . . 2·25 3·75

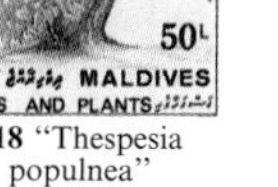

218 "Thespesia populnea"

219 "Precis octavia"

1987. Trees and Plants. Multicoloured.
1238 50l. Type **218** 10 10
1239 1r. "Cocos nucifera" 15 20
1240 2r. "Calophyllum mophyllum" 30 40
1241 3r. "Xanthosoma indica" (horiz) 45 60
1242 5r. "Ipomoea batatas" (horiz) . . . . 80 1·10
1243 7r. "Artocarpus altilis" . . . 1·10 1·75
MS1244 75 × 109 mm. 15r. "Cocos nucifera" (different) . . . . . 2·25 3·25
No. 1241 is inscr "Xyanthosomaindica" in error.

1987. America's Cup Yachting Championship. As T **218a** of Lesotho. Multicoloured.
1245 15l. "Intrepid", 1970 . . . 10 10
1246 1r. "France II", 1974 . . . 20 20
1247 2r. "Gretel", 1962 . . . . . 40 60
1248 12r. "Volunteer", 1887 . . . 2·00 3·00
MS1249 113 × 83 mm. 15r. Helmsman and crew on deck of "Defender", 1895 (horiz) . . . 2·25 3·25

1987. Butterflies. Multicoloured.
1250 15l. Type **219** 45 30
1251 20l. "Atrophaneura hector" 45 30
1252 50l. "Teinopalpus imperialis" 75 40
1253 1r. "Kallima horsfieldi" . . 1·00 45
1254 2r. "Cethosia biblis" . . . . 1·60 1·25
1255 4r. "Idea jasonia" . . . . . 2·50 2·25
1256 7r. "Papilio memnon" . . . 3·50 4·00
1257 10r. "Aeropetes tulbaghia" 4·00 5·00
MS1258 Two sheets, each 135 × 102 mm. (a) 15r. "Acraea violae". (b) 15r. "Hebomoia leucippe" Set of 2 sheets . . . 9·00 11·00

220 Isaac Newton experimenting with Spectrum

1988. Great Scientific Discoveries. Multicoloured.
1259 1r.50 Type **220** . . . . . . 1·25 1·00
1260 3r. Euclid composing "Principles of Geometry" (vert) . . . . 1·60 1·75
1261 4r. Mendel formulating theory of Genetic Evolution (vert) . . . . . 1·75 2·00
1262 5r. Galileo and moons of Jupiter . . . . 3·00 3·00
MS1263 102 × 72 mm. 15r. "Apollo" lunar module (vert) . . . . . 4·50 5·50

221 Donald Duck and Weather Satellite

1988. Space Exploration. Walt Disney cartoon characters. Multicoloured.
1264 3l. Type **221** 10 10
1265 4l. Minnie Mouse and navigation satellite . . . 10 10
1266 5l. Mickey Mouse's nephews talking via communication satellite 10 10
1267 10l. Goofy in lunar rover (vert) 10 10
1268 20l. Minnie Mouse delivering pizza to flying saucer (vert) 10 10
1269 13r. Mickey Mouse directing spacecraft docking (vert) 5·00 5·00
1270 14r. Mickey Mouse and "Voyager 2" . . . . . . 5·00 5·00
MS1271 Two sheets, each 127 × 102 mm. (a) 15r. Mickey Mouse at first Moon landing, 1969. (b) 15r. Mickey Mouse and nephews in space station swimming pool (vert) Set of 2 sheets . . . . 11·00 11·00

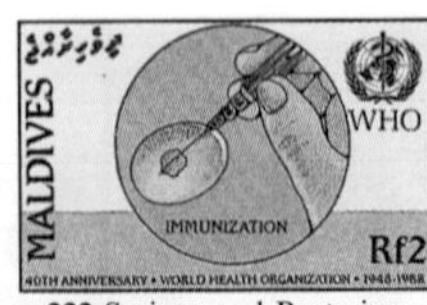

222 Syringe and Bacterium ("Immunization")

1988. 40th Anniv of W.H.O. Multicoloured.
1272 2r. Type **222** 40 40
1273 4r. Tap ("Clean Water") . . 60 85

223 Water Droplet and Atoll

1988. World Environment Day (1987). Mult.
1274 15l. Type **223** 10 10
1275 75l. Coral reef 20 40
1276 2r. Audubon's shearwaters in flight . . . . 85 1·40
MS1277 105 × 76 mm. 15r. Banyan tree (vert) . . . . 3·00 4·25

224 Globe, Carrier Pigeon and Letter **226** Discus-throwing

1988. Transport and Telecommunications Decade. Each showing central globe. Multicoloured.
1278 2r. Type **224** 60 65
1279 3r. Dish aerial and girl using telephone . . . . 1·00 1·10
1280 5r. Satellite, television, telephone and antenna tower . . . . 1·75 2·00
1281 10r. Car, ship and Lockheed TriStar airliner . . . . . 7·50 6·50

1988. Royal Ruby Wedding. Nos. 1170/3 optd **40TH WEDDING ANNIVERSARY H.M. QUEEN ELIZABETH II H.R.H. THE DUKE OF EDINBURGH**.
1282 1r. black and yellow 45 25
1283 2r. multicoloured 60 60
1284 12r. multicoloured . . . . . 2·75 3·50
MS1285 120 × 85 mm. 15r. black and brown . . . . 3·75 4·00

1988. Olympic Games, Seoul. Multicoloured.
1286 15l. Type **226** 10 10
1287 2r. 100 m race 40 40
1288 4r. Gymnastics (horiz) . . . 70 80
1289 12r. Three-day equestrian event (horiz) . . . . . . 2·25 3·25
MS1290 106 × 76 mm. 20r. Tennis (horiz) . . . . 3·75 4·50

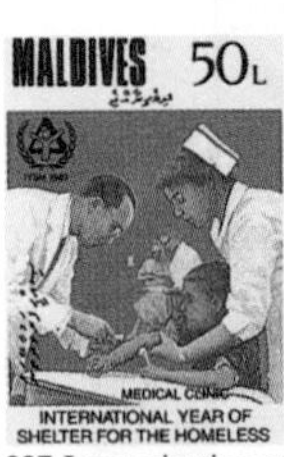

227 Immunization at Clinic **230** Pres. Kennedy and Launch of "Apollo" Spacecraft

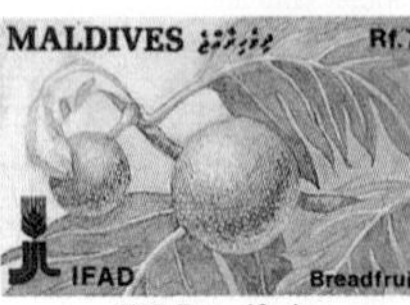

228 Breadfruit

1988. Int Year of Shelter for the Homeless. Mult.
1291 50l. Type **227** 30 30
1292 3r. Prefab housing estate . . 1·10 1·40
MS1293 63 × 105 mm. 15r. Building site . . . . 1·75 2·50

1988. 10th Anniv of International Fund for Agricultural Development. Multicoloured.
1294 7r. Type **228** . . . . 1·00 1·40
1295 10r. Mangoes (vert) . . . . 1·50 1·90
MS1296 103 × 74 mm. 15r. Coconut palm, fishing boat and yellowtail tuna . . . . 2·75 3·00

1988. World Aids Day. Nos. 1272/3 optd **WORLD AIDS DAY** and emblem.
1297 2r. Type **222** 35 45
1298 4r. "Tap" ("Clean Water") 65 80

1989. 25th Death Anniv (1988) of John F. Kennedy (American statesman). U.S. Space Achievements. Multicoloured.
1299 5r. Type **230** . . . . 1·90 2·00
1300 5r. Lunar module and astronaut on Moon . . . 1·90 2·00
1301 5r. Astronaut and buggy on Moon . . . . 1·90 2·00
1302 5r. President Kennedy and spacecraft . . . . 1·90 2·00
MS1303 108 × 77 mm. 15r. President Kennedy making speech . . . 3·50 4·25

1989. Olympic Medal Winners, Seoul. Nos. 1286/90 optd.
1304 15l. Type **226** (optd **J. SCHULT DDR**) 20 20
1305 2r. 100 m race (optd **C. LEWIS USA**) 65 65
1306 4r. Gymnastics (horiz) (optd **MEN'S ALL AROUND V. ARTEMOV USSR**) . . 1·40 1·40
1307 12r. Three-day equestrian event (horiz) (optd **TEAM SHOW JUMPING W. GERMANY**) . . . . 4·00 4·50
MS1308 106 × 76 mm. 20r. Tennis (horiz) (optd **OLYMPIC WINNERS MEN'S SINGLES GOLD M. MECIR CZECH SILVER T. MAYOTTE USA BRONZE B. GILBERT USA**) 5·00 6·00
On No. **MS**1308 the overprint appears on the sheet margin.

1989. 500th Birth Anniv of Titian (artist). As T **186a** of Lesotho, showing paintings. Multicoloured.
1309 15l. "Benedetto Varchi" . . 10 10
1310 1r. "Portrait of a Young Man" 20 15
1311 2r. "King Francis I of France" 40 40
1312 5r. "Pietro Aretino" . . . . 1·10 1·25
1313 15r. "The Bravo" . . . . . 3·50 5·00
1314 20r. "The Concert" (detail) 3·50 6·00
MS1315 Two sheets. (a) 112 × 96 mm. 20r. "An Allegory of Prudence" (detail). (b) 96 × 110 mm. 20r. "Francesco Maria della Rovere" Set of 2 sheets . . . . 6·50 8·00

1989. 10th Anniversary of Asia–Pacific Telecommunity. Nos. 1279/80 optd **ASIA-PACIFIC TELECOMMUNITY 10 YEARS** and emblem. Multicoloured.
1316 3r. Dish aerial and girl using telephone . . . . 1·25 1·50
1317 5r. Satellite, television, telephone and antenna tower . . . . 1·75 2·00

1989. Japanese Art. Paintings by Hokusai. As T **187a** of Lesotho. Multicoloured.
1318 15l. "Fuji from Hodogaya" (horiz) 10 10
1319 50l. "Fuji from Lake Kawaguchi" (horiz) . . . 15 15
1320 1r. "Fuji from Owari" (horiz) 25 15
1321 2r. "Fuji from Tsukudajima in Edo" (horiz) 50 40
1322 4r. "Fuji from a Teahouse at Yoshida" (horiz) . . . 80 90
1323 6r. "Fuji from Tagonoura" (horiz) . . . . 90 1·25
1324 10r. "Fuji from Mishima-goe" (horiz) . . . . . . 2·25 2·75
1325 12r. "Fuji from the Sumida River in Edo" (horiz) . . 2·25 2·75
MS1326 Two sheets, each 101 × 77 mm. (a) 18r. "Fuji from Inume Pass". (b) 18r. "Fuji from Fukagawa in Edo" Set of 2 sheets 8·50 9·00

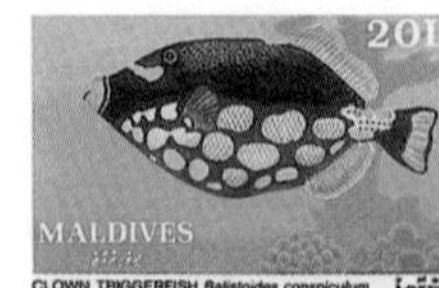

233 Clown Triggerfish

1989. Tropical Fishes. Multicoloured.
1327 20l. Type **233** 25 20
1328 50l. Blue-striped snapper . . 35 25
1329 1r. Powder-blue surgeonfish 45 30
1330 2r. Oriental sweetlips . . . 75 65
1331 3r. Six-barred wrasse . . . 1·00 85
1332 8r. Thread-finned butterflyfish . . . . . . 2·00 2·50
1333 10r. Bicoloured parrotfish 2·40 2·75
1334 12r. Scarlet-finned squirrelfish . . . . 2·40 2·75
MS1335 Two sheets, each 101 × 73 mm. (a) 15r. Butterfly perch. (b) 15r. Semicircle angelfish Set of 2 sheets . . . . 13·00 12·00

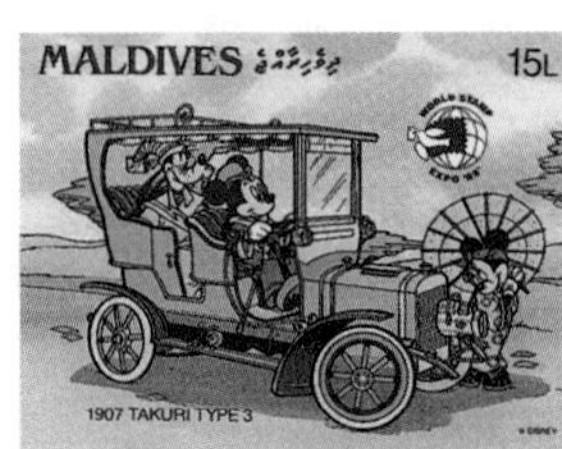

234 Goofy, Mickey and Minnie Mouse with Takuri "Type 3", 1907

1989. "World Stamp Expo '89" International Stamp Exhibition, Washington (1st issue). Designs showing Walt Disney cartoon characters with Japanese cars. Multicoloured.
1336 15l. Type **234** 20 15
1337 50l. Donald and Daisy Duck in Mitsubishi "Model A", 1917 . . . . 40 30
1338 1r. Goofy in Datsun "Roadstar", 1935 . . . . 70 50
1339 2r. Donald and Daisy Duck with Mazda, 1940 . . . . 1·00 75
1340 4r. Donald Duck with Nissan "Bluebird 310", 1959 . . . . 1·50 1·25
1341 6r. Donald and Daisy Duck with Subaru "360", 1958 1·75 1·75
1342 10r. Mickey Mouse and Pluto in Honda "5800", 1966 . . . . 3·25 3·75
1343 12r. Mickey Mouse and Goofy in Daihatsu "Fellow", 1966 . . . . . 3·75 4·25
MS1344 Two sheets, each 127 × 102 mm. (a) 20r. Daisy Duck with Chip n'Dale and Isuzu "Trooper II", 1981. (b) 20r. Mickey Mouse with tortoise and Toyota "Supra", 1985 Set of 2 sheets . . . . 11·00 13·00

1989. "World Stamp Expo '89" International Stamp Exhibition, Washington (2nd issue). Landmarks of Washington. Sheet 62 × 78 mm, containing multicoloured designs as T **193a** of Lesotho, but vert.
MS1345 8r. Marine Corps Memorial, Arlington National Cemetery . . . . 1·75 2·25

235 Lunar Module "Eagle"

1989. 20th Anniv of First Manned Landing on Moon. Multicoloured.
1346 1r. Type **235** 30 20
1347 2r. Astronaut Aldrin collecting dust samples . . 50 60
1348 6r. Aldrin setting up seismometer . . . . . . 1·25 1·75
1349 10r. Pres. Nixon congratulating "Apollo 11" astronauts 1·90 2·50
MS1350 107 × 75 mm. 18r. Television picture of Armstrong about to step onto Moon (34 × 47 mm) . . . . 4·00 4·75

236 Jawaharlal Nehru with Mahatma Gandhi

1989. Anniversaries and Events. Multicoloured.
1351 20l. Type **236** (birth cent) 2·25 80
1352 50l. Opium poppies and logo (anti-drugs campaign) (vert) . . . . 1·25 45
1353 1r. William Shakespeare (425th birth anniv) . . . 90 45
1354 2r. Storming the Bastille (bicent of French Revolution) (vert) . . . . 1·00 1·00
1355 3r. Concorde (20th anniv of first flight) . . . . 4·00 2·00
1356 8r. George Washington (bicent of inauguration) 2·00 3·00
1357 10r. William Bligh (bicent of mutiny on the "Bounty") 6·00 4·50
1358 12r. Hamburg harbour (800th anniv) (vert) . . . 3·75 5·00
MS1359 Two sheets. (a) 115 × 85 mm. 18r. Baseball players (50th anniv of first televised game) (vert). (b) 110 × 80 mm. 18r. Franz von Taxis (500th anniv of regular European postal services) (vert) Set of 2 sheets . . . . 12·00 14·00

237 Sir William van Horne (Chairman of Canadian Pacific), Locomotive and Map, 1894 **239** "Louis XVI in Coronation Robes" (Duplessis)

238 Bodu Thakurufaanu Memorial Centre, Utheemu

1989. Railway Pioneers. Multicoloured.
1360 10l. Type **237** 25 15
1361 25l. Matthew Murray (engineer) with Blenkinsop and Murray's rack locomotive, 1810 . . . . 35 20
1362 50l. Louis Favre (railway engineer) and steam locomotive entering tunnel 40 25
1363 2r. George Stephenson (engineer) and "Locomotion", 1825 . . . 75 55
1364 6r. Richard Trevithick and "Catch-Me-Who-Can", 1808 . . . . 1·50 1·50
1365 8r. George Nagelmackers and "Orient Express" dining car . . . . 1·75 1·75
1366 10r. William Jessop and horse-drawn wagon, Surrey Iron Railway, 1770 2·50 2·50
1367 12r. Isambard Brunel (engineer) and GWR steam locomotive, 1833 3·00 3·00
MS1368 Two sheets, each 71×103 mm. (a) 18r. George Pullman (inventor of sleeping cars), 1864. (b) 18r. Rudolf Diesel (engineer) and first oil engine Set of 2 sheets . . . . 7·50 8·50

1990. 25th Anniv of Independence. Multicoloured.
1369 20l. Type **238** 10 10
1370 25l. Islamic Centre, Male . . 10 10
1371 50l. National flag and logos of international organizations 10 10
1372 2r. Presidential Palace, Male 30 40
1373 5r. National Security Service 85 1·25
MS1374 128×90 mm. 10r. National emblem . . . . 2·75 3·25

1990. Bicentenary of French Revolution and "Philexfrance '89" International Stamp Exhibi-tion, Paris. French Paintings. Multicoloured.
1375 15l. Type **239** 15 15
1376 50l. "Monsieur Lavoisier and his Wife" (David) . . 30 25
1377 1r. "Madame Pastoret" (David) 45 35
1378 2r. "Oath of Lafayette, 14 July 1790" (anon) . . 70 70
1379 4r. "Madame Trudaine" (David) . . . . 1·25 1·50
1380 6r. "Chenard celebrating the Liberation of Savoy" (Boilly) . . . . 1·75 2·00
1381 10r. "An Officer swears Allegiance to the Constitution" (anon) . . 3·00 3·75
1382 12r. "Self Portrait" (David) 3·25 4·00
MS1383 Two sheets. (a) 104×79 mm. 20r. "The Oath of the Tennis Court, 20 June 1789" (David) (horiz). (b) 79×104 mm. 20r. "Rousseau and Symbols of the Revolution" (Jeaurat) Set of 2 sheets . . . . 9·50 11·00

239a Donald Duck, Mickey Mouse and Goofy Playing Rugby

1990. "Stamp World London '90" International Stamp Exhibition. Walt Disney cartoon characters playing British sports. Multicoloured.
1384 15l. Type **239a** 30 15
1385 50l. Donald Duck and Chip-n-Dale curling 45 25
1386 1r. Goofy playing polo . . . 65 40
1387 2r. Mickey Mouse and nephews playing soccer 90 70
1388 4r. Mickey Mouse playing cricket . . . . 1·75 1·50
1389 6r. Minnie and Mickey Mouse at Ascot races . . 2·25 1·90
1390 10r. Mickey Mouse and Goofy playing tennis . . 3·50 3·50
1391 12r. Donald Duck and Mickey Mouse playing bowls 3·50 3·50
MS1392 Two sheets, each 126×101 mm. (a) 20r. Minnie Mouse fox-hunting. (b) 20r. Mickey Mouse playing golf Set of 2 sheets . . . . . . 13·00 13·00

240 Silhouettes of Queen Elizabeth II and Queen Victoria

1990. 150th Anniv of the Penny Black.
1393 **240** 8r. black and green . . . 2·25 2·50
1394 – 12r. black and blue . . . 2·75 3·00
MS1395 109×84 mm. 18r. black and brown . . . . 4·00 4·75
DESIGN: 12r. As Type **240**, but with position of silhouettes reversed; 18r. Penny Black.

1990. 90th Birthday of Queen Elizabeth the Queen Mother. As T **198a** of Lesotho.
1396 6r. black, mauve and blue 90 1·10
1397 6r. black, mauve and blue 90 1·10
1398 6r. black, mauve and blue 90 1·10
MS1399 90×75 mm. 18r. multicoloured . . . . 2·75 3·25
DESIGNS: No. 1396, Lady Elizabeth Bowes-Lyon; 1397, Lady Elizabeth Bowes-Lyon wearing headband; 1398, Lady Elizabeth Bowes-Lyon leaving for her wedding; **MS**1399, Lady Elizabeth Bowes-Lyon wearing wedding dress.

241 Sultan's Tomb

1990. Islamic Heritage Year. Each black and blue.
1400 1r. Type **241** 25 35
1401 1r. Thakurufaan's Palace . . 25 35
1402 1r. Male Mosque 25 35
1403 2r. Veranda of Friday Mosque 25 35
1404 2r. Interior of Friday Mosque 25 35
1405 2r. Friday Mosque and Monument 25 35

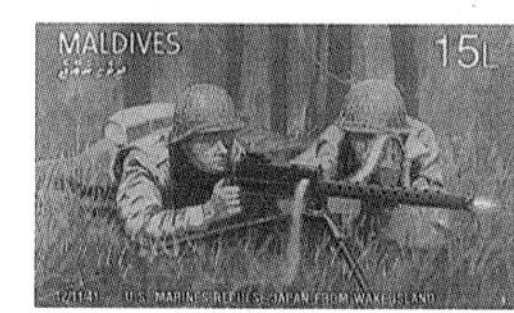

242 Defence of Wake Island, 1941

1990. 50th Anniv of Second World War. Mult.
1406 15l. Type **242** 15 15
1407 25l. Stilwell's army in Burma, 1944 . . . . . 20 20
1408 50l. Normandy offensive, 1944 . . . . 25 25
1409 1r. Capture of Saipan, 1944 40 40
1410 2r.50 D-Day landings, 1944 70 70
1411 3r.50 Allied landings in Norway, 1940 . . . . . 90 90
1412 4r. Lord Mountbatten, Head of Combined Operations, 1943 . . . . 1·10 1·10
1413 6r. Japanese surrender, Tokyo Bay, 1945 . . . . 1·50 1·50
1414 10r. Potsdam Conference, 1945 . . . . 2·50 2·50
1415 12r. Allied invasion of Sicily, 1943 . . . . 2·75 2·75
MS1416 115×87 mm. 18r. Atlantic convoy . . . . 5·00 6·00

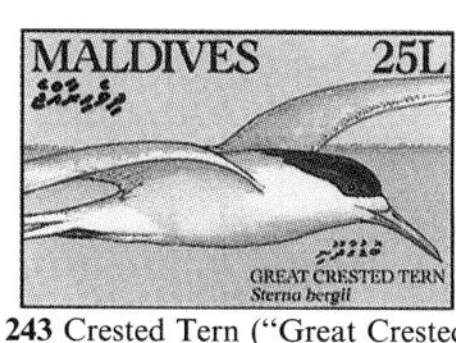

243 Crested Tern ("Great Crested Tern")

1990. Birds. Multicoloured.
1417 25l. Type **243** 15 15
1418 50l. Koel 25 25
1419 1r. White tern 35 35
1420 3r.50 Cinnamon bittern . . 90 1·00
1421 6r. Sooty tern . . . . . . 1·40 1·60
1422 8r. Audubon's shearwater . 1·60 2·00
1423 12r. Common noddy ("Brown Noddy") . . . 2·50 3·00
1424 15r. Lesser frigate bird . . . 2·75 3·25
MS1425 Two sheets, each 100×69 mm. (a) 18r. Grey heron. (b) 18r. White-tailed tropic bird Set of 2 sheets . . . . 8·00 10·00

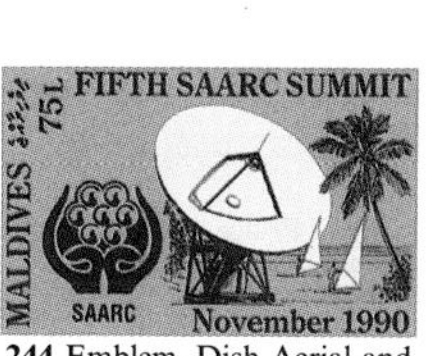

244 Emblem, Dish Aerial and Sailboards

245 "Spathoglottis plicata"

1990. 5th South Asian Association for Regional Co-operation Summit.
1426 **244** 75l. black and orange . . 20 25
1427 – 3r.50 multicoloured . . . 90 1·25
MS1428 112×82 mm. 20r. multicoloured . . . . 4·50 5·50
DESIGN: 3r.50, Flags of member nations; 20r. Global warming diagram.

1990. "EXPO '90" International Garden and Greenery Exhibition, Osaka. Flowers. Mult.
1429 20l. Type **245** 90 30
1430 75l. "Hippeastrum puniceum" . . . . . . 1·40 40
1431 2r. "Tecoma stans" (horiz) 1·60 90
1432 3r.50 "Catharanthus roseus" (horiz) . . . . 1·60 1·60
1433 10r. "Ixora coccinea" (horiz) 2·75 3·00
1434 12r. "Clitorea ternatea" (horiz) . . . . 3·00 3·25
1435 15r. "Caesalpinia pulcherrima" . . . . . . 3·00 3·50
MS1436 Four sheets, each 111×79 mm. (a) 20r. "Plumeria obtusa" (horiz). (b) 20r. "Jasminum grandiflorum" (horiz). (c) 20r. "Rosa" sp (horiz). (d) 20r. "Hibiscus tiliaceous" (horiz) Set of 4 sheets . . . . 13·00 13·00

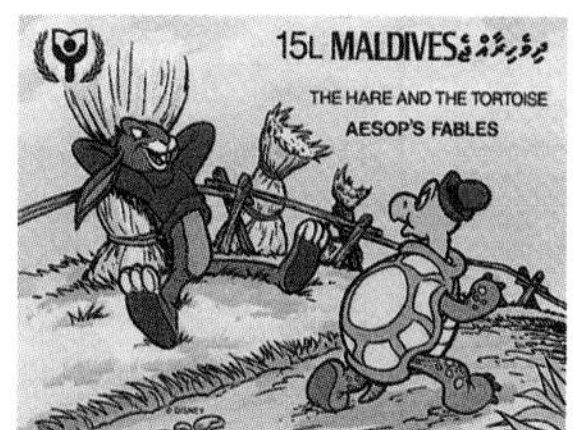

246 "The Hare and the Tortoise"

1990. International Literacy Year. Walt Disney cartoon characters illustrating fables by Aesop. Multicoloured.
1437 15l. Type **246** 30 15
1438 50l. "The Town Mouse and the Country Mouse" . . . 50 25
1439 1r. "The Fox and the Crow" 80 35
1440 3r.50 "The Travellers and the Bear" . . . . 1·60 1·60
1441 4r. "The Fox and the Lion" 1·75 1·75
1442 6r. "The Mice Meeting" . . 2·25 2·25
1443 10r. "The Fox and the Goat" . . . . 2·75 3·00
1444 12r. "The Dog in the Manger" . . . . 2·75 3·25
MS1445 Two sheets, each 127×102 mm. (a) 20r. "The Miller, his Son and the Ass" (vert). (b) 20r. "The Miser's Gold" (vert) Set of 2 sheets . . . . 12·00 12·00

247 East African Railways Class 31 Steam Locomotive

248 Ruud Gullit of Holland

1990. Railway Steam Locomotives. Multicoloured.
1446 20l. Type **247** 75 30
1447 50l. Steam locomotive, Sudan . . . . 1·00 45
1448 1r. Class GM Garratt, South Africa . . . . . . 1·40 60
1449 3r. 7th Class, Rhodesia . . 2·25 2·00
1450 5r. Central Pacific Class No. 229, U.S.A. . . . . 2·50 2·25
1451 8r. Reading Railroad No. 415, U.S.A. . . . . 2·75 2·75
1452 10r. Porter narrow gauge, Canada . . . . 2·75 2·75
1453 12r. Great Northern Railway No. 515, U.S.A. 2·75 3·00
MS1454 Two sheets, each 90×65 mm. (a) 20r. 19th-century standard American locomotive No. 315. (b) 20r. East African Railways Garratt locomotive No. 5950 Set of 2 sheets . . . 13·00 13·00

1990. World Cup Football Championship, Italy. Multicoloured.
1455 1r. Type **248** . . . . 1·50 50
1456 2r.50 Paul Gascoigne of England . . . . 2·00 1·25
1457 3r.50 Brazilian challenging Argentine player . . . . 2·00 1·60
1458 5r. Brazilian taking control of ball . . . . 2·25 2·00
1459 7r. Italian and Austrian jumping for header . . . 3·00 3·00
1460 10r. Russian being chased by Turkish player . . . . 3·25 3·25
1461 15r. Andres Brehme of West Germany . . . . 3·75 4·00
MS1462 Four sheets, each 77×92 mm. (a) 18r. Head of an Austrian player (horiz). (b) 18r. Head of a South Korean player (horiz). (c) 20r. Diego Maradona of Argentina (horiz). (d) 20r. Schilacci of Italy (horiz) Set of 4 sheets . . . . 16·00 16·00

249 Winged Euonymus

251 Greek Messenger from Marathon, 490 B.C. (2480th Anniv)

250 "Summer" (Rubens)

1991. Bonsai Trees and Shrubs. Multicoloured.
1463 20l. Type **249** 40 20
1464 50l. Japanese black pine . . 55 35
1465 1r. Japanese five needle pine 80 55
1466 3r.50 Flowering quince . . . 1·75 1·60
1467 5r. Chinese elm . . . . . . 2·25 2·25
1468 8r. Japanese persimmon . . 2·50 2·75
1469 10r. Japanese wisteria . . . 2·50 2·75
1470 12r. Satsuki azalea . . . . 2·50 3·00
MS1471 Two sheets, each 89×88 mm. (a) 20r. Trident maple. (b) 20r. Sargent juniper Set of 2 sheets . . . . 9·50 11·00

1991. 350th Death Anniv of Rubens. Mult.
1472 20l. Type **250** 20 15
1473 50l. "Landscape with Rainbow" (detail) 35 25
1474 1r. "Wreck of Aeneas" . . . 55 40
1475 2r.50 "Chateau de Steen" (detail) . . . . 1·00 1·00
1476 3r.50 "Landscape with Herd of Cows" . . . . 1·25 1·25
1477 7r. "Ruins on the Palantine" 2·00 2·50
1478 10r. "Landscape with Peasants and Cows" . . . 2·25 2·50
1479 12r. "Wagon fording Stream" . . . . 2·50 3·00
MS1480 Four sheets, each 100×71 mm. (a) 20r. "Landscape at Sunset". (b) 20r. "Peasants with Cattle by a Stream". (c) 20r. "Shepherd with Flock". (d) 20r. "Wagon in Stream" Set of 4 sheets 15·00 16·00

1991. Anniversaries and Events (1990). Mult.
1481 50l. Type **251** 45 25
1482 1r. Anthony Fokker in Haarlem Spin monoplane (birth centenary) 80 45
1483 3r.50 "Early Bird" satellite (25th anniv) . . . . . . 1·50 1·50
1484 7r. Signing Reunification of Germany agreement (horiz) . . . . 1·75 2·50
1485 8r. King John signing Magna Carta (775th anniv) . . . . 2·25 2·50
1486 10r. Dwight D. Eisenhower (birth centenary) . . . . 2·25 2·50

1487 12r. Sir Winston Churchill (25th death anniv) 3·25 3·50
1488 15r. Pres. Reagan at Berlin Wall (German reunification) (horiz) 2·75 3·75
MS1489 Two sheets. (a) 180×81 mm. 20r. German Junkers Ju88 bomber (50th anniv of Battle of Britain) (horiz). (b) 160×73 mm. 20r. Brandenburg Gate (German reunification) (horiz) Set of 2 sheets 13·00 13·00

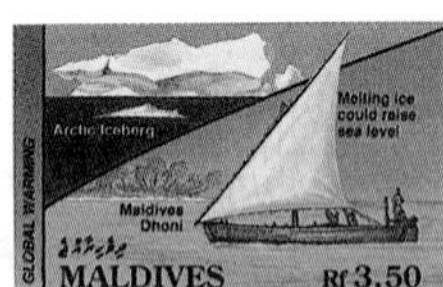

252 Arctic Iceberg and Maldives Dhoni

1991. Global Warming. Multicoloured.
1490 3r.50 Type **252** 1·25 1·25
1491 7r. Antarctic iceberg and "Maldive Trader" (freighter) 2·75 2·75

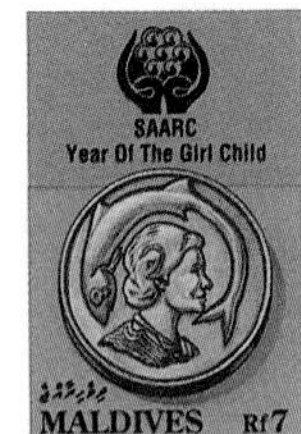

253 S.A.A.R.C. Emblem and Medal

1991. Year of the Girl Child.
1492 **253** 7r. multicoloured 1·75 1·75

254 Children on Beach

1991. Year of the Maldivian Child. Children's Paintings. Multicoloured.
1493 3r.50 Type **254** 2·25 1·40
1494 5r. Children in a park 2·75 2·25
1495 10r. Hungry child dreaming of food 3·75 4·00
1496 25r. Scuba diver 7·00 10·00

255 "Still Life: Japanese Vase with Roses and Anemones"

1991. Death Centenary (1990) of Vincent van Gogh (artist). Multicoloured.
1497 15l. Type **255** 50 25
1498 20l. "Still Life: Red Poppies and Daisies" 50 25
1499 2r. "Vincent's Bedroom in Arles" (horiz) 1·50 90
1500 3r.50 "The Mulberry Tree" 1·75 1·25
1501 7r. "Blossoming Chestnut Branches" (horiz) 2·75 3·00
1502 10r. "Peasant Couple going to Work" (horiz) 3·25 3·50
1503 12r. "Still Life: Pink Roses" (horiz) 3·50 3·75
1504 15r. "Child with Orange" 3·75 4·00
MS1505 Two sheets. (a) 77×101 mm. 25r. "Houses in Auvers" (70×94 mm). (b) 101×77 mm. 25r. "The Courtyard of the Hospital at Arles" (94×70 mm). Imperf Set of 2 sheets 12·00 13·00

1991. 65th Birthday of Queen Elizabeth II. As T **201** of Lesotho. Multicoloured.
1506 2r. Queen at Trooping the Colour, 1990 1·00 60
1507 5r. Queen with Queen Mother and Princess Margaret, 1973 2·00 1·50
1508 8r. Queen and Prince Philip in open carriage, 1986 2·75 2·50
1509 12r. Queen at Royal Estates Ball 3·00 3·25
MS1510 68×90 mm. 25r. Separate photographs of Queen and Prince Philip 5·75 6·50

1991. 10th Wedding Anniv of Prince and Princess of Wales. As T **210** of Lesotho. Multicoloured.
1511 1r. Prince and Princess skiing, 1986 80 20
1512 3r.50 Separate photographs of Prince, Princess and sons 1·75 1·10
1513 7r. Prince Henry in Christmas play and Prince William watching polo 2·00 2·00
1514 15r. Princess Diana at Ipswich, 1990, and Prince Charles playing polo 3·50 3·75
MS1515 68×90 mm. 25r. Prince and Princess of Wales in Hungary, and Princes William and Harry going to school 5·75 6·50

256 Boy painting **257** Class C57 Steam Locomotive

1991. Hummel Figurines. Multicoloured.
1516 10l. Type **256** 15 15
1517 25l. Boy reading at table 20 20
1518 50l. Boy with school satchel 30 30
1519 2r. Girl with basket 70 70
1520 3r.50 Boy reading 1·00 1·00
1521 8r. Girl and young child reading 2·25 2·50
1522 10r. School girls 2·25 2·50
1523 25r. School boys 4·75 6·50
MS1524 Two sheets, each 97×127 mm. (a) 5r. As No. 1519; 5r. As No. 1520; 5r. As No, 1521; 5r. As No. 1522. (b) 8r. As Type **256**; 8r. As No. 1517; 8r. As No. 1518; 8r. As No. 1523 Set of 2 sheets 9·00 11·00

1991. "Phila Nippon '91" International Stamp Exn, Tokyo. Japanese Steam Locomotives. Mult.
1525 15l. Type **257** 50 15
1526 25l. Class 6250 locomotive, 1915 (horiz) 65 25
1527 1r. Class D51 locomotive, 1936 1·25 40
1528 3r.50 Class 8620 locomotive, 1914 (horiz) 2·00 1·25
1529 5r. Class 10 locomotive, 1889 (horiz) 2·25 1·75
1530 7r. Class C61 locomotive, 1947 2·50 2·50
1531 10r. Class 9600 locomotive, 1913 (horiz) 2·50 2·75
1532 12r. Class D52 locomotive, 1943 (horiz) 2·75 3·50
MS1533 Two sheets, each 118×80 mm. (a) 20r. Class C56 locomotive, 1935 (horiz). (b) 20r. Class 1080 locomotive, 1925 (horiz) Set of 2 sheets 8·00 9·00

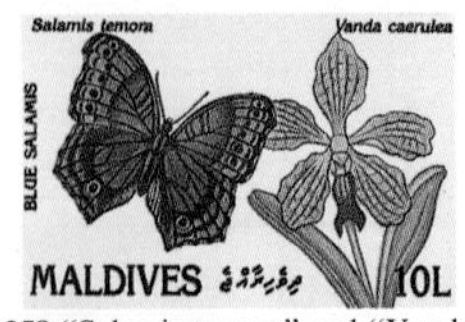

258 "Salamis temora" and "Vanda caerulea"

1991. Butterflies and Flowers. Multicoloured.
1534 10l. Type **258** 40 40
1535 25l. "Meneris tulbaghia" and "Incarvillea younghusbandii" 55 30
1536 50l. "Polyommatus icarus" and "Campsis grandiflora" 75 40
1537 2r. "Danaus plexippus" and "Thunbergia grandiflora" 1·25 90
1538 3r.50 "Colias interior" and "Medinilla magnifica" 1·75 1·75
1539 5r. "Ascalapha ordorata" and "Meconopsis horridula" 2·00 2·00
1540 8r. "Papilio memnon" and "Dillenia obovata" 2·50 3·00
1541 10r. "Precis octavia" and "Thespesia populnea" 2·50 3·00
MS1542 Two sheets, each 100×70 mm. (a) 20r. "Bombax ceiba" and "Plyciodes tharos". (b) 20r. "Amauris niavius" and "Bombax insigne" Set of 2 sheets 9·25 10·00

259 "H-II" Rocket

1991. Japanese Space Programme. Multicoloured.
1543 15l. Type **259** 40 20
1544 20l. Projected "H-II" orbiting plane 40 20
1545 2r. Satellite "GMS-5" 1·00 75
1546 3r.50 Satellite "MOMO-1" 1·40 1·40
1547 7r. Satellite "CS-3" 2·25 2·50
1548 10r. Satellite "BS-2a, 2b" 2·50 2·75
1549 12r. "H-I" Rocket (vert) 2·75 3·25
1550 15r. Space Flier unit and U.S. Space shuttle 2·75 3·25
MS1551 Two sheets. (a) 116×85 mm. 20r. Dish aerial, Katsura Tracking Station (vert). (b) 85×116 mm. 20r. "M-3SII" rocket (vert) Set of 2 sheets 11·00 11·00

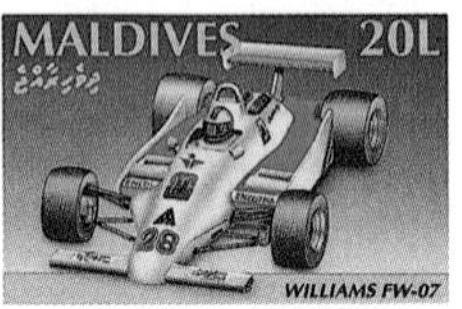

260 Williams "FW-07"

1991. Formula 1 Racing Cars. Multicoloured.
1552 20l. Type **260** 30 20
1553 50l. Brabham/BMW "BT50" turbo 40 30
1554 1r. Williams/Honda "FW-11" 60 45
1555 3r.50 Ferrari "312 T3" 1·25 1·25
1556 5r. Lotus/Honda "99T" 1·75 1·75
1557 7r. Benetton/Ford "B188" 2·00 2·25
1558 10r. Tyrrell "P34" six-wheeler 2·25 2·50
1559 21r. Renault "RE-30B" turbo 4·00 5·00
MS1560 Two sheets, each 84×56 mm. (a) 25r. Brabham/BMW "BT50" turbo (different). (b) 25r. Ferrari "F189" Set of 2 sheets 14·00 12·00

261 "Testa Rossa", 1957

1991. Ferrari Cars. Multicoloured.
1561 5r. Type **261** 1·90 2·00
1562 5r. "275GTB", 1966 1·90 2·00
1563 5r. "Aspirarta", 1951 1·90 2·00
1564 5r. "Testarossa" 1·90 2·00
1565 5r. Enzo Ferrari 1·90 2·00
1566 5r. "Dino 246", 1958 1·90 2·00
1567 5r. "Type 375", 1952 1·90 2·00
1568 5r. Nigel Mansell's Formula 1 racing car 1·90 2·00
1569 5r. "312T", 1975 1·90 2·00

262 Franklin D. Roosevelt

1991. 50th Anniv of Japanese Attack on Pearl Harbor. American War Leaders. Multicoloured.
1570 3r.50 Type **262** 1·50 1·50
1571 3r.50 Douglas MacArthur and map of Philippines 1·50 1·50
1572 3r.50 Chester Nimitz and Pacific island 1·50 1·50
1573 3r.50 Jonathan Wainwright and barbed wire 1·50 1·50
1574 3r.50 Ernest King and U.S.S. "Hornet" (aircraft carrier) 1·50 1·50
1575 3r.50 Claire Chennault and Curtiss Tomahawk II fighters 1·50 1·50
1576 3r.50 William Halsey and U.S.S. "Enterprise" (aircraft carrier) 1·50 1·50
1577 3r.50 Marc Mitscher and U.S.S. "Hornet" (aircraft carrier) 1·50 1·50
1578 3r.50 James Doolittle and North American B-25 Mitchell bomber 1·50 1·50
1579 3r.50 Raymond Spruance and Douglas Dauntless dive bomber 1·50 1·50

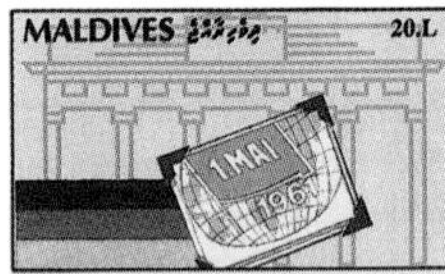

263 Brandenburg Gate and Postcard Commemorating Berlin Wall

1992. Anniversaries and Events. Multicoloured.
1580 20l. Type **263** 15 10
1581 50l. Schwarzenburg Palace 80 40
1582 1r. Spa at Baden 1·10 50
1583 1r.75 Berlin Wall and man holding child 50 50
1584 2r. Royal Palace, Berlin 1·00 80
1585 4r. Demonstrator and border guards 1·10 1·25
1586 5r. Viennese masonic seal 3·00 2·00
1587 6r. De Gaulle and Normandy landings, 1944 (vert) 2·50 2·25
1588 6r. Lilienthal's signature and "Flugzeug Nr. 16" 2·50 2·25
1589 7r. St. Marx 3·00 2·25
1590 7r. Trans-Siberian Railway Class VL80T electric locomotive No. 1406 (vert) 3·00 2·25
1591 8r. Kurt Schwitters (artist) and Landesmuseum 2·50 2·50
1592 9r. Map of Switzerland and man in Uri traditional costume 2·50 2·50
1593 10r. De Gaulle in Madagascar, 1958 2·50 2·50
1594 10r. Scouts exploring coral reef 2·50 2·50
1595 11r. Scout salute and badge (vert) 2·50 2·50
1596 12r. Trans-Siberian Railway steam locomotive 3·25 3·25
1597 15r. Imperial German badges 2·50 3·25
1598 20r. Josepsplatz, Vienna 3·50 3·50
MS1599 Eight sheets. (a) 76×116 mm. 15r. General de Gaulle during Second World War (vert). (b) 101×72 mm. 18r. Ancient German helmet. (c) 101×72 mm. 18r. 19th-century shako. (d) 101×72 mm. 18r. Helmet of 1939. (e) 90×117 mm. 18r. Postcard of Lord Baden-Powell carried by rocket, 1937 (grey, black and mauve) (vert). (f) 75×104 mm. 20r. Bust of Mozart (vert). (g) 115×85 mm. 20r. Trans-Siberian Railway Class P36 steam locomotive stopped at signal (57×43 mm). (h) 117×90 mm. 20r. Czechoslovakia 1918 10h. "Scout Post" stamp (vert) Set of 8 sheets 28·00 29·00

ANNIVERSARIES AND EVENTS: Nos. 1580, 1583, 1585, 1597, **MS**1599b/d, Bicentenary of Brandenburg Gate, Berlin; 1581/2, 1584, 1586, 1589, 1598, **MS**1599f, Death bicentenary of Mozart (1991); 1587, 1593, **MS**1599a, Birth centenary of Charles de Gaulle (French statesman) (1990); 1588, Centenary of Otto Lilienthal's first gliding experiments; 1590, 1596, **MS**1599g, Centenary of Trans-Siberian Railway; 1591, 750th anniv of Hannover; 1592, 700th anniv of Swiss Confederation; 1594/5, **MS**1599e,h, 17th World Scout Jamboree, Korea.

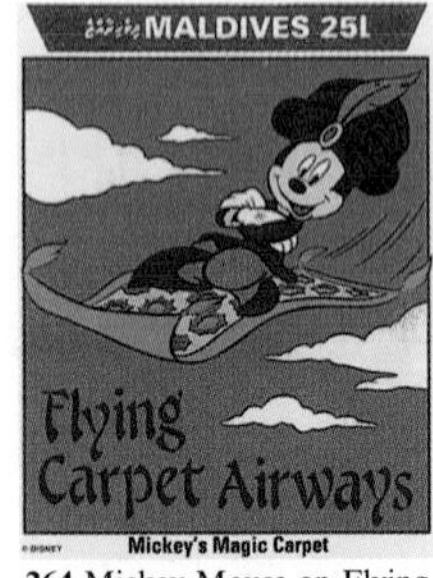

264 Mickey Mouse on Flying Carpet, Arabia

1992. Mickey's World Tour. Designs showing Walt Disney cartoon characters in different countries. Multicoloured.
1600 25l. Type **264** 45 20
1601 50l. Goofy and Big Ben, Great Britain 55 25
1602 1r. Mickey wearing clogs, Netherlands 75 35
1603 2r. Pluto eating pasta, Italy 1·25 75
1604 3r. Mickey and Donald doing Mexican hat dance 1·40 1·25
1605 3r.50 Mickey, Goofy and Donald as tiki, New Zealand 1·40 1·40
1606 5r. Goofy skiing in Austrian Alps 1·50 1·50
1607 7r. Mickey and city gate, Germany 1·75 2·00
1608 10r. Donald as samurai, Japan 2·00 2·25

1609 12r. Mickey as heroic statue, Russia . . . 2·25 2·75
1610 15r. Mickey, Donald, Goofy and Pluto as German band . . . 2·50 3·00
MS1611 Three sheets, each 83×104 mm. (a) 25r. Donald chasing leprechaun, Ireland (horiz). (b) 25r. Baby kangaroo surprising Pluto, Australia. (c) 25r. Mickey and globe Set of 3 sheets 13·00 14·00

265 Whimbrel **266** Powder-blue Surgeonfish

1992. Birds. Multicoloured.
1612 10l. Type **265** . . . 35 40
1613 25l. Great egret . . . 40 30
1614 50l. Grey heron . . . 50 35
1615 2r. Shag . . . 1·00 60
1616 3r.50 Roseate tern . . . 1·25 75
1617 5r. Greater greenshank . . . 1·25 80
1617a 6r.50+50l. Egyptian vulture 1·50 1·50
1618 8r. Hoopoe . . . 1·60 1·60
1619 10r. Black-shouldered kite 1·75 1·75
1620 25r. Scarlet ibis . . . 2·40 2·50
1620a 30r. Peregrine falcon . . . 3·00 3·25
1620b 40r. Black kite . . . 3·75 4·00
1621 50r. Grey plover . . . 4·75 5·00
1621a 100r. Common shoveler . . . 9·50 9·75
Nos. 1617a, 1620a/b and 1621a are larger, 23×32 mm.

1992. 40th Anniv of Queen Elizabeth II's Accession. As T **214** of Lesotho. Multicoloured.
1622 1r. Palm trees on beach . . . 50 25
1623 3r.50 Path leading to jetty 1·75 1·00
1624 7r. Tropical plant . . . 2·50 2·75
1625 10r. Palm trees on beach (different) . . . 2·75 3·00
MS1626 Two sheets, each 74×97 mm. (a) 18r. Dhow. (b) 18r. Palm trees on beach (different) Set of 2 sheets . . . 10·00 10·00

1992. Fishes. Multicoloured.
1627 7l. Type **266** . . . 30 20
1628 20l. Catalufa . . . 40 25
1629 50l. Yellow-finned tuna . . . 55 30
1630 1r. Twin-spotted red snapper 75 35
1631 3r.50 Hawaiian squirrelfish 1·50 1·25
1632 5r. Picasso triggerfish . . . 2·00 2·00
1633 8r. Bennet's butterflyfish . . . 2·25 2·50
1634 10r. Parrotfish . . . 2·50 2·75
1635 12r. Coral hind . . . 2·75 3·00
1636 15r. Skipjack tuna . . . 2·75 3·00
MS1637 Four sheets, each 116×76 mm. (a) 20r. Thread-finned butterflyfish. (b) 20r. Oriental sweetlips. (c) 20r. Two-banded anemonefish ("Clownfish"). (d) 20r. Clown triggerfish Set of 4 sheets . . . 13·00 15·00

1992. International Stamp Exhibitions. As T **215** of Lesotho showing Walt Disney cartoon characters. Multicoloured. (a) "Granada '92", Spain. The Alhambra.
1638 2r. Minnie Mouse in Court of the Lions . . . 90 70
1639 5r. Goofy in Lions Fountain 1·75 1·75
1640 8r. Mickey Mouse at the Gate of Justice . . . 2·25 2·75
1641 12r. Donald Duck serenading Daisy at the Vermilion Towers . . . 2·75 3·25
MS1642 127×102 mm. 25r. Goofy pushing Mickey in wheelbarrow 5·50 6·00

(b) "World Columbian Stamp Expo '92". Chicago Landmarks.
1643 1r. Mickey meeting Jean Baptiste du Sable (founder) . . . 80 40
1644 3r.50 Donald Duck at Old Chicago Post Office . . . 1·75 1·25
1645 7r. Donald at Old Fort Dearborn . . . 2·50 2·75
1646 15r. Goofy in Museum of Science and Industry . . . 3·25 3·75
MS1647 127×102 mm. 25r. Mickey and Minnie Mouse at Columbian Exposition, 1893 (horiz) . . . 5·50 6·00
On No. 1646 the design is wrongly captioned as the Science and Industry Museum.

267 Coastguard Patrol Boats

1992. Cent of National Security Service. Mult.
1648 3r.50 Type **267** . . . 2·00 1·25
1649 5r. Infantry in training . . . 2·00 1·75
1650 10r. Aakoatey fort . . . 2·25 2·50
1651 15r. Fire Service . . . 6·50 7·00
MS1652 100×68 mm. 20r. Ceremonial procession, 1892 6·00 7·00

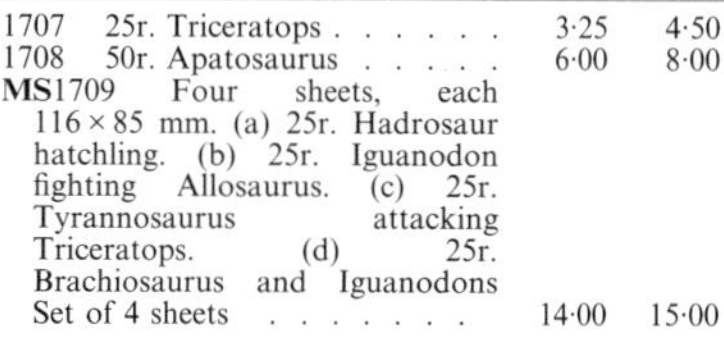

268 Flowers of the United States of America **269** "Laetiporus sulphureus"

1992. National Flowers. Multicoloured.
1653 25l. Type **268** . . . 50 30
1654 50l. Australia . . . 70 30
1655 2r. England . . . 1·40 1·10
1656 3r.50 Brazil . . . 1·75 1·50
1657 5r. Holland . . . 2·00 2·00
1658 8r. France . . . 2·25 3·00
1659 10r. Japan . . . 2·50 3·00
1660 15r. Africa . . . 3·00 4·00
MS1661 Two sheets, each 114×85 mm. (a) 25r. "Plumieria rubra", "Classia fistula" and "Eugenia malaccensis" (57×43 mm). (b) 25r. "Bauhinia variegata", "Catharanthus roseus" and "Plumieria alba" (57×43 mm) Set of 2 sheets . . . 9·00 10·00

1992. Fungi. Multicoloured.
1662 10l. Type **269** . . . 30 30
1663 25l. "Coprinus atramentarius" . . . 40 30
1664 50l. "Ganoderma lucidum" 60 40
1665 3r.50 "Russula aurata" . . . 1·25 1·00
1666 5r. "Grifola umbellata" ("Polyporus umbellatus") 1·75 1·75
1667 8r. "Suillus grevillei" . . . 2·25 2·50
1668 10r. "Clavaria zollingeri" . . . 2·50 2·50
1669 25r. "Boletus edulis" . . . 5·00 6·00
MS1670 Two sheets, each 100×70 mm. (a) 25r. "Marasmius oreades". (b) 25r. "Pycnoporus cinnabarinus" ("Trametes cinnabarina") Set of 2 sheets 12·00 13·00

1992. Olympic Games, Albertville and Barcelona (1st issue). As T **216** of Lesotho. Multicoloured.
1671 10l. Pole vault . . . 20 10
1672 25l. Men's pommel horse (horiz) . . . 25 15
1673 50l. Men's shot put . . . 30 25
1674 1r. Men's horizontal bar (horiz) . . . 35 30
1675 2r. Men's triple jump (horiz) 80 65
1676 3r.50 Table tennis . . . 1·10 1·10
1677 5r. Two-man bobsled . . . 1·40 1·40
1678 7r. Freestyle wrestling (horiz) . . . 1·75 2·00
1679 8r. Freestyle ski-jump . . . 1·75 2·00
1680 9r. Baseball . . . 2·00 2·25
1681 10r. Women's cross-country Nordic skiing . . . 2·00 2·25
1682 12r. Men's 200 m backstroke (horiz) 2·00 2·25
MS1683 Three sheets. (a) 100×70 mm. 25r. Decathalon (horiz). (b) 100×70 mm. 25r. Women's slalom skiing (horiz). (c) 70×100 mm. 25r. Men's figure skating Set of 3 sheets . . . 12·00 13·00
See also Nos. 1684/92.

270 Hurdling **271** Deinonychus

1992. Olympic Games, Barcelona (2nd issue). Multicoloured.
1684 10l. Type **270** . . . 10 10
1685 1r. Boxing . . . 30 30
1686 3r.50 Women's sprinting . . . 80 70
1687 5r. Discus . . . 1·25 1·25
1688 7r. Basketball . . . 3·00 2·50
1689 10r. Long-distance running 2·25 2·50
1690 12r. Aerobic gymnastics . . . 2·50 3·00
1691 20r. Fencing . . . 3·25 4·00
MS1692 Two sheets, each 70×100 mm. (a) 25r. Olympic symbol and national flags. (b) 25r. Olympic symbol and flame Set of 2 sheets . . . 8·50 9·00

1992. "Genova '92" International Thematic Stamp Exhibition. Prehistoric Animals. Multicoloured.
1693 5l. Type **271** . . . 40 20
1694 10l. Styracosaurus . . . 40 20
1695 25l. Mamenchisaurus . . . 50 30
1696 50l. Stenonychosaurus . . . 60 30
1697 1r. Parasaurolophus . . . 75 40
1698 1r.25 Scelidosaurus . . . 85 50
1699 1r.75 Tyrannosaurus . . . 1·10 55
1700 2r. Stegosaurus . . . 1·25 60
1701 3r.50 Iguanodon . . . 1·50 80
1702 4r. Anatosaurus . . . 1·50 1·00
1703 5r. Monoclonius . . . 1·60 1·10
1704 7r. Tenontosaurus . . . 1·90 1·90
1705 8r. Brachiosaurus . . . 1·90 1·90
1706 10r. Euoplocephalus . . . 2·00 2·00
1707 25r. Triceratops . . . 3·25 4·50
1708 50r. Apatosaurus . . . 6·00 8·00
MS1709 Four sheets, each 116×85 mm. (a) 25r. Hadrosaur hatchling. (b) 25r. Iguanodon fighting Allosaurus. (c) 25r. Tyrannosaurus attacking Triceratops. (d) 25r. Brachiosaurus and Iguanodons Set of 4 sheets . . . 14·00 15·00

1992. Postage Stamp Mega Event, New York. Sheet 100×70 mm, containing multicoloured design as T **219** of Lesotho, but horiz.
MS1710 20r. New York Public Library . . . 2·50 3·25

272 Destruction of LZ-129 "Hindenburg" (airship), 1937

1992. Mysteries of the Universe. T **272** and similar multicoloured designs, each in separate miniature sheet.
MS1711 Sixteen sheets, each 100×71 mm. (a) 25r. Type **272**. (b) 25r. Loch Ness Monster. (c) 25r. Crystal skull. (d) 25r. Space craft in Black Hole. (e) 25r. Ghosts (vert). (f) 25r. Flying saucer, 1947 (vert). (g) 25r. Bust of Plato (Atlantis). (h) 25r. U.F.O., 1973. (i) 25r. Crop circles. (j) 25r. Mil Mi-26 Russian helicopter at Chernobyl nuclear explosion. (k) 25r. Figure from Plain of Nazca. (l) 25r. Stonehenge (vert). (m) 25r. Yeti footprint (vert). (n) 25r. The Pyramid of Giza. (o) 25r. "Marie Celeste" (brigantine) (vert). (p) 25r. American Grumman TBF Avenger fighter aircraft (Bermuda Triangle) Set of 16 sheets . . . 55·00 55·00

273 Zubin Mehta (musical director) **274** Friedrich Schmiedl

1992. 150th Anniv of New York Philharmonic Orchestra. Sheet 100×70 mm.
MS1712 **273** 20r. multicoloured . . . 5·00 5·00

1992. 90th Birth Anniv of Friedrich Schmiedl (rocket mail pioneer). Sheet 104×69 mm.
MS1713 **274** 25r. multicoloured . . . 5·50 6·00

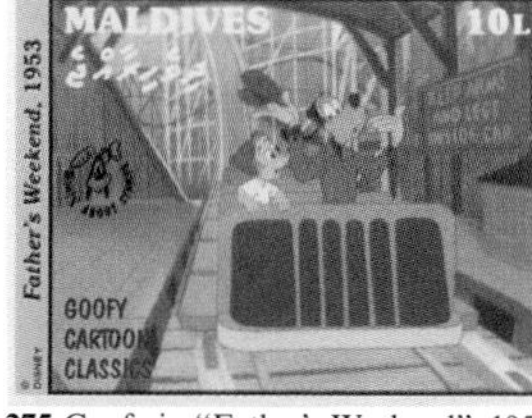

275 Goofy in "Father's Weekend", 1953

1992. 60th Anniv of Goofy (Disney cartoon character). Goofy in various cartoon films. Multicoloured.
1714 10l. Type **275** . . . 10 10
1715 50l. "Symphony Hour", 1942 . . . 35 20
1716 75l. "Frank Duck Brings 'Em Back Alive", 1946 . . . 45 20
1717 1r. "Crazy with the Heat", 1947 . . . 45 20
1718 2r. "The Big Wash", 1948 70 60
1719 3r.50 "How to Ride a Horse", 1950 . . . 1·25 1·25
1720 5r. "Two Gun Goofy", 1952 1·50 1·50
1721 8r. "Saludos Amigos", 1943 (vert) . . . 2·00 2·25
1722 10r. "How to be a Detective", 1952 . . . 2·00 2·25
1723 12r. "For Whom the Bulls Toil", 1953 . . . 2·25 2·50
1724 15r. "Double Dribble", 1946 (vert) . . . 2·25 2·50
MS1725 Three sheets, each 127×102 mm. (a) 20r. "Double Dribble", 1946 (different) (vert). (b) 20r. "The Goofy Success Story", 1955 (vert). (c) 20r. "Mickey and the Beanstalk", 1947 Set of 3 sheets . . . 9·00 9·50

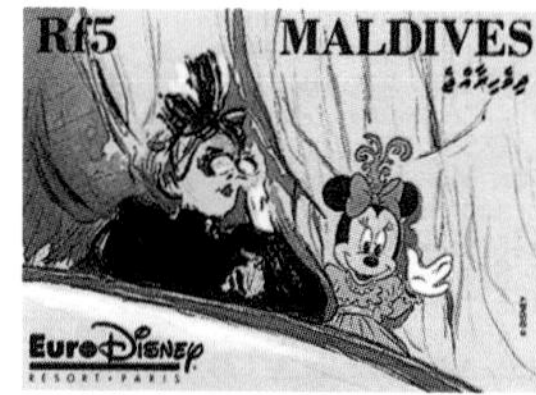

276 Minnie Mouse in "Le Missioner" (Toulouse-Lautrec)

1992. Opening of Euro-Disney Resort, France. Disney cartoon characters superimposed on Impressionist paintings. Multicoloured.
1726 5r. Type **276** . . . 1·40 1·50
1727 5r. Goofy in "The Card Players" (Cezanne) . . . 1·40 1·50
1728 5r. Mickey and Minnie Mouse in "The Cafe Terrace, Place du Forum" (Van Gogh) . . . 1·40 1·50
1729 5r. Mickey in "The Bridge at Langlois" (Van Gogh) 1·40 1·50
1730 5r. Goofy in "Chocolate Dancing" (Toulouse-Lautrec) . . . 1·40 1·50
1731 5r. Mickey and Minnie in "The Seine at Asnieres" (Renoir) . . . 1·40 1·50
1732 5r. Minnie in "Ball at the Moulin Rouge" (Toulouse-Lautrec) . . . 1·40 1·50
1733 5r. Mickey in "Wheatfield with Cypresses" (Van Gogh) . . . 1·40 1·50
1734 5r. Minnie in "When will you Marry?" (Gauguin) 1·40 1·50
MS1735 Four sheets. (a) 128×100 mm. 20r. Minnie as can-can dancer. (b) 128×100 mm. 20r. Goofy as cyclist. (c) 100×128 mm. 20r. Mickey as artist. (d) 100×128 mm. 20r. Donald as Frenchman (vert) Set of 4 sheets 12·00 13·00

277 Rivers

1992. South Asian Association for Regional Co-operation Year of the Environment. Natural and Polluted Environments. Multicoloured.
1736 25l. Type **277** . . . 15 10
1737 50l. Beaches . . . 25 10
1738 5r. Oceans . . . 80 1·00
1739 10r. Weather . . . 1·50 2·00

278 Jurgen Klinsmann (Germany) **280** Elvis Presley

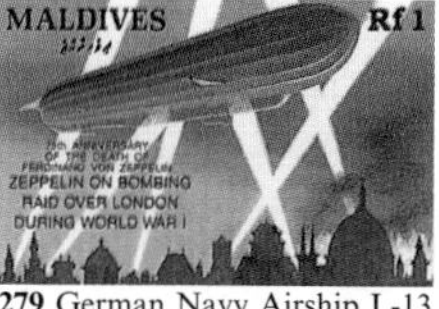

279 German Navy Airship L-13 bombing London, 1914–18

1993. World Cup Football Championship, U.S.A. (1994) (1st issue). German Players and Officials. Multicoloured.
1740 10l. Type **278** . . . 30 20
1741 25l. Pierre Littbarski . . . 35 20
1742 50l. Lothar Matthaus . . . 45 20
1743 1r. Rudi Voller . . . 65 25
1744 2r. Thomas Hassler . . . 1·00 60
1745 3r.50 Thomas Berthold . . . 1·40 1·00
1746 4r. Jurgen Kohler . . . 1·60 1·25
1747 5r. Berti Vogts . . . 1·75 1·40
1748 6r. Bodo Illgner . . . 1·90 1·90
1749 7r. Klaus Augenthaler . . . 1·90 2·00
1750 8r. Franz Beckenbauer . . . 1·90 2·00
1751 10r. Andreas Brehme . . . 2·25 2·50
1752 12r. Guido Buchwald . . . 2·25 2·75
MS1753 Two sheets, each 103×73 mm. (a) 35r. German players celebrating (horiz). (b) 35r. Rudi Voller (horiz) Set of 2 sheets 13·00 14·00
See also Nos. 1990/7 and 2089/2100.

1993. Anniversaries and Events. Multicoloured.
1754 1r. Type **279** . . . 80 30
1755 3r.50 Radio telescope . . . 70 80
1756 3r.50 Chancellor Adenauer and Pres. de Gaulle . . . 70 80
1757 6r. Indian rhinoceros . . . 2·75 1·75

1758	6r. Columbus and globe	2·00	1·50
1759	7r. Conference emblems	1·00	1·50
1760	8r. Green seaturtle	1·50	1·60
1761	10r. "America" (yacht), 1851	1·75	2·00
1762	10r. Melvin Jones (founder) and emblem	1·75	2·00
1763	12r. Columbus landing on San Salvador	2·75	3·00
1764	15r. "Voyager I" approaching Saturn	4·00	4·00
1765	15r. Adenauer, N.A.T.O. flag and Lockheed Starfighter aircraft	4·00	4·00
1766	20r. "Graf Zeppelin" over New York, 1929	4·00	4·00
MS1767	Five sheets, each 111×80 mm. (a) 20r. Count Ferdinand von Zeppelin. (b) 20r. "Landsat" satellite. (c) 20r. Konrad Adenauer. (d) 20r. Scarlet macaw. (e) 20r. "Santa Maria" Set of 5 sheets	19·00	20·00

ANNIVERSARIES AND EVENTS: 1754, 1766, **MS**1767a, 75th death anniv of Count Ferdinand von Zeppelin; 1755, 1764, **MS**1767b, International Space Year; 1756, 1765, **MS**1767c, 25th death anniv of Konrad Adenauer; 1757, 1760, **MS**1767d, Earth Summit '92, Rio; 1758, 1763, **MS**1767e, 500th anniv of discovery of America by Columbus; 1759, International Conference on Nutrition, Rome; 1761, Americas Cup Yachting Championship; 1762, 75th anniv of International Association of Lions Clubs.

1993. 15th Death Anniv of Elvis Presley (singer). Multicoloured.

1768	3r.50 Type **280**	90	70
1769	3r.50 Elvis with guitar	90	70
1770	3r.50 Elvis with microphone	90	70

1993. Bicentenary of the Louvre, Paris. As T **221a** of Lesotho. Multicoloured.

1771	8r. "The Study" (Fragonard)	90	1·10
1772	8r. "Denis Diderot" (Fragonard)	90	1·10
1773	8r. "Marie-Madelaine Guimard" (Fragonard)	90	1·10
1774	8r. "Inspiration" (Fragonard)	90	1·10
1775	8r. "Waterfalls, Tivoli" (Fragonard)	90	1·10
1776	8r. "The Music Lesson" (Fragonard)	90	1·10
1777	8r. "The Bolt" (Fragonard)	90	1·10
1778	8r. "Blind-man's Buff" (Fragonard)	90	1·10
1779	8r. "Self-portrait" (Corot)	90	1·10
1780	8r. "Woman in Blue" (Corot)	90	1·10
1781	8r. "Woman with a Pearl" (Corot)	90	1·10
1782	8r. "Young Girl at her Toilet" (Corot)	90	1·10
1783	8r. "Haydee" (Corot)	90	1·10
1784	8r. "Chartres Cathedral" (Corot)	90	1·10
1785	8r. "The Belfry of Douai" (Corot)	90	1·10
1786	8r. "The Bridge of Mantes" (Corot)	90	1·10
1787	8r. "Madame Seriziat" (David)	90	1·10
1788	8r. "Pierre Seriziat" (David)	90	1·10
1789	8r. "Madame De Verninac" (David)	90	1·10
1790	8r. "Madame Recamier" (David)	90	1·10
1791	8r. "Self-portrait" (David)	90	1·10
1792	8r. "General Bonaparte" (David)	90	1·10
1793	8r. "The Lictors bringing Brutus his Son's Body" (David) (left detail)	90	1·10
1794	8r. "The Lictors bringing Brutus his Son's Body" (David) (right detail)	90	1·10
MS1795	Two sheets, each 100×70 mm. (a) 20r. "Gardens of the Villa D'Este, Tivoli" (Corot) (85×52 mm). (b) 20r. "Tiger Cub playing with its Mother" (Delacroix) (85×52 mm) Set of 2 sheets	8·50	8·50

281 James Stewart and Marlene Dietrich ("Destry Rides Again")

1993. Famous Western Films. Multicoloured.

1796	5r. Type **281**	1·10	1·10
1797	5r. Gary Cooper ("The Westerner")	1·10	1·10
1798	5r. Henry Fonda ("My Darling Clementine")	1·10	1·10
1799	5r. Alan Ladd ("Shane")	1·10	1·10
1800	5r. Kirk Douglas and Burt Lancaster ("Gunfight at the O.K. Corral")	1·10	1·10
1801	5r. Steve McQueen ("The Magnificent Seven")	1·10	1·10
1802	5r. Robert Redford and Paul Newman ("Butch Cassidy and The Sundance Kid")	1·10	1·10
1803	5r. Jack Nicholson and Randy Quaid ("The Missouri Breaks")	1·10	1·10
MS1804	Two sheets, each 134×120 mm. (a) 20r. John Wayne ("The Searchers") (French poster). (b) 20r. Clint Eastwood ("Pale Rider") (French poster) Set of 2 sheets	7·00	7·00

1993. 40th Anniv of Coronation. As T **224** of Lesotho.

1805	3r.50 multicoloured	1·00	1·10
1806	5r. multicoloured	1·25	1·40
1807	10r. blue and black	1·50	1·75
1808	10r. blue and black	1·50	1·75

DESIGNS: No. 1805, Queen Elizabeth II at Coronation (photograph by Cecil Beaton); 1806, St. Edward's Crown; 1807, Guests in the Abbey; 1808, Queen Elizabeth II and Prince Philip.

282 Blue Goatfish

1993. Fishes. Multicoloured.

1809	3r.50 Type **282**	60	70
1810	3r.50 Emperor angelfish	60	70
1811	3r.50 Madagascar butterflyfish	60	70
1812	3r.50 Regal angelfish	60	70
1813	3r.50 Forceps fish ("Longnose butterflyfish")	60	70
1814	3r.50 Racoon butterflyfish	60	70
1815	3r.50 Harlequin filefish	60	70
1816	3r.50 Rectangle triggerfish	60	70
1817	3r.50 Yellow-tailed anemonefish	60	70
1818	3r.50 Clown triggerfish	60	70
1819	3r.50 Zebra lionfish	60	70
1820	3r.50 Maldive anemonefish ("Clownfish")	60	70
1821	3r.50 Black-faced butterflyfish	60	70
1822	3r.50 Bird wrasse	60	70
1823	3r.50 Checkerboard wrasse	60	70
1824	3r.50 Yellow-faced angelfish	60	70
1825	3r.50 Masked bannerfish	60	70
1826	3r.50 Thread-finned butterflyfish	60	70
1827	3r.50 Painted triggerfish	60	70
1828	3r.50 Coral hind	60	70
1829	3r.50 Pennant coralfish	60	70
1830	3r.50 Black-backed butterflyfish	60	70
1831	3r.50 Red-toothed triggerfish	60	70
1832	3r.50 Melon butterflyfish	60	70
MS1833	Two sheets. (a) 69×96 mm. 25r. Klein's butterflyfish (vert). (b) 96×69 mm. 25r. Brown anemonefish (vert) Set of 2 sheets	8·00	8·50

Nos. 1809/20 and 1821/32 were printed together, se-tenant, with the backgrounds forming composite designs.

Nos. 1810 and 1824 are both inscribed "Angelfish" in error.

283 Gull-billed Tern

1993. Birds. Multicoloured.

1834	3r.50 Type **283**	60	70
1835	3r.50 White-tailed tropic bird ("Long-tailed Tropicbird")	60	70
1836	3r.50 Great frigate bird ("Frigate Bird")	60	70
1837	3r.50 Wilson's storm petrel ("Wilson's Petrel")	60	70
1838	3r.50 White tern	60	70
1839	3r.50 Brown booby	60	70
1840	3r.50 Marsh harrier	60	70
1841	3r.50 Common noddy	60	70
1842	3r.50 Green-backed heron ("Little Heron")	60	70
1843	3r.50 Ruddy turnstone ("Turnstone")	60	70
1844	3r.50 Curlew	60	70
1845	3r.50 Crab plover	60	70
1846	3r.50 Pallid harrier (vert)	60	70
1847	3r.50 Cattle egret (vert)	60	70
1848	3r.50 Koel (vert)	60	70
1849	3r.50 Tree pipit (vert)	60	70
1850	3r.50 Short-eared owl (vert)	60	70
1851	3r.50 Common kestrel ("European Kestrel") (vert)	60	70
1852	3r.50 Yellow wagtail (vert)	60	70
1853	3r.50 Grey heron ("Common Heron") (vert)	60	70
1854	3r.50 Black bittern (vert)	60	70
1855	3r.50 Common snipe (vert)	60	70
1856	3r.50 Little egret (vert)	60	70
1857	3r.50 Little stint (vert)	60	70
MS1858	Two sheets, each 105×75 mm. (a) 25r. Caspian tern. (b) 25r. Audubon's shearwater Set of 2 sheets	8·50	9·00

Nos. 1834/45 and 1846/57 were printed together, se-tenant, with the backgrounds forming composite designs.

284 Precious Wentletrap

285 Sifaka Lemur

1993. Shells. Multicoloured.

1859	7l. Type **284**	30	30
1860	15l. Common purple janthina	35	30
1861	50l. Asiatic arabian cowrie	45	30
1862	3r.50 Common or major harp	1·50	1·00
1863	4r. Amplustre or royal paper bubble	1·75	1·25
1864	5r. Sieve cowrie	1·75	1·40
1865	6r. Episcopal mitre	2·00	2·00
1866	7r. Camp pitar venus	2·00	2·25
1867	8r. Spotted or eyed auger	2·25	2·50
1868	10r. Exposed cowrie	2·50	2·50
1869	12r. Geographic map cowrie	2·75	3·50
1870	20r. Bramble murex	3·50	4·50
MS1871	Three sheets, each 104×75 mm. (a) 25r. Black-striped triton. 25r. Scorpion conch. (c) 25r. Bull-mouth helmet Set of 3 sheets	17·00	19·00

1993. Endangered Species. Multicoloured.

1872	7l. Type **285**	50	30
1873	10l. Snow leopard	50	30
1874	15l. Numbat	50	30
1875	25l. Gorilla	90	40
1876	2r. Koala	1·00	70
1877	3r.50 Cheetah	1·25	1·10
1878	5r. Yellow-footed rock wallaby	1·40	1·40
1879	7r. Orang-utan	2·25	2·25
1880	8r. Black lemur	2·25	2·25
1881	10r. Black rhinoceros	2·75	2·75
1882	15r. Humpback whale	3·00	3·50
1883	20r. Mauritius parakeet	3·25	3·75
MS1884	Three sheets, each 104×75 mm. (a) 25r. Giant panda. (b) 25r. Tiger. (c) 25r. Indian elephant Set of 3 sheets	16·00	17·00

286 Symbolic Heads and Arrows

287 Early Astronomical Equipment

1993. Productivity Year. Multicoloured.

1885	7r. Type **286**	1·25	1·40
1886	10r. Abstract	1·60	1·75

1993. Anniversaries and Events. Multicoloured.

1887	3r.50 Type **287**	1·00	1·00
1888	3r.50 "Still Life with Pitcher and Apples" (Picasso)	1·00	1·00
1889	3r.50 "Zolte Roze" (Menasze Seidenbeurel)	1·00	1·00
1890	3r.50 Prince Naruhito and engagement photographs (horiz)	1·00	1·00
1891	5r. "Bowls and Jug" (Picasso)	1·25	1·25
1892	5r. Krysztofory Palace, Cracow	1·25	1·25
1893	8r. "Jabtka i Kotara" (Waclaw Borowski)	1·75	1·90
1894	8r. Marina Kiehl (Germany) (women's downhill skiing)	1·75	1·90
1895	10r. "Bowls of Fruit and Loaves on a Table" (Picasso)	1·90	2·00
1896	10r. Masako Owada and engagement photographs (horiz)	1·90	2·00
1897	15r. American astronaut in space	2·75	3·00
1898	15r. Vegard Ulvang (Norway) (30km cross-country skiing)	2·75	3·00
MS1899	Five sheets. (a) 105×75 mm. (a) 20r. Copernicus. (b) 105×75 mm. 20r. "Green Still Life" (detail) (Picasso) (horiz). (c) 105×75 mm. 25r. "Pejzaz Morski-Port z DoplywajacymStstkiem" (detail (Roman Sielski) (horiz). (d) 75×105 mm. 25r. Masako Owada. (e) 105×75 mm. 25r. Ice hockey goalkeeper Set of 5 sheets	16·00	18·00

ANNIVERSARIES AND EVENTS: Nos. 1887, 1897, **MS**1899a, 450th death anniv of Copernicus (astronomer); 1888, 1891, 1895, **MS**1899b, 20th death anniv of Picasso (artist); 1889, 1892/3, **MS**1899c, "Polska '93" International Stamp Exhibition, Poznan; 1890, 1896, **MS**1899d, Marriage of Crown Prince Naruhito of Japan; 1894, 1898, **MS**1899e, Winter Olympic Games '94, Lillehammer.

288 "Limenitis procris" and "Mussaenda"

1993. Butterflies and Flowers. Multicoloured.

1900	7l. Type **288**	30	20
1901	20l. "Danaus limniace" and "Thevetia neriifolia"	45	20
1902	25l. "Amblypodia centaurus" and "Clitoria ternatea"	45	20
1903	50l. "Papilio crino" and "Crossandra infundibuliformis"	60	20
1904	5r. "Mycalesis patnia" and "Thespesia populnia"	1·75	1·40
1905	6r.50+50l. "Idea jasonia" and "Cassia glauca"	2·00	2·25
1906	7r. "Catopsilia pomona" and "Calotropis"	2·00	2·25
1907	10r. "Precis orithyia" and "Thunbergia grandiflora"	2·25	2·50
1908	12r. "Vanessa cardui" and "Caesalpinia pulcherrima"	2·50	3·00
1909	15r. "Papilio polymnestor" and "Nerium oleander"	2·75	3·25
1910	18r. "Cirrochroa thais" and "Vinca rosea"	3·00	3·50
1911	20r. "Pachliopta hector" and "Ixora coccinea"	3·00	3·50
MS1912	Three sheets, each 105×72 mm. (a) 25r. "Cheritra freja" and "Bauhinia purpurea" (vert). (b) 25r. "Rohana parisatis" and "Plumeria acutifolia" (vert). (c) 25r. "Hebomoia glaucippe" and "Punica granatum" (vert) Set of 3 sheets	15·00	17·00

289 Airship "Graf Zeppelin" in Searchlights

1993. Aviation Anniversaries. Multicoloured.

1913	3r.50 Type **289**	1·50	65
1914	5r. Homing pigeon and message from Santa Catalina mail service, 1894	1·75	1·10
1915	10r. Eckener and airship "Graf Zeppelin"	2·25	2·25
1916	15r. Pilot's badge and loading Philadelphia–Washington mail, 1918	3·25	3·75
1917	20r. U.S.S. "Macon" (airship) and mooring mast, 1933	3·25	3·75
MS1918	Two sheets. (a) 70×100 mm. 25r. Santos Dumont's airship "Ballon No. 5" and Eiffel Tower, 1901. (b) 100×70 mm. 25r. Jean-Pierre Blanchard's balloon, 1793 (vert) Set of 2 sheets	6·00	7·00

ANNIVERSARIES: Nos. 1913, 1915, 1917, **MS**1918a, 125th birth anniv of Hugo Eckener (airship pioneer); 1914, 1916, **MS**1918b, Bicent of first airmail flight.

290 Ford Model "T"

1993. Centenaries of Henry Ford's First Petrol Engine (Nos. 1919/30) and Karl Benz's First Four-wheeled Car (others).

1919 **290**	3r.50 multicoloured	90	1·00
1920 –	3r.50 multicoloured	90	1·00
1921 –	3r.50 black and violet	90	1·00
1922 –	3r.50 multicoloured	90	1·00
1923 –	3r.50 multicoloured	90	1·00
1924 –	3r.50 multicoloured	90	1·00
1925 –	3r.50 multicoloured	90	1·00
1926 –	3r.50 multicoloured	90	1·00
1927 –	3r.50 multicoloured	90	1·00
1928 –	3r.50 multicoloured	90	1·00
1929 –	3r.50 multicoloured	90	1·00
1930 –	3r.50 black, brn & vio	90	1·00
1931 –	3r.50 multicoloured	90	1·00

1932 – 3r.50 multicoloured . . . 90 1·00
1933 – 3r.50 green, blk & vio 90 1·00
1934 – 3r.50 multicoloured . . . 90 1·00
1935 – 3r.50 multicoloured . . . 90 1·00
1936 – 3r.50 multicoloured . . . 90 1·00
1937 – 3r.50 multicoloured . . . 90 1·00
1938 – 3r.50 multicoloured . . . 90 1·00
1939 – 3r.50 multicoloured . . . 90 1·00
1940 – 3r.50 multicoloured . . . 90 1·00
1941 – 3r.50 multicoloured . . . 90 1·00
1942 – 3r.50 black, brn and violet . . . . 90 1·00
MS1943 Two sheets, each 100 × 70 mm. (a) 25r. multicoloured. (b) 25r. multicoloured Set of 2 sheets 9·00 10·00

DESIGNS: No. 1920, Henry Ford; 1921, Plans of first petrol engine; 1922, Ford "Probe GT", 1993; 1923, Front of Ford "Sportsman", 1947; 1924, Back of Ford "Sportsman"; 1925, Advertisement of 1915; 1926, Ford "Thunderbird", 1955; 1927, Ford logo; 1928, Ford "Edsel Citation", 1958; 1929, Ford half-ton pickup, 1941; 1930, Silhouette of early Ford car; 1931, Daimler-Benz "Straight 8", 1937; 1932, Karl Benz; 1933, Mercedes-Benz poster; 1934, Mercedes "38-250SS", 1929; 1935, Benz "Viktoria", 1893; 1936, Benz logo; 1937, Plan of Mercedes engine; 1938, Mercedes-Benz "300SL Gullwing", 1952; 1939, Mercedes-Benz "SL", 1993; 1940, Front of Benz 4-cylinder car, 1906; 1941, Back of Benz 4-cylinder car and advertisement; 1942, Silhouette of early Benz car; MS1943a, Ford Model "Y", 1933; MS1943b, Mercedes "300S", 1955.

Nos. 1919/30 and 1931/42 were printed together, se-tenant, forming a composite design.

291 Ivan, Sonia, Sasha and Peter in the Snow

1993. "Peter and the Wolf". Scenes from Walt Disney's cartoon film. Multicoloured.

1944 7l. Type **291** 25 25
1945 15l. Grandpa and Peter . . 30 25
1946 20l. Peter on bridge 30 25
1947 25l. Yascha, Vladimir and Mischa 30 25
1948 50l. Sasha on lookout . . . 45 30
1949 1r. The wolf 60 35
1950 3r.50 Peter dreaming . . . 70 80
1951 3r.50 Peter taking gun . . . 70 80
1952 3r.50 Peter with gun in snow 70 80
1953 3r.50 Sasha and Peter . . . 70 80
1954 3r.50 Sonia and Peter . . . 70 80
1955 3r.50 Peter with Ivan and Sasha 70 80
1956 3r.50 Ivan warning Peter of the wolf 70 80
1957 3r.50 Ivan, Peter and Sasha in tree 70 80
1958 3r.50 Wolf below tree . . . 70 80
1959 3r.50 Wolf and Sonia . . . 70 80
1960 3r.50 Sasha attacking the wolf 70 80
1961 3r.50 Sasha walking into wolf's mouth 70 80
1962 3r.50 Peter firing pop gun at wolf 70 80
1963 3r.50 Wolf chasing Sonia . . 70 80
1964 3r.50 Ivan tying rope to wolf's tail 70 80
1965 3r.50 Peter and Ivan hoisting wolf 70 80
1966 3r.50 Sasha and the hunters 70 80
1967 3r.50 Ivan and Peter on wolf hanging from tree 70 80
MS1968 Two sheets. (a) 102 × 127 mm. 25r. Sonia as an angel. (b) 127 × 102 mm. 25r. Ivan looking proud Set of 2 sheets 8·00 8·50

292 "Girl with a Broom" (Rembrandt)

1994. Famous Paintings by Rembrandt and Matisse. Multicoloured.

1969 50l. Type **292** 40 25
1970 2r. "Girl with Tulips" (Matisse) 90 70
1971 3r.50 "Young Girl at half-open Door" (Rembrandt) 1·25 1·10
1972 3r.50 "Portrait of Greta Moll" (Matisse) . . . . . 1·25 1·10
1973 5r. "The Prophetess Hannah" (Rembrandt) . . 1·50 1·25
1974 6r.50 "The Idol" (Matisse) 1·75 1·75
1975 7r. "Woman with a Pink Flower" (Rembrandt) . . 1·75 1·75
1976 9r. "Mme Matisse in a Japanese Robe" (Matisse) 2·00 2·25
1977 10r. "Portrait of Mme Matisse" (Matisse) . . . 2·00 2·25
1978 12r. "Lucretia" (Rembrandt) 2·25 2·50
1979 15r. "Lady with a Ostrich Feather Fan" (Rembrandt) . . . . . . 2·25 2·75
1980 15r. "The Woman with the Hat" (Matisse) . . . . . 2·25 2·75
MS1981 Three sheets. (a) 106 × 132 mm. 25r. "The Music-makers" (detail) (Rembrandt). (b) 132 × 106 mm. 25r. "Married Couple with Three Children" (detail) (Rembrandt) (horiz). (c) 132 × 106 mm. 25r. "The Painter's Family" (detail) (Matisse) Set of 3 sheets . . . . 15·00 15·00

No. 1979 is inscribed "The Lady with an Ostich Feather Fan" in error.

293 Hong Kong 1983 Space Museum Stamp and Moon-lantern Festival

1994. "Hong Kong '94" International Stamp Exn (1st issue). Multicoloured.

1982 4r. Type **293** 65 80
1983 4r. Maldive Islands 1976 5r. "Viking" space mission stamp and Moon-lantern festival 65 80

Nos. 1982/3 were printed together, se-tenant, forming a composite design.

294 Vase

295 Windischmann (U.S.A.) and Giannini (Italy)

1994. "Hong Kong '94" International Stamp Exhibition (2nd issue). Ching Dynasty Cloisonne Enamelware. Multicoloured.

1984 2r. Type **294** 65 65
1985 2r. Flower holder 65 65
1986 2r. Elephant with vase on back 65 65
1987 2r. Tibetan style lama's teapot 65 65
1988 2r. Fo-Dog 65 65
1989 2r. Teapot with swing handle 65 65

1994. World Cup Football Championship, U.S.A. (2nd issue). Multicoloured.

1990 7l. Type **295** 30 25
1991 20l. Carnevale (Italy) and Gascoigne (England) . . . 50 25
1992 25l. England players congratulating Platt . . . 50 25
1993 3r.50 Koeman (Holland) and Klinsmann (Germany) . . . . 1·25 80
1994 5r. Quinn (Ireland) and Maldini (Italy) . . . . . 1·40 1·00
1995 7r. Lineker (England) . . . 2·00 1·50
1996 15r. Hassam (Egypt) and Moran (Ireland) . . . . 3·00 3·50
1997 18r. Canniggia (Argentina) 3·25 3·50
MS1998 Two sheets, each 103 × 73 mm. 25r. Ogris (Austria). (b) 25r. Conejo (Costa Rica) (horiz) Set of 2 sheets . . . . 11·00 11·00

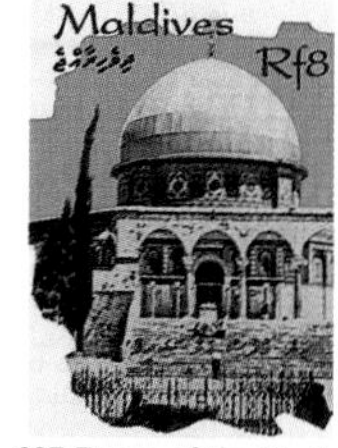

296 Humpback Whale

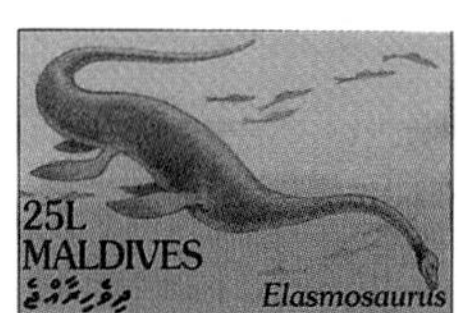

297 Dome of the Rock, Jerusalem

1994. Centenary (1992) of Sierra Club (environmental protection society). Endangered Species. Multicoloured.

1999 6r.50 Type **296** . . . . . . 1·60 1·60
2000 6r.50 Ocelot crouched in grass . . . . 1·60 1·60
2001 6r.50 Ocelot sitting . . . . 1·60 1·60
2002 6r.50 Snow monkey . . . . 1·60 1·60
2003 6r.50 Prairie dog . . . . . 1·60 1·60
2004 6r.50 Golden lion tamarin 1·60 1·60
2005 6r.50 Prairie dog eating (horiz) . . . . 1·60 1·60
2006 6r.50 Prairie dog outside burrow (horiz) . . . . . 1·60 1·60
2007 6r.50 Herd of woodland caribou (horiz) . . . . . 1·60 1·60
2008 6r.50 Woodland caribou facing left (horiz) . . . . 1·60 1·60
2009 6r.50 Woodland caribou facing right (horiz) . . . 1·60 1·60
2010 6r.50 Pair of Galapagos penguins (horiz) . . . . . 1·60 1·60
2011 6r.50 Galapagos penguin facing right . . . . 1·60 1·60
2012 6r.50 Galapagos penguin looking straight ahead . . 1·60 1·60
2013 6r.50 Bengal tiger looking straight ahead . . . . . 1·60 1·60
2014 6r.50 Bengal tiger looking right . . . . 1·60 1·60
2015 6r.50 Philippine tarsier with tree trunk at left . . . . 1·60 1·60
2016 6r.50 Philippine tarsier with tree trunk at right . . . . 1·60 1·60
2017 6r.50 Head of Philippine tarsier . . . . 1·60 1·60
2018 6r.50 Sierra Club centennial emblem (black, buff and green) . . . . 1·60 1·60
2019 6r.50 Golden lion tamarin between two branches (horiz) . . . . 1·60 1·60
2020 6r.50 Golden lion tamarin on tree trunk (horiz) . . . 1·60 1·60
2021 6r.50 Tail fin of humpback whale and coastline (horiz) . . . . 1·60 1·60
2022 6r.50 Tail fin of humpback whale at night (horiz) . . 1·60 1·60
2023 6r.50 Bengal tiger (horiz) . . 1·60 1·60
2024 5r.50 Ocelot (horiz) . . . . 1·60 1·60
2025 6r.50 Snow monkey in water climbing out of pool (horiz) . . . . 1·60 1·60
2026 6r.50 Snow monkey swimming (horiz) . . . . 1·60 1·60

1994. Solidarity with the Palestinians.

2027 **297** 8r. multicoloured . . . . 1·40 1·50

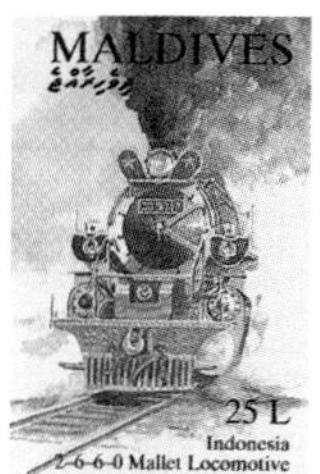

298 Elasmosaurus

1994. Prehistoric Animals. Multicoloured.

2028/59 25l., 50l., 1r., 3r. × 24, 5r., 8r., 10r., 15r., 20r. Set of 32 . . . . 30·00 28·00
MS2060 Two sheets, each 106 × 76 mm. (a) 25r. Gallimimus. (b) 25r. Plateosaurus (vert) Set of 2 sheets . . . . 8·00 8·50

Nos. 2031/42 and 2043/54 respectively were printed together, se-tenant, forming composite designs. The species depicted are, in addition to Type **298**, Dilophosaurus, Avimimus, Dimorphodon, Megalosaurus, Kuehneosaurus, Dryosaurus, Kentrosaurus, Baraposaurus, Tenontosaurus, Elaphrosaurus, Maiasaura, Huayangosaurus, Rutiodon, Pianitzkysaurus, Quetzalcoatlus, Daspletosaurus, Pleurocoelus, Baryonyx, Pentaceratops, Kritosaurus, Microvenator, Nodosaurus, Montanaceratops, Dromiceiomimus, Dryptosaurus, Parkosaurus, Chasmosaurus, Edmontonia, Anatosaurus, Velociraptor and Spinosaurus.

299 Mallet Steam Locomotive, Indonesia

1994. Railway Locomotives of Asia. Multicoloured.

2061 25l. Type **299** 20 20
2062 50l. Class C62 steam locomotive, Japan, 1948 25 20
2063 1r. Class D51 steam locomotive, Japan, 1936 (horiz) 30 20
2064 5r. Steam locomotive, India (horiz) 90 90
2065 6r.50+50l. Class W steam locomotive, India (horiz) 1·25 1·50
2066 6r.50+50l. Class C53 steam locomotive, Indonesia (horiz) . . . . 1·25 1·50
2067 6r.50+50l. Class C10 steam locomotive, Japan (horiz) 1·25 1·50
2068 6r.50+50l. Hanomag steam locomotive, India (horiz) 1·25 1·50
2069 6r.50+50l. "Hikari" express train, Japan (horiz) . . . 1·25 1·50
2070 6r.50+50l. Class C55 steam locomotive, Japan, 1935 (horiz) . . . . 1·25 1·50
2071 8r. Class 485 electric locomotive, Japan (horiz) 1·50 1·75
2072 10r. Class WP steam locomotive, India (horiz) 1·75 2·00
2073 15r. Class RM steam locomotive, China (horiz) 2·00 2·25
2074 20r. Class C57 steam locomotive, Japan, 1937 2·25 2·50
MS2075 Two sheets, each 110 × 80 mm. (a) 25r. Steam locomotive pulling goods train, Indonesia (horiz). (b) 25r. Class 8620 steam locomotive, Japan, 1914 (horiz) Set of 2 sheets . . 8·00 8·50

No. 2069 is inscribed "Hakari" in error.

300 Japanese Bobtail

1994. Cats. Multicoloured.

2076 7l. Type **300** 20 20
2077 20l. Siamese (vert) 35 20
2078 25l. Persian longhair 35 20
2079 50l. Somali (vert) 40 20
2080 3r.50 Oriental shorthair . . 1·00 80
2081 5r. Burmese . . . . 1·25 1·00
2082 7r. Bombay carrying kitten 1·50 1·50
2083 10r. Turkish van (vert) . . . 1·50 1·75
2084 12r. Javanese (vert) . . . . 1·75 2·00
2085 15r. Singapura . . . . . . 2·00 2·50
2086 18r. Turkish angora (vert) 2·25 2·75
2087 20r. Egyptian mau (vert) . . 2·25 2·75
MS2088 Three sheets. (a) 70 × 100 mm. 25r. Birman (vert). (b) 70 × 100 mm. 25r. Korat (vert). (c) 100 × 70 mm. 25r. Abyssinian (vert) Set of 3 sheets . . . . . 12·00 13·50

301 Franco Baresi (Italy) and Stuart McCall (Scotland)

1994. World Cup Football Championship, U.S.A. (3rd issue). Multicoloured. (a) Horiz designs.

2089 10l. Type **301** 40 40
2090 25l. Mick McCarthy (Ireland) and Gary Lineker (England) 50 50
2091 50l. J. Helt (Denmark) and R. Gordillo (Spain) . . . 50 50
2092 5r. Martin Vasquez (Spain) and Enzo Scifo (Belgium) 1·00 1·00
2093 10r. Championship emblem 1·40 1·40
2094 12r. Tomas Brolin (Sweden) and Gordon Durie (Scotland) . . . . 1·60 1·60

(b) Vert designs.

2095 6r.50 Bebeto (Brazil) . . . . 1·10 1·10
2096 6r.50 Lothar Matthaus (Germany) . . . . 1·10 1·10
2097 6r.50 Diego Maradona (Argentina) . . . . 1·10 1·10
2098 6r.50 Stephane Chapuasti (Switzerland) . . . . . . 1·10 1·10
2099 6r.50 George Hagi (Rumania) . . . . 1·10 1·10
2100 6r.50 Carlos Valderama (Colombia) . . . . 1·10 1·10
MS2101 100 × 70 mm. 10r. Egyptian players . . . . 3·75 3·75

302 Crew of "Apollo 11"

1994. 25th Anniv of First Manned Moon Landing. Multicoloured.

2102 5r. Type **302** 90 90
2103 5r. "Apollo 11" mission logo 90 90
2104 5r. Edwin Aldrin (astronaut) and "Eagle" 90 90
2105 5r. Crew of "Apollo 12" . . 90 90
2106 5r. "Apollo 12" mission logo 90 90
2107 5r. Alan Bean (astronaut) and equipment 90 90
2108 5r. Crew of "Apollo 16" . . 90 90
2109 5r. "Apollo 16" mission logo 90 90
2110 5r. Astronauts with U.S. flag 90 90
2111 5r. Crew of "Apollo 17" . . 90 90
2112 5r. "Apollo 17" mission logo 90 90
2113 5r. Launch of "Apollo 17" 90 90
MS2114 100 × 76 mm. 25r. Launch of Russian rocket from Baikonur (vert) . . . . 4·00 4·75

303 Linford Christie (Great Britain) (100 m), 1992

1994. Centenary of International Olympic Committee. Gold Medal Winners. Multicoloured.

2115 7r. Type **303** 1·50 1·25
2116 12r. Koji Gushiken (Japan) (gymnastics), 1984 1·75 2·00
MS2117 106 × 71 mm. 25r. George Hackl (Germany) (single luge), 1994 4·00 4·50

304 U.S. Amphibious DUKW

1994. 50th Anniv of D-Day. Multicoloured.

2118 2r. Type **304** 45 30
2119 4r. Tank landing craft unloading at Sword Beach 75 60
2120 18r. Infantry landing craft at Omaha Beach 3·00 4·25
MS2121 105 × 76 mm. 25r. Landing craft with Canadian commandos 4·50 4·75

305 Duckpond, Suwan Folk Village

1994. "Philakorea '94" International Stamp Exn, Seoul. Multicoloured.

2122 50l. Type **305** 50 30
2123 3r. Pear-shaped bottle (vert) 60 70
2124 3r. Vase with dragon decoration (vert) 60 70
2125 3r. Vase with repaired lip (vert) 60 70
2126 3r. Stoneware vase with floral decoration (vert) 60 70
2127 3r. Celadon-glazed vase (vert) 60 70
2128 3r. Unglazed stone vase (vert) 60 70
2129 3r. Ritual water sprinkler (vert) 60 70
2130 3r. Long-necked celadon-glazed vase (vert) 60 70
2131 3r.50 Yongduson Park 70 75
2132 20r. Ploughing with ox, Hahoe 8·00 9·50
MS2133 70 × 102 mm. 25r. "Hunting" (detail from eight-panel painted screen) (vert) 4·00 4·75

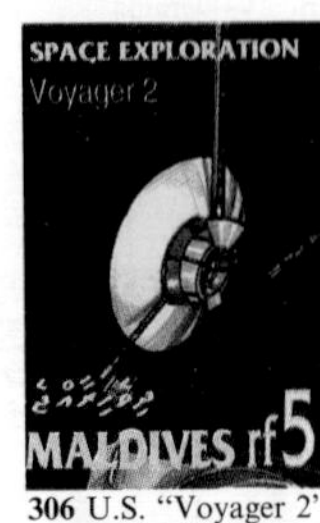

306 U.S. "Voyager 2" Satellite

1994. Space Exploration. Multicoloured.

2134 5r. Type **306** 1·25 1·25
2135 5r. Russian "Sputnik" satellite 1·25 1·25
2136 5r. "Apollo-Soyuz" mission 1·25 1·25
2137 5r. "Apollo 10" on parachutes 1·25 1·25
2138 5r. "Apollo 11" mission flag 1·25 1·25
2139 5r. Hubble space telescope 1·25 1·25
2140 5r. Edwin "Buzz" Aldrin (astronaut) 1·25 1·25
2141 5r. RCA lunar camera 1·25 1·25
2142 5r. Lunar Rover (space buggy) 1·25 1·25
2143 5r. Jim Irwin (astronaut) 1·25 1·25
2144 5r. "Apollo 12" lunar module 1·25 1·25
2145 5r. Astronaut holding equipment 1·25 1·25
MS2146 Two sheets. (a) 70 × 100 mm. 25r. David Scott (astronaut) in open hatch of "Apollo 9". (b) 100 × 70 mm. 25r. Alan Shepherd Jr. (astronaut) (horiz) Set of 2 sheets 12·00 12·00

307 Mother, Child, Old Man and Town Skyline

1994. United Nations Development Programme. Multicoloured.

2147 1r. Type **307** 15 10
2148 8r. Fisherman with son and island 1·40 1·75

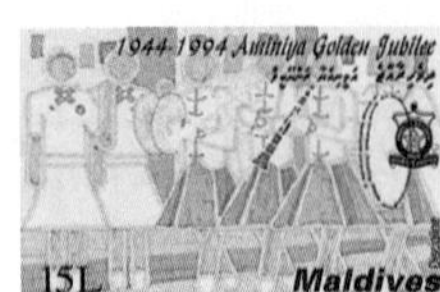

308 School Band

1994. 50th Anniv of Aminiya School. Children's Paintings. Multicoloured.

2149 15l. Type **308** 10 10
2150 50l. Classroom 20 15
2151 1r. School emblem and hand holding book (vert) 30 15
2152 8r. School girls holding books (vert) 1·75 2·00
2153 10r. Sporting activities 1·75 2·00
2154 11r. School girls holding crown (vert) 1·90 2·50
2155 13r. Science lesson 1·90 2·50

309 Boeing 747

1994. 50th Anniv of I.C.A.O. Multicoloured.

2156 50l. Type **309** 50 25
2157 1r. Hawker Siddeley ("de Havilland") Comet 4 60 25
2158 2r. Male International Airport 85 55
2159 3r. Lockheed L.1649 Super Star 1·25 85
2160 8r. European Airbus 2·00 2·50
2161 10r. Dornier Do-228 2·00 2·50
MS2162 100 × 70 mm. 25r. Concorde 4·00 4·50

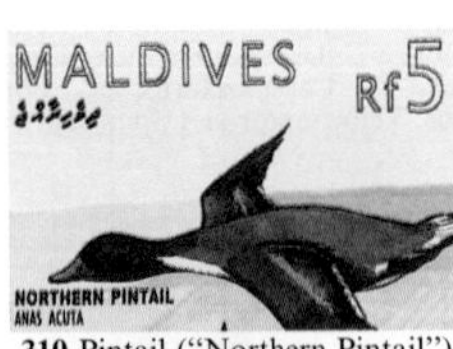

310 Pintail ("Northern Pintail")

1995. Ducks. Multicoloured.

2163 5r. Type **310** 90 1·00
2164 5r. Comb duck 90 1·00
2165 5r. Ruddy shelduck 90 1·00
2166 5r. Garganey 90 1·00
2167 5r. Indian whistling duck ("Lesser Whistling Duck") 90 1·00
2168 5r. Green-winged teal 90 1·00
2169 5r. Fulvous whistling duck 90 1·00
2170 5r. Common shoveler ("Northern Shoveler") 90 1·00
2171 5r. Cotton teal ("Cotton Pygmy Goose") 90 1·00
2172 6r.50+50l. Common pochard ("Pochard") (vert) 90 1·00
2173 6r.50+50l. Mallard (vert) 90 1·00
2174 6r.50+50l. European wigeon ("Wigeon") (vert) 90 1·00
2175 6r.50+50l. Common shoveler ("Northern Shoveler") (vert) 90 1·00
2176 6r.50+50l. Pintail ("Northern Pintail") (vert) 90 1·00
2177 6r.50+50l. Garganey (vert) 90 1·00
2178 6r.50+50l. Tufted duck (vert) 90 1·00
2179 6r.50+50l. Red-crested pochard ("Ferruginous Duck") (vert) 90 1·00
2180 6r.50+50l. Ferruginous duck ("Red-crested Pochard") (vert) 90 1·00
MS2181 Two sheets. (a) 100 × 71 mm. 25r. Spotbill duck ("Garganey"). (b) 73 × 100 mm. 25r. Cotton teal ("Cotton Pygmy Goose") (vert) Set of 2 sheets 7·50 8·50

Nos. 2163/71 and 2172/80 were printed together, se-tenant, forming composite designs.

311 Taj Mahal, India

1995. Famous Monuments of the World. Mult.

2182 7l. Type **311** 50 25
2183 10l. Washington Monument, U.S.A. 10 10
2184 15l. Mount Rushmore, U.S.A. 10 10
2185 25l. Arc de Triomphe, Paris (vert) 10 10
2186 50l. Sphinx, Egypt (vert) 50 20
2187 5r. El Castillo, Toltec pyramid, Yucatan 85 90
2188 8r. Toltec statue, Tula, Mexico (vert) 1·25 1·75
2189 12r. Victory Column, Berlin (vert) 1·60 2·25
MS2190 Two sheets, each 112 × 85 mm. (a) 25r. Easter Island statue (42 × 56 mm). (b) 25r. Stonehenge, Wiltshire (85 × 28 mm) Set of 2 sheets 7·50 8·50

312 Donald Duck driving Chariot

1995. History of Wheeled Transport. Scenes from Disney cartoon film "Donald and the Wheel". Multicoloured.

2191 3l. Type **312** 10 10
2192 4l. Donald with log 10 10
2193 5l. Donald driving Stephenson's "Rocket" 10 10
2194 10l. Donald pondering over circle (vert) 10 10
2195 20l. Donald in crashed car (vert) 10 10
2196 25l. Donald listening to early gramophone 10 10
2197 5r. Donald on mammoth 1·10 1·25
2198 20r. Donald pushing early car 3·25 4·25

313 Donald Duck playing Saxophone

1995. 60th Birthday of Donald Duck. Walt Disney cartoon characters. Multicoloured.

2199 5r. Type **313** 90 90
2200 5r. Moby Duck playing fiddle 90 90
2201 5r. Feathry Duck with banjo and drum 90 90
2202 5r. Daisy Duck playing harp 90 90
2203 5r. Gladstone Gander with clarinet 90 90
2204 5r. Huey, Dewey and Louie with bassoon 90 90
2205 5r. Gus Goose playing flute 90 90
2206 5r. Prof. Ludwig von Drake playing trombone 90 90
2207 5r. Daisy picking flowers 90 90
2208 5r. Donald with backpack 90 90
2209 5r. Grandma Duck with kitten 90 90
2210 5r. Gus Goose and pie 90 90
2211 5r. Gyro Gearloose in space 90 90
2212 5r. Huey, Dewey and Louie photographing porcupine 90 90
2213 5r. Prof. Ludwig von Drake 90 90
2214 5r. Scrooge McDuck with money 90 90
MS2215 Four sheets. (a) 108 × 130 mm. 25r. Donald playing banjo. (b) 133 × 108 mm. 25r. Donald posing for photo. (c) 108 × 130 mm. 25r. Donald conducting (horiz). (d) 102 × 121 mm. 25r. Huey, Dewey and Louie (horiz) Set of 4 sheets 14·00 15·00

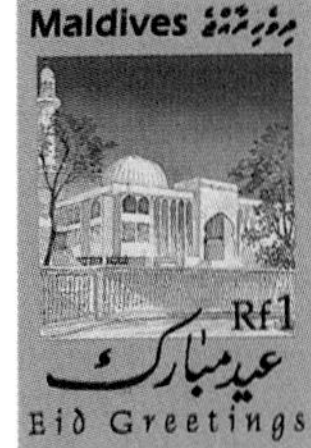

314 Islamic Centre, Male

1995. Eid Greetings. Multicoloured.

2216 1r. Type **314** 15 15
2217 1r. Rose 15 15
2218 8r. Orchid 1·50 1·50
2219 10r. Orchid (different) 1·50 1·50

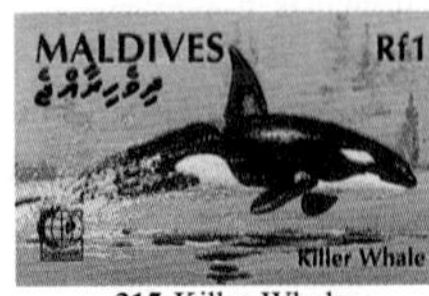

315 Killer Whale

1995. "Singapore '95" International Stamp Exhibition (1st issue). Whales, Dolphins and Porpoises. Multicoloured.

2220 1r. Type **315** 40 30
2221 2r. Bottlenose dolphins 45 35
2222 3r. Right whale 60 70
2223 3r. Pair of killer whales 60 70
2224 3r. Humpback whale 60 70
2225 3r. Pair of belugas 60 70
2226 3r. Narwhal 60 70
2227 3r. Head of blue whale 60 70
2228 3r. Bowhead whale 60 70
2229 3r. Head of fin whale 60 70
2230 3r. Pair of pilot whales 60 70
2231 3r. Grey whale 60 70
2232 3r. Sperm whale 60 70
2233 3r. Pair of goosebeaked whales 60 70
2234 3r. Hourglass dolphin 60 70
2235 3r. Bottlenose dolphin (different) 60 70
2236 3r. Dusky dolphin 60 70
2237 3r. Spectacled porpoise 60 70
2238 3r. Fraser's dolphin 60 70
2239 3r. Cameron's dolphin 60 70
2240 3r. Pair of spinner dolphins 60 70
2241 3r. Pair of Dalls dolphins 60 70
2242 3r. Spotted dolphin 60 70
2243 3r. Indus River dolphin 60 70
2244 3r. Hector's dolphin 60 70
2245 3r. Amazon River dolphin 60 70
2246 8r. Humpback whale and calf 1·25 1·50
2247 10r. Common dolphin 1·40 1·60
MS2248 Two sheets, each 100 × 70 mm. (a) 25r. Sperm whale (different). (b) 25r. Pair of hourglass dolphins Set of 2 sheets 9·00 9·00

See also Nos. 2302/10.

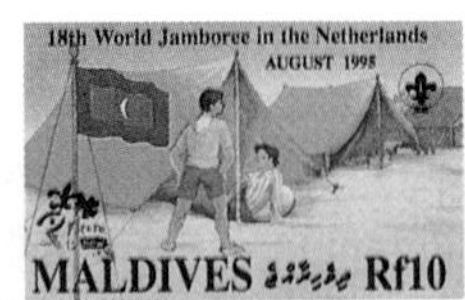

316 Scout Camp and National Flag

1995. 18th World Scout Jamboree, Netherlands. Multicoloured.

2249 10r. Type **316** 1·75 2·00
2250 12r. Campfire cooking 1·90 2·25
2251 15r. Scouts erecting tent 2·00 2·40
MS2252 102 × 72 mm. 25r. Scouts around camp fire (vert) 3·50 4·00

Nos. 2249/51 were printed together, se-tenant, forming a composite design.

317 Soviet Heavy Howitzer Battery

1995. 50th Anniv of End of Second World War in Europe. Multicoloured.

2253 5r. Type **317** 85 85
2254 5r. Ruins of Berchtesgaden 85 85
2255 5r. U.S. Boeing B-17 Flying Fortress dropping food over the Netherlands 85 85
2256 5r. Soviet Ilyushin Il-1 bomber 85 85
2257 5r. Liberation of Belsen 85 85
2258 5r. Supermarine Spitfire and V-1 flying bomb 85 85
2259 5r. U.S. tanks advancing through Cologne 85 85
2260 5r. Reichstag in ruins 85 85
MS2261 107 × 76 mm. 25r. Soviet and U.S. troops celebrating 3·50 3·75

318 Asian Child and Dove

320 Asian Child eating Rice

319 United Nations Emblem

1995. 50th Anniv of United Nations (1st issue). Multicoloured.

2262 6r.50+50l. Type **318** . . . . 90 1·25
2263 8r. Globe and dove . . . . 1·00 1·40
2264 10r. African child and dove 1·10 1·50
MS2265 72 × 102 mm. 25r. United Nations emblem and dove . . 2·75 3·75

Nos. 2262/4 were printed together, se-tenant, forming a composite design.

1995. 50th Anniv of United Nations (2nd issue).

2266 **319** 30l. black, blue & grn . . 10 10
2267 – 8r. multicoloured . . . . 1·00 1·25
2268 – 11r. multicoloured . . . 1·25 1·50
2269 – 13r. black, grey and red 1·60 1·90

DESIGNS: 8r. Symbolic women, flag and map; 11r. U.N. soldier and symbolic dove; 13r. Gun barrels, atomic explosion and bomb sight

1995. 50th Anniv of F.A.O. (1st issue). Mult

2270 6r.50+50l. Type **320** . . . . 90 1·10
2271 8r. F.A.O. emblem . . . . 1·00 1·25
2272 10r. African mother and child . . . . 1·10 1·40
MS2273 72 × 102 mm. 25r. African child and symbolic hand holding maize . . . . 2·75 3·75

See also Nos. 2311/12.

321 Queen Elizabeth the Queen Mother

1995. 95th Birthday of Queen Elizabeth the Queen Mother.

2274 **321** 5r. brown, lt brn & blk 1·00 1·10
2275 – 5r. multicoloured . . . . 1·00 1·10
2276 – 5r. multicoloured . . . . 1·00 1·10
2277 – 5r. multicoloured . . . . 1·00 1·10
MS2278 125 × 100 mm. 25r. multicoloured . . . . 4·25 4·50

DESIGNS: No. 2275, Without hat; 2276, At desk (oil painting); 2277, Queen Elizabeth the Queen Mother; **MS**2278, Wearing lilac hat and dress.

1995. 50th Anniv of End of Second World War in the Pacific. As T **317**. Multicoloured.

2279 6r.50+50l. Grumman F6F-3 Hellcat aircraft . . . . . 1·50 1·50
2280 6r.50+50l. F4-U1 fighter aircraft attacking beach 1·50 1·50
2281 6r.50+50l. Douglas SBD Dauntless aircraft . . . . 1·50 1·50
2282 6r.50+50l. American troops in landing craft, Guadalcanal . . . . . . 1·50 1·50
2283 6r.50+50l. U.S. marines in Alligator tanks . . . . . 1·50 1·50
2284 6r.50+50l. U.S. landing ship 1·50 1·50
MS2285 106 × 74 mm. 25r. F4-U1 fighter aircraft . . . . 4·00 4·50

322 Students using Library

1995. 50th Anniv of National Library. Mult.

2286 2r. Type **322** 25 25
2287 8r. Students using library (different) . . . . 1·00 1·50
MS2288 105 × 75 mm. 10r. Library entrance (100 × 70 mm). Imperf 1·40 1·60

323 Spur-thighed Tortoise

1995. Turtles and Tortoises. Multicoloured.

2289 3r. Type **323** 60 70
2290 3r. Aldabra turtle 60 70
2291 3r. Loggerhead turtle . . . 60 70
2292 3r. Olive Ridley turtle . . . 60 70
2293 3r. Leatherback turtle . . . 60 70
2294 3r. Green turtle 60 70
2295 3r. Atlantic Ridley turtle . . 60 70
2296 3r. Hawksbill turtle 60 70
2297 10r. Hawksbill turtle on beach . . . . 1·40 1·60
2298 10r. Pair of hawksbill turtles 1·40 1·60
2299 10r. Hawksbill turtle climbing out of water . . 1·40 1·60
2300 10r. Hawksbill turtle swimming . . . . 1·40 1·60
MS2301 100 × 70 mm. 25r. Green turtle . . . . 3·75 4·50

Nos. 2289/96 were printed together, se-tenant, forming a composite design.

Nos. 2297/2300 include the W.W.F. Panda emblem.

324 "Russula aurata" (fungi) and "Papilio demodocus" (butterfly)

1995. "Singapore '95" International Stamp Exhibition. Butterflies and Fungi. Multicoloured.

2302 2r. Type **324** 75 75
2303 2r. "Lepista saeva" and "Kallimoides rumia" . . 75 75
2304 2r. "Lepista nuda" and "Hypolimnas salmacis" 75 75
2305 2r. "Xerocomus subtomentosus" ("Boletus subtomentosus" and "Precis octavia") 75 75
2306 5r. "Gyroporus castaneus" and "Hypolimnas salmacis" . . . . 1·10 1·10
2307 8r. "Gomphidius glutinosus" and "Papilio dardanus" 1·25 1·25
2308 10r. "Russula olivacea" and "Precis octavia" . . . . . 1·40 1·40
2309 12r. "Boletus edulis" and "Prepona praeneste" . . . 1·40 1·40
MS2310 Two sheets, each 105 × 76 mm. (a) 25r. "Amanita muscaria" and "Kallimoides rumia" (vert). (b) 25r. "Boletus rhodoxanthus" and "Hypolimnas salmacis" (vert) Set of 2 sheets 8·00 8·00

Nos. 2302/5 and 2306/9 respectively were printed together, se-tenant, forming composite designs.

No. 2304 is inscribed "Lapista" in error.

325 Planting Kaashi

1995. 50th Anniv of F.A.O. (2nd issue). Mult.

2311 7r. Type **325** . . . . 90 1·10
2312 8r. Fishing boat . . . . . . 1·10 1·25

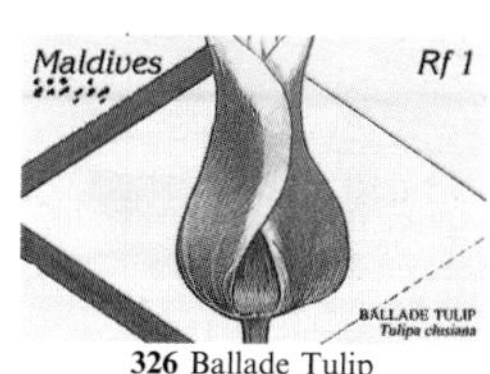

326 Ballade Tulip

1995. Flowers. Multicoloured.

2313 1r. Type **326** 20 15
2314 3r. White mallow 50 50
2315 5r. Regale trumpet lily . . . 1·00 1·00
2316 5r. "Dendrobium Waipahu Beauty" . . . . 1·00 1·00
2317 5r. "Brassocattleya Jean Murray" . . . . 1·00 1·00
2318 5r. "Cymbidium Fort George" . . . . 1·00 1·00
2319 5r. "Paphiopedilum malipoense" . . . . . . 1·00 1·00
2320 5r. "Cycnoches chlorochilon" . . . . . . 1·00 1·00
2321 5r. "Rhyncholaelia digbgana" . . . . 1·00 1·00
2322 5r. "Lycaste deppei" . . . . 1·00 1·00
2323 5r. "Masdevallia constricta" 1·00 1·00
2324 5r. "Paphiopedilum Clair de Lune" . . . . 1·00 1·00
2325 7r. "Lilactime dahlia" . . . 1·25 1·25
2326 8r. Blue ideal iris . . . . . 1·25 1·25
2327 10r. Red crown imperial . . 1·40 1·40
MS2328 Two sheets, each 106 × 76mm. (a) 25r. "Encyclia cochleata" (vert). (b) 25r. "Psychopsis kramerina" (vert) Set of 2 sheets . . . . 8·00 9·50

327 John Lennon with Microphone

329 Johannes van der Waals (1919 Physics)

328 Elvis Presley with Microphone

1995. 15th Death Anniv of John Lennon (musician). Multicoloured.

2329 5r. Type **327** . . . . 1·40 1·25
2330 5r. With glasses and moustache . . . . 1·40 1·25
2331 5r. With guitar . . . . . . 1·40 1·25
2332 5r. With guitar and wearing glasses . . . . 1·40 1·25
2333 5r. Wearing sun glasses and red jacket . . . . 1·40 1·25
2334 5r. Wearing headphones . . 1·40 1·25
MS2335 88 × 117 mm. 2, 3, 8, 10r. Different portraits of John Lennon 5·50 5·50
MS2236 102 × 72 mm. 25r. John Lennon performing . . . . . 5·50 5·50

1995. 60th Birth Anniv of Elvis Presley (entertainer). Multicoloured.

2337 5r. Type **328** 80 80
2338 5r. Wearing red jacket . . . 80 80
2339 5r. Wearing blue jacket . . 80 80
2340 5r. With microphone and wearing blue jacket . . . 80 80
2341 5r. In army uniform 80 80
2342 5r. Wearing yellow bow tie 80 80
2343 5r. In yellow shirt 80 80
2344 5r. In light blue shirt . . . 80 80
2345 5r. Wearing red and white high-collared jacket . . . 80 80
MS2346 80 × 110 mm. 25r. Elvis Presley (horiz) . . . . 3·75 4·00

1995. Cent of Nobel Prize Trust Fund. Mult.

2347/55 5r. × 9 (Type **329**; Charles Guillaume (1920 Physics); Sir James Chadwick (1935 Physics); Willem Einthoven (1924 Medicine); Henrik Dam (1943 Medicine); Sir Alexander Fleming (1945 Medicine); Hermann Muller (1946 Medicine); Rodney Porter (1972 Medicine); Werner Arber (1978 Medicine)) . . . . .
2356/64 5r. × 9 (Niels Bohr (1922 Physics); Ben Mottelson (1975 Physics); Patrick White (1973 Literature); Elias Canetti (1981 Literature); Theodor Kocher (1909 Medicine); August Krogh (1920 Medicine); William Murphy (1934 Medicine); John Northrop (1946 Chemistry); Luis Leloir (1970 Chemistry)) . . . .
2365/73 5r. × 9 (Dag Hammarskjold (1961 Peace); Alva Myrdal (1982 Peace); Archbishop Desmond Tutu (1984 Peace); Rudolf Eucken (1908 Literature); Aleksandr Solzhenitsyn (1970 Literature); Gabriel Marquez (1982 Literature); Chen Yang (1957 Physics); Karl Muller (1987 Physics); Melvin Schwartz (1988 Physics)) . . . . . .
2374/82 5r. × 9 (Robert Millikan (1923 Physics); Louis de Broglie (1929 Physics); Ernest Walton (1951 Physics); Richard Willstatter (1915 Chemistry); Lars Onsager (1968 Chemistry); Gerhard Herzberg (1971 Chemistry); William B. Yeats (1923 Literature); George Bernard Shaw (1925 Literature); Eugene O'Neill (1936 Literature)) . . . . .
2383/91 5r. × 9 (Bernardo Houssay (1947 Medicine); Paul Muller (1948 Medicine); Walter Hess (1949 Medicine); Sir MacFarlane Burnet (1960 Medicine); Baruch Blumberg (1976 Medicine); Daniel Nathans (1978 Medicine); Glenn Seaborg (1951 Chemistry); Ilya Prigogine (1977 Chemistry); Kenichi Fukui (1981 Chemistry)) . . . .
2392/2400 5r. × 9 (Carl Spitteler (1919 Literature); Henri Bergson (1927 Literature); Johannes Jensen (1944 Literature); Antoine-Henri Becquerel (1903 Physics); Sir William H. Bragg (1915 Physics); Sir William L. Bragg (1915 Physics); Frederik Bajer (1908 Peace); Leon Bourgeois (1920 Peace); Karl Benning (1921 Peace)) . . . .
Set of 54 . . . . 35·00 40·00
MS2401 Six sheets. (a) 80 × 110 mm. 25r. Konrad bloch (1964 Medicine). (b) 80 × 110 mm. 25r. Samuel Beckett (1969 Literature). (c) 80 × 110 mm. 25r. Otto Wallach (1910 Chemistry). (d) 110 × 80 mm. 25r. Hideki Yukawa (1949 Physics). (e) 110 × 80 mm. 25r. Eisaku Sato (1974 Peace). (f) 110 × 80 mm. 25r. Robert Koch (1905 Medicine) Set of 6 sheets 15·00 16·00

330 Rythmic Gymnast and Japanese Fan

1996. Olympic Games, Atlanta (1st issue). Mult.

2402 1r. Type **330** 20 10
2403 3r. Archer and Moscow Olympics logo 40 35
2404 5r. Diver and Swedish flag 65 70
2405 5r. Canadian Maple Leaf . . 65 70
2406 5r. Shot putting (decathlon) 65 70
2407 5r. Moscow Olympic medal and ribbon 65 70
2408 5r. Fencer 65 70
2409 5r. Gold medal 65 70
2410 5r. Equestrian competitor 65 70
2411 5r. Sydney Opera House . . 65 70
2412 5r. Athlete on starting blocks 65 70
2413 5r. South Korean flag . . . 65 70
2414 7r. High jumper and Tower Bridge, London 85 90
2415 10r. Athlete on starting blocks and Brandenburg Gate, Germany . . . . . 1·25 1·40
2416 12r. Hurdler and Amsterdam Olympic logo 1·40 1·60
MS2417 Two sheets, each 113 × 80 mm. (a) 25r. Red Olympic Flame (vert). (b) 25r. Multicoloured Olympic Flame (vert) Set of 2 sheets . . . . . 8·00 9·00

See also Nos. 2469/87.

331 "Self Portrait" (Degas)

1996. 125th Anniv of Metropolitan Museum of Art, New York. Multicoloured.
2418/25 4r. × 8 ("Self-Portrait" (Degas); "Andromache and Astyanax" (Prud'hon); "Rene Grenier" (Toulouse-Lautrec); "The Banks of the Bievre near Bicetre" (Rousseau); "The Repast of the Lion" (Rousseau); "Portrait of Yves Gobillard-Morisot" (Degas); "Sunflowers" (Van Gogh); "The Singer in Green" (Degas))
2426/33 4r. × 8 ("Still Life" (Fantin-Latour); "Portrait of a Lady in Grey" (Degas); "Apples and Grapes" (Monet); "The Englishman" (Toulouse-Lautrec); "Cypresses" (Van Gogh); "Flowers in a Chinese Vase" (Redon); "The Gardener" (Seurat); "Large Sunflowers I" (Nolde))
2434/41 4r. × 8 (All by Manet: "The Spanish Singer"; "Young Man in Costume of Majo"; "Mademoiselle Victorine"; "Boating"; "Peonies"; "Woman with a Parrot"; "George Moore"; "The Monet Family in their Garden")
2442/9 4r. × 8 ("Goldfish" (Matisse); "Spanish Woman: Harmony in Blue" (Matisse); "Nasturtiums and the "Dance" II" (Matisse); "The House behind Trees" (Braque); "Mada Primavesi" (Klimt); "Head of a Woman" (Picasso); "Woman in White" (Picasso); "Harlequin" (Picasso))
2418/49 Set of 32 . . . 23·00 25·00
MS2450 Four sheets, each 95 × 70 mm, containing horiz designs, 81 × 53 mm. (a) 25r. "Northeaster" (Homer). (b) 25r. "The Fortune Teller" (De La Tour). (c) 25r. "Santo (Sanzio), Ritratto de Andrea Navagero e Agostino Beazzano" (Raphael). (d) 25r. "Portrait of a Woman" (Rubens) Set of 4 sheets . . . 15·00 17·00

332 Mickey Mouse on Great Wall of China

1996. "CHINA '96" 9th Asian International Stamp Exhibition, Peking. Walt Disney cartoon characters in China. Multicoloured.
2451 2r. Type **332** . . . 80 80
2452 2r. Pluto with temple guardian . . . 80 80
2453 2r. Minnie Mouse with pandas . . . 80 80
2454 2r. Mickey windsurfing near junks . . . 80 80
2455 2r. Goofy cleaning grotto statue . . . 80 80
2456 2r. Donald and Daisy Duck at Marble Boat . . . 80 80
2457 2r. Mickey with terracotta warriors . . . 80 80
2458 2r. Goofy with geese and masks . . . 80 80
2459 2r. Donald and Goofy on traditional fishing boat . . 80 80
2460 2r. Mickey and Minnie in dragon boat . . . 80 80
2461 2r. Donald at Peking opera 80 80
2462 2r. Mickey and Minnie in Chinese garden . . . 80 80
2463 3r. Mickey and Minnie at the Ice Pagoda (vert) . . 1·00 1·00
2464 3r. Donald and Mickey flying Chinese kites (vert) 1·00 1·00
2465 3r. Goofy playing anyiwu (vert) . . . 1·00 1·00
2466 3r. Paper cutouts of Mickey and Goofy (vert) . . . 1·00 1·00
2467 3r. Donald and Mickey in dragon dance (vert) . . . 1·00 1·00
MS2468 Three sheets. (a) 108 × 133 mm. 5r. Mickey pointing. (b) 133 × 108 mm. 7r. Mickey and Minnie watching Moon. (c) 133 × 108 mm. 8r. Donald using chopsticks Set of 3 sheets . . . 4·50 5·00

333 Stella Walsh (Poland) (100 m sprint, 1932) on Medal

1996. Olympic Games, Atlanta (2nd issue). Previous Gold Medal Winners. Multicoloured.
2469 1r. Type **333** . . . 20 15
2470 3r. Emile Zatopek (Czechoslovakia) (10,000 m running, 1952) and Olympic torch (vert) 40 35
2471 5r. Yanko Rousseu (Bulgaria) (lightweight, 1980) (vert) . . . 65 70
2472 5r. Peter Baczako (Hungary) (middle heavyweight, 1980) (vert) . . . 65 70
2473 5r. Leonid Taranenko (Russia) (heavyweight, 1980) (vert) . . . 65 70
2474 5r. Aleksandr Kurlovich (Russia) (heavyweight, 1988) (vert) . . . 65 70
2475 5r. Assen Zlateu (Bulgaria) (middleweight, 1980) (vert) . . . 65 70
2476 5r. Zeng Guoqiang (China) (flyweight, 1984) (vert) . . 65 70
2477 5r. Yurik Vardanyan (Russia) (heavyweight, 1980) (vert) . . . 65 70
2478 5r. Sultan Rakhmanov (Russia) (super heavyweight, 1980) (vert) 65 70
2479 5r. Vassily Alexeev (Russia) (super heavyweight, 1972) (vert) . . . 65 70
2480 5r. Ethel Catherwood (Canada) (high jump, 1928) . . . 65 70
2481 5r. Mildred Didrikson (U.S.A.) (javelin, 1932) . . 65 70
2482 5r. Francina Blankers-Koen (Netherlands) (80 m hurdles, 1948) . . . 65 70
2483 5r. Tamara Press (Russia) (shot put, 1960) . . . 65 70
2484 5r. Lia Manoliu (Rumania) (discus, 1968) . . . 65 70
2485 5r. Rosa Mota (Portugal) (marathon, 1988) . . . 65 70
2486 10r. Olga Fikotova (Czechoslovakia) (discus, 1956) on medal . . . 1·25 1·40
2487 12r. Joan Benoit (U.S.A.) (marathon, 1984) on medal . . . 1·40 1·60
MS2488 Two sheets. (a) 76 × 106 mm. 25r. Naeem Suleymanoglu (Turkey) (weightlifting, 1988) (vert). (b) 105 × 75 mm. 25r. Irena Szewinska (Poland) (400 m running, 1976) on medal Set of 2 sheets . . . 8·00 9·00
No. 2469 identifies the event as 10 metres in error.

334 Queen Elizabeth II

1996. 70th Birthday of Queen Elizabeth II. Mult.
2489 8r. Type **334** . . . 1·25 1·40
2490 8r. Wearing hat . . . 1·25 1·40
2491 8r. At desk . . . 1·25 1·40
MS2492 125 × 103 mm. 25r. Queen Elizabeth and Queen Mother on Buckingham Palace balcony . . 4·50 4·50

335 African Child

1996. 50th Anniv of U.N.I.C.E.F. Multicoloured.
2493 5r. Type **335** . . . 60 55
2494 7r. European girl . . . 85 90
2495 7r. Maldivian boy . . . 85 90
2496 10r. Asian girl . . . 1·25 1·40
MS2497 114 × 74 mm. 25r. Baby with toy . . . 3·25 3·75

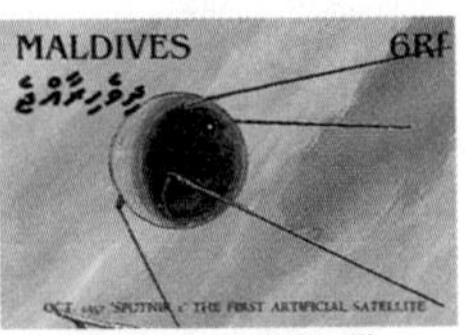

336 "Sputnik 1" Satellite

1996. Space Exploration. Multicoloured.
2498 6r. Type **336** . . . 85 90
2499 6r. "Apollo 11" command module . . . 85 90
2500 6r. "Skylab" . . . 85 90
2501 6r. Astronaut Edward White walking in space . . . 85 90
2502 6r. "Mariner 9" . . . 85 90
2503 6r. "Apollo" and "Soyuz" docking . . . 85 90
MS2504 104 × 74 mm. 25r. Launch of "Apollo 8" (vert) . . . 4·00 4·25

337 "Epiphora albida"

1996. Butterflies. Multicoloured.
2505 7r. Type **337** . . . 90 1·00
2506 7r. "Satyrus dryas" . . . 90 1·00
2507 7r. "Satyrus lena" . . . 90 1·00
2508 7r. "Papilio tynderaeus" . . 90 1·00
2509 7r. "Urota suraka" . . . 90 1·00
2510 7r. "Satyrus nercis" . . . 90 1·00
2511 7r. "Papilio troilus" (vert) 90 1·00
2512 7r. "Papilio cresphontes" (vert) . . . 90 1·00
2513 7r. Lime swallowtail caterpillar (vert) . . . 90 1·00
2514 7r. "Cynthia virginiensis" (vert) . . . 90 1·00
2515 7r. Monarch caterpillar (vert) . . . 90 1·00
2516 7r. "Danaus plexippus" (vert) . . . 90 1·00
2517 7r. Monarch caterpillar and pupa (vert) . . . 90 1·00
2518 7r. "Chlosyne harrisii" (vert) 90 1·00
2519 7r. "Cymothoe coccinata" (vert) . . . 90 1·00
2520 7r. "Morpho rhetenor" (vert) . . . 90 1·00
2521 7r. "Callicore lidwina" (vert) 90 1·00
2522 7r. "Heliconius erato reductimacula" (vert) . . 90 1·00
MS2523 Two sheets, each 106 × 76 mm. (a) 25r. "Heliconius charitonius" (vert). (b) 25r. "Heliconius cydno" (vert) Set of 2 sheets . . . 8·50 9·00

338 Amtrak F40H Diesel-electric Locomotive, U.S.A.

1996. Trains of the World. Multicoloured.
2524 3r. Type **338** . . . 60 60
2525 3r. Stephenson's "Experiment" . . . 60 60
2526 3r. Indian-Pacific Intercontinental, Australia 60 60
2527 3r. Stephenson's Killingworth type steam locomotive, 1815 . . . 60 60
2528 3r. George Stephenson . . . 60 60
2529 3r. Stephenson's "Rocket", 1829 . . . 60 60
2530 3r. High Speed Train 125, Great Britain . . . 60 60
2531 3r. First rail passenger coach "Experiment", 1825 60 60
2532 3r. Union Pacific Class U25B diesel locomotive (inscr "Tofac"), U.S.A. 60 60
2533 3r. Southern Pacific's "Daylight" express, 1952, U.S.A. . . . 60 60
2534 3r. Timothy Hackworth's "Sans Pareil", 1829 . . . 60 60
2535 3r. Chicago and North Western diesel locomotive, U.S.A. . . . 60 60
2536 3r. Richard Trevithick's "Pen-y-Darren" locomotive, 1804 . . . 60 60
2537 3r. Isambard Kingdom Brunel . . . 60 60
2538 3r. Great Western locomotive, 1838 . . . 60 60
2539 3r. Vistadome observation car, Canada . . . 60 60
2540 3r. Mohawk and Hudson Railroad "Experiment", 1832 . . . 60 60
2541 3r. ICE high speed train, Germany . . . 60 60
2542 3r. Electric container locomotive, Germany . . . 60 60
2543 3r. John Blenkinsop's rack locomotive, 1811 . . . 60 60
2544 3r. Diesel-electric locomotive, Western Australia . . . 60 60
2545 3r. Timothy Hackworth's "Royal George", 1827 . . 60 60
2546 3r. Robert Stephenson . . . 60 60
2547 3r. Trevithick's "Newcastle" 60 60
2548 3r. Deltic diesel-electric locomotive, Great Britain 60 60
2549 3r. Stockton and Darlington Railway locomotive No. 5 "Stockton", 1826 . . . 60 60
2550 3r. Channel Tunnel "Le Shuttle" train . . . 60 60
MS2551 Three sheets, each 96 × 91 mm. (a) 25r. Peter Cooper's "Tom Thumb", 1829. (b) 25r. John Jarvis's "De Witt Clinton", 1831. (c) 25r. William Hudson's "The General", 1855 Set of 3 sheets . . . 13·00 13·00
No. 2524 is inscribed "F4 OPH" in error.

339 Bongo

1996. Wildlife of the World. Multicoloured.
2552 5r. Type **339** . . . 80 80
2553 5r. Bushbuck . . . 80 80
2554 5r. Namaqua dove . . . 80 80
2555 5r. Hoopoe . . . 80 80
2556 5r. African fish eagle . . . 80 80
2557 5r. Egyptian goose . . . 80 80
2558 5r. Saddle-bill stork . . . 80 80
2559 5r. Blue-breasted kingfisher 80 80
2560 5r. Yellow baboon . . . 80 80
2561 5r. Banded duiker ("Zebra Duiker") . . . 80 80
2562 5r. Yellow-backed duiker . . 80 80
2563 5r. Pygmy hippopotamus . . 80 80
2564 5r. Large-spotted genet . . . 80 80
2565 5r. African spoonbill . . . 80 80
2566 5r. White-faced whistling duck . . . 80 80
2567 5r. Helmeted guineafowl . . 80 80
2568 7r. Cotton-headed tamarin (horiz) . . . 1·10 1·10
2569 7r. European bison (horiz) 1·10 1·10
2570 7r. Tiger (horiz) . . . 1·10 1·10
2571 7r. Western capercaillie (horiz) . . . 1·10 1·10
2572 7r. Giant panda (horiz) . . 1·10 1·10
2573 7r. "Trogonoptera brookiana" (butterfly) (horiz) . . . 1·10 1·10
2574 7r. American beaver (horiz) 1·10 1·10
2575 7r. "Leiopelma hamiltoni" (frog) (horiz) . . . 1·10 1·10
2576 7r. Manatee (horiz) . . . 1·10 1·10
MS2577 106 × 76 mm. 25r. Chimpanzee (horiz) . . . 3·50 4·00
Nos. 2552/9, 2560/7 and 2568/76 respectively were printed together, se-tenant, with the backgrounds forming composite designs.
No. 2553 is inscribed "BUSHBACK" in error.

340 Giant Panda

1996. Endangered Species. Multicoloured.
2578 5r. Type **340** . . . 85 85
2579 5r. Indian elephant . . . 85 85
2580 5r. Arrow-poison frog . . . 85 85
2581 5r. Mandrill . . . 85 85
2582 5r. Snow leopard . . . 85 85
2583 5r. California condor . . . 85 85
2584 5r. Whale-headed stork ("Shoebill Stork") . . . 85 85
2585 5r. Red-billed hornbill . . . 85 85
2586 5r. Hippopotamus . . . 85 85

2587 5r. Gorilla 85 85
2588 5r. Lion 85 85
2589 5r. South African crowned crane ("Gray Crowned Crane") 85 85
MS2590 Two sheets, each 110 × 80 mm. (a) 25r. Tiger (vert). (b) 25r. Leopard Set of 2 sheets 8·00 8·50

341 Mickey Mouse climbing out of Puddle

1996. Centenary of the Cinema. Cartoon Frames from "The Little Whirlwind" (Nos. 2591/2607) or "Pluto and the Flypaper" (Nos. 2608/24). Mult.

2591 4r. Type **341** 1·00 1·00
2592 4r. Frame 2 1·00 1·00
2593 4r. Frame 3 1·00 1·00
2594 4r. Frame 4 1·00 1·00
2595 4r. Frame 5 1·00 1·00
2596 4r. Frame 6 1·00 1·00
2597 4r. Frame 7 1·00 1·00
2598 4r. Frame 8 1·00 1·00
2599 4r. Frame 9 1·00 1·00
2600 4r. Frame 10 1·00 1·00
2601 4r. Frame 11 1·00 1·00
2602 4r. Frame 12 1·00 1·00
2603 4r. Frame 13 1·00 1·00
2604 4r. Frame 14 1·00 1·00
2605 4r. Frame 15 1·00 1·00
2606 4r. Frame 16 (Mickey holding fish above head) 1·00 1·00
2607 4r. Frame 17 (Mickey throwing fish into pool) 1·00 1·00
2608 4r. Frame 1 (Pluto) 1·00 1·00
2609 4r. Frame 2 1·00 1·00
2610 4r. Frame 3 1·00 1·00
2611 4r. Frame 4 1·00 1·00
2612 4r. Frame 5 1·00 1·00
2613 4r. Frame 6 1·00 1·00
2614 4r. Frame 7 1·00 1·00
2615 4r. Frame 8 1·00 1·00
2616 4r. Frame 9 1·00 1·00
2617 4r. Frame 10 1·00 1·00
2618 4r. Frame 11 1·00 1·00
2619 4r. Frame 12 1·00 1·00
2620 4r. Frame 13 1·00 1·00
2621 4r. Frame 14 1·00 1·00
2622 4r. Frame 15 1·00 1·00
2623 4r. Frame 16 1·00 1·00
2624 4r. Frame 17 1·00 1·00
MS2625 Two sheets, 111 × 131 mm. (a) 25r. Frame 18 ("The Little Whirlwind"). (b) 25r. Frame 18 ("Pluto and the Flypaper") Set of 2 sheets 12·00 12·50

342 Letter "O" with Chinese Character

1997. "HONG KONG '97" International Stamp Exhibition. Multicoloured.

2626 5r. Letter "H" and Chinese couple 75 75
2627 5r. Type **342** 75 75
2628 5r. Letter "N" and Chinese dragon 75 75
2629 5r. Letter "G" and carnival dragon 75 75
2630 5r. Letter "K" and modern office block 75 75
2631 5r. Letter "O" and Chinese character (different) 75 75
2632 5r. Letter "N" and Chinese fan cases 75 75
2633 5r. Letter "G" and Chinese junk 75 75
MS2634 106 × 125 mm. 25r. "HONG KONG" as on Nos. 2626/33 (76 × 38 mm) 3·50 4·00

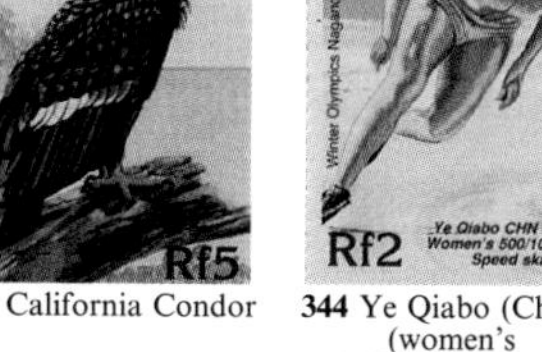

343 California Condor

344 Ye Qiabo (China) (women's 500/1000 m speed skating, 1992)

1997. Birds of the World. Multicoloured.

2635 5r. Type **343** 75 75
2636 5r. Audouin's gull 75 75
2637 5r. Atlantic puffin 75 75
2638 5r. Resplendent quetzal 75 75
2639 5r. Puerto Rican amazon 75 75
2640 5r. Lesser bird of paradise 75 75
2641 5r. Japanese crested ibis 75 75
2642 5r. Mauritius kestrel 75 75
2643 5r. Kakapo 75 75
MS2644 76 × 106 mm. 25r. Ivory-billed woodpecker 4·00 4·25

Nos. 2635/43 were printed together, se-tenant, with the backgrounds forming a composite design.

1997. Winter Olympic Games, Nagano, Japan (1998). Multicoloured.

2645 2r. Type **344** 30 25
2646 3r. Leonhard Stock (Austria) (downhill skiing, 1980) 45 35
2647 5r. Herma von Szabo-Planck (Austria) (figure skating, 1924) 65 70
2648 5r. Katarina Witt (Germany) (figure skating, 1988) 65 70
2649 5r. Natalia Bestemianova and Andrei Bukin (Russia) (pairs ice dancing, 1988) 65 70
2650 5r. Jayne Torvill and Christopher Dean (Great Britain) (pairs ice dancing, 1984) 65 70
2651 8r. Bjorn Daehlie (Norway) (cross-country skiing, 1992) 1·10 1·25
2652 12r. Wolfgang Hoppe (Germany) (bobsleigh, 1984) 1·50 1·75
MS2653 Two sheets, each 76 × 106 mm. (a) 25r. Sonja Henie (Norway) (figure skating, 1924). (b) 25r. Andree Joly and Pierre Brunet (France) (pairs ice dancing, 1932) Set of 2 sheets 8·00 9·00

345 Crowned Solitary Eagle

1997. Eagles. Multicoloured.

2654 1r. Type **345** 30 15
2655 2r. African hawk eagle (horiz) 40 30
2656 3r. Lesser spotted eagle 50 40
2657 5r. Stellar's sea eagle 65 70
2658 5r. Bald eagle attacking 65 70
2659 5r. Bald eagle on branch 65 70
2660 5r. Bald eagle looking left 65 70
2661 5r. Bald eagle looking right 65 70
2662 5r. Bald eagle sitting on branch with leaves 65 70
2663 5r. Bald eagle soaring 65 70
2664 8r. Imperial eagle ("Spanish Imperial Eagle") (horiz) 1·10 1·25
2665 10r. Harpy eagle 1·40 1·50
2666 12r. Crested serpent eagle (horiz) 1·50 1·75
MS2667 Two sheets. (a) 73 × 104 mm. 25r. Bald eagle. (b) 104 × 73 mm. 25r. American bald eagle (horiz) Set of 2 sheets 8·00 8·50

346 Blitzer Benz, 1911

1997. Classic Cars. Multicoloured.

2668 5r. Type **346** 70 75
2669 5r. Datsun, 1917 70 75
2670 5r. Auburn 8-120, 1929 70 75
2671 5r. Mercedes-Benz C280, 1996 70 75
2672 5r. Suzuki UR-1 70 75
2673 5r. Chrysler Atlantic 70 75
2674 5r. Mercedes-Benz 190SL, 1961 70 75
2675 5r. Kwaishinha D.A.T., 1916 70 75
2676 5r. Rolls-Royce Roadster 20/25 70 75
2677 5r. Mercedes-Benz SLK, 1997 70 75
2678 5r. Toyota Camry, 1996 70 75
2679 5r. Jaguar MK 2, 1959 70 75
MS2680 Two sheets, each 100 × 70 mm. (a) 25r. Volkswagen, 1939. (b) 25r. Mazda RX-01 Set of 2 sheets 7·50 8·50

347 "Patris II", Greece (1926)

1997. Passenger Ships. Multicoloured.

2681 1r. Type **347** 20 15
2682 2r. "Infanta Beatriz", Spain (1928) 30 25
2683 3r. "Vasilefs Constantinos", Greece (1914) 40 45
2684 3r. "Cunene", Portugal (1911) 40 45
2685 3r. "Selandia", Denmark (1912) 40 45
2686 3r. "President Harding", U.S.A. (1921) 40 45
2687 3r. "Ulster Monarch", Great Britain (1929) 40 45
2688 3r. "Matsonia", U.S.A. (1913) 40 45
2689 3r. "France", France (1911) 40 45
2690 3r. "Campania", Great Britain (1893) 40 45
2691 3r. "Klipfontein", Holland (1922) 40 45
2692 3r. "Eridan", France (1929) 40 45
2693 3r. "Mount Clinton", U.S.A. (1921) 40 45
2694 3r. "Infanta Isabel", Spain (1912) 40 45
2695 3r. "Suwa Maru", Japan (1914) 40 45
2696 3r. "Yorkshire", Great Britain (1920) 40 45
2697 3r. "Highland Chieftain", Great Britain (1929) 40 45
2698 3r. "Sardinia", Norway (1920) 40 45
2699 3r. "San Guglielmo", Italy (1911) 40 45
2700 3r. "Avila", Great Britain (1927) 40 45
2701 8r. "Stavangerfjord", Norway (1918) 1·10 1·25
2702 12r. "Baloeran", Netherlands (1929) 1·50 1·75
MS2703 Four sheets. (a) 69 × 69 mm. 25r. "Mauritania", Great Britain (1907). (b) 69 × 69 mm. 25r. "United States", U.S.A. (1952). (c) 69 × 69 mm. 25r. "Queen Mary", Great Britain (1930). (d) 91 × 76 mm. 25r. Royal Yacht "Britannia" amd Chinese junk, Hong Kong (56 × 42 mm) Set of 4 sheets 15·00 15·00

No. **MS**2703d is inscribed "BRITTANIA" in error.

348 Prayer Wheels, Lhasa

1997. 50th Anniv of U.N.E.S.C.O. Multicoloured.

2704 1r. Type **348** 20 15
2705 2r. Ruins of Roman Temple of Diana, Portugal (horiz) 30 25
2706 3r. Santa Maria Cathedral, Hildesheim, Germany (horiz) 45 35
2707 5r. Vivunga National Park, Zaire 65 70
2708 5r. Valley of Mai Nature Reserve, Seychelles 65 70
2709 5r. Kandy, Sri Lanka 65 70
2710 5r. Taj Mahal, India 65 70
2711 5r. Istanbul, Turkey 65 70
2712 5r. Sana'a, Yemen 65 70
2713 5r. Bleinheim Palace, England 65 70
2714 5r. Grand Canyon National Park, U.S.A. 65 70
2715 5r. Tombs, Gondar, Ethiopia 65 70
2716 5r. Bwindi National Park, Uganda 65 70
2717 5r. Bemaraha National Reserve, Madagascar 65 70
2718 5r. Buddhist ruins at Takht-I-Bahi, Pakistan 65 70
2719 5r. Anuradhapura, Sri Lanka 65 70
2720 5r. Cairo, Egypt 65 70
2721 5r. Ruins, Petra, Jordan 65 70
2722 5r. Volcano, Ujung Kulon National Park, Indonesia 65 70
2723 5r. Terrace, Mount Taishan, China 65 70
2724 5r. Temple, Mount Taishan, China 65 70
2725 5r. Temple turret, Mount Taishan, China 65 70
2726 5r. Standing stones, Mount Taishan, China 65 70
2727 5r. Courtyard, Mount Taishan, China 65 70
2728 5r. Staircase, Mount Taishan, China 65 70

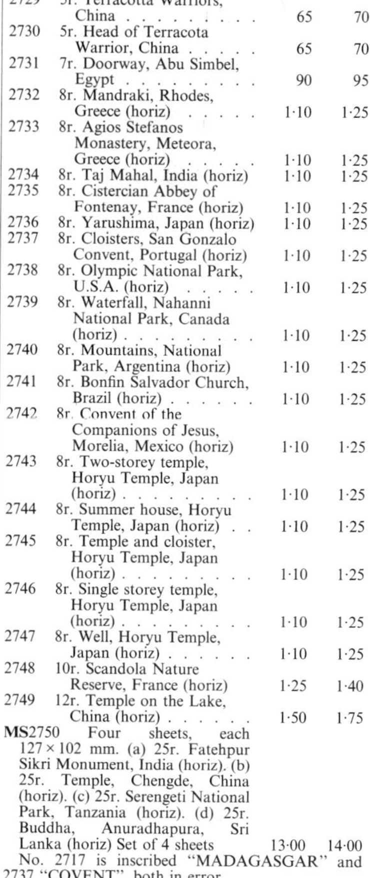

2729 5r. Terracotta Warriors, China 65 70
2730 5r. Head of Terracota Warrior, China 65 70
2731 7r. Doorway, Abu Simbel, Egypt 90 95
2732 8r. Mandraki, Rhodes, Greece (horiz) 1·10 1·25
2733 8r. Agios Stefanos Monastery, Meteora, Greece (horiz) 1·10 1·25
2734 8r. Taj Mahal, India (horiz) 1·10 1·25
2735 8r. Cistercian Abbey of Fontenay, France (horiz) 1·10 1·25
2736 8r. Yarushima, Japan (horiz) 1·10 1·25
2737 8r. Cloisters, San Gonzalo Convent, Portugal (horiz) 1·10 1·25
2738 8r. Olympic National Park, U.S.A. (horiz) 1·10 1·25
2739 8r. Waterfall, Nahanni National Park, Canada (horiz) 1·10 1·25
2740 8r. Mountains, National Park, Argentina (horiz) 1·10 1·25
2741 8r. Bonfin Salvador Church, Brazil (horiz) 1·10 1·25
2742 8r. Convent of the Companions of Jesus, Morelia, Mexico (horiz) 1·10 1·25
2743 8r. Two-storey temple, Horyu Temple, Japan (horiz) 1·10 1·25
2744 8r. Summer house, Horyu Temple, Japan (horiz) 1·10 1·25
2745 8r. Temple and cloister, Horyu Temple, Japan (horiz) 1·10 1·25
2746 8r. Single storey temple, Horyu Temple, Japan (horiz) 1·10 1·25
2747 8r. Well, Horyu Temple, Japan (horiz) 1·10 1·25
2748 10r. Scandola Nature Reserve, France (horiz) 1·25 1·40
2749 12r. Temple on the Lake, China (horiz) 1·50 1·75
MS2750 Four sheets, each 127 × 102 mm. (a) 25r. Fatehpur Sikri Monument, India (horiz). (b) 25r. Temple, Chengde, China (horiz). (c) 25r. Serengeti National Park, Tanzania (horiz). (d) 25r. Buddha, Anuradhapura, Sri Lanka (horiz) Set of 4 sheets 13·00 14·00

No. 2717 is inscribed "MADAGASGAR" and 2737 "COVENT", both in error.

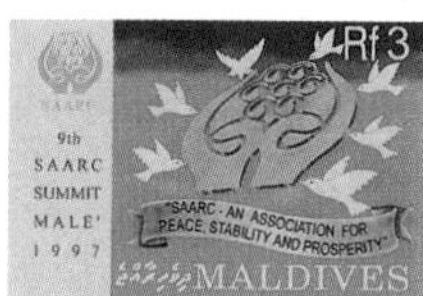

349 White Doves and S.A.A.R.C. Logo

1997. 9th South Asian Association for Regional Cooperation Summit, Male. Multicoloured.

2751 3r. Type **349** 40 35
2752 5r. Flags of member countries 1·00 75

350 Queen Elizabeth II

1997. Golden Wedding of Queen Elizabeth and Prince Philip. Multicoloured.

2753 5r. Type **350** 75 75
2754 5r. Royal coat of arms 75 75
2755 5r. Queen Elizabeth and Prince Philip at opening of Parliament 75 75
2756 5r. Queen Elizabeth and Prince Philip with Prince Charles, 1948 75 75
2757 5r. Buckingham Palace from the garden 75 75
2758 5r. Prince Philip 75 75
MS2759 100 × 70 mm. 25r. Queen Elizabeth II 3·50 3·50

351 Early Indian Mail Messenger

1997. "Pacific '97" International Stamp Exhibition, San Francisco. Death Centenary of Heinrich von Stephan (founder of the U.P.U.).

2760 **351** 2r. green and black 40 50
2761 – 2r. brown and black 40 50
2762 – 2r. violet 40 50

DESIGNS: No. 2761, Von Stephan and Mercury; 2762, Autogyro, Washington.

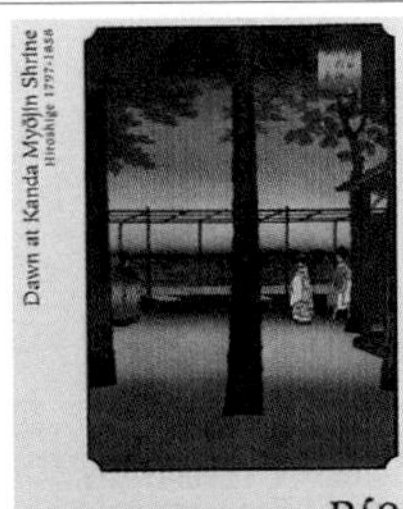

352 "Dawn at Kanda Myojn Shrine"

1997. Birth Bicentenary of Hiroshige (Japanese painter). "One Hundred Famous Views of Edo". Multicoloured.
2763 8r. Type **352** 1·25 1·25
2764 8r. "Kiyomizu Hall and Shinobazu Pond at Ueno" 1·25 1·25
2765 8r. "Ueno Yamashita" 1·25 1·25
2766 8r. "Moon Pine, Ueno" 1·25 1·25
2767 8r. "Flower Pavilion, Dango Slope, Sendagi" 1·25 1·25
2768 8r. "Shitaya Hirokoji" 1·25 1·25
MS2769 Two sheets, each 102 × 127 mm. (a) 25r. "Hilltop View, Yushima Tenjin Shrine". (b) 25r "Seido and Kanda River from Shohei Bridge" Set of 2 sheets 7·50 8·50

353 Common Noddy

354 "Canarina eminii"

1997. Birds. Multicoloured.
2770 30l. Type **353** 20 30
2771 1r. Spectacled owl 45 25
2772 2r. Malay fish owl 60 35
2773 3r. Peregrine falcon 70 50
2774 5r. Golden eagle 90 70
2775 7r. Ruppell's parrot 1·00 1·10
2776 7r. Blue-headed parrot 1·00 1·10
2777 7r. St Vincent amazon ("St Vincent Parrot") 1·00 1·10
2778 7r. Grey parrot 1·00 1·10
2779 7r. Masked lovebird 1·00 1·10
2780 7r. Sun conure ("Sun Parakeet") 1·00 1·10
2781 8r. Bateleur 1·25 1·25
2782 10r. Whiskered tern with chicks 1·50 1·50
2783 10r. Common caracara 1·50 1·50
2784 15r. Red-footed booby 2·00 2·25
MS2785 Two sheets, each 67 × 98 mm. (a) 25r. American bald eagle. (b) 25r. Secretary bird Set of 2 sheets 8·00 8·50

1997. Flowers. Multicoloured.
2786 1r. Type **354** 25 15
2787 2r. "Delphinium macrocentron" 40 25
2788 3r. "Leucadendron discolor" 55 40
2789 5r. "Nymphaea caerulea" 75 60
2790 7r. "Rosa multiflora polyantha" (20 × 23 mm) 1·00 1·00
2791 8r. "Bulbophyllum barbigerum" 1·25 1·40
2792 8r. "Acacia seyal" (horiz) 1·25 1·40
2793 8r. "Gloriosa superba" (horiz) 1·25 1·40
2794 8r. "Gnidia subcordata" (horiz) 1·25 1·40
2795 8r. "Platycelyphium voense" (horiz) 1·25 1·40
2796 8r. "Aspilia mossambicensis" (horiz) 1·25 1·40
2797 8r. "Adenium obesum" (horiz) 1·25 1·40
2798 12r. "Hibiscus vitifolius" 2·00 2·25
MS2799 Two sheets, each 105 × 76 mm. (a) 25r. "Aerangis rhodosticta" (horiz). (b) 25r. "Dichrostachys cinerea" and two sailing boats (horiz) Set of 2 sheets 11·00 11·00
Nos. 2792/7 were printed together, se-tenant, with the backgrounds forming a composite design.

355 Archaeopteryx

1997. Prehistoric Animals. Multicoloured. (a) Horiz designs.
2800 5r. Type **355** 90 65
2801 7r. Diplodocus 1·00 1·00
2802 7r. Tyrannosaurus rex 1·00 1·00
2803 7r. Pteranodon 1·00 1·00
2804 7r. Montanceratops 1·00 1·00
2805 7r. Dromaeosaurus 1·00 1·00
2806 7r. Oviraptor 1·00 1·00
2807 8r. Mosasaurus 1·25 1·25
2808 12r. Deinonychus 1·60 1·75
2809 15r. Triceratops 1·75 2·00

(b) Square designs, 31 × 31 mm.
2810 7r. Troodon 1·00 1·00
2811 7r. Brachiosaurus 1·00 1·00
2812 7r. Saltasaurus 1·00 1·00
2813 7r. Oviraptor 1·00 1·00
2814 7r. Parasaurolophus 1·00 1·00
2815 7r. Psittacosaurus 1·00 1·00
2816 7r. Triceratops 1·00 1·00
2817 7r. Pachycephalosaurus 1·00 1·00
2818 7r. Iguanodon 1·00 1·00
2819 7r. Tyrannosaurus rex 1·00 1·00
2820 7r. Corythosaurus 1·00 1·00
2821 7r. Stegosaurus 1·00 1·00
2822 7r. Euophlocephalus 1·00 1·00
2823 7r. Compsognathus 1·00 1·00
2824 7r. Herrerasaurus 1·00 1·00
2825 7r. Styracosaurus 1·00 1·00
2826 7r. Baryonyx 1·00 1·00
2827 7r. Lesothosaurus 1·00 1·00
MS2828 Two sheets. (a) 99 × 79 mm. 25r. Tyrannosaurus rex (42 × 28 mm). (b) 73 × 104 mm. 25r. Archaeopteryx (31 × 31 mm) Set of 2 sheets 17·00 17·00
Nos. 2801/6, 2810/15, 2816/21 and 2822/7 respectively were printed together, se-tenant, with the backgrounds of Nos. 2801/6 and 2810/15 forming composite designs.

1997. World Cup Football Championship, France. As T **246** of Lesotho.
2829 1r. black 25 15
2830 2r. black 35 25
2831 3r. multicoloured 45 35
2832/39 3r. × 8 (black; black; multicoloured; multicoloured; black; multicoloured; black; multicoloured) 3·50 3·75
2840/47 3r. × 8 (multicoloured; multicoloured; black; black; black; multicoloured; multicoloured; black) 3·50 3·75
2848/55 3r. × 8 (multicoloured; multicoloured; multicoloured; black; black; multicoloured; multicoloured; multicoloured) 3·50 3·75
2856 7r. black 1·00 1·00
2857 8r. black 1·25 1·40
2858 10r. multicoloured 1·40 1·50
MS2859 Three sheets. (a) 103 × 128 mm. 25r. multicoloured. (b) 103 × 128 mm. 25r. multicoloured. (c) 128 × 103 mm. 25r. multicoloured Set of 3 sheets 11·00 12·00
DESIGNS—HORIZ: No. 2829, Brazilian team, 1994; 2830, German player, 1954; 2831, Maradona holding World Cup, 1986; 2832, Brazilian team, 1958; 2833, Luis Bellini, Brazil, 1958; 2834, Brazilian team, 1962; 2835, Carlos Alberto, Brazil, 1970; 2836, Mauro, Brazil, 1962; 2837, Brazilian team, 1970; 2838, Dunga, Brazil, 1994; 2839, Brazilian team, 1994; 2840, Paulo Rossi, Italy, 1982; 2841, Zoff and Gentile, Italy, 1982; 2842, Angelo Schavio, Italy; 2843, Italian team, 1934; 2844, Italian team with flag, 1934; 2845, Italian team, 1982; 2846, San Paolo Stadium, Italy; 2847, Italian team, 1938; 2848, English player with ball, 1966; 2849, Wembley Stadium, London; 2850, English player heading ball, 1966; 2851, English players celebrating, 1966; 2852, English and German players chasing ball, 1966; 2853, English player wearing No. 21 shirt, 1966; 2854, English team with Jules Rimet trophy, 1966; 2855, German player wearing No. 5 shirt, 1966; 2856, Argentine player holding trophy, 1978; 2857, English players with Jules Rimet trophy, 1966; 2858, Brazilian player with trophy, 1970; **MS**2859c, Klinsmann, Germany. VERT: No. **MS**2859a, Ronaldo, Brazil; **MS**2892b, Schmeichel, Denmark.

1998. Diana, Princess of Wales Commemoration. As T **249** of Lesotho. Multicoloured (except Nos. 2864, 2870, 2872, 2877 and **MS**2878b).
2860 7r. Laughing 65 70
2861 7r. With Prince William and Prince Harry 65 70
2862 7r. Carrying bouquets 65 70
2863 7r. In white evening dress 65 70
2864 7r. Wearing bow tie (brown and black) 65 70
2865 7r. Wearing black jacket 65 70
2866 7r. With Indian child on lap 65 70
2867 7r. Wearing blue evening dress 65 70
2868 7r. Wearing blue jacket and poppy 65 70
2869 7r. Wearing cream jacket 65 70
2870 7r. Wearing blouse and jacket (brown and black) 65 70
2871 7r. Wearing red jacket 65 70
2872 7r. Wearing hat (blue and black) 65 70
2873 7r. Wearing red evening dress 65 70
2874 7r. With Sir Richard Attenborough 65 70
2875 7r. Wearing jeans and white shirt 65 70
2876 7r. Wearing white jacket 65 70
2877 7r. Carrying bouquet (brown and black) 65 70
MS2878 Three sheets. (a) 100 × 70 mm. 25r. On ski-lift. (b) 100 × 70 mm. 25r. Wearing polkadot dress (brown and black). (c) 70 × 100 mm. 25r. Wearing garland of flowers Set of 3 sheets 7·25 7·50

356 Pres. Nelson Mandela

357 Pres. John F. Kennedy

1998. 80th Birthday of Nelson Mandela (President of South Africa).
2879 **356** 7r. multicoloured 65 70

1998. Pres. John F. Kennedy Commemoration. Multicoloured, background colours given.
2880 **357** 5r. green 50 55
2881 – 5r. green 50 55
2882 – 5r. brown (inscr at right) 50 55
2883 – 5r. yellow 50 55
2884 – 5r. violet 50 55
2885 – 5r. blue 50 55
2886 – 5r. grey 50 55
2887 – 5r. brown (inscr at left) 50 55
2888 – 5r. blue (value at bottom right) 50 55
DESIGNS: Nos. 2881/8, Various portraits.

358 Yakovlev Yak-18 (from 1947)

1998. Aircraft in Longest Continuous Production. Multicoloured.
2889 5r. Type **358** 50 55
2890 5r. Beechcraft Bonanza (from 1947) 50 55
2891 5r. Piper Cub (1937–82) 50 55
2892 5r. Tupolev Tu-95 (1954–90) 50 55
2893 5r. Lockheed C-130 Hercules (from 1954) 50 55
2894 5r. Piper PA-28 Cherokee (from 1961) 50 55
2895 5r. Mikoyan Gurevich MiG-21 (from 1959) 50 55
2896 5r. Pilatus PC-6 Turbo Porter (from 1960) 50 55
2897 5r. Antonov An-2 (from 1949) 50 55
MS2898 120 × 90 mm. 25r. Boeing KC-135E (from 1956) (84 × 28 mm) 2·40 2·50

359 White American Shorthair

1998. Cats. Multicoloured.
2899 5r. Type **359** 50 55
2900 7r. American curl and Maine coon (horiz) 65 70
2901 7r. Maine coon (horiz) 65 70
2902 7r. Siberian (horiz) 65 70
2903 7r. Somali (horiz) 65 70
2904 7r. European Burmese (horiz) 65 70
2905 7r. Nebelung (horiz) 65 70
2906 7r. Bicolour British shorthair (horiz) 65 70
2907 7r. Manx (horiz) 65 70
2908 7r. Tabby American shorthair (horiz) 65 70
2909 7r. Silver tabby Persian (horiz) 65 70
2910 7r. Oriental white (horiz) 65 70
2911 7r. Norwegian forest cat (horiz) 65 70
2912 8r. Sphynx cat 75 80
2913 10r. Tabby American shorthair 95 1·00
2914 12r. Scottish fold 1·10 1·25
MS2915 Two sheets, each 98 × 68 mm. (a) 30r. Norwegian forest cat. (b) 30r. Snowshoe Set of 2 sheets 5·75 6·00
Nos. 2900/5 and 2906/11 respectively were printed together, se-tenant, forming composite designs.

360 Boeing 737 HS

1998. Aircraft. Multicoloured.
2916 2r. Type **360** 20 25
2917 5r. CL-215 (flying boat) 50 55
2918 5r. Orion 50 55
2919 5r. Yakolev Yak-54 50 55
2920 5r. Cessna sea plane 50 55
2921 5r. CL-215 (amphibian) 50 55
2922 5r. CL-215 SAR (amphibian) 50 55
2923 5r. Twin Otter 50 55
2924 5r. Rockwell Quail 50 55
2925 5r. F.S.W. fighter 50 55
2926 5r. V-Jet II 50 55
2927 5r. Pilatus PC-12 50 55
2928 5r. Citation Exel 50 55
2929 5r. Stutz Bearcat 50 55
2930 5r. Cessna T-37 (B) 50 55
2931 5r. Peregrine Business Jet 50 55
2932 5r. Beech 58 Baron 50 55
2933 7r. Boeing 727 65 70
2934 8r. Boeing 747-400 75 80
2935 10r. Boeing 737 95 1·00
MS2936 Two sheets, each 98 × 68 mm. (a) 25r. Beechcraft Model 18. (b) 25r. Falcon Jet Set of 2 sheets 4·75 5·00

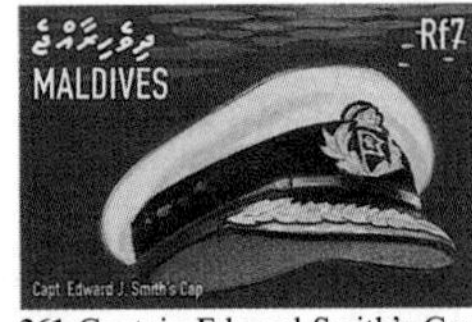

361 Captain Edward Smith's Cap

1998. Titanic Commemoration. Multicoloured.
2937 7r. Type **361** 65 70
2938 7r. Deck chair 65 70
2939 7r. Fifth Officer Harold Lowe's coat button 65 70
2940 7r. Lifeboat 65 70
2941 7r. "Titanic's" wheel 65 70
2942 7r. Passenger's lifejacket 65 70
MS2943 110 × 85 mm. 25r. "Titanic" from newspaper picture 2·40 2·50

362 Guava Tree

1998. 20th Anniv of International Fund of Agriculture. Multicoloured.
2944 1r. Type **362** 10 15
2945 5r. Selection of fruit 50 55
2946 7r. Fishing boat 65 70
2947 8r. Papaya tree 70 80
2948 10r. Vegetable produce 95 1·00

363 Thread-finned Butterflyfish

1998. Fish. Multicoloured.
2949 50l. Type **363** 10 10
2950 50l. Queen angelfish 10 10
2951 1r. Oriental sweetlips 10 15
2952 3r. Mandarin fish 30 35
2953 3r. Copper-banded butterflyfish 30 35
2954 3r. Harlequin tuskfish 30 35
2955 3r. Yellow-tailed demoiselle 30 35
2956 3r. Wimplefish 30 35
2957 3r. Red emperor snapper 30 35
2958 3r. Clown triggerfish 30 35
2959 3r. Common clown 30 35
2960 3r. Palette surgeonfish ("Regal Tang") 30 35
2961 5r. Emperor angelfish 50 55
2962 5r. Common squirrelfish ("Diadem Squirrelfish") 50 55
2963 5r. Lemon-peel angelfish 50 55
2964 5r. Powder-blue surgeonfish 50 55
2965 5r. Moorish idol 50 55
2966 5r. Bicolor angelfish ("Bicolor Cherub") 50 55
2967 5r. Doubulay's angelfish ("Scribbled Angelfish") 50 55
2968 5r. Two-banded anemonefish 50 55
2969 5r. Yellow tang 50 55
2970 7r. Red-tailed surgeonfish ("Achilles Tang") 65 70
2971 7r. Bandit angelfish 65 70

2972 8r. Hooded butterflyfish ("Red-headed Butterflyfish") 75 80
2973 50r. Blue-striped butterflyfish . . . . . . 4·75 5·00
MS2974 Two sheets, each 110 × 85 mm. (a) 25r. Long-nosed butterflyfish. (b) 25r. Porkfish Set of 2 sheets . . . . 4·75 5·00

364 Baden-Powell inspecting Scouts, Amesbury, 1909

1998. 19th World Scout Jamboree, Chile. Multicoloured.
2975 12r. Type **364** . . . . . . 1·10 1·25
2976 12r. Sir Robert and Lady Baden-Powell with children, 1927 . . . . . 1·10 1·25
2977 12r. Sir Robert Baden-Powell awarding merit badges, Chicago, 1926 . . 1·10 1·25

365 Diana, Princess of Wales

1998. 1st Death Anniv of Diana, Princess of Wales.
2978 **365** 10r. multicoloured . . . 95 1·00

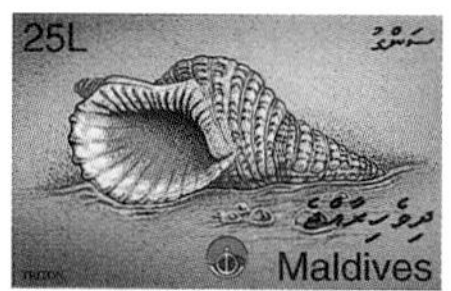

366 Triton Shell

1999. International Year of the Ocean. Marine Life. Multicoloured.
2979 25l. Type **366** 10 10
2980 50l. Napoleon wrasse . . . 10 10
2981 1r. Whale shark 10 15
2982 3r. Grey reef shark 30 35
2983 5r. Harp seal 50 55
2984 5r. Killer whale 50 55
2985 5r. Sea otter 50 55
2986 5r. Beluga 50 55
2987 5r. Narwhal 50 55
2988 5r. Walrus 50 55
2989 5r. Sea lion 50 55
2990 5r. Humpback salmon 50 55
2991 5r. Emperor penguin . . . 50 55
2992 7r. Blue whale 65 70
2993 7r. Skipjack tuna 65 70
2994 8r. Ocean sunfish 75 80
2995 8r. Opalescent squid 75 80
2996 8r. Electric ray 75 80
2997 8r. Corded neptune 75 80
MS2998 Three sheets, each 110 × 85 mm. (a) 25r. Horseshoe crab. (b) 25r. Blue whale. (c) 25r. Triton shell Set of 3 sheets . . 7·25 7·50
Nos. 2983/91 were printed together, se-tenant, with the backgrounds forming a composite design.

367 Broderip's Cowrie

1999. Marine Life. Multicoloured.
2999 30l. Type **367** 10 10
3000 1r. White tern ("Fairy Tern") 10 15
3001 3r. Green-backed heron ("Darker Maldivian Green Heron") 30 35
3002 5r. Manta ray 50 55
3003 5r. Green turtle 50 55
3004 5r. Spotted dolphins 50 55
3005 5r. Moorish idols 50 55
3006 5r. Threadfin anthias . . . 50 55
3007 5r. Goldbar wrasse 50 55
3008 5r. Palette surgeonfish . . . 50 55
3009 5r. Three-spotted angelfish 50 55
3010 5r. Oriental sweetlips . . . 50 55
3011 5r. Brown booby 50 55
3012 5r. Red-tailed tropic bird . . 50 55
3013 5r. Sooty tern 50 55
3014 5r. Striped dolphin 50 55
3015 5r. Spinner dolphin 50 55
3016 5r. Crab plover 50 55
3017 5r. Hawksbill turtle 50 55
3018 5r. Indo-Pacific sergeant . . 50 55
3019 5r. Yellow-finned tuna . . . 50 55
3020 7r. Blackflag sandperch . . 65 70
3021 8r. Coral hind 75 80
3022 10r. Olive Ridley turtle . . . 95 1·00
MS3023 Two sheets, each 110 × 85 mm. (a) 25r. Cinnamon bittern. (b) 25r. Blue-faced angelfish Set of 2 sheets . . . 4·75 5·00
Nos. 3002/10 and 3011/19 were each printed together, se-tenant, with the backgrounds forming composite designs.

368 Mickey Mouse

1999. 70th Anniv of Mickey Mouse (Disney cartoon character). Multicoloured.
3024/9 5r. × 6 (Mickey Mouse: Type **368**; laughing; looking tired; frowning; smiling; winking) . . .
3030/5 5r. × 6 (Minnie Mouse: facing left and smiling; with eyes closed; with hand on head; looking surprised; smiling; looking cross) . . . .
3036/41 7r. × 6 (Donald Duck: facing left and smiling; laughing; looking tired; looking cross; smiling; winking) . . . .
3042/7 7r. × 6 (Daisy Duck: with half closed eyes; laughing; looking shocked; looking cross; facing forwards; with head on one side) . . .
3048/53 7r. × 6 (Goofy: facing right and smiling; with eyes closed; with half closed eyes; looking shocked; looking puzzled; looking thoughtful) . . . . . .
3054/9 7r. × 6 (Pluto: looking shocked; with eyes closed; smiling; scowling; with tongue out (orange background); with tongue out (green background) . . . . .
3024/59 Set of 30 . . . . 27·00 28·00
MS3060 Six sheets, each 127 × 102 mm. (a) 25r. Minnie Mouse wearing necklace. (b) 25r. Mickey with hand on head. (c) 25r. Mickey wearing baseball hat. (d) 25r. Mickey facing right (horiz). (e) 25r. Minnie looking left (includes label showing Mickey with bouquet). (f) 25r. Minnie drinking through straw Set of 6 sheets . . . . 18·00 19·00

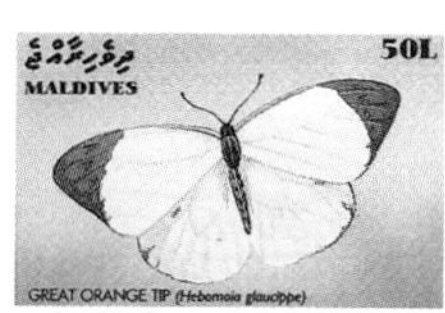

369 Great Orange Tip

1999. Butterflies. Multicoloured.
3061 50l. Type **369** 10 10
3062 1r. Large green aporandria 10 15
3063 2r. Common mormon . . . 20 25
3064 3r. African migrant 30 35
3065 5r. Common pierrot 50 55
3066 7r. Crimson tip (vert) . . . 65 70
3067 7r. Tawny rajah (vert) . . . 65 70
3068 7r. Leafwing butterfly (vert) 65 70
3069 7r. Great egg-fly (vert) . . . 65 70
3070 7r. Blue admiral (vert) . . . 65 70
3071 7r. African migrant (vert) 65 70
3072 7r. Common red flash (vert) 65 70
3073 7r. Burmese lascar (vert) . . 65 70
3074 7r. Common perriot (vert) 65 70
3075 7r. Baron (vert) 65 70
3076 7r. Leaf blue (vert) 65 70
3077 7r. Great orange tip (vert) 65 70
3078 10r. Giant red-eye . . . . . 95 1·00
MS3079 Two sheets, each 70 × 100 mm. (a) 25r. Crimson tip. (b) 25r. Large oak blue Set of 2 sheets . . . . 4·75 5·00
Nos. 3066/71 and 3072/7 were each printed together, se-tenant, with the backgrounds forming composite designs.

370 Scelidosaurus

1999. Prehistoric Animals. Multicoloured.
3080 1r. Type **370** 10 15
3081 3r. Yansudaurus 30 35
3082 5r. Ornitholestes 50 55
3083 7r. Dimorphodon (vert) . . 65 70
3084 7r. Rhamphorhynchus (vert) 65 70
3085 7r. Allosaurus (vert) 65 70
3086 7r. Leaellynasaura (vert) . . 65 70
3087 7r. Troodon (vert) 65 70
3088 7r. Syntarsus (vert) 65 70
3089 7r. Anchisaurus (vert) . . . 65 70
3090 7r. Pterenodon (vert) . . . 65 70
3091 7r. Barosaurus (vert) 65 70
3092 7r. Iguanodon (vert) 65 70
3093 7r. Archaeopteryx (vert) . . 65 70
3094 7r. Ceratosaurus (vert) . . . 65 70
3095 7r. Stegosaurus 65 70
3096 7r. Corythosaurus 65 70
3097 7r. Cetiosaurus 65 70
3098 7r. Avimimus 65 70
3099 7r. Styracosaurus 65 70
3100 7r. Massospondylus 65 70
3101 8r. Astrodon 75 80
MS3102 Two sheets, each 116 × 81 mm. (a) 25r. Megalosaurus (vert). (b) 25r. Brachiosaurus (vert) Set of 2 sheets . . . . 4·75 5·00
Nos. 3083/8, 3089/94 and 3095/100 were each printed together, se-tenant, forming composite designs.

371 Express Locomotive, Egypt, 1856

1999. Trains of the World. Multicoloured.
3103 50l. Type **371** 10 10
3104 1r. Channel Tunnel Le Shuttle, France, 1994 . . . 10 15
3105 2r. Gowan and Marx locomotive, U.S.A., 1839 . . 20 25
3106 3r. TGV train, France, 1981 30 35
3107 5r. "Ae 6/6" electric locomotive, Switzerland, 1954 50 55
3108 7r. Stephenson's long-boilered locomotive, Great Britain, 1846 (red livery) 65 70
3109 7r. "Cornwall", Great Britain, 1847 . . . . . . 65 70
3110 7r. First locomotive, Germany, 1848 . . . . . 65 70
3111 7r. Great Western locomotive, Great Britain, 1846 . . . . 65 70
3112 7r. Standard Stephenson locomotive, France, 1837 65 70
3113 7r. "Meteor", Great Britain, 1843 . . . . 65 70
3114 7r. Class 4T diesel-electric locomotive, Great Britain, 1940–65 . . . . 65 70
3115 7r. Mainline diesel-electric locomotive No. 20101, Malaya, 1940–65 . . . . 65 70
3116 7r. Class 7000 high-speed electric locomotive, France, 1949 . . . . . . 65 70
3117 7r. Diesel hydraulic express locomotive, Thailand, 1940–65 . . . . 65 70
3118 7r. Diesel hydraulic locomotive, Burma, 1940–65 . . . . 65 70
3119 7r. "Hikari" super express train, Japan, 1940–65 . . 65 70
3120 8r. Stephenson's long-boilered locomotive, Great Britain, 1846 (orange and green livery) 75 80
3121 10r. "Philadelphia", Austria, 1838 . . . . 95 1·00
3122 15r. S.E. and C.R. Class E steam locomotive, Great Britain, 1940 . . . . . . 1·40 1·50
MS3123 Two sheets, each 110 × 85 mm. (a) 25r. Passenger locomotive, France, 1846. (b) 25r. Southern Railway Class "King Arthur", steam locomotive, Great Britain, 1940 Set of 2 sheets . . 4·75 5·00

1999. "Queen Elizabeth the Queen Mother's Century". As T **267** of Lesotho.
3124 7r. black and gold 65 70
3125 7r. black and gold 65 70
3126 7r. multicoloured 65 70
3127 7r. multicoloured 65 70
MS3128 153 × 157 mm. 25r. multicoloured . . . . 2·40 2·50
DESIGNS: No. 3124, King George VI and Queen Elizabeth, 1936; 3125, Queen Elizabeth, 1941; 3126, Queen Elizabeth in evening dress, 1960; 3127, Queen Mother at Ascot, 1981. 37 × 50 mm: No. **MS**3128, Queen Mother in Garter robes.

1999. "iBRA '99" International Stamp Exhibition, Nuremberg. As T **262** of Lesotho. Multicoloured.
3129 12r. "Adler" (first German railway locomotive), 1833 1·10 1·25
3130 15r. "Drache" (Henshell and Sohn's first locomotive), 1848 . . . . 1·40 1·50
The captions on Nos. 3129/30 are transposed.

1999. 150th Death Anniv of Katsushika Hokusai (Japanese artist). As T **263** of Lesotho. Multicoloured (except No. 3133).
3131 7r. "Haunted House" . . . 65 70
3132 7r. "Juniso Shrine at Yotsuya" 65 70
3133 7r. Drawing of bird (black, green and gold) 65 70
3134 7r. Drawing of two women 65 70
3135 7r. "Lover in the Snow" . . 65 70
3136 7r. "Mountain Tea House" 65 70
3137 7r. "A Coastal View" . . . 65 70
3138 7r. "Bath House by a Lake" 65 70
3139 7r. Drawing of a horse . . . 65 70
3140 7r. Drawing of two birds on branch 65 70
3141 7r. "Evening Cool at Ryogoku" 65 70
3142 7r. "Girls boating" 65 70
MS3143 Two sheets, each 100 × 70 mm. (a) 25r. "Girls gathering Spring Herbs" (vert). (b) 25r. "Scene in the Yoshiwara" (vert) Set of 2 sheets . . . . . 4·75 5·00

1999. 10th Anniv of United Nations Rights of the Child Convention. As T **264** of Lesotho. Mult.
3144 10r. Baby boy and young mother . . . . 95 1·00
3145 10r. Young girl laughing . . 95 1·00
3146 10r. Three children . . . . 95 1·00
MS3147 110 × 85 mm. 25r. Sir Peter Ustinov (Goodwill ambassador for U.N.I.C.E.F.) . . . . . . 2·40 2·50

372 Standard Stephenson Railway Locomotive "Versailles", 1837

1999. "PhilexFrance '99" International Stamp Exhibition, Paris. Railway Locomotives. Two sheets, each 106 × 81 mm, containing T **372** and similar horiz design. Multicoloured.
MS3148 (a) 25r. Type **372**. (b) 25r. Stephenson long-boilered locomotive, 1841 Set of 2 sheets 4·75 5·00

373 Phobos and Demos (Martian Moons)

2000. Future Colonization of Mars. Multicoloured.
3149 5r. Type **373** 50 55
3150 5r. Improved Hubble Telescope 50 55
3151 5r. Passenger shuttle 50 55
3152 5r. Skyscrapers on Mars . . 50 55
3153 5r. Martian taxi 50 55
3154 5r. Martian landing facilities 50 55
3155 5r. Vegetation in Martian biosphere 50 55
3156 5r. Walking on Mars and biosphere 50 55
3157 5r. Mars rover 50 55
3158 5r. Russian Phobos 25 satellite 50 55
3159 5r. Earth and Moon 50 55
3160 5r. Space shuttle leaving Earth 50 55
3161 5r. Lighthouse on Mars . . 50 55
3162 5r. Mars excursion space liner 50 55
3163 5r. Mars shuttle and skyscrapers 50 55
3164 5r. Viking Lander 50 55
3165 5r. Mars air and water purification plant 50 55
3166 5r. Family picnic on Mars 50 55
MS3167 Two sheets, each 110 × 85 mm. (a) 25r. Astronaut with jet-pack. (b) 25r. Mars Set of 2 sheets . . . . . . 4·75 5·00
Nos. 3149/57 and 3158/66 were each printed together, se-tenant, with the backgrounds forming composite designs.

374 Coconuts

2000. "Destination 2000 – Maldives" Campaign. Multicoloured.
3168 7r. Type **374** 65 70
3169 7r. Shoal of skipjack tuna 65 70
3170 7r. Seaplane and traditional dhow 65 70
3171 7r. "Plumeria alba" 65 70
3172 7r. Lionfish 65 70
3173 7r. Windsurfers 65 70

2000. New Millennium. People and Events of Eighteenth Century (1750–1800). As T **268** of Lesotho. Multicoloured.
3174 3r. American bald eagle and American Declaration of Independence, 1776 . . . 30 35
3175 3r. Montgolfier brothers and first manned hot- air balloon flight, 1783 . . . 30 35
3176 3r. Napoleon and mob (French Revolution, 1789) 30 35
3177 3r. James Watt and drawing of steam engine, 1769 . . 30 35
3178 3r. Wolfgang Amadeus Mozart (born 1756) . . . 30 35
3179 3r. Front cover of The Dream of the Red Chamber (Chinese novel, published 1791) 30 35
3180 3r. Napoleon and pyramid (conquest of Egypt, 1798) 30 35
3181 3r. Empress Catherine the Great of Russia and St. Petersburg, 1762 . . . 30 35
3182 3r. Joseph Priestley (discovery of oxygen, 1774) 30 35
3183 3r. Benjamin Franklin (publication of work on electricity, 1751) 30 35
3184 3r. Edward Jenner (development of smallpox vaccine, 1796) 30 35
3185 3r. Death of General Wolfe, 1759 . . . . 30 35
3186 3r. "The Swing" (Jean Honore Fragonard), 1766 30 35
3187 3r. Ludwig von Beethoven (born 1770) 30 35
3188 3r. Marriage of Louis XVI of France and Marie Antoinette, 1770 . . . . 30 35
3189 3r. Captain James Cook (exploration of Australia, 1770) (59 × 39 mm) . . . 30 35
3190 3r. Luigi Galvani and frog (experiments into the effect of electricity on nerves and muscles, 1780) 30 35

The main design on No. 3184 may depict Sir William Jenner who undertook research into typhus.

On No. 3185 the uniforms are incorrectly shown as blue instead of red.

375 Sun and Moon over Forest

2000. Solar Eclipse Showing varying stages of eclipse as seen from Earth (Nos. 3191/6) or Space (Nos. 3197/202). Mult.
3191 7r. Type **375** 65 70
3192 7r. "Second Contact" . . . 65 70
3193 7r. "Totality" 65 70
3194 7r. "Third Contact" 65 70
3195 7r. "Fourth Contact" . . . 65 70
3196 7r. Observatory 65 70
3197 7r. "First Contact" 65 70
3198 7r. "Second Contact" . . . 65 70
3199 7r. "Totality" 65 70
3200 7r. "Third Contact" 65 70
3201 7r. "Fourth Contact" . . . 65 70
3202 7r. Solar and heliospheric observatory 65 70

Nos. 3191/6 and 3197/202 were each printed together, se-tenant, with the backgrounds forming composite designs.

376 Red Lacewing

2000. Butterflies of the Maldives. Multicoloured.
3203 5r. Type **376** 50 55
3204 5r. Large oak blue 50 55
3205 5r. Yellow coster 50 55
3206 5r. Great orange-tip 50 55
3207 5r. Common pierrot 50 55
3208 5r. Cruiser 50 55
3209 5r. Hedge blue 50 55
3210 5r. Common eggfly 50 55
3211 5r. Plain tiger 50 55
3212 5r. Common wall butterfly 50 55
3213 5r. Koh-i-Noor butterfly . . 50 55
3214 5r. Painted lady ("Indian Red Admiral") 50 55
3215 5r. Tawny rajah 50 55
3216 5r. Blue triangle 50 55
3217 5r. Orange albatross 50 55
3218 5r. Common rose swallowtail 50 55
3219 5r. Jewelled nawab 50 55
3220 5r. Striped blue crow . . . 50 55
MS3221 Two sheets. (a) 85 × 110 mm. 25r. Large tree nymph. (b) 110 × 85 mm. 25r. Blue pansy Set of 2 sheets . . . . . 4·75 5·00

Nos. 3203/11 and 3212/20 were each printed together, se-tenant, with the backgrounds forming composite designs.

No. 3219 is inscribed "JEWELED NAWAB" in error.

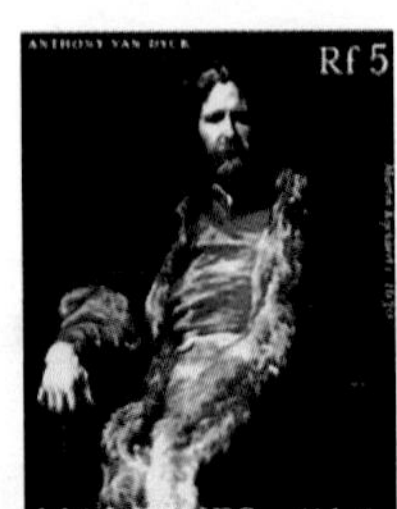

377 "Martin Rijckaert"

2000. 400th Birth Anniv of Sir Anthony Van Dyck (Flemish painter). Multicoloured.
3222 5r. Type **377** 50 55
3223 5r. "Frans Snyders" 50 55
3224 5r. "Quentin Simons" . . . 50 55
3225 5r. "Lucas van Uffel", 1632 50 55
3226 5r. "Nicolaes Rockox" . . . 50 55
3227 5r. "Nicholas Lamier" . . . 50 55
3228 5r. "Inigo Jones" 50 55
3229 5r. "Lucas van Uffel", c. 1622–25 . . . . 50 55
3230 5r. Detail of "Margaretha de Vos, Wife of Frans Snyders" 50 55
3231 5r. "Peter Brueghel the Younger" 50 55
3232 5r. "Cornelis van der Geest" 50 55
3233 5r. "Francois Langlois as a Savoyard" 50 55
3234 5r. "Portrait of a Family" 50 55
3235 5r. "Earl and Countess of Denby and Their Daughter" 50 55
3236 5r. "Family Portrait" . . . 50 55
3237 5r. "A Genoese Nobleman with his Children" . . . 50 55
3238 5r. "Thomas Howard, Earl of Arundel, and His Grandson" 50 55
3239 5r. "La dama d'oro" 50 55
MS3240 Six sheets. (a) 102 × 127 mm. 25r. "The Painter Jan de Wael and his Wife Gertrude de Jode". (b) 102 × 127 mm. 25r. "John, Count of Nassau-Siegen, and His Family". (c) 102 × 127 mm. 25r. "The Lomellini Family". (d) 102 × 127 mm. 25r. "Lucas and Cornelis de Wael". (e) 127 × 102 mm. 25r. "Sir Kenelm and Lady Digby with their two Eldest Sons". (f) 127 × 102 mm. 25r. "Sir Philip Herbert, 4th Earl of Pembroke, and His Family" (horiz) Set of 6 sheets . . . . 14·50 15·00

No. 3230 is inscribed "Margaretha de Vos, Wife of Frans Snders" in error.

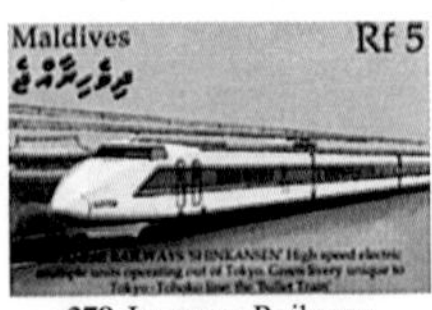

378 Japanese Railways "Shinkansen", High Speed Electric Train

2000. "The Stamp Show 2000" International Stamp Exhibition, London. Asian Railways. Mult.
3241 5r. Type **378** 50 55
3242 8r. Japanese Railways "Super Azusa", twelve-car train 75 80
3243 10r. Tobu Railway "Spacia", ten-car electric train, Japan . . . . . . 95 1·00
3244 10r. Shanghai-Nanking Railway passenger tank locomotive, China, 1909 95 1·00
3245 10r. Shanghai–Nanking Railway "Imperial Yellow" express mail locomotive, China, 1910 95 1·00
3246 10r. Manchurian Railway "Pacific" locomotive, China, 1914 . . . . . . 95 1·00
3247 10r. Hankow Line mixed traffic locomotive, China, 1934 . . . . 95 1·00
3248 10r. Chinese National Railway freight locomotive, 1949 . . . . 95 1·00
3249 10r. Chinese National Railway mixed traffic locomotive, 1949 . . . . 95 1·00
3250 10r. East Indian Railway passenger tank locomotive Fawn, 1856 . . . . . . 95 1·00
3251 10r. East Indian Railway express locomotive, 1893 95 1·00
3252 10r. Bengal–Nagpur Railway Atlantic Compound loco-motive, India, 1909 . . . . . . 95 1·00
3253 10r. Great Peninsular Railway passenger and mail locomotive, India, 1924 . . . . 95 1·00
3254 10r. North Western Class XS2 Pacific locomotive, India, 1932 . . . .
3255 10r. Indian National Railway Class YP Pacific locomotive, India, 1949–70 . . . . 95 1·00
3256 15r. Japanese Railway "Nozomi", high-speed electric train . . . . . . 1·40 1·50
MS3257 Two sheets, each 100 × 70 mm. (a) 25r. Indian National Railways Class WP locomotive (57 × 41 mm). (b) 25r. Chinese National Railway Class JS locomotive (57 × 41 mm) Set of 2 sheets . . . . 4·75 5·00

379 Republic Monument

2000. New Millennium (2nd issue). Multicoloured.
3258 10l. Type **379** 10 10
3259 30l. Bodu Thakurufaanu Memorial Centre 10 10
3260 1r. Modern medical facilities and new hospital 10 15
3261 7r. Male International Airport 65 70
3262 7r. Hukuru Miskiiy 65 70
3263 10r. Computer room, science lab and new school . . . 95 1·00
MS3264 Three sheets, each 106 × 77 mm. (a) 25r. Tourist resort and fish packing factory. (b) 25r. Islamic Centre. (c) 25r. People's Majlis (assembly) Set of 3 sheets . . . . 7·25 7·50

2000. 25th Anniv of "Apollo–Soyuz" Joint Project. As T **271** of Lesotho. Multicoloured.
3265 13r. "Apollo 18" and "Soyuz 19" docking (vert) 1·25 1·40
3266 13r. "Soyuz 19" (vert) . . . 1·25 1·40
3267 13r. "Apollo 18" (vert) . . . 1·25 1·40
MS3268 105 × 76 mm. 25r. "Soyuz 19" . . . . 2·50 2·75

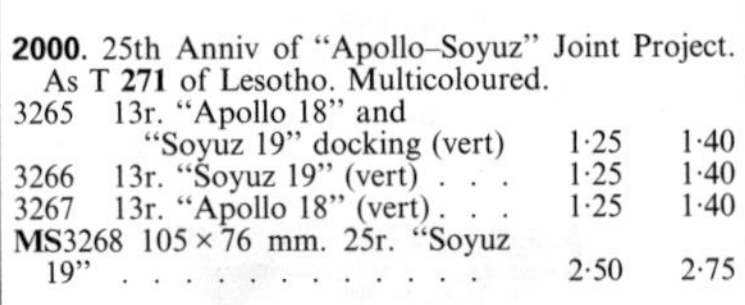

380 George Stephenson and *Locomotion No. 1*, 1825

2000. 175th Anniv of Stockton and Darlington Line (first public railway). Multicoloured.
3269 10r. Type **380** . . . . . . 95 1·00
3270 10r. William Hedley's *Puffing Billy* locomotive 95 1·00

2000. Centenary of First Zeppelin Flight. As T **276** of Lesotho. Multicoloured.
3271 13r. LZ-127 *Graf Zeppelin*, 1928 . . . . 1·25 1·40
3272 13r. LZ-130 *Graf Zeppelin II*, 1938 . . . . 1·25 1·40
3273 13r. LZ-9 *Ersatz*, 1911 . . . 1·25 1·40
MS3274 115 × 80 mm. 25r. LZ-88 (L-40), 1917 (37 × 50 mm) . . . 2·40 2·50

No. 3272 is inscribed "LZ-127" in error.

2000. Olympic Games, Sydney. As T **277** of Lesotho. Multicoloured.
3275 10r. Suzanne Lenglen, (French tennis player), 1920 . . . . 95 1·00
3276 10r. Fencing . . . . 95 1·00
3277 10r. Olympic Stadium, Tokyo, 1964, and Japanese flag . . . . . . 95 1·00
3278 10r. Ancient Greek long jumping . . . . 95 1·00

381 White Tern

2000. Tropical Birds. Multicoloured.
3279 15l. Type **381** 10 10
3280 25l. Brown booby 10 10
3281 30l. White-collared kingfisher (vert) 10 10
3282 1r. Black-winged stilt (vert) 10 15
3283 10r. White-collared kingfisher (different) (vert) 95 1·00
3284 10r. Island thrush (vert) . . 95 1·00
3285 10r. Red-tailed tropic bird (vert) . . . . 95 1·00
3286 10r. Peregrine falcon (vert) 95 1·00
3287 10r. Black-crowned night heron ("Night Heron") (vert) . . . . 95 1·00
3288 10r. Great egret (vert) . . . 95 1·00
3289 10r. Great frigate bird . . . 95 1·00
3290 10r. Common noddy . . . 95 1·00
3291 10r. Common tern . . . . 95 1·00
3292 10r. Red-footed booby ("Sula Sula") . . . . . . 95 1·00
3293 10r. Sooty tern . . . . . . 95 1·00
3294 10r. White-tailed tropic bird (*Phaethon lepturus*) . . . 95 1·00
3295 13r. Ringed plover . . . . 1·25 1·40
3296 13r. Ruddy turnstone ("Turnstone") . . . . . 1·25 1·40
3297 13r. Australian stone-curlew 1·25 1·40
3298 13r. Grey plover ("Black-bellied Plover") . . . . . 1·25 1·40
3299 13r. Crab lover . . . . . . 1·25 1·40
3300 13r. Western curlew ("Curlew") . . . . 1·25 1·40
MS3301 Two sheets, each 77 × 103 mm. (a) 25r. Great cormorant (vert). (b) 25r. Cattle egret (vert) Set of 2 sheets . . . 4·75 5·00

Nos. 3283/8, 3289/4 and 3295/300 were each printed together, se-tenant, with the backgrounds forming composite designs.

No. 3294 is inscribed "Leturus" in error.

382 *Dendrobium crepidatum* **384** Corn Lily

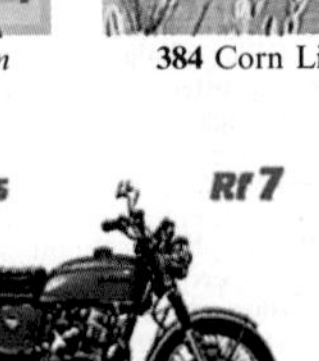

383 Honda CB 750 Motorcycle, 1969

2000. Orchids. Multicoloured.
3302 50l. Type **382** 10 10
3303 1r. *Eulophia guineensis* . . . 10 15
3304 2r.50 *Cymbidium finlaysonianum* 25 30
3305 3r.50 *Paphiopedilum druryi* 35 40
3306 10r. *Angraecum germinyanum* . . . . . . 95 1·00
3307 10r. *Phalaenopsis amabilis* 95 1·00
3308 10r. *Thrixspermum cantipeda* 95 1·00
3309 10r. *Phaius tankervilleae* . . 95 1·00
3310 10r. *Rhynchostylis gigantea* 95 1·00
3311 10r. *Papilionanthe teres* . . 95 1·00
3312 10r. Aerides odorata . . . . 95 1·00
3313 10r. *Dendrobium chrysotoxum* . . . . . . 95 1·00
3314 10r. *Dendrobium anosmum* 95 1·00
3315 10r. *Calypso bulbosa* . . . . 95 1·00
3316 10r. *Paphiopedilum fairrieanum* . . . . . . 95 1·00
3317 10r. *Cynorkis fastigiata* . . 95 1·00
MS3318 Two sheets, each 96 × 72 mm. (a) 25r. *Cymbidium dayanum*. (b) 25r. *Spathoglottis plicata* Set of 2 sheets . . . 4·75 5·00

Nos. 3306/11 and 3312/17 were each printed together, se-tenant, with the backgrounds forming composite designs.

2000. A Century of Motorcycles. Multicoloured.
3319 7r. Type **383** 65 70
3320 7r. Pioneer Harley Davidson, 1913 . . . . . 65 70
3321 7r. Bohmerland, 1925 . . . 65 70
3322 7r. American Indian, 1910 65 70
3323 7r. Triumph Trophy 1200, 1993 . . . . 65 70
3324 7r. Moto Guzzi 500S, 1928 65 70
3325 7r. Matchless, 1907 . . . . 65 70
3326 7r. Manch 4 1200 TTS, 1966 65 70
3327 7r. Lambretta LD-150, 1957 65 70
3328 7r. Yamaha XJP 1200, 1990's 65 70

3329 7r. Daimler, 1885 65 70
3330 7r. John Player Norton, 1950s–60's 65 70
MS3331 Two sheets, each 62×46 mm. (a) 25r. Harley Davidson, 1950. (b) 25r. Electra Glide, 1960 Set of 2 sheets 4·75 5·00

2000. Flowers of the Indian Ocean. Multicoloured.
3332 5r. Type **384** 50 55
3333 5r. Clivia 50 55
3334 5r. Red hot poker 50 55
3335 5r. Crown of Thorns 50 55
3336 5r. Cape daisy 50 55
3337 5r. Geranium 50 55
3338 5r. Fringed hibiscus (horiz) 50 55
3339 5r. *Erica vestita* (horiz) 50 55
3340 5r. Bird-of-paradise flower (horiz) 50 55
3341 5r. Peacock orchid (horiz) 50 55
3342 5r. Mesembryanthemums (horiz) 50 55
3343 5r. African violets (horiz) 50 55
MS3344 Two sheets, each 112×80 mm. (a) 25r. Gladiolus. (b) 25r. Calla lily (horiz) Set of 2 sheets 4·75 5·00
Nos. 3332/7 and 3338/43 were each printed together, se-tenant, with the backgrounds forming composite designs.

385 Racoon Butterflyfish (*Chaetodon lunula*)

2000. Marine Life of the Indian Ocean. Multicoloured.
3345 5r. Type **385** 50 55
3346 5r. Wrasse (*Stethojulis albovittata*) 50 55
3347 5r. Green turtle 50 55
3348 5r. Jobfish 50 55
3349 5r. Damsel fish 50 55
3350 5r. Meyer's butterflyfish (*Chaetodon meyeri*) 50 55
3351 5r. Wrasse (*Cirrhilabrus exquisitus*) 50 55
3352 5r. Maldive anemonefish 50 55
3353 5r. Hind (*Cephalopholis* sp) 50 55
3354 5r. Regal angelfish (*Pygopolites diacanthus*) (red face value) 50 55
3355 5r. Forceps butterflyfish (*Forcipiger flavissimus*) 50 55
3356 5r. Goatfish 50 55
3357 5r. Trumpet fish 50 55
3358 5r. Butterfly perch (*Pseudanthias squamipinnis*) 50 55
3359 5r. Two-spined angelfish (*Centropyge bispinosus*) 50 55
3360 5r. Sweetlips 50 55
3361 5r. Twin-spotted wrasse (*Coris aygula*) 50 55
3362 5r. Snapper 50 55
3363 5r. Sea bass 50 55
3364 5r. Bennett's butterflyfish (*Chaetodon bennetti*) 50 55
3365 5r. Pelagic snapper 50 55
3366 5r. Cardinalfish 50 55
3367 5r. Six-barred wrasse (*Thalassoma hardwicke*) 50 55
3368 5r. Surgeonfish 50 55
3369 5r. Longnosed filefish 50 55
3370 5r. Hawaiian squirrelfish 50 55
3371 5r. Freckled hawkfish 50 55
3372 5r. McCosker's flasher wrasse 50 55
3373 5r. Regal angelfish (*Pygoplites diacanthus*) (white face value) 50 55
3374 5r. Angelfish (*Parseentzopyge venusta*) 50 55
MS3375 Four sheets, each 108×80 mm. (a) 25r. Moray eel. (b) 25r. Yellow-bellied hamlet (*Hypoplectrus aberrans*). (c) 25r. Yellow-banded angelfish (*Pomacanthus maculosus*). (d) 25r. Spiny butterflyfish (*Pygoplites diacanthus*) Set of 4 sheets 9·50 9·75
Nos. 3345/52, 3353/60, 3361/8 and 3369/74 were each printed together, se-tenant, with the backgrounds forming composite designs.

385a "Nobleman with Golden Chain" (Tintoretto)

2000. "Espana 2000" International Stamp Exhibition, Madrid. Paintings from the Prado Museum. Multicoloured.
3376 7r. Type **385a** 65 70
3377 7r. "Triumphal Arch" (Domenichino) 65 70
3378 7r. "Don Garzia de'Medici" (Bronzino) 65 70
3379 7r. Man from "Micer Marsilio and his Wife" (Lorenzo Lotto) 65 70
3380 7r. "The Infanta Maria Antonieta Fernanda" (Jacopo Amigoni) 65 70
3381 7r. Woman from "Micer Marsilio and his Wife" 65 70
3382 7r. "Self-portrait" (Albrecht Durer) 65 70
3383 7r. "Woman and her Daughter" (Adriaen van Cronenburch) 65 70
3384 7r. "Portrait of a Man" (Albrecht Durer) 65 70
3385 7r. Wife and daughters from "The Artist and his Family" (Jacob Jordaens) 65 70
3386 7r. "Artemisia" (Rembrandt) 65 70
3387 7r. Man from "The Artist and his Family"
3388 7r. "The Painter Andrea Sacchi" (Carlo Maratta) 65 70
3389 7r. Two Turks from "The Turkish Embassy to the Court of Naples" (Giuseppe Bonito) 65 70
3390 7r. "Charles Cecil Roberts" (Pompeo Girolamo Batoni) 65 70
3391 7r. "Francesco Albani" (Andrea Sacchi) 65 70
3392 7r. Three Turks from "The Turkish Embassy to the Court of Naples" 65 70
3393 7r. "Sir William Hamilton" (Pompeo Girolamo Batoni) 65 70
3394 7r. Women from "Achilles amongst the Daughters of Lycomedes" (Rubens and Van Dyck) 65 70
3395 7r. Woman in red dress from "Achilles amongst the Daughters of Lycomedes" 65 70
3396 7r. Men from "Achilles amongst the Daughters of Lycomedes" 65 70
3397 7r. "The Duke of Lerma on Horseback" (Rubens) 65 70
3398 7r. "The Death of Seneca" (workshop of Rubens) 65 70

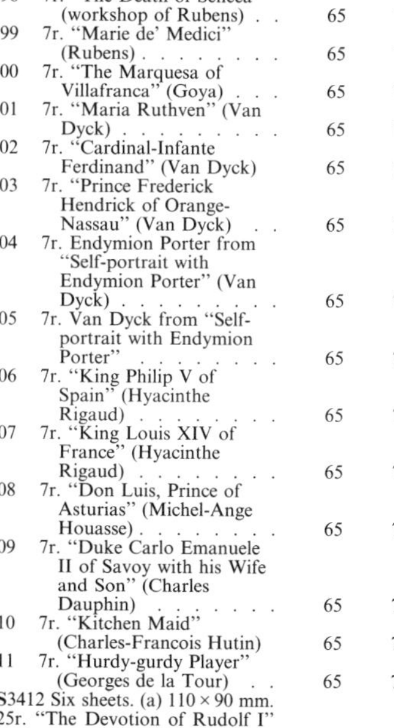

3399 7r. "Marie de' Medici" (Rubens) 65 70
3400 7r. "The Marquesa of Villafranca" (Goya) 65 70
3401 7r. "Maria Ruthven" (Van Dyck) 65 70
3402 7r. "Cardinal-Infante Ferdinand" (Van Dyck) 65 70
3403 7r. "Prince Frederick Hendrick of Orange-Nassau" (Van Dyck) 65 70
3404 7r. Endymion Porter from "Self-portrait with Endymion Porter" (Van Dyck) 65 70
3405 7r. Van Dyck from "Self-portrait with Endymion Porter" 65 70
3406 7r. "King Philip V of Spain" (Hyacinthe Rigaud) 65 70
3407 7r. "King Louis XIV of France" (Hyacinthe Rigaud) 65 70
3408 7r. "Don Luis, Prince of Asturias" (Michel-Ange Houasse) 65 70
3409 7r. "Duke Carlo Emanuele II of Savoy with his Wife and Son" (Charles Dauphin) 65 70

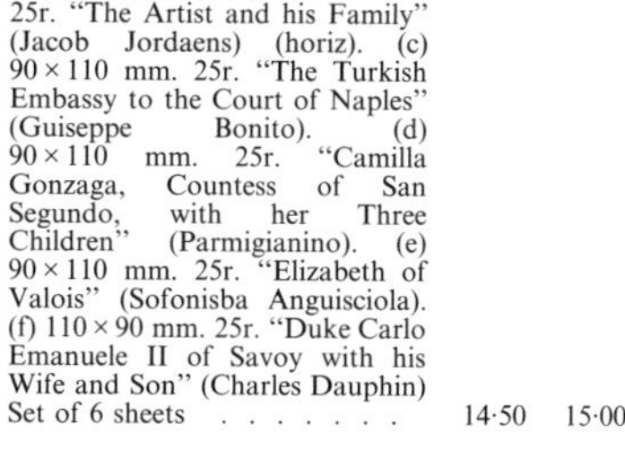

3410 7r. "Kitchen Maid" (Charles-Francois Hutin) 65 70
3411 7r. "Hurdy-gurdy Player" (Georges de la Tour) 65 70
MS3412 Six sheets. (a) 110×90 mm. 25r. "The Devotion of Rudolf I" (Peter Paul Rubens and Jan Wildens) (horiz). (b) 110×90 mm. 25r. "The Artist and his Family" (Jacob Jordaens) (horiz). (c) 90×110 mm. 25r. "The Turkish Embassy to the Court of Naples" (Guiseppe Bonito). (d) 90×110 mm. 25r. "Camilla Gonzaga, Countess of San Segundo, with her Three Children" (Parmigianino). (e) 90×110 mm. 25r. "Elizabeth of Valois" (Sofonisba Anguisciola). (f) 110×90 mm. 25r. "Duke Carlo Emanuele II of Savoy with his Wife and Son" (Charles Dauphin) Set of 6 sheets 14·50 15·00

386 Steam Locomotive *Hiawatha*, 1935

2000. Milestones in Twentieth-century Transport. Multicoloured.
3413 2r. 50 Steam locomotive *Papyrus*, 1934 (vert) 25 30
3414 3r. Type **386** 30 35
3415 5r. Thrust SSC rocket car, 1997 50 55
3416 5r. Curtiss R3C-2 seaplane, 1925 50 55
3417 5r. Steam locomotive *Rocket*, 1829 50 55
3418 5r. BB-9004 electric train, 1955 50 55
3419 5r. Steam locomotive *Mallard*, 1938 50 55
3420 5r. T.G.V. electric train, 1980 50 55

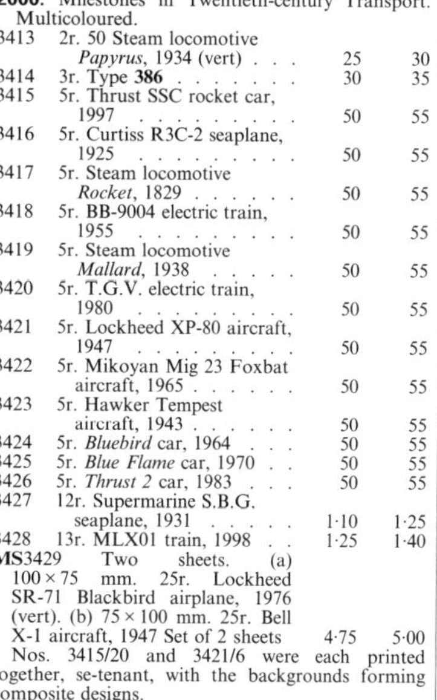

3421 5r. Lockheed XP-80 aircraft, 1947 50 55
3422 5r. Mikoyan Mig 23 Foxbat aircraft, 1965 50 55
3423 5r. Hawker Tempest aircraft, 1943 50 55
3424 5r. *Bluebird* car, 1964 50 55
3425 5r. *Blue Flame* car, 1970 50 55
3426 5r. *Thrust 2* car, 1983 50 55
3427 12r. Supermarine S.B.G. seaplane, 1931 1·10 1·25
3428 13r. MLX01 train, 1998 1·25 1·40
MS3429 Two sheets. (a) 100×75 mm. 25r. Lockheed SR-71 Blackbird airplane, 1976 (vert). (b) 75×100 mm. 25r. Bell X-1 aircraft, 1947 Set of 2 sheets 4·75 5·00
Nos. 3415/20 and 3421/6 were each printed together, se-tenant, with the backgrounds forming composite designs.

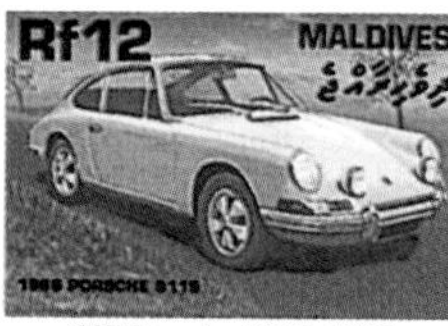

387 Porsche 911S, 1966

2000. "The World of Porsche". Multicoloured.
3430 12r. Type **387** 1·10 1·25
3431 12r. Model 959, 1988 1·10 1·25
3432 12r. Model 993 Carrera, 1995 1·10 1·25
3433 12r. Model 356 SC, 1963 1·10 1·25
3434 12r. Model 911 Turbo, 1975 1·10 1·25
3435 12r. Contemporary model 1·10 1·25
MS3436 110×85 mm. 25r. Model Boxter, 2000 (56×42 mm) 2·40 2·50

388 Limited Edition Trans-Am, 1976

2000. "The World of the Pontiac". Multicolourd.
3437 12r. Type **388** 1·10 1·25
3438 12r. Trans-Am, 1988 1·10 1·25
3439 12r. Trans-Am Coupe, 1988 1·10 1·25
3440 12r. Yellow Trans-Am, 1970–72 1·10 1·25
3441 12r. 25th Anniv Trans-Am, 1989 1·10 1·25
3442 12r. Trans-Am GT convertible, 1994 1·10 1·25
MS3443 110×85 mm. 25r. Trans-Am model, 1999 (56×42 mm) 2·40 2·50

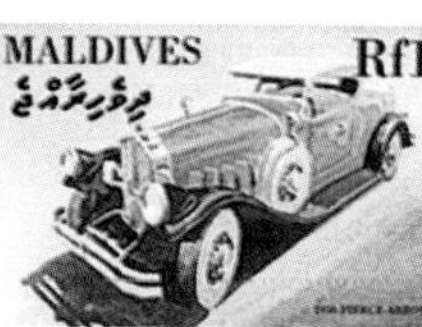

389 Pierce-Arrow

2000. Twentieth-century Classic Cars. Multicoloured.
3444 1r. Type **389** 10 15
3445 2r. Mercedes-Benz 540K (1938) 20 25
3446 7r. Auburn Convertible Sedan (1931) 65 70
3447 7r. Mercedes SSKL (1931) 65 70
3448 7r. Packard Roadster (1929) 65 70
3449 7r. Chevrolet (1940) 65 70
3450 7r. Mercer (1915) 65 70
3451 7r. Packard Sedan (1941) 65 70
3452 7r. Chevrolet Roadster (1932) 65 70
3453 7r. Cadillac Fleetwood Roadster (1929) 65 70
3454 7r. Bentley Speed Six (1928) 65 70
3455 7r. Cadillac Fleetwood (1930) 65 70
3456 7r. Ford Convertible (1936) 65 70
3457 7r. Hudson Phaeton (1929) 65 70
3458 8r. Duesenberg J (1934) 75 80
3459 10r. Bugatti Royale (1931) 95 1·00
MS3460 Two sheets, each 106×81 mm. (a) 25r. Rolls Royce P-1 (1931). (b) 25r. Cord Brougham (1930) Set of 2 sheets 4·75 5·00
No. 3457 is inscribed "HUDSIN" in error.

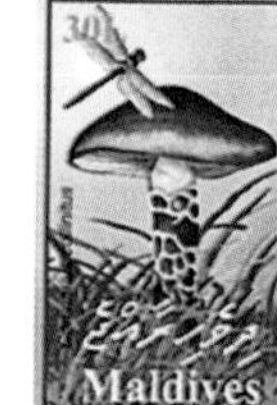

390 *Cortinarius collinitus*

2001. Fungi. Multicoloured.
3461 30l. Type **390** 10 10
3462 50l. *Russula ochroleuca* 10 10
3463 2r. *Lepiota acutesquamosa* 20 25
3464 3r. *Hebeloma radicosum* 30 35
3465 7r. *Tricholoma aurantium* 65 70
3466 7r. *Pholiota spectabilis* 65 70
3467 7r. *Russula caerulea* 65 70
3468 7r. *Amanita phalloides* 65 70
3469 7r. *Mycena strobilinoides* 65 70
3470 7r. *Boletus satanas* 65 70
3471 7r. *Amanita muscaria* 65 70
3472 7r. *Mycena lilacifolia* 65 70
3473 7r. *Coprinus comatus* 65 70
3474 7r. *Morchella crassipes* 65 70
3475 7r. *Russula nigricans* 65 70
3476 7r. *Lepiota procera* 65 70
3477 13r. *Amanita echinocephala* 1·25 1·40
3478 15r. *Collybia iocephala* 1·40 1·50
MS3479 Two sheets, each 112×82 mm. (a) 25r. *Tricholoma aurantium*. (b) 25r. *Lepiota procera* Set of 2 sheets 4·75 5·00

390a German Commanders looking across English Channel

2001. 60th Anniv of Battle of Britain. Multicoloured.
3480 5r. Type **390a** 50 55
3481 5r. Armourers with German bomber 50 55
3482 5r. German Stuka dive-bombers 50 55
3483 5r. Bombing the British coast 50 55
3484 5r. German bomber over Greenwich 50 55
3485 5r. St. Paul's Cathedral surrounded by fire 50 55
3486 5r. British fighter from German bomber 50 55
3487 5r. Spitfire on fire 50 55
3488 5r. Prime Minister Winston Churchill 50 55
3489 5r. British fighter pilots running to planes 50 55
3490 5r. R.A.F. planes taking off 50 55
3491 5r. British fighters in formation 50 55
3492 5r. German bomber crashing 50 55
3493 5r. British fighters attacking 50 55
3494 5r. German bomber in sea 50 55
3495 5r. Remains of German bomber in flames 50 55
MS3496 Two sheets, each 103×66 mm. (a) 25r. Hawker Hurricane. (b) 25r. Messerschmitt ME 109 Set of 2 sheets 4·75 5·00

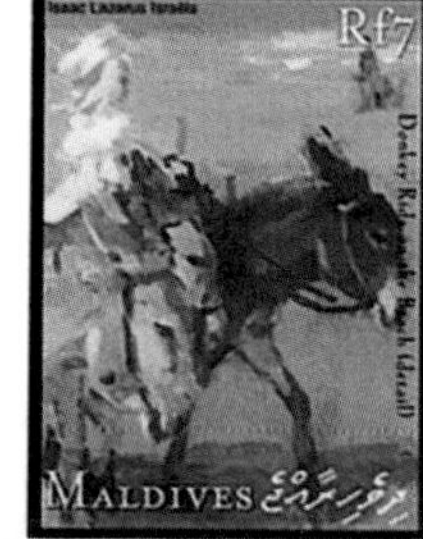

390b Donkeys from "Donkey Ride on the Beach" (Isaac Lazarus Israels)

2001. Bicentenary of Rijksmuseum, Amsterdam. Dutch Paintings. Multicoloured.
3497 7r. Type **390b** 65 70
3498 7r. "The Paternal Admonition" (Gerard ter Borch) 65 70
3499 7r. "The Sick Woman" (Jan Havicksz Steen) 65 70
3500 7r. Girls from "Donkey Ride on the Beach" 65 70
3501 7r. "Pompejus Occo" (Dick Jacobsz) 65 70
3502 7r. "The Pantry" (Pieter de Hooch) 65 70
3503 7r. Woman in doorway from "The Little Street" (Johannes Vermeer) 65 70
3504 7r. Woman with maid from "The Love Letter" (Johannes Vermeer) 65 70
3505 7r. "Woman in Blue Reading a Letter" (Johannes Vermeer) 65 70

3506 7r. Woman from "The Love Letter" 65 70
3507 7r. "The Milkmaid" (Johannes Vermeer) . . . 65 70
3508 7r. Woman in alley from "The Little Street" . . . 65 70
3509 7r. "Rembrandt's Mother" (Gerard Dou) 65 70
3510 7r. "Girl dressed in Blue" (Johannes Verspronck) . . 65 70
3511 7r. "Old Woman at Prayer" (Nicolaes Maes) 65 70
3512 7r. "Feeding the Hungry" (De Meester van Alkmaar) 65 70
3513 7r. "The Threatened Swan" (Jan Asselyn) 65 70
3514 7r. "The Daydreamer" (Nicolaes Maes) 65 70
3515 7r. "The Holy Kinship" (Geertgen Tot Sint Jans) 65 70
3516 7r. "Sir Thomas Gresham" (Anthonis Mor Vas Dashorst) 65 70
3517 7r. "Self portrait as St. Paul" (Rembrandt) . . 65 70
3518 7r. "Cleopatra's Banquet" (Gerard Lairesse) 65 70
3519 7r. "Flowers in a Glass" (Jan Brueghel the elder) 65 70
3520 7r. "Nicolaes Hasselaer" (Frans Hals) 65 70
MS3521 Four sheets. (a) 118 × 78 mm. 25r. "The Syndics" (Rembrandt). (b) 88 × 118 mm. 25r. "Johannes Wtenbogaert" (Rembrandt). (c) 118 × 88 mm. 25r. "The Night Watch" (Rembrandt). (d) 118 × 88 mm. 25r. "Shipwreck on a Rocky Coast" (Wijnandus Johannes Nuyen) (horiz) Set of 4 sheets 9·50 9·75

391 *Windfall* (schooner), 1962 **392** Roses

2001. Maritime Disasters. Multicoloured.
3522 5r. Type **391** 50 55
3523 5r. *Kobenhavn* (barque), 1928 . . . . 50 55
3524 5r. *Pearl* (schooner), 1874 50 55
3525 5r. H.M.S. *Bulwark* (battleship), 1914 . . . . 50 55
3526 5r. *Patriot* (brig), 1812 . . . 50 55
3527 5r. *Lusitania* (liner), 1915 . . 50 55
3528 5r. *Milton Iatrides* (coaster), 1970 . . . . 50 55
3529 5r. *Cyclops* (freighter), 1918 50 55
3530 5r. *Marine Sulphur Queen* (tanker), 1963 . . . . . 50 55
3531 5r. *Rosalie* (full-rigged ship), 1840 . . . . 50 55
3532 5r. *Mary Celeste* (sail merchantman), 1872 . . . 50 55
3533 5r. *Atlanta* (brig), 1880 . . . 50 55
MS3534 Two sheets, each 110 × 85 mm. (a) 25r. *L 'Astrolabe* and *La Boussole* (La Perouse, 1789). (b) 25r. *Titanic* (liner), 1912 Set of 2 sheets . . . . 4·75 5·00
Nos. 3522/7 and 3528/33 were printed together, se-tenant, with the backgrounds forming composite designs.
No. 3530 is inscribed "SULPHER" and No. **MS**3517a "LA BAUSSOLE", both in error.

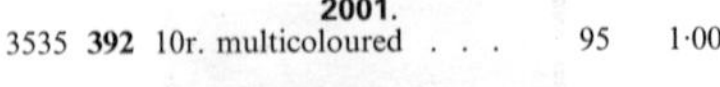

2001.
3535 **392** 10r. multicoloured . . . 95 1·00

393 Interior of Dharumavantha Rasgefaanu Mosque

2001. 848th Anniv of Introduction of Islam to the Maldives. Multicoloured (except Nos. 3537/8).
3536 10r. Type **393** . . . . . . 95 1·00
3537 10r. Plaque of Hukurumiskiiy (black and green) . . . . 95 1·00
3538 10r. Family studying the Holy Quran (black) . . . 95 1·00
3539 10r. Class at Institute of Islamic Studies . . . . . 95 1·00
3540 10r. Centre for the Holy Quran . . . . 95 1·00
3541 10r. Islamic Centre, Male 95 1·00
MS3542 116 × 90 mm. 25r. Tomb of Sultan Abdul Barakaat . . . . 2·40 2·50

394 Emperor Angelfish **395** "Young Women in Mist"

2001. Fish. Multicoloured.
3543 10r. Type **394** . . . . . . 95 1·00
3544 10r. Indian Ocean lionfish ("*Pterois miles*") . . . . 95 1·00

2001. "Philanippon '01" International Stamp Exhibition, Tokyo. Japanese Art. Multicoloured.
3545 7r. Type **395** 65 70
3546 7r. "Woman with Parasol" 65 70
3547 7r. "Courtesan" 65 70
3548 7r. "Comparison of Beauties" 65 70
3549 7r. "Barber" 65 70
3550 7r. Ichikawa Danjuro V in black robes (20 × 81 mm) 65 70
3551 7r. Ichikawa Danjuro V in brown robes with sword (20 × 81 mm) 65 70
3552 7r. Ichikawa Danjuro V with arms folded (20 × 81 mm) 65 70
3553 7r. Ichikawa Danjuro V seated in brown robes (20 × 81 mm) 65 70
3554 7r. Otani Tomoeman I and Bando Mitsugaro I (53 × 81 mm) 65 70
MS3555 Two sheets, each 88 × 124 mm. (a) 25r. "Courtesan Hinazuru" (Kitagawa Utamaro). (b) 25r. "Tsutsui Jmy and the Priest Ichirai" (Torii Kiyomasu I) Set of 2 sheets . . . . 4·75 5·00
Nos. 3545/9 show paintings of women by Kitagawa Utamaro, and Nos. 3550/4 show famous actors by Katsukawa Shunsho.

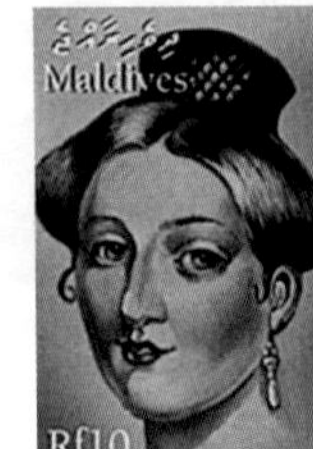

395a Victoria as a Young Girl (face value bottom left)

2001. Death Centenary of Queen Victoria. Multicoloured.
3556 10r. Type **395a** . . . . . . 95 1·00
3557 10r. Victoria in old age . . 95 1·00
3558 10r. Victoria as a young girl (face value top right) . . 95 1·00
3559 10r. Queen Victoria in mourning . . . . 95 1·00
MS3560 125 × 87 mm. 25r. Young Queen Victoria in evening dress 2·40 2·50

395b Mao as a teenager (brown background)

2001. 25th Death Anniv of Mao Tse-tung (Chinese leader). Multicoloured.
3561 15r. Type **395b** . . . . . . 1·40 1·50
3562 15r. Mao as leader of Communist Party in 1930s (violet background) . . . 1·40 1·50
3563 15r. Mao in 1940s (grey background) . . . . . . 1·40 1·50
MS3564 139 × 132 mm. 25r. Mao as leader of China in 1960s . . . 2·40 2·50

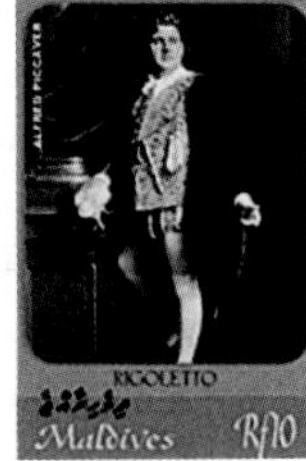

395c Portrait in Garter robes **395d** Alfred Piccaver (opera singer) after Annigoni as Duke of Mantua

2001. 75th Birthday of Queen Elizabeth II. Multicoloured.
3565 7r. Type **395c** 65 70
3566 7r. Queen at Coronation . . 65 70
3567 7r. In evening gown and tiara 65 70
3568 7r. In uniform for Trooping the Colour 65 70
3569 7r. In Garter robes and hat 65 70
3570 7r. Queen wearing cloak of kiwi feathers 65 70
MS3571 112 × 138 mm. 25r. Young Queen Elizabeth . . . . 2·40 2·50

2001. Death Centenary of Giuseppe Verdi (Italian composer). Multicoloured.
3572 10r. Type **395d** . . . . . . 95 1·00
3573 10r. Heinrich's costume from Rigoletto (opera) . . 95 1·00
3574 10r. Cologne's costume from Rigoletto . . . . 95 1·00
3575 10r. Cornell MacNeil (opera singer) as Rigoletto . . . 95 1·00
MS3576 79 × 119 mm. 25r. Matteo Manvgerri (opera singer) as Rigoletto . . . . 2·40 2·50

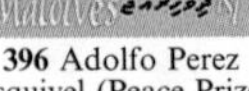

396 Adolfo Perez Esquivel (Peace Prize, 1980) **398** Eusebio and Portuguese Flag

397 Mercedes-Benz W165 Racing Car, 1939

2001. Centenary of Nobel Prizes. Prize Winners. Multicoloured.
3577 7r. Type **396** 65 70
3578 7r. Mikhail Gorbachev (Peace, 1990) 65 70
3579 7r. Betty Williams (Peace, 1976) 65 70
3580 7r. Alfonso Garcia Robles (Peace, 1982) 65 70
3581 7r. Paul d'Estournelles de Constant (Peace, 1909) . . 65 70
3582 7r. Louis Renault (Peace, 1907) 65 70
3583 7r. Ernesto Moneta (Peace, 1907) 65 70
3584 7r. Albert Luthuli (Peace, 1960) 65 70
3585 7r. Henri Dunant (Peace, 1901) 65 70
3586 7r. Albert Gobat (Peace, 1902) 65 70
3587 7r. Sean MacBride (Peace, 1974) 65 70
3588 7r. Elie Ducommun (Peace, 1902) 65 70
3589 7r. Simon Kuznets (Economics, 1971) 65 70
3590 7r. Wassily Leontief (Economics, 1973) 65 70
3591 7r. Lawrence Klein (Economics, 1980) 65 70
3592 7r. Friedrich von Hayek (Economics, 1974) 65 70
3593 7r. Leonid Kantorovich (Economics, 1975) 65 70
MS3594 Three sheets, each 108 × 127 mm. (a) 25r. Trygve Haavelmo (Economics, 1989). (b) 25r. Octavio Paz (Literature, 1990). (c) 25r. Vicente Aleixandre (Literature, 1977) Set of 3 sheets 7·25 7·50

2001. Centenary of Mercedes-Benz Cars. Multicoloured.
3595 2r.50 Type **397** 25 30
3596 5r. 460 Nurburg Sport-roadster, 1928 . . . . . . 50 55
3597 7r. 680S racing car, 1927 . . 65 70
3598 7r. 150, 1934 . . . . 65 70
3599 7r. 540K Roadster, 1936 . . 65 70

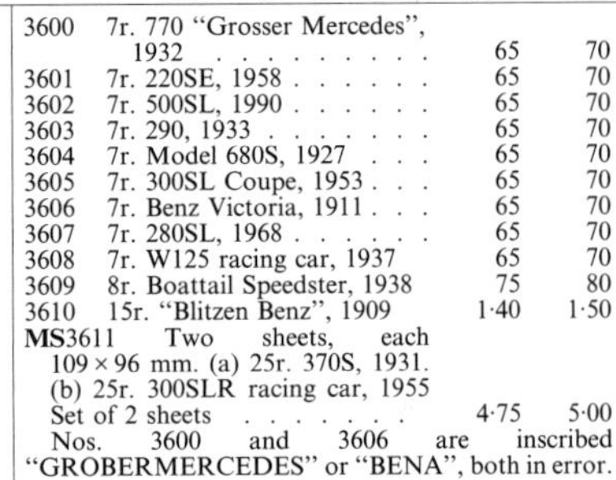

3600 7r. 770 "Grosser Mercedes", 1932 . . . . 65 70
3601 7r. 220SE, 1958 . . . . . . 65 70
3602 7r. 500SL, 1990 . . . . . . 65 70
3603 7r. 290, 1933 . . . . 65 70
3604 7r. Model 680S, 1927 . . . 65 70
3605 7r. 300SL Coupe, 1953 . . . 65 70
3606 7r. Benz Victoria, 1911 . . . 65 70
3607 7r. 280SL, 1968 . . . . . . 65 70
3608 7r. W125 racing car, 1937 65 70
3609 8r. Boattail Speedster, 1938 75 80
3610 15r. "Blitzen Benz", 1909 1·40 1·50
MS3611 Two sheets, each 109 × 96 mm. (a) 25r. 370S, 1931. (b) 25r. 300SLR racing car, 1955 Set of 2 sheets . . . . 4·75 5·00
Nos. 3600 and 3606 are inscribed "GROBERMERCEDES" or "BENA", both in error.

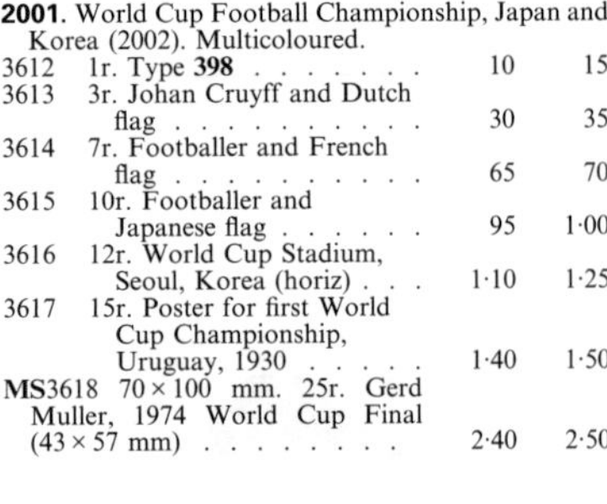

2001. World Cup Football Championship, Japan and Korea (2002). Multicoloured.
3612 1r. Type **398** 10 15
3613 3r. Johan Cruyff and Dutch flag 30 35
3614 7r. Footballer and French flag 65 70
3615 10r. Footballer and Japanese flag . . . . . . 95 1·00
3616 12r. World Cup Stadium, Seoul, Korea (horiz) . . . 1·10 1·25
3617 15r. Poster for first World Cup Championship, Uruguay, 1930 . . . . . 1·40 1·50
MS3618 70 × 100 mm. 25r. Gerd Muller, 1974 World Cup Final (43 × 57 mm) . . . . 2·40 2·50

399 *Cymothoe lucasi*

2001. Moths and Butterflies. Multicoloured.
3619 7r. Type **399** 65 70
3620 7r. *Milionia grandis* 65 70
3621 7r. *Ornithoptera croesus* . . 65 70
3622 7r. *Hyantis hodeva* 65 70
3623 7r. *Ammobiota festiva* . . . 65 70
3624 7r. *Salamis temora* 65 70
3625 7r. *Zygaena occitanica* . . . 65 70
3626 7r. *Campylotes desgodinsi* . . 65 70
3627 7r. *Bhutanitis thaidina* . . . 65 70
3628 7r. *Helicopsis endymion* . . 65 70
3629 7r. *Parnassius charitonius* . . 65 70
3630 7r. *Acaca ecucogiap* 65 70
3631 10r. *Papilio dardanus* . . . 95 1·00
3632 10r. *Baomisa hieroglyphica* 95 1·00
3633 10r. *Troides prattorum* . . . 95 1·00
3634 10r. *Funonia rhadama* . . . 95 1·00
MS3635 Two sheets. (a) 83 × 108 mm. 25r. *Hypolera cassotis*. (b) 108 × 83 mm. 25r. *Euphydryas maturna* (vert) . . 4·75 5·00
Nos. 3621 and 3629 are inscribed "eroesus" or "charltonius", both in error.

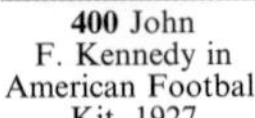

400 John F. Kennedy in American Football Kit, 1927 **401** Princess Diana wearing Pink Jacket

2001. John F. Kennedy (American President) Commemoration. Multicoloured.
3636 5r. Type **400** 50 55
3637 5r. John Kennedy at Harvard, 1935 . . . . . 50 55
3638 5r. As U.S. Navy officer, Solomon Islands, 1943 . . 50 55
3639 5r. On wedding day, 1953 50 55
3640 5r. With brother, Robert, 1956 . . . . 50 55
3641 5r. Presidential Inauguration, 1961 . . . . 50 55
3642 5r. With First Secretary Nikita Khrushchev of U.S.S.R., 1961 . . . . . 50 55
3643 5r. With Prime Minister Harold MacMillan of Great Britain 50 55
3644 5r. With Pres. Charles de Gaulle of France, 1961 . . 50 55
3645 5r. With Prime Minister Jawaharlal Nehru of India, 1962 . . . . 50 55

3646 5r. With Chancellor Konrad Adenauer of West Germany, 1963 . . . . . 50 55
3647 5r. With Martin Luther King (Civil Rights campaigner) 1963 . . . . 50 55
MS3648 Two sheets, each 82 × 112 mm. (a) 25r. John Kennedy. (b) 25r. With wife, Paris, 1961 . . . . 4·75 5·00
No. 3642 is inscribed "PRIMIER" in error.

2001. 40th Birth Anniv of Diana, Princess of Wales. Multicoloured.
3649 10r. Type **401** . . . . . . 95 1·00
3650 10r. In evening dress with tiara . . . . 95 1·00
3651 10r. Wearing matching yellow hat and coat . . . 95 1·00
3652 10r. In beige dress . . . . . 95 1·00
MS3653 73 × 109 mm. 25r. Princess Diana wearing pearls . . . . . 2·40 2·50

402 "Running Horse" (Xu Beihong)

404 Havana Brown

403 Swinhoe's Snipe

2001. Chinese New Year ("Year of the Horse"). Paintings by Xu Beihong. Multicoloured.
3654 5r. Type **402** 50 55
3655 5r. "Standing Horse" (from back, with head up) . . . 50 55
3656 5r. "Running Horse" (different) 50 55
3657 5r. "Standing Horse" (with head down) 50 55
3658 5r. "Horse" (with head up, from front) 50 55
MS3659 110 × 70 mm. 15r. "Six Horses running" (57 × 37 mm) 1·40 1·50

2002. Birds. Multicoloured.
3660 1r. Type **403** 10 15
3661 2r. Oriental honey buzzard 20 25
3662 3r. Asian koel 30 35
3663 5r. Red-throated pipet . . . 50 55
3664 5r. Cattle egret 50 55
3665 5r. Barn swallow 50 55
3666 5r. Osprey 50 55
3667 5r. Green-backed heron ("Little Heron") 50 55
3668 5r. Ruddy turnstone 50 55
3669 5r. Sooty tern 50 55
3670 5r. Lesser noddy 50 55
3671 5r. Roseate tern 50 55
3672 5r. Great frigate bird ("Frigate Minor") 50 55
3673 5r. Black-shafted tern ("Saunder's Tern") . . . 50 55
3674 5r. White-bellied storm petrel 50 55
3675 5r. Red-footed booby . . . 50 55
3676 7r. Rose-ringed parakeet . . 65 70
3677 7r. Common swift 65 70
3678 7r. Lesser kestrel 65 70
3679 7r. Golden oriole 65 70
3680 7r. Asian paradise flycatcher 65 70
3681 7r. Indian roller 65 70
3682 7r. Pallid harrier 65 70
3683 7r. Grey heron 65 70
3684 7r. Blue-tailed bee eater . . 65 70
3685 7r. White-breasted water hen 65 70
3686 7r. Cotton teal ("Cotton Pygmy Goose") 65 70
3687 7r. Maldivian pond heron 65 70
3688 7r. Short-eared owl 65 70
3689 10r. White spoonbill ("Eurasian Spoonbill") . . 95 1·00
3690 12r. Pied wheatear . . . . 1·10 1·25
3691 15r. Oriental pratincole . . 1·40 1·50
MS3692 Four sheets, each 114 × 57 mm. (a) 25r. White tern. (b) 25r. Greater flamingo. (c) 25r. Cinnamon bittern. (d) 25r. White-tailed tropicbird . . . . 9·50 9·75
Nos. 3664/9, 3670/5, 3676/81 and 3682/7 were each printed together, se-tenant, with the backgrounds forming composite designs.

2002. Cats. Multicoloured.
3693 3r. Type **404** 30 35
3694 5r. American wirehair . . . 50 55
3695 7r. Persian (horiz) 65 70
3696 7r. Exotic shorthair (horiz) 65 70
3697 7r. Ragdoll (horiz) 65 70
3698 7r. Manx (horiz) 65 70
3699 7r. Tonkinese (horiz) . . . 65 70
3700 7r. Scottish fold (horiz) . . 65 70
3701 7r. British blue 65 70
3702 7r. Red mackerel manx . . 65 70
3703 7r. Scottish fold 65 70
3704 7r. Somali 65 70
3705 7r. Balinese 65 70
3706 7r. Exotic shorthair 65 70
3707 8r. Norwegian forest cat . . 75 80
3708 10r. Seal point siamese . . . 95 1·00
MS3709 110 × 85 mm. 25r. Blue mackerel tabby cornish rex . . 2·40 2·50

405 Queen Elizabeth with Princess Margaret

2002. Golden Jubilee. Multicoloured.
3710 10r. Type **405** . . . . . . 95 1·00
3711 10r. Princess Elizabeth wearing white hat and coat . . . . 95 1·00
3712 10r. Queen Elizabeth in evening dress . . . . . . 95 1·00
3713 10r. Queen Elizabeth on visit to Canada . . . . . 95 1·00
MS3714 76 × 108 mm. 25r. Paying homage, at Coronation, 1953 2·40 1·00

406 Sivatherium

2002. Prehistoric Animals. Multicoloured.
3715 7r. Type **406** 65 70
3716 7r. Flat-headed peccary . . 65 70
3717 7r. Shasta ground sloth . . 65 70
3718 7r. Harlan's ground sloth 65 70
3719 7r. European woolly rhinoceros 65 70
3720 7r. Dwarf pronghorn . . . 65 70
3721 7r. Macrauchenia 65 70
3722 7r. Glyptodon 65 70
3723 7r. Nesodon 65 70
3724 7r. Imperial tapir and calf 65 70
3725 7r. Short-faced bear 65 70
3726 7r. Mastodon 65 70
MS3727 Two sheets, each 94 × 67 mm. (a) 25r. Sabre-toothed cat. (b) 25r. Mammoth . . . . 4·75 5·00
Nos. 3715/20 and 3721/6 were each printed together, se-tenant, with the backgrounds forming composite designs.
Nos. 3722 and 3726 are inscribed "GIYPTODON" and "MAMMOTH", both in error.

2002. International Year of Mountains. As T **219** of Lesotho, but vert. Multicoloured.
3728 15r. Ama Dablam, Nepal 1·40 1·50
3729 15r. Mount Clements, U.S.A. . . . . 1·40 1·50
3730 15r. Mount Artesonraju, Peru . . . . 1·40 1·50
3731 15r. Mount Cholatse, Nepal 1·40 1·50
MS3732 96 × 65 mm. 25r. Mount Jefferson, U.S.A., and balloon 2·40 1·50

407 Downhill Skiing

2002. Winter Olympic Games, Salt Lake City. Multicoloured.
3733 12r. Type **407** . . . . . . 1·10 1·25
3734 12r. Ski jumping . . . . . 1·10 1·25
MS3735 82 × 103 mm. Nos. 3733/4 2·25 2·40

2002. 20th World Scout Jamboree, Thailand. As T **295** of Lesotho. Multicoloured.
3736 15r. Buddhist pagoda, Thailand (vert) . . . . . 1·40 1·50
3737 15r. Thai scout (vert) . . . 1·40 1·50
3738 15r. Scout badges on Thai flag (vert) . . . . 1·40 1·50
MS3739 106 × 78 mm. 25r. Mountain-climbing badge and knot diagrams . . . . 2·40 2·50

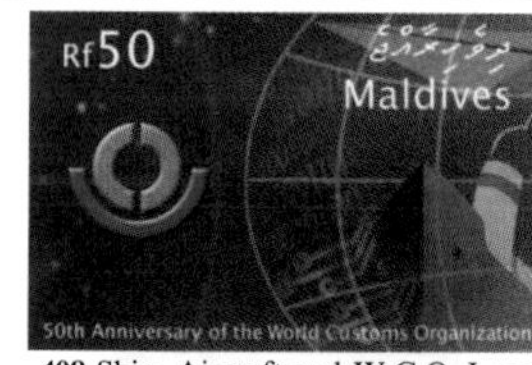
408 Ship, Aircraft and W.C.O. Logo

2002. 50th Anniv of World Customs Organization. Sheet 135 × 155 mm.
MS3740 **408** 50r. multicoloured 4·75 5·00

409 Elvis Presley

2002. 25th Death Anniv of Elvis Presley (American entertainer).
3741 **409** 5r. multicoloured 50 45

410 *Morpho menelaus*

2002. Flora and Fauna. Multicoloured.
3742 7r. Type **410** 65 70
3743 7r. *Heliconius erato* 65 70
3744 7r. *Thecla coronata* 65 70
3745 7r. *Battus philenor* 65 70
3746 7r. *Ornithoptera priamus* . . 65 70
3747 7r. *Danaus gilippus berenice* 65 70
3748 7r. *Ipomoea tricolor* Morning Glory 65 70
3749 7r. *Anemone coronaria* Wedding Bell 65 70
3750 7r. *Narcissus* Barrett Browning 65 70
3751 7r. *Nigella* Persian Jewel . . 65 70
3752 7r. *Osteospermum* Whirligig Pink 65 70
3753 7r. *Iris* Brown Lasso 65 70
3754 7r. *Laelia gouldiana* 65 70
3755 7r. *Cattleya* Louise Georgiana 65 70
3756 7r. *Laeliocattleya* Christopher Gubler . . . 65 70
3757 7r. *Miltoniopsis* Bert Field Crimson Glow 65 70
3758 7r. *Lemboglossum bictoniense* 65 70
3759 7r. *Derosara* Divine Victor 65 70
MS3760 Three sheets. (a) 72 × 50 mm. 25r. *Cymothoe lurida* (butterfly). (b) 66 × 45 mm. 25r. Perennial Aster Little Pink Beauty. (c) 50 × 72 mm. 25r. *Angraecum veitchii* (vert) . . . . 7·25 8·00
Nos. 3742/7 (butterflies), 3748/53 (flowers) and 3754/9 (orchids) were each printed together, se-tenant, with the backgrounds forming composite designs.
Nos. 3742 and 3748 are inscribed "Menelus" or "Impomoea", both in error.

411 Torsten Frings (Germany)

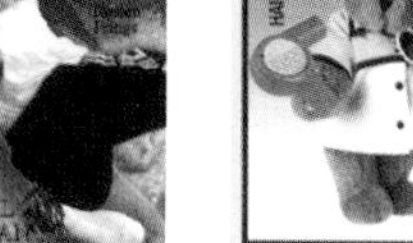
412 Hairdresser Bear

2002. World Cup Football Championship, Japan and Korea. Multicoloured.
3761 7r. Type **411** 65 70
3762 7r. Roberto Carlos (Brazil) 65 70
3763 7r. Torsten Frings (Germany) (different) . . 65 70
3764 7r. Ronaldo (Brazil), with one finger raised 65 70
3765 7r. Oliver Neuville (Germany) 65 70
3766 7r. Ronaldo (Brazil), heading ball 65 70
3767 7r. Eul Yong Lee (South Korea) and Alpay Ozalan (Turkey) 65 70
3768 7r. Myung Bo Hong (South Korea) and Hakan Sukur (Turkey) 65 70
3769 7r. Chong Gug Song (South Korea) and Emre Belozoglu (Turkey) . . . 65 70
3770 7r. Chong Gug Song (South Korea) and Ergun Penbe (Turkey) 65 70
3771 7r. Ki Hyeon Seol (South Korea) and Ergun Penbe (Turkey) 65 70
3772 7r. Chong Gug Song (South Korea) and Hakan Unsal (Turkey) 65 70
MS3773 Four sheets, each 82 × 82 mm. (a) 15r. Cafu (Brazil) and Oliver Neuville (Germany); 15r. World Cup Trophy. (b) 15r. Dietmar Hamann (Germany); 15r. Cafu (Brazil), holding Trophy. (c) 15r. Hakan Sukur (Turkey); 15r. Sang Chul Yoo (South Korea). (d) 15r. Ilhan Mansiz (Turkey); 15r. Young Pyo Lee (South Korea) 11·50 12·00

2002. Centenary of the Teddy Bear. Multicoloured.
3774 8r. Type **412** 75 80
3775 8r. Construction worker bear 75 80
3776 8r. Gardener bear 75 80
3777 8r. Chef bear 75 80
3778 12r. Nurse bear 75 80
3779 12r. Doctor bear 75 80
3780 12r. Dentist bear 75 80
3781 12r. Bride ("MOTHER") bear 75 80
3782 12r. Brother and sister bears 75 80
3783 12r. Groom ("FATHER") bear 75 80
MS3784 Three sheets, each 110 × 105 mm. (a) 30r. Golfer bear. (b) 30r. Footballer bear. (c) 30r. Skier bear ("SNOW BOARDER") . . . . 9·00 9·50

413 Charles Lindbergh and *Spirit of St. Louis*

414 Princess Diana

2002. 75th Anniv of First Solo Transatlantic Flight. Multicoloured.
3785 12r. Type **413** . . . . . . 1·10 1·25
3786 12r. Lindbergh in flying helmet and *Spirit of St. Louis* . . . . 1·10 1·25
3787 12r. Lindbergh holding propeller . . . . 1·10 1·25
3788 12r. Lindbergh in overalls and *Spirit of St. Louis* . . 1·10 1·25
3789 12r. Donald Hall (designer) 1·10 1·25
3790 12r. Charles Lindbergh (pilot) . . . . 1·10 1·25
3791 12r. Lindbergh under wing of *Spirit of St. Louis* . . . 1·10 1·25
3792 12r. Lindbergh, Mahoney and Hall at Ryan Airlines 1·10 1·25

2002. 5th Death Anniv of Diana, Princess of Wales. Multicoloured.
3793 12r. Type **414** . . . . . . 1·10 1·25
3794 12r. In evening dress and tiara . . . . 1·10 1·25

415 Joseph Kennedy with Sons Joseph Jr. and John, 1919

2002. Presidents John F. Kennedy and Ronald Reagan Commemoration. Multicoloured.
3795 7r. Type **415** 65 70
3796 7r. John F. Kennedy aged 11 . . . . 65 70
3797 7r. Kennedy inspecting Boston waterfront, 1951 65 70
3798 7r. Kennedy in naval ensign uniform, 1941 . . . . . 65 70
3799 7r. With sister Kathleen in London, 1939 . . . . . 65 70
3800 7r. Talking to Eleanor Roosevelt, 1951 . . . . . 65 70
3801 12r. Ronald Reagan facing right . . . . 1·10 1·25
3802 12r. Ronald Reagan (full-face portrait) . . . . . . 1·10 1·25

416 Wedding of Princess Juliana and Prince Bernhard, 1937

2002. "Amphilex '02" International Stamp Exhibition, Amsterdam. Dutch Royal Family.

3803	**416**	7r. blue and black	65	70
3804	–	7r. brown and black	65	70
3805	–	7r. red and black	65	70
3806	–	7r. brown and black	65	70
3807	–	7r. violet and black	65	70
3808	–	7r. green and black	65	70
3809	–	7r. multicoloured	65	70
3810	–	7r. brown and black	65	70
3811	–	7r. multicoloured	65	70
3812	–	7r. multicoloured	65	70
3813	–	7r. multicoloured	65	70
3814	–	7r. multicoloured	65	70

DESIGNS: No. 3804, Princess Juliana and Prince Bernhard with baby Princess Beatrix, 1938; 3805, Princess Juliana with her daughters in Canada, 1940–45; 3806, Inauguration of Queen Juliana, 1948; 3807, Royal Family inspecting Zeeland floods, 1953; 3808, Queen Juliana and Prince Bernhard; 3809, "Princess Beatrix as a Baby" (Pauline Hille); 3810, "Princess Beatrix in Flying Helmet" (John Klinkenberg); 3811, "Princess Beatrix" (Beatrice Filius); 3812, "Princess Beatrix and Prince Claus" (Will Kellermann); 3813, "Queen Beatrix in Royal Robes" (Graswinkel); 3814, "Queen Beatrix" (Marjolijn Spreeuwenberg).

417 Flame Basslet

2002. Marine Life. Multicoloured.

3815	10l. Type **417**	10	10
3816	15l. Teardrop butterflyfish	10	10
3817	20l. White-tailed damselfish ("Hambug Damselfish")	10	10
3818	25l. Bridled tern (23 × 27 mm)	10	10
3819	50l. Clown surgeonfish ("Blue-lined Surgeonfish")	10	10
3820	1r. Common tern (23 × 27 mm)	10	15
3821	2r. Common noddy (23 × 27 mm)	20	25
3822	2r.50 Yellow-breasted wrasse	25	30
3823	2r.50 Blue shark (23 × 27 mm)	25	30
3824	4r. Harlequin filefish	40	45
3825	5r. Masked unicornfish ("Orangespine Unicornfish")	50	55
3826	10r. Emperor angelfish	95	1·00
3827	12r. Catalufa ("Bullseye")	1·10	1·25
3828	20r. Scalloped hammerhead shark (23 × 27 mm)	1·90	2·00

No. 3822 is inscribed "wrass" in error.

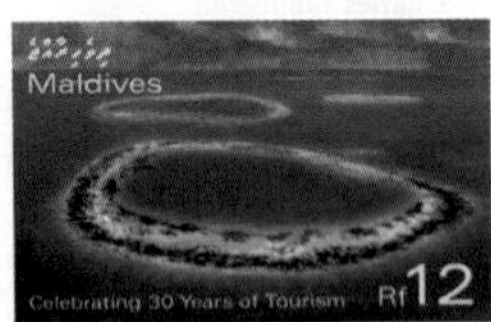

418 Atolls from the Air

2002. 30 Years of Maldives' Tourism Promotion. Multicoloured.

3829	12r. Type **418**	1·10	1·25
3830	12r. Island beach	1·10	1·25
3831	12r. Surfing	1·10	1·25
3832	12r. Scuba diving	1·10	1·25

419 Popeye diving

2003. "Popeye" (cartoon character). Multicoloured. Summer sports.

3833	7r. Type **419**	65	70
3834	7r. Surfing	65	70
3835	7r. Sailboarding	65	70
3836	7r. Baseball	65	70
3837	7r. Hurdling	65	70
3838	7r. Tennis	65	70
MS3839	120 × 90 mm. 25r. Volleyball (horiz)	2·40	2·50

Nos. 3833/8 were printed together, se-tenant, with the backgrounds forming a composite design.

420 Father with Baby

2003. UNICEF. "First Steps" Campaign. Multicoloured.

3840	2r.50 Type **420**	25	30
3841	5r. Mother and baby	50	55
3842	20r. Campaign emblem	1·90	2·00

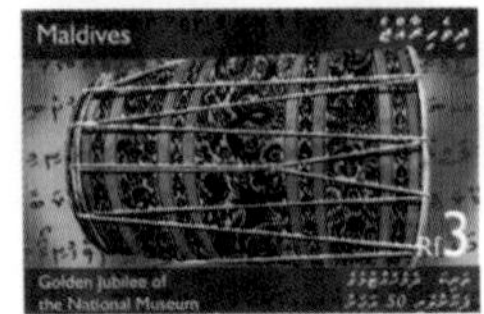

421 Decorated Drum

2003. 50th Anniv of National Museum. Multicoloured.

3843	3r. Type **421**	30	35
3844	3r.50 Carved covered bowl	35	40
3845	6r.50 Ceremonial sunshade	65	70
3846	22r. Ceremonial headdress	2·10	2·25

MALI Pt. 6; Pt. 13

Federation of French Sudan and Senegal, formed in 1959 as an autonomous republic within the French Community. In August 1960 the Federation was split up and the French Sudan part became the independent Mali Republic.

100 centimes = 1 franc.

A. FEDERATION.

1 Map, Flag, Mali and Torch

1959. Establishment of Mali Federation.
1 **1** 25f. multicoloured 35 25

2

1959. Air. 300th Anniv of St. Louis, Senegal.
2 **2** 85f. multicoloured 50 40

3 West African Parrotfish

4 Violet Starling

1960. (a) Postage. Fish as T **3**.
3 **3** 5f. orange, blue and bronze . . 40 15
4 – 10f. black, brown and turquoise 40 25
5 – 15f. brown, slate and blue . . 55 25
6 – 20f. black, bistre and green . . 65 35
7 – 25f. yellow, sepia and green 80 40
8 – 30f. red, purple and blue . . . 1·00 50
9 – 85f. red, blue and green . . . 3·00 1·75

(b) Air. Birds as T **4**.
10 **4** 100f. multicoloured . . . . . 5·50 1·25
11 – 200f. multicoloured . . . . . 12·00 3·75
12 – 500f. multicoloured . . . . . 32·00 11·50

DESIGNS—HORIZ: 10f. West African triggerfish; 15f. Guinean fingerfish; 20f. Threadfish; 25f. Shining butterflyfish; 30f. Monrovian surgeonfish; 85f. Pink dentex; 200f. Bateleur. VERT: 500f. Common gonolek.

1960. 10th Anniv of African Technical Co-operation Commission. As T **4** of Malagasy Republic.
13 25f. purple and violet . . . . 1·10 65

B. REPUBLIC.

1960. Nos. 6, 7, 9 and 10/12 optd **REPUBLIQUE DU MALI** and bar or bars or surch also.
14 20f. black, bistre and green (postage) . . . . 1·50 60
15 25f. red, purple and blue . . . 2·00 60
16 85f. red, blue and green . . . 3·75 1·50
17 100f. multicoloured (air) . . . 5·50 1·50
18 200f. multicoloured . . . . . 8·50 3·50
19 300f. on 500f. multicoloured 14·00 6·00
20 500f. multicoloured . . . . . 28·00 17·00

7 Pres. Mamadou Konate

1961.
21 **7** 20f. sepia and green (postage) 25 15
22 – 25f. black and purple 35 15
23 **7** 200f. sepia and red (air) . . . 3·00 1·00
24 – 300f. black and green . . . . 4·25 1·25

DESIGN: 25, 300f. President Keita. Nos. 23/4 are larger, 27 × 38 mm.

8 U.N. Emblem, Flag and Map

1961. Air. Proclamation of Independence and Admission into U.N.
25 **8** 100f. multicoloured . . . . . 1·60 95

9 Sankore Mosque, Timbuktu

1961. Air.
26 **9** 100f. brown, blue and sepia 1·75 55
27 – 200f. brown, red and green 4·50 1·50
28 – 500f. green, brown and blue 13·00 3·25

DESIGN: 200f. View of Timbuktu; 500f. Arms and view of Bamako.

10 Africans learning Vowels

1961. 1st Anniv of Independence.
29 **10** 25f. multicoloured 60 30

11 Sheep at Pool

12 African Map and King Mohammed V of Morocco

1961.
30 **11** 50c. sepia, myrtle and red 15 15
31 A 1f. bistre, green and blue . . 15 15
32 B 2f. red, green and blue . . . 15 15
33 C 3f. brown, green and blue 15 15
34 D 4f. blue, green and bistre . . 15 15
35 **11** 5f. purple, green and blue 20 15
36 A 10f. brown, myrtle and blue 20 15
37 B 15f. brown, green and blue 20 15
38 C 20f. red, green and blue . . 30 25
39 D 25f. brown and blue 40 20
40 **11** 30f. brown, green and violet 55 30
41 A 40f. brown, green and blue 1·25 30
42 B 50f. lake, green and blue . . 50 30
43 C 60f. brown, green and blue 15 15
44 D 85f. brown, bistre and blue 1·75 35

DESIGNS: A, Oxen at pool; B, House of Arts, Mali; C, Land tillage; D, Combine-harvester in rice field.

1962. 1st Anniv of African Conf, Casablanca.
45 **12** 25f. multicoloured 25 15
46 50f. multicoloured 50 20

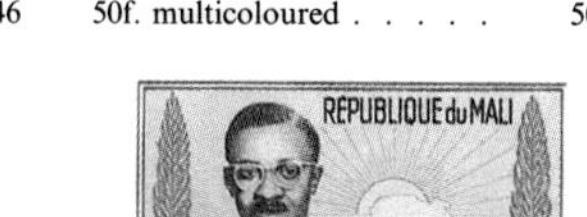

13 Patrice Lumumba

1962. 1st Death Anniv of Patrice Lumumba (Congo leader).
47 **13** 25f. brown and bistre . . . 20 20
48 100f. brown and green . . . 75 50

1962. Malaria Eradication. As T **43** of Mauritania.
49 25f.+5f. blue 50 60

14 Pegasus and U.P.U. Emblem

1962. 1st Anniv of Admission into U.P.U.
50 **14** 85f. multicoloured . . . . . 1·00 65

14a Posthorn on Map of Africa

15 Sansanding Dam

1962. African Postal Union Commem.
51 **14a** 25f. green and brown . . . 25 20
52 85f. orange and green . . . 75 50

1962.
53 **15** 25f. black, green and blue 40 20
54 – 45f. multicoloured . . . . . 1·25 50

DESIGN—HORIZ: 45f. Cotton plant.

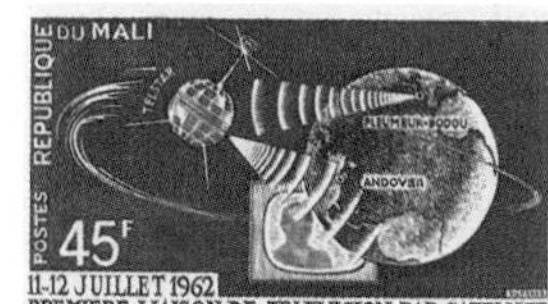

16 "Telstar" Satellite, Globe and Television Receiver

1962. 1st Trans-Atlantic Telecommunications Satellite Link.
55 **16** 45f. brown, violet and lake 80 40
56 55f. violet, olive and green 95 60

17 Soldier and Family

18 Bull's Head, Laboratory Equipment and Chicks

1962. Mali–Algerian Solidarity.
57 **17** 25f.+5f. multicoloured . . . 30 30

1963. Zoological Research Centre, Sobuta.
58 **18** 25f. turq & brn (postage) . . 35 25
59 – 200f. turquoise, purple and bistre (air) . . . . 3·50 1·25

DESIGN: 200f. As Type **18** but horiz, 47 × 27 mm.

19 Tractor and Campaign Emblem

1963. Freedom from Hunger.
60 **19** 25f. purple, black and blue 45 20
61 45f. brown, green & turq . . 80 35

20 Balloon and W.M.O. Emblem

1963. Atmospheric Research.
62 **20** 25f. multicoloured 40 20
63 45f. multicoloured 70 35
64 60f. multicoloured 95 50

21 Race Winners

22 Centenary Emblem and Globe

1963. Youth Week. Multicoloured.
65 5f. Type **21** 15 10
66 10f. Type **21** 20 15
67 20f. Acrobatic dance (horiz) 35 20
68 85f. Football (horiz) . . . . . 1·60 55

1963. Red Cross Centenary. Inscr in black.
69 **22** 5f. multicoloured 30 15
70 10f. red, yellow and grey . . 40 20
71 85f. red, yellow and grey . . 1·25 60

23 Stretcher case entering Aero 145 Ambulance Airplane

1963. Air.
72 **23** 25f. brown, blue and green 45 20
73 – 55f. blue, ochre and brown 1·25 40
74 – 100f. blue, brown and green 2·00 75

DESIGNS: 55f. Douglas DC-3 airliner on tarmac; 100f. Illyushin Il-18 airliner taking off.

24 South African Crowned Crane standing on Giant Tortoise

26 "Kaempferia aethiopica"

25 U.N. Emblem, Doves and Banner

1963. Air. Fauna Protection.
75 **24** 25f. brown, red and orange 1·50 50
76 200f. multicoloured . . . . 5·50 2·50

1963. Air. 15th Anniv of Declaration of Human Rights.
77 **25** 50f. yellow, red and green 75 40

1963. Tropical Flora. Multicoloured.
78 30f. Type **26** 60 25
79 70f. "Bombax costatum" . . . 1·75 50
80 100f. "Adenium honghel" . . 3·00 65

27 Pharaoh and Cleopatra, Philae

28 Locust on Map of Africa

1964. Air. Nubian Monuments Preservation.
81 **27** 25f. brown and purple . . . 75 25
82 55f. olive and purple . . . . 1·60 50

1964. Anti-locust Campaign.
83 **28** 5f. brown, green and purple 20 15
84 – 10f. brown, green and olive 30 20
85 – 20f. brown, green and bistre 75 25
DESIGNS—VERT: 10f. Locust and map. HORIZ: 20f. Air-spraying, locust and village.

29 Football

1964. Olympic Games, Tokyo.
86 **29** 5f. purple, green and red . . 15 10
87 – 10f. brown, blue and sepia 30 20
88 – 15f. red and violet 40 20
89 – 85f. green, brown and violet 1·25 70
DESIGNS—VERT: 10f. Boxing; 15f. Running and Olympic Flame. HORIZ: 85f. Hurdling. Each design has a stadium in the background.

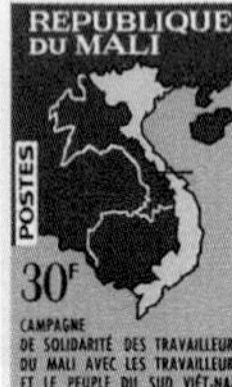

30 Solar Flares **32** Map of Vietnam

31 President Kennedy

1964. International Quiet Sun Years.
90 **30** 45f. olive, red and blue . . 1·00 35

1964. Air. 1st Death Anniv of Pres. Kennedy.
91 **31** 100f. multicoloured . . . . 1·75 1·25

1964. Mali–South Vietnam Workers' Solidarity Campaign.
92 **32** 30f. multicoloured 30 20

33 Greater Turacos ("Touraco")

1965. Air. Birds.
93 **33** 100f. green, blue and red . . 5·00 95
94 – 200f. black, red and blue . . 13·00 1·75
95 – 300f. black, ochre and green 18·00 2·50
96 – 500f. red, brown and green 29·00 4·75
BIRDS—VERT: 200f. Abyssinian ground hornbills; 300f. Egyptian vultures. HORIZ: 500f. Goliath herons.

34 I.C.Y. Emblem and U.N. Headquarters **36** Abraham Lincoln

35 African Buffalo

1965. Air. International Co-operation Year.
97 **34** 55f. ochre, purple and blue 75 40

1965. Animals.
98 – 1f. brown, blue and green 10 10
99 **35** 5f. brown, orange and green 15 10
100 – 10f. brown, mauve & green 40 25
101 – 30f. brown, green and red 75 30
102 – 90f. brown, grey and green 2·50 95
ANIMALS—VERT: 1f. Waterbuck; 10f. Scimitar oryx; 90f. Giraffe. HORIZ: 30f. Leopard.

1965. Death Centenary of Abraham Lincoln.
103 **36** 45f. multicoloured 60 40
104 55f. multicoloured 65 50

37 Hughes' Telegraph **38** "Lungs" and Mobile X-Ray Unit (Anti-T.B.)

1965. Centenary of I.T.U.
105 – 20f. black, blue and orange 30 25
106 **37** 30f. green, brown & orange 60 25
107 – 50f. green, brown & orange 90 45
DESIGNS—VERT: 20f. Denis's pneumatic tube; 50f. Lescurre's heliograph.

1965. Mali Health Service.
108 **38** 5f. violet, red and crimson 15 15
109 – 10f. green, bistre and red 25 15
110 – 25f. green and brown . . . 40 20
111 – 45f. green and brown . . . 75 40
DESIGNS: 10f. Mother and children (Maternal and Child Care); 25f. Examining patient (Marchoux Institute); 45f. Nurse (Biological Laboratory).

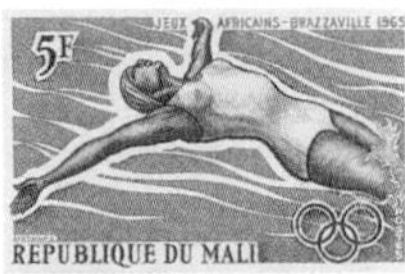

39 Diving

1965. 1st African Games, Brazzaville, Congo.
112 **39** 5f. red, brown and blue . . 25 10
113 – 15f. turquoise, brown and red (Judo) 75 30

40 Pope John XXIII

1965. Air. Pope John Commemoration.
114 **40** 100f. multicoloured . . . . 1·90 75

41 Sir Winston Churchill

1965. Air. Churchill Commemoration.
115 **41** 100f. blue and brown . . . 2·00 75

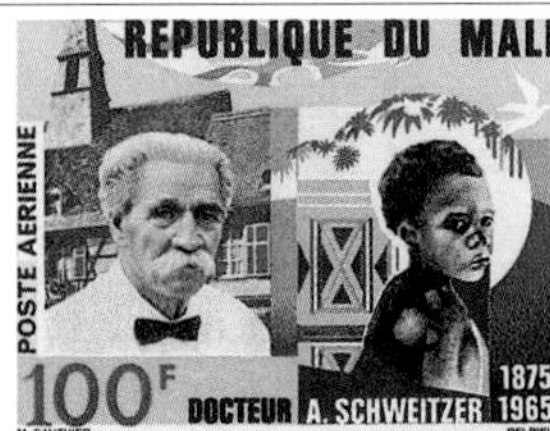

42 Dr. Schweitzer and Young African

1965. Air. Dr. Albert Schweitzer Commemoration.
116 **42** 100f. multicoloured . . . . 2·00 75

43 Leonov

1966. International Astronautic Conference, Athens (1965). Multicoloured.
117 100f. Type **43** . . . . 1·75 60
118 100f. White . . . . 1·75 60
119 300f. Cooper, Conrad, Leonov and Beliaiev (vert) 4·50 2·00

44 Vase, Quill and Cornet

1966. World Festival of Negro Arts, Dakar, Cameroun.
120 **44** 30f. black, red and ochre 30 20
121 – 55f. red, black and green 75 35
122 – 90f. brown, orange and blue . . . . 1·25 60
DESIGNS: 55f. Mask, brushes and palette, microphones; 90f. Dancers, mask and patterned cloth.

45 W.H.O. Building

1966. Inaug of W.H.O. Headquarters, Geneva.
123 **45** 30f. green, blue and yellow 40 20
124 45f. red, blue and yellow 60 35

46 Fisherman with Net

1966. River Fishing.
125 **46** 3f. brown and blue 15 15
126 – 4f. purple, blue and brown 20 15
127 – 20f. purple, green and blue 35 15
128 **46** 25f. purple, blue and green 75 20
129 – 60f. purple, lake and green 1·50 45
130 – 85f. plum, green and blue 1·50 50
DESIGNS: 4f., 60f. Collective shore fishing; 20f., 85f. Fishing pirogue.

47 Papal Arms, U.N. and Peace Emblems

1966. Air. Pope Paul's Visit to U.N.
131 **47** 200f. blue, green & turq . . 2·75 1·10

48 Initiation Ceremony **49** People and U.N.E.S.C.O. Emblem

1966. Mali Pioneers. Multicoloured.
132 5f. Type **48** 25 15
133 25f. Pioneers dancing 75 20

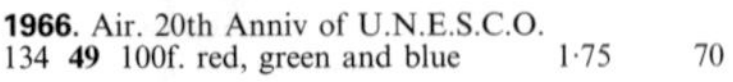

1966. Air. 20th Anniv of U.N.E.S.C.O.
134 **49** 100f. red, green and blue 1·75 70

50 Footballers, Globe, Cup and Football

1966. Air. World Cup Football Championship, England.
135 **50** 100f. multicoloured . . . . 1·75 70

51 Cancer ("The Crab") **52** U.N.I.C.E.F. Emblem and Children

1966. Air. 9th International Cancer Congress, Tokyo.
136 **51** 100f. multicoloured . . . . 1·75 55

1966. 20th Anniv of U.N.I.C.E.F.
137 **52** 45f. blue, purple and brown 60 25

53 Inoculating Cattle **55** "Diamant" Rocket and Francesco de Lana-Terzis's "Aerial Ship"

54 Desert Vehicles in Pass

1967. Campaign for Preventing Cattle Plague.
138 **53** 10f. multicoloured 25 10
139 30f. multicoloured 50 20

1967. Air. Crossing of the Hoggar (1924).
140 **54** 200f. green, brown & violet 4·75 2·25

1967. Air. French Space Rockets and Satellites.
141 **55** 50f. blue, turquoise & pur 85 30
142 – 100f. lake, purple & turq 1·60 50
143 – 200f. purple, olive and blue 2·60 1·00
DESIGNS: 100f. Satellite "A 1" and Jules Verne's "rocket"; 200f. Satellite "D 1" and Da Vinci's "bird-powered" flying machine.

56 Ancient City

1967. International Tourist Year.
144 **56** 25f. orange, blue and violet 30 20

57 Amelia Earhart and Mail Route-map

1967. Air. 30th Anniv of Amelia Earhart's Flight, via Gao.
145 **57** 500f. multicoloured . . . . 7·50 3·25

58 "The Bird Cage"

1967. Air. Picasso Commemoration. Designs showing paintings. Multicoloured.
146 50f. Type **58** . . . . 1·25 30
147 100f. "Paul as Harlequin" . . 2·00 70
148 250f. "The Pipes of Pan" . . 4·00 1·50
See also Nos. 158/9 and 164/7.

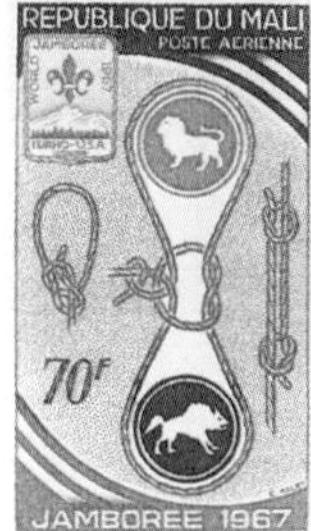

59 Scout Emblems and Rope Knots

1967. Air. World Scout Jamboree, Idaho.
149 **59** 70f. red and green . . . . 1·00 30
150 – 100f. black, lake and green 1·25 45
DESIGN: 100f. Scout with "walkie-talkie" radio.

60 "Chelorrhina polyphemus"

61 School Class

1967. Insects.
151 **60** 5f. green, brown and blue 40 20
152 – 15f. purple, brown & green 75 25
153 – 50f. red, brown and green 1·25 55
INSECTS—HORIZ: 15f. "Ugada grandicollis"; 50f. "Phymateus cinctus".

1967. International Literacy Day.
154 **61** 50f. black, red and green 60 20

62 "Europafrique"

1967. Europafrique.
155 **62** 45f. multicoloured 85 25

63 Lions Emblem and Crocodile

65 Block of Flats, Grenoble

64 "Water Resources"

1967. 50th Anniv of Lions International.
156 **63** 90f. multicoloured . . . . 1·10 55

1967. International Hydrological Decade.
157 **64** 25f. black, blue and bistre 70 20

1967. Air. Toulouse-Lautrec Commemoration. Paintings as T **58**. Multicoloured.
158 100f. "Gazelle" (horse's head) (horiz) . . . . 2·50 1·10
159 300f. "Gig drawn by Cob" (vert) . . . . 5·50 2·25

1968. Air. Winter Olympic Games, Grenoble.
160 **65** 50f. brown, green and blue 85 35
161 – 150f. brown, blue and ultramarine . . . . . . 1·75 65
DESIGN: 150f. Bobsleigh course, Huez mountain.

66 W.H.O. Emblem

1968. 20th Anniv of W.H.O.
162 **66** 90f. blue, lake and green 85 30

67 Human Figures and Entwined Hearts

1968. World "Twin Towns" Day.
163 **67** 50f. red, violet and green 40 15

1968. Air. Flower Paintings. As T **58**. Mult.
164 50f. "Roses and Anemones" (Van Gogh) 75 25
165 150f. "Vase of Flowers" (Manet) . . . . 1·75 55
166 300f. "Bouquet of Flowers" (Delacroix) . . . . 3·25 1·10
167 500f. "Marguerites" (Millet) 5·00 2·00
SIZES: 50f., 300f. 40 × 41½ mm; 150f. 36 × 47½ mm; 500f. 50 × 36 mm.

68 Dr. Martin Luther King

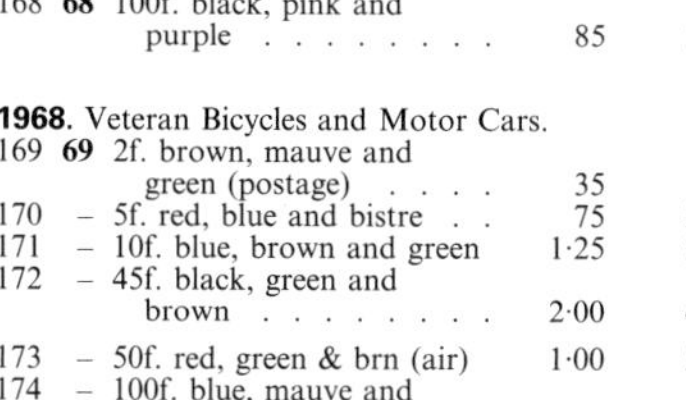

69 "Draisienne" Bicycle, 1809

1968. Air. Martin Luther King Commemoration.
168 **68** 100f. black, pink and purple 85 35

1968. Veteran Bicycles and Motor Cars.
169 **69** 2f. brown, mauve and green (postage) 35 15
170 – 5f. red, blue and bistre . . 75 20
171 – 10f. blue, brown and green 1·25 25
172 – 45f. black, green and brown . . . . 2·00 40
173 – 50f. red, green & brn (air) 1·00 25
174 – 100f. blue, mauve and bistre . . . . 2·00 60

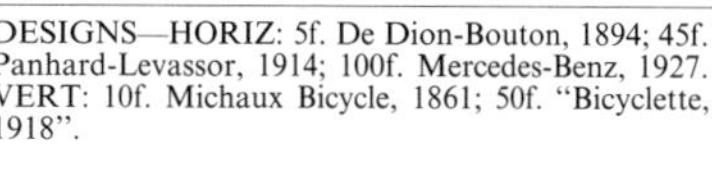
DESIGNS—HORIZ: 5f. De Dion-Bouton, 1894; 45f. Panhard-Levassor, 1914; 100f. Mercedes-Benz, 1927. VERT: 10f. Michaux Bicycle, 1861; 50f. "Bicyclette, 1918".

70 Books, Graph and A.D.B.A. Emblem

1968. 10th Anniv of International African Libraries and Archives Development Association.
175 **70** 100f. red, black and brown 65 30

71 Football

1968. Air. Olympic Games, Mexico. Multicoloured.
176 100f. Type **71** . . . . 1·00 40
177 150f. Long-jumping (vert) . . 1·50 60

1968. Air. "Philexafrique" Stamp Exhibition, Abidjan, Ivory Coast, 1969 (1st issue). As T **113a** of Mauritania. Multicoloured.
178 200f. "The Editors" (F. M. Granet) . . . . 2·00 1·50

1969. Air. "Philexafrique" Stamp Exn, Abidjan, Ivory Coast (2nd issue). As T **114a** of Mauritania.
179 100f. purple, red and violet 1·50 1·25
DESIGN: 100f. Carved animal and French Sudan stamp of 1931.

1969. Air. Birth Bicentenary of Napoleon Bonaparte. Multicoloured. As T **114b** of Mauritania.
180 150f. "Napoleon Bonaparte, First Consul" (Gros) . . . 2·50 1·25
181 200f. "The Bivouac – Battle of Austerlitz" (Lejeune) (horiz) . . . . 4·25 1·75

73 Montgolfier Balloon

1969. Air. Aviation History. Multicoloured.
182 50f. Type **73** 50 20
183 150f. Ferdinand Ferber's Glider No. 5 . . . . . . 1·75 40
184 300f. Concorde . . . . . . 3·50 1·40

74 African Tourist Emblem

1969. African Tourist Year.
185 **74** 50f. red, green and blue . . 25 20

75 "O.I.T." and I.L.O. Emblem

1969. 50th Anniv of I.L.O.
186 **75** 50f. violet, blue and green 30 20
187 60f. slate, red and brown 35 20

76 Panhard of 1897 and Model "24-CT"

1969. French Motor Industry.
188 **76** 25f. lake, black and bistre (postage) 50 20
189 – 30f. green and black . . . 75 20
190 – 55f. red, black and purple (air) . . . . 1·25 35
191 – 90f. blue, black and red . . 1·75 45
DESIGNS: 30f. Citroen of 1923 and Model "DS-21"; 55f. Renault of 1898 and Model "16"; 90f. Peugeot of 1893 and Model "404".

77 Clarke (Australia), 10,000 m (1965)

1969. Air. World Athletics Records.
192 **77** 60f. brown and blue . . . 30 25
193 – 90f. brown and red 45 25
194 – 120f. brown and green . . 55 35
195 – 140f. brown and slate . . . 70 35
196 – 150f. black and red 85 50
DESIGNS: 90f. Lusis (Russia), Javelin (1968); 120f. Miyake (Japan), Weightlifting (1967); 140f. Matson (U.S.A.), Shot-putting (1968); 150f. Keino (Kenya), 3,000 m (1965).

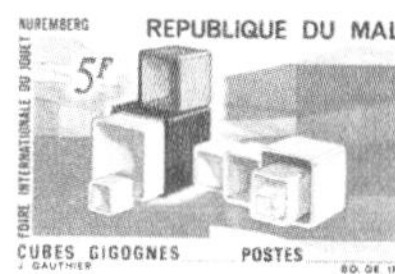

78 Hollow Blocks

1969. International Toy Fair, Nuremberg.
197 **78** 5f. red, yellow and grey . . 15 10
198 – 10f. multicoloured 15 10
199 – 15f. green, red and pink . . 30 10
200 – 20f. orange, blue and red 35 15
DESIGNS: 10f. Toy donkey on wheels; 15f. "Ducks"; 20f. Model car and race-track.

79 "Apollo 8", Earth and Moon

1969. Air. Moon Flight of "Apollo 8".
201 **79** 2,000f. gold . . . . 14·00 14·00
This stamp is embossed on gold foil.

1969. Air. 1st Man on the Moon. Nos. 182/4 optd **L'HOMME SUR LA LUNE JUILLET 1969** and Apollo 11.
202 50f. multicoloured 95 65
203 150f. multicoloured . . . . . 2·00 1·25
204 300f. multicoloured . . . . . 3·25 2·50

81 Sheep

1969. Domestic Animals.
205 **81** 1f. olive, brown and green 10 10
206 – 2f. brown, grey and red . . 10 10
207 – 10f. olive, brown and blue 20 10
208 – 35f. slate and red 60 30
209 – 90f. brown and blue . . . 1·25 55
ANIMALS: 2f. Goat; 10f. Donkey; 35f. Horse; 90f. Dromedary.

1969. 5th Anniv of African Development Bank. As T **122a** of Mauritania.
210 50f. brown, green and purple 25 20
211 90f. orange, green and brown 45 20

83 "Mona Lisa" (Leonardo da Vinci)

1969. Air. 450th Death Anniv of Leonardo da Vinci.
212 **83** 500f. multicoloured . . . . 4·50 3·25

84 Vaccination

1969. Campaign against Smallpox and Measles.
213 **84** 50f. slate, brown and green 40 15

85 Mahatma Gandhi

1969. Air. Birth Centenary of Mahatma Gandhi.
214 **85** 150f. brown and green . . 1·75 55

1969. 10th Anniv of Aerial Navigation Security Agency for Africa and Madagascar (A.S.E.C.N.A.). As T **94a** of Niger.
215 100f. green 75 25

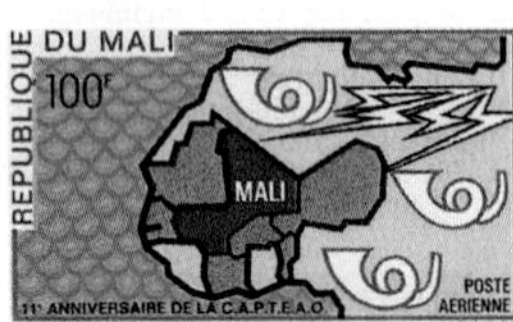

87 West African Map and Posthorns

1970. Air. 11th Anniv of West African Postal Union (C.A.P.T.E.A.O.).
216 **87** 100f. multicoloured 60 35

1970. Air. Religious Paintings. As T **83**. Mult.
217 100f. "Virgin and Child" (Van der Weydan School) 70 40
218 150f. "The Nativity" (The Master of Flamalle) . . . 1·10 65
219 250f. "Virgin, Child and St. John the Baptist" (Low Countries School) . . . . 2·40 1·40

89 Franklin D. Roosevelt

91 Lenin

90 Women of Mali and Japan

1970. Air. 25th Death Anniv of Franklin D. Roosevelt.
220 **89** 500f. black, red and blue 3·50 2·00

1970. "EXPO 70" World Fair, Osaka, Japan.
221 **90** 100f. orange, brown & blue 60 20
222 – 150f. red, green and yellow 80 30
DESIGN: 150f. Flags and maps of Mali and Japan.

1970. Air. Birth Centenary of Lenin.
223 **91** 300f. black, green and flesh 2·25 1·00

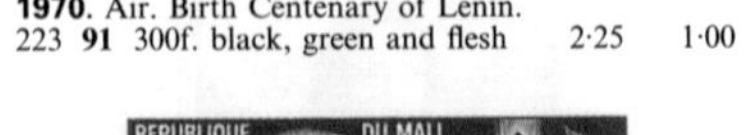

92 Verne and Moon Rockets

1970. Air. Jules Verne "Prophet of Space Travel". Multicoloured.
224 50f. Type **92** 75 25
225 150f. Moon orbit . . . . . 1·75 50
226 300f. Splashdown . . . . . 2·50 1·10

93 I.T.U. Emblem and Map

1970. World Telecommunications Day.
227 **93** 90f. red, brown and sepia 75 25

1970. New U.P.U. Headquarters Building, Berne. As Type **81** of New Caledonia.
228 50f. brown, green and red . . 40 20
229 60f. brown, blue and mauve 60 20

1970. Air. Space Flight of "Apollo 13". Nos. 224/6 optd **APOLLO XIII EPOPEE SPATIALE 11-17 AVRIL 1970** in three lines.
230 50f. multicoloured 50 25
231 150f. multicoloured . . . . . 1·25 45
232 300f. multicoloured . . . . . 2·25 1·25

96 "Intelstat 3" Satellite

1970. Air. Space Telecommunications.
233 **96** 100f. indigo, blue & orange 75 35
234 – 200f. purple, grey and blue 1·40 50
235 – 300f. brown, orange & slate . . . . 2·50 1·10
236 – 500f. brown, blue & indigo 3·75 1·60
DESIGNS: 200f. "Molnya I" satellite; 300f. Dish aerial, Type PB 2; 500f. "Symphony Project" satellite.

97 Auguste and Louis Lumiere, Jean Harlow and Marilyn Monroe

1970. Air. Lumiere Brothers (inventors of the cine camera) Commemoration.
237 **97** 250f. multicoloured . . . . 2·50 1·25

98 Footballers

1970. Air. World Cup Football Championship, Mexico.
238 **98** 80f. green, brown and red 50 25
239 200f. red, brown and blue 1·25 55

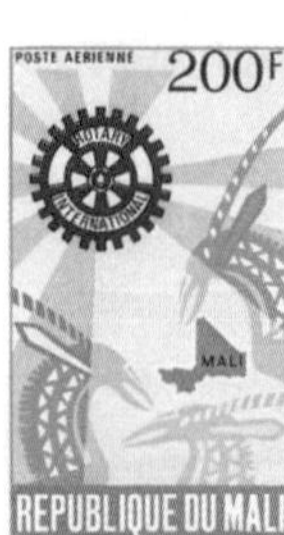

99 Rotary Emblem, Map and Antelope

100 "Supporting United Nations"

1970. Air. Rotary International.
240 **99** 200f. multicoloured . . . . 1·75 60

1970. Air. 25th Anniv of U.N.O.
241 **100** 100f. blue, brown & violet 70 35

101 Page from 11th century Baghdad Koran

1970. Air. Ancient Muslim Art. Multicoloured.
242 50f. Type **101** 50 25
243 200f. "Tree and wild Animals" (Jordanian mosaic, c.730) . . . . . . 1·25 55
244 250f. "The Scribe" (Baghdad miniature, 1287) . . . . . 2·00 90

1970. Air. Moon Landing of "Luna 16". Nos. 234/5 surch **LUNA 16 PREMIERS PRELEVEMENTS AUTOMATIQUES SUR LA LUNE SEPTEMBRE 1970** and new values.
245 150f. on 200f. purple, grey and blue . . . . 1·25 40
246 250f. on 300f. brown, orange and grey . . . . 1·75 60

103 G.P.O., Bamako

1970. Public Buildings.
247 **103** 30f. olive, green and brown 20 20
248 – 40f. purple, brown & green 30 20
249 – 60f. grey, green and red 40 20
250 – 80f. brown, green and grey 50 25
BUILDINGS: 40f. Chamber of Commerce, Bamako; 60f. Ministry of Public Works, Bamako; 80f. Town Hall, Segou.

104 Pres. Nasser

106 Gallet Steam Locomotive, 1882

105 "The Nativity" (Antwerp School 1530)

1970. Air. Pres. Gamal Nasser of Egypt. Commemoration.
251 **104** 1000f. gold . . . . 7·50 7·50

1970. Air. Christmas. Paintings. Multicoloured.
252 100f. Type **105** 70 40
253 250f. "Adoration of the Shepherds" (Memling) . . 1·60 95
254 300f. "Adoration of the Magi" (17th-century Flemish school) . . . . . 2·25 1·25

1970. Mali Railway Locomotives from the Steam Era (1st series).
255 **106** 20f. black, red and green 1·60 1·40
256 – 40f. black, green & brown 2·40 1·75
257 – 50f. black, green & brown 2·75 2·10
258 – 80f. black, red and green 4·00 3·00
259 – 100f. black, green & brn 4·75 4·00
LOCOMOTIVES: 40f. Felou, 1882; 50f. Bechevel, 1882; 80f. Series 1100, 1930 (inscr "Type 23"); 100f. Class 40, 1927 (incr "Type 141" and "vers 1930"). See also Nos. 367/70.

107 Scouts crossing Log-bridge

108 Bambara de San Mask

1970. Scouting in Mali. Multicoloured.
260 5f. Type **107** 20 15
261 30f. Bugler and scout camp (vert) 35 15
262 100f. Scouts canoeing 90 35

1971. Mali Masks and Ideograms. Multicoloured.
263 20f. Type **108** 15 10
264 25f. Dogon de Bandiagara mask 20 10
265 50f. Kanaga ideogram . . . 45 15
266 80f. Bambara ideogram . . . 60 25

109 General De Gaulle

1971. Air. Charles De Gaulle Commem. Die-stamped on gold foil.
267 **109** 2000f. gold, red and blue 30·00 30·00

110 Alfred Nobel

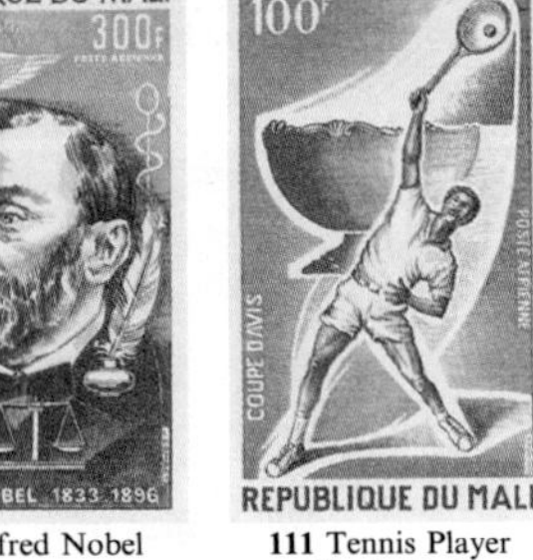

111 Tennis Player (Davis Cup)

1971. Air. 75th Death Anniv of Alfred Nobel (philanthropist).
268 **110** 300f. red, brown and green . . . . 2·50 1·25

1971. Air. World Sporting Events.
269 **111** 100f. slate, purple and blue 75 25
270 – 150f. olive, brown & green . . . . 1·40 40
271 – 200f. brown, olive and blue . . . . 2·00 60
DESIGNS—HORIZ: 150f. Steeplechase (inscr "Derby at Epsom" but probably represents the Grand National). VERT: 200f. Yacht (Americas Cup).

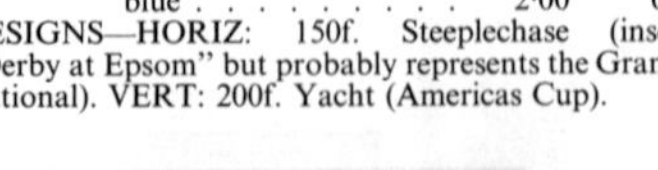

112 Youth, Sun and Microscope

1971. 50th Anniv of 1st B.C.G. Vaccine Innoculation.
272 **112** 100f. brown, green and red 85 40

113 "The Thousand and One Nights"

1971. Air. "Tales of the Arabian Nights". Mult.
273 120f. Type **113** 70 30
274 180f. "Ali Baba and the Forty Thieves" . . . . . 1·00 40
275 200f. "Aladdin's Lamp" . . . 1·40 50

114 Scouts, Japanese Horseman and Mt. Fuji

1971. 13th World Scout Jamboree, Asagiri, Japan.
276 **114** 80f. plum, green and blue 75 20

115 Rose between Hands

116 Rural Costume

1971. 25th Anniv of U.N.I.C.E.F.
277 **115** 50f. brown, red and orange 30 20
278 – 60f. blue, green and brown 40 20
DESIGN—VERT: 60f. Nurses and children.

1971. National Costumes. Multicoloured.
279 5f. Type **116** 15 10
280 10f. Rural costume (female) 20 15
281 15f. Tuareg 20 15
282 60f. Embroidered "boubou" 45 20
283 80f. Women's ceremonial costume 60 25

117 Olympic Rings and Events

1971. Air. Olympic Games Publicity.
284 **117** 80f. blue, purple and green 40 20

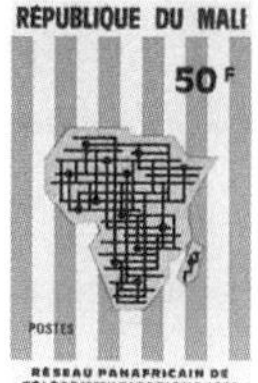

118 Telecommunications Map

1971. Pan-African Telecommunications Network Year.
285 **118** 50f. multicoloured 25 20

119 "Mariner 4" and Mars

1971. Air. Exploration of Outer Space.
286 **119** 200f. green, blue & brown 1·25 50
287 – 300f. blue, plum & purple 1·75 60
DESIGN: 300f. "Venera 5" and Venus.

120 "Santa Maria" (1492)

1971. Air. Famous Ships.
288 **120** 100f. brown, violet & blue 70 35
289 – 150f. violet, brown & grn 1·25 45
290 – 200f. green, blue and red 1·60 75
291 – 250f. red, blue and black 2·25 90
DESIGNS: 150f. "Mayflower" (1620); 200f. Battleship "Potemkin" (1905); 250f. Liner "Normandie" (1935).

121 "Hibiscus rosa-sinensis"

1971. Flowers. Multicoloured.
292 20f. Type **121** 20 10
293 50f. "Euphorbia pulcherrima" 55 15
294 60f. "Adenium obesum" . . 80 20
295 80f. "Allamanda cathartica" 1·25 25
296 100f. "Satanocrater berhautii" . . . . 1·50 35

122 Allegory of Justice

1971. 25th Anniv of Int Court of Justice, The Hague.
297 **122** 160f. chocolate, red & brn 80 35

123 Nat King Cole

124 Statue of Olympic Zeus (by Pheidias)

1971. Air. Famous Negro Musicians. Multicoloured.
298 130f. Type **123** . . . . 1·25 25
299 150f. Erroll Garner . . . . . 1·25 30
300 270f. Louis Armstrong . . . 1·75 45

1971. Air. "The Seven Wonders of the Ancient World".
301 **124** 70f. blue, brown & purple 35 20
302 – 80f. black, brown and blue 40 20
303 – 100f. blue, red and violet 50 25
304 – 130f. black, purple & blue 75 30
305 – 150f. brown, green & blue 1·10 35
306 – 270f. blue, brown & pur 1·60 75
307 – 280f. blue, purple & brn 2·00 85
DESIGNS—VERT: 80f. Pyramid of Cheops, Egypt; 130f. Pharos of Alexandria; 270f. Mausoleum of Halicarnassos; 280f. Colossus of Rhodes. HORIZ: 100f. Temple of Artemis, Ephesus; 150f. Hanging Gardens of Babylon.

125 "Family Life" (carving)

1971. 15th Anniv of Social Security Service.
308 **125** 70f. brown, green and red 40 20

126 Slalom-skiing and Japanese Girl

1972. Air. Winter Olympic Games, Sapporo, Japan.
309 **126** 150f. brown, green & orge 1·00 35
310 – 200f. green, brown and red . . . . 1·50 55
DESIGN: 200f. Ice-hockey and Japanese actor.

127 "Santa Maria della Salute" (Caffi)

1972. Air. U.N.E.S.C.O. "Save Venice" Campaign. Multicoloured.
312 130f. Type **127** 80 35
313 270f. "Rialto Bridge" . . . . 1·50 60
314 280f. "St. Mark's Square" (vert) . . . . 1·75 70

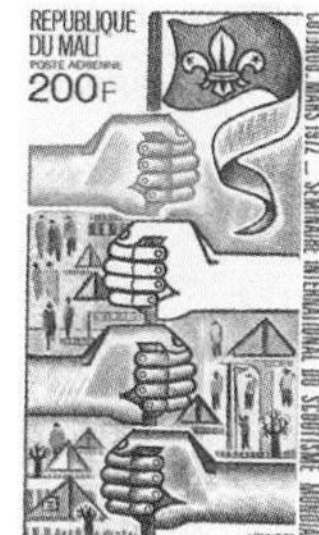

128 Hands clasping Flagpole

1972. Air. Int Scout Seminar, Cotonou, Dahomey.
315 **128** 200f. green, orange & brn 1·75 55

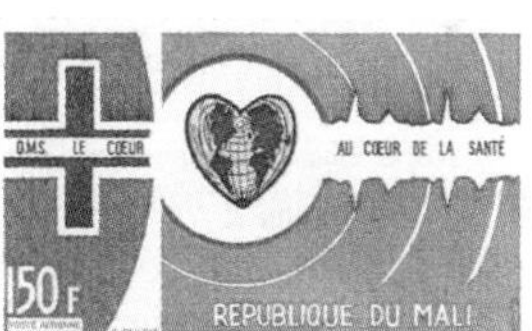

129 Heart and Red Cross Emblems

1972. Air. World Heart Month.
316 **129** 150f. red and blue . . . . 1·00 40

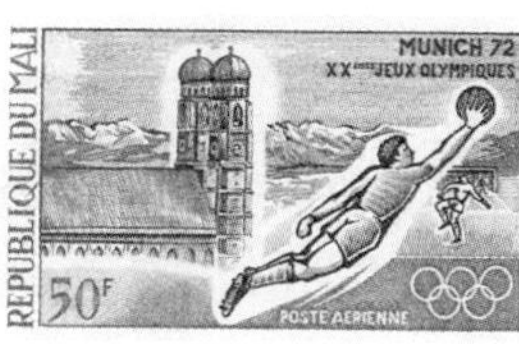

130 Football

1972. Air. Olympic Games, Munich (1st issue). Sports and Munich Buildings.
317 **130** 50f. blue, brown and green 25 20
318 – 150f. blue, brown & green 70 30
319 – 200f. blue, brown & green 80 50
320 – 300f. blue, brown & green 1·25 70
DESIGNS—VERT: 150f. Judo; 200f. Hurdling. HORIZ: 300f. Running.
See also Nos. 357/62.

131 "Apollo 15" and Lunar Rover

1972. Air. History of Transport Development.
322 **131** 150f. red, green and lake 80 40
323 – 250f. red, blue and green 2·00 1·00
DESIGN: 250f. Montgolfier's balloon and Cugnot's steam car.

132 "UIT" on T.V. Screen

1972. World Telecommunications Day.
324 **132** 70f. black, blue and red 40 20

133 Clay Funerary Statue

134 Samuel Morse and Early Telegraph

1972. Mali Archaeology. Multicoloured.
325 30f. Type **133** 20 15
326 40f. Female Figure (wood-carving) 30 20
327 50f. "Warrior" (stone-painting) 40 20
328 100f. Wrought-iron ritual figures . . . . 1·00 35

1972. Death Centenary of Samuel Morse (inventor of telegraph).
329 **134** 80f. purple, green and red 45 20

135 "Cinderella"

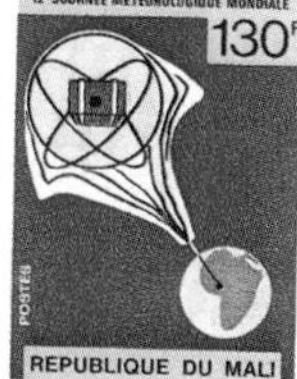

136 Weather Balloon

1972. Air. Charles Perrault's Fairy Tales.
330 **135** 70f. green, red and brown 45 20
331 – 80f. brown, red and green 50 25
332 – 150f. violet, purple & blue 1·10 35
DESIGNS: 80f. "Puss in Boots"; 150f. "The Sleeping Beauty".

1972. World Meteorological Day.
333 **136** 130f. multicoloured . . . 60 30

137 Astronauts and Lunar Rover

1972. Air. Moon Flight of "Apollo 16".
334 **137** 500f. brown, violet & grn 3·00 1·25

138 Book Year Emblem

1972. Air. International Book Year.
335 **138** 80f. gold, green and blue 40 25

139 Sarakole Dance, Kayes

140 Learning the Alphabet

1972. Traditional Dances. Multicoloured.
336 10f. Type **139** 25 15
337 20f. Malinke dance, Bamako 30 15
338 50f. Hunter's dance, Bougouni 55 20
339 70f. Bambara dance, Segou 70 20
340 80f. Dogon dance, Sanga . . 80 30
341 120f. Targuie dance, Timbukto . . . . 1·40 45

1972. International Literacy Day.
342 **140** 80f. black and green . . . 40 15

141 Statue and Musical Instruments

142 Club Banner

1972. 1st Anthology of Mali Music.
343 **141** 100f. multicoloured . . . 85 30

1972. Air. 10th Anniv of Bamako Rotary Club.
344 **142** 170f. purple, blue and red 1·00 40

143 Aries the Ram

1972. Signs of the Zodiac.
345 **143** 15f. brown and purple . . 30 20
346 – 15f. black and brown . . 30 20
347 – 35f. blue and red 50 25
348 – 35f. red and green 50 25
349 – 40f. brown and blue . . . 60 30
350 – 40f. brown and purple . . 60 30
351 – 45f. red and blue 70 35
352 – 45f. green and red 70 35
353 – 65f. blue and violet . . . 1·00 35
354 – 65f. brown and violet . . 1·00 35
355 – 90f. blue and mauve . . . 1·60 65
356 – 90f. green and mauve . . 1·60 65
DESIGNS: No. 346, Taurus the Bull; No. 347, Gemini the Twins; No. 348, Cancer the Crab; No. 349, Leo the Lion; No. 350, Virgo the Virgin; No. 351, Libra the Scales; No. 352, Scorpio the Scorpion; No. 353, Sagittarius the Archer; No. 354, Capricornus the Goat; No. 355, Aquarius the Water-carrier; No. 356, Pisces the Fish.

1972. Air. Olympic Games, Munich (2nd issue). Sports and Locations of Games since 1952. As Type **130**.
357 70f. blue, brown and red . . 1·75 40
358 90f. green, red and blue . . . 35 20
359 140f. olive, green and brown 60 20
360 150f. brown, green and red 65 25
361 170f. blue, brown and purple 75 30
362 210f. blue, red and green . . 90 40
DESIGNS—VERT: 70f. Boxing, Helsinki Games (1952); 150f. Weightlifting, Tokyo Games (1964). HORIZ: 90f. Hurdling, Melbourne Games (1956); 140f. 200 metres, Rome Games (1960); 170f. Swimming, Mexico Games (1968); 210f. Throwing the javelin, Munich Games (1972).

1972. Medal Winners, Munich Olympic Games. Nos. 318/20 and 362 optd with events and names, etc.
363 150f. blue, brown and green 70 30
364 200f. blue, brown and green 90 40
365 210f. blue, red and green . . 90 40
366 300f. blue, brown and green 1·25 70
OVERPRINTS: 150f. **JUDO RUSKA 2 MEDAILLES D'OR**; 200f. **STEEPLE KEINO MEDAILLE D'OR**; 210f. **MEDAILLE D'OR 90m. 48**; 300f. **100m. - 200m. BORZOV 2 MEDAILLES D'OR**.

1972. Mali Locomotives (2nd series). As T **106**.
367 10f. blue, green and red . . . 1·60 1·25
368 30f. blue, green and brown 3·25 2·50
369 60f. blue, brown and green 4·00 3·25
370 120f. purple, green and black 6·75 5·25
LOCOMOTIVES: 10f. First Locomotive to arrive at Bamako, 1906; 30f. Steam locomotive, Thies–Bamako line, 1920; 60f. Class 40 steam locomotive, Thies–Bamako line, 1927 (inscr "141");. 120f. Alsthom series BB 100 coupled diesel, Dakar–Bamako line, 1947.

146 Emperor Haile Selassie

1972. Air. 80th Birth Anniv of Emperor Haile Selassie.
371 **146** 70f. multicoloured 30 20

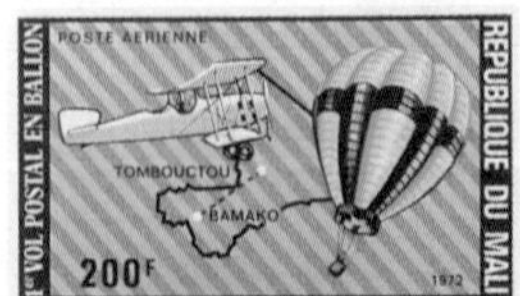

147 Balloon, Breguet 14T Biplane and Map

1972. Air. 1st Mali Airmail Flight by Balloon, Bamako to Timbuktu. Multicoloured.
372 200f. Type **147** . . . . 1·00 45
373 300f. Balloon, Concorde and map . . . . 1·40 60

148 High Jumping

1973. 2nd African Games, Lagos, Nigeria. Mult.
374 70f. Type **148** 30 20
375 270f. Throwing the discus . . 1·25 60
376 280f. Football . . . . 1·40 65

149 14th-century German Bishop

150 Interpol Headquarters, Paris

1973. Air. World Chess Championship, Reykjavik, Iceland.
377 **149** 100f. lt blue, blue & brown . . . . 1·25 35
378 – 200f. red, light red & black . . . . 2·50 75
DESIGN: 200f. 18th-century Indian knight (elephant).

1973. 50th Anniv of International Criminal Police Organization (Interpol).
379 **150** 80f. multicoloured 65 20

151 Emblem and Dove with letter

152 "Fauna Protection" Stamp of 1963

1973. 10th Anniv (1971) of African Postal Union.
380 **151** 70f. multicoloured 35 20

1973. Air. Stamp Day.
381 **152** 70f. orange, red and brown . . . . 1·10 65

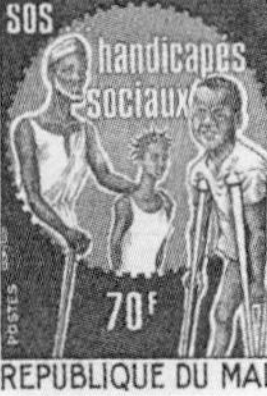

153 Astronauts on Moon

155 Handicapped Africans

154 Copernicus

1973. Moon Mission of "Apollo" 17.
382 **153** 250f. brown and blue . . 1·75 65

1973. 500th Birth Anniv of Copernicus.
384 **154** 300f. purple and blue . . 2·25 1·10

1973. "Help the Handicapped".
385 **155** 70f. orange, black and red 35 20

156 Dr. G. A. Hansen

1973. Centenary of Hansen's Identification of the Leprosy Bacillus.
386 **156** 200f. green, black and red 1·60 60

157 Bentley and Alfa Romeo, 1930

1973. 50th Anniv of Le Mans 24-hour Endurance Race.
387 **157** 50f. green, orange and blue 50 15
388 – 100f. green, blue and red 1·00 25
389 – 200f. blue, green and red 2·00 50
DESIGNS: 100f. Jaguar and Talbot, 1953; 200f. Matra and Porsche, 1952.

158 Scouts around Campfire

1973. International Scouting Congress, Addis Ababa and Nairobi.
390 **158** 50f. brown, red and blue 30 15
391 – 70f. brown, red and blue 50 20
392 – 80f. red, brown and green 60 20
393 – 130f. green, blue & brown 85 30
394 – 270f. red, violet and grey 1·75 60
DESIGNS—VERT: 70f. Scouts saluting flag; 130f. Lord Baden-Powell. HORIZ: 80f. Standard-bearers; 270f. Map of Africa and Scouts and Guides in ring.

159 Swimming and National Flags

1973. 1st Afro-American Sports Meeting, Bamako.
395 **159** 70f. green, red and blue 30 20
396 – 80f. green, red and blue 35 25
397 – 330f. blue and red . . . . 1·50 70
DESIGNS—VERT: 80f. Throwing the discus and javelin. HORIZ: 330f. Running.

1973. Pan-African Drought Relief. No. 296 surch **SECHERESSE SOLIDARITE AFRICAINE** and value.
398 200f. on 100f. multicoloured 1·10 65

1973. Air. African Fortnight, Brussels. As T **168a** of Niger.
399 70f. violet, blue and brown 30 20

162 "Perseus" (Cellini)

1973. Air. Famous Sculptures.
400 **162** 100f. green and red . . . 55 25
401 – 150f. purple and red . . . 85 35
402 – 250f. green and red . . . 1·50 65
DESIGNS: 150f. "Pieta" (Michelangelo); 250f. "Victory of Samothrace".

163 Stephenson's "Rocket" (1829) and French Buddicom Locomotive

1973. Air. Famous Locomotives.
403 **163** 100f. black, blue & brown 1·50 45
404 – 150f. multicoloured . . . 1·90 50
405 – 200f. blue, slate and brown . . . . 3·25 80
DESIGNS: 150f. Union Pacific steam locomotive No. 119 (1890) and Santa Fe Railroad steam locomotive "Blue Goose" (1937), U.S.A.; 200f. "Mistral" express (France) and "Hikari" express train (Japan).

164 "Apollo 11" First Landing

1973. Conquest of the Moon.
406 **164** 50f. purple, red and brown 25 20
407 – 75f. grey, blue and red . . 30 20
408 – 100f. slate, brown and blue 75 30
409 – 280f. blue, green and red 1·40 65
410 – 300f. blue, red and green 1·75 80
DESIGNS: 75f. "Apollo 13" Recovery capsule; 100f. "Apollo 14" Lunar trolley; 280f. "Apollo 15" Lunar rover; 300f. "Apollo 17" lift off from Moon.

165 Picasso

166 Pres. John Kennedy

1973. Air. Pablo Picasso (artist). Commem.
411 **165** 500f. multicoloured . . . 3·00 1·25

1973. Air. 10th Death Anniv of Pres. Kennedy.
412 **166** 500f. black, purple & gold 2·50 1·25

1973. Air. Christmas. As T **105** but dated "1973". Multicoloured.
413 100f. "The Annunciation" (V. Carpaccio) (horiz) . . . 50 25
414 200f. "Virgin of St. Simon" (F. Baroccio) . . . . . . 1·25 50
415 250f. "Flight into Egypt" (A. Solario) . . . . 1·60 70

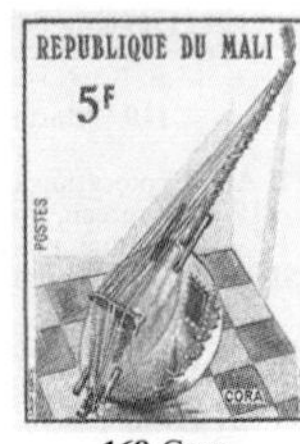

167 Player and Football

168 Cora

1973. Air. World Football Cup Championship, West Germany.
416 **167** 150f. red, brown and green 90 35
417 – 250f. green, brown & violet . . . . 1·75 60
DESIGN: 250f. Goalkeeper and ball.

1973. Musical Instruments.
419 **168** 5f. brown, red and green 20 10
420 – 10f. brown and blue . . . 25 10
421 – 15f. brown, red and yellow 35 15
422 – 20f. brown and red . . . 40 15
423 – 25f. brown, red and yellow 45 15

424 – 30f. black and blue . . . 60 20
425 – 35f. sepia, brown and red 70 20
426 – 40f. brown and red . . . 75 30
DESIGNS—HORIZ: 10f. Balafon. VERT: 15f. Djembe; 20f. Guitar; 25f. N'Djarka; 30f. M'Bolon; 35f. Dozo N'Goni; 40f. N'Tamani.

169 "Musicians" (mosaic)

1974. Roman Frescoes and Mosaics from Pompeii.
427 **169** 150f. red, brown and grey 75 35
428 – 250f. brown, red & orange 1·25 60
429 – 350f. brown, orange and olive . . . . 1·75 75
DESIGNS—VERT: 250f. "Alexander the Great" (mosaic); 350f. "Bacchante" (fresco).

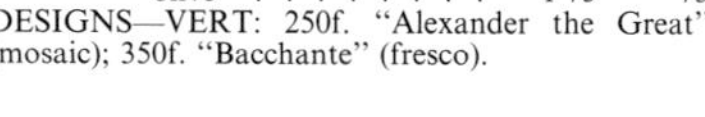

170 Corncob, Worker and "Kibaru" Newspaper

171 Sir Winston Churchill

1974. 2nd Anniv of Rural Press.
430 **170** 70f. brown and green . . 35 20

1974. Air. Birth Cent of Sir Winston Churchill.
431 **171** 500f. black . . . . 2·50 1·50

172 Chess-pieces on Board

1974. Air. 21st Chess Olympiad, Nice.
432 **172** 250f. indigo, red and blue 3·50 75

173 "The Crucifixion" (Alsace School c. 1380)

1974. Air. Easter. Multicoloured.
433 400f. Type **173** . . . . 1·60 1·00
434 500f. "The Entombment" (Titian) (horiz) . . . . . . 2·25 1·25

174 Lenin

1974. Air. 50th Death Anniv of Lenin.
435 **174** 150f. purple and violet . . 70 30

175 Goalkeeper and Globe

177 Full-rigged Sailing Ship and Modern Liner

176 Horse-jumping Scenes

1974. World Cup Football Championship, West Germany.
436 **175** 270f. red, green and lilac 1·25 80
437 – 280f. blue, brown and red 1·60 80
DESIGN: 280f. World Cup emblem on football.

1974. Air. World Equestrian Championships, La Baule.
438 **176** 130f. brown, lilac and blue . . . . 1·50 60

1974. Centenary of Universal Postal Union.
439 **177** 80f. purple, lilac & brown 55 25
440 – 90f. orange, grey and blue 40 30
441 – 270f. purple, olive & green . . . . 2·75 1·10
DESIGNS: 90f. Breguet 14T biplane and Douglas DC-8; 270f. Steam and electric mail trains.
See also Nos. 463/4.

178 "Skylab" over Africa

1974. Air. Survey of Africa by "Skylab" Space Station.
442 **178** 200f. indigo, blue & orge 1·00 40
443 – 250f. blue, purple & orge 1·25 60
DESIGN: 250f. Astronaut servicing cameras.

1974. Air. 11th Arab Scout Jamboree, Lebanon. Nos. 391/2 surch **130f. 11e JAMBOREE ARABE AOUT 1974 LIBAN** or **170f. CONGRES PAN-ARABE LIBAN AOUT 1974**.
444 130f. on 70f. brown, red & bl 70 40
445 170f. on 80f. blue, green & red 75 50

1974. Air. 5th Anniv of First Landing on Moon. Nos. 408/9 surch **130f. 1er DEBARQUEMENT SUR LA LUNE 20-VII-69** or **300f. 1er PAS SUR LA LUNE 21-VII-69**.
446 130f. on 100f. slate, brown and blue 70 45
447 300f. on 280f. blue, grn & red 1·40 70

1974. West Germany's Victory in World Cup Football Championship. Nos. 436/7 surch **R.F.A. 2 HOLLANDE 1** and value.
448 **175** 300f. on 270f. red, green and lilac . . . . 1·40 80
449 – 330f. on 280f. blue, brown and red . . . . 1·60 80

182 Weaver

183 River Niger near Gao

1974. Crafts and Craftsmen. Multicoloured.
450 50f. Type **182** 25 15
451 60f. Potter 30 15
452 70f. Smith 40 20
453 80f. Wood-carver 55 20

1974. Mali Views. Multicoloured.
454 10f. Type **183** 15 10
455 20f. "The Hand of Fatma" (rock formation, Hombori) (vert) 15 10
456 40f. Waterfall, Gouina . . . 35 15
457 70f. Hill-dwellings, Dogon (vert) 60 20

184 Class C No. 3 (1906) and Class P (1939) Steam Locomotives, France

1974. Air. Steam Locomotives.
458 **184** 90f. indigo, red and blue 1·25 50
459 – 120f. brown, orange & bl 1·40 60
460 – 210f. brown, orange & bl 2·75 90
461 – 330f. black, green and blue . . . . 4·00 1·90
DESIGNS: 120f. Baldwin (1870) and Pacific (1920) steam locomotives, U.S.A.; 210f. Class A1 (1925) and Buddicom (1847) steam locomotives; 330f. Hudson steam locomotive, 1938 (U.S.A.) and steam locomotive "Gironde", 1839.

185 Skiing

1974. Air. 50th Anniv of Winter Olympics.
462 **185** 300f. red, blue and green 1·40 80

1974. Berne Postal Convention. Cent, Nos. 439 and 441 surch **9 OCTOBRE 1974** and value.
463 **177** 250f. on 80f. purple, lilac and brown . . . . . . 1·40 80
464 – 300f. on 270f. purple, olive and green . . . . 3·00 1·25

187 Mao Tse-tung and Great Wall of China

1974. 25th Anniv of Chinese People's Republic.
465 **187** 100f. blue, red and green 50 30

188 "The Nativity" (Memling)

1974. Air. Christmas. Multicoloured.
466 290f. Type **188** . . . . . . 1·25 70
467 310f. "Virgin and Child" (Bourgogne School) . . . 1·50 75
468 400f. "Adoration of the Magi" (Schongauer) . . . 1·90 1·10

189 Raoul Follereau (missionary)

191 Dr. Schweitzer

190 Electric Train and Boeing 707

1974. Air. Raoul Follereau, "Apostle of the Lepers".
469 **189** 200f. blue . . . . 1·25 55
469a 200f. brown . . . . . . 1·75 1·10

1974. Air. Europafrique.
470 **190** 100f. green, brown & blue 2·75 70
471 110f. blue, violet & brown 3·00 70

1975. Birth Centenary of Dr Albert Schweitzer.
472 **191** 150f. turquoise, green & bl 90 40

192 Patients making Handicrafts and Lions International Emblem

1975. 5th Anniv of Samanko (Leprosy rehabilitation village). Multicoloured.
473 90f. Type **192** 50 20
474 100f. View of Samanko . . . 60 25

193 "The Pilgrims at Emmaus" (Champaigne)

1975. Air. Easter. Multicoloured.
475 200f. Type **193** 90 45
476 300f. "The Pilgrims at Emmaus" (Veronese) . . . 1·25 60
477 500f. "Christ in Majesty" (Limoges enamel) (vert) . . 2·25 1·25

194 "Journey to the Centre of the Earth"

1975. Air. 70th Death Anniv of Jules Verne.
478 **194** 100f. green, blue & brown 45 25
479 – 170f. brown, blue & lt brn 75 35
480 – 190f. blue, turquoise & brn . . . . 1·25 55
481 – 220f. brown, purple & blue . . . . 1·50 60
DESIGNS: 170f. Jules Verne and "From the Earth to the Moon"; 190f. Giant octopus–"Twenty Thousand Leagues Under the Sea"; 220f. "A Floating City".

195 Head of "Dawn" (Tomb of the Medici)

1975. Air. 500th Birth Anniv of Michelangelo (artist). Multicoloured.
482 400f. Type **195** . . . . 1·75 1·10
483 500f. "Moses" (marble statue, Rome) . . . . 2·25 1·25

196 Nile Pufferfish

1975. Fishes (1st series).
484 **196** 60f. brown, yellow & grn . . . 80 25
485 – 70f. black, brown and grey 90 35
486 – 80f. multicoloured . . . . 1·10 40
487 – 90f. blue, grey and green 1·60 50
488 – 110f. black and blue . . . 2·25 70
DESIGNS: 70f. Electric catfish; 80f. Deep-sided citharinid; 90f. Lesser tigerfish; 110f. Nile perch.
See also Nos. 544/8.

197 Astronaut

199 Woman with Bouquet

198 Einstein and Equation

1975. Air. Soviet–U.S. Space Co-operation.
489 **197** 290f. red, blue and black 1·10 50
490 – 300f. red, blue and black 1·10 60
491 – 370f. green, purple & black . . . . 1·40 80
DESIGNS: 300f. "America and Russia"; 370f. New York and Moscow landmarks.

1975. Air. 20th Death Anniv of Albert Einstein.
492 **198** 90f. blue, purple & brown 55 30
See also Nos. 504, 507 and 519.

1975. International Women's Year.
493 **199** 150f. red and green . . . 70 35

200 Morris "Oxford", 1913

1975. Early Motor-cars.
494 **200** 90f. violet, brown and blue 60 20
495 – 130f. red, grey and blue 95 25
496 – 190f. deep blue, green and blue . . . . 1·40 40
497 – 230f. brown, blue and red 1·75 45
DESIGNS—MOTOR-CARS: 130f. Franklin "E", 1907; 190f. Daimler, 1900; 230f. Panhard & Levassor, 1895.

201

1975. Air. "Nordjamb 75" World Scout Jamboree, Norway.
498 **201** 100f. blue, brown and lake 55 25
499 – 150f. green, brown & blue 75 30
500 – 290f. lake, brown and blue . . . . 1·40 75
DESIGNS: 150f., 290f. Scouts and emblem (different).

202 Lafayette and Battle Scene

1975. Air. Bicentenary of American Revolution. Mult.
501 290f. Type **202** . . . . 1·50 65
502 300f. Washington and battle scene . . . . 1·50 65
503 370f. De Grasse and Battle of the Chesapeake, 1781 . . . 1·90 95

1975. 20th Death Anniv of Sir Alexander Fleming (scientist). As T **198**.
504 150f. brown, purple and blue 80 35

204 Olympic Rings

1975. Air. "Pre-Olympic Year".
505 **204** 350f. violet and blue . . . 1·00 65
506 – 400f. blue . . . . 1·10 80
DESIGNS: 400f. Emblem of Montreal Olympics (1976).

1975. Birth Bicentenary of Andre-Marie Ampere. As T **198**.
507 90f. brown, red and violet . . 45 20

205 Tristater of Carthage

1975. Ancient Coins.
508 **205** 130f. black, blue & purple 50 25
509 – 170f. black, green & brn 70 35
510 – 190f. black, green and red 1·00 65
511 – 260f. black, blue & orange 1·75 1·25
COINS: 170f. Decadrachm of Syracuse; 190f. Tetradrachm of Acanthe; 260f. Didrachm of Eretrie.

1975. Air. "Apollo–Soyuz" Space Link. Nos. 489/91 optd **ARRIMAGE 17 Juil. 1975**.
512 **197** 290f. red, blue and black 1·25 65
513 – 300f. red, blue and black 1·25 65
514 – 370f. green, purple & black . . . . 1·50 95

207 U.N. Emblem and Names of Agencies forming "ONU"

1975. 30th Anniv of United Nations Charter.
515 **207** 200f. blue and green . . . 70 45

208 "The Visitation" (Ghirlandaio)

1975. Air. Christmas. Religious Paintings.
516 290f. Type **208** . . . . 1·40 55
517 300f. "Nativity" (Fra Filippo Lippi School) . . . . . . 1·40 65
518 370f. "Adoration of the Magi" (Velasquez) . . . . 1·60 1·10

1975. Air. 50th Death Anniv of Clement Ader (aviation pioneer). As T **198**.
519 100f. purple, red and blue . . 55 20

209 Concorde in Flight

1976. Air. Concorde's First Commercial Flight.
520 **209** 500f. multicoloured . . . 3·75 1·50

210 Figure-Skating

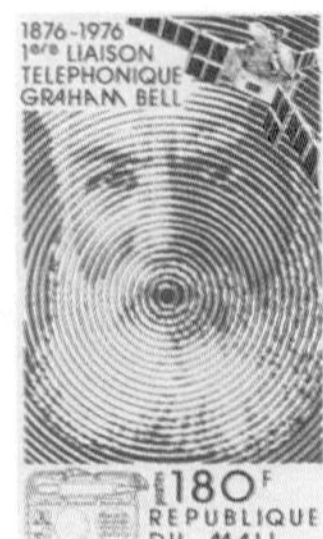

211 Alexander Graham Bell

1976. Air. Winter Olympic Games, Innsbruck. Multicoloured.
521 120f. Type **210** 50 25
522 420f. Ski-jumping . . . . . 1·50 65
523 430f. Skiing (slalom) . . . . 1·50 75

1976. Telephone Centenary.
524 **211** 180f. blue, brown and light brown 65 35

212 Chameleon

1976. Reptiles. Multicoloured.
525 20f. Type **212** 20 15
526 30f. Lizard 30 15
527 40f. Tortoise 35 20
528 90f. Python 75 25
529 120f. Crocodile . . . . . . 1·25 50

213 Nurse and Patient

1976. Air. World Health Day.
530 **213** 130f. multicoloured . . . 55 25

214 Dr. Adenauer and Cologne Cathedral

1976. Birth Centenary Dr. Konrad Adenauer.
531 **214** 180f. purple and brown 90 40

215 Constructing Orbital Space Station

1976. Air. "The Future in Space".
532 **215** 300f. deep blue, blue and orange . . . . 1·25 60
533 – 400f. blue, red and purple 1·90 90
DESIGN: 400f. Sun and space-ship with solar batteries.

216 American Bald Eagle and Liberty Bell

1976. Air. American Revolution Bicentenary and "Interphil '76" Int Stamp Exn, Philadelphia.
534 **216** 100f. blue, purple & black 70 20
535 – 400f. brown, blue & black 2·50 85
536 – 440f. violet, green & black 2·00 85
DESIGNS—HORIZ: 400f. Warships and American bald eagle. VERT: 440f. Red Indians and American bald eagle.

217 Running

1976. Air. Olympic Games, Montreal.
537 **217** 200f. black, brown and red 70 40
538 – 250f. brown, green & blue 80 50
539 – 300f. black, blue and green . . . . 1·25 60
540 – 400f. black, blue and green . . . . 1·60 90
DESIGNS: 250f. Swimming; 300f. Handball; 440f. Football.

218 Scouts marching

1976. Air. 1st All-African Scout Jamboree, Nigeria.
541 **218** 140f. brown, blue & green 70 35
542 – 180f. brown, green & grey 1·00 40
543 – 200f. violet and brown . . 1·10 50
DESIGNS—HORIZ: 180f. Scouts tending calf. VERT: 200f. Scout surveying camp at dusk.

1976. Fishes (2nd series). As T **196**.
544 100f. black and blue 80 25
545 120f. yellow, brown and green 90 35
546 130f. turquoise, brown & black . . . . 1·10 35
547 150f. yellow, drab and green 1·25 45
548 220f. black, green and brown 2·10 80
DESIGNS: 100f. African bonytongue; 120f. Budgett's upsidedown catfish; 130f. Double-dorsal catfish; 150f. Monod's tilapia; 220f. Big-scaled tetra.

220 Scenes from Children's Book

221 "Roi de L'Air"

1976. Literature for Children.
549 **220** 130f. grey, green and red 45 25

1976. 1st Issue of "L'Essor" Newspaper.
550 **221** 120f. multicoloured . . . 1·00 30

222 Fall from Scaffolding

1976. 20th Anniv of National Social Insurance.
551 **222** 120f. multicoloured . . . 35 25

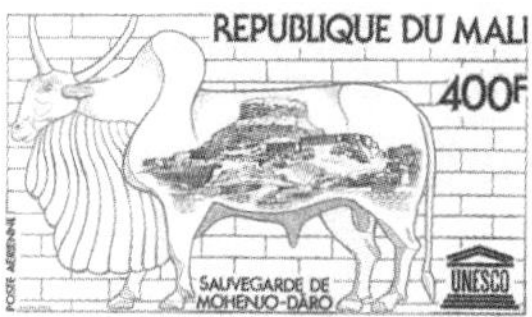

223 Moenjodaro

1976. Air. U.N.E.S.C.O. "Save Moenjodaro" (Pakistan) Campaign.
552 **223** 400f. purple, blue & black 1·75 80
553 – 500f. red, yellow and blue 2·00 1·25
DESIGN: 500f. Effigy, animals and remains.

224 Freighter, Vickers Viscount 800 and Map

1976. Air. Europafrique.
554 **224** 200f. purple and blue . . 1·10 45

225 Cascade of Letters

1976. 25th Anniv of U.N. Postal Administration.
555 **225** 120f. orange, green & lilac 45 25

226 Moto Guzzi "254" (Italy)

1976. Motorcycling.
556 **226** 90f. red, grey and brown 45 20
557 – 120f. violet, blue and black 55 25
558 – 130f. red, grey and green 70 25
559 – 140f. blue, green and grey 90 30
DESIGNS: 120f. B.M.W. "900" (Germany); 130f. Honda "Egli" (Japan); 140f. Motobecane "LT3" (France).

227 "The Nativity" (Taddeo Gaddi)

1976. Air. Christmas. Religious Paintings. Mult.
560 280f. Type **227** . . . . 1·25 50
561 300f. "Adoration of the Magi" (Hans Memling) . . 1·40 60
562 320f. "The Nativity" (Carlo Crivelli) . . . . 1·50 75

228 Muscat Fishing Boat

1976. Ships.
563 **228** 160f. purple, green & blue 75 30
564 – 180f. green, red and blue 75 35
565 – 190f. purple, blue & green 80 40
566 – 200f. green, red and blue 85 40
DESIGNS: 180f. Cochin Chinese junk; 190f. Dunkirk lightship "Ruytingen"; 200f. Nile felucca.

229 Rocket in Flight

1976. Air. Operation "Viking".
567 **229** 500f. blue, red and lake 1·75 1·25
568 – 1000f. lake, blue and deep blue . . . . 3·00 1·90
DESIGN: 1000f. Spacecraft on Mars.

230 Pres. Giscard d'Estaing and Sankore Mosque, Timbuktu

1977. Air. Visit of Pres. Giscard d'Estaing of France.
570 **230** 430f. multicoloured . . . 2·00 80

231 Rocket on Launch-pad, Newton and Apple

1977. Air. 250th Death Anniv of Isaac Newton.
571 **231** 400f. purple, red and green . . . . 2·00 75

232 Prince Philip and Queen Elizabeth II

1977. Air. "Personalities of Decolonization". Mult.
572 180f. Type **232** 65 35
573 200f. General De Gaulle (vert) . . . . 1·10 50
574 250f. Queen Wilhelmina of the Netherlands (vert) . . . 75 55
575 300f. King Baudouin and Queen Fabiola of Belgium 1·10 70
576 480f. Crowning of Queen Elizabeth II (vert) . . . . 2·00 1·25

233 Lindbergh and "Spirit of St. Louis"

1977. Air. 50th Anniv of Lindbergh's Transatlantic Flight.
577 **233** 420f. orange and violet . . 1·90 85
578 – 430f. blue, orange & green 1·90 85
DESIGN: 430f. "Spirit of St. Louis" crossing the Atlantic.

234 Village Indigobird

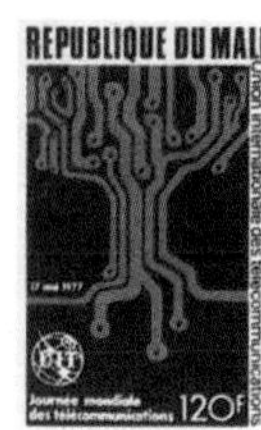

236 Printed Circuit

235 Louis Braille and Hands reading Book

1977. Mali Birds. Multicoloured.
579 15f. Type **234** 45 10
580 25f. Yellow-breasted barbet 75 10
581 30f. Vitelline masked weaver 75 25
582 40f. Carmine bee eater . . . 1·00 35
583 50f. Senegal parrot . . . . . 1·00 35

1977. 125th Death Anniv of Louis Braille (inventor of "Braille" system of reading and writing for the blind).
584 **235** 200f. blue, red and green 1·10 45

1977. World Telecommunications Day.
585 **236** 120f. red and brown . . . 35 20

236a Chateau Sassenage, Grenoble

1977. Air. 10th Anniv of International French Language Council.
586 **236a** 300f. multicoloured . . . 1·00 50

237 Airship LZ-1 over Lake Constance

1977. Air. History of the Zeppelin.
587 **237** 120f. green, brown & blue 55 25
588 – 130f. deep blue, brown and blue 65 25
589 – 350f. red, blue and deep blue . . . . 1·75 75
590 – 500f. deep blue, green and blue . . . . 2·50 95
DESIGNS: 130f. "Graf Zeppelin" over Atlantic; 350f. Burning of "Hindenburg" at Lakehurst; 500f. Count Ferdinand von Zeppelin and "Graf Zeppelin" at mooring mast.

238 "Anaz imperator"

1977. Insects. Multicoloured.
591 5f. Type **238** 20 15
592 10f. "Sphadromantis viridis" 25 15
593 20f. "Vespa tropica" 25 15
594 35f. "Melolontha melolantha" 30 15
595 60f. Stag beetle 55 20

239 Knight and Rook

1977. Chess Pieces.
596 **239** 120f. black, green & brn 1·10 30
597 – 130f. green, red and black 1·25 30
598 – 300f. green, red and blue 2·75 75
DESIGNS—VERT: 130f. Pawn and Bishop. HORIZ: 300f. King and Queen.

240 Henri Dunant

241 Ship

1977. Air. Nobel Peace Prize Winners. Multicoloured.
599 600f. Type **240** (founder of Red Cross) . . . . 2·00 1·00
600 700f. Martin Luther King . . 2·25 1·10

1977. Europafrique.
601 **241** 400f. multicoloured . . . 1·25 75

242 "Head of Horse"

1977. 525th Birth Anniv of Leonardo da Vinci.
602 **242** 200f. brown and black . . 75 50
603 – 300f. brown . . . . . . 1·10 60
604 – 500f. red . . . . 2·00 85
DESIGNS: 300f. "Head of Young Girl"; 500f. Self-portrait.

243 Footballers

245 Dome of the Rock

244 Friendship Hotel

1977. Air. Football Cup Elimination Rounds.
605 – 180f. brown, green & orge 50 30
606 **243** 200f. brown, green & orge 60 35
607 – 420f. grey, green and lilac 1·25 70
DESIGNS—HORIZ: 180f. Two footballers; 420f. Tackling.

1977. Inauguration of Friendship Hotel, Bamako.
608 **244** 120f. multicoloured . . . 35 25

1977. Palestinian Welfare.
609 **245** 120f. multicoloured . . . 55 20
610 180f. multicoloured . . . 70 30

246 Mao Tse-tung and "Comatex" Hall, Bamako

1977. Air. Mao Tse-tung Memorial.
611 **246** 300f. red . . . . 1·25 50

1977. Air. First Commercial Paris–New York Flight by Concorde. Optd **PARIS NEW - YORK 22.11.77.**
612 **209** 500f. multicoloured . . . 7·00 4·50

248 "Adoration of the Magi" (Rubens)

1977. Air. Christmas. Details from "Adoration of the Magi" by Rubens.
613 **248** 400f. multicoloured . . . 1·25 75
614 – 500f. multicoloured . . . 1·60 95
615 – 600f. multicoloured (horiz) 2·00 1·10

249 "Hercules and the Nemean Lion"

1978. 400th Birth Anniv of Peter Paul Rubens. Multicoloured.
616 200f. "Battle of the Amazons" (horiz) 70 35
617 300f. "Return from Labour in the Fields" (horiz) . . . 1·00 55
618 500f. Type **249** . . . . 1·75 95

250 Schubert and Mute Swans

1978. Air. 150th Death Anniv of Franz Schubert (composer). Multicoloured.
619 300f. Schubert and bars of music (vert) . . . . 1·75 60
620 420f. Type **250** . . . . 2·00 85

251 Cook and Shipboard Scene

1978. Air. 250th Birth Anniv of Captain James Cook.
621 **251** 200f. blue, red and violet 1·50 40
622 – 300f. brown, blue & green 3·00 70
DESIGN: 300f. Capt. Cook meeting natives.

252 African and Chained Building

1978. World Anti-Apartheid Year.
623 **252** 120f. violet, brown & blue 40 20
624 – 130f. violet, blue & orange 40 20
625 – 180f. brown, pur & orge 60 30
DESIGNS: 130f. Statue of Liberty and Africans walking to open door; 180f. African children and mule in fenced enclosure.

253 Players and Ball

1978. Air. World Cup Football Championship, Argentina.
626 **253** 150f. red, green and brown 60 30
627 – 250f. red, brown and green . . . . 1·25 45
628 – 300f. red, brown and blue 1·50 50
DESIGNS—VERT: 250f. HORIZ: 300f. Different football scenes.

254 "Head of Christ"

1978. Air. Easter. Works by Durer.
630 **254** 420f. green and brown . . 1·60 75
631 – 430f. blue and brown . . . 1·60 75
DESIGN: 430f. "The Resurrection".

255 Red-cheeked Cordon-bleu

1978. Birds. Multicoloured.
632 20f. Type **255** 10 10
633 30f. Masked fire finch 45 10
634 50f. Red-billed fire finch . . . 55 20
635 70f. African collared dove . . 1·00 20
636 80f. White-billed buffalo weaver . . . . 1·40 35

256 C-3 "Trefle"

1978. Air. Birth Centenary of Andre Citroen (automobile pioneer).
637 **256** 120f. brown, lake & green 70 20
638 – 130f. grey, orange and blue 85 25
639 – 180f. blue, green and red 1·25 30
640 – 200f. black, red and lake 1·50 40
DESIGNS: 130f. B-2 "Croisiere Noir" track-laying vehicle, 1924; 180f. B-14 G Saloon, 1927; 200f. Model-11 front-wheel drive car, 1934.

1978. 20th Anniv of Bamako Lions Club. Nos. 473/4 surch **XXe ANNIVERSAIRE DU LIONS CLUB DE BAMAKO 1958-1978** and value.
641 120f. on 90f. Type **192** . . . 45 20
642 130f. on 100f. View of Samanko 55 30

258 Names of 1978 U.P.U. members forming Map of the World

1978. Centenary of U.P.U. Foundation Congress, Paris.
643 **258** 120f. green, orange & mve 45 20
644 – 130f. yellow, red and green 45 20
DESIGN: 130f. Names of 1878 member states across globe.

259 Desert Scene

1978. Campaign against Desertification.
645 **259** 200f. multicoloured . . . 70 35

260 Mahatma Gandhi

262 Dominoes

261 "Dermestes bromius"

1978. 30th Anniv of Gandhi's Assassination.
646 **260** 140f. brown, red and black 85 30

1978. Insects. Multicoloured.
647 15f. Type **261** 20 15
648 25f. "Calosoma sp." 25 15
649 90f. "Lopocerus variegatus" 45 20
650 120f. "Coccinella septempunctata" 55 25
651 140f. "Goliathus giganteus" 70 30

1978. Social Games.
652 **262** 100f. black, green and red 40 20
653 – 130f. red, black and blue 85 25
DESIGN: 130f. Bridge hand.

263 Ostrich on Nest (Syrian Manuscript)

1978. Air. Europafrique. Multicoloured.
654 100f. Type **263** 80 25
655 110f. Common zebra (Mansur miniature) 50 30

1978. Air. World Cup Football Championship Finalists. Nos. 626/8 optd with results.
656 **253** 150f. red, green and brown 60 25
657 – 250f. red, brown and green . . . . 1·00 45
658 – 300f. red, brown and blue 1·25 60
OPTS: 150f. **CHAMPION 1978 ARGENTINE**; 250f. **2e HOLLANDE**; 300f. **3e BRESIL 4e ITALIE.**

265 Coronation Coach

1978. Air. 25th Anniv of Coronation of Queen Elizabeth II. Multicoloured.
660 500f. Type **265** . . . . 1·50 70
661 1000f. Queen Elizabeth II . . 2·75 1·40

266 Aristotle and African Animals

1978. 2300th Death Anniv of Aristotle (Greek philosopher).
662 **266** 200f. brown, red and green 90 35

267 Douglas DC-3 and U.S.A. 1918 24c. stamp

1978. Air. History of Aviation.
663 **267** 80f. deep blue, red & blue 35 15
664 – 100f. multicoloured . . . 50 20
665 – 120f. black, blue and red 60 25
666 – 130f. green, red and black 65 30
667 – 320f. violet, blue and red 1·50 65
DESIGNS: 100f. Stampe and Renard SV-4 and Belgium Balloon stamp of 1932; 120f. Clement Ader's Avion III and France Concorde stamp of 1976; 130f. Junkers Ju-52/3m and Germany Biplane stamp of 1919; 320f. Mitsubishi A6M Zero-Sen and Japan Pagoda stamp of 1951.

268 "The Annunciation"

1978. Air. Christmas. Works by Durer.
668 **268** 420f. brown and black . . 1·25 60
669 – 430f. brown and green . . 1·25 60
670 – 500f. black and brown . . 1·60 75
DESIGNS: 430f. "Virgin and Child"; 500f. "Adoration of the Magi".

269 Launch of "Apollo 8" and Moon

1978. Air. 10th Anniv of First Manned Flight around the Moon.
671 **269** 200f. red, green and violet 60 30
672 – 300f. violet, green and red 1·10 50
DESIGN: 300f. "Apollo 8" in orbit around the Moon.

30e ANNIVERSAIRE DE LA DECLARATION universelle DES DROITS DE L'HOMME
180F
XXX
REPUBLIQUE DU MALI

270 U.N. and Human Rights Emblems

1978. 30th Anniv of Declaration of Human Rights.
673 **270** 180f. red, blue and brown 60 35

271 Concorde and Clement Ader's "Eole"

1979. Air. 3rd Anniv of First Commercial Concorde Flight. Multicoloured.
674 120f. Type **271** 70 25
675 130f. Concorde and Wright Flyer I 85 30
676 200f. Concorde and "Spirit of St. Louis" . . . . 1·40 45

1979. Air. "Philexafrique" Stamp Exhibition, Libreville, Gabon (1st issue) and International Stamp Fair, Essen, West Germany. As T **262** of Niger. Multicoloured.
677 200f. Ruff (bird) and Lubeck 1859 ½s. stamp . . . . . . 2·00 90
678 200f. Dromedary and Mali 1965 200f. stamp . . . . . 3·00 1·75
See also Nos. 704/5.

1979. Air. Birth Centenary of Albert Einstein (physicist). No. 492 surch **"1879-1979" 130F**.
679 **198** 130f. on 90f. blue, purple and brown 55 30

273 "Christ carrying the Cross"

1979. Air. Easter. Works by Durer.
680 **273** 400f. black and turquoise 1·40 60
681 – 430f. black and red . . . 1·40 60
682 – 480f. black and blue . . 1·60 1·00
DESIGNS: 430f. "Christ on the Cross"; 480f. "The Great Lamentation".

274 Basketball and St. Basil's Cathedral, Moscow

275 African Manatee

1979. Air. Pre-Olympic Year. Multicoloured.
683 420f. Type **274** . . . . 1·50 75
684 430f. Footballer and Kremlin 1·50 75

1979. Endangered Animals. Multicoloured.
685 100f. Type **275** 45 20
686 120f. Chimpanzee 65 30
687 130f. Topi 75 35
688 180f. Gemsbok 90 40
689 200f. Giant eland . . . . . 1·00 55

276 Child and I.Y.C. Emblem

1979. International Year of the Child.
690 **276** 120f. green, red and brown 40 20
691 – 200f. purple and green . . 70 35
692 – 300f. brown, mauve and deep brown . . . . . 1·00 50
DESIGNS: 200f. Girl and scout with birds; 300f. Children with calf.

277 Judo

1979. World Judo Championships, Paris.
693 **277** 200f. sepia, red and ochre 80 40

278 Wave Pattern and Human Figures

279 Goat's Head and Lizard Fetishes

1979. World Telecommunications Day.
694 **278** 120f. multicoloured . . . 35 20

1979. World Museums Day. Multicoloured.
695 90f. Type **279** 30 15
696 120f. Seated figures (wood carving) 40 20
697 130f. Two animal heads and figurine (wood carving) . . 50 25

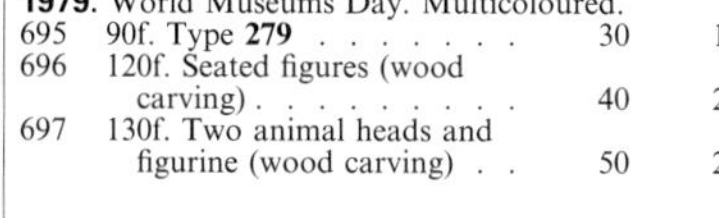

280 Rowland Hill and Mali 1961 25f. stamp

281 Cora Players

1979. Death Centenary of Sir Rowland Hill.
698 **280** 120f. multicoloured . . . 40 20
699 – 130f. red, blue and green 40 20
700 – 180f. black, green and blue 60 30
701 – 200f. black, red and purple 70 35
702 – 300f. blue, deep blue and red . . . . 1·25 50
DESIGNS: 130f. Airship "Graf Zeppelin" and Saxony stamp of 1850; 180f. Concorde and France stamp of 1849; 200f. Stage coach and U.S.A. stamp of 1849; 300f. U.P.U. emblem and Penny Black.

1979.
703 **281** 200f. multicoloured . . . 1·00 40

282 Sankore Mosque and "Adenium obesum"

1979. "Philexafrique" Exhibition, Libreville, Gabon (2nd issue).
704 **282** 120f. multicoloured . . . 90 55
705 – 300f. red, blue and orange 1·90 1·25
DESIGN: 300f. Horseman and satellite.

283 Map of Mali showing Conquest of Desert

1979. Operation "Sahel Vert". Multicoloured.
706 200f. Type **283** 70 30
707 300f. Planting a tree . . . . 1·10 50

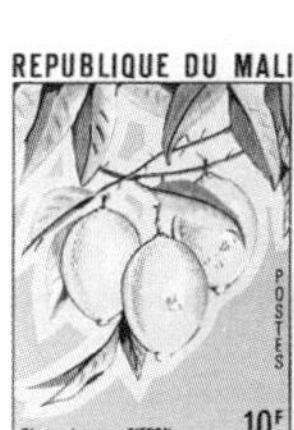

284 Lemons

285 Sigmund Freud

1979. Fruit (1st series). Multicoloured.
708 10f. Type **284** 15 10
709 60f. Pineapple 30 15
710 100f. Papaw 50 15
711 120f. Sweet-sops 55 20
712 130f. Mangoes 65 25
See also Nos. 777/81.

1979. 40th Death Anniv of Sigmund Freud (psychologist).
713 **285** 300f. sepia and violet . . 1·25 60

286 Caillie and Camel approaching Fort

1979. 180th Birth Anniv of Rene Caillie (explorer).
714 **286** 120f. sepia, brown & blue 50 20
715 – 130f. blue, green & brown 60 25
DESIGN: 130f. Rene Caillie and map of route across Sahara.

287 "Eurema brigitta"

1979. Butterflies and Moths (1st series). Mult.
716 100f. Type **287** 60 20
717 120f. "Papilio pylades" . . . 75 20
718 130f. "Melanitis leda satyridae" 90 40
719 180f. "Gonimbrasis belina occidentalis" . . . . 1·50 45
720 200f. "Bunaea alcinoe" . . . 1·75 50
See also Nos. 800/4.

288 Mali 1970 300f. Stamp and Modules orbiting Moon

1979. Air. 10th Anniv of First Moon Landing.
721 430f. Type **288** . . . . . . 1·40 60
722 500f. 1973 250f. stamp and rocket launch . . . . . . 1·60 95

289 Capt. Cook and H.M.S. "Resolution" off Kerguelen Islands

1979. Air. Death Bicent of Captain James Cook.
723 300f. Type **289** . . . . . . 1·75 80
724 400f. Capt. Cook and H.M.S. "Resolution" off Hawaii 2·50 1·10

290 Menaka Greyhound

1979. Dogs. Multicoloured.
725 20f. Type **290** 30 15
726 50f. Water spaniel 45 15
727 70f. Beagle 60 15
728 80f. Newfoundland 70 20
729 90f. Sheepdog 85 20

291 David Janowski

1979. Air. Chess Grand-masters.
730 **291** 100f. red and brown . . . 85 30
731 – 140f. red, brown and blue 1·25 30
732 – 200f. blue, violet and green . . . . 1·75 50
733 – 300f. brown, ochre and red . . . . 2·25 70
DESIGNS: 140f. Alexander Alekhine; 200f. Willi Schlage; 300f. Efim Bogoljubow.

292 "The Adoration of the Magi" 1511 (detail, Durer)

1979. Air. Christmas. Works by Durer.
734 **292** 300f. brown and orange 1·00 50
735 – 400f. brown and blue . . 1·25 75
736 – 500f. brown and green . . 1·60 95
DESIGNS: 400f. "Adoration of the Magi" (1503); 500f. "Adoration of the Magi" (1511, different).

1979. Air. 20th Anniv of ASECNA (African Air Safety Organization). As T **198** of Malagasy but 36 × 27 mm.
737 120f. multicoloured 40 20

293 Globe, Rotary Emblem and Diesel-electric Train

1980. Air. 75th Anniv of Rotary International. Multicoloured.
738 220f. Type **293** . . . . . . 2·75 80
739 250f. Globe, Rotary emblem and Douglas DC-10 airliner . . . . 1·00 45
740 430f. Bamako Rotary Club and emblem . . . . 1·40 75

294 African Ass

295 Speed Skating

1980. Protected Animals. Multicoloured.
741 90f. Type **294** 50 20
742 120f. Addax 60 20
743 130f. Cheetahs 75 35
744 140f. Barbary sheep 80 45
745 180f. African buffalo . . . . 1·00 50

1980. Air. Winter Olympic Games, Lake Placid. Multicoloured.
746 200f. Type **295** 70 30
747 300f. Ski jump . . . . 1·10 60

296 Stephenson's "Rocket" (1829) and Mali 30f. Stamp, 1972

1980. Air. 150th Anniv of Liverpool and Manchester Railway.
749 **296** 200f. blue, brown & green 1·25 45
750 – 300f. black, brown & turq 2·00 80
DESIGN: 300f. "Rocket" (1829) and Mali 50f. railway stamp, 1970.

297 Horse Jumping

1980. Air. Olympic Games, Moscow.
751 **297** 200f. green, brown & blue 70 30
752 – 300f. blue, brown & green 1·00 50
753 – 400f. red, green & lt green 1·50 75
DESIGN: 300f. Sailing. 400f. Football.

298 Solar Pumping Station, Koni

1980. Solar Energy. Multicoloured.
755 90f. Type **298** 30 15
756 100f. Solar capture tables, Dire 35 15
757 120f. Solar energy cooker . . 50 20
758 130f. Solar generating station, Dire 55 25

299 Nioro Horse

1980. Horses. Multicoloured.
759 100f. Mopti 50 15
760 120f. Type **299** 65 15
761 130f. Koro 75 20
762 180f. Lake zone horse . . . 90 35
763 200f. Banamba . . . . . . 1·10 40

300 "Head of Christ" (Maurice Denis)

1980. Air. Easter.
764 **300** 480f. red and brown . . . 1·60 95
765 – 500f. brown and red . . . 1·60 95
DESIGN: 500f. "Christ before Pilate" (Durer).

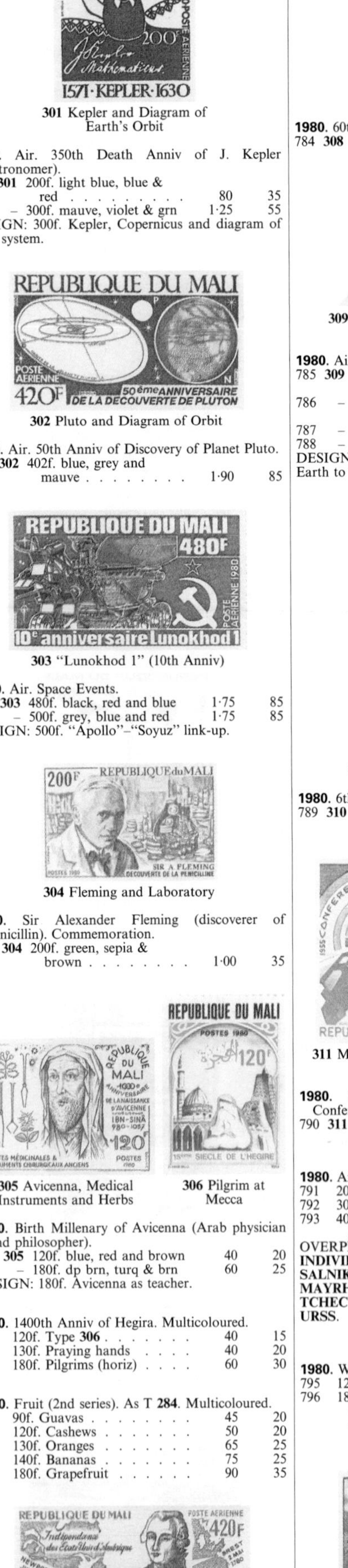

301 Kepler and Diagram of Earth's Orbit

1980. Air. 350th Death Anniv of J. Kepler (astronomer).
766 **301** 200f. light blue, blue & red 80 35
767 – 300f. mauve, violet & grn 1·25 55
DESIGN: 300f. Kepler, Copernicus and diagram of solar system.

302 Pluto and Diagram of Orbit

1980. Air. 50th Anniv of Discovery of Planet Pluto.
768 **302** 402f. blue, grey and mauve . . . . 1·90 85

303 "Lunokhod 1" (10th Anniv)

1980. Air. Space Events.
769 **303** 480f. black, red and blue 1·75 85
770 – 500f. grey, blue and red 1·75 85
DESIGN: 500f. "Apollo"–"Soyuz" link-up.

304 Fleming and Laboratory

1980. Sir Alexander Fleming (discoverer of penicillin). Commemoration.
771 **304** 200f. green, sepia & brown . . . . 1·00 35

305 Avicenna, Medical Instruments and Herbs

306 Pilgrim at Mecca

1980. Birth Millenary of Avicenna (Arab physician and philosopher).
772 **305** 120f. blue, red and brown 40 20
773 – 180f. dp brn, turq & brn 60 25
DESIGN: 180f. Avicenna as teacher.

1980. 1400th Anniv of Hegira. Multicoloured.
774 120f. Type **306** 40 15
775 130f. Praying hands 40 20
776 180f. Pilgrims (horiz) 60 30

1980. Fruit (2nd series). As T **284**. Multicoloured.
777 90f. Guavas 45 20
778 120f. Cashews 50 20
779 130f. Oranges 65 25
780 140f. Bananas 75 25
781 180f. Grapefruit 90 35

307 Rochambeau and French Fleet at Rhode Island, 1780

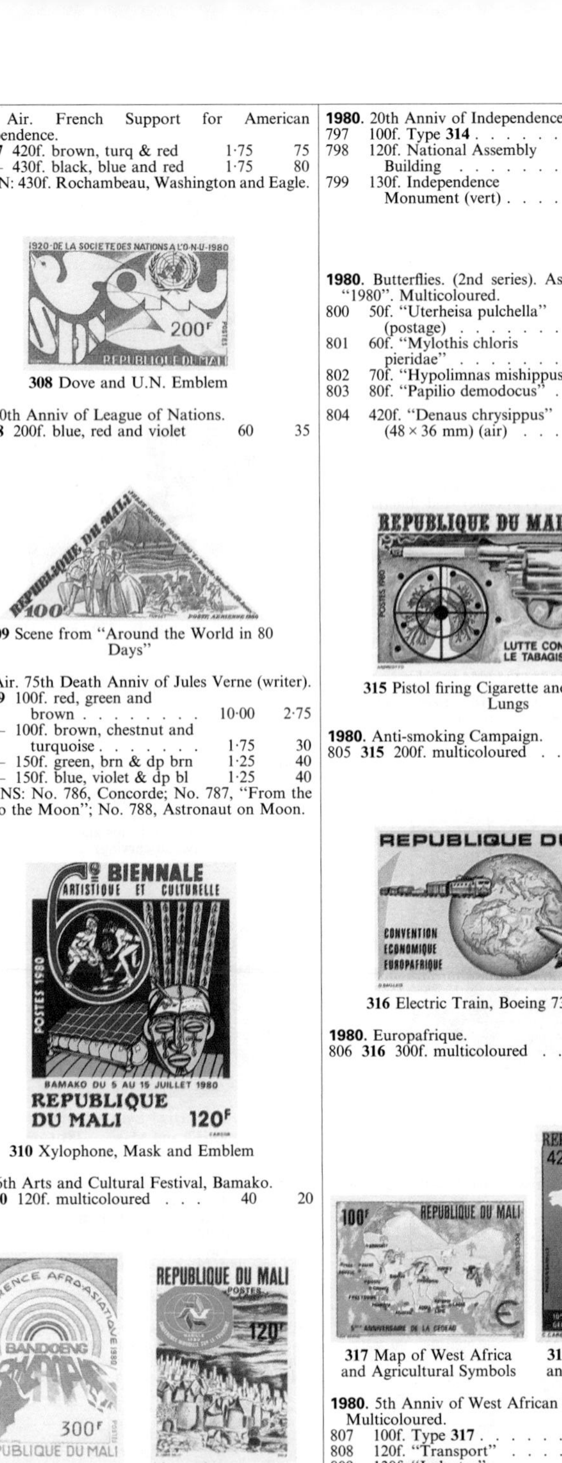

1980. Air. French Support for American Independence.
782 **307** 420f. brown, turq & red 1·75 75
783 – 430f. black, blue and red 1·75 80
DESIGN: 430f. Rochambeau, Washington and Eagle.

308 Dove and U.N. Emblem

1980. 60th Anniv of League of Nations.
784 **308** 200f. blue, red and violet 60 35

309 Scene from "Around the World in 80 Days"

1980. Air. 75th Death Anniv of Jules Verne (writer).
785 **309** 100f. red, green and brown . . . . 10·00 2·75
786 – 100f. brown, chestnut and turquoise . . . . 1·75 30
787 – 150f. green, brn & dp brn 1·25 40
788 – 150f. blue, violet & dp bl 1·25 40
DESIGNS: No. 786, Concorde; No. 787, "From the Earth to the Moon"; No. 788, Astronaut on Moon.

310 Xylophone, Mask and Emblem

1980. 6th Arts and Cultural Festival, Bamako.
789 **310** 120f. multicoloured . . . 40 20

311 Map of Africa and Asia

313 Conference Emblem

1980. 25th Anniv of Afro-Asian Bandung Conference.
790 **311** 300f. green, red and blue 90 55

1980. Air. Olympic Medal Winners. Nos. 751/3 optd.
791 200f. green, brown and blue 70 35
792 300f. blue, brown and green 1·00 55
793 400f. red, green and light green . . . . 1·40 75
OVERPRINTS: 200f. **CONCOURS COMPLET INDIVIDUEL ROMAN (It.) BLINOV (Urss) SALNIKOV (Urss)**; 300f. **FINN RECHARDT (Fin.) MAYRHOFER (Autr.) BALACHOV (Urss)**; 400f. **TCHECOSLOVAQUIE ALLEMAGNE DE L'EST URSS**.

1980. World Tourism Conference, Manila. Mult.
795 120f. Type **313** 35 15
796 180f. Encampment outside fort and Conference emblem 50 30

314 Dam and Rural Scene

1980. 20th Anniv of Independence. Multicoloured.
797 100f. Type **314** 40 15
798 120f. National Assembly Building 40 20
799 130f. Independence Monument (vert) 45 25

1980. Butterflies. (2nd series). As T **287** but dated "1980". Multicoloured.
800 50f. "Uterheisa pulchella" (postage) 40 20
801 60f. "Mylothis chloris pieridae" 50 20
802 70f. "Hypolimnas mishippus" 60 20
803 80f. "Papilio demodocus" . . 75 20
804 420f. "Denaus chrysippus" (48 × 36 mm) (air) . . . . 2·50 1·25

315 Pistol firing Cigarette and Target over Lungs

1980. Anti-smoking Campaign.
805 **315** 200f. multicoloured . . . 75 35

316 Electric Train, Boeing 737 and Globe

1980. Europafrique.
806 **316** 300f. multicoloured . . . 3·75 85

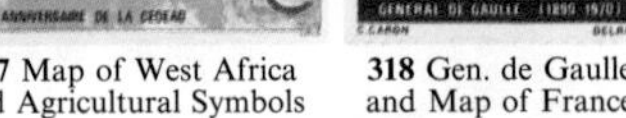

317 Map of West Africa and Agricultural Symbols

318 Gen. de Gaulle and Map of France

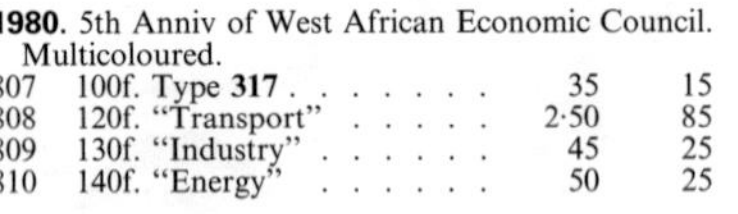

1980. 5th Anniv of West African Economic Council. Multicoloured.
807 100f. Type **317** 35 15
808 120f. "Transport" . . . . . 2·50 85
809 130f. "Industry" 45 25
810 140f. "Energy" 50 25

1980. Air. 10th Death Anniv of Gen. Charles de Gaulle. Multicoloured.
811 420f. Type **318** . . . . 1·75 75
812 430f. De Gaulle and Cross of Lorraine . . . . 1·75 75

319 "Hikari" Express Train (Japan) and Mali 1972 10f. Stamp

1980. Air. Locomotives.
813 **319** 120f. blue, green and red 95 20
814 – 130f. green, blue and red 1·25 25
815 – 200f. orange, black & grn 1·60 40
816 – 480f. black, red and green 4·25 95
DESIGNS—HORIZ: 130f. RTG train, U.S.A. and 20f. locomotive stamp of 1970; 200f. "Rembrandt" express, Germany, and 100f. locomotive stamp of 1970. VERT: 480f. TGV 001 turbotrain, France, and 80f. locomotive stamp of 1970.

320 "Flight into Egypt" (Rembrandt)

1980. Air. Christmas. Multicoloured.
817 300f. "St. Joseph showing the infant Jesus to St. Catherine" (Lorenzo Lotto) (horiz) . . . . . . 1·00 55
818 400f. Type **320** . . . . 1·40 80
819 500f. "Christmas Night" (Gauguin) (horiz) . . . . 1·60 90

1980. 5th Anniv of African Posts and Telecommunications Union. As T **292** of Niger.
820 130f. multicoloured 40 20

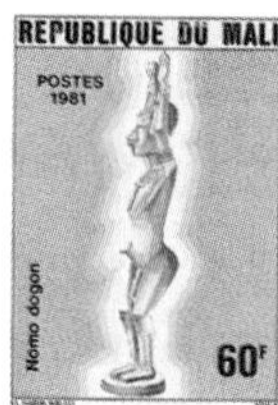

321 Nomo Dogon 323 Mambie Sidibe

322 "Self-portrait" (Blue Period)

1981. Statuettes. Multicoloured.
821 60f. Type **321** 20 15
822 70f. Senoufo fertility symbol 25 15
823 90f. Bamanan fertility statuette 35 15
824 100f. Senoufo captives snuff-box 40 15
825 120f. Dogon fertility statuette 50 20

1981. Birth Bicentenary of Pablo Picasso (artist).
826 **322** 1000f. multicoloured . . . 3·50 1·75

1981. Mali Thinkers and Savants.
827 **323** 120f. brown, buff and red 40 20
828 – 130f. brown, buff & black 40 25
DESIGN: 130f. Amadou Hampate Ba.

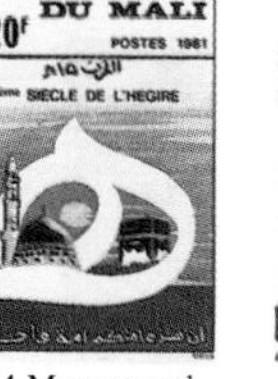

324 Mosque and Ka'aba 325 Tackle

1981. 1400th Anniv of Hejira.
829 **324** 120f. multicoloured . . . 40 20
830 180f. multicoloured . . . 60 30

1981. Air. World Cup Football Championship Eliminators. Multicoloured.
831 100f. Type **325** 40 20
832 200f. Heading the ball . . . 85 35
833 300f. Running for ball . . . 1·40 50

326 Kaarta Zebu 327 Crinum de Moore "Crinum moorei"

1981. Cattle. Multicoloured.
835 20f. Type **326** 15 15
836 30f. Peul du Macina sebu . . 15 15
837 40f. Maure zebu 25 15
838 80f. Touareg zebu 50 15
839 100f. N'Dama cow 60 20

1981. Flowers. Multicoloured.
840 50f. Type **327** 30 15
841 100f. Double rose hibiscus "Hibiscus rosa-sinensis" . . 80 15
842 120f. Pervenche "Catharanthus roseus" . . 90 20
843 130f. Frangipani "Plumeria rubra" 90 25
844 180f. Orgueil de Chine "Caesalpinia pulcherrima" 1·40 40

328 Mozart and Musical Instruments

1981. Air. 225th Birth Anniv of Mozart. Mult.
845 420f. Type **328** . . . . 2·00 85
846 430f. Mozart and musical instruments (different) . . 2·00 85

329 "The Fall on the Way to Calvary" (Raphael)

1981. Air. Easter.
847 500f. Type **329** . . . . 1·50 85
848 600f. "Ecce Homo" (Rembrandt) . . . . . . 2·00 1·25

330 Yuri Gagarin

1981. Air. Space Anniversaries and Events.
849 **330** 200f. blue, black and red 85 30
850 – 200f. blue, black & lt blue 85 30
851 – 380f. multicoloured . . . 1·40 55
852 – 430f. violet, black and blue . . . . 1·60 70
DESIGNS—VERT: No. 849, Type **330**: first man in space (20th anniv); No. 850, Alan Shepard, first American in space (20th anniv); No. 851, Saturn and moons (exploration of Saturn). HORIZ: No. 852, Sir William Herschel, and diagram of Uranus (discovery bicentenary).

331 Blind and Sighted Faces 332 Caduceus (Telecommunications and Health)

1981. International Year of Disabled People.
853 **331** 100f. light brown, brown and green 35 15
854 – 120f. violet, blue and purple 45 20
DESIGN: 120f. Mechanical hand and human hand with spanner.

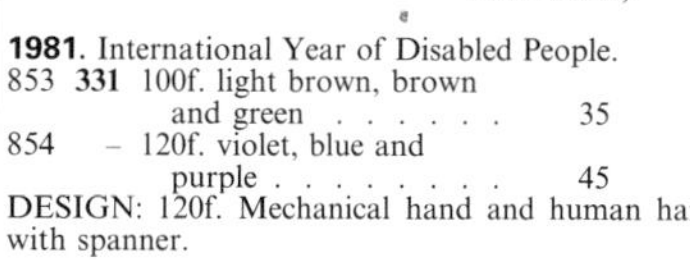

1981. World Telecommunications Day.
855 **332** 130f. multicoloured . . . 40 25

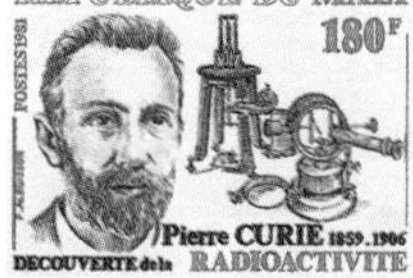

333 Pierre Curie and Instruments

1981. 75th Death Anniv of Pierre Curie (discoverer of radioactivity).
856 **333** 180f. blue, black & orange 90 30

334 Scouts at Well and Dorcas Gazelle

1981. 4th African Scouting Conference, Abidjan. Multicoloured.
857 110f. Type **334** 70 30
858 160f. Scouts signalling and patas monkey . . . . . . 1·25 60
859 300f. Scouts saluting and cheetah (vert) . . . . . . 1·75 85

1981. Air. World Railway Speed Record. No. 816 optd **26 fevrier 1981 Record du monde de vitesse–380 km/h.**
861 480f. black, red and blue . . 3·00 90

336 Columbus, Fleet and U.S. Columbus Stamp of 1892

1981. Air. 475th Death Anniv of Christopher Columbus.
862 **336** 180f. brown, black & blue 90 40
863 – 200f. green, blue & brown 1·10 40
864 – 260f. black, violet and red 1·60 60
865 – 300f. lilac, red and green 1·75 70
DESIGNS—VERT: 200f. "Nina" and 1c. Columbus stamp of Spain; 260f. "Pinta" and 5c. Columbus stamp of Spain. HORIZ: 300f. "Santa Maria" and U.S. 3c. Columbus stamp.

1981. 23rd World Scouting Conference, Dakar. Nos. 857/9 optd **DAKAR 8 AOUT 1981 28e CONFERENCE MONDIALE DU SCOUTISME.**
866 **334** 110f. multicoloured . . . 40 20
867 – 160f. multicoloured . . . 50 30
868 – 300f. multicoloured . . . 1·25 55

338 Space Shuttle after Launching

1981. Air. Space Shuttle. Multicoloured.
870 200f. Type **338** 90 30
871 500f. Space Shuttle in orbit 2·25 75
872 600f. Space Shuttle landing 2·50 1·25

339 "Harlequin on a Horse"

1981. Air. Birth Centenary of Pablo Picasso. Mult.
874 600f. Type **339** . . . . 2·75 1·25
875 750f. "Child with Pigeon" . . 3·25 1·40

340 Prince Charles, Lady Diana Spencer and St. Paul's Cathedral

1981. Air. British Royal Wedding. Multicoloured.
876 500f. Type **340** . . . . 1·25 75
877 700f. Prince Charles, Lady Diana Spencer and coach 1·75 1·10

342 Maure Sheep

1981. Sheep. Multicoloured.
886 10f. Type **342** 15 10
887 25f. Peul sheep 20 10
888 140f. Sahael sheep 50 25
889 180f. Touareg sheep 75 35
890 200f. Djallonke ram 85 35

343 Heinrich von Stephan (founder of U.P.U.), Latecoere 28 and Concorde

1981. Universal Postal Union Day.
891 **343** 400f. red and green . . . 1·60 70

344 Woman drinking from Bowl

1981. World Food Day.
892 **344** 200f. brown, orge & mve 65 30

345 "The Incarnation of the Son of God" (detail, Grunewald)

1981. Air. Christmas. Multicoloured.
893 500f. Type **345** . . . . 1·75 75
894 700f. "The Campori Madonna" (Correggio) . . 2·25 1·25

347 Transport and Hands holding Map of Europe and Africa

1981. Europafrique.
896 **347** 700f. blue, brown & orge 4·75 1·40

348 Guerin, Calmette, Syringe and Bacillus

1981. 60th Anniv of First B.C.G. Inoculation.
897 **348** 200f. brown, violet & blk 85 40

1982. Air. World Chess Championship, Merano. Nos. 731 and 733 optd.
898 140f. red, brown and blue . . 1·25 50
899 300f. brown, ochre and red 2·25 75
OPTS: 140f. **ANATOLI KARPOV VICTOR KORTCHNOI MERANO (ITALIE) Octobre-Novembre 1981**; 300f. **Octobre-Novembre 1981 ANATOLI KARPOV Champion du Monde 1981**.

350 "Nymphaea lotus"

1982. Flowers. Multicoloured.
900 170f. Type **350** 85 35
901 180f. "Bombax costatum" . . 90 35
902 200f. "Parkia biglobosa" . . 1·00 40
903 220f. "Gloriosa simplex" . . 1·25 45
904 270f. "Satanocrater berhautii" . . . . 1·40 50

351 Lewis Carroll and Characters from "Alice" Books

1982. Air. 150th Birth Anniv of Lewis Carroll (Revd. Charles Dodgson).
905 110f. Type **351** . . . . 1·00 25
906 130f. Characters from "Alice" books 75 30
907 140f. Characters from "Alice" books (different) 90 30

352 "George Washington" (Gilbert Stuart)

353 Ciwara Bamanan

1982. Air. 250th Birth Anniv of George Washington.
908 **352** 700f. multicoloured . . . 2·00 1·25

1982. Masks. Multicoloured.
909 5f. Type **353** 10 10
910 35f. Kanga Dogon 15 10
911 180f. N Domo Bamanan . . 1·00 40
912 200f. Cimier (Sogoninkum Bamanan) . . . . 1·00 40
913 250f. Kpelie Senoufo . . . . 1·10 45

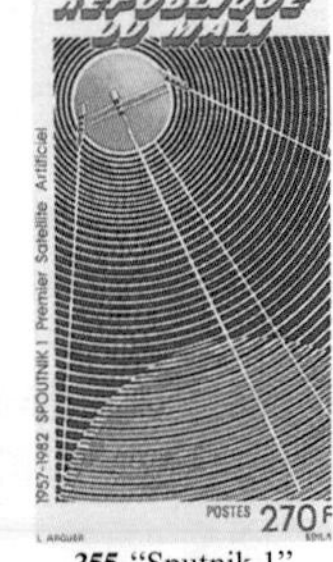

354 Football
355 "Sputnik 1"

1982. Air. World Cup Football Championship, Spain.
914 **354** 220f. multicoloured . . . 80 45
915 – 420f. multicoloured . . . 1·50 90
916 – 500f. multicoloured . . . 1·75 90
DESIGNS: 420f., 500f. Football scenes.

1982. 25th Anniv of First Artificial Satellite.
918 **355** 270f. violet, blue and red 1·25 50

356 Lord Baden-Powell, Tent and Scout Badge

1982. Air. 125th Birth Anniv of Lord Baden-Powell.
919 300f. Type **356** . . . . 1·50 50
920 500f. Saluting scout . . . . 2·25 90

357 "The Transfiguration" (Fra Angelico)

1982. Air. Easter. Multicoloured.
921 680f. Type **357** . . . . . . 2·00 1·25
922 1000f. "Pieta" (Giovanni Bellini) . . . . 3·00 1·90

358 Doctor giving Child Oral Vaccine
360 "En Bon Ami" (N'Teri)

359 Lions Emblem and Blind Person

1982. Anti-polio Campaign.
923 **358** 180f. multicoloured . . . 80 35

1982. Lions Club Blind Day.
924 **359** 260f. orange, blue and red 1·25 50

1982. Hairstyles. Multicoloured.
925 140f. Type **360** 35 30
926 150f. Tucked-in pony tail . . 60 35
927 160f. "Pour l'Art" 70 45
928 180f. "Bozo Kun" 75 50
929 270f. "Fulaw Kun" . . . . . 1·25 60

361 Arms Stamp of Mali and France

1982. Air. "Philexfrance 82" International Stamp Exhibition, Paris. Multicoloured.
930 180f. Type **361** 60 35
931 200f. Dromedary caravan and 1979 "Philexafrique II" stamp . . . . 1·00 40

362 Fire-engine, 1850

1982. Fire-engines. Multicoloured.
932 180f. Type **362** 95 35
933 200f. Fire-engine, 1921 . . . 1·40 40
934 270f. Fire-engine, 1982 . . . 1·60 50

363 Gobra

1982. Zebu Cattle. Multicoloured.
935 10f. Type **363** 10 10
936 60f. Azaouak 25 15
937 110f. Maure 35 25
938 180f. Toronke 65 35
939 200f. Peul Sambourou . . . 75 40

1982. Air. World Cup Football Championship Winners. Nos. 914/16 optd.
940 **354** 220f. multicoloured . . . 75 45
941 – 420f. multicoloured . . . 1·50 90
942 – 500f. multicoloured . . . 1·75 90
OPTS: 220f. **1 ITALIE 2 RFA 3 POLOGNE**; 420f. **POLOGNE FRANCE 3-2**; 500f. **ITALIE RFA 3-1**.

365 "Urchin with Cherries"

1982. Air. 150th Birth Anniv of Edouard Manet (painter).
944 **365** 680f. multicoloured . . . 2·75 1·25

366 "Virgin and Child" (detail) (Titian)

1982. Air. Christmas. Multicoloured.
945 500f. Type **366** . . . . 1·50 90
946 1000f. "Virgin and Child" (Giovanni Bellini) . . . . 2·75 1·90

367 Wind-surfing
368 Goethe

1982. Introduction of Wind-surfing as Olympic Event. Multicoloured.
947 200f. Type **367** 80 45
948 270f. Wind-surfer . . . . . 1·25 55
949 300f. Wind-surfer (different) 1·40 55

1982. Air. 150th Death Anniv of Goethe (poet).
950 **368** 500f. brown, light brown and black . . . . . . 2·00 90

369 Valentina Tereshkova
370 Transatlantic Balloon "Double Eagle II"

1983. Air. 20th Anniv of Launching of Vostok VI.
951 **369** 400f. multicoloured . . . 1·25 75

1983. Air. Bicentenary of Manned Flight. Mult.
952 500f. Type **370** . . . . 2·00 90
953 700f. Montgolfier balloon . . 2·50 1·25

371 Football

1983. Air. Olympic Games, Los Angeles. Mult.
954 180f. Type **371** 50 30
955 270f. Hurdles 75 40
956 300f. Windsurfing . . . . . 1·10 55

372 "The Transfiguration" (detail)

1983. Air. Easter. Multicoloured.
957 400f. Type **372** . . . . 1·25 75
958 600f. "The Entombment" (detail from Baglioni Retable) . . . . 2·00 1·10

373 Martin Luther King

374 Oua Hairstyle

1983. Celebrities.
959 **373** 800f. brown, blue & pur 2·50 1·40
960 – 800f. brown, red & dp red 3·00 1·25
DESIGN: No. 960, President Kennedy.

1983. Hairstyles. Multicoloured.
961 180f. Type **374** 60 30
962 200f. Nation (Diamani) . . . 70 30
963 270f. Rond Point 90 40
964 300f. Naamu-Naamu . . . . 1·00 45
965 500f. Bamba-Bamba . . . . 2·50 1·40

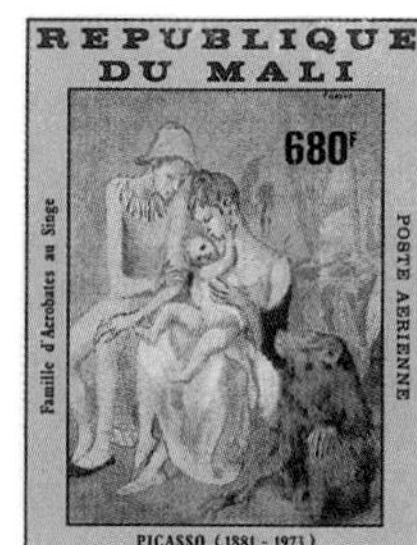

375 "Family of Acrobats with Monkey"

1983. Air. 10th Death Anniv of Picasso.
966 **375** 680f. multicoloured . . . 2·00 1·25

376 Lions Club Emblem and Lions

1983. Air. Lions and Rotary Clubs. Mult.
967 700f. Type **376** . . . . 2·25 2·00
968 700f. Rotary Club emblem, container ship, diesel railcar and Boeing 737 airliner . . . . 6·75 2·25

377 Satellite, Antenna and Telephone

1983. World Communications Year.
969 **377** 180f. multicoloured . . . 55 30

378 Lavoisier and Apparatus

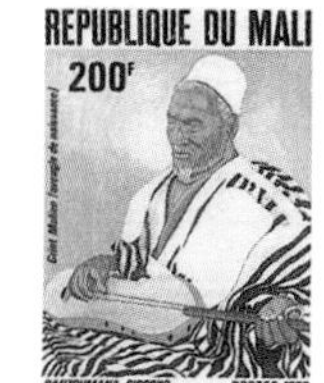

379 Banzoumana Sissoko

1983. Bicent of Lavoisier's Analysis of Water.
970 **378** 300f. green, brown & blue 1·10 50

1983. Mali Musicians. Multicoloured.
971 200f. Type **379** . . . . 1·00 30
972 300f. Batourou Sekou Kouyate . . . . 1·50 45

380 Nicephore Niepce and Camera

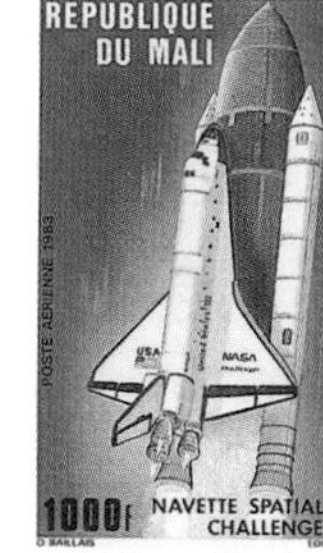

381 Space Shuttle "Challenger"

1983. 150th Death Anniv of Nicephore Niepce (pioneer of photography).
973 **380** 400f. blue, green & dp grn 1·75 65

1983. Air. Space Shuttle.
974 **381** 1000f. multicoloured . . . 3·25 1·75

382 Young People and Map of Africa

1983. 2nd Pan-African Youth Festival. Mult.
975 240f. Type **382** 75 40
976 270f. Hands reaching for map of Africa 75 40

383 Mercedes, 1914

1983. Air. Paris–Dakar Rally. Multicoloured.
977 240f. Type **383** . . . . . . 1·40 40
978 270f. Mercedes SSK, 1929 . . 1·50 50
979 500f. Mercedes W 196, 1954 2·50 80

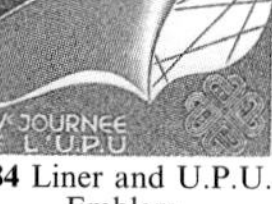

384 Liner and U.P.U. Emblem
385 Pawn and Bishop

1983. U.P.U. Day.
981 **384** 240f. red, black and blue 1·50 50

1983. Air. Chess Pieces.
982 **385** 300f. grey, violet and green . . . . 2·00 60
983 – 420f. green, pink and grey 2·50 85
984 – 500f. blue, dp blue & green . . . . 3·25 1·00
DESIGNS: 420f. Rook and knight; 500f. King and queen.

386 "Canigiani Madonna"

1983. Air. Christmas. 500th Birth Anniv of Raphael. Multicoloured.
986 700f. Type **386** . . . . 2·00 1·00
987 800f. "Madonna of the Lamb" . . . . 2·25 1·25

387 Sahara Goat

1984. Goats. Multicoloured.
988 20f. Type **387** 15 10
989 30f. Billy goat 20 10
990 50f. Billy goat (different) . . 25 15
991 240f. Kaarta goat . . . . . 1·00 40
992 350f. Southern goat . . . . 1·40 75

388 "Leopold Zborowski" (Modigliani)

1984. Air. Birth Centenary of Modigliani (painter).
993 **388** 700f. multicoloured . . . 2·75 1·25

389 Henri Dunant (founder of Red Cross)

390 Sidney Bechet

1984. Air. Celebrities.
994 **389** 400f. deep blue, red & blue . . . . 1·50 65
995 – 540f. deep blue, red & blue . . . . 1·60 85
DESIGN: 540f. Abraham Lincoln.

1984. Air. Jazz Musicians. Multicoloured.
996 470f. Type **390** . . . . 2·50 75
997 500f. Duke Ellington . . . . 2·50 80

391 Microlight Aircraft

1984. Air. Microlight Aircraft. Multicoloured.
998 270f. Type **391** . . . . . . 1·10 40
999 350f. Lazor Gemini motorized hang-glider . . . 1·40 55

392 Weightlifting

1984. Air. Olympic Games, Los Angeles. Multicoloured.
1000 265f. Type **392** 75 40
1001 440f. Show jumping 90 70
1002 500f. Hurdles . . . . 1·10 80

393 "Crucifixion" (Rubens)

1984. Air. Easter.
1004 **393** 940f. brown & dp brown 3·00 1·50
1005 – 970f. brown and red . . 3·00 1·50
DESIGN—HORIZ: 970f. "The Resurrection" (Mantegna).

1984. Currency revaluation. Various stamps surch. (i) U.P.U. Day (No. 981).
1006 **384** 120f. on 240f. red, black and blue (postage) . . 1·10 50

(ii) Goats (Nos. 988/92)
1007 **387** 10f. on 20f. mult 10 10
1008 – 15f. on 30f. mult 15 10
1009 – 25f. on 50f. mult 20 15
1010 – 125f. on 240f. mult . . . 95 40
1011 – 175f. on 350f. mult . . . 1·75 65

(iii) Paris–Dakar Rally (No. 977)
1012 **383** 120f. on 240f. mult (air) 1·25 40

395 Mercedes "Simplex"

1984. Air. 150th Birth Anniv of Gottlieb Daimler (motor car designer).
1035 **395** 350f. olive, blue and mauve . . . . 2·50 1·10
1036 – 470f. green, violet and plum . . . . 3·25 1·50
1037 – 485f. blue, violet and plum . . . . 3·50 1·75
DESIGNS: 470f. Mercedes-Benz Type "370 S"; 485f. Mercedes-Benz "500 S EC".

396 Farm Workers

1984. Progress in Countryside and Protected Essences. Multicoloured.
1038 5f. Type **396** 10 10
1039 90f. Carpentry 60 30
1040 100f. Tapestry making . . . 70 35
1041 135f. Metal work 80 40
1042 515f. "Borassus flabelifer" 3·25 1·90
1043 1225f. "Vitelaria paradoxa" 7·50 3·75

397 Emblem and Child

1984. United Nations Children's Fund.
1044 **397** 120f. red, brown and green 80 40
1045 – 135f. red, blue and brown 90 50
DESIGN: 135f. Emblem and two children.

398 U.P.U. Emblem, Anchor and Hamburg

1984. Universal Postal Union Congress, Hamburg.
1046 **398** 135f. mauve, green and blue 80 40

1984. Air. Olympic Winners, Los Angeles. No. 1000/1002 optd.
1047 135f. on 265f. Optd **HALTERES 56 KGS / 1. WU (CHINE). 2. LAI (CHINE). 3. KOTAKA (JAPON)** 80 40
1048 220f. on 440f. Optd **DRESSAGE / PAR EQUIPES / 1. RFA 2. SUISSE / 3. SUEDE** . . 1·10 75
1049 250f. on 500f. Optd **ATHLETISME 3000 METRES STEEPLE / 1. KORIR (KENYA). / 2. MAHMOUD (FRANCE). / 3. DIEMER (E-U)** . . . 1·40 1·00

400 Emblem

1984. 10th Anniv of Economic Community of West Africa.
1051 **400** 350f. multicoloured . . . 1·75 1·10

401 Dimetrodon

1984. Prehistoric Animals. Multicoloured.
1052 10f. Type **401** 15 15
1053 25f. Iguanodon (vert) . . . 25 15
1054 30f. Archaeopteryx (vert) . . 35 10
1055 120f. Type **401** . . . . . . 1·50 45
1056 175f. As No. 1053 . . . . . 1·75 70
1057 350f. As No. 1054 . . . . . 3·25 95
1058 470f. Triceratops . . . . . 5·00 2·50

402 "Virgin and Child between St. Joseph and St. Jerome" (detail, Lorenzo Lotto)

1984. Air. Christmas.
1059 **402** 500f. multicoloured . . . 3·00 1·60

1984. Drought Aid. No. 758 surch.
1060 **298** 470f. on 130f. mult . . . 2·75 1·75

404 Horse Galloping

405 "Clitocybe nebularis"

1985. Horses. Multicoloured.
1061 90f. Type **404** 70 35
1062 135f. Beledougou horse . . 1·25 40
1063 190f. Nara horse . . . . . 1·50 70
1064 530f. Trait horse . . . . . 4·50 2·00

1985. Fungi. Multicoloured.
1065 120f. Type **405** . . . . . . 1·75 65
1066 200f. "Lepiota cortinarius" 2·40 1·00
1067 485f. "Agaricus semotus" 6·00 2·40
1068 525f. "Lepiota procera" . . 6·50 2·75

406 Emile Marchoux and Marchoux Institute

1985. Health. Multicoloured.
1069 120f. Type **406** (World Lepers' Day and 40th anniv of Marchoux Institute) (postage) . . . 80 30
1070 135f. Lions' emblem and Samanto Village (15th anniv) 85 35
1071 470f. Laboratory technicians and polio victim (anti-polio campaign) (air) . . 3·50 1·50

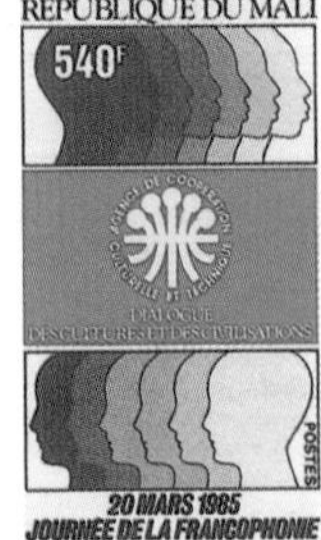
407 Profiles and Emblem

1985. 15th Anniv of Technical and Cultural Co-operation Agency.
1072 **407** 540f. green and brown 3·50 1·90

408 River Kingfisher

1985. Air. Birth Bicentenary of John J. Audubon (ornithologist). Multicoloured.
1073 180f. Type **408** . . . . . . 1·50 55
1074 300f. Great bustard (vert) 2·50 90
1075 470f. Ostrich (vert) . . . . 4·25 1·50
1076 540f. Ruppell's griffon . . . 4·50 2·00

409 National Pioneers Movement Emblem

1985. International Youth Year. Multicoloured.
1077 120f. Type **409** 80 40
1078 190f. Boy leading oxen . . . 1·40 70
1079 500f. Sports motifs and I.Y.Y. emblem . . . . . 3·50 1·75

410 Sud Aviation Caravelle, Boeing 727-200 and Agency Emblem

1985. Air. 25th Anniv of Aerial Navigation Security Agency for Africa and Madagascar (ASECNA).
1080 **410** 700f. multicoloured . . . 4·50 2·50

411 Lion, and Scouts collecting Wood

1985. Air. "Philexafrique" Stamp Exhibition, Lome. Multicoloured.
1081 200f. Type **411** . . . . . . 1·75 1·25
1082 200f. Satellite, dish aerial and globe . . . . 1·75 1·25

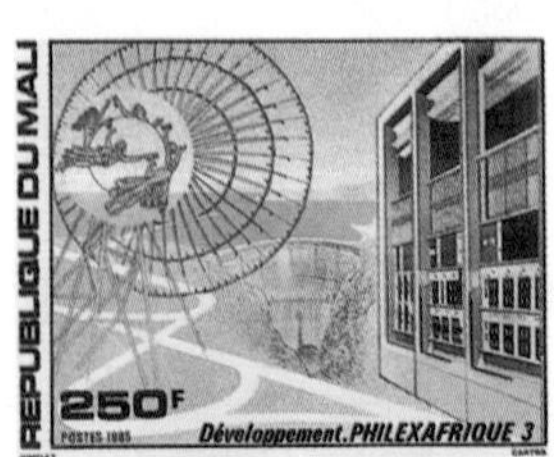
412 U.P.U. Emblem, Computer and Reservoir (Development)

1985. "Philexafrique" Stamp Exhibition, Lome, Togo (2nd issue). Multicoloured.
1083 250f. Type **412** . . . . . . 1·75 1·25
1084 250f. Satellite, girls writing and children learning from television (Youth) 1·75 1·25

413 Grey Cat

1986. Cats. Multicoloured.
1085 150f. Type **413** . . . . . . 1·50 60
1086 200f. White cat . . . . . . 2·25 80
1087 300f. Tabby cat . . . . . . 2·50 1·10

414 Hands releasing Doves and Globe

1986. Anti-apartheid Campaign. Multicoloured.
1088 100f. Type **414** 65 40
1089 120f. People breaking chain around world 85 50

415 Comet and Diagram of Orbit

1986. Air. Appearance of Halley's Comet.
1090 **415** 300f. multicoloured . . . 2·25 1·25

416 Internal Combustion Engine

1986. Air. Centenaries of First Motor Car with Internal Combustion Engine and Statue of Liberty. Multicoloured.
1091 400f. Type **416** . . . . . . 3·00 1·50
1092 600f. Head of statue, and French and American flags . . . . 4·00 2·25

417 Robeson

1986. Air. 10th Death Anniv of Paul Robeson (singer).
1093 **417** 500f. multicoloured . . . 4·00 2·00

418 Women tending Crop

1986. World Communications Day.
1094 **418** 200f. multicoloured . . . 1·50 80

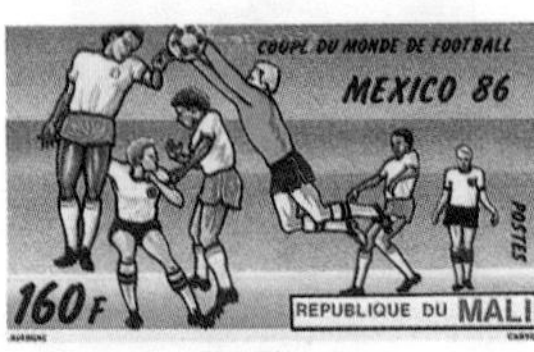
419 Players

1986. World Cup Football Championship, Mexico. Multicoloured.
1095 160f. Type **419** . . . . . . 1·40 65
1096 225f. Player capturing ball 1·90 90

420 Watt

1986. 250th Birth Anniv of James Watt (inventor).
1098 **420** 110f. multicoloured . . . 8·00 3·50

421 Eberth and Microscope

422 Chess Pieces on Board

1986. Air. 60th Death Anniv of Karl Eberth (discoverer of typhoid bacillus).
1099 **421** 550f. multicoloured . . . 4·00 1·90

1986. Air. World Chess Championship, London and Leningrad. Multicoloured.
1100 400f. Type **422** . . . . . . 3·75 1·75
1101 500f. Knight and board . . 4·75 2·25

1986. World Cup Winners. Nos. 1095/6 optd **ARGENTINE 3 R.F.A. 2**.
1102 160f. multicoloured . . . . 1·25 85
1103 225f. multicoloured . . . . 1·60 1·00

424 Head

1986. Endangered Animals. Giant Eland. Mult.
1105 5f. Type **424** 20 10
1106 20f. Standing by dead tree 40 10
1107 25f. Stepping over fallen branch 40 10
1108 200f. Mother and calf . . . 2·25 95

425 Mermoz and "Croix du Sud"

1986. Air. 50th Anniv of Disappearance of Jean Mermoz (aviator). Multicoloured.
1109 150f. Type **425** . . . . . . 1·25 60
1110 600f. CAMS 53 flying boat and monoplane . . . . . 4·25 2·25
1111 625f. Map and seaplane "Comte de la Vaulx" . . 4·50 2·50

1986. 10th Anniv of Concorde's First Commercial Flight. Nos. 674/6 surch **1986–10e Anniversaire du 1er Vol Commercial Supersonique**.
1112 175f. on 120f. Type **271** . . 1·40 80
1113 225f. on 130f. Concorde and Wright Flyer I . . . . . 1·75 1·00
1114 300f. on 200f. Concorde and Lindbergh's "Spirit of St. Louis" . . . . 2·75 1·50

427 Hansen and Follereau

1987. Air. 75th Death Anniv of Gerhard Hansen (discoverer of bacillus) and 10th Death Anniv of Raoul Follereau (leprosy pioneer).
1115 **427** 500f. multicoloured . . . 3·50 1·90

428 Model "A", 1903

1987. 40th Death Anniv of Henry Ford (motor car manufacturer). Multicoloured.

1116	150f. Type **428**	1·50	55
1117	200f. Model "T", 1923	2·00	75
1118	225f. "Thunderbird", 1968	2·00	95
1119	300f. "Continental", 1963	2·25	1·25

429 Konrad Adenauer **431** Scenes from "The Jazz Singer"

430 Runners and Buddha's Head

1987. Air. 20th Death Anniv of Konrad Adenauer (German statesman).

1120	**429** 625f. stone, brown and red	4·00	2·25

1987. Air. Olympic Games, Seoul (1988) (1st issue).

1121	**430** 400f. black and brown	2·00	1·40
1122	– 500f. dp green, grn & red	2·75	1·75

DESIGN: 500f. Footballers.

See also Nos. 1133/4.

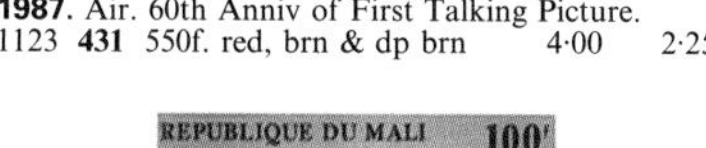

1987. Air. 60th Anniv of First Talking Picture.

1123	**431** 550f. red, brn & dp brn	4·00	2·25

432 "Apis florea"

1987. Bees. Multicoloured.

1124	100f. Type **432**	80	50
1125	150f. "Apis dorsata"	1·40	70
1126	175f. "Apis adonsonii"	1·60	80
1127	200f. "Apis mellifera"	1·75	1·00

433 Map, Dove and Luthuli

1987. Air. 20th Death Anniv of Albert John Luthuli (Nobel Peace Prize winner).

1128	**433** 400f. mauve, blue & brn	2·50	1·50

434 Profiles and Lions Emblem

1987. Air. Lions International and Rotary International. Multicoloured.

1129	500f. Type **434**	3·00	1·75
1130	500f. Clasped hands and Rotary emblem	3·00	1·75

435 Anniversary Emblem and Symbols of Activities

1988. 30th Anniv of Lions International in Mali.

1131	**435** 200f. multicoloured	1·25	75

436 Emblem and Doctor examining Boy

1988. 40th Anniv of W.H.O.

1132	**436** 150f. multicoloured	1·10	60

437 Coubertin and Ancient and Modern Athletes

1988. Air. Olympic Games, Seoul (2nd issue). 125th Birth Anniv of Pierre de Coubertin (founder of modern games). Multicoloured.

1133	240f. Type **437**	1·10	90
1134	400f. Stadium, Olympic rings and sports pictograms	1·90	1·40

438 "Harlequin"

1988. Air. 15th Death Anniv of Pablo Picasso (painter).

1135	**438** 600f. multicoloured	4·25	2·25

439 Concorde and Globe

1988. Air. 15th Anniv of First North Atlantic Crossing by Concorde.

1136	**439** 500f. multicoloured	4·00	2·00

440 Pres. Kennedy **442** Map

1988. 25th Death Anniv of John Fitzgerald Kennedy (American President).

1137	**440** 640f. multicoloured	4·00	2·40

1988. Mali Mission Hospital, Mopti. No. 1132 surch **MISSION MALI HOPITAL de MOPTI 300F** and **MEDECINS DU MONDE** emblem.

1138	**436** 300f. on 150f. mult	2·40	1·75

1988. 25th Anniv of Organization of African Unity.

1139	**442** 400f. multicoloured	2·50	1·25

443 Map, Leaf and Stove

1989. Air. "Improved Stoves: For a Green Mali". Multicoloured.

1140	5f. Type **443**	10	10
1141	10f. Tree and stove	10	10
1142	25f. Type **443**	15	10
1143	100f. As No. 1141	60	35

444 Astronauts on Moon

1989. Air. 20th Anniv of First Manned Moon Landing.

1144	**444** 300f. blue, purple & grn	2·00	1·25
1145	– 500f. purple, blue & brn	3·25	1·75

DESIGN: 500f. Astronauts on Moon (different).

445 Emblem and Crossed Syringes

1989. Vaccination Programme. Multicoloured.

1146	20f. Type **445**	15	10
1147	30f. Doctor vaccinating woman	20	10
1148	50f. Emblem and syringes	40	15
1149	175f. Doctor vaccinating child	1·40	65

446 Emblem

1989. 25th Anniv of International Law Institute of French-speaking Countries.

1150	**446** 150f. multicoloured	1·10	55
1151	200f. multicoloured	1·40	70

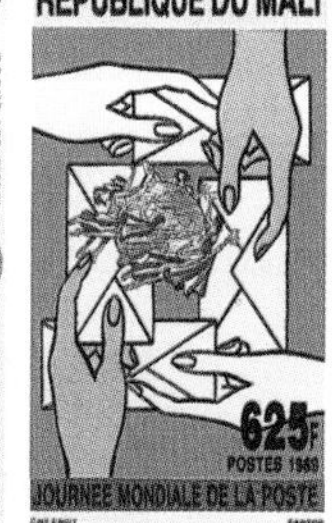

447 Crowd **448** U.P.U. Emblem and Hands holding Envelopes

1989. Air. Bicentenary of French Revolution and "Philexfrance 89" International Stamp Exn, Paris.

1152	**447** 400f. red, blue and purple	2·50	1·25
1153	– 600f. violet, pur & mve	3·50	2·00

DESIGN: 600f. Marianne and Storming of Bastille.

1989. World Post Day.

1154	**448** 625f. multicoloured	3·50	2·25

449 Pope and Cathedral

1990. Visit of Pope John Paul II.

1155	**449** 200f. multicoloured	1·60	80

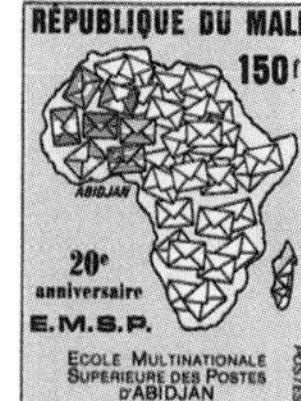

450 Envelopes on Map

1990. 20th Anniv of Multinational Postal Training School, Abidjan.

1156	**450** 150f. multicoloured	1·25	55

451 Footballers

1990. Air. World Cup Football Championship, Italy. Multicoloured.

1157	200f. Type **451**	1·50	75
1158	225f. Footballers (different)	1·75	85

1990. World Cup Result. Nos. 1157/8 optd. Mult.

1160	200f. **ITALIE : 2 / ANGLETERRE : 1**	1·50	85
1161	225f. **R.F.A. : 1 / ARGENTINE : 0**	1·75	85

453 Pres. Moussa Traore and Bamako Bridge

1990. 30th Anniv of Independence.

1163	**453** 400f. multicoloured	2·50	1·50

454 Man writing and Adults learning to Read **455** Woman carrying Water and Cattle at Well

1990. International Literacy Year.

1164	**454** 150f. multicoloured	1·25	55
1165	200f. multicoloured	1·50	75

1991. Lions Club (1166) and Rotary International (1167) Projects. Multicoloured.

1166	200f. Type **455** (6th anniv of wells project)	1·40	75
1167	200f. Bamako branch emblem and hand (30th anniv of anti-polio campaign)	1·40	75

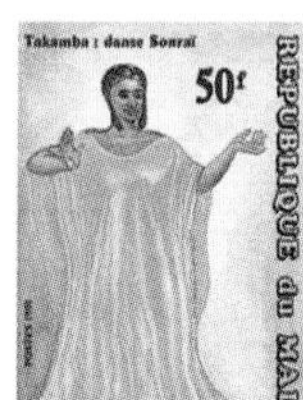

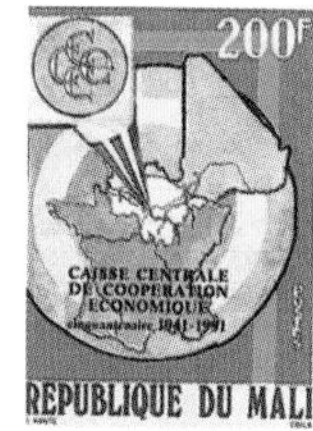

456 Sonrai Dance, Takamba **457** Bank Emblem and Map of France

1991. Dances. Multicoloured.

1168	50f. Type **456**	30	15
1169	100f. Malinke dance, Mandiani	60	30
1170	150f. Bamanan dance, Kono	90	50
1171	200f. Dogon dance, Songho	1·10	75

1991. 50th Anniv of Central Economic Co-operation Bank.

1172	**457** 200f. multicoloured	1·25	75

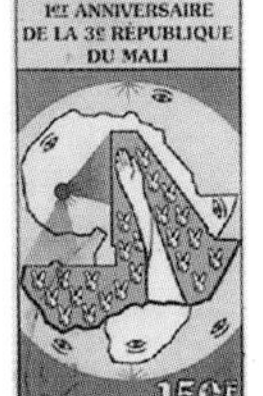
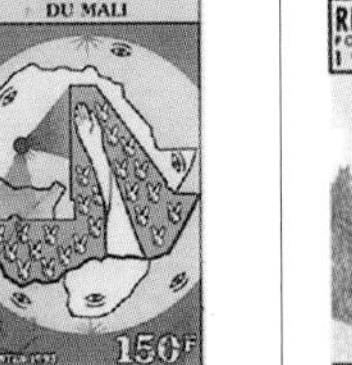

458 Women with Torch and Banner

461 Map of Africa

1992. National Women's Movement for the Safeguarding of Peace and National Unity.
1173 **458** 150f. multicoloured . . . 75 40

1992. Various stamps surch.
1174 – 25f. on 470f. mult (No. 1058) (postage) 15 10
1175 **420** 30f. on 110f. mult . . . 18·00 4·50
1176 – 50f. on 300f. mult (No. 1087) 25 15
1177 – 50f. on 1225f. mult (No. 1043) 25 15
1178 – 150f. on 135f. mult (No. 1070) 75 40
1179 – 150f. on 190f. mult (No. 1063) 75 40
1180 – 150f. on 190f. mult (No. 1078) 75 40
1181 **400** 150f. on 350f. mult . . . 75 40
1182 – 150f. on 485f. mult (No. 1067) . . . . . 1·25 50
1183 – 150f. on 525f. mult (No. 1068) . . . . . 1·25 50
1184 – 150f. on 530f. mult (No. 1064) 75 40
1185 **440** 200f. on 640f. mult . . . 1·00 50
1186 – 240f. on 350f. mult (No. 1057) . . . . . 1·90 1·40
1187 **448** 240f. on 625f. mult . . . 1·25 65
1188 **410** 20f. on 700f. mult (air) 10 10
1189 **415** 20f. on 300f. mult . . . 10 10
1190 – 25f. on 470f. mult (No. 1071) 15 10
1191 **408** 30f. on 180f. mult 15 10
1192 – 30f. on 500f. purple, blue and brown (No. 1145) 25 10
1193 – 100f. on 540f. mult (No. 1076) 80 50
1194 **438** 100f. on 600f. mult . . . 50 25
1195 **444** 150f. on 300f. blue, purple and green . . . 75 40
1196 **447** 150f. on 400f. red, blue and purple 75 40
1197 – 200f. on 300f. mult (No. 1074) . . . . . 1·60 1·00
1198 – 240f. on 600f. violet, purple and mauve (No. 1153) . . . . . 1·25 65

1992. (a) Postage. No. 1095 surch **150 f "Euro 92"**.
1199 **419** 150f. on 160f. mult . . . 75 40

(b) Air. No. 1134 surch **150F "Barcelone 92"**.
1200 150f. on 400f. multicoloured 75 40

1993. 1st Anniv of Third Republic.
1201 **461** 150f. multicoloured . . . 2·00 80

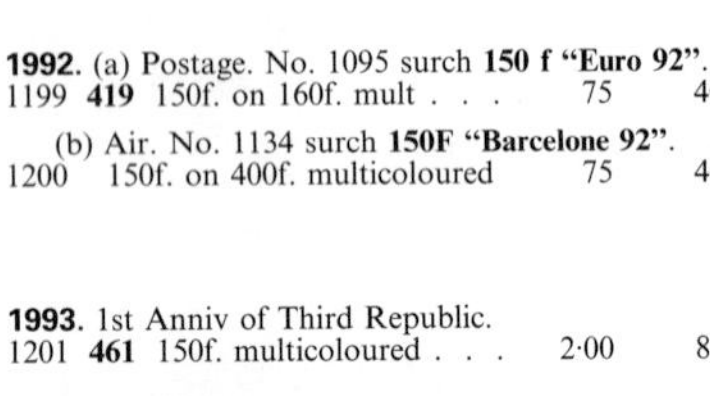

462 Blood, Memorial and Martyrs

463 Polio Victims

1993. 2nd Anniv of Martyrs' Day.
1203 **462** 150f. multicoloured . . . 70 35
1204 160f. multicoloured . . . 75 40

1993. Vaccination Campaign.
1205 **463** 150f. multicoloured . . . 2·00 1·00

464 Lecture on Problem Issues

1993. 35th Anniv of Lions International in Mali.
1207 **464** 200f. multicoloured . . . 90 45
1208 225f. multicoloured . . . 1·00 50

465 Place de la Liberte

466 Figure Skating

1993. Multicoloured, background colour of top panel given.
1209 **465** 20f. blue 10 10
1210 25f. yellow 10 10
1211 50f. pink 35 20
1212 100f. grey 65 20
1213 110f. yellow 65 35
1214 150f. green 90 35
1215 200f. yellow . . . . . . 1·40 55
1216 225f. flesh . . . . 1·40 65
1217 240f. lilac . . . . 1·75 65
1218 260f. lilac . . . . 1·75 65

1994. Winter Olympic Games, Lillehammer. Multicoloured.
1219 150f. Type **466** 35 20
1220 200f. Giant slalom 50 25
1221 225f. Ski jumping 55 30
1222 750f. Speed skating . . . . 1·75 90

467 Juan Schiaffino (Uruguay)

468 Scaphonyx

1994. World Cup Football Championship, U.S.A. Players from Different Teams. Multicoloured.
1224 200f. Type **467** 50 25
1225 240f. Diego Maradona (Argentine Republic) . . 60 30
1226 260f. Paolo Rossi (Italy) . . 65 35
1227 1000f. Franz Beckenbauer (Germany) . . . . 2·40 1·25

1994. Prehistoric Animals. Multicoloured.
1229 5f. Type **468** 10 10
1230 10f. Cynognathus 10 10
1231 15f. Lesothosaurus 10 10
1232 20f. Scutellosaurus 10 10
1233 25f. Ceratosaurus 10 10
1234 30f. Dilophosaurus 10 10
1235 40f. Dryosaurus 10 10
1236 50f. Heterodontosaurus . . 10 10
1237 60f. Anatosaurus 15 10
1238 70f. Saurornithoides 15 10
1239 80f. Avimimus 20 10
1240 90f. Saltasaurus 20 10
1241 300f. Dromaeosaurus . . . 75 40
1242 400f. Tsintaosaurus 95 50
1243 600f. Velociraptor . . . . . 1·50 75
1244 700f. Ouranosaurus . . . . 1·75 90

Nos. 1229/44 were issued together, se-tenant, forming a composite design.

469 "Sternuera castanea"

1994. Insects. Multicoloured.
1246 40f. Type **469** 20 10
1247 50f. "Eudicella gralli" (horiz) 20 10
1248 100f. "Homoderus mellyi" 35 15
1249 200f. "Kraussaria angulifera" (horiz) 60 25

470 Vaccinating Child

1994. Vaccination Campaign.
1250 **470** 150f. green and black . . 35 20
1251 200f. blue and black . . 50 25

471 Feral Rock Pigeons

1994. Birds. Multicoloured.
1252 25f. Type **471** 10 10
1253 30f. Helmeted guineafowl 10 10
1254 150f. South African crowned cranes (vert) 35 20
1255 200f. Red junglefowl (vert) 50 25

472 Family

473 Kirk Douglas in "Spartacus"

1994. International Year of the Family.
1256 **472** 200f. multicoloured . . . 50 25

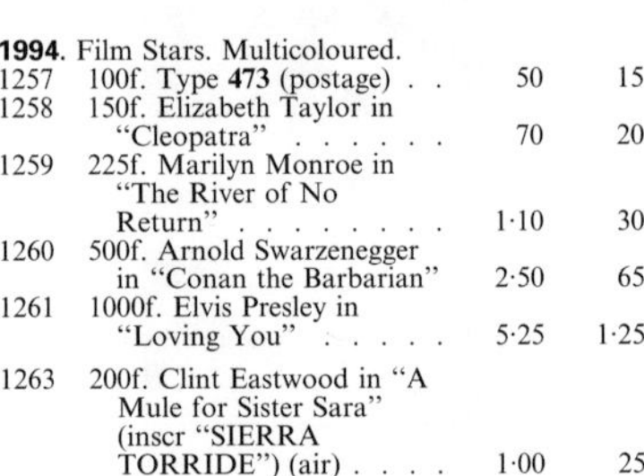

1994. Film Stars. Multicoloured.
1257 100f. Type **473** (postage) . . 50 15
1258 150f. Elizabeth Taylor in "Cleopatra" 70 20
1259 225f. Marilyn Monroe in "The River of No Return" . . . . 1·10 30
1260 500f. Arnold Swarzenegger in "Conan the Barbarian" 2·50 65
1261 1000f. Elvis Presley in "Loving You" . . . . . 5·25 1·25
1263 200f. Clint Eastwood in "A Mule for Sister Sara" (inscr "SIERRA TORRIDE") (air) . . . . 1·00 25

474 Ella Fitzgerald

1994. Jazz Singers. Multicoloured.
1264 200f. Type **474** 50 25
1265 225f. Lionel Hampton . . . 65 30
1266 240f. Sarah Vaughan . . . 75 30
1267 300f. Count Basie 90 40
1268 400f. Duke Ellington . . . 1·10 50
1269 600f. Miles Davis . . . . . 1·75 75

475 Soldiers caught in Explosion

1994. 50th Anniv of Second World War D-Day Landings. Multicoloured. (a) Villers-Bocage.
1271 200f. Type **475** 75 50
1272 200f. Tank (29 × 47 mm) . . 75 50
1273 200f. Troops beside tank . . 75 50

(b) Beaumont-sur-Sarthe.
1274 300f. Bombers and troops under fire . . . . 1·25 75
1275 300f. Bombers and tanks (29 × 47 mm) . . . . . . 1·25 75
1276 300f. Tank and soldier with machine gun . . . . . . 1·25 75

(c) Utah Beach (wrongly inscr "Utha").
1277 300f. Wounded troops and bow of boat . . . . . . 1·25 75
1278 300f. Troops in boat (29 × 47 mm) . . . . . . 1·25 75
1279 300f. Troops in boats . . . 1·25 75

(d) Air Battle.
1280 400f. Bombers . . . . 1·25 75
1281 400f. Aircraft (29 × 47 mm) 1·25 75
1282 400f. Airplane on fire . . . 1·25 75

(e) Sainte-Mere-Eglise.
1283 400f. Troops firing at paratrooper . . . . . . 1·25 75
1284 400f. Church and soldier (29 × 47 mm) . . . . . . 1·25 75
1285 400f. Paratroopers and German troops . . . . . 1·25 75

Nos. 1271/3, 1274/6, 1277/9, 1280/2 and 1283/5 respectively were issued together, se-tenant, forming composite designs.

476 Olympic Rings on National Flag

1994. Centenary of International Olympic Committee (1st issue).
1286 **476** 150f. multicoloured . . . 75 20
1287 200f. multicoloured . . . 1·25 25

See also Nos. 1342/5.

477 Couple holding Condoms

1994. Anti-AIDS Campaign. Multicoloured.
1288 150f. Type **477** 50 20
1289 225f. Nurse treating patient and laboratory worker . . 75 30

478 "Venus of Brassempoury"

1994. Ancient Art. Multicoloured.
1290 15f. Type **478** 10 10
1291 25f. Cave paintings, Tanum 10 10
1292 45f. Prehistoric men painting mural 10 10
1293 50f. Cave paintings, Lascaux (horiz) 10 10
1294 55f. Painting from tomb of Amonherkhopeshef . . . 15 10
1295 65f. God Anubis laying out Pharaoh (horiz) 15 10
1296 75f. Sphinx and pyramid, Mycerinus (horiz) 20 10
1297 85f. Bust of Nefertiti 20 10
1298 95f. Statue of Shibum . . . 25 15
1299 100f. Cavalry of Ur (horiz) 25 15
1300 130f. Head of Mesopotamian harp . . . 30 15
1301 135f. Mesopotamian tablet (horiz) 35 20
1302 140f. Assyrian dignitary . . 35 20
1303 180f. Enamel relief from Babylon (horiz) 45 25
1304 190f. Assyrians hunting . . 45 25
1305 200f. "Mona Lisa of Nimrod" 60 25
1306 225f. Phoenician coins (horiz) 65 30
1307 250f. Phoenician sphinx . . 70 30
1308 275f. Persian archer 75 35
1309 280f. Glass paste mask . . . 80 35

479 "Polyptychus roseus"

1994. Multicoloured. (a) Butterflies and Moths.
1310 20f. Type **479** 10 10
1311 30f. "Elymniopsis bammakoo" 10 10
1312 40f. Silver-striped hawk moth 20 10
1313 150f. Crimson-speckled moth 50 20
1314 180f. Foxy charaxes 60 25
1315 200f. Common dotted border 75 25

(b) Plants.
1316 25f. "Disa kewensis" 10 10
1317 50f. "Angraecum eburneum" 10 10
1318 100f. "Ansellia africana" 25 15
1319 140f. Sorghum 35 20
1320 150f. Onion 35 20
1321 190f. Maize 45 25
1322 200f. Clouded agaric 70 25
1323 225f. Parasol mushroom 75 30
1324 500f. "Lepiota aspera" 1·40 65

(c) Insects.
1325 225f. Goliath beetle 70 30
1326 240f. Cricket 75 30
1327 350f. Praying mantis 1·00 45

1994. Winter Olympic Games Medal Winners, Lillehammer. Nos. 1219/22 optd.
1328 150f. **O GRISHSHUK Y. PLATOV RUSSIE** 35 20
1329 150f. **Y. GORDEYEVA S. GRINKOV RUSSIE** 35 20
1330 200f. **M. WASMEIER ALLEMAGNE** 50 25
1331 200f. **D. COMPAGNONI ITALIE** 50 25
1332 225f. **T. WEISSFLOG ALLEMAGNE** 55 30
1333 225f. **E. BREDESEN NORVEGE** 55 30
1334 750f. **J.O. KOSS NORVEGE** 1·75 90
1335 750f. **B. BLAIR U.S.A.** 1·75 90

A sheetlet also exists containing Nos. 1219/22 each optd with both of the inscriptions for that value.

1994. Results of World Cup Football Championship. Nos. 1224/27 optd **1. BRESIL 2. ITALIE 3. SUEDE**.
1337 200f. multicoloured 80 25
1338 240f. multicoloured 90 30
1339 260f. multicoloured 95 35
1340 1000f. multicoloured 3·00 1·25

482 Pierre de Coubertin (founder) and Torchbearer

483 Statue and Village

1994. Centenary of International Olympic Committee (2nd issue). Multicoloured.
1342 225f. Type **482** 1·00 30
1343 240f. Coubertin designing Olympic rings 1·10 30
1344 300f. Athlete bearing torch and Coubertin (horiz) 1·40 40
1345 500f. Olympic rings and Coubertin at desk (horiz) 2·00 65

1994. 20th International Tourism Day. Multicoloured.
1347 150f. Type **483** 75 20
1348 200f. Sphinx, pyramids and Abu Simbel temple (horiz) 1·00 25

484 Reiner Klimker (dressage)

1995. Olympic Games, Atlanta (1996). Multicoloured.
1349 25f. Type **484** 10 10
1350 50f. Kristin Otto (swimming) 10 10
1351 100f. Gunther Winkler (show jumping) 30 10
1352 150f. Birgit Fischer-Schmidt (single kayak) 40 10
1353 200f. Nicole Uphoff (dressage) (vert) 60 20
1354 225f. Renate Stecher (athletics) (vert) 60 20
1355 230f. Michael Gross (swimming) 70 20
1356 240f. Karin Janz (gymnastics) 85 20
1357 550f. Anja Fichtel (fencing) (vert) 2·00 50
1358 700f. Heide Rosendahl-Ecker (long jump) (vert) 2·50 80

485 Ernst Opik, "Galileo" Probe, Shoemaker-Levy Comet and Jupiter

1995. Anniversaries and Events. Multicoloured.
1359 150f. Type **485** 40 10
1360 200f. Clyde Tombaugh (discoverer of Pluto, 1930) and "Pluto" probe 75 20
1361 500f. Henri Dunant (founder of Red Cross) 1·50 40
1362 650f. Astronauts and lunar rover (first manned moon landing, 1969) 2·00 40
1363 700f. Emblems of Lions International and Rotary International and child drinking from pump 3·00 40
1364 800f. Gary Kasparov (world chess champion, 1993) 4·50 50

486 Agriculture and Fishing (regional integration)

1995. 20th Anniv of Economic Community of West African States. Multicoloured.
1365 150f. Type **486** 50 20
1366 200f. Emblem and handshake (co-operation) (vert) 75 20
1367 220f. Emblem and banknotes (proposed common currency) 90 30
1368 225f. Emblem and doves (peace and security) 1·10 30

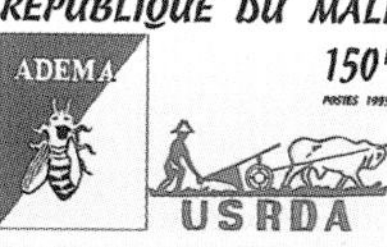

487 Emblems of Alliance for Democracy in Mali and Sudanese Union-RDA

1995. 3rd Anniv of New Constitution. Multicoloured.
1369 150f. Type **487** (second round of Presidential election) 40 20
1370 200f. President Alpha Oumar Konare (vert) 50 20
1371 225f. Emblems of competing parties (first round of Presidential election) 60 30
1372 240f. Map, flag and initials of parties (multi-party democracy) (vert) 70 30

488 Scout and Viennese Emperor Moth

1995. Scout Jamboree, Netherlands. Designs showing scouts and insects or fungi. Multicoloured.
1373 150f. Type **488** 40 10
1374 225f. Brimstone 60 20
1375 240f. Fig-tree blue 70 20
1376 500f. Clouded agaric 1·75 40
1377 650f. "Agaricus semotus" 2·00 50
1378 725f. Parasol mushroom 2·25 60

489 Paul Harris (founder) and Emblem

490 Imperial Woodpecker ("Campephilus imperialis")

1995. 90th Anniv of Rotary International.
1380 **489** 1000f. multicoloured 5·00 1·25

1995. Birds and Butterflies. Multicoloured.
1382 50f. Type **490** 10 10
1383 50f. Blue-crowned motmot ("Momotus momota") 10 10
1384 50f. Keel-billed toucan ("Ramphastos sulfuratus") 10 10
1385 50f. Blue-breasted kingfisher ("Halycon malimbica") 10 10
1386 50f. Streamertail ("Trochilus polytmus") 10 10
1387 50f. Common cardinal ("Cardinalis cardinalis") 10 10
1388 50f. Resplendent quetzal ("Pharomachrus mocinno") 10 10
1389 50f. Sun conure ("Aratinga solstitialis") 10 10
1390 50f. Red-necked amazon ("Amazona arausiaca") 10 10
1391 50f. Scarlet ibis ("Eudocimus ruber") 10 10
1392 50f. Red siskin ("Carduelis cucullatus") 10 10
1393 50f. Hyacinth macaw ("Anodorhynchus hyacinthinus") 10 10
1394 50f. Orange-breasted bunting ("Passerina leclancherii") 10 10
1395 50f. Red-capped manakin ("Pipra mentalis") 10 10
1396 50f. Guianan cock of the rock ("Rupicola rupicola") 10 10
1397 50f. Saffron finch ("Sicalis flaveola") 10 10
1398 100f. Black-spotted barbet ("Capito niger") 40 10
1399 100f. Amazon kingfisher ("Chloroceryle amazona") 40 10
1400 100f. Swallow tanager ("Tersina viridis") 40 10
1401 100f. Blue-crowned motmot ("Momotus momota") 40 10
1402 100f. Crimson-crested woodpecker ("Campephilus melanoleucos") 40 10
1403 100f. Red-breasted blackbird ("Leistes militaris") 40 10
1404 100f. King vulture ("Sarcorhamphus papa") 40 10
1405 100f. Capped heron ("Pilherodius pileatus") 40 10
1406 100f. Black-tailed tityra ("Tityra cayana") 40 10
1407 100f. Paradise tanager ("Tangara chilinsis") 40 10
1408 100f. Yellow-crowned amazon ("Amazona ochrocephala") 40 10
1409 100f. Buff-throated saltator ("Saltator maximus") 40 10
1410 100f. Red-cowled cardinal ("Paroaria dominicana") 40 10
1411 100f. Louisiana heron ("Egretta tricolor") 40 10
1412 100f. Black-bellied cuckoo ("Piaya melanogaster") 40 10
1413 100f. Barred antshrike ("Thamnophilus doliatus") 40 10

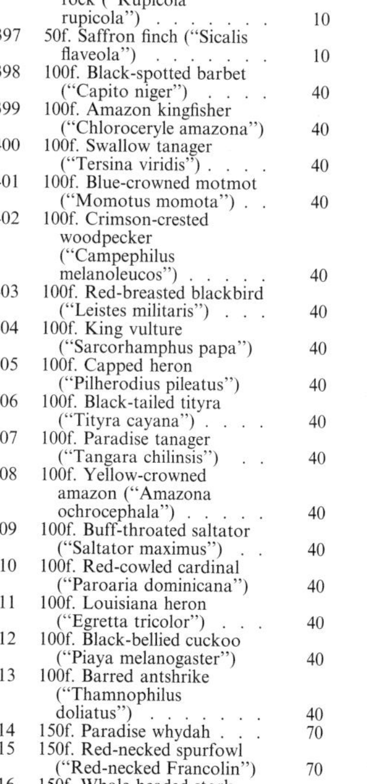

1414 150f. Paradise whydah 70 10
1415 150f. Red-necked spurfowl ("Red-necked Francolin") 70 10
1416 150f. Whale-headed stork (inscr "Shoebill") 70 10
1417 150f. Ruff 70 10
1418 150f. Marabou stork 70 10
1419 150f. Eastern white pelican ("White Pelican") 70 10
1420 150f. Western curlew 70 10
1421 150f. Scarlet ibis 70 10
1422 150f. Great crested grebe 70 10
1423 150f. White spoonbill 70 10
1424 150f. African jacana 70 10
1425 150f. African pygmy goose 70 10
1426 200f. Ruby-throated hummingbird 85 15
1427 200f. Grape shoemaker and blue morpho butterflies 85 15
1428 200f. Northern hobby 85 15
1429 200f. Black-mandibled toucan ("Cuvier Toucan") 85 15
1430 200f. Black-necked red cotinga and green-winged macaw 85 15
1431 200f. Green-winged macaws and blue and yellow macaw 85 15
1432 200f. Greater flamingo ("Flamingo") 85 15
1433 200f. Malachite kingfisher 85 15
1434 200f. Bushy-crested hornbill 85 15
1435 200f. Purple swamphen 85 15
1436 200f. Striped body 85 15
1437 200f. Painted lady 85 15

Stamps of the same value were issued together, in se-tenant sheetlets, each sheetlet forming a composite design.

491 Emblem and Scales of Justice

1995. 50th Anniv of U.N.O. Multicoloured.
1439 20f. Type **491** 10 10
1440 170f. Type **491** 70 30
1441 225f. Emblem, doves and men with linked arms (horiz) 80 30
1442 240f. As No. 1441 1·00 50

492 Food Jar

1995. Cooking Utensils. Multicoloured.
1443 5f. Type **492** 20 10
1444 50f. Pestle and mortar 20 10
1445 150f. Bowl (horiz) 1·00 10
1446 200f. Grain sack 1·10 15

493 Lennon

1995. 15th Death Anniv of John Lennon (musician).
1448 **493** 150f. multicoloured 2·50 10

494 George Barnes

1995. 40th Anniv of Rock Music (1461/6) and Centenary of Motion Pictures (others). Multicoloured. (a) Actors in Western Films.
1449 150f. Type **494** 80 40
1450 150f. William S. Hart 80 40
1451 150f. Tom Mix 80 40
1452 150f. Wallace Beery 80 40
1453 150f. Gary Cooper 80 40
1454 150f. John Wayne 80 40

(b) Leading Ladies and their Directors.
1455 200f. Marlene Dietrich and Josef von Sternberg ("The Blue Angel") 1·00 70
1456 200f. Jean Harlow and George Cukor ("Dinner at Eight") 1·00 70
1457 200f. Mary Astor and John Houston ("The Maltese Falcon") 1·00 70
1458 200f. Ingrid Bergman and Alfred Hitchcock ("Spellbound") 1·00 70
1459 200f. Claudette Colbert and Cecil B. de Mille ("Cleopatra") 1·00 70
1460 200f. Marilyn Monroe and Billy Wilder ("Some Like it Hot") 1·00 70

(c) Female Singers.
1461 225f. Connie Francis 1·25 70
1462 225f. The Ronettes 1·25 70
1463 225f. Janis Joplin 1·25 70
1464 225f. Debbie Harry 1·25 70

No.	Type	Description	Mint	Used
1465		225f. Cyndi Lauper	1·25	70
1466		225f. Carly Simon	1·25	70
		(d) Musicals.		
1467		240f. Gene Kelly in "Singin' in the Rain"	1·25	70
1468		240f. Cyd Charisse and Fred Astaire in "The Bandwagon"	1·25	70
1469		240f. Liza Minelli in "Cabaret"	1·25	70
1470		240f. Julie Andrews in "The Sound of Music"	1·25	70
1471		240f. Ginger Rogers and Fred Astaire in "Top Hat"	1·25	70
1472		240f. John Travolta and Karen Lynn Gorney in "Saturday Night Fever"	1·25	70

495 Charles de Gaulle (French statesman, 25th death anniv)

1995. Anniversaries. Multicoloured.

No.	Type	Description	Mint	Used
1474		150f. Type **495**	50	20
1475		200f. General de Gaulle (50th anniv of liberation of France)	70	20
1476		240f. Enzo Ferrari (car designer, 7th death anniv)	75	30
1477		500f. Ayrton Senna (racing driver, 1st death anniv)	1·50	20
1478		650f. Paul Emile Victor (explorer, 88th birthday)	2·25	30
1479		725f. Paul Harris (founder, 90th anniv of Rotary International)	3·50	40
1480		740f. Michael Schumacher (racing driver, 26th birth anniv) (wrongly dated "1970")	3·50	40
1481		1000f. Jerry Garcia (popular singer, death commemoration)	4·00	50

OFFICIAL STAMPS

O 9 Dogon Mask

O 30 Mali Flag and Emblems

1961.

No.	Type	Description	Mint	Used
O26	O 9	1f. violet	10	10
O27		2f. red	10	10
O28		3f. slate	10	10
O29		5f. turquoise	15	15
O30		10f. brown	20	15
O31		25f. blue	35	15
O32		30f. red	40	20
O33		50f. myrtle	70	25
O34		85f. purple	1·10	65
O35		100f. green	1·40	65
O36		200f. purple	2·75	1·40

1964. Centre and flag mult; frame colour given.

No.	Type	Description	Mint	Used
O 90	O 30	1f. green	10	10
O 91		2f. lavender	10	10
O 92		3f. slate	10	10
O 93		5f. purple	10	10
O 94		10f. blue	15	10
O 95		25f. ochre	20	15
O 96		30f. green	25	15
O 97		50f. orange	35	15
O 98		85f. brown	50	20
O 99		100f. red	65	30
O100		200f. blue	1·50	60

O 341 Arms of Gao

1981. Town Arms. Multicoloured.

No.	Type	Description	Mint	Used
O878		5f. Type O **341**	10	10
O879		15f. Tombouctou	10	10
O880		50f. Mopti	20	10
O881		180f. Segou	60	30
O882		200f. Sikasso	80	30
O883		680f. Koulikoro	2·50	95
O884		700f. Kayes	2·75	1·25
O885		1000f. Bamako	4·00	1·50

1984. Nos. O878/85 surch.

No.	Type	Description	Mint	Used
O1013		15f. on 5f. Type O **341**	15	10
O1014		50f. on 15f. Tombouctou	30	15
O1015		120f. on 50f. Mopti	70	25
O1016		295f. on 180f. Segou	2·00	90
O1017		470f. on 200f. Sikasso	3·00	1·50
O1018		515f. on 680f. Koulikoro	3·50	1·90
O1019		845f. on 700f. Kayes	6·00	2·50
O1020		1225f. on 1000f. Bamako	7·50	3·75

POSTAGE DUE STAMPS

D 9 Bambara Mask

1961.

No.	Type	Description	Mint	Used
D26	D 9	1f. black	10	10
D27		2f. blue	10	10
D28		5f. mauve	20	10
D29		10f. orange	25	15
D30		20f. turquoise	50	25
D31		25f. purple	65	30

D 28 "Polyptychus roseus"

1964. Butterflies and Moths. Multicoloured.

No.	Type	Description	Mint	Used
D83		1f. Type D **28**	10	10
D84		1f. "Deilephila nerii"	10	10
D85		2f. "Bunaea alcinoe"	15	15
D86		2f. "Gynanisa maja"	15	15
D87		3f. "Teracolus eris"	35	30
D88		3f. "Colotis antevippe"	35	30
D89		5f. "Manatha microcera"	35	30
D90		5f. "Charaxes epijasius"	35	30
D91		10f. "Hypokopelates otraeda"	45	35
D92		10f. "Lipaphnaeus leonina"	45	35
D93		20f. "Lobobunaea christyi"	75	70
D94		20f. "Gonimbrasia hecate"	75	70
D95		25f. "Hypolimnas misippus"	1·10	90
D96		25f. "Castopsilia florella"	1·10	90

1984. Nos. D83/96 surch.

No.	Type	Description	Mint	Used
D1021		5f. on 1f. Type D **28**	10	10
D1022		5f. on 1f. "Deilephila nerii"	10	10
D1023		10f. on 2f. "Bunaea alcinoe"	10	10
D1024		10f. on 2f. "Gynanisa maja"	10	10
D1025		15f. on 3f. "Teracolus eris"	15	10
D1026		15f. on 3f. "Colotis antevippe"	15	10
D1027		25f. on 5f. "Manatha microcera"	15	15
D1028		25f. on 5f. "Charaxes epijasius"	15	15
D1029		50f. on 10f. "Hypokopelates otraeda"	30	30
D1030		50f. on 10f. "Lipaphnaeus leonina"	30	30
D1031		100f. on 20f. "Lobobunaea christyi"	60	60
D1032		100f. on 20f. "Gonimbrasia hecate"	60	60
D1033		125f. on 25f. "Hypolimnas misippus"	75	75
D1034		125f. on 25f. "Catopsilia florella"	75	75

APPENDIX

The following stamps have either been issued in excess of postal needs or have not been available to the public in reasonable quantities at face value. Such stamps may later be given full listing if there is evidence of regular postal use.

All on gold foil.

1994.

World Cup Football Championship, U.S.A. Air. 3000f.

Film Stars. Air 3000f.

MALTA Pt. 1

An island in the Mediterranean Sea, south of Italy. After a period of self-government under various Constitutions, independence was attained on 21 September 1964. The island became a republic on 13 December 1974.

1860. 12 pence = 1 shilling;
20 shillings = 1 pound.
1972. 10 mils = 1 cent;
100 cents = M£1.

1 5

1860. Various frames.

No.	Type	Description	Mint	Used
18	1	½d. yellow	35·00	35·00
20		½d. green	2·25	50
22	–	1d. red	3·50	35
23	–	2d. grey	5·00	1·50
26	–	2½d. blue	35·00	1·00
27	–	4d. brown	11·00	3·00
28	–	1s. violet	35·00	9·00
30	5	5s. red	£110	80·00

6 Harbour of Valletta

7 Gozo Fishing Boat

8 Ancient Maltese Galley

9 Emblematic Figure of Malta

10 Shipwreck of St. Paul

12

1899.

No.	Type	Description	Mint	Used
31a	6	¼d. brown	1·50	40
79		4d. black	15·00	3·25
32	7	4½d. brown	16·00	10·00
58		4½d. orange	4·50	3·50
59	8	5d. red	26·00	5·00
60		5d. green	4·25	3·50
34	9	2s.6d. olive	40·00	12·00
35	10	10s. black	90·00	65·00

1902. No. 26 surch **One Penny**.

No.	Type	Description	Mint	Used
36		1d. on 2½d. blue	1·00	1·25

1903.

No.	Type	Description	Mint	Used
47b	12	½d. green	40·00	10
48		1d. black and red	16·00	20
49		1d. red	2·25	10
50		2d. purple and grey	8·00	2·25
51		2d. grey	3·25	5·50
52		2½d. purple and blue	16·00	60
53		2½d. blue	5·50	2·75
42		3d. grey and purple	1·75	50
54		4d. black and brown	11·00	5·50
55		4d. black and red on yellow	4·00	3·50
44		1s. grey and violet	16·00	7·00
62		1s. black on green	7·50	2·75
63		5s. green and red on yellow	65·00	75·00

13 15

17 18

1914.

No.	Type	Description	Mint	Used
69	13	¼d. brown	1·00	10
71		½d. green	2·25	30
73		1d. red	1·50	10
75		2d. grey	8·00	3·25
77		2½d. blue	2·25	50
78		3d. purple on yellow	2·50	8·00
80		6d. purple	11·00	17·00
81a		1s. black on green	12·00	14·00
86	15	2s. purple and blue on blue	50·00	30·00
88		5s. green and red on yellow	80·00	95·00
104	17	10s. black	£325	£600

1918. Optd **WAR TAX**.

No.	Type	Description	Mint	Used
92	13	½d. green	1·50	15
93	12	3d. grey and purple	1·75	7·50

1921.

No.	Type	Description	Mint	Used
100	18	2d. grey	4·25	1·75

1922. Optd **SELF-GOVERNMENT**.

No.	Type	Description	Mint	Used
114	13	¼d. brown	30	75
106		½d. green	1·00	1·75
116		1d. red	1·00	20
117	18	2d. grey	2·25	45
118	13	2½d. blue	1·10	1·00
108		3d. purple on yellow	2·75	16·00
109		6d. purple	2·50	16·00
110		1s. black on green	3·50	16·00
120	15	2s. purple and blue on blue	40·00	85·00
112	9	2s.6d. olive	22·00	45·00
113	15	5s. green and red on yellow	50·00	80·00
105	10	10s. black	£190	£350
121	17	10s. black	£130	£190

1922. Surch **One Farthing**.

No.	Type	Description	Mint	Used
122	18	¼d. on 2d. grey	85	30

22 23

1922.

No.	Type	Description	Mint	Used
123	22	¼d. brown	2·25	60
124		½d. green	2·25	15
125		1d. orange and purple	3·00	20
126		1d. violet	3·00	80
127		1½d. red	3·75	15
128		2d. brown and blue	2·75	1·25
129		2½d. blue	2·50	7·00
130		3d. blue	3·50	1·25
131		3d. black on yellow	2·75	13·00
132		4d. yellow and blue	1·75	2·25
133		6d. green and violet	3·25	2·25
134	23	1s. blue and brown	6·00	2·50
135		2s. brown and blue	9·50	9·00
136		2s.6d. purple and black	10·00	15·00
137		5s. orange and blue	21·00	40·00
138		10s. grey and brown	55·00	£150
140	22	£1 black and red	90·00	£275

1925. Surch **Two pence halfpenny**.

No.	Type	Description	Mint	Used
141	22	2½d. on 3d. blue	1·75	3·50

1926. Optd **POSTAGE**.

No.	Type	Description	Mint	Used
143	22	¼d. brown	70	3·75
144		½d. green	70	15
145		1d. violet	1·00	25
146		1½d. red	1·00	60
147		2d. brown and blue	75	80
148		2½d. blue	1·25	80
149		3d. black on yellow	75	80
150		4d. yellow and blue	6·50	16·00
151		6d. green and violet	2·75	3·25
152	23	1s. blue and brown	5·50	10·00
153		2s. brown and blue	50·00	£140
154		2s.6d. purple and black	12·00	32·00
155		5s. orange and blue	9·00	32·00
156		10s. grey and brown	7·00	17·00

26

27 Valletta Harbour

28 St. Publius

1926. Inscr "POSTAGE".
157 **26** ¼d. brown 80 15
158 ½d. green 60 15
159 1d. red 3·00 90
160 1½d. brown 2·00 10
161 2d. grey 4·50 9·00
162 2½d. blue 4·00 1·00
162a 3d. violet 4·25 2·50
163 4d. black and red 3·25 9·00
164 4½d. violet and yellow 3·50 2·75
165 6d. violet and red 4·25 3·50
166 **27** 1s. black 6·50 4·00
167 **28** 1s.6d. black and green 6·50 13·00
168 – 2s. black and purple 6·50 15·00
169 – 2s.6d. black and red 15·00 48·00
170 – 3s. black and blue 17·00 30·00
171 – 5s. black and green 22·00 60·00
172 – 10s. black and red 55·00 £100
DESIGNS—As Type **27**: 2s. Mdina (Notabile); 5s. Neolithic temple, Mnajdra. As Type **28**: 2s.6d. Gozo boat; 3s. Neptune; 10s. St. Paul.

1928. Air. Optd **AIR MAIL**.
173 **26** 6d. violet and red 1·75 1·00

1928. Optd **POSTAGE AND REVENUE**.
174 **26** ¼d. brown 1·50 10
175 ½d. green 1·50 10
176 1d. red 1·75 3·25
177 1d. brown 4·50 10
178 1½d. brown 2·00 85
179 1½d. red 4·25 10
180 2d. grey 4·25 9·00
181 2½d. blue 2·00 10
182 3d. violet 2·00 80
183 4d. black and red 2·00 1·75
184 4½d. violet and yellow 2·25 1·00
185 6d. violet and red 2·25 1·50
186 **27** 1s. black 5·50 2·50
187 **28** 1s.6d. black and green 6·50 9·50
188 – 2s. black and purple 24·00 50·00
189 – 2s.6d. black and red 17·00 23·00
190 – 3s. black and blue 19·00 30·00
191 – 5s. black and green 29·00 65·00
192 – 10s. black and red 55·00 90·00

1930. As Nos. 157/72, but inscr "POSTAGE & REVENUE".
193 ¼d. brown 60 10
194 ½d. green 60 10
195 1d. brown 60 10
196 1½d. red 70 10
197 2d. grey 1·25 50
198 2½d. blue 2·00 10
199 3d. violet 1·50 20
200 4d. black and red 1·25 4·00
201 4½d. violet and yellow 3·25 1·25
202 6d. violet and red 2·75 1·25
203 1s. black 10·00 14·00
204 1s.6d. black and green 8·50 19·00
205 2s. black and purple 10·00 19·00
206 2s.6d. black and red 17·00 48·00
207 3s. black and blue 26·00 55·00
208 5s. black and green 32·00 65·00
209 10s. black and red 70·00 £150

1935. Silver Jubilee. As T **14a** of Kenya, Uganda and Tanganyika.
210 ½d. black and green 50 50
211 2½d. brown and blue 2·50 4·50
212 6d. blue and olive 7·00 4·50
213 1s. grey and purple 11·00 16·00

1937. Coronation. As T **14b** of Kenya, Uganda and Tanganyika.
214 ½d. green 10 10
215 1½d. red 1·00 50
216 2½d. blue 90 60

37 Grand Harbour, Valletta

38 H.M.S. "St. Angelo"

39 Verdala Palace

1938. Various designs with medallion King George VI.
217 **37** ¼d. brown 10 10
218 **38** ½d. green 1·75 30
218a ½d. brown 55 30
219 **39** 1d. brown 4·25 40
219a 1d. green 60 10
220 – 1½d. red 1·00 30
220b – 1½d. black 30 15
221 – 2d. black 40 2·00
221a – 2d. red 40 30
222 – 2½d. blue 75 60
222a – 2½d. violet 60 10
223 – 3d. violet 55 80
223a – 3d. blue 30 20
224 – 4½d. olive and brown 50 30
225 – 6d. olive and red 75 30
226 – 1s. black 75 30
227 – 1s.6d. black and olive 7·00 4·00
228 – 2s. green and blue 4·50 4·00
229 – 2s.6d. black and red 8·00 5·50
230 – 5s. black and green 4·50 6·50
231 – 10s. black and red 15·00 15·00
DESIGNS—As Types **38/9**. VERT: 1½d. Hypogeum, Hal Saflieni; 3d. St. John's Co-Cathedral; 6d. Statue of Manoel de Vilhena; 1s. Maltese girl wearing faldetta; 5s. Palace Square, Valletta; 10s. St. Paul. HORIZ: 2d. Victoria and Citadel, Gozo; 2½d. De l'Isle Adam entering Mdina; 4½d. Ruins at Mnajdra; 1s.6d. St. Publius; 2s. Mdina Cathedral; 2s.6d. Statue of Neptune.

1946. Victory. As T **4a** of Pitcairn Islands.
232 1d. green 15 10
233 3d. blue 30 70

1948. Self-government. As 1938 issue optd **SELF-GOVERNMENT 1947**.
234 ¼d. brown 30 20
235 ½d. brown 30 10
236 1d. green 30 10
236a 1d. grey 30 10
237 1½d. black 1·25 10
237b 1½d. green 30 10
238 2d. red 1·25 10
238b 2d. yellow 30 10
239 2½d. violet 80 10
239a 2½d. red 50 1·50
240 3d. blue 1·00 15
240a 3d. violet 50 15
241 4½d. olive and brown 2·00 1·50
241a 4½d. olive and blue 50 90
242 6d. olive and red 2·50 15
243 1s. black 2·50 40
244 1s.6d. black and olive 2·50 50
245 2s. green and blue 5·00 2·50
246 2s.6d. black and red 12·00 2·50
247 5s. black and green 18·00 3·50
248 10s. black and red 18·00 22·00

1949. Silver Wedding. As T **4b/c** of Pitcairn Islands.
249 1d. green 50 10
250 £1 blue 38·00 35·00

1949. U.P.U. As T **4d/g** of Pitcairn Islands.
251 2½d. violet 30 10
252 3d. blue 2·75 60
253 6d. red 50 60
254 1s. black 50 2·25

53 Queen Elizabeth II when Princess

54 "Our Lady of Mount Carmel" (attrib Palladino)

1950. Visit of Princess Elizabeth.
255 **53** 1d. green 10 10
256 3d. blue 20 20
257 1s. black 55 1·10

1951. 7th Centenary of the Scapular.
258 **54** 1d. green 10 10
259 3d. violet 40 10
260 1s. black 90 75

1953. Coronation. As T **4h** of Pitcairn Islands.
261 1½d. black and green 50 10

55 St. John's Co-Cathedral

56 "Immaculate Conception" (Caruana) (altar-piece, Cospicua)

1954. Royal Visit.
262 **55** 3d. violet 30 10

1954. Centenary of Dogma of the Immaculate Conception.
263 **56** 1½d. green 10 10
264 3d. blue 10 10
265 1s. grey 35 20

57 Monument of the Great Siege, 1565

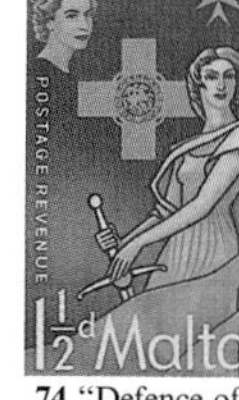
74 "Defence of Malta"

1956.
266 **57** ¼d. violet 20 10
267 – ½d. orange 50 10
314 – 1d. black 50 30
269 – 1½d. green 30 10
270 – 2d. sepia 1·50 10
271 – 2½d. brown 1·00 30
272 – 3d. red 1·50 10
273 – 4½d. blue 2·25 20
274 – 6d. blue 75 10
275 – 8d. ochre 3·00 1·00
276 – 1s. violet 1·00 10
277 – 1s.6d. turquoise 12·00 20
278 – 2s. olive 12·00 2·00
279 – 2s.6d. brown 8·00 2·25
280 – 5s. green 15·00 2·75
281 – 10s. red 38·00 11·00
282 – £1 brown 38·00 24·00
DESIGNS—VERT: ½d. Wignacourt aqueduct horsetrough; 1d. Victory church; 1½d. Second World War memorial; 2d. Mosta Church; 3d. The King's Scroll; 4½d. Roosevelt's Scroll; 8d. Vedette (tower); 1s. Mdina Gate; 1s.6d. "Les Gavroches" (statue); 2s. Monument of Christ the King; 2s.6d. Monument of Grand Master Cottoner; 5s. Grand Master Perellos's monument; 10s. St. Paul (statue); £1 Baptism of Christ (statue). HORIZ: 2½d. Auberge de Castile; 6d. Neolithic Temples at Tarxien.

1957. George Cross Commem. Cross in Silver.
283 **74** 1½d. green 15 10
284 – 3d. red 15 10
285 – 1s. brown 15 10
DESIGNS—HORIZ: 3d. Searchlights over Malta. VERT: 1s. Bombed buildings.

77 Design

81 Sea Raid on Grand Harbour, Valletta

1958. Technical Education in Malta. Inscr "TECHNICAL EDUCATION".
286 **77** 1½d. black and green 10 10
287 – 3d. black, red and grey 10 10
288 – 1s. grey, purple and black 15 10
DESIGNS—VERT: 3d. "Construction". HORIZ: 1s. Technical School, Paola.

1958. George Cross Commem. Cross in first colour outlined in silver.
289 – 1½d. green and black 15 10
290 **81** 3d. red and black 15 10
291 – 1s. mauve and black 15 10
DESIGNS—HORIZ: 1½d. Bombed-out family; 1s. Searchlight crew.

83 Air Raid Casualties

86 Shipwreck of St. Paul (after Palombi)

87 Statue of St. Paul, Rabat, Malta

1959. George Cross Commemoration.
292 **83** 1½d. green, black and gold 20 10
293 – 3d. mauve, black and gold 20 10
294 – 1s. grey, black and gold 70 95
DESIGNS—HORIZ: 3d. "For Gallantry". VERT: 1s. Maltese under bombardment.

1960. 19th Centenary of the Shipwreck of St. Paul. Inscr as in T **86/7**.
295 **86** 1½d. blue, gold and brown 15 10
296 – 3d. purple, gold and blue 15 10
297 – 6d. red, gold and grey 25 10
298 **87** 8d. black and gold 30 50
299 – 1s. purple and gold 25 10
300 – 2s.6d. blue, green and gold 1·00 2·00
DESIGNS—As Type **88**: 3d. Consecration of St. Publius, First Bishop of Malta; 6d. Departure of St. Paul (after Palombi). As Type **87**: 1s. Angel with the "Acts of the Apostles"; 2s.6d. St. Paul with the "Second Epistle to the Corinthians".

92 Stamp of 1860

1960. Centenary of Malta Stamps. Stamp in buff and blue.
301 **92** 1½d. green 25 10
302 3d. red 30 10
303 6d. blue 40 1·00

93 George Cross

1961. George Cross Commemoration.
304 **93** 1½d. black, cream and bistre 15 10
305 – 3d. brown and blue 30 10
306 – 1s. green, lilac and violet 75 1·75
DESIGNS: 3d. and 1s. show George Cross as Type **93** over backgrounds with different patterns.

96 "Madonna Damascena"

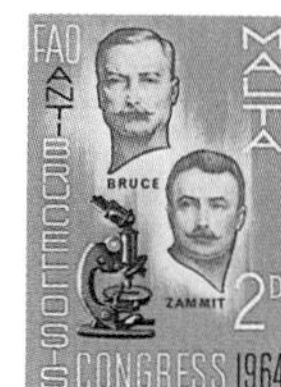

100 Bruce, Zammit and Microscope

1962. Great Siege Commemoration.
307 **96** 2d. blue 10 10
308 – 3d. red 10 10
309 – 6d. bronze 25 10
310 – 1s. purple 25 40
DESIGNS: 3d. Great Siege Monument; 6d. Grand Master La Valette; 1s. Assault on Fort St. Elmo.

1963. Freedom from Hunger. As T **20a** of Pitcairn Islands.
311 1s.6d. sepia 1·75 2·50

1963. Cent of Red Cross. As T **20b** of Pitcairn Islands.
312 2d. red on black 25 15
313 1s.6d. red and blue 1·75 4·00

1964. Anti-brucellosis Congress.
316 **100** 2d. brown, black and green 10 10
317 – 1s.6d. black and purple 90 90
DESIGN: 1s.6d. Goat and laboratory equipment.

102 "Nicola Cotoner tending Sick Man" (M. Preti)

1964. 1st European Catholic Doctors' Congress, Valletta. Multicoloured.
318 2d. Type **102** 20 10
319 6d. St. Luke and hospital 50 15
320 1s.6d. Sacra Infermeria, Valletta 1·10 1·90

106 Dove and British Crown

110 Neolithic Era

109 "The Nativity"

1964. Independence.
321 **106** 2d. olive, red and gold . . 30 10
322 – 3d. brown, red and gold 30 10
323 – 6d. slate, red and gold . . 70 15
324 **106** 1s. blue, red and gold . . 70 15
325 – 1s.6d. blue, red and gold 2·00 1·00
326 – 2s.6d. blue, red and gold 2·00 2·25
DESIGNS: 3d., 1s.6d. Dove and Pope's tiara; 6d., 2s.6d. Dove and U.N. emblem.

1964. Christmas.
327 **109** 2d. purple and gold . . . 10 10
328 4d. blue and gold 20 15
329 8d. green and gold . . . 45 45

1965. Multicoloured.
330 ½d. Type **110** 10 10
331 1d. Punic era 10 10
332 1½d. Roman era 30 10
333 2d. Proto Christian era . . 10 10
334 2½d. Saracenic era 80 10
335 3d. Siculo Norman era . . . 10 10
336 4d. Knights of Malta . . . 60 10
337 4½d. Maltese Navy . . . . 1·50 40
337b 5d. Fortifications 30 20
338 6d. French occupation . . . 30 10
339 8d. British rule 70 10
339c 10d. Naval Arsenal . . . . 50 1·90
340 1s. Maltese Corps of the British Army 30 10
341 1s.3d. International Eucharistic Congress, 1913 . . . . 2·00 1·40
342 1s.6d. Self-government, 1921 60 20
343 2s. Gozo Civic Council . . 70 10
344 2s.6d. State of Malta . . . 70 50
345 3s. Independence, 1964 . . 1·75 75
346 5s. HAFMED (Allied Forces, Mediterranean) 6·00 1·00
347 10s. The Maltese Islands (map) . . . . 3·00 4·00
348 £1 Patron Saints . . . . . 3·75 5·00
Nos. 339/48 are larger, 41 × 29 mm from perf to perf, and include portrait of Queen Elizabeth II.

129 "Dante" (Raphael)

131 Turkish Fleet

1965. 700th Birth Anniv of Dante.
349 **129** 2d. blue 10 10
350 6d. green 25 10
351 2s. brown . . . . 1·10 1·50

1965. 400th Anniv of Great Siege. Multicoloured.
352 2d. Turkish camp 30 10
353 3d. Battle scene 30 10
354 6d. Type **131** 50 10
355 8d. Arrival of relief force . . 90 90
356 1s. Grand Master J. de La Valette's arms 50 10
357 1s.6d. "Allegory of Victory" (from mural by M. Preti) 1·00 30
358 2s.6d. Victory medal . . . . 1·50 3·25
SIZES—As Type **131**: 1s. SQUARE (32½ × 32½ mm): others.

137 "The Three Kings"

1965. Christmas.
359 **137** 1d. purple and red . . . 10 10
360 4d. purple and blue . . . 30 25
361 1s.3d. slate and purple . . 30 30

138 Sir Winston Churchill

1966. Churchill Commemoration.
362 **138** 2d. black, red and gold 20 10
363 – 3d. green, olive and gold 20 10
364 **138** 1s. purple, red and gold 30 10
365 – 1s.6d. blue, ultram & gold 40 85
DESIGN : 3d., 1s.6d. Sir Winston Churchill and George Cross.

140 Grand Master La Valette

145 Pres. Kennedy and Memorial

1966. 400th Anniv of Valletta. Multicoloured.
366 2d. Type **140** 10 10
367 3d. Pope Pius V 10 10
368 6d. Map of Valletta 15 10
369 1s. F. Laparelli (architect) . . 15 10
370 2s.6d. G. Cassar (architect) 35 50

1966. Pres. Kennedy Commemoration.
371 **145** 3d. olive, gold and black 10 10
372 1s.6d. blue, gold and black 10 10

146 "Trade"

147 "The Child in the Manger"

1966. 10th Malta Trade Fair.
373 **146** 2d. multicoloured 10 10
374 8d. multicoloured 30 50
375 2s.6d. multicoloured . . . 30 50

1966. Christmas.
376 **147** 1d. multicoloured 10 10
377 4d. multicoloured 10 10
378 1s.3d. multicoloured . . . 10 10

148 George Cross

149 Crucifixion of St. Peter

1967. 25th Anniv of George Cross Award to Malta.
379 **148** 2d. multicoloured 10 10
380 4d. multicoloured 10 10
381 3s. multicoloured 15 15

1967. 1900th Anniv of Martyrdom of Saints Peter and Paul.
382 **149** 2d. brown, orange & black 10 10
383 – 8d. olive, gold and black 15 10
384 – 3s. blue and black . . . 20 15
DESIGNS—As Type **149**: 3s. Beheading of St. Paul. HORIZ (47 × 25 mm): 8d. Open Bible and episcopal emblems.

152 "St. Catherine of Siena"

156 Temple Ruins, Tarxien

1967. 300th Death Anniv of Melchior Gafa (sculptor). Multicoloured.
385 2d. Type **152** 10 10
386 4d. "St. Thomas of Villanova" 10 10
387 1s.6d. "Baptism of Christ" (detail) 15 10
388 2s.6d. "St. John the Baptist" (from "Baptism of Christ") 15 10

1967. 15th International Historical Architecture Congress, Valletta. Multicoloured.
389 2d. Type **156** 10 10
390 6d. Facade of Palazzo Falzon, Notabile 10 10
391 1s. Parish Church, Birkirkara 10 10
392 3s. Portal, Auberge de Castille 25 25

160 "Angels"

166 Human Rights Emblem and People

163 Queen Elizabeth II and Arms of Malta

1967. Christmas. Multicoloured.
393 1d. Type **160** 10 10
394 8d. "Crib" 20 10
395 1s.4d. "Angels" 20 10

1967. Royal Visit.
396 **163** 2d. multicoloured 10 10
397 – 4d. black, purple and gold 10 10
398 – 3s. multicoloured 20 25
DESIGNS—VERT: 4d. Queen in Robes of Order of St. Michael and St. George. HORIZ: 3s. Queen and outline of Malta.

1968. Human Rights Year. Multicoloured.
399 2d. Type **166** 10 10
400 6d. Human Rights emblem and people (different) . . . 10 10
401 2s. Type **166** (reversed) . . . 10 10

169 Fair "Products"

170 Arms of the Order of St. John and La Valette

1968. Malta International Trade Fair.
402 **169** 4d. multicoloured 10 10
403 8d. multicoloured 10 10
404 3s. multicoloured 15 10

1968. 4th Death Cent of Grand Master La Valette. Multicoloured.
405 1d. Type **170** 10 10
406 8d. "La Valette" (A. de Favray) (vert) 15 10
407 1s.6d. La Valette's tomb (28 × 23 mm) 15 10
408 2s.6d. Angels and scroll bearing date of death (vert) 20 20

174 Star of Bethlehem and Angel waking Shepherds

177 "Agriculture"

1968. Christmas. Multicoloured.
409 1d. Type **174** 10 10
410 8d. Mary and Joseph with shepherd watching over Cradle 15 10
411 1s.4d. Three Wise Men and Star of Bethlehem 15 20

1968. 6th Food and Agricultural Organization Regional Conference for Europe. Mult.
412 4d. Type **177** 10 10
413 1s. F.A.O. emblem and coin 10 10
414 2s.6d. "Agriculture" sowing Seeds 10 15

180 Mahatma Gandhi

181 ILO Emblem

1969. Birth Centenary of Mahatma Gandhi.
415 **180** 1s.6d. brown, black & gold 15 10

1969. 50th Anniv of Int Labour Organization.
416 **181** 2d. blue, gold & turquoise 10 10
417 6d. sepia, gold and brown 10 10

182 Robert Samut

1969. Birth Centenary of Robert Samut (composer of Maltese National Anthem).
418 **182** 2d. multicoloured 10 10

183 Dove of Peace, U.N. Emblem and Sea-bed

1969. United Nations Resolution on Oceanic Resources.
419 **183** 5d. multicoloured 10 10

184 "Swallows" returning to Malta

1969. Maltese Migrants' Convention.
420 **184** 10d. black, gold and olive 10 10

185 University Arms and Grand Master de Fonseca (founder)

1969. Bicentenary of University of Malta.
421 **185** 2s. multicoloured 15 20

187 Flag of Malta and Birds

1969. 5th Anniv of Independence.
422 – 2d. multicoloured 10 10
423 **187** 5d. black, red and gold 10 10
424 – 10d. black, blue and gold 10 10
425 – 1s.6d. multicoloured . . . 20 40
426 – 2s.6d. black, brown & gold 25 50
DESIGNS—SQUARE (31 × 31 mm): 2d. 1919 War Monument. VERT: 10d. "Tourism"; 1s.6d. U.N. and Council of Europe emblems; 2s.6d. "Trade and Industry".

191 Peasants playing Tambourine and Bagpipes

1969. Christmas. Children's Welfare Fund. Multicoloured.
427 1d.+1d. Type **191** 10 20
428 5d.+1d. Angels playing trumpet and harp 15 20
429 1s.6d.+3d. Choir boys singing 15 45

194 "The Beheading of St. John" (Caravaggio)

1970. 13th Council of Europe Art Exn. Mult.
430 1d. Type **194** 10 10
431 2d. "St. John the Baptist" (M. Preti) 10 10
432 5d. Interior of St. John's Co-Cathedral, Valletta 10 10

433 6d. "Allegory of the Order" (Neapolitan school) 10 10
434 8d. "St. Jerome" (Caravaggio) 15 50
435 10d. Articles from the Order of St. John in Malta 15 10
436 1s.6d. "The Blessed Gerard receiving Godfrey de Bouillon" (A. de Favray) 20 40
437 2s. Cape and Stolone (16th cent) 20 55
SIZES—HORIZ: 1d., 8d. 56×30 mm; 2d., 6d. 45×32 mm; 10d., 2s. 63×21 mm; 1s.6d. 45×34 mm. SQUARE: 5d. 39×39 mm.

202 Artist's Impression of Fujiyama

1970. World Fair, Osaka.
438 **202** 2d. multicoloured 10 10
439 5d. multicoloured 10 10
440 3s. multicoloured 15 15

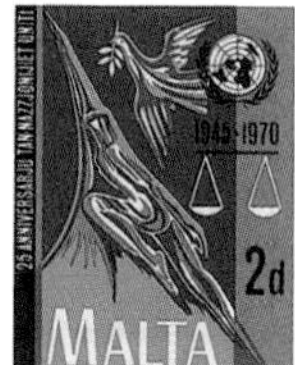
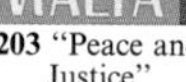
203 "Peace and Justice"
204 Carol-singers, Church and Star

1970. 25th Anniv of United Nations.
441 **203** 2d. multicoloured 10 10
442 5d. multicoloured 10 10
443 2s.6d. multicoloured 15 15

1970. Christmas. Multicoloured.
444 1d.+½d. Type **204** 10 10
445 10d.+2d. Church, star and angels with Infant 15 20
446 1s.6d.+3d. Church, star and nativity scene 20 35

207 Books and Quill

1971. Literary Anniversaries. Multicoloured.
447 1s.6d. Type **207** (De Soldanis (historian) death bicent) 10 10
448 2s. Dun Karm (poet), books, pens and lamp (birth cent) 10 15

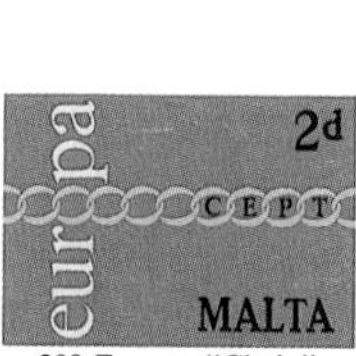
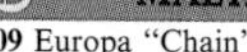

209 Europa "Chain"
211 "Centaurea spathulata"

210 "St. Joseph, Patron of the Universal Church" (G. Cali)

1971. Europa.
449 **209** 2d. orange, black and olive 10 10
450 5d. orange, black and red 10 10
451 1s.6d. orange, blk & slate 45 90

1971. Centenary of Proclamation of St. Joseph as Patron Saint of Catholic Church, and 50th Anniv of Coronation of the Statue of "Our Lady of Victories". Multicoloured.
452 2d. Type **210** 10 10
453 5d. Statue of "Our Lady of Victories" and galley 10 10
454 10d. Type **210** 15 10
455 1s.6d. As 5d. 30 40

1971. National Plant and Bird of Malta. Multicoloured.
456 2s. Type **211** 10 10
457 5d. Blue rock thrush (horiz) 20 10
458 10d. As 5d. 30 15
459 1s.6d. Type **211** 30 1·25

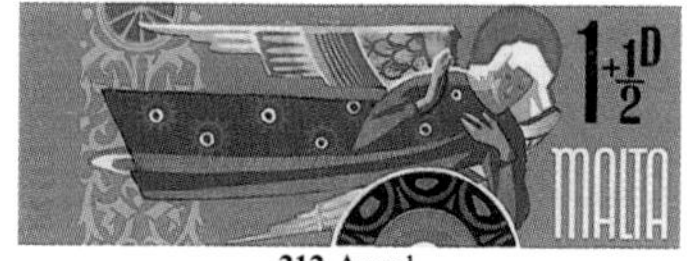
212 Angel

1971. Christmas. Multicoloured.
460 1d.+½d. Type **212** 10 10
461 10d.+2d. Mary and the Child Jesus 15 25
462 1s.6d.+3d. Joseph lying awake 20 40
MS463 131×113 mm. Nos. 460/2 75 2·50

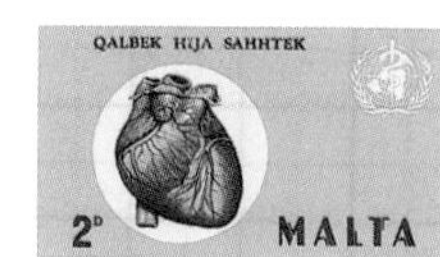
213 Heart and W.H.O. Emblem

1972. World Health Day.
464 **213** 2d. multicoloured 10 10
465 10d. multicoloured 15 10
466 2s.6d. multicoloured 40 80

214 Maltese Cross
216 "Communications"

1972. Decimal Currency. Coins. Multicoloured.
467 2m. Type **214** 10 10
468 3m. Bee on honeycomb 10 10
469 5m. Earthen lampstand 10 10
470 1c. George Cross 10 10
471 2c. Classical head 10 10
472 5c. Ritual altar 10 10
473 10c. Grandmaster's galley 20 10
474 50c. Great Siege Monument 1·25 1·25
SIZES: 3m., 2c. As Type **214**: 5m., 1c., 5c. 25×30 mm; 10c., 50c. 31×38 mm.

1972. Nos. 337a, 339 and 341 surch.
475 1c.3 on 5d. multicoloured 10 10
476 3c. on 8d. multicoloured 15 10
477 5c. on 1s.3d. multicoloured 15 20

1972. Europa.
478 **216** 1c.3 multicoloured 10 10
479 3c. multicoloured 10 10
480 5c. multicoloured 15 35
481 7c.5 multicoloured 20 75

217 Angel

1972. Christmas.
482 **217** 8m.+2m. brown, grey and gold 10 10
483 – 3c.+1c. purple, violet and gold 15 40
484 – 7c.5+1c.5 indigo, blue and gold 20 50
MS485 137×113 mm. Nos. 482/4 1·75 4·25
DESIGNS: No. 483, Angel with tambourine; No. 484, Singing angel.
See also Nos. 507/9.

218 Archaeology
219 Europa "Posthorn"

1973. Multicoloured.
486 2m. Type **218** 10 10
487 4m. History 10 10
488 5m. Folklore 10 10
489 8m. Industry 10 10
490 1c. Fishing industry 10 10
491 1c.3 Pottery 10 10
492 2c. Agriculture 10 10
493 3c. Sport 10 10
494 4c. Yacht marina 15 10
495 5c. Fiesta 15 10
496 7c.5 Regatta 25 10
497 10c. Voluntary service 25 10
498 50c. Education 1·25 50
499 £1 Religion 2·75 2·00
500 £2 Coat of arms (32×27 mm) 14·00 17·00
500b £2 National Emblem (32×27 mm) 9·00 14·00

1973. Europa.
501 **219** 3c. multicoloured 15 10
502 5c. multicoloured 15 35
503 7c.5 multicoloured 25 65

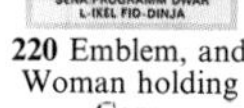

220 Emblem, and Woman holding Corn
221 Girolamo Cassar (architect)

1973. Anniversaries.
504 **220** 1c.3 multicoloured 10 10
505 – 7c.5 multicoloured 25 40
506 – 10c. multicoloured 30 50
ANNIVERSARIES: 1c.3, 10th anniv of World Food Programme; 7c.5, 25th anniv of W.H.O.; 10c. 25th anniv of Universal Declaration of Human Rights.

1973. Christmas. As T **217**. Multicoloured.
507 8m.+2m. Angels and organ pipes 15 10
508 3c.+1c. Madonna and Child 25 55
509 7c.5+1c.5 Buildings and Star 45 1·25
MS510 137×112 mm. Nos. 507/9 4·75 7·50

1973. Prominent Maltese.
511 **221** 1c.3 deep green, green and gold 10 10
512 – 3c. green, blue and gold 15 10
513 – 5c. brown, green and gold 20 15
514 – 7c.5 blue, lt blue & gold 20 30
515 – 10c. deep purple, purple and gold 20 40
DESIGNS: 3c. Giuseppe Barth (ophthalmologist); 5c. Nicolo' Isouard (composer); 7c.5, John Borg (botanist); 10c. Antonio Sciortino (sculptor).

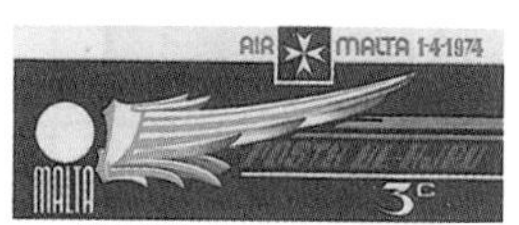
222 "Air Malta" Emblem

1974. Air. Multicoloured.
516 3c. Type **222** 15 10
517 4c. Boeing 720B 15 10
518 5c. Type **222** 20 10
519 7c.5 As 4c. 20 10
520 20c. Type **222** 45 60
521 25c. As 4c. 45 60
522 35c. Type **222** 60 1·40

223 Prehistoric Sculpture

1974. Europa.
523 **223** 1c.3 blue, black and gold 15 10
524 – 3c. brown, black and gold 20 15
525 – 5c. purple, black and gold 25 50
526 – 7c.5 green, black and gold 35 1·00
DESIGNS—VERT: 3c. Old Cathedral Door, Mdina; 7c.5, "Vetlina" (sculpture by A. Sciortino). HORIZ: 5c. Silver monstrance.

224 Heinrich von Stephan (founder) and Land Transport
225 Decorative Star and Nativity Scene

1974. Centenary of U.P.U.
527 **224** 1c.3 green, blue & orange 30 10
528 – 5c. brown, red and green 30 10
529 – 7c.5 blue, violet and green 35 20
530 – 50c. purple, red and orange 1·00 1·25
MS531 126×91 mm. Nos. 527/30 4·50 7·50
DESIGNS (each containing portrait as Type **224**): 5c. "Washington" (paddle-steamer) and "Royal Viking Star" (liner); 7c.5, Balloon and Boeing 747-100; 50c. U.P.U. Buildings, 1874 and 1974.

1974. Christmas. Multicoloured.
532 8m.+2m. Type **225** 10 10
533 3c.+1c. "Shepherds" 15 20
534 5c.+1c. "Shepherds with gifts" 20 35
535 7c.5+1c.5 "The Magi" 30 45

226 Swearing-in of Prime Minister

1975. Inauguration of Republic.
536 **226** 1c.3 multicoloured 10 10
537 – 5c. red and black 20 10
538 – 25c. multicoloured 60 1·00
DESIGNS: 5c. National flag; 25c. Minister of Justice, President and Prime Minister.

227 Mother and Child ("Family Life")

1975. International Women's Year.
539 **227** 1c.3 violet and gold 15 10
540 – 3c. blue and gold 15 10
541 **227** 5c. brown and gold 25 15
542 – 20c. brown and gold 80 2·50
DESIGN: 3c., 20c. Office secretary ("Public Life").

228 "Allegory of Malta" (Francesco de Mura)

1975. Europa. Multicoloured.
543 5c. Type **228** 30 10
544 15c. "Judith and Holofernes" (Valentin de Boulogne) 50 75
The 15c. is smaller, 47×23 mm.

229 Plan of Ggantija Temple

1975. European Architectural Heritage Year.
545 **229** 1c.3 black and red 10 10
546 – 3c. purple, red and brown 20 10
547 – 5c. brown and red 30 25
548 – 25c. green, red and black 1·10 3·00
DESIGNS: 3c. Mdina skyline; 5c. View of Victoria, Gozo; 25c. Silhouette of Fort St. Angelo.

230 Farm Animals
231 "The Right to Work"

1975. Christmas. Multicoloured.
549 8m.+2m. Type **230** 25 25
550 3c.+1c. Nativity scene (50×23 mm) 40 75
551 7c.5+1c.5 Approach of the Magi 45 1·40

1975. 1st Anniv of Republic.
552 **231** 1c.3 multicoloured 10 10
553 – 5c. multicoloured 20 10
554 – 25c. red, blue and black 70 1·10
DESIGNS: 5c. "Safeguarding the Environment"; 25c. National flag.

232 "Festa Tar-Rahal"
233 Water Polo

1976. Maltese Folklore. Multicoloured.
555 1c.3 Type **232** 10 10
556 5c. "L-Imnarja" (horiz) 15 10
557 7c.5 "Il-Karnival" (horiz) 35 70
558 10c. "Il-Gimgha L-Kbira" 55 1·40

1976. Olympic Games, Montreal. Multicoloured.
559 1c.7 Type **233** 10 10
560 5c. Sailing 25 10
561 30c. Athletics 85 1·50

234 Lace-making

1976. Europa. Multicoloured.
562 7c. Type **234** 20 35
563 15c. Stone carving 25 60

235 Nicola Cotoner

1976. 300th Anniv of School of Anatomy and Surgery. Multicoloured.
564 2c. Type **235** 10 10
565 5c. Arm 15 10
566 7c. Giuseppe Zammit 20 10
567 11c. Sacra Infermeria 35 65

236 St. John the Baptist and St. Michael
237 Jean de la Valette's Armour

1976. Christmas. Multicoloured.
568 1c.+5m. Type **236** 10 20
569 5c.+1c. Madonna and Child 15 60
570 7c.+1c.5 St. Christopher and St. Nicholas 20 80
571 10c.+2c. Complete painting (32 × 27 mm) . . . . . . 30 1·25
Nos. 568/71 show portions of "Madonna and Saints" by Domenico di Michelino.

1977. Suits of Armour. Multicoloured.
572 2c. Type **237** 10 10
573 7c. Aloph de Wignacourt's armour 20 10
574 11c. Jean Jacques de Verdelin's armour 25 50

1977. No. 336 surch **1c7**.
575 1c.7 on 4d. multicoloured . . 25 25

239 "Annunciation"

1977. 400th Birth Anniv of Rubens. Flemish Tapestries. Multicoloured.
576 2c. Type **239** 10 10
577 7c. "Four Evangelists" . . . 25 10
578 11c. "Nativity" 45 45
579 20c. "Adoration of the Magi" 80 1·00
See also Nos. 592/5, 615/18 and 638/9.

240 Map and Radio Aerial
242 "Aid to Handicapped Workers" (detail from Workers' Monument)

241 Ta' L-Isperanza

1977. World Telecommunications Day.
580 **240** 1c. black, green and red 10 10
581 6c. black, blue and red . . 20 10
582 – 8c. black, brown and red 30 10
583 – 17c. black, mauve and red 60 40

DESIGN—HORIZ: 8, 17c. Map, aerial and airplane tail-fin.

1977. Europa. Multicoloured.
584 7c. Type **241** 30 15
585 20c. Is-Salini . . . . 35 1·00

1977. Maltese Worker Commemoration.
586 **242** 2c. orange and brown . . 10 10
587 – 7c. light brown and brown 15 10
588 – 20c. multicoloured 40 60
DESIGNS—VERT: 7c. "Stoneworker, modern industry and ship-building" (monument detail). HORIZ: 20c. "Mother with Dead Son" and Service Medal.

243 The Shepherds

1977. Christmas. Multicoloured.
589 1c.+5m. Type **243** 10 35
590 7c.+1c. The Nativity 15 55
591 11c.+1c.5 The Flight into Egypt 20 70

1978. Flemish Tapestries. (2nd series). As T **239**. Multicoloured.
592 2c. "The Entry into Jerusalem" 10 10
593 7c. "The Last Supper" (after Poussin) 25 10
594 11c. "The Raising of the Cross" (after Rubens) . . . 30 25
595 25c. "The Resurrection" (after Rubens) 70 80

244 "Young Lady on Horseback and Trooper"

1978. 450th Death Anniv of Albrecht Durer.
596 **244** 1c.7 black, red and blue 10 10
597 – 8c. black, red and grey . . 15 10
598 – 17c. black, red and grey 40 45
DESIGNS: 8c. "The Bagpiper"; 17c. "The Virgin and Child with a Monkey".

245 Monument to Grand Master Nicola Cotoner (Foggini)
246 Goalkeeper

1978. Europa. Monuments. Multicoloured.
599 7c. Type **245** 15 10
600 25c. Monument to Grand Master Ramon Perellos (Mazzuoli) 35 90

1978. World Cup Football Championship, Argentina. Multicoloured.
601 2c. Type **246** 10 10
602 11c. Players heading ball . . 15 10
603 15c. Tackling 25 35
MS604 125 × 90 mm. Nos. 601/3 2·00 3·25

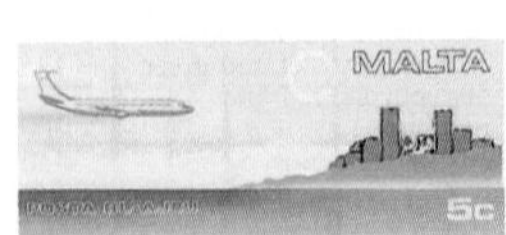

247 Boeing 707 over Megalithic Temple

1978. Air. Multicoloured.
605 5c. Type **247** 20 10
606 7c. Air Malta Boeing 720B 20 10
607 11c. Boeing 747 taking off from Luqa Airport 35 10
608 17c. Type **247** 45 30
609 20c. As 7c. 60 40
610 75c. As 11c. . . . . 1·75 2·75

248 Folk Musicians and Village Church
249 Fishing Boat and Aircraft Carrier

1978. Christmas. Multicoloured.
611 1c.+5m. Type **248** 10 10
612 5c.+1c. Choir of Angels . . . 15 20
613 7c.+1c.5 Carol singers . . . 20 35
614 11c.+3c. Folk musicians, church, angels and carol singers (58 × 22 mm) . . . 25 45

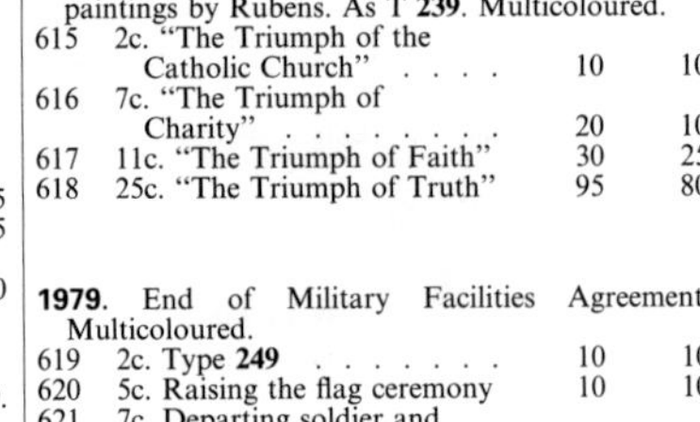

1979. Flemish Tapestries (3rd series) showing paintings by Rubens. As T **239**. Multicoloured.
615 2c. "The Triumph of the Catholic Church" 10 10
616 7c. "The Triumph of Charity" 20 10
617 11c. "The Triumph of Faith" 30 25
618 25c. "The Triumph of Truth" 95 80

1979. End of Military Facilities Agreement. Multicoloured.
619 2c. Type **249** 10 10
620 5c. Raising the flag ceremony 10 10
621 7c. Departing soldier and olive sprig 15 10
622 8c. Type **249** 40 40
623 17c. As 5c. 55 60
624 20c. As 7c. 55 60

250 Speronara (fishing boat) and Tail of Air Malta Airliner
251 Children on Globe

1979. Europa. Communications. Multicoloured.
625 7c. Type **250** 20 10
626 25c. Coastal watch tower and radio link towers 40 75

1979. International Year of the Child. Multicoloured.
627 2c. Type **251** 10 10
628 7c. Children flying kites (27 × 33 mm) 15 10
629 11c. Children in circle (27 × 33 mm) 20 35

252 Shells

1979. Marine Life. Multicoloured.
630 2c. Type **252** 10 10
631 5c. Loggerhead turtle 20 10
632 7c. Dolphin (fish) 25 10
633 25c. Noble pen shell . . . . 90 1·25

253 "The Nativity" (detail)

1979. Christmas. Paintings by Giuseppe Cali. Multicoloured.
634 1c.+5m. Type **253** 10 10
635 5c.+1c. "The Flight into Egypt" (detail) 10 15
636 7c.+1c.5 "The Nativity" . . . 15 20
637 11c.+3c. "The Flight into Egypt" 25 50

1980. Flemish Tapestries (4th series). As T **239**. Multicoloured.
638 2c. "The Institution of Corpus Domini" (Rubens) 10 10
639 8c. "The Destruction of Idolatry" (Rubens) 20 20
MS640 114 × 86 mm. 50c. "Grand Master Perelles with St. Jude and St. Simon (unknown Maltese artist) (vert) . . . . 80 1·60

254 Hal Saflieni Hypogeum, Paola
255 Dun Gorg Preca

1980. Int Restoration of Monuments Campaign. Multicoloured.
641 2c.5 Type **254** 10 15
642 6c. Vilhena Palace, Mdina . . 15 20
643 8c. Citadel of Victoria, Gozo (horiz) 20 40
644 12c. Fort St. Elmo, Valletta (horiz) 30 60

1980. Birth Centenary of Dun Gorg Preca (founder of Society of Christian Doctrine).
645 **255** 2c. 5 grey and black . . . 10 10

256 Ruzar Briffa (poet)

1980. Europa.
646 **256** 8c. yellow, brown & green 20 10
647 – 30c. green, brown and lake . . . . 55 1·25
DESIGN: 30c. Nikiol Anton Vassalli (scholar and patriot).

257 "Annunciation"
258 Rook and Pawn

1980. Christmas. Paintings by A. Inglott. Multicoloured.
648 2c.+5m. Type **257** 10 10
649 6c.+1c. "Conception" 20 20
650 8c.+1c.5 "Nativity" 25 40
651 12c.+3c. "Annunciation", "Conception" and "Nativity" (47 × 38 mm) 30 70

1980. 24th Chess Olympiad and International Chess Federation Congress. Multicoloured.
652 2c.5 Type **258** 25 20
653 8c. Bishop and pawn 65 20
654 30c. King, queen and pawn (vert) . . . . 1·00 1·50

259 Barn Owl
260 Traditional Horse Race

1981. Birds. Multicoloured.
655 3c. Type **259** 30 25
656 8c. Sardinian warbler 50 25
657 12c. Woodchat shrike 60 80
658 23c. British storm petrel . . . 1·10 1·75

1981. Europa. Folklore. Multicoloured.
659 8c. Type **260** 20 10
660 30c. Attempting to retrieve flag from end of "gostra" (greasy pole) 40 65

261 Stylized "25"
262 Disabled Artist at Work

1981. 25th Maltese International Trade Fair.
661 **261** 4c. multicoloured 15 15
662 25c. multicoloured 50 60

1981. International Year for Disabled Persons. Multicoloured.
663 3c. Type **262** 20 10
664 35c. Disabled child playing football 90 75

263 Wheat Ear in Conical Flask

264 Megalithic Building

1981. World Food Day.
665 **263** 8c. multicoloured 15 15
666 23c. multicoloured 60 50

1981. History of Maltese Industry. Multicoloured.
667 5m. Type **264** 10 85
668 1c. Cotton production . . . 10 10
669 2c. Early ship-building . . . 85 10
670 3c. Currency minting 30 10
671 5c. "Art" 30 25
672 6c. Fishing . . . . 1·25 25
673 7c. Agriculture . . . . 30 1·50
674 8c. Stone quarrying . . . . . 1·00 35
675 10c. Grape pressing 35 50
676 12c. Modern ship-building . . 2·00 2·00
677 15c. Energy . . . . 70 1·50
678 20c. Telecommunications . . 70 75
679 25c. "Industry" . . . . . . 1·00 2·00
680 50c. Drilling for Water . . . 2·50 2·75
681 £1 Sea transport . . . . . . 7·00 7·50
682 £3 Air transport . . . . . . 12·00 18·00

265 Children and Nativity Scene

266 Shipbuilding

1981. Christmas. Multicoloured.
683 2c.+1c. Type **265** 25 10
684 8c.+2c. Christmas Eve procession (horiz) 35 20
685 20c.+3c. Preaching midnight sermon . . . . 75 1·10

1982. Shipbuilding Industry.
686 **266** 3c. multicoloured 15 10
687 – 8c. multicoloured 30 30
688 – 13c. multicoloured 55 55
689 – 27c. multicoloured . . . . 1·25 1·25
DESIGNS: 8c. to 27c. Differing shipyard scenes.

267 Elderly Man and Has-Serh (home for elderly)

1982. Care of Elderly. Multicoloured.
690 8c. Type **267** 40 20
691 30c. Elderly woman and Has-Zmien (hospital for elderly) 1·40 1·40

268 Redemption of Islands by Maltese, 1428

1982. Europa. Historical Events. Multicoloured.
692 8c. Type **268** 40 20
693 30c. Declaration of rights by Maltese, 1802 . . . . . . 1·00 1·40

269 Stylized Footballer

1982. World Cup Football Championship, Spain.
694 **269** 3c. multicoloured 20 10
695 – 12c. multicoloured 60 55
696 – 15c. multicoloured 70 65
MS697 125 × 90 mm. Nos. 694/6 3·00 4·25
DESIGNS: 12c., 15c. Various stylized footballers.

270 Angel appearing to Shepherds

1982. Christmas. Multicoloured.
698 2c.+1c. Type **270** 15 20
699 8c.+2c. Nativity and Three Wise Men bearing gifts . . 50 60
700 20c.+3c. Nativity scene (45 × 37 mm) . . . . . . 1·00 1·25

271 "Ta Salvo Serafino" (oared brigantine), 1531

1982. Maltese Ships (1st series). Multicoloured.
701 3c. Type **271** 40 10
702 8c. "La Madonna del Rosaria" (tartane), 1740 . . 80 30
703 12c. "San Paulo" (xebec), 1743 . . . . 1·25 55
704 20c. "Ta' Pietro Saliba" (xprunara), 1798 . . . . . 1·60 90
See also Nos. 725/8, 772/5, 792/5 and 809/12.

272 Locomotive "Manning Wardle", 1883

1983. Centenary of Malta Railway. Multicoloured.
705 3c. Type **272** 45 15
706 13c. Locomotive "Black Hawthorn", 1884 . . . . 1·00 1·00
707 27c. Beyer Peacock locomotive, 1895 . . . . . 2·00 3·25

273 Peace Doves leaving Malta

1983. Commonwealth Day. Multicoloured.
708 8c. Type **273** 25 30
709 12c. Tourist landmarks . . . 40 60
710 15c. Holiday beach (vert) . . 45 75
711 23c. Ship-building (vert) . . . 70 1·00

274 Ggantija Megalithic Temples, Gozo

1983. Europa. Multicoloured.
712 8c. Type **274** 40 40
713 30c. Fort St. Angelo . . . . 1·00 2·40

275 Dish Aerials (World Communications Year)

1983. Anniversaries and Events. Multicoloured.
714 3c. Type **275** 45 15
715 7c. Ships' prows and badge (25th anniv of I.M.O. Convention) 70 55
716 13c. Container lorries and badge (30th anniv of Customs Co-operation Council) 90 90
717 20c. Stadium and emblem (9th Mediterranean Games) 1·00 2·25

276 Monsignor Giuseppe de Piro

277 Annunciation

1983. 50th Death Anniv of Monsignor Giuseppe de Piro.
718 **276** 3c. multicoloured 15 15

1983. Christmas. Multicoloured.
719 2c.+1c. Type **277** 35 15
720 8c.+2c. The Nativity 85 60
721 20c.+3c. Adoration of the Magi . . . . 1·60 2·25

278 Workers at Meeting

1983. 40th Anniv of General Workers' Union. Multicoloured.
722 3c. Type **278** 30 10
723 8c. Worker with family . . . 60 40
724 27c. Union H.Q. Building . . 1·60 1·75

1983. Maltese Ships (2nd series). As T **271**. Multicoloured.
725 2c. "Strangier" (full-rigged ship), 1813 . . . . 30 25
726 12c. "Tigre" (topsail schooner), 1839 . . . . . 1·25 1·25
727 13c. "La Speranza" (brig), 1844 . . . . 1·25 1·25
728 20c. "Wignacourt" (barque), 1844 . . . . 1·75 2·75

279 Boeing 737

1984. Air. Multicoloured.
729 7c. Type **279** 50 30
730 8c. Boeing 720B 60 35
731 16c. Vickers Vanguard . . . . 1·25 70
732 23c. Vickers Viscount . . . . 1·50 70
733 27c. Douglas DC-3 . . . . . 1·75 80
734 38c. Armstrong Whitworth Atalanta "Artemis" . . . 2·25 2·75
735 75c. "Marina" Fiat MF.5 flying boat . . . . 3·25 5·00

280 Bridge

1984. Europa. 25th Anniv of C.E.P.T.
736 **280** 8c. green, black and yellow 35 35
737 30c. red, black and yellow 1·25 1·25

281 Early Policeman

282 Running

1984. 170th Anniv of Malta Police Force. Multicoloured.
738 3c. Type **281** 65 15
739 8c. Mounted police . . . . . 1·50 65
740 11c. Motorcycle policeman . 1·75 2·00
741 25c. Policeman and firemen 2·75 3·75

1984. Olympic Games, Los Angeles. Multicoloured.
742 7c. Type **282** 25 30
743 12c. Gymnastics 50 70
744 23c. Swimming . . . . . . 85 1·25

283 "The Visitation" (Pietru Caruana)

284 Dove on Map

1984. Christmas. Paintings from Church of Our Lady of Porto Salvo, Valletta. Multicoloured.
745 2c.+1c. Type **283** 55 65
746 8c.+2c. "The Epiphany" (Rafel Caruana) (horiz) . . 1·00 1·40
747 20c.+3c. "Jesus among the Doctors" (Rafel Caruana) (horiz) . . . . 2·00 4·00

1984. 10th Anniv of Republic. Multicoloured.
748 3c. Type **284** 40 20
749 8c. Fort St. Angelo 75 65
750 30c. Hands . . . . 2·50 4·75

285 1885 ½d. Green Stamp

287 Nicolo Baldacchino (tenor)

286 Boy, and Hands planting Vine

1985. Centenary of Malta Post Office. Mult.
751 3c. Type **285** 45 15
752 8c. 1885 1d. rose 65 45
753 12c. 1885 2½d. blue . . . . 90 1·40
754 20c. 1885 4d. brown . . . . 1·40 3·00
MS755 165 × 90 mm. Nos. 751/4 3·50 6·00

1985. International Youth Year. Multicoloured.
756 2c. Type **286** 15 15
757 13c. Young people and flowers (vert) 85 60
758 27c. Girl holding flame in hand . . . . 1·75 1·40

1985. Europa. European Music Year. Mult.
759 8c. Type **287** . . . . 2·00 50
760 30c. Francesco Azopardi (composer) . . . . 3·50 5·00

288 Guzeppi Bajada and Manwel Attard (victims)

1985. 66th Anniv of 7 June 1919 Demonstrations. Multicoloured.
761 3c. Type **288** 35 15
762 7c. Karmnu Abela and Wenzu Dyer (victims) . . . 75 40
763 35c. Model of projected Demonstration monument by Anton Agius (vert) . . 2·50 2·75

289 Stylized Birds

1985. 40th Anniv of United Nations Organization. Multicoloured.
764 4c. Type **289** 25 15
765 11c. Arrow-headed ribbons . . 60 1·25
766 31c. Stylized figures . . . . 1·40 3·25

290 Giorgio Mitrovich (nationalist) (death centenary)

291 The Three Wise Men

1985. Celebrities' Anniversaries. Multicoloured.

767 8c. Type **290** . . . . 1·00 35
768 12c. Pietru Caxaru (poet and administrator) (400th death anniversary) . . . . 1·75 2·50

1985. Christmas. Designs showing details of terracotta relief by Ganni Bonnici. Multicoloured.

769 2c.+1c. Type **291** 55 75
770 8c.+2c. Virgin and Child . . 1·25 1·75
771 20c.+3c. Angels . . . . . . 2·50 4·00

1985. Maltese Ships (3rd series). Steamships. As T **271**. Multicoloured.

772 3c. "Scotia" (paddle-steamer), 1844 . . . . 85 20
773 7c. "Tagliaferro" (screw-steamer), 1822 . . . . . . 1·50 1·00
774 15c. "Gleneagles" (screw-steamer), 1885 . . . . . . 2·25 3·50
775 23c. "L'Isle Adam" (screw-steamer), 1886 . . . . . . 2·75 4·25

292 John XXIII Peace Laboratory and Statue of St. Francis of Assisi

1986. International Peace Year. Multicoloured.

776 8c. Type **292** . . . . 1·25 50
777 11c. Dove and hands holding olive branch (40 × 19 mm) 1·50 2·50
778 27c. Map of Africa, dove and two heads . . . . 3·25 4·75

293 Symbolic Plant and "Cynthia cardui", "Vanessa atalanta" and "Polyommatus icarus"

294 Heading the Ball

1986. Europa. Environmental Conservation. Multicoloured.

779 8c. Type **293** . . . . 1·50 50
780 35c. Island, Neolithic frieze, sea and sun . . . . 2·75 6·00

1986. World Cup Football Championship, Mexico. Multicoloured.

781 3c. Type **294** 60 20
782 7c. Saving a goal . . . . . . 1·25 1·00
783 23c. Controlling the ball . . 4·00 6·50
MS784 125 × 90 mm. Nos. 781/3 7·00 8·50

295 Father Diegu

1986. Maltese Philanthropists. Multicoloured.

785 2c. Type **295** 40 30
786 3c. Adelaide Cini 50 30
787 8c. Alfonso Maria Galea . . 1·25 60
788 27c. Vincenzo Bugeja . . . . 3·25 6·00

296 "Nativity"

1986. Christmas. Paintings by Giuseppe D'Arena. Multicoloured.

789 2c.+1c. Type **296** . . . . . 1·25 1·50
790 8c.+2c. "Nativity" (detail) (vert) . . . . 3·00 3·25
791 20c.+3c. "Epiphany" . . . . 4·25 6·50

1986. Maltese Ships (4th series). As T **271**. Multicoloured.

792 7c. "San Paul" (freighter), 1921 . . . . 1·25 50
793 10c. "Knight of Malta" (mail steamer), 1930 . . . . . . 1·50 1·75
794 12c. "Valetta City" (freighter), 1948 . . . . . 1·75 2·75
795 20c. "Saver" (freighter), 1959 3·00 4·50

297 European Robin

1987. 25th Anniv of Malta Ornithological Society. Multicoloured.

796 3c. Type **297** . . . . 1·25 50
797 8c. Peregrine falcon (vert) . . 2·50 1·00
798 13c. Hoopoe (vert) . . . . . 3·25 4·00
799 23c. Cory's shearwater . . . 3·75 6·00

298 Aquasun Lido

299 16th-century Pikeman

1987. Europa. Modern Architecture. Multicoloured.

800 8c. Type **298** . . . . 1·25 75
801 35c. Church of St. Joseph, Manikata . . . . 3·50 6·25

1987. Maltese Uniforms (1st series). Multicoloured.

802 3c. Type **299** 75 40
803 7c. 16th-century officer . . . 1·40 90
804 10c. 18th-century standard bearer . . . . 1·60 2·25
805 27c. 18th-century General of the Galleys . . . . 3·50 4·75

See also Nos. 832/5, 851/4, 880/3 and 893/6.

300 Maltese Scenes, Wheat Ears and Sun

1987. Anniversaries and Events. Multicoloured.

806 5c. Type **300** (European Environment Year) . . . . 1·25 50
807 8c. Esperanto star as comet (Centenary of Esperanto) 2·00 60
808 23c. Family at house door (International Year of Shelter for the Homeless) 3·00 3·00

1987. Maltese Ships (5th series). As T **271**. Multicoloured.

809 2c. "Medina" (freighter), 1969 . . . . 70 60
810 11c. "Rabat" (container ship), 1974 . . . . 2·50 2·50
811 13c. "Ghawdex" (passenger ferry), 1979 . . . . 2·75 2·75
812 20c. "Pinto" (car ferry), 1987 3·75 4·00

301 "The Visitation"

1987. Christmas. Illuminated illustrations, score and text from 16th-century choral manuscript. Multicoloured.

813 2c.+1c. Type **301** 50 50
814 8c.+2c. "The Nativity" . . . 2·00 2·75
815 20c.+3c. "The Adoration of the Magi" . . . . 3·25 4·50

302 Dr. Arvid Pardo (U.N. representative)

1987. 20th Anniv of United Nations Resolution on Peaceful Use of the Seabed. Multicoloured.

816 8c. Type **302** . . . . 1·00 75
817 12c. U.N. emblem and sea . . 1·75 3·00
MS818 125 × 90 mm. Nos. 816/17 3·50 4·00

303 Ven. Nazju Falzon (Catholic catechist)

304 "St. John Bosco with Youth" (statue)

1988. Maltese Personalities. Multicoloured.

819 2c. Type **303** 25 30
820 3c. Mgr. Sidor Formosa (philanthropist) 25 30
821 4c. Sir Luigi Preziosi (ophthalmologist) 40 30
822 10c. Fr. Anastasju Cuschieri (poet) 80 85
823 25c. Mgr. Pietru Pawl Saydon (Bible translator) 2·25 3·25

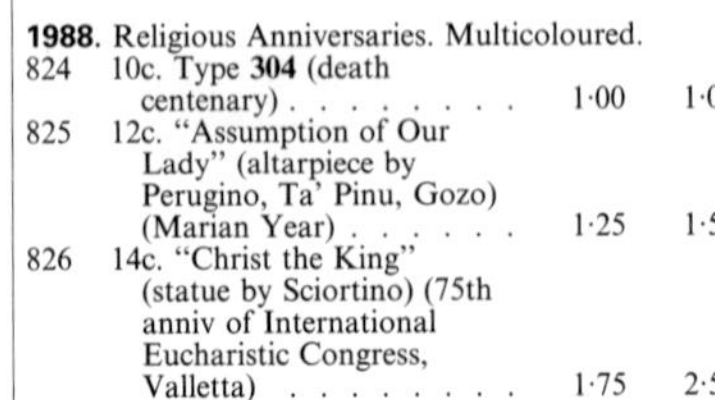

1988. Religious Anniversaries. Multicoloured.

824 10c. Type **304** (death centenary) . . . . 1·00 1·00
825 12c. "Assumption of Our Lady" (altarpiece by Perugino, Ta' Pinu, Gozo) (Marian Year) . . . . . . 1·25 1·50
826 14c. "Christ the King" (statue by Sciortino) (75th anniv of International Eucharistic Congress, Valletta) . . . . 1·75 2·50

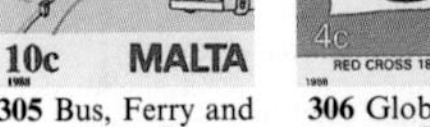

305 Bus, Ferry and Aircraft

306 Globe and Red Cross Emblems

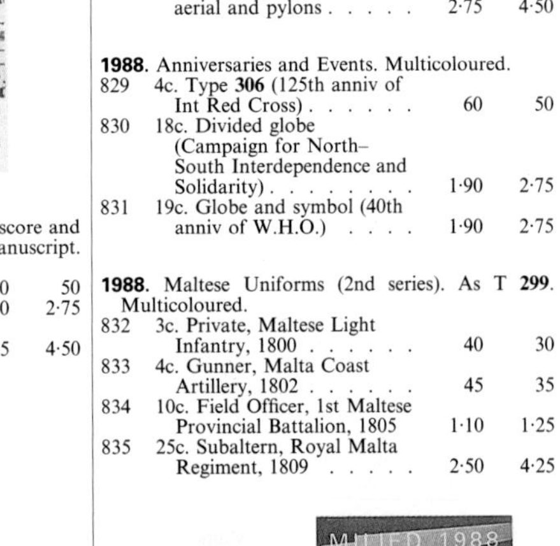

1988. Europa. Transport and Communications. Multicoloured.

827 10c. Type **305** . . . . 1·25 75
828 35c. Control panel, dish aerial and pylons . . . . . 2·75 4·50

1988. Anniversaries and Events. Multicoloured.

829 4c. Type **306** (125th anniv of Int Red Cross) 60 50
830 18c. Divided globe (Campaign for North–South Interdependence and Solidarity) . . . . 1·90 2·75
831 19c. Globe and symbol (40th anniv of W.H.O.) . . . . 1·90 2·75

1988. Maltese Uniforms (2nd series). As T **299**. Multicoloured.

832 3c. Private, Maltese Light Infantry, 1800 . . . . . . 40 30
833 4c. Gunner, Malta Coast Artillery, 1802 . . . . . . 45 35
834 10c. Field Officer, 1st Maltese Provincial Battalion, 1805 1·10 1·25
835 25c. Subaltern, Royal Malta Regiment, 1809 . . . . . 2·50 4·25

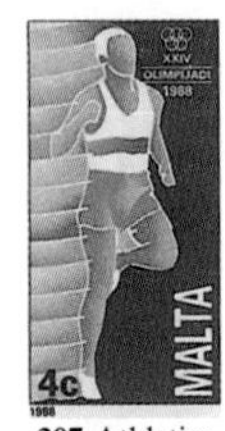

307 Athletics

308 Shepherd with Flock

1988. Olympic Games, Seoul. Multicoloured.

836 4c. Type **307** 30 30
837 10c. Diving 70 80
838 35c. Basketball . . . . 2·00 3·00

1988. Christmas. Multicoloured.

839 3c.+1c. Type **308** 30 30
840 10c.+2c. The Nativity . . . . 70 1·25
841 25c.+3c. Three Wise Men . . 1·75 2·75

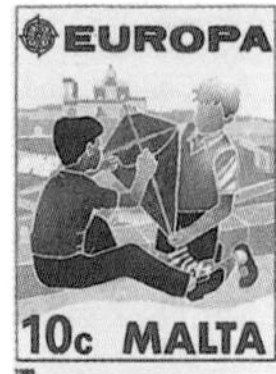

309 Commonwealth Emblem

311 Two Boys flying Kite

310 New State Arms

1989. 25th Anniv of Independence. Multicoloured.

842 2c. Type **309** 25 35
843 3c. Council of Europe flag . . 25 35
844 4c. U.N. flag 30 35
845 10c. Workers, hands gripping ring and national flag . . . 75 95
846 12c. Scales and allegorical figure of Justice . . . . . 90 1·40
847 25c. Prime Minister Borg Olivier with Independence constitution (42 × 28 mm) 1·90 3·25

1989.

848 **310** £1 multicoloured . . . . 4·00 4·50

1989. Europa. Children's Games. Multicoloured.

849 10c. Type **311** . . . . 1·25 75
850 35c. Two girls with dolls . . 3·25 4·50

1989. Maltese Uniforms (3rd series). As T **299**. Multicoloured.

851 3c. Officer, Maltese Veterans, 1815 . . . . 45 45
852 4c. Subaltern, Royal Malta Fencibles, 1839 . . . . . 50 50
853 10c. Private, Malta Militia, 1856 . . . . 1·50 1·50
854 25c. Colonel, Royal Malta Fencible Artillery, 1875 . . 2·75 3·75

312 Human Figures and Buildings

1989. Anniversaries and Commemorations. Designs showing logo and stylized human figures. Multicoloured.

855 3c. Type **312** (20th anniv of U.N. Declaration on Social Progress and Development) . . . 30 30
856 4c. Workers and figure in wheelchair (Malta's Ratification of European Social Charter) 35 35
857 10c. Family (40th anniv of Council of Europe) . . . . 80 1·25
858 14c. Teacher and children (70th anniv of Malta Union of Teachers) . . . . 1·00 1·75
859 25c. Symbolic knights (Knights of the Sovereign Military Order of Malta Assembly) . . . . 2·25 3·50

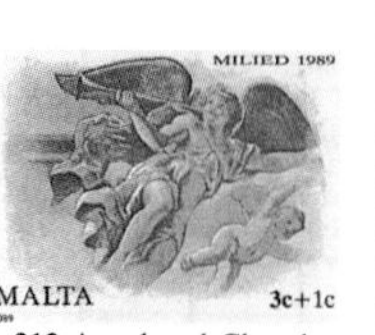

313 Angel and Cherub

315 General Post Office, Auberge d'Italie, Valletta

314 Presidents George H. Bush and Mikhail Gorbachev

1989. Christmas. Vault paintings by Mattia Preti from St. John's Co-Cathedral, Valletta.

860 3c.+1c. Type **313** 80 70
861 10c.+2c. Two angels . . . . 2·00 2·25
862 20c.+3c. Angel blowing trumpet . . . . 2·75 4·00

1989. U.S.A.–U.S.S.R. Summit Meeting, Malta.

863 **314** 10c. multicoloured . . . . 1·00 1·25

1990. Europa. Post Office Buildings. Multicoloured.

864 10c. Type **315** . . . . 1·00 50
865 35c. Branch Post Office, Zebbug (horiz) . . . . . . 2·50 3·75

316 Open Book and Letters from Different Alphabets (International Literacy Year)

318 St. Paul

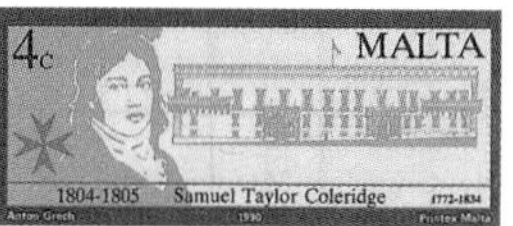

317 Samuel Taylor Coleridge (poet) and Government House

1990. Anniversaries and Events. Multicoloured.

866 3c. Type **316** 25 25
867 4c. Count Roger of Sicily and Norman soldiers (900th anniv of Sicilian rule) (horiz) 60 30
868 19c. Communications satellite (25th anniv of I.T.U.) (horiz) . . . . 2·25 2·50
869 20c. Football and map of Malta (Union of European Football Association 20th Ordinary Congress, Malta) 2·25 2·50

1990. British Authors. Multicoloured.

870 4c. Type **317** 50 30
871 10c. Lord Byron (poet) and map of Valletta 90 70
872 12c. Sir Walter Scott (novelist) and Great Siege 1·00 95
873 25c. William Makepeace Thackeray (novelist) and Naval Arsenal . . . . . . 2·00 2·25

1990. Visit of Pope John Paul II. Bronze Bas-reliefs.

874 **318** 4c. black, flesh and red 50 1·50
875 – 25c. black, flesh and red 1·50 1·75

DESIGN: 25c. Pope John Paul II.

319 Flags and Football

320 Innkeeper

1990. World Cup Football Championship, Italy. Multicoloured.

876 5c. Type **319** 35 30
877 10c. Football in net . . . . 65 1·00
878 14c. Scoreboard and football 1·00 1·75
MS879 123 × 90 mm. Nos. 876/8 3·00 4·00

1990. Maltese Uniforms (4th series). As T **299**. Multicoloured.

880 3c. Captain, Royal Malta Militia, 1889 . . . . . . 1·00 55
881 4c. Field officer, Royal Malta Artillery, 1905 . . . . . . 1·10 60
882 10c. Labourer, Malta Labour Corps, 1915 . . . . 2·25 1·50
883 25c. Lieutenant, King's Own Malta Regiment of Militia, 1918 . . . . 3·50 4·00

1990. Christmas. Figures from Crib by Austin Galea, Marco Bartolo and Rosario Zammit. Multicoloured.

884 3c.+1c. Type **320** 30 50
885 10c.+2c. Nativity (41 × 28 mm) . . . . . . 70 1·25
886 25c.+3c. Shepherd with sheep 1·60 2·50

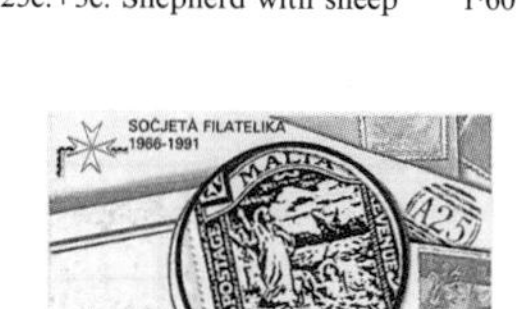

321 1919 10s. Stamp under Magnifying Glass

1991. 25th Anniv of Philatelic Society of Malta.

887 **321** 10c. multicoloured 60 70

322 "Eurostar" Satellite and V.D.U. Screen

324 Interlocking Arrows

323 St. Ignatius Loyola (founder of Jesuits) (500th birth anniv)

1991. Europa. Europe in Space. Multicoloured.

888 10c. Type **322** . . . . 1·00 70
889 35c. "Ariane 4" rocket and projected HOTOL aerospace-plane . . . . . 2·00 2·75

1991. Religious Commemorations. Multicoloured.

890 3c. Type **323** 30 20
891 4c. Abbess Venerable Maria Adeodata Pisani (185th birth anniversary) (vert) . . 35 25
892 30c. St. John of the Cross (400th death anniversary) 2·00 2·25

1991. Maltese Uniforms (5th series). As T **299**. Multicoloured.

893 3c. Officer with colour, Royal Malta Fencibles, 1860 . . 30 25
894 10c. Officer with colour, Royal Malta Regiment of Militia, 1903 . . . . 70 60
895 19c. Officer with Queen's colour, King's Own Malta Regiment, 1968 . . . . . 1·40 1·75
896 25c. Officer with colour, Malta Armed Forces, 1991 1·75 2·00

1991. 25th Anniv of Union Haddiema Maghqudin (public services union).

897 **324** 4c. multicoloured 30 30

325 Western Honey Buzzard

326 Three Wise Men

1991. Endangered Species. Birds. Multicoloured.

898 4c. Type **325** . . . . 1·75 2·00
899 4c. Marsh harrier . . . . . 1·75 2·00
900 10c. Eleonora's falcon . . . 1·75 2·00
901 10c. Lesser kestrel . . . . . 1·75 2·00

1991. Christmas. Multicoloured.

902 3c.+1c. Type **326** 45 50
903 10c.+2c. Holy Family . . . . 1·00 1·25
904 25c.+3c. Two shepherds . . . 2·00 3·00

327 Ta' Hagrat Neolithic Temple

1991. National Heritage of the Maltese Islands. Multicoloured.

905 1c. Type **327** 25 50
906 2c. Cottoner Gate 25 50
907 3c. St. Michael's Bastion, Valletta 25 50
908 4c. Spinola Palace, St. Julian's 25 15
909 5c. Birkirkara Church . . . 30 20
910 10c. Mellieha Bay 60 35
911 12c. Wied iz-Zurrieq 65 40
912 14c. Mgarr harbour, Gozo 75 45
913 20c. Yacht marina . . . . . 1·10 65
914 50c. Gozo Channel . . . . . 2·00 1·60
915 £1 "Arab Horses" (sculpture by Antonio Sciortino) . . . 4·25 3·25
916 £2 Independence Monument (Ganni Bonnici) (vert) . . 8·50 7·00

328 Aircraft Tailfins and Terminal

1992. Opening of Int Air Terminal. Mult.

917 4c. Type **328** 75 30
918 10c. National flags and terminal . . . . 1·25 70

329 Ships of Columbus

1992. Europa. 500th Anniv of Discovery of America by Columbus. Multicoloured.

919 10c. Type **329** . . . . 1·25 55
920 35c. Columbus and map of Americas . . . . 2·50 2·25

330 George Cross and Anti-aircraft Gun Crew

332 Church of the Flight into Egypt

331 Running

1992. 50th Anniv of Award of George Cross to Malta. Multicoloured.

921 4c. Type **330** . . . . 1·00 30
922 10c. George Cross and memorial bell . . . . . . 1·50 1·00
923 50c. Tanker "Ohio" entering Grand Harbour . . . . . 6·50 8·00

1992. Olympic Games, Barcelona. Multicoloured.

924 3c. Type **331** 65 20
925 10c. High jumping . . . . . 1·25 1·00
926 30c. Swimming . . . . . . 2·50 4·50

1992. Rehabilitation of Historical Buildings.

927 **332** 3c. black, stone and grey 40 30
928 – 4c. black, stone and pink 45 30
929 – 19c. black, stone and lilac 2·00 2·75
930 – 25c. black, stone and green . . . . 2·25 2·75

DESIGNS—HORIZ: 4c. St. John's Co-Cathedral; 25c. Auberge de Provence. VERT: 19c. Church of Madonna del Pillar.

333 "The Nativity" (Giuseppe Cali)

1992. Christmas. Religious Paintings by Giuseppe Cali from Mosta Church. Multicoloured.

931 3c.+1c. Type **333** 70 80
932 10c.+2c. "Adoration of the Magi" . . . . 1·75 2·00
933 25c.+3c. "Christ with the Elders in the Temple" . . 3·00 3·75

334 Malta College Building, Valletta

335 Lions Club Emblem

1992. 400th Anniv of University of Malta. Multicoloured.

934 4c. Type **334** 75 25
935 30c. Modern University complex, Tal-Qroqq (horiz) 2·75 4·00

1993. 75th Anniv of International Association of Lions Club. Multicoloured.

936 4c. Type **335** 50 25
937 50c. Eye (Sight First Campaign) . . . . 2·75 4·00

336 Untitled Painting by Paul Carbonaro

1993. Europa. Contemporary Art. Mult.

938 10c. Type **336** . . . . 1·00 50
939 35c. Untitled painting by Alfred Chircop (horiz) . . 2·50 4·25

337 Mascot holding Flame

1993. 5th Small States of Europe Games. Multicoloured.

940 3c. Type **337** 20 20
941 4c. Cycling 80 30
942 10c. Tennis . . . . 1·50 1·00
943 35c. Yachting . . . . 2·75 3·50
MS944 120 × 80 mm. Nos. 940/3 4·00 4·00

338 Learning First Aid **339** "Papilio machaon"

1993. 50th Anniv of Award of Bronze Cross to Maltese Scouts and Guides. Multicoloured.
945 3c. Type **338** 30 15
946 4c. Bronze Cross 30 20
947 10c. Scout building camp fire 80 80
948 35c. Governor Lord Gort presenting Bronze Cross, 1943 . . . . 2·25 3·25

1993. European Year of the Elderly. Butterflies. Multicoloured.
949 5c. Type **339** 35 20
950 35c. "Vanessa atalanta" . . . 1·75 2·25

340 G.W.U. Badge and Interlocking "50" **341** Child Jesus and Star

1993. 50th Anniv of General Workers Union.
951 **340** 4c. multicoloured 35 40

1993. Christmas. Multicoloured.
952 3c.+1c. Type **341** 30 35
953 10c.+2c. Christmas tree . . . 85 1·10
954 25c.+3c. Star in traditional window . . . . 1·60 2·50

342 Council Arms (face value top left)

1993. Inauguration of Local Community Councils. Sheet 110 × 93 mm, containing T **342** and similar horiz designs showing different Council Arms. Multicoloured.
MS955 5c. Type **342**; 5c. Face value top right; 5c. Face value bottom left; 5c. Face value bottom right 1·50 2·25

343 Symbolic Tooth and Probe **344** Sir Themistocles Zammit (discoverer of Brucella microbe)

1994. 50th Anniv of Maltese Dental Association. Multicoloured.
956 5c. Type **343** 35 30
957 44c. Symbolic mouth and dental mirror . . . . . . 3·00 3·00

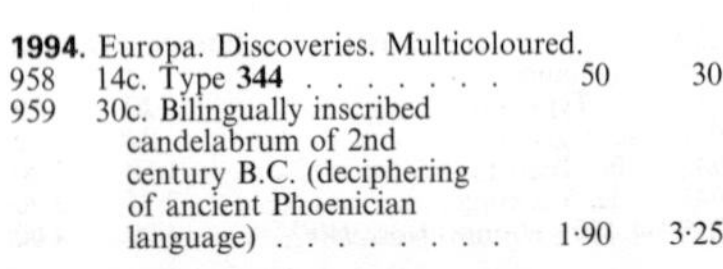
1994. Europa. Discoveries. Multicoloured.
958 14c. Type **344** 50 30
959 30c. Bilingually inscribed candelabrum of 2nd century B.C. (deciphering of ancient Phoenician language) . . . . 1·90 3·25

345 Family in Silhouette (International Year of the Family) **346** Football and Map

1994. Anniversaries and Events. Multicoloured.
960 5c. Type **345** 30 20
961 9c. Stylized Red Cross (International recognition of Malta Red Cross Society) 60 50
962 14c. Animals and crops (150th anniv of Agrarian Society) 90 80
963 20c. Worker in silhouette (75th anniv of I.L.O.) . . . 1·25 1·60
964 25c. St. Paul's Anglican Cathedral (155th anniv) (vert) . . . . 1·40 1·75

1994. World Cup Football Championship, U.S.A. Multicoloured.
965 5c. Type **346** 40 20
966 14c. Ball and goal . . . . . 1·00 80
967 30c. Ball and pitch superimposed on map . . 2·50 4·25
MS968 123 × 88 mm. Nos. 965/7 3·75 4·00

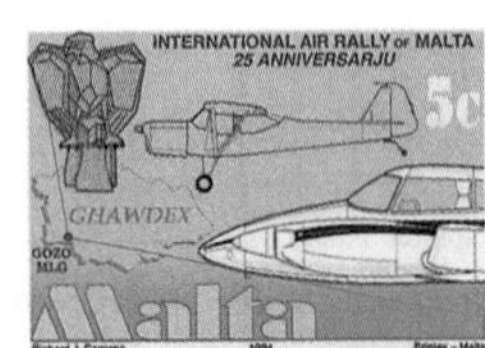
347 Falcon Trophy, Twin Comanche and Auster (25th anniv of Malta International Rally)

1994. Aviation Anniversaries and Events. Multicoloured.
969 5c. Type **347** 50 20
970 14c. Alouette helicopter, display teams and logo (Malta International Airshow) . . . . 1·75 85
971 20c. De Havilland Dove "City of Valetta" and Avro York aircraft with logo (50th anniv of I.C.A.O.) 1·90 1·75
972 25c. Airbus 320 "Nicolas Cottoner" and De Havilland Comet aircraft with logo (50th anniv of I.C.A.O.) . . . . 1·90 1·90

348 National Flags and Astronaut on Moon **350** Helmet-shaped Ewer

349 Virgin Mary and Child with Angels

1994. 25th Anniv of First Manned Moon Landing.
973 **348** 14c. multicoloured . . . . 1·10 1·25

1994. Christmas. Multicoloured.
974 5c. Type **349** 25 10
975 9c.+2c. Angel in pink (vert) 65 70
976 14c.+3c. Virgin Mary and Child (vert) . . . . 90 1·25
977 20c.+3c. Angel in green (vert) 1·60 2·50
Nos. 975/7 are larger, 28 × 41 mm, and depict details from Type **349**.

1994. Maltese Antique Silver Exhibition. Multicoloured.
978 5c. Type **350** 30 20
979 14c. Balsamina 80 80
980 20c. Coffee pot . . . . . . 1·40 1·75
981 25c. Sugar box . . . . 1·75 2·25

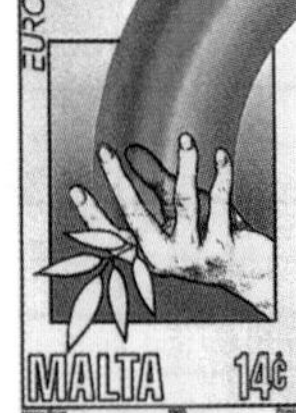
351 "60 plus" and Hands touching **352** Hand holding Leaf and Rainbow

1995. Anniversaries and Events. Multicoloured.
982 2c. Type **351** (25th anniv of National Association of Pensioners) 15 15
983 5c. Child's drawing (10th anniv of National Youth Council) 25 20
984 14c. Conference emblem (4th World Conference on Women, Peking, China) . . 70 80
985 20c. Nurse and thermometer (50th anniv of Malta Memorial District Nursing Association) . . . . 1·25 1·40
986 25c. Louis Pasteur (biologist) (death centenary) . . . . . 1·50 1·75

1995. Europa. Peace and Freedom. Multicoloured.
987 14c. Type **352** 75 55
988 30c. Peace doves (horiz) . . . 1·50 2·00

353 Junkers Ju 87B "Stuka" Dive Bombers over Valletta and Anti-aircraft Gun

1995. Anniversaries. Multicoloured.
989 5c. Type **353** (50th anniv of end of Second World War) 25 25
990 14c. Silhouetted people holding hands (50th anniv of United Nations) 70 80
991 35c. Hands holding bowl of wheat (50th anniv of F.A.O.) (vert) . . . . . . 2·00 2·25

354 Light Bulb **356** Pinto's Turret Clock

355 Rock Wall and Girna

1995. Maltese Electricity and Telecommunications. Multicoloured.
992 2c. Type **354** 15 15
993 5c. Symbolic owl and binary codes 25 25
994 9c. Dish aerial 45 50
995 14c. Sun and rainbow over trees 70 80
996 20c. Early telephone, satellite and Moon's surface . . . 1·25 1·50

1995. European Nature Conservation Year. Multicoloured.
997 5c. Type **355** 60 25
998 14c. Maltese wall lizards . . 1·75 80
999 44c. Aleppo pine . . . . . . 3·25 3·00

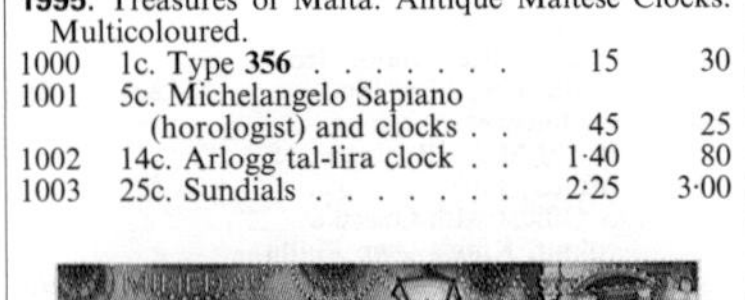
1995. Treasures of Malta. Antique Maltese Clocks. Multicoloured.
1000 1c. Type **356** 15 30
1001 5c. Michelangelo Sapiano (horologist) and clocks . . 45 25
1002 14c. Arlogg tal-lira clock . . 1·40 80
1003 25c. Sundials . . . . 2·25 3·00

357 Children's Christmas Eve Procession

1995. Christmas. Multicoloured.
1004 5c. Type **357** 25 10
1005 5c.+2c. Children with crib (vert) 30 50
1006 14c.+3c. Children with lanterns (vert) . . . . . 1·00 1·25
1007 25c.+3c. Boy with lantern and balustrade (vert) . . 1·75 2·75
Nos. 1005/7 are 27 × 32 mm and depict details from Type **357**.

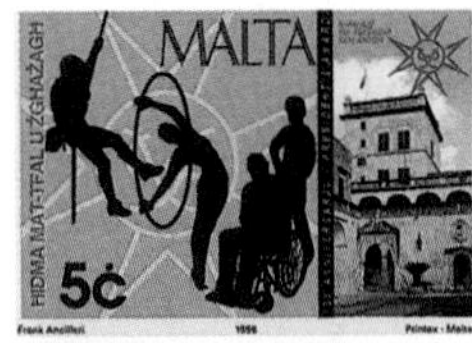
358 Silhouetted Children and President's Palace, San Anton

1996. Anniversaries. Multicoloured.
1008 5c. Type **358** (35th anniv of the President's Award) . . 25 25
1009 14c. Nazzareno Camilleri (priest) and St. Patrick's Church, Salesjani (90th birth anniv) 65 65
1010 20c. St. Mary Euphrasia and convent (birth bicentenary) . . . . . . 1·00 1·10
1011 25c. Silhouetted children and fountain (50th anniv of U.N.I.C.E.F.) . . . . 1·25 1·40

359 Carved Figures from Skorba

1996. Maltese Prehistoric Art Exhibition. Multicoloured.
1012 5c. Type **359** 30 20
1013 14c. Temple carving, Gozo 80 85
1014 20c. Carved figure of a woman, Skorba (vert) . . 1·10 1·25
1015 35c. Ghar Dalam pot (vert) 1·90 2·50

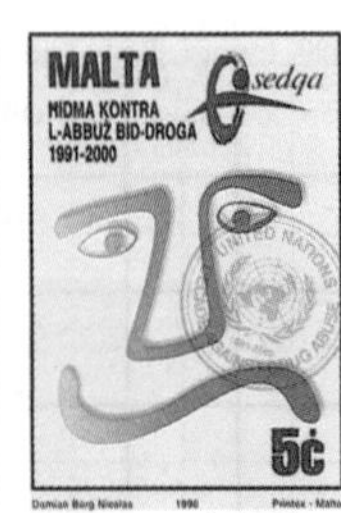
360 Mabel Strickland (politician and journalist) **361** Face and Emblem (United Nations Decade against Drug Abuse)

1996. Europa. Famous Women. Multicoloured.
1016 14c. Type **360** 75 55
1017 30c. Inez Soler (artist, musician and writer) . . . 2·00 2·00

1996. Anniversaries and Events. Multicoloured.
1018 5c. Type **361** 25 25
1019 5c. "Fi" and emblem (50th anniv of Malta Federation of Industry) 25 25
1020 14c. Commemorative plaque and national flag (75th anniv of self-government) 80 80
1021 44c. Guglielmo Marconi and early radio equipment (centenary of radio) . . . 2·25 2·50

362 Judo

1996. Olympic Games, Atlanta. Multicoloured.
1022 2c. Type **362** 10 10
1023 5c. Athletics 30 25
1024 14c. Diving 80 80
1025 25c. Rifle-shooting . . . . 1·40 1·60

363 "Harvest Time" (Cali)

1996. 150th Birth Anniv of Guiseppe Cali (painter). Multicoloured.
1026 5c. Type **363** 30 25
1027 14c. "Dog" (Cali) 80 70
1028 20c. "Countrywoman in a Field" (Cali) (vert) . . . 1·10 1·10
1029 25c. "Cali at his Easel" (Edward Dingli) (vert) . . 1·25 1·25

364 Bus No. 1990 "Diamond Star", 1920s

1996. Buses. Multicoloured.
1030 2c. Type **364** 30 10
1031 5c. No. 434 "Tom Mix", 1930s 60 25
1032 14c. No. 1764 "Verdala", 1940s . . . . 1·25 80
1033 30c. No. 3495, 1960s . . . 1·75 2·00

365 Stained Glass Window

1996. Christmas. Multicoloured.
1034 5c. Type **365** 35 10
1035 5c.+2c. Madonna and Child (29 × 35 mm) 40 50
1036 14c.+3c. Angel facing right (29 × 35 mm) . . . . . . 80 1·25
1037 25c.+3c. Angel facing left (29 × 35 mm) . . . . . . 1·25 1·90
Nos. 1035/7 show details from Type **365**.

366 Hompesch Arch and Arms, Zabbar
368 Gahan carrying Door

367 Captain-General of the Galleys' Sedan Chair

1997. Bicentenary of Maltese Cities. Multicoloured.
1038 6c. Type **366** 30 25
1039 16c. Statue, church and arms, Siggiewi 70 70
1040 26c. Seated statue and arms, Zejtun . . . . 1·10 1·10
MS1041 125 × 90 mm. Nos. 1038/40 3·25 3·00

1997. Treasures of Malta. Sedan Chairs. Multicoloured.
1042 2c. Type **367** 15 15
1043 6c. Cotoner Grandmasters' chair 30 30
1044 16c. Chair from Cathedral Museum, Mdina (vert) . . 70 70
1045 27c. Chevalier D'Arezzo's chair (vert) . . . . 1·10 1·10

1997. Europa. Tales and Legends. Multicoloured.
1046 16c. Type **368** . . . . . . 1·00 75
1047 35c. St. Dimitrius appearing from painting . . . . . . 1·75 1·50

369 Modern Sculpture (Antonio Sciortino)
370 Dr. Albert Laferla

1997. Anniversaries. Multicoloured.
1048 1c. Type **369** 10 15
1049 6c. Joseph Calleia and film reel (horiz) 40 40
1050 6c. Gozo Cathedral (horiz) 40 40
1051 11c. City of Gozo (horiz) . . 60 50
1052 16c. Sculpture of head (Sciortino) 80 70
1053 22c. Joseph Calleia and film camera (horiz) . . . . . 1·00 1·00
ANNIVERSARIES: 1, 16c. 50th death anniv of Antonio Sciortino (sculptor); 6 (No. 1049), 22c. Birth centenary of Joseph Calleia (actor); 6 (No. 1050), 11c. 300th anniv of construction of Gozo Cathedral.

1997. Pioneers of Education. Multicoloured.
1054 6c. Type **370** 30 25
1055 16c. Sister Emilie de Vialar 70 70
1056 19c. Mgr. Paolo Pullicino 80 80
1057 26c. Mgr. Tommaso Gargallo . . . . 1·00 1·10

371 The Nativity

1997. Christmas. Multicoloured.
1058 6c. Type **371** 30 10
1059 6c.+2c. Mary and baby Jesus (vert) 35 50
1060 16c.+3c. Joseph with donkey (vert) . . . . 1·00 1·40
1061 26c.+3c. Shepherd with lamb (vert) . . . . 1·50 2·50
Nos. 1059/61 show details from Type **371**.

372 Plan of Fort and Soldiers in Victoria Lines

1997. Anniversaries. Multicoloured (except 6c.).
1062 2c. Type **372** 20 10
1063 6c. Sir Paul Boffa making speech (black and red) . . 30 25
1064 16c. Plan of fort and gun crew 90 65
1065 37c. Queue of voters . . . . 1·50 2·00
ANNIVERSARIES: 2, 16c. Centenary of Victoria Lines; 6, 37c. 50th anniv of 1947 Self-government Constitution.

373 "Maria Amelia Grognet" (Antonine de Favray)

1998. Treasures of Malta. Costumes and Paintings.
1066 6c. Type **373** 60 50
1067 6c. Gentleman's waistcoat, c.1790–1810 . . . . . . 60 50
1068 16c. Lady's dinner dress, c.1880 . . . . 90 90
1069 16c. "Veneranda, Baroness Abela, and her Grandson" (De Favray) 90 90
MS1070 123 × 88 mm. 26c. City of Valletta from old print (39 × 47 mm) . . . . 1·60 1·60

374 Grand Master Ferdinand von Hompesch

1998. Bicentenary of Napoleon's Capture of Malta. Multicoloured.
1071 6c. Type **374** 60 70
1072 6c. French fleet 60 70
1073 16c. French landing . . . . 1·10 1·40
1074 16c. General Napoleon Bonaparte . . . . 1·10 1·40

375 Racing Two-man Luzzus
376 Dolphin and Diver

1998. Europa. Sailing Regatta, Grand Harbour. Multicoloured.
1075 16c. Type **375** . . . . . . 1·40 55
1076 35c. Racing four-man luzzus 1·90 2·50

1998. International Year of the Ocean. Multicoloured.
1077 2c. Type **376** 35 25
1078 6c. Diver and sea-urchin . . 55 25
1079 16c. Jacques Cousteau and diver (horiz) . . . . . . 1·40 80
1080 27c. Two divers (horiz) . . 1·75 2·25

377 Goalkeeper saving Goal
378 Ships' Wheels (50th anniv of Int Maritime Organization)

1998. World Cup Football Championship, France. Players and flags. Multicoloured.
1081 6c. Type **377** 70 25
1082 16c. Two players and referee 1·40 70
1083 22c. Two footballers . . . . 1·60 2·00
MS1084 122 × 87 mm. Nos. 1081/3 2·75 2·75

1998. Anniversaries. Multicoloured.
1085 1c. Type **378** 10 10
1086 6c. Symbolic family (50th anniv of Universal Declaration of Human Rights) 35 25
1087 11c. "GRTU" and cogwheels (50th anniv of General Retailers and Traders Union) 60 40
1088 19c. Mercury (50th anniv of Chamber of Commerce) 90 1·10
1089 26c. Aircraft tailfins (25th anniv of Air Malta) . . . 1·75 2·00

379 "Rest on the Flight to Egypt"

1998. Christmas. Paintings by Mattia Preti. Mult.
1090 6c. Type **379** 35 10
1091 6c.+2c. "Virgin and Child with Sts. Anthony and John the Baptist" 40 50
1092 16c.+3c. "Virgin and Child with Sts. Raphael, Nicholas and Gregory" 1·00 1·25
1093 26c.+3c. "Virgin and Child with Sts. John the Baptist and Nicholas" . . . . . 1·50 2·00

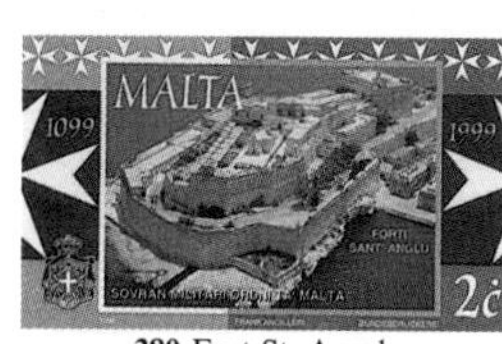

380 Fort St. Angelo

1999. 900th Anniv of the Sovereign Military Order of Malta. Multicoloured.
1094 2c. Type **380** 20 10
1095 6c. Grand Master De l'Isle Adam (vert) 40 25
1096 16c. Grand Master La Valette (vert) 80 55
1097 27c. Auberge de Castille et Leon . . . . 1·25 1·40

381 Little Ringed Plover, Ghadira Nature Reserve

1999. Europa. Parks and Gardens. Multicoloured.
1098 16c. Type **381** . . . . . . 1·25 55
1099 35c. River kingfisher, Simar Nature Reserve . . . . . 1·75 2·00

382 Council of Europe Assembly

1999. 50th Anniv of Council of Europe. Mult.
1100 6c. Type **382** 30 25
1101 16c. Council of Europe Headquarters, Strasbourg 70 75

383 U.P.U. Emblem and Marsamxett Harbour, Valletta

1999. 125th Anniv of Universal Postal Union. Multicoloured.
1102 6c. Type **383** . . . . 1·10 1·25
1103 16c. Nuremberg and "iBRA '99" International Stamp Exhibition emblem . . . 1·40 1·50
1104 22c. Paris and "Philexfrance '99" International Stamp Exhibition emblem . . . 1·50 1·60
1105 27c. Peking and "China '99" International Stamp Exhibition emblem . . . 1·60 1·75
1106 37c. Melbourne and "Australia '99" International Stamp Exhibition emblem . . . 1·75 1·90

384 Couple in Luzzu

1999. Tourism. Multicoloured.
1107 6c. Type **384** 45 25
1108 16c. Tourist taking photograph 85 55
1109 22c. Man sunbathing (horiz) 1·10 90
1110 27c. Couple with horse-drawn carriage (horiz) . . 1·60 1·00
1111 37c. Caveman at Ta' Hagrat Neolithic temple (horiz) 1·90 2·00

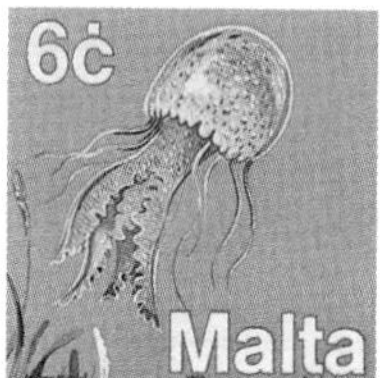

385 Common Jellyfish

1999. Marine Life of the Mediterranean. Mult.
1112 6c. Type **385** 60 60
1113 6c. Peacock wrasse 60 60
1114 6c. Common cuttlefish . . . 60 60
1115 6c. Violet sea-urchin 60 60
1116 6c. Dusky grouper 60 60
1117 6c. Common two-banded seabream 60 60
1118 6c. Star-coral 60 60
1119 6c. Spiny spider crab . . . 60 60
1120 6c. Rainbow wrasse 60 60
1121 6c. Octopus 60 60
1122 6c. Atlantic trumpet triton 60 60
1123 6c. Mediterranean parrotfish 60 60
1124 6c. Long-snouted seahorse 60 60

1125 6c. Deep-water hermit crab 60 60
1126 6c. Mediterranean moray . . 60 60
1127 6c. Common starfish 60 60

Nos. 1112/27 were printed together, se-tenant, forming a composite design.

386 Father Mikiel Scerri

1999. Bicentenary of Maltese Uprising against the French. Multicoloured.

1128 6c. Type **386** 55 55
1129 6c. "L-Eroj Maltin" (statue) 55 55
1130 16c. General Belgrand de Vaubois (French commander) . . . . . . 1·00 1·00
1131 16c. Captain Alexander Ball R.N. . . . . 1·00 1·00

387 "Wolfgang Philip Guttenberg interceding with The Virgin" (votive painting)

1999. Mellieha Sanctuary Commemoration. Mult.

1132 **387** 35c. multicoloured . . . 1·75 1·50
MS1133 123 × 88 mm. 6c. "Mellieha Virgin and Child" (rock painting) (vert) 60 70

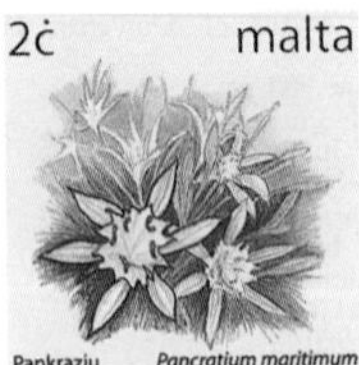

388 Sea Daffodil

1999. Maltese Flowers. Multicoloured.

1134 1c. *Helichrysum melitense* 10 10
1135 2c. Type **388** 10 10
1136 3c. *Cistus creticus* 10 15
1137 4c. Southern dwarf iris . . 10 15
1138 5c. *Papaver rhoeas* 15 20
1139 6c. French daffodil 20 25
1139a 7c. *Vitex angus-castus* . . . 25 30
1140 10c. *Rosa sempervirens* . . 30 35
1141 11c. *Silene colorata* 35 40
1142 12c. *Cynara cardunculus* . . 40 45
1143 16c. Yellow-throated crocus 50 55
1144 19c. *Anthemis arvensis* . . 60 65
1145 20c. *Anacamptis pyramidalis* 65 70
1145a 22c. *Spartium junceum* . . 70 75
1146 25c. Large Star of Bethlehem 80 85
1147 27c. *Borago officinalis* . . . 85 90
1147a 28c. *Crataegus azalorus* . . 90 95
1147b 37c. *Cercis siliquastrum* . . 1·25 1·40
1147c 45c. *Myrtus communis* . . 1·40 1·50
1148 46c. Wild tulip . . . . . . 1·40 1·50
1149 50c. *Chrysanthemum coronarium* . . . . . . 1·60 1·75
1149a 76c. *Pistacia lentiscus* . . . 2·10 2·25
1150 £1 *Malva sylvestris* . . . . 3·25 3·50
1151 £2 *Adonis microcarpa* . . . 6·25 6·50

389 Madonna and Child

1999. Christmas. Multicoloured.

1152 6c. Type **389** 45 10
1153 6c.+3c. Carol singers . . . 50 50
1154 16c.+3c. Santa Claus . . . 1·25 1·40
1155 26c.+3c. Christmas decorations . . . . 1·60 2·00

390 Parliament Chamber and Symbolic Luzzu

1999. 25th Anniv of Republic. Multicoloured.

1156 6c. Type **390** 35 25
1157 11c. Parliament in session and Council of Europe emblem 50 35
1158 16c. Church and Central Bank of Malta building 70 55
1159 19c. Aerial view of Gozo and emblems 90 75
1160 26c. Computer and shipyard 1·00 85

391 Gift and Flowers

2000. Greetings Stamps. Multicoloured.

1161 3c. Type **391** 20 15
1162 6c. Photograph, envelope and rose 30 25
1163 16c. Flowers and silver heart 70 55
1164 20c. Champagne and pocket watch 85 75
1165 22c. Wedding rings and roses 90 80

392 Luzzu and Cruise Liner

2000. Malta during the 20th Century. Multicoloured.

1166 6c. Type **392** 40 25
1167 16c. Street musicians and modern street carnival . . 75 55
1168 22c. Family in 1900 and illuminated quayside . . . 1·00 75
1169 27c. Rural occupations and Citadel, Victoria . . . . 1·40 1·25

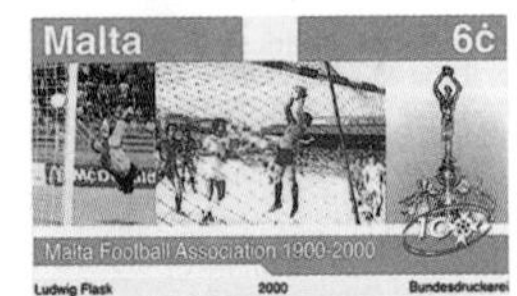

393 Footballers and Trophy (Centenary of Malta Football Association)

2000. Sporting Events. Multicoloured.

1170 6c. Type **393** 35 25
1171 16c. Swimming and sailing (Olympic Games, Sydney) 60 55
1172 26c. Judo, shooting and running (Olympic Games, Sydney) 90 90
1173 37c. Football (European Championship) . . . . . 1·10 1·50

394 "Building Europe"

2000. Europa.

1174 **394** 16c. multicoloured . . . 75 65
1175 46c. multicoloured . . . 2·25 2·00

395 D.H.66 Hercules, 1928

2000. Century of Air Transport, 1900–2000. Mult.

1176 6c. Type **395** 60 60
1177 6c. LZ 127 *Graf Zeppelin*, 1933 . . . . 60 60
1178 16c. Douglas DC-3 Dakota of Air Malta Ltd, 1949 1·10 1·10
1179 16c. Airbus A320 of Air Malta . . . . 1·10 1·10
MS1180 122 × 87 mm. Nos. 1176/9 2·50 2·50

Nos. 1176/7 and 1178/9 were each printed together, se-tenant, with the backgrounds forming composite designs.

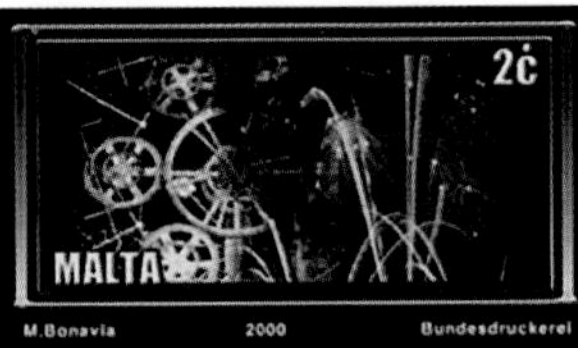

396 Catherine Wheel and Fireworks

2000. Fireworks. Multicoloured.

1181 2c. Type **396** 20 10
1182 6c. Exploding multicoloured fireworks 45 25
1183 16c. Catherine wheel 90 55
1184 20c. Exploding green fireworks . . . . 1·10 90
1185 50c. Numbered rockets in rack . . . . 2·25 2·50

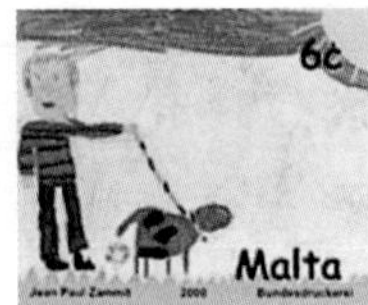

397 "Boy walking Dog" (Jean Paul Zammit)

2000. "Stampin' the Future" (Children's stamp design competition winners). Multicoloured.

1186 6c. Type **397** 40 30
1187 6c. "Stars and Woman in Megalithic Temple" (Chiara Borg) 40 30
1188 6c. "Sunny Day" (Bettina Paris) 40 30
1189 6c. "Hands holding Heart" (Roxana Caruana) . . . 40 30

398 Boy's Sermon, Nativity Play and Girl with Doll

2000. Christmas. Multicoloured.

1190 6c. Type **398** 40 10
1191 6c.+3c. Three Wise Men (23 × 27 mm) 50 50
1192 16c.+3c. Family with Father Christmas . . . . 1·00 1·25
1193 26c.+3c. Christmas tree, church and family . . . . 1·50 1·75
MS1194 174 × 45 mm. Nos. 1190/3 3·00 3·25

399 Crocodile Float

2001. Maltese Carnival. Multicoloured.

1195 6c. Type **399** 40 25
1196 11c. King Karnival in procession (vert) 55 40
1197 16c. Woman and children in costumes (vert) 70 55
1198 19c. Horseman carnival float (vert) . . . . 80 1·00
1199 27c. Carnival procession . . 1·10 1·40
MS1200 127 × 92 mm. 12c. Old-fashioned clowns; 37c. Women dressed as clowns (both 32 × 32 mm) . . . . 2·25 2·40

400 St. Elmo Lighthouse

401 "The Chicken Seller" (E. Caruana Dingli)

2001. Maltese Lighthouses. Multicoloured.

1201 6c. Type **400** 40 25
1202 16c. Gurdan Lighthouse . . 80 65
1203 22c. Delimara Lighthouse 1·00 1·00

2001. Edward Caruana Dingli (painter) Commemoration. Multicoloured.

1204 2c. Type **401** 10 15
1205 4c. "The Village Beau" . . 15 15
1206 6c. "The Faldetta" 25 25
1207 10c. "The Guitar Player" . . 45 45
1208 26c. "Wayside Orange Seller" . . . . 1·25 1·40

402 Nazju Falzon, Gorg Preca and Adeodata Pisani (candidates for Beatification)

2001. Visit of Pope John Paul II. Multicoloured.

1209 6c. Type **402** 40 25
1210 16c. Pope John Paul II and statue of St. Paul . . . . 1·00 85
MS1211 123 × 87 mm. 75c. Pope John Paul with Nazju Falzon, Gorg Preca and Adeodata Pisani 3·25 3·25

403 Painted Frog

2001. Europa. Pond Life. Multicoloured.

1212 16c. Type **403** 75 65
1213 46c. Red-veined darter (dragonfly) . . . . 1·75 2·00

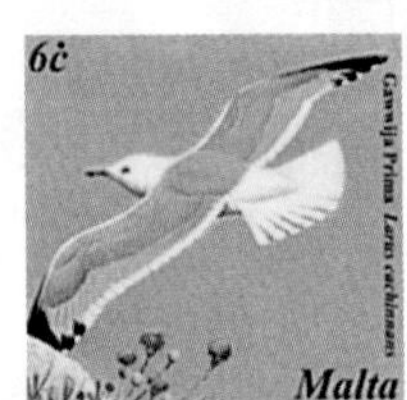

404 Herring Gull ("Yellow-legged Gull") (*Larus cachinnans*)

2001. Maltese Birds. Multicoloured.

1214 6c. Type **404** 40 40
1215 6c. Common kestrel (*Falco tinnunculus*) 40 40
1216 6c. Golden oriole (*Oriolus oriolus*) 40 40
1217 6c. Chaffinch (*Fringilla coelebs*) and Eurasian goldfinch (*Carduelis carduelis*) 40 40
1218 6c. Blue rock thrush (*Monticola solitarius*) . . 40 40
1219 6c. European bee-eater (*Merops apiaster*) 40 40
1220 6c. House martin (*Delichon urbica*) and barn swallow (*Hirundo rustica*) 40 40
1221 6c. Spanish sparrow (*Passer hispaniolensis*) 40 40
1222 6c. Spectacled warbler (*Sylvia conspicillata*) . . . 40 40
1223 6c. Turtle dove (*Streptopelia turtur*) 40 40
1224 6c. Northern pintail (*Anas acuta*) 40 40
1225 6c. Little bittern (*Ixobrychus minutus*) 40 40
1226 6c. Eurasian woodcock (*Scolopax rusticola*) . . . 40 40
1227 6c. Short-eared owl (*Asio flammeus*) 40 40
1228 6c. Northern lapwing (*Vanellus vanellus*) 40 40
1229 6c. Moorhen (*Gallinula chloropus*) 40 40

Nos 1214/29 were printed together, se-tenant, with the backgrounds forming a composite design.

405 Whistle Flute

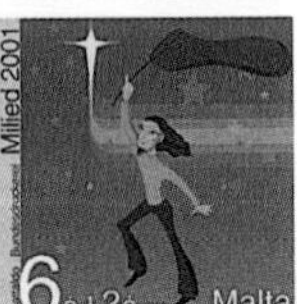

407 Man with Net chasing Star

406 Kelb tal-Fenek (Pharaoh Hound)

2001. Traditional Maltese Musical Instruments. Multicoloured.
1230 1c. Type **405** 10 20
1231 3c. Reed pipe 15 20
1232 14c. Maltese bagpipe 50 45
1233 20c. Friction drum 75 85
1234 25c. Frame drum 1·00 1·25

2001. Maltese Dogs. Multicoloured.
1235 6c. Type **406** 35 25
1236 16c. Kelb tal-Kacca 70 55
1237 19c. Maltese 80 85
1238 35c. Kelb tal-But 1·50 1·75

2001. Christmas. Multicoloured.
1239 6c.+2c. Type **407** 30 30
1240 15c.+2c. Father and children 65 75
1241 16c.+2c. Mother and daughter 70 80
1242 19c.+3c. Young woman with shopping bags 85 1·10

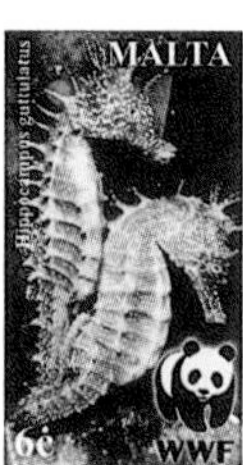

408 *Hippocampus guttulatus*

410 Child's Face painted as Clown

409 Sideboard

2002. Endangered Species. Mediterranean Seahorses. Multicoloured.
1243 6c. Type **408** 35 35
1244 6c. *Hippocampus hippocampus* 35 35
1245 16c. Close-up of *Hippocampus guttulatus* 75 80
1246 16c. *Hippocampus hippocampus* on seabed 75 80

2002. Antique Furniture. Multicoloured.
1247 2c. Type **409** 10 10
1248 4c. Bureau (vert) 10 15
1249 11c. Inlaid table (vert) 35 40
1250 26c. Cabinet (vert) 80 85
1251 60c. Carved chest 2·00 2·10

2002. Europa. Circus.
1252 **410** 16c. multicoloured 50 55

411 *Hyles sammuti*

2002. Moths and Butterflies. Multicoloured.
1253 6c. Type **411** 20 25
1254 6c. *Utetheisa pulchella* 20 25
1255 6c. *Ophiusa tirhaca* 20 25
1256 6c. *Phragmatobia fulginosa melitensis* 20 25
1257 6c. *Vanessa cardui* 20 25
1258 6c. *Polyommatus icarus* 20 25
1259 6c. *Gonepteryx cleopatra* 20 25
1260 6c. *Vanessa atlanta* 20 25
1261 6c. *Eucrostes indigenata* 20 25
1262 6c. *Macroglossum stellatarum* 20 25
1263 6c. *Lasiocampa quercus* 20 25
1264 6c. *Catocala electa* 20 25
1265 6c. *Maniola jurtina hyperhispulla* 20 25
1266 6c. *Pieris brassicae* 20 25
1267 6c. *Papilio machaon melitensis* 20 25
1268 6c. *Dainaus chrysippus* 20 25
No. 1260 is inscribed "atalania" and 1264 "elocata", both in error.

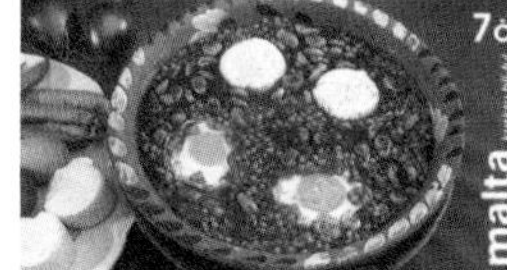

412 "Kusksu Bil-ful" (bean stew)

2002. Maltese Cookery. Multicoloured.
1269 7c. Type **412** 20 25
1270 12c. "Qaqocc mimli" (stuffed artichoke) 40 45
1271 16c. "Lampuki" (dorada with aubergines) 50 55
1272 27c. "Qaghqd Tal-kavatelli" (chestnut dessert) 85 90
MS1273 125 × 90 mm. 75c. "Stuffat Tal-fenek" (rabbit stew) 2·40 2·50

413 *Yavia cryptocarpa* (cactus)

414 Chief Justice Adrian Dingli,

2002. Cacti and Succulents. Multicoloured.
1274 1c. Type **413** 10 10
1275 7c. *Aztekium hintonii* (cactus) (vert) 20 25
1276 28c. *Pseudolithos migiurtinus* (succulent) 85 40
1277 37c. *Pierrebraunia brauniorum* (cactus) (vert) 1·10 1·25
1278 76c. *Euphorbia turbiniformis* (succulent) 2·40 2·50

2002. Personalities.
1279 **414** 3c. green and black 10 10
1280 – 7c. green and black 20 25
1281 – 15c. brown and agate 45 50
1282 – 35c. brown and sepia 1·10 1·25
1283 – 50c. light blue and blue 1·60 1·75
DESIGNS: 7c. Oreste Kirkop (opera singer); 15c. Athanasius Kircher (Jesuit scholar); 35c. Archpriest Saverio Cassar; 50c. Emmanuele Vitali (notary).

415 Mary and Joseph in Donkey Cart

2002. Christmas. Multicoloured.
1284 7c. Type **415** 20 25
1285 16c. Shepherds and Kings on a bus 50 55
1286 22c. Holy Family and angels in luzzu (boat) 70 75
1287 37c. Holy Family in horse-drawn carriage 1·10 1·25
1288 75c. Nativity on Maltese fishing boat 2·40 2·50

416 Vanden Plas Princess Landaulette, 1965

2003. Vintage Cars. Multicoloured.
1289 2c. Type **416** 10 10
1290 7c. Allard "M" type, 1948 20 25
1291 10c. Cadillac Model "B", 1904 30 35
1292 26c. Fiat Cinquecento Model "A" Topolino, 1936 80 85
1293 35c. Ford Anglia Super, 1965 1·10 1·25

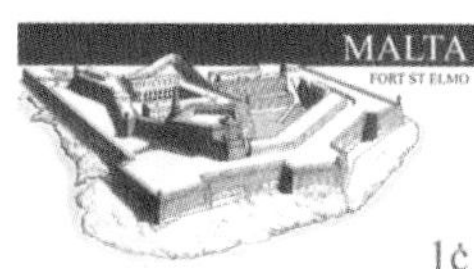

417 Fort St. Elmo

2003. Maltese Military Architecture. Multicoloured.
1294 1c. Type **417** 10 10
1295 4c. Rinella Battery 10 10
1296 11c. Fort St. Angelo 35 40
1297 16c. Section through Reserve Post R15 50 55
1298 44c. Fort Tigne 1·40 1·50

POSTAGE DUE STAMPS

D 1 D 2

1925. Imperf.
D 1 D **1** ½d. black 1·25 6·50
D 2 1d. black 3·25 3·00
D 3 1½d. black 3·00 3·75
D 4 2d. black 7·00 12·00
D 5 2½d. black 2·75 2·75
D 6 3d. black on grey 9·00 14·00
D 7 4d. black on yellow 5·00 9·50
D 8 6d. black on yellow 5·00 16·00
D 9 1s. black on yellow 7·50 21·00
D10 1s. 6d. black on yellow 14·00 55·00

1925. Perf.
D11 D **2** ½d. green 1·25 60
D12 1d. violet 1·25 45
D13 1½d. brown 1·50 80
D14 2d. grey 11·00 1·00
D35 2d. brown 85 70
D36 2½d. orange 60 70
D37 3d. blue 60 60
D38 4d. green 1·00 80
D39 6d. purple 75 1·50
D40 1s. black 90 1·50
D41 1s.6d. red 2·25 6·50

D 3 Maltese Lace D 4

1973.
D42 D **3** 2m. brown and red 10 10
D43 3m. orange and red 10 15
D44 5m. pink and red 15 20
D45 1c. blue and green 30 35
D46 2c. grey and black 40 35
D47 3c. light brown & brown 40 35
D48 5c. dull blue and blue 65 70
D49 10c. lilac and plum 85 1·00

1993.
D50 D **4** 1c. magenta and mauve 15 30
D51 2c. blue and light blue 20 40
D52 5c. green and turquoise 30 45
D53 10c. orange and yellow 45 55

MANAMA Pt. 19

A dependency of Ajman.

100 dirhams = 1 riyal.

1966. Nos. 10, 12, 14 and 18 of Ajman surch **Manama** in English and Arabic and new value.
1 40d. on 40n.p. multicoloured 25 15
2 70d. on 70n.p. multicoloured 50 15
3 1r.50 on 1r.50 multicoloured 1·40 45
4 10r. on 10r. multicoloured 8·25 7·50

1967. Nos. 140/8 of Ajman optd **MANAMA** in English and Arabic. (a) Postage.
5 15d. blue and brown 10 10
6 30d. brown and black 15 15
7 50d. black and brown 35 35
8 70d. violet and black 60 50

(b) Air.
9 1r. green and brown 40 25
10 2r. mauve and black 70 50
11 3r. black and brown 1·10 1·75
12 5r. brown and black 3·50 3·50
13 10r. blue and brown 6·50 6·50

APPENDIX

The following stamps have either been issued in excess of postal needs or have not been available to the public in reasonable quantities at face value. Such stamps may later be given full listing if there is evidence of regular postal use.

1966. New Currency Surcharges. Stamps of Ajman surch **Manama** in English and Arabic and new value.

(a) Nos. 19/20 and 22/4 (Kennedy). 10d. on 10n.p., 15d. on 15n.p., 1r. on 1r., 2r. on 2r., 3r. on 3r.

(b) Nos. 27, 30 and 35/6 (Olympics). 5d. on 5n.p., 25d. on 25n.p., 3r. on 3r., 5r. on 5r.

(c) Nos. 80/2 and 85 (Churchill). 50d. on 50n.p., 75d. on 75n.p., 1r. on 1r., 5r. on 5r.

(d) Nos. 95/8 (Space). Air 50d. on 50n.p., 1r. on 1r., 3r. on 3r., 5r. on 5r.

1967.

World Scout Jamboree, Idaho. Postage 30, 70d., 1r.; Air 2, 3, 4r.

Olympic Games, Mexico (1968). Postage 35, 65, 75d., 1r.; Air 1r.25, 2, 3, 4r.

Winter Olympic Games, Grenoble (1968). Postage 5, 35, 60, 75d.; Air 1, 1r.25, 2, 3r.

Paintings by Renoir and Terbrugghen. Air 35, 65d., 1, 2r. × 3.

1968.

Paintings by Velazquez. Air 1r. × 2, 2r. × 2.

Costumes. Air 30d. × 2, 70d. × 2, 1r. × 2, 2r. × 2.

Olympic Games, Mexico. Postage 1r. × 4; Air 2r. × 4.

Satellites and Spacecraft. Air 30d. × 2, 70d. × 2, 1r. × 2, 2r. × 2, 3r. × 2.

Human Rights Year. Kennedy Brothers and Martin Luther King. Air 1r. × 3, 2r. × 3.

Sports Champions, Famous Footballers. Postage 15, 20, 50, 75d., 1r.; Air 10r.

Heroes of Humanity. Circular designs on gold or silver foil. 60d. × 12.

Olympic Games, Mexico. Circular designs on gold or silver foil. Air 3r. × 8.

Mothers' Day. Paintings. Postage 1r. × 6.

Kennedy Brothers Commem. Postage 2r.; Air 5r.

Cats (1st series). Postage 1, 2, 3d.; Air 2, 3r.

5th Death Anniv of Pres. Kennedy. Air 10r.

Space Exploration. Postage 5, 10, 15, 20, 25d.; Air 15r.

Olympic Games, Mexico. Gold Medals. Postage 2r. × 4; Air 5r. × 4.

Christmas. Air 5r.

1969.

Sports Champions. Cyclists. Postage 1, 2, 5, 10, 15, 20d.; Air 12r.

Sports Champions. German Footballers. Postage 5, 10, 15, 20, 25d.; Air 10r.

Sports Champions. Motor-racing Drivers. Postage 1, 5, 10, 15, 25d.; Air 10r.

Motor-racing Cars. Postage 1, 5, 10, 15, 25d.; Air 10r.

Sports Champions. Boxers. Postage 5, 10, 15, 20d.; Air 10r.

Sports Champions. Baseball Players. Postage 1, 2, 5, 10, 15d.; Air 10r.

Birds. Air 1r. × 11.

Roses. Postage 1r. × 6.

Animals. Air 1r. × 6.

Paintings by Italian Artists. 5, 10, 15, 20d., 10r.

Great Composers. Air 5, 10, 25d., 10r.

Paintings by French Artists. 1r. × 4.

Nude Paintings. Air 2r. × 4.

Kennedy Brothers. Air 2, 3, 10r.

Olympic Games, Mexico. Gold Medal Winners. Postage 1, 2d., 10r.; Air 10d., 5, 10r.

Paintings of the Madonna. Postage 10d.; Air 10r.

Space Flight of "Apollo 9". Optd on 1968 Space Exploration issue. Air 15r.

Space Flight of "Apollo 10". Optd on 1968 Space Exploration issue. Air 15r.

1st Death Anniv of Gagarin. Optd on 1968 Space Exploration issue. 5d.

2nd Death Anniv of Edward White (astronaut). Optd on 1968 Space Exploration issue. 10d.

1st Death Anniv of Robert Kennedy. Optd on 1969 Kennedy Brothers issue. Air 2r.

Olympic Games, Munich (1972). Optd on 1969 Mexico Gold Medal Winners issue. Air 10d., 5, 10r.

Moon Mission of "Apollo 11". Air 1, 2, 3r.

Christmas. Paintings by Brueghel. Postage 1, 2, 4, 5, 10d.; Air 6r.

1970.

"Soyuz" and "Apollo" Space Programmes. Postage 1, 2, 4, 5, 10d.; Air 3, 5r.

Kennedy and Eisenhower Commem. Embossed on gold foil. Air 20r.

Lord Baden-Powell Commem. Embossed on gold foil. Air 20r.

World Cup Football Championship, Mexico. Postage 20, 40, 60, 80d., 1r.; Air 3r.

Brazil's Victory in World Cup Football Championship. Optd on 1970 World Cup issue. Postage 20, 40, 60, 80d., 1r.; Air 3r.

Paintings by Michelangelo. Postage 1, 2, 4, 5, 10d.; Air 6r.

World Fair "Expo 70", Osaka, Japan. Air 25, 50, 75d., 1, 2, 3, 12r.

Paintings by Renoir. Postage 1, 2, 5, 6, 10d.; Air 5, 12r.

Olympic Games, Rome, Tokyo, Mexico and Munich. Postage 15, 30, 50, 70d.; Air 2, 5r.

Winter Olympic Games, Sapporo (1972) (1st issue). Postage 2, 3, 4, 10d.; Air 2, 5r.

Christmas. Flower Paintings by Brueghel. Postage 5, 20, 25, 30, 50d.; Air 60d., 1, 2r.

1971.

Winter Olympic Games, Sapporo (2nd issue). Postage 1, 2, 3, 4, 5, 6, 8, 10, 12, 15, 20, 25, 30, 35, 40, 50d.; Air 75 d, 1, 2, 2r.50.

Roses. Postage 5, 20, 25, 30, 50d.; Air 60d., 1, 2r.

Birds. Postage 5, 20, 25, 30, 50d.; Air 60d., 1, 2r.

Paintings by Modigliani. Air 25, 50, 60, 75d., 1r.50, 3r.

Paintings by Rubens. Postage 1, 2, 3, 4, 5, 10d.; Air 2, 3r.

"Philatokyo '71" Stamp Exhibition, Paintings by Hokusai and Hiroshige. Postage 10, 15, 20, 25, 50, 75d.; Air 1, 2r.

25th Anniv of United Nations. Optd on 1970 Christmas issue. Postage 5, 20, 25, 30, 50d.; Air 60d., 1, 2r.

British Military Uniforms. Postage 5, 20, 25, 30, 50d.; Air 60d., 1, 2r.

Space Flight of "Apollo 14". Postage 15, 25, 50, 60, 70d.; Air 5r.

Space Flight of "Apollo 15". Postage 25, 40, 50, 60d.; Air 1, 6r.

13th World Scout Jamboree, Asagiri, Japan (1st issue). Postage 1, 2, 3, 5, 7, 10, 12, 15, 20, 25, 30, 35, 40, 50, 65, 80d.; Air 1, 1r.25, 1r.50, 2r.

World Wild Life Conservation. Postage 1, 2, 3, 5, 7, 10, 12, 15, 20, 25, 30, 35, 40, 50, 65, 80d.; Air 1r., 1r.25, 1r.50, 2r.

13th World Scout Jamboree, Asagiri, Japan (2nd issue). Stamps. Postage 10, 15, 20, 25, 50, 75d.; Air 1, 2r.

Winter Olympic Games, Sapporo (3rd issue). Postage 1, 2, 3, 4, 5, 10d.; Air 2, 3r.

Cats (2nd series). Postage 15, 25, 40, 60d.; Air 3, 10r.

Lions International Clubs. Optd on 1971 Uniforms issue. Postage 5, 20, 25, 30, 50d.; Air 60d., 1, 2r.

Paintings of Ships. Postage 15, 20, 25, 30, 50d.; Air 60d., 1, 2r.

Great Olympic Champions. Postage 25, 50, 75d., 1r.; Air 5r.

Prehistoric Animals. Postage 15, 20, 25, 30, 50, 60d.; Air 1, 2r.

Footballers. Postage 5, 10, 15, 20, 40d.; Air 5r.

Royal Visit of Queen Elizabeth II to Japan. Postage 10, 20, 30, 40, 50d.; Air 2, 3r.

Fairy Tales. Stories by Hans Andersen. Postage 1, 2, 4, 5, 10d.; Air 3r.

World Fair, Philadelphia (1976). American Paintings. Postage 20, 25, 50, 60, 75d.; Air 3r.

Fairy Tales. Well-known stories. Postage 1, 2, 4, 5, 10d.; Air 3r.

Space Flight of "Apollo 16". Postage 20, 30, 40, 50, 60d.; Air 3, 4r.

Tropical Fishes. Postage 1, 2, 3, 4, 5, 10d.; Air 2, 3r.

European Tour of Emperor Hirohito of Japan. Postage 1, 2, 4, 5, 10d.; Air 6r.

Meeting of Pres. Nixon and Emperor Hirohito of Japan in Alaska. Optd on 1971 Emperor's Tour issue. Air 6r.

2500th Anniv of Persian Empire. Postage 10, 20, 30, 40, 50d.; Air 3r.

Space Flight of "Apollo 15" and Future Developments in Space. Postage 10, 15, 20, 25, 50d.; Air 1, 2r.

1972.

150th Death Anniv (1971) of Napoleon. Postage 10, 20, 30, 40d.; Air 1, 2, 3, 4r.

1st Death Anniv of Gen. de Gaulle. Postage 10, 20, 30, 40d.; Air 1, 2, 3, 4r.

Paintings from the "Alte Pinakothek", Munich. Postage 5, 10, 15, 20, 25d.; Air 5r.

"Tour de France" Cycle Race. Postage 5, 10, 15, 20, 25, 30, 35, 40, 45, 50, 55, 60d.; Air 65, 70, 75, 80, 85, 90, 95d., 1r.

Cats and Dogs. Postage 10, 20, 30, 40, 50d.; Air 1r.

25th Anniv of U.N.I.C.E.F. Optd on 1971 World Scout Jamboree, Asagiri (2nd issue). Postage 10, 15, 20, 25, 50, 75d.; Air 1, 2r.

Past and Present Motorcars. Postage 10, 20, 30, 40, 50d.; Air 1r.

Military Uniforms. 1r. × 11.

The United Arab Emirates Ministry of Communications took over the Manama postal service on 1 August 1972. Further stamps inscribed "Manama" issued after that date were released without authority and had no validity.

MANCHUKUO Pt. 17

Issues for the Japanese puppet Government set up in 1932 under President (later Emperor) Pu Yi.

100 fen = 1 yuan.

1 White Pagoda, Liaoyang

2 Pu Yi, later Emperor Kang-teh

1932. (a) With five characters in top panel as T **1** and **2**.

1	**1**	½f. brown	75	25
2		1f. red	75	10
24		1f. brown	75	10
25		1½f. violet	1·50	75
4		2f. grey	2·25	20
26		2f. blue	3·50	50
27		3f. brown	2·50	10
6		4f. green	50	10
28		4f. brown	18·00	75
7		5f. green	75	15
8		6f. red	3·50	40
9		7f. grey	1·25	20
10		8f. brown	9·00	6·00
11		10f. orange	1·50	15
12	**2**	13f. brown	4·50	4·25
13		15f. red	15·00	75
14		16f. blue	14·00	2·25
15		20f. brown	2·75	40
16		30f. orange	3·25	1·25
17		50f. green	3·75	70
31		1y. violet	8·00	5·50

(b) With six characters in top panel.

40	**1**	½f. brown	25	10
41		1f. brown	25	10
42		1½f. violet	65	40
43		3f. brown	40	10
44		5f. blue	8·50	60
45		5f. slate	3·50	40
46		6f. red	1·00	15
47		7f. grey	1·25	40
48		9f. orange	1·25	20
55		10f. blue	4·25	10
56	**2**	13f. brown	3·75	4·25
49		15f. red	2·00	25
50		18f. green	12·00	3·50
51		20f. brown	2·25	20
52		30f. brown	3·35	35
53		50f. green	3·75	30
54		1y. violet	10·00	3·50

3 Map and Flags

6 Emperor's Palace

1933. 1st Anniv of Republic.

19	**3**	1f. orange	1·25	1·00
20	–	2f. green	8·50	7·50
21	**3**	4f. red	1·25	50
22	–	10f. blue	13·00	11·00

DESIGN: 2, 10f. Council Hall, Hsinking.

1934. Enthronement of Emperor.

32	**6**	1½f. brown	1·25	40
33	–	3f. red	1·75	20
34	**6**	6f. green	5·00	3·75
35	–	10f. blue	7·50	3·75

DESIGN: 3f., 10f. Phoenixes.

1934. Stamps of 1932 surch with four Japanese characters.

36	**1**	1f. on 4f. green (No. 6)	3·50	2·25
37		3f. on 4f. green	22·00	18·00
38		3f. on 4f. brown (No. 28)	4·25	2·50
39	**2**	3f. on 16f. blue (No. 14)	6·50	6·50

In No. 38 the left hand upper character of the surcharge consists of three horizontal lines.

12 Orchid Crest of Manchukuo

13 Changpai Mountain and Sacred Lake

1935. China Mail.

64	**12**	2f. green	45	15
65		2½f. violet	35	15
66	**13**	4f. green	1·00	30
67		5f. blue	25	10
68	**12**	8f. yellow	2·25	30
60	**13**	12f. red	4·50	2·25
70		13f. brown	50	15

15 Mt. Fuji

16 Phoenixes

1935. Visit of Emperor Kang-teh to Japan.

71	**15**	1½f. green	1·00	80
72	**16**	3f. orange	1·50	25
73	**15**	6f. red	3·25	3·25
74	**16**	10f. blue	5·00	2·50

17 Symbolic of Accord

19 State Council Building, Hsinking

20 Chengte Palace, Jehol

1936. Japan–Manchukuo Postal Agreement.

75	**17**	1½f. brown	1·75	1·50
76	–	3f. purple	1·50	25
77	**17**	6f. red	6·50	6·50
78	–	10f. blue	5·50	3·50

DESIGN—HORIZ: 3f., 10f. Department of Communications.

1936.

79	**19**	½f. brown	25	15
80		1f. red	25	10
81		1½f. lilac	2·50	2·00
82	A	2f. green	20	10
83	**19**	3f. brown	25	15
84	B	4f. green	20	10
149	**19**	5f. black	10	1·00
86	A	6f. red	75	10
87	B	7f. black	1·00	10
88		9f. red	75	20
89	**20**	10f. blue	40	10
90	B	12f. orange	25	10
91		13f. brown	10·00	20·00
92		15f. red	1·25	30
93	C	18f. green	7·50	7·50
94		19f. green	3·50	1·50
95	A	20f. brown	1·50	35
96	**20**	30f. brown	1·75	30
97	D	38f. blue	13·00	14·00
98		39f. blue	1·00	1·00
99	A	50f. green	2·25	30
154	**20**	1y. purple	45	2·75

DESIGNS: A, Carting soya-beans; B. Peiling Mausoleum; C, Airplane and grazing sheep (domestic and China air mail); D, Nakajima-built Fokker F.VIIb/3m airplane over Sungari River railway bridge (air mail to Japan).

21 Sun rising over Fields

22 Shadowgraph of old and new Hsinking

1937. 5th Anniv of Founding of State.

101	**21**	1½f. red	5·00	6·00
102	**22**	3f. green	1·50	1·75

1937. China Mail. Surch in Chinese characters.

108	**12**	2½f. on 2f. green	2·75	2·00
110	**13**	5f. on 4f. green	2·75	2·50
111		13f. on 12f. brown	9·50	7·00

27 Pouter Pigeon and Hsinking

1937. Completion of Five Year Reconstruction Plan for Hsinking.

112	**27**	2f. purple	2·00	1·00
113	–	4f. red	2·00	25
114	**27**	10f. green	6·50	4·00
115	–	20f. blue	7·50	5·00

DESIGN: 4, 20f. Flag over Imperial Palace.

29 Manchukuo

30 Japanese Residents Assn. Building

1937. Japan's Relinquishment of Extra-territorial Rights.

116	**29**	2f. red	1·00	25
117	**30**	4f. green	2·75	75
118		8f. orange	3·25	2·00
119	–	10f. blue	2·75	50
120	–	12f. violet	3·50	3·00
121	–	20f. brown	4·75	2·75

DESIGNS—As Type **30**: 10, 20f. Dept. of Communications Bldg. HORIZ: 12f. Ministry of Justice.

32 "Twofold Happiness"

33 Red Cross on Map and Globe

1937. New Year's Greetings.

122	**32**	2f. red and blue	3·00	30

1938. Inaug of Manchukuo Red Cross Society.

123	**33**	2f. red	1·00	1·25
124		4f. green	1·00	25

34 Map of Railway Lines

35 "Asia" Express

1939. Completion of 10,000 Kilometres of Manchurian Railways.

125	**34**	2f. blue and orange	2·75	1·60
126	**35**	4f. deep blue and blue	2·75	1·90

36 Manchurian Cranes over Shipmast

37 Census Official and Manchukuo

38 Census Slogans in Chinese and Mongolian

1940. 2nd Visit of Emperor Kang-teh to Japan.

127	**36**	2f. purple	65	35
128		4f. green	95	50

1940. National Census.

129	**37**	2f. brown and yellow	60	1·50
130	**38**	4f. deep green and green	60	1·50

39 Message of Congratulation

40 Dragon Dance

1940. 2600th Anniv of Founding of Japanese Empire.

131	**39**	2f. red	15	1·50
132	**40**	4f. blue	15	1 50

41 Recruit

(42)

1941. Enactment of Conscription Law.

133	**41**	2f. red	75	1·50
134		4f. blue	75	1·50

1942. Fall of Singapore. Stamps of 1936 optd with T **42**.

135	A	2f. green	1·00	2·00
136	B	4f. green	1·00	2·00

43 Kenkoku Shrine

44 Achievement of Fine Crops

45 Women of Five Races Dancing

46 Map of Manchukuo

1942. 10th Anniv of Founding of State.

137	**43**	2f. red	25	75
138	**44**	3f. orange	2·25	2·25
139	**43**	4f. lilac	40	75
140	**45**	6f. green	2·25	2·50
141	**46**	10f. red on yellow	75	1·50
142	–	20f. blue on yellow	1·00	1·50

DESIGN—HORIZ: 20f. Flag of Manchukuo.

1942. 1st Anniv of "Greater East Asia War". Stamps of 1936 optd with native characters above date **8.12.8**.

143	**19**	3f. brown	1·00	1·75
144	A	6f. red	1·00	1·75

1943. Labour Service Law Proclamation. Stamps of 1936 optd with native characters above heads of pick and shovel.

145	**19**	3f. brown	1·00	1·75
146	A	6f. red	1·00	1·75

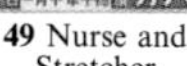

49 Nurse and Stretcher

50 Furnace at Anshan Plant

1943. 5th Anniv of Manchukuo Red Cross Society.
147 **49** 6f. green 75 2·50

1943. 2nd Anniv of "Greater East Asia War".
148 **50** 6f. red 75 2·50

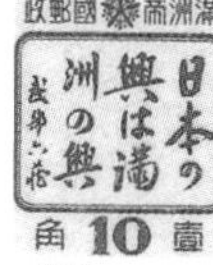

51 Chinese characters

52 Japanese characters

53 "One Heart One Soul"

1944. Friendship with Japan. (a) Chinese characters.
155 **51** 10f. red 25 75
156 40f. green 75 1·00

(b) Japanese characters.
157 **52** 10f. red 25 75
158 40f. green 75 1·00

1945. 10th Anniv of Emperor's Edict.
159 **53** 10f. red 1·25 4·50

MARIANA ISLANDS Pt. 7

A group of Spanish islands in the Pacific Ocean of which Guam was ceded to the U.S.A. and the others to Germany. The latter are now under U.S. Trusteeship.

100 pfennig = 1 mark.

1899. German stamps optd **Marianen**.
7 **8** 3pf. brown 12·00 22·00
8 5pf. green 15·00 22·00
9 **9** 10pf. red 12·00 32·00
10 20pf. blue 20·00 90·00
11 25pf. orange 55·00 £130
12 50pf. brown 60·00 £150

1901. "Yacht" key-type inscr "MARIANEN".
13 N 3pf. brown 75 1·25
14 5pf. green 75 1·90
15 10pf. red 75 2·75
16 20pf. blue 1·10 4·50
17 25pf. black & red on yellow 1·50 9·00
18 30pf. black & orge on buff 1·50 9·00
19 40pf. black and red 1·90 10·50
20 50pf. black & pur on buff 1·90 11·00
21 80pf. black and red on rose 2·40 18·00
22 O 1m. red 4·50 48·00
23 2m. blue 6·75 70·00
24 3m. black 7·50 £100
25 5m. red and black £120 £400

MARIENWERDER Pt. 7

A district of E. Prussia where a plebiscite was held in 1920. As a result the district remained part of Germany. After the War of 1939–45 it was returned to Poland and reverted to its original name of Kwidzyn.

100 pfennig = 1 mark.

1

1920.
1 **1** 5pf. green 70 50
2 10pf. red 70 50
3 15pf. grey 70 50
4 20pf. brown 50 45
5 25pf. blue 40 55
6 30pf. orange 95 1·00
7 40pf. brown 70 70
8 50pf. violet 70 70
9 60pf. brown 3·25 3·50
10 75pf. brown 85 1·00
11 1m. brown and green 1·00 1·00
12 2m. purple 4·25 3·50
13 3m. red 4·50 3·75
14 5m. blue and red 15·00 21·00

1920. Stamps of Germany inscr "DEUTSCHES REICH" optd or surch **Commission Interalliee Marienwerder**.
15 **10** 5pf. green 14·00 28·00
16 20pf. blue 5·50 17·00
17 50pf. black & purple on buff £350 £700
18 75pf. black and green 3·50 4·75
19 80pf. black and red on rose 70·00 £100
25 **12** 1m. red 2·75 5·00
21 **24** 1m. on 2pf. grey 17·00 35·00
26 **12** 1m.25 green 2·75 5·50
27 1m.50 brown 4·00 7·00
22 **24** 2m. on 2½pf. grey 8·50 14·00
28 **13** 2m.50 purple 2·50 5·00
23 **10** 3m. on 3pf. brown 11·50 14·00
24 **24** 5m. on 7½pf. orange 7·25 14·00

1920. As T **1**, with inscription at top changed to "PLEBISCITE".
29 5pf. green 2·50 2·10
30 10pf. red 2·50 1·70
31 15pf. grey 10·50 9·75
32 20pf. brown 1·70 1·40
33 25pf. blue 12·00 11·00
34 30pf. orange 1·20 1·00
35 40pf. brown 1·00 60
36 50pf. violet 1·50 75
37 60pf. brown 4·50 3·25
38 75pf. brown 5·50 5·00
39 1m. brown and green 1·00 60
40 2m. purple 1·40 75
41 3m. red 1·70 1·40
42 5m. blue and red 2·50 2·10

MARSHALL ISLANDS Pts. 7, 22

A group of islands in the Pacific Ocean, a German protectorate from 1885. From 1920 to 1947 it was a Japanese mandated territory and from 1947 part of the United States Trust Territory of the Pacific Islands, using United States stamps. In 1984 it assumed control of its postal services.

A. GERMAN PROTECTORATE

100 pfennig = 1 mark.

1897. Stamps of Germany (a) optd **Marschall-Inseln**.
G1 **8** 3pf. brown £110 £600
G2 5pf. green £425 £375
G3 **9** 10pf. red 42·00 80·00
G4 20pf. blue 42·00 70·00

(b) optd **Marshall-Inseln**.
G 5 **8** 3pf. brown 4·00 4·00
G 6 5pf. green 9·00 6·00
G 7 **9** 10pf. red 8·00 10·50
G 8 20pf. blue 14·00 18·00
G 9 25pf. orange 35·00 29·00
G10 50pf. brown 18·00 35·00

1901. "Yacht" key-type inscr "MARSHALL INSELN".
G11 N 3pf. brown 50 1·40
G12 5pf. green 55 1·10
G13 10pf. red 60 3·00
G14 20pf. blue 90 9·00
G15 25pf. black & red on yell 1·10 11·00
G16 30pf. black & orge on buff 1·10 11·00
G17 40pf. black and red 1·25 11·00
G18 50pf. black & pur on buff 1·90 18·00
G19 80pf. black & red on rose 2·40 28·00
G20 O 1m. red 3·75 55·00
G21 2m. blue 5·00 80·00
G22 3m. black 8·00 £150
G23 5m. red and black £120 £400

B. REPUBLIC

100 cents = 1 dollar.

1 Canoe

1984. Inauguration of Postal Independence. Multicoloured.
1 20c. Type **1** 55 30
2 20c. Fishes and net 55 30
3 20c. Navigational stick-chart 55 30
4 20c. Islet with coconut palms 55 30

2 Mili Atoll

3 German Marshall Islands 1900 3pf. Optd Stamp

1984. Maps. Multicoloured.
5 1c. Type **2** 10 10
6 3c. Likiep Atoll 10 10
7 5c. Ebon Atoll 15 10
8 10c. Jaluit Atoll 15 10
9 13c. Ailinginae Atoll 25 15
10 14c. Wotho Atoll 25 15
11 20c. Kwajalein and Ebeye Atolls 30 20
12 22c. Enewetak Atoll 30 20
13 28c. Ailinglaplap Atoll 45 35
14 30c. Majuro Atoll 45 25
15 33c. Namu Atoll 50 40
16 37c. Rongelap Atoll 55 45
16a 39c. Taka and Utirik Atolls 55 45
16b 44c. Ujelang Atoll 65 50
16c 50c. Aur and Maloclap Atolls 80 65
17 $1 Arno Atoll 1·75 75
18 $2 Wotje and Erikub Atolls 3·25 2·50
19 $5 Bikini Atoll 7·50 6·50
20 $10 Mashallese stick chart (31 × 31 mm) 12·00 10·50

1984. 19th Universal Postal Union Congress Philatelic Salon, Hamburg.
21 **3** 40c. brown, black and yellow 70 50
22 – 40c. brown, black and yellow 70 50
23 – 40c. blue, black and yellow 70 50
24 – 40c. multicoloured 70 50
DESIGNS: No. 22, German Marshall Islands 1901 3pf. "Yacht" stamp; 23, German Marshall Islands 1897 20pf. stamp; 24, German Marshall Islands 1901 5m. "Yacht" stamp.

4 Common Dolphin

1984. "Ausipex 84" International Stamp Exhibition, Melbourne. Dolphins. Multicoloured.
25 20c. Type **4** 50 35
26 20c. Risso's dolphin 50 35
27 20c. Spotter dolphins 50 35
28 20c. Bottle-nosed dolphin 50 35

5 Star over Bethlehem and Text

6 Traditional Chief and German and Marshallese Flags

1984. Christmas. Multicoloured.
29 20c. Type **5** 50 30
30 20c. Desert landscape 50 30
31 20c. Two kings on camels 50 30
32 20c. Third king on camel 50 30

1984. 5th Anniv of Constitution. Multicoloured.
33 20c. Type **6** 50 30
34 20c. Pres. Amata Kabua and American and Marshallese flags 50 30
35 20c. Admiral Chester W. Nimitz and Japanese and Marshallese flags 50 30
36 20c. Trygve H. Lie (first Secretary-General of United Nations) and U.N. and Marshallese flags 50 30

7 Leach's Storm Petrel ("Forked-tailed Petrel")

1985. Birth Bicentenary of John J. Audubon (ornithologist). Multicoloured.
37 22c. Type **7** (postage) 85 85
38 22c. Pectoral sandpiper 85 85
39 44c. Brown booby ("Booby Gannet") (air) 1·50 1·50
40 44c. Whimbrel ("Great Esquimaux Curlew") 1·50 1·50

8 Black-spotted Triton

1985. Sea Shells (1st series). Multicoloured.
41 22c. Type **8** 50 35
42 22c. Monodon murex 50 35
43 22c. Diana conch 50 35
44 22c. Great green turban 50 35
45 22c. Rose-branch murex 50 35
See also Nos. 85/9, 131/5 and 220/4.

9 Woman as Encourager and Drum

1985. International Decade for Women. Mult.
46 22c. Type **9** 40 30
47 22c. Woman as Peacemaker and palm branches 40 30
48 22c. Woman as Nurturer and pounding stone 40 30
49 22c. Woman as Benefactress and lesser frigate bird 65 65
Nos. 46/9 were printed together in se-tenant blocks of four within the sheet, each block forming a composite design.

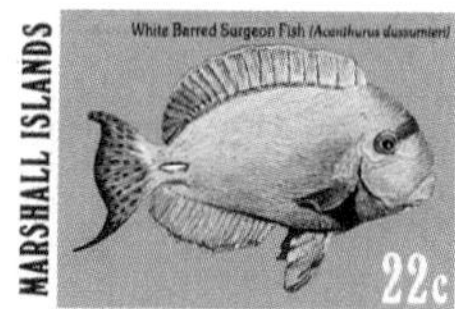

10 Palani ("White Barred Surgeon Fish")

1985. Lagoon Fishes. Multicoloured.
50 22c. Type **10** 60 40
51 22c. Silver-spotted squirrelfish ("White Blotched Squirrel Fish") 60 40
52 22c. Spotted boxfish 60 40
53 22c. Saddle butterflyfish 60 40

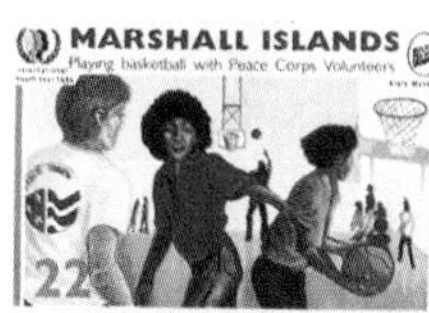

11 Basketball

1985. International Youth Year. Multicoloured.
54 22c. Type **11** 40 30
55 22c. Elderly woman recording for oral history project 40 30
56 22c. Islander explaining navigational stick charts 40 30
57 22c. Dancers at inter-atoll music and dance competition 40 30

12 American Board of Commissions for Foreign Missions Stock Certificate

1985. Christmas. "Morning Star I" (first Christian missionary ship to visit Marshall Islands). Multicoloured.
58 14c. Type **12** 15 30
59 22c. Launching of "Morning Star I", 1856 45 30
60 33c. Departure from Honolulu, 1857 70 50
61 44c. Entering Ebon Lagoon, 1857 80 60

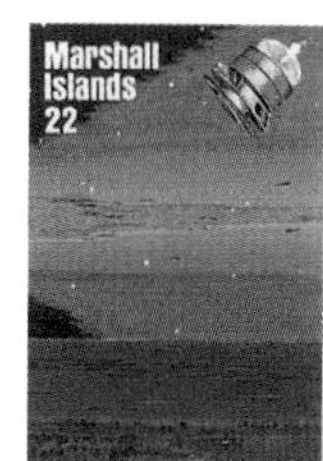

13 "Giotto" and Section of Comet Tail

1985. Appearance of Halley's Comet. Designs showing comet over Roi-Namur Island. Multicoloured.
62 22c. Space shuttle and comet 1·00 55
63 22c. "Planet A" space probe and dish aerial 1·00 55
64 22c. Type **13** 1·00 55
65 22c. "Vega" satellite and buildings on island 1·00 55
66 22c. Sir Edmund Halley, satellite communications ship and airplane 1·00 55
Nos. 62/6 were printed together, se-tenant, forming a composite design.

14 Mallow

1985. Medicinal Plants. Multicoloured.

67 22c. Type **14** 45 35
68 22c. Half-flower 45 35
69 22c. "Guettarda speciosa" . . 45 35
70 22c. Love-vine 45 35

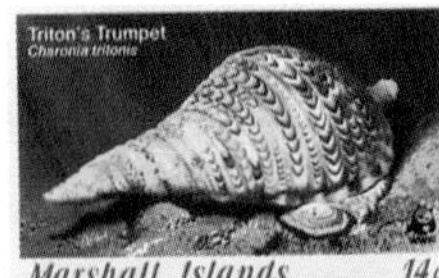

15 Trumpet Triton

1986. World Wildlife Fund. Marine Life. Mult.

71 14c. Type **15** 40 30
72 14c. Giant clam 40 30
73 14c. Small giant clam 40 30
74 14c. Coconut crab 40 30

16 Consolidated PBY-5A Catalina Amphibian

1986. Air. "Ameripex 86" International Stamp Exhibition, Chicago. Mail Planes. Multicoloured.

75 44c. Type **16** 85 65
76 44c. Grumman SA-16 Albatross 85 65
77 44c. Douglas DC-6B 85 65
78 44c. Boeing 727-100 . . . . . 85 65

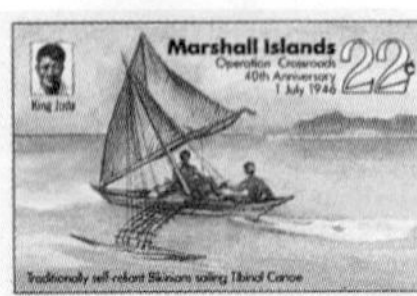

17 Islanders in Outrigger Canoe

1986. 40th Anniv of Operation Crossroads (atomic bomb tests on Bikini Atoll). Multicoloured.

80 22c. Type **17** 55 35
81 22c. Advance landing of amphibious DUKW from U.S.S. "Sumner" 55 35
82 22c. Loading "L.S.T. 1108" (tank landing ship) for islanders' departure 55 35
83 22c. Man planting coconuts as part of reclamation programme 55 35

1986. Sea Shells (2nd series). As T **8**. Multicoloured.

85 22c. Ramose ("Rose") murex 50 35
86 22c. Orange spider conch . . . 50 35
87 22c. Red-mouth frog shell . . 50 35
88 22c. Laciniate conch 50 35
89 22c. Giant frog shell 50 35

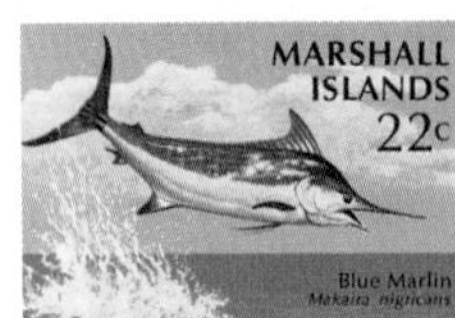

18 Blue Marlin

1986. Game Fishes. Multicoloured.

90 22c. Type **18** 50 40
91 22c. Wahoo 50 40
92 22c. Dolphin 50 40
93 22c. Yellow-finned tuna . . . 50 40

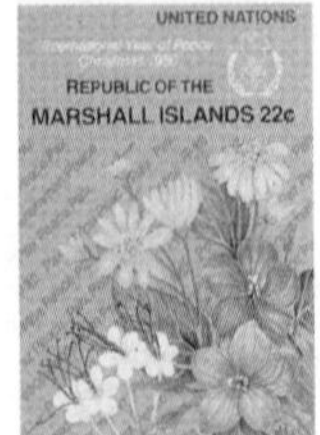

19 Flowers (top left)

1986. International Peace Year. Multicoloured.

94 22c. Type **19** (Christmas) (postage) 50 35
95 22c. Flowers (top right) . . . 50 35
96 22c. Flowers (bottom left) . . 50 35
97 22c. Flowers (bottom right) . . 50 35
98 44c. Head of Statue crowned with flowers (24 × 39 mm) (cent of Statue of Liberty) (air) . . . . 1·00 70

Nos. 94/7 were issued together, se-tenant, in blocks of four within the sheet, each block forming a composite design of mixed flower arrangement.

20 Girl Scout giving Plant to Patient

1986. Air. 20th Anniv of Marshall Island Girl Scouts and 75th Anniv (1987) of United States Girl Scout Movement. Multicoloured.

99 44c. Type **20** 75 55
100 44c. Giving salute 75 55
101 44c. Girl scouts holding hands in circle 75 55
102 44c. Weaving pandana and palm branch mats 75 55

21 Wedge-tailed Shearwater

1987. Air. Sea Birds. Multicoloured.

103 44c. Type **21** . . . . 1·10 1·10
104 44c. Red-footed booby . . . 1·10 1·10
105 44c. Red-tailed tropic bird . . 1·10 1·10
106 44c. Lesser frigate bird ("Great Frigatebird") . . . 1·10 1·00

22 "James T. Arnold", 1854

1987. Whaling Ships. Multicoloured.

107 22c. Type **22** 60 45
108 22c. "General Scott", 1859 60 45
109 22c. "Charles W. Morgan", 1865 . . . . 60 45
110 22c. "Lucretia", 1884 . . . . 60 45

23 Lindbergh's "Spirit of St. Louis" and Congressional Medal of Honour, 1927

1987. Aviators. Multicoloured.

111 33c. Type **23** 70 45
112 33c. Charles Lindbergh and Chance Vought F4U Corsair fighter, Marshall Islands, 1944 . . . . . . 70 45
113 39c. William Bridgeman and Consolidated B-24 Liberator bomber, Kwajalein, 1944 . . . . . 80 60
114 39c. Bridgeman and Douglas Skyrocket, 1951 . . . . . 80 60
115 44c. John Glenn and Chance Vought F4U Corsair fighters, Marshall Islands, 1944 . . . . 1·00 75
116 44c. Glenn and "Friendship 7" space capsule . . . . . 1·00 75

24 Earhart's Lockheed 10E Electra taking off from Lae, New Guinea

1987. Air. "Capex '87" International Stamp Exhibition, Toronto. 50th Anniv of Amelia Earhart's Round the World Flight Attempt. Multicoloured.

117 44c. Type **24** 90 65
118 44c. U.S. Coastguard cutter "Itasca" waiting off Howland Island for Electra 90 65
119 44c. Islanders and crashed Electra on Mili Atoll . . . 90 65
120 44c. Japanese patrol boat "Koshu" recovering Electra 90 65

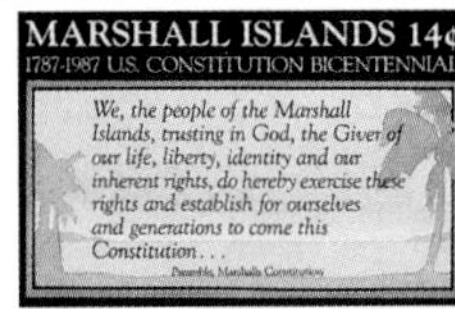

25 "We, the people of the Marshall Islands ..."

1987. Bicentenary of United States of America Constitution. Multicoloured.

122 14c. Type **25** 30 25
123 14c. Marshall Is. and U.S.A. emblems 30 25
124 14c. "We the people of the United States ..." 30 25
125 22c. "All we have and are today as a people ..." . . . 45 25
126 22c. Marshall Is. and U.S.A. flags 45 25
127 22c. "... to establish Justice ..." 45 25
128 44c. "With this Constitution ..." 85 75
129 44c. Marshall Is. stick chart and U.S. Liberty Bell . . . 85 75
130 44c. "... to promote the general Welfare ..." 85 75

The three designs of each value were printed together, se-tenant, the left hand stamp of each strip bearing quotations from the preamble to the Marshall Islands Constitution and the right hand stamp, quotations from the United States Constitution preamble.

1987. Sea Shells (3rd series). As T **8**. Multicoloured.

131 22c. Magnificent cone 50 35
132 22c. Pacific partridge tun . . 50 35
133 22c. Scorpion spider conch 50 35
134 22c. Common hairy triton . . 50 35
135 22c. Arthritic ("Chiragra") spider conch 50 35

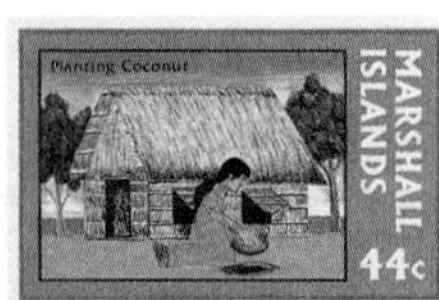

26 Planting Coconut

1987. Copra Industry. Multicoloured.

136 44c. Type **26** 70 55
137 44c. Making copra 70 55
138 44c. Bottling extracted coconut oil 70 55

27 "We have seen his star in the east ..."

1987. Christmas. Multicoloured.

139 14c. Type **27** 30 25
140 22c. "Glory to God in the highest; ..." 40 30
141 33c. "Sing unto the Lord a new song ..." 60 40
142 44c. "Praise him in the cymbals and dances; ..." 80 65

28 Reef Heron ("Pacific Reef Heron")

1988. Shore and Water Birds. Multicoloured.

143 44c. Type **28** . . . . 1·10 1·00
144 44c. Bar-tailed godwit . . . 1·10 1·00
145 44c. Blue-faced booby ("Masked Booby") . . . . 1·10 1·00
146 44c. Northern shoveler . . . 1·10 1·00

29 Maroon Anemonefish ("Damselfish") **30** Javelin Thrower

1988. Fishes. Multicoloured.

147 1c. Type **29** 10 10
148 3c. Black-faced butterflyfish 10 10
149 14c. Stocky hawkfish 20 10
150 15c. White-spotted puffer ("Balloonfish") 20 10
151 17c. Starry pufferfish ("Trunk Fish") 25 15
152 22c. Moon ("Lyretail") wrasse 30 20
153 25c. Six-banded parrotfish . . 30 20
154 33c. Spotted ("White-spotted") boxfish 40 25
155 36c. Yellow ("Spotted") boxfish 45 30
156 39c. Red-tailed surgeonfish 50 40
157 44c. Forceps ("Long-snouted") butterflyfish . . 55 45
158 45c. Oriental trumpetfish . . 55 45
159 56c. False-eyed pufferfish ("Sharp-nosed Puffer") . . 70 50
160 $1 Yellow seahorse . . . . . 1·50 70
161 $2 Ghost pipefish . . . . . 3·50 1·50
162 $5 Clown triggerfish ("Big-spotted Triggerfish") . . . 7·50 5·50
163 $10 Blue-finned trevally ("Blue Jack") (50 × 28 mm) 15·00 11·00

1988. Olympic Games, Seoul. Multicoloured.

166 15c. Type **30** 35 15
167 15c. Drawing javelin back and star 35 15
168 15c. Javelin drawn back fully (value at left) 35 15
169 15c. Commencing throw (value at right) 35 15
170 15c. Releasing javelin 35 15
171 25c. Runner and star (left half) 45 25
172 25c. Runner and star (right half) 45 25
173 25c. Runner (value at left) . . 45 25
174 25c. Runner (value at right) 45 25
175 25c. Finish of race 45 25

Nos. 166/70 were printed together, se-tenant, forming a composite design of a javelin throw with background of the Marshallese flag. Nos. 171/5 were similarly arranged forming a composite design of a runner and flag.

31 "Casco" sailing through Golden Gate of San Francisco

1988. Centenary of Robert Louis Stevenson's Pacific Voyages. Multicoloured.

176 25c. Type **31** 60 60
177 25c. "Casco" at the Needles of Ua-Pu, Marquesas . . . 60 40
178 25c. "Equator" leaving Honolulu 60 40
179 25c. Chieftain's canoe, Majuro Lagoon 60 40
180 25c. Bronze medallion depicting Stevenson by Augustus St. Gaudens, 1887 . . . . 60 40
181 25c. "Janet Nicoll" (inter-island steamer), Majuro Lagoon 60 40
182 25c. Stevenson's visit to maniap of King Tembinoka of Gilbert Islands 60 40
183 25c. Stevenson in Samoan canoe, Apia Harbour . . . 60 40
184 25c. Stevenson on horse Jack at Valima (Samoan home) 60 40

32 Spanish Ragged Cross Ensign (1516–1785) and Magellan's Ship "Vitoria"

1988. Exploration Ships and Flags. Multicoloured.

185 25c. Type **32** 50 35
186 25c. British red ensign (1707–1800), "Charlotte" and "Scarborough" (transports) 50 35
187 25c. American flag and ensign (1837–45), U.S.S. "Flying Fish" (schooner) and U.S.S. "Peacock" (sloop) 50 35
188 25c. German flag and ensign (1867–1919) and "Planet" (auxiliary schooner) . . . 50 35

33 Father Christmas in Sleigh

34 Nuclear Test on Bikini Atoll

1988. Christmas. Multicoloured.

189	25c. Type **33**	45	30
190	25c. Reindeer over island with palm huts and trees	45	30
191	25c. Reindeer over island with palm trees	45	30
192	25c. Reindeer and billfish	45	30
193	25c. Reindeer over island with outrigger canoe	45	30

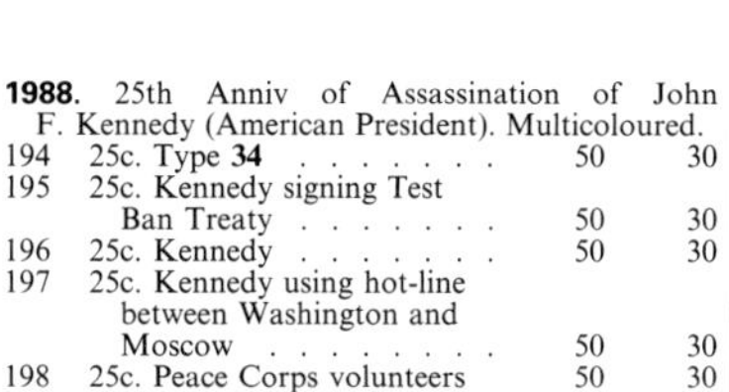

1988. 25th Anniv of Assassination of John F. Kennedy (American President). Multicoloured.

194	25c. Type **34**	50	30
195	25c. Kennedy signing Test Ban Treaty	50	30
196	25c. Kennedy	50	30
197	25c. Kennedy using hot-line between Washington and Moscow	50	30
198	25c. Peace Corps volunteers	50	30

35 "SV-5D PRIME" Vehicle Launch from Vandenberg Air Force Base

1988. Kwajalein Space Shuttle Tracking Station. Multicoloured.

199	25c. Type **35** (postage)	45	30
200	25c. Re-entry of "SV-5D"	45	30
201	25c. Recovery of "SV-5D" off Kwajalein	45	30
202	25c. Space shuttle "Discovery" over Kwajalein	45	30
203	45c. Shuttle and astronaut over Rongelap (air)	75	55

Nos. 199/202 were printed together, se-tenant, forming a composite design.

36 1918 Typhoon Monument, Majuro

1989. Links with Japan. Multicoloured.

204	45c. Type **36**	80	55
205	45c. Japanese seaplane base and railway, Djarret Islet, 1940s	1·25	90
206	45c. Japanese fishing boats	1·25	90
207	45c. Japanese skin-divers	80	55

37 "Island Woman"

1989. Links with Alaska. Oil Paintings by Claire Fejes. Multicoloured.

208	45c. Type **37**	75	55
209	45c. "Kotzebue, Alaska"	75	55
210	45c. "Marshallese Madonna"	75	55

38 Dornier Do-228

1989. Air. Airplanes. Multicoloured.

211	12c. Type **38**	30	20
212	36c. Boeing 737	55	40
213	39c. Hawker Siddeley H.S. 748	65	45
214	45c. Boeing 727	75	55

1989. Sea Shells (4th series). As T **8**. Mult.

220	25c. Pontifical mitre	55	35
221	25c. Tapestry turban	55	35
222	25c. Flame mouthed ("Bull-mouth") helmet	55	35
223	25c. Prickly Pacific drupe	55	35
224	25c. Blood-mouth conch	55	35

40 Wandering Tattler

1989. Birds. Multicoloured.

226	45c. Type **40**	1·10	95
227	45c. Ruddy turnstone	1·10	95
228	45c. Pacific golden plover	1·10	95
229	45c. Sanderling	1·10	95

41 "Bussard" (German cruiser) and 1897 Ship's Post Cancellation

1989. "Philexfrance 89" International Stamp Exhibition, Paris. Marshall Islands Postal History. Multicoloured.

230	25c. Type **41**	1·50	50
231	25c. First day cover bearing first Marshall Islands stamps and U.S. 10c. stamp	1·50	50
232	25c. Consolidated PBY-5 Catalina flying boats, floating Fleet Post Office ("L.S.T. 119"), Majuro, and 1944 U.S. Navy cancellation	1·50	50
233	25c. Nakajima A6M2 "Rufe" seaplane, mailboat off Mili Island and Japanese cancellation	1·50	50
234	25c. Majuro Post Office	1·50	50
235	25c. Consolidated PBY-5A Catalina amphibian, outrigger canoe and 1951 U.S. civilian mail cancellation	1·50	50
236	45c. "Morning Star V" (missionary ship) and 1905 Jaluit cancellation	1·75	55
237	45c. 1906 registered cover with Jaluit cancellation	1·75	55
238	45c. "Prinz Eitel Freiderich" (auxiliary cruiser) and 1914 German ship's post cancellation	1·75	55
239	45c. "Scharnhorst" (cruiser) leading German Asiatic Squadron and 1914 ship's post cancellation	1·75	55

Nos. 230/5 were printed together, se-tenant, Nos. 231 and 234 forming a composite design to commemorate the 5th anniversary of Marshall Islands Independent Postal Service.

42 Launch of Apollo "11"

1989. 20th Anniv of First Manned Moon Landing. Multicoloured.

241	25c. Type **42**	1·00	75
242	25c. Neil Armstrong	1·00	75
243	25c. Descent of lunar module to moon's surface	1·00	75
244	25c. Michael Collins	1·00	75
245	25c. Planting flag on Moon	1·00	75
246	25c. Edwin "Buzz" Aldrin	1·00	75

43 Polish Cavalry and German Tanks

1989. History of Second World War. Multicoloured.

(a) 1st issue. Invasion of Poland, 1939.

248	25c. Type **43**	45	35

(b) 2nd issue. Sinking of H.M.S. "Royal Oak", 1939.

249	45c. U-boat and burning battleship	75	55

(c) 3rd issue. Invasion of Finland, 1939.

250	45c. Troops on skis and tanks	75	55

(d) 4th issue. Battle of the River Plate, 1939.

251	45c. H.M.S. "Exeter" (cruiser)	75	55
252	45c. H.M.S. "Ajax" (cruiser)	75	55
253	45c. "Admiral Graf Spee" (German battleship)	75	55
254	45c. H.M.N.Z.S. "Achilles" (cruiser)	75	55

See also Nos. 320/44, 359/84, 409/40, 458/77, 523/48 and 575/95.

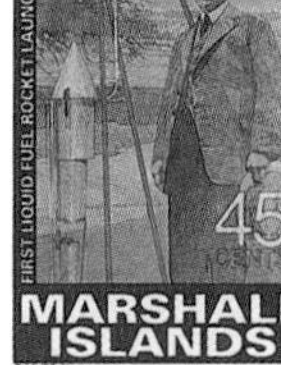

44 Angel with Horn

45 Dr. Robert Goddard

1989. Christmas. Multicoloured.

255	25c. Type **44**	70	50
256	25c. Angel singing	70	50
257	25c. Angel with lute	70	50
258	25c. Angel with lyre	70	50

1989. Milestones in Space Exploration. Multicoloured.

259	45c. Type **45** (first liquid fuel rocket launch, 1926)	90	55
260	45c. "Sputnik 1" (first man-made satellite, 1957)	90	55
261	45c. Rocket lifting off (first American satellite, 1958)	90	55
262	45c. Yuri Gagarin (first man in space, 1961)	90	55
263	45c. John Glenn (first American in Earth orbit, 1962)	90	55
264	45c. Valentina Tereshkova (first woman in space, 1963)	90	55
265	45c. Aleksei Leonov (first space walk, 1965)	90	55
266	45c. Edward White (first American space walk, 1965)	90	55
267	45c. "Gemini 6" and "7" (first rendezvous in space, 1965)	90	55
268	45c. "Luna 9" (first soft landing on the Moon, 1966)	90	55
269	45c. "Gemini 8" (first docking in space, 1966)	90	55
270	45c. "Venera 4" (first successful Venus probe, 1967)	90	55
271	45c. Moon seen from "Apollo 8" (first manned orbit of Moon, 1968)	90	55
272	45c. Neil Armstrong and U.S. flag (first man on Moon, 1969)	90	55
273	45c. "Soyuz 11" and "Salyut 1" space station (first space station crew, 1971)	90	55
274	45c. Lunar rover of "Apollo 15" (first manned lunar vehicle, 1971)	90	55
275	45c. "Skylab 1" (first American space station, 1973)	90	55
276	45c. "Pioneer 10" and Jupiter (first flight past Jupiter, 1973)	90	55
277	45c. "Apollo" and "Soyuz" craft approaching each other (first international joint space flight, 1975)	90	55
278	45c. "Viking 1" on Mars (first landing on Mars, 1976)	90	55
279	45c. "Voyager 1" and Saturn's rings (first flight past Saturn, 1979)	90	55
280	45c. "Columbia" (first space shuttle flight, 1981)	90	55
281	45c. Satellite in outer space (first probe beyond the solar system, 1983)	90	55
282	45c. Astronaut (first untethered space walk, 1984)	90	55
283	45c. Launch of space shuttle "Discovery", 1988	90	55

46 White-capped Noddy ("Black Noddy")

1990. Birds. Multicoloured.

284	1c. Type **46**	20	20
285	5c. Red-tailed tropic bird	20	20
286	9c. Whimbrel	20	20
287	10c. Sanderling	25	25
288	12c. Black-naped tern	25	25
289	15c. Wandering tattler	30	30
290	20c. Bristle-thighed curlew	35	35
291	22c. Greater scaup	40	40
292	23c. Common (inscr "Northern") shoveler	40	40
293	25c. Common (inscr "Brown") noddy	50	50
294	27c. Sooty tern	50	50
295	28c. Sharp-tailed sandpiper	50	50
296	29c. Wedge-tailed shearwater	55	50
297	30c. Pacific golden plover	55	55
298	35c. Brown booby	60	60
299	36c. Red-footed booby	65	65
300	40c. White tern	75	75
301	45c. Green-winged (inscr "Common") teal	85	85
302	50c. Great frigate bird	95	95
303	52c. Crested tern (inscr "Great Crested Tern")	1·10	1·10
304	65c. Lesser sand plover	1·25	1·25
305	75c. Little tern	1·50	1·50
306	$1 Reef heron (inscr "Pacific")	2·25	2·25
307	$2 Blue-faced (inscr "Masked") booby	4·50	4·50

47 Lodidean (coconut-palm leaf windmill)

1990. Children's Games. Multicoloured.

309	25c. Type **47**	70	55
310	25c. Lejonjon (juggling green coconuts)	70	55
311	25c. Etobobo (coconut leaf musical instrument)	70	55
312	25c. Didmakol (pandanus leaf flying-toy)	70	55

48 Penny Black

1990. 150th Anniv of the Penny Black. Multicoloured.

313	25c. Type **48**	75	75
314	25c. Essay of James Chalmers's cancellation	75	75
315	25c. Stamp essay by Robert Sievier	75	75
316	25c. Stamp essay by Charles Whiting	75	75
317	25c. Stamp essay by George Dickinson	75	75
318	25c. "City" medal by William Wyon (struck to commemorate Queen Victoria's first visit to City of London)	75	75

1990. History of Second World War. As T **43**. Multicoloured. (a) 5th issue. Invasions of Denmark and Norway, 1940.

320 25c. German soldier and "Stuka" dive bombers in Copenhagen 45 35
321 25c. Norwegian soldiers, burning building and German column 45 35

(b) 6th issue. Katyn Forest Massacre of Polish Prisoners, 1940.

322 25c. Bound hands and grave (vert) 45 35

(c) 7th issue. Appointment of Winston Churchill as Prime Minister of Great Britain, 1940.

323 45c. Union Jack, Churchill and war scenes 70 50

(d) 8th issue. Invasion of Low Countries, 1940.

324 25c. Bombing of Rotterdam 45 35
325 25c. Invasion of Belgium . . 45 35

(e) 9th issue. Evacuation at Dunkirk, 1940.

326 45c. British bren-gunner on beach 70 50
327 45c. Soldiers queueing for boats 70 50

Nos. 326/7 were issued together, se-tenant, forming a composite design.

(f) 10th issue. German Occupation of Paris, 1940.

328 45c. German soldiers marching through Arc de Triomphe (vert) 70 50

(g) 11th issue. Battle of Mers-el-Kebir, 1940.

329 25c. Vice-Admiral Sir James Somerville, Vice-Admiral Marcel Gensoul and British and French battleships . . 45 35

(h) 12th issue. The Burma Road, 1940.

330 25c. Allied and Japanese forces (vert) 45 35

(i) 13th issue. British Bases and American Destroyers Lend-lease Agreement, 1940.

331 45c. H.M.S. "Georgetown" (formerly U.S.S. "Maddox") 70 50
332 45c. H.M.S. "Banff" (formerly U.S.C.G.C. "Saranac") 70 50
333 45c. H.M.S. "Buxton" (formerly U.S.S. "Edwards") 70 50
334 45c. H.M.S. "Rockingham" (formerly U.S.S. "Swasey") 70 50

(j) 14th issue. Battle of Britain, 1940.

335 45c. Supermarine Spitfire Mk 1A fighters 70 50
336 45c. Hawker Hurricane Mk 1 and Spitfire fighters 70 50
337 45c. Messerschmitt Bf 109E fighters 70 50
338 45c. Junkers Ju 87B-2 "Stuka" dive bomber . . . 70 50

Nos. 335/8 were issued together, se-tenant, forming a composite design.

(k) 15th issue. Tripartite Pact, 1940.

339 45c. Officers' caps of Germany, Italy and Japan (vert) 70 50

(l) 16th issue. Election of Franklin D. Roosevelt for Third United States Presidential Term, 1940.

340 25c. Roosevelt (vert) 45 35

(m) 17th issue. Battle of Taranto, 1940.

341 25c. H.M.S. "Illustrious" (aircraft carrier) 45 35
342 25c. Fairey Swordfish bomber 45 35
343 25c. "Andrea Doria" (Italian battleship) 45 35
344 25c. "Conte di Cavour" (Italian battleship) 45 35

Nos. 341/4 were issued together, se-tenant, forming a composite design.

49 Pacific Green Turtles

1990. Endangered Turtles. Multicoloured.

345 25c. Type **49** . . . . 1·10 75
346 25c. Pacific green turtle swimming . . . . 1·10 75
347 25c. Hawksbill turtle hatching 1·10 75
348 25c. Hawksbill turtle swimming . . . . 1·10 75

50 Stick Chart, Outrigger Canoe and Flag

1990. 4th Anniv of Ratification of Compact of Free Association with United States.

349 **50** 25c. multicoloured 75 45

51 Brandenburg Gate, Berlin

1990. Re-unification of Germany.

350 **51** 45c. multicoloured . . . . 1·00 70

52 Outrigger Canoe and Stick Chart

1990. Christmas. Multicoloured.

351 25c. Type **52** 70 50
352 25c. Missionary preaching and "Morning Star" (missionary ship) 70 50
353 25c. British sailors dancing 70 50
354 25c. Electric guitar and couple dancing 70 50

53 Harvesting Breadfruit

1990. Breadfruit. Multicoloured.

355 25c. Type **53** 70 50
356 25c. Peeling breadfruit . . . 70 50
357 25c. Soaking breadfruit . . . 70 50
358 25c. Kneading dough 70 50

1991. History of Second World War. As T **43**. Multicoloured. (a) 18th issue. Four Freedoms Speech to U.S. Congress by President Franklin Roosevelt, 1941.

359 30c. Freedom of Speech . . . 50 40
360 30c. Freedom from Want . . 50 40
361 30c. Freedom of Worship . . 50 40
362 30c. Freedom from Fear . . 50 40

(b) 19th issue. Battle of Beda Fomm, 1941.

363 30c. Tank battle 50 40

(c) 20th issue. German Invasion of Balkans, 1941.

364 29c. German Dornier DO-17Z bombers over Acropolis, Athens (Greece) (vert) 50 40
365 29c. German tank and Yugoslavian Parliament building (vert) 50 40

(d) 21st issue. Sinking of the "Bismarck" (German battleship), 1941.

366 50c. H.M.S. "Prince of Wales" (battleship) 75 60
367 50c. H.M.S. "Hood" (battle cruiser) 75 60
368 50c. "Bismarck" 75 60
369 50c. Fairey Swordfish torpedo bombers 75 60

(e) 22nd issue. German Invasion of Russia, 1941.

370 30c. German tanks 50 40

(f) 23rd issue. Declaration of Atlantic Charter by United States and Great Britain, 1941.

371 29c. U.S.S. "Augusta" (cruiser) and Pres. Roosevelt of United States (vert) 50 40
372 29c. H.M.S. "Prince of Wales" (battleship) and Winston Churchill (vert) 50 40

Nos. 371/2 were issued together, se-tenant, forming a composite design.

(g) 24th issue. Siege of Moscow, 1941.

373 29c. German tanks crossing snow-covered plain 50 40

(h) 25th issue. Sinking of U.S.S. "Reuben James", 1941.

374 30c. U.S.S. "Reuben James" (destroyer) 50 40
375 30c. German U-boat 562 (submarine) 50 40

Nos. 374/5 were issued together, se-tenant, forming a composite design.

(i) 26th issue. Japanese Attack on Pearl Harbor, 1941.

376 50c. American airplanes (inscr "Peal Harbor") (vert) 75 60
376b As No. 376 but inscr "Pearl Harbor" 75 60
377 50c. Japanese dive bombers (vert) 75 60
378 50c. U.S.S. "Arizona" (battleship) (vert) 75 60
379 50c. "Akagi" (Japanese aircraft carrier) (vert) . . 75 60

Nos. 376/9 were issued together, se-tenant, forming a composite design.

(j) 27th issue. Japanese Capture of Guam, 1941.

380 29c. Japanese troops (vert) 50 40

(k) 28th issue. Fall of Singapore to Japan, 1941.

381 29c. Japanese soldiers with Japanese flag, Union Jack and white flag 50 40

(l) 29th issue. Formation of "Flying Tigers" (American volunteer group), 1941.

382 50c. American Curtiss Tomahawk fighters 75 60
383 50c. Japanese Mitsubishi Ki-21 "Sally" bombers . . 75 60

Nos. 382/3 were issued together, se-tenant, forming a composite design.

(m) 30th issue. Fall of Wake Island to Japan, 1941.

384 29c. American Grumman Wildcat fighters and Japanese Mitsubishi G3M "Nell" bombers over Wake Island 50 40

54 Boeing 747 carrying "Columbia" to Launch Site

1991. Ten Years of Space Shuttle Flights. Multicoloured.

385 50c. Type **54** 90 70
386 50c. Orbital release of Long Duration Exposure Facility from "Challenger", 1984 90 70
387 50c. Shuttle launch at Cape Canaveral 90 70
388 50c. Shuttle landing at Edwards Air Force Base 90 70

Nos. 385/8 were issued together, se-tenant, the backgrounds forming a composite design.

55 "Ixora carolinensis"

1991. Native Flowers. Multicoloured.

389 52c. Type **55** 90 70
390 52c. Glory-bower ("Clerodendum inerme") 90 70
391 52c. "Messerschmidia argentea" 90 70
392 52c. "Vigna marina" 90 70

56 American Bald Eagle and Marshall Islands and U.S. Flags

1991. United States Participation in Operation Desert Storm (campaign to liberate Kuwait).

394 **56** 29c. multicoloured 60 45

57 Red-footed Booby

1991. Birds. Multicoloured.

395 29c. Type **57** 90 40
396 29c. Great frigate bird (facing right) 90 40
397 29c. Brown booby 90 40
398 29c. White tern 90 40
399 29c. Great frigate bird (facing left) 90 40
400 29c. White-capped noddy ("Black Noddy") 90 40

58 Dornier Do-228

1991. Passenger Aircraft. Multicoloured.

402 12c. Type **58** 35 20
403 29c. Douglas DC-8 jetliner 75 50
404 50c. Hawker Siddeley H.S. 748 airliner . . . . 1·25 90
405 50c. Saab 2000 . . . . . . 1·25 90

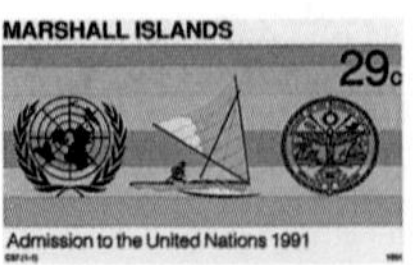

59 U.N. and State Emblems and Outrigger Canoe

1991. Admission of Marshall Islands to the United Nations.

406 **59** 29c. multicoloured 60 45

60 Dove and Glory-bower Flowers

1991. Christmas.

407 **60** 30c. multicoloured 65 50

61 State Flag and Dove

1991. 25th Anniv of Peace Corps in Marshall Islands.

408 **61** 29c. multicoloured 55 45

1992. History of Second World War. As T **43**. Multicoloured. (a) 31st issue. Arcadia Conference, Washington D.C., 1942.

409 29c. Pres. Franklin Roosevelt of U.S.A., Winston Churchill of Great Britain, White House and United Nations emblem 50 40

(b) 32nd issue. Fall of Manila to Japan, 1942.

410 50c. Japanese tank moving through Manila 75 60

(c) 33rd issue. Capture of Rabaul by Japan, 1942.

411 29c. Japanese flag, Admiral Yamamoto, General Douglas MacArthur and U.S. flag 50 40

(d) 34th issue. Battle of the Java Sea, 1942.

412 29c. Sinking of the "De Ruyter" (Dutch cruiser) . . 50 40

(e) 35th issue. Capture of Rangoon by Japan, 1942.

413 50c. Japanese tank and soldiers in Rangoon (vert) 75 60

(f) 36th issue. Japanese Landing on New Guinea, 1942.

414 29c. Japanese soldiers coming ashore 50 40

(g) 37th issue. Evacuation of General Douglas MacArthur from Corregidor, 1942.

415 29c. MacArthur 50 40

(h) 38th issue. British Raid on Saint Nazaire, 1942.

416 29c. H.M.S. "Campbeltown" (destroyer) and motor torpedo boat 50 40

(i) 39th issue. Surrender of Bataan, 1942.

417 29c. Prisoners on "death" march (vert) 50 40

(j) 40th issue. Doolittle Raid on Tokyo, 1942.

418 50c. North American B-25 Mitchell bomber taking off from U.S.S. "Hornet" (aircraft carrier) (vert) . . 75 60

(k) 41st issue. Fall of Corregidor to Japan, 1942.

419 29c. Lt.-Gen. Jonathan Wainwright 50 40

(l) 42nd issue. Battle of the Coral Sea, 1942.

420 50c. U.S.S. "Lexington" (aircraft carrier) and Grumman F4F-3 Wildcat fighter (inscr "U.S.S. Lexington") 75 60
420b As No. 420 but additionally inscr with aircraft name 75 60

421 50c. Japanese Aichi D3A 1 "Val" and Nakajima B5N2 "Kate" dive bombers (wrongly inscr 'Mitsubishi A6M2 "Zero" ') . . . 75 60
421a As No. 421 but inscr corrected . . . 75 60
422 50c. American Douglas TBD-1 Devastator torpedo bombers (wrongly inscr "U.S. Douglas SBD Dauntless") . . . 75 60
422a As No. 422 but with inscr corrected . . . 75 60
423 50c. "Shoho" (Japanese aircraft carrier) and Mitsubishi A6M2 Zero-Sen fighters (inscr "Japanese carrier Shoho") 75 60
423a As No. 423 but additionally inscr with aircraft name 75 60

The four designs were issued together, se-tenant, each pair forming a composite design.

(m) 43rd issue. Battle of Midway, 1942.
424 50c. "Akagi" (Japanese aircraft carrier) . . . 75 60
425 50c. U.S.S. "Yorktown" (aircraft carrier) . . . 75 60
426 50c. American Douglas SBD Dauntless dive bombers . . 75 60
427 50c. Japanese Nakajima B5N2 "Kate" dive bombers . . . 75 60

Nos. 424/7 were issued together, se-tenant, forming a composite design.

(n) 44th issue. Destruction of Lidice (Czechoslovakian village), 1942.
428 29c. Cross and memorial at Lidice . . . 50 40

(o) 45th issue. German Capture of Sevastopol, 1942.
429 29c. German siege gun "Dora" (vert) . . . 50 40

(p) 46th issue. Destruction of Convoy PQ-17, 1942.
430 29c. British merchant ship . . 50 40
431 29c. German U-boat . . . 50 40

(q) 47th issue. Marine Landing on Guadalcanal, 1942.
432 29c. American marines landing on beach . . . 50 40

(r) 48th issue. Battle of Savo Island, 1942.
433 29c. Admiral Mikawa of Japan (vert) . . . 50 40

(s) 49th issue. Dieppe Raid, 1942.
434 29c. Soldiers landing at Dieppe . . . 50 40

(t) 50th issue. Battle of Stalingrad, 1942.
435 50c. Heroes monument and burning buildings (vert) . . 75 60

(u) 51st issue. Battle of Eastern Solomon Islands, 1942.
436 29c. Aircraft over U.S.S. "Enterprise" (aircraft carrier) . . . 50 40

(v) 52nd issue. Battle of Cape Esperance, 1942.
437 50c. American cruiser firing guns at night . . . 75 60

(w) 53rd issue. Battle of El Alamein, 1942.
438 29c. Gen. Bernard Montgomery of Great Britain and Gen. Erwin Rommel of Germany . . . 50 40

(x) 54th issue. Battle of Barents Sea, 1942.
439 29c. H.M.S. "Sheffield" (cruiser) . . . 50 40
440 29c. "Admiral Hipper" (German cruiser) . . . 50 40

62 "Emlain" (bulk carrier)

63 Northern Pintail

1992. Ships flying the Marshall Islands Flag. Multicoloured.
441 29c. Type **62** . . . 70 50
442 29c. "CSK Valiant" (tanker) 70 50
443 29c. "Ionmeto" (fisheries protection vessel) . . . 70 50
444 29c. "Micro Pilot" (inter-island freighter) . . . 70 50

1992. Nature Protection.
445 **63** 29c. multicoloured . . . 60 45

64 Tipnol (outrigger canoe)

65 Basket Making

1992. Legends of Discovery. Multicoloured.
446 50c. Type **64** . . . 75 75
447 50c. "Santa Maria" (reconstruction of Columbus's flagship) . . . 75 75
448 50c. Constellation Argo Navis . . . 75 75
449 50c. Sailor and tipnol . . . 75 75
450 50c. Christopher Columbus and "Santa Maria" . . . 75 75
451 50c. Astronaut and Argo Navis constellation . . . 75 75

1992. Handicrafts. Multicoloured.
453 29c. Type **65** . . . 50 40
454 29c. Boy holding model outrigger canoe . . . 50 40
455 29c. Man carving boat . . . 50 40
456 29c. Fan making . . . 50 40

66 Christmas Offering

1992. Christmas.
457 **66** 29c. multicoloured . . . 50 40

1993. History of Second World War. As T **43**. Multicoloured. (a) 55th issue. Casablanca Conference, 1943.
458 29c. Pres. Franklin Roosevelt and Winston Churchill . . 50 40

(b) 56th issue. Liberation of Kharkov, 1943.
459 29c. Russian tank in Kharkov . . . 50 40

(c) 57th issue. Battle of the Bismarck Sea, 1943.
460 50c. Japanese Mitsubishi A6M Zero-Sen fighters and "Arashio" (Japanese destroyer) . . . 75 60
461 50c. American Lockheed P-38 Lightnings and Australian Bristol Beaufighter fighters 75 60
462 50c. "Shirayuki" (Japanese destroyer) . . . 75 60
463 50c. American A-20 Havoc and North American B-52 Mitchell bombers . . . 75 60

Nos 460/63 were issued together, se-tenant, forming a composite design.

(d) 58th issue. Interception of Yamamoto, 1943.
464 50c. Admiral Yamamoto . . 75 60

(e) 59th issue. Battle of Kursk, 1943.
465 29c. German "Tiger 1" tank 50 40
466 29c. Soviet "T-34" tank . . . 50 40

Nos. 465/6 were issued together, se-tenant, forming a composite design.

(f) 60th issue. Allied Invasion of Sicily, 1943.
467 52c. Gen. George Patton, Jr 85 60
468 52c. Gen. Bernard Montgomery . . . 85 65
469 52c. Americans landing at Licata . . . 85 65
470 52c. British landing south of Syracuse . . . 85 65

(g) 61st issue. Raids on Schweinfurt, 1943.
471 50c. American Boeing B-17F Flying Fortress bombers and German Messerschmitt Bf 109 fighter . . . 75 60

(h) 62nd issue. Liberation of Smolensk, 1943.
472 29c. Russian soldier and burning buildings (vert) . . 50 40

(i) 63rd issue. Landing at Bougainville, 1943.
473 29c. American Marines on beach at Empress Augusta Bay . . . 50 40

(j) 64th issue. U.S. Invasion of Tarawa, 1943.
474 50c. American Marines . . . 75 60

(k) 65th issue. Teheran Allied Conference, 1943.
475 52c. Winston Churchill of Great Britain, Pres. Franklin Roosevelt of U.S.A. and Josef Stalin of Russia (vert) . . . 85 65

(l) 66th issue. Battle of North Cape, 1943.
476 29c. H.M.S. "Duke of York" (British battleship) . . . 50 40
477 29c. "Scharnhorst" (German battleship) . . . 50 40

67 Atoll Butterflyfish

1993. Reef Life. Multicoloured.
478 50c. Type **67** . . . 90 60
479 50c. Brick soldierfish . . . 90 60
480 50c. Caerulean damselfish . . 90 60
481 50c. Japanese inflator-filefish 90 60
482 50c. Arc-eyed hawkfish . . . 90 60
483 50c. Powder-blue surgeonfish 90 60

68 "Britannia" (full-rigged ship)

1993. Ships. Multicoloured. (a) Size 35 × 20 mm.
485 10c. "San Jeronimo" (Spanish galleon) . . . 10 10
486 14c. U.S.C.G. "Cape Corwin" (fisheries patrol vessel) . . . 15 10
487 15c. Type **68** . . . 20 15
488 19c. "Micro Palm" (inter-island freighter) . . . 25 15
489 20c. "Eendracht" (Dirk Hartog's ship) . . . 30 15
490 23c. H.M.S "Cornwallis" (sail frigate) . . . 35 20
491 24c. U.S.S. "Dolphin" (schooner) . . . 40 20
492 29c. "Morning Star I" (missionary brigantine) . . 45 25
493 30c. "Rurik" (Otto von Kotzebue's brig) (inscr "Rurick") . . . 50 25
494 32c. "Vitoria" (Magellan's flagship) . . . 55 25
669 32c. As Type **68** . . . 50 40
670 32c. U.S.S. "Dolphin" (schooner) . . . 50 40
671 32c. "Morning Star I" (missionary brigantine) . . 50 40
672 32c. U.S.S. "Lexington" (aircraft carrier) . . . 50 40
673 32c. "Micro Palm" (inter-island freighter) . . . 50 40
674 32c. H.M.S. "Cornwallis" (sail frigate) . . . 50 40
675 32c. H.M.S. "Serpent" (brig) 50 40
676 32c. "Scarborough" (transport) . . . 50 40
677 32c. "San Jeronimo" (Spanish galleon) . . . 50 40
678 32c. "Rurik" (Otto van Kotzebue's brig) (inscr "Rurick") . . . 50 40
679 32c. "Nautilus" (German gunboat) . . . 50 40
680 32c. Fishing vessels . . . 50 40
681 32c. Malmel outrigger canoe 50 40
682 32c. "Eendracht" (Dirk Hartog's ship) . . . 50 40
683 32c. "Nautilus" (brig) . . . 50 40
684 32c. "Nagara" and "Isuzu" (Japanese cruisers) . . . 50 40
685 32c. "Potomac" (whaling ship) . . . 50 40
687 32c. U.S.C.G. "Assateague" (cutter) . . . 50 40
688 32c. "Charles W. Morgan" (whaling ship) . . . 50 40
689 32c. "Victoria" (whaling ship) 50 40
690 32c. U.S.C.G. "Cape Corwin" (fisheries patrol vessel) . . . 50 40
691 32c. "Equator" (schooner) . . 50 40
692 32c. "Tanager" (inter-island steamer) . . . 50 40
693 32c. "Tole Mour" (hospital schooner) . . . 50 40
495 35c. "Nautilus" (German gunboat) . . . 60 30
496 40c. "Nautilus" (British brig) 65 30
497 45c. "Nagara" and "Isuzu" (Japanese cruisers) . . . 70 35
498 46c. "Equator" (schooner) . . 75 35
499 50c. U.S.S. "Lexington" (aircraft carrier) . . . 80 40
500 52c. H.M.S. "Serpent" (brig) 85 45
501 55c. "Potomac" (whaling ship) . . . 90 50
502 60c. U.S.C.G. "Assateague" (cutter) . . . 1·00 70
503 75c. "Scarborough" (transport) . . . 1·10 75
504 78c. "Charles W. Morgan" (whaling ship) . . . 1·25 90
505 95c. "Tanager" (inter-island steamer) . . . 1·40 1·00
506 $1 "Tole Mour" (hospital schooner) . . . 1·50 1·10
507 $2.90 Fishing vessels . . . 4·25 2·75
508 $3.00 "Victoria" (whaling ship) . . . 4·50 3·00

(b) Size 46 × 26 mm.
509 $1 Enewetak outrigger canoe 1·50 1·00
510 $2 Jaluit outrigger canoe . . 4·00 3·00
511 $5 Ailuk outrigger canoe . . 7·00 5·00
512 $10 Racing outrigger canoes 14·00 10·00

69 Capitol Complex

1993. Inauguration of New Capitol Complex, Majuro. Multicoloured.
513 29c. Type **69** . . . 40 25
514 29c. Parliament building . . 40 25
515 29c. National seal (vert) . . . 40 25
516 29c. National flag (vert) . . . 40 25

71 Woman with Breadfruit

1993. Marshallese Life in the 1800s. Designs adapted from sketches by Louis Choris. Multicoloured.
518 29c. Type **71** . . . 50 35
519 29c. Canoes and warrior . . 50 35
520 29c. Chief and islanders . . . 50 35
521 29c. Drummer and dancers 50 35

72 Singing Silent Night

1993. Christmas.
522 **72** 29c. multicoloured . . . 50 35

1994. History of Second World War. As T **43**. Multicoloured. (a) 67th issue. Appointment of Gen. Dwight D. Eisenhower as Commander of Supreme Headquarters, Allied Expeditionary Force, 1944.
523 29c. Eisenhower . . . 50 40

(b) 68th issue. Invasion of Anzio, 1944.
524 50c. Troops landing . . . 70 60

(c) 69th issue. Lifting of Siege of Leningrad, 1944.
525 52c. St. Isaac's Cathedral and soldier with Soviet flag . . 85 65

(d) 70th issue. U.S. Liberation of Marshall Islands, 1944.
526 29c. Douglas SBD Dauntless dive bombers . . . 50 40

(e) 71st issue. Japanese Defeat at Truk, 1944.
527 29c. Admirals Spruance and Marc Mitscher (vert) . . . 50 40

(f) 72nd issue. U.S. Bombing of Germany, 1944.
528 52c. Boeing B-17 Flying Fortress bombers . . . 85 65

(g) 73rd issue. Allied Liberation of Rome, 1944.
529 50c. Lt.-Gen. Mark Clark and flowers in gun barrel (vert) . . . 75 60

(h) 74th issue. Allied Landings in Normandy, 1944.
530 75c. Airspeed A.S.51 Horsa gliders (inscr "Horsa Gliders") . . . 1·10 80
530b As No. 530 but inscr "Horsa Gliders, Parachute Troops" . . . 1·10 80
531 75c. Hawker Typhoon 1B and North American P-51B Mustang fighters (wrongly inscr "U.S. P51B Mustangs, British Hurricanes") . . . 1·10 80
531a As No. 531 but inscr corrected . . . 1·10 80
532 75c. German gun defences (inscr "German Gun Defenses") . . . 1·10 80
532a As No. 523 but inscr "German Gun Defenses, Pointe du Hoc" . . . 1·10 80
533 75c. Allied amphibious landing . . . 1·10 80

The four designs were issued together, se-tenant, forming a composite design.

(i) 75th issue. V-1 Bombardment of England, 1944.
534 50c. V-1 flying bomb over River Thames . . . 75 60

(j) 76th issue. U.S. Marines Land on Saipan, 1944.
535 29c. U.S. and Japanese troops . . . 50 40

(k) 77th issue. First Battle of the Philippine Sea, 1944.
536 50c. Grumman F6F-3 Hellcat fighter . . . 75 60

(l) 78th issue. U.S. Liberation of Guam, 1944.
537 29c. Naval bombardment . . . 50 40

(m) 79th issue. Warsaw Uprising, 1944.
538 50c. Polish Home Army fighter . . . 75 60

(n) 80th issue. Liberation of Paris, 1944.
539 50c. Allied troops marching along Champs Elysee . . . 75 60

(o) 81st issue. U.S. Marines Land on Peleliu, 1944.
540 29c. Amphibious armoured tracked vehicle . . . 50 40

(p) 82nd issue. General Douglas MacArthur's Return to Philippines, 1944.
541 52c. McArthur and soldiers 85 65

(q) 83rd issue. Battle of Leyte Gulf, 1944.
542 52c. American motor torpedo boat and Japanese warships . . . 85 65

(r) 84th issue. Sinking of the "Tirpitz" (German battleship), 1944.
543 50c. Avro Lancaster bombers 75 60
544 50c. Tirpitz burning . . . 75 60

(s) 85th issue. Battle of the Bulge, 1944.
545 50c. Infantrymen . . . 75 60
546 50c. Tank driver and tanks 75 60
547 50c. Pilot and aircraft . . . 75 60
548 50c. Lt.-Col. Creighton Abrams and Brig.-Gen. Anthony McAuliffe shaking hands . . . 75 60

75 Footballers

76 Neil Armstrong stepping onto Moon

1994. World Cup Football Championship, U.S.A. Multicoloured.

552 50c. Type **75** . . . . 1·40 60
553 50c. Footballers (different) 1·40 60

Nos. 552/53 were issued together, se-tenant, forming a composite design.

1994. 25th Anniv of First Manned Moon Landing. Multicoloured.

554 75c. Type **76** 95 70
555 75c. Planting U.S. flag on Moon 95 70
556 75c. Astronauts saluting . . . 95 70
557 75c. Pres. John F. Kennedy and Armstrong 95 70

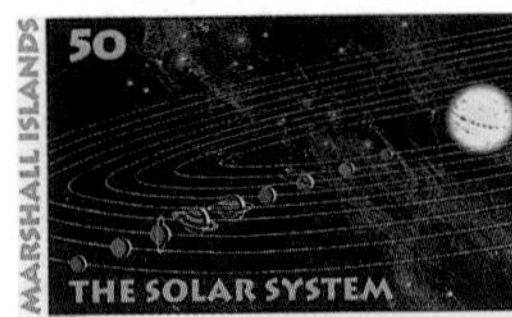

77 Solar System

1994. The Solar System. Multicoloured.

559 50c. Type **77** 85 65
560 50c. Sun 85 65
561 50c. Moon 85 65
562 50c. Mercury 85 65
563 50c. Venus 85 65
564 50c. Earth 85 65
565 50c. Mars 85 65
566 50c. Jupiter 85 65
567 50c. Saturn 85 65
568 50c. Uranus 85 65
569 50c. Neptune 85 65
570 50c. Pluto 85 65

79 Church and Christmas Tree (Ringo Baso)

1994. Christmas.

573 **79** 29c. multicoloured 50 40

1995. History of Second World War. As T **43**. Multicoloured. (a) 86th issue. Yalta Conference, 1945.

575 32c. Josef Stalin of U.S.S.R., Winston Churchill of Great Britain and Franklin Roosevelt of U.S.A. (vert) 55 45

(b) 87th issue. Allied Bombing of Dresden, 1945.

576 55c. "Europe" (Meissen porcelain statuette), flames and bombers (vert) 90 70

(c) 88th issue. U.S. Marine Invasion of Iwo Jima, 1945.

577 $1 Marines planting flag on Mt. Suribachi (vert) . . . 1·60 1·25

(d) 89th issue. U.S. Capture of Remagen Bridge, Germany, 1945.

578 32c. Troops and tanks crossing bridge (vert) . . . 55 45

(e) 90th issue. U.S. Invasion of Okinawa, 1945.

579 55c. Soldiers throwing grenades (vert) 90 70

(f) 91st issue. Death of Franklin D. Roosevelt, 1945.

580 50c. Funeral cortege 75 60

(g) 92nd issue. U.S. and U.S.S.R. Troops meet at Elbe, 1945.

581 32c. American and Soviet troops 55 45

(h) 93rd issue. Capture of Berlin by Soviet Troops, 1945.

582 60c. Soviet Marshal Georgi Zhukov and Berlin landmarks 95 75

(i) 94th issue. Allied Liberation of Concentration Camps, 1945.

583 55c. Inmates and soldier cutting barbed-wire fence 90 70

(j) 95th issue. V-E (Victory in Europe) Day, 1945.

584 75c. Signing of German surrender, Rheims . . . . 1·10 80
585 75c. Soldier kissing girl, Times Square, New York 1·10 80

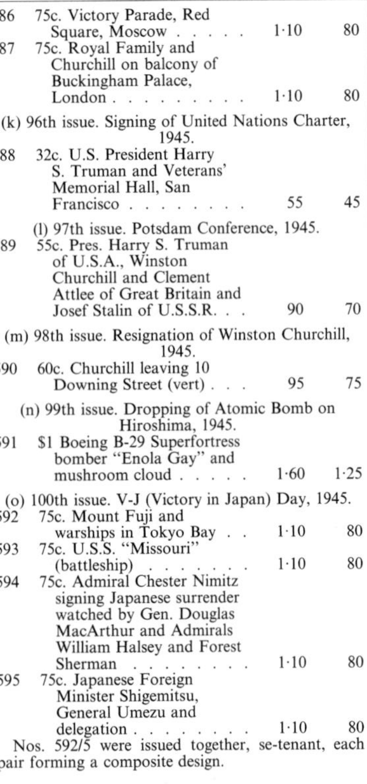

586 75c. Victory Parade, Red Square, Moscow . . . . . 1·10 80
587 75c. Royal Family and Churchill on balcony of Buckingham Palace, London . . . . 1·10 80

(k) 96th issue. Signing of United Nations Charter, 1945.

588 32c. U.S. President Harry S. Truman and Veterans' Memorial Hall, San Francisco 55 45

(l) 97th issue. Potsdam Conference, 1945.

589 55c. Pres. Harry S. Truman of U.S.A., Winston Churchill and Clement Attlee of Great Britain and Josef Stalin of U.S.S.R. . . 90 70

(m) 98th issue. Resignation of Winston Churchill, 1945.

590 60c. Churchill leaving 10 Downing Street (vert) . . . 95 75

(n) 99th issue. Dropping of Atomic Bomb on Hiroshima, 1945.

591 $1 Boeing B-29 Superfortress bomber "Enola Gay" and mushroom cloud . . . . . 1·60 1·25

(o) 100th issue. V-J (Victory in Japan) Day, 1945.

592 75c. Mount Fuji and warships in Tokyo Bay . . 1·10 80
593 75c. U.S.S. "Missouri" (battleship) . . . . 1·10 80
594 75c. Admiral Chester Nimitz signing Japanese surrender watched by Gen. Douglas MacArthur and Admirals William Halsey and Forest Sherman . . . . 1·10 80
595 75c. Japanese Foreign Minister Shigemitsu, General Umezu and delegation . . . . 1·10 80

Nos. 592/5 were issued together, se-tenant, each pair forming a composite design.

81 Scuba Diver, Meyer's Butterflyfish and Red-tailed Surgeonfish ("Achilles Tang")

1995. Undersea World (1st series). Multicoloured.

596 55c. Type **81** 90 70
597 55c. Moorish idols and scuba diver 90 70
598 55c. Pacific green turtle and anthias ("Fairy Basslet") 90 70
599 55c. Anthias ("Fairy Basslet"), emperor angelfish and orange-finned anemonefish 90 70

Nos. 596/9 were issued together, se-tenant, forming a composite design.

See also Nos. 865/8.

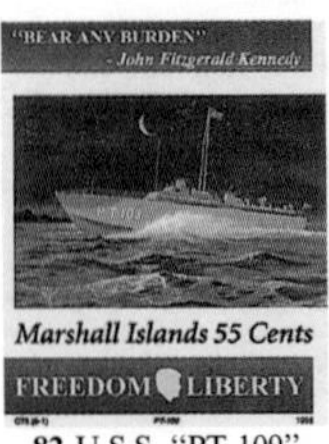

82 U.S.S. "PT 109" (motor torpedo boat)

83 Marilyn Monroe

1995. 35th Anniv of Election of John F. Kennedy as U.S. President. Multicoloured.

600 55c. Type **82** (Second World War command) 80 65
601 55c. Presidential inauguration 80 65
602 55c. Peace corps on agricultural project in Marshall Islands 80 65
603 55c. U.S. airplane and warships superintending removal of Soviet missiles from Cuba 80 65
604 55c. Kennedy signing Nuclear Test Ban Treaty, 1963 . . 80 65
605 55c. Eternal flame on Kennedy's grave, Arlington National Cemetery, Washington D.C. 80 65

1995. 69th Birth Anniv of Marilyn Monroe (actress). Multicoloured.

606 75c. Type **83** . . . . 1·10 80
607 75c. Monroe (face value top right) . . . . 1·10 80
608 75c. Monroe (face value bottom left) . . . . 1·10 80
609 75c. Monroe (face value bottom right) . . . . . . 1·10 80

85 "Mir" (Soviet space station)

86 Siamese and Exotic Shorthair

1995. Docking of Atlantis with "Mir" Space Station (611/12) and 20th Anniv of "Apollo"–"Soyuz" Space Link (613/14). Multicoloured.

611 75c. Type **85** . . . . 1·10 80
612 75c. "Atlantis" (U.S. space shuttle) . . . . 1·10 80
613 75c. "Apollo" (U.S. spacecraft) . . . . 1·10 80
614 75c. "Soyuz" (Soviet spacecraft) . . . . 1·10 80

Nos. 611/14 were issued together, se-tenant, forming a composite design.

1995. Cats. Multicoloured.

615 32c. Type **86** 55 45
616 32c. American shorthair tabby and red Persian . . 55 45
617 32c. Maine coon and Burmese 55 45
618 32c. Himalayan and Abyssinian 55 45

87 Sailfish and Tuna

1995. Pacific Game Fish. Multicoloured.

619 60c. Type **87** . . . . 1·00 75
620 60c. Albacores . . . . 1·00 75
621 60c. Wahoo . . . . 1·00 75
622 60c. Blue marlin . . . . . . 1·00 75
623 60c. Yellow-finned tunas . . 1·00 75
624 60c. Giant trevally . . . . . 1·00 75
625 60c. Dolphin (fish) . . . . . 1·00 75
626 60c. Short-finned mako . . . 1·00 75

Nos. 619/26 were issued together, se-tenant, forming a composite design.

88 Inedel's Magic Kite

91 Shepherds gazing at Sky

1995. Folk Legends (1st series). Multicoloured.

627 32c. Type **88** 60 45
628 32c. Lijebake rescues her granddaughter 60 45
629 32c. Jebro's mother invents the sail 60 45
630 32c. Limajnon escapes to the moon 60 45

See also Nos. 727/30 and 861/4.

1995. Christmas.

633 **91** 32c. multicoloured 45 25

92 Messerschmit Me 262-1a Schwalbe

93 Rabin

1995. Jet Fighters. Multicoloured.

634 32c. Type **92** 50 40
635 32c. Gloster Meteor F Mk 8 50 40
636 32c. Lockheed F-80 Shooting Star 50 40
637 32c. North American F-86 Sabre 50 40
638 32c. F9F-2 Panther 50 40
639 32c. Mikoyan Gurevich MiG-15 . . . . 50 40
640 32c. North American F-100 Super Sabre 50 40
641 32c. Convair TF-102A Delta Dagger 50 40
642 32c. Lockheed F-104 Starfighter 50 40
643 32c. Mikoyan Gurevich MiG-21 MT 50 40
644 32c. F8U Crusader 50 40
645 32c. Republic F-105 Thunderchief 50 40
646 32c. Saab J35 Draken 50 40
647 32c. Fiat G-91Y 50 40
648 32c. McDonnell Douglas F-4 Phantom II 50 40
649 32c. Saab JA 37 Viggen . . . 50 40
650 32c. Dassault Mirage F1C . . 50 40
651 32c. Grumman F-14 Tomcat 50 40
652 32c. F-15 Eagle 50 40
653 32c. General Dynamics F-16 Fighting Falcon 50 40
654 32c. Panavia Tornado F Mk 3 . . . . 50 40
655 32c. Sukhoi Su-27UB 50 40
656 32c. Dassault Mirage 2000C 50 40
657 32c. Hawker Siddeley Sea Harrier FRS.MK1 . . . . 50 40
658 32c. F-117 Nighthawk . . . 50 40

1995. Yitzhak Rabin (Israeli Prime Minister) Commemoration.

659 **93** 32c. multicoloured 45 35

95 Blue-grey Noddy

1996. Birds. Multicoloured.

661 32c. Type **95** 70 55
662 32c. Spectacled tern ("Gray-backed Tern") 70 55
663 32c. Blue-faced booby ("Masked Booby") 70 55
664 32c. Black-footed albatross 70 55

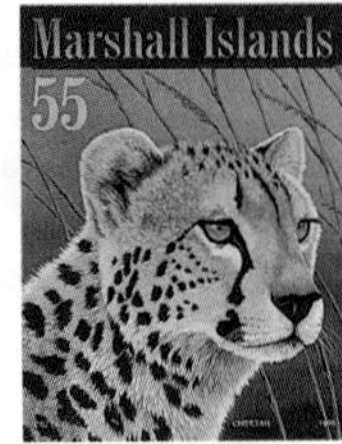

96 Cheetah

1996. Big Cats. Multicoloured.

665 55c. Type **96** 90 70
666 55c. Tiger 90 70
667 55c. Lion 90 70
668 55c. Jaguar 90 70

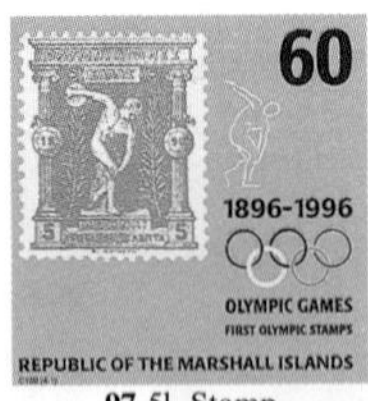

97 5l. Stamp

1996. Centenary of Modern Olympic Games. Designs reproducing 1896 Greek Olympic stamps. Multicoloured.

694 60c. Type **97** 90 70
695 60c. 60l. stamp 90 70
696 60c. 40l. stamp 90 70
697 60c. 1d. stamp 90 70

98 Undersea Eruptions form Islands

99 Presley

1996. History of Marshall Islands. Multicoloured.

698 55c. Type **98** 75 60
699 55c. Coral reefs grow around islands 75 60
700 55c. Storm-driven birds carry seeds to atolls 75 60
701 55c. First human inhabitants arrive, 1500 B.C. 75 60
702 55c. Spanish explorers discover islands, 1527 . . . 75 60
703 55c. John Marshall charts islands, 1788 . . . . . . 75 60
704 55c. German Protectorate, 1885 . . . . 75 60

705 55c. Japanese soldier on beach, 1914 . . . . 75 60
706 55c. American soldiers liberate islands, 1944 . . . 75 60
707 55c. Evacuation of Bikini Atoll for nuclear testing, 1946 . . . . 75 60
708 55c. Marshall Islands becomes United Nations Trust Territory, 1947 . . . 75 60
709 55c. People and national flag (independence, 1986) . . . 75 60

1996. 40th Anniv of Elvis Presley's First Number One Hit Record "Heartbreak Hotel".
710 **99** 32c. multicoloured 50 40

101 Dean

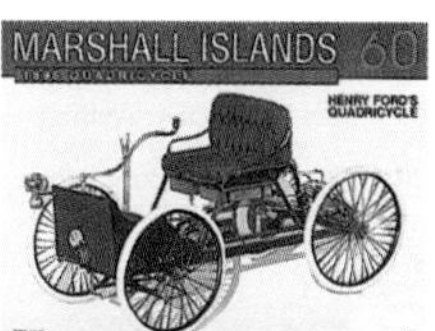

102 1896 Quadricycle

1996. 65th Birth Anniv of James Dean (actor).
712 **101** 32c. multicoloured 50 40

1996. Centenary of Ford Motor Vehicle Production. Multicoloured.
713 60c. Type **102** 80 60
714 60c. 1903 Model A Roadster 80 60
715 60c. 1909 Model T touring car 80 60
716 60c. 1929 Model A station wagon 80 60
717 60c. 1955 "Thunderbird" . . 80 60
718 60c. 1964 "Mustang" convertible 80 60
719 60c. 1995 "Explorer" 80 60
720 60c. 1996 "Taurus" 80 60

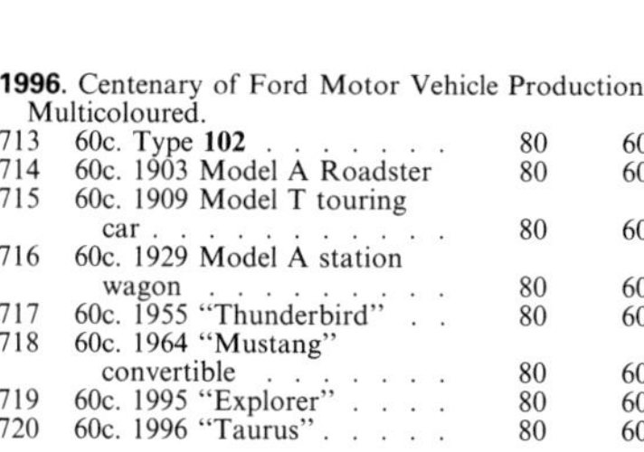

103 Evacuees boarding "L.S.T. 1108" (tank landing ship)

1996. 50th Anniv of Operation Crossroads (nuclear testing) at Bikini Atoll. Multicoloured.
721 32c.+8c. Type **103** 60 60
722 32c.+8c. U.S. Navy preparation of site 60 60
723 32c.+8c. Explosion of "Able" (first test) 60 60
724 32c.+8c. Explosion of "Baker" (first underwater test) 60 60
725 32c.+8c. Ghost fleet (targets) 60 60
726 32c.+8c. Bikinian family . . 60 60

1996. Folk Legends (2nd series). As T **88**. Multicoloured.
727 32c. Letao gives gift of fire 50 40
728 32c. Mennin Jobwodda flying on giant bird 50 40
729 32c. Koko chasing Letao in canoe 50 40
730 32c. Mother and girl catching Kouj (octopus) to cook . . 50 40

104 Pennsylvania Railroad Class K4, U.S.A.

1996. Steam Railway Locomotives. Multicoloured.
731 55c. Type **104** 75 75
732 55c. Big Boy, U.S.A. 75 75
733 55c. Class A4 "Mallard", Great Britain 75 75
734 55c. Class 242, Spain 75 75
735 55c. Class 01 No. 052, Germany 75 75
736 55c. Class 691 No. 031, Italy 75 75
737 55c. "Royal Hudson", Canada 75 75
738 55c. "Evening Star", Great Britain 75 75
739 55c. Class 520, South Australia 75 75
740 55c. Class 232.U.2, France 75 75
741 55c. Class QJ "Advance Forward", China 75 75
742 55c. Class C62 "Swallow", Japan 75 75

105 Stick Chart, Outrigger Canoe and Flag

1996. 10th Anniv of Ratification of Compact of Free Association with U.S.A.
744 **105** $3 multicoloured . . . . 4·50 3·50

106 "Madonna and Child with Four Saints" (detail, Rosso Fiorentino)

1996. Christmas.
745 **106** 32c. multicoloured 50 40

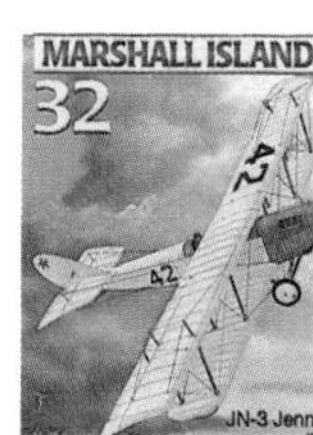

107 Curtiss JN-4 "Jenny"

1996. Biplanes. Multicoloured.
746 32c. Type **107** 50 40
747 32c. SPAD XIII 50 40
748 32c. Albatros 50 40
749 32c. De Havilland D.H.4 Liberty 50 40
750 32c. Fokker Dr-1 . . . . . 50 40
751 32c. Sopwith Camel 50 40
752 32c. Martin MB-2 . . . . . 50 40
753 32c. Martin MB-3A Tommy 50 40
754 32c. Curtiss TS-1 . . . . . . 50 40
755 32c. P-1 Hawk 50 40
756 32c. Boeing PW-9 . . . . . 50 40
757 32c. Douglas O-2-H 50 40
758 32c. LB-5 Pirate 50 40
759 32c. O2U-1 Corsair 50 40
760 32c. Curtiss F8C Helldiver 50 40
761 32c. Boeing F4B-4 . . . . . 50 40
762 32c. J6B Gerfalcon 50 40
763 32c. Martin BM 50 40
764 32c. FF-1 Fifi 50 40
765 32c. C.R.32 Cricket 50 40
766 32c. Polikarpov I-15 Gull . . 50 40
767 32c. Fairey Swordfish 50 40
768 32c. Aichi D1A2 . . . . . . 50 40
769 32c. Grumman F3F 50 40
770 32c. SOC-3 Seagull 50 40

108 Fan-making

1996. Traditional Crafts. Multicoloured. Self-adhesive gum (780, 782); ordinary or self-adhesive gum (others).
771 32c. Type **108** 50 40
772 32c. Boys sailing model outrigger canoes (country name at right) 50 40
773 32c. Carving canoes 50 40
774 32c. Weaving baskets (country name at right) . . 50 40
780 32c. As No. 772 but with country name at left . . . 55 45
782 32c. As No. 774 but with country name at left . . . 55 45

110 "Rocking '50s"

1997. 20th Death Anniv of Elvis Presley (entertainer). Different portraits. Multicoloured.
784 32c. Type **110** 55 45
785 32c. "Soaring '60s" 55 45
786 32c. "Sensational '70s" . . . 55 45

111 Kabua

113 St. Andrew

1997. President Amata Kabua Commemoration. Multicoloured.
787 32c. Type **111** 50 40
788 60c. As Type **111** but inscr in English at left and right and in Marshallese at foot 1·00 75

1997. Easter. 140th Anniv of Introduction of Christianity to the Marshall Islands. The Twelve Disciples. Multicoloured.
790 60c. Type **113** 90 70
791 60c. St. Matthew 90 70
792 60c. St. Philip 90 70
793 60c. St. Simon 90 70
794 60c. St. Thaddeus 90 70
795 60c. St. Thomas 90 70
796 60c. St. Bartholomew 90 70
797 60c. St. John 90 70
798 60c. St. James the Lesser . . 90 70
799 60c. St. James the Greater . . 90 70
800 60c. St. Paul 90 70
801 60c. St. Peter 90 70

114 Immigrants arriving at Ellis Island, New York, 1900

1997. The Twentieth Century (1st series). "Decade of New Possibilities, 1900–1909". Multicoloured.
803 60c. Type **114** 90 70
804 60c. Chinese and Dowager Empress Ci Xi, 1900 (Boxer Rebellion) 90 70
805 60c. George Eastman (inventor of box camera) photographing family, 1900 90 70
806 60c. Walter Reed (discoverer of yellow fever transmission by mosquito), 1900 . . . . 90 70
807 60c. Sigmund Freud (pioneer of psychoanalysis) (publication of "Interpretation of Dreams", 1900) 90 70
808 60c. Guglielmo Marconi sending first transatlantic wireless message, 1901 . . 90 70
809 60c. Enrico Caruso (opera singer) (first award of Gold Disc for one million record sales, 1903) 90 70
810 60c. Wright Brothers' Flyer I (first powered flight, Kitty Hawk, 1903) 90 70
811 60c. Albert Einstein and formula (development of Theory of Relativity, 1905) 90 70
812 60c. White ensign and H.M.S. "Dreadnought" (battleship), 1906 . . . . . 90 70
813 60c. San Francisco earthquake, 1906 . . . . . 90 70
814 60c. Mohandas Gandhi and protestors, Johannesburg, South Africa, 1906 . . . . 90 70
815 60c. Pablo Picasso and "Les Demoiselles d'Avignon", 1907 . . . . 90 70
816 60c. First Paris–Peking motor car race, 1907 . . . . . . 90 70
817 60c. Masjik-i-Salaman oil field, Persia, 1908 . . . . 90 70

See also Nos. 872/86, 948/62, 975//89, 1067/81, 1165/79, 1218/32, 1239/55, 1256/70 and 1303/17.

115 Deng Xiaoping

1997. Deng Xiaoping (Chinese statesman) Commemoration.
818 **115** 60c. multicoloured 85 65

116 German Marshall Islands 1899 3pf. Stamp

1997. "Pacific 97" International Stamp Exhibition, San Francisco. Centenary of Marshall Islands Postage Stamps. Multicoloured.
819 50c. Type **116** 70 70
820 50c. German Marshall Islands 1899 5pf. stamp . . 70 70
821 50c. German Marshall Islands 1897 10pf. stamp 70 70
822 50c. German Marshall Islands 1897 20pf. stamp 70 70
823 50c. Unissued German Marshall Islands 25pf. stamp 70 70
824 50c. Unissued German Marshall Islands 50pf. stamp 70 70

117 Curlew on Seashore

1997. The Bristle-thighed Curlew. Multicoloured.
826 16c. Type **117** 30 20
827 16c. Flying 30 20
828 16c. Running 30 20
829 16c. Standing on branch . . 30 20

119 Pacific Arts Festival Canoe, Enewetak

1997. Traditional Outrigger Canoes. Multicoloured.
831 32c. Type **119** 55 45
832 32c. Kor Kor racing canoes 55 45
833 32c. Large voyaging canoe, Jaluit 55 45
834 32c. Sailing canoe, Ailuk . . 55 45

120 Douglas C-54 Skymaster Transport

1997. Aircraft of United States Air Force (1st series). Multicoloured.
835 32c. Type **120** 50 40
836 32c. Boeing B-36 Peacemaker 50 40
837 32c. North American F-86 Sabre jet fighter 50 40
838 32c. Boeing B-47 Stratojet jet bomber 50 40
839 32c. Douglas C-124 Globemaster II transport 50 40
840 32c. Lockheed C-121 Constellation 50 40
841 32c. Boeing B-52 Stratofortress jet bomber 50 40
842 32c. North American F-100 Super Sabre jet fighter . . 50 40
843 32c. Lockheed F-104 Starfighter jet fighter . . . 50 40
844 32c. Lockheed C-130 Hercules transport 50 40
845 32c. Republic F-105 Thunderchief jet fighter . . 50 40
846 32c. KC-135 Stratotanker . . 50 40
847 32c. Convair B-58 Hustler jet bomber 50 40
848 32c. McDonnell Douglas F-4 Phantom II jet fighter . . . 50 40
849 32c. Northrop T-38 Talon trainer 50 40
850 32c. Lockheed C-141 StarLifter jet transport . . 50 40
851 32c. General Dynamics F-111 Aardvark jet fighter . . . 50 40
852 32c. SR-71 "Blackbird" . . . 50 40
853 32c. Lockheed C-5 Galaxy jet transport 50 40
854 32c. A-10 Thunderbolt II bomber 50 40
855 32c. F-15 Eagle fighter . . . 50 40
856 32c. General Dynamics F-16 Fighting Falcon jet fighter 50 40

857 32c. Lockheed F-117 "Nighthawk" Stealth bomber 50 40
858 32c. B-2 Spirit 50 40
859 32c. C-17 Globemaster III transport 50 40
See also Nos. 1272/96.

121 U.S.S. "Constitution"

1997. Bicentenary of Launch of U.S.S. "Constitution" (frigate).
860 **121** 32c. multicoloured 50 40

1997. Folk Legends (3rd series). As T **88**. Multicoloured.
861 32c. The Large Pool of Mejit 55 45
862 32c. The Beautiful Woman of Kwajalein 55 45
863 32c. Sharks and Lowakalle Reef 55 45
864 32c. The Demon of Adrie . . 55 45

1997. Undersea World (2nd series). As T **81**. Multicoloured.
865 60c. Watanabe's angelfish, blue-finned trevallys ("Bluefin Jack"), grey reef shark and scuba diver . . 95 75
866 60c. Scuba diver, anchor and racoon butterflyfish 95 75
867 60c. Lionfish and flame angelfish 95 75
868 60c. Square-spotted anthias ("Fairy Basslet"), anchor, scuba diver with torch and orange-finned anemonefish 95 75
Nos. 865/8 were issued together, se-tenant, forming a composite design.

122 Diana, Princess of Wales, aged 20

1997. Diana, Princess of Wales Commemoration. Multicoloured.
869 60c. Type **122** . . . . 1·00 75
870 60c. Wearing pearl drop earrings (aged 27) . . . . 1·00 75
871 60c. Wearing pearl choker (aged 36) . . . . 1·00 75

123 Flags and Suffragettes

1997. The Twentieth Century (2nd series). "Decade of Revolution and Great War, 1910–1919". Mult.
872 60c. Type **123** 75 55
873 60c. Nobel Prize medal, Ernest Rutherford and diagram of atom, 1911 . . 75 55
874 60c. Sun Yat-Sen (Chinese Revolution, 1911–12) . . . 75 55
875 60c. Sinking of the "Titanic" (liner), 1912 . . . . 75 55
876 60c. Igor Stravinsky (composer) and score of "The Rite of Spring", 1913 75 55
877 60c. Building motor car (introduction of assembly line construction of motor vehicles by Ford Motor Company), 1913 . . . . . 75 55
878 60c. Countess Sophie Chotek and Archduke Franz Ferdinand of Austria, 1914 (assassination in Sarajevo leads to First World War) 75 55
879 60c. Torpedo striking "Lusitania" (liner), 1915 75 55
880 60c. Battle of Verdun, 1916 75 55
881 60c. Patrick Pearse and proclamation of Irish Republic (Easter Rebellion, 1916) 75 55
882 60c. Western wall, Jerusalem (Balfour Declaration of Jewish Homeland, 1917) 75 55
883 60c. "Aurora" (cruiser) signals start of Russian Revolution, 1917 . . . . . 75 55
884 60c. Biplanes and "Red" Baron Manfred von Richthofen (fighter pilot), 1918 . . . . 75 55
885 60c. Armed revolutionaries, Berlin, 1918 . . . . 75 55
886 60c. Meeting of heads of state (Treaty of Versailles, 1919) 75 55

124 Cherub

1997. Christmas. Details of "Sistine Madonna" by Raphael. Multicoloured.
887 32c. Type **124** 45 35
888 32c. Cherub resting head on folded arms 45 35

125 U.S.S. "Alabama" (battleship), 1942

1997. Ships named after U.S. States. Multicoloured.
889 20c. Type **125** 30 20
890 20c. U.S.S. "Alaska" (cruiser), 1869, and junk 30 20
891 20c. U.S.S. "Arizona" (battleship), 1916 . . . . 30 20
892 20c. U.S.S. "Arkansas" (battleship), 1912 . . . . . 30 20
893 20c. U.S.S. "California" (cruiser), 1974 . . . . . . 30 20
894 20c. U.S.S. "Colorado" (battleship), 1921, and landing craft 30 20
895 20c. U.S.S. "Connecticut" (gunboat), 1776, with fleet 30 20
896 20c. U.S.S. "Delaware" (ship of the line), 1828 . . . . . 30 20
897 20c. U.S.S. "Florida" (cruiser), 1967 . . . . . . 30 20
898 20c. U.S.S. "Georgia" (battleship), 1906 . . . . . 30 20
899 20c. U.S.S. "Honolulu" (cruiser), 1938 . . . . . . 30 20
900 20c. U.S.S. "Idaho" (battleship), 1919 . . . . . 30 20
901 20c. U.S.S. "Illinois" (battleship), 1901 . . . . . 30 20
902 20c. U.S.S. "Indiana" (battleship), 1895 . . . . . 30 20
903 20c. U.S.S. "Iowa" (battleship), 1943 . . . . . 30 20
904 20c. U.S.S. "Kansas" (battleship), 1907 . . . . . 30 20
905 20c. U.S.S. "Kentucky" (battleship), 1900 . . . . . 30 20
906 20c. U.S.S. "Louisiana" (frigate), 1812 . . . . . . 30 20
907 20c. U.S.S. "Maine" (battleship), 1895 . . . . . 30 20
908 20c. U.S.S. "Maryland" (frigate), 1799 . . . . . . 30 20
909 20c. U.S.S. "Massachusetts" (battleship), 1942 . . . . . 30 20
910 20c. U.S.S. "Michigan" (paddle gunboat), 1843 . . 30 20
911 20c. U.S.S. "Minnesota" (corvette), 1857 . . . . . 30 20
912 20c. U.S.S. "Mississippi" (paddle gunboat), 1841, and junk 30 20
913 20c. U.S.S. "Missouri" (battleship), 1944, in Tokyo Bay 30 20
914 20c. U.S.S. "Montana" (battleship), 1908 . . . . . 30 20
915 20c. U.S.S. "Nebraska" (battleship), 1907 . . . . . 30 20
916 20c. U.S.S. "Nevada" (battleship), 1916, at Pearl Harbor 30 20
917 20c. U.S.S. "New Hampshire" (battleship), 1908, and Statue of Liberty 30 20
918 20c. U.S.S. "New Jersey" (battleship), 1943 . . . . . 30 20
919 20c. U.S.S. "New Mexico" (battleship), 1918, in Tokyo Bay 30 20
920 20c. U.S.S. "New York" (frigate), 1800, and felucca 30 20
921 20c. U.S.S. "North Carolina" (battleship), 1941 . . . . . 30 20
922 20c. U.S.S. "North Dakota" (battleship), 1910 . . . . . 30 20
923 20c. U.S.S. "Ohio" (ship of the line), 1838 . . . . . . 30 20
924 20c. U.S.S. "Oklahoma" (battleship), 1916 . . . . . 30 20
925 20c. U.S.S. "Oregon" (battleship), 1896 . . . . . 30 20
926 20c. U.S.S. "Pennsylvania" (battleship), 1905 . . . . . 30 20
927 20c. U.S.S. "Rhode Island" (paddle gunboat), 1861 . . 30 20
928 20c. U.S.S. "South Carolina" (frigate), 1783 . . . . . . 30 20
929 20c. U.S.S. "South Dakota" (battleship), 1942 . . . . . 30 20
930 20c. U.S.S. "Tennessee" (battleship), 1906 . . . . . 30 20
931 20c. U.S.S. "Texas" (battleship), 1914 . . . . . 30 20
932 20c. U.S.S. "Utah" (battleship), 1911 . . . . . 30 20
933 20c. U.S.S. "Vermont" (battleship), 1907 . . . . . 30 20
934 20c. U.S.S. "Virginia" (schooner), 1798 . . . . . 30 20
935 20c. U.S.S. "Washington" (battleship), 1941 . . . . . 30 20
936 20c. U.S.S. "West Virginia" (battleship), 1923 . . . . . 30 20
937 20c. U.S.S. "Wisconsin" (battleship), 1944 . . . . . 30 20
938 20c. U.S.S. "Wyoming" (monitor), 1902 . . . . . 30 20
Dates given are those of either launch or commission.

128 Presley

1998. 30th Anniv of First Television Special by Elvis Presley (entertainer). Multicoloured.
941 32c. Type **128** 45 35
942 32c. Presley in black leather jacket 45 35
943 32c. Presley in white suit in front of "ELVIS" in lights 45 35

129 Chiragra Spider Conch ("Lambis chiragra")

1998. Sea Shells. Multicoloured.
944 32c. Type **129** 50 40
945 32c. Fluted giant clam ("Tridacna squamosa") . . 50 40
946 32c. Adusta murex ("Chicoreus brunneus") . . 50 40
947 32c. Golden cowrie ("Cypraea aurantium") . . 50 40

130 Family listening to Radio

1998. The Twentieth Century (3rd series). "Decade of Optimism and Disillusionment, 1920–1929". Multicoloured.
948 60c. Type **130** 75 55
949 60c. Leaders from Japan, United States, France, Great Britain and Italy (Washington Conference, 1920) 75 55
950 60c. Ludwig Mies van der Rohe (architect), 1922 . . 75 55
951 60c. Mummiform coffin of Tutankhamun (discovery of tomb, 1922) 75 55
952 60c. Workers from U.S.S.R., 1923 (emergence of U.S.S.R. as communist state) 75 55
953 60c. Kemal Ataturk (first president of modern Turkey, 1923) (break-up of Turkish Empire) 75 55
954 60c. Bix Beiderbecke (trumpeter) and flappers (dancers), 1924 (Jazz Age) 75 55
955 60c. Robert Goddard demonstrates first liquid-propelled rocket, 1926 . . 75 55
956 60c. Poster for "The Jazz Singer" (second talking picture, 1926) 75 55
957 60c. Benito Mussolini assumes total power in Italy, 1926 . . . . 75 55
958 60c. Explosive glare and Leonardo da Vinci's "Proportion of Man" (Big Bang Theory of beginning of Universe, 1927) 75 55
959 60c. Sir Alexander Fleming discovers penicillin, 1928 75 55
960 60c. John Logie Baird invents television, 1926 . . . . . 75 55
961 60c. Airship "Graf Zeppelin" above Mt. Fuji, Japan (first round the world flight, 1929) 75 55
962 60c. U.S. stock market crash, 1929 (economic depression) 75 55

131 Pahi Sailing Canoe, Tuamotu Archipelago

1998. Canoes of the Pacific. Multicoloured.
963 32c. Type **131** 45 35
964 32c. Maori war canoe, New Zealand 45 35
965 32c. Wa'a Kaukahi fishing canoe, Hawaii 45 35
966 32c. Amatasi sailing canoe, Samoa 45 35
967 32c. Ndrua sailing canoe, Fiji Islands 45 35
968 32c. Tongiaki voyaging canoe, Tonga 45 35
969 32c. Tipairua travelling canoe, Tahiti 45 35
970 32c. Walap sailing canoe, Marshall Islands 45 35

132 Douglas C-54 Skymaster Transport

1998. 50th Anniv of Berlin Airlift (relief of Berlin during Soviet blockade). Multicoloured.
971 60c. Type **132** 75 55
972 60c. Avro Type 685 York transport 75 55
973 60c. Crowd and building . . 75 55
974 60c. Crowd 75 55
Nos. 971/4 were issued together, se-tenant, forming a composite design.

133 Soup Kitchens, 1930 (depression)

1998. The Twentieth Century (4th series). "Decade of the Great Depression, 1930–1939". Multicoloured.
975 60c. Type **133** 75 55
976 60c. Ernest Lawrence and first cyclotron, 1931 (splitting of atom) 75 55
977 60c. Forced collectivization of farms in Soviet Union, 1932 (Stalin era) 75 55
978 60c. Torchlight Parade celebrates rise of Hitler to power, 1933 (fascism) . . . 75 55
979 60c. Dneproges Dam on Dnepr River, 1933 (harnessing of nature) . . . 75 55
980 60c. Streamlined locomotive "Zephyr" (record-breaking run, Denver to Chicago, 1934) 75 55
981 60c. Douglas DC-3 airliner (first all-metal airliner, 1936) 75 55
982 60c. Pablo Picasso (artist) and "Guernica" (German bombing during Spanish Civil War, 1937) 75 55
983 60c. "Hindenburg" (airship disaster), 1937 (media reporting) 75 55
984 60c. Families fleeing ruins (Japanese assault on Nanjing, 1937) 75 55
985 60c. Neville Chamberlain declares "Peace in our Time", 1938 (appeasement) 75 55
986 60c. Chester Carlson (invention of xerography, 1938) 75 55
987 60c. Jew and Star of David (Kristallnacht (Nazi violence against Jews), 1938) 75 55
988 60c. Junkers "Stuka" bombers over Poland, 1939 (start of Second World War) 75 55
989 60c. Audience (premiere of "Gone with the Wind", 1939) (movies) 75 55

134 Coronation of Tsar Nicholas II, 1896

1998. 80th Death Anniv of Tsar Nicholas II and his Family. Multicoloured.
990 60c. Type **134** 75 55
991 60c. "Varyag" (cruiser) and Tsar (Russo-Japanese war, 1904–05) 75 55
992 60c. Troops firing on crowd, Tsar and October manifesto, 1905 . . . . . 75 55
993 60c. Peasant sowing, Tsar and Rasputin, 1905 . . . . 75 55
994 60c. Mounted troops, Tsar and Nicholas II at strategy meeting, 1915 . . . . . . 75 55
995 60c. Abdication, Tsar and Ipateva House, Ekaterinburg, 1917 . . . . 75 55

135 Babe Ruth

1998. 50th Death Anniv of Babe Ruth (baseball player).
997 **135** 132c. multicoloured . . . 50 40

136 NC-4

1998. Aircraft of United States Navy. Mult.
998 32c. Type **136** 45 35
999 32c. Consolidated PBY-5 Catalina flying boat . . . 45 35
1000 32c. TBD Devastator . . . 45 35
1001 32c. SB2U Vindicator . . . 45 35
1002 32c. Grumman F4F Wildcat fighter 45 35
1003 32c. Vought-Sikorsky OS2U Kingfisher seaplane . . . 45 35
1004 32c. Douglas SBD Dauntless bomber 45 35
1005 32c. Chance Vought F4U Corsair fighter 45 35
1006 32c. Curtiss SB2C Helldiver bomber 45 35
1007 32c. Lockheed PV-1 Ventura bomber 45 35
1008 32c. Grumman TBM Avenger bomber 45 35
1009 32c. Grumman F6F Hellcat fighter 45 35
1010 32c. PB4Y-2 Privateer . . . 45 35
1011 32c. A-1J Skyraider 45 35
1012 32c. McDonnell F2H-2P Banshee 45 35
1013 32c. F9F-2B Panther . . . 45 35
1014 32c. P5M Marlin 45 35
1015 32c. F-8 Crusader 45 35
1016 32c. McDonnell Douglas F-4 Phantom II fighter . . 45 35
1017 32c. A-6 Intruder 45 35
1018 32c. Lockheed P-3 Orion reconnaissance 45 35
1019 32c. Vought A-70 Corsair II 45 35
1020 32c. Douglas A-4 Skyhawk bomber 45 35
1021 32c. S-3 Viking 45 35
1022 32c. F/A-18 Hornet 45 35

137 Classic Six, 1912

1998. Chevrolet Vehicles. Multicoloured.
1023 60c. Type **137** 75 55
1024 60c. Sport Roadster, 1931 75 55
1025 60c. Special Deluxe, 1941 75 55
1026 60c. Cameo Carrier Fleetside, 1955 . . . . . 75 55
1027 60c. Corvette, 1957 . . . . 75 55
1028 60c. Bel Air, 1957 . . . . . 75 55
1029 60c. Camaro, 1967 . . . . 75 55
1030 60c. Chevelle SS 454, 1970 75 55

138 Letter "A" and Pres. Amata Kabua

1998. Marshallese Alphabet and Language. Mult.
1031 33c. Type **138** 45 35
1032 33c. Letter "A" and woman weaving 45 35
1033 33c. Letter "B" and butterfly 45 35
1034 33c. Letter "D" and woman wearing garland of flowers 45 35
1035 33c. Letter "E" and fish . . 45 35
1036 33c. Letter "I" and couple in front of rainbow . . . 45 35
1037 33c. Letter "J" and woven mat 45 35
1038 33c. Letter "K" and Government House . . . 45 35
1039 33c. Letter "L" and night sky 45 35
1040 33c. Letter "L" and red-tailed tropicbird 45 35
1041 33c. Letter "M" and breadfruit 45 35
1042 33c. Letter "M" and arrowroot plant 45 35
1043 33c. Letter "N" and coconut tree 45 35
1044 33c. Letter "N" and wave 45 35
1045 33c. Letter "N" and shark 45 35
1046 33c. Letter "O" and fisherman 45 35
1047 33c. Letter "O" and tattooed woman 45 35
1048 33c. Letter "O" and lionfish 45 35
1049 33c. Letter "P" and visitor's hut 45 35
1050 33c. Letter "R" and whale 45 35
1051 33c. Letter "T" and outrigger sailing canoe . . 45 35
1052 33c. Letter "U" and fire . . 45 35
1053 33c. Letter "U" and whale's fin 45 35
1054 33c. Letter "W" and woven leaf sail 45 35

139 Trust Company of the Marshall Islands Offices, 1998

1998. New Buildings. Multicoloured.
1055 33c. Type **139** 45 35
1056 33c. Embassy of the People's Republic of China, 1996 45 35
1057 33c. Outrigger Marshall Islands Resort, 1996 . . . 45 35

140 Midnight Angel

1998. Christmas.
1058 **140** 33c. multicoloured . . . 45 35

141 Launch of "Friendship 7", 1962

1998. John Glenn's (astronaut) Return to Space. Multicoloured.
1059 60c. Type **141** 75 55
1060 60c. John Glenn, 1962, and Earth 75 55
1061 60c. "Friendship 7" orbiting Earth 75 55
1062 60c. Launch of space shuttle "Discovery", 1998 . . . . 75 55
1063 60c. John Glenn, 1998, and flag 75 55
1064 60c. "Discovery" orbiting Earth, 1998 . . . . . . 75 55

143 British and German Planes over St. Paul's Cathedral (Battle of Britain, 1940)

1998. The Twentieth Century (5th series). "Decade of War and Peace, 1940–1949". Multicoloured.
1067 60c. Type **143** 75 55
1068 60c. Japanese aircraft attack American battleship (Pearl Harbor, 1941) (global warfare) 75 55
1069 60c. Wernher von Braun and missiles (first surface to surface guided missile, 1942) 75 55
1070 60c. The Dorsey Brothers (Big Bands, 1942) 75 55
1071 60c. Soviet worker building weaponry (fight for survival against Germans, 1943) 75 55
1072 60c. Concentration camp prisoners (the Holocaust, 1945) 75 55
1073 60c. Mushroom cloud and skull (first atomic bomb tested, Alamogordo, New Mexico, 1945) 75 55
1074 60c. Families reunited (end of war, 1945) 75 55
1075 60c. Eniac computer and worker (first electronic digital computer goes into operation, 1946) 75 55
1076 60c. American delegate (United Nations, 1946) . . 75 55
1077 60c. Nuremberg Tribunal (trials of Germans for war crimes 1946) 75 55
1078 60c. George Marshall (U.S. Secretary of State) and Europeans (Marshall Plan, 1947) 75 55
1079 60c. William Shockley, John Bardeen and Walter Brattain (development of transistor, 1948) 75 55
1080 60c. Berlin Airlift, 1948–49 (Cold War) 75 55
1081 60c. Mao Tse-tung proclaiming People's Republic of China, 1949 75 55

144 Trireme

1998. Warships. Multicoloured.
1082 33c. Type **144** 45 35
1083 33c. Roman galley ("Trireme Romano") . . 45 35
1084 33c. Viking longship 45 35
1085 33c. Ming treasure ship . . 45 35
1086 33c. "Mary Rose" (English galleon) 45 35
1087 33c. "Nuestra Senora del Rosario" (Spanish galleon) 45 35
1088 33c. Korean "turtle" ship 45 35
1089 33c. "Brederode" (Dutch ship of the line) 45 35
1090 33c. Venetian galley 45 35
1091 33c. "Santissima Trinidad" (Spanish ship of the line) 45 35
1092 33c. "Ville de Paris" (French ship of the line) 45 35
1093 33c. H.M.S. "Victory" (ship of the line) 45 35
1094 33c. "Bonhomme Richard" (American sail frigate) . . 45 35
1095 33c. U.S.S. "Constellation" (sail frigate) 45 35
1096 33c. U.S.S. "Hartford" (steam frigate) 45 35
1097 33c. Fijian Ndrua canoe . . 45 35
1098 33c. H.M.S. "Dreadnought" (battleship) 45 35
1099 33c. H.M.A.S. "Australia" (battle cruiser) 45 35
1100 33c. H.M.S. "Dorsetshire" (cruiser) 45 35
1101 33c. "Admiral Graf Spee" (German battleship) . . . 45 35
1102 33c. "Yamato" (Japanese battleship) 45 35
1103 33c. U.S.S. "Tautog" (sub-marine) 45 35
1104 33c. "Bismarck" (German battleship) 45 35
1105 33c. U.S.S. "Hornet" (aircraft carrier) 45 35
1106 33c. U.S.S. "Missouri" (battleship) 45 35

146 Pacific Golden Plover ("Lesser Golden Plover")

147 Tecumseh

1999. Birds. Multicoloured.
1108 1c. Type **146** 10 10
1109 3c. Grey-rumped sandpiper ("Siberian (gray-tailed) Tattler") 10 10
1110 5c. Black-tailed godwit . . . 10 10
1113 20c. Common noddy ("Brown Noddy") 25 20
1114 22c. White tern ("Common Fairy Tern") 30 25
1116 33c. Micronesian pigeon . . 40 30
1117 40c. Franklin's gull 50 40
1118 45c. Rufous-necked sandpiper ("Rufous-necked Stint") 55 40
1119 55c. Long-tailed koel ("Long-tailed Cuckoo") 70 55
1121 75c. Kermadec petrel . . . 95 70
1122 $1 Christmas Island shearwater ("Christmas Shearwater") . . . . . . 1·25 95
1123 $1.20 Purple-capped fruit dove . . . . 1·50 1·25
1124 $2 Lesser sand plover ("Mongolian Plover") . . 2·50 1·90
1125 $3.20 Cattle egret . . . . . 4·00 3·00
1127 $5 Dunlin . . . . 6·25 4·75
1129 $10 Eurasian tree sparrow 12·50 9·50

1999. Canoes of the Pacific. Multicoloured. (a) Size 49 × 30 mm.
1130 33c. Type **131** 40 30
1131 33c. As No. 964 . . . . . 40 30
1132 33c. As No. 965 . . . . . 40 30
1133 33c. As No. 966 but inscr changed to "Tongiaki voyaging canoe, Tonga" 40 30
1134 33c. As No. 967 . . . . . 40 30
1135 33c. As No. 968 but inscr changed to "Amatasi sailing canoe, Samoa" . . 40 30
1136 33c. As No. 969 . . . . . 40 30
1137 33c. As No. 970 . . . . . 40 30

(b) Size 39 × 24 mm.
1138 33c. Type **131** 40 30
1139 33c. As No. 1131 . . . . . 40 30
1140 33c. As No. 1132 . . . . . 40 30
1141 33c. As No. 1133 . . . . . 40 30
1142 33c. As No. 1134 . . . . . 40 30
1143 33c. As No. 1135 . . . . . 40 30
1144 33c. As No. 1136 . . . . . 40 30
1145 33c. As No. 1137 . . . . . 40 30
Nos. 1138/45 were self-adhesive.

1999. Great American Indian Chiefs. Multicoloured.
1146 60c. Type **147** 75 55
1147 60c. Powhatan 75 55
1148 60c. Hiawatha 75 55
1149 60c. Dull Knife 75 55
1150 60c. Sequoyah 75 55
1151 60c. Sitting Bull 75 55
1152 60c. Cochise 75 55
1153 60c. Red Cloud 75 55
1154 60c. Geronimo 75 55
1155 60c. Chief Joseph 75 55
1156 60c. Pontiac 75 55
1157 60c. Crazy Horse 75 55

148 State Flag

1999.
1158 **148** 33c. multicoloured . . . 40 30

149 Plumeria

1999. Flowers of the Pacific. Multicoloured.
1159 33c. Type **149** 40 30
1160 33c. Vanda 40 30
1161 33c. Ilima 40 30
1162 33c. Tiare 40 30
1163 33c. White ginger 40 30
1164 33c. Hibiscus 40 30

150 Family watching Television

1999. The Twentieth Century (6th series). "Decade of Peril and Progress, 1950–1959". Multicoloured.
1165 60c. Type **150** 75 55
1166 60c. U.N. landing at Inchon, Korea, 1950 (Cold War) 75 55
1167 60c. Vaccination against polio, 1952 . . . . 75 55
1168 60c. American hydrogen bomb test, Enewetak Atoll, 1952 (Arms race) 75 55
1169 60c. James Watson and Francis Crick (scientists) and DNA double helix, 1953 (unravelling of genetic code) 75 55
1170 60c. Sir Edmund Hillary, Tenzing Norgay and Mt. Everest, 1953 . . . . . . 75 55
1171 60c. Coronation of Queen Elizabeth II, Westminster Abbey, 1953 . . . . . . 75 55
1172 60c. Singer and dancers, 1954 (rock 'n' roll music) 75 55
1173 60c. Ho Chi Minh and Vietnamese troops celebrating victory over French garrison at Dien Bien Phu, 1954 (end of colonial empires) 75 55
1174 60c. People of different races on bus, 1955 (condemnation of racial discrimination) 75 55
1175 60c. Hungarians firing on Russian tanks, Budapest, 1956 (challenge to Communism) 75 55
1176 60c. Signing of Treaty of Rome, 1957 (European union) 75 55
1177 60c. Launch of Russian sputnik, 1957 (space race) 75 55
1178 60c. De Havilland Comet (first commercial jet airline service, 1958) . . . 75 55
1179 60c. Jack Kilby (inventor) and first microchip, 1959 75 55

152 Presley

1999. Elvis Presley, "Artist of the Century".
1181 **152** 33c. multicoloured . . . 40 30

153 5m. Stamp

1999. "iBRA '99" International Stamp Exhibition, Nuremberg, Germany. Multicoloured.
1182 60c. Type **153** 75 55
1183 60c. 3m. stamp 75 55
1184 60c. 2m. stamp 75 55
1185 60c. 1m. stamp 75 55

154 Magnifying Glass over Committee Members

1999. 20th Anniv of Marshall Islands Constitution.
1186 **154** 33c. multicoloured . . . 40 30

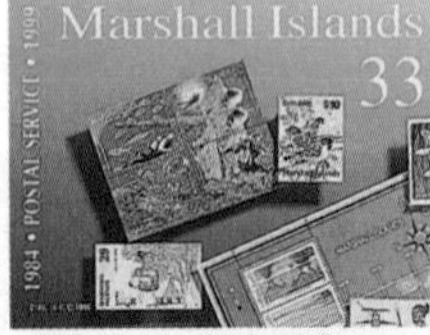

155 Marshall Island Stamps

1999. 15th Anniv of Marshall Islands Postal Service. Multicoloured.
1187 33c. Type **155** 40 30
1188 33c. Butterfly, fish, canoe and flower stamps 40 30
1189 33c. Pres. Amata Kabua, flower and legend stamps 40 30
1190 33c. Stamps and magnifying glass 40 30
Nos. 1187/90 were issued together, se-tenant, forming a composite design.

156 B-10 B

1999. Legendary Aircraft. Multicoloured.
1191 33c. Type **156** 40 30
1192 33c. A-17A Nomad 40 30
1193 33c. Douglas B-18 Bolo bomber 40 30
1194 33c. Boeing B-17F Flying Fortress bomber 40 30
1195 33c. A-20 Havoc 40 30
1196 33c. North American B-25B Mitchell bomber 40 30
1197 33c. Consolidated B-24D Liberator bomber 40 30
1198 33c. North American P-51B Mustang fighter 40 30
1199 33c. Martin B-26 Marauder bomber 40 30
1200 33c. A-26B Invader 40 30
1201 33c. P-59 Airacomet 40 30
1202 33c. KC-97 Stratofreighter 40 30
1203 33c. A-1J Skyraider 40 30
1204 33c. P2V-7 Neptune 40 30
1205 33c. B-45 Tornado 40 30
1206 33c. Boeing B-50 Superfortress 40 30
1207 33c. AJ-2 Savage 40 30
1208 33c. F9F Cougar 40 30
1209 33c. Douglas A-3 Skywarrior jet bomber . . 40 30
1210 33c. English Electric B-57E Canberra jet bomber . . 40 30
1211 33c. EB-66 Destroyer . . . 40 30
1212 33c. E-2A Hawkeye 40 30
1213 33c. Northrop F-5E Tiger II jet fighter 40 30
1214 33c. AV-8B Harrier II . . . 40 30
1215 33c. B-1B Lancer 40 30

159 T. H. Maiman and Ruby Crystal Laser, 1960

1999. The Twentieth Century (7th series). "Decade of Upheaval and Exploration 1960–1969". Mult.
1218 60c. Type **159** 75 55
1219 60c. Young couple (birth control pill, 1960) 75 55
1220 60c. Yuri Gagarin (first man in space, 1961) 75 55
1221 60c. John F. Kennedy (President of U.S.A., 1960–63) making speech in Berlin, 1961 (failures of Communism) 75 55
1222 60c. Rachel Carson and endangered species (publication of "Silent Spring", 1962) 75 55
1223 60c. John F. Kennedy and Russian President Nikita Khrushchev (Cuban missile crisis, 1962) . . . 75 55
1224 60c. Pope John XXIII and crowds (Spirit of Ecumenism) 75 55
1225 60c. "Hikari" express train, Japan (new railway record speeds, 1964) 75 55
1226 60c. Chinese workers waving banners (Chinese cultural revolution, 1965) 75 55
1227 60c. Soldier with gun (Arab–Israeli six-day war, 1967) 75 55
1228 60c. Surgeons (first human heart transplants, 1967) 75 55
1229 60c. American soldiers in jungle (Vietnam war) . . 75 55
1230 60c. Robert F. Kennedy (U.S. presidential candidate) and statue of Abraham Lincoln (political assassinations) 75 55
1231 60c. British Aerospace/ Aerospatiale Concorde supersonic jetliner (maiden flight, 1969) 75 55
1232 60c. Neil Armstrong and Buzz Aldrin planting American flag (first men on Moon, 1969) 75 55

161 "Los Reyes" (Alvarao de Menana de Neyra's galleon, 1568)

1999. European Exploration of Marshall Islands. Multicoloured.
1234 33c. Type **161** 40 30
1235 33c. H.M.S. "Dolphin" (Samuel Wallis's frigate, 1767) 40 30
1236 33c. "Scarborough" (John Marshall's transport, 1788) 40 30
1237 33c. "Rurik" (Otto van Kotzebue's brig, 1817) . . 40 30
No. 1236 is wrongly inscribed "Scarsborough" and No. 1237 "Rurick".

162 Nativity

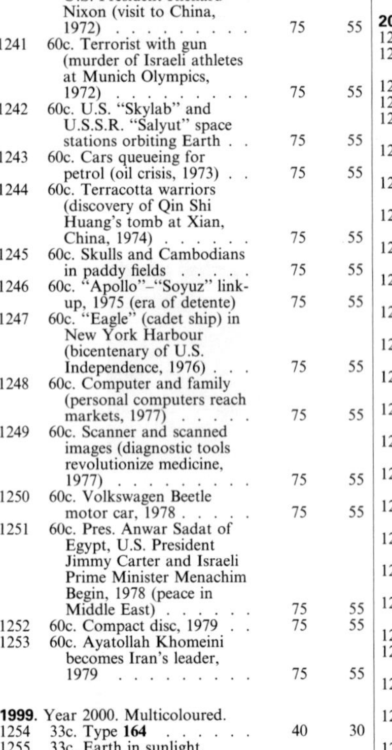

164 Earth in Darkness, December 31, 1999

163 First Scheduled Transatlantic Flight of Boeing 747 Jetliner, 1970

1999. Christmas.
1238 **162** 33c. multicoloured . . . 40 30

1999. The Twentieth Century (8th series). "Decade of Detente and Discovery 1970–1979". Multicoloured.
1239 60c. Type **163** 75 55
1240 60c. Mao Tse Tung and U.S. President Richard Nixon (visit to China, 1972) 75 55
1241 60c. Terrorist with gun (murder of Israeli athletes at Munich Olympics, 1972) 75 55
1242 60c. U.S. "Skylab" and U.S.S.R. "Salyut" space stations orbiting Earth . . 75 55
1243 60c. Cars queueing for petrol (oil crisis, 1973) . . 75 55
1244 60c. Terracotta warriors (discovery of Qin Shi Huang's tomb at Xian, China, 1974) 75 55
1245 60c. Skulls and Cambodians in paddy fields 75 55
1246 60c. "Apollo"–"Soyuz" link-up, 1975 (era of detente) 75 55
1247 60c. "Eagle" (cadet ship) in New York Harbour (bicentenary of U.S. Independence, 1976) . . . 75 55
1248 60c. Computer and family (personal computers reach markets, 1977) 75 55
1249 60c. Scanner and scanned images (diagnostic tools revolutionize medicine, 1977) 75 55
1250 60c. Volkswagen Beetle motor car, 1978 . . . . . 75 55
1251 60c. Pres. Anwar Sadat of Egypt, U.S. President Jimmy Carter and Israeli Prime Minister Menachim Begin, 1978 (peace in Middle East) 75 55
1252 60c. Compact disc, 1979 . . 75 55
1253 60c. Ayatollah Khomeini becomes Iran's leader, 1979 . . . . 75 55

1999. Year 2000. Multicoloured.
1254 33c. Type **164** 40 30
1255 33c. Earth in sunlight, 1 January 2000 . . . . . 40 30
Nos. 1254/5 were issued together, se-tenant, forming a composite design.

165 Lech Walesa and Protestors at Gdansk Shipyard, Poland, 1980

2000. The Twentieth Century (9th series). "Decade of People and Democracy, 1980–1989". Multicoloured.
1256 60c. Type **165** 85 65
1257 60c. Doctor treating AIDS patient, 1981 . . . . . . 85 65
1258 60c. Prince and Princess of Wales (Royal wedding, 1981) 85 65
1259 60c. Man and computer (IBM personal computers introduced 1981) 85 65
1260 60c. British jet fighter and warships (Falkland Islands war, 1982) 85 65
1261 60c. Man using mobile phone (first commercial wireless cellular system, Chicago, 1983) 85 65
1262 60c. Girl playing football (camcorders, 1983) . . . 85 65
1263 60c. Astronauts (space shuttle *Challenger* explodes, 1986) 85 65
1264 60c. Power station and man wearing protective clothing (Chernobyl Nuclear Power Station disaster, 1986) 85 65
1265 60c. Mikhail Gorbachev and workers (era of Glasnost (openness) and Perestroika (restructuring) in U.S.S.R., 1987) 85 65
1266 60c. American B-2 stealth bomber, 1988 . . . . . . 85 65
1267 60c. Aircraft wreckage (bombing of Pan-American flight 103 over Lockerbie, Scotland, 1988) 85 65
1268 60c. *Exxon Valdez* (oil-tanker) and whales (oil spill off Alaskan Coast, 1989) 85 65
1269 60c. Student demonstrators and police in Tiananmen Square, China, 1989 . . . 85 65
1270 60c. German breaking down wall (dismantling of Berlin Wall, 1989) 85 65

167 Boeing P-26A "Peashooter" fighter

2000. Legendary Aircraft (2nd series). Multicoloured.
1272 33c. Type **167** 45 35
1273 33c. Stearman N2S-1 Kaydett biplane 45 35
1274 33c. Seversky P-35A 45 35
1275 33c. Curtiss P-36A Hawk 45 35
1276 33c. Curtiss P-40B Warhawk fighter 45 35
1277 33c. Lockheed P-38 Lightning fighter 45 35
1278 33c. Bell P-39D Airacobra fighter 45 35
1279 33c. Curtiss C-46 Commando airliner . . . 45 35
1280 33c. Republic P-47D Thunderbolt fighter . . . 45 35
1281 33c. Northrop P-61A Black Widow 45 35
1282 33c. Boeing B-29 Superfortress bomber . . 45 35
1283 33c. Grumman F7F-3N Tigercat 45 35
1284 33c. Grumman F8F-2 Bearcat 45 35
1285 33c. North American F-82 Twin Mustang 45 35
1286 33c. Republic F-84G Thunderjet jet fighter . . 45 35
1287 33c. North American FJ-1 Fury 45 35
1288 33c. Fairchild C-119C Flying Boxcar 45 35
1289 33c. Douglas F3D-2 Skynight 45 35
1290 33c. Northrop F-89D Scorpion 45 35
1291 33c. Lockheed F-94B Starfire 45 35
1292 33c. Douglas F4D Skyray 45 35
1293 33c. McDonnell F3H-2 Demon 45 35
1294 33c. McDonnell RF-101A/C Voodoo 45 35
1295 33c. Lockheed U-2F Dragon Lady 45 35
1296 33c. Rockwell OV-10 Bronco 45 35

168 "Masquerade"

2000. Garden Roses. Multicoloured.

1297	33c. Type **168**	45	35
1298	33c. "Tuscany Superb"	45	35
1299	33c. "Frau Dagmar Hastrup"	45	35
1300	33c. "Ivory Fashion"	45	35
1301	33c. "Charles de Mills"	45	35
1302	33c. "Peace"	45	35

169 Container Ships (political reform in Poland, 1990)

2000. The Twentieth Century (10th series). "Decade of Globalization and Hope, 1990–1999". Multicoloured.

1303	60c. Type **169**	85	65
1304	60c. Fighter planes over burning oil wells, 1991	85	65
1305	60c. Nelson Mandela and F. W. de Klerk (abolition of apartheid, 1991)	85	65
1306	60c. Tim Berners-Lee and computer (creator of World Wide Web, 1991)	85	65
1307	60c. Boris Yeltsin (President of Russian Federation, 1991)	85	65
1308	60c. Yitzhak Rabin, Bill Clinton and Yasir Arafat (signing of Middle East Peace Accord, Washington D.C., 1993)	85	65
1309	60c. High-speed train (inauguration of the "Channel Tunnel" between United Kingdom and France, 1994)	85	65
1310	60c. Family (Bosnian civil war, 1995)	85	65
1311	60c. Athletes (Atlanta Olympic Games, 1996)	85	65
1312	60c. Sheep (researchers clone Dolly, 1997)	85	65
1313	60c. Hong Kong and Chinese flag (return of Hong Kong to Chinese rule, 1997)	85	65
1314	60c. Sojourner (roving vehicle) (Mars "Pathfinder" mission, 1997)	85	65
1315	60c. Deaths of Diana, Princess of Wales and Mother Teresa, 1997	85	65
1316	60c. Rebuilding of German Reichstag, 1999	85	65
1317	60c. People of different races (birth of World's sixth billionth inhabitant, 1999)	85	65

170 Panda

2000. Giant Pandas. Multicoloured.

1318	33c. Type **170**	45	35
1319	33c. Adult facing cub	45	35
1320	33c. Adult holding cub	45	35
1321	33c. Two adults	45	35
1322	33c. Moving rock	45	35
1323	33c. Cub beside adult eating bamboo	45	35

171 George Washington

2000. American Presidents. Multicoloured.

1324	1c. Type **171**	10	10
1325	2c. John Adams	10	10
1326	3c. Thomas Jefferson	10	10
1327	4c. James Madison	10	10
1328	5c. James Monroe	10	10
1329	6c. John Quincy Adams	10	10
1330	7c. Andrew Jackson	10	10
1331	8c. Martin van Buren	10	10
1332	9c. William Henry Harrison	10	10
1333	10c. John Tyler	15	10
1334	11c. James K. Polk	15	10
1335	12c. Zachary Taylor	15	10
1336	13c. Millard Filmore	20	15
1337	14c. Franklin Pierce	20	15
1338	15c. James Buchanan	20	15
1339	16c. Abraham Lincoln	20	15
1340	17c. Andrew Johnson	25	20
1341	18c. Ulysses S. Grant	25	20
1342	19c. Rutherford B. Hayes	25	20
1343	20c. James A. Garfield	30	25
1344	21c. Chester A. Arthur	30	25
1345	22c. Grover Cleveland	30	25
1346	23c. Benjamin Harrison	30	25
1347	24c. The White House	30	25
1348	25c. William McKinley	35	25
1349	26c. Theodore Roosevelt	35	25
1350	27c. William H. Taft	35	25
1351	28c. Woodrow Wilson	40	30
1352	29c. Warren G. Harding	40	30
1353	30c. Calvin Coolidge	40	30
1354	31c. Herbert C. Hoover	40	30
1355	32c. Franklin D. Roosevelt	45	35
1356	33c. Harry S. Truman	45	35
1357	34c. Dwight D. Eisenhower	45	35
1358	35c. John F. Kennedy	50	40
1359	36c. Lyndon B. Johnson	50	40
1360	37c. Richard M. Nixon	50	40
1361	38c. Gerald R. Ford	50	40
1362	39c. James E. Carter	50	40
1363	40c. Ronald W. Reagan	55	45
1364	41c. George H. Bush	55	45
1365	42c. William J. Clinton	60	45

172 LZ-1 (first Zeppelin airship), 1900

2000. Centenary of Zeppelin Airships. Multicoloured.

1366	33c. Type **172**	45	35
1367	33c. *Graf Zeppelin I*, 1928	45	35
1368	33c. *Hindenburg*, 1936	45	35
1369	33c. *Graf Zeppelin II*, 1937	45	35

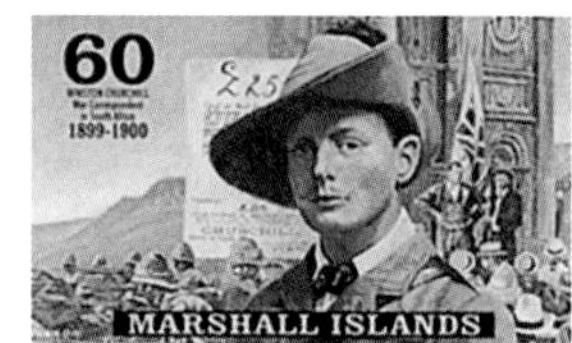

173 Churchill in South Africa as War Correspondent, 1899–1900

2000. 35th Death Anniv of Winston Churchill (British Prime Minister, 1940–45 and 1951–55). Multicoloured.

1370	60c. Type **173**	85	65
1371	60c. Churchill and Clementine Hozier on wedding day, 1908	85	65
1372	60c. Kaiser Wilhelm II, Churchill and clock tower, Houses of Parliament	85	65
1373	60c. Various portraits of Churchill between 1898 and 1960	85	65
1374	60c. Wearing naval cap (First Lord of the Admiralty, 1939–40)	85	65
1375	60c. Churchill giving "Victory" sign and St. Paul's Cathedral (Prime Minister, 1940–45)	85	65

174 Cannon, Flag and Soldier preparing to Fire (Army)

2000. 225th Anniv of United States Military Forces. Multicoloured.

1377	33c. Type **174**	45	35
1378	33c. Ship, flag and officer looking through telescope (Navy)	45	35
1379	33c. Ship, cannon and mariner drawing sword (Marines)	45	35

175 Nitijela (elected lower house) Complex

2000. Multicoloured.

1380	33c. Type **175**	45	35
1381	33c. Capitol building	45	35
1382	33c. National Seal and Nitijela Complex (vert)	45	35
1383	33c. National Flag and Nitijela Complex (vert)	45	35

176 *Half Moon* (Hudson)

2000. Sailing Ships. Multicoloured.

1384	60c. Type **176**	85	65
1385	60c. *Grande Hermine* (Cartier)	85	65
1386	60c. *Golden Hind* (Drake)	85	65
1387	60c. *Matthew* (Cabot) (wrongly inscr "Mathew")	85	65
1388	60c. *Vitoria* (Magellan) (inscr "Victoria")	85	65
1389	60c. *Sao Gabriel* (Vasco da Gama)	85	65

177 As a Young Girl, 1904

2000. "Queen Elizabeth the Queen Mother's Century". Multicoloured.

1390	60c. Type **177**	85	65
1391	60c. Wearing a turquoise hat, 1923	85	65
1392	60c. Wearing pearl necklace, 1940	85	65
1393	60c. Wearing purple hat, 1990	85	65

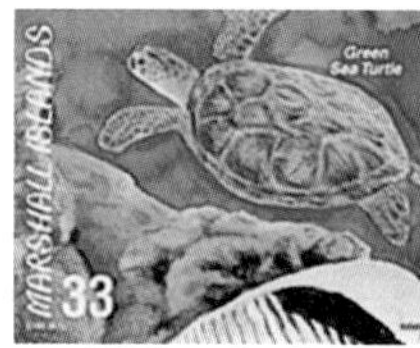

178 Green Sea Turtle

2000. Marine Life. Multicoloured.

1394	33c. Type **178**	45	35
1395	33c. Blue-girdled angelfish	45	35
1396	33c. Clown triggerfish	45	35
1397	33c. Harlequin tuskfish	45	35
1398	33c. Lined butterflyfishes	45	35
1399	33c. Whitebonnet anemonefish	45	35
1400	33c. Long-nose filefish	45	35
1401	33c. Emperor angelfish	45	35

Nos. 1394/1401 were issued together, se-tenant, forming the composite design of the reef.

179 Holly Blue Butterfly

2000. Butterflies. Multicoloured.

1402	60c. Type **179**	85	65
1403	60c. Swallowtail butterfly	85	65
1404	60c. Clouded yellow butterfly	85	65
1405	60c. Small tortoiseshell butterfly	85	65
1406	60c. Nettle-tree butterfly	85	65
1407	60c. Long tailed blue butterfly	85	65
1408	60c. Cranberry blue butterfly	85	65
1409	60c. Small heath butterfly	85	65
1410	60c. Pontic blue butterfly	85	65
1411	60c. Lapland fritillary butterfly	85	65
1412	60c. Large blue butterfly	85	65
1413	60c. Monarch butterfly	85	65

180 Brandenburg Gate, Berlin and Flag

182 Decorated Trees

181 S-44 Submarine, 1925 (½ size illustration)

2000. 10th Anniv of Reunification of Germany.

1414	**180** 33c. multicoloured	45	35

2000. Centenary of United States Submarine Fleet. Multicoloured.

1415	33c. Type **181**	45	35
1416	33c. Gato, 1941	45	35
1417	33c. Wyoming, 1996	45	35
1418	33c. Cheyenne, 1997	45	35

2000. Christmas.

1419	**182** 33c. multicoloured	45	35

183 Sun Yat-sen as Young Boy, 1866

2000. 75th Death Anniv of Dr. Sun Yat-sen (President of Republic of China, 1912–25). Multicoloured.

1420	60c. Type **183**	85	65
1421	60c. With family in Honolulu, 1879 and amongst other students in Hong Kong	85	65
1422	60c. As President of Tong Meng Hui, 1905	85	65
1423	60c. Empress Dowager (Revolution, 1911)	85	65
1424	60c. As President of Republic of China, 1912	85	65
1425	60c. Flag and various portraits of Sun Yat-sen	85	65

184 Snake (½-size illustration)

2001. New Year. Year of the Snake. Sheet 111 × 88 mm.

1427	**184** 80c. multicoloured	95	55

185 Carnations

2001. Flowers. Multicoloured.

1428	34c. Type **185**	40	25
1429	34c. Violet	40	25
1430	34c. Jonquil	40	25

186 Walap (canoe), Jaluit

187 Amata Kabua (first President)

2001. Sailing Canoes.
1440 **186** $5 green 6·00 3·50
1441 – $10 blue 12·00 7·25
DESIGN: $10 Walap, Enewetak.

2001. Personalities. Multicoloured.
1442 35c. Type **187** 40 25
1443 55c. Robert Reimers (entrepreneur) 65 40
1444 80c. Father Leonard Hacker (humanitarian) 95 55
1445 $1 Dwight Heine (educator) 1·25 75

188 Red Admiral

2001. Butterflies. Multicoloured.
1450 80c. Type **188** 95 55
1451 80c. Moroccan orange tip 95 55
1452 80c. Silver-studded blue 95 55
1453 80c. Marbled white 95 55
1454 80c. False Apollo 95 55
1455 80c. Ringlet 95 55
1456 80c. Map 95 55
1457 80c. Fenton's wood white 95 55
1458 80c. Grecian copper 95 55
1459 80c. Pale Arctic clouded yellow 95 55
1460 80c. Great banded greyling 95 55
1461 80c. Cardinal 95 55

189 *Tom Thumb*

2001. Fairytales. Multicoloured.
1462 34c. Type **189** 40 25
1463 34c. *Three Little Pigs* 40 25
1464 34c. *Gulliver's Travels* 40 25
1465 34c. *Cinderella* 40 25
1466 34c. *Gallant John* 40 25
1467 34c. *The Ugly Duckling* 40 25
1468 34c. *Fisher and the Goldfish* 40 25

MARTINIQUE Pt. 6

An island in the West Indies, now an overseas department using the stamps of France.

100 centimes = 1 franc.

1886. Stamp of French Colonies, "Commerce" type.
(a) Surch **MARTINIQUE** and new value.
3 J 01 on 20c. red on green 10·00 13·50
1 5 on 20c. red on green 38·00 45·00
4 05 on 20c. red on green 8·25 7·75
2 5c. on 20c. red on green £11000 £11000
6 015 on 20c. red on green 42·00 55·00
5 15 on 20c. red on green £140 £120

(b) Surch **MQE 15 c.**
7 J 15c. on 20c. red on green 65·00 65·00

1888. Stamps of French Colonies, "Commerce" type, surch **MARTINIQUE** and value, thus **01 c.**
10 01c. on 4c. brown on grey 8·25 3·00
11 05c. on 4c. brown on grey £950 £800
12 05c. on 10c. black and lilac 85·00 38·00
13 05c. on 20c. red on green 20·00 16·00
14 05c. on 30c. brown on drab 16·00 21·00
15 05c. on 35c. black on yellow 18·00 11·50
16 05c. on 40c. red on yellow 50·00 32·00
17 15c. on 4c. brown on grey £7250 £6750
18 15c. on 20c. red on green £110 60·00
19 15c. on 25c. black on pink 10·00 7·25
20 15c. on 75c. red on pink £130 £120

1891. Postage Due stamps of French Colonies surch **TIMBRE-POSTE MARTINIQUE** and value in figures.
21 U 05c. on 5c. black 10·00 12·00
25 05c. on 10c. black 5·25 5·75
22 05c. on 15c. black 6·50 6·00
23 15c. on 20c. black 13·00 9·25
24 15c. on 30c. black 17·00 9·25

1891. Stamp of French Colonies, "Commerce" type, surch **TIMBRE-POSTE 01c. MARTINIQUE**.
9 01c. on 2c. brown on buff 80 1·00

1892. Stamp of French Colonies, "Commerce" type, surch **1892 MARTINIQUE** and new value.
31 15c. on 25c. black on pink 20·00 20·00

1892. "Tablet" key-type inscr "MARTINIQUE", in red (1, 5, 15, 25, 75c., 1f.) or blue (others).
33 D 1c. black on blue 1·00 1·00
34 2c. brown on buff 1·25 1·40
35 4c. brown on grey 1·60 1·75
36 5c. green on green 3·50 50
37 10c. black on lilac 8·50 70
47 10c. red 3·75 30
38 15c. blue 34·00 2·25
48 15c. grey 11·50 75
39 20c. red on green 17·00 7·75
40 25c. black on pink 12·00 1·00
49 25c. blue 14·00 19·00
41 30c. brown on drab 17·00 12·50
50 35c. black on yellow 16·00 5·50
42 40c. red on yellow 30·00 13·00
43 50c. red on pink 25·00 14·00
51 50c. brown on blue 16·00 28·00
44 75c. brown on orange 25·00 17·00
45 1f. green 24·00 16·00
52 2f. violet on pink 80·00 65·00
53 5f. mauve on lilac 85·00 80·00

1903. Postage Due stamp of French Colonies surch **TIMBRE POSTE 5 F. MARTINIQUE COLIS POSTAUX**.
53a U 5f. on 60c. brown on buff £450 £475
Despite the surcharge No. 53a was for use on letters as well as parcels.

1904. Nos. 41 and 43 surch **10 c**.
54 10c. on 30c. brown and drab 9·25 12·00
55 10c. on 5f. mauve on lilac 8·75 15·00

1904. Surch **1904 0f10**.
56 0f.10 on 30c. brown on drab 14·50 18·00
57 0f.10 on 40c. red on yellow 15·00 18·00
58 0f.10 on 50c. red on pink 14·50 18·00
59 0f.10 on 75c. brown on orange 11·50 17·00
60 0f.10 on 1f. green 17·00 18·00
61 0f.10 on 5f. mauve on lilac £150 £150

13 Martinique Woman

15 Woman and Sugar Cane

14 Fort-de-France

1908.
62 **13** 1c. chocolate and brown 15 20
63 2c. brown and green 15 45
64 4c. brown and purple 40 65
65 5c. brown and green 50 15
87 5c. brown and orange 15 15
66 10c. brown and red 2·75 15
88 10c. olive and green 1·60 1·00
89 10c. red and purple 1·25 60
67 15c. red and purple 1·00 1·10
90 15c. olive and green 15 20
91 15c. red and blue 2·00 95
68 20c. brown and lilac 2·50 1·40
69 **14** 25c. brown and blue 3·00 45
92 25c. brown and orange 35 15
93 30c. brown and red 2·25 2·75
94 30c. red and carmine 55 2·75
95 30c. brown and light brown 40 1·00
96 30c. green and blue 3·00 1·25
71 35c. brown and lilac 1·00 1·50
72 40c. brown and green 1·25 45
73 45c. chocolate and brown 2·25 2·50
74 50c. brown and red 2·75 3·00
97 50c. brown and blue 1·90 2·50
98 50c. green and red 1·75 20
99 60c. pink and blue 85 2·75
100 65c. brown and violet 3·00 3·50
75 75c. brown and black 85 3·25
101 75c. blue and deep blue 2·00 2·25
102 75c. blue and brown 3·75 3·50
103 90c. carmine and red 7·00 8·50
76 **15** 1f. brown and red 2·50 3·00
104 1f. blue 2·25 2·25
105 1f. green and red 2·50 2·00
106 1f.10 brown and violet 4·50 6·00
107 1f.50 light blue and blue 8·00 8·75
77 2f. brown and grey 4·00 3·25
108 3f. mauve on pink 12·00 14·00
78 5f. brown and red 12·00 15·00

1912. Stamps of 1892 surch.
79 05 on 15c. grey 30 25
80 05 on 25c. black on pink 45 3·00
81 10 on 40c. red on yellow 2·25 2·50
82 10 on 5f. mauve on lilac 2·75 4·00

1915. Surch **5c** and red cross.
83 **13** 10c.+5c. brown and red 1·90 2·00

1920. Surch in figures.
115 **13** 0,01 on 2c. brown & green 3·00 4·25
109 0,01 on 15c. red and purple 45 30
110 0,02 on 15c. red and purple 45 2·75
84 05 on 1c. chocolate & brn 3·50 3·25
111 0,05 on 15c. red and purple 15 2·75
116 0,05 on 20c. brown and lilac 3·50 4·25
85 10 on 2c. brown and green 85 80
117 **14** 0,15 on 30c. brown and red 3·50 18·00
86 **13** 25 on 15c. red and purple 2·50 2·75
121 25c. on 15c. red and purple 15 2·75
119 **14** 0,25 on 50c. brown and red £200 £200
120 0,25 on 50c. brown and blue 4·25 5·00
122 **15** 25c. on 2f. brown and grey 50 2·75
123 25c. on 5f. brown and red 2·00 3·25
112 **14** 60 on 75c. pink and blue 10 40
113 65 on 45c. brown & lt brn 1·75 3·25
114 85 on 75c. brown and black 2·25 3·50
124 90c. on 75c. carmine and red 2·75 4·50
125 **15** 1f.25 on 1f. blue 75 2·50
126 1f.50 on 1f. ultram & bl 2·50 1·75
127 3f. on 5f. green and red 3·00 2·50
128 10f. on 5f. red and green 10·50 14·50
129 20f. on 5f. violet & brown 17·00 21·00

1931. "Colonial Exhibition" key-types inscr "MARTINIQUE".
130 E 40c. black and green 4·50 5·50
131 F 50c. black and mauve 4·00 3·00
132 G 90c. black and red 4·50 5·50
133 H 1f.50 black and blue 4·75 5·25

26 Basse Pointe Village

27 Government House, Fort-de-France

28 Martinique Woman

1933.
134 **26** 1c. red on pink 15 2·00
135 **27** 2c. blue 15 2·50
136 3c. purple 30 2·75
137 **26** 4c. green 15 2·75
138 **27** 5c. purple 15 35
139 **26** 10c. black on pink 15 30
140 **27** 15c. black on red 15 30
141 **28** 20c. brown 15 30
142 **26** 25c. purple 40 30
143 **27** 30c. green 55 30
144 30c. blue 45 2·75
145 **28** 35c. green 60 1·40
146 40c. brown 15 70
147 **27** 45c. brown 2·75 3·50
148 45c. green 70 2·25
149 50c. red 70 35
150 **26** 55c. red 1·50 2·25
151 60c. blue 40 2·75
152 **28** 65c. red on blue 1·00 1·75
153 70c. purple 1·25 2·25
154 **26** 75c. brown 2·00 2·00
155 **27** 80c. violet 1·10 1·75
156 **26** 90c. red 3·00 80
157 90c. purple 1·60 1·75
158 **27** 1f. black on green 1·75 1·10
159 1f. red 90 2·10
160 **28** 1f.25 violet 2·50 2·50
161 1f.25 red 2·00 2·50
162 1f.40 blue 1·90 2·25
163 **27** 1f.50 blue 95 75
164 1f.60 brown 2·00 2·25
165 **28** 1f.75 green 12·00 6·00
166 1f.75 blue 2·00 1·60
167 **26** 2f. blue on green 2·50 1·00
168 **28** 2f.25 blue 2·50 3·00
169 **26** 2f.50 purple 2·00 2·50
170 **28** 3f. purple 2·25 1·50
171 5f. red on pink 2·50 1·50
172 **26** 10f. blue on blue 1·75 1·50
173 **27** 20f. red on yellow 2·25 2·00

30 Belain d'Esnambuc, 1635

31 Schoelcher and Abolition of Slavery, 1848

1935. West Indies Tercentenary.
174 **30** 40c. brown 3·75 3·50
175 50c. red 3·75 3·75
176 1f.50 blue 13·00 16·00
177 **31** 1f.75 red 16·00 13·00
178 5f. brown 14·50 16·00
179 10f. green 11·00 9·75

1937. International Exhibition, Paris. As T **16** of Mauritania.
180 20c. violet 80 2·75
181 30c. green 1·10 2·75
182 40c. red 45 2·25
183 50c. brown and agate 45 1·60
184 90c. red 60 3·25
185 1f.50 blue 75 2·25

1938. Int Anti-cancer Fund. As T **22** of Mauritania.
186 1f.75+50c. blue 7·00 14·00

1939. New York World's Fair. As T **28** of Mauritania.
187 1f.25 red 2·00 3·25
188 2f.25 blue 2·25 3·25

1939. 150th Anniv of French Revolution. As T **29** of Mauritania.
189 45c.+25c. green and black 7·50 11·00
190 70c.+30c. brown and black 7·50 11·00
191 90c.+35c. orange and black 6·75 11·00
192 1f.25+1f. red and black 6·75 11·00
193 2f.25+2f. blue and black 6·75 11·00

1944. Mutual Aid and Red Cross Funds. As T **19b** of Oceanic Settlements.
194 5f.+20f. violet 90 3·50

1945. Eboue. As T **20a** of Oceanic Settlements.
195 2f. black 10 40
196 25f. green 1·10 2·50

1945. Surch.
197 **27** 1f. on 2c. blue 2·50 1·25
198 **26** 2f. on 4c. olive 50 1·40
199 **27** 3f. on 2c. blue 2·25 90
200 **28** 5f. on 65c. red on blue 70 2·00
201 10f. (DIX f.) on 65c. red on blue 2·50 2·00
202 **27** 20f. (VINGT f.) on 3c. pur 2·50 2·75

33 Victor Schoelcher

1945.
203 **33** 10c. blue and violet 15 2·75
204 30c. brown and red 20 2·00
205 40c. blue and light blue 40 2·25
206 50c. red and purple 40 2·50
207 60c. orange and yellow 30 1·75
208 70c. purple and brown 95 3·00
209 80c. green and light green 95 2·75
210 1f. blue and light blue 30 1·60
211 1f.20 violet and purple 90 3·00
212 1f.50 red and orange 55 1·40
213 2f. black and grey 60 1·25
214 2f.40 red and pink 1·10 3·25
215 3f. pink and light pink 85 1·00
216 4f. ultramarine and blue 70 2·00
217 4f.50 turquoise and green 85 1·25
218 5f. light brown and brown 95 1·50
219 10f. purple and mauve 1·10 1·25
220 15f. red and pink 90 1·50
221 20f. olive and green 60 1·60

1945. Air. As No. 299 of New Caledonia.
222 50f. green 60 1·75
223 100f. red 55 2·75

1946. Air. Victory. As T **20b** of Oceanic Settlements.
224 8f. blue 25 3·25

1946. Air. From Chad to the Rhine. As T **25a** of Madagascar.
225 5f. orange 80 2·75
226 10f. green 40 2·75
227 15f. red 80 3·25
228 20f. brown 1·00 2·50
229 25f. blue 55 3·25
230 50f. grey 1·10 2·25

34 Martinique Woman

39 Mountains and Palms

35 Local Fishing Boats and Rocks

40 West Indians and Latecoere 611 (flying boat)

1947.

231 **34** 10c. lake (postage) . . . . 20 2·50
232 30c. blue . . . . 15 2·50
233 50c. brown . . . . 15 2·75
234 **35** 60c. green . . . . 30 2·75
235 1f. lake . . . . 30 1·00
236 1f.50 violet . . . . 45 2·75
237 – 2f. green . . . . 80 2·25
238 – 2f.50 brown . . . . 80 3·00
239 – 3f. blue . . . . 95 1·50
240 – 4f. brown . . . . 80 2·00
241 – 5f. green . . . . 75 1·50
242 – 6f. mauve 90 50
243 – 10f. blue . . . . 2·00 1·75
244 – 15f. lake . . . . 2·25 2·00
245 – 20f. brown . . . . 1·75 1·90
246 **39** 25f. violet . . . . 1·90 2·00
247 40f. green . . . . 1·90 3·50

248 **40** 50f. purple (air) . . . . . 4·50 4·00
249 – 100f. green . . . . 5·50 6·25
250 – 200f. violet . . . . 32·00 22·00

DESIGNS—HORIZ: As Type **35**: 2f. to 3f. Gathering sugar cane; 4f. to 6f. Mount Pele; 10f. to 20f. Fruit products. As Type **40**—VERT: 100f. Aeroplane over landscape. HORIZ: 200f. Wandering albatross in flight.

POSTAGE DUE STAMPS

1927. Postage Due stamps of France optd **MARTINIQUE**.

D130 **D 11** 5c. blue . . . . 25 3·25
D131 10c. brown . . . . . 40 3·75
D132 20c. olive . . . . . . 65 3·75
D133 25c. red . . . . 1·00 4·25
D134 30c. red . . . . 1·25 4·50
D135 45c. green . . . . . . 1·75 4·75
D136 50c. purple . . . . . 2·25 9·00
D137 60c. green . . . . . . 3·25 9·75
D138 1f. red on yellow . . . 4·75 12·00
D139 2f. mauve . . . . . . 6·75 18·00
D140 3f. red . . . . 6·25 21·00

D **29** Fruit

D **43** Map of Martinique

1933.

D174 **D 29** 5c. blue on green . . . 35 1·60
D175 10c. brown . . . . . 15 2·75
D176 20c. blue . . . . . . 95 3·00
D177 25c. red on pink . . . 65 3·00
D178 30c. purple . . . . . 65 2·75
D179 45c. red on yellow . . 85 2·50
D180 50c. brown . . . . . 50 3·25
D181 60c. green . . . . . . 1·00 3·25
D182 1f. black on red . . . 85 3·75
D183 2f. purple . . . . . . 90 3·50
D184 3f. blue on blue . . . 1·25 3·75

1947.

D251 **D 43** 10c. blue . . . . . . 15 2·75
D252 30c. green . . . . . . 15 2·75
D253 50c. blue . . . . . . 15 3·00
D254 1f. orange . . . . . . 15 3·00
D255 2f. purple . . . . . . 1·25 3·25
D256 3f. purple . . . . . . 1·25 3·25
D257 4f. brown . . . . . . 2·25 3·50
D258 5f. red . . . . 2·25 3·50
D259 10f. black . . . . . . 2·50 4·25
D260 20f. green . . . . . . 3·25 4·25

MAURITANIA Pt. 6; Pt. 13

A French colony extending inland to the Sahara, incorporated in French West Africa from 1945 to 1959. In 1960 Mauritania became an independent Islamic republic.

1906. 100 centimes = 1 franc.
1973. 100 cents = 1 ouguiya (um).

1906. "Faidherbe", "Palms" and "Balay" key-types inscr "MAURITANIE" in blue (10, 40c., 5f.) or red (others).

1 I 1c. grey 90 80
2 2c. brown . . . . 80 1·00
3 4c. brown on blue . . . . 2·50 2·25
4 5c. green . . . . 2·75 2·25
5 10c. pink . . . . 10·00 7·00
6 J 20c. black on blue . . . . 17·00 18·00
7 25c. blue . . . . 9·00 7·50
8 30c. brown on pink . . . . £100 60·00
9 35c. black on yellow . . . 5·75 6·00
10 40c. red on blue . . . . . 8·50 8·25
11 45c. brown on green . . . 8·25 8·25
12 50c. violet . . . . 8·75 8·00
13 75c. green on orange . . . 8·00 6·75
14 K 1f. black on blue . . . . 21·00 19·00
15 2f. blue on pink . . . . . 55·00 70·00
16 5f. red on yellow £130 £110

6 Merchants crossing Desert

1913.

18 **6** 1c. brown and lilac 10 20
19 2c. blue and black . . . . 10 1·25
20 4c. black and violet . . . . 10 1·50
21 5c. green and light green . . 1·75 2·25
37 5c. red and purple . . . . 30 2·50
22 10c. orange and pink . . . 2·50 2·75
38 10c. green and light green . . 10 2·50
39 10c. pink on blue . . . . 15 2·75
23 15c. black and brown . . . 95 2·75
24 20c. orange and brown . . . 2·00 3·00
25 25c. ultramarine and blue . . 3·00 3·25
40 25c. red and green . . . . 1·75 2·25
26 30c. pink and green . . . 2·50 3·25
41 30c. orange and red . . . 2·25 2·50
42 30c. yellow and black . . . 15 2·50
43 30c. light green and green . . 2·75 3·75
27 35c. violet and brown . . . 1·25 3·25
44 35c. light green and green . . 1·00 3·00
28 40c. green and brown . . . 2·50 3·50
29 45c. brown and orange . . . 1·60 2·75
30 50c. pink and lilac . . . . 75 3·25
45 50c. ultramarine and blue . . 1·10 2·75
46 50c. blue and green . . . . 1·90 2·75
47 60c. violet on pink . . . . 1·50 2·75
48 65c. blue and brown . . . 2·25 3·25
31 75c. brown and blue . . . 1·50 3·25
49 85c. brown and green . . . 45 3·00
50 90c. pink and red . . . . 3·00 3·75
32 1f. black and red . . . . . 1·60 2·50
51 1f.10 red and mauve . . . 9·50 15·00
52 1f.25 brown and blue . . . 3·50 4·00
53 1f.50 blue and light blue . . 1·75 3·00
54 1f.75 red and green . . . . 2·50 3·25
55 1f.75 ultramarine and blue . 1·25 3·25
33 2f. violet and orange . . . 1·60 3·75
56 3f. mauve on pink . . . . 1·90 3·75
34 5f. blue and violet . . . . 3·00 4·25

1915. Surch **5c** and red cross.

35 **6** 10c.+5c. orange and pink . . 1·25 2·25
36 15c.+5c. black and brown . . 95 3·25

1922. Surch in figures and bars (some colours changed).

60 **6** 25c. on 2f. violet and orange 2·75 3·25
57 60 on 75c. violet on pink . . 1·60 2·75
58 65 on 15c. black and brown 3·00 4·25
59 85 on 75c. brown and blue 2·00 4·00
61 90c. on 75c. pink and red . . 3·00 4·00
62 1f.25 on 1f. ultram & blue . . 2·00 3·25
63 1f.50 on 1f. blue & light blue 1·25 3·00
64 3f. on 5f. mauve and brown 9·75 12·00
65 10f. on 5f. green and mauve 9·00 10·50
66 20f. on 5f. orange and blue 5·75 11·00

1931. "Colonial Exhibition" key-types inscr "MAURITANIE".

67 E 40c. green and black . . . . 9·25 13·00
68 F 50c. purple and black . . . 5·00 6·00
69 G 90c. red and black . . . . 5·00 6·50
70 H 1f.50 blue and black . . . . 5·00 6·50

16 Commerce

22 Pierre and Marie Curie

1937. International Exhibition, Paris.

71 **16** 20c. violet . . . . 45 2·50
72 30c. green . . . . 80 3·25
73 40c. red . . . . 40 3·00
74 50c. brown . . . . 35 1·40
75 90c. red . . . . 30 2·00
76 1f.50 blue . . . . 35 3·25

1938. International Anti-cancer Fund.

76b **22** 1f.75+50c. blue . . . . . 3·00 12·50

23 Man on Camel

24 Warriors

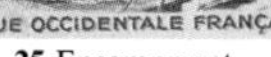

25 Encampment

26 Mauritanians

1938.

77 **23** 2c. purple . . . . 15 2·50
78 3c. blue . . . . 10 2·25
79 4c. lilac . . . . 45 2·50
80 5c. red . . . . 10 2·00
81 10c. red . . . . 80 3·00
82 15c. violet . . . . 1·10 2·50
83 **24** 20c. red 35 80
84 25c. blue . . . . 80 2·25
85 30c. purple . . . . 75 2·50
86 35c. green . . . . 60 2·75
87 40c. red . . . . 90 3·00
88 45c. green . . . . 1·75 3·00
89 50c. violet . . . . 55 3·25
90 **25** 55c. lilac . . . . 55 2·50
91 60c. violet . . . . 2·00 3·00
92 65c. green . . . . 45 3·00
93 70c. red . . . . 2·00 3·25
94 80c. blue . . . . 1·50 4·00
95 90c. lilac . . . . 1·10 2·75
96 1f. red . . . . 70 3·50
97 1f. green . . . . 10 2·50
98 1f.25 red . . . . 1·60 3·50
99 1f.40 blue . . . . 2·25 3·25
100 1f.50 violet . . . . 1·25 3·00
100a 1f.50 red £110 £100
101 1f.60 brown . . . . 3·00 3·50
102 **26** 1f.75 blue . . . . 95 2·00
103 2f. lilac . . . . 85 3·00
104 2f.25 blue . . . . 2·00 3·25
105 2f.50 brown . . . . 2·00 3·00
106 3f. green . . . . 75 3·50
107 5f. red . . . . 2·00 3·25
108 10f. purple . . . . 1·25 4·00
109 20f. red . . . . 1·50 3·25

27 Rene Caillie (explorer)

1939. Death Centenary of Caillie.

110 **27** 90c. orange . . . . 30 2·75
111 2f. violet . . . . 40 2·00
112 2f.25 blue . . . . 50 3·50

28

1939. New York World's Fair.

113 **28** 1f.25 red . . . . 1·00 3·25
114 2f.25 blue . . . . 1·10 3·25

29 Storming the Bastille

1939. 150th Anniv of French Revolution.

115 **29** 45c.+25c. green and black 7·75 13·00
116 70c.+30c. brown and black 7·75 13·00
117 90c.+35c. orange and black 7·75 13·00
118 1f.25+1f. red and black . . 8·00 13·00
119 2f.25+2f. blue and black 7·75 13·00

30 Twin-engine Airliner over Jungle

1940. Air.

120 **30** 1f.90 blue . . . . 85 2·75
121 2f.90 red . . . . 35 3·25
122 4f.50 green . . . . 45 3·00
123 4f.90 olive . . . . 1·25 2·25
124 6f.90 orange . . . . . . 80 2·75

1941. National Defence Fund. Surch **SECOURS NATIONAL** and value.

124a +1f. on 50c. (No. 89) . . . 4·75 4·75
124b +2f. on 80c. (No. 94) . . . 8·50 9·50
124c +2f. on 1f.50 (No. 100) . . 8·25 9·50
124d +3f. on 2f. (No. 103) . . . 8·50 9·50

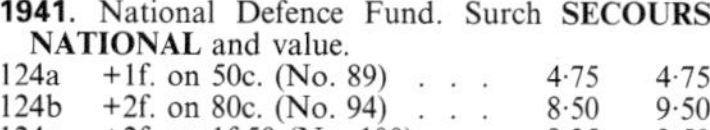

31a Ox Caravan

1942. Marshal Petain issue.

124e **31a** 1f. green . . . . 60 4·00
124f 2f.50 blue . . . . 15 4·00

1942. Air. Colonial Child Welfare Fund. As Nos. 98g/i of Niger.

124g 1f.50+3f.50 green . . . . . 15 3·25
124h 2f.+6f. brown . . . . . . 15 3·25
124i 3f.+9f. red . . . . 15 3·25

1942. Air. Imperial Fortnight. As No. 98j of Niger.

124j 1f.20+1f.80 blue and red . . 50 3·25

32 Twin-engine Airliner over Camel Caravan

1942. Air. T **32** inscr "MAURITANIE" at foot.

124k **32** 50f. orange and yellow . . 2·00 3·50

1944. Surch.

125 **25** 3f.50 on 65c. green 10 15
126 4f. on 65c. green 15 35
127 5f. on 65c. green 20 65
128 10f. on 65c. green 25 40
129 **27** 15f. on 90c. orange . . . . 75 1·25

ISLAMIC REPUBLIC

35 Flag of Republic

37 Well

38 Slender-billed Gull

1960. Inauguration of Islamic Republic.

130 **35** 25f. bistre, grn & brn on rose . . . . 2·00 2·00

1960. 10th Anniv of African Technical Co-operation Commission. As T **4** of Malagasy Republic.

131 25f. blue and turquoise . . . 2·00 2·00

1960.

132 **37** 50c. purple & brn (postage) 10 10
133 – 1f. bistre, brown and green 10 10
134 – 2f. brown, green and blue 15 10
135 – 3f. red, sepia and turquoise 20 20
136 – 4f. buff and green 20 20
137 – 5f. chocolate, brown and red 15 10
138 – 10f. blue, black and brown 20 15
139 – 15f. multicoloured 40 15
140 – 20f. brown and green . . . 30 15
141 – 25f. blue and green 50 15
142 – 30f. blue, violet and bistre 50 15
143 – 50f. brown and green . . . 80 40
144 – 60f. purple, red and green 1·25 40
145 – 85f. brown, sepia and blue 3·50 1·50

146 – 100f. brn, choc & bl (air) 6·75 2·40
147 – 200f. myrtle, brown & sepia . . . . 14·00 4·25
148 **38** 500f. sepia, blue and brown 32·00 8·75

DESIGNS—VERT: (As Type **37**) 2f. Harvesting dates; 5f. Harvesting millet; 25, 30f. Seated dance; 50f. "Telmidi" (symbolic figure); 60f. Metalsmith; 85f. Scimitar oryx; 100f. Greater flamingo; 200f. African spoonbill. HORIZ: 3f. Barbary sheep; 4f. Fennec foxes; 10f. Cordwainer; 15f. Fishing-boat; 20f. Nomad school.

39 Flag and Map

43 Campaign Emblem

42 European, African and Boeing 707 Airliners

1960. Proclamation of Independence.
149 **39** 25f. green, brown & chest . . . 50 50

1962. Air. Air Afrique Airline.
150 **42** 100f. green, brown & bistre . . 1·75 1·10

1962. Malaria Eradication.
151 **43** 25f.+5f. olive 50 50

44 U.N. Headquarters and View of Nouakchott

1962. Admission to U.N.O.
152 **44** 15f. brown, black and blue . . 20 20
153 25f. brown, myrtle and blue 35 35
154 85f. brown, purple and blue . . . . 1·00 1·00

45 Union Flag

1962. 1st Anniv of Union of African and Malagasy States.
155 **45** 30f. blue 45 45

46 Eagle and Crescent over Nouakchott

1962. 8th Endemic Diseases Eradication Conference, Nouakchott.
156 **46** 30f. green, brown and blue . . 45 35

47 Diesel Mineral Train

1962.
157 **47** 50f. multicoloured . . . . 3·75 1·25

1962. Air. 1st Anniv of Admission to U.N.O. As T **44** but views from different angles and inscr "1 er ANNIVERSAIRE 27 OCTOBRE 1962".
158 100f. blue, brown & turquoise . . 1·10 90

49 Map and Agriculture

1962. 2nd Anniv of Independence.
159 **49** 30f. green and purple . . . 45 30

50 Congress Representatives

1962. 1st Anniv of Unity Congress.
160 **50** 25f. brown, myrtle and blue 45 40

51 Globe and Emblem

1962. Freedom from Hunger.
161 **51** 25f.+5f. blue, brown & pur . . 55 55

52 Douglas DC-3 Airliner over Nouakchott Airport

1963. Air. Creation of National Airline.
162 **52** 500f. myrtle, brown & blue . 12·00 4·50

53 Open-cast Mining, Zouerate

1963. Air. Mining Development. Multicoloured.
163 100f. Type **53** . . . . 2·50 60
164 200f. Port-Etienne . . . . . 5·25 2·50

54 Striped Hyena

56 "Posts and Telecommunications"

1963. Animals.
165 **54** 50c. black, brown & myrtle . . 10 10
166 – 1f. black, blue and buff . . 10 10
167 – 1f.50 brown, olive & pur . . 20 15
168 – 2f. purple, green and red . . 15 15
169 – 5f. bistre, blue and ochre . . 25 20
170 – 10f. black and ochre . . . 50 20
171 – 15f. purple and blue . . . 50 20
172 – 20f. bistre, purple and blue . 60 20
173 – 25f. ochre, brown & turq . . 85 25
174 – 30f. bistre, brown and blue . 1·50 30
175 – 50f. bistre, brown and green . . . . 2·00 60
176 – 60f. bistre, brown & turq . . 2·50 90
ANIMALS—HORIZ: 1f. Spotted hyena; 2f. Guinea baboons; 10f. Leopard; 15f. Bongos; 20f. Aardvark; 30f. North African crested porcupine; 60f. Chameleon. VERT: 1f.50, Cheetah; 5f. Dromedaries; 25f. Patas monkeys; 50f. Dorcas gazelle.

1963. Air. African and Malagasy Posts and Telecommunications Union.
177 **56** 85f. multicoloured . . . . 1·00 65

57 "Telstar" Satellite

1963. Air. Space Telecommunications.
178 **57** 50f. brown, purple & green . . 65 45
179 – 100f. blue, brown and red . . 1·25 80
180 – 150f. turquoise and brown . . 2·25 1·50
DESIGNS: 100f. "Syncom" satellite; 150f. "Relay" satellite.

58 "Tiros" Satellite

60 U.N. Emblem, Sun and Birds

59 Airline Emblem

1963. Air. World Meteorological Day.
181 **58** 200f. brown, blue and green . . . . 3·50 1·75

1963. Air. 1st Anniv of "Air Afrique" and DC-8 Service Inauguration.
182 **59** 25f. multicoloured 50 25

1963. Air. 15th Anniv of Declaration of Human Rights.
183 **60** 100f. blue, violet and purple . . . . 1·25 85

61 Cogwheels and Wheat

62 Lichtenstein's Sandgrouse

1964. Air. European-African Economic Convention.
184 **61** 50f. multicoloured . . . . 1·10 70

1964. Air. Birds.
185 **62** 100f. ochre, brown & green . . 8·50 1·00
186 – 200f. black, brown and blue . . . . 12·00 2·50
187 – 500f. slate, red and green . 29·00 7·00
DESIGNS: 200f. Reed cormorant; 500f. Dark chanting goshawk.

63 Temple, Philae

1964. Air. Nubian Monuments Preservation.
188 **63** 10f. brown, black and blue . . 45 30
189 25f. slate, brown and blue . . 70 60
190 60f. chocolate, brown & bl . . 1·50 1·10

64 W.M.O. Emblem, Sun and Lightning

65 Radar Antennae and Sun Emblem

1964. World Meteorological Day.
191 **64** 85f. blue, orange and brown . . . . 1·25 80

1964. International Quiet Sun Years.
192 **65** 25f. red, green and blue . . 35 25

66 Bowl depicting Horse-racing

1964. Air. Olympic Games, Tokyo.
193 **66** 15f. brown and bistre . . . 30 25
194 – 50f. brown and blue . . . 60 50
195 – 85f. brown and red . . . . 1·10 1·00
196 – 100f. brown and green . . 1·50 1·25
DESIGNS—VERT: 50f. Running (vase); 85f. Wrestling (vase). HORIZ: 100f. Chariot-racing (bowl).

67 Flat-headed Grey Mullet

1964. Marine Fauna.
197 **67** 1f. green, blue and brown . . 25 15
198 – 5f. purple, green and brown 40 15
199 – 10f. green, ochre and blue . . 50 20
200 – 60f. slate, green and brown . 3·50 1·10
DESIGNS—VERT: 5f. Lobster ("Panulirus mauritanicus"); 10f. Lobster ("Panulirus regius"). HORIZ: 60f. Meagre.

68 "Co-operation"

69 Pres. Kennedy

1964. French, African and Malagasy Co-operation.
201 **68** 25f. brown, green & mauve . . 40 30

1964. Air. 1st Death Anniv of Pres. Kennedy.
202 **69** 100f. multicoloured . . . . 1·75 1·00

70 "Nymphaea lotus"

1965. Mauritanian Flowers.
203 **70** 5f. green, red and blue . . 25 15
204 – 10f. green, ochre and purple 40 15
205 – 20f. brown, red and sepia . . 60 20
206 – 45f. turquoise, purple & grn . . . . 1·25 60
FLOWERS—VERT: 10f. "Acacia gommier"; 45f. "Caralluma retrospiciens". HORIZ: 20f. "Adenium obesum".

71 "Hardine"

72 Abraham Lincoln

1965. Musical Instruments and Musicians.
207 **71** 2f. brown, bistre and blue . . 25 15
208 – 8f. brown, bistre and red . . 50 15
209 – 25f. brown, black and green 85 20
210 – 40f. black, blue and violet . . 1·10 35
DESIGNS: 8f. "Tobol" (drums); 25f. "Tidinit" ("Violins"); 40f. Native band.

1965. Death Centenary of Abraham Lincoln.
211 **72** 50f. multicoloured 70 35

73 Early Telegraph and Relay Satellite

1965. Air. Centenary of I.T.U.
212 **73** 250f. green, mauve and blue . . . . 4·25 3·25

74 Palms in the Adrar

1965. "Tourism and Archaeology" (1st series).
213 **74** 1f. green, brown and blue 10 10
214 – 4f. brown, red and blue . . 15 10
215 – 15f. multicoloured 30 20
216 – 60f. sepia, brown and green 90 45
DESIGNS—VERT: 4f. Chinguetti Mosque. HORIZ: 15f. Clay-pits; 60f. Carved doorway, Qualata.
See also Nos. 255/8.

75 "Attack on Cancer" (the Crab)

1965. Air. Campaign against Cancer.
217 **75** 100f. red, blue and ochre 1·50 60

76 Wooden Tea Service

1965. Native Handicrafts.
218 **76** 3f. brown, ochre and slate 15 15
219 – 7f. purple, orange and blue 20 20
220 – 25f. brown, black and red 35 20
221 – 50f. red, green and orange 75 35
DESIGNS—VERT: 7f. Snuff-box and pipe; 25f. Damasquine dagger. HORIZ: 50f. Mederdra chest.

77 Nouakchott Wharf 78 Sir Winston Churchill

1965. Mauritanian Development.
222 – 5f. green and brown . . . 1·75 90
223 **77** 10f. red, turquoise and blue 15 10
224 – 30f. red, brown and purple 3·50 1·10
225 – 85f. violet, lake and blue 1·25 55
DESIGNS—VERT: 5f., 30f. Choum Tunnel. HORIZ: 85f. Nouakchott Hospital.

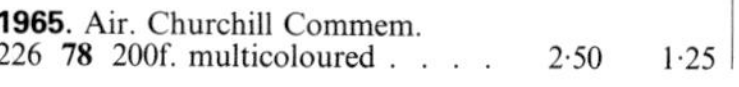

1965. Air. Churchill Commem.
226 **78** 200f. multicoloured . . . . 2·50 1·25

79 Rocket "Diamant"

1966. Air. French Satellites.
227 **79** 30f. green, red and blue . . 50 25
228 – 60f. purple, blue & turquoise . . . . 1·00 45
229 – 90f. lake, violet and blue 1·50 75
DESIGNS—HORIZ: 60f. Satellite "A 1" and Globe; 90f. Rocket "Scout" and satellite "FR 1".

80 Dr. Schweitzer and Hospital Scene

1966. Air. Schweitzer Commem.
230 **80** 50f. multicoloured . . . . 1·10 50

81 Stafford, Schirra and "Gemini 6"

1966. Air. Space Flights. Multicoloured.
231 50f. Type **81** 60 25
232 100f. Borman, Lovell and "Gemini 7" . . . . 1·25 60
233 200f. Beliaiev, Leonov and "Voskhod 2" . . . . . . 2·50 1·25

82 African Woman and Carved Head

1966. World Festival of Negro Arts, Dakar.
234 **82** 10f. black, brown and green 20 10
235 – 30f. purple, black and blue 35 20
236 – 60f. purple, red and orange 75 45
DESIGNS: 30f. Dancers and hands playing cornet; 60f. Cine-camera and village huts.

83 "Dove" over Map of Africa 84 Satellite "D 1"

1966. Air. Organization of African Unity (O.A.U.).
237 **83** 100f. multicoloured . . . . 1·00 50

1966. Air. Launching of Satellite "D 1".
238 **84** 100f. plum, brown and blue . . . . 1·10 75

85 Breguet 14T2 Salon

1966. Air. Early Aircraft.
239 **85** 50f. indigo, blue and bistre 1·00 25
240 – 100f. green, purple and blue . . . . 2·00 50
241 – 150f. turquoise, brown & bl . . . . 3·00 75
242 – 200f. indigo, blue & purple 4·00 1·25
AIRCRAFT: 100f. Farman Goliath; 150f. Couzinet "Arc en Ciel"; 200f. Latecoere 28-3 seaplane "Comte de la Vaulx".

86 "Acacia ehrenbergiana"

1966. Mauritanian Flowers. Multicoloured.
243 10f. Type **86** 25 15
244 15f. "Schouwia purpurea" . . 50 15
245 20f. "Ipomaea asarifolia" . . 65 20
246 25f. "Grewia bicolor" 75 25
247 30f. "Pancratium trianthum" 1·10 25
248 60f. "Blepharis linariifolia" 1·75 55

87 DC-8F and "Air Afrique" Emblem

1966. Air. Inauguration of Douglas DC-8F Air Services.
249 **87** 30f. grey, black and red . . 75 15

88 "Raft of the Medusa" (after Gericault)

1966. Air. 150th Anniv of Shipwreck of the "Medusa".
250 **88** 500f. multicoloured . . . . 9·00 6·50

89 "Myrina silenus" 90 "Hunting" (petroglyph from Tenses, Adrar)

1966. Butterflies. Multicoloured.
251 5f. Type **89** 50 20
252 30f. "Colotis danae" . . . . 1·25 40
253 45f. "Hypolimnas misippus" 2·00 60
254 60f. "Danaus chrysippus" . . 2·75 85

1966. Tourism and Archaeology (2nd series).
255 **90** 2f. chestnut and brown . . 15 15
256 – 3f. brown and blue 20 20
257 – 30f. green and red 55 25
258 – 50f. brown, green & purple 1·25 80
DESIGNS: 3f. "Fighting" (petroglyph from Tenses, Adrar); 30f. Copper jug (from Le Mreyer, Adrar); 50f. Camel and caravan.

91 Cogwheels and Ears of Wheat

1966. Air. Europafrique.
259 **91** 50f. multicoloured 70 40

92 U.N.E.S.C.O. Emblem

1966. 20th Anniv of U.N.E.S.C.O.
260 **92** 30f. multicoloured 45 20

93 Olympic Village, Grenoble

1967. Publicity for Olympic Games (1968).
261 – 20f. brown, blue and green 30 20
262 **93** 30f. brown, green and blue 40 30
263 – 40f. brown, purple and blue 60 40
264 – 100f. brown, green & black 1·10 70
DESIGNS—VERT: 20f. Old and new buildings, Mexico City; 40f. Ice rink, Grenoble and Olympic torch. HORIZ: 100f. Olympic stadium, Mexico City.

94 South African Crowned Crane 95 Globe, Rockets and Eye

1967. Air. Birds. Multicoloured.
265 100f. Type **94** . . . . 3·75 1·10
266 200f. Great egret . . . . . . 8·00 1·50
267 500f. Ostrich . . . . 18·00 5·25

1967. Air. World Fair, Montreal.
268 **95** 250f. brown, blue and black . . . . 2·25 1·25

96 Prosopis 97 Jamboree Emblem and Scout Kit

1967. Trees.
269 **96** 10f. green, blue and brown 20 10
270 – 15f. green, blue and purple 25 15
271 – 20f. green, purple and blue 30 15
272 – 25f. brown and green . . . 40 20
273 – 30f. brown, green and red 55 25
TREES: 15f. Jujube; 20f. Date palm; 25f. Peltophorum; 30f. Baobab.

1967. World Scout Jamboree, Idaho.
274 **97** 60f. blue, green and brown 85 35
275 – 90f. blue, green and red . . 1·40 50
DESIGN—HORIZ: 90f. Jamboree emblem and scouts.

98 Weaving 99 Atomic Symbol

1967. Advancement of Mauritanian Women.
276 **98** 5f. red, black and violet . . 15 10
277 – 10f. black, violet and green 20 10
278 – 20f. black, purple and blue 35 15
279 – 30f. blue, black and brown 45 25
280 – 50f. black, violet and indigo 70 30
DESIGNS—VERT: 10f. Needlework; 30f. Laundering. HORIZ: 20f. Nursing; 50f. Sewing (with machines).

1967. Air. International Atomic Energy Agency.
281 **99** 200f. blue, green and red 2·25 1·10

100 Cattle

1967. Campaign for Prevention of Cattle Plague.
282 **100** 30f. red, blue and green 35 25

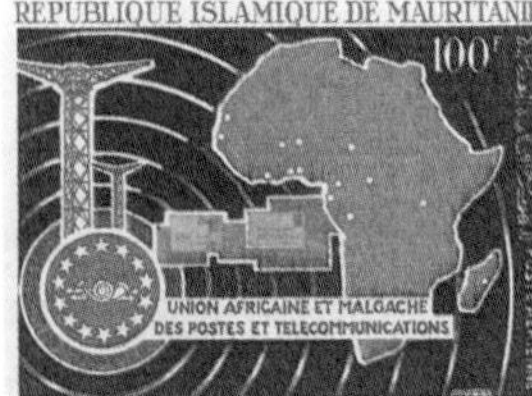

101 Map of Africa, Letters and Pylons

1967. Air. 5th Anniv of U.A.M.P.T.
283 **101** 100f. green, brown & pur 1·00 60

102 "Francois of Rimini" (Ingres) **103** Currency Tokens

1967. Air. Death Centenary of Jean Ingres (painter). Multicoloured.
284 90f. Type **102** 1·25 60
285 200f. "Ingres in his Studio" (Alaux) 2·50 1·25
See also Nos. 306/8.

1967. 5th Anniv of West African Monetary Union.
286 **103** 30f. grey and orange 35 15

104 "Hyphaene thebaica" **105** Human Rights Emblem

1967. Mauritanian Fruits.
287 **104** 1f. brown, green & purple 15 10
288 – 2f. yellow, green & brown 15 10
289 – 3f. olive, green and violet 15 10
290 – 4f. red, green and brown 15 10
291 – 5f. orange, brown & green 20 10
FRUITS—HORIZ: 2f. "Balanites aegyptiaca"; 4f. "Ziziphus lotus". VERT: 3f. "Adansonia digitata"; 5f. "Phoenix dactylifera".

1968. Human Rights Year.
292 **105** 30f. yellow, green & black 30 20
293 50f. yellow, brown & black 55 35

106 Chancellor Adenauer **108** Mosque, Nouakchott

107 Skiing

1968. Air. Adenauer Commemoration.
294 **106** 100f. sepia, brown & blue 1·25 60

1968. Air. Olympic Games, Grenoble and Mexico.
296 **107** 20f. purple, indigo & blue 30 10
297 – 30f. brown, green & plum 35 15
298 – 50f. green, blue and ochre 55 25
299 – 100f. green, red and brown 1·00 50
DESIGNS—VERT: 30f. Horse-vaulting; 50f. Ski-jumping. HORIZ: 100f. Hurdling.

1968. Tourism. Multicoloured.
300 30f. Type **108** 25 20
301 45f. Amogjar Pass 35 20
302 90f. Cavaliers' Tower, Boutilimit 65 35

109 Man and W.H.O. Emblem

1968. Air. 20th Anniv of W.H.O.
303 **109** 150f. blue, purple & brown 1·50 75

110 U.N.E.S.C.O. Emblem and "Movement of Water"

1968. International Hydrological Decade.
304 **110** 90f. green and lake 70 40

111 U.P.U. Building, Berne

1968. Admission of Mauritania to U.P.U.
305 **111** 30f. brown and red 35 20

1968. Air. Paintings by Ingres. As T **102**. Mult.
306 100f. "Man's Torso" 1·10 65
307 150f. "The Iliad" 1·75 95
308 250f. "The Odyssey" 2·75 1·60

112 Land-yachts crossing Desert **113** Dr. Martin Luther King

1968. Land-yacht Racing.
309 **112** 30f. blue, yellow & orange 45 25
310 – 40f. purple, blue & orange 55 30
311 – 60f. green, yellow & orange 85 50
DESIGNS—HORIZ: 40f. Racing on shore. VERT: 60f. Crew making repairs.

1968. Air. "Apostles of Peace".
312 **113** 50f. brown, blue and olive 1·00 40
313 – 50f. brown and blue 60 25
DESIGN: No. 313, Mahatma Gandhi.

113a "Surprise Letter" (C. A. Coypel) **114** Donkey and Foal

1968. Air. "Philexafrique" Stamp Exn, Abidjan, Ivory Coast (1969) (1st issue).
315 **113a** 100f. multicoloured 1·75 1·75

1968. Domestic Animals. Multicoloured.
316 5f. Type **114** 15 10
317 10f. Ewe and lamb 20 15
318 15f. Dromedary and calf 25 15
319 30f. Mare and foal 45 25
320 50f. Cow and calf 70 35
321 90f. Goat and kid 1·40 50

114a Forest Scene and Stamp of 1938

1969. Air. "Philexafrique" Stamp Exhibition, Abidjan, Ivory Coast (2nd issue).
322 **114a** 50f. purple, green & brown 1·10 1·10

114b "Napoleon at Council of Five Hundred" (Bouchot) **115** Map and I.L.O. Emblem

1969. Air. Birth Bicentenary of Napoleon Bonaparte. Multicoloured.
323 50f. **114b** 1·50 90
324 90f. "Napoleon's Installation by the Council of State" (Conder) 2·00 1·25
325 250f. "The Farewell of Fontainebleau" (Vernet) 5·00 3·25

1969. 50th Anniv of I.L.O.
326 **115** 50f. multicoloured 50 25

116 Monitor Lizard **117** Date Palm, "Parlatoria blanchardi" and "Pharoscymus anchorage"

1969. Reptiles. Multicoloured.
327 5f. Type **116** 35 20
328 10f. Horned viper 55 30
329 30f. Black-collared cobra 1·25 35
330 60f. Rock python 2·00 1·10
331 85f. Nile crocodile 3·00 1·40

1969. Date-palms. Protection Campaign.
332 **117** 30f. blue, red and green 30 15

118 Camel and Emblem

1969. Air. African Tourist Year.
333 **118** 50f. purple, blue & orange 85 35

119 Dancers and Baalbek Columns

1969. Baalbek Festival, Lebanon.
334 **119** 100f. brown, red and blue 1·50 55

120 "Apollo 8" and Moon

1969. Air. Moon Flight of "Apollo 8". Embossed on gold foil.
335 **120** 1,000f. gold 14·00 14·00

121 Wolde (marathon) **122a** Bank Emblem

122 London-Istanbul Route-Map

1969. Air. Gold Medal Winners, Mexico Olympic Games.
336 **121** 30f. red, brown and blue 25 15
337 – 70f. red, brown and green 50 30
338 – 150f. green, bistre and red 1·25 70
DESIGNS: 70f. Beamon (athletics); 150f. Vera Caslavska (gymnastics).

1969. Air. London–Sydney Motor Rally.
339 **122** 10f. brown, blue & purple 25 10
340 – 20f. brown, blue & purple 50 15
341 – 50f. brown, blue & purple 85 25
342 – 70f. brown, blue & purple 1·10 30
ROUTE—MAPS: 20f. Ankara–Teheran; 50f. Kandahar–Bombay; 70f. Perth–Sydney.

1969. 5th Anniv of African Development Bank. Multicoloured.
344 **122a** 30f. brown, green & blue 30 15

123 Pendant **124** Sea-water Desalination Plant, Nouakchott

1969. Native Handicrafts.
345 **123** 10f. brown and purple 20 15
346 – 20f. red, black and blue 40 20
DESIGN—HORIZ: 20f. Rahla headdress.

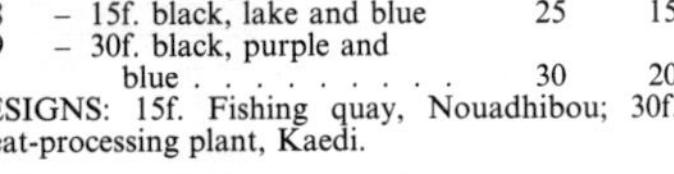
1969. Economic Development.
347 **124** 10f. blue, purple and red 20 15
348 – 15f. black, lake and blue 25 15
349 – 30f. black, purple and blue 30 20
DESIGNS: 15f. Fishing quay, Nouadhibou; 30f. Meat-processing plant, Kaedi.

125 Lenin **126** "Sternocera interrupta"

1970. Birth Centenary of Lenin.
350 **125** 30f. black, red and blue 30 20

1970. Insects.
351 **126** 5f. black, buff and brown 25 15
352 – 10f. brown, yellow & lake 35 15
353 – 20f. olive, purple & brown 50 25

354 – 30f. violet, green & brown 80 45
355 – 40f. brown, blue and lake 1·50 70
INSECTS: 10f. "Anoplocnemis curvipes"; 20f. "Julodis aequinoctialis"; 30f. "Thermophilum sexmaculatum marginatum"; 40f. "Plocaederus denticornis".

127 Footballers and Hemispheres **128** Japanese Musician, Emblem and Map on Palette

1970. World Cup Football Championship, Mexico.
356 **127** 25f. multicoloured 30 20
357 – 30f. multicoloured 35 20
358 – 70f. multicoloured 70 30
359 – 150f. multicoloured . . . 1·60 75
DESIGNS: 30, 70, 150f. As Type **127**, but with different players.

1970. New U.P.U. Headquarters Building. As T **81** of New Caledonia.
360 30f. red, brown and green . . 35 20

1970. Air. "EXPO 70" World Fair, Osaka, Japan. Multicoloured.
361 50f. Type **128** 50 20
362 75f. Japanese fan 75 35
363 150f. Stylised bird, map and boat . . . . 1·40 80

129 U.N. Emblem and Examples of Progress

1970. Air. 25th Anniv of U.N.O.
364 **129** 100f. green, brown & blue 1·25 60

130 Vladimir Komarov **131** Descent of "Apollo 13"

1970. Air. "Lost Heroes of Space" (1st series).
365 **130** 150f. brown, orge & slate 1·50 70
366 – 150f. brown, blue and slate . . . . 1·50 70
367 – 150f. brown, orge & slate 1·50 70
HEROES: No. 366, Elliott See; 367, Yuri Gagarin.
See also Nos. 376/8.

1970. Air. Space Flight of "Apollo 13".
369 **131** 500f. red, blue and gold 5·00 5·00

132 Woman in Traditional Costume **133** Arms and State House

1970. Traditional Costumes. As T **132**.
370 **132** 10f. orange and brown . . 20 15
371 – 30f. blue, red and brown 40 20
372 – 40f. brown, purple and red 50 30
373 – 50f. blue and brown . . . 70 35
374 – 70f. brown, choc & bl . . 90 45

1970. Air. 10th Anniv of Independence.
375 **133** 100f. multicoloured . . . 1·00 45

1970. Air. "Lost Heroes of Space" (2nd series). As T **130**.
376 150f. brown, blue & turquoise 1·50 70
377 150f. brown, blue & turquoise 1·50 70
378 150f. brown, blue and orange 1·50 70
HEROES: No. 376, Roger Chaffee; No. 377, Virgil Grissom; No. 378, Edward White.

134 Greek Wrestling

1971. Air. "Pre-Olympics Year".
380 **134** 100f. brown, purple & blue . . . . 1·10 75

135 People of Different Races

1971. Racial Equality Year.
381 **135** 30f. plum, blue and brown 30 15
382 – 40f. black, red and blue 35 20
DESIGN—VERT: 40f. European and African hands.

136 Pres. Nasser

1971. Air. Pres. Gamal Nasser of Egypt Commemoration.
383 **136** 100f. multicoloured . . . 85 40

137 Gen. De Gaulle in Uniform

1971. De Gaulle Commem. Multicoloured.
384 40f. Type **137** . . . . 1·25 60
385 100f. De Gaulle as President of France . . . . 2·75 1·40

138 Scout Badge, Scout and Map

1971. Air. 13th World Scout Jamboree, Asagiri, Japan.
387 **138** 35f. multicoloured 40 20
388 40f. multicoloured . . . 50 20
389 100f. multicoloured . . . 1·25 45

139 Diesel Locomotive

1971. Miferma Iron-ore Mines. Multicoloured.
390 35f. Iron ore train . . . . . 2·25 1·00
391 100f. Type **139** . . . . . . 5·00 2·50
Nos. 390/1 were issued together, se-tenant, forming a composite design.

139a Headquarters, Brazzaville, and Ardin Musicians

1971. Air. 10th Anniv of African and Malagasy Posts and Telecommunications Union.
392 **139a** 100f. multicoloured . . . 1·10 60

140 A.P.U. Emblem and Airmail Envelope

1971. Air. 10th Anniv of African Postal Union.
393 **140** 35f. multicoloured 40 25

141 U.N.I.C.E.F. Emblem and Child

1971. 25th Anniv of U.N.I.C.E.F.
394 **141** 35f. black, brown and blue 35 20

142 "Moslem King" (c. 1218)

1972. Air. Moslem Miniatures. Multicoloured.
395 35f. Type **142** 45 20
396 40f. "Enthroned Prince" (Egypt, c. 1334) 60 25
397 100f. "Pilgrims' Caravan" (Maquamat, Baghdad, 1237) . . . . 1·50 70

1972. Air. U.N.E.S.C.O. "Save Venice" Campaign. As T **127** of Mali. Multicoloured.
398 45f. "Quay and Ducal Palace" (Carlevaris) (vert) 60 25
399 100f. "Grand Canal" (Canaletto) . . . . 1·40 60
400 250f. "Santa Maria della Salute" (Canaletto) . . . . 3·00 1·50

143 Hurdling

1972. Air. Olympic Games, Munich.
401 **143** 75f. purple, orange & grn 55 30
402 100f. purple, blue & brn 75 40
403 200f. purple, lake & green 1·60 70

144 Nurse tending Baby

1972. Mauritanian Red Crescent Fund.
405 **144** 35f.+5f. multicoloured . . 60 60

145 Samuel Morse and Morse Key

1972. World Telecommunications Day. Mult.
406 35f. Type **145** 35 20
407 40f. "Relay" satellite and hemispheres 45 20
408 75f. Alexander Graham Bell and early telephone 70 35

146 Spirifer Shell

1972. Fossil Shells. Multicoloured.
409 25f. Type **146** . . . . 1·00 35
410 75f. Trilobite . . . . 2·75 1·10

147 "Luna 16" and Moon Probe **151** Mediterranean Monk Seal with Young

149 Africans and 500f. Coin

1972. Air. Russian Exploration of the Moon.
411 **147** 75f. brown, blue and green 60 30
412 – 100f. brown, grey & violet 90 50
DESIGN—HORIZ: 100f. "Lunokhod 1".

1972. Air. Gold Medal Winners, Munich. Nos. 401/3 optd as listed below.
413 **143** 75f. purple, orange & grn 60 30
414 100f. purple, blue & brn 80 50
415 200f. purple, lake & green 1·60 1·00
OVERPRINTS: 75f. **110m. HAIES MILBURN MEDAILLE D'OR**; 100f. **400m. HAIES AKII-BUA MEDAILLE D'OR**; 200f. **3,000m. STEEPLE KEINO MEDAILLE D'OR**.

1972. 10th Anniv of West African Monetary Union.
416 **149** 35f. grey, brown and green 30 20

1973. Air. Moon Flight of "Apollo 17". No. 267 surch **Apollo XVII Decembre 1972** and value.
417 250f. on 500f. multicoloured 4·00 2·00

1973. Seals. Multicoloured.
418 40f. Type **151** (postage) . . . 1·50 50
419 135f. Head of Mediterranean monk seal (air) . . . . . 3·00 1·60

152 "Lion and Crocodile" (Delacroix)

1973. Air. Paintings by Delacroix. Mult.
420 100f. Type **152** . . . . . . 1·50 75
421 250f. "Lion attacking Forest Hog" . . . . 3·25 2·00

153 "Horns of Plenty"

1973. 10th Anniv of World Food Programme.
422 **153** 35f. multicoloured 30 20

154 U.P.U. Monument, Berne, and Globe

1973. World U.P.U. Day.
423 **154** 100f. blue, orange & green 1·00 65

155 Nomad Encampment and Eclipse

1973. Total Eclipse of the Sun.
424 **155** 35f. purple and green . . 35 20
425 – 40f. purple, red and blue 45 20
426 – 140f. purple and red . . . 1·60 75
DESIGNS—VERT: 40f. Rocket and Concorde. HORIZ: 140f. Observation team.

1973. "Drought Relief". African Solidarity. No. 320 surch **SECHERESSE SOLIDARITE AFRICAINE** and value.
428 20um. on 50f. multicoloured 65 45

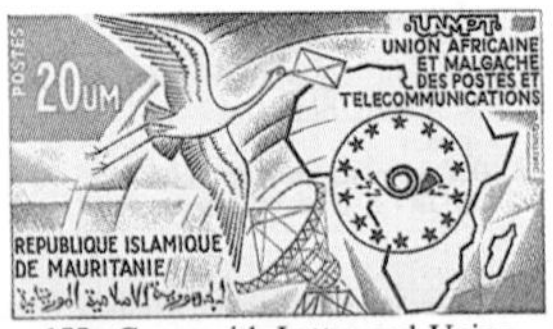

155a Crane with Letter and Union Emblem

1973. 12th Anniv of African and Malagasy Posts and Telecommunications Union.
429 **155a** 20um. brown, lt brn & orge . . . . 1·00 45

157 Detective making Arrest and Fingerprint

1973. 50th Anniv of International Criminal Police Organization (Interpol).
430 **157** 15um. violet, red & brown 1·10 45

1974. Various stamps surch with values in new currency. (a) Postage. (i) Nos. 345/6.
431 **123** 27um. on 10f. brn & pur 1·50 70
432 – 28um. on 20f. red, blk & bl . . . . 1·75 90
(ii) Nos. 351/5.
433 **126** 5um. on 5f. black, buff and brown 70 50
434 – 7um. on 10f. brown, yellow and lake 60 30
435 – 8um. on 20f. olive, purple and brown 70 35
436 – 10um. on 30f. violet, purple and brown . . . 1·00 45
437 – 20um. on 40f. brown, blue and lake . . . . 2·00 1·10
(iii) Nos. 409/10.
438 **146** 5um. on 25f. multicoloured 60 40
439 – 15um. on 75f. mult . . . 1·75 1·00
(iv) No. 418.
440 **151** 8um. on 40f. multicoloured 90 45
(b) Air. (i) Nos. 395/7.
441 **142** 7um. on 35f. mult 40 20
442 – 8um. on 40f. mult 40 20
443 – 20um. on 100f. mult . . . 1·50 70
(ii) No. 419.
444 – 27um. on 135f. mult . . . . 2·25 85
(iii) Nos. 420/1.
445 **152** 20um. on 100f. mult . . . 1·60 70
446 – 50um. on 250f. mult . . . 3·75 2·00
(iv) Nos. 424/6.
447 **155** 7um. on 35f. purple & grn 45 20
448 – 8um. on 40f. pur, red & bl 45 20
449 – 28um. on 140f. pur & red 1·90 70

159 Footballers

161 Sir Winston Churchill

160 Jules Verne and Scenes from Books

1974. Air. World Cup Football Championship, West Germany.
450 **159** 7um. multicoloured . . . 40 20
451 8um. multicoloured . . . 40 20
452 20um. multicoloured . . . 1·10 50

1974. Air. Jules Verne "Prophet of Space Travel" and "Skylab" Flights Commemoration.
454 **160** 70um. silver . . . . . . 4·50 4·50
455 – 70um. silver . . . . . . 4·50 4·50
456 **160** 250um. gold . . . . . 12·00 12·00
457 – 250um. gold . . . . . 12·00 12·00
DESIGNS: Nos. 455, 457, "Skylab" in Space.

1974. Air. Birth Centenary of Sir Winston Churchill.
458 **161** 40um. red and purple . . 1·75 95

162 U.P.U. Monument and Globes

1974. Centenary of U.P.U.
459 **162** 30um. red, green & dp grn . . . . 1·25 75
460 50um. red, lt blue & blue 2·00 1·25

163 5 Ouguiya Coin and Banknote

1974. 1st Anniv of Introduction of Ouguiya Currency.
461 **163** 7um. black, green and blue 35 20
462 – 8um. black, mauve and green 40 20
463 – 20um. black, blue and red 1·00 50
DESIGNS: 8um. 10 ouguiya coin and banknote; 20um. 20 ouguiya coin and banknote.

164 Lenin

166 Two Hunters

1974. Air. 50th Death Anniv of Lenin.
464 **164** 40um. green and red . . . 2·00 95

1974. Treaty of Berne Centenary. Nos. 459/60 optd **9 OCTOBRE 100 ANS D'UNION POSTALE INTERNATIONALE.**
465 **162** 30um. red, green and deep green . . . . 1·60 80
466 50um. red, light blue and blue . . . . 2·00 1·25

1975. Nos. 287/91 surch in new currency.
467 – 1um. on 5f. orange, brown and green . . . 10 10
468 – 2um. on 4f. red, green and brown 15 15
469 – 3um. on 2f. yellow, green and brown 20 15
470 **104** 10um. on 1f. brown, green and purple 60 20
471 – 12um. on 3f. olive, green and violet 75 30

1975. Rock-carvings, Zemmour.
472 **166** 4um. red and brown . . . 40 15
473 – 5um. purple 45 25
474 – 10um. blue and light blue 80 35
DESIGNS—VERT: 5um. Ostrich. HORIZ: 10um. Elephant.

167 Mauritanian Women

1975. Air. International Women's Year.
475 **167** 12um. purple, brown & bl 50 25
476 – 40um. purple, brown & bl 1·75 85
DESIGNS: 40um. Head of Mauritanian woman.

168 Combined European and African Heads

169 Dr. Schweitzer

1975. Europafrique.
477 **168** 40um. brown, red & bistre 1·60 95

1975. Birth Centenary of Dr. Albert Schweitzer.
478 **169** 60um. olive, brown & green . . . . 2·50 1·50

1975. Pan-African Drought Relief. Nos. 301/2 surch **SECHERESSE SOLIDARITE AFRICAINE** and value.
479 15um. on 45f. multicoloured 1·00 50
480 25um. on 90f. multicoloured 1·40 75

171 Akoujt Plant and Man with Camel

172 Fair Emblem

1975. Mining Industry.
481 **171** 10um. brown, blue & orge 1·25 30
482 – 12um. blue, red and brown . . . . 1·50 40
DESIGN: 12um. Mining operations.

1975. Nouakchott National Fair.
483 **172** 10um. multicoloured . . . 40 25

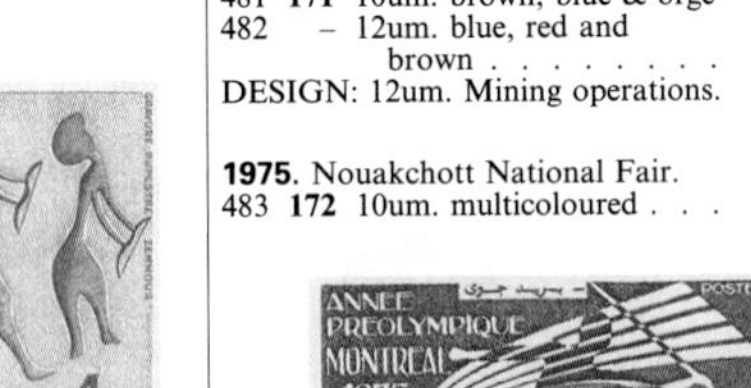

173 Throwing the Javelin

1975. Air. "Pre-Olympic Year". Olympic Games, Montreal (1976).
484 **173** 50um. red, green & brown 1·60 1·40
485 – 52um. blue, brown and red . . . . 1·75 1·40
DESIGN: 52um. Running.

174 Commemorative Medal

1975. 15th Anniv of Independence. Multicoloured.
486 10um. Type **174** 50 30
487 12um. Map of Mauritania . . 1·60 60

175 "Soyuz" Cosmonauts Leonov and Kubasov

1975. "Apollo–Soyuz" Space Link. Multicoloured.
488 8um. Type **175** (postage) . . 45 20
489 10um. "Soyuz" on launch-pad 55 25
490 20um. "Apollo" on launch-pad (air) 70 45
491 50um. Cosmonauts meeting astronauts . . . . 2·00 1·00
492 60um. Parachute splashdown 2·25 1·25

176 Foot-soldier of Lauzun's Legion

1976. Bicentenary of American Independence. Mult.
494 8um. Type **176** (postage) . . 60 20
495 10um. "Green Mountain" infantryman 70 20
496 20um. Lauzun Hussars officer (air) 90 40
497 50um. Artillery officer of 3rd Continental Regiment . . . 2·40 1·00
498 60um. Grenadier of Gatinais' Regiment 3·00 1·25

1976. 10th Anniv of Arab Labour Charter. No. 408 surch **10e ANNIVERSAIRE DE LA CHARTE ARABE DU TRAVAIL** in French and Arabic.
500 12um. on 75f. blue, blk & grn 55 30

178 Commemorative Text on Map

1976. Reunification of Mauritania.
501 **178** 10um. green, lilac and deep green 45 30

181 Running

1976. Air. Olympic Games, Montreal.

514	**181**	10um. brown, green and violet	40	25
515	–	12um. brown, green and violet	50	35
516	–	52um. brown, green and violet	1·75	1·25

DESIGNS: 12um. Vaulting (gymnastics); 52um. Fencing.

182 LZ-4 at Friedrichshafen

1976. 75th Anniv of Zeppelin Airship. Mult.

517		5um. Type **182** (postage)	25	15
518		10um. "Schwaben" over German Landscape	40	20
519		12um. "Hansa" over Heligoland	50	25
520		20um. "Bodensee" and Doctor H. Durr	1·10	50
521		50um. "Graf Zeppelin" over Capitol, Washington (air)	2·25	90
522		60um. "Graf Zeppelin II" crossing Swiss Alps	3·00	1·25

183 Temple and Bas-relief

1976. U.N.E.S.C.O. "Save Moenjodaro" (Pakistan) Campaign.

524	**183**	15um. multicoloured	80	40

184 Sacred Ibis and Yellow-billed Stork

1976. Air. Mauritanian Birds. Multicoloured.

525		50um. Type **184**	5·00	1·25
526		100um. Marabou storks (horiz)	8·50	2·75
527		200um. Long-crested and Martial eagles	18·00	5·00

185 Alexander Graham Bell, Early Telephone and Satellite

1976. Telephone Centenary.

528	**185**	10um. blue, lake and red	50	25

186 Mohammed Ali Jinnah

1976. Birth Centenary of Mohammed Ali Jinnah (first Governor-General of Pakistan).

529	**186**	10um. multicoloured	35	20

187 Capsule Assembly

1977. "Viking" Space Mission. Multicoloured.

530		10um. Misson Control (horiz) (postage)	50	15
531		12um. Type **187**	55	20
532		20um. "Viking" in flight (horiz) (air)	80	25
533		50um. "Viking" over Mars (horiz)	2·00	60
534		60um. Parachute descent	2·25	65

188 Bush Hare

1977. Mauritanian Animals. Multicoloured.

536		5um. Type **188**	30	15
537		10um. Golden jackals	65	30
538		12um. Warthogs	90	40
539		14um. Lion and lioness	1·00	50
540		15um. African elephants	1·90	80

189 Frederic and Irene Joliot-Curie (Chemistry, 1935)

1977. Nobel Prize-winners. Multicoloured.

541		12um. Type **189** (postage)	75	15
542		15um. Emil von Behring and nurse inoculating patient (1901)	75	20
543		14um. George Bernard Shaw and scene from "Androcles and the Lion" (1925) (air)	75	30
544		55um. Thomas Mann and scene from "Joseph and his Brethren" (1929)	1·90	60
545		60um. International Red Cross and scene on Western Front (Peace Prize) (1917)	2·25	70

190 A.P.U. Emblem

1977. 25th Anniv of Arab Postal Union.

547	**190**	12um. multicoloured	45	30

191 Oil Lamp

1977. Pottery from Tegdaoust.

548	**191**	1um. olive, brown and blue	10	10
549	–	2um. mauve, brown & blue	15	10
550	–	5um. orange, brown & blue	25	10
551	–	12um. brown, green and red	55	20

DESIGNS: 2um. Four-handled tureen; 5um. Large jar; 12um. Narrow-necked jug.

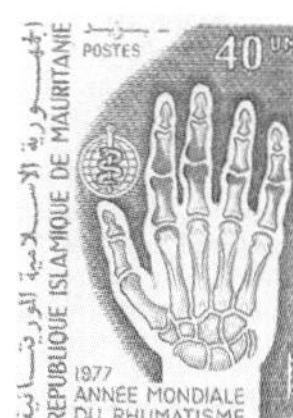

192 Skeleton of Hand

1977. World Rheumatism Year.

552	**192**	40um. orange, brown & grn	2·00	1·25

193 Holy Kaaba, Mecca

1977. Air. Pilgrimage to Mecca.

553	**193**	12um. multicoloured	60	40

194 Charles Lindbergh and "Spirit of St. Louis"

1977. History of Aviation. Multicoloured.

554		12um. Type **194**	60	15
555		14um. Clement Ader and "Eole"	70	25
556		15um. Louis Bleriot and Bleriot XI	85	25
557		55um. General Italo Balbo and Savoia Marchetti S-55X flying boats	2·50	70
558		60um. Concorde	2·75	85

195 Dome of the Rock

1977. Palestinian Welfare.

560	**195**	12um. multicoloured	70	30
561		14um. multicoloured	80	35

196 Two Players

1977. World Cup Football Championship—Elimination Rounds. Multicoloured.

562		12um. Type **196** (postage)	40	15
563		14um. Sir Alf Ramsey and Wembley Stadium	50	20
564		15um. A "throw-in"	60	20
565		50um. Football and emblems (air)	2·00	60
566		60um. Eusebio Ferreira	2·40	1·00

197 "Helene Fourment and Her Children" (Rubens)

1977. 400th Birth Anniv of Rubens. Paintings. Multicoloured.

568		12um. Type **197**	50	15
569		14um. "The Marquis of Spinola"	60	20
570		67um. "The Four Philosophers"	2·25	75
571		69um. "Steen Castle and Park" (horiz)	2·50	85

198 Addra Gazelles

1978. Endangered Animals. Multicoloured.

573		5um. Scimitar oryx (horiz)	35	15
574		12um. Type **198**	65	25
575		14um. African manatee (horiz)	80	35
576		55um. Barbary sheep	3·00	1·00
577		60um. African elephant (horiz)	3·25	1·25
578		100um. Ostrich	4·50	1·75

199 Clasped Hands and President Giscard d'Estaing of France

1978. Air. Franco-African Co-operation. Embossed on foil.

579	**199**	250um. silver	7·00	7·00
580		500um. gold	14·00	14·00

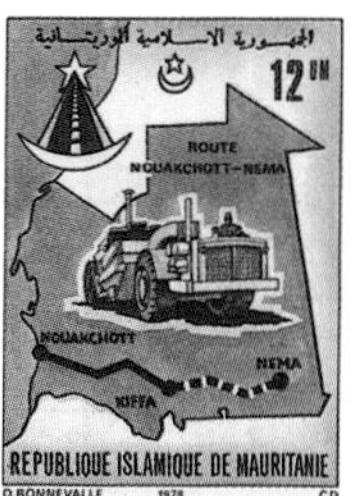

199a Earth-mover and Route Map

200 Footballers

1978. Nouakchott–Nema Highway. Mult.
580a 12um. Type **199a** . . . . . 2·00 1·50
580b 14um. Bulldozer and route map . . . . 2·25 1·75

1978. World Cup Football Championship, Argentina. Multicoloured.
581 12um. Type **200** 40 20
582 14um. World Cup 50 25
583 20um. F.I.F.A. flag and football 85 35

201 Raoul Follereau and St. George fighting Dragon

1978. 25th Anniv of Raoul Follereau Foundation.
585 **201** 12um. brown and green 70 40

202 Emblem and People holding Hands

1978. International Anti-Apartheid Year.
586 – 25um. brown, blue and red 90 60
587 **202** 30um. brown, blue & green . . . . 1·10 70
DESIGN—HORIZ: 25um. Emblem and people behind fence.

203 Charles de Gaulle

1978. Personalities. Multicoloured.
588 12um. Type **203** 90 30
589 14um. King Baudouin of Belgium 90 30
590 55um. Queen Elizabeth II (25th anniv of Coronation) 2·00 90

1978. Air. "Philexafrique" Stamp Exhibition, Libreville (Gabon) (1st issue), and 2nd International Stamp Fair, Essen (West Germany). As T **262** of Niger. Multicoloured.
591 20um. Water rail and Hamburg 1859 ½s. stamp 2·10 1·50
592 20um. Spotted hyena and Mauritania 1967 100f. South African crowned crane stamp . . . . 2·10 1·50
See also Nos. 619/20.

1978. Argentina's Victory in World Cup Football Championship. Nos. 562/6 optd **ARGENTINE–PAYS BAS 3-1** in English and Arabic.
593 **196** 12um. mult (postage) . . 50 25
594 – 14um. multicoloured . . . 55 30
595 – 15um. multicoloured . . . 65 30
596 – 50um. multicoloured (air) 1·75 1·10
597 – 60um. multicoloured . . . 2·25 1·40

205 View of Nouakchott

1978. 20th Anniv of Nouakchott.
599 **205** 12um. multicoloured . . . 45 30

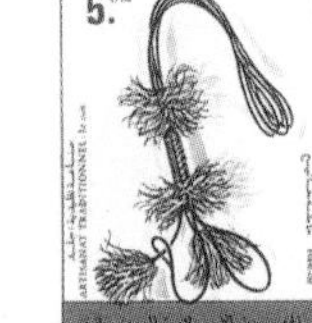

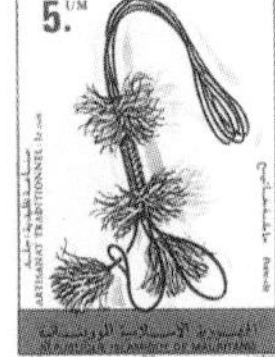

206 Human Rights Emblem **208** Key Chain

207 Wright Flyer I and Clement Ader's Avion III

1978. 30th Anniv of Declaration of Human Rights.
600 **206** 55um. red and blue . . . 1·60 1·25

1979. Air. 75th Anniv of First Powered Flight.
601 **207** 15um. grey, red and blue 1·00 35
602 – 40um. violet, blue & brn 2·00 1·10
DESIGN: 40um. Concorde and Wright Flyer I.

1979. Handicrafts. Multicoloured.
603 5um. Type **208** 25 15
604 7um. Tooth-brush case . . . 30 20
605 10um. Knife sheath 45 25

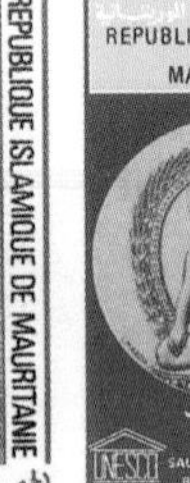

209 "Market Peasant and Wife" **210** Seated Buddha, Temple of Borobudur

1979. 450th Birth Anniv of Albrecht Durer (artist).
606 **209** 12um. black and red . . . 70 30
607 – 14um. black and red . . . 60 25
608 – 55um. black and red . . . 1·60 75
609 – 60um. black and red . . . 1·90 1·00
DESIGNS: 14um. "Young Peasant and his Wife"; 55um. "Mercenary with Banner"; 60um. "St. George and the Dragon".

1979. U.N.E.S.C.O. Campaign for Preservation of Historic Monuments. Multicoloured.
611 12um. Type **210** 50 30
612 14um. Carthaginian warrior and hunting dog 60 30
613 55um. Erechtheum Caryatid, Acropolis . . . . 1·75 1·25

211 Rowland Hill and Paddle-steamer "Sirius"

1979. Death Centenary of Sir Rowland Hill. Multicoloured.
614 12um. Type **211** 50 25
615 14um. Hill and "Great Republic" (paddle-steamer) 65 25
616 55um. Hill and "Mauretania I" (liner) . . . . 2·00 60
617 60um. Hill and "Stirling Castle" (liner) . . . . . . 2·50 85

212 Satellite over Earth

1979. "Philexafrique" Exhibition, Libreville (2nd issue).
619 – 12um. multicoloured . . . 60 50
620 **212** 30um. red, blue and lilac 1·40 1·25
DESIGN—HORIZ: 12um. Embossed leather cushion cover.

213 Mother and Children **215** Sprinter on Starting-blocks

1979. International Year of the Child. Multicoloured.
621 12um. Type **213** 45 25
622 14um. Mother with sleeping baby 55 35
623 40um. Children playing with ball . . . . 1·50 90

1979. 10th Anniv of "Apollo 11" Moon Landing. Nos. 530/4 optd **ALUNISSAGE APOLLO XI JUILLET 1969**, with Lunar module, or surch also.
624 10um. Mission Control (horiz) (postage) 40 25
625 12um. Type **187** 45 30
626 14um. on 20um. "Viking" in flight (horiz) (air) 60 25
627 50um. "Viking" over Mars (horiz) . . . . 1·60 1·00
628 60um. Parachute descent . . 1·90 1·10

1979. Pre-Olympic Year. Multicoloured.
630 12um. Type **215** 35 15
631 14um. Female runner 40 15
632 55um. Male runner leaving start . . . . 1·50 60
633 60um. Hurdling . . . . . . 1·60 60

215a Skipper

1979. Fishes. Multicoloured.
634a 1um. Type **215a** 10 10
634b 2um. Swordfish 25 15
634c 5um. Tub gurnard 40 20

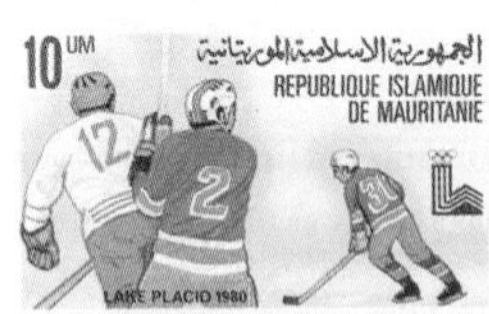

216 Ice Hockey

1979. Winter Olympic Games, Lake Placid (1980). Ice Hockey. Multicoloured.
635 10um. Type **216** 40 20
636 12um. Saving a goal 45 25
637 14um. Goalkeeper and player 55 25
638 55um. Two players . . . . . 2·00 60
639 60um. Goalkeeper . . . . . 2·25 65
640 100um. Tackle . . . . 3·50 1·25

217 Woman pouring out Tea

1980. Taking Tea.
641 **217** 1um. multicoloured . . . 10 10
642 5um. multicoloured . . . 20 10
643 12um. multicoloured . . . 45 20

218 Koran, World Map and Symbols of Arab Achievements

1980. The Arabs.
644 **218** 12um. multicoloured . . . 40 25
645 15um. multicoloured . . . 50 30

1980. Winter Olympics Medal Winners. Nos. 635/40 optd.
646 10um. **Medaille de bronze SUEDE** 35 20
647 12um. **MEDAILLE DE BRONZE SUEDE** 40 20
648 14um. **Medaille d'argent U.R.S.S.** 45 25
649 55um. **MEDAILLE D'ARGENT U.R.S.S.** . . . 1·50 80
650 60um. **MEDAILLE D'OR ETATS-UNIS** . . . . . . 1·75 90
651 100um. **Medaille d'or ETATS-UNIS** . . . . . . 3·00 1·50

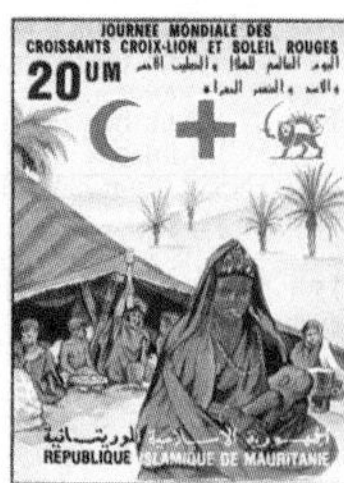

220 Holy Kaaba, Mecca **221** Mother and Child

1980. Pilgrimage to Mecca. Multicoloured.
652 10um. Type **220** 40 20
653 50um. Pilgrims outside Mosque . . . . 1·60 1·10

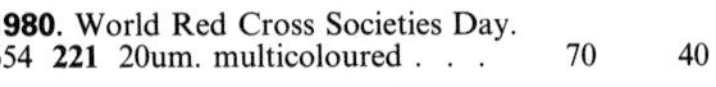

1980. World Red Cross Societies Day.
654 **221** 20um. multicoloured . . . 70 40

222 Crowd greeting Armed Forces

1980. Armed Forces Festival.
655 **222** 12um. multicoloured . . . 35 20
656 14um. multicoloured . . . 40 25

223 Horse jumping Bar **224** Trees on Map of Mauritania

1980. Olympic Games, Moscow. Multicoloured.
657 10um. Type **223** 30 20
658 20um. Water polo 55 30
659 50um. Horse jumping brick wall (horiz) . . . . 1·40 55
660 70um. Horse jumping stone wall . . . . 1·90 75

1980. Tree Day.
662 **224** 12um. multicoloured . . . 35 20

225 "Rembrandt's Mother"

1980. Paintings by Rembrandt. Multicoloured.
663 10um. "Self-portrait" 30 20
664 20um. Type **225** 75 30
665 50um. "Portrait of a Man in Oriental Costume" . . . . 1·75 55
666 70um. "Titus Lisant" . . . . 2·25 75

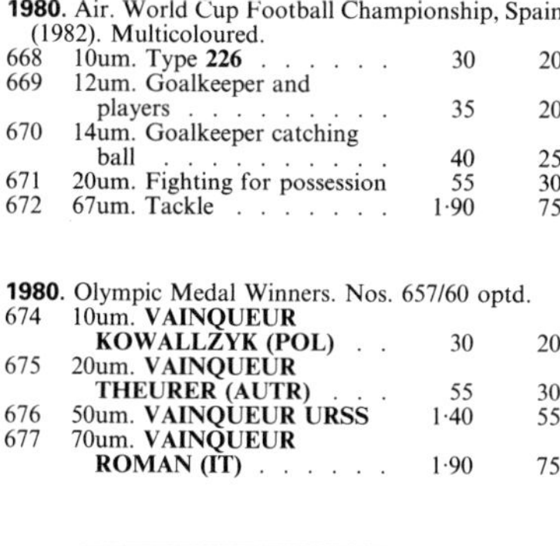

226 Footballers

1980. Air. World Cup Football Championship, Spain (1982). Multicoloured.

668 10um. Type **226** 30 20
669 12um. Goalkeeper and players 35 20
670 14um. Goalkeeper catching ball 40 25
671 20um. Fighting for possession 55 30
672 67um. Tackle . . . . 1·90 75

1980. Olympic Medal Winners. Nos. 657/60 optd.

674 10um. **VAINQUEUR KOWALLZYK (POL)** . . 30 20
675 20um. **VAINQUEUR THEURER (AUTR)** . . . 55 30
676 50um. **VAINQUEUR URSS** 1·40 55
677 70um. **VAINQUEUR ROMAN (IT)** . . . . . . 1·90 75

228 "Mastodonte del Giovi", 1853, Italy

1980. Steam Locomotives. Multicoloured.

679 10um. Type **228** 55 15
680 12um. Diesel ore train . . . 60 15
681 14um. Chicago, Milwaukee and St. Paul Railway locomotive No. 810, U.S.A. 75 20
682 20um. Bury steam locomotive, 1837, Great Britain . . . . 1·00 25
683 67um. Locomotive No. 170, France . . . . 3·50 55
684 100um. Berlin–Potsdam line, Germany . . . . 5·25 95

229 Palm Tree, Crescent and Star, Maize and Map

1980. 20th Anniv of Independence.

685 **229** 12um. multicoloured . . . 40 20
686 15um. multicoloured . . . 50 30

230 El Haram Mosque

1981. 15th Century of Hegira. Multicoloured.

687 2um. Type **230** 10 10
688 12um. Medine Mosque . . . 40 20
689 14um. Chinguetti Mosque . . 50 30

231 Space Shuttle in Orbit

1981. Air. Space Shuttle. Multicoloured.

690 12um. Type **231** 40 20
691 20um. Shuttle and space station 85 30
692 50um. Shuttle performing experiment . . . . 1·75 75
693 70um. Shuttle landing . . . . 2·50 1·00

232 "The Harlequin"

1981. Air. Birth Centenary of Pablo Picasso. Multicoloured.

695 12um. Type **232** 50 20
696 20um. "Vase of Flowers" . . 75 30
697 50um. "Three Women at a Fountain" (horiz) . . . . 1·40 75
698 70um. "Dinard Landscape" (horiz) . . . . 2·25 1·00
699 100um. "Le Dejeuner sur l'Herbe" (horiz) . . . . . 3·00 1·50

233 I.Y.D.P. Emblem

1981. International Year of Disabled People.

700 **233** 12um. violet, gold and blue 45 30

234 Open Landau

1981. British Royal Wedding. Multicoloured.

701 14um. Type **234** 40 20
702 18um. Light carriage 45 20
703 77um. Closed coupe . . . . 1·40 1·10

235 George Washington

1981. Bicentenary of Battles of Yorktown and Chesapeake Bay. Multicoloured.

705 14um. Type **235** 45 25
706 18um. Admiral de Grasse . . 55 25
707 63um. Surrender of Cornwallis at Yorktown (horiz) . . . . 1·75 95
708 81um. Battle of Chesapeake Bay (horiz) . . . . 2·25 1·50

236 Columbus and "Pinta"

1981. 450th Death Anniv of Christopher Columbus. Multicoloured.

709 19um. Type **236** . . . . . . 1·00 40
710 55um. Columbus and "Santa Maria" . . . . 2·75 1·10

237 Wheat and F.A.O. Emblem

238 Kemal Ataturk

1981. World Food Day.

711 **237** 19um. multicoloured . . . 60 40

1981. Birth Centenary of Kemal Ataturk (Turkish statesman).

712 **238** 63um. multicoloured . . . 2·00 1·25

239 Eastern White Pelicans

1981. Birds of the Arguin. Multicoloured.

713 2um. Type **239** 40 15
714 18um. Greater flamingoes . . 1·75 80

240 Hand holding Torn Flag

1981. Battle of Karameh Commemoration.

715 **240** 14um. multicoloured . . . 45 30

241 "Dermochelys coiacer"

1981. Turtles. Multicoloured.

716 1um. Type **241** 30 15
717 3um. "Chelonia mydas" . . . 40 15
718 4um. "Eretmochelys imbricata" 50 15

242 Sea Scouts

1982. 75th Anniv of Boy Scout Movement. Multicoloured.

719 14um. Type **242** 55 25
720 19um. Scouts boarding rowing boat 90 35
721 22um. Scouts in rowing boat 1·00 40
722 92um. Scouts in yacht . . . 3·00 1·25

243 Deusenberg, 1921

1982. 75th Anniv of French Grand Prix Motor Race. Multicoloured.

724 7um. Type **243** 50 20
725 12um. Alfa Romeo, 1932 . . 60 20
726 14um. Juan Fangio 75 35
727 18um. Renault, 1979 . . . . 1·00 40
728 19um. Niki Lauda . . . . . 1·00 45

244 A.P.U. Emblem

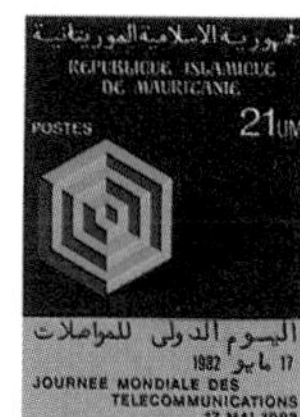

245 Hexagonal Pattern

1982. 30th Anniv of Arab Postal Union.

730 **244** 14um. orange and brown 45 30

1982. World Telecommunications Day.

731 **245** 21um. multicoloured . . . 65 45

246 Environmental Emblem on Map

1982. 10th Anniv of U.N. Environmental Programme.

732 **246** 14um. blue and light blue 45 30

247 Princess of Wales

1982. 21st Birthday of Princess of Wales. Mult.

733 21um. Type **247** 75 35
734 77um. Princess of Wales (different) . . . . 2·40 1·10

248 Straw Hut

1982. Traditional Houses. Multicoloured.

736 14um. Type **248** 45 30
737 18um. Thatched hut 55 45
738 19um. Tent 60 45

1982. Birth of Prince William of Wales. Nos. 701/3 surch **NAISSANCE ROYALE 1982**.

739 14um. Type **234** 45 35
740 18um. Light carriage 55 40
741 77um. Closed coupe . . . . 2·40 1·25

1982. Air. World Cup Football Championship Results. Nos. 668/72 optd **ITALIE 3 ALLEMAGNE (R.F.A.) 1.**

743 10um. Type **226** 40 25
744 12um. Goalkeeper punching ball 40 30
745 14um. Goalkeeper catching ball 45 30
746 20um. Three players 70 40
747 67um. Tackle . . . . 2·25 1·40

251 Cattle at Collinaire Dam, Hodh El Gharbi

1982. Agricultural Development.

749 14um. Type **251** . . . . . . 1·25 1·10
750 18um. Irrigation canal, Gorgol . . . . 1·75 1·25

252 Desert Rose

1982. Desert Rose.
751 **252** 21um. multicoloured . . . 1·50 1·00

253 Montgolfier Balloon, 1783

1983. Bicent of Manned Flight. Multicoloured.
752 14um. Type **253** 65 20
753 18um. Charles's hydrogen balloon ascent, 1783 (horiz) 65 30
754 19um. Goodyear Aerospace airship 65 30
755 55um. Nieuport 11 "Bebe" biplane (horiz) . . . . . . 1·75 70
756 63um. Concorde (horiz) . . . 3·00 1·00
757 77um. "Apollo 11" on Moon 2·50 1·00
No. 754 is wrongly inscribed "Zeppelin".

254 Ouadane

1983. Protection of Ancient Sites. Multicoloured.
758 14um. Type **254** 40 25
759 18um. Chinguetti 50 30
760 24um. Oualata 70 45
761 30um. Tichitt . . . . 1·00 55

255 Manuscript

256 I.M.O. Emblem

1983. Ancient Manuscripts. Multicoloured.
762 2um. Type **255** 10 10
763 5um. Decorated manuscript 15 15
764 7um. Shield-shaped patterned manuscript 25 20

1983. 25th Anniv of I.M.O.
765 **256** 18um. multicoloured . . . 50 30

257 W.C.Y. Emblem

1983. World Communications Year.
766 **257** 14um. multicoloured . . . 55 30

258 Customs Emblems

1983. 30th Anniv of Customs Co-operation Council.
767 **258** 14um. multicoloured . . . 45 30

259 Pilatre de Rozier and Montgolfier Balloon

260 Grinding Stone

1983. Bicentenary of Manned Flight. Mult.
768 10um. Type **259** (postage) . . 40 20
769 14um. John Wise and balloon "Atlantic" 50 30
770 25um. Charles Renard and Renard and Krebs' airship "La France" (horiz) . . . 85 35
771 100um. Henri Juillot and Lebaudy-Juillot airship "Patrie" (horiz) (air) . . . 3·75 1·25

1983. Prehistoric Grindstones. Multicoloured.
773 10um. Type **260** 50 30
774 14um. Pestle and mortar . . 75 40
775 18um. Grinding dish . . . . 1·00 60

261 Basketball

1983. Pre-Olympic Year. Multicoloured.
776 1um. Type **261** (postage) . . 10 10
777 20um. Wrestling 60 25
778 50um. Show-jumping . . . . 1·50 80
779 77um. Running (air) . . . . 2·25 1·25

262 Lord Baden-Powell (founder of Scout Movement)

1984. Celebrities. Multicoloured.
781 5um. Type **262** (postage) . . 15 10
782 14um. Goethe (poet) 45 20
783 25um. Rubens and detail of painting "The Virgin and Child" 75 45
784 100um. P. Harris (founder of Rotary International) (air) 3·00 1·40

263 Blue-finned Tuna

1984. Fishing Resources. Multicoloured.
786 1um. Type **263** 10 10
787 2um. Atlantic mackerel . . . 15 10
788 5um. European hake 40 15
789 14um. Atlantic horse-mackerel . . . . 1·10 45
790 18um. Building a fishing boat 1·25 55

264 Durer and "Madonna and Child"

1984. Multicoloured.
791 10um. Type **264** (postage) . . 35 20
792 12um. "Apollo 11" and astronaut (15th anniv of first manned Moon landing) 40 25
793 50um. Chess pieces and globe 2·00 80
794 77um. Prince and Princess of Wales (air) . . . . 2·25 1·40

265 Start of Race

1984. Olympic Games, Los Angeles. Multicoloured.
796 14um. Type **265** 40 25
797 18um. Putting the shot (vert) 55 25
798 19um. Hurdling (vert) . . . 55 25
799 44um. Throwing the javelin (vert) . . . . 1·25 65
800 77um. High jumping . . . . 2·00 1·25

266 Feeding Dehydrated Child from Glass

1984. Infant Survival Campaign. Multicoloured.
802 1um. Type **266** 10 10
803 4um. Breast-feeding baby . . 15 10
804 10um. Vaccinating baby . . . 30 20
805 14um. Weighing baby 45 30

267 Aerial View of Complex

1984. Nouakchott Olympic Complex.
806 **267** 14um. multicoloured . . . 50 40

268 Tents and Mosque Courtyard

1984. Pilgrimage to Mecca. Multicoloured.
807 14um. Type **268** 50 30
808 18um. Tents and courtyard (different) 75 40

269 Emblem

1984. 10th Anniv of West African Economic Community.
809 **269** 14um. multicoloured . . . 45 30

270 S. van den Berg (windsurfing)

1984. Air. Olympic Games Sailing Gold Medallists. Multicoloured.
810 14um. Type **270** 55 25
811 18um. R. Coutts ("Finn" class) 75 25
812 19um. Spain ("470" class) . . 1·00 25
813 44um. U.S.A. ("Soling" class) 1·90 60

1984. Drought Relief. No. 537 surch **Aide au Sahel 84**.
815 18um. on 10um. multicoloured 70 50

272 Profiles and Emblem

1985. 15th Anniv of Technical and Cultural Co-operation Agency.
816 **272** 18um. blue, deep blue and red 60 45

273 Animal drinking in Water Droplet and Skeletons

1985. Campaign against Drought. Multicoloured.
817 14um. Type **273** . . . . . . 1·10 50
818 18um. Lush trees by river in water droplet and dead trees . . . . 1·10 50

274 Replanting Trees

1985. Anti-desertification Campaign. Multicoloured.
819 10um. Type **274** 35 25
820 14um. Animals fleeing from forest fire . . . . 1·60 85
821 18um. Planting grass to hold sand dunes 65 50

275 Emblem

1985. 30th Anniv (1984) of Arab League.
822 **275** 14um. green and black . . 45 30

276 Map, I.Y.Y. Emblem and Youths

1985. Air. "Philexafrique" Stamp Exhibition, Lome. Multicoloured.
823 40um. Type **276** (International Youth Year) 1·50 1·25
824 40um. Nouadhibou oil refinery . . . . 1·50 1·25

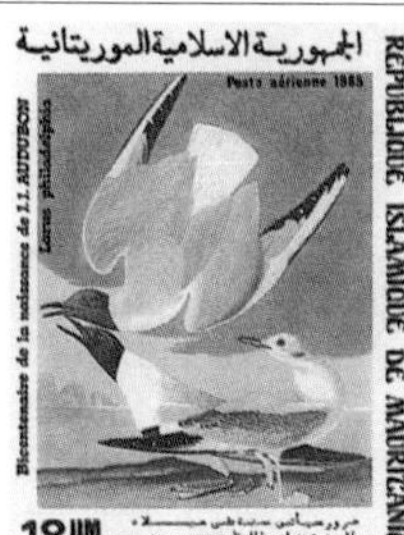
277 Bonaparte's Gulls

1985. Air. Birth Bicentenary of John J. Audubon (ornithologist). Multicoloured.
825 14um. Wester tanager and scarlet tanager . . . . . . 1·25 20
826 18um. Type **277** . . . . . . 1·50 25
827 19um. Blue jays . . . . . . 1·75 35
828 44um. Black skimmer . . . . 4·50 1·40

278 Locomotive "Adler", 1835

1985. Anniversaries. Multicoloured.
830 12um. Type **278** (150th anniv of German railways) . . . 2·25 60
831 18um. Class 10 steam locomotive, 1956 (150th anniv of German railways) 2·50 60
832 44um. Johann Sebastian Bach (composer, 300th birth anniv European Music Year) . . . . 1·60 70
833 77um. Georg Frederick Handel (composer, 300th birth anniv European Music Year) . . . . 2·75 1·25
834 90um. Statue of Liberty (centenary) (vert) . . . . . 2·75 1·40

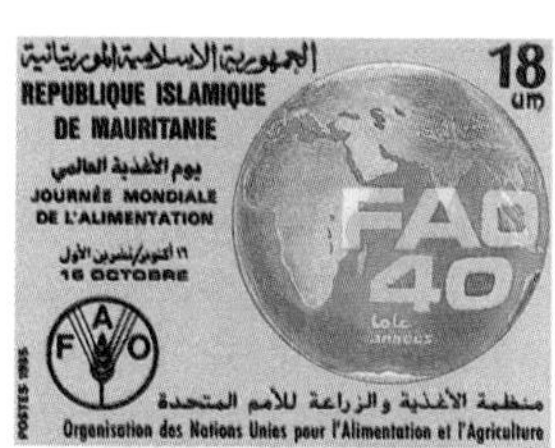
279 Globe and Emblem

1985. World Food Day.
836 **279** 18um. multicoloured . . . 55 35

280 Tending Sheep and reading Book

1985. Air. "Philexafrique" Stamp Exhibition, Lome, Togo (2nd issue). Multicoloured.
837 50um. Type **280** . . . . . . 2·00 1·50
838 50um. Dock, iron ore mine and diesel train . . . . . 3·50 90

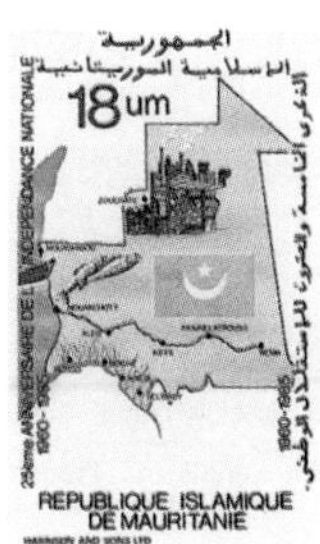
281 Map showing Industries

1985. 25th Anniv of Independence.
839 **281** 18um. multicoloured . . . 60 40

282 Development

1986. International Youth Year. Multicoloured.
840 18um. Type **282** 60 30
841 22um. Re-afforestation (voluntary work) 70 40
842 25um. Hands reaching from globe to dove (peace) (vert) 75 50

283 Latecoere Seaplane "Comte de la Vaulx" and Map

1986. Air. 55th Anniv (1985) of First Commercial South Atlantic Flight. Multicoloured.
843 18um. Type **283** 75 35
844 50um. Piper Twin Commanche airplanes crossing between maps of Africa and South America 2·00 1·25

284 Toujounine Earth Receiving Station

1986.
845 **284** 25um. multicoloured . . . 90 50

285 Heads of Mother and Pup

1986. World Wildlife Fund. Mediterranean Monk Seal. Multicoloured.
846 2um. Type **285** 50 30
847 5um. Mother and pup on land 75 50
848 10um. Mother and pup swimming . . . . 1·00 75
849 18um. Seal family . . . . . 2·00 1·00

286 Player and 1970 25f. Stamp

1986. Air. World Cup Football Championship, Mexico. Multicoloured.
851 8um. Type **286** 25 10
852 18um. Player and 1970 30f. stamp 60 20
853 22um. Player and 1970 70f. stamp 70 30
854 25um. Player and 1970 150f. stamp 85 35
855 40um. Player and World Cup trophy on "stamp" . . . . 1·25 60

287 Weaving

1986.
857 **287** 18um. multicoloured . . . 60 35

288 Emblem, Boeing 737, Douglas DC-10 and Map

1986. Air. 25th Anniv of Air Afrique.
858 **288** 26um. multicoloured . . . 1·00 40

289 Indian, "Santa Maria" and Route Map

1986. 500th Anniv (1992) of Discovery of America by Christopher Columbus. Multicoloured.
859 2um. Type **289** (postage) . . 10 10
860 22um. Indian, "Nina" and map 65 30
861 35um. Indian, "Pinta" and map . . . . 1·10 50
862 150um. Indian, map and Christopher Columbus (air) 4·50 1·60

290 J. H. Dort, Comet Picture and Space Probe "Giotto"

1986. Appearance of Halley's Comet. Multicoloured.
864 5um. Type **290** (postage) . . 15 10
865 18um. William Huggins (astronomer) and "Ariane" space rocket 60 20
866 26um. E. J. Opik and space probes "Giotto" and "Vega" 80 30
867 80um. F. L. Whipple and "Planet A" space probe (air) . . . . 2·75 1·25

291 Astronauts

1986. "Challenger" Astronauts Commemoration. Multicoloured.
869 7um. Type **291** (postage) . . 20 10
870 22um. Judith Resnik and astronaut 60 30
871 32um. Ellison Onizuka and Ronald McNair . . . . . 1·00 45
872 43um. Christa Corrigan McAuliffe (air) . . . . . . 1·50 60

292 Red Seabream

1986. Fishes and Birds. Multicoloured.
874 4um. Type **292** 30 15
875 22um. White spoonbills . . . 1·75 65
876 32um. Bridled terns . . . . . 2·00 1·00
877 98um. Sea-trout . . . . . . 5·50 3·00
See also Nos. 896/900.

293 Arrow through Victim

294 Fisherman

1986. 4th Anniv of Massacre of Palestinian Refugees in Sabra and Shatila Camps, Lebanon.
878 **293** 22um. black, gold and red 80 40

1986. World Food Day.
879 **294** 22um. multicoloured . . . 1·25 40

295 Dome of the Rock

1987. "Arab Jerusalem".
880 **295** 22um. multicoloured . . . 80 40

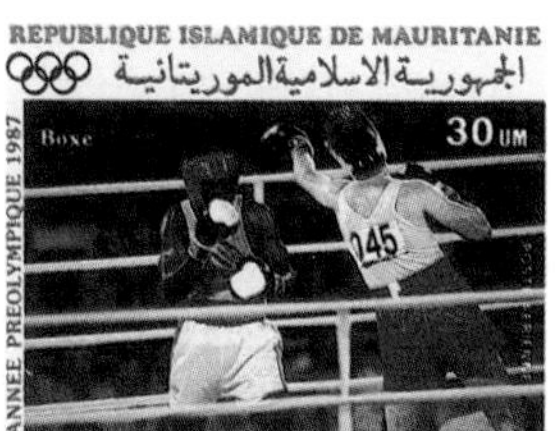
296 Boxing

1987. Air. Olympic Games, Seoul (1988) (1st issue). Multicoloured.
881 30um. Type **296** 80 40
882 40um. Judo . . . . 1·00 55
883 50um. Fencing . . . . 1·25 70
884 75um. Wrestling . . . . . . 2·00 1·10
See also Nos. 902/5.

297 Cordoue Mosque

1987. 1200th Anniv of Cordoue Mosque.
886 **297** 30um. multicoloured . . . 1·00 50

298 Women's Slalom

1987. Air. Winter Olympic Games, Calgary (1988). Multicoloured.
887 30um. Type **298** . . . . . . 1·10 40
888 40um. Men's speed skating 1·40 55
889 50um. Ice hockey . . . . . 1·60 75
890 75um. Women's downhill skiing . . . . 2·50 1·10

299 Adults at Desk

1987. Literacy Campaign. Multicoloured.
892 18um. Type **299** 60 40
893 20um. Adults and children reading 80 50

300 People queueing for Treatment

1987. World Health Day.
894 **300** 18um. multicoloured . . . 70 40

301 Map within Circle

1988. National Population and Housing Census.
895 **301** 20um. multicoloured . . . 60 35

1988. Fishes and Birds. Horiz designs as T **292**. Multicoloured.
896 1um. Small-horned blenny . . 10 10
897 7um. Grey triggerfish 40 15
898 15um. Skipjack tuna 70 30
899 18um. Great cormorants . . 95 65
900 80um. Royal terns . . . . . 4·00 2·75

302 People with Candles
303 Hammer Throwing

1988. 40th Anniv of W.H.O.
901 **302** 30um. multicoloured . . . 1·00 40

1988. Air. Olympic Games, Seoul (2nd issue). Multicoloured.
902 20um. Type **303** 50 25
903 24um. Discus 60 30
904 30um. Putting the shot . . . 80 40
905 150um. Javelin throwing . . 4·00 2·10

1988. Winter Olympic Games Gold Medal Winners. Nos. 887/90 optd.
907 30um. Optd **Medaille d'or Vreni Schneider (Suisse)** . . 1·00 50
908 40um. Optd **Medaille d'or 1500m. Andre Hoffman (R.D.A.)** . . . . 1·10 75
909 50um. Optd **Medaille d'or U.R.S.S.** . . . . 1·50 1·00
910 75um. Optd **Medaille d'or Marina Kiehl (R.F.A.)** . . . 2·25 1·50

305 Flags and Globe

1988. 75th Anniv of Arab Scout Movement.
912 **305** 35um. multicoloured . . . 1·50 55

306 Men at Ballot Box

1988. 1st Municipal Elections. Multicoloured.
913 20um. Type **306** 60 30
914 24um. Woman at ballot box 80 40

307 Emblem
308 Ploughing with Oxen

1988. 25th Anniv of Organization of African Unity.
915 **307** 40um. multicoloured . . . 1·25 60

1988. 10th Anniv of International Agricultural Development Fund.
916 **308** 35um. multicoloured . . . 1·10 70

309 Port Activities

1989. 1st Anniv of Nouakchott Free Port.
917 **309** 24um. multicoloured . . . 1·25 65

310 "Heliothis armigera"
311 "Nomadacris septemfasciata"

1989. Plant Pests. Multicoloured.
918 2um. Type **310** 15 15
919 6um. "Aphis gossypii" . . . 20 15
920 10um. "Agrotis ypsilon" . . 35 15
921 20um. "Chilo" sp. 75 30
922 24um. "Plitella xylostella" . . 85 40
923 30um. "Henosepilachna elaterii" . . . . 1·25 55
924 42um. "Trichoplusia ni" . . 1·50 70

1989. Locusts. Multicoloured.
925 5um. Type **311** 15 10
926 20um. Locusts mating . . . 60 30
927 24um. Locusts emerging from chrysallis 70 40
928 40um. Locusts flying . . . . 1·25 75
929 88um. Locust (different) . . . 3·00 1·25

312 Men of Different Races embracing
313 Footballers

1989. "Philexfrance '89" Int Stamp Exn, Paris, and Bicent of French Revolution.
930 **312** 35um. multicoloured . . . 1·10 60

1989. World Cup Football Championship, Italy (1990) (1st issue).
931 **313** 20um. multicoloured . . . 1·00 40
See also Nos. 937/41.

314 Attan'eem Migat, Mecca

1989. Pilgrimage to Mecca.
932 **314** 20um. multicoloured . . . 75 30

315 Emblem
317 Youths

316 Carpet

1989. 25th Anniv of African Development Bank.
933 **315** 37um. black and mauve 1·00 50

1989.
934 **316** 50um. multicoloured . . . 1·50 80

1989. 2nd Anniv of Palestinian "Intifada" Movement.
935 **317** 35um. multicoloured . . . 1·25 50

318 Member Countries' Leaders (½-size illustration)

1990. 1st Anniv of Arab Maghreb Union.
936 **318** 50um. multicoloured . . . 1·50 70

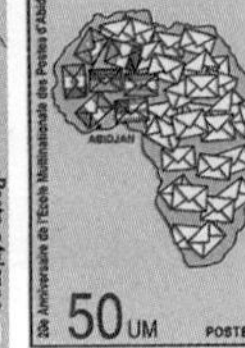

319 Players
320 Envelopes on Map

1990. Air. World Cup Football Championship, Italy (2nd issue).
937 **319** 50um. multicoloured . . . 1·50 50
938 – 60um. multicoloured . . . 1·90 60
939 – 70um. multicoloured . . . 2·00 75
940 – 90um. multicoloured . . . 2·75 75
941 – 150um. multicoloured . . 4·50 1·25
DESIGNS: 60 to 150um. Show footballers.

1990. 20th Anniv of Multinational Postal Training School, Abidjan.
942 **320** 50um. multicoloured . . . 1·10 50

321 Books and Desk

1990. International Literacy Year.
943 **321** 60um. multicoloured . . . 1·75 1·00

322 Maps and Earth-moving Vehicles

1990. Mineral Resources.
944 **322** 60um. multicoloured . . . 2·75 1·25

323 Dressage
324 Emblem

1990. Olympic Games, Barcelona (1992). Mult.
945 5um. Type **323** (postage) . . 20 15
946 50um. Archery . . . . 1·40 40
947 60um. Throwing the hammer 1·50 50
948 75um. Football . . . . . . 2·00 50
949 90um. Basketball . . . . . . 2·75 65
950 220um. Table tennis (air) . . 6·00 1·40

1990. 2nd Anniv of Declaration of State of Palestine.
952 **324** 85um. multicoloured . . . 1·75 1·10

325 Camp

1990. Integration of Repatriates from Senegal. Multicoloured.
953 50um. Type **325** 90 60
954 75um. Women's sewing group 1·25 1·00
955 85um. Water collection . . . 1·40 1·00

326 Map, Dove and Mandela

1990. Release from South African Prison of Nelson Mandela.
956 **326** 85um. multicoloured . . . 1·60 1·10

327 Downhill skiing

1990. Winter Olympic Games, Albertville (1992). Multicoloured.
957 60um. Type **327** (postage) . . 1·00 60
958 75um. Cross-country skiing 1·50 75
959 90um. Ice hockey . . . . . 1·75 95
960 220um. Figure skating (pairs) (air) . . . . 3·75 2·25

328 Blue Leg
330 Woman carrying Bucket of Water

329 Dish Aerials and Transmitting Tower

1991. Scouts, Fungi and Butterflies. Multicoloured.
962 5um. Type **328** (postage) . . 40 20
963 50um. "Agaricus bitorquis edulis" . . . . 2·50 80

964		60um. "Bunea alcinoe" (butterfly)	2·25	75
965		90um. "Salamis cytora" (butterfly)	2·75	1·10
966		220um. "Bronze boletus"	6·50	3·00
967		75um. "Cyrestis camillus" (butterfly) (air)	2·50	85

1991. 30th Anniv of Independence. Multicoloured.

968		50um. Type **329**	1·00	65
969		60um. Container ship in dock	2·00	85
970		100um. Workers in field	1·75	1·00

1991. World Meteorological Day.

972	**330**	100um. multicoloured	1·75	1·10

331 Health Centre

1991. 20th Anniv of Medecins sans Frontieres (international medical relief organization).

973	**331**	60um. multicoloured	70	45

332 Cats

1991. Domestic Animals. Multicoloured.

974		50um. Type **332**	75	35
975		60um. Basenji dog	1·00	45

333 Globe and Stylized Figures

1991. World Population Day.

976	**333**	90um. multicoloured	1·00	60

334 Blind Woman with Sight restored

1991. Anti-blindness Campaign.

977	**334**	50um. multicoloured	55	35

335 Nouakchott Electricity Station

1991. 2nd Anniv of Nouakchott Electricity Station.

978	**335**	50um. multicoloured	55	35

336 Quarrying

1993. Mineral Exploitation, Haoudat. Multicoloured.

979		50um. Type **336**	75	35
980		60um. Dry land	85	40

337 Camel Train

338 Palestinians

1993.

981	**337**	50um. multicoloured	55	35
982		60um. multicoloured	65	40

1993. Palestinian "Intifada" Movement. Multicoloured.

983		50um. Type **338**	55	35
984		60um. Palestinian children by fire (horiz)	65	40

339 Four-man Bobsleighing

340 Soldier Field, Chicago

1993. Winter Olympic Games, Lillehammer. Multicoloured.

985		10um. Type **339**	10	10
986		50um. Luge	55	35
987		60um. Figure skating	65	40
988		80um. Skiing	85	55
989		220um. Cross-country skiing	2·40	1·50

1994. World Cup Football Championship, U.S.A. Players and Stadiums. Multicoloured.

991		10um. Type **340**	10	10
992		50um. Foxboro Stadium, Boston	50	30
993		60um. Robert F. Kennedy Stadium, Washington D.C.	65	40
994		90um. Stanford Stadium, San Francisco	95	60
995		220um. Giant Stadium, New York	2·25	1·40

341 Anniversary Emblem and 1962 15f. Stamp

1995. 50th Anniv of U.N.O.

997	**341**	60um. multicoloured	60	40

342 Stabilizing Desert

345 Weaving

1995. 50th Anniv of F.A.O. Multicoloured.

998		50um. Type **342**	50	30
999		60um. Fishermen launching boat	60	40
1000		90um. Planting crops	85	55

1995. Crafts. Multicoloured.

1006		50um. Type **345**	30	15
1007		60um. Metalwork	35	20

346 Door

347 Start of Race

1995. Tourism. Re-vitalization of Ancient Towns. Multicoloured.

1008		10um. Type **346**	10	10
1009		20um. Arch and rubble	10	10
1010		40um. Town in desert	25	15
1011		50um. Door in ornate wall	30	15

1996. Olympic Games, Atlanta, U.S.A. Mult.

1012		20um. Type **347**	10	10
1013		30um. Start of race (horiz)	15	10
1014		40um. Running in lane	25	15
1015		50um. Long-distance race (horiz)	30	15

348 Beaded Locks and Headdress

349 Ball-in-Pot Game

1996. Traditional Hairstyles. Multicoloured.

1016		50um. Type **348**	30	15
1017		60um. Woman with hair adornments	35	20

1996. Traditional Games. Multicoloured.

1018		50um. Type **349**	30	15
1019		60um. Strategy game with spherical and conical pieces (horiz)	35	20
1020		90um. Pegs-in-board game (horiz)	50	30

350 Family

1996. 50th Anniv of United Nations Children's Fund. The Rights of the Child. Showing children's drawings. Multicoloured.

1021		50um. Type **350**	30	15
1022		60um. Boy in wheelchair	35	20

OFFICIAL STAMPS

O 41 Cross of Trarza

O 179

1961.

O150	**O 41**	1f. purple and blue	10	10
O151		3f. myrtle and red	10	10
O152		5f. brown and green	10	10
O153		10f. blue and turquoise	20	10
O154		15f. orange and blue	30	15
O155		20f. green and myrtle	35	20
O156		25f. red and orange	40	30
O157		30f. green and purple	45	30
O158		50f. sepia and red	1·00	45
O159		100f. blue and orange	1·60	75
O160		200f. red and green	3·00	1·60

1976.

O502	**O 179**	1um. multicoloured	10	10
O503		2um. multicoloured	15	10
O504		5um. multicoloured	20	15
O505		10um. multicoloured	40	20
O506		12um. multicoloured	55	30
O507		40um. multicoloured	1·75	1·00
O508		50um. multicoloured	2·25	1·25

POSTAGE DUE STAMPS

1906. Stamps of 1906 optd **T** in a triangle.

D18	I	5c. green and red	—	32·00
D19		10c. pink and blue	—	32·00
D20	J	20c. black and red on blue	—	52·00
D21		25c. blue and red	—	52·00
D22		30c. brown & red on pink	—	£120
D23		40c. red on blue	—	£500
D24		50c. violet and red	—	£120
D25	K	1f. black and red on blue	—	£180

1906. "Natives" key-type inscr "MAURITANIE" in blue (10, 30c.) or red (others).

D25	L	5c. green	1·25	1·10
D26		10c. purple	2·00	1·90
D27		15c. blue on blue	4·00	2·50
D28		20c. black on yellow	4·75	7·75
D29		30c. red on cream	6·75	14·50
D30		50c. violet	10·00	21·00
D31		60c. black on buff	7·25	11·50
D32		1f. black on pink	14·00	23·00

1914. "Figure" key-type inscr "MAURITANIE".

D35	M	5c. green	10	65
D36		10c. red	15	25
D37		15c. grey	15	1·75
D38		20c. brown	15	2·25
D39		30c. blue	30	2·50
D40		50c. black	30	2·25
D41		60c. orange	20	1·90
D42		1f. violet	35	2·25

1927. Surch in figures.

D67	M	2f. on 1f. purple	70	4·25
D68		3f. on 1f. brown	65	4·50

D 40 Qualata Motif

D 180

D 55 Ruppell's Griffon

1961.

D150	**D 40**	1f. yellow and purple	10	10
D151		2f. grey and red	10	10
D152		5f. pink and red	20	15
D153		10f. green and myrtle	25	15
D154		15f. brown and drab	30	15
D155		20f. blue and red	35	20
D156		25f. red and green	55	35

1963. Birds. Multicoloured.

D177		50c. Type **D 55**	45	15
D178		50c. Common crane	45	15
D179		1f. Eastern white pelican	55	20
D180		1f. Garganey	55	20
D181		2f. Golden oriole	80	25
D182		2f. Variable sunbird	80	25
D183		5f. Great snipe	85	45
D184		5f. Common shoveler	85	45
D185		10f. Vulturine guineafowl	1·40	80
D186		10f. Black stork	1·40	80
D187		15f. Grey heron	1·60	1·25
D188		15f. White stork	1·60	1·25
D189		20f. Paradise whydah	2·10	1·40
D190		20f. Red-legged partridge	2·10	1·40
D191		25f. Little stint	2·75	1·75
D192		25f. Arabian bustard	2·75	1·75

1976.

D509	**D 180**	1um. multicoloured	10	10
D510		3um. multicoloured	15	15
D511		10um. multicoloured	35	35
D512		12um. multicoloured	40	40
D513		20um. multicoloured	70	70

APPENDIX

The following stamps have either been issued in excess of postal needs or have not been available to the public in a reasonable quantities at face value. Such stamps may later be given full listing if there is evidence of regular postal use.

1962.

World Refugee Year (1960). Optd on 1960 Definitive issue, 30, 50, 60f.

Olympic Games in Rome (1960) and Tokyo (1964). Surch on 1960 Definitive issue 75f. on 15f., 75f. on 20f.

European Steel and Coal Community and Exploration of Iron-ore in Mauritania. Optd on 1960 Definitive issue. Air 500f.

Malaria Eradication. Optd on 1960 Definitive issue. Air. 100, 200f.

MAURITIUS Pt. 1

An island in the Indian Ocean, east of Madagascar. Attained self-government on 1 September 1967, and became independent on 12 March 1968.

1847. 12 pence = 1 shilling;
20 shillings = 1 pound.
1878. 100 cents = 1 rupee.

1 ("POST OFFICE")

2 ("POST PAID")

1847. Imperf.

1	**1**	1d. red	—	£450000
2		2d. blue	—	£550000

1848. Imperf.

23	**2**	1d. red	£1500	£375
25		2d. blue	£2000	£550

3 5

1854. Surch **FOUR-PENCE**. Imperf.
26 **3** 4d. green £750 £375

1858. No value on stamps. Imperf.
27 **3** (4d.) green £425 £200
28 (6d.) red . . . . 30·00 55·00
29 (9d.) purple £550 £200

1859. Imperf.
32 **5** 6d. blue . . . . £600 35·00
33 6d. black . . . . 21·00 40·00
34 1s. red . . . . £2000 45·00
35 1s. green £475 £110

6 8

1859. Imperf.
39 **6** 2d. blue £1200 £425

1859. Imperf.
42 **8** 1d. red £3500 £750
44 2d. blue £1800 £400

9 10

1860.
56 **9** 1d. purple . . . . 60·00 10·00
57 1d. brown . . . . 80·00 6·50
60 2d. blue . . . . 75·00 7·50
61a 3d. red . . . . 48·00 9·00
62 4d. red . . . . 80·00 3·25
65 6d. green . . . . £120 4·50
50 6d. grey . . . . £225 85·00
63 6d. violet . . . . £190 26·00
51 9d. purple . . . . £100 38·00
66 9d. green £120 £190
67 **10** 10d. red . . . . £225 35·00
70 **9** 1s. yellow . . . . £170 12·00
53 1s. green £550 £150
69 1s. blue . . . . £130 20·00
71 5s. mauve . . . . £160 50·00

1862. Perf.
54 **5** 6d. black . . . . 20·00 55·00
55 1s. green £1800 £325

HALF PENNY (11) HALF PENNY (13)

1876. Surcharged with T **11**.
76 **9** ½d. on 9d. purple . . . . . 8·00 12·00
77 **10** ½d. on 10d. red . . . . . . 1·75 17·00

1877. Surch with T **13**.
79 **10** ½d. on 10d. red . . . . . . 4·00 29·00

1877. Surch in words.
80 **9** 1d. on 4d. red . . . . 8·50 13·00
82 1s. on 5s. mauve £200 £100

1878. Surch.
83 **10** 2c. red . . . . 7·00 4·75
84 **9** 4c. on 1d. brown . . . . . 12·00 4·75
85 8c. on 2d. blue . . . . . . 70·00 1·50
86 13c. on 3d. red . . . . . . 11·00 26·00
87 17c. on 4d. red . . . . . . £150 2·25
88 25c. on 6d. blue . . . . . . £190 4·75
89 38c. on 9d. purple . . . . . 19·00 55·00
90 50c. on 1s. green . . . . . 85·00 2·50
91 2r.50 on 5s. mauve . . . . 12·00 15·00

18 19

1879. Various frames.
101 **18** 1c. violet . . . . 1·75 50
102 2c. red . . . . 30·00 4·75
103 2c. green . . . . 2·25 60
104 **19** 4c. orange . . . . 70·00 2·75
105 4c. red . . . . 2·75 60
106 – 8c. blue . . . . 2·00 90
95 – 13c. grey £120 £160
107 – 15c. brown . . . . 4·00 1·25
108 – 15c. blue . . . . 5·50 90
109 – 16c. brown . . . . 4·00 1·00
96 – 17c. red . . . . 55·00 4·75
110 – 25c. olive . . . . 4·75 1·75
98 – 38c. purple £150 £200
99 – 50c. green . . . . 3·75 2·75
111 – 50c. orange . . . . 28·00 8·00
100 – 2r.50 purple . . . . 32·00 55·00

1883. No. 96 surch **16 CENTS**.
112 16c. on 17c. red . . . . . . £130 50·00

1883. No. 96 surch **SIXTEEN CENTS**.
115 16c. on 17c. red . . . . . . 75·00 1·25

1885. No. 98 surch **2 CENTS** with bar.
116 2c. on 38c. purple . . . . . 95·00 35·00

1887. No. 95 surch **2 CENTS** without bar.
117 2c. on 13c. grey . . . . . . 45·00 80·00

1891. Surch in words with or without bar.
123 **18** 1c. on 2c. violet . . . . . 1·25 50
124 – 1c. on 16c. brown (No. 109) . . . . 1·25 2·75
118 **19** 2c. on 4c. red . . . . . . 1·50 60
119 – 2c. on 17c. red (No. 96) . . 95·00 £100
120 **9** 2c. on 38c. on 9d. purple (No. 89) . . . . 2·50 3·50
121 – 2c. on 38c. purple (No. 98) 3·50 4·75

36 37

1895.
127 **36** 1c. purple and blue . . . . 75 1·50
128 2c. purple and orange . . . 2·75 50
129 3c. purple 70 50
130 4c. purple and green . . . 3·75 50
131 6c. green and red . . . . 4·50 4·00
132 18c. green and blue . . . . 9·00 3·50

1898. Diamond Jubilee.
133 **37** 36c. orange and blue . . . 11·00 17·00

1900. Surch in figures and words.
137 – 4c. on 16c. brown (No. 109) . . . . 2·75 12·00
134 **36** 6c. on 18c. (No. 132) . . . 1·00 1·00
156 12c. on 18c. (No. 132) . . 2·00 5·00
163 **37** 12c. on 36c. (No. 133) . . 1·25 1·25
135 15c. on 36c. (No. 133) . . 1·40 1·75

40 Admiral Mahe de Labourdonnais, Governor of Mauritius 1735–46

42

1899. Birth Bicentenary of Labourdonnais.
136 **40** 15c. blue . . . . 11·00 3·25

1900.
138 **36** 1c. grey and black 50 10
139 2c. purple 75 20
140 3c. green & red on yellow 3·75 1·25
141 4c. purple & red on yellow . . . . 1·50 40
142 4c. green and violet . . . 75 2·00
167a 4c. black and red on blue 2·75 10
144 5c. purple on buff . . . . 6·50 50·00
145 5c. purple & black on buff . . . . 2·50 2·50
168a 6c. purple and red on red 3·50 10
147 8c. green & black on buff 2·00 7·00
148 12c. black and red . . . . 1·75 2·25
149 15c. green and orange . . 12·00 6·00
171 15c. black & blue on blue 4·00 35
151a 25c. green & red on green 3·25 13·00
174 50c. green on yellow . . . 1·75 2·50
175 **42** 1r. grey and red . . . . . 20·00 45·00
154 2r.50 green & blk on blue 18·00 80·00
155 5r. purple and red on red 60·00 80·00

1902. Optd **Postage & Revenue**.
157 **36** 4c. purple and red on yellow . . . . 1·25 20
158 6c. green and red . . . . 1·25 2·75
159 15c. green and orange . . 2·25 75
160 – 25c. olive (No. 110) . . . 2·75 2·75
161 – 50c. green (No. 99) . . . 4·00 3·00
162 – 2r.50 purple (No. 100) . . 85·00 £120

46 47

1910.
205 **46** 1c. black . . . . 1·00 1·00
206 2c. brown . . . . 1·00 10
207 2c. purple on yellow . . . 1·00 20
183 3c. green . . . . 3·00 10
184 4c. green and red . . . . 3·50 10
210 4c. green . . . . 1·00 10
211 4c. brown . . . . 2·75 1·50
186 6c. red . . . . 2·25 20
213 6c. mauve . . . . 1·25 10
187 8c. orange . . . . 3·00 1·25
215 10c. grey . . . . 2·00 3·25
216 10c. red . . . . 4·00 1·50
217 12c. red . . . . 1·50 40
218 12c. grey . . . . 1·75 3·50
219b 15c. blue 75 25
220 20c. blue . . . . 2·00 80
221 20c. purple . . . . 8·50 10·00

1910.
185 **47** 5c. grey and red . . . . . 2·75 3·00
188 12c. grey . . . . 2·00 2·75
190 25c. black & red on yellow 2·00 12·00
191 50c. purple and black . . . 2·00 18·00
192 1r. black on green . . . . 6·50 12·00
193 2r.50 black and red on blue 13·00 70·00
194 5r. green and red on yellow 26·00 95·00
195 10r. green and red on green 90·00 £180

48 51

1913.
223 **48** 1c. black . . . . 80 1·25
224 2c. brown 70 10
225 3c. green 70 40
226 4c. green and red 60 30
226c 4c. green . . . . 6·00 45
227 5c. grey and red 90 10
228 6c. brown . . . . 1·75 60
229 8c. orange . . . . 75 10·00
230 10c. red . . . . 1·25 20
232b 12c. grey . . . . 4·75 20
232 12c. red . . . . 30 3·50
233 15c. blue . . . . 1·00 20
234 20c. purple 70 40
235 20c. blue . . . . 9·50 90
236 25c. black & red on yellow 50 15
237 50c. purple and black . . 7·50 3·50
238 1r. black on green . . . . 3·50 50
239 2r.50 black & red on blue 20·00 6·50
240 5r. green and red on yellow . . . . 28·00 70·00
204d 10r. green & red on green 26·00 £100

1924. As T **42** but Arms similar to T **46**.
222 50r. purple and green £700 £1300

1925. Surch with figures, words and bar.
242 **46** 3c. on 4c. green . . . . . 3·00 3·75
243 10c. on 12c. red 30 30
244 15c. on 20c. blue 55 20

1935. Silver Jubilee. As T **14a** of Kenya, Uganda and Tanganyika.
245 5c. blue and grey 50 10
246 12c. green and blue . . . . . 4·50 10
247 20c. brown and blue . . . . 5·50 20
248 1r. grey and purple . . . . . 29·00 42·00

1937. Coronation. As T **14b** of Kenya, Uganda and Tanganyika.
249 5c. violet 40 10
250 12c. red . . . . 40 1·75
251 20c. blue 40 10

1938.
252 **51** 2c. grey 30 10
253 3c. purple and red . . . . 2·00 2·00
254b 4c. green . . . . 2·00 2·00
255a 5c. violet . . . . 3·25 20
256b 10c. red . . . . 2·50 20
257 12c. orange . . . . 1·00 20
258 20c. blue . . . . 1·00 10
259b 25c. purple . . . . 6·00 10
260b 1r. brown . . . . 19·00 1·25
261a 2r.50 violet . . . . 29·00 13·00
262a 5r. olive . . . . 27·00 23·00
263a 10r. purple . . . . 12·00 24·00

1946. Victory. As T **4a** of Pitcairn Islands.
264 5c. violet 10 30
265 20c. blue 10 10

52 1d. "Post Office" Mauritius and King George VI

1948. Cent of First British Colonial Stamp.
266 **52** 5c. orange and mauve . . 10 30
267 12c. orange and green . . 15 10
268 – 20c. blue 15 10
269 – 1r. blue and brown 15 30
DESIGN: 20c., 1r. As Type **52**, but showing 2d. "Post Office" Mauritius.

1948. Silver Wedding. As T **4b/c** of Pitcairn Islands.
270 5c. violet 10 10
271 10r. mauve . . . . 10·00 23·00

1949. U.P.U. As T **4d/g** of Pitcairn Islands.
272 12c. red . . . . 50 1·00
273 20c. blue . . . . 2·00 2·00
274 35c. purple 50 85
275 1r. brown 50 20

55 Aloe Plant

60 Legend of Paul and Virginie

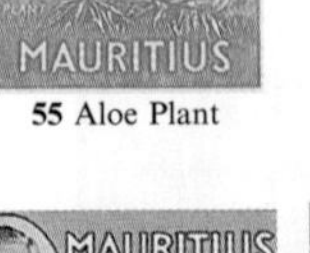
67 Arms of Mauritius

69 Historical Museum, Mahebourg

1950.
276 – 1c. purple 10 50
277 – 2c. red 15 10
278 **55** 3c. green . . . . 60 2·75
279 – 4c. green . . . . 20 1·50
280 – 5c. blue 15 10
281 – 10c. red 30 75
282 – 12c. green . . . . 1·50 2·25
283 **60** 20c. blue . . . . 1·00 15
284 – 25c. red . . . . 1·75 40
285 – 35c. violet 30 10
286 – 50c. green . . . . 2·75 50
287 – 1r. brown . . . . 4·50 10
288 – 2r.50 orange . . . . 17·00 8·50
289 – 5r. brown . . . . 14·00 15·00
290 **67** 10r. blue . . . . 14·00 21·00
DESIGNS—HORIZ: 1c. Labourdonnais sugar factory; 2c. Grand Port; 5c. Rempart Mountain; 10c. Transporting cane; 12c. Mauritius dodo and map; 35c. Government House, Reduit; 1r. Timor deer; 2r.50, Port Louis; 5r. Beach scene. VERT: 4c. Tamarind Falls; 25c. Labourdonnais statue; 50c. Pieter Both Mountain.

1953. Coronation. As T **4h** of Pitcairn Islands.
291 10c. black and green . . . . 1·25 15

1953. As 1950 but portrait of Queen Elizabeth II. Designs as for corresponding values except where stated.
293 – 2c. red 10 10
294 – 3c. green 30 40
295 – 4c. purple (as 1c.) . . . . 10 1·00
296 – 5c. blue 10 10
314 – 10c. green (as 4c.) 15 10
298 **69** 15c. red 10 10
299 – 20c. red (as 25c.) 15 20
300 – 25c. blue (as 20c.) . . . . 1·50 10
301 – 35c. violet 20 10
302 – 50c. green 55 85
315 – 60c. green (as 12c.) . . . 1·75 10
303 – 1r. sepia 30 10
316 – 2r.50 orange . . . . 6·50 8·50
305 – 5r. brown . . . . 14·00 10·00
306 – 10r. blue . . . . 13·00 1·75

70 Queen Elizabeth II and King George III (after Lawrence)

1961. 150th Anniv of British Post Office in Mauritius.
307 **70** 10c. black and red 10 10
308 20c. ultramarine and blue 30 35
309 35c. black and yellow . . . 40 35
310 1r. purple and green . . . 60 30

1963. Freedom from Hunger. As T **20a** of Pitcairn Islands.
311 60c. violet 40 10

1963. Cent of Red Cross. As T **20b** of Pitcairn Islands.
312 10c. red and black 15 10
313 60c. red and blue 60 20

71 Bourbon White-eye

1965. Birds. Multicoloured.

317 2c. Type **71** (yellow background) 40 15
318 3c. Rodriguez fody ("Rodrigues Fody") (brown background) . . . 1·00 15
319 4c. Mauritius olive white-eye ("Olive White-Eye") . . . 30 15
340 5c. Mascarene paradise flycatcher ("Paradise Flycatcher") 70 15
321 10c. Mauritius fody 30 10
322 15c. Mauritius parakeet ("Parrakeet") (grey background) . . . . 2·00 40
323 20c. Mauritius greybird ("Cuckoo-Shrike") (yellow background) . . . . 2·00 10
324 25c. Mauritius kestrel ("Kestrel") . . . . 2·00 30
341 35c. Pink pigeon 30 15
326 50c. Reunion bulbul ("Mascarene Bul-Bul") . . 50 40
327 60c. Mauritius blue pigeon (extinct) ("Dutch Pigeon") (yellow background) . . . 60 10
328 1r. Mauritius dodo (extinct) (olive background) . . . . 5·50 10
329 2r.50 Rodriguez solitaire (extinct) ("Rodrigues Solitaire") . . . . 5·00 6·00
330 5r. Mauritius red rail (extinct) ("Red Rail") . . . . . . 14·00 12·00
331 10r. Broad-billed parrot (extinct) . . . . 28·00 23·00

For some values with background colours changed see Nos. 370/5.

1965. Centenary of I.T.U. As T **24a** of Pitcairn Islands.

332 10c. orange and green . . . 20 10
333 60c. yellow and violet 70 20

1965. I.C.Y. As T **24b** of Pitcairn Islands.

334 10c. purple and turquoise . . 15 10
335 60c. green and violet 30 20

1966. Churchill Commemoration. As T **24c** of Pitcairn Islands.

336 2c. blue . . . . 10 2·75
337 10c. green 25 10
338 60c. brown . . . . 1·10 20
339 1r. violet . . . . 1·25 20

1966. 20th Anniv of U.N.E.S.C.O. As T **25b/d** of Pitcairn Islands.

342 5c. multicoloured 25 30
343 10c. yellow, violet and green 30 10
344 60c. black, purple and orange 1·40 15

86 Red-tailed Tropic Bird

1967. Self-Government. Multicoloured.

345 2c. Type **86** . . . . 20 1·75
346 10c. Rodriguez brush warbler 60 10
347 60c. Rose-ringed parakeet (extinct) ("Rodrigues Parakeet") 70 10
348 1r. Grey-rumped swiftlet ("Mauritius Swiftlet") . . . 70 10

1967. Self-Government. Nos. 317/31 optd **SELF GOVERNMENT 1967**.

349 **71** 2c. multicoloured 10 50
350 – 3c. multicoloured 10 50
351 – 4c. multicoloured 10 50
352 – 5c. multicoloured 10 10
353 – 10c. multicoloured 10 10
354 – 15c. multicoloured 10 30
355 – 20c. multicoloured 15 10
356 – 25c. multicoloured 15 10
357 – 35c. multicoloured 20 10
358 – 50c. multicoloured 30 15
359 – 60c. multicoloured 30 10
360 – 1r. multicoloured . . . . . 1·00 10
361 – 2r.50 multicoloured . . . . 1·00 2·25
362 – 5r. multicoloured . . . . . 6·00 3·25
363 – 10r. multicoloured . . . . 8·00 14·00

91 Flag of Mauritius

1968. Independence. Multicoloured.

364 2c. Type **91** . . . . 10 1·50
365 3c. Arms and Mauritius dodo emblem . . . . 15 1·50
366 15c. Type **91** 20 10
367 20c. As 3c. 50 10
368 60c. Type **91** 60 10
369 1r. As 3c. 95 10

1968. As Nos. 317/8, 322/3 and 327/8 but background colours changed as below.

370 **71** 2c. olive . . . . 20 2·50
371 – 3c. blue . . . . 1·75 5·00
372 – 15c. brown 55 20
373 – 20c. buff . . . . 3·50 3·50
374 – 60c. red . . . . 1·50 15
375 – 1r. purple . . . . 3·00 1·50

93 Dominique rescues Paul and Virginie

1968. Bicentenary of Bernardin de St. Pierre's Visit to Mauritius. Multicoloured.

376 2c. Type **93** . . . . 10 1·25
377 15c. Paul and Virginie crossing the river (vert) . . 35 10
378 50c. Visit of Labourdonnais to Madame de la Tour . . 50 10
379 60c. Meeting of Paul and Virginie in Confidence (vert) 50 10
380 1r. Departure of Virginie for Europe 50 20
381 2r.50 Bernardin de St. Pierre (vert) . . . . 1·50 3·75

99 Black-spotted Emperor

1969. Multicoloured (except 10, 15, 25, 60c.).

382 2c. Type **99** . . . . 10 2·25
383 3c. Red reef crab . . . . . 10 3·00
384 4c. Episcopal mitre . . . . 1·75 3·25
385 5c. Black-saddled pufferfish ("Bourse") 30 10
386 10c. Starfish (red, black and flesh) . . . . 1·50 10
387 15c. Sea urchin (brown, black and blue) 30 10
480 20c. Fiddler crab . . . . . 1·25 30
389 25c. Spiny shrimp (red, black and green) . . . . 30 3·00
390 30c. Single harp shells and double harp shell . . . . 1·50 1·75
483 35c. Common paper nautilus . . . . 1·75 15
484 40c. Spanish dancer . . . . 1·00 60
448 50c. Orange spider conch and violet spider conch 45 10
449b 60c. Blue marlin (black, pink and blue) 65 10
487 75c. "Conus clytospira" . . 1·25 1·50
396 1r. Dolphin (fish) 60 10
452 2r.50 Spiny lobster . . . . 2·00 4·00
453 5r. Ruby snapper ("Sacre chien rouge") . . . . . 3·00 2·00
399w 10r. Yellow-edged lyretail ("Croissant queue jaune") 2·50 3·00

117 Gandhi as Law Student

1969. Birth Cent of Mahatma Gandhi. Mult.

400 2c. Type **117** 10 20
401 15c. Gandhi as stretcher-bearer during Zulu Revolt 20 10
402 50c. Gandhi as Satyagrahi in South Africa 20 50
403 60c. Gandhi at No. 10 Downing Street, London 20 10
404 1r. Gandhi in Mauritius, 1901 . . . . 20 10
405 2r.50 Gandhi, the "Apostle of Truth and Non-Violence" 45 2·00
MS406 153 × 153 mm. Nos. 400/5 2·00 7·50

124 Frangourinier Cane-crusher (18th cent)

1969. 150th Anniv of Telfair's Improvements to the Sugar Industry. Multicoloured.

407 2c. Three-roller Vertical Mill 10 20
408 15c. Type **124** 10 10
409 60c. Beau Rivage Factory, 1867 . . . . 10 10
410 1r. Mon Desert-Alma Factory, 1969 . . . . . . 10 10
411 2r.50 Dr. Charles Telfair (vert) . . . . 25 1·25
MS412 159 × 88 mm. Nos. 407/11 1·25 2·25

1970. Expo '70. Nos. 394 and 396 optd **EXPO '70' OSAKA**.

413 60c. black, red and blue . . . 10 10
414 1r. multicoloured 10 10

129 Morne Plage, Mountain and Boeing 707

1970. Inauguration of Lufthansa Flight, Mauritius–Frankfurt. Multicoloured.

415 25c. Type **129** 10 10
416 50c. Boeing 707 and map (vert) 10 10

131 Lenin as a Student

1970. Birth Centenary of Lenin.

417 **131** 15c. green and silver . . . 10 10
418 – 75c. brown 20 20

DESIGN: 75c. Lenin as founder of U.S.S.R.

133 2d. "Post Office" Mauritius and original Post Office

1970. Port Louis, Old and New. Multicoloured.

419 5c. Type **133** 10 10
420 15c. G.P.O. Building (built 1870) 10 10
421 50c. Mail coach (c. 1870) . . 40 10
422 75c. Port Louis Harbour (1970) 55 10
423 2r.50 Arrival of Pierre A. de Suffren (1783) 70 70
MS424 165 × 95 mm. Nos. 419/23 2·75 7·00

138 U.N. Emblem and Symbols

1970. 25th Anniv of U.N.

425 **138** 10c. multicoloured 10 10
426 60c. multicoloured 40 10

139 Rainbow over Waterfall

1971. Tourism. Multicoloured.

427 10c. Type **139** 25 10
428 15c. Trois Mamelles Mountains 25 10
429 60c. Beach scene 35 10
430 2r.50 Marine life . . . . . . 50 1·50

Nos. 427/30 have inscriptions on the reverse.

140 "Crossroads" of Indian Ocean

1971. 25th Anniv of Plaisance Airport. Multicoloured.

431 15c. Type **140** 20 10
432 60c. Boeing 707 and Terminal buildings 40 10
433 1r. Air hostesses on gangway 45 10
434 2r.50 Farman F.190, "Roland Garros" airplane, Choisy Airfield, 1937 . . . . . . 1·75 4·00

141 Princess Margaret Orthopaedic Centre

1971. 3rd Commonwealth Medical Conference. Multicoloured.

435 10c. Type **141** 10 10
436 75c. Operating theatre in National Hospital 20 20

142 Queen Elizabeth II and Prince Philip

1972. Royal Visit. Multicoloured.

455 15c. Type **142** 15 10
456 2r.50 Queen Elizabeth II (vert) . . . . 2·00 2·00

143 Theatre Facade

1972. 150th Anniv of Port Louis Theatre. Multicoloured.

457 10c. Type **143** 10 10
458 1r. Theatre auditorium . . . 40 20

144 Pirate Dhow

1972. Pirates and Privateers. Multicoloured.

459 15c. Type **144** 65 15
460 60c. Treasure chest (vert) . . 1·00 20
461 1r. Lemene and "L'Hirondelle" (vert) . . . 1·25 20
462 2r.50 Robert Surcouf . . . . 4·50 8·00

145 Mauritius University

1973. 5th Anniv of Independence. Multicoloured.

463 15c. Type **145** 10 10
464 60c. Tea development 15 15
465 1r. Bank of Mauritius . . . 15 15

146 Map and Hands

1973. O.C.A.M. Conference. Multicoloured.

466 10c. O.C.A.M. emblem (horiz) 10 10
467 2r.50 Type **146** 40 45

O.C.A.M. = Organisation Commune Africaine Malgache et Mauricienne.

147 W.H.O. Emblem

1973. 25th Anniv of W.H.O.
468 **147** 1r. multicoloured 10 10

148 Meteorological Station, Vacoas

1973. Centenary of I.M.O./W.M.O.
469 **148** 75c. multicoloured 30 70

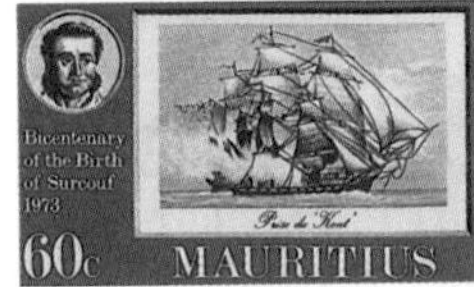

149 Capture of the "Kent" 1800

1973. Birth Bicentenary of Robert Surcouf (privateer).
470 **149** 60c. multicoloured 50 85

150 P. Commerson

1974. Death Bicentenary (1973) of Philibert Commerson (naturalist).
471 **150** 2r.50 multicoloured . . . 30 40

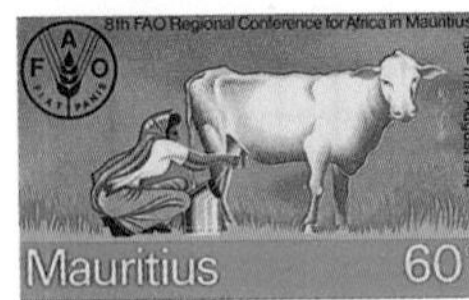

151 Cow being Milked

1974. 8th F.A.O. Regional Conf for Africa, Mauritius.
472 **151** 60c. multicoloured 20 20

152 Mail Train

1974. Centenary of U.P.U. Multicoloured.
473 15c. Type **152** 40 15
474 1r. New G.P.O., Port Louis 40 20

153 "Cottage Life" (F. Leroy)

1975. Aspects of Mauritian Life. Paintings. Mult.
493 15c. Type **153** 10 10
494 60c. "Milk Seller" (A. Richard) (vert) 25 10
495 1r. "Entrance of Port Louis Market" (Thuillier) 25 10
496 2r.50 "Washerwoman" (Max Boullee) (vert) 80 80

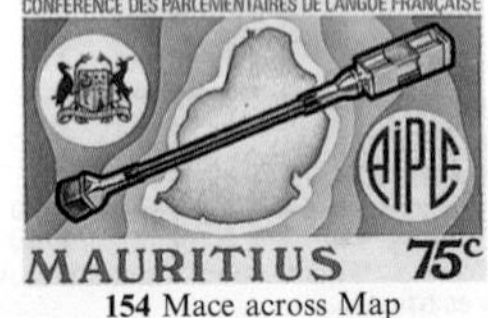

154 Mace across Map

1975. French-speaking Parliamentary Assemblies Conference, Port Louis.
497 **154** 75c. multicoloured . . . . 30 1·25

155 Woman with Lamp ("The Light of the World")

1976. International Women's Year.
498 **155** 2r.50 multicoloured . . . 35 2·00

156 Parched Landscape

1976. Drought in Africa. Multicoloured.
499 50c. Type **156** 15 30
500 60c. Map of Africa and carcass (vert) 15 30

157 "Pierre Loti", 1953–70

1976. Mail Carriers to Mauritius. Multicoloured.
501 10c. Type **157** 60 10
502 15c. "Secunder", 1907 . . . 85 10
503 50c. "Hindoostan", 1842 . . 1·40 15
504 60c. "St. Geran", 1740 . . . 1·50 15
505 2r.50 "Maen", 1638 . . . . 3·50 7·00
MS506 115 × 138 mm. Nos. 501/5 7·50 10·00

158 "The Flame of Hindi carried across the Seas"

1976. 2nd World Hindi Convention. Multicoloured.
507 10c. Type **158** 10 10
508 75c. Type **158** 10 30
509 1r.20 Hindi script . . . . . 20 1·25

159 Conference Logo and Map of Mauritius

160 King Priest and Breastplate

1976. 22nd Commonwealth Parliamentary Association Conference. Multicoloured.
510 1r. Type **159** 25 10
511 2r.50 Conference logo . . . 50 1·75

1976. Moenjodaro Excavations, Pakistan. Mult.
512 60c. Type **160** 30 10
513 1r. House with well and goblet 50 10
514 2r.50 Terracotta figurine and necklace . . . . 1·25 80

161 Sega Scene

1977. 2nd World Black and African Festival of Arts and Culture, Nigeria.
515 **161** 1r. multicoloured 30 15

162 The Queen with Sceptre and Rod

1977. Silver Jubilee. Multicoloured.
516 50c. The Queen at Mauritius Legislative Assembly, 1972 15 10
517 75c. Type **162** 20 10
518 5r. Presentation of Sceptre and Rod 55 75

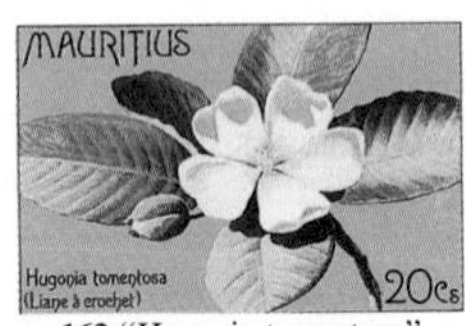

163 "Hugonia tomentosa"

1977. Indigenous Flowers. Multicoloured.
519 20c. Type **163** 20 10
520 1r. "Ochna mauritiana" (vert) 40 10
521 1r.50 "Dombeya acutangula" 50 20
522 5r. "Trochetia blackburniana" (vert) . . . 1·10 1·50
MS523 130 × 130 mm. Nos. 519/22 3·00 6·50

164 De Havilland Twin Otter 200/300

1977. Inaugural International Flight of Air Mauritius. Multicoloured.
524 25c. Type **164** 60 10
525 50c. De Havilland Twin Otter 200/300 and Air Mauritius emblem 80 10
526 75c. Piper Navajo and Boeing 747-100 . . . . 95 20
527 5r. Boeing 707 . . . . 3·00 3·75
MS528 110 × 152 mm. Nos. 524/7 7·50 7·50

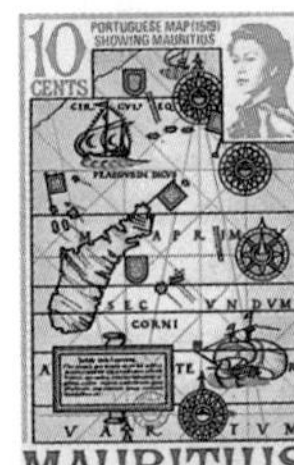

165 Portuguese Map of Mauritius, 1519

166 Mauritius Dodo

1978.
529B **165** 10c. multicoloured . . . 75 1·00
530A – 15c. multicoloured . . . 1·50 2·50
531A – 20c. multicoloured . . . 80 2·50
532A – 25c. multicoloured . . . 60 1·75
533B – 35c. multicoloured . . . 1·00 20
534A – 50c. multicoloured . . . 50 75
535A – 60c. multicoloured . . . 60 2·50
536A – 70c. multicoloured . . . 2·75 3·75
537B – 75c. multicoloured . . . 1·75 3·50
538A – 90c. multicoloured . . . 4·00 3·75
539A – 1r. multicoloured . . . 60 50
540A – 1r.20 multicoloured . . 1·75 3·75
541B – 1r.25 multicoloured . . 1·50 20
542A – 1r.50 multicoloured . . 1·00 2·50
543A – 2r. multicoloured . . . 60 70
544A – 3r. multicoloured . . . 60 50
545A – 5r. multicoloured . . . 60 1·50
546A – 10r. multicoloured . . . 1·00 1·00
547A – 15r. multicoloured . . . 1·50 3·00
548A – 25r. green, black & brn 2·00 3·25

DESIGNS—HORIZ: 15c. Dutch Occupation, 1638–1710; 20c. Map by Van Keulen, c. 1700; 50c. Construction of Port Louis, c. 1736; 70c. Map by Bellin, 1763; 90c. Battle of Grand Port, 1810; 1r. Landing of the British, 1810; 1r.20, Government House, c. 1840; 1r.50, Indian immigration, 1835; 2r. Race Course, c. 1870; 3r. Place d'Armes, c. 1880; 5r. Royal Visit postcard, 1901; 10r. Royal College, 1914; 25r. First Mauritian Governor-General and Prime Minister. VERT: 25c. Settlement on Rodriguez, 1691; 35c. French settlers Charter, 1715; 60c. Pierre Poivre, c. 1767; 75c. First coinage, 1794; 1r.25 Lady Gomm's Ball, 1847; 15r. Unfurling of Mauritian flag.

1978. 25th Anniv of Coronation.
549 – 3r. grey, black and blue 25 45
550 – 3r. multicoloured 25 45
551 **166** 3r. grey, black and blue 25 45

DESIGNS: No. 549, Antelope of Bohun; No. 550, Queen Elizabeth II.

167 Problem of Infection, World War I

1978. 50th Anniv of Discovery of Penicillin.
552 **167** 20c. multicoloured 60 10
553 – 1r. multicoloured . . . . 1·25 10
554 – 1r.50 black, brown & grn 2·00 1·40
555 – 5r. multicoloured . . . . 2·75 5·50
MS556 150 × 90 mm. Nos. 552/5 8·00 8·50

DESIGNS: 1r. First mould growth, 1928; 1r.50, "Penicillium chrysogenum" ("notatum"); 5r. Sir Alexander Fleming.

168 "Papilio manlius" (butterfly)

1978. Endangered Species. Multicoloured.
557 20c. Type **168** . . . . 1·75 30
558 1r. Geckos 90 10
559 1r.50 Greater Mascarene flying fox . . . . 1·25 1·00
560 5r. Mauritius kestrel . . . . 13·00 9·00
MS561 154 × 148 mm. Nos. 557/60 38·00 17·00

169 Ornate Table

171 Father Laval and Crucifix

170 Whitcomb Diesel Locomotive 65H.P., 1949

1978. Bicentenary of Reconstruction of Chateau Le Reduit. Multicoloured.
562 15c. Type **169** 10 10
563 75c. Chateau Le Reduit . . . 10 10
564 3r. Le Reduit gardens 40 45

1979. Railway Locomotives. Multicoloured.
565 20c. Type **170** 20 10
566 1r. "Sir William", 1922 . . . 40 10
567 1r.50 Kitson type 1930 . . 60 45
568 2r. Garratt type, 1927 . . . . 75 85
MS569 128 × 128 mm. Nos. 565/8 2·00 4·00

1979. Beatification of Father Laval (missionary). Multicoloured.
570 20c. Type **171** 10 10
571 1r.50 Father Laval 10 10
572 5r. Father Laval's tomb (horiz) 35 50
MS573 150 × 96 mm. Nos. 570/2 2·25 2·75

172 Astronaut descending from Lunar Module

173 Great Britain 1855 4d. Stamp and Sir Rowland Hill

1979. 10th Anniv of Moon Landing. Multicoloured. Self-adhesive.
574 20c. Type **172** 30 40
575 3r. Astronaut performing experiment on Moon . . . 80 1·10
576 5r. Astronaut on Moon . . . 2·75 5·00

1979. Death Cent of Sir Rowland Hill. Mult.
577 25c. Type **173** 10 10
578 2r. 1954 60c. definitive . . . 55 50
579 5r. 1847 1d. "POST OFFICE" . . . . 1·00 1·50
MS580 120 × 89 mm. 3r. 1847 2d. "POST OFFICE" . . . . . . 1·10 1·75

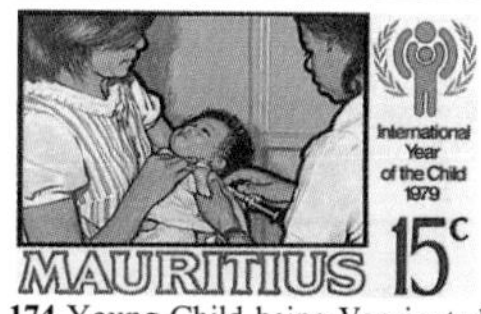

174 Young Child being Vaccinated

1979. International Year of the Child.
581 **174** 15c. multicoloured 10 10
582 – 25c. multicoloured 10 10
583 – 1r. black, blue and light blue 15 10
584 – 1r.50 multicoloured 30 30
585 – 3r. multicoloured 50 90
DESIGNS—HORIZ: 25c. Children playing; 1r.50, Girls in chemistry laboratory; 3r. Boy operating lathe. VERT: 1r. I.Y.C. emblem.

175 The Lienard Obelisk

1980. Pamplemousses Botanical Gardens. Multicoloured.
586 20c. Type **175** 10 10
587 25c. Poivre Avenue 10 10
588 1r. Varieties of Vacoas 20 10
589 2r. Giant water lilies 45 55
590 5r. Mon Plaisir (mansion) 80 2·75
MS591 152 × 105 mm. Nos. 586/90 3·25 4·00

176 "Emirne" (French steam packet)

1980. "London 1980" International Stamp Exhibition. Mail-carrying Ships. Multicoloured.
592 25c. Type **176** 25 10
593 1r. "Boissevain" (cargo liner) 40 10
594 2r. "La Boudeuse" (Bougainville's ship) 60 60
595 5r. "Sea Breeze" (English clipper) 70 2·25

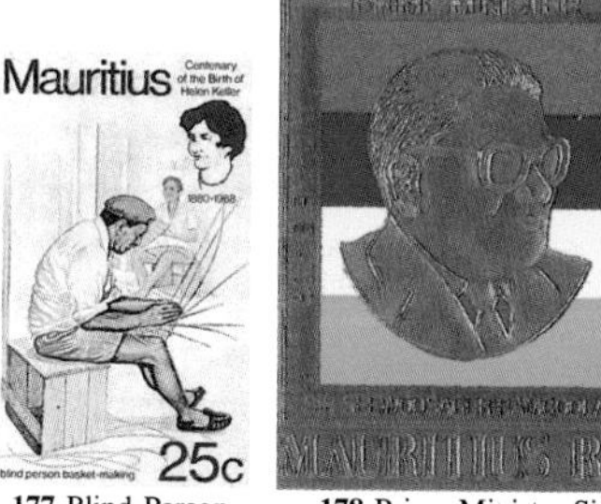

177 Blind Person Basket-making **178** Prime Minister Sir Seewoosagur Ramgoolam

1980. Birth Centenary of Helen Keller (campaigner for the handicapped). Multicoloured.
596 25c. Type **177** 20 10
597 1r. Deaf child under instruction 45 10
598 2r.50 Helen reading braille 70 35
599 5r. Helen at graduation, 1904 1·25 1·25

1980. 80th Birthday and 40th Year in Parliament of Prime Minister Sir Seewoosagur Ramgoolam.
600 **178** 15r. multicoloured 1·00 1·40

179 Headquarters, Mauritius Institute

1980. Centenary of Mauritius Institute. Mult.
601 25c. Type **179** 15 10
602 2r. Rare copy of Veda 40 20
603 2r. Glory of India cone shell 55 25
604 5r. "Le Torrent" (painting by Harpignies) 65 1·25

180 "Hibiscus liliiflorus" **181** Beau-Bassin/Rose Hill

1981. Flowers. Multicoloured.
605 25c. Type **180** 20 10
606 2r. "Erythrospermum monticolum" 60 65
607 2r.50 "Chasalia boryana" 65 1·25
608 5r. "Hibiscus columnaris" 1·00 3·25

1981. Coats of Arms of Mauritius Towns. Multicoloured.
609 25c. Type **181** 10 10
610 1r.50 Curepipe 25 20
611 2r. Quatre-Bornes 30 25
612 2r.50 Vacoas/Phoenix 35 30
613 5r. Port Louis 55 75
MS614 130 × 130 mm. Nos. 609/13 1·75 5·00

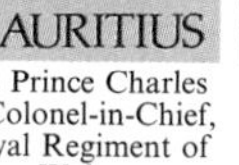

182 Prince Charles as Colonel-in-Chief, Royal Regiment of Wales **184** Drummer and Piper

183 Emmanuel Anquetil and Guy Rozemont

1981. Royal Wedding. Multicoloured
615 25c. Wedding bouquet from Mauritius 10 10
616 2r.50 Type **182** 40 15
617 10r. Prince Charles and Lady Diana Spencer 80 90

1981. Famous Politicians and Physician.
618 **183** 20c. black and red 10 10
619 – 25c. black and yellow 10 10
620 – 1r.25 black and green 30 30
621 – 1r.50 black and red 35 15
622 – 2r. black and blue 45 20
623 – 2r.50 black and brown 50 60
624 – 5r. black and blue 1·25 1·50
DESIGNS: 25c. Remy Ollier and Sookdeo Bissoondoyal; 1r.25, Maurice Cure and Barthelemy Ohsan; 1r.50, Sir Guy Forget and Renganaden Seeneevassen; 2r. Sir Abdul Razak Mohamed and Jules Koenig; 2r.50, Abdoollatiff Mahomed Osman and Dazzi Rama (Pandit Sahadeo); 5r. Sir Thomas Lewis (physician) and electrocardiogram.

1981. Religion and Culture. Multicoloured.
625 20c. Type **184** 10 10
626 2r. Swami Sivananda (vert) 1·00 1·00
627 5r. Chinese Pagoda 1·25 3·25
The 20c. value commemorates the World Tamil Culture Conference (1980).

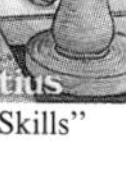

185 "Skills" **186** Ka'aba (sacred shrine, Great Mosque of Mecca)

1981. 25th Anniv of Duke of Edinburgh Award Scheme. Multicoloured.
628 25c. Type **185** 10 10
629 1r.25 "Service" 10 10
630 5r. "Expeditions" 20 30
631 10r. Duke of Edinburgh 40 70

1981. Moslem Year 1400 A.H. Commemoration. Multicoloured.
632 25c. Type **186** 30 10
633 2r. Mecca 80 80
634 5r. Mecca and Ka'aba 1·40 2·75

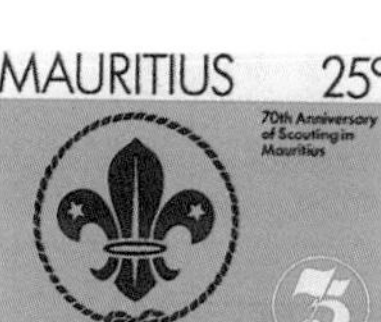

187 Scout Emblem **189** Bride and Groom at Buckingham Palace

188 Charles Darwin

1982. 75th Anniv of Boy Scout Movement and 70th Anniv of Scouting in Mauritius.
635 **187** 25c. lilac and green 10 10
636 – 2r. brown and ochre 40 30
637 – 5r. green and olive 85 1·00
638 – 10r. green and blue 1·25 2·00
DESIGNS: 2r. Lord Baden-Powell and Baden-Powell House; 5r. Grand Howl; 10r. Ascent of Pieter Both.

1982. 150th Anniv of Charles Darwin's Voyage. Multicoloured.
639 25c. Type **188** 20 10
640 2r. Darwin's telescope 40 45
641 2r.50 Darwin's elephant ride 70 55
642 10r. H.M.S. "Beagle" beached for repairs 1·50 2·75

1982. 21st Birthday of Princess of Wales. Mult.
643 25c. Mauritius coat of arms 10 10
644 2r.50 Princess Diana in Chesterfield, November 1981 60 45
645 5r. Type **189** 75 1·25
646 10r. Formal portrait 2·75 3·00

190 Prince and Princess of Wales with Prince William

1982. Birth of Prince William of Wales.
647 **190** 2r.50 multicoloured 1·00 50

191 Bois Fandamane Plant **193** Early Wall-mounted Telephone

192 Arms and Flag of Mauritius

1982. Centenary of Robert Koch's Discovery of Tubercle Bacillus. Multicoloured.
648 25c. Type **191** 10 10
649 1r.25 Central market, Port Louis 35 40
650 2r. Bois Banane plant 50 75
651 5r. Platte de Lezard plant 60 2·25
652 10r. Dr. Robert Koch 90 3·75

1983. Commonwealth Day. Multicoloured.
653 25c. Type **192** 10 10
654 2r.50 Satellite view of Mauritius 20 30
655 5r. Harvesting sugar cane 30 75
656 10r. Port Louis harbour 95 1·50

1983. World Communications Year. Mult.
657 25c. Type **193** 10 10
658 1r.25 Early telegraph apparatus (horiz) 35 20
659 2r. Earth satellite station 45 50
660 10r. First hot-air balloon in Mauritius, 1784 (horiz) 80 2·75

194 Map of Namibia **195** Fish Trap

1983. Namibia Day. Multicoloured.
661 25c. Type **194** 45 10
662 2r.50 Hand breaking chains 1·50 75
663 5r. Family and settlement 2·00 2·25
664 10r. Diamond mining 4·75 3·75

1983. Fishery Resources. Multicoloured.
665 25c. Type **195** 15 10
666 1r. Fishing boat (horiz) 30 15
667 5r. Game fishing 55 2·25
668 10r. Octopus drying (horiz) 80 4·00

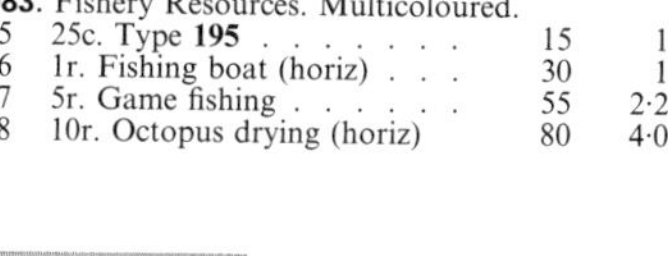

196 Swami Dayananda **197** Adolf von Plevitz

1983. Death Centenary of Swami Dayananda. Multicoloured.
669 25c. Type **196** 10 10
670 35c. Last meeting with father 10 10
671 2r. Receiving religious instruction 50 65
672 5r. Swami demonstrating strength 90 2·50
673 10r. At a religious gathering 1·40 3·75

1983. 125th Anniv of Arrival in Mauritius of Adolf von Plevitz (social reformer). Multicoloured.
674 25c. Type **197** 10 10
675 1r.25 La Laura, Government school 30 30
676 5r. Von Plevitz addressing Commission of Enquiry, 1872 1·00 2·50
677 10r. Von Plevitz with Indian farm workers 1·75 3·75

198 Courtship Chase

1984. The Mauritius Kestrel. Multicoloured.
678 25c. Type **198** 85 30
679 2r. Kestrel in tree (vert) 2·00 1·25
680 2r.50 Young kestrel 2·25 2·25
681 10r. Head (vert) 3·25 8·50

199 Wreck of S.S. "Tayeb" **200** Blue Latan Palm

1984. 250th Anniv of "Lloyd's List" (newspaper). Multicoloured.
682 25c. Type **199** 30 10
683 1r. S.S. "Taher" 95 15
684 5r. East Indiaman "Triton" 3·00 3·25
685 10r. M.S. "Astor" 3·50 6·50

1984. Palm Trees. Multicoloured.
686 25c. Type **200** 10 10
687 50c. "Hyophorbe vaughanii" 20 20
688 2r.50 "Tectiphiala ferox" 1·25 1·50
689 5r. Round Island bottle-palm 2·00 3·25
690 10r. "Hyophorbe amaricaulis" 3·25 6·50

201 Slave Girl

203 The Queen Mother on Clarence House Balcony, 1980

202 75th Anniversary Production of "Faust" and Leoville L'Homme

1984. 150th Anniv of Abolition of Slavery and Introduction of Indian Immigrants.
691 **201** 25c. purple, lilac and brown 15 10
692 – 1r. purple, lilac and brown 70 10
693 – 2r. purple and lilac . . . 1·50 1·00
694 – 10r. purple and lilac . . . 6·50 10·00
DESIGNS—VERT: 1r. Slave market. HORIZ: 2r. Indian immigrant family; 10r. Arrival of Indian immigrants.

1984. Centenary of Alliance Francaise (cultural organization). Multicoloured.
695 25c. Type **202** 20 10
696 1r.25 Prize-giving ceremony and Aunauth Beejadbur . . 70 50
697 5r. First headquarters and Hector Clarenc . . . . . 2·00 3·00
698 10r. Lion Mountain and [illegible] . . . . 2·50 5·50

1985. Life and Times of Queen Elizabeth the Queen Mother. Multicoloured.
699 25c. The Queen Mother in 1926 . . . . 35 10
700 2r. With Princess Margaret at Trooping the Colour . . . 1·10 45
701 5r. Type **203** . . . . 1·25 1·50
702 10r. With Prince Henry at his christening (from photo by Lord Snowdon) . . . . . 1·60 3·50
MS703 91 × 73 mm. 15r. Reopening the Stratford Canal, 1964 . . . 4·75 3·50

204 High Jumping

205 Adult and Fledgling Pink Pigeons

1985. 2nd Indian Ocean Islands Games. Multicoloured.
704 25c. Type **204** 20 10
705 50c. Javelin-throwing 50 30
706 1r.25 Cycling . . . . 3·75 1·75
707 10r. Wind surfing . . . . . 6·50 11·00

1985. Pink Pigeon. Multicoloured.
708 25c. Type **205** . . . . 2·75 50
709 2r. Pink pigeon displaying at nest . . . . 6·00 1·75
710 2r.50 On nest . . . . 6·50 3·50
711 5r. Pair preening . . . . . . 11·00 11·00

206 Caverne Patates, Rodrigues

1985. 10th Anniv of World Tourism Organization. Multicoloured.
712 25c. Type **206** 50 10
713 35c. Coloured soils, Chamarel 50 40
714 5r. Serpent Island . . . . . 4·50 5·00
715 10r. Coin de Mire Island . . 6·50 10·00

207 Old Town Hall, Port Louis

1985. 250th Anniv of Port Louis. Multicoloured.
716 25c. Type **207** 10 10
717 1r. Al-Aqsa Mosque (180th anniv) . . . . 1·00 10
718 2r.50 Vase and trees (250th anniv of settlement of Tamil-speaking Indians) . . 1·25 1·75
719 10r. Port Louis Harbour . . 6·50 11·00

208 Edmond Halley and Diagram

1986. Appearance of Halley's Comet. Mult.
720 25c. Type **208** 40 10
721 1r.25 Halley's Comet (1682) and Newton's Reflector . . 1·10 50
722 3r. Halley's Comet passing Earth . . . . 1·60 2·25
723 10r. "Giotto" spacecraft . . 3·50 7·00

1986. 60th Birthday of Queen Elizabeth II. As T **246a** of Papua New Guinea. Multicoloured.
724 25c. Princess Elizabeth wearing badge of Grenadier Guards, 1942 . . 10 10
725 75c. Investiture of Prince of Wales, 1969 . . . . 10 10
726 2r. With Prime Minister of Mauritius, 1972 . . . . . 20 25
727 3r. In Germany, 1978 . . . . 30 40
728 15r. At Crown Agents Head Office, London, 1983 . . . 1·25 2·00

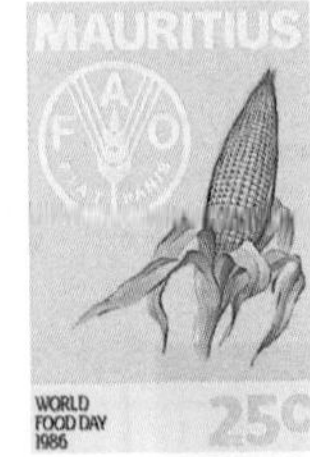

209 Maize (World Food Day)

210 "Cryptopus elatus"

1986. International Events. Multicoloured.
729 25c. Type **209** 10 10
730 1r. African Regional Industrial Property Organization emblem (10th anniv) 30 10
731 1r.25 International Peace Year emblem 65 50
732 10r. Footballer and Mauritius Football Association emblem (World Cup Football Championship, Mexico) . . . . 5·50 10·00

1986. Orchids. Multicoloured.
733 25c. Type **210** 50 10
734 2r. "Jumellea recta" . . . . 1·25 45
735 2r.50 "Angraecum mauritianum" . . . . . . 1·40 60
736 10r. "Bulbophyllum longiflorum" . . . . 2·25 3·50

211 Hesketh Bell Bridge

1987. Mauritius Bridges. Multicoloured.
758 25c. Type **211** 25 10
759 50c. Sir Colville Deverell Bridge 35 20
760 2r.50 Cavendish Bridge . . . 70 75
761 5r. Tamarin Bridge . . . . . 90 2·00
762 10r. Grand River North West Bridge . . . . 1·25 2·50

212 Supreme Court, Port Louis

213 Mauritius Dodo Mascot

1987. Bicentenary of the Mauritius Bar. Mult.
763 25c. Type **212** 10 10
764 1r. District Court, Flacq . . 40 10
765 1r.25 Statue of Justice . . . 50 20
766 10r. Barristers of 1787 and 1987 . . . . 2·00 2·25

1987. International Festival of the Sea. Mult.
767 25c. Type **213** 40 10
768 1r.50 Yacht regatta (horiz) 1·50 1·00
769 3r. Water skiing (horiz) . . . 2·50 3·25
770 5r. "Svanen" (barquentine) 3·00 6·50

214 Toys

1987. Industrialization. Multicoloured.
771 20c. Type **214** 10 10
772 35c. Spinning factory 10 10
773 50c. Rattan furniture 10 10
774 2r.50 Spectacle factory . . . 85 80
775 10r. Stone carving . . . . . 2·50 2·75

215 Maison Ouvriere (Int Year of Shelter for the Homeless)

1987. Art and Architecture.
776 **215** 25c. multicoloured 10 10
777 – 1r. black and grey 25 10
778 – 1r.25 multicoloured . . . 30 30
779 – 2r. multicoloured 55 55
780 – 5r. multicoloured . . . . 1·00 1·25
DESIGNS: 1r. "Paul et Virginie" (lithograph); 1r.25, Chateau de Rosnay; 2r. "Vieille Ferme" (Boulle); 5r. "Trois Mamelles".

216 University of Mauritius

1988. 20th Anniv of Independence. Mult.
781 25c. Type **216** 10 10
782 75c. Anniversary gymnastic display 20 10
783 2r.50 Hurdlers and aerial view of Sir Maurice Rault Stadium 70 55
784 5r. Air Mauritius aircraft at Sir Seewoosagur Ramgoolam International Airport . . . . 1·40 1·60
785 10r. Governor-General Sir Veerasamy Ringadoo and Prime Minister Anerood Jugnauth . . . . 2·25 2·75

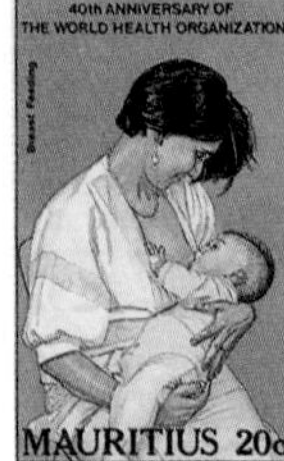

217 Breast Feeding

218 Modern Bank Building

1988. 40th Anniv of W.H.O. Multicoloured.
786 20c. Type **217** 15 10
787 2r. Baby under vaccination umbrella and germ droplets 1·25 70
788 3r. Nutritious food . . . . 1·40 1·25
789 10r. W.H.O. logo . . . . . 2·75 3·75

1988. 150th Anniv of Mauritius Commercial Bank Ltd.
790 **218** 25c. black, green and blue 10 10
791 – 1r. black and red 15 10
792 – 1r.25 multicoloured . . . 30 30
793 – 25r. multicoloured . . . 6·00 7·50
DESIGNS—HORIZ: 1r. Mauritius Commercial Bank, 1897; 25r. Fifteen dollar bank note of 1838. VERT: 1r.25, Bank arms.

219 Olympic Rings and Athlete

1988. Olympic Games, Seoul. Multicoloured.
794 25c. Type **219** 10 10
795 35c. Wrestling 15 15
796 1r.50 Long distance running 75 60
797 10r. Swimming . . . . 2·50 4·00

220 Nature Park

1989. Protection of the Environment. Mult.
798B 15c. Underwater view . . 15 80
799B 20c. As 15c. 15 80
800B 30c. Common greenshank ("Greenshank") . . . . 1·00 1·00
801B 40c. Type **220** 15 35
810A 50c. Round Island (vert) 15 10
801cB 60c. As 50c. 20 10
811A 75c. Bassin Blanc 20 10
812A 1r. Mangrove (vert) . . . 20 10
802A 1r.50 Whimbrel . . . . . 1·00 35
813A 2r. Le Morne 30 20
803A 3r. Marine life 50 20
804B 4r. Fern tree (vert) 50 60
814A 5r. Riviere du Poste estuary 60 50
805A 6r. Ecological scenery (vert) 60 50
806B 10r. "Phelsuma ornata" (gecko) on plant (vert) 85 1·10
806aB 15r. Benares waves . . . . 1·50 2·25
807B 25r. Migratory birds and map (vert) . . . . . . 3·50 3·25

221 La Tour Sumeire, Port Louis

222 Cardinal Jean Margeot

1989. Bicentenary of the French Revolution.
818 **221** 30c. black, green & yellow 10 10
819 – 1r. black, brown and light brown 25 10
820 – 8r. multicoloured . . . . 1·75 2·00
821 – 15r. multicoloured . . . . 2·25 2·75
DESIGNS: 1r. Salle de Spectacle du Jardin; 8r. Portrait of Comte de Malartic; 15r. Bicentenary logo.

1989. Visit of Pope John Paul II. Multicoloured.
822 30c. Type **222** 30 10
823 40c. Pope John Paul II and Prime Minister Jugnauth, Vatican, 1988 . . . . . . 70 25
824 3r. Mere Marie Magdeleine de la Croix and Chapelle des Filles de Marie, Port Louis, 1864 . . . . 1·25 1·25
825 6r. St. Francois d'Assise Church, Pamplemousses, 1756 . . . . 2·00 2·25
826 10r. Pope John Paul II . . . 4·50 5·00

223 Nehru

1989. Birth Centenary of Jawaharlal Nehru (Indian statesman). Multicoloured.
827 40c. Type **223** 85 20
828 1r.50 Nehru with daughter, Indira, and grandsons . . 2·25 70
829 3r. Nehru and Gandhi . . . 3·50 2·50
830 4r. Nehru with Presidents Nasser and Tito . . . . . 3·00 3·75
831 10r. Nehru with children . . 4·75 8·50

224 Cane Cutting

1990. 350th Anniv of Introduction of Sugar Cane to Mauritius. Multicoloured.
832 30c. Type **224** 10 10
833 40c. Sugar factory, 1867 . . . 15 10
834 1r. Mechanical loading of cane 30 10
835 25r. Modern sugar factory . . 10·00 12·00

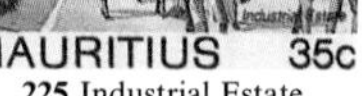

225 Industrial Estate

226 Desjardins (naturalist) (150th death anniv)

1990. 60th Birthday of Prime Minister Sir Anerood Jugnauth. Multicoloured.

836	35c. Type **225**	10	10
837	40c. Sir Anerood Jugnauth at desk	10	10
838	1r.50 Mauritius Stock Exchange symbol	30	30
839	4r. Jugnauth with Governor-General Sir Seewoosagur Ramgoolam	1·50	2·25
840	10r. Jugnauth greeting Pope John Paul II	8·50	10·00

1990. Anniversaries. Multicoloured.

841	30c. Type **226**	30	10
842	35c. Logo on TV screen (25th anniv of Mauritius Broadcasting Corporation) (horiz)	30	10
843	6r. Line Barracks (now Police Headquarters) (250th anniv)	4·50	4·50
844	8r. Town Hall, Curepipe (centenary of municipality) (horiz)	3·50	4·75

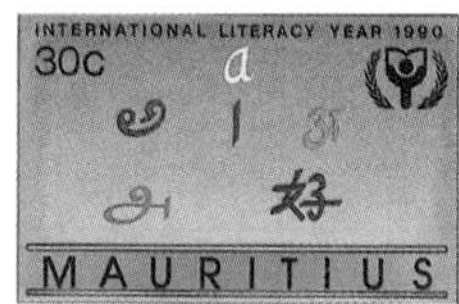

227 Letters from Alphabets

1990. International Literacy Year. Multicoloured.

845	30c. Type **227**	20	10
846	1r. Blind child reading Braille	1·50	15
847	3r. Open book and globe	2·50	2·00
848	10r. Book showing world map with quill pen	7·00	9·50

1991. 65th Birthday of Queen Elizabeth II and 70th Birthday of Prince Philip. As T **58** of Kiribati. Multicoloured.

849	8r. Queen Elizabeth II	1·40	2·50
850	8r. Prince Philip in Grenadier Guards ceremonial uniform	1·40	2·50

228 City Hall, Port Louis (25th anniv of City status)

1991. Anniversaries and Events. Multicoloured.

851	40c. Type **228**	10	10
852	4r. Colonel Draper (race course founder) (150th death anniv) (vert)	1·75	1·75
853	6r. Joseph Barnard (engraver) and "POST PAID" 2d. stamp (175th birth anniv) (vert)	2·00	2·50
854	10r. Supermarine Spitfire "Mauritius II" (50th anniv of Second World War)	4·50	7·00

229 "Euploea euphon"

1991. "Phila Nippon '91" International Stamp Exn, Tokyo. Butterflies. Multicoloured.

855	40c. Type **229**	60	20
856	3r. "Hypolimnas misippus" (female)	1·90	1·00
857	8r. "Papilio manlius"	3·50	4·25
858	10r. "Hypolimnas misippus" (male)	3·50	4·50

230 Green Turtle, Tromelin

1991. Indian Ocean Islands. Multicoloured.

859	40c. Type **230**	50	20
860	1r. Glossy ibis ("Ibis"), Agalega	1·50	40
861	2r. Takamaka flowers, Chagos Archipelago	1·60	1·10
862	15r. Violet spider conch sea shell, St. Brandon	7·00	9·50

231 Pres. Veerasamy Ringadoo and President's Residence

1992. Proclamation of Republic. Multicoloured.

863	40c. Type **231**	10	10
864	4r. Prime Minister Anerood Jugnauth and Government House	90	1·25
865	8r. Children and rainbow	2·00	3·50
866	10r. Presidential flag	3·50	4·00

232 Ticolo (mascot)

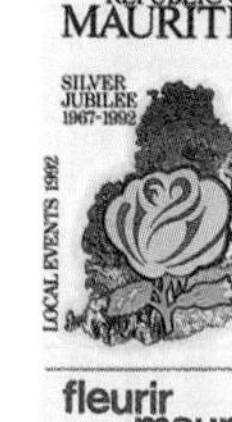

233 Bouquet (25th anniv of Fleurir Maurice)

1992. 8th African Athletics Championships, Port Louis. Multicoloured.

867	40c. Type **232**	10	10
868	4r. Sir Anerood Jugnauth Stadium (horiz)	75	1·10
869	5r. High jumping (horiz)	90	1·25
870	6r. Championships emblem	1·25	1·75

1992. Local Events and Anniversaries. Mult.

871	40c. Type **233**	15	10
872	1r. Swami Krishnanandji Maharaj (25th anniv of arrival)	50	10
873	2r. Boy with dog (humane education) (horiz)	1·40	75
874	3r. Commission Headquarters (10th anniv of Indian Ocean Commission) (horiz)	1·25	1·00
875	15r. Radio telescope antenna, Bras d'Eau (project inauguration) (horiz)	4·50	7·50

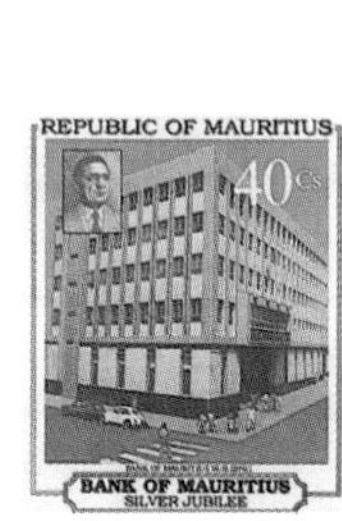

234 Bank of Mauritius Headquarters

235 Housing Development

1992. 25th Anniv of Bank of Mauritius. Mult.

876	40c. Type **234**	10	10
877	4r. Dodo gold coin (horiz)	1·75	1·10
878	8r. First bank note issue (horiz)	2·50	3·25
879	15r. Graph of foreign exchange reserves, 1967–92 (horiz)	4·50	7·00

1993. 25th Anniv of National Day. Multicoloured.

880	30c. Type **235**	10	10
881	40c. Gross domestic product graph on computer screen	10	10
882	3r. National colours on map of Mauritius	40	50
883	4r. Ballot box	45	70
884	15r. Grand Commander's insignia for Order of Star and Key of the Indian Ocean	2·00	4·00

236 Bell 206 B JetRanger Helicopter

1993. 25th Anniv of Air Mauritius Ltd. Mult.

885	40c. Type **236**	70	30
886	3r. Boeing 747SP	1·25	1·10
887	4r. Aerospatiale/Aeritalia ATR 42	1·40	1·40
888	10r. Boeing 767-200ER	3·00	6·00
MS889	150 × 91 mm. Nos. 885/8	7·00	8·00

1993. No. 811 surch **40cs**.

890	40c. on 75c. Bassin Blanc	60	50

238 French Royal Charter, 1715, and Act of Capitulation, 1810

239 "Scotia" (cable ship) and Map of Cable Route

1993. 5th Summit of French-speaking Nations. Multicoloured.

891	1r. Type **238**	60	10
892	5r. Road signs	2·50	2·25
893	6r. Code Napoleon	2·50	2·75
894	7r. Early Mauritius newspapers	2·50	3·00

1993. Centenary of Telecommunications. Mult.

895	40c. Type **239**	50	20
896	3r. Morse key and code	1·00	80
897	4r. Signal Mountain Earth station	1·25	1·25
898	8r. Communications satellite	2·25	3·50

240 Indian Mongoose

1994. Mammals. Multicoloured.

899	40c. Type **240**	30	10
900	2r. Indian black-naped hare	95	40
901	8r. Pair of crab-eating macaques	2·50	3·25
902	10r. Adult and infant common tenrec	2·75	3·50

241 Dr Edouard Brown-Sequard (physiologist) (death cent)

1994. Anniversaries and Events. Multicoloured.

903	40c. Type **241**	15	10
904	4r. Family in silhouette (International Year of the Family)	45	55
905	8r. World Cup and map of U.S.A. (World Cup Football Championship, U.S.A.)	1·25	2·00
906	10r. Control tower, SSR International Airport (50th anniv of Civil Aviation Organization)	1·50	2·25

242 "St. Geran" leaving L'Orient for Isle de France, 1744

1994. 250th Anniv of Wreck of "St. Geran" (sailing packet). Multicoloured.

907	40c. Type **242**	25	10
908	5r. In rough seas off Isle de France	75	80
909	6r. Bell and main mast	85	1·25
910	10r. Artifacts from wreck	1·40	2·75
MS911	119 × 89 mm. 15r. "St. Geran" leaving L'Orient (vert)	3·00	4·25

243 Ring-a-ring-a-roses

1994. Children's Games and Pastimes. Children's paintings. Multicoloured.

912	30c. Type **243**	10	10
913	40c. Skipping and ball games	10	10
914	8r. Water sports	1·25	2·00
915	10r. Blind man's buff	1·25	2·00

244 Nutmeg

245 Mare Longue Reservoir

1995. Spices. Multicoloured.

916	40c. Type **244**	10	10
917	4r. Coriander	55	65
918	5r. Cloves	65	80
919	10r. Cardamom	1·25	2·50

1995. 50th Anniv of End of Second World War. As T **75** of Kiribati, but 35 × 28 mm. Mult.

920	5r. H.M.S. "Mauritius" (cruiser)	1·50	2·00
921	5r. Mauritian soldiers and map of North Africa	1·50	2·00
922	5r. Consolidated PBY-5 Catalina flying boat, Tombeau Bay	1·50	2·00

1995. Anniversaries. Multicoloured.

923	40c. Type **245** (50th anniv of construction)	10	10
924	4r. Mahebourg to Curepipe road (bicentenary of construction)	90	1·10
925	10r. Buildings on fire (centenary of Great Fire of Port Louis)	1·75	2·75

246 Ile Plate Lighthouse

247 Symbolic Children under U.N.I.C.E.F. Umbrella

1995. Lighthouses. Multicoloured.

926	30c. Type **246**	60	20
927	40c. Pointe aux Caves	60	20
928	8r. Ile aux Fouquets	2·25	2·75
929	10r. Pointe aux Canonniers	2·50	2·75
MS930	130 × 100 mm. Nos. 926/9	5·50	6·50

1995. 50th Anniv of United Nations. Multicoloured.

931	40c. Type **247**	10	10
932	4r. Hard hat and building construction (I.L.O.)	35	50
933	8r. Satellite picture of cyclone (W.M.O.)	70	1·25
934	10r. Bread and grain (F.A.O.)	90	1·50

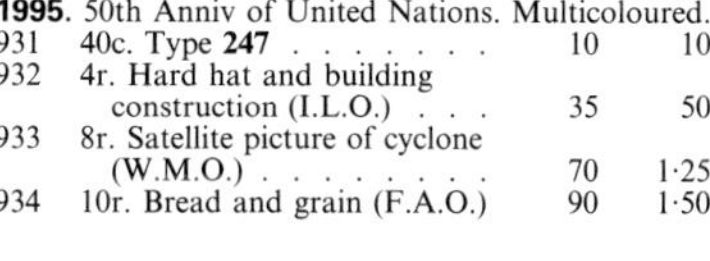

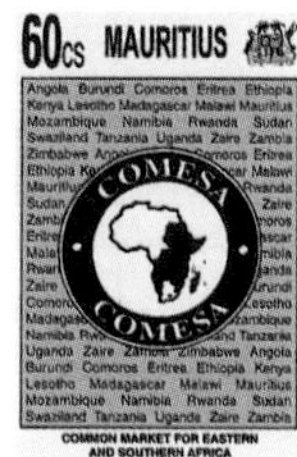

248 C.O.M.E.S.A. Emblem

1995. Inauguration of Common Market for Eastern and Southern Africa.

935 **248**	60c. black and pink	10	10
936	4r. black and blue	35	50
937	8r. black and yellow	70	1·25
938	10r. black and green	90	1·50

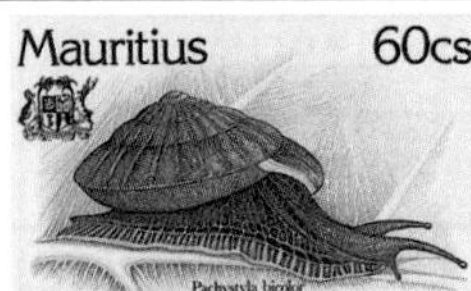

249 "Pachystyla bicolor"

1996. Snails. Multicoloured.
939 60c. Type **249** 15 10
940 4r. "Gonidomus pagodus" 55 50
941 5r. "Harmogenanina implicata" 55 60
942 10r. "Tropidophora eugeniae" . . . . 95 1·60

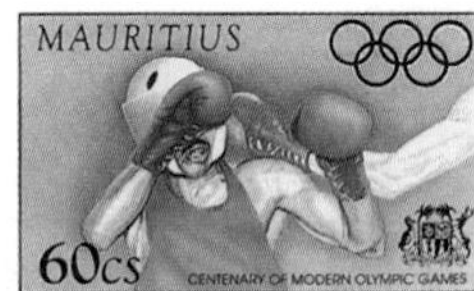

250 Boxing

1996. Centenary of Modern Olympic Games. Mult.
943 60c. Type **250** 10 10
944 4r. Badminton 50 50
945 5r. Basketball 80 70
946 10r. Table tennis . . . . . . 1·25 1·75

251 "Zambezia" (freighter)

1996. Ships. Multicoloured.
947 60c. Type **251** 20 10
948 4r. "Sir Jules" (coastal freighter) 65 55
949 5r. "Mauritius" (cargo liner) 75 75
950 10r. "Mauritius Pride" (container ship) . . . . . 1·50 2·00
MS951 125 × 91 mm. Nos. 947/50 2·75 3·50

252 Posting a Letter

1996. 150th Anniv of the Post Office Ordinance. Multicoloured.
952 60c. Type **252** 10 10
953 4r. "B53" duplex postmark 45 50
954 5r. Modern mobile post office 55 60
955 10r. Carriole (19th-century horse-drawn postal carriage) . . . . 1·00 1·50

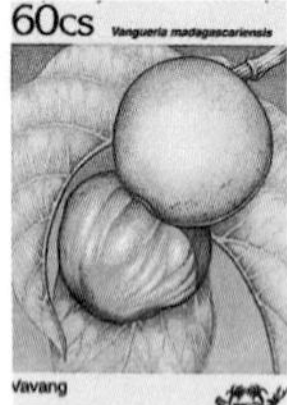

253 Vavang

1997. Fruits. Multicoloured.
956 60c. Type **253** 10 10
957 4r. Pom zako 45 50
958 5r. Zambos 55 60
959 10r. Sapot negro . . . . . . 1·00 1·50

254 Governor Mahe de la Bourdonnais and Map

1997. Aspects of Mauritius History. Multicoloured.
960 60c. Type **254** 30 15
961 1r. La Perouse and map of Pacific 40 15
962 4r. Governor Sir William Gomm and Lady Gomm's Ball, 1847 . . . . 70 50
963 6r. George Clark discovering skeleton of dodo, 1865 . . 1·10 1·25
964 10r. Professor Brian Abel-Smith and Social Policies report of 1960 . . . . . . 1·25 2·00

255 1d. "POST OFFICE" Mauritius

1997. 150th Anniv of "POST OFFICE" Stamps. Multicoloured.
965 60c. Type **255** 25 10
966 4r.2d. "POST OFFICE" Mauritius 60 60
967 5r. "POST OFFICE" 1d. and 2d. on gold background . . 85 1·00
968 10r. "POST OFFICE" 2d. and 1d. on silver background . . . . 1·60 2·25
MS969 127 × 90 mm. 20r. "POST OFFICE" stamps on cover to Bordeaux . . . . 2·25 2·50

256 Wheelwright

1997. Small Businesses. Multicoloured.
970 60c. Type **256** 10 10
971 4r. Laundryman 40 35
972 5r. Shipwright 55 55
973 15r. Quarryman . . . . . . 1·75 2·75

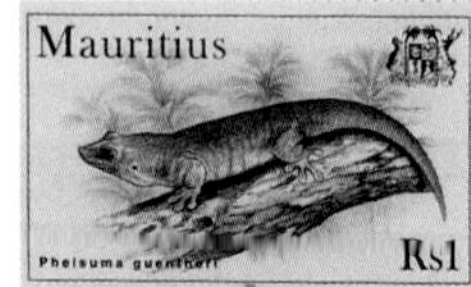

257 "Phelsuma guentheri" (gecko)

1998. Geckos. Multicoloured.
974 1r. Type **257** 20 10
975 6r. "Nactus serpensinsula durrelli" 55 65
976 7r. "Nactus coindemirensis" 65 1·25
977 8r. "Phelsuma edwardnewtonii" . . . . . 75 1·25

258 Steam Train on Viaduct

1998. Inland Transport. Multicoloured.
978 40c. Type **258** 25 10
979 5r. Early lorry 60 50
980 6r. Bus in town street 75 80
981 10r. Sailing barge at wharf 1·50 2·50

259 President Nelson Mandela

1998. State Visit of President Nelson Mandela of South Africa.
982 **259** 25r. multicoloured . . . . 2·00 2·75

260 Count Maurice of Nassau and Dutch Landing

1998. 400th Anniv of Dutch Landing on Mauritius. Multicoloured.
983 50c. Type **260** 20 10
984 1r. Fort Frederik Hendrik and sugar cane 20 10
985 7r. Dutch map of Mauritius (1670) . . . . 1·25 1·50
986 8r. Diagram of landing . . . 1·25 1·50
MS987 105 × 80 mm. 25r. Two Dutch ships . . . . 3·00 3·50

261 Cascade Balfour

1998. Waterfalls. Multicoloured.
988 1r. Type **261** 25 10
989 5r. Rochester Falls 60 45
990 6r. Cascade G.R.S.E. (vert) 70 70
991 10r. 500ft. Cascade (vert) . . 1·25 1·75

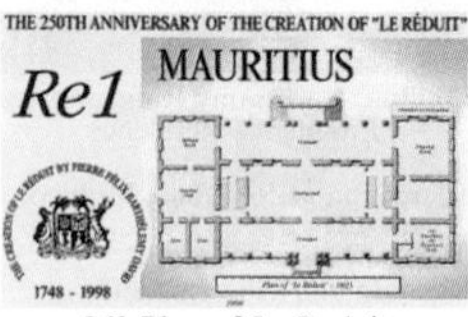

262 Plan of Le Reduit

1998. 250th Anniv of Chateau Le Reduit. Multicoloured.
992 1r. Type **262** 10 10
993 4r. "Le Chateau du Reduit, 1814" (P. Thuillier) 30 30
994 5r. "Le Reduit, 1998" (Hassen Edun) 40 40
995 15r. Commemorative monument . . . . 1·10 2·00

263 Governor Mahe de la Bourdonnais on 15c. Stamp of 1899

1999. 300th Birth Anniv of Governor Mahe de la Bourdonnais.
996 **263** 7r. blue, black and red . . 50 70

264 "Clerodendron laciniatum"

1999. Local Plants. Multicoloured.
997 1r. Type **264** 10 10
998 2r. "Senecio lamarckianus" 15 15
999 5r. "Cylindrocline commersonii" 40 45
1000 9r. "Psiadia pollicina" . . . 75 1·40

265 "The Washerwomen" (Herve Masson)

1999. Mauritius through Local Artists' Eyes. Multicoloured.
1001 1r. Type **265** 10 10
1002 3r. "The Casino" (Gaetan de Rosnay) 30 30
1003 4r. "The Four Elements" (Andree Poilly) 35 45
1004 6r. "Going to Mass" (Xavier Le Juge de Segrais) 45 80

266 Old Chimney, Alma

1999. Old Sugar Mill Chimneys. Multicoloured.
1005 1r. Type **266** 10 10
1006 2r. Antoinette 20 15
1007 5r. Belle Mare 40 50
1008 7r. Grande Rosalie . . . . . 50 1·00
MS1009 132 × 100 mm. Nos. 1005/8 1·50 2·00

267 Mosquito and Sprayer (Eradication of Malaria)

1999. 20th-century Achievements. Multicoloured.
1010 1r. Type **267** 25 10
1011 2r. Judge's robes, silhouette and airliner (emancipation of women) 40 20
1012 5r. Conference room (international conference centre) 65 60
1013 9r. Spoons full of sugar (development of sugar industry) . . . . 1·10 1·60

268 Crest

2000. 150th Anniv of Mauritius Chamber of Commerce and Industry. Multicoloured.
1014 1r. Type **268** 20 15
1015 2r. Unity, Vision and Service logos 30 20
1016 7r. Francis Channell (First Secretary, 1850–72) . . . 85 1·10
1017 15r. Louis Lechelle (First President, 1850) . . . . . 1·40 2·50

269 "Cratopus striga" (beetle)

2000. Beetles. Multicoloured.
1018 1r. Type **269** 10 10
1019 2r. "Cratopus armatus" . . 15 15
1020 3r. "Cratopus chrysochlorus" 25 25
1021 15r. "Cratopus nigrogranatus" . . . . . 1·00 1·50
MS1022 130 × 100 mm. Nos. 1018/21 1·25 1·50

270 Handball

2000. Olympic Games, Sydney. Multicoloured.
1023 1r. Type **270** 15 10
1024 2r. Archery 20 15
1025 5r. Sailing 50 50
1026 15r. Judo . . . . 1·10 1·50

271 Sir Seewoosagur Ramgoolam greeting Mother Teresa, 1984

2000. Birth Centenary of Sir Seewoosagur Ramgoolam (former Prime Minister). Multicoloured.
1027 1r. Type **271** 50 10
1028 2r. Election as member of Legislative Council, 1948 (vert) 25 15
1029 5r. As a student, 1926 (vert) 60 60
1030 15r. As Prime Minister, 1968 (vert) . . . . 1·25 1·50

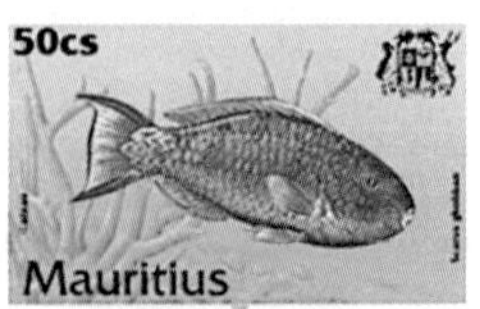

272 *Scarus ghobban*

2000. Fish. Multicoloured.
1031 50c. Type **272** 10 10
1032 1r. *Cephalopholis sonnerati* 10 10
1033 2r. *Naso brevirostris* 10 15
1034 3r. *Lethrinus nebulosus* . . . 15 20
1035 4r. *Centropyge debelius* . . . 20 25
1036 5r. *Amphiprion chrysogaster* 20 25
1037 6r. *Forcipiger flavissimus* . . 25 30

1038 7r. *Acanthurus leucosternon* 30 35
1039 8r. *Pterois volitans* 35 40
1040 10r. *Siderea grisea* 45 50
1041 15r. *Carcharhinus wheeleri* 65 70
1042 25r. *Istiophrous platypterus* 1·10 1·25
MS1043 Three sheets, each 132 × 102 mm. (a) Nos. 1031/3 and 1042. (b) Nos. 1035 and 1038/40. (c) Nos. 1034, 1036/7 and 1041 Set of 3 sheets 6·00 7·00

273 Affan Tank Wen

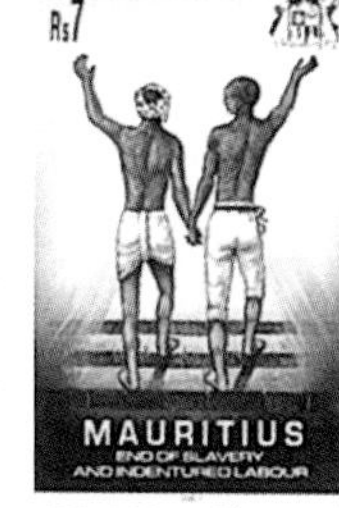

275 African Slave and Indian Indentured Labourer

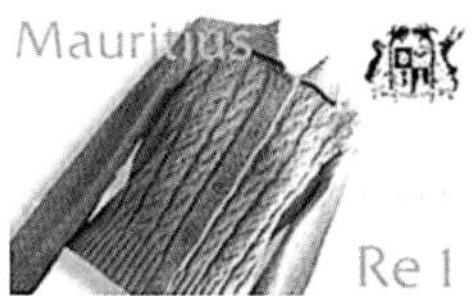

274 Finished Pullover

2000. Famous Mauritians. Multicoloured.
1044 1r. Type **273** 20 10
1045 5r. Alphonse Ravatoni 60 50
1046 7r. Dr. Idrice Goumany 80 90
1047 9r. Anjalay Coopen 1·00 1·25

2001. Textile Industry. Multicoloured.
1048 1r. Type **274** 20 10
1049 3r. Computer-aided machinery 35 50
1050 6r. T-shirt folding 70 70
1051 10r. Embroidery machine 1·10 1·40

2001. Anti-slavery and Indentured Labour Campaign Commemoration.
1052 **275** 7r. multicoloured 75 80

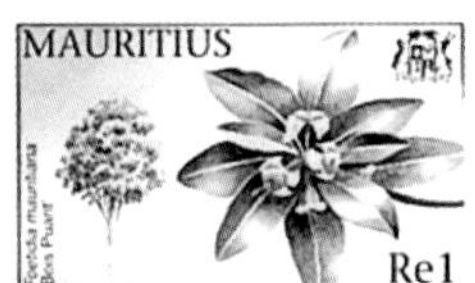

276 *Foetidia mauritiana*

2001. Trees. Multicoloured.
1053 1r. Type **276** 20 10
1054 3r. *Diospyros tessellaria* 40 20
1055 5r. *Sideroxylon puberulum* 60 55
1056 15r. *Gastonia mauritiana* 1·40 1·75

277 *Geographe* and *Naturaliste* (French corvettes)

2001. Bicentenary of Baudin's Expedition to New Holland (Australia). Multicoloured.
1057 1r. Type **277** 20 10
1058 4r. Capt. Nicholas Baudin and map of voyage 50 30
1059 6r. Mascarene martin (bird) 75 70
1060 10r. M. F. Peron and title page of book (vert) 1·10 1·40

278 Hotel School

2001. Mauritius Economic Achievements during the 20th Century. Multicoloured.
1061 2r. Type **278** 20 15
1062 3r. Steel bar milling 25 20
1063 6r. Solar energy panels, Agalega 50 45
1064 10r. Indian Ocean Rim Association for Regional Co-operation 90 1·10

279 Gandhi on Mauritius Stamp of 1969

280 De-husking Coconuts

2001. Centenary of Gandhi's Visit to Mauritius.
1065 **279** 15r. multicoloured 1·25 1·40

2001. Coconut Industry. Multicoloured.
1066 1r. Type **280** 15 10
1067 5r. Shelling coconuts (horiz) 45 35
1068 6r. Drying copra (horiz) 50 50
1069 10r. Extracting coconut oil 80 1·00

281 New Container Port

2002. 10th Anniv of Republic. Multicoloured.
1070 1r. Type **281** 15 10
1071 4r. Symbols of Mauritius stock exchange 35 30
1072 5r. New reservoir under construction 45 40
1073 9r. Motorway junction 75 90

282 *Abricta*

284 Constellation of Orion

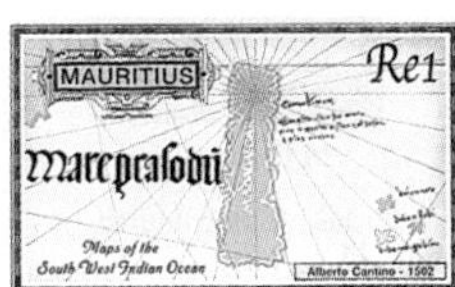

283 Map by Alberto Cantino, 1502

2002. Cicadas. Multicoloured.
1074 1r. Type **282** 10 10
1075 6r. *Fractuosella darwini* 25 30
1076 7r. *Distantada thomaseti* 30 35
1077 8r. *Dinarobia claudeae* 35 40
MS1078 130 × 100 mm. Nos. 1074/7 1·00 1·10

2002. 16th-century Maps of the South-west Indian Ocean. Multicoloured.
1079 1r. Type **283** 10 10
1080 3r. Map by Jorge Reinel, 1520 15 20
1081 4r. Map by Diogo Ribeiro, 1529 20 25
1082 10r. Map by Gerard Mercator, 1569 45 50

2002. Constellations. Multicoloured.
1083 1r. Type **284** 10 10
1084 7r. Sagittarius 30 35
1085 8r. Scorpius 35 40
1086 9r. Southern Cross 40 45

285 African Growth and Opportunity Act Logo

286 Echo Parakeet Chick

2003. 2nd United States/Sub-Saharan Africa Trade and Economic Co-operation Forum.
1087 **285** 1r. red, blue and yellow 10 10
1088 25r. red, ultramarine and blue 1·25 1·40

2003. Endangered Species. Echo Parakeet. Multicoloured.
1089 1r. Type **286** 10 10
1090 2r. Fledgling 10 15
1091 5r. Female parakeet 20 25
1092 15r. Male parakeet 65 70

EXPRESS DELIVERY STAMPS

1903. No. 136 surch **EXPRESS DELIVERY 15c**.
E1 **40** 15c. on 15c. blue 8·00 22·00

1903. No. 136 surch **EXPRESS DELIVERY (INLAND) 15c**.
E3 **40** 15c. on 15c. blue 7·50 3·00

1904. T **42** without value in label. (a) Surch **(FOREIGN) EXPRESS DELIVERY 18 CENTS**.
E5 **42** 18c. green 1·50 23·00

(b) Surch **EXPRESS DELIVERY (INLAND) 15c**.
E6 **42** 15c. green 3·75 4·00

POSTAGE DUE STAMPS

D 1

1933.
D 1 **D 1** 2c. black 1·25 50
D 2 4c. violet 50 65
D 3 6c. red 60 80
D 4 10c. green 70 1·00
D 5 20c. blue 50 1·25
D13 50c. purple 75 12·00
D 7 1r. orange 70 15·00

1982. Nos. 530/1, 535, 540, 542 and 547 surch **POSTAGE DUE** and value.
D14 10c. on 15c. Dutch Occupation, 1638–1710 20 50
D15 20c. on 20c. Van Keulen's map, c. 1700 30 50
D16 50c. on 60c. Pierre Poivre, c. 1767 (vert) 30 30
D17 1r. on 1r.20 Government House, c. 1840 40 30
D18 1r.50 on 1r.50 Indian immigration, 1835 50 75
D19 5r. on 15r. Unfurling Mauritian flag, 1968 1·00 2·25

MAYOTTE Pt. 6

One of the Comoro Islands adjacent to Madagascar.

In 1974 (when the other islands became an independent state) Mayotte was made an Overseas Department of France, using French stamps. From 1997 it again had its own issues.

100 centimes = 1 franc.

1892. "Tablet" key-type inscr "MAYOTTE".
1 D 1c. black and red on blue 1·25 75
2 2c. brown and blue on buff 1·75 1·90
3 4c. brown and blue on grey 2·25 2·25
4 5c. green and red on green 2·50 2·75
5 10c. black and blue on lilac 4·75 4·50
15 10c. red and blue 30·00 45·00
6 15c. blue and red 10·50 9·50
16 15c. grey and red 90·00 75·00
7 20c. red and blue on green 11·00 11·00
8 25c. black and red on pink 6·50 5·50
17 25c. blue and red 7·00 8·50
9 30c. brown and blue on drab 14·50 14·50
18 35c. black and red on yellow 4·50 4·00
10 40c. red and blue on yellow 13·50 13·00
19 45c. black on green 14·00 14·00
11 50c. red and blue on pink 22·00 18·00
20 50c. brown and red on blue 10·50 20·00
12 75c. brown & red on orange 19·00 22·00
13 1f. green and red 15·00 19·00
14 5f. mauve and blue on lilac 95·00 10·00

1912. Surch in figures.
21 D 05 on 20c. brown and blue on buff 1·10 3·75
22 05 on 4c. brown and blue on grey 1·60 2·25
23 05 on 15c. blue and red 1·60 2·00
24 05 on 20c. red and blue on green 1·50 2·75
25 05 on 25c. black and red on pink 1·25 2·75
26 05 on 30c. brown and blue on drab 1·40 3·00
27 10 on 40c. red and blue on yellow 1·00 2·75
28 10 on 45c. black and red on green 1·50 1·40
29 10 on 50c. red and blue on pink 2·75 4·75
30 10 on 75c. brown and red on orange 1·90 3·75
31 10 on 1f. green and red 2·75 3·25

1997. Stamps of France optd **MAYOTTE**. (a) Nos. 2907/10, 2912, 2917, 2924 and 2929/30.
40 **1118** 10c. brown 15 10
41 20c. green 15 10
42 50c. violet 15 10
43 1f. orange 35 15
44 2f. blue 60 35
45 2f.70 green 80 45
46 3f.80 blue 1·00 55
47 5f. blue 1·75 70
48 10f. violet 3·50 1·50

(b) No. 3121. No value expressed.
49 **1118** (–) red 75 55
No. 49 was sold at 3f.

6 Ylang-ylang

1997.
50 **6** 2f.70 multicoloured 85 50

7 Arms

1997.
51 **7** 3f. multicoloured 70 40

8 Terminal Building and Airplane

1997. Air. Inauguration of New Airport.
52 **8** 20f. indigo, red and blue 6·00 2·75

9 Le Banga

1997.
53 **9** 3f.80 multicoloured 95 55

10 Dzen-dze (musical instrument)

1997.
54 **10** 5f.20 multicoloured 1·40 70

1997. Stamps of France optd **MAYOTTE**. (a) On Nos. 3415/20, 3425, 3430 and 3432.
55 **1318** 10c. brown 15 10
56 20c. green 15 10
57 50c. violet 15 10
58 1f. orange 30 15
59 2f. blue 50 35
60 2f.70 green 55 40
62 3f.80 blue 80 55
66 5f. blue 1·10 65
68 10f. violet 2·40 1·25

(b) On No. 3407. No value expressed. Ordinary or self-adhesive gum.
69 **1318** (3f.) red 75 35

11 Lemur

1997.
71 **11** 3f. brown and red 80 45

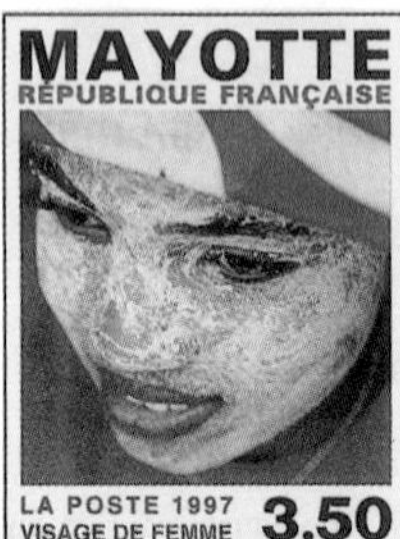

12 Woman's Face

1997.
72 **12** 3f.50 multicoloured 85 55

13 Fishes and Corals

1997. Marine Life.
73 **13** 3f. multicoloured 75 45

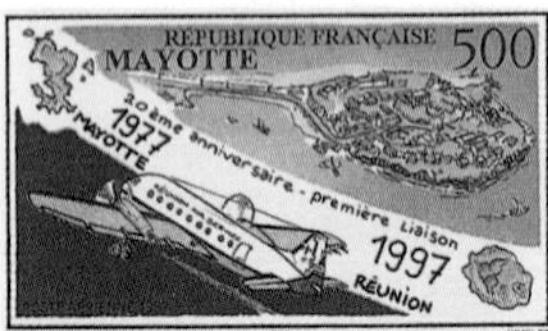

14 Reunion, Maps and Airplane

1997. Air. 20th Anniv of First Mayotte–Reunion Air Flight.
74 **14** 5f. black, blue and green . . 1·25 75

15 Longoni Port

1998.
75 **15** 2f.70 multicoloured 70 40

16 Indian Ocean Green Turtle

1998.
76 **16** 3f. multicoloured 75 45

17 Family on Island 18 Cattle Egret on Zebu's Head

1998. Family Planning.
77 **17** 1f. multicoloured 25 10

1998. Air.
78 **18** 30f. multicoloured . . . . . 7·50 3·75

19 Children in Costume

1998. Children's Carnival.
79 **19** 3f. multicoloured 75 40

20 "Salama Djema II" (ferry)

1998. Mamoudzou–Dzaoudzi Ferry.
80 **20** 3f.80 multicoloured 90 50

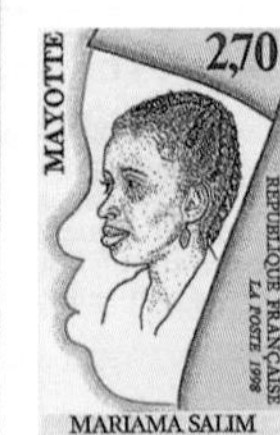

21 Tsingoni Mosque 22 Mariama Salim

1998.
81 **21** 3f. multicoloured 75 40

1998. 2nd Death Anniv of Mariama Salim (women's rights activist).
82 **22** 2f.70 multicoloured 65 35

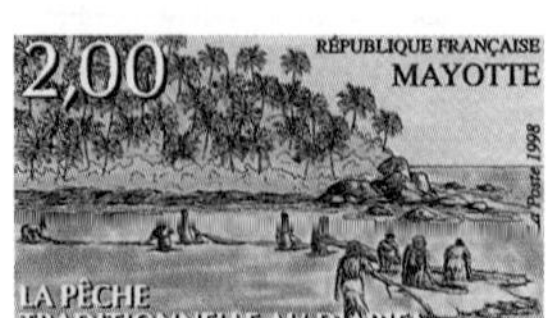

23 Spreading Nets

1998. Traditional Fishing, Djarifa.
83 **23** 2f. multicoloured 50 25

24 Emperor Angelfish

1998.
84 **24** 3f. multicoloured 70 40

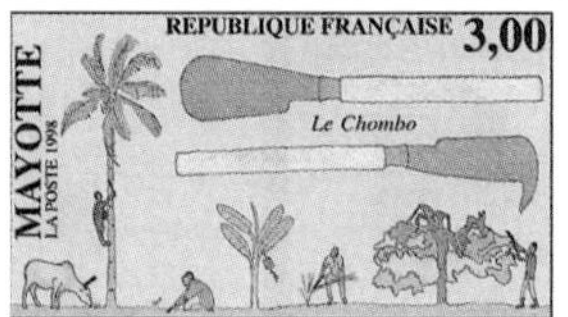

25 Chombos and Workers

1998. The Chombo (agricultural tool).
85 **25** 3f. multicoloured 65 40

26 Map of Mayotte

1999.
86 **26** 3f. multicoloured 65 40

27 Reservoir, Combani

1999.
87 **27** 8f. multicoloured . . . . . 1·90 1·00

28 Coral Hind

1999. Lagoon Fishes. Multicoloured.
88 2f.70 Type **28** 60 30
89 3f. Lionfish (horiz) 70 35
90 5f.20 Regal angelfish (horiz) 1·00 60
91 10f. Powder-blue surgeonfish (horiz) . . . . 2·25 1·10

1999. The Euro (European currency). No. 3553 of France optd **MAYOTTE**.
92 3f. red and blue 75 35

29 Genet

1999.
93 **29** 5f.40 orange, black & stone 1·40 70

30 Baobab Tree

1999.
94 **30** 8f. multicoloured . . . . . 1·90 1·00

31 Prefecture Building

1999. Dzaoudzi Prefecture.
96 **31** 3f. multicoloured 70 40

33 Vanilla

1999.
98 **33** 4f.50 multicoloured 95 50

34 "Le Deba"

1999. Air.
99 **34** 10f. multicoloured . . . . . 2·10 1·10

35 Map of Mayotte, Arrow and "2000"

1999. Year 2000.
100 **35** 3f. multicoloured 65 40

36 Soulou Waterfall

1999.
101 **36** 10f. multicoloured . . . . 2·00 1·10

37 Sailing Boat

2000. Indian Ocean.
102 **37** 3f. multicoloured 65 40

38 Two Whales

2000. Whales.
103 **38** 5f.20 multicoloured . . . . 1·10 60

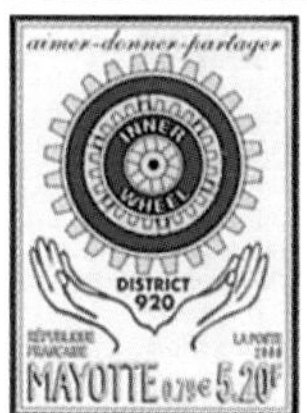

39 Emblem

2000. District 920 of Inner Wheel (women's section of Rotary International).

104	**39**	5f.20 multicoloured	1·00	60

40 L'île au Lagon

2000.

105	**40**	3f. multicoloured	65	40

42 Tyre Race

2000.

107	**42**	3f. multicoloured	65	40

43 Sultan Andriantsouli's Tomb

2000.

108	**43**	5f.40 multicoloured	1·00	60

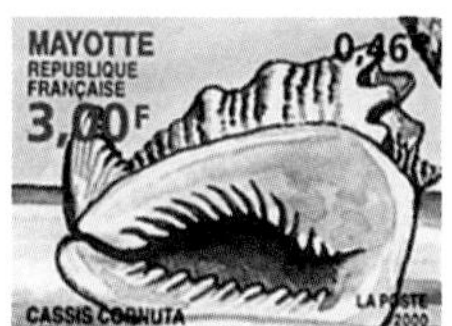

44 Horned Helmet

2000. Shells. Multicoloured.

109	3f. Type **44**	65	40
110	3f. Trumpet triton (*Charonia tritonis*)	65	40
111	3f. Bullmouth helmet (*Cypraecassis rufa*)	65	40
112	3f. Humpback cowrie (*Cyprae mauritiana*) (wrongly inscr "mauritania") and tiger cowrie (*Cyprae tigris*)	65	40

Nos. 109/12 were issued together, se-tenant, with the backgrounds forming a composite design of a beach.

45 M'Dere

2000. 1st Death Anniv of Zena M'Dere.

113	**45**	3f. multicoloured	65	40

46 Distillery

2000. Ylang-ylang Distillery.

114	**46**	2f.70 multicoloured	60	35

47 Building

48 Map of Mayotte

2000. New Hospital.

115	**47**	10f. multicoloured	2·00	1·10

2001.

116	**48**	2f.70 black and green	60	35

2001. No value expressed. As T **48**.

120	**48**	(3f.) black and red	65	40

49 Mother breast-feeding

2001. Breast-feeding.

130	**49**	3f. multicoloured	65	40

50 Pilgrims

2001. Pilgrimage to Mecca.

131	**50**	2f.70 multicoloured	60	35

51 Bush Taxi

2001.

132	**51**	3f. multicoloured	65	40

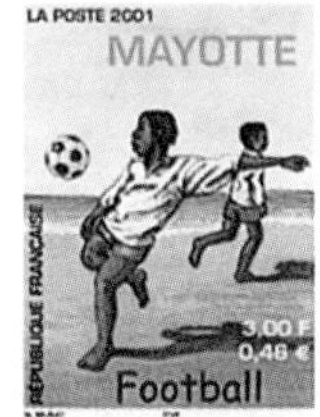

52 Children playing Football

2001.

133	**52**	3f. multicoloured	60	35

53 Pyjama Cardinalfish

2001.

134	**53**	10f. multicoloured	2·00	1·25

54 Legionnaire, Map and Market Scene

2001. 25th Anniv of Mayotte Foreign Legion Detachment.

135	**54**	5f.20 multicoloured	1·00	60

56 Airplanes and Club House

2001. Air. Dzaoudzi Flying Club.

137	**56**	20f. multicoloured	4·00	2·40

57 Military Personnel and Building

2001. 1st Anniv of Adapted Military Service Units.

138	**57**	3f. multicoloured	60	35

58 *Protea* sp.

2001. Flower and Fruit. Multicoloured.

139	3f. Type **58**	60	35
140	5f.40 Selection of fruit	1·00	60

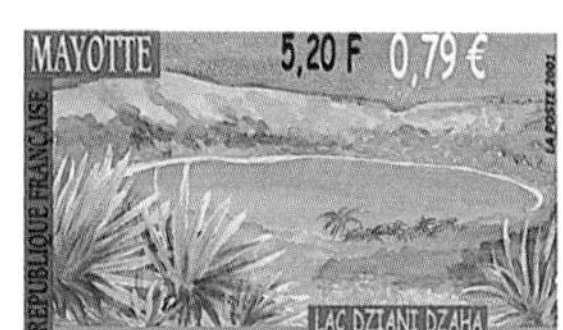

59 Dziani Dzaha Lake

2001.

141	**59**	5f.20 multicoloured	1·00	60

60 Mayotte Post Office

2001.

142	**60**	10f. multicoloured	2·00	1·25

2002. Stamps of France optd **MAYOTTE**. (a) Nos. 3770/85.

143	**1318**	1c. yellow	10	10
144		2c. brown	10	10
145		5c. green	10	10
146		10c. violet	15	10
147		20c. orange	30	15
148		41c. green	55	35
149		50c. blue	70	40
150		53c. green	75	45
151		58c. blue	80	50
152		64c. orange	90	55
153		67c. blue	95	60
154		69c. mauve	95	60
155		€1 turquoise	1·40	85
156		€1.02 green	1·40	85
157		€2 violet	2·75	1·60

(b) No value expressed. No. 3752.

166		(41c.) red	55	35

No. 166 was sold at the rate for inland letters up to 20 grammes.

61 Arms

2002. Attainment of Department Status within France (11 July 2001).

167	**61**	46c. multicoloured	65	40

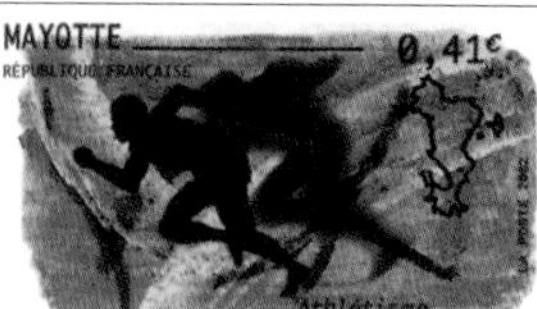

62 Runners

2002. Athletics.

168	**62**	41c. multicoloured	55	35

63 Mangroves, Kaweni Basin

2002.

169	**63**	€1.52 multicoloured	2·10	1·60

64 Building Facade   **66** House and People

65 Women processing Salt (½-size illustration)

2002. 25th Anniv of Mayotte Commune.

170	**64**	46c. multicoloured	65	40

2002. Salt Production at Bandrele.

171	**65**	79c. multicoloured	1·10	65

2002. National Census.

171	**66**	46c. multicoloured	65	40

MECKLENBURG-SCHWERIN Pt. 7

In northern Germany. Formerly a Grand Duchy, Mecklenburg-Schwerin joined the North German Confederation in 1868.

48 schilling = 1 thaler.

1

2

1856. Imperf.

1a	**1**	4/4s. red	£130	£110
1		4/4s. red	£130	95·00
2	**2**	3s. yellow	85·00	50·00
4		5s. blue	£200	£250

See note below No. 7.

1864. Roul.

5a	**1**	¼s. red	£2500	£1600
6a		¼s. red	£375	65·00
5		4/4s. red	£2250	£1800
6		4/4s. red	60·00	60·00
11	**2**	2s. purple	£225	£225
9		3s. yellow	£150	£110
7		5s. bistre	£130	£225

Nos. 1, 1a, 5, 5a have a dotted background, Nos. 6 and 6a a plain background. Prices for Nos. 1a, 5a and 6a are for quarter stamps; prices for Nos. 1, 5 and 6 are for the complete on cover stamp (four quarters) as illustrated in Type **1**.

MECKLENBURG-STRELITZ Pt. 7

In northern Germany. Formerly a Grand Duchy, Mecklenburg-Strelitz joined the North German Confederation in 1868.

30 silbergroschen = 1 thaler.

1

2

1864. Roul. Various frames.
2 **1** ¼sgr. orange £160 £1700
3 ⅓sgr. green . . . . 65·00 £1200
6 1sch. mauve £275 £3000
7 **2** 1sgr. red £140 £170
9 2sgr. blue . . . . 32·00 £650
11 3sgr. bistre . . . . 32·00 £1200

MEMEL Pt. 7

A seaport and district on the Baltic Sea, formerly part of Germany. Under Allied control after the 1914–18 war, it was captured and absorbed by Lithuania in 1923 and returned to Germany in 1939. From 1945 the area has been part of Lithuania.

1920. 100 pfennig = 1 mark.
1923. 100 centu = 1 litas.

1920. Stamps of France surch **MEMEL** and **pfennig** or **mark** with figure of value.
1 **18** 5pf. on 5c. green 10 20
2 10pf. on 10c. red 10 15
3 20pf. on 25c. blue 10 20
4 30pf. on 30c. orange 10 20
19 40pf. on 20c. brown 10 15
5 50pf. on 35c. violet 10 65
6 **13** 60pf. on 40c. red and blue 20 60
7 80pf. on 45c. green and blue 50 60
8 1m. on 50c. brown and lilac 15 40
9 1m.25 on 60c. violet & blue 95 2·25
10 2m. on 1f. red and green . . 15 35
11 3m. on 2f. orange and green 9·50 28·00
12 3m. on 5f. blue and buff . . 11·00 28·00
13 4m. on 2f. orange and green 30 40
14 10m. on 5f. blue and buff 1·75 5·50
15 20m. on 5f. blue and buff 25·00 80·00

1920. Stamps of Germany inscr "DEUTSCHES REICH" optd **Memel- gebiet** or **Memelgebiet**.
25 **10** 5pf. green . . . . 30 1·00
26 10pf. red . . . . 2·10 6·00
27 10pf. orange 15 40
28 **24** 15pf. brown . . . . 2·40 6·00
29 **10** 20pf. blue . . . . 30 1·50
30 30pf. black & orange on buff . . . . 4·25 10·00
31 30pf. blue . . . . 25 3·75
32 40pf. black and red . . . . 30 2·40
33 50pf. black & purple on buff 25 85
34 60pf. green . . . . 55 1·60
35 75pf. black and green . . . 2·00 6·75
36 80pf. blue . . . . 1·20 2·50
37 **12** 1m. red . . . . 65 1·40
38 1m.25 green . . . . 12·00 31·00
39 1m.50 brown . . . . 4·75 11·00
40 **13** 2m. blue . . . . 2·30 3·25
41 2m.50 purple . . . . 12·50 23·00

1921. Nos. 2/3, 5, 8, 10, 19 and 49 further surch in large figures.
42 **18** 15 on 10pf. on 10c. red . . 65 80
43 15 on 20pf. on 25c. blue . . 75 1·00
44 15 on 50pf. on 35c. violet 50 1·00
45 60 on 40pf. on 20c. brown 60 90
46 **13** 75 on 60pf. on 40c. red and blue (49) . . . . 1·20 1·60
47 1,25 on 1m. on 50c. brown and lilac . . . . 35 1·10
48 5,00 on 2m. on 1f. red and green . . . . 1·20 2·00

1921. Surch **MEMEL** and **Pfennig** or **Mark** with figure of value.
60 **18** 5pf. on 5c. orange 30 80
61 10pf. on 10c. red . . . . . 1·20 2·50
62 10pf. on 10c. green 45 65
63 15pf. on 10c. green . . . . 35 1·10
64 20pf. on 20c. brown . . . 5·75 16·00
65 20pf. on 25c. blue . . . . 5·75 16·00
66 25pf. on 5c. orange 10 60
67 30pf. on 30c. red . . . . . 90 2·75
68 35pf. on 35c. violet 35 70
77 **13** 40pf. on 40c. red and blue 30 90
69 **15** 50pf. on 50c. blue 20 55
49 **13** 60pf. on 40c. red and blue 3·50 9·00
71 **15** 75pf. on 15c. green 25 95
70 **18** 75pf. on 35c. violet 25 45
78 **13** 80pf. on 45c. green & blue 20 75
72 **18** 1m. on 25c. blue 30 85
79 **13** 1m. on 40c. red and blue 15 55
73 **18** 1¼m. on 30c. red 30 75
80 **13** 1m.25 on 60c. violet & bl 40 55
81 1m.50 on 45c. green & bl 35 90
82 2m. on 45c. green and blue 50 70
83 2m. on 1f. red and green 25 60
84 2¼m. on 40c. red and blue 50 80
85 2¼m. on 60c. violet and blue . . . . 60 1·30
74 **18** 3m. on 5c. orange . . . . 20 1·50
86 **13** 3m. on 60c. violet and blue 75 1·40
87 4m. on 45c. green and blue 30 1·00
88 5m. on 1f. red and green 50 1·00
75 **15** 6m. on 15c. green . . . . 30 1·60
89 **13** 6m. on 60c. violet and blue 80 95
90 6m. on 2f. orange & green 60 1·40
76 **18** 8m. on 30c. red . . . . . 55 4·50
91 **13** 9m. on 1f. red and green 45 1·00
92 9m. on 5f. blue and buff 45 1·50
93 10m. on 45c. green & blue 60 1·90
51 10m. on 5f. blue and buff 80 1·70
94 12m. on 40c. red and blue 30 1·20
95 20m. on 40c. red and blue 1·00 2·10
52 20m. on 45c. green & blue 3·50 12·00
96 20m. on 2f. orange & green 50 1·10
97 30m. on 60c. violet & blue 65 2·10
98 30m. on 5f. blue and buff 3·75 8·50
90 40m. on 1f. red and green 35 1·60
100 50m. on 2f. orange & green 9·00 21·00
101 80m. on 2f. orange & green 65 2·00
102 100m. on 5f. blue and buff 1·20 3·75

1921. Air. Nos. 6/8, 10, 13 and 49/50 optd **FLUGPOST** in double-lined letters.
53 **13** 60pf. on 40c. red and blue 30·00 50·00
54 60pf. on 40c. red and blue (No. 49) . . . . 3·75 8·00
55 80pf. on 45c. green and blue 2·75 7·00
56 1m. on 50c. brown and lilac 2·50 5·50
57 2m. on 1f. red and green . . 2·75 6·00
58 3m. on 60c. violet and blue (No. 50) . . . . 3·00 7·75
59 4m. on 2f. orange and green 3·75 11·50

1922. Air. Nos. 13, 50, 77/81, 83, 86, 88, 90 and 92 further optd **Flugpost** in script letters.
103 **13** 40pf. on 40c. red and blue (No. 77) . . . . 95 1·60
104 80pf. on 45c. green and blue (No. 78) . . . . . 85 1·60
105 1m. on 40c. red and blue (No. 68) . . . . 1·00 1·50
106 1m.25 on 60c. violet and blue (No. 80) . . . . . 1·00 2·20
107 1m.50 on 45c. green and blue (No. 81) . . . . . 95 2·40
108 2m. on 1f. red and green (No. 83) . . . . 1·30 2·40
110 3m. on 60c. violet and blue (No. 86) . . . . 1·30 2·00
111 4m. on 2f. orange and green (No. 13) . . . . . 1·10 2·20
112 5m. on 1f. red and green (No. 88) . . . . 1·20 2·10
113 6m. on 2f. orange and green (No. 90) . . . . . 1·10 2·30
114 9m. on 5f. blue and buff (No. 92) . . . . 1·40 2·20

1922. Air. Surch as in 1921 and optd **FLUGPOST** in ordinary capitals.
115 **13** 40pf. on 40c. red and blue 1·20 5·00
116 1m. on 40c. red and blue 1·20 5·50
117 1m.25 on 60c. violet and blue . . . . 1·20 5·25
118 1m.50 on 45c. green and blue . . . . 1·20 4·75
119 2m. on 1f. red and green 1·10 7·00
120 3m. on 60c. violet and blue 1·00 6·00
121 4m. on 2f. orange & green 1·20 6·50
122 5m. on 1f. red and green 1·30 6·25
123 6m. on 2f. orange & green 1·20 6·50
124 9m. on 5f. blue and buff 1·40 6·00

1922. Nos. 62, 64 and 69 further surch as in 1921 but with additional surch **Mark** obliterating **Pfennig**.
125 **18** 10m. on 10pf. on 10c. green (No. 62) . . . . . 80 3·75
126 20m. on 20pf. on 20c. brown (No. 64) . . . . 65 1·40
127 **15** 50m. on 50pf. on 50c. blue (No. 69) . . . . 2·00 7·50

1923. Nos. 77 and 80 with additional surch.
128 **13** 40m. on 40pf. on 40c. red and blue . . . . 1·00 2·10
129 80m. on 1m.25 on 60c. violet and blue . . . . . 1·00 2·75

1923. Nos. 72 and 82 surch with large figures.
130 **13** 10m. on 2m. on 45c. green and blue . . . . 1·70 5·00
131 **18** 25m. on 1m. on 25c. blue 1·80 5·75

LITHUANIAN OCCUPATION

The port and district of Memel was captured by Lithuanian forces in 1923 and incorporated in Lithuania.

1

5

1923. (a) Surch **KLAIPEDA (MEMEL)** and value over curved line and **MARKIU**.
1 **1** 10m. on 5c. blue . . . . . . 40 1·30
2 25m. on 5c. blue . . . . . . 40 1·30
3 50m. on 25c. red . . . . . . 40 1·30
4 100m. on 25c. red . . . . . 55 1·90
5 400m. on 1l. brown . . . . 1·10 3·50

(b) Surch **Klaipeda (Memel)** and value over two straight lines and **Markiu**.
6 **1** 10m. on 5c. blue . . . . . . 75 3·00
7 25m. on 5c. blue . . . . . . 75 3·00
8 50m. on 25c. red . . . . . . 75 3·00
9 100m. on 25c. red . . . . . 75 3·00
10 400m. on 1l. brown . . . . 1·00 4·00
11 500m. on 1l. brown . . . . 1·00 4·00

(c) Surch **KLAIPEDA (Memel)** and value over four stars and **MARKIU**.
12 **1** 10m. on 5c. blue . . . . . . 1·30 5·00
13 20m. on 5c. blue . . . . . . 1·30 5·00
14 25m. on 25c. red . . . . . . 1·30 5·75
15 50m. on 25c. red . . . . . . 1·90 6·50
16 100m. on 1l. brown . . . . 2·50 7·75
17 200m. on 1l. brown . . . . 2·75 7·75

1923.
18 **5** 10m. brown 30 55
19 20m. yellow 30 55
20 25m. orange 30 55
21 40m. violet 30 55
22 50m. green . . . . 65 1·10
23 100m. red 50 55
24 300m. green . . . . 4·50 70·00
25 400m. brown 50 75
26 500m. purple . . . . 4·50 70·00
27 1000m. blue . . . . 75 1·90

7 Liner, Memel Port

8 Memel Arms

9 Memel Lighthouse

1923. Uniting of Memel with Lithuania and Amalgamation of Memel Harbours.
28 **7** 40m. green . . . . 2·75 16·00
29 50m. brown . . . . 2·75 16·00
30 80m. green . . . . 2·75 16·00
31 100m. red . . . . 2·75 16·00
32 **8** 200m. blue . . . . 2·75 16·00
33 300m. brown . . . . 2·75 16·00
34 400m. purple . . . . 2·75 16·00
35 500m. orange . . . . 2·75 16·00
36 600m. green . . . . 2·75 16·00
37 **9** 800m. blue . . . . 2·75 16·00
38 1000m. purple . . . . . . 2·75 16·00
39 2000m. red . . . . 2·75 16·00
40 3000m. green . . . . 2·75 16·00

1923. No. 123 of Memel surch **Klaipeda**, value and large **M** between bars, sideways.
41 100m. on 80 on 1m.25 on 60c. . . . . 4·25 15·00
42 400m. on 80 on 1m.25 on 60c. . . . . 4·25 15·00
43 500m. on 80 on 1m.25 on 60c. . . . . 4·25 15·00

1923. Surch in **CENTU**.
44 **5** 2c. on 300m. green . . . . . 5·75 7·75
45 3c. on 300m. green . . . . . 6·00 9·50
46 10c. on 25m. orange . . . . 7·75 7·75
47 15c. on 25m. orange . . . . 7·75 7·75
48 20c. on 500m. purple . . . . 9·25 17·00
49 30c. on 500m. purple . . . . 7·75 7·75
50 50c. on 500m. purple . . . . 11·50 21·00

1923. Surch (thin or thick figures) in **CENT.** or **LITAS**.
60 **5** 2c. on 10m. brown . . . . . 1·50 6·00
51 2c. on 20m. yellow . . . . . 3·00 11·50
52 2c. on 50m. green . . . . . 3·00 9·50
63 3c. on 10m. brown . . . . . 2·50 7·75
53 3c. on 40m. violet . . . . . 3·75 9·50
54 3c. on 300m. green . . . . . 2·75 4·50
55 5c. on 100m. red . . . . . . 3·50 4·50
56 5c. on 300m. green . . . . . 3·75 9·50
57 10c. on 400m. brown . . . . 7·75 13·50
67 15c. on 25m. orange . . . . 85·00 £450
58 30c. on 500m. purple . . . . 7·75 7·75
68 50c. on 1000m. blue . . . . 2·10 7·75
69 1l. on 1000m. blue . . . . . 4·25 13·50

1923. Surch in **CENT.** or **LITAS**.
70 **7** 15c. on 40m. green . . . . . 4·25 14·00
71 30c. on 50m. brown . . . . 4·25 7·25
72 30c. on 80m. green . . . . . 4·25 17·00
73 30c. on 100m. red . . . . . 4·25 7·25
74 **8** 50c. on 200m. blue . . . . . 4·25 14·00
75 50c. on 300m. brown . . . . 4·25 7·25
76 50c. on 400m. purple . . . . 4·25 12·50
77 50c. on 500m. orange . . . . 4·25 7·25
78 1l. on 600m. green . . . . . 5·00 14·00
79 **9** 1l. on 800m. blue . . . . . . 5·00 14·00
80 1l. on 1000m. purple . . . . 5·00 14·00
81 1l. on 2000m. red . . . . . . 5·00 15·00
82 1l. on 3000m. green . . . . 5·00 14·00

1923. Surch in large figures and **Centu** and bars reading upwards.
83 **1** 10c. on 25m. on 5c. blue (No. 2) . . . . 21·00 42·00
84 15c. on 100m. on 25c. red (No. 4) . . . . 21·00 £140
85 30c. on 400m. on 1l. brown (No. 5) . . . . 7·75 27·00
86 60c. on 50m. on 25c. red (No. 8) . . . . 21·00 £170

1923. Surch in large figures and **CENT.** and bars.
87 **7** 15c. on 50m. brown £170 £2000
88 25c. on 100m. red . . . . . 65·00 £1100
89 **8** 30c. on 300m. brown £130 £1200
90 60c. on 500m. orange . . . . 65·00 £1100

1923. Surch in **Centu** or **Centai** (25c.) between bars.
91 **5** 15c. on 10m. brown . . . . 5·75 25·00
92 15c. on 20m. yellow . . . . 2·75 13·50
93 15c. on 25m. orange . . . . 2·75 15·00
94 15c. on 40m. violet . . . . 2·75 13·50
95 15c. on 50m. green . . . . 2·10 11·50
96 15c. on 100m. red . . . . . 2·10 11·50
97 15c. on 400m. brown . . . . 1·90 9·50
98 15c. on 1000m. blue . . . . 55·00 £300
99 25c. on 10m. brown . . . . 3·50 21·00
100 25c. on 20m. yellow . . . . 2·75 13·50
101 25c. on 25m. orange . . . . 2·75 15·00
102 25c. on 40m. violet . . . . 3·50 21·00
103 25c. on 50m. green . . . . 2·10 10·50
104 25c. on 100m. red . . . . . 1·90 10·50
105 25c. on 400m. brown . . . . 1·90 10·50
106 25c. on 1000m. blue . . . . 55·00 £350
107 30c. on 10m. brown . . . . 5·75 27·00
108 30c. on 20m. yellow . . . . 2·75 17·00
109 30c. on 25m. orange . . . . 3·75 21·00
110 30c. on 40m. violet . . . . 3·00 15·00
111 30c. on 50m. green . . . . 2·10 11·50
112 30c. on 100m. red . . . . . 2·10 11·50
113 30c. on 400m. brown . . . . 2·10 11·50
114 30c. on 1000m. blue . . . . 55·00 £325

MEXICO Pt. 15

A republic of Central America. From 1864–67 an Empire under Maximilian of Austria.

8 reales = 100 centavos = 1 peso.

1 Miguel Hidalgo y Costilla

2

1856. With or without optd district name. Imperf.
1c **1** ½r. blue . . . . 12·50 14·00
8c ½r. black on buff . . . . 12·50 17·00
6 1r. orange . . . . 11·00 1·60
9b 1r. black on green . . . . 2·50 2·75
7b 2r. green . . . . 10·50 1·60
10c 2r. black on red . . . . . 1·40 3·25
4b 4r. red . . . . 55·00 75·00
11b 4r. black on yellow . . . 22·00 35·00
12a 4r. red on yellow . . . . 50·00 60·00
5c 8r. lilac . . . . 75·00 95·00
13a 8r. black on brown . . . . 48·00 95·00
14a 8r. green on brown . . . . 60·00 80·00

1864. Perf.
15a **2** 1r. red 10
16a 2r. blue 15
17a 4r. brown 25
18a 1p. black 95

3 Arms of Mexico

4 Emperor Maximilian

1864. Imperf.
30 **3** 3c. brown £600 £1200
19a ½r. brown . . . . 85·00 £225
31 ½r. purple . . . . 35·00 28·00
31c ½r. grey . . . . 40·00 40·00
32b 1r. blue . . . . 8·25 5·00
33 2r. orange . . . . 2·50 1·60
34 4r. green . . . . 55·00 32·00
35b 8r. red . . . . 80·00 48·00

1864. Imperf.
40 **4** 7c. purple £225 £2500
36c 7c. grey . . . . 32·00 60·00
41 13c. blue . . . . 3·75 5·50
42 25c. orange . . . . 3·25 5·00
39c 50c. green . . . . 11·50 11·50

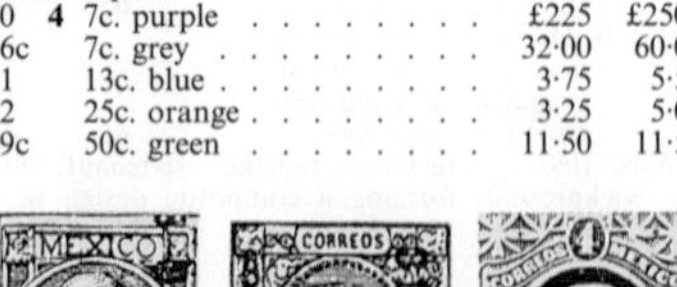

7 Hidalgo 8 Hidalgo 9 Hidalgo

10 Hidalgo 15 Benito Juarez 16

1868. Imperf or perf.
67 **7** 6c. black on brown . . . . 4·50 2·50
68 12c. black on green . . . . 1·90 60
69 25c. blue on pink . . . . . 3·50 45
70b 50c. black on yellow . . . 60·00 7·50
71 100c. black on brown . . . 60·00 22·00
76 100c. brown on brown . . . 95·00 28·00

1872. Imperf or perf.
87 **8** 6c. green . . . . 6·25 6·25
88 12c. blue 80 65
94 25c. red . . . . 3·50 75
90 50c. yellow . . . . 70·00 16·00
91 100c. lilac . . . . 48·00 25·00

1874. Various frames. Perf.

102a	**9**	4c. orange	3·50	6·25
97	**10**	5c. brown	2·10	1·40
98	**9**	10c. black	85	50
105		10c. orange	85	50
99	**10**	25c. blue	35	30
107	**9**	50c. green	7·00	6·25
108		100c. red	9·50	8·25

1879.

115	**15**	1c. brown	1·90	1·75
116		2c. violet	1·75	1·50
117		5c. orange	1·25	60
118		10c. blue	1·60	1·25
127a		10c. brown	1·25	
128		12c. brown	3·25	3·25
129		18c. brown	3·75	3·25
130		24c. mauve	3·75	3·25
119		25c. red	4·00	4·75
132		25c. brown	2·10	
120		50c. green	6·25	6·00
134		50c. yellow	35·00	38·00
121		85c. violet	11·00	9·50
122		100c. black	12·50	11·00
137		100c. orange	40·00	48·00

1882.

138	**16**	2c. green	3·25	2·50
139		3c. red	3·25	2·50
140		6c. blue	2·50	1·90

17 Hidalgo

18

1884.

141	**17**	1c. green	1·25	15
142		2c. green	1·90	25
157		2c. red	6·25	1·40
143		3c. green	3·75	80
158		3c. brown	8·75	2·50
144		4c. green	5·00	80
159		4c. red	12·50	7·50
145		5c. green	5·00	60
160		5c. blue	8·75	1·60
146		6c. green	4·50	45
161		6c. brown	10·00	2·50
147		10c. green	4·75	15
162		10c. orange	7·50	45
148		12c. green	8·75	1·25
163		12c. brown	16·00	3·75
149		20c. green	25·00	95
150		25c. green	45·00	1·90
164		25c. blue	55·00	8·75
151		50c. green	40	1·25
152		1p. blue	40	4·75
153		2p. blue	40	8·75
154		5p. blue	£120	80·00
155		10p. blue	£170	95·00

1886.

196	**18**	1c. green	30	10
209		2c. red	35	10
167		3c. lilac	2·50	1·25
189		3c. red	30	10
198		3c. orange	95	35
168		4c. lilac	4·50	95
211		4c. red	75	50
199		4c. orange	1·10	50
191		5c. blue	20	10
170		6c. lilac	5·00	60
213		6c. red	95	10
200		6c. orange	1·40	35
171		10c. lilac	5·00	15
193		10c. red	10	10
185a		10c. brown	8·75	1·90
201		10c. orange	7·50	35
172		12c. lilac	5·00	3·25
215		12c. red	3·25	3·75
173		20c. lilac	40·00	22·00
194		20c. red	50	20
202		20c. orange	12·50	1·60
174		25c. lilac	16·00	3·75
217		25c. red	95	25
203		25c. orange	4·00	1·10
206		5p. red	£350	£225
207		10p. red	£550	£350

19 Foot Postman

20 Mounted Postman and Pack Mules

21 Statue of Cuauhtemoc

22 Mailcoach

23 Steam Mail Train

1895.

253	**19**	1c. green	20	10
219		2c. red	30	10
220		3c. brown	30	10
221	**20**	4c. orange	1·50	25
257	**21**	5c. blue	35	10
223	**22**	10c. purple	50	10
224	**20**	12c. olive	8·25	3·75
225	**22**	15c. blue	4·00	80
226		20c. red	4·00	40
227		50c. mauve	12·00	4·75
228	**23**	1p. brown	32·00	10·00
229		5p. red	£150	60·00
230		10p. blue	£190	90·00

27

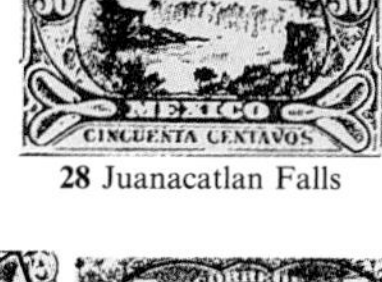

28 Juanacatlan Falls

29 Popocatepetl

30 Cathedral, Mexico

1899. Various frames for T **27**.

266	**27**	1c. green	80	10
276		1c. purple	60	10
267		2c. red	2·40	10
277		2c. green	80	10
268		3c. brown	1·60	10
278		4c. red	2·50	20
269		5c. blue	2·50	10
279		5c. orange	45	10
270		10c. brown and purple	3·25	15
280		10c. orange and blue	2·50	10
271		15c. purple and lavender	4·25	10
272		20c. blue and red	4·75	15
273a	**28**	50c. black and purple	19·00	1·25
281		50c. black and red	40·00	3·50
274	**29**	1p. black and blue	42·00	1·90
275	**30**	5p. black and red	£130	6·25

32 Josefa Ortiz

40 Hidalgo at Dolores

1910. Centenary of First Independence Movement.

282	**32**	1c. purple	10	10
283	–	2c. green	10	10
284	–	3c. brown	25	10
285	–	4c. red	1·25	20
286	–	5c. orange	10	10
287	–	10c. orange and blue	80	10
288	–	15c. lake and slate	4·50	20
289	–	20c. blue and lake	2·50	10
290	**40**	50c. black and brown	6·25	95
291	–	1p. black and blue	7·50	1·10
292	–	5p. black and red	28·00	2·75

DESIGNS: As Type **32**: 2c. L. Vicario; 3c. L. Rayon; 4c. J. Aldama; 5c. M. Hidalgo; 10c. I. Allende; 15c. E. Gonzalez; 20c. M. Abasolo. As Type **40**: 1p. Mass on Mt. of Crosses; 5p. Capture of Granaditas.

REVOLUTIONARY PROVISIONALS

For full list of the provisional issues made during the Civil War from 1913 onwards, see the Stanley Gibbons Part 15 (Central America) Catalogue.

CONSTITUTIONALIST GENERAL ISSUES

CT 1

1914. "Transitorio".

CT1	CT **1**	1c. blue	20	15
CT2		2c. green	30	15
CT3		4c. blue	7·00	1·60
CT4		5c. green	7·00	1·90
CT9		5c. green	10	10
CT5		10c. red	15	15
CT6		20c. brown	25	25
CT7		50c. red	1·60	2·10
CT8		1p. violet	8·75	10·00

The words of value on No. CT4 are 2 × 14 mm and on No. CT9 are 2½ × 16 mm.

1914. Victory of Torreon. Nos. CT1/7 optd **Victoria de TORREON ABRIL 2-1914**.

CT10	CT **1**	1c. blue	95·00	80·00
CT11		2c. green	£110	95·00
CT12		4c. blue	£130	£160
CT13		5c. green	11·50	12·50
CT14		10c. red	60·00	60·00
CT15		20c. brown	£1100	£1200
CT16		50c. red	£1200	£1200

CT 3

CT 4

1914. Handstamped with Type CT **3**. (a) Nos. D282/6.

CT17	D **32**	1c. blue	8·75	10·00
CT18		2c. blue	8·75	10·00
CT19		4c. blue	8·75	10·00
CT20		5c. blue	8·75	10·00
CT21		10c. blue	8·75	10·00

(b) Nos. 282/92.

CT22	**32**	1c. purple	35	30
CT23	–	2c. green	95	80
CT24	–	3c. brown	95	80
CT25	–	4c. red	1·60	1·25
CT26	–	5c. orange	20	10
CT27	–	10c. orange and blue	1·90	1·25
CT28	–	15c. lake and slate	3·25	1·90
CT29	–	20c. blue and lake	6·25	3·75
CT30	**40**	50c. black and brown	7·50	5·00
CT31	–	1p. black and blue	16·00	6·25
CT32	–	5p. black and red	£100	95·00

1914.

CT33	CT **4**	1c. pink	80	12·50
CT34		2c. green	80	11·50
CT35		3c. orange	80	12·50
CT36		5c. red	60	5·00
CT37		10c. green	60	22·00
CT38		25c. blue	10·00	

CT 5

1914. "Denver" issue.

CT39	CT **5**	1c. blue	15	20
CT40		2c. green	15	15
CT41		3c. orange	25	15
CT42		5c. red	25	15
CT43		10c. red	35	40
CT44		15c. mauve	60	1·10
CT45		50c. yellow	1·25	1·60
CT46		1p. violet	5·25	7·50

1914. Optd **GOBIERNO CONSTITUCIONALISTA**. (a) Nos. 279 and 271/2.

CT50	–	5c. orange	48·00	35·00
CT51	–	15c. purple and lavender	95·00	95·00
CT52	–	20c. blue and red	£300	£250

(b) Nos. D282/6.

CT53	D **32**	1c. blue	1·10	1·10
CT54		2c. blue	1·25	1·25
CT55		4c. blue	9·50	9·50
CT56		5c. blue	9·50	9·50
CT57		10c. blue	1·60	1·60

(c) Nos. 282/92.

CT58	**32**	1c. purple	10	10
CT59	–	2c. green	10	10
CT60	–	3c. brown	20	20
CT61	–	4c. red	25	25
CT62	–	5c. orange	10	10
CT63	–	10c. orange and blue	10	10
CT64	–	15c. lake and slate	35	30
CT65	–	20c. blue and lake	35	35
CT66	**40**	50c. black and brown	1·10	75
CT67	–	1p. black and blue	4·75	3·25
CT68	–	5p. black and red	25·00	19·00

CONVENTIONIST ISSUES

(CV **1**) Villa–Zapata Monogram

1914. Optd with Type CV **1**. (a) Nos. 266/75.

CV 1	**27**	1c. green	60·00	
CV 2		2c. red	60·00	
CV 3		3c. brown	32·00	
CV 4		5c. blue	60·00	
CV 5		10c. brown and purple	60·00	
CV 6		15c. purple and lavender	60·00	
CV 7		20c. blue and red	60·00	
CV 8	**28**	50c. black and red	£160	
CV 9	**29**	1p. black and blue	£160	
CV10	**30**	5p. black and red	£300	

(b) Nos. 276/80.

CV11	**27**	1c. purple	60·00	
CV12		2c. green	60·00	
CV13		4c. red	60·00	
CV14		5c. orange	7·75	
CV15		10c. orange and blue	48·00	

(c) Nos. D282/6.

CV16	D **32**	1c. blue	6·00	6·25
CV17		2c. blue	6·00	6·25
CV18		4c. blue	6·00	6·25
CV19		5c. blue	6·00	6·25
CV20		10c. blue	60·00	6·25

(d) Nos. 282/92.

CV21	**32**	1c. purple	40	40
CV22	–	2c. green	45	20
CV23	–	3c. brown	30	30
CV24	–	4c. red	1·25	1·25
CV25	–	5c. orange	10	10
CV26	–	10c. orange and blue	95	95
CV27	–	15c. lake and slate	95	95
CV28	–	20c. blue and lake	95	95
CV29	**40**	50c. black and brown	6·25	6·25
CV30	–	1p. black and blue	9·50	9·50
CV31	–	5p. black and red	95·00	95·00

CONSTITUTIONALIST PROVISIONAL ISSUES

CT 10

CT 11 Carranza Monogram

1914. Nos. 282/92 handstamped with Type CT **10**.

CT69	**32**	1c. purple	6·00	5·50
CT70	–	2c. green	6·00	5·50
CT71	–	3c. brown	6·00	5·50
CT72	–	4c. red	7·50	7·00
CT73	–	5c. orange	90	90
CT74	–	10c. orange and blue	7·00	6·25
CT75	–	15c. lake and slate	7·00	6·25
CT76	–	20c. blue and lake	8·75	5·75
CT77	**40**	50c. black and brown	19·00	19·00
CT78	–	1p. black and blue	28·00	
CT79	–	5p. black and red	£100	

1915. Optd with Type CT **11**. (a) No. 271.

CT80	–	15c. purple and lavender	50·00	50·00

(b) No. 279.

CT81	–	5c. orange	12·50	12·50

(c) Nos. D282/6.

CT82	D **32**	1c. blue	7·00	
CT83		2c. blue	7·00	
CT84		4c. blue	7·00	
CT85		5c. blue	7·00	
CT86		10c. blue	7·00	

(d) Nos. 282/92.

CT87	**32**	1c. purple	35	35
CT88	–	2c. green	35	30
CT89	–	3c. brown	35	35
CT90	–	4c. red	1·25	1·25
CT91	–	5c. orange	10	10
CT92	–	10c. orange and blue	75	75
CT93	–	15c. lake and slate	75	75
CT94	–	20c. blue and lake	75	75
CT95	**40**	50c. black and brown	6·25	6·25
CT96	–	1p. black and blue	9·50	9·50
CT97	–	5p. black and red	95·00	95·00

GENERAL ISSUES.

43 Coat of Arms

44 Statue of Cuauhtemoc

45 Ignacio Zaragoza

1915. Portraits as T **45**. Roul or perf.

293	**43**	1c. violet	10	10
294	**44**	2c. green	20	15
304	**45**	3c. brown	20	15
305		4c. red (Morelos)	20	20
306		5c. orange (Madero)	25	15
307		10c. blue (Juarez)	15	10

46 Map of Mexico

47 Lighthouse, Veracruz

48 Post Office, Mexico City

1915.

299	**46**	40c. grey	2·25	70
433		40c. mauve	1·75	25
300	**47**	1p. grey and brown	35	60
411		1p. grey and blue	22·00	60
301	**48**	5p. blue and lake	5·00	5·50
412		5p. grey and green	1·25	1·50

(49)

50 V. Carranza

1916. Silver Currency. Optd with T **49**. (a) No. 271.
309 – 15c. purple and lavender £250 £250
(b) No. 279.
309a – 5c. orange 55·00 55·00
(c) Nos. 282/92.
310 **32** 1c. purple 2·10 3·25
311 – 2c. green 25 15
312 – 3c. brown 25 15
313 – 4c. red 3·75 5·00
314 – 5c. orange 10 10
315 – 10c. orange and blue 60 95
316 – 15c. lake and slate 1·10 1·90
317 – 20c. blue and lake 1·10 1·90
318 **40** 50c. black and brown 5·25 3·25
319 – 1p. black and blue 9·50 4·00
320 – 5p. black and red 95·00 80·00
(d) Nos. CT1/3 and CT5/8.
320b CT **1** 1c. blue 15·00
320c 2c. green 7·50
320d 4c. blue £160
320e 10c. red 1·40
320f 20c. brown 1·90
320g 50c. red 9·50
320h 1p. violet 15·00
(e) Nos. CT39/46.
321 CT **5** 1c. blue 2·40 12·00
322 2c. green 2·40 7·00
323 3c. orange 45 7·00
324 5c. red 45 7·00
325 10c. red 45 3·25
326 15c. mauve 45 7·00
327 50c. yellow 70 8·00
328 1p. violet 6·00 15·00
(f) Nos. CT58/68.
329 **32** 1c. purple 1·60 2·50
330 – 2c. green 35 30
331 – 3c. brown 30 30
332 – 4c. red 30 30
333 – 5c. orange 50 15
334 – 10c. orange and blue 35 30
335 – 15c. lake and slate 40 40
336 – 20c. blue and lake 40 40
337 **40** 50c. black and brown 4·75 3·75
338 – 1p. black and blue 10·00 10·00
339 – 5p. black and red 95·00 85·00
(g) Nos. CV22/9.
340 **32** 1c. purple 7·00 9·50
341 – 2c. green 75 45
342 – 3c. brown 2·00 2·75
343 – 4c. red 8·25 9·50
344 – 5c. orange 2·75 3·75
345 – 10c. orange and blue 7·50 8·75
346 – 15c. lake and slate 7·50 8·75
347 – 20c. blue and lake 7·50 8·75
(h) Nos. CT87/97.
348 **32** 1c. purple 1·60 2·10
349 – 2c. green 30 30
350 – 3c. brown 25 20
351 – 4c. red 3·25 3·75
352 – 5c. orange 40 10
353 – 10c. orange and blue 75 1·25
354 – 15c. lake and slate 60 30
355 – 20c. blue and red 60 55
356 **40** 50c. black and brown 4·75 5·50
357 – 1p. black and blue 7·00 7·50

1916. Carranza's Triumphal Entry into Mexico City.
358 **50** 10c. brown 7·50 8·25
359 10c. blue 60 30

(51)

1916. Optd with T **51**. (a) Nos. D282/6.
360 D **32** 5c. on 1c. blue 1·60 1·60
361 10c. on 2c. blue 1·60 1·60
362 20c. on 4c. blue 1·60 1·60
363 25c. on 5c. blue 1·60 1·60
364 60c. on 10c. blue 75 75
365 1p. on 1c. blue 75 75
366 1p. on 2c. blue 75 75
367 1p. on 4c. blue 75 40
368 1p. on 5c. blue 1·60 1·60
369 1p. on 10c. blue 1·60 1·60
(b) Nos. 282, 286 and 283.
370 **32** 5c. on 1c. purple 10 10
371 10c. on 1c. purple 10 10
372 – 20c. on 5c. orange 10 10
373 – 25c. on 5c. orange 15 15
374 – 60c. on 2c. green 10·50 12·50
(c) Nos. CT39/40.
375 CT **5** 60c. on 1c. blue 1·90 3·75
376 60c. on 2c. green 1·90 3·75
(d) Nos. CT58, CT62 and CT59.
377 **32** 5c. on 1c. purple 10 10
378 – 10c. on 1c. purple 60 60
379 – 25c. on 5c. purple 15 15
380 – 60c. on 2c. green £130 £170
(e) No. CV25.
381 – 25c. on 5c. orange 15 10
(f) Nos. CT87, CT91 and CT88.
382 **32** 5c. on 1c. purple 9·50 12·50
383 – 10c. on 1c. purple 3·25 4·75
385 – 25c. on 5c. orange 50 95
386 – 60c. on 2c. green £140

1916. Nos. D282/6 surch **GPM** and value.
387 D **32** $2.50 on 1c. blue 60 60
388 $2.50 on 2c. blue 6·25 6·25
389 $2.50 on 4c. blue 6·25 6·25
390 $2.50 on 5c. blue 6·25 6·25
391 $2.50 on 10c. blue 6·25 6·25

52a Arms **53** Zaragoza

1916.
392 **52a** 1c. purple 15 15

1917. Portraits. Roul or perf.
393 **53** 1c. violet 25 10
393a 1c. grey 70 20
394 – 2c. green (Vazquez) 35 10
395 – 3c. brown (Suarez) 35 10
396 – 4c. red (Carranza) 60 20
397 – 5c. blue (Herrera) 85 10
398 – 10c. blue (Madero) 1·40 10
399 – 20c. lake (Dominguez) 14·00 35
400 – 30c. purple (Serdan) 38·00 60
401 – 30c. black (Serdan) 45·00 60

1919. Red Cross Fund. Surch with cross and premium.
413 5c.+3c. blue (No. 397) 9·00 9·50
414 10c.+5c. blue (No. 398) 11·00 9·50

56 Meeting of Iturbide and Guerrero

1921. Centenary of Declaration of Independence.
415 **56** 10c. brown and blue 9·50 1·90
416 – 10p. black and brown 9·50 22·00
DESIGN: 10p. Entry into Mexico City.

58 Golden Eagle

1922. Air.
454 **58** 25c. sepia and lake 50 25
455 25c. sepia and green 55 30
456 50c. red and blue 70 40

59 Morelos Monument **60** Fountain and Aqueduct

61 Pyramid of the Sun, Teotihuacan **62** Castle of Chapultepec

63 Columbus Monument **74** Benito Juarez

64 Juarez Colonnade **65** Monument to Dona Josefa Ortiz de Dominguez

66 Cuauhtemoc Monument **68** Ministry of Communications

69 National Theatre and Palace of Fine Arts

1923. Roul or perf.
436 **59** 1c. brown 25 10
437 **60** 2c. red 15 10
438 **61** 3c. brown 10 10
429 **62** 4c. green 60 10
440 **63** 4c. green 15 10
441 5c. orange 10 10
453 **74** 8c. orange 15 10
423 **64** 10c. brown 4·75 10
442 **66** 10c. lake 15 10
443 **65** 20c. blue 35 10
426 **66** 30c. green 35·00 2·50
432 **64** 30c. green 45 10
434 **68** 50c. brown 30 10
435 **69** 1p. blue and lake 50 25

70 **72** Sr. Francisco Garcia y Santos

73 Post Office, Mexico City

1926. 2nd Pan-American Postal Congress. Inscr as in T **70/3**.
445 **70** 2c. red 1·25 35
446 – 4c. green 1·25 40
447 **70** 5c. orange 1·25 25
448 – 10c. red 1·90 25
449 **72** 20c. blue 1·90 50
450 30c. green 3·25 1·90
451 40c. mauve 6·25 1·60
452 **73** 1p. blue and brown 17·00 3·75
DESIGN—As Type **70**: 4c., 10c. Map of North and South America.

1929. Child Welfare. Optd **Proteccion a la Infancia**.
457 **59** 1c. brown 25 15

77 **79** Capt. Emilio Carranza

1929. Obligatory Tax. Child Welfare.
459 **77** 1c. violet 10 10
461 2c. green 20 10
462 5c. brown 15 10

1929. Air. 1st Death Anniv of Carranza (airman).
463 **79** 5c. sepia and green 55 30
464 10c. red and sepia 65 35
465 15c. green and violet 1·90 60
466 20c. black and sepia 60 35
467 50c. black and red 3·75 1·25
468 1p. sepia and black 7·75 1·75

80

1929. Air. Perf or roul (10, 15, 20, 50c.), roul (5, 25c.), perf (others).
476a **80** 5c. blue 10 10
477 10c. violet 10 10
478 15c. red 15 10
479 20c. brown 75 10
480 25c. purple 45 40
472 30c. black 10 10
473 35c. blue 15 10
481 50c. red 45 35
474 1p. blue and black 60 30
475 5p. blue and red 2·50 2·10
476 10p. brown and violet 3·75 4·50

81 **87**

1929. Air. Aviation Week.
482 **81** 20c. violet 60 50
483 40c. green 55·00 48·00

1930. 2nd Pan-American Postal Congress issue optd **HABILITADO 1930.**
484 **70** 2c. red 2·10 1·40
485 – 4c. green 2·10 1·25
486 **70** 5c. orange 2·10 1·10
487 – 10c. red 3·75 1·25
488 **72** 20c. blue 5·00 1·90
489 30c. green 4·50 2·10
490 40c. mauve 6·25 4·50
491 **73** 1p. blue and brown 5·50 3·75

1930. Air. National Tourist Congress. Optd **Primer Congreso Nacional de Turismo. Mexico. Abril 20-27 de 1930.**
492 **80** 10c. violet (No. 477) 1·25 60

1930. Obligatory Tax. Child Welfare. Surch **HABILITADO $0.01.**
494 **77** 1c. on 2c. green 30 15
495 1c. on 5c. brown 60 15

1930. Air. Optd **HABILITADO 1930.**
496 **79** 5c. sepia and green 3·50 2·75
497 15c. green and violet 5·50 4·75

1930. Air. Optd **HABILITADO Aereo 1930-1931.**
498 **79** 5c. sepia and green 3·75 4·00
499 10c. red and sepia 2·10 2·50
500 15c. green and violet 4·00 4·50
501 20c. black and sepia 4·50 3·50
502 50c. black and red 8·75 6·25
503 1p. sepia and black 2·50 1·75

1931. Obligatory Tax. Child Welfare. No. CT58 optd **PRO INFANCIA.**
504 **32** 1c. purple 20 15

1931. Fourth Centenary of Puebla.
505 **87** 10c. brown and blue 1·60 25

88

1931. Air. Aeronautic Exhibition.
506 **88** 25c. lake 2·00 1·60

1931. Nos. 446/52 optd **HABILITADO 1931.**
508 – 4c. green 35·00
509 **70** 5c. orange 6·25
510 – 10c. red 6·25
511 **72** 20c. blue 6·25
512 30c. green 11·00
513 40c. mauve 16·00
514 **73** 1p. blue and brown 19·00

1931. Air. Surch **HABILITADO Quince centavos.** Perf or rouletted.
516 **80** 15c. on 20c. sepia 20 10

1932. Air. Surch in words and figures. Perf. or roul.
517 **88** 20c. on 25c. lake 30 15
521 **80** 30c. on 20c. sepia 15 10
519 **58** 40c. on 25c. sepia and lake 2·10 1·10
520 40c. on 25c. sepia & green 40·00 40·00
522 **80** 80c. on 25c. (No. 480) 90 60

1932. Air. 4th Death Anniv of Emilio Carranza. Optd **HABILITADO AEREO-1932.**
523 **79** 5c. sepia and green 3·75 3·25
524 10c. red and sepia 3·25 1·90
525 15c. green and violet 3·75 2·50
526 20c. black and sepia 3·25 1·75
527 50c. black and red 22·00 22·00

92 Fray Bartolome de las Casas

1933. Roul.
528 **92** 15c. blue 15 10

93 Mexican Geographical and Statistical Society's Arms
94 National Theatre and Palace of Fine Arts

1933. 21st Int Statistical Congress and Centenary of Mexican Geographical and Statistical Society.
529 **93** 2c. green (postage) 75 20
530 5c. brown 1·10 25
531 10c. blue 35 10
532 1p. violet 32·00 38·00

533 **94** 20c. violet and red (air) 2·10 85
534 30c. violet and brown 4·25 3·75
535 1p. violet and green 42·00 45·00

95 Mother and Child
98 Nevada de Toluca

1934. National University. Inscr "PRO-UNIVERSIDAD".
543 **95** 1c. orange (postage) 10 10
544 – 5c. green 1·00 15
545 – 10c. lake 1·25 30
546 – 20c. blue 5·00 3·25
547 – 30c. black 8·75 7·50
548 – 40c. brown 15·00 10·00
549 – 50c. blue 28·00 32·00
550 – 1p. black and red 32·00 30·00
551 – 5p. brown and black £120 £160
552 – 10p. violet and brown £500 £650
DESIGNS: 5c. Archer; 10c. Festive headdress; 20c. Woman decorating pot; 30c. Indian and Inca Lily; 40c. Potter; 50c. Sculptor; 1p. Gold craftsman; 5p. Girl offering fruit; 10p. Youth burning incense.

553 **98** 20c. orange (air) 1·75 1·75
554 – 30c. purple and mauve 3·50 4·25
555 – 50c. brown and green 4·00 6·25
556 – 75c. green and black 4·75 8·75
557 – 1p. blue and green 5·00 6·25
558 – 5p. blue and brown 26·00 60·00
559 – 10p. red and blue 80·00 £130
560 – 20p. red and brown £475 £750
DESIGNS—Airplane over: 30c. Pyramids of the Sun and Moon, Teotihuacan; 50c. Mt. Ajusco; 75c. Mts. Ixtaccihuatl and Popocatepetl; 1p. Bridge over R. Papagallo; 5p. Chapultepec Castle entrance; 10p. Orizaba Peak, Mt. Citlaltepetl; 20p. Girl and Aztec calendar stone.

101 Zapoteca Indian Woman
110 Coat of Arms

1934. Pres. Cardenas' Assumption of Office. Designs as Type **101** and **110**. Imprint "OFICINA IMPRESORA DE HACIENDA-MEXICO" at foot of stamp. (a) Postage.
561 – 1c. orange 30 10
562 **101** 2c. green 30 10
563 – 4c. red 45 15
564 – 5c. brown 30 10
565 – 10c. blue 40 10
565a – 10c. violet 80 10
566 – 15c. blue 2·50 15
567 – 20c. green 1·25 10
567a – 20c. blue 85 10
568 – 30c. red 35 10
653 – 30c. blue 40 10
569 – 40c. brown 40 10
570 – 50c. black 45 10
571 **110** 1p. red and brown 1·60 10
572 – 5p. violet and orange 4·75 55
DESIGNS: 1c. Yalalteca Indian; 4c. Revolution Monument; 5c. Los Remedios Tower; 10c. Cross of Palenque; 15c. Independence Monument, Mexico City; 20c. Independence Monument, Puebla; 30c. "Heroic Children" Monument, Mexico City; 40c. Sacrificial Stone; 50c. Ruins of Mitla, Oaxaca; 5p. Mexican "Charro" (Horseman).

112 Mictlantecuhtli
120 "Peasant admiration"

(b) Air.
573 **112** 5c. black 20 10
574 – 10c. brown 45 10
575 – 15c. green 90 10
576 – 20c. red 1·90 10
577 – 30c. olive 35 10
577a – 40c. blue 60 10
578 – 50c. green 1·60 10
579 – 1p. red and green 2·50 10
580 **120** 5p. black and red 4·50 25
DESIGNS—HORIZ: 10c. Temple at Quetzalcoatl; 15c. Aeroplane over Citlaltepetl; 20c. Popocatepetl; 30c. Pegasus; 50c. Uruapan pottery; 1p. "Warrior Eagle". VERT: 40c. Aztec idol.

121 Tractor
122 Arms of Chiapas

1935. Industrial Census.
581 **121** 10c. violet 2·50 25

1935. Air. Amelia Earhart Flight to Mexico. No. 576 optd **AMELIA EARHART VUELO DE BUENA VOLUNTAD MEXICO 1935**.
581a 20c. red £1900 £2500

1935. Annexation of Chiapas Centenary.
582 **122** 10c. blue 35 15

123 E. Zapata
124 Francisco Madero

1935. 25th Anniv of Revolutionary Plans of Ayala and San Luis Potosi.
583 **123** 10c. violet (postage) 35 10
584 **124** 20c. red (air) 20 10

129 Nuevo Laredo Road
131 Rio Corona Bridge

1936. Opening of Nuevo Laredo Highway (Mexico City–U.S.A.).
591 – 5c. red and green (postage) 15 10
592 – 10c. grey 25 10
593 **129** 20c. green and brown 75 50
DESIGNS: As Type **129**: 5c. Symbolical Map of Mexico–U.S.A. road; 10c. Matalote Bridge.

594 – 10c. blue (air) 30 10
595 **131** 20c. orange and violet 30 10
596 – 40c. green and blue 40 30
DESIGNS: As Type **131**: 10c. Tasquillo Bridge over Rio Tula; 40c. Guayalejo Bridge.

1936. 1st Congress of Industrial Medicine and Hygiene. Optd **PRIMER CONGRESO NAL. DE HIGIENE Y. MED. DEL TRABAJO**.
597 – 10c. violet (No. 565a) 30 20

1937. As Nos. 561/4, 565a and 576, but smaller. Imprint at foot changed to "TALLERES DE IMP.(RESION) DE EST. (AMPILLAS) Y VALORES-MEXICO".
708 1c. orange (postage) 25 10
709 2c. green 25 10
600 4c. red 40 10
601 5c. brown 35 10
602 10c. violet 25 10
603 20c. red (air) 80 10

134 Blacksmith

1938. Carranza's "Plan of Guadelupe". 25th Anniv. Inscr "CONMEMORATIVO PLAN DE GUADALUPE", etc.
604 **134** 5c. brown & blk (postage) 30 10
605 – 10c. brown 10 10
606 – 20c. orange and brown 3·25 50
607 – 20c. blue and red (air) 20 10
608 – 40c. red and blue 45 15
609 – 1p. blue and yellow 3·00 1·40
DESIGNS—VERT: 10c. Peasant revolutionary; 20c. Preaching revolt. HORIZ: 20c. Horseman; 40c. Biplane; 1p. Mounted horseman.

140 Arch of the Revolution
141 Cathedral and Constitution Square

1938. 16th International Town Planning and Housing Congress, Mexico City. Inscr as in T **140/1**.
610 **140** 5c. brown (postage) 80 30
611 – 5c. olive 1·60 1·40
612 – 10c. orange 8·75 7·00
613 – 10c. brown 30 10
614 – 20c. black 2·10 2·50
615 – 20c. lake 11·50 9·50
DESIGNS: As Type **140**: 10c. National Theatre; 20c. Independence Column.

616 **141** 20c. red (air) 15 10
617 – 20c. violet 8·75 6·25
619 – 40c. green 4·50 3·25
620 – 1p. slate 4·50 3·25
621 – 1p. light blue 4·50 3·25
DESIGNS: As Type **141**: 40c. Chichen Itza Ruins (Yucatan); 1p. Acapulco Beach.

142 Mosquito and Malaria Victim

1939. Obligatory Tax. Anti-malaria Campaign.
622 **142** 1c. blue 95 10

143 Statue of an Indian
144 Statue of Woman Pioneer and Child

1939. Tulsa Philatelic Convention, Oklahoma.
623 **143** 10c. red (postage) 20 10
624 **144** 20c. brown (air) 50 20
625 40c. green 1·25 60
626 1p. violet 80 45

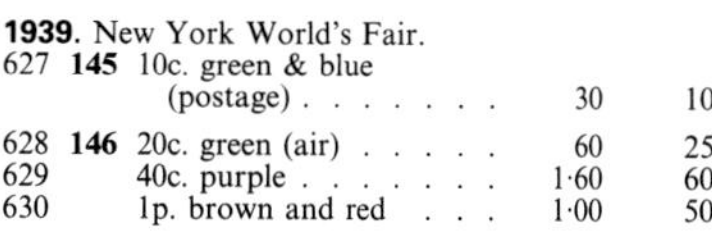
145 Mexican Pavilion, World's Fair
146 Morelos Statue on Mexican Pavilion

1939. Air. F. Sarabia non-stop Flight to New York. Optd **SARABIA Vuelo MEXICO-NUEVA YORK**.
626a **146** 20c. blue and red £160 £300

1939. New York World's Fair.
627 **145** 10c. green & blue (postage) 30 10
628 **146** 20c. green (air) 60 25
629 40c. purple 1·60 60
630 1p. brown and red 1·00 50

147 J. de Zumarraga
152 "Building"

154 "Transport"

1939. 400th Anniv of Printing in Mexico.
631 **147** 2c. black (postage) 35 10
632 – 5c. green 35 10
633 – 10c. red 10 10
634 – 20c. blue (air) 10 10
635 – 40c. green 30 10
636 – 1p. red and brown 55 35
DESIGNS: 5c. First printing works in Mexico; 10c. Antonio D. Mendoza; 20c. Book frontispiece; 40c. Title page of first law book printed in America; 1p. Oldest Mexican Colophon.

1939. National Census. Inscr "CENSOS 1939 1940".
637 **152** 2c. red (postage) 60 10
638 – 5c. green 10 10
639 – 10c. brown 10 10
640 **154** 20c. blue (air) 2·50 40
641 – 40c. orange 35 10
642 – 1p. violet and blue 1·75 35
DESIGNS: As Type **152**: 5c. "Agriculture"; 10c. "Commerce". As Type **154**: 40c. "Industry"; 1p. "Seven Censuses".

155 "Penny Black"
156 Roadside Monument

1940. Centenary of First Adhesive Postage Stamps.
643 **155** 5c. yellow & black (postage) 45 25
644 10c. purple 10 10
645 20c. red and blue 15 10
646 1p. red and grey 4·50 2·50
647 5p. blue and black 23·00 19·00
648 5c. green and black (air) 45 30
649 10c. blue and brown 35 10
650 20c. violet and red 25 10
651 1p. brown and red 2·10 3·25
652 5p. brown and green 25·00 35·00

1940. Opening of Highway from Mexico City to Guadalajara.
654 **156** 6c. green 35 10

159 Original College at Patzcuaro

1940. 4th Centenary of National College of St. Nicholas de Hidalgo.
655 – 2c. violet (postage) 65 25
656 – 5c. red 40 10
657 – 10c. olive 40 10
658 **159** 20c. green (air) 20 10
659 – 40c. orange 25 10
660 – 1p. violet, brown & orange 60 45
DESIGNS—VERT: 2c. V. de Quiroga; 5c. M. Ocampo; 10c. St. Nicholas College Arms; 40c. Former College at Morelia. HORIZ: 1p. Present College at Morelia.

163 Pirate Galleon

1940. 400th Anniv of Campeche. Inscr as in T **163**.
661 – 10c. red & brown (postage) 1·90 60
662 **163** 20c. brown and red (air) 90 35
663 – 40c. green and black 75 25
664 – 1p. black and blue 3·25 1·90
DESIGNS: 10c. Campeche City Arms; 40c. St. Miguel Castel; 1p. Temple of San Francisco.

165 Helmsman 166 Miguel Hidalgo y Costilla

1940. Inauguration of Pres. Camacho.
665 **165** 2c. orange & black (postage) . . . . 1·00 30
666 5c. blue and brown . . . 3·75 2·10
667 10c. olive and brown . . 1·40 40
668 20c. grey and orange (air) 1·25 60
669 40c. brown and green . . 1·25 95
670 1p. purple and red . . . 2·10 1·25

1940. Compulsory Tax. Dolores Hidalgo Memorial Fund.
671 **166** 1c. red 30 10

168 Javelin throwing 169 Dark Nebula in Orion

1941. National Athletic Meeting.
675 **168** 10c. green . . . . 2·10 25

1942. Inauguration of Astro-physical Observatory at Tonanzintla, Puebla.
676 **169** 2c. blue & violet (postage) 80 50
677 – 5c. blue . . . . 5·50 1·25
678 – 10c. blue and orange . . 5·50 25
679 – 20c. blue and green (air) 7·75 1·90
680 – 40c. blue and red . . . . 7·00 2·50
681 – 1p. black and orange . . 7·00 2·75
DESIGNS: 5c. Solar Eclipse; 10c. Spiral Galaxy of the "Hunting Dog"; 20c. Extra-Galactic Nebula in Virgo; 40c. Ring Nebula in Lyra; 1p. Russell Diagram.

171 Ruins of Chichen-Itza 172 Merida Nunnery

1942. 400th Anniv of Merida. Inscr as in T **171/2**.
682 **171** 2c. brown (postage) . . . 70 30
683 – 5c. red . . . . 1·40 30
684 – 10c. violet 80 10
685 **172** 20c. blue (air) 95 25
686 – 40c. green . . . . 1·40 1·25
687 – 1p. red . . . . 1·60 1·25
DESIGNS–VERT: 5c. Mayan sculpture; 10c. Arms of Merida; 40c. Montejo University Gateway. HORIZ: 1p. Campanile of Merida Cathedral

173 "Mother Earth" 175 Hidalgo Monument

1942. 2nd Inter-American Agricultural Conference.
688 **173** 2c. brown (postage) . . . 40 20
689 – 5c. blue . . . . 1·90 55
690 – 10c. orange 60 25
691 – 20c. green (air) . . . . . 1·25 25
692 – 40c. brown 75 25
693 – 1p. violet . . . . 1·60 1·25
DESIGNS: 5c. Sowing wheat; 10c. Western Hemisphere carrying torch; 20c. Corn; 40c. Coffee; 1p. Bananas.

1942. 400th Anniv of Guadalajara.
694 **175** 2c. brown & blue (postage) 15 15
695 – 5c. red and black 60 25
696 – 10c. blue and red 60 20
697 – 20c. black and green (air) 80 35
698 – 40c. green and olive . . . 1·10 50
699 – 1p. violet and brown . . 80 60
DESIGNS—VERT: 5c. Government Palace; 10c. Guadalajara. HORIZ: 20c. St. Paul's Church, Zapopan; 40c. Sanctuary of Our Lady of Guadalupe; 1p. Arms of Guadalajara.

186 Saltillo Athenaeum, Coahuila

1942. 75th Anniv of Saltillo Athenaeum.
700 **186** 10c. black 90 20

189 Birthplace of Allende 190 "Liberty"

1943. 400th Anniv of San Miguel de Allende.
701 – 2c. blue (postage) 50 15
702 – 5c. brown 55 15
703 – 10c. black . . . . 2·10 50
704 – 20c. green (air) 45 30
705 **189** 40c. purple 60 30
706 – 1p. red . . . . 1·75 1·60
DESIGNS—VERT: 2c. Cupola de las Monjas; 5c. Gothic Church; 10c. Gen. de Allende. HORIZ: 20c. San Miguel de Allende; 1p. Church seen through cloisters.

1944.
707 **190** 12c. brown 20 10

192 Dr. de Castorena 194 "Flight"

1944. 3rd National Book Fair.
732 **192** 12c. brown (postage) . . 40 10
733 – 25c. green (air) 45 10
DESIGN: 25c. Microphone, book and camera.

1944. Air.
734 **194** 25c. brown 30 10

195 Hands clasping Globe

1945. Inter-American Conference.
735 **195** 12c. red (postage) 25 10
736 1p. green 45 10
737 5p. brown . . . . 3·50 2·75
738 10p. black . . . . 6·25 5·00
739 25c. orange (air) 10 10
740 1p. green 15 10
741 5p. blue . . . . 1·50 1·10
742 10p. red . . . . 4·00 3·25
743 20p. blue . . . . 8·75 8·00

196 La Paz Theatre, San Luis Potosi

1945. Reconstruction of La Paz Theatre, San Luis Potosi.
744 **196** 12c. pur & blk (postage) 20 10
745 1p. blue and black . . . 30 10
746 5p. red and black . . . . 3·75 3·25
747 10p. green and black . . 8·25 7·50
748 30c. green (air) 10 10
749 1p. purple and green . . . 15 10
750 5p. black and green . . . 1·40 1·25
751 10p. blue and green . . . 2·75 2·10
752 20p. green and black . . 6·00 5·25

197 Fountain of Diana the Huntress 198 Removing Bandage

1945.
753 **197** 3c. violet 40 10

1945. Literacy Campaign.
754 **198** 2c. blue (postage) 15 10
755 6c. orange 20 10
756 12c. blue 20 10
757 1p. olive 25 10
758 5p. red and black . . . . 2·40 1·90
759 10p. green and blue . . . 13·00 12·50
760 30c. green (air) 10 10
761 1p. red 15 10
762 5p. blue . . . . 1·60 1·40
763 10p. red . . . . 2·75 2·75
764 20p. brown and green . . 13·00 12·50

199 Founder of National Post Office 200 O.N.U., Olive Branch and Globe

201 O.N.U. and Flags of United Nations

1946. Foundation of Posts in Mexico in 1580.
765 **199** 8c. black 60 10

1946. United Nations.
766 **200** 2c. olive (postage) 15 10
767 6c. brown 15 10
768 12c. blue 10 10
769 1p. green 30 10
770 5p. red . . . . 3·25 3·25
771 10p. blue . . . . 14·00 12·50
772 **201** 3c. brown (air) 10 10
773 1p. grey 10 10
774 5p. green and brown . . . 70 50
775 10p. brown and sepia . . 2·75 2·50
776 20p. red and slate . . . . 6·75 4·75

202 Zacatecas City Arms 205 Don Genaro Codina and Zacatecas

1946. 400th Anniv of Zacatecas.
777 **202** 2c. brown (postage) . . . 25 10
778 – 12c. blue 15 10
779 – 1p. mauve 30 10
780 – 5p. red . . . . 3·50 1·90
781 – 10p. black and blue . . . 20·00 6·25
DESIGNS: 1p. Statue of Gen. Ortega; 5p. R. L. Velarde (poet); 10p. F. G. Salinas.

782 – 30c. grey (air) 10 10
783 **205** 1p. green and brown . . . 15 10
784 – 5p. green and red . . . . 1·90 1·60
785 – 10p. brown and green . . 7·50 2·75
PORTRAITS: 30c. Fr. Margil de Jesus; 5p. Gen. Enrique Estrada; 10p. D. Fernando Villalpando.

207 Learning Vowels 208 Postman

1946. Education Plan.
786 **207** 1c. sepia 20 10

1947.
787 **208** 15c. blue 15 10

209 Roosevelt and First Mexican Stamp 210 10c. U.S.A. 1847 and Mexican Eagle

1947. U.S.A. Postage Stamp Centenary.
788 **209** 10c. brown (postage) . . 1·10 60
789 – 15c. green 10 10
790 – 25c. blue (air) 35 20
791 **210** 30c. black 25 10
792 – 1p. blue and red 80 15
DESIGNS: 15c. as Type **209** but vert; 25c., 1p. as Type **210** but horiz.

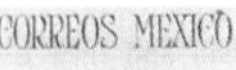

213 Justo Sierra 214 Ministry of Communications

212 Douglas DC-4

1947.
795 **213** 10p. green and brown (postage) . . . . 65·00 8·50
796 **214** 20p. mauve and green . . 1·10 90
793 – 10p. red and brown (air) 75 80
794 **212** 20p. red and blue . . . . 1·50 1·25
DESIGN—HORIZ: 10p. E. Carranza.

215 Manuel Rincon 217 Vicente Suarez

1947. Battle Centenaries. Portraits of "Child Heroes" etc. Inscr "1er CENTENARIO CHAPULTEPEC ("CHURUBUSCO" or "MOLINO DEL REY") 1847 1947".
797 – 2c. black (postage) . . . 30 10
798 – 5c. red 15 10
799 – 10c. brown 15 10
800 – 15c. green 15 10
801 **215** 30c. olive 20 10
802 – 1p. blue 30 15
803 – 5p. red and blue . . . . 1·25 1·25
DESIGNS—VERT: 2c. Francisco Marquez; 5c. Fernando Montes de Oca; 10c. Juan Escutin; 15c. Agustin Melgar; 1p. Lucas Balderas; 5p. Flag of San Blas Battalion.

804 **217** 25c. violet (air) 15 10
805 – 30c. blue 15 10
806 – 50c. green 25 10
807 – 1p. violet 30 10
808 – 5p. brown and blue . . . 1·25 1·25
DESIGNS—HORIZ: 30c. Juan de la Barrera; 50c. Military Academy; 1p. Pedro Maria Anaya; 5p. Antonio de Leon.

218 Puebla Cathedral

221 Dance of the Half Moons, Puebla

1950. (a) Postage. As T **218**.
835 – 3c. blue 15 10
874 – 5c. brown 25 10
875a – 10c. green 40 10
876a – 15c. green 20 10
877e **218** 20c. blue 30 10
840 – 30c. red 25 10
879 – 30c. brown 35 10
880b – 40c. orange 95 10
1346b – 50c. blue 10 10
1327b – 80c. green 35 10
843 – 1p. brown . . . . . . 2·75 10
1346f – 1p. green 10 10
1011ab – 1p. grey 30 10
1327d – 3p. red 55 10
1012a – 5p. blue and green . . 1·50 60
1013ab – 10p. black and blue 2·50 1·25
846 – 20p. violet and green 6·25 6·25
1014 – 20p. violet and black 5·75 4·50
1327e – 50p. orange and green 6·25 4·75
DESIGNS: 3 c, 3p. La Purisima Church, Monterrey; 5c. Modern building, Mexico City; 10c. Convent of the Nativity, Tepoztlan; 15 c, 50p. Benito Juarez; 30c., 80c. Indian dancer, Michoacan; 40c. Sculpture, Tabasco; 50c. Carved head, Veracruz; 1p. Actopan Convent and carved head; 5p. Galleon, Campeche; 10p. Francisco Madero; 20p. Modern building, Mexico City.

(b) Air. As T **221**.
897 – 5c. blue 15 10
898a – 10c. brown 25 15
899a – 20c. red 35 10
850 – 25c. brown 60 10
851 – 30c. olive 15 10
902 – 35c. violet 55 10
1327f – 40c. blue 10 10
904c – 50c. green 35 10
1056 – 80c. red 60 70
906a **221** 1p. grey 45 10
1327h – 1p.60 red 60 10
1327i – 1p.90 red 35 10
907ab – 2p. brown 65 25
908 – 2p.25 purple 60 45
1327j – 4p.30 blue 45 10
1017a – 5p. orange and brown 2·75 35
1327k – 5p.20 lilac 70 25
1327l – 5p.60 green . . . . . 1·40 30
895 – 10p. blue and black 3·75 60
859a – 20p. blue and red . . 5·25 5·75
DESIGNS: 5c., 1p.90 Bay of Acapulco; 10c., 4p.30, Dance of the Plumes, Oaxaca; 20c. Mayan frescoes, Chiapas; 25c., 2p.25, 5p.60, Masks, Michoacan; 30c. Cuauhtemoc; 35c., 2p., 5p.20, Taxco, Guerrero; 40c. Sculpture, San Luis Potosi; 50c., 1p.60, Ancient carvings, Chiapas; 80c. University City, Mexico City; 5p. Architecture, Queretaro; 10p. Hidalgo; 20p. National Music Conservatoire, Mexico City.

222 Arterial Road

224 Diesel Locomotive and Map

1950. Opening of Mexican Section of Pan-American Highway. Inscr "CARRETERA INTERNACIONAL 1950".
860 – 15c. violet (postage) . . . 30 10
861 **222** 20c. blue 20 10
862 – 25c. pink (air) . . . . . 1·60 20
863 – 35c. green 10 10
DESIGNS—HORIZ: 15c. Bridge; 25c. Pres. M. Aleman, bridge and map; 35c. B. Juarez and map.

1950. Inauguration of Mexico–Yucatan Railway.
864 – 15c. purple (postage) . . 1·75 30
865 **224** 20c. red 70 35
866 – 25c. green (air) 70 35
867 – 35c. blue 70 40
DESIGNS—VERT: 15c. Rail-laying. HORIZ: 25c. Diesel trains crossing Isthmus of Tehuantepac; 35c. M. Aleman and railway bridge at Coatzacoalcos.

227 Hands and Globe

1950. 75th Anniv of U.P.U.
868 – 50c. violet (postage) . . . 25 10
869 – 25c. red (air) 55 25
870 **227** 80c. blue 30 20
DESIGNS—HORIZ: 25c. Aztec runner. VERT: 50c. Letters "U.P.U.".

228 Miguel Hidalgo

229

1953. Birth Bicentenary of Hidalgo.
871 **228** 20c. sepia & blue (postage) . . . . 1·10 10
872 – 25c. lake and blue (air) 35 10
873 **229** 35c. green 35 10
DESIGN: As Type **229**: 25c. Full face portrait.

231 Aztec Athlete

232 View and Mayan Bas-relief

1954. 7th Central American and Caribbean Games.
918 **231** 20c. blue & pink (postage) 55 10
919 **232** 25c. brown and green (air) 35 15
920 – 35c. turquoise and purple 30 10
DESIGN: 35c. Stadium.

233

234

1954. Mexican National Anthem Centenary.
921 **233** 5c. lilac and blue (postage) 45 15
922 20c. brown and purple . . 55 10
923 1p. green and red 30 20
924 **234** 25c. blue and lake (air) 45 15
925 35c. purple and blue . . . 20 10
926 80c. green and blue . . . 25 15

235 Torchbearer and Stadium

236 Aztec God and Map

1955. 2nd Pan-American Games, Mexico City. Inscr "II JUEGOS DEPORTIVOS PANAMERICANOS".
927 **235** 20c. green & brn (postage) 40 10
928 **236** 25c. blue and brown (air) 30 10
929 – 35c. brown and red . . . 30 10
DESIGN: As Type **236**: 35c. Stadium and map.

237 Olin Design

238 Feathered Serpent and Mask

1956. Mexican Stamp Centenary.
930 **237** 5c. green & brn (postage) 30 10
931 – 10c. blue and grey . . . 30 10
932 – 30c. purple and red . . . 20 10
933 – 50c. brown and blue . . . 25 10
934 – 1p. black and green . . . 35 10
935 – 5p. sepia and bistre . . . 1·60 1·40
DESIGNS: As Type **237**: 10c. Tohtli bird; 30c. Zochitl flower; 50c. Centli corn; 1p. Mazatl deer; 5p. Teheutli man's head.

937 **238** 5c. black (air) 15 10
938 – 10c. blue 15 10
939 – 50c. purple 10 10
940 – 1p. violet 15 10
941 – 1p.20 mauve 15 10
942 – 5p. turquoise 80 80
DESIGNS: As Type **238**: 10c. Bell tower, coach and Viceroy Enriquez de Almanza; 50c. Morelos and cannon; 1p. Mother, child and mounted horseman; 1p.20, Sombrero and spurs; 5p. Emblems of food and education and pointing hand.

239 Stamp of 1856

1956. Centenary Int Philatelic Exn, Mexico City.
944 **239** 30c. blue and brown . . . 45 15

240 F. Zarco

241 V. Gomez Farias and M. Ocampo

1956. Inscr "CONSTITUYENTE(S) DE 1857".
945 – 25c. brown (postage) 35 10
946 – 45c. blue 15 10
947 – 60c. purple 15 10
1346d **240** 70c. blue 20 10
1327c – 2p.30 blue 55 10
949 **241** 15c. blue (air) 20 10
1327g – 60c. green 15 15
950 – 1p.20 violet and green 35 15
951 **241** 2p.75 purple 50 30
PORTRAITS: As T **240** (postage): 25, 45c., 2p.30, G. Prieto; 60c. P. Arriagan. As T **41** (air): 60c., 1p.20, L. Guzman and I. Ramirez.

242 Paricutin Volcano

1956. Air. 20th International Geological Congress.
952 **242** 50c. violet 30 10

243 Map of Central America and the Caribbean

1956. Air. 4th Inter-American Congress of Caribbean Tourism.
953 **243** 25c. blue and grey 20 10

244 Assembly of 1857

245 Mexican Eagle and Scales

1957. Centenary of 1857 Constitution.
958 – 30c. gold & lake (postage) 35 10
959 **244** 1p. green and sepia . . . 25 10
960 **245** 50c. brown and green (air) 20 10
961 – 1p. lilac and blue 30 15
DESIGNS—VERT: 30c. Emblem of Constitution. HORIZ: 1p. (Air), "Mexico" drafting the Constitution.

246 Globe, Weights and Dials

1957. Air. Centenary of Adoption of Metric System in Mexico.
962 **246** 50c. black and silver . . . 30 10

247 Train Disaster

248 Oil Derrick

1957. Air. 50th Anniv of Heroic Death of Jesus Garcia (engine driver) at Nacozari.
963 **247** 50c. purple and red . . . 90 25

1958. 20th Anniv of Nationalization of Oil Industry.
964 **248** 30c. black & blue (postage) 25 10
965 – 5p. red and blue . . . . 3·50 2·50
966 – 50c. green and black (air) 10 10
967 – 1p. black and red 20 10
DESIGNS—HORIZ: 50c. Oil storage tank and "AL SERVICIO DE LA PATRIA" ("At the service of the Fatherland"); 1p. Oil refinery at night. VERT: 5p. Map of Mexico and silhouette of oil refinery.

249 Angel, Independence Monument, Mexico City

250 U.N.E.S.C.O. Headquarters, Paris

1958. Air. 10th Anniv of Declaration of Human Rights.
968 **249** 50c. blue 20 10

1959. Inauguration of U.N.E.S.C.O. Headquarters Building, Paris.
969 **250** 30c. black and purple . . 30 10

251 U.N. Headquarters, New York

252 President Carranza

1959. U.N. Economic and Social Council Meeting, Mexico City.
970 **251** 30c. blue and yellow . . . 30 10

1960. "President Carranza Year" (1959) and his Birth Centenary.
971 **252** 30c. pur & grn (postage) 20 10
972 – 50c. violet and salmon (air) 20 10
DESIGN—HORIZ: 50c. Inscription "Plan de Guadalupe Constitucion de 1917" and portrait as Type **252**.

253 Alexander von Humboldt (statue)

254 Alberto Braniff's Voisin "Boxkite" and Bristol Britannia

1960. Death Centenary of Alexander von Humboldt (naturalist).
973 **253** 40c. green and brown . . 20 10

1960. Air. 50th Anniv of Mexican Aviation.
974 **254** 50c. brown and violet . . 40 10
975 1p. brown and green . . . 40 15

255 Francisco I. Madero

257 Dolores Bell

1960. Visit to Mexico of Members of Elmhurst Philatelic Society (American Society of Mexican Specialists). Inscr "HOMENAJE AL COLECCIONISTA".

976 **255** 10p. sepia, green and purple (postage) . . . . 27·00 45·00
977 – 20p. sepia, green and purple (air) . . . . . . 38·00 50·00
DESIGN: As No. 1019a 20p. National Music Conservatoire inscr "MEX. D.F.".

1960. 150th Anniv of Independence.

978 **257** 30c. red & green (postage) 60 10
979 – 1p. sepia and green . . . 25 10
980 – 5p. blue and purple . . . 3·25 3·25
981 – 50c. red and green (air) 15 10
982 – 1p.20 sepia and blue . . . 20 10
983 – 5p. sepia and green . . . 3·50 1·40
DESIGNS—VERT: No. 979, Independence Column; 980, Hidalgo, Dolores Bell and Mexican Eagle. HORIZ: No. 981, Mexican Flag; 982, Eagle breaking chain and bell tolling; 983, Dolores Church.

259 Children at Desk, University and School Buildings

261 Count S. de Revillagigedo

1960. 50th Anniv of Mexican Revolution.

984 – 10c. multicoloured (postage) 30 10
985 – 15c. brown and green . . 1·75 10
986 – 20c. blue and brown . . . 50 10
987 – 30c. violet and sepia . . . 20 10
988 **259** 1p. slate and purple . . . 25 10
989 – 5p. grey and purple . . . 2·10 2·10
990 – 50c. black and blue (air) 20 10
991 – 1p. green and red 20 10
992 – 1p.20 sepia and green . . 20 10
993 – 5p. lt blue, blue & mauve 2·00 90
DESIGNS: No. 984, Pastoral scene (35½ × 45½ mm). As Type **259** VERT: No. 985, Worker and hospital buildings; 986, Peasant, soldier and marine; 987, Power lines and pylons; 989, Coins, banknotes and bank entrance. HORIZ: No. 990, Douglas DC-8 airliner; 991, Riggers on oil derrick; 992, Main highway and map; 993, Barrage.

1960. Air. National Census.

994 **261** 60c. black and lake . . . 35 10

262 Railway Tunnel

263 Mosquito Globe and Instruments

1961. Opening of Chihuahua State Railway.

995 **262** 40c. black & grn (postage) 75 30
996 – 60c. blue and black (air) 75 30
997 – 70c. black and blue . . . 75 30
DESIGNS—HORIZ: 60c. Railway tracks and map of railway; 70c. Railway viaduct.

1962. Malaria Eradication.

998 **263** 40c. brown and blue . . . 25 10

264 Pres. Goulart of Brazil

265 Soldier and Memorial Stone

1962. Visit of President of Brazil.

999 **264** 40c. bistre 65 10

1962. Centenary of Battle of Puebla.

1000 **265** 40c. sepia and green (postage) 25 10
1001 – 1p. olive and green (air) 35 10
DESIGN—HORIZ: 1p. Statue of Gen. Zaragoza.

266 Draughtsman and Surveyor

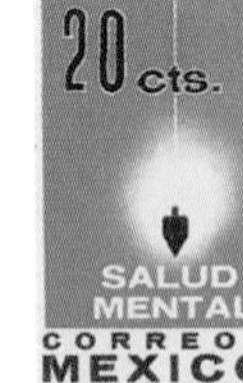

267 Plumb-line

1962. 25th Anniv of National Polytechnic Institute.

1002 **266** 40c. turquoise and blue (postage) 65 10
1003 – 1p. olive and blue (air) 35 10
DESIGN—HORIZ: 1p. Scientist and laboratory assistant.

1962. Mental Health.

1004 **267** 20c. blue and black . . . 90 15

268 Pres. J. F. Kennedy

269 Tower and Cogwheels

1962. Air. Visit of U.S. President.

1005 **268** 80c. blue and red . . . . 1·00 15

1962. "Century 21" Exn ("World's Fair"), Seattle.

1006 **269** 40c. black and green . . 35 10

270 Globe and O.E.A. Emblem

271 Pres. Alessandri of Chile

1962. Inter-American Economic and Social Council.

1007 **270** 40c. sepia and grey (postage) 25 10
1008 – 1p.20 sepia & violet (air) 35 15
DESIGN—HORIZ: 1p.20, Globe, Scroll and O.E.A. emblem.

1962. Visit of President of Chile.

1009 **271** 20c. brown 45 10

272 Balloon over Mexico City

273 "ALALC" Emblem

1962. Air. 1st Mexican Balloon Flight Centenary.

1010 **272** 80c. black and blue . . . 90 25

1963. Air. 2nd "ALALC" Session.

1023 **273** 80c. purple and orange 65 20

274 Pres. Betancourt of Venezuela

275 Petroleum Refinery

1963. Visit of President of Venezuela.

1024 **274** 20c. blue 35 10

1963. Air. 25th Anniv of Nationalization of Mexican Petroleum Industry.

1025 **275** 80c. slate and orange . . 35 10

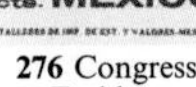

276 Congress Emblem

277 Campaign Emblem

1963. 19th International Chamber of Commerce Congress, Mexico City.

1026 **276** 40c. brown and black (postage) 45 10
1027 – 80c. black and blue (air) 55 20
DESIGN—HORIZ: 80c. World map and "C.I.C." emblem.

1963. Freedom from Hunger.

1028 **277** 40c. red and blue 45 15

278 Arms and Mountain

279 B. Dominguez

1963. 4th Centenary of Durango.

1029 **278** 20c. brown and blue . . 45 15

1963. Birth Centenary of B. Dominguez (revolutionary).

1030 **279** 20c. olive and green . . 45 15

280 Exhibition Stamp of 1956

281 Pres. Tito

1963. 77th American Philatelic Society Convention, Mexico City.

1031 **280** 1p. brown & bl (postage) 60 45
1032 – 5p. red (air) . . . . . . 1·40 1·00
DESIGN—HORIZ: 5p. EXMEX "stamp" and "postmark".

1963. Air. Visit of President of Yugoslavia.

1033 **281** 2p. green and violet . . 1·10 30

283 Part of U.I.A. Building

284 Red Cross on Tree

1963. Air. International Architects' Day.

1034 **283** 80c. grey and blue . . . 45 15

1963. Red Cross Centenary.

1035 **284** 20c. red & grn (postage) 30 15
1036 – 80c. red and green (air) 70 25
DESIGN—HORIZ: 80c. Red Cross on dove.

285 Pres. Estenssoro

286 Jose Morelos

1963. Visit of President of Bolivia.

1037 **285** 40c. purple and brown 45 15

1963. 150th Anniv of First Anahuac Congress.

1038 **286** 40c. bronze and green 40 15

287 Don Quixote as Skeleton

288 University Arms

1963. Air. 50th Death Anniv of Jose Posada (satirical artist).

1039 **287** 1p.20 black 75 20

1963. 90th Anniv of Sinaloa University.

1040 **288** 40c. bistre and green . . 45 15

289 Diesel-electric Train

290 "F.S.T.S.E." Emblem

1963. 11th Pan-American Railways Congress, Mexico City.

1041 **289** 20c. brn & blk (postage) 1·25 70
1042 – 1p.20 blue and violet (air) . . . . 1·25 55
DESIGN: 1p.20, Steam and diesel-electric locomotives and horse-drawn tramcar.

1964. 25th Anniv of Workers' Statute.

1075 **290** 20c. sepia and orange . . 30 10

291 Mrs. Roosevelt, Flame and U.N. Emblem

1964. Air. 15th Anniv of Declaration of Human Rights.

1076 **291** 80c. blue and orange . . 50 10

292 Pres. De Gaulle

1964. Air. Visit of President of France.

1077 **292** 2p. blue and brown . . . 1·25 35

293 Pres. Kennedy and Pres. A. Lopez Mateos

1964. Air. Ratification of Chamizal Treaty (1963).

1078 **293** 80c. black and blue . . . 55 15

294 Queen Juliana and Arms

295 Academy Emblem

1964. Air. Visit of Queen Juliana of the Netherlands.
1079 **294** 20c. bistre and blue . . . 70 15

1964. Centenary of National Academy of Medicine.
1080 **295** 20c. gold and black . . . 30 10

296 Lieut. Jose Azueto and Cadet Virgillo Uribe

1964. Air. 50th Anniv of Heroic Defence of Veracruz.
1081 **296** 40c. green and brown . . 30 10

297 Arms and World Map

298 Colonel G. Mendez

1964. Air. International Bar Assn Conf, Mexico City.
1082 **297** 40c. blue and brown . . 45 10

1964. Centenary of Battle of the Jahuactal Tabasco.
1083 **298** 40c. olive and brown . . 35 10

299 Dr. Jose Rizal

300 Zacatecas

1964. 400 Years of Mexican–Philippine Friendship. Inscr "1564 AMISTAD MEXICANO–FILIPINA 1964".
1084 **299** 20c. blue & grn (postage) 35 10
1085 – 40c. blue and violet . . . 40 10
1086 – 80c. blue & lt blue (air) 1·75 25
1087 – 2p.75 black and yellow 1·75 70
DESIGNS—As Type **299**: VERT: 40c. Legaspi. HORIZ: 80c. "San Pedro" (16th-century Spanish galleon). LARGER (44 × 36 mm): 2p.75, Ancient map of Pacific Ocean.

1964. 50th Anniv of Conquest of Zacatecas.
1088 **300** 40c. green and red . . . 40 10

301 Morelos Theatre, Aguascalientes

302 Andres Manuel del Rio

1965. 50th Anniv of Aguascalientes Convention.
1089 **301** 20c. purple and grey . . 30 10

1965. Andres M. del Rio Commemoration.
1090 **302** 30c. black 35 10

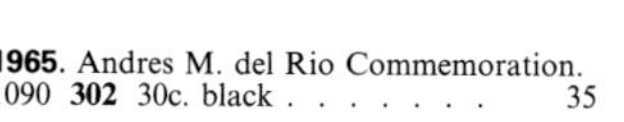

303 Netzahualcoyotl Dam

304 J. Morelos (statue)

1965. Air. Inauguration of Netzahualcoyotl Dam.
1091 **303** 80c. slate and purple . . 30 10

1965. 150th Anniv (1964) of First Constitution.
1092 **304** 40c. brown and green . . 40 10

305 Microwave Tower

306 Fir Trees

1965. Air. Centenary of I.T.U.
1093 **305** 80c. blue and indigo . . 40 20
1094 – 1p.20 green and black 45 20
DESIGN: 1p.20, Radio-electric station.

1965. Forest Conservation.
1095 **306** 20c. green and blue . . . 30 10
The inscription "¡CUIDALOS!" means "CARE FOR THEM!".

307 I.C.Y. Emblem

1965. International Co-operation Year.
1096 **307** 40c. brown and green . . 25 10

308 Camp Fire and Tent

1965. Air. World Scout Conference, Mexico City.
1097 **308** 30c. ultramarine and blue 40 20

309 King Baudouin and Queen Fabiola

1965. Air. Visit of Belgian King and Queen.
1098 **309** 2p. blue and green . . . 75 20

310 Mexican Antiquities and Unisphere

311 Dante (after R. Sanzio)

1965. Air. New York World's Fair.
1099 **310** 80c. green and yellow . . 30 15

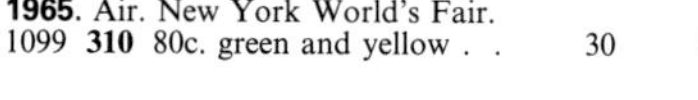

1965. Air. Dante's 700th Birth Anniv.
1100 **311** 2p. red . . . . 1·00 55

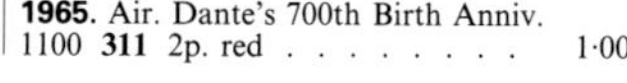

312 Sling-thrower

313 Jose M. Morelos y Pavon (leader of independence movement)

1965. Olympic Games (1968) Propaganda (1st series). Museum pieces.
1101 **312** 20c. blue & olive (postage) 45 10
1102 – 40c. sepia and red . . . 15 10
1103 – 80c. slate and red (air) 35 10
1104 – 1p.20 indigo and blue . . 45 15
1105 – 2p. brown and blue . . . 35 10
DESIGNS—As Type **312**: VERT: 40c. Batsman. HORIZ: 2p. Ball game. HORIZ (36 × 20 mm): 80c. Fieldsman. 1p.20, Scoreboard.

1965. 150th Anniv of Morelos's Execution.
1108 **313** 20c. black and blue . . . 30 10

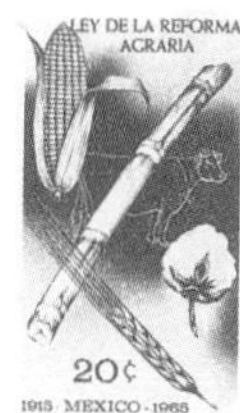

314 Agricultural Produce

315 Ruben Dario

1966. Centenary of Agrarian Reform Law.
1109 **314** 20c. red 30 10
1110 – 40c. black 40 10
DESIGN: 40c. Emilio Zapata, pioneer of agrarian reform.

1966. Air. 50th Death Anniv of Ruben Dario (Nicaraguan poet).
1111 **315** 1p.20 sepia 55 20

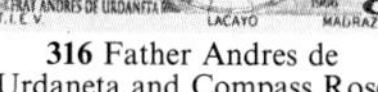

316 Father Andres de Urdaneta and Compass Rose

317 Flag and Postal Emblem

1966. Air. 400th Anniv of Father Andres de Urdaneta's Return from the Philippines.
1112 **316** 2p.75 black 85 45

1966. 9th Postal Union of Americas and Spain Congress (U.P.A.E.), Mexico City.
1113 **317** 40c. blk & grn (postage) 35 10
1114 – 80c. blck & mauve (air) 30 15
1115 – 1p.20 black and blue . . 35 15
DESIGNS—VERT: 80c. Flag and posthorn. HORIZ: 1p.20, U.P.A.E. emblem and flag.

318 Friar B. de Las Casas

319 E.S.I.M.E. Emblem and Diagram

1966. 400th Death Anniv of Friar Bartolome de Las Casas ("Apostle of the Indies").
1116 **318** 20c. black on buff . . . 35 10

1966. 50th Anniv of Higher School of Mechanical and Electrical Engineering.
1117 **319** 20c. green and grey . . . 30 10

320 U Thant and U.N. Emblem

321 "1966 Friendship Year"

1966. Air. U.N. Secretary-General U Thant's Visit to Mexico.
1118 **320** 80c. black and blue . . . 30 15

1966. Air. "Year of Friendship" with Central American States.
1119 **321** 80c. green and red . . . 25 10

322 F.A.O. Emblem

323 Running and Jumping

1966. International Rice Year.
1120 **322** 40c. green 30 10

1966. Olympic Games (1968) Propaganda (2nd series).
1121 **323** 20c. black & bl (postage) 55 10
1122 – 40c. black and lake . . . 25 10
1124 – 80c. black & brown (air) 35 10
1125 – 2p.25 black and green 55 25
1126 – 2p.75 black and violet 60 35
DESIGNS: 40c. Wrestling. LARGER (57 × 20 mm): 80c. Obstacle race; 2p.25, American football; 2p.75, Lighting Olympic flame.

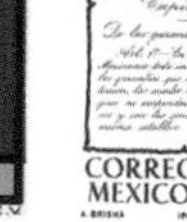

324 U.N.E.S.C.O. Emblem

325 Constitution of 1917

1966. Air. 20th Anniv of U.N.E.S.C.O.
1128 **324** 80c. multicoloured . . . 30 10

1967. 50th Anniv of Mexican Constitution.
1129 **325** 40c. black (postage) . . 45 10
1130 – 80c. brown & ochre (air) 35 10
DESIGN: 80c. President V. Carranza.

326 Earth and Satellite

327 Oil Refinery

1967. Air. World Meteorological Day.
1131 **326** 80c. blue and black . . . 30 20

1967. 7th World Petroleum Congress, Mexico City.
1132 **327** 40c. black and blue . . . 30 10

328 Nayarit Indian

329 Degollado Theatre

1967. 50th Anniv of Nayarit State.
1133 **328** 20c. black and green . . 30 10

1967. Cent of Degollado Theatre, Guadalajara.
1134 **329** 40c. brown and mauve 10 10

330 Mexican Eagle and Crown

331 School Emblem

1967. Centenary of Triumph over the Empire.
1135 **330** 20c. black and ochre . . 30 10

1967. Air. 50th Anniv of Military Medical School.
1136 **331** 80c. green and yellow . . 35 15

332 Capt. H. Ruiz Gavino

333 Marco Polo

1967. Air. 50th Anniv of 1st Mexican Airmail Flight, Pachuca–Mexico City.
1137 **332** 80c. brown and black . . 30 10
1138 – 2p. brown and black . . 70 20
DESIGN—HORIZ: 2p. De Havilland D.H.6A biplane.

1967. Air. International Tourist Year.
1139 **333** 80c. red and black . . . 20 10

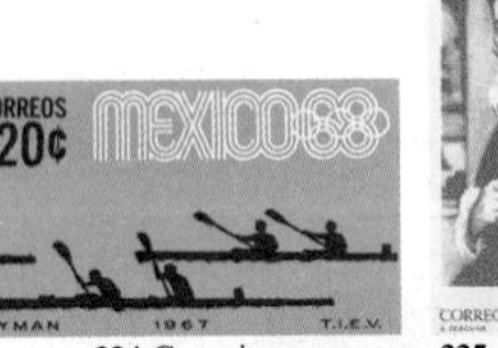

334 Canoeing

335 A. del Valle-Arizpe (writer)

1967. Olympic Games (1968) Propaganda (3rd series).
1140 **334** 20c. black & bl (postage) 20 10
1141 – 40c. black and red . . . 15 10
1142 – 50c. black and green . . 15 10
1143 – 80c. black and violet . . 25 10
1144 – 2p. black and orange . . 40 15

1146 – 80c. black & mauve (air) 15 10
1147 – 1p.20 black and green 15 10
1148 – 2p. black and lemon . . 60 20
1149 – 5p. black and yellow . . 1·00 35
DESIGNS: 40c. Basketball; 50c. Hockey; 80c. (No. 1143), Cycling; 80c. (No. 1146), Diving; 1p.20, Running; 2p. (No. 1144), Fencing; 2p. (No. 1148), Weightlifting; 5p. Football.

1967. Centenary of Fuente Athenaeum, Saltillo.
1151 **335** 20c. slate and brown . . 30 10

336 Hertz and Clark Maxwell

337 P. Moreno

1967. Air. International Telecommunications Plan Conference, Mexico City.
1152 **336** 80c. green and black . . 30 10

1967. 150th Death Anniv of Pedro Moreno (revolutionary).
1153 **337** 40c. black and blue . . . 30 15

338 Gabino Berreda (founder of Preparatory School)

339 Exhibition Emblem

1968. Centenary of National Preparatory and Engineering Schools.
1154 **338** 40c. red and blue 35 10
1155 – 40c. blue and black . . . 35 10
DESIGN: No. 1155, Staircase, Palace of Mining.

1968. Air. "Efimex '68" International Stamp Exn, Mexico City.
1156 **339** 80c. green and black . . 25 30
1157 2p. red and black . . . 25 30
The emblem reproduces the "Hidalgo" Official stamp design of 1884.

1968. Olympic Games (1968) Propaganda (4th series). Designs as T **334**, but inscr "1968".
1158 20c. black and olive (postage) 25 10
1159 40c. black and purple . . 25 10
1160 50c. black and green . . . 25 10
1161 80c. black and mauve . . . 25 10
1162 1p. black and brown . . . . 1·50 25
1163 2p. black and grey . . . . 1·75 95

1165 80c. black and blue (air) . . 30 10
1166 1p. black and turquoise . . 35 15
1167 2p. black and yellow 35 20
1168 5p. black and brown 80 70
DESIGNS: 20c. Wrestling; 40c. Various sports; 50c. Water-polo; 80c. (No. 1161), Gymnastics; 80c. (No. 1165), Yachting; 1p. (No. 1162), Boxing; 1p. (No. 1166), Rowing; 2p. (No. 1163), Pistol-shooting; 2p. (No. 1167), Volleyball; 5p. Horse-racing.

340 Dr. Martin Luther King

1968. Air. Martin Luther King Commemorative.
1170 **340** 80c. black and grey . . . 35 15

341 Olympic Flame

342 Emblems of Games

1968. Olympic Games, Mexico. (i) Inaug Issue.
1171 **341** 10p. multicoloured . . . 2·00 1·25

(ii) Games Issue. Multicoloured designs as T **341** (20, 40, 50c. postage and 80c., 1, 2p. air) or as T **342** (others).
1172 20c. Dove of Peace on map (postage) 25 10
1173 40c. Stadium 30 10
1174 50c. Telecommunications Tower, Mexico City . . . 30 10
1175 2p. Palace of Sport, Mexico City . . . . 1·40 25
1176 5p. Cultural symbols of Games . . . . 2·75 80

1178 80c. Dove and Olympic rings (air) 15 10
1179 1p. "The Discus-thrower" 15 10
1180 2p. Olympic medals 45 25
1181 5p. Type **342** . . . . 1·75 85
1182 10p. Line-pattern based on "Mexico 68" and rings . . 1·50 95

343 Arms of Vera Cruz

344 "Father Palou" (M. Guerrero)

1969. 450th Anniv of Vera Cruz.
1185 **343** 40c. multicoloured . . . 30 10

1969. Air. 220th Anniv of Arrival in Mexico of Father Serra (colonizer of California).
1186 **344** 80c. multicoloured . . . 35 10
It was intended to depict Father Serra in this design, but the wrong detail of the painting by Guerrero, which showed both priests, was used.

345 Football and Spectators

1969. Air. World Cup Football Championship (1st issue). Multicoloured.
1187 80c. Type **345** 25 10
1188 2p. Foot kicking ball . . . 35 10
See also Nos. 1209/10.

346 Underground Train

1969. Inauguration of Mexico City Underground Railway System.
1189 **346** 40c. multicoloured . . . 60 20

347 Mahatma Gandhi

348 Footprint on Moon

1969. Air. Birth Centenary of Mahatma Gandhi.
1190 **347** 80c. multicoloured . . . 30 10

1969. Air. 1st Man on the Moon.
1191 **348** 2p. black 30 25

349 Bee and Honeycomb

350 "Flying" Dancers and Los Nichos Pyramid, El Tajin

1969. 50th Anniv of I.L.O.
1192 **349** 40c. brown, blue & yell 20 10

1969. Tourism (1st series). Multicoloured.
1193 40c. Type **350**(postage) . . 25 10
1193a 40c. Puerto Vallarta, Jalisco (vert) 25 10

1194 80c. Acapulco (air) 80 15
1195 80c. Pyramid, Teotihuacan 60 15
1196 80c. "El Caracol" (Maya ruin), Yucatan 60 15
See also Nos. 1200/2 and 1274/7.

351 Red Crosses and Sun

352 "General Allende" (D. Rivera)

1969. Air. 50th Anniv of League of Red Cross Societies.
1197 **351** 80c. multicoloured . . . 30 10

1969. Birth Bicentenary of General Ignacio Allende ("Father of Mexican Independence").
1198 **352** 40c. multicoloured . . . 20 10

353 Dish Aerial

354 Question Marks

1969. Air. Inauguration of Satellite Communications Station, Tulancingo.
1199 **353** 80c. multicoloured . . . 35 10

1969. Tourism (2nd series). As T **350** but dated "1970". Multicoloured.
1200 40c. Puebla Cathedral . . . 40 10
1201 40c. Anthropological Museum, Mexico City . . 40 10
1202 40c. Belaunzaran Street, Guanajuato 40 10

1970. 9th National and 5th Agricultural Census. Multicoloured.
1204 20c. Type **354** 30 10
1205 40c. Horse's head and agricultural symbols . . . 25 10

355 Diagram of Human Eye

1970. 21st International Ophthalmological Congress, Mexico City.
1206 **355** 40c. multicoloured . . . 25 10

356 Cadet Ceremonial Helmet and Kepi

357 Jose Pino Suarez

1970. 50th Anniv of Military College Reorganization.
1207 **356** 40c. multicoloured . . . 20 10

1970. Birth Centenary (1969) of Jose Maria Pino Suarez (statesman).
1208 **357** 40c. multicoloured . . . 20 10

358 Football and Masks

361 Arms of Celaya

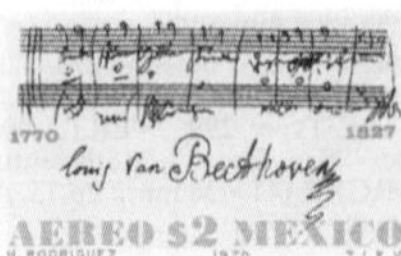

360 Composition by Beethoven

1970. Air. World Cup Football Championship (2nd issue). Multicoloured.
1209 80c. Type **358** 30 15
1210 2p. Football and Mexican idols 25 25

1970. Air. Birth Bicentenary of Beethoven.
1212 **360** 2p. multicoloured . . . 50 25

1970. 400th Anniv of Celaya.
1213 **361** 40c. multicoloured . . . 20 10

362 "General Assembly"

1970. Air. 25th Anniv of U.N.O.
1214 **362** 80c. multicoloured . . . 30 10

363 "Eclipse de Sol" **364** "Galileo" (Susterman)

1970. Total Eclipse of the Sun.
1215 **363** 40c. black 20 10

1971. Air. Conquest of Space. Early Astronomers. Multicoloured.
1216 2p. Type **364** 25 10
1217 2p. "Kepler" (unknown artist) 25 10
1218 2p. "Sir Isaac Newton" (Kneller) 25 10

365 "Sister Juana" (M. Cabrera)

1971. Air. Mexican Arts and Sciences (1st series). Paintings. Multicoloured.
1219 80c. Type **365** 40 15
1220 80c. "El Paricutin" (volcano) (G. Murillo) 40 15
1221 80c. "Men of Flames" (J. C. Orozco) 40 15
1222 80c. "Self-portrait" (J. M. Velasco) 40 15
1223 80c. "Mayan Warriors" ("Dresden Codex") . . . 40 15

See also Nos. 1243/7, 1284/8, 1323/7, 1351/5, 1390/4, 1417/21, 1523/7, 1540/4, 1650/4, 1688/92, 1834 and 1845.

366 Stamps from Venezuela, Mexico and Colombia

1971. Air. "Philately for Peace". Latin-American Stamp Exhibitions.
1224 **366** 80c. multicoloured . . . 35 15

367 Lottery Balls

1971. Bicentenary of National Lottery.
1225 **367** 40c. black and green . . 25 10

368 "Francisco Clavijero" (P. Carlin)

1971. Air. Return of the Remains of Francisco Javier Clavijero (historian) to Mexico (1970).
1226 **368** 2p. brown and green . . 50 25

369 Vasco de Quiroga and "Utopia" (O'Gorman) **370** "Amado Nervo" (artist unknown)

1971. 500th Birth Anniv of Vasco de Quiroga, Archbishop of Michoacan.
1227 **369** 40c. multicoloured . . . 20 10

1971. Birth Centenary of Amado Nervo (writer).
1228 **370** 80c. multicoloured . . . 20 10

371 I.T.U. Emblem **372** "Mariano Matamoros" (D. Rivera)

1971. Air. World Telecommunications Day.
1229 **371** 80c. multicoloured . . . 25 10

1971. Air. Birth Bicentenary of Mariano Matamoros (patriot).
1230 **372** 2p. multicoloured . . . 45 25

373 "General Guerrero" (O'Gorman) **374** Loudspeaker and Sound Waves

1971. Air. 150th Anniv of Independence from Spain.
1231 **373** 2p. multicoloured . . . 45 25

1971. 50th Anniv of Radio Broadcasting in Mexico.
1232 **374** 40c. black, blue and green 25 10

375 Pres. Cardenas and Banners **376** Stamps of Venezuela, Mexico, Colombia and Peru

1971. 1st Death Anniv of General Lazaro Cardenas.
1233 **375** 40c. black and lilac . . . 25 10

1971. Air. "EXFILIMA 71" Stamp Exhibition Lima, Peru.
1234 **376** 80c. multicoloured . . . 45 15

377 Abstract of Circles **378** Piano Keyboard

1971. Air. 25th Anniv of U.N.E.S.C.O.
1235 **377** 80c. multicoloured . . . 30 15

1971. 1st Death Anniv of Agustin Lara (composer).
1236 **378** 40c. black, blue & yellow 30 10

379 "Mental Patients" **380** City Arms of Monterrey

1971. Air. 5th World Psychiatric Congress, Mexico City.
1237 **379** 2p. multicoloured . . . 25 20

1971. 375th Anniv of Monterrey.
1238 **380** 40c. multicoloured . . . 10 10

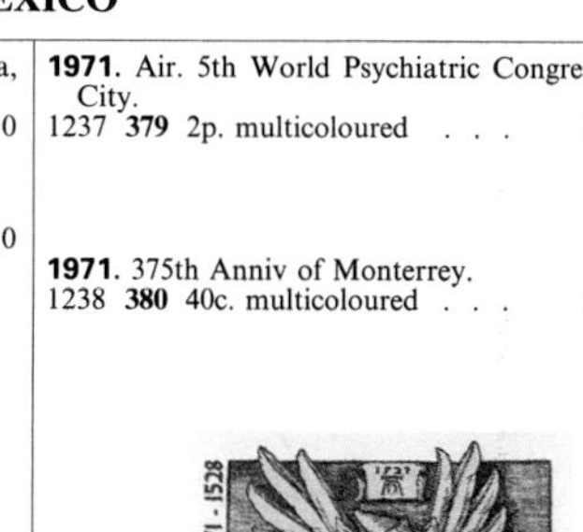

381 Durer's Bookplate

1971. Air. 500th Anniv of Albrecht Durer (artist).
1239 **381** 2p. black and brown . . 40 25

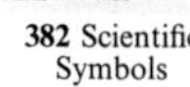

382 Scientific Symbols **383** Emblem of Mexican Cardiological Institute

1972. Air. 1st Anniv of National Council of Science and Technology.
1240 **382** 2p. multicoloured . . . 20 10

1972. World Health Month. Multicoloured.
1241 40c. Type **383** (postage) . . 10 10
1242 80c. Heart specialists (air) 10 10

1972. Air. Mexican Arts and Sciences (2nd series). Portraits. As T **365**.
1243 80c. brown and black . . . 75 15
1244 80c. green and black . . . 75 15
1245 80c. brown and black . . . 75 15
1246 80c. blue and black 75 15
1247 80c. red and black 75 15

PORTRAITS: Nos. 1243, King Netzahualcoyotl of Texcoco (patron of the arts); No. 1244, J. R. de Alarcon (lawyer); No. 1245, J. J. Fernandez de Lizardi (writer); No. 1246, E. G. Martinez (poet); No. 1247, R. L. Velardo (author).

384 Rotary Emblems **385** Indian Laurel and Fruit

1972. Air. 50th Anniv of Rotary Movement in Mexico.
1248 **384** 80c. multicoloured . . . 10 10

1972. Centenary of Chilpancingo as Capital of Guerrero State.
1249 **385** 40c. black, gold and green 10 10

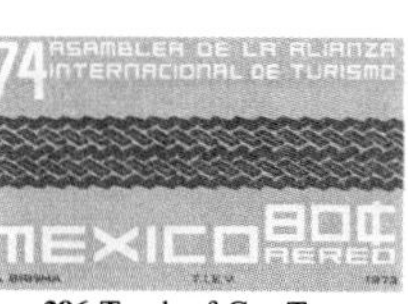

386 Track of Car Tyre

1972. Air. 74th Assembly of International Tourist Alliance, Mexico City.
1250 **386** 80c. black and grey . . . 10 10

387 First issue of "Gaceta De Mexico" **388** Emblem of Lions Organization

1972. 250th Anniv of Publication of "Gaceta De Mexico" (1st newspaper to be published in Latin America).
1251 **387** 40c. multicoloured . . . 10 10

1972. Lions' Clubs Convention, Mexico City.
1252 **388** 40c. multicoloured . . . 10 10

389 "Zaragoza" (cadet sail corvette) **390** "Margarita Maza de Juarez" (artist unknown)

1972. 75th Anniv of Naval Academy, Veracruz.
1253 **389** 40c. multicoloured . . . 60 10

1972. Death Centenary of Pres. Benito Juarez.
1254 **390** 20c. mult (postage) . . . 35 10
1255 – 40c. multicoloured . . . 35 10
1256 – 80c. black and blue (air) 10 10
1257 – 1p.20 multicoloured . . 15 10
1258 – 2p. multicoloured . . . 20 10

DESIGNS: 40c. "Benito Juarez" (D. Rivera); 80c. Page of Civil Register with Juarez signature; 1p.20, "Benito Juarez" (P. Clave); 2p. "Benito Juarez" (J. C. Orozco).

391 "Emperor Justinian I" (mosaic) **392** Atomic Emblem

1972. 50th Anniv of Mexican Bar Association.
1259 **391** 40c. multicoloured . . . 55 10

1972. Air. 16th General Conference of Int Atomic Energy Organization, Mexico City.
1260 **392** 2p. black, blue and grey 15 10

393 Caravel on "Stamp" **394** "Sobre las Olas" (sheet-music cover by O'Brandstetter)

1972. Stamp Day of the Americas.
1261 **393** 80c. violet and brown . . 15 10

1972. Air. 28th International Authors' and Composers' Society Congress, Mexico City.
1262 **394** 80c. brown 15 10

395 "Mother and Child" (G. Galvin)

1972. Air. 25th Anniv of U.N.I.C.E.F.
1263 **395** 80c. multicoloured . . . 50 10

396 "Father Pedro de Gante" (Rodriguez y Arangorti)
397 Olympic Emblems

1972. Air. 400th Death Anniv of Father Pedro de Gante (founder of first school in Mexico).
1264 **396** 2p. multicoloured . . . 25 10

1972. Olympic Games, Munich.
1265 **397** 40c. multicoloured (postage) 10 10
1266 – 80c. multicoloured (air) 15 10
1267 – 2p. black, green and blue 25 10
DESIGNS—HORIZ: 80c. Football. VERT: 2p. Similar to Type **397**.

398 Books on Shelves
400 "Footprints on the Americas"

399 Common Snook ("Pure Water")

1972. International Book Year.
1268 **398** 40c. multicoloured . . . 10 10

1972. Anti-pollution Campaign.
1269 **399** 40c. black & bl (postage) 20 10
1270 – 80c. black and blue (air) 15 10
DESIGN—VERT: 80c. Pigeon on cornice ("Pure Air").

1972. Air. Tourist Year of the Americas.
1271 **400** 80c. multicoloured . . . 15 10

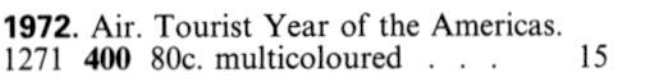

401 Stamps of Mexico, Colombia, Venezuela, Peru and Brazil

1973. Air. "EXFILBRA 72" Stamp Exhibition, Rio de Janeiro, Brazil.
1272 **401** 80c. multicoloured . . . 15 10

402 "Metlac Viaduct" (J. M. Velasco)

1973. Centenary of Mexican Railways.
1273 **402** 40c. multicoloured . . . 1·25 25

403 Ocotlan Abbey

1973. Tourism (3rd series). Multicoloured.
1274 40c. Type **403** (postage) . . 20 10
1275 40c. Indian hunting dance, Sonora (vert) 20 10
1276 80c. Girl in local costume (vert) (air) 35 15
1277 80c. Sport fishing, Lower California 35 10

404 "God of the Winds"

1973. Air. Centenary of W.M.O.
1278 **404** 80c. black, blue & mauve 35 10

405 Copernicus
406 Cadet

1973. Air. 500th Birth Anniv of Copernicus (astronomer).
1279 **405** 80c. green 15 10

1973. 150th Anniv of Military College.
1280 **406** 40c. multicoloured . . . 10 10

407 "Francisco Madero" (D. Rivera)
408 Antonio Narro (founder)

1973. Birth Centenary of Pres. Francisco Madero.
1281 **407** 40c. multicoloured . . . 10 10

1973. 50th Anniv of "Antonio Narro" Agricultural School, Saltillo.
1282 **408** 40c. grey 10 10

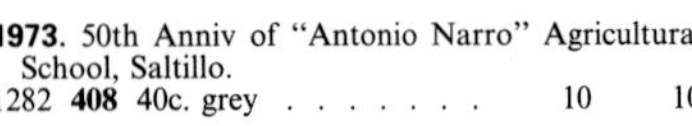

409 San Martin Statue
410 Caryon Molecules

1973. Air. Argentina's Gift of San Martin Statue to Mexico City.
1283 **409** 80c. multicoloured . . . 15 10

1973. Air. "Mexican Arts and Sciences" (3rd series). Astronomers. As T **365** but dated "1973".
1284 80c. green and red 10 10
1285 80c. multicoloured 10 10
1286 80c. multicoloured 10 10
1287 80c. multicoloured 10 10
1288 80c. multicoloured 10 10
DESIGNS: No. 1284, Aztec "Sun" stone; No. 1285, Carlos de Siguenza y Gongora; No. 1286, Francisco Diaz Covarrubias; No. 1287, Joaquin Gallo; No. 1288, Luis Enrique Erro.

1973. 25th Anniv of Chemical Engineering School.
1289 **410** 40c. black, yellow and red 10 10

411 Fist with Pointing Finger
412 "EXMEX 73" Emblem

1974. Promotion of Exports.
1294 **411** 40c. black and green . . 10 10

1974. "EXMEX 73" National Stamp Exhibition, Cuernavaca.
1295 **412** 40c. black (postage) . . 10 10
1296 – 80c. multicoloured (air) 15 10
DESIGN: 80c. Cortes' Palace, Cuernavaca.

413 Manuel Ponce

1974. 25th Death Anniv (1973) of Manuel M. Ponce (composer).
1297 **413** 40c. multicoloured . . . 10 10

414 Gold Brooch, Mochica Culture

1974. Air. Exhibition of Peruvian Gold Treasures, Mexico City.
1298 **414** 80c. multicoloured . . . 15 10

415 C.E.P.A.L. Emblem and Flags
416 Baggage

1974. Air. 25th Anniv of U.N. Economic Commission for Latin America (C.E.P.A.L.).
1299 **415** 80c. multicoloured . . . 15 10

1974. Air. 16th Confederation of Latin American Tourist Organizations (C.O.T.A.L.) Convention, Acapulco.
1300 **416** 80c. multicoloured . . . 15 10

417 Silver Statuette
419 "Dancing Dogs" (Indian statuette)

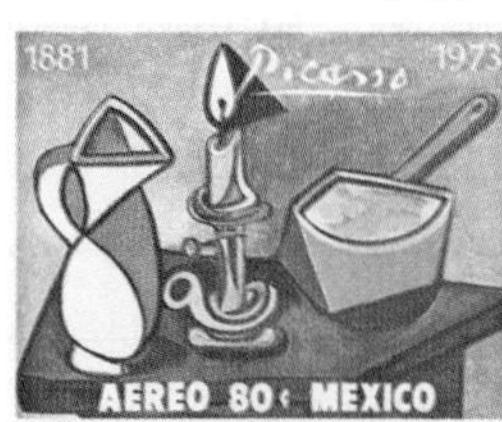

418 "The Enamelled Saucepan" (Picasso)

1974. 1st International Silver Fair, Mexico City.
1301 **417** 40c. multicoloured . . . 10 10

1974. Air. 1st Death Anniv of Pablo Picasso (artist).
1302 **418** 80c. multicoloured . . . 15 10

1974. 6th Season of Dog Shows.
1303 **419** 40c. multicoloured . . . 10 10

420 Mariano Azuela

1974. Birth Cent (1973) of Mariano Azuela (writer).
1304 **420** 40c. multicoloured . . . 10 10

421 Tepotzotlan Viaduct

1974. National Engineers' Day.
1305 **421** 40c. black and blue . . . 55 15

422 R. Robles (surgeon)

1974. 25th Anniv of W.H.O.
1306 **422** 40c. brown and green . . 10 10

423 U.P.U. Emblem

1974. "Exfilmex 74" Inter-American Stamp Exhibition, Mexico City.
1307 **423** 40c. black and green on yellow (postage) . . . 10 10
1308 80c. black and brown on yellow (air) 15 10

424 Demosthenes   426 Map and Indian Head

425 Lincoln Standard Biplane

1974. 2nd Spanish-American Reading and Writing Studies Congress, Mexico City.
1309 **424** 20c. green and brown . . 35 10

1974. Air. 50th Anniv of "Mexicana" (Mexican Airlines). Multicoloured.
1310 80c. Type **425** 15 10
1311 2p. Boeing 727-200 jetliner 40 10

1974. 150th Anniv of Union with Chiapas.
1312 **426** 20c. green and brown . . 10 10

427 "Sonar Waves"

1974. Air. 1st International Electrical and Electronic Communications Congress, Mexico City.
1313 **427** 2p. multicoloured . . . 15 10

428 S. Lerdo de Tejada   429 Manuscript of Constitution

1974. Centenary of Restoration of Senate.
1314 **428** 40c. black and blue . . . 10 10

1974. 150th Anniv of Federal Republic.
1315 **429** 40c. black and green . . 10 10

430 Ball in Play

1974. Air. 8th World Volleyball Championships, Mexico City.
1316 **430** 2p. black, brown & orge 15 10

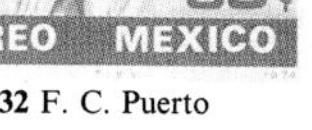

432 F. C. Puerto   433 Mask, Bat and Catcher's Glove

1974. Air. Birth Centenary of Felipe Carrillo Puerto (politician and journalist).
1318 **432** 80c. brown and green . . 10 10

1974. Air. 50th Anniv of Mexican Baseball League.
1319 **433** 80c. brown and green . . 10 10

434 U.P.U. Monument

1974. Centenary of U.P.U.
1320 **434** 40c. brown and blue (postage) 10 10
1321 – 80c. multicoloured (air) 10 10
1322 – 2p. brown and green . . 20 10
DESIGNS: 80c. Man's face as letter-box, Colonial period; 2p. Heinrich von Stephan, founder of U.P.U.

1974. Air. Mexican Arts and Sciences (4th series). Music and Musicians. As T **365** but dated "1974". Multicoloured.
1323 80c. "Musicians" – Mayan painting, Bonampak . . . 15 10
1324 80c. First Mexican-printed score, 1556 . . . . 15 10
1325 80c. Angela Peralta (soprano and composer) 15 10
1326 80c. "Miguel Lerdo de Tejada" (composer) . . . 15 10
1327 80c. "Silvestre Revueltas" (composer) (bronze by Carlos Bracho) 15 10

435 I.W.Y. Emblem   436 Economic Charter

1975. Air. International Women's Year.
1328 **435** 1p.60 black and red . . 15 10

1975. Air. U.N. Declaration of Nations' Economic Rights and Duties.
1329 **436** 1p.60 multicoloured . . 15 10

437 Jose Maria Mora   439 Dr. M. Jimenez

438 Trans-Atlantic Balsa Raft "Acali"

1975. 150th Anniv of Federal Republic.
1330 **437** 20c. multicoloured . . . 10 10

1975. Air. Trans-Atlantic Voyage of "Acali", Canary Islands to Yucatan (1973).
1331 **438** 80c. multicoloured . . . 50 10

1975. Air. 5th World Gastroenterological Congress.
1332 **439** 2p. multicoloured . . . 15 10

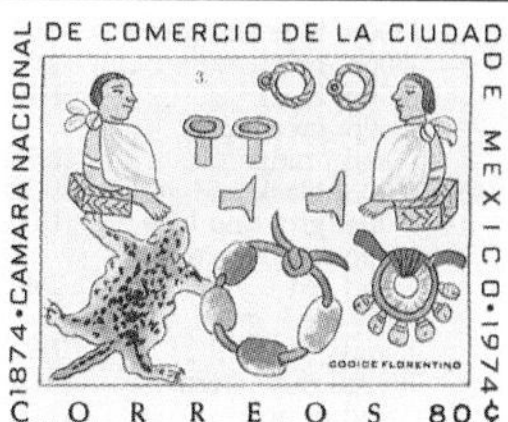

440 Aztec Merchants with Goods ("Codex Florentino")

1975. Centenary (1974) of Mexican Chamber of Commerce.
1333 **440** 80c. multicoloured . . . 10 10

441 Miguel de Cervantes Saavedra (Spanish author)   443 Salvador Novo

442 4-reales Coin of 1675

1975. Air. 3rd International Cervantes Festival, Guanajuato.
1334 **441** 1p.60 red and black . . 15 10

1975. Air. International Numismatics Convention "Mexico 74".
1335 **442** 1p.60 bronze and blue 15 10

1975. Air. 1st Death Anniv of Salvador Novo (poet and writer).
1336 **443** 1p.60 multicoloured . . 15 10

444 "Self-portrait" (Siqueiros)

1975. Air. 1st Death Anniv of David Alfaro Siqueiros (painter).
1337 **444** 1p.60 multicoloured . . 15 10

445 General Juan Aldama (detail from mural by Diego Rivera)

1975. Birth Bicentenary (1974) of General Aldama.
1338 **445** 80c. multicoloured . . . 10 10

446 U.N. and I.W.Y. Emblems

1975. Air. International Women's Year and World Conference.
1339 **446** 1p.60 blue and pink . . 15 10

447 Eagle and Snake ("Codex Duran")

1975. 650th Anniv of Tenochtitlan (now Mexico City). Multicoloured.
1340 80c. Type **447** (postage) . . 10 10
1341 1p.60 Arms of Mexico City (air) 15 10

448 Domingo F. Sarmiento (educator and statesman)   449 Teachers' Monument, Mexico City

1975. Air. 1st International Congress of "Third World" Educators, Acapulco.
1342 **448** 1p.60 green and brown 15 10

1975. Air. Mexican–Lebanese Friendship.
1343 **449** 4p.30 green and brown 25 10

450 Games' Emblem

1975. Air. 7th Pan-American Games, Mexico City.
1344 **450** 1p.60 multicoloured . . 15 10

451 Julian Carrillo (composer)   452 Academy Emblem

1975. Birth Centenary of J. Carrillo.
1345 **451** 80c. brown and green . . 10 10

1975. Cent of Mexican Languages Academy.
1346 **452** 80c. yellow and brown 10 10

453 University Building

1975. 50th Anniv of Guadalajara University.
1347 **453** 80c. black, brown & pink 10 10

454 Dr. Atl   455 Road Builders

1975. Air. Atl (Gerardo Murillo, painter and writer). Birth Centenary.
1348 **454** 4p.30 multicoloured . . 25 10

1975. "50 Years of Road Construction" and 15th World Road Congress, Mexico City.
1349 **455** 80c. black & grn (postage) 10 10
1350 – 1p.60 black & blue (air) 15 10
DESIGN: 1p.60, Congress emblem.

1975. Air. Mexican Arts and Sciences (5th series). As T **365**, but dated "1975". Multicoloured.
1351 1p.60 Title page, F. Hernandez' "History of New Spain" 15 10
1352 1p.60 A. L. Herrera (naturalist) 15 10
1353 1p.60 Page from "Badiano Codex" (Aztec herbal) . . 15 10
1354 1p.60 A. Rosenblueth Stearns (neurophysiologist) . . . 15 10
1355 1p.60 A. A. Duges (botanist and zoologist) 15 10

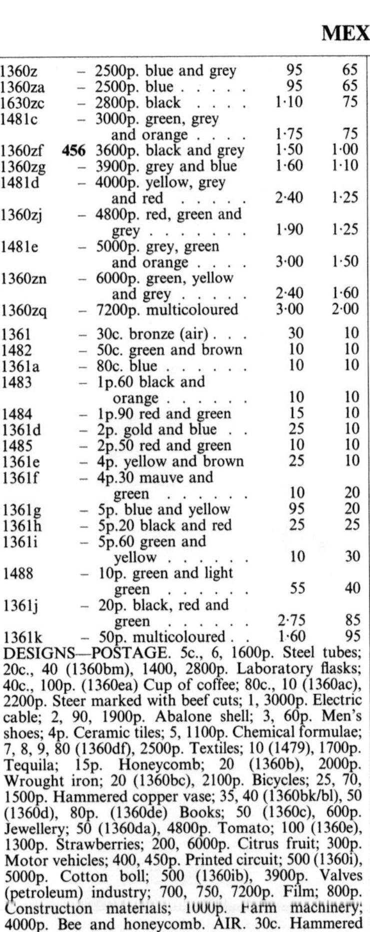

456 Car Engine Parts **457** Aguascalientes Cathedral

1975. Mexican Exports. Multicoloured.
1356 – 5c. blue (postage) . . 35 10
1471 – 20c. black 35 10
1356b – 40c. brown 30 10
1356c **456** 50c. blue 35 10
1472 50c. black 10 10
1473 – 80c. red 10 10
1474 – 1p. violet and yellow 10 10
1358a – 1p. black and orange 10 10
1475 – 2p. blue and turquoise 55 10
1476 – 3p. brown 25 10
1359b – 4p. red and brown . . 25 10
1359e – 5p. brown 10 10
1359ed – 6p. red 10 10
1359ee – 6p. grey 10 10
1359f – 7p. blue 10 10
1359g – 8p. brown 10 10
1359h – 9p. blue 10 10
1479 – 10p. lt green & green 95 45
1360ac – 10p. red 10 10
1360ad – 15p. orange and brown 15 10
1360b – 20p. black 15 10
1360bc – 20p. black and red . . 10 10
1360be – 25p. brown 25 10
1360bh – 35p. yellow and mauve 25 10
1360bk – 40p. yellow and brown 25 10
1360bl – 40p. gold and green 25 10
1360bm – 40p. black 10 10
1360c – 50p. multicoloured . . 1·25 35
1360d – 50p. yellow and blue 35 20
1360da – 50p. red and green . . 35 20
1360db – 60p. brown 30 15
1360dc – 70p. brown 35 20
1360de – 80p. gold and mauve 20 50
1360df – 80p. blue 80 50
1360dg – 90p. blue and green 1·25 55
1360e – 100p. red, green and grey 70 35
1360ea – 100p. brown 10 10
1360f – 200p. yellow, green and grey . . . . . 1·90 30
1360fb – 200p. yellow and green 10 10
1360g – 300p. blue, red and grey 60 60
1360gb – 300p. blue and red . . 15 10
1360h – 400p. bistre, brown and grey 95 35
1360hb – 450p. brown and mauve 20 10
1360i – 500p. green, orange and grey . . . . . 1·90 30
1360ib – 500p. grey and blue 20 10
1360j – 600p. multicoloured 30 10
1360k – 700p. black, red and green 35 10
1360kb – 750p. black, red and green 30 10
1360l – 800p. brown & dp brown 40 10
1360m **456** 900p. black 50 10
1360n 950p. blue 40 20
1481a – 1000p. black, red and grey 50 20
1360pa – 1000p. red and black 40 10
1360q – 1100p. grey 60 30
1360r – 1300p. red, green and grey 60 30
1360rb – 1300p. red and green 50 25
1360rg – 1400p. black 50 20
1360s – 1500p. brown 55 45
1360t – 1600p. orange 65 30
1360u – 1700p. green and deep green 70 30
1360w – 1900p. blue and green 2·25 75
1481b – 2000p. black and grey 1·25 50
1360xa – 2000p. black 80 55
1360y – 2100p. black, orange and grey 80 55
1360ya – 2100p. black and red 80 55
1360yb – 2200p. red 90 60
1360z – 2500p. blue and grey 95 65
1360za – 2500p. blue 95 65
1630zc – 2800p. black . . . . 1·10 75
1481c – 3000p. green, grey and orange . . . . 1·75 75
1360zf **456** 3600p. black and grey 1·50 1·00
1360zg – 3900p. grey and blue 1·60 1·10
1481d – 4000p. yellow, grey and red . . . . . 2·40 1·25
1360zj – 4800p. red, green and grey . . . . 1·90 1·25
1481e – 5000p. grey, green and orange . . . . 3·00 1·50
1360zn – 6000p. green, yellow and grey . . . . . 2·40 1·60
1360zq – 7200p. multicoloured 3·00 2·00
1361 – 30c. bronze (air) . . . 30 10
1482 – 50c. green and brown 10 10
1361a – 80c. blue 10 10
1483 – 1p.60 black and orange 10 10
1484 – 1p.90 red and green 15 10
1361d – 2p. gold and blue . . 25 10
1485 – 2p.50 red and green 10 10
1361e – 4p. yellow and brown 25 10
1361f – 4p.30 mauve and green 10 20
1361g – 5p. blue and yellow 95 20
1361h – 5p.20 black and red 25 25
1361i – 5p.60 green and yellow 10 30
1488 – 10p. green and light green 55 40
1361j – 20p. black, red and green . . . . . . 2·75 85
1361k – 50p. multicoloured . . 1·60 95
DESIGNS—POSTAGE. 5c., 6, 1600p. Steel tubes; 20c., 40 (1360bm), 1400, 2800p. Laboratory flasks; 40c., 100p. (1360ea) Cup of coffee; 80c., 10 (1360ac), 2200p. Steer marked with beef cuts; 1, 3000p. Electric cable; 2, 90, 1900p. Abalone shell; 3, 60p. Men's shoes; 4p. Ceramic tiles; 5, 1100p. Chemical formulae; 7, 8, 9, 80 (1360df), 2500p. Textiles; 10 (1479), 1700p. Tequila; 15p. Honeycomb; 20 (1360b), 2000p. Wrought iron; 20 (1360bc), 2100p. Bicycles; 25, 70, 1500p. Hammered copper vase; 35, 40 (1360bk/bl), 50 (1360d), 80p. (1360de) Books; 50 (1360c), 600p. Jewellery; 50 (1360da), 4800p. Tomato; 100 (1360e), 1300p. Strawberries; 200, 6000p. Citrus fruit; 300p. Motor vehicles; 400, 450p. Printed circuit; 500 (1360i), 5000p. Cotton boll; 500 (1360ib), 3900p. Valves (petroleum) industry; 700, 750, 7200p. Film; 800p. Construction materials; 1000p. Farm machinery; 4000p. Bee and honeycomb. AIR. 30c. Hammered copper vase; 50c. Electronic components; 80c. Textiles; 1p.60, Bicycles; 1p.90, Valves (petroleum) industry; 2p. Books; 2p.50, Tomato; 4p. Bee and honeycomb; 4p.30, Strawberry; 5p. Motor vehicles; 5p.20, Farm machinery; 5p.60, Cotton boll; 10p. Citrus fruit; 20p. Film; 50p. Cotton.

1975. 400th Anniv of Aguascalientes.
1362 **457** 50c. black and green . . 35 10

458 J. T. Bodet **460** "Death of Cuautemoc" (Chavez Morado)

459 "Fresco" (J. C. Orozco)

1975. 1st Death Anniv of Jaime T. Bodet (author and late Director-General of U.N.E.S.C.O.).
1363 **458** 80c. brown and blue . . 10 10

1975. 150th Anniv of Mexican Supreme Court of Justice.
1364 **459** 80c. multicoloured . . . 10 10

1975. 450th Death Anniv of Emperor Cuautemoc.
1365 **460** 80c. multicoloured . . . 10 10

461 Allegory of Irrigation

1976. 50th Anniv of Nat Irrigation Commission.
1366 **461** 80c. deep blue and blue 10 10

462 City Gateway

1976. 400th Anniv of Leon de los Aldamas, Guanajuato.
1367 **462** 80c. yellow and purple 10 10

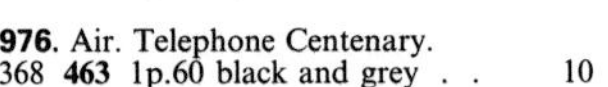

463 Early Telephone **464** Gold Coin

1976. Air. Telephone Centenary.
1368 **463** 1p.60 black and grey . . 10 10

1976. Air. 4th Int Numismatics Convention.
1369 **464** 1p.60 gold, brown & blk 10 10

465 Tlaloc (Aztec god of rain) and Calles Dam

1976. Air. 12th Int Great Dams Congress.
1370 **465** 1p.60 purple and green 20 10

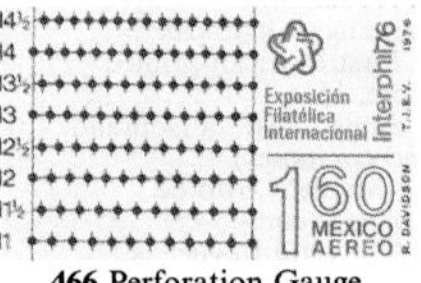

466 Perforation Gauge

1976. Air. "Interphil '76" International Stamp Exhibition, Philadelphia.
1371 **466** 1p.60 black, red and blue 20 10

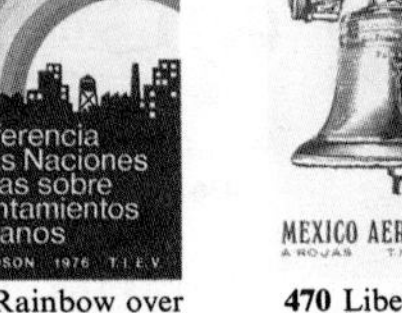

467 Rainbow over Industrial Skyline **470** Liberty Bell

1976. Air. U.N. Conf on Human Settlements.
1372 **467** 1p.60 multicoloured . . 20 10

1976. Air. Bicentenary of American War of Independence.
1378 **470** 1p.60 blue and mauve 20 10

471 Forest Fire

1976. Fire Prevention Campaign.
1379 **471** 80c. multicoloured . . . 10 10

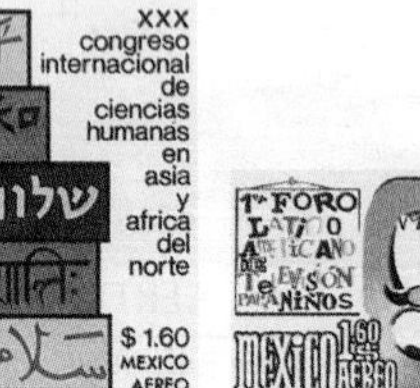
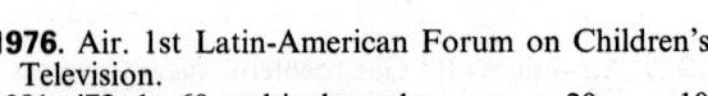

472 Peace Texts **473** Children on TV Screen

1976. Air. 30th International Asian and North American Science and Humanities Congress, Mexico City.
1380 **472** 1p.60 multicoloured . . 15 10

1976. Air. 1st Latin-American Forum on Children's Television.
1381 **473** 1p.60 multicoloured . . 20 10

474 Scout's Hat **475** Exhibition Emblem

1976. 50th Anniv of Mexican Boy Scout Movement.
1382 **474** 80c. olive and brown . . 10 10

1976. "Mexico Today and Tomorrow" Exhibition.
1383 **475** 80c. black, red & turq 10 10

476 New Buildings **477** Dr. R. Vertiz

1976. Inaug of New Military College Buildings.
1384 **476** 50c. brown and ochre . . 10 10

1976. Centenary of Ophthalmological Hospital of Our Lady of the Light.
1385 **477** 80c. brown and black . . 10 10

478 Guadalupe Basilica

1976. Inauguration of Guadalupe Basilica.
1386 **478** 50c. bistre and black . . 10 10

479 "40" and Emblem

1976. 40th Anniv of National Polytechnic Institute.
1387 **479** 80c. black, red and green 10 10

480 Blast Furnace

1976. Inauguration of Lazaro Cardenas Steel Mill, Las Truchas.
1388 **480** 50c. multicoloured . . . 10 10

481 Natural Elements

1976. Air. World Urbanization Day.
1389 **481** 1p.60 multicoloured . . 10 10

1976. Air. Mexican Arts and Sciences (6th series). As T **365** but dated "1976". Multicoloured.
1390 1p.60 black and red 10 10
1391 1p.60 multicoloured 10 10
1392 1p.60 black and yellow . . . 10 10
1393 1p.60 multicoloured 10 10
1394 1p.60 brown and black . . . 10 10

DESIGNS: No. 1390, "The Signal" (Angela Gurria); No. 1391, "The God of Today" (L. Ortiz Monasterio); No. 1392, "The God Coatlicue" (traditional Mexican sculpture); No. 1393, "Tiahuicole" (Manuel Vilar); No. 1394, "The Horseman" (Manuel Tolsa).

482 Score of "El Pesebre"

1977. Air. Birth Centenary of Pablo Casals (cellist).
1395 **482** 4p.30 blue and brown . . 15 10

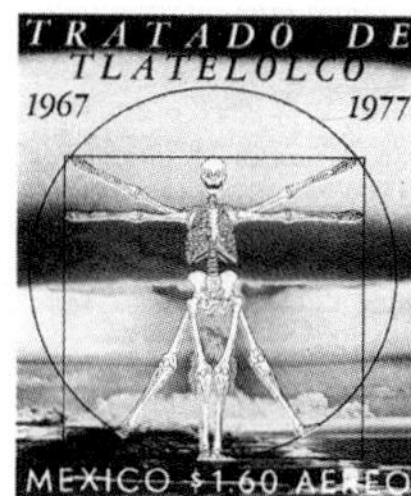

483 "Man's Destruction"

1977. Air. 10th Anniv of Treaty of Tlatelolco.
1396 **483** 1p.60 multicoloured . . 10 10

484 Saltillo Cathedral

485 Light Switch, Pylon and Engineers

1977. 400th Anniv of Founding of Saltillo.
1397 **484** 80c. brown and yellow 10 10

1977. 40 Years of Development in Mexico. Federal Electricity Commission.
1398 **485** 80c. multicoloured . . . 10 10

486 Footballers

1977. Air. 50th Anniv of Mexican Football Federation.
1399 **486** 1p.60 multicoloured . . 10 10
1400 – 4p.30 yellow, blue & blk 15 10
DESIGN: 4p.30, Football emblem.

487 Hands and Scales

1977. Air. 50th Anniv of Federal Council of Reconciliation and Arbitration.
1401 **487** 1p.60 orange, brn & blk 10 10

488 Flags of Spain and Mexico

489 Tlaloc (weather god)

1977. Resumption of Diplomatic Relations with Spain.
1402 **488** 50c. multicoloured (postage) 10 10
1403 80c. multicoloured . . . 10 10
1404 – 1p.60 black and grey (air) 10 10
1405 – 1p.90 red, green & lt grn 10 10
1406 – 4p.30 grey, brown & grn 15 10

DESIGNS: 1p.60, Arms of Mexico and Spain; 1p.90, Maps of Mexico and Spain; 4p.30, President Jose Lopez Portillo and King Juan Carlos.

1977. Air. Centenary of Central Meterological Observatory.
1407 **489** 1p.60 multicoloured . . 10 10

490 Ludwig van Beethoven

491 A. Serdan

1977. Air. 150th Death Anniv of Beethoven.
1408 **490** 1p.60 green and brown 10 10
1409 4p.30 red and blue . . . 15 10

1977. Birth Centenary of Aquiles Serdan (revolutionary martyr).
1410 **491** 80c. black, turq & grn 10 10

492 Mexico City–Guernavaca Highway

1977. Air. 25th Anniv of First National Highway.
1411 **492** 1p.60 multicoloured . . 10 10

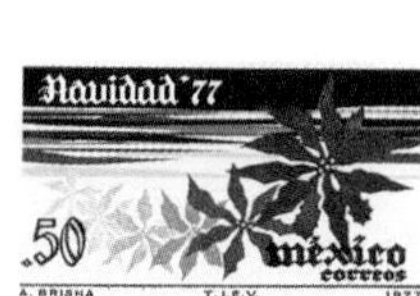

493 Poinsettia

494 Arms of Campeche

1977. Christmas.
1412 **493** 50c. multicoloured . . . 10 10

1977. Air. Bicentenary of Naming of Campeche.
1413 **494** 1p.60 multicoloured . . 10 10

495 Tractor and Dam

1977. Air. U.N. Desertification Conference, Mexico City.
1414 **495** 1p.60 multicoloured . . 10 10

496 Congress Emblem

1977. Air. 20th World Education, Hygiene and Recreation Congress.
1415 **496** 1p.60 multicoloured . . 10 10

497 Freighter "Rio Yaqui"

498 Mayan Dancer

1977. Air. 60th Anniv of National Merchant Marine.
1416 **497** 1p.60 multicoloured . . 60 10

1977. Air. Mexican Arts and Sciences (7th series). Pre-colonial statuettes.
1417 **498** 1p.60 red, black and pink 10 10
1418 – 1p.60 blue, black and light blue 10 10
1419 – 1p.60 grey, black and yellow 10 10
1420 – 1p.60 green, black and turquoise 10 10
1421 – 1p.60 red, black and grey 10 10
DESIGNS: No. 1418, Aztec god of dance; No. 1419, Snake dance; No. 1420, Dancer, Monte Alban; No. 1421, Dancer, Totonaca.

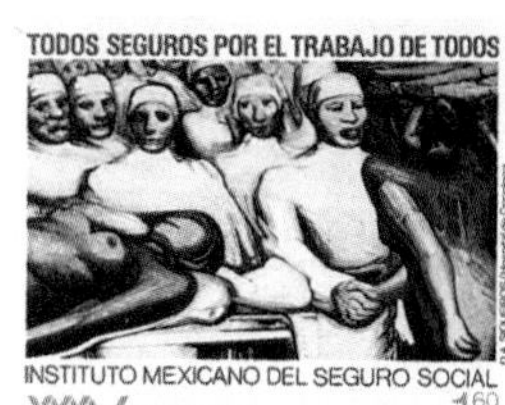

499 Hospital Scene

1978. Air. 35th Anniv of Mexican Social Insurance Institute. Multicoloured.
1422 1p.60 Type **499** 10 10
1423 4p.30 Workers drawing benefits 15 10

500 Moorish Fountain

1978. Air. 450th Anniv of Chiapa de Corzo, Chiapas.
1424 **500** 1p.60 multicoloured . . 10 10

501 Telephones, 1878 and 1978

502 Oilwell

1978. Centenary of Mexican Telephone.
1425 **501** 80c. red and salmon . . 10 10

1978. 40th Anniv of Nationalization of Oil Resources.
1426 **502** 80c. red and salmon (postage) 10 10
1427 – 1p.60 blue and red (air) 10 10
1428 – 4p.30 black, light blue and blue 55 20
DESIGNS: 1p.60, General I. Cardenas (President, 1938); 4p.30, Oil rig, Gulf of Mexico.

503 Arms of San Cristobal de las Casas

1978. Air. 450th Anniv of San Cristobal de las Casas, Chiapas.
1429 **503** 1p.60 purple, pink and black 10 10

504 Fairchild FC-71 Mail Plane

506 Blood Pressure Gauge and Map of Mexico

505 Globe and Cogwheel

1978. Air. 50th Anniv of First Mexican Airmail Route.
1430 **504** 1p.60 multicoloured . . 20 10
1431 4p.30 multicoloured . . 30 10

1978. Air. World Conference on Technical Co-operation between Underdeveloped Countries. Multicoloured.
1432 1p.60 Type **505** 10 10
1433 4p.30 Globe and cogwheel joined by flags 15 10

1978. Air. World Hypertension Month and World Health Day.
1434 **506** 1p.60 blue and red . . . 10 10
1435 – 4p.30 salmon and blue 15 10
DESIGN: 4p.30, Hand with stethoscope.

507 Kicking Ball

508 Francisco (Pancho) Villa

1978. Air. World Cup Football Championship, Argentina.
1436 **507** 1p.60 bl, lt orge & orge 10 10
1437 – 1p.90 blue, brn & orge 10 10
1438 – 4p.30 blue, grn & orge 15 10
DESIGNS: 1p.90, Saving a goal; 4p.30, Footballer.

1978. Air. Birth Centenary of Francisco Villa (revolutionary leader).
1439 **508** 1p.60 multicoloured . . 10 10

509 Emilio Carranza Stamp of 1929

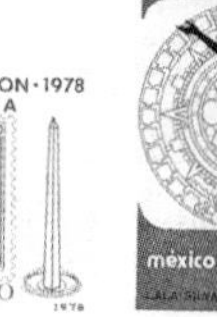

510 Woman and Calendar Stone

1978. Air. 50th Anniv of Mexico–Washington Flight by Emilio Carranza.
1440 **509** 1p.60 red and brown . . 10 10

1978. Air. Miss Universe Contest, Acapulco.
1441 **510** 1p.60 black, brn & red 10 10
1442 1p.90 black, brn & grn 10 10
1443 4p.30 black, brn & red 15 10

511 Alvaro Obregon (J. Romero)

1978. Air. 50th Death Anniv of Alvaro Obregon (statesman).
1444 **511** 1p.60 multicoloured . . 10 10

512 Institute Emblem

1978. 50th Anniv of Pan-American Institute for Geography and History.
1445 **512** 80c. blue and black (postage) 10 10
1446 – 1p.60 green and black (air) 10 10
1447 – 4p.30 brown and black 15 10
DESIGNS: 1p.60, 4p.30, Designs as Type **512**, showing emblem.

513 Sun rising over Ciudad Obregon

514 Mayan Statue, Rook and Pawn

1978. Air. 50th Anniv of Ciudad Obregon.
1448 **513** 1p.60 multicoloured . . 10 10

1978. Air. World Youth Team Chess Championship, Mexico City.
1449 **514** 1p.60 multicoloured . . 10 10
1450 4p.30 multicoloured . . 20 10

515 Aristotle

516 Mule Deer

1978. Air. 2300th Death Anniv of Aristotle.
1451 **515** 1p.60 grey, blue and yellow 10 10
1452 – 4p.30 grey, red and yellow 20 10
DESIGN: 4p.30, Statue of Aristotle.

1978. Air. World Youth Team Chess Championship, Mexico City.
1453 1p.60 Type **516** 20 10
1454 1p.60 Ocelot 20 10
See also Nos. 1548/9, 1591/2, 1638/9 and 1683/4.

517 Man's Head and Dove

518 "Dahlia coccinea". ("Dalia" on stamp)

1978. Air. International Anti-Apartheid Year.
1455 **517** 1p.60 grey, red and black 10 10
1456 – 4p.30 grey, lilac and black 15 10
DESIGN: 4p.30, Woman's head and dove.

1978. Mexican Flowers (1st series). Multicoloured.
1457 50c. Type **518** 10 10
1458 80c. "Plumeria rubra" . . . 10 10
See also Nos. 1550/1, 1593/4, 1645/6, 1681/2, 1791/2 and 1913/14.

519 Emblem

520 Dr. Rafael Lucio

1978. Air. 12th World Architects' Congress.
1459 **519** 1p.60 red, black and orange 10 10

1978. Air. 11th International Leprosy Congress.
1460 **520** 1p.60 green 10 10

521 Franz Schubert and "Death and the Maiden"

522 Decorations and Candles

1978. Air. 150th Death Anniv of Franz Schubert (composer).
1461 **521** 4p.30 brown, black and green 15 10

1978. Christmas. Multicoloured.
1462 50c. Type **522** (postage) . . 10 10
1463 1p.60 Children and decoration (air) 10 10

523 Antonio Vivaldi

524 Wright Flyer III

1978. Air. 300th Birth Anniv of Antonio Vivaldi (composer).
1464 **523** 4p.30 red, stone and brown 15 10

1978. Air. 75th Anniv of First Powered Flight.
1465 **524** 1p.60 orange, yell & mve 15 10
1466 – 4p.30 yellow, red & flesh 30 10
DESIGN: 4p.30, Side view of Wright Flyer I.

525 Albert Einstein and Equation

1979. Air. Birth Centenary of Albert Einstein (physicist).
1467 **525** 1p.60 multicoloured . . 10 10

526 Arms of Hermosillo

527 Sir Rowland Hill

1979. Centenary of Hermosillo, Sonora.
1468 **526** 80c. multicoloured . . . 10 10

1979. Air. Death Centenary of Sir Rowland Hill.
1469 **527** 1p.60 multicoloured . . 10 10

528 "Children" (Adriana Blas Casas)

1979. Air. International Year of the Child.
1470 **528** 1p.60 multicoloured . . 10 10

529 Registered Letter from Mexico to Rome, 1880

1979. Air. "Mepsipex 79", Third International Exhibition of Elmhurst Philatelic Society, Mexico City.
1499 **529** 1p.60 multicoloured . . 10 10

530 Football

531 Josefa Ortiz de Dominguez

1979. "Universiada 79", 10th World University Games, Mexico City (1st issue).
1500 **530** 50c. grey, black and blue (postage) 10 10
1501 – 80c. multicoloured . . . 10 10
1502 – 1p. multicoloured . . . 10 10
1504 – 1p.60 multicoloured (air) 10 10
1505 – 4p.30 multicoloured . . 15 10
DESIGNS—VERT: 80c. Aztec ball player; 1p. Wall painting of athletes; 1p.60, Games emblem; 4p.30, Flame and doves.
See also Nos. 1514/19.

1979. 150th Death Anniv of Josefa Ortiz de Dominguez (Mayor of Queretaro).
1507 **531** 80c. pink, black and bright pink 10 10

532 "Allegory of National Culture" (Alfaro Siqueiros)

1979. 50th Anniv of National University's Autonomy. Multicoloured.
1508 80c. Type **532** (postage) . . 10 10
1509 3p. "The Conquest of Energy" (Chavez Morado) 20 10
1510 1p.60 "The Return of Quetzalcoatl" (Chavez Morado) (air) 10 10
1511 4p.30 "Students reaching for Culture" (Alfaro Siqueiros) 15 10

533 Messenger and U.P.U. Emblem

534 Emiliano Zapata (after Diego Rivera)

1979. Air. Centenary of Mexico's Admission to U.P.U.
1512 **533** 1p.60 yellow, black and brown 10 10

1979. Birth Centenary of Emiliano Zapata (revolutionary).
1513 **534** 80c. multicoloured . . . 10 10

535 Football

536 Tepoztlan, Morelos

1979. "Universiada '79", 10th World University Games, Mexico City (2nd issue). Multicoloured.
1514 50c. Type **535** (postage) . . 10 10
1515 80c. Volleyball 10 10
1516 1p. Basketball 10 10
1518 1p.60 Tennis (air) 10 10
1519 5p.50 Swimming 30 20

1979. Tourism (1st series). Multicoloured.
1526 80c. Type **536** (postage) . . 10 10
1527 80c. Mexacaltitan, Nayarit 10 10
1528 1p.60 Agua Azul waterfall, Chipas (air) 10 10
1529 1p.60 King Coliman statue, Colima 10 10
See also Nos. 1631/4 and 1675/8.

537 Congress Emblem

538 Edison Lamp

1979. Air. 11th Congress and Assembly of International Industrial Design Council.
1530 **537** 1p.60 black, mauve and turquoise 10 10

1979. Air. Centenary of Electric Light.
1531 **538** 1p.60 multicoloured . . 10 10

539 Martin de Olivares (postmaster)

540 Assembly Emblem

1979. 400th Anniv of Royal Proclamation of Mail Services in the New World. Multicoloured.
1532 80c. Type **539** (postage) . . 10 10
1533 1p.60 Martin Enriquez de Almanza (viceroy of New Spain) (air) 10 10
1534 5p.50 King Philip II of Spain 35 20

1979. Air. 8th General Assembly of Latin American Universities Union.
1536 **540** 1p.60 multicoloured . . 10 10

541 Shepherd

542 Moon Symbol from Mexican Codex

1979. Christmas. Multicoloured.
1537 50c. Type **541** (postage) . . 10 10
1538 1p.60 Girl and Christmas tree (air) 10 10

1979. Air. 10th Anniv of First Man on Moon.
1539 **542** 2p.50 multicoloured . . 15 10

543 Church, Yanhuitlan

1980. Air. Mexican Arts and Sciences (8th series). Multicoloured.
1540 1p.60 Type **543** 10 10
1541 1p.60 Monastery, Yuriria . . 10 10
1542 1p.60 Church, Tlayacapan 10 10
1543 1p.60 Church, Actopan . . 10 10
1544 1p.60 Church, Acolman . . 10 10

544 Steps and Snake's Head

1980. National Pre-Hispanic Monuments (1st series). Multicoloured.
1545 80c. Type **544** (postage) . . 10 10
1546 1p.60 Doble Tlaloc (rain god) (air) 10 10
1547 5p.50 Coyolzauhqui (moon goddess) 35 20
See also Nos. 1565/7 and 1605/7.

1980. Mexican Fauna (2nd series). As T **516**. Multicoloured.
1548 80c. Common turkey (postage) 90 15
1549 1p.60 Greater flamingo (air) 90 40

1980. Mexican Flowers (2nd series). As T **518**. Multicoloured.
1550 80c. "Tajetes erecta" (postage) 15 10
1551 1p.60 "Vanilla planifolia" (air) 25 10

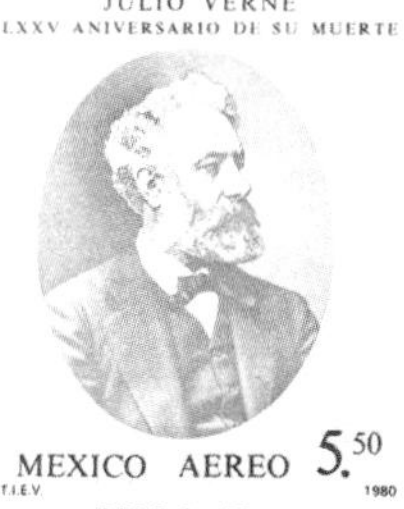

545 Jules Verne

1980. Air. 75th Death Anniv of Jules Verne (author).
1552 **545** 5p.50 brown and black 35 20

546 Skeleton smoking Cigar (after Guadalupe Posada)

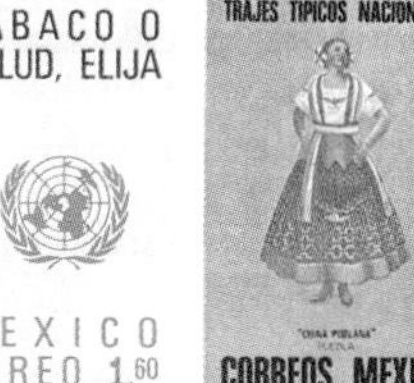

547 China Poblana, Puebla

1980. Air. World Health Day. Anti-smoking Campaign.
1553 **546** 1p.60 purple, blue & red 10 10

1980. National Costumes (1st series). Multicoloured.
1554 50c. Type **547** (postage) . . 10 10
1555 80c. Jarocha, Veracruz . . . 10 10
1556 1p.60 Chiapaneca, Chiapas (air) 10 10
See also Nos. 1588/90.

548 Family

549 Cuauhtemoc (last Aztec Emperor)

1980. 10th Population and Housing Census.
1557 **548** 3p. black and silver . . . 20 10

1980. Pre-Hispanic Personalities (1st series). Multicoloured.
1558 80c. Type **549** 10 10
1559 1p.60 Nezahualcoyotl (governor of Tetzcoco) . . 10 10
1560 5p.50 Eight Deer Tiger's Claw (11th Mixtec king) 35 20
See also Nos. 1642/4 and 1846/8.

550 Xipe (Aztec god of medicine)

551 Bronze Medal

1980. 22nd World Biennial Congress of International College of Surgeons, Mexico City.
1561 **550** 1p.60 multicoloured . . 10 10

1980. Olympic Games, Moscow.
1562 **551** 1p.60 bronze, black and turquoise 10 10
1563 – 3p. silver, black and blue 20 10
1564 – 5p.50 gold, black and red 35 20
DESIGNS: 3p. Silver medal; 5p.50, Gold medal.

1980. National Pre-Hispanic Monuments (2nd series). As T **554**. Multicoloured.
1565 80c. Sacred glass 10 10
1566 1p.60 Stone snail 10 10
1567 5p.50 Chac Mool (god) . . 35 20

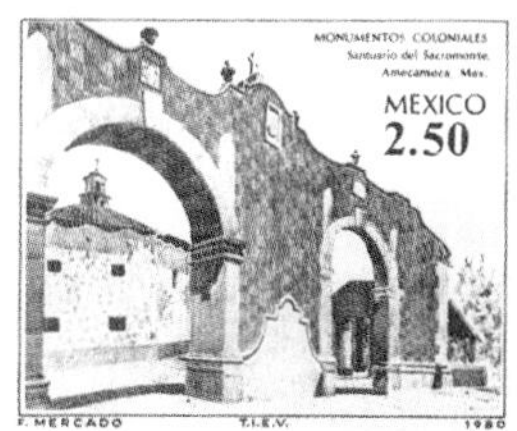

552 Sacromonte Sanctuary, Amecameca

1980. Colonial Architecture (1st series).
1568 **552** 2p.50 grey and black . . 20 10
1569 – 2p.50 grey and black . . 20 10
1570 – 3p. grey and black . . . 25 10
1571 – 3p. grey and black . . . 25 10
DESIGNS—HORIZ: No. 1552, St. Catherine's Convent, Patzcuaro; No. 1554, Hermitage, Cuernavaca. VERT: No. 1553, Basilica, Culiapan.
See also Nos. 1617/20, 1660/3, 1695/8 and 1784/7.

553 Quetzalcoatl (god)

554 Arms of Sinaloa

1980. World Tourism Conference, Manila, Philippines.
1572 **553** 2p.50 multicoloured . . 15 10

1980. 150th Anniv of Sinaloa State.
1573 **554** 1p.60 multicoloured . . 10 10

555 Straw Angel

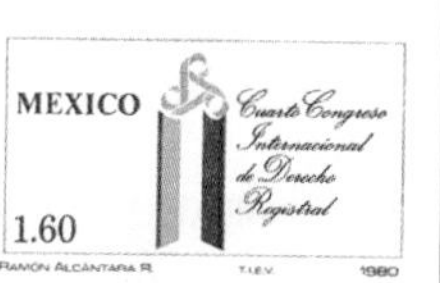

556 Congress Emblem

1980. Christmas. Multicoloured.
1574 50c. Type **555** 10 10
1575 1p.60 Poinsettia in a jug . . 10 10

1980. 4th International Civil Justice Congress.
1576 **556** 1p.60 multicoloured . . 10 10

557 Glass Demijohn and Animals

558 "Simon Bolivar" (after Paulin Guerin)

1980. Mexican Crafts (1st series). Multicoloured.
1577 50c. Type **557** 10 10
1578 1p. Poncho 10 10
1579 3p. Wooden mask 20 15
See also Nos. 1624/6.

1980. 150th Death Anniv of Simon Bolivar.
1580 **558** 4p. multicoloured . . . 30 20

559 Vicente Guerrero

560 Valentin Gomez Farias

1981. 150th Death Anniv of Vicente Guerrero (liberator).
1581 **559** 80c. multicoloured . . . 10 10

1981. Birth Bicentenary of Valentin Gomez Farias.
1582 **560** 80c. black and green . . 10 10

561 Table Tennis Balls in Flight

1981. 1st Latin-American Table Tennis Cup.
1583 **561** 4p. multicoloured . . . 30 20

562 Jesus Gonzalez Ortega

563 Gabino Barreda

1981. Death Centenary of Jesus Gonzalez Ortega.
1584 **562** 80c. light brown & brown 10 10

1981. Death Centenary of Gabino Barreda (politician).
1585 **563** 80c. pink, black and green 10 10

564 Benito Juarez

565 Foundation Monument

1981. 175th Birth Anniv of Benito Juarez (patriot).
1586 **564** 1p.60 green, brn & lt brn 15 10

1981. 450th Anniv of Puebla City.
1587 **565** 80c. multicoloured . . . 10 10

1981. National Costumes (2nd series). Vert designs as T **547**. Multicoloured.
1588 50c. Purepecha, Michoacan 10 10
1589 80c. Charra, Jalisco 10 10
1590 1p.60 Mestiza, Yucatan . . 15 10

1981. Mexican Fauna (3rd series). Vert designs as T **516**. Multicoloured.
1591 80c. Northern mockingbird 65 20
1592 1p.60 Mexican trogon . . . 1·25 40

1981. Mexican Flowers (3rd series). Vert designs as T **518**. Multicoloured.
1593 80c. Avocado 10 10
1594 1p.60 Cacao 15 10

566 "Martyrs of Cananea" (David A. Siqueiros)

1981. 75th Anniv of Martyrs of Cananea.
1595 **566** 1p.60 multicoloured . . 15 10

567 Toy Drummer with One Arm

568 Arms of Queretaro

1981. International Year of Disabled People.
1596 **567** 4p. multicoloured . . . 30 20

1981. 450th Anniv of Queretaro City.
1597 **568** 80c. multicoloured . . . 10 10

569 Mexican Stamp of 1856 and Postal Service Emblem

1981. 125th Anniv of First Mexican Stamp.
1598 **569** 4p. multicoloured . . . 30 20

570 Sir Alexander Fleming

572 St. Francisco Xavier Claver

571 Union Congress Building and Emblem

1981. Birth Centenary of Sir Alexander Fleming (discoverer of penicillin).
1599 **570** 5p. blue and orange . . 35 10

1981. Opening of New Union Congress Building.
1600 **571** 1p.60 green and red . . 10 10

1981. 250th Birth Anniv of St. Francis Xavier Claver.
1601 **572** 80c. multicoloured . . . 10 10

573 "Desislava" (detail of Bulgarian Fresco)

1981. 1300th Anniv of Bulgarian State. Mult.
1602 1p.60 Type **573** 10 10
1603 4p. Horse-headed cup from Thrace 25 20
1604 7p. Madara Horseman (relief) 45 30

1981. Pre-Hispanic Monuments. As T **544**. Multicoloured.
1605 80c. Seated God 10 10
1606 1p.60 Alabaster deer's head 15 10
1607 4p. Jade fish 45 20

574 Pablo Picasso

1981. Birth Centenary of Pablo Picasso (artist).
1608 **574** 5p. deep green and green 35 20

575 Shepherd **576** Wheatsheaf

1981. Christmas. Multicoloured.
1609 50c. Type **575** 10 10
1610 1p.60 Praying girl 15 10

1981. World Food Day.
1611 **576** 4p. multicoloured . . . 25 15

577 Thomas Edison, Lightbulb and Gramophone

1981. 50th Death Anniv of Thomas Edison (inventor).
1612 **577** 4p. stone, brown & green 25 15

578 Co-operation Emblem and Wheat

1981. International Meeting on Co-operation and Development, Cancun.
1613 **578** 4p. blue, grey and black 25 20

579 Globe and Diesel Locomotive

1981. 15th Pan-American Railway Congress.
1614 **579** 1p.60 multicoloured . . 50 25

580 Film Frame

1981. 50th Anniv of Mexican Sound Movies.
1615 **580** 4p. grey, black and green 25 20

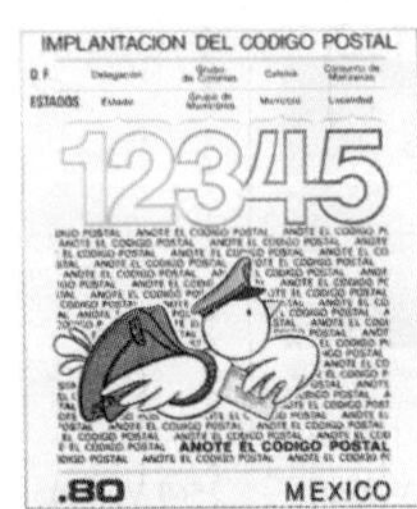

581 Postcode and Bird delivering Letter

1981. Inauguration of Postcodes.
1616 **581** 80c. multicoloured . . . 10 10

1981. Colonial Architecture (2nd series). As T **552**. Multicoloured.
1617 4p. Mascarones House . . . 25 15
1618 4p. La Merced Convent . . 25 15
1619 5p. Chapel of the Third Order, Texcoco 30 20
1620 5p. Father Tembleque Aqueduct, Otumba . . . 30 20

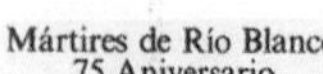

582 "Martyrs of Rio Blanco" (Orozco)

1982. 75th Anniv of Martyrs of Rio Blanco.
1621 **582** 80c. multicoloured . . . 10 10

583 Ignacio Lopez Rayon

1982. 150th Death Anniv of Ignacio Lopez Rayon.
1622 **583** 1p.60 green, red & black 10 10

584 Postal Headquarters

1982. 75th Anniv of Postal Headquarters.
1623 **584** 4p. pink and green . . . 25 20

1982. Mexican Crafts (2nd series). As T **557**. Multicoloured.
1624 50c. "God's Eye" (Huichol art) 10 10
1625 1p. Ceramic snail 10 10
1626 3p. Tiger mask 20 15

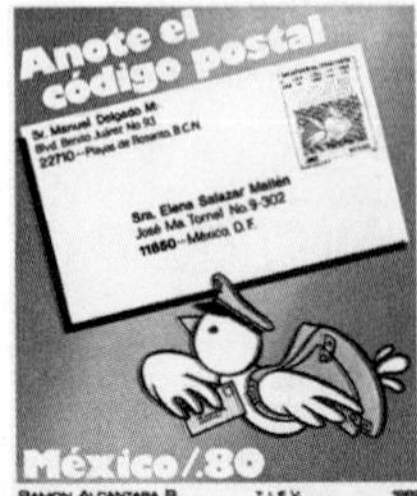

585 Postcoded Letter and Bird

1982. Postcode Publicity.
1627 **585** 80c. multicoloured . . . 10 10

586 Dr. Robert Koch and Cross of Lorraine

1982. Centenary of Discovery of Tubercle Bacillus.
1628 **586** 4p. multicoloured . . . 15 10

587 Military Academy **588** Arms of Oaxaca

1982. 50th Anniv of Military Academy.
1629 **587** 80c. yellow, black & gold 10 10

1982. 450th Anniv of Oaxaca City.
1630 **588** 1p.60 multicoloured . . 10 10

1982. Tourism (2nd series). As T **563**. Multicoloured.
1631 80c. Basaseachic Falls, Chihuahua 10 10
1632 80c. Natural rock formation, Pueblo Nuevo, Durango 10 10
1633 1p.60 Mayan City of Edzna, Campeche 10 10
1634 1p.60 La Venta (Olmeca sculpture, Tabasco) . . . 10 10

589 Footballers

1982. World Cup Football Championship, Spain. Multicoloured.
1635 1p.60 Type **589** 10 10
1636 4p. Dribbling 15 10
1637 7p. Tackling 25 15

590 Hawksbill Turtles

1982. Mexican Fauna. Multicoloured.
1638 1p.60 Type **590** 10 10
1639 4p. Grey Whales 15 30

591 Vicente Guerrero

1982. Birth Bicentenary of Vicente Guerrero (independence fighter).
1640 **591** 80c. multicoloured . . . 10 10

592 Symbols of Peace and Communication

1982. Second U.N. Conference on the Exploration and Peaceful Uses of Outer Space, Vienna.
1641 **592** 4p. multicoloured . . . 10 10

1982. Pre-Hispanic Personalities (2nd series). As T **549**. Multicoloured.
1642 80c. Tariacuri 10 10
1643 1p.60 Acamapichtli 10 10
1644 4p. Ten Deer Tiger's breastplate 10 10

593 Pawpaw ("Carica papaya")

1982. Mexican Flora. Multicoloured.
1645 80c. Type **593** 10 10
1646 1p.60 Maize ("Zea mays") 10 10

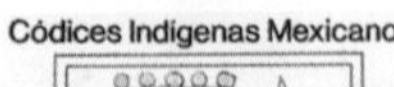

594 Astrologer

1982. Native Mexican Codices. Florentine Codex. Multicoloured.
1647 80c. Type **594** 10 10
1648 1p.60 Arriving at School . . 10 10
1649 4p. Musicians 10 10

595 Manuel Gamio (anthropologist)

1982. Mexican Arts and Scientists. Multicoloured.
1650 1p.60 Type **595** 10 10
1651 1p.60 Isaac Ochoterena (biologist) 10 10
1652 1p.60 Angel Maria Garibay (philologist) 10 10
1653 1p.60 Manuel Sandoval Vallarta (nuclear physicist) 10 10
1654 1p.60 Guillermo Gonzalez Camarena (electronics engineer) 10 10

596 State Archives Building

1982. Inaug of State Archives Building.
1655 **596** 1p.60 black and green 10 10

597 Dove and Peace Text

1982. Christmas. Multicoloured.
1656 50c. Type **597** 10 10
1657 1p.60 Dove and Peace text (different) 10 10

598 Hands holding Food

1982. Mexican Food System.
1658 **598** 1p.60 multicoloured . . 20 10

599 "Revolutionary Mexico" Stamp, 1956

1982. Inauguration of Revolution Museum, Chihuahua.
1659 **599** 1p.60 grey and green . . 10 10

1982. Colonial Architecture (3rd series). As T **552**. Multicoloured.
1660 1p.60 College of Sts. Peter and Paul, Mexico City . . 10 10
1661 8p. Convent of Jesus Maria, Mexico City 15 10
1662 10p. Open Chapel, Tlalmanalco 20 15
1663 14p. Convent, Actopan . . 25 20

600 Alfonso Garcia Robles and Laurel

601 Jose Vasconcelos

1982. Alfonso Garcia Robles (Nobel Peace Prize Winner) Commemoration.
1664 **600** 1p.60 grey, black & gold 10 10
1665 – 14p. pink, black and gold 25 20
DESIGN: 14p. Robles and medal.

1982. Birth Centenary of Jose Vasconcelos (philosopher).
1666 **601** 1p.60 black and blue . . 10 10

602 W.C.Y. Emblem and Methods of Communication

1983. World Communications Year.
1667 **602** 16p. multicoloured . . . 20 15

603 Sonora State Civil War Stamp, 1913

1983. "Herfilex 83" Mexican Revolution Stamp Exhibition.
1668 **603** 6p. brown, black & green 10 10

604 "Nauticas Mexico" (container ship), World Map and I.M.O. Emblem

1983. 25th Anniv of International Maritime Organization.
1669 **604** 16p. multicoloured . . . 1·25 30

605 Doctor treating Patient

1983. Constitutional Right to Health Protection.
1670 **605** 6p. green and red . . . 10 10

606 Valentin Gomez Farias (founder) and Arms of Society

1983. 150th Anniv of Mexican Geographical and Statistical Society.
1671 **606** 6p. multicoloured . . . 10 10

607 Football

1983. 2nd World Youth Football Championship, Mexico.
1672 **607** 6p. black and green . . 10 10
1673 13p. black and red . . . 15 10
1674 14p. black and blue . . 20 15

1983. Tourism. As T **536**. Multicoloured.
1675 6p. Federal Palace, Queretaro 10 10
1676 6p. Water tank, San Luis Potosi 10 10
1677 13p. Cable car, Zacatecas 15 10
1678 14p. Carved head of Kohunlich, Quintana Roo 20 15

608 Bolivar on Horseback

1983. Birth Bicentenary of Simon Bolivar.
1679 **608** 21p. multicoloured . . . 25 15

609 Angela Peralta

610 Agave

1983. Death Centenary of Angela Peralta (opera singer).
1680 **609** 9p. light brown & brown 10 10

1983. Mexican Flora and Fauna (5th series). Multicoloured.
1681 9p. Type **610** 10 10
1682 9p. Sapodilla 10 10
1683 9p. Swallowtail 30 10
1684 9p. Boa constrictor 10 10

611 Two Candles

1983. Christmas. Multicoloured.
1685 9p. Type **611** 10 10
1686 20p. Three candles 25 15

612 S.C.T. Emblem

1983. Integral Communications and Transport System.
1687 **612** 13p. blue and black . . 15 10

613 Carlos Chavez (musician)

1983. Mexican Arts and Sciences (10th series). Contemporary Artists. Multicoloured.
1688 **613** 9p. brown, light brown and deep brown . . . 10 10
1689 – 9p. brown, light brown and deep brown . . . 10 10
1690 – 9p. deep brown, light brown and brown . . 10 10
1691 – 9p. light brown, deep brown and brown . . 10 10
1692 – 9p. deep brown, stone and brown 10 10
DESIGNS: No. 1689, Francisco Goitia (painter); No. 1690, S. Diaz Miron (poet); No. 1691, Carlos Bracho (sculptor); No. 1692, Fanny Anitua (singer).

614 Orozco (self-portrait)

1983. Birth Centenary of Jose Clemente Orozco (artist).
1693 **614** 9p. multicoloured . . . 10 10

615 Human Rights Emblem

1983. 35th Anniv of Human Rights Declaration.
1694 **615** 20p. deep blue, yellow and blue 25 15

1983. Colonial Architecture (4th series). As T **552**. Each grey and black.
1695 9p. Convent, Malinalco . . 10 10
1696 20p. Cathedral, Cuernavaca 25 15
1697 21p. Convent, Tepeji del Rio 25 15
1698 24p. Convent, Atlatlahucan 30 20

616 Antonio Caso and Books

1983. Birth Centenary of Antonio Caso (philospher).
1699 **616** 9p. blue, lilac and red . . 10 10

617 Joaquin Velazquez

1983. Bicentenary of Royal Legislation on Mining.
1700 **617** 9p. multicoloured . . . 10 10

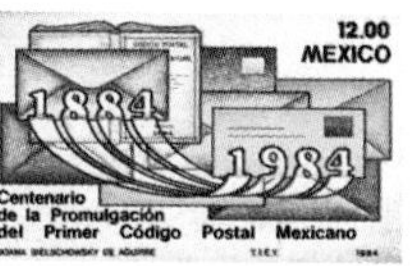

618 Book and Envelopes

1984. Centenary of First Postal Laws.
1701 **618** 12p. multicoloured . . . 15 10

619 Children dancing around Drops of Anti-Polio Serum

1984. World Anti-polio Campaign.
1702 **619** 12p. multicoloured . . . 15 10

620 Muscovy Duck

1984. Mexican Fauna (6th series). Multicoloured.
1703 12p. Type **620** 70 65
1704 20p. Red-billed whistling duck . . . . 1·40 1·25

621 Xoloitzcuintle Dog

1984. World Dog Show.
1705 **621** 12p. multicoloured . . . 15 10

622 Bank Headquarters

1984. Centenary of National Bank.
1706 **622** 12p. multicoloured . . . 15 10

623 Hands holding Trees

624 Putting the Shot

1984. Protection of Forest Resources.
1707 **623** 20p. multicoloured . . . 20 15

1984. Olympic Games, Los Angeles. Multicoloured.
1708 14p. Type **624** 15 15
1709 20p. Show jumping 20 15
1710 23p. Gymnastics (floor exercise) 25 20
1711 24p. Diving 25 20
1712 25p. Boxing 25 20
1713 26p. Fencing 25 20

625 Mexican and Russian Flags

1984. 60th Anniv of Diplomatic Relations with U.S.S.R.
1715 **625** 23p. multicoloured . . . 25 20

626 Hand holding U.N. emblem

1984. International Population Conference.
1716 **626** 20p. multicoloured . . . 20 15

627 Gen. Mugica

1984. Birth Centenary of General Francisco Mugica (politician).
1717 **627** 14p. brown and black . . 15 15

628 Emblem and Dates

629 Airline Emblem

1984. 50th Anniv of Economic Culture Fund.
1718 **628** 14p. brown, black and red 15 15

1984. 50th Anniv of Aeromexico (state airline).
1719 – 14p. multicoloured . . . 15 15
1720 **629** 20p. black and red . . . 20 15
DESIGN—36 × 44 mm: 14p. "Red Cactus" (sculpture, Sebastian).

630 Palace of Fine Arts

1984. 50th Anniv of Palace of Fine Arts.
1721 **630** 14p. blue, black and brown 15 15

631 Metropolitan Cathedral (detail of facade)

633 Dove and Hand holding Flame

632 Coatzacoalcos Bridge

1984. 275th Anniv of Chihuahua City.
1722 **631** 14p. brown and black . . 15 15

1984. Inaug of Coatzacoalcos Bridge.
1723 **632** 14p. multicoloured . . . 15 15

1984. World Disarmament Week.
1724 **633** 20p. multicoloured . . . 20 15

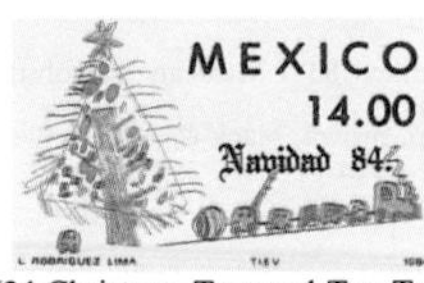

634 Christmas Tree and Toy Train

1984. Christmas. Multicoloured.
1725 14p. Type **634** 50 25
1726 20p. Breaking the pinata (balloon filled with gifts) (vert) 20 15

635 Ignacio Manuel Altamirano

1984. 150th Birth Anniv of Ignacio Manuel Altamirano (politician and journalist).
1727 **635** 14p. red and black . . . 15 15

636 Maps, Graph and Text

1984. 160th Anniv of State Audit Office.
1728 **636** 14p. multicoloured . . . 15 15

637 Half a Football and Mexican Colours

1984. Mexico, Site of 1986 World Cup Football Championship. Multicoloured.
1729 20p. Type **637** 20 15
1730 24p. Football and Mexican colours 25 20

638 Romulo Gallegos

639 State Arms and Open Register

1984. Birth Centenary of Romulo Gallegos.
1731 **638** 20p. black and blue . . 20 15

1984. 125th Anniv of Mexican Civil Register.
1732 **639** 24p. blue 25 20

640 Mexican Flag

641 Johann Sebastian Bach

1985. 50th Anniv of National Flag.
1733 **640** 22p. multicoloured . . . 25 20

1985. 300th Birth Anniv of Johann Sebastian Bach (composer).
1734 **641** 35p. red and black . . . 15 30

642 I.Y.Y. Emblem

643 Children and Fruit within Book

1985. International Youth Year.
1735 **642** 35p. purple, gold and black 15 30

1985. Child Survival Campaign.
1736 **643** 36p. multicoloured . . . 15 10

644 Commemorative Medallion

1985. 450th Anniv of State Mint.
1737 **644** 35p. gold, mauve & blue 15 10

645 Victor Hugo, Text and Gateway

1985. Death Centenary of Victor Hugo (novelist).
1738 **645** 35p. grey 15 10

646 Hidalgo 8r. Stamp, 1856

1985. "Mexifil 85" Stamp Exhibition.
1739 **646** 22p. grey, black and purple 10 10
1740 – 35p. grey, black and blue 15 10
1741 – 36p. multicoloured . . . 15 10
DESIGNS: 35p. Carranza 10c. stamp, 1916; 36p. Juarez 50p. stamp, 1975.

647 Rockets, Satellite, Nurse and Computer Operator

1985. Launching of First Morelos Satellite. Mult.
1743 22p. Type **647** 10 10
1744 36p. Camera, dish aerial, satellite and computers . . 15 10
1745 90p. Camera, dish aerial, satellite, television and couple telephoning . . . 25 20
Nos. 1743/5 were printed together, se-tenant, forming a composite design.

648 Conifer

1985. 9th World Forestry Congress, Mexico.
1747 **648** 22p. brown, black and green 10 10
1748 – 35p. brown, black and green 15 10
1749 – 36p. brown, black and green 15 10
DESIGNS: 35p. Silk-cotton trees; 36p. Mahogany tree.

649 Martin Luis Guzman

1985. Mexican Arts and Sciences (11th series). Contemporary Writers.
1750 **649** 22p. grey and blue . . . 10 10
1751 – 22p. grey and blue . . . 10 10
1752 – 22p. grey and blue . . . 10 10
1753 – 22p. grey and blue . . . 10 10
1754 – 22p. grey and blue . . . 10 10
DESIGNS: No. 1751, Augustin Yanez; 1752, Alfonso Reyes; 1753, Jose Ruben Romero; 1754, Artemio de Valle-Arizpe.

650 Miguel Hidalgo

1985. 175th Anniv of Independence Movement. Each green, black and red.
1755 22p. Type **650** 10 10
1756 35p. Jose Ma. Morelos . . . 10 10
1757 35p. Ignacio Allende 10 10
1758 36p. Leona Vigario 10 10
1759 110p. Vicente Guerrero . . 20 15

651 San Ildefonso

1985. 75th Anniv of National University. Mult.
1761 26p. Type **651** 10 10
1762 26p. Emblem 10 10
1763 40p. Modern building . . . 10 10
1764 45p. 1910 crest and Justo Sierra (founder) 10 10
1765 90p. University crest 15 10

652 Rural and Industrial Landscapes

1985. 25th Anniv of Inter-American Development Bank.
1766 **652** 26p. multicoloured . . . 10 10

653 Guns and Doves **654** Hands and Dove

1985. United Nations Disarmament Week.
1767 **653** 36p. multicoloured . . . 10 10

1985. 40th Anniv of U.N.O.
1768 **654** 26p. multicoloured . . . 10 10

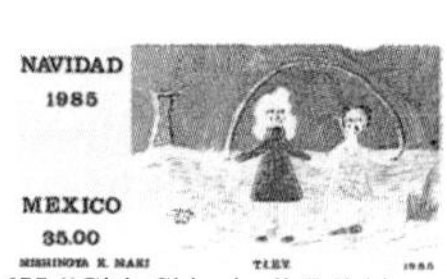

655 "Girls Skipping" (Mishinoya K. Maki)

1985. Christmas. Children's Paintings. Mult.
1769 26p. Disabled and able-bodied children playing (Margarita Salazar) . . . 10 10
1770 35p. Type **655** 10 10

656 Soldadera

1985. 75th Anniv of 1910 Revolution. Each red, black and green.
1771 26p. Type **656** 10 10
1772 35p. Pancho Villa 10 10
1773 40p. Emiliano Zapata . . . 10 10
1774 45p. Venustiano Carranza 10 10
1775 110p. Francisco Madero . . 20 15

657 "Vigilante" (Federico Silva)

1985. 2nd "Morelos" Telecommunications Satellite Launch.
1777 – 26p. black and blue . . 10 10
1778 **657** 35p. grey, pink and black 10 10
1779 – 45p. multicoloured . . . 10 10
DESIGNS—VERT: 26p. "Cosmonaut" (sculpture by Sebastian). HORIZ: 45p. "Mexican Astronaut" (painting by Cauduro).

658 "Mexico" holding Book

1985. 25th Anniv of Free Textbooks National Commission.
1781 **658** 26p. multicoloured . . . 10 10

659 Olympic Stadium, University City

1985. World Cup Football Championship, Mexico. Each grey and black.
1782 26p. Type **659** 10 10
1783 45p. Azteca Stadium 10 10

1985. Colonial Architecture (5th series). Vert designs as T **552**. Each brown and black.
1784 26p. Vizcayan College, Mexico City 10 10
1785 35p. Counts of Heras y Soto Palace, Mexico City . . . 10 10
1786 40p. Counts of Calimaya Palace, Mexico City . . . 10 10
1787 45p. St. Carlos Academy, Mexico City 10 10

661 Luis Enrique Erro Planetarium

1986. 50th Anniv of National Polytechnic Institute. Multicoloured.
1788 40p. Type **661** 10 10
1789 65p. National School of Arts and Crafts 10 10
1790 75p. Founders, emblem and "50" 10 10

1986. Mexican Flowers (6th series). As T **518**. Multicoloured.
1791 40p. Calabash 10 10
1792 65p. "Nopalea coccinellifera" (cactus) . . 10 10

663 Doll

1986. World Health Day.
1793 **663** 65p. multicoloured . . . 10 10

664 Halley and Comet

1986. Appearance of Halley's Comet.
1794 **664** 90p. multicoloured . . . 15 10

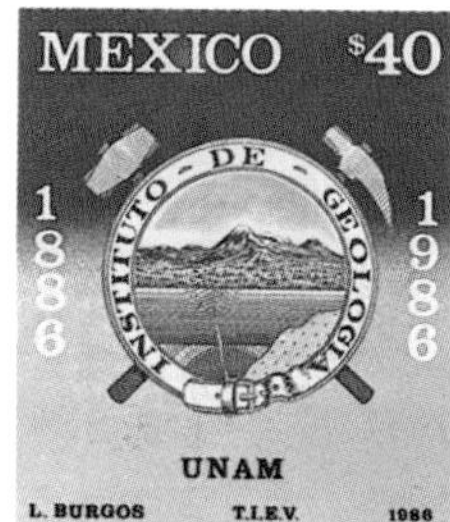

665 Emblem

1986. Centenary of Geological Institute.
1795 **665** 40p. multicoloured . . . 10 10

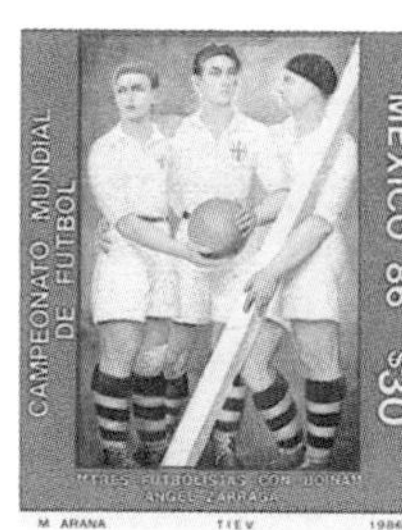

666 "Three Footballers with Berets"

1986. World Cup Football Championship, Mexico (2nd issue). Paintings by Angel Zarraga. Multicoloured.
1796 30p. Type **666** 10 10
1797 40p. "Portrait of Ramon Novaro" 10 10
1798 65p. "Sunday" 10 10
1799 70p. "Portrait of Ernest Charles Gimpel" 10 10
1800 90p. "Three Footballers" . . 15 10

667 Ignacio Allende

1986. 175th Death Annivs of Independence Heroes. Multicoloured.
1802 40p. Type **667** 10 10
1803 40p. Miguel Hidalgo (after J. C. Orozco) 10 10
1804 65p. Juan Aldama 10 10
1805 75p. Mariano Jimenez . . . 10 10

668 Mexican Arms over "FTF" **669** Nicolas Bravo

1986. 50th Anniv of Fiscal Tribunal.
1806 **668** 40p. black, blue and grey 10 10

1986. Birth Bicentenary of Nicolas Bravo (independence fighter).
1807 **669** 40p. multicoloured . . . 10 10

670 "Zapata Landscape"

1986. Paintings by Diego Rivera. Multicoloured.
1808 50p. Type **670** 10 10
1809 80p. "Nude with Arum Lilies" 10 10
1810 110p. "Vision of a Sunday Afternoon Walk on Central Avenue" (horiz) 20 15

671 Guadalupe Victoria

1986. Birth Bicentenary of Guadalupe Victoria (first President).
1811 **671** 50p. multicoloured . . . 10 10

672 People depositing Produce

1986. 50th Anniv of National Depositories.
1812 **672** 40p. multicoloured . . . 10 10

673 Pigeon above Hands holding Posthorn

674 Emblem

1986. World Post Day.
1813 **673** 120p. multicoloured . . 20 15

1986. Foundation of National Commission to Mark 500th Anniv (1992) of Discovery of America.
1814 **674** 50p. black and red . . . 10 10

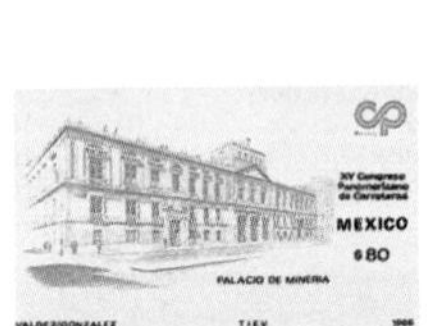

675 Ministry of Mines

676 Liszt

1986. 15th Pan-American Roads Congress.
1815 **675** 80p. grey and black . . 10 10

1986. 175th Birth Anniv of Franz Liszt (composer).
1816 **676** 100p. brown and black 15 10

677 U.N. and "Pax Cultura" Emblems

1986. International Peace Year.
1817 **677** 80p. blue, red and black 10 10

678 Jose Maria Pino Suarez (1st Vice-President of Revolutionary Govt.)

1986. Famous Mexicans buried in The Rotunda of Illustrious Men (1st series).
1818 **678** 50p. multicoloured . . . 10 10
See also Nos. 1823/4, 1838 and 1899.

679 King

680 "Self-portrait"

1986. Christmas. Multicoloured.
1819 50p. Type **679** 10 10
1820 80p. Angel 10 10

1986. Birth Centenary of Diego Rivera (artist).
1821 **680** 80p. multicoloured . . . 10 10

681 Baby receiving Vaccination

682 Perez de Leon College

1987. National Days for Poliomyelitis Vaccination.
1822 **681** 50p. multicoloured . . . 10 10

1987. Famous Mexicans buried in The Rotunda of Illustrious Men (2nd series). As T **678**. Mult.
1823 100p. Jose Maria Iglesias . . 10 10
1824 100p. Pedro Sainz de Baranda 10 10

1987. Centenary of Higher Education.
1825 **682** 100p. multicoloured . . 10 10

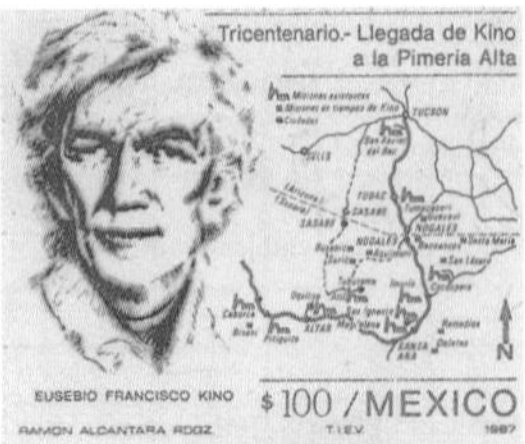

683 Kino and Map

1987. 300th Anniv of Father Eusebio Francisco Kino's Mission to Pimeria Alta.
1826 **683** 100p. multicoloured . . 10 10

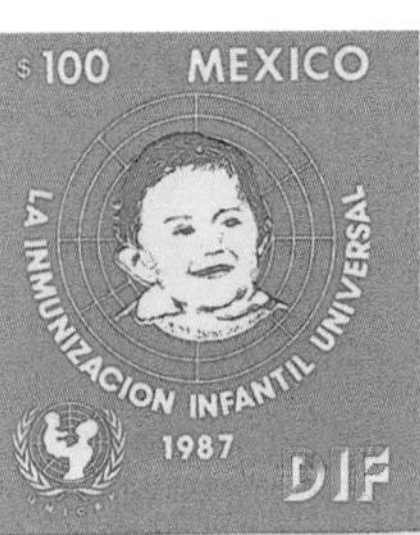

684 Baby's Head

1987. Child Immunization Campaign.
1827 **684** 100p. deep blue and blue 10 10

685 Staircase

686 "5th of May, 1862, and the Siege of Puebla" Exhibition Poster, 1887

1987. 50th Anniv of Puebla Independent University.
1828 **685** 200p. grey, pink and black 10 10

1987. 125th Anniv of Battle of Puebla.
1829 **686** 100p. multicoloured . . 10 10

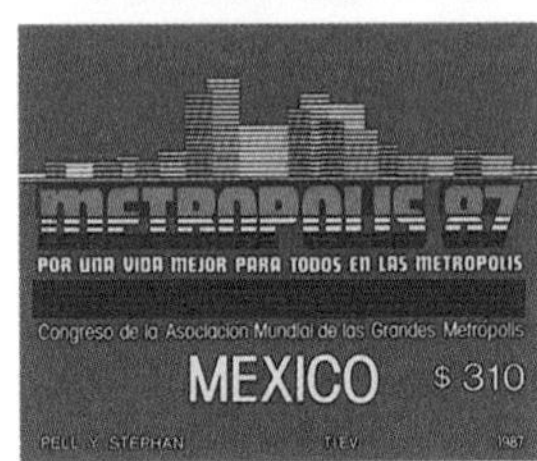

687 Stylized City

1987. "Metropolis 87" World Association of Large Cities Congress.
1830 **687** 310p. red, black and green 45 30

688 Lacquerware Tray, Uruapan, Michoacan

689 Genaro Estrada (author and pioneer of democracy)

1987. Handicrafts. Multicoloured.
1831 100p. Type **688** 10 10
1832 200p. Woven blanket, Santa Ana Chiautempan, Tlaxcala 10 10
1833 230p. Ceramic jar with lid, Puebla, Puebla 15 10

1987. Mexican Arts and Sciences (12th series).
1834 **689** 100p. brown, black and pink 10 10
See also Nos. 1845, 1880 and 1904/5.

690 "Native Traders" (mural, P. O'Higgins)

1987. 50th Anniv of National Foreign Trade Bank.
1835 **690** 100p. multicoloured . . 10 10

691 Diagram of Longitudinal Section through Ship's Hull

1987. 400th Anniv of Publication of First Shipbuilding Manual in America, Diego Garcia de Palacio's "Instrucion Nautica".
1836 **691** 100p. green, blue & brn 10 10

692 Man carrying Sack of Maize Flour

1987. 50th Anniv of National Food Programme.
1837 **692** 100p. multicoloured . . 10 10

1987. Mexicans in Rotunda of Illustrious Men (3rd series). As T **678**. Multicoloured.
1838 100p. Leandro Valle 10 10

693 "Self-portrait with Skull"

1987. Paintings by Saturnino Herran.
1839 **693** 100p. brown and black 15 10
1840 – 100p. multicoloured . . 15 10
1841 – 400p. multicoloured . . 60 50
DESIGNS: No. 1840, "The Offering"; 1841, "Creole with Shawl".

694 Flags of Competing Countries

1987. 10th Pan-American Games, Indianapolis.
1842 **694** 100p. multicoloured . . 10 10
1843 – 200p. black, red and green 10 10
DESIGN: 200p. Running.

695 Electricity Pylon

1987. 50th Anniv of Federal Electricity Commission.
1844 **695** 200p. multicoloured . . 10 10

1987. Mexican Arts and Sciences (13th series). As T **689**. Multicoloured.
1845 100p. J. E. Hernandez y Davalos (author) 10 10

1987. Pre-Hispanic Personalities (3rd series). As T **549**. Multicoloured.
1846 100p. Xolotl (Chichimeca commander) 10 10
1847 200p. Nezahualpilli (leader of Tezcoco tribe) 10 10
1848 400p. Motecuhzoma Ilhuicamina (leader of Tenochtitlan tribe) . . . 45 10

696 Stylized Racing Car

1987. Mexico Formula One Grand Prix.
1849 **696** 100p. multicoloured . . 10 10

697 Mexican Cultural Centre, Mexico City

698 "Santa Maria" and 1922 Mexican Festival Emblem

1987. Mexican Tourism.
1850 **697** 100p. multicoloured . . 10 10

1987. 500th Anniv of "Meeting of Two Worlds" (discovery of America by Columbus) (1st issue).
1851 **698** 150p. multicoloured . . 65 20
See also Nos. 1902, 1941, 1979, 2038 and 2062/6.

699 16th-century Spanish Map of Mexico City

1987. 13th International Cartography Conference.
1852 **699** 150p. multicoloured . . 10 10

1987. Mexican Tourism. As T **697**. Multicoloured.
1853 150p. Michoacan 30 10
1854 150p. Garcia Caves, Nuevo Leon 10 10
1855 150p. View of Mazatlan, Sinaloa 10 10

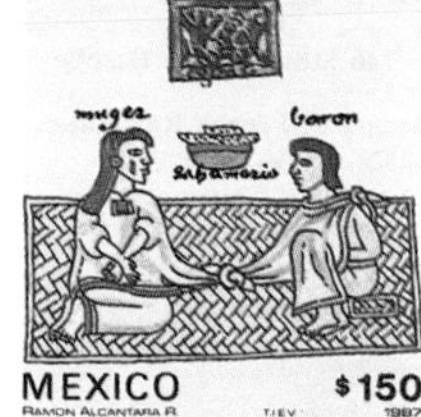

700 Pre-Hispanic Wedding Ceremony

1987. Native Codices. Mendocino Codex. Mult.
1856 150p. Type **700** 10 10
1857 150p. Moctezuma's council chamber 10 10
1858 150p. Foundation of Tenochtitlan 10 10

701 Dove with Olive Twig

1987. Christmas.
1859 **701** 150p. mauve 10 10
1860 – 150p. blue 10 10
DESIGN: No. 1860, As T **701** but dove facing left.

702 "Royal Ordinance for the Carriage of Maritime Mail" Title Page

1987. World Post Day.
1861 **702** 150p. green and grey . . 10 10

703 Circle of Flags

1987. 1st Meeting of Eight Latin-American Presidents, Acapulco. Multicoloured.
1863 250p. Type **703** 10 10
1864 500p. Flags and doves . . . 25 10

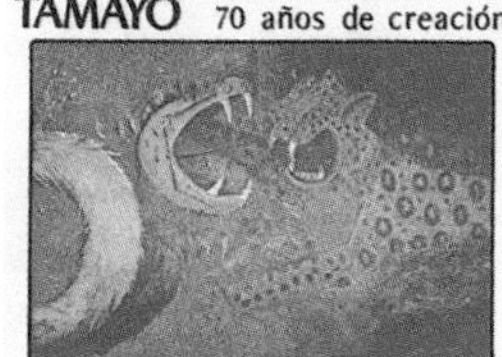

704 "Dualidad 1964"

1987. Rufino Tamayo (painter). "70 Years of Creativity".
1865 **704** 150p. multicoloured . . 10 10

705 Train on Metlac Viaduct

1987. 50th Anniv of Railway Nationalization.
1866 **705** 150p. multicoloured . . 40 15

706 Stradivarius at Work (detail, 19th-century engraving)

1987. 250th Death Anniv of Antonio Stradivarius (violin-maker).
1867 **706** 150p. light violet and violet 10 10

707 Statue of Manuel Crescensio Rejon (promulgator of Yucatan State Constitution)

1988. Constitutional Tribunal, Supreme Court of Justice.
1868 **707** 300p. multicoloured . . 15 10

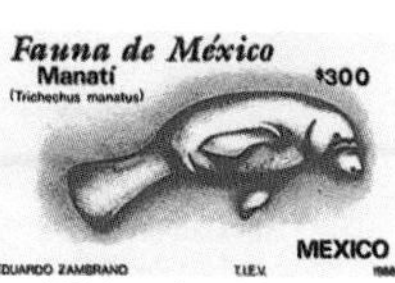

708 American Manatee

1988. Animals. Multicoloured.
1869 300p. Type **708** 15 10
1870 300p. Mexican mole salamander 15 10

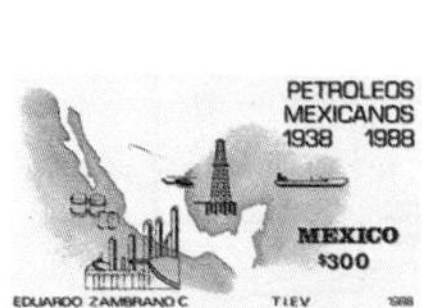

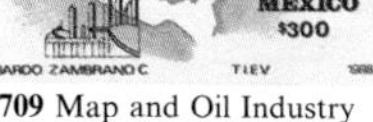
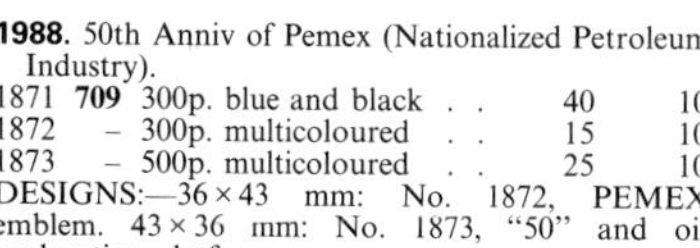

709 Map and Oil Industry Symbols

710 "The Vaccination"

1988. 50th Anniv of Pemex (Nationalized Petroleum Industry).
1871 **709** 300p. blue and black . . 40 10
1872 – 300p. multicoloured . . 15 10
1873 – 500p. multicoloured . . 25 10
DESIGNS:—36 × 43 mm: No. 1872, PEMEX emblem. 43 × 36 mm: No. 1873, "50" and oil exploration platform.

1988. World Health Day (1874) and 40th Anniv of W.H.O. (1875). Paintings by Diego Rivera.
1874 **710** 300p. brown and green 15 10
1875 – 300p. multicoloured . . 15 10
DESIGN:—43 × 36 mm: No. 1875, "The People demand Health".

711 "Death Portrait" (Victor Delfin)

1988. 50th Death Anniv of Cesar Vallejo (painter and poet). Multicoloured.
1876 300p. Type **711** 15 10
1877 300p. Portrait by Arnold Belkin and "Hoy me palpo ..." 15 10
1878 300p. Portrait as in T **711** but larger (30 × 35 mm) 15 10
1879 300p. Portrait as in No. 1877 but larger (23 × 35 mm) 15 10

1988. Mexican Arts and Sciences (14th series). As T **689**.
1880 300p. brown, black and violet 15 10
DESIGN: 300p. Carlos Pellicer (poet).

712 Girl and Boy holding Stamp in Tweezers

1988. "Mepsirrey '88" Stamp Exhibition, Monterrey. Multicoloured.
1881 300p. Type **712** 15 10
1882 300p. Envelope with "Monterrey" handstamp 15 10
1883 500p. Exhibition emblem . . 25 10

713 Hernandos Rodriguez Racing Circuit, Mexico City

1988. Mexico Formula One Grand Prix.
1884 **713** 500p. multicoloured . . 25 10

714 Lopez Verlarde and Rose

715 Emblem

1988. Birth Centenary of Ramon Lopez Verlarde (poet). Multicoloured.
1885 300p. Type **714** 15 10
1886 300p. Abstract 15 10

1988. 50th Anniv of Military Sports.
1887 **715** 300p. multicoloured . . 15 10

716 Chrysanthemum, Container Ship and Flags

1988. Centenary of Mexico–Japan Friendship, Trade and Navigation Treaty.
1888 **716** 500p. multicoloured . . 45 10

717 Map

1988. Oceanographical Assembly.
1889 **717** 500p. multicoloured . . 25 10

718 Runners

719 Boxer and Flags

1988. Olympic Games, Seoul.
1890 **718** 500p. multicoloured . . 25 10

1988. 25th Anniv of World Boxing Council.
1892 **719** 500p. multicoloured . . 25 10

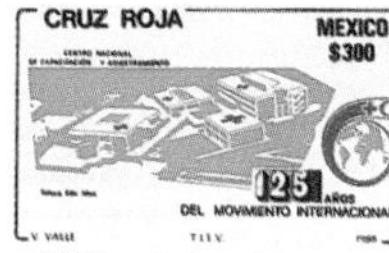

720 Hospital and Emblem

1988. 125th Anniv of Red Cross.
1893 **720** 300p. grey, red and black 15 10

721 Posada

1988. 75th Death Anniv of Jose Guadalupe Posada (painter).
1894 **721** 300p. black and silver . . 15 10

722 "Danaus plexippus"

1988. Endangered Insects. The Monarch Butterfly. Multicoloured.
1895 300p. Type **722** . . . . . . 1·00 10
1896 300p. Butterflies on wall . . 1·00 10
1897 300p. Butterflies on leaves 1·00 10
1898 300p. Caterpillar, butterfly and chrysalis . . . . . . 1·00 10

1988. Mexicans in Rotunda of Illustrious Persons (4th series). As T **678**. Multicoloured.
1899 300p. Manuel Sandoval Vallarta 15 10

723 Envelopes forming Map

1988. World Post Day.
1900 **723** 500p. black and blue . . 20 10

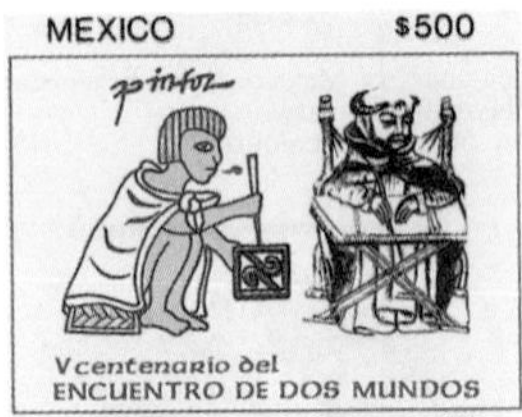

724 Indian and Monk writing

1988. 500th Anniv of "Meeting of Two Worlds" (2nd issue). Yanhuitian Codex.
1902 **724** 500p. multicoloured . . 20 10

725 Man watering Plant

1988. World Food Day. "Rural Youth".
1903 **725** 500p. multicoloured . . 20 10

1988. Mexican Arts and Sciences (15th series). As T **689**.
1904 300p. black and grey . . . 15 10
1905 300p. brown, black & yellow 15 10
DESIGNS: No. 1904, Alfonso Caso; 1905, Vito Alessio Robles.

726 Act

1988. 175th Anniv of Promulgation of Act of Independence.
1906 **726** 300p. flesh and brown 15 10

727 "Self-portrait 1925"

728 Children and Kites

1988. 25th Death Anniv of Antonio Ruiz (painter). Multicoloured.
1907 300p. Type **727** 15 10
1908 300p. "La Malinche" . . . 15 10
1909 300p. "March Past" 15 10

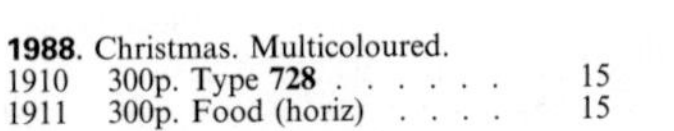

1988. Christmas. Multicoloured.
1910 300p. Type **728** 15 10
1911 300p. Food (horiz) 15 10

729 Emblem

1988. 50th Anniv of Municipal Workers Trade Union.
1912 **729** 300p. black and brown 15 10

1988. Mexican Flowers (7th series). As T **518**. Multicoloured.
1913 300p. "Mimosa tenuiflora" 15 10
1914 300p. "Ustilago maydis" . . 30 10

731 "50" and Emblem

1989. 50th Anniv of State Printing Works.
1915 **731** 450p. brown, grey and red 20 10

732 Arms and Score of National Anthem

1989. 145th Anniv of Dominican Independence.
1916 **732** 450p. multicoloured . . 20 10

733 Emblem

1989. Centenary of International Boundary and Water Commission.
1917 **733** 1100p. multicoloured . . 50 50

734 Emblem

1989. 10th International Book Fair, Mineria.
1918 **734** 450p. multicoloured . . 20 10

735 Composer at Work

1989. 25th Anniv of Society of Authors and Composers.
1919 **735** 450p. multicoloured . . 20 10

736 People

1989. Anti-AIDS Campaign.
1920 **736** 450p. multicoloured . . 20 10

737 Vicario

738 Statue of Reyes

1989. Birth Bicentenary of Leona Vicario (Independence fighter).
1921 **737** 450p. brown, deep brown and black . . . 20 10

1989. Birth Centenary of Alfonso Reyes (writer).
1922 **738** 450p. multicoloured . . 20 10

739 Speeding Cars

1989. Mexico Formula One Grand Prix.
1923 **739** 450p. multicoloured . . 20 10

740 Sea and Mountains

741 Huehuetcotl (god)

1989. 14th Travel Agents' Meeting, Acapulco.
1924 **740** 1100p. multicoloured . . 50 50

1989. 14th International Congress on Ageing.
1925 **741** 450p. pink, black and stone 20 10

742 Revolutionary and Battle Site

1989. 75th Anniv of Battle of Zacatecas.
1926 **742** 450p. black 20 10

743 Catchers

1989. Baseball Professionals' Hall of Fame. Multicoloured.
1927 550p. Type **743** 20 10
1928 550p. Striker 20 10
Nos. 1927/8 were printed together, se-tenant, forming a composite design.

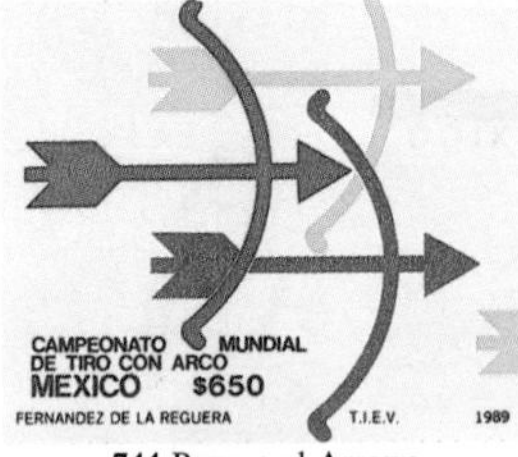

744 Bows and Arrows

1989. World Archery Championships, Switzerland. Multicoloured.
1929 650p. Type **744** 25 10
1920 650p. Arrows and target . . 25 10
Nos. 1929/30 were printed together, se-tenant, forming a composite design.

745 Arms

1989. Centenary of Tijuana.
1931 **745** 1100p. multicoloured . . 50 20

746 Storming the Bastille

1989. Bicentenary of French Revolution.
1932 **746** 1300p. multicoloured . . 60 50

747 Mina

1989. Birth Bicentenary of Francisco Xavier Mina (independence fighter).
1933 **747** 450p. multicoloured . . 20 10

748 Cave Paintings

1989. 25th Anniv of National Anthropological Museum, Chapultepec.
1934 **748** 450p. multicoloured . . 20 10

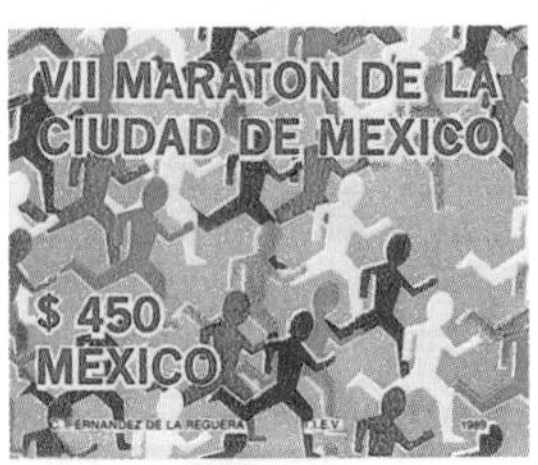

749 Runners

1989. 7th Mexico City Marathon.
1935 **749** 450p. multicoloured . . 20 10

750 Printed Page

1989. 450th Anniv of First American and Mexican Printed Work.
1936 **750** 450p. multicoloured . . 20 10

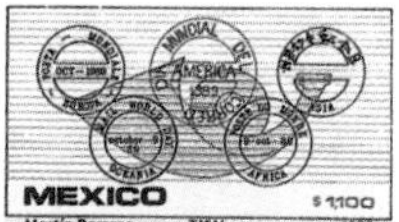

751 Posthorn and Cancellations

1989. World Post Day.
1937 **751** 1100p. multicoloured . . 50 20

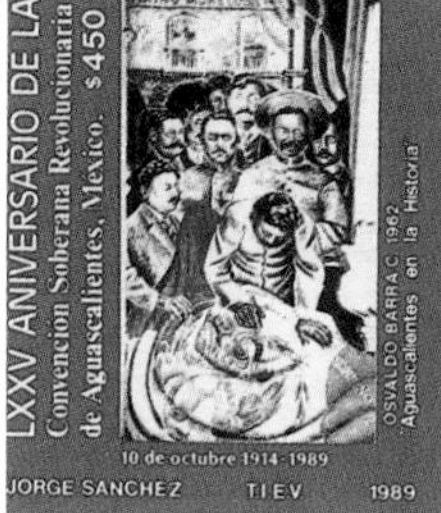

752 "Aguascalientes in History" (Osvaldo Barra)

1989. 75th Anniv of Aguascalientes Revolutionary Convention.
1936 **752** 450p. multicoloured . . 20 10

753 Patterns

1989. America. Pre-Columbian Culture.
1939 450p. Type **753** 20 10
1940 450p. Traditional writing . . 20 10

754 Old and New World Symbols

755 Cross of Lorraine

1989. 500th Anniv of "Meeting of Two Worlds" (3rd issue).
1941 **754** 1300p. multicoloured . . 60 25

1989. 50th Anniv of Anti-tuberculosis National Committee.
1942 **755** 450p. multicoloured . . 20 10

756 Mask of God Murcielago

1989.
1943 **756** 450p. green, black & mve 20 10

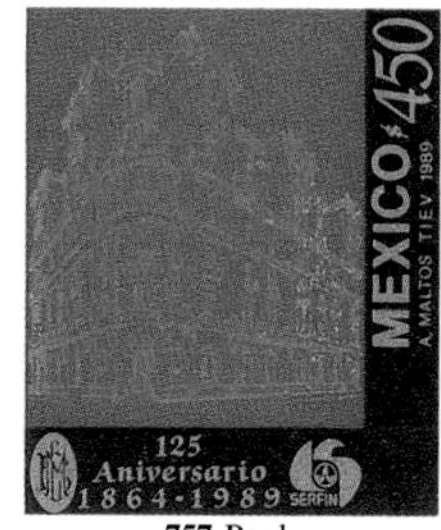

757 Bank

1989. 125th Anniv of Serfin Commercial Bank.
1944 **757** 450p. blue, gold and black 20 10

758 Cortines

759 Man with Sparkler

1989. Birth Centenary of Adolfo Ruiz Cortines (President, 1952–58).
1945 **758** 450p. multicoloured . . 20 10

1989. Christmas. Multicoloured.
1946 450p. Type **759** 20 10
1947 450p. People holding candles (horiz) 20 10

760 Emblem

1989. 50th Anniv of National Institute of Anthropology and History.
1948 **760** 450p. gold, red and black 20 10

761 Steam Locomotive, Diesel Train and Felipe Pescador

1989. 80th Anniv of Nationalization of Railways.
1949 **761** 450p. multicoloured . . 50 15

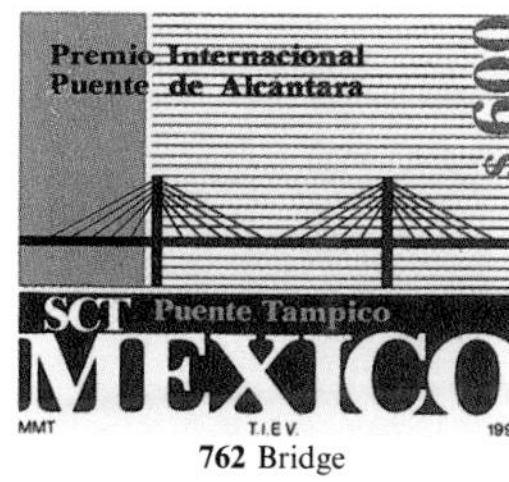

762 Bridge

1990. Opening of Tampico Bridge.
1950 **762** 600p. black, gold and red 20 10

763 Smiling Children

1990. Child Vaccination Campaign.
1951 **763** 700p. multicoloured . . 25 10

764 People in Houses

1990. 11th General Population and Housing Census.
1952 **764** 700p. green, yell & lt grn 25 10

765 Stamp under Magnifying Glass

1990. 10th Anniv of Mexican Philatelic Association.
1953 **765** 700p. multicoloured . . 25 10

766 Archive

1990. Bicentenary of National Archive.
1954 **766** 700p. blue 25 10

767 Emblem and "90"

1990. 1st International Poster Biennale.
1955 **767** 700p. multicoloured . . 25 10

768 Messenger, 1790

1990. "Stamp World London 90" International Stamp Exhibition.
1956 **768** 700p. yellow, red & black 25 10

769 Penny Black

1990. 150th Anniv of the Penny Black.
1957 **769** 700p. black, red and gold 25 10

770 National Colours and Pope John Paul II

1990. Papal Visit.
1958 **770** 700p. multicoloured . . 25 10

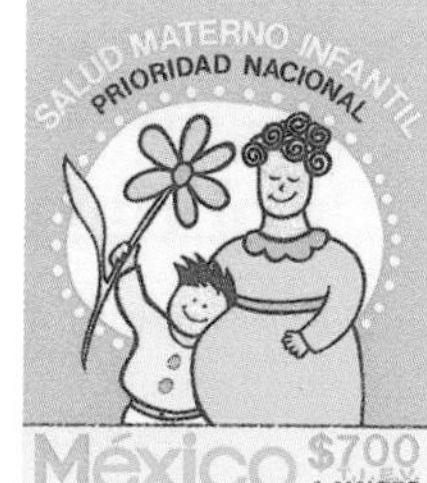

771 Church

772 Mother and Child

1990. 15th Travel Agents' Congress.
1959 **771** 700p. multicoloured . . 25 10

1990. Mother and Child Health Campaign.
1960 **772** 700p. multicoloured . . 25 10

773 Smoke Rings forming Birds

774 Globe as Tree

1990. World Anti-Smoking Day.
1961 **773** 700p. multicoloured . . 25 10

1990. World Environment Day.
1962 **774** 700p. multicoloured . . 25 10

775 Racing Car and Chequered Flag

1990. Mexico Formula One Grand Prix.
1963 **775** 700p. black, red and green 25 10

776 Aircraft Tailfin

1990. 25th Anniv of Airports and Auxiliary Services.
1964 **776** 700p. multicoloured . . 25 10

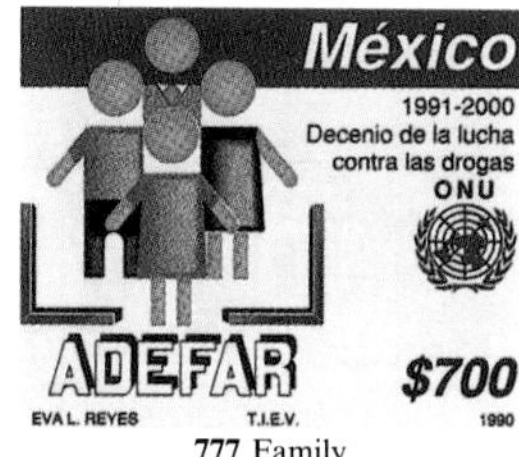

777 Family

1990. United Nations Anti-drugs Decade.
1965 **777** 700p. multicoloured . . 25 10

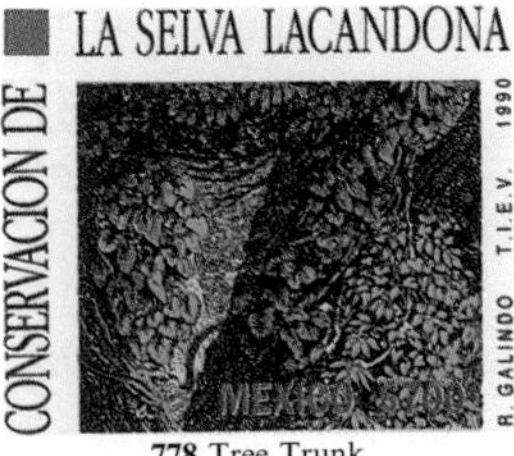

778 Tree Trunk

1990. Forest Conservation.
1966 **778** 700p. multicoloured . . 25 10

779 Emblem

1990. "Solidarity".
1967 **779** 700p. multicoloured . . 25 10
See also No. 2047.

780 Columns and Native Decoration

1990. World Heritage Site. Oaxaca.
1968 **780** 700p. multicoloured . . 25 10

781 Elegant Tern

1990. Conservation of Rasa Island, Gulf of California.
1969 **781** 700p. grey, black and red 1·10 40

782 Institute Activities

1990. 25th Anniv of Mexican Petroleum Institute.
1970 **782** 700p. blue and black . . 25 10

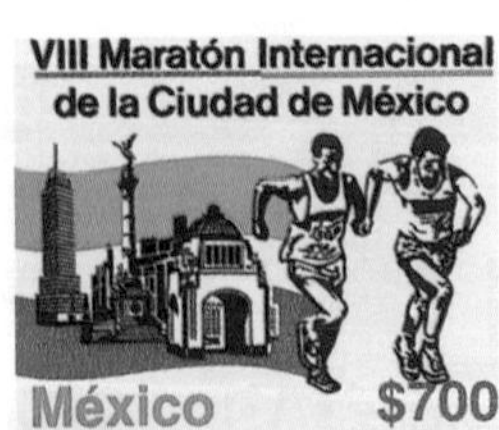

783 National Colours, City Monuments and Runners

1990. 18th International Mexico City Marathon.
1971 **783** 700p. black, red & green 25 10

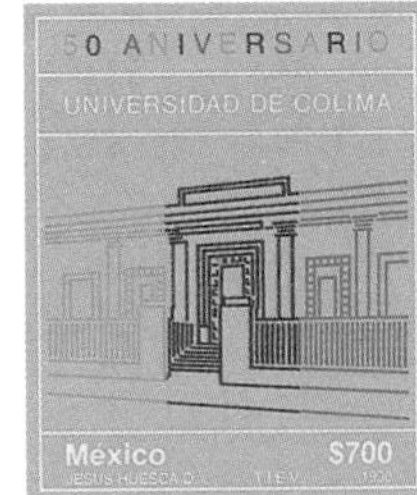

784 Facade

1990. 50th Anniv of Colima University.
1972 **784** 700p. multicoloured . . 25 10

785 Abstract

1990. Mexico City Consultative Council.
1973 **785** 700p. multicoloured . . 25 10

786 Electricity Worker

1990. 30th Anniv of Nationalization of Electricity Industry.
1974 **786** 700p. multicoloured . . 25 10

787 Violin and Bow

1990. 50th Death Anniv of Silvestre Revueltas (violinist).
1975 **787** 700p. multicoloured . . 25 10

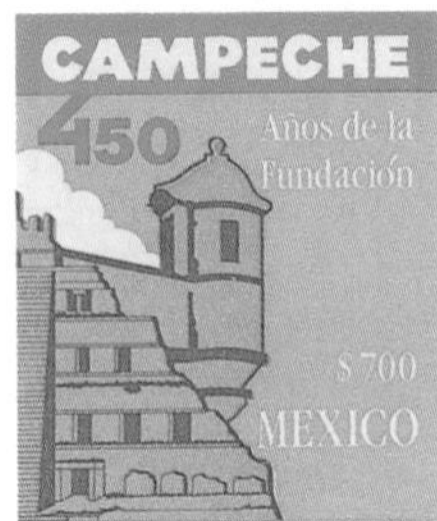

788 Building

1990. 450th Anniv of Campeche.
1976 **788** 700p. multicoloured . . 25 15

789 Crossed Rifle and Pen **790** Emblem

1990. 80th Anniv of San Luis Plan.
1977 **789** 700p. multicoloured . . 25 15

1990. 14th World Supreme Councils Conference.
1978 **790** 1500p. multicoloured . . 55 35

791 Spanish Tower and Mexican Pyramid

1990. 500th Anniv of "Meeting of Two Worlds" (4th issue).
1979 **791** 700p. multicoloured . . 25 15

792 Glass of Beer, Ear of Barley and Hop **793** Carving

1990. Centenary of Brewing Industry.
1980 **792** 700p. multicoloured . . 25 15

1990. Bicentenary of Archaeology in Mexico.
1981 **793** 1500p. multicoloured . . 55 35

794 Ball-game Field **795** Globe and Poinsettia

1990. 16th Central American and Caribbean Games. Multicoloured.
1982 750p. Type **794** . . . . . . 1·10 20
1983 750p. Amerindian ball-game player . . . . 1·10 20
1984 750p. Amerindian ball-game player (different) (horiz) 1·10 20
1985 750p. Yutsil and Balam (mascots) (horiz) . . . . 1·10 20

1990. Christmas. Multicoloured.
1986 700p. Type **795** 25 15
1987 700p. Fireworks and candles 25 15

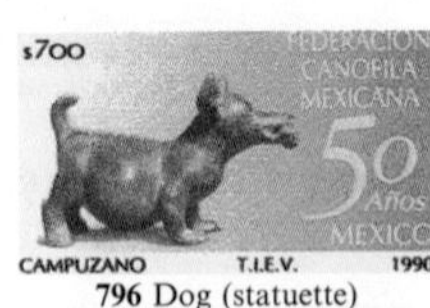

796 Dog (statuette)

1990. 50th Anniv of Mexican Canine Federation.
1988 **796** 700p. multicoloured . . 25 15

797 Microscope, Dolphin and Hand holding Map

1991. 50th Anniv of Naval Secretariat.
1989 **797** 1000p. gold, black & blue 40 25

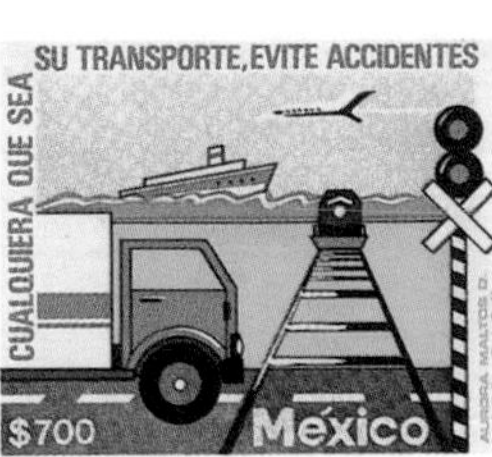

798 Means of Transport

1991. Accident Prevention.
1990 **798** 700p. multicoloured . . 65 20

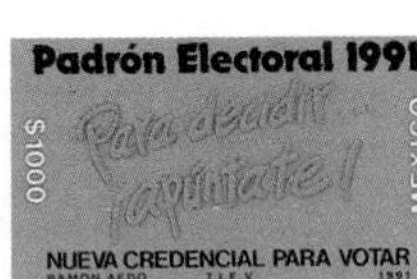

799 Products in Bags **800** "In order to Decide, Register"

1991. 15th Anniv of National Consumer Institute.
1991 **799** 1000p. multicoloured . . 40 25

1991. Electoral Register.
1992 **800** 1000p. orange, grn & blk 40 25

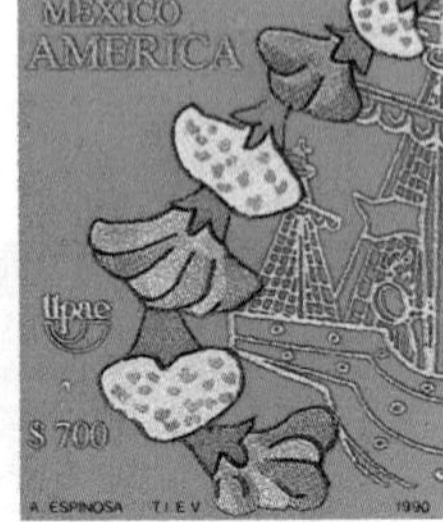

801 Basketball Player **802** Flowers and Caravel

1991. Olympic Games, Barcelona (1992) (1st issue).
1993 **801** 1000p. black and yellow 40 25
See also Nos. 2050, 2057 and 2080/9.

1991. America (1990). Natural World. Mult.
1994 700p. Type **802** 75 20
1995 700p. Right half of caravel, blue and yellow macaw and flowers 75 40
Nos. 1994/5 were issued together, se-tenant, forming a composite design.

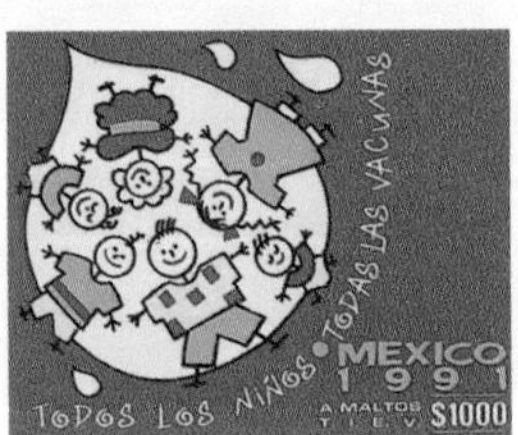

803 Children in Droplet

1991. Children's Month. Vaccination Campaign.
1996 **803** 1000p. multicoloured . . 40 25

804 Map **805** Dove and Children

1991. World Post Day (1990).
1997 **804** 1500p. multicoloured . . 55 35

1991. Children's Days for Peace and Development.
1998 **805** 1000p. multicoloured . . 40 25

806 Dove **807** Mining

1991. Family Health and Unity.
1999 **806** 1000p. multicoloured . . 40 25

1991. 500th Anniv of Mining.
2000 **807** 1000p. multicoloured . . 40 25

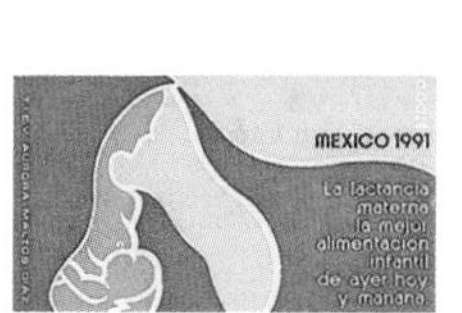

808 Mother feeding Baby

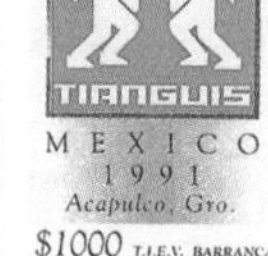

809 Emblem

1991. Breastfeeding Campaign.
2001 **808** 1000p. buff, blue & brn 40 25

1991. 16th Tourism Fair, Acapulco.
2002 **809** 1000p. green & dp green 40 25

810 Rotary Emblem and Independence Monument, Mexico City

811 "Communication"

1991. Rotary International Convention. "Let us Preserve the Planet Earth".
2003 **810** 1000p. gold and blue . . 40 25

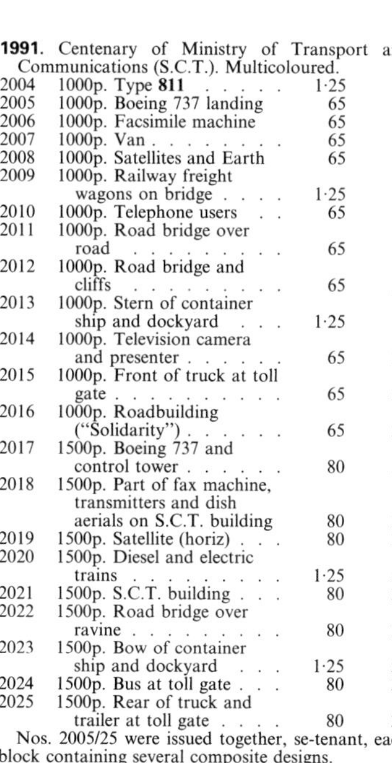

1991. Centenary of Ministry of Transport and Communications (S.C.T.). Multicoloured.
2004 1000p. Type **811** . . . . . 1·25 50
2005 1000p. Boeing 737 landing 65 25
2006 1000p. Facsimile machine 65 25
2007 1000p. Van 65 25
2008 1000p. Satellites and Earth 65 25
2009 1000p. Railway freight wagons on bridge . . . . 1·25 35
2010 1000p. Telephone users . . 65 25
2011 1000p. Road bridge over road 65 25
2012 1000p. Road bridge and cliffs 65 25
2013 1000p. Stern of container ship and dockyard . . . 1·25 35
2014 1000p. Television camera and presenter 65 25
2015 1000p. Front of truck at toll gate 65 25
2016 1000p. Roadbuilding ("Solidarity") 65 25
2017 1500p. Boeing 737 and control tower 80 35
2018 1500p. Part of fax machine, transmitters and dish aerials on S.C.T. building 80 35
2019 1500p. Satellite (horiz) . . . 80 35
2020 1500p. Diesel and electric trains . . . . 1·25 50
2021 1500p. S.C.T. building . . . 80 35
2022 1500p. Road bridge over ravine 80 35
2023 1500p. Bow of container ship and dockyard . . . 1·25 50
2024 1500p. Bus at toll gate . . . 80 35
2025 1500p. Rear of truck and trailer at toll gate 80 35
Nos. 2005/25 were issued together, se-tenant, each block containing several composite designs.

812 Jaguar

1991. Lacandona Jungle Conservation.
2026 **812** 1000p. black, orge & red 40 25

813 Driver and Car

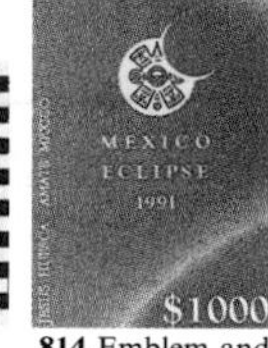

814 Emblem and Left-hand Sections of Sun and Earth

1991. Mexico Formula 1 Grand Prix.
2027 **813** 1000p. multicoloured . . 40 25

1991. Total Eclipse of the Sun. Multicoloured.
2028 1000p. Type **814** . . . . . 1·00 25
2029 1000p. Emblem and right-hand sections of sun and Earth . . . . 1·00 25
2030 1500p. Emblem and centre of sun and Earth showing north and central America 1·50 35
Nos. 2028/30 were issued together, se-tenant, forming a composite design.

815 "Solidarity" (Rufino Tamayo)

816 Bridge

1991. 1st Latin American Presidential Summit, Guadalajara.
2031 **815** 1500p. black, orge & yell 55 35

1991. Solidarity between Nuevo Leon and Texas.
2032 **816** 2000p. multicoloured . . 1·10 75

817 Runners

819 Emblem

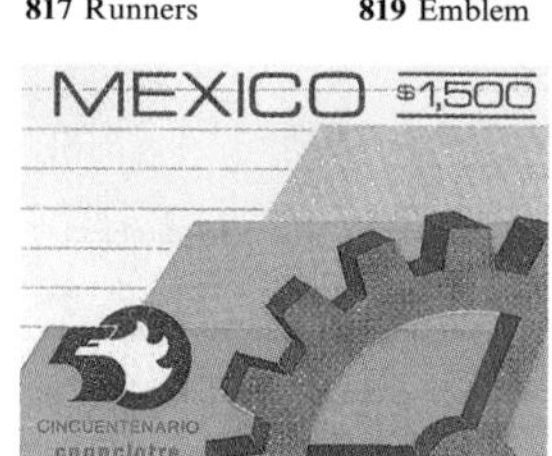

818 Cogwheel

1991. 9th Mexico City Marathon.
2033 **817** 1000p. multicoloured . . 40 25

1991. 50th Anniv (1990) of National Chambers of Industry and Commerce.
2034 **818** 1500p. multicoloured . . 55 35

1991. 55th Anniv of Federation Fiscal Tribunal.
2035 **819** 1000p. silver and blue . . 40 25

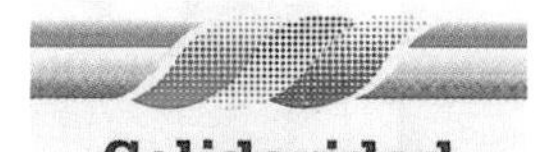

820 National Colours forming Emblem

1991. "Solidarity—Let us Unite in order to Progress".
2036 **820** 1000p. multicoloured . . 40 25

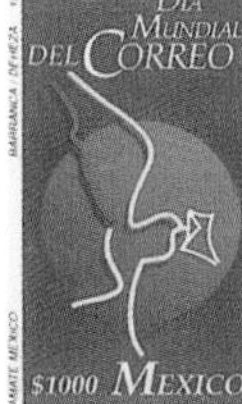

821 Dove with Letter

822 World Map

1991. World Post Day.
2037 **821** 1000p. multicoloured . . 40 25

1991. 500th Anniv of "Meeting of Two Worlds" (5th issue).
2038 **822** 1000p. multicoloured . . 95 25

823 Caravel, Sun and Trees

1991. America. Voyages of Discovery. Mult.
2039 1000p. Type **823** 75 25
2040 1000p. Storm cloud, caravel and broken snake 75 25

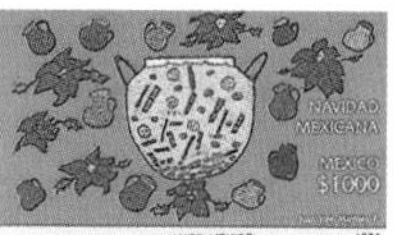
824 Flowers and Pots

1991. Christmas. Multicoloured.
2041 1000p. Type **824** 40 25
2042 1000p. Children with decoration 40 25

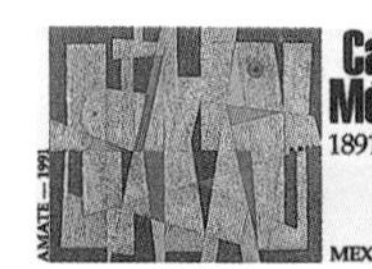

825 Abstract

1991. Carlos Merida (artist) Commemoration.
2043 **825** 1000p. multicoloured . . 40 25

826 Score and Portrait

1991. Death Bicentenary of Wolfgang Amadeus Mozart (composer).
2044 **826** 1000p. multicoloured . . 40 25

827 Kidney Beans and Maize

1991. Self-sufficiency in Kidney Beans and Maize.
2045 **827** 1000p. multicoloured . . 40 25

828 City Plan

1991. 450th Anniv of Morelia.
2046 **828** 1000p. brown, stone and red 40 25

1991. "Solidarity". As No. 1967 but new value.
2047 **779** 1000p. multicoloured . . 40 25

829 Merida

1992. 450th Anniv of Merida.
2048 **829** 1300p. multicoloured . . 60 40

830 Colonnade

1992. Bicentenary of Engineering Training in Mexico.
2049 **830** 1300p. blue and red . . 60 40

831 Horse Rider

1992. Olympic Games, Barcelona (2nd issue).
2050 **831** 2000p. multicoloured . . 90 60

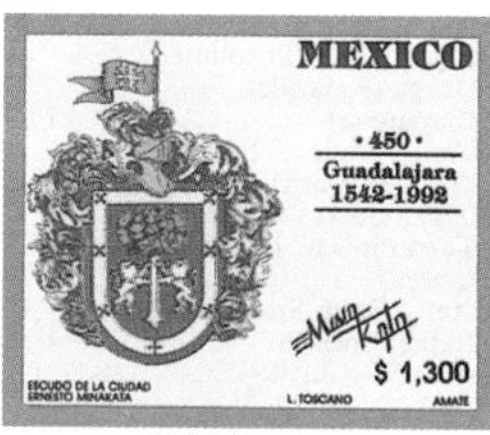

832 City Arms

1992. 450th Anniv of Guadalajara. Multicoloured.
2051 1300p. Type **832** . . . . . 1·10 40
2052 1300p. "Guadalajara Town Hall" (Jorge Navarro) . . 1·10 40
2053 1300p. "Guadalajara Cathedral" (Gabriel Flores) . . . . 1·10 40
2054 1900p. "Founding of Guadalajara" (Rafael Zamarripa) . . . . 1·60 55
2055 1900p. Anniversary emblem (Ignacio Vazquez) . . . . 1·60 55

833 Children and Height Gauge

834 Olympic Torch and Rings

1992. Child Health Campaign.
2056 **833** 2000p. multicoloured . . 90 60

1992. Olympic Games, Barcelona (3rd issue).
2057 **834** 2000p. multicoloured . . 90 60

835 Horse and Racing Car

1992. "500th Anniv of the Wheel and the Horse in America". Mexico Formula 1 Grand Prix.
2058 **835** 1300p. multicoloured . . 60 40

836 Satellite and Map of Americas

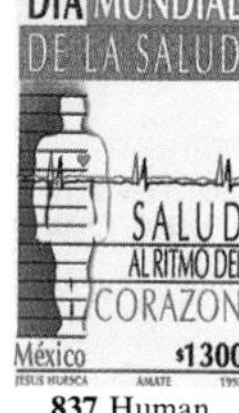

837 Human Figure and Cardiograph

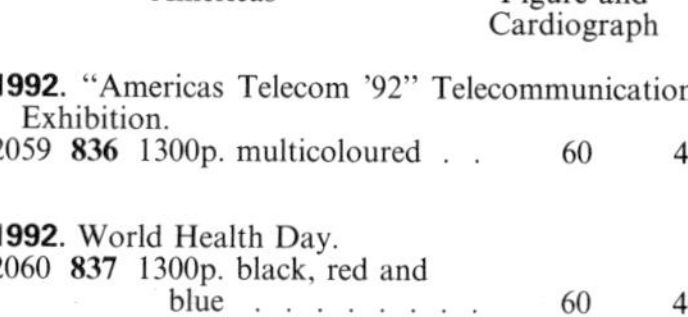

1992. "Americas Telecom '92" Telecommunications Exhibition.
2059 **836** 1300p. multicoloured . . 60 40

1992. World Health Day.
2060 **837** 1300p. black, red and blue 60 40

838 Emblem

1992. 60th Anniv of Military Academy.

2061	**838** 1300p. red, yellow & blk	60	40

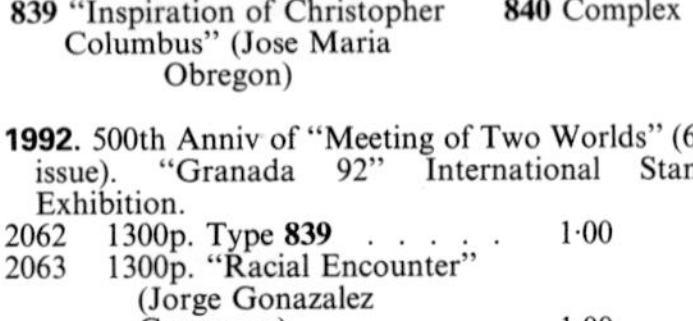

839 "Inspiration of Christopher Columbus" (Jose Maria Obregon) **840** Complex

1992. 500th Anniv of "Meeting of Two Worlds" (6th issue). "Granada 92" International Stamp Exhibition.

2062	1300p. Type **839**	1·00	40
2063	1300p. "Racial Encounter" (Jorge Gonazalez Camarena)	1·00	40
2064	2000p. "Origin of the Sky" (Selden Codex)	1·75	60
2065	2000p. "Quetzalcoatl and Tezcatlipoca" (Borhomico Codex)	1·75	60
2066	2000p. "From Spaniard and Indian, mestizo"	1·75	60

1992. National Medical Centre.

2068	**840** 1300p. multicoloured	60	40

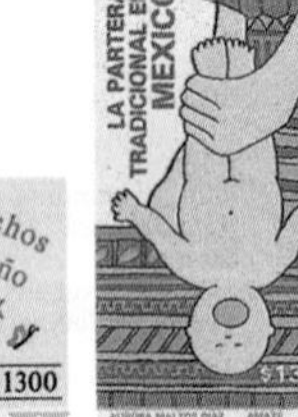

841 Children, Dove and Globe **842** New-born Baby

1992. Children's Rights.

2069	**841** 1300p. multicoloured	60	40

1992. Traditional Childbirth.

2070	**842** 1300p. multicoloured	60	40

1992. "World Columbian Stamp Expo '92", Chicago. Nos. 2062/6 optd **WORLD COLUMBIAN STAMP EXPO '92 MAY 22-31, 1992 - CHICAGO** and emblem.

2071	1300p. mult (No. 2062)	2·00	2·00
2072	1300p. mult (No. 2063)	2·00	2·00
2073	2000p. mult (No. 2064)	5·00	5·00
2074	2000p. mult (No. 2065)	5·00	5·00
2075	2000p. mult (No. 2066)	5·00	5·00

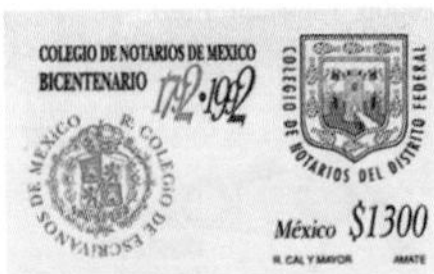

845 Arms of Colleges

1992. Bicentenary of Mexico Notary College.

2078	**845** 1300p. multicoloured	50	35

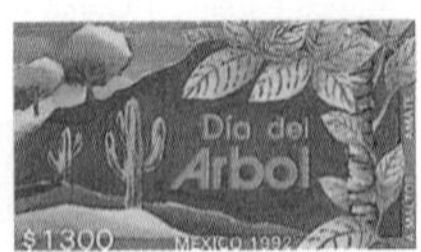

846 Trees and Cacti

1992. Tree Day.

2079	**846** 1300p. multicoloured	50	35

847 Boxing **848** Athlete

1992. Olympic Games, Barcelona (4th issue). Mult.

2080	1300p. Type **847**	80	35
2081	1300p. High jumping	80	35
2082	1300p. Fencing	80	35
2083	1300p. Shooting	80	35
2084	1300p. Gymnastics	80	35
2085	1900p. Rowing	1·60	50
2086	1900p. Running	1·60	50
2087	1900p. Football	1·60	50
2088	1900p. Swimming	1·60	50
2089	2000p. Equestrian	1·60	55

1992. 10th Mexico City Marathon.

2091	**848** 1300p. multicoloured	50	35

849 Emblem

1992. "Solidarity".

2092	**849** 1300p. multicoloured	50	35

851 Television, Map and Radio

1992. 50th Anniv of National Chamber of Television and Radio Industry.

2094	**851** 1300p. multicoloured	50	35

852 Letter orbiting Globe

1992. World Post Day.

2095	**852** 1300p. multicoloured	50	35

853 Satellite above South and Central America and Flags

1992. American Cadena Communications System.

2096	**853** 2000p. multicoloured	1·10	55

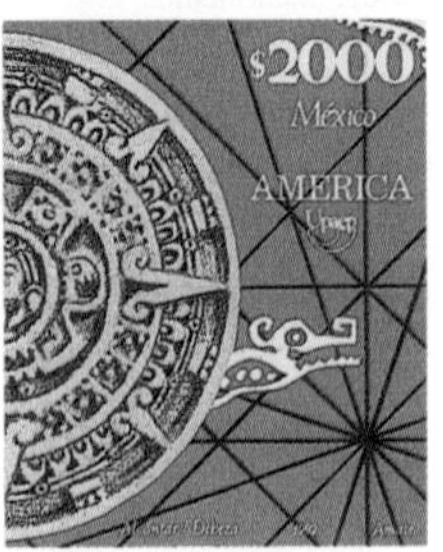

854 Gold Compass Rose

1992. America. 500th Anniv of Discovery of America by Columbus. Multicoloured.

2097	2000p. Type **854**	1·25	55
2098	2000p. Compass rose (different) and fish	1·25	55

Nos. 2097/8 were issued together, se-tenant, forming a composite design.

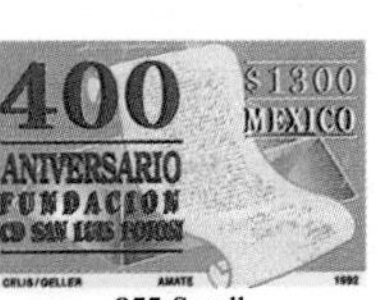

855 Scroll

1992. 400th Anniv of San Luis Potosi.

2099	**855** 1300p. black and mauve	50	35

856 Berrendos Deer

1992. Conservation.

2100	**856** 1300p. multicoloured	50	35

857 Schooner, Landing Ship, Emblem and Sailors **858** Christmas Tree, Children and Crib

1992. Navy Day.

2101	**857** 1300p. multicoloured	50	35

1992. Christmas. Children's Drawings. Mult.

2102	1300p. Type **858**	50	35
2103	2000p. Street celebration (horiz)	1·25	55

Currency Reform. 1 (new) peso = 1000 (old) pesos.

859 Anniversary Emblem **860** Emblem

1993. 50th Anniv of Mexican Social Security Institute (1st issue).

2104	**859** 1p.50 green, gold & blk	60	40

See also Nos. 2110 and 2152/3.

1993. Centenary of Mexican Ophthalmological Society.

2105	**860** 1p.30 multicoloured	50	35

861 Children **862** Society Arms and Founders

1993. Children's Month.

2106	**861** 1p.30 multicoloured	50	35

1993. 160th Anniv of Mexican Geographical and Statistical Society.

2107	**862** 1p.30 multicoloured	50	35

863 1824 Constitution **864** Gomez, Children and Hospital

1993. 150th Death Anniv of Miguel Ramos Arizpe, "Father of Federalism".

2108	**863** 1p.30 multicoloured	50	35

1993. 50th Anniv of Federico Gomez Children's Hospital.

2109	**864** 1p.30 multicoloured	50	35

865 Doctor with Child

1993. 50th Anniv of Mexican Social Security Institute (2nd issue). Medical Services.

2110	**865** 1p.30 multicoloured	50	35

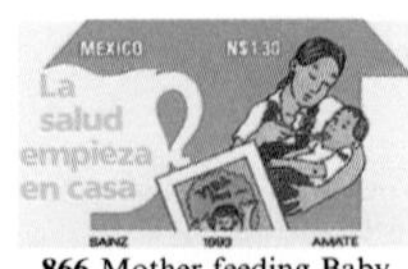

866 Mother feeding Baby

1993. "Health begins at Home".

2111	**866** 1p.30 multicoloured	50	35

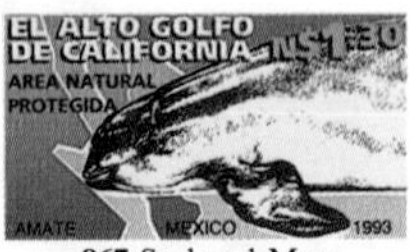

867 Seal and Map

1993. Upper Gulf of California Nature Reserve.

2112	**867** 1p.30 multicoloured	50	35

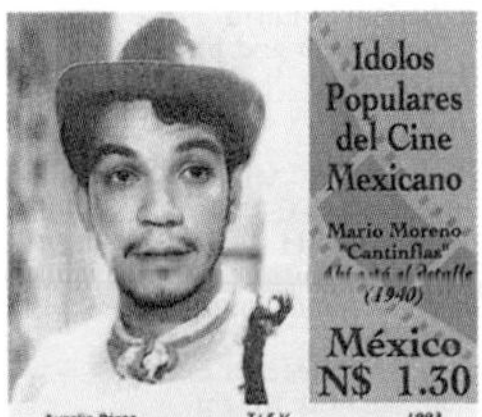

868 Cantinflas

1993. Mexican Film Stars. Mario Moreno (Cantinflas).

2113	**868** 1p.30 black and blue	50	35

See also Nos. 2156/60.

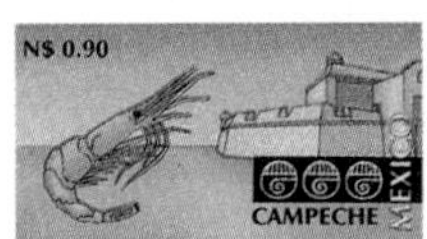

869 Campeche

1993. Tourism. Value expressed as "NS". Mult.

2114	90c. Type **869**	65	25
2115	1p. Guanajuato	70	25
2263	1p.10 As No. 2115	70	10
2116	1p.30 Colima	80	35
2264	1p.80 As No. 2124	55	20
2265	1p.80 As No. 2118	65	20
2266	1p.80 As No. 2116	55	20
2267	1p.80 As Type **869**	55	20
2117	1p.90 Michoacan (vert)	1·25	50
2118	2p. Coahuila	1·25	55
2269	2p. As No. 2266	90	20
2119	2p.20 Queretaro	1·60	60
2271	2p.30 As No. 2122	70	25
2272	2p.40 As No. 2123	80	25
2120	2p.50 Sonora	2·00	65
2274	2p.70 As No. 2145	1·25	25
2121	2p.80 Zacatecas (vert)	2·25	75
2276	3p. Type **869**	1·40	30
2278	3p.40 As No. 2271	1·40	35
2122	3p.70 Sinaloa	3·25	1·25
2280	3p.80 As No. 2272	1·25	40
2123	4p.40 Yucatan	3·50	1·50
2124	4p.80 Chiapas	3·75	1·60
2145	6p. Mexico City	4·00	2·00
2290	6p.80 As No. 2120	2·50	90

See also Nos. 2410/29.

870 Dr. Maximiliano Ruiz Castaneda

1993. 50th Anniv of Health Service. Multicoloured.

2126	1p.30 Type **870**	50	35
2127	1p.30 Dr. Bernardo Sepulveda Gutierrez	50	35
2128	1p.30 Dr. Ignacio Chavez Sanchez	50	35
2129	1p.30 Dr. Mario Salazar Mallen	50	35
2130	1p.30 Dr. Gustavo Baz Prada	50	35

871 Brazil 30r. "Bull's Eye" Stamp

872 Runners

1993. 150th Anniv of First Brazilian Stamps.
2131 **871** 2p. multicoloured . . . 80 55

1993. 11th Mexico City Marathon.
2132 **872** 1p.30 multicoloured . . 1·40 55

873 Emblem

874 Open Book and Symbols

1993. "Solidarity".
2133 **873** 1p.30 multicoloured . . 50 35

1993. 50th Anniv of Monterrey Institute of Technology and Higher Education. Multicoloured.
2134 1p.30 Type **874** 50 35
2135 2p. Buildings and mountains 80 55
Nos. 2134/5 were issued together, se-tenant, forming a composite design.

875 Cogwheels and Emblem

876 Torreon

1993. 75th Anniv of Concamin.
2136 **875** 1p.30 multicoloured . . 50 35

1993. Centenary of Torreon.
2137 **876** 1p.30 multicoloured . . 50 35

877 Emblem

1993. "Europalia 93 Mexico" Festival.
2138 **877** 2p. multicoloured . . . 80 55

878 Globe in Envelope

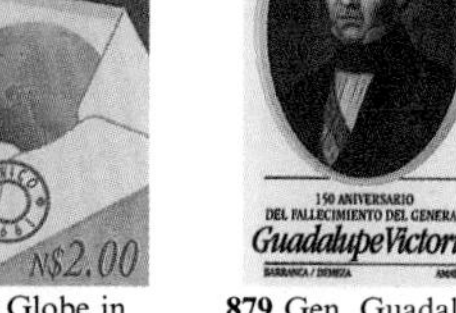

879 Gen. Guadalupe Victoria

1993. World Post Day.
2139 **878** 2p. multicoloured . . . 80 55

1993. 150th Death Anniv of General Manuel Guadalupe Victoria (first President, 1824–28).
2140 **879** 1p.30 multicoloured . . 50 35

880 Emblem

881 Hands protecting Foetus

1993. National Civil Protection System and International Day for Reduction of Natural Disasters.
2141 **880** 1p.30 red, black & yell 50 35

1993. United Nations Decade of International Law.
2142 **881** 2p. multicoloured . . . 80 55

882 Torch Carrier

1993. 20th National Wheelchair Games.
2143 **882** 1p.30 multicoloured . . 50 35

883 Peon y Contreras

1993. 150th Birth Anniv of Jose Peon y Contreras (poet, dramatist and founder of National Romantic Theatre).
2144 **883** 1p.30 violet and black 50 35

884 Horned Guan

885 Presents around Trees

1993. America. Endangered Birds. Multicoloured.
2145 2p. Type **884** . . . . 2·50 1·25
2146 2p. Resplendent quetzal on branch (horiz) . . . . . 2·50 1·25

1993. Christmas. Multicoloured.
2147 1p.30 Type **885** 50 35
2148 1p.30 Three wise men (horiz) 50 35

886 Satellites orbiting Earth

1993. "Solidarity".
2149 **886** 1p.30 multicoloured . . 50 35

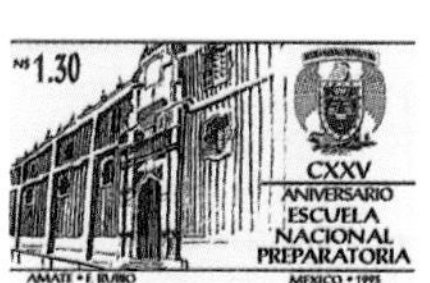

887 School and Arms

1993. 125th Anniv of National Preparatory School.
2150 **887** 1p.30 multicoloured . . 50 35

888 Emblem on Map

1993. 55th Anniv of Municipal Workers Trade Union.
2151 **888** 1p.30 multicoloured . . 50 35

889 Hands

1993. 50th Anniv of Mexican Social Security Institute (3rd issue). Multicoloured.
2152 1p.30 Type **889** (social security) 50 35
2153 1p.30 Ball, building blocks, child's painting and dummy (day nurseries) . . 50 35

890 Mezcala Solidarity Bridge

1993. Tourism. Multicoloured.
2154 1p.30 Type **890** 50 35
2155 1p.30 Mexico City–Acapulco motorway 50 35

1993. Mexican Film Stars. As T **868**.
2156 1p.30 black and blue . . . 50 35
2157 1p.30 black and orange . . 50 35
2158 1p.30 black and green . . . 50 35
2159 1p.30 black and violet . . 50 35
2160 1p.30 black and pink . . . 50 35
DESIGNS:—No, 2156, Pedro Armendariz in "Juan Charrasqueado"; 2157, Maria Felix in "The Lover"; 2158, Pedro Infante in "Necesito dinero"; 2159, Jorge Negrete in "It is not enough to be a Peasant"; 2160, Dolores del Rio in "Flor Silvestre".

891 Estefania Castaneda Nunez

1994. 72nd Anniv of Secretariat of Public Education. Educationists. Multicoloured.
2161 1p.30 Type **891** 50 35
2162 1p.30 Lauro Aguirre Espinosa 50 35
2163 1p.30 Rafael Ramirez Castaneda 50 35
2164 1p.30 Moises Saenz Garza 50 35
2165 1p.30 Gregorio Torres Quintero 50 35
2166 1p.30 Jose Vasconcelos . . 50 35
2167 1p.30 Rosaura Zapato Cano 50 35

892 Zapata (after H. Velarde)

893 Emblem and Worker

1994. 75th Death Anniv of Emiliano Zapata (revolutionary).
2168 **892** 1p.30 multicoloured . . 50 35

1994. 75th Anniv of I.L.O.
2169 **893** 2p. multicoloured . . . 80 50

894 Map and Emblem

895 "Earth and Communication" (frieze, detail)

1994. 50th Anniv of National Schools Building Programme Committee.
2170 **894** 1p.30 multicoloured . . 50 35

1994. 3rd Death Anniv of Francisco Zuniga (sculptor).
2171 **895** 1p.30 multicoloured . . 50 35

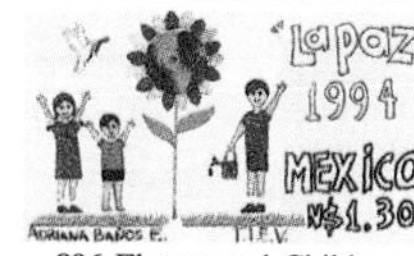

896 Flower and Children

1994. Children's Organization for Peace and Development.
2172 **896** 1p.30 multicoloured . . 50 35

897 Greater Flamingo

1994. DUMAC Nature Protection Organization.
2173 **897** 1p.30 multicoloured . . 1·50 85

898 Children and Silhouette of Absentee

1994. Care and Control of Minors.
2174 **898** 1p.30 black and green 50 35

899 Man and Letters

900 Route Map

1994. 34th World Advertising Congress, Cancun.
2175 **899** 2p. multicoloured . . . 80 35

1994. 50th Anniv of National Association of Importers and Exporters.
2176 **900** 1p.30 multicoloured . . 50 35

901 Head and Emblem

1994. International Telecommunications Day.
2177 **901** 2p. multicoloured . . . 80 55

902 Animals

1994. Yumka Wildlife Centre, Villahermosa.
2178 **902** 1p.30 multicoloured . . 1·25 85

903 Town Centre

904 Mother and Baby

1994. U.N.E.S.C.O. World Heritage Site, Zacatecas.
2179 **903** 1p.30 multicoloured . . 50 35

1994. Friendship Hospital. Mother and Child Health Month.
2180 **904** 1p.30 multicoloured . . 55 45

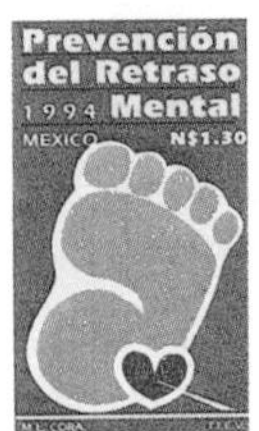

905 Foot and Heart **906** Song and Ornamental Birds

1994. Prevention of Mental Retardation.
2181 **905** 1p.30 multicoloured . . 55 45

1994. Nature Conservation. Multicoloured.
2182 1p.30 Type **906** . . . . . . 1·25 85
2183 1p.30 Game birds (silhouettes) . . . . . . 1·25 85
2184 1p.30 Threatened animals (silhouettes) . . . . . . 1·25 85
2185 1p.30 Animals in danger of extinction (silhouettes) . . 1·25 85
2186 1p.30 Orange-fronted conures . . . . 1·25 85
2187 1p.30 Yellow-tailed oriole 1·25 85
2188 1p.30 Pyrrhuloxias . . . . 1·25 85
2189 1p.30 Loggerhead shrike . . 1·25 85
2190 1p.30 Northern mockingbird 1·25 85
2191 1p.30 Common turkey . . . 1·25 85
2192 1p.30 White-winged dove . . 1·25 85
2193 1p.30 Red-billed whistling duck . . . . 1·25 85
2194 1p.30 Snow goose . . . . . 1·25 85
2195 1p.30 Gambel's quail . . . 1·25 85
2196 1p.30 Peregrine falcon . . . 1·25 85
2197 1p.30 Jaguar 80 50
2198 1p.30 Jaguarundi 80 50
2199 1p.30 Mantled howler monkey 80 50
2200 1p.30 Californian sealions 80 50
2201 1p.30 Pronghorn 80 50
2202 1p.30 Scarlet macaw . . . . 1·25 85
2203 1p.30 Mexican prairie dogs 80 50
2204 1p.30 Wolf 80 50
2205 1p.30 American manatee . . 80 50

907 Player **908** Fish

1994. World Cup Football Championship, U.S.A. Multicoloured.
2206 2p. Type **907** . . . . 1·00 70
2207 2p. Goalkeeper . . . . . . 1·00 70
Nos. 2206/7 were issued together, se-tenant, forming a composite design.

1994. International Fishing Festival, Veracruz.
2208 **908** 1p.30 multicoloured . . 55 45

909 Stylized Figure and Emblem **910** "Butterflies" (Carmen Parra)

1994. 25th Anniv of Juvenile Integration Centres.
2209 **909** 1p.30 multicoloured . . 55 45

1994. 50th Anniv of Diplomatic Relations with Canada.
2210 **910** 2p. multicoloured . . . 90 65

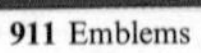

911 Emblems **912** Emblem and Family

1994. 20th Anniv of National Population Council.
2211 **911** 1p.30 multicoloured . . 55 45

1994. International Year of the Family.
2212 **912** 2p. multicoloured . . . 90 60

913 Runner breasting Tape **914** Giant Panda

1994. 12th Mexico City International Marathon.
2213 **913** 1p.30 multicoloured . . 55 45

1994. Chapultepec Zoo.
2214 **914** 1p.30 multicoloured . . 80 45

915 Tree **916** Anniversary Emblem

1994. Tree Day.
2215 **915** 1p.30 brown and green 55 45

1994. 60th Anniv of Economic Culture Fund.
2216 **916** 1p.30 multicoloured . . 55 45

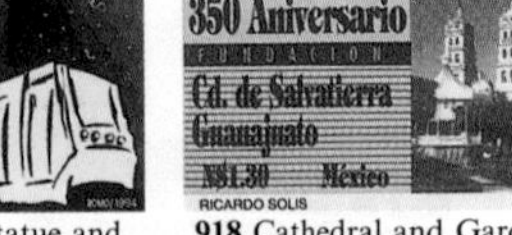

917 Statue and Light Rail Transit Train **918** Cathedral and Gardens

1994. 25th Anniv of Mexico City Transport System.
2217 **917** 1p.30 multicoloured . . 65 45

1994. 350th Anniv of Salvatierra City, Guanajuato.
2218 **918** 1p.30 purple, grey and black 55 45

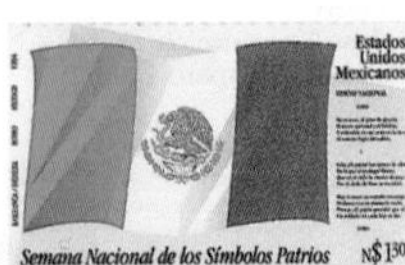

919 State Flag and National Anthem

1994. National Symbols Week.
2219 **919** 1p.30 multicoloured . . 55 45

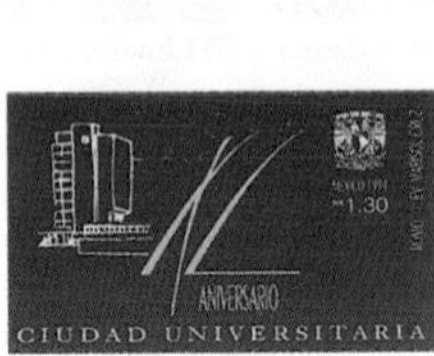

920 Building and Anniversary Emblem **921** Figures with Flags

1994. 40th Anniv of University City.
2220 **920** 1p.30 multicoloured . . 55 45

1994. 5th Solidarity Week.
2221 **921** 1p.30 black, red and green 55 45

922 Lopez Mateos **923** Palace Facade

1994. 25th Death Anniv of Adolfo Lopez Mateos (President, 1958–64).
2222 **922** 1p.30 multicoloured . . 55 45

1994. 60th Anniv of Palace of Fine Arts.
2223 **923** 1p.30 black and grey . . 55 45

924 Rings and "100"

1994. Centenary of International Olympic Committee.
2224 **924** 2p. multicoloured . . . 90 60

925 Quarter Horse (Juan Rayas)

1994. Horses. Paintings by artists named. Multicoloured.
2225 1p.30 Aztec horse (Heladio Velarde) 80 45
2226 1p.30 Type **925** 80 45
2227 1p.30 Quarter horse (Rayas) (different) 80 45
2228 1p.30 Vaquero on horseback (Velarde) 80 45
2229 1p.30 Aztec horse (Velarde) 80 45
2230 1p.30 Rider with lance (Velarde) 80 45

926 Emblem **927** Saint-Exupery and The Little Prince (book character)

1994. Inauguration of 20 November National Medical Centre.
2231 **926** 1p.30 multicoloured . . 55 45

1994. 50th Death Anniv of Antoine de Saint-Exupery (pilot and writer).
2232 **927** 2p. multicoloured . . . 90 60

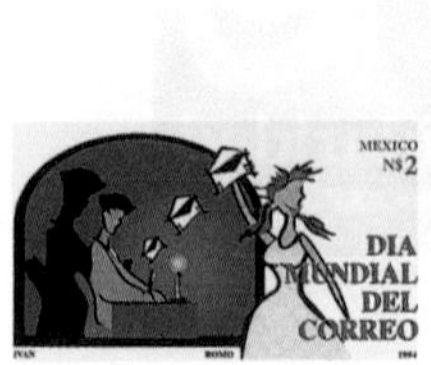

928 Man writing Letters to Woman **929** Urban Postman on Bicycle

1994. World Post Day.
2233 **928** 2p. multicoloured . . . 90 60

1994. America. Postal Transport. Multicoloured.
2234 2p. Type **929** 85 50
2235 2p. Rural postman on rail tricycle . . . . 1·40 75
Nos. 2234/5 were issued together, se-tenant, forming a composite design.

930 Couple (Sofia Bassi)

1994. Ancestors' Day.
2236 **930** 1p.30 multicoloured . . 55 45

931 Water Drop and Hand **932** Dr. Mora

1994. National Clean Water Programme.
2237 **931** 1p.30 multicoloured . . 55 45

1994. Birth Bicentenary of Dr. Jose Maria Luis Mora (journalist and politician).
2238 **932** 1p.30 multicoloured . . 55 45

933 Theatre and Soler (actor)

1994. 15th Anniv of Fernando Soler Theatre, Saltillo, Coahuila.
2239 **933** 1p.30 multicoloured . . 55 45

934 Allegory of Flight **935** Museum's Central Pillar

1994. 50th Anniv of I.C.A.O.
2240 **934** 2p. multicoloured . . . 1·10 60

1994. 30th Anniv of National Anthropological Museum.
2241 **935** 1p.30 multicoloured . . 55 45

936 Theatrical Masks **937** Allende

1994. 60th Anniv of National Association of Actors.
2242 **936** 1p.30 multicoloured . . 55 45

1994. 225th Birth Anniv of Ignacio Allende (independence hero).
2243 **937** 1p.30 multicoloured . . 55 45

938 Chapultepec Castle

1994. 50th Anniv of National History Museum.
2244 **938** 1p.30 multicoloured . . 55 45

939 Dome **940** Anniversary Emblem

1994. Centenary of Coahuila School.
2245 **939** 1p.30 multicoloured . . 55 45

1994. 40th Anniv of Pumas University Football Club.
2246 **940** 1p.30 blue and gold . . 55 45

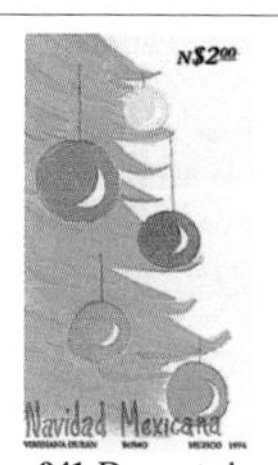

941 Decorated Tree

942 Valley

1994. Christmas. Multicoloured.
2247 2p. Type **941** 80 60
2248 2p. Couple watching shooting star (horiz) . . . 80 60

1994. "Solidarity". Chalco Valley.
2249 **942** 1p.30 multicoloured . . 20 15

943 Ines de la Cruz (after Miguel de Cabrera)

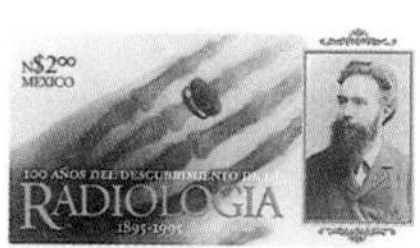

944 X-Ray of Hand and Rontgen

1995. 300th Birth Anniv of Juana Ines de la Cruz (mystic poet).
2250 **943** 1p.80 multicoloured . . 30 20

1995. Centenary of Discovery of X-Rays by Wilhelm Rontgen.
2251 **944** 2p. multicoloured . . . 35 25

945 Ignacio Altamirano
946 Emblem

1995. Teachers' Day.
2252 **945** 1p.80 black, green & bl 30 20

1995. World Telecommunications Day. "Telecommunications and the Environment".
2253 **946** 2p.70 multicoloured . . 70 55

947 Anniversary Emblem

948 Marti

1995. 40th Anniv of National Institute of Public Administration.
2254 **947** 1p.80 green, mve & lilac 30 20

1995. Death Centenary of Jose Marti (Cuban writer and revolutionary).
2255 **948** 2p.70 multicoloured . . 70 55

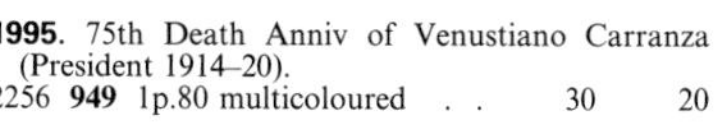
949 Carranza
950 Kite

1995. 75th Death Anniv of Venustiano Carranza (President 1914–20).
2256 **949** 1p.80 multicoloured . . 30 20

1995. 20th Anniv of National Tourist Organization.
2257 **950** 2p.70 multicoloured . . 70 55

951 Drugs, Skull and Unhappy Face

952 Cardenas del Rio

1995. International Day against Drug Abuse and Trafficking. Multicoloured.
2258 1p.80 Type **951** 85 20
2259 1p.80 Drug addict on swing 85 20
2260 1p.80 Faces behind bars . . 85 20

1995. Birth Centenary of Gen. Lazaro Cardenas del Rio (President 1934–40).
2261 **952** 1p.80 black 30 20

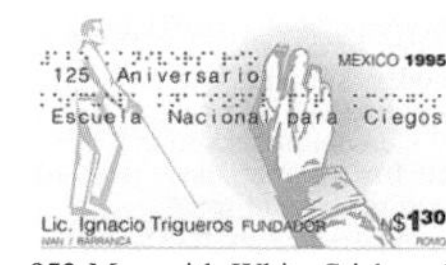

953 Man with White Stick and Hand reading Braille

1995. 125th Anniv of National Blind School. Mult.
2262 **953** 1p.30 brown and black 20 15

954 Northern Pintails

1995. Animals. Multicoloured.
2295 2p.70 Type **954** 90 50
2296 2p.70 Belted kingfisher . . . 90 50
2297 2p.70 Orange tiger 90 50
2298 2p.70 Hoary bat 90 50

955 Runners

956 Envelopes

1995. 13th International Marathon, Mexico City.
2299 **955** 2p.70 multicoloured . . 40 25

1995. 16th Congress of Postal Union of the Americas, Spain and Portugal, Mexico City.
2300 **956** 2p.70 multicoloured . . 40 25

957 Pasteur

958 Hands holding Envelopes

1995. Death Centenary of Louis Pasteur (chemist).
2301 **957** 2p.70 blue, black and green 40 25

1995. World Post Day.
2302 **958** 2p.70 multicoloured . . 40 25

959 Basket of Shopping

960 Anniversary Emblem

1995. World Food Day.
2303 **959** 1p.80 multicoloured . . 30 20

1995. 50th Anniv of F.A.O.
2304 **960** 2p.70 multicoloured . . 40 25

961 Elias Calles

962 Cuauhtemoc

1995. 50th Death Anniv of General Plutarco Elias Calles (President 1924–28).
2305 **961** 1p.80 multicoloured . . 30 20

1995. 500th Birth Anniv of Cuauhtemoc (Aztec Emperor of Tenochtitlan).
2306 **962** 1p.80 multicoloured . . 30 20

963 National Flag, National Anthem and Constitution

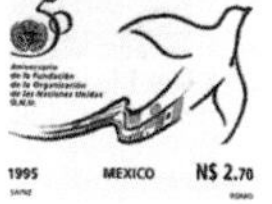

964 Flags as Tail of Dove

1995. National Constitution and Patriotic Symbols Day.
2307 **963** 1p.80 multicoloured . . 30 20

1995. 50th Anniv of U.N.O.
2308 **964** 2p.70 multicoloured . . 40 25

965 Airplane, Streamlined Train and Motor Vehicle

1995. International Passenger Travel Year.
2309 **965** 2p.70 multicoloured . . 80 25

966 "The Holy Family" (Andres de Concha)

1995. 30th Anniv of Museum of Mexican Art in the Vice-regency Period.
2310 **966** 1p.80 multicoloured . . 30 20

967 Pedro Maria Anaya

1995. Generals in Mexican History. Each black, yellow and gold.
2311 1p.80 Type **967** 30 20
2312 1p.80 Felipe Berriozabal . . 30 20
2313 1p.80 Santos Degollado . . 30 20
2314 1p.80 Sostenes Rocha . . . 30 20
2315 1p.80 Leandro Valle 30 20
2316 1p.80 Ignacio Zaragoza . . 30 20

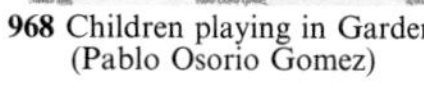
968 Children playing in Garden (Pablo Osorio Gomez)

969 Emblem

1995. Christmas. Children's Drawings. Multicoloured.
2317 1p.80 Type **968** 30 20
2318 2p.70 Adoration of the Wise Men (Oscar Enrique Carrillo) 40 25

1995. 10th Anniv of Mexican Health Foundation.
2319 **969** 1p.80 multicoloured . . 30 20

970 Ocelot
971 Louis Lumiere and Cine-camera

1995. Nature Conservation.
2320 **970** 1p.80 multicoloured . . 30 20

1995. Centenary of Motion Pictures.
2321 **971** 1p.80 black, mauve and blue 30 20

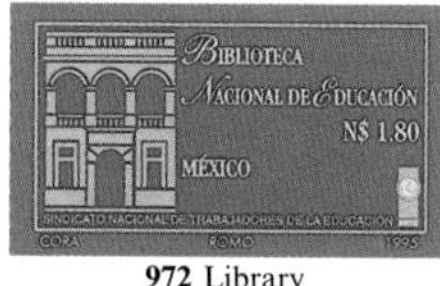

972 Library

1995. National Education Library, Mexico City.
2322 **972** 1p.80 green, blue and yellow 30 20

973 "Proportions of Man" (Leonardo da Vinci)

974 Pedro Vargas

1995. 50th Anniv of National Science and Arts Prize.
2323 **973** 1p.80 multicoloured . . 30 20

1995. Radio Personalities. Multicoloured.
2324 1p.80 Type **974** 85 20
2325 1p.80 Agustin Lara 85 20
2326 1p.80 Aguila Sisters 85 20
2327 1p.80 Tona "La Negra" . . 85 20
2328 1p.80 F. Gabilondo Soler "Cri-Cri" 85 20
2329 1p.80 Emilio Teuro 85 20
2330 1p.80 Gonzalo Curiel . . . 85 20
2331 1p.80 Lola Beltran 85 20

975 Robot Hand holding Optic Fibres

1995. 25th Anniv of Science and Technology Council.
2332 **975** 1p.80 multicoloured . . 30 20

976 Airplane

1996. National Aviation Day. Multicoloured.
2333 1p.80 Type **976** 70 20
2334 1p.80 Squadron 201, 1945 70 20
2335 2p.70 Ley Airport 90 25
2336 2p.70 Modern jetliner and biplane 90 25

977 Child and Caso

1996. Birth Centenary of Dr. Alfonso Caso (anthropologist).
2337 **977** 1p.80 multicoloured . . 30 20

978 Silverio Perez, Carlos Arruza and Manolo Martinez

1996. 50th Anniv of Plaza Mexico (bullring). Matadors. Multicoloured.
2338 1p.80 Type **978** 30 20
2339 2p.70 Roldolfo Gaona, Fermin Espinosa and Lorenzo Garza 40 25
Nos. 2338/9 were issued together, se-tenant, forming a composite design of the bullring.

979 Bag of Groceries

1996. 20th Anniv of Federal Consumer Council.
2340 **979** 1p.80 multicoloured . . 30 20

980 "Treatment of Fracture" (from Sahagun Codex)

1996. 50th Anniv of Mexican Society of Orthopaedics.
2341 **980** 1p.80 multicoloured . . 30 20

981 Rulfo

1996. 10th Death Anniv of Juan Rulfo (writer).
2342 **981** 1p.80 multicoloured . . 30 20

982 Anniversary Emblem and Map of Mexico

983 Healthy Hand reaching for Sick Hand

1996. 60th Anniv of National Polytechnic Institute.
2343 **982** 1p.80 grey, black and red 30 20

1996. United Nations Decade against the Abuse and Illicit Trafficking of Drugs. Multicoloured.
2344 1p.80 Type **983** 60 15
2345 1p.80 Man helping addict out of dark hole 60 15
2346 2p.70 Stylized figures . . . 90 25

984 Gymnastics

985 Cameraman and Film Frames of Couples

1996. Olympic Games, Atlanta, U.S.A. Multicoloured.
2347 1p.80 Type **984** 45 15
2348 1p.80 Hurdling 45 15
2349 2p.70 Football 65 25
2350 2p.70 Running 65 25
2351 2p.70 Show jumping 65 25

1996. Centenary of Mexican Films. Multicoloured.
2352 1p.80 Type **985** 25 15
2353 1p.80 Camera and film frames of individuals . . 25 15

986 Scales

1996. 60th Anniv of Fiscal Tribunal.
2354 **986** 1p.80 multicoloured . . 25 15

987 Runners' Feet

1996. 14th Mexico City International Marathon.
2355 **987** 2p.70 multicoloured . . 40 25

988 Flask, Open Books, Atomic Model and Microscope

1996. Science.
2356 **988** 1p.80 multicoloured . . 25 15

989 "Allegory of Foundation of Zacatecas" (anon)

1996. 450th Anniv of Zacatecas.
2357 **989** 1p.80 multicoloured . . 25 15

990 Rural Education

992 Emblem

1996. 25th Anniv of National Council for the Improvement of Education.
2358 **990** 1p.80 multicoloured . . 25 15

1996. Family Planning Month.
2360 **992** 1p.80 green, mauve and blue 25 15

993 Flag of the "Three Guarantees", 1821

1996. 175th Anniv of Declaration of Independence.
2361 **993** 1p.80 multicoloured . . 25 15

994 Blue Morpho, Monkey, Harpy Eagle and other Birds

1996. Nature Conservation. Multicoloured.
2362 1p.80 Type **994** 55 15
2363 1p.80 Turtle dove, yellow grosbeak with chicks in nest, trogon and hummingbird 55 15
2364 1p.80 Mountains, monarchs (butterflies) in air and American black bear with cub 55 15
2365 1p.80 Fishing buzzard, mule deer, lupins and monarchs (butterflies) on plant . . . 55 15
2366 1p.80 Scarlet macaws, monarchs, toucan, peafowl and spider monkey hanging from tree 55 15
2367 1p.80 Resplendent quetzal, emerald toucanet, bromeliads and tiger-cat 55 15
2368 1p.80 Parrots, white-tailed deer and rabbit by river 55 15
2369 1p.80 Snake, wolf, puma and lizard on rock and blue-capped bird 55 15
2370 1p.80 Coyote, prairie dogs at burrow, quail on branch, deer, horned viper and caracara on cactus . . 55 15
2371 1p.80 Jaguar, euphonias, long-tailed bird, crested bird and bat 55 15
2372 1p.80 "Martucha", peacock, porcupine, butterfly and green snake 55 15
2373 1p.80 Blue magpie, green-headed bird, owl, woodpecker and hummingbird by river . . 55 15
2374 1p.80 Cinnamon cuckoo in tree, fox by river and green macaws in tree . . 55 15
2375 1p.80 Wild sheep by rocks, bird on ocotillo plant, bats, owl, lynx and woodpecker on cactus . . 55 15
2376 1p.80 Ant-eater climbing sloping tree, jaguarundi, bat, orchid and ocellated turkey in undergrowth . . 55 15
2377 1p.80 Ocelot, "grison", coral snake, "temazate", paca and otter by river 55 15
2378 1p.80 Grey squirrel in tree, salamander, beaver, bird, shrew-mole, mountain hen and racoon by river . . . 55 15
2379 1p.80 Butterfly, trogon in red tree, "chachalaca", crested magpie and "tejon" 55 15
2380 1p.80 Bat, "tlalcoyote", "rata neotoma", "chichimoco", hare, cardinal (bird), lizard, kangaroo rat and tortoise 55 15
2381 1p.80 Beetle on leaf, tapir, tree frog and "tunpache" 55 15
2382 1p.80 Crocodile, insect, cup fungus, boa constrictor and butterfly 55 15
2383 1p.80 Armadillo, "tlacuache", iguana, turkey and butterfly . . . 55 15
2384 1p.80 Turkey, collared peccary, zorilla, lizard, rattlesnake and mouse . . 55 15
2385 1p.80 Cacomistle, "matraca", lark, collared lizard and cacti 55 15
Nos. 2362/85 were issued together, se-tenant, forming a composite design of habitats and wildlife under threat.

995 Bird with Letter in Beak

996 Institute

1996. World Post Day.
2386 **995** 2p.70 multicoloured . . 40 25

1996. 50th Anniv of Salvador Zubiran National Nutrition Institute.
2387 **996** 1p.80 multicoloured . . 25 15

997 Constantino de Tarnava

998 "Portrait of a Woman" (Baltasar de Echave Ibia)

1996. 75th Anniv of Radio Broadcasting in Mexico.
2388 **997** 1p.80 multicoloured . . 25 15

1996. Virreinal Art Gallery. Multicoloured.
2389 1p.80 Type **998** 50 15
2390 1p.80 "Portrait of the Child Joaquin Manuel Fernandez de Santa Cruz" (Nicolas Rodriguez Xuarez) 50 15
2391 1p.80 "Portrait of Dona Maria Luisa Gonzaga Foncerrada y Labarrieta" (Jose Maria Vazquez) . . 50 15
2392 1p.80 "Archangel Michael" (Luis Juarez) 50 15
2393 2p.70 "Virgin of the Apocalypse" (Miguel Cabrera) 65 25

999 Isidro Fabela and Genaro Estrada

1000 Maize

1996. "Precursors of Foreign Policy".
2394 **999** 1p.80 multicoloured . . 25 15

1996. World Food Day.
2395 **1000** 2p.70 multicoloured . . 40 25

1001 Underground Train around Globe

1996. International Metros Conference.
2396 **1001** 2p.70 multicoloured . . 40 25

1002 Star (Elias Martin del Campo)

1996. Christmas. Multicoloured.
2397 1p. Type **1002** 15 10
2398 1p.80 Man with star-shaped bundles on stick (Ehecatl Cabrera Franco) (vert) . . 25 15

1003 Henestrosa

1996. Andres Henestrosa (writer) Commemoration.
2399 **1003** 1p.80 multicoloured . . 25 15

1004 Old and New Institute Buildings

1005 Emblem

1996. 50th Anniv of National Cancer Institute.
2400 **1004** 1p.80 multicoloured . . 25 15

1996. Paisano Programme.
2401 **1005** 2p.70 multicoloured . . 40 25

1006 Painting

1996. Birth Centenary of David Alfaro Siqueiros (painter).
2402 **1006** 1p.80 multicoloured . . 25 15

1007 Dr. Jose Maria Barcelo de Villagran

1996. 32nd National Assembly of Surgeons.
2403 **1007** 1p.80 multicoloured . . 25 15

1008 Black Bears

1996. Nature Conservation.
2404 **1008** 1p.80 multicoloured . . 25 15

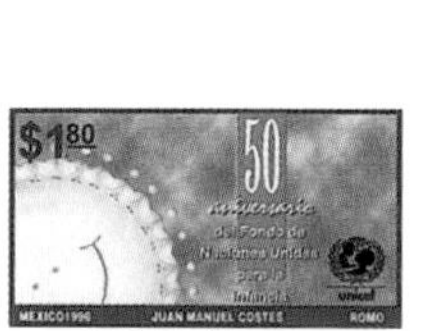

1009 Smiling Sun

1010 Library

1996. 50th Anniv of U.N.I.C.E.F.
2405 **1009** 1p.80 multicoloured . . 25 15

1996. 350th Anniv of Palafoxiana Library, Puebla.
2406 **1010** 1p.80 multicoloured . . 25 15

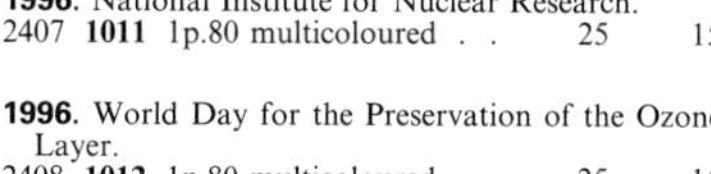

1011 Sphere and Atomic Symbol

1012 Sun's Rays and Earth

1996. National Institute for Nuclear Research.
2407 **1011** 1p.80 multicoloured . . 25 15

1996. World Day for the Preservation of the Ozone Layer.
2408 **1012** 1p.80 multicoloured . . 25 15

1013 Sculpture

1014 Pellicer (after D. Rivera)

1996. 30 Years of Work by Sebastian (sculptor).
2409 **1013** 1p.80 multicoloured . . 25 15

1997. Tourism. As Nos. 2263 etc but with value expressed as "$".
2410 1p. Colima 15 10
2411 1p.80 Chiapas 25 15
2412 2p. Colima 30 20
2413 2p. Guanajuato 30 20
2413a 2p. Coahiula 30 20
2414 2p.30 Chiapas 35 25
2415 2p.50 Queretaro 35 25
2416 2p.60 Colima 40 25
2417 2p.70 Mexico City . . . 40 25
2418 3p. Type **869** 45 30
2419 3p.10 Coahuila 45 30
2420 3p.40 Sinaloa 50 35
2421 3p.50 Mexico City . . . 50 35
2421a 3p.60 Sonora 50 35
2421b 3p.60 Coahuila 50 35
2421c 3p.70 Campeche 50 35
2422 4p. Michoacan (vert) . . . 60 40
2422a 4p.20 Guanajuato . . . 55 35
2423 4p.40 Yucatan 65 45
2424 4p.90 Sonora 70 45
2425 5p. Queretaro 70 45
2426 5p. Colima 65 45
2426a 5p.30 Michoacan (vert) . . 70 45
2426b 5p.90 Queretaro 80 55
2427 6p. Zacatacas (vert) . . . 85 55
2427a 6p. Sinaloa 85 55
2427b 6p.50 Sinaloa 85 50
2428 7p. Sonora . . . . . . 1·00 65
2428a 8p. Zacatecas (vert) . . . 1·10 75
2429 8p.50 Mexico City . . . 1·25 85

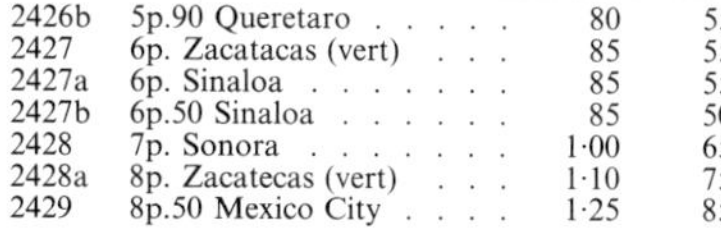

1997. Birth Centenary of Carlos Pellicer (lyricist).
2435 **1014** 2p.30 multicoloured . . 35 25

1015 Eloy Blanco (after Oswaldo)

1997. Birth Centenary (1996) of Andres Eloy Blanco (poet).
2436 **1015** 3p.40 multicoloured . . 50 35

1016 Book, Inkwell and Pencil

1017 Tree, Globe and Atomic Cloud

1997. Confederation of American Educationalists' International Summit Conference.
2437 **1016** 3p.40 multicoloured . . 50 35

1997. 30th Anniv of Tlatelolco Treaty (Latin American and Caribbean treaty banning nuclear weapons).
2438 **1017** 3p.40 multicoloured . . 50 35

1019 Felipe Angeles

1020 Woman dancing

1997. Noted Generals. Multicoloured.
2440 2p.30 Type **1019** 35 25
2441 2p.30 Joaquin Amaro Dominguez 35 25
2442 2p.30 Mariano Escobedo . . 35 25
2443 2p.30 Jacinto Trevino Glez 35 25
2444 2p.30 Candido Aguilar Vargas 35 25
2445 2p.30 Francisco Urquizo . . 35 25

1997. International Women's Day.
2446 **1020** 2p.30 multicoloured . . 35 25

1021 "Grammar" (Juan Correa)

1997. 1st International Spanish Language Congress.
2447 **1021** 3p.40 multicoloured . . 50 35

1022 Chavez

1997. Birth Centenary of Dr. Ignacio Chavez.
2448 **1022** 2p.30 multicoloured . . 35 25

1023 State Emblem and Venustiano Carranza (President 1915–20)

1997. 80th Anniv of 1917 Constitution.
2449 **1023** 2p.30 multicoloured . . 35 25

1024 Yanez

1997. 50th Anniv of First Edition of "At the Water's Edge" by Agustin Yanez.
2450 **1024** 2p.30 multicoloured . . 35 25

1025 Mexican Mythological Figures (Luis Nishizawa)

1997. Centenary of Japanese Immigration.
2451 **1025** 3p.40 red, gold and black 50 35

1026 Rafael Ramirez

1027 University

1997. Teachers' Day.
2452 **1026** 2p.30 green and black 35 25

1997. 40th Anniv of Autonomous University of Lower California.
2453 **1027** 2p.30 multicoloured . . 35 25

1028 Dove flying Free

1029 Freud

1997. International Day against Illegal Use and Illicit Trafficking of Drugs. Multicoloured.
2454 2p.30 Type **1028** 35 25
2455 3p.40 Dove imprisoned behind bars 50 35
2456 3p.40 Man opening cage . . 50 35
Nos. 2454/6 were issued together, se-tenant, forming a composite design.

1997. 58th Death Anniv of Sigmund Freud (pioneer of psychoanalysis).
2457 **1029** 2p.30 blue, green and violet 35 25

1030 School Arms

1031 Emblem

1997. Centenary of Naval School.
2458 **1030** 2p.30 multicoloured . . 35 25

1997. Introduction of New Social Security Law.
2459 **1031** 2p.30 multicoloured . . 30 20

1032 Globes and Anniversary Emblem

1997. 60th Anniv of National Bank of Foreign Commerce.
2460 **1032** 3p.40 multicoloured . . 40 25

1033 Common Porpoises

1997. Nature Conservation.
2461 **1033** 2p.30 multicoloured . . 30 20

1034 Passenger Airliners, 1947 and 1997

1997. 50th Anniv of Mexican Air Pilots' College.
2462 **1034** 2p.30 multicoloured . . 30 20

1035 Runners

1997. 15th Mexico City Marathon.
2463 **1035** 3p.40 multicoloured . . 40 25

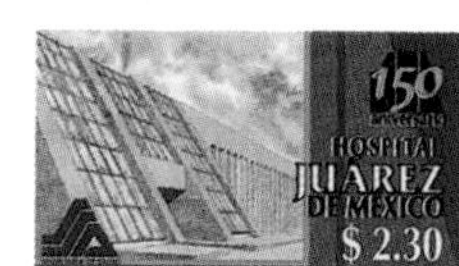

1036 Hospital Entrance

1997. 150th Anniv of Juarez Hospital.
2464 **1036** 2p.30 multicoloured . . 30 20

1037 Battle of Padierna

1997. 150th Anniversaries of Battles. Multicoloured.
2465 2p.30 Type **1037** 30 20
2466 2p.30 Battle of Churubusco 30 20
2467 2p.30 Battle of Molino del Rey 30 20
2468 2p.30 Defence of Chapultepec Fort 30 20

1038 Prieto

1039 Commemorative Cross

1997. Death Centenary of Guillermo Prieto (writer).
2469 **1038** 2p.30 blue 30 20

1997. 150th Anniv of Mexican St. Patrick's Battalion.
2470 **1039** 3p.40 multicoloured . . 40 25

1040 Emblem 1041 Bird carrying Letter

1997. Adolescent Reproductive Health Month.
2471 **1040** 2p.30 multicoloured . . 30 20

1997. World Post Day. Multicoloured.
2472 3p.40 Type **1041** 40 25
2473 3p.40 Heinrich von Stephan (founder of U.P.U.) (horiz) 40 25

1042 Gomez Morin 1043 Hospital

1997. Birth Centenary of Manuel Gomez Morin (politician).
2474 **1042** 2p.30 multicoloured . . 30 20

1997. 50th Anniv of Dr. Manuel Gea Gonzalez General Hospital.
2475 **1043** 2p.30 multicoloured . . 30 20

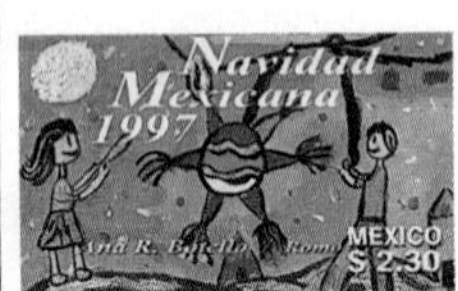

1044 Emblem 1045 Children celebrating Christmas (Ana Botello)

1997. 75th Anniv of Mexican Bar College of Law.
2476 **1044** 2p.30 red and black . . 30 20

1997. Christmas. Children's Paintings. Multicoloured.
2477 2p.30 Type **1045** 30 20
2478 2p.30 Children playing blind-man's-buff (Adrian Laris) 30 20

1046 Emblem and Hospital Facade

1997. Centenary of Central University Hospital, Chihuahua.
2479 **1046** 2p.30 multicoloured . . 30 20

1047 Molina and Nobel Medal

1997. Dr. Mario Molina (winner of Nobel Prize for Chemistry, 1995).
2480 **1047** 3p.40 multicoloured . . 40 25

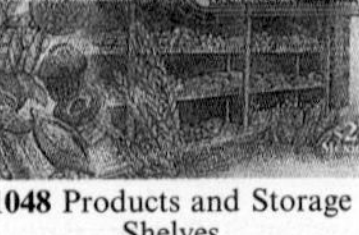

1048 Products and Storage Shelves 1049 "Buildings" (Jose Chavez Morado)

1997. National Chamber of Baking Industry. Multicoloured.
2481 2p.30 Type **1048** 30 20
2482 2p.30 Baker putting loaves in oven 30 20
2483 2p.30 Wedding cake, ingredients and baker . . 30 20
Nos. 2481/3 were issued together, se-tenant, forming a composite design.

1997. 25th Cervantes Festival, Guanajuato.
2484 **1049** 2p.30 multicoloured . . 30 20

1050 Galleon and Map of Loreto, California 1051 Sword and Rifle

1997. 300th Anniv of Loreto.
2485 **1050** 2p.30 multicoloured . . 30 20

1998. 50th Anniv of Military Academy, Puebla.
2486 **1051** 2p.30 multicoloured . . 30 20

1052 Hands holding Children on Heart 1053 Dancers (5th of May Festival)

1998. International Women's Day.
2487 **1052** 2p.30 multicoloured . . 30 20

1998. Festivals.
2488 **1053** 3p.50 multicoloured . . 45 30

1054 Eiffel Tower, Player and Flag 1055 Sierra

1998. World Cup Football Championship, France. Multicoloured.
2489 2p.30 Type **1054** 30 20
2490 2p.30 Mascot, Eiffel Tower and flag 30 20

1998. 150th Birth Anniv of Justo Sierra (educationist).
2492 **1055** 2p.30 multicoloured . . 30 20

1056 Zubiran

1998. Birth Centenary of Salvador Zubiran (physician).
2493 **1056** 2p.30 multicoloured . . 30 20

1057 Emblem

1998. 50th Anniv of Organization of American States.
2494 **1057** 3p.40 multicoloured . . 40 25

1058 University Emblem 1059 Soledad Anaya Solorzano

1998. 25th Anniv of People's Autonomous University of Puebla State.
2495 **1058** 2p.30 red, silver and black 30 20

1998. Teachers' Day.
2496 **1059** 2p.30 bistre, black and cream 30 20

1060 Crops

1998. 250th Anniv of Tamaulipas (formerly New Santander) (1st issue).
2497 **1060** 2p.30 multicoloured . . 30 20
See also Nos. 2548.

1061 Macuilxochitl

1998. 20th Anniv of Sports Lottery.
2498 **1061** 2p.30 multicoloured . . 30 20

1062 Manila Galleon

1998. Centenary of Philippine Independence.
2499 **1062** 3p.40 multicoloured . . 45 30

1063 Garcia Lorca

1998. Birth Centenary of Federico Garcia Lorca (poet).
2501 **1063** 3p.40 multicoloured . . 40 25

1064 Emblems

1998. 50th Anniv of Universal Declaration of Human Rights.
2502 **1064** 3p.40 green and black 45 30

1065 Open Book and Dove 1067 Tree

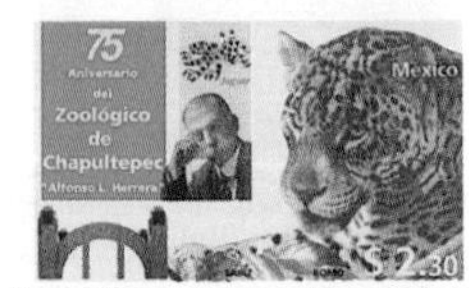

1066 Alfonso Herrera (founder) and Leopard

1998. International Day against the Use and Illegal Trafficking of Drugs.
2503 **1065** 2p.30 multicoloured . . 30 20

1998. 75th Anniv of Chapultepec Zoo.
2504 **1066** 2p.30 multicoloured . . 30 20

1998. Tree Day.
2505 **1067** 2p.30 multicoloured . . 30 20

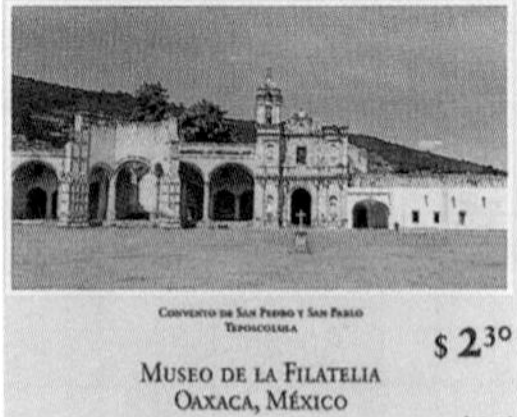

1068 St. Peter and St. Paul's Monastery, Teposcolula

1998. Inauguration of Philatelic Museum, Oaxaca. Multicoloured.
2506 2p.30 Type **1068** 30 20
2507 2p.30 Clay pot, San Bartolo Coyotepec 30 20
2508 2p.30 "The Road" (painting, Francisco Toledo) 30 20
2509 2p.30 Gold pectoral from Tomb 7, Monte Alban . . 30 20

1069 Juarez

1998. 126th Death Anniv of Benito Juarez (President 1859–64 and 1867–72).
2510 **1069** 2p.30 stone, black and brown 30 20

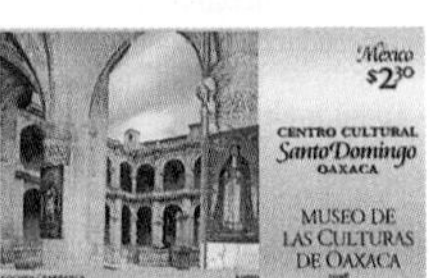

1070 Cultural Museum

1998. St. Dominic's Cultural Centre, Oaxaca. Multicoloured.
2511 2p.30 Type **1070** 30 20
2512 2p.30 Francisco de Burgoa Library 30 20
2513 2p.30 Historical botanic garden 30 20
2514 3p.40 St. Dominic's Monastery (after Teodoro Velasco) 45 30

1071 Frigate Bird, Blue-footed Booby, Whales and Cacti

1998. Marine Life. Multicoloured.
2515 2p.30 Type **1071** 30 20
2516 2p.30 Albatross, humpback whale and seagulls . . . 30 20
2517 2p.30 Tail of whale and swordfish 30 20
2518 2p.30 Fish eagle, flamingo, herons and dolphins . . . 30 20
2519 2p.30 Turtles, flamingoes, cormorant and palm tree 30 20
2520 2p.30 Oystercatcher, turnstone, elephant seal and sealions 30 20
2521 2p.30 Dolphin, turtle, seagulls and swallows . . 30 20
2522 2p.30 Killer whale, dolphins and ray 30 20
2523 2p.30 Flamingoes, pelican, kingfishers and spider . . 30 20
2524 2p.30 Crocodile, roseate spoonbill and tiger heron 30 20
2525 2p.30 Schools of sardines and anchovies 30 20
2526 2p.30 Turtle, squid, gold-finned tunnyfish and shark 30 20
2527 2p.30 Jellyfish, dolphins and fishes 30 20
2528 2p.30 Dolphin (fish), barracudas and haddock 30 20
2529 2p.30 Manatee, fishes, anemone and coral . . . 30 20
2530 2p.30 Seaweed, starfish, coral and fishes 30 20

2531 2p.30 Hammerhead shark, angelfish, gudgeon, eels and coral 30 20
2532 2p.30 Shrimps, ray and other fishes 30 20
2533 2p.30 Octopus, bass, crayfish and other fishes 30 20
2534 2p.30 Turtle, porcupinefish, coral, angelfish and other fishes 30 20
2535 2p.30 Abalone, clams, razor clam, crayfish and anemone 30 20
2536 2p.30 Seahorses, angelfishes, coral and shells 30 20
2537 2p.30 Octopus, turtle, crab and moray eel 30 20
2538 2p.30 Butterflyfishes and other fishes 30 20
2539 2p.30 Reef shark, angelfish and corals 30 20

Nos. 2515/39 were issued together, se-tenant, forming a composite design.

1072 Runners

1998. 16th International Marathon, Mexico City.
2540 **1072** 3p.40 multicoloured . . 45 30

1073 Aztec Deity

1998. World Tourism Day.
2541 **1073** 3p.40 multicoloured . . 45 30

1074 Lucas Alaman (founder)

1998. 175th Anniv of National Archives.
2542 **1074** 2p.30 green, red and black 30 20

1075 Emblem

1076 Stylized Couple

1998. 75th Anniv of Interpol.
2543 **1075** 3p.40 multicoloured . . 45 30

1998. Healthy Pregnancy Month.
2544 **1076** 2p.30 multicoloured . . 30 20

1077 Painting by Luis Nishizawa

1998.
2545 **1077** 2p.30 multicoloured . . 30 20

1078 Key and Globe

1998. World Post Day.
2546 **1078** 3p.40 multicoloured . . 45 30

1079 College Campus

1998. 175th Anniv of Military College.
2547 **1079** 2p.30 multicoloured . . 30 20

1080 Map

1998. 250th Anniv of Tamaulipas (formerly New Santander) (2nd issue).
2548 **1080** 2p.30 multicoloured . . 30 20

1081 Golden Eagle

1998. Nature Conservation.
2549 **1081** 2p.30 multicoloured . . 30 20

1082 Woman and Potatoes

1998. World Food Day.
2550 **1082** 3p.30 multicoloured . . 45 30

1083 Mexico arrowed on Globe

1998. National Migration Week.
2551 **1083** 2p.30 multicoloured . . 30 20

1084 Jimenez

1998. 25th Death Anniv of Jose Alfredo Jimenez (writer).
2552 **1084** 2p.30 multicoloured . . 30 20

1085 Oil Rig and Emblem

1087 Franciscan Monastery, Colima

1086 Mexican Stone Carving and Eiffel Tower

1998. 25th Anniv of Mexican Petroleum Engineers' Association.
2553 **1085** 3p.40 multicoloured . . 45 30

1998. Mexican–French Economic and Cultural Co-operation.
2554 **1086** 3p.40 multicoloured . . 45 30

1998. 475th Anniv of Colima.
2555 **1087** 2p.30 multicoloured . . 30 20

1088 Wise Men approaching Stable

1998. Christmas. Multicoloured. Self-adhesive.
2556 2p.30 Type **1088** 30 20
2557 3p.40 Decorations and pot (vert) 45 30

1089 Woman with Baby

1998. 50th Anniv of National Institute of Indigenous Peoples.
2558 **1089** 2p.30 multicoloured . . 30 20

1090 Eagle holding Statute

1998. 60th Anniv of Federation of Civil Servants' Trade Unions.
2559 **1090** 2p.30 multicoloured . . 30 20

1091 Airplane and Aztec Bird-man

1092 University Arms

1998. 25th Anniv of Latin-American Civil Aviation Commission.
2560 **1091** 3p.40 multicoloured . . 45 30

1998. 125th Anniv of Sinaloa Autonomous University.
2561 **1092** 2p.30 multicoloured . . 30 20

1094 "Satmex 5" and Earth

1999. Launch of "Satmex 5" Satellite.
2563 **1094** 3p. multicoloured . . . 40 25

1095 Maracas Player and Streamers

1096 Couple in Hammock

1999. Veracruz Carnival.
2564 **1095** 3p. multicoloured . . . 40 25

1999. Bicentenary of Acapulco, Guerrero. Mult.
2565 3p. Type **1096** 40 25
2566 4p.20 Diving from cliff . . . 55 30

Nos. 2565/6 were issued together, se-tenant, forming a composite design.

1097 Internet Website

1999. International Women's Day.
2567 **1097** 4p.20 multicoloured . . 55 30

1098 "Mexico" (Jorge Gonzalez Camarena)

1999. 40th Anniv of National Commission for Free Textbooks.
2568 **1098** 3p. multicoloured . . . 40 25

1099 Family Members

1999. 25th Anniv of National Population Council.
2569 **1099** 3p. multicoloured . . . 40 25

1101 Guadalupe Ceniceros de Perez

1999. Teachers' Day.
2571 **1101** 3p. multicoloured . . . 40 25

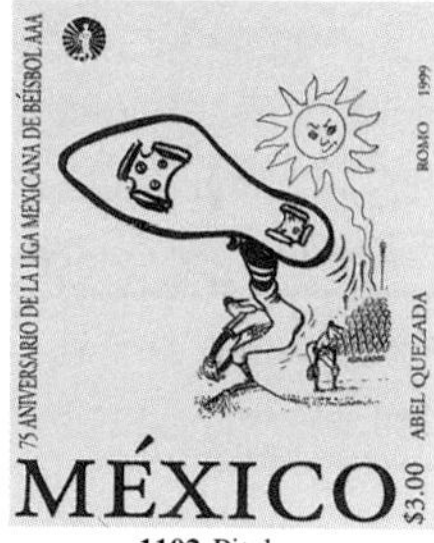

1102 Pitcher

1999. 75th Anniv of Mexican Baseball League. Each black and grey.
2572 3p. Type **1102** 40 25
2573 3p. Catcher 40 25
2574 3p. Skeletal pitcher 40 25
2575 3p. Pitcher (different) . . . 40 25

1103 10p. Banknote

1999. 115th Anniv of National Bank of Mexico. Multicoloured.
2576 3p. Type **1103** 40 25
2577 3p. Former and current headquarters 40 25

1105 Couple holding Hands

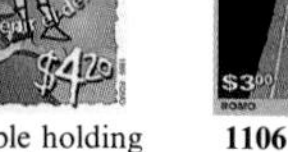

1106 Skyscraper

1999. International Day against Illegal Use and Illicit Trafficking of Drugs.
2579 **1105** 4p.20 multicoloured . . 60 40

1999. 65th Anniv of National Financial Institute.
2580 **1106** 3p. multicoloured . . . 45 30

1107 Tree

1999. Tree Day.
2581 **1107** 3p. multicoloured . . . 45 30

1108 Registration Documents and Fingerprint

1999. 140th Anniv of National Civil Register.
2582 **1108** 3p. multicoloured . . . 45 30

1109 Runner's Feet

1999. 17th International Marathon, Mexico City.
2583 **1109** 4p.20 multicoloured . . 60 40

1110 Children, Flag and Book on Island ("Conoce nuestra Constitucion")

1999. 40th Anniv of National Commission for Free Textbooks (2nd issue). Multicoloured.
2584 3p. Type **1110** 45 30
2585 3p. Children dancing ("Tsuni tsame") 45 30
2586 3p. Bird on flower ("Ciencias naturales") . . 45 30

1111 "Self-portrait"

1999. Birth Centenary of Rufino Tamayo (artist).
2587 **1111** 3p. multicoloured . . . 45 30

1112 Building

1999. Bicentenary of Toluca City.
2588 **1112** 3p. black and copper 45 30

1113 State Arms, Model Figures and Signature

1999. 175th Anniv of State of Mexico.
2589 **1113** 3p. multicoloured . . . 45 30

1114 "50" and Map of Americas

1999. 50th Anniv of Union of Universities of Latin America.
2590 **1114** 4p.20 multicoloured . . 60 40

1115 Emblem

1999. 40th Anniv of Institute of Security and Social Services of State Workers (I.S.S.S.T.E.).
2591 **1115** 3p. multicoloured . . . 45 30

1116 Map and State Emblem

1999. 25th Anniv of State of Baja California Sur.
2592 **1116** 3p. multicoloured . . . 45 30

1117 Emblem, "25" and Map

1999. 25th Anniv of Mexican Family Planning.
2593 **1117** 3p. multicoloured . . . 45 30

1118 Harpy Eagle

1999. Nature Conservation.
2594 **1118** 3p. multicoloured . . . 45 30

1119 Stone Carving and Arms

1120 U.P.U. Messengers

1999. 25th Anniv of State of Quintana Roo.
2595 **1119** 3p. multicoloured . . . 45 30

1999. 125th Anniv of Universal Postal Union.
2596 **1120** 4p.20 multicoloured . . 60 40

1121 Globe and Stamps

1999. World Post Day.
2597 **1121** 4p.20 multicoloured . . 60 40

1122 Emblem and Monument

1999. 12th General Assembly of International Council on Monuments and Sites.
2598 **1122** 4p.20 silver, blue and black 60 40

1123 Chavez and Revueltas

1999. Birth Centenaries of Carlos Chavez and Silvestre Revueltas (composers).
2599 **1123** 3p. multicoloured . . . 45 30

1124 Emblem

1126 "Mexico 1999" in Star and Children (Alfredo Carciarreal)

1125 Map, Cave Painting and State Arms

1999. 25th Anniv of Autonomous Metropolitan University.
2600 **1124** 3p. multicoloured . . . 45 30

1999. 150th Anniv of State of Guerrero.
2601 **1125** 3p. multicoloured . . . 45 30

1999. Christmas. Children's Drawings. Multicoloured.
2602 3p. Type **1126** 45 30
2603 4p.20 Christmas decorations (Rodrigo Santiago Salazar) 60 40

1127 Anniversary Emblem

1999. 20th Anniv of National Commission on Professional Education.
2604 **1127** 3p. green, ultramarine and black 45 30

1128 Humboldt (naturalist)

1999. Bicentenary of Alexander von Humboldt's Exploration of South America.
2605 **1128** 3p. multicoloured . . . 45 30

1130 Emblem and Crowd

1131 Woman ascending Stairs

2000. Census.
2607 **1130** 3p. multicoloured . . . 45 30

2000. International Women's Day.
2608 **1131** 4p.20 multicoloured . . 60 40

1134 Totonaca Temple, El Tajin

2000.
2611 **1134** 3p. multicoloured . . . 45 30

1135 Emblem, Books and Keyboard

2000. 50th Anniv of National Association of Universities and Institutes of Higher Education.
2612 **1135** 3p. multicoloured . . . 45 30

1136 Emblem

2000. 25th Tourism Fair, Acapulco.
2613 **1136** 4p.20 multicoloured . . 60 40

1137 Men in Canoe and Sailing Ship

2000. 500th Anniv of the Discovery of Brazil.
2614 **1137** 4p.20 multicoloured . . 60 40

1138 Luis Alvarez Barret

2000. Teachers' Day.
2615 **1138** 3p. multicoloured . . . 45 30

1139 Flying Cars and Boy with Dog (Alejandro Guerra Millan)

2000. "Stampin the Future". Winning Entries in Children's International Painting Competition. Mult.
2616 3p. Type **1139** 45 30
2617 4p.20 Houses and space ships (Carlos Hernandez Garcia) 60 40

1140 Emblem

2000. 4th Asian–Pacific Telecommunications and Information Industry Economic Co-operation Forum.
2618 **1140** 4p.20 multicoloured . . 60 40

1141 Young Children

1144 Pictograms

2000. International Anti-drugs Day.
2619 **1141** 4p.20 multicoloured . . 60 40

2000. Convive (disabled persons' organization).
2622 **1144** 3p. multicoloured . . . 45 25

1145 Globe and Member Flags

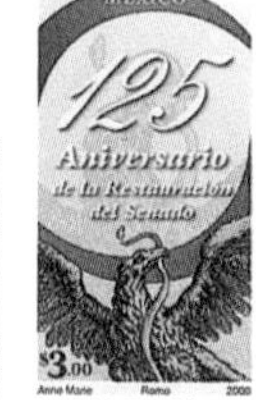
1146 Emblem

2000. 20th Anniv of Association of Latin American Integration.
2623 **1145** 4p.20 multicoloured . . 65 40

2000. 125th Anniv of Restoration of Senate.
2624 **1146** 3p. multicoloured . . . 45 25

1149 Runners crossing Finishing Line

2000. 18th International Marathon, Mexico City.
2627 **1149** 4p.20 multicoloured . . 65 40

1150 Athletes and Sydney Opera House

2000. Olympic Games, Sydney.
2628 **1150** 4p.20 multicoloured . . 65 40

1151 Emblem and Family

2000. Paisano Programme (support for Mexicans returning home from abroad).
2629 **1151** 4p.20 multicoloured . . 65 40

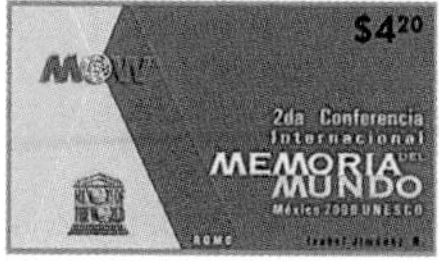
1152 Emblem

2000. 2nd International U.N.E.S.C.O. World Conference, Colima.
2630 **1152** 4p.20 multicoloured . . 65 40

1153 Profiles

1155 Bird holding Letter

1154 Building and Emblem

2000. Women's Health Month.
2631 **1153** 3p. multicoloured . . . 35 20

2000. 250th Anniv of Ciudad Victoria, Tamaulipas.
2632 **1154** 3p. multicoloured . . . 35 20

2000. World Post Day.
2633 **1155** 4p.20 multicoloured . . 50 30

1156 Emblem

2000. 50th Anniv of National Human Rights Commission.
2634 **1156** 3p. silver and blue . . . 35 20

1157 Doctors and Ambulance

2000. New Millennium. Sheet 223 × 135 mm in shape of flag, containing T **1157** and similar multicoloured designs.
MS2635 3p. Type **1157**; 3p. Posters, doctors and globe (79 × 25 mm); 3p. Children receiving injections; 3p. Poster showing tractor and crowd demonstrating (79 × 25 mm); 4p.20, Modern medical technology (oval- shaped, 39 × 49 mm) . . . . 2·00 1·25

1158 Clouds and Emblem

2000. 50th Anniv of World Meteorological Organization.
2636 **1158** 3p. multicoloured . . . 35 20

1159 Emblem

2000. 50th Anniv of International Diabetes Federation.
2637 **1159** 4p.20 gold and red . . 50 30

1160 Contemporary Art with Sculpture (½-size illustration)

2000. Art. Sheet 223 × 39 mm in shape of flag, containing T **1160** and similar multicoloured designs.
MS2638 3p. Type **1160**; 3p. Photographs (39 × 25 mm); 3p. Opera singer and movie actors; 3p. Dancers (39 × 25 mm); 4p.20 Ballet dancers and musicians (oval-shaped, 39 × 49 mm) . . 2·00 1·25

1161 Samuel Morse, Juan de la Granja and Telegraph Apparatus

2000. 150th Anniv of Telegraph in Mexico.
2639 **1161** 3p. multicoloured . . . 35 20
Samuel Morse invented the telegraph and Morse code system and Juan de la Granja introduced the telegraph to Mexico.

1162 Bunuel

2000. Birth Centenary of Luis Bunuel (film director).
2640 **1162** 3p. silver, black and red 35 20

1163 Lightning

2000. 25th Anniv of Electric Investigation Institute.
2641 **1163** 3p. multicoloured . . . 35 20

1164 Building Customs House, and Bridge

2000. Centenary of Customs.
2642 **1164** 3p. multicoloured . . . 35 20

1165 Star and Girl (Maria Carina Lona Martinez)

2000. Christmas. Children's paintings. Multicoloured.
2643 3p. Type **1165** 35 20
2644 4p.20 Poinsettia (Daniela Escamilla Rodriguez) . . 50 30

1166 Television Set and Emblem

2000. 50th Anniv of Television in Mexico.
2645 **1166** 3p. multicoloured . . . 35 20

1167 Adamo Boari (architect)

2000. Centenary of Commencement of Construction of Postal Headquarters, Mexico City. Sheet 92 × 100 mm, containing T **1167** and similar designs. Multicoloured.
MS2646 3p. multicoloured; 3p. black, brown and red; 3p. multicoloured; 10p. black, brown and red (71 × 39 mm) . . . . 2·10 1·25
DESIGNS: As Type **1167**—3p. Building facade; 3p. Gonzalo Garita y Frontera (engineer). 71 × 39 mm—10p. Completed building.

1168 Coiled Mattress (Manuel Alvarez Bravo)

2000. Photography. Sheet 223 × 135 mm in shape of flag, containing T **1168** and similar multicoloured designs.
MS2647 3p. Type **1168**; 3p. Various portraits (79 × 25 mm); 3p. Roses (Tina Modotti); 3p. Various photographs including a lift, a lake, a 1925 car, a helicopter, a ruined building, a street scene, men in costume and boot heels (79 × 25 mm); 4p.20 Men in gas masks (oval-shaped, 39 × 49 mm) 2·00 1·25

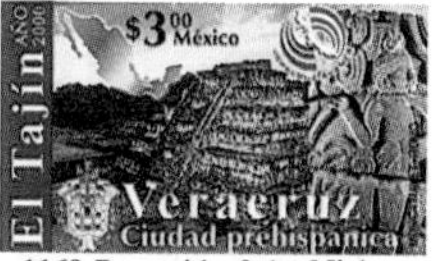
1169 Pyramid of the Niches

2000. El Tajin.
2648 **1169** 3p. multicoloured . . . 35 20

1170 Manatee

2000. Nature Conservation.
2649 **1170** 3p. multicoloured . . . 35 20

1171 Sarabia

2000. Birth Centenary of Francisco Sarabia (aviator).
2650 **1171** 3p. multicoloured . . . 35 20

1172 Telephone Exchange and Fabric Shops (½-size illustration)

2000. Industry. Sheet 223 × 135 mm in shape of flag, containing T **1172** and similar multicoloured designs.
MS2651 3p. Type **1172**; 3p. Tractor and modern farming (39 × 25 mm); 3p. Traditional farming methods and car; 3p. Manufacturing and industrial plant (39 × 25 mm); 4p.20 Globe and industries (oval-shaped, 39 × 49 mm) . . . . 2·00 1·60

1173 Stamps and Post Collection (½-size illustration)

2000. Forms of Communication. Sheet 223 × 135 mm in shape of flag, containing T **1173** and similar multicoloured designs.
MS2652 3p. Type **1173**; 3p. Telephone operators and telegraph clerk (39 × 25 mm); 3p. Old and modern train and station; 3p. Motorway (39 × 25 mm); 4p.20 Globe and satellite and satellite dish (oval-shaped, 39 × 49 mm) 2·00 1·60

2001. Tourism. As Nos. 2410 etc but with face value changed.
2658 6p.50 Queretaro 75 45

1174 Chiapas

2001. Tourism.
2670 **1174** 1p.50 multicoloured . . 20 15
2673 8p.50 multicoloured . . 1·00 60

1175 Emblem, Book and Building

2001. 50th Anniv of National Autonomous University.
2680 **1175** 3p. multicoloured . . . 35 20

1176 Woman

2001. International Women's Day.
2681 **1176** 4p.20 multicoloured . . 50 30

1177 Cement Factory

2001. 53rd Anniv of National Cement Chamber.
2682 **1177** 3p. multicoloured . . . 35 20

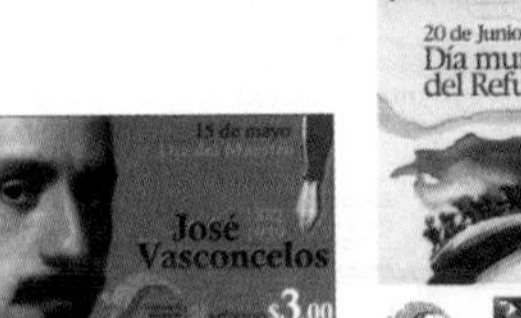
1178 Vasconcelos and Ink Pen

1179 People Running and Flames

2001. 42nd Death Anniv of Jose Vasconcelos (lawyer).
2683 **1178** 3p. multicoloured . . . 35 20

2001. 50th Anniv of United Nations High Commissioner for Refugees.
2684 **1179** 4p.20 multicoloured . . 50 30

1180 "Self-portrait wearing Jade Necklace"

1181 Stylized Bird

2001. Frida Kahlo (artist) Commemoration.
2685 **1180** 4p.20 multicoloured . . 50 30
A stamp of similar design was issued by the United States of America.

2001. Anti-drugs Campaign.
2686 **1181** 4p.20 multicoloured . . 50 30

1182 De la Cueva

2001. Birth Centenary of Mario de la Cueva (university director).
2687 **1182** 3p. blue and gold . . . 35 20

1183 Emblem

2001. International Year of Volunteers.
2688 **1183** 4p.20 multicoloured . . 50 30

1184 Women and Flowers (painting)

2001. Rodolfo Morales (artist) Commemoration. Sheet 121 × 60 mm.
MS2689 **1184** 10p. multicoloured 1·10 65

EXPRESS LETTER STAMPS

E 55 Express Service Messenger

1919.
E445 **E 55** 20c. black and red . . 35 15

E 95

1934.
E536 **E 95** 10c. blue and red . . . 15 30

E 121 Indian Archer

E 222

1934. New President's Assumption of Office. Imprint "OFICINA IMPRESORA DE HACIENDA–MEXICO".
E581 **E 121** 10c. violet . . . . . 1·00 20

1938. Imprint "TALLERES DE IMP. DE EST. Y VALORES-MEXICO".
E610 **E 121** 10c. violet 55 20
E731 20c. orange 25 30

1940. Optd **1940**.
E665 **E 55** 20c. black and red . . 20 15

1950.
E860 **E 222** 25c. orange 20 10
E910 – 60c. green . . . . . 1·10 35
DESIGN: 60c. Hands and letter.

E 244

E 245

1956.
E 954 **E 244** 35c. purple 25 10
E1065 50c. green 45 10
E 956 **E 245** 80c. red 50 80
E1066 1p.20 lilac . . . . 1·50 75
E1346p **E 244** 2p. orange 20 15
E1346q **E 245** 5p. blue 20 60

E 468 Watch Face

1979.
E1373 **E 468** 2p. black and orange 10 60

INSURED LETTER STAMPS

IN **125** Safe

IN **222** P.O. Treasury Vault

1935. Inscr as in Type IN **125**.
IN583 – 10c. red . . . . . 1·10 30
IN733 – 50c. blue 75 25
IN734 IN **125** 1p. green 75 35
DESIGNS: 10c. Bundle of insured letters; 50c. Registered mailbag.

1950.
IN911 IN **222** 20c. blue 15 10
IN912 40c. purple 15 10
IN913 1p. green 20 10
IN914 5p. green and blue 65 60
IN915 10p. blue and red 3·00 1·50

IN **469** Padlock

1976.
IN1374 IN **469** 40c. black & turq 10 10
IN1522 1p. black & turq 10 10
IN1376 2p. black and blue 10 10
IN1380 5p. black & turq 10 10
IN1524 10p. black & turq 10 10
IN1525 20p. black & turq 10 10
IN1383 50p. black & turq 95 95
IN1384 100p. black & turq 65 60
The 5, 10, 20p. exist with the padlock either 31 or 32½ mm high.

OFFICIAL STAMPS

O 18 Hidalgo

1884. No value shown.
O156 **O 18** Red 30 20
O157 Brown 15 10
O158 Orange 80 15
O159 Green 30 15
O160 Blue 45 35

1894. Stamps of 1895 handstamped **OFICIAL**.
O231 **19** 1c. green . . . . 3·75 1·25
O232 2c. red . . . . 4·50 1·25
O233 3c. brown . . . . 3·75 1·25
O234 **20** 4c. orange . . . . . . 5·50 2·50
O235 **21** 5c. blue . . . . 7·50 2·50
O236 **22** 10c. purple . . . . . . 7·00 50
O237 **20** 12c. olive . . . . . . 15·00 6·25
O238 **22** 15c. blue . . . . 8·75 3·75
O239 20c. red . . . . 8·75 3·75
O240 50c. mauve . . . . . . 19·00 9·50
O241 **23** 1p. brown . . . . 48·00 19·00
O242 5p. red . . . . £200 95·00
O243 10p. blue £275 £150

1899. Stamps of 1899 handstamped **OFICIAL**.
O276 **27** 1c. green . . . . 9·50 60
O286 1c. purple . . . . 8·75 95
O277 2c. red . . . . 12·50 95
O287 2c. green . . . . 8·75 95
O278 3c. brown . . . . 12·50 60
O288 4c. red . . . . 16·00 45
O279 5c. blue . . . . 12·50 1·10
O289 5c. orange . . . . . . 16·00 3·25
O280 10c. brown and purple 16·00 1·40
O290 10c. orange and blue 19·00 95
O281 15c. purple and lavender 16·00 1·40
O282 20c. blue and red . . . . 19·00 45
O283 **28** 50c. black and purple . . 38·00 6·25
O291 50c. black and red . . . 48·00 6·25
O284 **29** 1p. black and blue . . . 80·00 6·25
O285 **30** 5p. black and red . . . . 50·00 19·00

1911. Independence stamps optd **OFICIAL**.
O301 **32** 1c. purple . . . . 1·25 1·25
O302 – 2c. green 75 45
O303 – 3c. brown . . . . 1·25 45
O304 – 4c. red . . . . 1·90 45
O305 – 5c. orange . . . . . . 3·25 1·75
O306 – 10c. orange and blue . . 1·90 45
O307 – 15c. lake and slate . . . 3·25 2·00
O308 – 20c. blue and lake . . . 2·50 45
O309 **40** 50c. black and brown . . 8·75 3·75
O310 – 1p. black and blue . . . 15·00 6·25
O311 – 5p. black and red . . . . 55·00 32·00

1915. Stamps of 1915 optd **OFICIAL**.
O321 **43** 1c. violet 30 55
O322 **44** 2c. green 30 55
O323 **45** 3c. brown 30 55
O324 4c. red 30 55
O325 5c. orange 30 55
O326 10c. blue 30 55

1915. Stamps of 1915 optd **OFICIAL**.
O318 **46** 40c. grey . . . . 4·75 3·25
O455 40c. mauve . . . . . . 3·75 1·90
O319 **47** 1p. grey and brown . . . 3·25 3·75
O456 1p. grey and blue . . . . 9·50 6·25
O320 **48** 5p. blue and lake . . . . 19·00 16·00
O457 5p. grey and green . . . 55·00 95·00

1916. Nos. O301/11 optd with T **49**.
O358 **32** 1c. purple . . . . 1·90
O359 – 2c. green 30
O360 – 3c. brown 35
O361 – 4c. red . . . . 2·00
O362 – 5c. orange 35
O363 – 10c. orange and blue . . 35
O364 – 15c. lake and slate . . . 35
O365 – 20c. blue and lake . . . 40
O366 **40** 50c. black and brown . . 55·00
O367 – 1p. black and blue . . . 3·25
O368 – 5p. black and red £1600

1918. Stamps of 1917 optd **OFICIAL**.
O424 **53** 1c. violet . . . . 1·25 60
O446 1c. grey 30 20
O447 – 2c. green 20 20
O448 – 3c. brown 25 20
O449 – 4c. red . . . . 3·75 45
O450 – 5c. blue 20 20
O451 – 10c. blue 30 15
O452 – 20c. lake . . . . 2·50 2·50
O454 – 30c. black . . . . 3·75 1·40

1923. No. 416 optd **OFICIAL**.
O485 10p. black and brown . . . 60·00 95·00

1923. Stamps of 1923 optd **OFICIAL**.
O471 **59** 1c. brown 20 20
O473 **60** 2c. red 25 25
O475 **61** 3c. brown 55 40
O461 **62** 4c. green . . . . 1·90 1·90
O476 **63** 4c. green 40 40
O477 5c. orange 70 65
O489 **74** 8c. orange . . . . 3·75 2·50
O479 **66** 10c. lake 55 55
O480 **65** 20c. blue . . . . 3·25 2·50
O464 **64** 30c. green 35 25
O467 **68** 50c. brown 55 55
O469 **69** 1p. blue and lake . . . . 4·75 4·75

1929. Air. Optd **OFICIAL**.
O501 **80** 5c. blue (roul) 45 25
O502 **81** 20c. violet 55 55
O492 **58** 25c. sepia and lake . . . 6·50 7·50
O490 25c. sepia and green . . 2·50 3·00

1929. Air. As 1926 Postal Congress stamp optd **HABILITADO Servicio Oficial Aereo**.
O493 **70** 2c. black . . . . 26·00 26·00
O494 – 4c. black . . . . 26·00 26·00
O495 **70** 5c. black . . . . 26·00 26·00
O496 – 10c. black . . . . 26·00 26·00
O497 **72** 20c. black . . . . 26·00 26·00
O498 30c. black . . . . 26·00 26·00
O499 40c. black . . . . 26·00 26·00
O500 **73** 1p. black £950 £950

O 85

1930. Air.
O503 **O 85** 20c. grey . . . . . . 2·75 2·75
O504 35c. violet 40 95
O505 40c. blue and brown 50 90
O506 70c. sepia and violet 50 95

1931. Air. Surch **HABILITADO Quince centavos**.
O515 **O 85** 15c. on 20c. grey . . . 45 45

1932. Air. Optd **SERVICIO OFICIAL** in one line.
O532 **80** 10c. violet (perf or roul) 30 30
O533 15c. red (perf or roul) . . 85 85
O534 20c. sepia (roul) 85 85
O531 **58** 50c. red and blue . . . . 1·25 1·25

1932. Stamps of 1923 optd **SERVICIO OFICIAL** in two lines.
O535 **59** 1c. brown 15 15
O536 **60** 2c. red 10 10
O537 **61** 3c. brown 95 95
O538 **63** 4c. green . . . . 3·25 2·50
O539 5c. red . . . . 3·75 2·50
O540 **66** 10c. lake . . . . 1·10 75
O541 **65** 20c. blue . . . . 4·75 3·25
O544 **64** 30c. green . . . . 2·50 95
O545 **46** 40c. mauve . . . . . . 4·75 3·25
O546 **68** 50c. brown 80 95
O547 **69** 1p. blue and lake 95 95

1933. Air. Optd **SERVICIO OFICIAL** in two lines.
O553 **58** 50c. red and blue . . . . 1·40 1·25

1933. Air. Optd **SERVICIO OFICIAL** in two lines.
O548 **80** 5c. blue (No. 476a) . . . 30 30
O549 10c. violet (No. 477) . . 30 30

O550 20c. sepia (No. 479) 30 60
O551 50c. lake (No. 481) 40 95

1934. Optd **OFICIAL**.
O565 **92** 15c. blue 35 35

1938. Nos. 561/71 optd **OFICIAL**.
O622 1c. orange 70 1·25
O623 2c. green 45 45
O624 4c. red 45 45
O625 10c. violet 45 80
O626 20c. blue 55 80
O627 30c. red 70 1·25
O628 40c. brown 70 1·25
O629 50c. black 1·00 1·00
O630 1p. red and brown 2·50 3·75

PARCEL POST STAMPS

P 167 Steam Mail Train

1941.
P732 **P 167** 10c. red 2·25 55
P733 20c. violet 2·75 70

P 228 Class DE-10 Diesel-electric Locomotive

1951.
P916 **P 228** 10c. pink 1·50 20
P917 20c. violet 2·00 40

POSTAGE DUE STAMPS

D 32

1908.
D282 **D 32** 1c. blue 1·00 1·00
D283 2c. blue 1·00 1·00
D284 4c. blue 1·00 1·00
D285 5c. blue 1·00 1·00
D286 10c. blue 1·00 1·00

MICRONESIA Pt. 22

A group of islands in the Pacific, from 1899 to 1914 part of the German Caroline Islands. Occupied by the Japanese in 1914 the islands were from 1920 a Japanese mandated territory, and from 1947 part of the United States Trust Territory of the Pacific Islands, using United States stamps. Micronesia assumed control of its postal services in 1984.

100 cents = 1 dollar.

1 Yap

1984. Inauguration of Postal Independence. Maps. Multicoloured.
1 20c. Type **1** 50 40
2 20c. Truk 50 40
3 20c. Pohnpei 50 40
4 20c. Kosrae 50 40

2 Fernandez de Quiros

3 Boeing 727-100

1984.
5 **2** 1c. blue 10 10
6 – 2c. brown 10 10
7 – 3c. blue 10 10
8 – 4c. green 10 10
9 – 5c. brown and olive 10 10
10 – 10c. purple 15 10
11 – 13c. blue 20 10
11a – 15c. red 20 10
12 – 17c. brown 25 10
13 **2** 19c. purple 30 10
14 – 20c. green 30 10
14a – 22c. green 30 15
14b – 25c. orange 30 15
15 – 30c. red 45 15
15a – 36c. blue 50 20
16 – 37c. violet 50 20
16a – 45c. green 60 30
17 – 50c. brown and sepia 80 35
18 – $1 olive 1·25 85
19 – $2 blue 2·50 1·50
20 – $5 brown 6·00 4·50
20a – $10 blue 12·50 11·00

DESIGNS: 2, 20c. Louis Duperrey; 3, 30c. Fyodor Lutke; 4, 37c. Jules Dumont d'Urville; 5c. Men's house, Yap; 10, 45c. Sleeping Lady (mountains), Kosrae; 13, 15c. Liduduhriap waterfall, Pohnpei; 17, 25c. Tonachau Peak, Truk; 22, 36c. "Senyavin" (full-rigged sailing ship); 50c. Devil mask, Truk; $1 Sokehs Rock, Pohnpei; $2 Outrigger canoes, Kosrae; $5 Stone money, Yap; $10 Official seal.

1984. Air. Multicoloured.
21 28c. Type **3** 55 30
22 35c. Grumman SA-16 Albatros flying boat 70 50
23 40c. Consolidated PBY-5A Catalina amphibian 95 60

4 Truk Post Office

1984. "Ausipex 84" International Stamp Exhibition, Melbourne. Multicoloured.
24 20c. Type **4** (postage) 50 20
25 28c. German Caroline Islands 1919 3pf. yacht stamp (air) 60 40
26 35c. German 1900 20pf. stamp optd for Caroline Islands 70 50
27 40c. German Caroline Islands 1915 5m. yacht stamp 80 65

5 Baby in Basket

1984. Christmas. Multicoloured.
28 20c. Type **5** (postage) 55 25
29 28c. Open book showing Christmas scenes (air) 65 40
30 35c. Palm tree decorated with lights 85 50
31 40c. Women preparing food 1·00 65

6 U.S.S. "Jamestown" (warship)

1985. Ships.
32 **6** 22c. black & brown (postage) 65 35
33 – 33c. black and lilac (air) 85 50
34 – 39c. black and green 1·00 75
35 – 44c. black and red 1·40 90

DESIGNS: 33c. "L'Astrolabe" (D'Urville's ship); 39c. "La Coquille" (Duperrey's ship); 44c. "Shenandoah" (Confederate warship).

7 Lelu Protestant Church, Kosrae

1985. Christmas.
36 **7** 22c. black and orange (postage) 55 30
37 – 33c. black and violet (air) 80 50
38 – 44c. black and green 1·10 70

DESIGNS: 33c. Dublon Protestant Church; 44c. Pohnpei Catholic Church.

8 "Noddy Tern"

1985. Birth Bicentenary of John J. Audubon (ornithologist). Multicoloured.
39 22c. Type **8** (postage) 80 80
40 22c. "Turnstone" 80 80
41 22c. "Golden Plover" 80 80
42 22c. "Black-bellied Plover" 80 80
43 44c. "Sooty Tern" (air) 1·50 1·50

9 Land of Sacred Masonry

1985. Nan Madol, Pohnpei. Multicoloured.
44 22c. Type **9** (postage) 45 25
45 33c. Nan Tauas inner courtyard (air) 60 45
46 39c. Nan Tauas outer wall 75 60
47 44c. Nan Tauas burial vault 90 70

10 Doves, "LOVE" and Hands

12 Bully Hayes

1986. Anniversaries and Events. Multicoloured.
48 22c. Type **10** (International Peace Year) 50 35
49 44c. Halley's comet 1·25 80
50 44c. "Trienza" (cargo liner) arriving at jetty (40th anniv of return of Nauruans from Truk) 1·25 80

1986. Nos. 1/4 surch.
51 22c. on 20c. Type **1** 45 45
52 22c. on 20c. Truk 45 45
53 22c. on 20c. Pohnpei 45 45
54 22c. on 20c. Kosrae 45 45

1986. "Ameripex 86" International Stamp Exhibition, Chicago. Bully Hayes (buccaneer). Multicoloured.
55 22c. Type **12** (postage) 50 30
56 33c. Angelo (crew member) forging Hawaii 5c. blue stamp (air) 65 50
57 39c. "Leonora" sinking off Kosrae 75 60
58 44c. Hayes escaping capture on Kosrae 95 75
59 75c. Cover of book "Bully Hayes, Buccaneer" by Louis Becke 1·50 1·25

13 "Madonna and Child"

1986. Christmas. "Madonna and Child" Paintings.
61 – 5c. multicoloured (postage) 15 10
62 – 22c. multicoloured 70 30
63 – 33c. multicoloured (air) 95 65
64 **13** 44c. multicoloured 1·25 1·00

14 Passports on Globe

1986. 1st Micronesian Passport.
65 **14** 22c. blue, black and yellow 50 35

15 Emblem (International Year of Shelter for the Homeless)

1987. Anniversaries and Events.
66 **15** 22c. blue, red and black (postage) 50 40
67 – 33c. green, red and black (air) 75 50
68 – 39c. blue, black and red 90 60
69 – 44c. blue, red and black 1·25 75

DESIGNS: 33c. Dollar sign (bicentenary of dollar currency); 39c. Space capsule (25th anniv of first American to orbit Earth); 44c. "200 USA" (bicentenary of US constitution).

16 Archangel Gabriel appearing to Mary

1987. Christmas. Multicoloured.
71 22c. Type **16** (postage) 40 30
72 33c. Joseph praying and Mary with baby Jesus (air) 60 45
73 39c. Shepherds with their sheep 75 60
74 44c. Wise men 90 75

17 Spanish Missionary and Flag

1988. Micronesian History. Multicoloured.
75 22c. Type **17** (postage) 50 35
76 22c. Natives producing copra and German flag 50 35
77 22c. School pupils and Japanese flag 50 35
78 22c. General store and U.S. flag 50 35
79 44c. Traditional boatbuilding and fishing skills (air) 1·00 75
80 44c. Welcoming tourists from Douglas DC-10 airliner and divers investigating World War II wreckage 1·00 75

18 Ponape White Eye

19 Marathon

1988. Birds. Multicoloured.
81 3c. Type **18** (postage) 10 10
82 14c. Truk monarch 25 10
83 22c. Ponape starling 35 20
84 33c. Truk white eye (air) 55 35
85 44c. Blue-faced parrot finch 75 65
86 $1 Yap monarch 1·50 1·40

1988. Olympic Games, Seoul. Multicoloured.
87 25c. Type **19** 45 25
88 25c. Hurdling 45 25
89 45c. Basketball 70 55
90 45c. Volleyball 70 55

20 Girls decorating Tree

1988. Christmas. Multicoloured.
91 25c. Type **20** 45 30
92 25c. Dove with mistletoe in beak and children holding decorations 45 30
93 25c. Boy in native clothing and girl in floral dress sitting at base of tree 45 30
94 25c. Boy in T-shirt and shorts and girl in native clothing sitting at base of tree 45 30

Nos. 91/4 were printed together in blocks of four, se-tenant, forming a composite design.

21 Blue-girdled Angelfish

1988. Truk Lagoon, "Micronesia's Living War Memorial". Multicoloured.
95 25c. Type **21** 50 40
96 25c. Jellyfish and shoal of small fishes 50 40
97 25c. Snorkel divers 50 40
98 25c. Two golden trevally (black-striped fishes facing left) 50 40
99 25c. Blackfinned reef shark 50 40

100 25c. Deck railings of wreck and fishes . . . 50 40
101 25c. Soldierfish (red fish) and damselfish . . . 50 40
102 25c. Damselfish, narrow-banded batfish and aircraft cockpit . . . 50 40
103 25c. Three Moorish idols (fishes with long dorsal fins) . . . 50 40
104 25c. Four pickhandle barracuda and shoal . . . 50 40
105 25c. Spot-banded butterflyfish and damselfish (facing alternate directions) . . . 50 40
106 25c. Three-spotted dascyllus and aircraft propeller . . . 50 40
107 25c. Fox-faced rabbitfish and shoal . . . 50 40
108 25c. Lionfish (fish with spines) . . . 50 40
109 25c. Scuba diver and white-tailed damselfish . . . 50 40
110 25c. Tubular corals . . . 50 40
111 25c. White-tailed damselfish, ornate butterflyfish and brain coral . . . 50 40
112 25c. Pink anemonefish, giant clam and sea plants . . . 50 40

Nos. 95/112 were printed together, se-tenant, in sheetlets of 18 stamps, the backgrounds of the stamps forming an overall design of the remains of a Japanese ship and "Zero" fighter plane on the Lagoon bed colonized by marine life.

22 Flag of Pohnpei

1989. Air. State Flags. Multicoloured.
113 45c. Type **22** . . . 65 50
114 45c. Truk . . . 65 50
115 45c. Kosrae . . . 65 50
116 45c. Yap . . . 65 50

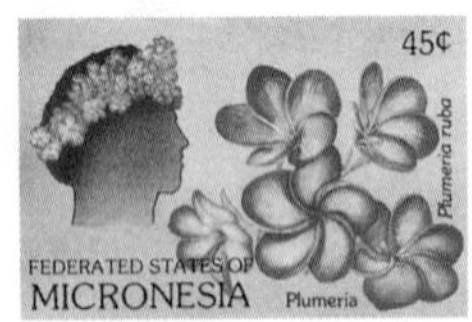

23 Plumeria and Headdress

1989. Mwarmwarms (floral decorations). Mult.
117 45c. Type **23** . . . 65 50
118 45c. Hibiscus and lei . . . 65 50
119 45c. Jasmine and Yap religious mwarmwarm . . . 65 50
120 45c. Bougainvillea and Truk dance mwarmwarm . . . 65 50

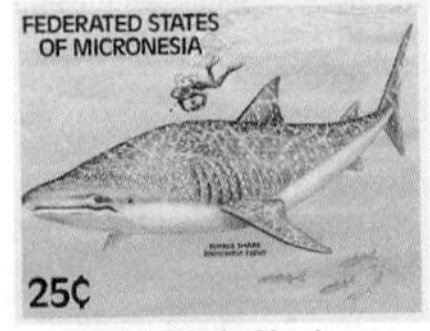

24 Whale Shark

1989. Sharks. Multicoloured.
121 25c. Type **24** . . . 70 40
122 25c. Smooth hammerhead . . . 70 40
123 45c. Tiger shark (vert) . . . 1·10 75
124 45c. Great white shark (vert) . . . 1·10 75

26 "Explorer 1" Satellite over North America

1989. 20th Anniv of First Manned Landing on the Moon. Multicoloured.
126 25c. Bell XS-15 rocket plane . . . 40 30
127 25c. Type **26** . . . 40 30
128 25c. Ed White on space walk during "Gemini 4" mission . . . 40 30
129 25c. "Apollo 18" spacecraft . . . 40 30
130 25c. "Gemini 4" space capsule over South America . . . 40 30
131 25c. Space Shuttle "Challenger" . . . 40 30
132 25c. Italian "San Marco 2" satellite . . . 40 30
133 25c. Russian "Soyuz 19" spacecraft . . . 40 30
134 25c. Neil Armstrong descending ladder to Moon's surface during "Apollo 11" mission . . . 40 30
135 $2.40 Lunar module "Eagle" on Moon (34 × 46 mm) . . . 3·50 2·75

Nos. 126/34 were printed together in se-tenant sheetlets of nine stamps, the backgrounds of the stamps forming an overall design of Earth as viewed from the Moon.

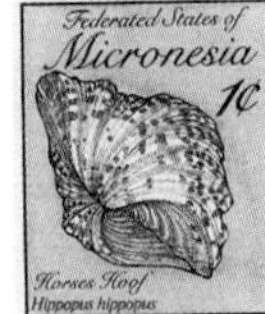

27 Horse's Hoof

1989. Sea Shells. Multicoloured.
136 1c. Type **27** . . . 10 10
137 3c. Rare spotted cowrie . . . 10 10
138 15c. Commercial trochus . . . 20 10
139 20c. General cone . . . 25 10
140 25c. Trumpet triton . . . 30 20
141 30c. Laciniate conch . . . 35 25
142 36c. Red-mouth olive . . . 45 35
143 45c. All-red map cowrie . . . 55 45
144 50c. Textile cone . . . 60 50
145 $1 Orange spider conch . . . 1·40 1·00
146 $2 Golden cowrie . . . 2·75 2·00
147 $5 Episcopal mitre . . . 6·50 4·50

28 Oranges

1989. "World Stamp Expo '89" International Stamp Exhibition, Washington D.C. "Kosrae–The Garden State". Multicoloured.
155 25c. Type **28** . . . 40 30
156 25c. Limes . . . 40 30
157 25c. Tangerines . . . 40 30
158 25c. Mangoes . . . 40 30
159 25c. Coconuts . . . 40 30
160 25c. Breadfruit . . . 40 30
161 25c. Sugar cane . . . 40 30
162 25c. Kosrae house . . . 40 30
163 25c. Bananas . . . 40 30
164 25c. Children with fruit and flowers . . . 40 30
165 25c. Pineapples . . . 40 30
166 25c. Taro . . . 40 30
167 25c. Hibiscus . . . 40 30
168 25c. Ylang ylang . . . 40 30
169 25c. White ginger . . . 40 30
170 25c. Plumeria . . . 40 30
171 25c. Royal poinciana . . . 40 30
172 25c. Yellow allamanda . . . 40 30

29 Angel over Micronesian Village

1989. Christmas. Multicoloured.
173 25c. Type **29** . . . 30 20
174 45c. Truk children dressed as Three Kings . . . 65 50

30 Young Kingfisher and Sokehs Rock, Pohnpei

1990. Endangered Species. Micronesian Kingfisher and Micronesian Pigeon.
175 10c. Type **30** . . . 35 25
176 15c. Adult kingfisher and rain forest, Pohnpei . . . 55 35
177 20c. Pigeon flying over lake at Sleeping Lady, Kosrae . . . 90 65
178 25c. Pigeon perched on leaf, Tol Island, Truk . . . 1·25 1·10

31 Wooden Whale Stamp and "Lyra"

1990. "Stamp World London 90" International Stamp Exhibition. 19th-century British Whaling Ships. Multicoloured.
179 45c. Type **31** . . . 65 45
180 45c. Harpoon heads and "Prudent" . . . 65 45
181 45c. Carved whale bone and "Rhone" . . . 65 45
182 45c. Carved whale tooth and "Sussex" . . . 65 45

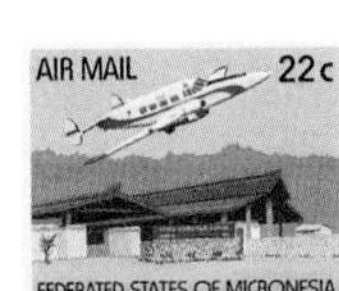

33 Beech 18 over Kosrae Airport
34 School Building

1990. Air. Aircraft. Multicoloured.
185 22c. Type **33** . . . 30 15
186 36c. Boeing 727 landing at Truk . . . 50 30
187 39c. Britten Norman Islander over Pohnpei . . . 50 30
188 45c. Beech Queen Air over Yap . . . 60 35

1990. 25th Anniv of Pohnpei Agriculture and Trade School. Multicoloured.
190 25c. Type **34** . . . 30 20
191 25c. Fr. Costigan (founder) and students . . . 30 20
192 25c. Fr. Hugh Costigan . . . 30 20
193 25c. Ispahu Samuel Hadley (Metelanim chief) and Fr. Costigan . . . 30 20
194 25c. Statue of Liberty, New York City Police Department badge and Empire State Building . . . 30 20

36 Loading Mail Plane at Pohnpei Airport

1990. Pacific Postal Transport. Multicoloured.
196 25c. Type **36** . . . 35 20
197 45c. Launch meeting "Nantaku" (inter-island freighter) in Truk Lagoon to exchange mail, 1940 . . . 65 40

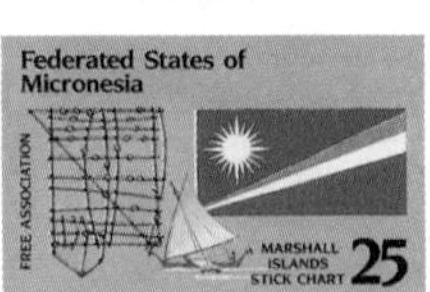

37 Marshallese Stick Chart, Outrigger Canoe and Flag

1990. 4th Anniv of Ratification of Micronesia and Marshall Islands Compacts of Free Association. Multicoloured.
198 25c. Type **37** . . . 45 20
199 25c. Great frigate bird, U.S.S. "Constitution" (frigate), U.S. flag and American bald eagle . . . 55 55
200 25c. Micronesian outrigger canoe and flag . . . 45 20

38 "Caloptilia sp." and New Moon

1990. Moths. Multicoloured.
201 45c. Type **38** . . . 60 50
202 45c. "Anticrates sp." (inscr "Yponomeatidae") and waxing moon . . . 60 50
203 45c. "Cosmopterigidae" family and full moon . . . 60 50
204 45c. "Cosmopteridigae" family and waning moon . . . 60 50

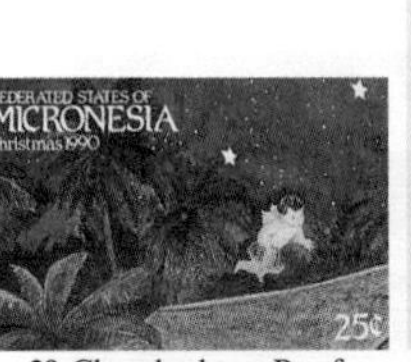

39 Cherub above Roof
41 Hawksbill Turtle returning to Sea

1990. Christmas. "Micronesian Holy Night". Multicoloured.
205 25c. Type **39** . . . 30 20
206 25c. Two cherubs and Star of Bethlehem . . . 30 20
207 25c. Cherub blowing horn . . . 30 20
208 25c. Lambs, goat, pig and chickens . . . 30 20
209 25c. Native wise men offering gifts to Child . . . 30 20
210 25c. Children and dog beside lake . . . 30 20
211 25c. Man blowing trumpet triton . . . 30 20
212 25c. Adults and children on path . . . 30 20
213 25c. Man and children carrying gifts . . . 30 20

Nos. 205/13 were printed together, se-tenant, forming a composite design.

1991. Sea Turtles. Multicoloured.
215 29c. Type **41** . . . 50 30
216 29c. Green turtles swimming underwater . . . 50 30
217 50c. Hawksbill turtle swimming underwater . . . 90 50
218 50c. Leatherback turtle swimming underwater . . . 90 50

42 Boeing E-3 Sentry

1991. Operations Desert Shield and Desert Storm (liberation of Kuwait). Multicoloured.
219 29c. Type **42** . . . 40 25
220 29c. Grumman F-14 Tomcat fighter . . . 40 25
221 29c. U.S.S. "Missouri" (battleship) . . . 40 25
222 29c. Multiple Launch Rocket System . . . 40 25
223 $2.90 Great frigate bird with yellow ribbon and flag of Micronesia (50 × 37 mm) . . . 5·50 5·50

43 "Evening Flowers, Toloas, Truk"

1991. "Phila Nippon '91" International Stamp Exhibition, Tokyo. 90th Birth Anniv (1992) of Paul Jacoulet (artist). Micronesian Ukiyo-e Prints by Jacoulet. Multicoloured.
225 29c. Type **43** . . . 40 25
226 29c. "The Chief's Daughter, Mogomog" . . . 40 25
227 29c. "Yagourouh and Mio, Yap" . . . 40 25
228 50c. "Yap Beauty and Orchids" . . . 70 45
229 50c. "The Yellow-Eyed Boys, Ohlol" . . . 70 45
230 50c. "Violet Flowers, Tomil, Yap" . . . 70 45

44 Sheep and Holy Family

1991. Christmas. Shell Cribs. Multicoloured.
232 29c. Type **44** . . . 40 25
233 40c. Three Kings arriving at Bethlehem . . . 55 35
234 50c. Sheep around manger . . . 65 45

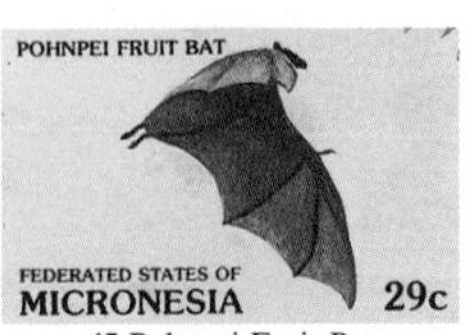

45 Pohnpei Fruit Bat

1991. Pohnpei Rain Forest. Multicoloured.
235 29c. Type **45** . . . 55 55
236 29c. Purple-capped fruit dove . . . 55 55
237 29c. Micronesian kingfisher . . . 55 55
238 29c. Birdnest fern . . . 55 55
239 29c. Caroline swiftlets ("Island Swiftlet") . . . 55 55
240 29c. Ponape white-eye ("Long-billed White-eye") . . . 55 55

241 29c. Common noddy ("Brown Noddy") 55 55
242 29c. Ponape lory ("Pohnpei Lory") 55 55
243 29c. Micronesian flycatcher ("Pohnpei Flycatcher") . . 55 55
244 29c. Truk Island ground dove ("Caroline Ground-Dove") 55 55
245 29c. White-tailed tropic bird 55 55
246 29c. Cardinal honeyeater ("Micronesian Honeyeater") 55 55
247 29c. Ixora 55 55
248 29c. Rufous fantail ("Pohnpei Fantail") 55 55
249 29c. Grey-brown white-eye ("Grey White-eye") 55 55
250 29c. Blue-faced parrot finch 55 55
251 29c. Common Cicadabird ("Cicadabird") 55 55
252 29c. Green skink 55 55

Nos. 235/52 were issued together, se-tenant, forming a composite design.

46 Britten Norman Islander and Outrigger Canoe

47 Volunteers learning Crop Planting

1992. Air. Multicoloured.
253 40c. Type **46** 55 35
254 50c. Boeing 727-200 airliner and outrigger canoe (different) 65 45

1992. 25th Anniv of Presence of United States Peace Corps in Micronesia. Multicoloured.
255 29c. Type **47** 40 25
256 29c. Education 40 25
257 29c. Pres. John Kennedy announcing formation of Peace Corps 40 25
258 29c. Public health nurses . . 40 25
259 29c. Recreation 40 25

48 Queen Isabella of Spain

1992. 500th Anniv of Discovery of America by Christopher Columbus. Multicoloured.
260 29c. Type **48** . . . . 1·10 50
261 29c. "Santa Maria" . . . . 1·10 50
262 29c. Christopher Columbus 1·10 50

49 Flags

1992. 1st Anniv of U.N. Membership.
264 **49** 29c. multicoloured 40 25
265 50c. multicoloured 65 45

50 Bouquet

1992. Christmas.
266 **50** 29c. multicoloured 40 25

51 Edward Rickenbacker (fighter pilot)

1993. Pioneers of Flight (1st series). Pioneers and aircraft. Multicoloured.
267 29c. Type **51** 45 30
268 29c. Manfred von Richthofen (fighter pilot) 45 30
269 29c. Andrei Tupolev (aeronautical engineer) . . 45 30
270 29c. John Macready (first non-stop crossing of U.S.A.) 45 30
271 29c. Sir Charles Kingsford-Smith (first trans-Pacific flight) 45 30
272 29c. Igor Sikorsky (aeronautical engineer) . . 45 30
273 29c. Lord Trenchard ("Father of the Royal Air Force") 45 30
274 29c. Glenn Curtiss (builder of U.S. Navy's first aircraft) 45 30

See also Nos. 322/9, 364/71, 395/402, 418/25, 441/8, 453/60 and 514/21.

52 Big-scaled Soldierfish

1993. Fishes. Multicoloured.
275 10c. Type **52** 15 10
276 19c. Bennett's butterflyfish 25 15
277 20c. Peacock hind ("Peacock Grouper") 25 15
278 22c. Great barracuda . . . 30 20
278a 23c. Yellow-finned tuna . . 30 20
279 25c. Coral hind ("Coral Grouper") 30 20
280 29c. Regal angelfish 40 25
281 30c. Bleeker's parrotfish . . 40 25
282 32c. Saddle butterflyfish (dated "1995") 40 25
283 35c. Picasso triggerfish ("Picassofish") 45 30
284 40c. Mandarin fish 50 35
285 45c. Clown ("Bluebanded") surgeonfish 60 40
285a 46c. Red-tailed surgeonfish ("Achilles Tang") 60 40
286 50c. Undulate ("Orange-striped") triggerfish . . . 65 45
287 52c. Palette surgeonfish . . 70 45
288 55c. Moorish idol 70 45
288a 60c. Skipjack tuna 80 55
289 75c. Oriental sweetlips . . . 95 65
290 78c. Square-spotted anthias ("Square-spot Fairy Basslet") . . . . 1·00 65
290a 95c. Blue-striped ("Blue-lined") snapper . . . . . 1·25 85
291 $1 Zebra moray . . . . . . 1·25 85
292 $2 Fox-faced rabbitfish . . 2·50 1·60
293 $2.90 Masked ("Orangespine") unicornfish . . . . 3·75 2·50
294 $3 Flame angelfish . . . . 3·75 2·50
295 $5 Six-blotched hind ("Cave Grouper") . . . . 6·50 4·25

See also Nos. 465/89 and 522/5.

53 "Great Republic"

54 Jefferson

1993. American Clipper Ships. Multicoloured.
301 29c. Type **53** 50 35
302 29c. "Benjamin F. Packard" 50 35
303 29c. "Stag Hound" 50 35
304 29c. "Herald of the Morning" 50 35
305 29c. "Rainbow" and junk . . 50 35
306 29c. "Flying Cloud" 50 35
307 29c. "Lightning" 50 35
308 29c. "Sea Witch" 50 35
309 29c. "Columbia" 50 35
310 29c. "New World" 50 35
311 29c. "Young America" . . . 50 35
312 29c. "Courier" 50 35

1993. 250th Birth Anniv of Thomas Jefferson (U.S. President, 1801–09).
313 **54** 29c. multicoloured 45 25

55 Yap Outrigger Canoe

1993. Traditional Canoes. Multicoloured.
314 29c. Type **55** 50 35
315 29c. Kosrae outrigger canoe 50 35
316 29c. Pohnpei lagoon outrigger canoe 50 35
317 29c. Chuuk war canoe . . . 50 35

56 Ambilos Iehsi

57 Kepirohi Falls

1993. Local Leaders (1st series). Multicoloured.
318 29c. Type **56** (Pohnpei) . . . 45 25
319 29c. Andrew Roboman (Yap) 45 25
320 29c. Joab Sigrah (Kosrae) . . 45 25
321 29c. Petrus Mailo (Chuuk) 45 25

See also Nos. 409/12.

1993. Pioneers of Flight (2nd series). As T **51**. Multicoloured.
322 50c. Lawrence Sperry (inventor of the gyro) . . . 75 50
323 50c. Alberto Santos-Dumont (first powered flight in Europe) 75 50
324 50c. Hugh Dryden (developer of first guided missile) . . 75 50
325 50c. Theodore von Karman (space pioneer) 75 50
326 50c. Orville Wright (first powered flight) 75 50
327 50c. Wilbur Wright (second powered flight) 75 50
328 50c. Otto Lilienthal (first heavier-than-air flight) . . 75 50
329 50c. Sir Thomas Sopwith (aircraft designer) 75 50

1993. Pohnpei Tourist Sites. Multicoloured.
330 29c. Type **57** 40 25
331 50c. Spanish Wall 65 45

See also Nos. 357/9.

58 Female Common ("Great") Eggfly

59 "We Three Kings"

1993. Butterflies. Multicoloured.
333 29c. Type **58** 50 30
334 29c. Female common ("great") eggfly (variant) 50 30
335 50c. Male monarch 90 50
336 50c. Male common ("great") eggfly 90 50

See also Nos. 360/3.

1993. Christmas. Carols. Multicoloured.
337 29c. Type **59** 40 25
338 50c. "Silent Night, Holy Night" 65 45

60 Baby Basket

1993. Yap. Multicoloured.
339 29c. Type **60** 40 25
340 29c. Bamboo raft 40 25
341 29c. Basketry 40 25
342 29c. Fruit bat 40 25
343 29c. Forest 40 25
344 29c. Outrigger canoes 40 25
345 29c. Dioscorea yams 40 25
346 29c. Mangroves 40 25
347 29c. Manta ray 40 25
348 29c. "Cyrtosperma taro" . . 40 25
349 29c. Fish weir 40 25
350 29c. Seagrass, golden rabbitfish and masked rabbitfish 40 25
351 29c. Taro bowl 40 25
352 29c. Thatched house 40 25
353 29c. Coral reef 40 25
354 29c. Lavalava 40 25
355 29c. Dancers 40 25
356 29c. Stone money 40 25

1994. Kosrae Tourist Sites. As T **57** but horiz. Multicoloured.
357 29c. Sleeping Lady (mountains) 40 25
358 40c. Walung 50 35
359 50c. Lelu Ruins 65 45

1994. "Hong Kong '94" International Stamp Exhibition. Designs as Nos. 333/6 but with inscriptions in brown and additionally inscribed "Hong Kong '94 Stamp Exhibition" in English (361/2) or Chinese (others).
360 29c. As No. 333 . . . . . . 50 25
361 29c. As No. 334 . . . . . . 50 25
362 50c. As No. 335 . . . . . . 75 50
363 50c. As No. 336 . . . . . . 75 50

1994. Pioneers of Flight (3rd series). As T **51**. Multicoloured.
364 29c. Octave Chanute (early glider designer) 45 25
365 29c. T. Claude Ryan (founder of first commercial airline) 45 25
366 29c. Edwin (Buzz) Aldrin ("Apollo 11" crew member and second man to step onto moon) 45 25
367 29c. Neil Armstrong (commander of "Apollo 11" and first man on moon) 45 25
368 29c. Frank Whittle (developer of jet engine) 45 25
369 29c. Waldo Waterman (aircraft designer) 45 25
370 29c. Michael Collins ("Apollo 11" crew member) 45 25
371 29c. Wernher von Braun (rocket designer) 45 25

61 Spearfishing

1994. 3rd Micronesian Games. Multicoloured.
372 29c. Type **61** 45 25
373 29c. Basketball 45 25
374 29c. Coconut husking 45 25
375 29c. Tree climbing 45 25

62 Pohnpei

64 "Fagraea berteriana" (Kosrae)

63 People

1994. Traditional Costumes. Multicoloured.
376 29c. Type **62** 45 25
377 29c. Kosrae 45 25
378 29c. Chuuk 45 25
379 29c. Yap 45 25

1994. 15th Anniv of Constitution.
380 **63** 29c. multicoloured 45 25

1994. Native Flowers. Multicoloured.
381 29c. Type **64** 45 25
382 29c. "Pangium edule" (Yap) 45 25
383 29c. "Pittosporum ferrugineum" (Chuuk) . . 45 25
384 29c. "Sonneratia caseolaris" (Pohnpei) 45 25

Nos. 381/4 were issued together, se-tenant, forming a composite design.

65 1985 $10 Definitive under Magnifying Glass

1994. 10th Anniv of Postal Independence. Multicoloured.
385 29c. Type **65** 50 30
386 29c. 1993 traditional canoes block 50 30
387 29c. 1984 postal independence block 50 30
388 29c. 1994 native costumes block 50 30
Nos. 385/8 were issued together, se-tenant, forming a composite design of various Micronesian stamps. Nos. 386/8 are identified by the block in the centre of the design.

66 Players **69** Oriental Cuckoo

68 Iguanodons

1994. World Cup Football Championship, U.S.A. Multicoloured.
389 50c. Type **66** 70 45
390 50c. Ball and players 70 45
Nos. 389/90 were issued together, se-tenant, forming a composite design.

1994. "Philakorea 1994" International Stamp Exhibition, Seoul. Prehistoric Animals. Multicoloured.
392 29c. Type **68** 50 30
393 52c. Iguanodons and coelurosaurs . . . . 1·00 1·00
394 $1 Camarasaurus . . . . . 1·60 1·00
Nos. 392/4 were issued together, se-tenant, forming a composite design.

1994. Pioneers of Flight (4th series). As T **51**. Multicoloured.
395 50c. Yuri Gagarin (first man in space) 75 50
396 50c. Alan Shepard Jr. (first American in space) 75 50
397 50c. William Bishop (fighter pilot) 75 50
398 50c. "Atlas" (first U.S. intercontinental ballistic missile) and Karel Bossart (aerospace engineer) . . . 75 50
399 50c. John Towers (world endurance record, 1912) . . 75 50
400 50c. Hermann Oberth (space flight pioneer) 75 50
401 50c. Marcel Dassault (aircraft producer) 75 50
402 50c. Geoffrey de Havilland (aircraft designer) 75 50

1994. Migratory Birds. Multicoloured.
403 29c. Type **69** 65 65
404 29c. Long-tailed koel ("Long-tailed Cuckoo") 65 65
405 29c. Short-eared owl 65 65
406 29c. Eastern broad-billed roller ("Dollarbird") . . . 65 65

70 Doves

1994. Christmas. Multicoloured.
407 29c. Type **70** 50 30
408 50c. Angels 90 60

1994. Local Leaders (2nd series). As T **56**. Mult.
409 32c. Anron Ring Buas . . . 55 35
410 32c. Belarmino Hatheylul . . 55 35
411 32c. Johnny Moses 55 35
412 32c. Paliknoa Sigrah (King John) 55 35

72 Diver, Coral, Clown Triggerfish and Black-backed Butterflyfish

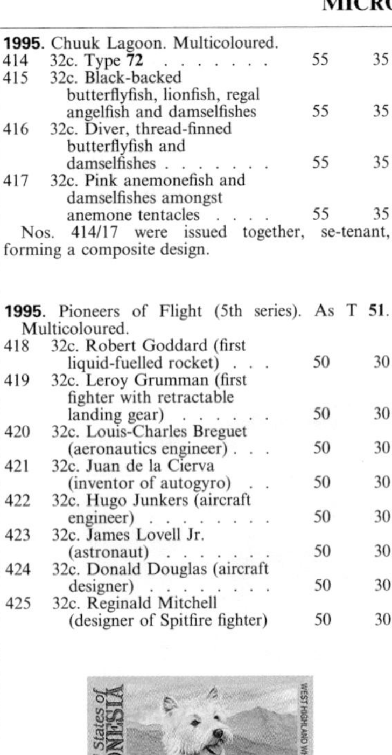

1995. Chuuk Lagoon. Multicoloured.
414 32c. Type **72** 55 35
415 32c. Black-backed butterflyfish, lionfish, regal angelfish and damselfishes 55 35
416 32c. Diver, thread-finned butterflyfish and damselfishes 55 35
417 32c. Pink anemonefish and damselfishes amongst anemone tentacles 55 35
Nos. 414/17 were issued together, se-tenant, forming a composite design.

1995. Pioneers of Flight (5th series). As T **51**. Multicoloured.
418 32c. Robert Goddard (first liquid-fuelled rocket) . . . 50 30
419 32c. Leroy Grumman (first fighter with retractable landing gear) 50 30
420 32c. Louis-Charles Breguet (aeronautics engineer) . . . 50 30
421 32c. Juan de la Cierva (inventor of autogyro) . . 50 30
422 32c. Hugo Junkers (aircraft engineer) 50 30
423 32c. James Lovell Jr. (astronaut) 50 30
424 32c. Donald Douglas (aircraft designer) 50 30
425 32c. Reginald Mitchell (designer of Spitfire fighter) 50 30

73 West Highland White Terrier

1995. Dogs. Multicoloured.
426 32c. Type **73** 55 35
427 32c. Welsh springer spaniel 55 35
428 32c. Irish setter 55 35
429 32c. Old English sheepdog . . 55 35

74 "Hibiscus tiliaceus"

1995. Hibiscus. Multicoloured.
430 32c. Type **74** 50 30
431 32c. "Hibiscus huegelii" . . . 50 30
432 32c. "Hibiscus trionum" . . 50 30
433 32c. "Hibiscus splendens" . . 50 30
Nos. 430/3 were issued together, se-tenant, forming a composite design.

77 U.S.S. "Portland" (cruiser)

1995. 50th Anniv of End of Second World War. Liberation of Micronesia. Multicoloured.
436 60c. Type **77** (liberation of Chuuk) . . . . 1·00 70
437 60c. U.S.S. "Tillman" (destroyer) (Yap) . . . . . 1·00 70
438 60c. U.S.S. "Soley" (destroyer) (Kosrae) . . . 1·00 70
439 60c. U.S.S. "Hyman" (destroyer) (Pohnpei) . . . 1·00 70

1995. Pioneers of Flight (6th series). As T **51**. Multicoloured.
441 60c. Frederick Rohr (developer of mass-production techniques) . . 90 60
442 60c. Juan Trippe (founder of Pan-American Airways) . . 90 60
443 60c. Konstantin Tsiolkovsky (rocket pioneer) 90 60
444 60c. Count Ferdinand von Zeppelin (airship inventor) 90 60
445 60c. Air Chief Marshal Hugh Dowding (commander of R.A.F. Fighter Command, 1940) 90 60
446 60c. William Mitchell (pioneer of aerial bombing) 90 60
447 60c. John Northrop (aircraft designer) 90 60
448 60c. Frederick Handley Page (producer of first twin-engine bomber) 90 60

79 Poinsettia **80** Rabin

1995. Christmas.
449 **79** 32c. multicoloured 40 25
450 60c. multicoloured 80 55

1995. Yitzhak Rabin (Israeli Prime Minister) Commemoration.
451 **80** 32c. multicoloured 55 35

1995. Pioneers of Flight (7th series). As T **51**. Multicoloured.
453 32c. James Doolittle (leader of America's Second World War bomb raid on Japan) 50 30
454 32c. Claude Dornier (aircraft designer) 50 30
455 32c. Ira Eaker (leader of air effort against occupied Europe during Second World War) 50 30
456 32c. Jacob Ellehammer (first European manned flight) 50 30
457 32c. Henry Arnold (Commander of U.S. air operations during Second World War) 50 30
458 32c. Louis Bleriot (first flight across the English Channel) 50 30
459 32c. William Boeing (founder of Boeing Corporation) . . 50 30
460 32c. Sydney Camm (aircraft designer) 50 30

82 Meeting House

1995. Tourism in Yap. Multicoloured.
461 32c. Type **82** 50 30
462 32c. Stone money 50 30
463 32c. Churu dancing 50 30
464 32c. Traditional canoe . . . 50 30

1995. Fishes. As Nos. 275/95 but face values changed. Multicoloured.
465 32c. Bennett's butterflyfish . . 55 25
466 32c. Regal angelfish 55 25
467 32c. Undulate ("Orange-striped") triggerfish 55 25
468 32c. Zebra moray 55 25
469 32c. Great barracuda 55 25
470 32c. Bleeker's parrotfish . . . 55 25
471 32c. Mandarin fish 55 25
472 32c. Clown ("Blue-banded") surgeonfish 55 25
473 32c. Big-scaled soldierfish . . 55 25
474 32c. Peacock hind ("Peacock Grouper") 55 25
475 32c. Picasso triggerfish ("Picassofish") 55 25
476 32c. Masked ("Orangespine") unicornfish 55 25
477 32c. Red-tailed surgeonfish . 55 25
478 32c. Coral hind ("Coral Grouper") 55 25
479 32c. Palette surgeonfish . . . 55 25
480 32c. Oriental sweetlips . . . 55 25
481 32c. Fox-faced rabbitfish . . 55 25
482 32c. Saddle butterflyfish (dated "1996") 55 25
483 32c. Moorish idol 55 25
484 32c. Square-spotted anthias ("Square-spot Fairy Basslet") 55 25
485 32c. Flame angelfish 55 25
486 32c. Yellow-finned tuna . . . 55 25
487 32c. Skipjack tuna 55 25
488 32c. Blue-striped ("Blue-lined") snapper 55 25
489 32c. Six-blotched hind ("Cave Grouper") 55 25
See also Nos. 522/5.

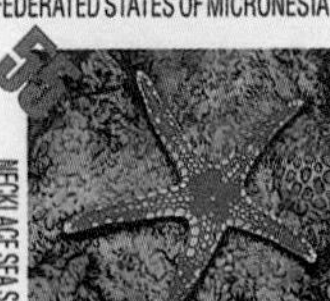

83 Necklace Sea Star

1996. Starfishes. Multicoloured.
490 55c. Type **83** 85 55
491 55c. Rhinoceros sea star . . 85 55
492 55c. Blue sea star 85 55
493 55c. Thick-skinned sea star 85 55
Nos. 490/3 were issued together, se-tenant, forming a composite design.

84 10l. Stamp

1996. Centenary of Modern Olympic Games. Designs reproducing 1896 Greek Olympic Issue. Multicoloured.
494 60c. Type **84** . . . . 1·10 70
495 60c. 25l. stamp . . . . . . 1·10 70
496 60c. 20l. stamp . . . . . . 1·10 70
497 60c. 10d. stamp . . . . . . 1·10 70

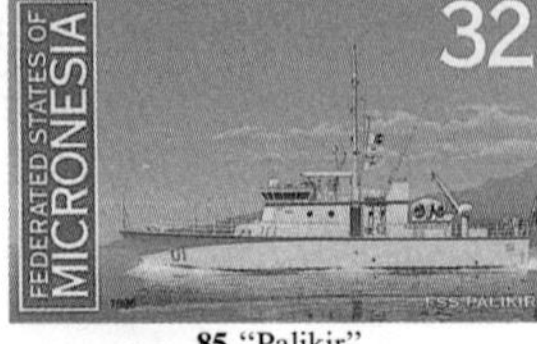

85 "Palikir"

1996. Patrol Boats. Multicoloured.
498 32c. Type **85** 45 25
499 32c. "Micronesia" 45 25
Nos. 498/9 were issued together, se-tenant, forming a composite design.

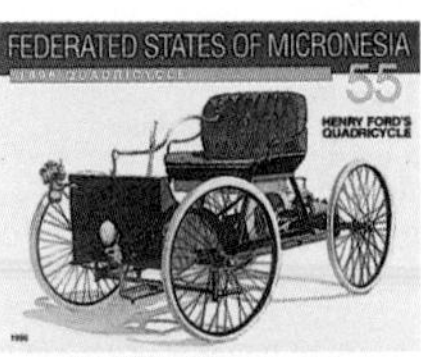

87 1896 Quadricycle

1996. Centenary of Ford Motor Vehicle Production. Multicoloured.
501 55c. Type **87** 90 60
502 55c. 1917 Model T Truck . . 90 60
503 55c. 1928 Model A Tudor Sedan 90 60
504 55c. 1932 V-8 Sport Roadster 90 60
505 55c. 1941 Lincoln Continental 90 60
506 55c. 1953 F-100 Truck . . . 90 60
507 55c. 1958 Thunderbird convertible 90 60
508 55c. 1996 Mercury Sable . . 90 60

88 Reza **89** Oranges

1996. Reza (National Police Drug Enforcement Unit's dog).
509 **88** 32c. multicoloured 50 30

1996. Citrus Fruits. Multicoloured.
510 50c. Type **89** 90 60
511 50c. Limes 90 60
512 50c. Lemons 90 60
513 50c. Tangerines 90 60
Nos. 510/13 were issued together, se-tenant, forming a composite design.

1996. Pioneers of Flight (8th series). As T **51**. Multicoloured.
514 60c. Curtis LeMay (commander of Strategic Air Command) 90 60
515 60c. Grover Loening (first American graduate in aeronautical engineering) 90 60
516 60c. Gianni Caproni (aircraft producer) 90 60
517 60c. Henri Farman (founder of Farman Airlines) . . . 90 60
518 60c. Glenn Martin (aircraft producer) 90 60
519 60c. Alliot Verdon Roe (aircraft designer) 90 60
520 60c. Sergei Korolyov (rocket scientist) 90 60
521 60c. Isaac Laddon (aircraft designer) 90 60

1996. 10th Asian International Stamp Exhibition, Taipeh. Fishes. As previous designs but additionally inscr for the exhibition in English (522, 525) or Chinese (523/4).
522 32c. As No. 465 . . . . . . 55 35
523 32c. As No. 468 . . . . . . 55 35
524 32c. As No. 475 . . . . . . 55 35
525 32c. As No. 483 . . . . . . 55 35

90 Wise Men following Star

1996. Christmas.
526 **90** 32c. multicoloured 50 35
527 60c. multicoloured 90 60

91 Outrigger Canoe and State Flag

1996. 10th Anniv of Ratification of Compact of Free Association with U.S.A.
528 **91** $3 multicoloured 4·50 3·25

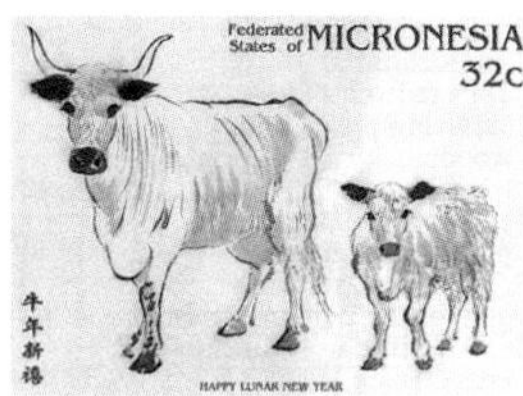

92 Water Buffalo

1997. New Year. Year of the Ox.
529 **92** 32c. multicoloured 50 35

93 Walutahanga, Melanesia

94 Deng Xiaoping

1997. "Pacific 97" International Stamp Exhibition, San Francisco. Sea Goddesses of the Pacific. Multicoloured.
531 32c. Type **93** 50 30
532 32c. Tien-Hou holding lantern, China 50 30
533 32c. Lorop diving in ocean, Micronesia 50 30
534 32c. Oto-Hime with fisherman, Japan 50 30
535 32c. Nomoi holding shell, Micronesia 50 30
536 32c. Junkgowa Sisters in canoe, Australia 50 30

1997. Deng Xiaoping (Chinese statesman) Commemoration. Multicoloured.
537 60c. Type **94** 85 50
538 60c. Facing left (bare-headed) 85 50
539 60c. Facing right 85 50
540 60c. Facing left wearing cap 85 50

95 "Melia azedarach"

1997. Return of Hong Kong to China. Multicoloured.
542 60c. Type **95** 85 50
543 60c. Victoria Peak 85 50
544 60c. "Dendrobium chrysotoxum" 85 50
545 60c. "Bauhinia blakeana" 85 50
546 60c. "Cassia surattensis" 85 50
547 60c. Sacred lotus ("Nelumbo nucifera") 85 50

96 Tennis

1997. 2nd National Games. Multicoloured.
549 32c. Type **96** 50 30
550 32c. Throwing the discus 50 30
551 32c. Swimming 50 30
552 32c. Canoeing 50 30

97 Rapids

1997. Birth Bicentenary of Hiroshige Ando (painter). Designs depicting details from "Whirlpools at Naruto in Awa Province" (Nos. 553/5), "Tail of Genji: Viewing the Plum Blossoms" (Nos. 556/8) and "Snow on the Sumida River" (Nos. 559/61). Multicoloured.
553 20c. Type **97** 30 20
554 20c. Whirlpools (rocky island at left) 30 20
555 20c. Whirlpools (rocky island at right) 30 20
556 50c. Woman on stepping stones 65 40
557 50c. Woman 65 40
558 50c. Woman on balcony of house 65 40
559 60c. House and junks 1·00 60
560 60c. Two women 1·00 60
561 60c. Woman alighting from junk 1·00 60
Nos. 553/5, 556/8 and 559/61 respectively, were issued, se-tenant, forming composite designs of the paintings depicted.

98 Presley from High School Graduation Yearbook

1997. 20th Death Anniv of Elvis Presley (entertainer). Multicoloured.
563 50c. Type **98** 85 55
564 50c. With hound dog Nipper (R.C.A. Records mascot) 85 55
565 50c. Wearing red striped shirt in publicity photograph for "Loving You" (film), 1957 85 55
566 50c. Wearing sailor's cap in scene from "Girls, Girls, Girls!" (film), 1963 85 55
567 50c. Wearing knitted jacket with collar turned up, 1957 85 55
568 50c. Wearing stetson in scene from "Flaming Star" (film), 1960 85 55

99 Simon Lake and his Submarine "Argonaut", 1897

1997. Ocean Exploration: Pioneers of the Deep. Multicoloured.
569 32c. Type **99** 40 25
570 32c. William Beebe and Otis Barton's bathysphere (record depth, 1934) 40 25
571 32c. Auguste Piccard and his bathyscaphe, 1954 40 25
572 32c. Harold Edgerton and his deep sea camera, 1954 40 25
573 32c. Jacques Piccard and U.S. Navy bathyscaphe "Trieste" (designed by Auguste Piccard) (record depth with Don Walsh, 1960) 40 25
574 32c. Edwin Link and diving chamber ("Man-in-Sea" projects, 1962) 40 25
575 32c. Melvin Fisher and diver (discovery of "Atocha" and "Santa Margarita" (Spanish galleons), 1971) 40 25
576 32c. Robert Ballard and submersible "Alvin", 1978 40 25
577 32c. Sylvia Earle and submersible "Deep Rover" (record dive in armoured suit, 1979) 40 25

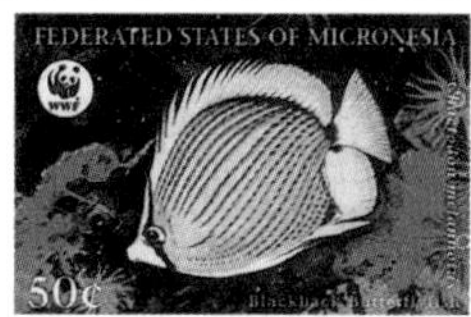

100 Black-backed Butterflyfish

1997. Butterflyfishes. Multicoloured.
579 50c. Type **100** 75 50
580 50c. Saddle butterflyfish 75 50
581 50c. Thread-finned butterflyfish 75 50
582 50c. Bennett's butterflyfish 75 50

101 "Christ Glorified in the Court of Heaven" (Fra Angelico) (left detail)

102 Diana, Princess of Wales

1997. Christmas. Multicoloured.
583 32c. Type **101** 50 35
584 32c. "Christ Glorified in the Court of Heaven" (right detail) 50 35
585 60c . "A Choir of Angels" (detail, Simon Marmion) 75 50
586 60c. "A Choir of Angels" (different detail) 75 50

1997. Diana, Princess of Wales Commemoration.
587 **102** 60c. multicoloured 75 50

105 Rabbit

1998. Children's Libraries. The Hundred Acre Wood. Featuring characters from the Winnie the Pooh children's books. Multicoloured.
590 32c. Type **105** 55 35
591 32c. Owl 55 35
592 32c. Eeyore 55 35
593 32c. Kanga and Roo 55 35
594 32c. Piglet 55 35
595 32c. Tigger 55 35
596 32c. Pooh 55 35
597 32c. Christopher Robin 55 35
Nos. 590/7 were issued together, se-tenant, forming a composite design.

106 Player celebrating Goal

1998. World Cup Football Championship, France. Multicoloured.
599 32c. Type **106** 50 30
600 32c. Player in green shirt kicking ball 50 30
601 32c. Player in yellow shirt tackling another player 50 30
602 32c. Goalkeeper throwing ball 50 30
603 32c. Player in yellow shirt kicking ball overhead 50 30
604 32c. Goalkeeper in red shirt 50 30
605 32c. Player in yellow shirt with ball between legs 50 30
606 32c. Player in red shirt and player on ground 50 30
Nos. 599/606 were issued together, se-tenant, forming a composite design of a pitch.

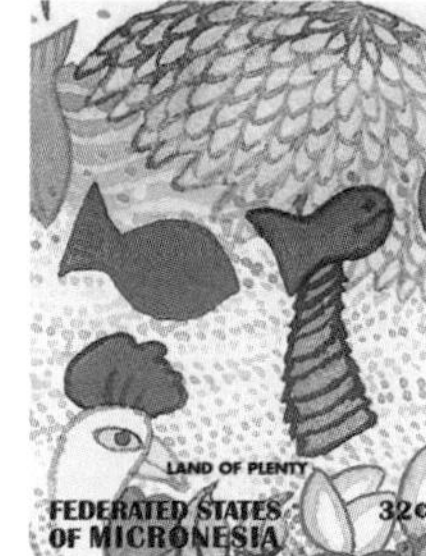

108 Land of Plenty

1998. Old Testament Stories. Multicoloured.
609 32c. Type **108** 50 30
610 32c. Adam and Eve 50 30
611 32c. Serpent of Temptation 50 30
612 40c. Three of Joseph's brothers 60 40
613 40c. Joseph and merchants 60 40
614 40c. Ishmaelites 60 40
615 60c. Rebekah in front of well 80 50
616 60c. Eliezer, Abraham's servant 80 50
617 60c. Angel 80 50

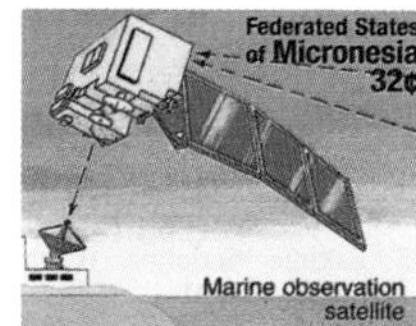

109 Marine Observation Satellite

1998. International Year of the Ocean. Deep Sea Research. Multicoloured.
619 32c. Type **109** 55 35
620 32c. "Natsushima" (support vessel) 55 35
621 32c. "Kaiyo" (research vessel) 55 35
622 32c. Anemone 55 35
623 32c. "Shinkai 2000" (deep-sea research vessel) 55 35
624 32c. Deep-towed research vessel 55 35
625 32c. Tripod fish 55 35
626 32c. Towed deep-survey system 55 35
627 32c. Black smokers 55 35
Nos. 619/27 were issued together, se-tenant, forming a composite design.

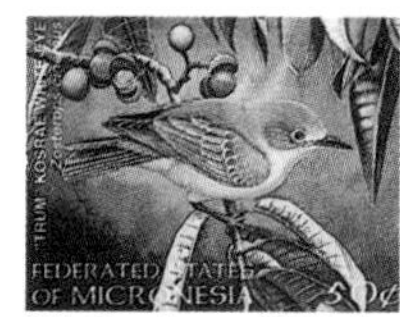
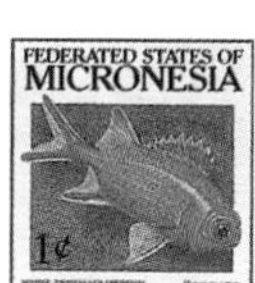

110 Grey-brown White-Eye ("Kosrae White-eye")

111 Ribbon-striped ("White-tipped") Soldierfish

1998. Birds. Multicoloured.
629 50c. Type **110** 60 40
630 50c. Truk monarch ("Chuuk Monarch") 60 40
631 50c. Yap monarch 60 40
632 50c. Pohnpei starling 60 40

1998. Fishes. Multicoloured.
634 1c. Type **111** 10 10
635 2c. Red-breasted wrasse 10 10
636 3c. Bicoloured ("Bicolor") angelfish 10 10
637 4c. Falco hawkfish 10 10
638 5c. Convict tang 10 10
639 10c. Square-spotted anthias ("Square-spot Fairy Basslet") 10 10
640 13c. Orange-spotted ("Orangeband") surgeonfish 15 10
641 15c. Multibarred goatfish 20 15
642 17c. Masked rabbitfish 20 15
643 20c. White-spotted surgeonfish 25 15
644 22c. Blue-girdled angelfish 30 20
645 32c. Rectangle triggerfish ("Wedge Picassofish") 40 25
646 33c. Black jack 40 25
647 39c. Red parrotfish 50 35
648 40c. Lemon-peel angelfish 50 35
649 50c. White-cheeked ("Whitecheek") surgeonfish 60 40
650 55c. Scarlet-finned ("Long-jawed") squirrelfish 65 45
651 60c. Hump-headed ("Humphead") wrasse 75 50
652 77c. Onespot snapper 95 65
653 78c. Blue ("Sapphire") damselfish 95 65
654 $1 Blue-finned ("Bluefin") trevally 1·25 85
655 $3 Whitespot hawkfish 3·75 2·25
656 $3.20 Tan-faced parrotfish 4·00 2·75
657 $5 Spotted boxfish ("Trunkfish") 6·25 4·25
658 $10.75 Pink-tailed ("Pinktail") triggerfish 13·50 9·00
659 $11.75 Yellow-faced angelfish (48 × 25 mm) 14·50 9·75

112 Fala being stroked

1998. Fala (Scottish terrier owned by Franklin D. Roosevelt). Multicoloured.
665 32c. Type **112** 40 25
666 32c. Fala and left half of wireless 40 25
667 32c. Fala and right half of wireless 40 25
668 32c. Fala and Roosevelt in car 40 25
669 32c. Fala's seal 40 25
670 32c. Fala 40 25

113 "Eskimo Madonna" (Claire Fejes)

1998. Christmas. Works of Art. Multicoloured.
671 32c. Type **113** 40 25
672 32c. "Madonna" (Man Ray) 40 25
673 32c. "Peasant Mother" (David Siquerios) 40 25
674 60c. "Mother and Child" (Pablo Picasso) 40 25
675 60c. "Gypsy Woman with Baby" (Amedeo Modigliani) 40 25
676 60c. "Mother and Child" (Jose Orozco) 40 25

114 Glenn

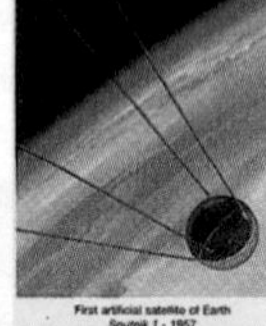

115 "Sputnik 1"

1998. John Glenn's (first American to orbit Earth) Return to Space. Multicoloured.
678 60c. Type **114** 75 50
679 60c. Launch of "Friendship 7" 75 50
680 60c. Glenn (bare-headed and in spacesuit) and United States flag on spaceship . . 75 50
681 60c. Glenn (in spacesuit) and "Friendship" space capsule 75 50
682 60c. Glenn (in spacesuit) and United States flag on pole 75 50
683 60c. Head and shoulders of Glenn in civilian clothes and stars (dated "1992") 75 50
684 60c. "Friendship 7" 75 50
685 60c. John Glenn with President Kennedy 75 50
686 60c. Glenn in overalls 75 50
687 60c. Launch of "Discovery" (space shuttle) 75 50
688 60c. Glenn in cockpit 75 50
689 60c. Head of Glenn in civilian suit 75 50
690 60c. Glenn fastening inner helmet 75 50
691 60c. Glenn with full helmet on 75 50
692 60c. Model of "Discovery" 75 50
693 60c. Head of Glenn smiling (bare-headed) in spacesuit 75 50

1999. Exploration of the Solar System. Multicoloured. (a) Space Achievements of Russia.
695 33c. Type **115** (first artificial satellite, 1957) 40 25
696 33c. Space dog Laika (first animal in space, 1957) (wrongly inscr "Leika") . . 40 25
697 33c. "Luna 1", 1959 . . . . 40 25
698 33c. "Luna 3", 1959 . . . . 40 25
699 33c. Yuri Gagarin (first man in space, 1961) 40 25
700 33c. "Venera 1" probe, 1961 40 25
701 33c. "Mars 1" probe, 1962 40 25
702 33c. Valentina Tereshkova (first woman in space, 1963) 40 25
703 33c. "Voskhod 1", 1964 . . . 40 25
704 33c. Aleksei Leonov and "Voskhod 2" (first space walk, 1965) 40 25
705 33c. "Venera 3" probe, 1966 40 25
706 33c. "Luna 10", 1966 . . . . 40 25
707 33c. "Luna 9" (first landing on moon, 1966) 40 25
708 33c. "Lunokhod 1" moon-vehicle from "Luna 17" (first roving vehicle on Moon, 1970) (wrongly inscr "First robot mission ... Luna 16") 40 25
709 33c. "Luna 16" on Moon's surface (first robot mission, 1970) (wrongly inscr "First roving vehicle ... Luna 17") 40 25
710 33c. "Mars 3", 1971 . . . . 40 25
711 33c. Leonid Popov, "Soyuz 35" and Valery Ryumin (first long manned space mission, 1980) 40 25
712 33c. Balloon ("Vega 1" Venus-Halley's Comet probe, 1985–86) 40 25
713 33c. "Vega 1" and Halley's Comet, 1986 . . . . 40 25
714 33c. "Mir" space station . . 40 25

(b) Achievements of the United States of America
715 33c. "Explorer 1", 1958 . . . 40 25
716 33c. Space observatory "OSO-1", 1962 . . . . . 40 25
717 33c. "Mariner 2" Venus probe, 1962 (first scientifically successful planetary mission) 40 25
718 33c. "Mariner 2" Venus probe, 1962 (first scientific interplanetary space discovery) 40 25
719 33c. "Apollo 8" above Moon's surface 40 25
720 33c. Astronaut descending ladder on "Apollo 11" mission (first manned Moon landing, 1969) . . . 40 25
721 33c. Astronaut taking Moon samples, 1969 . . . . . . 40 25
722 33c. Lunar Rover of "Apollo 15", 1971 . . . . 40 25
723 33c. "Mariner 9" Mars probe, 1971 . . . . 40 25
724 33c. "Pioneer 10" passing Jupiter, 1973 . . . . . . 40 25
725 33c. "Mariner 10" passing Mercury, 1974 . . . . . . 40 25
726 33c. "Viking 1" on Mars, 1976 . . . . 40 25
727 33c. "Pioneer 11" passing Saturn, 1979 . . . . . . 40 25
728 33c. "STS-1" (first re-usable spacecraft, 1981) 40 25
729 33c. "Pioneer 10" (first man-made object to leave solar system, 1983) 40 25
730 33c. Solar Maximum Mission, 1984 . . . . . . 40 25
731 33c. "Cometary Explorer", 1985 . . . . 40 25
732 33c. "Voyager 2" passing Neptune, 1989 . . . . . . 40 25
733 33c. "Galileo" space probe, 1992 . . . . 40 25
734 33c. "Sojourner" (Mars rover), 1997 . . . . 40 25

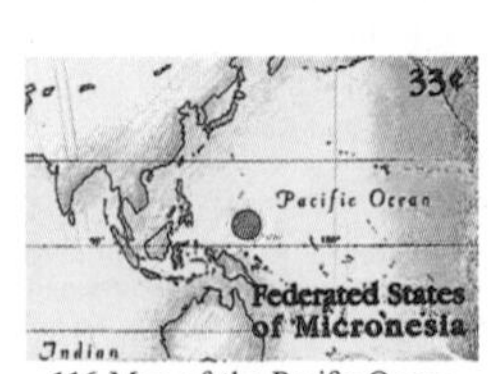

116 Map of the Pacific Ocean

1999. Voyages of the Pacific. Multicoloured.
736 33c. Type **116** 40 25
737 33c. Black-fronted parakeet 40 25
738 33c. Red-tailed tropic bird . . 40 25
739 33c. Plan of ship's hull . . . 40 25
740 33c. Sketches of winches . . 40 25
741 33c. Yellow flowers 40 25
742 33c. Full-rigged sailing ship 40 25
743 33c. Three flowers growing from seeds and top of compass rose 40 25
744 33c. Fish (background of ship's planking) 40 25
745 33c. Flag of Yap 40 25
746 33c. Flag of Truk (palm tree) 40 25
747 33c. Flag of Kosrae (four stars) and bottom of compass rose 40 25
748 33c. Sketches of fruit 40 25
749 33c. Three plants and leaves 40 25
750 33c. Fish (leaves at left) . . . 40 25
751 33c. Flag of Pohnpei and equator 40 25
752 33c. Sextant 40 25
753 33c. Red plant 40 25
754 33c. Fish and left side of compass rose 40 25
755 33c. Right side of compass rose and full-rigged sailing ship 40 25

Nos. 736/55 were issued together, se-tenant, forming a composite design.

117 Couple Meeting

1999. "Romance of the Three Kingdoms" (Chinese novel by Luo Guanzhong). Multicoloured.
756 33c. Type **117** 40 25
757 33c. Four men (one with lance) in room 40 25
758 33c. Two riders in combat . . 40 25
759 33c. Four men watching fifth man walking through room 40 25
760 33c. Captives before man on wheeled throne 40 25
761 50c. Riders approaching castle 40 25
762 50c. Warrior pointing at fire 40 25
763 50c. Opposing warriors riding through thick smoke . . . 40 25
764 50c. Couple kneeling before man on dais 40 25
765 50c. Cauldron on fire 40 25

118 Carriage of Leipzig–Dresden Railway and Caroline Islands 1900 20pf. Stamp

1999. "iBRA" International Stamp Fair, Nuremberg, Germany. Multicoloured.
767 55c. Type **118** 65 45
768 55c. Golsdorf steam railway locomotive and Caroline Islands 1m. "Yacht" stamp 65 45

119 Black Rhinoceros

121 Deep-drilling for Brine Salt

120 "Ghost of O-Iwa"

1999. Earth Day. Multicoloured.
770 33c. Type **119** 40 25
771 33c. Cheetah 40 25
772 33c. Jackass penguin 40 25
773 33c. Blue whale 40 25
774 33c. Red-headed woodpecker 40 25
775 33c. African elephant 40 25
776 33c. Aurrochs 40 25
777 33c. Dodo 40 25
778 33c. Tasmanian wolf 40 25
779 33c. Giant lemur 40 25
780 33c. Quagga 40 25
781 33c. Steller's sea cow 40 25
782 33c. Pteranodon 40 25
783 33c. Shonisaurus 40 25
784 33c. Stegosaurus 40 25
785 33c. Gallimimus 40 25
786 33c. Tyrannosaurus 40 25
787 33c. Archelon 40 25
788 33c. Brachiosaurus 40 25
789 33c. Triceratops 40 25

1999. 150th Death Anniv of Hokusai Katsushika (Japanese artist). Multicoloured.
791 33c. Type **120** 40 25
792 33c. Spotted horse with head lowered 40 25
793 33c. "Abe Nakamaro" . . . 40 25
794 33c. "Ghost of Kasane" . . . 40 25
795 33c. Bay horse with head held up 40 25
796 33c. "The Ghost of Kiku and the Priest Mitazuki" . . . 40 25
797 33c. "Belly Band Float" . . 40 25
798 33c. Woman washing herself 40 25
799 33c. "Swimmers" 40 25
800 33c. "Eel Climb" 40 25
801 33c. Woman playing lute . . 40 25
802 33c. "Kimo Ga Imo ni Naru" 40 25

Nos. 792 and 795 are inscribed "Hores Drawings".

1999. New Millennium. Multicoloured. (a) Science and Technology of Ancient China.
804 33c. Type **121** 40 25
805 33c. Chain pump 40 25
806 33c. Magic lantern 40 25
807 33c. Chang Heng's seismograph 40 25
808 33c. Dial and pointer devices 40 25
809 33c. Page of Lui Hui's mathematics treatise (value of Pi) 40 25
810 33c. Porcelain production . . 40 25
811 33c. Water mill 40 25
812 33c. Relief of horse from tomb of Tang Tai-Tsung (the stirrup) 40 25
813 33c. Page of Lu Yu's tea treatise and detail of Liu Songnian's painting of tea-making 40 25
814 33c. Umbrella 40 25
815 33c. Brandy and whisky production 40 25
816 33c. Page from oldest surviving printed book, woodblock and its print (printing) 40 25
817 33c. Copper plate and its print (paper money) . . . 40 25
818 33c. Woodcut showing gunpowder demonstration 40 25
819 33c. Anji Bridge (segmented arch) (56½ × 36 mm) . . . 40 25
820 33c. Mercator's star map and star diagram on bronze mirror 40 25

(b) People and Events of the Twelfth Century (1100–1150)
821 20c. Holy Roman Emperor Henry IV (death, 1106) . . 30 20
822 20c. Chastisement of monks of Enryakuji Temple, Kyoto, 1108 . . . . 30 20
823 20c. Founding of Knights of the Hospital of St. John, 1113 . . . . 30 20
824 20c. Invention of nautical compass, 1117 . . . . . . 30 20
825 20c. Drowning of Prince William, heir of King Henry I of England, 1120 30 20
826 20c. Pope Callixtus II (Treaty of Worms, 1122, between Papacy and Holy Roman Emperor Henry V) 30 20
827 20c. Death of Omar Khayyam (Persian poet), 1126 . . . . 30 20
828 20c. Death of Duke Guilhem IX, Count of Poitiers and Duke of Aquitaine (earliest known troubadour, 1127) 30 20
829 20c. Coronation of King Roger II of Sicily, 1130 . . 30 20
830 20c. King Stephen and Queen Matilda (start of English civil war, 1135) 30 20
831 20c. Moses Maimonides (philosopher, birth, 1138) 30 20
832 20c. Abelard and Heloise (Church's censure of Abelard, 1140) 30 20
833 20c. Defeat of French and German crusaders at Damascus, 1148 . . . . . 30 20
834 20c. Fall of Mexican city of Tula, 1150s 30 20
835 20c. Completion of Angkor Vat, Cambodia, 1150 . . . 30 20
836 20c. Rise of Kingdom of Chimu, Peru, 1150s (56½ × 36 mm) 30 20
837 20c. Honen (Buddhist monk) becomes hermit, 1150 . . . 30 20

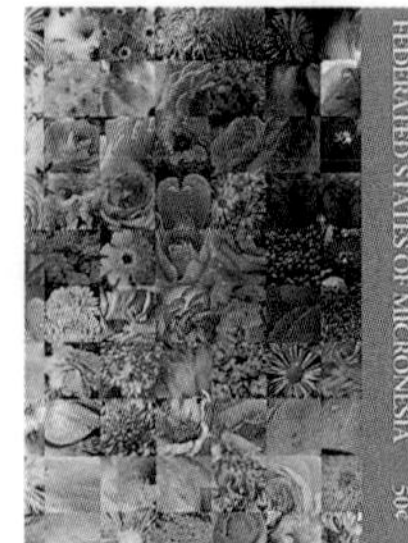

122 Flowers

1999. Faces of the Millennium: Diana, Princess of Wales. Showing collage of miniature flower photographs. Multicoloured, country panel at left (a) or right (b).
838 50c. Deep red shades (a) . . 60 40
839 50c. Deep red shades (b) . . 60 40
840 50c. Deep red shades with violet shades at bottom left (a) 60 40
841 50c. Blackish shades in bottom left corner (b) . . . 40 60

842 50c. Violet shades at left and bottom, pinkish shades at right (a) 60 40
843 50c. Lemon and pink shades (b) 60 40
844 50c. Violet shades (a) 60 40
845 50c. Type **122** (rose in bottom row) (b) 60 40

Nos. 838/45 were issued together, se-tenant, and when viewed as a whole, form a portrait of Diana, Princess of Wales.

123 Face of Woman

1999. Costumes of the World. Multicoloured.
846 33c. Type **123** 30 20
847 33c. Tools for fabric making 30 20
848 33c. Head of African Masai warrior and textile pattern 30 20
849 33c. Head of woman and textile pattern (inscr "French Renaissance costume") 30 20
850 33c. Head of woman in hat with black feathers ("French princess gown 1900–1910") 30 20
851 33c. Head of Micronesian woman in wedding costume 30 20
852 33c. Body of African Masai warrior and head of woman 30 20
853 33c. Body of woman ("Textile patterns of French Renaissance costume") 30 20
854 33c. Body of woman ("1900–1910 French princess gown") 30 20
855 33c. Body and head of two Micronesian women in wedding costumes 30 20
856 33c. Hem of costume and body of woman ("Details of woman costume from African fabrics") 30 20
857 33c. Lower part of dress and head of woman ("French Renaissance costume") 30 20
858 33c. Hem of dress and furled umbrella 30 20
859 33c. Body and legs of two Micronesian women in wedding costumes 30 20
860 33c. Head of woman in Japanese Kabuki costume 30 20
861 33c. Rulers for tailoring 30 20
862 33c. Scissors 30 20
863 33c. Japanese fabrics 30 20
864 33c. Head and body of two women in Japanese Kabuki costumes 30 20
865 33c. Iron 30 20

Nos. 846/65 were issued together, se-tenant, forming several composite designs.

124 "Holy Family with St. John"

1999. Christmas. Paintings by Anthony van Dyck. Multicoloured.
866 33c. Type **124** 30 20
867 60c. "Madonna and Child" 75 50
868 $2 "Virgin and Child with Two Donors" (detail) 2·50 1·60

125 Wright "Flyer I"

1999. Man's First Century of Flight. Multicoloured
870 33c. Type **125** 30 20
871 33c. Bleriot XI and Notre Dame Cathedral, Paris 30 20
872 33c. Fokker D.VII biplane and Brandenburg Gate, Berlin 30 20
873 33c. Dornier Komet I (numbered B 240) and Amsterdam 30 20
874 33c. Charles Lindbergh's Ryan NYP Special "Spirit of St. Louis" and steeple 30 20
875 33c. Mitsubishi A6M Zero-Sen fighter and Mt. Fuji 30 20
876 33c. Boeing B-29 Superfortress bomber and roof of building 30 20
877 33c. Messerschmitt Me 262A jet fighter (swastika on tail) 30 20
878 33c. Chuck Yeager's Bell X-1 rocket plane and Grand Canyon 30 20
879 33c. Mikoyan Gurevich MiG-19 over Russian church 30 20
880 33c. Lockheed U-2 reconnaissance plane over building at night 30 20
881 33c. Boeing 707 jetliner and head of Statue of Liberty, New York 30 20
882 33c. British Aerospace/Aerospatiale Concorde supersonic jetliner and top of Eiffel Tower, Paris 30 20
883 33c. McDonnell Douglas DC-10 jetliner and Sydney Opera House 30 20
884 33c. B-2 Spirit stealth bomber and globe 30 20

Nos. 870/84 were issued together, se-tenant, forming a composite design of the globe.

126 *Oncidium obryzatum*

127 Martin Luther King (civil rights leader)

2000. Orchids. Multicoloured.
886 33c. Type **126** 45 30
887 33c. *Oncidium phalaenopsis* 45 30
888 33c. *Oncidium pulvinatum* 45 30
889 33c. *Paphiodedilum armeniacum* 45 30
890 33c. *Paphiopedilum dayanum* 45 30
891 33c. *Paphiopedilum druryi* 45 30
892 33c. *Baptistonia echinata* 45 30
893 33c. *Bulbophyllum lobbii* 45 30
894 33c. *Cattleya bicolor* 45 30
895 33c. *Cischweinfia dasyandra* 45 30
896 33c. *Cochleanthes discolor* 45 30
897 33c. *Dendrobium bellatulum* 45 30
898 33c. *Esmeralda clarkei* 45 30
899 33c. *Gomesa crispa* 45 30
900 33c. *Masdevallia elephanticeps* 45 30
901 33c. *Maxillaria variabilis* 45 30
902 33c. *Mitoniopsis roezlii* 45 30
903 33c. *Oncidium cavendishianum* 45 30

2000. Personalities of the Twentieth Century. Multicoloured.
905 33c. Type **127** 45 30
906 33c. Dr. Albert Schweitzer (philosopher and missionary) 45 30
907 33c. Pope John Paul II 45 30
908 33c. Sarvepalli Radhakrishnan (philosopher and Indian statesman) 45 30
909 33c. Toyohiko Kagawa (social reformer) 45 30
910 33c. Mahatma Gandhi (Indian leader) 45 30
911 33c. Mother Teresa (nun and missionary) 45 30
912 33c. Khyentse Rinpoche (poet and philosopher) 45 30
913 33c. Desmond Tutu (religious leader) 45 30
914 33c. Chiara Lubich (founder of Focolare movement) 45 30
915 33c. Dalai Lama (religious leader) 45 30
916 33c. Abraham Heschel (theologian) 45 30

129 Mother-of-Pearl (*Salamis parhassus*)

2000. Butterflies. Multicoloured.
918 20c. Type **129** 30 20
919 20c. Blue morpho (*Morpho rhetenor*) 30 20
920 20c. Monarch (*Danaus plexippus*) 30 20
921 20c. *Phyciodes actinote* 30 20
922 20c. *Idea leuconoe* 30 20
923 20c. *Actinote negra sobrina* 30 20
924 55c. Blue triangle (*Graphium sarpedon*) 80 50
925 55c. Swallowtail (*Papilio machaon*) 80 50
926 55c. Cairn's birdwing (*Ornithoptera priamus*) 80 50
927 55c. *Ornithoptera chimaera* 80 50
928 55c. Five-bar swallowtail (*Graphium antiphates*) 80 50
929 55c. *Pachliopta aristolochiae* 80 50

130 Mahatma Gandhi (Indian leader)

131 Mikhail Gorbachev (statesman)

2000. New Millennium. Multicoloured.
931 20c. Type **130** 30 20
932 20c. Poster (Dada Art fair, Berlin, 1920) 30 20
933 20c. Women with American flags (female suffrage, 1930) 30 20
934 20c. Nicola Sacco and Bartolomeo Vanzetti (anarchists) (international controversy over murder conviction, 1921) 30 20
935 20c. Hermann Rorschach (psychiatrist and neurologist) (developed inkblot test, 1921) 30 20
936 20c. George W. Watson (incorporation of I.B.M., 1924) 30 20
937 20c. Leica camera (first commercial 35 mm camera, 1925) 30 20
938 20c. Scientists and John Thomas Scopes (brought to trial for teaching Darwin's theory of evolution, 1925) 30 20
939 20c. Charles Lindbergh (aviator) and Ryan NYP Special Spirit of St. Louis (first solo transatlantic flight, 1927) 30 20
940 20c. "Big Bang" (George Henri Lemaitre) (astrophysicist and cosmologist) (formulated "Big Bang" theory, 1927) 30 20
941 20c. Chiang Kai-Shek (Chinese nationalist leader)
942 20c. Werner Heisenberg (theoretical physicist) developed "Uncertainty Principle", 1927 30 20
943 20c. Sir Alexander Fleming (bacteriologist) and microscope (discovery of penicillin, 1928) 30 20
944 20c. Emperor Hirohito of Japan 30 20
945 20c. Car and man (U.S. Stock Market crash causes Great Depression) 30 20
946 20c. Douglas World Cruiser seaplanes and men (round-the-world formation flight, 1924) (59 × 39 mm) 30 20
947 20c. *All Quiet on the Western Front* (novel by Erich Maria Remarque published 1929) 30 20

2000. International Relations in the Twentieth Century. Multicoloured.
948 33c. Type **131** 45 30
949 33c. U.S.S.R. and U.S. flags, Gorbachev and Reagan (end of Cold War) 45 30
950 33c. Ronald Reagan (U.S. President, 1980–88) 45 30
951 33c. Le Duc Tho (Vietnamese politician) 45 30
952 33c. Le Duc Tho and Henry Kissinger (resolution to Vietnam conflict) 45 30
953 33c. Henry Kissinger (U.S. Secretary of State) 45 30
954 33c. Linus Pauling (chemist) 45 30
955 33c. Pauling at protest against nuclear weapons 45 30
956 33c. Peter Benenson (founder of Amnesty International, 1961) 45 30
957 33c. Amnesty International emblem and prisoners 45 30
958 33c. Mahatma Gandhi (Indian leader) 45 30
959 33c. Gandhi fasting 45 30
960 33c. John F. Kennedy (U.S. President, 1960–3) making speech initiating Peace Corps 45 30
961 33c. President Kennedy 45 30
962 33c. Dalai Lama (Tibetan religious leader) praying 45 30
963 33c. Dalai Lama 45 30
964 33c. United Nations Headquarters, New York 45 30
965 33c. Cordell Hull (U.S. Secretary of State 1933–44) (active in creation of United Nations) 45 30
966 33c. Frederick Willem de Klerk (South African politician) 45 30
967 33c. De Klerk and Nelson Mandela (end of Apartheid) 45 30
968 33c. Nelson Mandela 45 30
969 33c. Franklin D. Roosevelt (U.S. President) 45 30
970 33c. Winston Churchill, Roosevelt and Josef Stalin (Soviet leader) (Yalta Conference, 1945) 45 30
971 33c. Winston Churchill (British Prime Minister) 45 30

132 Andrew Carnegie (industrialist)

2000. Philanthropists of the Twentieth Century. Multicoloured.
972 33c. Type **132** 45 30
973 33c. John D. Rockefeller (oil magnate) 45 30
974 33c. Henry Ford (motor manufacturer) 45 30
975 33c. C. J. Walker 45 30
976 33c. James B. Duke 45 30
977 33c. Andrew Mellon (financier) 45 30
978 33c. Charles F. Kettering (engineer) 45 30
979 33c. R. W. Woodruff 45 30
980 33c. Brooke Astor 45 30
981 33c. Howard Hughes (businessman and aviator) 45 30
982 33c. Jesse H. Jones 45 30
983 33c. Paul Mellon 45 30
984 33c. Jean Paul Getty (oil exectutive) 45 30
985 33c. George Soros 45 30
986 33c. Phyllis Wattis 45 30
987 33c. Ted (Robert Edward) Turner (entrepreneur) 45 30

133 Fairies' Bonnets (*Coprinus disseminatus*)

2000. Fungi. Multicoloured.
988 33c. Type **133** 45 30
989 33c. Black Bulgar (*Bulgaria inquinans*) 45 30
990 33c. Amethyst deceiver (*Laccaria amethystina*) (inscr "amethystea") 45 30
991 33c. Common morel (*Morchella esculenta*) 45 30
992 33c. Common bird's nest (*Crucibulum laeve*) 45 30
993 33c. Trumpet agaric (*Clitocybe geotropa*) 45 30
994 33c. Bonnet mycena (*Mycena galericulata*) 45 30
995 33c. Underside of horse mushroom (*Agaricus arvensis*) 45 30
996 33c. Part of *Boletus subtomento* 45 30
997 33c. Oyster mushroom (*Pleurotus ostreatus*) 45 30
998 33c. Fly agaric (*Amanita muscaria*) 45 30
999 33c. Aztec mushroom mandala design 45 30

134 *Freycinetia arborea*

2000. Flowers. Multicoloured.
1001 33c. Type **134** 40 25
1002 33c. Mount Cook lily (*Ranunculus lyallii*) (inscr "lyalli") 40 25
1003 33c. Sun orchid (*Thelymitra nuda*) 40 25
1004 33c. *Bossiaea ensata* 40 25
1005 33c. Swamp hibiscus (*Hibiscus diversifolius*) 40 25
1006 33c. *Gardenia brighamii* 40 25
1007 33c. Elegant brodiaea (Brodiaea elegans) 40 25
1008 33c. Skyrocket (*Ipomopsis aggregata*) 40 25
1009 33c. Hedge bindweed (*Convovulus sepium*) 40 25
1010 33c. Woods' rose (*Rosa woodsii*) 40 25

1011 33c. Swamp rose (*Rosa palustris*) 40 25
1012 33c. Wake robin (*Trillium erectum*) 40 25
MS1013 Two sheets. (a) 95 × 80 mm. $2 Black-eyed susan (*Tetratheca juncea*). (b) 108 × 80 mm. $2 Yellow meadow lily (*Lilium canadense*) Set of 2 sheets . . . 4·75 2·75

135 Two Siamese Cats

2000. Cats and Dogs. Multicoloured.
1014 33c. Type **135** 40 25
1015 33c. Red mackerel tabbies 40 25
1016 33c. British shorthair . . . 40 25
1017 33c. Red Persian 40 25
1018 33c. Turkish angora 40 25
1019 33c. Calico 40 25
1020 33c. Afghan hounds 40 25
1021 33c. Yellow labrador retriever 40 25
1022 33c. Greyhound 40 25
1023 33c. German shepherd . . . 40 25
1024 33c. King Charles spaniel 40 25
1025 33c. Jack Russell terrier . . 40 25
MS1026 Two sheets, each 85 × 110 mm. (a) $2 Tortoiseshell and white cat watching bird. (b) $2 Setter and trees Set of 2 sheets 4·75 2·75
Nos. 1014/19 (cats) and 1020/5 (dogs) respectively were issued together, se-tenant, each sheetlet forming a composite design.

136 Henry Taylor (Great Britain) preparing to Dive, 1908, London

2000. Olympic Games, Sydney. Multicoloured.
1027 33c. Type **136** 40 25
1028 33c. Cyclist 40 25
1029 33c. Munich stadium and flag, West Germany . . . 40 25
1030 33c. Ancient Greek wrestlers 40 25

137 Zodiac Airship *Capitaine Ferber*

2000. Centenary of First Zeppelin Flight and Airship Development. Multicoloured.
1031 33c. Type **137** 40 25
1032 33c. Astra airship *Adjutant Reau* 40 25
1033 33c. Airship 1A, Italy . . . 40 25
1034 33c. Astra-Torres No. 14 . . 40 25
1035 33c. Front of Astra-Torres No. 14, Schuttle-Lanz SL3 and front of Siemens-Schukert airship 40 25
1036 33c. Siemens-Schukert airship 40 25
MS1037 Two sheets, each 110 × 85 mm. (a) $2 LZ-130 *Graf Zeppelin II*. (b) $2 Dupuy de Lome airship Set of 2 sheets . . . . 4·75 2·75
Nos. 1031/6 were issued together, se-tenant, forming a composite design.

138 Top of Head

2000. 100th Birthday of Queen Elizabeth the Queen Mother. T **138** and similar vert designs showing collage of miniature flower photographs. Multicoloured, country inscription and face value at left (a) or right (b).
1038 33c. Type **138** 40 25
1039 33c. Top of head (b) 40 25
1040 33c. Eye and temple (a) . . 40 25
1041 33c. Temple (b) 40 25
1042 33c. Cheek (a) 40 25
1043 33c. Cheek (b) 40 25
1044 33c. Chin (a) 40 25
1045 33c. Chin and neck (b) . . . 40 25
Nos. 1038/45 were issued together in se-tenant sheetlets of eight with the stamps arranged in two vertical columns separated by a gutter also containing miniature photographs. When viewed as a whole, the sheetlet forms a portrait of Queen Elizabeth the Queen Mother.

139 Woman Weightlifter and Traditional Cloth

2000. "OLYMPHILEX 2000" International Olympic Stamp Exhibition, Sydney. Sheet 137 × 82 mm, containing T **139** and similar vert designs. Multicoloured.
MS1046 33c. Type **139**; 33c. Woman playing basketball; $1 Male weightlifter . . . . 2·00 1·25

140 Blue-streaked Cleaner Wrasse (*Labroides dimidiatus*)

2000. Coral Reef. Multicoloured.
1047 33c. Type **140** 40 25
1048 33c. Pennant coralfish (*Heniochus acuminatus*) . . 40 25
1049 33c. Chevron butterflyfish (*Chaetodon trifascialis*) . . 40 25
1050 33c. Rock beauty (*Holacanthus tricolor*) . . 40 25
1051 33c. Mandarin fish (*Synchiropus splendidus*) 40 25
1052 33c. Emperor snapper (*Lutjanus sebae*) (wrongly inscr "timorensis") . . . 40 25
1053 33c. Copper-banded butterflyfish (*rostratus*) . . 40 25
1054 33c. Chevron butterflyfish (*Chaetodon trifascialis*) (different) 40 25
1055 33c. Lemon-peel angelfish (*Centropyge flavissimus*) 40 25
1056 33c. Lemon-peel angelfish and harlequin tuskfish (*Choerodon fasciatus*) . . 40 25
1057 33c. Crown triggerfish (*Balistoides conspicillum*) 40 25
1058 33c. Coral hind (*Cephalopholis miniata*) . . 40 25
1059 33c. Pennant coralfish (*Heniochus acuminatus*) (different) 40 25
1060 33c. Scuba diver and six-blotched hind (*Cephalopholis sexmaculata*) 40 25
1061 33c. Common jellyfish (*Aurelia aurita*) 40 25
1062 33c. Palette surgeonfish (*Paracanthurus hepatus*) and common jellyfish . . 40 25
1063 33c. Bicoloured angelfish (*Centropyge bicolor*) . . . 40 25
1064 33c. Thread-finned butterflyfish (*Chaetodon auriga*) and clown anemonefish 40 25
1065 33c. Clown anemonefish (*Amphiprion percula*) . . . 40 25
1066 33c. Three-banded damselfish (*Chrysiptera tricincta*) 40 25
1067 33c. Three-banded damselfish and grey reef shark (*Carcharhinus amblyrhynchs*) (inscr "amblyrhynchos") 40 25
1068 33c. Tail of grey reef shark and starfish (*Luidia ciliaris*) 40 25
MS1069 Two sheets, each 98 × 68 mm. (a) $2 Forceps butterflyfish (*Forcipiger flavissimus*). (b) $2 Emperor angelfish (*Pomacanthus imperator*) Set of 2 sheets . . . . 4·75 2·75
Nos. 1051/59 and 1060/8 respectively were issued, se-tenant, forming a composite design.

141 Back of Head

2000. 80th Birthday of Pope John Paul II. T **141** and similar vert designs showing collage of miniature religious photographs. Multicoloured, country Inscription and face value at left (a) or right (b).
1070 50c. Type **141** 60 35
1071 50c. Forehead (b) 60 35
1072 50c. Ear (a) 60 35
1073 50c. Forehead and eye (b) 60 35
1074 50c. Neck and collar (a) . . 60 35
1075 50c. Nose and cheek (b) . . 60 35
1076 50c. Shoulder (a) 60 35
1077 50c. Hands (b) 60 35
Nos. 1070/7 were issued together in se-tenant sheetlets of eight with the stamps arranged in two vertical columns separated by a gutter also containing miniature photographs. When viewed as a whole, the sheetlet forms a portrait of Pope John Paul II.

142 "The Holy Trinity" (Titian)

2000. Christmas. Multicoloured.
1078 20c. Type **142** 25 10
1079 33c. "Adoration of the Magi" (Diego de Silva y Velasquez) 40 25
1080 60c. "Holy Nereus" (Peter Paul Rubens) 75 45
1081 $3.20 "St. Gregory, St. Maurus, St. Papianus and St. Domitilla" (Rubens) . . . . 4·00 2·40

143 Snake

2001. New Year. Year of the Snake. Two sheets, each 72 × 101 mm, containing horiz design as T **143**. Multicoloured.
MS1082 (a) 60c. Type **143**. (b) 60c. Brown snake . . . . 1·50 90

144 Weepinbell

2001. Pokemon (children's computer game). Showing various Pokemon characters. Multicoloured.
1083 50c. Type **144** 60 35
1084 50c. Snorlax 60 35
1085 50c. Seel 60 35
1086 50c. Hitmonchan 60 35
1087 50c. Jynx 60 35
1088 50c. Pontya 60 35
MS1089 74 × 114 mm. $2 Farfetch'd (37 × 50 mm) . . . . 2·50 1·40

145 Coral Reef

2001. Environmental Protection. Multicoloured.
1090 34c. Type **145** 40 25
1091 34c. Galapagos turtle . . . 40 25
1092 34c. Tasmanian tiger . . . 40 25
1093 34c. Yanomami 40 25
1094 34c. Pelican and Florida Keys 40 25
1095 34c. Bird of prey 40 25
1096 60c. Factory chimneys (Pollution) 75 45
1097 60c. Desert and tree stump (Deforestation) 75 45
1098 60c. Forest (Acid rain) . . . 75 45
1099 60c. Horse, mother and child, tree and Globe (Greenhouse effect) . . . 75 45
MS1100 Two sheets each 110 × 77 mm. (a) $2 Sea bird (visit by Jacques Cousteau); (b) $2 Chimpanzee (Jane Goodall Institute) Set of 2 sheets . . . 4·75 2·75

146 Fin Whale (*Balaenoptera physalus*)

2001. Whales of the Pacific. Multicoloured.
1101 50c. Type **146** 60 35
1102 50c. Right whale (*Balaena galacials*) 60 35
1103 50c. Pygmy right whale (*Caperea marginata*) . . . 60 35
1104 50c. Humpback whale (*Megaptera novaeangliae*) (inscr "novaeangliae") . . 60 35
1105 50c. Blue whale (*Balaenoptera musculus*) 60 35
1106 50c. Bowhead whale (*Balaena mysticetus*) . . . 60 35
1107 60c. True's beaked whale (*Mesoplodon mirus*) . . . 75 45
1108 60c. Cuvier's beaked whale (*Ziphius cavirostris*) . . . 75 45
1109 60c. Shepherd's beaked whale (*Tasmacetus shepherdi*) 75 45
1110 60c. Baird's beaked whale (*Berardius bairdii*) 75 45
1111 60c. Northern bottlenose whale (*Hyperodon ampullatus*) 75 45
1112 60c. Pygmy sperm whale (*Kogia breviceps*) 75 45
MS1113 Two sheets each 100 × 70 mm. (a) $2 Killer whale (*Orcinus orca*); (b) $2 Sperm whale (*Physeter macrocephalus*) Set of 2 sheets . . . . 4·75 2·75
Nos. 1101/6 and 1107/12 respectively were issued together, se-tenant, forming a composite design.

147 Three-spotted ("Yellow") Damselfish (*Stegastes planifrons*)

148 "The Courtesan Hinazuru of the Choji-ya" (Chokosai Eisho)

2001. Fishes. Multicoloured.
1114 11c. Type **147** 10 10
1115 34c. Rainbow runner (*Elegatis bipinnulatus*) . . 40 25
1118 70c. Whitelined grouper (*Anyperodon leucogrammicus*) 80 50
1119 80c. Purple queen anthias (*Pseudanthias pascalus*) . . 85 55
1123 $3.50 Eibl's angelfish (*Centropye eibli*) . . . . 4·25 2·50
1127 $12.25 Spotted ("Blue-spotted") boxfish (*Ostracion meleagris*) . . . 14·00 6·00

2001. "PHILANIPPON '01" International Stamp Exhibition, Tokyo. Japanese Art. Multicoloured.
1130 34c. Type **148** 40 25
1131 34c. "The Iris Garden" (Torii Kiyonaga) 40 25
1132 34c. "Girl tying her Hair Ribbon" (Tori Kiyomine) 40 25
1133 34c. "The Courtesan of the Mayuzumi of the Daimonji-ya" (Katsukawa Shuncho) 40 25

1134 34c. "Parody of the Allegory of the Sage Chin Kao Riding a Carp" (Suzuki Harunobo) 40 25
1135 34c. "Bath-house Scene" (Utagawa Toyokuni) 40 25
1136 34c. "Dance of Kamisha" (Kitagawa Utamaro) 40 25
1137 34c. "The Courtesan Hinazura at the Keizetsuro" (Kitagawa Utamaro) 40 25
1138 34c. "Toilet Scene" (Kitagawa Utamaro) 40 25
1139 34c. "Applying Lip Rouge" (Kitagawa Utamaro) 40 25
1140 34c. "Beauty reading a Letter" (Kitagawa Utamaro) 40 25
1141 34c. "The Geisha Kamekichi" (Kitagawa Utamaro) 40 25
MS1142 Two sheets each 118 × 88 mm. (a) $2 "Girl seated by a Brook at Sunset" (Suzuki Harunobu). Imperf; (b) $2 "Allegory of Ariwara No Narihira" (Kikugawa Eizan). Imperf Set of 2 shets 4·75 2·75

149 "Oscar Wilde"

2001. Death Centenary of Henri de Toulouse-Lautrec (artist). Multicoloured.
1143 60c. Type **149** 75 45
1144 60c. "Doctor Tapié in a Theatre Corridor" 75 45
1145 60c. "Monsieur Delaporte" 75 45
MS1146 54 × 84 mm. $2 "The Clowness Cha-U-Kao" 2·40 1·40

150 Queen Victoria **151** Queen Elizabeth

2001. Death Centenary of Queen Victoria. Each black (except **MS**1151 multicoloured).
1147 60c. Type **150** 75 45
1148 60c. Facing right 75 45
1149 60c. Facing left wearing black decorated hat 75 45
1150 60c. Facing forwards 75 45
1151 60c. Holding baby 75 45
1152 60c. Facing left wearing lace headdress 75 45
MS1153 84 × 110 mm. $2 Queen Victoria (37 × 50 mm) 2·40 1·40

2001. 75th Birthday of Queen Elizabeth II. Each black (except No. 1153 and **MS**1158 multicoloured).
1154 60c. Type **151** 75 45
1155 60c. Wearing blue jacket 75 45
1156 60c. As young girl 75 45
1157 60c. As infant 75 45
1158 60c. With dog 75 45
1159 60c. In profile 75 45
MS1160 78 × 108 mm. $2 Princess Elizabeth 2·40 1·40

MIDDLE CONGO Pt. 6

One of three colonies into which Fr. Congo was divided in 1906. Became part of Fr. Equatorial Africa in 1937. Became part of the Congo Republic within the French Community on 28 November 1958.

100 centimes = 1 franc.

1 Leopard in Ambush

2 Bakalois Woman **3** Coconut Palms, Libreville

1907.
1 **1** 1c. olive and brown 50 25
2 2c. violet and brown 55 55
3 4c. blue and brown 1·00 1·60
4 5c. green and blue 1·25 50
21 5c. yellow and blue 1·60 3·00
5 10c. red and blue 1·10 80
22 10c. green and light green 3·25 4·25
6 15c. purple and pink 65 2·25
7 20c. brown and blue 3·00 4·25
8 **2** 25c. blue and green 2·50 85
23 25c. green and grey 2·50 3·25
9 30c. pink and green 1·50 3·25
24 30c. red 95 3·00
10 35c. brown and blue 2·25 2·50
11 40c. green and brown 2·75 3·25
12 45c. violet and orange 4·25 6·25
13 50c. green and orange 2·50 3·50
25 50c. blue and green 1·60 2·75
14 75c. brown and blue 6·00 8·00
15 **3** 1f. green and violet 9·00 11·00
16 2f. violet and green 6·50 10·50
17 5f. blue and pink 38·00 35·00

1916. Surch **5c** and red cross.
20 **1** 10c.+5c. red and blue 60 2·50

1924. Surch **AFRIQUE EQUATORIALE FRANCAISE** and new value.
26 **3** 25c. on 2f. green and violet 70 2·75
27 25c. on 5f. pink and blue 45 80
28 65 on 1f. brown and orange 50 3·00
29 85 on 1f. brown and orange 80 3·00
30 **2** 90 on 75c. scarlet and red 2·50 3·00
31 1f.25 on 1f. ultramarine & bl 80 2·50
32 1f.50 on 1f. blue & ultram 1·75 2·75
33 3f. on 5f. pink and brown 4·00 3·75
34 10f. on 5f. green and red 10·00 12·50
35 20f. on 5f. purple and brown 17·00 10·50

1924. Optd **AFRIQUE EQUATORIALE FRANCAISE.**
36 **1** 1c. olive and brown 15 2·25
37 2c. violet and brown 20 2·25
38 4c. blue and brown 20 2·25
39 5c. yellow and blue 40 2·25
40 10c. green and light green 80 2·75
41 10c. red and grey 55 2·25
42 15c. purple and pink 1·10 2·25
43 20c. brown and blue 25 2·75
44 20c. green and light green 40 2·75
45 20c. brown and mauve 2·50 2·75
46 **2** 25c. green and grey 50 50
47 30c. red 55 3·25
48 30c. grey and mauve 60 1·00
49 30c. deep green and green 2·25 3·25
50 35c. brown and blue 40 3·00
51 40c. green and brown 55 2·75
52 45c. violet and orange 35 3·00
53 50c. blue and green 60 1·25
54 50c. yellow and black 85 30
55 65c. brown and blue 2·75 4·00
56 75c. brown and blue 1·25 2·75
57 90c. red and pink 3·75 5·00
58 **3** 1f. green and violet 1·60 1·75
59 1f.10 mauve and brown 4·00 5·00
60 1f.50 ultramarine and blue 7·25 7·75
61 2f. violet and green 1·75 2·25
62 3f. mauve on pink 7·50 6·00
63 5f. blue and pink 2·00 2·50

1931. "Colonial Exhibition" key-types inscr "MOYEN CONGO".
65 E 40c. green and black 4·50 5·50
66 F 50c. mauve and black 2·75 3·75
67 G 90c. red and black 2·00 4·00
68 H 1f.50 blue and black 5·00 4·25

15 Mindouli Viaduct

1933.
69 **15** 1c. brown 10 2·25
70 2c. blue 10 2·50
71 4c. olive 20 50
72 5c. red 50 1·75
73 10c. green 1·60 2·50
74 15c. purple 2·00 2·75
75 20c. red on rose 7·75 8·00
76 25c. orange 1·90 2·75
77 30c. green 2·50 2·50
78 – 40c. brown 2·75 3·75
79 – 45c. black on green 2·75 3·50
80 – 50c. purple 2·25 45
81 – 65c. red on green 2·75 3·25
82 – 75c. black on red 10·00 8·50
83 – 90c. red 2·75 3·25
84 – 1f. red 1·75 1·50
85 – 1f.25 green 2·50 2·25
86 – 1f.50 blue 6·75 3·75
87 – 1f.75 violet 3·00 2·50
88 – 2f. olive 2·50 2·25
89 – 3f. black on red 4·00 3·00
90 – 5f. grey 15·00 16·00
91 – 10f. black 50·00 26·00
92 – 20f. brown 30·00 17·00
DESIGNS: 40c. to 1f.50 Pasteur Institute, Brazzaville; 1f.75 to 20f. Government Building, Brazzaville.

POSTAGE DUE STAMPS

1928. Postage Due type of France optd **MOYEN-CONGO A. E. F.**
D64 D **11** 5c. blue 20 2·50
D65 10c. brown 45 2·75
D66 20c. olive 45 3·00
D67 25c. red 85 3·25
D68 30c. red 50 3·00
D69 45c. green 60 3·00
D70 50c. purple 70 3·75
D71 60c. brown on cream 95 4·00
D72 1f. red on cream 1·25 3·75
D73 2f. red 1·60 5·00
D74 3f. violet 2·75 8·75

D 13 Village

1930.
D75 D **13** 5c. olive and blue 65 2·50
D76 10c. brown and red 65 3·00
D77 20c. brown and green 2·25 4·25
D78 25c. brown and blue 2·50 4·50
D79 30c. green and brown 1·75 7·75
D80 45c. olive and green 3·00 6·75
D81 50c. brown and mauve 3·50 7·75
D82 60c. black and violet 4·00 8·00
D83 – 1f. black and brown 11·00 16·00
D84 – 2f. brown and mauve 9·50 18·00
D85 – 3f. brown and red 8·75 16·00
DESIGN: 1 to 3f. "William Guinet" (steamer) on the River Congo.

D 17 "Le Djoue"

1933.
D 93 D **17** 5c. green 25 2·75
D 94 10c. blue on blue 1·25 2·75
D 95 20c. red on yellow 2·00 3·00
D 96 25c. red 2·25 3·25
D 97 30c. red 2·00 3·50
D 98 45c. purple 2·25 3·50
D 99 50c. black 2·50 4·50
D100 60c. black on red 3·00 5·50
D101 1f. red 2·75 7·25
D102 2f. orange 6·75 11·00
D103 3f. blue 11·50 15·00

For later issues see **FRENCH EQUATORIAL AFRICA**.

MODENA Pt. 8

A state in Upper Italy, formerly a duchy and now part of Italy. Used stamps of Sardinia after the cessation of its own issues in 1860. Now uses Italian stamps.

100 centesimi = 1 lira.

1 Arms of Este **5** Cross of Savoy

1852. Imperf.
9 **1** 5c. black on green 25·00 44·00
3 10c. black on pink £325 65·00
4 15c. black on yellow 40·00 25·00
5 25c. black on buff 42·00 29·00
12 40c. black on blue 40·00 £120
13 1l. black on white 55·00 £2250

1859. Imperf.
18 **5** 5c. green £1300 £600
19 15c. brown £2500 £3500
20 15c. grey £300
21 20c. black £1800 £150
22 20c. lilac 60·00 £1000
23 40c. red £180 £1200
24 80c. brown £180 £19000

NEWSPAPER STAMPS

1853. As T **1** but in the value tablet inscr "B.G. CEN" and value. Imperf.
N15 **1** 9c. black on mauve £600 75·00
N16 10c. black on lilac 55·00 £275

N 4

1859. Imperf.
N17 N **4** 10c. black £1000 £2000

MOHELI Pt. 6

An island in the Comoro Archipelago adjacent to Madagascar. A separate French dependency until 1914 when the whole archipelago was placed under Madagascar whose stamps were used until 1950. Now part of the Comoro Islands.

100 centimes = 1 franc.

1906. "Tablet" key-type inscr "MOHELI" in blue (2, 4, 10, 20, 30, 40c., 5f.) or red (others).
1 D 1c. black on blue 2·25 2·00
2 2c. brown on buff 1·25 2·00
3 4c. brown on grey 2·25 3·25
4 5c. green 3·00 2·50
5 10c. red 2·75 1·90
6 20c. red on green 9·75 9·25
7 25c. blue 9·25 5·25
8 30c. brown on drab 17·00 7·00
9 35c. black on yellow 7·00 2·75
10 40c. red on yellow 13·50 10·50
11 45c. black on green 55·00 52·00
12 50c. brown on blue 23·00 14·00
13 75c. brown on orange 30·00 29·00
14 1f. green 15·00 20·00
15 2f. violet on pink 32·00 42·00
16 5f. mauve on lilac £110 £120

1912. Surch in figures.
17 D 05 on 4c. brown & bl on grey 2·00 3·25
18 05 on 20c. red & blue on grn 1·90 5·00
19 05 on 30c. brn & bl on drab 1·75 3·75
20 10 on 40c. red & blue on yell 1·90 3·50
21 10 on 45c. blk & red on grn 1·10 2·50
22 10 on 50c. brown & red on bl 1·75 4·00

MOLDOVA Pt. 10

Formerly Moldavia, a constituent republic of the Soviet Union. Moldova declared its sovereignty within the Union in 1990 and became independent in 1991.

1991. 100 kopeks = 1 rouble.
1993. Kupon (temporary currency).
1993. 100 bani = 1 leu.

1 Arms **2** Codrii Nature Reserve

1991. 1st Anniv of Declaration of Sovereignty. Multicoloured. Imperf.
1 7k. Type **1** 10 10
2 13k. Type **1** 10 10
3 30k. Flag (35 × 23 mm) 15 10

1992.
4 **2** 25k. multicoloured 55 25

3 Arms **4** Tupolev Tu-144

1992.
5 **3** 35k. green 10 10
6 50k. red 10 10
7 65k. brown 10 10
8 1r. purple 15 10
9 1r.50 blue 25 10

1992. Air.
15 **4** 1r.75 red 10 10
16 2r.50 mauve 15 10
17 7r.75 violet 60 30
18 8r.50 green 80 40
See also Nos. 70/3.

5 European Bee Eater

6 St. Panteleimon's Church

1992. Birds. Multicoloured.
19 50k. Type **5** 20 20
20 65k. Golden oriole 20 20
21 2r.50 Green woodpecker . . . 40 40
22 6r. European roller . . . . . 1·00 1·00
23 7r.50 Hoopoe . . . . 1·25 1·25
24 15r. European cuckoo . . . . 2·75 2·75
See also Nos. 63/9.

1992. Centenary (1991) of St. Panteleimon's Church, Chisinau.
25 **6** 1r.50 multicoloured 15 10

7 Wolf suckling Romulus and Remus

9 High Jumping

1992. Trajan Memorial, Chisinau.
26 **7** 5r. multicoloured 15 10

1992. Various stamps of Russia surch **MOLDOVA** and value.
27 2r.50 on 4k. red (No. 4672) . . 10 10
28 6r. on 3k. red (No. 4671) . . . 10 10
29 8r.50 on 4k. red (No. 4672) . . 30 15
30 10r. on 3k. green (No. 6074) 50 25

1992. Olympic Games, Barcelona. Multicoloured.
31 35k. Type **9** 10 10
32 65k. Wrestling 10 10
33 1r. Archery 10 10
34 2r.50 Swimming 30 15
35 10r. Show jumping . . . . . 1·10 55

1992. Nos. 4669/71 of Russia surch **MOLDOVA**, new value and bunch of grapes.
37 45k. on 2k. mauve 10 10
38 46k. on 2k. mauve 10 10
39 63k. on 1k. green 10 10
40 63k. on 3k. red 10 10
41 70k. on 1k. green 10 10
42 4r. on 1k. green 30 15

1992. Moldovan Olympic Games Medal Winners. Nos. 33/4 optd.
43 1r. Archery (optd **NATALIA VALEEVbronz** and emblem) 40 20
44 2r.50 Swimming (optd **IURIE BASCATOVargint** and emblem) . . . . 1·10 55

13 Moldovan Flag, Statue of Liberty and U.N. Emblem and Building

1992. Admission of Moldova to U.N.O. Mult.
46 1r.30 Type **13** 10 10
47 12r. As Type **13** but with motifs differently arranged 40 20

14 Moldovan Flag and Prague Castle

1992. Admission of Moldova to European Security and Co-operation Conference. Multicoloured.
48 2r.50 Type **14** 15 10
49 25r. Helsinki Cathedral and Moldovan flag 50 25

15 Carpet and Pottery

16 Galleon

1992. Folk Art.
50 **15** 7r.50 multicoloured 25 15

1992. 500th Anniv of Discovery of America by Columbus. Multicoloured.
51 1r. Type **16** 15 10
52 6r. Carrack 80 40
53 6r. Caravel 80 40

17 Letter Sorter, Diesel Train, State Flag and U.P.U. Emblem

1992. Admission to U.P.U. Multicoloured.
55 5r. Type **17** 75 40
56 10r. Douglas DC-10 jetliner, computerized letter sorting equipment, state flag and U.P.U. emblem 95 50

18 Aesculapius Snake

1993. Protected Animals. Snakes. Multicoloured.
57 3r. Type **18** 20 10
58 3r. Aesculapius in tree 20 10
59 3r. Aesculapius on path . . . 20 10
60 3r. Aesculapius on rock . . . 20 10
61 15r. Grass snake 75 40
62 25r. Adder . . . . 1·25 60
Nos. 57/60 were issued together, se-tenant, forming a composite design.

1993. Birds. As Nos. 19/24 but with values changed and additional design. Multicoloured.
63 2r. Type **5** 20 20
64 3r. As No. 20 . . . . 20 20
65 5r. As No. 21 . . . . 20 20
66 10r. As No. 22 . . . . 30 20
67 15r. As No. 23 . . . . 40 30
68 50r. As No. 24 . . . . 1·50 1·40
69 100r. Barn swallow . . . . . 3·25 2·75

1993. Air.
70 **4** 25r. red 20 10
71 45r. brown 35 20
72 50r. green 40 20
73 90r. blue 70 35

19 Arms

20 Arms

1993.
74 **19** 2k. blue 10 10
75 3k. purple 10 10
76 6k. green 10 10
77 – 10k. violet and green . . . 10 10
78 – 15k. violet and green . . . 10 10
79 – 20k. violet and grey 10 10
80 – 30k. violet and yellow . . . 15 10
81 – 50k. violet and red 20 10
82 **20** 100k. multicoloured 40 20
83 250k. multicoloured 90 45
DESIGN: 10 to 50k. Similar to Type **19** but with inscription and value at foot differently arranged.

21 Red Admiral

22 "Tulipa bibersteiniana"

1993. Butterflies and Moths. Multicoloured.
94 6b. Type **21** 10 10
95 10b. Swallowtail 10 10
96 50b. Peacock 35 20
97 250b. Emperor moth . . . . 1·90 80

1993. Flowers. Multicoloured.
98 6b. Type **22** 10 10
99 15b. Lily of the valley . . . 10 10
100 25b. Snowdrop 15 10
101 30b. Peony 20 10
102 50b. Snowdrop 30 15
103 90b. Pasque flower 60 30

23 Dragos Voda (1352–53)

24 "Story of One Life" (M. Grecu)

1993. 14th-century Princes of Moldavia. Mult.
105 6b. Type **23** 10 10
106 25b. Bogdan Voda I (1359–65) 10 10
107 50b. Latcu Voda (1365–75) 20 10
108 100b. Petru I Musat (1375–91) 45 25
109 150b. Roman Voda Musat (1391–94) 65 35
110 200b. Stefan I (1394–99) . . 90 45

1993. Europa. Contemporary Art. Multicoloured.
111 3b. Type **24** 10 10
112 150b. "Coming of Spring" (I. Vieru) . . . . 1·60 80

25 Biathletes

27 State Arms

1994. Winter Olympic Games, Lillehammer, Norway. Multicoloured.
113 3b. Type **25** 10 10
114 150b. Close-up of biathlete shooting . . . . 1·25 60

1994. No. 4669 of Russia surch **MOLDOVA**, grapes and value.
115 3b. on 1k. green 10 10
116 25b. on 1k. green 10 10
117 50b. on 1k. green 15 10

1994.
118 **27** 1b. multicoloured 10 10
119 10b. multicoloured 10 10
120 30b. multicoloured 10 10
121 38b. multicoloured 15 10
122 45b. multicoloured 15 10
123 75b. multicoloured 30 15
124 1l.50 multicoloured 60 30
125 1l.80 multicoloured 70 35
126 2l.50 mult (24 × 29 mm) . . 95 50
127 4l.50 multicoloured . . . . 1·75 1·25
128 5l.40 multicoloured . . . . 2·00 1·40
129 6l.90 multicoloured . . . . 2·50 1·50
130 7l.20 mult (24 × 29 mm) . . 2·75 1·75
131 13l. mult (24 × 29 mm) . . 5·25 3·50
132 24l. mult (24 × 29 mm) . . 9·25 6·00

28 Launch of "Titan II" Rocket

29 Maria Cibotari (singer)

1994. Europa. Inventions and Discoveries. 25th Anniv of First Manned Moon Landing. Multicoloured.
136 1b. Type **28** 10 10
137 45b. Ed White (astronaut) on space walk ("Gemini 4" flight, 1965) 65 35
138 2l.50 Lunar module landing, 1969 . . . . 2·25 1·25

1994. Entertainers' Death Anniversaries. Mult.
139 3b. Type **29** (45th) 10 10
140 90b. Dumitru Caraciobanu (actor, 14th) 40 20
141 150b. Eugeniu Coca (composer, 40th) 70 35
142 250b. Igor Vieru (actor, 11th) 1·10 55

30 Preparing Stamp Design

1994. Stamp Day.
143 **30** 10b. black, blue and mauve 10 10
144 – 45b. black, mauve and yellow 30 15
145 – 2l. multicoloured . . . . . 1·25 65
DESIGNS: 45b. Printing stamps; 2l. Checking finished sheets.

31 Pierre de Coubertin (founder)

32 Map

1994. Centenary of International Olympic Committee. Multicoloured.
146 60b. Type **31** 20 10
147 1l.50 Rings and "Paris 1994" centenary congress emblem 65 35

1994. Partnership for Peace Programme (co-operation of N.A.T.O. and Warsaw Pact members).
148 – 60b. black, ultram and bl 20 20
149 **32** 2l.50 multicoloured 30 30
DESIGN: 60b. Manfred Worner (Secretary-General of N.A.T.O.) and President Mircea Snegur of Moldova.

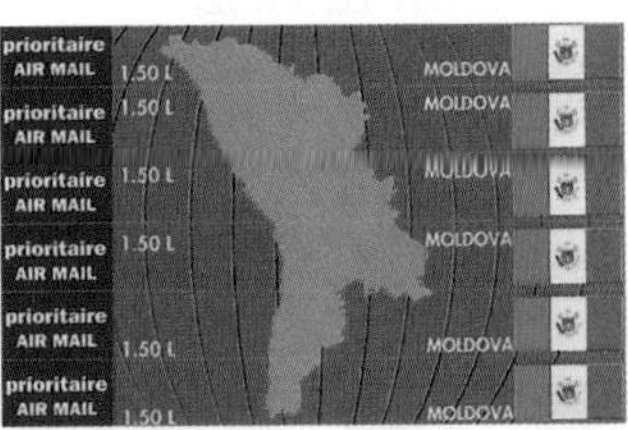

34 Map (½-size illustration)

1994. Air. Self-adhesive. Roul.
152 **34** 1l.50 multicoloured 50 25
153 4l.50 multicoloured . . . . 1·50 75
The individual stamps are peeled directly from the card backing. Each card contains six different designs with the same face value forming the composite design illustrated. Each stamp is a horizontal strip with a label indicating the main class of mail covered by the rate at the left, separated by a vertical line of rouletting. The outer edges of the cards are imperforate.

35 Family

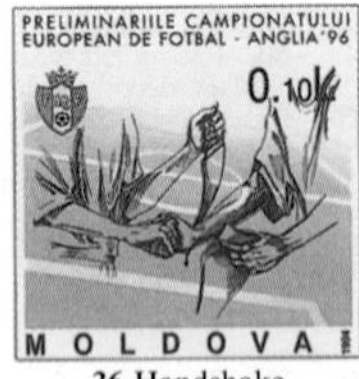

36 Handshake

1994. International Year of the Family. Multicoloured.
154 30b. Type **35** 20 10
155 60b. Mother breast-feeding baby 40 20
156 1l.50 Child drawing . . . . 1·50 90

1994. Preliminary Rounds of European Football Championship, England (1996). Multicoloured.
157 10b. Type **36** 10 10
158 40b. Players competing for ball 25 15
159 2l.40 Goalkeeper making save 1·50 90

37 "Birth of Jesus Christ" (anon)

38 Cracked Green Russula

1994. Christmas. Multicoloured.

161	20b. Type **37**	15	10
162	3l.60 "Birth of Jesus Christ" (Gherasim)	1·90	1·00

1995. Fungi. Multicoloured.

163	4b. Type **38**	10	10
164	10b. Oak mushroom	25	15
165	20b. Chanterelle	45	25
166	90b. Red-capped scaber stalk	2·10	1·10
167	1l.80 "Leccinum duriusculum"	4·25	2·25

39 Booted Eagle

1995. European Nature Conservation Year. Multicoloured.

168	4b. Type **39**	15	15
169	45b. Roe deer	1·00	50
170	90b. Wild boar	2·00	1·10

40 Earthenware Urns and Necklace

1995. National Museum Exhibits. Multicoloured.

171	4b. Type **40**	10	10
172	10b.+2b. Representation and skeleton of "Dinotherium gigantissimum"	25	15
173	1l.80+30b. Silver coins	2·75	1·75

41 "May 1945" (Igor Vieru)

1995. Europa. Peace and Freedom. Paintings. Multicoloured.

174	10b. Type **41**	15	10
175	40b. "Peace" (Sergiu Cuciuc)	35	20
176	2l.20 "Spring 1944" (Cuciuc)	2·00	1·10

42 Constantin Stere (writer, 130th birth)

43 Alexandru cel Bun (1400–32)

1995. Anniversaries.

177	**42** 9b. brown and grey	15	10
178	– 10b. purple and grey	15	10
179	– 40b. lilac and grey	55	30
180	– 1l.80 green and grey	2·50	1·50

DESIGNS: 10b. Tamara Ceban (singer, 5th death); 40b. Alexandru Plamadeala (sculptor, 55th death); 1l.80, Lucian Blaga (philosopher, birth centenary).

1995. 15th and 16th-century Princes of Moldavia. Multicoloured.

181	10b. Type **43**	15	10
182	10b. Petru Aron (1451–52 and 1454–57)	15	10
183	10b. Stefan cel Mare (1457–1504)	15	10
184	45b. Petru Rares (1527–38 and 1541–46)	65	35
185	90b. Alexandru Lapusneanu (1552–61 and 1564–68)	1·40	70
186	1l.80 Ioan Voda cel Cumplit (1572–74)	3·00	1·50

44 Soroca Castle

1995. Castles. Multicoloured.

188	10b. Type **44**	15	10
189	20b. Tighina Castle	35	15
190	60b. Alba Castle	1·00	60
191	1l.30 Hotin Castle	2·40	1·60

45 Seal in Eye

46 "50" and Emblem

1995. 50th Anniv of U.N.O. Multicoloured.

(a) Ordinary gum. Perf.

192	10b. Type **45**	20	10
193	10b. Airplane in eye	20	10
194	1l.50 Child's face and barbed wire in eye	3·25	2·00

(b) Self-adhesive. Rouletted.

195	90b. Type **46**	30	15
196	1l.50 Type **46**	45	25

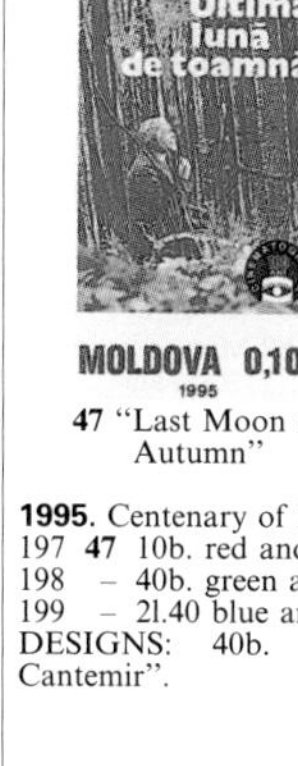

47 "Last Moon of Autumn"

48 Fly Agaric

1995. Centenary of Motion Pictures.

197	**47** 10b. red and black	15	10
198	– 40b. green and black	50	25
199	– 2l.40 blue and black	3·00	2·00

DESIGNS: 40b. "Lautarii"; 2l.40, "Dimitrie Cantemir".

1996. Fungi. Multicoloured.

200	10b. Type **48**	10	10
201	10b. Satan's mushroom	10	10
202	65b. Death cap	65	35
203	1l.30 Clustered woodlover	1·25	70
204	2l.40 Destroying angel	2·40	1·25

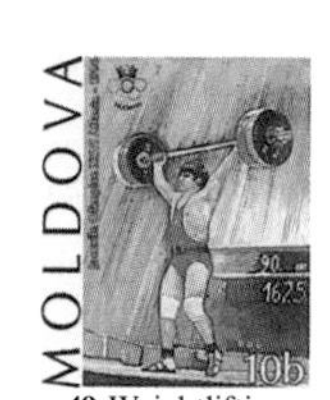

49 Weightlifting

50 Rudi Monastery

1996. Olympic Games, Atlanta, U.S.A. Mult.

205	10b. Type **49**	10	10
206	20b.+5b. Judo	35	15
207	45b.+10b. Running	65	35
208	2l.40+30b. Kayaking	3·00	1·75

1996. Monasteries. Multicoloured.

210	10b. Type **50**	10	10
211	90b. Japca	40	20
212	1l.30 Curchi	60	30
213	2l.80 Saharna	1·25	70
214	4l.40 Capriana	2·10	1·25

51 Moorhens

52 Elena Alistar (president of Women's League)

1996. Birds. Multicoloured.

215	9b. Type **51**	15	10
216	10b. Greylag geese	15	10
217	2l.20 Turtle doves	1·75	1·10
218	4l.40 Mallard	3·50	2·10

1996. Europa. Famous Women. Multicoloured.

220	10b. Type **52**	15	10
221	3l.70 Marie Sklodowska-Curie (physicist)	2·75	1·90

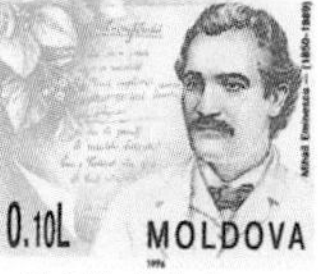

53 Mihail Eminescu (poet) (146th birth anniv)

54 Town Hall

1996. Birth Anniversaries.

223	**53** 10b. brown and deep brown	10	10
224	– 10b. sepia and brown	10	10
225	– 2l.20 green and brown	90	45
226	– 3l.30 green and deep brown	1·40	75
227	– 5l.40 brown and deep brown	2·25	1·40

DESIGNS: 10b. Gavriil Banulescu-Bodoni (Metropolitan of Chisinau, 250th); 2l.20, Ion Creanga (writer, 159th); 3l.30, Vasile Alecsandri (writer, 172nd); 5l.40, Petru Movila and printing press (400th).

1996. 560th Anniv of Chisinau. Multicoloured.

229	10b. Type **54**	10	10
230	1l.30 Cultural Palace	1·25	60
231	2l.40 Mazarache Church	2·25	1·40

55 Carol Singers with Star

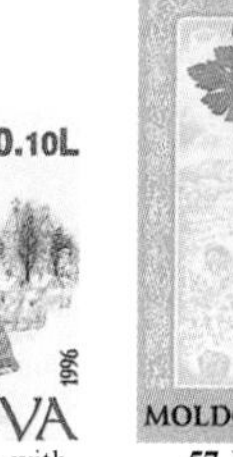

57 Feteasca

1996. Christmas. Multicoloured.

232	10b. Type **55**	10	10
233	2l.20+30b. Mother and child at centre of star	1·25	60
234	2l.80+50b. Children decorating Christmas tree	1·60	1·00

1997. Moldovan Wines. Each showing a grape variety and bottle of wine. Multicoloured.

236	10b. Type **57**	10	10
237	45b. Cabernet Sauvignon	30	15
238	65b. Sauvignon	45	25
239	3l.70 Rara Neagra	2·50	1·50

58 Franz Schubert

1997. Composers. Each green and grey.

240	10b. Type **58** (birth bicentenary)	10	10
241	10b. Gavriil Musicescu (150th birth anniv)	10	10
242	45b. Sergei Rachmaninov	40	20
243	4l.40 Georges Enesco	3·75	2·40

59 Girl with Eggs

1997. Easter. Multicoloured.

244	10b. Type **59**	10	10
245	3l.30 Easter dish	1·75	1·10

60 White Stork flying over Battlements

61 Praying Mantis

1997. Europa. Tales and Legends. Multicoloured.

247	10b. Type **60**	10	10
248	2l.80 Master Manole	1·25	75

1997. Insects in the Red Book. Multicoloured.

250	25b. Type **61**	10	10
251	80b. "Ascalaphus macaronius" (owl-fly)	45	20
252	1l. Searcher	55	30
253	2l.20 "Liometopum microcephalum" (ant)	1·25	70

62 Post Office No. 12, Chisinau

63 Nicolai Zelinski School, Tiraspol

1997. World Post Day.

255	**62** 10b. green and olive	10	10
256	– 2l.20 green and brown	1·60	80
257	– 3l.30 olive and green	2·40	1·40

DESIGNS HORIZ: 2l.20, District Head Post and Telegraph Office, Chisinau. VERT: 3l.30, Heinrich von Stephan (founder of U.P.U.) (death centenary).

1997. Protection of Buildings.

258	**63** 7b. black and violet	10	10
259	– 10b. black and purple	10	10
260	– 10b. black and blue	10	10
261	– 90b. black and yellow	50	25
262	– 1l.30 black and blue	75	40
263	– 3l.30 black and grey	1·90	90

DESIGNS: No. 259, Railway station, Tighina; 260, Sts. Constantine and Elena Cathedral, Balti; 261, Church, Causeni; 262, Archangel Michael Cathedral, Cahul; 263, Academy of Art, Chisinau.

64 Noul Neamt Monastery, Chitcani

65 Petru Schiopul (1574–77, 1578–79 and 1582–91)

1997. Christmas. Multicoloured.

264	10b. Type **64**	10	10
265	45b. "Birth of Our Lord Jesus Christ"	25	15
266	5l. "Birth of Jesus Christ" (different)	2·75	1·75

1997. 16th and 17th-century Princes of Moldavia. Multicoloured.

267	10b. Type **65**	10	10
268	10b. Ieremia Movila (1595–1606)	10	10
269	45b. Stefan Tomsa (1611–15 and 1621–23)	25	15
270	1l.80 Radu Mihnea (1616–19 and 1623–26)	95	55
271	2l.20 Miron Barnovschi Movila (1626–29 and 1633)	1·10	70
272	2l.80 Bogdan Orbul (1504–1517)	1·50	90

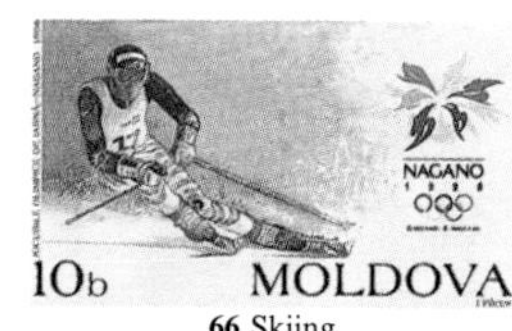

66 Skiing

1998. Winter Olympic Games, Nagano, Japan. Multicoloured.

274	10b. Type **66**	10	10
275	45b. Pairs figure skating	35	15
276	2l.20 Biathlon	1·75	1·10

67 Alexei Mateeici

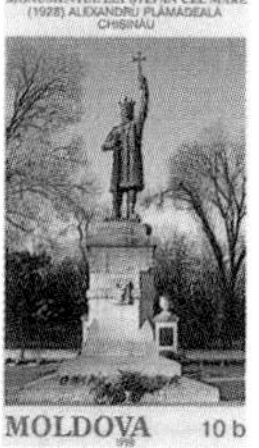

68 Statue of Stefan cel Mare (Alexandru Plamadeala), Chisinau

1998. Anniversaries. Multicoloured.

277	10b. Type **67** (110th birth anniv)	10	10
278	40b. Pantelimon Halippa (115th birth anniv)	20	10

279 60b. Stefan Ciobanu (115th birth anniv) 35 20
280 2l. Constantin Stamati-Ciurea (death centenary) 90 45

1998. Art. Multicoloured.
282 10b. Type **68** 10 10
283 60b. "The Resurrection of Christ" (icon) 35 20
284 1l. Modern sculpture (Constantin Brancusi), Targu-Jiu 55 30
285 2l.60 Trajan's Column, Rome 1·25 65

69 Masks and Eye **70** Cherries

1998. Europa. National Festivals. Multicoloured.
286 10b. Type **69** (Eugene Ionescu Theatre Festival) 10 10
287 2l.20 Medallion showing potter (Cermanics Fair) . . 1·10 55

1998. Fruits. Multicoloured.
289 7b. Type **70** 10 10
290 10b. Plums 10 10
291 1l. Apples 55 30
292 2l. Pears 90 45

72 Chilia

1998. Medieval Towns.
294 **72** 10b. grey and black . . . 10 10
295 – 60b. brown and black . . . 35 20
296 – 1l. red and black 50 25
297 – 2l. blue and black 95 50
DESIGNS: 60b. Orhei; 1l. Suceava; 2l. Ismail.

73 1858 Moldavia Stamps

1998. 140th Anniv of Stamp Issues for Moldavia. Multicoloured.
298 10b. Type **73** 10 10
299 90b. 1858 Moldavia 54p. and 1928 Rumania 1 and 5l. stamps 40 20
300 2l.20 1858 Moldavia 81p. and Russian stamps . . . . . . 1·10 55
301 2l.40 1858 Moldavia 108p. and Moldova 1996 10b. and 1994 45b. stamps . . . 1·25 65

74 Northern Eagle Owl **75** Couple from Vara

1998. Birds. Multicoloured.
302 25b. Type **74** 30 15
303 2l. Demoiselle crane (horiz) 1·25 65

1998. Regional Costumes. Multicoloured.
304 25b. Type **75** 15 10
305 90b. Couple from Vara (different) 60 30
306 1l.80 Couple from Iarna . . 1·25 65
307 2l. Couple from Iarna (different) . . . . 1·40 70

76 Anniversary Emblem and "Proportions of Man" (Leonardo da Vinci)

1998. 50th Anniv of Universal Declaration of Human Rights.
308 **76** 2l.40 multicoloured . . . . 1·60 80

77 Conference Members

1998. 80th Anniv of Union of Bessarabia and Rumania.
309 **77** 90b. brown, blue and black 60 30

78 Mail Coach

1999. Anniversaries. Multicoloured.
310 25b. Type **78** (125th anniv of U.P.U.) 15 10
311 2l.20 Map of Europe and Council of Europe emblem (50th anniv) . . . . 1·50 75

79 Prutul de Jos Park

1999. Europa. Parks and Gardens. Multicoloured.
312 25b. Type **79** 15 10
313 2l.40 Padurea Domneasca Park . . . . 1·60 80

80 Balzac **81** "Aleksandr Pushkin and Constantin Stamati" (B. Lebedev)

1999. Birth Bicent of Honore de Balzac (writer).
315 **80** 90b. multicoloured 60 30

1999. Birth Bicentenary of Aleksandr Pushkin (poet).
316 **81** 65b. brown, deep brown and black 45 25

82 Tranta

1999. National Sports.
317 **82** 25b. green and light green 15 10
318 – 1l.80 green and yellow . . 1·25 60
DESIGN: 1l.80, Oina.

83 Neil Armstrong (first man on Moon)

1999. 30th Anniv of First Manned Moon Landing. Multicoloured.
319 25b. Type **83** 15 10
320 25b. Michael Collins (pilot of Command Module) 15 10
321 5l. Edwin Aldrin (pilot of Lunar Module) . . . . . 3·25 1·75

84 Military Merit **85** Embroidered Shirt

1999. Orders and Medals. Multicoloured.
322 25b. Type **84** 15 10
323 25b. For Valour 15 10
324 25b. Civil Merit 15 10
325 90b. Mihai Eminescu Medal 60 30
326 1l.10 Order of Gloria Muncii 75 40
327 2l.40 Order of Stefan al Mare 1·60 80

1999. Crafts. Multicoloured.
329 5b. Inlaid wine flask 10 10
330 25b. Type **85** 15 10
331 95b. Ceramic jugs 60 30
332 1l.80 Wicker table and chairs 1·25 60

86 Goethe

1999. 250th Birth Anniv of Johann Wolfgang von Goethe (poet).
333 **86** 1l.10 multicoloured 40 20

87 Emblem **88** Metropolitan Varlaam

1999. 10th Anniv of Adoption of Latin Alphabet.
334 **87** 25b. multicoloured 10 10

1999. Patriarchs of the Orthodox Church. Mult.
335 25b. Type **88** 10 10
336 2l.40 Metropolitan Gurie Grosu 80 40

89 Bogdan II (1449–51) **91** Player and Chessboard

90 European Otter ("Lutra lutra")

1999. 15th to 17th-century Princes of Moldavia. Multicoloured.
337 25b. Type **89** 10 10
338 25b. Bogdan IV (1568–72) . . 10 10
339 25b. Constantin Cantemir (1685–93) 10 10
340 1l.50 Simon Movila (1606–07) 55 25
341 3l. Gheorghe III Duca (1665–66, 1668–72 and 1678–84) 1·00 50
342 3l.90 Ilias Alexandru (1666–68) . . . . 1·25 65

1999. Animals in the Red Book. Multicoloured.
344 25b. Type **90** 10 10
345 1l.80 Beluga ("Huso huso") 65 30
346 3l.60 Greater horseshoe bat ("Rhinolophus ferrumequinum") . . . . . 1·10 55

1999. World Women's Chess Championship, Chisinau. Multicoloured.
347 25b. Type **91** 10 10
348 2l.20+30b. Championship venue and emblem 85 40

92 4th-century B.C. Bronze Helmet and Candle Holder **95** Henri Coanda (aeronautical engineer)

94 Ileana Cosinzeana

1999. National History Museum Exhibits. Mult.
349 25b. Type **92** 10 10
350 1l.80 10th-century B.C. ceramic pot 65 30
351 3l.60 Gospel, 1855 . . . . . 1·10 55

2000. Folk Heroes. Multicoloured.
353 25b. Type **94** 10 10
354 1l.50 Fat-Frumos 55 25
355 1l.80 Harap Alb 65 30

2000. Birth Anniversaries. Each pink and black.
356 25b. Type **95** (114th anniv) 10 10
357 25b. Toma Ciorba (physician, 136th) 10 10
358 2l. Guglielmo Marconi (physicist, 126th) 70 35
359 3l.60 Norbert Wiener (mathematician, 106th) . . 1·10 55

96 Globe in Palm and Astronaut on Moon **97** "Resurrection" (anon)

2000. The Twentieth Century. Multicoloured.
360 25b. Type **96** (first manned moon landing, 1969) . . . 10 10
361 1l. Model of nuclear fission and hand (use of nuclear energy) 10 10
362 3l. Computer and mouse (development of electronic data processing) 35 15
363 3l.90 P. F. Teoctist (patriarch) and Pope John Paul II (consultation between Eastern and Roman churches) (horiz) 45 20

2000. Easter. Paintings in the National Gallery. Mult.
364 25b. Type **97** 10 10
365 3l. "Resurrection" (anon) . . 35 15

98 "Building Europe" **99** Emblem and Profiles

2000. Europa.
366 **98** 3l. multicoloured 35 15

2000. "EXPO 2000" World's Fair, Hanover, Germany (367) and "WIPA 2000" International Stamp Exhibition, Vienna, Austria (368). Mult.
367 25b. Type **99** 10 10
368 3l.60+30b. Hands holding tweezers and 1994 1b. State Arms stamp 20 10

100 Monastery, Tipova

2000. Churches and Monasteries. Multicoloured.
369 25b. Type **100** 10 10
370 1l.50 St. Nicolas's Church (vert) 15 10
371 1l.80 Palanca Church (vert) 20 10
372 3l. Butucheni Monastery . . 35 15

101 Judo

2000. Olympic Games, Sydney. Multicoloured.
373 25b. Type **101** 10 10
374 1l.80 Wrestling 20 10
375 5l. Weightlifting 55 25

102 Child and Schoolroom

2000. International Teachers' Day.
376 **102** 25b. grey and green . . . 10 10
377 – 3l.60 blue and lilac . . . 40 20
DESIGN: 3l.60, Teacher holding book.

103 Adoration of the Shepherds (icon)

2000. Christmas. Multicoloured.
378 25b. Type **103** 10 10
379 1l.50 The Nativity (icon) . . 15 10

104 Mother and Child

2001. 50th Anniv of United Nations High Commissioner for Refugees.
381 **104** 3l. multicoloured 30 15

105 Corncrake

2001. Endangered Species. The Corncrake. Multicoloured.
382 3l. Type **105** 30 15
383 3l. Singing 30 15
384 3l. In reeds 30 15
385 3l. With chicks 30 15
Nos. 382/5 were issued together, se-tenant, forming a composite design.

106 Yuri Gagarin and *Vostok* (spacecraft)

2001. 40th Anniv of First Manned Space Flight.
386 **106** 1l.80 multicoloured . . . 20 10

107 Maria Dragan

2001. Anniversaries. Multicoloured.
387 25b. Type **107** (singer, 15th death anniv) 10 10
388 1l. Marlene Dietrich (actress, birth centenary) 10 10
389 2l. Ruxandra Lupu (314th death anniv) 20 10
390 3l. Lidia Lipkovski (opera singer, 43rd death anniv) 30 15

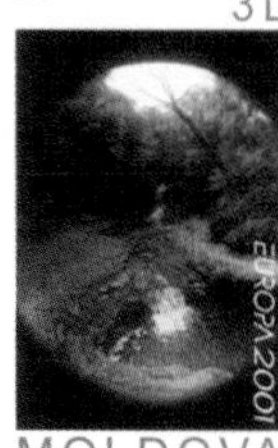

108 Waterfall

110 Stylized Humans (Aliona Valeria Samburic)

109 Prunariu

2001. Europa. Water Resources.
391 **108** 3l. multicoloured 25 15

2001. 20th Anniv of Space Flight by Dumitru Prunariu (first Rumanian cosmonaut).
392 **109** 1l.80 multicoloured . . . 15 10

2001. Winning Entries in Children's Painting Competition. Designs by named artist. Multicoloured.
393 25b. Type **110** 10 10
394 25b. Cars inside house and sun (Ion Sestacovschi) . . 10 10
395 25b. House, balloons and sun (Cristina Mereacre) 10 10
396 1l.80 Abstract painting (Andrei Sestacovschi) . . . 15 10

111 1991 7k. Arms Stamp

112 Tiger (*Panthera tigris*)

2001. 10th Anniv of First Moldovan Stamps. Sheet 100 × 74 mm, containing T **111** and similar multicoloured designs.
MS397 40b. Type **111**; 2l. 1991 13k. Arms stamp; 3l. 30k. 1991 Flag stamp (42 × 25 mm) 45 25

2001. Chisinau Zoo. Multicoloured.
398 40b. Type **112** 10 10
399 1l. Quagga (*Equus quagga*) 10 10
400 1l.50 Brown bear (*Ursus arctos*) 15 10
401 3l. + 30b. *Antilopa nilgau* . . 30 15
MS402 84 × 70 mm. 5l. Lion (*Panthera leo*) 45 25

113 Flag and Buildings

2001. 10th Anniv of Independence.
403 **113** 1l. multicoloured 10 10

114 Cimpoi

116 Nicolai Mavrocordat (1711–15)

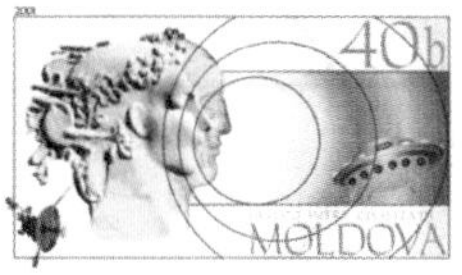

115 Women's Profiles and Space Ship

2001. Musical Instruments. Multicoloured.
404 40b. Type **114** 10 10
405 1l. Fluier 10 10
406 1l.80 Nai 15 10
407 3l. Tar'agot 25 15

2001. United Nations Year of Dialogue among Civilizations. Multicoloured.
408 40b. Type **115** 10 10
409 3l.60 Children encircling globe (vert) 30 15

2001. Rulers. Multicoloured (except **MS**416).
410 40b. Type **116** 10 10
411 40b. Mihai Racovita (1716–26) 10 10
412 40b. Constantin Mavrocordat (1748–49) 10 10
413 40b. Grigore Callimachi (1767–69) 10 10
414 1l. Grigore Alexandru Gnica (1774–77) 10 10
415 3l. Anton Cantemir (1705–7) 25 15
MS416 61 × 88 mm. 5l. Dimitrie Cantemir (1710–11) (black, yellow and red) (horiz) 45 25

117 St. Treime Basilica, Manastirea Saharna

2001. Christmas. Multicoloured.
417 40b. Type **117** 10 10
418 1l. Adormirea Maicii Domnului Basilica, Manastirea Hancu 10 10
419 3l. St. Dumitru Basilica, Orhei 25 15
420 3l.90 Nasterea Domnului Cathedral, Chisinau . . . 35 20

118 Emblem

2001. 10th Anniv of Union of Independent States.
421 **118** 1l.50 multicoloured . . . 15 10

POSTAGE DUE STAMPS

D 33 Postal Emblems

1994.
D150 **D 33** 30b. brown and green 50 50
D151 40b. green and lilac . . 65 65
One stamp in the pair was put on insufficiently franked mail, the other stamp on associated documents.

MONACO Pt. 6

A principality on the S. coast of France including the town of Monte Carlo.

1885. 100 centimes = 1 French franc.
2002. 100 cents = 1 euro.

1 Prince Charles III

2 Prince Albert

4 War Widow and Monaco

1885.
1 **1** 1c. olive . . . . 22·00 13·00
2 2c. lilac . . . . 42·00 19·00
3 5c. blue . . . . 50·00 26·00
4 10c. brown on yellow . . . 65·00 26·00
5 15c. red . . . . £275 8·50
6 25c. green . . . . £500 48·00
7 40c. blue on red . . . . . 60·00 35·00
8 75c. black on red . . . . . £225 85·00
9 1f. black on yellow £1400 £400
10 5f. red on green £2500 £1700

1891.
11 **2** 1c. green 50 50
12 2c. purple 55 60
13 5c. blue . . . . 38·00 4·25
22 5c. green 35 30
14 10c. brown on yellow . . . 85·00 9·50
23 10c. red . . . . 2·50 40
15a 15c. pink . . . . £150 6·50
24 15c. brown on yellow . . . 2·50 70
25 15c. green . . . . 1·50 2·10
16 25c. green . . . . £225 19·00
26 25c. blue . . . . 14·00 3·00
17 40c. black on pink . . . . 2·50 1·90
18 50c. brown on orange . . . 5·25 3·25
19a 75c. brown on buff . . . . 24·00 15·00
20 1f. black on yellow . . . . 15·00 8·50
21 5f. red on green . . . . . £100 70·00
28 5f. mauve £200 £200
29 5f. green . . . . 18·00 22·00

1914. Surcharged **+5c**.
30 **2** 10c.+5c. red . . . . 5·50 5·00

1919. War Orphans Fund.
31 **4** 2c.+3c. mauve . . . . 27·00 23·00
32 5c.+5c. green . . . . 15·00 13·00
33 15c.+10c. red . . . . 15·00 13·00
34 25c.+15c. blue . . . . 32·00 29·00
35 50c.+50c. brown on orange £150 £130
36 1f.+1f. black on yellow . . . £275 £275
37 5f.+5f. red £850 £950

1920. Princess Charlotte's Marriage. Nos. 33/7 optd **20 mars 1920** or surch also.
38 **4** 2c.+3c. on 15c.+10c. red . . 35·00 35·00
39 2c.+3c. on 25c.+15c. blue . . 35·00 35·00
40 2c.+3c. on 50c.+50c. brown on orange . . . . 35·00 35·00
41 5c.+5c. on 1f.+1f. black on yellow . . . . 35·00 35·00
42 5c.+5c.on 5f.+ 5f. red . . . . 35·00 35·00
43 15c.+10c. red . . . . 22·00 22·00
44 25c.+15c. blue . . . . 11·00 10·50
45 50c.+50c. brown on orange 45·00 45·00
46 1f.+1f. black on yellow . . . 60·00 60·00
47 5f.+5f. red £5500 £5500

1921. Princess Antoinette's Baptism. Optd **28 DECEMBRE 1920** or surch also.
48 **2** 5c. green 55 55
49 75c. brown on buff . . . . . 4·00 5·00
50 2f. on 5f. mauve . . . . . . 30·00 38·00

1922. Surch.
51 **2** 20c. on 15c. green . . . . . 1·00 1·50
52 25c. on 10c. red 60 80
53 50c. on 1f. black on yellow 4·50 8·00

8 Prince Albert I

9 St. Devote Viaduct

1922.
54 **8** 25c. brown . . . . 3·00 3·50
55 – 30c. green . . . . 85 1·40
56 – 30c. red 40 40
57 **9** 40c. brown 45 55
58 – 50c. blue . . . . 3·50 3·25
59 – 60c. grey 35 30
60 – 1f. black on yellow 25 20
61a – 2f. red 45 40
62 – 5f. brown . . . . 28·00 30·00
63 – 5f. green on blue . . . . . 8·00 8·00
64 – 10f. red . . . . 11·00 12·50
DESIGNS:—As Type **9**: 30, 50c. Oceanographic Museum; 60c., 1, 2f. The Rock; 5, 10f. Prince's Palace, Monaco.

12 Prince Louis

13 Prince Louis and Palace

1923.
65 **12** 10c. green 35 45
66 15c. red 50 60
67 20c. brown 30 45
68 25c. purple 25 45
69 **13** 50c. blue 25 45

1924. Surch with new value and bars.
70 **2** 45c. on 50c. brown on orange 50 65
71 75c. on 1f. black on yellow 45 45
72 85c. on 5f. green 30 45

14

15

16

17 St. Devote Viaduct

1924.

No.	Type	Description	Unused	Used
73	**14**	1c. grey	10	10
74		2c. brown	10	10
75		3c. mauve	1·90	1·90
76		5c. orange	30	20
77		10c. blue	10	10
78	**15**	15c. green	10	10
79		15c. violet	1·90	1·40
80		20c. mauve	15	10
81		20c. pink	20	10
82		25c. pink	10	10
83		25c. red on yellow	15	15
84		30c. orange	10	10
85		40c. brown	15	10
86		40c. blue on blue	25	20
87		45c. black	50	30
88	**16**	50c. green	15	20
89	**15**	50c. brown on yellow	10	10
90	**16**	60c. brown	10	20
91	**15**	60c. green on green	10	20
92		75c. green on green	20	20
93		75c. red on yellow	30	15
94		75c. black	60	30
95		80c. red on yellow	30	20
96		90c. red on yellow	1·25	95
97	**17**	1f. black on yellow	30	25
98		1f.05 mauve	30	25
99		1f.10 green	7·50	5·25
100	**15**	1f.25 blue on blue	10	25
101		1f.50 blue on blue	3·50	1·25
102	–	2f. brown and mauve	95	60
103	–	3f. lilac and red on yellow	16·00	7·75
104	–	5f. red and green	5·75	4·00
105	–	10f. blue and brown	16·00	15·00

DESIGN—As Type **17**: 2f. to 10f. Monaco.

1926. Surch.

No.	Type	Description	Unused	Used
106	**15**	30c. on 25c. pink	25	20
107		50c. on 60c. green on green	90	25
108	**17**	50c. on 1f.05 mauve	70	65
109		50c. on 1f.10 green	9·25	5·00
110	**15**	50c. on 1f.25 blue on blue	90	40
111		1f.25 on 1f. blue on blue	45	40
112	–	1f.50 on 2f. brown and mauve (No. 102)	3·75	3·25

20 Prince Charles III, Louis II and Albert I

1928. International Philatelic Exn, Monte Carlo.

No.	Type	Description	Unused	Used
113	**20**	50c. red	1·75	3·75
114		1f.50 blue	1·75	3·75
115		3f. violet	1·75	3·75

20a

21 Palace Entrance

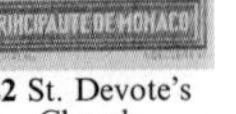

22 St. Devote's Church

23 Prince Louis II

1933.

No.	Type	Description	Unused	Used
116	**20a**	1c. plum	10	10
117		2c. green	10	10
118		3c. purple	10	10
119		5c. red	10	10
120		10c. blue	10	10
121		15c. violet	70	1·10
122	**21**	15c. red	75	25
123		20c. brown	75	25
124	A	25c. sepia	1·10	35
125	**22**	30c. green	1·25	35
126	**23**	40c. sepia	2·50	1·50
127	B	45c. brown	2·25	1·40
128	**23**	50c. violet	2·10	85
129	C	65c. green	2·50	60
130	D	75c. blue	3·00	1·60
131	**23**	90c. red	5·25	2·40
132	**22**	1f. brown	21·00	5·75
133	D	1f.25 red	5·00	3·00
134	**23**	1f.50 blue	29·00	7·00
135	A	1f.75 red	27·00	6·75
136		1f.75 red	17·00	9·50
137	B	2f. blue	9·50	3·25
138	**21**	3f. violet	14·50	5·50
139	A	3f.50 orange	38·00	28·00
140	**22**	5f. purple	19·00	11·00
141	A	10f. blue	£100	60·00
142	C	20f. black	£275	£110

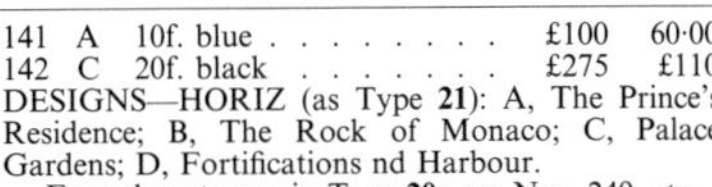

DESIGNS—HORIZ (as Type **21**): A, The Prince's Residence; B, The Rock of Monaco; C, Palace Gardens; D, Fortifications nd Harbour.

For other stamps in Type **20a** see Nos. 249, etc.

1933. Air. Surch with Bleriot XI airplane and **1f50.**

No.	Type	Description	Unused	Used
143		1f.50 on 5f. red & grn (No. 104)	21·00	19·00

28 Palace Gardens

1937. Charity.

No.	Type	Description	Unused	Used
144	**28**	50c.+50c. green	2·25	2·00
145	–	90c.+90c. red	2·25	2·00
146	–	1f.50+1f.50 blue	5·50	7·50
147	–	2f.+2f. violet	6·50	9·50
148	–	5f.+5f. red	95·00	90·00

DESIGNS—HORIZ: 90c. Exotic gardens; 1f.50, The Bay of Monaco. VERT: 2, 5f. Prince Louis II.

1937. Postage Due stamps optd **POSTES** or surch also.

No.	Type	Description	Unused	Used
149	D **18**	5 on 10c. violet	80	1·00
150		10c. violet	80	1·00
151		15 on 30c. bistre	80	1·00
152		20 on 30c. bistre	80	1·00
153		25 on 60c. red	1·00	1·25
154		30c. bistre	2·00	2·25
155		40 on 60c. red	1·75	1·75
156		50 on 60c. red	2·50	3·25
157		65 on 1f. blue	1·90	2·25
158		85 on 1f. blue	4·50	5·00
159		1f. blue	6·00	6·50
160		2f.15 on 2f. red	6·00	6·50
161		2f.25 on 2f. red	15·00	16·00
162		2f.50 on 2f. red	21·00	25·00

31 Prince Louis II

33 Monaco Hospital

1938.

No.	Type	Description	Unused	Used
164	**31**	55c. brown	4·50	1·75
165		65c. violet	21·00	17·00
166		70c. brown	15	15
167		90c. violet	15	15
168		1f. red	13·00	6·00
169		1f.25 red	20	20
170		1f.75 blue	13·00	7·75
171		2f.25 blue	20	15

1938. Anti-cancer Fund. 40th Anniv of Discovery of Radium.

No.	Type	Description	Unused	Used
172	–	65c.+25c. green	8·50	7·75
173	**33**	1f.75+50c. blue	8·50	9·50

DESIGN—VERT: 65c. Pierre and Marie Curie.

34 The Cathedral

38 Monaco Harbour

1939.

No.	Type	Description	Unused	Used
174	**34**	20c. mauve	15	15
175	–	25c. brown	30	20
176	–	30c. green	20	20
177	–	40c. red	20	20
178	–	45c. purple	35	20
179	–	50c. green	25	15
180	–	60c. red	20	20
181	–	60c. green	20	50
182	**38**	70c. lilac	35	20
183		75c. green	35	20
184	–	1f. black	20	20
185	–	1f.30 brown	20	20
186	–	2f. purple	20	20
187	–	2f.50 red	18·00	19·00
188	–	2f.50 blue	1·25	1·10
189	**38**	3f. red	40	20
190	**34**	5f. blue	2·25	2·75
191	–	10f. green	95	1·10
192	–	20f. blue	1·10	1·10

DESIGNS—VERT: 25, 40c., 2f. Place St. Nicholas; 30, 60c., 20f. Palace Gateway; 50c., 1f., 1f.30, Palace of Monaco. HORIZ: 45c., 2f.50, 10f. Aerial view of Monaco.

40 Louis II Stadium

41 Lucien

1939. Inauguration of Louis II Stadium, Monaco.

No.	Type	Description	Unused	Used
198	**40**	10f. green	80·00	90·00

1939. National Relief. 16th–18th-century portrait designs and view.

No.	Type	Description	Unused	Used
199	**41**	5c.+5c. black	1·50	1·00
200	–	10c.+10c. purple	1·50	1·00
201	–	45c.+15c. green	5·75	5·00
202	–	70c.+30c. mauve	8·75	7·75
203	–	90c.+35c. violet	8·75	7·75
204	–	1f.+1f. blue	22·00	22·00
205	–	2f.+2f. red	22·00	22·00
206	–	2f.25+1f.25 blue	25·00	29·00
207	–	3f.+3f. red	32·00	42·00
208	–	5f.+5f. red	55·00	80·00

DESIGNS—VERT: 10c. Honore II; 45c. Louis I; 70c. Charlotte de Gramont; 90c. Antoine I; 1f. Marie de Lorraine; 2f. Jacques I; 2f.25, Louise-Hippolyte; 3f. Honore III. HORIZ: 5f. The Rock of Monaco.

1939. 8th International University Games. As T **40** but inscr "VIIIeme JEUX UNIVERSITAIRES INTERNATIONAUX 1939".

No.	Type	Description	Unused	Used
209		40c. green	90	1·25
210		70c. brown	1·25	1·50
211		90c. violet	1·40	2·25
212		1f.25 red	2·10	3·00
213		2f.25 blue	3·00	4·50

1940. Red Cross Ambulance Fund. As Nos. 174/92 in new colours surch with Red Cross and premium.

No.	Type	Description	Unused	Used
214	**34**	20c.+1f. violet	2·75	2·75
215	–	25c.+1f. green	2·75	2·75
216	–	30c.+1f. red	2·75	2·75
217	–	40c.+1f. blue	2·75	2·75
218	–	45c.+1f. red	3·00	3·00
219	–	50c.+1f. brown	3·00	3·00
220	–	60c.+1f. green	3·00	3·00
221	**38**	75c.+1f. black	3·50	3·50
222	–	1f.+1f. red	4·00	4·25
223	–	2f.+1f. slate	4·00	4·75
224	–	2f.50+1f. green	9·00	10·50
225	**38**	3f.+1f. blue	11·00	11·00
226	**34**	5f.+1f. black	12·00	13·00
227	–	10f.+5f. blue	24·00	22·00
228	–	20f.+5f. purple	24·00	33·00

44 Prince Louis II

1941.

No.	Type	Description	Unused	Used
229	**44**	40c. red	40	40
230		80c. green	40	40
231		1f. violet	10	10
232		1f.20 green	10	10
233		1f.50 red	10	10
234		1f.50 violet	10	10
235		2f. green	10	10
236		2f.40 red	10	10
237		2f.50 blue	70	70
238		4f. blue	10	10

45

46

1941. National Relief Fund.

No.	Type	Description	Unused	Used
239	**45**	25c.+25c. purple	60	1·10
240	**46**	50c.+25c. brown	60	1·10
241		75c.+50c. purple	1·60	1·50
242	**45**	1f.+1f. blue	1·60	1·50
243	**46**	1f.50+1f.50 red	1·75	2·75
244	**45**	2f.+2f. green	1·75	2·75
245	**46**	2f.50+2f. blue	2·25	3·50
246	**45**	3f.+3f. brown	2·25	3·50
247	**46**	5f.+5f. green	6·25	7·00
248	**45**	10f.+8f. sepia	13·50	14·00

1941. New values and colours.

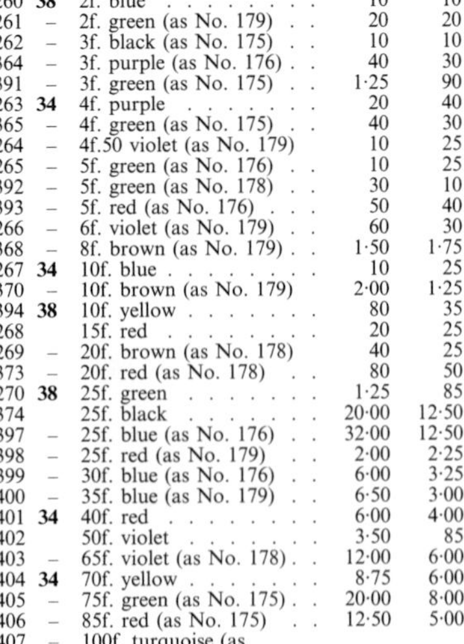

No.	Type	Description	Unused	Used
249	**20a**	10c. black	10	10
250	–	30c. red (as No. 176)	20	25
251	**20a**	30c. green	10	10
252		40c. red	10	10
253		50c. violet	10	10
362	**34**	50c. brown	15	25
254	**20a**	60c. blue	10	10
363	–	60c. pink (as No. 175)	15	25
255	**20a**	70c. brown	10	10
256	**34**	80c. green	10	20
257	–	1f. brown (as Nos. 178)	10	10
258	**38**	1f.20 blue	15	15
259	–	1f.50 blue (as Nos. 175)	20	20
260	**38**	2f. blue	10	10
261	–	2f. green (as No. 179)	20	20
262	–	3f. black (as No. 175)	10	10
364	–	3f. purple (as No. 176)	40	30
391	–	3f. green (as No. 175)	1·25	90
263	**34**	4f. purple	20	40
365	–	4f. green (as No. 175)	40	30
264	–	4f.50 violet (as No. 179)	10	25
265	–	5f. green (as No. 176)	10	25
392	–	5f. green (as No. 178)	30	10
393	–	5f. red (as No. 176)	50	40
266	–	6f. violet (as No. 179)	60	30
368	–	8f. brown (as No. 179)	1·50	1·75
267	**34**	10f. blue	10	25
370	–	10f. brown (as No. 179)	2·00	1·25
394	**38**	10f. yellow	80	35
268		15f. red	20	25
269	–	20f. brown (as No. 178)	40	25
373	–	20f. red (as No. 178)	80	50
270	**38**	25f. green	1·25	85
374		25f. black	20·00	12·50
397	–	25f. blue (as No. 176)	32·00	12·50
398	–	25f. red (as No. 179)	2·00	2·25
399	–	30f. blue (as No. 176)	6·00	3·25
400	–	35f. blue (as No. 179)	6·50	3·00
401	**34**	40f. red	6·00	4·00
402		50f. violet	3·50	85
403	–	65f. violet (as No. 178)	12·00	6·00
404	**34**	70f. yellow	8·75	6·00
405	–	75f. green (as No. 175)	20·00	8·00
406	–	85f. red (as No. 175)	12·50	5·00
407	–	100f. turquoise (as No. 178)	12·00	5·50

47 Caudron Rafale over Monaco

48 Propeller and Palace

49 Arms, Airplane and Globe

50 Charles II

1942. Air.

No.	Type	Description	Unused	Used
271	**47**	5f. green	30	30
272		10f. blue	30	30
273	**48**	15f. brown	40	60
274	–	20f. brown	50	90
275	–	50f. purple	2·40	3·00
276	**49**	100f. red and purple	2·40	3·00

DESIGNS—VERT: 20f. Pegasus. HORIZ: 50f. Mew gull over Bay of Monaco.

1942. National Relief Fund. Royal Personages.

No.	Type	Description	Unused	Used
277	–	2c.+3c. blue	20	30
278	**50**	5c.+5c. red	20	30
279	–	10c.+5c. black	20	30
280	–	20c.+10c. green	20	30
281	–	30c.+30c. purple	20	30
282	–	40c.+40c. red	20	30
283	–	50c.+50c. violet	20	30
284	–	75c.+75c. purple	20	30
285	–	1f.+1f. green	20	30
286	–	1f.50+1f. red	20	30
287	–	2f.50+2f.50 violet	1·90	3·75
288	–	3f.+3f. blue	1·90	3·75
289	–	5f.+5f. sepia	2·50	5·25
290	–	10f.+5f. purple	3·00	5·25
291	–	20f.+5f. blue	3·00	6·00

PORTRAITS: 2c. Rainier Grimaldi; 10c. Jeanne Grimaldi; 20c. Charles Auguste, Goyon de Matignon; 30c. Jacques I; 40c. Louise-Hippolyte; 50c. Charlotte Grimaldi; 75c. Marie Charles Grimaldi; 1f. Honore III; 1f.50, Honore IV; 2f.50, Honore V; 3f. Florestan I; 5f. Charles III; 10f. Albert I; 20f. Princess Marie-Victoire.

52 Prince Louis II

1943.

No.	Type	Description	Unused	Used
292	**52**	50f. violet	45	75

53 St. Devote

54 Blessing the Sea

55 Arrival of St. Devote at Monaco

1944. Charity. Festival of St. Devote.

293	**53**	50c.+50c. brown	20	20
294	–	70c.+80c. blue	20	20
295	–	80c.+70c. green	20	20
296	–	1f.+1f. purple	20	20
297	–	1f.50+1f.50 red	30	45
298	**54**	2f.+2f. purple	40	60
299	–	5f.+2f. violet	45	60
300	–	10f.+40f. blue	45	60
301	**55**	20f.+60f. blue	3·00	5·50

DESIGNS—VERT: 70c., 1f. Various processional scenes; 1f.50, Burning the boat; 10f. Trial scene. HORIZ: 80c. Procession; 5f. St. Devote's Church.

1945. Air. For War Dead and Deported Workers. As Nos. 272/6 (colours changed) surch.

302	1f.+4f. on 10f. red	50	45
303	1f.+4f. on 15f. brown	50	45
304	1f.+4f. on 20f. brown	50	45
305	1f.+4f. on 50f. blue	50	45
306	1f.+4f. on 100f. purple	50	45

57 Prince Louis II

58 Prince Louis II

1946.

361	**57**	30c. black	15	10
389		50c. olive	15	25
390		1f. violet	20	10
307		2f.50 green	30	30
308		3f. mauve	30	30
366		5f. brown	40	30
309		6f. red	30	30
367		6f. purple	3·50	1·75
310		10f. blue	30	30
369		10f. orange	40	25
371		12f. red	4·00	2·10
395		12f. slate	6·00	5·00
396		15f. lake	6·00	3·50
372		18f. blue	7·00	5·50
311	**58**	50f. grey	2·50	1·50
312		100f. red	3·50	2·25

59 Child Praying

60 Nurse and Baby

1946. Child Welfare Fund.

313	**59**	1f.+3f. green	30	30
314		2f.+4f. red	30	30
315		4f.+6f. blue	30	30
316		5f.+40f. mauve	80	75
317		10f.+60f. red	80	75
318		15f.+100f. blue	1·25	1·25

1946. Anti-tuberculosis Fund.

319	**60**	2f.+8f. blue	40	65

1946. Air. Optd **POSTE AERIENNE** over Sud Ouest Cassiopees airplane.

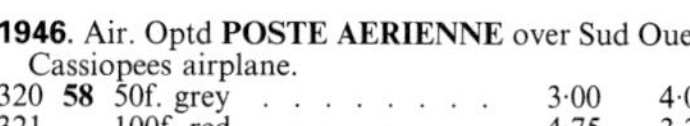

320	**58**	50f. grey	3·00	4·00
321		100f. red	4·75	3·25

62 Steamship and Chart

1946. Stamp Day.

322	**62**	3f.+2f. blue	30	40

63

1946. Air.

323	**63**	40f. red	60	75
324		50f. brown	1·50	90
325		100f. green	2·50	1·75
326		200f. violet	2·50	2·00
326a		300f. blue and ultramarine	55·00	50·00
326b		500f. green and deep green	35·00	30·00
326c		1000f. violet and brown	60·00	55·00

64 Pres. Roosevelt and Palace of Monaco

66 Pres. Roosevelt

1946. President Roosevelt Commemoration.

327	**66**	10c. mauve (postage)	30	25
328	–	30c. blue	30	15
329	**64**	60c. green	30	25
330	–	1f. sepia	80	85
331	–	2f.+3f. green	80	95
332	–	3f. violet	1·25	1·25
333	–	5f. red (air)	40	50
334	–	10f. black	70	45
335	**66**	15f.+10f. orange	1·50	1·25

DESIGNS—HORIZ: 30c., 5f. Rock of Monaco; 2f. Viaduct and St. Devote. VERT: 1, 3, 10f. Map of Monaco.

67 Prince Louis II

68 Pres. Roosevelt as a Philatelist

69 Statue of Liberty and New York Harbour

1947. Participation in the Centenary International Philatelic Exhibition, New York. (a) Postage.

336	**67**	10f. blue	3·25	3·25

(b) Air. Dated "1847 1947"

337	**68**	50c. violet	80	90
338	–	1f.50 mauve	30	40
339	–	3f. orange	40	45
340	–	10f. blue	2·75	2·75
341	**69**	15f. red	4·50	4·50

DESIGNS—HORIZ: As Type **68**: 1f.50, G.P.O., New York; 3f. Oceanographic Museum, Monte Carlo. As Type **69**: 10f. Bay of Monaco.

70 Prince Charles III

1948. Stamp Day.

342	**70**	6f.+4f. green on blue	40	40

71 Diving

72 Tennis

1948. Olympic Games, Wembley. Inscr "JEUX OLYMPIQUES 1948".

343	–	50c. green (postage)	20	20
344	–	1f. red	20	20
345	–	2f. blue	70	55
346	–	2f.50 red	1·75	3·50
347	**71**	4f. slate	1·90	1·75
348	–	5f.+5f. brown (air)	7·25	7·25
349	–	6f.+9f. violet	12·00	10·00
350	**72**	10f.+15f. red	20·00	18·00
351	–	15f.+25f. blue	24·00	25·00

DESIGNS—HORIZ: 50c. Hurdling; 15f. Yachting. VERT: 1f. Running; 2f. Throwing the discus; 2f.50, Basketball; 5f. Rowing; 6f. Skiing.

75 The Salmacis Nymph

77 F. J. Bosio (wrongly inscr "J. F.")

1948. Death Centenary of Francois Joseph Bosio (sculptor).

352	**75**	50c. green (postage)	40	25
353	–	1f. red	40	25
354	–	2f. blue	80	55
355	–	2f.50 violet	2·25	1·60
356	**77**	4f. mauve	2·25	1·90
357	–	5f.+5f. blue (air)	12·00	14·00
358	–	6f.+9f. green	12·00	14·00
359	–	10f.+15f. red	13·00	14·00
360	–	15f.+25f. brown	16·00	18·00

DESIGNS—VERT: 1, 5f. Hercules struggling with Achelous; 2, 6f. Aristaeus (Garden God); 15f. The Salmacis Nymph (36×48 mm). HORIZ: 2f.50, 10f. Hyacinthus awaiting his turn to throw a quoit.

79 Exotic Gardens

80 "Princess Alice II"

1949. Birth Centenary of Prince Albert I.

375	–	2f. blue (postage)	20	20
376	**79**	3f. green	20	20
377	–	4f. brown and blue	30	25
378	**80**	5f. red	80	85
379	–	6f. violet	50	55
380	–	10f. sepia	70	1·85
381	–	12f. pink	1·40	1·40
382	–	18f. orange and brown	2·50	2·75
383	–	20f. brown (air)	50	65
384	–	25f. blue	50	65
385	–	40f. green	95	1·40
386	–	50f. green, brown and black	1·50	1·75
387	–	100f. red	5·75	6·50
388	–	200f. orange	11·00	10·50

DESIGNS—HORIZ: 2f. Yacht "Hirondelle I" (1870); 4f. Oceanographic Museum, Monaco; 10f. "Hirondelle II" (1914); 12f. Albert harpooning whale; 18f. Buffalo (Palaeolithic mural); 20f. Constitution Day, 1911; 25f. Paris Institute of Palaeontology; 200f. Coin with effigy of Albert. VERT: 6f. Statue of Albert at tiller; 40f. Anthropological Museum; 50f. Prince Albert I; 100f. Oceanographic Institute, Paris.

83 Palace of Monaco and Globe

1949. 75th Anniv of U.P.U.

410	**83**	5f. green (postage)	30	35
411		10f. orange	3·50	4·00
412		15f. red	45	55
413		25f. blue (air)	50	55
414		40f. sepia and brown	1·50	1·60
415		50f. blue and green	2·50	2·75
416		100f. blue and red	3·50	4·00

84 Prince Rainier III and Monaco Palace

85 Prince Rainier III

1950. Accession of Prince Rainier III.

417	**84**	10c. purple & red (postage)	10	10
418		50c. brown, lt brn & orge	10	10
419		1f. violet	20	25
420		5f. deep green and green	1·60	1·40
421		15f. carmine and red	3·00	3·00
422		25f. blue, green & ultram	3·00	3·75
423		50f. brown and black (air)	4·75	5·25
424		100f. blue, dp brn & brn	7·75	6·75

1950.

425	**85**	50c. violet	20	10
426		1f. brown	20	10
434		5f. green	6·75	3·75
427		6f. green	95	60
428		8f. green	4·50	1·75
429		8f. orange	1·10	70
435		10f. orange	10·50	5·50
430		12f. blue	1·10	30
431		15f. red	2·00	50
432		15f. blue	1·40	40
433		18f. red	3·50	1·10

86 Prince Albert I

87 Edmond and Jules de Goncourt

1951. Unveiling of Prince Albert Statue.

436	**86**	15f. blue	5·75	5·75

1951. 50th Anniv of Goncourt Academy.

437	**87**	15f. purple	5·75	5·25

88 St. Vincent de Paul

90 St. Peter's Keys and Papal Bull

89 Judgement of St. Devote

1951. Holy Year.

438	**88**	10c. blue, ultramarine & red	20	20
439	–	50c. violet and red	20	20
440	**89**	1f. green and brown	20	25
441	**90**	2f. red and purple	30	45
442	–	5f. green	30	30
443	–	12f. violet	40	45
444	–	15f. red	3·00	3·00
445	–	20f. brown	4·50	5·25
446	–	25f. blue	5·75	7·25
447	–	40f. violet and mauve	7·75	8·25

448 – 50f. brown and olive . . . 9·50 11·00
449 – 100f. brown . . . . . . 20·00 22·00
DESIGNS—TRIANGULAR: 50c. Pope Pius XII. HORIZ (as Type **90**): 5f. Mosaic. VERT (as Type **90**): 12f. Prince Rainier III in St. Peter's; 15f. St. Nicholas of Patara; 20f. St. Romain; 25f. St. Charles Borromeo; 40f. Coliseum; 50f. Chapel of St. Devote. VERT (as Type **89**): 100f. Rainier of Westphalia.

93 Wireless Mast and Monaco
94 Seal of Prince Rainier III

1951. Monte Carlo Radio Station.
450 **93** 1f. orange, red and blue . . 50 25
451 15f. purple, red and violet 2·50 80
452 30f. brown and blue . . . 11·50 4·50

1951.
453 **94** 1f. violet 60 50
454 5f. black . . . . 2·10 1·40
512 5f. violet . . . . 3·00 70
513 6f. red . . . . 3·50 1·10
455 8f. red . . . . 5·25 3·00
514 8f. brown . . . . 4·00 2·75
456 15f. green . . . . 7·75 5·75
515 15f. blue . . . . 11·50 3·50
457 30f. blue . . . . 15·00 11·50
516 30f. green . . . . 14·50 11·00

95 Gallery of Hercules

1952. Monaco Postal Museum.
460 **95** 5f. chestnut and brown . . 30 35
461 15f. violet and purple . . . 60 35
462 30f. indigo and blue . . . 1·10 40

96 Football

1953. 15th Olympic Games, Helsinki. Inscr "HELSINKI 1952".
463 – 1f. mauve & violet (postage) 20 25
464 **96** 2f. blue and green 20 25
465 – 3f. pale and deep blue . . 20 25
466 – 5f. green and brown . . . 60 30
467 – 8f. red and lake . . . . . 1·50 85
468 – 15f. brown, green and blue 80 70
469 – 40f. black (air) . . . . . . 7·75 6·75
470 – 50f. violet . . . . 9·00 6·75
471 – 100f. green . . . . 13·00 11·00
472 – 200f. red . . . . 17·00 11·50
DESIGNS: 1f. Basketball; 3f. Sailing; 5f. Cycling; 8f. Gymnastics; 15f. Louis II Stadium, Monaco; 40f. Running; 50f. Fencing; 100f. Rifle target and Arms of Monaco; 200f. Olympic torch.

97 "Journal Inedit"

1953. Centenary of Publication of Journal by E. and J. de Goncourt.
473 **97** 5f. green 50 35
474 15f. brown . . . . 2·25 1·25

98 Physalia, Yacht "Princess Alice", Prince Albert, Richet and Portier

1953. 50th Anniv of Discovery of Anaphylaxis.
475 **98** 2f. violet, green and brown 20 20
476 5f. red, lake and green . . 50 20
477 15f. lilac, blue and green 2·25 1·25

99 F. Ozanam
100 St. Jean-Baptiste de la Salle

1954. Death Centenary of Ozanam (founder of St. Vincent de Paul Conferences).
478 **99** 1f. red 20 25
479 – 5f. blue 30 35
480 **99** 15f. black . . . . 1·50 1·25
DESIGN: 5f. Outline drawing of Sister of Charity.

1954. St. J.-B. de la Salle (educationist).
481 **100** 1f. red 20 25
482 – 5f. sepia 30 45
483 **100** 15f. blue . . . . 1·50 1·25
DESIGN: 5f. Outline drawing of De la Salle and two children.

101 **102** **103**

1954. Arms.
484 – 50c. red, black and mauve 10 10
485 – 70c. red, black and blue 10 10
486 **101** 80c. red, black and green 10 10
487 – 1f. red, black and blue . . 10 10
488 **102** 2f. red, black and orange 10 10
489 – 3f. red, black and green 10 10
490 **103** 5f. multicoloured 20 25
DESIGNS—HORIZ: 50c. as Type **101**. VERT: 70c., 1, 3f. as Type **102**.

104 Seal of Prince Rainier III
105 Lambarene

106 Dr. Albert Schweitzer

1954. Precancelled.
491 **104** 4f. red . . . . 1·25 60
492 5f. blue 30 20
493 8f. green . . . . 1·25 80
494 8f. purple 80 45
495 10f. green 20 20
496 12f. violet . . . . 4·00 2·75
497 15f. orange 80 60
498 20f. green . . . . 1·25 80
499 24f. brown . . . . 6·75 3·25
500 30f. blue . . . . 1·40 95
501 40f. brown . . . . 2·00 1·60
502 45f. red . . . . 2·00 1·25
503 55f. blue . . . . 5·00 3·50
See also Nos. 680/3.

1955. 80th Birthday of Dr. Schweitzer (humanitarian).
504 **105** 2f. grn, turq & bl (postage) 20 20
505 **106** 5f. blue and green 70 95
506 – 15f. purple, black and green . . . . 2·10 2·00
507 – 200f. slate, grn & bl (air) 22·00 25·00
DESIGNS—As Type **106**: 15f. Lambarene Hospital. HORIZ (48 × 27 mm): 200f. Schweitzer and jungle scene.

107 Great Cormorants

1955. Air.
508a – 100f. indigo and blue . . 15·00 15·00
509 – 200f. black and blue . . 17·00 9·50
510 – 500f. grey and green . . 29·00 20·00
511a **107** 1,000f. black, turq & grn 70·00 50·00
DESIGNS—As Type **107**: 100f. Roseate tern; 200f. Herring gull; 500f. Wandering albatrosses.

108 Eight Starting Points
109 Prince Rainier III

1955. 25th Monte Carlo Car Rally.
517 **108** 100f. red and brown . . . 60·00 60·00

1955.
518 **109** 6f. purple and green . . . 30 25
519 8f. violet and red 30 25
520 12f. green and red 30 25
521 15f. blue and purple . . . 70 25
522 18f. blue and orange . . . 3·00 25
523 20f. turquoise . . . . . . 1·40 45
524 25f. black and orange . . 70 40
525 30f. sepia and blue . . . 9·75 5·00
526 30f. violet . . . . 3·00 1·75
527 35f. brown . . . . 2·50 1·90
528 50f. lake and green . . . 3·50 1·25
See also Nos. 627/41.

110 "La Maison a Vapeur"

111 "The 500 Millions of the Begum"
113 U.S.S. "Nautilus"

112 "Round the World in Eighty Days"

1955. 50th Death Anniv of Jules Verne (author). Designs illustrating his works.
529 – 1f. blue & brown (postage) 10 10
530 – 2f. sepia, indigo and blue 10 10
531 **110** 3f. blue, black and brown 30 30
532 – 5f. sepia and red 30 30
533 **111** 6f. grey and sepia 70 60
534 – 8f. turquoise and olive . . 30 30
535 – 10f. sepia, turquoise & ind 70 60
536 **112** 15f. red and brown . . . 60 50
537 – 25f. black and green . . . 1·75 1·25
538 **113** 30f. black, purple & turq 4·00 3·25
539 – 200f. indigo and blue (air) 21·00 20·00
DESIGNS—VERT (as Type **111**): 1f. "Five Weeks in a Balloon". HORIZ (as Type **110**): 2f. "A Floating Island"; 10f. "Journey to the Centre of the Earth"; 25f. "20,000 Leagues under the Sea"; 200f. "From the Earth to the Moon". (as Type **111**): 5f. "Michael Strogoff"; 8f. "Le Superbe Orenoque".

114 "The Immaculate Virgin" (F. Brea)

1955. Marian Year.
540 **114** 5f. green, grey and brown 20 20
541 – 10f. green, grey and brown 30 30
542 – 15f. brown and sepia . . 40 40
DESIGNS—As Type **114**: 10f. "Madonna" (L. Brea). As Type **113**: 15f. Bienheureux Rainier.

115 Rotary Emblem

1955. 50th Anniv of Rotary International.
543 **115** 30f. blue and yellow . . . 70 85

116 George Washington
118 President Eisenhower

117 Abraham Lincoln

1956. 5th International Stamp Exhibition, New York.
544 **116** 1f. violet and lilac 10 10
545 – 2f. lilac and purple . . . 20 20
546 **117** 3f. blue and violet 20 20
547 **118** 5f. red 20 20
548 – 15f. brown and chocolate 50 40
549 – 30f. black, indigo and blue . . . . 2·25 1·25
550 – 40f. brown . . . . 3·00 1·50
551 – 50f. red . . . . 3·50 1·50
552 – 100f. green . . . . 3·50 2·50
DESIGNS—As Type **117**: 2f. F. D. Roosevelt. HORIZ (as Type **116**): 15f. Monaco Palace in the 18th century; 30f. Landing of Columbus. (48 × 36 mm): 50f. Aerial view of Monaco Palace in the 18th century; 100f. Louisiana landscape in 18th century. VERT (as Type **118**): 40f. Prince Rainier III.

120

1956. 7th Winter Olympic Games, Cortina d'Ampezzo and 16th Olympic Games, Melbourne.
553 – 15f. brown, green & pur . . . 80 60
554 **120** 30f. red . . . . 1·40 1·40
DESIGN: 15f. "Italia" ski-jump.

1956. Nos. D482/95 with "TIMBRE TAXE" barred out and some surch also. (a) Postage.
555 2f. on 4f. slate and brown . . 30 30
556 2f. on 4f. brown and slate . . 30 30
557 3f. lake and green 30 30
558 3f. green and lake 30 30
559 5f. on 4f. slate and brown . . 50 40
560 5f. on 4f. brown and slate . . 50 40
561 10f. on 4f. slate and brown 70 60
562 10f. on 4f. brown and slate 70 60
563 15f. on 5f. violet and blue . . 1·10 1·40
564 15f. on 5f. blue and violet . . 1·10 1·40
565 20f. violet and blue . . . . . 1·75 2·25
566 20f. blue and violet . . . . . 1·75 2·25
567 25f. on 20f. violet and blue 3·50 2·50
568 25f. on 20f. blue and violet 3·50 2·50
569 30f. on 10f. indigo and blue 5·50 4·00
570 30f. on 10f. blue and indigo 5·50 4·00
571 40f. on 50f. brown and red 7·75 6·00
572 40f. on 50f. red and brown 7·75 6·00
573 50f. on 100f. green and purple . . . . 11·00 8·75
574 50f. on 100f. purple and green . . . . 11·00 8·75
(b) Air. Optd **POSTE AERIENNE** also.
575 100f. on 20f. violet and blue 6·75 7·75
576 100f. on 20f. blue and violet 6·75 7·75

121 Route Map from Glasgow

1956. 26th Monte Carlo Car Rally.
577 **121** 100f. brown and red . . . 17·00 19·00

122 Princess Grace and Prince Rainier III

1956. Royal Wedding.
578 **122** 1f. black & grn (postage) 10 10
579 2f. black and red 10 10
580 3f. black and blue 10 20
581 5f. black and green . . . 20 25
582 15f. black and brown . . 20 40
583 100f. brown & purple (air) 60 40
584 200f. brown and red . . . 60 40
585 500f. brown and grey . . 2·00 1·60

123 Princess Grace **124** Princess Grace with Princess Caroline

1957. Birth of Princess Caroline.
586 **123** 1f. grey 10 10
587 2f. olive 10 10
588 3f. brown 10 10
589 5f. red 20 20
590 15f. pink 20 25
591 25f. blue 60 55
592 30f. violet 60 55
593 50f. red . . . . 1·10 65
594 75f. orange . . . . 2·00 1·60

1958. Birth of Prince Albert.
595 **124** 100f. black . . . . 5·50 4·00

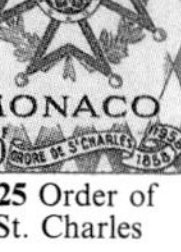

125 Order of St. Charles **126** Route Map from Munich

1958. Centenary of Creation of National Order of St. Charles.
596 **125** 100f. multicoloured . . . 1·50 1·60

1958. 27th Monte Carlo Rally.
597 **126** 100f. multicoloured . . . 5·00 5·50

127 Statue of the Holy Virgin and Popes Pius IX and Pius XII

1958. Centenary of Apparition of Virgin Mary at Lourdes.
598 **127** 1f. grey & brown (postage) 10 10
599 – 2f. violet and blue 10 10
600 – 3f. sepia and green . . . 10 10
601 – 5f. blue and sepia 10 10
602 – 8f. multicoloured 20 25
603 – 10f. multicoloured 20 20
604 – 12f. multicoloured 30 25
605 – 20f. myrtle and purple . . 30 25
606 – 35f. myrtle, bistre and brown 40 35
607 – 50f. blue, green and lake 60 55
608 – 65f. turquoise and blue 80 70
609 – 100f. grey, myrtle and blue (air) . . . . . . 1·40 1·10
610 – 200f. brown and chestnut 1·90 1·75
DESIGNS—VERT ($26\frac{1}{2} \times 36$ mm): 2f. St. Bernadette; 3f. St. Bernadette at Bartres; 5f. The Miracle of Bourriette; 20f. St. Bernadette at prayer; 35f. St. Bernadette's canonization. (22×36 mm): 8f. Stained-glass window. As Type **127**: 50f. St. Bernadette, Pope Pius XI, Mgr. Laurence and Abbe Peyramale. HORIZ (48×36 mm): 10f. Lourdes grotto; 12f. Interior of Lourdes grotto. ($36 \times 26\frac{1}{2}$ mm): 65f. Shrine of St. Bernadette; (48×27 mm): 100f. Lourdes Basilica; 200f. Pope Pius X and subterranean interior of Basilica.

128 Princess Grace and Clinic

1959. Opening of new Hospital Block in "Princess Grace" Clinic, Monaco.
611 **128** 100f. grey, brown & green 2·50 1·50

129 U.N.E.S.C.O. Headquarters, Paris, and Cultural Emblems

1959. Inaug of U.N.E.S.C.O. Headquarters Building.
612 **129** 25f. multicoloured 20 20
613 – 50f. turquoise, black & ol 30 35
DESIGN: 50f. As Type **129** but with heads of children and letters of various alphabets in place of the emblems.

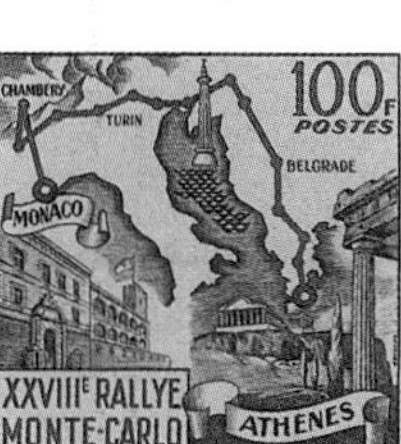

130 Route Map from Athens

1959. 28th Monte Carlo Rally.
614 **130** 100f. blue, red & grn on bl . . . . 4·50 3·50

131 Prince Rainier and Princess Grace

1959. Air.
615 **131** 300f. violet . . . . 9·50 6·75
616 500f. blue . . . . 14·50 12·50
See also Nos. 642/3.

132 "Princess Caroline" Carnation

1959. Flowers.
617 **132** 5f. mauve, green & brown 10 10
618 – 10f. on 3f. pink, green and brown 10 10
619 – 15f. on 1f. yellow & green 20 25
620 – 20f. purple and green . . 50 40
621 – 25f. on 6f. red, yellow and green 70 65
622 – 35f. pink and green . . . 1·40 1·60
623 – 50f. green and sepia . . . 2·25 1·75
624 – 85f. on 65f. lavender, bronze and green . . . 2·75 2·00
625 – 100f. red and green . . . 4·50 3·00
FLOWERS—As Type **132**: 10f. "Princess Grace" carnation; 100f. "Grace of Monaco" rose. VERT (22×36 mm): 15f. Mimosa; 25f. Geranium. HORIZ (36×22 mm): 20f. Bougainvillea; 35f. "Laurier" rose; 50f. Jasmine; 85f. Lavender.

(New currency. 100 (old) francs = 1 (new franc.)

133 "Uprooted Tree" **134** Oceanographic Museum

1960. World Refugee Year.
626 **133** 25c. green, blue and black 20 25

1960. Prince Rainier types with values in new currency.
627 **109** 25c. blk & orge (postage) 30 10
628 30c. violet 40 10
629 40c. red and brown . . . 40 20
630 45c. brown and grey . . . 40 20
631 50c. red and green 50 25
632 50c. red and brown . . . 50 30
633 60c. brown and green . . 1·25 40
634 60c. brown and purple . . 1·60 55
635 65c. blue and brown . . . 9·25 4·00
636 70c. blue and plum . . . 1·00 55
637 85c. green and violet . . . 1·40 90
638 95c. blue 95 85
639 1f.10 blue and brown . . 2·00 1·60
640 1f.30 brown and red . . . 2·40 1·75
641 2f.30 purple and orange 2·00 65
642 **131** 3f. violet (air) . . . . . 35·00 14·00
643 5f. blue . . . . 35·00 20·00

1960.
644 – 5c. green, black and blue 15 15
645 **134** 10c. brown and blue . . . 30 25
646 – 10c. blue, violet and green 15 10
647 – 40c. purple, grn & dp grn 55 20
648 – 45c. brown, green and blue . . . . 4·50 60
649 – 70c. brown, red and green 40 30
650 – 80c. red, green and blue 1·40 60
651 – 85c. black, brown and grey . . . . 6·00 1·90
652 – 90c. red, blue and black 1·50 65
653 – 1f. multicoloured . . . . 1·25 30
654 – 1f.15 black, red and blue 2·10 1·25
655 – 1f.30 brown, green & blue 75 55
656 – 1f.40 orange, green & vio 2·25 1·90
DESIGNS—HORIZ: 5c. Palace of Monaco; 10c. (No. 646), Aquatic Stadium; 40, 45, 80c., 1f.40, Aerial view of Palace; 70, 85, 90c., 1f.15, 1f.30, Court of Honour, Monaco Palace; 1f. Palace floodlit.

134a St. Devote

1960. Air.
668 **134a** 2f. violet, blue and green 1·25 90
669 3f. brown, green and blue . . . . 1·90 1·25
670 5f. red . . . . 3·50 1·75
671 10f. brown, grey and green . . . . 5·00 3·25

135 Long-snouted Seahorse **136** Route Map from Lisbon

1960. Marine Life and Plants. (a) Marine Life.
672 – 1c. red and turquoise . . 10 10
673 – 12c. brown and blue . . . 35 20
674 **135** 15c. green and red 45 20
675 – 20c. multicoloured 55 20
DESIGNS—HORIZ: 1c. "Macrocheira kampferi" (crab); 20c. Lionfish. VERT: 12c. Trapezium horse conch.
(b) Plants.
676 – 2c. multicoloured 25 10
677 – 15c. orange, brown and olive 60 10
678 – 18c. multicoloured 45 10
679 – 20c. red, olive and brown 45 20
PLANTS—VERT: 2c. "Selenicereus sp."; 15c. "Cereus sp."; 18c. "Aloe ciliaris"; 20c. "Nopalea dejecta".

1960. Prince Rainier Seal type with values in new currency. Precancelled.
680 **104** 8c. purple . . . . 1·40 70
681 20c. green . . . . 1·75 85
682 40c. brown . . . . 3·50 1·40
683 55c. blue . . . . 5·00 2·75

1960. 29th Monte Carlo Rally.
684 **136** 25c. black, red & bl on bl 1·50 1·50

137 Stamps of Monaco 1885, France and Sardinia, 1860

1960. 75th Anniv of First Monaco Stamp.
685 **137** 25c. bistre, blue and violet 70 75

138 Aquarium

1960. 50th Anniv of Oceanographic Museum, Monaco.
686 – 5c. black, blue and purple 30 25
687 **138** 10c. grey, brown and green 40 30
688 – 15c. black, bistre and blue 40 30
689 – 20c. black, blue and mauve 70 40
690 – 25c. turquoise . . . . . 1·50 1·00
691 – 50c. brown and blue . . . 1·75 1·75
DESIGNS—VERT: 5c. Oceanographic Museum (similar to Type **134**). HORIZ: 15c. Conference Hall; 20c. Hauling-in catch; 25c. Museum, aquarium and underwater research equipment; 50c. Prince Albert, "Hirondelle I" (schooner) and "Princess Alice" (steam yacht).

139 Horse-jumping

1960. Olympic Games.
692 **139** 5c. brown, red and green 10 10
693 – 10c. brown, blue and green 20 25
694 – 15c. red, brown and purple 20 25
695 – 20c. black, blue and green 2·00 2·25
696 – 25c. purple, turq & grn 70 60
697 – 50c. purple, blue & turq 1·10 90
DESIGNS: 10c. Swimming; 15c. Long-jumping; 20c. Throwing the javelin; 25c. Free-skating; 50c. Skiing.

140 Rally Badge, Old and Modern Cars

1961. 50th Anniv of Monte Carlo Rally.
698 **140** 1f. violet, red and brown 1·40 1·40

MONACO 1961 1er CONGRES MONDIAL D'AQUARIOLOGIE NOV. 1960 0,25

141 Route Map from Stockholm **142** Marine Life

1961. 30th Monte Carlo Rally.
699 **141** 1f. multicoloured 80 90

1961. World Aquariological Congress. Orange network background.
700 **142** 25c. red, sepia and violet 20 25

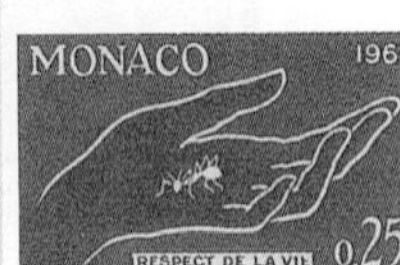

143 Leper in Town of Middle Ages **145** Insect within Protective Hand

144 Semi-submerged Sphinx of Ouadi-es-Saboua

1961. Sovereign Order of Malta.
701 **143** 25c. black, red and brown 20 25

1961. U.N.E.S.C.O. Campaign for Preservation of Nubian Monuments.
702 **144** 50c. purple, blue & brown 70 75

1962. Nature Preservation.
703 **145** 25c. mauve and purple . . 20 25

146 Chevrolet, 1912

1961. Veteran Motor Cars.
704 **146** 1c. brown, green and chestnut 10 10
705 – 2c. blue, purple and red 10 10
706 – 3c. purple, black and mauve 10 10
707 – 4c. blue, brown and violet 10 10
708 – 5c. green, red and olive 10 10
709 – 10c. brown, red and blue 10 10
710 – 15c. green and turquoise 20 25
711 – 20c. brown, red and violet 20 25
712 – 25c. violet, red and brown 30 35
713 – 30c. lilac and green . . . 70 80
714 – 45c. green, purple and brown . . . . 1·50 1·90
715 – 50c. blue, red and brown 1·50 1·90
716 – 65c. brown, red and grey 2·25 1·75
717 – 1f. blue, red and violet . . 2·50 2·75
MOTOR CARS: 2c. Peugeot, 1898; 3c. Fiat, 1901; 4c. Mercedes, 1901; 5c. Rolls Royce, 1903;. 10c. Panhard-Lavassor, 1899; 15c. Renault, 1898; 20c. Ford "N", 1906 (wrongly inscr "FORD-S-1908"); 25c. Rochet-Schneider, 1894; 30c. FN-Herstal, 1901; 45c. De Dion Bouton, 1900; 50c. Buick, 1910; 65c. Delahaye, 1901; 1f. Cadillac, 1906.

147 Racing Car and Race Route

1962. 20th Monaco Motor Grand Prix.
718 **147** 1f. purple . . . . 1·25 90

148 Route Map from Oslo

1962. 31st Monte Carlo Rally.
719 **148** 1f. multicoloured 95 80

149 Louis XII and Lucien Grimaldi

1962. 450th Anniv of Recognition of Monegasque Sovereignty by Louis XII.
720 **149** 25c. black, red and blue 20 25
721 – 50c. brown, lake and blue 30 30
722 – 1f. red, green and brown 50 55
DESIGNS: 50c. Parchment bearing declaration of sovereignty; 1f. Seals of two Sovereigns.

150 Mosquito and Swamp

1962. Malaria Eradication.
723 **150** 1f. green and olive . . . 40 45

151 Sun, Bouquet and "Hope Chest"

1962. National Multiple Sclerosis Society, New York.
724 **151** 20c. multicoloured 20 20

152 Harvest Scene

1962. Europa.
725 **152** 25c. brown, green and blue (postage) 10 10
726 50c. olive and turquoise 20 25
727 1f. olive and purple . . . 40 50
728 – 2f. slate, brown & green (air) 90 90
DESIGN: 2f. Mercury in flight over Europe.

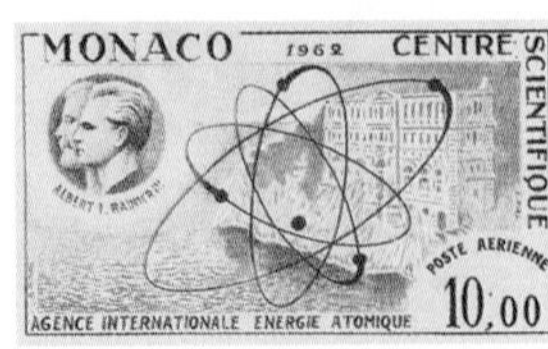

153 Atomic Symbol and Scientific Centre, Monaco

1962. Air. Scientific Centre, Monaco.
729 **153** 10f. violet, brown and blue . . . . 4·75 4·75

154 Yellow Wagtails **155** Galeazzi's Diving Turret

1962. Protection of Birds useful to Agriculture.
730 **154** 5c. yellow, brown & green 10 20
731 – 10c. red, bistre and purple 10 20
732 – 15c. multicoloured 25 20
733 – 20c. sepia, green & mauve 30 30
734 – 25c. multicoloured 40 35
735 – 30c. brown, blue & myrtle 55 45
736 – 45c. brown and violet . . 95 90
737 – 50c. black, olive & turq 1·25 1·10
738 – 85c. multicoloured . . . . 1·75 1·50
739 – 1f. sepia, red and green 2·00 1·75
BIRDS: 10c. European robins; 15c. Eurasian goldfinches; 20c. Blackcaps; 25c. Greater spotted woodpeckers; 30c. Nightingale; 45c. Barn owls; 50c. Common starlings; 85c. Red crossbills; 1f. White storks.

1962. Underwater Exploration.
740 – 5c. black, violet and blue 10 10
741 **155** 10c. blue, violet and brown 10 10
742 – 25c. bistre, green and blue 10 10
743 – 45c. black, blue and green 30 35
744 – 50c. green, bistre and blue 50 55
745 – 85c. blue and turquoise 80 85
746 – 1f. brown, green and blue 1·40 1·25
DESIGNS—HORIZ: 5c. Divers; 25c. Williamson's photosphere (1914) and bathyscaphe "Trieste"; 45c. Klingert's diving-suit (1797) and modern diving-suit; 50c. Diving saucer; 85c. Fulton's "Nautilus" (1800) and modern submarine; 1f. Alexander the Great's diving bell and Beebe's bathysphere.

156 Donor's Arm and Globe **158** Feeding Chicks in Nest

157 "Ring-a-ring o' Roses"

1962. 3rd Int Blood Donors' Congress Monaco.
747 **156** 1f. red, sepia and orange 50 65

1963. U.N. Children's Charter.
748 **157** 5c. red, blue and ochre . . 10 10
749 **158** 10c. green, sepia and blue 10 10
750 – 15c. blue, red and green 10 20
751 – 20c. multicoloured 10 20
752 – 25c. blue, purple & brown 25 25
753 – 50c. multicoloured 50 35
754 – 95c. multicoloured 80 55
755 – 1f. purple, red & turquoise . . . . 1·75 1·10
DESIGNS—As Type **157**: 1f. Prince Albert and Princess Caroline; Children's paintings as Type **158**: HORIZ: 15c. Children on scales; 50c. House and child. VERT: 20c. Sun's rays and children of three races; 25c. Mother and child; 95c. Negress and child.

159 Ship's Figurehead

1963. International Red Cross Centenary.
756 **159** 50c. red, brown & turquoise 30 35
757 – 1f. multicoloured 55 60
DESIGN—HORIZ: 1f. Moynier, Dunant and Dufour.

160 Racing Cars

1963. European Motor Grand Prix.
758 **160** 50c. multicoloured 55 40

161 Emblem and Charter

1963. Founding of Lions Club of Monaco.
759 **161** 50c. blue, bistre and violet 80 65

162 Hotel des Postes and U.P.U. Monument, Berne

1963. Paris Postal Conference Centenary.
760 **162** 50c. lake, green and yellow 30 45

163 "Telstar" Satellite and Globe

1963. 1st Link Trans-Atlantic T.V. Satellite.
761 **163** 50c. brown, green & purple 45 45

164 Route Map from Warsaw

1963. 32nd Monte Carlo Rally.
762 **164** 1f. multicoloured . . . . 1·00 1·10

165 Feeding Chicks

1963. Freedom from Hunger.
763 **165** 1f. multicoloured 50 50

166 Allegory

1963. 2nd Ecumenical Council, Vatican City.
764 **166** 1f. turquoise, green and red 45 45

167 Henry Ford and Ford "A" Car of 1903

1963. Birth Centenary of Henry Ford (motor pioneer).
765 **167** 20c. green and purple . . 25 25

168 H. Garin (winner of 1903 race) cycling through Village

1963. 50th "Tour de France" Cycle Race.
766 **168** 25c. green, brown and blue 30 30
767 – 50c. sepia, green and blue 30 35
DESIGN: 50c. Cyclist passing Desgrange Monument, Col du Galibier, 1963.

169 P. de Coubertin and Discus-thrower

1963. Birth Centenary of Pierre de Coubertin (reviver of Olympic Games).
768 **169** 1f. brown, red and lake 40 60

170 Roland Garros and Morane Saulnier Type I

1963. Air. 50th Anniv of 1st Aerial Crossing of Mediterranean Sea.
769 **170** 2f. sepia and blue . . . . 1·25 90

171 Route Map from Paris **173** "Europa"

172 Children with Stamp Album

1963. 33rd Monte Carlo Rally.
770 **171** 1f. red, turquoise and blue 80 70

1963. "Scolatex" International Stamp Exn, Monaco.
771 **172** 50c. blue, violet and red 20 25

1963. Europa.
772 **173** 25c. brown, red and green 30 25
773 50c. sepia, red and blue 50 50

174 Wembley Stadium

1963. Cent of (English) Football Association.
774 **174** 1c. violet, green and red 10 10
775 – 2c. red, black and green 10 10
776 – 3c. orange, olive and red 10 10
777 – 4c. multicoloured 10 10

Multicoloured horiz designs depicting (a) "Football through the Centuries".
778 10c. "Calcio", Florence (16th cent) 10 10
779 15c. "Soule", Brittany (19th cent) 10 10
780 20c. English military college (after Cruickshank, 1827) 10 10
781 25c. English game (after Overend, 1890) 10 10

(b) "Modern Football".
782 30c. Tackling 20 20
783 50c. Saving goal 50 50
784 95c. Heading ball 70 70
785 1f. Corner kick . . . . . . 1·00 1·00

DESIGNS—As Type **174**: 4c. Louis II Stadium, Monaco. This stamp is optd in commemoration of the Association Sportive de Monaco football teams in the French Championships and in the Coupe de France, 1962–63. HORIZ (36 × 22 mm): 2c. Footballer making return kick; 3c. Goalkeeper saving ball.

Nos. 778/81 and 782/5 were respectively issued together in sheets and arranged in blocks of 4 with a football in the centre of each block.

175 Communications in Ancient Egypt, and Rocket

1964. "PHILATEC 1964" Int Stamp Exn, Paris.
786 **175** 1f. brown, indigo and blue 40 40

176 Reproduction of Rally Postcard Design

1964. 50th Anniv of 1st Aerial Rally, Monte Carlo.
787 **176** 1c. olive, blue & grn (postage) 10 10
788 – 2c. bistre, brown and blue 10 10
789 – 3c. brown, blue and green 10 10
790 – 4c. red, turquoise and blue 10 10
791 – 5c. brown, red and violet 10 10
792 – 10c. violet, brown and blue 10 10
793 – 15c. orange, brown and blue 10 10
794 – 20c. sepia, green and blue 20 10
795 – 25c. brown, blue and red 30 10
796 – 30c. myrtle, purple and blue 40 20
797 – 45c. sepia, turquoise and brown 70 30
798 – 50c. ochre, olive and violet 70 45
799 – 65c. red, slate and turquoise 70 85
800 – 95c. turquoise, red and bistre . . . . 1·25 95
801 – 1f. brown, blue and turquoise . . . . 1·60 1·25
802 – 5f. sepia, blue and brown (air) . . . . 2·40 2·40

DESIGNS: 48 × 27 mm—Rally planes: 2c. Renaux's Farman M.F.7 floatplane; 3c. Espanet's Nieuport 4 seaplane; 4c. Moineau's Breguet HU-3 seaplane; 5c. Roland Garros' Morane Saulnier Type I seaplane; 10c. Hirth's WDD Albatros seaplane; 15c. Prevost's Deperdussin Monocoque Racer. Famous planes and flights: 20c. Vickers-Vimy (Ross Smith: London–Port Darwin, 1919); 25c. Douglas World Cruiser seaplane (U.S. World Flight, 1924); 30c. Savoia Marchetti S-55M flying boat "Santa Maria" (De Pinedo's World Flight, 1925); 45c. Fokker F. VIIa/3m "Josephine Ford" (Flight over North Pole, Byrd and Bennett, 1925); 50c. Ryan NYP Special "Spirit of St. Louis" (1st solo crossing of N. Atlantic, Lindbergh, 1927); 65c. Breguet 19 "Point d'Interrogation" (Paris–New York, Coste and Bellonte, 1930); 95c. Latecoere 28-3 seaplane "Comte de la Vaulx" (Dakar–Natal, first S. Atlantic airmail flight, Mermoz, 1930); 1f. Dornier Do-X flying boat (Germany–Rio de Janeiro, Christiansen, 1930); 5f. Convair B-58 Hustler (New York–Paris in 3 hours, 19' 41" Major Payne, U.S.A.F., 1961).

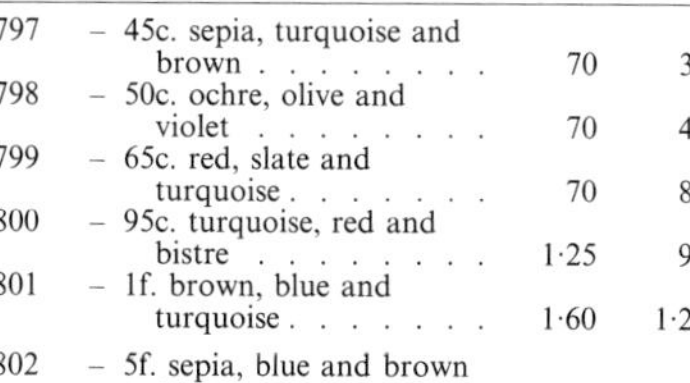

177 Aquatic Stadium **178** Europa "Flower"

1964. Precancelled.
803 **177** 10c. multicoloured . . . 1·40 90
803a 15c. multicoloured . . . 70 50
804 25c. turquoise, blue & blk 70 50
805 50c. violet, turq & blk 1·40 70

The "1962" date has been obliterated with two bars.

See also Nos. 949/51a and 1227/30.

1964. Europa.
806 **178** 25c. red, green and blue 20 25
807 50c. brown, bistre and blue 35 50

179 Weightlifting

1964. Olympic Games, Tokyo and Innsbruck.
808 **179** 1c. red, brown and blue (postage) 10 10
809 – 2c. red, green and olive 10 10
810 – 3c. blue, brown and red 10 10
811 – 4c. green, olive and red 10 10
812 – 5f. red, brown and blue (air) . . . . 2·00 1·90

DESIGNS: 2c. Judo; 3c. Pole vaulting; 4c. Archery; 5f. Bobsleighing.

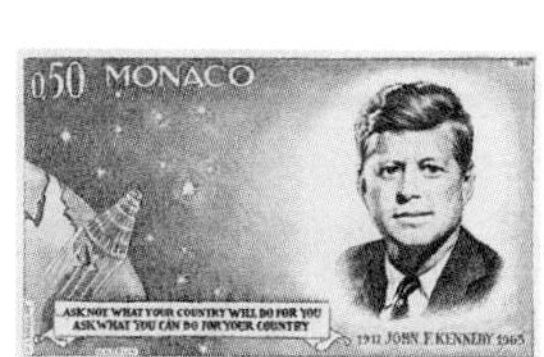

180 Pres. Kennedy and Space Capsule

1964. Pres. Kennedy Commemoration.
813 **180** 50c. indigo and blue . . . 40 50

181 Monaco and Television Set

1964. 5th Int Television Festival, Monte Carlo.
814 **181** 50c. brown, blue and red 30 40

182 F. Mistral and Statue

1964. 50th Death Anniv of Frederic Mistral (poet).
815 **182** 1f. brown and olive . . . 40 50

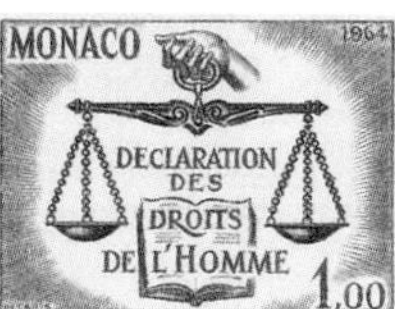

183 Scales of Justice

1964. 15th Anniv of Declaration of Human Rights.
816 **183** 1f. green and brown . . . 40 50

184 Route Map from Minsk

1964. 34th Monte Carlo Rally.
817 **184** 1f. brown, turq & ochre 70 70

185 FIFA Emblem

1964. 60th Anniv of Federation Internationale de Football Association (FIFA).
818 **185** 1f. bistre, blue and red . . 60 65

186 "Syncom 2" and Globe

1965. Centenary of I.T.U.
819 **186** 5c. grn & ultram (postage) 10 10
820 – 10c. chestnut, brown & bl 10 10
821 – 12c. purple, red and grey 10 10
822 – 18c. blue, red and purple 10 20
823 – 25c. violet, bistre & purple 10 20
824 – 30c. bistre, brown & sepia 20 25
825 – 50c. blue and green . . . 30 35
826 – 60c. blue and brown . . . 40 45
827 – 70c. sepia, orange and blue 60 60
828 – 95c. black, indigo and blue 80 80
829 – 1f. brown and blue . . . 95 90
830 – 10f. green, bl & brn (air) 1·60 2·50

DESIGNS—HORIZ (as Type **186**): 10c. "Echo 2"; 18c. "Lunik 3"; 30c. A. G. Bell and telephone; 50c. S. Morse and telegraph; 60c. E. Belin and "belinograph". (48½ × 27 mm): 25c. "Telstar" and Pleumeur-Bodou Station; 70c. Roman beacon and Chappe's telegraph; 95c. Cable ships "Great Eastern" and "Alsace"; 1f. E. Branly, G. Marconi and English Channel. VERT (as Type **186**): 12c. "Relay"; 10f. Monte Carlo television transmitter.

187 Europa "Sprig"

1965. Europa.
831 **187** 30c. brown and green . . 35 25
832 60c. violet and red . . . 1·00 45

188 Monaco Palace (18th cent)

1966. 750th Anniv of Monaco Palace.
833 **188** 10c. violet, green and blue 10 10
834 – 12c. bistre, blue and black 10 10
835 – 18c. green, black and blue 10 10
836 – 30c. brown, black and blue 30 30
837 – 60c. green, blue and bistre 40 55
838 – 1f.30 brown and green . . 90 1·10
DESIGNS (Different views of Palace): 12c. 17th century; 18c. 18th century; 30c. 19th century; 60c. 19th century; 1f.30, 20th century.

189 Dante

1966. 700th Anniv of Dante's Birth.
839 **189** 30c. green, deep green and red 20 25
840 – 60c. blue, turquoise & grn 40 50
841 – 70c. black, green and red 50 60
842 – 95c. blue, violet and purple 70 80
843 – 1f. turquoise, blue & dp bl 70 85
DESIGNS (Scenes from Dante's works): 60c. Dante harassed by the panther (envy); 70c. Crossing the 5th circle; 95c. Punishment of the arrogant; 1f. Invocation of St. Bernard.

190 "The Nativity"

1966. World Association of Children's Friends (A.M.A.D.E.).
844 **190** 30c. brown 20 25

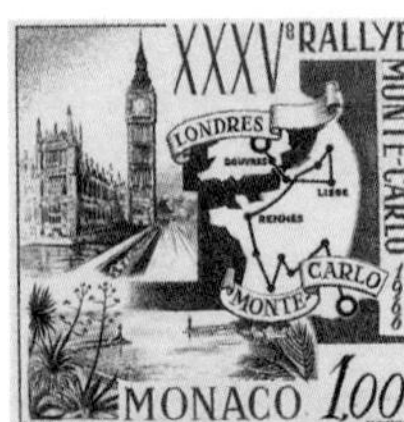

191 Route Map from London

1966. 35th Monte Carlo Rally.
845 **191** 1f. blue, purple and red 60 70

192 Princess Grace with Children

1966. Air. Princess Stephanie's 1st Birthday.
846 **192** 3f. brown, blue and violet 2·00 2·00

193 Casino in 19th Century **194** Europa "Ship"

1966. Centenary of Monte Carlo.
847 – 12c. black, red and blue (postage) 10 10
848 **193** 25c. multicoloured 10 10
849 – 30c. multicoloured 10 10
850 – 40c. multicoloured 25 25
851 – 60c. multicoloured 30 25
852 – 70c. blue and lake 30 35
853 – 95c. black and purple . . 60 60
854 – 1f.30 purple, brown and chestnut 95 80
855 – 5f. lake, ochre and blue (air) . . . . 2·00 2·00
DESIGNS—VERT: 12c. Prince Charles III. HORIZ (as Type **143**): 40c. Charles III Monument; 95c. Massenet and Saint-Saens; 1f.30, Faure and Ravel. (48 × 27 mm): 30c. F. Blanc, originator of Monte Carlo, and view of 1860; 60c. Prince Rainier III and projected esplanade; 70c. Rene Blum and Diaghilev, ballet character from "Petrouchka". (36 × 36 mm): 5f. Interior of Opera House, 1879.

1966. Europa.
856 **194** 30c. orange 20 25
857 60c. green 30 35

195 Prince Rainier and Princess Grace **197** "Learning to Write"

196 Prince Albert I and Yachts "Hirondelle I" and "Princess Alice"

1966. Air.
858 **195** 2f. slate and red 85 40
859 3f. slate and green . . . 1·75 65
860 5f. slate and blue . . . . 2·25 1·00
860a 10f. slate and bistre . . 4·50 2·75
860b 20f. brown and orange 48·00 27·00

1966. 1st International Oceanographic History Congress, Monaco.
861 **196** 1f. lilac and blue 50 60

1966. 20th Anniv of U.N.E.S.C.O.
862 **197** 30c. purple and mauve . . 10 10
863 60c. brown and blue . . . 30 30

198 T.V. Screen, Cross and Monaco Harbour

1966. 10th Meeting of International Catholic Television Association (U.N.D.A.), Monaco.
864 **198** 60c. red, purple & crimson 20 25

199 "Precontinent III"

1966. 1st Anniv of Underwater Research Craft "Precontinent III".
865 **199** 1f. yellow, brown and blue 40 35

200 W.H.O. Building

1966. Inaug of W.H.O. Headquarters, Geneva.
866 **200** 30c. brown, green and blue 15 15
867 60c. brown, red and green 20 15

201 Bugatti, 1931 **202** Dog (Egyptian bronze)

1967. 25th Motor Grand Prix, Monaco. Multicoloured. (a) Postage.
868 1c. Type **201** 10 10
869 2c. Alfa-Romeo, 1932 . . . . 10 10
870 5c. Mercedes, 1936 . . . . . 10 10
871 10c. Maserati, 1948 . . . . . 10 10
872 18c. Ferrari, 1955 . . . . . 20 20
873 20c. Alfa-Romeo, 1950 . . . 10 10
874 25c. Maserati, 1957 . . . . . 20 10
875 30c. Cooper-Climax, 1958 . . 30 20
876 40c. Lotus-Climax, 1960 . . 30 30
877 50c. Lotus-Climax, 1961 . . 50 45
878 60c. Cooper-Climax, 1962 . . 80 45
879 70c. B.R.M., 1963–6 . . . . 90 70
880 1f. Walter Christie, 1907 . . 1·10 90
881 2f.30 Peugeot, 1910 . . . . . 2·00 1·60

(b) Air. Diamond. 50 × 50 mm.
882 3f. black and blue . . . . . 1·40 1·75
DESIGN: 3f. Panhard-Phenix, 1895.

1967. Int Cynological Federation Congress, Monaco.
883 **202** 30c. black, purple & green 35 35

203 View of Monte Carlo

1967. International Tourist Year.
884 **203** 30c. brown, green and blue 20 25

204 Pieces on Chessboard

1967. Int Chess Grand Prix, Monaco.
885 **204** 60c. black, plum and blue 50 40

205 Melvin Jones (founder), Lions Emblem and Monte Carlo

1967. 50th Anniv of Lions International.
886 **205** 60c. blue, ultramarine and brown 30 30

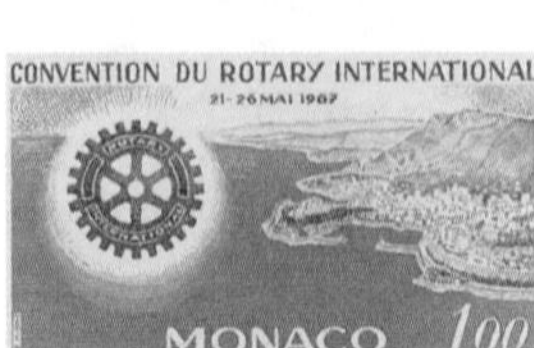

206 Rotary Emblem and Monte Carlo

1967. Rotary International Convention.
887 **206** 1f. bistre, blue and green 40 30

207 Fair Buildings

1967. World Fair, Montreal.
888 **207** 1f. red, slate and blue . . 40 45

208 Squiggle on Map of Europe

1967. European Migration Committee (C.I.M.E.).
889 **208** 1f. brown, bistre and blue 40 30

209 Cogwheels

1967. Europa.
890 **209** 30c. violet, purple and red 30 25
891 60c. green, turq & emer 50 35

210 Dredger and Coastal Chart

1967. 9th Int Hydrographic Congress, Monaco.
892 **210** 1f. brown, blue and green 40 35

211 Marie Curie and Scientific Equipment

1967. Birth Centenary of Marie Curie.
893 **211** 1f. blue, olive and brown 50 40

212 Skiing

1967. Winter Olympic Games, Grenoble.
894 **212** 2f.30 brown, blue & slate 90 90

213 "Prince Rainier I" (E. Charpentier)

1967. Paintings. "Princes and Princesses of Monaco". Multicoloured.
895 1f. Type **213** 40 40
896 1f. "Lucien Grimaldi" (A. di Predis) 55 55
See also Nos. 932/3, 958/9, 1005/6, 1023/4, 1070/1, 1108/9, 1213/14, 1271/2, 1325, 1380/1, 1405/6, 1460/1 and 1531/2.

214 Putting the Shot

1968. Olympic Games, Mexico.
897 **214** 20c. blue, brown and green (postage) 10 10
898 – 30c. brown, blue and plum 10 10
899 – 60c. blue, purple and red 20 25
900 – 70c. red, blue and ochre 30 30
901 – 1f. blue, brown and orange 50 50
902 – 2f.30 olive, blue and lake 1·00 1·25
903 – 3f. blue, violet & grn (air) 1·40 1·25
DESIGNS: 30c. High-jumping; 60c. Gymnastics; 70c. Water-polo; 1f. Greco-Roman wrestling; 2f.30, Gymnastics (different); 3f. Hockey.

215 "St. Martin"

1968. 20th Anniv of Monaco Red Cross.
904 **215** 2f.30 blue and brown . . 80 90

216 "Anemones" (after Raoul Dufy) **217** Insignia of Prince Charles III and Pope Pius IX

1968. Monte Carlo Floral Exhibitions.
905 **216** 1f. multicoloured 50 50

1968. Centenary of "Nullius Diocesis" Abbey.
906 **217** 10c. brown and red . . . 10 10
907 – 20c. red, green and brown 10 10
908 – 30c. brown and blue . . . 20 25
909 – 60c. brown, blue and green 30 30
910 – 1f. indigo, bistre and blue 40 40
DESIGNS—VERT: 20c. "St. Nicholas" (after Louis Brea); 30c. "St. Benedict" (after Simone Martini); 60c. Subiaco Abbey. HORIZ: 1f. Old St. Nicholas' Church (on site of present cathedral).

218 Europa "Key"

1968. Europa.
911 **218** 30c. red and orange . . . 40 25
912 60c. blue and red 70 60
913 1f. brown and green . . . 70 85

219 First Locomotive on Monaco Line, 1868

1968. Centenary of Nice–Monaco Railway.
914 **219** 20c. black, blue and purple 30 30
915 – 30c. black, blue and olive 50 50
916 – 60c. black, blue and ochre 70 70
917 – 70c. black, violet & brown 1·25 1·00
918 – 1f. black, blue and red . . 2·40 1·60
919 – 2f.30 blue, black and red 3·25 2·75

DESIGNS: 30c. Class 220-C steam locomotive, 1898; 60c. Class 230-C steam locomotive, 1910; 70c. Class 231-F steam locomotive, 1925; 1f. Class 241-A steam locomotive, 1932; 2f.30, Class BB 25200 electric locomotive, 1968.

220 Chateaubriand and Combourg Castle

1968. Birth Centenary of Chateaubriand (novelist).
920 **220** 10c. plum, green & myrtle 10 10
921 – 20c. violet, purple and blue 10 10
922 – 25c. brown, violet and blue 10 10
923 – 30c. violet, choc & brn . . 20 20
924 – 60c. brown, green and red 30 20
925 – 2f.30 brown, mauve & bl 85 1·00
Scenes from Chateaubriand's novels: 20c. "Le Genie du Christianisme"; 25c. "Rene"; 30c. "Le Dernier Abencerage"; 60c. "Les Martyrs"; 2f.30, "Atala".

221 Law Courts, Paris, and statues–"La France et la Fidelite"

1968. Birth Centenary of J. F. Bosio (Monegasque sculptor).
926 **221** 20c. brown and purple . . 10 10
927 – 25c. brown and red . . . 10 10
928 – 30c. blue and green . . . 20 10
929 – 60c. green and myrtle . . 40 20
930 – 2f.30 black and slate . . . 70 75
DESIGNS—VERT (26 × 36 mm): 25c. "Henry IV as a Child"; 30c. "J. F. Bosio" (lithograph); 60c. "Louis XIV". HORIZ (as Type **221**): 2f.30, "Napoleon I, Louis XVIII and Charles X".

222 W.H.O. Emblem

1968. 20th Anniv of W.H.O.
931 **222** 60c. multicoloured 30 25

1968. Paintings. "Princes and Princesses of Monaco". As T **213**. Multicoloured.
932 1f. "Prince Charles II" (Mimault) 40 35
933 2f.30 "Princess Jeanne Grimaldi" (Mimault) . . . 70 85

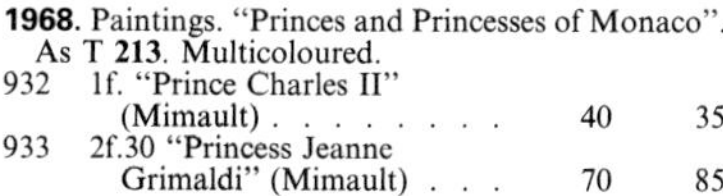

223 The Hungarian March

1969. Death Centenary of Hector Berlioz (composer).
934 **223** 10c. brown, violet and green (postage) 10 10
935 – 20c. brown, olive & mauve 10 10
936 – 25c. brown, blue & mauve 10 10
937 – 30c. black, green and blue 10 20
938 – 40c. red, black and slate 10 20
939 – 50c. brown, slate & purple 20 25
940 – 70c. brown, slate and green 30 25
941 – 1f. black, mauve & brown 30 35
942 – 1f.15 black, blue & turq 50 45
943 – 2f. black, blue & grn (air) 90 90
DESIGNS—HORIZ: 20c. Mephistopheles appears to Faust; 25c. Auerbach's tavern; 30c. Sylphs' ballet; 40c. Minuet of the goblins; 50c. Marguerite's bedroom; 70c. "Forests and caverns"; 1f. The journey to Hell; 1f.15, Heaven; All scenes from Berlioz's "The Damnation of Faust". VERT: 2f. Bust of Berlioz.

224 "St. Elisabeth of Hungary"

1969. Monaco Red Cross.
944 **224** 3f. blue, brown and red 1·10 1·25

225 "Napoleon I" (P. Delaroche)

1969. Birth Bicentenary of Napoleon Bonaparte.
945 **225** 3f. multicoloured . . . . 1·10 1·10

226 Colonnade

1969. Europa.
946 **226** 40c. red and purple . . . 40 30
947 70c. blue, brown and black 60 45
948 1f. ochre, brown and blue 90 65

1969. Precancelled. As T **177**. No date.
949 22c. brown, blue and black 30 30
949a 26c. violet, blue and black 40 25
949b 30c. multicoloured 50 35
950 35c. multicoloured 40 35
950a 45c. multicoloured 60 55
951 70c. black and blue 60 55
951a 90c. green, blue and black 1·10 70

227 "Head of Woman" (Da Vinci) **228** Marine Fauna, King Alfonso XIII of Spain and Prince Albert I of Monaco

1969. 450th Death Anniv of Leonardo da Vinci.
952 **227** 30c. brown 10 10
953 – 40c. red and brown . . . 20 10
954 – 70c. green 30 20
955 – 80c. sepia 40 20
956 – 1f.15 brown 60 40
957 – 3f. brown . . . . 1·40 90
DRAWINGS: 40c. Self-portrait; 70c. "Head of an Old Man"; 80c. "Head of St. Madeleine"; 1f.15, "Man's Head"; 3f. "The Condottiere".

1969. Paintings. "Princes and Princesses of Monaco". As T **213**. Multicoloured.
958 1f. "Prince Honore II" (Champaigne) 30 50
959 3f. "Princess Louise-Hippolyte" (Champaigne) 90 1·00

1969. 50th Anniv of Int Commission for Scientific Exploration of the Mediterranean, Madrid.
960 **228** 40c. blue and black . . . 20 20

229 I.L.O. Emblem

1969. 50th Anniv of I.L.O.
961 **229** 40c. multicoloured 20 25

230 Aerial View of Monaco and T.V. Camera

1969. 10th International Television Festival.
962 **230** 40c. purple, lake and blue 20 20

231 J.C.C. Emblem

1969. 25th Anniv of Junior Chamber of Commerce.
963 **231** 40c. violet, bistre and blue 20 25

232 Alphonse Daudet and Scenes from "Lettres"

1969. Centenary of Daudet's "Lettres de Mon Moulin".
964 **232** 30c. lake, violet and green 10 10
965 – 40c. green, brown and blue 20 20
966 – 70c. multicoloured 30 30
967 – 80c. violet, brown & green 40 30
968 – 1f.15 brown, orange & bl 50 50
DESIGNS (Scenes from the book): 40c. "Installation" (Daudet writing); 70c. "Mule, Goat and Wolf"; 80c. "Gaucher's Elixir" and "The Three Low Masses"; 1f.15, Daudet drinking, "The Old Man" and "The Country Sub-Prefect".

233 Conference Building, Albert I and Rainier III

1970. Interparliamentary Union's Spring Meeting, Monaco.
969 **233** 40c. black, red and purple 20 20

234 Baby Common Seal

1970. Protection of Baby Seals.
970 **234** 40c. drab, blue and purple 40 50

235 Japanese Print **236** Dobermann

1970. Expo 70.
971 **235** 20c. brown, green and red . . . 10 10
972 – 30c. brown, buff and green 20 20
973 – 40c. bistre and violet . . 20 20
974 – 70c. grey and red 50 60
975 – 1f.15 red, green & purple 60 75
DESIGNS—VERT: 30c. Manchurian Cranes (birds); 40c. Shinto temple gateway. HORIZ: 70c. Cherry blossom; 1f.15, Monaco Palace and Osaka Castle.

1970. International Dog Show, Monte Carlo.
976 **236** 40c. black and brown . . 80 85

237 Apollo

1970. 20th Anniv of World Federation for Protection of Animals.
977 **237** 30c. black, red and blue 20 25
978 – 40c. brown, blue and green 40 30
979 – 50c. brown, ochre and blue 60 50
980 – 80c. brown, blue and green . . . . 1·10 90
981 – 1f. brown, bistre and slate 1·60 1·90
982 – 1f.15 brown, green & blue 2·25 2·10
DESIGNS—HORIZ: 40c. Basque ponies; 50c. Common seal. VERT: 80c. Chamois; 1f. White-tailed sea eagles; 1f.15, European otter.

238 "St. Louis" (King of France)

1970. Monaco Red Cross.
983 **238** 3f. green, brown and slate 1·10 1·60
See also Nos. 1022, 1041, 1114, 1189 and 1270.

239 "Roses and Anemones" (Van Gogh)

1970. Monte Carlo Flower Show.
984 **239** 3f. multicoloured . . . . 1·50 2·00
See also Nos. 1042 and 1073.

240 Moon Plaque, Presidents Kennedy and Nixon

1970. 1st Man on the Moon (1969). Multicoloured.
985 40c. Type **240** 40 40
986 80c. Astronauts on Moon . . 60 55

241 New U.P.U. Building and Monument
242 "Flaming Sun"

1970. New U.P.U. Headquarters Building.
987 **241** 40c. brown, black & green 20 20

1970. Europa.
988 **242** 40c. purple 30 25
989 80c. green . . . . 1·10 80
990 1f. blue . . . . 1·60 1·25

243 Camargue Horse

1970. Horses.
991 **243** 10c. slate, olive and blue (postage) 10 10
992 – 20c. brown, olive and blue 20 20
993 – 30c. brown, green and blue 50 30
994 – 40c. grey, brown and slate 70 55
995 – 50c. brown, olive and blue 1·10 80
996 – 70c. brown, orange & grn 2·00 1·25
997 – 85c. blue, green and olive 2·00 1·75
998 – 1f.15 black, green & blue 2·10 2·10
999 – 3f. multicoloured (air) . . 1·50 1·75
HORSES—HORIZ: 20c. Anglo-Arab; 30c. French saddle-horse; 40c. Lippizaner; 50c. Trotter; 70c. English thoroughbred; 85c. Arab; 1f.15, Barbary. DIAMOND (50 × 50 mm): 3f. Rock-drawings of horses in Lascaux grotto.

244 Dumas, D'Artagnan and the Three Musketeers

1970. Death Centenary of Alexandre Dumas (pere) (author).
1000 **244** 30c. slate, brown and blue 20 20

245 Henri Rougier and Voisin "Boxkite"

1970. 60th Anniv of First Mediterranean Flight.
1001 **245** 40c. brown, blue and slate 20 20

246 De Lamartine and scene from "Meditations Poetiques"

1970. 150th Anniv of "Meditations Poetiques" by Alphonse de Lamartine (writer).
1002 **246** 80c. brown, blue & turq 30 30

247 Beethoven

1970. Birth Bicentenary of Beethoven.
1003 **247** 1f.30 brown and red . . 1·60 1·10

1970. 50th Death Anniv of Modigliani. Vert Painting as T **213**. Multicoloured.
1004 3f. "Portrait of Dedie" . . . 2·00 2·00

1970. Paintings. "Princes and Princesses of Monaco". As T **213**.
1005 1f. red and black 30 45
1006 3f. multicoloured . . . . . 90 1·25
PORTRAITS: 1f. "Prince Louis I" (F. de Troy); 3f. "Princess Charlotte de Gramont" (S. Bourdon).

248 Cocker Spaniel **249** Razorbill

1971. International Dog Show, Monte Carlo.
1007 **248** 50c. multicoloured . . . 2·00 1·50
See also Nos. 1036, 1082, 1119, 1218 and 1239.

1971. Campaign Against Pollution of the Sea.
1008 **249** 50c. indigo and blue . . 40 45

250 Hand holding Emblem

1971. 7th Int Blood Donors Federation Congress.
1009 **250** 80c. red, violet and grey 40 45

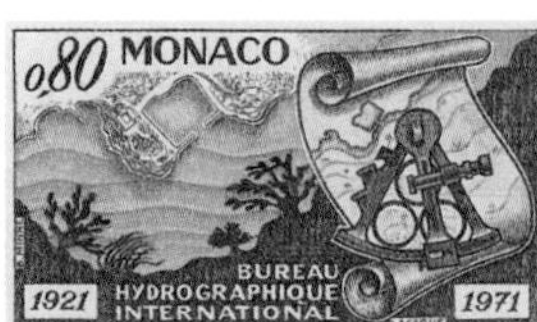

251 Sextant, Scroll and Underwater Scene

1971. 50th Anniv of Int Hydrographic Bureau.
1010 **251** 80c. brown, green & slate 40 45

252 Detail of Michelangelo Painting ("The Arts")

1971. 25th Anniv of U.N.E.S.C.O.
1011 **252** 30c. brown, blue & violet 10 20
1012 – 50c. blue and brown . . 20 20
1013 – 80c. brown and green . . 30 30
1014 – 1f.30 green 50 50
DESIGNS—VERT: 50c. Alchemist and dish aerial ("Sciences"); 1f.30, Prince Pierre of Monaco (National U.N.E.S.C.O. Commission). HORIZ: 80c. Ancient scribe, book and T.V. screen ("Culture").

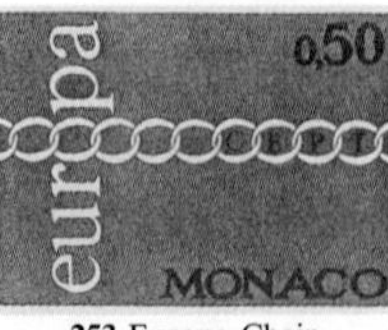

253 Europa Chain

1971. Europa.
1015 **253** 50c. red 70 45
1016 80c. blue . . . . 1·25 80
1017 1f.30 green . . . . . . 2·10 1·50

254 Old Bridge, Sospel

1971. Protection of Historic Monuments.
1018 **254** 50c. brown, blue & green 20 20
1019 – 80c. brown, green & grey 30 25
1020 – 1f.30 red, green & brown 50 50
1021 – 3f. slate, blue and olive 1·25 1·10

DESIGNS—HORIZ: 80c. Roquebrune Chateau; 1f.30, Grimaldi Chateau, Cagnes-sur-Mer. VERT: 3f. Roman "Trophy of the Alps", La Turbie.

1971. Monaco Red Cross. As T **238**.
1022 3f. brown, olive and green 1·25 1·40
DESIGN: 3f. St. Vincent de Paul.

1972. Paintings. "Princes and Princesses of Monaco". As T **213**. Multicoloured.
1023 1f. "Prince Antoine I" (Rigaud) 40 45
1024 3f. "Princess Marie de Lorraine" (18th-century French School) . . . . . 1·25 1·40

255 La Fontaine and Animal Fables (350th)

1972. Birth Anniversaries (1971).
1025 **255** 50c. brown, emer & grn 40 30
1026 – 1f.30 purple, black & red 65 60
DESIGN: 1f.30, Baudelaire, nudes and cats (150th).

256 Saint-Saens and scene from Opera, "Samson and Delilah"

1972. 50th Death Anniv (1971) of Camile Saint-Saens.
1027 **256** 90c. brown and sepia . . 40 35

257 Battle Scene

1972. 400th Anniv (1971) of Battle of Lepanto.
1028 **257** 1f. blue, brown and red 40 35

258 "Christ before Pilate" (engraving by Durer)

1972. 500th Birth Anniv (1971) of Albrecht Durer.
1029 **258** 2f. black and brown . . 1·10 1·25

259 "The Cradle" (B. Morisot)

1972. 25th Anniv (1971) of U.N.I.C.E.F.
1030 **259** 2f. multicoloured . . . . 1·10 1·10

260 "Gilles" (Watteau)

1972. 250th Death Anniv (1971) of Watteau.
1031 **260** 3f. multicoloured . . . . 1·60 1·60

261 Santa Claus

1972. Christmas (1971).
1032 **261** 30c. red, blue and brown 10 20
1033 50c. red, green & orange 20 20
1034 90c. red, blue and brown 45 30

262 Class 743 Steam Locomotive, Italy, and TGV 001 Turbotrain, France

1972. 50th Anniv of International Railway Union.
1035 **262** 50c. purple, lilac and red 70 60

1972. Int Dog Show, Monte Carlo. As T **248**.
1036 60c. multicoloured . . . . . 1·60 1·60
DESIGN: 60c. Great Dane.

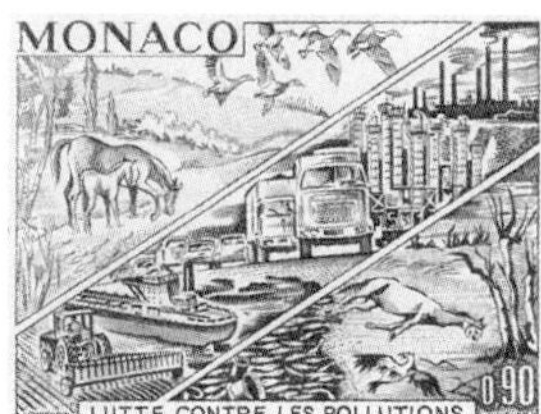

263 "Pollution Kills"

1972. Anti-pollution Campaign.
1037 **263** 90c. brown, green & black 40 35

264 Ski-jumping

1972. Winter Olympic Games, Sapporo, Japan.
1038 **264** 90c. black, red and green 55 50

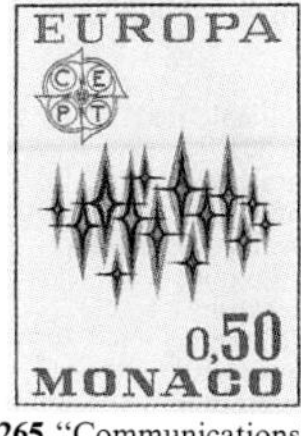

265 "Communications"

1972. Europa.
1039 **265** 50c. blue and orange . . 80 60
1040 90c. blue and green . . . 1·60 1·50

1972. Monaco Red Cross. As T **238**.
1041 3f. brown and purple . . . 1·25 1·40
DESIGN: 3f. St. Francis of Assisi.

1972. Monte Carlo Flower Show. As T **239**.
1042 3f. multicoloured . . . . . 2·40 2·00
DESIGN: 3f. "Vase of Flowers" (Cezanne).

266 "SS. Giovanni e Paolo" (detail, Canaletto)

1972. U.N.E.S.C.O. "Save Venice" Campaign.
1043 **266** 30c. red 20 25
1044 – 60c. violet 30 30
1045 – 2f. blue . . . . 1·25 1·40
DESIGNS—27 × 48 mm: 60c. "S. Pietro di Castello" (F. Guradi). As Type **266**: 2f. "Piazetta S. Marco" (B. Bellotto).

267 Dressage

1972. Olympic Games, Munich. Equestrian Events.
1046 **267** 60c. brown, blue and lake 40 55
1047 – 90c. lake, brown and blue . . . . 80 1·00
1048 – 1f.10 blue, lake & brown 1·25 1·50
1049 – 1f.40 brown, lake & blue 2·10 2·40
DESIGNS: 90c. Cross country; 1f.10, Show jumping (wall); 1f.40, Show jumping (parallel bars).

268 Escoffier and Birthplace

1972. 125th Birth Anniv of Auguste Escoffier (master chef).
1050 **268** 45c. black and brown . . 20 25

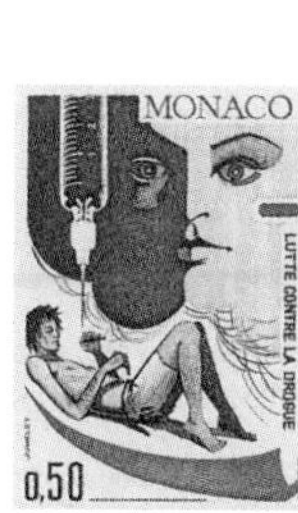

269 Drug Addiction

270 Globe, Birds and Animals

1972. Campaign Against Drugs.
1051 **269** 50c. red, brown & orange 30 25
1052 90c. green, brown & blue 40 45
See also Nos. 1088/91 and 1280/1.

1972. 17th Int Congress of Zoology, Monaco.
1053 **270** 30c. green, brown and red 10 10
1054 – 50c. brown, purple and red 20 20
1055 – 90c. blue, brown and red 40 30
DESIGNS—HORIZ: 50c. VERT: 90c. Similar symbolic design.

271 Bouquet

272 "The Nativity" and Child's face

1972. Monte Carlo Flower Show, 1973 (1st issue). Multicoloured.
1056 30c. Lilies in vase 40 30
1057 50c. Type **271** 70 45
1058 90c. Flowers in vase . . . . 1·25 90
See also Nos. 1073, 1105/7, 1143/4, 1225/6, 1244, 1282/3 and 1316/17.

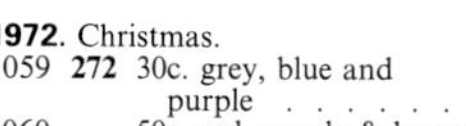

1972. Christmas.
1059 **272** 30c. grey, blue and purple 10 10
1060 50c. red, purple & brown 20 10
1061 90c. violet, plum & pur 40 30

273 Louis Bleriot and Bleriot XI (Birth cent)

1972. Birth Anniversaries.
1062 **273** 30c. blue and brown . . 20 10
1063 – 50c. blue, turq & new blue 60 60
1064 – 90c. brown and buff . . 80 55
DESIGNS AND ANNIVERSARIES: 50c. Amundsen and polar scene (birth centenary); 90c. Pasteur and laboratory scene (150th birth anniv).

274 "Gethsemane"

1972. Protection of Historical Monuments. Frescoes by J. Canavesio, Chapel of Notre-Dame des Fontaines, La Brigue.
1065 **274** 30c. red 10 10
1066 – 50c. grey 20 25
1067 – 90c. green 40 40
1068 – 1f.40 red 60 55
1069 – 2f. purple . . . . 1·10 80
DESIGNS: 50c. "Christ Outraged"; 90c. "Ascent to Calvary"; 1f.40, "The Resurrection"; 2f. "The Crucifixion".

1972. Paintings. "Princes and Princesses of Monaco". As T **213**. Multicoloured.
1070 1f. "Prince Jacques 1" (N. Largillière) 40 45
1071 3f. "Princess Louise-Hippolyte" (J. B. Vanloo) 1·25 1·50

1973. Monte Carlo Flower Show (2nd issue). As T **239**.
1073 3f.50 multicoloured . . . . 3·50 3·25
DESIGN: 3f.50, "Bouquet of Flowers".

276 Europa "Posthorn"

1973. Europa.
1074 **276** 50c. orange . . . . . . 2·75 1·25
1075 90c. green . . . . 4·25 2·50

277 Moliere and Characters from "Le Malade Imaginaire"

1973. 300th Death Anniv of Moliere.
1076 **277** 20c. red, brown and blue 35 30

278 Colette, Cat and Books

1973. Birth Anniversaries.
1077 **278** 30c. black, blue and red 70 45
1078 – 45c. multicoloured . . . 1·75 1·25
1079 – 50c. lilac, purple and blue 35 25
1080 – 90c. multicoloured . . . 40 50
DESIGNS AND ANNIVERSARIES—HORIZ: 30c., Type **278** (nature writer, birth cent); 45c. J.-H. Fabre and insects (entomologists, 150th birth anniv); 90c. Sir George Cayley and his "convertiplane" (aviation pioneer, birth bicent). VERT: 50c. Blaise Pascal (philosopher and writer, 350th birth anniv).

279 E. Ducretet, "Les Invalides" and Eiffel Tower

1973. 75th Anniv of Eugene Ducretet's First Hertzian Radio Link.
1081 **279** 30c. purple and brown 20 25

1973. International Dog Show, Monte Carlo. As T **248**. Inscr "1973". Multicoloured.
1082 45c. Alsatian . . . . 7·25 4·25

280 C. Peguy and Chartres Cathedral

1973. Birth Bicentenary of Charles Peguy (writer).
1083 **280** 50c. brown, mauve & grey 30 35

281 Telecommunications Equipment

1973. 5th World Telecommunications Day.
1084 **281** 60c. violet, blue & brown 30 30

282 Stage Characters

1973. 5th World Amateur Theatre Festival.
1085 **282** 60c. lilac, blue and red 30 35

283 Ellis and Rugby Tackle

1973. 150th Anniv of Founding of Rugby Football by William Webb Ellis.
1086 **283** 90c. red, lake and brown 50 50

284 St. Theresa

1973. Birth Centenary of St. Theresa of Lisieux.
1087 **284** 1f.40 multicoloured . . . 60 55

285 Drug Addiction

1973. Campaign Against Drugs.
1088 **285** 50c. red, green and blue 20 25
1089 – 50c. multicoloured . . . 20 25
1090 **285** 90c. violet, green and red 40 45
1091 – 90c. multicoloured . . . 50 50
DESIGN: Nos. 1089, 1091, Children, syringes and addicts.

286 "Institution of the Creche" (Giotto)

1973. 750th Anniv of St. Francis of Assisi Creche.
1092 **286** 30c. purple (postage) . . 30 30
1093 – 45c. red 60 55
1094 – 50c. brown 70 70
1095 – 1f. green . . . . 1·60 1·25
1096 – 2f. brown . . . . 3·00 2·75
1097 – 3f. blue (air) . . . . . . 1·75 1·60
DESIGN—HORIZ: 45c. "The Nativity" (School of F. Lippi); 50c. "The Birth of Jesus Christ" (Giotto). VERT: 1f. "The Nativity" (15th-century miniature); 2f. "The Birth of Jesus" (Fra Angelico); 3f. "The Nativity" (Flemish school).

287 Country Picnic

1973. 50th Anniv of National Committee for Monegasque Traditions.
1098 **287** 10c. blue, green & brown 10 10
1099 – 20c. violet, blue and green 10 10
1100 – 30c. sepia, brown & green 20 25
1101 – 45c. red, violet and purple 40 35
1102 – 50c. black, red and brown 50 40
1103 – 60c. red, violet and blue 50 60
1104 – 1f. violet, blue and brown . . . . 95 1·10
DESIGNS—VERT: 20c. Maypole dance. HORIZ: 30c. "U Bradi" (local dance); 45c. St. Jean fire-dance; 50c. Blessing the Christmas loaf; 60c. Blessing the sea, Festival of St. Devote; 1f. Corpus Christi procession.

1973. Monte Carlo Flower Show, 1974. As T **271**. Multicoloured.
1105 45c. Roses and Strelitzia . . 80 55
1106 60c. Mimosa and myosotis 1·25 90
1107 1f. "Vase of Flowers" (Odilon Redon) . . . . . 2·00 1·60

1973. Paintings. "Princes and Princesses of Monaco". As T **213**. Multicoloured.
1108 2f. "Charlotte Grimaldi" (in day dress, P. Gobert) . . 1·40 1·40
1109 2f. "Charlotte Grimaldi" (in evening dress, P. Gobert) 1·40 1·40

289 U.P.U. Emblem and Symbolic Heads

1974. Centenary of Universal Postal Union.
1111 **289** 50c. purple and brown 30 25
1112 – 70c. multicoloured . . . 40 30
1113 – 1f.10 multicoloured . . . 70 55
DESIGNS: 70c. Hands holding letters; 1f.10, "Countries of the World" (famous buildings).

1974. Monaco Red Cross. As T **238**.
1114 3f. blue, green and purple 1·40 1·25
DESIGN: 3f. St. Bernard of Menthon.

290 Farman, Farman F.60 Goliath and Farman H.F.III

1974. Birth Centenary of Henry Farman (aviation pioneer).
1115 **290** 30c. brown, purple & blue 10 10

291 Marconi, Circuit Plan and Destroyer

1974. Birth Centenary of Guglielmo Marconi (radio pioneer).
1116 **291** 40c. red, deep blue & blue 20 10

292 Duchesne and "Penicillium glaucum"

1974. Birth Centenary of Ernest Duchesne (microbiologist).
1117 **292** 45c. black, blue & purple 30 20

293 Forest and Engine

1974. 60th Death Anniv of Fernand Forest (motor engineer and inventor).
1118 **293** 50c. purple, red and black 30 25

1974. International Dog Show, Monte Carlo. As T **248**, inscr "1974".
1119 60c. multicoloured . . . . . 2·75 2·00
DESIGN: 60c. Schnauzer.

294 Ronsard and Characters from "Sonnet to Helene"

1974. 450th Birth Anniv of Pierre de Ronsard (poet).
1120 **294** 70c. brown and red . . . 40 45

295 Sir Winston Churchill (after bust by O. Nemon)

297 "The King of Rome" (Bosio)

296 Interpol Emblem, and Views of Monaco and Vienna

1974. Birth Centenary of Sir Winston Churchill.
1121 **295** 1f. brown and grey . . . 55 45

1974. 60th Anniv of 1st International Police Judiciary Congress and 50th Anniv of International Criminal Police Organization (Interpol).
1122 **296** 2f. blue, brown and green . . . . 1·10 90

1974. Europa. Sculptures by J. F. Bosio.
1123 **297** 45c. green and brown . . 1·00 75
1124 – 1f.10 bistre and brown 1·75 1·40
DESIGN: 1f.10, "Madame Elizabeth".

298 "The Box" (A. Renoir)

1974. "The Impressionists". Multicoloured.
1126 1f. Type **298** . . . . 1·40 1·40
1127 1f. "The Dance Class" (E. Degas) . . . . 1·40 1·40
1128 2f. "Impression-Sunrise" (C. Monet) (horiz) . . . . 2·75 2·75
1129 2f. "Entrance to Voisins Village" (C. Pissarro) (horiz) . . . . 2·75 2·75
1130 2f. "The Hanged Man's House" (P. Cezanne) (horiz) . . . . 2·75 2·75
1131 2f. "Floods at Port Marly" (A. Sisley) (horiz) . . . . 2·75 2·75

299 Tigers and Trainer

1974. 1st International Circus Festival, Monaco.
1132 **299** 2c. brown, green and blue 10 10
1133 – 3c. brown and purple . . 10 10
1134 – 5c. blue, brown and red 10 10
1135 – 45c. brown, black and red 40 35
1136 – 70c. multicoloured . . . 60 45
1137 – 1f.10 brown, green and red . . . . 1·40 75
1138 – 5f. green, blue and brown . . . . 4·00 3·25
DESIGNS—VERT: 3c. Performing horse; 45c. Equestrian act; 1f.10, Acrobats; 5f. Trapeze act. HORIZ: 5c. Performing elephants; 70c. Clowns.

300 Honore II on Medal

1974. 350th Anniv of Monegasque Numismatic Art.
1139 **300** 60c. green and red . . . 40 35

301 Marine Flora and Fauna

1974. 24th Congress of the International Commission for the Scientific Exploration of the Mediterranean. Multicoloured.
1140 45c. Type **301** 80 60
1141 70c. Sea-bed flora and fauna 1·40 90
1142 1f.10 Sea-bed flora and fauna (different) . . . . 2·00 1·40
Nos. 1141/2 are larger, size 52 × 31 mm.

1974. Monte Carlo Flower Show. As T **271**. Multicoloured.
1143 70c. Honeysuckle and violets 70 60
1144 1f.10 Iris and chrysanthemums . . . . 1·00 1·00

302 Prince Rainier III (F. Messina)

303

1974.
1145 **302** 60c. green (postage) . . 70 30
1146 80c. red 80 45
1147 80c. green 40 10
1148 1f. brown . . . . . . 2·00 85
1149 1f. red 50 20
1149a 1f. green 40 20
1149b 1f.10 green 40 20
1150 1f.20 violet . . . . . . 4·25 2·00
1150a 1f.20 red 60 20
1150b 1f.20 green 70 20
1151 1f.25 blue . . . . . . 1·00 85
1151a 1f.30 red 70 25
1152 1f.40 red 80 20
1152a 1f.50 black 80 60
1153 1f.60 grey 80 50
1153a 1f.70 blue 90 60
1153b 1f.80 blue . . . . . . 1·40 1·40
1154 2f. mauve . . . . . . 1·50 1·50
1154a 2f.10 brown . . . . . 1·40 75
1155 2f.30 violet . . . . . . 1·75 1·25
1156 2f.50 black . . . . . . 1·75 1·40
1157 9f. violet . . . . 5·00 3·25
1158 **303** 10f. violet (air) . . . . 6·00 2·50
1159 15f. red . . . . 9·00 5·50
1160 20f. blue . . . . 11·00 6·00

304 Coastline, Monte Carlo **305** "Haagocereus chosicensis"

1974.
1161 **304** 25c. blue, green & brown 1·50 45
1162 – 25c. brown, green & blue 30 20
1163 – 50c. brown and blue . . 1·50 45
1164 **304** 65c. blue, brown & green 30 25
1165 – 70c. multicoloured . . . 40 40
1166 **304** 1f.10 brown, green & bl 1·75 65
1167 – 1f.10 black, brown & bl 60 70
1168 – 1f.30 brown, green & bl 60 40
1169 – 1f.40 green, grey & brn 2·00 1·00
1170 – 1f.50 green, blue & black 1·00 90
1171 – 1f.70 brown, green & bl 3·00 2·00
1172 – 1f.80 brown, green & bl 1·10 85
1173 – 2f.30 brown, grey & blue 1·75 1·40
1174 – 3f. brown, grey and green . . . . 4·75 2·00
1175 – 5f.50 brown, green & blue . . . . 6·25 4·25
1176 – 6f.50 brown, blue & grn 3·00 2·40
DESIGNS—VERT: 50c. Palace clock tower; 70c. Botanical gardens; 1f.30, Monaco Cathedral; 1f.40, 1f.50, Prince Albert I statue and Museum; 3f. Fort Antoine. HORIZ: 25c. (1162), 1f.70, "All Saints" Tower; 1f.10 (1167), Palais de Justice; 1f.80, 5f.50, La Condamine; 2f.30, North Galleries of Palace; 6f.50, Aerial view of hotels and harbour.

1975. Plants. Multicoloured.
1180 10c. Type **305** 10 10
1181 20c. "Matucana madisoniarum" 20 20
1182 30c. "Parodia scopaioides" 40 25
1183 85c. "Mediolobivia arachnacantha" . . . . . 1·50 80
1184 1f.90 "Matucana yanganucensis" . . . . . 2·75 2·10
1185 4f. "Echinocereus marksianus" . . . . . . 5·25 3·75

306 "Portrait of a Sailor" (P. Florence)

308 "Prologue"

307 "St. Bernardin de Sienne"

1975. Europa.
1186 **306** 80c. purple . . . . . . 1·10 60
1187 – 1f.20 blue . . . . 1·60 80
DESIGN: 1f.20, "St. Devote" (Ludovic Brea).

1975. Monaco Red Cross.
1189 **307** 4f. blue and purple . . . 1·90 1·75

1975. Centenary of "Carmen" (opera by Georges Bizet).
1190 **308** 30c. violet, brown & blk 10 10
1191 – 60c. grey, green and red 20 10
1192 – 80c. green, brown & blk 50 35
1193 – 1f.40 purple, brn & ochre 80 70
DESIGNS—HORIZ: 60c. Lilla Pastia's tavern; 80c. "The Smuggler's Den"; 1f.40, "Confrontation at Seville".

309 Saint-Simon

310 Dr. Albert Schweitzer

1975. 300th Birth Anniv of Louis de Saint-Simon (writer).
1194 **309** 40c. blue 30 25

1975. Birth Centenary of Dr. Schweitzer (Nobel Peace Prize Winner).
1195 **310** 60c. red and brown . . . 50 35

311 "Stamp" and Calligraphy

1975. "Arphila 75" International Stamp Exhibition, Paris.
1196 **311** 80c. brown and orange 50 45

312 Seagull and Sunrise

1975. International Exposition, Okinawa.
1197 **312** 85c. blue, green & orange 60 50

313 Pike smashing Crab

1975. Anti-cancer Campaign.
1198 **313** 1f. multicoloured 60 50

314 Christ with Crown of Thorns

1975. Holy Year.
1199 **314** 1f.15 black, brn & pur 85 60

315 Villa Sauber, Monte Carlo

1975. European Architectural Heritage Year.
1200 **315** 1f.20 green, brown & bl 80 60

316 Woman's Head and Globe

1975. International Women's Year.
1201 **316** 1f.20 multicoloured . . . 80 60

317 Rolls-Royce "Silver Ghost" (1907)

1975. History of the Motor Car.
1202 **317** 5c. blue, green and brown 10 10
1203 – 10c. indigo and blue . . 10 10
1204 – 20c. blue, ultram & black 20 10
1205 – 30c. purple and mauve 40 20
1206 – 50c. blue, purple & mauve 70 50
1207 – 60c. red and green . . . 1·00 70
1208 – 80c. indigo and blue . . 1·75 1·10
1209 – 85c. brown, orange & grn . . . . 2·00 1·50
1210 – 1f.20 blue, red and green 3·00 2·40
1211 – 1f.40 green and blue . . 4·25 2·75
1212 – 5f.50 blue, emerald and green . . . . 9·50 7·00
DESIGNS: 10c. Hispano-Suiza "H.6B" (1926); 20c. Isotta Fraschini "8A" (1928); 30c. Cord "L.29"; 50c. Voisin "V12" (1930); 60c. Duesenberg "SJ" (1933); 80c. Bugatti "57 C" (1938); 85c. Delahaye "135 M" (1940); 1f.20, Cisitalia "Pininfarina" (1945); 1f.40, Mercedes-Benz "300 SL" (1955); 5f.50, Lamborghini "Countach" (1974).

1975. Paintings. "Princes and Princesses of Monaco". As T **213**. Multicoloured.
1213 2f. "Prince Honore III" . . 1·25 85
1214 4f. "Princess Catherine de Brignole" . . . . 2·50 2·40

318 Dog behind Bars

1975. 125th Birth Anniv of Gen. J. P. Delmas de Grammont (author of Animal Protection Code).
1215 **318** 60c. black and brown . . 80 80
1216 – 80c. black and brown . . 1·10 85
1217 – 1f.20 green and purple 1·90 1·50
DESIGNS—VERT: 80c. Cat chased up tree. HORIZ: 1f.20, Horse being ill-treated.

1975. International Dog Show, Monte Carlo. As T **248**, but inscr "1975". Multicoloured.
1218 60c. black and purple . . . 3·50 2·75
DESIGN: 60c. French poodle.

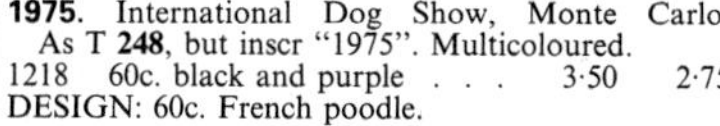

319 Maurice Ravel

1975. Birth Centenaries of Musicians.
1219 **319** 60c. brown and purple 70 55
1220 – 1f.20 black and purple 1·50 1·25
DESIGN: 1f.20, Johann Strauss (the younger).

320 Circus Clown

322 Andre Ampere with Electrical Meter

321 Monaco Florin Coin, 1640

1975. 2nd International Circus Festival.
1221 **320** 80c. multicoloured . . . 80 55

1975. Monaco Numismatics.
1222 **321** 80c. brown and blue . . 50 50
See also Nos. 1275, 1320 and 1448.

1975. Birth Centenary of Andre Ampere (physicist).
1223 **322** 85c. indigo and blue . . 50 50

323 "Lamentations for the Dead Christ"

1975. 500th Birth Anniv of Michelangelo.
1224 **323** 1f.40 olive and black . . 80 80

1975. Monte Carlo Flower Show (1976). As T **271**. Multicoloured.
1225 60c. Bouquet of wild flowers 80 55
1226 80c. Ikebana flower arrangement . . . . . . 1·40 90

1975. Precancelled. Surch.
1227 42c. on 26c. violet, blue and black (No. 949a) . . . . 1·60 1·40
1228 48c. on 30c. multicoloured (No. 949b) . . . . 1·90 1·90
1229 70c. on 45c. multicoloured (No. 950a) . . . . 3·25 2·75
1230 1f.35 on 90c. green, blue and black (No. 951a) . . 4·25 3·75

325 Prince Pierre de Monaco

1976. 25th Anniv of Literary Council of Monaco.
1231 **325** 10c. black 10 10
1232 – 20c. blue and red 20 20
1233 – 25c. blue and red 20 20
1234 – 30c. brown 20 30
1235 – 50c. blue, red and purple 40 30
1236 – 60c. brown, grn & lt brn 50 35
1237 – 80c. purple and blue . . 80 75
1238 – 1f.20 violet, blue & mve 1·60 1·10
COUNCIL MEMBERS—HORIZ: 20c. A. Maurois and Colette; 25c. Jean and Jerome Tharaud; 30c. E. Henriot, M. Pagnol and G. Duhamel; 50c. Ph. Heriat, J. Supervielle and L. Pierard; 60c. R. Dorgeles, M. Achard and G. Bauer; 80c. F. Hellens, A. Billy and Mgr. Grente; 1f.20, J. Giono, L. Pasteur Vallery-Radot and M. Garcon.

326 Dachshunds

1976. International Dog Show, Monte Carlo.
1239 **326** 60c. multicoloured . . . 4·00 3·25

327 Bridge Table and Monte Carlo Coast

1976. 5th Bridge Olympiad, Monte Carlo.
1240 **327** 60c. brown, green and red 50 40

328 Alexander Graham Bell and Early Telephone

1976. Telephone Centenary.
1241 **328** 80c. brown, light brown and grey 50 30

329 Federation Emblem on Globe

1976. 50th Anniv of International Philatelic Federation.
1242 **329** 1f.20 red, blue and green 70 55

330 U.S.A. 2c. Stamp, 1926

1976. Bicent of American Revolution.
1243 **330** 1f.70 black and purple 80 55

331 "The Fritillaries" (Van Gogh)

1976. Monte Carlo Flower Show.
1244 **331** 3f. multicoloured . . . . 7·00 5·00

332 Diving 333 Decorative Plate

1976. Olympic Games, Montreal.
1245 **332** 60c. brown and blue . . 30 30
1246 – 80c. blue, brown & green 40 35
1247 – 85c. blue, green & brown 50 40
1248 – 1f.20 brown, green & bl 70 60
1249 – 1f.70 brown, blue & grn 1·00 1·00
DESIGNS—VERT: 80c. Gymnastics; 85c. Hammer-throwing. HORIZ: 1f.20, Rowing; 1f.70, Boxing.

1976. Europa. Monegasque Ceramics. Multicoloured.
1251 80c. Type **333** 70 70
1252 1f.20 Grape-harvester (statuette) . . . . 1·25 1·10

334 Palace Clock Tower 335 "St. Louise de Marillac" (altar painting)

1976. Precancelled.
1254 **334** 50c. red 50 45
1255 52c. orange 30 20
1256 54c. green 40 20
1257 60c. green 50 55
1258 62c. mauve 40 40
1259 68c. yellow 50 45
1260 90c. violet 80 80
1261 95c. red 80 65
1262 1f.05 brown 80 60
1263 1f.60 blue . . . . 1·40 1·25
1264 1f.70 turquoise . . . . . 1·40 1·00
1265 1f.85 brown . . . . . . 1·40 1·25

1976. Monaco Red Cross.
1270 **335** 4f. black, purple & green 2·00 1·90

1976. Paintings. "Princes and Princesses of Monaco". As T **213**.
1271 2f. purple . . . . 1·60 1·50
1272 4f. multicoloured . . . . . 3·00 2·10
DESIGNS: 2f. "Prince Honore IV"; 4f. "Princess Louise d'Aumont-Mazarin".

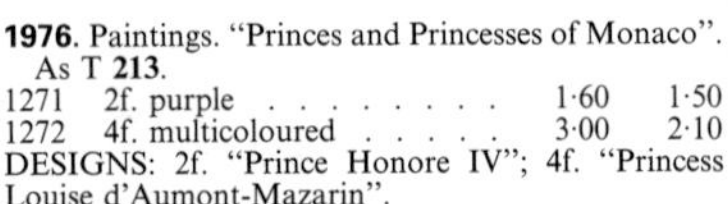

336 St. Vincent-de-Paul 337 Marie de Rabutin Chantal

1976. Centenary of St. Vincent-de-Paul Conference, Monaco.
1273 **336** 60c. black, brown & blue 35 25

1976. 350th Birth Anniv of Marquise de Sevigne (writer).
1274 **337** 80c. black, violet and red 40 30

338 Monaco 2g. "Honore II" Coin, 1640

1976. Monaco Numismatics.
1275 **338** 80c. blue and green . . . 50 40

339 Richard Byrd, "Josephine Ford", Airship "Norge" and Roald Amundsen

1976. 50th Anniv of First Flights over North Pole.
1276 **339** 85c. black, blue and green . . . . 1·25 1·10

340 Gulliver and Lilliputians

1976. 250th Anniv of Jonathan Swift's "Gulliver's Travels".
1277 **340** 1f.20 multicoloured . . . 60 45

341 Girl's Head and Christmas Decorations

1976. Christmas.
1278 **341** 60c. multicoloured . . . 40 25
1279 1f.20 green, orge & pur 60 40

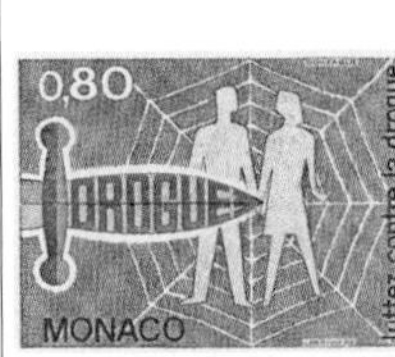

342 "Drug" Dagger piercing Man and Woman 343 Circus Clown

1976. Campaign against Drug Abuse.
1280 **342** 80c. blue, orge & bronze 50 30
1281 1f.20 lilac, purple & brn 70 50

1976. Monte Carlo Flower Show (1977). As T **271**. Multicoloured.
1282 80c. Flower arrangement . . 1·00 75
1283 1f. Bouquet of flowers . . . 1·50 1·25

1976. 3rd International Circus Festival, Monte Carlo.
1284 **343** 1f. multicoloured . . . . 1·40 1·00

344 Schooner "Hirondelle I"

1977. 75th Anniv of Publication of "Career of a Navigator" by Prince Albert I (1st issue). Illustrations by L. Tinayre.
1285 **344** 10c. brown, blue & turq 10 10
1286 – 20c. black, brown & lake 10 20
1287 – 30c. green, blue & orange 20 25
1288 – 80c. black, blue and red 40 40
1289 – 1f. black and brown . . 60 50
1290 – 1f.25 olive, green & violet 80 75
1291 – 1f.40 brown, olive & grn 1·25 1·25
1292 – 1f.90 blue, lt blue & red 2·25 1·60
1293 – 2f.50 brown, blue and turquoise . . . . . . 3·25 2·75
DESIGNS—VERT: 20c. Prince Albert I; 1f. Helmsman; 1f.90, Bringing in the trawl. HORIZ: 30c. Crew-members; 80c. "Hirondelle" in a gale; 1f.25, Securing the lifeboat; 1f.40, Shrimp fishing; 2f.50, Capture of an oceanic sunfish.
See also Nos. 1305/13.

345 Pyrenean Sheep and Mountain Dogs

1977. International Dog Show, Monte Carlo.
1294 **345** 80c. multicoloured . . . 3·75 2·75

346 "Maternity" (M. Cassatt)

1977. World Association of the "Friends of Children".
1295 **346** 80c. deep brown, brown and black 95 70

347 Archers

1977. 10th International Archery Championships.
1296 **347** 1f.10 black, brown & bl 70 50

348 Charles Lindbergh and "Spirit of St. Louis"

1977. 50th Anniv of Lindbergh's Transatlantic Flight.
1297 **348** 1f.90 light blue, blue and brown . . . . 1·40 1·10

349 "Harbour, Deauville"

1977. Birth Centenary of Raoul Dufy (painter).
1298 **349** 2f. multicoloured . . . . 3·00 2·50

350 "Portrait of a Young Girl" 351 "L'Oreillon" Tower

1977. 400th Birth Anniv of Peter Paul Rubens (painter).
1299 **350** 80c. orange, brown & blk 50 45
1300 – 1f. red 85 60
1301 – 1f.40 orange and red . . 1·75 1·25
DESIGNS: 1f. "Duke of Buckingham"; 1f.40, "Portrait of a Child".

1977. Europa. Views.
1302 **351** 1f. brown and blue . . . 80 60
1303 – 1f.40 blue, brown and bistre . . . . 1·25 1·10
DESIGN: 1f.40, St. Michael's Church, Menton.

1977. 75th Anniv of Publication of "Career of a Navigator" by Prince Albert I (2nd issue). Illustrations by L. Tinayre. As T **344**.
1305 10c. black and blue 10 10
1306 20c. blue 10 15
1307 30c. blue, light blue and green 20 25
1308 80c. brown, black and green 40 35
1309 1f. grey and green 50 50
1310 1f.25 black, brown and lilac 80 75
1311 1f.40 purple, blue and brown . . . . 1·25 1·25
1312 1f.90 black, blue and light blue . . . . 2·10 1·75
1313 3f. blue, brown and green 3·00 2·75
DESIGNS—HORIZ: 10c. "Princess Alice" (steam yacht) at Kiel; 20c. Ship's laboratory; 30c. "Princess Alice" in ice floes; 1f. Polar scene; 1f.25, Bridge of "Princess Alice" during snowstorm; 1f.40, Arctic camp; 1f.90, Ship's steam launch in floating ice; 3f. "Princess Alice" passing iceberg. VERT: 80c. Crewmen in Arctic dress.

352 Santa Claus & Sledge 353 Face, Poppy and Syringe

1977. Christmas.
1314 **352** 80c. red, green and blue 40 30
1315 1f.40 multicoloured . . . 60 40

1977. Monte Carlo Flower Show. As T **271**. Mult.
1316 80c. Snapdragons and campanula 80 70
1317 1f. Ikebana . . . . 1·25 1·00

1977. Campaign Against Drug Abuse.
1318 **353** 1f. black, red and violet 50 40

354 Clown and Flags

1977. 4th International Festival of Circus, Monaco.
1319 **354** 1f. multicoloured . . . . 1·40 1·10

355 Gold Coin of Honore II

1977. Monaco Numismatics.
1320 **355** 80c. brown and red . . . 50 45

356 Mediterranean divided by Industry

1977. Protection of the Mediterranean Environment.
1321 **356** 1f. black, green and blue 60 50

357 Dr. Guglielminetti and Road Tarrers

1977. 75th Anniv of First Experiments at Road Tarring in Monaco.
1322 **357** 1f.10 black, bistre and brown 60 45

358 F.M.L.T. Badge and Monte Carlo

1977. 50th Anniv of Monaco Lawn Tennis Federation.
1323 **358** 1f. blue, red and brown 1·00 50

359 Wimbledon and First Championships

1977. Centenary of Wimbledon Lawn Tennis Championships.
1324 **359** 1f.40 grey, green & brown . . . . 1·10 95

1977. Paintings. "Princes and Princesses of Monaco". As T **213**. Multicoloured.
1325 6f. "Prince Honore V" . . . 4·00 2·75

360 St. Jean Bosco

1977. Monaco Red Cross. Monegasque Art.
1326 **360** 4f. green, brown and blue . . . . 1·90 1·75

1978. Precancelled. Surch.
1327 **334** 58c. on 54c. green . . . 50 45
1328 73c. on 68c. yellow . . . 70 60
1329 1f.15 on 1f.05 brown . . 1·00 95
1330 2f. on 1f.85 brown . . . 1·75 1·75

362 Aerial Shipwreck from "L'Ile Mysterieuse"

1978. 150th Birth Anniv of Jules Verne.
1331 **362** 5c. brown, red and olive 10 10
1332 – 25c. turquoise, blue & red 10 10
1333 – 30c. blue, brown & lt blue 20 10
1334 – 80c. black, green & orge 30 30
1335 – 1f. brown, lake and blue 60 50
1336 – 1f.40 bistre, brown and green 80 70
1337 – 1f.70 brown, light blue and blue . . . . . . 1·10 1·25
1338 – 5f.50 violet and blue . . 2·75 2·75
DESIGNS: 25c. The abandoned ship from "L'Ile Mysterieuse"; 30c. The secret of the island from "L'Ile Mysterieuse"; 80c. "Robur the Conqueror"; 1f. "Master Zacharius"; 1f.40, "The Castle in the Carpathians"; 1f.70, "The Children of Captain Grant"; 5f.50, Jules Verne and allegories.

363 Aerial View of Congress Centre

1978. Inauguration of Monaco Congress Centre.
1339 **363** 1f. brown, blue and green 40 40
1340 – 1f.40 blue, brown & grn 60 50
DESIGN: 1f.40, View of Congress Centre from sea.

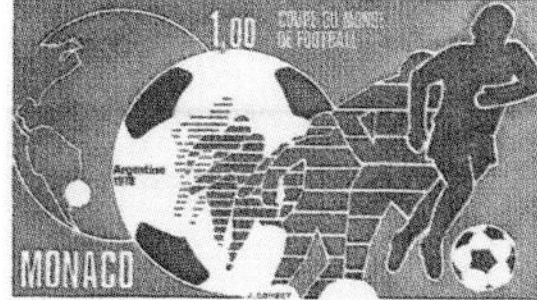

364 Footballers and Globe

1978. World Cup Football Championship, Argentina.
1341 **364** 1f. blue, slate and green 60 55

365 Antonio Vivaldi

366 "Ramoge" (research vessel) and Grimaldi Palace

1978. 300th Birth Anniv of Antonio Vivaldi (composer).
1342 **365** 1f. brown and red . . . 70 70

1978. Environment Protection. "RAMOGE" Agreement.
1343 **366** 80c. multicoloured . . . 40 35
1344 – 1f. red, blue and green 60 40
DESIGN—HORIZ (48 × 27 mm): 1f. Map of coastline between St. Raphael and Genes.

367 Monaco Cathedral

1978. Europa. Monaco Views.
1345 **367** 1f. green, brown and blue 70 60
1346 – 1f.40 brown, green & bl 1·40 1·00
DESIGN: 1f.40, View of Monaco from the east.

368 Monaco Congress Centre

1978. Precancelled.
1348 **368** 61c. orange 30 25
1349 64c. green 30 25
1350 68c. blue 30 25
1351 78c. purple 40 40
1352 83c. violet 40 40
1353 88c. orange 40 40
1354 1f.25 brown 70 60
1355 1f.30 red 70 60
1356 1f.40 green 70 60
1357 2f.10 blue . . . . . . 1·00 1·10
1358 2f.25 orange . . . . . 1·00 1·10
1359 2f.35 mauve . . . . . 1·10 95

369 "Cinderella"

1978. 350th Birth Anniv of Charles Perrault (writer).
1360 **369** 5c. red, olive and violet 10 10
1361 – 25c. black, brown & mve 10 10
1362 – 30c. green, lake & brown 20 10
1363 – 80c. multicoloured . . . 40 30
1364 – 1f. red, brown and olive 60 55
1365 – 1f.40 mauve, ultramarine and blue 80 65
1366 – 1f.70 green, blue & grey 1·00 85
1367 – 1f.90 multicoloured . . 1·40 1·10
1368 – 2f.50 blue, orange & grn 1·60 1·50
DESIGNS: 25c. "Puss in Boots"; 30c. "The Sleeping Beauty"; 80c. "Donkey's Skin"; 1f. "Little Red Riding Hood"; 1f.40, "Bluebeard"; 1f.70, "Tom Thumb"; 1f.90, "Riquet with a Tuft"; 2f.50, "The Fairies".

370 "The Sunflowers" (Van Gogh)

372 Girl with Letter

371 Afghan Hound

1978. Monte Carlo Flower Show (1979) and 125th Birth Anniv of Vincent Van Gogh. Multicoloured.
1369 1f. Type **370** . . . . 2·00 1·75
1370 1f.70 "The Iris" (Van Gogh) 3·00 1·90

1978. International Dog Show, Monte Carlo. Multicoloured.
1371 1f. Type **371** . . . . 2·75 1·90
1372 1f.20 Borzoi . . . . 3·25 2·50

1978. Christmas.
1373 **372** 1f. brown, blue and red 50 40

373 Catherine and William Booth

1978. Centenary of Salvation Army.
1374 **373** 1f.70 multicoloured . . . 90 85

374 Juggling Seals

1978. 5th International Circus Festival, Monaco.
1375 **374** 80c. orange, black & blue 40 45
1376 – 1f. multicoloured 60 55
1377 – 1f.40 brown, mauve and bistre 90 90
1378 – 1f.90 blue, lilac and mauve . . . . 1·60 1·60
1379 – 2f.40 multicoloured . . . 2·50 1·90
DESIGNS—HORIZ: 1f.40, Horseback acrobatics; 1f.90, Musical monkeys; 2f.40, Trapeze. VERT: 1f. Lion tamer.

1978. Paintings. "Princes and Princesses of Monaco". As T **213**. Multicoloured.
1380 2f. "Prince Florestan I" (G. Dauphin) . . . . . . 1·60 1·50
1381 4f. "Princess Caroline Gilbert de la Metz" (Marie Verroust) . . . . 3·00 2·50

377 "Jongleur de Notre-Dame" (Massenet)

1979. Centenary of "Salle Garnier" (Opera House) (1st issue).
1384 **377** 1f. blue, orange & mauve 40 35
1385 – 1f.20 violet, black & turq 60 45
1386 – 1f.50 maroon, grn & turq 70 75
1387 – 1f.70 multicoloured . . . 1·25 1·40
1388 – 2f.10 turquoise and violet . . . . 1·75 1·75
1389 – 3f. multicoloured . . . . 2·50 2·40
DESIGNS—HORIZ: 1f.20, "Hans the Flute Player" (L. Ganne); 1f.50, "Don Quixote" (J. Massenet); 2f.10, "The Child and the Sorcerer" (M. Ravel); 3f. Charles Garnier (architect) and south facade of Opera House. VERT: 1f.70, "L'Aiglon" (A. Honegger and J. Ibert).
See also Nos. 1399/1404.

378 Flower, Bird and Butterfly

1979. International Year of the Child. Children's Paintings.
1390 **378** 50c. pink, green and black 25 25
1391 – 1f. slate, green and orange 40 40
1392 – 1f.20 slate, orange & mve 60 60
1393 – 1f.50 yellow, brown & bl 1·00 1·00
1394 – 1f.70 multicoloured . . . 1·25 1·25
DESIGNS: 1f. Horse and Child; 1f.20, "The Gift of Love"; 1f.50, "Peace in the World"; 1f.70, "Down with Pollution".

379 Armed Foot Messenger

1979. Europa.
1395 **379** 1f.20 brown, green & bl 60 45
1396 – 1f.50 brown, turq & bl 70 45
1397 – 1f.70 brown, green & bl 80 75
DESIGNS: 1f.50, 18th-cent felucca; 1f.70, Arrival of first train at Monaco.

380 "Instrumental Music" (G. Boulanger) (detail of Opera House interior)

1979. Centenary of "Salle Garnier" (Opera House) (2nd issue).
1399 – 1f. brown, orange & turq 50 40
1400 – 1f.20 multicoloured . . . 60 50
1401 – 1f.50 multicoloured . . . 1·00 80
1402 – 1f.70 blue, brown and red . . . . 1·40 1·25
1403 – 2f.10 red, violet & black 1·75 1·75
1404 **380** 3f. green, brown and light green . . . . . 2·75 2·50
DESIGNS (as Type **377**)—HORIZ: 1f. "Les Biches" (F. Poulenc); 1f.20, "The Sailors" (G. Auric); 1f.70, "Gaiete Parisienne" (J. Offenbach). VERT: 1f.50, "La Spectre de la Rose" (C. M. Weber) (after poster by Jean Cocteau); 2f.10, "Salome" (R. Strauss).

1979. Paintings. "Princes and Princesses of Monaco". As T **213**. Multicoloured.
1405 3f. "Prince Charles III" (B. Biard) . . . . 1·60 1·40
1406 4f. "Antoinette de Merode" 2·40 1·60

381 St. Pierre Claver

382 "Princess Grace" Orchid

1979. Monaco Red Cross.
1407 **381** 5f. multicoloured . . . . 2·25 2·25

1979. Monte Carlo Flora 1980.
1408 **382** 1f. multicoloured . . . . 1·75 1·40

383 "Princess Grace" Rose

384 Clown balancing on Ball

1979. Monte Carlo Flower Show.
1409 **383** 1f.20 multicoloured . . . 1·60 1·40

1979. 6th International Circus Festival.
1410 **384** 1f.20 multicoloured . . . 70 80

385 Sir Rowland Hill and Penny Black

386 Albert Einstein

1979. Death Centenary of Sir Rowland Hill.
1411 **385** 1f.70 brown, blue & blk 60 55

1979. Birth Centenary of Albert Einstein (physicist).
1412 **386** 1f.70 brown, grey and red 70 55

387 St. Patrick's Cathedral

1979. Centenary of St. Patrick's Cathedral, New York.
1413 **387** 2f.10 black, blue & brn 90 70

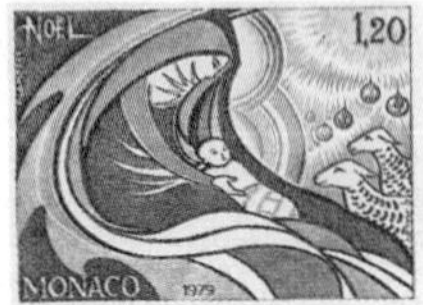

388 Nativity Scene

1979. Christmas.
1414 **388** 1f.20 blue, orange & mve 50 55

389 Early Racing Cars

1979. 50th Anniv of Grand Prix Motor Racing.
1415 **389** 1f. multicoloured 70 50

390 Arms of Charles V and Monaco

1979. 450th Anniv of Visit of Emperor Charles V.
1416 **390** 1f.50 brown, blue & blk 60 50

391 Setter and Pointer

1979. International Dog Show, Monte Carlo.
1417 **391** 1f.20 multicoloured . . . 3·00 2·50

392 Spring

1980. Precancels. The Seasons.
1418 **392** 76c. brown and green . . 30 20
1419 88c. olive, emerald & grn 30 20
1420 – 99c. green and brown . . 50 30
1421 – 1f.14 green, emer & brn 30 30
1422 – 1f.60 brown, grey and deep brown 80 60
1423 – 1f.84 lake, grey & brown 80 60
1424 – 2f.65 brown, lt blue & bl 1·40 85
1425 – 3f.05 brown, bl & slate 1·40 85
DESIGNS: 99c., 1f.14, Summer; 1f.60, 1f.84, Autumn; 2f.65, 3f.05, Winter.

394 Paul P. Harris (founder) and View of Chicago

1980. 75th Anniv of Rotary International.
1434 **394** 1f.80 olive, blue & turq 80 65

395 Gymnastics

1980. Olympic Games, Moscow and Lake Placid.
1435 **395** 1f.10 blue, brown & grey 30 25
1436 – 1f.30 red, brown & blue 40 30
1437 – 1f.60 red, blue & brown 50 40
1438 – 1f.80 brown, bis & grn 60 50
1439 – 2f.30 grey, violet & mve 90 75
1440 – 4f. green, blue and brown . . . . 1·40 1·25
DESIGNS: 1f.30, Handball; 1f.60, Pistol-shooting; 1f.80, Volleyball; 2f.30, Ice hockey; 4f. Skiing.

396 Colette (novelist)

1980. Europa. Each black, green and red.
1441 1f.30 Type **396** 40 30
1442 1f.80 Marcel Pagnol (writer) 50 45

397 "La Source"

1980. Birth Bicentenary of Jean Ingres (artist).
1444 **397** 4f. multicoloured . . . . 5·00 3·75

398 Montaigne **399** Guillaume Apollinaire (after G. Pieret)

1980. 400th Anniv of Publication of Montaigne's "Essays".
1445 **398** 1f.30 black, red and blue 55 40

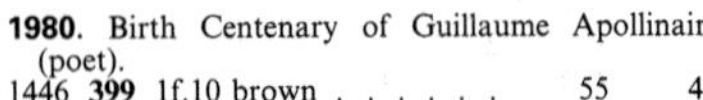
1980. Birth Centenary of Guillaume Apollinaire (poet).
1446 **399** 1f.10 brown 55 40

400 Congress Centre

1980. Kiwanis International European Convention.
1447 **400** 1f.30 black, blue and red 55 40

401 Honore II Silver Ecu, 1649

1980. Numismatics.
1448 **401** 1f.50 black and blue . . 60 55

402 Lhassa Apso and Shih Tzu

1980. International Dog Show, Monte Carlo.
1449 **402** 1f.30 multicoloured . . . 3·50 2·75

403 "The Princess and the Pea"

1980. 175th Birth Anniv of Hans Christian Andersen.
1450 **403** 70c. sepia, red and brown 30 25
1451 – 1f.30 blue, turq & red . . 40 45
1452 – 1f.50 black, blue & turq 70 65
1453 – 1f.60 red, black & brown 80 80
1454 – 1f.80 yellow, brn & turq 1·00 1·00
1455 – 2f.30 brown, pur & vio 1·40 1·25
DESIGNS: 1f.30, "The Little Mermaid"; 1f.50, "The Chimneysweep and Shepherdess"; 1f.60, "The Brave Little Lead Soldier"; 1f.80, "The Little Match Girl"; 2f.30, "The Nightingale".

404 "The Road" (M. Vlaminck)

1980. 75th Anniv of 1905 Autumn Art Exhibition. Multicoloured.
1456 2f. Type **404** . . . . 1·50 1·25
1457 3f. "Woman at Balustrade" (Van Dongen) . . . . . 2·50 1·25
1458 4f. "The Reader" (Henri Matisse) . . . . 3·00 3·00
1459 5f. "Three Figures in a Meadow" (A. Derain) . . 4·50 3·75

1980. Paintings. "Princes and Princesses of Monaco". As T **213**. Multicoloured.
1460 4f. "Prince Albert I" (L. Bonnat) . . . . . . 2·00 1·75
1461 4f. "Princess Marie Alice Heine" (L. Maeterlinck) 2·00 1·75

405 "Sunbirds"

1980. Monaco Red Cross.
1462 **405** 6f. red, bistre and brown 2·50 2·50

406 "MONACO" balanced on Tightrope

1980. 7th International Circus Festival, Monaco.
1463 **406** 1f.30 red, turquoise & blue . . . . 1·40 85

407 Children and Nativity

1980. Christmas.
1464 **407** 1f.10 blue, carmine and red 45 40
1465 2f.30 violet, orange and pink 95 60

1980. Monte Carlo Flower Show, 1981. As T **383**. Multicoloured.
1466 1f.30 "Princess Stephanie" rose 80 60
1467 1f.80 Ikebana . . . . 1·50 1·00

408 "Alcyonium" **409** Fish with Hand for Tail

1980. Marine Fauna. Multicoloured.
1468 5c. "Spirographis spallanzanli" 10 10
1469 10c. "Anemonia sulcata" . . 10 10
1470 15c. "Leptopsammia pruvoit" 10 10
1471 20c. "Pteroides" 10 20
1472 30c. "Paramuricea clavata" (horiz) 30 20
1473 40c. Type **408** 30 20
1474 50c. "Corallium rubrum" . . 40 30
1475 60c. Trunculus murex ("Calliactis parasitica") (horiz) 70 65
1476 70c. "Cerianthus membranaceus" (horiz) 90 80
1477 1f. "Actinia equina" (horiz) 1·00 80
1478 2f. "Protula" (horiz) . . . . 2·00 1·10

1981. "Respect the Sea".
1479 **409** 1f.20 multicoloured . . . 70 55

410 Prince Rainier and Princess Grace

1981. Royal Silver Wedding.
1480 **410** 1f.20 black and green . . 1·00 75
1481 1f.40 black and red . . . 1·40 1·25
1482 1f.70 black and green . . 1·60 1·40
1483 1f.80 black and brown 2·00 1·60
1484 2f. black and blue . . . 3·25 1·90

411 Mozart (after Lorenz Vogel) **412** Palm Cross

1981. 225th Birth Anniv of Wolfgang Amadeus Mozart (composer).
1485 **411** 2f. brown, dp brown & bl . . . . 1·25 85
1486 – 2f.50 blue, brn & dp brn 1·75 1·40
1487 – 3f.50 dp brown, bl & brn 2·75 1·75
DESIGNS—HORIZ: 2f.50, "Mozart at 7 with his Father and Sister" (engraving by Delafoose after drawing by Carmontelle); 3f.50 "Mozart directing Requiem two Days before his Death" (painting by Baude).

1981. Europa. Multicoloured.
1488 **412** 1f.40 green, brown & red 50 40
1489 – 2f. multicoloured 60 55
DESIGN: 2f. Children carrying palm crosses.

413 Paris Football Stadium, Cup and Footballer

1981. 25th Anniv of European Football Cup.
1491 **413** 2f. black and blue . . . 95 70

414 I.Y.D.P. Emblem and Girl in Wheelchair

1981. International Year of Disabled Persons.
1492 **414** 1f.40 blue and green . . 70 55

415 Palace flying Old Flag, National Flag and Monte Carlo

1981. Centenary of National Flag.
1493 **415** 2f. red, blue and brown 90 65

416 Oceanographic Institute, Paris and Oceanographic Museum, Monaco

1981. 75th Anniv of Oceanographic Institute.
1494 **416** 1f.20 blue, black & brn 60 60

417 Bureau Building and "Faddey Bellingshausen" (hydrographic research ship)

1981. 50th Anniv of Int Hydrographic Bureau.
1495 **417** 2f.50 sepia, brown and light brown . . . . . 1·40 1·25

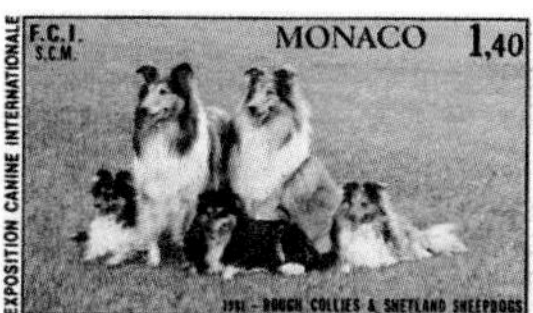

418 Rough Collies and Shetland Sheepdogs

1981. International Dog Show, Monte Carlo.
1496 **418** 1f.40 multicoloured . . . 3·50 3·25

419 Rainier III and Prince Albert

421 Arctic Scene and Map

1981. (a) 23 × 28 mm.
1497 **419** 1f.40 green (postage) . . 70 20
1498 1f.60 red 95 15
1499 1f.60 green 50 20
1500 1f.70 green 80 25
1501 1f.80 red 60 40
1502 1f.80 green 70 20
1503 1f.90 green 1·40 50
1504 2f. red 1·25 40
1505 2f. green 85 25
1506 2f.10 red 90 25
1507 2f.20 red 80 40
1508 2f.30 blue 2·75 2·40
1509 2f.50 brown 1·00 60
1510 2f.60 blue 1·90 1·75
1511 2f.80 blue 1·75 1·50
1512 3f. blue 1·75 1·25
1513 3f.20 blue 1·75 1·75
1514 3f.40 blue 2·75 1·60
1515 3f.60 blue 1·75 1·25
1516 4f. brown 1·40 75
1517 5f.50 black 1·90 1·40
1518 10f. purple 2·75 1·10
1519 15f. green 6·50 1·75
1520 20f. blue 6·50 2·50

(b) 36 × 27 mm.
1521 – 5f. violet (air) 1·60 75
1522 – 10f. red 3·75 1·50
1523 – 15f. green 5·00 1·60
1524 – 20f. blue 6·00 3·00
1525 – 30f. brown 8·00 4·00
DESIGN: Nos. 1521/5, Double portrait and monograms.

1981. 1st International Congress on Discovery and History of Northern Polar Regions, Rome.
1530 **421** 1f.50 multicoloured . . . 1·25 95

1981. Paintings. "Princes and Princesses of Monaco". Vert designs as T **213**. Multicoloured.
1531 3f. "Prince Louis II" (P.-A. de Laszlo) 1·60 1·00
1532 5f. "Princess Charlotte" (P.-A. de Laszlo) 3·25 1·90

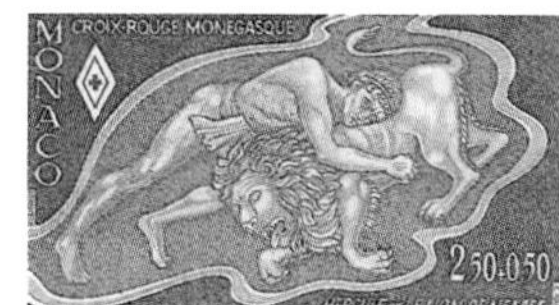

422 Hercules fighting the Nemean Lion

1981. Monaco Red Cross. The Twelve Labours of Hercules (1st series).
1533 **422** 2f.50+50c. green, brown and red 1·00 1·25
1534 – 3f.50+50c. blue, green and red 1·25 1·25
DESIGN: 3f.50, Slaying the Hydra of Lerna.
See also Nos. 1584/5, 1631/2, 1699/1700, 1761/2 and 1794/5.

423 Ettore Bugatti (racing car designer) (Cent)

424 Eglantines and Morning Glory

1981. Birth Anniversaries.
1535 **423** 1f. indigo, blue and red 80 50
1536 – 2f. black, blue and brown 80 75
1537 – 2f.50 brown, black and red 1·10 80
1538 – 4f. multicoloured 2·50 2·40
1539 – 4f. multicoloured 2·50 2·40
DESIGNS: No. 1536, George Bernard Shaw (dramatist, 125th anniv); 1537, Fernand Leger (painter, centenary). LARGER: (37 × 48 mm): 1538, Pablo Picasso (self-portrait) (centenary); 1539, Rembrandt (self-portrait) (375th anniv).

1981. Monte Carlo Flower Show (1982). Mult.
1540 1f.40 Type **424** 1·00 75
1541 2f. "Ikebana" (painting by Ikenobo) 1·75 1·40

425 "Catherine Deneuve"

426 Tiger, Clown, Acrobat and Elephants

1981. 1st International Rose Show, Monte Carlo.
1542 **425** 1f.80 multicoloured . . . 2·50 1·90

1981. 8th International Circus Festival, Monaco.
1543 **426** 1f.40 violet, mauve & blk 1·90 1·50

427 Praying Children and Nativity

1981. Christmas.
1544 **427** 1f.20 blue, mauve & brn 50 50

428 "Lancia-Stratos" Rally Car

1981. 50th Monte Carlo Rally (1982).
1545 **428** 1f. blue, red & turquoise 90 80

430 "Hoya bella"

431 Spring

1981. Plants in Exotic Garden. Multicoloured.
1547 1f.40 Type **430** 2·50 1·40
1548 1f.60 "Bolivicereus samaipatanus" 2·00 1·25
1549 1f.80 "Trichocereus grandiflorus" (horiz) 2·50 1·50
1550 2f. "Argyroderma roseum" 1·25 40
1551 2f.30 "Euphorbia milii" 2·00 1·75
1552 2f.60 "Echinocereus fitchii" (horiz) 2·00 1·75
1553 2f.90 "Rebutia heliosa" (horiz) 2·00 1·90
1554 4f.10 "Echinopsis multiplex cristata" (horiz) 3·00 2·50

1982. Precancels. The Seasons of the Peach Tree.
1555 **431** 97c. mauve and green 30 20
1556 – 1f.25 green, orge & mve 50 30
1557 – 2f.03 brown 80 60
1558 – 3f.36 brown and blue 1·40 90
DESIGNS: 1f.25, Summer; 2f.03, Autumn; 3f.36, Winter.

432 Common Nutcracker

433 Capture of Monaco Fortress, 1297

1982. Birds from Mercantour National Park.
1559 **432** 60c. black, brown & grn 60 70
1560 – 70c. black and mauve 70 70
1561 – 80c. red, black & orange 80 80
1562 – 90c. black, red and blue 1·40 1·25
1563 – 1f.40 brown, black & red 2·40 1·75
1564 – 1f.60 brown, black & blue 2·75 2·10
DESIGNS—VERT: 70c. Black grouse; 80c. Rock partridge; 1f.60, Golden eagle. HORIZ: 90c. Wallcreeper; 1f.40, Rock ptarmigan.

1982. Europa.
1565 **433** 1f.60 blue, brown and red 50 40
1566 – 2f.30 blue, brown and red 70 45
DESIGN: 2f.30, Signing the Treaty of Peronne, 1641.

434 Old Quarter

1982. Fontvieille.
1568 **434** 1f.40 blue, brown & grn 60 40
1569 – 1f.60 light brown, brown and red 70 60
1570 – 2f.30 purple 1·25 80
DESIGNS: 1f.60, Land reclamation; 2f.30, Urban development.

435 Stadium

1982. Fontvieille Sports Stadium (1st series).
1571 **435** 2f.30 green, brown & blue 1·00 80
See also No. 1616.

436 Arms of Paris

1982. "Philexfrance" International Stamp Exhibition, Paris.
1572 **436** 1f.40 red, grey and deep red 70 60

437 Old English Sheepdog

1982. International Dog Show, Monte Carlo. Multicoloured.
1573 60c. Type **437** 2·00 1·50
1574 1f. Briard 2·50 1·90

438 Monaco Cathedral and Arms

1982. Creation of Archbishopric of Monaco (1981).
1575 **438** 1f.60 black, blue and red 60 60

439 St. Francis of Assisi

440 Dr. Robert Koch

1982. 800th Birth Anniv of St. Francis of Assisi.
1576 **439** 1f.40 grey and light grey 70 65

1982. Centenary of Discovery of Tubercle Bacillus.
1577 **440** 1f.40 purple and lilac . . 70 70

441 Lord Baden-Powell

443 St. Hubert (18th-century medallion)

1982. 125th Birth Anniv of Lord Baden-Powell (founder of Boy Scout Movement).
1578 **441** 1f.60 brown and black 1·00 90

1982. 29th Meeting of International Hunting Council, Monte Carlo.
1580 **443** 1f.60 multicoloured . . . 90 75

444 Books, Reader and Globe

1982. International Bibliophile Association General Assembly, Monte Carlo.
1581 **444** 1f.60 blue, purple & red 60 55

445 "Casino, 1870"

1982. Monaco in the "Belle Epoque" (1st series). Paintings by Hubert Clerissi. Multicoloured.
1582 3f. Type **445** . . . . 1·25 1·10
1583 5f. "Porte d'Honneur, Royal Palace, 1893" . . . . . . 2·50 1·60
See also Nos. 1629/30, 1701/2, 1763/4, 1801/2, 1851/2, 1889/90 and 1965/6.

1982. Monaco Red Cross. The Twelve Labours of Hercules (2nd series). As T **422**.
1584 2f.50+50c. green, red and bright red . . . . 1·25 1·40
1585 3f.50+50c. brown, blue and red . . . . 1·40 1·50
DESIGNS: 2f.50, Capturing the Erymanthine Boar; 3f.50, Shooting the Stymphalian Birds.

446 Nicolo Paganini (violinist and composer, bicent) **447** Vase of Flowers

1982. Birth Anniversaries.
1586 **446** 1f.60 brown and purple 90 60
1587 – 1f.80 red, mauve & brn 1·25 80
1588 – 2f.60 green and red . . . 1·40 1·25
1589 – 4f. multicoloured . . . . 2·75 2·40
1590 – 4f. multicoloured . . . . 2·75 2·40
DESIGNS—VERT: No. 1587, Anna Pavlova (ballerina, centenary); 1588, Igor Stravinsky (composer, centenary). HORIZ (47 × 36 mm): 1589, "In a Boat" (Edouard Manet, 150th anniv); 1590, "The Black Fish" (Georges Braque, centenary).

1982. Monte Carlo Flower Show (1983). Mult.
1591 1f.60 Type **447** . . . . . . 1·40 90
1592 2f.60 Ikebana arrangement 1·75 1·50

448 Bowl of Flowers **449** The Three Kings

1982.
1593 **448** 1f.60 multicoloured . . . 1·40 90

1982. Christmas.
1594 **449** 1f.60 green, blue & orge 50 35
1595 – 1f.80 green, blue & orge 60 35
1596 – 2f.60 green, blue & orge 90 50
DESIGNS: 1f.80, The Holy Family; 2f.60, Shepherds and angels.

450 Prince Albert I and Polar Scene

1982. Centenary of First International Polar Year.
1598 **450** 1f.60 brown, green & bl 1·75 1·40

451 Viking Longships off Greenland

1982. Millenary of Discovery of Greenland by Erik the Red.
1599 **451** 1f.60 blue, brown & blk 1·75 1·40

452 Julius Caesar in the Port of Monaco ("Aeneid", Book VI)

1982. 2000th Death Anniv of Virgil (poet).
1600 **452** 1f.80 deep blue, blue and brown . . . . 1·75 1·40

453 Spring **454** Tourism

1983. Precancels. The Seasons of the Apple Tree.
1601 **453** 1f.05 purple, green and yellow 40 50
1602 – 1f.35 light green, deep green and turquoise 50 55
1603 – 2f.19 red, brown & grey 1·00 1·10
1604 – 3f.63 yellow and brown 1·60 1·50
DESIGNS: 1f.35, Summer; 2f.19, Autumn; 3f.63, Winter.

1983. 50th Anniv of Exotic Garden. Mult.
1605 1f.80 Type **454** 90 85
1606 2f. Cactus plants (botanical collections) . . . . 1·25 80
1607 2f.30 Cactus plants (international flower shows) . . . . 1·40 1·40
1608 2f.60 Observatory grotto (horiz) . . . . 1·75 1·50
1609 3f.30 Museum of Prehistoric Anthropology (horiz) . . 2·25 2·00

455 Alaskan Malamute **457** St. Charles Borromee and Church

1983. International Dog Show, Monte Carlo.
1610 **455** 1f.80 multicoloured . . . 4·50 3·75

1983. Centenary of St. Charles Church, Monte Carlo.
1612 **457** 2f.60 deep blue, blue and green 95 80

458 Montgolfier Balloon, 1783 **459** Franciscan College

1983. Europa.
1613 **458** 1f.80 blue, brown & grey 50 35
1614 – 2f.60 grey, blue & brown 70 60
DESIGN: 2f.60, Space shuttle.

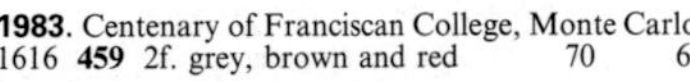

1983. Centenary of Franciscan College, Monte Carlo.
1616 **459** 2f. grey, brown and red 70 60

460 Stadium

1983. Fontvieille Sports Stadium (2nd series).
1617 **460** 2f. green, blue and brown 70 55

461 Early and Modern Cars

1983. Centenary of Petrol-driven Motor Car.
1618 **461** 2f.90 blue, brown & green . . . . 2·00 1·40

462 Blue Whale

1983. International Commission for the Protection of Whales.
1619 **462** 3f.30 blue, light blue and grey . . . . 2·75 2·50

463 Dish Aerial, Pigeon, W.C.Y. Emblem and Satellite

1983. World Communications Year.
1620 **463** 4f. lilac and mauve . . . 1·25 1·10

464 Smoking Moor **466** Circus Performers

465 Johannes Brahms (composer)

1983. Nineteenth Century Automata from the Galea Collection. Multicoloured.
1621 50c. Type **464** 20 20
1622 60c. Clown with diabolo . . 20 20
1623 70c. Smoking monkey . . . 20 20
1624 80c. Peasant with pig . . . 40 40
1625 90c. Buffalo Bill smoking 50 45
1626 1f. Snake charmer 50 45
1627 1f.50 Pianist 80 60
1628 2f. Young girl powdering herself . . . . 1·25 1·00

1983. Monaco in the "Belle Epoque" (2nd series). As T **445**. Multicoloured.
1629 3f. "The Beach, 1902" . . . 2·00 1·60
1630 5f. "Cafe de Paris, 1905" . . 3·25 2·75

1983. Monaco Red Cross. The Twelve Labours of Hercules (3rd series). As T **422**.
1631 2f.50+50c. brn, bl & red . . 1·25 1·00
1632 3f.50+50c. violet, mve & red 1·40 1·25
DESIGNS: 2f.50, Capturing the Hind of Ceryneia; 3f.50, Cleaning the Augean stables.

1983. Birth Anniversaries.
1633 **465** 3f. deep brown, brown and green . . . . . . 1·00 80
1634 – 3f. black, brown and red 1·00 80
1635 – 4f. multicoloured . . . . 2·25 1·90
1636 – 4f. multicoloured . . . . 2·25 1·90
DESIGNS—HORIZ: No. 1633, Type **465** (150th anniv); 1634, Giacomo Puccini (composer) and scene from "Madame Butterfly" (125th anniv). VERT (37 × 48 mm): 1635, "Portrait of a Young Man" (Raphael (artist), 500th anniv); 1636, "Cottin Passage" (Utrillo (artist), centenary).

1983. 9th International Circus Festival, Monaco.
1637 **466** 2f. blue, red and green 1·40 1·25

467 Bouquet **468** Provencale Creche

1983. Monte Carlo Flower Show (1984). Mult.
1638 1f.60 Type **467** . . . . . . 1·00 70
1639 2f.60 Arrangement of poppies . . . . 1·50 1·10

1983. Christmas.
1640 **468** 2f. multicoloured . . . . 1·10 70

469 Nobel Literature Prize Medal

1983. 150th Birth Anniv of Alfred Nobel (inventor of dynamite and founder of Nobel Prizes).
1641 **469** 2f. black, grey and red 90 80

470 O. F. Ozanam (founder) and Paris Headquarters

1983. 150th Anniv of Society of St. Vincent de Paul.
1642 **470** 1f.80 violet and purple 70 50

471 "Tazerka" (oil rig)

1983. Oil Industry.
1643 **471** 5f. blue, brown & turq 1·75 1·25

474 Skater and Stadium

1984. Winter Olympic Games, Sarajevo.
1646 **474** 2f. blue, green and turquoise 70 55
1647 – 4f. blue, violet and purple . . . . 1·40 1·00
DESIGN: 4f. Skater and snowflake.

475 Bridge

1984. Europa. 25th Anniv of European Post and Telecommunications Conference.
1648 **475** 2f. blue 70 50
1649 3f. green . . . . 1·10 95

476 Balkan Fritillary

478 Sanctuary and Statue of Virgin

477 Auvergne Pointer

1984. Butterflies and Moths in Mercantour National Park. Multicoloured.
1651 1f.60 Type **476** . . . . . . 1·00 1·00
1652 2f. "Zygaena vesubiana" . . 1·50 1·10
1653 2f.80 False mnestra ringlet 1·60 1·40
1654 3f. Small apollo (horiz) . . 1·90 1·60
1655 3f.60 Southern swallowtail (horiz) . . . . 2·75 1·90

1984. International Dog Show, Monte Carlo.
1656 **477** 1f.60 multicoloured . . . 2·50 1·75

1984. Our Lady of Laghet Sanctuary.
1657 **478** 2f. blue, brown and green 70 45

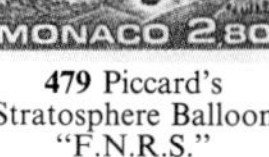

479 Piccard's Stratosphere Balloon "F.N.R.S."

481 Place de la Visitation

480 Concert

1984. Birth Centenary of Auguste Piccard (physicist).
1658 **479** 2f.80 black, green & blue 80 55
1659 – 4f. blue, green & turq . . 1·25 80
DESIGN: 4f. Bathyscaphe.

1984. 25th Anniv of Palace Concerts.
1660 **480** 3f.60 blue and deep blue 1·25 80

1984. Bygone Monaco (1st series). Paintings by Hubert Clerissi.
1661 **481** 5c. brown 10 10
1662 – 10c. red 10 10
1663 – 15c. violet 10 10
1664 – 20c. blue 10 10
1665 – 30c. blue 10 10
1666 – 40c. green 40 20
1667 – 50c. red 10 10
1668 – 60c. blue 10 10
1669 – 70c. orange 50 35
1670 – 80c. green 20 20
1671 – 90c. mauve 30 25
1672 – 1f. blue 30 20
1673 – 2f. black 60 40
1674 – 3f. red . . . . 1·75 80
1675 – 4f. blue . . . . 1·40 75
1676 – 5f. green . . . . 1·40 75
1677 – 6f. green . . . . 2·10 1·10
DESIGNS: 10c. Town Hall; 15c. Rue Basse; 20c. Place Saint-Nicolas; 30c. Quai du Commerce; 40c. Rue des Iris; 50c. Ships in harbour; 60c. St. Charles's Church; 70c. Religious procession; 80c. Olive tree overlooking harbour; 90c. Quayside; 1f. Palace Square; 2f. Fishing boats in harbour; 3f. Bandstand; 4f. Railway station; 5f. Mail coach; 6f. Monte Carlo Opera House.
See also Nos. 2015/27.

482 Spring

1984. Precancels. The Seasons of the Quince.
1678 **482** 1f.14 red and green . . . 40 50
1679 – 1f.47 deep green & green 60 55
1680 – 2f.38 olive, turquoise and green . . . . 1·00 1·00
1681 – 3f.95 green . . . . . . 1·75 1·50
DESIGNS: 1f.47, Summer; 2f.38, Autumn; 3f.95, Winter.

483 Shepherd

485 Bowl of Mixed Flowers

484 Gargantua and Cattle

1984. Christmas. Crib Figures from Provence. Multicoloured.
1682 70c. Type **483** 30 20
1683 1f. Blind man 40 30
1684 1f.70 Happy man 70 50
1685 2f. Spinner 80 70
1686 2f.10 Angel playing trumpet 90 1·10
1687 2f.40 Garlic seller . . . . . 1·10 1·25
1688 3f. Drummer . . . . 1·25 1·25
1689 3f.70 Knife grinder . . . . 1·50 1·25
1690 4f. Elderly couple . . . . . 1·90 1·60

1984. 450th Anniv of First Edition of "Gargantua" by Francois Rabelais.
1691 **484** 2f. black, red and brown 70 50
1692 – 2f. black, red and blue 70 50
1693 – 4f. green . . . . 1·40 1·25
DESIGNS—As T **484**: No. 1692, Panurge's sheep. 36 × 48 mm: 1693, Francois Rabelais.

1984. Monte Carlo Flower Show (1985). Mult.
1694 2f.10 Type **485** . . . . . . 1·00 80
1695 3f. Ikebana arrangement . . 1·60 1·10

486 Television Lights and Emblem

1984. 25th Int Television Festival, Monte Carlo.
1696 **486** 2f.10 blue, grey and mauve 70 55
1697 – 3f. grey, blue and red . . 1·00 80
DESIGN: 3f. "Golden Nymph" (Grand Prix).

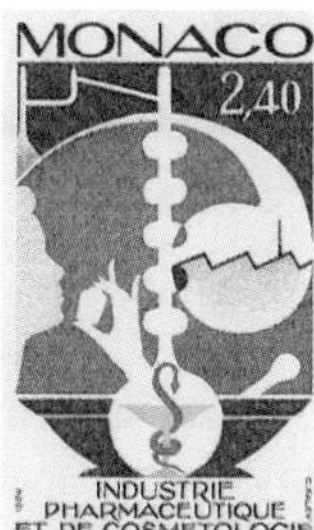

487 Chemical Equipment

1984. Pharmaceutical and Cosmetics Industry.
1698 **487** 2f.40 blue, deep blue and green 80 50

1984. Monaco Red Cross. The Twelve Labours of Hercules (4th series). As T **422**.
1699 3f.+50c. brown, light brown and red . . . . 1·00 1·25
1700 4f.+50c. green, brown and red . . . . 1·40 1·50
DESIGNS: 3f. Killing the Cretan bull; 4f. Capturing the Mares of Diomedes.

1984. Monaco in the "Belle Epoque" (3rd series). Paintings by Hubert Clerissi. As T **445**. Mult.
1701 4f. "Grimaldi Street, 1908" (vert) . . . . 2·25 1·90
1702 5f. "Railway Station, 1910" (vert) . . . . 3·50 2·75

489 "Woman with Chinese Vase"

1984. 150th Birth Anniv of Edgar Degas (artist).
1704 **489** 6f. multicoloured . . . . 3·50 2·50

490 Spring

1985. Precancels. Seasons of the Cherry.
1705 **490** 1f.22 olive, green and blue 40 50
1706 – 1f.57 red, green and yellow 60 55
1707 – 2f.55 orange and brown 1·10 1·10
1708 – 4f.23 purple, green and blue . . . . 1·75 1·60
DESIGNS: 1f.57, Summer; 2f.55, Autumn; 4f.23, Winter.

491 First Stamp

1985. Centenary of First Monaco Stamps.
1709 **491** 1f.70 green 60 40
1710 2f.10 red 70 20
1711 3f. blue . . . . 1·25 65

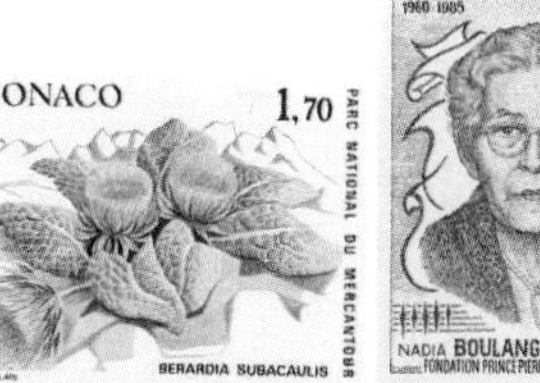

493 "Berardia subacaulis"

495 Nadia Boulanger (composer)

1985. Flowers in Mercantour National Park. Mult.
1724 1f.70 Type **493** 60 45
1725 2f.10 "Saxifraga florulenta" (vert) 70 55
1726 2f.40 "Fritillaria moggridgei" (vert) . . . . 1·00 75
1727 3f. "Sempervivum allionii" (vert) . . . . 1·25 1·10
1728 3f.60 "Silene cordifolia" (vert) . . . . 1·60 1·25
1729 4f. "Primula allionii" . . . 1·95 1·60

1985. 25th Anniv of First Musical Composition Competition.
1731 **495** 1f.70 brown 70 50
1732 – 2f.10 blue 90 90
DESIGN: 2f.10, Georges Auric (composer).

496 Stadium and Runners

1985. Inauguration of Louis II Stadium, Fontvieille, and Athletics and Swimming Championships.
1733 **496** 1f.70 brown, red and violet 50 40
1734 – 2f.10 blue, brown and green 85 50
DESIGN: 2f.10, Stadium and swimmers.

497 Prince Antoine I

1985. Europa.
1735 **497** 2f.10 blue 70 50
1736 – 3f. red 90 85
DESIGN: 3f. John-Baptiste Lully (composer).

498 Museum, "Hirondelle I" (schooner) and "Denise" (midget submarine)

1985. 75th Anniv of Oceanographic Museum.
1738 **498** 2f.10 black, green and blue 70 65

499 Boxer

1985. International Dog Show, Monte Carlo.
1739 **499** 2f.10 multicoloured . . . 1·90 1·50

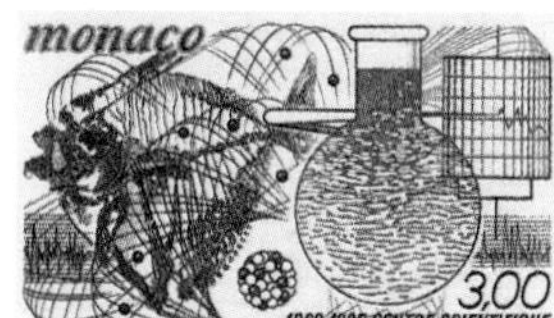

500 Scientific Motifs

1985. 25th Anniv of Scientific Centre.
1740 **500** 3f. blue, black and violet 1·00 70

501 Children and Hands holding Seedling and Emblem

1985. International Youth Year.
1741 **501** 3f. brown, green and light brown . . . . . 1·00 70

502 Regal Angelfish

1985. Fishes in Oceanographic Museum Aquarium (1st series). Multicoloured.
1742 1f.80 Type **502** 90 80
1743 1f.90 Type **502** . . . . . . 1·50 80
1744 2f.20 Powder blue surgeonfish 90 75
1745 3f.20 Red-tailed butterflyfish 1·25 1·25
1746 3f.40 As No. 1745 . . . . . 2·75 1·90
1747 3f.90 Clown triggerfish . . . 1·90 1·75
1748 7f. Fishes in aquarium (36 × 48 mm) . . . . . . 3·25 2·75
See also Nos. 1857/62.

504 Rome Buildings and Emblem

1985. "Italia '85" International Stamp Exhibition, Rome.
1750 **504** 4f. black, green and red 1·25 85

505 Clown **506** Decorations

1985. 11th International Circus Festival, Monaco.
1751 **505** 1f.80 multicoloured . . . 1·25 85

1985. Christmas.
1752 **506** 2f.20 multicoloured . . . 80 45

507 Ship and Marine Life **508** Arrangement of Roses, Tulips and Jonquil

1985. Fish Processing Industry.
1753 **507** 2f.20 blue, turquoise and brown 70 45

1985. Monte Carlo Flower Show (1986). Mult.
1754 2f.20 Type **508** 90 80
1755 3f.20 Arrangement of chrysanthemums and heather . . . . 1·50 1·40

509 Globe and Satellite

1985. European Telecommunications Satellite Organization.
1756 **509** 3f. black, blue and violet 1·00 1·00

510 Sacha Guitry (actor, centenary)

1985. Birth Anniversaries.
1757 **510** 3f. orange and brown . . 1·00 95
1758 – 4f. blue, brown and mauve . . . . 1·25 1·10
1759 – 5f. turquoise, blue and grey . . . . 1·50 1·25
1760 – 6f. blue, brown and black . . . . 1·90 1·50
DESIGNS: 4f. Wilhelm and Jacob Grimm (folklorists, bicentenaries); 5f. Frederic Chopin and Robert Schumann (composers, 175th annivs); 6f. Johann Sebastian Bach and Georg Friedrich Handel (composers, 300th annivs).

1985. Monaco Red Cross. The Twelve Labours of Hercules (5th series). As T **422**.
1761 3f.+70c. green, deep red and red . . . . 1·00 90
1762 4f.+80c. brown, blue & red 1·25 1·25
DESIGNS: 3f. The Cattle of Geryon; 4f. The Girdle of Hippolyte.

1985. Monaco in the "Belle Epoque" (4th series). As T **445**, showing paintings by Hubert Clerissi. Multicoloured.
1763 4f. "Port of Monaco, 1912" 2·00 1·25
1764 6f. "Avenue de la Gare 1920" . . . . 2·50 2·00

512 Spring

1986. Precancels. Seasons of the Hazel Tree.
1766 **512** 1f.28 brown, green & bl 40 50
1767 – 1f.65 green, brown & yell 60 55
1768 – 2f.67 grey, brown and deep brown . . . . . 1·00 1·10
1769 – 4f.44 green and brown 1·60 1·60
DESIGNS: 1f.65, Summer; 2f.67, Autumn; 4f.44, Winter.

513 Ancient Monaco

1986. 10th Anniv of "Annales Monegasques" (historical review).
1770 **513** 2f.20 grey, blue and brown 70 45

514 Scotch Terriers

1986. International Dog Show, Monte Carlo.
1771 **514** 1f.80 multicoloured . . . 3·00 2·10

515 Mouflon

1986. Mammals in Mercantour National Park. Multicoloured.
1772 2f.20 Type **515** 80 40
1773 2f.50 Ibex 90 60
1774 3f.20 Chamois . . . . . . 1·25 1·00
1775 3f.90 Alpine marmot (vert) 1·90 1·25
1776 5f. Arctic hare (vert) . . . . 2·25 1·75
1777 7f.20 Stoat (vert) . . . . . 2·75 2·25

516 Research Vessel "Ramoge"

1986. Europa. Each green, blue and red.
1778 2f.20 Type **516** 70 50
1779 3f.20 Underwater nature reserve, Larvotto beach 1·10 75

517 Prince Albert I and National Council Building

1986. Anniversaries and Events.
1781 **517** 2f.50 brown and green 80 80
1782 – 3f.20 brown, red and black . . . . 1·40 1·25
1783 – 3f.90 purple and red . . 1·75 1·75
1784 – 5f. green, red and blue 1·60 1·50
DESIGNS—HORIZ: 2f.50, Type **517** (75th anniv of First Constitution); 3f.20, Serge Diaghilev and dancers (creation of new Monte Carlo ballet company); 3f.90, Henri Rougier and Turcat-Mery car (75th Anniv of first Monte Carlo Rally). VERT: 5f. Flags and Statue of Liberty (centenary).

518 Chicago and Flags

1986. "Ameripex '86" International Stamp Exhibition, Chicago.
1785 **518** 5f. black, red and blue 1·60 1·10

520 Comet, Telescopes and 1532 Chart by Apian

1986. Appearance of Halley's Comet.
1787 **520** 10f. blue, brown & green 3·00 2·50

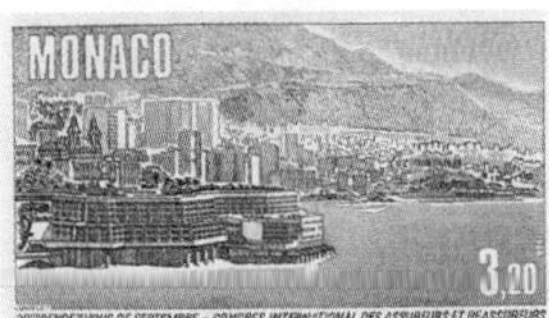

521 Monte Carlo and Congress Centre

1986. 30th International Insurance Congress.
1788 **521** 3f.20 blue, brown & grn 1·00 80

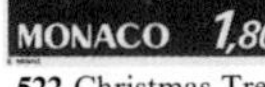

522 Christmas Tree Branch and Holly **523** Clown's Face and Elephant on Ball

1986. Christmas. Multicoloured.
1789 1f.80 Type **522** 60 25
1790 2f.50 Christmas tree branch and poinsettia 80 40

1986. 12th International Circus Festival, Monaco.
1791 **523** 2f.20 multicoloured . . . 1·10 95

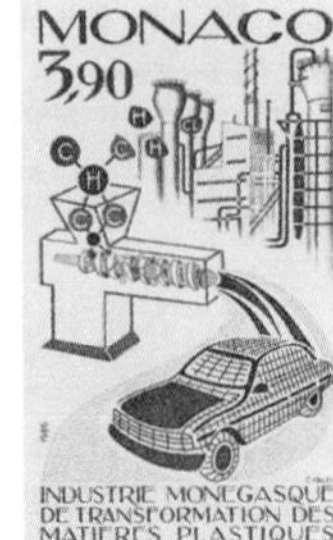

524 Posy of Roses and Acidanthera **525** Making Plastic Mouldings for Car Bodies

1986. Monte Carlo Flower Show (1987). Mult.
1792 2f.20 Type **524** . . . . . . 1·00 65
1793 3f.90 Lilies and beech in vase . . . . 1·60 1·50

1986. Monaco Red Cross. The Twelve Labours of Hercules (6th series). As T **422**.
1794 3f.+70c. green, yell & red 1·25 1·25
1795 4f.+80c. blue, brown & red 1·40 1·50
DESIGNS: 3f. The Golden Apples of the Hesperides; 4f. Capturing Cerberus.

1986. Plastics Industry.
1796 **525** 3f.90 turquoise, red and grey . . . . 1·25 80

526 Scenes from "Le Cid" (Pierre Corneille)

1986. Anniversaries.
1797 **526** 4f. deep brown & brown 1·25 1·00
1798 – 5f. brown and blue . . . 1·50 1·10
DESIGNS: 4f. Type **526** (350th anniv of first performance); 5f. Franz Liszt (composer) and bible (175th birth anniv).

527 Horace de Saussure, Mont Blanc and Climbers

1986. Bicentenary of First Ascent of Mont Blanc by Dr. Paccard and Jacques Balmat.
1799 **527** 5f.80 blue, red and black 1·75 1·50

528 "The Olympic Diver" (Emma de Sigaldi)

1986. 25th Anniv of Unveiling of "The Olympic Diver" (statue).
1800 **528** 6f. multicoloured . . . . 1·75 1·40

1986. Monaco in the "Belle Epoque" (5th series). Paintings by Hubert Clerissi. As T **445**. Mult.
1801 6f. "Bandstand and Casino, 1920" (vert) . . . . . . 2·50 1·90
1802 7f. "Avenue du Beau Rivage, 1925" (vert) . . . 4·25 3·25

530 Spring

1987. Precancels. Seasons of the Chestnut.
1804 **530** 1f.31 green, yellow & brn 40 35
1805 – 1f.69 green and brown 60 45
1806 – 2f.74 brown, yellow & bl 1·00 85
1807 – 4f.56 brown, grn & grey 1·60 1·40
DESIGNS: 1f.69, Summer; 2f.74, Autumn; 4f.56, Winter.

531 Golden Hunter

1987. Insects in Mercantour National Park. Multicoloured.
1808 1f. Type **531** 40 35
1809 1f.90 Golden wasp (vert) . . 70 65
1810 2f. Green tiger beetle . . . 90 90
1811 2f.20 Brown aeshna (vert) 1·25 80
1812 3f. Leaf beetle . . . . . . 1·75 1·50
1813 3f.40 Grasshopper (vert) . . 2·50 1·90

532 St. Devote Church

1987. Centenary of St. Devote Parish Church.
1814 **532** 1f.90 brown 70 45

533 Dogs

1987. International Dog Show, Monte Carlo.
1815 **533** 1f.90 grey, black & brn . . . 1·40 1·00
1816 – 2f.70 black and green . . 2·00 1·75
DESIGN: 2f.70, Poodle.

534 Stamp Album

1987. Stamp Day.
1817 **534** 2f.20 red, purple and mauve 70 45

535 Louis II Stadium, Fontvieille

536 Cathedral

1987. Europa. Each blue, green and red.
1818 2f.20 Type **535** 70 55
1819 3f.40 Crown Prince Albert Olympic swimming pool 1·25 85

1987. Centenary of Monaco Diocese.
1821 **536** 2f.50 green 70 50

538 Lawn Tennis

1987. 2nd European Small States Games, Monaco.
1823 **538** 3f. black, red and purple 1·50 1·40
1824 – 5f. blue and black . . . 1·90 1·60
DESIGN: 5f. Sailing dinghies and windsurfer.

539 "Red Curly Tail" (Alexander Calder)

1987. "Monte Carlo Sculpture 1987" Exhibition.
1825 **539** 3f.70 multicoloured . . . 1·50 95

540 Prince Rainier III

542 Festival Poster (J. Ramel)

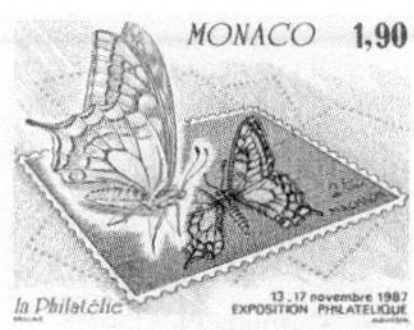

541 Swallowtail on Stamp

1987. 50th Anniv of Monaco Stamp Issuing Office.
1826 **540** 4f. blue . . . . 1·25 1·25
1827 – 4f. red . . . . 1·25 1·25
1828 – 8f. black . . . . 2·75 2·75
DESIGNS: No. 1827, Prince Louis II. (47 × 37 mm): 1828, Villa Miraflores.

1987. International Stamp Exhibition.
1829 **541** 1f.90 deep green and green 60 40
1830 2f.20 purple and red . . 70 45
1831 2f.50 purple and mauve 80 55
1832 3f.40 deep blue and blue 1·25 75

1987. 13th International Circus Festival, Monaco (1988).
1833 **542** 2f.20 multicoloured . . . 1·40 95

543 Christmas Scenes

1987. Christmas.
1834 **543** 2f.20 red 85 45

544 Strawberry Plants and Campanulas in Bowl

1987. Monte Carlo Flower Show (1988). Mult.
1835 2f.20 Type **544** 80 60
1836 3f.40 Ikebana arrangement of water lilies and dog roses (horiz) . . . . . . 1·40 1·10

545 Obverse and Reverse of Honore V 5f. Silver Coin

1987. 150th Anniv of Revival of Monaco Coinage.
1837 **545** 2f.50 black and red . . . 80 55

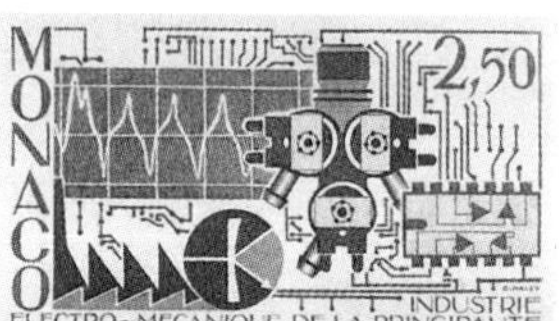

546 Graph, Factory, Electron Microscope and Printed Circuit

1987. Electro-Mechanical Industry.
1838 **546** 2f.50 blue, green and red 95 65

547 St. Devote

1987. Monaco Red Cross. St. Devote, Patron Saint of Monaco (1st series). Multicoloured.
1839 4f. Type **547** . . . . 1·25 80
1840 5f. St. Devote and her nurse 1·50 1·10
See also Nos. 1898/9, 1956/7, 1980/1, 2062/3 and 2101/2.

548 Oceanographic Museum and I.A.E.A. Headquarters, Vienna

1987. 25th Anniv of International Marine Radioactivity Laboratory, Monaco.
1842 **548** 5f. black, brown and blue . . . . 1·50 1·25

549 Jouvet

1987. Birth Centenary of Louis Jouvet (actor).
1843 **549** 3f. black . . . . 1·00 95

550 River Crossing

1987. Bicentenary of First Edition of "Paul and Virginia" by Bernardin de Saint-Pierre.
1844 **550** 3f. green, orange and blue . . . . 1·00 85

551 Marc Chagall (painter)

1987. Anniversaries.
1845 **551** 4f. black and red . . . . 1·25 1·10
1846 – 4f. purple, red and brown . . . . 1·25 1·10
1847 – 4f. red, blue and brown 1·25 1·10
1848 – 4f. green, brown & purple . . . . 1·25 1·10
1849 – 5f. blue, brown and green . . . . 1·60 1·25
1850 – 5f. brown, green and blue . . . . 1·60 1·25
DESIGNS: No. 1845, Type **551** (birth centenary); 1846, Chapel of Ronchamp and Charles Edouard Jeanneret (Le Corbusier) (architect, birth centenary); 1847, Sir Isaac Newton (mathematician) and diagram (300th anniv of publication of "Principia Mathematica"); 1848, Key and Samuel Morse (inventor, 150th Anniv of Morse telegraph); 1849, Wolfgang Amadeus Mozart and scene from "Don Juan" (opera, bicentenary of composition); 1850, Hector Berlioz (composer) and scene from "Mass for the Dead" (150th anniv of composition).

1987. Monaco in the "Belle Epoque" (6th series). As T **445** showing paintings by Hubert Clerissi. Multicoloured.
1851 6f. "Main Ramp to Palace Square, 1925" (vert) . . . 2·50 1·60
1852 7f. "Monte Carlo Railway Station, 1925" (vert) . . . 3·25 2·75

552 Coat of Arms

553 Spanish Hogfish

1987.
1853 **552** 2f. multicoloured 65 35
1854 2f.20 multicoloured . . . 65 30

1988. Fishes in Oceanographic Museum Aquarium (2nd series). Multicoloured.
1857 2f. Type **553** 80 65
1858 2f.20 Copper-banded butterflyfish . . . . . . 1·10 50
1859 2f.50 Harlequin filefish . . . 1·40 95
1860 3f. Blue boxfish . . . . . . 1·40 75
1861 3f.70 Lionfish . . . . 2·10 1·60
1862 7f. Moon wrasse (horiz) . . 3·00 1·75

554 Spring

556 Dachshunds

1988. Precancels. Seasons of the Pear Tree. Multicoloured.
1863 1f.36 Type **554** 40 50
1864 1f.75 Summer 60 65
1865 2f.83 Autumn . . . . 1·10 1·10
1866 4f.72 Winter . . . . 1·60 1·60
Scc also Nos. 1952/5.

1988. European Dachshunds Show, Monte Carlo.
1868 **556** 3f. multicoloured . . . . 1·75 1·60

557 Children of different Races around Globe

1988. 25th Anniv of World Association of Friends of Children.
1869 **557** 5f. green, brown and blue . . . . 1·60 1·60

558 Satellite Camera above Man with World as Brain

560 Jean Monnet (statesman)

559 Coxless Four

1988. Europa. Transport and Communications. Each black, brown and red.
1870 2f.20 Type **558** . . . . . . 1·10 70
1871 3f.60 Atlantique high speed mail train and aircraft propeller . . . . 1·75 1·40

1988. Centenary of Monaco Nautical Society (formerly Regatta Society).
1873 **559** 2f. blue, green and red 80 55

1988. Birth Centenaries.
1874 **560** 2f. black, brown and blue . . . . 1·75 1·25
1875 – 2f. black and blue . . . 1·75 1·25
DESIGN: No. 1875, Maurice Chevalier (entertainer).

561 "Leccinum rotundifoliae"

1988. Fungi in Mercantour National Park. Multicoloured.
1876 2f. Type **561** 70 60
1877 2f.20 Crimson wax cap . . . 90 60
1878 2f.50 "Pholiota flammans" 1·00 1·25
1879 2f.70 "Lactarius lignyotus" 1·25 1·40
1880 3f. Goaty smell (vert) . . . 1·40 1·60
1881 7f. "Russula olivacea" (vert) 2·75 3·25

562 Nansen

563 Church and "Miraculous Virgin"

1988. Centenary of First Crossing of Greenland by Fridtjof Nansen (Norwegian explorer).
1882 **562** 4f. violet . . . . 1·75 1·40

1988. Restoration of Sanctuary of Our Lady of Laghet.
1883 **563** 5f. multicoloured . . . . 1·50 1·25

564 Anniversary Emblem

1988. 40th Anniv of W.H.O.

1884 **564** 6f. red and blue . . . . 1·75 1·40

565 Anniversary Emblem

1988. 125th Anniv of Red Cross.

1885 **565** 6f. red, grey and black 1·75 1·25

566 Congress Centre

1988. 10th Anniv of Monte Carlo Congress Centre.

1886 **566** 2f. green 70 75

1887 – 3f. red . . . . 90 1·10

DESIGN: 3f. Auditorium.

1988. Monaco in the "Belle Epoque" (7th series). Paintings by Hubert Clerissi. As T **445**. Mult.

1889 6f. "Steam packet in Monte Carlo Harbour, 1910" . . 2·50 1·90

1890 7f. "Place de la Gare, 1910" 2·75 2·50

568 Festival Poster (J. Ramel) **569** Star Decoration

1988. 14th International Circus Festival, Monaco (1989).

1891 **568** 2f. multicoloured . . . . 1·00 55

1988. Christmas.

1892 **569** 2f. multicoloured 80 60

570 Arrangement of Fuchsias, Irises, Roses and Petunias **571** Models

1988. Monte Carlo Flower Show (1989).

1893 **570** 3f. multicoloured . . . . 1·40 85

1988. Ready-to-Wear Clothing Industry.

1894 **571** 3f. green, orange & black 90 75

572 Lord Byron (bicentenary)

1988. Writers' Birth Anniversaries.

1895 **572** 3f. black, brown and blue 90 80

1896 – 3f. purple and blue . . . 90 80

DESIGN: No. 1896, Pierre de Marivaux (300th anniv).

1988. Monaco Red Cross. St. Devote, Patron Saint of Monaco (2nd series). As T **547**. Multicoloured.

1898 4f. Roman governor Barbarus arriving at Corsica . . . . 1·25 80

1899 5f. St. Devote at the Roman senator Eutychius's house 1·90 1·25

574 "Le Nain and his Brothers" (Antoine Le Nain)

1988. Artists' Birth Anniversaries.

1900 **574** 5f. brown, olive and red 1·90 1·40

1901 – 5f. black, green and blue 1·90 1·40

DESIGNS: No. 1900, Type **574** (400th anniv); 1901, "The Great Archaeologists" (bronze statue, Giorgio de Chirico) (centenary).

575 Sorcerer

1989. Rock Carvings in Mercantour National Park. Multicoloured.

1902 2f. Type **575** 65 45

1903 2f.20 Oxen in yoke 75 55

1904 3f. Hunting implements . . 1·00 85

1905 3f.60 Tribal chief . . . . . 1·40 1·10

1906 4f. Puppet (vert) . . . . . 1·60 1·25

1907 5f. Jesus Christ (vert) . . . 2·00 1·40

576 Rue des Spelugues **577** Prince Rainier

1989. Old Monaco (1st series). Multicoloured.

1908 2f. Type **576** 60 45

1909 2f.20 Place Saint Nicolas . . 70 55

See also Nos. 1969/70 and 2090/1.

1989.

1910 **577** 2f. blue and azure . . . 70 20

1911 2f.10 blue and azure . . 70 25

1912 2f.20 brown and pink . . 90 30

1913 2f.20 blue and azure . . 70 20

1914 2f.30 brown and pink . . 80 30

1915 2f.40 blue and azure . . 70 25

1916 2f.50 brown and pink . . 80 30

1917 2f.70 blue 70 65

1918 2f.80 brown and pink . . 85 35

1919 3f. brown and pink . . . 85 25

1920 3f.20 blue and cobalt . . 1·10 75

1922 3f.40 blue and cobalt . . 1·40 95

1923 3f.60 blue and cobalt . . 1·60 1·25

1924 3f.70 blue and cobalt . . 1·10 70

1925 3f.80 purple and lilac . . 1·50 50

1926 3f.80 blue and cobalt . . 95 45

1927 4f. purple and lilac . . . 1·00 95

1930 5f. brown and pink . . . 1·50 65

1932 10f. deep green and green . . . . 2·25 90

1934 15f. blue and grey . . . 3·75 1·25

1936 20f. red and pink . . . 4·50 1·75

1938 25f. black and grey . . . 6·00 2·10

1940 40f. brown and pink . . 8·00 4·25

See also Nos. 2388/90.

578 Yorkshire Terrier

1989. International Dog Show, Monte Carlo.

1941 **578** 2f.20 multicoloured . . . 90 65

579 Magician, Dove and Cards

1989. 5th Grand Prix of Magic, Monte Carlo.

1942 **579** 2f.20 black, blue and red 90 55

580 Nuns and Monks around "Our Lady of Misericorde"

1989. 350th Anniv of Archiconfrerie de la Misericorde.

1943 **580** 3f. brown, black and red 90 60

581 Charlie Chaplin (actor) and Film Scenes

1989. Birth Centenaries.

1944 – 3f. green, blue and mauve . . . . 1·00 95

1945 **581** 4f. purple, green and red 1·50 1·25

DESIGN: 3f. Jean Cocteau (writer and painter), scene from "The Double-headed Eagle" and frescoes in Villefrance-sur-Mer chapel.

583 Boys playing Marbles **587** Poinsettia, Christmas Roses and Holly

586 "Artist's Mother" (Philibert Florence)

1989. Europa. Children's Games. Each mauve, brown and grey.

1947 2f.20 Type **583** 70 60

1948 3f.60 Girls skipping . . . . 1·10 1·00

1989. Precancels. As Nos. 1863/6 but values changed. Multicoloured.

1952 1f.39 Type **554** 40 50

1953 1f.79 Summer 60 65

1954 2f.90 Autumn . . . . 1·40 1·10

1955 4f.84 Winter . . . . 1·90 1·60

1989. Monaco Red Cross. St. Devote, Patron Saint of Monaco (3rd series). As T **547**. Multicoloured.

1956 4f. St. Devote beside the dying Eutychius . . . . . 1·25 85

1957 5f. Barbarus condemns St. Devote to torture for refusing to make a sacrifice to the gods . . . 1·60 1·10

1989. Artists' 150th Birth Anniversaries.

1958 **586** 4f. brown . . . . 1·60 1·40

1959 – 6f. multicoloured . . . . 2·00 1·60

1960 – 8f. multicoloured . . . . 2·75 2·00

DESIGNS—HORIZ: 6f. "Molesey Regatta" (Alfred Sisley). VERT: 8f. "Farmyard at Auvers" (Paul Cezanne).

1989. Christmas.

1961 **587** 2f. multicoloured . . . . 1·60 70

588 Map and Emblem

1989. Centenary of Interparliamentary Union.

1962 **588** 4f. black, green and red 1·50 80

590 Monaco Palace, White House, Washington, and Emblem

1989. 20th U.P.U. Congress, Washington D.C.

1964 **590** 6f. blue, brown and black . . . . 1·60 1·25

1989. Monaco in the "Belle Epoque" (8th series). Paintings by Hubert Clerissi. As T **445**. Mult.

1965 7f. "Barque in Monte Carlo Harbour, 1915" (vert) . . 2·50 1·90

1966 8f. "Gaming Tables, Casino, 1915" (vert) . . . . . . 2·75 2·50

591 World Map

1989. 10th Anniv of Monaco Aide et Presence (welfare organization).

1967 **591** 2f.20 brown and red . . 1·50 1·10

592 Clown and Horses **593** Phalaenopsis "Princess Grace"

1989. 15th International Circus Festival, Monte Carlo.

1968 **592** 2f.20 multicoloured . . . 1·60 1·40

1990. Old Monaco (2nd series). Paintings by Claude Rosticher. As T **576**. Multicoloured.

1969 2f.10 La Rampe Major . . 70 45

1970 2f.30 Town Hall Courtyard 80 50

1990. International Garden and Greenery Exposition, Osaka, Japan. Multicoloured.

1971 2f. Type **593** 75 55

1972 3f. Iris "Grace Patricia" . . 1·00 70

1973 3f. "Paphiopedilum" "Prince Rainier III" . . . . 1·00 75

1974 4f. "Cattleya" "Principessa Grace" . . . . 1·40 80

1975 5f. Rose "Caroline of Monaco" . . . . 2·25 1·50

594 Bearded Collie

1990. International Dog Show, Monte Carlo.
1976 **594** 2f.30 multicoloured . . . 1·25 1·00

595 Noghes and Racing Car

1990. Birth Centenary of Antony Noghes (founder of Monaco Grand Prix and Monte Carlo Rally).
1977 **595** 3f. red, lilac and black 1·10 75

596 Cyclist and Lancia Rally Car

1990. Centenary of Automobile Club of Monaco (founded as Cycling Racing Club).
1978 **596** 4f. blue, brown & purple 1·50 1·25

597 Telephone, Satellite and Dish Aerial

1990. 125th Anniv of I.T.U.
1979 **597** 4f. lilac, mauve and blue 1·25 1·25

1990. Monaco Red Cross. St. Devote, Patron Saint of Monaco (4th series). As T **547**. Multicoloured.
1980 4f. St. Devote being flogged 1·25 1·00
1981 5f. Placing body of St. Devote in fishing boat 1·75 1·25

598 Sir Rowland Hill and Penny Black

1990. 150th Anniv of Penny Black.
1982 **598** 5f. blue and black . . . 2·00 1·50

599 "Post Office, Place de la Mairie"

1990. Europa. Post Office Buildings. Paintings by Hubert Clerissi. Multicoloured.
1983 2f.30 Type **599** 70 50
1984 3f.70 "Post Office, Avenue d'Ostende" . . . . 1·25 85

601 Anatase

1990. Minerals in Mercantour National Park. Mult.
1987 2f.10 Type **601** 60 35
1988 2f.30 Albite 70 45
1989 3f.20 Rutile . . . . 1·00 85
1990 3f.80 Chlorite . . . . . . 1·40 85
1991 4f. Brookite (vert) . . . . . 1·75 1·40
1992 6f. Quartz (vert) . . . . . 2·50 1·90

602 Powerboat

603 Pierrot writing (mechanical toy)

1990. World Offshore Powerboat Racing Championship.
1993 **602** 2f.30 brown, red & blue 90 60

1990. Philatelic Round Table.
1994 **603** 3f. blue . . . . 1·00 60

604 Christian Samuel Hahnemann (founding of homeopathy)

1990. Bicentenaries.
1995 **604** 3f. purple, green & black 1·00 75
1996 – 5f. chestnut, brown & bl 1·75 1·25
DESIGN: 5f. Jean-Francois Champollion (Egyptologist) and hieroglyphics (birth bicentenary).

605 Monaco Heliport, Fontvieille

1990. 30th International Civil Airports Association Congress, Monte Carlo.
1997 **605** 3f. black, red and brown 90 50
1998 – 5f. black, blue and brown . . . . 1·75 1·25
DESIGN: 5f. Aerospatiale Ecureuil helicopters over Monte Carlo Congress Centre.

606 Petanque Player

608 Miller on Donkey

607 Spring

1990. 26th World Petanque Championship.
1999 **606** 6f. blue, brown & orange 2·00 1·25

1990. Precancels. Seasons of the Plum Tree. Multicoloured.
2000 1f.46 Type **607** 45 35
2001 1f.89 Summer 65 45
2002 3f.06 Autumn . . . . 1·25 85
2003 5f.10 Winter . . . . 1·90 1·40

1990. Christmas. Crib figures from Provence. Multicoloured.
2004 2f.30 Type **608** 80 40
2005 3f.20 Woman carrying faggots . . . . 1·00 70
2006 3f.80 Baker . . . . 1·40 95
See also Nos. 2052/4, 2097/9, 2146/8 and 2191/3.

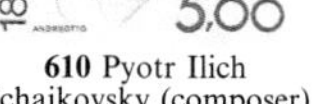

610 Pyotr Ilich Tchaikovsky (composer)

611 Clown playing Concertina

1990. 150th Birth Anniversaries.
2008 **610** 5f. blue and green . . . 1·75 1·10
2009 – 5f. bistre and blue . . . 1·75 1·10
2010 – 7f. multicoloured . . . . 3·50 3·00
DESIGNS—As T **610**: No. 2009, "Cathedral" (Auguste Rodin, sculptor). 48 × 37 mm: "The Magpie" (Claude Monet, painter).

1991. 16th International Circus Festival, Monte Carlo.
2011 **611** 2f.30 multicoloured . . . 95 75
See also No. 2069.

1991. Bygone Monaco (2nd series). Paintings by Hubert Clerissi. As T **481**.
2015 20c. purple 10 10
2017 40c. green 10 10
2018 50c. red 10 10
2019 60c. blue 20 10
2020 70c. green 20 10
2021 80c. blue 20 20
2022 90c. lilac 20 20
2023 1f. blue 30 20
2024 2f. red 50 25
2025 3f. black 80 30
2027 7f. grey and black . . . . . 1·60 80
DESIGNS: 20c. Rock of Monaco and Fontvieille; 40c. Place du Casino; 50c. Place de la Cremaillere and railway station; 60c. National Council building; 70c. Palace and Rampe Major; 80c. Avenue du Beau Rivage; 90c. Fishing boats, Fontvieille; 1f. Place d'Armes; 2f. Marche de la Condamine; 3f. Yacht; 7f. Oceanographic Museum.

612 Abdim's Stork

613 Phytoplankton

1991. International Symposium on Bird Migration. Multicoloured.
2029 2f. Type **612** 70 55
2030 3f. Broad-tailed hummingbirds 90 80
2031 4f. Garganeys . . . . . . 1·40 1·10
2032 5f. Eastern broad-billed roller . . . . 1·75 1·50
2033 6f. European bee eaters . . 2·25 1·90

1991. Oceanographic Museum (1st series).
2034 **613** 2f.10 multicoloured . . . 95 55
See also Nos. 2095/6.

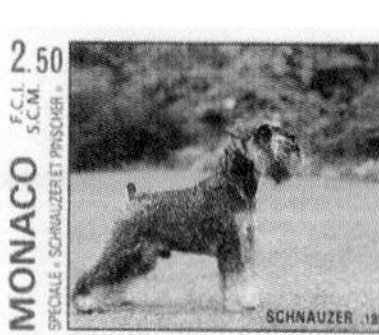

614 Schnauzer

1991. International Dog Show, Monte Carlo.
2035 **614** 2f.50 multicoloured . . . 1·25 85

615 Cyclamen, Lily-of-the-Valley and Pine Twig in Fir-cone

616 Corals

1991. Monte Carlo Flower Show.
2036 **615** 3f. multicoloured . . . . 1·10 65

1991. "Joys of the Sea" Exhibition. Multicoloured.
2037 2f.20 Type **616** 85 65
2038 2f.40 Coral necklace 95 75

617 Control Room, "Eutelsat" Satellite and Globe

1991. Europa. Europe in Space. Each blue, black and green.
2039 2f.30 Type **617** 85 50
2040 3f.20 Computer terminal, "Inmarsat" satellite, research ship transmitting signal and man with receiving equipment . . . 1·10 70

618 Cross-country Skiers and Statue of Skiers by Emma de Sigaldi

1991. 1992 Olympic Games. (a) Winter Olympics, Albertville.
2042 **618** 3f. green, blue and olive 1·00 1·10
2043 – 4f. green, blue and olive 1·40 1·40

(b) Olympic Games, Barcelona.
2044 – 3f. green, lt brown & brown . . . . 1·00 1·25
2045 – 5f. black, brown and green 1·50 1·75
DESIGNS: No. 2043, Right-hand part of statue and cross-country skiers; 2044, Track, relay runners and left part of statue of relay runners by Emma de Sigaldi; 2045, Right part of statue, view of Barcelona and track.

619 Head of "David" (Michelangelo), Computer Image and Artist at Work

620 Prince Pierre, Open Book and Lyre

1991. 25th International Contemporary Art Prize.
2046 **619** 4f. green, dp green & lilac . . . . 1·40 95

1991. 25th Anniv of Prince Pierre Foundation.
2047 **620** 5f. black, blue and brown . . . . 1·50 1·25

621 Tortoises

1991. Endangered Species. Hermann's Tortoise. Multicoloured.
2048 1f.25 Type **621** 85 70
2049 1f.25 Head of tortoise . . . 85 70
2050 1f.25 Tortoise in grass . . . 85 70
2051 1f.25 Tortoise emerging from among plants . . . 85 70

1991. Christmas. As T **608** showing crib figures from Provence. Multicoloured.
2052 2f.50 Consul 80 35
2053 3f.50 Arlesian woman . . . 1·25 85
2054 4f. Mayor . . . . 1·50 1·10

622 Norway Spruce

1991. Conifers in Mercantour National Park. Multicoloured.
2055 2f.50 Type **622** 85 30
2056 3f.50 Silver fir . . . . . . 1·25 65

2057 4f. "Pinus uncinata" . . . . 1·25 80
2058 5f. Scots pine (vert) . . . . 1·50 1·00
2059 6f. Arolla pine . . . . . . 1·75 1·25
2060 7f. European larch (vert) . . 2·00 1·50

1991. Monaco Red Cross. St. Devote, Patron Saint of Monaco (5th series). As T **547**. Multicoloured.
2062 4f.50 Fishing boat carrying body caught in storm . . 1·50 80
2063 5f.50 Dove guiding boatman to port of Monaco . . . 1·75 1·10

624 "Portrait of Claude Monet"

1991. 150th Birth Anniv of Auguste Renoir (painter).
2064 **624** 5f. multicoloured . . . . 1·60 1·25

625 Prince Honore II of Monaco

1991. 350th Anniv of Treaty of Peronne (giving French recognition of sovereignty of Monaco). Paintings by Philippe de Champaigne. Mult.
2065 6f. Type **625** . . . . 2·10 1·60
2066 7f. King Louis XIII of France . . . . 2·50 1·75

626 Princess Grace (after R. Samini)

1991. 10th Anniv of Princess Grace Theatre.
2067 **626** 8f. multicoloured . . . . 3·25 2·40

1992. 16th International Circus Festival, Monte Carlo. As No. 2011 but value and dates changed.
2069 **611** 2f.50 multicoloured . . . 95 75
The 1991 Festival was cancelled.

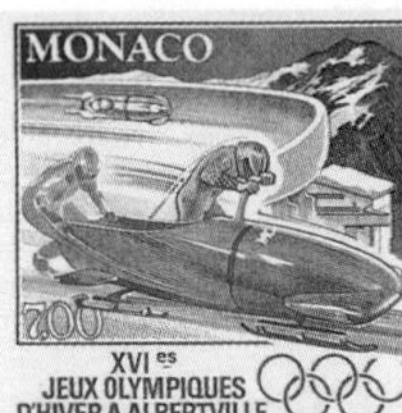

628 Two-man Bobsleighs

1992. Winter Olympic Games, Albertville (7f.), and Summer Games, Barcelona (8f.).
2070 **628** 7f. blue, turquoise & blk 2·10 1·40
2071 – 8f. purple, blue and green . . . . 2·50 1·50
DESIGN: 8f. Football.

630 Spring

1992. Precancels. Seasons of the Walnut Tree. Mult.
2073 1f.60 Type **630** 50 60
2074 2f.08 Summer 60 70
2075 2f.98 Autumn . . . . 1·10 1·10
2076 5f.28 Winter . . . . 1·75 1·75

631 Golden Labrador

1992. International Dog Show, Monte Carlo.
2077 **631** 2f.20 multicoloured . . . 1·25 80

632 Racing along Seafront

1992. 50th Monaco Grand Prix.
2078 **632** 2f.50 black, purple & bl 85 55

633 Mixed Bouquet

1992. 25th Monte Carlo Flower Show.
2079 **633** 3f.40 multicoloured . . . 1·40 85

634 Ford Sierra Rally Car

1992. 60th Monte Carlo Car Rally.
2080 **634** 4f. black, green and red 1·50 1·10

636 "Pinta" off Palos

1992. Europa. 500th Anniv of Discovery of America by Columbus. Multicoloured.
2082 2f.50 Type **636** 80 65
2083 3f.40 "Santa Maria" in the Antilles . . . . 1·40 1·10
2084 4f. "Nina" off Lisbon . . . 1·50 1·25

637 Produce

1992. "Ameriflora" Horticultural Show, Columbus, Ohio. Multicoloured.
2086 4f. Type **637** . . . . . . 1·25 95
2087 5f. Vase of mixed flowers . . 1·60 1·50

638 Prince Rainier I and Fleet (detail of fresco by E. Charpentier, Spinola Palace, Genoa)

1992. Columbus Exhibition, Genoa (6f.), and "Expo '92" World's Fair, Seville (7f.).
2088 **638** 6f. brown, red and blue 2·00 1·40
2089 – 7f. brown, red and blue 2·10 1·60
DESIGN: 7f. Monaco pavilion.

1992. Old Monaco (3rd series). Paintings by Claude Rosticher. As T **576**. Multicoloured.
2090 2f.20 La Porte Neuve (horiz) 75 25
2091 2f.50 La Placette Bosio (horiz) 85 25

639 "Christopher Columbus"

1992. "Genova '92" International Thematic Stamp Exhibition. Roses. Multicoloured.
2092 3f. Type **639** . . . . 1·25 1·00
2093 4f. "Prince of Monaco" . . 1·40 1·10

640 Lammergeier

1992.
2094 **640** 2f.20 orange, blk & grn 85 80

1992. Oceanographic Museum (2nd series). As T **613**. Multicoloured.
2095 2f.20 "Ceratium ranipes" . . 85 60
2096 2f.50 "Ceratium hexacanthum" 95 70

1992. Christmas. As T **608** showing crib figures from Provence. Multicoloured.
2097 2f.50 Basket-maker 85 30
2098 3f.40 Fishwife . . . . . . 1·25 65
2099 5f. Rural constable . . . . 1·75 1·40

641 "Seabus" (projected tourist submarine)

1992.
2100 **641** 4f. blue, red and brown 1·40 1·25

642 Burning Boat Ceremony, St. Devote's Eve

1992. Monaco Red Cross. St. Devote, Patron Saint of Monaco (6th series).
2101 **642** 6f. red, blue and brown 1·75 1·10
2102 – 8f. purple, orange and red . . . . 2·40 1·60
DESIGN: 8f. Procession of reliquary, St. Devote's Day.

643 Athletes, Sorbonne University and Coubertin

1992. Centenary of Pierre de Coubertin's Proposal for Revival of Olympic Games.
2103 **643** 10f. blue . . . . 3·00 1·90

644 Baux de Provence and St. Catherine's Chapel

1992. Titles of Princes of Monaco. Marquis of Baux de Provence.
2104 **644** 15f. multicoloured . . . 4·25 2·75

646 Clown and Tiger

1993. 17th Int Circus Festival, Monte Carlo.
2106 **646** 2f.50 multicoloured . . . 85 55

647 Short-toed Eagles

1993. Birds of Prey in Mercantour National Park.
2107 **647** 2f. chestnut, brown and orange 65 50
2108 – 3f. indigo, orange & blue 1·10 65
2109 – 4f. brown, ochre and blue . . . . 1·25 1·10
2110 – 5f. brown, chestnut and green . . . . 1·60 1·40
2111 – 6f. brown, mauve & grn 1·90 1·60
DESIGNS—HORIZ: 3f. Peregrine falcon. VERT: 4f. Eagle owl; 5f. Western honey buzzard; 6f. Tengmalm's owl.

650 Mixed Bouquet

652 Fire Fighting and Rescue

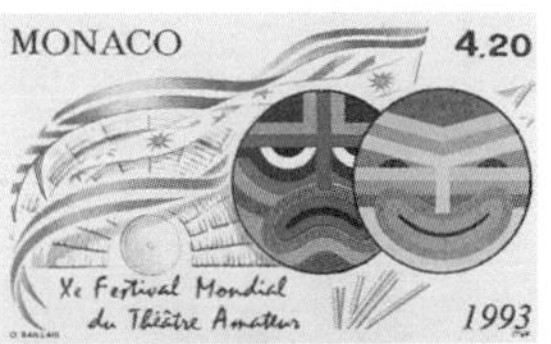

651 Pennants, Auditorium and Masks

1993. Monte Carlo Flower Show.
2114 **650** 3f.40 multicoloured . . . 1·10 75

1993. 10th International Amateur Theatre Festival.
2115 **651** 4f.20 multicoloured . . . 1·40 75

1993. World Civil Protection Day.
2116 **652** 6f. black, red and green 1·90 1·40

653 Newfoundland

1993. International Dog Show, Monte Carlo.
2117 **653** 2f.20 multicoloured . . . 90 70

654 Golfer

1993. 10th Monte Carlo Open Golf Tournament.
2118 **654** 2f.20 multicoloured . . . 70 65

655 Princess Grace **656** Mirror and Candelabra

1993. 10th Death Anniv (1992) of Princess Grace.
2119 **655** 5f. blue . . . . 1·50 1·25

1993. 10th Antiques Biennale.
2120 **656** 7f. multicoloured . . . . 2·10 1·40

657 "Echinopsis multiplex" **658** Monte Carlo Ballets

1993. Cacti.
2121 **657** 2f.50 green, purple & yell 70 60
2122 – 2f.50 green and purple 70 60
2123 – 2f.50 green, purple & yell 70 60
2124 – 2f.50 green and yellow 70 60
DESIGNS: No. 2122, "Zygocactus truncatus"; 2123, "Echinocereus procumbens"; 2124, "Euphorbia virosa".
See also Nos. 2154/66.

1993. Europa. Contemporary Art.
2125 **658** 2f.50 black, brn & pink 70 50
2126 – 4f.20 grey and brown . . 1·25 95
DESIGN: 4f.20, "Evolution" (sculpture, Emma de Sigaldi).

660 State Arms and Olympic Rings

1993. 110th International Olympic Committee Session, Monaco.
2129 **660** 2f.80 red, brown & blue 80 85
2130 – 2f.80 blue, lt blue & red 80 85
2131 – 2f.80 brown, blue & red 80 85
2132 – 2f.80 blue, lt blue & red 80 85
2133 – 2f.80 brown, blue & red 80 85
2134 – 2f.80 blue, lt blue & red 80 85
2135 – 2f.80 brown, blue & red 80 85
2136 **660** 2f.80 blue, lt blue & red 80 85
2137 – 4f.50 multicoloured . . . 1·25 1·40
2138 – 4f.50 black, yellow & bl 1·25 1·40
2139 – 4f.50 red, yellow & blue 1·25 1·40
2140 – 4f.50 black, yellow & bl 1·25 1·40
2141 – 4f.50 red, yellow & blue 1·25 1·40
2142 – 4f.50 black, yellow & bl 1·25 1·40
2143 – 4f.50 red, yellow & blue 1·25 1·40
2144 – 4f.50 red, yellow & blue 1·25 1·40
DESIGNS: 2130, Bobsleighing; 2131, Skiing; 2132, Yachting; 2133, Rowing; 2134, Swimming; 2135, Cycling; 2136, 2144, Commemorative inscription; 2138, Gymnastics (rings exercise); 2139, Judo; 2140, Fencing; 2141, Hurdling; 2142, Archery; 2143, Weightlifting.

661 Examining 1891 1c. Stamp

1993. Centenary of Monaco Philatelic Union.
2145 **661** 2f.40 multicoloured . . . 70 45

1993. Christmas. Crib figures from Provence. As T **608**. Multicoloured.
2146 2f.80 Donkey 80 35
2147 3f.70 Shepherd holding lamb 1·00 90
2148 4f.40 Ox lying down in barn 1·25 1·25

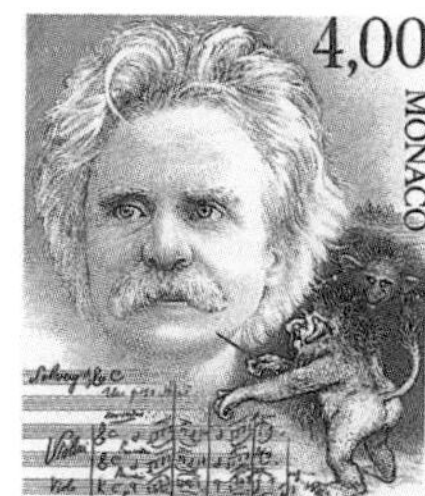

662 Grieg, Music and Trolls

1993. 150th Birth Anniv of Edvard Grieg (composer).
2149 **662** 4f. blue . . . . 1·60 1·10

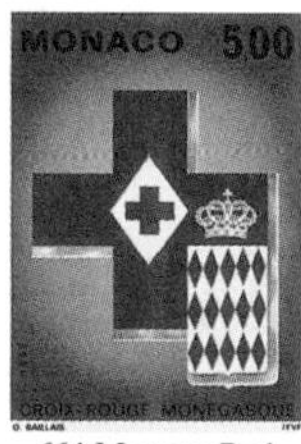

663 Abstract Lithograph **664** Monaco Red Cross Emblem

1993. Birth Centenary of Joan Miro (painter and sculptor).
2150 **663** 5f. multicoloured . . . . 1·60 1·40

1993. Monaco Red Cross.
2151 **664** 5f. red, yellow and black 1·40 1·10
2152 – 6f. red and black . . . . 1·90 1·60
DESIGN: 6f. Crosses inscribed with fundamental principles of the International Red Cross.

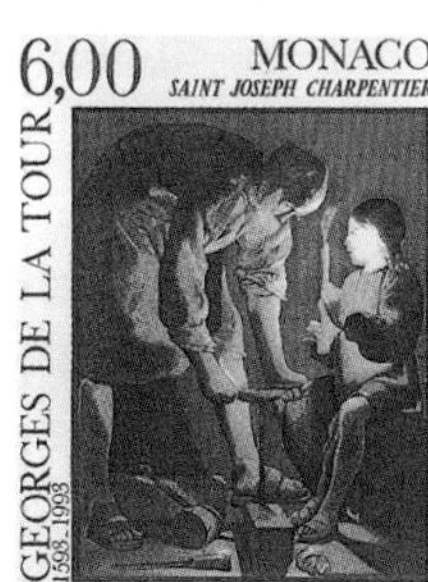

665 "St. Joseph the Carpenter"

1993. 400th Birth Anniv of Georges de la Tour (painter).
2153 **665** 6f. multicoloured . . . . 1·75 1·40

1994. Cacti. As Nos. 2121/4 but values changed and additional designs.
2153a – 10c. green, orange and red 10 10
2154 **657** 20c. green, purple and yellow 10 10
2155 – 30c. green and purple 10 10
2156 – 40c. green and yellow 10 10
2157 – 50c. green, red and olive 10 10
2158 – 60c. green, red and yellow 20 25
2159 – 70c. green, red and blue 20 25
2160 – 80c. green, orange and red 20 25
2162 – 1f. green, brown and yellow 25 25
2164 – 2f. green, red and yellow 50 45
2165 – 2f.70 green, red and yellow 70 50
2166 – 4f. green, purple and yellow . . . . 1·00 60
2166a – 4f. green, red and yellow 80 70
2167 – 5f. green, mauve and brown . . . . 1·25 85
2167a – 6f. brown, green and red . . . . 1·50 1·25
2167b – 7f. green, brown and red . . . . 1·90 1·50
DESIGNS: 10c. "Bromelia brevifolia"; 30c. "Zygocactus truncatus"; 40c. "Euphorbia virosa"; 50c. "Selenicereus grandiflorus"; 60c. "Opuntia basilaris"; 70c. "Aloe plicatilis"; 80c. "Opuntia hybride"; 1f. "Stapelia flavirostris"; 2f. "Aporocactus flagelliformis"; 2f.70, "Opuntia dejecta"; 4f. (2166), "Echinocereus procumbens"; 4f. (2166a), "Echinocereus blanckii"; 5f. "Cereus peruvianus"; 6f. "Euphorbia milii; 7f. "Stapelia variegata.

666 Festival Poster **667** Artist/Poet

1994. 18th Int Circus Festival, Monte Carlo.
2168 **666** 2f.80 multicoloured . . . 95 70

1994. Mechanical Toys.
2169 **667** 2f.80 blue 70 75
2170 – 2f.80 red 70 75
2171 – 2f.80 purple 70 75
2172 – 2f.80 green 70 75
DESIGNS: No. 2170, Bust of Japanese woman; 2171, Shepherdess with sheep; 2172, Young Parisienne.

669 King Charles Spaniels

1994. International Dog Show, Monte Carlo.
2175 **669** 2f.40 multicoloured . . . 95 45

670 Couple, Leaves and Pollution **671** Iris

1994. Monaco Committee of Anti-tuberculosis and Respiratory Diseases Campaign.
2176 **670** 2f.40+60c. mult 85 75

1994. Monte Carlo Flower Show.
2177 **671** 4f.40 multicoloured . . . 1·40 85

672 Levitation Trick

1994. 10th Monte Carlo Magic Grand Prix.
2178 **672** 5f. blue, black and red 1·50 95

673 Ingredients and Dining Table overlooking Harbour

1994. 35th Anniv of Brotherhood of Cordon d'Or French Chefs.
2179 **673** 6f. multicoloured . . . . 1·75 1·25

674 Isfjord, Prince Albert I, Map of Spitzbergen and "Princess Alice II"

1994. Europa. Discoveries made by Prince Albert I. Each black, blue and red.
2180 2f.80 Type **674** 85 70
2181 4f.50 Oceanographic Museum, Grimaldi's spookfish and "Eryoneicus alberti" (crustacean) . . . . . . 1·40 1·10

675 Olympic Flag and Sorbonne University **676** Dolphins through Porthole

1994. Centenary of International Olympic Committee.
2183 **675** 3f. multicoloured 95 75

1994. Economic Institute of the Rights of the Sea Conference, Monaco.
2184 **676** 6f. multicoloured . . . . 1·75 1·50

677 Family around Tree of Hearts **678** Footballer's Legs and Ball

1994. International Year of the Family.
2185 **677** 7f. green, orange and blue . . . . 1·90 1·50

1994. World Cup Football Championship, U.S.A.
2186 **678** 8f. red and black . . . . 2·25 1·50

679 Athletes and Villa Miraflores

1994. Inauguration of New Seat of International Amateur Athletics Federation.
2187 **679** 8f. blue, purple and bistre . . . . 2·10 2·00

680 De Dion Bouton, 1903

1994. Vintage Car Collection of Prince Rainier III.
2188 **680** 2f.80 black, brown and mauve 85 80

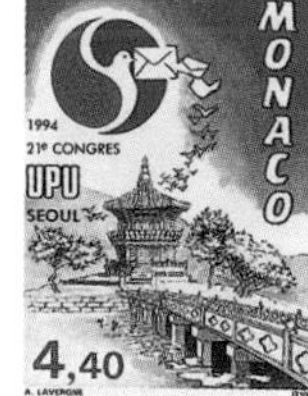

681 Emblem and Monte Carlo **682** Emblem and Korean Scene

1994. 1st Association of Postage Stamp Catalogue Editors and Philatelic Publications Grand Prix.
2189 **681** 3f. multicoloured 95 55

1994. 21st Universal Postal Union Congress, Seoul.
2190 **682** 4f.40 black, blue and red 1·40 85

1994. Christmas. As T **608** showing crib figures from Provence. Multicoloured.
2191 2f.80 Virgin Mary 70 60
2192 4f.50 Baby Jesus . . . . . 1·25 85
2193 6f. Joseph . . . . 1·60 1·10

683 Prince Albert I

684 Three Ages of Voltaire (writer, 300th anniv)

1994. Inaug of Stamp and Coin Museum (1st issue). Coins.
2194 **683** 3f. stone, brown and red 85 65
2195 – 4f. grey, brown and red 1·25 95
2196 – 7f. stone, brown and red 1·90 1·50
DESIGNS: 4f. Arms of House of Grimaldi; 7f. Prince Rainier III.
See also Nos. 2265/7 and 2283/5.

1994. Birth Anniversaries.
2198 **684** 5f. green 1·50 1·10
2199 – 6f. brown and purple 1·75 1·40
DESIGN—HORIZ: 6f. Sarah Bernhardt (actress, 150th anniv).

685 Heliport and Helicopter

1994. 50th Anniv of International Civil Aviation Organization.
2200 **685** 5f. green, black and blue 1·40 1·00
2201 – 7f. brown, black and red 1·90 1·60
DESIGN: 7f. Harbour and helicopter.

687 Blood Vessels on Woman (anti-cancer)

1994. Monaco Red Cross. Health Campaigns.
2203 **687** 6f. blue, black and red 1·60 1·10
2204 – 8f. green, black and red 2·10 1·60
DESIGN: 8f. Tree and woman (anti-AIDS).

688 Robinson Crusoe and Friday

1994. Anniversaries. Multicoloured.
2205 7f. Type **688** (275th anniv of publication of "Robinson Crusoe" by Daniel Defoe) 2·10 1·50
2206 9f. "The Snake Charmer" (150th birth anniv of Henri Rousseau, painter) 2·50 1·75

689 Clown playing Trombone

690 Crown Prince Albert

1995. 19th Int Circus Festival, Monte Carlo.
2207 **689** 2f.80 multicoloured 70 65

1995. 35th Television Festival, Monte Carlo.
2208 **690** 8f. brown 2·00 2·00

691 Fontvieille

1995. European Nature Conservation Year.
2209 **691** 2f.40 multicoloured 60 45

692 American Cocker Spaniel

1995. International Dog Show, Monte Carlo.
2210 **692** 4f. multicoloured 1·00 1·00

693 Parrot Tulips

1995. Monte Carlo Flower Show.
2211 **693** 5f. multicoloured 1·50 1·00

694 "Acer palmatum"

1995. European Bonsai Congress.
2212 **694** 6f. multicoloured 1·50 85

695 Alfred Nobel (founder of Nobel Prizes) and Dove

1995. Europa. Peace and Freedom. Multicoloured.
2213 2f.80 Type **695** 75 70
2214 5f. Roses, broken chain and watchtower 1·40 1·00

696 Emblem of Monagasque Disabled Children Association

1995. Int Special Olympics, New Haven, U.S.A.
2215 **696** 3f. multicoloured 75 55

697 Emblem

1995. Rotary International Convention, Nice.
2216 **697** 4f. blue 1·10 1·00

699 Jean Giono

701 Princess Caroline (President)

700 Saint Hubert (patron saint of hunting)

1995. Writers' Birth Centenaries.
2218 **699** 5f. lilac, brown and green 1·40 90
2219 – 6f. brown, violet and green 1·50 1·10
DESIGN: 6f. Marcel Pagnol.

1995. General Assembly of International Council for Hunting and Conservation of Game.
2220 **700** 6f. blue 1·50 1·40

1995. World Association of Friends of Children General Assembly, Monaco.
2221 **701** 7f. blue 1·60 1·40

702 Athletes and Medal

1995. International Amateur Athletics Federation Grand Prix, Monaco.
2222 **702** 7f. mauve, purple and grey 1·75 1·40

703 "Trophee des Alpes" (Hubert Clerissi)

1995. 2000th Anniv of Emperor Augustus Monument, La Turbie.
2223 **703** 8f. multicoloured 1·90 1·75

704 Prince Pierre (after Philip Laszlo de Lombos)

706 St. Antony (wooden statue)

1995. Birth Centenary of Prince Pierre of Monaco.
2224 **704** 10f. purple 2·50 1·75

1995. 800th Birth Anniv of St. Antony of Padua.
2226 **706** 2f.80 multicoloured 65 55

707 United Nations Charter and Peacekeeping Soldiers

1995. 50th Anniv of U.N.O.
2227 **707** 2f.50 multicoloured 65 55
2228 – 2f.50 multicoloured 65 55
2229 – 2f.50 multicoloured 65 55
2230 – 2f.50 blue, black and brown 65 55
2231 – 3f. black, brown and blue 75 75
2232 – 3f. multicoloured 75 75
2233 – 3f. multicoloured 75 75
2234 – 3f. multicoloured 75 75
DESIGNS: No. 2228, Wheat ears, boy and arid ground; 2229, Children from different nationalities; 2230, Head of Colossus, Abu Simbel Temple; 2231, United Nations meeting; 2232, Growing crops and hand holding seeds; 2233, Figures and alphabetic characters; 2234, Lute and U.N.E.S.C.O. headquarters, Paris.
Nos. 2228 and 2232 commemorate the F.A.O., Nos. 2229 and 2233 International Year of Tolerance, Nos. 2230 and 2234 U.N.E.S.C.O.

708 Rose "Grace de Monaco"

709 Balthazar

1995. Flowers. Multicoloured.
2236 3f. Type **708** 65 50
2237 3f. Fuchsia "Lakeland Princess" 65 50
2238 3f. Carnation "Centenaire de Monte-Carlo" 65 50
2239 3f. Fuchsia "Grace" 65 50
2240 3f. Rose "Princesse de Monaco" 65 50
2241 3f. Alstroemeria "Gracia" 65 50
2242 3f. Lily "Princess Gracia" 65 50
2243 3f. Carnation "Princesse Caroline" 65 50
2244 3f. Rose "Stephanie de Monaco" 65 50
2245 3f. Carnation "Prince Albert" 65 50
2246 3f. Sweet pea "Grace de Monaco" 65 50
2247 3f. Gerbera "Gracia" 65 50

1995. Christmas. Crib Figures from Provence of the Three Wise Men. Multicoloured.
2248 3f. Type **709** 75 55
2249 5f. Gaspard 1·25 75
2250 6f. Melchior 1·50 1·10

710 Tree, Bird, Seahorse and Association Emblem

1995. 20th Anniv of Monaco Association for Nature Protection.
2251 **710** 4f. green, black and red 90 70

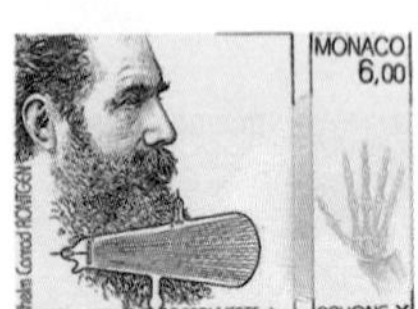

711 Rontgen and X-Ray of Hand

1995. Centenary of Discovery of X-Rays by Wilhelm Rontgen.
2252 **711** 6f. black, yellow and green 1·40 75

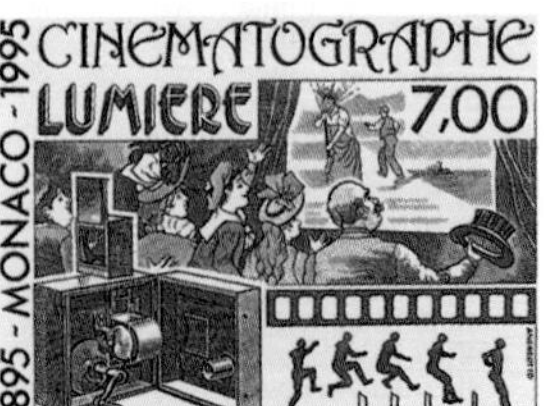

712 First Screening to Paying Public, Paris, December 1895

1995. Centenary of Motion Pictures.
2253 **712** 7f. blue 1·60 85

713 Allegory of Anti-leprosy Campaign

1995. Monaco Red Cross. Multicoloured.
2254 7f. Type **713** . . . . 1·75 1·40
2255 8f. Doctors Prakash and Mandakini Amte (anti-leprosy campaign in India) . . . . 1·90 1·75

714 First Car with Tyres

1995. Centenary of Invention of Inflatable Tyres.
2256 **714** 8f. purple and claret . . 1·90 1·40

715 "Spring"

1995. 550th Birth Anniv of Sandro Botticelli (artist).
2257 **715** 15f. blue . . . . 3·75 3·50

716 Poster

718 Rhododendron

717 Illusion

1996. 20th International Circus Festival, Monte Carlo.
2258 **716** 2f.40 multicoloured . . . 70 55

1996. Magic Festival, Monte Carlo.
2259 **717** 2f.80 black 85 55

1996. Monte Carlo Flower Show.
2260 **718** 3f. multicoloured 85 55

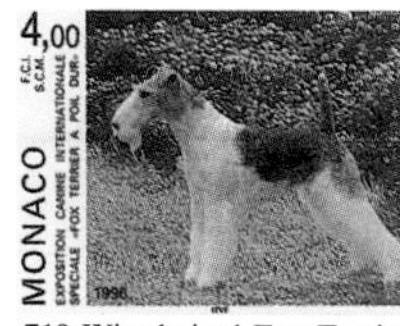
719 Wire-haired Fox Terrier

1996. International Dog Show, Monte Carlo.
2261 **719** 4f. multicoloured . . . . 1·25 95

720 "Chapel" (Hubert Clerissi)

1996. 300th Anniv of Chapel of Our Lady of Mercy.
2262 **720** 6f. multicoloured . . . . 1·75 1·60

721 Prince Albert I of Monaco (½-size illustration)

1996. Centenary of Oceanographic Expeditions. Multicoloured.
2263 3f. Type **721** 85 55
2264 4f.50 King Carlos I of Portugal . . . . 1·40 85

722 Prince Rainier III (after F. Messina)

723 Princess Grace

1996. Inauguration of Stamp and Coin Museum (2nd issue). 1974 Prince Rainier design.
2265 **722** 10f. violet . . . . 2·00 1·40
2266 15f. brown . . . . . . 3·25 1·75
2267 20f. blue . . . . 4·00 2·40

1996. Europa. Famous Women.
2268 **723** 3f. brown and red . . . 85 60

724 Fishes, Sea and Coastline

1996. 20th Anniv of Ramoge Agreement on Environmental Protection of Mediterranean.
2269 **724** 3f. multicoloured 85 60

727 Code and Monaco

728 Throwing the Javelin

1996. Introduction of International Dialling Code "377".
2272 **727** 3f. blue 85 60
2273 3f.80 red . . . . 1·10 85

1996. Olympic Games, Atlanta. Multicoloured.
2274 3f. Type **728** 85 80
2275 3f. Baseball 85 80
2276 4f.50 Running . . . . . . 1·40 1·40
2277 4f.50 Cycling . . . . . . 1·40 1·40

729 Children of Different Races with Balloon

730 Angel and Star

1996. 50th Anniv of U.N.I.C.E.F.
2278 **729** 3f. brown, blue and lilac 85 70

1996. Christmas. Multicoloured.
2279 3f. Type **730** 85 60
2280 6f. Angels heralding . . . . 1·50 1·25

731 Planet and Neptune, God of the Sea (after Roman mosaic, Sousse)

1996. Anniversaries.
2281 **731** 4f. red, blue and black 1·00 95
2282 – 5f. blue and red . . . . 1·25 1·10
DESIGNS—4f. Type **731** (150th anniv of discovery of planet Neptune by Johann Galle); 5f. Rene Descartes (after Franz Hals) (philosopher and scientist, 400th birth anniv).

732 Coins and Press

1996. Inauguration of Stamp and Coin Museum (3rd issue).
2283 **732** 5f. brown and blue . . . 1·25 1·40
2284 – 5f. brown and purple . . 1·25 1·40
2285 – 10f. blue and brown . . 3·00 2·75
DESIGNS—As T **733**: 5f. Stamp press and engraver. 48 × 37 mm: 10f. Museum entrance.

733 Camille Corot (bicentenary)

1996. Artists' Birth Anniversaries. Self-portraits. Multicoloured.
2287 6f. Type **733** . . . . 1·50 1·40
2288 7f. Francisco Goya (250th anniv) . . . . 1·75 1·75

734 Allegory

1996. Monaco Red Cross. Anti-tuberculosis Campaign. Multicoloured.
2289 7f. Type **734** . . . . 1·75 1·25
2290 8f. Camille Guerin and Albert Calmette (developers of vaccine) . . 2·00 1·40

736 "Gloria" (cadet barque), Club, Motorboat and "Tuiga" (royal yacht)

1996. Monaco Yacht Club.
2292 **736** 3f. multicoloured 80 65

737 Seal of Prince Rainer III

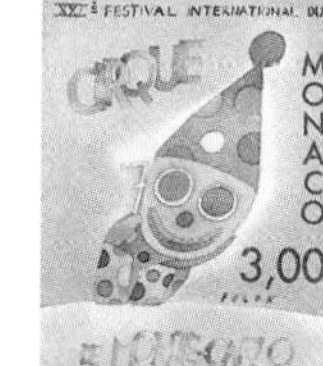
738 Clown

1996. 700th Anniv of Grimaldi Dynasty (1st issue).
2293 **737** 2f.70 red, brown and blue 80 55
See also Nos. 2302/14 and 2326/38.

1996. 21st International Circus Festival, Monte Carlo (1997).
2294 **738** 3f. multicoloured 80 55

739 Old and New Racing and Rally Cars

1996. Motor Sport.
2295 **739** 3f. multicoloured 80 55

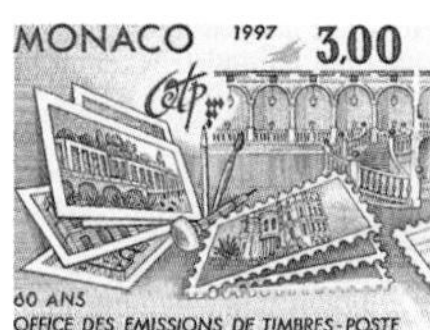
740 Pictures, Engraving Tools and "Stamps"

1996. 60th Anniv of Stamp Issuing Office (2296) and "Monaco 97" International Stamp Exhibition, Monte Carlo (2297). Each brown, mauve and blue.
2296 3f. Type **740** 80 55
2297 3f. Stamp, magnifying glass and letters 80 55
Nos. 2296/7 were issued together, se-tenant, forming a composite design featuring the Grand Staircase of the Prince's Palace.

741 Double Red Camellia

1996. Monte Carlo Flower Show (1997).
2298 **741** 3f.80 multicoloured . . . 1·00 70

742 Afghan Hound

1996. International Dog Show, Monte Carlo.
2299 **742** 4f.40 multicoloured . . . 1·40 1·25

743 Award

744 Giant Bellflower and Carob Pods and Leaves

1996. 37th Television Festival, Monte Carlo (1997).
2300 **743** 4f.90 multicoloured . . . 1·25 1·10

1996.
2301 **744** 5f. multicoloured . . . . 1·40 1·10

745 Rainier I, Battle of Zerikzee, Arms of his wife Andriola Grillo and Chateau de Cagnes

1997. 700th Anniv of Grimaldi Dynasty (2nd issue). The Seigneurs. Multicoloured.
2302 1f. Type **745** 35 35
2303 1f. Seal of Charles I, Battle of Crecy, Chateau de Roquebrune and Rocher fortifications 35 35
2304 1f. Siege of Rocher by Boccanegra, seal of Rainier II, arms of his two wives Ilaria del Caretto and Isabelle Asinari, Vatican and Papal Palace, Avignon . . 35 35
2305 2f. Defeat of combined fleets of Venice and Florence and Jean I on horseback and with his wife Pomelline Fregoso 55 60
2306 2f. Claudine, acclamation by crowd of her husband Lambert, seals of Lambert and his father Nicolas and strengthening of Monaco Castle 55 60
2307 7f. Statue of Francois Grimaldi disguised as Franciscan monk and clashes between Ghibellines and Guelphs at Genoa . . . . 1·90 1·75
2308 7f. Honore I flanked by Pope Paul III and Duke of Savoy and Battle of Lepanto . . . . 1·90 1·75
2309 7f. Charles II, flags of Genoa and Savoy and attack on Rocher by Capt. Cartier . . . . . . 1·90 1·75
2310 7f. Hercule I, flags of Savoy, Nice and Provence, assassination of Hercule and acclamation of his infant son Honore II . . 1·90 1·75
2311 9f. Catalan aiding Doge of Venice in war against Aragon, exercising "Right of the Sea" and entrusting education of his heiress Claudine to his wife Pomelline . . . . 2·75 2·75
2312 9f. Jean II with his wife Antoinette of Savoy, retable in Chapel of St. Nicholas and assassination of Jean by his brother Lucien . . . . 2·75 2·75
2313 9f. Lucien and siege of Monaco by Genoa . . . 2·75 2·75
2314 9f. Seal of Augustin, Treaty of Tordesillas, visit by King Charles V and Augustin as bishop with his nephew and heir Honore . . . . 2·75 2·75

746 Tennis Match and Players

1997. Centenary of Monaco Tennis Championships.
2316 **746** 4f.60 multicoloured . . . 1·25 95

747 Prince Rainier, Trophy and Stamp and Coin Museum

1997. Award to Prince Rainier of International Philately Grand Prix (made to "Person who has Contributed Most to Philately") by Association of Catalogue Editors.
2317 **747** 4f.60 multicoloured . . . 1·25 1·10

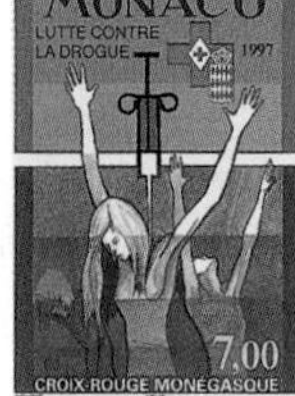

748 Images of St.Devote (patron saint) **749** Syringe and Drug Addicts

1997. Europa. Tales and Legends.
2318 **748** 3f. orange and brown . . 80 70
2319 – 3f. blue 80 70
DESIGN: No. 2319, Hercules.

1997. Monaco Red Cross. Anti-drugs Campaign.
2320 **749** 7f. black, blue and red 2·00 1·40

750 First Stamps of United States and Monaco 1996 15f. Stamp

1997. "Pacific 97" International Stamp Exhibiton, San Francisco. 150th Anniv of First United States Stamps.
2321 **750** 4f.90 multicoloured . . . 1·40 1·10

751 Winter and Summer Uniforms, 1997

1997. The Palace Guard. Multicoloured.
2322 3f. Type **751** 80 65
2323 3f.50 Uniforms of 1750, 1815, 1818, 1830 and 1853 1·00 70
2324 5f.20 Uniforms of 1865, 1870, 1904, 1916 and 1935 1·40 1·10

1997. Victory of Marcelo M. Rios at Monaco Tennis Championships. No. 2316 optd **M. RIOS**.
2325 **746** 4f.60 multicoloured . . . 1·40 1·25

1997. 700th Anniv of Grimaldi Dynasty (3rd issue). The Princes. As T **745**. Multicoloured.
2326 1f. Honore II 35 35
2327 1f. Louis I 35 35
2328 1f. Antoine I 35 35
2329 2f. Jacques I 65 65
2330 7f. Charles III . . . . . . 1·90 1·90
2331 7f. Albert I . . . . 1·90 1·90
2332 7f. Louis II . . . . 1·90 1·90
2333 7f. Rainier III . . . . . . 1·90 1·90
2334 9f. Louise-Hippolyte . . . . 2·50 2·50
2335 9f. Honore IV (wrongly inscr "Honore III") . . . 2·50 2·50
2336 9f. Honore III (wrongly inscr "Honore IV") . . . 2·50 2·50
2337 9f. Honore V . . . . 2·50 2·50
2338 9f. Florestan I . . . . . . 2·50 2·50

753 Club Badge, Ball as Globe and Stadium

1997. Monaco, Football Champion of France, 1996–97
2339 **753** 3f. multicoloured 80 75

754 Magic Wand, Hands and Stars

1997. 13th Magic Grand Prix, Monte Carlo.
2340 **754** 4f.40 black and gold . . 1·25 1·10

755 "Francois Grimaldi" (Ernando Venanzi)

1997. Paintings. Multicoloured.
2341 8f. Type **755** . . . . 2·10 1·75
2342 9f. "St. Peter and St. Paul" (Peter Paul Rubens) . . . 2·25 2·25

757 Map of Europe and Blue Whales

1997. 49th Session of International Whaling Commission, Monaco.
2344 **757** 6f.70 multicoloured . . . 1·40 1·25

758 Princess Charlotte

1997. 20th Death Anniv of Princess Charlotte.
2346 **758** 3f.80 brown . . . . . . 1·00 1·00

759 Dancer of Russian Ballet and Kremlin, Moscow **761** Diamond-Man (Ribeiro)

760 Trees in Monaco

1997. "Moskva 97" International Stamp Exhbition, Moscow.
2347 **759** 5f. multicoloured . . . . 1·25 1·25

1997. 10th Anniv of Marcel Korenlein Arboretum.
2348 **760** 9f. multicoloured . . . . 2·50 2·25

1997. Winning Entries in Schoolchildren's Drawing Competition.
2349 **761** 4f. multicoloured . . . . 1·00 90
2350 – 4f.50 blue, ultramarine and red . . . . 1·25 1·00
DESIGN—HORIZ: 4f.50, Flying diamonds (Testa).

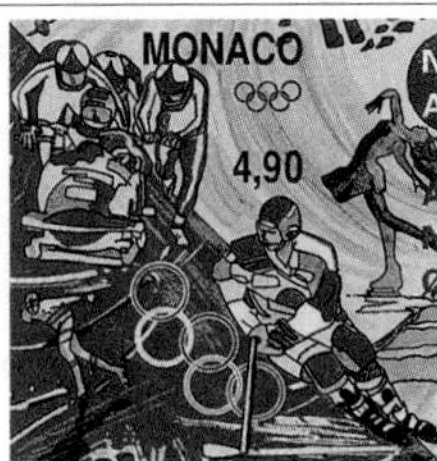

762 Four-man Bobsleighing, Speed and Figure Skating and Ice Hockey

1997. Winter Olympic Games, Nagano, Japan (1998). Multicoloured.
2351 4f.90 Type **762** . . . . . 1·40 1·40
2352 4f.90 Alpine skiing, biathlon, two-man bobsleighing and ski-jumping . . . . 1·40 1·40
Nos. 2351/2 were issued together, se-tenant, forming a composite design.

763 Albert I (statue) ($\frac{1}{2}$-size illustration)

1997. 150th Birth Anniv of Prince Albert I (1st issue).
2353 **763** 8f. multicoloured . . . . 2·10 2·10
See also No. 2368.

764 Clown and Horse **765** Pink Campanula and Carob Plant

1997. 22nd International Circus Festival, Monte Carlo (1998).
2354 **764** 3f. multicoloured 80 75

1997. Monte Carlo Flower Show (1998).
2355 **765** 4f.40 multicoloured . . . 1·25 1·10

766 "The Departure of Marcus Attilius Regulus for Carthage" **768** Baseball Hat, Television Controller, Ballet Shoe and Football Boot

767 Pope Innocent IV

1997. 250th Birth Anniv of Louis David (painter).
2356 **766** 5f.20 green and red . . . 1·40 1·25

1997. 750th Anniv of Creation of Parish of Monaco by Papal Bull.
2357 **767** 7f.50 brown and blue . . 1·90 1·85

1998. 38th Television Festival.
2358 **768** 4f.50 multicoloured . . . 1·10 1·00

769 Past and Present Presidents

1998. 50th Anniv of Monaco Red Cross.
2359 **769** 5f. brown and red . . . 1·40 1·40

770 Boxer and Dobermann

1998. International Dog Show, Monte Carlo.
2360 **770** 2f.70 multicoloured . . . 80 70

771 White Doves and Laurel Wreath

1998. 30th Meeting of Academy of Peace and International Security.
2361 **771** 3f. green and blue . . . 80 70

772 Ballet Dancer, Piano Keys, Music Score and Violin

1998. 15th Spring Arts Festival.
2362 **772** 4f. multicoloured . . . . 1·00 65

773 Pierre and Marie Curie

1998. Centenary of Discovery of Radium.
2363 **773** 6f. blue and mauve . . . 1·60 1·50

774 Caravel and Globe

1998. "Expo '98" World's Fair, Lisbon. International Year of the Ocean.
2364 **774** 2f.70 multicoloured . . . 80 75

775 St. Devote (stained glass window, Palace Chapel) (½-size illustration)

1998. Europa (1st issue). National Festivals.
2365 **775** 3f. multicoloured 80 70
See also No. 2372.

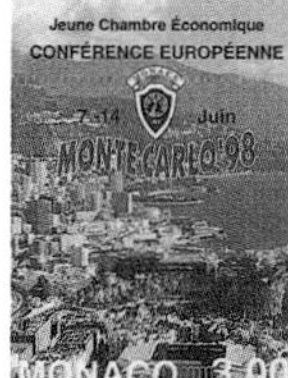

776 Monte Carlo

777 Kessel

1998. Junior Chamber of Commerce European Conference, Monte Carlo.
2366 **776** 3f. multicoloured 80 75

1998. Birth Centenary of Joseph Kessel (writer).
2367 **777** 3f.90 multicoloured . . . 1·00 1·00

778 Prince Albert I at different Ages (½-size illustration)

1998. 150th Birth Anniv of Prince Albert I (2nd issue).
2368 **778** 7f. brown . . . . 1·75 1·60

779 Garnier and Monte Carlo Casino

780 Trophy and Monte Carlo

1998. Death Centenary of Charles Garnier (architect).
2369 **779** 10f. multicoloured . . . 2·75 2·25

1998. 10th World Music Awards, Monte Carlo.
2370 **780** 10f. multicoloured . . . 2·75 2·50

781 Racing Cars

1998. 1st Formula 3000 Grand Prix, Monte Carlo.
2371 **781** 3f. red and black 85 45

782 Prince Rainier III, Prince Albert and Royal Palace (½-size illustration)

1998. Europa (2nd issue). National Festivals.
2372 **782** 3f. multicoloured 85 70

783 Porcelain Teapot and Figure of Francois Grimaldi

1998. Fine Arts. Multicoloured.
2373 8f. Type **783** . . . . 2·00 1·90
2374 9f. Fine-bound books and illustration . . . . 2·25 1·40

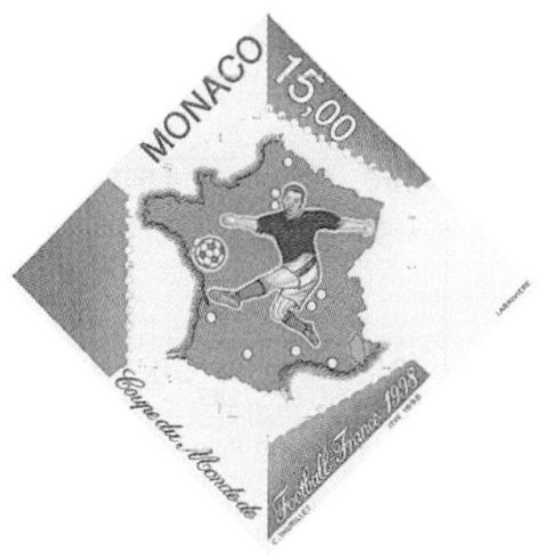

784 Player on Map of France

1998. World Cup Football Championship, France.
2375 **784** 15f. multicoloured . . . 4·25 4·00

785 Modern and Old Motor Cars and Ferrari

1998. Birth Centenary of Enzio Ferrari (motor manufacturer).
2376 **785** 7f. multicoloured . . . . 1·90 1·75

786 Gershwin, Trumpeter, Dancers and Opening Bars of "Rhapsody in Blue"

1998. Birth Cent of George Gershwin (composer).
2377 **786** 7f.50 ultramarine, blue and black . . . . . . 1·90 1·75

787 Int Marine Pollution College and Marine Environment Laboratory

1998. Int Marine Pollution Conference, Monaco.
2378 **787** 4f.50 multicoloured . . . 1·40 1·10

788 Venue

1998. Post Europ (successor to C.E.P.T.) Plenary Assembly, Monaco.
2379 **788** 5f. multicoloured . . . . 1·40 1·10

789 Belem Tower, Lisbon, and Palace, Monaco

1998. "Expo '98" World's Fair and Stamp Exhibition, Lisbon.
2380 **789** 6f.70 multicoloured . . . 1·75 1·75

790 Sportsmen

1998. 30th Anniv of International Association against Violence in Sport.
2381 **790** 4f.20 multicoloured . . . 1·10 1·00

791 Magician

1998. "Magic Stars" Magic Festival, Monte Carlo.
2382 **791** 3f.50 gold and red . . . 90 90

792 Statue and Vatican Colonnade

1998. 400th Birth Anniv of Giovanni Lorenzo Bernini (architect and sculptor).
2383 **792** 11f.50 blue and brown 3·00 3·25

793 Milan Cathedral

794 Christmas Tree Decoration

1998. "Italia 98" Int Stamp Exhibition, Milan.
2384 **793** 4f.90 green and red . . . 1·25 1·25

1998. Christmas. Multicoloured.
2385 3f. Type **794** 80 65
2386 6f.70 "The Nativity" (detail of icon) (horiz) . . . . . 1·75 1·75

1998. As Nos. 1910 etc but no value expressed.
2388 **577** (2f.70) turquoise & blue 60 25
2389 (3f.) red and pink . . . 60 25
2390 (3f.80) blue and cobalt 80 40

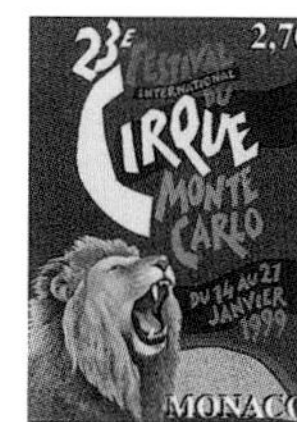

795 Lion

1998. 23rd International Circus Festival, Monte Carlo (1999).
2391 **795** 2f.70 multicoloured . . . 70 55

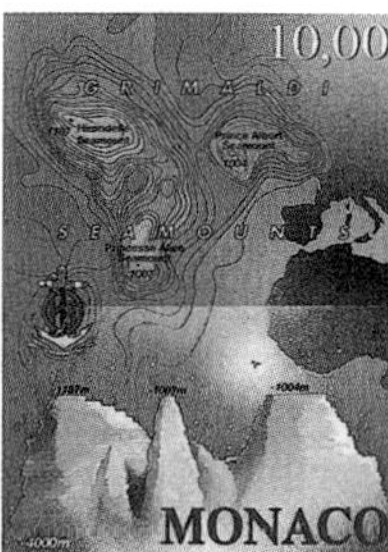

796 Map and Elevation of Seamounts

1998. Grimaldi Seamounts.
2392 **796** 10f. multicoloured . . . 2·50 2·00

798 1860 Cover and Stamp and Coin Museum

1999. "Monaco 99" International Stamp Exhibition.
2394 **798** 3f. multicoloured 80 50

799 Festival Poster

1999. 39th Television Festival.
2396 **799** 3f.80 multicoloured . . . 1·00 60

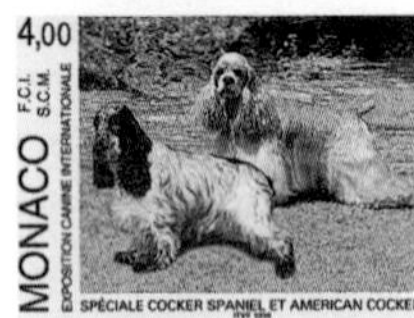

800 Cocker Spaniel and American Cocker

1999. International Dog Show, Fontvieille.
2397 **800** 4f. multicoloured . . . . 1·00 65

801 World Map

1999. 50th Anniv of Geneva Conventions.
2398 **801** 4f.40 red, brown and black . . . . 1·10 60

802 Arrangement of Flowers named after Grimaldi Family Members

1999. Monte Carlo Flower Show.
2399 **802** 4f.50 multicoloured . . . 1·10 60

803 Children and Heart

1999. 20th Anniv of Monaco Aid and Presence.
2400 **803** 6f.70 multicoloured . . . 1·75 1·00
No. 2400 is also denominated in euros.

804 Palace and Centre

1999. 20th Anniv of Congress Centre Auditorium.
2401 **804** 2f.70 multicoloured . . . 70 50

DENOMINATION. From No. 2402 Monaco stamps are denominated both in francs and in euros. As no cash for the latter was in circulation until 2002, the catalogue continues to use the franc value.

805 Globe and Piano Keys

1999. 10th Piano Masters, Monte Carlo.
2402 **805** 4f.60 multicoloured . . . 1·25 65

806 Rose "Jubile du Prince de Monaco"

808 Olympic Rings and Trophy

807 Williams's Bugatti (winner of first race) and Michael Schumacher's Car (winner of 1999 race)

1999. Flowers. Multicoloured.
2403 4f.90 Type **806** . . . . . . 1·25 70
2404 6f. Rose "Prince de Monaco", rose "Grimaldi" and orchid "Prince Rainier III" . . . 1·50 85

1999. 70th Anniv of Monaco Motor Racing Grand Prix.
2405 **807** 3f. multicoloured 85 50

1999. 3rd Association of Postage Stamp Catalogue Editors and Philatelic Publications Grand Prix.
2406 **808** 4f.40 multicoloured . . . 1·10 75

809 Riders jumping over Monte Carlo (½-size illustration)

1999. 5th International Show Jumping Competition, Monte Carlo.
2407 **809** 5f.20 red, black and blue 1·40 95

810 Footballer, Runner and Palace (½-size illustration)

1999. 75th Anniv of Monaco Sports Association. Multicoloured.
2408 7f. Type **810** . . . . 1·75 1·10
2409 7f. Boxer, footballer, harbour, runner and handballer . . . . 1·75 1·10

811 Architect's Drawing of Forum

1999. Construction of Grimaldi Forum (congress and exhibition centre).
2410 **811** 3f. multicoloured 80 50

812 Facade and Construction

1999. Centenary of Laying of First Stone of Oceanographic Museum.
2411 **812** 5f. multicoloured . . . . 1·25 1·10

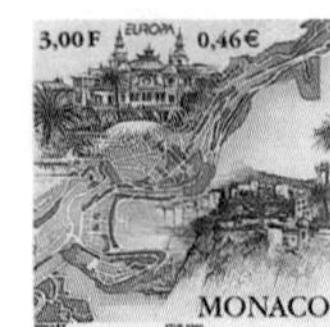

813 Eiffel Tower on Map of France, 1849 20c. "Ceres" Stamp and Emblem

814 Casino and Rock

1999. "Philexfrance 99" International Stamp Exhibition, Paris (1st issue). 150th Anniv of First French Stamps.
2412 **813** 2f.70 multicoloured . . . 70 55
See also No. 2423.

1999. Europa. Parks and Gardens. Multicoloured.
2413 3f. Type **814** 70 60
2414 3f. Fontvieille (48 × 27 mm) 70 60

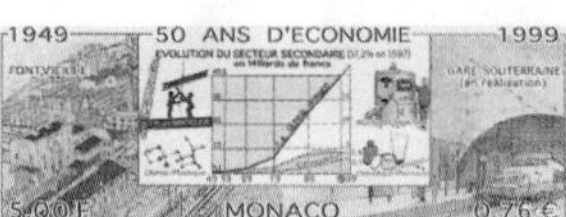

815 Fontvieille in 1949, Line Graph and Underground Station in 1999 (½-size illustration)

1999. 50 Years of the Economy. Multicoloured.
2415 5f. Type **815** (second sector) 1·25 1·10
2416 5f. Le Larvotto in 1949, line graph and Grimaldi Forum in 1999 (third sector) . . . . 1·25 1·10

817 Honore de Balzac

818 Emblem and Chinese Drawing

1999. Writers' Birth Bicentenaries.
2418 **817** 4f.50 blue and scarlet . . 1·10 70
2419 – 5f.20 brown, blue and red . . . . 1·25 85
DESIGN: 5f.20, Sophie Rostopchine, Comtesse de Segur.

1999. 125th Anniv of Universal Postal Union.
2420 **818** 3f. blue, red and yellow 70 55

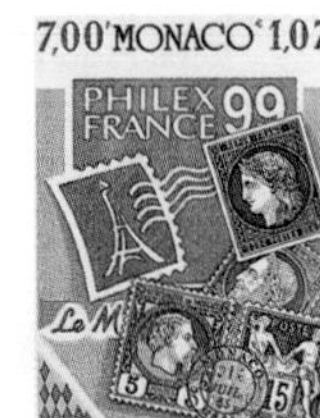

819 Iris "Rainier III" and Rose "Rainier III"

821 Emblem and Monaco 1885 and French 1878 Stamps

820 Anniversary Emblem

1999. Flowers.
2421 **819** 4f. multicoloured 90 75

1999. 50th Anniv of Monaco's Admission to United Nations Educational, Scientific and Educational Organization.
2422 **820** 4f.20 multicoloured . . . 1·00 80

1999. "Philexfrance 99" International Stamp Exhibition, Paris (2nd issue).
2423 **821** 7f. black, blue and mauve . . . . 1·60 1·50

822 Athletes

1999. 10th Sportel (sport and television) Congress, Fontvieille.
2424 **822** 10f. multicoloured . . . 2·25 2·00

823 Maltese Cross, Knights and Valletta

1999. 900th Anniv of Sovereign Military Order of Malta and 25th Anniv of National Association of the Order.
2425 **823** 11f.50 red, brown and blue . . . . 2·50 2·50

824 1999 Postcard of Monaco, 1989 Definitive Design and Obverse of Jubilee Coin

1999. Postcard, Coin and Stamp Exhibition, Fontvieille (1st issue).
2426 **824** 3f. multicoloured 70 55
See also No. 2429.

1999. "Magic Stars" Magic Festival, Monte Carlo. As No. 2382 but face value and date changed.
2427 **791** 4f.50 gold and red . . . 1·10 90

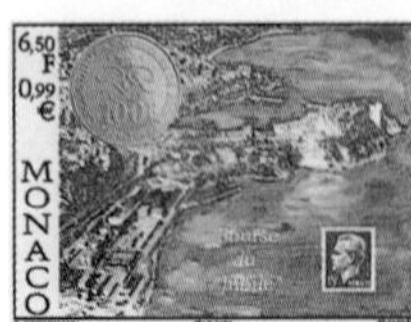

826 1949 Postcard of Monaco, Reverse of Jubilee Coin and 1950 Definitive

1999. Postcard, Coin and Stamp Exhibition, Fontvieille (2nd issue).
2429 **826** 6f.50 multicoloured . . . 1·60 1·40

827 Pierrot juggling "2000"

828 "Madonna and Child" (Simone Cantarini)

1999. 24th International Circus Festival, Monte Carlo (2000).
2430 **827** 2f.70 multicoloured . . . 65 55

1999. Christmas.
2431 **828** 3f. multicoloured 75 55

829 Blessing and Holy Door, St. Peter's Cathedral, Rome

1999. Holy Year 2000.
2432 **829** 3f.50 multicoloured . . . 80 65

830 Mixed Arrangement **831** Emblem

1999. 33rd Monte Carlo Flower Show.
2433 **830** 4f.50 multicoloured . . . 1·10 90

1999. "Monaco 2000" International Stamp Exhibitions.
2434 **831** 3f. multicoloured 75 55

832 Bust of Napoleon (Antonio Canova) **833** Festival Emblem

2000. 30th Anniv of Napoleonic Museum.
2435 **832** 4f.20 multicoloured . . . 1·00 80

2000. 40th Television Festival, Monte Carlo.
2436 **833** 4f.90 multicoloured . . . 1·10 95

834 St. Peter and St. James the Major

2000. The Twelve Apostles. Multicoloured.
2437 **834** 4f. blue, orange and gold 80 75
2438 – 5f. red and gold . . . . 1·00 95
2439 – 6f. violet and gold . . . 1·25 1·10
2440 – 7f. brown and gold . . 1·50 1·40
2441 – 8f. green and gold . . . 1·75 1·50
2442 – 9f. red, orange and gold 1·90 1·75
DESIGNS: 5f. St. John and St. Andrew; 6f. St. Philip and St. Bartholomew; 7f. St. Matthew and St. Thomas; 8f. St. James the Minor and St. Jude; 9f. St. Simon and St. Mathias.

835 Golden Labrador and Golden Retriever

2000. International Dog Show, Monte Carlo.
2443 **835** 6f.50 multicoloured . . . 1·60 1·40

836 Man's Head, Drawings and Key (Adami)

2000. Monaco and the Sea. Multicoloured.
2444 6f.55 Type **836** . . . . . . 1·50 1·40
2445 6f.55 "Monaco" above sea (Arman) . . . . 1·50 1·40
2446 6f.55 Abstract designs (Cane) . . . . 1·50 1·40
2447 6f.55 Hand touching sun in sky (Folon) . . . . . . 1·50 1·40
2448 6f.55 Angel sleeping and boats (Fuchs) . . . . . . 1·50 1·40
2449 6f.55 Harbour (E. de Sigaldi) . . . . 1·50 1·40
2450 6f.55 Views of harbour on silhouettes of yachts (Sosno) . . . . 1·50 1·40
2451 6f.55 Waves and floating ball (Verkade) . . . . . 1·50 1·40

837 Olympic Rings on Globe and Flags

2000. Olympic Games, Sydney, Australia.
2452 **837** 7f. multicoloured . . . . 1·50 1·40

838 "Building Europe" **839** Racing Cars

2000. Europa. Multicoloured.
2453 3f. Type **838** 75 70
2454 3f. Map of Europe and Post Europ member countries' flags (56 × 37 mm) 75 70

2000. 2nd Historic Vehicles Grand Prix.
2455 **839** 4f.40 multicoloured . . . 90 80

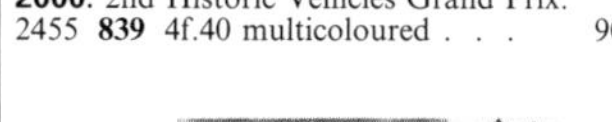

840 Monaco Pavilion and Emblem

2000. "EXPO 2000" World's Fair, Hanover.
2456 **840** 5f. multicoloured . . . . 1·00 95

841 Sts. Mark, Matthew, John and Luke

2000. The Four Evangelists.
2457 **841** 20f. black, flesh and green . . . . 4·25 4·25

842 St. Stephen and Emblem **843** Golfer

2000. "WIPA 2000" International Stamp Exhibition, Vienna.
2458 **842** 4f.50 black, blue and red 90 85

2000. Pro-celebrity Golf Tournament, Monte Carlo.
2459 **843** 4f.40 multicoloured . . . 90 85

844 Fencing

2000. Olympic Games, Sydney. Multicoloured.
2460 2f.70 Type **844** 65 35
2461 4f.50 Rowing 90 55

845 Humber Beeston and Woman with Parasol, 1911

2000. Motor Cars and Fashion. Motor cars from the Royal Collection. Multicoloured.
2462 3f. Type **845** 65 45
2463 6f.70 Jaguar 4-cylinder and woman, 1947 . . . . . . 1·50 85
2464 10f. Rolls Royce Silver Cloud and woman wearing swing coat, 1956 2·00 1·25
2465 15f. Lamborghini Countach and woman wearing large hat, 1986 . . . . 3·25 1·60

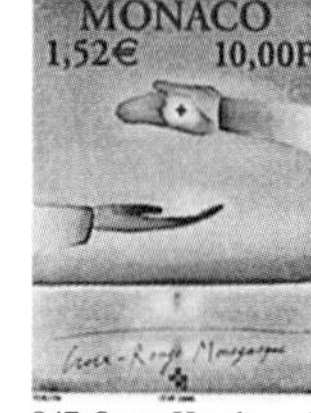

846 Entrance to Museum **847** Open Hands and Emblem

2000. Philatelic Rarities Exhibition (1999), Stamp and Coin Museum, Monte Carlo.
2466 **846** 3f.50 multicoloured . . . 75 65

2000. Monaco Red Cross.
2467 **847** 10f. multicoloured . . . 2·10 1·90

848 Magnifying Glass, Stamps and Exhibition Hall **849** Magician

2000. "WORLD STAMP USA" International Exhibition, Anaheim, California.
2468 **848** 4f.40 multicoloured . . . 95 55

2000. "Magic Stars" Magic Festival, Monte Carlo.
2469 **849** 4f.60 multicoloured . . . 95 55

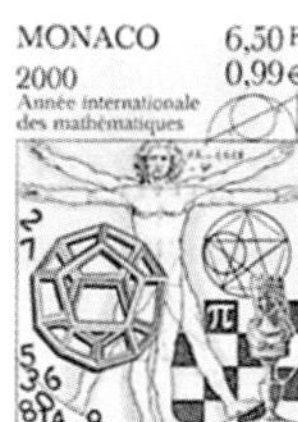

850 Da Vinci's "Man" and Mathematical Symbols

2000. World Mathematics Year.
2470 **850** 6f.50 brown . . . . . . 1·40 65

852 Shark and Museum Facade

2000. Opening of New Aquarium, Oceanographical Museum.
2472 **852** 3f. multicoloured 65 35

853 Cathedral and Statue of Bear

2000. "ESPANA 2000" International Stamp Exhibition, Madrid.
2473 **853** 3f.80 multicoloured . . . 85 45

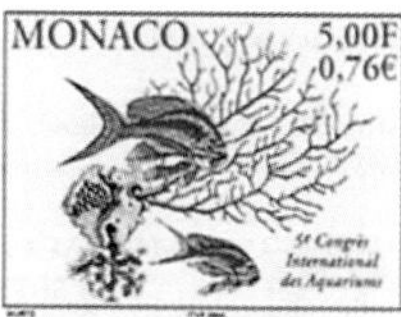

854 Fishes and Corals

2000. 5th International Congress on Aquaria (5f.) and 25th Anniv of Monaco Nature Protection Association (9f.). Multicoloured.
2474 5f. Type **854** . . . . 1·10 55
2475 9f. Starfish, water plant and fish . . . . 1·90 95

855 Museum Facade and Plants

2000. 50th Anniv of Observatory Cave and 40th Anniv of Anthropological Museum.
2476 **855** 5f.20 purple, green and brown . . . . 1·00 55

856 Fresco, Oceanography Museum (½-size illustration)

2000. International Aquariological Congress.
2477 **856** 7f. multicoloured . . . . 1·50 65

857 18th-century Crib **858** Princess Stephanie (President)

2000. Christmas.
2478 **857** 3f. multicoloured 65 25

2000. Motor Cars and Fashion. Motor cars from the Royal Collection. As T **845**. Multicoloured.
2479 5f. Ferrari Formula 1 racing car and woman in racing clothes, 1989 . . . . . . 1·10 55
2480 6f. Fiat 600 "Jolly" and woman wearing swimming costume, 1955 . . . . . 1·25 65
2481 8f. Citroen C4F "Autochenille" and woman wearing coat and hat, 1929 . . . . 1·75 85

2000. Association for Help and Protection of Disabled Children (A.M.A.P.E.I.).
2482 **858** 11f.50 blue and red . . . 2·40 1·10

860 Warrior kneeling **861** Museum Building

2000. Terracotta Warrior Exhibition, Grimaldi Forum (2001).
2484 **860** 2f.70 black and red . . . 65 25

2000. 50th Anniv of Postal Museum.
2485 **861** 3f. multicoloured 65 25

862 Arms

863 Iris "Princess Caroline of Monaco"

2000. Self-adhesive.
2486 **862** (3f.) black and red . . . 65 25

2000. 34th Monte Carlo Flower Show.
2487 **863** 3f.80 multicoloured . . . 85 35

864 Sardinian 1851 5c., 20c. and 40c. Stamps

2000. 150th Anniv (2001) of First Sardinian Stamp.
2488 **864** 6f.50 blue, red and black 1·40 65

865 Seahorse, Marine Life and Life Belt

2000. 25th Anniv (2001) of the Ramoge Agreement on Environmental Protection of Mediterranean.
2489 **865** 6f.70 multicoloured . . . 1·50 65

866 Breitling Orbiter and 1984 2f.80 Stamp

867 Clown with Seal balancing Ball

2000. 1st Non-Stop Balloon Circumnavigation of Globe (1999). Award to Bertrand Picard of International Philately Grand Prix by Association of Catalogue Editors.
2490 **866** 9f. multicoloured . . . . 1·90 95

2000. 25th International Circus Festival, Monte Carlo (2001). Different poster designs by artist named. Multicoloured (except No. 2492).
2491 2f.70 Type **867** 65 35
2492 6f. Clown playing guitar (Hodge) (black, red and blue) . . . . 1·25 65
2493 6f. Clown resting head (Knie) . . . . 1·25 65
2494 6f. Tiger and circus tent (P. Merot) . . . . 1·25 65
2495 6f. Lions, horses and trapeze artists (Poulet) . . . . . 1·25 65
2496 6f. Monkey and circus tents (T. Mordant) . . . . . . 1·25 65

868 Player kicking Ball

2000. Monaco, Football Champion of France, 1999–2000.
2497 **868** 4f.50 multicoloured . . . 1·00 45

869 Sea Mammals and Mediterranean Sea

2000. Mediterranean Sea Marine Mammals Sanctuary.
2498 **869** 5f.20 multicoloured . . . 1·10 55

870 Nativity Scene (½-size illustration)

2000. Christmas.
2499 **870** 10f. multicoloured . . . 2·00 1·10

871 Poster

873 Flower Arrangement

872 Leonberger and Newfoundland Dogs

2001. 41st Television Festival, Monte Carlo.
2500 **871** 3f.50 multicoloured . . . 70 50

2001. International Dog Show, Monte Carlo.
2501 **872** 6f.50 multicoloured . . . 1·25 95

2001. Flower Show, Genoa.
2502 **873** 6f.70 multicoloured . . . 1·25 95

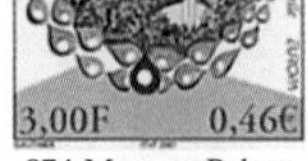

874 Monaco Palace

875 Princess Caroline and Portrait of Prince Pierre of Monaco (founder)

2001. Europa. Water Resources. Multicoloured.
2503 3f. Type **874** 60 45
2504 3f. Undercover washing area 60 45

2001. 50th Anniv of Literary Council of Monaco.
2505 **875** 2f.70 black, brown and green 50 25

876 Malraux

877 Town Hall

2001. Birth Centenary of Andre Malraux (writer).
2506 **876** 10f. black and red . . . 1·90 1·40

2001. "BELGICA 2001" International Stamp Exhibition, Brussels.
2507 **877** 4f. blue and red 75 60

878 Coins, Stamp and Book

879 Princess Grace and Ballet Dancer

2001. Postcard, Coin and Stamp Exhibition, Fontvielle.
2508 **878** 2f.70 multicoloured . . . 50 40

2001. 25th Anniv of Princess Grace Dance Academy.
2509 **879** 4f.40 multicoloured . . . 85 65

880 Model

2001. Naval Museum, Fontvielle.
2510 **880** 4f.50 multicoloured . . . 85 65

881 Petanque Ball

2001. World Petanque Championships.
2511 **881** 5f. multicoloured 75 70

882 Fireplace, Throne Room

2001. Royal Palace (1st series). Multicoloured.
2512 3f. Type **882** 60 40
2513 4f.50 Blue Room 85 65
2514 6f.70 York Chamber . . . . 1·25 95
2515 15f. Throne room ceiling fresco . . . . 3·00 2·25
See also Nos. 2541/3.

883 Littre and Diderot

2001. 250th Anniv of *Encyclopaedia or Critical Dictionary of Sciences, Arts and Trades* (Denis Diderot) and Birth Bicentenary of Emile Littre (compiler of *Dictionary of the French Language*).
2516 **883** 4f.20 black, blue and green 80 60

884 Medal and Steam Yacht

2001. 30th Anniv of Prince Albert Oceanography Prize.
2517 **884** 9f. blue . . . . 1·75 1·25

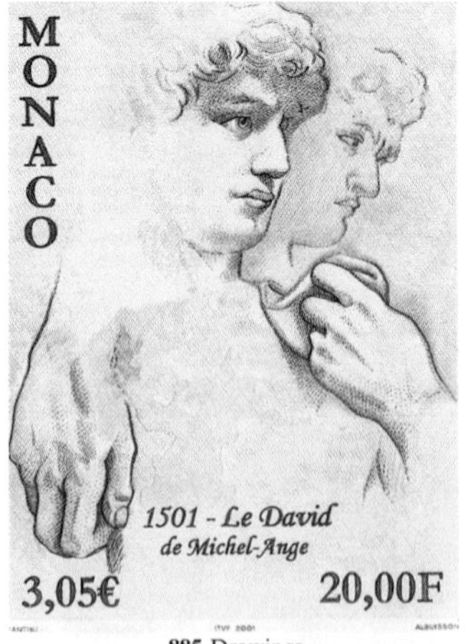

885 Drawings

2001. 500th Anniv of David (sculpture, Michaelangelo).
2518 **885** 20f. multicoloured . . . 3·75 3·00

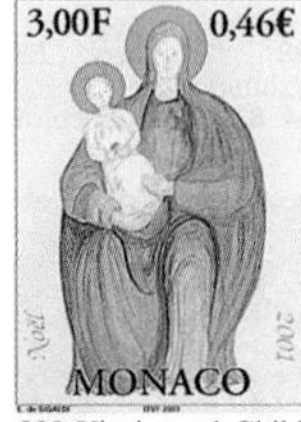

886 Alfred Nobel (prize fund founder)

888 Virgin and Child

887 Prince Rainer, Prince Albert, Map, Satellite, Ship, and Submarine

2001. Centenary of the Nobel Prize. Multicoloured.
2519 5f. Type **886** 95 70
2520 8f. Henri Dunant (founder of Red Cross and winner of Peace Prize, 1901) . . 1·50 1·10
2521 11f.50 Enrico Fermi (physicist and winner of Physics Prize, 1938) . . . 2·25 1·75

2001. 36th International Commission for Scientific Exploration of the Mediterranean Meeting.
2522 **887** 3f. multicoloured 60 45

2001. Christmas.
2523 **888** 3f. multicoloured 60 45

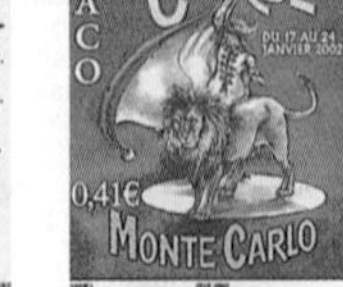

889 Garden Tiger Moth (*Artica caja*)

890 Lion and Ringmaster

2002. Flora and Fauna.
2524 **889** 1c. black, red and sepia 10 10
2525 – 2c. multicoloured 10 10
2526 – 5c. multicoloured 10 10
2527 – 10c. black, green and yellow 15 10
2528 – 20c. red, yellow and black 25 20
2529 – 41c. multicoloured . . . 65 45
2530 – 50c. multicoloured . . . 60 45
2531 – €1 multicoloured . . . 1·25 1·00
2532 – €2 multicoloured . . . 2·50 2·00
2533 – €5 brown, green and black . . . . 6·25 4·75
2534 – €10 green, red and black . . . . 12·50 9·50

DESIGNS—VERT: 5c. Blue trumpet vine (*Thunbergia grandiflora*); 41c. *Helix aspera*; 50c. Foxy charaxes (*Charaxes jasius*); €2 Red thorn apple (*Datura sanguinea*); €5 Crested tit (*Parus crisatus*). HORIZ: 2c. *Luria lurida*; 10c. Great tit (*Parus major*); 20c. Common barberfish (*Anthias anthias*); €1 Zoned mitre (*Mitra zonata*); €10 Common snipefish (*Macroramphosus scolopax*).

2002. 26th International Circus Festival, Monte Carlo.
2540 **890** 41c. multicoloured . . . 50 40

891 Crystal Gallery

2002. Royal Palace (2nd series). Multicoloured.
2541 41c. Type **891** 50 40
2542 46c. Throne room (horiz) 60 45
2543 58c. Landscape painting in Crystal Gallery (horiz) . . 75 60

892 Rocking Horse of Flowers

2002. 35th Monte Carlo Flower Show.
2544 **892** 53c. multicoloured . . . 65 50

893 Old and Modern Rally Cars

2002. Motoring Events in Monaco. Sheet 124×95 mm, containing T **893** and similar vert design. Multicoloured.
MS2545 €1.07, Type **893** (70th Monte Carlo car rally); €1.22, Old racing car (Historic Vehicles third Grand Prix) and modern Formula 1 racing car (60th Monaco Grand Prix) . . . . . 3·25 2·40

894 Skiers, Ice Skater and Ice Hockey Player

2002. Winter Olympic Games, Salt Lake City, U.S.A. Multicoloured.
2546 23c. Type **894** 35 25
2547 23c. Bobsleigh, luge and skiers (face value, emblem and country inscription at right) 35 25
Nos. 2446/7 were issued together, se-tenant, forming a composite design.

895 Exhibition Cases and Prince Albert I

2002. Anniversaries. Multicoloured.
2548 64c. Type **895** (centenary of Prehistoric Anthropology Museum) 90 65
2549 67c. Title page, Prince Albert I and ship (centenary of publication of "La Carriere d'un Navigateur" (memoirs) by Prince Albert I) 95 70

896 Mazarin (painting, Phillippe de Champaigne)

2002. 400th Birth Anniv of Jules Mazarin (cardinal to Louis XIV).
2550 **896** 69c. multicoloured . . . 1·00 75

897 Bust of Napoleon Bonaparte and Medal

2002. Bicentenary of Legion d'Honneur.
2551 **897** 70c. multicoloured . . . 1·00 75

898 Whales and Dolphins

2002. 1st Meeting of Signatories to Agreement on the Conservation of Cetaceans of the Black Sea, Mediterranean Sea and Contiguous Atlantic Area (ACCOBAMS), Monaco.
2552 **898** 75c. multicoloured . . . 1·80 80

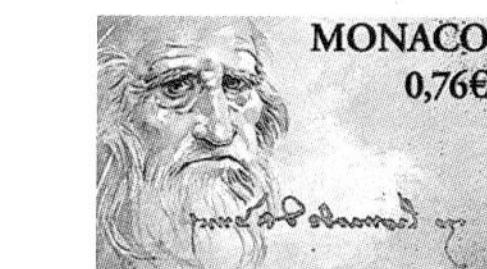
899 Da Vinci

2002. 550th Birth Anniv of Leonardo da Vinci (artist).
2553 **899** 76c. multicoloured . . . 1·10 80

900 St. Bernard and Bouvier

2002. International Dog Show, Monte Carlo.
2554 **900** 99c. multicoloured . . . 1·40 1·00

901 Police Officers and Badge

2002. Centenary of Police Force.
2555 **901** 53c. multicoloured . . . 75 55

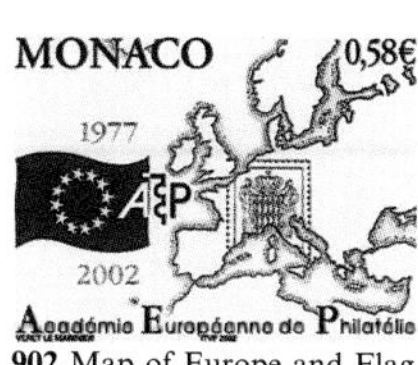
902 Map of Europe and Flag

2002. 25th Anniv of European Academy of Postal Studies.
2556 **902** 58c. multicoloured . . . 85 60

903 Circus and Globe **904** Emblem

2002. Europa. Circus. Multicoloured.
2557 46c. Type **903** 65 45
2558 46c. "JOURS DE CIRQUE" and performers 65 45

2002. 20th International Swimming Competition.
2559 **904** 64c. multicoloured . . . 95 65

905 Tarmac Roads

2002. Centenary of First Tarmac Roads.
2560 **905** 41c. red, black and brown 60 45

906 Exhibition Hall and Displays **907** Emblem

2002. "Monacophil 2002" International Stamp Exhibition.
2561 **906** 46c. green, violet and red 65 45

2002. 42nd Television Festival, Monte Carlo.
2562 **907** 70c. multicoloured . . . 1·00 75

908 Footballers and Globe

2002. World Cup Football Championship, Japan and South Korea.
2563 **908** 75c. green, blue and red 1·10 80

909 Obverse of 1, 2 and 5 cent Coins and Reverse

2002. Coins.
2564 **909** 46c. copper, red and black 65 45
2565 – 46c. gold, red and black 65 45
2566 – €1.50 multicoloured . . 2·10 1·50
2567 – €1.50 multicoloured . . 2·10 1·50
DESIGNS: Type **909**; 46c. Obverse of 10, 20 and 50 cent coins and reverse; €1.50, Obverse and reverse of 1 euro coin; €1.50, Obverse and reverse of 2 euro coin.

910 Debussy, Pelleas and Melisande

2002. Centenary of First Performance of Claude Debussy's Opera "Pelleas and Melisande".
2568 **910** 69c. green, blue and red 1·00 75

911 Saint Devote, Boat and Dove

2002. Monaco Red Cross.
2569 **911** €1.02 red, greenish blue and black . . . . . . 1·50 1·10

912 Aerial View of Monaco

2002. International Year of Mountains.
2570 **912** €1.37 multicoloured . . 2·00 1·50

913 Hugo **914** Dumas

2002. Birth Bicentenary of Victor Hugo (writer). Each blue, brown and red.
2571 50c. Type **913** 70 50
2572 57c. Scenes from his books 80 60
Nos. 2571/2 were issued together, se-tenant, forming a composite design.

2002. Birth Bicentenary of Alexandre Dumas (writer). Multicoloured.
2573 61c. Type **914** 90 65
2574 61c. Scenes from his books 90 65
Nos. 2573/4 were issued together, se-tenant, forming a composite design.

915 Princess Grace **916** Star-shaped Flower

2002. 26th Publication of "Annales Monegasques" (archives).
2575 **915** €1.75 multicoloured . . 2·50 1·80

2002. Christmas.
2576 **916** 50c. multicoloured . . . 70 50

917 Frame from Film and Melies **918** Magician

2002. Centenary of "Le Voyage dans la Lune" (film by Georges Melies).
2577 **917** 76c. multicoloured . . . 1·10 80

2002. "Magic Stars" Magic Festival, Monte Carlo.
2578 **918** €1.52 multicoloured . . 2·20 1·60

919 1949 Mercedes 220A Cabriolet

2002. Motor Cars from the Royal Collection. Multicoloured.
2579 46c. Type **919** 65 45
2580 69c. 1956 Rolls Royce Silver Cloud . . . . 1·75 75
2581 €1.40 1974 Citroen DS 21 2·00 1·50

920 Spring

2002. Royal Palace (3rd series). Frescoes. Sheet 120 × 100 mm containing T **920** and similar horiz designs showing the Four Seasons. Multicoloured.
MS2582 50c. Type **920**; €1 Summer; €1.50, Autumn; €2 Winter 7·00 5·25

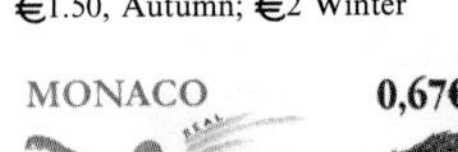

921 Footballer and Golden Ball

923 Flower Arrangement

922 Exhibition Poster

2002. Award of International Philatelic Grand Prix to Luis Figo (footballer and 2001 Golden Ball winner). Centenary of Real Madrid Football Club.
2583 **921** 91c. multicoloured . . . 1·80 30

2002. "MonacoPhil 2002" Stamp Exhibition (2nd issue). Sheet 120 × 82 mm, containing T **922** and similar vert design. Multicoloured. Imperf.
MS2584 €3 Type **922**; €3 Exhibition emblem . . . . . . 8·50 6·50

2002. 36th Monte Carlo Flower Show.
2585 **923** 67c. multicoloured . . . 95 70

924 Princesses Caroline and Stephanie (presidents)

2002. 40th Anniv of "Association Mondiale des Amis de l'Enfance" (children's society).
2586 **924** €1.25 multicoloured . . 1·80 1·30

925 St. George (statue)

926 Prince Louis II, Flag, Arch and Building

2002. 1700th Anniv of St. George's Martyrdom.
2587 **925** 53c. multicoloured . . . 75 55

2002. Bicentenary of Saint-Cyr Imperial Military School.
2588 **926** 61c. multicoloured . . . 90 65

POSTAGE DUE STAMPS

D 3

D 4

D 18

1906.

D 29a **D 3** 1c. green 30 45
D 30 5c. green 40 55
D 31a 10c. red 30 55
D 32 10c. brown £350 £110
D 33 15c. purple on cream 1·75 1·40
D113 20c. bistre on buff . . 30 30
D 34 30c. blue 30 55
D114 40c. mauve 30 30
D 35 50c. brown on buff . . 3·00 3·25
D115 50c. green 30 30
D116 60c. black 30 50
D117 60c. mauve . . . . . 15·00 19·00
D118 1f. purple on cream . . 25 25
D119 2f. red . . . . 60 1·00
D120 3f. red . . . . 60 1·00
D121 5f. blue 60 75

1910.

D36 **D 4** 1c. olive 20 40
D37 10c. lilac 30 40
D38 30c. bistre £150 £150

1919. Surch.
D39 **D 4** 20c. on 10c. lilac . . . . 3·00 4·50
D40 40c. on 30c. bistre . . . 3·00 5·50

1925.

D106 **D 18** 1c. olive 30 35
D107 10c. violet 20 45
D108 30c. bistre 30 55
D109 60c. red 45 65
D110 1f. blue . . . . 60·00 55·00
D111 2f. red . . . . 70·00 75·00

1925. Surch **1 franc a percevoir**.
D112 **D 3** 1f. on 50c. brown on buff 60 70

D 64

D 65

1946.

D327 **D 64** 10c. black 10 10
D328 30c. violet 10 10
D329 30c. blue 10 10
D330 1f. green 20 20
D331 2f. brown 20 25
D332 3f. mauve 20 25
D333 4f. red 30 35
D334 **D 65** 5f. brown 30 25
D335 10f. blue 50 25
D336 20f. turquoise 50 55
D337 50f. red and mauve . . 40·00 48·00
D338 100f. red and green . . 7·50 8·00

D 99 Buddicom Locomotive, 1843

1953.

D478 – 1f. red and green . . . 10 10
D479 – 1f. green and red . . . 10 10
D480 – 2f. turquoise and blue 10 10
D481 – 2f. blue and turquoise 10 10
D482 **D 99** 3f. lake and green . . 10 10
D483 – 3f. green and lake . . 10 10
D484 – 4f. slate and brown . . 25 25
D485 – 4f. brown and slate . . 25 25
D486 – 5f. violet and blue . . 45 45
D487 – 5f. blue and violet . . 45 45
D488 – 10f. indigo and blue 5·00 6·50
D489 – 10f. blue and indigo 5·00 6·50
D490 – 20f. violet and blue . . 2·00 3·00
D491 – 20f. blue and violet . . 2·00 3·00
D492 – 50f. brown and red . . 5·00 7·50
D493 – 50f. red and brown . . 5·00 7·50
D494 – 100f. green and purple 8·50 12·00
D495 – 100f. purple and green 8·50 12·00

TRIANGULAR DESIGNS: Nos. D478, Pigeons released from mobile loft; D479, Sikorsky S-51 helicopter; D480, Brig; D481, "United States" (liner); D483, Streamlined steam locomotive; D484, Santos-Dumont's monoplane No. 20 Demoiselle; D485, De Havilland Comet 1 airliner; D486, Old motor car; D487, "Sabre" racing-car; D488, Leonardo da Vinci's flying machine; D489, Postal rocket; D490, Mail balloon, Paris, 1870; D491, Airship "Graf Zeppelin"; D492, Postilion; D493, Motor cycle messenger; D494, Mail coach; D495, Railway mail van.

D 140 18th-century Felucca

1960.

D698 **D 140** 1c. brown, green & bl 55 55
D699 – 2c. sepia, blue & grn 10 10
D700 – 5c. purple, blk & turq 10 10
D701 – 10c. black, green & bl 10 10
D702 – 20c. purple, grn & bl 1·25 1·25
D703 – 30c. brown, bl & grn 80 80
D704 – 50c. blue, brn & myrtle . . . . . . 1·25 1·50
D705 – 1f. brown, myrtle & bl . . . . 1·75 1·75

DESIGNS: 2c. Paddle-steamer "La Palmaria"; 5c. Arrival of first railway train at Monaco; 10c. 15th–16th-century armed messenger; 20c. 18th-century postman; 30c. "Charles III" (paddle-steamer); 50c. 17th-century courier; 1f. Mail coach (19th-century).

D 393 Prince's Seal

D 492 Coat of Arms

1980.

D1426 **D 393** 5c. red and brown 10 10
D1427 10c. orange and red 10 10
D1428 15c. violet and red 10 10
D1429 20c. green and red 10 10
D1430 30c. blue and red . . 20 20
D1431 40c. bistre and red 20 20
D1432 50c. violet and red 30 30
D1433 1f. grey and blue . . 65 65
D1434 2f. brown and black 80 75
D1435 3f. red and green . . 1·25 1·00
D1436 4f. green and red . . 1·75 1·50
D1437 5f. brown and mauve . . . . . 2·10 1·60

1985.

D1712 **D 492** 5c. multicoloured . . 10 10
D1713 10c. multicoloured 10 10
D1714 15c. multicoloured 10 10
D1715 20c. multicoloured 10 10
D1716 30c. multicoloured 10 10
D1717 40c. multicoloured 10 20
D1718 50c. multicoloured 10 20
D1719 1f. multicoloured . . 30 45
D1720 2f. multicoloured . . 60 65
D1721 3f. multicoloured . . 1·00 1·25
D1722 4f. multicoloured . . 1·25 1·40
D1723 5f. multicoloured . . 1·75 2·00

MONGOLIA Pt. 10

A republic in Central Asia between China and Russia, independent since 1921.

1924. 100 cents = 1 dollar (Chinese).
1926. 100 mung = 1 tugrik.

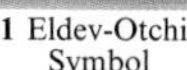

1 Eldev-Otchir Symbol — 2 Soyombo Symbol

1924. Inscr in black.

No.	Type	Description	Unused	Used
1	1	1c. brown, pink and grey on bistre	4·00	4·00
2		2c. brown, blue and red on brown	5·00	3·50
3		5c. grey, red and yellow	25·00	20·00
4		10c. blue and brown on blue	9·00	7·00
5		20c. grey, blue and white on blue	18·00	10·00
6		50c. red and orange on pink	30·00	18·00
7		$1 bistre, red and white on yellow	45·00	28·00

Stamps vary in size according to the face value.

1926. Fiscal stamps as T **2** optd **POSTAGE** in frame in English and Mongolian.

No.	Type	Description	Unused	Used
8	2	1c. blue	10·00	10·00
9		2c. buff	10·00	10·00
10		5c. purple	14·00	12·00
11		10c. green	18·00	15·00
12		20c. brown	20·00	17·00
13		50c. brown and yellow	£175	£160
14		$1 brown and pink	£400	£325
15		$5 red and olive	£600	

Stamps vary in size according to the face value.

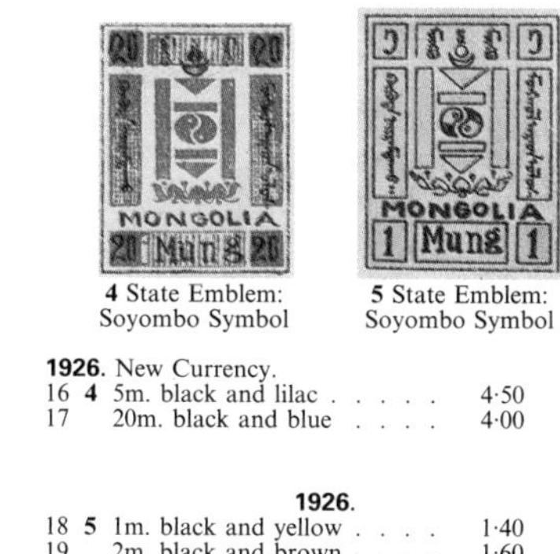

4 State Emblem: Soyombo Symbol — 5 State Emblem: Soyombo Symbol

1926. New Currency.

No.	Type	Description	Unused	Used
16	4	5m. black and lilac	4·50	4·50
17		20m. black and blue	4·00	4·00

1926.

No.	Type	Description	Unused	Used
18	5	1m. black and yellow	1·40	80
19		2m. black and brown	1·60	90
20		5m. black and lilac (A)	2·50	1·40
28		5m. black and lilac (B)	13·00	9·50
21		10m. black and blue	1·60	1·10
30		20m. black and blue	14·00	8·00
22		25m. black and green	4·00	1·75
23		40m. black and yellow	5·75	2·00
24		50m. black and brown	7·00	3·25
25		1t. black, green and brown	18·00	6·50
26		3t. black, yellow and red	38·00	30·00
27		5t. black, red and purple	60·00	48·00

In (A) the Mongolian numerals are in the upper and in (B) in the lower value tablets.

These stamps vary in size according to the face value.

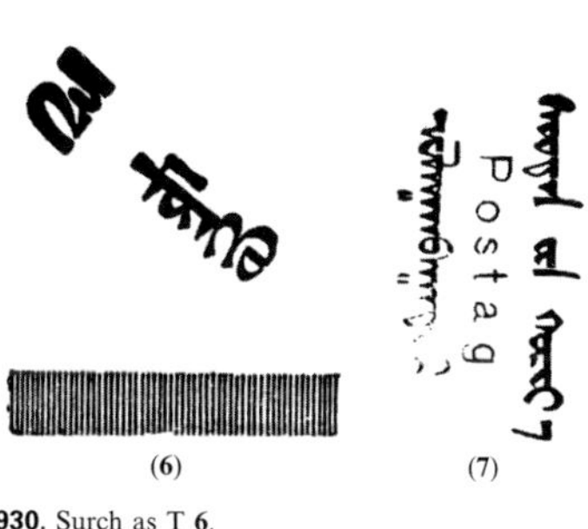

(6) (7)

1930. Surch as T **6**.

No.	Type	Description	Unused	Used
32	5	10m. on 1m. black & yellow	25·00	25·00
33		20m. on 2m. black & brown	35·00	30·00
34		25m. on 40m. black & yellow	40·00	35·00

1931. Optd with T **7**.

No.	Type	Description	Unused	Used
35	2	1c. blue	17·00	8·00
36		2c. buff	18·00	6·00
37		5c. purple	25·00	6·00
38		10c. green	20·00	6·00
39		20c. brown	32·00	8·50
40		50c. brown and yellow	—	—
41		$1 brown and pink	—	—

1931. Surch **Postage** and value in **menge**.

No.	Type	Description	Unused	Used
43	2	5m. on 5c. purple	25·00	8·00
44		10m. on 10c. green	38·00	20·00
45		20m. on 20c. brown	50·00	25·00

9 Govt Building, Ulan Bator — 11 Sukhe Bator

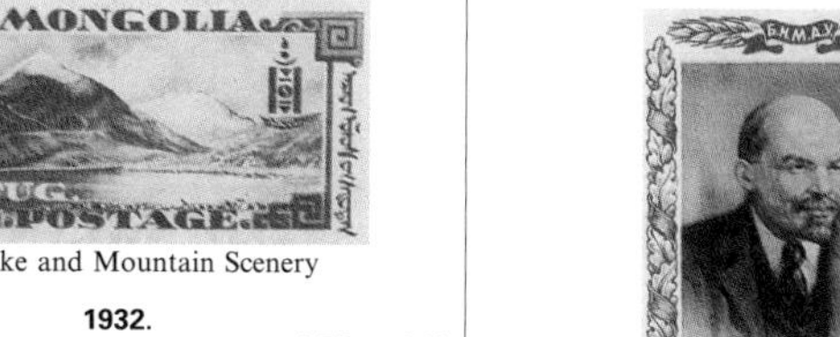

12 Lake and Mountain Scenery

1932.

No.	Type	Description	Unused	Used
46	–	1m. brown	1·75	1·00
47	–	2m. red	1·75	1·00
48	–	5m. blue	50	30
49	9	10m. green	50	30
50	–	15m. brown	50	30
51	–	20m. red	50	30
52	–	25m. violet	75	30
53	11	40m. black	75	40
54	–	50m. blue	50	30
55	12	1t. green	90	50
56	–	3t. violet	2·00	1·25
57	–	5t. brown	12·00	7·50
58	–	10t. blue	20·00	13·00

DESIGNS—As Type **9**: 1m. Weavers; 5m. Machinist. As Type **11**: 2m. Telegraphist; 15m. Revolutionary soldier carrying flag; 20m. Mongols learning Latin alphabet; 25m. Soldier; 50m. Sukhe Bator's monument. As Type **12**: 3t. Sheep-shearing; 5t. Camel caravan; 10t. Lassoing wild horses (after painting by Sampilon).

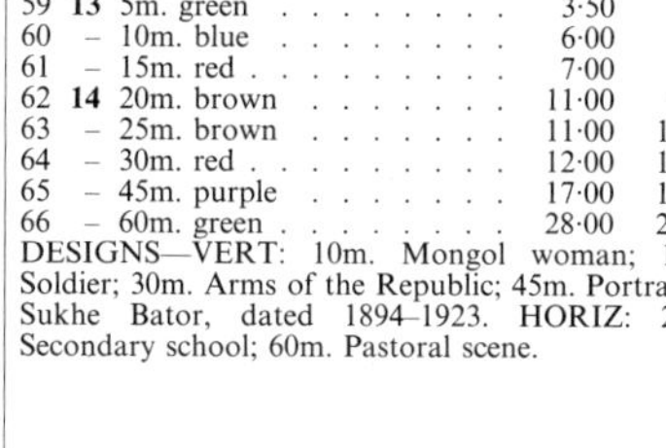

13 Mongol Man — 14 Camel Caravan

1943. Network background in similar colour to stamps.

No.	Type	Description	Unused	Used
59	13	5m. green	3·50	3·50
60	–	10m. blue	6·00	3·75
61	–	15m. red	7·00	5·00
62	14	20m. brown	11·00	9·00
63	–	25m. brown	11·00	11·00
64	–	30m. red	12·00	12·00
65	–	45m. purple	17·00	17·00
66	–	60m. green	28·00	28·00

DESIGNS—VERT: 10m. Mongol woman; 15m. Soldier; 30m. Arms of the Republic; 45m. Portrait of Sukhe Bator, dated 1894–1923. HORIZ: 25m. Secondary school; 60m. Pastoral scene.

15 Marshal Kharloin Choibalsan — 17 Victory Medal

16 Choibalsan and Sukhe Bator

1945. 50th Birthday of Choibalsan.

No.	Type	Description	Unused	Used
67	15	1t. black	9·00	8·00

1946. 25th Anniv of Independence. As T **16/17**.

No.	Type	Description	Unused	Used
68	–	30m. bistre	4·50	3·50
69	16	50m. purple	5·50	4·00
70	–	60m. brown	5·50	5·50
71	–	60m. black	8·00	5·50
72	17	80m. brown	7·50	7·50
73	–	1t. blue	11·00	12·00
74	–	2t. brown	14·00	16·00

DESIGNS—VERT: (21½ × 32 mm): 30m. Choibalsan, aged four. As Type **17**: 60m. (No. 71), Choibalsan when young man; 1t. 25th Anniversary Medal; 2t. Sukhe Bator. HORIZ: As Type **16**: 60m. (No. 70), Choibalsan University.

17a Flags of Communist Bloc

1951. Struggle for Peace.

No.	Type	Description	Unused	Used
75	17a	1t. multicoloured	7·50	7·50

17b Lenin (after P. Vasilev)

1951. Honouring Lenin.

No.	Type	Description	Unused	Used
76	17b	3t. multicoloured	17·00	17·00

18 State Shop

19 Sukhe Bator

1951. 30th Anniv of Independence.

No.	Type	Description	Unused	Used
77	–	15m. green on azure	3·25	3·25
78	18	20m. orange	3·25	3·25
79	–	20m. multicoloured	3·75	3·75
80	–	25m. blue on azure	3·75	3·75
81	–	30m. multicoloured	4·25	4·25
82	–	40m. violet on pink	4·50	4·50
83	–	50m. brown on azure	9·00	9·00
84	–	60m. black on pink	8·00	8·00
85	19	2t. brown	15·00	15·00

DESIGNS—HORIZ: (As Type **18**): 15m. Alti Hotel; 40m. State Theatre, Ulan Bator; 50m. Pedagogical Institute. 55½ × 26 mm: 25m. Choibalsan University. VERT: (As Type **19**): 20m. (No. 79); 30m. Arms and flag; 60m. Sukhe Bator Monument.

20 Schoolchildren

1952. Culture.

No.	Type	Description	Unused	Used
86	–	5m. brown on pink	2·00	1·75
87	20	10m. blue on pink	2·50	2·50

DESIGN: 5m. New houses.

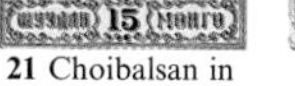

21 Choibalsan in National Costume — 22 Choibalsan and Farm Worker

1953. 1st Death Anniv of Marshal Choibalsan. As T **21/22**.

No.	Type	Description	Unused	Used
88	21	15m. blue	2·50	2·75
89	22	15m. green	2·50	2·75
90	21	20m. green	5·00	6·00
91	22	20m. sepia	2·50	2·50
92	–	20m. blue	2·50	2·50
93	–	30m. sepia	3·25	3·25
94	–	50m. brown	3·25	3·25
95	–	1t. red	4·00	4·00
96	–	1t. purple	4·00	4·00
97	–	2t. red	4·00	4·00
98	–	3t. purple	5·00	5·00
99	–	5t. red	19·00	19·00

DESIGNS: As Type **21**: 1t. (96); 2t. Choibalsan in uniform. 33 × 48 mm: 3, 5t. Busts of Choibalsan and Sukhe Bator. 33 × 46 mm: 50m., 1t. (95), Choibalsan and young pioneer. 48 × 33 mm: 20m. (92); 30m. Choibalsan and factory hand.

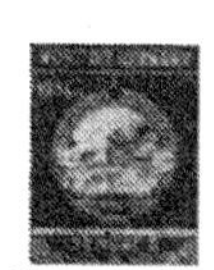

23 Arms of the Republic — 23a Lenin

1954.

No.	Type	Description	Unused	Used
100	23	10m. red	6·50	4·00
101		20m. red	13·00	5·00
102		30m. red	6·00	4·50
103		40m. red	7·00	4·50
104		60m. red	6·50	4·50

1955. 85th Birth Anniv of Lenin.

No.	Type	Description	Unused	Used
105	23a	2t. blue	3·75	2·00

23b Flags of the Communist Bloc — 24 Sukhe Bator and Choibalsan

1955. Struggle for Peace.

No.	Type	Description	Unused	Used
106	23b	60m. multicoloured	1·25	65

1955.

No.	Type	Description	Unused	Used
107	24	30m. green	30	20
108	–	30m. blue	50	20
109	–	30m. red	40	20
110	–	40m. purple	1·00	40
111	–	50m. brown	1·00	45
112	–	1t. multicoloured	2·75	1·25

DESIGNS—HORIZ: 30m. blue, Lake Khobsogol; 50m. Choibalsan University. VERT: 30m. red, Lenin Statue, Ulan Bator; 40m. Sukhe Bator and dog; 1t. Arms and flag of the Republic.

24a Steam Train linking Ulan Bator and Moscow — 25 Arms of the Republic

1956. Mongol–Soviet Friendship. Multicoloured.

No.	Type	Description	Unused	Used
113		1t. Type **24a**	25·00	13·00
114		2t. Flags of Mongolia and Russia	4·50	2·75

1956.

No.	Type	Description	Unused	Used
115	25	20m. brown	50	30
116		30m. brown	65	35
117		40m. blue	80	45
118		60m. green	1·00	65
119		1t. red	1·60	80

26 Hunter and Golden Eagle — 27 Arms

27a Wrestlers

1956. 35th Anniv of Independence.

No.	Type	Description	Unused	Used
120	26	30m. brown	25·00	21·00
121	27	30m. blue	5·00	4·00
122	27a	60m. green	15·00	15·00
123	–	60m. orange	15·00	15·00

DESIGN: As Type **26**: 60m. (No. 123), Children. Also inscr "xxxv".

28 29

1958. With or without gum.
124 **28** 20m. red . . . . 1·50 1·00

1958. 13th Mongol People's Revolutionary Party Congress. With or without gum.
125 **29** 30m. red and salmon . . . 3·00 2·25

1958. As T **27a** but without "xxxv". With or without gum.
126 50m. brown on pink . . . . 5·00 3·75

30 Dove and Globe

1958. 4th Congress of International Women's Federation, Vienna. With or without gum.
127 **30** 60m. blue . . . . 3·25 2·00

31 Ibex **32** Yak

1958. Mongolian Animals. As T **31/2**.
128 – 30m. pale blue . . . . . . 6·50 2·10
129 – 30m. turquoise . . . . . . 4·50 2·10
130 **31** 30m. green . . . . 3·00 1·50
131 30m. turquoise . . . . . . 3·00 1·00
132 **32** 60m. bistre . . . . 3·50 2·00
133 60m. orange . . . . 3·50 1·25
134 – 1t. blue . . . . 5·00 2·50
135 – 1t. light blue . . . . 4·00 1·75
136 – 1t. red . . . . 5·00 3·25
137 – 1t. red . . . . 4·00 2·00
DESIGNS—VERT: 30m. (Nos. 128/9), Dalmatian pelicans. HORIZ: 1t. (Nos. 134/5), Yak, facing right; 1t. (Nos. 136/7), Bactrian camels.

33 Goat **34** "Tulaga"

1958. Mongolian Animals.
138 **33** 5m. sepia and yellow . . . 15 10
139 – 10m. sepia and green . . . 20 10
140 – 15m. sepia and lilac . . . 35 10
141 – 20m. sepia and blue . . . 35 10
142 – 25m. sepia and red 40 10
143 – 30m. purple and mauve . . 50 10
144 **33** 40m. green 50 10
145 – 50m. brown and salmon 60 20
146 – 60m. blue 80 20
147 – 1t. bistre and yellow . . . 1·75 50
ANIMALS: 10, 30m. Ram; 15, 60m. Stallion; 20, 50m. Bull; 25m., 1t. Bactrian camel.

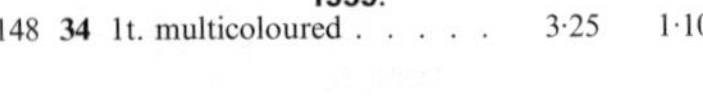

1959.
148 **34** 1t. multicoloured . . . . . 3·25 1·10

35 Taming a Wild Horse

1959. Mongolian Sports. Centres and inscriptions multicoloured: frame colours given below.
149 **35** 5m. yellow and orange . . 20 10
150 – 10m. purple 20 10
151 – 15m. yellow and green . . 20 10
152 – 20m. lake and red 25 10
153 – 25m. blue 40 15
154 – 30m. yellow, green & turq 55 15
155 – 70m. red and yellow . . . 70 30
156 – 80m. purple . . . . 1·10 60
DESIGNS: 10m. Wrestlers; 15m. Introducing young rider; 20m. Archer; 25m. Galloping horseman; 30m. Archery contest; 70m. Hunting a wild horse; 80m. Proclaiming a champion.

36 Child Musician

1959. Mongolian Youth Festival (1st issue).
157 **36** 5m. purple and blue . . . 20 10
158 – 10m. brown and green . . 25 10
159 – 20m. green and purple . . 25 10
160 – 25m. blue and green . . . 50 25
161 – 40m. violet and myrtle . . 95 40
DESIGNS—VERT: 10m. Young wrestlers; 20m. Youth on horse; 25m. Artists in national costume. HORIZ: 40m. Festival parade.

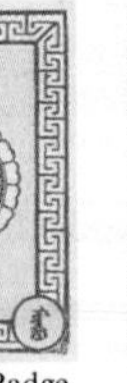

37 Festival Badge **38** Kalmuck Script

1959. Mongolian Youth Festival (2nd issue).
162 **37** 30m. purple and blue . . . 30 20

1959. Mongolists' Congress. Designs as T **38** incorporating "MONGOL" in various scripts.
163 – 30m. multicoloured . . . . 5·00 5·00
164 – 40m. red, blue and yellow 5·00 5·00
165 **38** 50m. multicoloured . . . . 7·00 7·00
166 – 60m. red, blue and yellow 11·00 11·00
167 – 1t. yellow, turquoise & orge . . . . 14·00 14·00
SCRIPTS (29½ × 42½ mm): 30m. Stylized Ulghur; 40m. Soyombo; 60m. Square (Pagspa). (21½ × 31 mm): 1t. Cyrillic.

39 Military Monument **40** Herdswoman and Lamb

1959. 20th Anniv of Battle of Khalka River.
168 – 40m. red, brown and yellow 55 15
169 **39** 50m. multicoloured 55 15
DESIGN: 40m. Mounted horseman with flag (emblem), inscr "AUGUST 1959 HALHIN GOL".

1959. 2nd Meeting of Rural Economy Co-operatives.
170 **40** 30m. green . . . . 3·50 3·50

41 Sable

1959. Mongolian Fauna.
171 **41** 5m. purple, yellow and blue 15 10
172 – 10m. multicoloured 55 10
173 – 15m. black, green and red 45 10
174 – 20m. purple, blue and red 55 15
175 – 30m. myrtle, purple & grn 50 15
176 – 50m. black, blue and green 1·10 30
177 – 1t. black, green and red . . 1·75 40
ANIMALS—HORIZ: (58 × 21 mm): 10m. Common pheasants; 20m. European otter; 50m. Saiga; 1t. Siberian musk deer. As Type **41**: 15m. Muskrat; 30m. Argali.

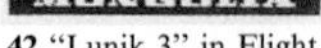

42 "Lunik 3" in Flight **44** "Flower" Emblem

43 Motherhood Badge

1959. Launching of "Lunik 3" Rocket.
178 **42** 30m. yellow and violet . . 65 25
179 – 50m. red, green and blue 80 35
DESIGN—HORIZ: 50m. Trajectory of "Lunik 3" around the Moon.

1960. International Women's Day.
180 **43** 40m. bistre and blue . . . 40 15
181 **44** 50m. yellow, green and blue 70 20

45 Lenin **46** Larkspur

1960. 90th Birth Anniv of Lenin.
182 **45** 40m. red 40 15
183 50m. violet 60 30

1960. Flowers.
184 **46** 5m. blue, green and bistre 10 10
185 – 10m. red, green and orange 10 10
186 – 15m. violet, green and bistre 10 10
187 – 20m. yellow, green and olive 15 10
188 – 30m. violet, green & emer 15 10
189 – 40m. orange, green & violet 35 15
190 – 50m. violet, green and blue 45 20
191 – 1t. mauve, green & lt green 80 40
FLOWERS: 10m. Tulip; 15m. Jacob's ladder; 20m. Asiatic globe flower; 30m. Clustered bellflower; 40m. Grass of Parnassus; 50m. Meadow cranesbill; 1t. "Begonia vansiana".

47 Horse-jumping

1960. Olympic Games. Inscr "ROMA 1960" or "ROMA MCMLX". Centres in greenish grey.
192 **47** 5m. red, black & turquoise 10 10
193 – 10m. violet and yellow . . 10 10
194 – 15m. turquoise, black & red 10 10
195 – 20m. red and blue 10 10
196 – 30m. ochre, black and green 10 10
197 – 50m. blue and turquoise 15 10
198 – 70m. green, black and violet 25 20
199 – 1t. mauve and green . . . 35 25
DESIGNS—DIAMOND SHAPED: 10m. Running; 20m. Wrestling; 50m. Gymnastics; 1t. Throwing the discus. As Type **47**: 15m. Diving; 30m. Hurdling; 70m. High-jumping.

48

1960. Red Cross.
200 **48** 20m. red, yellow and blue 70 25

49 Newspapers

1960. 40th Anniv of Mongolian Newspaper "Unen" ("Truth").
201 **49** 20m. buff, green and red 15 10
202 30m. red, yellow and green 20 15

50 Hoopoe

1961. Mongolian Songbirds.
203 – 5m. mauve, black and green 75 10
204 **50** 10m. red, black and green 85 10
205 – 15m. yellow, black & green 1·00 10
206 – 20m. green, black and bistre . . . . 1·25 15
207 – 50m. blue, black and red 1·75 30
208 – 70m. yellow, black & mauve . . . . 2·00 50
209 – 1t. mauve, orange and black . . . . 2·40 70
BIRDS: As Type **50**: 15m. Golden oriole; 20m. Black-billed capercaillie. Inverted triangulars: 5m. Rose-coloured starling; 50m. Eastern broad-billed roller; 70m. Tibetan sandgrouse; 1t. Mandarin.

51 Foundry Worker **52** Patrice Lumumba

1961. 15th Anniv of World Federation of Trade Unions.
210 **51** 30m. red and black 15 10
211 – 50m. red and violet 20 10
DESIGN—HORIZ: 50m. Hemispheres.

1961. Patrice Lumumba (Congolese politician) Commemoration.
212 **52** 30m. brown . . . . 1·50 1·00
213 50m. purple . . . . 2·00 1·25

53 Bridge **54** Yuri Gagarin with Capsule

1961. 40th Anniv of Independence (1st issue). Mongolian Modernization.
214 **53** 5m. green 10 10
215 – 10m. blue 10 10
216 – 15m. red 10 10
217 – 20m. brown 10 10
218 – 30m. blue 15 15

219 – 50m. green 25 15
220 – 1t. violet 50 30

DESIGNS: 10m. Shoe-maker; 15m. Store at Ulan Bator; 30m. Government Building, Ulan Bator; 50m. Machinist; 1t. Ancient and modern houses. (59 × 20½ mm): 20m. Choibalsan University.

See also Nos. 225/32, 233/41, 242/8 and 249/56.

1961. World's First Manned Space Flight. Mult.

221 20m. Type **54** 15 10
222 30m. Gagarin and globe (horiz) 30 10
223 50m. Gagarin in capsule making parachute descent 30 20
224 1t. Globe and Gagarin (horiz) 50 35

55 Postman with Reindeer

1961. 40th Anniv of Independence (2nd issue). Mongolian Postal Service.

225 **55** 5m. red, brown and blue (postage) 15 10
226 – 15m. violet, brown & bistre 30 10
227 – 20m. blue, black and green 20 10
228 – 25m. violet, bistre and green 30 15
229 – 30m. green, black & lav . . 5·00 1·25
230 – 10m. orange, black and green (air) 35 10
231 – 50m. black, pink and green 1·00 25
232 – 1t. multicoloured . . . . . 1·10 35

DESIGNS: Postman with—10m. Horses; 15m. Camels; 20m. Yaks; 25m. "Sukhe Bator" (lake steamer); 30m. Diesel mail train; 50m. Ilyushin Il-14M mail plane over map; 1t. Postal emblem.

56 Rams

1961. 40th Anniv of Independence (3rd issue). Animal Husbandry.

233 **56** 5m. black, red and blue . . 10 10
234 – 10m. black, green & purple 10 10
235 – 15m. black, red and green 10 10
236 – 20m. sepia, blue and brown 10 10
237 – 25m. black, yellow & green 15 10
238 – 30m. black, red and violet 15 10
239 – 40m. black, green and red 25 15
240 – 50m. black, brown and blue 30 25
241 – 1t. black, violet and olive 55 40

DESIGNS: 10m. Oxen; 15m. Camels; 20m. Pigs and poultry; 25m. Angora goats; 30m. Mongolian horses; 40m. Ewes; 50m. Cows; 1t. Combine-harvester.

57 Children Wrestling

1961. 40th Anniv of Independence (5th issue). Mongolian Sports.

242 **57** 5m. multicoloured 10 10
243 – 10m. sepia, red and green 10 10
244 – 15m. purple blue and yellow 10 10
245 – 20m. red, black and green 1·10 30
246 – 30m. purple, green & lav 15 10
247 – 50m. indigo, orange & blue 30 20
248 – 1t. purple, blue and grey 35 20

DESIGNS: 10m. Horse-riding; 15m. Children on camel and pony; 20m. Falconry; 30m. Skiing; 50m. Archery; 1t. Dancing.

58 Young Mongol

1961. 40th Anniv of Independence (6th issue). Mongolian Culture.

249 **58** 5m. purple and green . . . 10 10
250 – 10m. blue and red 10 10
251 – 15m. brown and blue . . . 10 10
252 – 20m. green and violet . . . 15 10
253 – 30m. red and blue 20 15
254 – 50m. violet and bistre . . . 40 20
255 – 70m. green and mauve . . 45 25
256 – 1t. red and blue 65 60

DESIGNS—HORIZ: 10m. Mongol chief; 70m. Orchestra; 1t. Gymnast. VERT: 15m. Sukhe Bator Monument; 20m. Young singer; 30m. Young dancer; 50m. Dombra-player.

59 Mongol Arms

60 Congress Emblem

1961. Arms multicoloured; inscr in blue; background colours given.

257 **59** 5m. salmon 10 10
258 10m. lilac 10 10
259 15m. brown 10 10
260 20m. turquoise 10 10
261 30m. ochre 10 10
262 50m. mauve 15 10
263 70m. olive 20 10
264 1t. orange 30 15

1961. 5th World Federation of Trade Unions Congress, Moscow.

265 **60** 30m. red, yellow and blue 15 10
266 50m. red, yellow and sepia 20 10

61 Dove, Map and Globe

1962. Admission of Mongolia to U.N.O.

267 **61** 10m. multicoloured 10 10
268 – 30m. multicoloured 15 10
269 – 50m. multicoloured 20 15
270 – 60m. multicoloured 30 20
271 – 70m. multicoloured 35 30

DESIGNS: 30m. U.N. Emblem and Mongol Arms; 50m. U.N. and Mongol flags; 60m. U.N. Headquarters and Mongolian Parliament building; 70m. U.N. and Mongol flags, and Assembly.

62 Football, Globe and Flags

1962. World Cup Football Championship, Chile. Multicoloured.

272 10m. Type **62** 10 10
273 30m. Footballers, globe and ball 10 10
274 50m. Footballers playing in stadium 20 15
275 60m. Goalkeeper saving goal 25 20
276 70m. Stadium 50 30

63 D. Natsagdorj

64 Torch and Handclasp

1962. 3rd Congress of Mongolian Writers.

277 **63** 30m. brown 15 10
278 50m. green 20 10

1962. Afro-Asian People's Solidarity.

279 **64** 20m. multicoloured 15 10
280 30m. multicoloured 20 10

65 Flags of Mongolia and U.S.S.R.

67 Victory Banner

1962. Mongol–Soviet Friendship.

281 **65** 30m. multicoloured 15 10
282 50m. multicoloured 20 10

1962. Malaria Eradication. Nos. 184/91 optd with Campaign emblem and **LUTTE CONTRE LE PALUDISME**.

283 **46** 5m. 20 20
284 – 10m. 20 20
285 – 15m. 20 20
286 – 20m. 20 20
287 – 30m. 30 30
288 – 40m. 30 30
289 – 50m. 50 50
290 – 1t. 80 80

1962. 800th Birth Anniv of Genghis Khan.

291 **67** 20m. multicoloured . . . . 5·50 5·50
292 – 30m. multicoloured . . . . 5·50 5·50
293 – 50m. black, brown and red 12·00 12·00
294 – 60m. buff, blue and brown 12·00 12·00

DESIGNS: 30m. Engraved lacquer tablets; 50m. Obelisk; 60m. Genghis Khan.

68 Eurasian Perch

1962. Fishes. Multicoloured.

295 5m. Type **68** 10 10
296 10m. Burbot 20 10
297 15m. Arctic grayling 30 10
298 20m. Short-spined seascorpion 40 15
299 30m. Estuarine zander . . . 60 20
300 50m. Siberian sturgeon . . . 95 30
301 70m. Waleck's dace . . . . 1·25 45
302 1t.50 Yellow-winged bullhead 2·25 70

69 Sukhe Bator

1963. 70th Birth Anniv of Sukhe Bator.

303 **69** 30m. blue 15 10
304 60m. lake 20 10

70 Dog "Laika" and "Sputnik 2"

1963. Space Flights. Multicoloured.

305 5m. Type **70** 10 10
306 15m. Rocket blasting off . . 15 10
307 25m. "Lunik 2" (1959) . . . 15 10
308 70m. Nikolaev and Popovich 30 25
309 1t. Rocket "Mars" (1962) . . 40 35

SIZES: As Type **70**: 70m., 1t. VERT: (21 × 70 mm): 15m., 25m.

71 Children packing Red Cross Parcels

1963. Red Cross Centenary Multicoloured.

310 20m. Type **71** 10 10
311 30m. Blood transfusion . . . 15 10
312 50m. Doctor treating child 20 15
313 60m. Ambulance at street accident 25 15
314 1t.30 Centenary emblem . . . 40 20

72 Karl Marx

73 Woman

1963. 145th Birth Anniv of Karl Marx.

315 **72** 30m. blue 15 10
316 60m. lake 20 10

1963. 5th World Congress of Democratic Women, Moscow.

317 **73** 30m. multicoloured 15 10

74 Peacock

1963. Mongolian Butterflies. Multicoloured.

318 5m. Type **74** 30 10
319 10m. Brimstone 35 10
320 15m. Small tortoiseshell . . . 35 15
321 20m. Apollo 55 20
322 30m. Swallowtail 85 25
323 60m. Damon blue . . . . . 1·25 50
324 1t. Poplar admiral . . . . . 1·75 65

75 Globe and Scales of Justice

1963. 15th Anniv of Declaration of Human Rights.

325 **75** 30m. red, blue and brown 15 20
326 60m. black, blue and yellow 25 10

76 Shaggy Ink Cap

1964. Fungi. Multicoloured.

327 5m. Type **76** 25 10
328 10m. Woolly milk cap . . . 35 10
329 15m. Field mushroom . . . 45 15
330 20m. Milk-white russula . . . 50 20
331 30m. Granulated boletus . . 75 30
332 50m. "Lactarius scrobiculatus" . . . . . . 1·00 45
333 70m. Saffron milk cap . . . 1·40 65
334 1t. Variegated boletus . . . . 1·90 85

77 Lenin when a Young Man

1964. 60th Anniv of London Bolshevik (Communist) Party.
335 **77** 30m. red and brown . . . 45 10
336 50m. ultramarine and blue 50 10

78 Gymnastics

1964. Olympic Games, Tokyo. Multicoloured.
337 5m. Type **78** 10 10
338 10m. Throwing the javelin . . 10 10
339 15m. Wrestling 10 10
340 20m. Running 10 10
341 30m. Horse-jumping 10 10
342 50m. High-diving 20 15
343 60m. Cycling 25 20
344 1t. Emblem of Tokyo Games 40 30

79 Congress Emblem

1964. 4th Mongolian Women's Congress.
345 **79** 30m. multicoloured 20 10

80 "Lunik 1"

1964. Space Research. Multicoloured.
346 5m. Type **80** 10 10
347 10m. "Vostoks 1 and 2" . . 10 10
348 15m. "Tiros" (vert) 10 10
349 20m. "Cosmos" (vert) . . . 10 10
350 30m. "Mars Probe" (vert) . . 10 10
351 60m. "Luna 4" (vert) 20 15
352 80m. "Echo 2" 30 20
353 1t. Radio telescope 35 25

81 Horseman and Flag

1964. 40th Anniv of Mongolian Constitution.
354 **81** 25m. multicoloured 20 10
355 50m. multicoloured 30 10

82 Marine Exploration

1965. International Quiet Sun Year. Multicoloured.
356 5m. Type **82** (postage) . . . 40 10
357 10m. Weather balloon . . . 15 10
358 60m. Northern Lights 60 20
359 80m. Geomagnetic emblems 70 25
360 1t. Globe and I.Q.S.Y. emblem . . . . 1·10 50
361 15m. Weather satellite (air) 40 10
362 20m. Antarctic exploration 3·00 55
363 30m. Space exploration . . . 55 15

83 Horses Grazing

1965. Mongolian Horses. Multicoloured.
364 5m. Type **83** 15 10
365 10m. Hunting with golden eagles 50 20
366 15m. Breaking-in wild horse 20 10
367 20m. Horses racing 20 10
368 30m. Horses jumping 25 10
369 60m. Hunting wolves 30 25
370 80m. Milking a mare 40 30
371 1t. Mare and colt 70 40

84 Farm Girl with Lambs

1965. 40th Anniv of Mongolian Youth Movement.
372 **84** 5m. orange, bistre and green 10 10
373 – 10m. bistre, blue and red 10 10
374 – 20m. ochre, red and violet 20 15
375 – 30m. lilac, brown and green 30 20
376 – 50m. orange, buff and blue 55 35
DESIGNS: 10m. Young drummers; 20m. Children around campfire; 30m. Young wrestlers; 50m. Emblem.

85 Chinese Perch

1965. Mongolian Fishes. Multicoloured.
377 5m. Type **85** 25 10
378 10m. Lenok 25 10
379 15m. Siberian sturgeon . . . 30 15
380 20m. Taimen 45 15
381 30m. Banded catfish 75 20
382 60m. Amur catfish . . . . . 1·10 20
383 80m. Northern pike . . . . 1·25 40
384 1t. Eurasian perch . . . . . 1·75 60

86 Marx and Lenin

87 I.T.U. Emblem and Symbols

1965. Organization of Socialist Countries' Postal Administrations Conference, Peking.
385 **86** 10m. black and red 15 10

1965. Air. I.T.U. Centenary.
386 **87** 30m. blue and bistre . . . 15 10
387 50m. red, bistre and blue 20 10

88 Sable

1966. Mongolian Fur Industry.
388 **88** 5m. purple, black & yellow 10 10
389 – 10m. brown, black and grey 10 10
390 – 15m. brown, black and blue 35 10
391 – 20m. multicoloured 20 10
392 – 30m. brown, black & mauve 25 10
393 – 60m. brown, black & green 40 25
394 – 80m. multicoloured 60 40
395 – 1t. blue, black and olive . . 1·40 50
DESIGNS (Fur animals): HORIZ: 10m. Red fox; 30m. Pallas's cat; 60m. Beech marten. VERT: 15m. European otter; 20m. Cheetah; 80m. Stoat; 1t. Woman in fur coat.

89 W.H.O. Building

1966. Inauguration of W.H.O. Headquarters, Geneva.
396 **89** 30m. blue, gold and green 15 10
397 50m. blue, gold and red . . 25 10

90 Footballers

1966. World Cup Football Championship. Multicoloured.
398 10m. Type **90** 10 10
399 30m. Footballers (different) 10 10
400 60m. Goalkeeper saving goal 15 15
401 80m. Footballers (different) 30 20
402 1t. World Cup flag 50 35

92 Sukhe Bator and Parliament Buildings, Ulan Bator

1966. 15th Mongolian Communist Party Congress.
404 **92** 30m. multicoloured 20 10

93 Wrestling

95 State Emblem

1966. World Wrestling Championships, Toledo (Spain). Similar wrestling designs.
405 **93** 10m. black, mauve & purple 10 10
406 – 30m. black, mauve and grey 10 15
407 – 60m. black, mauve & brown 20 15
408 – 80m. black, mauve and lilac 30 20
409 – 1t. black, mauve & turq . . 40 20

1966. 45th Anniv of Independence. Mult.
411 30m. Type **95** . . . . 1·25 50
412 50m. Sukhe Bator, emblems of agriculture and industry (horiz) . . . . 2·75 75

96 "Physochlaena physaloides"

1966. Flowers. Multicoloured.
413 5m. Type **96** 10 10
414 10m. Onion 15 10
415 15m. Red lily 20 10
416 20m. "Thermopsis lanceolata" 25 10
417 30m. "Amygdalus mongolica" 40 20
418 60m. Bluebeard 50 30
419 80m. "Piptanthus mongolicus" 60 40
420 1t. "Iris bungei" 85 55

1966. 60th Birth Anniv of D. Natsagdorj. Nos. 277/8 optd **1906 1966**.
420a **63** 30m. brown . . . . . . 6·50 6·50
420b 50m. green . . . . 6·50 6·50

97 Child with Dove

1966. Children's Day. Multicoloured.
421 10m. Type **97** 10 10
422 15m. Children with reindeer (horiz) 10 10
423 20m. Boys wrestling 10 10
424 30m. Boy riding horse (horiz) 20 10
425 60m. Children on camel . . . 30 15
426 80m. Shepherd boy with sheep (horiz) 35 15
427 1t. Boy archer 70 40

98 "Proton 1"

1966. Space Satellites. Multicoloured.
428 5m. "Vostok 2" (vert) . . . 10 10
429 10m. Type **98** 10 10
430 15m. "Telstar 1" (vert) . . . 10 10
431 20m. "Molniya 1" (vert) . . 10 10
432 30m. "Syncom 3" (vert) . . . 10 10
433 60m. "Luna 9" (vert) 20 15
434 80m. "Luna 12" (vert) . . . 30 20
435 1t. Mars and photographs taken by "Mariner 4" . . . 35 25

99 Tarbosaurus

1966. Prehistoric Animals. Multicoloured.
436 5m. Type **99** 20 10
437 10m. Talararus 20 10
438 15m. Protoceratops 30 15
439 20m. Indricotherium 30 15
440 30m. Saurolophus 50 20
441 60m. Mastodon 75 30
442 80m. Mongolotherium . . . 90 45
443 1t. Mammuthus . . . . . . 1·00 70

100 Congress Emblem

101 Sukhe Bator and Mongolian and Soviet Soldiers

1967. 9th International Students' Union Congress.
444 **100** 30m. ultramarine and blue . . . 15 10
445 50m. blue and pink . . . 25 15

1967. 50th Anniv of October Revolution.
446 **101** 40m. multicoloured . . . 25 20
447 – 60m. multicoloured . . . 35 25
DESIGN: 60m. Lenin, and soldiers with sword.

102 Vietnamese Mother and Child

1967. Help for Vietnam.
448 **102** 30m.+20m. brown, red and blue 20 10
449 50m.+30m. brown, blue and red 30 15

103 Figure Skating

1967. Winter Olympic Games, Grenoble. Mult.
450 5m. Type **103** 10 10
451 10m. Speed skating 10 10
452 15m. Ice hockey 10 10
453 20m. Skijumping 15 10
454 30m. Bob sleighing 15 10
455 60m. Figure skating (pairs) 30 25
456 80m. Downhill skiing 40 30

104 Bactrian Camel and Calf

1968. Young Animals. Multicoloured.
458 5m. Type **104** 15 10
459 10m. Yak 15 10
460 15m. Lamb 20 10
461 20m. Foal 30 10
462 30m. Calf 30 10
463 60m. Bison 40 15
464 80m. Roe deer 55 30
465 1t. Reindeer 80 40

105 Prickly Rose

ДЭХБ
20 ЖИЛ
WHO
(106)

1968. Mongolian Berries.
466 **105** 5m. ultramarine on blue 15 10
467 – 10m. brown on buff . . . 15 10
468 – 15m. emerald on green . . 20 10
469 – 20m. red on cream . . . 20 10
470 – 30m. red on pink 25 10
471 – 60m. brown on orange . . 45 20
472 – 80m. turquoise on blue 60 25
473 – 1t. red on cream 80 40

DESIGNS: 10m. Blackcurrant; 15m. Gooseberry; 20m. Crab-apple; 30m. Strawberry; 60m. Redcurrant; 80m. Cowberry; 1t. Sea buckthorn.

1968. 20th Anniv of World Health Organization. Nos. 396/7 optd with T **106**.
474 **89** 30m. blue, gold and green 2·50 2·50
475 50m. blue, gold and red . . 2·50 2·50

107 Human Rights Emblem

1968. Human Rights Year.
476 **107** 30m. green and blue . . . 15 10

108 "Das Kapital"

1968. 150th Birth Anniv of Karl Marx. Mult.
477 30m. Type **108** 15 10
478 50m. Karl Marx 25 15

109 "Portrait of Artist Sharab" (A. Sangatzohyo)

1968. Mongolian Paintings. Multicoloured.
479 5m. Type **109** 15 10
480 10m. "On Remote Roads" (A. Sangatzohyo) 20 10
481 15m. "Camel Calf" (B. Avarzad) 30 10
482 20m. "The Milk" (B. Avarzad) 40 15
483 30m. "The Bowman" (B. Gombosuren) 55 30
484 80m. "Girl Sitting on a Yak" (A. Sangatzohyo) 95 55
485 1t.40 "Cagan Dara Ekke" (Janaivajara) . . . . . . 1·90 1·00

110 Volleyball

1968. Olympic Games, Mexico. Multicoloured.
487 5m. Type **110** 10 10
488 10m. Wrestling 10 10
489 15m. Cycling 10 10
490 20m. Throwing the javelin . . 10 10
491 30m. Football 10 10
492 60m. Running 20 15
493 80m. Gymnastics 30 20
494 1t. Weightlifting 35 25

111 Hammer and Spade

112 Gorky

1968. 7th Anniv of Darkhan Town.
496 **111** 50m. orange and blue . . 15 10

1968. Birth Centenary of Maksim Gorky (writer).
497 **112** 60m. ochre and blue . . . 15 10

113 "Madonna and Child" (Boltraffio)

1968. 20th Anniv (1966) of U.N.E.S.C.O. Paintings by European Masters in National Gallery, Budapest. Multicoloured.
498 5m. Type **113** 20 10
499 10m. "St. Roch healed by an angel" (Moretto of Brescia) 25 10
500 15m. "Madonna and Child with St. Anne" (Macchietti) 35 10
501 20m. "St. John on Patmos" (Cano) 45 15
502 30m. "Young lady with viola da gamba" (Kupetzky) . . 50 15
503 80m. "Study of a head" (Amerling) 80 50
504 1t.40 "The death of Adonis" (Furini) . . . . 1·60 75

114 Paavo Nurmi (running)

1969. Olympic Games' Gold-medal Winners. Multicoloured.
506 5m. Type **114** 10 10
507 10m. Jesse Owens (running) 10 10
508 15m. F. Blankers-Koen (hurdling) 10 10
509 20m. Laszlo Papp (boxing) 10 10
510 30m. Wilma Rudolph (running) 10 10
511 60m. Boris Sahlin (gymnastics) 20 10
512 80m. D. Schollander (swimming) 25 15
513 1t. A. Nakayama (ring exercises) 35 25

115 Bayit Costume (woman)

1969. Mongolian Costumes. Multicoloured.
515 5m. Type **115** 10 10
516 10m. Torgut (man) 15 10
517 15m. Sakhchin (woman) . . . 20 10
518 20m. Khalka (woman) . . . 30 10
519 30m. Daringanga (woman) 35 15
520 60m. Mingat (woman) . . . 50 20
521 80m. Khalka (man) 65 25
522 1t. Barga (woman) . . . . . 1·10 40

116 Emblem and Helicopter Rescue

1969. 30th Anniv of Mongolian Red Cross.
523 **116** 30m. red and blue 60 20
524 – 50m. red and violet . . . 50 25
DESIGN: 50m. Shepherd and ambulance.

117 Yellow Lion's-foot

1969. Landscapes and Flowers. Multicoloured.
525 5m. Type **117** 15 10
526 10m. Variegated pink 15 10
527 15m. Superb pink 25 10
528 20m. Meadow cranesbill . . 25 10
529 30m. Mongolian pink 45 15
530 60m. Asiatic globe flower . . 50 15
531 80m. Long-lipped larkspur 70 30
532 1t. Saxaul 85 40

118 "Bullfight" (O. Tsewegdjaw)

1969. 10th Anniv of Co-operative Movement. Paintings in National Gallery, Ulan Bator. Mult.
533 5m. Type **118** 10 10
534 10m. "Colts Fighting" (O. Tsewegdjaw) 10 10
535 15m. "Horse-herd" (A. Sengetsohyo) 20 10
536 20m. "Camel Caravan" (D. Damdinsuren) 20 10
537 30m. "On the Steppe" (N. Tsultem) 35 15
538 60m. "Milking Mares" (O. Tsewegdjaw) 40 15
539 80m. "Off to School" (B. Avarzad) 50 30
540 1t. "After Work" (G. Odon) 80 40

120 Army Crest

БНМАУ-ыг
тунхагласны
45
жилийн ой
1969—XI—26
(121)

1969. 30th Anniv of Battle of Khalka River.
543 **120** 50m. multicoloured . . . 15 10

1969. 45th Anniv of Mongolian People's Republic. Nos. 411/12 optd with T **121**.
544 **95** 30m. multicoloured . . . . 3·75 3·75
545 – 50m. multicoloured . . . . 5·25 5·25

122 "Sputnik 3"

1969. Exploration of Space. Multicoloured.
546 5m. Type **122** 10 10
547 10m. "Vostok 1" 10 10
548 15m. "Mercury 7" 10 10
549 20m. Space-walk from "Voskhod 2" 10 10
550 30m. "Apollo 8" in Moon orbit 15 10
551 60m. Space-walk from "Soyuz 5" 30 20
552 80m. "Apollo 12" and Moon landing 40 30

123 Wolf

1970. Wild Animals. Multicoloured.
554 5m. Type **123** 20 10
555 10m. Brown bear 40 10

556 15m. Lynx 50 10
557 20m. Wild boar 50 10
558 30m. Elk 55 20
559 60m. Bobak marmot 65 20
560 80m. Argali 75 35
561 1t. "Hun Hunter and Hound" (tapestry) 90 50

124 "Lenin Centenary" (silk panel, Cerenhuu)

1970. Birth Centenary of Lenin. Multicoloured.
562 20m. Type **124** 15 10
563 50m. "Mongolians meeting Lenin" (Sangatzohyo) (horiz) 20 10
564 1t. "Lenin" (Mazhig) 35 15

125 "Fairy Tale" Pavilion

1970. "EXPO 70" World Fair, Osaka, Japan.
565 **125** 1t.50 multicoloured . . . 50 45

126 Footballers

1970. World Cup Football Championship, Mexico.
567 **126** 10m. multicoloured . . . 10 10
568 – 20m. multicoloured . . . 10 10
569 – 30m. multicoloured . . . 10 10
570 – 50m. multicoloured . . . 10 10
571 – 60m. multicoloured . . . 15 10
572 – 1t. multicoloured 30 20
573 – 1t.30 multicoloured . . . 35 25
DESIGNS: Nos. 568/73, Different football scenes.

127 Common Buzzard

1970. Birds of Prey. Multicoloured.
575 10m. Type **127** 75 15
576 20m. Tawny owls . . . . . 1·00 15
577 30m. Northern goshawk . . 1·25 20
578 50m. White-tailed sea eagle 1·90 30
579 60m. Peregrine falcon . . . . 1·90 60
580 1t. Common kestrels . . . . 2·10 65
581 1t.30 Black kite . . . . . . 2·50 80

128 Soviet Memorial, Berlin-Treptow

1970. 25th Anniv of Victory in Second World War.
582 **128** 60m. multicoloured . . . 15 10

129 Mongol Archery

1970. Mongolian Traditional Life. Multicoloured.
583 10m. Type **129** 30 15
584 20m. Bodg-gegeen's Palace, Ulan Bator 30 15
585 30m. Mongol horsemen . . . 30 20
586 40m. "The White Goddess-Mother" 30 25
587 50m. Girl in National costume 65 45
588 60m. "Lion's Head" (statue) 75 45
589 70m. Dancer's mask 85 65
590 80m. Gateway, Bogd-gegeen's Palace . . . . 1·00 1·00

131 I.E.Y. and U.N. Emblems with Flag

1970. International Education Year.
592 **131** 60m. multicoloured . . . 35 15

132 Horseman, "50" and Sunrise

1970. 50th Anniv of National Press.
593 **132** 30m. multicoloured . . . 25 10

133 "Vostok 3" and "4"

1971. Space Research. Multicoloured.
594 10m. Type **133** 10 10
595 20m. Space-walk from "Voskhod 2" 10 10
596 30m. "Gemini 6" and "7" . . 10 10
597 50m. Docking of "Soyuz 4" and "5" 10 10
598 60m. "Soyuz 6", "7" and "8" 15 10
599 80m. "Apollo 11" and lunar module 20 15
600 1t. "Apollo 13" damaged . . 25 20
601 1t.30 "Luna 16" 30 25
No. 594 is incorrectly inscribed "Vostok 2-3". The date refers to flight of "Vostoks 3" and "4".

134 Sukhe Bator addressing Meeting

1971. 50th Anniv of Revolutionary Party. Mult.
603 30m. Type **134** 10 10
604 60m. Horseman with flag . . 15 10
605 90m. Sukhe Bator with Lenin 25 15
606 1t.20 Mongolians with banner 40 25

136 Tsam Mask

1971. Mongol Tsam Masks.
608 **136** 10m. multicoloured . . . 15 10
609 – 20m. multicoloured . . . 25 10
610 – 30m. multicoloured . . . 30 10
611 – 50m. multicoloured . . . 35 15
612 – 60m. multicoloured . . . 45 20
613 – 1t. multicoloured 80 30
614 – 1t.30 multicoloured . . . 1·00 50
DESIGNS: Nos. 609/14, Different dance masks.

137 Banner and Party Emblems

1971. 16th Revolutionary Party Congress.
615 **137** 60m. multicoloured . . . 15 10

138 Steam Locomotive

1971. "50 Years of Transport Development". Multicoloured.
616 20m. Type **138** 70 10
617 30m. Diesel locomotive . . . 70 10
618 40m. Russian "Urals" lorry 65 15
619 50m. Russian "Moskovich 412" car 75 15
620 60m. Polikarpov Po-2 biplane 90 25
621 80m. Antonov An-24B airliner . . . . 1·10 40
622 1t. Lake steamer "Sukhe Bator" . . . . 2·00 70

139 Soldier

1971. 50th Anniv of People's Army and Police. Multicoloured.
623 60m. Type **139** 10 10
624 1t.50 Policeman and child . . 40 15

140 Emblem and Red Flag

1971. 50th Anniv of Revolutionary Youth Organization.
625 **140** 60m. multicoloured . . . 20 10

141 Mongolian Flag and Year Emblem

1971. Racial Equality Year.
626 **141** 60m. multicoloured . . . 15 10

142 "The Old Man and the Tiger"

1971. Mongolian Folk Tales. Multicoloured.
627 10m. Type **142** 20 10
628 20m. "The Boy Giant-killer" 20 10
629 30m. Cat and mice 20 10
630 50m. Mongolians riding on eagle 25 10
631 60m. Girl on horseback ("The Wise Bride") 40 15
632 80m. King and courtiers with donkey 55 20
633 1t. Couple kneeling before empty throne ("Story of the Throne") 80 25
634 1t.30 "The Wise Bird" . . . 95 40

143 Yaks

1971. Livestock Breeding. Multicoloured.
635 20m. Type **143** 20 10
636 30m. Bactrian camels 20 10
637 40m. Sheep 25 10
638 50m. Goats 40 10
639 60m. Cattle 50 20
640 80m. Horses 60 25
641 1t. Pony 95 45

144 Cross-country Skiing

1972. Winter Olympic Games, Sapporo, Japan. Multicoloured.
642 10m. Type **144** 10 10
643 20m. Bobsleighing 10 10
644 30m. Figure skating 10 10
645 50m. Slalom skiing 10 10
646 60m. Speed skating 15 10
647 80m. Downhill skiing 20 15
648 1t. Ice hockey 25 15
649 1t.30 Pairs figure skating . . 30 20

145 "Horse-breaking" (A. Sengatzohyo)

1972. Paintings by Contemporary Artists from the National Gallery, Ulan Bator. Multicoloured.
651 10m. Type **145** 15 10
652 20m. "Black Camel" (A. Sengatzohyo) 20 10
653 30m. "Jousting" (A. Sengatzohyo) 25 10
654 50m. "Wrestling Match" (A. Sengatzohyo) 30 10
655 60m. "Waterfall" (A. Sengatzohyo) 40 10
656 80m. "Old Musician" (U. Yadamsuren) 50 20
657 1t. "Young Musician" (U. Yadamsuren) 60 25
658 1t.30 "Ancient Prophet" (B. Avarzad) 85 40

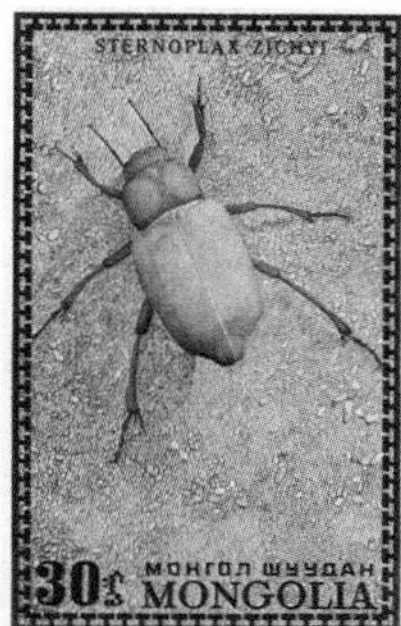

147 "Calosoma fischeri" (ground beetle)

1972. Beetles. Multicoloured.
660 10m. Type **147** 20 10
661 20m. "Mylabris mongolica" (blister beetle) 25 10
662 30m. "Sternoplax zichyi" (mealworm beetle) 30 10
663 50m. "Rhaebus komarovi" (snout weevil) 40 15
664 60m. "Meloe centripubens" (oil beetle) 55 15
665 80m. "Eodorcadion mongolicum" (longhorn beetle) 75 25
666 1t. "Platyope maongolica" (mealworm beetle) 90 30
667 1t.30 "Lixus nigrolineatus" (weevil) . . . . 1·40 50

149 Satellite and Dish Aerial ("Telecommunications")

1972. Air. National Achievements. Multicoloured.
669 20m. Type **149** 10 10
670 30m. Horse-herd ("Livestock Breeding") 20 10
671 40m. Diesel train and Tupolev Tu-144 jetliner ("Transport") 95 10
672 50m. Corncob and farm ("Agriculture") 25 15
673 60m. Ambulance and hospital ("Public Health") 60 15
674 80m. Actors ("Culture") . . 60 20
675 1t. Factory ("Industry") . . . 65 30

150 Globe, Flag and Dish Aerial

1972. Air. World Telecommunications Day.
676 **150** 60m. multicoloured . . . 25 15

151 Running

1972. Olympic Games, Munich. Multicoloured.
677 10m. Type **151** 10 10
678 15m. Boxing 10 10
679 20m. Judo 10 10
680 25m. High jumping 10 10
681 30m. Rifle-shooting 10 10
682 60m. Wrestling 20 15
683 80m. Weightlifting 25 20
684 1t. Mongolian flag and Olympic emblems 35 25

152 E.C.A.F.E. Emblem

1972. 25th Anniv of E.C.A.F.E.
686 **152** 60m. blue, gold and red 20 10

153 Mongolian Racerunner

1972. Reptiles. Multicoloured.
687 10m. Type **153** 20 10
688 15m. Radde's toad 25 10
689 20m. Halys viper 35 10
690 25m. Toad-headed agama . . 40 15
691 30m. Asiatic grass frog . . . 55 15
692 60m. Plate-tailed geckol . . . 70 25
693 80m. Steppe ribbon snake . . 85 35
694 1t. Mongolian agama . . . . 1·25 55

154 "Technical Knowledge"

1972. 30th Anniv of Mongolian State University. Multicoloured.
695 50m. Type **154** 15 10
696 60m. University building . . 20 10

155 "Madonna and Child with St. John the Baptist and a Holy Woman" (Bellini)

1972. Air. U.N.E.S.C.O. "Save Venice" Campaign. Paintings. Multicoloured.
697 10m. Type **155** 15 10
698 20m. "The Transfiguration" (Bellini) (vert) 20 10
699 30m. "Blessed Virgin with the Child" (Bellini) (vert) . . . 25 10
700 50m. "Presentation of the Christ in the Temple" (Bellini) 40 15
701 60m. "St. George" (Bellini) (vert) 50 20
702 80m. "Departure of Ursula" (detail, Carpacclo) (vert) 65 35
703 1t. "Departure of Ursula" (different detail, Carpaccio) 85 45

156 Manlay-Bator Damdinsuren

157 Spassky Tower, Moscow Kremlin

1972. National Heroes. Multicoloured.
705 10m. Type **156** 10 10
706 20m. Ard Ayus in chains (horiz) 20 10
707 50m. Hatan-Bator Magsarzhav 30 15
708 60m. Has-Bator on the march (horiz) 40 20
709 1t. Sukhe Bator 70 30

1972. 50th Anniv of U.S.S.R.
710 **157** 60m. multicoloured . . . 25 15

158 Snake and "Mars 1"

1972. Air. Animal Signs of the Mongolian Calendar and Progress in Space Exploration. Multicoloured.
711 60m. Type **158** 70 25
712 60m. Horse and "Apollo 8" (square) 70 25
713 60m. Sheep and "Electron 2" (square) 70 25
714 60m. Monkey and "Explorer 6" 70 25
715 60m. Dragon and "Mariner 2" 70 25
716 60m. Pig and "Cosmos 110" (square) 70 25
717 60m. Dog and "Ariel 2" (square) 70 25
718 60m. Cockerel and "Venus 1" 70 25
719 60m. Hare and "Soyuz 5" . . 70 25
720 60m. Tiger and "Gemini 7" (square) 70 25
721 60m. Ox and "Venus 4" (square) 70 25
722 60m. Rat and "Apollo 15" lunar rover 70 25
The square designs are size 40 × 40 mm.

159 Swimming Gold Medal (Mark Spitz, U.S.A.)

1972. Gold Medal Winners, Munich Olympic Games. Multicoloured.
723 5m. Type **159** 10 10
724 10m. High jumping (Ulrike Meyfarth, West Germany) 10 10
725 20m. Gymnastics (Savao Kato, Japan) 10 10
726 30m. Show jumping (Andras Balczo, Hungary) 10 10
727 60m. Running (Lasse Viren, Finland) 25 15
728 80m. Swimming (Shane Gould, Australia) 35 20
729 1t. Putting the shot (Anatoli Bondarchuk, U.S.S.R.) . . 40 25

160 Monkey on Cycle

1973. Mongolian Circus (1st series). Mult.
731 5m. Type **160** 10 10
732 10m. Seal with ball 15 10
733 15m. Bear on mono-wheel . . 20 10
734 20m. Acrobat on camel . . . 25 10
735 30m. Acrobat on horse . . . 40 10
736 50m. Clown playing flute . . 50 20
737 60m. Contortionist 60 25
738 1t. New Circus Hall, Ulan Bator 80 40
See also Nos. 824/30.

161 Mounted Postman **162** Sukhe Bator receiving Traditional Gifts

1973.
739 **161** 50m. brown (postage) . . 60 10
740 – 60m. green . . . . 2·50 15
741 – 1t. purple . . . . 1·00 20
742 – 1t.50 blue (air) . . . . . 1·75 25
DESIGNS: 60m. Diesel train; 1t. Mail truck; 1t.50, Antonov An-24 airliner.

1973. 80th Birth Anniv of Sukhe Bator. Mult.
743 10m. Type **162** 10 10
744 20m. Holding reception . . . 10 10
745 50m. Leading army 20 10
746 60m. Addressing council . . 25 10
747 1t. Giving audience (horiz) 45 20

163 W.M.O. Emblem and Meteorological Symbols

1973. Air. Centenary of World Meteorological Organization.
748 **163** 60m. multicoloured . . . 30 10

164 "Copernicus" (anon)

167 Marx and Lenin

Нэгдлийн Холбооны IV Их Хурал 1973—6—11

(**166**)

1973. 500th Birth Anniv of Nicholas Copernicus (astronomer). Multicoloured.
749 50m. Type **164** 15 10
750 60m. "Copernicus in his Observatory" (J. Matejko) (55 × 35 mm) 25 10
751 1t. "Copernicus" (Jan Matejko) 35 15

1973. 4th Agricultural Co-operative Congress, Ulan Bator. No. 538 optd with T **166**.
754 60m. multicoloured . . . . .

1973. 9th Organization of Socialist States Postal Ministers Congress, Ulan Bator.
755 **167** 60m. multicoloured . . . 30 10

168 Russian Stamp and Emblems

1973. Air. Council for Mutual Economic Aid Posts and Telecommunications Conference, Ulan Bator. Multicoloured.
756 30m. Type **168** . . . . 1·25 30
757 30m. Mongolia 45 20
758 30m. Bulgaria 45 20

759	30m. Hungary	45	20
760	30m. Czechoslovakia	45	20
761	30m. German Democratic Republic	45	20
762	30m. Cuba	45	20
763	30m. Rumania	45	20
764	30m. Poland	1·25	30

169 Common Shelduck

1973. Aquatic Birds. Multicoloured.

765	5m. Type **169**	50	10
766	10m. Black-throated diver	70	10
767	15m. Bar-headed geese	1·10	15
768	30m. Great crested grebe	1·50	25
769	50m. Mallard	2·00	50
770	60m. Mute swan	2·40	50
771	1t. Greater scaups	2·75	70

170 Siberian Weasel

1973. Small Fur Animals. Multicoloured.

772	5m. Type **170**	20	10
773	10m. Siberian chipmunk	20	10
774	15m. Siberian flying squirrel	20	10
775	20m. Eurasian badger	25	15
776	30m. Eurasian red squirrel	35	15
777	60m. Wolverine	70	30
778	80m. American mink	85	45
779	1t. Arctic hare	1·25	60

171 Launching "Soyuz" Spacecraft

1973. Air. "Apollo" and "Soyuz" Space Programmes. Multicoloured.

780	5m. Type **171**	10	10
781	10m. "Apollo 8"	10	10
782	15m. "Soyuz 4" and "5" linked	10	10
783	20m. "Apollo 11" module on Moon	10	10
784	30m. "Apollo 14" after splashdown	10	10
785	50m. Triple flight by "Soyuz 6", "7" and "8"	20	15
786	60m. "Apollo 16" lunar rover	25	15
787	1t. "Lunokhod 1"	40	30

172 Global Emblem

1973. 15th Anniv of Review "Problems of Peace and Socialism".

789	**172** 60m. red, gold and blue	25	10

173 Alpine Aster

1973. Mongolian Flowers. Multicoloured.

790	5m. Type **173**	10	10
791	10m. Mongolian catchfly	20	10
792	15m. "Rosa davurica"	25	10
793	20m. Mongolian dandelion	30	15
794	30m. "Rhododendron dahuricum"	45	25
795	50m. "Clematis tangutica"	55	40
796	60m. Siberian primrose	65	45
797	1t. Pasque flower	85	75

174 Poplar Admiral

1974. Butterflies and Moths. Multicoloured.

798	5m. Type **174**	30	10
799	10m. Hebe tiger moth	35	10
800	15m. Purple tiger moth	40	10
801	20m. Rosy underwing	55	10
802	30m. "Isoceras kaszabi" (moth)	70	15
803	50m. Spurge hawk moth	1·00	30
804	60m. Garden tiger moth	1·10	40
805	1t. Clouded buff	1·50	50

175 "Hebe Namshil" (L. Merdorsh)

1974. Mongolian Opera and Drama. Multicoloured.

806	15m. Type **175**	15	10
807	20m. "Sive Hiagt" (D. Luvsansharav) (horiz)	15	10
808	25m. "Edre" (D. Namdag)	20	10
809	30m. "The Three Khans of Sara-gol" (horiz)	25	15
810	60m. "Amarsana" (B. Damdinsuren)	40	20
811	80m. "Edre" (different scene)	55	25
812	1t. "Edre" (different scene)	85	55

176 Comecon Headquarters, Moscow

1974. Air. 25th Anniv of Communist Council for Mutual Economic Aid ("Comecon").

813	**176** 60m. multicoloured	30	20

177 Government Building and Sukhe Bator Monument, Ulan Bator

1974. 50th Anniv of Renaming of Capital as Ulan Bator.

814	**177** 60m. multicoloured	20	10

179 Mounted Courier

1974. Air. Centenary of U.P.U. Multicoloured.

816	50m. Type **179**	1·50	40
817	50m. Reindeer mail sledge	1·50	40
818	50m. Mail coach	1·50	40
819	50m. Balloon post	2·00	40
820	50m. Lake steamer "Sukhe Bator" and Polikarpov Po-2 biplane	2·25	40
821	50m. Diesel train and P.O. truck	2·25	40
822	50m. Rocket in orbit	1·50	40

180 Performing Horses

1974. Mongolian Circus (2nd series). Multicoloured.

824	10m. Type **180** (postage)	10	10
825	20m. Juggler (vert)	15	10
826	30m. Elephant on ball (vert)	20	10
827	40m. Performing yak	30	15
828	60m. Acrobats (vert)	45	20
829	80m. Trick cyclist (vert)	60	25
830	1t. Contortionist (vert) (air)	70	35

181 "Training a Young Horse"

1974. International Children's Day. Drawings by Lhamsurem. Multicoloured.

831	10m. Type **181**	10	10
832	20m. "Boy with Calf"	15	10
833	30m. "Riding untamed Horse"	20	10
834	40m. "Boy with Foal"	25	10
835	60m. "Girl dancing with Doves"	30	15
836	80m. "Wrestling"	35	25
837	1t. "Hobby-horse Dance"	60	30

182 Archer on Foot

1974. "Nadam" Sports Festival. Multicoloured.

838	10m. Type **182**	10	10
839	20m. "Kazlodanie" (Kazakh mounted game)	15	10
840	30m. Mounted archer	20	10
841	40m. Horse-racing	25	10
842	60m. Bucking horse-riding	30	15
843	80m. Capturing wild horse	35	25
844	1t. Wrestling	60	30

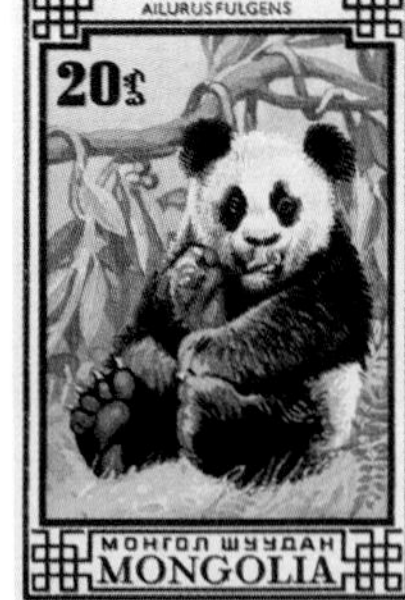

183 Giant Panda

1974. Bears. Multicoloured.

845	10m. Brown bear	25	10
846	20m. Type **183**	25	10
847	30m. Giant Panda	45	15
848	40m. Brown bear	45	20
849	60m. Sloth bear	70	30
850	80m. Asiatic black bear	80	50
851	1t. Brown bear	1·50	65

184 Red Deer

1974. Games Reserves. Fauna. Multicoloured.

852	10m. Type **184**	15	10
853	20m. Eurasian beaver	30	10
854	30m. Leopard	40	15
855	40m. Herring gull	85	35
856	60m. Roe deer	80	30
857	80m. Argali	85	35
858	1t. Siberian musk deer	1·25	55

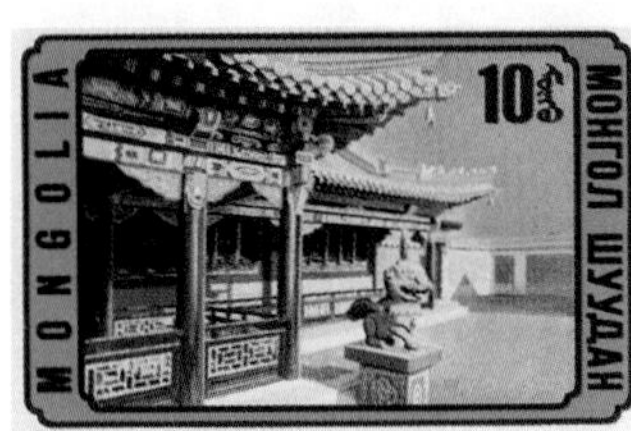

185 Detail of Buddhist Temple, Palace of Bogdo Gegen

1974. Mongolian Architecture. Multicoloured.

859	10m. Type **185**	10	10
860	15m. Buddhist temple (now museum)	10	10
861	30m. "Charity" Temple, Ulan Bator	20	10
862	50m. Yurt (tent)	30	20
863	80m. Arbour in court-yard	50	30

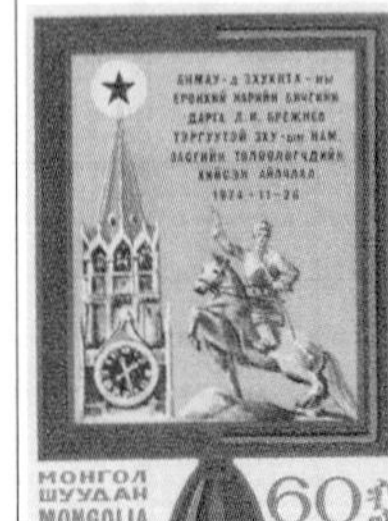
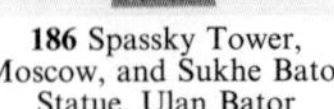

186 Spassky Tower, Moscow, and Sukhe Bator Statue, Ulan Bator

187 Proclamation of the Republic

1974. Brezhnev's Visit to Mongolia.

864	**186** 60m. multicoloured	30	10

1974. 50th Anniv of Mongolian People's Republic. Multicoloured.

865	60m. Type **187**	30	10
866	60m. "First Constitution" (embroidery)	30	10
867	60m. Mongolian flag	30	10

188 Gold Decanter

1974. Goldsmiths' Treasures of the 19th Century. Multicoloured.

868	10m. Type **188**	15	10
869	20m. Silver jug	20	10
870	30m. Night lamp	25	10
871	40m. Tea jug	35	20
872	60m. Candelabra	45	20
873	80m. Teapot	60	30
874	1t. Silver bowl on stand	80	40

189 Northern Lapwing

1974. Protection of Water and Nature Conservation. Multicoloured.

875	10m. Type **189** (postage)	40	10
876	20m. Lenok (fish)	45	10
877	30m. Marsh marigolds	40	15
878	40m. Dalmatian pelican	80	25
879	60m. Eurasian perch	75	25
880	80m. Sable	75	25
881	1t. Hydrologist with jar of water (air)	80	30

190 U.S. Mail Coach

1974. Centenary of U.P.U. Multicoloured.

883	10m. Type **190**	15	10
884	20m. French postal cart	20	10
885	30m. Changing horses, Russian mail and passenger carriage	35	15
886	40m. Swedish postal coach with caterpillar tracks	45	20
887	50m. First Hungarian mail van	50	25
888	60m. German Daimler-Benz mail van and trailer	65	40
889	1t. Mongolian postal courier	95	55

191 Red Flag

193 Mongolian Woman

192 "Zygophyllum xanthoxylon" (½-size illustration)

1975. 30th Anniv of Victory.

891	**191** 60m. multicoloured	30	10

1975. 12th International Botanical Conference. Rare Medicinal Plants. Multicoloured.

892	10m. Type **192**	20	10
893	20m. "Incarvillea potaninii"	30	10
894	30m. "Lancea tibetica"	45	15
895	40m. "Jurinea mongolica"	45	20
896	50m. "Saussurea involucrata"	55	20
897	60m. "Allium mongolicum"	65	30
898	1t. "Adonis mongolica"	1·25	40

1975. International Women's Year.

899	**193** 60m. multicoloured	30	10

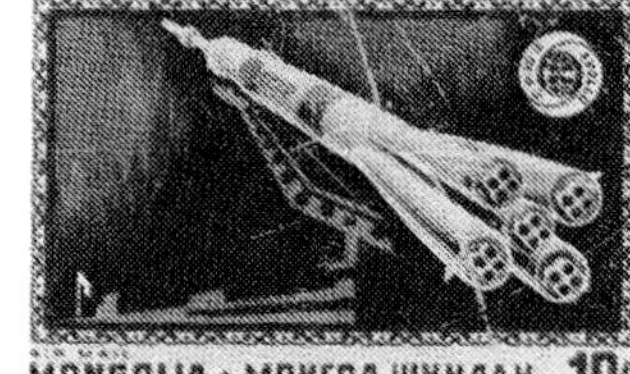

194 "Soyuz" on Launch-pad

1975. Air. Joint Soviet–American Space Project. Multicoloured.

900	10m. Type **194**	20	10
901	20m. Launch of "Apollo"	15	10
902	30m. "Apollo" and "Soyuz" spacecraft	30	10
903	40m. Docking manoeuvre	35	20
904	50m. Spacecraft docked together	50	20
905	60m. "Soyuz" in orbit	60	30
906	1t. "Apollo" and "Soyuz" spacecraft and communications satellite	95	40

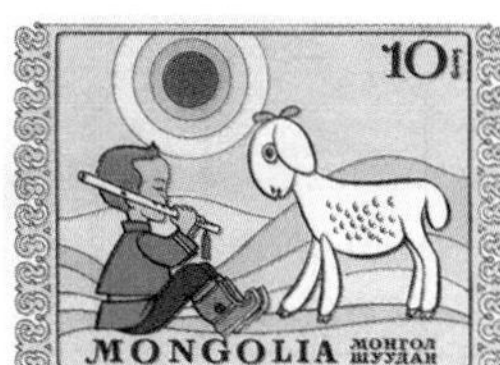

195 Child and Lamb

1975. International Children's Day. Multicoloured.

908	10m. Type **195**	10	10
909	20m. Child riding horse	20	10
910	30m. Child with calf	20	10
911	40m. Child and "orphan camel"	25	15
912	50m. "The Obedient Yak"	30	20
913	60m. Child riding on swan	35	25
914	1t. Two children singing	55	40

See also Nos. 979/85.

196 Pioneers tending Tree

Тээвэр—50
1975—7—15.
(197)

1975. 50th Anniv of Mongolian Pioneer Organization. Multicoloured.

915	50m. Type **196**	20	10
916	60m. Children's study circle	30	10
917	1t. New emblem of Mongolian pioneers	40	20

1975. 50th Anniv of Public Transport. Nos. 616/22 optd with T **197**.

918	**138** 20m. multicoloured	2·50	2·50
919	– 30m. multicoloured	2·50	2·50
920	– 40m. multicoloured	1·90	1·90
921	– 50m. multicoloured	1·90	1·90
922	– 60m. multicoloured	2·50	2·50
923	– 80m. multicoloured	3·00	3·00
924	– 1t. multicoloured	3·75	3·75

198 Argali

1975. Air. South Asia Tourist Year.

925	**198** 1t.50 multicoloured	90	40

199 Golden Eagle attacking Red Fox

1975. Hunting Scenes. Multicoloured.

926	10m. Type **199**	50	10
927	20m. Lynx-hunting (vert)	45	10
928	30m. Hunter stalking bobak marmots	50	15
929	40m. Hunter riding on reindeer (vert)	60	20
930	50m. Shooting wild boar	60	25
931	60m. Wolf in trap (vert)	75	35
932	1t. Hunters with brown bear	1·00	50

200 Haite's Bullhead

1975. Fishes. Multicoloured.

933	10m. Type **200**	25	10
934	20m. Flat-headed asp	40	10
935	30m. Altai osman	45	15
936	40m. Tench	55	20
937	50m. Hump-backed whitefish	80	25
938	60m. Mongolian redfin	95	30
939	1t. Goldfish	1·60	60

201 "Morin Hur" (musical instrument)

1975. Mongolian Handicrafts. Multicoloured.

940	10m. Type **201**	10	10
941	20m. Saddle	15	10
942	30m. Headdress	20	10
943	40m. Boots	30	15
944	50m. Cap	40	15
945	60m. Pipe and tobacco pouch	45	20
946	1t. Fur hat	75	30

202 Revolutionary with Banner

1975. 70th Anniv of 1905 Russian Revolution.

947	**202** 60m. multicoloured	25	10

203 "Taming a Wild Horse"

1975. Mongolian Paintings. Multicoloured.

948	10m. Type **203**	10	10
949	20m. "Camel Caravan" (horiz)	25	10
950	30m. "Man playing Lute"	35	10
951	40m. "Woman adjusting Headdress" (horiz)	40	15
952	50m. "Woman in ceremonial Costume"	40	25
953	60m. "Woman fetching Water"	50	30
954	1t. "Woman playing Yaga" (musical instrument)	75	40

204 Ski Jumping

1975. Winter Olympic Games, Innsbruck. Multicoloured.

956	10m. Type **204**	10	10
957	20m. Ice hockey	10	10
958	30m. Slalom skiing	10	10
959	40m. Bobsleighing	15	10
960	50m. Rifle shooting (biathlon)	20	10
961	60m. Speed skating	20	15
962	1t. Figure skating	35	25

205 "House of Young Technicians"

1975. Public Buildings.

964	**205** 50m. blue	40	10
965	– 60m. green	50	15
966	– 1t. brown	70	25

DESIGNS: 60m. Hotel, Ulan Bator; 1t. "Museum of the Revolution".

206 "Molniya" Satellite

1976. Air. 40th Anniv of Mongolian Meteorological Office.

967	**206** 60m. blue and yellow	40	15

209 "National Economy" Star

1976. 17th Mongolian People's Revolutionary Party Congress, Ulan Bator.

970	**209** 60m. multicoloured	30	10

210 Archery

1976. Olympic Games, Montreal. Multicoloured.
971 10m. Type **210** 10 10
972 20m. Judo 10 10
973 30m. Boxing 10 10
974 40m. Gymnastics 15 10
975 60m. Weightlifting 20 15
976 80m. High jumping 25 20
977 1t. Rifle shooting 35 25

1976. Int Children's Day. As T **195**. Mult.
979 10m. Gobi Desert landscape 15 10
980 20m. Horse-taming 20 10
981 30m. Horse-riding 25 10
982 40m. Pioneers' camp 35 10
983 60m. Young musician 50 20
984 80m. Children's party 70 25
985 1t. Mongolian wrestling . . . 90 30

211 Cavalry Charge

1976. 55th Anniv of Revolution. Multicoloured.
986 60m. Type **211** (postage) . . 40 10
987 60m. Man and emblem (vert) 40 10
988 60m. "Industry and Agriculture" (air) 40 10

213 Osprey

1976. Protected Birds. Multicoloured.
990 10m. Type **213** . . . . 1·50 40
991 20m. Griffon vulture . . . . 1·00 20
992 30m. Lammergeier . . . . . 1·40 25
993 40m. Marsh harrier . . . . . 1·75 25
994 60m. Cinerous vulture . . . 2·00 40
995 80m. Golden eagle . . . . . 2·50 45
996 1t. Tawny eagle . . . . . . 2·75 55

214 "Rider on Wild Horse"

1976. Paintings by O. Tsewegdjaw. Multicoloured.
997 10m. Type **214** 15 10
998 20m. "The First Nadam" (game on horse-back) (horiz) 20 10
999 30m. "Harbour on Khobsogol Lake" (horiz) 55 15
1000 40m. "Awakening the Steppe" (horiz) 45 20
1001 80m. "Wrestling" (horiz) . . 60 25
1002 1t. "The Descent" (yak hauling timber) . . . . . 1·10 50

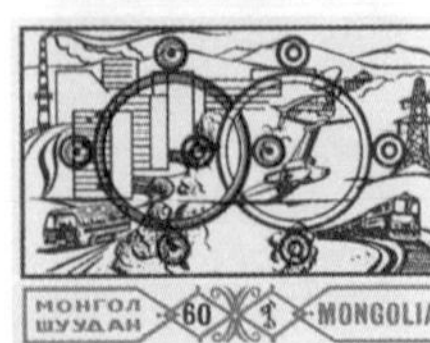

215 "Industrial Development"

1976. Mongolian–Soviet Friendship.
1003 **215** 60m. multicoloured . . . 1·25 20

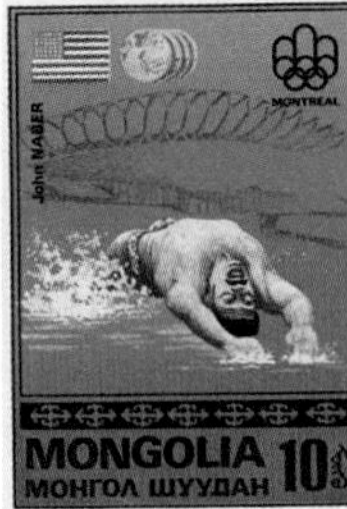

216 John Naber of U.S.A. (Swimming) **217** Tablet on Tortoise

1976. Olympic Games, Montreal. Gold Medal Winners. Multicoloured.
1004 10m. Type **216** 10 10
1005 20m. Nadia Comaneci of Rumania (gymnastics) . . 10 10
1006 30m. Kornelia Ender of East Germany (swimming) 10 10
1007 40m. Mitsuo Tsukahara of Japan (gymnastics) . . . 15 10
1008 60m. Gregor Braun of West Germany (cycling) 20 15
1009 80m. Lasse Viren of Finland (running) 25 20
1010 1t. Nikolai Andrianov of U.S.S.R. (gymnastics) . . 35 25

1976. Archaeology.
1012 **217** 50m. brown and blue . . 80 15
1013 – 60m. black and green . . 1·10 15
DESIGN: 60m. 6th-century stele.

218 R-1 Biplane

1976. Aircraft. Multicoloured.
1014 10m. Type **218** 20 10
1015 20m. Polikarpov R-5 biplane 30 10
1016 30m. Kalinin K-5 monoplane 40 10
1017 40m. Polikarpov Po-2 biplane 45 15
1018 60m. Polikarpov I-16 jet fighter 60 25
1019 80m. Yakovlev Ya-6 Air 6 monoplane 75 35
1020 1t. Junkers F-13 monoplane 95 40

219 Dancers in Folk Costume

1977. Mongolian Folk Dances. Multicoloured.
1021 10m. Type **219** 25 10
1022 20m. Dancing girls in 13th-century costume . . 35 10
1023 30m. West Mongolian dance 45 10
1024 40m. "Ekachi" dance . . . 50 15
1025 60m. "Bielge" ("Trunk") dance 80 20
1026 80m. "Hodak" dance . . . 95 30
1027 1t. "Dojarka" dance . . . . 1·10 45

220 Gravitational Effects on "Pioneer"

1977. 250th Death Anniv of Sir Isaac Newton (mathematician). Multicoloured.
1028 60m. Type **220** (postage) . . 25 15
1029 60m. Apple tree (25 × 32 mm) 25 15
1030 60m. Planetary motion and sextant 25 15
1031 60m. Sir Isaac Newton (25 × 32 mm) 25 15
1032 60m. Spectrum of light . . . 25 15
1033 60m. Attraction of Earth . . 25 15
1034 60m. Laws of motion of celestial bodies (25 × 32 mm) 25 15
1035 60m. Space-walking (air) . . 25 15
1036 60m. "Pioneer 10" and Jupiter 25 15

221 Natsagdorj, Mongolian Scenes and Extract from poem "Mother" (½-size illustration)

1977. Natsagdorj (poet) Commem. Mult.
1037 60m. Type **221** 40 25
1038 60m. Border stone, landscape and extract from poem "My Homeland" 40 25

222 Horse Race

1977. Horses. Multicoloured.
1039 10m. Type **222** 25 10
1040 20m. Girl on white horse . . 30 10
1041 30m. Rangeman on brown horse 40 10
1042 40m. Tethered horses . . . 55 20
1043 60m. White mare with foal 70 20
1044 80m. Brown horse with shepherd . . . . 1·00 30
1045 1t. White horse . . . . . . 1·25 45

223 "Mongolemys elegans"

1977. Prehistoric Animals. Multicoloured.
1046 10m. Type **223** 30 10
1047 20m. "Embolotherium ergiliense" 45 10
1048 30m. "Psittacosaurus mongoliensis" 55 15
1049 40m. Enthelodon 70 20
1050 60m. "Spirocerus kiakhtensis" . . . . . . 1·00 25
1051 80m. Hipparion . . . . . . 1·40 40
1052 1t. "Bos primigenius" . . . 1·60 55

225 Child feeding Lambs

1977. Children's Day and 1st Balloon Flight in Mongolia. Multicoloured.
1054 10m.+5m. Type **225** 30 15
1055 20m.+5m. Boy playing flute and girl dancing 45 15
1056 30m.+5m. Girl chasing butterflies 55 20
1057 40m.+5m. Girl with ribbon 60 25
1058 60m.+5m. Girl with flowers 70 40
1059 80m.+5m. Girl with bucket 90 50
1060 1t.+5m. Boy going to school 1·25 60

226 Industrial Plant and Transport

1977. Erdenet (New Town).
1062 **226** 60m. multicoloured . . . 1·25 20

227 Trade Unions Emblem

1977. Air. 11th Mongolian Trade Unions Congress.
1063 **227** 60m. multicoloured . . . 1·00 15

228 Mounting Bell-shaped Gear on Rocket (⅔-size illustration)

1977. Air. 11th Anniv of "Intercosmos" Co-operation. Multicoloured.
1064 10m. Type **228** 10 10
1065 20m. Launch of "Intercosmos 3" 10 10
1066 30m. Research ship "Kosmonavt Yury Gargarin" 40 15
1067 40m. Observation of lunar eclipse 15 10
1068 60m. Earth station's multiple antennae 15 15
1069 80m. Magnetosphere examination, Van Allen Zone 20 20
1070 1t. Meteorological satellites 30 25

229 Fire-fighters' Bucket Chain

1977. Mongolian Fire-fighting Services. Multicoloured.
1072 10m. Type **229** 10 10
1073 20m. Horse-drawn hand pump 10 10
1074 30m. Horse-drawn steam pump 10 10
1075 40m. Fighting forest fire . . 15 10
1076 60m. Mobile foam extinguisher 20 15
1077 80m. Modern fire engine . . 25 20
1078 1t. Mil Mi-8 helicopter spraying fire 35 25

230 "Molniya" Satellite and Dish Aerial on TV Screen

1977. 40th Anniv of Technical Institute.
1079 **230** 60m. blue, black and grey 30 10

231 Black-veined White

1977. Butterflies and Moths. Multicoloured.
1080 10m. Type **231** 20 10
1081 20m. Lappet moth 35 10
1082 30m. Lesser clouded yellow 50 20
1083 40m. Dark tussock moth . . 70 20
1084 60m. Lackey moth . . . . 1·00 25
1085 80m. Clouded buff . . . . 1·40 35
1086 1t. Scarce copper . . . . . 1·60 50

232 Lenin Museum

1977. Inauguration of Lenin Museum, Ulan Bator.
1087 **232** 60m. multicoloured . . . 40 20

233 Cruiser "Aurora" and Soviet Flag

1977. 60th Anniv of Russian Revolution. Mult.
1088 50m. Type **233** 60 15
1089 60m. Dove and globe (horiz) 50 15
1090 1t.50 Freedom banner around the globe (horiz) 75 35

234 Giant Pandas

1977. Giant Pandas. Multicoloured.
1091 10m. Eating bamboo shoot (vert) 20 10
1092 20m. Type **234** 35 10
1093 30m. Female and cub in washtub (vert) 45 15
1094 40m. Male and cub with bamboo shoot 60 20
1095 60m. Female and cub (vert) 80 30
1096 80m. Family (horiz) . . . . 1·40 50
1097 1t. Male on hind legs (vert) 1·60 65

236 Montgolfier Brothers' Balloon

1977. Air. Airships and Balloons. Multicoloured.
1099 20m. Type **236** 10 10
1100 30m. Airship "Graf Zeppelin" over North Pole 10 10
1101 40m. Airship "Osoaviakhim" over the Arctic 20 10
1102 50m. Soviet Airship "Sever" 30 15
1103 60m. Aereon 340 airship . . 40 20
1104 80m. Nestrenko's planned airship 45 20
1105 1t.20 "Flying Crane" airship 70 35

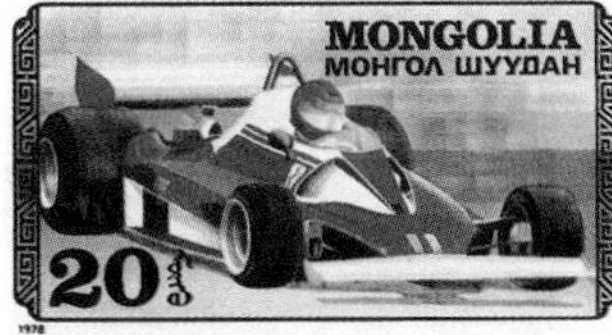

237 Ferrari "312-T2"

1978. Racing Cars. Multicoloured.
1107 20m. Type **237** 25 10
1108 30m. Ford McLaren "M-23" 30 10
1109 40m. Soviet experimental car 40 20
1110 50m. Japanese Mazda . . . 50 20
1111 60m. Porsche "936-Turbo" 60 25
1112 80m. Model of Soviet car 65 25
1113 1t.20 American rocket car "Blue Flame" 95 40

238 Variegated Boletus (½-size illustration)

1978. Mushrooms. Multicoloured.
1114 20m. Type **238** 50 15
1115 30m. The charcoal burner 75 20
1116 40m. Red cap 80 25
1117 50m. Brown birch bolete . . 1·00 30
1118 60m. Yellow swamp russula 1·25 35
1119 80m. "Lactarius resimus" 1·50 50
1120 1t.20 "Flammula spumosa" 2·00 75

239 Aleksandr Mozhaisky and his Monoplane, 1884

1978. Air. History of Aviation. Multicoloured.
1121 20m. Type **239** 10 10
1122 30m. Henri Farman and Farman H.F.III biplane 10 10
1123 40m. Geoffrey de Havilland and De Havilland FE-1 biplane 20 10
1124 50m. Charles Lindbergh and "Spirit of St. Louis" . . . 30 15
1125 60m. Shagdarsuren, Demberel, biplane and glider 40 20
1126 80m. Chkalov, Baidukov, Belyakov and Tupolev ANT-25 airliner 45 25
1127 1t.20 A. N. Tupolev and Tupolev Tu-154 jetliner 70 35

240 Footballers and View of Rio de Janeiro

1978. World Cup Football Championship, Argentina. Multicoloured.
1129 20m. Type **240** 10 10
1130 30m. Footballers and Old Town Tower, Berne . . . 10 10
1131 40m. Footballers and Stockholm Town Hall . . 15 10
1132 50m. Footballers and University of Chile . . . 20 10
1133 60m. Footballers, Houses of Parliament and Tower of London 30 15
1134 80m. Footballers and Theatre Degolladeo of Guadalajara, Mexico . . 35 15
1135 1t.20 Footballers and Munich Town Hall . . . 45 25

241 Mongolian Youth and Girl

1978. Mongolian Youth Congress, Ulan Bator.
1137 **241** 60m. multicoloured . . . 35 15

242 Eurasian Beaver and 1954 Canadian Beaver Stamp

1978. "CAPEX '78". International Stamp Exhibition, Toronto. Multicoloured.
1138 20m. Type **242** 20 10
1139 30m. Tibetan sandgrouse and Canada S.G. 620 . . 50 35
1140 40m. Black-throated diver and Canada S.G. 495 . . 65 40
1141 50m. Argali and Canada S.G. 449 . . . . 70 15
1142 60m. Brown bear and Canada S.G. 447 . . . . 80 15
1143 80m. Elk and Canada S.G. 448 . . . . 90 25
1144 1t.20 Herring gull and Canada S.G. 474 . . . . 1·90 75

243 Marx, Engels and Lenin

1978. 20th Anniv of Review "Problems of Peace and Socialism".
1146 **243** 60m. red, gold and black 35 15

244 Map of Cuba, Liner, Tupolev Tu-134 Jetliner and Emblem (½-size illustration)

1978. Air. 11th World Youth Festival, Havana.
1147 **244** 1t. multicoloured 90 20

245 "Open-air Repose"

1978. 20th Anniv of Philatelic Co-operation between Mongolia and Hungary. Paintings by P. Angalan. Multicoloured.
1148 1t.50 Type **245** 40 40
1149 1t.50 "Winter Night" . . . 40 40
1150 1t.50 "Saddling" 40 40

247 Butterfly Dog

1978. Dogs. Multicoloured.
1152 10m. Type **247** 20 10
1153 20m. Black Mongolian sheepdog 25 10
1154 30m. Puli (Hungarian sheepdog) 35 15
1155 40m. St. Bernard 40 20
1156 50m. German shepherd dog 55 25
1157 60m. Mongolian watchdog 65 25
1158 70m. Semoyedic spitz . . . 75 35
1159 80m. Laika (space dog) . . 90 35
1160 1t.20 Black and white poodles and cocker spaniel . . . . 1·10 55

248 Open Book showing Scenes from Mongolian Literary Works

1978. 50th Anniv of Mongolian Writers' Association.
1161 **248** 60m. blue and red . . . 35 15

249 "Dressed Maja" (Goya, 150th death anniv)

1978. Painters' Anniversaries. Multicoloured.
1162 1t.50 Type **249** . . . . . . 1·25 1·25
1163 1t.50 "Ta Matete" (Gaugin – 75th death anniv) . . . 1·25 1·25
1164 1t.50 "Bridge at Arles" (Van Gogh – 125th birth anniv) 1·25 1·25

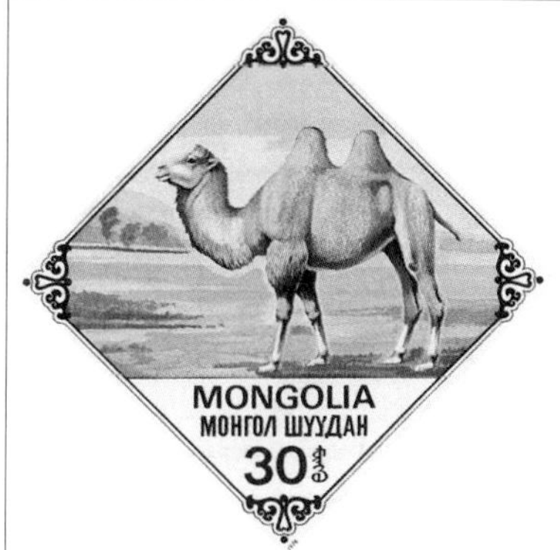

250 Young Bactrian Camel

1978. Bactrian Camels. Multicoloured.
1166 20m. Camel with Foal . . . 25 15
1167 30m. Type **250** 30 15
1168 40m. Two camels 45 20
1169 50m. Woman leading loaded camel 55 25
1170 60m. Camel in winter coat 70 30
1171 80m. Camel-drawn water waggon 90 45
1172 1t.20 Camel racing . . . . 1·25 60

251 Flags of COMECON Countries

1979. 30th Anniv of Council of Mutual Economic Assistance.
1173 **251** 60m. multicoloured . . . 35 15

252 Children riding Camel

1979. International Year of the Child. Multicoloured.
1174 10m.+5m. Type **252** 20 15
1175 30m.+5m. Children feeding chickens 30 15
1176 50m.+5m. Children with deer 45 15
1177 60m.+5m. Children picking flowers 55 20
1178 70m.+5m. Children watering tree 65 25
1179 80m.+5m. Young scientists 75 35
1180 1t.+5m. Making music and dancing . . . . 1·00 50

253 Silver Tabby

1978. Domestic Cats. Multicoloured.
1182 10m. Type **253** 20 10
1183 30m. White Persian 35 15
1184 50m. Red Persian 55 15
1185 60m. Blue-cream Persian . . 70 20
1186 70m. Siamese 80 30
1187 80m. Smoke Persian 90 35
1188 1t. Birman . . . . 1·25 50

254 "Potaninia mongolica"

1979. Flowers. Multicoloured.

1189	10m. Type **254**	20	10
1190	30m. "Sophora alopecuroides"	30	10
1191	50m. "Halimodendron halodendron"	35	15
1192	60m. "Myosotis asiatica"	50	20
1193	70m. "Scabiosa comosa"	50	30
1194	80m. "Leucanthemum sibiricum"	60	30
1195	1t. "Leontopodium ochroleucum"	80	45

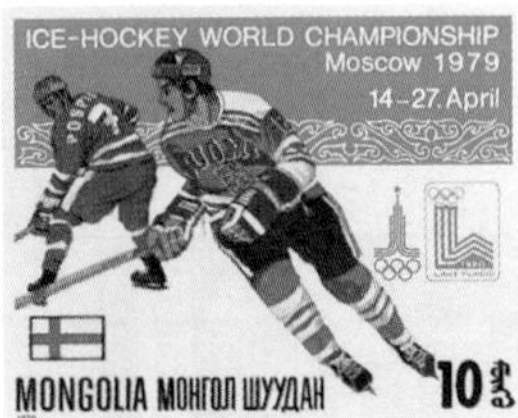

255 Finland v. Czechoslovakia

1979. World Ice Hockey Championships, Moscow. Multicoloured.

1196	10m. Type **255**	10	10
1197	30m. West Germany v. Sweden	10	10
1198	50m. U.S.A. v. Canada	15	10
1199	60m. Russia v. Sweden	15	10
1200	70m. Canada v. Russia	20	15
1201	80m. Swedish goalkeeper	20	15
1202	1t. Czechoslovakia v. Russia	30	20

256 Lambs (Sanzhid)

1979. Agriculture Paintings. Multicoloured.

1203	10m. Type **256**	10	10
1204	30m. "Milking camels" (Budbazar)	20	10
1205	50m. "Aircraft bringing help" (Radnabazar)	40	15
1206	60m. "Herdsmen" (Budbazar)	40	15
1207	70m. "Milkmaids" "Nanzadsguren) (vert)	55	30
1208	80m. "Summer Evening" (Sanzhid)	75	40
1209	1t. "Country Landscape" (Tserendondog)	90	50

257 First Mongolian and Bulgarian Stamps

1979. Death Centenary of Sir Rowland Hill, and "Philaserdica 79" International Stamp Exn, Sofia. Each black, grey and brown.

1211	1t. Type **257**	1·50	1·00
1212	1t. American mail coach	1·50	1·00
1213	1t. Travelling post office, London–Birmingham railway	2·00	1·25
1214	1t. Paddle-steamer "Hindoostan"	1·75	1·00

258 Stephenson's "Rocket"

1979. Development of Railways. Multicoloured.

1215	10m. Type **258**	30	10
1216	20m. Locomotive "Adler", 1835, Germany	35	10
1217	30m. Steam locomotive, 1860, U.S.A.	45	10
1218	40m. Class KB4 steam locomotive, 1931, Mongolia	55	15
1219	50m. Class Er steam locomotive, 1936, Mongolia	60	20
1220	60m. Diesel train, 1970, Mongolia	70	25
1221	70m. "Hikari" express train, 1963, Japan	90	30
1222	80m. Monorail aerotrain "Orleans", France	95	40
1223	1t.20 Experimental jet train "Rapidity", Russia	1·10	50

259 Flags of Mongolia and Russia

262 East German Flag, Berlin Buildings and "Soyuz 31"

260 Pallas's Cat

1979. 40th Anniv of Battle of Khalka River.

1224 **259**	60m. gold, red and yellow	30	20
1225 –	60m. red, yellow and blue	30	20

DESIGN: No. 1225, Ribbons, badge and military scene.

1979. Wild Cats. Multicoloured.

1226	10m. Type **260**	15	10
1227	30m. Lynx	30	15
1228	50m. Tiger	55	25
1229	60m. Snow leopard	65	25
1230	70m. Leopard	75	35
1231	80m. Cheetah	80	35
1232	1t. Lion	1·25	50

1979. 30th Anniv of German Democratic Republic (East Germany).

1234 **262**	60m. multicoloured	35	10

263 Demoiselle Crane

1979. Air. Protected Birds. Multicoloured.

1235	10m. Type **263**	40	25
1236	30m. Barred warbler	60	25
1237	50m. Ruddy shelduck	70	35
1238	60m. Azure-winged magpie	85	50
1239	70m. Goldfinch	85	50
1240	80m. Great tit	95	65
1241	1t. Golden oriole	1·40	75

264 "Venus 5" and "6"

1979. Air. Space Research. Multicoloured.

1242	10m. Type **264**	10	10
1243	30m. "Mariner 5"	10	10
1244	50m. "Mars 3"	15	10
1245	60m. "Viking 1" and "2"	15	10
1246	70m. "Luna 1", "2" and "3"	20	15
1247	80m. "Lunokhod 2"	20	15
1248	1t. "Apollo 15" Moon-rover	30	20

265 Cross-country Skiing

1980. Winter Olympic Games, Lake Placid. Multicoloured.

1250	20m. Type **265**	10	10
1251	30m. Biathlon	10	10
1252	40m. Ice hockey	15	10
1253	50m. Ski jumping	15	10
1254	60m. Slalom	20	15
1255	80m. Speed skating	20	15
1256	1t.20 Four-man bobsleigh	30	20

266 "Andrena scita" (mining bee)

1980. Air. Wasps and Bees. Multicoloured.

1258	20m. Type **266**	10	10
1259	30m. "Paravespula germanica" (wasp)	10	10
1260	40m. "Perilampus ruficornis" (parasitic wasp)	20	10
1261	50m. Buff-tailed bumble bee	30	15
1262	60m. Honey bee	40	20
1263	80m. "Stilbum cyanurum" (cuckoo wasp)	45	25
1264	1t.20 "Parnopes grandior" (cuckoo wasp)	70	35

267 Weightlifting

1980. Olympic Games, Moscow. Multicoloured.

1266	20m. Type **267**	10	10
1267	30m. Archery	10	10
1268	40m. Gymnastics	15	10
1269	50m. Running	15	10
1270	60m. Boxing	20	15
1271	80m. Judo	20	15
1272	1t.20 Cycling	30	20

268 Zlin Z-526 AFs Akrobat Special

1980. Air. World Acrobatic Championship, Oshkosh, Wisconsin. Multicoloured.

1274	20m. Type **268**	10	10
1275	30m. Socata RF-6B Sportsman (inscr "RS-180")	15	10
1276	40m. Grumman A-1 Yankee	20	10
1277	50m. MJ-2 Tempete	30	15
1278	60m. Pitts S-2A biplane (inscr "Pits")	35	20
1279	80m. Hirth Acrostar	45	25
1280	1t.20 Yakovlev Yak-50	65	35

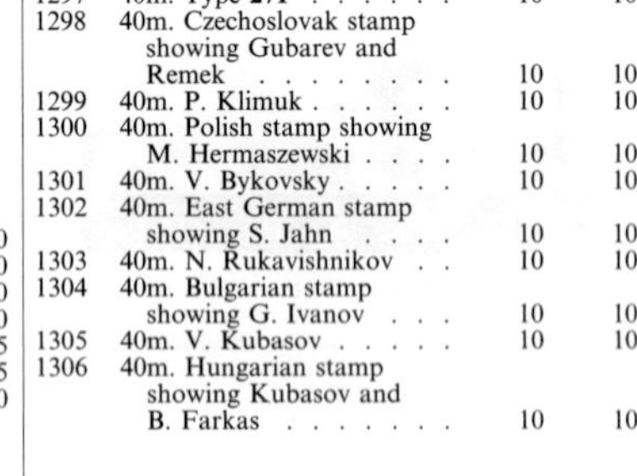

269 Swimming

1980. Olympic Medal Winners. Multicoloured.

1282	20m. Type **269**	10	10
1283	30m. Fencing	10	10
1284	50m. Judo	10	10
1285	60m. Athletics	15	10
1286	80m. Boxing	20	10
1287	1t. Weightlifting	25	15
1288	1t.20 Kayak-canoe	30	20

270 Sukhe Bator

271 Gubarev

1980. Mongolian Politicians.

1290 **270**	60m. brown	15	10
1291 –	60m. blue	15	10
1292 –	60m. turquoise	15	10
1293 –	60m. bronze	15	10
1294 –	60m. green	15	10
1295 –	60m. red	15	10
1296 –	60m. brown	15	10

DESIGNS—VERT: No. 1291, Marshal Choibalsan; 1292, Yu. Tsedenbal aged 13; 1293, Tsedenbal as soldier, 1941; 1294, Pres. Tsedenbal in 1979; 1295, Tsedenbal with children. HORIZ: No. 1296, Tsedenbal and President Brezhnev of Russia.

1980. "Intercosmos" Space Programme. Multicoloured.

1297	40m. Type **271**	10	10
1298	40m. Czechoslovak stamp showing Gubarev and Remek	10	10
1299	40m. P. Klimuk	10	10
1300	40m. Polish stamp showing M. Hermaszewski	10	10
1301	40m. V. Bykovsky	10	10
1302	40m. East German stamp showing S. Jahn	10	10
1303	40m. N. Rukavishnikov	10	10
1304	40m. Bulgarian stamp showing G. Ivanov	10	10
1305	40m. V. Kubasov	10	10
1306	40m. Hungarian stamp showing Kubasov and B. Farkas	10	10

272 Benz, 1885

1980. Classic Cars. Multicoloured.

1307	20m. Type **272**	25	10
1308	30m. "President" Czechoslovakia, 1897	30	10
1309	40m. Armstrong Siddeley, 1904	35	25
1310	50m. Russo-Balt, 1909	45	20
1311	60m. Packard, 1909	50	20
1312	80m. Lancia, 1911	70	30
1313	1t.60 "Marne" taxi, 1914	1·60	60

273 Adelie Penguin

1980. Antarctic Exploration. Multicoloured.

No.	Description	Mint	Used
1315	20m. Type **273**	1·25	20
1316	30m. Blue whales	70	15
1317	40m. Wandering albatross and Jacques Cousteau's ship "Calypso" and bathysphere	1·90	40
1318	50m. Weddell seals and mobile research station	90	20
1319	60m. Emperor penguins	2·75	45
1320	70m. Great skuas	3·25	60
1321	80m. Killer whales	1·75	50
1322	1t.20 Adelie penguins, research station, Ilyushin Il-18B airplane and tracked vehicle	5·00	1·00

276 "The Shepherd speaking the Truth"

1980. Nursery Tales. Multicoloured.

No.	Description	Mint	Used
1326	20m. Type **276**	10	10
1327	30m. Children under umbrella and rainbow ("Above them the Sky is always clear")	10	10
1328	40m. Children on sledge and skis ("Winter's Joys")	10	10
1329	50m. Girl watching boy playing flute ("Little Musicians")	15	10
1330	60m. Boys giving girl leaves ("Happy Birthday")	15	10
1331	80m. Children with flowers and briefcase ("First Schoolday")	20	15
1332	1t.20 Girls dancing ("May Day")	35	25

277 Soldier

1981. 60th Anniv of Mongolian People's Army.

No.	Description	Mint	Used
1334	**277** 60m. multicoloured	40	15

278 Economy Emblems within Party Initials

1981. 60th Anniv of Mongolian Revolutionary People's Party.

No.	Description	Mint	Used
1335	**278** 60m. gold, red and black	30	15

279 Motocross

1981. Motor Cycle Sports. Multicoloured.

No.	Description	Mint	Used
1336	10m. Type **279**	10	10
1337	20m. Tour racing	10	10
1338	30m. Ice racing	10	10
1339	40m. Road racing	15	10
1340	50m. Motocross (different)	15	10
1341	60m. Road racing (different)	20	10
1342	70m. Speedway	20	10
1343	80m. Sidecar racing	25	15
1344	1t.20 Road racing (different)	40	20

280 Cosmonauts entering Space Capsule

1981. Soviet–Mongolian Space Flight. Mult.

No.	Description	Mint	Used
1345	20m. Type **280**	10	10
1346	30m. Rocket and designer S. P. Korolev	10	10
1347	40m. "Vostok 1" and Yuri Gagarin	10	10
1348	50m. "Soyuz"–"Salyut" space station	15	10
1349	60m. Spectral photography	15	10
1350	80m. Crystal and space station	20	15
1351	1t.20 Space complex, Moscow Kremlin and Sukhe Bator statue, Ulan Bator	35	25

281 Ulan Bator Buildings and 1961 Mongolian Stamp

1981. Stamp Exhibitions.

No.	Description	Mint	Used
1353	**281** 1t. multicoloured	2·25	1·00
1354	– 1t. multicoloured	1·75	80
1355	– 1t. black, blue and magenta	1·75	80
1356	– 1t. multicoloured	2·25	1·00

DESIGNS: No. 1353, Type **281** (Mongolian stamp exhibition); 1354, Wurttemberg stamps of 1947 and 1949 and view of Old Stuttgart ("Naposta '81" exhibition); 1355, Parliament building and sculpture, Vienna, and Austrian stamp of 1933 ("WIPA 1981" exhibition); 1356, Japanese stamp of 1964, cherry blossom and girls in Japanese costume ("Japex '81" exhibition, Tokyo).

282 Star and Industrial and Agricultural Scenes

1981. 18th Mongolian Revolutionary People's Party Congress.

No.	Description	Mint	Used
1357	**282** 60m. multicoloured	30	10

284 Sheep Farming

1981. "Results of the People's Economy". Multicoloured.

No.	Description	Mint	Used
1359	20m. Type **284**	10	10
1360	30m. Transport	1·25	15
1361	40m. Telecommunications	60	15
1362	50m. Public health service	20	10
1363	60m. Agriculture	30	10
1364	80m. Electrical industry	35	15
1365	1t.20 Housing	50	20

286 Pharaonic Ship (15th century B.C.)

1981. Sailing Ships. Multicoloured.

No.	Description	Mint	Used
1367	10m. Type **286**	15	10
1368	20m. Mediterranean sailing ship (9th century)	20	10
1369	40m. Hanse kogge (12th century) (vert)	30	10
1370	50m. Venetian felucca (13th century) (vert)	40	15
1371	60m. Columbus's "Santa Maria" (vert)	45	25
1372	80m. Cook's H.M.S. "Endeavour" (vert)	50	30
1373	1t. "Poltava" (Russian ship of the line) (vert)	70	35
1374	1t.20 American schooner (19th century) (vert)	80	40

287 Arms of Mongolia and Russia

1981. Soviet–Mongolian Friendship Pact.

No.	Description	Mint	Used
1375	**287** 60m. red, blue and gold	35	10

288 "Hendrickje in Bed"

1981. 375th Birth Anniv of Rembrandt (artist). Multicoloured.

No.	Description	Mint	Used
1376	20m. "Flora"	20	10
1377	30m. Type **288**	25	15
1378	40m. "Young Woman with Earrings"	45	20
1379	50m. "Young girl in the Window"	50	25
1380	60m. "Hendrickje like Flora"	60	30
1381	80m. "Saskia with Red Flower"	80	35
1382	1t.20 "The Holy Family with Drape" (detail)	1·10	45

289 Billy Goat (pawn)

1981. Mongolian Chess Pieces. Multicoloured.

No.	Description	Mint	Used
1384	20m. Type **289**	20	10
1385	40m. Horse-drawn cart (rook)	30	15
1386	50m. Camel (bishop)	40	20
1387	60m. Horse (knight)	60	25
1388	80m. Lion (queen)	75	30
1389	1t.20 Man with dog (king)	1·10	40

290 White-tailed Sea Eagle and German 1m. "Zeppelin" Stamp

1981. Air. 50th Anniv of "Graf Zeppelin" Polar Flight. Multicoloured.

No.	Description	Mint	Used
1391	20m. Type **290**	75	25
1392	30m. Arctic fox and German 2m. "Zeppelin" stamp	40	15
1393	40m. Walrus and German 4m. "Zeppelin" stamp	50	15
1394	50m. Polar bear and Russian 30k. "Zeppelin" stamp	60	15
1395	60m. Snowy owl and Russian 35k. "Zeppelin" stamp	1·90	70
1396	80m. Atlantic puffin and Russian 1r. "Zeppelin" stamp	2·25	90
1397	1t.20 Northern sealion and Russian 2r. "Zeppelin" stamp	1·50	30

291 Circus Camel and Circus Building, Ulan Bator

1981. Mongolian Sport and Art. Multicoloured.

No.	Description	Mint	Used
1399	10m. Type **291**	10	10
1400	20m. Horsemen and stadium (National holiday cavalcade)	15	10
1401	40m. Wrestling and Ulan Bator stadium	25	15
1402	50m. Archers and stadium	35	20
1403	60m. Folk singer-dancer and House of Culture	45	20
1404	80m. Girl playing jatga (folk instrument) and Ulan Bator Drama Theatre	60	30
1405	1t. Ballet dancers and Opera House	90	40
1406	1t.20 Exhibition Hall and statue of man on bucking horse	1·10	65

292 Mozart and scene from "The Magic Flute"

1981. Composers. Multicoloured.

No.	Description	Mint	Used
1407	20m. Type **292**	15	10
1408	30m. Beethoven and scene from "Fidelio"	20	10
1409	40m. Bartok and scene from "The Miraculous Mandarin"	20	10
1410	50m. Verdi and scene from "Aida"	30	15
1411	60m. Tchaikovsky and scene from "The Sleeping Beauty"	35	15

1412 80m. Dvorak and score of "New World" symphony 45 25
1413 1t.20 Chopin, piano, score and quill pens 60 30

293 "Mongolian Women in Everyday Life" (detail, Davaakhuu)

294 Gorbatko

1981. International Decade for Women. Mult.

1414 20m. Type **293** 25 10
1415 30m. "Mongolian Women in Everyday Life" (different detail) 35 15
1416 40m. "National Day" (detail, Khishigbaiar) 40 20
1417 50m. "National Day" (detail) (different) 50 25
1418 60m. "National Day" (detail) (different) 60 35
1419 80m. "Ribbon Weaver" (Ts. Baidi) 85 40
1420 1t.20 "Expectant Mother" (Senghesokhio) 1·25 65

1981. "Intercosmos" Space Programme. Mult.

1422 50m. Type **294** 15 10
1423 50m. Vietnam stamp showing Gorbatko and Pham Tuan 15 10
1424 50m. Romanenko 15 10
1425 50m. Cuban stamp showing Tamayo 15 10
1426 50m. Dzhanibekov 15 10
1427 50m. Mongolian stamp showing Dzhanibekov and Gurrugchaa 15 10
1428 50m. Popov 15 10
1429 50m. Rumanian stamp showing "Salyut" space station and "Soyuz" space ship 15 10

295 Karl von Drais Bicycle, 1816

1982. History of the Bicycle. Multicoloured.

1430 10m. Type **295** 10 10
1431 20m. Macmillan bicycle, 1838 10 10
1432 40m. First American pedal bicycle by Pierre Lallament, 1866 15 10
1433 50m. First European pedal bicycle by Ernest Michaux 20 10
1434 60m. "Kangaroo" bicycle, 1877 20 10
1435 80m. Coventry Rotary Tandem, 1870s 30 10
1436 1t. Chain-driven bicycle, 1878 35 15
1437 1t.20 Modern bicycle 40 20

296 Footballers (Brazil, 1950)

1982. World Cup Football Championship, Spain. Multicoloured.

1439 10m. Type **296** 10 10
1440 20m. Switzerland, 1954 10 10
1441 40m. Sweden, 1958 15 10
1442 50m. Chile, 1962 20 10
1443 60m. England, 1966 20 10
1444 80m. Mexico, 1970 30 10
1445 1t. West Germany, 1974 35 15
1446 1t.20 Argentina, 1978 40 20

297 Trade Union Emblem and Economic Symbols

299 Dimitrov

1982. 12th Mongolian Trade Unions Congress.

1448 **297** 60m. multicoloured 1·00 30

1982. Birth Centenary of Georgi Dimitrov (Bulgarian statesman).

1450 **299** 60m. black, grey and gold 35 10

300 Chicks

1982. Young Animals. Multicoloured.

1451 10m. Type **300** 10 10
1452 20m. Colt 10 10
1453 30m. Lamb 15 10
1454 40m. Roe deer fawn 20 10
1455 50m. Bactrian camel 20 10
1456 60m. Kid 25 10
1457 70m. Calf 30 15
1458 1t.20 Wild piglet 40 20

301 Coal-fired Industry

1982. Coal Mining.

1459 **301** 60m. multicoloured 35 10

302 Emblem

304 Revsomol Emblem within "Flower"

303 Siberian Pine

1982. 18th Revsomol Youth Congress.

1460 **302** 60m. multicoloured 35 10

1982. Trees. Multicoloured.

1461 20m. Type **303** 10 10
1462 30m. Siberian fir 10 10
1463 40m. Poplar 20 10
1464 50m. Siberian larch 20 10
1465 60m. Scots pine 25 10
1466 80m. Birch 30 15
1467 1t.20 Spruce 50 25

1982. 60th Anniv of Revsomol Youth Organization.

1468 **304** 60m. multicoloured 35 10

305 World Map and Satellite

1982. Air. I.T.U. Delegates' Conference, Nairobi.

1469 **305** 60m. multicoloured 45 15

306 Japanese "Iseki-6500" Tractor

1982. Tractors. Multicoloured.

1470 10m. Type **306** 10 10
1471 20m. West German "Deutz-DX230" 10 10
1472 40m. British "Bonser" 15 10
1473 50m. American "International-884" 20 10
1474 60m. French Renault "TX 145-14" 20 10
1475 80m. Russian "Belarus-611" 25 10
1476 1t. Russian "K-7100" 30 15
1477 1t.20 Russian "DT-75" 40 20

307 Hump-backed Whitefish and Lake Hevsgel

1982. Landscapes and Animals. Multicoloured.

1478 20m. Type **307** 50 15
1479 30m. Zavkhan Highlands and sheep 30 10
1480 40m. Lake Hovd and Eurasian beaver 40 10
1481 50m. Lake Uvs and horses 50 15
1482 60m. Bajankhongor Steppe and goitred gazelle 60 20
1483 80m. Bajan-Elgii Highlands and rider with golden eagle 65 20
1484 1t.20 Gobi Desert and bactrian camels 1·00 50

308 "Sputnik 1"

1982. Air. Second U.N. Conference on the Exploration and Peaceful Uses of Outer Space. Multicoloured.

1485 60m. Type **308** 15 10
1486 60m. "Sputnik 2" and Laika (first dog in space) 15 10
1487 60m. "Vostok 1" and Yuri Gagarin (first man in space) 15 10
1488 60m. "Venera 8" 15 10
1489 60m. "Vostok 6" and V. Tereshkova (first woman in space) 15 10
1490 60m. Aleksei Leonov and space walker 15 10
1491 60m. Neil Armstrong and astronaut on Moon's surface 15 10
1492 60m. V. Dzhanibekov, Jean-Loup Chretien and "Soyuz T-6" 15 10

309 Montgolfier Brothers' Balloon, 1783

1982. Air. Bicentenary of Manned Flight. Mult.

1494 20m. Type **309** 10 10
1495 30m. Jean-Pierre Blanchard and John Jeffries crossing the channel, 1785 15 10
1496 40m. Charles Green's flight to Germany in balloon "Royal Vauxhall", 1836 20 10
1497 50m. Salomon Andree's North Pole flight in balloon "Ornen", 1897 25 10
1498 60m. First Gordon Bennett balloon race, Paris, 1906 30 15
1499 80m. First stratosphere flight by Auguste Piccard in balloon "F.N.R.S.", Switzerland, 1931 40 20
1500 1t.20 Stratosphere balloon USSR-VR-62 flight, 1933 55 25

310 Sorcerer tells Mickey Mouse to clean up Quarters

1983. Drawings from "The Sorcerer's Apprentice" (section of Walt Disney's film "Fantasia"). Mult.

1502 25m. Type **310** 20 10
1503 35m. Mickey notices Sorcerer has left his cap behind 30 15
1504 45m. Mickey puts cap on and commands broom to fetch water 35 20
1505 55m. Broom carrying water 40 25
1506 65m. Mickey sleeps while broom continues to fetch water, flooding the room 50 30
1507 75m. Mickey uses axe on broom to try to stop it 55 35
1508 85m. Each splinter becomes a broom which continues to fetch water 65 40
1509 1t.40 Mickey, clinging to Sorcerer's Book of Spells, caught in whirlpool 1·00 55
1510 2t. Mickey handing cap back to Sorcerer 1·40 75

311 Foal with Mother

1983. "The Foal and the Hare" (folk tale). Mult.

1512 10m. Type **311** 10 10
1513 20m. Foal wanders off alone 15 10
1514 30m. Foal finds sack 25 15
1515 40m. Foal unties sack 30 15
1516 50m. Wolf jumps out of sack 40 20
1517 60m. Hare appears as wolf is about to eat foal 45 25
1518 70m. Hare tricks wolf into re-entering sack 50 30
1519 80m. Hare ties up sack with wolf inside 60 35
1520 1t.20 Hare and foal look for foal's mother 90 50

312 Antonov An-24B Aircraft

1983. Tourism. Multicoloured.
1524 20m. Type **312** 20 10
1525 30m. Skin tent 10 10
1526 40m. Roe deer 15 10
1527 50m. Argali 25 10
1528 60m. Imperial eagle 85 40
1529 80m. Khan Museum, Ulan Bator 40 20
1530 1t.20 Sukhe Bator statue, Ulan Bator 55 25

313 Rose

1983. Flowers. Multicoloured.
1531 20m. Type **313** 10 10
1532 30m. Dahlia 15 10
1533 40m. Marigold 20 10
1534 50m. Narcissus 25 10
1535 60m. Viola 30 10
1536 80m. Tulip 40 15
1537 1t.20 Sunflower 50 25

314 Border Guard

1983. 50th Anniv of Border Guards.
1538 **314** 60m. multicoloured 40 10

316 Karl Marx

1983. Death Centenary of Karl Marx.
1540 **316** 60m. red, gold and blue 35 10

317 Agriculture

1983. 18th Communist Party Congress Five Year Plan. Multicoloured.
1541 10m. Type **317** 10 10
1542 20m. Power industry 10 10
1543 30m. Textile industry 10 10
1544 40m. Science in industry and agriculture 15 10
1545 60m. Improvement of living standards 20 10
1546 80m. Communications 2·00 50
1547 1t. Children (education) 40 20

318 Young Inventors

1983. Children's Year. Multicoloured.
1548 10m. Type **318** 15 10
1549 20m. In school 25 10
1550 30m. Archery 40 15
1551 40m. Shepherdess playing flute 50 20
1552 50m. Girl with deer 65 30
1553 70m. Collecting rocks and mushrooms 2·25 50
1554 1t.20 Girl playing lute and boy singing 1·25 60

319 Skating

1983. 10th Anniv of Children's Fund. Mult.
1555 20m. Type **319** 10 10
1556 30m. Shepherds 10 10
1557 40m. Tree-planting 15 10
1558 50m. Playing by the sea 20 10
1559 60m. Carrying water 25 15
1560 80m. Folk dancing 30 20
1561 1t.20 Ballet 55 25

320 Pallas's Pika

1983. Small Mammals. Multicoloured.
1563 20m. Type **320** 35 20
1564 30m. Long-eared jerboa 45 25
1565 40m. Eurasian red squirrel 55 30
1566 50m. Daurian hedgehog 65 40
1567 60m. Harvest mouse 80 45
1568 80m. Eurasian water shrew 1·25 70
1569 1t.20 Siberian chipmunk 1·75 95

322 Bobsleighing

1984. Winter Olympic Games, Sarajevo. Mult.
1571 20m. Type **322** 10 10
1572 30m. Cross-country skiing 10 10
1573 40m. Ice hockey 10 10
1574 50m. Speed skating 15 10
1575 60m. Ski jumping 15 10
1576 80m. Ice dancing 20 15
1577 1t.20 Biathlon (horiz) 35 25

323 Mail Van

1984. World Communications Year. Multicoloured.
1579 10m. Type **323** 10 10
1580 20m. Earth receiving station 10 10
1581 40m. Airliner 40 15
1582 50m. Central Post Office, Ulan Bator 25 10
1583 1t. Transmitter 40 15
1584 1t.20 Diesel train 3·50 1·25

325 Cycling

326 Flag, Rocket and Coastal Scene

1984. Olympic Games, Los Angeles. Multicoloured.
1587 20m. Gymnastics (horiz) 10 10
1588 30m. Type **325** 10 10
1589 40m. Weightlifting 10 10
1590 50m. Judo 10 10
1591 60m. Archery 15 10
1592 80m. Boxing 20 15
1593 1t.20 High jumping (horiz) 35 25

1984. 25th Anniv of Cuban Revolution.
1595 **326** 60m. multicoloured 25 10

328 Douglas DC-10

329 Speaker, Radio and Transmitter

1984. Air. Civil Aviation. Multicoloured.
1597 20m. Type **328** 10 10
1598 30m. Airbus Industrie A300B2 20 10
1599 40m. Concorde supersonic jetliner 25 10
1600 50m. Boeing 747-200 30 15
1601 60m. Ilyushin Il-62M 30 20
1602 80m. Tupolev Tu-154 50 25
1603 1t.20 Ilyushin Il-86 60 35

1984. 50th Anniv of Mongolian Broadcasting.
1605 **329** 60m. multicoloured 60 20

330 Silver and Gold Coins

1984. 60th Anniv of State Bank.
1606 **330** 60m. multicoloured 25 10

331 Donshy Mask

333 Sukhe Bator Statue

332 Golden Harp

1984. Traditional Masks. Multicoloured.
1607 20m. Type **331** 10 10
1608 30m. Zamandi 25 10
1609 40m. Ulaan-Yadam 30 10
1610 50m. Lkham 45 15
1611 60m. Damdinchoizhoo 55 20
1612 80m. Ochirvaan 75 25
1613 1t.20 Namsrai 1·25 40

1984. Scenes from Walt Disney's "Mickey and the Beanstalk" (cartoon film). Multicoloured.
1615 25m. Type **332** 20 10
1616 35m. Mickey holding box of magic beans 30 15
1617 45m. Mickey about to eat bean 40 20
1618 55m. Mickey looking for magic bean 50 25
1619 65m. Goofy, Mickey and Donald at top of beanstalk 55 30
1620 75m. Giant holding Mickey 60 35
1621 85m. Giant threatening Mickey 80 40
1622 140m. Goofy, Mickey and Donald cutting down beanstalk 1·40 65
1623 2t. Goofy and Donald rescuing golden harp 1·60 75

1984. 60th Anniv of Ulan Bator City.
1625 **333** 60m. multicoloured 60 20

334 Arms, Flag and Landscape

335 Rider carrying Flag

1984. 60th Anniv of Mongolian People's Republic.
1626 **334** 60m. multicoloured 60 20

1984. 60th Anniv of Mongolian People's Revolutionary Party.
1627 **335** 60m. multicoloured 35 10

336 Collie

1984. Dogs. Multicoloured.
1628 20m. Type **336** 10 10
1629 30m. German shepherd 25 10
1630 40m. Papillon 35 10
1631 50m. Cocker spaniel 50 15
1632 60m. Terrier puppy (diamond-shaped) 60 20
1633 80m. Dalmatians (diamond-shaped) 75 25
1634 1t.20 Mongolian shepherd 1·25 40

337 Gaetan Boucher (speed skating)

1984. Winter Olympic Gold Medal Winners. Multicoloured.
1635 20m. Type **337** 10 10
1636 30m. Eirik Kvalfoss (biathlon) 10 10
1637 40m. Marja-Liisa Hamalainen (cross-country skiing) 10 10
1638 50m. Max Julen (slalom) 15 10
1639 60m. Jens Weissflog (ski jumping) (vert) 15 10
1640 80m. W. Hoppe and D. Schauerhammer (two-man bobsleigh) (vert) 20 15
1641 1t.20 J. Valova and O. Vassiliev (pairs figure skating) (vert) 35 25

338 Four Animals and Tree

1984. "The Four Friendly Animals" (fairy tale). Multicoloured.

No.	Description		
1643	10m. Type **338**	15	10
1644	20m. Animals discussing who was the oldest	20	10
1645	30m. Monkey and elephant beside tree	20	10
1646	40m. Elephant as calf and young tree	25	10
1647	50m. Monkey and young tree	40	15
1648	60m. Hare and young tree	50	20
1649	70m. Dove and sapling	55	20
1650	80m. Animals around mature tree	70	30
1651	1t.20 Animals supporting each other so that dove could reach fruit	95	40

339 Fawn

1984. Red Deer. Multicoloured.

No.	Description		
1653	50m. Type **339**	40	20
1654	50m. Stag	40	20
1655	50m. Adults and fawn by river	40	20
1656	50m. Doe in woodland	40	20

340 Flag and Pioneers **342** Black Stork

341 Shar Tarlan

1985. 60th Anniv of Mongolian Pioneer Organization.

No.	Description		
1657	**340** 60m. multicoloured	40	15

1985. Cattle. Multicoloured.

No.	Description		
1658	20m. Type **341**	10	10
1659	30m. Bor khalium	20	10
1660	40m. Sarlag	30	10
1661	50m. Dornod talin bukh	45	15
1662	60m. Char tarlan	55	20
1663	80m. Nutgiin uulderiin unee	65	20
1664	1t.20 Tsagaan tolgoit	1·10	35

1985. Birds. Multicoloured.

No.	Description		
1666	20m. Type **342**	30	45
1667	30m. White-tailed sea eagle	40	45
1668	40m. Great white crane	55	45
1669	50m. Heude's parrotbill	85	90
1670	60m. Hooded crane	1·00	90
1671	80m. Japanese white-naped crane	1·25	1·25
1672	1t.20 Rough-legged buzzard	2·10	2·25

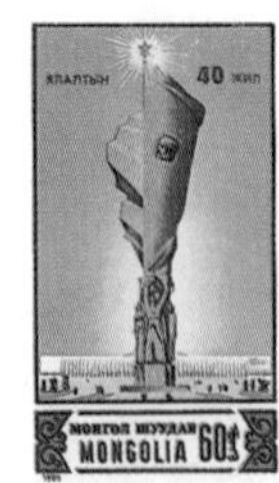

343 Footballers **344** Monument

1985. World Junior Football Championship, U.S.S.R.

No.	Description		
1674	**343** 20m. multicoloured	10	10
1675	– 30m. multicoloured	10	10
1676	– 40m. multicoloured	15	10
1677	– 50m. multicoloured	20	10
1678	– 60m. multicoloured	25	10
1679	– 80m. multicoloured	30	15
1680	– 1t.20 multicoloured	50	25

DESIGNS: 30m. to 1t.20, Different footballing scenes.

1985. 40th Anniv of Victory in Europe.

No.	Description		
1682	**344** 60m. multicoloured	30	10

345 Snow Leopards

1985. The Snow Leopard. Multicoloured.

No.	Description		
1683	50m. Type **345**	40	20
1684	50m. Leopard	40	20
1685	50m. Leopard on cliff ledge	40	20
1686	50m. Mother and cubs	40	20

346 Moscow Kremlin and Girls of Different Races **347** Monument

1985. 12th World Youth and Students' Festival, Moscow.

No.	Description		
1687	**346** 60m. multicoloured	30	10

1985. 40th Anniv of Victory in Asia.

No.	Description		
1688	**347** 60m. multicoloured	35	10

348 "Rosa dahurica"

1985. Plants. Multicoloured.

No.	Description		
1689	20m. Type **348**	10	10
1690	30m. False chamomile	20	10
1691	40m. Dandelion	30	10
1692	50m. "Saxzitraga nirculus"	45	15
1693	60m. Cowberry	55	20
1694	80m. "Sanguisorba officinalis"	65	20
1695	1t.20 "Plantago major"	1·10	35

See also Nos. 1719/25.

349 Camel

1985. The Bactrian Camel. Multicoloured.

No.	Description		
1697	50m. Type **349**	40	20
1698	50m. Adults and calf	40	20
1699	50m. Calf	40	20
1700	50m. Adult	40	20

350 "Soyuz" Spacecraft

1985. Space. Multicoloured.

No.	Description		
1701	20m. Type **350**	10	10
1702	30m. "Kosmos" satellite	10	10
1703	40m. "Venera-9" satellite	10	10
1704	50m. "Salyut" space station	15	10
1705	60m. "Luna-9" landing vehicle	15	10
1706	80m. "Soyuz" rocket on transporter	1·10	50
1707	1t.20 Dish aerial receiving transmission from "Soyuz"	30	15

352 U.N. and Mongolian Flags and U.N. Headquarters, New York **354** Congress Emblem

353 "Tricholoma mongolica"

1985. 40th Anniv of U.N.O.

No.	Description		
1710	**352** 60m. multicoloured	30	10

1985. Fungi. Multicoloured.

No.	Description		
1711	20m. Type **353**	20	10
1712	30m. Chanterelle	25	10
1713	40m. Honey fungus	30	10
1714	50m. Caesar's mushroom	55	15
1715	70m. Chestnut mushroom	80	20
1716	80m. Red-staining mushroom	90	25
1717	1t.20 Cep	1·40	35

1986. 19th Mongolian Revolutionary People's Party Congress.

No.	Description		
1718	**354** 60m. multicoloured	25	10

1986. Plants. As T **348**. Multicoloured.

No.	Description		
1719	20m. "Valeriana officinalis"	10	10
1720	30m. "Hyoscymus niger"	20	10
1721	40m. "Ephedra sinica"	30	10
1722	50m. "Thymus gobica"	45	15
1723	60m. "Paeonia anomalia"	55	20
1724	80m. "Achilea millefolium"	65	25
1725	1t.20 "Rhododendron adamsii"	1·10	35

355 Scene from Play

1986. 80th Birth Anniv of D. Natsagdorj (writer).

No.	Description		
1726	**355** 60m. multicoloured	25	10

356 Thalmann **357** Man wearing Patterned Robe

1986. Birth Centenary of Ernst Thalmann (German politician).

No.	Description		
1727	**356** 60m. multicoloured	25	10

1986. Costumes. Multicoloured.

No.	Description		
1728	60m. Type **357**	25	10
1729	60m. Man in blue robe and fur-lined hat with ear flaps	25	10
1730	60m. Woman in black and yellow dress and bolero	25	10
1731	60m. Woman in pink dress patterned with stars	25	10
1732	60m. Man in cream robe with fur cuffs	25	10
1733	60m. Man in brown robe and mauve and yellow tunic	25	10
1734	60m. Woman in blue dress with black, yellow and red overtunic	25	10

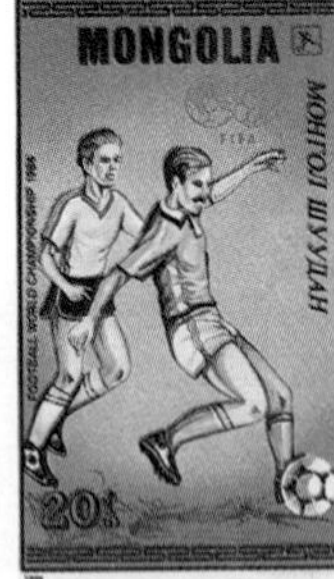

358 Footballers

1986. World Cup Football Championship, Mexico.

No.	Description		
1735	**358** 20m. multicoloured	10	10
1736	– 30m. multicoloured	10	10
1737	– 40m. multicoloured	10	10
1738	– 50m. multicoloured	15	10
1739	– 60m. multicoloured	15	10
1740	– 80m. multicoloured	20	15
1741	– 1t.20 multicoloured	35	25

DESIGNS: 30m. to 1t.20, Different footballing scenes.

359 Mink

1986. Mink. Multicoloured.

No.	Description		
1743	60m. Type **359**	45	15
1744	60m. Mink on rock	45	15
1745	60m. Mink on snow-covered branch	45	15
1746	60m. Two mink	45	15

See also Nos. 1771/4, 1800/3, 1804/7, 1840/3 and 1844/7.

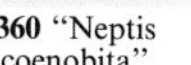

360 "Neptis coenobita" **361** Sukhe Bator Statue

1986. Butterflies and Moths. Multicoloured.

1747	20m. Type **360**	10	10
1748	30m. "Colias tycha"	15	10
1749	40m. "Leptidea amurensis"	20	10
1750	50m. "Oeneis tarpenledevi"	30	15
1751	60m. "Mesoacidalia charlotta"	40	20
1752	80m. Eyed hawk moth	45	25
1753	1t.20 Large tiger moth	75	40

1986. 65th Anniv of Independence.

1754	**361** 60m. multicoloured	25	10

362 Yak and Goats Act

1986. Circus. Multicoloured.

1755	20m. Type **362**	10	10
1756	30m. Acrobat	10	10
1757	40m. Yak act	15	10
1758	50m. Acrobats (vert)	20	10
1759	60m. High wire act (vert)	25	15
1760	80m. Fire juggler on camel (vert)	30	15
1761	1t.20 Acrobats on camel-drawn cart (vert)	50	25

363 Morin Khuur **364** Flag and Emblem

1986. Musical Instruments. Multicoloured.

1762	20m. Type **363**	10	10
1763	30m. Bishguur (wind instrument)	20	10
1764	40m. Ever buree (wind)	30	10
1765	50m. Shudarga (string)	45	15
1766	60m. Khiil (string)	55	20
1767	80m. Janchir (string) (horiz)	65	25
1768	1t.20 Jatga (string) (horiz)	1·10	35

1986. International Peace Year.

1770	**364** 10m. multicoloured	50	20

1986. Przewalski's Horse. As T **359**. Mult.

1771	50m. Horses grazing on sparsely grassed plain	45	15
1772	50m. Horses grazing on grassy plain	45	15
1773	50m. Adults with foal	45	15
1774	50m. Horses in snow	45	15

365 Temple

1986. Ancient Buildings. Multicoloured.

1775	60m. Type **365**	60	20
1776	60m. Temple with light green roof and white doors	60	20
1777	60m. Temple with porch	60	20
1778	60m. White building with three porches	60	20

366 Redhead ("Aythya americana")

1986. Birds. Multicoloured.

1779	60m. Type **366**	85	55
1780	60m. Ruffed grouse ("Bonasa umbellus")	85	55
1781	60m. Tundra swan ("Olor columbianus")	85	55
1782	60m. Water pipit ("Anthus spinoletta")	85	55

367 Alfa Romeo "RL Sport", 1922

1986. Cars. Multicoloured.

1783	20m. Type **367**	10	10
1784	30m. Stutz "Bearcat", 1912	15	10
1785	40m. Mercedes "Simplex", 1902	20	10
1786	50m. Tatra "11", 1923	25	10
1787	60m. Ford Model "T", 1908	30	15
1788	80m. Vauxhall, 1905	40	20
1789	1t.20 Russo-Balt "K", 1913	60	30

368 Wilhelm Steinitz and Curt von Bardeleben Game, 1895

1986. World Chess Champions. Multicoloured.

1791	20m. Type **368**	10	10
1792	30m. Emanuel Lasker and Harry Pilsberi game, 1895	15	10
1793	40m. Alexander Alekhine and Richard Retti game, 1925	20	10
1794	50m. Mikhail Botvinnik and Capablanca game, 1938	25	10
1795	60m. Anatoly Karpov and Wolfgang Untsiker game, 1975	30	15
1796	80m. Nona Gaprindashvili and Lasarevich game, 1961	40	20
1797	1t.20 Maia Chirburdanidze and Irina Levitina game, 1984	60	30

1986. Saiga Antelope. As T **359**. Multicoloured.

1800	60m. Male	45	15
1801	60m. Female with calf	45	15
1802	60m. Male and female	45	15
1803	60m. Male and female in snow	45	15

1986. Pelicans. As T **359**. Multicoloured.

1804	60m. Dalmatian pelican ("Pelecanus crispus")	1·10	55
1805	60m. Dalmatian pelican preening	1·10	55
1806	60m. Eastern white pelican ("Pelecanus onocrotalus")	1·10	55
1807	60m. Eastern white pelicans in flight	1·10	55

370 Siamese Fighting Fish

1987. Aquarium Fishes. Multicoloured.

1808	20m. Type **370**	10	10
1809	30m. Goldfish	15	10
1810	40m. Glowlight rasbora	25	10
1811	50m. Acara	35	10
1812	60m. Platy	40	15
1813	80m. Green swordtail	55	20
1814	1t.20 Freshwater angelfish (vert)	95	30

371 Lassoing Horse

1987. Traditional Equestrian Sports. Mult.

1816	20m. Type **371**	10	10
1817	30m. Breaking horse	15	10
1818	40m. Mounted archer	20	10
1819	50m. Race	25	10
1820	60m. Horseman snatching flag from ground	35	15
1821	80m. Tug of war	40	20
1822	1t.20 Racing wolf	70	25

372 Grey-headed Woodpecker **373** Butterfly Hunting

1987. Woodpeckers. Multicoloured.

1823	20m. Type **372**	30	20
1824	30m. Wryneck	45	25
1825	40m. Great spotted woodpecker	75	25
1826	50m. White-backed woodpecker	1·10	35
1827	60m. Lesser spotted woodpecker	1·25	35
1828	80m. Black woodpecker	1·75	50
1829	1t.20 Three-toed woodpecker	3·25	85

1987. Children's Activities. Multicoloured.

1831	20m. Type **373**	10	10
1832	30m. Feeding calves	10	10
1833	40m. Drawing on ground in chalk	15	10
1834	50m. Football	20	10
1835	60m. Go-carting	25	15
1836	80m. Growing vegetables	30	15
1837	1t.20 Playing string instrument	45	25

374 Industry and Agriculture

1987. 13th Congress and 60th Anniv of Mongolian Trade Union.

1838	**374** 60m. multicoloured	1·00	30

375 Women in Traditional Costume **376** Flags of Member Countries

1987. 40th Anniv of Mongol–Soviet Friendship.

1839	**375** 60m. multicoloured	40	10

1987. Argali. As T **359**. Multicoloured.

1840	60m. On grassy rock (full face)	45	15
1841	60m. On rock (three-quarter face)	45	15
1842	60m. Family	45	15
1843	60m. Close-up of head and upper body	45	15

1987. Swans. As T **359**. Multicoloured.

1844	60m. Mute Swan ("Cygnus olor") in water	85	55
1845	60m. Mute swan on land	85	55
1846	60m. Tundra swan ("Cygnus bewickii")	85	55
1847	60m. Tundra swan, ("Cygnus gunus") and mute swan	85	55

1987. 25th Anniv of Membership of Council for Mutual Economic Aid.

1848	**376** 60m. multicoloured	35	10

377 Sea Buckthorn **378** Couple in Traditional Costume

1987. Fruits. Multicoloured.

1849	20m. Type **377**	10	10
1850	30m. Blackcurrants	10	10
1851	40m. Redcurrants	15	10
1852	50m. Redcurrants	20	10
1853	60m. Raspberries	25	15
1854	80m. "Padus asiatica"	30	15
1855	1t.20 Strawberries	45	25

1987. Folk Art. Multicoloured.

1857	20m. Type **378**	10	10
1858	30m. Gold-inlaid baton and pouch	15	10
1859	40m. Gold and jewelled ornaments	20	10
1860	50m. Bag and dish	30	10
1861	60m. Earrings	35	15
1862	80m. Pipe, pouch and bottle	45	20
1863	1t.20 Decorative headdress	65	25

379 Dancer

1987. Dances.

1864	**379** 20m. multicoloured	10	10
1865	– 30m. multicoloured	15	10
1866	– 40m. multicoloured	20	10
1867	– 50m. multicoloured	30	10
1868	– 60m. multicoloured	35	15
1869	– 80m. multicoloured	45	20
1870	– 1t.20 multicoloured	65	25

DESIGNS: 30m. to 1t.20, Different dances.

381 Scottish Fold

1987. Cats. Multicoloured.

1872	20m. Type **381**	10	10
1873	30m. Grey	15	10
1874	40m. Oriental	20	10
1875	50m. Abyssinian (horiz)	30	10
1876	60m. Manx (horiz)	35	15
1877	80m. Black shorthair (horiz)	45	20
1878	1t.20 Spotted (horiz)	65	25

382 Mil Mi-V12

1987. Helicopters. Multicoloured.

1880	20m. Type **382**	10	10
1881	30m. Westland WG-30	15	10
1882	40m. Bell 206L LongRanger II	20	10
1883	50m. Kawasaki-Hughes 369HS	25	10

1884 60m. Kamov Ka-32 . . . . 30 10
1885 80m. Mil Mi-17 . . . . . 35 15
1886 1t.20 Mil Mi-10K 60 25

383 City Scene

384 Kremlin, Lenin and Revolutionaries

1987. 19th Mongolian People's Revolutionary Party Congress. Multicoloured.
1887 60m. Type **383** 25 10
1888 60m. Clothing and mining industries . . . . 1·00 25
1889 60m. Agriculture 25 10
1890 60m. Family 25 10
1891 60m. Workers, factories and fields 25 10
1892 60m. Building construction 25 10
1893 60m. Scientist 25 10

1987. 70th Anniv of Russian October Revolution.
1894 **384** 60m. multicoloured . . . 35 10

385 Seven with One Blow

1987. Walt Disney Cartoons. Multicoloured (a) "The Brave Little Tailor" (Grimm Brothers).
1895 25m. Type **385** 10 10
1896 35m. Brought before the King 20 10
1897 45m. Rewards for bravery 25 10
1898 55m. Fight between Mickey and the giant 30 15
1899 2t. Happy ending . . . . . 1·00 50

(b) "The Celebrated Jumping Frog of Calaveras County" (Mark Twain).
1901 65m. "He'd bet on anything" 30 15
1902 75m. "He never done nothing but ... learn that frog to jump" 45 20
1903 85m. "What might it be that you've got in that box?" 50 25
1904 1t. "40 He got the frog out and filled him full of quail shot" 80 40

386 Head

1987. The Red Fox. Multicoloured.
1906 60m. Type **386** 45 15
1907 60m. Vixen and cubs . . . 45 15
1908 60m. Stalking 45 15
1909 60m. In the snow 45 15

388 Bobsleighing

389 Sukhe Bator

1988. Air. Winter Olympic Games, Calgary. Mult.
1911 20m. Type **388** 10 10
1912 30m. Ski jumping 10 10
1913 40m. Skiing 15 10
1914 50m. Biathlon 20 10
1915 60m. Speed skating 25 10
1916 80m. Figure skating 30 15
1917 1t.20 Ice hockey 50 25

1988. 95th Birth Anniv of Sukhe Bator.
1919 **389** 60m. multicoloured . . . 40 10

390 "Invitation"

1988. Roses. Multicoloured.
1920 20m. Type **390** 10 10
1921 30m. "Meilland" 10 10
1922 40m. "Pascali" 15 10
1923 50m. "Tropicana" 20 10
1924 60m. "Wendy Cussons" . . 25 10
1925 80m. "Rosa sp. " (wrongly inscr "Blue Moon") . . . 30 15
1926 1t.20 "Diorama" 50 25

391 "Ukhaant Ekhner"

1988. Puppets. Multicoloured.
1928 20m. Type **391** 10 10
1929 30m. "Altan Everte Mungun Turuut" 10 10
1930 40m. "Aduuchyn Khuu" . . 15 10
1931 50m. "Suulenkhuu" 20 10
1932 60m. "Khonchyn Khuu" . . 25 10
1933 80m. "Argat Byatskhan Baatar" 30 15
1934 1t.20 "Botgochyn Khuu" . . 50 25

393 Judo

394 Marx

1988. Olympic Games, Seoul. Multicoloured.
1936 20m. Type **393** 10 10
1937 30m. Archery 10 10
1938 40m. Weightlifting 15 10
1939 50m. Gymnastics 20 10
1940 60m. Cycling 25 10
1941 80m. Running 30 15
1942 1t.20 Wrestling 50 25

1988. 170th Birth Anniv of Karl Marx.
1944 **394** 60m. multicoloured . . . 50 20

395 Couple and Congress Banner

396 "Kosmos"

1988. 19th Revsomol Youth Congress.
1945 **395** 60m. multicoloured . . . 1·00 30

1988. Spacecraft and Satellites. Multicoloured.
1946 20m. Type **396** 10 10
1947 30m. "Meteor" 10 10
1948 40m. "Salyut"–"Soyuz" space complex 10 10
1949 50m. "Prognoz-6" 15 10
1950 60m. "Molniya-1" 15 10
1951 80m. "Soyuz" 20 15
1952 1t.20 "Vostok" 35 20

397 Buddha

398 Emblem

1988. Religious Sculptures.
1954 **397** 20m. multicoloured . . . 10 10
1955 – 30m. multicoloured . . . 10 10
1956 – 40m. multicoloured . . . 20 10
1957 – 50m. multicoloured . . . 25 10
1958 – 60m. multicoloured . . . 30 10
1959 – 70m. multicoloured . . . 35 10
1960 – 80m. multicoloured . . . 40 15
1961 – 1t.20 multicoloured . . . 65 25
DESIGNS: 30m. to 1t.20, Different buddhas.

1988. 30th Anniv of Problems of "Peace and Socialism" (magazine).
1962 **398** 60m. multicoloured . . . 50 10

399 Eagle

1988. White-tailed Sea Eagle. Multicoloured.
1963 60m. Type **399** 90 60
1964 60m. Eagle on fallen branch and eagle landing 90 60
1965 60m. Eagle on rock 90 60
1966 60m. Eagle (horiz) 90 60

400 Ass

1988. Asiatic Wild Ass. Multicoloured.
1967 60m. Type **400** 40 15
1968 60m. Head of ass 40 15
1969 60m. Two adults 40 15
1970 60m. Mare and foal 40 15

401 Athlete

403 U.S.S.R. (ice hockey)

1988. Traditional Sports. Multicoloured.
1971 10m. Type **401** 10 10
1972 20m. Horseman 15 10
1973 30m. Archery 20 10
1974 40m. Wrestling 25 10
1975 50m. Archery (different) . . 35 15
1976 70m. Horsemen (national holiday cavalcade) 60 30
1977 1t.20 Horsemen, wrestlers and archers 95 45

1988. Winter Olympic Games Gold Medal Winners. Multicoloured.
1979 1t.50 Type **403** 30 10
1980 1t.50 Bonnie Blair (speed skating) 30 10
1981 1t.50 Alberto Tomba (slalom) 30 10
1982 1t.50 Matti Nykanen (ski jumping) (horiz) 30 10

404 Brown Goat

1988. Goats. Multicoloured.
1984 20m. Type **404** 10 10
1985 30m. Black goat 10 10
1986 40m. White long-haired goats 15 10
1987 50m. Black long-haired goat 20 10
1988 60m. White goat 25 10
1989 80m. Black short-haired goat 30 15
1990 1t.20 Nanny and kid . . . 50 25

405 Emblem

1989. 60th Anniv of Mongolian Writers' Association.
1992 **405** 60m. multicoloured . . . 40 10

406 Beaver gnawing Trees

1989. Eurasian Beaver. Multicoloured.
1993 60m. Type **406** 40 15
1994 60m. Beaver with young . . 40 15
1995 60m. Beavers beside tree stump and in water . . . 40 15
1996 60m. Beaver rolling log . . 40 15

407 Dancers

1989. Ballet.
1997 **407** 20m. multicoloured . . . 10 10
1998 – 30m. multicoloured . . . 10 10
1999 – 40m. multicoloured (vert) 15 10
2000 – 50m. multicoloured . . . 20 10
2001 – 60m. multicoloured . . . 25 10
2002 – 80m. multicoloured (vert) 30 15
2003 – 1t.20 multicoloured (vert) 50 25
DESIGNS: 30m. to 1t.20, Different dancing scenes.

408 "Ursus pruinosis"

1989. Bears. Multicoloured.
2004 20m. Type **408** 10 10
2005 30m. Brown bear 20 10
2006 40m. Asiatic black bear . . 30 15
2007 50m. Polar bear 40 20
2008 60m. Brown bear 55 25
2009 80m. Giant panda 70 35
2010 1t.20 Brown bear . . . . . 1·10 55

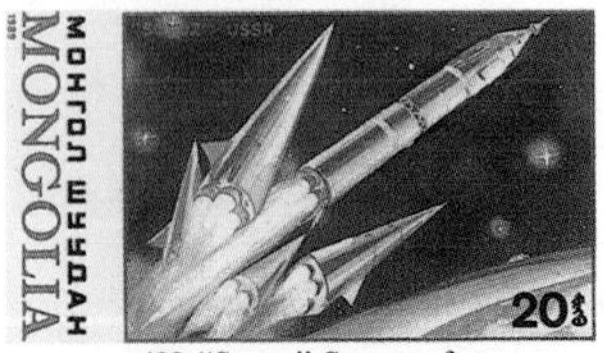

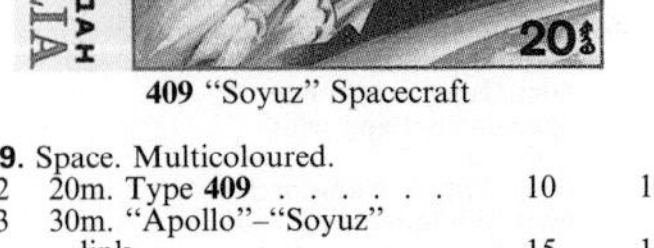

409 "Soyuz" Spacecraft

1989. Space. Multicoloured.
2012 20m. Type **409** 10 10
2013 30m. "Apollo"–"Soyuz" link 15 10

2014 40m. "Columbia" space shuttle (vert) 20 10
2015 50m. "Hermes" spacecraft 30 15
2016 60m. "Nippon" spacecraft (vert) 45 20
2017 80m. "Energy" rocket (vert) 65 30
2018 1t.20 "Buran" space shuttle (vert) 95 45

411 Nehru

412 "Opuntia microdasys"

1989. Birth Centenary of Jawaharial Nehru (Indian statesman).
2021 **411** 10m. multicoloured . . . 50 15

1989. Cacti. Multicoloured.
2022 20m. Type **412** 10 10
2023 30m. "Echinopsis multipiex" 10 10
2024 40m. "Rebutia tephracanthus" 15 10
2025 50m. "Brasilicactus haselbergii" 20 10
2026 60m. "Gymnocalycium mihanovichii" 25 10
2027 80m. "C. strausii" 30 15
2028 1t.20 "Horridocactus tuberisvicatus" 50 25

1989. 800th Anniv of Coronation of Genghis Khan. Nos. 291/4 optd **CHINGGIS KHAN CROWNATION 1189**.
2030 **67** 20m. multicoloured . . . 2·75 2·75
2031 – 30m. multicoloured . . . 4·25 4·25
2032 – 50m. black, brown and red . . . . 6·50 6·50
2033 – 60m. buff, blue and brown . . . . 8·50 8·50

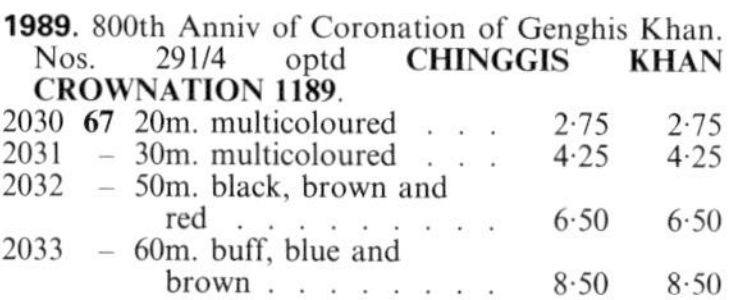

415 Citroen "BX"

1989. Motor Cars. Multicoloured.
2035 20m. Type **415** 10 10
2036 30m. Volvo "760 GLF" . . 10 10
2037 40m. Honda "Civic" 60 25
2038 50m. Volga 20 10
2039 60m. Ford "Granada" . . . 25 10
2040 80m. Baz "21099" 30 15
2041 1t.20 Mercedes "190" . . . 50 20

416 Monument

417 Florence Griffith-Joyner (running)

1989. 50th Anniv of Battle of Khalka River.
2043 **416** 60m. multicoloured . . . 55 15

1989. Olympic Games Medal Winners. Mult.
2044 60m. Type **417** (wrongly inscr "Joyner-Griffith") 25 10
2045 60m. Stefano Cerioni (fencing) 25 10
2046 60m. Gintautas Umaras (cycling) 25 10
2047 60m. Kristin Otto (swimming) 25 10

418 "Malchin Zaluus" (N. Sandagsuren)

1989. 30th Anniv of Co-operative Movement. Paintings. Multicoloured.
2049 20m. Type **418** 10 10
2050 30m. "Tsaatny Tukhai Dursamkh" (N. Sandagsuren) (vert) 20 10
2051 40m. "Uul Shig Tushigtei" (D. Amgalan) 30 15
2052 50m. "Goviin Egshig" (D. Amgalan) 40 20
2053 60m. "Tsagaan Sar" (Ts. Dagvanyam) 55 25
2054 80m. "Tumen Aduuny Bayar" (M. Butemkh) (vert) 65 30
2055 1t.20 "Bilcheer Deer" (N. Tsultem) . . . . . . 1·10 50

419 Four-man Bobsleighing

420 Victory Medal

1989. Ice Sports. Multicoloured.
2057 20m. Type **419** 10 10
2058 30m. Luge 10 10
2059 40m. Figure skating 15 10
2060 50m. Two-man bobsleighing 20 10
2061 60m. Ice dancing 25 10
2062 80m. Speed skating 30 15
2063 1t.20 Ice speedway 50 25

1989. Orders. Designs showing different badges and medals. Multicoloured, background colour given.
2065 **420** 60m. blue 25 10
2066 – 60m. orange 25 10
2067 – 60m. mauve 25 10
2068 – 60m. violet 25 10
2069 – 60m. green 25 10
2070 – 60m. blue 25 10
2071 – 60m. red 25 10

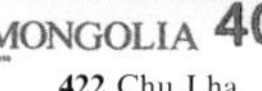

422 Chu Lha

423 Sukhe Bator Statue

1989. Buddhas. Multicoloured.
2073 20m. Damdin Sandub . . . 10 10
2074 30m. Pagwa Lama 20 10
2075 40m. Type **422** 30 15
2076 50m. Agwanglobsan 40 20
2077 60m. Dorje Dags Dan . . . 55 25
2078 80m. Wangchikdorje 65 30
2079 1t.20 Buddha . . . . 1·10 50

1990. New Year.
2081 **423** 10m. multicoloured . . . 75 35

424 Newspapers and City

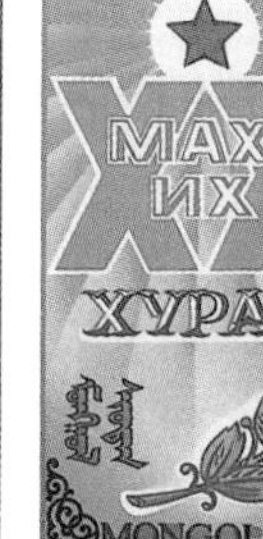

425 Emblem

1990. 70th Anniv of "Khuvisgalt Khevlel" (newspaper).
2082 **424** 60m. multicoloured . . . 65 30

1990. 20th Mongolian People's Revolutionary Party Congress.
2083 **425** 60m. multicoloured . . . 50 25

426 Male Character

1990. "Mandukhai the Wise" (film).
2084 **426** 20m. multicoloured . . . 20 10
2085 – 30m. multicoloured . . . 30 15
2086 – 40m. multicoloured . . . 45 20
2087 – 50m. multicoloured . . . 55 30
2088 – 60m. multicoloured . . . 75 35
2089 – 80m. multicoloured . . . 90 45
2090 – 1t.20 multicoloured . . . 1·25 65
DESIGNS: 30m. to 1t.20, Different characters from the film.

427 Trophy and Players

1990. World Cup Football Championship, Italy.
2092 **427** 20m. multicoloured . . . 10 10
2093 – 30m. multicoloured . . . 10 10
2094 – 40m. multicoloured . . . 10 10
2095 – 50m. multicoloured . . . 15 10
2096 – 60m. multicoloured . . . 15 10
2097 – 80m. multicoloured . . . 20 10
2098 – 1t.20 multicoloured . . . 35 20
DESIGNS: 30m. to 1t.20, Trophy and different players.

428 Lenin

1990. 120th Birth Anniv of Lenin.
2100 **428** 60m. black, red and gold 65 30

429 Mother with Fawn

1990. Siberian Musk Deer. Multicoloured.
2101 60m. Type **429** 65 30
2102 60m. Deer in wood 65 30
2103 60m. Deer on river bank . . 65 30
2104 60m. Deer in winter landscape 65 30

433 Russian Victory Medal

434 Crane

1990. 45th Anniv of End of Second World War.
2108 **433** 60m. multicoloured . . . 65 30

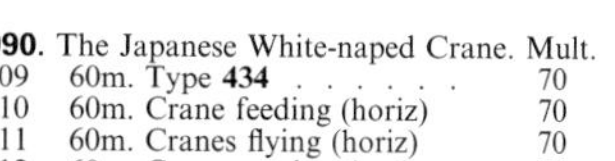

1990. The Japanese White-naped Crane. Mult.
2109 60m. Type **434** 70 70
2110 60m. Crane feeding (horiz) 70 70
2111 60m. Cranes flying (horiz) 70 70
2112 60m. Crane on river bank 70 70

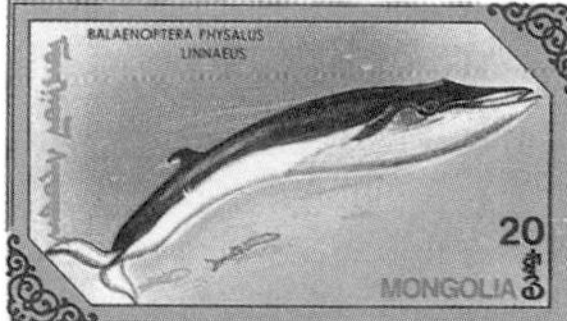

435 Fin Whale

1990. Marine Mammals. Multicoloured.
2113 20m. Type **435** 15 10
2114 30m. Humpback whale . . 30 15
2115 40m. Narwhal 40 20
2116 50m. Risso's dolphin . . . 50 25
2117 60m. Bottle-nosed dolphin 60 30
2118 80m. Atlantic white-sided dolphin 85 40
2119 1t.20 Bowhead whale . . . 1·10 55

436 Weapons and Black Standard

437 Panda

1990. 750th Anniv of "Secret History of the Mongols" (book). Multicoloured.
2121 10m. Type **436** 10 10
2122 10m. Weapons and white standard 10 10
2123 40m. Brazier (17½ × 22 mm) 40 20
2124 60m. Genghis Khan (17½ × 22 mm) 60 30
2125 60m. Horses galloping . . . 60 30
2126 60m. Tartar camp 60 30
2127 80m. Men kneeling to ruler 75 35
2128 80m. Court 75 35

1990. The Giant Panda. Multicoloured.
2129 10m. Type **437** 15 10
2130 20m. Panda eating bamboo 25 10
2131 30m. Adult eating bamboo, and cub 40 20
2132 40m. Panda on tree branch (horiz) 45 25
2133 50m. Adult and cub resting (horiz) 55 25
2134 60m. Panda and mountains (horiz) 75 35
2135 80m. Adult and cub playing (horiz) 85 45
2136 1t.20 Panda on snow-covered river bank (horiz) 1·60 80

438 Chasmosaurus

1990. Prehistoric Animals. Multicoloured.
2138 20m. Type **438** 15 10
2139 30m. Stegosaurus 25 10
2140 40m. Probactrosaurus . . . 35 15
2141 50m. Opisthocoelicaudia . . 55 25
2142 60m. Iguanodon (vert) . . . 65 30
2143 80m. Tarbosaurus 90 45
2144 1t.20 Mamenchisaurus (after Mark Hallett) (60 × 22 mm) . . . . . . 1·10 55

439 Lighthouse, Alexandria, Egypt

440 Kea

1990. Seven Wonders of the World. Mult.
2146 20m. Type **439** 15 10
2147 30m. Pyramids of Egypt (horiz) 25 10
2148 40m. Statue of Zeus, Olympia 35 20
2149 50m. Colossus of Rhodes 55 25

2150 60m. Mausoleum, Halicarnassus 65 35
2151 80m. Temple of Artemis, Ephesus (horiz) 90 45
2152 1t.20 Hanging Gardens of Babylon 1·10 55

1990. Parrots. Multicoloured.
2154 20m. Type **440** 20 20
2155 30m. Hyacinth macaw 35 35
2156 40m. Australian king parrot 50 50
2157 50m. Grey parrot 65 65
2158 60m. Kakapo 75 75
2159 80m. Alexandrine parakeet 1·10 1·10
2160 1t.20 Scarlet macaw 1·25 1·25

441 Purple Tiger Moth

1990. Moths and Butterflies. Multicoloured.
2162 20m. Type **441** 15 10
2163 30m. Viennese emperor moth 25 10
2164 40m. Comma 40 20
2165 50m. Magpie moth 50 25
2166 60m. Chequered moth 60 30
2167 80m. Swallowtail 85 45
2168 1t.20 Orange-tip

442 Jetsons in Flying Saucer

1991. The Jetsons (cartoon characters). Mult.
2170 20m. Type **442** 10 10
2171 25m. Family walking on planet, and dragon (horiz) 15 10
2172 30m. Jane, George, Elroy and dog Astro 20 10
2173 40m. George, Judy, Elroy and Astro crossing river 25 10
2174 50m. Flying in saucer (horiz) 30 15
2175 60m. Jetsons and Cosmo Spacely (horiz) 35 20
2176 70m. George and Elroy flying with jetpacks 45 20
2177 80m. Elroy (horiz) 50 25
2178 1t.20 Judy and Astro watching Elroy doing acrobatics on tree 75 40

443 Dino and Bam-Bam meeting Mongolian Boy with Camel

1991. The Flintstones (cartoon characters). Mult.
2180 25m. Type **443** 10 10
2181 35m. Bam-Bam and Dino posing with boy (vert) 15 10
2182 45m. Mongolian mother greeting Betty Rubble, Wilma Flintstone and children 20 10
2183 55m. Barney Rubble and Fred riding dinosaurs 25 10
2184 65m. Flintstones and Rubbles by river 30 15
2185 75m. Bam-Bam and Dino racing boy on camel 40 20
2186 85m. Fred, Barney and Bam-Bam with Mongolian boy 55 25
2187 1t.40 Flintstones and Rubbles in car 90 45
2188 2t. Fred and Barney taking refreshments with Mongolian 1·40 70

444 Party Emblem

445 Black-capped Chickadee

1991. 70th Anniv of Mongolian People's Revolutionary Party.
2190 **444** 60m. multicoloured 50 25

1991. "Stamp World London 90" International Stamp Exhibition. Multicoloured.
2191 25m. Type **445** 15 15
2192 35m. Common cardinal 20 20
2193 45m. Crested shelduck 30 30
2194 55m. Mountain bluebird 35 35
2195 65m. Northern oriole 45 45
2196 75m. Bluethroat (horiz) 50 50
2197 85m. Eastern bluebird 65 65
2198 1t.40 Great reed warbler 1·25 1·25
2199 2t. Golden eagle 1·60 1·60

446 Black Grouse

1991. Birds. Multicoloured.
2201 20m. Type **446** 25 25
2202 30m. Common shelduck 35 35
2203 40m. Common pheasant 45 45
2204 50m. Long-tailed duck 60 60
2205 60m. Hazel grouse 65 65
2206 80m. Red-breasted merganser 1·00 1·00
2207 1t.20 Goldeneye 1·75 1·75

447 Emblem

448 Superb Pink

1991. 70th Anniv of Mongolian People's Army.
2209 **447** 60m. multicoloured 50 25

1991. Flowers. Multicoloured.
2210 20m. Type **448** 15 10
2211 30m. "Gentiana pneumonanthe" (wrongly inscr "puenmonanthe") 25 10
2212 40m. Dandelion 40 20
2213 50m. Siberian iris 55 25
2214 60m. Turk's-cap lily 65 30
2215 80m. "Aster amellus" 90 45
2216 1t.20 Thistle 1·25 60

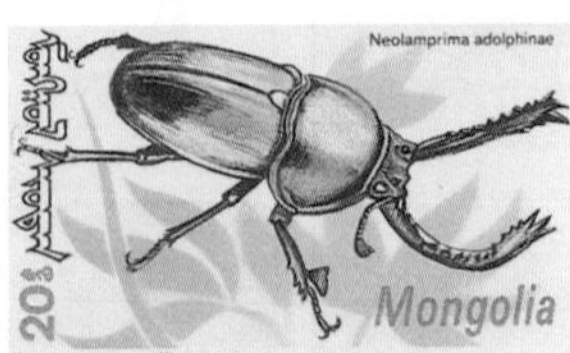

449 Stag Beetle

1991. Beetles. Multicoloured.
2218 20m. Type **449** 15 10
2219 30m. "Chelorrhina polyphemus" 25 10
2220 40m. "Coptolabrus coelestis" 40 20
2221 50m. "Epepeotes togatus" 55 25
2222 60m. Tiger beetle 65 30
2223 80m. "Macrodontia cervicornis" 90 45
2224 1t.20 Hercules beetle 1·25 60

450 Defend

1991. Buddhas. Multicoloured.
2226 20m. Type **450** 15 10
2227 30m. Badmasanhava 25 10
2228 40m. Avalokitecvara 35 15
2229 50m. Buddha 50 25
2230 60m. Mintugwa 60 30
2231 80m. Shyamatara 70 35
2232 1t.20 Samvara 1·10 55

451 Zebras

1991. African Wildlife. Multicoloured.
2234 20m. Type **451** 15 10
2235 30m. Cheetah (wrongly inscr "Cheetan") 25 10
2236 40m. Black rhinoceros 40 20
2237 50m. Giraffe (vert) 55 25
2238 60m. Gorilla 65 35
2239 80m. Elephants 90 45
2240 1t.20 Lion (vert) 1·25 60

452 Communications

1991. Meiso Mizuhara Stamp Exhibition, Ulan Bator.
2242 **452** 1t.20 multicoloured 2·00 60

453 Scotch Bonnet

1991. Fungi. Multicoloured.
2243 20m. Type **453** 15 10
2244 30m. Oak mushroom 20 10
2245 40m. "Hygrophorus marzuelus" 30 15
2246 50m. Chanterelle 40 20
2247 60m. Field mushroom 55 25
2248 80m. Bronze boletus 70 35
2249 1t.20 Caesar's mushroom 1·25 60
2250 2t. "Tricholoma terreum" 2·10 1·00

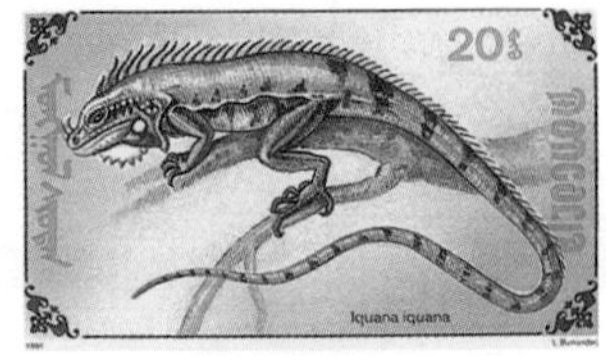

455 Green Iguana

1991. Reptiles. Multicoloured.
2253 20m. Type **455** 15 10
2254 30m. Flying gecko 30 15
2255 40m. Frilled lizard 40 20
2256 50m. Common cape lizard 55 25
2257 60m. Common basilisk 65 30
2258 80m. Common tegu 90 45
2259 1t.20 Marine iguana 1·50 50

456 Warrior

1991. Masked Costumes. Multicoloured.
2261 35m. Type **456** 20 10
2262 45m. Mask with fangs 30 15
2263 55m. Bull mask 40 20
2264 65m. Dragon mask 55 25
2265 85m. Mask with beak 65 30
2266 1t.40 Old man 1·25 60
2267 2t. Gold mask with earrings 1·50 75

457 German Shepherd

1991. Dogs. Multicoloured.
2269 20m. Type **457** 15 10
2270 30m. Dachshund (vert) 30 15
2271 40m. Yorkshire terrier (vert) 40 20
2272 50m. Standard poodle 50 25
2273 60m. Springer spaniel 70 35
2274 80m. Norfolk terrier 90 45
2275 1t.20 Keeshund 1·50 75

458 Siamese

1991. Cats. Multicoloured.
2277 20m. Type **458** 15 10
2278 30m. Black and white longhaired (vert) 30 15
2279 40m. Ginger red 40 20
2280 50m. Tabby (vert) 50 30
2281 60m. Red and white (vert) 70 35
2282 80m. Maine coon (vert) 90 45
2283 1t.20 Blue-eyed white persian (vert) 1·50 65

459 Pagoda

460 "Zegris fausti"

1991. "Phila Nippon '91" International Stamp Exhibition, Tokyo. Multicoloured.
2285 1t. Type **459** 30 10
2286 2t. Japanese woman 55 25
2287 3t. Mongolian woman 85 40
2288 4t. Temple 1·40 65

1991. Butterflies and Flowers. Multicoloured.
2289 20m. Type **460** 10 10
2290 25m. Yellow roses 15 10
2291 30m. Apollo 20 10
2292 40m. Purple tiger moth 25 10
2293 50m. "Pseudochazara regeli" 30 15
2294 60m. "Colotis fausta" 35 15
2295 70m. Red rose 40 20
2296 80m. Marguerites 50 25
2297 1t.20 Lily 75 35

1991. "Expo '90" International Garden and Greenery Exhibition, Osaka. Nos. 2289/97 optd **EXPO '90** and symbol.
2298 20m. multicoloured 10 10
2299 25m. multicoloured 15 10
2300 30m. multicoloured 20 10
2301 40m. multicoloured 25 10
2302 50m. multicoloured 30 15
2303 60m. multicoloured 35 15
2304 70m. multicoloured 40 20
2305 80m. multicoloured 50 25
2306 1t.20 multicoloured 75 35

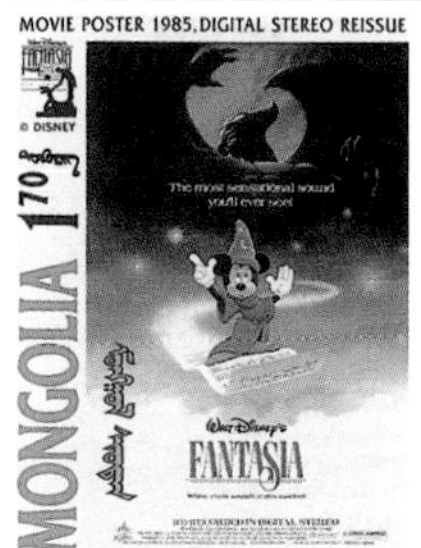

462 Poster for 1985 Digital Stereo Re-issue

1991. 50th Anniv (1990) of Original Release of Walt Disney's "Fantasia" (cartoon film). Mult.

2308 1t.70 Type **462** 15 10
2309 2t. 1940 poster for original release 20 10
2310 2t.30 Poster for 1982 digital re-issue 25 10
2311 2t.60 Poster for 1981 stereo re-issue 35 15
2312 4t.20 Poster for 1969 "Psychedelic Sixties" release 60 30
2313 10t. 1941 poster for original release 1·50 75
2314 15t. Mlle. Upanova (sketch by Campbell Grant) 2·00 90
2315 16t. Mickey as the Sorcerer's Apprentice (original sketch) 2·40 1·25

463 Speed Skating **465** Elk

1992. Winter Olympic Games, Albertville. Mult.

2317 60m. Type **463** 10 10
2318 80m. Ski jumping 10 10
2319 1t. Ice hockey 15 10
2320 1t.20 Ice skating 15 10
2321 1t.50 Biathlon (horiz) 15 10
2322 2t. Skiing (horiz) 20 15
2323 2t.40 Two-man bobsleigh (horiz) 25 15

1992. The Elk. Multicoloured.

2326 3t. Type **465** 70 30
2327 3t. Female with young (horiz) 70 30
2328 3t. Adult male (horiz) 70 30
2329 3t. Female 70 30

466 Steam Locomotive, Darjeeling–Himalaya Railway, India

1992. Multicoloured. (a) Railways of the World.

2330 3t. Type **466** 70 25
2331 3t. The "Royal Scot", Great Britain 70 25
2332 6t. Steam train on bridge over River Kwai, Burma–Siam Railway 1·60 60
2333 6t. Baltic steam locomotive No. 767, Burma 1·60 60
2334 8t. Baldwin steam locomotive, Thailand 2·10 70
2335 8t. Western Railways steam locomotive, Pakistan 2·10 70
2336 16t. Class P36 locomotive, Russia 4·50 1·50
2337 16t. Shanghai–Peking express, China 4·50 1·50

(b) "Orient Express".

2339 3t. 1931 advertising poster 70 25
2340 3t. 1928 advertising poster 70 25
2341 6t. Dawn departure 1·60 60
2342 6t. The "Golden Arrow" leaving Victoria Station, London 1·60 60
2343 8t. Standing in station, Yugoslavia 2·10 70
2344 8t. Train passing through mountainous landcape, early 1900s 2·10 70
2345 16t. "Fleche d'Or" approaching Etaples 4·50 1·50
2346 16t. Arrival in Istanbul 4·50 1·50

468 Black-billed Magpie

1992. Multicoloured. (a) Birds.

2349 3t. Type **468** 40 20
2350 3t. Northern eagle owl 40 20
2351 6t. Relict gull (horiz) 80 40
2352 6t. Redstart (horiz) 80 40
2353 8t. Demoiselle crane 1·10 55
2354 8t. Black stork (horiz) 1·10 55
2355 16t. Rough-legged buzzard 2·25 1·10
2356 16t. Golden eagle (horiz) 2·25 1·10

(b) Butterflies and Moths.

2358 3t. Scarce swallowtail (horiz) 40 20
2359 3t. Small tortoiseshell 40 20
2360 6t. "Thyria jacobaeae" (value at right) (horiz) 80 40
2361 6t. Peacock (value at left) (horiz) 80 40
2362 8t. Camberwell beauty (value at left) (horiz) 1·10 55
2363 8t. Red admiral (value at right) (horiz) 1·10 55
2364 16t. "Hyporhaia audica" (horiz) 2·25 1·10
2365 16t. Large tortoiseshell (flying over river) (horiz) 2·25 1·10

472 Fleet

1992. 500th Anniv of Discovery of America by Columbus (2nd issue). Multicoloured.

2370 3t. Type **472** 15 10
2371 7t. Amerindians' canoe approaching "Santa Maria" 25 10
2372 10t. "Pinta" 35 15
2373 16t. "Santa Maria" in open sea (vert) 55 25
2374 30t. "Santa Maria" passing coastline 1·10 50
2375 40t. Dolphins and "Santa Maria" 1·50 75
2376 50t. "Nina" 1·90 90

474 Long Jumping

1992. Olympic Games, Barcelona. Multicoloured.

2379 3t. Type **474** 10 10
2380 6t. Gymnastics (pommel exercise) 10 10
2381 8t. Boxing 10 10
2382 16t. Wrestling 10 10
2383 20t. Archery (vert) 10 10
2384 30t. Cycling 10 10
2385 40t. Show jumping 15 10
2386 50t. High jumping 20 10
2387 60t. Weightlifting 20 10

Eight designs, each 200t. and embossed on both gold and silver foil and accompanied by matching miniature sheets, were issued in 1993 in limited printings, depicting animals, sports or transport.

476 Black Grouse

1993. Birds. Multicoloured.

2390 3t. Type **476** 10 10
2391 8t. Moorhen 30 15
2392 10t. Golden-crowned kinglet 40 20
2393 16t. River kingfisher 60 30
2394 30t. Red-throated diver 1·10 50
2395 40t. Grey heron 1·50 75
2396 50t. Hoopoe 1·90 90
2397 60t. Blue-throated niltava 2·25 1·10

477 Orange-tip

1993. Butterflies and Moths. Multicoloured.

2399 3t. Type **477** 10 10
2400 8t. Peacock 30 15
2401 10t. High brown fritillary 40 20
2402 16t. "Limenitis reducta" 60 30
2403 30t. Common burnet 1·10 50
2404 40t. Common blue 1·50 75
2405 50t. Apollo 1·90 90
2406 60t. Great peacock 2·25 1·10

1993. No. 1221 surch **XXX 15Ter**.

2408 15t. on 70m. multicoloured 2·75 1·00

479 Nicolas Copernicus (astronomer)

1993. "Polska'93" International Stamp Exhibition, Poznan. Multicoloured.

2409 30t. Type **479** (520th birth anniv) 2·00 90
2410 30t. Frederic Chopin (composer) 2·00 90
2411 30t. Pope John Paul II 2·00 90

1993. No. 263 surch **8-Ter**.

2413 8t. on 70m. multicoloured 40 20

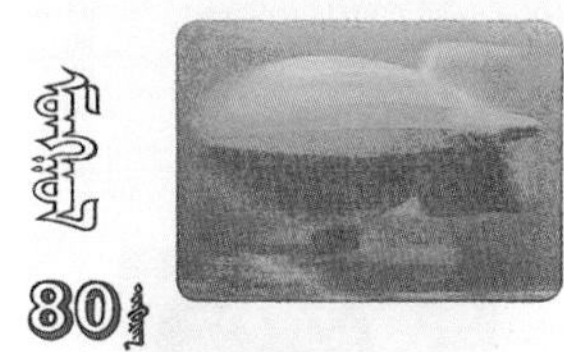

482 Hologram of Airship

1993. Airship Flight over Ulan Bator.

2415 **482** 80t. multicoloured 1·00 50

483 Buddha

1993. "Bangkok 1993" International Stamp Exhibition. Multicoloured.

2416 50t. Buddha on throne 55 25
2417 100t. Buddha (different) 1·10 50
2418 150t. Type **483** 1·60 80
2419 200t. Multi-armed Buddha 2·25 1·10

484 Clouds, Mountains and Dog

1994. New Year. Year of the Dog. Multicoloured.

2421 60t. Type **484** 45 20
2422 60t. Dog reclining between mountains and waves (horiz) 45 20

485 Uruguay (1930, 1950)

1994. World Cup Football Championship, U.S.A. Previous Winners. Multicoloured.

2423 150t. Type **485** 30 15
2424 150t. Italy (1934) 30 15
2425 150t. German Federal Republic (1954) 30 15
2426 150t. Brazil (1958) 30 15
2427 150t. Argentina (1978, 1986) 30 15
2428 200t. Italy (1938) 40 20
2429 200t. Brazil (1962) 40 20
2430 200t. German Federal Republic (1974) 40 20
2431 250t. Brazil (1970) 50 25
2432 250t. Italy (1982) 50 25
2433 250t. German Federal Republic (1990) 50 25

488 Biathlon

1994. Winter Olympic Games, Lillehammer, Norway. Multicoloured.

2437 50t. Type **488** 30 15
2438 60t. Two-man bobsleigh 35 15
2439 80t. Skiing 45 20
2440 100t. Ski jumping 60 30
2441 120t. Ice skating 70 35
2442 200t. Speed skating 1·25 60

490 Lammergeier

1994. Wildlife. Multicoloured.

2445 60t. Type **490** 45 20
2446 60t. Grey-headed woodpecker on tree trunk 45 20
2447 60t. Japanese white-naped cranes 45 20
2448 60t. Western marsh harrier 45 20
2449 60t. Golden oriole on branch 45 20
2450 60t. Bank swallows 45 20
2451 60t. Montagu's harrier perched on rock 45 20
2452 60t. Pallid harriers in flight 45 20
2453 60t. Squirrel on branch 45 20
2454 60t. Dragonfly 45 20
2455 60t. Black stork 45 20
2456 60t. Northern pintail 45 20
2457 60t. Spotted nutcracker standing on rock 45 20
2458 60t. Marmot 45 20
2459 60t. Ladybird on flower 45 20
2460 60t. Clutch of eggs in ground nest 45 20
2461 60t. Grasshopper 45 20
2462 60t. Butterfly 45 20

Nos. 2445/62 were issued together, se-tenant, forming a composite design.

491 Command Module **492** Flowers

1994. 25th Anniv of First Manned Moon Landing. Multicoloured.

2463 200t. Type **491** 65 30
2464 200t. Earth, astronaut in chair and shuttle wing 65 30

2465 200t. Shuttle approaching Earth 65 30
2466 200t. Astronaut on Moon 65 30

1994.
2468 **492** 10t. green and black . . 10 10
2469 – 18t. purple and black . . 10 10
2470 – 22t. blue and black . . . 15 10
2471 – 44t. purple and black . . 25 10
DESIGNS: 18, 44t. Argali; 22t. Airplane.

493 Korean Empire 1884 5m. Stamp

1994. "Philakorea 1994" International Stamp Exhibition, Seoul. Multicoloured.
2472 600t. Type **493** . . . . . . 2·25 1·00
2473 600t. Mongolia 1924 1c. stamp . . . . 2·25 1·00
2474 600t. Mongolia 1966 Children's Day 15 m. stamp (47 × 34 mm) . . . 2·25 1·00
2475 600t. South Korea 1993 New Year 110 w. stamp (47 × 34 mm) . . . . . . 2·25 1·00

494 Butterfly

1994. "Singpex '94" National Stamp Exhibition, Singapore. Year of the Dog.
2477 **494** 300t. multicoloured . . . 1·00 50

496 Mammoth

1994. Prehistoric Animals. Multicoloured.
2480 60t. Type **496** 35 15
2481 80t. Stegosaurus 50 25
2482 100t. Talararus (horiz) . . . 75 35
2483 120t. Gorythosaurus (horiz) 90 45
2484 200t. Tyrannosaurus (horiz) 1·50 75

497 National Flags

1994. Mongolia–Japan Friendship and Co-operation.
2486 **497** 20t. multicoloured . . . 15 10

498 Boar and Mountains

1995. New Year. Year of the Pig. Multicoloured.
2487 200t. Type **498** 65 30
2488 200t. Boar reclining amongst clouds (vert) 65 30

499 Dancer

1995. Tsam Religious Mask Dance.
2489 **499** 20t. multicoloured . . . 10 10
2490 – 50t. multicoloured . . . 20 10
2491 – 60t. multicoloured . . . 30 15
2492 – 100t. multicoloured . . . 50 25
2493 – 120t. multicoloured . . . 60 30
2494 – 150t. multicoloured . . . 65 30
2495 – 200t. multicoloured . . . 95 40
DESIGNS: 50t. to 200t. Different masked characters.

500 Saiga

1995. The Saiga. Multicoloured.
2497 40t. Type **500** 20 10
2498 50t. Male and female . . . 30 15
2499 70t. Male running 45 20
2500 200t. Head and neck of male . . . . 1·00 50

502 Yellow Oranda

1995. Goldfish. Multicoloured.
2502 20t. Type **502** 20 10
2503 50t. Red and white veil-tailed wen-yu 35 15
2504 60t. Brown oranda red-head 45 20
2505 100t. Pearl-scaled 80 30
2506 120t. Red lion-head . . . . 1·00 45
2507 150t. Brown oranda . . . . 1·40 55
2508 200t. Red and white oranda with narial . . . . 1·90 75

503 Bishop

1995. X-Men (comic strip). Designs showing characters. Multicoloured.
2511 30t. Type **503** 10 10
2512 50t. Beast 15 10
2513 60t. Rogue 25 10
2514 70t. Gambit 30 15
2515 80t. Cyclops 40 20
2516 100t. Storm 50 25
2517 200t. Professor X 95 45
2518 250t. Wolverine . . . . . . 1·25 60

505 Presley

1995. 60th Birth Anniv of Elvis Presley (entertainer). Multicoloured.
2521 60t. Type **505** 30 15
2522 80t. Wearing cap 35 15
2523 100t. Holding microphone 45 20
2524 120t. Wearing blue and white striped T-shirt . . . 60 30
2525 150t. With guitar and microphone 70 35
2526 200t. On motor bike with girl 85 40
2527 250t. On surfboard . . . . 1·10 50
2528 300t. Pointing with left hand 1·50 70
2529 350t. Playing guitar and girl clapping . . . . 1·90 85
Nos. 2521/9 were issued together, se-tenant, forming a composite design.

506 Monroe smiling

1995. 70th Birth Anniv (1996) of Marilyn Monroe (actress). Multicoloured.
2531 60t. Type **506** 30 15
2532 80t. Wearing white dress . . 35 15
2533 100t. Pouting 45 20
2534 120t. With naval officer and cello player 60 30
2535 150t. Wearing off-the-shoulder blouse 70 35
2536 200t. Using telephone and wearing magenta dress . . 85 40
2537 250t. Man kissing Monroe's shoulder . . . . 1·10 50
2538 300t. With white fur collar 1·50 70
2539 350t. With Clark Gable . . 1·90 85
Nos. 2531/9 were issued together, se-tenant, forming a composite design.

507 Rat sitting between Mountains

1996. New Year. Year of the Rat. Multicoloured.
2541 150t. Type **507** 70 35
2542 200t. Rat crouching between mountains and waves (horiz) 85 40

510 Cycling

1996. Olympic Games, Atlanta, U.S.A. Mult.
2548 30t. Type **510** 10 10
2549 60t. Shooting 10 10
2550 80t. Weightlifting 15 10
2551 100t. Boxing 20 10
2552 120t. Archery (vert) 25 10
2553 150t. Rhythmic gymnastics (vert) 30 15
2554 200t. Hurdling (vert) 40 20
2555 350t. Show jumping 70 35
2556 400t. Wrestling 80 40

Since the above, further issues have appeared inscribed either "Mongolia" or "Mongol Post". It has so far proved impossible to discover the dates on which these stamps were issued and, indeed, if any of them were available for postal purposes in Mongolia.

MONG-TSEU (MENGTSZ) Pt. 17

An Indo-Chinese P.O. in Yunnan province, China, closed in 1922.

1903. 100 centimes = 1 franc.
1919. 100 cents = 1 piastre.

Stamps of Indo-China surcharged.

1903. "Tablet" key-type surch **MONGTZE** and value in Chinese.
1 D 1c. black and red on buff . . 5·75 8·75
2 2c. brown and blue on buff 3·50 5·50
3 4c. brown and blue on grey 5·75 8·25
4 5c. green and red . . . . . 3·75 4·75
5 10c. red and blue . . . . . 5·75 11·00
6 15c. grey and red . . . . . 9·25 11·00
7 20c. red and blue on green 11·00 17·00
8 25c. blue and red . . . . . 10·50 11·50
9 25c. black and red on pink £500 £500
10 30c. brown & blue on drab 8·25 16·00
11 40c. red and blue on yellow 60·00 65·00
12 50c. red and blue on pink £275 £275
13 50c. brown and red on blue £100 £100
14 75c. brown and red on orge £120 £100
15 1f. green and red £120 £100
16 5f. mauve and blue on lilac £120 £100

1906. Surch **Mong-Tseu** and value in Chinese.
17 **8** 1c. green . . . . 80 3·50
18 2c. purple on yellow . . . . 90 3·75
19 4c. mauve on blue . . . . . 75 3·75
20 5c. green . . . . 1·25 4·25
21 10c. pink . . . . 1·25 5·00
22 15c. brown on blue . . . . 1·40 5·00
23 20c. red on green . . . . . 4·75 5·75
24 25c. blue . . . . 6·00 6·25
25 30c. brown on cream . . . . 8·00 11·00
26 35c. black on yellow . . . . 6·25 7·75
27 40c. black on grey . . . . . 2·00 10·00
28 50c. brown . . . . 11·50 20·00
29 D 75c. brown & red on orange 45·00 45·00
30 **8** 1f. green . . . . 16·00 20·00
31 2f. brown on yellow . . . . 48·00 50·00
32 D 5f. mauve and blue on lilac £100 £110
34 **8** 10f. red on green . . . . . 90·00 90·00

1908. Surch **MONGTSEU** and value in Chinese.
35 **10** 1c. black and brown . . . . 1·10 80
36 2c. black and brown . . . . 1·40 95
37 4c. black and blue . . . . . 1·90 1·90
38 5c. black and green . . . . 1·90 80
39 10c. black and red . . . . 1·75 2·75
40 15c. black and violet . . . . 2·75 3·25
41 **11** 20c. black and violet . . . . 4·00 5·25
42 25c. black and blue . . . . 3·75 7·75
43 30c. black and brown . . . 4·00 4·75
44 35c. black and green . . . . 5·00 4·75
45 40c. black and brown . . . 3·50 4·50
46 50c. black and red . . . . 5·00 5·50
47 **12** 75c. black and orange . . . 9·25 12·50
48 – 1f. black and red . . . . . 13·50 12·00
49 – 2f. black and green . . . . 15·00 18·00
50 – 5f. black and blue £100 £110
51 – 10f. black and violet £100 £110

1919. Nos. 35/51 further surch in figures and words.
52 **10** $\frac{2}{5}$ c. on 1c. black and brown 1·25 3·00
53 $\frac{4}{5}$ c. on 2c. black and brown 1·25 3·00
54 $1\frac{3}{5}$ c. on 4c. black and blue 1·75 2·75
55 2c. on 5c. black and green 2·00 3·00
56 4c. on 10c. black and red 3·00 3·25
57 6c. on 15c. black and violet 2·50 3·25
58 **11** 8c. on 20c. black and violet 5·00 5·00
59 10c. on 25c. black and blue 4·25 4·00
60 12c. on 30c. black & brown 3·50 4·00
61 14c. on 35c. black & green 3·00 3·75
62 16c. on 40c. black & brown 3·00 4·00
63 20c. on 50c. black and red 3·50 4·00
64 **12** 30c. on 75c. black & orange 4·00 4·75
65 – 40c. on 1f. black and red . . 7·50 9·50
66 – 80c. on 2f. black and green 6·00 6·50
67 – 2p. on 5f. black and blue . . £120 £120
68 – 4p. on 10f. black and violet 18·00 26·00

MONTENEGRO Pt. 3

Formerly a monarchy on the Adriatic Sea, now part of Yugoslavia. In Italian and German occupation during 1939–45 war.

1874. 100 novcic = 1 florin.
1902. 100 heller = 1 krone.
1907. 100 para = 1 krone (1910 = 1 perper).

1 Prince Nicholas

Прослава
1493 1893
Штампарије
(**2**)

1874.
45 **1** 1n. blue 40 45
38 2n. yellow . . . . 2·00 2·00
51 2n. green 20 15
39 3n. green 50 50
52 3n. red 20 15
40 5n. red 50 50
53 5n. orange 45 20
19 7n. mauve . . . . 35·00 30·00
41 7n. pink 50 50
54 7n. grey 35 45
42 10n. blue 50 50
55 10n. purple 30 45
56 15n. brown 30 45
46 20n. brown 25 25
7 25n. purple £250 £275
44 25n. brown . . . . 50 2·75
57 25n. blue 30 45
47 30n. brown 40 45
48 50n. blue 40 45
49 1f. green . . . . 1·25 2·75
50 2f. red . . . . 1·25 4·00

1893. 400th Anniv of Introduction of Printing into Montenegro. Optd with T **2**.
81 **1** 2n. yellow . . . . 24·00 2·75
82 3n. green . . . . 1·50 1·50
83 5n. red . . . . 1·25 1·25
84 7n. pink . . . . 1·00 1·00
86 10n. blue . . . . 1·75 1·75
87 15n. bistre . . . . 1·50 1·50
89 25n. brown . . . . 1·90 1·90

3 Monastery near Cetinje, Royal Mausoleum

1896. Bicentenary of Petrovich Niegush Dynasty.
90 **3** 1n. brown and blue . . . . 30 1·00
91 2n. yellow and purple . . . 30 1·00
92 3n. green and brown . . . . 30 1·00
93 5n. brown and green . . . . 30 1·00
94 10n. blue and yellow . . . . 30 1·00
95 15n. green and blue . . . . 30 1·00
96 20n. blue and green . . . . 40 1·25
97 25n. yellow and blue . . . . 40 1·25
98 30n. brown and purple . . . 45 1·25
99 50n. blue and red . . . . . 50 1·50
100 1f. blue and pink . . . . . 90 1·75
101 2f. black and brown . . . . 1·00 1·50

4

УСТАВ
Constitution
1905
Никољдан
(5)

7

1902.
102 **4** 1h. blue 30 30
103 2h. mauve 30 30
104 5h. green 30 20
105 10h. red 30 30
106 25h. blue 30 50
107 50h. green 40 50
108 1k. brown 35 35
109 2k. brown 50 50
110 5k. brown . . . . 75 1·50

1905. Granting of Constitution. Optd with T **5**.
111 **4** 1h. blue 15 20
112 2h. mauve 15 20
113 5h. green 15 20
114 10h. red 50 50
124a 25h. blue 15 25
125a 50h. green 15 25
126a 1k. brown 15 25
127a 2k. brown 15 25
119 5k. orange . . . . 75 2·50

1907. New Currency.
129 **7** 1pa. yellow 15 20
130 2pa. black 15 20
131 5pa. green . . . . 1·00 10
132 10pa. red . . . . 1·50 10
133 15pa. blue 20 15
134 20pa. orange 20 20
135 25pa. blue . . . . 20 1·25
136 35pa. brown 25 15
137 50pa. lilac 45 35
138 1k. red 45 60
139 2k. green 45 60
140 5k. red . . . . 90 2·00

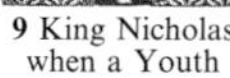
9 King Nicholas when a Youth

10 King Nicholas and Queen Milena

11 Prince Nicholas

12 Nicholas I

1910. Proclamation of Kingdom and 50th Anniv of Reign of Prince Nicholas.
141 **9** 1pa. black 35 15
142 **10** 2pa. purple 35 15
143 – 5pa. green 30 15
144 – 10pa. red 30 15
145 – 15pa. blue 30 15
146 **10** 20pa. olive 65 15
147 – 25pa. blue 65 15
148 – 35pa. brown 85 85
149 – 50pa. violet 65 35
150 – 1per. lake 65 35
151 – 2per. green 85 50
152 **11** 5per. blue . . . . 1·25 1·00
DESIGNS: As Type **9**: 5, 10, 25, 35pa. Nicholas I in 1910; 15pa. Nicholas I in 1878; 50pa., 1, 2per. Nicholas I in 1890.

1913.
153 **12** 1pa. orange 15 15
154 2pa. purple 15 15
155 5pa. green 15 15
156 10pa. red 15 15
157 15pa. blue 20 20
158 20pa. brown 20 20
159 25pa. blue 20 20
160 35pa. red 50 50
161 50pa. blue 25 25
162 1per. brown 25 25
163 2per. purple 65 65
164 5per. green 65 65

ITALIAN OCCUPATION

Montenegro
Црна Гора
17-IV-41-XIX
(1)

ЦРНА ГОРА
(2)

1941. Stamps of Yugoslavia optd with T **1**. (a) Postage. On Nos. 414, etc.
1 **99** 25p. black 30 65
2 1d. green 30 65
3 1d.50 red 30 65
4 2d. mauve 30 65
5 3d. brown 30 65
6 4d. blue 30 65
7 5d. blue . . . . 1·50 4·75
8 5d.50 violet . . . . 1·50 4·75
9 6d. blue . . . . 1·50 4·75
10 8d. brown . . . . 1·75 5·50
11 12d. violet . . . . 1·50 4·75
12 16d. purple . . . . 1·50 4·75
13 20d. blue . . . . 90·00 £140
14 30d. pink . . . . 40·00 65·00

(b) Air. On Nos. 360/7.
15 **80** 50p. brown . . . . 8·00 6·00
16 – 1d. green . . . . 2·00 5·00
17 – 2d. blue . . . . 2·00 5·50
18 – 2d.50 red . . . . 3·00 6·00
19 **80** 5d. violet . . . . 22·00 45·00
20 – 10d. red . . . . 22·00 45·00
21 – 20d. green . . . . 22·00 50·00
22 – 30d. blue . . . . 22·00 48·00

1941. Stamps of Italy optd with T **2**. (a) On Postage stamps of 1929.
28 **98** 5c. brown 15 50
29 – 10c. brown 15 50
30 – 15c. green 15 50
31 **99** 20c. red 15 50
32 – 25c. green 15 50
33 **103** 30c. brown 15 50
34 50c. violet 15 50
35 – 75c. red 15 50
36 – 1l.25 blue 15 50

(b) On Air stamp of 1930.
37 **110** 50c. brown 15 50

1942. Nos. 416 etc of Yugoslavia optd **Governatorato del Montenegro Valore LIRE**.
43 **99** 1d. green . . . . 75 1·40
44 1d.50 red . . . . 25·00 30·00
45 3d. brown . . . . 75 1·40
46 4d. blue . . . . 75 1·40
47 5d.50 violet . . . . 75 1·40
48 6d. blue . . . . 75 1·40
49 8d. brown . . . . 75 1·40
50 12d. violet . . . . 75 1·40
51 16d. purple . . . . 75 1·40

1942. Air. Nos. 360/7 of Yugoslavia optd **Governatorato del Montenegro Valore in Lire**.
52 **80** 0.50l. brown . . . . 2·50 3·50
53 – 1l. green . . . . 2·50 3·50
54 – 2l. blue . . . . 2·50 3·50
55 – 2.50l. red . . . . 2·50 3·50
56 **80** 5l. violet . . . . 2·50 3·50
57 – 10l. brown . . . . 2·50 3·50
58 – 20l. green . . . . 65·00 £100
59 – 30l. blue . . . . 20·00 32·00

4 Prince Bishop Peter Njegos and View

1943. National Poem Commemoratives. Each stamp has fragment of poetry inscr at back.
60 **4** 5c. violet 25 75
61 – 10c. green 25 75
62 – 15c. brown 25 75
63 – 20c. orange 25 75
64 – 25c. green 25 75
65 – 50c. mauve 25 75
66 – 1l.25 blue 25 75
67 – 2l. green . . . . 1·00 2·00
68 – 5l. red on buff . . . . . 2·50 6·00
69 – 20l. purple on grey . . . . 5·00 13·00
DESIGNS—HORIZ: 10c. Meadow near Mt. Lovcen; 15c. Country Chapel; 20c. Chiefs Meeting; 25, 50c. Folk Dancing; 1l.25, Taking the Oath; 2l. Moslem wedding procession; 5l. Watch over wounded standard-bearer. VERT: 20l. Portrait of Prince Bishop Peter Njegos.

5 Cetinje

1943. Air. With Junkers G31 airplane (2, 20l.) or Fokker F.VIIa/3m airplane (others).
70 **5** 50c. brown . . . . 35 1·25
71 – 1l. blue . . . . 35 1·25
72 – 2l. mauve . . . . 35 1·25
73 – 5l. green . . . . 70 2·50
74 – 10l. purple on buff . . . . 4·00 9·00
75 – 20l. blue on pink . . . . . 6·25 16·00
DESIGNS—HORIZ. 1l. Coastline; 2l. Budva; 5l. Mt. Lovcen; 10l. Lake of Scutari. VERT: 20l. Mt. Durmitor.

GERMAN OCCUPATION

1943. Nos. 419/20 of Yugoslavia surch **Deutsche Militaer-Verwaltung Montenegro** and new value in lire.
76 **99** 50c. on 3d. brown . . . . . 3·00 24·00
77 1l. on 3d. brown . . . . . 3·00 24·00
78 1l.50 on 3d. brown . . . . 3·00 24·00
79 2l. on 3d. brown . . . . . 4·50 45·00
80 4l. on 3d. brown . . . . . 4·50 45·00
81 5l. on 4d. blue . . . . . . 5·00 45·00
82 8l. on 4d. blue . . . . . . 9·75 90·00
83 10l. on 4d. blue . . . . . 14·00 £150
84 20l. on 4d. blue . . . . . 30·00 £325

1943. Appointment of National Administrative Committee. Optd **Nationaler Verwaltungsausschuss 10.XI.1943**. (a) Postage. On Nos. 64/8.
85 25c. green . . . . 5·75 £190
86 50c. mauve . . . . 5·75 £190
87 1l.25 blue . . . . 5·75 £190
88 2l. green . . . . 5·75 £190
89 5l. red on buff £160 £2250

(b) Air. On Nos. 70/4.
90 **5** 50c. brown . . . . 9·50 £190
91 1l. blue . . . . 9·50 £190
92 2l. mauve . . . . 9·50 £190
93 5l. green . . . . 9·50 £190
94 10l. purple on buff £2000 £16000

1944. Refugees Fund. Surch **Flüchtlingshilfe Montenegro** and new value in German currency. (a) On Nos. 419/20 of Yugoslavia.
95 **99** 0.15+0.85Rm. on 3d. . . . 7·75 £170
96 0.15+0.85Rm. on 4d. . . . 7·75 £170

(b) On Nos. 46/9.
97 – 0.15+0.85Rm. on 25c. . . . 7·75 £170
98 – 0.15+1.35Rm. on 50c. . . . 7·75 £170
99 – 0.25+1.75Rm. on 1l.25 . . 7·75 £170
100 – 0.25+1.75Rm. on 2l. . . . 7·75 £170

(c) Air. On Nos. A52/4.
101 **5** 0.15+0.85Rm. on 50c. . . . 7·75 £180
102 – 0.25+1.25Rm. on 1l. . . . 7·75 £180
103 – 0.50+1.50Rm. on 2l. . . . 7·75 £180

1944. Red Cross. Surch **+Crveni krst Montenegro** and new value in German currency. (a) On Nos. 419/20 of Yugoslavia.
104 **99** 0.50+2.50Rm. on 3d. . . . 6·50 £170
105 0.50+2.50Rm. on 4d. . . . 6·50 £170

(b) On Nos. 64/5.
106 – 0.15+0.85Rm. on 25c. . . . 6·50 £170
107 – 0.15+1.35Rm. on 50c. . . . 6·50 £170

(c) Air. On Nos. 70/2.
108 **5** 0.25+1.75Rm. on 50c. . . . 6·50 £170
109 – 0.25+2.75Rm. on 1l. . . . 6·50 £170
110 – 0.50+2Rm. on 2l. . . . . 6·50 £170

ACKNOWLEDGEMENT OF RECEIPT STAMPS

A 3

A 4

1895.
A90 **A 3** 10n. blue and red . . . 85 1·00

1902.
A111 **A 4** 25h. orange and red . . 75 75

1905. Optd with T **5**.
A120 **A 4** 25h. orange and red . . 60 60

1907. As T **7**, but letters "A" and "R" in top corners.
A141 **7** 25p. olive 50 65

1913. As T **12**, but letters "A" and "R" in top corners.
A169 **12** 25p. olive 40 70

POSTAGE DUE STAMPS

D 3

D 4

D 8

1894.
D90 **D 3** 1n. red . . . . 2·25 1·40
D91 2n. green 50 20
D92 3n. orange 50 20
D93 5n. green 50 20
D94 10n. purple 50 30
D95 20n. blue 50 30
D96 30n. green 50 30
D97 50n. pale green 50 30

1902.
D111 **D 4** 5h. orange 20 20
D112 10h. green 30 30
D113 25h. purple 30 30
D114 50h. green 30 30
D115 1k. grey 35 35

1905. Optd with T **5**.
D120 **D 4** 5h. orange 35 50
D121 10h. olive . . . . . . 50 1·00
D122 25h. purple 35 50
D123 50h. green 35 50
D124 1k. pale green 50 75

1907.
D141 **D 8** 5p. brown 25 35
D142 10p. violet 25 35
D143 25p. red 25 35
D144 50p. green 25 35

1913. As T **12** but inscr "HOPTOMAPKA" at top.
D165 5p. grey 75 75
D166 10p. lilac 50 50
D167 25p. blue 50 50
D168 50p. red 65 65

ITALIAN OCCUPATION

1941. Postage Due stamps of Yugoslavia optd **Montenegro Upha 17-IV-41-XIX**.
D23 **D 56** 50p. violet . . . . . . 50 1·00
D24 1d. mauve . . . . . . 50 1·00
D25 2d. blue . . . . 50 1·00
D26 5d. orange . . . . . . 30·00 50·00
D27 10d. brown . . . . . . 3·00 6·00

1942. Postage Due stamps of Italy optd **UPHATOPA**.
D38 **D 141** 10c. blue . . . . . . 15 1·25
D39 20c. red . . . . 15 1·25
D40 30c. orange . . . . . . 15 1·25
D41 50c. violet . . . . . . 15 1·25
D42 1l. orange . . . . . . 25 1·25

MONTSERRAT Pt. 1

One of the Leeward Is., Br. W. Indies. Used general issues for Leeward Is. concurrently with Montserrat stamps until 1 July 1956, when Leeward Is. stamps were withdrawn.

1876. 12 pence = 1 shilling;
20 shillings = 1 pound.
1951. 100 cents = 1 West Indian dollar.

1876. Stamps of Antigua as T **1** optd **MONTSERRAT**.
8c 1d. red . . . . 17·00 14·00
2 6d. green . . . . 60·00 42·00

3

1880.
7 **3** ½d. green . . . . 1·00 7·50
9 2½d. brown . . . . £225 65·00
10 2½d. blue . . . . 21·00 19·00
5 4d. blue . . . . £140 40·00
12 4d. mauve . . . . 4·75 3·00

4 Device of the Colony

5

1903.
24a **4** ½d. green . . . . 80 1·25
15 1d. grey and red 75 40
26a 2d. grey and brown . . . 2·25 1·25
17 2½d. grey and blue . . . 1·50 1·75
28a 3d. orange and purple . . 9·50 2·50
29a 6d. purple and olive . . . 10·00 5·50
30 1s. green and purple . . . 10·00 7·00
21 2s. green and brown . . . 25·00 17·00
22 2s.6d. green and black . . 18·00 35·00
33 **5** 5s. black and red . . . . 95·00 £110

1908.
36 **4** 1d. red . . . . 1·40 30
38 2d. grey . . . . 1·75 15·00
39 2½d. blue . . . . 2·25 3·50
40 3d. purple on yellow . . . 1·00 18·00
43 6d. purple . . . . 6·50 50·00
44 1s. black on green . . . . 8·50 45·00
45 2s. purple and blue on blue 25·00 55·00
46 2s.6d. black and red on blue 30·00 70·00
47 **5** 5s. red and green on yellow 50·00 70·00

1914. As T **5**, but portrait of King George V.
48 5s. red and green on yellow . . 65·00 90·00

8

10 Plymouth

1916.
63 **8** ½d. brown 15 5·50
64 ½d. green 30 30
50 1d. red 1·00 75
65 1d. violet 30 60
67 1½d. yellow 1·75 9·50
68 1½d. red 30 3·75
69 1½d. brown 1·75 50
70 2d. grey 50 2·00
71a 2½d. blue 60 90
72 2½d. yellow 1·25 19·00
74 3d. purple on yellow 1·10 4·75
73 3d. blue 60 16·00
75 4d. black and red on yellow 60 12·00
76 5d. purple and olive 3·50 10·00
77 6d. purple 3·00 7·50
78 1s. black on green 3·00 7·00
79 2s. purple and blue on blue 7·00 14·00
80 2s.6d. black and red on blue 12·00 50·00
81 3s. green and violet 12·00 19·00
82 4s. black and red 15·00 38·00
83 5s. green and red on yellow 26·00 42·00

1917. Optd **WAR STAMP**.
60 **8** ½d. green 10 1·50
62 1½d. black and orange 10 30

1932. 300th Anniv of Settlement of Montserrat.
84 **10** ½d. green 75 7·50
85 1d. red 75 5·50
86 1½d. brown 1·25 2·50
87 2d. grey 1·50 16·00
88 2½d. blue 1·25 15·00
89 3d. orange 1·50 16·00
90 6d. violet 2·25 27·00
91 1s. olive 12·00 35·00
92 2s.6d. purple 48·00 70·00
93 5s. brown £100 £160

1935. Silver Jubilee. As T **14a** of Kenya, Uganda and Tanganyika.
94 1d. blue and red 85 3·25
95 1½d. blue and grey 1·50 2·75
96 2½d. brown and blue 2·25 3·25
97 1s. grey and purple 3·00 14·00

1937. Coronation. As T **14b** of Kenya, Uganda and Tanganyika.
98 1d. red 30 1·00
99 1½d. brown 40 30
100 2½d. blue 40 1·10

11 Carr's Bay

1938. King George VI.
101a **11** ½d. green 15 20
102a – 1d. red 50 30
103a – 1½d. purple 50 50
104a – 2d. orange 1·50 70
105a – 2½d. blue 50 30
106a **11** 3d. brown 2·00 40
107a – 6d. violet 2·50 60
108a **11** 1s. red 2·25 30
109a – 2s.6d. blue 17·00 2·50
110a **11** 5s. red 21·00 3·00
111 – 10s. blue 13·00 19·00
112 **11** £1 black 13·00 27·00
DESIGNS: 1d., 1½d., 2½d. Sea Island cotton; 2d., 6d., 2s.6d., 10s. Botanic station.

1946. Victory. As T **4a** of Pitcairn Islands.
113 1½d. purple 10 10
114 3d. brown 10 10

1949. Silver Wedding. As T **4b/c** of Pitcairn Islands.
115 2½d. blue 10 10
116 5s. red 4·75 8·50

1949. U.P.U. As T **4d/g** of Pitcairn Islands.
117 2½d. blue 15 75
118 3d. brown 1·50 50
119 6d. purple 30 50
120 1s. purple 30 50

1951. Inauguration of B.W.I. University College. As T **15a/b** of Leeward Islands.
121 3c. black and purple 20 75
122 12c. black and violet 20 75

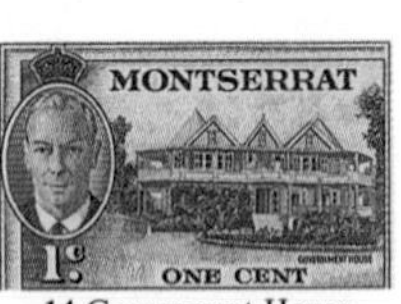

14 Government House

1951.
123 **14** 1c. black 10 2·00
124 – 2c. green 15 70
125 – 3c. brown 30 70
126 – 4c. red 30 70
127 – 5c. violet 30 70
128 – 6c. brown 30 30
129 – 8c. blue 70 20
130 – 12c. blue and brown 50 30
131 – 24c. red and green 1·25 30
132 – 60c. black and red 6·50 2·75
133 – $1.20 green and blue 6·50 6·00
134 – $2.40 black and green 7·00 12·00
135 – $4.80 black and purple 17·00 16·00
DESIGNS: 2c., $1.20, Sea Island cotton: cultivation; 3c. Map; 4c., 24c. Picking tomatoes; 5c., 12c. St. Anthony's Church; 6c., $4.80, Badge; 8c., 60c. Sea Island cotton: ginning; $2.40, Government House (portrait on right).

1953. Coronation. As T **4h** of Pitcairn Islands.
136 2c. black and green 50 30

1953. As 1951 but portrait of Queen Elizabeth II.
136a ½c. violet (As 3c.) (I) 50 10
136b ½c. violet (II) 80 10
137 1c. black 10 10
138 2c. green 15 10
139 3c. brown (I) 50 10
139a 3c. brown (II) 80 2·00
140 4c. red 30 20
141 5c. violet 30 50
142 6c. brown (I) 30 10
142a 6c. brown (II) 55 15
143 8c. blue 1·00 10
144 12c. blue and brown 1·50 10
145 24c. red and green 1·50 20
145a 48c. olive and purple (As 2c.) 12·00 2·25
146 60c. black and red 8·00 2·25
147 $1.20 green and blue 15·00 6·00
148 $2.40 black and green 13·00 12·00
149 $4.80 black and purple (I) 5·00 10·00
149a $4.80 black and purple (II) 16·00 7·50
I. Inscr "Presidency". II. Inscr "Colony".

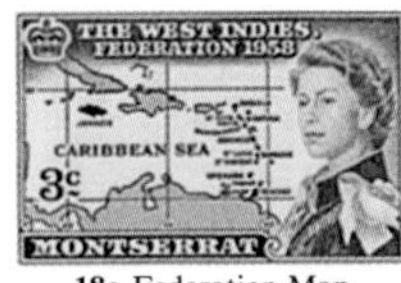

18a Federation Map

1958. Inauguration of British Caribbean Federation.
150 **18a** 3c. green 55 20
151 6c. blue 75 60
152 12c. red 90 15

1963. Freedom from Hunger. As T **20a** of Pitcairn Islands.
153 12c. violet 30 15

1963. Cent of Red Cross. As T **20b** of Pitcairn Islands.
154 4c. red and black 15 20
155 12c. red and blue 35 50

20 Shakespeare and Memorial Theatre, Stratford-upon-Avon

1964. 400th Birth Anniv of Shakespeare.
156 **20** 12c. blue 10 10

1965. Cent of I.T.U. As T **24a** of Pitcairn Islands.
158 4c. red and violet 15 10
159 48c. green and red 30 20

21 Pineapple

1965. Multicoloured.
160 1c. Type **21** 10 10
161 2c. Avocado 10 10
162 3c. Soursop 10 10
163 4c. Pepper 10 10
164 5c. Mango 10 10
165 6c. Tomato 10 10
166 8c. Guava 10 10
167 10c. Ochro 10 10
168 12c. Lime 15 40
169 20c. Orange 20 10
170 24c. Banana 20 10
171 42c. Onion 75 60
172 48c. Cabbage 1·50 75
173 60c. Pawpaw 3·00 1·10
174 $1.20 Pumpkin 2·00 4·00
175 $2.40 Sweet potato 6·00 8·00
176 $4.80 Egg plant 6·00 10·00

1965. I.C.Y. As T **24b** of Pitcairn Islands.
177 2c. purple and turquoise 10 20
178 12c. green and lavender 25 10

1966. Churchill Commem. As T **24c** of Pitcairn Islands.
179 1c. blue 10 60
180 2c. green 10 10
181 24c. brown 20 10
182 42c. violet 25 30

23 Queen Elizabeth II and Duke of Edinburgh

1966. Royal Visit.
183 **23** 14c. black and blue 75 15
184 24c. black and mauve 1·00 15

24 W.H.O. Building

1966. Inauguration of W.H.O. Headquarters, Geneva.
185 **24** 12c. black, green and blue 15 25
186 60c. black, pur & ochre 35 75

1966. 20th Anniv of U.N.E.S.C.O. As T **25b/d** of Pitcairn Islands.
187 4c. multicoloured 10 10
188 60c. yellow, violet and olive 35 10
189 $1.80 black, purple and orange 1·40 70

25 Sailing Dinghies

1967. International Tourist Year. Multicoloured.
190 5c. Type **25** 15 10
191 15c. Waterfall near Chance Mountain (vert) 20 10
192 16c. Fishing, skin diving and swimming 25 70
193 24c. Playing golf 1·60 45

1968. Nos. 168, 170, 172, 174/6 surch.
194 15c. on 12c. Lime 20 15
195 25c. on 24c. Banana 25 15
196 50c. on 48c. Cabbage 45 15
197 $1 on $1.20 Pumpkin 80 40
198 $2.50 on $2.40 Sweet potato 1·00 4·25
199 $5 on $4.80 Egg plant 1·10 4·25

27 Sprinting

1968. Olympic Games, Mexico.
200 **27** 15c. mauve, green and gold 10 10
201 – 25c. blue, orange and gold 15 10
202 – 50c. green, red and gold 25 10
203 – $1 multicoloured 35 30
DESIGNS—HORIZ: 25c. Weightlifting; 50c. Gymnastics. VERT: $1 Sprinting and Aztec pillars.

31 Alexander Hamilton

1968. Human Rights Year. Multicoloured.
204 5c. Type **31** 10 10
205 15c. Albert T. Marryshow 10 10
206 25c. William Wilberforce 10 10
207 50c. Dag Hammarskjold 10 10
208 $1 Dr. Martin Luther King 25 30

32 "The Two Trinities" (Murillo)

34 Map showing CARIFTA Countries

1968. Christmas.
209 **32** 5c. multicoloured 10 10
210 – 15c. multicoloured 10 10
211 **32** 25c. multicoloured 10 10
212 – 50c. multicoloured 25 20
DESIGN: 15, 50c. "The Adoration of the Kings" (detail, Botticelli).

1969. 1st Anniv of CARIFTA (Caribbean Free Trade Area). Multicoloured.
223 15c. Type **34** 10 10
224 20c. Type **34** 10 10
225 35c. "Strength in Unity" (horiz) 10 20
226 50c. As 35c. (horiz) 15 20

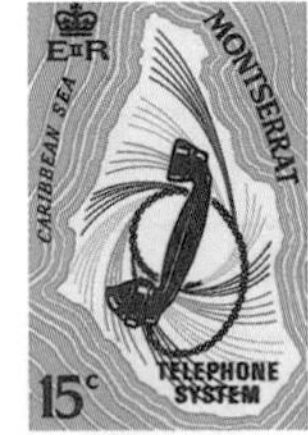

36 Telephone Receiver and Map of Montserrat

41 King Caspar before the Virgin and Child (detail) (Norman 16th-cent stained glass window)

40 Dolphin (fish)

1969. Development Projects. Multicoloured.
227 15c. Type **36** 10 10
228 25c. School symbols and map 10 10
229 50c. Hawker Siddeley H.S.748 aircraft and map 15 10
230 $1 Electricity pylon and map 25 70

1969. Game Fish. Multicoloured.
231 5c. Type **40** 35 10
232 15c. Atlantic sailfish 50 10
233 25c. Blackfin tuna 60 10
234 40c. Spanish mackerel 80 55

1969. Christmas. Paintings multicoloured; frame colours given.
235 **41** 15c. black, gold and violet 10 10
236 25c. black and red 10 10
237 – 50c. black, blue and orange 15 15
DESIGN—HORIZ: 50c. "Nativity" (Leonard Limosin).

43 "Red Cross Sale"

1970. Centenary of British Red Cross. Mult.
238 3c. Type **43** 10 25
239 4c. School for deaf children 10 25
240 15c. Transport services for disabled 10 20
241 20c. Workshop 10 60

44 Red-footed Booby

1970. Birds. Multicoloured.
242 1c. Type **44** 10 10
243 2c. American kestrel (vert) 15 15
244 3c. Magnificent frigate bird (vert) 15 15
245 4c. Great egret (vert) 1·00 15
299a 5c. Brown pelican (vert) 60 55
247 10c. Bananaquit (vert) 40 10
248 15c. Smooth-billed ani 30 15
249 20c. Red-billed tropic bird 35 15
250 25c. Montserrat oriole 50 50
251 50c. Green-throated carib (vert) 5·00 1·50
252 $1 Antillean crested hummingbird 6·50 1·00
253 $2.50 Little blue heron (vert) 5·50 12·00
254 $5 Purple-throated carib 7·50 15·00
254c $10 Forest thrush 15·00 15·00

45 "Madonna and Child with Animals" (Brueghel the Elder, after Durer)

1970. Christmas. Multicoloured.
255 5c. Type **45** 10 10
256 15c. "The Adoration of the Shepherds" (Domenichino) 10 10
257 20c. Type **45** 10 10
258 $1 As 15c. . . . . 35 1·50

46 War Memorial

1970. Tourism. Multicoloured.
259 5c. Type **46** 10 10
260 15c. Plymouth from Fort St. George 10 10
261 25c. Carr's Bay 15 15
262 50c. Golf Fairway . . . . . 1·00 2·00
MS263 135 × 109 mm. Nos. 259/62 2·50 2·00

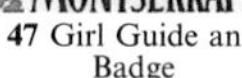

47 Girl Guide and Badge **48** "Descent from the Cross" (Van Hemessen)

1970. Diamond Jubilee of Montserrat Girl Guides. Multicoloured.
264 10c. Type **47** 10 10
265 15c. Brownie and badge . . . 10 10
266 25c. As 15c. 15 15
267 40c. Type **47** 20 75

1971. Easter. Multicoloured.
268 5c. Type **48** 10 10
269 15c. "Noli me tangere" (Orcagna) 10 10
270 20c. Type **48** 10 10
271 40c. As 15c. 15 80

49 D.F.C. and D.F.M. in Searchlights **50** "The Nativity with Saints" (Romanino)

1971. Golden Jubilee of Commonwealth Ex-Services League. Multicoloured.
272 10c. Type **49** 10 10
273 20c. M.C., M.M. and jungle patrol 15 10
274 40c. D.S.C., D.S.M. and submarine action 15 15
275 $1 V.C. and soldier attacking bunker 30 70

1971. Christmas. Multicoloured.
276 5c. Type **50** 10 10
277 15c. "Choir of Angels" (Simon Marmion) 10 10
278 20c. Type **50** 10 10
279 $1 As 15c. 35 40

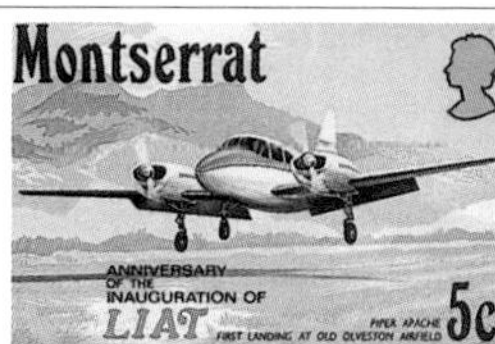

51 Piper Apache

1971. 14th Anniv of Inauguration of L.I.A.T. (Leeward Islands Air Transport). Multicoloured.
280 5c. Type **51** 10 10
281 10c. Beech 50 Twin Bonanza 15 15
282 15c. De Havilland Heron . . 30 15
283 20c. Britten Norman Islander 35 15
284 40c. De Havilland Twin Otter 100 . . . . 50 45
285 75c. Hawker Siddeley H.S.748 . . . . 1·40 2·25
MS286 203 × 102 mm. Nos. 280/5 7·00 13·00

52 "Chapel of Christ in Gethsemane", Coventry Cathedral

1972. Easter. Multicoloured.
287 5c. Type **52** 10 10
288 10c. "The Agony in the Garden" (Bellini) 10 10
289 20c. Type **52** 10 10
290 75c. As 10c. 35 50

53 Lizard **54** "Madonna of the Chair" (Raphael)

1972. Reptiles. Multicoloured.
291 15c. Type **53** 15 10
292 20c. Mountain chicken (frog) 20 10
293 40c. Iguana (horiz) 35 20
294 $1 Tortoise (horiz) . . . . . 1·00 1·00

1972. Christmas. Multicoloured.
303 10c. Type **54** 10 10
304 35c. "Virgin and Child with Cherub" (Fungai) 15 10
305 50c. "Madonna of the Magnificat" (Botticelli) . . 20 30
306 $1 "Virgin and Child with St. John and an Angel" (Botticelli) 30 65

55 Lime, Tomatoes and Pawpaw

1972. Royal Silver Wedding. Multicoloured, background colour given.
307 **55** 35c. pink 10 10
308 $1 blue 20 20

56 "Passiflora herbertiana" **58** "Virgin and Child" (School of Gerard David)

57 Montserrat Monastery, Spain

1973. Easter. Passion-flowers. Multicoloured.
309 20c. Type **56** 20 10
310 35c. "P. vitifolia" 25 10
311 75c. "P. amabilis" 35 75
312 $1 "P. alata-caerulea" . . . 50 80

1973. 480th Anniv of Columbus's Discovery of Montserrat. Multicoloured.
313 10c. Type **57** 15 10
314 35c. Columbus sighting Montserrat 30 15
315 60c. "Santa Maria" off Montserrat 70 60
316 $1 Island badge and map of voyage 80 70
MS317 126 × 134 mm. Nos. 313/16 9·00 13·00

1973. Christmas. Multicoloured.
318 20c. Type **58** 15 10
319 35c. "The Holy Family with St. John" (Jordaens) . . . 20 10
320 50c. "Virgin and Child" (Bellini) 25 30
321 90c. "Virgin and Child with Flowers" (Dolci) 50 70

58a Princess Anne and Captain Mark Phillips

1973. Royal Wedding. Multicoloured, background colour given.
322 **58a** 35c. green 10 10
323 $1 blue 20 20

59 Steel Band

1974. 25th Anniv of University of West Indies. Multicoloured.
324 20c. Type **59** 15 10
325 35c. Masqueraders (vert) . . 15 10
326 60c. Student weaving (vert) 25 45
327 $1 University Centre, Montserrat 30 55
MS328 130 × 89 mm. Nos. 324/7 1·75 6·00

60 Hands with Letters

1974. Centenary of U.P.U.
329 **60** 1c. multicoloured 10 10
330 – 2c. red, orange and black 10 10
331 **60** 3c. multicoloured 10 10
332 – 5c. orange, red and black 10 10
333 **60** 50c. multicoloured 20 20
334 – $1 blue, green and black 40 65
DESIGN: 2, 5c., $1 Figures from U.P.U. Monument.

1974. Various stamps surch.
335 2c. on $1 mult (No. 252) . . 30 2·25
336 5c. on 50c. mult (No. 333) . . 30 60
337 10c. on 60c. mult (No. 326) 65 1·75
338 20c. on $1 mult (No. 252) . . 30 2·00
339 35c. on $1 blue, green and black (No. 334) . . . . . 40 1·25

62 Churchill and Houses of Parliament

1974. Birth Cent of Sir Winston Churchill. Mult.
340 35c. Type **62** 15 10
341 70c. Churchill and Blenheim Palace 20 20
MS342 81 × 85 mm. Nos. 340/1 50 70

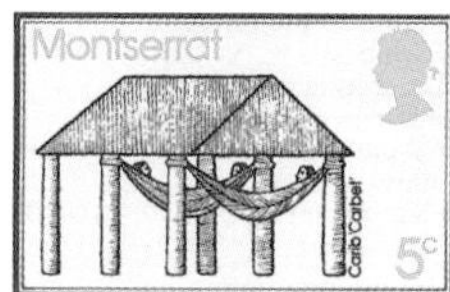

63 Carib "Carbet"

1975. Carib Artefacts. Self-adhesive or ordinary gum.
343 **63** 5c. brown, yellow and black 10 10
344 – 20c. black, brown & yellow 10 10
345 – 35c. black, yellow & brown 15 10
346 – 70c. yellow, brown & black 45 40
DESIGNS: 20c. "Caracoli"; 35c. Club or mace; 70c. Carib canoe.

64 One-Bitt Coin

1975. Local Coinage, 1785–1801.
351 **64** 5c. black, blue and silver 10 10
352 – 10c. black, pink and silver 15 10
353 – 35c. black, green and silver 20 15
354 – $2 black, red and silver . . 70 1·50
MS355 142 × 142 mm. Nos. 351/4 1·25 2·75
DESIGNS: 10c. Eighth dollar; 35c. Quarter dollar; $2 One dollar.

65 1d. and 6d. Stamps of 1876

1976. Centenary of First Montserrat Postage Stamp.
356 **65** 5c. red, green and black . . 15 10
357 – 10c. yellow, red and black 20 10
358 – 40c. multicoloured 50 40
359 – 55c. mauve, green and black 60 50
360 – 70c. multicoloured 70 70
361 – $1.10 green, blue and black 1·00 1·00
MS362 170 × 159 mm. Nos. 356/61 3·00 5·50
DESIGNS: 10c. G.P.O. and bisected 1d. stamp; 40c. Bisects on cover; 55c. G.B. 6d. used in Montserrat and local 6d. of 1876; 70c. Stamps for 2½d. rate, 1876; $1.10, Packet boat "Antelope" and 6d. stamp.

66 "The Trinity" **69** Mary and Joseph

68 White Frangipani

1976. Easter. Paintings by Orcagna. Multicoloured.

363	15c. Type **66**	10	10
364	40c. "The Resurrection"	15	15
365	55c. "The Ascension"	15	15
366	$1.10 "Pentecost"	30	40
MS367	160 × 142 mm. Nos. 363/6	1·25	2·25

1976. Nos. 244, 246 and 247 surch.

368	2c. on 5c. multicoloured	10	90
369	30c. on 10c. multicoloured	30	30
370	45c. on 3c. multicoloured	40	50

1976. Flowering Trees. Multicoloured.

371	1c. Type **68**	10	10
372	2c. Cannon-ball tree	10	10
373	3c. Lignum vitae	10	10
374	5c. Malay apple	15	10
375	10c. Jacaranda	30	10
376	15c. Orchid tree	50	10
377	20c. Manjak	30	10
378	25c. Tamarind	60	75
379	40c. Flame of the forest	30	30
380	55c. Pink cassia	40	40
381	70c. Long john	40	30
382	$1 Saman	50	80
383	$2.50 Immortelle	1·00	1·50
384	$5 Yellow poui	1·40	2·25
385	$10 Flamboyant	2·00	4·25

1976. Christmas. Multicoloured.

386	5c. Type **69**	10	10
387	20c. The Shepherds	10	10
388	55c. Mary and Jesus	15	15
389	$1.10 The Magi	30	50
MS390	95 × 135 mm. Nos. 386/9	60	2·25

70 Hudson River Review, 1976

1976. Bicent of American Revolution. Mult.

391	15c. Type **70**	55	20
392	40c. "Raleigh" (American frigate), 1777*	90	40
393	75c. H.M.S. "Druid" (frigate), 1777*	90	40
394	$1.25 Hudson River Review (different detail)	1·25	60
MS395	95 × 145 mm. Nos. 391/4	3·25	2·75

*The date is wrongly given on the stamps as "1776".

Nos. 391 and 394 and 392/3 respectively were issued in se-tenant pairs, each pair forming a composite design.

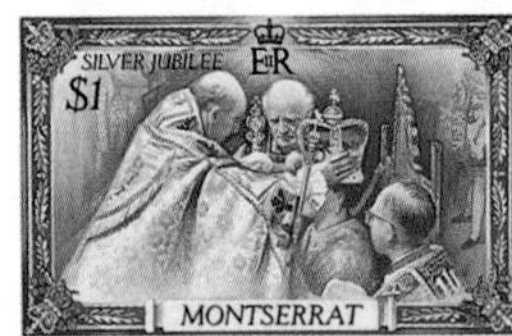

71 The Crowning

1977. Silver Jubilee. Multicoloured.

396	30c. Royal Visit, 1966	10	10
397	45c. Cannons firing salute	15	10
398	$1 Type **71**	25	50

72 "Ipomoea alba" **75** The Stable at Bethlehem

73 Princess Anne laying Foundation Stone of Glendon Hospital

1977. Flowers of the Night. Multicoloured.

399	15c. Type **72**	15	10
400	40c. "Epiphyllum hookeri" (horiz)	25	30
401	55c. "Cereus hexagonus" (horiz)	25	30
402	$1.50 "Cestrum nocturnum"	60	1·40
MS403	126 × 130 mm. Nos. 399/402	1·25	3·25

1977. Development. Multicoloured.

404	20c. Type **73**	30	10
405	40c. "Statesman" (freighter) in Plymouth Port	35	15
406	55c. Glendon Hospital	35	20
407	$1.50 Jetty at Plymouth Port	1·00	1·50
MS408	146 × 105 mm. Nos. 404/7	1·75	2·50

1977. Royal Visit. Nos. 380/1 and 383 surch **$1.00 SILVER JUBILEE 1977 ROYAL VISIT TO THE CARIBBEAN**.

409	$1 on 55c. Pink cassia	25	45
410	$1 on 70c. Long john	25	45
411	$1 on $2.50 Immortelle	25	45

1977. Christmas. Multicoloured.

412	5c. Type **75**	10	10
413	40c. The Three Kings	10	10
414	55c. Three Ships	15	10
415	$2 Three Angels	40	1·75
MS416	119 × 115 mm. Nos. 412/15	1·00	2·25

76 Four-eyed Butterflyfish

1978. Fish. Multicoloured.

417	30c. Type **76**	55	10
418	40c. French angelfish	60	15
419	55c. Blue tang	70	15
420	$1.50 Queen triggerfish	1·10	1·25
MS421	152 × 102 mm. Nos. 417/20	3·50	3·00

77 St. Paul's Cathedral

1978. 25th Anniv of Coronation. Multicoloured.

422	40c. Type **77**	10	10
423	55c. Chichester Cathedral	10	10
424	$1 Lincoln Cathedral	20	25
425	$2.50 Llandaff Cathedral	40	50
MS426	130 × 102 mm. Nos. 422/5	70	1·25

78 "Alpinia speciosa"

79 Private, 21st (Royal North British Fusiliers), 1786

1978. Flowers. Multicoloured.

427	40c. Type **78**	20	10
428	55c. "Allamanda cathartica"	20	15
429	$1 "Petrea volubilis"	35	45
430	$2 "Hippeastrum puniceum"	55	80

1978. Military Uniforms (1st series). British Infantry Regiments. Multicoloured.

431	30c. Type **79**	15	15
432	40c. Corporal, 86th (Royal County Down), 1831	20	15
433	55c. Sergeant, 14th (Buckinghamshire), 1837	25	15
434	$1.50 Officer, 55th (Westmorland), 1784	50	80
MS435	140 × 89 mm. Nos. 431/4	1·50	2·75

See also Nos. 441/5.

80 Cub Scouts

1979. 50th Anniv of Boy Scout Movement on Montserrat. Multicoloured.

436	40c. Type **80**	20	10
437	55c. Scouts with signalling equipment	20	15
438	$1.25 Camp fire (vert)	35	60
439	$2 Oath ceremony (vert)	45	1·00
MS440	120 × 110 mm. Nos. 436/9	1·25	2·25

1979. Military Uniforms (2nd series). As T **79**. Multicoloured.

441	30c. Private, 60th (Royal American), 1783	15	15
442	40c. Private, 1st West India, 1819	20	15
443	55c. Officer, 5th (Northumberland), 1819	20	15
444	$2.50 Officer, 93rd (Sutherland Highlanders), 1830	60	1·25
MS445	139 × 89 mm. Nos. 441/4	1·25	2·50

81 Child reaching out to Adult

1979. International Year of the Child.

446	**81** $2 black, brown and flesh	50	55
MS447	85 × 99 mm. No. 446	50	1·10

82 Sir Rowland Hill with Penny Black and Montserrat 1876 1d. Stamp

1979. Death Cent of Sir Rowland Hill and Cent of U.P.U. Membership. Multicoloured.

448	40c. Type **82**	20	10
449	55c. U.P.U. emblem and notice announcing Leeward Islands entry into Union	20	15
450	$1 1883 letter following U.P.U. membership	30	50
451	$2 Great Britain Post Office Regulations Notice and Sir Rowland Hill	40	1·25
MS452	135 × 154 mm. Nos. 448/51	1·00	2·25

83 Plume Worm

1979. Marine Life. Multicoloured.

453	40c. Type **83**	30	15
454	55c. Sea fans	40	20
455	$2 Sponge and coral	1·00	2·50

84 Tree Frog

1980. Reptiles and Amphibians. Mult.

456	40c. Type **84**	15	15
457	55c. Tree lizard	15	15
458	$1 Crapaud	30	50
459	$2 Wood slave	50	1·00

85 "Marquess of Salisbury" and 1838 Handstamps

1980. "London 1980" Int Stamp Exhibition. Mult.

460	40c. Type **85**	20	15
461	55c. Hawker Siddeley H.S.748 aircraft and 1976 55c. definitive	25	25
462	$1.20 "La Plata" (liner) and 1903 5s. stamp	30	45
463	$1.20 "Lady Hawkins" (packet steamer) and 1932 Tercentenary 5s. commemorative	30	45
464	$1.20 "Avon I" (paddle-steamer) and Penny Red stamp with "A 08" postmark	30	45
465	$1.20 Aeronca Champion 17 airplane and 1953 $1.20 definitive	30	45
MS466	115 × 110 mm. Nos. 460/5	1·25	2·50

1980. 75th Anniv of Rotary International. No. 383 optd **75th Anniversary of Rotary International**.

467	$2.50 Immortelle	55	85

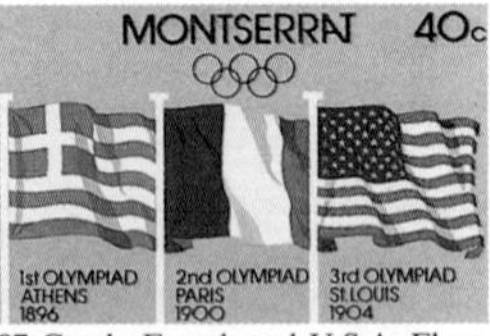

87 Greek, French and U.S.A. Flags

1980. Olympic Games, Moscow. Multicoloured.

468	40c. Type **87**	20	55
469	55c. Union, Swedish and Belgian flags	20	55
470	70c. French, Dutch and U.S.A. flags	25	70
471	$1 German, Union and Finnish flags	30	70
472	$1.50 Australian, Italian and Japanese flags	35	90
473	$2 Mexican, West German and Canadian flags	40	90
474	$2.50 "The Discus Thrower" (sculpture, Miron)	40	1·00
MS475	150 × 100 mm. Nos. 468/74	1·75	3·50

1980. Nos. 371, 373, 376 and 379 surch.

476	5c. on 3c. Lignum vitae	10	10
477	35c. on 1c. Type **68**	15	15
478	35c. on 3c. Lignum vitae	15	15
479	35c. on 15c. Orchid tree	15	15
480	55c. on 40c. Flame of the forest	15	15
481	$5 on 40c. Flame of the forest	60	2·00

89 "Lady Nelson", 1928

1980. Mail Packet Boats (1st series). Mult.

482	40c. Type **89**	30	15
483	55c. "Chignecto", 1913	30	15
484	$1 "Solent II", 1878	50	65
485	$2 "Dee", 1841	70	1·25

See also Nos. 615/19.

90 "Heliconius charithonia"

91 Atlantic Spadefish

1981. Butterflies. Multicoloured.

486	50c. Type **90**	50	40
487	65c. "Pyrgus oileus"	60	45
488	$1.50 "Phoebis agarithe"	70	85
489	$2.50 "Danaus plexippus"	1·00	1·10

1981. Fishes. Multicoloured.

555	5c. Type **91**	20	10
556	10c. Hogfish and neon goby	25	10
492	15c. Creole wrasse	80	30
493	20c. Three-spotted damselfish	70	10
559	25c. Sergeant major	35	20
560	35c. Fin-spot wrasse	45	30
496	45c. Schoolmaster	80	40
497	55c. Striped parrotfish	1·10	45
498	65c. Bigeye	80	60
564	75c. French grunt	75	55
565	$1 Rock beauty	85	65
501	$2 Blue chromis	1·50	1·10
502	$3 Royal gramma ("Fairy basslet") and blueheads	1·60	1·75
503	$5 Cherub angelfish	2·00	2·75
504	$7.50 Long-jawed squirrelfish	2·50	4·75
570	$10 Caribbean long-nosed butterflyfish	2·50	6·00

92 Fort St. George

1981. Montserrat National Trust. Multicoloured.
506 50c. Type **92** 25 20
507 65c. Bird sanctuary, Fox's Bay 45 35
508 $1.50 Museum 50 65
509 $2.50 Bransby Point Battery, c. 1780 60 1·10

1981. Royal Wedding. Royal Yachts. As T **26/27** of Kiribati. Multicoloured.
510 90c. "Charlotte" 25 25
511 90c. Prince Charles and Lady Diana Spencer 85 85
512 $3 "Portsmouth" 60 60
513 $3 As No. 511 1·50 1·50
514 $4 "Britannia" 75 75
515 $4 As No. 511 1·75 1·75
MS516 120 × 109 mm. $5 As No. 511 1·00 1·00

93 H.M.S. "Dorsetshire" and Fairey Firefly Seaplane

1981. 50th Anniv of Montserrat Airmail Service. Multicoloured.
519 50c. Type **93** 30 30
520 65c. Beech 50 Twin Bonanza 40 30
521 $1.50 De Havilland Dragon Rapide "Lord Shaftesbury" 60 1·50
522 $2.50 Hawker Siddeley H.S.748 and maps of Montserrat and Antigua 80 2·75

94 Methodist Church, Bethel

95 Rubiaceae ("Rondeletia buxifolia")

1981. Christmas. Churches. Multicoloured.
523 50c. Type **94** 15 15
524 65c. St. George's Anglican Church, Harris 15 15
525 $1.50 St. Peter's Anglican Church, St. Peter's 30 60
526 $2.50 St. Patrick's R.C. Church, Plymouth 50 1·00
MS527 176 × 120 mm. Nos. 523/6 1·75 3·00

1982. Plant Life. Multicoloured.
528 50c. Type **95** 20 30
529 65c. Boraginaceae ("Heliotropium ternatum") (horiz) 25 40
530 $1.50 Simarubaceae ("Picramnia pentandra") 50 85
531 $2.50 Ebenaceae ("Diospyrus revoluta") (horiz) 70 1·25

96 Plymouth

1982. 350th Anniv of Settlement of Montserrat by Sir Thomas Warner.
532 **96** 40c. green 25 30
533 55c. red 20 35
534 65c. brown 30 50
535 75c. grey 30 60
536 85c. blue 30 75
537 95c. orange 30 80
538 $1 violet 30 80
539 $1.50 olive 35 1·25
540 $2 claret 45 1·50
541 $2.50 brown 50 1·50
The design of Nos. 532/41 is based on the 1932 Tercentenary set.

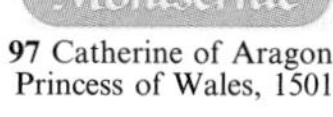

97 Catherine of Aragon, Princess of Wales, 1501

98 Local Scout

1982. 21st Birthday of Princess of Wales. Mult.
542 75c. Type **97** 15 15
543 $1 Coat of Arms of Catherine of Aragon 15 15
544 $5 Diana, Princess of Wales 80 1·25

1982. 75th Anniv of Boy Scout Movement. Mult.
545 $1.50 Type **98** 50 50
546 $2.20 Lord Baden-Powell 60 75

99 Annunciation

1982. Christmas. Multicoloured.
547 35c. Type **99** 15 15
548 75c. Shepherds' Vision 25 35
549 $1.50 The Stable 45 85
550 $2.50 Flight into Egypt 55 1·10

100 "Lepthemis vesiculosa"

1983. Dragonflies. Multicoloured.
551 50c. Type **100** 40 20
552 65c. "Orthemis ferruginea" 50 25
553 $1.50 "Triacanthagyna trifida" 1·00 1·25
554 $2.50 "Erythrodiplax umbrata" 1·40 2·50

101 Blue-headed Hummingbird

102 Montserrat Emblem

1983. Hummingbirds. Multicoloured.
571 35c. Type **101** 1·50 35
572 75c. Green-throated carib 1·75 85
573 $2 Antilean crested hummingbird 2·75 2·75
574 $3 Purple-throated carib 3·00 3·75

1983.
575 **102** $12 blue and red 3·50 5·00
576 $30 red and blue 6·50 12·00

1983. Various stamps surch. (a) Nos. 491, 494, 498/9 and 501.
577 40c. on 25c. Sergeant major (No. 494) 30 35
578 70c. on 10c. Hogfish and neon goby (No. 491) 45 50
579 90c. on 65c. Bigeye (No. 498) 55 70
580 $1.15 on 75c. French grunt (No. 499) 65 80
581 $1.50 on $2 Blue chromis (No. 501) 85 1·00

(b) Nos. 512/15.
582 70c. on $3 "Portsmouth" 50 1·00
583 70c. on $3 Prince Charles and Lady Diana Spencer 1·50 2·75
584 $1.15 on $4 "Britannia" 65 1·50
585 $1.15 on $4 As No. 583 1·75 3·25

104 Montgolfier Balloon, 1783

106 Statue of Discus Thrower

105 Boys dressed as Clowns

1983. Bicentenary of Manned Flight. Mult.
586 35c. Type **104** 15 15
587 75c. De Havilland Twin Otter 200/300 (horiz) 25 30
588 $1.50 Lockheed Vega V (horiz) 40 75
589 $2 Beardmore airship R.34 (horiz) 60 1·25
MS590 109 × 145 mm. Nos. 586/9 1·25 2·75

1983. Christmas. Carnival. Multicoloured.
591 55c. Type **105** 10 10
592 90c. Girls dressed as silver star bursts 15 20
593 $1.15 Flower girls 20 35
594 $2 Masqueraders 35 80

1984. Olympic Games, Los Angeles. Mult.
595 90c. Type **106** 30 35
596 $1 Olympic torch 35 45
597 $1.25 Los Angeles Olympic stadium 40 50
598 $2.50 Olympic and American flags 65 1·00
MS599 110 × 110 mm. Nos. 595/8 1·50 2·25

107 Cattle Egret

1984. Birds of Montserrat. Multicoloured.
600 5c. Type **107** 30 50
601 10c. Carib grackle 30 50
602 15c. Moorhen ("Common Gallinule") 30 50
603 20c. Brown booby 40 50
604 25c. Black-whiskered vireo 40 50
605 40c. Scaly-breasted thrasher 60 60
606 55c. Laughing gull 75 30
607 70c. Glossy ibis 90 50
608 90c. Green-backed heron ("Green Heron") 1·00 60
609 $1 Belted kingfisher (vert) 1·25 70
610 $1.15 Bananaquit (vert) 1·50 1·40
611 $3 American kestrel ("Sparrow Hawk") (vert) 3·25 5·50
612 $5 Forest thrush (vert) 4·50 7·50
613 $7.50 Black-crowned night heron (vert) 5·00 13·00
614 $10 Bridled quail dove (vert) 5·50 13·00

1984. Mail Packet Boats (2nd series). As T **89**. Multicoloured.
615 55c. "Tagus II", 1907 20 40
616 90c. "Cobequid", 1913 30 50
617 $1.15 "Lady Drake", 1942 40 70
618 $2 "Factor", 1948 60 1·25
MS619 152 × 100 mm. Nos. 615/18 2·00 5·00
No. **MS**619 also commemorates the 250th anniversary of "Lloyd's List" (newspaper).

108 Hermit Crab and West Indian Top Shell

1984. Marine Life. Multicoloured.
620 90c. Type **108** 1·50 1·00
621 $1.15 Rough file shell 1·75 1·40
622 $1.50 True tulip 2·50 3·00
623 $2.50 Queen or pink conch 3·25 4·75

109 "Bull Man"

1984. Christmas. Carnival Costumes. Mult.
624 55c. Type **109** 50 25
625 $1.15 Masquerader Captain 1·50 1·25
626 $1.50 "Fantasy" Carnival Queen 1·75 2·25
627 $2.30 "Ebony and Ivory" Carnival Queen 2·50 4·00

110 Mango

111 "Oncidium urophyllum"

1985. National Emblems. Multicoloured.
628 $1.15 Type **110** 30 60
629 $1.50 Lobster claw 40 1·00
630 $3 Montserrat oriole 60 2·50

1985. Orchids of Montserrat. Multicoloured.
631 90c. Type **111** 40 55
632 $1.15 "Epidendrum difforme" 40 80
633 $1.50 "Epidendrum ciliare" 45 1·10
634 $2.50 "Brassavola cucullata" 55 2·50
MS635 120 × 140 mm. Nos. 631/4 3·75 6·50

112 Queen Elizabeth the Queen Mother

115 Black-throated Blue Warbler

113 Cotton Plants

1985. Life and Times of Queen Elizabeth the Queen Mother. Various vertical portraits.
636 **112** 55c. multicoloured 25 40
637 – 55c. multicoloured 25 40
638 – 90c. multicoloured 25 50
639 – 90c. multicoloured 25 50
640 – $1.15 multicoloured 25 50
641 – $1.15 multicoloured 25 50
642 – $1.50 multicoloured 30 55
643 – $1.50 multicoloured 30 55
MS644 85 × 113 mm. $2 multicoloured; $2 multicoloured 65 1·90
Each value was issued in pairs showing a floral pattern across the bottom of the portraits which stops short of the left-hand edge on the first stamp and of the right-hand edge on the second.

1985. Montserrat Sea Island Cotton Industry. Multicoloured.
645 90c. Type **113** 25 45
646 $1 Operator at carding machine 25 50
647 $1.15 Threading loom 25 65
648 $2.50 Weaving with hand loom 50 2·50
MS649 148 × 103 mm. Nos. 645/8 3·00 3·75

1985. Royal Visit. Nos. 514/15, 543, 587/8 and 640/1 optd **CARIBBEAN ROYAL VISIT 1985** or surch also.
650 75c. multicoloured (No. 587) 3·00 2·50
651 $1 multicoloured (No. 543) 4·50 3·50
652 $1.15 multicoloured (No. 640) 4·25 6·00
653 $1.15 multicoloured (No. 641) 4·25 6·00
654 $1.50 multicoloured (No. 588) 7·00 7·00
655 $1.60 on $4 mult (No. 514) 2·00 4·00
656 $1.60 on $4 mult (No. 515) 17·00 20·00
No. 656 shows a new face value only, "CARIBBEAN ROYAL VISIT 1985" being omitted from the surcharge.

1985. Leaders of the World. Birth Bicentenary of John J. Audubon (ornithologist). Designs showing original paintings. Multicoloured.
657 15c. Type **115** 15 35
658 15c. Palm warbler 15 35
659 30c. Bobolink 15 40
660 30c. Lark sparrow 15 40
661 55c. Chipping sparrow 20 40
662 55c. Northern oriole 20 40
663 $2.50 American goldfinch 40 1·25
664 $2.50 Blue grosbeak 40 1·25

116 Herald Angel appearing to Goatherds

1985. Christmas. Designs showing Caribbean Nativity. Multicoloured.
665 70c. Type **116** 15 15
666 $1.15 Three Wise Men following Star 25 40
667 $1.50 Carol singing around War Memorial, Plymouth 30 70
668 $2.30 Praying to "Our Lady of Montserrat", Church of Our Lady, St. Patrick's Village 45 1·75

117 Lord Baden-Powell

1986. 50th Anniv of Montserrat Girl Guide Movement. Multicoloured.
669 20c. Type **117** 15 60
670 20c. Girl Guide saluting . . . 15 60
671 75c. Lady Baden-Powell . . . 25 75
672 75c. Guide assisting in old people's home 25 75
673 90c. Lord and Lady Baden-Powell 30 75
674 90c. Guides serving meal in old people's home 30 75
675 $1.15 Girl Guides of 1936 . . 40 80
676 $1.15 Two guides saluting . . 40 80

117a Queen Elizabeth II

1986. 60th Birthday of Queen Elizabeth II. Multicoloured.
677 10c. Type **117a** 10 10
678 $1.50 Princess Elizabeth in 1928 . . . . 25 50
679 $3 In Antigua, 1977 . . . . 40 1·00
680 $6 In Canberra, 1982 (vert) 65 2·00
MS681 85 × 115 mm. $8 Queen with bouquet . . . . 3·25 5·50

118 King Harold and Halley's Comet, 1066 (from Bayeux Tapestry)

1986. Appearance of Halley's Comet. Mult.
682 35c. Type **118** 20 25
683 50c. Comet of 1301 (from Giotto's "Adoration of the Magi") 25 30
684 70c. Edmond Halley and Comet of 1531 . . . . . 25 40
685 $1 Comets of 1066 and 1910 25 40
686 $1.15 Comet of 1910 . . . . 30 50
687 $1.50 E.S.A. "Giotto" spacecraft and Comet . . . 30 80
688 $2.30 U.S. space telescope and Comet . . . . 40 1·75
689 $4 Computer reconstruction of 1910 Comet . . . . . . 50 3·25
MS690 Two sheets, each 140 × 115 mm. (a) 40c. Type **118**; $1.75, As No. 683; $2 As No. 684; $3 As No. 685. (b) 55c. As No. 686; 60c. As No. 687; 80c. As No. 688; $5 As No. 689 Set of 2 sheets . . . . 2·75 9·00

118a Prince Andrew

1986. Royal Wedding (1st issue). Multicoloured.
691 70c. Type **118a** 25 35
692 70c. Miss Sarah Ferguson . . 25 35
693 $2 Prince Andrew wearing stetson (horiz) 40 80
694 $2 Miss Sarah Ferguson on skiing holiday (horiz) . . . 40 80
MS695 115 × 85 mm. $10 Duke and Duchess of York on Palace balcony after wedding (horiz) 3·00 4·75
See also Nos. 705/8.

119 "Antelope" being attacked by "L'Atalante"

1986. Mail Packet Sailing Ships. Mult.
696 90c. Type **119** . . . . 2·00 1·50
697 $1.15 "Montagu" (1810) . . 2·25 2·00
698 $1.50 "Little Catherine" being pursued by "L'Etoile" (1813) . . . . . 2·75 2·75
699 $2.30 "Hinchingbrook I" (1813) . . . . 3·50 5·00
MS700 165 × 123 mm. Nos. 696/9 10·00 11·00

120 Radio Montserrat Building, Dagenham

1986. Communications. Multicoloured.
701 70c. Type **120** . . . . 1·00 70
702 $1.15 Radio Gem dish aerial, Plymouth . . . . 1·00 1·50
703 $1.50 Radio Antilles studio, O'Garro's . . . . 1·75 2·25
704 $2.30 Cable and Wireless building, Plymouth . . . . 2·25 4·25

1986. Royal Wedding (2nd issue). Nos. 691/4 optd **Congratulations to T.R.H. The Duke & Duchess of York**.
705 70c. Prince Andrew . . . . . 70 1·25
706 70c. Miss Sarah Ferguson . . 70 1·25
707 $2 Prince Andrew wearing stetson (horiz) . . . . . . 1·25 1·75
708 $2 Miss Sarah Ferguson on skiing holiday (horiz) . . . 1·25 1·75

121a Statue of Liberty

123 Christmas Rose

122 Sailing and Windsurfing

1986. Centenary of Statue of Liberty. Vert views of Statue as T **121a** in separate miniature sheets. Multicoloured.
MS709 Three sheets, each 85 × 115 mm. $3; $4.50; $5 Set of 3 sheets . . . . 3·75 9·00

1986. Tourism. Multicoloured.
710 70c. Type **122** 40 70
711 $1.15 Golf . . . . 70 1·50
712 $1.50 Plymouth market . . . 70 2·00
713 $2.30 Air Recording Studios 80 3·00

1986. Christmas. Flowering Shrubs. Mult.
714 70c. Type **123** 70 40
715 $1.15 Candle flower 95 85
716 $1.50 Christmas tree kalanchoe . . . . 1·50 1·50
717 $2.30 Snow on the mountain 2·00 4·50
MS718 150 × 110 mm. Nos. 714/17 7·50 8·00

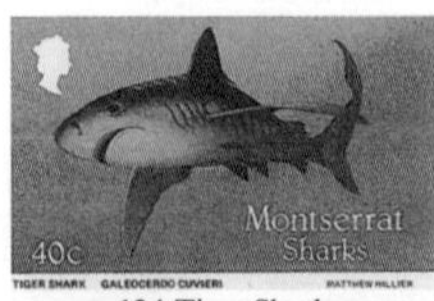

124 Tiger Shark

1987. Sharks. Multicoloured.
719 40c. Type **124** . . . . 1·50 55
720 90c. Lemon shark . . . . . 2·50 1·50
721 $1.15 Great white shark . . . 2·75 2·00
722 $3.50 Whale shark . . . . . 5·50 8·00
MS723 150 × 102 mm. Nos. 719/22 12·00 14·00

1987. Nos. 601, 603, 607/8 and 611 surch.
724 5c. on 70c. Glossy ibis . . . 50 2·25
725 $1 on 20c. Brown booby . . 1·75 1·00
726 $1.15 on 10c. Carib grackle 2·00 1·40
727 $1.50 on 90c. Green-backed heron . . . . 2·25 2·50
728 $2.30 on $3 American kestrel (vert) . . . . 3·25 7·50

1987. "Capex '87" International Stamp Exhibition, Toronto. No. **MS**690 optd with **CAPEX 87** logo.
MS729 Two sheets. As No. **MS**690 Set of 2 sheets . . . . 4·00 10·00
No. **MS**729 also carries an overprint commemorating the exhibition on the lower sheet margins.

127 "Phoebis trite"

128 "Oncidium variegatum"

1987. Butterflies. Multicoloured.
730 90c. Type **127** . . . . 2·00 1·10
731 $1.15 "Biblis hyperia" . . . 2·50 1·60
732 $1.50 "Polygonus leo" . . . 3·00 2·50
733 $2.50 "Hypolimnas misippus" 4·50 6·50

1987. Christmas. Orchids. Multicoloured.
734 90c. Type **128** 60 45
735 $1.15 "Vanilla planifolia" (horiz) 85 55
736 $1.50 "Gongora quinquenervis" . . . . . . 1·10 1·10
737 $3.50 "Brassavola nodosa" (horiz) . . . . 2·00 5·00
MS738 100 × 75 mm. $5 "Oncidium lanceanum" (horiz) . . . . . 10·00 12·00

1987. Royal Ruby Wedding. Nos. 601, 604/5 and 608 surch **40th Wedding Anniversary HM Queen Elizabeth II HRH Duke of Edinburgh. November 1987.** and value.
739B 5c. on 90c. Green-backed heron 30 40
740B $1.15 on 10c. Carib grackle 1·00 1·00
741B $2.30 on 25c. Black-whiskered vireo . . . . . 1·75 2·25
742B $5 on 40c. Scaly-breasted thrasher . . . . 3·50 5·00

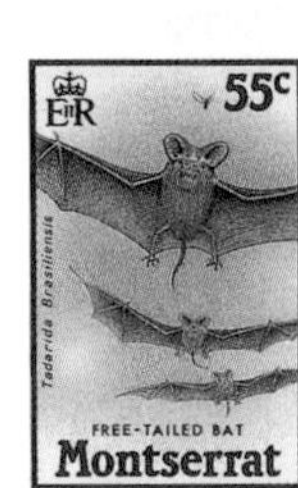

130 Free-tailed Bat

131 Magnificent Frigate Bird

1988. Bats. Multicoloured.
743 55c. Type **130** 80 40
744 90c. "Chiroderma improvisum" (fruit bat) . . 1·25 90
745 $1.15 Fisherman bat . . . . 1·60 1·50
746 $2.30 "Brachyphylla cavernarum" (fruit bat) . . 3·00 5·50
MS747 133 × 110 mm. $2.50 Funnel-eared bat . . . . 6·50 8·00

1988. Easter. Birds. Multicoloured.
748 90c. Type **131** 60 45
749 $1.15 Caribbean elaenia . . . 80 75
750 $1.50 Glossy ibis . . . . . . 1·00 1·50
751 $3.50 Purple-throated carib 2·00 4·00
MS752 100 × 75 mm. $5 Brown pelican . . . . 2·50 3·50

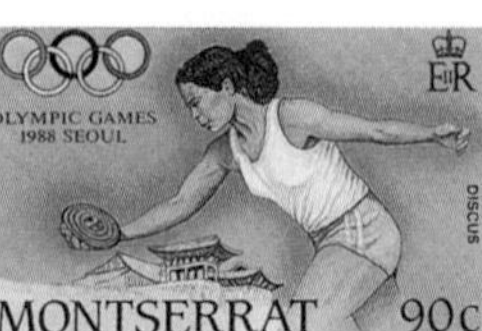

132 Discus throwing

1988. Olympic Games, Seoul. Multicoloured.
753 90c. Type **132** 70 50
754 $1.15 High jumping 80 55
755 $3.50 Athletics . . . . 2·00 3·25
MS756 103 × 77 mm. $5 Rowing 3·00 3·00

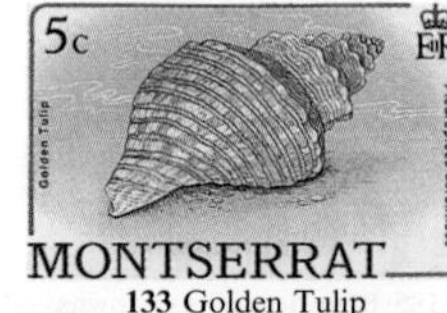

133 Golden Tulip

1988. Sea Shells. Multicoloured.
757 5c. Type **133** 30 50
758 10c. Little knobbed scallop 40 50
759 15c. Sozoni's cone 40 50
760 20c. Globular coral shell . . 50 50
761 25c. American or common sundial 50 50
762 40c. King helmet 60 50
763 55c. Channelled turban . . . 80 50
764 70c. True tulip . . . . 1·00 75
765 90c. Music volute . . . . . 1·25 75
766 $1 Flame auger . . . . . . 1·40 80
767 $1.15 Rooster-tail conch . . 1·50 90
768 $1.50 Queen or pink conch 1·60 1·40
769 $3 Teramachi's slit shell . . . 2·50 4·25
770 $5 Common or Florida crown conch . . . . 3·50 6·50
771 $7.50 Beau's murex . . . . . 4·50 11·00
772 $10 Atlantic trumpet triton 5·50 11·00

134 University Crest

1988. 40th Anniv of University of West Indies.
773 **134** $5 multicoloured . . . . 2·40 3·50

1988. Princess Alexandra's Visit. Nos. 763, 766 and 769/70 surch **HRH PRINCESS ALEXANDRA'S VISIT NOVEMBER 1988** and new value.
774 40c. on 55c. Channelled turban 45 45
775 90c. on $1 Flame auger . . . 70 80
776 $1.15 on $3 Teramachi's slit shell 85 95
777 $1.50 on $5 Common or Florida crown conch . . . 1·10 1·50

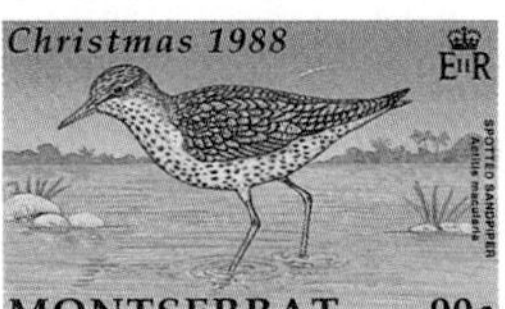

136 Spotted Sandpiper

1988. Christmas. Sea Birds. Multicoloured.
778 90c. Type **136** 70 55
779 $1.15 Ruddy turnstone . . . 85 70
780 $3.50 Red-footed booby . . . 2·00 3·75
MS781 105 × 79 mm. $5 Audubon's shearwater . . . . 2·75 4·00

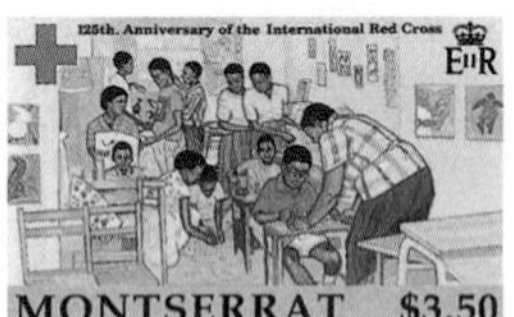

137 Handicapped Children in Classroom

1988. 125th Anniv of International Red Cross.
782 **137** $3.50 multicoloured . . . 1·50 2·25

138 Drum Major in Ceremonial Uniform

1989. 75th Anniv (1986) of Montserrat Defence Force. Uniforms. Multicoloured.
783 90c. Type **138** 70 50
784 $1.15 Field training uniform 85 75
785 $1.50 Cadet in ceremonial uniform . . . . 1·25 1·75
786 $3.50 Gazetted Police Officer in ceremonial uniform . . 2·50 3·75
MS787 102 × 76 mm. $5 Island Girl Guide Commissioner and brownie 3·50 4·25

139 Amazon Lily

1989. Easter. Lilies. Multicoloured.
788 90c. Type **139** 50 50
789 $1.15 Salmon blood lily (vert) 70 70
790 $1.50 Amaryllis (vert) . . . . 85 1·25
791 $3.50 Amaryllis (vert) . . . . 1·90 3·00
MS792 103 × 77 mm. $5 Resurrection lily (vert) . . . . 4·25 6·50

140 "Morning Prince" (schooner), 1942

1989. Shipbuilding in Montserrat. Mult.
793 90c. Type **140** . . . . 1·00 60
794 $1.15 "Western Sun" (inter-island freighter) . . . . . 1·50 1·10
795 $1.50 "Kim G" (inter-island freighter) under construction . . . . 1·75 2·25
796 $3.50 "Romaris" (inter-island ferry), c. 1942 . . . . . . 3·00 5·00

141 The Scarecrow

1989. 50th Anniv of "The Wizard of Oz" (film). Multicoloured.
797 90c. Type **141** 40 45
798 $1.15 The Lion 55 60
799 $1.50 The Tin Man 70 85
800 $3.50 Dorothy . . . . 1·60 2·50
MS801 113 × 84 mm. $5 Characters from film (horiz) . . . . . . 2·40 3·75

1989. Hurricane Hugo Relief Fund. Nos. 795/6 surch **Hurricane Hugo Relief Surcharge $2.50**.
802 $1.50+$2.50 "Kim G" (inter-island freighter under construction) . . . . . . 2·75 4·00
803 $3.50+$2.50 "Romaris" (inter-island ferry), c. 1942 3·00 5·00

143 "Apollo 11" above Lunar Surface

1989. 20th Anniv of First Manned Landing on Moon. Multicoloured.
804 90c. Type **143** 35 40
805 $1.15 Astronaut alighting from lunar module "Eagle" 45 50
806 $1.50 "Eagle" and astronaut conducting experiment . . 60 80
807 $3.50 Opening "Apollo 11" hatch after splashdown . . 1·40 2·50
MS808 101 × 76 mm. $5 Astronaut on Moon . . . . 4·75 6·00

144 "Yamato" (Japanese battleship)

1990. World War II Capital Ships. Multicoloured.
809 70c. Type **144** . . . . 2·25 70
810 $1.15 U.S.S."Arizona" at Pearl Harbor . . . . . . 2·75 95
811 $1.50 "Bismarck" (German battleship) in action . . . 3·50 2·50
812 $3.50 H.M.S. "Hood" (battle cruiser) . . . . 5·00 8·00
MS813 118 × 90 mm. $5 "Bismarck" and map of North Atlantic . . 11·00 11·00

145 The Empty Tomb

1990. Easter. Stained glass windows from St. Michael's Parish Church, Bray, Berkshire. Multicoloured.
814 $1.15 Type **145** . . . . . . 1·75 2·00
815 $1.50 The Ascension . . . . 1·75 2·00
816 $3.50 The Risen Christ with Disciples . . . . 2·50 3·00
MS817 65 × 103 mm. $5 The Crucifixion . . . . 4·50 6·00

1990. "Stamp World London '90" International Stamp Exhibition. Nos. 460/4 surch **Stamp World London 90**, emblem and value.
818 70c. on 40c. Type **85** 60 60
819 90c. on 55c. Hawker Siddeley H.S.748 aircraft and 1976 55c. definitive 80 80
820 $1 on $1.20 "La Plata" (liner) and 1903 5s. stamp 90 90
821 $1.15 on $1.20 "Lady Hawkins" (packet steamer) and 1932 Tercentenary 5s. commemorative . . . . . 1·10 1·10
822 $1.50 on $1.20 "Avon I" (paddle-steamer) and Penny Red stamp with "A 08" postmark . . . . 1·50 2·00

147 General Office, Montserrat and 1884 ½d. Stamp

1990. 150th Anniv of the Penny Black. Mult.
823 90c. Type **147** 65 65
824 $1.15 Sorting letters and Montserrat 1d. stamp of 1876 (vert) 85 90
825 $1.50 Posting letters and Penny Black (vert) . . . . 1·25 1·75
826 $3.50 Postman delivering letters and 1840 Twopence Blue . . . . 3·00 4·50
MS827 102 × 75 mm. $5 Montserrat soldier's letter of 1836 and Penny Black . . . . 7·50 9·00

148 Montserrat v. Antigua Match

1990. World Cup Football Championship, Italy. Multicoloured.
828 90c. Type **148** 65 55
829 $1.15 U.S.A. v. Trinidad match 85 75
830 $1.50 Montserrat team . . . 1·25 1·50
831 $3.50 West Germany v. Wales match . . . . 2·25 3·50
MS832 77 × 101 mm. $5 World Cup trophy (vert) . . . . 6·00 7·50

149 Spinner Dolphin

1990. Dolphins. Multicoloured.
833 90c. Type **149** . . . . 1·50 85
834 $1.15 Common dolphin . . . 1·75 1·25
835 $1.50 Striped dolphin . . . . 2·50 2·50
836 $3.50 Atlantic spotted dolphin . . . . 3·75 5·00
MS837 103 × 76 mm. $5 Atlantic white-sided dolphin . . . . . 8·50 9·50

150 Spotted Goatfish

1991. Tropical Fishes. Multicoloured.
838 90c. Type **150** . . . . 1·50 95
839 $1.15 Cushion star . . . . . 1·75 1·25
840 $1.50 Rock beauty . . . . . 2·50 2·75
841 $3.50 French grunt . . . . . 3·75 5·50
MS842 103 × 76 mm. $5 Buffalo trunkfish . . . . 5·50 7·00

1991. Nos. 760/1, 768 and 771 surch.
843 5c. on 20c. Globular coral shell . . . . 65 1·75
844 5c. on 25c. American or common sundial . . . . . 65 1·75
845 $1.15 on $1.50 Queen or pink conch . . . . 2·75 3·25
846 $1.15 on $7.50 Beau's murex 2·75 3·25

152 Duck

1991. Domestic Birds. Multicoloured.
847 90c. Type **152** 60 60
848 $1.15 Hen and chicks 80 90
849 $1.50 Red junglefowl ("Rooster") . . . . 1·10 1·50
850 $3.50 Helmeted guineafowl 2·40 3·50

153 "Panaeolus antillarum"

1991. Fungi.
851 **153** 90c. grey . . . . 1·25 1·00
852 – $1.15 red . . . . 1·50 1·25
853 – $1.50 brown . . . . . . 2·25 2·25
854 – $2 purple . . . . 2·50 3·25
855 – $3.50 blue . . . . 3·75 5·00
DESIGNS: $1.15, "Cantharellus cinnabarinus"; $1.50, "Gymnopilus chrysopellus"; $2 "Psilocybe cubensis"; $3.50, "Leptonia caeruleocapitata".

154 Red Water Lily

155 Tree Frog

1991. Lilies. Multicoloured.
856 90c. Type **154** 65 65
857 $1.15 Shell ginger 75 85
858 $1.50 Early day lily . . . . . 1·00 1·60
859 $3.50 Anthurium . . . . . . 2·50 3·75

1991. Frogs and Toad. Multicoloured.
860 $1.15 Type **155** . . . . . . 2·75 1·25
861 $2 Crapaud toad . . . . . . 4·00 4·00
862 $3.50 Mountain chicken (frog) . . . . 6·50 7·00
MS863 110 × 110 mm. $5 Tree frog, crapaud toad and mountain chicken (76½ × 44 mm) . . . . 9·00 9·50

156 Black British Shorthair Cat

1991. Cats. Multicoloured.
864 90c. Type **156** . . . . 1·50 90
865 $1.15 Seal point Siamese . . 1·75 1·10
866 $1.50 Silver tabby Persian . . 2·25 2·25
867 $2.50 Birman temple cat . . 3·00 3·75
868 $3.50 Egyptain mau . . . . 4·00 5·00

157 Navigational Instruments

1992. 500th Anniv of Discovery of America by Columbus. Multicoloured.
869 $1.50 Type **157** . . . . . . 1·25 1·50
870 $1.50 Columbus and coat of arms . . . . 1·25 1·50
871 $1.50 Landfall on the Bahamas . . . . 1·25 1·50
872 $1.50 Petitioning Queen Isabella . . . . 1·25 1·50
873 $1.50 Tropical birds . . . . 1·25 1·50
874 $1.50 Tropical fruits . . . . 1·25 1·50
875 $3 Ships of Columbus (81 × 26 mm) . . . . . . 1·75 2·00

158 Runner with Olympic Flame

1992. Olympic Games, Barcelona. Multicoloured.
876 $1 Type **158** 90 60
877 $1.15 Montserrat, Olympic and Spanish flags . . . . 1·25 90
878 $2.30 Olympic flame on map of Montserrat . . . . . . 2·25 2·75
879 $3.60 Olympic events . . . . 2·75 4·25

159 Tyrannosaurus

1992. Death Centenary of Sir Richard Owen (zoologist). Multicoloured.
880 $1 Type **159** . . . . 2·00 1·25
881 $1.15 Diplodocus . . . . . 2·25 1·40
882 $1.50 Apatosaurus . . . . . 2·75 2·75
883 $3.45 Dimetrodon . . . . . 5·50 8·00
MS884 114 × 84 mm. $4.60, Sir Richard Owen and dinosaur bone (vert) . . . . 8·50 10·00

160 Male Montserrat Oriole

1992. Montserrat Oriole. Multicoloured.
885 $1 Type **160** . . . . 1·10 1·10
886 $1.15 Male and female orioles 1·40 1·40
887 $1.50 Female oriole with chicks . . . . 1·75 2·00
888 $3.60 Map of Montserrat and male oriole . . . . 3·50 5·00

161 "Psophus stridulus" (grasshopper)

1992. Insects. Multicoloured.
889 5c. Type **161** 30 40
890 10c. "Gryllus campestris" (field cricket) 35 40
891 15c. "Lepthemis vesiculosa" (dragonfly) 40 40
892 20c. "Orthemis ferruginea" (red skimmer) 45 45
893 25c. "Gerris lacustris" (pond skater) 45 45
894 40c. "Byctiscus betulae" (leaf weevil) 60 50
895 55c. "Atta texana" (leaf-cutter ants) 60 40
896 70c. "Polistes fuscatus" (paper wasp) 70 60
897 90c. "Sparmopolius fulvus" (bee fly) 80 60
898 $1 "Chrysopa carnea" (lace wing) . . . . 1·25 65
899 $1.15 "Phoebis philea" (butterfly) . . . . 2·00 90
900 $1.50 "Cynthia cardui" (butterfly) . . . . 2·25 1·75
901 $3 "Utetheisa bella" (moth) 3·00 4·25

902 $5 "Alucita pentadactyla" (moth) . . . . 4·25 6·00
903 $7.50 "Anartia jatropha" (butterfly) . . . . 5·50 8·50
904 $10 "Heliconius melpomene" (butterfly) . . . . 5·50 8·50

162 Adoration of the Magi

1992. Christmas. Multicoloured.
905 $1.15 Type **162** . . . . . . 2·00 75
906 $4.60 Appearance of angel to shepherds . . . . 4·50 6·50

163 $1 Coin and $20 Banknote
164 Columbus meeting Amerindians

1993. East Caribbean Currency. Multicoloured.
907 $1 Type **163** 90 70
908 $1.15 10c. and 25c. coins with $10 banknote . . . . . . 1·25 85
909 $1.50 5c. coin and $5 banknote . . . . 1·75 2·00
910 $3.60 1c. and 2c. coins with $1 banknote . . . . 4·00 6·00

1993. Organization of East Caribbean States. 500th Anniv of Discovery of America by Columbus. Multicoloured.
911 $1 Type **164** . . . . 1·10 90
912 $2 Ships approaching island 2·00 2·75

165 Queen Elizabeth II on Montserrat with Chief Minister W. H. Bramble, 1966

1993. 40th Anniv of Coronation. Multicoloured.
913 $1.15 Type **165** . . . . . . 1·50 75
914 $4.60 Queen Elizabeth II in State Coach, 1953 . . . . 4·50 5·50

1993. 500th Anniv of Discovery of Montserrat. As Nos. 869/75, some with new values, each showing "500th ANNIVERSARY DISCOVERY OF MONTSERRAT" at foot and with additional historical inscr across the centre.
915 $1.15 mult (As Type **157**) . . 1·75 2·00
916 $1.15 multicoloured (As No. 870) . . . . 1·75 2·00
917 $1.15 multicoloured (As No. 871) . . . . 1·75 2·00
918 $1.50 multicoloured (As No. 872) . . . . 2·00 2·25
919 $1.50 multicoloured (As No. 873) . . . . 2·00 2·25
920 $1.50 multicoloured (As No. 874) . . . . 2·00 2·25
921 $3.45 multicoloured (As No. 875) . . . . 2·75 3·50

Additional inscriptions: No. 915, "PRE-COLUMBUS CARIB NAME OF ISLAND ALLIOUGANA"; 916, "COLUMBUS NAMED ISLAND SANTA MARIA DE MONTSERRATE"; 917, "COLUMBUS SAILED ALONG COASTLINE 11th NOV. 1493"; 918, "ISLAND OCCUPIED BY FRENCH BRIEFLY IN 1667"; 919, "ISLAND DECLARED ENGLISH BY TREATY OF BREDA 1667"; 920, "AFRICAN SLAVES BROUGHT IN DURING 1600's"; 921, "IRISH CATHOLICS FROM ST. KITTS AND VIRGINIA SETTLED ON ISLAND BETWEEN 1628–1634".

166 Boeing Sentry, 1993

1993. 75th Anniv of Royal Air Force. Mult.
922 15c. Type **166** 45 20
923 55c. Vickers Valiant B Mk 1, 1962 . . . . 65 40
924 $1.15 Handley Page Hastings C Mk 2, 1958 . . . . . . 1·25 75
925 $3 Lockheed Ventura, 1943 2·50 4·25
MS926 117×78 mm. $1.50 Felixstowe F5, 1921; $1.50 Armstrong Whitworth Atlas, 1934; $1.50 Fairey Gordon, 1935; $1.50 Boulton & Paul Overstrand, 1936 . . . . 4·50 6·00

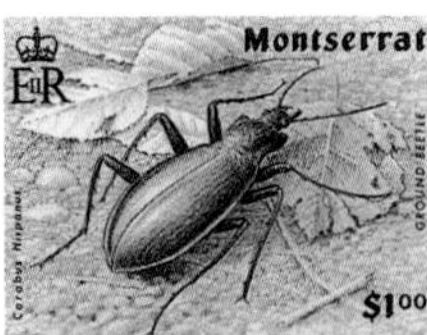

167 Ground Beetle

1994. Beetles. Multicoloured.
927 $1 Type **167** 65 65
928 $1.15 Click beetle 80 80
929 $1.50 Harlequin beetle . . . 1·25 1·50
930 $3.45 Leaf beetle . . . . . . 3·00 4·50
MS931 68×85 mm. $4.50 Scarab beetle . . . . 3·50 4·00

168 "Gossypium barbadense"

1994. Flowers. Multicoloured.
932 90c. Type **168** . . . . 1·25 80
933 $1.15 "Hibiscus sabdariffa" 1·50 1·00
934 $1.50 "Hibiscus esculentus" 1·75 1·75
935 $3.50 "Hibiscus rosa-sinensis" 3·75 6·00

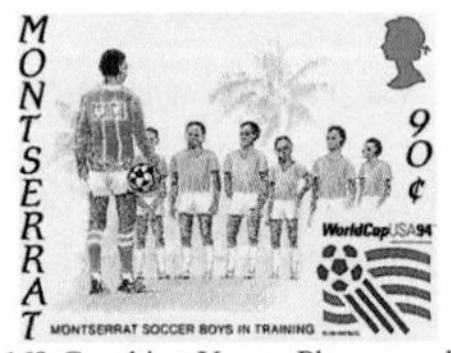

169 Coaching Young Players and Logo

1994. World Cup Football Championship, U.S.A. Multicoloured.
936 90c. Type **169** . . . . 1·90 2·25
937 $1 United States scoring against England, 1950 . . 1·90 2·25
938 $1.15 Rose Bowl stadium, Los Angeles, and trophy 1·90 2·25
939 $3.45 German players celebrating with trophy, 1990 . . . . 3·00 3·50
MS940 114×85 mm. $2 Jules Rimet (founder) and Jules Rimet Trophy; $2 Bobby Moore (England) holding trophy, 1966; $2 Lew Jaschin (U.S.S.R.); $2 Sepp Herberger (Germany) and German players celebrating, 1990 7·00 8·00

170 Elasmosaurus

1994. Aquatic Dinosaurs. Multicoloured.
941 $1 Type **170** . . . . 2·25 2·25
942 $1.15 Plesiosaurus . . . . . 2·25 2·25
943 $1.50 Nothosaurus . . . . . 2·75 2·75
944 $3.45 Mosasaurus . . . . . 3·50 4·25

1994. Space Anniversaries. Nos. 804/7 variously surch or optd, each including **Space Anniversaries**.
945 40c. on 90c. Type **143** . . . 1·50 80
946 $1.15 Astronaut alighting from lunar module "Eagle" 2·25 1·50
947 $1.50 "Eagle" and astronaut conducting experiment . . 2·75 2·75
948 $2.30 on $3.50 Opening "Apollo 11" hatch after splashdown . . . . 4·25 6·00

Surcharges and overprints: No. 945, **Juri Gagarin First man in space April 12, 1961**; 946, **First Joint US Soviet Mission July 15, 1975**; 947 **25th Anniversary First Moon Landing Apollo XI – July 20, 1994**; 948, **Columbia First Space Shuttle April 12, 1981.**

172 1969 Festival Logo

1994. 25th Anniv of Woodstock Music Festival. Multicoloured.
949 $1.15 Type **172** . . . . . . 1·00 1·00
950 $1.50 1994 anniversary festival logo . . . . 1·25 1·25

173 Sea Fan

1995. Marine Life. Multicoloured.
951 $1 Type **173** 60 50
952 $1.15 Sea lily 70 60
953 $1.50 Sea pen . . . . 90 1·00
954 $3.45 Sea fern . . . . 2·00 3·00
MS955 88×96 mm. $4.50 Sea rose 3·00 3·75

174 Marilyn Monroe

1995. Centenary of Cinema. Portraits of Marilyn Monroe (film star). Multicoloured.
956 $1.15 Type **174** . . . . . . 90 1·00
957 $1.15 Puckering lips . . . . 90 1·00
958 $1.15 Laughing in brown evening dress and earrings 90 1·00
959 $1.15 Wearing red earrings 90 1·00
960 $1.15 In brown dress without earrings . . . . 90 1·00
961 $1.15 With white boa . . . . 90 1·00
962 $1.15 In red dress . . . . . 90 1·00
963 $1.15 Wearing white jumper 90 1·00
964 $1.15 Looking over left shoulder . . . . 90 1·00
MS965 102×132 mm. $6 With Elvis Presley (50×56 mm) . . . . . 4·50 5·00

175 Jesse Owens (U.S.A.)
177 Ears of Wheat ("Food")

176 Atmospheric Sounding Experiments using V2 Rockets

1995. 5th International Amateur Athletic Federation Games, Göteborg. Sheet 181×103 mm, containing T **175** and similar vert designs.
MS966 $1.50 black and pink (Type **175**); $1.50 black and orange (Eric Lemming (Sweden)); $1.50 black and yellow (Rudolf Harbig (Germany)); $1.50 black and green (young Montserrat athletes) . . . . 4·50 5·50

1995. 50th Anniv of End of Second World War. Scientific Achievements. Multicoloured.
967 $1.15 Type **176** . . . . . . 80 1·00
968 $1.15 American space shuttle "Challenger" . . . . . . 80 1·00
969 $1.15 Nuclear experiment, Chicago, 1942 . . . . . . 80 1·00
970 $1.15 Calder Hall Atomic Power Station, 1956 . . . 80 1·00
971 $1.50 Radar-equipped Ju 88G 7a nightfighter . . . . . . 1·25 1·50
972 $1.50 Boeing E6 A.W.A.C.S. aircraft . . . . 1·25 1·50
973 $1.50 Gloster G.41 Meteor Mk III jet fighter . . . . 1·25 1·50
974 $1.50 Concorde (airliner) . . 1·25 1·50

1995. 50th Anniv of United Nations. Multicoloured.
975 $1.15 Type **177** 90 75
976 $1.50 Open book ("Education") . . . . . . 1·25 1·00
977 $2.30 P.T. class ("Health") 1·75 2·25
978 $3 Dove ("Peace") . . . . . 2·25 3·50
MS979 105×75 mm. $6 Scales ("Justice") . . . . 3·75 5·50

178 Headquarters Building

1995. 25th Anniv of Montserrat National Trust. Multicoloured.
980 $1.15 Type **178** 80 75
981 $1.50 17th-century cannon, Bransby Point . . . . . . 1·25 1·00
982 $2.30 Impression of Galways Sugar Mill (vert) . . . . . 2·25 2·50
983 $3 Great Alps Falls (vert) . . 4·00 5·00

1995. 25th Anniv of Air Recording Studios. No. 713 surch **air 25TH ANNIVERSARY 1970 - 1995.**
984 $2.30+$5 Air Recording Studios . . . . 4·25 5·50

The $5 premium on No. 984 was for relief following a volcanic eruption.

180 Bull Shark

1996. Scavengers of the Sea. Multicoloured.
985 $1 Type **180** 80 70
986 $1.15 Sea mouse 90 80
987 $1.50 Bristleworm . . . . . 1·25 1·50
988 $3.45 Prawn "Xiphocaris" . . 2·50 3·50
MS989 69×95 mm. $4.50 Man of war fish . . . . 3·00 3·75

181 Marconi and Radio Equipment, 1901

1996. Centenary of Radio. Multicoloured.
990 $1.15 Type **181** 90 80
991 $1.50 Marconi's steam yacht "Elettra" . . . . 1·25 1·00
992 $2.30 Receiving first Transatlantic radio message, Newfoundland, 1901 . . . . 1·75 2·25
993 $3 Imperial Airways airplane at Croydon Airport, 1920 2·25 3·50
MS994 74×105 mm. $4.50 Radio telescope, Jodrell Bank . . . . 3·00 3·75

182 Paul Masson (France) (Cycling)

1996. Olympic Games, Atlanta. Gold Medal Winners of 1896. Multicoloured.
995 $1.15 Type **182** 80 80
996 $1.50 Robert Garrett (U.S.A.) (Discus) . . . . . 1·00 1·00
997 $2.30 Spyridon Louis (Greece) (Marathon) . . . 1·50 1·75
998 $3 John Boland (Great Britain) (Tennis) . . . . . 2·00 3·25

183 James Dean

1996. James Dean (film star) Commemoration. Multicoloured.
999 $1.15 Type **183** 80 95
1000 $1.15 Wearing stetson facing right 80 95
1001 $1.15 Wearing blue sweater 80 95
1002 $1.15 Wearing black sweater 80 95
1003 $1.15 Full face portrait wearing stetson 80 95
1004 $1.15 Wearing fawn jacket 80 95
1005 $1.15 Wearing red wind-cheater 80 95
1006 $1.15 Smoking a cigarette 80 95
1007 $1.15 In open-necked shirt and green jumper 80 95
MS1008 169 × 133 mm. $6 As No. 1000 (51 × 57 mm) . . . . 4·50 5·50

184 Leprechaun

185 Blue and Green Teddybears

1996. Mythical Creatures. Multicoloured.
1009 5c. Type **184** 10 30
1010 10c. Pegasus 10 30
1011 15c. Griffin 15 30
1012 20c. Unicorn 20 30
1013 25c. Gnomes 25 30
1014 40c. Mermaid 40 40
1015 55c. Cockatrice 50 40
1016 70c. Fairy 65 40
1017 90c. Goblin 80 50
1018 $1 Faun 90 55
1019 $1.15 Dragon . . . . 1·00 65
1020 $1.50 Giant . . . . 1·25 85
1021 $3 Elves . . . . 2·00 2·50
1022 $5 Centaur . . . . 3·25 3·75
1023 $7.50 Phoenix . . . . . . 4·75 6·00
1024 $10 Erin . . . . 5·50 6·50

1996. Jerry Garcia and the Grateful Dead (rock group) Commemoration. Multicoloured.
1025 $1.15 Type **185** . . . . . . 1·00 1·00
1026 $1.15 Green and yellow teddybears . . . . 1·00 1·00
1027 $1.15 Brown and pink teddybears . . . . 1·00 1·00
1028 $6 Jerry Garcia (37 × 50 mm) . . . . . . 5·50 5·50
Nos. 1025/7 were printed together, se-tenant, forming a composite design.

186 Turkey Vulture

1997. Scavengers of the Sky. Multicoloured.
1029 $1 Type **186** 75 70
1030 $1.15 American crow . . . 90 70
1031 $1.50 Great skua . . . . . 1·25 1·50
1032 $3.45 Black-legged kittiwake ("Kittiwake") . . . . . . 2·25 3·75
MS1033 74 × 95 mm. $4.50 King vulture . . . . 2·75 3·50

1997. "HONG KONG '97" International Stamp Exhibition. Nos. 1025/7 optd **HONG KONG '97**.
1034 $1.15 Type **185** . . . . . . 70 1·00
1035 $1.15 Green and yellow teddybears . . . . 70 1·00
1036 $1.15 Brown and pink teddybears . . . . 70 1·00

1997. "PACIFIC '97" International Stamp Exhibition, San Francisco. Nos. 999/1007 optd **PACIFIC 97 World Philatelic Exhibition San Francisco, California 29 May - 8 June**.
1037 $1.15 Type **183** 80 95
1038 $1.15 Wearing stetson facing right 80 95
1039 $1.15 Wearing blue sweater 80 95
1040 $1.15 Wearing black sweater 80 95
1041 $1.15 Full-face portrait wearing stetson 80 95
1042 $1.15 Wearing fawn jacket 80 95
1043 $1.15 Wearing red wind-cheater 80 95
1044 $1.15 Smoking a cigarette 80 95
1045 $1.15 In open-necked shirt and green jumper 80 95

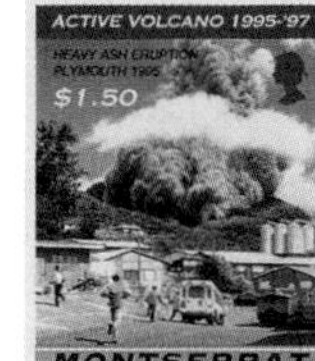

189 Heavy Ash Eruption over Plymouth, 1995

1997. Eruption of Soufriere Volcano. Mult.
1046 $1.50 Type **189** . . . . . . 1·10 1·25
1047 $1.50 Burning rock flow entering sea . . . . . . 1·10 1·25
1048 $1.50 Double venting at Castle Peak . . . . . . 1·10 1·25
1049 $1.50 Mangrove cuckoo . . 1·10 1·25
1050 $1.50 Lava flow at night, 1996 . . . . 1·10 1·25
1051 $1.50 Antillean crested hummingbird . . . . . . 1·10 1·25
1052 $1.50 Ash cloud over Plymouth . . . . 1·10 1·25
1053 $1.50 Lava spine, 1996 . . . 1·10 1·25
1054 $1.50 Burning rock flows forming new land . . . . 1·10 1·25

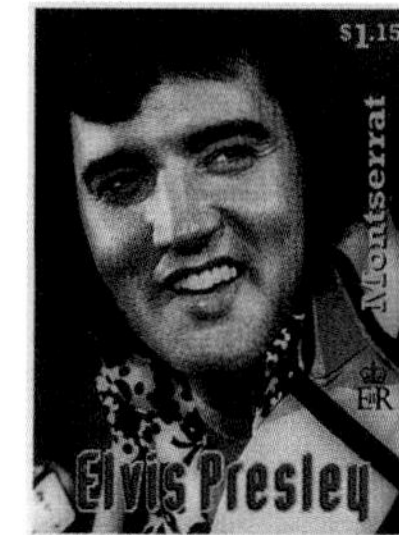

190 Elvis Presley

1997. Rock Legends. Multicoloured.
1055 $1.15 Type **190** . . . . . . 1·40 1·40
1056 $1.15 Jimi Hendrix . . . . 1·40 1·40
1057 $1.15 Jerry Garcia . . . . . 1·40 1·40
1058 $1.15 Janis Joplin . . . . . 1·40 1·40

191 Untitled Painting by Frama

1997. Frama Exhibition at Guggenheim Museum, New York.
1059 **191** $1.50 multicoloured . . 1·00 1·25

1997. No. 1028 surch **$1.50**.
1060 $1.50 on $6 Jerry Garcia (37 × 50 mm) . . . . . . 1·00 1·25

193 Prickly Pear

MONTSERRAT
194 Eva and Juan Peron (Argentine politicians)

1998. Medicinal Plants. Multicoloured.
1061 $1 Type **193** 65 50
1062 $1.15 Pomme coolie 70 55
1063 $1.50 Aloe 85 90
1064 $3.45 Bird pepper . . . . . 1·75 2·50

1998. Famous People of the 20th Century. Mult.
1065 $1.15 Type **194** . . . . . . 1·00 1·10
1066 $1.15 Pablo Picasso (painter) 1·00 1·10
1067 $1.15 Wernher von Braun (space scientist) . . . . . 1·00 1·10
1068 $1.15 David Ben Gurion (Israeli statesman) . . . . 1·00 1·10
1069 $1.15 Jean Henri Dunant (founder of Red Cross) 1·00 1·10
1070 $1.15 Dwight Eisenhower (President of U.S.A.) . . 1·00 1·10
1071 $1.15 Mahatma Gandhi (leader of Indian Independence movement) 1·00 1·10
1072 $1.15 King Leopold III and Queen Astrid of Belgium 1·00 1·10
1073 $1.15 Grand Duchess Charlotte and Prince Felix of Luxembourg . . . . . 1·00 1·10
1074 $1.50 Charles Augustus Lindbergh (pioneer aviator) . . . . 1·00 1·10
1075 $1.50 Mao Tse-tung (Chinese communist leader) . . . . 1·00 1·10
1076 $1.50 Earl Mountbatten (last Viceroy of India) . . 1·00 1·10
1077 $1.50 Konrad Adenauer (German statesman) . . . 1·00 1·10
1078 $1.50 Anne Frank (Holocaust victim) . . . . 1·00 1·10
1079 $1.50 Queen Wilhelmina of the Netherlands . . . . . 1·00 1·10
1080 $1.50 King George VI of Great Britain . . . . . . 1·00 1·10
1081 $1.50 King Christian X of Denmark . . . . 1·00 1·10
1082 $1.50 King Haakon VII and Crown Prince Olav of Norway . . . . 1·00 1·10
1083 $1.50 King Alfonso XIII of Spain . . . . 1·00 1·10
1084 $1.50 King Gustavus V of Sweden . . . . 1·00 1·10
MS1085 115 × 63 mm. $3 John F. Kennedy (Resident of U.S.A.) (50 × 32 mm) . . . . 1·75 2·50

195 Jerry Garcia

1998. Rock Music Legends. Multicoloured. (a) Jerry Garcia.
1086 $1.15 In long-sleeved blue shirt 80 95
1087 $1.15 With drum kit in background 80 95
1088 $1.15 Type **195** 80 95
1089 $1.15 Wearing long-sleeved black t-shirt 80 95
1090 $1.15 Close-up with left hand in foreground . . . 80 95
1091 $1.15 With purple and black background 80 95
1092 $1.15 Holding microphone 80 95
1093 $1.15 In short-sleeved blue t-shirt 80 95
1094 $1.15 In sunglasses with cymbal in background . . 80 95

(b) Bob Marley. Predominant colour for each design given.
1095 $1.15 Pointing (green) . . . 80 95
1096 $1.15 Wearing neck chain (green) 80 95
1097 $1.15 Singing into microphone (green) . . . 80 95
1098 $1.15 Singing with eyes closed (yellow) 80 90
1099 $1.15 Facing audience (yellow) 80 90
1100 $1.15 In striped t-shirt with fingers on chin (red) . . . 80 90
1101 $1.15 In Rastafarian hat (red) 80 95
1102 $1.15 In striped t-shirt with hand closed (red) 80 95
MS1103 152 × 101 mm. $5 Jerry Garcia (50 × 75 mm) . . . . . 2·50 3·00

196 Ash Eruption from Soufriere Hills Volcano

1998. Total Eclipse of the Sun. Multicoloured.
1104 $1.15 Type **196** . . . . . . 1·25 1·25
1105 $1.15 Volcano emitting black cloud . . . . 1·25 1·25
1106 $1.15 Village below volcano 1·25 1·25
1107 $1.15 Lava flow and wrecked house . . . . . 1·25 1·25
MS1108 152 × 102 mm. $6 Solar eclipse (vert) . . . . 4·25 4·50

197 Princess Diana on Wedding Day, 1981

1998. Diana, Princess of Wales Commemoration. Multicoloured.
1109 $1.15 Type **197** . . . . . . 1·25 70
1110 $1.50 Accepting bouquet from children . . . . . . 1·40 1·10
1111 $3 At Royal Ascot . . . . 2·50 3·50
MS1112 133 × 100 mm. $6 Diana and "Princess of Wales" rose (50 × 37 mm) . . . . 4·00 4·50

1998. 19th World Scout Jamboree, Chile. Nos. 669/72 optd **19th WORLD JAMBOREE MONDIAL CHILE 1999** and emblem.
1113 20c. Type **117** 30 40
1114 20c. Girl Guide saluting . . . 30 40
1115 75c. Lady Baden-Powell . . 70 1·00
1116 75c. Guide assisting in old people's home . . . . . 70 1·00

199 Jerry Garcia

1999. Jerry Garcia (rock musician) Commem. Mult.
1117 $1.15 Type **199** . . . . . . 90 1·00
1118 $1.15 In front of drum kit (violet background) . . . 90 1·00
1119 $1.15 Singing into microphone . . . . 90 1·00
1120 $1.15 Playing guitar, facing right (vert) . . . . 90 1·00
1121 $1.15 Singing with eyes closed (vert) . . . . . . 90 1·00
1122 $1.15 Singing in white spotlight (vert) . . . . . 90 1·00
1123 $1.15 In front of drum kit (green background) . . . 90 1·00
1124 $1.15 In long-sleeved black shirt . . . . 90 1·00
1125 $1.15 In red shirt . . . . . 90 1·00
1126 $1.15 In short-sleeved black t-shirt (without frame) (vert) . . . . 90 1·00
1127 $1.15 In blue t-shirt (oval frame) (vert) . . . . . . 90 1·00
1128 $1.15 In short-sleeved black t-shirt (oval frame) (vert) 90 1·00
MS1129 Two sheets. (a) 115 × 153 mm. $6 Jerry Garcia in concert (50 × 75 mm). (b) 153 × 115 mm. $6 Singing into microphone (75 × 50 mm) Set of 2 sheets . . . . 7·00 8·00

1999. "iBRA '99" International Stamp Exhibition, Nuremberg. Nos. 975/6 optd **iBRA INTERNATIONALE BRIEFMARKEN WELTAUSSTELLUNG NURNBERG 27.4.-4.5.99.**
1130 $1.15 Type **177** . . . . . . 1·25 1·25
1131 $1.50 Open book ("Education") . . . . . 1·50 1·75

201 Mango

1999. Tropical Caribbean Fruits. Multicoloured.
1132 $1.15 Type **201** 75 70
1133 $1.50 Breadfruit 90 85
1134 $2.30 Papaya . . . . 1·40 1·60
1135 $3 Lime . . . . 1·75 2·25
1136 $6 Akee . . . . 3·50 5·00
MS1137 134 × 95 mm. Nos. 1132/6 8·50 10·00

202 Yorkshire Terrier

1999. Dogs. Each black.
1138 70c. Type **202** . . . . . . 1·00 65
1139 $1 Welsh corgi . . . . . . 1·10 75
1140 $1.15 King Charles spaniel 1·25 85
1141 $1.50 Poodle . . . . 1·40 1·25
1142 $3 Beagle . . . . 2·50 3·50
MS1143 133 × 95 mm. Nos. 1138/42 6·50 7·00

203 Pupil's Equipment and World Map

1999. World Teachers' Day. Multicoloured.
1144 $1 Type **203** . . . . 1·00 70
1145 $1.15 Teacher and class . . 1·00 80
1146 $1.50 Emblems of vocational training . . . . 1·25 1·10
1147 $5 Scientific equipment . . . 4·00 5·50

204 Great Hammerhead Shark

1999. Endangered Species. Great Hammerhead Shark. Multicoloured.
1148 50c. Type **204** 35 50
1149 50c. Two hammerhead sharks among fish 35 50
1150 50c. Two hammerhead sharks on sea-bed 35 50
1151 50c. Three hammerhead sharks 35 50

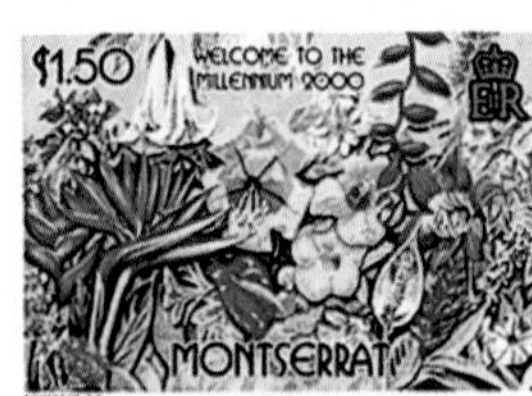

205 Flowers

2000. New Millennium.
1152 **205** $1.50 multicoloured . . 1·25 1·25

206 Alfred Valentine

2000. West Indies Cricket Tour and 100th Test Match at Lord's. Multicoloured.
1153 $1 Type **206** . . . . 1·50 60
1154 $5 George Headley batting 3·00 4·00
MS1155 119 × 101 mm. $6 Lord's Cricket Ground (horiz) . . . . 4·00 4·50

207 Spitfire Squadron taking-off

2000. "The Stamp Show 2000" International Stamp Exhibition, London. 60th Anniv of Battle of Britain. Multicoloured.
1156 70c. Type **207** 75 50
1157 $1.15 Overhauling Hurricane Mk I . . . . 1·00 65
1158 $1.50 Hurricane MK I attacking . . . . 1·25 1·25
1159 $5 Flt. Lt. Frank Howell's Spitfire Mk IA . . . . . 3·25 4·25
MS1160 110 × 87 mm. $6 Hawker Hurricane . . . . 4·00 4·50

208 Statue of Liberty and Carnival Scene

2000. New Millennium. Landmarks. Each including carnival scene. Multicoloured.
1161 90c. Type **208** 65 50
1162 $1.15 Great Wall of China 80 60
1163 $1.50 Eiffel Tower . . . . . 1·10 1·10
1164 $3.50 Millennium Dome . . 2·25 3·00

209 Queen Elizabeth the Queen Mother and W.H. Bramble Airport

2000. Queen Elizabeth the Queen Mother's 100th Birthday. Each showing different portrait. Mult.
1165 70c. Type **209** 65 40
1166 $1.15 Government House 1·00 65
1167 $3 Court House . . . . . . 2·25 2·25
1168 $6 War Memorial Clock Tower . . . . 4·00 4·50
MS1169 120 × 75 mm. Nos. 1165/8 7·50 8·00

210 Three Wise Men following Star
211 Golden Swallow

2000. Christmas. Multicoloured.
1170 $1 Type **210** 75 55
1171 $1.15 Cavalla Hill Methodist Church 80 65
1172 $1.50 Shepherds with flocks 1·00 85
1173 $3 Mary and Joseph arriving at Bethlehem . . 1·75 2·25
MS1174 105 × 75 mm. $6 As $3 4·25 4·75

2001. Caribbean Birds. Multicoloured.
1175 $1 Type **211** 90 65
1176 $1.15 Crested quail dove (horiz) 95 75
1177 $1.50 Red-legged thrush (horiz) . . . . 1·25 95
1178 $5 Fernandina's flicker . . . 3·75 4·50
MS1179 95 × 68 mm. $8 St. Vincent amazon (horiz) . . . . 6·50 7·00

212 Edward Stanley Gibbons, Charles J. Phillips and 391 Strand Shop

2001. Famous Stamp Personalities. Multicoloured.
1180 $1 Type **212** 80 60
1181 $1.15 John Lister and Montserrat stamps . . . 85 70
1182 $1.50 Theodore Champion and French postilion . . 1·00 90
1183 $3 Thomas De La Rue and De La Rue's stand at Great Exhibition, 1851 . . 2·00 2·25
MS1184 95 × 68 mm. $8 Sir Rowland Hill and Bruce Castle 5·00 6·00

213 Princess Elizabeth at International Horse Show, 1950

2001. Queen Elizabeth II's 75th Birthday. Mult.
1185 90c. Type **213** 70 55
1186 $1.15 Queen Elizabeth II, 1986 . . . . 80 70
1187 $1.50 Queen Elizabeth II, 1967 . . . . 1·00 1·00
1188 $5 Queen Elizabeth, 1976 3·50 4·25
MS1189 90 × 68 mm. $6 Queen Elizabeth, 2000 . . . . 4·50 4·75

214 Look Out Village

2001. Reconstruction. Multicoloured.
1190 70c. Type **214** 45 50
1191 $1 St. John's Hospital . . . 65 65
1192 $1.15 Tropical Mansions Suites Hotel 70 70
1193 $1.50 Montserrat Secondary School 90 90
1194 $3 Golden Years Care Home . . . . 1·75 2·00

215 West Indian Cherry

2001. Caribbean Fruits. Multicoloured.
1195 5c. Type **215** 10 10
1196 10c. Mammee apple 10 10
1197 15c. Lime 10 10
1198 20c. Grapefruit 10 15
1199 25c. Orange 10 15
1200 40c. Passion fruit 20 25
1201 55c. Banana 25 30
1202 70c. Pawpaw 35 40
1203 90c. Pomegranate 45 50
1204 $1 Guava 50 55
1205 $1.15 Mango 55 60
1206 $1.50 Sugar apple 70 75
1207 $3 Cashew . . . . 1·40 1·50
1208 $5 Soursop . . . . 2·40 2·50
1209 $7.50 Watermelon . . . . . 3·50 3·75
1210 $10 Pineapple . . . . 4·75 5·00

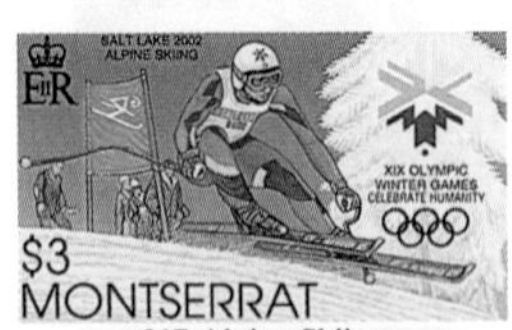

216 Common Long-tail Skipper (butterfly)

2001. Caribbean Butterflies. Multicoloured.
1211 $1 Type **216** 75 60
1212 $1.15 Straight-line sulphur 80 70
1213 $1.50 Giant hairstreak . . . 90 90
1214 $3 Monarch . . . . 1·75 2·00
MS1215 115 × 115 mm. $10 Painted Lady . . . . 6·50 7·50
The overall design of No. **MS**1215 is butterfly-shaped

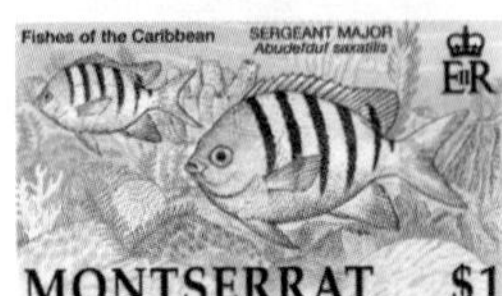

217 Alpine Skiing

2002. Winter Olympic Games, Salt Lake City. Mult.
1216 $3 Type **217** . . . . 2·00 2·25
1217 $5 Four man bobsleigh . . 3·00 3·50

218 Sergeant Major (fish)

2002. Fishes of the Caribbean. Multicoloured.
1218 $1 Type **218** 50 55
1219 $1.15 Mutton snapper . . . 55 60
1220 $1.50 Lantern bass 70 75
1221 $5 Shy Hamlet . . . . . . 2·40 2·50
MS1222 102 × 70 mm. $8 Queen angelfish . . . . 3·75 4·00

2002. Queen Elizabeth the Queen Mother Commemoration. Nos. 1165/8 optd **Life and Death of Her Majesty Queen Elizabeth The Queen Mother 1900 2002.**
1223 70c. Type **209** 35 40
1224 $1.15 Government House 55 60
1225 $3 Court House . . . . . . 1·40 1·50
1226 $6 War Memorial Clock Tower . . . . 3·00 3·25

OFFICIAL STAMPS

1976. Various stamps, some already surch, optd **O.H.M.S.**
O1 5c. multicoloured (No. 246) † 65
O2 10c. multicoloured (No. 247) † 75
O3 30c. on 10c. mult (No. 369) † 1·50
O4 45c. on 3c. mult (No. 370) . . † 2·00
O5 $5 multicoloured (No. 254) † £100
O6 $10 multicoloured (No. 254a) † £550
These stamps were issued for use on mail from the Montserrat Philatelic Bureau. They were not sold to the public, either unused or used.

1976. Nos. 372, 374/82, 384/5 and 476 optd **O.H.M.S.** or surch also.
O17 5c. Malay apple . . . . . . † 10
O28 5c. on 3c. Lignum vitae . . † 20
O18 10c. Jacaranda . . . . . . † 10
O19 15c. Orchid tree . . . . . . † 10
O20 20c. Manjak . . . . † 10
O21 25c. Tamarind . . . . . . † 15
O33 30c. on 15c. Orchid tree . . † 30
O34 35c. on 2c. Cannon-ball tree † 30
O35 40c. Flame of the forest . . † 40
O22 55c. Pink cassia . . . . . . † 35
O23 70c. Long john . . . . . . † 45
O24 $1 Saman . . . . † 60
O39 $2.50 on 40c. Flame of the forest . . . . † 2·00
O25 $5 Yellow poui . . . . . . † 1·50
O16 $10 Flamboyant . . . . . . † 3·75

1981. Nos. 490/4, 496, 498, 500, 502/3 and 505 optd **O.H.M.S.**
O42 5c. Type **91** 10 10
O43 10c. Hogfish and neon goby 10 10
O44 15c. Creole wrasse 10 10
O45 20c. Three-spotted damselfish 15 15
O46 25c. Sergeant major 15 15
O47 45c. Schoolmaster 25 20
O48 65c. Bigeye 35 30
O49 $1 Rock beauty 65 65
O50 $3 Royal gramma ("Fairy basslet") and blueheads . . 1·50 1·75
O51 $5 Cherub angelfish . . . . 2·00 2·25
O52 $10 Caribbean long-nosed butterflyfish . . . . 3·00 2·25

1983. Nos. 510/15 surch **O.H.M.S.** and value.
O53 45c. on 90c. "Charlotte" . . 20 30
O54 45c. on 90c. Prince Charles and Lady Diana Spencer 60 1·00
O55 75c. on $3 "Portsmouth" . . 25 35
O56 75c. on $3 Prince Charles and Lady Diana Spencer 90 1·40
O57 $1 on $4 "Britannia" 35 50
O58 $1 on $4 Prince Charles and Lady Diana Spencer . . . 1·00 1·50

1983. Nos. 542/4 surch **O.H.M.S.**
O59 70c. on 75c. Type **97** 60 40
O60 $1 Coat of Arms of Catherine of Aragon . . . 70 50
O61 $1.50 on $5 Diana, Princess of Wales . . . . 1·00 80

1985. Nos. 600/12 and 614 optd **O H M S**.
O62 5c. Type **107** . . . . 1·00 1·00
O63 10c. Carib grackle . . . . . 1·00 1·00
O64 15c. Moorhen . . . . 1·25 1·00
O65 20c. Brown booby . . . . . 1·25 70
O66 25c. Black-whiskered vireo 1·25 70
O67 40c. Scaly-breasted thrasher 1·75 70
O68 55c. Laughing gull . . . . . 2·00 70
O69 70c. Glossy ibis . . . . . . 2·25 90
O70 90c. Green-backed heron . . 2·50 90
O71 $1 Belted kingfisher . . . . 2·50 90
O72 $1.15 Bananaquit . . . . . 2·75 90
O73 $3 American kestrel . . . . 4·25 2·50
O74 $5 Forest thrush . . . . . . 5·00 2·50
O75 $10 Bridled quail dove . . . 6·50 2·50

1989. Nos. 757/70 and 772 optd **O H M S**.
O76 5c. Type **133** 40 60
O77 10c. Little knobbed scallop 40 60
O78 15c. Sozoni's cone 50 60
O79 20c. Globular coral shell . . 55 50
O80 25c. American or common sundial 55 50
O81 40c. King helmet 60 55
O82 55c. Channelled turban . . . 70 50
O83 70c. True tulip shell 90 75
O84 90c. Music volute . . . . . 1·00 90
O85 $1 Flame auger . . . . . . 1·00 80
O86 $1.15 Rooster-tail conch . . 1·25 85
O87 $1.50 Queen or pink conch 1·40 1·40
O88 $3 Teramachi's slit shell . . 2·00 2·50
O89 $5 Common or Florida crown conch . . . . . . 3·25 3·25
O90 $10 Atlantic trumpet triton 5·50 5·50

1989. Nos. 578 and 580/1 surch **OHMS**.
O91 70c. on 10c. Hogfish and neon goby . . . . 2·00 1·75
O92 $1.15 on 75c. French grunt 2·50 1·75
O93 $1.50 on $2 Blue chromis . . 2·75 3·00

1992. Nos. 838/41, 847/50, 856/9 surch or optd **OHMS**.
O 94 70c. on 90c. Type **150** . . . 1·40 1·40
O 95 70c. on 90c. Type **152** . . . 1·40 1·40
O 96 70c. on 90c. Type **154** . . . 1·40 1·40
O 97 70c. on $3.50 French grunt 1·40 1·40
O 98 $1 on $3.50 Helmeted guineafowl . . . . 1·50 1·50
O 99 $1 on $3.50 Anthurium . . 1·50 1·50
O100 $1.15 Cushion star . . . . 1·50 1·50
O101 $1.15 Hen and chicks . . . 1·50 1·50
O102 $1.15 Shell ginger . . . . . 1·50 1·50
O103 $1.50 Rock beauty . . . . 1·60 1·60
O104 $1.50 Red junglefowl . . . 1·60 1·60
O105 $1.50 Early day lily . . . . 1·60 1·60

1993. Nos. 889/902 and 904 optd **OHMS**.
O106 5c. Type **161** 60 80
O107 10c. "Gryllus campestris" (field cricket) 60 80
O108 15c. "Lepthemis vesiculosa" (dragonfly) 70 80
O109 20c. "Orthemis ferruginea" (red skimmer) 70 60
O110 25c. "Gerris lacustris" (pond skater) 70 60
O111 40c. "Byctiscus betulae" (leaf weevil) 85 40
O112 55c. "Atta texana" (leaf-cutter ants) 90 40
O113 70c. "Polistes fuscatus" (paper wasp) . . . . . . 1·00 70
O114 90c. "Sparmopolius fulvus" (bee fly) . . . . 1·10 70
O115 $1 "Chrysopa carnea" (lace wing) . . . . 1·25 70
O116 $1.15 "Phoebis philea" (butterfly) . . . . 2·00 1·50
O117 $1.50 "Cynthia cardui" (butterfly) . . . . 2·25 2·25
O118 $3 "Utetheisa bella" (moth) 3·00 3·50
O119 $5 "Alucita pentadactyla" (moth) . . . . 3·75 4·25
O120 $10 "Heliconius melpomene" (butterfly) 6·00 6·50

1997. Nos. 1009/22 and 1024 optd **O.H.M.S.**
O121 5c. Type **184** 15 50
O122 10c. Pegasus 25 50
O123 15c. Griffin 35 50
O124 20c. Unicorn 35 50
O125 25c. Gnomes 35 50
O126 40c. Mermaid 50 50
O127 55c. Cockatrice 60 50
O128 70c. Fairy 70 55
O129 90c. Goblin 90 60
O130 $1 Faun . . . . 1·00 60
O131 $1.15 Dragon . . . . 1·25 65
O132 $1.50 Giant . . . . 1·40 85
O133 $3 Elves . . . . 2·50 2·75
O134 $5 Centaur . . . . 4·00 4·25
O135 $10 Erin . . . . 6·00 6·50

2002. Nos. 1195/1208 and 1210 optd **OHMS**.
O137 5c. Type **215** 10 10
O138 10c. Mammee apple 10 10
O139 15c. Lime 10 10
O140 20c. Grapefruit 10 10
O141 25c. Orange 10 15
O142 40c. Passion fruit 20 25
O143 55c. Banana 25 30
O144 70c. Pawpaw 35 40
O145 90c. Pomegranate 45 50
O146 $1 Guava 50 55
O147 $1.15 Mango 55 60
O148 $1.50 Sugar apple 70 75
O149 $3 Cashew . . . . 1·60 1·75
O150 $5 Soursop . . . . 2·40 2·50
O151 $10 Pineapple . . . . . . 4·75 5·00

MOROCCO Pt. 13

An independent kingdom, established in 1956, comprising the former French and Spanish International Zones.

A. NORTHERN ZONE

100 centimes = 1 peseta.

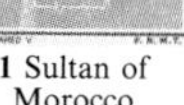
1 Sultan of Morocco

2 Polytechnic

1956.
1 **1** 10c. brown 10 10
2 – 15c. brown 10 10
3 **2** 25c. violet 10 10
4 – 50c. green 25 25
5 **1** 80c. green 90 90
6 – 2p. lilac . . . . 7·50 7·50
7 **2** 3p. blue . . . . 15·00 15·00
8 – 10p. green . . . . 31·00 31·00
DESIGNS—HORIZ: 15c., 2p. Villa Sanjurjo harbour. VERT: 50c., 10p. Cultural Delegation building, Tetuan.

3 Lockheed Super Constellation over Lau Dam

1956. Air.
9 **3** 25c. purple 20 15
10 – 1p.40 mauve 90 60
11 **3** 3p.40 red . . . . 1·90 1·50
12 – 4p.80 purple . . . . 3·50 2·50
DESIGN: 1p.40, 4p.80, Lockheed Super Constellation over Rio Nekor Bridge.

1957. 1st Anniv of Independence. As T **7** but with Spanish inscriptions and currency.
13 80c. green 65 50
14 1p.50 olive . . . . 1·90 1·40
15 3p. red . . . . 4·25 3·25

1957. As T **5** but with Spanish inscriptions and currency.
16 30c. indigo and blue 10 10
17 70c. purple and brown 20 10
18 80c. purple . . . . 1·60 40
19 1p.50 lake and green 50 15
20 3p. green 75 50
21 7p. red . . . . 5·25 1·50

1957. Investiture of Prince Moulay el Hassan. As T **9** but with Spanish inscriptions and currency.
22 80c. blue 65 25
23 1p.50 green . . . . 1·60 80
24 3p. red . . . . 4·75 2·50

1957. Nos. 17 and 19 surch.
25 15c. on 70c. purple and brown 75 75
26 1p.20 on 1p.50 lake and green 1·40 1·40

1957. 30th Anniv of Coronation of Sultan Sidi Mohammed ben Yusuf. As T **10** but with Spanish inscription and currency.
27 1p.20 green and black 65 50
28 1p.80 red and black 90 75
29 3p. violet and black . . . . . 1·60 1·50

B. SOUTHERN ZONE

100 centimes = 1 franc.

5 Sultan of Morocco

6 Classroom

1956.
30 **5** 5f. indigo and blue 20 10
31 10f. sepia and brown 15 10
32 15f. lake and green 25 10
33 25f. purple . . . . 1·10 10
34 30f. green . . . . 1·90 10
35 50f. red . . . . 3·00 15
36 70f. brown and sepia . . . . 4·25 60

1956. Education Campaign.
37 – 10f. violet and purple . . . . 1·90 1·25
38 – 15f. lake and red . . . . . . 2·40 1·50
39 **6** 20f. green and turquoise . . 2·50 2·50
40 – 30f. red and lake . . . . . . 4·50 2·75
41 – 50f. blue and indigo . . . . 7·50 5·00
DESIGNS: 10f. Peasants reading book; 15f. Two girls reading; 30f. Child reading to old man; 50f. Child teaching parents the alphabet.

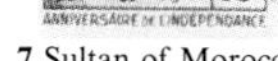
7 Sultan of Morocco

8 Emblem over Casablanca

1957. 1st Anniv of Independence.
42 **7** 15f. green . . . . 1·60 1·25
43 25f. olive . . . . 2·25 1·25
44 30f. red . . . . 4·00 1·90

1957. Air. International Fair, Casablanca.
45 **8** 15f. green and red . . . . . 1·25 1·00
46 25f. turquoise . . . . 2·25 1·40
47 30f. brown . . . . 2·75 1·75

9 Crown Prince Moulay el Hassan

10 King Mohammed V

1957. Investiture of Crown Prince Moulay el Hassan.
48 **9** 15f. blue . . . . 1·50 95
49 25f. green . . . . 1·75 1·25
50 30f. red . . . . 2·75 1·60

1957. 30th Anniv of Coronation of King Mohammed V.
51 **10** 15f. green and black 95 50
52 25f. red and black . . . . . 1·50 1·00
53 30f. violet and black . . . . 1·60 1·10

C. ISSUES FOR THE WHOLE OF MOROCCO

1958. 100 centimes = 1 franc.
1962. 100 francs = 1 dirham.

11 Moroccan Pavilion

1958. Brussels International Exhibition.
54 **11** 15f. turquoise 25 20
55 25f. red 25 25
56 30f. blue 35 30

12 King Mohammed V and U.N.E.S.C.O. Headquarters, Paris

1958. Inauguration of U.N.E.S.C.O. Headquarters Building, Paris.
57 **12** 15f. green 25 20
58 25f. lake 25 25
59 30f. blue 35 30

13 Ben-Smine Sanatorium

14 King Mohammed V on Horseback

1959. "National Aid".
60 **13** 50f. bistre, green and red . . 70 35

1959. King Mohammed V's 50th Birthday.
61 **14** 15f. lake 65 30
62 25f. blue 95 35
63 45f. green . . . . 1·10 45

15 Princess Lalla Amina

16

1959. Children's Week.
64 **15** 15f. blue 25 20
65 25f. green 30 25
66 45f. purple 60 30

1960. Meeting of U.N. African Economic Commission, Tangier.
67 **16** 45f. green, brown and violet 1·10 50

+10f

اعانة ضحايا
الزيوت المسممة
أكتوبر 1959
(17)

18 Arab Refugees

1960. Adulterated Cooking Oil Victims Relief Fund. Surch as T **17**.
68 **5** 5f.+10f. indigo and blue . . . 35 30
69 10f.+10f. sepia and brown . . . 70 45
70 15f.+10f. lake and green . . 1·25 95
71 25f.+15f. purple . . . . . . 1·40 1·10
72 30f.+20f. green . . . . . . 2·25 2·00

1960. World Refugee Year.
73 **18** 15f. black, green and ochre 25 20
74 – 45f. green and black 65 35
DESIGNS: 45f. "Uprooted tree" and Arab refugees.

19 Marrakesh

20 Lantern

1960. 900th Anniv of Marrakesh.
75 **19** 100f. green, brown and blue 1·40 95

1960. 1100th Anniv of Karaouiyne University.
76 **20** 15f. purple 60 50
77 – 25f. blue 65 55
78 – 30f. brown . . . . 1·25 60
79 – 35f. black . . . . 1·60 80
80 – 45f. green . . . . 2·25 1·40
DESIGNS: 25f. Fountain; 30f. Minaret; 35f. Frescoes; 45f. Courtyard.

21 Arab League Centre and King Mohammed V

1960. Inauguration of Arab League Centre, Cairo.
81 **21** 15f. black and green 20 20

اسبوعا
التضامن
1380
1960
+5f
(22)

23 Wrestling

1960. Solidarity Fund. Nos. 458/9 (Mahakma, Casablanca) of French Morocco surch as T **22**.
82 **106** 15f.+3f. on 18f. myrtle . . 55 55
83 +5f. on 20f. lake 80 80

1960. Olympic Games.
84 **23** 5f. purple, green and violet 10 10
85 – 10f. chocolate, blue & brown 15 10
86 – 15f. brown, blue and green 20 15
87 – 20f. purple, blue and bistre 25 20
88 – 30f. brown, violet and red 30 25
89 – 40f. brown, blue and violet 60 25
90 – 45f. blue, green and purple 75 35
91 – 70f. black, blue and brown 1·40 45
DESIGNS: 10f. Gymnastics; 15f. Cycling; 20f. Weightlifting; 30f. Running; 40f. Boxing; 45f. Sailing; 70f. Fencing.

24 Runner

25 Post Office and Letters

1961. 3rd Pan-Arab Games, Casablanca.
92 **24** 20f. green 20 15
93 30f. lake 65 20
94 50f. blue 75 60

1961. African Postal and Telecommunications Conference, Tangier.
95 **25** 20f. purple and mauve . . . 35 30
96 – 30f. turquoise and green . . 45 35
97 – 90f. ultramarine and blue 85 60
DESIGNS—VERT: 30f. Telephone operator. HORIZ: 90f. Sud Aviation Caravelle mail plane over Tangier.

26 King Mohammed V and African Map

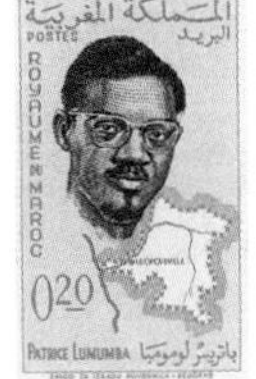
27 Lumumba and Congo Map

1962. 1st Anniv of African Charter of Casablanca.
98 **26** 20f. purple and buff 20 20
99 30f. indigo and blue 25 25

1962. Patrice Lumumba Commemoration.
100 **27** 20f. black and bistre . . . 20 20
101 30f. black and brown . . . 30 25

28 King Hassan II

29 "Pupils of the Nation"

1962. Air.
102 **28** 90f. black 75 15
103 1d. red 90 15
104 2d. blue . . . . 1·10 45
105 3d. green . . . . 2·25 1·10
106 5d. violet . . . . 4·50 1·60

1962. Children's Education.
107 **29** 20f. blue, red and green . . 35 25
108 30f. sepia, brown and green 40 35
109 90f. blue, purple and green 90 50

1962. Arab League Week. As T **76** of Libya.
110 20f. brown 20 15

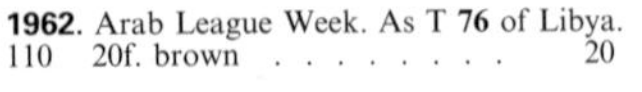

30 King Hassan II

31 Scout with Banner

1962.
111 **30** 1f. olive 10 10
112 2f. violet 10 10
113 5f. sepia 10 10
114 10f. brown 10 10
115 15f. turquoise 15 10
116 20f. purple (18 × 22 mm) 20 10
116a 20f. purple ($17\frac{1}{2} \times 23\frac{1}{2}$ mm) 30 10
116b 25f. red 20 10
117 30f. green 25 10
117a 35f. slate 65 10
117b 40f. blue 65 10
118 50f. purple 80 10
118a 60f. purple . . . . 1·10 10
119 70f. blue . . . . 1·25 10
120 80f. lake . . . . 2·10 15

1962. 5th Arab Scout Jamboree, Rabat.
121 **31** 20f. purple and blue . . . 20 15

32 Campaign Emblem and Swamp

33 Aquarium, Brown Trout and Fish

1962. Malaria Eradication Campaign.
122 **32** 20f. blue and green 20 15
123 – 50f. lake and green 35 25
DESIGN—VERT: 50f. Sword piercing mosquito.

1962. Casablanca Aquarium. Multicoloured.
124 20f. Type **33** 85 25
125 30f. Aquarium and Mediterranean moray . . . 90 25

34 Mounted Postman and 1912 Sherifian Stamp

(35)

1962. First National Philatelic Exhibition, Rabat, and Stamp Day.
126 **34** 20f. green and brown . . . 75 35
127 – 30f. black and red 90 40
128 – 50f. bistre and blue . . . . 1·25 50
DESIGNS: 30f. Postman and circular postmark; 50f. Sultan Hassan I and octagonal postmark. (Both stamps commemorate 70th anniv of Sherifian post.)

1963. Flood Relief Fund. Surch as T **35**.
129 **5** 20+5f. on 5f. indigo & bl . . 90 85
130 30+10f. on 50f. red . . . . 1·00 85

36 King Moulay Ismail

37 Ibn Batota (voyager)

1963. 300th Anniv of Meknes.
131 **36** 20f. sepia 25 20

1963. "Famous Men of Maghreb".
132 **37** 20f. purple 45 20
133 – 20f. black 45 20
134 – 20f. myrtle 25 25
134a **37** 40f. blue 30 10
PORTRAITS: No. 133, Ibn Khaldoun (historian); 134, Al Idrissi (geographer).

38 Sugar Beet and Refinery

39 Isis (bas relief)

1963. Freedom from Hunger.
135 **38** 20f. black, brown and green 25 20
136 – 50f. black, brown and blue 65 35
DESIGN—VERT: 50f. Fisherman and tuna.

1963. Nubian Monuments Preservation.
137 – 20f. black and grey 20 15
138 **39** 30f. violet 25 25
139 – 50f. purple 60 35
DESIGNS—HORIZ: 20f. Heads of Colossi, Abu Simbel; 50f. Philae Temple.

40 Agadir before Earthquake

1963. Reconstruction of Agadir.
140 **40** 20f. red and blue 35 35
141 30f. red and blue 45 35
142 – 50f. red and blue 80 40
DESIGNS: 30f. is optd with large red cross and date of earthquake, 29th February, 1960; 50f. Reconstructed Agadir.

41 Plan of new Agadir Hospital

42 Emblems of Morocco and Rabat

1963. Centenary of International Red Cross.
143 **41** 30f. multicoloured 50 20

1963. Opening of Parliament.
144 **42** 20f. multicoloured 45 20

43 Hands breaking Chain

44 National Flag

1963. 15th Anniv of Declaration of Human Rights.
145 **43** 20f. brown, sepia and green 45 20

1963. Evacuation of Foreign Troops from Morocco.
146 **44** 20f. red, green and black 25 25

45 "Moulay Abdurrahman" (after Delacroix)

1964. 3rd Anniv of King Hassan's Coronation.
147 **45** 1d. multicoloured . . . . 2·75 1·90

46 Map, Chart and W.M.O. Emblem

1964. World Meteorological Day. Multicoloured.
148 20f. African weather map (vert) (postage) 25 20
149 30f. Type **46** 40 35
150 90f. Globe and weather vane (vert) (air) 90 45

47 Fair Entrance

1964. Air. 20th Anniv of Casablanca Int Fair.
151 **47** 1d. red, drab and blue . . 95 60

48 Moroccan Pavilion at Fair

1964. Air. New York World's Fair.
152 **48** 1d. multicoloured . . . . 1·25 65

49 Children Playing in the Sun

50 Olympic Torch

1964. Postal Employees' Holiday Settlements.
153 **49** 20f. multicoloured 25 20
154 – 30f. multicoloured 35 25
DESIGN: 30f. Boy, girl and holiday settlement.

1964. Olympic Games, Tokyo.
155 **50** 20f. green, violet and red 25 25
156 30f. purple, blue and green 35 30
157 50f. red, blue and green . . 75 35

51 Lighthouse and Sultan Mohamed ben Abdurrahman (founder)

52 Tangier Iris

1964. Centenary of Cape Spartel Lighthouse.
158 **51** 25f. multicoloured 55 45

1965. Flowers. Multicoloured.
159 25f. Type **52** . . . . 1·00 45
160 40f. Gladiolus (vert) . . . . 1·25 55
161 60f. Caper (horiz) . . . . . 1·90 1·40

53 Return of King Mohammed

54 Early Telegraph Receiver

1965. 10th Anniv of Return of King Mohammed V from Exile.
162 **53** 25f. green 50 20

1965. Centenary of I.T.U. Multicoloured.
163 25f. Type **54** 20 20
164 40f. "TIROS" weather satellite 35 30

55 I.C.Y. Emblem

59 Corn

1965. International Co-operation Year.
165 **55** 25f. black and green . . . 25 20
166 60f. lake 40 35

1965. Sea Shells. As T **52**. Mult, background colours given.
167 25f. violet 55 25
168 25f. blue 55 25
169 25f. yellow 55 25
SEASHELLS: No. 167, Knobbed triton ("Charonia nodifera"); 168, Smooth callista ("Pitaria chione"); 169, "Cymbium tritonis".

1965. Shellfish. As T **52**. Multicoloured.
170 25f. Helmet crab 70 50
171 40f. Mantis shrimp . . . . . 1·60 95
172 1d. Royal prawn (horiz) . . . 2·25 1·40

1965. Orchids. As T **52**. Multicoloured.
173 25f. "Ophrys speculum" (vert) 60 45
174 40f. "Ophrys fusca" (vert) . . 95 50
175 60f. "Ophrys tenthredinifera" (horiz) . . . . 1·75 1·25

1966. Agricultural Products (1st issue).
176 **59** 25f. black and ochre . . . 20 15
See also Nos. 188/9 and 211.

60 Flag, Map and Dove

1966. 10th Anniv of Independence.
177 **60** 25f. red and green 20 15

61 King Hassan II and Crown

1966. 5th Anniv of King Hassan's Coronation.
178 **61** 25f. blue, green and red . . 20 15

62 Cross-country Runner

1966. 53rd "Cross des Nations" (Cross-country Race).

No.	Type	Description	Mint	Used
179	**62**	25f. green	20	15

63 W.H.O. Building

1966. Inaug of W.H.O. Headquarters, Geneva.

No.	Type	Description	Mint	Used
180	**63**	25f. black and purple	20	15
181	–	40f. black and blue	25	20

DESIGN: 40f. W.H.O. Building (different view).

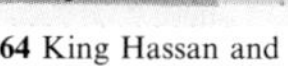

64 King Hassan and Parachutist　65 Brooch

1966. 10th Anniv of Royal Armed Forces.

No.	Type	Description	Mint	Used
182	**64**	25f. black and gold	60	25
183	–	40f. black and gold	60	25

DESIGN: 40f. Crown Prince Hassan kissing hand of King Mohammed.

1966. Palestine Week. As No. 110 but inscr "SEMAINE DE LA PALESTINE" at foot and dated "1966".

No.	Type	Description	Mint	Used
184		25f. blue	20	15

1966. Red Cross Seminar. Moroccan Jewellery. Multicoloured.

No.	Type	Description	Mint	Used
185		25f.+5f. Type **65**	90	45
186		40f.+10f. Pendant	1·25	55

See also Nos. 203/4, 246/7, 274/5, 287/8, 303/4, 324/5, 370/1, 397/8, 414/15, 450/1 and 493.

66 Rameses II, Abu Simbel　67 Class XDd Diesel Train

1966. Air. 20th Anniv of U.N.E.S.C.O.

No.	Type	Description	Mint	Used
187	**66**	1d. red and yellow	1·25	75

1966. Agricultural Products (2nd and 3rd issue). As T **59**.

No.	Type	Description	Mint	Used
188		40f. multicoloured	25	10
189		60f. multicoloured	35	20

DESIGNS—VERT: 40f. Citrus fruits. HORIZ: 60f. Olives.

1966. Moroccan Transport. Multicoloured.

No.	Type	Description	Mint	Used
190		25f. Type **67** (postage)	1·50	60
191		40f. Liner "Maroc"	80	40
192		1d. Tourist coach	95	60
193		3d. Sud Aviation Caravelle of Royal Air Maroc (48 × 27½ mm) (air)	4·50	1·90

68 Twaite Shad

1967. Fishes. Multicoloured.

No.	Type	Description	Mint	Used
194		25f. Type **68**	1·10	25
195		40f. Plain bonito	1·40	30
196		1d. Bluefish	3·00	1·40

69 Hilton Hotel, Ancient Ruin and Map

1967. Opening of Hilton Hotel, Rabat.

No.	Type	Description	Mint	Used
197	**69**	25f. black and blue	20	15
198		1d. purple and blue	50	20

70 Ait Aadel Dam

1967. Inauguration of Ait Aadel Dam.

No.	Type	Description	Mint	Used
199	**70**	25f. grey, blue and green	25	15
200		40f. bistre and blue	65	20

71 Moroccan Scene and Lions Emblem

1967. 50th Anniv of Lions International.

No.	Type	Description	Mint	Used
201	**71**	40f. blue and gold	50	20
202		1d. green and gold	1·00	25

1967. Moroccan Red Cross. As T **65**. Mult.

No.	Type	Description	Mint	Used
203		60f.+5f. Necklace	95	95
204		1d.+10f. Two bracelets	1·90	1·90

72 Three Hands and Pickaxe　73 I.T.Y. Emblem

1967. Communal Development Campaign.

No.	Type	Description	Mint	Used
205	**72**	25f. green	20	15

1967. International Tourist Year.

No.	Type	Description	Mint	Used
206	**73**	1d. blue and cobalt	80	35

74 Arrow and Map　75 Horse-jumping

1967. Mediterranean Games, Tunis.

No.	Type	Description	Mint	Used
207	**74**	25f. multicoloured	25	20
208		40f. multicoloured	30	20

1967. International Horse Show.

No.	Type	Description	Mint	Used
209	**75**	40f. multicoloured	30	20
210		1d. multicoloured	75	35

1967. Agricultural Products (4th issue). As T **59**.

No.	Type	Description	Mint	Used
211		40f. mult (Cotton plant)	65	15

76 Human Rights Emblem　77 Msouffa Woman

1968. Human Rights Year.

No.	Type	Description	Mint	Used
212	**76**	25f. slate	20	20
213		1d. lake	35	25

1968. Moroccan Costumes. Multicoloured.

No.	Type	Description	Mint	Used
214		10f. Ait Moussa or Ali	65	25
215		15f. Ait Mouhad	90	30
216		25f. Barquemaster of Rabat-Sale	1·00	35
217		25f. Townsman	1·90	75
218		40f. Townswoman	1·10	45
219		60f. Royal Mokhazni	1·50	60
220		1d. Type **77**	1·50	95
221		1d. Riff	1·50	95
222		1d. Zemmour woman	1·90	1·25
223		1d. Meknassa	1·90	60

78 King Hassan　79 Red Crescent Nurse and Child

1968.

No.	Type	Description	Mint	Used
224	**78**	1f. multicoloured	10	10
225		2f. multicoloured	10	10
226		5f. multicoloured	10	10
227		10f. multicoloured	10	10
228		15f. multicoloured	10	10
229		20f. multicoloured	10	10
230		25f. multicoloured	15	10
231		30f. multicoloured	15	10
232		35f. multicoloured	45	10
233		40f. multicoloured	45	10
234		50f. multicoloured	50	10
235		60f. multicoloured	50	10
236		70f. multicoloured	4·00	90
237		75f. multicoloured	1·00	15
238		80f. multicoloured	70	20
239	–	90f. multicoloured	1·40	20
240	–	1d. multicoloured	2·00	20
241	–	2d. multicoloured	2·50	35
242	–	3d. multicoloured	5·00	80
243	–	5d. multicoloured	8·75	2·50

Nos. 239/43 bear a similar portrait of King Hassan, but are larger, 26½ × 40½ mm.

1968. 20th Anniv of W.H.O.

No.	Type	Description	Mint	Used
244	**79**	25f. brown, red and blue	20	10
245		40f. brown, red and slate	25	15

1968. Red Crescent. Moroccan Jewellery. As T **65**. Multicoloured.

No.	Type	Description	Mint	Used
246		25f. Pendant brooch	80	40
247		40f. Bracelet	1·25	50

80 Rotary Emblem, Conference Building and Map

1968. Rotary Int District Conf, Casablanca.

No.	Type	Description	Mint	Used
248	**80**	40f. gold, blue and green	65	20
249		1d. gold, ultramarine and blue	75	30

81 Belt Pattern　82 Princess Lalla Meryem

1968. "The Belts of Fez". Designs showing ornamental patterns.

No.	Type	Description	Mint	Used
250	**81**	25f. multicoloured	1·90	70
251	–	40f. multicoloured	2·25	1·25
252	–	60f. multicoloured	3·50	1·75
253	–	1d. multicoloured	6·00	3·25

1968. World Children's Day. Multicoloured.

No.	Type	Description	Mint	Used
254		25f. Type **82**	25	20
255		40f. Princess Lalla Asmaa	65	25
256		1d. Crown Prince Sidi Mohammed	1·10	55

83 Wrestling

1968. Olympic Games, Mexico. Multicoloured.

No.	Type	Description	Mint	Used
257		15f. Type **83**	15	15
258		20f. Basketball	15	15
259		25f. Cycling	50	15
260		40f. Boxing	60	15
261		60f. Running	75	15
262		1d. Football	1·25	45

84 Silver Crown　85 Costumes of Zagora, South Morocco

1968. Ancient Moroccan Coins.

No.	Type	Description	Mint	Used
263	**84**	20f. silver and purple	55	20
264	–	25f. gold and purple	80	25
265	–	40f. silver and green	1·40	65
266	–	60f. gold and red	1·60	65

COINS: 25f. Gold dinar; 40f. Silver dirham; 60f. Gold piece.

See also Nos. 270/1.

1969. Traditional Women's Costumes. Mult.

No.	Type	Description	Mint	Used
267		15f. Type **85** (postage)	1·25	75
268		25f. Ait Adidou costumes	1·90	1·10
269		1d. Ait Ouaouzguit costumes (air)	2·50	1·25

1969. 8th Anniv of Coronation of Hassan II. As T **84** (silver coins).

No.	Type	Description	Mint	Used
270		1d. silver and blue	4·25	1·60
271		5d. silver and violet	10·00	6·00

COINS: 1d. One dirham coin of King Mohammed V; 5d. One dirham coin of King Hassan II.

86 Hands "reading" Braille on Map

1969. Protection of the Blind Week.

No.	Type	Description	Mint	Used
272	**86**	25f.+10f. multicoloured	45	15

87 "Actor"　89 King Hassan II

1969. World Theatre Day.

No.	Type	Description	Mint	Used
273	**87**	1d. multicoloured	45	25

1969. 50th Anniv of League of Red Cross Societies. Moroccan Jewellery as T **65**. Mult.

No.	Type	Description	Mint	Used
274		25f.+5f. Bracelets	90	45
275		40f.+10f. Pendant	1·25	55

1969. King Hassan's 40th Birthday.

No.	Type	Description	Mint	Used
276	**89**	1d. multicoloured	1·25	35

مؤتمر القمة الاسلامي
الرباط ١٥ رجب 1389

(90)

91 Mahatma Gandhi

1969. Islamic Summit Conf, Rabat (1st issue). No. 240 optd with T **90**.
278 1d. multicoloured . . . . . 5·00 4·00

1969. Birth Centenary of Mahatma Gandhi.
279 **91** 40f. brown and lavender 60 15

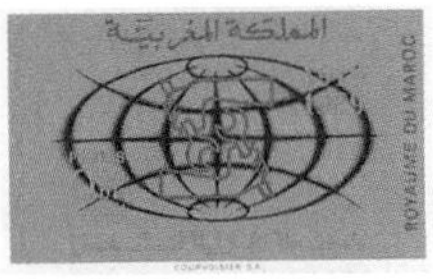

92 I.L.O. Emblem

1969. 50th Anniv of I.L.O.
280 **92** 50f. multicoloured 50 20

93 King Hassan on Horseback

1969. Islamic Summit Conference, Rabat (2nd issue).
281 **93** 1d. multicoloured . . . . 1·10 35

94 "Spahi Horseman" (Haram al Glaoui)

1970. Moroccan Art.
282 **94** 1d. multicoloured . . . . 1·10 30

1970. Flood Victims Relief Fund. Nos. 227/8 surch.
283 **78** 10f.+25f. multicoloured . . 3·50 3·50
284 15f.+25f. multicoloured . . 3·50 3·50

96 Drainage System, Fez

97 "Dance of the Guedra" (P. Beaubrun)

1970. 50th Congress of Public and Municipal Health Officials, Rabat.
285 **96** 60f. multicoloured 35 20

1970. Folklore Festival, Marrakesh.
286 **97** 40f. multicoloured 75 20

1970. Red Crescent. Moroccan Jewellery as T **65**. Multicoloured.
287 25f.+5f. Necklace . . . . . 1·00 65
288 50f.+10t. Pendant . . . . . 1·50 1·40

1970. Population Census. No. 189 surch **1970 0,25** and Arabic inscr.
290 25f. on 60f. multicoloured . . 50 10

99 Dish Aerial, Souk el Arba des Sehoul Communications Station

100 Ruddy Shelduck

1970. 17th Anniv of Revolution.
291 **99** 1d. multicoloured 80 35

1970. Nature Protection. Wild Birds. Mult.
292 25f. Type **100** 75 45
293 40f. Houbara bustard . . . . 1·75 65

101 I.E.Y. Emblem and Moroccan with Book

1970. International Education Year.
294 **101** 60f. multicoloured 65 20

102 Symbols of U.N.

1970. 25th Anniv of U.N.O.
295 **102** 50f. multicoloured 55 15

103 League Emblem, Map and Laurel

1970. 25th Anniv of Arab League.
296 **103** 50f. multicoloured 50 15

104 Olive Grove and Extraction Plant

1970. World Olive-oil Production Year.
297 **104** 50f. black, brown & green 55 15

105 Es Sounna Mosque

1971. Restoration of Es Sounna Mosque, Rabat.
298 **105** 60f. multicoloured 60 15

106 "Heart" within Horse

107 King Hassan II and Dam

1971. European and North African Heart Week.
299 **106** 50f. multicoloured 50 20

1971. 10th Anniv of King Hassan's Accession.
300 **107** 25f. multicoloured 45 10

108 Palestine on Globe

1971. Palestine Week.
302 **108** 25f.+10f. multicoloured 25 20

1971. Red Crescent, Moroccan Jewellery. As T **65**. Multicoloured.
303 25f.+5f. "Arrow-head" brooch 75 50
304 40f.+10f. Square pendant . . 1·10 90

109 Hands holding Peace Dove

1971. Racial Equality Year.
305 **109** 50f. multicoloured 50 15

110 Musical Instrument

1971. Protection of the Blind Week.
306 **110** 40f.+10f. multicoloured 60 20

111 Children at Play

112 Shah Mohammed Reza Pahlavi of Iran

1971. International Children's Day.
307 **111** 40f. multicoloured 45 15

1971. 2,500th Anniv of Persian Empire.
308 **112** 1d. multicoloured 70 30

113 Aerial View of Mausoleum

1971. Mausoleum of Mohammed V. Multicoloured.
309 25f. Type **113** 15 15
310 50f. Tomb of Mohammed V 20 20
311 1d. Interior of Mausoleum (vert) 80 50

114 Football and Emblem

1971. Mediterranean Games, Izmir, Turkey. Mult.
312 40f. Type **114** 55 15
313 60f. Athlete and emblem . . 70 20

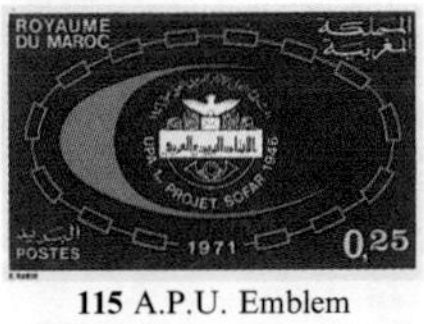

115 A.P.U. Emblem

1971. 25th Anniv of Founding of Arab Postal Union at Sofar Conference.
314 **115** 25f. red, blue & light blue 15 10

116 Sun and Landscape

1971. 50th Anniv of Sherifian Phosphates Office.
315 **116** 70f. multicoloured 55 20

117 Torch and Book Year Emblem

118 Lottery Symbol

1972. International Book Year.
316 **117** 1d. multicoloured 65 25

1972. Creation of National Lottery.
317 **118** 25f. gold, black and brown 15 10

119 Bridge of Sighs

120 Mizmar (double-horned flute)

1972. U.N.E.S.C.O. "Save Venice" Campaign. Multicoloured.
318 25f. Type **119** 15 15
319 50f. St. Mark's Basilica (horiz) 20 15
320 1d. Lion of St. Marks (horiz) 65 20

1972. Protection of the Blind Week.
321 **120** 25f.+10f. multicoloured 60 20

121 Bridge and Motorway

1972. 2nd African Highways Conference, Rabat.
322 **121** 75f. multicoloured 75 20

122 Moroccan Stamp of 1969, and Postmark

1972. Stamp Day.
323 **122** 1d. multicoloured 65 20

1972. Red Crescent. Moroccan Jewellery. As T **65**. Multicoloured.
324 25f.+5f. Jewelled bangles . . 75 75
325 70f.+10f. Filigree pendant . . 1·10 1·10

123 "Betrothal of Imilchil" (Tayeb Lahlou) 124 Dove on African Map

1972. Folklore Festival, Marrakesh.
326 **123** 60f. multicoloured 90 35

1972. 9th Organization of African Unity Summit Conference, Rabat.
327 **124** 25f. multicoloured 15 15

125 Polluted Beach

1972. U.N. Environmental Conservation Conf, Stockholm.
328 **125** 50f. multicoloured 50 20

126 Running 127 "Sonchus pinnatifidus"

1972. Olympic Games, Munich.
329 **126** 25f. red, pink and black 15 15
330 – 50f. violet, lilac and black 20 15
331 – 75f. green, yellow & black 60 20
332 – 1d. blue, lt blue & black 75 25
DESIGNS: 50f. Wrestling; 75f. Football; 1d. Cycling.

1972. Moroccan Flowers (1st series). Mult.
333 25f. Type **127** 45 15
334 40f. "Amberboa crupinoides" 55 15
See also Nos. 375/6.

128 Sand Gazelle 129 Rabat Carpet

1972. Nature Protection. Fauna. Multicoloured.
335 25f. Type **128** 75 25
336 40f. Barbary sheep . . . . . 1·00 60

1972. Moroccan Carpets (1st series). Mult.
337 50f. Type **129** . . . . 1·00 35
338 75f. Rabat carpet with "star-shaped" centre . . . . . . 1·50 50
See also Nos. 380/1, 406/7, 433/4, 485/7 and 513.

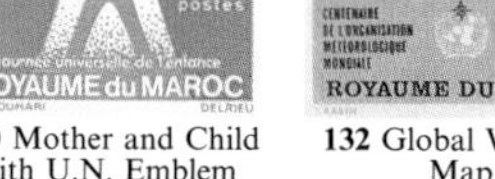

130 Mother and Child with U.N. Emblem 132 Global Weather Map

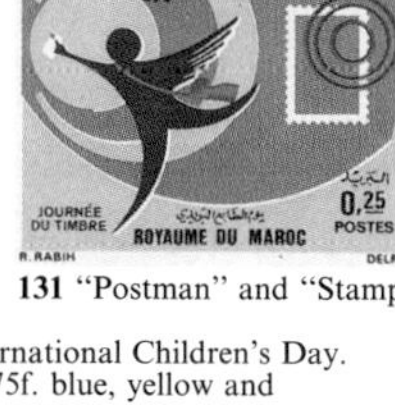

131 "Postman" and "Stamp"

1972. International Children's Day.
339 **130** 75f. blue, yellow and green 35 30

1973. Stamp Day.
340 **131** 25f. multicoloured 15 10

1973. Centenary of W.M.O.
341 **132** 70f. multicoloured 70 20

133 King Hassan and Arms

1973.

342	**133**	1f. multicoloured	10	10
343		2f. multicoloured	10	10
344		5f. multicoloured	10	10
345		10f. multicoloured . . .	10	10
346		15f. multicoloured . . .	10	10
347		20f. multicoloured . . .	10	10
348		25f. multicoloured . . .	10	10
349		30f. multicoloured . . .	15	10
350		35f. multicoloured . . .	15	10
351		40f. multicoloured . . .	5·00	70
352		50f. multicoloured . . .	50	10
353		60f. multicoloured . . .	60	15
354		70f. multicoloured . . .	25	15
355		75f. multicoloured . . .	30	15
356		80f. multicoloured . . .	60	20
357		90f. multicoloured . . .	75	15
358		1d. multicoloured . . .	2·00	20
359		2d. multicoloured . . .	4·25	55
360		3d. multicoloured . . .	6·25	1·25
361		5d. multicoloured (brown background)	4·25	1·25
361a		5d. multicoloured (pink background)	4·00	90

مناظرة
السياحة
1973

(134)

1973. Nat Tourist Conf. Nos. 324/5 surch with T **134**.
362 **65** 25f. on 5f. multicoloured 2·50 2·50
363 70f. on 10f. multicoloured 2·50 2·50
On No. 363 the Arabic text is arranged in one line.

135 Tambours

1973. Protection of the Blind Week.
364 **135** 70f.+10f. multicoloured 75 55

136 Kaaba, Mecca, and Mosque, Rabat

1973. Prophet Mohammed's Birthday.
365 **136** 25f. multicoloured 15 10

137 Roses and M'Gouna

1973. M'Gouna Rose Festival.
366 **137** 25f. multicoloured 45 10

138 Handclasp and Torch 139 Folk-dancers

1973. 10th Anniv of Organization of African Unity.
367 **138** 70f. multicoloured 30 15

1973. Folklore Festival, Marrakesh. Multicoloured.
368 50f. Type **139** 50 15
369 1d. Folk-musicians 75 25

1973. Red Crescent. Moroccan Jewellery. As T **65**. Multicoloured.
370 25f.+5f. Locket . . . . . . 1·00 50
371 70f.+10f. Bracelet inlaid with pearls . . . . 1·10 60

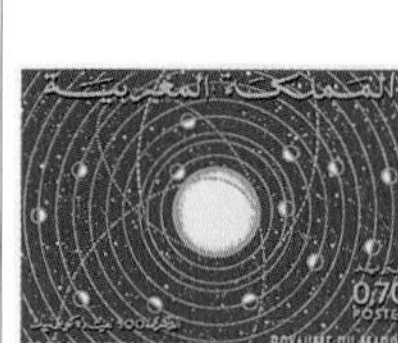

140 Solar System 141 Microscope

1973. 500th Birth Anniv of Nicholas Copernicus.
372 **140** 70f. multicoloured 60 20

1973. 25th Anniv of W.H.O.
373 **141** 70f. multicoloured 55 20

142 Interpol Emblem and Fingerprint

1973. 50th Anniv of International Criminal Police Organization (Interpol).
374 **142** 70f. multicoloured 30 25

1973. Moroccan Flowers (2nd series). As T **127**. Multicoloured.
375 25f. "Chrysanthemum carinatum" (horiz) 75 35
376 1d. "Amberboa muricata" . . 1·25 55

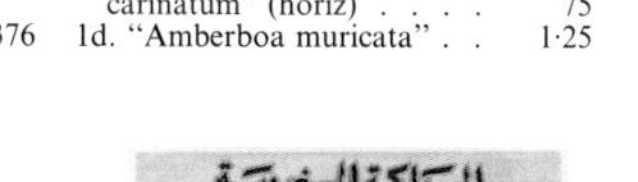

143 Striped Hyena

1973. Nature Protection. Multicoloured.
377 25f. Type **143** 95 40
378 50f. Eleonora's falcon (vert) 3·00 1·00

144 Map and Arrows

1973. Meeting of Maghreb Committee for Co-ordination of Posts and Telecommunications, Tunis.
379 **144** 25f. multicoloured 15 10

1973. Moroccan Carpets (2nd series). As T **129**. Multicoloured.
380 25f. Carpet from the High Atlas . . . . 1·00 25
381 70f. Tazenakht carpet . . . . 1·50 50

المؤتمر الاسلامي - لاهور
1394

145 Golf Club and Ball (146)

1974. International "Hassan II Trophy" Golf Grand Prix, Rabat.
382 **145** 70f. multicoloured . . . . 1·25 60

1974. Islamic Summit Conference, Lahore, Pakistan. No. 281 optd with T **146**.
383 1d. multicoloured . . . . . 2·75 1·60

147 Human Rights Emblem 148 Vanadinite

1974. 25th Anniv (1973) of Declaration of Human Rights.
384 **147** 70f. multicoloured 50 20

1974. Moroccan Mineral Sources. Multicoloured.
385 25f. Type **148** 95 50
386 70f. Erythrine . . . . 1·90 1·00

149 Marrakesh Minaret 150 U.P.U. Emblem and Congress Dates

1974. 173rd District of Rotary International Annual Conference, Marrakesh.
387 **149** 70f. multicoloured 70 20

1974. Centenary of U.P.U.
388 **150** 25f. black, red and green 15 10
389 – 1d. multicoloured 70 25
DESIGN—HORIZ: 1d. Commemorative scroll.

151 Drummers and Dancers

1974. 15th Folklore Festival, Marrakesh. Mult.
390 25f. Type **151** 35 15
391 70f. Juggler with woman . . 1·25 30

152 Environmental Emblem and Scenes 154 Flintlock Pistol

1974. World Environmental Day.
392 **152** 25f. multicoloured 20 15

1974. Red Crescent. Moroccan Firearms. Mult.
397 25f.+5f. Type **154** 75 75
398 70f.+10f. Gunpowder box . . 1·10 1·10

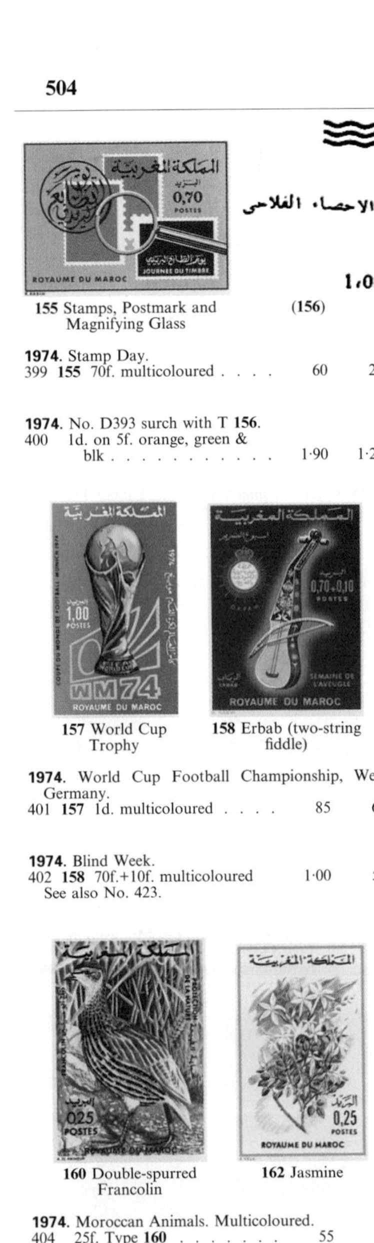

155 Stamps, Postmark and Magnifying Glass (156)

1974. Stamp Day.
399 **155** 70f. multicoloured 60 20

1974. No. D393 surch with T **156**.
400 1d. on 5f. orange, green & blk . . . . 1·90 1·25

157 World Cup Trophy

158 Erbab (two-string fiddle)

1974. World Cup Football Championship, West Germany.
401 **157** 1d. multicoloured 85 65

1974. Blind Week.
402 **158** 70f.+10f. multicoloured 1·00 50
See also No. 423.

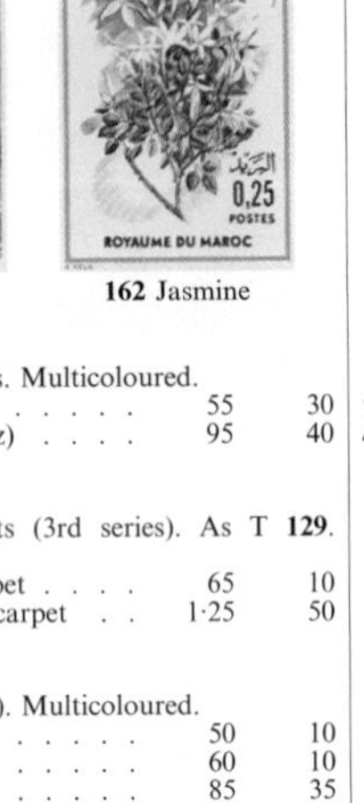

160 Double-spurred Francolin

162 Jasmine

1974. Moroccan Animals. Multicoloured.
404 25f. Type **160** 55 30
405 70f. Leopard (horiz) 95 40

1974. Moroccan Carpets (3rd series). As T **129**. Multicoloured.
406 25f. Zemmour carpet 65 10
407 1d. Beni M'Guild carpet . . 1·25 50

1975. Flowers (1st series). Multicoloured.
408 25f. Type **162** 50 10
409 35f. Orange lilies 60 10
410 70f. Poppies 85 35
411 90f. Carnations . . . . . . 1·10 50
See also Nos. 417/20.

163 Aragonite

165 "The Water-carrier" (Feu Taieb-Lalou)

1975. Minerals. Multicoloured.
412 50f. Type **163** 75 40
413 1d. Agate . . . . 1·50 75
See also Nos. 543 and 563/4.

1975. Red Crescent. Moroccan Jewellery. As T **65**. Multicoloured.
414 25f.+5f. Pendant 75 75
415 70f.+10f. Earring . . . . . . 1·10 1·00

1975. "Moroccan Painters".
416 **165** 1d. multicoloured . . . . 1·10 30

1975. Flowers (2nd series). As T **162**. Mult.
417 10f. Daisies 10 10
418 50f. Pelargoniums 60 10
419 60f. Orange blossom 75 30
420 1d. Pansies . . . . 1·10 60

166 Collector with Stamp Album

167 Dancer with Rifle

1975. Stamp Day.
421 **166** 40f. multicoloured 20 10

1975. 16th Nat Folklore Festival, Marrakesh.
422 **167** 1d. multicoloured 65 30

1975. Blind Week. As T **158**. Multicoloured.
423 1d. Mandolin 85 25

168 "Animals in Forest" (child's drawing)

1975. Children's Week.
424 **168** 25f. multicoloured 15 10

169 Games Emblem and Athletes

1975. 7th Mediterranean Games, Algiers.
425 **169** 40f. multicoloured 45 10

170 Waldrapp

1975. Fauna. Multicoloured.
426 40f. Type **170** . . . . 2·50 50
427 1d. Caracal (vert) . . . . . 1·50 75
See also Nos. 470/1.

1975. "Green March" (1st issue). Nos. 370/1 optd **1975** and Arabic inscr.
428 25f. (+ 5f.) multicoloured . . 2·50 2·50
429 70f. (+ 10f.) multicoloured . . 2·50 2·50
The premiums on the stamps are obliterated.

172 King Mohammed V greeting Crowd

1975. 20th Anniv of Independence. Mult.
430 40f. Type **172** 15 10
431 1d. King Hassan (vert) . . . 75 45
432 1d. King Hassan V wearing fez (vert) 75 45

1975. Moroccan Carpets (4th series). As T **129**. Multicoloured.
433 25f. Ouled Besseba carpet . . 60 35
434 1d. Ait Ouaouzguid carpet 90 45
See also Nos. 485/7 and 513.

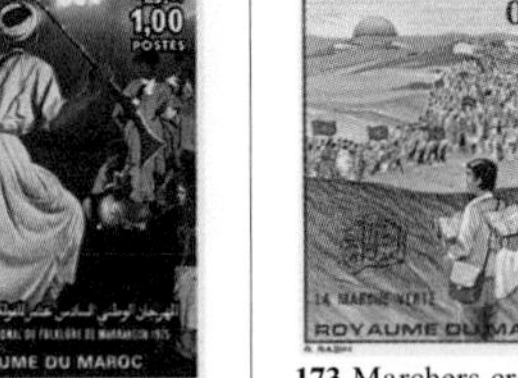

173 Marchers crossing Desert

174 Fez Coin of 1883/4

1975. "Green March" (2nd issue).
435 **173** 40f. multicoloured 15 10

1976. Moroccan Coins (1st series). Multicoloured.
436 5f. Type **174** 10 10
437 15f. Rabat silver coin 1774/5 10 10
438 35f. Sabta coin, 13/14th centuries 75 35
439 40f. Type **174** 50 10
440 50f. As No. 437 . . . . . . 75 35
441 65f. As No. 438 . . . . . . 75 50
442 1d. Sabta coin, 12/13th centuries . . . . 1·10 60
See also Nos. 458/67a.
For Nos. 439/40 in smaller size, see Nos. 520/b.

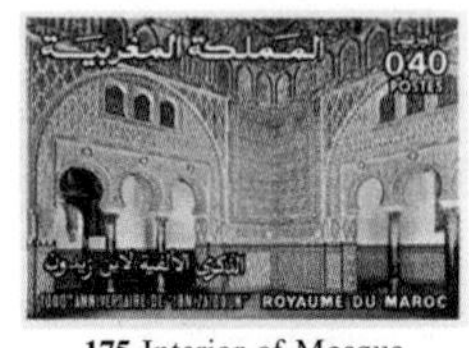

175 Interior of Mosque

1976. Millennium of Ibn Zaidoun Mosque. Mult.
443 40f. Type **175** 15 10
444 65f. Interior archways (vert) 50 15

176 Moroccan Family

1976. Family Planning.
445 **176** 40f. multicoloured 15 10

177 Bou Anania College, Fez

1976. Moroccan Architecture.
446 **177** 1d. multicoloured 70 20

178 Temple Sculpture

1976. Borobudur Temple Preservation Campaign. Multicoloured.
447 40f. Type **178** 15 15
448 1d. View of Temple 60 20

179 Dome of the Rock, Jerusalem

1976. 6th Anniv of Islamic Conference.
449 **179** 1d. multicoloured 70 20

1976. Red Crescent. Moroccan Jewellery. As T **65**. Multicoloured.
450 40f. Jewelled purse 15 10
451 1d. Jewelled pectoral 65 25

180 George Washington, King Hassan I, Statue of Liberty and Mausoleum of Mohammed V

181 Wrestling

1976. Bicentenary of American Revolution. Mult.
452 40f. Flags of U.S.A. and Morocco (horiz) 45 15
453 1d. Type **180** 65 25

1976. Olympic Games, Montreal. Multicoloured.
454 35f. Type **181** 10 10
455 40f. Cycling 15 10
456 50f. Boxing 50 15
457 1d. Running 70 25

1976. Moroccan Coins (2nd series). As T **174**. Multicoloured.
458 5f. Medieval silver mohur 10 10
459 10f. Gold mohur 10 10
460 15f. Gold coin 10 10
461 20f. Gold coin (different) . . 10 10
461a 25f. As No. 437 . . . . . . 1·25 50
462 30f. As No. 459 . . . . . . 35 10
463 35f. Silver dinar 45 10
464 60f. As No. 458 . . . . . . 50 15
465 70f. Copper coin 80 15
466 75f. As No. 463 . . . . . . 50 15
466a 80f. As No. 460 . . . . . . 2·50 75
467 2d. As No. 465 . . . . . . 60 35
467a 3d. As No. 461 . . . . . . 3·75 1·25

182 Early and Modern Telephones with Dish Aerial

1976. Telephone Centenary.
468 **182** 1d. multicoloured 70 25

183 Gold Medallion

1976. Blind Week.
469 **183** 50f. multicoloured 50 10

1976. Birds. As T **170**. Multicoloured.
470 40f. Dark chanting goshawk (vert) . . . . 2·25 75
471 1d. Purple swamphen (vert) 3·50 1·40

185 King Hassan, Emblems and Map

(186)

1976. 1st Anniv of "Green March".
472 **185** 40f. multicoloured 45 10

1976. Fifth African Tuberculosis Conference. Nos. 414/15 optd with T **186**.
473 25f. multicoloured . . . . . 1·90 1·90
474 70f. multicoloured . . . . . 2·25 2·25

187 Globe and Peace Dove

188 African Nations Cup

1976. Conference of Non-Aligned Countries, Colombo.
475 **187** 1d. red, black and blue 30 20

1976. African Nations Football Championship.
476 **188** 1d. multicoloured 65 20

189 Letters encircling Globe

1977. Stamp Day.
477 **189** 40f. multicoloured 40 10

190 "Aeonium arboreum"

موسم حب الملوك
1977
0,40

(**192**)

191 Ornamental Candle Lamps

1977. Flowers. Multicoloured.
478 40f. Type **190** 30 10
479 50f. "Malope trifida" (24 × 38 mm) 95 30
480 1d. "Hesperolaburnum platyclarpum" . . . . . . 1·10 30

1977. Procession of the Candles, Sale.
481 **191** 40f. multicoloured 45 10

1977. Cherry Festival. No. D394 surch with T **192**.
482 40f. on 10f. Cherries 75 30

193 Map and Emblem

1977. 5th Congress. Organization of Arab Towns.
483 **193** 50f. multicoloured 15 10

194 A.P.U. Emblem

1977. 25th Anniv of Arab Postal Union.
484 **194** 1d. multicoloured 60 20

1977. Moroccan Carpets (5th series). As T **129**. Multicoloured.
486 40f. Ait Haddou carpet . . . 40 20
487 1d. Henbel rug, Sale 95 30

195 Zither

196 Mohammed Ali Jinnah

1977. Blind Week.
488 **195** 1d. multicoloured 85 25

1977. Birth Centenary of Mohammed Ali Jinnah.
489 **196** 70f. multicoloured 50 20

197 Marcher with Flag

1977. 2nd Anniv of "Green March".
490 **197** 1d. multicoloured 60 20

198 Assembly Hall

1977. Opening of House of Representatives.
491 **198** 1d. multicoloured 65 20

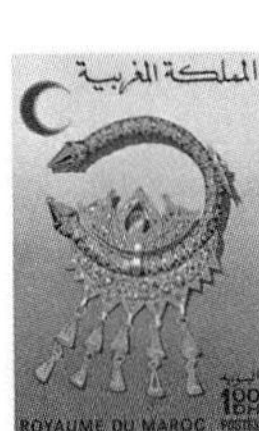
199 Silver Brooch

200 Bowl with Funnel

1977. Red Crescent.
493 **199** 1d. multicoloured . . . . 1·25 60

1978. Moroccan Copperware. Multicoloured.
494 40f. Type **200** 35 10
495 1d. Bowl with cover 70 20

201 Development Emblem

202 Decorative Pot with Lid

1978. Sahara Development. Multicoloured.
496 40f. Type **201** 35 10
497 1d. Fishes in net and camels at oasis (horiz) 60 20

1978. Blind Week. Multicoloured.
498 1d. Type **202** 90 30
499 1d. Decorative jar 90 30

203 Map and Red Cross within Red Crescent

1978. 10th Conference of Arab Red Crescent and Red Cross Societies.
500 **203** 1d. red and black 65 20

204 View of Fez

205 Dome of the Rock

1978. Rotary International Meeting, Fez.
501 **204** 1d. multicoloured 65 20

1978. Palestine Welfare.
502 **205** 5f. multicoloured 10 10
503 10f. multicoloured 10 10

206 Flautist and Folk Dancers

208 Yacht

207 Sugar Field and Crushing Plant

1978. National Folklore Festival, Marrakesh.
504 **206** 1d. multicoloured 55 20

1978. Sugar Industry.
505 **207** 40f. multicoloured 15 10

1978. World Sailing Championships.
506 **208** 1d. multicoloured 60 20

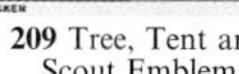
209 Tree, Tent and Scout Emblem

211 Human Rights Emblem

210 Moulay Idriss

1978. Pan-Arab Scout Festival, Rabat.
507 **209** 40f. multicoloured 15 10

1978. Moulay Idriss Great Festival.
508 **210** 40f. multicoloured 15 10

1978. 30th Anniv of Declaration of Human Rights.
509 **211** 1d. multicoloured 65 20

212 Houses in Agadir

214 Decorated Pot

213 Player, Football and Cup

1979. Southern Moroccan Architecture (1st series). Multicoloured.
510 40f. Type **212** 15 10
511 1d. Old fort at Marrakesh . . 60 15
See also Nos. 536 and 562.

1979. Mohammed V Football Cup.
512 **213** 40f. multicoloured 15 10

1979. Moroccan Carpets (6th series). As T **129**. Multicoloured.
513 40f. Marmoucha carpet . . . 40 15

1979. Blind Week.
514 **214** 1d. multicoloured 65 20

215 "Procession from a Mosque"

216 Coffee Pot and Heater

1979. Paintings by Mohamed Ben Ali Rbati. Mult.
515 40f. Type **215** 15 10
516 1d. "Religious Ceremony in a Mosque" (horiz) 55 20

1979. Red Cresent. Brassware. Multicoloured.
517 40f. Engraved circular boxes 25 15
518 1d. Type **216** 85 30

217 Costumed Girls

218 Curved Dagger in Jewelled Sheath

1979. National Folklore Festival, Marrakesh.
519 **217** 40f. multicoloured 15 10

1979. Moroccan Coins. As T **174**, but smaller, $17\frac{1}{2} \times 22\frac{1}{2}$ mm.
520 40f. multicoloured 10 10
520b 50f. multicoloured 10 10

1979. Ancient Weapons.
521 **218** 1d. black and yellow . . . 75 20

219 King Hassan II

221 King Hassan II

220 Festival Emblem

1979. King Hassan's 50th Birthday.
522 **219** 1d. multicoloured 70 20

1979. 4th Arab Youth Festival, Rabat.
523 **220** 1d. multicoloured 70 20

1979. "25th Anniv of Revolution of King and People".
524 **221** 1d. multicoloured 30 20

222 World Map superimposed on Open Book

1979. 50th Anniv of Int Bureau of Education.
525 **222** 1d. brown and yellow . . 60 20

223 Pilgrims in Wuquf, Arafat

1979. Pilgrimage to Mecca.
526 **223** 1d. multicoloured 70 20

استرجاع اقليم وادى الذهب
1979–8–14
(224)

1979. Recovery of Oued Eddahab Province. Design as No. 497, with face value amended (40f.), optd with T **224**.
527 40f. multicoloured 15 10
528 1d. multicoloured 65 20

225 Centaurium **226** Children around Globe

1979. Flowers. Multicoloured.
529 40f. Type **225** 15 10
530 1d. "Leucanthemum catanance" 55 20

1979. International Year of the Child.
531 **226** 40f. multicoloured 60 25

227 European Otter **228** Traffic Signs

1979. Wildlife. Multicoloured.
532 40f. Type **227** 50 15
533 1d. Moussier's redstart . . . 1·60 50

1980. Road Safety. Multicoloured.
534 40f. Type **228** 15 10
535 1d. Children at crossing . . . 30 20

229 Fortress

1980. South Moroccan Architecture (2nd series).
536 **229** 1d. multicoloured 55 20

230 Copper Bowl with Lid **231** Pot

1980. Red Crescent. Multicoloured.
537 50f. Type **230** 50 15
538 70f. Copper kettle and brazier 60 20

1980. Blind Week.
539 **231** 40f. multicoloured 15 10

232 Mechanized Sorting Office, Rabat

1980. Stamp Day.
540 **232** 40f. multicoloured 15 10

233 World Map and Rotary Emblem **234** Leather Bag and Cloth

1980. 75th Anniv of Rotary International.
541 **233** 1d. multicoloured 55 20

1980. 4th Textile and Leather Exhibition, Casablanca.
542 **234** 1d. multicoloured 55 20

1980. Minerals (2nd series). As T **163**. Mult.
543 40f. Gypsum 85 10

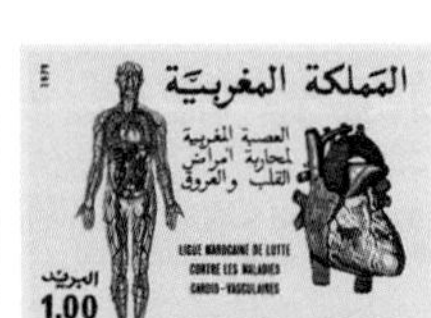

235 Peregrine Falcon **236** Diagram of Blood Circulation and Heart

1980. Hunting with Falcon.
544 **235** 40f. multicoloured . . . . 1·25 65

1980. Campaign against Cardiovascular Diseases.
545 **236** 1d. multicoloured 65 20

237 Decade Emblem and Human Figures **238** Harnessed Horse

1980. Decade for Women.
546 **237** 40f. mauve and blue . . . 15 10
547 – 1d. multicoloured 55 20
DESIGN: 1d. Decade and United Nations emblems.

1980. Ornamental Harnesses. Multicoloured.
548 40f. Harnessed horse (different) 15 10
549 1d. Type **238** 75 20

239 Satellite orbiting Earth and Dish Aerial **241** Conference Emblem

240 Light Bulb and Fuel Can

1980. World Meteorological Day.
550 **239** 40f. multicoloured 15 10

1980. Energy Conservation. Multicoloured.
551 40f. Type **240** 15 10
552 1d. Hand holding petrol pump 55 20

1980. World Tourism Conference, Manila.
553 **241** 40f. multicoloured 15 10

242 Tree bridging Straits of Gibraltar

1980. European–African Liaison over the Straits of Gibraltar.
554 **242** 1d. multicoloured 60 20

243 Flame and Marchers

1980. 5th Anniv of "The Green March".
555 **243** 1d. multicoloured 60 20

244 Holy Kaaba, Mecca **245** "Senecio antheuphorbium"

1980. 1400th Anniv of Hegira. Multicoloured.
556 40f. Type **244** 15 10
557 1d. Mosque, Mecca 60 20

1980. Flowers. Multicoloured.
558 40f. Type **245** 60 10
559 1d. "Periploca laevigata" . . 1·25 50

246 Painting by Aherdan **247** Nejjarine Fountain, Fez

1980. Paintings.
560 – 40f. bistre and brown . . 15 10
561 **246** 1d. multicoloured 60 20
DESIGN: 40f. Composition of bird and feathers.

1981. Moroccan Architecture (3rd series).
562 **247** 40f. multicoloured 10 10

1981. Minerals (3rd series). Vert designs as T **163**. Multicoloured.
563 40f. Onyx 95 35
564 1d. Malachite-azurite . . . . 1·60 75

248 King Hassan II

1981. 25th Anniv of Independence. Mult.
565 60f. Type **248** 35 10
566 60f. Map, flags, broken chains and "25" 35 10
567 60f. King Mohammed V. . . 35 10

249 King Hassan II

1981. 20th Anniv of King Hassan's Coronation.
568 **249** 1d.30 multicoloured . . . 50 25

250 "Source" (Jillali Gharbaoul)

1981. Moroccan Painting.
569 **250** 1d.30 multicoloured . . . 75 25

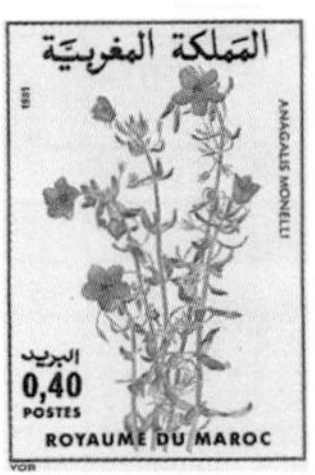

251 "Anagalis monelli" **252** King Hassan as Major General

1981. Flowers. Multicoloured.
570 40f. Type **251** 20 10
571 70f. "Bubonium intricatum" 40 15

1981. 25th Anniv of Moroccan Armed Forces.
572 **252** 60f. lilac, gold and green 35 10
573 – 60f. multicoloured 35 10
574 – 60f. lilac, gold and green 35 10
DESIGNS: No. 573, Army badge; 574, King Mohammed V (founder).

253 Caduceus (Telecommunications and Health) **254** Plate with Pattern

1981. World Telecommunications Day.
575 **253** 1d.30 multicoloured . . . 70 20

1981. Blind Week. Multicoloured.
576 50f. Type **254** 10 10
577 1d.30 Plate with ship pattern 60 20

255 Musicians and Dancers **256** "Seboula" Dagger

1981. 22nd National Folklore Festival, Marrakesh.
578 **255** 1d.30 multicoloured . . . 85 25

1981. Ancient Weapons.
579 **256** 1d.30 multicoloured . . . 75 20

257 Pestle and Mortar
258 Hands holding I.Y.D.P. Emblem

1981. Red Crescent. Moroccan Copperware. Mult.
580 60f. Type **257** 25 15
581 1d.30 Tripod brazier 80 25

1981. International Year of Disabled People.
582 **258** 60f. multicoloured 35 10

259 "Iphiclides feisthamelii Lotteri"
260 King Hassan and Marchers

1981. Butterflies (1st series). Multicoloured.
583 60f. Type **259** 50 25
584 1d.30 "Zerynthina rumina africana" . . . . 1·25 60
See also Nos. 609/10.

1981. 6th Anniv of "Green March".
585 **260** 1d.30 multicoloured . . . 70 20

261 Town Buildings and Congress Emblem

1981. 10th International Twinned Towns Congress, Casablanca.
586 **261** 1d.30 multicoloured . . . 20 20

262 Dome of the Rock
264 Terminal Building and Runway

1981. Palestinian Solidarity Day.
587 **262** 60f. multicoloured 35 10

1981. 12th Arab Summit Conference, Fez. Nos. 502/3 surch **1981 0,40**.
588 **205** 40f. on 5f. multicoloured 4·00 4·00
588a 40f. on 10f. multicoloured . . . . 2·75 2·75

1981. 1st Anniv of Mohammed V Airport.
589 **264** 1d.30 multicoloured . . . 70 20

265 Al Massira Dam
266 King Hassan II

1981. Al Massira Dam.
590 **265** 60f. multicoloured 35 10

1981.
591 **266** 5f. red, blue and gold . . 10 10
592 10f. red, yellow and gold 10 10
593 15f. red, green and gold 10 10
594 20f. red, pink and gold 10 10
595 25f. red, lilac and gold 10 10
596 30f. blue, lt blue & gold 10 10
597 35f. blue, yellow and gold 10 10
598 40f. blue, green and gold 10 10
599 50f. blue, pink and gold 10 10
600 60f. blue, lilac and gold 10 10
601 65f. blue, lilac and gold 10 10
602 70f. violet, yellow and gold 10 10
603 75f. violet, green and gold 15 15
604 80f. violet, pink and gold 15 15
605 90f. violet, lilac and gold 15 15
605a 1d.25 red, mauve & gold 20 15
605b 4d. brown, yell & gold 1·10 55
See also Nos. 624/9, 718/22, 759/61, 866, 895/6 and 930.

267 Horse Jumping

1981. Equestrian Sports.
606 **267** 1d.30 multicoloured . . . 1·25 25

268 Ait Quaquzguit

1982. Carpets (1st series). Multicoloured.
607 50f. Type **268** 10 10
608 1d.30 Ouled Besseba 60 30
See also Nos. 653/4.

1982. Butterflies and Moths (2nd series). As T **259**. Multicoloured.
609 60f. "Celerio oken lineata" 70 25
610 1d.30 "Mesoacidalia aglaja lyauteyi" . . . . 1·50 55

269 Tree and Emblem
270 Jug

1982. World Forestry Day.
611 **269** 40f. multicoloured 10 10

1982. Blind Week.
612 **270** 1d. multicoloured 50 25

271 Dancers
272 Candlestick

1982. Popular Art.
613 **271** 1d.40 multicoloured . . . 60 35

1982. Red Crescent.
614 **272** 1d.40 multicoloured . . . 60 35

273 Painting by M. Mezian
274 Buildings and People on Graph

1982. Moroccan Painting.
615 **273** 1d.40 multicoloured . . . 60 35

1982. Population and Housing Census.
616 **274** 60f. multicoloured 15 15

275 Dr. Koch, Lungs and Apparatus
276 I.T.U. Emblem

1982. Centenary of Discovery of Tubercle Bacillus.
617 **275** 1d.40 multicoloured . . . 75 35

1982. I.T.U. Delegates' Conference, Nairobi.
618 **276** 1d.40 multicoloured . . . 60 35

277 Wheat, Globe, Sea and F.A.O. Emblem

1982. World Food Day.
619 **277** 60f. multicoloured 15 15

278 Class XDd Diesel Locomotive (1956) and Route Map

1982. Unity Railway.
620 **278** 1d.40 multicoloured . . . 1·25 70

279 A.P.U. Emblem

1982. 30th Anniv of Arab Postal Union.
621 **279** 1d.40 multicoloured . . . 40 15

280 Dome of the Rock and Map of Palestine
281 Red Coral

1982. Palestinian Solidarity.
622 **280** 1d.40 multicoloured . . . 40 15

1982. Red Coral of Al Hoceima.
623 **281** 1d.40 multicoloured . . . 70 25

1983. Size 25 × 32 mm but inscribed "1982".
624 **266** 1d. red, blue and gold . . 25 10
625 1d.40 brown, lt brown & gold 35 10
626 2d. red, green and gold 45 15
627 3d. brown, yellow and gold 65 25
628 5d. brown, green and gold 1·40 50
629 10d. brown, orange and gold . . . . 2·75 90

282 Moroccan Stamps
283 King Hassan II

1983. Stamp Day.
630 **282** 1d.40 multicoloured . . . 60 20

1983.
631 **283** 1d.40 multicoloured . . . 25 20
632 2d. multicoloured 35 30
633 3d. multicoloured 80 50
634 5d. multicoloured . . . . 1·40 45
635 10d. multicoloured . . . 2·75 1·10

284 Decorated Pot
286 Ornamental Stand

285 Musicians

1983. Blind Week.
636 **284** 1d.40 multicoloured . . . 60 20

1983. Popular Arts.
637 **285** 1d.40 multicoloured . . . 75 20

1983. Red Crescent.
638 **286** 1d.40 multicoloured . . . 75 20

287 Commission Emblem

1983. 25th Anniv of Economic Commission for Africa.
639 **287** 1d.40 multicoloured . . . 55 20

288 "Tecoma sp."
290 Games Emblem and Stylized Sports

289 King Hassan II, Map and Sultan of Morocco

1983. Flowers. Multicoloured.
640 60c. Type **288** 10 10
641 1d.40 "Strelitzia sp." 75 20

1983. 30th Anniv of Revolution.
642 **289** 80c. multicoloured 20 20

1983. 9th Mediterranean Games, Casablanca.
644 **290** 80c. blue, silver and gold 20 20
645 – 1d. multicoloured 20 20
646 – 2d. multicoloured 60 30
DESIGNS—VERT: 1d. Games emblem. HORIZ: 2d. Stylized runner.

291 Ploughing

1983. Touiza.
648 **291** 80c. multicoloured 20 20

292 Symbol of "Green March"

293 Palestinian formed from Map and Globe

1983. 8th Anniv of "Green March".
649 **292** 80f. multicoloured 20 15

1983. Palestinian Welfare.
650 **293** 80f. multicoloured 20 15

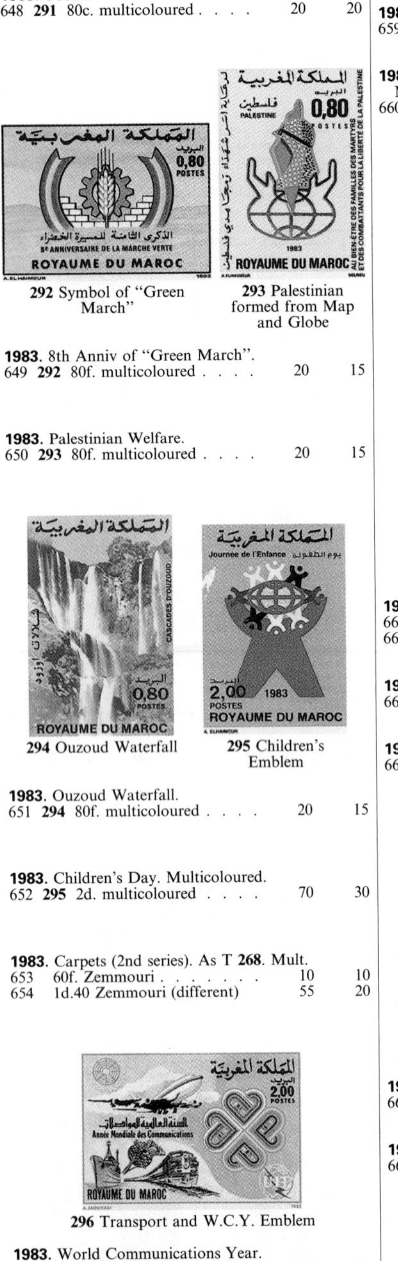

294 Ouzoud Waterfall

295 Children's Emblem

1983. Ouzoud Waterfall.
651 **294** 80f. multicoloured 20 15

1983. Children's Day. Multicoloured.
652 **295** 2d. multicoloured 70 30

1983. Carpets (2nd series). As T **268**. Mult.
653 60f. Zemmouri 10 10
654 1d.40 Zemmouri (different) 55 20

296 Transport and W.C.Y. Emblem

1983. World Communications Year.
655 **296** 2d. multicoloured . . . . 1·75 70

297 Views of Jerusalem and Fez

1984. Twinned Towns.
656 **297** 2d. multicoloured 95 20

298 Fennec Fox

1984. Animals. Multicoloured.
657 80f. Type **298** 30 25
658 2d. Lesser Egyptian jerboa 60 35

299 Map of League Members and Emblem

المهرجان 25

(300)

1984. 39th Anniv of League of Arab States.
659 **299** 2d. multicoloured 70 20

1984. 25th National Folklore Festival, Marrakesh. No. 578 optd with T **300**.
660 **255** 1d.30 multicoloured . . . 75 15

301 "Metha viridis"

303 Lidded Container

302 Decorated Bowl

1984. Flowers. Multicoloured.
661 80f. Type **301** 20 15
662 2d. Aloe 75 30

1984. Blind Week.
663 **302** 80f. multicoloured 20 15

1984. Red Crescent.
664 **303** 2d. multicoloured 75 30

304 Sports Pictograms

305 Dove carrying Children

1984. Olympic Games, Los Angeles.
665 **304** 2d. multicoloured 75 30

1984. International Child Victims' Day.
666 **305** 2d. multicoloured 70 30

306 U.P.U. Emblem and Ribbons

307 Hands holding Ears of Wheat

1984. Universal Postal Union Day.
667 **306** 2d. multicoloured 40 30

1984. World Food Day.
668 **307** 80f. multicoloured 20 15

308 Stylized Bird, Airplane and Emblem

309 Inscribed Scroll

1984. 40th Anniv of I.C.A.O.
669 **308** 2d. multicoloured 40 30

1984. 9th Anniv of "Green March".
670 **309** 80f. multicoloured 20 15

311 Flag and Dome of the Rock

312 Emblem and People

1984. Palestinian Welfare.
672 **311** 2d. multicoloured 60 25

1984. 36th Anniv of Human Rights Declaration.
673 **312** 2d. multicoloured 60 25

313 Aidi

314 Weighing Baby

1984. Dogs. Multicoloured.
674 80f. Type **313** 50 10
675 2d. Sloughi . . . . 1·10 25

1985. Infant Survival Campaign.
676 **314** 80f. multicoloured 15 10

315 Children playing in Garden

316 Sherifian Mail Postal Cancellation, 1892

1985. 1st Moroccan S.O.S. Children's Village.
677 **315** 2d. multicoloured 60 25

1985. Stamp Day.
678 **316** 2d. grey, pink and black 60 25
See also Nos. 698/9, 715/16, 757/8, 778/9, 796/7, 818/19, 841/2, 877/8, 910/11 and 924/5.

317 Emblem, Birds, Landscape and Fish

318 Musicians

1985. World Environment Day.
680 **317** 80f. multicoloured 20 10

1985. National Folklore Festival, Marrakesh.
681 **318** 2d. multicoloured 75 25

319 Decorated Plate

320 Bougainvillea

1985. Blind Week.
682 **319** 80f. multicoloured 15 10

1985. Flowers. Multicoloured.
683 80f. Type **320** 60 10
684 2d. "Hibiscus rosasinensis" 1·25 50

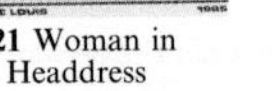

321 Woman in Headdress

323 Map and Emblem

322 Musicians and Dancers

1985. Red Crescent.
685 **321** 2d. multicoloured . . . . 1·25 50

1985. National Folklore Festival, Marrakesh.
686 **322** 2d. multicoloured 95 25

1985. 6th Pan-Arab Games.
687 **323** 2d. multicoloured 95 25

324 Emblem on Globe

325 Emblem

1985. 40th Anniv of U.N.O.
688 **324** 2d. multicoloured 60 25

1986. International Youth Year.
689 **325** 2d. multicoloured 60 25

326 Medal

327 Clasped Hands around Flag

1985. 10th Anniv of "Green March".
690 **326** 2d. multicoloured 60 25

1985. Palestinian Welfare.
691 **327** 2d. multicoloured 60 25

328 "Euphydryas desfontainii"

329 Arms

1985. Butterflies (1st series). Multicoloured.
692 80f. Type **328** 45 30
693 2d. "Colotis evagore" . . . . 1·40 90
See also Nos. 713/14.

1986. 25th Anniv of King Hassan's Coronation. Multicoloured.
694 80f. Type **329** 15 10
695 2d. King Hassan II (horiz) 60 25

330 Emblem

331 Vase

1986. 26th International Military Medicine Congress.
697 **330** 2d. multicoloured 60 25

1986. Stamp Day. As T **316**.
698 80f. orange and black 15 10
699 2d. green and black 60 25
DESIGNS: 80f. Sherifian postal seal of Maghzen-Safi; 2d. Sherifian postal seal of Maghzen-Safi (different).

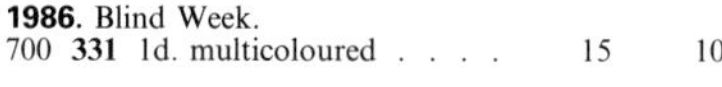

1986. Blind Week.
700 **331** 1d. multicoloured 15 10

332 Footballer and Emblem

1986. World Cup Football Championship, Mexico. Multicoloured.
701 1d. Type **332** 50 10
702 2d. Cup, pictogram of footballer and emblem . . 1·00 25

333 Copper Coffee Pot

334 "Warionia saharae"

1986. Red Crescent.
703 **333** 2d. multicoloured . . . . 1·25 50

1986. Flowers. Multicoloured.
704 1d. Type **334** 60 10
705 2d. "Mandragora autumnalis" . . . . 1·25 50

335 Emblem

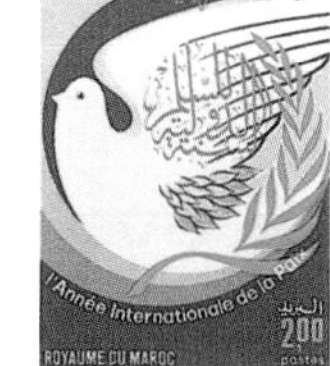
336 Dove and Olive Branch

1986. 18th Parachute Championships.
706 **335** 2d. multicoloured 90 25

1986. International Peace Year.
707 **336** 2d. multicoloured 60 25

337 Horsemen

338 Book

1986. Horse Week.
708 **337** 1d. light brown, pink and brown 60 10

1986. 11th Anniv of "Green March".
709 **338** 1d. multicoloured 15 10

339 Stylized People and Wheat

340 Marrakesh

1986. Fight against Hunger.
710 **339** 2d. multicoloured 60 25

1986. Aga Khan Architecture Prize.
711 **340** 2d. multicoloured 60 25

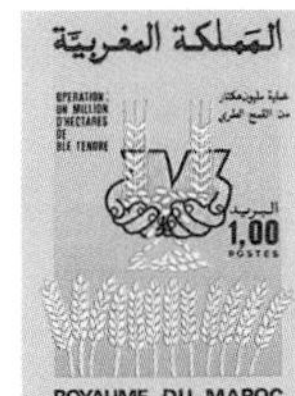
341 Hands holding Wheat

الملتقى العالمي الاول
لخطباء الجمعة
(342)

1986. "1,000,000 Hectares of Grain".
712 **341** 1d. multicoloured 15 10

1986. Butterflies (2nd series). As T **328**. Mult.
713 1d. "Elphinstonia charlonia" 65 35
714 2d. "Anthocharis belia" . . . 90 85

1987. Stamp Day. As T **316**.
715 1d. blue and black 15 10
716 2d. red and black 60 25
DESIGNS: 1d. Circular postal cancellation of Tetouan; 2d. Octagonal postal cancellation of Tetouan.

1987. Air. 1st World Reunion of Friday Preachers. Optd with T **342**.
717 **283** 2d. multicoloured 90 60

1987. Size 25 × 32 mm but inscr "1986".
718 **266** 1d.60 red, brown and gold 25 20
719 2d.50 red, grey and gold 60 25
720 6d.50 red, brown and gold 1·50 35
721 7d. red, brown and gold 1·75 45
722 8d.50 red, lilac and gold 2·00 50

343 Sidi Muhammad ben Yusuf addressing Crowd

1987. 40th Anniv of Tangier Conference. Each blue, silver and black.
723 1d. Type **343** 15 10
724 1d. King Hassan II making speech 15 10

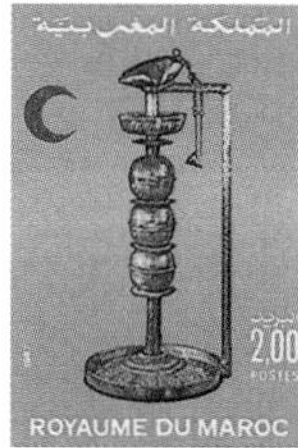
344 Copper Lamp

345 Woman with Baby and Packet of Salt being emptied into Beaker

1987. Red Crescent.
726 **344** 2d. multicoloured 60 25

1987. U.N.I.C.E.F. Child Survival Campaign.
727 **345** 1d. multicoloured 15 10

346 Decorated Pottery Jug

347 "Zygophyllum fontanesii"

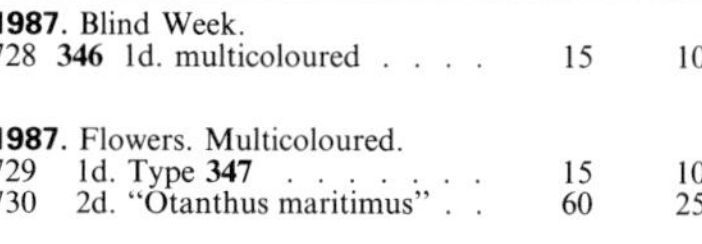

1987. Blind Week.
728 **346** 1d. multicoloured 15 10

1987. Flowers. Multicoloured.
729 1d. Type **347** 15 10
730 2d. "Otanthus maritimus" . . 60 25

348 Arabesque from Door, Dar Batha Palace, Fez

349 Map and King Hassan giving Blood

1987. Bicentenary of Diplomatic Relations with United States of America.
731 **348** 1d. blue, red and black 15 10

1987. Blood Transfusion Service.
732 **349** 2d. multicoloured 95 25

350 Woman from Melhfa

351 Emblem and Irrigated Field

1987. Sahara Costumes. Multicoloured.
733 1d. Type **350** 15 10
734 2d. Man from Derraa 60 25

1987. 13th International Irrigation and Drainage Congress.
735 **351** 1d. multicoloured 15 10

352 Baby on Hand and Syringe

353 Azurite

1987. United Nations Children's Fund Child Survival Campaign.
736 **352** 1d. multicoloured 15 10

1987. Mineral Industries Congress, Marrakesh. Multicoloured.
737 1d. Type **353** 50 10
738 2d. Wulfenite . . . . 1·00 50

354 "12" on Scroll

1987. 12th Anniv of "Green March".
739 **354** 1d. multicoloured 15 10

355 Activities

356 Desert Sparrow

1987. Armed Forces Social Services Month.
740 **355** 1d. multicoloured 15 10

1987. Birds. Multicoloured.
741 1d. Type **356** . . . . 1·10 45
742 2d. Barbary partridge . . . . 2·00 95

357 1912 25m. Stamp and Postmark

1987. 75th Anniv of Moroccan Stamps.
743 **357** 3d. mauve, black and green 80 40

358 "Cetiosaurus mogrebiensis"

1988. Dinosaur of Tilougguite.
744 **358** 2d. multicoloured . . . . 1·40 50

359 King Mohammed V

360 Map and Player in Arabesque Frame

1988. International Conf on King Mohammed V, Rabat.
745 **359** 2d. multicoloured 60 25

1988. 16th African Nations Cup Football Competition.
746 **360** 3d. multicoloured 75 40

361 Boy with Horse

1988. Horse Week.
747 **361** 3d. multicoloured . . . . 1·50 60

362 Pottery Flask

363 Anniversary Emblem

1988. Blind Week.
748 **362** 3d. multicoloured 75 35

1988. 125th Anniv of Red Cross.
749 **363** 3d. black, red and pink 75 35

364 "Citrullus colocynthis"

365 Breastfeeding Baby

1988. Flowers. Multicoloured.
750 3d.60 Type **364** 90 45
751 3d.60 "Calotropis procera" 90 45

1988. U.N.I.C.E.F. Child Survival Campaign.
752 **365** 3d. multicoloured 95 35

366 Olympic Medals and Rings

367 Greater Bustard

1988. Olympic Games, Seoul.
753 **366** 2d. multicoloured 30 25

1988. Birds. Multicoloured.
754 3d.60 Type **367** . . . . . . 1·90 80
755 3d.60 Greater flamingo . . . 1·90 80

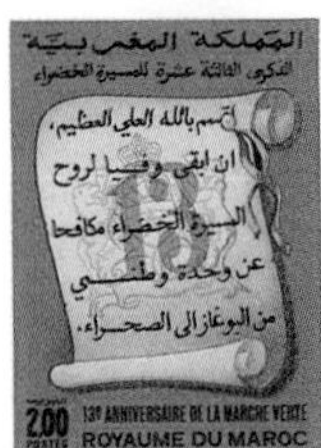

368 "13" on Scroll

اتحاد المغرب العربي
مراكش - فبراير 89

(370)

369 Housing of the Ksours and Csbaha

1988. 13th Anniv of "Green March".
756 **368** 2d. multicoloured 60 25

1988. Stamp Day. As T **316**.
757 3d. brown and black 95 35
758 3d. violet and black 95 35
DESIGNS: No. 757, Octagonal postal cancellation of Maghzen el Jadida; 758, Circular postal cancel-lation of Maghzen el Jadida.

1988. Size 25 × 32 mm but inscr "1988".
759 **266** 1d.20 blue, lilac and gold 15 10
760 3d.60 red and gold . . . 75 20
761 5d.20 brown, bis & gold 1·25 30

1989. Architecture.
762 **369** 2d. multicoloured 60 25

1989. Union of Arab Maghreb. No. 631 optd with T **370**.
763 **283** 1d.40 multicoloured . . . 50 15

371 King and Bishop with Chess Symbols

1989. 25th Anniv of Royal Moroccan Chess Federation.
764 **371** 2d. multicoloured 85 25

372 Copper Vase

374 King Hassan

375 "Cerinthe major"

1989. 60th Birthday of King Hassan II. Mult.
767 2d. Type **374** 75 25
768 2d. King Hassan in robes . . 75 25

1989. Flowers. Multicoloured.
770 2d. Type **375** 75 25
771 2d. "Narcissus papyraceus" 75 25

376 Telephone Handset linking Landmarks

1989. World Telecommunications Day.
772 **376** 2d. multicoloured 60 25

377 Gender Symbols forming Globe, Woman and Eggs

1989. 1st World Fertility and Sterility Congress.
773 **377** 2d. multicoloured 75 25

378 Desert Wheatear

1989. Birds. Multicoloured.
774 2d. Type **378** 50 50
775 3d. Shore lark . . . . 1·75 75

379 House of Representatives

1989. Centenary of Interparliamentary Union.
776 **379** 2d. multicoloured 60 25

380 Scroll

1989. 14th Anniv of "Green March".
777 **380** 3d. multicoloured 70 35

1990. Stamp Day. As T **316**.
778 2d. orange and black 60 20
779 3d. green and black 70 35
DESIGNS: 2d. Round postal cancellation of Casablanca; 3d. Octagonal postal cancellation of Casablanca.

381 Flags forming Map

1990. 1st Anniv of Union of Arab Maghreb.
780 **381** 2d. multicoloured 65 20

382 Oil Press

1990. 3rd World Olive Year. Multicoloured.
782 2d. Type **382** 60 15
783 3d. King Hassan and olives 85 25

383 Decorated Pot

1990. Blind Week.
784 **383** 2d. multicoloured 55 15

384 Silver Teapot

1990. Red Crescent.
785 **384** 2d. multicoloured 60 15

385 Arabic Script and Open Book

386 Turtle Dove

1990. International Literacy Year.
786 **385** 3d. green, yellow and black 80 25

1990. Birds. Multicoloured.
787 2d. Type **386** . . . . 1·10 35
788 3d. Hoopoe (horiz) . . . . . 1·90 65

387 "15" on Scroll

388 "35", Sun's Rays and Flag

1990. 15th Anniv of "Green March".
789 **387** 3d. multicoloured 80 25

1990. 35th Anniv of Independence.
790 **388** 3d. multicoloured 80 25

389 Dam

1990.
791 **389** 3d. multicoloured 80 25

390 Emblem

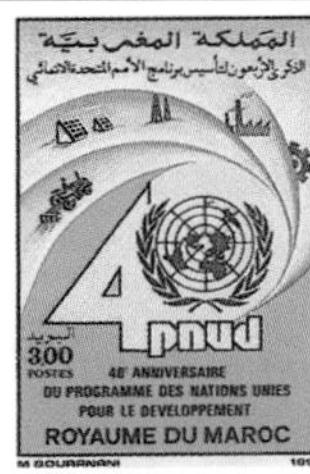

392 Projects and Emblem

391 Morse Code Apparatus

1990. 10th Anniv of Royal Academy of Morocco.
792 **390** 3d. multicoloured 85 25

1990. 20th Anniv of National Postal Museum. Multicoloured.
793 2d. Type **391** 60 15
794 3d. Horse-drawn mail wagon, 1913 . . . . 85 25

1991. Stamp Day. As T **316**.
796 2d. red and black 60 15
797 3d. blue and black 85 25
DESIGNS: 2d. Round postal cancellation of Rabat; 3d. Octagonal postal cancellation of Rabat.

1991. 40th Anniv of United Nations Development Programme.
798 **392** 3d. turquoise, yellow & blk 85 25

393 King Hassan

394 Mining

1991. 30th Anniv of Enthronement of King Hassan II. Multicoloured.
799 3d. Type **393** 85 25
800 3d. King Hassan in robes . . 85 25

1991. 70th Anniv of Mineral Exploitation by Sherifian Phosphates Office.
802 **394** 3d. multicoloured 85 25

395 Kettle on Stand

396 Lantern

1991. Blind Week.
803 **395** 3d. multicoloured 85 25

1991. Red Crescent.
804 **396** 3d. multicoloured 85 25

397 "Cynara humilis"

398 Man

373 Ceramic Vase

1989. Red Crescent.
765 **372** 2d. multicoloured 60 25

1989. Blind Week.
766 **373** 2d. multicoloured 60 25

1991. Flowers. Multicoloured.
805 3d. Type **397** 85 25
806 3d. "Pyrus mamorensis" . . 85 25

1991. Ouarzazate Costumes. Multicoloured.
807 3d. Type **398** 85 20
808 3d. Woman 85 20

1991. Inscribed "1991".
809 **266** 1d.35 red, green and gold 20 10

399 Road

400 Members' Flags and Map

1991. 19th World Roads Congress, Marrakesh.
810 **399** 3d. multicoloured 85 20

1991. 4th Ordinary Session of Arab Maghreb Union Presidential Council, Casablanca.
811 **400** 3d. multicoloured 85 20

401 "16" on Scroll

402 White Stork

1991. 16th Anniv of "Green March".
812 **401** 3d. multicoloured 85 20

1991. Birds. Multicoloured.
813 3d. Type **402** . . . . 1·50 50
814 3d. European bee eater . . . 1·50 50

403 Figures and Blood Splash

405 Zebra and Map of Africa

404 Emblem

1991. World AIDS Day.
815 **403** 3d. multicoloured 85 20

1991. 20th Anniv of Islamic Conf Organization.
816 **404** 3d. multicoloured 85 20

1991. African Tourism Year.
817 **405** 3d. multicoloured 85 20

1992. Stamp Day. As T **316**.
818 3d. green and black 85 20
819 3d. violet and black 85 20
DESIGNS: No. 818, Circular postal cancellation of Essaouira; No. 819, Octagonal postal cancellation of Essaouira.

406 Satellites around Earth

407 Bottle

1992. International Space Year.
820 **406** 3d. multicoloured 85 20

1992. Blind Week.
821 **407** 3d. multicoloured 85 20

408 Brass Jug

409 Quartz

1992. Red Crescent.
822 **408** 3d. multicoloured 85 50

1992. Minerals. Multicoloured.
823 1d.35 Type **409** 45 10
824 3d.40 Calcite . . . . 1·10 60

410 Woman

411 "Campanula afra"

1992. Tata Costumes. Multicoloured.
825 1d.35 Type **410** 20 10
826 3d.40 Man . . . . 1·10 60

1992. Flowers. Multicoloured.
827 1d.35 Type **411** 20 10
828 3d.40 "Thymus broussonetii" 1·10 60

412 Olympic Rings and Torch

414 La Koutoubia, La Giralda (cathedral bell-tower) and Exhibition Emblem

413 Map of Africa and Methods of Transport and Communication

1992. Olympic Games, Barcelona.
829 **412** 3d.40 multicoloured . . . 1·10 20

1992. Decade of Transport and Communications in Africa.
830 **413** 3d.40 multicoloured . . . 3·00 1·00

1992. "Expo '92" World's Fair, Seville.
831 **414** 3d.40 multicoloured . . . 1·10 50

415 Columbus's Fleet and Route Map

1992. 500th Anniv of Discovery of America by Columbus.
832 **415** 3d.40 multicoloured . . . 1·25 50

416 Pin-tailed Sandgrouse

1992. Birds. Multicoloured.
833 3d. Type **416** . . . . 1·10 40
834 3d. Griffon vulture ("Gyps fulvus") (vert) . . . . . . 1·10 40

417 "17" on Scroll

1992. 17th Anniv of "Green March".
835 **417** 3d.40 multicoloured . . . 1·10 20

418 Postal Messenger, Route Map and Cancellations

1992. Centenary of Sherifian Post. Multicoloured.
836 1d.35 Type **418** 20 10
837 3d.40 Postal cancellation, "100" on scroll and Sultan Mulay al-Hassan . . . . . 1·10 50

419 Conference Emblem

1992. International Nutrition Conference, Rome.
839 **419** 3d.40 multicoloured . . . 1·10 50

420 Douglas DC-9 Airliners on Runway

422 Satellite orbiting Earth

421 Dishes

1992. Al Massira Airport, Agadir.
840 **420** 3d.40 multicoloured . . . 1·10 20

1993. Stamp Day. As T **316**.
841 1d.70 green and black . . . 25 10
842 3d.80 orange and black . . . 1·10 50
DESIGNS: 1d.70, Round postal cancellation of Tangier; 3d.80, Octagonal postal cancellation of Tangier.

1993. Blind Week.
843 **421** 4d.40 multicoloured . . . 1·25 25

1993. World Meteorological Day.
844 **422** 4d.40 multicoloured . . . 1·25 25

423 Kettle on Stand

424 Emblem

1993. Red Crescent.
845 **423** 4d.40 multicoloured . . . 1·25 25

1993. World Telecommunications Day.
846 **424** 4d.40 multicoloured . . . 60 25

425 Woman extracting Argan Oil

426 Prince Sidi Mohammed

1993. Argan Oil. Multicoloured.
847 1d.70 Type **425** 25 10
848 4d.80 Branch and fruit of argan tree 70 30

1993. 30th Birthday of Prince Sidi Mohammed.
849 **426** 4d.80 multicoloured . . . 70 30

427 King Hassan and Mosque

428 Canopy, Sceptres, Flag and "40" on Sun

1993. Inauguration of King Hassan II Mosque.
850 **427** 4d.80 multicoloured . . . 70 30

1993. 40th Anniv of Revolution.
851 **428** 4d.80 multicoloured . . . 70 30

429 Post Box and Globe

430 Emblem

1993. World Post Day.
852 **429** 4d.80 multicoloured . . . 70 30

1993. Islamic Summer University.
853 **430** 4d.80 multicoloured . . . 70 30

431 "18" on Scroll

433 Flags, Scroll and "50"

432 Marbled Teal

1993. 18th Anniv of "Green March".
854 **431** 4d.80 multicoloured . . . 70 30

1993. Waterfowl. Multicoloured.
855 1d.70 Type **432** 25 10
856 4d.80 Red-knobbed coot . . 70 30

1994. 50th Anniv of Istaqlal (Independence) Party.
857 **433** 4d.80 multicoloured . . . 70 30

434 House

435 Decorated Vase

1994. Signing of Uruguay Round Final Act of General Agreement on Tariffs and Trade, Marrakesh.
858 **434** 1d.70 multicoloured . . . 25 10
859 – 4d.80 multicoloured . . . 70 30
DESIGN: 4d.80, Mosque.

1994. Blind Week.
861 **435** 4d.80 multicoloured . . . 70 30

436 Copper Vessel

437 Couple

1994. Red Crescent.
862 **436** 4d.80 multicoloured . . . 70 30

1994. National Congress on Children's Rights. Children's Drawings. Multicoloured.
863 1d.70 Type **437** 25 10
864 4d.80 Couple under sun . . . 70 30

438 Ball, Moroccan and U.S.A. Flags, Pictogram and Trophy

1994. World Cup Football Championship, U.S.A.
865 **438** 4d.80 multicoloured . . . 70 30

1994. Size 25 × 32 mm but inscr "1994".
866 **266** 1d.70 red, blue and gold 25 10

439 King Hassan II and Arms

1994. 65th Birthday of King Hassan II. Mult.
867 1d.70 Type **439** 25 10
868 4d.80 King Hassan II (vert) 70 30

440 "100" and Rings

441 Saint-Exupery, Route Map and Biplane

1994. Centenary of International Olympic Committee.
869 **440** 4d.80 multicoloured . . . 70 30

1994. 50th Death Anniv of Antoine de Saint-Exupery (writer and pilot).
870 **441** 4d.80 multicoloured . . . 70 30

442 "Chamaeleon gummifer"

1994. Flowers. Multicoloured.
871 1d.70 Type **442** 25 10
872 4d.80 "Pancratium maritimum" (vert) 70 30

443 Slender-billed Curlew

1994. Birds. Multicoloured.
873 1d.70 Type **443** 25 10
874 4d.80 Audouin's gull 70 30

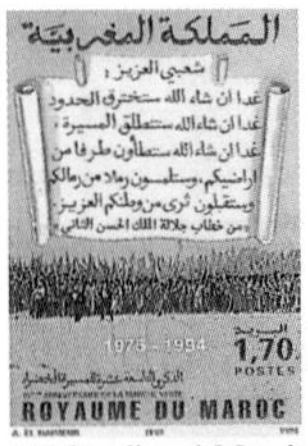

444 Scroll and March

445 Decorated Vase

1994. 19th Anniv of "Green March". Mult.
875 1d.70 Type **444** 25 10
876 4d.80 Marchers and Moroccan coastline 70 30

1994. Stamp Day. As T **316**.
877 1d.70 blue and black 25 10
878 4d.80 red and black 70 30
DESIGNS: 1d.70, Round postal cancellation of Marrakesh; 4d.80, Octagonal postal cancellation of Marrakesh.

1995. Blind Week.
879 **445** 4d.80 multicoloured . . . 70 30

446 Anniversary Emblem

447 Copper Vessel

1995. 50th Anniv of League of Arab States.
880 **446** 4d.80 multicoloured . . . 70 30

1995. Red Crescent.
881 **447** 4d.80 multicoloured . . . 70 30

448 "Malva hispanica"

449 European Roller

1995. Flowers. Multicoloured.
882 2d. Type **448** 30 10
883 4d.80 "Phlomis crinita" . . . 70 30

1995. Birds. Multicoloured.
884 1d.70 Type **449** 25 10
885 4d.80 Eurasian goldfinch . . 70 30

450 Anniversary Emblem, Building and Map

1995. 50th Anniv of F.A.O.
886 **450** 4d.80 multicoloured . . . 70 30

451 "50" and Flags

1995. 50th Anniv of U.N.O. Multicoloured.
887 1d.70 Type **451** 25 10
888 4d.80 U.N. emblem, doves and map 70 30

452 "20" on Scroll

453 "40", National Flag and Crown

1995. 20th Anniv of "Green March". Mult.
889 1d.70 Type **452** 25 10
890 4d.80 National flag, book and medal 70 30

1995. 40th Anniv of Independence.
891 **453** 4d.80 multicoloured . . . 70 30

1995. Stamp Day. As T **316**.
893 1d.70 bistre and black . . . 25 10
894 4d.80 lilac and black 70 30
DESIGNS: 1d.70, Round postal cancellation of Meknes; 4d.80, Octagonal cancellation of Meknes.

1996. Size 25 × 32 mm but inscr "1996".
895 **266** 5d.50 brown, red and gold 80 35
896 20d. brown, blue and gold 2·75 1·10

454 National Arms

455 Decorated Vase

1996. 35th Anniv of Enthronement of King Hassan II. Multicoloured.
897 2d. Type **454** 30 15
898 5d.50 King Hassan II 80 35

1996.
900 **455** 5d.50 multicoloured . . . 80 35

456 Leather Flask

457 "Cleonia lusitanica"

1996.
901 **456** 5d.50 multicoloured . . . 80 35

1996. Flowers. Multicoloured.
902 2d. Type **457** 30 15
903 5d.50 "Tulipa sylvestris" . . 80 35

458 King Hassan II wearing Military Uniform

459 Emblem and Runners

1996. 40th Anniv of Royal Armed Forces. Mult.
904 2d. Type **458** 30 15
905 5d.50 King Hassan II and globe 80 35

1996. Centenary of Modern Olympic Games. Olympic Games, Atlanta, U.S.A.
906 **459** 5d.50 multicoloured . . . 70 30

460 Osprey

461 "21" on Scroll

1996. Birds. Multicoloured.
907 2d. Type **460** 25 10
908 5d.50 Little egret 70 30

1996. 21st Anniv of "Green March".
909 **461** 5d.50 multicoloured . . . 70 30

1996. Stamp Day. As T **316**.
910 2d. orange and black 25 10
911 5d.50 green and black . . . 70 30
DESIGNS: 2d. Round postal cancellation of Maghzen-Fes; 5d.50, Octagonal postal cancellation of Maghzen-Fes.

462 Rainbow and Emblem

1996. 50th Anniv of U.N.I.C.E.F.
912 **462** 5d.50 multicoloured . . . 70 30

463 Terracotta Vessel

1997.
913 **463** 5d.50 multicoloured . . . 70 30

464 Lupin

465 King Mohammed V

1997. Flowers. Multicoloured.
914 2d. Type **464** 25 10
915 5d.50 Milk thistle 70 30

1997. 50th Anniv of Tangier Talks (determining future status of Tangier).
916 2d. Type **465** 25 10
917 2d. King Hassan II 25 10

466 Map in Open Book and Quill

468 Copper Door Knocker

467 Ibn Battuta and Globe

1997. World Book Day.
918 **466** 5d.50 multicoloured . . . 70 30

1997. International Conference on Ibn Battuta (explorer).
919 **467** 5d.50 multicoloured . . . 70 30

1997.
920 **468** 5d.50 multicoloured . . . 70 30

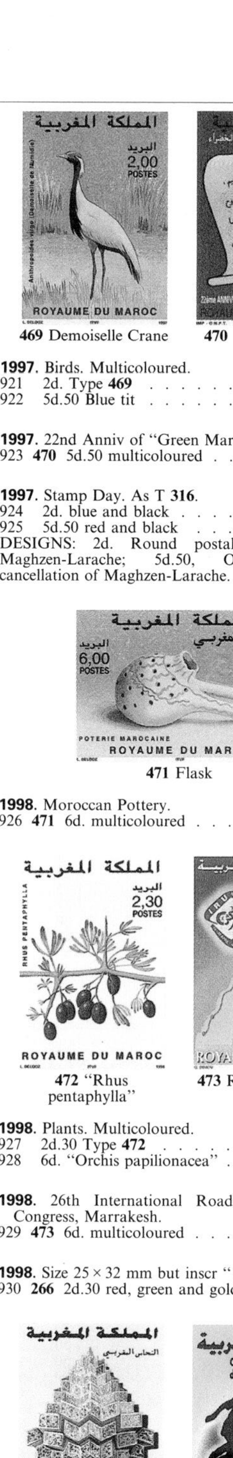

469 Demoiselle Crane 470 "22" on Scroll

1997. Birds. Multicoloured.
921 2d. Type **469** 25 10
922 5d.50 Blue tit 70 30

1997. 22nd Anniv of "Green March".
923 **470** 5d.50 multicoloured . . . 70 30

1997. Stamp Day. As T **316**.
924 2d. blue and black 25 10
925 5d.50 red and black 70 30
DESIGNS: 2d. Round postal cancellation of Maghzen-Larache; 5d.50, Octagonal postal cancellation of Maghzen-Larache.

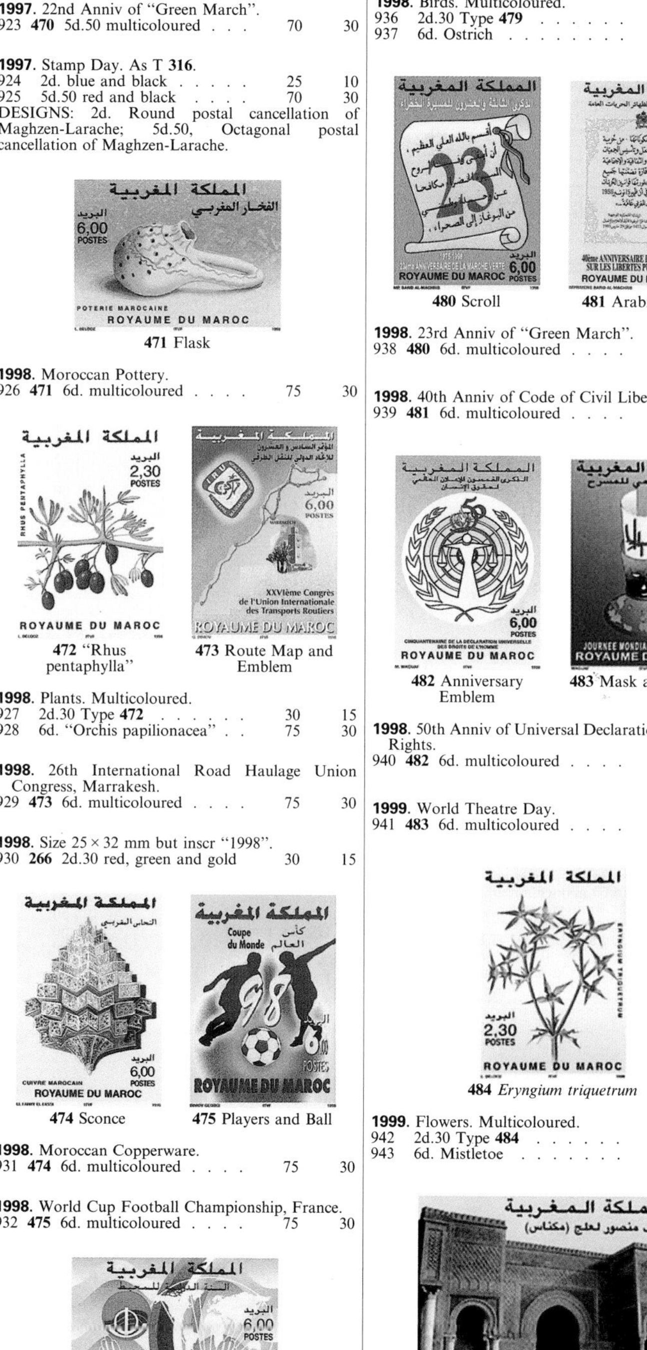

471 Flask

1998. Moroccan Pottery.
926 **471** 6d. multicoloured 75 30

472 "Rhus pentaphylla" 473 Route Map and Emblem

1998. Plants. Multicoloured.
927 2d.30 Type **472** 30 15
928 6d. "Orchis papilionacea" . . 75 30

1998. 26th International Road Haulage Union Congress, Marrakesh.
929 **473** 6d. multicoloured 75 30

1998. Size 25 × 32 mm but inscr "1998".
930 **266** 2d.30 red, green and gold 30 15

474 Sconce 475 Players and Ball

1998. Moroccan Copperware.
931 **474** 6d. multicoloured 75 30

1998. World Cup Football Championship, France.
932 **475** 6d. multicoloured 75 30

476 Emblem, Rainbow, World Map and Hands

1998. International Year of the Ocean.
933 **476** 6d. multicoloured 75 30

477 King Mohammed V and King Hassan II

1998. 45th Anniv of Revolution.
934 **477** 6d. multicoloured 75 30

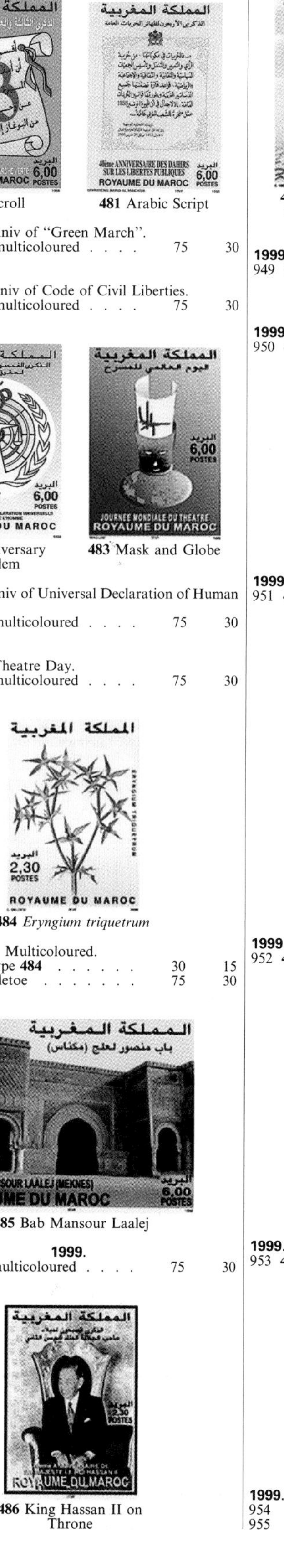

478 Globe and Letter 479 Nightingale

1998. World Stamp Day.
935 **478** 6d. multicoloured 75 30

1998. Birds. Multicoloured.
936 2d.30 Type **479** 30 15
937 6d. Ostrich 75 30

480 Scroll 481 Arabic Script

1998. 23rd Anniv of "Green March".
938 **480** 6d. multicoloured 75 30

1998. 40th Anniv of Code of Civil Liberties.
939 **481** 6d. multicoloured 75 30

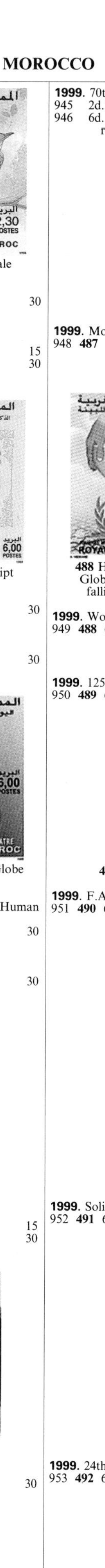

482 Anniversary Emblem 483 Mask and Globe

1998. 50th Anniv of Universal Declaration of Human Rights.
940 **482** 6d. multicoloured 75 30

1999. World Theatre Day.
941 **483** 6d. multicoloured 75 30

484 *Eryngium triquetrum*

1999. Flowers. Multicoloured.
942 2d.30 Type **484** 30 15
943 6d. Mistletoe 75 30

485 Bab Mansour Laalej

1999.
944 **485** 6d. multicoloured 75 30

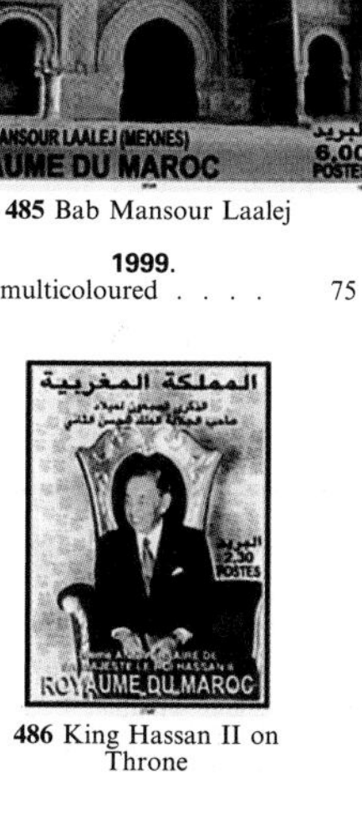

486 King Hassan II on Throne

1999. 70th Birthday of King Hassan II. Mult.
945 2d.30 Type **486** 30 15
946 6d. King Hassan wearing robes 75 30

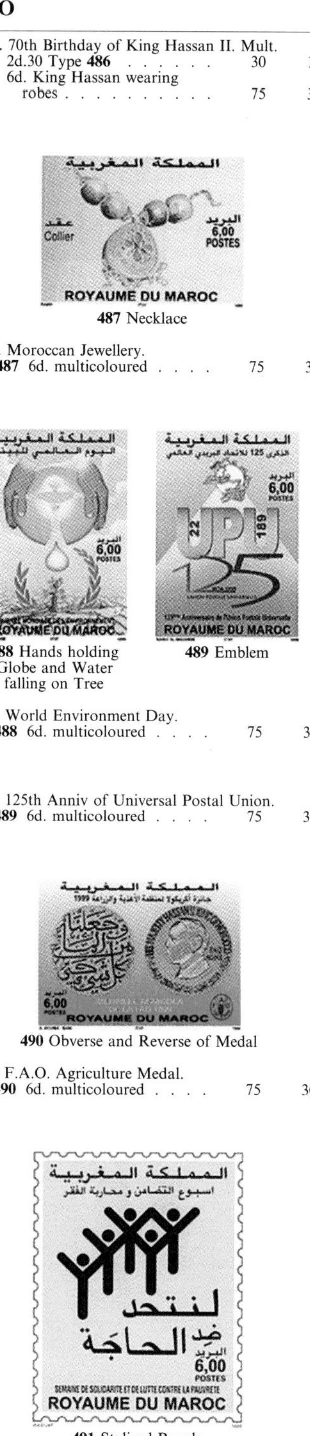

487 Necklace

1999. Moroccan Jewellery.
948 **487** 6d. multicoloured 75 30

488 Hands holding Globe and Water falling on Tree 489 Emblem

1999. World Environment Day.
949 **488** 6d. multicoloured 75 30

1999. 125th Anniv of Universal Postal Union.
950 **489** 6d. multicoloured 75 30

490 Obverse and Reverse of Medal

1999. F.A.O. Agriculture Medal.
951 **490** 6d. multicoloured 75 30

491 Stylized People

1999. Solidarity Week.
952 **491** 6d. blue, yellow and black 75 30

492 "24" on Scroll

1999. 24th Anniv of "Green March".
953 **492** 6d. multicoloured 75 30

493 Zebra Seabream

1999. Fishes. Multicoloured.
954 2d.30 Type **493** 30 15
955 6d. Opah 75 30

494 Stork on Nest (A. Slaoui)

1999. "Year of Morocco in France". Paintings. Multicoloured.
956 6d. Type **494** 75 30
957 6d. Women sitting on mat (Afif Bennani) 75 30
958 6d. Guitar (Abdelkader Rhorbal) 75 30
959 6d. View of harbour (A. Slaoui) 75 30

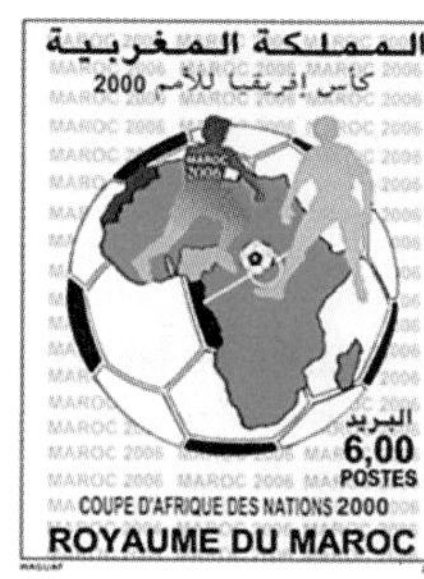

495 Players and Globe

2000. African Nations' Cup Football Championship.
960 **495** 6d. multicoloured 75 30

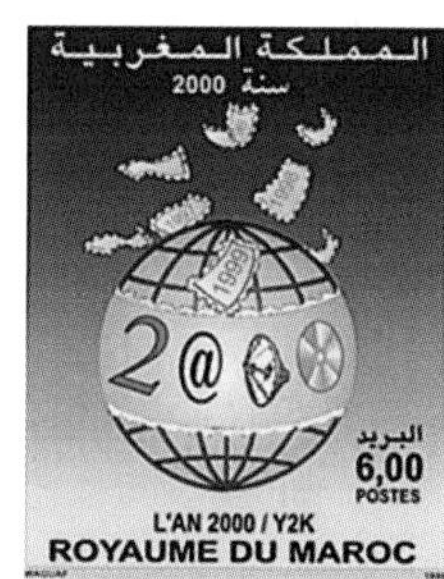

496 Globe and "2000"

2000. New Year
961 **496** 6d. multicoloured 75 30

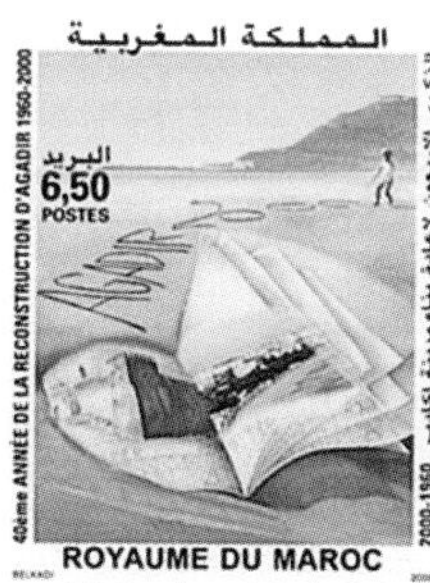

497 Beach and Calendar

2000. 40th Anniv of the Reconstruction of Agadir.
962 **497** 6d.50 multicoloured . . . 80 35

498 Emblem and Building

2000. 25th Anniv of Islamic Development Bank.
963 **498** 6d.50 multicoloured . . . 80 35

499 Stylized People

2000. National Disabled Persons Day.

964	**499**	6d.50 multicoloured . . .	80	35

500 *Jasione montana*

2000. Flowers. Multicoloured.

965	2d.50 Type **500**	30	10
966	6d.60 *Pistorica breviflora* . .	80	30

501 Emblem

2000. 50th Anniv of World Meteorological Organization.

967	**501**	6d.50 multicoloured . . .	80	30

502 People dancing

2000. National Festival of Popular Arts, Marrakesh.

968	**502**	6d.50 multicoloured . . .	80	30

503 Open Book and White Dove

2000. International Year of Culture and Peace.

969	**503**	6d.50 multicoloured . . .	80	30

(**504**) **505** King Mohammed VI

2000. Air. International Conference on Hassan II. No. 631 optd with T **504**.

970	6d.50 on 1d.40 multicoloured	80	30

2000. 1st Anniv of Enthronement of King Mohammed VI. Multicoloured.

971	2d.50 Type **505**	30	10
972	6d.50 King Mohammed VI	80	30

506 Ruins, Volubis and Performers

2000. Mediterranean Song and Dance Festival.

974	**506**	6d.50 multicoloured . . .	80	30

507 Emblem and Olympic Torch **508** Emblem, House and Children

2000. Olympic Games, Sydney.

975	**507**	6d.50 multicoloured . . .	80	30

2000. 50th Anniv of S.O.S. Children's Villages.

976	**508**	6d.50 multicoloured . . .	80	30

509 Quill, Globe and Emblem **511** "25" on Scroll

510 Emblem

2000. International Teachers' Day.

977	**509**	6d.50 multicoloured . . .	80	30

2000. King Mohammed VI Solidarity Foundation.

978	**510**	6d.50 blue, yellow and black	80	30

2000. 25th Anniv of "Green March". Mult.

979	2d.50 Type **511**	30	10
980	6d.50 "25" and text	80	30

512 St. Exupery and Plane **513** "45" and National Flag

2000. Birth Centenary of Antonie de Saint.-Exupery (author).

981	**512**	6d.50 multicoloured . . .	80	30

2000. 45th Anniv of Independence.

982	**513**	6d.50 multicoloured . . .	80	30

514 Mediterranean Cardinalfish (*Apogon imberbis*)

2000. Fishes. Multicoloured.

983	2d.50 Type **514**	30	10
984	6d.50 Cadenat's rockfish (*Scorpaena loppei*)	80	30

POSTAGE DUE STAMPS

D 53

1965.

D162	**D 53**	5f. green	3·00	1·25
D163		10f. brown	50	25
D164		20f. red	50	25
D165		30f. sepia	1·25	50

D 153 Peaches

1974.

D393	–	5f. orange, grn & blk	10	10
D394	–	10f. green, red & blk	10	10
D395	–	20f. green and black	50	10
D396	**D 153**	30f. orge, grn & blk	60	35
D397	–	40f. green and black	15	10
D398	–	60f. orge, grn & blk	20	15
D399	–	80f. orge, grn & blk	50	20
D399a	–	1d. multicoloured	20	15
D400	–	1d.20 multicoloured	50	15
D401	–	1d.60 multicoloured	60	20
D402	–	2d. multicoloured	55	25
D403	–	5d. multicoloured	65	30

DESIGNS: 60f., 1d.60, Peaches. VERT: 5f. Oranges; 10f., 1d.20, Cherries; 20f. Raisins; 40f. Grapes; 80f. Oranges; 1, 5d. Apples; 2d. Strawberries.

MOROCCO AGENCIES Pt. 1

Stamps used at British postal agencies in Morocco, N. Africa, the last of which closed on 30 April 1957.

I. GIBRALTAR ISSUES OVERPRINTED.

For use at all British Post Offices in Morocco.

All British P.O.s in Morocco were under the control of the Gibraltar P.O. until 1907 when control was assumed by H.M. Postmaster-General.

1898. Stamps of Gibraltar (Queen Victoria) optd **Morocco Agencies**.

9	**7**	5c. green	50	60
10		10c. red	1·75	30
11		20c. olive	5·50	70
3		20c. olive and brown	6·50	1·75
4		25c. blue	3·50	60
5		40c. brown	5·00	3·25
14		50c. lilac	8·50	3·50
7		1p. brown and blue	16·00	27·00
8		2p. black and red	19·00	27·00

1903. Stamps of Gibraltar (King Edward VII) optd **Morocco Agencies**.

24	**8**	5c. light green and green . .	7·50	2·75
18		10c. purple on red	7·50	40
26		20c. green and red	4·25	28·00
20		25c. purple and black on blue	7·50	30
28		50c. purple and violet	7·00	40·00
29		1p. black and red	27·00	75·00
30		2p. black and blue	15·00	35·00

II. BRITISH CURRENCY.

On sale at British P.O.s throughout Morocco, including Tangier, until 1937.

PRICES. Our prices for used stamps with these overprints are for examples used in Morocco. These stamps could also be used in the United Kingdom, with official sanction, from the summer of 1950 onwards, and with U.K. postmarks are worth about 50 per cent less.

Stamps of Great Britain optd **MOROCCO AGENCIES**.

1907. King Edward VII.

31	**83**	½d. green	2·25	8·00
32		1d. red	9·00	5·00
33	–	2d. green and red	8·50	5·00
34	–	4d. green and brown	3·75	3·75
35	–	4d. orange	9·50	10·00
36	–	6d. purple	14·00	18·00
37	–	1s. green and red	26·00	18·00
38	–	2s.6d. purple	70·00	£110

1914. King George V.

55	**105**	½d. green	1·25	50
43	**104**	1d. red	85	20
44	**105**	1½d. brown	2·75	12·00
45	**106**	2d. orange	3·25	50
58	**104**	2½d. blue	2·00	5·00
46	**106**	3d. violet	1·25	35
47		4d. green	3·00	1·25
60b	**107**	6d. purple	1·00	60
49	**108**	1s. brown	5·50	1·25
53	**109**	2s.6d. brown	38·00	25·00
74		5s. red	23·00	95·00

1935. Silver Jubilee.

62	**123**	½d. green	1·25	6·50
63		1d. red	1·25	6·50
64		1½d. brown	2·25	9·00
65		2½d. blue	2·50	2·50

1935. King George V.

66	**119**	1d. red	3·25	12·00
67	**118**	1½d. brown	3·25	15·00
68	**120**	2d. orange	1·25	6·50
69	**119**	2½d. blue	1·75	4·25
70	**120**	3d. violet	50	30
71		4d. green	50	30
72	**122**	1s. brown	80	2·50

1936. King Edward VIII.

75	**124**	1d. red	10	30
76		2½d. blue	10	15

In 1937 unoverprinted Great Britain stamps replaced overprinted **MOROCCO AGENCIES** issues as stocks became exhausted. In 1949 overprinted issues reappeared and were in use at Tetuan (Spanish Zone), the only remaining British P.O. apart from that at Tangier.

1949. King George VI.

77	**128**	½d. green	1·75	7·00
94		½d. orange	1·75	85
78		1d. red	2·75	9·00
95		1d. blue	1·75	1·25
79		1½d. brown	2·75	8·50
96		1½d. green	1·75	2·25
80		2d. orange	3·00	9·00
97		2d. brown	2·00	3·75
81		2½d. blue	3·25	10·00
98		2½d. red	1·75	3·75
82		3d. violet	1·50	1·60
83	**129**	4d. green	50	1·25
84		5d. brown	3·00	15·00
85		6d. purple	1·50	1·25
86	**130**	7d. green	50	16·00
87		8d. red	3·00	6·50
88		9d. olive	50	11·00
89		10d. blue	50	6·00
90		11d. plum	70	6·50
91		1s. brown	2·75	6·00
92	**131**	2s.6d. green	15·00	35·00
93		5s. red	28·00	60·00

1951. Pictorials.

99	**147**	2s.6d. green	13·00	20·00
100	–	5s. red (No. 510)	13·00	21·00

1952. Queen Elizabeth II.

101	**154**	½d. orange	10	10
102		1d. blue	15	1·40
103		1½d. green	15	20
104		2d. brown	20	1·60
105	**155**	2½d. red	15	80
106		4d. blue	85	3·50
107	**156**	5d. brown	65	60
108		6d. purple	85	3·50
109	**158**	8d. mauve	70	70
110	**159**	1s. bistre	70	60

III. SPANISH CURRENCY.

Stamps surcharged in Spanish currency were sold at British P.O.s throughout Morocco until the establishment of the French Zone and the Tangier International Zone, when their use was confined to the Spanish Zone.

Stamps of Great Britain surch **MOROCCO AGENCIES** and value in Spanish currency.

1907. King Edward VII.

112	**83**	5c. on ½d. green	6·00	20
113		10c. on 1d. red	10·00	10
114a	–	15c. on 1½d. purple and green	2·25	20
115	–	20c. on 2d. green and red	1·75	20
116a	**83**	25c. on 2½d. blue	1·50	20
117	–	40c. on 4d. green & brown	1·00	2·75
118a	–	40c. on 4d. orange . . .	1·00	60
119a	–	50c. on 5d. purple and blue	1·50	2·75

120a – 1p. on 10d. purple and red 21·00 11·00
121 – 3p. on 2s.6d. purple 20·00 25·00
122 – 6p. on 5s. red 35·00 45·00
123 – 12p. on 10s. blue 75·00 75·00

1912. King George V.
126 **101** 5c. on ½d. green 3·00 20
127 **102** 10c. on 1d. red 1·00 10

1914. King George V.
128 **105** 3c. on ½d. green 85 4·00
129 5c. on ½d. green 50 10
130 **104** 10c. on 1d. red 1·00 10
131 **105** 15c. on 1½d. brown 80 10
132 **106** 20c. on 2d. orange 90 25
133 **104** 25c. on 2½d. blue 1·75 25
148 **106** 40c. on 4d. green 1·75 2·00
135 **108** 1p. on 10d. blue 2·50 6·00
142 **109** 3p. on 2s.6d. brown 23·00 75·00
136 6p. on 5s. red 29·00 48·00
138 12p. on 10s. blue £110 £160

1935. Silver Jubilee.
149 **123** 5c. on ½d. green 1·00 80
150 10c. on 1d. red 2·75 2·25
151 15c. on 1½d. brown 5·50 16·00
152 25c. on 2½d. blue 3·50 2·25

1935. King George V.
153 **118** 5c. on ½d. green 85 17·00
154 **119** 10c. on 1d. red 2·50 8·50
155 **118** 15c. on 1½d. brown 5·00 3·25
156 **120** 20c. on 2d. orange 50 25
157 **119** 25c. on 2½d. blue 1·25 4·00
158 **120** 40c. on 4d. green 50 3·00
159 **122** 1p. on 10d. blue 5·00 30

1936. King Edward VIII.
160 **124** 5c. on ½d. green 10 10
161 10c. on 1d. red 50 2·00
162 15c. on 1½d. brown 10 15
163 25c. on 2½d. blue 10 10

1937. Coronation.
164 **126** 15c. on 1½d. brown 50 30

1937. King George VI.
165 **128** 5c. on ½d. green 85 20
182 5c. on ½d. orange 2·00 3·50
166 10c. on 1d. red 70 10
183 10c. on 1d. blue 3·25 6·50
167 15c. on 1½d. brown 85 25
184 15c. on 1½d. green 1·75 15·00
168 25c. on 2½d. blue 1·25 60
185 25c. on 2½d. red 1·75 7·50
169 **129** 40c. on 4d. green 29·00 12·00
186 40c. on 4d. blue 60 9·00
170 **130** 70c. on 7d. green 1·00 11·00
171 1p. on 10d. blue 1·75 3·50

1940. Stamp Centenary.
172 **134** 5c. on ½d. green 30 2·00
173 10c. on 1d. red 3·00 2·00
174 15c. on 1½d. brown 50 2·00
175 25c. on 2½d. blue 50 60

1948. Silver Wedding.
176 **137** 25c. on 2½d. blue 75 15
177 **138** 45p. on £1 blue 17·00 22·00

1948. Olympic Games.
178 **139** 25c. on 2½d. blue 40 70
179 **140** 30c. on 3d. violet 40 70
180 – 60c. on 6d. purple 40 70
181 – 1p.20 on 1s. brown 55 70

1954. Queen Elizabeth II.
189 **154** 5c. on ½d. orange 15 2·00
188 10c. on 1d. blue 50 1·00
190 **155** 40c. on 4d. blue 70 1·75

IV. FRENCH CURRENCY.

Stamps surch in French currency were sold at British P.O.s in the French Zone.

Stamps of Great Britain surch **MOROCCO AGENCIES** and value in French currency.

1917. King George V.
191 **105** 3c. on ½d. green 80 2·50
192 5c. on ½d. green 30 20
203 **104** 10c. on 1d. red 30 1·50
194 **105** 15c. on 1½d. brown 2·50 20
205 **104** 25c. on 2½d. blue 70 50
206 **106** 40c. on 4d. green 50 80
207 **107** 50c. on 5d. brown 1·00 10
198 **108** 75c. on 9d. green 1·00 75
209 90c. on 9d. green 14·00 6·50
210 1f. on 10d. blue 1·00 10
211 1f.50 on 1s. brown 8·50 2·25
200 **109** 3f. on 2s.6d. brown 7·50 1·50
226 6f. on 5s. red 6·00 21·00

1935. Silver Jubilee.
212 **123** 5c. on ½d. green 15 15
213 10c. on 1d. red 2·25 50
214 15c. on 1½d. brown 30 50
215 25c. on 2½d. blue 30 25

1935. King George V.
216 **118** 5c. on ½d. green 50 4·50
217 **119** 10c. on 1d. red 35 30
218 **118** 15c. on 1½d. brown 4·25 5·00
219 **119** 25c. on 2½d. blue 30 15
220 **120** 40c. on 4d. green 30 15
221 **121** 50c. on 5d. brown 30 15
222 **122** 90c. on 9d. olive 35 1·50
223 1f. on 10d. blue 30 30
224 1f.50 on 1s. brown 65 3·00

1936. King Edward VIII.
227 **124** 5c. on ½d. green 10 15
228 15c. on 1½d. brown 10 15

1937. Coronation.
229 **126** 15c. on 1½d. brown 30 20

1937. King George VI.
230 **128** 5c. on ½d. green 1·75 2·00

V. TANGIER INTERNATIONAL ZONE.

This Zone was established in 1924 and the first specially overprinted stamps issued in 1927.

PRICES. Our note re U.K. usage (at beginning of Section II) also applies to **TANGIER** optd stamps.

Stamps of Great Britain optd **TANGIER**.

1927. King George V.
231 **105** ½d. green 2·50 20
232 **104** 1d. red 2·75 20
233 **105** 1½d. brown 4·75 3·25
234 **106** 2d. orange 3·25 20

1934. King George V.
235 **118** ½d. green 1·00 1·60
236 **119** 1d. red 3·25 2·00
237 **118** 1½d. brown 50 20

1935. Silver Jubilee optd **TANGIER TANGIER**.
238 **123** ½d. green 1·00 4·00
239 1d. red 13·50 13·00
240 1½d. brown 1·25 70

1936. King Edward VIII.
241 **124** ½d. green 10 20
242 1d. red 10 10
243 1½d. brown 15 10

1937. Coronation optd **TANGIER TANGIER**.
244 **126** 1½d. brown 50 30

1937. King George VI.
245 **128** ½d. green 2·00 80
280 ½d. orange 70 1·50
246 1d. red 5·00 60
281 1d. blue 90 2·75
247 1½d. brown 2·00 20
282 1½d. green 90 14·00
261 2d. orange 5·00 5·00
283 2d. brown 90 2·25
262 2½d. blue 1·75 4·00
284 2½d. red 90 4·50
263 3d. violet 70 80
264 **129** 4d. green 11·00 10·00
285 4d. blue 2·75 2·75
265 5d. brown 3·75 16·00
266 6d. purple 70 30
267 **130** 7d. green 1·25 11·00
268 8d. red 3·75 8·50
269 9d. olive 1·25 11·00
270 10d. blue 1·25 11·00
271 11d. plum 1·25 9·00
272 1s. brown 1·25 2·25
273 **131** 2s.6d. green 4·50 11·00
274 5s. red 13·00 38·00
275 – 10s. blue (No. 478a) 38·00 £100

1940. Stamp Centenary.
248 **134** ½d. green 30 4·00
249 1d. red 45 50
250 1½d. brown 2·00 4·25

1946. Victory.
253 **135** 2½d. blue 40 30
254 – 3d. violet 40 1·50

1948. Silver Wedding.
255 **137** 2½d. blue 50 15
256 **138** £1 blue 20·00 25·00

1948. Olympic Games.
257 **139** 2½d. blue 75 1·50
258 **140** 3d. violet 75 1·50
259 – 6d. purple 75 1·50
260 – 1s. brown 75 70

1949. U.P.U.
276 **143** 2½d. blue 55 2·25
277 **144** 3d. violet 55 1·25
278 – 6d. purple 55 1·00
279 – 1s. brown 55 2·75

1951. Pictorial stamps.
286 **147** 2s.6d. green 8·50 4·75
287 – 5s. red (No. 510) 14·00 16·00
288 – 10s. blue (No. 511) 19·00 16·00

1952. Queen Elizabeth II.
313 **154** ½d. orange 10 30
314 1d. blue 20 40
291 1½d. green 10 30
292 2d. brown 20 60
293 **155** 2½d. red 10 70
294 3d. lilac 20 80
320 4d. blue 65 2·00
296 **157** 5d. brown 60 1·00
297 6d. purple 45 15
298 7d. green 80 2·50
299 **158** 8d. mauve 60 1·50
300 9d. olive 1·40 75
301 10d. blue 1·40 2·75
302 11d. purple 1·40 3·25
303 **159** 1s. brown 50 70
304 1s.3d. green 65 3·50
305 1s.6d. blue 1·00 1·75

1953. Coronation.
306 **161** 2½d. red 40 30
307 – 4d. blue 1·00 30
308 **163** 1s.3d. green 1·00 1·25
309 – 1s.6d. blue 1·00 1·00

1955. Pictorials.
310 **166** 2s.6d. brown 3·50 7·50
311 – 5s. red 4·50 14·00
312 – 10s. blue 16·00 21·00

1957. Cent of British Post Office in Tangier. Queen Elizabeth II stamps optd **1857-1957 TANGIER**.
323 **154** ½d. orange 10 10
324 1d. blue 10 10
325 1½d. green 10 10
326 2d. brown 10 10
327 **155** 2½d. red 15 1·00
328 3d. lilac 15 40
329 4d. blue 30 20
330 **157** 5d. brown 30 35
331 6d. purple 30 35
332 7d. green 30 35
333 **158** 8d. mauve 30 1·00
334 9d. olive 30 30
335 10d. blue 30 30
336 11d. plum 30 30
337 **159** 1s. bistre 30 30
338 1s.3d. green 45 3·75
339 1s.6d. blue 50 1·40
340 **166** 2s.6d. brown 2·00 3·50
341 – 5s. red (No. 596a) 2·75 5·00
342 – 10s. blue (No. 597a) 3·75 6·50

MORVI Pt. 1

A state of India, Bombay district. Now uses Indian stamps.

12 pies = 1 anna.

1 Maharaja Lakhdirji

3 Maharaja Lakhdirji

1931.
8 **1** 3p. red 3·25 9·00
9b 6p. green 3·75 9·00
5 ½a. blue 2·50 12·00
6 1a. brown 3·25 22·00
10 1a. blue 3·00 9·50
7 2a. brown 4·00 30·00
11 2a. violet 10·00 29·00

1934.
16 **3** 3p. red 1·00 3·00
17 6p. green 75 2·25
14 1a. brown 1·10 9·50
19 2a. violet 2·50 15·00

MOSUL Pt.1

Stamps used by Indian forces in Mesopotamia (now Iraq) at the close of the 1914–18 war.

12 pies = 1 anna; 16 annas = 1 rupee.

1919. Turkish Fiscal stamps surch **POSTAGE I.E.F. 'D'** and value in annas.
1 ½a. on 1pi. green and red 2·25 1·90
2 1a. on 20pa. black on red 1·40 1·75
4 2½a. on 1pi. mauve and yellow 1·50 1·50
5 3a. on 20pa. green 1·50 4·00
6 3a. on 20pa. green and orange 32·00 50·00
7 4a. on 1pi. violet 3·00 3·50
8 8a. on 10pa. red 4·00 5·00

MOZAMBIQUE Pt. 9; Pt. 13; Pt. 1

Former Overseas Province of Portugal in East Africa, granted independence in 1975. The Republic of Mozambique joined the Commonwealth on 12 November 1995.

1876. 1000 reis = 1 milreis.
1913. 100 centavos = 1 escudo.
1980. 100 centavos = 1 metical.

1876. "Crown" key-type inscr "MOCAMBIQUE".
1 P 5r. black 50 40
11 10r. yellow 1·60 1·40
19 10r. green 40 30
3 20r. bistre 50 30
20 20r. red £100 75·00
4a 25r. red 25 15
21 25r. lilac 1·10 60
14 40r. blue 4·00 2·50
22 40r. buff 75 65
6 50r. green 35·00 11·00
23 50r. blue 40 30
7 100r. lilac 40 25
8 200r. orange 1·25 70
9 300r. brown 95 65

1886. "Embossed" key-type inscr "PROVINCIA DE MOCAMBIQUE".
30 Q 5r. black 50 35
32 10r. green 45 35
34 20r. red 50 35
48 25r. lilac 3·25 1·75
37 40r. brown 45 30
38 50r. blue 70 35
40 100r. brown 50 30
42 200r. violet 1·10 75
43 300r. orange 1·40 45

1893. No. 37 surch **PROVISORIO 5 5**.
53 Q 5 on 40r. brown 32·00 23·00

1894. "Figures" key-type inscr "MOCAMBIQUE".
56 R 5r. orange 30 20
57 10r. mauve 30 20
58 15r. brown 35 25
59 20r. lilac 35 20
65 25r. green 30 15
60 50r. blue 1·10 25
67 75r. pink 65 45
61 80r. green 1·10 65
62 100r. brown on buff 70 50
68 150r. red on pink 3·00 1·60
64 200r. blue on blue 1·10 90
69 300r. blue on brown 1·60 1·25

1895. "Embossed" key-type of Mozambique optd **1195 CENTENARIO ANTONINO 1895**.
71 Q 5r. black 2·25 1·60
72 10r. green 2·25 1·75
73 20r. red 2·40 2·00
74 25r. purple 2·40 2·00
75 40r. brown 2·40 2·25
76 50r. blue 2·40 2·25
77 100r. brown 2·40 2·25
78 200r. lilac 7·50 5·50
79 300r. orange 7·50 5·50

1897. No. 69 surch **50 reis**.
82 R 50r. on 300r. blue on brown 60·00 45·00

1898. Nos. 34 and 37 surch **MOCAMBIQUE** and value.
84 Q 2½r. on 20r. red 7·00 5·50
85 5r. on 40r. brown 6·00 5·50

1898. "King Carlos" key type inscr "MOCAMBIQUE". Name and value in red (500r.) or black (others).
86 S 2½r. grey 15 15
87 5r. red 15 15
88 10r. green 15 15
89 15r. brown 1·50 75
138 15r. green 50 40
90 20r. lilac 50 25
91 25r. green 50 25
139 25r. red 40 15
92 50r. blue 55 30
140 50r. brown 1·25 85
141 65r. blue 3·00 3·00
93 75r. pink 2·50 1·50
142 75r. purple 1·00 85
94 80r. mauve 2·50 1·50
95 100r. blue on blue 1·25 65
143 115r. brown on pink 3·00 2·50
144 130r. brown on yellow 3·00 2·50
96 150r. brown on yellow 2·25 1·50
97 200r. purple on pink 1·00 70
98 300r. blue on pink 2·00 1·25
145 400r. blue on cream 4·50 3·25
99 500r. black on blue 4·75 3·00
100 700r. mauve on yellow 5·50 3·50

1902. Various types surch.
146 S 50r. on 65r. blue 1·10 1·00
101 R 65r. on 10r. mauve 95 85
102 65r. on 15r. brown 95 85
105 Q 65r. on 20r. red 1·40 1·00
106 R 65r. on 20r. lilac 95 85
108 Q 65r. on 40r. brown 1·25 1·25
110 65r. on 200r. violet 1·50 1·00
111 V 115r. on 2½r. brown 95 90
113 Q 115r. on 5r. black 65 55
114 R 115r. on 5r. orange 90 75
115 115r. on 25r. green 95 85
117 Q 115r. on 50r. blue 60 50
120 130r. on 25r. mauve 70 45
121 R 130r. on 75r. red 95 90
122 130r. on 100r. brn on buff 2·25 2·25
123 130r. on 150r. red on pink 1·00 1·00
124 130r. on 200r. blue on bl 2·00 2·00
126 Q 130r. on 300r. orange 75 45
128 400r. on 10r. green 1·75 1·60
129 R 400r. on 50r. blue 60 50
130 400r. on 80r. green 60 50
132 Q 400r. on 100r. brown 12·50 8·50
133 R 400r. on 300r. bl on brn 60 50

1902. "King Carlos" key-type of Mozambique optd **PROVISORIO**.
134 S 15r. brown 75 45
135 25r. green 75 45
136 50r. blue 1·25 95
137 75r. pink 2·10 1·25

1911. "King Carlos" key-type of Mozambique optd **REPUBLICA**.
147 S 2½r. grey 10 15
148 5r. orange 15 15
149 10r. green 40 25
150 15r. green 15 10
151 20r. lilac 40 20
152 25r. red 15 10
153 50r. brown 15 15
154 75r. purple 30 25
155 100r. blue on blue 30 25
156 115r. brown on pink 40 30

157 130r. brown on yellow . . . 40 30
158 200r. purple on pink . . . 75 50
159 400r. blue on yellow 70 45
160 500r. black on blue 70 45
161 700r. mauve on yellow . . . 70 45

1912. "King Manoel" key-type inscr "MOCAMBIQUE" with opt **REPUBLICA**.
162 T 2½r. lilac 15 10
163 5r. black 15 10
164 10r. green 15 10
165 20r. red 35 25
166 25r. brown 15 10
167 50r. blue 20 15
168 75r. brown 20 15
169 100r. brown on green . . . 20 15
170 200r. green on orange . . . 45 40
171 300r. black on blue 45 40
172 500r. brown and green . . 90 80

1913. Surch **REPUBLICA MOCAMBIQUE** and value on "Vasco da Gama" issues. (a) Portuguese Colonies.
173 ¼c. on 2½r. green 45 30
174 ½c. on 5r. red 40 30
175 1c. on 10r. purple 35 30
176 2½c. on 25r. green 35 30
177 5c. on 50r. blue 40 30
178 7½c. on 75r. brown 70 55
179 10c. on 100r. brown 50 45
180 15c. on 150r. brown 45 40

(b) Macao.
181 ¼c. on ½a. green 60 50
182 ½c. on 1a. red 55 50
183 1c. on 2a. purple 55 45
184 2½c. on 4a. green 55 45
185 5c. on 8a. blue . . . . 1·50 1·25
186 7½c. on 12a. brown 85 75
187 10c. on 16a. brown 60 50
188 15c. on 24a. brown 55 45

(c) Timor.
189 ¼c. on ½a. green 60 50
190 ½c. on 1a. red 60 50
191 1c. on 2a. purple 55 45
192 2½c. on 4a. green 55 45
193 5c. on 8a. blue 90 70
194 7½c. on 12a. brown 65 50
195 10c. on 16a. brown 50 45
196 15c. on 24a. brown 45 35

1914. "Ceres" key-type inscr "MOCAMBIQUE".
197 U ¼c. green 10 10
198 ½c. black 10 10
199 1c. green 10 10
200 1½c. brown 10 10
201 2c. red 10 10
270 2c. grey 10 10
202 2½c. violet 10 10
255 3c. orange 10 10
256 4c. pink 10 10
257 4½c. grey 10 10
203 5c. blue 10 10
275 6c. mauve 10 10
259 7c. blue 10 10
260 7½c. brown 10 10
278 8c. grey 10 10
279 10c. red 10 10
280 12c. brown 10 10
281 12c. green 10 10
283 15c. purple 10 10
284 20c. green 15 15
285 24c. blue 15 15
286 25c. brown 20 20
209 30c. brown on green . . . 70 50
287 30c. green 15 15
295 30c. lilac on pink 70 55
210 40c. brown on pink 75 60
288 40c. turquoise 40 15
211 50c. orange on orange . . . 1·40 1·10
289 50c. mauve 15 10
297 60c. brown on pink 70 55
290 60c. blue 45 25
291 60c. pink 45 25
298 80c. brown on blue 65 45
293 80c. red 45 25
299 1e. green on blue . . . . . 1·10 65
264 1e. pink 50 40
301 1e. blue 70 45
300 2e. mauve on pink 80 50
302 2e. purple 40 30
303 5e. brown . . . . 4·50 1·90
304 10e. pink . . . . 6·75 2·50
305 20e. green . . . . 18·00 8·25

1915. Provisional issues of 1902 optd **REPUBLICA**.
226 S 50r. blue (No. 136) 30 20
227 50r. on 65r. blue 30 25
213 75r. pink (No. 137) 70 40
228 V 115r. on 2½r. brown 30 25
216 Q 115r. on 5r. black . . . . 9·00 8·50
229 R 115r. on 5r. orange 30 25
230 115r. on 25r. green 30 25
231 130r. on 75r. red 30 25
220 130r. on 100r. brown on buff 55 45
232 130r. on 150r. red on pink 30 25
233 130r. on 200r. blue on bl 30 25
223 400r. on 50r. blue 65 60
224 400r. on 80r. green 65 60
225 400r. on 300r. blue on brn 65 60

1918. Charity Tax stamp surch **2½ CENTAVOS**. Roul or perf.
248 C 16 2½c. on 5c. red 40 25

1920. Charity Tax stamps surch. (a) **CORREIOS** and value in figures.
306 C 15 1c. on 1c. green 30 30
307 C 16 1½c. on 5c. red 30 25

(b) **SEIS CENTAVOS**.
308 C 16 6c. on 5c. red 40 30

1921. "Ceres" stamps of 1913 surch.
309 U 10c. on ½c. black 70 60
310 30c. on 1½c. brown 70 60
316 50c. on 4c. pink 55 35
311 60c. on 2½c. violet 90 70
328 70c. on 2e. purple 30 20
329 1e.40 on 2e. purple 35 20

1922. "Ceres" key-type of Lourenco Marques surch.
312 U 10c. on ¼c. black 50 45
314 30c. on 1½c. brown 50 45

1922. Charity Tax stamp surch **2$00**.
315 C 16 $2 on 5c. red 60 35

1924. 4th Death Centenary of Vasco da Gama. "Ceres" key-type of Mozambique optd **Vasco da Gama 1924**.
317 U 80c. pink 50 35

1925. Nos. 129 and 130 surch **Republica 40 C.**
318 R 40c. on 400r. on 50r. . . . 35 25
319 40c. on 400r. on 80r. . . . 35 30

1929. "Due" key-type inscr "MOCAMBIQUE" optd **CORREIOS**.
320 W 50c. lilac 55 45

23 Mousinho de Albuquerque

25 "Portugal" and Camoens' "The Lusiads"

1930. Albuquerque's Victories Commemorative. Vignette in grey.
321 23 50c. lake and red (Macontene) . . . . . . 2·75 2·50
322 50c. orge & red (Mujenga) 2·75 2·50
323 50c. mve & brn (Coolela) 2·25 1·90
324 50c. grey and green (Chaimite) . . . . . . 2·75 2·50
325 50c. bl & ind (Ibrahimo) 2·25 1·90
326 50c. blue and black (Mucuto-muno) . . . . 2·25 1·90
327 50c. vio & lilac (Naguema) 2·25 1·90

The above were for compulsory use throughout Mozambique in place of ordinary postage stamps on certain days in 1930 and 1931. They are not listed among the Charity Tax stamps as the revenue was not applied to any charitable fund.

1938. Value in red (1, 15c., 1e.40) or black (others).
330 25 1c. brown 10 10
331 5c. brown 10 10
332 10c. purple 10 10
333 15c. black 10 10
334 20c. grey 10 10
335 30c. green 10 10
336 35c. green . . . . 2·50 1·40
337 40c. red 10 10
338 45c. blue 20 20
339 50c. brown 15 10
340 60c. green 20 15
341 70c. brown 20 15
342 80c. green 20 15
343 85c. red 55 40
344 1e. purple 25 15
345 1e.40 blue . . . . 3·75 1·25
346 1e.75 blue . . . . 2·40 1·10
347 2e. lilac 65 25
348 5e. green . . . . 1·25 30
349 10e. brown . . . . 2·75 50
350 20e. orange . . . . 12·50 80

1938. As 1938 issue of Macao. Name and value in black.
351 54 1c. green (postage) 10 10
352 5c. brown 10 10
353 10c. red 10 10
354 15c. purple 10 10
355 20c. grey 10 10
356 – 30c. purple 15 10
357 – 35c. green 20 15
358 – 40c. brown 20 15
359 – 50c. mauve 20 10
360 – 60c. black 20 10
361 – 70c. violet 25 15
362 – 80c. orange 25 15
363 – 1e. red 30 15
364 – 1e.75 blue 90 30
365 – 2e. red 90 30
366 – 5e. green . . . . 2·25 30
367 – 10e. blue . . . . 4·50 60
368 – 20e. brown . . . . 11·00 1·00
369 56 10c. red (air) 10 10
370 20c. violet 10 10
371 50c. orange 15 10
372 1e. blue 20 10
373 2e. red 40 15
374 3e. green 60 20
375 5e. brown . . . . 1·00 35
376 9e. red . . . . 1·90 45
377 10e. mauve . . . . 3·00 60

DESIGNS: 30 to 50c. Mousinho de Albuquerque; 60c. to 1e. Dam; 1e.75 to 5e. Henry the Navigator; 10, 20e. Afonso de Albuquerque.

1938. No. 338 surch **40 centavos**.
378 25 40c. on 45c. blue . . . . . 1·75 1·50

26a Route of President's Tour

27 New Cathedral, Lourenco Marques

1938. President Carmona's 2nd Colonial Tour.
379 26a 80c. violet on mauve . . . 3·25 1·40
380 1e.75 blue on blue . . . . 10·00 3·50
381 3e. green on green . . . . 15·00 6·50
382 20e. brown on cream . . 70·00 30·00

1944. 400th Anniv of Lourenco Marques.
383 27 50c. brown . . . . 1·60 60
384 – 50c. green . . . . 1·60 60
385 – 1e.75 blue . . . . 11·00 2·10
386a – 20e. black . . . . 6·75 60

DESIGNS—HORIZ: 1e.75, Lourenco Marques Central Railway Station; 20e. Town Hall, Lourenco Marques.
See also No. 405.

1946. Nos. 354, 364 and 375 surch.
387 10c. on 15c. purple (postage) 40 30
388 60c. on 1e.75 blue 60 35
389 3e. on 5e. brown (air) . . . . 4·00 1·75

1947. No. 386a surch.
390 2e. on 20e. black . . . . . . 1·25 1·10

30 Lockheed L.18 Lodestar

1940. Air. Values in black.
391 30 1e.20 red . . . . 1·00 65
392 1e.60 blue . . . . 1·50 80
393 1e.70 purple . . . . . . 2·10 1·20
394 2e.90 brown . . . . . . 3·75 1·40
395 3e. green . . . . 2·75 1·60

1947. Air. Optd **Taxe percue**. Values in red (50c.) or black (others).
397 30 50c. black 40 30
398 1e. pink 50 30
399 3e. green 80 40
400 4e.50 green . . . . 1·40 55
401 5e. red . . . . 2·00 80
402 10e. blue . . . . 5·50 1·90
403 20e. violet . . . . 13·50 5·25
404 50e. orange . . . . 30·00 12·00

1948. As T **27** but without commemorative inscr.
405 4e.50 red . . . . 1·25 40

31 Antonio Enes

33 Lourenco Marques

1948. Birth Centenary of Antonio Enes.
406 31 50c. black and cream . . . 1·00 20
407 5e. purple and cream . . . 4·25 80

1948.
408 – 5c. brown 55 15
409 – 10c. purple . . . . 1·10 15
410 – 20c. brown 55 15
411 – 30c. purple 55 15
412 – 40c. green 55 15
413 33 50c. grey 55 15
414 – 60c. purple 70 15
415 33 80c. violet 55 15
416 – 1e. red 75 15
417 – 1e.20 grey . . . . 4·50 45
418 – 1e.50 violet 75 20
419 – 1e.75 blue . . . . 2·10 25
420 – 2e. brown . . . . 1·25 15
421 – 2e.50 blue . . . . 4·75 20
422 – 3e. green . . . . 2·00 20
423 – 3e.50 green . . . . 3·50 20
424 – 5e. green . . . . 3·00 20
425 – 10e. brown . . . . 7·25 35
426 – 15e. red . . . . 18·00 1·50
427 – 20e. orange . . . . 32·00 1·75

DESIGNS—VERT: 5, 30c. Gogogo Peak; 20, 40c. Zumbo River; 60c., 3e.50, Nhanhangare Waterfall. HORIZ: 10c., 1e.20, Railway bridge over River Zambesi at Sena; 1, 5e. Gathering coconuts; 1e.50, 2e. River Pungue at Beira; 1e.75, 3e. Polana beach, Lourenco Marques; 2e.50, 10e. Bird's eye view of Lourenco Marques; 15, 20e. Malema River.

1949. Honouring the Statue of Our Lady of Fatima. As T **62** of Macao.
428 50c. blue . . . . 5·25 90
429 1e.20 mauve . . . . 10·50 1·75
430 4e.50 green . . . . 40·00 6·25
431 20e. brown . . . . 75·00 9·25

35 Aircraft and Globe

36 Clown Triggerfish

1949. Air.
432 35 50c. brown 55 25
433 1e.20 violet . . . . 1·10 50
434 4e.50 blue . . . . 2·50 90
435 5e. green . . . . 4·50 1·10
436 20e. brown . . . . 13·00 2·50

1949. 75th Anniv of U.P.U. As T **64** of Macao.
437 4e.50 blue . . . . 1·50 60

1950. Holy Year. As Nos. 425/6 of Macao.
438 1e.50 orange 65 30
439 3e. blue 90 45

1951. Fishes. Multicoloured.
440 5c. Type **36** 35 15
441 10c. Thread-finned butterflyfish 25 15
442 15c. Racoon butterflyfish . . 85 25
443 20c. Lionfish 35 15
444 30c. Pearl puffer 35 15
445 40c. Golden filefish 25 15
446 50c. Spot-cheeked surgeonfish 25 15
447 1e. Pennant coralfish (vert) 35 15
448 1e.50 Seagrass wrasse 35 15
449 2e. Sombre sweetlips 35 15
450 2e.50 Blue-striped snapper . . 1·00 20
451 3e. Convict tang . . . . . . 1·00 20
452 3e.50 Starry triggerfish . . . 1·10 15
453 4e. Cornetfish . . . . 1·75 25
454 4e.50 Vagabond butterflyfish 2·50 20
455 5e. Sail-backed mailcheek . . 2·50 15
456 6e. Dusky batfish (vert) . . . 2·50 15
457 8e. Moorish idol (vert) . . . 4·25 35
458 9e. Triangulate boxfish . . . 4·25 30
459 10e. Eastern flying gurnard 10·50 1·50
460 15e. Red-toothed triggerfish 70·00 10·50
461 20e. Picasso triggerfish . . . 35·00 4·50
462 30e. Long-horned cowfish . . 42·00 6·50
463 50e. Spotted cowfish . . . . 65·00 14·00

1951. Termination of Holy Year. As T **69** of Macao.
464 5e. red and orange . . . . . 1·90 90

37 Victor Cordon (colonist)

39 Liner and Lockheed Constellation Airliner

1951. Birth Centenary of Cordon.
465 37 1e. brown and light brown 1·25 30
466 5e. black and blue . . . . 6·00 85

1952. 1st Tropical Medicine Congress, Lisbon. As T **71** of Macao.
467 3e. orange and blue . . . . 1·25 35

DESIGN: 3e. Miguela Bombarda Hospital.

1952. 4th African Tourist Congress.
468 39 1e.50 multicoloured . . . . 1·25 35

40 Missionary

41 Citrus Butterfly

1953. Missionary Art Exhibition.
469 40 10c. red and lilac 10 10
470 1e. red and green 70 20
471 5e. black and blue . . . . 1·40 40

1953. Butterflies and Moths. Multicoloured.
472 10c. Type **41** 10 10
473 15c. "Amphicallia thelwalli" 10 10
474 20c. Forest queen 10 10
475 30c. Western scarlet 10 10
476 40c. Black-barred red-tip . . 10 10
477 50c. Mocker swallowtail . . . 10 10
478 80c. "Nudaurelia hersilia dido" 15 15
479 1e. African moon moth . . . 15 10
480 1e.50 Large striped swallowtail 15 10
481 2e. "Athletes ethica" . . . . 4·50 30
482 2e.30 African monarch . . . 3·00 25
483 2e.50 Green swallowtail . . . 7·50 25
484 3e. "Arniocera ericata" . . . 95 10
485 4e. Apollo moth 50 10
486 4e.50 Peach moth 50 10
487 5e. "Metarctica lateritia" . . 50 10
488 6e. "Xanthospilopteryx mozambica" 55 15
489 7e.50 White bear . . . . . . 3·00 30
490 10e. Flame-coloured charaxes 7·50 1·00
491 20e. Fervid tiger moth . . . 11·00 1·00

42 Stamps

43 Map of Mozambique

1953. Philatelic Exhibition, Lourenco Marques.
492 **42** 1e. multicoloured . . . . . 1·25 30
493 3e. multicoloured . . . . . 3·25 1·10

1953. Portuguese Postage Stamp Centenary. As T **75** of Macao.
494 50c. multicoloured 50 35

1954. 4th Centenary of Sao Paulo. As T **76** of Macao.
495 3e.50 multicoloured 30 20

1954. Multicoloured map; Mozambique territory in colours given.
496 **43** 10c. lilac 10 10
497 20c. yellow 10 10
498 50c. blue 10 10
499 1e. yellow 10 10
500 2e.30 white 65 35
501 4e. orange 65 25
502 10e. green . . . . 1·90 25
503 20e. brown . . . . 2·75 35

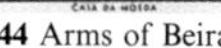
44 Arms of Beira

45 Mousinho de Albuquerque

1954. 1st Philatelic Exhibition, Manica and Sofala.
504 **44** 1e.50 multicoloured 35 20
505 3e.50 multicoloured 90 35

1955. Birth Centenary of M. de Albuquerque.
506 **45** 2e. brown and grey 50 30
507 – 2e.50 multicoloured . . . . 1·10 55
DESIGN: 2e.50, Equestrian statue of Albuquerque.

46 Arms and Inhabitants

47 Beira

1956. Visit of President to Mozambique. Multicoloured. Background in colours given.
508 **46** 1e. cream 25 15
509 2e.50 blue 65 30

1957. 50th Anniv of Beira.
510 **47** 2e.50 multicoloured 65 25

1958. 6th International Congress of Tropical Medicine. As T **79** of Macao.
511 1e.50 multicoloured . . . . . 1·25 70
DESIGN: 1e.50, "Strophanthus grandiflorus" (plant).

1958. Brussels International Exn. As T **78** of Macao.
512 3e.50 multicoloured 25 15

48 Caravel

49 "Arts and Crafts"

1960. 500th Death Anniv of Prince Henry the Navigator.
513 **48** 5e. multicoloured 45 20

1960. 10th Anniv of African Technical Co-operation Commission.
514 **49** 3e. multicoloured 45 20

50 Arms of Lourenco Marques

51 Fokker F.27 Friendship and De Havilland D.H.89 Dragon Rapide over Route Map

1961. Arms. Multicoloured.
515 5c. Type **50** 15 10
516 15c. Chibuto 15 10
517 20c. Nampula 15 10
518 30c. Inhambane 15 10
519 50c. Mozambique (city) . . . 15 10
520 1e. Matola 30 15
521 1e.50 Quelimane 30 15
522 2e. Mocuba 50 15
523 2e.50 Antonio Enes . . . . . 1·10 15
524 3e. Cabral 50 15
525 4e. Manica 50 20
526 4e.50 Pery 50 15
527 5e. St. Tiago de Tete 60 20
528 7e.50 Porto Amelia 80 35
529 10e. Chinde . . . . 1·40 35
530 20e. Joao Belo . . . . 2·75 50
531 50e. Beira . . . . 4·50 1·25

1962. Sports. As T **82** of Macao. Multicoloured.
532 50c. Water-skiing 10 10
533 1e. Wrestling 75 20
534 1e.50 Gymnastics 35 15
535 2e.50 Hockey 60 15
536 4e.50 Netball 90 40
537 15e. Outboard speedboat racing . . . . 1·60 90

1962. Malaria Eradication. Mosquito design as T **83** of Macao. Multicoloured.
538 2e.50 "Anopheles funestus" 50 30

1962. 25th Anniv of D.E.T.A. (Mozambique Airline).
539 **51** 3e. multicoloured 45 20

52 Lourenco Marques in 1887 and 1962

53 Oil Refinery, Sonarep

1962. 75th Anniv of Lourenco Marques.
540 **52** 1e. multicoloured 40 20

1962. Air. Multicoloured.
541 1e.50 Type **53** 50 10
542 2e. Salazar Academy 30 10
543 3e.50 Aerial view of Lourenco Marques Port . . 40 15
544 4e.50 Salazar Barrage 35 15
545 5e. Trigo de Morais Bridge and Dam 40 15
546 20e. Marcelo Caetano Bridge and Dam . . . . 1·10 50
Each design includes an airplane in flight.

54 Arms of Mozambique and Statue of Vasco da Gama

55 Nef, 1430

1963. Bicentenary of City of Mozambique.
547 **54** 3e. multicoloured 35 20

1963. 10th Anniv of T.A.P. Airline. As T **52** of Portuguese Guinea.
548 2e.50 multicoloured 35 15

1963. Evolution of Sailing Ships. Multicoloured.
549 10c. Type **55** 10 10
550 20c. Caravel, 1436 (vert) . . 10 10
551 30c. Lateen-rigged caravel, 1460 (vert) 15 10
552 50c. Vasco da Gama's ship "Sao Gabriel", 1497 (vert) 30 10
553 1e. Don Manuel's nau, 1498 (vert) 55 10
554 1e.50 Galleon, 1530 (vert) . . 40 15
555 2e. Nau "Flor de la Mer", 1511 (vert) 40 15
556 2e.50 Caravel "Redonda", 1519 . . . . 45 15
557 3e.50 Nau, 1520 (vert) . . . 45 15
558 4e. Portuguese Indies galley, 1521 . . . . 50 20
559 4e.50 Galleon "Santa Tereza", 1639 (vert) . . . 50 20
560 5e. Nau "N. Senhora da Conceicao", 1716 (vert) . . 10·00 30
561 6e. Warship "N. Senhora do Bom Sucesso", 1764 . . . 80 25
562 7e.50 Bomb launch, 1788 . . 90 35
563 8e. Naval brigantine "Lebre", 1793 . . . . 90 35
564 10e. Corvette "Andorinha", 1799 . . . . 95 35
565 12e.50 Naval schooner "Maria Teresa", 1820 . . . 1·25 60
566 15e. Warship "Vasco da Gama", 1841 . . . . . . 1·60 60
567 20e. Sail frigate "Don Fernando II e Gloria", 1843 (vert) . . . . . . 2·00 75
568 30e. Cadet barque "Sagres I", 1924 (vert) . . . . 3·50 1·25

1964. Centenary of National Overseas Bank. As T **84** of Macao but view of Bank building, Lourenco Marques.
569 1e.50 multicoloured 20 15

56 Pres. Tomas

57 State Barge of Joao V, 1728

1964. Presidential Visit.
570 **56** 2e.50 multicoloured 15 10

1964. Portuguese Marine, 18th and 19th Centuries. Multicoloured.
571 15c. Type **57** 10 10
572 35c. State barge of Jose I, 1753 . . . . 10 10
573 1e. Barge of Alfandega, 1768 35 10
574 1e.50 Oarsman of 1780 (vert) 30 15
575 2e.50 State barge "Pinto da Fonseca", 1780 . . . . . 20 10
576 5e. State barge of Carlota Joaquina, 1790 . . . . . 25 20
577 9e. Don Miguel's state barge, 1831 . . . . 60 40

1965. I.T.U. Centenary. As T **85** of Macao.
578 1e. multicoloured 30 20

1966. 40th Anniv of Portuguese National Revolution. As T **86** of Macao, but showing different building. Multicoloured.
579 1e. Beira railway station and Antonio Enes Academy . . 85 50

58 Arquebusier, 1560

59 Luis de Camoens (poet)

1967. Portuguese Military Uniforms. Mult.
580 20c. Type **58** 10 10
581 30c. Arquebusier, 1640 . . . 10 10
582 40c. Infantryman, 1777 . . . 15 10
583 50c. Infantry officer, 1777 . . 15 10
584 80c. Drummer, 1777 . . . . 35 20
585 1e. Infantry sergeant, 1777 30 10
586 2e. Infantry major, 1784 . . 30 15
587 2e.50 Colonial officer, 1788 40 15
588 3e. Infantryman, 1789 . . . 40 20
589 5e. Colonial bugler, 1801 . . 50 30
590 10e. Colonial officer, 1807 . . 70 30
591 15e. Infantryman, 1817 . . . 85 55

1967. Centenary of Military Naval Association. As T **88** of Macao. Multicoloured.
592 3e. A. Coutinho and paddle-gunboat "Tete" 35 15
593 10e. J. Roby and paddle-gunboat "Granada" . . . 65 35

1967. 50th Anniv of Fatima Apparitions. As T **89** of Macao.
594 50c. "Golden Crown" . . . 15 10

1968. 500th Birth Anniv of Pedro Cabral (explorer). As T **90** of Macao.
595 1e. Erecting the Cross at Porto Sequro (horiz) . . . 10 10
596 1e.50 First mission service in Brazil (horiz) 20 10
597 3e. Church of Grace, Santarem 40 15

1969. Birth Centenary of Admiral Gago Coutinho. As T **91** of Macao.
598 70c. Admiral Gago Coutinho Airport, Lourenco Marques (horiz) 25 10

1969. 400th Anniv of Camoens' Visit to Mozambique. Multicoloured.
599 15c. Type **59** 10 10
600 50c. Nau of 1553 (horiz) . . 15 10
601 1e.50 Map of Mozambique, 1554 . . . . 20 15
602 2e.50 Chapel of Our Lady of Baluarte (horiz) 25 20
603 5e. Part of the "Lusiad" (poem) 40 30

1969. 500th Birth Anniv of Vasco da Gama (explorer). As T **92** of Macao. Multicoloured.
604 1e. Route map of Da Gama's Voyage to India (horiz) . . 15 10

1969. Centenary of Overseas Administrative Reforms. As T **93** of Macao.
605 1e.50 multicoloured 15 10

1969. 500th Birth Anniv of King Manoel I. As T **95** of Macao. Multicoloured.
606 80c. Illuminated arms (horiz) 15 10

1970. Birth Centenary of Marshal Carmona. As T **96** of Macao. Multicoloured.
607 5e. Portrait in ceremonial dress 25 15

60 Fossilized Fern

1971. Rocks, Minerals and Fossils. Mult.
608 15c. Type **60** 15 10
609 50c. "Lytodiscoides conduciensis " (fossilized snail) 20 10
610 1e. Stibnite 20 10
611 1e.50 Pink beryl 20 10
612 2e. Endothiodon and fossil skeleton 25 10
613 3e. Tantalocolumbite 30 10
614 3e.50 Verdelite 40 15
615 4e. Zircon 50 30
616 10e. Petrified tree-stump . . . 1·25 65

1972. 400th Anniv of Camoens' "The Lusiads" (epic poem). As T **98** of Macao. Multicoloured.
617 4e. Mozambique Island in 16th century . . . . 1·25 30

1972. Olympic Games, Munich. As T **99** of Macao. Multicoloured.
618 3e. Hurdling and swimming 15 10

1972. 50th Anniv of 1st Flight, Lisbon–Rio de Janeiro. As T **100** of Macao. Multicoloured.
619 1e. Fairey IIID seaplane "Santa Cruz" at Recife . . 15 10

61 Racing Dinghies

1973. World Championships for "Vauriens" Class Yachts, Lourenco Marques.
620 **61** 1e. multicoloured 15 10
621 – 1e.50 multicoloured 15 10
622 – 3e. multicoloured 30 20
DESIGNS: Nos. 621/2 similar to Type **61**.

1973. Centenary of I.M.O./W.M.O. As T **102** of Macao.
623 2e. multicoloured 20 20

62 Dish Aerials

1974. Inauguration of Satellite Communications Station Network.
624 **62** 50c. multicoloured 20 20

63 Bird with "Flag" Wings

1975. Implementation of Lusaka Agreement.
625 **63** 1e. multicoloured 10 10
626 1e.50 multicoloured 10 10
627 2e. multicoloured 15 10
628 3e.50 multicoloured 25 15
629 6e. multicoloured 65 30

1975. Independence. Optd **INDEPENDENCIA 25 JUN 75**.
631 **43** 10c. multicoloured (postage) 50 50
632 – 40c. mult (No. 476) 10 10
633 **62** 50c. multicoloured 20 15
634 **61** 1e. multicoloured 30 25
635 – 1e.50 mult (No. 621) . . . 85 75
636 – 2e. multicoloured (No. 623) 2·40 2·40
637 – 2e.50 mult (No. 535) . . . 35 30
638 – 3e. multicoloured (No. 618) 40 35
639 – 3e. multicoloured (No. 622) 45 40
640 – 3e.50 mult (No. 614) . . . 2·40 2·40
641 – 4e.50 mult (No. 536) . . . 2·75 1·50
642 – 7e.50 mult (No. 489) . . . 80 30
643 – 10e. mult (No. 616) . . . . 1·40 35
644 – 15e. mult (No. 537) . . . . 1·75 1·50
645 **43** 20e. multicoloured . . . . 4·75 4·25
646 – 3e.50 multicoloured (No. 543) (air) 35 25
647 – 4e.50 mult (No. 544) . . . 40 25
648 – 5e. multicoloured (No. 545) 1·25 50
649 – 20e. mult (No. 546) . . . . 2·00 4·25

66 Workers, Farmers and Children

67 Farm Worker

1975. "Vigilance, Unity, Work". Multicoloured.
650 20c. Type **66** 10 10
651 30c. Type **66** 10 10
652 50c. Type **66** 10 10
653 2e.50 Type **66** 15 10
654 4e.50 Armed family, workers and dancers 25 15
655 5e. As No. 654 . . . . 35 15
656 10e. As No. 654 . . . . . . 95 30
657 50e. As No. 654 . . . . . . 4·25 2·10

1976. Women's Day.
659 **67** 1e. black and green 10 10
660 – 1e.50 black and brown . . 10 10
661 – 2e.50 black and blue . . . 15 10
662 – 10e. black and red 90 40
DESIGNS: 1e.50, Teaching; 2e.50, Nurse; 10e. Mother.

1976. Pres. Kaunda's First Visit to Mozambique. Optd **PRESIDENTE KENNETH KAUNDA PREMEIRA VISITA 20/4/1976**.
663 **63** 2e. multicoloured 15 10
664 3e.50 multicoloured 25 15
665 6e. multicoloured 50 30

69 Arrival of President Machel

70 Mozambique Stamp of 1876 and Emblem

1976. 1st Anniv of Independence. Mult.
666 50c. Type **69** 10 10
667 1e. Proclamation ceremony 10 10
668 2e.50 Signing ceremony . . . 15 10
669 7e.50 Soldiers on parade . . 40 20
670 20e. Independence flame . . 1·50 1·10

1976. Stamp Centenary.
671 **70** 1e.50 multicoloured 10 10
672 6e. multicoloured 30 20

1976. "FACIM" Industrial Fair. Optd **FACIM 1976**.
673 **66** 2e.50 multicoloured 30 15

72 Weapons and Flag

73 Thick-tailed Bush baby

1976. Army Day.
674 **72** 3e. multicoloured 20 10

1977. Animals. Multicoloured.
675 50c. Type **73** 15 10
676 1e. Ratel (horiz) 15 10
677 1e.50 Temminck's ground pangolin 20 10
678 2e. Steenbok (horiz) 20 10
679 2e.50 Diademed monkey . . 25 10
680 3e. Hunting dog (horiz) . . 25 10
681 4e. Cheetah (horiz) 35 10
682 5e. Spotted hyena 50 15
683 7e.50 Warthog (horiz) . . . 1·00 25
684 8e. Hippopotamus (horiz) . . 1·10 30
685 10e. White rhinoceros (horiz) 1·10 30
686 15e. Sable antelope . . . . . 1·60 65

74 Congress Emblem

75 "Women" (child's drawing)

1977. 3rd Frelimo Congress, Maputo. Mult.
687 3e. Type **74** 15 10
688 3e.50 Macheje Monument (site of 2nd Congress) (34 × 24 mm) 20 10
689 20e. Maputo Monument (23 × 34 mm) . . . . . . 1·40 50

1977. Mozambique Women's Day.
690 **75** 5e. multicoloured 25 10
691 15e. multicoloured 65 25

76 Labourer and Farmer

77 Crowd with Arms and Crops

1977. Labour Day.
692 **76** 5e. multicoloured 25 10

1977. 2nd Anniv of Independence.
693 **77** 50c. multicoloured 10 10
694 1e.50 multicoloured 10 10
695 3e. multicoloured 15 10
696 15e. multicoloured 60 25

78 "Encephalartos ferox"

79 "Chariesthes bella"

1978. Stamp Day. Nature Protection. Mult.
697 1e. Type **78** 10 10
698 10e. Nyala 50 20

1978. Beetles. Multicoloured.
699 50c. Type **79** 10 10
700 1e. "Tragocephalus variegata" 10 10
701 1e.50 "Monochamus leuconotus" 10 10
702 3e. "Prosopocera lactator" 25 10
703 5e. "Dinocephalus ornatus" 40 10
704 10e. "Tragiscoschema nigroscriptus" 60 20

80 Violet-crested Turaco

81 Mother and Child

1978. Birds. Multicoloured.
705 50c. Type **80** 35 15
706 1e. Lilac-breasted roller . . . 45 15
707 1e.50 Red-headed weaver . . 45 15
708 2e.50 Violet starling 50 25
709 3e. Peters's twin-spot . . . . 1·00 35
710 15e. European bee eater . . . 2·50 70

1978. Global Eradication of Smallpox.
711 **81** 15e. multicoloured 45 25

82 "Crinum delagoense"

83 First Stamps of Mozambique and Canada

1978. Flowers. Multicoloured.
712 50c. Type **82** 10 10
713 1e. "Gloriosa superba" . . . 10 10
714 1e.50 "Eulophia speciosa" . . 10 10
715 3e. "Erithrina humeana" . . 15 10
716 5e. "Astripomoea malvacea" 80 15
717 10e. "Kigelia africana" . . . 1·00 60

1978. "CAPEX '78" International Stamp Exhibition, Toronto.
718 **83** 15e. multicoloured 45 25

84 Mozambique Flag

85 Boy with Books

1978. 3rd Anniv of Independence. Multicoloured.
719 1e. Type **84** 10 10
720 1e.50 Coat of Arms 10 10
721 7e.50 People and Constitution 25 15
722 10e. Band and National Anthem 30 20

1978. 11th World Youth Festival, Havana. Mult.
724 2e.50 Type **85** 10 10
725 3e. Soldiers 15 10
726 7e.50 Harvesting wheat . . . 25 20

86 Czechoslovakian 50h. Stamp, 1919

1978. "PRAGA '78" International Stamp Exhibition.
727 **86** 15e. blue, ochre and red . . 45 30

87 Football

1978. Stamp Day. Sports. Multicoloured.
729 50c. Type **87** 10 10
730 1e.50 Putting the shot 10 10
731 3e. Hurdling 15 10
732 7e.50 Basketball 35 20
733 12e.50 Swimming 45 35
734 25e. Roller-skate hockey . . 1·25 60

88 U.P.U. Emblem and Dove

1979. Membership of U.P.U.
735 **88** 20e. multicoloured . . . . 1·00 45

89 Eduardo Mondlane

1979. 10th Death Anniv of Eduardo Mondlane (founder of FRELIMO). Multicoloured.
736 1e. Soldier handing gourd to woman 10 10
737 3e. FRELIMO soldiers . . . 15 10
738 7e.50 Children learning to write 30 20
739 12e.50 Type **89** 40 30

90 Shaded Silver

91 I.Y.C. Emblem

1979. Domestic Cats. Multicoloured.
740 50c. Type **90** 10 10
741 1e.50 Manx cat 10 10
742 2e.50 British blue 15 10
743 3e. Turkish cat 20 10
744 12e.50 Long-haired tabby . . 85 55
745 20e. African wild cat . . . . 1·50 90

1979. Obligatory Tax. International Year of the Child.
746 **91** 50c. red 15 10

92 Wrestling

1979. Olympic Games, Moscow (1980). Mult.
747 1e. Type **92** 10 10
748 2e. Running 10 10
749 3e. Horse jumping 15 10
750 5e. Canoeing 15 10
751 10e. High jump 30 20
752 15e. Archery 50 40

93 Flowers

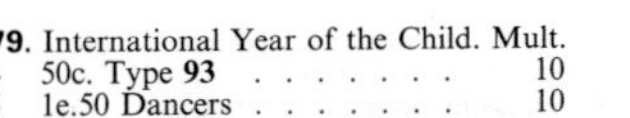

1979. International Year of the Child. Mult.
754 50c. Type **93** 10 10
755 1e.50 Dancers 10 10

756	3e. In the city	15	10
757	5e. Working in the country	15	10
758	7e.50 Houses	25	15
759	12e.50 Transport	1·50	50

94 Flight from Colonialism

1979. 4th Anniv of Independence. Multicoloured.

760	50c. Type **94**	10	10
761	2e. Eduardo Mondlane (founder of FRELIMO)	10	10
762	3e. Armed struggle, death of Mondlane	15	10
763	7e.50 Final fight for liberation	25	15
764	15e. President Samora Machel proclaims victory	45	35

95 Golden Scorpionfish

1979. Tropical Fish. Multicoloured.

766	50c. Type **95**	10	10
767	1e.50 Golden trevally	15	10
768	2e.50 Brick goby	20	10
769	3e. Clown surgeonfish	25	15
770	10e. Lace goby	60	25
771	12e.50 Yellow-edged lyretail	95	40

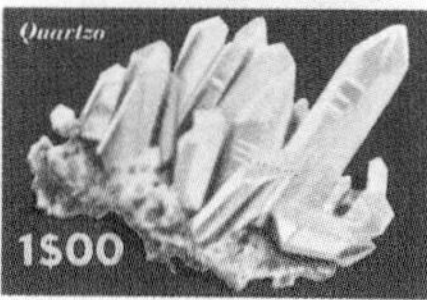

96 Quartz

1979. Minerals. Multicoloured.

772	1e. Type **96**	10	10
773	1e.50 Beryl	10	10
774	2e.50 Magnetite	15	10
775	5e. Tourmaline	30	10
776	10e. Euxenite	60	20
777	20e. Fluorite	1·40	45

97 Soldier handing out Guns

1979. 15th Anniv of Fight for Independence.

778	**97**	5e. multicoloured	25	15

98 Locomotive No. 1, 1914

1979. Early Locomotives. Multicoloured.

779	50c. Type **98**	15	10
780	1e.50 Gaza Railway locomotive No. 1, 1898	20	10
781	3e. Cape Government Railway 1st Class locomotive, 1878	45	10
782	7e.50 Delagoa Bay Railway locomotive No. 9, 1892	75	20
783	12e.50 Locomotive No. 41, 1896	1·25	30
784	15e. Trans Zambesia Railway Class D steam locomotive	1·40	35

99 Dalmatian

1979. Dogs. Multicoloured.

785	50c. Basenji (vert)	10	10
786	1e.50 Type **99**	15	10
787	3e. Boxer	15	10
788	7e.50 Blue gascon pointer	35	15
789	12e.50 English cocker spaniel	85	25
790	15e. Pointer	1·25	30

100 "Papilio nireus"

1979. Stamp Day. Butterflies. Multicoloured.

791	1e. Type **100**	10	10
792	1e.50 "Amauris ochlea"	10	10
793	2e.50 "Pinacopterix eriphia"	15	10
794	5e. "Junonia hierta"	35	10
795	10e. "Nephronia argia"	1·00	20
796	20e. "Catacroptera cloanthe"	2·10	90

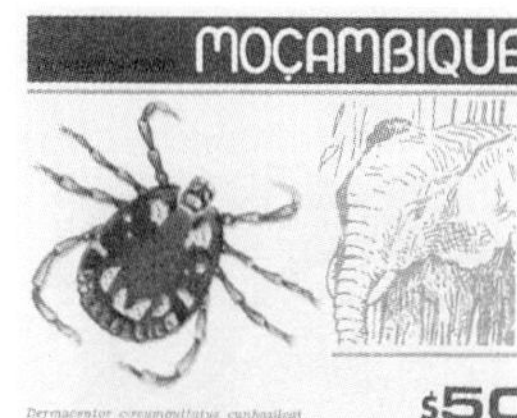

101 "Dermacentor circumguttatus cunhasilvai" and African Elephant

1980. Ticks. Multicoloured.

797	50c. Type **101**	20	10
798	1e.50 "Dermacentor rhinocerinos" and black rhinoceros	30	10
799	2e.50 "Amblyomma hebraeum" and giraffe	40	15
800	3e. "Amblyomma pomposum" and eland	50	15
801	5e. "Amblyomma theilerae" and cow	60	15
802	7e.50 "Amblyomma eburneum" and African buffalo	85	30

102 Ford "Hercules" Bus, 1950

1980. Road Transport. Multicoloured.

803	50c. Type **102**	10	10
804	1e.50 Scania "Marco-Polo" bus, 1978	10	10
805	3e. Bussing Nag Bus, 1936	15	10
806	5e. Ikarus articulated bus, 1978	20	10
807	7e.50 Ford Taxi, 1929	40	15
808	12e.50 Fiat "131" Taxi, 1978	80	20

103 Soldier and Map of Southern Africa

1980. Zimbabwe Independence.

809	**103**	10e. blue and brown	40	15

104 Marx, Engels and Lenin

1980. International Workers' Day.

810	**104**	10e. multicoloured	40	15

105 "Market" (Moises Simbine)

1980. "London 1980" International Stamp Exhibition. Multicoloured.

811	50c. "Heads" (Malangatana)	10	10
812	1e.50 Type **105**	10	10
813	3e. "Heads with Helmets" (Malangatana)	15	10
814	5e. "Women with Goods" (Machiana)	20	10
815	7e.50 "Crowd with Masks" (Malangatana)	25	15
816	12e.50 "Man and Woman with Spear" (Mankeu)	50	25

106 Telephone

1980. World Telecommunications Day.

817	**106**	15e. multicoloured	60	25

107 Mueda Massacre **108** Crowd waving Tools

1980. 20th Anniv of Mueda Massacre.

818	**107**	15e. green, brown and red	60	25

1980. 5th Anniv of Independence.

819	–	1e. black and red	10	10
820	**108**	2e. multicoloured	10	10
821	–	3e. multicoloured	15	10
822	–	4e. multicoloured	20	10
823	–	5e. black, yellow and red	20	10
824	–	10e. multicoloured	40	15

DESIGNS—As T **108**: 1e. Crowd, doctor tending patient, soldier and workers tilling land; 3e. Crowd with flags and tools; 4e. Stylized figures raising right hand; 5e. Hand grasping flags, book and plants; 10e. Figures carrying banners each with year date. 55 × 37 mm: 30e. Soldiers.

109 Gymnastics

1980. Olympic Games, Moscow. Multicoloured.

826	50c. Type **109**	10	10
827	1e.50 Football	10	10
828	2e.50 Running	10	10
829	3e. Volleyball	20	10
830	10e. Cycling	40	15
831	12e.50 Boxing	45	20

110 Narina's Trogon

1980. Birds. Multicoloured.

832	1m. Type **110**	35	10
833	1m.50 South African crowned crane	40	10
834	2m.50 Red-necked spurfowl	45	10
835	5m. Ostrich	85	20
836	7m.50 Spur-winged goose	1·00	25
837	12m.50 African fish eagle	1·40	35

111 Family and Census Officer

1980. First General Census.

838	**111**	3m.50 multicoloured	25	10

112 Animals fleeing from Fire

1980. Campaign against Bush Fires.

839	**112**	3m.50 multicoloured	25	10

113 Common Harp

1980. Stamp Day. Shells. Multicoloured.

840	1m. Type **113**	10	10
841	1m.50 Arthritic spider conch	15	10
842	2m.50 Venus comb murex	20	10
843	5m. Clear sundial	40	15
844	7m.50 Ramose murex	50	20
845	12m.50 Diana conch	1·10	35

114 Pres. Machel, Electricity Pylons, Aircraft and Lorry

1981. "Decade for Victory over Underdevelopment".

846	**114**	3m.50 blue and red	2·00	75
847	–	7m.50 brown and green	25	15
848	–	12m.50 mauve and blue	50	30

DESIGNS: 7m.50, Pres. Machel and armed forces on parade; 12m.50, Pres. Machel and classroom scenes.

115 Footballer and *Athletic de Bilbao* Stadium

1981. World Cup Football Championship, Spain (1982). Multicoloured.

849	1m. Type **115**	10	10
850	1m.50 Valencia, C.F.	10	10
851	2m.50 Oviedo C.F.	10	10
852	5m. R. Betis Balompie	20	10
853	7m.50 Real Zaragoza	25	15
854	12m.50 R.C.D. Espanol	50	25

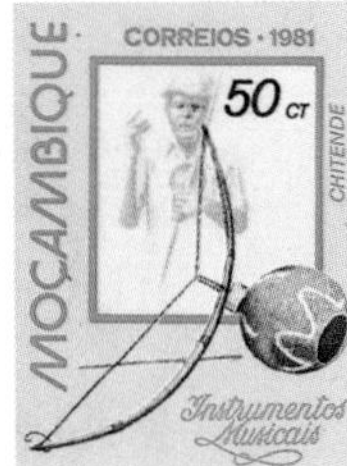

116 Giraffe **117** Chitende

1981. Protected Animals. Multicoloured.
856 50c. Type **116** 10 10
857 1m.50 Topi 10 10
858 2m.50 Aardvark 10 10
859 3m. African python 10 10
860 5m. Loggerhead turtle . . . 20 15
861 10m. Marabou stork . . . . 1·10 45
862 12m.50 Saddle-bill stork . . . 1·40 55
863 15m. Kori bustard . . . . . 1·90 65

1981. Musical Instruments. Multicoloured.
864 50c. Type **117** 10 10
865 2m. Pankwe (horiz) 10 10
866 2m.50 Kanyembe 10 10
867 7m. Nyanga (horiz) 30 20
868 10m. Likuti and M'Petheni (horiz) 70 25

118 Disabled Persons making Baskets

1981. International Year of Disabled People.
869 **118** 5m. multicoloured 25 15

119 De Havilland Dragon Rapide

1981. Air. Mozambique Aviation History. Mult.
870 50c. Type **119** 10 10
871 1m.50 Junkers Ju 52/3m . . . 10 10
872 3m. Lockheed Super Electra 20 15
873 7m.50 De Havilland Dove . . 35 30
874 10m. Douglas DC-3 . . . . 50 35
875 12m.50 Fokker Friendship 75 50

120 Controlled Killing, Marromeu

1981. World Hunting Exhibition, Plovdiv. Mult.
876 2m. Type **120** 30 15
877 5m. Traditional hunting Cheringoma 20 15
878 6m. Tourist hunting, Save . . 40 30
879 7m.60 Marksmanship, Gorongosa 40 20
880 12m.50 African elephants, Gorongosa . . . . 1·50 60
881 20m. Trap, Cabo Delgado . . 80 50

121 50 Centavos Coin **122** Sunflower

1981. 1st Anniv of New Currency. Mult.
883 50c. Type **121** 10 10
884 1m. One metical coin 10 10
885 2m.50 Two meticals 50 coin 10 10
886 5m. Five meticals coin . . . 20 15
887 10m. Ten meticals coin . . . 50 25
888 20m. Twenty meticals coin 1·40 55

1981. Agricultural Resources.
890 **122** 50c. orange and red . . . 10 10
891 – 1m. black and red 10 10
892 – 1m.50 blue and red . . . 10 10
893 – 2m.50 yellow and red . . 10 10
894 – 3m.50 green and red . . . 15 10
895 – 4m.50 grey and red . . . 15 10
896 – 10m. blue and red 40 15
897 – 12m.50 brown and red . . 50 20
898 – 15m. brown and red . . . 60 25
899 – 25m. green and red . . . 1·40 40
900 – 40m. orange and red . . . 2·00 60
901 – 60m. brown and red . . . 2·75 1·00

DESIGNS: 1m. Cotton; 1m.50, Sisal; 2m.50, Cashew; 3m.50, Tea; 4m.50, Sugar cane; 10m. Castor oil; 12m.50, Coconut; 15m. Tobacco; 25m. Rice; 40m. Maize; 60m. Groundnut.

123 Archaeological Excavation, Manyikeni

1981. Archaeological Excavation. Mult.
902 1m. Type **123** 10 10
903 1m.50 Hand-axe (Massingir Dam) 10 10
904 2m.50 Ninth century bowl (Chibuene) 10 10
905 7m.50 Ninth century pot (Chibuene) 30 20
906 12m.50 Gold beads (Manyikeni) 50 30
907 20m. Gong (Manyikeni) . . . 80 50

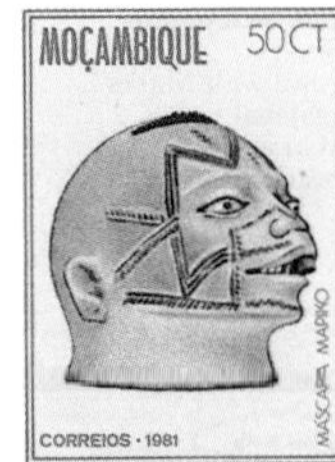

124 Mapiko Mask

1981. Sculptures. Multicoloured.
908 50c. Type **124** 10 10
909 1m. Woman who suffers . . 10 10
910 2m.50 Woman with a child 10 10
911 3m.50 The man who makes fire 15 10
912 5m. Chietane 20 15
913 12m.50 Chietane (different) 70 30

125 Broken Loaf on Globe

1981. World Food Day.
914 **125** 10m. multicoloured . . . 45 25

126 Tanker "Matchedje"

1981. Mozambique Ships. Multicoloured.
915 50c. Type **126** 15 15
916 1m.50 Tug "Macuti" 15 15
917 3m. Trawler "Vega 7" . . . 25 15
918 5m. Freighter "Linde" . . . 35 25
919 7m.50 Freighter "Pemba" . . 55 30
920 12m.50 Dredger "Rovuma" 95 55

127 "Portunus pelagicus"

1981. Crustaceans. Multicoloured.
921 50c. Type **127** 10 10
922 1m.50 "Scylla serrata" . . . 10 10
923 3m. "Penacus indicus" . . . 15 10
924 7m.50 "Palinurus delagoae" 35 20
925 12m.50 "Lysiosquilla maculata" 55 35
926 15m. "Panulirus ornatus" . . 80 45

128 "Hypoxis multiceps" **129** Telex Tape, Telephone and Globe

1981. Flowers. Multicoloured.
927 1m. Type **128** 10 10
928 1m.50 "Pelargonium luridun" 10 10
929 2m.50 "Caralluma melanathera" 10 10
930 7m.50 "Ansellia gigantea" . . 35 20
931 12m.50 "Stapelia leendertsiae" 60 35
932 25m. "Adenium multiflorum" 1·50 70

1982. 1st Anniv of Mozambique Post and Telecommunications. Multicoloured.
933 6m. Type **129** 35 20
934 15m. Winged envelope and envelope forming railway wagon . . . . 3·00 1·50

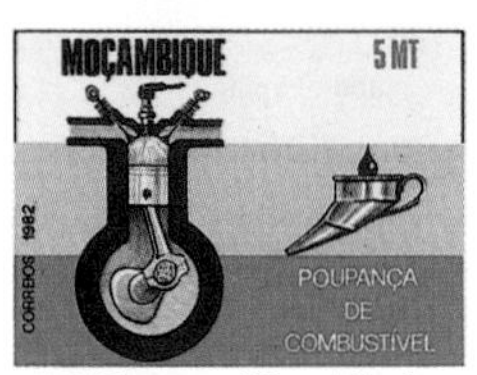

130 Diagram of Petrol Engine

1982. Fuel Saving. Multicoloured.
935 5m. Type **130** 30 15
936 7m.50 Speeding car 45 25
937 10m. Loaded truck 60 35

131 Sea-snake

1982. Reptiles. Multicoloured.
938 50c. Type **131** 20 10
939 1m.50 "Naja mossambica mossambica" 10 10
940 3m. "Thelotornis capensis mossambica" 20 15
941 6m. "Dendroaspis polylepis polylepis" 35 25
942 15m. "Dispholidus typus" . . 80 50
943 20m. "Bitis arietans arietans" 1·50 75

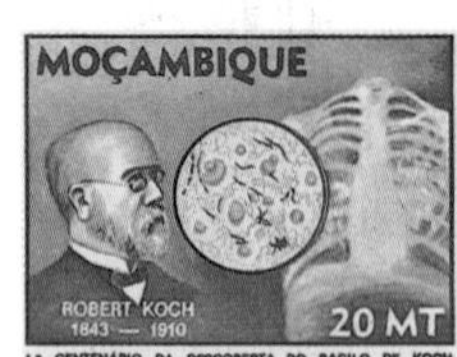

132 Dr. Robert Koch, Bacillus and X-Ray

1982. Centenary of Discovery of Tubercle Bacillus.
944 **132** 20m. multicoloured . . . 1·75 1·00

133 Telephone Line **134** Player with Ball

1982. International Telecommunications Union. Plenipotentiary Conference.
945 **133** 20m. multicoloured . . . 1·00 75

1982. World Cup Football Championship, Spain. Multicoloured.
946 1m.50 Type **134** 10 10
947 3m.50 Player heading ball . . 25 15
948 7m. Two players fighting for ball 40 20
949 10m. Player receiving ball . . 60 30
950 20m. Goalkeeper . . . . . . 1·25 1·00

135 Political Rally **137** "Vangueria infausta"

1982. 25th Anniv of FRELIMO. Multicoloured.
953 4m. Type **135** 25 15
954 8m. Agriculture 45 25
955 12m. Marching workers . . . 70 35

1982. Fruits. Multicoloured.
956 1m. Type **137** 10 10
957 2m. "Mimusops caffra" . . . 10 10
958 4m. "Sclerocarya caffra" . . 25 15
959 8m. "Strychnos spinosa" . . 45 25
960 12m. "Salacia kraussi" . . . 70 40
961 32m. "Trichilia emetica" . . 1·90 85

138 "Sputnik I"

1982. 25th Anniv of First Artificial Satellite. Multicoloured.
962 1m. Type **138** 10 10
963 2m. First manned space flight 10 10
964 4m. First walk in space . . 25 15
965 8m. First manned flight to the Moon 45 25
966 16m. "Soyuz"–"Apollo" mission . . . . 1·25 70
967 20m. "Intercosmos" rocket 1·50 70

139 Vigilantes

1982. People's Surveillance Day.
968 **139** 4m. multicoloured 25 15

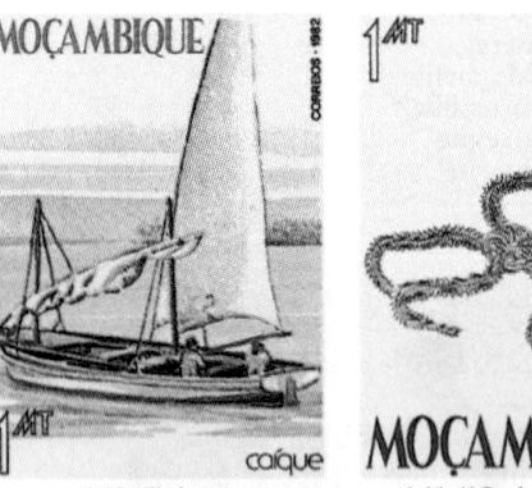

140 Caique **141** "Ophiomostix venosa"

1982. Traditional Boats. Multicoloured.
969 1m. Type **140** 10 10
970 2m. Machua 15 10
971 4m. Calaua (horiz) 30 15
972 8m. Chitatarro (horiz) . . . 60 25
973 12m. Cangaia (horiz) 80 35
974 16m. Chata (horiz) . . . . . 1·75 60

1982. Starfishes and Sea Urchins. Multicoloured.
975 1m. Type **141** 10 10
976 2m. "Protoreaster lincki" . . 10 10
977 4m. "Tropiometra carinata" 15 10
978 8m. "Holothuria scabra" . . 35 20
979 12m. "Prionocidaris baculosa" 60 35
980 16m. "Colobocentrotus atnatus" 80 40

142 Soldiers defending Mozambique

1983. 4th Frelimo Party Congress. Multicoloured.
981 4m. Type **142** 15 10
982 8m. Crowd waving voting papers 30 20
983 16m. Agriculture, industry and education 65 40

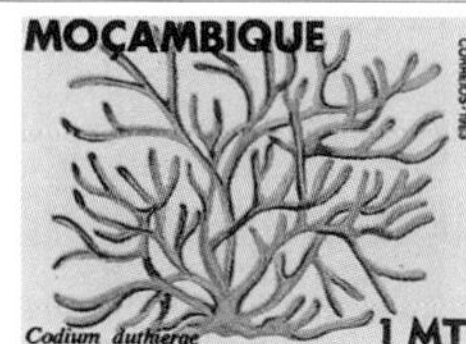
143 "Codium duthierae"

1983. Seaweeds. Multicoloured.
984 1m. Type **143** 10 10
985 2m. "Halimeda cunata" . . . 10 10
986 4m. "Dictyota liturata" . . . 15 10
987 8m. "Endorachne binghamiae" 40 20
988 12m. "Laurencia flexuosa" 60 30
989 20m. "Acrosorium sp." . . . 1·25 55

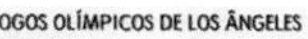
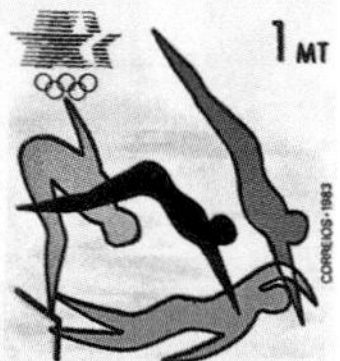
144 Diving and Swimming

1983. Olympic Games, Los Angeles (1st issue). Multicoloured.
990 1m. Type **144** 10 10
991 2m. Boxing 10 10
992 4m. Basketball 20 10
993 8m. Handball 35 20
994 12m. Volleyball 55 30
995 16m. Running 65 40
996 20m. Yachting . . . . 1·25 65
See also Nos. 1029/34.

145 Mallet Type Locomotive

1983. Steam Locomotives. Multicoloured.
998 1m. Type **145** 10 10
999 2m. Baldwin, 1915–45 . . . 20 10
1000 4m. Class 141-148, 1950 . . 40 15
1001 8m. Baldwin, 1926 . . . . 75 25
1002 16m. Henschel Garratt type, 1956 . . . . 1·40 50
1003 32m. Natal Government Class H, 1899–1903 . . . 3·00 1·00

146 O.A.U. Emblem

1983. 20th Anniv of Organization of African Unity.
1004 **146** 4m. multicoloured . . . 20 15

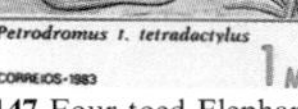
147 Four-toed Elephant-shrew
150 "Communications"

148 Aiding Flood Victims

1983. Mozambique Mammals. Multicoloured.
1005 1m. Type **147** 10 10
1006 2m. Four-striped grass mouse 15 10
1007 4m. Vincent's bush squirrel 25 15
1008 8m. Hottentot mole-rat . . 50 25
1009 12m. Natal red hare 75 40
1010 16m. Straw-coloured fruit bat . . . . 1·25 75

1983. 2nd Anniv of Mozambique Red Cross. Multicoloured.
1011 4m. Type **148** 20 10
1012 8m. Red Cross lorry 40 20
1013 16m. First aid demonstration 75 40
1014 32m. Agricultural worker performing first aid . . . 1·90 75

1983. World Communications Year.
1016 **150** 8m. multicoloured . . . 1·50 75

151 Line Fishing

1983. Fishery Resources. Multicoloured.
1017 50c. Type **151** 10 10
1018 2m. Chifonho (basket trap) 10 10
1019 4m. Spear fishing 25 15
1020 8m. Gamboa (fence trap) . . 40 25
1021 16m. Mono (basket trap) . . 1·50 40
1022 20m. Lema (basket trap) . . 1·60 55

152 Kudu Horn
153 Swimming

1983. Stamp Day. Multicoloured.
1023 50c. Type **152** 10 10
1024 1m. Drum communication 10 10
1025 4m. Postal runners 20 15
1026 8m. Mail canoe 40 40
1027 16m. Mail van 75 40
1028 20m. Steam mail train . . . 3·25 1·50

1984. Olympic Games, Los Angeles (2nd issue). Multicoloured.
1029 50c. Type **153** 10 10
1030 4m. Football 20 10
1031 8m. Hurdling 35 20
1032 16m. Basketball 90 50
1033 32m. Handball . . . . . . 1·90 80
1034 60m. Boxing . . . . 3·00 1·75

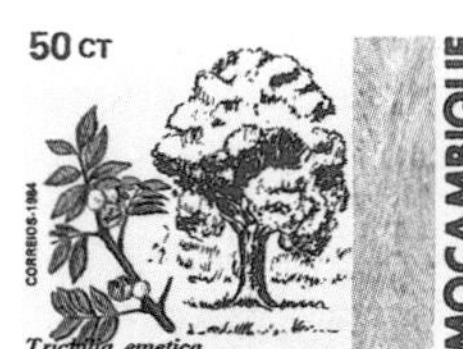
154 "Trichilia emetica"

1984. Indigenous Trees. Multicoloured.
1035 50c. Type **154** 10 10
1036 2m. "Brachystegia spiciformis" 10 10
1037 4m. "Androstachys johnsonii" 20 10
1038 8m. "Pterocarpus angolensis" 35 20
1039 16m. "Milletia stuhlmannii" 80 40
1040 50m. "Dalbergia melanoxylon" . . . . . 2·75 1·75

155 Dove with Olive Sprig

1984. Nkomati South Africa–Mozambique Non-aggression Pact.
1041 **155** 4m. multicoloured . . . 25 10

156 State Arms

1984. Emblems of the Republic. Multicoloured.
1042 4m. Type **156** 20 10
1043 8m. State Flag 40 20

157 Makway Dance

1984. "Lubrapex '84" Portuguese–Brazilian Stamp Exhibition, Lisbon. Traditional Mozambican dances. Multicoloured.
1044 4m. Type **157** 20 10
1045 8m. Mapiko dance 40 20
1046 16m. Wadjaba dance . . . 1·40 50

158 Nampula Museum and Statuette of Woman with Water Jug

1984. Museums. Multicoloured.
1047 50c. Type **158** 10 10
1048 4m. Natural History Museum and secretary bird 35 10
1049 8m. Revolution Museum and soldier carrying wounded comrade 35 20
1050 16m. Colonial History Museum and cannon . . 65 40
1051 20m. National Numismatic Museum and coins . . . 1·25 65
1052 30m. St. Paul's Palace and antique chair . . . . . . 1·50 95

159 Imber's Tetra

1984. Fishes. Multicoloured.
1053 50c. Type **159** 10 10
1054 4m. Purple labeo 25 10
1055 12m. Brown squeaker . . . 75 35
1056 16m. Blue-finned notho . . 95 55
1057 40m. Slender serrate barb 2·50 1·40
1058 60m. Barred minnow . . . 3·75 1·90

160 Badge and Laurels
162 Knife and Club

161 Rural Landscape and Emblem

1984. International Fair, Maputo.
1059 **160** 16m. multicoloured . . . 70 50

1984. 20th Anniv of African Development Bank.
1060 **161** 4m. multicoloured . . . 30 10

1984. Traditional Weapons. Multicoloured.
1061 50c. Type **162** 10 10
1062 4m. Axes 20 10
1063 8m. Spear and shield . . . 35 15
1064 16m. Bow and arrow . . . 75 35
1065 32m. Rifle . . . . 1·90 95
1066 50m. Assegai and arrow . . 2·75 1·90

163 Workers and Emblem

1984. 1st Anniv of Organization of Mozambican Workers.
1067 **163** 4m. multicoloured . . . 20 10

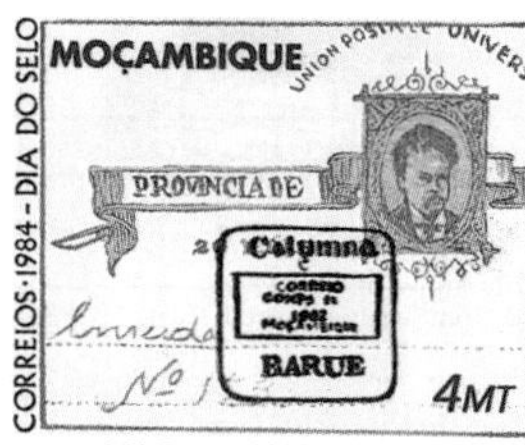
164 Barue 1902 Postmark

1984. Stamp Day. Postmarks. Multicoloured.
1068 4m. Type **164** 15 10
1069 8m. Zumbo postmark and King Carlos 15r. Mozambique "key type" stamp 35 20
1070 12m. Mozambique Company postmark and 1935 airmail stamp . . . 55 30
1071 16m. Macequece postmark and 1937 2e. Mozambique Company stamp 70 40

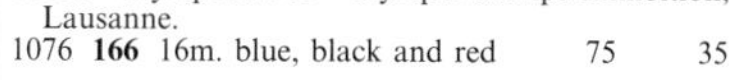
165 Keeper and Hive
166 Shot-putter and Emblem

1985. Bee-keeping. Multicoloured.
1072 4m. Type **165** 15 10
1073 8m. Worker bee 45 20
1074 16m. Drone . . . . 1·25 40
1075 20m. Queen bee . . . . . . 1·75 60

1985. "Olymphilex 85" Olympic Stamps Exhibition, Lausanne.
1076 **166** 16m. blue, black and red 75 35

167 Forecasting Equipment and Desert

1985. World Meteorology Day.
1077 **167** 4m. multicoloured . . . 35 10

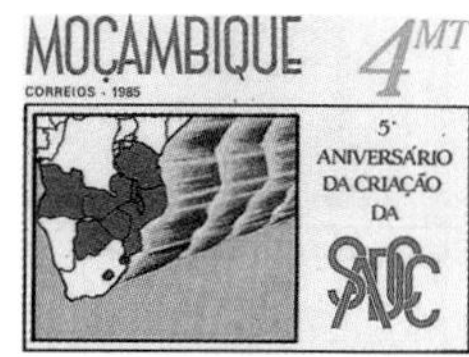
168 Map

1985. 5th Anniv of Southern African Development Co-ordination Conference. Multicoloured.
1078 4m. Type **168** 15 10
1079 8m. Map and pylon 45 20
1080 16m. Industry and transport 2·50 1·25
1081 32m. Member states' flags 1·90 95

169 Battle of Mujenga, 1896

1985. 10th Anniv of Independence. Mult.
1082 1m. Type **169** 10 10
1083 4m. Attack on Barue by Macombe, 1917 . . . . . 25 10
1084 8m. Attack on Massangano, 1868 . . . . 55 20
1085 16m. Battle of Marracuene, 1895, and Gungunhana 1·50 50

170 U.N. Building, New York and Flag

1985. 40th Anniv of U.N.O.
1086 **170** 16m. multicoloured . . . 80 50

171 Mathacuzana

1985. Traditional Games and Sports. Multicoloured.
1087 50c. Type **171** 10 10
1088 4m. Mudzobo 20 10
1089 8m. Muravarava (board game) 40 20
1090 16m. N'tshuwa 90 50

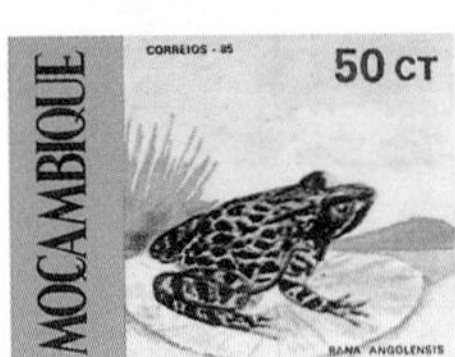

172 "Rana angolensis"

1985. Frogs and Toads. Multicoloured.
1091 50c. Type **172** 10 10
1092 1m. "Hyperolius pictus" . . 10 10
1093 4m. "Ptychadena porosissima" 15 10
1094 8m. "Afrixalus formasinii" 50 20
1095 16m. "Bufo regularis" . . . 95 50
1096 32m. "Hyperolius marmoratus" . . . . . . 2·40 95

174 "Aloe ferox" **176** Comet and "Giotto" Space Probe

175 Mozambique Company 1918 10c. Stamp

1985. Medicinal Plants. Multicoloured.
1099 50c. Type **174** 10 10
1100 1m. "Boophone disticha" 10 10
1101 3m.50 "Gloriosa superba" 15 10
1102 4m. "Cotyledon orbiculata" 15 10
1103 8m. "Homeria breyniana" 55 20
1104 50m. "Haemanthus coccineus" . . . . 3·75 1·90

1985. Stamp Day. Multicoloured.
1105 1m. Type **175** . . . . 1·25 75
1106 4m. Nyassa Co. 1911 25r. stamp 15 10
1107 8m. Mozambique Co. 1918 ½c. stamp 50 20
1108 16m. Nyassa Co. 1924 1c. Postage Due stamp . . . 1·25 50

1986. Appearance of Halley's Comet.
1109 **176** 4m. blue and light blue 20 10
1110 – 8m. violet and light violet 50 20
1111 – 16m. multicoloured . . . 95 50
1112 – 30m. multicoloured . . . 2·00 95
DESIGNS: 8m. Comet orbits; 16m. Small and large telescopes, comet and space probe; 30m. Comet, stars and globe.

177 Vicente

1986. World Cup Football Championship, Mexico. Multicoloured.
1113 3m. Type **177** 15 10
1114 4m. Coluna 20 10
1115 8m. Costa Pereira 40 20
1116 12m. Hilario 65 35
1117 16m. Matateu 95 50
1118 50m. Eusebio . . . . 3·25 1·90

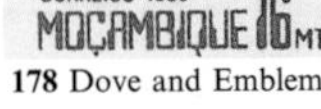

178 Dove and Emblem **179** "Amanita muscaria"

1986. International Peace Year.
1119 **178** 16m. multicoloured . . . 85 45

1986. Fungi. Multicoloured.
1120 4m. Type **179** 50 20
1121 8m. "Lactarius deliciosus" 95 30
1122 16m. "Amanita phaloides" 2·00 65
1123 30m. "Tricholoma nudum" 4·25 1·25

181 Spiky Style

1986. Women's Hairstyles. Multicoloured.
1125 1m. Type **181** 10 10
1126 4m. Beaded plaits 25 10
1127 8m. Plaited tightly to head 50 20
1128 16m. Plaited tightly to head with ponytail . . . . . . 1·25 55

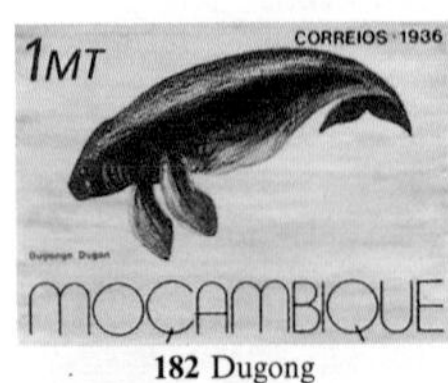

182 Dugong

1986. Marine Mammals. Multicoloured.
1129 1m. Type **182** 10 10
1130 8m. Common dolphin . . . 35 20
1131 16m. "Neobalena marginata" . . . . 1·25 85
1132 50f. Fin whale . . . . . . 4·25 2·75

183 Children Studying

1986. 1st Anniv of Continuadores Youth Organization.
1133 **183** 4m. multicoloured . . . 30 15

184 50m. Notes

1986. Savings. Multicoloured.
1134 4m. Type **184** 25 10
1135 8m. 100m. notes 50 20
1136 16m. 500m. notes . . . . . 1·40 50
1137 30m. 1000m. notes . . . . 2·75 1·25

185 Quelimane Post Office

1986. Stamp Day. Post Offices. Multicoloured.
1138 3m. Type **185** 20 10
1139 4m. Maputo 30 10
1140 8m. Beira 65 20
1141 16m. Nampula . . . . . . 1·40 50

186 Pyrite

1987. Minerals. Multicoloured.
1142 4m. Type **186** 30 10
1143 8m. Emerald 60 20
1144 12m. Agate 85 40
1145 16m. Malachite . . . . . . 1·40 50
1146 30m. Garnet . . . . 2·50 1·25
1147 50m. Amethyst . . . . . . 4·25 2·00

187 Crowd beneath Flag

1987. 10th Anniv of Mozambique Liberation Front.
1148 **187** 4m. multicoloured . . . 30 15

188 Little Libombos Dam

1987.
1149 **188** 16m. multicoloured . . . 1·40 60

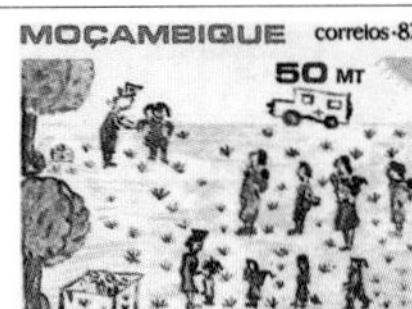

189 Children being Vaccinated

1987. World Health Day. Vaccination Campaign.
1150 **189** 50m. multicoloured . . . 1·90 1·50

190 Common Grenadier **191** Football

1987. Birds. Multicoloured.
1151 3m. Type **190** 25 15
1152 4m. Woodland kingfisher . . 30 20
1153 8m. White-fronted bee eater 65 40
1154 12m. Lesser seedcracker . . 1·10 60
1155 16m. African broad-billed roller . . . . 1·25 90
1156 30m. Neergaard's sunbird 2·50 1·60

1987. Olympic Games, Seoul (1988) (1st issue). Multicoloured.
1157 12m.50 Type **191** 10 10
1158 25m. Running 20 10
1159 50m. Handball 40 20
1160 75m. Chess . . . . 1·25 30
1161 100m. Basketball . . . . . 1·25 35
1162 200m. Swimming . . . . . 2·00 65
See also Nos. 1176/81.

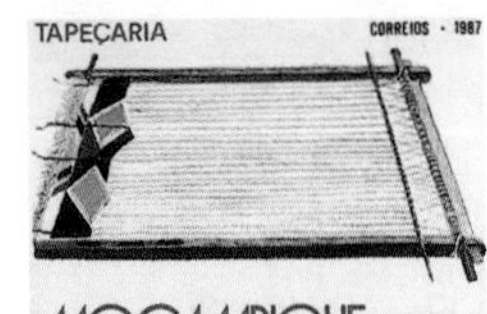

193 Work on Loom

1987. Weaving. Multicoloured.
1164 20m. Type **193** 15 10
1165 40m. Triangle and diamond design 40 10
1166 80m. "Eye" design 70 20
1167 200m. Red carpet . . . . . 2·00 60

194 Piper "Navajo"

1987. Air. History of Aviation in Mozambique. Multicoloured.
1168 20m. Type **194** 15 10
1169 40m. De Havilland Hornet moth 25 10
1170 80m. Boeing 737 . . . . . 50 20
1171 120m. Beechcraft King Air 75 20
1172 160m. Piper Aztec . . . . . 1·00 35
1173 320m. Douglas DC-10 . . . 2·00 75

195 Early Plan

1987. Centenary of Maputo as City.
1174 **195** 20m. multicoloured . . . 20 15

1987. No. 895 surch **4,00 MT.**
1175 4m. on 4m.50 grey and red 15 10

197 Javelin throwing

198 "Boophane disticha"

1988. Olympic Games, Seoul (2nd issue). Mult.

1176 10m. Type **197** 10 10
1177 20m. Baseball 10 10
1178 40m. Boxing 10 10
1179 80m. Hockey 40 10
1180 100m. Gymnastics 50 15
1181 400m. Cycling . . . . . . 1·50 75

1988. Flowers. Multicoloured.

1182 10m. "Heamanthus nelsonii" 10 10
1183 20m. "Crinum polyphyllum" 15 10
1184 40m. Type **198** 15 10
1185 80m. "Cyrtanthus contractus" 35 10
1186 100m. "Nerine angustifolia" 50 15
1187 400m. "Cyrtanthus galpinnii" . . . . 2·00 75

199 Man refusing Cigarette

1988. 40th Anniv of W.H.O. Anti-smoking Campaign.

1188 **199** 20m. multicoloured . . . 20 10

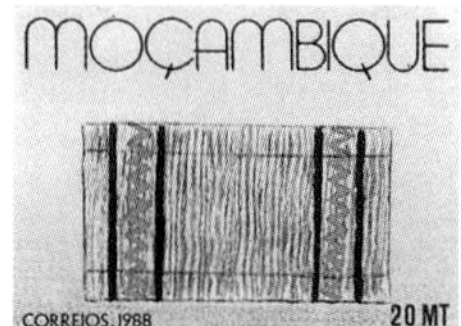

201 Mat

1988. Basketry. Multicoloured.

1190 20m. Type **201** 10 10
1191 25m. Basket with lid 10 10
1192 80m. Basket with handle . . 20 10
1193 100m. Fan 30 10
1194 400m. Dish . . . . 1·50 1·00
1195 500m. Conical basket . . . 1·90 1·40

203 Percheron

1988. Horses. Multicoloured.

1197 20m. Type **203** 15 10
1198 40m. Arab 20 10
1199 80m. Pure blood 40 10
1200 100m. Pony 50 15

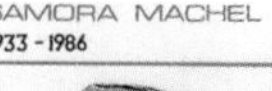

204 Machel

1988. 2nd Death Anniv of Samora Machel (President 1975–86).

1201 **204** 20m. multicoloured . . . 15 10

205 Inhambane

1988. Ports. Multicoloured.

1202 20m. Type **205** 15 10
1203 50m. Quelimane (vert) . . . 40 10
1204 75m. Pemba 50 10
1205 100m. Beira 55 20
1206 250m. Nacali (vert) . . . . 1·10 50
1207 500m. Maputo . . . . . . 2·75 1·25

206 Mobile Post Office

1988. Stamp Day. Multicoloured.

1208 20m. Type **206** 10 10
1209 40m. Posting box (vert) . . 15 10

207 Maize

208 Mondlane

1989. 5th FRELIMO Congress. Multicoloured.

1210 25m. Type **207** 10 10
1211 50m. Hoe 10 10
1212 75m. Abstract 10 10
1213 100m. Cogwheels 20 10
1214 250m. Right-half of cogwheel 50 25

Nos. 1210/14 were printed together, se-tenant, forming a composite design.

1989. 20th Anniv of Assassination of Pres. Mondlane.

1215 **208** 25m. black, gold and red 15 10

209 "Storming the Bastille" (Thevenin)

1989. Bicentenary of French Revolution. Mult.

1216 100m. Type **209** 25 10
1217 250m. "Liberty guiding the People" (Delacroix) . . . 60 35

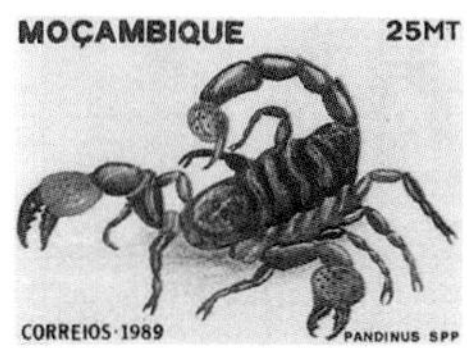

210 "Pandinus sp."

1989. Venomous Animals. Multicoloured.

1219 25m. Type **210** 10 10
1220 50m. Egyptian cobra 10 10
1221 75m. "Bombus sp." (bee) . . 15 10
1222 100m. "Paraphysa sp." (spider) 25 10
1223 250m. Marble cone 90 40
1224 500m. Lionfish . . . . . . 1·90 70

211 "Acropora pulchra"

1989. Corals. Multicoloured.

1225 25m. Type **211** 10 10
1226 50m. "Eunicella papilosa" 15 10
1227 100m. "Dendrophyla migrantus" 30 10
1228 250m. "Favia fragum" . . . 50 35

212 Footballers

213 Macuti Lighthouse

1989. World Cup Football Championship, Italy (1990). Designs showing various footballing scenes.

1229 **212** 30m. multicoloured . . . 10 10
1230 – 60m. multicoloured . . . 15 10
1231 – 125m. multicoloured . . 30 10
1232 – 200m. multicoloured . . 50 25
1233 – 250m. multicoloured . . 65 35
1234 – 500m. multicoloured . . 1·50 70

1989. Lighthouses. Multicoloured.

1235 30m. Type **213** 15 10
1236 60m. Pinda 15 10
1237 125m. Cape Delgado . . . 30 10
1238 200m. Goa Island 60 25
1239 250m. Caldeira Point . . . 80 35
1240 500m. Vilhena . . . . . . 1·50 70

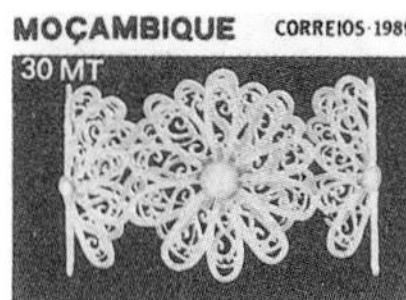

214 Bracelet

1989. Silver Filigree Work.

1241 **214** 30m. grey, red and black 10 10
1242 – 60m. grey, blue and black 15 10
1243 – 125m. grey, red and black 25 10
1244 – 200m. grey, blue & black 40 25
1245 – 250m. grey, purple & blk 55 35
1246 – 500m. grey, green & blk 1·25 70

DESIGNS: 60m. Flower belt; 125m. Necklace; 200m. Casket; 250m. Spoons; 500m. Butterfly.

215 Flag and Soldiers

216 Rain Gauge

1989. 25th Anniv of Fight for Independence.

1247 **215** 30m. multicoloured . . . 15 10

1989. Meteorological Instruments. Multicoloured.

1248 30m. Type **216** 10 10
1249 60m. Radar graph 15 10
1250 125m. Sheltered measuring instruments 30 10
1251 200m. Computer terminal 55 25

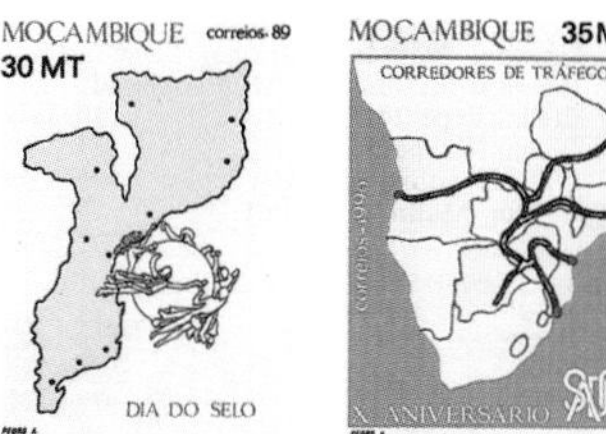

218 Map and U.P.U. Emblem

219 Railway Map

1989. Stamp Day.

1253 **218** 30m. multicoloured . . . 15 10
1254 – 60m. black, green and red 15 10

DESIGN: 60m. Map and Mozambique postal emblem.

1990. 10th Anniv of Southern Africa Development Co-ordination Conference.

1255 **219** 35m. multicoloured . . . 1·00 50

220 Cloth and Woman wearing Dress

1990. Traditional Dresses. Designs showing women wearing different dresses and details of cloth used.

1256 **220** 42m. multicoloured . . . 10 10
1257 – 90m. multicoloured . . . 15 10
1258 – 150m. multicoloured . . 20 10
1259 – 200m. multicoloured . . 25 15
1260 – 400m. multicoloured . . 55 40
1261 – 500m. multicoloured . . 65 50

221 Sena Fortress, Sofala

1990. Fortresses.

1262 **221** 45m. blue and black . . 10 10
1263 – 90m. blue and black . . 15 10
1264 – 150m. multicoloured . . 20 10
1265 – 200m. multicoloured . . 30 15
1266 – 400m. red and black . . 55 40
1267 – 500m. red and black . . 70 40

DESIGNS: 90m. Sto. Antonio, Ibo Island; 150m. S. Sebastiao, Mozambique Island; 200m. S. Caetano, Sofala; 400m. Our Lady of Conception, Maputo; 500m. S. Luis, Tete.

223 Obverse and Reverse of 50m. Coin

1990. 15th Anniv of Bank of Mozambique.

1269 **223** 100m. multicoloured . . 20 10

224 Statue of Eduardo Mondlane (founder of FRELIMO)

1990. 15th Anniv of Independence. Mult.

1270 42m.50 Type **224** 10 10
1271 150m. Statue of Samora Machel (President, 1975–86) 25 15

225 White Rhinoceros

1990. Endangered Animals. Multicoloured.

1272 42m.50 Type **225** 15 10
1273 100m. Dugong 20 10
1274 150m. African elephant . . 35 15
1275 200m. Cheetah 40 15
1276 400m. Spotted-necked otter 70 40
1277 500m. Hawksbill turtle . . . 85 50

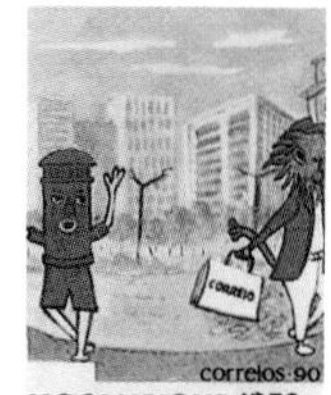

226 "Dichrostachys cinerea"

227 Pillar Box waving to Kurika

1990. Environmental Protection. Plants. Mult.

1278 42m.50 Type **226** 10 10
1279 100m. Forest fire 20 10
1280 150m. Horsetail tree 25 10
1281 200m. Mangrove 30 15
1282 400m. "Estrato herbaceo" (grass) 65 40
1283 500m. Pod mahogany . . . 80 50

1990. Kurika (post mascot) at Work. Mult.

1284 42m.50 Type **227** 15 10
1285 42m.50 Hand cancelling envelopes 15 10
1286 42m.50 Leaping across hurdles 15 10
1287 42m.50 Delivering post to chicken 15 10

228 "10" and Posts Emblem

229 Bird-of-Paradise Flower

1991. 10th Anniv of National Posts and Telecommunications Enterprises, Mozambique.
1288 **228** 50m. blue, red and black 15 10
1289 – 50m. brown, green & black 15 10
DESIGN: No. 1289, "10" and telecommunications emblem.

1991. Flowers. Multicoloured.
1290 50m. Type **229** 15 10
1291 125m. Flamingo lily 25 15
1292 250m. Calla lily 50 30
1293 300m. Canna lily 55 35

230 Two Hartebeest

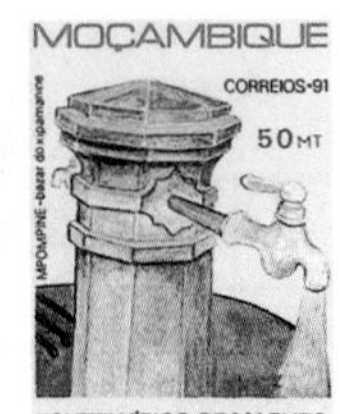

231 Mpompine

1991. Lichtenstein's Hartebeest. Multicoloured.
1294 50m. Type **230** 15 10
1295 100m. Alert hartebeest 20 10
1296 250m. Hartebeest grazing 1·50 70
1297 500m. Mother feeding young 2·10 1·40

1991. Maputo Drinking Fountains. Mult.
1298 50m. Type **231** 10 10
1299 125m. Chinhambanine 15 10
1300 250m. S. Pedro-Zaza 25 10
1301 300m. Xipamanine 35 15

232 Painting by Samate

233 Diving

1991. Paintings by Mozambican Artists. Mult.
1302 180m. Type **232** 15 10
1303 250m. Malangatana Ngwenya 20 15
1304 560m. Malangatana Ngwenya (different) 40 30

1991. Olympic Games, Barcelona (1992). Mult.
1305 10m. Type **233** 10 10
1306 50m. Roller hockey 15 10
1307 100m. Tennis 20 10
1308 200m. Table tennis 30 10
1309 500m. Running 50 20
1310 1000m. Badminton 1·10 40

234 Proposed Boundaries in 1890 Treaty

236 Skipping

1991. Centenary of Settling of Mozambique Borders. Multicoloured.
1311 600m. Type **234** 50 25
1312 800m. Frontiers settled in English–Portuguese 1891 treaty 75 35

1991. Stamp Day. Children's Games. Mult.
1314 40m. Type **236** 10 10
1315 150m. Spinning top 10 10
1316 400m. Marbles 20 10
1317 900m. Hopscotch 45 20

237 "Christ"

238 "Rhisophora mucronata"

1992. Stained Glass Windows. Multicoloured.
1318 40m. Type **237** 10 10
1319 150m. "Faith" 10 10
1320 400m. "IC XC" 20 10
1321 900m. Window in three sections 45 20

1992. Marine Flowers. Multicoloured.
1322 300m. Type **238** 15 10
1323 600m. "Cymodocea ciliata" 30 15
1324 1000m. "Sophora inhambanensis" 85 25

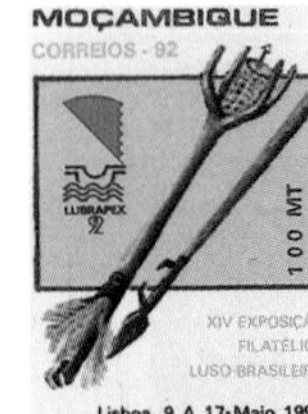

239 Spears

240 Amethyst Sunbird

1992. "Lubrapex 92" Brazilian–Portuguese Stamp Exhibition, Lisbon. Weapons. Multicoloured.
1325 100m. Type **239** 10 10
1326 300m. Tridents 15 10
1327 500m. Axe 25 10
1328 1000m. Dagger 85 25

1992. Birds. Multicoloured.
1329 150m. Type **240** 30 30
1330 200m. Mosque swallow 30 30
1331 300m. Red-capped robin chat 45 30
1332 400m. Lesser blue-eared glossy starling 60 30
1333 500m. Grey-headed bush shrike 1·50 30
1334 800m. African golden oriole 2·25 70

241 Emblem

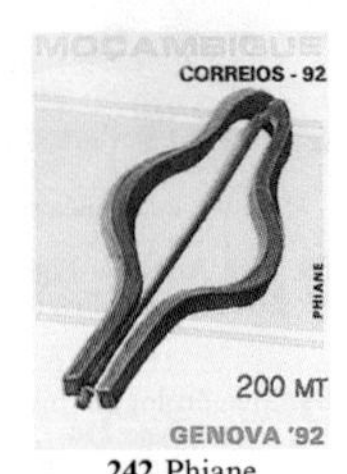

242 Phiane

1992. 30th Anniv of Eduardo Mondlane University.
1335 **241** 150m. green and brown 10 10

1992. "Genova '92" International Thematic Stamp Exn. Musical Instruments. Multicoloured.
1336 200m. Type **242** 10 10
1337 300m. Xirupe (rattle) 15 10
1338 500m. Ngulula (drum) 25 10
1339 1500m. Malimba (drum) 75 35

243 Children Eating

244 Parachutist

1992. International Nutrition Conference, Rome.
1341 **243** 450m. multicoloured 20 10

1992. Parachuting. Multicoloured.
1342 50m. Type **244** 10 10
1343 400m. Parachutist and buildings 20 10
1344 500m. Airplane dropping parachutists 25 10
1345 1500m. Parachutist (different) 1·10 1·10

1992. No. 890 surch **50MT**.
1346 **122** 50m. on 50c. orge & red 10 10

246 Order of Peace and Friendship

1993. Mozambique Decorations. Multicoloured.
1347 400m. Type **246** 20 10
1348 800m. Bagamoyo Medal 40 20
1349 1000m. Order of Eduardo Mondlane 50 25
1350 1500m. Veteran of the Struggle for National Liberation Medal 70 35

247 Tree Stumps and Girl carrying Wood

1993. Pollution. Multicoloured.
1351 200m. Type **247** 10 10
1352 750m. Chimneys smoking 35 15
1353 1000m. Tanker sinking 50 25
1354 1500m. Car exhaust fumes 70 35

248 Lion (Gorongosa Park, Sofala)

1993. National Parks. Multicoloured.
1355 200m. Type **248** 10 10
1356 800m. Giraffes (Banhine Park, Gaza) 40 20
1357 1000m. Dugongs (Bazoruto Park, Inhambane) 50 25
1358 1500m. Ostriches (Zinave Park, Inhambane) 1·75 75

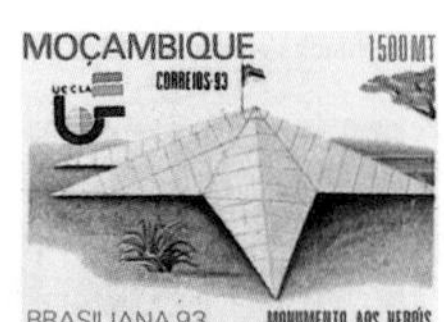

249 Heroes Monument, Maputo

1993. "Brasiliana 93" International Stamp Exhibition, Rio de Janeiro.
1359 **249** 1500m. multicoloured 55 25

250 Conference Emblem

251 "Cycas cercinalis"

1993. National Culture Conference, Maputo.
1360 **250** 200m. multicoloured 10 10

1993. Forest Plants. Multicoloured.
1361 200m. Type **251** 10 10
1362 250m. "Cycas revoluta" 10 10
1363 900m. "Encephalartos ferox" 25 10
1364 2000m. "Equisetum ramosissimum" 50 25

252 "Anacardium occidentale"

254 Mozambique Rough-scaled Sand Lizard

1994. Medicinal Plants. Multicoloured.
1365 200m. Type **252** 10 10
1366 250m. "Sclerocarya caffra" 10 10
1367 900m. "Annona senegalensis" 25 10
1368 2000m. "Crinum delagoense" 50 25

1994. Various stamps surch.
1369 50m. on 7m.50 mult (No. 905) 10 10
1370 50m. on 7m.50 mult (No. 924) 10 10
1371 50m. on 7m.50 mult (No. 930) 10 10
1372 100m. on 10m. blue and red (No. 896) 10 10
1373 100m. on 12m.50 mult (No. 931) 10 10
1374 200m. on 12m.50 brown and red (No. 897) 10 10
1375 250m. on 12m.50 mult (No. 925) 10 10

1994. "Philakorea 1994" International Stamp Exhibition, Seoul. Reptiles. Multicoloured.
1376 300m. Type **254** 10 10
1377 500m. Olive loggerhead turtle 10 10
1378 2000m. Northern coppery snake 40 20
1379 3500m. Marshall's chameleon 75 35

255 Crop-spraying

1994. 50th Anniv of I.C.A.O. Multicoloured.
1381 300m. Type **255** 10 10
1382 500m. Airport 10 10
1383 2000m. Air transport 40 20
1384 3500m. Aircraft maintenance 75 35

256 Bean Plant

257 Queue of Voters

1994. "Lubrapex'94" Portuguese–Brazilian Stamp Exhibition. World Food Day.
1385 **256** 2000m. multicoloured 40 20

1994. 1st Multiparty Elections.
1386 **257** 900m. multicoloured 20 10

258 Document and Handshake

259 Couple using Drugs

1994. 20th Anniv of Lusaka Accord (establishing independence).
1387 **258** 1500m. multicoloured 30 15

1994. Anti-drugs Campaign. Multicoloured.
1388 500m. Type **259** 10 10
1389 1000m. Couple, syringe, cigarette and skeleton 20 10
1390 2000m. Addict 40 20
1391 5000m. Sniffer dog capturing man with drugs 1·00 50

260 Basket

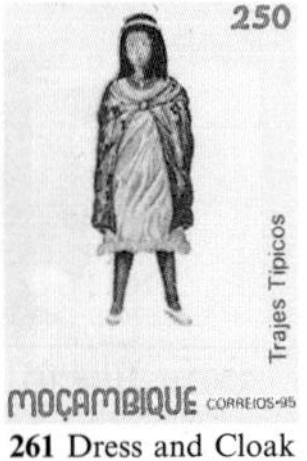

261 Dress and Cloak

1995. Baskets and Bags. Multicoloured.
1392 250m. Type **260** 10 10
1393 300m. Bag with two handles 10 10

1394 1200m. Circular bag with one handle 20 10
1395 5000m. Bag with flap 85 40

1995. Women's Costumes. Multicoloured.
1396 250m. Type **261** 10 10
1397 300m. Blouse and calf-length skirt 10 10
1398 1200m. Blouse and ankle-length skirt 20 10
1399 5000m. Strapless top and skirt 85 40

262 State Arms
263 Bushbaby

1995. Investiture (1994) of President Joaquim Chissano. Multicoloured.
1400 900m. Type **262** 15 10
1401 2500m. National flag 45 20
1402 5000m. Pres. Chissano 85 40
Nos. 1400/2 were issued together, se-tenant, the commemorative inscription at the foot extending across the strip.

1995. Mammals. Multicoloured.
1403 500m. Type **263** 10 10
1404 2000m. Greater kudu (horiz) 25 10
1405 3000m. Bush pig (horiz) 40 20
1406 5000m. Bushbuck 65 30

1995. Various stamps surch.
1407 250m. on 12m.50 multicoloured (No. 931) 10 10
1408 300m. on 10m. blue and red (No. 896) 10 10
1409 500m. on 12m.50 multicoloured (No. 925) 10 10
1410 900m. on 12e.50 multicoloured (No. 771) 10 10
1411 1000m. on 12m.50 multicoloured (No. 837) 15 10
1412 1500m. on 16m. multicoloured (No. 1064) 20 10
1413 2000m. on 16m. multicoloured (No. 995) 25 10
1414 2500m. on 12m. multicoloured (No. 880) 35 15

265 Family carrying Foodstuffs
266 Emblem

1995. 50th Anniv of F.A.O.
1415 **265** 5000m. multicoloured 65 30

1995. 50th Anniv of United Nations Organization.
1416 **266** 5000m. blue and black 65 30

267 Child wearing Blue Cloak

1995. 20th Anniv of U.N.I.C.E.F. in Mozambique.
1417 **267** 5000m. multicoloured 60 65

268 Player scoring Goal

1996. Football. Multicoloured.
1418 1000m. Type **268** 25 15
1419 2000m. Goalkeeper holding ball 40 25
1420 4000m. Referee admonishing players 60 70
1421 6000m. Two players tackling for ball 75 75

269 Mask
270 "Mae Africa" (De Malangatana)

1996. Local Masks.
1422 **269** 1000m. multicoloured 10 15
1423 – 2000m. multicoloured 20 25
1424 – 4000m. multicoloured 40 45
1425 – 6000m. multicoloured 60 65
DESIGNS: 2000 to 6000m. Different masks.

1996. 15th Anniv of Mozambique Red Cross.
1426 **270** 5000m. multicoloured 50 55

271 African Elephant
272 Mine Field

1996. Wild Animals. Multicoloured.
1427 1000m. Type **271** 65 30
1428 2000m. White rhinoceros 85 55
1429 4000m. Leopard 90 90
1430 6000m. Pel's fishing owl 1·75 1·50

1996. Land Mine Clearance Campaign. Mult.
1431 2000m. Type **272** 30 25
1432 6000m. Warning sign 75 65
1433 8000m. Soldier with mine detector 90 90
1434 10000m. Soldier lifting mine 1·25 1·25

273 City Street
274 5r. Stamp of 1876 and Magnifying Glass

1996. "Keeping the City Clean".
1435 **273** 2000m. multicoloured 30 25

1996. 120th Anniv of Mozambique Stamps.
1436 **274** 2000m. multicoloured 30 25

275 Mitumbui

1997. Local Boats. Multicoloured.
1437 2000m. Type **275** 20 25
1438 6000m. Muterere 60 65
1439 8000m. Lancha 80 85
1440 10000m. Dhow 1·00 1·10

276 Village Scene

1997. International Children's Day.
1441 **276** 2000m. multicoloured 30 25

277 "Enaretta conitera"

1997. Beetles. Multicoloured.
1442 2000m. Type **277** 30 25
1443 6000m. "Zographus hieroglyphicus 70 65
1444 8000m. "Tragiscoschema bertolonii" 90 90
1445 10000m. "Tragocephala ducalis" 1·25 1·25
MS1446 97 × 105 mm. Nos. 1442/5 2·50 2·75
No. **MS**1446 also commemorates the "LUBRAPEX 97" International Stamp Exhibition, Brazil.

278 Yellow-billed Stork
280 Sun and Globe

279 Abstract Patterns

1997. Aquatic Birds. Multicoloured.
1447 2000m. Type **278** 50 25
1448 4000m. Black-winged stilt 70 45
1449 8000m. Long-toed stint (horiz) 1·25 1·10
1450 10000m. Eastern white pelican 1·40 1·40

1997. Centenary of Joao Ferreira dos Santos Group.
1451 **279** 2000m. multicoloured 30 25

1997. Protection of Ozone Layer.
1452 **280** 2000m. multicoloured 30 25

282 Coelacanth

1998. "EXPO '98" International Stamp Exhibition, Lisbon.
1454 **282** 2000m. multicoloured 55 25

283 Woman with Food Products

1998. Food Production.
1455 **283** 2000m. multicoloured 30 25

CHARITY TAX STAMPS

The notes under this heading in Portugal also apply here.

C **15** Arms of Portugal and Mozambique and Allegorical Figures

C **16** Prow of Galley of Discoveries and Symbols of Declaration of War

1916. War Tax Fund. Imperf, roul or perf.
C234 C **15** 1c. green 35 25
C235 C **16** 5c. red 35 30

C **18** "Charity"
C **22** Society's Emblem

1920. 280th Anniv of Restoration of Portugal. Wounded Soldiers and Social Assistance Funds.
C309 C **18** ¼c. green 70 70
C310 ½c. black 75 70
C311 1c. brown 75 70
C312 2c. brown 75 75
C313 3c. lilac 75 75
C314 4c. green 75 75
C315 – 5c. green 85 75
C316 – 6c. blue 85 75
C317 – 7½c. brown 85 75
C318 – 8c. yellow 85 75
C319 – 10c. lilac 85 85
C320 – 12c. pink 85 85
C321 – 18c. red 85 85
C322 – 24c. brown 1·10 85
C323 – 30c. green 1·10 85
C324 – 40c. red 1·10 85
C325 – 50c. yellow 1·10 85
C326 – 1e. blue 1·10 85
DESIGNS: 5c. to 12c. Wounded soldier and nurse; 18c. to 1e. Family scene.

1925. Marquis de Pombal stamps of Portugal, but inscr "MOCAMBIQUE".
C327 C **73** 15c. brown 15 15
C328 – 15c. brown 15 15
C329 C **75** 15c. brown 15 15

1925. Red Cross. Surch **50 CENTAVOS**.
C330 C **22** 50c. yellow and grey 55 40

1926. Surch **CORREIOS** and value.
C337 C **22** 5c. yellow and red 75 60
C338 10c. yellow and green 75 60
C339 20c. yellow and grey 75 60
C340 30c. yellow and blue 75 60
C331 40c. yellow and grey 80 75
C341 40c. yellow and violet 75 60
C332 50c. yellow and grey 80 75
C342 50c. yellow and red 75 60
C333 60c. yellow and grey 80 75
C343 60c. yellow and brown 75 60
C334 80c. yellow and grey 80 75
C344 80c. yellow and blue 75 60
C335 1e. yellow and grey 90 75
C345 1e. yellow and green 75 60
C336 2e. yellow and grey 90 75
C346 2e. yellow and brown 75 60

C **25**

1928. Surch **CORREIOS** and value in black, as in Type C **25**.
C347 C **25** 5c. yellow and green 1·10 1·00
C348 10c. yellow and blue 1·10 1·00
C349 20c. yellow and black 1·10 1·00
C350 30c. yellow and red 1·10 1·00
C351 40c. yellow and purple 1·10 1·00
C352 50c. yellow and red 1·10 1·00
C353 60c. yellow and brown 1·10 1·00
C354 80c. yellow and brown 1·10 1·00
C355 1e. yellow and grey 1·10 1·00
C356 2e. yellow and red 1·10 1·00

C **27**
C **29** Pelican

C **28** "Charity"

1929. Value in black.
C357 C **27** 40c. purple and blue 85 85
C358 40c. violet and red 85 85
C359 40c. violet and green 85 85
C360 40c. red and brown 85 85
C361 (No value) red & green 1·10 1·10
C362 40c. blue and orange 1·10 1·10
C363 40c. blue and brown 85 85
C364 40c. purple and green 1·10 1·00
C365 40c. black and yellow 1·10 1·10
C366 40c. black and brown 1·10 1·10

1942.

C383 C 28	50c. pink and black	2·00	90

1943. Inscr "Colonia de Mocambique". Value in black.

C390 C 29	50c. red	1·50	75
C389	50c. blue	1·50	75
C386	50c. violet	1·50	75
C387	50c. brown	1·50	75
C393	50c. green	1·50	75

1952. Inscr "Provincia de Mocambique". Value in black.

C514 C 29	30c. yellow	45	35
C515	50c. orange	45	35
C469	50c. green	75	40
C470	50c. brown	75	40

1957. No. C470 surch **$30.**

C511 C 29	30c. on 50c. brown	45	25

C 56 Women and Children

C 58 Telegraph Poles and Map

1963.

C569 C 56	30c. black, green & red	15	15
C570	50c. black, bistre & red	20	15
C571	50c. black, pink & red	20	15
C572	50c. black, green & red	20	15
C573	50c. black, blue & red	20	15
C574	50c. black, buff & red	20	15
C575	50c. black, grey & red	20	15
C576	50c. black, yell & red	20	15
C577	1e. grey, black and red	50	25
C578	1e. black, buff and red	15	10
C578a	1e. black, mauve & red	15	10

1965. Mozambique Telecommunications Improvement.

C579 C 58	30c. black, pink & vio	10	10
C580	– 50c. black, brown & blue	10	10
C581	– 1e. black, orange & green	20	20

DESIGN—19½ × 36 mm: 50c., 1e. Telegraph linesman.

A 2e.50 in Type C 58 was also issued for compulsory use on telegrams.

NEWSPAPER STAMPS

1893. "Embossed" key-type of Mozambique surch.

(a) **JORNAES 2½ 2½.**

N53 Q	2½r. on 40r. brown	9·50	7·50

(b) **JORNAES 2½ REIS.**

N54 Q	2½r. on 40r. brown	45·00	30·00
N57	5r. on 40r. brown	28·00	24·00

1893. "Newspaper" key-type inscribed "MOCAMBIQUE".

N58 V	2½r. brown	25	20

POSTAGE DUE STAMPS

1904. "Due" key-type inscr "MOCAMBIQUE".

D146 W	5r. green	15	15
D147	10r. grey	15	15
D148	20r. brown	15	15
D149	30r. orange	30	20
D150	50r. brown	30	20
D151	60r. brown	1·25	75
D152	100r. mauve	1·25	75
D153	130r. blue	70	65
D154	200r. red	1·25	65
D155	500r. violet	1·25	65

1911. "Due" key-type of Mozambique optd **REPUBLICA.**

D162 W	5r. green	15	15
D163	10r. grey	15	15
D164	20r. brown	20	15
D165	30r. orange	20	15
D166	50r. brown	20	15
D167	60r. brown	30	20
D168	100r. mauve	30	20
D169	130r. blue	50	40
D170	200r. red	65	60
D171	500r. lilac	65	60

1917. "Due" key-type of Mozambique, but currency changed.

D246 W	½c. green	15	15
D247	1c. grey	15	15
D248	2c. brown	15	15
D249	3c. orange	15	15
D250	5c. brown	15	15
D251	6c. brown	15	15
D252	10c. mauve	15	15
D253	13c. blue	30	25
D254	20c. red	30	25
D255	50c. lilac	30	25

1918. Charity Tax stamps optd **PORTEADO.**

D256 C 15	1c. green	50	40
D257 C 16	5c. red	50	40

1922. "Ceres" key-type of Lourenco Marques (¼, 1½c.) and of Mozambique (1, 2½, 4c.) surch **PORTEADO** and value and bar.

D316 U	5c. on ¼c. black	55	40
D318	6c. on 1c. green	60	40
D317	10c. on 1½c. brown	55	40
D319	20c. on 2½c. violet	60	40
D320	50c. on 4c. pink	60	40

1924. "Ceres" key-type of Mozambique surch **Porteado** and value.

D321 U	20c. on 30c. green	35	30
D323	50c. on 60c. blue	55	40

1925. Marquis de Pombal charity tax designs as Nos. C327/9, optd **MULTA.**

D327 C 73	30c. brown	15	15
D328	– 30c. brown	15	15
D329 C 75	30c. brown	15	15

1952. As Type D **70** of Macao, but inscr "MOCAMBIQUE".

D468	10c. multicoloured	10	10
D469	30c. multicoloured	10	10
D470	50c. multicoloured	10	10
D471	1e. multicoloured	20	20
D472	2e. multicoloured	20	20
D473	5e. multicoloured	25	25

MOZAMBIQUE COMPANY Pt. 9

The Mozambique Company was responsible from 1891 until 1942 for the administration of Manica and Sofala territory in Portuguese East Africa. Now part of Mozambique.

1899. 1000 reis = 1 milreis.
1913. 100 centavos = 1 escudo.

1892. "Embossed" key-type inscr "PROVINCA DE MOCAMBIQUE" optd **COMPA. DE MOCAMBIQUE.**

10 Q	5r. black	25	20
2	10r. green	35	15
3	20r. red	45	15
4	25r. mauve	30	20
5	40r. brown	30	15
6	50r. blue	35	20
7	100r. brown	30	45
8	200r. violet	60	45
9	300r. orange	60	45

2

1895. Value in black or red (500, 1000r.).

33 2	2½r. yellow	10	10
114	2½r. grey	50	25
17	5r. orange	15	10
36	10r. mauve	15	15
115	10r. green	30	25
39	15r. brown	15	15
116	15r. green	30	25
20	20r. lilac	15	15
45	25r. green	15	15
117	25r. red	45	20
46	50r. blue	20	15
118	50r. brown	45	30
109	65r. blue	30	25
48	75r. red	20	15
119	75r. mauve	90	75
50	80r. green	20	15
52	100r. brown on buff	25	15
120	100r. blue on blue	90	75
110	115r. pink on pink	80	70
121	115r. brown on pink	1·40	90
111	130r. green on pink	80	70
122	130r. brown on yellow	1·40	90
54	150r. orange on pink	25	15
55	200r. blue on blue	25	15
123	200r. lilac on pink	1·40	90
56	300r. blue on brown	25	15
112	400r. black on blue	80	70
124	400r. blue on yellow	1·75	1·40
58	500r. black	35	25
125	500r. black on blue	1·75	40
126	700r. mauve on buff	1·90	1·60
59	1000r. mauve	45	25

1895. Surch **PROVISORIO 25.**

77 2	25 on 80r. green	6·50	4·50

1895. No. 6 optd **PROVISORIO.**

78 Q	50r. blue	1·60	1·25

1898. Vasco da Gama. Optd **1498 Centenario da India 1898.**

80 2	2½r. yellow	55	55
81	5r. orange	65	60
82	10r. mauve	65	55
84	15r. brown	80	70
86	20r. lilac	90	80
87	25r. green	1·50	90
99	50r. blue	85	80
89	75r. red	1·50	1·25
91	80r. green	1·50	1·10
101	100r. brown on buff	1·60	1·40
102	150r. orange on pink	1·60	1·50
94	200r. blue on blue	2·00	1·75
104	300r. blue on brown	3·00	2·25

1899. Surch **25 PROVISORIO.**

105 2	25 on 75r. red	1·25	1·10

1900. Surch **25 Reis** and bar.

106 2	25r. on 5r. orange	1·10	65

1900. Perforated through centre and surch **50 REIS.**

108 2	50r. on half of 20r. lilac	40	40

1911. Optd **REPUBLICA.**

145 2	2½r. grey	15	10
147	5r. orange	15	10
148	10r. green	10	10
150	15r. green	10	10
151	20r. lilac	15	10
153	25r. red	10	10
155	50r. brown	10	10
156	75r. mauve	15	10
157	100r. blue on blue	20	10
159	115r. brown on pink	30	20
160	130r. brown on yellow	30	20
161	200r. lilac on pink	30	15
162	400r. blue on yellow	30	15
163	500r. black on blue	30	15
164	700r. mauve on yellow	35	30

1916. Surch **REPUBLICA** and value in figures.

166 2	¼c. on 2½r. grey	10	10
168	½c. on 5r. orange	10	10
170	1c. on 10r. green	15	15
173	1½c. on 15r. green	15	15
175	2c. on 20r. lilac	15	15
178	2½c. on 25r. red	15	15
180	5c. on 50r. brown	15	15
181	7½c. on 75r. mauve	25	15
182	10c. on 100r. blue on blue	25	15
183	11½c. on 115r. brown on pink	50	30
184	13c. on 130r. brown on yell	60	35
185	20c. on 200r. lilac on pink	40	30
186	40c. on 400r. blue on yellow	40	30
187	50c. on 500r. black on blue	50	35
188	70c. on 700r. mauve on yell	50	35

1917. Red Cross Fund. Stamps of 1911 (optd **REPUBLICA**) optd with red cross and **31.7.17.**

189 2	2½r. grey	1·50	1·25
190	10r. green	2·00	1·75
191	20r. lilac	2·00	1·75
192	50r. brown	4·50	2·75
193	75r. mauve	10·50	8·75
194	100r. blue on blue	13·50	11·25
195	700r. mauve on yellow	42·00	29·00

1918. Stamps of 1911 (optd **REPUBLICA**) surch with new value.

196 2	¼c. on 700r. mauve on yellow	80	70
197	2½c. on 500r. black on blue	80	70
198	5c. on 400r. blue on yellow	80	70

14 Native Village

15 Ivory

1918.

199 14	¼c. green and brown	15	15
233	¼c. black and green	15	15
200 15	½c. black	15	15
201	– 1c. black and green	15	15
202	– 1½c. green and black	15	15
203	– 2c. black and red	15	15
235	– 2c. black and grey	15	15
204	– 2½c. black and lilac	15	15
236	– 3c. black and orange	15	15
205	– 4c. brown and green	15	15
237	– 4c. black and red	15	15
227 14	4½c. black and grey	20	15
206	– 5c. black and blue	25	15
207	– 6c. blue and purple	25	20
238	– 6c. black and mauve	15	15
228	– 7c. black and blue	75	25
208	– 7½c. green and orange	35	30
239	– 8c. black and lilac	30	25
210	– 10c. black and red	45	30
229	– 12c. black and brown	65	45
241	– 12c. black and green	30	20
242	– 15c. black and red	55	40
212	– 20c. black and green	20	15
213	– 30c. black and brown	40	30
244	– 30c. black and green	40	30
214	– 40c. black and green	30	20
246	– 40c. black and blue	45	30
215	– 50c. black and orange	40	30
247	– 50c. black and mauve	60	40
230	– 60c. brown and red	75	50
231	– 80c. brown and blue	1·75	70
248	– 80c. black and red	1·00	50
216	– 1e. black and green	70	50
249	– 1e. black and blue	60	50
232	– 2e. violet and red	2·25	80
250	– 2e. black and lilac	5·00	55

DESIGNS—HORIZ: 1, 3c. Maize field; 2c. Sugar factory; 5c., 2e. Beira; 20c. Law Court; 40c. Mangrove swamp. VERT: 1½c. India-rubber; 2½c. River Buzi; 4c. Tobacco bushes; 6c. Coffee bushes; 7, 15c. Steam train, Amatongas Forest; 7½c. Orange tree; 8, 12c. Cotton plants; 10, 80c. Sisal plantation; 30c. Coconut palm; 50, 60c. Cattle breeding; 1e. Mozambique Co's Arms.

1920. Pictorial issue surch in words.

217	¼c. on 30c. (No. 213)	1·10	95
218	½c. on 1e. (No. 216)	1·10	95
219	1½c. on 2½c. (No. 204)	90	90
220	1½c. on 5c. (No. 206)	3·25	3·25
221	2c. on 2½c. (No. 204)	70	55
222	4c. on 20c. (No. 212)	1·10	75
223	4c. on 40c. (No. 214)	1·10	75
224	6c. on 8c. (No. 239)	1·10	75
225	6c. on 50c. (No. 215)	1·10	75

33

36 Tea

1925.

251 33	24c. black and blue	80	65
252	– 25c. blue and brown	80	65
253 33	85c. black and red	60	50
254	– 1e.40 black and blue	1·25	40
255	– 5e. blue and brown	65	35
256 36	10e. black and red	65	35
257	– 20e. black and green	80	35

DESIGNS—VERT: 25c., 1e.40, Beira; 5e. Tapping rubber. HORIZ: 20e. River Zambesi.

38 Ivory

1931.

258 38	45c. blue	1·50	80
259	– 70c. brown	1·00	50

DESIGN—VERT: 70c. Gold mining.

40 Zambesi Bridge

1935. Opening of River Zambesi Railway Bridge at Sena.

260 40	1e. black and blue	2·50	35

41 Armstrong-Whitworth Atalanta Airliner over Beira

1935. Inauguration of Blantyre–Beira–Salisbury Air Route.

261 41	5c. black and blue	70	50
262	10c. black and red	70	50
263	15c. black and red	70	50
264	20c. black and green	70	50
265	30c. black and green	70	50
266	40c. black and blue	90	70
267	45c. black and blue	90	70
268	50c. black and purple	90	70
269	60c. brown and red	1·40	80
270	80c. black and red	1·40	80

42 Armstrong-Whitworth Atalanta Airliner over Beira

1935. Air.

271 42	5c. black and blue	15	15
272	10c. black and red	15	15
273	15c. black and red	15	15
274	20c. black and green	15	15
275	30c. black and green	15	15
276	40c. black and green	15	15
277	45c. black and blue	15	15
278	50c. black and purple	15	15
279	60c. brown and red	15	15
280	80c. black and red	15	15
281	1e. black and blue	20	15
282	2e. black and lilac	50	35
283	5e. blue and brown	90	55
284	10e. black and red	95	65
285	20e. black and green	2·10	1·40

43 Coastal Dhow

46 Palms at Beira

45 Crocodile

1937.

286 – 1c. lilac and green 10 10
287 – 5c. green and blue 10 10
288 **43** 10c. blue and red 10 10
289 – 15c. black and red 10 10
290 – 20c. blue and green 10 10
291 – 30c. blue and green 10 10
292 – 40c. black and blue 10 10
293 – 45c. brown and blue . . . 10 10
294 **45** 50c. green and violet . . . 15 15
295 – 60c. blue and red 15 15
296 – 70c. green and brown . . . 15 15
297 – 80c. green and red 15 15
298 – 85c. black and red 20 15
299 – 1e. black and blue 15 15
300 **46** 1e.40 green and blue . . . 20 15
301 – 2e. brown and lilac 40 20
302 – 5e. blue and brown 90 80
303 – 10e. black and red 55 35
304 – 20e. purple and green . . . 85 50

DESIGNS—VERT: 21 × 29 mm—1c. Giraffe; 20c. Common zebra; 70c. Native woman. 23 × 31 mm—10e. Old Portuguese gate, Sena; 20e. Arms. HORIZ: 29 × 21 mm—5c. Native huts; 15c. S. Caetano fortress, Sofala; 60c. Leopard; 80c. Hippopotami. 37 × 22 mm—5e. Railway bridge over River Zambesi. TRIANGULAR: 30c. Python; 40c. White rhinoceros; 45c. Lion; 85c. Vasco da Gama's flagship "Sao Gabriel"; 1e. Native in dugout canoe; 2e. Greater kudu.

1939. President Carmona's Colonial Tour. Optd **28-VII-1939 Visita Presidencial**.

305 – 30c. (No. 291) . . . . . . 1·40 70
306 – 40c. (No. 292) . . . . . . 1·40 70
307 – 45c. (No. 293) . . . . . . 1·40 70
308 **45** 50c. green and violet . . . 1·40 70
309 – 85c. (No. 298) . . . . . . 1·40 70
310 – 1e. (No. 299) . . . . . . 2·25 1·25
311 – 2e. (No. 301) . . . . . . 2·75 1·60

49 King Afonso Henriques

51 "Don John IV" after Alberto de Souza

1940. 800th Anniv of Portuguese Independence.

312 **49** 1e.75 light blue and blue 70 40

1940. Tercentenary of Restoration of Independence.

313 **51** 40c. black and blue 20 15
314 50c. green and violet . . . 20 15
315 60c. blue and red 20 15
316 70c. green and brown . . . 20 15
317 80c. green and red 20 15
318 1e. black and blue 20 15

CHARITY TAX STAMPS

The notes under this heading in Portugal also apply here.

1932. No. 236 surch **Assistencia Publica 2 Ctvos. 2.**

C260 2c. on 3c. black and orange 35 35

C 41 "Charity" C 50

1934.

C261 C **41** 2c. black and mauve 45 1·10

1940.

C313 C **50** 2c. blue and black . . 2·75 2·40

C 52

1941.

C319 C **52** 2c. red and black . . . 2·75 2·40

NEWSPAPER STAMPS

1894. "Newspaper" key-type inscr "MOCAMBIQUE" optd **COMPA. DE MOCAMBIQUE**.

N15 V 2½r. brown 25 20

POSTAGE DUE STAMPS

D 9 D 32

1906.

D114 D **9** 5r. green 20 20
D115 10r. grey 20 20
D116 20r. brown 20 20
D117 30r. orange 35 25
D118 50r. brown 35 25
D119 60r. brown . . . . . . 1·75 1·60
D120 100r. mauve 50 50
D121 130r. blue . . . . . . 2·50 1·75
D122 200r. red . . . . . . 1·10 70
D123 500r. lilac . . . . . . 1·40 1·10

1911. Optd **REPUBLICA**.

D166 D **9** 5r. green 15 15
D167 10r. grey 15 15
D168 20r. brown 15 15
D169 30r. orange 15 15
D170 50r. brown 15 15
D171 60r. brown 30 20
D172 100r. mauve 30 20
D173 130r. blue 70 75
D174 200r. red 80 70
D175 500r. lilac 90 80

1916. Currency changed.

D189 D **9** ½c. green 15 15
D190 1c. grey 15 15
D191 2c. brown 15 15
D192 3c. orange 15 15
D193 5c. brown 15 15
D194 6c. brown 15 15
D195 10c. mauve 35 35
D196 13c. blue 70 70
D197 20c. red 70 70
D198 50c. lilac 90 90

1919.

D217 D **32** ½c. green 10 10
D218 1c. black 10 10
D219 2c. brown 10 10
D220 3c. orange 10 10
D221 5c. brown 15 10
D222 6c. brown 20 20
D223 10c. red 20 20
D224 13c. blue 25 25
D225 20c. red 25 20
D226 50c. grey 30 30

MUSCAT Pt. 1

Independent Sultanate in Eastern Arabia with Indian and, subsequently, British postal administration.

12 pies = 1 anna; 16 annas = 1 rupee.

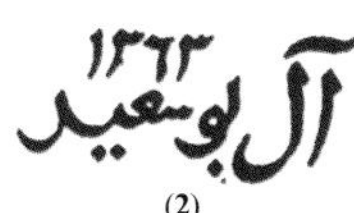

(2)

1944. Bicentenary of Al-Busaid Dynasty. Stamps of India (King George VI) optd as T **2**.

1 **100a** 3p. slate . . . . 30 5·50
2 ½a. mauve . . . . 30 5·50
3 9p. green . . . . 30 5·50
4 1a. red . . . . 30 5·50
5 **101** 1½a. plum . . . . 30 5·50
6 2a. red . . . . 30 5·50
7 3a. violet . . . . 70 5·50
8 3½a. blue . . . . 70 5·50
9 **102** 4a. brown . . . . . . 70 5·50
10 6a. green . . . . 75 5·50
11 8a. violet . . . . 75 5·50
12 12a. red . . . . 90 5·50
13 – 14a. purple (No. 277) . . 3·25 8·50
14 **93** 1r. slate and brown . . 1·25 9·00
15 2r. purple and brown . . 2·50 15·00

OFFICIAL STAMPS

1944. Bicentenary of Al-Busaid Dynasty. Official stamps of India optd as T **2**.

O 1 O **20** 3p. slate . . . . 50 10·00
O 2 ½a. purple . . . . . . 50 10·00
O 3 9p. green . . . . 50 10·00
O 4 1a. red . . . . 50 10·00
O 5 1½a. violet . . . . . . 50 10·00
O 6 2a. orange . . . . . . 60 10·00
O 7 2½a. violet . . . . . . 3·00 10·00
O 8 4a. brown . . . . . . 1·50 10·00
O 9 8a. violet . . . . . . 3·25 12·00
O10 **93** 1r. slate and brown (No. O138) . . . . . 2·50 20·00

For later issues see **BRITISH POSTAL AGENCIES IN EASTERN ARABIA**.

MUSCAT AND OMAN Pt. 19

Independent Sultanate in Eastern Arabia. The title of the Sultanate was changed in 1971 to Oman.

1966. 64 baizas = 1 rupee.
1970. 1000 baizas = 1 rial saidi.

12 Sultan's Crest

14 Nakhal Fort

1966.

94 **12** 3b. purple 10 10
95 5b. brown 10 10
96 10b. brown 10 10
97 A 15b. black and violet . . . 20 15
98 20b. black and blue . . . 30 20
99 25b. black and orange . . 35 20
100 **14** 30b. mauve and blue . . . 45 30
101 B 50b. green and brown . . . 70 40
102 C 1r. blue and orange . . . . 1·40 75
103 D 2r. brown and green . . . 2·75 1·50
104 E 5r. violet and red . . . . . 6·75 4·50
105 F 10r. red and violet . . . . 11·00 9·50

DESIGNS—VERT: 21½ × 25½ mm: A, Crest and Muscat harbour. HORIZ (as Type **14**): B, Samail Fort; C, Sohar Fort; D, Nizwa Fort; E, Matrah Fort; F, Mirani Fort.

15 Mina el Fahal

1969. 1st Oil Shipment (July 1967). Multicoloured.

106 20b. Type **15** 80 40
107 25b. Storage tanks 70 50
108 40b. Desert oil-rig . . . . . 1·10 85
109 1r. Aerial view from "Gemini 4" . . . . 2·75 2·00

1970. Designs as issue of 1966, but inscribed in new currency.

110 **12** 5b. purple 10 10
111 10b. brown 10 10
112 20b. brown 20 10
113 A 25b. black and violet . . . 25 15
114 30b. black and blue . . . 35 20
115 40b. black and orange . . 45 25
116 **14** 50b. mauve and blue . . . 50 30
117 B 75b. green and brown . . . 75 50
118 C 100b. blue and orange . . 1·10 65
119 D ¼r. brown and green . . . 3·00 1·90
120 E ½r. violet and red . . . . . 6·00 3·75
121 F 1r. red and violet . . . . . 11·00 7·75

For later issues see **OMAN**.

MYANMAR Pt. 21

Formerly known as Burma.

100 pyas = 1 kyat.

81 Fountain, National Assembly Park (½-size illustration)

1990. State Law and Order Restoration Council.

312 **81** 1k. multicoloured . . . . 1·00 65

1990. As Nos. 258/61 of Burma but inscr "UNION OF MYANMAR".

313 15p. deep green and green . . 20 15
314 20p. black, brown and blue . . 25 20
315 50p. violet and brown . . . 45 25
316 1k. violet, mauve and black . 90 65

82 Map and Emblem

83 Nawata Ruby

1990. 40th Anniv of United Nations Development Programme.

322 **82** 2k. blue, yellow and black 1·90 1·25

1991. Gem Emporium.

323 **83** 50p. multicoloured 95 65

84 "Grandfather giving Sword to Grandson" (statuette, Nan Win)

85 Emblem

1992. 44th Anniv of Independence. Multicoloured.

324 50p. Warrior defending personification of Myanmar and map (poster, Khin Thein) 50 40
325 2k. Type **84** . . . . 2·00 1·50

1992. National Sports Festival.

326 **85** 50p. multicoloured 55 40

86 Campaign Emblem

87 Fish, Water Droplet and Leaf

1992. Anti-AIDS Campaign.

327 **86** 50p. red 40 30

1992. International Nutrition Conference, Rome.

328 **87** 50p. multicoloured 30 20
329 1k. multicoloured 55 40
330 3k. multicoloured . . . . 1·60 1·10
331 5k. multicoloured . . . . 2·75 1·90

88 Statue

89 Hintha (legendary bird)

1993. National Convention for Drafting of New Constitution.

332 **88** 50p. multicoloured 25 20
333 3k. multicoloured . . . . 1·50 1·00

1993. Statuettes. Multicoloured.

334 5k. Type **89** . . . . 2·50 1·75
335 10k. Lawkanat . . . . 5·00 3·50

90 Horseman aiming Spear at Target

1993. Festival of Traditional Equestrian Sports, Sittwe.

336 **90** 3k. multicoloured . . . . 1·60 1·10

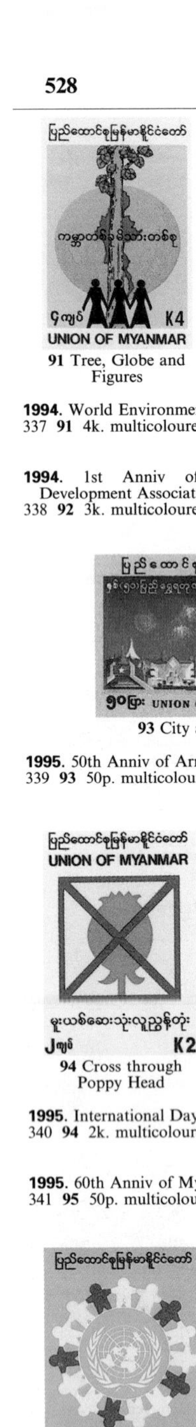

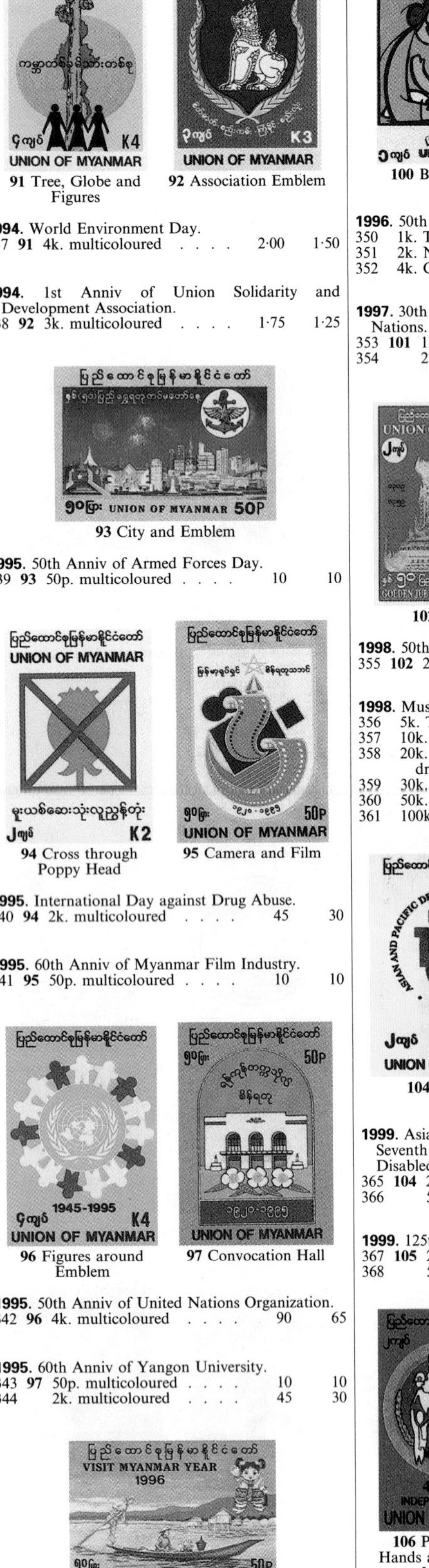

91 Tree, Globe and Figures

92 Association Emblem

1994. World Environment Day.
337 **91** 4k. multicoloured . . . . 2·00 1·50

1994. 1st Anniv of Union Solidarity and Development Association.
338 **92** 3k. multicoloured . . . . 1·75 1·25

93 City and Emblem

1995. 50th Anniv of Armed Forces Day.
339 **93** 50p. multicoloured 10 10

94 Cross through Poppy Head

95 Camera and Film

1995. International Day against Drug Abuse.
340 **94** 2k. multicoloured 45 30

1995. 60th Anniv of Myanmar Film Industry.
341 **95** 50p. multicoloured 10 10

96 Figures around Emblem

97 Convocation Hall

1995. 50th Anniv of United Nations Organization.
342 **96** 4k. multicoloured 90 65

1995. 60th Anniv of Yangon University.
343 **97** 50p. multicoloured 10 10
344 2k. multicoloured 45 30

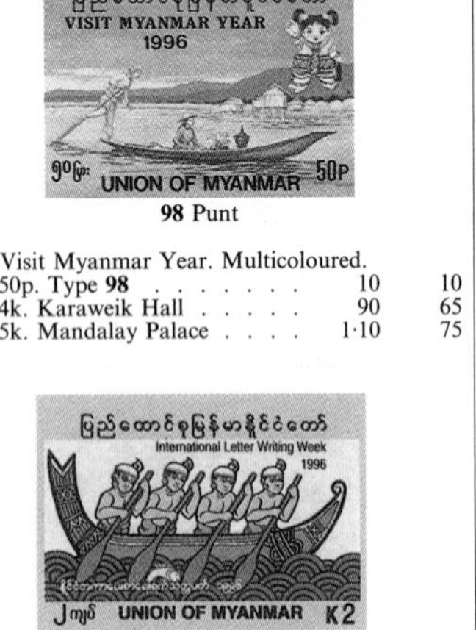

98 Punt

1996. Visit Myanmar Year. Multicoloured.
345 50p. Type **98** 10 10
346 4k. Karaweik Hall 90 65
347 5k. Mandalay Palace . . . . 1·10 75

99 Four-man Canoe

1996. International Letter Writing Week. "Unity equals Success". Multicoloured.
348 2k. Type **99** 40 30
349 5k. Human pyramid holding flag aloft (vert) . . . . . 1·10 75

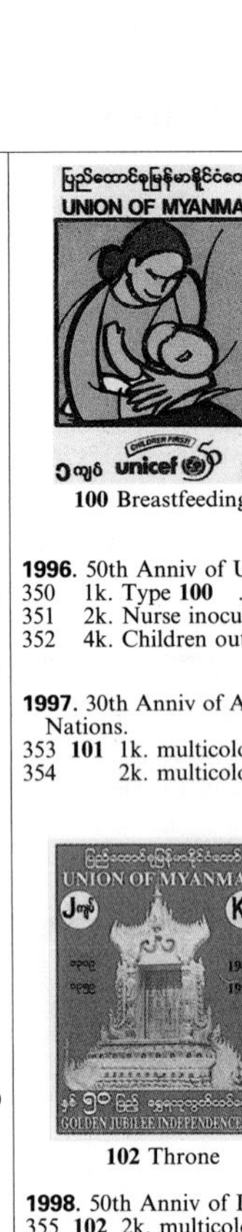

100 Breastfeeding

101 Emblem and Map of Myanmar

1996. 50th Anniv of U.N.I.C.E.F. Multicoloured.
350 1k. Type **100** 20 15
351 2k. Nurse inoculating child 40 30
352 4k. Children outside school 85 60

1997. 30th Anniv of Association of South-East Asian Nations.
353 **101** 1k. multicoloured 25 15
354 2k. multicoloured 40 30

102 Throne

103 Xylophone

1998. 50th Anniv of Independence.
355 **102** 2k. multicoloured 40 30

1998. Musical Instruments. Multicoloured.
356 5k. Type **103** . . . . 1·00 70
357 10k. Mon brass gongs . . . 2·00 1·40
358 20k. Rakhine auspicious drum . . . . 4·00 2·75
359 30k. Myanmar harp . . . . 6·00 4·25
360 50k. Shan pot drum . . . . 10·00 7·00
361 100k. Kachin brass gong . . 20·00 14·00

104 Emblem

105 Dove and U.P.U. Emblem

1999. Asian and Pacific Decade of Disabled Persons. Seventh Far East and South Pacific Region Disabled Games.
365 **104** 2k. multicoloured 40 30
366 5k. multicoloured . . . . 1·00 70

1999. 125th Anniv of Universal Postal Union.
367 **105** 2k. multicoloured 40 30
368 5k. multicoloured . . . . 1·00 70

106 People linking Hands around Map of Myanmar

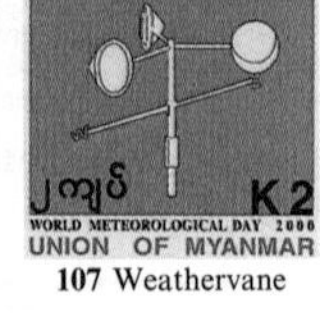

107 Weathervane

2000. 52nd Anniv of Independence.
369 **106** 2k. multicoloured 40 30

2000. World Meteorological Day. 50th Anniv of World Meteorological Organization.
370 **107** 2k. black and blue . . . 40 30
371 – 5k. multicoloured . . . . 1·00 70
372 – 10k. multicoloured . . . 2·10 1·50
DESIGNS—HORIZ: 5k. Emblem and globe; 10k. Emblem and symbols for rain and sunshine.

108 Royal Palace Gate, Burma and Great Wall of China (½-size illustration)

2000. 50th Anniv of Burma–China Relations.
373 **108** 5k. multicoloured . . . . 1·00 70

109 Burning Poppy Heads and Needles

2000. Anti-drugs Campaign.
374 **109** 2k. multicoloured 40 30

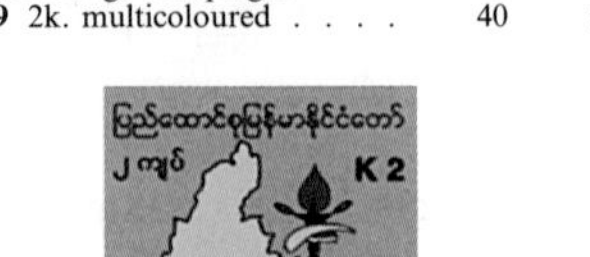

110 Television Set and Map of Myanmar

2001. 53rd Anniv of Independence.
375 **110** 2k. multicoloured 40 30

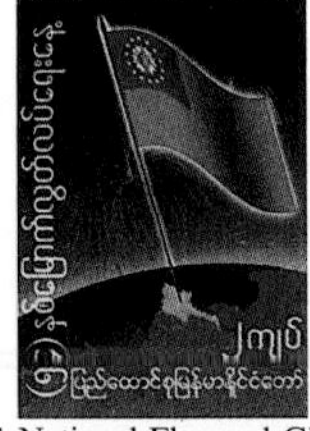

111 National Flag and Globe

2002. 54th Anniv of Independence. Multicoloured.
376 2k. Type **111** 40 30
377 30k. As No. 376 but inscriptions and face value in English . . . . 6·00 4·25

NABHA Pt. 1

A "Convention" state in the Punjab, India.

12 pies = 1 anna; 16 annas = 1 rupee.

Stamps of India optd **NABHA STATE**.

1885. Queen Victoria. Vert opt.
1 **23** ½a. turquoise . . . . 3·00 4·25
2 – 1a. purple . . . . 38·00 £140
3 – 2a. blue . . . . 15·00 42·00
4 – 4a. green (No. 96) . . . . . 75·00 £180
5 – 8a. mauve £300
6 – 1r. grey (No. 79) £325

1885. Queen Victoria. Horiz opt.
36 **40** 3p. red 20 20
14 **23** ½a. turquoise 30 10
15 – 9p. red . . . . 1·25 3·00
17 – 1a. purple . . . . 1·50 70
18 – 1a.6p. brown . . . . . . 1·25 2·75
20 – 2a. blue . . . . 1·75 1·25
22 – 3a. orange . . . . 2·75 1·75
12 – 4a. green (No. 69) . . . . . 32·00 £160
24 – 4a. green (No. 96) . . . . . 4·50 2·00
26 – 6a. brown (No. 80) . . . . 2·00 2·50
27 – 8a. mauve . . . . 2·00 1·75
28 – 12a. purple on red . . . . 3·25 3·75
29 – 1r. grey (No. 101) . . . . . 10·00 42·00
30 **37** 1r. green and red . . . . 9·00 4·00
31 **38** 2r. red and orange £100 £200
32 3r. brown and green £100 £275
33 5r. blue and violet £100 £400

1903. King Edward VII.
37 3p. grey 60 15
38 ½a. green (No. 122) 60 35
39 1a. red (No. 123) . . . . . 1·40 70
40a 2a. lilac . . . . 2·50 35
40b 2½a. blue . . . . 18·00 85·00
41 3a. orange 75 40
42 4a. olive . . . . 2·25 1·75
43 6a. bistre . . . . 2·00 14·00
44 8a. mauve . . . . 8·00 18·00
45 12a. purple on red . . . . 3·25 19·00
46 1r. green and red . . . . . 8·00 11·00

1907. As last, but inscr "INDIA POSTAGE & REVENUE".
47 ½a. green (No. 149) . . . . . 1·25 1·25
48 1a. red (No. 150) 75 70

1913. King George V. Optd in two lines.
49a **55** 3p. grey 20 20
50 **56** ½a. green 30 10
51 **57** 1a. red 85 10
59 1a. brown . . . . 4·25 2·25
52 **59** 2a. lilac 50 50
53 **62** 3a. orange 50 35
54 **63** 4a. olive . . . . 65 1·10
55 **64** 6a. bistre . . . . 75 4·50
56a **65** 8a. mauve . . . . 3·00 3·00
57 **66** 12a. red . . . . 1·75 19·00
58 **67** 1r. brown and green . . . 7·50 4·00

1928. King George V. Optd in one line.
60 **55** 3p. grey . . . . 1·25 15
61 **56** ½a. green 60 20
73 **79** ½a. green 50 40
61a **80** 9p. green . . . . 10·00 10·00
62 **57** 1a. brown . . . . 1·25 15
74 **81** 1a. brown 40 30
63 **82** 1¼a. mauve . . . . 1·50 5·00
64 **70** 2a. lilac . . . . 2·50 35
65 **61** 2½a. orange . . . . 80 7·50
66 **62** 3a. blue . . . . 2·25 1·10
75 **57** 3a. red . . . . 4·00 12·00
76 **63** 4a. olive . . . . 4·00 3·25
67 **71** 4a. green . . . . 2·50 1·75
71 **67** 2r. red and orange . . . . 25·00 90·00
72 5r. blue and purple . . . . 70·00 £275

1938. King George VI. Nos. 247/63.
77 **91** 3p. slate . . . . 7·00 60
78 ½a. brown . . . . 5·00 90
79 9p. green . . . . 19·00 4·00
80 1a. red . . . . 2·50 60
81 **92** 2a. red . . . . 1·25 5·50
82 – 2a.6p. violet . . . . 1·25 8·50
83 – 3a. green . . . . 1·40 5·00
84 – 3a.6p. blue . . . . 1·40 18·00
85 – 4a. brown . . . . 7·00 7·00
86 – 6a. green . . . . 3·00 18·00
87 – 8a. violet . . . . 2·25 18·00
88 – 12a. red . . . . 2·50 18·00
89 **93** 1r. slate and brown . . . . 11·00 25·00
90 2r. purple and brown . . . 24·00 85·00
91 5r. green and blue . . . . . 35·00 £170
92 10r. purple and red . . . . 55·00 £350
93 15r. brown and green . . . £160 £650
94 25r. slate and purple £140 £650

1942. King George VI. Optd **NABHA** only.
95 **91** 3p. slate . . . . 30·00 3·75
105 **100a** 3p. slate 90 90
96 **91** ½a. brown . . . . 70·00 4·75
106 **100a** ½a. mauve . . . . . . 3·00 1·00
97 **91** 9p. green . . . . 10·00 12·00
107 **100a** 9p. green . . . . . . 2·50 1·00
98 **91** 1a. red . . . . 10·00 2·50
108 **100a** 1a. red . . . . 90 3·00
109 **101** 1a.3p. brown . . . . . . 90 2·50
110 1½a. violet . . . . 1·75 1·75
111 2a. red . . . . 1·10 3·75
112 3a. violet . . . . 4·50 3·50
113 3½a. blue . . . . 14·00 45·00
114 **102** 4a. brown . . . . 1·75 1·00
115 6a. green . . . . 9·50 42·00
116 8a. violet . . . . 8·00 32·00
117 12a. purple . . . . 5·50 45·00

OFFICIAL STAMPS

Stamps of Nabha optd **SERVICE**.

1885. Nos. 1/3 (Queen Victoria).
O1 ½a. turquoise . . . . 3·00 90
O2 1a. purple 50 20
O3 2a. blue . . . . 65·00 £130

1885. Nos. 14/30 (Queen Victoria).
O 6 ½a. turquoise 30 10
O 8 1a. purple . . . . 1·00 25
O 9 2a. blue . . . . 2·00 90
O11 3a. orange . . . . 22·00 70·00
O13 4a. green (No. 4) . . . . . 2·50 1·00
O15 6a. brown . . . . 16·00 26·00
O17 8a. mauve . . . . 2·25 85
O18 12a. purple on red . . . . . 6·50 17·00
O19 1r. grey . . . . 35·00 £225
O20 1r. green and red . . . . . 29·00 70·00

1903. Nos. 37/46 (King Edward VII).
O25 3p. grey . . . . 1·00 12·00
O26 ½a. green 70 30
O27 1a. red 50 10
O29 2a. lilac . . . . 1·60 40
O30 4a. olive . . . . 1·60 50
O32 8a. mauve . . . . 1·40 1·50
O34 1r. green and red . . . . . 1·60 2·25

1907. Nos. 47/8 (King Edward VII inscr "INDIA POSTAGE & REVENUE").
O35 ½a. green 50 50
O36 1a. red 50 30

1913. Nos. 54 and 58 (King George V).
O37 **63** 4a. olive . . . . 10·00 50·00
O38 **67** 1r. brown and green . . . 55·00 £375

1913. Official stamps of India (King George V) optd **NABHA STATE**.
O39a **55** 3p. grey . . . . 60 7·00
O40 **56** ½a. green 30 15
O41 **57** 1a. red 25 10
O42 **59** 2a. purple 40 40
O43 **63** 4a. olive 40 50
O44 **65** 8a. mauve . . . . 75 1·25
O46 **67** 1r. brown and green . . 3·75 2·50

1932. Stamps of India (King George V) optd **NABHA STATE SERVICE**.
O47 **55** 3p. grey 10 15
O48 **81** 1a. brown 15 15

O49 **63** 4a. olive . . . . 20·00 2·50
O50 **65** 8a. mauve . . . . 1·00 2·00

1938. Stamps of India (King George VI) optd **NABHA STATE SERVICE.**
O53 **91** 9p. green . . . . 3·00 3·25
O54 1a. red . . . . 13·00 75

1943. Stamps of India (King George VI) optd **NABHA.**
O55 **O 20** 3p. slate . . . . 80 1·00
O56 ½a. brown 90 30
O57 ½a. purple . . . . . . 3·50 70
O58 9p. green . . . . 1·25 20
O59 1a. red 60 20
O61 1½a. violet 70 40
O62 2a. orange . . . . . . 2·00 1·00
O64 4a. brown . . . . . . 3·50 2·75
O65 8a. violet . . . . 5·50 16·00

1943. Stamps of India (King George VI) optd **NABHA SERVICE.**
O66 **93** 1r. slate and brown . . . 8·50 32·00
O67 2r. purple and brown . . 26·00 £150
O68 5r. green and blue £170 £500

NAGORNO-KARABAKH Pt. 10

The mountainous area of Nagorno-Karabakh, mainly populated by Armenians, was declared an Autonomous Region within the Azerbaijan Soviet Socialist Republic on 7 July 1923.

Following agitation for union with Armenia in 1988 Nagorno-Karabakh was placed under direct U.S.S.R. rule in 1989. On 2 September 1991 the Regional Soviet declared its independence and this was confirmed by popular vote on 10 December. By 1993 fighting between Azerbaijan forces and those of Nagorno-Karabakh, supported by Armenia, led to the occupation of all Azerbaijan territory separating Nagorno-Karabakh from the border with Armenia. A ceasefire under Russian auspices was signed on 18 February 1994.

1993. 100 kopeks = 1 rouble.
1995. 100 louma = 1 dram.

1 National Flag

1993. Inscr "REPUBLIC OF MOUNTAINOUS KARABAKH".
1 **1** 1r. multicoloured 20 20
2 – 3r. blue, purple and brown . . 60 60
3 – 15r. red and blue . . . . . . 3·00 3·00
DESIGNS: 3r. President Arthur Mkrtchian; 15r. "We are Our Mountains" (sculpture of man and woman).

Ա Բ Գ
(**2** "A") (**2a** "P") (**2b** "K")

1995. Nos. 1 and 3 surch in Armenian script as T **2/2b**.
6 **2** (50d.) on 1r. multicoloured 1·25 1·25
7 **2a** (100d.) on 15r. red and blue 2·25 2·25
8 **2b** (200d.) on 15r. red and blue 4·75 4·75

3 Dadiwank Monastery

1996. 5th Anniv of Independence. Multicoloured.
9 50d. Type **3** 50 50
10 100d. Parliament Building, Stepanakert 90 90
11 200d. "We are Our Mountains" (sculpture of man and woman) . . . . . 1·60 1·60

4 Boy playing Drum and Fawn (Erna Arshakyan)

1997. Festivals. Multicoloured.
13 50d. Type **4** (New Year) . . . 35 35
14 200d. Madonna and Child with angels (Mihran Akopyan) (Christmas) (vert) 1·75 1·75

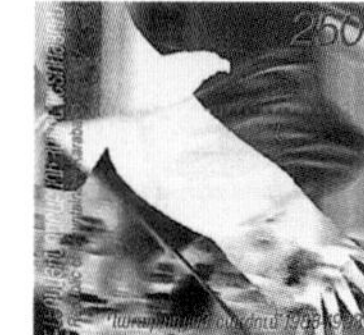
5 Eagle and Demonstrator with Flag

1998. 10th Anniv of Karabakh Movement.
15 **5** 250d. multicoloured 75 75

6 Parliament Summer Palace

1998. 5th Anniv of Liberation of Shushi. Mult.
16 100d. Type **6** 30 30
17 250d. Church of the Saviour (vert) 75 75

NAKHICHEVAN Pt. 10

An autonomous province of Azerbaijan, separated from the remainder of the republic by Armenian territory. Nos. 1 and 2 were issued during a period when the administration of Nakhichevan was in dispute with the central government.

100 qopik = 1 manat.

1 President Aliev

1993. 70th Birthday of President H. Aliev of Nakhichevan.
1 **1** 5m. black and red . . . . . . 3·75 3·75
2 – 5m. multicoloured . . . . . . 3·75 3·75
DESIGN: No. 2, Map of Nakhichevan.

NAMIBIA Pt. 1

Formerly South West Africa, which became independent on 21 March 1990.

1990. 100 cents = 1 rand.
1993. 100 cents = 1 Namibia dollar.

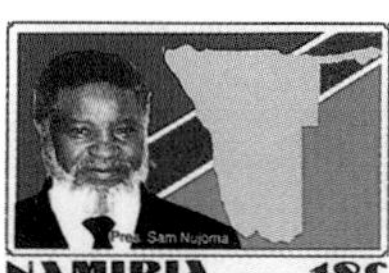

141 Pres. Sam Nujoma, Map of Namibia and National Flag

1990. Independence. Multicoloured.
538 18c. Type **141** 20 15
539 45c. Hands releasing dove and map of Namibia (vert) 50 75
540 60c. National flag and map of Africa . . . . 1·00 1·50

142 Fish River Canyon

1990. Namibia Landscapes. Multicoloured.
541 18c. Type **142** 25 20
542 35c. Quiver-tree forest, Keetmanshoop 50 35
543 45c. Tsaris Mountains . . . 60 55
544 60c. Dolerite boulders, Keetmanshoop 70 65

143 Stores on Kaiser Street, c. 1899

1990. Centenary of Windhoek. Multicoloured.
545 18c. Type **143** 20 20
546 35c. Kaiser Street, 1990 . . . 30 35
547 45c. City Hall, 1914 . . . . 40 65
548 60c. City Hall, 1990 . . . . 50 1·00

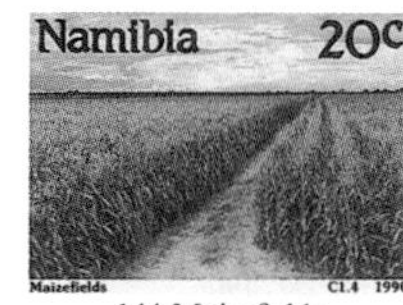

144 Maizefields **145** Gypsum

1990. Farming. Multicoloured.
549 20c. Type **144** 15 20
550 35c. Sanga bull 30 35
551 50c. Damara ram 40 45
552 65c. Irrigation in Okavango 50 60

1991. Minerals. As Nos. 519/21 and 523/33 of South West Africa, some with values changed and new design (5r.), inscr "Namibia" as T **145**. Multicoloured.
553 1c. Type **145** 10 10
554 2c. Fluorite 15 10
555 5c. Mimetite 20 10
556 10c. Azurite 30 10
557 20c. Dioptase 35 10
558 25c. Type **139** 35 15
559 30c. Tsumeb lead and copper complex 50 20
560 35c. Rosh Pinah zinc mine 50 20
561 40c. Diamonds 65 25
562 50c. Uis tin mine 65 25
563 65c. Boltwoodite 65 35
564 1r. Rossing uranium mine . . 70 50
565 1r.50 Wulfenite . . . . . . 1·10 70
566 2r. Gold . . . . 1·50 1·10
567 5r. Willemite (vert as T **145**) 3·00 2·75

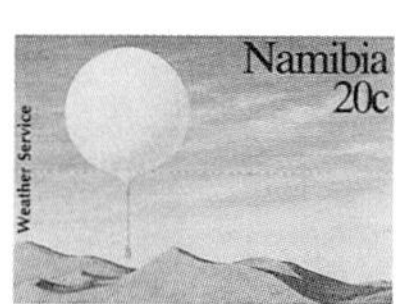

146 Radiosonde Weather Balloon

1991. Centenary of Weather Service. Mult.
568 20c. Type **146** 20 20
569 35c. Sunshine recorder . . . 35 30
570 50c. Measuring equipment . . 45 50
571 65c. Meteorological station, Gobabeb 50 60

147 Herd of Zebras

1991. Endangered Species. Mountain Zebra. Mult.
572 20c. Type **147** . . . . 1·10 60
573 25c. Mare and foal . . . . . 1·25 70
574 45c. Zebras and foal . . . . 2·00 1·75
575 60c. Two zebras . . . . . . 2·50 3·00

148 Karas Mountains

1991. Mountains of Namibia. Multicoloured.
576 20c. Type **148** 20 20
577 25c. Gamsberg Mountains . . 30 30
578 45c. Mount Brukkaros . . . 45 70
579 60c. Erongo Mountains . . . 65 1·00

149 Bernabe de la Bat Camp

1991. Tourist Camps. Multicoloured.
580 20c. Type **149** 45 30
581 25c. Von Bach Dam Recreation Resort 55 45

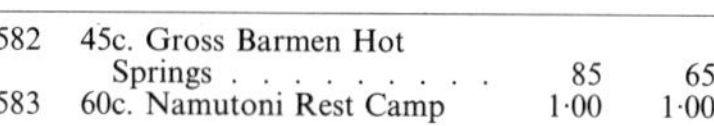
582 45c. Gross Barmen Hot Springs 85 65
583 60c. Namutoni Rest Camp 1·00 1·00

150 Artist's Pallet

1992. 21st Anniv of Windhoek Conservatoire. Multicoloured.
584 20c. Type **150** 20 15
585 25c. French horn and cello 25 20
586 45c. Theatrical masks 50 60
587 60c. Ballet dancers 65 60

151 Mozambique Mouthbrooder

1992. Freshwater Angling. Multicoloured.
588 20c. Type **151** 45 20
589 25c. Large-mouthed yellowfish 50 20
590 45c. Common carp 95 50
591 60c. Sharp-toothed catfish . . 1·10 65

152 Old Jetty

1992. Centenary of Swakopmund. Mult.
592 20c. Type **152** 25 25
593 25c. Recreation centre . . . 25 25
594 45c. State House and lighthouse 80 60
595 60c. Sea front 85 75
MS596 118 × 93 mm. Nos. 592/5 2·75 2·75

153 Running **154** Wrapping English Cucumbers

1992. Olympic Games, Barcelona. Mult.
597 20c. Type **153** 25 20
598 25c. Map of Namibia, Namibian flag and Olympic rings 30 20
599 45c. Swimming 50 40
600 60c. Olympic Stadium, Barcelona 65 55
MS601 115 × 75 mm. Nos. 597/600 (sold at 2r.) . . . . 2·25 2·75

1992. Integration of the Disabled. Mult.
602 20c. Type **154** 20 15
603 25c. Weaving mats 20 15
604 45c. Spinning thread 40 30
605 60c. Preparing pot plants . . 55 50

155 Elephants in Desert

1993. Namibia Nature Foundation. Rare and Endangered Species. Multicoloured.
606 20c. Type **155** 40 20
607 25c. Sitatunga in swamp . . 30 20
608 45c. Black rhinoceros 65 50
609 60c. Hunting dogs 65 60
MS610 217 × 59 mm. Nos. 606/9 (sold at 2r.50) . . . . 3·50 3·50

156 Herd of Simmentaler Cattle

1993. Centenary of Simmentalar Cattle in Namibia. Multicoloured.
611 20c. Type **156** 30 10
612 25c. Cow and calf 30 15
613 45c. Bull 60 40
614 60c. Cattle on barge 85 75

157 Sand Dunes, Sossusvlei

1993. Namib Desert Scenery. Multicoloured.
615 30c. Type **157** 25 20
616 40c. Blutkuppe 25 20
617 65c. River Kuiseb, Homeb 40 45
618 85c. Desert landscape 60 65

158 Smiling Child

1993. S.O.S. Child Care in Namibia. Mult.
619 30c. Type **158** 20 20
620 40c. Family 25 20
621 65c. Modern house 45 55
622 85c. Young artist with mural 65 80

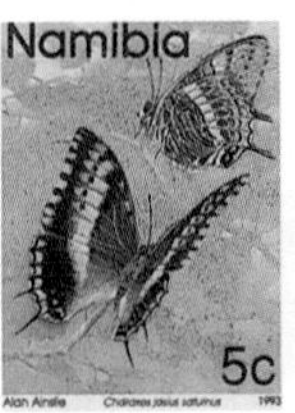

159 "Charaxes jasius" **160** White Seabream

1993. Butterflies. Multicoloured.
707 5c. Type **159** 50 50
624 10c. "Acraea anemosa" . . . 20 20
625 20c. "Papilio nireus" 30 10
626 30c. "Junonia octavia" . . . 30 10
627 40c. "Hypolimnus misippus" 30 10
708 50c. "Physcaeneura panda" 60 40
629 65c. "Charaxes candiope" . . 40 30
630 85c. "Junonia hierta" 50 40
631 90c. "Colotis cellmene" . . . 50 40
632 $1 "Cacyreus dicksoni" . . . 55 35
633 $2 "Charaxes bohemani" . . 80 80
634 $2.50 "Stugeta bowkeri" . . 80 1·10
635 $5 "Byblia anvatara" . . . . 1·25 1·75
See also No. 648.

1994. Coastal Angling. Multicoloured.
636 30c. Type **160** 25 25
637 40c. Kob 25 25
638 65c. West coast steenbras . . 40 40
639 85c. Galjoen 60 60
MS640 134 × 89 mm. Nos. 636/9 (sold at $2.50) . . . . 2·00 2·50

161 Container Ship at Wharf

1994. Incorporation of Walvis Bay Territory into Namibia. Multicoloured.
641 30c. Type **161** 40 30
642 65c. Aerial view of Walvis Bay 60 80
643 85c. Map of Namibia . . . . 95 1·25

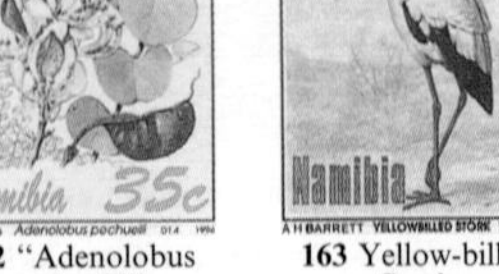

162 "Adenolobus pechuelii" **163** Yellow-billed Stork

1994. Flowers. Multicoloured.
644 35c. Type **162** 25 25
645 40c. "Hibiscus elliottiae" . . 25 25
646 65c. "Pelargonium cortusifolium" 40 40
647 85c. "Hoodia macrantha" . . 50 60

1994. Butterflies. As T **159**, but inscr "STANDARDISED MAIL". Multicoloured.
648 (–) "Graphium antheus" . . 25 20
No. 648 was initially sold at 35c., but this was subsequently increased to reflect changes in postal rates.

1994. Storks. Multicoloured.
649 35c. Type **163** 40 30
650 40c. Abdim's stork 40 30
651 80c. African open-bill stork 70 50
652 $1.10 White stork 80 65

164 Steam Railcar, 1908

1994. Steam Locomotives. Multicoloured.
653 35c. Type **164** 45 30
654 70c. Krauss side-tank locomotive No. 106, 1904 70 50
655 80c. Class 24 locomotive, 1948 . . . . 75 55
656 $1.10 Class 7C locomotive, 1914 . . . . 1·10 80

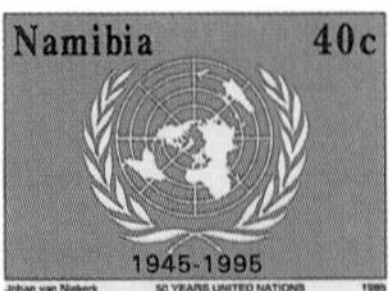

165 Cape Cross Locomotive No. 84 "Prince Edward", 1895

1995. Cent of Railways in Namibia. Mult.
657 35c. Type **165** 55 25
658 70c. Steam locomotive, German South West Africa 90 35
659 80c. South African Railways Class 8 steam locomotive 85 40
660 $1.10 Trans-Namib Class 33-400 diesel-electric locomotive . . . . 1·25 55
MS661 101 × 94 mm. Nos. 657/60 3·00 1·75

166 National Arms **167** Living Tortoise and "Geochelone stromeri" (fossil)

1995. 5th Anniv of Independence.
662 **166** (–) multicoloured 40 30
No. 662 is inscribed "STANDARDISED MAIL" and was initially sold for 35c., but this was subsequently increased to reflect changes in postal rates.

1995. Fossils. Multicoloured.
663 40c. Type **167** 60 25
664 80c. Ward's diamond bird and "Diamantornis wardi" (fossil eggs) 90 70
665 90c. Hyraxes and "Prohyrax hendeyi" skull . . . . . . 1·00 80
666 $1.20 Crocodiles and "Crocodylus lloydi" skull 1·25 1·10

168 Martii Rautanen and Church **169** Ivory Buttons

1995. 125th Anniv of Finnish Missionaries in Namibia. Multicoloured.
667 40c. Type **168** 25 20
668 80c. Albin Savola and hand printing press 50 50
669 90c. Karl Weikkolin and wagon 60 65
670 $1.20 Dr. Selma Rainio and Onandjokwe Hospital . . . 85 95

1995. Personal Ornaments. Multicoloured.
671 40c. Type **169** 20 20
672 80c. Conus shell pendant . . 45 45
673 90c. Cowrie shell headdress 55 55
674 $1.20 Shell button pendant 85 95

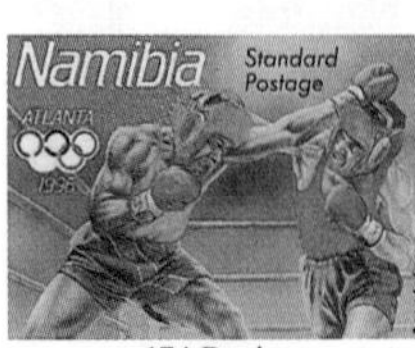

169a Warthog

1995. "Singapore '95" International Stamp Exhibition. Sheet 110 × 52 mm, containing design as No. 359b of South West Africa.
MS675 **169a** $1.20 multicoloured 1·10 1·25

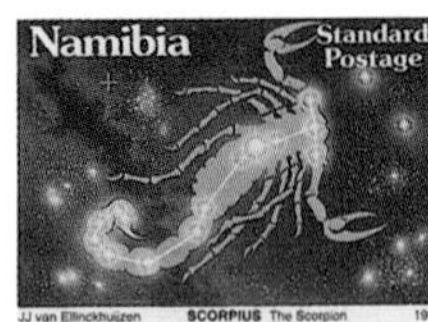

170 U.N. Flag

1995. 50th Anniv of the United Nations.
676 **170** 40c. blue and black . . . 20 20

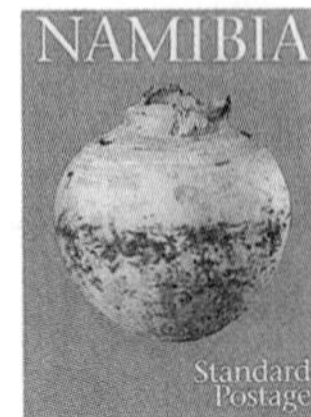

171 Bogenfels Arch

1996. Tourism. Multicoloured.
677 (–) Type **171** 15 15
678 90c. Ruacana Falls 30 30
679 $1 Epupa Falls 30 30
680 $1.30 Herd of wild horses . . 35 50
No. 677 is inscribed "Standardised Mail" and was initially sold at 45c.

172 Sister Leoni Kreitmeier and Dobra Education and Training Centre

1996. Centenary of Catholic Missions in Namibia. Multicoloured.
681 50c. Type **172** 20 20
682 95c. Father Johann Malinowski and Heirachabis Mission . . . 30 40
683 $1 St. Mary's Cathedral, Windhoek 30 40
684 $1.30 Archbishop Joseph Gotthardt and early church, Ovamboland . . . 35 80

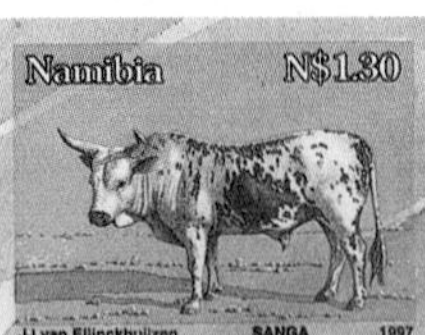

172a Caracal

1996. "CAPEX '96" International Stamp Exhibition, Toronto. Sheet 105 × 45 mm, containing design as No. 358c of South West Africa.
MS685 **172a** $1.30 multicoloured 85 90

173 Children and U.N.I.C.E.F. Volunteer

1996. 50th Anniv of U.N.I.C.E.F. Multicoloured.
686 (–) Type **173** 15 15
687 $1.30 Girls in school 60 60
No. 686 is inscribed "STANDARD POSTAGE" and was initially sold at 50c.

174 Boxing

1996. Centennial Olympic Games, Atlanta. Mult.
688 (–) Type **174** 15 15
689 90c. Cycling 30 40
690 $1 Swimming 30 40
691 $1.30 Running 35 55
No. 688 is inscribed "Standard Postage" and was initially sold at 50c.

175 Scorpius

1996. Stars in the Namibian Sky. Multicoloured.
692 (–) Type **175** 15 15
693 90c. Sagittarius 25 30
694 $1 Southern Cross 30 30
695 $1.30 Orion 35 50
MS696 100 × 80 mm. No. 694 . . 1·50 1·75
No. 692 is inscribed "Standard Postage" and was initially sold at 50c.
See also No. **MS**706.

176 Urn-shaped Pot

1996. Early Pottery. Multicoloured.
697 (–) Type **176** 15 15
698 90c. Decorated storage pot 30 40
699 $1 Reconstructed cooking pot 30 40
700 $1.30 Storage pot 35 70
No. 697 is inscribed "Standard Postage" and was initially sold at 50c.

177 Khauxa!nas Ruins

1997. Khaux!nas Ruins.
701 **177** (–) multicoloured 30 20
702 – $1 multicoloured 70 50
703 – $1.10 multicoloured . . . 80 80
704 – $1.50 multicoloured . . . 1·10 1·60
DESIGNS: $1 to $1.50, Different views.
No. 701 is inscribed "Standard postage" and was initially sold at 50c.

178 Ox

1997. "HONG KONG '97" International Stamp Exhibition and Chinese New Year ("Year of the Ox"). Sheet 103 × 67 mm.
MS705 **178** $1.30 multicoloured 1·10 1·10

1997. Support for Organised Philately. No. **MS**696 with margin additionally inscr "Reprint February 17 1997. Sold in aid of organised philately N$3.50".
MS706 $1 Southern Cross (sold at $3.50) . . . . 1·75 2·00

179 Heinrich von Stephan **180** Cinderella Waxbill

1997. Death Centenary of Heinrich von Stephan (founder of U.P.U.).
709 **179** $2 multicoloured . . . . 1·10 1·10

1997. Waxbills. Multicoloured.
710 50c. Type **180** 10 10
711 60c. Black-cheeked waxbill 10 10

181 Helmeted Guineafowl

1997. Greetings Stamp.
712 **181** $1.20 multicoloured . . . 30 35
For similar designs see Nos. 743/6.

182 Jackass Penguins Calling

1997. Endangered Species. Jackass Penguin. Mult.
713 (–) Type **182** 25 30
714 $1 Incubating egg 40 40
715 $1.10 Adult with chick . . . 50 50
716 $1.50 Penguins swimming . . 55 60
MS717 101 × 92 mm. As Nos. 713/16, but without WWF symbol (sold at $5) . . . . . 1·50 1·50
No. 713 is inscribed "STANDARD POSTAGE" and was initially sold at 50c.

183 Caracal

1997. Wildcats. Multicoloured.
718 (–) Type **183** 20 20
719 $1 "Felis lybic" 40 30
720 $1.10 Serval 50 40
721 $1.50 Black-footed cat . . . 60 55
MS722 100 × 80 mm. $5 As No. 721 2·00 2·25
No. **MS**722 was sold in aid of organised philately in Southern Africa.
No. 718 is inscribed "STANDARD POSTAGE" and was initially sold at 50c.

184 "Catophractes alexandri"

1997. Greeting Stamps. Flowers and Helmeted Guineafowl. Multicoloured.
723 (–) Type **184** 40 40
724 (–) "Crinum paludosum" . . 40 40
725 (–) "Gloriosa superba" . . . 40 40
726 (–) "Tribulus zeyheri" . . . 40 40
727 (–) "Aptosimum pubescens" 40 40
728 50c. Helmeted guineafowl raising hat 10 10
729 50c. Holding bouquet 10 10
730 50c. Ill in bed 10 10
731 $1 With heart round neck . . 15 20
732 $1 With suitcase and backpack 15 20
Nos. 723/7 are inscribed "Standard Postage" and were initially sold at 50c. each.

185 Collecting Bag

1997. Basket Work. Multicoloured.
733 50c. Type **185** 20 20
734 90c. Powder basket 30 30
735 $1.20 Fruit basket 35 35
736 $2 Grain basket 70 75

186 Veterinary Association Coat of Arms

1997. 50th Anniv of Namibian Veterinary Association.
737 **186** $1.50 multicoloured . . . 50 50

187 Head of Triceratops

1997. Youth Philately. Dinosaurs. Sheet 82 × 56 mm.
MS738 **187** $5 multicoloured . . 1·50 1·75

188 German South West Africa Postman

189 False Mopane

1997. World Post Day.
739 **188** (–) multicoloured 20 20
No. 739 is inscribed "STANDARD POSTAGE" and was initially sold at 50c.

1997. Trees. Multicoloured.
740 (–) Type **189** 15 20
741 $1 Ana tree 30 40
742 $1.10 Shepherd's tree 35 55
743 $1.50 Kiaat 50 70
No. 740 is inscribed "STANDARD POSTAGE" and was initially sold at 50c.

1997. Christmas. As T **181**, showing Helmeted Guineafowl, each with festive frame. Mult.
744 (–) Guineafowl facing right 15 20
745 $1 Guineafowl in grass . . . 30 30
746 $1.10 Guineafowl on rock . . 35 40
747 $1.50 Guineafowl in desert 50 55
MS748 110 × 80 mm. $5 Helmeted guineafowl (vert) . . . . . 2·25 2·25
No. 744 is inscribed "standard postage" and was initially sold at 50c.

190 Flame Lily

191 John Muafangejo

1997. Flora and Fauna. Multicoloured.
749 5c. Type **190** 10 10
750 10c. Bushman poison . . . 10 10
751 20c. Camel's foot 10 10
752 30c. Western rhigozum . . . 10 10
753 40c. Blue-cheeked bee-eater 10 10
754 50c. Laughing dove 10 10
755 (–) Peach-faced lovebird ("Roseyfaced Lovebird") 10 10
756 60c. Lappet-faced vulture . . 10 10
757a 90c. Southern yellow-billed hornbill ("Yellow-billed Hornbill") 15 20
758a $1 Lilac-breasted roller . . . 15 20
759a $1.10 Hippopotamus . . . 15 20
760 $1.20 Giraffe 20 25
761 (–) Leopard 20 25
762 $1.50 Elephant 25 30
763 $2 Lion 30 35
764 $4 Buffalo 60 65
765 $5 Black rhinoceros 75 80
766 $10 Cheetah . . . . 1·50 1·60
No. 755 is inscribed "standard postage" and was initially sold at 50c.; No. 761 is inscribed "postcard rate" and was initially sold at $1.20.
Nos. 755, 758 and 761 exist with ordinary or self-adhesive gum.

1997. 10th Death Anniv of John Muafangejo (artist).
770 **191** (50c.) multicoloured . . . 65 30
No. 770 is inscribed "STANDARD POSTAGE" and was initially sold at 50c.

192 Gabriel B. Taapopi

1998. Gabriel B. Taapopi (writer) Commemoration.
771 **192** (–) silver and brown . . . 50 20
No. 771 is inscribed "STANDARD POSTAGE" and was initially sold at 50c.

193 Year of the Tiger

1998. International Stamp and Coin Exhibition, 1997, Shanghai. Sheets 165 × 125 mm or 97 × 85 mm, containing multicoloured designs as T **193**. (a) Lunar New Year.
MS772 165 × 125 mm. $2.50 × 6. Type **193**; Light green tiger and circular symbol; Yellow tiger and head symbol; Blue tiger and square symbol; Emerald tiger and square symbol; Mauve tiger and triangular symbol (61 × 29 mm) 2·50 3·25
MS773 97 × 85 mm. $6 Symbolic tiger designs (71 × 40 mm) . . 1·25 1·40

(b) Chinese Calendar.
MS774 165 × 125 mm. $2.50 × 6. Various calendar symbols (24 × 80 mm) . . . . 2·50 3·25
MS775 97 × 85 mm. $6 Soft toy tigers (71 × 36 mm) . . . . . 1·25 1·40

(c) 25th Anniv of Shanghai Communique.
MS776 165 × 125 mm. $3.50 × 4. Pres. Nixon's visit to China, 1972; Vice Premier Deng Xiaoping's visit to U.S.A., 1979; Pres. Reagan's visit to China, 1984; Pres. Bush's visit to China, 1989 (61 × 32 mm) . . . . 2·50 3·00
MS777 97 × 85 mm. $6 China–U.S.A. Communique, 1972 (69 × 36 mm) . . . . 1·25 1·40

(d) Pres. Deng Xiaoping's Project for Unification of China.
MS778 165 × 125 mm. $3.50 × 4. Beijing as national capital; Return of Hong Kong; Return of Macao; Links with Taiwan (37 × 65 mm) 2·50 3·00
MS779 97 × 85 mm. $6 Reunified China (71 × 41 mm) . . . . . 1·25 1·40

(e) Return of Macao to China, 1999.
MS780 Two sheets, each 165 × 120 mm. (a) $4.50 × 3 Carnival dragon and modern Macao (44 × 33 mm). (b) $4.50 × 3 Ruins of St. Paul's Church, Macao (62 × 29 mm) Set of 2 sheets . . 4·00 5·50
MS781 Two sheets, each 97 × 85 mm. (a) $6 Carnival dragon and modern Macao (62 × 32 mm). (b) $6 Deng Xiaoping and ruins of St. Paul's Church, Macao (71 × 36 mm) Set of 2 sheets . . . . 2·00 2·75

194 Leopard

1998. Large Wild Cats. Multicoloured.
782 $1.20 Type **194** 50 25
783 $1.90 Lioness and cub . . . 70 55
784 $2 Lion 70 60
785 $2.50 Cheetah 80 90
MS786 112 × 98 mm. Nos. 782/5 2·50 2·50

195 Narra Plant
196 Collecting Rain Water

1998. Narra Cultivation.
787 **195** $2.40 multicoloured . . . 50 60

1998. World Water Day.
788 **196** (–) multicoloured 50 30

No. 788 is inscribed "STANDARD POSTAGE" and was initially sold at 50c. On 1 April 1998 the standard postage rate was increased to 55c.

1998. Diana, Princess of Wales Commemoration. Sheet 145 × 70 mm, containing vert designs as T **91** of Kiribati. Multicoloured.
MS789 $1 Princess Diana wearing protective mask; $1 Wearing Red Cross badge; $1 Wearing white shirt; $1 Comforting crippled child 1·60 1·75

197 White-faced Scops Owl ("Whitefaced Owl")

1998. Owls of Namibia. Multicoloured.
790 55c. Black-tailed tree rat (20 × 24 mm) 10 10
791 $1.50 Type **197** 25 30
792 $1.50 African barred owl ("Barred Owl") 25 30
793 $1.90 Spotted eagle owl . . . 30 35
794 $1.90 Barn owl (61 × 24 mm) 30 35
See also No. **MS**850.

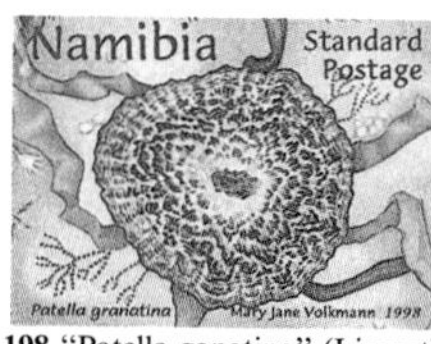

198 "Patella granatina" (Limpet)

1998. Shells. Multicoloured.
795 (–) Type **198** 30 10
796 $1.10 "Cymatium cutaceum africanum" (Triton) . . . 65 30
797 $1.50 "Conus mozambicus" (Cone) 85 65
798 $6 "Venus verrucosa" (Venus clam) . . . . 2·50 3·00
MS799 109 × 84 mm. Nos. 795/8 3·50 3·50
No. 795 is inscribed "Standard Postage" and was initially sold at 55c.

199 Underwater Diamond Excavator

1998. Marine Technology. Sheet 70 × 90 mm.
MS800 **199** $2.50 multicoloured 1·25 1·25

200 "Chinga" (cheetah)

1998. Wildlife Conservation. "Racing for Survival" (Olympic sprinter Frank Frederiks v cheetah). Sheet 108 × 80 mm.
MS801 **200** $5 multicoloured . . 1·25 1·40

201 Namibian Beach

1998. World Environment Day. Multicoloured.
802 (–) Type **201** 10 10
803 $1.10 Okavango sunset . . . 20 25
804 $1.50 Sossusvlei 30 35
805 $1.90 African Moringo tree 40 45
No. 802 is inscribed "STANDARD POSTAGE" and was initially sold at 55c.

202 Two Footballers

203 Chacma Baboon

1998. World Cup Football Championship, France. Sheet 80 × 56 mm.
MS806 **202** $5 multicoloured . . 1·00 1·10

1998. Animals with their Young. Sheet 176 × 60 mm, containing T **203** and similar vert designs.
MS807 $1.50, Type **203**; $1.50, Blue Wildebeest; $1.50, Meercat (suricate); $1.50, African Elephant; $1.50, Burchell's Zebra 1·50 1·60

204 Carmine Bee Eater

1998. Wildlife of the Caprivi Strip. Multicoloured.
808 60c. Type **204** 25 25
809 60c. Sable antelope (40 × 40 mm) 25 25
810 60c. Lechwe (40 × 40 mm) . . 25 25
811 60c. Woodland waterberry . . 25 25
812 60c. Nile monitor (40 × 40 mm) 25 25
813 60c. African jacana 25 25
814 60c. African fish eagle . . . 25 25
815 60c. Woodland kingfisher . . 25 25
816 60c. Nile crocodile (55 × 30 mm) 25 25
817 60c. Black mamba (32 × 30 mm) 25 25
Nos. 808/17 were printed together, se-tenant, with the backgrounds forming a composite design.

205 Black Rhinoceros and Calf

1998. "ILSAPEX '98" International Stamp Exhibition, Johannesburg. Sheet 103 × 68 mm.
MS818 **205** $5 multicoloured . . 1·00 1·10

206 Blue Whale

1998. Whales of the Southern Oceans (joint issue with Norfolk Island and South Africa). Sheet 103 × 70 mm.
MS819 **206** $5 multicoloured . . 1·25 1·40

207 Damara Dik-dik **208** Yoka perplexed

1999. "Fun Stamps for Children". Animals. Mult.
820 $1.80 Type **207** 75 75
821 $2.65 Striped tree squirrel (26 × 36 mm) . . . . . . 1·00 1·00

1999. "Yoka the Snake" (cartoon). Multicoloured. Self-adhesive.
822 $1.60 Type **208** 25 30
823 $1.60 Yoka under attack (33 × 27 mm) 25 30
824 $1.60 Yoka caught on branch 25 30
825 $1.60 Yoka and wasps (33 × 27 mm) 25 30
826 $1.60 Yoka and footprint . . 25 30
827 $1.60 Yoka and tail of red and white snake 25 30
828 $1.60 Mouse hunt (33 × 27 mm) 25 30
829 $1.60 Snakes entwined . . . 25 30
830 $1.60 Red and white snake singing 25 30
831 $1.60 Yoka sulking (33 × 27 mm) 25 30

209 "Windhuk" (liner)

1999. "Windhuk" (liner) Commemoration. Sheet 110 × 90 mm.
MS832 **209** $5.50 multicoloured 85 90

210 Zogling Glider, 1928

1999. Gliding in Namibia. Multicoloured.
833 $1.60 Type **210** 25 30
834 $1.80 Schleicher glider, 1998 25 30

211 Yoka the Snake with Toy Zebra

1999. "iBRA '99" International Stamp Exhibition, Nuremberg. Sheet 110 × 84 mm.
MS835 **211** $5.50 multicoloured 85 90

212 Greater Kestrel

1999. Birds of Prey. Multicoloured.
836 60c. Type **212** 25 15
837 $1.60 Common kestrel ("Rock Kestrel") 50 40
838 $1.80 Red-headed falcon ("Red-necked Falcon") . . 50 45
839 $2.65 Lanner falcon 70 95

213 Wattled Crane

1999. Wetland Birds. Multicoloured.
840 $1.60 Type **213** 25 30
841 $1.80 Variegated sandgrouse ("Burchell's Sandgrouse") 25 30
842 $1.90 White-collared pratincole ("Rock Pratincole") 30 35
843 $2.65 Eastern white pelican 40 45

214 "Termitomyces schimperi" (fungus) **216** Johanna Gertze

215 "Eulophia hereroensis" (orchid)

1999. "PhilexFrance '99" International Stamp Exhibition, Paris. Sheet 79 × 54 mm.
MS844 **214** $5.50 multicoloured 85 90

1999. "China '99" International Philatelic Exhibition, Beijing. Orchids. Multicoloured.
845 $1.60 Type **215** 25 30
846 $1.80 "Ansellia africana" . . 25 30
847 $2.65 "Eulophia leachii" . . 40 45
848 $3.90 "Eulophia speciosa" . . 60 65
MS849 72 × 72 mm. $5.50 "Eulophia walleri" 85 90

1999. Winning entry in 5th Stamp World Cup, France. Sheet 120 × 67 mm, design as No. 794, but with changed face value. Multicoloured.
MS850 $11 Barn owl (61 × 24 mm) 1·60 1·75

1999. Johanna Gertze Commemoration.
851 **216** $20 red, pink and blue . . 2·75 3·50

217 Sunset over Namibia

1999. New Millennium. Multicoloured.
852 $2.20 Type **217** 35 40
853 $2.40 Sunrise over Namibia 35 40
MS854 77 × 54 mm. $9 Globe (hologram) (37 × 44 mm) . . . 1·40 1·50

218 South African Shelduck

2000. Ducks of Namibia. Multicoloured.
855 $2 Type **218** 30 35
856 $2.40 White-faced whistling duck 35 40
857 $3 Comb duck ("Knobbilled duck") 45 50
858 $7 Cape shoveler . . . . . . 1·10 1·25
No. 858 is inscribed "Cape shoveller" in error.

2000. Nos. 749/52 surch with **standard postage** (859) or new values (others).
859 (–) on 5c. Type **190** 20 25
860 $1.80 on 30c. Western rhigozum 25 30
861 $3 on 10c. Bushman poison 45 50
862 $6 on 20c. Camel's foot . . . 90 95
No. 859 was initially sold at 65c. The other surcharges show face values.

220 Namibian Children

2000. 10th Anniv of Independence. Multicoloured.
863 65c. Type **220** 10 15
864 $3 Namibian flag 45 50

221 Actor playing Jesus wearing Crown of Thorns

2000. Easter Passion Play. Multicoloured.
865 $2.10 Type **221** 30 35
866 $2.40 On the way to Calvary 35 40

222 Tenebrionid Beetle **223** *Welwitschia mirabilis*

2000. "The Stamp Show 2000" International Stamp Exhibition, London. Wildlife of Namibian Dunes. Sheet 165 × 73 mm, containing T **222** and similar multicoloured designs.
MS867 $2 Type **222**; $2 Namib golden mole; $2 Brown hyena; $2 Shovel-snouted lizard (49 × 30 mm); $2 Dune lark (25 × 36 mm); $6 Namib side-winding adder (25 × 36 mm) . . 2·40 2·50

2000. *Welwitschia mirabilis* (prehistoric plant). Multicoloured.
868 (–) Type **223** 20 25
869 $2.20 *Welwitschia mirabilis* from above 35 40
870 $3 Seed pods 45 50
871 $4 Flats covered by *Welwitschia mirabilis* . . . 60 65
No. 868 is inscribed "Standard inland mail" and was originally sold for 65c.

224 High Energy Stereoscopic System Telescopes

2000. High Energy Stereoscopic System Telescopes Project. Namibian Khomas Highlands. Sheet 100 × 70 mm.
MS872 **224** $11 multicoloured . . 1·60 1·75

225 Jackal-berry Tree

2000. Trees with Nutritional Value. Multicoloured.
873 (–) Type **225** 20 25
874 $2 Sycamore fig 30 35
875 $2.20 Bird plum 35 40
876 $7 Marula . . . . 1·10 1·25
No. 873 is inscribed "Standard inland mail" and was originally sold for 65c.

226 Yoka and Nero the Elephant

2000. "Yoka the Snake" (cartoon) (2nd series). Sheet 103 × 68 mm.
MS877 **226** $11 multicoloured . . 1·60 1·75

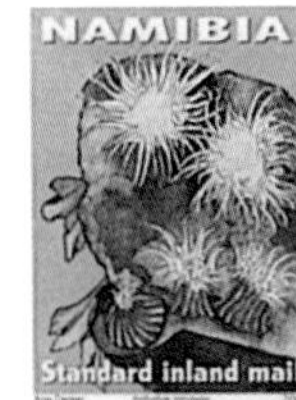

227 Striped Anemone **229** Wood-burning Stove

228 Cessna 210 Turbo Aircraft

2001. Sea Anemone. Multicoloured.
878 (–) Type **227** 20 25
879 $2.45 Violet-spotted anemone 35 40
880 $3.50 Knobbly anemone . . 50 55
881 $6.60 False plum anemone 1·00 1·10
No. 878 is inscribed "Standard inland mail" and was originally sold for 70c.

2001. Civil Aviation. Multicoloured.
882 (–) Type **228** 20 25
883 $2.20 Douglas DC-6B airliner 35 40
884 $2.50 Pitts S2A bi-plane . . . 40 45
885 $13.20 Bell 407 helicopter . . 2·00 2·10
No. 882 is inscribed "Standard inland mail" and was originally sold for 70c.

2001. Renewable Energy Sources. Multicoloured.
886 (–) Type **229** 20 25
887 (–) Biogas digester 20 25
888 (–) Solar cooker 20 25
889 (–) Re-cycled tyre 20 25
890 (–) Solar water pump 20 25
891 $3.50 Solar panel above traditional hut 50 55
892 $3.50 Solar street light . . . 50 55
893 $3.50 Solar panels on hospital building 50 55
894 $3.50 Solar telephone 50 55
895 $3.50 Wind pump 50 55
Nos. 886/95 were printed together, se-tenant, with the backgrounds forming a composite design.
Nos. 886/90 are inscribed "Standard Mail" and were originally sold for $1 each.

230 Ruppell's Parrot

231 Plaited Hair, Mbalantu

2001. Flora and Fauna from the Central Highlands. Multicoloured.

No.	Description	Mint	Used
896	(–) Type **230**	20	25
897	(–) Flap-necked chameleon (40 × 30 mm)	20	25
898	(–) Klipspringer (40 × 30 mm)	20	25
899	(–) Rockrunner (40 × 30 mm)	20	25
900	(–) Pangolin (40 × 40 mm)	20	25
901	$3.50 Camel thorn (55 × 30 mm)	50	55
902	$3.50 Berg aloe (40 × 30 mm)	50	55
903	$3.50 Kudu (40 × 40 mm)	50	55
904	$3.50 Rock agama (40 × 40 mm)	50	55
905	$3.50 Armoured ground cricket (40 × 30 mm)	50	55

Nos. 896/905 were printed together, se-tenant, with the backgrounds forming a composite design.

Nos. 896/900 are inscribed "Standard Mail" and were originally sold for $1 each.

2002. Traditional Women's Hairstyles and Headdresses. Multicoloured.

No.	Description	Mint	Used
906	(–) Type **231**	15	20
907	(–) Cloth headdress, Damara	15	20
908	(–) Beaded hair ornaments, San	15	20
909	(–) Leather ekori headdress, Herero	15	20
910	(–) Bonnet, Baster	15	20
911	(–) Seed necklaces, Mafue	15	20
912	(–) Thihukeka hairstyle, Mbukushu	15	20
913	(–) Triangular cloth headdress, Herero	15	20
914	(–) Goat-skin headdress, Himba	15	20
915	(–) Horned headdress, Kwanyama	15	20
916	(–) Headscarf, Nama	15	20
917	(–) Plaits and oshikoma, Ngandjera/Kwaluudhi	15	20

Nos. 906/17 are inscribed "STANDARD MAIL" and were originally sold for $1 each.

232 African Hoopoe

2002. Birds. Multicoloured.

No.	Description	Mint	Used
918	(–) Type **232**	15	20
919	$2.20 Paradise flycatcher	35	40
920	$2.60 Swallowtailed bee eater	40	45
921	$2.80 Malachite kingfisher	45	50

No. 918 is inscribed "Standard Mail" and was originally sold for $1.

NANDGAON — Pt. 1

A state of central India. Now uses Indian stamps.

12 pies = 1 anna; 16 annas = 1 rupee.

1

2 (½a.)

1891. Imperf.

No.	Type	Description	Mint	Used
1	**1**	½a. blue	4·75	£140
2		2a. pink	21·00	£425

1893. Imperf.

No.	Type	Description	Mint	Used
3	**2**	½a. green	10·00	70·00
6		1a. red	48·00	£110
4		2a. red	9·00	70·00

OFFICIAL STAMPS

1893. Optd **M.B.D.** in oval.

No.	Type	Description	Mint	Used
O1	**1**	½a. blue	£350	
O4	**2**	½a. green	5·00	9·00
O5		1a. red	8·00	30·00
O6		2a. red	7·50	19·00

NAPLES — Pt. 8

A state on the S.W. coast of Central Italy, formerly part of the Kingdom of Sicily, but now part of Italy.

200 tornesi = 100 grano = 1 ducato.

1 Arms under Bourbon Dynasty

4 Cross of Savoy

1858. The frames differ in each value. Imperf.

No.	Type	Description	Mint	Used
8	**1**	½t. blue	£150000	£10000
1a		½g. red	£2250	£475
2		1g. red	£450	40·00
3		2g. red	£275	12·00
4a		5g. red	£4500	£9500
5a		10g. red	£5000	£32000
6a		20g. red	£6500	£1300
7a		50g. red	£10000	£3000

1860. Imperf.

No.	Type	Description	Mint	Used
9	**4**	½t. blue	£38000	£3750

NATAL — Pt. 1

On the east coast of S. Africa. Formerly a British Colony, later a province of the Union of S. Africa.

12 pence = 1 shilling;
20 shillings = 1 pound.

1

1857. Embossed stamps. Various designs.

No.	Type	Description	Mint	Used
1	**1**	1d. blue	—	£1100
2		1d. red	—	£1700
3		1d. buff	—	£1000
4	–	3d. red	—	£400
5	–	6d. green	—	£1100
6	–	9d. blue	—	£7000
7	–	1s. buff	—	£5500

The 3d., 6d., 9d. and 1s. are larger. Beware of reprints.

6

7

1859.

No.	Type	Description	Mint	Used
19	**6**	1d. red	85·00	27·00
12		3d. blue	£100	32·00
13		6d. grey	£160	50·00
24		6d. violet	48·00	28·00

1867.

No.	Type	Description	Mint	Used
25	**7**	1s. green	£130	28·00

1869. Variously optd **POSTAGE** or **Postage**.

No.	Type	Description	Mint	Used
50	**6**	1d. red	85·00	38·00
82		1d. yellow	70·00	70·00
53		3d. blue	£140	42·00
83		6d. violet	55·00	6·50
84	**7**	1s. green	80·00	5·50

1870. Optd **POSTAGE** in a curve.

No.	Type	Description	Mint	Used
59	**7**	1s. green	70·00	10·00
108		1s. orange	3·75	85

1870. Optd **POSTAGE** twice, reading up and down.

No.	Type	Description	Mint	Used
60	**6**	1d. red	70·00	13·00
61		3d. blue	75·00	13·00
62		6d. violet	£150	25·00

1873. Optd **POSTAGE** once, reading up.

No.	Type	Description	Mint	Used
63	**7**	1s. brown	£180	18·00

23

28

16

1874. Queen Victoria. Various frames.

No.	Type	Description	Mint	Used
97a	**23**	½d. green	2·50	60
99	–	1d. red	2·75	10
107	–	2d. olive	2·50	1·40
113	**28**	2½d. blue	4·50	60
68	–	3d. blue	95·00	18·00
101	–	3d. grey	3·50	1·00
102	–	4d. brown	4·25	75
103	–	6d. lilac	3·75	80
73	**16**	5s. red	65·00	27·00

1877. No. 99 surch ½ **HALF**.

No.	Type	Description	Mint	Used
85		½d. on 1d. red	25·00	65·00

POSTAGE
Half-penny
(21)

POSTAGE.
Half-Penny
(29)

1877. Surch as T **21**.

No.	Type	Description	Mint	Used
91	**6**	½d. on 1d. yellow	8·00	12·00
92		1d. on 6d. violet	50·00	8·50
93		1d. on 6d. red	95·00	38·00

1885. Surch in words.

No.	Type	Description	Mint	Used
104		½d. on 1d. red (No. 99)	16·00	11·00
105		2d. on 3d. grey (No. 101)	18·00	5·50
109		2½d. on 4d. brown (No. 102)	10·00	9·00

1895. No. 23 surch with T **29**.

No.	Type	Description	Mint	Used
114	**6**	½d. on 6d. violet	1·50	3·50

1895. No. 99 surch **HALF**.

No.	Type	Description	Mint	Used
125		HALF on 1d. red	1·75	1·25

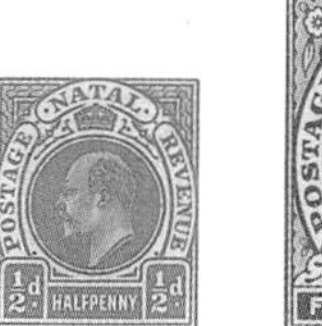

31

32

1902.

No.	Type	Description	Mint	Used
127	**31**	½d. green	2·25	20
128		1d. red	6·00	15
129		1½d. green and black	2·75	2·00
130		2d. red and olive	1·50	25
131		2½d. blue	1·25	3·00
132		3d. purple and grey	1·00	1·00
152		4d. red and brown	2·75	1·25
134		5d. black and orange	1·75	2·75
135		6d. green and purple	1·75	1·75
136		1s. red and blue	2·75	2·25
137		2s. green and violet	48·00	9·00
138		2s.6d. purple	40·00	12·00
139		4s. red and yellow	65·00	70·00
140	**32**	5s. blue and red	25·00	9·00
141		10s. red and purple	65·00	26·00
142		£1 black and blue	£160	50·00
143		£1.10s. green and violet	£350	90·00
162		£1.10s. orange and purple	£1000	£1800
144		£5 mauve and black	£2250	£550
145		£10 green and orange	£6500	£2500
145b		£20 red and green	£14000	£6500

1908. As T **31/2** but inscr "POSTAGE POSTAGE".

No.	Type	Description	Mint	Used
165	**31**	6d. purple	4·50	2·75
166		1s. black on green	6·00	2·00
167		2s. purple and blue on blue	15·00	3·00
168		2s.6d. black and red on blue	25·00	3·00
169	**32**	5s. green and red on yellow	18·00	20·00
170		10s. green and red on green	65·00	70·00
171		£1 purple and black on red	£225	£225

OFFICIAL STAMPS

1904. Optd **OFFICIAL**.

No.	Type	Description	Mint	Used
O1	**31**	½d. green	3·00	35
O2		1d. red	3·25	70
O3		2d. red and olive	20·00	9·50
O4		3d. purple and grey	11·00	4·00
O5		6d. green and purple	40·00	50·00
O6		1s. red and blue	£120	£180

NAURU — Pt. 1

An island in the W. Pacific Ocean, formerly a German possession and then administered by Australia under trusteeship. Became a republic on 31 January 1968.

1916. 12 pence = 1 shilling;
20 shillings = 1 pound.
1966. 100 cents = 1 Australian dollar.

1916. Stamps of Gt. Britain (King George V) optd **NAURU**.

No.	Type	Description	Mint	Used
1	**105**	½d. green	2·25	7·00
2	**104**	1d. red	1·75	5·50
15	**105**	1½d. brown	24·00	42·00
4	**106**	2d. orange	2·00	13·00
6	**104**	2½d. blue	2·75	7·00
7	**106**	3d. violet	2·00	3·75
8		4d. green	2·00	8·50
9	**107**	5d. brown	2·25	9·00
10		6d. purple	3·75	10·00
11	**108**	9d. black	8·50	22·00
12		1s. brown	7·00	19·00
25	**109**	2s.6d. brown	70·00	£100
22		5s. red	£100	£140
23		10s. blue	£250	£325

4

6

1924.

No.	Type	Description	Mint	Used
26A	**4**	½d. brown	1·75	2·75
27B		1d. green	2·50	3·00
28B		1½d. red	1·00	1·50
29B		2d. orange	2·25	8·00
30dB		2½d. blue	3·00	4·00
31cB		3d. blue	3·50	12·00
32B		4d. green	4·25	13·00
33B		5d. brown	3·75	4·00
34B		6d. violet	3·75	5·00
35A		9d. brown	9·50	19·00
36B		1s. red	6·50	2·75
37B		2s.6d. green	28·00	35·00
38B		5s. purple	38·00	50·00
39B		10s. yellow	£100	£130

1935. Silver Jubilee. Optd **HIS MAJESTY'S JUBILEE. 1910-1935.**

No.	Type	Description	Mint	Used
40	**4**	1½d. red	75	80
41		2d. orange	1·50	4·25
42		2½d. blue	1·50	1·50
43		1s. red	5·00	3·50

1937. Coronation.

No.	Type	Description	Mint	Used
44	**6**	1½d. red	45	1·75
45		2d. orange	45	2·50
46		2½d. blue	45	1·50
47		1s. purple	65	1·50

8 Anibare Bay

18 "Iyo" ("calophyllum")

21 White Tern

1954.

No.	Type	Description	Mint	Used
48	–	½d. violet	20	60
49a	**8**	1d. green	20	40
50	–	3½d. red	1·75	75
51	–	4d. blue	1·75	1·50
52	–	6d. orange	70	20
53	–	9d. red	60	20
54	–	1s. purple	30	30
55	–	2s.6d. green	2·75	1·00
56	–	5s. mauve	9·00	2·25

DESIGNS—HORIZ: ½d. Nauruan netting fish; 3½d. Loading phosphate from cantilever; 4d. Great frigate bird; 6d. Canoe; 9d. Domaneab (meeting house); 2s.6d. Buada Lagoon. VERT: 1s. Palm trees; 5s. Map of Nauru.

1963.

No.	Type	Description	Mint	Used
57	–	2d. multicoloured	75	2·25
58	–	3d. multicoloured	40	35
59	**18**	5d. multicoloured	40	75
60	–	8d. black and green	2·00	80
61	–	10d. black	40	30
62	**21**	1s.3d. blue, black and green	2·25	4·50
63	–	2s.3d. blue	3·25	55
64	–	3s.3d. multicoloured	2·25	2·75

DESIGNS—VERT (As Type **21**): 2d. Micronesian pigeon. (26 × 29 mm): 10d. Capparis (flower). HORIZ (As Type **18**): 3d. Poison nut (flower); 8d. Black lizard; 2s.3d. Coral pinnacles; 3s.3d. Nightingale reed warbler ("Red Warbler").

22 "Simpson and his Donkey"

1965. 50th Anniv of Gallipoli Landing.
65 **22** 5d. sepia, black and green . . . 15 10

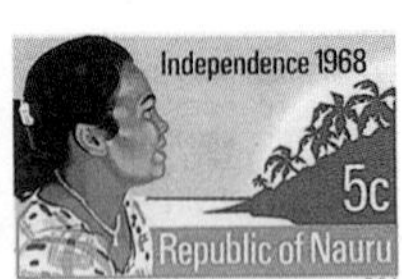

24 Anibare Bay **27** "Towards the Sunrise"

1966. Decimal Currency. As earlier issues but with values in cents and dollars as in T **24**. Some colours changed.
66 **24** 1c. blue 15 10
67 – 2c. purple (as No. 48) . . . 15 40
68 – 3c. green (as No. 50) . . . 30 1·75
69 – 4c. multicoloured (as T **18**) 20 10
70 – 5c. blue (as No. 54) 25 60
71 – 7c. black & brn (as No. 60) 30 10
72 – 8c. green (as No. 61) . . . 20 10
73 – 10c. red (as No. 51) 40 10
74 – 15c. bl, blk and grn (as T **21**) . . . . 60 1·75
75 – 25c. brown (as No. 63) . . 30 1·00
76 – 30c. mult (as No. 58) . . . 45 30
77 – 35c. mult (as No. 64) . . . 75 35
78 – 50c. mult (as No. 57) . . . 1·50 80
79 – $1 mauve (as No. 56) . . . 75 1·00
The 25c. is as No. 63 but larger, 27½ × 25 mm.

1968. Nos. 66/79 optd **REPUBLIC OF NAURU**.
80 **24** 1c. blue 10 30
81 – 2c. purple 10 10
82 – 3c. green 15 10
83 – 4c. multicoloured 15 10
84 – 5c. blue 10 10
85 – 7c. black and brown 25 10
86 – 8c. green 15 10
87 – 10c. red 30 15
88 – 15c. blue, black and green 1·25 2·50
89 – 25c. brown 20 15
90 – 30c. multicoloured 55 15
91 – 35c. multicoloured . . . . . 1·25 30
92 – 50c. multicoloured . . . . . 1·25 35
93 – $1 purple 75 50

1968. Independence.
94 **27** 5c. multicoloured 10 10
95 – 10c. black, green and blue 10 10
DESIGN: 10c. Planting seedling, and map.

29 Flag of Independent Nauru

1969.
96 **29** 15c. yellow, orange and blue 50 15

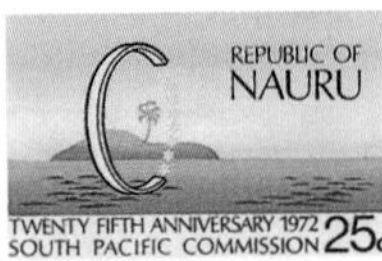

30 Island, "C" and Stars

1972. 25th Anniv of South Pacific Commission.
97 **30** 25c. multicoloured 30 30

1973. 5th Anniv of Independence. No. 96 optd **Independence 1968-1973**.
98 **29** 15c. yellow, orange and blue 20 30

32 Denea **33** Artefacts and Map

1973. Multicoloured.
99 1c. Ekwenababae 40 20
100 2c. Kauwe iud 45 20
101 3c. Rimone 45 20
102 4c. Type **32** 45 40
103 5c. Erekogo 45 40
104 7c. Racoon butterflyfish ("Ikimago") (horiz) 50 70
105 8c. Catching flying fish (horiz) 30 20
106 10c. Itsibweb (ball game) (horiz) 30 20
107 15c. Nauruan wrestling . . . 35 20
108 20c. Snaring great frigate birds ("Frigate Birds") . . 50 70
109 25c. Nauruan girl 40 30
110 30c. Catching common noddy birds ("Noddy Birds") (horiz) 60 40
111 50c. Great frigate birds ("Frigate Birds") (horiz) 80 75
112 $1 Type **33** 80 75

34 Co-op Store

1973. 50th Anniv of Nauru Co-operative Society. Multicoloured.
113 5c. Type **34** 20 30
114 25c. Timothy Detudamo (founder) 20 15
115 50c. N.C.S. trademark (vert) 45 55

35 Phosphate Mining

1974. 175th Anniv of First Contact with the Outside World. Multicoloured.
116 7c. M.V. "Eigamoiya" (bulk carrier) 80 90
117 10c. Type **35** 60 25
118 15c. Fokker Fellowship "Nauru Chief" 80 30
119 25c. Nauruan chief in early times 60 35
120 35c. Capt. Fearn and 18th-century frigate (70 × 22 mm) . . . . . . 3·00 2·50
121 50c. 18th-century frigate off Nauru (70 × 22 mm) . . . 1·50 1·40
The ship on the 35c. and 50c. is wrongly identified as the "Hunter" (snow).

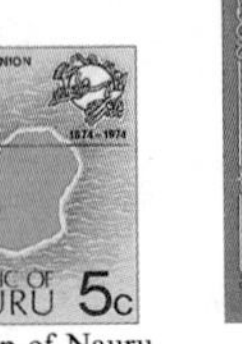

36 Map of Nauru **37** Rev. P. A. Delaporte

1974. Centenary of U.P.U. Multicoloured.
122 5c. Type **36** 15 20
123 8c. Nauru Post Office 15 20
124 20c. Nauruan postman . . . 15 10
125 $1 U.P.U. Building and Nauruan flag 40 60
MS126 157 × 105 mm. Nos. 122/5. Imperf . . . . 2·00 5·50

1974. Christmas and 75th Anniv of Rev. Delaporte's Arrival.
127 **37** 15c. multicoloured 20 20
128 20c. multicoloured 30 30

38 Map of Nauru, Lump of Phosphate Rock and Albert Ellis

1975. Phosphate Mining Anniversaries. Mult.
129 5c. Type **38** 25 40
130 7c. Coolies and mine 35 40
131 15c. Electric phosphate train, barges and ship . . . . . 1·00 1·40
132 25c. Modern ore extraction 1·25 1·50
ANNIVERSARIES: 5c. 75th anniv of discovery; 7c. 70th anniv of Mining Agreement; 15c. 55th anniv of British Phosphate Commissioners; 25c. 5th anniv of Nauru Phosphate Corporation.

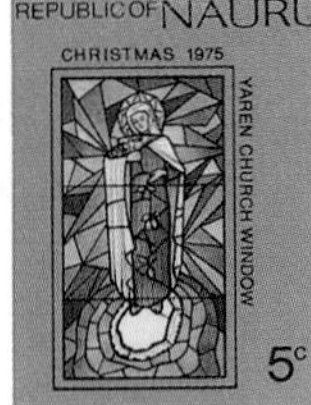

39 Micronesian Outrigger **41** "Our Lady" (Yaren Church)

40 New Civic Centre

1975. South Pacific Commission Conf, Nauru (1st issue). Multicoloured.
133 20c. Type **39** 75 40
134 20c. Polynesian double-hull 75 40
135 20c. Melanesian outrigger . . 75 40
136 20c. Polynesian outrigger . . 75 40

1975. South Pacific Commission Conf, Nauru (2nd issue). Multicoloured.
137 30c. Type **40** 15 15
138 50c. Domaneab (meeting-house) 30 30

1975. Christmas. Stained-glass Windows. Mult.
139 5c. Type **41** 15 25
140 7c. "Suffer little children" (Orro Church) 15 25
141 15c. As 7c. 20 55
142 25c. Type **41** 25 70

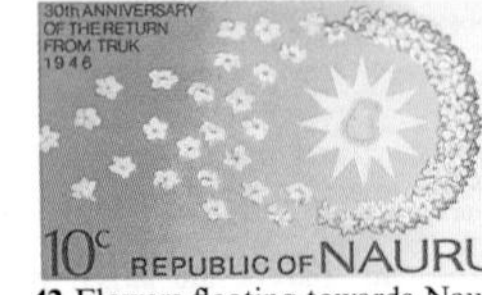

42 Flowers floating towards Nauru

1976. 30th Anniv of Islanders' Return from Truk. Multicoloured.
143 10c. Type **42** 10 10
144 14c. Nauru encircled by garland 15 10
145 25c. Nightingale reed warbler and maps 65 25
146 40c. Return of the islanders 45 35

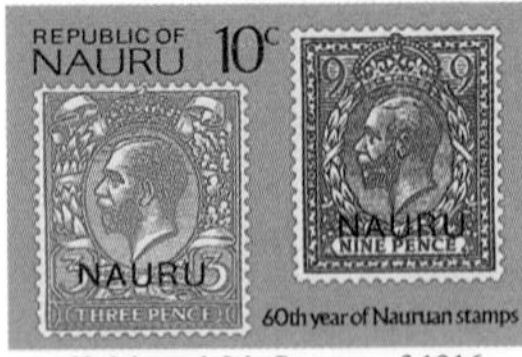

43 3d. and 9d. Stamps of 1916

1976. 60th Anniv of Nauruan Stamps. Mult.
147 10c. Type **43** 15 15
148 15c. 6d. and 1s. stamps . . . 15 15
149 25c. 2s.6d. stamp 20 25
150 50c. 5s. "Specimen" stamp 25 35

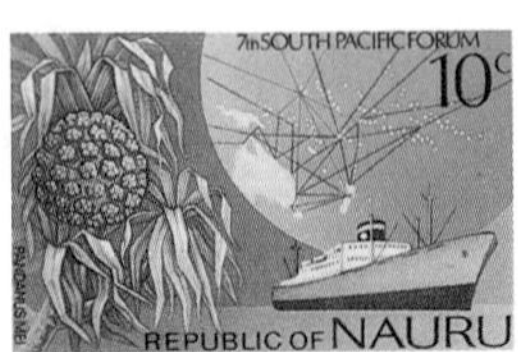

44 "Pandanus mei" and "Enna G" (cargo liner)

1976. South Pacific Forum, Nauru. Mult.
151 10c. Type **44** 20 10
152 20c. "Tournefortia argentea" with Boeing 737 and Fokker Fellowship aircraft 30 15
153 30c. "Thespesia populnea" and Nauru Tracking Station 30 15
154 40c. "Cordia subcordata" and produce 35 25

45 Nauruan Choir **46** Nauru House and Coral Pinnacles

1976. Christmas. Multicoloured.
155 15c. Type **45** 10 10
156 15c. Nauruan choir 10 10
157 20c. Angel in white dress . . 15 15
158 20c. Angel in red dress . . . 15 15

1977. Opening of Nauru House, Melbourne. Mult.
159 15c. Type **46** 15 15
160 30c. Nauru House and Melbourne skyline 25 25

47 Cable Ship "Anglia" **48** Father Kayser and First Catholic Church

1977. 75th Anniv of First Trans-Pacific Cable and 20th Anniv of First Artificial Earth Satellite.
161 **47** 7c. multicoloured 20 10
162 – 15c. blue, grey and black 30 15
163 – 20c. blue, grey and black 30 20
164 – 25c. multicoloured 30 20
DESIGNS: 15c. Tracking station, Nauru; 20c. Stern of "Anglia"; 25c. Dish aerial.

1977. Christmas. Multicoloured.
165 15c. Type **48** 10 10
166 25c. Congregational Church, Orro 15 15
167 30c. Catholic Church, Arubo 15 15

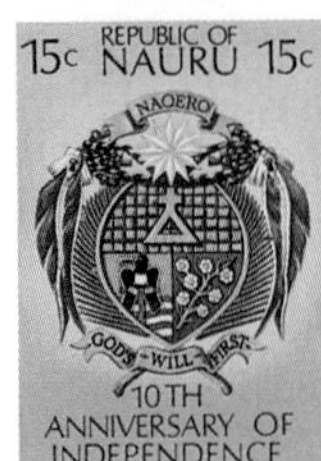

49 Arms of Nauru

1978. 10th Anniv of Independence.
168 **49** 15c. multicoloured 20 15
169 60c. multicoloured 35 30

1978. Nos. 159/60 surch.
170 **46** 4c. on 15c. multicoloured 55 1·50
171 5c. on 15c. multicoloured 55 1·50
172 – 8c. on 30c. multicoloured 55 1·50
173 – 10c. on 30c. multicoloured 55 1·50

51 Collecting Shellfish

1978.
174 **51** 1c. multicoloured 50 30
175 – 2c. multicoloured 50 30
176 – 3c. multicoloured . . . . . 1·75 1·00
177 – 4c. brown, blue and black 50 30
178 – 5c. multicoloured . . . . . 2·00 1·00
179 – 7c. multicoloured . . . . . 30 1·25
180 – 10c. multicoloured 30 20
181 – 15c. multicoloured 40 30
182 – 20c. grey, black and blue 30 30
183 – 25c. multicoloured 30 30
184 – 30c. multicoloured . . . . 1·50 45
185 – 32c. multicoloured . . . . 2·75 1·00
186 – 40c. multicoloured . . . . 1·50 2·00
187 – 50c. multicoloured . . . . 1·00 1·00
188 – $1 multicoloured . . . . . 70 1·00
189 – $2 multicoloured . . . . . 80 1·00
190 – $5 grey, black and blue . . 1·50 2·25

DESIGNS: 2c. Coral outcrop; 3c. Reef scene; 4c. Girl with fish; 5c. Reef heron; 7c. Catching fish, Buada Lagoon; 10c. Ijuw Lagoon; 15c. Girl framed by coral; 20c. Pinnacles, Anibare Bay reef; 25c. Pinnacle at Meneng; 30c. Head of great frigate bird; 32c. White-capped noddy birds in coconut palm; 40c. Wandering tattler; 50c. Great frigate birds on perch; $1 Old coral pinnacles at Topside; $2 New pinnacles at Topside; $5 Blackened pinnacles at Topside.

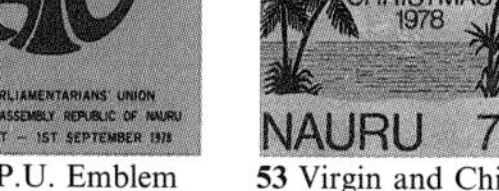

52 A.P.U. Emblem **53** Virgin and Child

1978. 14th General Assembly of Asian Parliamentarians' Union. Nauru.
191 **52** 15c. multicoloured 20 25
192 – 20c. black, blue and gold 20 25
DESIGN: 20c. As Type **52**, but with different background.

1978. Christmas. Multicoloured.
193 7c. Type **53** 10 10
194 15c. Angel in sunrise scene (horiz) 10 10
195 20c. As 15c. 15 15
196 30c. Type **53** 20 20

54 Baden-Powell and Cub Scout

1978. 70th Anniv of Boy Scout Movement. Mult.
197 20c. Type **54** 20 15
198 30c. Scout 25 20
199 50c. Rover Scout 35 30

55 Wright Flyer I over Nauru

1979. Flight Anniversaries. Multicoloured.
200 10c. Type **55** 20 15
201 15c. Fokker F.VIIa/3m "Southern Cross" superimposed on nose of Boeing 737 . . . . 30 20
202 15c. "Southern Cross" and Boeing 737 (front view) . . 30 20
203 30c. Wright Flyer I over Nauru airfield 55 30
ANNIVERSARIES: Nos. 200, 203, 75th anniv of powered flight; 201/2, 50th anniv of Kingsford-Smith's Pacific flight.

56 Sir Rowland Hill and Marshall Islands 10pf. stamp of 1901

1979. Death Cent of Sir Rowland Hill. Mult.
204 5c. Type **56** 15 10
205 15c. Sir Rowland Hill and "Nauru" opt on G.B. 10s. "Seahorse" stamp of 1916–23 . . . . 25 20
206 60c. Sir Rowland Hill and Nauru 60c. 10th anniv of Independence stamp, 1978 55 40
MS207 159 × 101 mm. Nos. 204/6 85 1·25

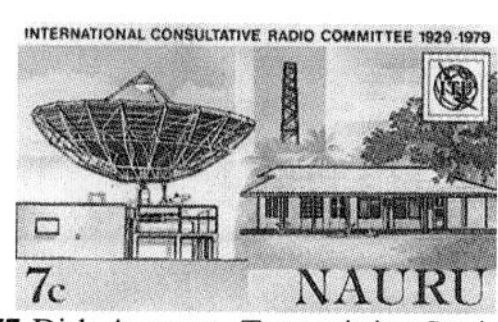

57 Dish Antenna, Transmitting Station and Radio Mast

1979. 50th Anniv of International Consultative Radio Committee. Multicoloured.
208 7c. Type **57** 15 10
209 32c. Telex operator 35 25
210 40c. Radio operator 40 25

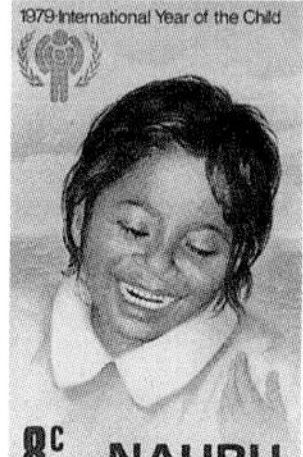

58 Smiling Child

1979. International Year of the Child.
211 **58** 8c. multicoloured 10 10
212 – 15c. multicoloured 15 15
213 – 25c. multicoloured 20 20
214 – 32c. multicoloured 20 20
215 – 50c. multicoloured 25 25
DESIGNS: 15c. to 50c. Smiling children.

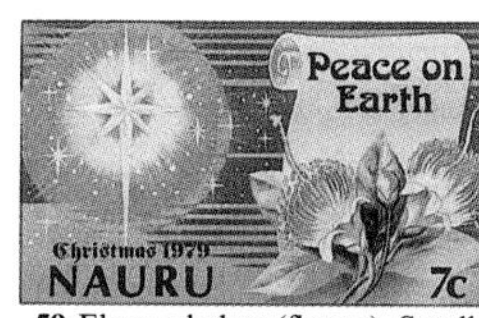

59 Ekwenababae (flower), Scroll inscribed "Peace on Earth" and Star

1979. Christmas. Multicoloured.
216 7c. Type **59** 10 10
217 15c. "Thespia populnea" (flower), scroll inscribed "Goodwill towards Men" and star 10 10
218 20c. Denea (flower), scroll inscribed "Peace on Earth" and star 10 10
219 30c. Erekogo (flower), scroll inscribed "Goodwill toward Men" and star 20 20

60 Dassault Bregeut Mystere Falcon 50 over Melbourne

1980. 10th Anniv of Air Nauru. Multicoloured.
220 15c. Type **60** 35 15
221 20c. Fokker F.28 Fellowship over Tarawa 40 15
222 25c. Boeing 727-100 over Hong Kong 40 15
223 30c. Boeing 737 over Auckland 40 15

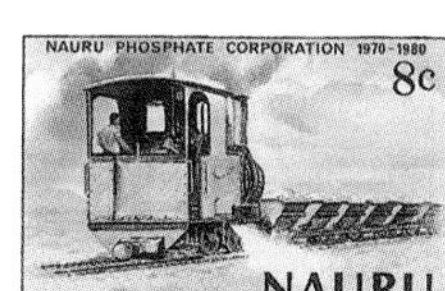

61 Steam Locomotive

1980. 10th Anniv of Nauru Phosphate Corporation. Multicoloured.
224 8c. Type **61** 10 10
225 32c. Electric locomotive . . . 20 20
226 60c. Diesel-hydraulic locomotive 35 35
MS227 168 × 118 mm. Nos. 224/6 1·00 2·50
No. **MS**227 also commemorates the "London 1980" International Stamp Exhibition.

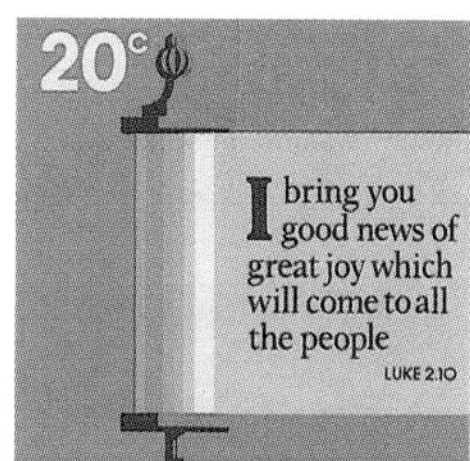

62 Verse 10 from Luke, Chapter 2 in English

1980. Christmas. Verses from Luke, Chapter 2. Multicoloured.
228 20c. Type **62** 10 10
229 20c. Verse 10 in Nauruan . . 10 10
230 30c. Verse 14 in English . . . 15 15
231 30c. Verse 14 in Nauruan . . 15 15
See also Nos. 248/51.

63 Nauruan, Australia, Union and New Zealand Flags on Aerial View of Nauru

1980. 20th Anniv of U.N. Declaration on the Granting of Independence to Colonial Countries and Peoples. Multicoloured.
232 25c. Type **63** 15 15
233 50c. U.N. Trusteeship Council (72 × 23 mm) . . . 15 15
234 50c. Nauru independence ceremony, 1968 (72 × 23 mm) 25 25

64 Timothy Detudamo

1981. 30th Anniv of Nauru Local Government Council. Head Chiefs. Multicoloured.
235 20c. Type **64** 15 15
236 30c. Raymond Gadabu . . . 15 15
237 50c. Hammer DeRoburt . . 25 25

65 Casting Net by Hand

1981. Fishing. Multicoloured.
238 8c. Type **65** 15 10
239 20c. Outrigger canoe 25 15
240 32c. Outboard motor boat . . 35 20
241 40c. Trawler 35 25
MS242 167 × 116 mm. No. 241 × 4 2·25 2·00
No. **MS**242 was issued to commemorate the "WIPA 1981" International Stamp Exhibition, Vienna.

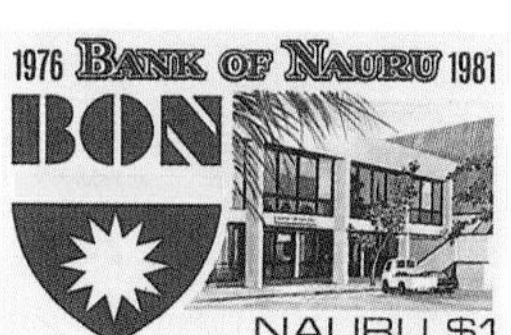

66 Bank of Nauru Emblem and Building

1981. 5th Anniv of Bank of Nauru.
243 **66** $1 multicoloured 60 60

67 Inaugural Speech

1981. U.N. Day. E.S.C.A.P. (United Nations Economic and Social Commission for Asia and the Pacific) Events. Multicoloured.
244 15c. Type **67** 15 15
245 20c. Presenting credentials . . 15 15
246 25c. Unveiling plaque 20 20
247 30c. Raising U.N. flag . . . 25 25

1981. Christmas. Bible Verses. Designs as T **62**. Multicoloured.
248 20c. Matthew 1, 23 in English 15 15
249 20c. Matthew 1, 23 in Nauruan 15 15
250 30c. Luke 2, 11 in English . . 20 20
251 30c. Luke 2, 11 in Nauruan 20 20

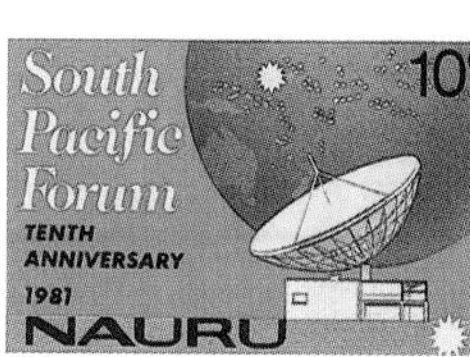

68 Earth Satellite Station

1981. 10th Anniv of South Pacific Forum. Mult.
252 10c. Type **68** 20 15
253 20c. "Enna G" (cargo liner) 25 20
254 30c. Boeing 737 airliner . . . 25 25
255 40c. Local produce 25 30

69 Nauru Scouts leaving for 1935 Frankston Scout Jamboree

1982. 75th Anniv of Boy Scout Movement. Mult.
256 7c. Type **69** 15 15
257 8c. Two Nauru scouts on "Nauru Chief", 1935 (vert) 15 15
258 15c. Nauru scouts making pottery, 1935 (vert) 15 20
259 20c. Lord Huntingfield addressing Nauru scouts, Frankston Jamboree, 1935 20 25
260 25c. Nauru cub and scout, 1982 . . . . 20 30
261 40c. Nauru cubs, scouts and scouters, 1982 . . . . . . 30 45
MS262 152 × 114 mm. Nos. 256/61. Imperf . . . . 1·25 2·25
No. **MS**262 also commemorates Nauru's participation in the "Stampex" National Stamp Exhibition, London.

70 100 kw Electricity Generating Plant under Construction (left side)

1982. Ocean Thermal Energy Conversion. Mult.
263 25c. Type **70** 50 30
264 25c. 100 kw Electricity Generating Plant under construction (right side) . . 50 30
265 40c. Completed plant (left) 70 40
266 40c. Completed plant (right) 70 40
Nos. 263/4 and 265/6 were each issued as horizontal se-tenant pairs, forming composite designs.

71 S.S. "Fido"

1982. 75th Anniv of Phosphate Shipments. Mult.
267 5c. Type **71** 40 10
268 10c. Steam locomotive "Nellie" 50 20
269 30c. Class "Clyde" diesel locomotive 60 50
270 60c. M.V. "Eigamoiya" (bulk carrier) 65 80
MS271 165 × 107 mm. $1 "Eigamoiya", "Rosie-D" and "Kolle-D" (bulk carriers) (67 × 27 mm) . . . . 1·50 2·25
No. **MS**271 was issued to commemorate "ANPEX 82" National Stamp Exhibition, Brisbane.

72 Queen Elizabeth II on Horseback

1982. Royal Visit. Multicoloured.
272 20c. Type **72** 30 20
273 50c. Prince Philip, Duke of Edinburgh 40 45
274 $1 Queen Elizabeth II and Prince Philip (horiz) . . . 45 1·00

73 Father Bernard Lahn

1982. Christmas. Multicoloured.
275 10c. Type **73** 20 30
276 30c. Reverend Itubwa Amram 20 45
277 40c. Pastor James Aingimen 25 70
278 50c. Bishop Paul Mea . . . 30 1·00

74 Speaker of the Nauruan Parliament

75 Nauru Satellite Earth Station

1983. 15th Anniv of Independence. Mult.

279	15c. Type **74**	20	20
280	20c. Family Court in session	25	25
281	30c. Law Courts building (horiz)	25	25
282	50c. Parliamentary chamber (horiz)	40	40

1983. World Communications Year. Mult.

283	5c. Type **75**	20	10
284	10c. Omni-directional range installation	20	15
285	20c. Emergency short-wave radio	25	25
286	25c. Radio Nauru control room	40	30
287	40c. Unloading air mail	90	45

76 Return of Exiles from Truk on M.V. "Trienza", 1946

1983. Angam Day. Multicoloured.

288	15c. Type **76**	20	25
289	20c. Mrs. Elsie Agio (exile community leader) (vert) (25 × 41 mm)	20	25
290	30c. Child on scales (vert) (25 × 41 mm)	35	40
291	40c. Nauruan children (vert) (25 × 41 mm)	45	50

77 "The Holy Virgin, Holy Child and St. John" (School of Raphael)

78 S.S. "Ocean Queen"

1983. Christmas. Multicoloured.

292	5c. Type **77**	10	10
293	15c. "Madonna on the Throne, surrounded by Angels" (School of Sevilla)	20	15
294	50c. "The Mystical Betrothal of St. Catherine with Jesus" (School of Veronese) (horiz)	60	40

1984. 250th Anniv of "Lloyd's List" (newspaper). Multicoloured.

295	20c. Type **78**	30	20
296	25c. M.V "Enna G"	35	25
297	30c. M.V "Baron Minto"	40	30
298	40c. Sinking of M.V. "Triadic", 1940	50	45

79 1974 U.P.U. $1 Stamp

1984. Universal Postal Union Congress, Hamburg.

299	**79**	$1 multicoloured	70	1·25

80 "Hypolimnas bolina" (female)

1984. Butterflies. Multicoloured.

300	25c. Type **80**	35	40
301	30c. "Hypolimnas bolina" (male)	35	55
302	50c. "Danaus plexippus"	40	85

81 Coastal Scene

1984. Life in Nauru. Multicoloured.

303	1c. Type **81**	10	40
304	3c. Nauruan woman (vert)	15	40
305	5c. Modern trawler	40	50
306	10c. Golfer on the links	90	50
307	15c. Excavating phosphate (vert)	90	65
308	20c. Surveyor (vert)	65	55
309	25c. Air Nauru Boeing 727 airliner	80	55
310	30c. Elderly Nauruan (vert)	50	50
311	40c. Loading hospital patient onto Boeing 727 aircraft	90	55
312	50c. Skin-diver with fish (vert)	1·00	80
313	$1 Tennis player (vert)	2·50	3·25
314	$2 Anabar Lagoon	2·50	3·75

82 Buada Chapel

1984. Christmas. Multicoloured.

315	30c. Type **82**	40	50
316	40c. Detudamo Memorial Church	50	65
317	50c. Candle-light service, Kayser College (horiz)	60	70

83 Air Nauru Boeing 737 Jet on Tarmac

1985. 15th Anniv of Air Nauru. Multicoloured.

318	20c. Type **83**	50	35
319	30c. Stewardesses on Boeing 737 aircraft steps (vert)	60	60
320	40c. Fokker F.28 Fellowship over Nauru	75	75
321	50c. Freight being loaded onto Boeing 727 (vert)	85	85

84 Open Cut Mining

1985. 15th Anniv of Nauru Phosphate Corporation. Multicoloured.

322	20c. Type **84**	1·00	60
323	25c. Diesel locomotive hauling crushed ore	2·00	1·00
324	30c. Phosphate drying plant	1·75	1·00
325	50c. Early steam locomotive	2·50	1·75

85 Mother and Baby on Beach

86 Adult Common Noddy with Juvenile

1985. Christmas. Multicoloured.

326	50c. Beach scene	1·50	2·25
327	50c. Type **85**	1·50	2·25

Nos. 326/7 were printed together, se-tenant, forming a composite design.

1985. Birth Bicentenary of John J. Audubon (ornithologist). Common ("Brown") Noddy. Mult.

328	10c. Type **86**	35	35
329	20c. Adult and immature birds in flight	50	70
330	30c. Adults in flight	65	85
331	50c. "Brown Noddy" (John J. Audubon)	80	1·10

87 Douglas Motor Cycle

1986. Early Transport on Nauru. Multicoloured.

332	15c. Type **87**	80	70
333	20c. Primitive lorry	95	95
334	30c. German-built steam locomotive, 1910	1·50	1·50
335	40c. "Baby" Austin car	1·75	1·75

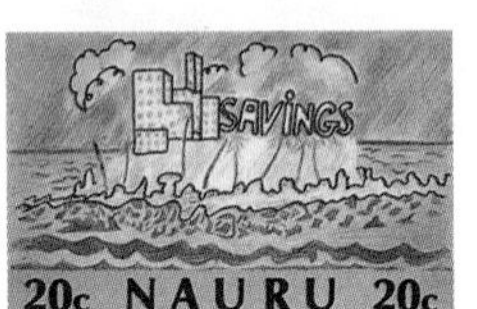

88 Island and Bank of Nauru

1986. 10th Anniv of Bank of Nauru. Children's Paintings. Multicoloured.

336	20c. Type **88**	20	30
337	25c. Borrower with notes and coins	25	35
338	30c. Savers	30	40
339	40c. Customers at bank counter	35	55

89 "Plumeria rubra"

1986. Flowers. Multicoloured.

340	20c. Type **89**	55	70
341	25c. "Tristellateia australis"	65	85
342	30c. "Bougainvillea cultivar"	75	1·00
343	40c. "Delonix regia"	1·00	1·25

90 Carol Singers

1986. Christmas. Multicoloured.

344	20c. Type **90**	40	30
345	$1 Carol singers and hospital patient	1·60	3·50

91 Young Girls Dancing

1987. Nauruan Dancers. Multicoloured.

346	20c. Type **91**	80	80
347	30c. Stick dance	1·00	1·25
348	50c. Boy doing war dance (vert)	1·75	2·50

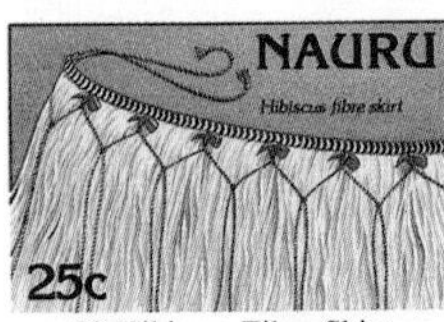
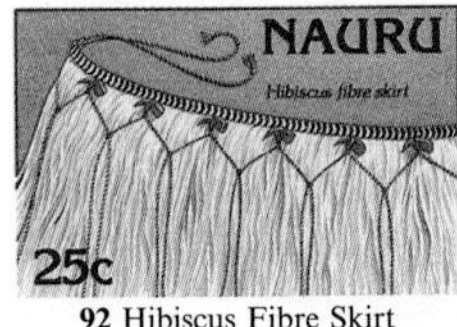

92 Hibiscus Fibre Skirt

1987. Personal Artefacts. Multicoloured.

349	25c. Type **92**	75	75
350	30c. Headband and necklets	85	85
351	45c. Decorative necklets	1·10	1·10
352	60c. Pandanus leaf fan	1·60	1·60

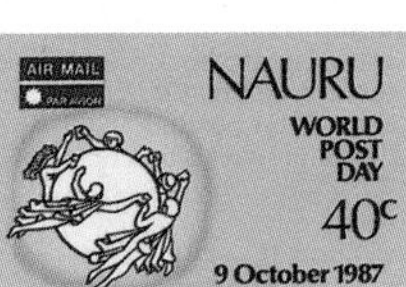

93 U.P.U. Emblem and Air Mail Label

94 Open Bible

1987. World Post Day.

353	**93**	40c. multicoloured	1·25	1·25
MS354		122 × 82 mm. $1 U.P.U. emblem and map of Pacific showing mail routes (114 × 74 mm)	2·50	3·25

1987. Centenary of Nauru Congregational Church.

355	**94**	40c. multicoloured	1·25	1·50

95 Nauruan Children's Party

1987. Christmas. Multicoloured.

356	20c. Type **95**	75	50
357	$1 Nauruan Christmas dinner	2·75	3·25

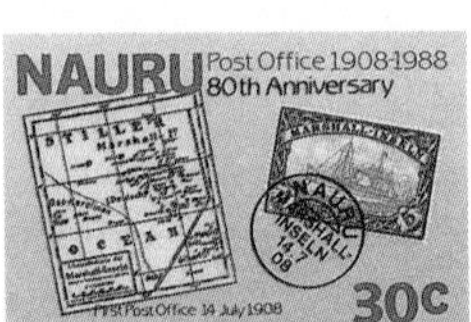

96 Loading Phosphate on Ship

1988. 20th Anniv of Independence. Mult.

358	25c. Type **96**	1·00	1·00
359	40c. Tomano flower (vert)	1·50	1·50
360	55c. Great frigate bird (vert)	2·25	2·25
361	$1 Arms of Republic (35 × 35 mm)	2·50	3·50

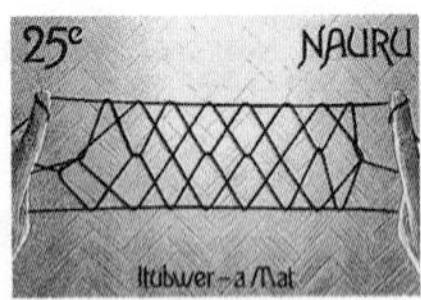

97 Map of German Marshall Is. and 1901 5m. Yacht Definitive

1988. 80th Anniv of Nauru Post Office. Mult.

362	30c. Type **97**	75	75
363	50c. Letter and post office of 1908	1·00	1·25
364	70c. Nauru Post Office and airmail letter	1·25	1·50

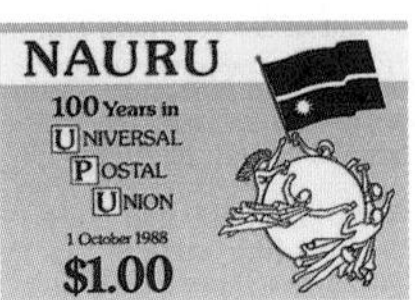

98 "Itubwer" (mat)

1988. String Figures. Multicoloured.

365	25c. Type **98**	35	35
366	40c. "Etegerer – the Pursuer"	50	60
367	55c. "Holding up the Sky"	65	70
368	80c. "Manujie's Sword"	1·00	1·75

99 U.P.U. Emblem and National Flag

1988. Cent of Nauru's Membership of U.P.U.

369	**99**	$1 multicoloured	1·25	1·25

100 "Hark the Herald Angels"

1988. Christmas. Designs showing words and music from "Hark the Herald Angels Sing".
370 **100** 20c. black, red and yellow . . . 50 30
371 – 60c. black, red and mauve . . . 1·25 1·00
372 – $1 black, red and green . . . 1·90 1·90

101 Logo (15th anniv of Nauru Insurance Corporation)

102 Mother and Baby

1989. Anniversaries and Events. Multicoloured.
373 15c. Type **101** 30 30
374 50c. Logos (World Telecommunications Day and 10th anniv of Asian-Pacific Telecommunity) . . 75 85
375 $1 Photograph of island scene (150 years of photography) . . . . . . 1·75 2·00
376 $2 Capitol and U.P.U. emblem (20th U.P.U. Congress, Washington) . . 2·75 4·00

1989. Christmas. Multicoloured.
377 20c. Type **102** 50 30
378 $1 Children opening presents 2·25 3·25

103 Eigigu working while Sisters play

104 Early Mining by Hand

1989. 20th Anniv of First Manned Landing on Moon. Legend of "Eigigu, the Girl in the Moon". Multicoloured.
379 25c. Type **103** . . . . 3·00 2·75
380 30c. Eigigu climbing tree . . 3·25 3·00
381 50c. Eigigu stealing toddy from blind woman . . . . 6·00 5·50
382 $1 Eigigu on Moon . . . . 8·00 7·50

1990. 20th Anniv of Nauru Phosphate Corporation. Multicoloured.
383 50c. Type **104** 75 75
384 $1 Modern mining by excavator . . . . 1·25 2·00

105 Sunday School Class

106 Eoiyepiang laying Baby on Mat

1990. Christmas. Multicoloured.
385 25c. Type **105** . . . . 90 1·25
386 25c. Teacher telling Christmas story . . . . . 90 1·25

Nos. 385/6 were printed together, se-tenant, forming a composite design.

1990. Legend of "Eoiyepiang, the Daughter of Thunder and Lightning". Multicoloured.
387 25c. Type **106** . . . . 1·25 60
388 30c. Eoiyepiang making floral decoration . . . . 1·50 70
389 50c. Eoiyepiang left on snow-covered mountain . . . . 2·00 2·00
390 $1 Eoiyepiang and warrior 3·00 3·50

107 Oleander

1991. Flowers. Multicoloured.
391 15c. Type **107** 10 15
392 20c. Lily 15 20
393 25c. Passion flower 20 25
394 30c. Lily (different) 20 25
395 35c. Caesalpinia 25 30
396 40c. Clerodendron 30 35
397 45c. "Baubina pinnata" . . . 30 35
398 50c. Hibiscus (vert) 35 40
399 75c. Apocymaceae 55 60
400 $1 Bindweed (vert) 70 75
401 $2 Tristellateia (vert) . . . . 1·40 1·50
402 $3 Impala lily (vert) . . . . 2·10 2·25

108 Jesus Christ and Children (stained glass window)

1991. Christmas. Sheet 124 × 82 mm.
MS403 **108** $2 multicoloured . . 4·00 4·50

109 Star and Symbol of Asian Development Bank

1992. 25th Annual Meeting of Asian Development Bank.
404 **109** $1.50 multicoloured . . . 2·00 2·50

110 Gifts under Christmas Tree

1992. Christmas. Children's Paintings. Mult.
405 45c. Type **110** 75 75
406 60c. Father Christmas in sleigh . . . . 1·00 1·50

111 Hammer DeRoburt

112 Running, Constitution Day Sports

1993. 25th Anniv of Independence and Hammer DeRoburt (former President) Commemoration.
407 **111** $1 multicoloured . . . . 2·50 3·00

1993. 15th Anniv of Constitution Day. Mult.
408 70c. Type **112** . . . . 1·40 1·40
409 80c. Part of Independence Proclamation . . . . . . 1·40 1·40

113 Great Frigate Birds, Flying Fish and Island

1993. 24th South Pacific Forum Meeting, Nauru. Multicoloured.
410 60c. Type **113** . . . . 1·40 1·50
411 60c. Red-tailed tropic bird, great frigate bird, dolphin and island . . . . 1·40 1·50
412 60c. Racoon butterflyfish ("Ikimago"), coral and sea urchins . . . . 1·40 1·50
413 60c. Three different types of fish with corals . . . . . 1·40 1·50
MS414 140 × 130 mm. Nos. 410/13 7·00 8·00

Nos. 410/13 were printed together, se-tenant, forming a composite design.

114 "Peace on Earth, Goodwill to Men" and Star

1993. Christmas. Multicoloured.
415 55c. Type **114** 85 85
416 65c. "Hark the Herald Angels Sing" and star 90 90

115 Girls with Dogs

1994. "Hong Kong '94" International Stamp Exhibition. Chinese New Year ("Year of the Dog"). Multicoloured.
417 $1 Type **115** . . . . 1·50 2·00
418 $1 Boys with dogs . . . . . 1·50 2·00
MS419 100 × 75 mm. Nos. 417/18 3·00 3·75

1994. "Singpex '94" National Stamp Exhibition, Singapore. No. **MS**419 optd "SINGPEX '94" and emblem in gold on sheet margin.
MS420 100 × 75 mm. Nos. 417/18 3·00 3·75

116 Weightlifting

117 Peace Dove and Star over Island

1994. 15th Commonwealth Games, Victoria, Canada.
421 **116** $1.50 multicoloured . . . 1·40 2·00

1994. Christmas. Multicoloured.
422 65c. Type **117** 60 65
423 75c. Star over Bethlehem . . 70 85

118 Air Nauru Airliner and Emblems

1994. 50th Anniv of I.C.A.O. Multicoloured.
424 55c. Type **118** 50 55
425 65c. Control tower, Nauru International Airport . . . 60 65
426 80c. D.V.O.R. equipment . . 70 1·00
427 $1 Crash tenders . . . . . . 90 1·10
MS428 165 × 127 mm. Nos. 424/7 4·00 4·50

119 Emblem and Olympic Rings

1994. Nauru's Entry into Int Olympic Committee.
429 **119** 50c. multicoloured 50 50

120 Nauruan Flag

1995. 50th Anniv of United Nations (1st issue). Multicoloured.
430 75c. Type **120** . . . . 1·40 1·40
431 75c. Arms of Nauru . . . . 1·40 1·40
432 75c. Outrigger canoe on coastline . . . . 1·40 1·40
433 75c. Airliner over phosphate freighter . . . . 1·40 1·40
MS434 110 × 85 mm. Nos. 430/3 4·50 5·50

Nos. 430/3 were printed together, se-tenant, forming a composite design.
See also Nos. 444/5.

121 Signing Phosphate Agreement, 1967

1995. 25th Anniv of Nauru Phosphate Corporation. Multicoloured.
435 60c. Type **121** . . . . 80 1·00
436 60c. Pres. Bernard Dowiyogo and Prime Minister Keating of Australia shaking hands . . . . . . 80 1·00
MS437 120 × 80 mm. $2 Excavating phosphate . . . . 2·75 3·25

1995. International Stamp Exhibitions. No. 309 surch.
438 50c. on 25c. multicoloured (surch **at Beijing**) . . . . . 1·40 1·40
439 $1 on 25c. multicoloured (surch **at Jakarta**) . . . . 1·40 1·75
440 $1 on 25c. multicoloured (surch **at Singapore**) . . . 1·40 1·75

123 Sea Birds (face value at top right)

1995. Olympic Games, Atlanta. Sheet 140 × 121 mm, containing T **123** and similar vert designs. Multicoloured.
MS441 60c.+15c. Type **123**; 60c.+15c. Sea brids (face value at top left); 60c.+15c. Four dolphins; 60c.+15c. Pair of dolphins . . 4·00 4·50

The premiums on No. **MS**441 were for Nauru sport development.

124 Children playing on Gun

1995. 50th Anniv of Peace. Multicoloured
442 75c. Type **124** . . . . 1·75 2·00
443 $1.50 Children making floral garlands . . . . 1·75 2·00

125 Nauru Crest, Coastline and U.N. Anniversary Emblem

126 Young Girl praying

1995. 50th Anniv of United Nations (2nd issue). Multicoloured.
444 75c. Type **125** . . . . 90 1·00
445 $1.50 Aerial view of Nauru and U.N. Headquarters, New York . . . . 1·60 2·00

1995. Christmas. Multicoloured.
446 60c. Type **126** . . . . 90 1·00
447 70c. Man praying . . . . . 90 1·00

127 Returning Refugees and Head Chief Timothy Detudamo

1996. 50th Anniv of Nauruans' Return from Truk.
448 **127** 75c. multicoloured . . . . 90 1·00
449 $1.25 multicoloured . . . 1·60 2·00
MS450 120 × 80 mm. Nos. 448/9 3·00 3·50

128 Nanjing Stone Lion

1996. "CHINA '96" 9th Asian International Stamp Exhibition, Peking. Sheet 130 × 110 mm.
MS451 **128** 45c. multicoloured 80 1·00

129 Symbolic Athlete

1996. Centenary of Modern Olympic Games. Mult.
452 40c. Type **129** 90 70
453 50c. Symbolic weightlifter . . 1·00 90
454 60c. Weightlifter (horiz) . . . 1·10 1·00
455 $1 Athlete (horiz) . . . . . 1·50 2·00

130 The Nativity and Angel

1996. Christmas. Multicoloured.
456 50c. Type **130** 60 60
457 70c. Angel, world map and wild animals . . . . 80 1·00

131 Dolphin (fish)

1997. Endangered Species. Fishes. Multicoloured.
458 20c. Type **131** 75 75
459 30c. Wahoo 80 80
460 40c. Sailfish 85 85
461 50c. Yellow-finned tuna . . . 90 90

132 Statue of Worshipper with Offering

133 Princess Elizabeth and Lieut. Philip Mountbatten, 1947

1997. "HONG KONG '97" International Stamp Exhibition. Statues of different worshippers (1c. to 15c.) or Giant Buddha of Hong Kong (25c.).
462 **132** 1c. multicoloured 20 20
463 – 2c. multicoloured 20 20
464 – 5c. multicoloured 25 25
465 – 10c. multicoloured 30 30
466 – 12c. multicoloured 30 30
467 – 15c. multicoloured 30 30
468 – 25c. multicoloured 40 40

1997. Golden Wedding of Queen Elizabeth and Prince Philip.
469 **133** 80c. black and gold . . . 90 1·00
470 – $1.20 multicoloured . . . 1·40 1·60
MS471 150 × 110 mm. Nos. 469/70 (sold at $3) . . . . 3·00 3·50
DESIGN: $1.20, Queen Elizabeth and Prince Philip, 1997.

134 Conference Building

1997. 28th Parliamentary Conference of Presiding Officers and Clerks. Sheet 150 × 100 mm.
MS472 **134** $2 multicoloured . . 1·75 2·00

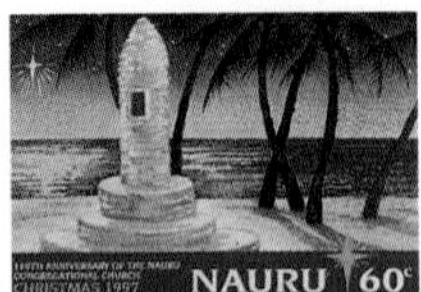

135 Commemorative Pillar

1997. Christmas. 110th Anniv of Nauru Congregational Church. Multicoloured.
473 60c. Type **135** 60 55
474 80c. Congregational Church 80 90

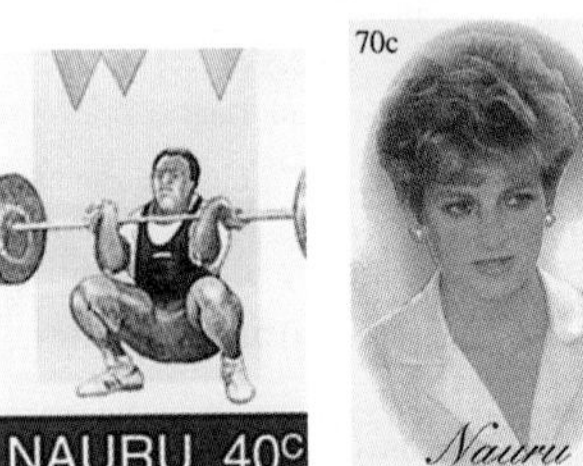

136 Weightlifter

138 Diana, Princess of Wales

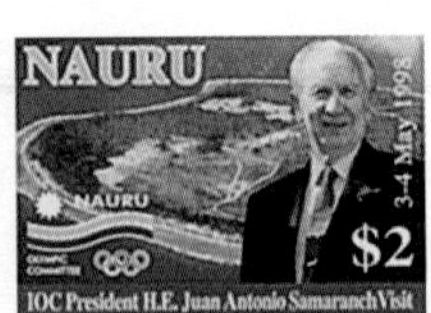

137 Juan Antonio Samaranch and Aerial View

1998. Commonwealth, Oceania and South Pacific Weightlifting Championships, Nauru. Sheet 180 × 100 mm, containing T **136** and similar vert designs showing weightlifters.
MS475 40c., 60c., 80c., $1.20 multicoloured . . . . 2·25 2·75

1998. Visit of International Olympic Committee President.
476 **137** $2 multicoloured . . . . 1·75 2·00

1998. Diana, Princess of Wales Commemoration. Multicoloured.
477 70c. Type **138** 55 60
478 70c. Wearing white shirt . . 55 60
479 70c. With tiara 55 60
480 70c. In white jacket 55 60
481 70c. Wearing pink hat . . . 55 60
482 70c. In white suit 55 60

139 Gymnastics

140 Sqn. Ldr. Hicks (Composer of Nauru's National Anthem) conducting

1998. 16th Commonwealth Games, Kuala Lumpur, Malaysia. Multicoloured.
483 40c. Type **139** 40 40
484 60c. Athletics 55 60
485 70c. Sprinting 65 70
486 80c. Weightlifting 70 80
MS487 153 × 130 mm. Nos. 483/6 1·90 2·40

1998. 30th Anniv of Independence. Multicoloured.
488 $1 Type **140** 85 80
489 $2 Sqn. Ldr. Hicks and score 1·75 2·25
MS490 175 × 110 mm. Nos. 488/9 2·50 3·00

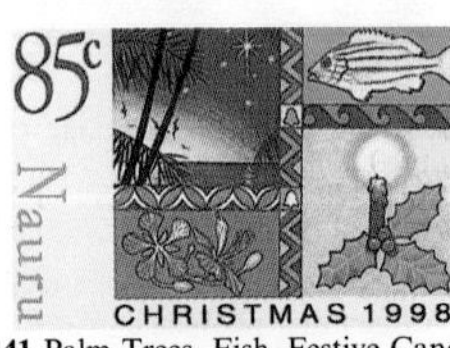

141 Palm Trees, Fish, Festive Candle and Flower

1998. Christmas. Multicoloured.
491 85c. Type **141** . . . . 80 1·00
492 95c. Flower, present, fruit and island scene . . . . . 85 1·00

142 18th-century Frigate

1998. Bicentenary of First Contact with the Outside World. Multicoloured.
493 $1.50 Type **142** . . . . . . 1·50 1·75
494 $1.50 Capt. John Fearn . . . 1·50 1·75
MS495 173 × 131 mm. Nos. 493/4 3·00 3·50
No. 493 is wrongly identified as "Hunter" (snow).

143 H.M.A.S. "Melbourne" (cruiser)

1999. "Australia '99" World Stamp Exhibition, Melbourne. Ships. Sheet 101 × 120 mm, containing T **143** and similar multicoloured designs.
MS496 70c. Type **143**; 80c. H.M.A.S. "D'Amantina" (frigate); 90c. "Alcyone" (experimental ship); $1 "Rosie-D" (bulk carrier); $1.10 Outrigger canoe (80 × 30 mm) . . . . 4·25 4·75

1999. 30th Anniv of First Manned Landing on Moon. As T **98a** of Kiribati. Multicoloured.
497 70c. Neil Armstrong (astronaut) 65 70
498 80c. Service and lunar module on way to Moon 70 80
499 90c. Aldrin and "Apollo 11" on Moon's surface . . . . 85 1·00
500 $1 Command module entering Earth's atmosphere . . . . 90 1·25
MS501 90 × 80 mm. $2 Earth as seen from Moon (circular, 40 mm diam) . . . . 1·90 2·40

144 Emblem and Forms of Transport

1999. 125th Anniv of Universal Postal Union.
502 **144** $1 multicoloured . . . . 1·00 1·25

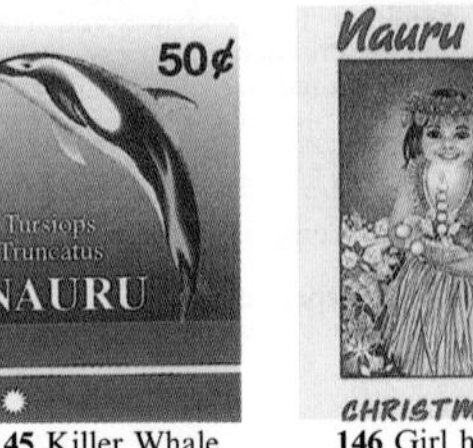

145 Killer Whale

146 Girl holding Candle

1999. "China '99" International Philatelic Exhibition, Beijing. Sheet 185 × 85 mm, containing T **145** and similar vert design. Multicoloured.
MS503 50c. Type **145**; 50c. Swordfish . . . . 1·00 1·40

1999. Christmas. Multicoloured.
504 65c. Type **146** 70 75
505 70c. Candle and Christmas tree 80 85

147 Nauruan Woman in Traditional Dress and Canoes

2000. New Millennium. Multicoloured.
506 70c. Type **147** 90 90
507 $1.10 Aspects of modern Nauru . . . . 1·50 1·50
508 $1.20 Woman holding globe and man at computer . . . 1·50 1·50
MS509 149 × 88 mm. Nos. 506/8 2·25 2·75

148 Power Plant

2000. Centenary of Phosphate Discovery. Mult.
510 $1.20 Type **148** . . . . . . 1·25 1·25
511 $1.80 Phosphate train . . . . 2·00 2·00
512 $2 Albert Ellis and phosphate sample . . . . 2·00 2·25
MS513 79 × 131 mm. Nos. 510/12 3·50 3·75

149 Queen Mother in Royal Blue Hat and Coat

150 Running and Sydney Opera House

2000. 100th Birthday of Queen Elizabeth the Queen Mother. Sheet 150 × 106 mm, containing T **149** and similar horiz designs, each including photograph of Queen Mother as a child. Multicoloured.
MS514 150 × 106 mm. $1 Type **149**; $1.10 In lilac hat and coat; $1.20 In turquoise hat and coat; $1.40 In greenish blue hat and coat with maple leaf brooch . . . . . . 3·25 3·50

2000. Olympic Games, Sydney. Multicoloured.
515 90c. Type **150** 85 85
516 $1 Basketball . . . . 1·00 90
517 $1.10 Weightlifting and cycling . . . . 1·25 1·10
518 $1.20 Running and Olympic Torch . . . . 1·25 1·40

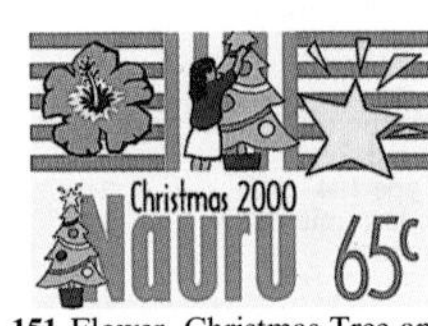

151 Flower, Christmas Tree and Star

2000. Christmas. Multicoloured.
519 65c. Type **151** 45 50
520 75c. Decorations, toy engine and palm tree 55 60
MS521 134 × 95 mm. Nos. 519/20 1·00 1·10

152 Noddy and Part of Island

2001. 32nd Pacific Islands Forum, Nauru. Multicoloured.
522 90c. Type **152** 65 70
523 $1 Frigate bird in flight and part of island 70 75
524 $1.10 Two frigate birds and part of island 80 85
525 $2 Frigate bird and Nauru airport . . . . 1·40 1·50
MS526 145 × 130 mm. Nos. 522/5 3·50 3·75
Nos. 522/5 were printed together, se-tenant, forming a composite view of Nauru.

153 Princess Elizabeth in A.T.S. Uniform, 1946

2002. Golden Jubilee.
527 **153** 70c. black, mauve and gold 50 55
528 – 80c. multicoloured 60 65

529 – 90c. black, mauve and gold 65 70
530 – $1 multicoloured 70 75
MS531 162 × 95 mm. Nos. 527/30 and $4 multicoloured . . . . . 5·50 5·75
DESIGNS—HORIZ: 80c. Queen Elizabeth in multicoloured hat; 90c. Princess Elizabeth at Cheltenham Races, 1951; $1 Queen Elizabeth in evening dress, 1997. VERT (38 x 51 mm)—$4 Queen Elizabeth after Annigoni.
Designs as Nos. 527/30 in No. **MS**531 omit the gold frame around each stamp and the "Golden Jubilee 1952–2002" inscription.

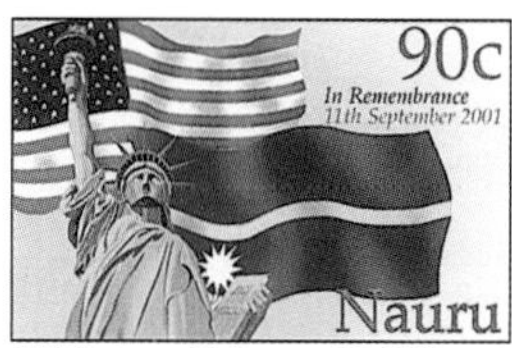

154 Statue of Liberty with U.S. and Nauru Flags

2002. In Remembrance. Victims of Terrorist Attacks on U.S.A. (11 September 2001).
532 **154** 90c. multicoloured 65 70
533 $1 multicoloured 70 75
534 $1.10 multicoloured . . . 80 85
535 $2 multicoloured . . . . 1·40 1·50

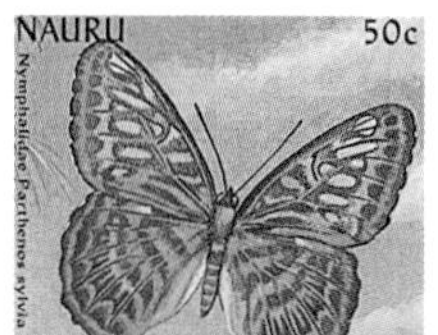

155 *Parthenos sylvia*

2002. Butterflies of the Pacific. Multicoloured.
536 50c. Type **155** 35 40
537 50c. *Delias madetes* 35 40
538 50c. *Danaus philene* 35 40
539 50c. *Arhopala hercules* . . . 35 40
540 50c. *Papilio canopus* 35 40
541 50c. *Danaus schenkii* 35 40
542 50c. *Pairthenos tigrina* . . . 35 40
543 50c. *Mycalesis phidon* 35 40
544 50c. *Vindula sapor* 35 40
MS545 85 × 60 mm. $2 *Graphium agamemnon* . . . . 1·40 1·50
Nos. 536/44 were printed together, se-tenant, forming a composite design.

156 Queen Elizabeth in London, 1940

2002. Queen Elizabeth the Queen Mother Commemoration.
546 **156** $1.50 black, gold and purple . . . . 1·10 1·25
547 – $1.50 multicoloured . . . 1·10 1·25
MS548 145 × 70 mm. Nos. 546/7 2·25 2·50
DESIGNS: No. 547, Queen Mother in Norwich, 1990.
Designs as Nos. 546/7 in No. **MS**548 omit the "1900--2002" inscription and the coloured frame.

157 Turntable Ladder and Burning Building

2002. International Firefighters. Multicoloured.
549 20c. Type **157** 15 20
550 50c. Firefighting tug and burning ship 35 40
551 90c. Fighting a forest fire . . 65 70
552 $1 Old and new helmets . . . 75 80
553 $1.10 Steam-driven pump and modern fire engine 80 85
554 $2 19th-century and present day hose teams . . . . . 1·40 1·50
MS555 110 × 90 mm. $5 Airport fire engine . . . . 3·50 3·75

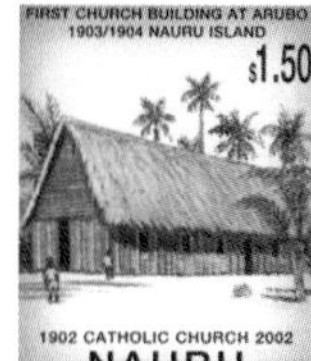

158 First Catholic Church, Arubo

2002. Centenary of Catholic Church on Nauru.
556 **158** $1.50 brown and black . . 1·10 1·25
557 – $1.50 violet and black . . 1·10 1·25
558 – $1.50 blue and black . . . 1·10 1·25
559 – $1.50 green and black . . 1·10 1·25
560 – $1.50 blue and black . . . 1·10 1·25
561 – $1.50 red and black . . . 1·10 1·25
DESIGNS: No. 557, Father Friedrich Gründl (first missionary); 558, Sister Stanisla; 559, Second Catholic church, Ibwenape; 560, Brother Kalixtus Bader (lay brother); 561, Father Alois Kayser (missionary).

159 "Holy Family with dancing Angels" (Van Dyck)

2002. Christmas. Religious Art. Multicoloured.
562 15c. Type **159** 10 15
563 $1 "Holy Virgin with Child" (Cornelis Bloemaert after Lucas Cangiasius) 70 75
564 $1.20 "Holy Family with Cat" (Rembrandt) 85 90
565 $3 "Holy Family with St. John" (Pierre Brebiette after Raphael) . . . . . . 2·10 2·25

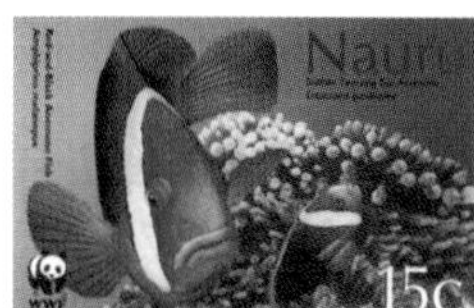

160 Bubble Tentacle Sea Anemone and Fire Anemonefish ("Red-and-Black Anemone Fish")

2003. Endangered Species. Sea Anemones and Anemonefish. Multicoloured.
566 15c. Type **160** 10 15
567 $1 Leathery sea anemone and orange-finned anemonefish 70 75
568 $1.20 Magnificent sea anemone and pink anemonefish 85 90
569 $3 Merten's sea anemone and yellow-tailed anemonefish ("Clark's Anemone Fish") 2·10 2·25

NAWANAGAR Pt. 1

A state of India, Bombay District. Now uses Indian stamps.

6 docra = 1 anna.

1 (1 docra) **2** (2 docra)

1877. Imperf or perf.
1 **1** 1doc. blue . . . . 50 22·00

1880. Imperf.
6ab **2** 1doc. lilac . . . . 2·75 6·00
8 c 2doc. green . . . . 3·50 8·50
9 b 3doc. yellow . . . . 4·75 9·50

4 (1 docra)

1893. Imperf or perf.
13 **4** 1doc. black . . . . 1·00 4·50
14 2doc. green . . . . 1·25 5·00
15b 3doc. yellow . . . . 1·25 8·50

NEAPOLITAN PROVINCES Pt. 8

Temporary issues for Naples and other parts of S. Italy which adhered to the new Kingdom of Italy in 1860.

200 tornesi = 100 grano = 1 ducato.

1

1861. Embossed. Imperf.
2 **1** $\frac{1}{2}$t. green . . . . 9·25 £140
5 $\frac{1}{2}$g. brown £130 £150
9 1g. black . . . . £325 19·00
10 2g. blue . . . . 80·00 9·50
15 5g. red . . . . £140 90·00
18 10g. orange £100 £170
19 20g. yellow £425 £1600
23 50g. slate . . . . 23·00 £7000

NEGRI SEMBILAN Pt. 1

A state of the Federation of Malaya, incorporated in Malaysia in 1963.

100 cents = 1 dollar (Straits or Malayan).

1891. Stamp of Straits Settlements optd **Negri Sembilan**.
1 **5** 2c. red . . . . 3·00 4·75

2 Tiger **3**

1891.
2 **2** 1c. green . . . . 3·00 1·00
3 2c. red . . . . 3·25 7·00
4 5c. blue . . . . 30·00 40·00

1896.
5 **3** 1c. purple and green . . . . 8·50 4·50
6 2c. purple and brown . . . . 35·00 £110
7 3c. purple and red . . . . . 13·00 1·00
8 5c. purple and yellow . . . . 8·00 7·00
9 8c. purple and blue . . . . . 29·00 16·00
10 10c. purple and orange . . . 27·00 14·00
11 15c. green and violet . . . . 40·00 75·00
12 20c. green and olive . . . . 60·00 38·00
13 25c. green and red . . . . . 70·00 90·00
14 50c. green and black . . . . 65·00 65·00

1898. Surch in words and bar.
15 **3** 1c. on 15c. green and violet 90·00 £180
16 **2** 4c. on 1c. green . . . . . . 1·75 15·00
17 **3** 4c. on 3c. purple and red . . 3·00 15·00
18 **2** 4c. on 5c. blue . . . . 1·25 15·00

1898. Surch in words only.
19 **3** 4c. on 8c. purple and blue . . 4·25 4·25

6 Arms of Negri Sembilan **7** Arms of Negri Sembilan

1935.
21 **6** 1c. black . . . . 1·00 20
22 2c. green . . . . 1·00 20
23 2c. orange . . . . 4·25 65·00
24 3c. green . . . . 8·00 8·00
25 4c. orange . . . . 1·00 10
26 5c. brown . . . . 1·75 10
27 6c. red . . . . 13·00 2·50
28 6c. grey . . . . 4·75 75·00
29 8c. grey . . . . 2·00 10
30 10c. purple 80 10
31 12c. blue . . . . 1·60 50
32 15c. blue . . . . 10·00 50·00
33 25c. purple and red . . . . . 1·25 70
34 30c. purple and orange . . . 3·50 2·00
35 40c. red and purple . . . . . 1·50 2·00
36 50c. black on green . . . . . 4·00 2·25
37 $1 black and red on blue . . 3·50 3·25
38 $2 green and red . . . . . . 30·00 16·00
39 $5 green and red on green . . 18·00 50·00

1948. Silver Wedding. As T **4b/c** of Pitcairn Islands.
40 10c. violet 15 50
41 $5 green . . . . 18·00 28·00

1949.
42 **7** 1c. black 20 10
43 2c. orange 20 10
44 3c. green 20 30
45 4c. brown 20 10
46a 5c. purple 30 45
47 6c. grey 50 10
48 8c. red 50 75
49 8c. green . . . . 1·75 1·60
50 10c. mauve 20 10
51 12c. red . . . . 1·75 2·75
52 15c. blue . . . . 3·00 10
53 20c. black and green 50 75
54 20c. blue . . . . 1·00 10
55 25c. purple and orange . . . 50 10
56 30c. red and purple . . . . 1·25 2·50
57 35c. red and purple . . . . 1·00 1·00
58 40c. red and purple . . . . 1·25 4·75
59 50c. black and blue . . . . 1·75 20
60 $1 blue and purple . . . . . 3·75 2·25
61 $2 green and red . . . . . 12·00 16·00
62 $5 green and brown . . . . 50·00 40·00

1949. U.P.U. As T **4d/g** of Pitcairn Islands.
63 10c. purple 20 10
64 15c. blue . . . . 1·10 2·50
65 25c. orange . . . . 30 2·25
66 50c. black . . . . 60 3·00

1953. Coronation. As T **4h** of Pitcairn Islands.
67 10c. black and purple . . . . 1·00 40

1957. As Nos. 92/102 of Kedah but inset Arms of Negri Sembilan.
68 1c. black 10 10
69 2c. red 10 10
70 4c. sepia 10 10
71 5c. lake 10 10
72 8c. green . . . . 1·00 1·40
73 10c. sepia . . . . 1·50 10
74 10c. purple . . . . 4·00 10
75 20c. blue 75 10
76a 50c. black and blue 60 10
77 $1 blue and purple . . . . . 1·50 2·00
78 $2 green and red . . . . . . 6·50 15·00
79 $5 brown and green . . . . 11·00 17·00

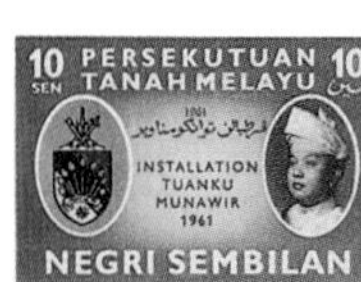

8 Tuanku Munawir

1961. Installation of Tuanku Munawir as Yang di-Pertuan Besar of Negri Sembilan.
80 **8** 10c. multicoloured 30 60

9 "Vanda hookeriana"

1965. As Nos. 115/21 of Kedah but with Arms of Negri Sembilan inset and inscr "NEGERI SEMBILAN" as in T **6**.
81 **9** 1c. multicoloured . . . . . 10 1·40
82 – 2c. multicoloured . . . . . 10 1·40
83 – 5c. multicoloured 40 10
84 – 6c. multicoloured 40 60
85 – 10c. multicoloured 40 10
86 – 15c. multicoloured 80 10
87 – 20c. multicoloured . . . . . 1·25 1·00
The higher values used in Negri Sembilan were Nos. 20/7 of Malaysia (National Issues).

10 Negri Sembilan Crest and Tuanku Ja'afar

1968. Installation of Tuanku Ja'afar as Yang di-Pertuan Besar of Negri Sembilan.
88 **10** 15c. multicoloured 15 70
89 50c. multicoloured . . . . . 30 1·40

11 "Hebomoia glaucippe"

1971. Butterflies. As Nos. 124/30 of Kedah but with Arms of Negri Sembilan inset as T **11** and inscr "negeri sembilan".
91 – 1c. multicoloured . . . . . 40 1·75
92 – 2c. multicoloured . . . . . 60 1·75
93 – 5c. multicoloured 90 20
94 – 6c. multicoloured . . . . . 90 1·75
95 **11** 10c. multicoloured 90 10
96 – 15c. multicoloured . . . . . 1·25 10
97 – 20c. multicoloured . . . . . 1·25 50
The higher values in use with this issue were Nos. 64/71 of Malaysia (National Issues).

12 "Hibiscus rosa-sinensis" **13** Oil Palm

1979. Flowers. As Nos. 135/41 of Kedah but with Arms of Negri Sembilan and inscr "negeri sembilan" as in T **12**.

103		1c. "Rafflesia hasseltii"	10	1·00
104		2c. "Pterocarpus indicus"	10	1·00
105		5c. "Lagerstroemia speciosa"	15	30
106		10c. "Durio zibethinus"	20	10
107		15c. Type **12**	20	10
108		20c. "Rhododendron scortechinii"	25	10
109		25c. "Etlingera elatior" (inscr "Phaeomeria speciosa")	45	25

1986. As Nos. 152/8 of Kedah but with Arms of Negri Sembilan and inscr "NEGERI SEMBILAN" as T **13**.

117		1c. Coffee	10	10
118		2c. Coconuts	10	10
119		5c. Cocoa	10	10
120		10c. Black pepper	10	10
121		15c. Rubber	10	10
122		20c. Type **13**	10	15
123		30c. Rice	10	15

NEPAL Pt. 21

An independent kingdom in the Himalayas N. of India.

1861. 16 annas = 1 rupee.
1907. 64 pice = 1 rupee.
1954. 100 paisa = 1 rupee.

1 (1a.) Crown and Kukris **2** (½a.) Bow and Arrow and Kukris **3** Siva Mahadeva (2p.)

1881. Imperf or pin-perf.

34	**2**	½a. black	2·00	1·00
35		½a. orange	£300	£120
42	**1**	1a. blue	4·00	1·60
14		1a. green	26·00	26·00
16c		2a. violet	12·00	12·00
40		2a. brown	5·00	3·00
41		4a. green	4·00	4·00

1907. Various sizes.

57	**3**	2p. brown	20	20
58		4p. green	60	40
59		8p. red	40	30
60		16p. purple	3·00	1·50
61		24p. orange	3·00	1·00
62		32p. blue	5·00	1·25
63		1r. red	9·00	4·00
50		5r. black and brown	14·00	8·00

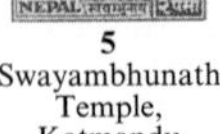

5 Swayambhunath Temple, Katmandu **7** Guheswari Temple, Patan

8 Sri Pashupati (Siva Mahadeva)

1949.

64	**5**	2p. brown	50	40
65	–	4p. green	50	40
66	–	6p. pink	1·00	40
67	–	8p. red	1·00	60
68	–	16p. purple	1·00	60
69	–	20p. blue	2·00	1·00
70	**7**	24p. red	1·60	60
71	–	32p. blue	3·00	1·00
72	**8**	1r. orange	12·00	6·00

DESIGNS—As Type **5**: 4p. Pashupatinath Temple, Katmandu; 6p. Tri-Chundra College; 8p. Mahabuddha Temple. 26 × 30 mm: 16p. Krishna Mandir Temple, Patan. As Type **7**: 20p. View of Katmandu; 32p. The twenty-two fountains, Balaju.

9 King Tribhuvana **10** Map of Nepal

1954. (a) Size 18 × 22 mm.

73	**9**	2p. brown	1·00	20
74		4p. green	2·00	60
75		6p. red	80	20
76		8p. lilac	60	20
77		12p. orange	4·00	1·00
		(b) Size 25½ × 29½ mm.		
78	**9**	16p. brown	80	20
79		20p. red	1·60	60
80		24p. purple	1·40	60
81		32p. blue	2·00	60
82		50p. mauve	9·00	3·00
83		1r. red	18·00	5·00
84		2r. orange	9·00	4·00
		(c) Size 30 × 18 mm.		
85	**10**	2p. brown	80	40
86		4p. green	2·00	60
87		6p. red	6·00	1·00
88		8p. lilac	60	40
89		12p. orange	6·00	1·00
		(d) Size 38 × 21½ mm.		
90	**10**	16p. brown	1·00	40
91		20p. red	1·60	40
92		24p. purple	1·25	40
93		32p. blue	3·00	80
94		50p. mauve	11·00	3·00
95		1r. red	20·00	4·00
96		2r. orange	9·00	4·00

11 Mechanization of Agriculture **13** Hanuman Dhoka, Katmandu

1956. Coronation.

97	**11**	4p. green	2·00	1·25
98	–	6p. red and yellow	1·25	60
99	–	8p. violet	80	40
100	**13**	24p. red	2·00	80
101	–	1r. red	55·00	48·00

DESIGNS—As Type **11**: 8p. Processional elephant. As Type **13**: 6p. Throne; 1r. King and Queen and mountains.

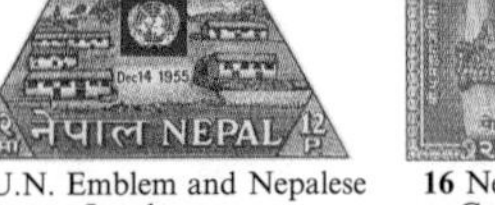

15 U.N. Emblem and Nepalese Landscape **16** Nepalese Crown

1956. 1st Anniv of Admission into U.N.O.

102	**15**	12p. blue and brown	2·75	1·60

1957. (a) Size 18 × 22 mm.

103	**16**	2p. brown	40	25
104		4p. green	60	40
105		6p. red	40	40
106		8p. violet	40	40
107		12p. red	2·25	60
		(b) Size 25½ × 29½ mm.		
108	**16**	16p. brown	3·00	1·00
109		20p. red	5·00	1·40
110		24p. mauve	3·00	1·25
111		32p. blue	4·00	1·40
112		50p. pink	7·00	3·00
113		1r. salmon	15·00	6·00
114		2r. orange	7·00	4·00

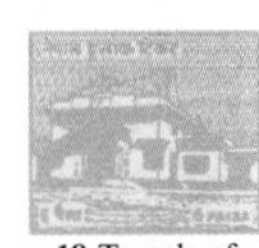

17 Gaunthali carrying Letter **18** Temple of Lumbini

1958. Air. Inauguration of Nepalese Internal Airmail Service.

115	**17**	10p. blue	1·10	1·10

1958. Human Rights Day.

116	**18**	6p. yellow	80	80

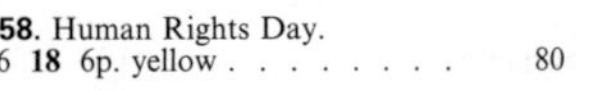

19 Nepalese Map and Flag

1959. 1st Nepalese Elections.

117	**19**	6p. red and green	30	25

20 Spinning Wheel **21** King Mahendra

1959. Cottage Industries.

118	**20**	2p. brown	25	25

1959. Admission of Nepal to U.P.U.

119	**21**	12p. blue	30	25

22 Vishnu **23** Nyatopol Temple, Bhaktapur

1959.

120	**22**	1p. brown	10	10
121	–	2p. violet	10	10
122	–	4p. blue	30	20
123	–	6p. pink	30	15
124	–	8p. brown	20	10
125	–	12p. grey	30	10
126	**23**	16p. violet and brown	30	10
127	–	20p. red and blue	1·00	40
128	**23**	24p. red and green	1·00	40
129		32p. blue and lilac	60	40
130		50p. green and red	1·00	40
131	–	1r. blue and brown	11·00	4·25
132	–	2r. blue and purple	13·00	6·25
133	–	5r. red and violet	90·00	75·00

DESIGNS—As Type **22**. HORIZ: 2p. Krishna; 8p. Siberian musk deer; 12p. Indian rhinoceros. VERT: 4p. Himalayas; 6p. Gateway, Bhaktapur Palace. As Type **23**. VERT: 1r., 2r. Himalayan monal pheasant; 5r. Satyr tragopan.

24 King Mahendra opening Parliament

1959. Opening of 1st Nepalese Parliament.

134	**24**	6p. red	60	60

25 Sri Pashupatinath **26** Children, Pagoda and Mt. Everest

1959. Renovation of Sri Pashupatinath Temple, Katmandu.

135	**25**	4p. green (18 × 25 mm)	40	40
136		8p. red (21 × 28½ mm)	60	40
137		1r. blue (24½ × 33½ mm)	5·00	3·25

1960. Children's Day.

137a	**26**	6p. blue	8·00	6·00

27 King Mahendra **28** Mt. Everest

1960. King Mahendra's 41st Birthday.

138	**27**	1r. purple	90	60

See also Nos. 163/4a.

1960. Mountain Views.

139	–	5p. brown and purple	20	10
140	**28**	10p. purple and blue	30	15
141	–	40p. brown and violet	70	45

DESIGNS: 5p. Machha Puchhre; 40p. Manaslu (wrongly inscr "MANSALU").

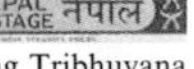

29 King Tribhuvana **30** Prince Gyanendra cancelling Children's Day Stamps of 1960

1961. 10th Democracy Day.

142	**29**	10p. orange and brown	10	10

1961. Children's Day.

143	**30**	12p. orange	20·00	20·00

31 King Mahendra **32** Campaign Emblem and House

1961. King Mahendra's 42nd Birthday.

144	**31**	6p. green	20	20
145		12p. blue	30	30
146		50p. red	60	60
147		1r. brown	1·00	1·00

1962. Malaria Eradication.

148	**32**	12p. blue	20	20
149	–	1r. orange and red	60	60

DESIGN: 1r. Emblem and Nepalese flag.

33 King Mahendra on Horseback **34** Bhana Bhakta Acharya

1962. King Mahendra's 43rd Birthday.

150	**33**	10p. blue	15	15
151		15p. brown	20	20
152		45p. brown	40	40
153		1r. grey	60	60

1962. Nepalese Poets.

154	**34**	5p. brown	20	20
155	–	10p. turquoise	20	20
156	–	40p. green	30	30

PORTRAITS: 10p. Moti Ram Bhakta; 40p. Sambhu Prasad.

35 King Mahendra **36** King Mahendra

1962.

157	**35**	1p. red	10	10
158		2p. blue	10	10
158a		3p. grey	30	20
159		5p. brown	10	10
160	**36**	10p. purple	10	10
161		40p. brown	20	20
162		75p. green	6·00	6·00
162a	**35**	75p. green	80	40
163	**27**	2r. red	80	80
164		5r. green	1·60	1·60
164a		10r. violet	6·00	5·00

No. 162a is smaller, 17½ × 20 mm.

37 Emblems of Learning

1963. U.N.E.S.C.O. "Education for All" Campaign.
165 **37** 10p. black 20 10
166 15p. brown 30 20
167 50p. blue 50 40

38 Hands holding Lamps

1963. National Day.
168 **38** 5p. blue 10 10
169 10p. brown 10 10
170 50p. purple 40 30
171 1r. green 80 40

39 Campaign Symbols

40 Map of Nepal and Open Hand

1963. Freedom from Hunger.
172 **39** 10p. orange 20 10
173 15p. blue 30 20
174 50p. green 60 40
175 1r. brown 80 70

1963. Rastruya Panchayat.
176 **40** 10p. green 10 10
177 15p. purple 20 20
178 50p. grey 50 30
179 1r. blue 80 50

41 King Mahendra

42 King Mahendra and Highway Map

1963. King Mahendra's 44th Birthday.
180 **41** 5p. violet 10 10
181 10p. brown 20 10
182 15p. green 30 20

1964. Inauguration of East–West Highway.
183 **42** 10p. orange and blue . . . 10 10
184 15p. orange and blue . . . 20 10
185 50p. brown and green . . . 30 20

43 King Mahendra at Microphone

44 Crown Prince Birendra

1964. King Mahendra's 45th Birthday.
186 **43** 1p. brown 10 10
187 2p. grey 10 10
188 2r. brown 60 60

1964. Crown Prince's 19th Birthday.
189 **44** 10p. green 50 40
190 15p. brown 50 40

45 Flag, Kukris, Rings and Torch

46 Nepalese Family

1964. Olympic Games, Tokyo.
191 **45** 10p. blue, red and pink . . 50 40

1965. Land Reform.
192 – 2p. black and green . . . 20 20
193 – 5p. brown and green . . . 20 20
194 – 10p. purple and grey . . . 20 20
195 **46** 15p. brown and yellow . . 30 30
DESIGNS: 2p. Farmer ploughing; 5p. Ears of wheat; 10p. Grain elevator.

47 Globe and Letters

48 King Mahendra

1965. Introduction of International Insured and Parcel Service.
196 **47** 15p. violet 20 20

1965. King Mahendra's 46th Birthday.
197 **48** 50p. purple 50 40

49 Four Martyrs

50 I.T.U. Emblem

1965. "Nepalese Martyrs".
198 **49** 15p. green 25 20

1965. I.T.U. Centenary.
199 **50** 15p. black and purple . . . 30 20

51 I.C.Y. Emblem

52 Devkota (poet)

1965. International Co-operation Year.
200 **51** 1r. multicoloured 60 50

1965. Devkota Commemoration.
201 **52** 15p. brown 20 20

54 Flag and King Mahendra

1966. Democracy Day.
202 **54** 15p. red and blue 40 30

55 Siva Parvati and Pashuvati Temple

1966. Maha Siva-Ratri Festival.
203 **55** 15p. violet 25 20

56 "Stamp" Emblem

1966. Nepalese Philatelic Exhibition, Katmandu.
204 **56** 15p. orange and green . . 30 20

57 King Mahendra

58 Queen Mother

1966. King Mahendra's 47th Birthday.
205 **57** 15p. brown and yellow . . 25 20

1966. Queen Mother's 60th Birthday.
206 **58** 15p. brown 20 20

59 Queen Ratna

60 Flute-player and Dancer

1966. Children's Day.
207 **59** 15p. brown and yellow . . 25 20

1966. Krishna Anniv.
208 **60** 15p. violet and yellow . . 25 20

61 "To render service..."

1966. 1st Anniv of Nepalese Red Cross.
209 **61** 50p. red and green . . . . 2·40 80

62 W.H.O. Building on Flag

63 Paudyal

1966. Inaug of W.H.O. Headquarters, Geneva.
210 **62** 1r. violet . . . . 1·25 80

1966. Leknath Paudyal (poet) Commemoration.
211 **63** 15p. blue 25 20

64 Rama and Sita

65 Buddha

1967. Rama Navami, 2024, birthday of Rama.
212 **64** 15p. brown and yellow . . 25 20

1967. Buddha Jayanti, birthday of Buddha.
213 **65** 75p. purple and orange . . 50 50

66 King Mahendra addressing Nepalese

1967. King Mahendra's 48th Birthday.
214 **66** 15p. brown and blue . . . 25 25

67 Queen Ratna and Children

68 Ama Dablam (mountain)

1967. Children's Day.
215 **67** 15p. brown and cream . . 25 20

1967. International Tourist Year.
216 **68** 5p. violet (postage) 20 20
217 – 65p. brown 40 40
218 – 1r.80 red and blue (air) . . 1·00 80
DESIGNS—38 × 20 mm: 65p. Bhaktapur Durbar Square. 35½ × 25½ mm: 1r.80, Plane over Katmandu.

69 Open-air Class

1967. Constitution Day. "Go to the Village" Educational Campaign.
219 **69** 15p. multicoloured 25 20

70 Crown Prince Birendra, Campfire and Scout Emblem

1967. Diamond Jubilee of World Scouting.
220 **70** 15p. blue 40 30

71 Prithvi Narayan Shah (founder of Kingdom)

72 Arms of Nepal

1968. Bicentenary of the Kingdom.
221 **71** 15p. blue and red 40 30

1968. National Day.
222 **72** 15p. blue and red 40 30

73 W.H.O. Emblem and Nepalese Flag

1968. 20th Anniv of W.H.O.
223 **73** 1r.20 blue, red and yellow 1·75 1·25

74 Sita and Janaki Temple

1968. Sita Jayanti.
224 **74** 15p. brown and violet . . 30 20

75 King Mahendra, Mountains and Himalayan Monal Pheasant

1968. King Mahendra's 49th Birthday.
225 **75** 15p. multicoloured . . . . 2·00 45

76 Garuda and Airline Emblem

1968. Air. 10th Anniv of Royal Nepalese Airlines.
226 **76** 15p. brown and blue . . . 20 20
227 – 65p. blue 40 40
228 – 2r.50 blue and orange . . . 1·50 1·25
DESIGNS—DIAMOND (25½ × 25½ mm): 65p. Route-map. As Type **76**: 2r.50, Convair Metropolitan airliner over Mount Dhaulagiri.

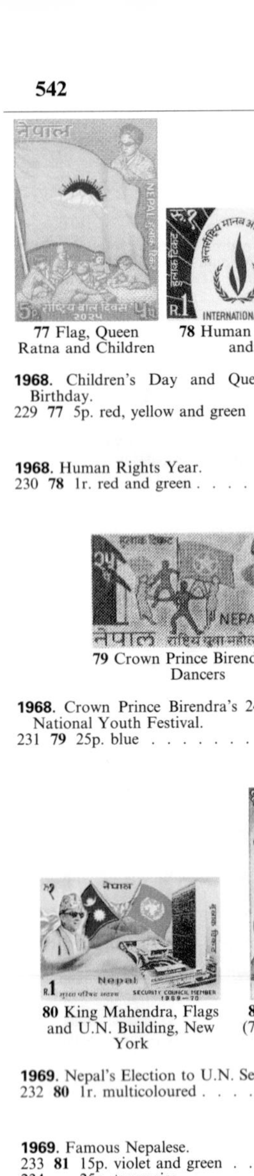

77 Flag, Queen Ratna and Children

78 Human Rights Emblem and Buddha

1968. Children's Day and Queen Ratna's 41st Birthday.
229 **77** 5p. red, yellow and green 20 15

1968. Human Rights Year.
230 **78** 1r. red and green . . . . . 1·60 1·25

79 Crown Prince Birendra and Dancers

1968. Crown Prince Birendra's 24th Birthday, and National Youth Festival.
231 **79** 25p. blue 40 30

80 King Mahendra, Flags and U.N. Building, New York

81 Amsu Varma (7th-century ruler)

1969. Nepal's Election to U.N. Security Council.
232 **80** 1r. multicoloured 60 50

1969. Famous Nepalese.
233 **81** 15p. violet and green . . . 30 30
234 – 25p. turquoise 40 40
235 – 50p. brown 50 50
236 – 1r. purple and brown . . . 60 50
DESIGNS—VERT: 25p. Ram Shah (17th-century King of Gurkha); 50p. Bhimsen Thapa (19th-century Prime Minister). HORIZ: 1r. Bal Bhadra Kunwar (19th-century warrior).

82 I.L.O. Emblem

1969. 50th Anniv of I.L.O.
237 **82** 1r. brown and mauve . . . 3·00 2·00

83 King Mahendra

85 Queen Ratna, and Child with Toy

84 King Tribhuvana and Queens

1969. King Mahendra's 50th Birthday.
238 **83** 25p. multicoloured 25 25

1969. 64th Birth Anniv of King Tribhuvana.
239 **84** 25p. brown and yellow . . 25 25

1969. National Children's Day.
240 **85** 25p. mauve and brown . . 25 25

86 Rhododendron

87 Durga, Goddess of Victory

1969. Flowers. Multicoloured.
241 25p. Type **86** 35 30
242 25p. Narcissus 35 30
243 25p. Marigold 35 30
244 25p. Poinsettia 35 30

1969. Durga Pooja Festival.
245 **87** 15p. black and orange . . 20 20
246 50p. violet and brown . . 45 40

88 Crown Prince Birendra and Princess Aishwarya

1970. Royal Wedding.
247 **88** 25p. multicoloured 25 20

89 Produce, Cow and Landscape

1970. Agricultural Year.
248 **89** 25p. multicoloured 25 20

90 King Mahendra, Mt. Everest and Nepalese Crown

1970. King Mahendra's 51st Birthday.
249 **90** 50p. multicoloured 40 30

91 Lake Gosainkunda

1970. Nepalese Lakes. Multicoloured.
250 5p. Type **91** 20 20
251 25p. Lake Phewa Tal 30 30
252 1r. Lake Rara Daha 50 50

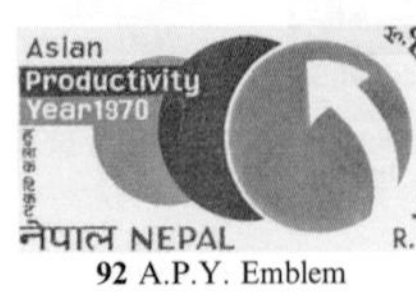

92 A.P.Y. Emblem

1970. Asian Productivity Year.
253 **92** 1r. blue 50 40

93 Queen Ratna and Children's Palace, Taulihawa

1970. National Children's Day.
254 **93** 25p. grey and brown . . . 25 20

94 New Headquarters Building

1970. New U.P.U. Headquarters, Berne.
255 **94** 2r.50 grey and brown . . . 1·00 80

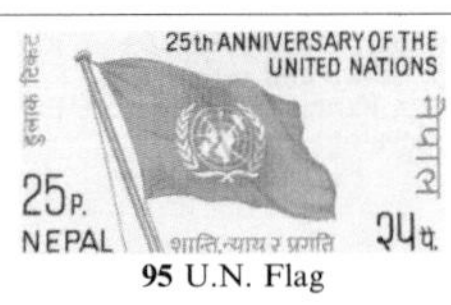

95 U.N. Flag

1970. 25th Anniv of United Nations.
256 **95** 25p. blue and purple . . . 25 20

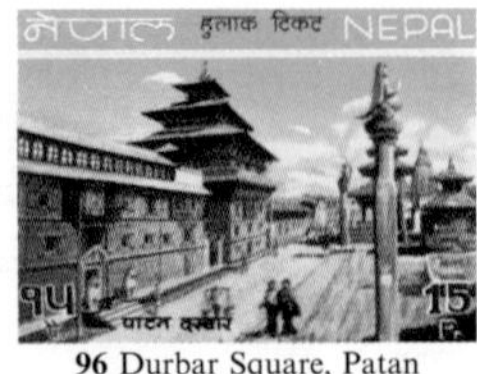

96 Durbar Square, Patan

1970. Tourism. Multicoloured.
257 15p. Type **96** 20 10
258 25p. Boudhanath Stupa (temple) (vert) 30 20
259 1r. Mt. Gauri Shankar . . . 50 40

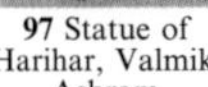

97 Statue of Harihar, Valmiki Ashram

98 Torch within Spiral

1971. Nepalese Religious Art.
260 **97** 25p. black and brown . . . 25 20

1971. Racial Equality Year.
261 **98** 1r. red and blue 60 45

99 King Mahendra taking Salute

1971. King Mahendra's 52nd Birthday.
262 **99** 15p. purple and blue . . . 25 20

100 Sweta Bhairab

1971. Bhairab Statues of Shiva.
263 **100** 15p. brown and chestnut 20 20
264 – 25p. brown and green . . 20 20
265 – 50p. brown and blue . . . 40 40
DESIGNS: 25p. Mahankal Bhairab; 50p. Kal Bhairab.

101 Child presenting Queen Ratna with Garland

1971. National Children's Day.
266 **101** 25p. multicoloured . . . 25 15

102 Iranian and Nepalese Flags on Map of Iran

1971. 2,500th Anniv of Persian Empire.
267 **102** 1r. multicoloured 60 40

103 Mother and Child

1971. 25th Anniv of U.N.I.C.E.F.
268 **103** 1r. blue 60 40

104 Mt. Everest

1971. Tourism. Himalayan Peaks.
269 **104** 25p. dp brown, brn and bl 20 10
270 – 1r. black, brown and blue 40 30
271 – 1r.80 green, brown & blue 70 50
DESIGNS: 1r. Mt. Kanchenjunga; 1r.80, Mt. Annapurna I.

105 Royal Standard

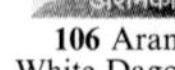

106 Araniko and White Dagoba, Peking

1972. National Day.
272 **105** 25p. black and red . . . 25 15

1972. Araniko (13th-century architect) Commem.
273 **106** 15p. brown and blue . . . 15 10

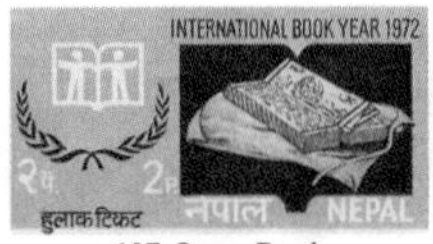

107 Open Book

1972. International Book Year.
274 **107** 2p. brown and buff . . . 10 10
275 5p. black and brown . . . 10 10
276 1r. black and blue 50 40

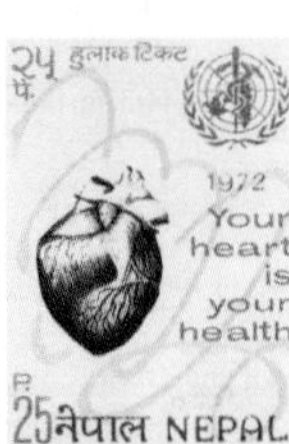

108 Human Heart

1972. World Heart Month.
277 **108** 25p. red and green . . . 25 20

109 King Mahendra

110 King Birendra

1972. 1st Death Anniv of King Mahendra.
278 **109** 25p. brown and black . . 25 15

1972. King Birendra's 28th Birthday.
279 **110** 50p. purple and brown . . 30 25

111 Northern Border Costumes

112 Sri Baburam Acharya

1973. National Costumes. Multicoloured.
280 25p. Type **111** 20 10
281 50p. Hill-dwellers 25 20

282 75p. Katmandu Valley . . . 35 25
283 1r. Inner Terai 50 35

1973. 85th Birth Anniv of Sri Baburam Acharya (historian).
284 **112** 25p. grey and red 20 15

113 Nepalese Family

1973. 25th Anniv of W.H.O.
285 **113** 1r. blue and orange . . . 50 40

114 Birthplace of Buddha, Lumbini

1973. Tourism. Multicoloured.
286 25p. Type **114** 20 10
287 75p. Mt. Makalu 30 20
288 1r. Castle, Gurkha 40 40

115 Transplanting Rice

1973. 10th Anniv of World Food Programme.
289 **115** 10p. brown and violet . . 10 10

116 Interpol H.Q., Paris

1973. 50th Anniv of International Criminal Police Organization (Interpol).
290 **116** 25p. blue and brown . . . 20 15

117 Shri Shom Nath Sigdyal

118 Cow

1973. 1st Death Anniv of Shri Shom Nath Sigdyal (scholar).
291 **117** 1r.25 violet 50 40

1973. Domestic Animals. Multicoloured.
292 2p. Type **118** 10 10
293 3r.25 Yak 90 60

119 King Birendra

1974. King Birendra's 29th Birthday.
294 **119** 5p. brown and black . . . 10 10
295 15p. brown and black . . 15 10
296 1r. brown and black . . . 40 30

120 Text of National Anthem

121 King Janak seated on Throne

1974. National Day.
297 **120** 25p. purple 20 10
298 – 1r. green 30 25
DESIGN: 1r. Anthem musical score.

1974. King Janak Commemoration.
299 **121** 2r.50 multicoloured . . . 1·00 80

122 Emblem and Village

1974. 25th Anniv of SOS Children's Village International.
300 **122** 25p. blue and red 15 15

123 Football

124 W.P.Y. Emblem

1974. Nepalese Games. Multicoloured.
301 2p. Type **123** 10 10
302 2r.75 Baghchal (diagram) . . 60 50

1974. World Population Year.
303 **124** 5p. blue and brown . . . 10 10

125 U.P.U. Monument, Berne

126 Red Lacewing

1974. Centenary of U.P.U.
304 **125** 1r. black and green . . . 40 30

1974. Nepalese Butterflies. Multicoloured.
305 10p. Type **126** 10 10
306 15p. Leaf buttefly 40 15
307 1r.25 Leaf butterfly (underside) . . . . 1·00 70
308 1r.75 Red-breasted jezebel . . 1·25 1·00

127 King Birendra

128 Muktinath

1974. King Birendra's 30th Birthday.
309 **127** 25p. black and green . . 15 15

1974. "Visit Nepal" Tourism. Multicoloured.
310 25p. Type **128** 20 10
311 1r. Peacock window, Bhaktapur (horiz) 40 25

129 Guheswari Temple

1975. Coronation of King Birendra. Multicoloured.
312 25p. Type **129** 20 10
313 50p. Lake Rara (37 × 30 mm) 20 10
314 1r. Throne and sceptre (46 × 26 mm) 30 20
315 1r.25 Royal Palace, Katmandu (46 × 26 mm) 60 30
316 1r.75 Pashupatinath Temple (25 × 31 mm) 40 40
317 2r.75 King Birendra and Queen Aishwarya (46 × 25 mm) 60 50

130 Tourism Year Emblem

1975. South Asia Tourism Year. Multicoloured.
319 2p. Type **130** 10 10
320 25p. Temple stupa (vert) . . 20 20

131 Tiger

1975. Wildlife Conservation. Multicoloured.
321 2p. Type **131** 20 20
322 5p. Swamp deer (vert) . . . 20 20
323 1r. Lesser panda 40 40

132 Queen Aishwarya and I.W.Y. Emblem

1975. International Women's Year.
324 **132** 1r. multicoloured 30 20

133 Rupse Falls

134 King Birendra

1975. Tourism. Multicoloured.
325 2p. Mt. Ganesh Himal (horiz) 10 10
326 25p. Type **133** 10 10
327 50p. Kumari ("Living Goddess") 30 20

1975. King Birendra's 31st Birthday.
328 **134** 25p. violet and mauve . . 15 10

136 Flag and Map

138 Flags of Nepal and Colombo Plan

137 Transplanting Rice

1976. Silver Jubilee of National Democracy Day.
330 **136** 2r.50 red and blue 10 10

1976. Agriculture Year.
331 **137** 25p. multicoloured . . . 15 10

1976. 25th Anniv of Colombo Plan.
332 **138** 1r. multicoloured 30 25

139 Running

140 "Dove of Peace"

1976. Olympic Games, Montreal.
333 **139** 3r.25 black and blue . . . 80 60

1976. 5th Non-aligned Countries' Summit Conf.
334 **140** 5r. blue, yellow and black 15 15

141 Lakhe Dance

1976. Nepalese Dances. Multicoloured.
335 10p. Type **141** 10 10
336 15p. Maruni dance 10 10
337 30p. Jhangad dance 20 10
338 1r. Sebru dance 30 20

142 Nepalese Lily

143 King Birendra

1976. Flowers. Multicoloured.
339 30p. Type **142** 30 10
340 30p. "Meconopsis grandis" 30 10
341 30p. "Cardiocrinum giganteum" (horiz) 30 10
342 30p. "Megacodon stylophorus" (horiz) . . . 30 10

1976. King Birendra's 32nd Birthday.
343 **143** 5p. green 10 10
344 30p. dp brown, brn & yell 15 10

144 Liberty Bell

1976. Bicentenary of American Revolution.
345 **144** 10r. multicoloured . . . . 1·50 1·40

145 Kaji Amarsingh Thapa

1977. Kaji Amarsingh Thapa (19th-century warrior) Commemoration.
346 **145** 10p. green and brown . . 10 10

146 Terracotta Figurine and Kapilavastu

1977. Tourism.
347 **146** 30p. violet 10 10
348 – 5r. green and brown . . . 80 60
DESIGN: 5r. Ashokan pillar, Lumbini.

147 Great Indian Hornbill

1977. Birds. Multicoloured.
349 5p. Type **147** 50 15
350 15p. Cheer pheasant (horiz) 90 20
351 1r. Green magpie (horiz) . . 1·40 55
352 2r.30 Spiny babbler . . . . 2·50 1·40

148 Tukuche Himal and Police Flag

1977. 1st Anniv of Ascent of Tukuche Himal by Police Team.
353 **148** 1r.25 multicoloured . . . 30 20

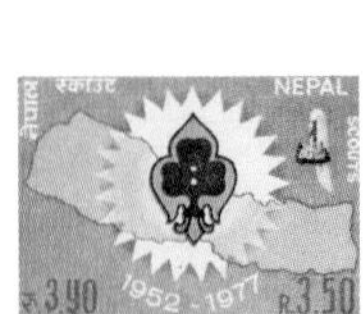

149 Map of Nepal and Scout Emblem
150 Dhanwantari, the Health-giver

1977. 25th Anniv of Scouting in Nepal.
354 **149** 3r.50 multicoloured . . . 60 40

1977. Health Day.
355 **150** 30p. green 15 10

151 Map of Nepal and Flags
152 King Birendra

1977. 26th Consultative Committee Meeting of Colombo Plan, Katmandu.
356 **151** 1r. multicoloured 20 15

1977. King Birendra's 33rd Birthday.
357 **152** 5p. brown 10 10
358 1r. brown 20 20

153 General Post Office, Katmandu, and Seal

1978. Centenary of Nepalese Post Office.
359 **153** 25p. brown and agate . . 10 10
360 – 75p. brown and agate . . 10 10
DESIGN: 75p. General Post Office, Katmandu, and early postmark.

154 South-west Face of Mt. Everest

1978. 25th Anniv of First Ascent of Mt. Everest.
361 **154** 2r.30 grey and brown . . 50 30
362 – 4r. blue and green 70 60
DESIGN: 4r. South face of Mt. Everest.

155 Sun, Ankh and Landscape

1978. World Environment Day.
363 **155** 1r. green and orange . . . 10 10

156 Queen Mother Ratna
157 Rapids, Tripsuli River

1978. Queen Mother's 50th Birthday.
364 **156** 2r.30 green 10 10

1978. Tourism. Multicoloured.
365 10p. Type **157** 10 10
366 50p. Window, Nara Devi, Katmandu 15 10
367 1r. Mahakali dance (vert) . . 25 20

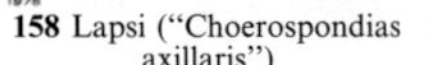

158 Lapsi ("Choerospondias axillaris")
159 Lamp and U.N. Emblem

1978. Fruits. Multicoloured.
368 5p. Type **158** 15 10
369 1r. Katus (vert) 25 20
370 1r.25 Rudrakshya 40 25

1978. 30th Anniv of Human Rights Declaration.
371 **159** 25p. brown and red . . . 10 10
372 1r. blue and red 20 15

160 Wright Flyer I and Boeing 727-100
161 King Birendra

1978. Air. 75th Anniv of First Powered Flight.
373 **160** 2r.30 blue and brown . . 45 30

1978. King Birendra's 34th Birthday.
374 **161** 30p. blue and brown . . . 10 10
375 2r. brown and violet . . . 10 10

162 Red Machchhindranath and Kamroop and Patan Temples

1979. Red Machchhindranath (guardian deity) Festival.
376 **162** 75p. brown and green . . 20 15

163 "Buddha's Birth" (carving, Maya Devi Temple)
164 Planting a Sapling

1979. Lumbini Year.
377 **163** 1r. yellow and brown . . 20 15

1979. Tree Planting Festival.
378 **164** 2r.30 brown, green & yellow 10 10

165 Chariot of Red Machchhindranath
166 Nepalese Scouts and Guides

1979. Bhoto Jatra (Vest Exhibition) Festival.
379 **165** 1r.25 multicoloured . . . 25 20

1979. International Year of the Child.
380 **166** 1r. brown 10 10

167 Mount Pabil
168 Great Grey Shrike

1979. Tourism.
381 **167** 30p. green 10 10
382 – 50p. red and blue 10 10
383 – 1r.25 multicoloured . . . 25 25
DESIGNS: 50p. Yajnashala, Swargadwari. 1r.25, Shiva-Parbati (wood carving, Gaddi Baithak Temple).

1979. International World Pheasant Association Symposium, Katmandu. Multicoloured.
384 10p. Type **168** (postage) . . . 15 20
385 10r. Fire-tailed sunbird . . . 6·50 3·50
386 3r.50 Himalayan monal pheasant (horiz) (air) . . . 2·10 1·90

169 Lichchhavi Coin (obverse)
170 King Birendra

1979. Coins.
387 **169** 5p. orange and brown . . 10 10
388 – 5p. orange and brown . . 10 10
389 – 15p. blue and indigo . . . 10 10
390 – 15p. blue and indigo . . . 10 10
391 – 1r. blue and deep blue . . 20 20
392 – 1r. blue and deep blue . . 20 20
DESIGNS: No. 388, Lichchhavi coin (reverse); 389, Malla coin (obverse); 390, Malla coin (reverse); 391, Prithvi Narayan Shah coin (obverse); 392, Prithvi Narayan Shah coin (reverse).

1979. King Birendra's 35th Birthday. Mult.
393 25p. Type **170** 10 10
394 2r.30 Reservoir 40 30

171 Samyak Pooja Festival

1980. Samyak Pooja Festival, Katmandu.
395 **171** 30p. brown, grey & purple 10 10

172 Sacred Basil

1980. Herbs. Multicoloured.
396 5p. Type **172** 10 10
397 30p. Valerian 10 10
398 1r. Nepalese pepper 20 15
399 2r.30 Himalayan rhubarb . . 40 25

173 Gyandil Das
174 Everlasting Flame and Temple, Shirsasthan

1980. Nepalese Writers.
400 **173** 5p. lilac and brown . . . 10 10
401 – 30p. purple and brown . . 10 10
402 – 1r. green and blue 15 15
403 – 2r.30 blue and green . . . 55 25
DESIGNS: 30p. Siddhidas Amatya; 1r. Pahalman Singh Swanr; 2r.30, Jay Prithvi Bahadur Singh.

1980. Tourism. Multicoloured.
404 10p. Type **174** 10 10
405 1r. Godavari Pond 20 15
406 5r. Mount Dhaulagiri 70 50

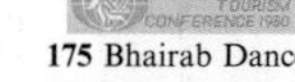

175 Bhairab Dancer
176 King Birendra

1980. World Tourism Conf, Manila, Philippines.
407 **175** 25r. multicoloured . . . . 3·00 2·25

1980. King Birendra's 36th Birthday.
408 **176** 1r. multicoloured 20 15

177 I.Y.D.P. Emblem and Nepalese Flag

1981. International Year of Disabled Persons.
409 **177** 5r. multicoloured 80 60

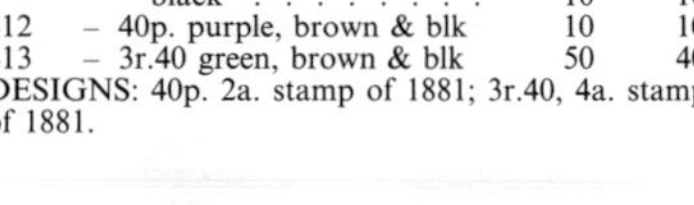

178 Nepal Rastra Bank
179 One Anna Stamp of 1881

1981. 25th Anniv of Nepal Rastra Bank.
410 **178** 1r.75 multicoloured . . . 10 10

1981. Nepalese Postage Stamp Centenary.
411 **179** 10p. blue, brown and black 10 10
412 – 40p. purple, brown & blk 10 10
413 – 3r.40 green, brown & blk 50 40
DESIGNS: 40p. 2a. stamp of 1881; 3r.40, 4a. stamp of 1881.

180 Nepalese Flag and Association Emblem
181 Hand holding Stamp

1981. 70th Council Meeting of International Hotel Association, Katmandu.
415 **180** 1r.75 multicoloured . . . 10 10

1981. "Nepal 81" Stamp Exhibition, Katmandu.
416 **181** 40p. multicoloured . . . 10 10

182 King Birendra
183 Image of Hrishikesh, Ridi

1981. King Birendra's 37th Birthday.
417 **182** 1r. multicoloured 10 10

1981. Tourism. Multicoloured.
418 5p. Type **183** 10 10
419 25p. Tripura Sundari Temple, Baitadi 10 10
420 2r. Mt. Langtang Lirung . . 10 10

184 Academy Building
185 Balakrishna Sama

1982. 25th Anniv of Royal Nepal Academy.
421 **184** 40p. multicoloured . . . 10 10

1982. 1st Death Anniv of Balakrishna Sama (writer).
422 **185** 1r. multicoloured 10 10

186 "Intelsat V" and Dish Aerial　**187** Mount Nuptse

1982. Sagarmatha Satellite Earth Station, Balambu.
423 **186** 5r. multicoloured 75 40

1982. 50th Anniv of Union of International Alpinist Associations. Multicoloured.
424 25p. Type **187** 10 10
425 2r. Mount Lhotse (31 × 31 mm) 30 20
426 3r. Mount Everest (39 × 31 mm) 60 30
Nos. 424/6 were issued together, se-tenant, forming a composite design.

188 Games Emblem and Weights　**189** Indra Sarobar Lake

1982. 9th Asian Games, New Delhi.
427 **188** 3r.40 multicoloured . . . 50 40

1982. Kulekhani Hydro-electric Project.
428 **189** 2r. multicoloured 10 10

190 King Birendra　**191** N.I.D.C. Emblem

1982. King Birendra's 38th Birthday.
429 **190** 5p. multicoloured 10 10

1983. 25th Anniv (1984) of Nepal Industrial Development Corporation.
430 **191** 50p. multicoloured . . . 10 10

192 Boeing 727 over Himalayas

1983. 25th Anniv of Royal Nepal Airlines.
431 **192** 1r. multicoloured 40 15

193 W.C.Y. Emblem and Nepalese Flag　**194** Sarangi

1983. World Communications Year.
432 **193** 10p. multicoloured . . . 10 10

1983. Musical Instruments. Multicoloured.
433 5p. Type **194** 10 10
434 10p. Kwota (drum) 10 10
435 50p. Narashinga (horn) . . . 10 10
436 1r. Murchunga 20 20

195 Chakrapani Chalise　**196** King Birendra and Doves

1983. Birth Centenary of Chakrapani Chalise (poet).
437 **195** 4r.50 multicoloured . . . 60 45

1983. King Birendra's 39th Birthday.
438 **196** 5r. multicoloured 70 40

197 Barahkshetra Temple and Image of Barah

1983. Tourism. Multicoloured.
439 1r. Type **197** 15 10
440 2r.20 Temple, Triveni 15 15
441 6r. Mount Cho-oyu 15 15

198 Auditing Accounts

1984. 25th Anniv of Auditor General.
442 **198** 25p. multicoloured . . . 10 10

199 Antenna and Emblem

1984. 20th Anniv of Asia-Pacific Broadcasting Union.
443 **199** 5r. multicoloured 70 60

200 University Emblem　**201** Boxing

1984. 25th Anniv of Tribhuvan University.
444 **200** 50p. multicoloured . . . 15 10

1984. Olympic Games, Los Angeles.
445 **201** 10r. multicoloured 30 30

202 Family and Emblem　**203** National Flag and Emblem

1984. 25th Anniv of Nepal Family Planning Association.
446 **202** 1r. multicoloured 15 10

1984. Social Service Day.
447 **203** 5p. multicoloured 10 10

204 Gharial　**205** "Vishnu as Giant" (stone carving)

1984. Wildlife. Multicoloured.
448 10p. Type **204** 10 10
449 25p. Snow leopard 10 10
450 50p. Blackbuck 20 20

1984. Tourism. Multicoloured.
451 10p. Type **205** 10 10
452 1r. Temple of Chhinna Masta Bhagavati and sculpture (horiz) 15 10
453 5r. Mount Api 70 45

206 King Birendra

1984. King Birendra's 40th Birthday.
454 **206** 1r. multicoloured 15 10

207 Animals and Mountains　**208** Shiva

1985. Sagarmatha (Mt. Everest) National Park.
455 **207** 10r. multicoloured . . . . 3·25 1·60

1985. Traditional Paintings. Details of cover of "Shiva Dharma Purana". Multicoloured.
456 50p. Type **208** 10 10
457 50p. Multi-headed Shiva talking to woman 10 10
458 50p. Brahma and Vishnu making offering (15 × 22 mm) 10 10
459 50p. Shiva in single- and multi-headed forms 10 10
460 50p. Shiva talking to woman 10 10
Nos. 456/60 were printed together, se-tenant, forming a composite design.

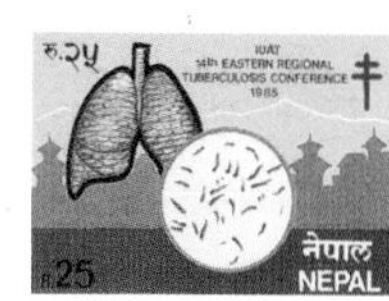

209 U.N. Flag　**210** Lungs and Bacilli

1985. 40th Anniv of U.N.O.
461 **209** 5r. multicoloured 15 15

1985. 14th Eastern Regional Tuberculosis Conf, Katmandu.
462 **210** 25r. multicoloured 50 50

211 Flags of Member Countries

1985. 1st South Asian Association for Regional Co-operation Summit.
463 **211** 5r. multicoloured 60 40

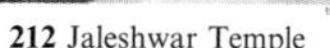

212 Jaleshwar Temple　**213** I.Y.Y. Emblem

1985. Tourism. Multicoloured.
464 10p. Type **212** 10 10
465 1r. Temple of Goddess Shaileshwari, Silgadi . . . 10 10
466 2r. Phoksundo Lake 10 10

1985. International Youth Year.
467 **213** 1r. multicoloured 15 10

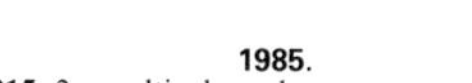

214 King Birendra　**215** Devi Ghat Hydro-electric Project

1985. King Birendra's 41st Birthday.
468 **214** 50p. multicoloured . . . 10 10

1985.
469 **215** 2r. multicoloured 10 10

216 Emblem　**217** Royal Crown

1986. 25th Anniv of Panchayat System (partyless government).
470 **216** 4r. multicoloured 50 40

1986.
471 **217** 5p. brown and deep brown 10 10
472 – 10p. blue 10 10
474 – 50p. blue 10 10
476 – 1r. brown and ochre . . . 15 10
DESIGNS: 10p. Mayadevi Temple of Lumbini (Buddha's birthplace); 50p. Pashupati Temple; 1r. Royal Crown.

218 Pharping Hydro-electric Station

1986. 75th Anniv of Pharping Hydro-electric Power Station.
480 **218** 15p. multicoloured . . . 10 10

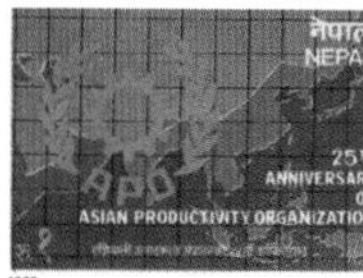

219 Emblem and Map

1986. 25th Anniv of Asian Productivity Organization.
481 **219** 1r. multicoloured 15 10

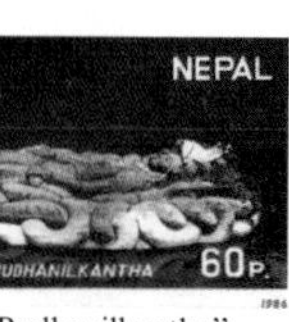

220 "Budhanilkantha" (sculpture of reclining Vishnu), Katmandu Valley　**221** King Birendra

1986. Tourism. Multicoloured.
482 60p. Type **220** 10 10
483 8r. Mt. Pumori, Himalayas (35 × 22 mm) 15 15

1986. King Birendra's 42nd Birthday.
484 **221** 1r. multicoloured 10 10

222 I.P.Y. Emblem　**223** National Flag and Council Emblem

1986. International Peace Year.
485 **222** 10r. multicoloured 25 25

1987. 10th Anniv of National Social Service Co-ordination Council.
486 **223** 1r. multicoloured 10 10

224 Emblem and Forest

1987. 1st Nepal Scout Jamboree, Katmandu.
487 **224** 1r. brown, orange and blue 10 10

225 Ashokan Pillar and Maya Devi

1987. Lumbini (Buddha's Birthplace) Development Project.
488 **225** 4r. multicoloured 40 30

226 Emblem **227** Emblem

1987. 3rd South Asian Association for Regional Co-operation Summit, Katmandu.
489 **226** 60p. gold and red 10 10

1987. 25th Anniv of Rastriya Samachar Samiti (news service).
490 **227** 4r. purple, blue and red 10 10

228 Kashthamandap, Katmandu **229** Gyawali

1987.
491 **228** 25p. multicoloured . . . 10 10

1987. 89th Birth Anniv of Surya Bikram Gyawali.
492 **229** 60p. multicoloured . . . 10 10

230 Emblem **231** King Birendra

1987. International Year of Shelter for the Homeless.
493 **230** 5r. multicoloured 10 10

1987. King Birendra's 43rd Birthday.
494 **231** 25p. multicoloured . . . 10 10

232 Mt. Kanjiroba

1987.
495 **232** 10r. multicoloured 25 25

233 Crown Prince Dipendra

1988. Crown Prince Dipendra's 17th Birthday.
496 **233** 1r. multicoloured 10 10

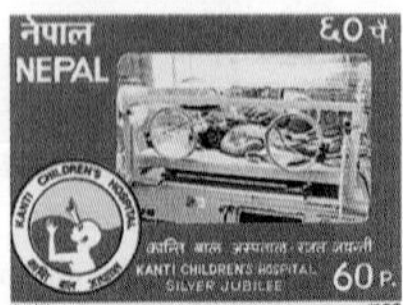

234 Baby in Incubator

1988. 25th Anniv of Kanti Children's Hospital, Katmandu.
497 **234** 60p. multicoloured . . . 10 10

235 Swamp Deer **236** Laxmi, Goddess of Wealth

1988. 12th Anniv of Royal Shukla Phanta Wildlife Reserve.
498 **235** 60p. multicoloured . . . 20 10

1988. 50th Anniv of Nepal Bank Ltd.
499 **236** 2r. multicoloured 10 10

237 Queen Mother **238** Hands protecting Blood Droplet

1988. 60th Birthday of Queen Mother.
500 **237** 5r. multicoloured 15 15

1988. 25th Anniv of Nepal Red Cross Society.
501 **238** 1r. red and brown 10 10

239 Temple and Statue

1988. Temple of Goddess Bindhyabasini, Pokhara.
502 **239** 15p. multicoloured . . . 10 10

240 King Birendra **241** Temple

1988. King Birendra's 44th Birthday.
503 **240** 4r. multicoloured 10 10

1989. Pashupati Area Development Trust.
504 **241** 1r. multicoloured 10 10

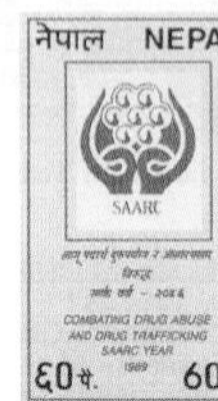

242 Emblem **243** S.A.A.R.C. Emblem

1989. 10th Anniv of Asia-Pacific Telecommunity.
505 **242** 4r. green, black and violet 15 15

1989. South Asian Association for Regional Co-operation Year against Drug Abuse and Trafficking.
506 **243** 60p. multicoloured . . . 10 10

244 King Birendra **245** Child Survival Measures

1989. King Birendra's 45th Birthday.
507 **244** 2r. multicoloured 20 10

1989. Child Survival Campaign.
508 **245** 1r. multicoloured 10 10

246 Lake Rara

1989. Rara National Park.
509 **246** 4r. multicoloured 15 15

247 Mt. Amadablam

1989.
510 **247** 5r. multicoloured 20 20

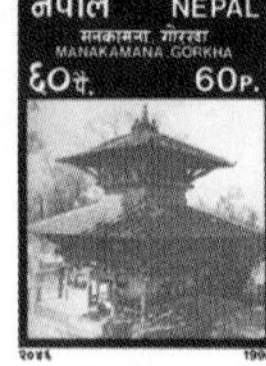

248 Crown Prince Dipendra **249** Temple of Manakamana, Gorkha

1989. Crown Prince Dipendra's Coming-of-Age.
511 **248** 1r. multicoloured 10 10

1990.
512 **249** 60p. black and violet . . 10 10

250 Emblem and Children **251** Emblem

1990. 25th Anniv of Nepal Children's Organization.
513 **250** 1r. multicoloured 10 10

1990. Centenary of Bir Hospital.
514 **251** 60p. red, blue and yellow 10 10

252 Emblem **253** Goddess and Bageshwori Temple, Nepalgunj

1990. 20th Anniv of Asian–Pacific Postal Training Centre, Bangkok.
515 **252** 4r. multicoloured 30 15

1990. Tourism. Multicoloured.
516 1r. Type **253** 10 10
517 5r. Mt. Saipal (36 × 27 mm) 35 25

254 Leisure Activities

1990. South Asian Association for Regional Co-operation Girls' Year.
518 **254** 4r.60 multicoloured . . . 35 20

255 King Birendra **256** Koirala

1990. King Birendra's 46th Birthday.
519 **255** 2r. multicoloured 15 10

1990. 76th Birth Anniv of Bisweswar Prasad Koirala (Prime Minister, 1959–60).
520 **256** 60p. black, orange and red 10 10

257 Indian Rhinoceros and Lake **258** Flower and Crowd

1991. Royal Chitwan National Park.
521 **257** 4r. multicoloured 15 15

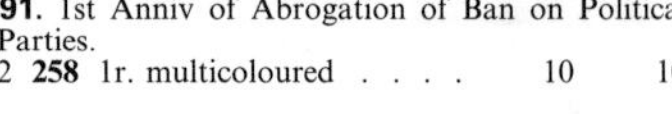

1991. 1st Anniv of Abrogation of Ban on Political Parties.
522 **258** 1r. multicoloured 10 10

259 Official and Villagers **260** Federation and Jubilee Emblems

1991. National Population Census.
523 **259** 60p. multicoloured . . . 10 10

1991. 25th Anniv of Federation of Nepalese Chambers of Commerce and Industry.
524 **260** 3r. multicoloured 15 15

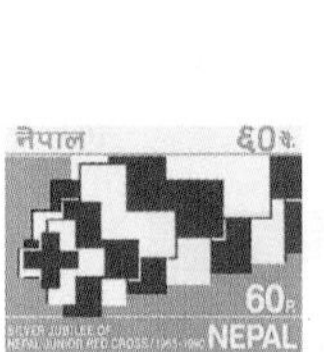

261 Crosses **262** Delegates

1991. 25th Anniv (1990) of Nepal Junior Red Cross.
525 **261** 60p. red and grey 10 10

1991. 1st Session of Revived Parliament.
526 **262** 1r. multicoloured 10 10

263 King Birendra making Speech

1991. Constitution Day.
527 **263** 50p. multicoloured . . . 10 10

264 Rama and Janaki (statues) and Vivaha Mandap **266** King Birendra

265 Mt. Kumbhakarna

1991. 5th Anniv of Rebuilt Vivaha Mandap Pavilion, Janaki Temple.
528 **264** 1r. multicoloured 10 10

1991. Tourism.
529 **265** 4r.60 multicoloured . . . 15 15

1991. King Birendra's 47th Birthday.
530 **266** 8r. multicoloured 15 15

267 Houses

268 Glass magnifying Society Emblem

1991. South Asian Association for Regional Co-operation Year of Shelter.
531 **267** 9r. multicoloured 25 25

1992. 25th Anniv (1991) of Nepal Philatelic Society.
532 **268** 4r. multicoloured 10 10

269 Rainbow over River and Trees

1992. Environmental Protection.
533 **269** 60p. multicoloured . . . 10 10

270 Nutrition, Education and Health Care

1992. Rights of the Child.
534 **270** 1r. multicoloured 10 10

271 Thakurdwara Temple, Bardiya

272 Bank Emblem

1992. Temples. Multicoloured.
535 75p. Type **271** (postage) . . . 10 10
536 1r. Namo Buddha Temple, Kavre 10 10
537 2r. Narijhowa Temple, Mustang 10 10
538 11r. Dantakali Temple, Bijayapur (air) 20 20

1992. 25th Anniv of Agricultural Development Bank.
539 **272** 40p. brown and green . . 10 10

273 Pin-tailed Green Pigeon

1992. Birds. Multicoloured.
540 1r. Type **273** 30 30
541 3r. Bohemian waxwing . . . 45 30
542 25r. Rufous-tailed desert (inscr "Finch") lark . . . 2·00 1·60

274 King Birendra exchanging Swords with Goddess Sree Bhadrakali

275 Pandit Kulchandra Gautam

1992. King Birendra's 48th Birthday.
543 **274** 7r. multicoloured 20 20

1992. Poets. Multicoloured, frame colour given in brackets.
544 1r. Type **275** 10 10
545 1r. Chittadhar Hridaya (drab) 10 10
546 1r. Vidyapati (stone) 10 10
547 1r. Teongsi Sirijunga (grey) 10 10

276 Shooting and Marathon

277 Golden Mahseer

1992. Olympic Games, Barcelona.
548 **276** 25r. multicoloured 50 50

1993. Fishes. Multicoloured.
549 25p. Type **277** 15 10
550 1r. Marinka 15 10
551 5r. Indian eel 40 20
552 10r. False loach 85 45

278 Antibodies attacking Globe

279 Tanka Prasad Acharya (Prime Minister, 1956–57)

1993. World AIDS Day.
554 **278** 1r. multicoloured 10 10

1993. Death Anniversaries. Multicoloured.
555 25p. Type **279** (1st anniv) . . 10 10
556 1r. Sungdare Sherpa (mountaineer) (4th anniv) 10 10
557 7r. Siddhi Charan Shrestha (poet) (1st anniv) 20 10
558 15r. Falgunanda (religious leader) (44th anniv) 30 20

280 Halesi Mahadev Cave (hiding place of Shiva), Khotang

1993. Holy Places. Multicoloured.
559 1r.50 Type **280** 10 10
560 5r. Devghat (gods' bathing place), Tanahun 10 10
561 8r. Bagh Bairab Temple, Kirtipur 20 15

281 Tushahiti Fountain, Sundari Chowk, Patan

282 King Birendra

1993. Tourism. Multicoloured.
562 5r. Type **281** 10 10
563 8r. White-water rafting . . . 20 10

1993. King Birendra's 49th Birthday.
564 **282** 10r. multicoloured 25 20

283 Monument

284 Mt. Everest

1994.
565 **283** 20p. brown 10 10
566 – 25p. red 10 10
567 – 30p. green 10 10
568 **284** 1r. multicoloured 10 10
569 – 5r. multicoloured 20 10
DESIGNS—20 × 22 mm: 25p. State arms. 22 × 20 mm: 30p. Lumbini. 25 × 15 mm: 5r. Map of Nepal, crown and state arms and flag.

285 Pasang Sherpa

1994. 1st Death Anniv of Pasang Sherpa (mountaineer).
570 **285** 10r. multicoloured 25 20

286 Cigarette, Lungs and Crab's Claws

287 Postal Delivery

1994. Anti-smoking Campaign.
571 **286** 1r. multicoloured 10 10

1994.
572 **287** 1r.50 multicoloured . . . 10 10

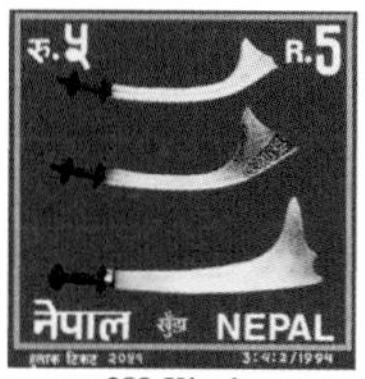

288 Khuda

1994. Weapons. Multicoloured.
573 5r. Kukris (three swords and two scabbards) 15 10
574 5r. Type **288** 15 10
575 5r. Dhaal (swords and shield) 15 10
576 5r. Katari (two daggers) . . . 15 10

289 Workers and Emblem

1994. 75th Anniv of I.L.O.
577 **289** 15r. gold, blue & ultram 30 25

290 Landscape

1994. World Food Day.
578 **290** 25r. multicoloured 50 40

291 "Dendrobium densiflorum"

292 Family

1994. Orchids. Multicoloured.
579 10r. Type **291** 25 15
580 10r. "Coelogyne flaccida" . . 25 15
581 10r. "Cymbidium devonianum" 25 15
582 10r. "Coelogyne corymbosa" 25 15

1994. International Year of the Family.
583 **292** 9r. emerald, green and red 20 15

293 Emblem and Airplane

294 "Russula nepalensis"

1994. 50th Anniv of I.C.A.O.
584 **293** 11r. blue, gold and deep blue 20 15

1994. Fungi. Multicoloured.
585 7r. Type **294** 35 10
586 7r. Morels ("Morchella conica") 35 10
587 7r. Caesar's mushroom ("Amanita caesarea") . . . 35 10
588 7r. "Cordyceps sinensis" . . 35 10

295 Dharanidhar Koirala (poet)

1994. Celebrities. Multicoloured.
589 1r. Type **295** 10 10
590 2r. Narayan Gopal Guruwacharya (singer) . . 10 10
591 6r. Bahadur Shah (vert) . . . 10 10
592 7r. Balaguru Shadananda . . 15 10

296 King Birendra, Flag, Map and Crown

1994. King Birendra's 50th Birthday (1st issue).
593 **296** 9r. multicoloured 20 15
See also No. 621.

297 Lake Tilicho, Manang

1994. Tourism. Multicoloured.
594 9r. Type **297** 20 15
595 11r. Taleju Temple, Katmandu (vert) 20 15

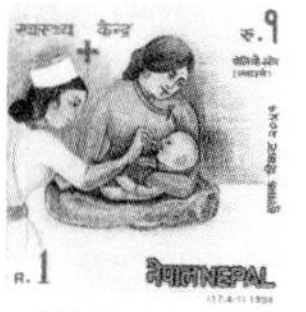

298 Health Care

1994. Children's Activities. Multicoloured.
596 1r. Type **298** 10 10
597 1r. Classroom 10 10
598 1r. Playground equipment . . 10 10
599 1r. Stamp collecting 10 10

299 Singhaduarbar

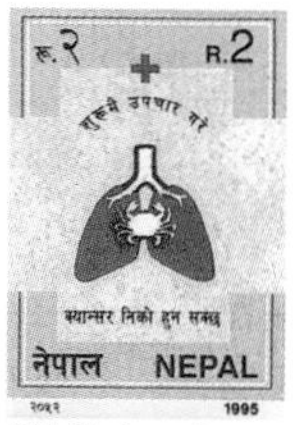

300 Crab on Lungs

1995.
600 **299** 10p. green 10 10
601 – 50p. blue 10 10
DESIGN—VERT: 50p. Pashupati.

1995. Anti-cancer Campaign.
602 **300** 2r. multicoloured 10 10

301 Chandra Man Singh Maskey (artist)

302 Bhakti Thapa (soldier)

1995. Celebrities. Multicoloured.
603 3r. Type **301** 10 10
604 3r. Parijat (writer) 10 10
605 3r. Bhim Nidhi Tiwari (writer) 10 10
606 3r. Yuddha Prasad Mishra (writer) 10 10

1995. Celebrities. Multicoloured.
607 15p. Type **302** 10 10
608 1r. Madan Bhandari (politician) 10 10
609 4r. Prakash Raj Kaphley (human rights activist) . . 10 10

303 Gaur ("Bos gaurus")

1995. "Singapore '95" International Stamp Exhibition. Mammals. Multicoloured.
610 10r. Type **303** 20 10
611 10r. Lynx ("Felis lynx") . . . 20 10
612 10r. Assam macaque ("Macaca assamensis") . . 20 10
613 10r. Striped hyena ("Hyaena hyaena") 20 10

304 Anniversary Emblem

1995. 50th Anniv of F.A.O.
614 **304** 7r. multicoloured 15 10

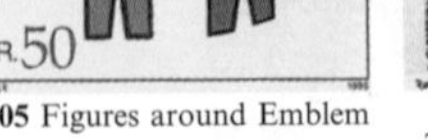
305 Figures around Emblem

306 Bhimeswor Temple, Dolakha

1995. 50th Anniv of U.N.O.
615 **305** 50r. multicoloured 95 35

1995. Tourism. Multicoloured.
616 1r. Type **306** 10 10
617 5r. Ugra Tara Temple, Dadeldhura (horiz) 10 10
618 7r. Mt. Nampa (horiz) . . . 15 10
619 18r. Nrity Aswora (traditional Pauba painting) (27 × 39 mm) 35 10
620 20r. Lumbini (Buddha's birthplace) (28 × 28 mm) 40 15

307 King Birendra

309 King Birendra

308 Anniversary Emblem

1995. King Birendra's 50th Birthday (1994) (2nd issue).
621 **307** 1r. multicoloured 10 10

1995. 10th Anniv of South Asian Association for Regional Co-operation.
622 **308** 10r. multicoloured 20 10

1995. King Birendra's 51st Birthday.
623 **309** 12r. multicoloured 25 10

310 Karnali Bridge

1996.
624 **310** 7r. multicoloured 15 10

311 State Arms

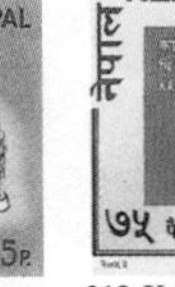
312 Kaji Kalu Pande (soldier and royal adviser)

1996.
625 **311** 25p. red 10 10

1996. Political Figures. Multicoloured.
626 75p. Type **312** 10 10
627 1r. Pushpa Lal Shrestha (Nepal Communist Party General-Secretary) 10 10
628 5r. Suvarna Shamsher Rana (founder of Nepal Democratic Congress Party) 10 10

313 Hem Raj Sharma (grammarian)

314 Runner and Track

1996. Writers. Multicoloured.
629 1r. Type **313** 10 10
630 3r. Padma Prasad Bhattarai (Sanskrit scholar) 10 10
631 5r. Bhawani Bhikshu (novelist) 10 10

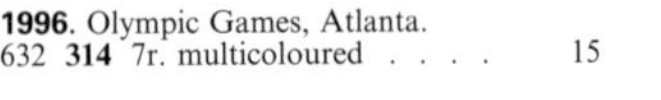
1996. Olympic Games, Atlanta.
632 **314** 7r. multicoloured 15 10

315 Kasthamandap, Katmandu

316 Hindu Temple, Arjundhara

1996. Temples.
633 **315** 10p. red and black . . . 10 10
634 50p. black and red . . . 10 10
635 – 1r. red and blue 10 10
DESIGN—VERT: 1r. Nyata Pola temple, Bhaktapur.

1996. Tourism. Multicoloured.
636 1r. Type **316** 10 10
637 2r. Durbar, Nuwakot 10 10
638 8r. Gaijatra Festival, Bhaktapur 15 10
639 10r. Lake Beganas, Kaski . . 20 10

317 Krishna Peacock

318 Ashoka Pillar

1996. Butterflies and Birds. Multicoloured.
640 5r. Type **317** 10 10
641 5r. Great barbet ("Great Himalayan Barbet") . . . 10 10
642 5r. Sarus crane 10 10
643 5r. Northern jungle queen . . 10 10
Nos. 640/3 were issued together, se-tenant, forming a composite design.

1996. Centenary of Rediscovery of Ashoka Pillar, Lumbini (birthplace of Buddha).
644 **318** 12r. multicoloured 25 10

319 King Birendra

1996. King Birendra's 52nd Birthday.
645 **319** 10r. multicoloured 20 10

320 Mt. Annapurna South and Mt. Annapurna I

1996. The Himalayas.
646 18r. Type **320** 35 10
647 18r. Mt. Machhapuchhre and Mt. Annapurna III 35 10
648 18r. Mt. Annapurna IV and Mt. Annapurna II 35 10
Nos. 646/8 were issued together, se-tenant, forming a composite design.

321 King Birendra before Throne

1997. Silver Jubilee of King Birendra's Accession.
649 **321** 2r. multicoloured 10 10

322 Mountains and National Flags

323 Postal Emblem

1997. 40th Anniv of Nepal–Japan Diplomatic Relations.
650 **322** 18r. multicoloured 35 10

1997.
651 **323** 2r. red and brown 10 10

324 Campaign Emblem

1997. National Tourism Year.
652 **324** 2r. red and blue 10 10
653 – 10r. multicoloured 20 10
654 – 18r. multicoloured 35 10
655 – 20r. multicoloured 40 10
DESIGNS—HORIZ: 10r. Upper Mustang mountain peak; 18r. Rafting, River Sunkoshi. VERT: 20r. Changunarayan.

325 Chepang Couple

326 National Flags and Handshake

1997. Ethnic Groups. Multicoloured.
656 5r. Type **325** 10 10
657 5r. Gurung couple 10 10
658 5r. Rana Tharu couple . . . 10 10

1997. 50th Anniv of Nepal United States Diplomatic Relations.
659 **326** 20r. multicoloured 40 10

327 Riddhi Bahadur Malla (writer)

328 "Jasminum gracile"

1997. Celebrities. Multicoloured.
660 2r. Type **327** 10 10
661 2r. Dr. K. I. Singh (politician) 10 10

1997. Flowers. Multicoloured.
662 40p. Type **328** 10 10
663 1r. China aster 10 10
664 2r. "Manglietia insignis" . . 10 10
665 15r. "Luculia gratissima" . . 30 10

329 Dhiki (corn crusher)

1997. Traditional Technology. Multicoloured.
666 5r. Type **329** 10 10
667 5r. Janto (mill stone) 10 10
668 5r. Kol (oil mill) (vert) . . . 10 10
669 5r. Okhal (implement for pounding rice) (vert) . . . 10 10

330 King Birendra

331 Sunrise, Shree Antudanda, Ilam

1997. King Birendra's 53rd Birthday.
670 **330** 10r. multicoloured 20 10

1998. Tourism. Multicoloured.
671 2r. Type **331** 10 10
672 10r. Maitidevi Temple, Katmandu 20 10
673 18r. Great Renunciation Gate, Kapilavastu 35 10
674 20r. Mt. Cholatse, Solukhumbu (vert) 35 10

332 Ram Prasad Rai (nationalist)

1998. Personalities.
675 **332** 75p. black and brown . . 10 10
676 – 1r. black and mauve . . . 10 10
677 – 2r. black and green . . . 10 10
678 – 2r. black and blue 10 10
679 – 5r.40 black and red . . . 10 10
DESIGNS: No. 676, Imansing Chemjong (Kiranti language specialist); 677, Tulsi Meher Shrestha (social worker); 678, Maha Pundit Dadhi Ram Marasini (poet); 679, Mahananda Sapkota (educationalist and writer).

333 Match Scenes

1998. World Cup Football Championship, France.
680 **333** 12r. multicoloured 20 10

334 Ganesh Man Singh

1998. 1st Death Anniv of Ganesh Man Singh (politician).
681 **334** 5r. multicoloured 10 10

335 World Map and Nepalese Soldiers

1998. 40 Years of Nepalese Army Involvement in United Nations Peace Keeping Missions.
682 **335** 10r. multicoloured 20 10

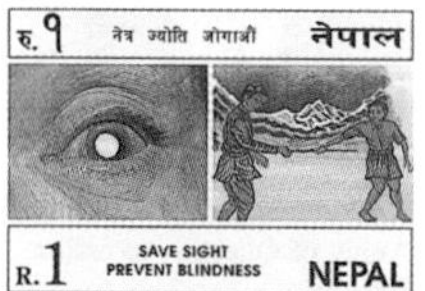

336 Cataract and Guiding of Blind Man

1998. Cataract Awareness Campaign.
683 **336** 1r. multicoloured 10 10

337 King Cobra

1998. Snakes. Multicoloured.
684 1r.70 Type **337** 10 10
685 2r. Golden tree snake 10 10
686 5r. Asiatic rock python . . . 10 10
687 10r. Karan's pit viper 20 10

338 Dove and Profile

1998. 50th Anniv of Universal Declaration of Human Rights.
688 **338** 10r. multicoloured 20 10

339 Disabled Persons

R.2 NEPAL

340 King Birendra

1998. Asian and Pacific Decade of Disabled Persons.
689 **339** 10r. multicoloured 20 10

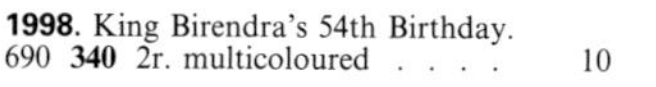

1998. King Birendra's 54th Birthday.
690 **340** 2r. multicoloured 10 10

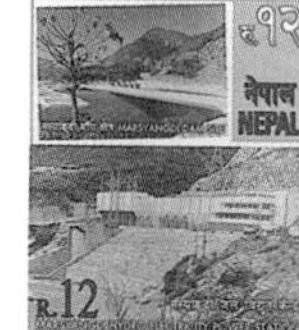

341 Dam and Power House

1998. River Marsyangdi Hydro-electric Power Station.
691 **341** 12r. multicoloured 20 10

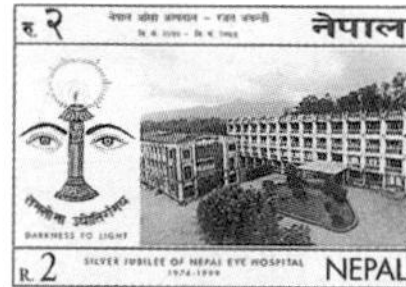

342 Hospital and Emblem

1999. 25th Anniv of Nepal Eye Hospital.
692 **342** 2r. multicoloured 10 10

343 Kalika Bhagawati Temple, Baglung

1999. Tourism. Multicoloured.
693 2r. Type **343** 10 10
694 2r. Chandan Nath Temple, Jumla (vert) 10 10
695 12r. Bajrayogini Temple, Sankhu (vert) 20 10
696 15r. Mt. Everest 25 10
697 15r. Ashokan Pillar, Lumbini, and English translation of its inscription (39 × 27 mm) 25 10

344 Four-horned Antelope

125th ANNIVERSARY OF THE UPU 1874-1999
NEPAL R.15

346 U.P.U. Emblem and Cockerel

345 Him Kanchha (mascot) and Games Emblem

1999. Mammals. Multicoloured.
698 10r. Type **344** 10 10
699 10r. Argali (Ovis ammon) . . 10 10

1999. 8th South Asian Sports Federation Games, Katmandu.
700 **345** 10r. multicoloured 10 10

1999. 125th Anniv of Universal Postal Union.
701 **346** 15r. multicoloured 25 10

347 Ramnarayan Mishra (revolutionary, 1922–67)

1999. Personalities.
702 **347** 1r. green and black . . . 10 10
703 – 1r. brown and black . . . 10 10
704 – 1r. blue and black 10 10
705 – 2r. red and black 10 10
706 – 2r. blue and black 10 10
707 – 2r. buff and black 10 10
DESIGNS: No. 703, Master Mitrasen (writer, 1895–1946); 704, Bhupi Sherchan (poet, 1935–89); 705, Rudraraj Pandey (writer, 1901–87); 706, Gopalprasad Rimal (writer, 1917–73); 707, Mangaladevi Singh (revolutionary, 1924–96).

348 Sorathi Dance

1999. Local Dances. Multicoloured.
708 5r. Type **348** 10 10
709 5r. Bhairav dance 10 10
710 5r. Jhijhiya dance 10 10

349 Children working and writing

1999. Nepal's involvement in International Programme on the Elimination of Child Labour.
711 **349** 12r. multicoloured 20 10

350 King Birendra

1999. King Birendra's 55th Birthday.
712 **350** 5r. multicoloured 10 10

351 Headquarters

2000. 60th Anniv of Radio Nepal.
713 **351** 2r. multicoloured 10 10

352 Queen Aishwarya

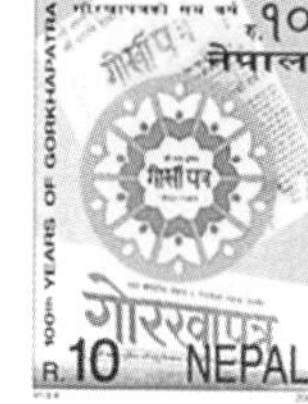

353 Front Page of Newspaper and Emblem

2000. Queen Aishwarya's 50th Birthday.
714 **352** 15r. multicoloured 30 10

2000. Centenary of *Gorkhapatra* (newspaper).
715 **353** 10r. multicoloured 20 10

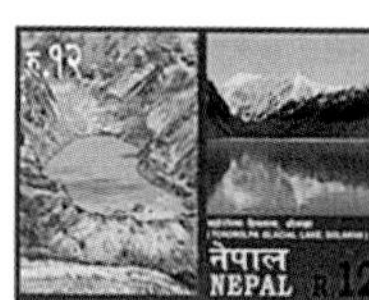

354 Tchorolpa Glacial Lake, Dolakha

2000. Tourist Sights. Multicoloured.
716 12r. Type **354** 20 10
717 15r. Dakshinkali Temple, Kathmandu 30 10
718 18r. Mount Annapurna (50th anniv of first ascent) . . . 35 10

355 Ranipokhari Pagoda, Kathmandu

2000.
719 **355** 50p. black and orange . . 10 10
720 1r. black and blue 10 10
721 2r. black and brown . . . 10 10

356 Soldier and Child

2000. 50th Anniv of Geneva Convention.
725 **356** 5r. multicoloured 10 10

357 Runners

2000. Olympic Games, Sydney.
726 **357** 25r. multicoloured 45 15

358 Hridayachandra Singh Pradhan (writer)

NEPAL R.10

359 Indian Rhinoceros (male)

2000. Personalities.
727 **358** 2r. black and yellow . . . 10 10
728 – 2r. black and brown . . . 10 10
729 – 5r. black and blue 10 10
730 – 5r. black and red 10 10
DESIGNS: No. 728, Thir Barn Malla (revolutionary); 729, Krishna Prasad Koirala (social reformer); 730, Manamohan Adhikari (polititian).

2000. Wildlife. Multicoloured.
731 10r. Type **359** 20 10
732 10r. Indian rhinoceros (*Rhinoceros unicornis*) (female) 20 10
733 10r. Lesser adjutant stork (*Leptoptilos javanicus*) . . . 20 10
734 10r. Bengal florican (*Houbaropsis bengalensis*) 20 10

360 Orchid (*Dactylorhiza hatagirea*)

R.5 NEPAL

361 King Birendra

2000. Flowers. Multicoloured.
735 5r. Type **360** 10 10
736 5r. *Mahonia napaulensis* (horiz) 10 10
737 5r. *Talauma hodgsonii* (horiz) 10 10

2000. King Birendra's 56th Birthday.
738 **361** 5r. multicoloured 10 10

362 King Tribhuvana and Crowd

2001. 50th Anniv of Constitutional Monarchy.
739 **362** 5r. multicoloured 10 10

363 Crowd and Emblem

2001. Population Census.
740 **363** 2r. multicoloured 10 10

364 Khaptad Baba (religious leader)

365 Asiatic Coinwort (*Centella asiatica*)

2001. Personalities.

No.	Type	Description	Unused	Used
741	**364**	2r. pink and black	10	10
742	–	2r. mauve and black	10	10
743	–	2r. magenta and black	10	10
744	–	2r. red and black	10	10
745	–	2r. blue and black	10	10

DESIGNS: No. 742, Bhikkhu Pragyananda Mahathera (Buddhist writer and teacher); 743, Guru Prasad Mainali (author); 744, Tulsi Lal Amatya Politician); 745, Madan Lal Agrawal (industrialist).

2001. Plants. Multicoloured.

No.	Type	Description	Unused	Used
746		5r. Type **365**	10	10
747		15r. *Bergenia ciliata*	25	10
748		30r. Himalayan yew (*Taxus baccata wallichania*)	55	25

366 Pipal Tree (*Ficus religiosa*)

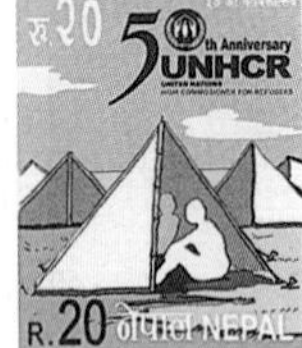
367 Tents

2001.

No.	Type	Description	Unused	Used
749	**366**	10r. multicoloured	20	10

2001. 50th Anniv of United Nations High Commissioner for Refugees.

No.	Type	Description	Unused	Used
750	**367**	20r. multicoloured	40	20

368 National Flag

369 Amargadi Fort

2001.

No.	Type	Description	Unused	Used
751	**368**	10p. red and blue	10	10

2001. Tourism. Multicoloured.

No.	Type	Description	Unused	Used
752		2r. Type **369**	10	10
753		5r. Hiranyavarna Mahavihar (Golden Temple) (vert)	10	10
754		15r. Jugal mountain range	25	10

370 King Birendra

2001. 57th Birth Anniv of King Birendra.

No.	Type	Description	Unused	Used
755	**370**	15r. multicoloured	25	10

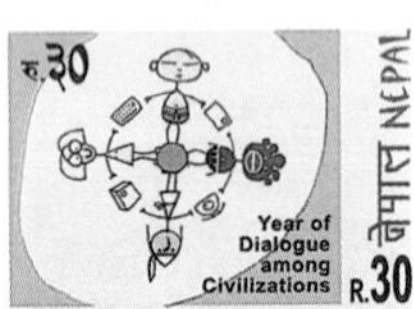
371 Children encircling Globe

2001. United Nations Year of Dialogue among Civilizations.

No.	Type	Description	Unused	Used
756	**371**	30r. multicoloured	50	25

OFFICIAL STAMPS

O 25 Nepalese Arms and Soldiers

काज सरकारी
(O 28)

1960. (a) Size 30 × 18 mm.

No.	Type	Description	Unused	Used
O135	**O 25**	2p. brown	10	10
O136		4p. green	10	10
O137		6p. red	10	10
O138		8p. violet	10	10
O139		12p. orange	15	15

(b) Size 38 × 27 mm.

No.	Type	Description	Unused	Used
O140	**O 25**	16p. brown	20	20
O141		24p. red	35	25
O142		32p. purple	35	35
O143		50p. blue	65	55
O144		1r. red	1·40	1·25
O145		2r. orange	2·50	2·25

1960. Optd as Type O **28**.

No.	Type	Description	Unused	Used
O146	**27**	1r. purple	50	

1961. Optd with Type O **28**.

No.	Type	Description	Unused	Used
O148	**35**	1p. red	10	10
O149		2p. blue	10	10
O150		5p. brown	10	10
O151	**36**	10p. purple	10	10
O152		40p. brown	10	10
O153		75p. green	15	15
O154	**27**	2r. red	30	30
O155		5r. green	80	80

NETHERLANDS Pt. 4

A kingdom in the N.W. of Europe on the North Sea.

1852. 100 cents = 1 gulden (florin).
2002. 100 cents = 1 euro.

1

3 King William III

4

1852. Imperf.

No.	Type	Description	Unused	Used
1	**1**	5c. blue	£225	30·00
2		10c. red	£225	27·00
3b		15c. orange	£600	£100

1864. Perf.

No.	Type	Description	Unused	Used
8	**3**	5c. blue	£200	16·00
9		10c. red	£300	7·50
10		15c. orange	£500	90·00

1867.

No.	Type	Description	Unused	Used
17d	**4**	5c. blue	85·00	2·40
18c		10c. red	£150	3·00
19c		15c. brown	£650	30·00
20		20c. green	£600	23·00
15		25c. purple	£2250	£100
22		50c. gold	£2750	£160

5

6

1869.

No.	Type	Description	Unused	Used
58	**5**	½c. brown	24·020	4·00
53		1c. black	£190	70·00
59		1c. green	11·50	2·40
55a		1½c. red	£130	80·00
56a		2c. yellow	42·00	12·00
62		2½c. mauve	£500	70·00

1872.

No.	Type	Description	Unused	Used
80	**6**	5c. blue	9·00	30
81		7½c. brown	38·00	17·00
82		10c. red	60·00	1·60
83		12½c. grey	65·00	2·40
84		15c. brown	£375	5·00
85		20c. green	£450	5·00
86		22½c. green	80·00	45·00
87		25c. lilac	£575	4·00
97		50c. bistre	£750	10·00
90		1g. violet	£500	40·00
75	–	2g.50 blue and red	£950	£110

No. 75 is similar to Type **6** but larger and with value and country scrolls transposed.

8

9 Queen Wilhelmina

1876.

No.	Type	Description	Unused	Used
133	**8**	½c. red	3·00	10
134		1c. green	9·50	10
137		2c. yellow	38·00	2·75
139		2½c. mauve	15·00	30

1891.

No.	Type	Description	Unused	Used
147a	**9**	3c. orange	8·75	2·00
148a		5c. blue	5·00	25
149b		7½c. brown	17·00	5·25
150b		10c. red	25·00	1·40
151b		12½c. grey	25·00	1·50
152a		15c. brown	50·00	4·00
153b		20c. green	65·00	3·00
154a		22½c. green	32·00	11·50
155		25c. mauve	£110	5·25
156a		50c. bistre	£500	16·00
159	–	50c. brown and green	75·00	9·50
157	**9**	1g. violet	£550	65·00
160	–	1g. green and brown	£190	19·00
161	–	2g.50 blue and red	£450	£140
165	–	5g. red and green	£700	£400

Nos. 159, 160, 161 and 165 are as Type **9** but larger and with value and country scrolls transposed.

11

12

13

14

1898. Nos. 174 and 176 also exist imperf.

No.	Type	Description	Unused	Used
167	**12**	½c. lilac	60	20
168		1c. red	1·10	15
170		1½c. blue	3·00	35
171		2c. brown	4·50	20
172		2½c. green	3·75	20
173	**13**	3c. orange	17·00	3·50
174		3c. green	1·50	15
175		4c. purple	1·50	90
176		4½c. mauve	3·75	3·75
177b		5c. red	1·75	15
178		7½c. brown	75	20
179		10c. grey	7·50	15
180		12½c. blue	4·00	25
181		15c. brown	95·00	3·50
182		15c. red and blue	7·50	15
183		17½c. mauve	50·00	12·00
184		17½c. brown and blue	18·00	90
185		20c. green	£120	70
186		20c. grey and green	12·00	45
187		22½c. green and brown	11·50	50
188		25c. blue and pink	11·50	30
189		30c. purple and mauve	25·00	50
190		40c. orange and green	38·00	90
191		50c. red and green	£110	95
192		50c. violet and grey	65·00	90
193		60c. green and olive	38·00	1·10
194a	**11**	1g. green	50·00	75
195b		2½g. lilac	95·00	3·50
196a		5g. red	£225	5·50
197		10g. red	£750	£700

1906. Society for the Prevention of Tuberculosis.

No.	Type	Description	Unused	Used
208	**14**	1c. (+1c.) red	18·00	10·00
209		3c. (+3c.) green	32·00	22·00
210		5c. (+5c.) violet	30·00	15·00

15 Admiral M. A. de Ruyter

16 William I

1907. Birth Tercentenary of Admiral de Ruyter.

No.	Type	Description	Unused	Used
211	**15**	½c. blue	2·10	1·40
212		1c. red	4·00	2·50
213		2½c. red	7·00	2·50

1913. Independence Centenary.

No.	Type	Description	Unused	Used
214	**16**	2½c. green on green	90	85
215	–	3c. yellow on cream	1·40	1·25
216	–	5c. red on buff	1·40	90
217	–	10c. grey	4·25	2·40
218	**16**	12½c. blue on blue	3·25	2·25
219	–	20c. brown	12·50	10·00
220	–	25c. blue	15·00	8·75
221	–	50c. green	32·00	28·00
222	**16**	1g. red	48·00	20·00
223	–	2½g. lilac	£120	48·00
224	–	5g. yellow on cream	£250	40·00
225	–	10g. orange	£750	£750

DESIGNS: 3c., 20c., 2½g. William II; 5c., 25c., 5g. William III; 10c., 50c., 10g. Queen Wilhelmina.

1919. Surch **Veertig Cent** (40c.) or **Zestig Cent** (60c.).

No.	Type	Description	Unused	Used
234	**13**	40c. on 30c. purple & mve	32·00	3·75
235		60c. on 30c. purple & mve	32·00	3·50

1920. Surch in figures.

No.	Type	Description	Unused	Used
238	**13**	4c. on 4½c. mauve	5·25	1·75
236	**11**	2.50 on 10g. red	£140	£120
237	–	2.50 on 10g. red (No. 225)	£150	£110

23

24

1921. Air.

No.	Type	Description	Unused	Used
239	**23**	10c. red	1·75	1·40
240		15c. green	6·25	2·25
241		60c. blue	19·00	20

1921.

No.	Type	Description	Unused	Used
242	**24**	5c. green	8·75	20
243		12½c. red	20·00	3·25
244		20c. blue	26·00	25

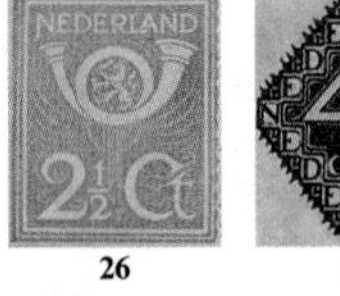
25 Lion in Dutch Garden and Orange Tree (emblematical of Netherlands) 26 27

1923.

No.	Type	Description	Unused	Used
248	**25**	1c. violet	65	65
249		2c. orange	6·00	20
250	**26**	2½c. green	2·10	70
251	**27**	4c. blue	1·50	60

1923. Surch.

No.	Type	Description	Unused	Used
252	**12**	2c. on 1c. red	60	20
253		2c. on 1½c. blue	60	25
254	**13**	10c. on 3c. green	5·00	20
255		10c. on 5c. red	10·00	55
256		10c. on 12½c. blue	8·25	60
257a		10c. on 17½c. brown & blue	4·50	4·00
258a		10c. on 22½c. olive & brown	4·50	4·00

30

31

1923. 25th Anniv of Queen's Accession.

No.	Type	Description	Unused	Used
259	**31**	2c. green	30	10
260	**30**	5c. green	40	25
261	**31**	7½c. red	50	25
262		10c. red	40	10
263		20c. blue	4·25	80
264		25c. yellow	7·50	1·60
265b		35c. orange	8·00	3·50
266a		50c. black	18·00	50
267	**30**	1g. red	35·00	7·25
268		2½g. black	£250	£200
269		5g. blue	£225	£170

1923. Surch **DIENST ZEGEL PORTEN AAN TEEKEN RECHT** and value.

No.	Type	Description	Unused	Used
270	**13**	10c. on 3c. green	1·25	1·10
271		1g. on 17½c. brown & blue	80·00	17·00

33

1923. Culture Fund.

No.	Type	Description	Unused	Used
272	**33**	2c. (+5c.) blue on pink	20·00	17·00
273	–	10c. (+5c.) red on pink	20·00	17·00

DESIGN: 10c. Two women.

35 Carrier Pigeon

36 Queen Wilhelmina

1924.

No.	Type	Description	Unused	Used
304C	**35**	½c. grey	45	30
305A		1c. red	20	10
306C		1½c. mauve	40	10
424a		1½c. grey	20	80
425		2c. orange	20	10
426a		2½c. green	1·60	20
427		3c. green	20	10
427a		4c. blue	20	10
428	**36**	5c. green	20	10
429		6c. brown	20	10
279A		7½c. yellow	60	10
313A		7½c. violet	4·00	10
314A		7½c. red	30	10
279cA		9c. red and black	1·60	1·50
281A		10c. red	1·75	10
317A		10c. blue	2·75	10
282A		12½c. red	2·10	40
319A		12½c. blue	35	10
320A		15c. blue	7·25	20
321C		15c. yellow	85	60
322C		20c. blue	5·50	2·50
434		21c. brown	25·00	90
324B		22½c. brown	6·75	2·40
434a		22½c. orange	15·00	18·00

435 25c. green . . . . . . 5·00 15
326A 27½c. grey . . . . . . 4·50 20
437 30c. violet . . . . . . 6·00 20
286cA 35c. brown . . . . . . 35·00 7·00
437a 40c. brown . . . . . . 9·50 20
330A 50c. green . . . . . . 5·50 20
289A 60c. violet . . . . . . 30·00 95
331A 60c. black . . . . . . 23·00 1·00
301 1g. blue (23 × 29 mm) 8·75 50
302 2½g. red (23 × 29 mm) 90·00 5·25
303 5g. black (23 × 29 mm) £180 2·75
For further stamps in Type **35**, see Nos. 546/57.

1924. International Philatelic Exn, The Hague.
290 **36** 10c. green . . . . 38·00 38·00
291 15c. black . . . . 42·00 42·00
292 35c. red . . . . 38·00 38·00

37 **38**

1924. Dutch Lifeboat Centenary.
293 **37** 2c. brown . . . . 4·00 3·00
294 **38** 10c. brown on yellow . . . 7·00 2·50

39 **40** Arms of South Holland

1924. Child Welfare.
295 **39** 2c. (+2c.) green . . . . . 2·10 2·10
296 7½c. (+3½c.) brown . . . . 5·25 6·25
297 10c. (+2½c.) red . . . . . 4·50 1·75

1925. Child Welfare. Arms as T **40**.
298A – 2c. (+2c.) green and yellow 90 85
299A – 7½c. (+3½c.) violet and blue . . . . 4·50 4·75
300A **40** 10c. (+2½c.) red and yellow . . . . 3·50 60
ARMS: 2c. North Brabant; 7½c. Gelderland.
See also Nos. 350/3A and 359/62A.

1926. Child Welfare. Arms as T **40**.
350A 2c. (+2c.) red and silver . . 55 50
351A 5c. (+3c.) green and blue 1·60 1·40
352A 10c. (+3c.) red and green 2·40 30
353A 15c. (+3c.) yellow and blue 6·25 5·75
ARMS: 2c. Utrecht; 5c. Zeeland; 10c. North Holland; 15c. Friesland.

46 Queen Wilhelmina **47** Red Cross Allegory

1927. 60th Anniv of Dutch Red Cross Society.
354a **46** 2c. (+2c.) red . . . . . . 3·25 2·40
355 – 3c. (+2c.) green . . . . . 6·29 9·00
356 – 5c. (+3c.) blue . . . . . 1·10 1·10
357a – 7½c. (+3½c.) blue . . . . 5·50 2·25
358 **47** 15c. (+5c.) red and blue 9·75 10·00
PORTRAITS: 2c. King William III; 3c. Queen Emma; 5c. Henry, Prince Consort.

1927. Child Welfare. Arms as T **40**.
359A 2c. (+2c.) red and lilac . . 45 45
360A 5c. (+3c.) green and yellow 1·75 1·60
361A 7½c. (+3½c.) red and black 4·00 40
362A 15c. (+3c.) blue and brown 6·00 5·50
ARMS: 2c. Drente; 5c. Groningen; 7½c. Limburg; 15c. Overyssel.

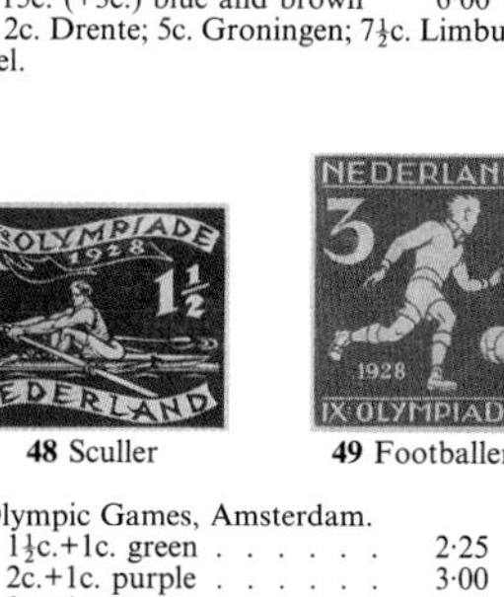

48 Sculler **49** Footballer

1928. Olympic Games, Amsterdam.
363 **48** 1½c.+1c. green . . . . . . 2·25 1·60
364 – 2c.+1c. purple . . . . . . 3·00 2·00
365 **49** 3c.+1c. green . . . . . . 2·50 2·40
366 – 5c.+1c. blue . . . . 3·00 1·60
367 – 7½c.+2½c. orange . . . . . 3·00 1·90
368 – 10c.+2c. red . . . . 8·00 6·00
369 – 15c.+2c. blue . . . . . . 8·00 4·50
370 – 30c.+3c. sepia . . . . . . 25·00 24·00
DESIGNS—HORIZ: 2c. Fencing. VERT: 5c. Sailing; 7½c. Putting the shot; 10c. Running; 15c. Show-jumping; 30c. Boxing.

50 Lieut. Koppen

1928. Air.
371 **50** 40c. red 60 60
372 – 75c. green 60 60
DESIGN: 75c. Van der Hoop.

52 J. P. Minckelers **53** Mercury

1928. Child Welfare.
373 **52** 1½c.+1½c. violet 60 50
374 – 5c.+3c. green . . . . . . 1·90 70
375a – 7½c.+2½c. red . . . . . . 3·50 35
376a – 12½c.+3½c. blue . . . . . 10·00 7·50
PORTRAITS: 5c. Boerhaave; 7½c. H. A. Lorentz; 12½c. G. Huygens.

1929. Air.
377 **53** 1½g. black . . . . 2·75 1·60
378 4½g. red . . . . 1·60 3·00
379 7½g. green . . . . 25·00 4·00

1929. Surch **21**.
380 **36** 21c. on 22½c. brown . . . 21·00 1·40

55 "Friendship and Security" **56** Rembrandt and "De Staalmeesters"

1929. Child Welfare.
381A **55** 1½c. (+1½c.) grey . . . . 2·25 50
382C 5c. (+3c.) green . . . . . 3·75 80
383A 6c. (+4c.) red . . . . . 2·25 35
384A 12½c. (+3½c.) blue . . . . 15·00 13·00

1930. Rembrandt Society.
385 **56** 5c. (+5c.) green . . . . . 8·00 7·50
386 6c. (+5c.) black . . . . . 5·50 3·75
387 12½c. (+5c.) blue . . . . . 8·50 8·50

57 Spring **58** **59** Queen Wilhelmina

1930. Child Welfare.
388A **57** 1½c. (+1½c.) red . . . . 1·60 50
389A – 5c. (+3c.) green . . . . . 2·75 65
390A – 6c. (+4c.) purple . . . . 2·40 40
391A – 12½c. (+3½c.) blue . . . . 19·00 9·50
DESIGNS (allegorical): 5c. Summer; 6c. Autumn; 12½c. Winter.

1931. Gouda Church Restoration Fund.
392 **58** 1½c.+1½c. green . . . . . 17·50 15·00
393 – 6c.+4c. red . . . . 21·00 18·00
DESIGN: No. 393, Church facade.

1931.
395 – 70c. blue and red (postage) . . . . 30·00 45
395b – 80c. green and red . . . £110 3·25
394 **59** 36c. red and blue (air) . . 12·50 75
DESIGNS: 70c. Portrait and factory; 80c. Portrait and shipyard.

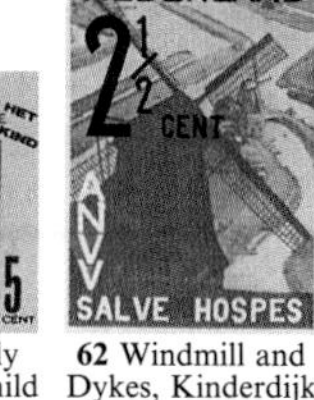

61 Mentally Deficient Child **62** Windmill and Dykes, Kinderdijk **63** Gorse (Spring)

1931. Child Welfare.
396A – 1½c. (+1½c.) red and blue 1·60 1·50
397A **61** 5c. (+3c.) green and purple . . . . 5·25 1·50
398A – 6c. (+4c.) purple and green . . . . 5·25 1·50
399A – 12½c. (+3½c.) blue and red . . . . 30·00 22·00
DESIGNS: 1½c. Deaf mute; 6c. Blind girl; 12½c. Sick child.

1932. Tourist Propaganda.
400 **62** 2½c.+1½c. green and black 7·75 4·75
401 – 6c.+4c. grey and black . . 10·75 4·75
402 – 7½c.+3½c. red and black . . 30·00 15·00
403 – 12½c.+2½c. blue and black 35·00 22·00
DESIGNS: 6c. Aerial view of Town Hall, Zierikzee; 7½c. Bridges at Schipluiden and Moerdijk; 12½c. Tulips.

1932. Child Welfare.
404A **63** 1½c. (+1½c.) brown & yell 2·50 45
405A – 5c. (+3c.) blue and red 3·25 80
406A – 6c. (+4c.) green and orange . . . . 2·50 40
407A – 12½c. (+3½c.) blue & orange . . . . 27·00 22·00
DESIGNS: Child and: 5c. Cornflower (Summer); 6c. Sunflower (Autumn); 12½c. Christmas rose (Winter).

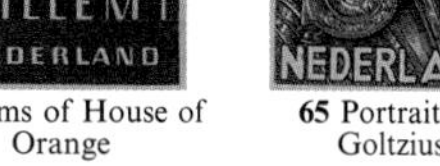

64 Arms of House of Orange **65** Portrait by Goltzius

1933. 4th Birth Centenary of William I of Orange. T **64** and portraits of William I inscr "1533", as T **65**.
408 **64** 1½c. black 60 30
409 **65** 5c. green . . . . 1·75 30
410 – 6c. purple . . . . 2·75 15
411 – 12½c. blue . . . . 16·00 3·00
DESIGNS: 6c. Portrait by Key; 12½c. Portrait attributed to Moro.

68 Dove of Peace **69** Projected Monument at Den Helder **70** "De Hoop" (hospital ship)

1933. Peace Propaganda.
412 **68** 12½c. blue . . . . 8·75 35

1933. Seamen's Fund.
413 **69** 1½c. (+1½c.) red . . . . . 3·25 1·60
414 **70** 5c. (+3c.) green and red . . 10·25 3·00
415 – 6c. (+4c.) green . . . . . 16·00 2·40
416 – 12½c. (+3½c.) blue . . . . 23·00 17·00
DESIGNS: 6c. Lifeboat; 12½c. Seaman and Seamen's Home.

73 Pander S.4 Postjager

1933. Air. Special Flights.
417 **73** 30c. green 75 70

74 Child and Star of Epiphany **75** Princess Juliana

1933. Child Welfare.
418A **74** 1½c. (+1½c.) orange and grey . . . . 1·60 50
419A 5c. (+3c.) yellow and brown . . . . 2·25 65
420A 6c. (+4c.) gold and green 3·25 60
421A 12½c. (+3½c.) silver and blue . . . . 25·00 17·00

1934. Crisis stamps.
438 – 5c. (+4c.) purple . . . . . 12·50 3·00
439 **75** 6c. (+5c.) blue . . . . . . 10·50 4·25
DESIGN: 5c. Queen Wilhelmina.

76 Dutch Warship **77** Dowager Queen Emma

1934. Tercentenary of Curacao.
440 – 6c. black . . . . 3·25 15
441 **76** 12½c. blue . . . . 22·00 2·50
DESIGN: 6c. Willemstad Harbour.

1934. Anti-T.B. Fund.
442 **77** 6c. (+2c.) blue . . . . . . 12·50 1·50

78 Destitute child **79** H. D. Guyot

1934. Child Welfare.
443 **78** 1½c. (+1½c.) brown . . . . 1·60 50
444 5c. (+3c.) red . . . . . . 2·50 1·00
445 6c. (+4c.) green . . . . . 2·50 30
446 12½c. (+3½c.) blue . . . . 25·00 16·00

1935. Cultural and Social Relief Fund.
447 **79** 1½c. (+1½c.) red . . . . . 1·75 1·60
448 – 5c. (+3c.) brown . . . . . 4·50 5·00
449 – 6c. (+4c.) green . . . . . 5·50 85
450 – 12½c. (+3½c.) blue . . . . 27·00 5·75
PORTRAITS: 5c. A. J. M. Diepenbrock; 6c. F. C. Donders; 12½c. J. P. Sweelinck.
See also Nos. 456/9, 469/72, 478/82 and 492/6.

80 Aerial Map of Netherlands **81** Child picking Fruit

1935. Air Fund.
451 **80** 6c. (+4c.) brown . . . . . 27·00 9·25

1935. Child Welfare.
452 **81** 1½c. (+1½c.) red 65 45
453 5c. (+3c.) green . . . . . 1·60 1·40
454 6c. (+4c.) brown . . . . . 1·60 40
455 12½c. (+3½c.) blue . . . . 23·00 8·25

1936. Cultural and Social Relief Fund. As T **79**.
456 1½c. (+1½c.) sepia . . . . . 90 1·00
457 5c. (+3c.) green . . . . . . 4·25 3·50
458 6c. (+4c.) red . . . . 3·75 55
459 12½c. (+3½c.) blue . . . . . 14·00 3·25
PORTRAITS: 1½c. H. Kamerlingh Onnes; 5c. Dr. A. S. Talma; 6c. Mgr. Dr. H. J. A. M. Schaepman; 12½c. Desiderius Erasmus.

83 Pallas Athene

1936. Tercentenary of Utrecht University Foundation.
460 **83** 6c. red . . . . 1·75 25
461 – 12½c. blue . . . . 5·50 8·75
DESIGN: 12½c. Gisbertus Voetius.

84 Child Herald **85** Scout Movement

1936. Child Welfare.
462 **84** 1½c. (+1½c.) slate 60 35
463 5c. (+3c.) green . . . . . 2·25 75
464 6c. (+4c.) brown . . . . . 2·00 30
465 12½c. (+3½c.) blue . . . . 15·00 4·25

1937. Scout Jamboree.
466 – 1½c. black and green . . . 20 15
467 **85** 6c. brown and black . . . 1·50 15
468 – 12½c. black and blue . . . 4·50 1·25
DESIGNS: 1½c. Scout Tenderfoot Badge; 12½c. Hermes.

1937. Cultural and Social Relief Fund. Portraits as T **79**.

469		1½c.+1½c. sepia	60	60
470		5c.+3c. green	5·50	4·00
471		6c.+4c. purple	1·25	40
472		12½c.+3½c. blue	8·25	1·00

PORTRAITS: 1½c. Jacob Maris; 5c. F. de la B. Sylvius; 6c. J. van den Vondel; 12½c. A. van Leeuwenhoek.

86 "Laughing Child" by Frans Hals **87** Queen Wilhelmina

1937. Child Welfare.

473	**86**	1½c. (+1½c.) black	20	15
474		3c. (+2c.) green	1·60	1·10
475		4c. (+2c.) red	65	50
476		5c. (+3c.) green	60	15
477		12½c. (+3½c.) blue	7·50	1·25

1938. Cultural and Social Relief Fund. As T **79**.

478		1½c.+1½c. sepia	40	50
479		3c.+2c. green	65	35
480		4c.+2c. red	2·00	2·10
481		5c.+3c. green	2·50	35
482		12½c.+3½c. blue	9·25	1·10

PORTRAITS: 1½c. M. van St. Aldegonde; 3c. O. G. Heldring; 4c. Maria Tesselschade; 5c. Rembrandt; 12½c. H. Boerhaave.

1938. 40th Anniv of Coronation.

483	**87**	1½c. black	20	15
484		5c. red	30	15
485		12½c. blue	3·75	1·50

88 Carrion Crow **89** Boy with Flute

1938. Air. Special Flights.

486	**88**	12½c. blue and grey	65	65
790a		25c. blue and grey	4·00	1·75

1938. Child Welfare.

487	**89**	1½c.+1½c. black	20	30
488		3c.+2c. brown	50	40
489		4c.+2c. green	90	85
490		5c.+3c. red	45	20
491		12½c.+3½c. blue	10·00	2·00

1939. Cultural and Social Relief Fund. As T **79**.

492		1½c.+1½c. brown	65	60
493		2½c.+2½c. green	3·50	2·75
494		3c.+3c. red	90	1·25
495		5c.+3c. green	2·75	35
496		12½c.+3½c. blue	6·75	1·10

PORTRAITS: 1½c. M. Maris; 2½c. Anton Mauve; 3c. Gerardus van Swieten; 5c. Nicolas Beets; 12½c. Pieter Stuyvesant.

91 St. Willibrord's landing in the Netherlands **92** Replica of Locomotive "De Arend" **93** Child and Cornucopia

1939. 12th Death Centenary of St. Willibrord.

497	**91**	5c. green	75	15
498	–	12½c. blue	5·50	3·00

DESIGN: 12½c. St. Willibrord as Bishop of Utrecht.

1939. Centenary of Netherlands Railway.

499	**92**	5c. green	80	15
500	–	12½c. blue	8·25	4·25

DESIGN: 12½c. Electric railcar.

1939. Child Welfare.

501	**93**	1½c.+1½c. black	20	25
502		2½c.+2½c. green	5·50	3·00
503		3c.+3c. red	75	30
504		5c.+3c. green	1·10	25
505		12½c.+3½c. blue	4·50	1·50

94 Queen Wilhelmina **95** Vincent Van Gogh **98** Girl with Dandelion

1940.

506	**94**	5c. green	30	10
506a		6c. brown	70	15
507		7½c. red	30	10
508		10c. purple	30	10
509		12½c. blue	30	10
510		15c. blue	30	10
510a		17½c. blue	1·25	85
511		20c. violet	65	15
512		22½c. olive	1·25	1·00
513		25c. red	50	15
514		30c. ochre	1·00	40
515		40c. green	2·00	85
515a		50c. orange	8·00	65
515b		60c. purple	8·00	2·50

1940. Cultural and Social Relief Fund.

516	**95**	1½c.+1½c. brown	2·00	50
517	–	2½c.+2½c. green	6·00	1·10
518	–	3c.+3c. red	3·50	1·10
519	–	5c.+3c. green	7·50	40
520	–	12½c.+3½c. blue	6·75	85

PORTRAITS: 1½c. E. J. Potgieter; 3c. Petrus Camper; 5c. Jan Steen; 12½c. Joseph Scaliger.

See also Nos. 558/62 and 656/60.

1940. As No. 519, colour changed. Surch.

521		7½c.+2½c. on 5c.+3c. red	65	40

1940. Surch with large figures and network.

522	**35**	2½ on 3c. red	3·00	40
523		5 on 3c. green	20	15
524		7½ on 3c. red	20	10
525		10 on 3c. green	20	15
526		12½ on 3c. blue	40	30
527		17½ on 3c. green	70	65
528		20 on 3c. green	50	15
529		22½ on 3c. green	90	1·00
530		25 on 3c. green	55	35
531		30 on 3c. green	70	45
532		40 on 3c. green	85	65
533		50 on 3c. green	1·00	65
534		60 on 3c. green	1·90	1·40
535		70 on 3c. green	4·00	2·40
536		80 on 3c. green	6·00	5·25
537		100 on 3c. green	35·00	35·00
538		250 on 3c. green	42·00	40·00
539		500 on 3c. green	40·00	38·00

1940. Child Welfare.

540	**98**	1½c.+1½c. violet	90	30
541		2½c.+2½c. olive	2·50	85
542		4c.+3c. blue	3·00	95
543		5c.+3c. green	3·25	15
544		7½c.+3½c. red	95	15

1941.

546	**35**	5c. green	10	10
547		7½c. red	10	10
548		10c. violet	80	15
549		12½c. blue	30	30
550		15c. blue	80	35
551		17½c. red	15	15
552		20c. violet	85	15
553		22½c. olive	15	25
554		25c. lake	35	30
555		30c. brown	3·00	30
556		40c. green	15	30
557		50c. brown	15	15

1941. Cultural and Social Relief Fund. As T **95** but inscr "ZOMERZEGEL 31.12.46".

558		1½c.+1½c. brown	85	30
559		2½c.+2½c. green	85	30
560		4c.+3c. red	85	30
561		5c.+3c. green	85	30
562		7½c.+3½c. purple	85	30

PORTRAITS: 1½c. Dr. A. Mathijsen; 2½c. J. Ingenhousz; 4c. Aagje Deken; 5c. Johan Bosboom; 7½c. A. C. W. Staring.

100 "Titus Rembrandt" **101** Legionary

1941. Child Welfare.

563	**100**	1½c.+1½c. black	50	30
564		2½c.+2½c. olive	50	30
565		4c.+3c. blue	50	30
566		5c.+3c. green	50	30
567		7½c.+3½c. red	50	30

1942. Netherlands Legion Fund.

568	**101**	7½c.+2½c. red	75	60
569	–	12½c.+87½c. blue	6·25	6·00

DESIGN—HORIZ: 12½c. Legionary with similar inscription.

1943. 1st European Postal Congress. As T **26** but larger (21 × 27½ mm) surch **EUROPEESCHE P T T VEREENIGING 19 OCTOBER 1942 10 CENT.**

570	**26**	10c. on 2½c. yellow	20	25

103 Seahorse **104** Michiel A. de Ruyter

1943. Old Germanic Symbols.

571	**103**	1c. black	10	10
572	–	1½c. red	10	10
573	–	2c. blue	10	10
574	–	2½c. green	10	10
575	–	3c. red	10	10
576	–	4c. brown	10	10
577	–	5c. olive	10	10

DESIGNS—VERT: 1½c. Triple crowned tree; 2½c. Birds in ornamental tree; 4c. Horse and rider. HORIZ: 2c. Swans; 3c. Trees and serpentine roots; 5c. Prancing horses.

1943. Dutch Naval Heroes.

578	**104**	7½c. red	10	10
579	–	10c. green	15	10
580	–	12½c. blue	15	15
581	–	15c. violet	15	15
582	–	17½c. grey	15	15
583	–	20c. brown	15	15
584	–	22½c. red	15	20
585	–	25c. purple	45	55
586	–	30c. blue	15	20
587	–	40c. grey	15	15

PORTRAITS: 10c. Johan Evertsen; 12½c. Maarten H. Tromp; 15c. Piet Hein; 17½c. Wilhelm Joseph van Gent; 20c. Witte de With; 22½c. Cornelis Evertsen; 25c. Tjerk Hiddes de Fries; 30c. Cornelis Tromp; 40c. Cornelis Evertsen the younger.

105 Mail Cart **106** Child and Doll's House

1943. Stamp Day.

589	**105**	7½c.+7½c. red	15	15

1944. Child Welfare and Winter Help Funds. Inscr "WINTERHULP" (1½c. and 7½c.) or "VOLKSDIENST" (others).

590	**106**	1½c.+3½c. black	15	20
591	–	4c.+3½c. brown	15	20
592	–	5c.+5c. green	15	20
593	–	7½c.+7½c. red	15	20
594	–	10c.+40c. blue	15	20

DESIGNS: 4c. Mother and child; 5c., 10c. Mother and children; 7½c. Child and wheatsheaf.

107 Infantryman **111** Queen Wilhelmina

1944.

595	**107**	1½c. black	10	10
596	–	2½c. green	10	10
597	–	3c. brown	10	10
598	–	5c. blue	10	10
599	**111**	7½c. red	10	10
600		10c. orange	10	10
601		12½c. blue	10	10
602		15c. red	1·40	1·25
603		17½c. green	1·10	1·10
604		20c. violet	50	30
605		22½c. red	1·10	90
606		25c. brown	1·75	1·40
607		30c. green	30	20
608		40c. purple	2·10	1·90
609		50c. mauve	1·40	1·00

DESIGNS—HORIZ: 2½c. "Nieuw Amsterdam" (liner); 3c. Airman. VERT: 5c. "De Ruyter" (cruiser).

The above set was originally for use on Netherlands warships serving with the Allied Fleet, and was used after liberation in the Netherlands.

112 Lion and Dragon **113**

1945. Liberation.

610	**112**	7½c. orange	20	15

1945. Child Welfare.

611	**113**	1½c.+2½c. grey	30	30
612		2½c.+3½c. green	30	30
613		5c.+5c. brown	30	30
614		7½c.+4½c. red	30	30
615		12½c.+5½c. blue	30	30

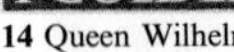

114 Queen Wilhelmina **115** Emblem of Abundance

1946.

616	**114**	1g. blue	1·75	50
617		2½g. red	£130	10·50
618		5g. green	£130	27·00
619		10g. violet	£130	26·00

1946. War Victims' Relief Fund.

620	**115**	1½c.+3½c. black	50	30
621		2½c.+5c. green	60	55
622		5c.+10c. violet	60	55
623		7½c.+15c. red	50	30
624		12½c.+37½c. blue	95	55

116 Princess Irene **117** Boy on Roundabout

1946. Child Welfare.

625	**116**	1½c.+1½c. brown	60	55
626	–	2½c.+1½c. green	60	55
627	**116**	4c.+2c. red	70	55
628	–	5c.+2c. brown	70	55
629	–	7½c.+2½c. red	60	15
630	–	12½c.+7½c. blue	60	55

PORTRAITS: 2½c., 5c. Princess Margriet; 7½c., 12½c. Princess Beatrix.

1946. Child Welfare.

631	**117**	2c.+2c. violet	60	45
632		4c.+2c. green	60	45
633		7½c.+2½c. red	60	45
634		10c.+5c. purple	70	15
635		20c.+5c. blue	95	65

118 Numeral **119** Queen Wilhelmina **122** Children

1946.

636	**118**	1c. red	10	10
637		2c. blue	10	10
638		2½c. orange	7·50	1·60
638a		3c. brown	10	10
639		4c. green	35	10
639a		5c. orange	10	10
639c		6c. grey	35	15
639d		7c. red	15	10
639f		8c. mauve	15	10

1947.

640	**119**	5c. green	1·10	10
641		6c. black	40	10
642		6c. blue	60	10
643		7½c. red	40	20
644		10c. purple	70	10
645		12½c. red	70	40
646		15c. violet	8·25	10
647		20c. blue	8·75	10
648		22½c. green	70	65
649		25c. blue	16·00	10
650		30c. orange	16·00	25
651		35c. blue	16·00	55
652		40c. brown	19·00	55
653	–	45c. blue	22·00	12·00
654	–	50c. brown	14·50	30
655	–	60c. red	18·00	2·25

Nos. 653/5 are as Type **119** but have the inscriptions in colour on white ground.

1947. Cultural and Social Relief Fund. As T **95** but inscr "ZOMERZEGEL ... 13.12.48".
656 2c.+2c. red 85 45
657 4c.+2c. green . . . . . . 1·40 65
658 7½c.+2½c. violet . . . . . 1·90 85
659 10c.+5c. brown . . . . . . 1·75 35
660 20c.+5c. blue . . . . 1·40 65
PORTRAITS: 2c. H. van Deventer; 4c. P. C. Hooft; 7½c. Johan de Witt; 10c. J. F. van Royen; 20c. Hugo Grotius.

1947. Child Welfare.
661 **122** 2c.+2c. brown 15 15
662 – 4c.+2c. green . . . . . 1·10 55
663 – 7½c.+2½c. brown . . . . 1·10 85
664 – 10c.+5c. lake . . . . . 1·25 15
665 **122** 20c.+5c. blue . . . . . 1·40 85
DESIGN: 4c. to 10c. Baby.

124 Ridderzaal, The Hague
125 Queen Wilhelmina

1948. Cultural and Social Relief Fund.
666 **124** 2c.+2c. brown . . . . . 1·90 45
667 – 6c.+4c. green . . . . . 2·00 55
668 – 10c.+5c. red . . . . . . 1·40 30
669 – 20c.+5c. blue . . . . . 2·00 85
BUILDINGS: 6c. Palace on the Dam; 10c. Kneuterdijk Palace; 20c. Nieuwe Kerk, Amsterdam.

1948. Queen Wilhelmina's Golden Jubilee.
670 **125** 10c. red 15 10
671 20c. blue . . . . 2·25 1·90

126 Queen Juliana
127 Boy in Canoe

1948. Coronation.
672 **126** 10c. brown . . . . 1·60 10
673 20c. blue . . . . 2·00 50

1948. Child Welfare.
674 **127** 2c.+2c. green 15 15
675 – 5c.+3c. green . . . . . . 2·25 70
676 – 6c.+4c. grey . . . . . . 1·25 15
677 – 10c.+5c. red 50 15
678 – 20c.+8c. blue . . . . . . 2·25 1·00
DESIGNS: 5c. Girl swimming; 6c. Boy on toboggan; 10c. Girl on swing; 20c. Boy skating.

128 Terrace near Beach

1949. Cultural and Social Relief Fund.
679 **128** 2c.+2c. yellow and blue 2·00 20
680 – 5c.+3c. yellow and blue 3·50 1·90
681 – 6c.+4c. green . . . . . . 3·00 45
682 – 10c.+5c. yellow and blue 3·75 10
683 – 20c.+5c. blue . . . . . . 3·50 1·90
DESIGNS: 5c. Hikers in cornfield; 6c. Campers by fire; 10c. Gathering wheat; 20c. Yachts.

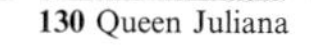

129 Queen Juliana
130 Queen Juliana
131 Hands reaching for Sunflower

1949.
684 **129** 5c. green 65 10
685 6c. blue 40 10
686 10c. orange 40 10
687 12c. red . . . . 1·90 1·75
688 15c. green . . . . 5·75 40
689 20c. blue . . . . 4·25 10
690 25c. brown . . . . 12·50 10
691 30c. violet . . . . 8·75 10
692 35c. blue . . . . 23·00 15
693 40c. purple . . . . 40·00 30
694 45c. orange . . . . 1·90 80
695 45c. violet . . . . 55·00 55
696 50c. green . . . . 10·00 25
697 60c. brown . . . . 15·00 20
697a 75c. red . . . . 70·00 1·25
698 **130** 1g. red . . . . 4·00 15
699 2½g. brown . . . . . . £250 2·00
700a 5g. brown . . . . £450 3·50
701 10g. violet . . . . £300 15·00

1949. Red Cross and Indonesian Relief Fund.
702 **131** 2c.+3c. yellow and grey 95 30
703 6c.+4c. yellow and red . . 60 35
704 10c.+5c. yellow and blue 3·75 25
705 30c.+10c. yellow & brn 9·50 3·00

132 Posthorns and Globe
133 "Autumn"

1949. 75th Anniv of U.P.U.
706 **132** 10c. lake 95 10
707 20c. blue . . . . 9·50 2·25

1949. Child Welfare Fund. Inscr "VOOR HET KIND".
708 **133** 2c.+3c. brown 40 15
709 – 5c.+3c. red . . . . 6·50 1·90
710 – 6c.+4c. green . . . . . . 3·50 40
711 – 10c.+5c. grey 40 15
712 – 20c.+7c. blue . . . . . . 5·50 1·50
DESIGNS: 5c. "Summer"; 6c. "Spring"; 10c. "Winter"; 20c. "New Year".

134 Resistance Monument
135 Section of Moerdijk Bridge

1950. Cultural and Social Relief Fund. Inscr "ZOMERZEGEL 1950".
713 **134** 2c.+2c. brown . . . . . 2·00 1·10
714 – 4c.+2c. green . . . . . . 11·50 10·50
715 – 5c.+3c. grey . . . . . . 8·75 3·25
716 – 6c.+4c. violet . . . . . 4·50 65
717 **135** 10c.+5c. slate . . . . . 6·00 35
718 – 20c.+5c. blue . . . . . 17·00 14·00
DESIGNS—VERT: 4c. Sealing dykes; 5c. Rotterdam skyscraper. HORIZ: 6c. Harvesting; 20c. "Overijssel" (canal freighter).

1950. Surch with bold figure **6**.
719 **119** 6c. on 7½c. red . . . . . 2·25 15

137 Good Samaritan and Bombed Church
138 Janus Dousa

1950. Bombed Churches Rebuilding Fund.
720 **137** 2c.+2c. olive . . . . . . 7·25 1·75
721 5c.+3c. brown . . . . . 10·50 10·25
722 6c.+4c. green . . . . . . 7·25 3·00
723 10c.+5c. red . . . . . . 17·50 65
724 20c.+5c. blue . . . . . . 32·00 29·00

1950. 375th Anniv of Leyden University.
725 **138** 10c. olive . . . . 4·25 15
726 – 20c. blue . . . . 4·25 1·25
PORTRAIT: 20c. Jan van Hout.

139 Baby and Bees
140 Bergh Castle

1950. Child Welfare. Inscr "VOOR HET KIND".
727 **139** 2c.+3c. red 30 15
728 – 5c.+3c. olive . . . . . . 10·00 3·75
729 – 6c.+4c. green . . . . . . 3·50 65
730 – 10c.+5c. purple 40 15
731 – 20c.+7c. blue . . . . . . 10·50 9.00.
DESIGNS: 5c. Boy and fowl; 6c. Girl and birds; 10c. Boy and fish; 20c. Girl, butterfly and frog.

1951. Cultural and Social Relief Fund. Castles.
732 – 2c.+2c. violet . . . . . . 2·50 1·25
733 **140** 5c.+3c. red . . . . 8·75 5·50
734 – 6c.+4c. sepia . . . . . . 3·00 55
735 – 10c.+5c. green . . . . . 6·00 30
736 – 20c.+5c. blue . . . . . 8·50 7·50
DESIGNS—HORIZ: 2c. Hillenraad; 6c. Hernen. VERT: 10c. Rechteren; 20c. Moermond.

141 Girl and Windmill
142 Gull

1951. Child Welfare.
737 **141** 2c.+3c. green 60 15
738 – 5c.+3c. blue . . . . . . 7·50 4·25
739 – 6c.+4c. brown . . . . . 5·50 65
740 – 10c.+5c. lake 35 15
741 – 20c.+7c. blue . . . . . . 7·50 6·50
DESIGNS: Each shows boy or girl: 5c. Crane; 6c. Fishing nets; 10c. Factory chimneys; 20c. Flats.

1951. Air.
742 **142** 15g. brown £275 £125
743 25g. black £275 £125

143 Jan van Riebeeck

1952. Tercentenary of Landing in South Africa and Van Riebeeck Monument Fund.
744 **143** 2c.+3c. violet . . . . . . 5·50 3·75
745 6c.+4c. green . . . . . . 6·25 4·50
746 10c.+5c. red . . . . . . 7·25 4·50
747 20c.+5c. blue . . . . . . 5·50 3·50

144 Miner
145 Wild Rose

1952. 50th Anniv of State Mines, Limburg.
748 **144** 10c. blue . . . . 2·25 10

1952. Cultural and Social Relief Fund. Floral designs inscr "ZOMERZEGEL 1952".
749 **145** 2c.+2c. green and red . . 70 50
750 – 5c.+3c. yellow and green 2·50 2·75
751 – 6c.+4c. green and red . . 2·25 1·00
752 – 10c.+5c. green & orange 1·90 35
753 – 20c.+5c. green and blue 10·50 8·50
FLOWERS: 5c. Marsh marigold; 6c. Tulip; 10c. Marguerite; 20c. Cornflower.

146 Radio Masts
147 Boy feeding Goat

1952. Netherlands Stamp Centenary and Centenary of Telegraph Service.
754 – 2c. violet 50 10
755 **146** 6c. red 60 15
756 – 10c. green 50 10
757 – 20c. slate . . . . 7·50 1·90
DESIGNS: 2c. Telegraph poles and steam train; 10c. Postman delivering letters, 1852; 20c. Postman delivering letters, 1952.

1952. International Postage Stamp Exn, Utrecht ("ITEP"). Nos. 754/7 but colours changed.
757a – 2c. brown . . . . 20·00 15·00
757b **146** 6c. blue . . . . 20·00 15·00
757c – 10c. lake . . . . 20·00 15·00
757d – 20c. blue . . . . 20·00 15·00
Nos. 757a/d were sold only in sets at the Exhibition at face plus 1g. entrance fee.

1952. Child Welfare.
758 **147** 2c.+3c. black and olive 20 20
759 – 5c.+3c. black and pink . . 3·00 1·25
760 – 6c.+4c. black and green 2·50 45
761 – 10c.+5c. black & orange 15 15
762 – 20c.+7c. black and blue 7·50 6·00
DESIGNS: 5c. Girl riding donkey; 6c. Girl playing with dog; 10c. Boy and cat; 20c. Boy and rabbit.

1953. Flood Relief Fund. Surch **19 53 10c +10 WATERSNOOD**.
763 **129** 10c.+10c. orange 65 15

149 Hyacinth
150 Red Cross

1953. Cultural and Social Relief Fund.
764 **149** 2c.+2c. green and violet 70 40
765 – 5c.+3c. green & orange 2·10 1·75
766 – 6c.+4c. yellow and green 2·00 55
767 – 10c.+5c. green and red . . 3·25 15
768 – 20c.+5c. green and blue 13·15 12·00
FLOWERS: 5c. African marigold; 6c. Daffodil; 10c. Anemone; 20c. Dutch iris.

1953. Red Cross Fund. Inscr "RODE KRUIS".
769 **150** 2c.+3c. red and sepia . . 95 45
770 – 6c.+4c. red and brown . . 3·75 2·50
771 – 7c.+5c. red and olive . . 1·10 45
772 – 10c.+5c. red 65 15
773 – 25c.+8c. red and blue . . 8·25 5·00
DESIGNS: 6c. Man with lamp; 7c. Rescue worker in flooded area; 10c. Nurse giving blood transfusion; 25c. Red Cross flags.

151 Queen Juliana
152 Queen Juliana

1953.
775 **151** 10c. brown 15 10
776 12c. turquoise 15 10
777 15c. red 15 10
777b 18c. turquoise 15 10
778 20c. purple 15 10
778b 24c. olive 25 20
779 25c. blue 25 10
780a 30c. orange 40 10
781 35c. brown 70 10
781a 37c. turquoise 50 15
782 40c. slate 40 10
783 45c. red 40 10
784 50c. green 55 10
785 60c. brown 65 10
785a 62c. red . . . . 3·00 2·50
785b 70c. blue 65 10
786 75c. purple 65 10
786a 80c. violet 65 10
786b 85c. green . . . . 1·10 10
786c 95c. brown . . . . 1·40 25
787 **152** 1g. red . . . . 1·90 20
788 2½g. green . . . . 8·75 15
789 5g. black . . . . 3·75 30
790 10g. blue . . . . 17·50 1·75

153 Girl with Pigeon
154 M. Nijhoff (poet)

1953. Child Welfare. Inscr "VOOR HET KIND".
791 – 2c.+3c. blue and yellow 15 15
792 – 5c.+3c. lake and green . . 3·25 2·25
793 **153** 7c.+5c. brown and blue 3·75 85
794 – 10c.+5c. lilac and bistre 15 15
795 – 25c.+8c. turq & pink . . 11·00 10·00
DESIGNS: 2c. Girl, bucket and spade; 5c. Boy and apple; 10c. Boy and tjalk (sailing boat); 25c. Girl and tulip.

1954. Cultural and Social Relief Fund.
796 **154** 2c.+3c. blue . . . . . . 1·90 1·60
797 – 5c.+3c. brown . . . . . 2·75 1·75
798 – 7c.+5c. red . . . . 3·75 1·40
799 – 10c.+5c. green . . . . . 7·25 60
800 – 25c.+8c. purple . . . . . 10·50 11·00
PORTRAITS: 5c. W. Pijper (composer); 7c. H. P. Berlage (architect); 10c. J. Huizinga (historian); 25c. Vincent van Gogh (painter).

155 St. Boniface
156 Boy and Model Glider

1954. 1200th Anniv of Martyrdom of St. Boniface.
801 **155** 10c. blue . . . . 2·75 10

1954. National Aviation Fund.
802 **156** 2c.+2c. green . . . . . . 1·40 1·00
803 – 10c.+4c. blue . . . . . 3·50 65
PORTRAIT: 10c. Dr. A. Plesman (aeronautical pioneer).

157 Making Paperchains 158 Queen Juliana

1954. Child Welfare.
804 **157** 2c.+3c. brown 15 15
805 – 5c.+3c. olive . . . . . . 1·75 1·50
806 – 7c.+5c. blue . . . . . . 1·60 55
807 – 10c.+5c. red 15 15
808 – 25c.+8c. blue . . . . . . 9·25 5·75
DESIGNS—VERT: 5c. Girl brushing her teeth; 7c. Boy and toy boat; 10c. Nurse and child. HORIZ: 25c. Invalid boy drawing in bed.

1954. Ratification of Statute for the Kingdom.
809 **158** 10c. red . . . . 1·00 15

159 Factory, Rotterdam 160 "The Victory of Peace"

1955. Cultural and Social Relief Fund.
810 **159** 2c.+3c. brown . . . . . 1·25 1·10
811 – 5c.+3c. green . . . . . . 1·40 95
812 – 7c.+5c. red . . . . 1·25 95
813 – 10c.+5c. blue . . . . . . 2·10 20
814 – 25c.+8c. brown . . . . . 11·50 9·50
DESIGNS—HORIZ: 5c. Post Office, The Hague; 10c. Town Hall, Hilversum; 25c. Office Building, The Hague. VERT: 7c. Stock Exchange, Amsterdam.

1955. 10th Anniv of Liberation.
815 **160** 10c. red . . . . 1·60 15

161 Microscope and Emblem of Cancer 162 "Willem van Loon" (D. Dircks)

1955. Queen Wilhelmina Anti-cancer Fund.
816 **161** 2c.+3c. black and red . . 60 55
817 5c.+3c. green and red . . 1·60 1·25
818 7c.+5c. purple and red . . 1·40 65
819 10c.+5c. blue and red . . 90 15
820 25c.+8c. olive and red . . 5·75 5·75

1955. Child Welfare Fund.
821 **162** 2c.+3c. green 45 15
822 – 5c.+3c. red . . . . 2·25 95
823 – 7c.+5c. brown . . . . . . 4·00 80
824 – 10c.+5c. blue 40 15
825 – 25c.+8c. lilac . . . . . . 9·25 7·75
PORTRAITS: 5c. "Portrait of a Boy" (J. A. Backer); 7c. "Portrait of a Girl" (unknown); 10c. "Philips Huygens" (A. Hanneman); 25c. "Constantin Huygens" (A. Hanneman).

163 "Farmer"

1956. Cultural and Social Relief Fund and 350th Birth Anniv of Rembrandt. Details from Rembrandt's paintings.
826 **163** 2c.+3c. slate . . . . . . 2·75 2·50
827 – 5c.+3c. olive . . . . . . 1·75 1·40
828 – 7c.+5c. brown . . . . . . 4·25 4·00
829 – 10c.+5c. green . . . . . 12·50 65
830 – 25c.+8c. brown . . . . . 18·00 16·00
PAINTINGS: 5c. "Young Tobias with Angel"; 7c. "Persian wearing Fur Cap"; 10c. "Old Blind Tobias"; 25c. Self-portrait, 1639.

164 Yacht 165 Amphora

1956. 16th Olympic Games, Melbourne.
831 **164** 2c.+3c. black and blue . . 75 65
832 – 5c.+3c. black and yellow 1·25 95
833 **165** 7c.+5c. black and brown 1·40 95
834 – 10c.+5c. black and grey 2·75 55
835 – 25c.+8c. black and green 6·50 5·75
DESIGNS: As Type **164**: 5c. Runner; 10c. Hockey player; 25c. Water polo player.

1956. Europa. As T **110** of Luxembourg.
836 10c. black and lake . . . . . 2·25 10
837 25c. black and blue . . . . . 50·00 1·60

167 "Portrait of a Boy" (Van Scorel)

1956. Child Welfare Fund. 16th-century Dutch Paintings.
838 **167** 2c.+3c. grey and cream 40 10
839 – 5c.+3c. olive and cream 1·25 1·10
840 – 7c.+5c. purple & cream 3·50 1·50
841 – 10c.+5c. red and cream 40 15
842 – 25c.+8c. blue and cream 7·25 3·75
PAINTINGS: 5c. "Portrait of a Boy"; 7c. "Portrait of a Girl"; 10c. "Portrait of a Girl"; 25c. "Portrait of Eechie Pieters".

168 "Curacao" (trawler) and Fish Barrels 169 Admiral M. A. de Ruyter

1957. Cultural and Social Relief Fund. Ships.
843 – 4c.+3c. blue . . . . . . 1·25 1·00
844 – 6c.+4c. lilac . . . . . . 2·25 1·90
845 – 7c.+5c. red . . . . 1·90 1·25
846 **168** 10c.+8c. green . . . . . 3·75 35
847 – 30c.+8c. brown . . . . . 4·75 4·25
DESIGNS: 4c. "Gaasterland" (freighter); 6c. Coaster; 7c. "Willem Barendsz" (whale factory ship) and whale; 30c. "Nieuw Amsterdam" (liner).

1957. 350th Birth Anniv of M. A. de Ruyter.
848 **169** 10c. orange 70 15
849 – 30c. blue . . . . 4·75 1·90
DESIGN: 30c. De Ruyter's flagship, "De Zeven Provincien".

170 Blood Donors' Emblem 171 "Europa" Star

1957. 90th Anniv of Netherlands Red Cross Society and Red Cross Fund.
850 **170** 4c.+3c. blue and red . . . 1·10 1·10
851 – 6c.+4c. green and red . . 1·40 1·25
852 – 7c.+5c. red and green . . 1·40 1·25
853 – 10c.+8c. red and ochre . . 1·25 15
854 – 30c.+8c. red and blue . . 2·75 2·50
DESIGNS: 6c. "J. Henry Dunant" (hospital ship); 7c. Red Cross; 10c. Red Cross emblem; 30c. Red Cross on globe.

1957. Europa.
855 **171** 10c. black and blue . . . 60 10
856 30c. green and blue . . . 7·00 1·50

172 Portrait by B. J. Blommers 173 Walcheren Costume

1957. Child Fund Welfare. 19th- and 20th-Century Paintings by Dutch Masters.
857 **172** 4c.+4c. red 40 15
858 – 6c.+4c. green . . . . . . 2·50 1·90
859 – 8c.+4c. sepia . . . . . . 3·25 1·90
860 – 12c.+9c. purple 40 15
861 – 30c.+9c. blue . . . . . . 8·25 6·75
PORTRAITS: Child paintings by: W. B. Tholen (6c.); J. Sluyters (8c.); M. Maris (12c.); C. Kruseman (30c.).

1958. Cultural and Social Relief Fund. Provincial Costumes.
862 **173** 4c.+4c. blue 70 55
863 – 6c.+4c. ochre . . . . . 1·60 1·00
864 – 8c.+4c. red . . . . 4·75 1·60
865 – 12c.+9c. brown . . . . . 1·75 20
866 – 30c.+9c. lilac . . . . . . 7·50 6·25
COSTUMES: 6c. Marken; 8c. Scheveningen; 12c. Friesland; 30c. Volendam.

1958. Surch **12 C**.
867 **151** 12c. on 10c. brown . . . 1·25 10

1958. Europa. As T **119a** of Luxembourg.
868 12c. blue and red 20 10
869 30c. red and blue . . . . . 1·00 65

176 Girl on Stilts and Boy on Tricycle 177 Cranes

1958. Child Welfare Fund. Children's Games.
870 **176** 4c.+4c. blue 20 15
871 – 6c.+4c. red . . . . 2·50 1·75
872 – 8c.+4c. green . . . . . . 1·75 1·00
873 – 12c.+9c. red 20 15
874 – 30c.+9c. blue . . . . . . 6·00 4·75
DESIGNS: 6c. Boy and girl on scooter; 8c. Boys playing leap-frog; 12c. Boys on roller-skates; 30c. Girl skipping and boy in toy car.

1959. 10th Anniv of N.A.T.O. As T **123** of Luxembourg (N.A.T.O. emblem).
875 12c. blue and yellow 20 10
876 30c. blue and red . . . . . 1·00 60

1959. Cultural and Social Relief Fund. Prevention of Sea Encroachment.
877 – 4c.+4c. blue on green . . 1·40 1·25
878 – 6c.+4c. brown on grey . . 95 90
879 – 8c.+4c. violet on blue . . 2·25 1·40
880 **177** 12c.+9c. green on yell . . 4·25 20
881 – 30c.+9c. black on red . . 6·50 6·00
DESIGNS: 4c. Tugs and caisson; 6c. Dredger; 8c. Labourers making fascine mattresses; 30c. Sand-spouter and scoop.

1959. Europa. As T **123a** of Luxembourg.
882 12c. red 20 10
883 30c. green . . . . 3·60 3·25

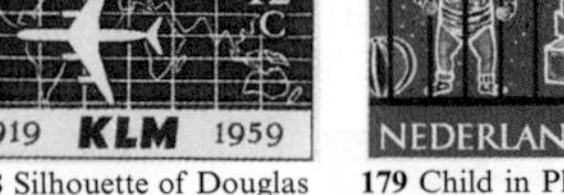

178 Silhouette of Douglas DC-8 Airliner and World Map 179 Child in Play-pen

1959. 40th Anniv of K.L.M. (Royal Dutch Airlines).
884 **178** 12c. blue and red 20 10
885 – 30c. blue and green . . . 1·60 1·25
DESIGN: 30c. Silhouette of Douglas DC-8 airliner.

1959. Child Welfare Fund.
886 **179** 4c.+4c. blue and brown 20 15
887 – 6c.+4c. brown and green 1·75 1·40
888 – 8c.+4c. blue and red . . . 2·75 1·75
889 – 12c.+9c. red, black and blue 20 10
890 – 30c.+9c. turquoise and yellow . . . . 4·25 3·50
DESIGNS: 6c. Boy as "Red Indian" with bow and arrow; 8c. Boy feeding geese; 12c. Traffic warden escorting children; 30c. Girl doing homework.

180 Refugee Woman 181 White Water-lily

1960. World Refugee Year.
891 **180** 12c.+8c. purple 35 15
892 30c.+10c. green . . . . . 3·50 2·25

1960. Cultural and Social Relief Fund. Flowers.
893 – 4c.+4c. red, green and grey 95 60
894 – 6c.+4c. yellow, green and salmon . . . . 1·40 1·25
895 **181** 8c.+4c. multicoloured . . 3·25 1·90
896 – 12c.+8c. red, green and buff . . . . 2·75 30
897 – 30c.+10c. blue, green and yellow . . . . 6·00 5·00
FLOWERS—VERT: 4c. "The Princess" tulip; 6c. Gorse; 12c. Poppy; 30c. Blue sea-holly.

182 J. van der Kolk 183 Marken Costume

1960. World Mental Health Year.
898 **182** 12c. red 85 15
899 – 30c. blue (J. Wier) . . . . 6·50 2·40

1960. Europa. As T **113a** of Norway.
900 12c. yellow and red 20 10
901 30c. yellow and blue . . . . 3·00 1·90

1960. Child Welfare Fund. Costumes. Mult portraits.
902 **183** 4c.+4c. slate 35 15
903 – 6c.+4c. ochre . . . . . . 2·40 1·25
904 – 8c.+4c. turquoise . . . . 5·00 1·75
905 – 12c.+9c. violet 30 10
906 – 30c.+9c. grey . . . . . . 7·25 5·75
DESIGNS: Costumes of: 6c. Volendam; 8c. Bunschoten; 12c. Hindeloopen; 30c. Huizen.

184 Herring Gull 185 Doves

1961. Cultural and Social Relief Fund. Beach and Meadow Birds.
907 **184** 4c.+4c. slate and yellow 1·25 1·25
908 – 6c.+4c. sepia and brown 1·40 1·40
909 – 8c.+4c. brown and olive 1·10 2·00
910 – 12c.+8c. black and blue 2·40 40
911 – 30c.+10c. black & green 3·00 2·75
BIRDS—HORIZ: 6c. Oystercatcher; 12c. Pied avocet. VERT: 8c. Curlew; 30c. Northern lapwing.

1961. Europa.
912 **185** 12c. brown 10 10
913 30c. turquoise 30 30

186 St. Nicholas 187 Queen Juliana and Prince Bernhard

1961. Child Welfare.
914 **186** 4c.+4c. red 20 15
915 – 6c.+4c. blue . . . . . . 1·25 90
916 – 8c.+4c. bistre . . . . . . 1·25 1·00
917 – 12c.+9c. green 20 10
918 – 30c.+9c. orange . . . . . 3·50 3·00
DESIGNS: 6c. Epiphany; 8c. Palm Sunday; 12c. Whitsuntide; 30c. Martinmas.

1962. Silver Wedding.
919 **187** 12c. red 20 10
920 30c. green . . . . 1·40 75

188 Detail of "The Repast of the Officers of the St. Jorisdoelen" after Frans Hals 189 Telephone Dial

1962. Cultural, Health and Social Welfare Funds.
921 – 4c.+4c. green . . . . . . 1·10 90
922 – 6c.+4c. black 90 90
923 – 8c.+4c. purple . . . . . 1·40 1·25
924 – 12c.+8c. bistre . . . . . 1·40 40
925 **188** 30c.+10c. blue . . . . . 1·60 1·40
DESIGNS—HORIZ: 4c. Roman cat (sculpture). VERT: 6c. "Pleuroceras spinatus" (ammonite); 8c. Pendulum clock (after principle of Huygens); 12c. Ship's figurehead.

1962. Completion of Netherlands Automatic Telephone System. Inscr "1962".
926 **189** 4c. red and black 20 10
927 – 12c. drab and black . . . 55 10
928 – 30c. ochre, blue and black 2·25 1·60
DESIGNS—VERT: 12c. Diagram of telephone network. HORIZ: 30c. Arch and telephone dial.

190 Europa "Tree"   **191** "Polder" Landscape (reclaimed area)

1962. Europa.
929 **190** 12c. black, yellow & bistre 10 10
930 30c. black, yellow and blue . . . . 1·00 1·25

1962.
935 – 4c. deep blue and blue . . 10 10
937 **191** 6c. deep green and green 40 15
938 – 10c. deep purple and purple 10 10
DESIGNS: 4c. Cooling towers, State mines, Limburg; 10c. Delta excavation works.

192 Children cooking Meal   **193** Ears of Wheat

1962. Child Welfare.
940 **192** 4c.+4c. red 20 15
941 – 6c.+4c. bistre 95 55
942 – 8c.+4c. blue . . . . . . 1·60 1·40
943 – 12c.+9c. green 20 10
944 – 30c.+9c. lake . . . . . . 2·75 2·50
DESIGNS—Children: 6c. Cycling; 8c. Watering flowers; 12c. Feeding poultry; 30c. Making music.

1963. Freedom from Hunger.
945 **193** 12c. ochre and blue . . . 20 10
946 30c. ochre and red . . . 1·25 1·00

194 "Gallery" Windmill   **195**

1963. Cultural, Health and Social Welfare Funds. Windmill types.
947 **194** 4c.+4c. blue . . . . . . 1·10 1·00
948 – 6c.+4c. violet . . . . . . 1·10 1·00
949 – 8c.+4c. green . . . . . . 1·40 1·40
950 – 12c.+8c. brown . . . . . 1·40 30
951 – 30c.+10c. red . . . . . . 1·75 1·90
WINDMILLS—VERT: 6c. North Holland polder; 12c. "Post"; 30c. "Wip". HORIZ: 8c. South Holland polder.

1963. Paris Postal Conference Centenary.
952 **195** 30c. blue, green & blk . . 1·40 1·25

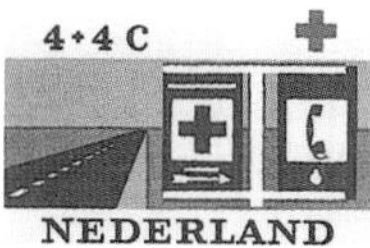

196 Wayside First Aid Post

1963. Red Cross Fund and Centenary (8c.).
953 **196** 4c.+4c. blue and red . . 40 40
954 – 6c.+4c. violet and red . . 35 30
955 – 8c.+4c. red and black . . 1·10 80
956 – 12c.+9c. brown and red 20 10
957 – 30c.+9c. green and red . . 1·60 1·40
DESIGNS: 6c. "Books" collection-box; 8c. Crosses; 12c. "International Aid" (Negro children at meal); 30c. First aid party tending casualty.

197 "Co-operation"   **198** "Auntie Luce sat on a goose ..."

1963. Europa.
958 **197** 12c. orange and brown . . 20 10
959 30c. orange and green . . 1·40 1·10

1963. Child Welfare.
960 **198** 4c.+4c. ultramarine & bl 20 15
961 – 6c.+4c. green and red . . 70 65
962 – 8c.+4c. brown & green . . 95 60
963 – 12c.+9c. violet & yellow 20 10
964 – 30c.+8c. blue and pink . . 1·60 1·40
DESIGNS (Nursery rhymes): 6c. "In the Hague there lives a count ..."; 8c. "One day I passed a puppet's fair ..."; 12c. "Storky, storky, Billy Spoon ..."; 30c. "Ride on a little pram ...".

199 William, Prince of Orange, landing at Scheveningen   **200** Knights' Hall, The Hague

1963. 150th Anniv of Kingdom of the Netherlands.
965 **199** 4c. black, bistre and blue 10 10
966 5c. black, red and green 20 10
967 – 12c. bistre, blue and black 10 10
968 – 30c. red and black 75 60
DESIGNS: 12c. Triumvirate: Van Hogendorp, Van Limburg, and Van der Duyn van Maasdam; 30c. William I taking oath of allegiance.

1964. 500th Anniv of 1st States-General Meeting.
969 **200** 12c. black and olive . . . 20 10

201 Guide Dog for the Blind

1964. Cultural, Health and Social Welfare Funds. Animals.
970 **201** 5c.+5c. red, black and olive 60 45
971 – 8c.+5c. brown, black and red 40 30
972 – 12c.+9c. black, grey and bistre 60 20
973 – 30c.+9c. multicoloured . . 70 65
DESIGNS: 8c. Three red deer; 12c. Three kittens; 30c. European bison and calf.

202 University Arms   **203** Signal No. 144, Amersfoort Station

1964. 350th Anniv of Groningen University.
974 **202** 12c. slate 10 10
975 – 30c. brown 25 25
DESIGN: 30c. "AG" monogram.

1964. 125th Anniv of Netherlands Railways.
976 **203** 15c. black and green . . . 20 10
977 – 40c. black and yellow . . 75 70
DESIGN: 40c. Class ELD-4 electric train.

204 Bible and Dove

1964. 150th Anniv of Netherlands Bible Society.
978 **204** 15c. brown 20 10

205 Europa "Flower"   **206** Young Artist

1964. Europa.
979 **205** 15c. green 20 10
980 20c. brown 40 40

1964. 20th Anniv of "BENELUX". As T **150a** of Luxembourg, but smaller 35 × 22 mm.
981 15c. violet and flesh 20 10

1964. Child Welfare.
982 **206** 7c.+3c. blue and green . . 50 45
983 – 10c.+5c. red, pink and green 40 40
984 – 15c.+10c. yellow, black and bistre 20 10
985 – 20c.+10c. red, sepia and mauve 60 45
986 – 40c.+15c. green & blue . 1·00 80
DESIGNS: 10c. Ballet-dancing; 15c. Playing the recorder; 20c. Masquerading; 40c. Toy-making.

207 Queen Juliana   **208** "Killed in Action" (Waalwijk) and "Destroyed Town" (Rotterdam) (monuments)

1964. 10th Anniv of Statute for the Kingdom.
987 **207** 15c. green 20 10

1965. "Resistance" Commemoration.
988 **208** 7c. black and red 20 10
989 – 15c. black and olive . . . 20 10
990 – 40c. black and red 95 85
MONUMENTS: 15c. "Docker" (Amsterdam) and "Killed in Action" (Waalwijk); 40c. "Destroyed Town" (Rotterdam) and "Docker" (Amsterdam).

209 Medal of Knight (Class IV)   **210** I.T.U. Emblem and "Lines of Communication"

1965. 150th Anniv of Military William Order.
991 **209** 1g. grey . . . . 1·60 65

1965. Centenary of I.T.U.
992 **210** 20c. blue and drab . . . 20 25
993 40c. brown and blue . . . 60 45

211 Veere

1965. Cultural, Health and Social Welfare Funds.
994 **211** 8c.+6c. black and yellow 35 25
995 – 10c.+6c. black & turq . . 50 40
996 – 18c.+12c. black & brn . . 40 25
997 – 20c.+10c. black & blue . . 50 40
998 – 40c.+10c. black & green 55 45
DESIGNS: (Dutch towns): 10c. Thorn; 18c. Dordrecht; 20c. Staveren; 40c. Medemblik.

212 Europa "Sprig"

1965. Europa.
999 **212** 18c. black, red and brown 20 10
1000 20c. black, red and blue 30 30

213 Girl's Head

1965. Child Welfare. Multicoloured.
1001 8c.+6c. Type **213** 20 15
1002 10c.+6c. Ship 50 50
1003 18c.+12c. Boy (vert) . . . 20 15
1004 20c.+10c. Duck-pond . . . 65 55
1005 40c.+10c. Tractor . . . . . 1·90 75

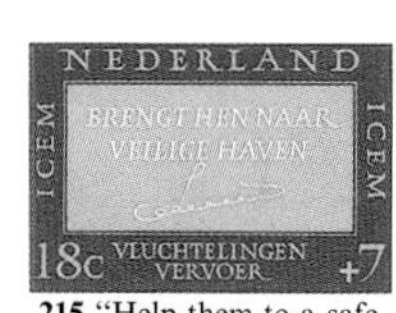

214 Marines of 1665 and 1965   **215** "Help them to a safe Haven" (Queen Juliana)

1965. Tercentenary of Marine Corps.
1007 **214** 18c. blue and red 20 10

1966. Intergovernmental Committee for European Migration (I.C.E.M.) Fund.
1008 **215** 10c.+7c. yellow & blk . . 50 35
1009 40c.+20c. red & black 40 25

216 Writing Materials   **217** Aircraft in Flight

1966. Cultural, Health and Social Welfare Funds. Gysbert Japicx Commem and 200th Anniv of Netherlands Literary Society. Multicoloured.
1011 10c.+5c. Type **216** 40 40
1012 12c.+8c. Part of MS, Japicx's poem "Wobbelke" 40 40
1013 20c.+10c. Part of miniature, "Knight Walewein" . . . 55 40
1014 25c.+10c. Initial "D" and part of MS, novel, "Ferguut" 70 55
1015 40c.+20c. 16th-century printery (woodcut) . . . 55 55

1966. Air (Special Flights).
1016 **217** 25c. multicoloured . . . 20 45

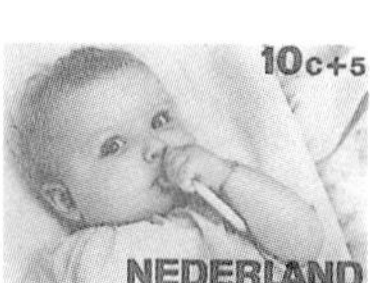

218 Europa "Ship"   **219** Infant

1966. Europa.
1017 **218** 20c. green and yellow . . 20 10
1018 40c. deep blue and blue 35 25

1966. Child Welfare.
1019 **219** 10c.+5c. red and blue . . 20 15
1020 – 12c.+8c. green and red 20 15
1021 – 20c.+10c. blue and red 20 15
1022 – 25c.+10c. purple & bl . . 95 85
1023 – 40c.+20c. red & green 90 80
DESIGNS: 12c. Young girl; 20c. Boy in water; 25c. Girl with moped; 40c. Young man with horse.

220 Assembly Hall

1967. 125th Anniv of Delft Technological University.
1025 **220** 20c. sepia and yellow . . 20 10

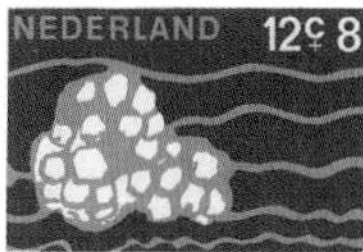

221 Common Northern Whelk Eggs

1967. Cultural, Health and Social Welfare Funds. Marine Fauna.
1026 **221** 12c.+8c. brown & grn 30 30
1027 – 15c.+10c. blue, light blue and deep blue 30 30
1028 – 20c.+10c. mult 30 25
1029 – 25c.+10c. brown, purple and bistre 60 55
1030 – 45c.+20c. mult 80 65
DESIGNS: 15c. Common northern whelk; 20c. Common blue mussel; 25c. Jellyfish; 45c. Crab.

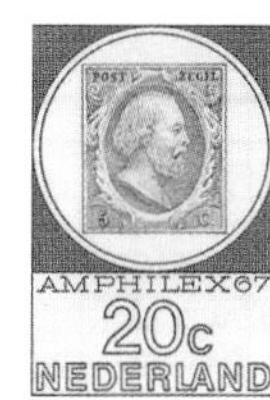

222 Cogwheels   **223** Netherlands 5c. Stamp of 1852

1967. Europa.
1031 **222** 20c. blue and light blue 40 10
1032 45c. purple & light purple . . . . 1·10 80

1967. "Amphilex 67" Stamp Exn, Amsterdam.
1035 **223** 20c. blue and black . . . 2·25 1·90
1036 – 25c. red and black . . . 2·25 1·90
1037 – 75c. green and black . . 2·25 1·90
DESIGNS: 25c. Netherlands 10c. stamp of 1864; 75c. Netherlands 20c. stamp of 1867.

Nos. 1035/7 were sold at the exhibition and at post offices at 3g.70, which included entrance fee to the exhibition.

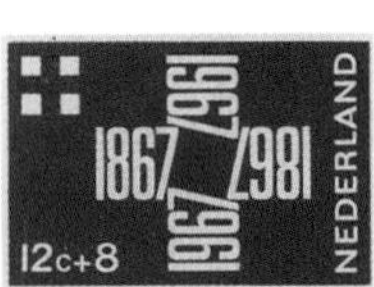

224 "1867–1967" **225** "Porcupine Lullaby"

1967. Centenary of Dutch Red Cross.

1038 12c.+8c. blue and red . . . 30 30
1039 15c.+10c. red 50 40
1040 20c.+10c. olive and red . . 30 20
1041 25c.+10c. green and red . . 50 50
1042 45c.+20c. grey and red . . . 70 65

DESIGNS: 12c. Type **224**; 15c. Red crosses; 20c. "NRK" ("Nederlandsche Rood Kruis") in the form of a cross; 25c. Maltese cross and "red" crosses; 45c. "100" in the form of a cross.

1967. Child Welfare. Multicoloured.

1043 12c.+8c. Type **225** 20 20
1044 15c.+10c. "The Whistling Kettle" 20 20
1045 20c.+10c. "Dikkertje Dap" (giraffe) 20 20
1046 25c.+10c. "The Flower-seller" . . . . 1·25 80
1047 45c.+20c. "Pippeloentje" (bear) . . . . 1·10 85

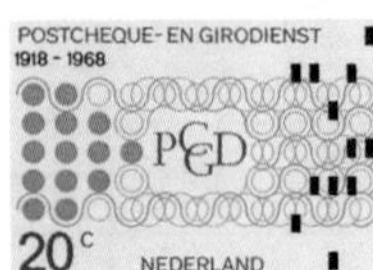

226 "Financial Automation"

1968. 50th Anniv of Netherlands Postal Cheque and Clearing Service.

1049 **226** 20c. red, black and yellow 20 10

227 St. Servatius' Bridge, Maastricht

1968. Cultural, Health and Social Welfare Funds. Dutch Bridges.

1050 **227** 12c.+8c. green . . . . . 1·40 95
1051 – 15c.+10c. brown 70 65
1052 – 20c.+10c. red 50 25
1053 – 25c.+10c. blue 55 55
1054 – 45c.+20c. blue 90 85

BRIDGES: 15c. Magere ("Narrow"), Amsterdam; 20c. Railway, Culemborg; 25c. Van Brienenoord, Rotterdam; 45c. Oosterschelde, Zeeland.

228 Europa "Key"

1968. Europa.

1055 **228** 20c. blue 30 10
1056 45c. red 95 80

229 "Wilhelmus van Nassouwe" **230** Wright Type A and Cessna 150F

1968. 400th Anniv of Dutch National Anthem, "Wilhelmus".

1057 **229** 20c. multicoloured . . . 20 10

1968. Dutch Aviation Anniversaries.

1058 12c. black, red and mauve 20 10
1059 20c. black, emerald and green 20 10
1060 45c. black, blue and green 1·25 1·10

DESIGNS AND EVENTS: 12c. T **230** (60th anniv (1967) of Royal Netherlands Aeronautical Assn); 20c. Fokker F.II and Fellowship aircraft (50th anniv (1969) of Royal Netherlands Aircraft Factories "Fokker"); 45c. De Havilland D.H.9B biplane and Douglas DC-9 airliner (50th anniv (1969) of Royal Dutch Airlines "KLM").

231 "Goblin"

1968. Child Welfare.

1061 **231** 12c.+8c. pink, black and green 20 15
1062 – 15c.+10c. pink, blue and black 20 15
1063 – 20c.+10c. blue, green and black 20 15
1064 – 25c.+10c. red, yellow and black . . . . . . 1·60 1·10
1065 – 45c.+20c. yellow, orange and black . . . . . . 1·60 1·25

DESIGNS: 15c. "Giant"; 20c. "Witch"; 25c. "Dragon"; 45c. "Sorcerer".

232 "I A O" (Internationale Arbeidsorganisatie)

1969. 50th Anniv of I.L.O.

1067 **232** 25c. red and black . . . 60 10
1068 45c. blue and black . . . 1·00 90

233 Queen Juliana **234** Villa, Huis ter Heide (1915)

1969. (a) Type **233**.

1069 **233** 25c. red . . . . 1·40 20
1069c 30c. brown 15 20
1070a 35c. blue 20 10
1071a 40c. red 30 10
1072a 45c. blue 30 10
1073a 50c. purple 25 10
1073c 55c. red 20 10
1074a 60c. blue 20 10
1075 70c. brown 50 10
1076 75c. green 60 10
1077 80c. red 65 10
1077a 90c. grey 65 10

(b) Size 22 × 33 mm.

1078 – 1g. green 70 10
1079 – 1g.25 lake 95 10
1080 – 1g.50 brown . . . . 1·10 10
1081 – 2g. mauve . . . . 1·40 10
1082 – 2g.50 blue . . . . 1·75 10
1083 – 5g. grey . . . . 3·50 10
1084 – 10g. blue . . . . 7·00 1·10

DESIGN: 1g.to 10g. similar to Type **233**.

1969. Cultural, Health and Social Welfare Funds. 20th-century Dutch Architecture.

1085 **234** 12c.+8c. black & brn . . 70 70
1086 – 15c.+10c. black, red and blue 70 70
1087 – 20c.+10c. black & vio . . 70 70
1088 – 25c.+10c. brown & grn 70 30
1089 – 45c.+20c. black, blue and yellow 70 70

DESIGNS: 15c. Private House, Utrecht (1924); 20c. Open-air School, Amsterdam (1930); 25c. Orphanage, Amsterdam (1960); 45c. Congress Building, The Hague (1969).

235 Colonnade **236** Stylized "Crab" (of Cancer)

1969. Europa.

1090 **235** 25c. blue 40 10
1091 45c. red . . . . 1·40 1·10

1969. 20th Anniv of Queen Wilhelmina Cancer Fund.

1092 **236** 12c.+8c. violet 65 60
1093 25c.+10c. orange 95 40
1094 45c.+20c. green . . . . 1·75 1·50

1969. 25th Anniv of "BENELUX" Customs Union. As T **186** of Luxembourg.

1095 25c. multicoloured 30 10

238 Erasmus **239** Child with Violin

1969. 500th Birth Anniv of Desiderius Erasmus.

1096 **238** 25c. purple on green . . 30 10

1969. Child Welfare.

1097 – 12c.+8c. black, yellow and blue 20 15
1098 **239** 15c.+10c. black and red 20 15
1099 – 20c.+10c. black, yellow and red . . . . 1·75 1·40
1100 – 25c.+10c. black, red and yellow 20 15
1101 – 45c.+20c. black, red and green . . . . 2·00 1·75

DESIGNS—VERT: 12c. Child with recorder; 20c. Child with drum. HORIZ: 25c. Three choristers; 45c. Two dancers.

240 Queen Juliana and "Sunlit Road"

1969. 25th Anniv of Statute for the Kingdom.

1103 **240** 25c. multicoloured . . . 30 10

241 Prof. E. M. Meijers (author of "Burgerlijk Wetboek")

1970. Introduction of New Netherlands Civil Code ("Burgerlijk Wetboek").

1104 **241** 25c. ultramarine, green and blue 30 10

242 Netherlands Pavilion **243** "Circle to Square"

1970. Expo 70 World Fair, Osaka, Japan.

1105 **242** 25c. grey, blue and red 30 15

1970. Cultural, Health and Social Welfare Funds.

1106 **243** 12c.+8c. black on yell . . 1·10 1·25
1107 – 15c.+10c. black on silver 1·10 1·25
1108 – 20c.+10c. black . . . . 1·10 1·25
1109 – 25c.+10c. black on bl . . 1·10 75
1110 – 45c.+20c. white on grey 1·10 1·25

DESIGNS: 15c. Parallel planes in cube; 20c. Overlapping scales; 25c. Concentric circles in transition; 45c. Spirals.

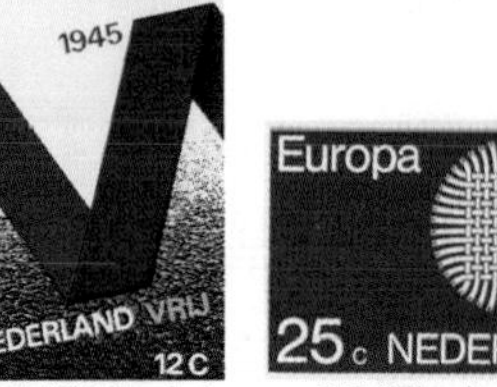

244 "V" Symbol **245** "Flaming Sun"

1970. 25th Anniv of Liberation.

1111 **244** 12c. red, blue and brown 40 10

1970. Europa.

1112 **245** 25c. red 40 10
1113 45c. blue . . . . 1·60 1·00

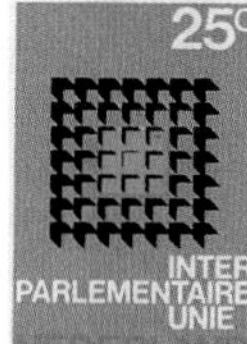

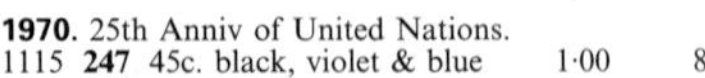

246 "Work and Co-operation" **247** Globe on Plinth

1970. Inter-Parliamentary Union Conference.

1114 **246** 25c. green, black and grey 60 10

1970. 25th Anniv of United Nations.

1115 **247** 45c. black, violet & blue 1·00 85

248 Human Heart **249** Toy Block

1970. Netherlands Heart Foundation.

1116 **248** 12c.+8c. red, black and yellow 70 75
1117 25c.+10c. red, black and mauve 70 65
1118 45c.+20c. red, black and green 70 60

1970. Child Welfare. "The Child and the Cube".

1119 **249** 12c.+8c. blue, violet and green 20 15
1120 – 15c.+10c. green, blue and yellow . . . . . 1·40 1·40
1121 **249** 20c.+10c. mauve, red and violet . . . . . . 1·40 1·40
1122 – 25c.+10c. red, yellow and mauve 20 15
1123 **249** 45c.+20c. grey, cream and black . . . . . . 1·75 1·60

DESIGN: 15c., 25c. As Type **249**, but showing underside of block.

250 "Fourteenth Census 1971"

1971. 14th Netherlands Census.

1125 **250** 15c. purple 20 10

251 "50 years of Adult University Education" **252** Europa Chain

1971. Cultural, Health and Social Welfare Funds. Other designs show 15th-century wooden statues by unknown artists.

1126 **251** 15c.+10c. black, red and yellow . . . . 1·40 1·40
1127 – 20c.+10c. black and green on green . . . . 1·25 1·00
1128 – 25c.+10c. black and orange on orange . . 1·25 60
1129 – 30c.+15c. black and blue on blue . . . . 1·40 1·40
1130 – 45c.+20c. black and red on pink . . . . 1·40 1·40

STATUES: 20c. "Apostle Paul"; 25c. "Joachim and Ann"; 30c. "John the Baptist and Scribes"; 45c. "Ann, Mary and Christ-Child" (detail).

1971. Europa.

1131 **252** 25c. yellow, red and black 40 10
1132 45c. yellow, blue & black 1·40 1·25

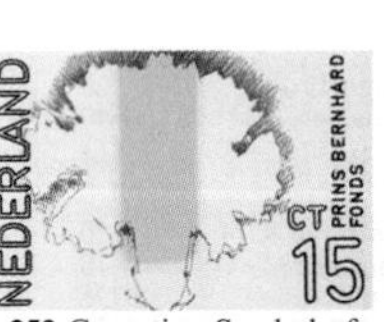

253 Carnation Symbol of Prince Bernhard Fund **254** "The Good Earth"

1971. Prince Bernhard's 60th Birthday.
1133 **253** 15c. yellow, grey & black 20 15
1134 – 20c. multicoloured . . . 65 40
1135 – 25c. multicoloured . . . 30 15
1136 – 45c.+20c. black, purple and yellow . . . . . 2·50 2·25
DESIGNS—HORIZ: 20c. Panda symbol of World Wildlife Fund. VERT: 25c. Prince Bernhard; 45c. Statue, Borobudur Temple, Indonesia.

1971. Child Welfare.
1137 **254** 15c.+10c. red, purple and black 20 15
1138 – 20c.+10c. mult 30 20
1139 – 25c.+10c. mult 20 20
1140 – 30c.+15c. blue, violet and black . . . . . . 1·10 65
1141 – 45c.+20c. blue, green and black . . . . . . 1·90 1·40
DESIGNS—VERT: 20c. Butterfly; 45c. Reflecting water. HORIZ: 25c. Sun waving; 30c. Moon winking.

255 Delta Map

256 "Fruits"

1972. Delta Sea-Defences Plan.
1143 **255** 20c. multicoloured . . . 20 10

1972. Cultural, Health and Social Welfare Funds. "Floriade Flower Show" (20c., 25c.) and "Holland Arts Festival" (30c., 45c.). Multicoloured.
1144 20c.+10c. Type **256** . . . . 1·10 90
1145 25c.+10c. "Flower" . . . . 1·10 90
1146 30c.+15c. "Sunlit Landscape" . . . . . . 1·10 65
1147 45c.+25c. "Music" . . . . 1·10 90

257 "Communications"

258 "There is more to be done in the world than ever before" (Thorbecke)

1972. Europa.
1148 **257** 30c. brown and blue . . 95 10
1149 45c. brown and orange 1·40 1·10

1972. Death Centenary of J. R. Thorbecke (statesman).
1150 **258** 30c. black and blue . . . 70 15

259 Netherlands Flag

260 Hurdling

1972. 400th Anniv of Netherlands Flag.
1151 **259** 20c. multicoloured . . . 50 20
1152 25c. multicoloured . . . 1·25 15

1972. Olympic Games, Munich. Multicoloured.
1153 20c. Type **260** 20 15
1154 30c. Diving 20 15
1155 45c. Cycling . . . . 1·10 1·10

261 Red Cross

262 Prince Willem-Alexander

1972. Netherlands Red Cross.
1156 **261** 5c. red 20 15
1157 – 20c.+10c. red and pink 55 55
1158 – 25c.+10c. red & orange 95 85
1159 – 30c.+15c. red & black 70 55
1160 – 45c.+25c. red and blue 1·00 90
DESIGNS: 20c. Accident services; 25c. Blood transfusion; 30c. Refugee relief; 45c. Child care.

1972. Child Welfare. Multicoloured.
1161 25c.+15c. Type **262** 20 15
1162 30c.+10c. Prince Johan Friso (horiz) 70 65
1163 35c.+15c. Prince Constantin (horiz) 70 15
1164 50c.+20c. The Three Princes (horiz) . . . . 2·40 2·00

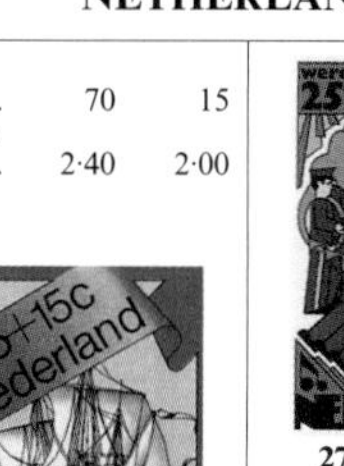

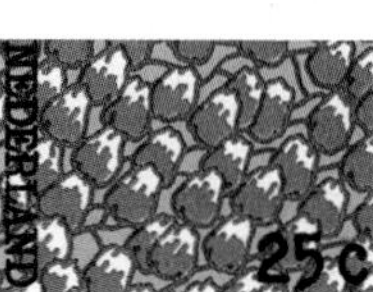

263 Tulips in Bloom

264 "De Zeven Provincien" (De Ruyter's flagship)

1973. Tulip Exports.
1166 **263** 25c. multicoloured . . . 65 10

1973. Cultural, Health and Social Welfare Funds. Dutch Ships. Multicoloured.
1167 25c.+15c. Type **264** 95 90
1168 30c.+10c. "W.A. Scholten" (steamship) (horiz) . . . 95 90
1169 35c.+15c. "Veendam" (liner) (horiz) . . . . 1·10 75
1170 50c.+20c. Fishing boat (from etching by R. Nooms) . . . . 1·25 1·25

265 Europa "Posthorn"

266 Hockey-players

1973. Europa.
1171 **265** 35c. light blue and blue 55 10
1172 50c. blue and violet . . . 95 85

1973. Events and Anniversaries. Multicoloured.
1173 25c. Type **266** 40 25
1174 30c. Gymnastics . . . . . 2·00 60
1175 35c. Dish aerial (vert) . . . 50 15
1176 50c. Rainbow 85 75
EVENTS—VERT: 25c. 75th anniv of Royal Netherlands Hockey Association; 30c. World Gymnastics Championships, Rotterdam. HORIZ: 35c. Opening of Satellite Station, Burum; 50c. Centenary of World Meteorological Organization.

267 Queen Juliana

268 "Co-operation"

1973. Silver Jubilee of Queen Juliana's Accession.
1177 **267** 40c. multicoloured . . . 50 15

1973. International Development Co-operation.
1178 **268** 40c. multicoloured . . . 95 10

269 "Chess"

270 Northern Goshawk

1973. Child Welfare.
1179 **269** 25c.+15c. red, yellow and black 40 20
1180 – 30c.+10c. green, mauve and black . . . . . . 1·60 65
1181 – 40c.+20c. yellow, green and black 40 15
1182 – 50c.+20c. blue, yellow and black . . . . . . 1·60 2·00
DESIGNS: 30c. "Noughts and crosses"; 40c. "Maze"; 50c. "Dominoes".

1974. "Nature and Environment". Multicoloured.
1184 25c. Type **270** . . . . . . 1·10 55
1185 25c. Tree . . . . 1·10 55
1186 25c. Fisherman and frog . . 1·10 55
Nos. 1184/6 were issued together, se-tenant, forming a composite design.

271 Bandsmen (World Band Contest, Kerkrade)

272 Football on Pitch

1974. Cultural, Health and Social Welfare Funds.
1187 **271** 25c.+15c. mult 95 85
1188 – 30c.+10c. mult 95 85
1189 – 40c.+20c. brown, black and red 95 65
1190 – 50c.+20c. purple, black and red 95 85
DESIGNS: 30c. Dancers and traffic-lights ("Modern Ballet"); 40c. Herman Heijermans; 50c. "Kniertje" (character from Heijermans' play "Op hoop van zegan"). The 40c. and 50c. commemorate the 50th death anniv of the playwright.

1974. Sporting Events.
1191 **272** 25c. multicoloured . . . 20 15
1192 – 40c. yellow, red & mauve 35 15
DESIGNS AND EVENTS—HORIZ: 25c. (World Cup Football Championship, West Germany). VERT: 40c. Hand holding tennis ball (75th anniv of Royal Dutch Lawn Tennis Association).

273 Netherlands Cattle

274 "BENELUX" (30th Anniv of Benelux (Customs Union))

1974. Anniversaries. Multicoloured.
1193 25c. Type **273** . . . . . . 8·75 1·90
1194 25c. "Cancer" 95 20
1195 40c. "Suzanna" (lifeboat) seen through binoculars 70 20
EVENTS AND ANNIVERSARIES: No. 1193, Cent of Netherlands Cattle Herdbook Society; 1194, 25th anniv of Queen Wilhelmina Cancer Research Fund; 1195, 150th anniv of Dutch Lifeboat Service.

1974. International Anniversaries.
1196 **274** 30c. green, turquoise & blue 30 15
1197 – 45c. deep blue, silver & blue 50 15
1198 – 45c. yellow, blue & black 50 15
DESIGNS—VERT: No. 1197, NATO emblem (25th anniv); 1198, Council of Europe emblem (25th anniv).

275 Hands with Letters

276 Boy with Hoop

1974. Centenary of Universal Postal Union.
1199 **275** 60c. multicoloured . . . 55 45

1974. 50th Anniv of Child Welfare Issues. Early Photographs.
1200 **276** 30c.+15c. brown & blk 20 15
1201 – 35c.+20c. brown 55 55
1202 – 45c.+20c. black 55 25
1203 – 60c.+20c. black . . . . 1·25 1·40
DESIGNS: 35c. Child and baby; 45c. Two young girls; 60c. Girl sitting on balustrade.

277 Amsterdam

278 St. Hubertus Hunting Lodge, De Hoge Veluwe National Park

1975. Anniversaries. Multicoloured.
1205 30c. Type **277** 30 30
1206 30c. Synagogue and map . . 30 30
1207 35c. Type **277** 40 15
1208 45c. "Window" in human brain 35 45
ANNIVERSARIES: Nos. 1205, 1207, Amsterdam (700th anniv); 1206, Portuguese-Israelite Synagogue, Amsterdam (300th anniv); 1208, Leyden University and university education (400th anniv).

1975. Cultural, Health and Social Welfare Funds. National Monument Year. Preserved Monuments. Multicoloured.
1209 35c.+20c. Type **278** 55 55
1210 40c.+15c. Bergijnhof (Beguinage), Amsterdam (vert) 55 55
1211 50c.+20c. "Kuiperspoort" (Cooper's gate), Middelburg (vert) 70 55
1212 60c.+20c. Orvelte village, Drenthe 95 85

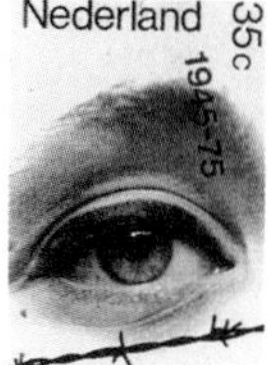

279 Eye and Barbed Wire

280 Company Emblem and "Stad Middelburg" (schooner)

1975. 30th Anniv of Liberation.
1213 **279** 35c. black and red . . . 35 10

1975. Centenary of Zeeland Shipping Company.
1214 **280** 35c. multicoloured . . . 35 15

281 Dr. Albert Schweitzer crossing Lambarene River

1975. Birth Centenary of Dr. Schweitzer (medical missionary).
1215 **281** 50c. multicoloured . . . 40 10

282 Man and Woman on "Playing-card"

283 Braille Reading

1975. International Events. Multicoloured.
1216 35c. Type **282** (Int Women's Year) 35 15
1217 50c. Metric scale (Metre Convention cent) (horiz) 40 10

1975. 150th Anniv of Invention of Braille.
1218 **283** 35c. multicoloured . . . 35 15

284 Dutch 25c. Coins

285 "Four Orphans" (C. Simons), Torenstraat Orphanage, Medemblik

1975. Savings Campaign.
1219 **284** 50c. grey, green and blue 40 10

1975. Child Welfare. Historic Ornamental Stones. Multicoloured.
1220 35c.+15c. Type **285** 20 15
1221 40c.+15c. "Milkmaid" Kooltuin Alkmaar . . . 50 50
1222 50c.+25c. "Four Sons of Aymon seated on Beyaert", Herengracht . . 40 20
1223 60c.+25c. "Life at the Orphanage", Molenstraat Orphanage, Gorinchem 1·00 75

286 18th-century Lottery Ticket

287 Numeral

1976. 250th Anniv of National Lottery.
1225 **286** 35c. multicoloured . . . 35 15

1976. (a) Ordinary gum.
1226 **287** 5c. grey 10 10
1227 10c. blue 10 10

1228 25c. violet 20 10
1229 40c. brown 40 10
1230 45c. blue 40 10
1231 50c. mauve 40 10
1232 55c. green 65 10
1233 60c. yellow 70 10
1234 65c. brown . . . . . 1·00 10
1235 70c. violet 85 10
1236 80c. mauve . . . . . . 1·50 10

(b) Self-adhesive gum.

1237 **287** 5c. grey 10 10
1238 10c. blue 10 10
1239 25c. violet 15 10

288 West European Hedgehog

1976. Cultural, Health and Social Welfare Funds. Nature Protection (40, 75c.) and Anniversaries. Multicoloured.
1241 40c.+20c. Type **288** 60 45
1242 45c.+20c. Open book (vert) 60 45
1243 55c.+20c. People and organization initials . . . 65 30
1244 75c.+25c. Frog and spawn (vert) 85 80
ANNIVERSARIES: No. 1242, 175th anniv of Primary education and centenary of Agricultural education; 1243, 75th anniv of Social Security Bank and legislation.

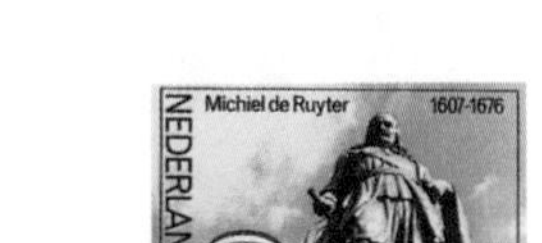

289 Admiral Michiel de Ruyter (statue)

1976. 300th Death Anniv of Admiral Michiel de Ruyter.
1245 **289** 55c. multicoloured . . . 40 15

290 Guillaume Groen van Prinsterer

1976. Death Centenary of Guillaume Groen van Prinsterer (statesman).
1246 **290** 55c. multicoloured . . . 40 15

291 Detail of 18th-century Calendar

1976. Bicentenary of American Revolution.
1247 **291** 75c. multicoloured . . . 55 35

292 Long-distance Marchers

293 The Art of Printing

1976. Sport and Recreation Anniversaries. Mult.
1248 40c. Type **292** 30 25
1249 55c. Runners "photo-finish" 65 25
ANNIVERSARIES: 40c. 60th Nijmegen Long-distance March; 55c. Royal Dutch Athletics Society (75th anniv).

1976. Anniversaries.
1250 **293** 45c. red and blue 30 25
1251 – 55c.+25c. mult 50 45
DESIGNS AND EVENTS: 45c. Type **293** (75th anniv of Netherlands Printers' organization); 55c. Rheumatic patient "Within Care" (50th anniv of Dutch Anti-Rheumatism Association).

294 Dutch Tjalk and Reclaimed Land

295 Queen Wilhelmina 4½c. Stamp, 1919

1976. Zuider Zee Project—Reclamation and Urbanization. Multicoloured.
1252 **294** 40c. blue, olive and red 30 15
1253 – 75c. yellow, red and blue 55 45
DESIGN: 75c. Duck flying over reclaimed land.

1976. "Amphilex '77" International Stamp Exhibition, Amsterdam (1977) (1st series). Stamp Portraits of Queen Wilhelmina. Multicoloured.
1254 – 55c.+55c. blue, deep grey and grey 95 80
1255 **295** 55c.+55c. purple, deep grey and grey 95 80
1256 – 55c.+55c. brown, deep grey and grey 95 80
1257 – 75c.+75c. turquoise, deep grey and grey 95 80
1258 – 75c.+75c. blue, deep grey and grey 95 80
DESIGNS: No. 1254, 5c. stamp, 1891; 1256, 25c. stamp, 1924; 1257, 15c. stamp, 1940; 1258, 25c. stamp, 1947.
See also Nos. 1273/6.

296 "Football" (J. Raats)

1976. Child Welfare. Children's Paintings. Mult
1259 40c.+20c. Type **296** 30 25
1260 45c.+20c. "Boat" (L. Jacobs) 30 30
1261 55c.+20c. "Elephant" (M. Lugtenburg) 40 15
1262 75c.+25c. "Caravan" (A. Seeleman) 70 85

297 Ballot-paper and Pencil

1977. National Events. Multicoloured.
1264 40c. "Energy" (vert) 30 10
1265 45c. Type **297** 40 15
EVENTS: 40c. "Be wise with energy" campaign; 45c. Elections to Lower House of States-General.
See also No. 1268.

298 Spinoza

299 Early Type Faces and "a" on Bible Script

1977. 300th Death Anniv of Barach (Benedictus) de Spinoza (philosopher).
1266 **298** 75c. multicoloured . . . 55 35

1977. 500th Anniv of Printing of "Delft Bible".
1267 **299** 55c. multicoloured . . . 45 35

1977. Elections to Lower House of States-General. As T **297** but also inscribed "25 MEI '77".
1268 45c. multicoloured 40 20

300 Altar of Goddess Nehalennia

301 "Kaleidoscope"

1977. Cultural, Health and Social Welfare Funds. Roman Archaeological Discoveries.
1269 – 40c.+20c. mult 40 30
1270 **300** 45c.+20c. black, stone and green 50 30
1271 – 55c.+20c. black, blue and red 50 30
1272 – 75c.+25c. black, grey and yellow 65 50

DESIGNS: 40c. Baths, Heerlen; 55c. Remains of Zwammerdam ship; 75c. Parade helmet.

1977. "Amphilex 1977" International Stamp Exhibition, Amsterdam (2nd series). As T **295**.
1273 55c.+45c. grn, brn & grey 55 35
1274 55c.+45c. blue, brn & grey 55 45
1275 55c.+45c. blue, brn & grey 55 45
1276 55c.+45c. red, brn & grey 55 35
DESIGNS: No. 1273, Queen Wilhelmina 1g. stamp, 1898; 1274, Queen Wilhelmina 20c. stamp, 1923; 1275, Queen Wilhelmina 12½c. stamp, 1938; 1276, Queen Wilhelmina 10c. stamp, 1948.

1977. Bicentenary of Netherlands Society for Industry and Commerce.
1278 **301** 55c. multicoloured . . . 45 10

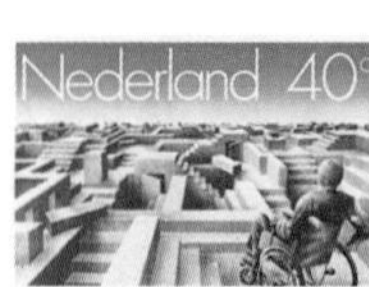

302 Man in Wheelchair and Maze of Steps

303 Risk of Drowning

1977. Anniversaries.
1279 **302** 40c. brown, green & blue 30 15
1280 – 45c. multicoloured . . . 30 20
1281 – 55c. multicoloured . . . 40 10
DESIGNS—HORIZ: 40c. Type **302** (50th anniv of A.V.O. Nederland); 45c. Diagram of water current (50th anniv of Delft Hydraulic Laboratory). VERT: 55c. Teeth (centenary of dentists' training in Netherlands).

1977. Child Welfare. Dangers to Children. Mult.
1282 40c.+20c. Type **303** 35 20
1283 45c.+20c. Medicine cabinet (poisons) 35 20
1284 55c.+20c. Balls in road (traffic) 35 20
1285 75c.+25c. Matches (fire) . . 65 65

304 "Postcode"

305 Makkum Dish

1978. Introduction of Postcodes.
1287 **304** 40c. red and blue 30 10
1288 45c. red and blue 30 10

1978. Cultural, Health and Social Welfare Funds. Multicoloured.
1289 40c.+20c. Anna Maria van Schurman (writer) 40 30
1290 45c.+20c. Passage from letter by Belle de Zuylen (Mme. de Charriere) . . . 50 30
1291 55c.+20c. Delft dish 50 30
1292 75c.+25c. Type **305** 65 50

306 "Human Rights" Treaty

307 Chess

1978. European Series.
1293 **306** 45c. grey, black and blue 30 15
1294 – 55c. black, stone and orange 45 10
DESIGN: 55c. Haarlem Town Hall (Europa).

1978. Sports.
1295 **307** 40c. multicoloured . . . 30 15
1296 – 45c. red and blue 30 20
DESIGN: 45c. The word "Korfbal".

308 Kidney Donor

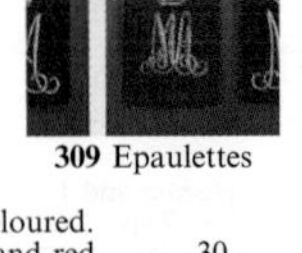

309 Epaulettes

1978. Health Care. Multicoloured.
1297 **308** 40c. black, blue and red 30 20
1298 – 45c. multicoloured . . . 30 20
1299 – 55c.+25c. red, grey and black 50 45

DESIGNS—VERT: 45c. Heart and torch. HORIZ: 55c. Red crosses on world map.

1978. 150th Anniv of Royal Military Academy, Breda.
1301 **309** 55c. multicoloured . . . 40 10

310 Verkade as Hamlet

1978. Birth Centenary of Eduard Rutger Verkade (actor and producer).
1302 **310** 45c. multicoloured . . . 30 20

311 Boy ringing Doorbell

1978. Child Welfare. Multicoloured.
1303 40c.+20c. Type **311** 40 20
1304 45c.+20c. Child reading . . 50 20
1305 55c.+20c. Boy writing (vert) 50 20
1306 75c.+25c. Girl and blackboard 65 65

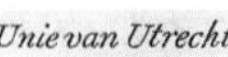

312 Clasped Hands and Arrows

313 Names of European Community Members

1979. 400th Anniv of Treaty of Utrecht.
1308 **312** 55c. blue 40 20

1979. First Direct Elections to European Assembly.
1309 **313** 45c. red, blue and black 30 15

314 Queen Juliana

1979. Queen Juliana's 70th Birthday.
1310 **314** 55c. multicoloured . . . 40 15

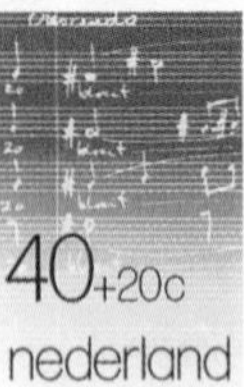

315 Fragment of "Psalmen Trilogie" (J. Andriessen)

316 Netherlands Stamps and Magnifying Glass

1979. Cultural, Health and Social Welfare Funds.
1311 **315** 40c.+20c. grey and red 40 30
1312 – 45c.+20c. grey and red 50 30
1313 – 55c.+20c. mult 50 25
1314 – 75c.+25c. mult 65 45
DESIGNS AND EVENTS: 150th anniv of Musical Society; 45c. Choir. Restoration of St. John's Church, Gouda (stained glass windows); 55c. Mary (detail, "Birth of Christ"); 75c. William of Orange (detail, "Relief of Leyden").

1979. Europa and 75th Anniv of Scheveningen Radio. Multicoloured.
1315 55c. Type **316** 40 15
1316 75c. Liner and Morse Key 55 40

317 Map of Chambers of Commerce

318 Action Shot of Football Match

1979. 175th Anniv of First Dutch Chamber of Commerce, Maastricht.
1317 **317** 45c. multicoloured . . . 30 20

1979. Anniversaries. Multicoloured.
1318 45c. Type **318** (centenary of organized football) . . . 30 20
1319 55c. Women's suffrage meeting (60th anniv of Women's suffrage) (vert) 40 15

319 Porch of Old Amsterdam Theatre

1979. 300th Death Annivs of Joost van den Vondel (poet) and Jan Steen (painter). Multicoloured.
1320 40c. Type **319** 30 20
1321 45c. "Gay Company" (detail) (Jan Steen) . . . 30 20

320 Hindustani Girl on Father's Shoulder (The Right to Love)

1979. Child Welfare. International Year of the Child
1322 **320** 40c.+20c. grey, red and yellow 40 20
1323 – 45c.+20c. grey, red and black 50 20
1324 – 55c.+20c. grey, black and yellow 50 20
1325 – 75c.+25c. black, blue and red 65 65
DESIGNS—HORIZ: 45c. Chilean child from refugee camp (The Right to Medical Care). VERT: 55c. Senegalese boy from Sahel area (The Right to Food); 75c. Class from Albert Cuyp School, Amsterdam (The Right to Education).

321 A. F. de Savornin Lohman
322 Dunes

1980. Dutch Politicians. Multicoloured.
1327 45c. Type **321** (Christian Historical Union) 30 20
1328 50c. P. J. Troelstra (Socialist Party) 30 20
1329 60c. P. J. Oud (Liberal Party) 50 20

1980. Cultural, Health and Social Welfare Funds. Multicoloured.
1330 45c.+20c. Type **322** 50 30
1331 50c.+20c. Country estate (vert) 50 30
1332 60c.+25c. Lake District . . 55 30
1333 80c.+35c. Moorland 70 50

323 Avro Type 683 Lancaster dropping Food Parcels
324 Queen Beatrix and New Church, Amsterdam

1980. 35th Anniv of Liberation. Multicoloured.
1334 45c. Type **323** 40 20
1335 60c. Anne Frank (horiz) . . 50 10

1980. Installation of Queen Beatrix.
1336 **324** 60c. blue, red and yellow 1·00 30
1337 65c. blue, red and yellow 1·40 10

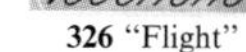

325 Young Stamp Collectors
326 "Flight"

1980. "Jupostex 1980" Stamp Exhibition, Eindhoven, and Dutch Society of Stamp Dealers Show, The Hague.
1338 **325** 50c. multicoloured . . . 40 30

1980. Air. (Special Flights).
1339 **326** 1g. blue and black . . . 80 65

327 Bridge Players and Cards
328 Road Haulage

1980. Sports Events. Multicoloured.
1340 50c. Type **327** (Bridge Olympiad, Valkenburg) 40 20
1341 60c.+25c. Sportswoman in wheelchair (Olympics for the Disabled, Arnhem and Veenendaal) 55 40

1980. Transport.
1342 **328** 50c. multicoloured . . . 40 15
1343 – 60c. blue, brown & black 50 15
1344 – 80c. multicoloured . . . 65 30
DESIGNS: 60c. Rail transport; 80c. Motorized canal barge.

329 Queen Wilhelmina

1980. Europa.
1345 **329** 60c. black, red and blue 50 10
1346 – 80c. black, red and blue 65 30
DESIGN: 80c. Sir Winston Churchill.

330 Abraham Kuyper (first rector) and University Seal

1980. Centenary of Amsterdam Free University.
1347 **330** 50c. multicoloured . . . 40 15

331 "Pop-up" Book
332 Saltmarsh

1980. Child Welfare. Multicoloured.
1348 45c.+20c. Type **331** 40 20
1349 50c.+20c. Child flying on a book (vert) 50 40
1350 60c.+30c. Boy reading "Kikkerkoning" (vert) . . 55 10
1351 80c.+30c. Dreaming in a book 65 65

1981. Cultural, Health and Social Welfare Funds. Multicoloured.
1353 45c.+20c. Type **332** 40 30
1354 55c.+25c. Dyke 50 30
1355 60c.+25c. Drain 55 30
1356 65c.+30c. Cultivated land 65 30

333 Parcel (Parcel Post)

1981. P.T.T. Centenaries. Multicoloured.
1357 45c. Type **333** 40 15
1358 55c. Telephone, dish aerial and telephone directory page (public telephone service) 45 15
1359 65c. Savings bank books, deposit transfer card and savings bank stamps (National Savings Bank) 50 10

334 Huis ten Bosch Royal Palace, The Hague

1981.
1361 **334** 55c. multicoloured . . . 45 15

335 Carillon

1981. Europa. Multicoloured.
1362 45c. Type **335** 40 20
1363 65c. Barrel organ 50 15

336 Council of State Emblem and Maps of 1531 and 1981

1981. 450th Anniv of Council of State.
1364 **336** 65c. orange, deep orange and red 50 10

337 Marshalling Yard, Excavator and Ship's Screw

1981. Industrial and Agricultural Exports. Mult.
1365 45c. Type **337** 40 15
1366 55c. Inner port, cast-iron component and weighing machine 45 20
1367 60c. Airport, tomato and lettuce 50 40
1368 65c. Motorway interchange, egg and cheese 50 10

338 "Integration in Society"

1981. Child Welfare. Integration of Handicapped Children. Multicoloured.
1369 45c.+25c. Type **338** 40 10
1370 55c.+20c. "Integration in the Family" (vert) 50 50
1371 60c.+25c. Child vaccinated against polio (Upper Volta project) (vert) . . . 55 50
1372 65c.+30c. "Integration among Friends" 65 10

339 Queen Beatrix
340 Agnieten Chapel and Banners

1981.
1374 **339** 65c. brown and black . . 55 10
1375 70c. lilac and black . . 70 10
1376 75c. pink and black . . 70 10
1377 90c. green and black . . 1·10 10
1378 1g. lilac and black . . . 70 15
1379 1g.20 bistre and black 1·25 20
1380 1g.40 green and black . . 1·75 20
1381 1g.50 lilac and black . . 1·10 20
1382 2g. bistre and black . . 1·40 15
1383 2g.50 orange and black 1·75 30
1384 3g. blue and black . . . 2·10 20
1385 4g. green and black . . . 3·00 20
1386 5g. blue and black . . . 3·75 20
1387 6g.50 lilac and black . . 5·75 20
1388 7g. blue and black . . . 4·75 30
1389 7g.50 green and black . . 5·75 50
For this design but on uncoloured background see Nos. 1594/1605.

1982. 350th Anniv of University of Amsterdam.
1395 **340** 65c. multicoloured . . . 50 10

341 Skater
342 Apple Blossom

1982. Centenary of Royal Dutch Skating Association.
1396 **341** 45c. multicoloured . . . 40 20

1982. Cultural, Health and Social Welfare Funds. Multicoloured.
1397 50c.+20c. Type **342** 50 30
1398 60c.+25c. Anemones 55 30
1399 65c.+25c. Roses 55 30
1400 70c.+30c. African violets . . 65 55

343 Stripes in National Colours

1982. Bicentenary of Netherlands–United States Diplomatic Relations.
1401 **343** 50c. red, blue and black 40 20
1402 65c. red, blue and black 55 15

344 Sandwich Tern and Eider
345 Zebra Crossing

1982. Waddenzee. Multicoloured.
1403 50c. Type **344** 40 20
1404 70c. Barnacle Geese 55 10

1982. 50th Anniv of Dutch Road Safety Organization.
1405 **345** 60c. multicoloured . . . 50 30

346 Ground Plan of Enkhuizen Fortifications
347 Aerial view of Palace and Liberation Monument

1982. Europa. Multicoloured.
1406 50c. Type **346** 40 20
1407 70c. Part of ground plan of Coevorden fortifications 55 10

1982. Royal Palace, Dam Square, Amsterdam. Mult.
1408 50c. Facade, ground plan and cross-section of palace 40 10
1409 60c. Type **347** 50 10

348 Great Tits and Child
349 Touring Club Activities

1982. Child Welfare. Child and Animal. Mult.
1410 50c.+30c. Type **348** 40 15
1411 60c.+20c. Child arm-in-arm with cat 50 15
1412 65c.+20c. Child with drawing of rabbit . . . 65 45
1413 70c.+30c. Child with palm cockatoo 70 70

1983. Centenary of Royal Dutch Touring Club.
1415 **349** 70c. multicoloured . . . 60 10

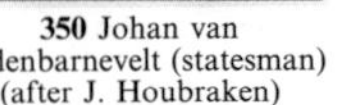

350 Johan van Oldenbarnevelt (statesman) (after J. Houbraken)

351 Newspaper

1983. Cultural, Health and Social Welfare Funds.

1416 **350** 50c.+20c. pink, blue and black 50 40
1417 – 60c.+25c. mult 65 40
1418 – 65c.+25c. mult 70 55
1419 – 70c.+30c. grey, black and gold 70 55

DESIGNS: 60c. Willem Jansz Blaeu (cartographer) (after Thomas de Keijser); 65c. Hugo de Groot (statesman) (after J. van Ravesteyn); 70c. "Saskia van Uylenburch" (portrait of his wife by Rembrandt).

1983. Europa. Multicoloured.

1420 50c. Type **351** (75th anniv of Netherlands Newspaper Publishers Association) 40 20
1421 70c. European Communications Satellite and European Telecommunication Satellites Organization members' flags 55 10

352 "Composition 1922" (P. Mondriaan)

353 "Geneva Conventions"

1983. De Stijl Art Movement. Multicoloured.

1422 50c. Type **352** 40 15
1423 65c. Contra construction from "Maison Particuliere" (C. van Eesteren and T. van Doesburg) 50 30

1983. Red Cross.

1424 **353** 50c.+25c. mult 50 45
1425 – 60c.+20c. mult 55 45
1426 – 65c.+25c. mult 65 45
1427 – 70c.+30c. grey, black and red 70 65

DESIGNS: 60c. Red Cross and text "charity, independence, impartiality"; 65c. "Socio-medical work"; 70c. Red Cross and text "For Peace".

354 Luther's Signature

355 Child looking at Donkey and Ox through Window

1983. 500th Birth Anniv of Martin Luther (Protestant Reformer).

1428 **354** 70c. multicoloured . . . 55 10

1983. Child Welfare. Child and Christmas. Mult.

1429 50c.+10c. Type **355** 50 45
1430 50c.+25c. Child riding flying snowman 55 15
1431 60c.+30c. Child in bed and star 65 70
1432 70c.+30c. Children dressed as the three kings 70 15

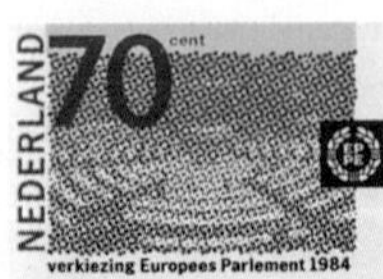

356 Parliament

1984. Second Elections to European Parliament.

1434 **356** 70c. multicoloured . . . 50 10

357 Northern Lapwings

358 St. Servaas

1984. Cultural, Health and Social Welfare Funds. Pasture Birds. Multicoloured.

1435 50c.+20c. Type **357** 50 40
1436 60c.+25c. Ruffs 55 40
1437 65c.+25c. Redshanks (vert) 65 55
1438 70c.+30c. Black-tailed godwits (vert) 70 55

1984. 1600th Death Anniv of St. Servaas (Bishop of Tongeren and Maastricht).

1439 **358** 60c. multicoloured . . . 50 15

359 Bridge

1984. Europa. 25th Anniv of European Post and Telecommunications Conference.

1440 **359** 50c. deep blue and blue 40 15
1441 70c. green and light green 55 10

360 Eye and Magnifying Glass

1984. Centenary of Organized Philately in the Netherlands and "Filacento" International Stamp Exhibition, The Hague. Multicoloured.

1442 50c.+20c. Type **360** 55 45
1443 60c.+25c. 1909 cover . . . 65 55
1444 70c.+30c. Stamp club meeting, 1949 . . . . . . 65 65

361 William of Orange (after Adriaen Thomaszoon Key)

1984. 400th Death Anniv of William of Orange.

1446 **361** 70c. multicoloured . . . 55 15

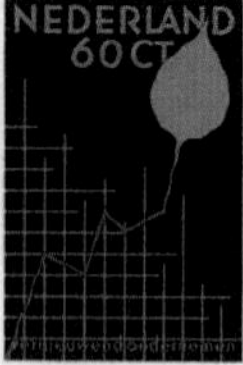

362 Giant Pandas and Globe

363 Graph and Leaf

1984. World Wildlife Fund.

1447 **362** 70c. multicoloured . . . 70 15

1984. 11th International Small Business Congress, Amsterdam.

1448 **363** 60c. multicoloured . . . 50 20

364 Violin Lesson

365 Sunny, First Dutch Guide-Dog

1984. Child Welfare. Strip Cartoons. Mult.

1449 50c.+25c. Type **364** 40 30
1450 60c.+20c. At the dentist . . 70 55
1451 65c.+20c. The plumber . . . 85 75
1452 70c.+30c. The king and money chest 65 30

1985. 50th Anniv of Royal Dutch Guide-Dog Fund.

1454 **365** 60c. black, ochre and red 50 20

366 Plates and Cutlery on Place-mat

367 Saint Martin's Church, Zaltbommel

1985. Tourism. Multicoloured.

1455 50c. Type **366** (centenary of Travel and Holidays Association) 40 20
1456 70c. Kroller-Muller museum emblem, antlers and landscape (50th anniv of De Hoge Veluwe National Park) 55 10

1985. Cultural, Health and Social Welfare Funds. Religious Buildings. Multicoloured.

1457 50c.+20c. Type **367** 55 45
1458 60c.+25c. Winterswijk synagogue and Holy Ark (horiz) 65 55
1459 65c.+25c. Bolsward Baptist church 70 55
1460 70c.+30c. Saint John's Cathedral, 's-Hertogenbosch (horiz) 70 40

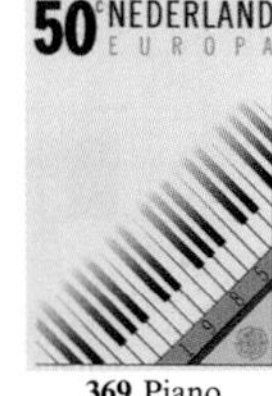

368 Star of David, Illegal Newspapers and Rifle Practice (Resistance Movement)

369 Piano Keyboard

1985. 40th Anniv of Liberation.

1461 **368** 50c. black, stone and red 45 20
1462 – 60c. black, stone and blue 50 15
1463 – 65c. black, stone & orge 55 45
1464 – 70c. black, stone & green 55 20

DESIGNS: 60c. Bombers over houses, "De Vliegende Hollander" (newspaper) and soldier (Allied Forces); 65c. Soldiers and civilians, "Parool" (newspaper) and American war cemetery, Margraten (Liberation); 70c. Women prisoners, prison money and Burma Railway (Dutch East Indies).

1985. Europa. Music Year. Multicoloured.

1465 50c. Type **369** 40 20
1466 70c. Organ 55 10

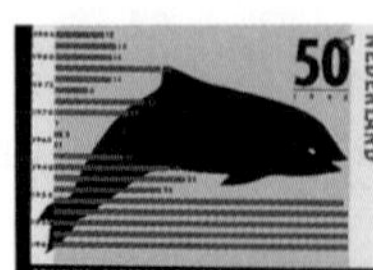

370 National Museum, Amsterdam (centenary)

1985. Anniversaries and Events. Multicoloured.

1467 50c. Type **370** 40 20
1468a 60c. Teacher with students (bicentenary of Amsterdam Nautical College) 50 25
1469 70c. Ship's mast and rigging ("Sail '85", Amsterdam) 55 10

371 Porpoise and Graph

1985. Endangered Animals.

1470 **371** 50c. black, blue and red 40 20
1471 – 70c. black, blue and red 55 15

DESIGN: 70c. Seal and PCB molecule structure.

372 Ignition Key and Framed Photograph ("Think of Me")

1985. Child Welfare. Road Safety. Multicoloured.

1472 50c.+25c. Type **372** 55 20
1473 60c.+20c. Child holding target showing speeds . . 55 65
1474 65c.+20c. Girl holding red warning triangle 65 75
1475 70c.+30c. Boy holding "Children Crossing" sign 90 20

373 Penal Code Extract

1986. Centenary of Penal Code.

1477 **373** 50c. black, yellow & purple 40 15

374 Surveyor with Pole and N.A.P. Water Gauge

1986. 300th Anniv of Height Gauging Marks at Amsterdam.

1478 **374** 60c. multicoloured . . . 45 15

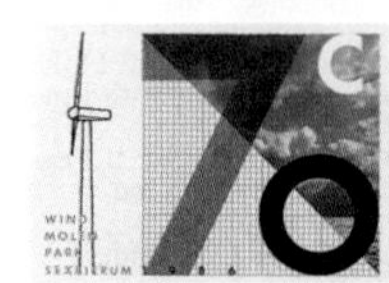

375 Windmill, Graph and Cloudy Sky

1986. Inaug of Windmill Test Station, Sexbierum.

1479 **375** 70c. multicoloured . . . 55 10

376 Scales

377 Het Loo Palace Garden, Apeldoorn

1986. Cultural, Health and Social Welfare Funds. Antique Measuring Instruments. Multicoloured.

1480 50c.+20c. Type **376** 55 35
1481 60c.+25c. Clock (vert) . . . 55 35
1482 65c.+25c. Barometer (vert) 65 65
1483 70c.+30c. Jacob's staff . . . 70 85

1986. Europa. Multicoloured.

1484 50c. Type **377** 40 20
1485 70c. Tree with discoloured crown 50 10

378 Cathedral

379 Drees at Binnenhof, 1947

1986. Utrecht Events.

1486 **378** 50c. multicoloured . . . 50 30
1487 – 60c. blue, pink and black 55 30
1488 – 70c. multicoloured . . . 70 20

DESIGNS—VERT: 50c. Type **378** (completion of interior restoration); 60c. German House (75th anniv of Heemschut Conservation Society). HORIZ: 70c. Extract from foundation document (350th anniv of Utrecht University).

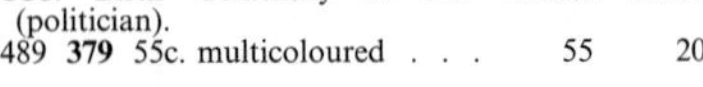

1986. Birth Centenary of Dr. Willem Drees (politician).

1489 **379** 55c. multicoloured . . . 55 20

380 Draughts as Biscuits in Saucer

381 Map of Flood Barrier

1986. 75th Anniversary of Royal Dutch Draughts Association (1490) and Royal Dutch Billiards Association (1491). Multicoloured.
1490 75c. Type **380** 65 65
1491 75c. Player in ball preparing to play 20 20

1986. Delta Project Completion. Multicoloured.
1492 65c. Type **381** 55 30
1493 75c. Flood barrier 65 20

382 Children listening to Music (experiencing)

383 Engagement Picture

1986. Child Welfare. Child and Culture.
1494 55c.+25c. Type **382** 70 65
1495 65c.+35c. Boy drawing (achieving) 75 45
1496 75c.+35c. Children at theatre (understanding) 85 20

1987. Golden Wedding of Princess Juliana and Prince Bernhard.
1498 **383** 75c. orange, black and gold 70 20

384 Block of Flats and Hut

1987. International Year of Shelter for the Homeless (65c.) and Centenary of Netherlands Salvation Army (75c.). Multicoloured.
1499 65c. Type **384** 55 30
1500 75c. Army officer, meeting and tramp 65 20

385 Eduard Douwes Dekker (Multatuli) and De Harmonie Club

1987. Writers' Death Annivs. Multicoloured.
1501 55c. Type **385** (centenary) 50 30
1502 75c. Constantijn Huygens and Scheveningseweg, The Hague (300th anniv) . . . 1·00 20

386 Steam Pumping Station, Nijerk

1987. Cultural Health and Social Welfare Funds. Industrial Buildings.
1503 **386** 55c.+30c. red, grey and black 90 80
1504 – 65c.+35c. grey, black and blue . . . . . . 1·00 80
1505 – 75c.+35c. grey, yellow and black . . . . . . 1·10 65
DESIGNS: 65c. Water tower, Deventer; 75c. Brass foundry, Joure.

387 Dance Theatre, Scheveningen (Rem Koolhaas)

1987. Europa. Architecture. Multicoloured.
1506 55c. Type **387** 50 30
1507 75c. Montessori School, Amsterdam (Herman Hertzberger) 65 20

388 Auction at Broek op Langedijk

1987. Centenary of Auction Sales (55, 75c.) and 150th Anniv of Groningen Agricultural Society (65c.). Multicoloured.
1508 55c. Type **388** 50 30
1509 65c. Groningen landscape and founders' signatures 70 30
1510 75c. Auction sale and clock 70 20

389 Telephone Care Circles

390 Map of Holland

1987. Dutch Red Cross. Multicoloured.
1511 55c.+30c. Type **389** 70 70
1512 65c.+35c. Red cross and hands (Welfare work) . . 80 60
1513 75c.+35c. Red cross and drip (Blood transfusion) 90 50

1987. 75th Anniv of Netherlands Municipalities Union.
1514 **390** 75c. multicoloured . . . 65 20

391 Noordeinde Palace, The Hague

392 Woodcutter

1987.
1515 **391** 65c. multicoloured . . . 55 10

1987. Child Welfare. Child and Profession. Mult.
1516 55c.+25c. Type **392** 65 70
1517 65c.+35c. Woman sailor . . 80 50
1518 75c.+35c. Woman pilot . . 90 30

393 Star

394 "Narcissus cyclamineus" "Peeping Tom" and Extract from "I Call You Flowers" (Jan Hanlo)

1987. Christmas.
1520 **393** 50c. red, blue and green 65 25
1521 50c. yellow, red and blue 65 25
1522 50c. red, blue and yellow 65 20
1523 50c. yellow, red and green 65 20
1524 50c. blue, green and red 65 20
The first colour described is that of the St. George's Cross.

1988. "Filacept" European Stamp Exhibition, The Hague. Flowers. Multicoloured.
1525 55c.+55c. Type **394** 90 85
1526 75c.+70c. "Rosa gallica" "Versicolor" and "Roses" (Daan van Golden) . . . 1·10 1·10
1527 75c.+70c. Sea holly and 1270 map of The Hague 1·10 1·10

395 Quagga

1988. Cultural, Health and Social Welfare Funds. 150th Anniv of Natura Artis Magistra Zoological Society. Multicoloured.
1528 55c.+30c. Type **395** 65 70
1529 65c.+35c. American manatee 85 85
1530 75c.+35c. Orang-utan (vert) 90 50

396 Man's Shoulder

397 Traffic Scene with Lead Symbol crossed Through

1988. 75th Anniv of Netherlands Cancer Institute.
1531 **396** 75c. multicoloured . . . 60 20

1988. Europa. Transport. Multicoloured.
1532 55c. Type **397** (lead-free petrol) 50 20
1533 75c. Cyclists reflected in car wing mirror (horiz) . . . 85 20

398 Pendulum, Prism and Saturn

1988. 300th Anniv of England's Glorious Revolution. Multicoloured.
1534 65c. Type **398** 55 20
1535 75c. Queen Mary, King William III and 17th-century warship . . 70 20

399 "Cobra Cat" (Appel)

400 Sailing Ship and Map of Australia

1988. 40th Anniv of Founding of Cobra Painters Group. Multicoloured.
1536 55c. Type **399** 65 65
1537 65c. "Kite" (Corneille) . . . 65 65
1538 75c. "Stumbling Horse" (Constant) 70 35

1988. Bicentenary of Australian Settlement.
1539 **400** 75c. multicoloured . . . 70 20

401 Statue of Erasmus, Rotterdam

402 "Rain"

1988. 75th Anniv of Erasmus University, Rotterdam (1540) and Centenary of Concertgebouw Concert Hall and Orchestra (1541).
1540 **401** 75c. deep green and green 65 20
1541 – 75c. violet 65 20
DESIGN: No. 1541, Violin and Concertgebouw concert hall.

1988. Child Welfare. Centenary of Royal Netherlands Swimming Federation. Children's drawings. Multicoloured.
1543 55c.+25c. Type **402** 65 55
1544 65c.+35c. "Getting Ready for the Race" 85 50
1545 75c.+35c. "Swimming Test" 85 35

403 Stars

1988. Christmas.
1547 **403** 50c. multicoloured . . . 55 10

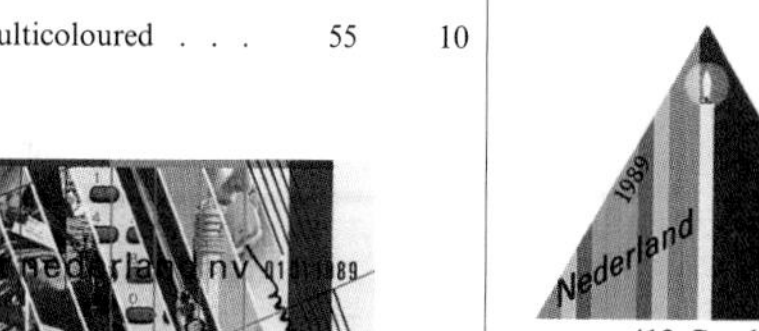

404 Postal and Telecommunications Services

1989. Privatization of Netherlands PTT.
1548 **404** 75c. multicoloured . . . 70 20

405 "Solidarity"

406 Members' Flags

1989. Trade Unions. Multicoloured.
1549 55c. Type **405** 50 20
1550 75c. Talking mouths on hands 65 20

1989. 40th Anniv of N.A.T.O.
1551 **406** 75c. multicoloured . . . 65 20

407 Boier

408 Boy with Homemade Telephone

1989. Cultural, Health and Social Welfare Funds. Old Sailing Vessels.
1552 **407** 55c.+30c. green & blk 70 75
1553 – 65c.+35c. blue & black 85 75
1554 – 75c.+35c. brown & blk 1·00 75
DESIGNS: 65c. Fishing smack; 75c. Clipper.

1989. Europa. Children's Games. Multicoloured.
1555 55c. Type **408** 50 20
1556 75c. Girl with homemade telephone 75 20

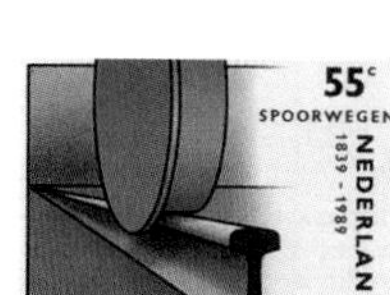

409 Wheel on Rail

410 Boy with Ball and Diagram of Goal Scored in European Championship

1989. 150th Anniv of Netherlands' Railways. Mult.
1557 55c. Type **409** 50 30
1558 65c. Steam, electric and diesel locomotives 50 30
1559 75c. Diesel train, station clock and "The Kiss" (sculpture by Rodin) . . . 55 20

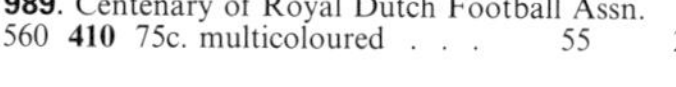

1989. Centenary of Royal Dutch Football Assn.
1560 **410** 75c. multicoloured . . . 55 20

411 Map

412 Right to Housing

1989. 150th Anniv of Division of Limburg between Netherlands and Belgium.
1561 **411** 75c. multicoloured . . . 55 20

1989. Child Welfare. 30th Anniv of Declaration of Rights of the Child. Multicoloured.
1562 55c.+25c. Type **412** 65 65
1563 65c.+35c. Right to food . . 70 55
1564 75c.+35c. Right to education 85 30

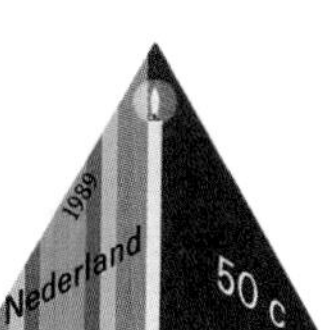

413 Candle

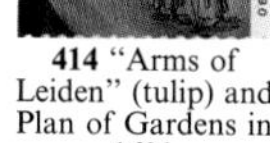

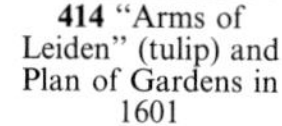

414 "Arms of Leiden" (tulip) and Plan of Gardens in 1601

1989. Christmas.
1566 **413** 50c. multicoloured . . . 55 10

1990. 400th Anniv of Hortus Botanicus (botanical gardens), Leiden.
1567 **414** 65c. multicoloured . . . 50 30

415 Pointer on Graduated Scale

416 "Self-portrait" (detail)

1990. Centenary of Labour Inspectorate.
1568 **415** 75c. multicoloured . . . 65 20

1990. Death Centenary of Vincent van Gogh (painter). Multicoloured.
1569 55c. Type **416** 60 20
1570 75c. "Green Vineyard" (detail) 70 20

417 Summer's Day

1990. Cultural, Health and Social Welfare Funds. The Weather. Multicoloured.
1571 55c.+30c. Type **417** 70 65
1572 65c.+35c. Clouds and isobars (vert) 90 75
1573 75c.+35c. Satellite weather picture (vert) . . . . . . 1·00 70

418 Zuiderkerk Ruins

1990. 50th Anniv of German Bombing of Rotterdam.
1574 **418** 55c. deep brown, brown and black 50 30
1575 – 65c. multicoloured . . . 60 20
1576 – 75c. multicoloured . . . 65 20
DESIGNS: 65c. City plan as stage; 75c. Girder and plans for future construction.

419 Postal Headquarters, Groningen, and Veere Post Office

420 Construction of Indiaman and Wreck of "Amsterdam"

1990. Europa. Post Office Buildings.
1577 – 55c. grey, mauve & brn 50 30
1578 **419** 75c. blue, green and grey 65 20
DESIGN: 55c. As Type **419** but inscr "Postkantoor Veere".

1990. 3rd Anniv of Dutch East India Company Ships Association (replica ship project) (1579) and "Sail 90", Amsterdam (1580). Multicoloured.
1579 65c. Type **420** 60 35
1580 75c. Crew manning yards on sailing ship 65 20

421 Queens Emma, Wilhelmina, Juliana and Beatrix

422 Flames, Telephone Handset and Number

1990. Netherlands Queens of the House of Orange.
1581 **421** 150c. multicoloured . . . 1·40 65

1990. Introduction of National Emergency Number.
1582 **422** 65c. multicoloured . . . 60 30

423 Girl riding Horse

424 Falling Snow

1990. Child Welfare. Hobbies. Multicoloured.
1583 55c.+25c. Type **423** 65 60
1584 65c.+35c. Girl at computer 85 50
1585 75c.+35c. Young philatelist 90 40

1990. Christmas.
1587 **424** 50c. multicoloured . . . 45 10

425 Industrial Chimneys, Exhaust Pipes and Aerosol Can (Air Pollution)

1991. Environmental Protection. Multicoloured.
1588 55c. Type **425** 60 30
1589 65c. Outfall pipes and chemicals (sea pollution) 65 30
1590 75c. Agricultural chemicals, leaking drums and household landfill waste (soil pollution) 70 20

426 German Raid on Amsterdam Jewish Quarter and Open Hand

1991. 50th Anniv of Amsterdam General Strike.
1591 **426** 75c. multicoloured . . . 65 20

427 Princess Beatrix and Prince Claus on Wedding Day

428 Queen Beatrix

1991. Royal Silver Wedding Anniversary. Mult.
1592 75c. Type **427** 70 20
1593 75c. Queen Beatrix and Prince Claus on horseback 70 20

1991. (a) Ordinary gum.
1594 **428** 75c. deep green & green 1·40 30
1595 80c. brown & lt brown 50 10
1597 90c. blue 65 20
1598 1g. violet 70 20
1599 1g.10 blue 85 20
1600 1g.30 blue and violet 90 20
1601 1g.40 green and olive 90 15
1601a 1g.50 green . . . . . . 5·50 1·60
1602 1g.60 purple and mauve 1·00 20
1603 2g. brown . . . . . . 1·10 20
1603a 2g.50 purple . . . . . 2·50 85
1604 3g. blue . . . . 2·00 20
1605 5g. red . . . . 1·75 20
1706 7g.50 violet . . . . . 5·25 1·40
1708 10g. green . . . . . . 6·75 65

(b) Self-adhesive gum.
1606 **428** 1g. violet . . . . 1·00 80
1607 1g.10 blue . . . . . . 1·10 90
1608 1g.45 green . . . . . . 1·25 1·10
1609 2g.50 purple . . . . . 2·50 2·10
1609a 5g. red . . . . 5·25 4·50

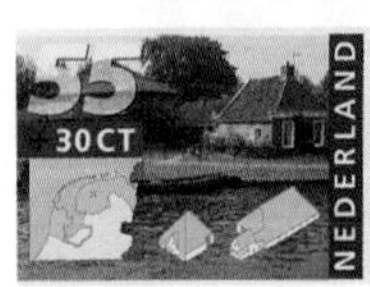

429 "Meadow" Farm, Wartena, Friesland

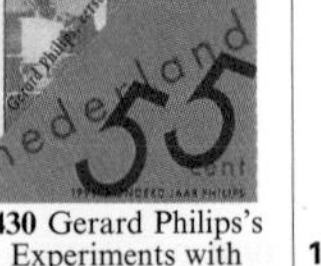

430 Gerard Philips's Experiments with Carbon Filaments

1991. Cultural, Health and Social Welfare Funds. Traditional Farmhouses. Multicoloured.
1610 55c.+30c. Type **429** 85 80
1611 65c.+35c. "T-house" farm, Kesteren, Gelderland . . 90 80
1612 75c.+35c. "Courtyard" farm, Nuth, Limburg . . 1·00 80

1991. 75th Anniv of Netherlands Standards Institute (65c.) and Centenary of Philips Organization (others). Multicoloured.
1615 55c. Type **430** 60 35
1616 65c. Wiring to Standard NEN 1010 (horiz) 65 20
1617 75c. Laser beams reading video disc 70 20

431 Man raising Hat to Space

432 Sticking Plaster over Medal

1991. Europa. Europe in Space. Multicoloured.
1618 55c. Type **431** 55 40
1619 75c. Ladders stretching into space 70 20

1991. 75th Anniv of Nijmegen International Four Day Marches.
1620 **432** 80c. multicoloured . . . 65 20

433 Jacobus Hendericus van't Hoff

1991. Dutch Nobel Prize Winners (1st series). Multicoloured.
1621 60c. Type **433** (chemistry, 1901) 60 35
1622 70c. Pieter Zeeman (physics, 1902) 65 30
1623 80c. Tobias Michael Carel Asser (peace, 1911) . . . 70 20
See also Nos. 1690/2 and 1773/5.

434 Children and Open Book

1991. Centenary (1992) of Public Libraries in the Netherlands.
1624 **434** 70c. drab, black & mauve 65 25
1625 – 80c. multicoloured . . . 70 20
DESIGN: 80c. Books on shelf.

435 Girls with Doll and Robot

436 "Greetings Cards keep People in Touch"

1991. Child Welfare. Outdoor Play. Multicoloured.
1626 60c.+30c. Type **435** 70 40
1627 70c.+35c. Bicycle race . . . 1·00 90
1628 80c.+40c. Hide and seek . . 90 40

1991. Christmas.
1630 **436** 55c. multicoloured . . . 45 10

437 Artificial Lightning, Microchip and Oscilloscope

1992. 150th Anniv of Delft University of Technology.
1631 **437** 60c. multicoloured . . . 55 30

438 Extract from Code

440 Tulips ("Mondrian does not like Green")

1992. Implementation of Property Provisions of New Civil Code.
1632 **438** 80c. multicoloured . . . 70 20

1992. "Expo '92" World's Fair, Seville. Mult.
1634 70c. Type **440** 65 30
1635 80c. "Netherland Expo '92" 70 20

441 Tasman's Map of Staete Landt (New Zealand)

1992. 350th Anniv of Discovery of Tasmania and New Zealand by Abel Tasman.
1636 **441** 70c. multicoloured . . . 65 30

442 Yellow and Purple Flowers

443 Geometric Planes

1992. Cultural, Health and Social Welfare Funds. "Floriade" Flower Show, Zoetermeer. Mult.
1637 60c.+30c. Water lilies . . . 90 80
1638 70c.+35c. Orange and purple flowers . . . . . 1·10 90
1639 80c.+40c. Type **442** . . . . 1·25 65

1992. 150th Anniv of Royal Association of Netherlands Architects (60c.) and Inauguration of New States General Lower House (80c.). Mult.
1643 60c. Type **443** 55 30
1644 80c. Atrium and blue sky (symbolizing sending of information into society) 70 20

444 Globe and Columbus

445 Moneta (Goddess of Money)

1992. Europa. 500th Anniv of Discovery of America by Columbus.
1645 **444** 60c. multicoloured . . . 65 30
1646 – 80c. black, mauve & yellow 85 20
DESIGN—VERT: 80c. Galleon.

1992. Centenary of Royal Netherlands Numismatics Society.
1647 **445** 70c. multicoloured . . . 65 25

446 Teddy Bear wearing Stethoscope

447 List of Relatives and Friends

1992. Centenary of Netherlands Paediatrics Society.
1648 **446** 80c. multicoloured . . . 70 20

1992. 50th Anniv of Departure of First Deportation Train from Westerbork Concentration Camp.
1649 **447** 70c. multicoloured . . . 65 25

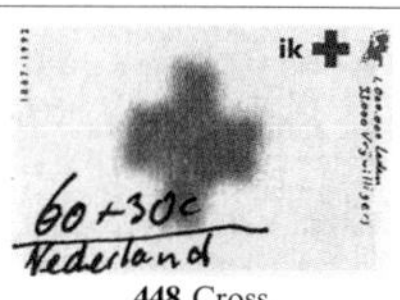
448 Cross

1992. 125th Anniv of Netherlands Red Cross. Multicoloured.
1650 60c.+30c. Type **448** 90 80
1651 70c.+35c. Supporting injured person . . . . 1·10 90
1652 80c.+40c. Red cross on dirty bandage . . . . 1·25 65

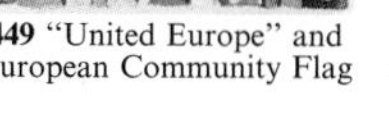

449 "United Europe" and European Community Flag

450 Queen Beatrix on Official Birthday, 1992, and at Investiture

1992. European Single Market.
1656 **449** 80c. multicoloured . . . 70 20

1992. 12½ Years since Accession to the Throne of Queen Beatrix.
1657 **450** 80c. multicoloured . . . 70 20

451 Saxophone Player

452 Poinsettia

1992. Child Welfare. Child and Music. Mult.
1658 60c.+30c. Type **451** 85 50
1659 70c.+35c. Piano player . . . 90 60
1660 80c.+40c. Double bass player . . . . 1·00 75

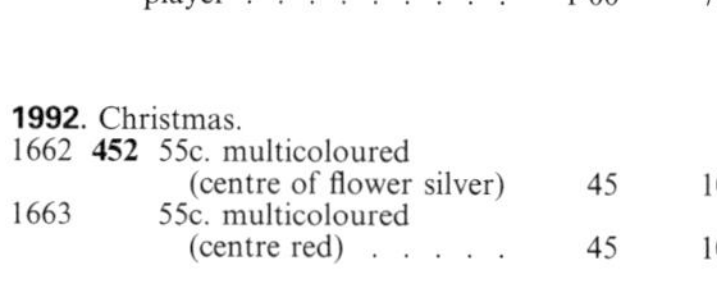

1992. Christmas.
1662 **452** 55c. multicoloured (centre of flower silver) 45 10
1663 55c. multicoloured (centre red) 45 10

453 Cycling

1993. Centenary of Netherlands Cycle and Motor Industry Association.
1664 **453** 70c. multicoloured . . . 65 35
1665 – 80c. brown, grey & yell 70 20
DESIGN: 80c. Car.

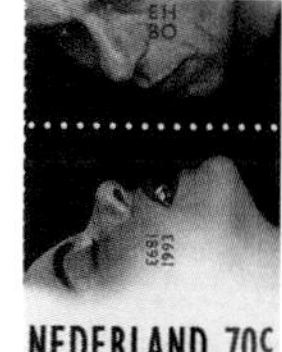
454 Collages

455 Mouth to Mouth Resuscitation

1993. Greetings Stamps. Multicoloured.
1666 70c. Type **454** 60 20
1667 70c. Collages (different) . . 60 20

1993. Anniversaries. Multicoloured.
1668 70c. Type **455** (centenary of Royal Netherlands First Aid Association) 65 35
1669 80c. Pests on leaf (75th anniv of Wageningen University of Agriculture) 70 20
1670 80c. Lead driver and horses (bicentenary of Royal Horse Artillery) 70 20

456 Emblems

1993. 150th Anniv of Royal Dutch Notaries Association. Each red and violet.
1671 80c. Type **456** ("150 Jaar" reading up) 70 20
1672 80c. As Type **456** but emblems inverted and "150 Jaar" reading down 70 20
Nos. 1671/2 were issued together in horizontal tete-beche pairs, each pair forming a composite design.

457 Large White

458 Elderly Couple

1993. Butterflies. Multicoloured.
1673 70c. Pearl-bordered fritillary 70 35
1674 80c. Large tortoiseshell . . . 80 20
1675 90c. Type **457** 90 80

1993. Cultural, Health and Social Welfare Funds. Senior Citizens' Independence.
1677 70c.+35c. Type **458** . . . . 1·10 1·10
1678 70c.+35c. Elderly man . . . 1·10 1·10
1679 80c.+40c. Elderly woman with dog . . . . 1·25 85

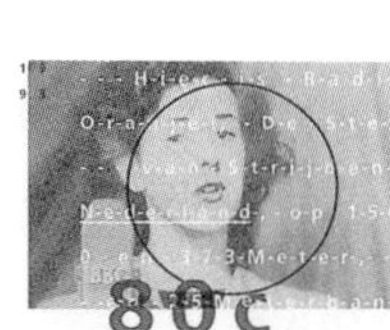

459 Broadcaster

460 Sports Pictograms

1993. Radio Orange (Dutch broadcasts from London during Second World War). Mult.
1683 80c. Type **459** 70 20
1684 80c. Man listening to radio in secret 70 20

1993. 2nd European Youth Olympic Days. Mult.
1685 70c. Type **460** 70 30
1686 80c. Sports pictograms (different) 80 20

461 "The Embodiment of Unity" (Wessel Couzijn)

462 Johannes Diderik van der Waals (Physics, 1910)

1993. Europa. Contemporary Art. Multicoloured.
1687 70c. Type **461** 70 35
1688 80c. Architectonic sculpture (Per Kirkeby) 80 20
1689 160c. Sculpture (Naum Gabo) (vert) . . . . . . 1·40 1·10

1993. Dutch Nobel Prize Winners (2nd series).
1690 **462** 70c. blue, black and red 65 30
1691 – 80c. mauve, black & red 70 20
1692 – 90c. multicoloured . . . 90 75
DESIGNS: 80c. Willem Einthoven (medicine, 1924); 90c. Christiaan Eijkman (medicine, 1929).

463 Pen and Pencils

1993. Letter Writing Campaign. Multicoloured.
1693 80c. Type **463** 65 20
1694 80c. Envelope 65 20

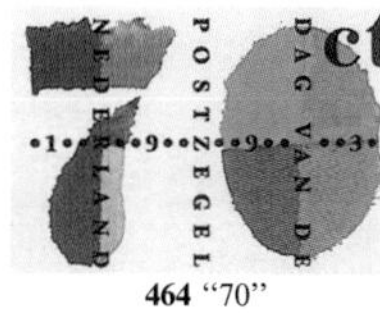
464 "70"

1993. Stamp Day (70c.) and Netherlands PTT (80c.). Multicoloured.
1695 70c. Type **464** 65 30
1696 80c. Dish aerial and dove carrying letter 70 20

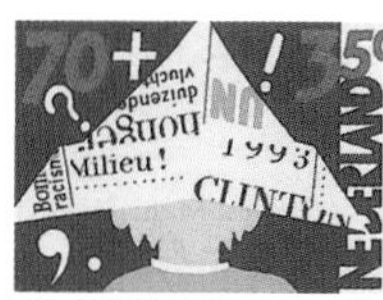
465 Child in Newspaper Hat

1993. Child Welfare. Child and the Media. Mult.
1697 70c.+35c. Type **465** 90 65
1698 70c.+35c. Elephant using headphones 90 65
1699 80c.+40c. Television . . . . 1·10 50

466 Candle

1993. Christmas. Multicoloured.
1711 55c. Type **466** 45 10
1712 55c. Fireworks 45 10
Both designs have a number of punched holes.

467 "Composition"

1994. 50th Death Anniv of Piet Mondriaan (artist). Multicoloured.
1713 70c. "The Red Mill" (detail) 65 30
1714 80c. Type **467** 70 20
1715 90c. "Broadway Boogie Woogie" (detail) 90 60

468 Barnacle Goose

1994. "Fepapost 94" European Stamp Exhibition, The Hague. Multicoloured.
1716 70c.+60c. Type **468** . . . . 1·00 85
1717 80c.+70c. Bluethroat . . . . 1·10 1·25
1718 90c.+80c. Garganey . . . . 1·25 1·10

469 Downy Rose

1994. Wild Flowers. Multicoloured.
1719 70c. Type **469** 65 30
1720 80c. Daisies 70 20
1721 90c. Wood forgetmenot . . 90 75

470 Airplane

1994. 75th Aircraft Industry Anniversaries.
1723 **470** 80c. blue and black . . . 70 20
1724 – 80c. grey, red and black 70 20
1725 – 80c. multicoloured . . . 70 20
DESIGNS: No. 1723, Type **470** (KLM (Royal Dutch Airlines)); 1724, Plan and outline of aircraft and clouds (Royal Netherlands Fokker Aircraft Industries); 1725, Airplane and clouds (National Aerospace Laboratory).

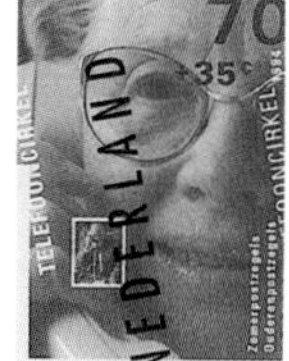

471 Woman using Telephone

472 Eisinga's Planetarium

1994. Cultural, Health and Social Welfare Funds. Senior Citizens' Security. Multicoloured.
1726 70c.+35c. Type **471** 90 90
1727 80c.+40c. Man using telephone . . . . 1·10 1·10
1728 90c.+35c. Man using telephone (different) . . . 1·25 1·10

1994. Anniversaries. Multicoloured.
1732 80c. Type **472** (250th birth anniv of Eise Eisinga) . . 70 20
1733 90c. Astronaut and boot print on Moon surface (25th anniv of first manned Moon landing) 1·10 65

473 Players Celebrating

1994. World Cup Football Championship, U.S.A.
1734 **473** 80c. multicoloured . . . 70 30

474 Stock Exchange

1994. Quotation of Netherlands PTT (KPN) on Stock Exchange.
1735 **474** 80c. multicoloured . . . 70 20

475 Road Sign, Car and Bicycle

1994. Anniversaries and Events. Multicoloured.
1736 70c. Type **475** (centenary of provision of road signs by Netherlands Motoring Association) 65 40
1737 80c. Equestrian sports (World Equestrian Games, The Hague) . . . 70 20

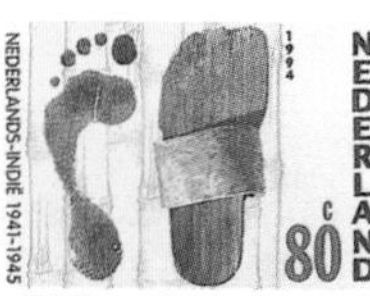
476 Footprint and Sandal

1994. Second World War. Multicoloured.
1738 80c. Type **476** (war in Netherlands Indies, 1941–45) 70 20
1739 90c. Soldier, children and aircraft dropping paratroops (50th anniv of Operation Market Garden (Battle of Arnhem)) (vert) 90 60

477 Brandaris Lighthouse, Terschelling

1994. Lighthouses. Multicoloured.
1740 70c. Type **477** 65 40
1741 80c. Ameland (vert) 70 20
1742 90c. Vlieland (vert) 90 75

478 Decorating

479 Star and Christmas Tree

1994. Child Welfare. "Together". Multicoloured.

1744	70c.+35c. Type **478**	90	65
1745	80c.+40c. Girl on swing knocking fruit off tree (vert)	1·10	60
1746	90c.+35c. Girl helping boy onto playhouse roof (vert)	1·10	1·10

1994. Christmas. Multicoloured.

1748	55c. Type **479**	45	10
1749	55c. Candle and star	45	10

480 Flying Cow

1995.

1750 **480**	100c. multicoloured	1·10	30

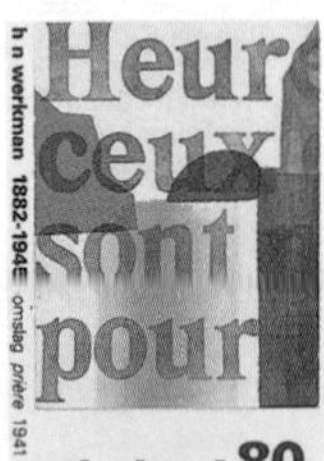
481 "Prayer" (detail)

1995. Anniversary and Events.

1751 **481**	80c. multicoloured	70	30
1752 –	80c. multicoloured	70	30
1753 –	80c. black and red	70	30

DESIGNS—VERT: No. 1751, Type **481** (50th death anniv of Hendrik Werkman (graphic designer); 1752, "Mesdag Panorama" (detail) (re-opening of Mesdag Museum). HORIZ: No. 1753, Mauritius 1847 2d. "POST OFFICE" stamp (purchase of remaining mint example in private hands by PTT Museum).

482 Joriz Ivens (documentary maker)

1995. Year of the Film (centenary of motion pictures). Multicoloured.

1754	70c. Type **482**	65	30
1755	80c. Scene from "Turkish Delight"	70	20

483 Mahler and Score of 7th Symphony

1995. Mahler Festival, Amsterdam.

1756 **483**	80c. black and blue	70	30

484 Dates and Acronym

1995. Centenaries. Multicoloured.

1757	80c. Type **484** (Netherlands Institute of Chartered Accountants)	70	20
1758	80c. Builders, bricklayer's trowel and saw (Netherlands Association of Building Contractors)	70	20

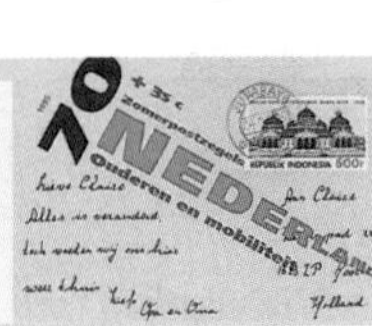
485 Postcard from Indonesia

486 "40 45"

1995. Cultural, Health and Social Welfare Funds. Mobility of the Elderly. Multicoloured.

1759	70c.+35c. Type **485**	90	85
1760	80c.+40c. Couple reflected in mirror	1·10	85
1761	100c.+45c. Couple with granddaughter at zoo	1·25	1·25

1995. 50th Anniversaries. Multicoloured.

1763	80c. Type **486** (end of Second World War)	70	30
1764	80c. "45 95" (liberation)	70	30
1765	80c. "50" (U.N.O.)	70	30

487 Birthday Cake and Signs of the Zodiac

488 Scout

1995. Birthday Greetings.

1766 **487**	70c. multicoloured	1·75	30

1995. Events. Multicoloured.

1767	70c. Type **488** (World Scout Jamboree, Dronten)	70	30
1768	80c. Amsterdam harbour ("Sail '95" and finish of Tall Ships Race) (horiz)	70	20

489 Common Kestrel

490 Petrus Debye (Chemistry, 1936)

1995. Birds of Prey. Multicoloured.

1769	70c. Type **489**	65	30
1770	80c. Face of hen harrier (horiz)	70	20
1771	100c. Red kite (horiz)	90	75

1995. Dutch Nobel Prize Winners (3rd series). Multicoloured.

1773	80c. Type **490**	70	20
1774	80c. Frederik Zernike (Physics, 1953)	70	20
1775	80c. Jan Tinbergen (Economics, 1969)	70	20

491 Eduard Jacobs and Jean-Louis Pisuisse

1995. Centenary of Dutch Cabaret. Multicoloured.

1776	70c. Type **491**	70	30
1777	80c. Wim Kan and Freek de Jonge	1·10	20

492 "The Schoolteacher" (Leonie Ensing)

493 Children with Stars

1995. Child Welfare. "Children and Fantasy". Children's Computer Drawings. Multicoloured.

1778	70c.+35c. "Dino" (Sjoerd Stegeman) (horiz)	85	85
1779	80c.+40c. Type **492**	1·00	85
1780	100c.+50c. "Children and Colours" (Marcel Jansen) (horiz)	1·25	1·40

1995. Christmas. Self-adhesive.

1782 **493**	55c. red, yellow and black	60	10
1783 –	55c. blue, yellow and black	60	10

DESIGN: No. 1783, Children looking at star through window.

494 "Woman in Blue reading a Letter"

495 Trowel, Daffodil Bulb and Glove

1996. Johannes Vermeer Exhibition, Washington and The Hague. Details of his Paintings. Mult.

1784	70c. "Lady writing a Letter with her Maid"	65	40
1785	80c. "The Love Letter"	70	30
1786	100c. Type **494**	1·10	90

1996. Spring Flowers. Multicoloured.

1788	70c. Type **495**	65	40
1789	80c. Tulips "kissing" woman	70	20
1790	100c. Snake's-head fritillary (detail of painting, Charles Mackintosh)	1·75	85

496 Putting up "MOVED" sign

497 Swimming

1996. Change of Address Stamp.

1792 **496**	70c. multicoloured	1·00	40

For 80c. self-adhesive version of this design see No. 1826.

1996. Cultural, Health and Social Welfare Funds. The Elderly in the Community. Multicoloured.

1793	70c.+35c. Type **497**	85	80
1794	80c.+40c. Grandad bottle-feeding baby	1·00	90
1795	100c.+50c. Playing piano	1·40	1·25

499 Cycling

1996. Tourism. Multicoloured.

1798	70c. Type **499**	65	10
1799	70c. Paddling in sea	65	20
1800	80c. Traditional architecture, Amsterdam	70	20
1801	100c. Windmills, Zaanse Schand Open-Air Museum	85	30

500 Parade in Traditional Costumes

1996. Bicentenary of Province of North Brabant.

1802 **500**	80c. multicoloured	70	20

501 Lighting Olympic Torch

502 Erasmus Bridge

1996. Sporting Events. Multicoloured.

1803	70c. Type **501** (Olympic Games, Atlanta)	65	20
1804	80c. Flag and cyclists (Tour de France cycling championship)	70	20
1805	100c. Player, ball and Wembley Stadium (European Football Championship, England)	85	55
1806	160c. Olympic rings and athlete on starting block (Olympic Games, Atlanta)	1·25	55

1996. Bridges and Tunnels. Multicoloured.

1807	80c. Type **502**	65	20
1808	80c. Wijker Tunnel (horiz)	65	20
1809	80c. Martinus Nijhoff Bridge (horiz)	65	20

503 Children in School Uniforms

504 Bert and Ernie

1996. 50th Anniv of U.N.I.C.E.F. Multicoloured.

1810	70c. Type **503**	65	20
1811	80c. Girl carrying platter on head	65	20

1996. Sesame Street (children's television programme). Multicoloured.

1812	70c. Type **504**	65	20
1813	80c. Bears holding Big Bird's foot	60	15

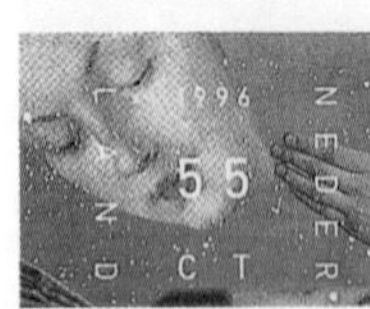

505 Petrus Plancius

506 Books and Baby

1996. 16th-century Voyages of Discovery.

1814 **505**	70c. black, yellow and red	60	40
1815 –	80c. multicoloured	65	20
1816 –	80c. multicoloured	65	20
1817 –	100c. multicoloured	65	65

DESIGNS: No. 1815, Cornelis de Houtman; 1816, Willem Barentsz; 1817, Mahu en De Cordes.

1996. Child Welfare. Multicoloured.

1818	70c.+35c. Type **506**	65	75
1819	80c.+40c. Animals and boy	90	85
1820	80c.+40c. Tools and girl	90	60

507 Woman's Face and Hand

1996. Christmas. Multicoloured. Self-adhesive.

1822	55c. Type **507**	50	20
1823	55c. Woman's eyes and man shouting	50	20
1824	55c. Bird's wing, hands and detail of man's face	50	20
1825	55c. Men's faces and bird's wing	50	20

Nos. 1822/5 were issued together, se-tenant, forming a composite design.

1997. Change of Address Stamp. Self-adhesive.

1826 **496**	80c. multicoloured	60	30

No. 1826 was intended for use by people moving house.

508 Numeral on Envelope with Top Flap

1997. Business Stamps. Multicoloured. Self-adhesive.

1827	80c. Type **508**	50	20
1828	160c. Numeral on envelope with side flap	1·00	40

509 Skaters

1997. 15th Eleven Cities Skating Race.
1829 **509** 80c. multicoloured . . . 65 20

510 Heart

1997. Greetings Stamps.
1830 **510** 80c. multicoloured . . . 50 30
The price quoted for No. 1830 is for an example with the heart intact. The heart can be scratched away to reveal different messages.

511 Pony

1997. Nature and the Environment. Multicoloured.
1831 80c. Type **511** 65 20
1832 100c. Cow 90 65

512 Suske, Wiske, Lambik and Aunt Sidonia

1997. Suske and Wiske (cartoon by Willy Vandersteen).
1834 **512** 80c. multicoloured . . . 50 20

513 Rosebud

1997. Cultural, Health and Social Welfare Funds. The Elderly and their Image. Multicoloured.
1836 80c.+40c. Type **513** 90 80
1837 80c.+40c. Rose stem 90 80
1838 80c.+40c. Rose 90 80

514 Birthday Cake

1997. Greetings Stamps. Multicoloured.
1840 80c. Type **514** 50 20
1841 80c. Cup of coffee, glasses of wine, candles, writing letter, and amaryllis . . . 50 20
See also No. 1959.

515 "REKENKAMER ..." (550th anniv of Court of Audit)
516 Clasped Hands over Red Cross

1997. Anniversaries.
1842 **515** 80c. multicoloured . . . 65 25
1843 – 80c. red, yellow and black 65 25
1844 – 80c. red, black and blue 65 25
DESIGNS—50th anniv of Marshall Plan (post-war American aid for Europe): No. 1843, Map of Europe; 1844, Star and stripes.

1997. Red Cross.
1845 **516** 80c.+40c. mult . . . . . 1·10 1·10

517 "eu" and Globe

1997. European Council of Ministers' Summit, Amsterdam.
1846 **517** 100c. multicoloured . . . 1·00 40

518 Children playing in Boat

1997. Water Activities. Multicoloured.
1847 80c. Type **518** 60 25
1848 1g. Skutsje (sailing barges) race, Friesland 80 40

519 "vernuft"

1997. Anniversaries. Multicoloured.
1849 **519** 80c. ultramarine and blue 60 25
1850 – 80c. ultramarine and blue 60 25
1851 – 80c. multicoloured . . . 60 30
1852 – 80c. multicoloured . . . 60 25
DESIGNS: No. 1849, Type **519** (150th anniv of Royal Institute of Engineers); 1850, "adem" (centenary of Netherlands Asthma Centre, Davos, Switzerland); 1851, Flower (centenary of Florens College (horticultural college) and 125th anniv of Royal Botanical and Horticultural Society); 1852, Pianist accompanying singer (birth bicentenary of Franz Schubert (composer)).

520 "Nederland80"

1997. Youth. Multicoloured.
1853 **520** 80c. red and blue 50 25
1854 – 80c. multicoloured . . . 50 25
DESIGN: No. 1854, "NEDERLAND80" in style of computer games giving appearance of three-dimensional block on race track.

521 Stork with Bundle

1997. New Baby Stamp. Self-adhesive gum.
1855 **521** 80c. multicoloured . . . 50 30
See also Nos. 1960, 2120 amd 2189.

522 "Little Red Riding Hood"
523 Heads and Star

1997. Child Welfare. Fairy Tales. Multicoloured.
1856 80c.+40c. Type **522** . . . . 1·00 65
1857 80c.+40c. Man laying loaves on ground ("Tom Thumb") . . . . 1·00 65
1858 80c.+40c. Woodman with bottle ("Genie in the Bottle") . . . . 1·00 65

1997. Christmas. Multicoloured, colour of background given.
1860 **523** 55c. yellow 50 25
1861 55c. blue 50 25
1862 – 55c. orange 50 25
1863 – 55c. red 50 25
1864 – 55c. green 50 25
1865 **523** 55c. green 50 25
DESIGN: Nos. 1862/4, Heads and heart.

524 Light across Darkness
525 Cow and "Ship" Tiles

1998. Bereavement Stamp.
1866 **524** 80c. blue 50 35

1998. Delft Faience.
1867 **525** 100c. multicoloured . . . 65 35
1868 – 160c. blue . . . . 1·00 90
DESIGN: 160c. Ceramic tile showing boy standing on head.

526 Strawberries in Bloom (Spring)
527 Handshake

1998. The Four Seasons. Multicoloured.
1869 80c. Type **526** 65 65
1870 80c. Strawberry, flan and strawberry plants (Summer) 65 65
1871 80c. Bare trees and pruning diagram (Winter) 65 65
1872 80c. Orchard and apple (Autumn) 65 65

1998. Anniversaries. Multicoloured.
1873 80c. Type **527** (350th anniv of Treaty of Munster) . . 60 40
1874 80c. Statue of Johan Thorbecke (politician) (150th anniv of Constitution) 60 40
1875 80c. Child on swing (50th anniv of Declaration of Human Rights) 60 40

528 Bride and Groom
529 Shopping List

1998. Wedding Stamp. Self-adhesive gum.
1876 **528** 80c. multicoloured . . . 50 35
See also No. 1961.

1998. Cultural, Health and Social Welfare Funds. Care and the Elderly.
1877 80c.+40c. Type **529** . . . . 1·00 95
1878 80c.+40c. Sweet . . . . . . 1·00 95
1879 80c.+40c. Training shoe . . 1·00 95

530 Letters blowing in Wind

1998. Letters to the Future.
1881 **530** 80c. multicoloured . . . 60 40

531 Customers

1998. Centenary of Rabobank.
1882 **531** 80c. yellow, green and blue 60 40

532 Goalkeeper catching Boot

1998. Sport. Multicoloured.
1883 80c. Type **532** (World Cup Football Championship, France) 50 40
1884 80c. Family hockey team (centenary of Royal Netherlands Hockey Federation) (35 × 24 mm) 60 30

533 Map of Friesland, c. 1600

1998. 500th Anniv of Central Administration of Friesland.
1885 **533** 80c. multicoloured . . . 60 40

534 River Defences

1998. Bicentenary of Directorate-General of Public Works and Water Management. Multicoloured.
1886 80c. Type **534** 60 40
1887 1g. Sea defences 80 55

535 "tnt post groep"

1998. Separation of Royal Netherlands PTT into TNT Post Groep and KPN NV (telecommunications).
1888 **535** 80c. black, blue and red 60 45
1889 – 80c. black, blue and green 60 45
DESIGN: No. 1889, "kpn nv".
Nos. 1888/9 were issued together, se-tenant, forming a composite design of the complete "160".

536 Books and Keyboard

1998. Cultural Anniversaries. Multicoloured.
1890 80c. Type **536** (bicentenary of National Library) . . . 60 40
1891 80c. Maurits Escher (graphic artist, birth centenary) looking at his mural "Metamorphose" in The Hague Post Office (vert) 60 40
1892 80c. Simon Vestdijk (writer, birth centenary) and page from "Fantoches" (vert) 60 40

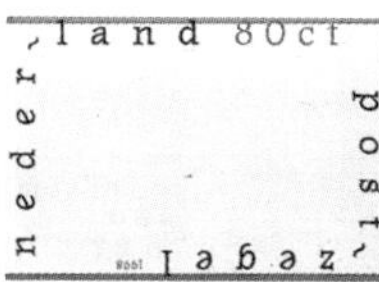

538 "land 80 ct"

1998. Greetings Stamps. Multicoloured. Self-adhesive.
1894 80c. Type **538** (top of frame red) 70 50
1895 80c. "80 ct post" (top of frame mauve) 70 50
1896 80c. Type **538** (top of frame orange) 70 50
1897 80c. "80 ct post" (top of frame orange) 70 50
1898 80c. Type **538** (top of frame yellow) 70 50
The part of the frame used for identification purposes is above the face value.
Nos. 1894/8 were only available in sheetlets of ten stamps and 20 labels (five stamps and ten labels on each side of the card). It was intended that the sender should insert the appropriate greetings label into the rectangular space on each stamp before use.

539 Rabbits

1998. Domestic Pets. Multicoloured.
1899 80c. Type **539** 60 45
1900 80c. Drent partridge dog . . 50 45
1901 80c. Kittens 50 40

540 Cathy and Jeremy writing a Letter

1998. 25th Anniv of Jack, Jacky and the Juniors (comic strip characters).
1902 **540** 80c. multicoloured . . . 50 40

541 St. Nicholas on Horseback

1998. Child Welfare. Celebrations. Multicoloured.
1904 80c.+40c. Type **541** . . . . 1·00 70
1905 80c.+40c. Making birthday cake . . . . 1·00 70
1906 80c.+40c. Carnival parade 1·00 70

542 Hare and Snowball **543** House and Tree on Snowball

1998. Christmas. Self-adhesive.
1908 **542** 55c. blue, red and black 75 35
1909 – 55c. multicoloured . . . 75 35
1910 – 55c. blue, red and black 75 35
1911 – 55c. multicoloured . . . 75 35
1912 – 55c. blue, red and black 75 35
1913 – 55c. green, blue and red 75 35
1914 – 55c. green, blue and red 75 35
1915 – 55c. green, blue and red 75 35
1916 – 55c. green, blue and red 75 35
1917 – 55c. green, blue and red 75 35
1918 – 55c. blue, green and red 75 35
1919 – 55c. red, green and black 75 35
1920 – 55c. blue, green and red 75 35
1921 – 55c. green, red and black 75 35
1922 – 55c. blue, green and red 75 35
1923 – 55c. blue, green and red 75 35
1924 – 55c. blue, green and red 75 35
1925 – 55c. blue, green and red 75 35
1926 – 55c. blue, green and red 75 35
1927 – 55c. blue, green and red 75 35
DESIGNS: No. 1909, House and snowball; 1910, Dove and snowball; 1911, Christmas tree and snowball; 1912, Reindeer and snowball; 1913, Hare; 1914, House; 1915, Dove; 1916, Christmas tree; 1917, Reindeer; 1918, House and hare; 1919, House and heart; 1920, Dove and house; 1921, Christmas tree and house; 1922, House and reindeer; 1923, Christmas tree and hare; 1924, Christmas tree and house; 1925, Christmas tree and dove; 1926, Christmas tree and heart; 1927, Christmas tree and reindeer.

1999. Make-up Rate Stamp.
1928 **543** 25c. red and black . . . 25 20

544 Euro Coin

1999. Introduction of the Euro (European currency).
1929 **544** 80c. multicoloured . . . 60 30

545 Pillar Box, 1850

1999. Bicentenary of Netherlands Postal Service.
1930 **545** 80c. multicoloured . . . 60 60

546 Richard Krajicek serving **547** White Spoonbill

1999. Centenary of Royal Dutch Lawn Tennis Federation.
1931 **546** 80c. multicoloured . . . 50 45

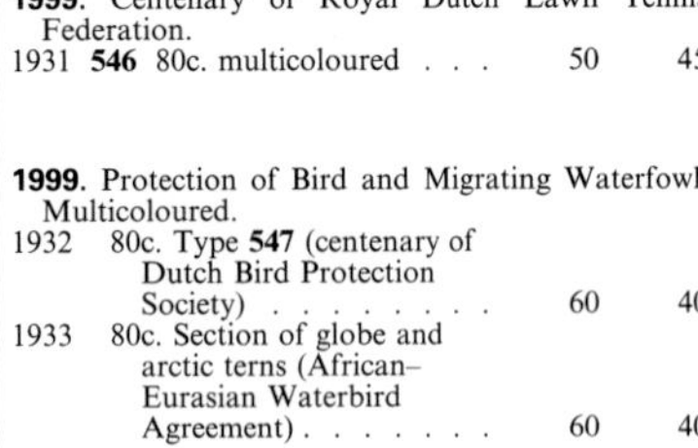

1999. Protection of Bird and Migrating Waterfowl. Multicoloured.
1932 80c. Type **547** (centenary of Dutch Bird Protection Society) 60 40
1933 80c. Section of globe and arctic terns (African–Eurasian Waterbird Agreement) 60 40

548 Haarlemmerhout in Autumn **549** Woman

1999. Parks during the Seasons. Multicoloured.
1934 80c. Type **548** 50 60
1935 80c. Sonsbeek in winter . . 50 60
1936 80c. Weerribben in summer 50 60
1937 80c. Keukenhof in spring . . 50 60

1999. Cultural, Health and Social Welfare Funds. International Year of the Elderly. Multicoloured.
1938 80c.+40c. Type **549** . . . . 1·00 95
1939 80c.+40c. Man (green background) . . . . . . 1·00 95
1940 80c.+40c. Man (blue background) . . . . . . 1·00 95

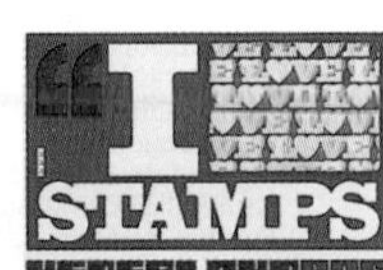

550 Lifeboats on Rough Sea **551** "I Love Stamps"

1999. Water Anniversaries. Multicoloured.
1942 80c. Type **550** (175th Anniv of Royal Netherlands Lifeboat Association) . . 60 45
1943 80c. Freighters in canal (150th Anniv of Royal Association of Ships' Masters "Schuttevaer") 60 45

1999.
1944 **551** 80c. blue and red 50 50
1945 – 80c. red and blue 50 50
DESIGN: No. 1945, "Stamps love Me".

552 "The Goldfinch" (Carel Fabritius)

1999. 17th-century Dutch Art. Multicoloured. Self-adhesive gum (1g.).
1946 80c. Type **552** 70 65
1947 80c. "Self-portrait" (Rembrandt) 70 65
1948 80c. "Self-portrait" (Judith Leyster) 70 65
1949 80c. "St. Sebastian" (Hendrick ter Brugghen) 70 65
1950 80c. "Beware of Luxury" (Jan Steen) 70 65
1951 80c. "The Sick Child" (Gabriel Metsu) 70 65
1952 80c. "Gooseberries" (Adriaen Coorte) 70 65
1953 80c. "View of Haarlem" (Jacob van Ruisdael) . . 70 65
1954 80c. "Mariaplaats, Utrecht" (Pieter Saenredam) . . . 70 65
1955 80c. "Danae" (Rembrandt) 70 65
1956 1g. "The Jewish Bride" (Rembrandt) 65 55

553 "80" on Computer Screen

1999. Ordinary or self-adhesive gum.
1957 **553** 80c. multicoloured . . . 50 40

554 Amaryllis, Coffee Cup, Candles, Letter Writing and Wine Glasses

1999. Greetings Stamp. Self-adhesive.
1959 **554** 80c. multicoloured . . . 50 40

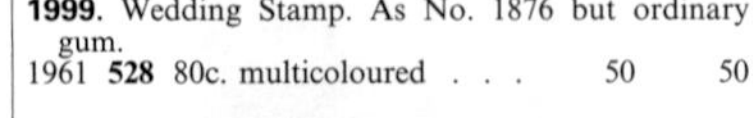

1999. New Baby Stamp. As No. 1855 but ordinary gum.
1960 **521** 80c. multicoloured . . . 50 50

1999. Wedding Stamp. As No. 1876 but ordinary gum.
1961 **528** 80c. multicoloured . . . 50 50

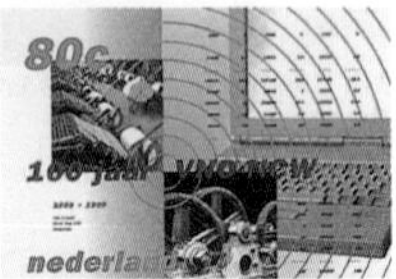

555 Victorian Heavy Machinery and Modern Computer

1999. Centenary of Confederation of Netherlands Industry and Employers.
1962 **555** 80c. multicoloured . . . 60 50

556 Tintin and Snowy wearing Space Suits

1999. 70th Anniv of Tintin (comic strip character by Herge). Scenes from "Explorers on the Moon". Multicoloured.
1963 **556** 80c. multicoloured . . . 50 50

558 Digger (completion of Afsluitdijk, 1932)

1999. The Twentieth Century. Multicoloured.
1966 80c. Type **558** . . . . . . 1·10 80
1967 80c. Space satellite . . . . 1·10 80
1968 80c. Berlage Commodity Exchange, Amsterdam (inauguration, 1903) . . . 1·10 80
1969 80c. Empty motorway (car-free Sundays during oil crisis, 1973–74) . . . . . 1·10 80
1970 80c. Old man (Old Age Pensions Act, 1947) . . . 1·10 80
1971 80c. Delta Flood Project, 1953–97 . . . . 1·10 80
1972 80c. Players celebrating (victory of Netherlands in European Cup Football Championship, 1998) . . 1·10 80
1973 80c. Four riders on one motor cycle (liberation and end of Second World War, 1945) . . . . . . 1·10 80
1974 80c. Woman posting vote (Women's Franchise, 1919) . . . . 1·10 80
1975 80c. Ice skaters (eleven cities race) . . . . 1·10 80

559 Pluk van de Pettevlet on Fire Engine

1999. Child Welfare. Characters created by Fiep Westendorp. Multicoloured.
1976 80c.+40c. Type **559** . . . . 1·00 75
1977 80c.+40c. Otje drinking through straw . . . . . 1·00 75
1978 80c.+40c. Jip and Janneke with cat . . . . 1·00 75

560 Father Christmas (Robin Knegt) **561** "25"

1999. Christmas. Winning entries in design competition. Multicoloured.
1980 55c. Type **560** 50 25
1981 55c. Angel singing (Davinia Bovenlander) (vert) . . . 50 25
1982 55c. Dutch doughnuts in box (Henk Drenth) . . . 50 25
1983 55c. Moon wearing Christmas hat (Lizet van den Berg) (vert) 50 25
1984 55c. Father Christmas carrying sacks (Noortje Kruse) 50 25
1985 55c. Clock striking midnight (Hucky de Haas) (vert) . . 50 25
1986 55c. Ice skater (Marleen Bos) 50 25
1987 55c. Human Christmas tree (Mariette Strik) (vert) . . 50 25
1988 55c. Woman wearing Christmas tree earrings (Saskia van Oversteeg) . . 50 25
1989 55c. Woman vacuuming pine needles (Frans Koenis) (vert) 50 25
1990 55c. Angel with harp and music score (Evelyn de Zeeuw) 50 25
1991 55c. Hand balancing candle, star, hot drink, hat and Christmas tree on fingers (Aafke van Ewijk) (vert) 50 25
1992 55c. Christmas tree (Daan Roepman) (vert) 50 25
1993 55c. Cat wearing crown (Sjoerd van der Zee) (vert) 50 25
1994 55c. Bird flying over house (Barbara Vollers) 50 25
1995 55c. Baby with angel wings (Rosmarijn Schmink) (vert) 50 25
1996 55c. Dog wearing Christmas hat (Casper Heijstek and Mirjam Cnosser) 50 25
1997 55c. Angel flying (Patricia van der Neut) (vert) . . . 50 25
1998 55c. Nativity (Marco Cockx) 50 25
1999 55c. Christmas tree with decorations (Matthias Meiling) (vert) 50 25

2000. Make-up Rate Stamp.
2000 **561** 25c. red, blue and yellow 20 25

562 1 Guilder Coin, Margaret of Austria (Regent of Netherlands) (after Bernard van Orley) and "Coronation of Charles V" (Juan de la Coate)

2000. 500th Birth Anniv of Charles V, Holy Roman Emperor. Multicoloured.
2001 80c. Type **562** 60 50
2002 80c. Map of the Seventeen Provinces, "Charles V after the Battle of Muehlberg" (Titian) and Margaret of Parma (Regent of Netherlands) (after Antonius Mohr) . . 60 50

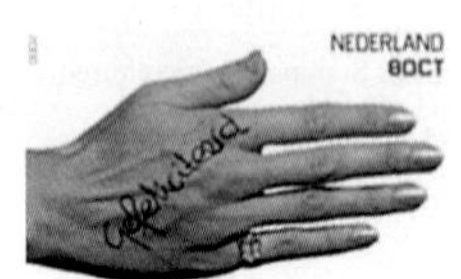

563 "Gefeliciteerd" ("Congratulations")

2000. Greetings stamps. Showing greetings messages on hands. Multicoloured.
2003 80c. Type **563** 60 55
2004 80c. "Succes met je nieuwe baan" ("Good luck with your new job") 60 55
2005 80c. "gefeliciteerd met je huis" ("Congratulations on your new home") . . 60 55
2006 80c. "PROFICIAT" ("Congratulations") . . . 60 55
2007 80c. "Succes" ("Hope you have success") 60 55
2008 80c. "Veel geluk samen" ("Good luck together") 60 55
2009 80c. "Proficiat met je diploma" ("Congratulations on passing your exam") . . . 60 55
2010 80c. "Geluk" ("Good luck") 60 55
2011 80c. "Van Harte" ("Cordially") 60 55
2012 80c. "GEFELICITEERD MET JE RUBEWIUS!" ("Congratulations on passing your driving test!") 60 55

564 Players celebrating

565 Man and Woman passing Ball

2000. European Football Championship, Netherlands and Belgium. Multicoloured.
2013 80c. Type **564** 50 30
2014 80c. Football 50 30

2000. Cultural, Health and Social Welfare Funds. Senior Citizens. Multicoloured.
2015 80c.+40c. Type **565** 90 60
2016 80c.+40c. Woman picking apples 90 60
2017 80c.+40c. Woman wearing swimming costume . . . 90 60

566 "Feigned Sadness" (C. Troost)

2000. Bicentenary of the Rijksmuseum, Amsterdam. Multicoloured. (a) Ordinary gum.
2019 80c. Type **566** 60 55
2020 80c. "Harlequin and Columbine" (porcelain figurine) (J. J. Kandler) 60 55
2021 80c. "Ichikawa Ebizo IV" (woodcut) (T. Sharaku) 60 55
2022 80c. "Heavenly Beauty" (sandstone sculpture) . . 60 55
2023 80c. "St. Vitus" (wood sculpture) 60 55
2024 80c. "Woman in Turkish Costume" (J. E. Liotard) 60 55
2025 80c. "J. van Speyk" (J. Schoemaker Doyer) . . 60 55
2026 80c. "King Saul" (engraving) (L. van Leyden) 60 55
2027 80c. "L'Amour Menacant" (marble sculpture) (E. M. Falconet) 60 55
2028 80c. "Sunday" (photograph) (C. Ariens) 60 55

(b) Self-adhesive.
2029 80c. "The Nightwatch" (Rembrandt) 60 55

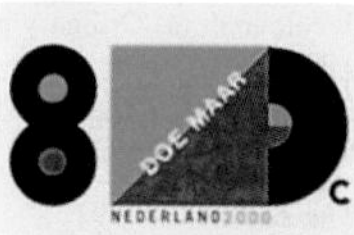

567 "80" and "Doe Maar" Record Cover

2000. Doe Maar (Dutch pop group). Multicoloured.
2030 80c. Type **567** 50 45
2031 80c. "80" and song titles . . 50 45

568 "Dutch Landscape" (Jeroen Krabb)

2000. Priority Mail. Contemporary Art. Self-adhesive.
2033 **568** 110c. multicoloured . . . 60 50

569 "The Nightwatch" (Rembrandt)

2000. Priority Mail. Self-adhesive.
2034 **569** 110c. multicoloured . . . 65 65

570 *Libertad* (full-rigged cadet ship)

2000. "Sail Amsterdam 2000". Sailing Ships. Multicoloured.
2036 80c. Type **570** 45 20
2037 80c. *Amerigo Vespucci* (cadet ship) and figurehead . . . 45 20
2038 80c. *Dar Mlodziezy* (full-rigged cadet ship) and sail 45 20
2039 80c. *Europa* (cadet ship) and wheel 45 20
2040 80c. *Kruzenshtern* (cadet barque) and bell 45 20
2041 80c. *Sagres II* (cadet barque) and sail 45 20
2042 80c. *Alexander von Humboldt* (barque) and sail 45 20
2043 80c. *Sedov* (cadet barque) and sailors dropping sail 45 20
2044 80c. *Mir* (square-rigged training ship) 45 20
2045 80c. *Oosterschelde* (schooner) and rope . . . 45 20

571 Roller Skating

2000. Sjors and Sjimmie (comic strip characters by Frans Piet). Multicoloured.
2046 80c. Type **571** 45 20
2047 80c. In car 45 20
2049 80c. Listening to radio . . . 45 20
2050 80c. Swinging on rope . . . 45 20

2000. Bereavement Stamp. As No. 1866 but self-adhesive.
2051 **524** 80c. blue 45 20

572 Green Dragonfly

2000. Endangered Species. Multicoloured.
2052 80c. Type **572** 45 20
2053 80c. Weather loach 45 20

574 Children wearing Monster Hats

575 Couple with Christmas Tree

2000. Child Welfare. Multicoloured. Self-adhesive gum.
2055 80c.+40c. Type **574** 65 40
2056 80c.+40c. Boy sailing bath-tub 65 40
2057 80c.+40c. Children brewing magical stew 65 40

2000. Christmas. Multicoloured.
2059 60c. Type **575** 35 15
2060 60c. Children making snow balls 35 15
2061 60c. Couple dancing 35 15
2062 60c. Man playing French horn 35 15
2063 60c. Man carrying Christmas tree 35 15
2064 60c. Man carrying young child 35 15
2065 60c. Woman reading book 35 15
2066 60c. Couple kissing 35 15
2067 60c. Man playing piano . . 35 15
2068 60c. Woman watching from window 35 15
2069 60c. Woman sitting in chair 35 15
2070 60c. Man sitting beside fire 35 15
2071 60c. Snowman flying 35 15
2072 60c. Couple in street 35 15
2073 60c. Child playing violin . . 35 15
2074 60c. Children on sledge . . 35 15
2075 60c. Man writing letter . . . 35 15
2076 60c. Woman carrying plate of food 35 15
2077 60c. Family 35 15
2078 60c. Woman sleeping . . . 35 15

576 Moon

577 Whinchat

2001. Make-up Rate Stamp.
2079 **576** 20c. multicoloured . . . 15 10

2001. Centenary of Royal Dutch Nature Society. Multicoloured.
2080 80c. Type **577** 45 20
2081 80c. Family in rowing boat 45 20
2082 80c. Fox 45 20
2083 80c. Couple bird watching 45 20
2084 80c. Flowers 45 20

578 Poem (by E. du Perron)

2001. "Between Two Cultures". National Book Week. Multicoloured.
2085 80c. Type **578** 45 20
2086 80c. Men in street 45 20
2087 80c. Poem (by Hafid Bouazza) 45 20
2088 80c. Woman and young men 45 20
2089 80c. Poem (by Adriaan van Dis) 45 20
2090 80c. Profiles of two women 45 20
2091 80c. Poem (by Kader Abdolah) 45 20
2092 80c. Two young girls . . . 45 20
2093 80c. Poem (by Ellen Ombre) 45 20
2094 80c. Boy carrying map . . . 45 20

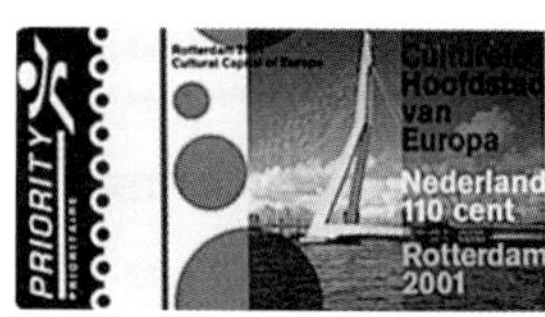

579 Rotterdam Bridge

2001. Priority Mail. Rotterdam, European City of Culture. Self-adhesive gum.
2095 **579** 110c. multicoloured . . . 65 25

582 Helen's Flower (*Helenium rubinzwerg*)

2001. Flowers. Multicoloured. Self-adhesive gum.
2098 80c.+40c. Type **582** 65 40
2099 80c.+40c. Russian hollyhock (*Alcea rugosa*) 65 40
2100 80c.+40c. Persian cornflower (*Centaurea dealbata*) . . . 65 40

583 "Autumn" (detail) (L. Gestel)

2001. Art Nouveau. Multicoloured.
2102 80c. Type **583** . . . 45 20
2103 80c. Book cover by C. Lebeau for *De Stille Kracht* . . . 45 20
2104 80c. Burcht Federal Council Hall, Amsterdam (R. N. Roland Holst and H. P. Berlage) 45 20
2105 80c. "O Grave Where is Thy Victory" (painting) (J. Throop) . . . 45 20
2106 80c. Vases by C. J. van der Hoef from Amphora factory 45 20
2107 80c. Capital from staircase of Utrecht building (J. Mendes da Costa) 45 20
2108 80c. Illustration of common peafowl from *The Happy Owls* (T. van Hoytema) 45 20
2109 80c. "The Bride" (detail) (painting) (J. Thorn Prikker) 45 20
2110 80c. Factory-printed cotton fabric (M. Duco Crop) 45 20
2111 80c. Dentz van Schaik room (L. Zyl) 45 20

2001. As T **428** but with face value expressed in euros and cents. Self-adhesive gum.
2112 85c. blue 50 20

584 Sky and Landscape

2001. Self-adhesive gum.
2113 **584** 85c. multicoloured . . . 50 20

585 Arrows

2001. Business Coil Stamp. Self-adhesive gum.
2114 **585** 85c. purple and silver . . 50 20

586 Reclaimed Land

2001. Multicoloured. Self-adhesive gum.
2115 85c. Type **586** (postage) . . 50 20
2116 1g.20 Beach (priority mail) 65 25
2117 1g.65 Town and canal . . . 90 35

587 House carrying Suitcase

2001. Greetings Stamps. Self-adhesive gum.
2118 **587** 85c. black and yellow . . 50 20
2119 – 85c. red, yellow and gold 50 20
2120 – 85c. multicoloured . . . 50 20
2121 – 85c. multicoloured . . . 50 20
DESIGNS: No. 2118, Type **587** (change of address stamp); 2119, Couple (wedding stamp); 2120, As Type **521** (new baby); 2121, As Type **524** (bereavement stamp).

588 Tom and Jerry

589 "Veel Geluk" ("Good Luck")

2001. Cartoon Characters. Multicoloured.
2122 85c. Type **588** 50 20
2123 85c. Fred Flintstone and Barney Rubble 50 20
2124 85c. Johnny Bravo 50 20
2125 85c. Dexter posting letter . . 50 20
2126 85c. Powerpuff Girls 50 20

2001. Greetings Stamps. Multicoloured. Self-adhesive gum.
2127 85c. Type **589** 50 20
2128 85c. "Gefeliciteerd!" ("Congratulations!") . . . 50 20
2129 85c. "Veel Geluk" with envelope flap (horiz) . . . 50 20
2130 85c. "Gefeliciteerd!" with envelope flap (horiz) . . . 50 20
2131 85c. "Proficiat" ("Congratulations") . . . 50 20
2132 85c. "Succes !" ("Success") 50 20
2133 85c. "Van Harte ..." ("Cordially ...") 50 20
2134 85c. "Proficiat" with envelope flap (horiz) . . . 50 50
2135 85c. "Succes !" with envelope flap (horiz) . . . 50 20
2136 85c. "Van Harte ..." with envelope flap (horiz) . . . 50 20

590 Guilder Coins

2001. Replacement of the Guilder. Self-adhesive.
2137 **590** 12g.75 silver . . . . . . 7·00 3·00

593 Computer Figure and River

2001. Child Welfare. Multicoloured. Self-adhesive gum.
2140 **593** 85c.+40c. mult 80 65

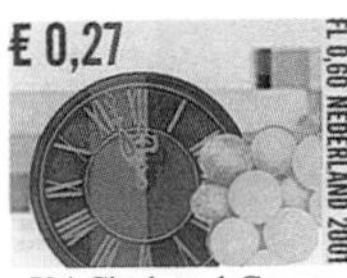

594 Clock and Grapes

595 "12"

2001. Christmas. Multicoloured. Self-adhesive gum.
2142 60c. Type **594** 35 15
2143 60c. Stars and bun 35 15
2144 60c. Steeple and buns . . . 35 15
2145 60c. Cherub and coins . . . 35 15
2146 60c. Champagne bottle . . . 35 15
2147 60c. Wreath around chimney 35 15
2148 60c. Tower 35 15
2149 60c. Christmas tree bauble 35 15
2150 60c. Playing card with Christmas tree as sign . . 35 15
2151 60c. Cake seen through window 35 15
2152 60c. Decorated Christmas tree 35 15
2153 60c. Father Christmas . . . 35 15
2154 60c. Sign displaying hot drink 35 15
2155 60c. Candles seen through window 35 15
2156 60c. Illuminated roof-tops 35 15
2157 60c. Reindeer 35 15
2158 60c. Snowman 35 15
2159 60c. Parcel 35 15
2160 60c. Bonfire 35 15
2161 60c. Children on toboggan 35 15

2002. Make-up Rate Stamp. (a) Self-adhesive gum.
2162 **595** 2c. red 15 10
2166 12c. green 15 10

(b) Ordinary gum.
2169 **595** 2c. red 15 10
2170 5c. mauve 10 10
2171 10c. blue 15 10

596 Queen Beatrix

597 Arrows

2002. Queen Beatrix. Self-adhesive gum.
2175 **596** 25c. brown and green . . 35 15
2176 39c. blue and pink . . . 50 20
2177 40c. blue and brown . . 50 20
2178 50c. pink and green . . 65 25
2179 55c. mauve and brown 75 45
2181 65c. green and violet . . 85 35
2182 70c. deep green and green 95 60
2183 78c. blue and brown . . 1·00 40
2185 €1 green and blue . . . 1·25 50
2187 €3 mauve and green . . 3·75 1·50

2002. Business Coil Stamps. Self-adhesive gum.
2195 **597** 39c. purple and silver . . 50 20
2196 78c. blue and gold . . . 1·00 40

598 Prince Willem-Alexander and Máxima Zorreguieta

2002. Marriage of Prince Willem-Alexander and Maxima Zorreguieta. Sheet 145 × 75 mm, containing T **598** and similar horiz design.
MS2197 **598** 39c. black, silver and orange; 39c. multicoloured . . 1·25 1·25
DESIGN: 39c. "Willem-Alexander Maxima" and "222".

599 Sky and Landscape

2002. Self-adhesive gum.
2198 **599** 39c. multicoloured . . . 55 25

600 Couple

601 "Veel Geluk" ("Good Luck")

2002. Greetings Stamps. Face values in euros. Self-adhesive gum.
2199 – 39c. black and yellow . . 55 25
2200 **600** 39c. red, yelow and gold 55 25
2201 – 39c. multicoloured . . . 55 25
2202 – 39c. blue 55 25
DESIGNS: No. 2199, As Type **587** (change of address stamp); 2200, Type **600** (wedding stamp); 2201, As Type **521** (new baby); 2202, As Type **524** (bereavement stamp).

2001. Greetings Stamps. Face values in euros. Multicoloured. Self-adhesive gum.
2203 39c. Type **601** 55 25
2204 39c. "Gefeliciteerd!" ("Congratulations!") . . . 55 25
2205 39c. "Veel Geluk" ("Good Luck") (horiz) 55 25
2206 39c. "Gefeliciteerd!" with envelope flap (horiz) . . . 55 25
2207 39c. "Proficiat" ("Congratulations") . . . 55 25
2208 39c. "Succes !" ("Success") 55 25
2209 39c. "Van Harte..." ("Cordially ...") 55 25
2210 39c. "Proficiat" with envelope flap (horiz) . . . 55 25
2211 39c. "Succes !" with envelope flap (horiz) . . . 55 25
2212 39c. "Van Harte..." with envelope flap (horiz) . . . 55 25

602 Reclaimed Land

2002. Landscapes. Face values in euros. Multicoloured. Self-adhesive gum.
2213 39c. Type **603** (postage) . . 55 25
2214 54c. Beach (priority mail) 70 30
2215 75c. Town and canal . . . 1·00 40

603 Water Lily

604 Flowers and Red Crosses

2002. "Floriade 2002" International Horticultural Exhibition, Harlemmermeer. Flowers. Multicoloured.
2216 39c. + 19c. Type **603** . . . 80 50
2217 39c. + 19c. Dahlia 80 50
2218 39c. + 19c. Japanese cherry blossom 80 50
2219 39c. + 19c. Rose 80 50
2220 39c. + 19c. Orchid 80 50
2221 39c. + 19c. Tulip 80 50
Nos. 2216/21 were printed on paper impregnated with perfume which was released when the stamps were scratched.

2002. Red Cross. 10th Annual Blossom Walk.
2222 **604** 39c. + 19c. multicoloured 80 50

605 Langnek

2002. 50th Anniv of Efteling Theme Park. Multicoloured. Self-adhesive gum.
2223 39c. Type **605** 55 25
2224 39c. Pardoes de Tovernar 55 25
2225 39c. Droomvlucht Elfje . . 55 25
2226 39c. Kleine Boodschap . . . 55 25
2227 39c. Holle Bolle Gijs 55 25

606 "West Indies Landscape" (Jan Mostaert)

2002. Landscape Paintings. Showing paintings and enlarged detail in foreground. Multicoloured.
2228 39c. Type **606** 55 25
2229 39c. "Riverbank with Cows" (Aelbert Cuyp) 55 25
2230 39c. "Cornfield" (Jacob van Ruisdael) 55 25
2231 39c. "Avenue at Middelharnis" (Meindert Hobbema) 55 25
2232 39c. "Italian Landscape with Umbrella Pines" (Hendrik Voogd) 55 25
2233 39c. "Landscape in Normandy" (Andreas Schelfhout) 55 25
2234 39c. "Landscape with Waterway" (Jan Toorop) 55 25
2235 39c. "Landscape" (Jan Sluijters) 55 25
2236 39c. "Kismet" (Michael Raedecker) 55 25
2237 39c. "Untitled" (Robert Zandvliet) 55 25

607 Circus Performers

608 Circles

2002. Priority Mail. Europa. Circus. Multicoloured.
2238 54c. Type **607** 70 30
2239 54c. Lions and Big Top . . 70 30

2002. Business Coil Stamp. Self-adhesive gum.
2240 **608** 39c. deep blue, blue and red 55 25
2241 78c. green, light green and red . . . . 1·10 45

609 Dutch East Indiaman and 1852 Stamps

2002. 150th Anniv of Netherlands Stamps. 400th Anniv of Dutch East India Company (V. O. C.). Sheet 108 × 50 mm, containing T **609** and similar horiz design. Multicoloured.
MS2250 Type **609**; 39c. Two Dutch East Indiamen and and stamps of 1852 . . . . 1·10 45

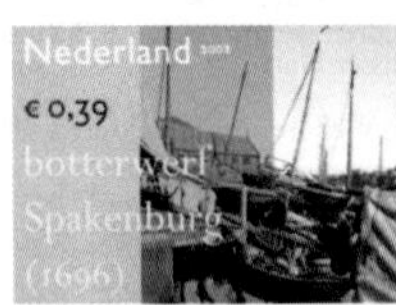

610 Boatyard, Spakenburg

2002. Industrial Heritage. Multicoloured.
2251 39c. Type **610** 55 25
2252 39c. Limekiln, Dedemsvaart 55 25
2253 39c. Steam-driven pumping station, Cruquius 55 25
2254 39c. Mine-shaft winding gear, Heerlen 55 25
2255 39c. Salt drilling tower, Hengelo 55 25
2256 39c. Windmill, Weidum . . 55 25
2257 39c. Brick-works, Zevenaar 55 25
2258 39c. "Drie Hoefijzers" brewery, Breda 55 25
2259 39c. Water-treatment plant, Tilburg 55 25
2260 39c. "Nodding-donkey" oil pump, Schoonebeck . . . 55 25

611 Cat and Child

2002. Child Welfare. Sheet 147 × 76 mm, containing T **611** and similar horiz designs. Multicoloured.
MS2261 Type **611**, 39c.+19c. Blue figure and upper part of child with green head; 39c.+19c. Child and ball; 39c.+19c. Child with yellow head and raised arms; 39c.+19c. Child with brown head and left arm raised; 39c.+19c. Dog and child . . . . 4·00 2·20

612 Woman and Child

2002. Christmas. Multicoloured. Self-adhesive gum.
2262 29c. Type **612** 40 15
2263 29c. Seated man facing left 40 15
2264 29c. Profile with raised collar 40 15
2265 29c. Stream and figure wearing scarf 40 15
2266 29c. Woman, tree and snowflakes 40 15
2267 29c. Snowflakes and man wearing knee-length coat beside grasses 40 15
2268 29c. Snowflakes, man, and gate and stream 40 15
2269 29c. Snowflakes, windmill, stream and woman . . . 40 15
2270 29c. Seated man facing right 40 15
2271 29c. Willow tree and profile of child facing left 40 15
2272 29c. Man leaning against tree 40 15
2273 29c. Man with hands in pockets 40 15
2274 29c. Seated couple 40 15
2275 29c. Fir tree and man's profile facing left 40 15
2276 29c. Man carrying child on shoulders 40 15
2277 29c. Profile of boy facing right 40 15
2278 29c. Standing child facing left 40 15
2279 29c. Snowflakes, sea and upper part of man with raised collar 40 15
2280 29c. Sea behind man wearing hat and glasses 40 15
2281 29c. Figure with out-stretched arms 40 15
Nos 2262/81 were issued together, se-tenant, the stamps arranged in strips of five, each strip forming a composite design.

613 "Landscape with Four Trees"

614 "Self-portrait with Straw Hat"

2003. 150th Birth Anniv of Vincent Van Gogh (artist). Multicoloured. (a) Ordinary gum.
2282 39c. Type **613** 55 25
2283 39c. "The Potato Eaters" . . 55 25
2284 39c. "Four Cut Sunflowers" 55 25
2285 39c. "Self-portrait with Grey Felt Hat" 55 25
2286 39c. "The Zouave" 55 25
2287 39c. "Place Du Forum Cafe Terrace by Night, Arles" 55 25
2288 39c. "Tree Trunks in Long Grass" 55 25
2289 39c. "Almond Blossom" . . 55 25
2290 39c. "Auvers-sur-Oise" . . . 55 25
2291 39c. "Wheatfield with Crows, Auvers-sur-Oise" 55 25

(b) Self-adhesive gum.
2292 39c. Type **614** 55 25
2293 59c. "Vase with Sunflowers" 55 25
2294 75c. "The Sower" 55 25

615 North Pier, Ijmuiden

2003. 50th Anniv of Floods in Zeeland, North Brabant and South Holland. Designs showing photographs from national archives. Each grey and black.
2295 39c. Type **615** 55 25
2296 39c. Hansweert Lock . . . 55 55
2297 39c. Building dam, Wieringermeer 55 25
2298 39c. Ijsselmeer Dam 55 25
2299 39c. Breached dyke, Willemstad 55 25
2300 39c. Repairing dyke, Stavenisse 55 25
2301 39c. Building dam, Zandkreek 55 25
2302 39c. Building dam, Grevelingen 55 25
2303 39c. Flood barrier, Oosterschelde 55 25
2304 39c. Floods, Roermond . . 55 25

616 See-through Register (security feature)

2003. 300th Anniv of Joh. Enschede (printers). Multicoloured.
2305 39c. Type **616** 55 25
2306 39c. Fleischman's musical notation 55 25
No. 2305 has the remaining symbols of the see-through register printed on the back over the gum. This forms a complete design when held up to the light.
No. 2305 was embossed with a notional barcode and No. 2306 with a security device.

MARINE INSURANCE STAMPS

M 22

1921.
M238 M **22** 15c. green . . . . . 9·25 45·00
M239 60c. red . . . . . 11·00 55·00
M240 75c. brown . . . . . 12·50 65·00
M241 – 1g.50 blue . . . . . 65·00 £500
M242 – 2g.25 brown £110 £700
M243 – 4½g. black £180 £850
M244 – 7½g. red £250 £1200
DESIGNS (inscr "DRIJVENDE BRANDKAST"): 1g.50, 2g.25, "Explosion"; 4½g., 7½g. Lifebelt.

OFFICIAL STAMPS

1913. Stamps of 1898 optd **ARMENWET**.
O214 **12** 1c. red . . . . 3·50 3·00
O215 1½c. blue . . . . 95 2·25
O216 2c. brown . . . . . . 6·25 7·00
O217 2½c. green . . . . . . 16·00 12·50
O218 **13** 3c. green . . . . . . 3·50 1·25
O219 5c. red . . . . 3·50 4·75
O220 10c. grey . . . . 35·00 40·00

POSTAGE DUE STAMPS

D 8

D 9

1870.
D76 D **8** 5c. brown on yellow . . 55·00 11·75
D77 10c. purple on blue . . . £110 15·00
For same stamps in other colours, see Netherlands Indies, Nos. D1/5.

1881.
D174 D **9** ½c. black and blue . . . 40 40
D175 1c. black and blue . . . 1·25 40
D176 1½c. black and blue . . 65 50
D177 2½c. black and blue . . 1·75 40
D178 3c. black and blue . . . 1·60 1·00
D179 4c. black and blue . . . 1·60 1·60
D180 5c. black and blue . . . 9·75 40
D181 6½c. black and blue . . 35·00 32·00
D182 7½c. black and blue . . 1·75 60
D183 10c. black and blue . . 28·00 50
D184 12½c. black and blue . . 23·00 1·25
D185 15c. black and blue . . 28·00 95
D186 20c. black and blue . . 24·00 6·25
D187 25c. black and blue . . 35·00 60
D188 1g. red and blue . . . 90·00 29·00
No. D188 is inscribed "EEN GULDEN".

1906. Surch.
D213 D **9** 3c. on 1g. red and blue 28·00 28·00
D215 4 on 6½c. black and blue . . . . 4·50 5·50
D216 6½ on 20c. black & blue 3·75 4·50
D214 50c. on 1g. red & blue £125 £125

1907. De Ruyter Commemoration. stamps surch **PORTZEGEL** and value.
D217A **15** ½c. on 1c. red . . . . . 1·25 1·25
D218A 1c. on 1c. red 70 70
D219A 1½c. on 1c. red 70 70
D220A 2½c. on 1c. red . . . . 1·60 1·60
D221A 5c. on 2½c. red . . . . 1·60 70
D222A 6½c. on 2½c. red . . . 3·00 3·00
D223A 7½c. on ½c. blue . . . 1·90 1·40
D224A 10c. on ½c. blue . . . 1·90 95
D225A 12½c. on ½c. blue . . . 4·50 4·50
D226A 15c. on 2½c. red . . . 6·25 3·75
D227A 25c. on ½c. blue . . . 8·25 7·50
D228A 50c. on ½c. blue . . . 40·00 35·00
D229A 1g. on ½c. blue . . . . 60·00 48·00

1912. Re-issue of Type D **9** in one colour.
D230 D **9** ½c. blue 40 40
D231 1c. blue 40 40
D232 1½c. blue . . . . 2·00 1·75
D233 2½c. blue 60 40
D234 3c. blue . . . . 1·10 70
D235 4c. blue 55 55
D236 4½c. blue . . . . . . 5·00 4·75
D237 5c. blue 65 55
D238 5½c. blue . . . . . . 4·75 4·50
D239 7c. blue . . . . 2·25 2·25
D240 7½c. blue . . . . . . 3·25 1·60
D241 10c. blue . . . . . . 1·10 55
D242 12½c. blue 55 55
D453 15c. blue 55 55
D244 20c. blue 55 40
D245 25c. blue . . . . . . 65·00 95
D246 50c. blue 55 40

D 25

D 121

1921.
D442 D **25** 3c. blue 75 20
D445 6c. blue 40 40
D446 7c. blue 55 55
D447 7½c. blue 55 50
D448 8c. blue 70 40
D449 9c. blue 65 65
D450 11c. blue . . . . . . 9·50 3·25
D247 12c. blue 50 40
D455 25c. blue 50 40
D456 30c. blue 50 40
D458 1g. red 70 40

1923. Surch in white figures in black circle.
D272 D **9** 1c. on 3c. blue 70 70
D273 2½c. on 7c. blue . . . 1·10 55
D274 25c. on 1½c. blue . . . 8·25 70
D275 25c. on 7½c. blue . . . 9·25 55

1924. Stamps of 1898 surch **TE BETALEN PORT** and value in white figures in black circle.
D295 **13** 4c. on 3c. green . . . . 1·40 1·25
D296 **12** 5c. on 1c. red 70 40
D297 10c. on 1½c. blue . . . . 1·10 50
D298 **13** 12½c. on 5c. red . . . . 1·25 50

1947.
D656 D **121** 1c. blue 20 20
D657 3c. blue 20 25
D658 4c. blue . . . . . . 9·25 95
D659 5c. blue 20 20
D660 6c. blue 40 40
D661 7c. blue 25 25
D662 8c. blue 25 25
D663 10c. blue 25 20
D664 11c. blue 50 50
D665 12c. blue 95 85
D666 14c. blue 95 70
D667 15c. blue 40 20
D668 16c. blue 85 85
D669 20c. blue 35 25
D670 24c. blue . . . . . . 1·25 1·25
D671 25c. blue 40 25
D672 26c. blue . . . . . . 1·40 1·60
D673 30c. blue 60 20
D674 35c. blue 70 20
D675 40c. blue 70 20
D676 50c. blue 95 25
D677 60c. blue . . . . . . 1·00 50
D678 85c. blue . . . . . . 15·00 55
D679 90c. blue . . . . . . 3·00 65
D680 95c. blue . . . . . . 3·00 65
D681 1g. red . . . . 2·25 20
D682 1g.75 red . . . . . . 5·50 35
For stamps as Types D **121**, but in violet, see under Surinam.

INTERNATIONAL COURT OF JUSTICE

Stamps specially issued for use by the Headquarters of the Court of International Justice. Nos. J1 to J36 were not sold to the public in unused condition.

1934. Optd **COUR PER- MANENTE DE JUSTICE INTER- NATIONALE**.
J1 **35** 1½c. mauve . . . . — 55
J2 2½c. green . . . . — 55
J3 **36** 7½c. red . . . . — 95
J4 **68** 12½c. blue . . . . — 25·00
J7 **36** 12½c. blue . . . . — 18·00
J5 15c. yellow . . . . — 1·25
J6 3c. purple . . . . — 2·25

1940. Optd **COUR PER- MANANTE DE JUSTICE INTER- NATIONALE**.
J 9 **94** 7½c. red . . . . — 9·25
J10 12½c. blue . . . . — 9·25
J11 15c. blue . . . . — 9·25
J12 30c. bistre . . . . — 9·25

1947. Optd **COUR INTERNATIONALE DE JUSTICE**.
J13 **94** 7½c. red . . . . — 1·10
J14 10c. purple . . . . — 1·10
J15 12½c. blue . . . . — 1·10
J16 20c. violet . . . . — 1·10
J17 25c. red . . . . — 1·10

J 3

J 4 Peace Palace, The Hague

J 5 Queen Juliana

1950.
J18 J **3** 2c. blue . . . . — 8·25
J19 4c. green . . . . — 8·25

1951.
J20 J **4** 2c. lake . . . . — 60
J21 3c. blue . . . . — 60
J22 4c. green . . . . — 60
J23 5c. brown . . . . — 60
J24 J **5** 6c. mauve . . . . — 2·10
J25 J **4** 6c. green . . . . — 90
J26 7c. red . . . . — 90
J27 J **5** 10c. green . . . . — 20
J28 12c. red . . . . — 1·75
J29 15c. red . . . . — 20
J30 20c. blue . . . . — 25
J31 25c. brown . . . . — 25
J32 30c. purple . . . . — 40
J33 J **4** 40c. blue . . . . — 35
J34 45c. red . . . . — 50
J35 50c. mauve . . . . — 55
J36 J **5** 1g. grey . . . . — 65

J 6 Olive Branch and Peace Palace, The Hague

1989.
J37 J **6** 5c. black and yellow . . . 15 15
J38 10c. black and blue . . . 15 15
J39 25c. black and red 20 20
J41 50c. black and green . . . 35 40
J42 55c. black and mauve . . 40 35
J43 60c. black and bistre . . . 40 45
J44 65c. black and green . . . 40 45
J45 70c. black and blue . . . 45 50
J46 75c. black and yellow . . 45 60
J47 80c. black and green . . . 50 65
J49 1g. black and orange . . . 65 75
J50 1g.50 black and blue . . . 95 1·25
J51 1g.60 black and brown . . 1·00 1·25
J54 – 5g. multicoloured . . . . 3·50 3·75
J56 – 7g. multicoloured . . . . 4·25 5·00
DESIGNS: 5, 7g. Olive branch and column.

NETHERLANDS ANTILLES Pt. 4

Curacao and other Netherlands islands in the Caribbean Sea. In December 1954 these were placed on an equal footing with Netherlands under the Crown.

100 cents = 1 gulden.

48 Spanish Galleon

49 Alonso de Ojeda

1949. 450th Anniv of Discovery of Curacao.
306 **48** 6c. green . . . . 3·25 2·00
307 **49** 12½c. red . . . . 4·00 3·25
308 **48** 15c. blue . . . . 4·00 2·50

50 Posthorns and Globe 51 Leap-frog

1949. 75th Anniv of U.P.U.
309 **50** 6c. red . . . . 4·00 2·75
310 25c. blue . . . . 4·00 1·25

1950. As numeral and portrait types of Netherlands but inscr "NED. ANTILLEN".
325 **118** 1c. brown 10 10
326 1½c. blue 10 10
327 2c. orange 10 10
328 2½c. green 90 20
329 3c. violet 20 10
329a 4c. green 60 35
330 5c. red 10 10
310a **129** 5c. yellow 20 10
311 6c. purple . . . . 1·40 10
311a 7½c. brown . . . . 5·50 10
312a 10c. red . . . . 1·60 1·60
313 12½c. green . . . . 2·50 20
314a 15c. blue 30 10
315a 20c. orange 40 25
316 21c. black . . . . 2·50 1·60
316a 22½c. green . . . . 6·25 10
317a 25c. violet 50 35
318 27½c. brown . . . . 7·25 1·50
319a 30c. sepia . . . . 1·10 70
319b 40c. blue 55 45
320 50c. olive . . . . 11·00 10
321 **130** 1½g. green . . . . 45·00 25
322 2½g. brown . . . . 50·00 1·60
323 5g. red . . . . 65·00 11·00
324 10g. purple . . . . £200 65·00

1951. Child Welfare.
331 **51** 1½c.+1c. violet . . . . . . 7·25 1·10
332 – 5c.+2½c. brown . . . . . 9·50 3·25
333 – 6c.+2½c. blue . . . . . . 9·50 3·75
334 – 12½c.+5c. red . . . . . . 11·00 4·25
335 – 25c.+10c. turquoise . . . . 10·50 3·25
DESIGNS: 5c. Kite-flying; 6c. Girl on swing; 12½c. Girls playing "Oranges and Lemons"; 25c. Bowling hoops.

52 Gull over Ship

54 Fort Beekenburg

1952. Seamen's Welfare Fund. Inscr "ZEEMANSWELVAREN".
336 **52** 1½c.+1c. green . . . . . . 7·25 1·25
337 – 6c.+4c. brown . . . . . . 9·00 3·25
338 – 12½c.+7c. mauve . . . . . 9·00 3·50
339 – 15c.+10c. blue . . . . . . 11·00 4·25
340 – 25c.+15c. red . . . . . . 10·50 4·25
DESIGNS: 6c. Sailor and lighthouse; 12½c. Sailor on ship's prow; 15c. Tanker in harbour; 25c. Anchor and compass.

1953. Netherlands Flood Relief Fund. No. 321 surch **22½ Ct. +7½ Ct. WATERSNOOD NEDERLAND 1953.**
341 **130** 22½c.+7½c. on 1½g. green 1·25 1·25

1953. 250th Anniv of Fort Beekenburg.
342 **54** 22½c. brown . . . . 5·00 50

55 Aruba Beach

1954. 3rd Caribbean Tourist Assn Meeting.
343 **55** 15c. blue and buff . . . . 5·00 2·75

1954. Ratification of Statute of the Kingdom. As No. 809 of Netherlands.
344 **158** 7½c. green 90 85

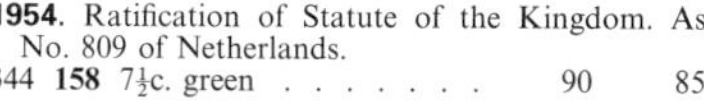

56 "Anglo" Flower

1955. Child Welfare.
345 **56** 1½c.+1c. bl, yell & turq . . 1·75 80
346 – 7½c.+5c. red, yellow & vio 3·75 2·25
347 – 15c.+5c. red, grn & olive 3·75 2·40
348 – 22½c.+7½c. red, yell & bl 3·75 2·25
349 – 25c.+10c. red, yell & grey 3·75 2·40
FLOWERS: 7½c. White Cayenne; 15c. "French" flower; 22½c. Cactus; 25c. Red Cayenne.

57 Prince Bernhard and Queen Juliana

1955. Royal Visit.
350 **57** 7½c.+2½c. red 20 20
351 22½c.+7½c. blue . . . . . 1·10 1·10

59 Oil Refinery

1955. 21st Meeting of Caribbean Commission.
352 – 15c. blue, green and brown 3·75 2·40
353 **59** 25c. blue, green and brown 4·50 2·75
DESIGN (rectangle, 36 × 25 mm): 15c. Aruba Beach.

60 St. Anne Bay

1956. 10th Anniv of Caribbean Commission.
354 **60** 15c. blue, red and black 35 35

61 Lord Baden-Powell

1957. 50th Anniv of Boy Scout Movement.
355 **61** 6c.+1½c. yellow 60 55
356 7½c.+2½c. green 60 55
357 15c.+5c. red 60 55

62 "Dawn of Health"

1957. 1st Caribbean Mental Health Congress, Aruba.
358 **62** 15c. black and yellow 35 35

63 Saba

1957. Tourist Publicity. Multicoloured.
359 7½c. Type **63** 45 45
360 15c. St. Maarten 45 45
361 25c. St. Eustatius 45 45

64 Footballer

65 Curacao Intercontinental Hotel

1957. 8th Central American and Caribbean Football Championships.
362 **64** 6c.+2½c. orange 95 75
363 – 7½c.+5c. red 1·40 1·10
364 – 15c.+5c. green 1·40 1·10
365 – 22½c.+7½c. blue 1·40 90
DESIGNS—HORIZ: 7½c. Caribbean map. VERT: 15c. Goalkeeper saving ball; 22½c. Footballers with ball.

1957. Opening of Curacao Intercontinental Hotel.
366 **65** 15c. blue 35 35

66 Map of Curacao

67 American Kestrel

1957. International Geophysical Year.
367 **66** 15c. deep blue and blue 75 75

1958. Child Welfare. Bird design inscr "VOOR HET KIND". Multicoloured.
368 2½c.+1c. Type **67** 50 30
369 7½c.+1½c. Yellow oriole 95 80
370 15c.+2½c. Scaly-breasted ground doves 1·10 1·00
371 22½c.+2½c. Brown-throated conure 1·25 90

68 Greater Flamingoes (Bonaire)

1958. Size 33½ × 22 mm.
372 **68** 6c. pink and green 1·90 15
373 A 7½c. yellow and brown 20 15
374 8c. yellow and blue 20 15
375 B 10c. yellow and grey 20 15
376 C 12c. grey and green 20 15
377 D 15c. blue and green 20 15
377a 15c. lilac and green 15 10
378 E 20c. grey and red 20 15
379 A 25c. green and blue 30 15
380 D 30c. green and brown 30 15
381 E 35c. pink and grey 35 15
382 C 40c. green and mauve 50 15
383 B 45c. blue and violet 50 15
384 **68** 50c. pink and brown 50 15
385 E 55c. green and red 55 25
386 **68** 65c. pink and green 65 30
387 D 70c. orange and purple 1·25 50
388 **68** 75c. pink and violet 70 50
389 B 85c. green and brown 80 70
390 E 90c. orange and blue 90 90
391 C 95c. yellow and orange 1·10 1·00
392 D 1g. grey and red 1·00 15
393 A 1½g. brown and violet 1·40 20
394 C 2½g. yellow and blue 2·40 40
395 B 5g. mauve and brown 5·00 75
396 **68** 10g. pink and blue 9·00 5·00
DESIGNS: A. Dutch Colonial houses (Curacao); B. Mountain and palms (Saba); C. Town Hall (St. Maarten); D. Church tower (Aruba); E. Memorial obelisk (St. Eustatius).
For larger versions of some values see Nos. 653/6.

69

1958. 50th Anniv of Netherlands Antilles Radio and Telegraph Administration.
397 **69** 7½c. lake and blue 20 20
398 15c. blue and red 35 35

70 Red Cross Flag and Antilles Map

71 Aruba Caribbean Hotel

1958. Neth. Antilles Red Cross Fund. Cross in red.
399 **70** 6c.+2c. brown 30 30
400 7½c.+2½c. green 55 55
401 15c.+5c. yellow 55 55
402 22½c.+7½c. blue 55 55

1959. Opening of Aruba Caribbean Hotel.
403 **71** 15c. multicoloured 35 35

72 Zeeland

1959. Curacao Monuments Preservation Fund. Multicoloured.
404 6c.+1½c. Type **72** 1·25 90
405 7½c.+2½c. Saba Island 1·25 90
406 15c.+5c. Molenplein (vert) 1·25 90
407 22½c.+7½c. Scharloobrug 1·25 90
408 25c.+7½c. Brievengat 1·25 90

73 Water-distillation Plant

74 Antilles Flag

1959. Inauguration of Aruba Water-distillation Plant.
409 **73** 20c. light blue and blue 50 50

1959. 5th Anniv of Ratification of Statute of the Kingdom.
410 **74** 10c. red, blue and light blue 50 35
411 20c. red, blue and yellow 50 35
412 25c. red, blue and green 50 35

75 Fokker F.XVIII "De Snip" over Caribbean

76 Mgr. Niewindt

1959. 25th Anniv of K.L.M. Netherlands–Curacao Air Service. Each yellow, deep blue and blue.
413 10c. Type **75** 50 35
414 20c. Fokker F.XVIII "De Snip" over globe 50 35
415 25c. Douglas DC-7C "Seven Seas" over Handelskade (bridge), Willemstad 50 15
416 35c. Douglas DC-8 at Aruba Airport 50 55

1960. Death Centenary of Mgr. M. J. Niewindt.
417 **76** 10c. purple 55 45
418 20c. violet 55 55
419 25c. olive 55 55

77 Flag and Oil-worker

78 Frogman

1960. Labour Day.
420 **77** 20c. multicoloured 45 45

1960. Princess Wilhelmina Cancer Relief Fund. Inscr "KANKERBESTRIJDING".
421 **78** 10c.+2c. blue 1·40 1·10
422 – 20c.+3c. multicoloured 1·40 1·40
423 – 25c.+5c. red, blue & blk 1·40 1·40
DESIGNS—HORIZ: 20c. Queen angelfish; 25c. Big-scaled soldierfish.

79 Child on Bed

1961. Child Welfare. Inscr "voor het kind".
424 6c.+2c. black and green 35 30
425 10c.+3c. black and red 35 30
426 20c.+6c. black and yellow 35 30
427 25c.+8c. black and orange 35 30
DESIGNS: 6c. Type **79**; 10c. Girl with doll; 20c. Boy with bucket; 25c. Children in classroom.

80 Governor's Salute to the American Naval Brig "Andrew Doria" at St. Eustatius

1961. 185th Anniv of 1st Salute to the American Flag.
428 **80** 20c. multicoloured 65 65

1962. Royal Silver Wedding. As T **187** of Netherlands.
429 10c. orange 30 30
430 25c. blue 30 30

81 Jaja (nursemaid) and Child 82 Knight and World Map

1962. Cultural Series.
431 – 6c. brown and yellow 35 30
432 – 10c. multicoloured 35 30
433 – 20c. multicoloured 35 35
434 **81** 25c. brown, green and black 35 35
DESIGNS: 6c. Corn-masher; 10c. Benta player; 20c. Petji kerchief.

1962. 5th International Candidates Chess Tournament, Curacao.
436 **82** 10c.+5c. green 95 70
437 20c.+10c. red 95 70
438 25c.+10c. blue 95 70

1963. Freedom from Hunger. No. 378 surch **TEGEN DE HONGER** wheat sprig and **+10c.**
439 20c.+10c. grey and red 55 55

84 Family Group

1963. 4th Caribbean Mental Health Congress, Curacao.
440 **84** 20c. buff and blue 30 30
441 – 25c. red and blue 30 30
DESIGN: 25c. Egyptian Cross emblem.

85 "Freedom"

1963. Centenary of Abolition of Slavery in Dutch West Indies.
442 **85** 25c. brown and yellow 35 30

86 Hotel Bonaire

1963. Opening of Hotel Bonaire.
443 **86** 20c. brown 35 30

87 Child and Flowers

88 Test-tube and Flask

1963. Child Welfare. Child Art. Multicoloured.
444 5c.+2c. Type **87** 35 30
445 6c.+3c. Children and flowers (horiz) 35 30
446 10c.+5c. Girl with ball (horiz) 35 30
447 20c.+10c. Men with flags (horiz) 35 30
448 25c.+12c. Schoolboy 35 30

1963. 150th Anniv of Kingdom of the Netherlands. As No. 968 of Netherlands, but smaller, 26 × 27 mm.
449 25c. green, red and black 35 30

1963. Chemical Industry, Aruba.
450 **88** 20c. red, light green and green 45 45

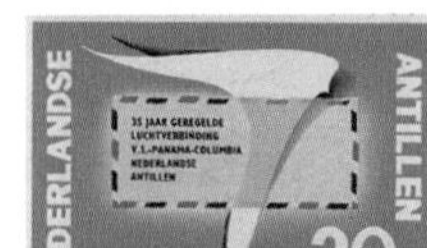

89 Winged Letter

1964. 35th Anniv of 1st U.S.–Curacao Flight. Multicoloured.
451 20c. Type **89** 35 35
452 25c. Route map, Sikorsky S-38 flying boat and Boeing 707 35 35

90 Trinitaria

1964. Child Welfare. Multicoloured.
453 6c.+3c. Type **90** 30 30
454 10c.+5c. Magdalena 30 30
455 20c.+10c. Yellow keiki . . . 30 30
456 25c.+11c. Bellisima 30 30

91 Caribbean Map

1964. 5th Caribbean Council Assembly.
457 **91** 20c. yellow, red and blue 35 30

92 "Six Islands" **93** Princess Beatrix

1964. 10th Anniv of Statute for the Kingdom.
458 **92** 25c. multicoloured 35 30

1965. Visit of Princess Beatrix.
459 **93** 25c. red 35 35

94 I.T.U. Emblem and Symbols

1965. Centenary of I.T.U.
460 **94** 10c. deep blue and blue . . 20 20

95 "Asperalla" (tanker) at Curacao

1965. 50th Anniv of Curacao's Oil Industry. Multicoloured.
461 10c. Catalytic cracking plant (vert) 30 20
462 20c. Type **95** 30 20
463 25c. Super fractionating plant (vert) 30 30

96 Flag and Fruit Market, Curacao

1965.
464 **96** 1c. blue, red and green . . 10 10
465 – 2c. blue, red and yellow . . 10 10
466 – 3c. blue, red and cobalt . . 10 10
467 – 4c. blue, red and orange 10 10
468 – 5c. blue, red and blue . . . 20 10
469 – 6c. blue, red and pink . . 20 10
DESIGNS (Flag and): 2c. Divi-divi tree; 3c. Lace; 4c. Greater flamingoes; 5c. Church; 6c. Lobster.
Each is inscr with a different place-name.

97 Cup Sponges

1965. Child Welfare. Marine Life. Multicoloured.
470 6c.+3c. Type **97** 20 20
471 10c.+5c. Cup sponges (diff) 20 20
472 20c.+10c. Sea anemones on star coral 30 20
473 25c.+11c. Basket sponge, blue chromis and "Brain" coral 35 30

98 Marine and Seascape **99** Budgerigars and Wedding Rings

1965. Tercentenary of Marine Corps.
474 **98** 25c. multicoloured 20 20

1966. Intergovernmental Committee for European Migration (I.C.E.M.) Fund. As T **215** of Netherlands.
475 35c.+15c. bistre and brown 30 30

1966. Marriage of Crown Princess Beatrix and Herr Claus von Amsberg.
476 **99** 25c. multicoloured 30 20

100 Admiral de Ruyter and Map

1966. 300th Anniv of Admiral de Ruyter's Visit to St. Eustatius.
477 **100** 25c. ochre, violet and blue 20 20

101 "Grammar" **102** Cooking

1966. 25 Years of Secondary Education.
478 **101** 6c. black, blue and yellow 20 20
479 – 10c. black, red and green 20 20
480 – 20c. black, blue and yellow 30 20
481 – 25c. black, red and green 30 20
DESIGNS: The "Free Arts", figures representing: 10c. "Rhetoric" and "Dialect"; 20c. "Arithmetic" and "Geometry"; 25c. "Astronomy" and "Music".

1966. Child Welfare. Multicoloured.
482 6c.+3c. Type **102** 20 20
483 10c.+5c. Nursing 20 20
484 20c.+10c. Metal-work fitting 30 20
485 25c.+11c. Ironing 30 20

103 "Gelderland" (cruiser)

1967. 60th Anniv of Royal Netherlands Navy League.
486 **103** 6c. bronze and green . . 20 20
487 – 10c. ochre and yellow . . 20 20
488 – 20c. brown and sepia . . 30 20
489 – 25c. blue and indigo . . . 30 20
SHIPS: 10c. "Pioneer" (schooner); 20c. "Oscilla" (tanker); 25c. "Santa Rosa" (liner).

104 M. C. Piar **105** "Heads in Hands"

1967. 150th Death Anniv of Manuel Piar (patriot).
490 **104** 20c. brown and red . . . 30 20

1967. Cultural and Social Relief Funds.
491 **105** 6c.+3c. black and blue . . 20 20
492 10c.+5c. black & mauve 20 20
493 20c.+10c. purple 30 20
494 25c.+11c. blue 30 20

106 "The Turtle and the Monkey" **107** Olympic Flame and Rings

1967. Child Welfare. "Nanzi" Fairy Tales. Mult.
495 6c.+3c. "Princess Long Nose" (vert) 20 20
496 10c.+5c. Type **106** 20 20
497 20c.+10c. "Nanzi (spider) and the Tiger" 30 20
498 25c.+11c. "Shon Arey's Balloon" (vert) 90 70

1968. Olympic Games, Mexico. Multicoloured.
499 10c. Type **107** 30 30
500 20c. "Throwing the discus" (statue) 30 30
501 25c. Stadium and doves . . . 30 30

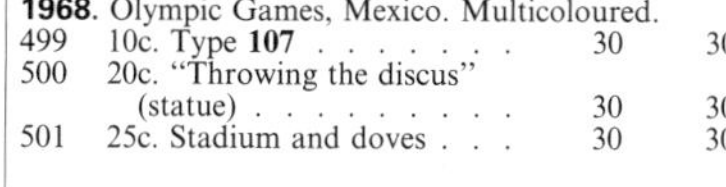

108 "Dance of the Ribbons"

1968. Cultural and Social Relief Funds.
502 **108** 10c.+5c. multicoloured . . 20 20
503 15c.+5c. multicoloured . . 20 20
504 20c.+10c. multicoloured 30 20
505 25c.+10c. multicoloured 30 20

109 Boy with Goat

1968. Child Welfare Fund. Multicoloured.
506 6c.+3c. Type **109** 20 20
507 10c.+5c. Girl with dog . . . 20 20
508 20c.+10c. Boy with cat . . . 30 20
509 25c.+11c. Girl with duck . . 30 20

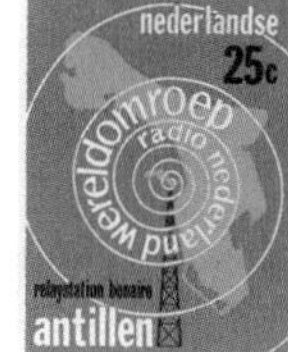

110 Fokker Friendship 500 **111** Radio Pylon, "Waves" and Map

1968. Dutch Antillean Airlines.
510 **110** 10c. blue, black and yellow 30 30
511 – 20c. blue, black and brown 30 30
512 – 25c. blue, black and pink 30 30
DESIGNS: 20c. Douglas DC-9; 25c. Fokker Friendship 500 in flight and Douglas DC-9 on ground.

1969. Opening of Broadcast Relay Station, Bonaire.
513 **111** 25c. green, dp blue & blue 30 30

112 "Code of Laws" **113** "Carnival"

1969. Centenary of Netherlands Antilles Court of Justice.
514 **112** 20c. green, gold & lt green 30 30
515 – 25c. multicoloured 30 30
DESIGN: 25c. "Scales of Justice".

1969. Cultural and Social Relief Funds. Antilles' Festivals. Multicoloured.
516 10c.+5c. Type **113** 35 35
517 15c.+5c. "Harvest Festival" 35 35
518 20c.+10c. "San Juan Day" 35 35
519 25c.+10c. "New Years' Day" 35 35

114 I.L.O. Emblem, "Koenoekoe" House and Cacti

1969. 50th Anniv of I.L.O.
520 **114** 10c. black and blue . . . 20 20
521 25c. black and red 30 20

115 Boy playing Guitar **118** St. Anna Church, Otrabanda, Curacao

117 Radio Station, Bonaire

1969. Child Welfare.
522 **115** 6c.+3c. violet & orange 30 30
523 – 10c.+5c. green & yellow 35 35
524 – 20c.+10c. red and blue . . 35 35
525 – 25c.+11c. brown & pink 40 40
DESIGNS: 10c. Girl playing recorder; 20c. Boy playing "marimula"; 25c. Girl playing piano.

1969. 15th Anniv of Statute of the Kingdom. As T **240** of the Netherlands, but inscr "NEDERLANDSE ANTILLEN".
526 25c. multicoloured 30 30

1970. 5th Anniv of Trans-World Religious Radio Station, Bonaire. Multicoloured.
527 10c. Type **117** 20 20
528 15c. Trans-World Radio emblem 20 20

1970. Churches of the Netherlands Antilles. Mult.
529 10c. Type **118** 35 30
530 20c. "Mikve Israel-Emanuel" Synagogue, Punda, Curacao (horiz) 35 30
531 25c. Pulpit Fort Church Curacao 35 30

119 "The Press" **120** Mother and Child

1970. Cultural and Social Relief Funds. "Mass-media". Multicoloured.
532 10c.+5c. Type **119** 50 50
533 15c.+5c. "Films" 50 50
534 20c.+10c. "Radio" 50 50
535 25c.+10c. "Television" . . . 50 50

1970. Child Welfare. Multicoloured.
536 6c.+3c. Type **120** 50 50
537 10c.+5c. Child with piggy-bank 50 50
538 20c.+10c. Children's Judo . . 50 50
539 25c.+11c. "Pick-a-back" . . . 50 50

121 St. Theresia's Church, St. Nicolaas, Aruba **122** Lions Emblem

1971. 40th Anniv of St. Theresia Parish, Aruba.
540 **121** 20c. multicoloured 30 30

1971. 25th Anniv of Curacao Lions Club.
541 **122** 25c. multicoloured 35 35

123 Charcoal Stove

125 Admiral Brion

1971. Cultural and Social Relief Funds. Household Utensils. Multicoloured.

542 10c.+5c. Type **123** 55 55
543 15c.+5c. Earthenware water vessel 55 55
544 20c.+10c. Baking oven . . . 55 55
545 25c.+10c. Kitchen implements 55 55

1971. Prince Bernhard's 60th Birthday. Design as No. 1135 of Netherlands.

546 45c. multicoloured 55 55

1971. 150th Death Anniv of Admiral Pedro Luis Brion.

547 **125** 40c. multicoloured 35 35

126 Bottle Doll

127 Queen Emma Bridge, Curacao

1971. Child Welfare. Home-made Toys. Mult.

548 15c.+5c. Type **126** 65 65
549 20c.+10c. Simple cart 65 65
550 30c.+15c. Spinning-tops . . . 65 65

1971. Views of the Islands. Multicoloured.

551 1c. Type **127** 10 10
552 2c. The Bottom, Saba 10 10
553 3c. Greater flamingoes, Bonaire 10 10
554 4c. Distillation plant, Aruba 10 10
555 5c. Fort Amsterdam, St. Maarten 20 10
556 6c. Fort Oranje, St. Eustatius 20 10

128 Ship in Dock

129 Steel Band

1972. Inauguration of New Dry Dock Complex, Willemstad, Curacao.

557 **128** 30c. multicoloured 35 35

1972. Cultural and Social Relief Funds. Folklore. Multicoloured.

558 15c.+5c. Type **129** 70 70
559 20c.+10c. "Seu" festival . . . 70 70
560 30c.+15c. "Tambu" dance . . 70 70

130 J. E. Irausquin

131 Dr. M. F. da Costa Gomez

1972. 10th Death Anniv of Juan Enrique Irausquin (Antilles statesman).

561 **130** 30c. red 35 35

1972. 65th Birth Anniv of Moises F. da Costa Gomez (statesman).

562 **131** 30c. black and green . . . 35 35

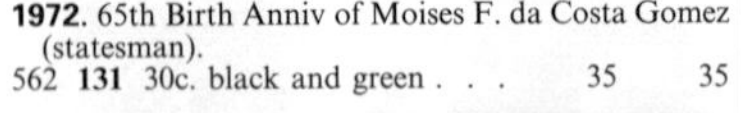

132 Child playing with Earth

133 Pedestrian Crossing

1972. Child Welfare. Multicoloured.

563 15c.+5c. Type **132** 75 75
564 20c.+10c. Child playing in water 75 75
565 30c.+15c. Child throwing ball into the air 75 75

1973. Cultural and Social Relief Funds. Road Safety.

566 **133** 12c.+6c. multicoloured . . 80 80
567 – 15c.+7c. grn, orge & red 80 80
568 – 40c.+20c. multicoloured 80 80

DESIGNS: 15c. Road-crossing patrol; 40c. Traffic lights.

134 William III (portrait from stamp of 1873)

135 Map of Aruba, Curacao and Bonaire

1973. Stamp Centenary.

569 **134** 15c. violet, mauve and gold 35 25
570 – 20c. multicoloured 50 35
571 – 30c. multicoloured 50 35

DESIGNS: 20c. Antilles postman; 30c. Postal Service emblem.

1973. Inauguration of Submarine Cable and Microwave Telecommunications Link. Multicoloured.

572 15c. Type **135** 50 45
573 30c. Six stars ("The Antilles") 50 45
574 45c. Map of Saba, St. Maarten and St. Eustatius 50 45

136 Queen Juliana

137 Jan Eman

1973. Silver Jubilee of Queen Juliana's Reign.

576 **136** 15c. multicoloured 55 55

1973. 16th Death Anniv of Jan Eman (Aruba statesman).

577 **137** 30c. black and green . . . 35 35

138 "1948–1973"

139 L. B. Scott

1973. Child Welfare Fund. 25th Anniv of 1st Child Welfare Stamps.

578 **138** 15c.+5c. light green, green and blue 70 70
579 – 20c.+10c. brown, green and blue 70 70
580 – 30c.+15c. violet, blue and light blue 70 70

DESIGNS: No. 579, Three Children; 580, Mother and child.

1974. 8th Death Anniv of Lionel B. Scott (St. Maarten statesman).

582 **139** 30c. multicoloured 35 35

140 Family Meal

141 Girl combing Hair

1974. Family Planning Campaign. Multicoloured.

583 6c. Type **140** 20 20
584 12c. Family at home 30 30
585 15c. Family in garden 35 30

1974. Cultural and Social Relief Funds. "The Younger Generation". Multicoloured.

586 12c.+6c. Type **141** . . . . . 1·00 90
587 15c.+7c. "Pop dancers" . . . 1·00 90
588 40c.+20c. Group drummer 1·00 90

142 Desulphurisation Plant

1974. 50th Anniv of Lago Oil Co, Aruba. Mult.

589 15c. Type **142** 30 30
590 30c. Fractionating towers . . 35 35
591 45c. Lago refinery at night 55 55

143 U.P.U. Emblem

144 "A Carpenter outranks a King"

1974. Centenary of Universal Postal Union.

592 **143** 15c. gold, green and black 50 45
593 30c. gold, blue and black 50 45

1974. Child Welfare. Children's Songs. Mult.

594 15c.+5c. Type **144** 80 80
595 20c.+10c. Footprints ("Let's Do a Ring-dance") 80 80
596 30c.+15c. "Moon and Sun" 80 80

145 Queen Emma Bridge

146 Ornamental Ventilation Grid

1975. Antillean Bridges. Multicoloured.

597 20c. Type **145** 45 45
598 30c. Queen Juliana Bridge . . 45 45
599 40c. Queen Wilhelmina Bridge 55 55

1975. Cultural and Social Welfare Funds.

600 **146** 12c.+6c. multicoloured . . 70 70
601 – 15c.+7c. brown & stone 70 70
602 – 40c.+20c. multicoloured 70 70

DESIGNS: 15c. Knight accompanied by buglers (tombstone detail); 40c. Foundation stone.

147 Sodium Chloride Molecules

1975. Bonaire Salt Industry. Multicoloured.

603 15c. Type **147** 50 35
604 20c. Salt incrustation and blocks 50 45
605 40c. Map of salt area (vert) 55 45

148 Fokker F.XVIII "De Snip" and Old Control Tower

1975. 40th Anniv of Aruba Airport. Mult.

606 15c. Type **148** 35 25
607 30c. Douglas DC-9-30 and modern control tower . . . 50 35
608 40c. Tail of Boeing 727-200 and "Princess Beatrix" Airport buildings 50 45

149 I.W.Y. Emblem

1975. International Women's Year. Multicoloured.

609 6c. Type **149** 20 20
610 12c. "Social Development" 35 25
611 20c. "Equality of Sexes" . . 50 35

150 Children making Windmill

1975. Child Welfare. Multicoloured.

612 15c.+5c. Type **150** 70 70
613 20c.+10c. Child modelling clay 70 70
614 30c.+15c. Children drawing pictures 70 70

151 Beach, Aruba

152 J. A. Abraham (statesman)

1976. Tourism. Multicoloured.

615 40c. Type **151** 55 55
616 40c. Fish Kiosk, Bonaire . . 55 55
617 40c. "Table Mountain", Curacao 55 55

1976. Abraham Commemoration.

618 **152** 30c. purple on brown . . 45 45

153 Dyke Produce

154 Arm holding Child

1976. Agriculture, Animal Husbandry and Fisheries. Multicoloured.

619 15c. Type **153** 35 25
620 35c. Cattle 55 45
621 45c. Fishes 55 50

1976. Child Welfare. "Carrying the Child".

622 **154** 20c.+10c. multicoloured 70 65
623 – 25c.+12c. multicoloured 70 65
624 – 40c.+18c. multicoloured 70 65

DESIGNS—HORIZ: 25c. VERT: 40c. Both similar to Type **154** showing arm holding child.

155 "Andrew Doria" (naval brig) receiving Salute

156 Carnival Costume

1976. Bicentenary of American Revolution. Multicoloured.

625 25c. Flags and plaque, Fort Oranje 70 45
626 40c. Type **155** 70 45
627 55c. Johannes de Graaff, Governor of St. Eustatius 70 70

1977. Carnival.

628 – 25c. multicoloured 55 50
629 **156** 35c. multicoloured 55 50
630 – 40c. multicoloured 55 50

DESIGNS: 25c., 40c. Women in Carnival costumes.

157 Tortoise (Bonaire)

158 "Ace" Playing Card

1977. Rock Paintings. Multicoloured.

631 25c. Bird (Aruba) 50 35
632 35c. Abstract (Curaca) . . . 50 45
633 40c. Type **157** 55 45

1977. Sixth Central American and Caribbean Bridge Championships. Multicoloured.

634 **158** 20c.+10c. red and black 50 35
635 – 25c.+12c. multicoloured 50 50
636 – 40c.+18c. multicoloured 65 65

DESIGNS—VERT: 25c. "King" playing card. HORIZ: 40c. Bridge hand.

159 "Cordia sebestena" **160** Bells outside Main Store

1977. Flowers. Multicoloured.

639 25c. Type **159** 50 35
640 40c. "Albizzia lebbeck" (vert) 55 40
641 55c. "Tamarindus indica" . . 65 65

1977. 50th Anniv of Spritzer and Fuhrmann (jewellers). Multicoloured.

642 20c. Type **160** 50 35
643 40c. Globe basking in sun . . 55 50
644 55c. Antillean flag and diamond ring 65 65

161 Children with Toy Animal

1977. Child Welfare. Multicoloured.

645 15c.+15c. Type **161** 25 20
646 20c.+10c. Children with toy rabbit 50 50
647 25c.+12c. Children with toy cat 55 55
648 40c.+18c. Children with toy beetle 65 55

162 "The Unspoiled Queen" (Saba)

1977. Tourism. Multicoloured.

650 25c. Type **162** 20 10
651 35c. "The Golden Rock" (St. Eustatius) 25 20
652 40c. "The Friendly Island" (St. Maarten) 25 25

1977. As Nos. 378, 381/2 and 385, but larger, (39 × 22 mm).

653 E 20c. grey and red . . . . . 1·60 65
654 35c. pink and brown . . . 3·50 3·00
655 C 40c. green and mauve . . . 55 35
656 E 55c. green and red 75 50

163 19th-century Chest **164** Water-skiing

1978. 150th Anniv of Netherlands Antilles' Bank. Multicoloured.

657 **163** 15c. blue and light blue 20 10
658 – 20c. orange and gold . . 20 20
659 – 40c. green and deep green 25 25

DESIGNS: 20c. Bank emblem; 40c. Strong-room door.

1978. Sports Funds. Multicoloured.

660 15c.+5c. Type **164** 20 20
661 20c.+10c. Yachting 20 20
662 25c.+12c. Football 20 20
663 40c.+18c. Baseball 35 30

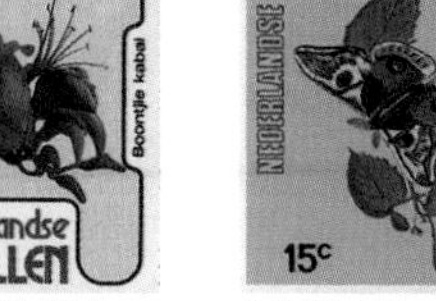

165 "Erythrina velutina" **166** "Polythysana rubrescens"

1978. Flora of Netherlands Antilles. Multicoloured.

664 15c. "Delconix regia" 20 20
665 25c. Type **165** 25 20
666 50c. "Gualacum officinale" (horiz) 35 35
667 55c. "Gilricidia sepium" (horiz) 50 50

1978. Butterflies. Multicoloured.

668 15c. Type **166** 20 20
669 25c. "Caligo sp." 25 20
670 35c. "Prepona praeneste" . . 35 35
671 40c. "Morpho sp." 50 45

167 "Conserve Energy" (English) **168** Red Cross

1978. Energy Conservation.

672 **167** 15c. orange and black . . 20 20
673 – 20c. green and black . . . 25 20
674 – 40c. red and black 50 40

DESIGNS: As No. 672 but text in Dutch (20c.) or in Papiamento (40c.).

1978. 150th Birth Anniv of Henri Dunant (founder of Red Cross).

675 **168** 55c.+25c. red and blue . . 25 25

169 Curacao from Sea, and Punched Tape **170** Boy Rollerskating

1978. 70th Anniv of Antilles Telecommunications Corporation (Landsradio). Multicoloured.

677 20c. Type **169** 25 25
678 40c. Ship's bridge, punched tape and radio mast . . . 35 35
679 55c. Satellite and aerial (vert) 55 55

1978. Child Welfare. Multicoloured.

680 15c.+5c. Type **170** 50 35
681 20c.+10c. Boy and girl flying kite 55 45
682 25c.+12c. Boy and girl playing marbles 55 50
683 40c.+18c. Girl riding bicycle 65 55

171 Ca'i Awa (pumping station) **172** Aruba Coat of Arms (float)

1978. 80th Death Anniv of Leonard Burlington Smith (entrepreneur and U.S. Consul).

685 **171** 25c. multicoloured 20 20
686 – 35c. black, greenish yellow and yellow 25 25
687 – 40c. multicoloured 50 25

DESIGNS—VERT: 35c. Leonard Burlington Smith. HORIZ: 40c. Opening ceremony of Queen Emma Bridge, 1888.

1979. 25th Aruba Carnival. Multicoloured.

688 40c.+10c. Float representing heraldic fantasy 50 35
689 75c.+20c. Type **172** 70 70

173 Goat and P.A.H.O. Emblem **174** Yacht and Sun

1979. 12th Inter-American Ministerial Meeting on Foot and Mouth Disease and Zoonosis Control, Curacao. Multicoloured.

690 50c. Type **173** 35 35
691 75c. Horse and conference emblem 45 45
692 150c. Cows, flag and Pan-American Health Organization (P.A.H.O.) and W.H.O. emblems . . . 1·00 1·00

1979. 12th International Sailing Regatta, Bonaire. Multicoloured.

694 15c.+5c. Type **174** 20 20
695 35c.+25c. Yachts 35 35
696 40c.+15c. Yacht and globe (horiz) 50 45
697 55c.+25c. Yacht, sun and flamingo 65 50

175 Corps Members **176** "Melochia tomentosa"

1979. 50th Anniv of Curacao Volunteer Corps.

699 **175** 15c.+10c. blue, red and ultramarine 20 20
700 – 40c.+20c. blue, violet and gold 55 55
701 – 1g. multicoloured 70 65

DESIGNS: 40c. Sentry in battle dress and emblem; 1g. Corps emblem, flag and soldier in ceremonial uniform.

1979. Flowers. Multicoloured.

702 25c. "Casearia tremula" . . . 30 20
703 40c. "Cordia cylindrostachya" 35 35
704 1g.50 Type **176** . . . . . . 1·10 1·10

177 Girls reading Book **178** Dove and Netherlands Flag

1979. International Year of the Child.

705 **177** 20c.+10c. multicoloured 25 25
706 – 25c.+12c. multicoloured 35 35
707 – 35c.+15c. violet, brown and black 55 45
708 – 50c.+20c. multicoloured 65 65

DESIGNS: 25c. Toddler and cat; 35c. Girls carrying basket; 50c. Boy and girl dressing-up.

1979. 25th Anniv of Statute of the Kingdom. Multicoloured.

710 65c. Type **178** 65 55
711 1g.50 Dove and Netherlands Antilles flag . . . . 1·10 1·10

179 Map of Aruba and Foundation Emblem

1979. 30th Anniv of Aruba Cultural Centre Foundation. Multicoloured.

712 95c. Type **179** 80 80
713 1g. Foundation headquarters 90 90

180 Brass Chandelier

1980. 210th Anniv of Fort Church, Curacao.

714 **180** 20c.+10c. yellow, black and brown 25 25
715 – 50c.+25c. multicoloured 55 55
716 – 100c. multicoloured . . . 80 80

DESIGNS: 50c. Pipe organ; 100c. Cupola tower, 1910.

181 Rotary Emblem and Cogwheel

1980. 75th Anniv of Rotary International. Multicoloured.

717 45c. Rotary emblem 35 35
718 50c. Globe and cogwheels . . 50 35
719 85c. Type **181** 70 70

182 Savings Box

1980. 75th Anniv of Post Office Savings Bank. Multicoloured.

721 25c. Type **182** 25 20
722 150c. Savings box (different) 1·25 1·25

183 Queen Juliana Accession Stamp

1980. Accession of Queen Beatrix.

723 **183** 25c. red, green and gold 20 20
724 – 60c. green, red and gold 50 45

DESIGN: 60c. 1965 Royal Visit stamp.

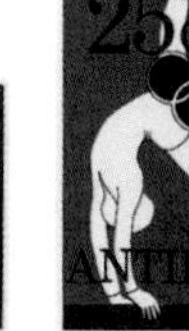

184 Sir Rowland Hill **185** Gymnastics (beam exercise)

1980. "London 1980" International Stamp Exhibition.

725 **184** 45c. black and green . . . 35 35
726 – 60c. black and red 50 50
727 – 1g. red, black and blue . . 90 90

DESIGNS: 60c. "London 1980" logo; 1g. Airmail label.

1980. Sports Funds.

729 **185** 25c.+10c. red and black 25 25
730 – 30c.+15c. yellow & blk . . 35 35
731 – 45c.+20c. light green, green and black 55 50
732 – 60c.+25c. pink, orange and black 70 65

DESIGNS: 30c. Gymnastics (horse vaulting); 45c. Volleyball; 60c. Basketball.

186 White-fronted Dove

1980. Birds. Multicoloured.

734 25c. Type **186** 25 25
735 60c. Tropical mockingbird . . 65 55
736 85c. Bananaquit 90 70

187 "St. Maarten Landscape" **188** Rudolf Theodorus Palm

1980. Child Welfare. Children's Drawings. Multicoloured.

737 25c.+10c. Type **187** 35 25
738 30c.+15c. "Bonaire House" 50 50

739 40c.+20c. "Child writing on Board" 55 55
740 60c.+25c. "Dancing Couple" (vert) 70 65

1981. Birth Centenary (1980) of Rudolf Theodorus Palm (musician).
742 **188** 60c. brown and yellow 55 55
743 – 1g. buff and blue 1·00 90
DESIGN: 1g. Musical score and hands playing piano.

189 Map of Aruba and TEAM Emblem
190 Boy in Wheelchair

1981. 50th Anniv of Evangelical Alliance Mission (TEAM) in Antilles. Multicoloured.
744 30c. Type **189** 25 25
745 50c. Map of Curacao and emblem 55 45
746 1g. Map of Bonaire and emblem 1·00 90

1981. International Year of Disabled Persons. Multicoloured.
747 25c.+10c. Blind woman 35 35
748 30c.+15c. Type **190** 50 45
749 45c.+20c. Child in walking frame 70 70
750 60c.+25c. Deaf girl 80 80

191 Tennis

192 Gateway

1981. Sports Funds. Multicoloured.
751 30c.+15c. Type **191** 55 45
752 50c.+20c. Swimming 70 70
753 70c.+25c. Boxing 1·00 90

1981. 125th Anniv of St. Elisabeth's Hospital. Multicoloured.
755 60c. Type **192** 55 55
756 1g.50 St. Elisabeth's Hospital 1·40 1·40

193 Marinus van der Maarel (promoter)

194 Mother and Child

1981. 50th Anniv (1980) of Antillean Boy Scouts Association. Multicoloured.
757 45c.+20c. Wolf Cub and leader 80 80
758 70c.+25c. Type **193** 1·10 1·10
759 1g.+50c. Headquarters, Ronde Klip 1·60 1·60

1981. Child Welfare. Multicoloured.
761 35c.+15c. Type **194** 45 45
762 45c.+20c. Boy and girl 65 65
763 55c.+25c. Child with cat 80 80
764 85c.+40c. Girl with teddy bear 1·25 1·25

195 "Jatropha gossypifolia"

196 Pilot Gig approaching Ship

1981. Flowers. Multicoloured.
766 45c. "Cordia globosa" 40 35
767 70c. Type **195** 75 70
768 100c. "Croton flavens" 90 90

1982. Centenary of Pilotage Service. Mult.
769 70c. Type **196** 90 90
770 85c. Modern liner and map of Antilles 1·10 1·00
771 1g. Pilot boarding ship 1·25 1·10

197 Fencing

198 Holy Ark

1982. Sports Funds.
772 **197** 35c.+15c. mauve and violet 70 65
773 – 45c.+20c. blue and deep blue 90 80
774 – 70c.+35c. multicoloured 1·40 1·25
775 – 85c.+40c. brown and deep brown 1·60 1·40
DESIGNS: 45c. Judo; 70c. Football; 85c. Cycling.

1982. 250th Anniv of Dedication of Mikve Israel-Emanuel Synagogue, Curacao. Mult.
777 75c. Type **198** 1·00 80
778 85c. Synagogue facade 1·10 80
779 150c. Tebah (raised platform) 1·60 1·40

199 Peter Stuyvesant (Governor) and Flags of Netherlands, Netherlands Antilles and United States

200 Airport Control Tower

1982. Bicentenary of Netherlands–United States Diplomatic Relations.
780 **199** 75c. multicoloured 1·10 90

1982. International Federation of Air Traffic Controllers.
782 – 35c. black, ultramarine and blue 55 35
783 **200** 75c. black, green and light green 1·00 80
784 – 150c. black, orange and salmon 1·60 1·40
DESIGNS: 35c. Radar plot trace; 150c. Radar aerials.

201 Mail Bag

202 Brown Chromis

1982. "Philexfrance 82" International Stamp Exhibition, Paris. Multicoloured.
785 45c. Exhibition emblem 65 50
786 85c. Type **201** 1·00 60
787 150c. Netherlands Antilles and French flags 1·60 1·40

1982. Fishes. Multicoloured.
789 35c. Type **202** 70 45
790 75c. Spotted trunkfish 1·25 90
791 85c. Blue tang 1·40 1·10
792 100c. French angelfish 1·50 1·10

203 Girl playing Accordion

1982. Child Welfare. Multicoloured.
793 35c.+15c. Type **203** 80 65
794 75c.+35c. Boy playing guitar 1·40 1·25
795 85c.+40c. Boy playing violin 1·60 1·40

204 Saba House

1982. Cultural and Social Relief Funds. Local Houses. Multicoloured.
797 35c.+15c. Type **204** 90 65
798 75c.+35c. Aruba House 1·50 1·25
799 85c.+40c. Curacao House 1·75 1·40

205 High Jumping

1983. Sports Funds. Multicoloured.
801 35c.+15c. Type **205** 70 55
802 45c.+20c. Weightlifting 1·10 90
803 85c.+40c. Wind-surfing 1·60 1·40

206 Natural Bridge, Aruba

207 W.C.Y. Emblem and Means of Communication

1983. Tourism. Multicoloured.
804 35c. Type **206** 65 55
805 45c. Lac Bay, Bonaire 70 65
806 100c. Willemstad, Curacao 1·40 1·25

1983. World Communications Year.
807 **207** 1g. multicoloured 1·40 1·25

208 "Curacao" (paddle-steamer) and Post Office Building

209 Mango ("Mangifera indica")

1983. "Brasiliana 83" International Stamp Exhibition, Rio de Janeiro. Multicoloured.
809 45c. Type **208** 80 70
810 55c. Brazil flag, exhibition emblem and Netherlands Antilles flag and postal service emblem 90 80
811 100c. Governor's Palace, Netherlands Antilles, and Sugarloaf Mountain, Rio de Janeiro 1·50 1·40

1983. Flowers. Multicoloured.
813 45c. Type **209** 90 70
814 55c. "Malpighia punicifolia" 1·00 80
815 100c. "Citrus aurantifolia" 1·60 1·40

210 Boy and Lizard

1983. Child Welfare. Multicoloured.
816 45c.+20c. Type **210** 1·10 90
817 55c.+25c. Girl watching ants 1·25 1·10
818 100c.+50c. Girl feeding donkey 2·10 1·90

211 Aruba Water Jar

212 Saba

1983. Cultural and Social Relief Funds. Pre-Columbian Pottery.
820 **211** 45c.+20c. light blue, blue and black 1·25 1·00
821 – 55c.+25c. pink, red and black 1·40 1·25
822 – 85c.+40c. stone, green and black 1·60 1·40
823 – 100c.+50c. light brown, brown and black 2·10 2·00
DESIGNS: 55c. Aruba decorated bowl; 85c. Curacao human figurine; 100c. Fragment of Curacao female figurine.

1983. Local Government Buildings. Multicoloured.
824 20c. Type **212** 25 25
825 25c. St. Eustatius 25 25
826 30c. St. Maarten 35 35
827 35c. Aruba 2·40 45
828 45c. Bonaire 55 55
829 55c. Curacao 70 65
830 60c. Type **212** 65 65
831 65c. As No. 825 70 70
832 70c. Type **212** 65 45
833 75c. As No. 826 90 90
834 85c. As No. 827 3·00 1·10
835 85c. As No. 828 80 55
836 90c. As No. 828 1·10 1·10
837 95c. As No. 829 1·25 1·25
838 1g. Type **212** 1·25 1·10
839 1g.50 As No. 825 1·50 1·40
841 2g.50 As No. 826 2·50 1·75
842 5g. As No. 828 5·50 3·50
843 10g. As No. 829 9·50 6·00
844 15g. Type **212** 14·00 9·50

213 Note-taking, Typesetting and Front Page of "Amigoe"

1984. Centenary of "Amigoe de Curacao" (newspaper). Multicoloured.
845 45c. Type **213** 70 65
846 55c. Printing press and newspapers 80 70
847 85c. Reading newspaper 1·40 1·25

214 W.I.A. and I.C.A.O. Emblems

1984. 40th Anniv of I.C.A.O.
848 **214** 25c. multicoloured 45 35
849 – 45c. violet, blue and black 90 65
850 – 55c. multicoloured 1·00 75
851 – 100c. multicoloured 1·60 1·25
DESIGNS: 45c. I.C.A.O. anniversary emblem; 55c. A.L.M. and I.C.A.O. emblems; 100c. Fokker F.XIII airplane "De Snip".

215 Fielder

1984. Sports Funds. 50th Anniv of Curacao Baseball Federation. Multicoloured.
852 25c.+10c. Type **215** 90 65
853 45c.+20c. Batter 1·40 1·10
854 55c.+25c. Pitcher 1·60 1·40
855 85c.+40c. Running for base 1·90 1·60

216 Microphones and Radio

1984. Cultural and Social Relief Funds. Radio and Gramophone. Multicoloured.
857 45c.+20c. Type **216** 1·40 1·10
858 55c.+25c. Gramophones and record 1·90 1·40
859 100c.+50c. Gramophone with horn 2·10 1·90

217 Bonnet-maker

1984. Centenary of Curacao Chamber of Commerce and Industry. Multicoloured.
860 45c. Type **217** 1·25 90
861 55c. Chamber emblem 1·25 90
862 1g. "Southward" (liner) passing under bridge 1·75 1·40
No. 861 is an inverted triangle.

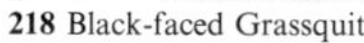

218 Black-faced Grassquit

219 Eleanor Roosevelt and Val-Kill, Hyde Park, New York

1984. Birds. Multicoloured.
863 45c. Type **218** . . . . 1·00 80
864 55c. Rufous-collared sparrow 1·25 1·40
865 150c. Blue-tailed emerald . . 1·90 1·90

1984. Birth Centenary of Eleanor Roosevelt.
866 **219** 45c. multicoloured 80 65
867 – 85c. black, gold and bistre 1·25 1·10
868 – 100c. black, yellow and red . . . . 1·10 1·25
DESIGNS: 85c. Portrait in oval frame; 100c. Eleanor Roosevelt with children.

220 Child Reading

221 Adult Flamingo and Chicks

1984. Child Welfare. Multicoloured.
869 45c.+20c. Type **220** . . . . 1·10 1·00
870 55c.+25c. Family reading . . 1·40 1·40
871 100c.+50c. Family in church 1·90 1·90

1985. Greater Flamingoes. Multicoloured.
873 25c. Type **221** 70 55
874 45c. Young flamingoes . . . 1·10 75
875 55c. Adult flamingoes . . . . 1·10 90
876 100c. Flamingoes in various flight positions . . . . . . 1·90 1·40

222 Symbols of Entered Apprentice

223 Players with Ball

1985. Bicentenary of De Vergenoeging Masonic Lodge, Curacao. Multicoloured.
877 45c. Type **222** . . . . 1·00 70
878 55c. Symbols of the Fellow Craft . . . . 1·10 1·00
879 100c. Symbols of the Master Mason . . . . 1·90 1·60

1985. Sports Funds. Football. Multicoloured.
880 10c.+5c. Type **223** 55 35
881 15c.+5c. Dribbling ball . . . 55 45
882 45c.+20c. Running with ball 1·10 1·00
883 55c.+25c. Tackling . . . . . 1·40 1·25
884 85c.+40c. Marking player with ball . . . . 1·90 1·75

224 Boy using Computer

1985. Cultural and Social Welfare Funds. International Youth Year. Multicoloured.
885 45c.+20c. Type **224** . . . . 1·25 1·10
886 55c.+25c. Girl listening to records . . . . 1·50 1·40
887 100c.+50c. Boy break-dancing . . . . 2·25 2·10

225 U.N. Emblem

1985. 40th Anniv of U.N.O.
888 **225** 55c. multicoloured . . . . 1·00 90
889 1g. multicoloured . . . . 1·50 1·40

226 Pierre Lauffer and Poem

227 Eskimo

1985. Papiamentu (Creole language). Multicoloured.
890 45c. Type **226** 55 55
891 55c. Wave inscribed "Papiamentu" 75 75

1985. Child Welfare. Multicoloured.
892 5c.+5c. Type **227** 35 20
893 10c.+5c. African child . . . 50 25
894 25c.+10c. Chinese girl 70 50
895 45c.+20c. Dutch girl . . . . 1·10 90
896 55c.+25c. Red Indian girl . . 1·25 1·10

228 "Calotropis procera"

229 Courthouse

1985. Flowers. Multicoloured.
898 5c. Type **228** 35 20
899 10c. "Capparis flexuosa" . . 35 20
900 20c. "Mimosa distachya" . . 55 35
901 45c. "Ipomoea nil" 90 65
902 55c. "Heliotropium ternatum" . . . . 1·10 70
903 150c. "Ipomoea incarnata" 1·90 1·60

1986. 125th Anniv of Curacao Courthouse. Multicoloured.
904 5c. Type **229** 25 20
905 15c. States room (vert) . . . 35 20
906 25c. Court room 55 35
907 55c. Entrance (vert) 90 70

230 Sprinting

231 Girls watching Artist at work

1986. Sports Funds. Multicoloured.
908 15c.+5c. Type **230** 90 45
909 25c.+10c. Horse racing . . . 1·10 70
910 45c.+20c. Motor racing . . . 1·40 1·00
911 55c.+25c. Football . . . . . 1·50 1·25

1986. Curacao Youth Care Foundation. Multicoloured.
912 30c.+15c. Type **231** 90 65
913 45c.+20c. Children watching sculptor at work . . . . . 1·10 80
914 55c.+25c. Children watching potter at work . . . . . . 1·40 1·10

232 Chained Man

1986. 25th Anniv of Amnesty International. Multicoloured.
915 45c. Type **232** 80 55
916 55c. Dove behind bars . . . 90 65
917 100c. Man behind bars . . . 1·40 1·10

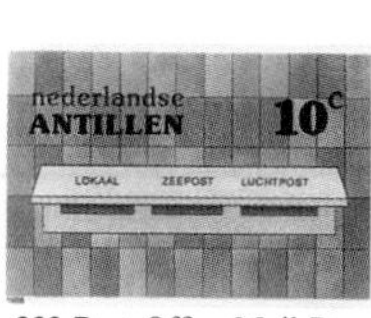

233 Post Office Mail Box

234 Boy playing Football

1986. Mail Boxes. Multicoloured.
918 10c. Type **233** 20 20
919 25c. Street mail box on pole 35 25
920 45c. Street mail box in brick column 65 55
921 55c. Street mail box 80 65

1986. Child Welfare. Multicoloured.
922 20c.+10c. Type **234** 55 50
923 25c.+15c. Girl playing tennis 70 55
924 45c.+20c. Boy practising judo 90 80
925 55c.+25c. Boy playing baseball . . . . 1·10 1·00

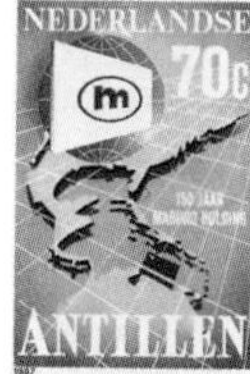

235 Brothers' First House and Mauritius Vliegendehond

236 Engagement Picture

1986. Centenary of Friars of Tilburg Mission. Multicoloured.
927 10c. Type **235** 30 20
928 45c. St. Thomas College and Mgr. Ferdinand E. C. Kieckens 75 55
929 55c. St. Thomas College courtyard and Fr. F.S. de Beer 85 70

1987. Golden Wedding of Princess Juliana and Prince Bernhard.
930 **236** 1g.35 orange, blk & gold 2·10 1·60

237 Map

238 Girls playing Instruments

1987. 150th Anniv of Maduro Holding Inc. Multicoloured.
932 70c. Type **237** 70 65
933 85c. Group activities 90 80
934 1g.55 Saloman Elias Levy Maduro (founder) . . . . 1·60 1·60

1987. Cultural and Social Relief Funds.
935 **238** 35c.+15c. multicoloured 70 65
936 – 45c.+25c. light green, green and blue . . . . 1·10 80
937 – 85c.+40c. multicoloured 1·40 1·25
DESIGNS: 45c. Woman pushing man in wheelchair. 85c. Bandstand.

239 Map and Emblem

1987. 50th Anniv of Curacao Rotary Club. Multicoloured.
938 15c. Type **239** 20 20
939 50c. Zeelandia country house (meeting venue) 65 55
940 65c. Emblem on map of Curacao 75 70

240 Octagon (house where Bolivar's sisters lived)

1987. 175th Anniv of Simon Bolivar's Exile on Curacao (60, 80c.) and 50th Anniv of Bolivarian Society (70, 90c.). Multicoloured.
941 60c. Type **240** 70 65
942 70c. Society headquarters, Willemstad, Curacao . . . 80 70
943 80c. Room in Octagon . . . 1·00 90
944 90c. Portraits of Manuel Carlos Piar, Simon Bolivar and Pedro Luis Brion . . . 1·10 1·00

241 Baby

1987. Child Welfare. Multicoloured.
945 40c.+15c. Type **241** . . . . 1·00 70
946 55c.+25c. Child . . . . . . 1·25 1·00
947 115c.+50c. Youth . . . . . 1·75 1·50

242 White-tailed Tropic Birds

1987. 25th Anniv of Netherlands Antilles National Parks Foundation. Multicoloured.
949 70c. Type **242** 70 65
950 85c. White-tailed deer 90 80
951 155c. Iguana . . . . 1·60 1·50

243 Printing Press and Type

1987. 175th Anniv of "De Curacaosche Courant" (periodical and printing shop). Multicoloured.
952 55c. Type **243** 70 55
953 70c. Keyboard and modern printing press 85 65

244 William Godden (founder)

1988. 75th Anniv of Curacao Mining Company. Multicoloured.
954 40c. Type **244** 70 45
955 105c. Phosphate processing plant . . . . 1·50 1·10
956 155c. Tafelberg (source of phosphate) . . . . 2·25 1·60

245 Flags, Minutes and John Horris Sprockel (first President)

246 Bridge through "100"

1988. 50th Anniv of Netherlands Antilles Staten (legislative body). Multicoloured.
957 65c. Type **245** 70 70
958 70c. Ballot paper and schematic representation of extension of voting rights 90 70
959 155c. Antilles and Netherlands flags and birds representing five Antilles islands and Aruba . . . . 1·60 1·40

1988. Cultural and Social Relief Funds. Centenary of Queen Emma Bridge, Curacao. Mult.
960 55c.+25c. Type **246** . . . . 1·10 65
961 115c.+55c. Willemstad harbour (horiz) . . . . . 1·75 1·40
962 190c.+60c. Leonard B. Smith (engineer) and flags (horiz) 2·75 2·50

247 Broken Chain

1988. 125th Anniv of Abolition of Slavery. Mult.
963 155c. Type **247** . . . . . . 1·50 1·40
964 190c. Breach in slave wall . . 1·75 1·40

248 Flags and Map

249 Charles Hellmund (Bonaire councillor)

1988. 3rd Inter-American Foundation of Cities "Let us Build Bridges" Conference, Curacao. Multicoloured.

965 80c. Type **248** . . . . 1·00 70
966 155c. Bridge and globe . . . 1·40 1·25

1988. Celebrities. Multicoloured.

967 55c. Type **249** 65 45
968 65c. Atthelo Maud Edwards-Jackson (founder of Saba Electric Company) 70 50
969 90c. Nicolaas Debrot (Governor of Antilles, 1962–69) . . . . 1·10 90
970 120c. William Charles de la Try Ellis (lawyer and politician) . . . . 1·25 1·10

250 Child watching Television

251 "Cereus hexagonus"

1988. Child Welfare. Multicoloured.

971 55c.+25c. Type **250** . . . . 1·00 65
972 65c.+30c. Boy with radio . . 1·10 90
973 115c.+55c. Girl using computer . . . . 1·60 1·40

1988. Cacti. Multicoloured.

975 55c. Type **251** 70 50
976 115c. Melocactus . . . . . . 1·25 90
977 125c. "Opuntia wentiana" . . 1·25 1·10

252 Magnifying Glass over 1936 and 1980 Stamps

253 Crested Bobwhite

1989. Cultural and Social Relief Funds. 50th Anniv of Curacao Stamp Association. Multicoloured.

978 30c.+10c. Type **252** 80 45
979 55c.+20c. Picking up stamp with tweezers (winning design by X. Rico in drawing competition) . . . 1·10 80
980 80c.+30c. Barn owl and stamp album . . . . . . 1·25 1·00

Nos. 978/80 were printed together, se-tenant, forming a composite design.

1989. 40th Anniv of Curacao Foundation for Prevention of Cruelty to Animals. Multicoloured.

981 65c. Type **253** 90 70
982 115c. Dogs and cats . . . . 1·25 1·10

254 "Sun Viking" in Great Bay Harbour, St. Maarten

255 Paula Clementina Dorner (teacher)

1989. Tourism. Cruise Liners. Multicoloured.

983 70c. Type **254** 90 70
984 155c. "Eugenio C" entering harbour, St. Annabay, Curacao . . . . 1·60 1·10

1989. Celebrities. Multicoloured.

985 40c. Type **255** 65 45
986 55c. John Aniseto de Jongh (pharmacist and politician) 70 50
987 90c. Jacobo Jesus Maria Palm (musician) . . . . . 1·00 80
988 120c. Abraham Mendes Chumaceiro (lawyer and social campaigner) . . . . 1·25 1·10

256 Boy and Girl under Tree

257 Hand holding "7"

1989. Child Welfare. Multicoloured.

989 40c.+15c. Type **256** 90 65
990 65c.+30c. Two children playing on shore . . . . . 1·10 90
991 115c.+35c. Adult carrying child . . . . 1·60 1·40

1989. 40th Anniv of Queen Wilhelmina Foundation for Cancer Care. Multicoloured.

993 30c. Type **257** 55 45
994 60c. Seated figure and figure receiving radiation treatment 80 70
995 80c. Figure exercising and Foundation emblem . . . 1·00 70

258 Fireworks

259 "Tephrosia cinerea"

1989. Christmas. Multicoloured.

997 30c. Type **258** 50 35
998 100c. Christmas tree decorations . . . . 1·10 90

1990. Flowers. Multicoloured.

999 30c. Type **259** 35 35
1000 55c. "Erithalis fruticosa" . . 65 55
1001 65c. "Evolvulus antillanus" 70 65
1002 70c. "Jacquinia arborea" . . 80 70
1003 125c. "Tournefortia onaphalodes" . . . . . . 1·40 1·40
1004 155c. "Sesuvium portulacastrum" . . . . 1·90 1·40

260 Girl Guides

261 Nun with Child, Flag and Map

1990. Cultural and Social Relief Funds. Mult.

1005 30c.+10c. Type **260** (60th anniv) 70 50
1006 40c.+15c. Totolika (care of mentally handicapped organization) (17th anniv) 90 70
1007 155c.+65c. Boy scout (60th anniv) . . . . 2·50 2·50

1990. Centenary of Arrival of Dominican Nuns in Netherlands Antilles. Multicoloured.

1008 10c. Type **261** 20 20
1009 55c. St. Rose Hospital and St. Martin's Home, St. Maarten 65 50
1010 60c. St. Joseph School, St. Maarten 70 65

262 Goal Net, Ball and Shield

263 Carlos Nicolaas-Perez (philologist and poet)

1990. Multicoloured.

1011 65c.+30c. Type **262** (65th anniv of Sport Unie Brion Trappers football club) . . 1·10 1·00
1012 115c.+55c. Guiding addict from darkness towards sun (anti-drugs campaign) 1·75 1·75

1990. Meritorious Antilleans. Multicoloured.

1013 40c. Type **263** 50 35
1014 60c. Evert Kruythoff (writer) 70 65
1015 80c. John de Pool (writer) 90 80
1016 150c. Joseph Sickman Corsen (poet and composer) . . . . 1·75 1·60

264 Queen Emma

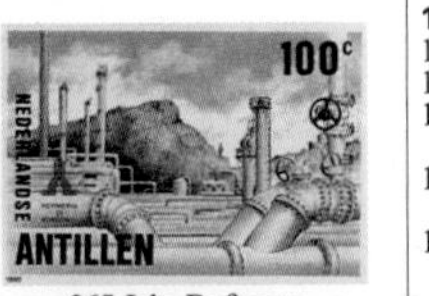

265 Isla Refinery

1990. Dutch Queens of the House of Orange. Multicoloured.

1017 100c. Type **264** . . . . . 1·40 1·10
1018 100c. Queen Wilhelmina . . 1·40 1·10
1019 100c. Queen Juliana . . . . 1·40 1·10
1020 100c. Queen Beatrix . . . . 1·40 1·10

1990. 75th Anniv of Oil Refining on Curacao.

1022 **265** 100c. multicoloured . . . 1·25 1·25

266 Flower and Bees

267 Parcels

1990. Child Welfare. International Literacy Year. Designs illustrating letters of alphabet. Multicoloured.

1023 30c.+5c. Type **266** 65 45
1024 55c.+10c. Dolphins and sun 1·00 70
1025 65c.+15c. Donkey with bicycle . . . . 1·10 90
1026 100c.+20c. Goat dreaming of house . . . . 1·50 1·75
1027 115c.+25c. Rabbit carrying food on yoke . . . . . 1·75 1·50
1028 155c.+55c. Lizard, moon and cactus . . . . 2·75 2·40

1990. Christmas. Multicoloured.

1029 30c. Type **267** (25th anniv of Curacao Lions Club's Good Neighbour project) 55 35
1030 100c. Mother and child . . 1·40 1·10

268 Flag, Map and Distribution of Mail

269 Scuba Diver and French Grunt

1991. 6th Anniv of Express Mail Service.

1031 **268** 20g. multicoloured . . . 23·00 22·00

1991. Fishes. Multicoloured.

1032 10c. Type **269** 35 20
1033 40c. Spotted trunkfish . . . 65 45
1034 55c. Copper sweepers . . . 85 70
1035 75c. Skindiver and yellow goatfishes . . . . . . 1·10 90
1036 100c. Black-barred soldier-fishes . . . . 1·50 1·25

270 Children and Stamps

1991. Cultural and Social Relief Funds. Mult.

1037 30c.+10c. Type **270** (12th anniv of Philatelic Club of Curacao) 70 55
1038 65c.+25c. St. Vincentius Brass Band (50th anniv) 1·25 1·10
1039 155c.+55c. Games and leisure pursuits (30th anniv of FESEBAKO) (Curacao community centres) . . . . 2·75 2·50

271 "Good Luck"

272 Westpoint Lighthouse, Curacao

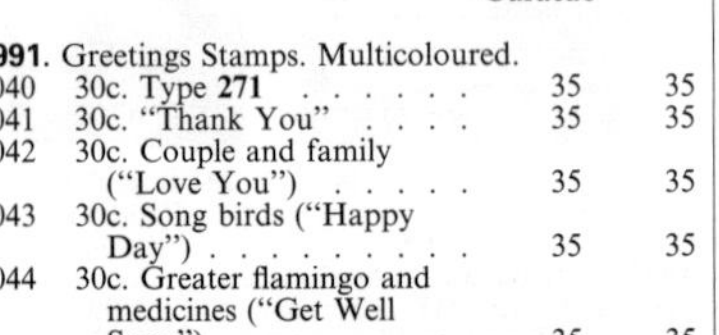

1991. Greetings Stamps. Multicoloured.

1040 30c. Type **271** 35 35
1041 30c. "Thank You" 35 35
1042 30c. Couple and family ("Love You") 35 35
1043 30c. Song birds ("Happy Day") 35 35
1044 30c. Greater flamingo and medicines ("Get Well Soon") 35 35

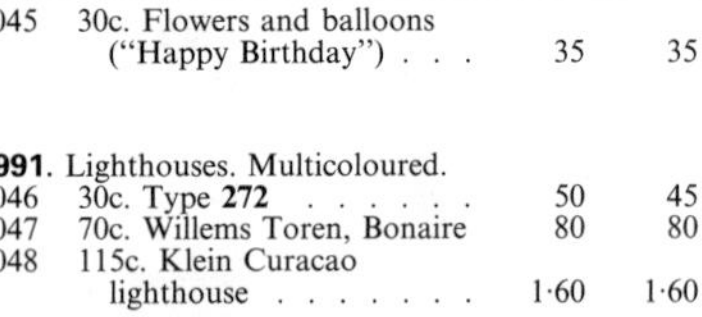

1045 30c. Flowers and balloons ("Happy Birthday") . . . 35 35

1991. Lighthouses. Multicoloured.

1046 30c. Type **272** 50 45
1047 70c. Willems Toren, Bonaire 80 80
1048 115c. Klein Curacao lighthouse . . . . 1·60 1·60

273 Peter Stuyvesant College

1991. 50th Anniv of Secondary Education in Netherlands Antilles (65c.) and "Espamer '91" Spain–Latin America Stamp Exhibition, Buenos Aires (125c.). Multicoloured.

1049 65c. Type **273** 70 70
1050 125c. Dancers of Netherlands Antilles, Argentina and Portugal (vert) . . . . 1·40 1·40

274 Octopus with Letters and Numbers

275 Nativity

1991. Child Welfare. Multicoloured.

1051 40c.+15c. Type **274** 90 70
1052 65c.+30c. Parents teaching arithmetic . . . . 1·40 1·25
1053 155c.+65c. Bird and tortoise with clock . . . . 2·75 2·75

1991. Christmas. Multicoloured.

1055 30c. Type **275** 35 35
1056 100c. Angel appearing to shepherds . . . . 1·10 1·10

276 Joseph Alvarez Correa (founder) and Headquarters of S.E.L. Maduro and Sons

277 Fawn

1991. 75th Anniv of Maduro and Curiel's Bank. Multicoloured.

1057 30c. Type **276** 65 50
1058 70c. Lion rampant (bank's emblem) and "75" . . . 1·10 90
1059 155c. Isaac Haim Capriles (Managing Director, 1954–74) and Scharloo bank branch . . . . . . 1·90 1·75

1992. The White-tailed Deer. Multicoloured.

1060 5c. Type **277** (postage) . . . 20 20
1061 10c. Young adults 25 20
1062 30c. Stag 50 35
1063 40c. Stag and hind in water 65 45
1064 200c. Stag drinking (air) . . 2·40 2·40
1065 355c. Stag calling . . . . . 4·25 4·00

278 Windsurfer

280 "Santa Maria"

1992. Cultural and Social Relief Funds. Olympic Games, Barcelona. Multicoloured.

1066 30c.+10c. Type **278** (award of silver medal to Jan Boersma, 1988 Games) . . 74 55
1067 55c.+25c. Globe, national flag and Olympic rings . . 1·10 90
1068 115c.+55c. Emblem of National Olympic Committee (60th anniv) 2·10 2·00

Nos. 1066/8 were issued together, se-tenant, forming a composite design.

1992. "World Columbian Stamp Expo '92", Chicago. Multicoloured.

1070	250c. Type **280**	3·00	2·75
1071	500c. Chart and Columbus	5·75	5·50

281 View of Dock and Town **282** Angela de Lannoy-Willems

1992. Curacao Port Container Terminal. Mult.

1072	80c. Type **281**	90	90
1073	125c. Crane and ship	1·40	1·40

1992. Celebrities.

1074	**282** 30c. black, brown & grn	35	35
1075	– 40c. black, brown & blue	55	45
1076	– 55c. black, brown & orge	70	65
1077	– 70c. black, brown and red	80	70
1078	– 100c. black, brown & blue	1·10	1·10

DESIGNS: 30c. Type **282** (first woman Member of Parliament); 40c. Lodewijk Daniel Gerharts (entrepreneur on Bonaire); 55c. Cyrus Wilberforce Wathey (entrepreneur on St. Maarten); 70c. Christian Winkel (Deputy Governor of Antilles); 100c. Mother Joseph (founder of Roosendaal Congregation (Franciscan welfare sisterhood)).

283 Spaceship **284** Queen Beatrix and Prince Claus

1992. Child Welfare. Multicoloured.

1079	30c.+10c. Type **283**	55	45
1080	70c.+30c. Robot	1·10	1·10
1081	100c.+40c. Extra-terrestrial being	1·60	1·50

1992. 12½ Years since Accession to the Throne of Queen Beatrix (100c.) and Royal Visit to Netherlands Antilles (others). Designs showing photos of previous visits to the Antilles. Multi.

1083	70c. Type **284**	80	80
1084	100c. Queen Beatrix signing book	1·10	1·10
1085	175c. Queen Beatrix and Prince Claus with girl	1·90	1·90

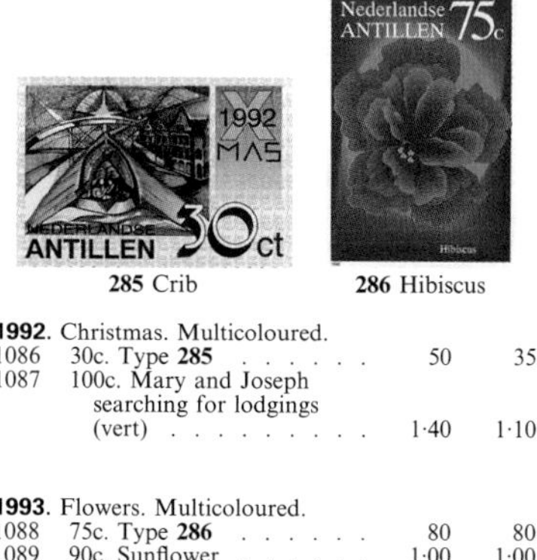

285 Crib **286** Hibiscus

1992. Christmas. Multicoloured.

1086	30c. Type **285**	50	35
1087	100c. Mary and Joseph searching for lodgings (vert)	1·40	1·10

1993. Flowers. Multicoloured.

1088	75c. Type **286**	80	80
1089	90c. Sunflower	1·00	1·00
1090	175c. Ixora	1·90	1·90
1091	195c. Rose	2·25	2·25

287 De Havilland Twin Otter and Flight Paths

288 Pekingese

1993. Anniversaries. Multicoloured.

1092	65c. Type **287** (50th anniv of Princess Juliana International Airport, St. Maarten)	70	70
1093	75c. Laboratory worker and National Health Laboratory (75th anniv)	80	80
1094	90c. De Havilland Twin Otter on runway at Princess Juliana International Airport	1·00	1·00
1095	175c. White and yellow cross (50th anniv of Princess Margriet White and Yellow Cross Foundation for District Nursing)	1·90	1·90

1993. Dogs. Multicoloured.

1096	65c. Type **288**	80	70
1097	90c. Standard poodle	1·10	1·00
1098	100c. Pomeranian	1·25	1·10
1099	175c. Papillon	2·00	1·90

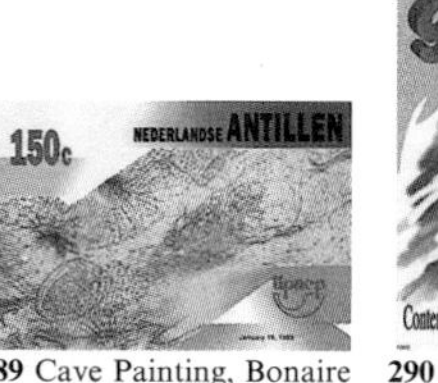

289 Cave Painting, Bonaire

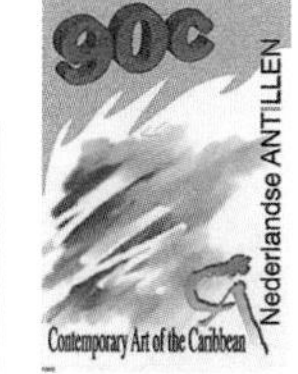

290 "Sun and Sea"

1993. "Brasiliana '93" International Stamp Exhibition, Rio de Janeiro, and Admittance of Antilles to Postal Union of the Americas, Spain and Portugal. Multicoloured.

1100	150c. Type **289**	1·60	1·60
1101	200c. Exhibition emblem and Antilles flag	2·10	2·10
1102	250c. Globe and hand signing U.P.A.E.P. agreement	2·75	2·75

1993. "Carib-Art" Exhibition, Curacao. Multicoloured.

1103	90c. Type **290**	1·00	1·00
1104	150c. "Heaven and Earth"	1·60	1·60

291 "Safety in the Home"

1993. Child Welfare. Child and Danger. Mult.

1105	65c.+25c. Type **291**	1·10	1·00
1106	90c.+35c. Child using seat belt ("Safety in the Car") (vert)	1·40	1·40
1107	175c.+75c. Child wearing armbands ("Safety in the Water")	2·75	2·75

292 Consulate, Curacao

293 "Mother and Child" (mosaic)

1993. Bicentenary of United States Consul General to the Antilles. Multicoloured.

1109	65c. Type **292**	80	70
1110	90c. Arms of Netherlands Antilles and U.S.A	1·10	1·00
1111	175c. American bald eagle	2·00	1·90

1993. Christmas. Works by Lucila Engels-Boskaljon. Multicoloured.

1112	30c. Type **293**	40	30
1113	115c. "Madonna and Christ" (painting)	1·25	1·25

294 Basset Hound

295 Common Caracara

1994. Dogs. Multicoloured.

1114	65c. Type **294**	95	75
1115	75c. Pit bull terrier	1·10	80
1116	90c. Cocker spaniel	1·25	1·00
1117	175c. Chow-chow	2·10	1·90

1994. Birds. Multicoloured.

1118	50c. Type **295**	90	55
1119	95c. Green peafowl	1·50	1·25
1120	100c. Scarlet macaw	1·40	1·25
1121	125c. Troupial	1·75	1·40

296 Joseph Husurell Lake

297 Players' Legs

1994. Celebrities. Multicoloured.

1122	65c. Type **296** (founder of United People's Liberation Front)	70	70
1123	75c. Efrain Jonckheer (politician and diplomat)	90	80
1124	100c. Michiel Martinus Romer (teacher)	1·10	1·10
1125	175c. Carel Nicolaas Winkel (social reformer)	2·00	1·90

1994. World Cup Football Championship, U.S.A. Multicoloured.

1126	90c. Type **297**	1·10	1·00
1127	150c. Foot and ball	1·75	1·60
1128	175c. Referee's whistle and cards	2·00	1·90

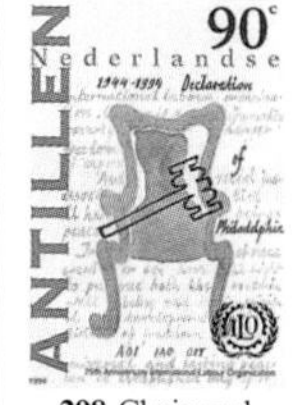

298 Chair and Hammer

299 Birds and Dolphin

1994. 75th Anniv of International Labour Organization. Multicoloured.

1129	90c. Type **298**	1·25	1·10
1130	110c. Heart and "75"	1·40	1·25
1131	200c. Tree	2·50	2·50

1994. Nature Protection. Multicoloured.

1132	10c. Type **299**	30	30
1133	35c. Dolphin, magnificent frigate bird, brown pelican and troupial	50	50
1134	50c. Coral, iguana, lobster and fish	65	65
1135	125c. Fish, turtle, queen conch, greater flamingoes and American wigeons	1·60	1·60

300 1945 7½c. Netherlands Stamp

301 Mother and Child

1994. "Fepapost '94" European Stamp Exhibition, The Hague. Multicoloured.

1137	2g.50 Type **300**	2·75	2·50
1138	5g. Curacao 1933 6c. stamp	5·50	5·25

1994. Child Welfare. International Year of the Family. Multicoloured.

1140	35c.+15c. Type **301**	60	50
1141	65c.+25c. Father and daughter reading together	1·25	1·10
1142	90c.+35c. Grandparents	2·10	2·00

302 Dove in Hands

1994. Christmas. Multicoloured.

1144	30c. Type **302**	50	35
1145	115c. Globe and planets in hands	1·50	1·25

303 Carnival and Houses

304 Handicapped and Able-bodied Children

1995. Carnival. Multicoloured.

1146	125c. Type **303**	1·50	1·40
1147	175c. Carnival and harbour	2·10	1·90
1148	250c. Carnival and rural house	3·00	2·75

1995. 50th Anniv of Mgr. Verriet Institute (for the physically handicapped). Multicoloured.

1149	65c. Type **304**	80	70
1150	90c. Cedric Virginie (wheelchair-bound bookbinder)	1·10	1·00

305 Dobermann

1995. Dogs. Multicoloured.

1151	75c. Type **305**	1·10	85
1152	85c. German shepherd	1·25	1·00
1153	100c. Bouvier	1·40	1·10
1154	175c. St. Bernard	2·40	1·90

306 Bonaire

1995. Flags and Arms of the Constituent Islands of the Netherlands Antilles. Multicoloured.

1155	10c. Type **306**	20	10
1156	35c. Curacao	50	35
1157	50c. St. Maarten	70	55
1158	65c. Saba	90	70
1159	75c. St. Eustatius (also state flag and arms)	1·00	80
1160	90c. Island flags and state arms	1·10	1·00

307 Monument to Slave Revolt of 1795

309 Sealpoint Siamese

1995. Cultural and Social Relief Funds. Bicentenary of Abolition of Slavery in the Antilles (1161/2) and Children's Drawings on Philately (1163/4). Multicoloured.

1161	30c.+10c. Type **307**	55	50
1162	45c.+15c. Magnificent frigate bird and slave bell	70	65
1163	65c.+25c. "Stamps" from Curacao and Bonaire (Nicole Wever and Sabine Anthonio)	1·10	1·00
1164	75c.+35c. "Stamps" from St. Maarten, St. Eustatius and Saba (Chad Jacobs, Martha Hassell and Dion Humphreys)	1·25	1·10

1995. Hurricane Relief Fund. Nos. 831, 833 and 838 surch **ORKAAN LUIS** and premium.

1165	65c.+65c. multicoloured	1·60	1·50
1166	75c.+75c. multicoloured	1·75	1·60
1167	1g.+1g. multicoloured	2·40	2·10

1995. Cats. Multicoloured.

1168	25c. Type **309**	50	30
1169	60c. Maine coon	90	65
1170	65c. Silver Egyptian mau	1·00	75
1171	90c. Angora	1·25	1·00
1172	150c. Blue smoke Persian	2·00	1·60

310 Helping Elderly Woman across Road

1995. Child Welfare. Children and Good Deeds. Multicoloured.

1173	35c.+15c. Type **310**	60	55
1174	65c.+25c. Reading newspaper to blind person	1·10	1·00
1175	90c.+35c. Helping younger brother	1·40	1·25
1176	175c.+75c. Giving flowers to the sick	2·75	2·50

311 Wise Men on Camels

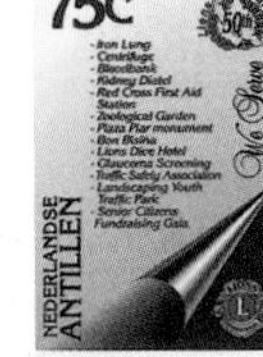

312 Serving the Community

1995. Christmas. Multicoloured.

1177	30c. Type **311**	50	35
1178	115c. Fireworks over houses	1·40	1·25

1996. 50th Anniv of Curacao Lions Club. Multicoloured.

1179	75c. Type **312**	1·10	80
1180	105c. Anniversary emblem	1·40	1·25
1181	250c. Handshake	3·25	2·75

313 Disease on Half of Leaf

314 Dish Aerial and Face

1996. 60th Anniv of Capriles Psychiatric Clinic, Otrabanda on Rif. Multicoloured.

1182	60c. Type **313**	70	65
1183	75c. Tornado and sun over house	1·10	80

1996. Centenary of Guglielmo Marconi's Patented Wireless Telegraph. Multicoloured.

1184	85c. Type **314**	1·00	90
1185	175c. Dish aerial and morse transmitter	2·10	1·90

315 Letters and Buildings

316 Gulf Fritillary

1996. Translation of Bible into Papiamentu (Creole language). Multicoloured.

1186	85c. Type **315**	1·00	90
1187	225c. Bible and alphabets	2·75	2·40

1996. "Capex '96" International Stamp Exhibition, Toronto, Canada. Butterflies. Multicoloured.

1188	5c. Type **316**	20	10
1189	110c. "Callithea philotima"	1·25	1·10
1190	300c. Clipper	3·50	3·25
1191	750c. "Euphaedra francina"	8·75	8·25

317 Mary Johnson-Hassell (introducer of drawn-thread work to Saba, 57th death)

1996. Anniversaries.

1193 **317**	40c. orange and black on grey	60	50
1194 –	50c. green and black on grey	70	55
1195 –	75c. red and black on grey	1·00	80
1196 –	80c. blue and black on grey	1·10	1·00

DESIGNS: 40c. Type **317** (introducer of drawn-thread work to Saba); 50c. Cornelius Marten (Papa Cornes) (pastor to Bonaire); 75c. Phelippi Chakutoe (union leader); 85c. Chris Engels (physician, artist, author and fencing champion).

318 Shire

1996. Horses. Multicoloured.

1197	110c. Type **318**	1·50	1·25
1198	225c. Shetland ponies	2·75	2·50
1199	275c. British thoroughbred	2·25	3·00
1200	350c. Przewalski mare and foal	4·50	4·00

319 Street Child and Shanty Town

320 Straw Hat with Poinsettias and Gifts

1996. Child Welfare. 50th Anniv of U.N.I.C.E.F. Multicoloured.

1201	40c.+15c. Type **319**	70	65
1202	75c.+25c. Asian child weaver	1·25	1·10
1203	110c.+45c. Child in war zone of former Yugoslavia (vert)	1·90	1·75
1204	225c.+100c. Impoverished Caribbean mother and child (vert)	3·75	3·50

1996. Christmas. Multicoloured. Self-adhesive.

1205	35c. Type **320**	60	35
1206	150c. Father Christmas	2·00	1·60

321 Emblem

322 Deadly Galerina

1997. Cultural and Social Relief Funds.

1207 **321**	40c.+15c. black and yellow	70	65
1208 –	75c.+30c. blue, mauve and black	1·25	1·10
1209 –	85c.+40c. red and black	1·60	1·50
1210 –	110c.+50c. black, green and red	1·90	1·90

DESIGNS: 40c. Type **321** (50th anniv of Curacao Foundation for Care and Resettlement of Ex-prisoners); 75c. Emblem (60th anniv (1996) of General Union of Public Servants (ABVO)); 85c. Flag of Red Cross (65th anniv of Curacao division); 110c. National Red Cross emblem (65th anniv of Curacao division).

1997. Fungi. Multicoloured.

1211	40c. Type **322**	60	50
1212	50c. Destroying angel	75	55
1213	75c. Cep	1·10	80
1214	175c. Fly agaric	2·25	1·90

323 Budgerigars

1997. Birds. Multicoloured.

1215	5c. Type **323**	25	10
1216	25c. Sulphur-crested cockatoo	70	30
1217	50c. Yellow-shouldered Amazon	95	55
1218	75c. Purple heron	1·10	80
1219	85c. Ruby topaz hummingbird	1·40	90
1220	100c. South African crowned crane	1·60	1·10
1221	110c. Vermilion flycatcher	1·75	1·10
1222	125c. Greater flamingo	1·75	1·40
1223	200c. Osprey	2·50	2·25
1224	225c. Keel-billed toucan	3·00	2·50

324 Parrots ("Love")

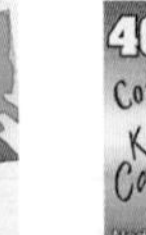

325 "Correspondence"

1997. Greetings Stamps. Multicoloured. (a) As T **324**.

1225	40c. Type **324**	50	45
1226	75c. Waterfall ("Positivism")	95	80
1227	85c. Roses ("Mothers' Day")	1·10	1·00
1228	100c. Quill pen ("Correspondence")	1·25	1·10
1229	110c. Leaves, rainbow and heart ("Success")	1·40	1·25
1230	225c. Ant on flower ("Congratulations")	2·75	2·50

(b) As T **325**.

1231	40c. Motif as in Type **324**	80	80
1232	40c. Type **325**	80	80
1233	75c. Petals and moon ("Positivism")	1·10	1·10
1234	75c. Motif as No. 1226	1·10	1·10
1235	75c. Sun and moon ("Success")	1·10	1·10
1236	85c. Motif as No. 1227	1·10	1·10
1237	100c. Motif as No. 1228	1·60	1·40
1238	110c. Motif as No. 1229	1·40	1·40
1239	110c. Heart between couple ("Love")	1·40	1·25
1240	225c. Motif as No. 1230	3·25	3·25

326 Rat

327 2½ Cent Coin (Plaka)

1997. "Pacific '97" International Stamp Exhibition, San Francisco. Chinese Zodiac. Designs showing Tangram (puzzle) representations and Chinese symbols for each animal. Multicoloured.

1241	5c. Type **326**	15	10
1242	5c. Ox	15	10
1243	5c. Tiger	15	10
1244	40c. Rabbit	60	50
1245	40c. Dragon	60	50
1246	40c. Snake	60	50
1247	75c. Horse	1·00	80
1248	75c. Goat	1·00	80
1249	75c. Monkey	1·00	80
1250	100c. Rooster	1·25	1·10
1251	100c. Dog	1·25	1·10
1252	100c. Pig	1·25	1·10

1997. Coins. Obverse and reverse of coins. Multicoloured.

1254	85c. Type **327**	1·25	1·00
1255	175c. 5 cent (Stuiver)	2·10	2·00
1256	225c. 2½ gulden (Fuerte)	3·25	2·50

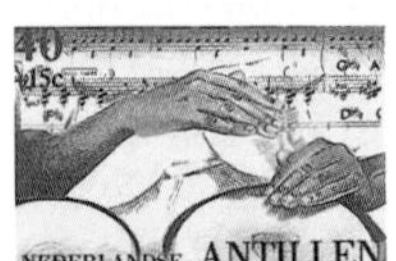

328 Score of "Atras de Nos" and Salsa Drummer

1997. Child Welfare. The Child and Music. Multicoloured.

1257	40c.+15c. Type **328**	65	60
1258	75c.+25c. Score of "For Elise" and pianist	1·10	1·00
1259	110c.+45c. Score of "Blues for Alice" and flautist	1·90	1·75
1260	225c.+100c. Score of "Yesterday" and guitarist	2·75	2·50

329 Nampu Grand Bridge, Shanghai

330 Worshippers (detail of mural by Marcolino Maas in Church of the Holy Family, Willemstad, Curacao)

1997. "Shanghai 1997" International Stamp and Coin Exhibition, China. Multicoloured.

1261	15c. Type **329**	20	20
1262	40c. Giant panda	70	55
1263	75c. Tiger (New Year) (vert)	1·10	90

1997. Christmas and New Year. Multicoloured.

1265	35c. Type **330**	60	40
1266	150c. Popping champagne cork and calendar (New Year)	2·00	1·60

331 Partial Eclipse

332 Camera and Painting

1998. Total Solar Eclipse, Curacao. Multicoloured.

1267	85c. Type **331**	1·10	1·00
1268	110c. Close-up of sun in total eclipse	1·60	1·25
1269	225c. Total eclipse	3·00	2·76

1998. Cultural and Social Relief Funds. Mult.

1271	40c.+15c. Type **332** (50th anniv of Curacao Museum)	70	65
1272	40c.+15c. Desalination plant and drinking water (70 years of seawater desalination)	70	65
1273	75c.+25c. Mangrove roots and shells (Lac Cai wetlands, Bonaire) (vert)	1·40	1·10
1274	85c.+40c. Lake and underwater marine life (Little Bonaire wetlands) (vert)	1·75	1·60

333 Salt Deposit, Dead Sea

334 Superior, 1923, and Elias Moreno Brandao

1998. "Israel 98" International Stamp Exhibition, Tel Aviv. Multicoloured.

1275	40c. Type **333**	45	45
1276	75c. Zion Gate, Jerusalem	90	80
1277	110c. Masada	1·25	1·10

1998. 75th Anniv of E. Moreno Brandao and Sons (car dealers). Chevrolet Motor Cars. Multicoloured.

1279	40c. Type **334**	1·60	1·00
1280	55c. Roadster, 1934	1·75	1·40
1281	75c. Styleline deluxe sedan, 1949	2·10	1·75
1282	110c. Bel Air convertible, 1957	3·25	2·50
1283	225c. Corvette Stingray coupe, 1963	5·50	5·25
1284	500c. Chevelle SS-454 2-door hardtop, 1970	13·50	12·00

335 State Flag and Arms

336 Christina Flanders (philanthropic worker)

1998. 50th Anniv of Netherlands Antilles Advisory Council. Multicoloured.

1285	75c. Type **335**	90	80
1286	85c. Gavel	1·00	95

1998. Death Anniversaries. Multicoloured.

1287	40c. Type **336** (second anniv)	50	45
1288	75c. Abraham Jesurun (writer and first president of Curacao Chamber of Commerce, 80th anniv)	95	80
1289	85c. Capt. Gerrit Newton (seaman and shipyard manager, 50th anniv (1999))	1·00	95
1290	110c. Eduardo Adriana (sportsman, first anniv)	1·40	1·10

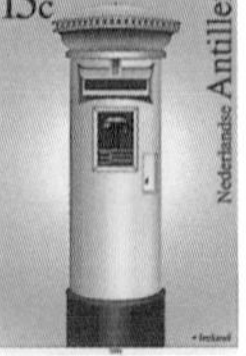

337 Ireland Pillar Box

338 Globe and New Post Emblem

1998. Postboxes (1st series). Multicoloured.

1291	15c. Type **337**	25	15
1292	40c. Nepal postbox	60	45
1293	75c. Uruguay postbox	1·00	80
1294	85c. Curacao postbox	1·00	1·00

See also Nos. 1413/16.

1998. Privatization of Postal Services.

1295 **338**	75c. black, blue and red	90	80
1296 –	110c. multicoloured	1·40	1·10
1297 –	225c. multicoloured	2·50	2·40

DESIGNS—VERT: 110c. Tree and binary code. HORIZ: 225c. 1949 25c. U.P.U. stamp, reproduction of No. 1296 and binary code.

339 Black Rhinoceros

1998. Endangered Species. Multicoloured.

1298	5c. Type **339**	40	10
1299	75c. White-tailed hawk (vert)	1·10	80
1300	125c. White-tailed deer	1·75	1·40
1301	250c. Tiger ("Tigris") (vert)	3·25	2·75

340 Short-finned Mako ("Mako Shark")

1998. Fishes. Multicoloured.

1302	275c. Type **340**	3·75	3·00
1303	350c. Manta ray	4·50	3·75

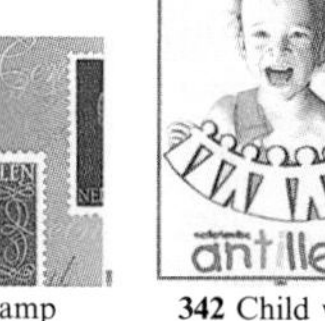

341 1950 5c. Stamp

342 Child with Family Paper Chain

1998. "70th Anniv of Dutch Stamp Dealers Club" Stamp Exhibition, The Hague. Multicoloured.

1304	225c. Type **341**	2·50	60
1305	500c. 1950 Queen Juliana 15c. stamp	5·50	5·50

1998. Child Welfare. Universal Rights of the Child. Multicoloured.

1307	40c.+15c. Type **342** (right to name and nationality)	65	60
1308	75c.+25c. Children eating water melons (right to health care)	1·10	1·00
1309	110c.+45c. Children painting (right of handicapped children to special care)	1·90	1·75
1310	225c.+100c. Children playing with can telephones (right to freedom of expression)	3·75	3·50

343 Former Office, Curacao

1998. 60th Anniv of PriceWaterhouseCoopers (accountancy firm). Multicoloured.

1311	75c. Type **343**	1·50	85
1312	225c. Modern office, Curacao	3·00	2·40

344 "Christmas Tree" (Theodora van Ierland)

345 Avila Beach Hotel and Dr. Pieter Maal (founder)

1998. Christmas. Children's Paintings. Multicoloured.

1313	35c. Type **344**	40	50
1314	150c. "Post in mail box" (Anna Sordam)	1·75	1·60

1999. 50th Anniv of Avila Beach Hotel. Mult.

1315	75c. Type **345**	1·00	80
1316	110c. Beach and flamboyant tree	1·40	1·25
1317	225c. Mesquite tree	2·75	2·40

346 Rabbit and Great Wall of China

347 Girls hugging and Wiri

1999. "China 1999" International Stamp Exhibition, Peking. Year of the Rabbit. Multicoloured.

1318	75c. Type **346**	60	80
1319	225c. Rabbit and Jade Pagoda (vert)	2·75	2·40

1999. 50th Anniv of Government Correctional Institute. Musical instruments. Multicoloured.

1321	40c. Type **347**	60	45
1322	75c. Institute building and bamba	1·00	80
1323	85c. Boy at lathe and triangle (horiz)	1·00	90

348 Launch of Ship

349 Godett

1999. 500th Anniv of First Written Record (by Amerigo Vespucci) of Curacao. Multicoloured.

1324	75c. Type **348**	1·10	80
1325	110c. Otrobanda, 1906	1·50	1·25
1326	175c. Nos. 1324/5 and anniversary emblem	2·25	2·00
1327	225c. Fort Beeckenburg, Caracasbaai	2·75	2·40
1328	500c. 1949 12½c. stamp and sailing ship	5·75	5·50

1999. Fourth Death Anniv of Wilson Godett (politician).

1329	**349** 75c. multicoloured	1·10	80

350 Amerindians and Old Map

1999. The Millennium. Multicoloured. (a) Size 35½ × 35½ mm. Ordinary gum.

1330	5c. Type **350** (arrival of Alonso de Ojeda, Amerigo Vespucci and Juan de la Cosa, 1499)	40	40
1331	10c. Dutch ship, indian and soldier on horseback (Dutch conquest, 1634)	40	40
1332	40c. Flags of constituent islands of Netherlands Antilles, Autonomy Monument in Curacao and document granting autonomy, 1954	60	60
1333	75c. Telephone and Curacao 1873 25c. King William III stamp (installation of telephones on Curacao, 1892)	1·00	1·00
1334	85c. Fokker F.XVIII airplane "De Snip" (first Amsterdam–Curacao flight, 1934)	1·10	1·10
1335	100c. Oil refinery, Curacao (inauguration, 1915)	1·10	1·10
1336	110c. Dish aerial, undersea fibre optic cable and dolphins (telecommunications)	1·40	1·40
1337	125c. Curacao harbour, bridge and bow of cruise liner (tourism)	1·75	1·75
1338	225c. Ka'i orgel (musical instrument) and couple in folk costume (culture)	2·75	2·75
1339	350c. Brown-throated conure, common caracara, yellow-shouldered amazon and greater flamingoes (nature)	4·25	4·25

(b) Size 29 × 29 mm. Self-adhesive.

1340	5c. Type **350**	40	40
1341	10c. As No. 1331	40	40
1342	40c. As No. 1332	60	60
1343	75c. As No. 1333	1·00	1·00
1344	85c. As No. 1334	1·10	1·10
1345	100c. As No. 1335	1·10	1·10
1346	110c. As No. 1336	1·40	1·40
1347	125c. As No. 1337	1·75	1·75
1348	225c. As No. 1338	2·75	2·75
1349	350c. As No. 1339	4·25	4·25

351 Ijzerstraat, Otrobanda

1999. Cultural and Social Relief Funds. Willemstad, World Heritage Site. Multicoloured.

1350	40c.+15c. Type **351**	70	65
1351	75c.+30c. Oldest house in Punda (now Postal Museum) (vert)	1·40	1·10
1352	110c.+50c. "The Bridal Cake" (now Central National Archives), Scharloo	2·00	1·75

352 St. Paul's Roman Catholic Church, Saba

1999. Tourist Attractions. Multicoloured.

1357	150c. Type **352**	2·40	1·60
1359	250c. Greater flamingoes, Bonaire	3·25	2·75
1361	500c. Courthouse, St. Maarten	6·00	5·50

353 Basketball

1999. Child Welfare. Sports. Multicoloured.

1370	40c.+15c. Type **353**	1·00	65
1371	75c.+25c. Golf	1·60	1·10
1372	110c.+45c. Fencing	2·10	1·60
1373	225c.+100c. Tennis	4·25	3·50

354 *Saintpaulia ionantha*

1999. Flowers. Multicoloured.

1374	40c. Type **354**	80	80
1375	40c. *Gardenia jasminioides*	80	80
1376	40c. Allamanda	80	80
1377	40c. Bougainvillea	80	80
1378	75c. Strelitzia	1·00	1·00
1379	75c. Cymbidium	1·00	1·00
1380	75c. Phalaenopsis	1·00	1·00
1381	75c. *Cassia fistula*	1·00	1·00
1382	110c. Doritaenopsis	1·60	1·60
1383	110c. Guzmania	1·60	1·60
1384	225c. *Catharanthus roseus*	2·75	2·75
1385	225c. *Caralluma hexagona*	2·75	2·75

355 Children wearing Hats

356 Man, Baby and Building Blocks (Fathers' Day)

1999. Christmas. Multicoloured.

1386	35c. Type **355**	50	40
1387	150c. Clock face and islands	1·90	1·60

2000. Greetings Stamps. Multicoloured.

1388	40c. Type **356**	55	50
1389	40c. Women and globe (Mothers' Day)	55	50
1390	40c. Hearts and flowers (Valentine's Day)	55	50
1391	75c. Puppy and present ("Thank You")	95	90
1392	110c. Butterfly and vase of flowers (Special Occasions)	1·10	1·00
1393	150c. As No. 1389	2·25	2·10
1394	150c. As No. 1390	2·25	2·10
1395	225c. Hands and wedding rings (Anniversary)	2·75	2·75

357 Dragon

2000. Chinese New Year. Year of the Dragon.

1396	**357** 110c. multicoloured	1·10	1·00

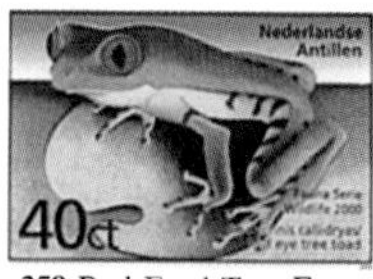

358 Red Eyed Tree Frog

2000. Endangered Animals. Multicoloured.

1398	40c. Type **358**	1·00	1·00
1399	75c. King penguin (vert)	1·60	1·60
1400	85c. Killer whale (vert)	1·60	1·60
1401	100c. African elephant (vert)	1·60	1·60
1402	110c. Chimpanzee (vert)	1·60	1·60
1403	225c. Tiger	3·00	3·00

359 Children playing

360 Space Shuttle Launch

2000. Cultural and Social Relief Funds. Mult.

1404	75c.+30c. Type **359**	1·00	95
1405	110c.+50c. Schoolchildren performing science experiments	2·10	2·00
1406	225c.+100c. Teacher giving lesson (vert)	3·75	3·75

2000. "World Stamp Expo 2000", Anaheim, California. Space Exploration. Multicoloured.

1407	75c. Type **360**	1·40	1·00
1408	225c. Astronaut, Moon and space station	3·00	3·00

361 Cycling

362 People

2000. Olympic Games, Sydney. Multicoloured.

1410	75c. Type **361**	1·10	1·10
1411	225c. Athletics	3·00	3·00

2000. Postboxes (2nd series). As T **337**. Multicoloured.

1413	110c. Mexico postbox	1·40	1·40
1414	175c. Dubai postbox	2·25	2·25
1415	350c. Great Britain postbox	4·25	4·25
1416	500c. United States of America postbox	6·00	6·00

2000. Social Insurance Bank. Multicoloured.

1417	75c. Type **362**	1·00	1·00
1418	110c. Adult holding child's hand (horiz)	1·40	1·40
1419	225c. Anniversary emblem	3·25	3·25

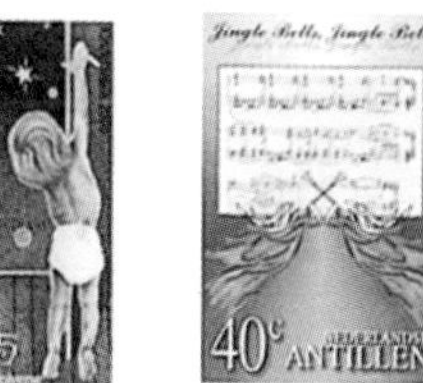

363 Child reaching towards Night Sky

364 Angels and Score of *Jingle Bells* (carol)

2000. Child Welfare. Multicoloured.

1420	40c.+15c. Type **363**	1·00	1·00
1421	75c.+25c. Children using Internet (horiz)	1·60	1·60
1422	110c.+45c. Children playing with toy boat (horiz)	2·40	2·40
1423	225c.+100c. Children consulting map	4·00	4·00

2000. Christmas. Multicoloured.

1424	40c. Type **364**	70	70
1425	150c. Seasonal messages in different languages (horiz)	2·10	2·10

365 Red King Snake **366** Forest

2001. Chinese New Year. Year of the Snake.

1426 **365**	110c. multicoloured	1·40	1·40

2001. "HONG KONG 2001" World Stamp Exhibition. Landscapes. Multicoloured.

1428	25c. Type **366**	55	55
1429	40c. Palm trees and waterfall	75	75
1430	110c. Spinner dolphins (*Stenella longirostris*)	1·25	1·25

367 Persian Shaded Golden Cat **368** *Mars* (Dutch ship of the line)

2001. Cats and Dogs. Multicoloured.

1431	55c. Type **367**	1·10	1·10
1432	75c. Burmese bluepoint cat and kittens	1·40	1·40
1433	110c. American wirehair	1·75	1·75
1434	175c. Golden retriever dog	2·10	2·10
1435	225c. German shepherd dog	3·00	3·00
1436	750c. British shorthair silver tabby	9·00	9·00

2001. Ships. Multicoloured.

1437	110c. Type **368**	1·40	1·40
1438	275c. *Alphen* (frigate)	3·50	3·50
1439	350c. *Curacao* (paddle-steamer) (horiz)	4·50	4·50
1440	500c. *Pioneer* (schooner) (horiz)	6·25	6·25

369 Pen and Emblem **370** Fedjai riding Bicycle

2001. 5th Anniv of Caribbean Postal Union. Multicoloured.

1441	75c. + 25c. Type **369**	75	75
1442	110c. + 45c. Emblem	1·10	1·10
1443	225c. + 100c. Silhouettes encircling globe	2·40	2·40

2001. Fedjai (cartoon postman) (1st series). Multicoloured.

1444	5c. Type **370**	10	10
1445	40c. Fedjai and children	30	25
1446	75c. Fedjai and post box containing bird's nest and chicks	55	45
1447	85c. Fedjai and elderly woman	60	50
1448	100c. Barking dog and Fedjai sitting on postbox	75	60
1449	110c. Fedjai and boy reading comic	80	65

See also Nos. 1487/90.

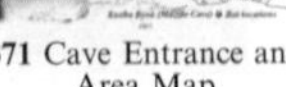

371 Cave Entrance and Area Map **372** Streamertail (*Trochilus polytmus*)

2001. Kueba Boza (Muzzle Cave). Multicoloured.

1450	85c. Type **371**	60	50
1451	110c. *Leptonycteris nivalis cursoae* (bat)	80	65
1452	225c. *Glosophaga elongata* (bat)	1·60	1·25

2001. Birds. Multicoloured.

1453	10c. Type **372**	10	10
1454	85c. Eastern white pelican (*Pelecanus onocrotalus*)	60	50
1455	110c. Gouldian finch (*Erythrura gouldiae*)	80	65
1456	175c. Painted bunting (*Passerina ciris*)	1·25	1·00
1457	250c. Atlantic puffin (*Fratercula artica*)	1·90	1·50
1458	350c. American darter (*Anhinga anhinga*)	2·50	2·00

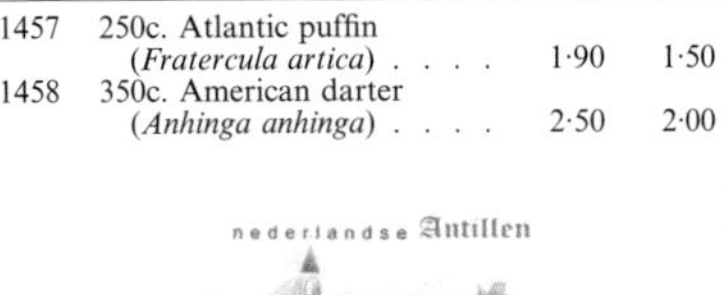

373 Chapel Facade and Map of St. Maarten Island

2001. 150th Anniv of Philipsburg Methodist Chapel. Multicoloured.

1459	75c. Type **373**	55	45
1460	110c. Rainbow, open Bible and map of St. Maarten	80	65

374 Boy feeding Toddler

2001. Child Welfare. Youth Volunteers. Multicoloured.

1461	40c. + 15c. Type **374**	40	35
1462	75c. + 25c. Girls dancing (vert)	75	60
1463	110c. + 45c. Boy and elderly woman (vert)	1·10	90

375 Children of Different Nations **376** Prince Willem-Alexander

2001. Christmas. Multicoloured.

1464	40c. Type **375**	30	25
1465	150c. Children and Infant Jesus (vert)	1·10	90

2002. Wedding of Crown Prince Willem-Alexander to Maxima Zorreguieta. Multicoloured.

1466	75c. Type **376**	55	45
1467	110c. Princess Maxima	80	65
MS1468	75 × 72 mm. 2g.25, Prince Willem-Alexander facing left; 2g.75, Princess Maxima facing left	3·75	3·75

377 Horse **378** Blue-tailed Emerald (*Chlorostilbon mellisugus*) and Passion Flower (*Passiflora foetida*)

2002. Chinese New Year. Year of the Horse. Multicoloured.

1469	25c. Type **377**	20	15
MS1470	52 × 86 mm. 95c. Horse's head	75	75

2002. Flora and Fauna. Multicoloured.

1471	50c. Type **378**	35	30
1472	95c. Lineated anole (*Anolis lineatus*) and *Cordia sebestena* (flower) (horiz)	65	55
1473	120c. Dragonfly (*Odonata*) (horiz)	90	75
1474	145c. Hermit crab (*Coenobita clypeatus*) (horiz)	1·10	90
1475	285c. Paper wasp (*Polistes versicolor*)	2·10	1·75

379 Flambeau (*Dryas julia*) **380** Flags as Football

2002. Butterflies. Multicoloured.

1480	25c. Type **379**	20	15
1481	145c. Monarch (*Danaus plexippus*) (horiz)	1·10	90
1482	400c. *Mechanitis polymnia* (horiz)	2·75	2·25
1483	500c. *Pyrrhopygopsis socrates* (wrongly inscr "Pyrhapygopsis socrates") (horiz)	3·50	2·75

2002. World Cup Football Championship, Japan and South Korea. Multicoloured.

1484	95c. + 35c. Type **380**	95	75
1485	145c. + 55c. Player and globe as football	1·50	1·25
1486	240c. + 110c. Player and ball	2·50	2·00

381 Fedjai skipping

2002. Fedjai (cartoon postman) (2nd series). Multicoloured.

1487	10c. Type **381**	10	10
1488	55c. Fedjai and dog in rubbish bin (vert)	40	35
1489	95c. Fedjai presenting envelope on tray (vert)	70	55
1490	240c. Fedjai helping elderly woman across road (vert)	90	70

POSTAGE DUE STAMPS

1952. As Type D **121** of Netherlands but inscr "NEDERLANDSE ANTILLEN".

D336	1c. green	10	10
D337	2½c. green	65	65
D338	5c. green	20	10
D339	6c. green	55	50
D340	7c. green	55	50
D341	8c. green	55	50
D342	9c. green	55	50
D343	10c. green	30	20
D344	12½c. green	30	20
D345	15c. green	35	30
D346	20c. green	35	50
D347	25c. green	55	10
D348	30c. green	1·25	1·50
D349	35c. green	1·60	1·50
D350	40c. green	1·25	1·50
D351	45c. green	1·50	1·50
D352	50c. green	1·25	1·25

PROVINCIAL STAMPS

The following stamps, although valid for postage throughout Netherlands, were only available from Post Offices within the province depicted and from the Philatelic Bureau.

V 1 Freisland

2002. Multicoloured.

V 1	39c. Type **V 1**	55	25
V 2	39c. Drenthe	55	25
V 3	39c. North Holland	55	25
V 4	39c. Gelderland	55	25
V 5	39c. North Brabant	55	25
V 6	39c. Groningen	55	25
V 7	39c. South Holland	55	25
V 8	39c. Utrecht	55	25
V 9	39c. Limburg	55	25
V10	39c. Zeeland	55	25
V11	39c. Flevoland	55	25
V12	39c. Overijssel	55	25

NETHERLANDS INDIES Pt. 4

A former Dutch colony, consisting of numerous settlements in the East Indies, of which the islands of Java and Sumatra and parts of Borneo and New Guinea are the most important. Renamed Indonesia in 1948, Independence was granted during 1949. Netherlands New Guinea remained a Dutch possession until 1962 when it was placed under U.N. control, being incorporated with Indonesia in 1963.

100 cents = 1 gulden.

1 King William III **2**

1864. Imperf.

1 **1**	10c. red	£325	£100

1868. Perf.

2 **1**	10c. red	£1000	£180

1870. Perf.

27 **2**	1c. green	5·50	3·50
28	2c. purple	£100	90·00
29	2c. brown	8·00	4·50
30	2½c. buff	45·00	23·00
12	5c. green	65·00	7·00
32	10c. brown	18·00	1·10
40	12½c. drab	5·25	2·50
34	15c. brown	23·00	2·50
5	20c. blue	£110	3·50
36	25c. purple	24·00	1·40
44	30c. green	40·00	4·50
17	50c. red	27·00	3·25
38	2g.50 green and purple	90·00	16·00

5 **6** Queen Wilhelmina

1883.

87 **5**	1c. green	1·40	20
88	2c. brown	1·40	20
89	2½c. buff	1·40	70
90	3c. purple	1·75	20
86	5c. green	45·00	26·00
91	5c. blue	14·00	20

1892.

94 **6**	10c. brown	7·00	40
95	12½c. grey	12·00	24·00
96	15c. brown	17·00	1·60
97	20c. blue	38·00	1·60
98	25c. purple	32·00	1·60
99	30c. green	48·00	2·00
100	50c. red	35·00	1·60
101	2g.50 blue and brown	£130	38·00

1900. Netherlands stamps of 1898 surch **NED.-INDIE** and value.

111 **13**	10c. on 10c. lilac	2·40	40
112	12½c. on 12½c. blue	3·00	80
113	15c. on 15c. brown	4·00	80
114	20c. on 20c. green	20·00	80
115	25c. on 25c. blue and pink	17·00	80
116	50c. on 50c. red and green	32·00	1·10
117 **11**	2½g. on 2½g. lilac	50·00	19·00

1902. Surch.

118 **5**	½ on 2c. brown	50	35
119	2½ on 3c. purple	55	50

11 **12**

13

1902.

120 **11**	½c. lilac	60	30
121	1c. olive	60	30
122	2c. brown	4·00	35
123	2½c. green	2·40	20
124	3c. orange	2·75	1·25
125	4c. blue	17·00	9·00
126	5c. red	6·00	20
127	7½c. grey	4·00	35
128 **12**	10c. slate	1·60	20
129	12½c. blue	2·00	20
130	15c. brown	9·75	2·10
131	17½c. bistre	4·00	30
132	20c. grey	2·00	1·50
133	20c. olive	27·00	25
134	22½c. olive and brown	4·75	30
135	25c. mauve	11·50	30
136	30c. brown	32·00	30
137	50c. red	25·00	30
138 **13**	1g. lilac	60·00	40
206	1g. lilac on blue	42·00	4·75
139	2½g. grey	70·00	1·60
207	2½g. grey on blue	60·00	26·00

1902. No. 130 optd with horiz bars.

140	15c. brown	2·00	70

1905. No. 132 surch **10 cent**.

141	10c. on 20c. grey	2·75	1·25

1908. Stamps of 1902 optd **JAVA**.

142	½c. lilac	35	20
143	1c. olive	60	30
144	2c. brown	2·50	2·50
145	2½c. green	1·50	20
146	3c. orange	1·10	1·00
147	5c. red	2·50	20
148	7½c. grey	2·00	1·75

149 10c. slate 1·00 20
150 12½c. blue 2·10 70
151 15c. brown 3·25 3·00
152 17½c. bistre 1·75 65
153 20c. olive 10·00 70
154 22½c. olive and brown 4·75 2·75
155 25c. mauve 4·75 30
156 30c. brown 28·00 2·50
157 50c. red 19·00 70
158 1g. lilac 45·00 3·00
159 2½g. grey 65·00 50·00

1908. Stamps of 1902 optd **BUITEN BEZIT**.
160 ½c. lilac 45 35
161 1c. olive 55 35
162 2c. brown 1·90 2·50
163 2½c. green 1·10 35
164 3c. orange 1·00 1·10
165 5c. red 3·10 50
166 7½c. grey 3·00 2·50
167 10c. slate 1·10 20
168 12½c. blue 9·75 2·25
169 15c. brown 4·50 2·50
170 17½c. bistre 2·10 1·75
171 20c. olive 8·75 2·10
172 22½c. olive and brown 6·25 4·50
173 25c. mauve 7·00 35
174 30c. brown 15·00 2·10
175 50c. red 7·00 80
176 1g. lilac 55·00 4·50
177 2½g. grey 85·00 55·00

19 **20**

1912.
208 **19** ½c. lilac 30 20
209 1c. green 30 20
210 2c. brown 55 20
264 2c. grey 55 20
211 2½c. green 1·40 20
265 2½c. pink 70 20
212 3c. brown 55 20
266 3c. green 1·10 20
213 4c. blue 1·10 20
267 4c. green 1·10 20
268 4c. bistre 9·00 4·00
214 5c. pink 1·25 20
269 5c. green 1·10 20
270 5c. blue 70 20
215 7½c. brown 70 20
271 7½c. bistre 70 20
216 **20** 10c. red 1·10 20
272 **19** 10c. lilac 1·75 20
217 **20** 12½c. blue 1·25 20
273 12½c. red 1·25 35
274 15c. blue 7·00 30
218 17½c. brown 1·25 20
219 20c. green 2·10 20
275 20c. blue 2·10 20
276 20c. orange 12·50 20
220 22½c. orange 2·10 75
221 25c. mauve 2·10 20
222 30c. grey 2·10 20
277 32½c. violet and orange 2·10 30
278 35c. brown 7·25 55
279 40c. green 2·75 20

21

1913.
223 **21** 50c. green 4·75 20
280 60c. blue 6·00 20
281 80c. orange 4·75 35
224 1g. brown 4·00 20
283 1g.75 lilac 20·00 1·75
225 2½g. pink 16·00 1·25

1915. Red Cross. Stamps of 1912 surch **+5 cts.** and red cross.
243 1c.+5c. green 5·50 5·50
244 5c.+5c. pink 5·50 5·50
245 10c.+5c. red 7·00 7·00

1917. Stamps of 1902, 1912 and 1913 surch.
246 ½c. on 2½c. (No. 211) 35 35
247 1c. on 4c. (No. 213) 35 55
250 12½c. on 17½c. (No. 218) 30 20
251 12½c. on 22½c. (No. 220) 35 20
248 17½c. on 22½c. (No. 134) 1·75 70
252 20c. on 22½c. (No. 220) 35 20
249 30c. on 1g. (No. 138) 6·25 1·75
253 32½c. on 50c. (No. 223) 1·00 20
254 40c. on 50c. (No. 223) 3·50 50
255 60c. on 1g. (No. 224) 5·75 35
256 80c. on 1g. (No. 224) 6·25 80

1922. Bandoeng Industrial Fair. Stamps of 1912 and 1917 optd **3de N. I. JAARBEURS BANDOENG 1922.**
285 1c. green 7·00 7·00
286 2c. brown 7·00 7·00
287 2½c. pink 55·00 60·00
288 3c. yellow 7·00 8·00
289 4c. blue 35 35
290 5c. green 12·50 10·00
291 7½c. brown 9·50 8·00
292 10c. lilac 65·00 80·00
293 12½c. on 22½c. orge (No. 251) 8·00 9·00
294 17½c. brown 5·50 7·00
295 20c. blue 7·00 7·00
Nos. 285/95 were sold at a premium for 3, 4, 5, 6, 8, 9, 10, 12½, 15, 20 and 22c. respectively.

33 **36** Fokker F.VIIa

1923. Queen's Silver Jubilee.
296 **33** 5c. green 35 35
297 12½c. red 35 35
298 20c. blue 70 35
299 50c. orange 2·50 90
300 1g. purple 4·25 60
301 2½g. grey 38·00 32·00
302 5g. brown £120 £110

1928. Air. Stamps of 1912 and 1913 surch **LUCHTPOST**, Fokker F.VII airplane and value.
303 10c. on 12½c. red 1·25 1·25
304 20c. on 25c. mauve 2·75 2·75
305 40c. on 80c. orange 2·10 2·10
306 75c. on 1g. sepia 1·10 1·10
307 1½g. on 2½g. red 7·25 7·25

1928. Air.
308 **36** 10c. purple 35 35
309 20c. brown 90 75
310 40c. red 1·10 75
311 75c. green 2·40 35
312 1g.50 orange 4·25 75

1930. Air. Surch **30** between bars.
313 **36** 30c. on 40c. red 1·10 40

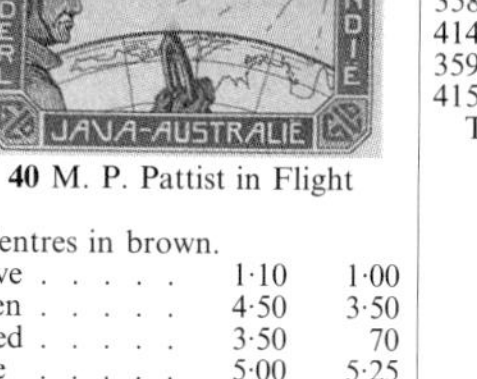

38 Watch-tower **40** M. P. Pattist in Flight

1930. Child Welfare. Centres in brown.
315 – 2c. (+1c.) mauve 1·10 1·00
316 **38** 5c. (+2½c.) green 4·50 3·50
317 – 12½c. (+2½c.) red 3·50 70
318 – 15c. (+5c.) blue 5·00 5·25
DESIGNS—VERT: 2c. Bali Temple. HORIZ: 12½c. Minangkabau Compound; 15c. Buddhist Temple, Borobudur.

1930. No. 275 surch **12½**.
319 12½c. on 20c. blue 80 20

1931. Air. 1st Java–Australia Mail.
320 **40** 1g. brown and blue 15·00 12·50

41

1931. Air.
321 **41** 30c. red 2·75 35
322 4½g. blue 9·00 2·75
323 7½g. green 11·50 3·50

42 Ploughing

1931. Lepers' Colony.
324 **42** 2c. (+1c.) brown 2·50 2·00
325 – 5c. (+2½c.) green 4·00 4·00
326 – 12½c. (+2½c.) red 3·25 65
327 – 15c. (+5c.) blue 7·75 6·75
DESIGNS: 5c. Fishing; 12½c. Native actors; 15c. Native musicians.

1932. Air. Surch **50** on Fokker F.VIIa/3m airplane.
328 **36** 50c. on 1g.50 orange 3·25 55

44 Plaiting Rattan

45 William of Orange

1932. Salvation Army. Centres in brown.
329 – 2c. (+1c.) purple 55 55
330 **44** 5c. (+2½c.) green 3·00 2·25
331 – 12½c. (+2½c.) red 90 35
332 – 15c. (+5c.) blue 4·25 3·50
DESIGNS: 2c. Weaving; 12½c. Textile worker; 15c. Metal worker.

1933. 400th Birth Anniv of William I of Orange.
333 **45** 12½c. red 1·60 40

46 Rice Cultivation

47 Queen Wilhelmina

1933.
335 **46** 1c. violet 30 20
397 2c. purple 10 40
337 2½c. bistre 30 20
338 3c. green 30 20
339 3½c. grey 30 20
340 4c. green 90 20
401 5c. blue 10 10
342 7½c. violet 1·10 20
343 10c. red 2·00 20
403 **47** 10c. red 10 10
334 12½c. brown 8·00 35
345 12½c. red 55 20
404 15c. blue 10 10
405 20c. purple 35 10
348 25c. green 2·10 20
349 30c. blue 3·50 20
350 32½c. bistre 9·00 8·25
408 35c. violet 5·00 1·50
352 40c. green 2·75 20
353 42½c. yellow 2·75 35
354 50c. blue 5·00 35
355 60c. blue 5·50 70
356 80c. red 7·00 1·10
357 1g. violet 8·75 35
358 1g.75 green 18·00 10·00
414 2g. green 25·00 12·50
359 2g.50 purple 21·00 1·75
415 5g. bistre 24·00 6·25
The 50c. to 5g. are larger, 30 × 30 mm.

48 Pander S.4 Postjager

1933. Air. Special Flights.
360 **48** 30c. blue 1·50 1·50

49 Woman and Lotus Blossom

53 Cavalryman and Wounded Soldier

1933. Y.M.C.A. Charity.
361 **49** 2c. (+1c.) brown & purple 70 45
362 – 5c. (+2½c.) brown and green 2·40 2·00
363 – 12½c. (+2½c.) brown & orge 2·75 30
364 – 15c. (+5c.) brown and blue 3·25 2·75
DESIGNS: 5c. Symbolizing the sea of life; 12½c. Y.M.C.A. emblem; 15c. Unemployed man.

1934. Surch.
365 **36** 2c. on 10c. purple 35 50
366 2c. on 20c. brown 35 30
367 **41** 2c. on 30c. red 35 65
368 **36** 42½c. on 75c. green 4·75 35
369 42½c. on 1g.50 orange 4·75 50

1934. Anti-tuberculosis Fund. As T **77** of Netherlands.
370 12½c. (+2½c.) brown 1·75 55

1935. Christian Military Home.
371 – 2c. (+1c.) brown and purple 1·75 1·25
372 **53** 5c. (+2½c.) brown and green 3·50 3·50
373 – 12½c. (+2½c.) brown & orge 3·50 30
374 – 15c. (+5c.) brown and blue 5·25 5·25
DESIGNS: 2c. Engineer chopping wood; 12½c. Artilleryman and volcano victim; 15c. Infantry bugler.

54 Dinner-time **55** Boy Scouts

1936. Salvation Army.
375 **54** 2c. (+1c.) purple 1·25 70
376 5c. (+2½c.) blue 1·50 1·25
377 7½c. (+2½c.) violet 1·50 1·60
378 12½c. (+2½c.) orange 1·50 40
379 15c. (+5c.) blue 2·50 2·40
Nos. 376/9 are larger, 30 × 27 mm.

1937. Scouts' Jamboree.
380 **55** 7½c. (+2½c.) green 1·00 95
381 12½c. (+2½c.) red 1·00 55

1937. Nos. 222 and 277 surch in figures.
382 10c. on 30c. slate 2·50 30
383 10c. on 32½c. violet and orange 2·75 35

59 Sifting Rice

62 Douglas DC-2 Airliner

1937. Relief Fund. Inscr "A.S.I.B.".
385 **59** 2c. (+1c.) sepia and orange 1·40 80
386 – 3½c. (+1½c.) grey 1·40 90
387 – 7½c. (+2½c.) green & orange 1·50 1·10
388 – 10c. (+2½c.) red and orange 1·50 30
389 – 20c. (+5c.) blue 1·40 1·40
DESIGNS: 3½c. Mother and children; 7½c. Ox-team ploughing rice-field; 10c. Ox-team and cart; 20c. Man and woman.

1938. 40th Anniv of Coronation. As T **87** of Netherlands.
390 2c. violet 10 10
391 10c. red 10 10
392 15c. blue 1·40 70
393 20c. red 70 35

1938. Air Service Fund. 10th Anniv of Royal Netherlands Indies Air Lines.
394 **62** 17½c. (+5c.) brown 90 90
395 – 20c. (+5c.) slate 90 90
DESIGN: 20c. As Type **62**, but reverse side of airliner.

63 Nurse and Child

1938. Child Welfare. Inscr "CENTRAAL MISSIE-BUREAU".
416 **63** 2c. (+1c.) violet 80 55
417 – 3½c. (+1½c.) green 1·25 1·10
418 – 7½c. (+2½c.) red 90 90
419 – 10c. (+2½c.) red 1·00 30
420 – 20c. (+5c.) blue 1·25 1·10
DESIGNS—(23 × 23 mm): Nurse with child suffering from injuries to eye (3½c.), arm (7½c.), head (20c.) and nurse bathing a baby (10c.).

63a Group of Natives

64 European Nurse and Patient

1939. Netherlands Indies Social Bureau and Protestant Church Funds.
421 – 2c. (+1c.) violet 30 30
422 – 3½c. (+1½c.) green 35 30
423 **63a** 7½c. (+2½c.) brown 35 30
424 – 10c. (+2½c.) red 1·60 1·00
425 **64** 10c. (+2½c.) red 1·60 90
426 – 20c. (+5c.) blue 55 50
DESIGNS—VERT: 2c. as Type **63a** but group in European clothes. HORIZ: 3½c., 10c. (No. 424) as Type **64**, but Native nurse and patient.

1940. Red Cross Fund. No. 345 surch **10+5 ct** and cross.
428 **47** 10c.+5c. on 12½c. red 3·50 55

68 Queen Wilhelmina **69** Netherlands Coat of Arms

1941. As T **94** of Netherlands but inscr "NED. INDIE" and T **68**.
429 – 10c. red 55 35
430 – 15c. blue 2·50 1·75
431 – 17½c. orange 1·00 70
432 – 20c. mauve 30·00 32·00
433 – 25c. green 40·00 42·00
434 – 30c. brown 4·50 1·40
435 – 35c. purple £160 £350
436 – 40c. green 12·00 3·50
437 – 50c. red 3·50 75
438 – 60c. blue 3·00 75
439 – 80c. red 3·00 75
440 – 1g. violet 3·00 75
441 – 2g. green 16·00 1·75
442 – 5g. bistre £300 £600
443 – 10g. green 42·00 18·00
444 **68** 25g. orange £250 £140
Nos 429/36 measure 18×23 mm, Nos. 431/43 20½×26 mm.

1941. Prince Bernhard Fund for Dutch Forces.
453 **69** 5c.+5c. blue and orange 75 15
454 10c.+10c. blue and red 75 15
455 1g.+1g. blue and grey 16·00 10·75

70 Doctor and Child **71** Wayangwong Dancer

1941. Indigent Mohammedans' Relief Fund.
456 **70** 2c. (+1c.) green 1·10 55
457 – 3½c. (+1½c.) brown 5·25 2·75
458 – 7½c. (+2½c.) violet 4·50 3·50
459 – 10c. (+2½c.) red 1·75 35
460 – 15c. (+5c.) blue 13·00 7·00
DESIGNS: 3½c. Native eating rice; 7½c. Nurse and patient; 10c. Nurse and children; 15c. Basket-weaver.

1941.
461 – 2c. red 30 15
462 – 2½c. purple 55 15
463 – 3c. green 55 35
464 **71** 4c. green 50 35
465 – 5c. blue 10 10
466 – 7½c. violet 55 10
DESIGNS (dancers): 2c. Menari; 2½c. Nias; 3c. Legon; 5c. Padjoge; 7½c. Dyak.
See also Nos. 514/16.

72 Paddyfield **73** Queen Wilhelmina

1945.
467 **72** 1c. green 55 15
468 – 2c. mauve 55 30
469 – 2½c. purple 55 15
470 – 5c. blue 35 15
471 – 7½c. olive 75 15
472 **73** 10c. brown 35 15
473 15c. blue 35 15
474 17½c. red 35 15
475 20c. purple 35 15
476 30c. grey 35 15
477 – 60c. grey 75 15
478 – 1g. green 1·10 15
479 – 2½g. orange 3·50 70
DESIGNS: As Type **72**: 2c. Lake in W. Java; 2½c. Medical School, Batavia; 5c. Seashore; 7½c. Douglas DC-2 airplane over Bromo Volcano. (30×30 mm): 60c. to 2½g. Portrait as Type **73** but different frame.

76 Railway Viaduct near Soekaboemi **81** Queen Wilhelmina

1946.
484 **76** 1c. green 30 20
485 – 2c. brown 30 20
486 – 2½c. red 30 20
487 – 5c. blue 30 20
488 – 7½c. blue 30 20
DESIGNS: 2c. Power station; 3c. Minangkabau house; 5c. Tondano scene (Celebes); 7½c. Buddhist Stupas, Java.

1947. Surch in figures.
502 – 3c. on 2½c. red (No. 486) 30 20
503 – 3c. on 7½c. blue (No. 488) 30 20
504 **76** 4c. on 1c. green 30 20
505 – 45c. on 60c. blue (No. 355) 1·40 95
No. 505 has three bars.

1947. Optd **1947**.
506 **47** 12½c. red 35 20
507 25c. green 35 20
508 – 40c. green (No. 436) 55 20
509 **47** 50c. blue 75 30
510 80c. red 1·10 65
511 – 2g. green (No. 441) 4·00 55
512 – 5g. brown (No. 442) 10·75 6·75

1948. Relief for Victims of the Terror. Surch **PELITA 15+10 Ct.** and lamp.
513 **47** 15c.+10c. on 10c. red 30 30

1948. Dancers. As T **71**.
514 3c. red (Menari) 35 20
515 4c. green (Legon) 35 20
516 7½c. brown (Dyak) 70 65

1948.
517 **81** 15c. orange 90 70
518 20c. blue 35 35
519 25c. green 35 35
520 40c. green 35 35
521 45c. mauve 55 70
522 50c. lake 50 35
523 80c. red 55 35
524 1g. violet 50 35
525 10g. green 30·00 12·50
526 25g. orange 60·00 50·00
Nos. 524/6 are larger, 21×26 mm.

1948. Queen Wilhelmina's Golden Jubilee. As T **81** but inscr "1898 1948".
528 15c. orange 40 30
529 20c. blue 40 30

1948. As T **126** of Netherlands.
530 15c. red 50 35
531 20c. blue 50 35

MARINE INSURANCE STAMPS

1921. As Type M **22** of the Netherlands, but inscribed "NED. INDIE".
M257 15c. green 9·00 28·00
M258 60c. red 9·00 45·00
M259 75c. brown 9·00 48·00
M260 1g.50 blue 27·00 £225
M261 2g.25 brown 32·00 £275
M262 4½g. black 60·00 £550
M263 7½g. red 75·00 £600

OFFICIAL STAMPS

1911. Stamps of 1892 optd **D** in white on a black circle.
O178 **6** 10c. brown 2·40 1·40
O179 12½c. grey 4·00 5·25
O180 15c. bistre 4·00 3·50
O181 20c. blue 3·50 2·10
O182 25c. mauve 13·00 9·75
O183 50c. red 3·00 2·00
O184 2g.50 blue and brown 55·00 55·00

1911. Stamps of 1902 (except No. O185) optd **DIENST**.
O186 ½c. lilac 35 70
O187 1c. olive 35 35
O188 2c. brown 35 35
O185 2½c. yellow (No. 91) 90 1·90
O189 2½c. green 1·75 1·75
O190 3c. orange 55 50
O191 4c. blue 35 35
O192 5c. red 1·10 90
O193 7½c. grey 2·75 2·75
O194 10c. slate 35 35
O195 12½c. blue 2·50 2·50
O196 15c. brown 90 90
O197 15c. brown (No. 140) 35·00
O198 17½c. bistre 3·50 2·75
O199 20c. olive 90 55
O200 22½c. olive and brown 3·50 3·50
O201 25c. mauve 2·10 1·90
O202 30c. brown 1·10 65
O203 50c. red 14·00 9·00
O204 1g. lilac 3·50 1·60
O205 2½g. grey 32·00 35·00

POSTAGE DUE STAMPS

1874. As Postage Due stamps of Netherlands. Colours changed.
D56 **D 8** 5c. yellow £300 £250
D57 10c. green on yellow £110 90·00
D59 15c. orange on yellow 22·00 18·00
D60 20c. green on blue 35·00 14·50

1882. As Type D **10** of Netherlands.
D63b 2½c. black and red 55 1·10
D64b 5c. black and red 55 1·10
D65 10c. black and red 4·50 5·00
D70 15c. black and red 4·50 4·50
D71c 20c. black and red 90·00 55
D76b 30c. black and red 3·50 4·50
D72b 40c. black and red 2·50 1·25
D73b 50c. black and pink 1·40 1·60
D67 75c. black and red 1·10 1·40

1892. As Type D **9** of Netherlands.
D102 2½c. black and pink 1·10 35
D103 5c. black and pink 3·50 30
D104b 10c. black and pink 4·50 2·50
D105 15c. black and pink 15·00 2·50
D106b 20c. black and pink 5·50 2·00
D107 30c. black and pink 23·00 8·00
D108 40c. black and pink 20·00 3·00
D109 50c. black and pink 12·50 1·25
D110 75c. black and pink 25·00 5·50

1913. As Type D **9** of Netherlands.
D226 1c. orange 10 1·75
D489 1c. violet 75 90
D227 2½c. orange 10 10
D527 2½c. brown 1·10 1·25
D228 3½c. orange 10 1·75
D491 3½c. blue 70 90
D229 5c. orange 10 10
D230 7½c. orange 10 10
D493 7½c. green 90 90
D231 10c. orange 10 10
D494 10c. mauve 90 90
D232 12½c. orange 2·75 10
D448 15c. orange 1·90 1·25
D234 20c. orange 20 10
D495 20c. blue 90 1·10
D235 25c. orange 20 10
D496 25c. yellow 90 1·10
D236 30c. orange 20 20
D497 30c. brown 1·10 1·10
D237 37½c. orange 18·00 14·50
D238 40c. orange 20 20
D498 40c. green 1·10 1·25
D239 50c. orange 2·10 10
D499 50c. yellow 1·50 1·50
D240 75c. orange 2·75 20
D500 75c. blue 1·50 1·50
D241 1g. orange 5·00 7·25
D452 1g. blue 1·40 90
D501 100c. green 1·50 1·50

1937. Surch **20**.
D384 **D 5** 20c. on 37½c. red 90 50

1946. Optd **TE BETALEN PORT** or surch also.
D480 2½c. on 10c. red (No. 429) 90 90
D481 10c. red (No. 429) 2·00 2·00
D482 20c. mauve (No. 432) 5·50 5·50
D483 40c. green (No. 436) 45·00 45·00

For later issues see **INDONESIA**.

NETHERLANDS NEW GUINEA Pt. 4

The Western half of the island of New Guinea was governed by the Netherlands until 1962, when control was transferred to the U.N. (see West New Guinea). The territory later became part of Indonesia as West Irian (q.v.).

100 cents = 1 gulden.

1950. As numeral and portrait types of Netherlands but inscr "NIEUW GUINEA".
1 **118** 1c. grey 25 20
2 2c. orange 25 20
3 2½c. olive 50 20
4 3c. mauve 1·90 1·40
5 4c. green 1·90 1·25
6 5c. blue 3·25 20
7 7½c. brown 50 20
8 10c. violet 1·90 20
9 12½c. red 1·90 1·60
10 **129** 15c. brown 2·25 75
11 20c. blue 90 20
12 25c. red 90 20
13 30c. blue 11·00 20
14 40c. green 1·50 20
15 45c. brown 5·00 75
16 50c. orange 1·10 20
17 55c. grey 10·00 55
18 80c. purple 10·50 3·25
19 **130** 1g. red 11·50 20
20 2g. brown 9·00 1·40
21 5g. green 12·50 1·25

1953. Netherlands Flood Relief Fund. Nos. 6, 10 and 12 surch **hulp nederland 1953** and premium.
22 **118** 5c.+5c. blue 9·00 9·00
23 **129** 15c.+10c. brown 9·00 9·00
24 25c.+10c. red 9·00 9·00

5 Lesser Bird of Paradise **6** Queen Juliana

1954.
25 **5** 1c. yellow and red 15 15
26 5c. yellow and brown 20 20
27 – 10c. brown and blue 20 20
28 – 15c. brown and yellow 25 20
29 – 20c. brown and green 1·10 65
DESIGN: 10, 15, 20c. Greater bird of paradise.

1954.
30 **6** 25c. red 25 25
31 30c. blue 25 25
32 40c. orange 2·25 2·25
33 45c. green 75 1·25
34 55c. turquoise 55 25
35 80c. grey 90 35
36 85c. brown 1·25 50
37 1g. purple 4·75 2·25

1955. Red Cross. Nos. 26/8 surch with cross and premium.
38 **5** 5c.+5c. yellow and sepia 1·25 1·10
39 – 10c.+10c. brown and blue 1·25 1·10
40 – 15c.+10c. brown and lemon 1·25 1·10

8 Child and Native Hut **10** Papuan Girl and Beach Scene

1956. Anti-leprosy Fund.
41 – 5c.+5c. green 1·10 1·00
42 **8** 10c.+5c. purple 1·10 1·00
43 – 25c.+10c. blue 1·10 1·00
44 **8** 30c.+10c. buff 1·10 1·00
DESIGN: 5c., 25c. Palm-trees and native hut.

1957. Child Welfare Fund.
51 **10** 5c.+5c. lake 1·10 1·00
52 – 10c.+5c. green 1·10 1·00
53 **10** 25c.+10c. brown 1·10 1·00
54 – 30c.+10c. blue 1·10 1·00
DESIGN: 10c., 30c. Papuan child and native hut.

11 Red Cross and Idol **12** Papuan and Helicopter

1958. Red Cross Fund.
55 **11** 5c.+5c. multicoloured 1·10 1·10
56 – 10c.+5c. multicoloured 1·10 1·10
57 **11** 25c.+10c. multicoloured 1·10 1·10
58 – 30c.+10c. multicoloured 1·10 1·10
DESIGN: 10c., 30c. Red Cross and Asman-Papuan bowl in form of human figure.

1959. Stars Mountains Expedition, 1959.
59 **12** 55c. brown and blue 1·25 90

13 Blue-crowned Pigeon **14** "Tecomanthe dendrophila"

1959.
60 **13** 7c. purple, blue and brown 35 35
61 12c. purple, blue and green 35 35
62 17c. purple and blue 35 35

1959. Social Welfare. Inscr "SOCIALE ZORG".
63 **14** 5c.+5c. red and green 75 65
64 – 10c.+5c. purple, yellow and olive 75 65
65 – 25c.+10c. yellow, green and red 75 65
66 – 30c.+10c. green and violet 75 65
DESIGNS: 10c. "Dendrobium attennatum Lindley"; 25c. "Rhododendron zoelleri Warburg"; 30c. "Boea cf. urvillei".

1960. World Refugee Year. As T **180** of Netherlands.
67 25c. blue 65 65
68 30c. ochre 65 65

16 Paradise Birdwing

1960. Social Welfare Funds. Butterflies.
69 **16** 5c.+5c. multicoloured 90 90
70 – 10c.+5c. bl, blk & salmon 90 90
71 – 25c.+10c. red, sepia & yell 90 90
72 – 30c.+10c. multicoloured 90 90
BUTTERFLIES: 10c. Large green-banded blue; 25c. Red lacewing; 30c. Catops owl butterfly.

17 Council Building, Hollandia

1961. Opening of Netherlands New Guinea Council.
73 **17** 25c. turquoise 25 35
74 30c. red 25 35

18 "Scapanes australis" 19 Children's Road Crossing

1961. Social Welfare Funds. Beetles.
75 **18** 5c.+5c. multicoloured . . . 50 35
76 – 10c.+5c. multicoloured . . . 50 35
77 – 25c.+10c. multicoloured . . 50 35
78 – 30c.+10c. multicoloured . . 50 35
BEETLES: 10c. Brenthid weevil; 25c. "Neolamprima adolphinae" (stag beetle); 30c. "Aspidomorpha aurata" (leaf beetle).

1962. Road Safety Campaign. Triangle in red.
79 **19** 25c. blue 25 35
80 – 30c. green (Adults at road crossing) 25 35

1962. Silver Wedding of Queen Juliana and Prince Bernhard. As T **187** of Netherlands.
81 55c. brown 35 50

21 Shadow of Palm on Beach

1962. 5th South Pacific Conference, Pago Pago. Multicoloured.
82 25c. Type **21** 25 40
83 30c. Palms on beach 25 40

22 Lobster

1962. Social Welfare Funds. Shellfish. Multicoloured.
84 5c.+5c. Crab (horiz) 20 20
85 10c.+5c. Type **22** 20 20
86 25c.+10c. Spiny lobster . . . 25 25
87 30c.+10c. Shrimp (horiz) . . . 25 35

POSTAGE DUE STAMPS

1957. As Type D **121** of Netherlands but inscr "NEDERLANDS NIEUW GUINEA".
D45 1c. red 20 25
D46 5c. red . . . . 75 1·25
D47 10c. red . . . . 1·90 2·40
D48 25c. red . . . . 2·75 1·10
D49 40c. red . . . . 2·75 1·25
D50 1g. blue . . . . 3·50 4·50

For later issues see **WEST NEW GUINEA** and **WEST IRIAN**.

NEVIS Pt. 1

One of the Leeward Islands, Br. W. Indies. Used stamps of St. Kitts–Nevis from 1903 until June 1980 when Nevis, although remaining part of St. Kitts–Nevis, had a separate postal administration.

1861. 12 pence = 1 shilling; 20 shillings = 1 pound.
1980. 100 cents = 1 dollar.

1 2 5

(The design on the stamps refers to a medicinal spring on the Island).

1861. Various frames.
15 **1** 1d. red . . . . 19·00 14·00
6 **2** 4d. red . . . . 95·00 60·00
12 4d. orange . . . . £100 20·00
7 – 6d. lilac . . . . 95·00 48·00
20 – 1s. green . . . . 80·00 95·00

1879.
25 **5** ½d. green . . . . 4·25 12·00
23 1d. mauve . . . . 65·00 30·00
27a 1d. red . . . . 8·00 8·00
28 2½d. brown . . . . £100 48·00
29 2½d. blue . . . . 16·00 15·00
30 4d. blue . . . . £275 48·00
31 4d. grey . . . . 8·50 3·25
32 6d. green £350 £350
33 6d. brown . . . . 20·00 55·00
34 1s. violet £100 £180

1883. Half of No. 23 surch **NEVIS. ½d.**
35 **5** ½d. on half 1d. mauve . . . £800 42·00

1980. Nos. 394/406 of St. Christopher, Nevis and Anguilla with "St. Christopher" and "Anguilla" obliterated.
37 5c. Radio and T.V. station . . 10 10
38 10c. Technical college 10 10
39 12c. T.V. assembly plant . . . 10 30
40 15c. Sugar cane harvesting . . 10 10
41 25c. Crafthouse (craft centre) 10 10
42 30c. "Europa" (liner) 20 15
43 40c. Lobster and sea crab . . 15 40
44 45c. Royal St. Kitts Hotel and golf course 80 70
45 50c. Pinney's Beach, Nevis . . 15 30
46 55c. New runway at Golden Rock 60 15
47 $1 Picking cotton 15 30
48 $5 Brewery 30 75
49 $10 Pineapples and peanuts . . 40 1·00

7a Queen Elizabeth the Queen Mother

1980. 80th Birthday of Queen Elizabeth the Queen Mother.
50 **7a** $2 multicoloured 20 30

8 Nevis Lighter 9 Virgin and Child

1980. Boats. Multicoloured.
51 5c. Type **8** 10 10
52 30c. Local fishing boat 15 10
53 55c. "Caona" (catamaran) . . 15 10
54 $3 "Polynesia" (cruise schooner) (39 × 53 mm) . . 40 40

1980. Christmas. Multicoloured.
55 5c. Type **9** 10 10
56 30c. Angel 10 10
57 $2.50 The Wise Men 20 30

10 Charlestown Pier 11 New River Mill

1981. Multicoloured.
58A 5c. Type **10** 10 10
59A 10c. Court House and Library 10 10
60A 15c. Type **11** 10 10
61A 20c. Nelson Museum 10 10
62A 25c. St. James' Parish Church 15 15
63A 30c. Nevis Lane 15 15
64A 40c. Zetland Plantation . . . 20 20
65A 45c. Nisbet Plantation . . . 20 25
66A 50c. Pinney's Beach 25 25
67A 55c. Eva Wilkin's Studio . . 25 30
68A $1 Nevis at dawn 30 45
69A $2.50 Ruins of Fort Charles 35 80
70A $5 Old Bath House . . . . 40 1·00
71A $10 Beach at Nisbet's . . . 50 2·00

1981. Royal Wedding. Royal Yachts. As T **26/27** of Kiribati. Multicoloured.
72 55c. "Royal Caroline" 15 15
73 55c. Prince Charles and Lady Diana Spencer 40 40
74 $2 "Royal Sovereign" 30 30
75 $2 As No. 73 . . . . 80 1·25
76 $5 "Britannia" 45 80
77 $5 As No. 73 . . . . 1·00 2·00
MS78 120 × 109 mm. $4.50 As No. 73 . . . . 1·10 1·25

12 "Heliconius charithonia"

1982. Butterflies (1st series). Multicoloured.
81 5c. Type **12** 10 10
82 30c. "Siproeta stelenes" . . . 20 10
83 55c. "Marpesia petreus" . . . 25 15
84 $2 "Phoebis agarithe" 60 80
See also Nos. 105/8.

13 Caroline of Brunswick, Princess of Wales, 1793

1982. 21st Birthday of Princess of Wales. Mult.
85 30c. Type **13** 10 10
86 55c. Coat of arms of Caroline of Brunswick 15 15
87 $5 Diana, Princess of Wales 1·10 1·00

1982. Birth of Prince William of Wales. Nos. 85/7 optd **ROYAL BABY**.
88 30c. As Type **13** 10 10
89 55c. Coat of arms of Caroline of Brunswick 15 15
90 $5 Diana, Princess of Wales 60 1·00

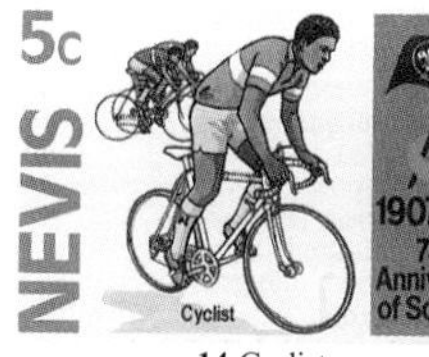

14 Cyclist

1982. 75th Anniv of Boy Scout Movement. Multicoloured.
91 5c. Type **14** 20 10
92 30c. Athlete 25 10
93 $2.50 Camp cook 50 65

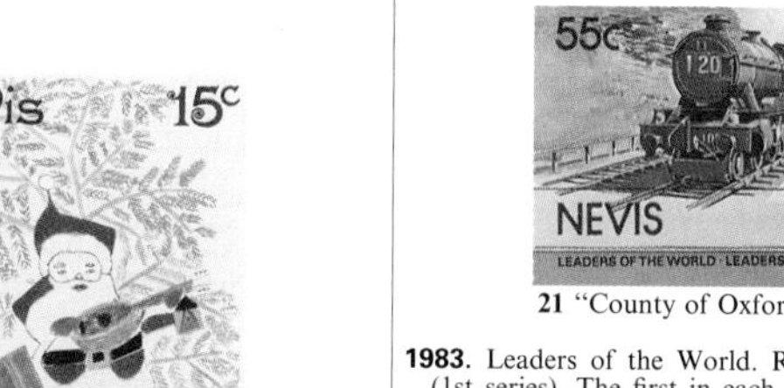

15 Santa Claus

1982. Christmas. Children's Paintings. Mult.
94 15c. Type **15** 10 10
95 30c. Carollers 10 10
96 $1.50 Decorated house and local band (horiz) 15 25
97 $2.50 Adoration of the Shepherds (horiz) 25 40

16 Tube Sponge 19 Montgolfier Balloon, 1783

17 H.M.S. "Boreas" off Nevis

1983. Corals (1st series). Multicoloured.
98 15c. Type **16** 10 10
99 30c. Stinging coral 15 10
100 55c. Flower coral 15 10
101 $3 Sea rod and red fire sponge 50 80
MS102 82 × 115 mm. Nos. 98/101 1·40 2·50
See also Nos. 423/6.

1983. Commonwealth Day. Multicoloured.
103 55c. Type **17** 15 10
104 $2 Capt. Horatio Nelson and H.M.S. "Boreas" at anchor 45 60

1983. Butterflies (2nd series). As T **12**. Mult.
105 30c. "Pyrgus oileus" 20 10
106 55c. "Junonia evarete" (vert) 20 10
107 $1.10 "Urbanus proteus" (vert) 30 40
108 $2 "Hypolimnas misippus" 40 75

1983. Nos. 58 and 60/71 optd **INDEPENDENCE 1983**.
109B 5c. Type **10** 10 10
110B 15c. Type **11** 10 10
111B 20c. Nelson Museum . . . 10 10
112B 25c. St. James' Parish Church 10 15
113B 30c. Nevis Lane 15 15
114B 40c. Zetland Plantation . . 15 20
115B 45c. Nisbet Plantation . . . 15 25
116B 50c. Pinney's Beach 15 25
117B 55c. Eva Wilkin's Studio . . 15 30
118B $1 Nevis at dawn 15 30
119B $2.50 Ruins of Fort Charles 25 45
120B $5 Old Bath House 30 55
121B $10 Beach at Nisbet's . . . 40 70

1983. Bicentenary of Manned Flight. Mult.
122 10c. Type **19** 10 10
123 45c. Sikorsky S-38 flying boat (horiz) 15 10
124 50c. Beech 50 Twin Bonanza (horiz) 15 10
125 $2.50 Hawker Siddeley Sea Harrier (horiz) 30 90
MS126 118 × 145 mm. Nos. 122/5 75 1·00

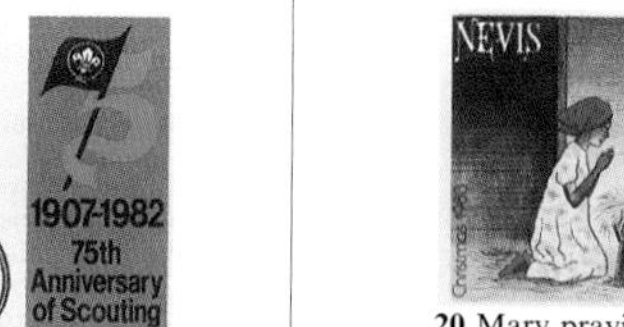

20 Mary praying over Holy Child

1983. Christmas. Multicoloured.
127 5c. Type **20** 10 10
128 30c. Shepherds with flock . . 10 10
129 55c. Three Angels 10 10
130 $3 Boy with two girls 30 60
MS131 135 × 149 mm. Nos. 127/30 85 2·00

21 "County of Oxford" (1945)

1983. Leaders of the World. Railway Locomotives (1st series). The first in each pair shows technical drawings and the second the locomotive at work.
132 **21** 55c. multicoloured 10 20
133 – 55c. multicoloured 10 20
134 – $1 red, blue and black . . 10 20
135 – $1 multicoloured 10 20
136 – $1 purple, blue and black 10 20
137 – $1 multicoloured 10 20
138 – $1 red, black and yellow 10 20
139 – $1 multicoloured 10 20
140 – $1 multicoloured 10 20
141 – $1 multicoloured 10 20
142 – $1 yellow, black and blue 10 20
143 – $1 multicoloured 10 20
144 – $1 yellow, black and purple 10 20
145 – $1 multicoloured 10 20

146 – $1 multicoloured 10 20
147 – $1 multicoloured 10 20

DESIGNS: Nos. 132/3, "County of Oxford", Great Britain (1945); 134/5, "Evening Star", Great Britain (1960); 136/7, Stanier Class 5 No. 44806, Great Britain (1934); 138/9, "Pendennis Castle", Great Britain (1924); 140/1, "Winston Churchill", Great Britain (1946); 142/3, "Mallard", Great Britain (1938) (inscr "1935" in error); 144/5, "Britannia", Great Britain (1951); 146/7, "King George V", Great Britain.

See also Nos. 219/26, 277/84, 297/308, 352/9 and 427/42.

22 Boer War

1984. Leaders of the World. British Monarchs (1st series). Multicoloured.

148 5c. Type **22** 10 10
149 5c. Queen Victoria 10 10
150 50c. Queen Victoria at Osborne House 10 30
151 50c. Osborne House 10 30
152 60c. Battle of Dettingen 10 30
153 60c. George II 10 30
154 75c. George II at the Bank of England 10 30
155 75c. Bank of England 10 30
156 $1 Coat of Arms of George II 10 30
157 $1 George II (different) 10 30
158 $3 Coat of Arms of Queen Victoria 20 50
159 $3 Queen Victoria (different) 20 50

See also Nos. 231/6.

23 Golden Rock Inn

1984. Tourism (1st series). Multicoloured.

160 55c. Type **23** 25 20
161 55c. Rest Haven Inn 25 20
162 55c. Cliffdwellers Hotel 25 20
163 55c. Pinney's Beach Hotel 25 20

See also Nos. 245/8.

24 Early Seal of Colony

1984.

164 **24** $15 red 1·40 4·00

25 Cadillac

1984. Leaders of the World Automobiles (1st series). As T **25**. The first design in each pair shows technical drawings and the second paintings.

165 1c. yellow, black and mauve 10 10
166 1c. multicoloured 10 10
167 5c. blue, mauve and black 10 10
168 5c. multicoloured 10 10
169 15c. multicoloured 10 15
170 15c. multicoloured 10 15
171 35c. mauve, yellow and black 10 25
172 35c. multicoloured 10 25
173 45c. blue, mauve and black 10 25
174 45c. multicoloured 10 25
175 55c. multicoloured 10 25
176 55c. multicoloured 10 25
177 $2.50 mauve, black and yellow 20 40
178 $2.50 multicoloured 20 40
179 $3 blue, yellow and black 20 40
180 $3 multicoloured 20 40

DESIGNS: No. 165/6, Cadillac "V16 Fleetwood Convertible" (1932); 167/8, Packard "Twin Six Touring Car" (1916); 169/70, Daimler "2 Cylinder" (1886); 171/2, Porsche "911 S Targa" (1970); 173/4, Benz "Three Wheeler" (1885); 175/6, M.G. "TC" (1947); 177/8, Cobra "Roadster 289" (1966); 179/80, Aston Martin "DB6 Hardtop" (1966).

See also Nos. 203/10, 249/64, 326/37, 360/371 and 411/22.

26 Carpentry

1984. 10th Anniv of Culturama Celebrations. Multicoloured.

181 30c. Type **26** 10 10
182 55c. Grass mat and basket making 10 10
183 $1 Pottery firing 15 25
184 $3 Culturama Queen and dancers 40 55

27 Yellow Bell

29 C. P. Mead

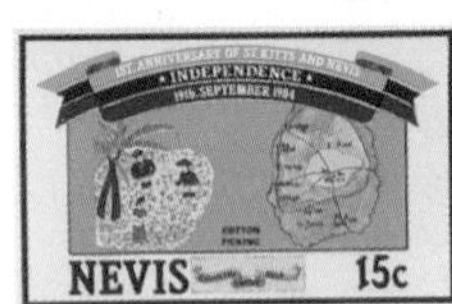

28 Cotton-picking and Map

1984. Flowers. Multicoloured.

185A 5c. Type **27** 10 10
186A 10c. Plumbago 10 10
187A 15c. Flamboyant 10 10
188B 20c. Eyelash orchid 60 30
189A 30c. Bougainvillea 10 15
190B 40c. Hibiscus 30 30
191A 50c. Night-blooming cereus 15 20
192A 55c. Yellow mahoe 15 25
193A 60c. Spider-lily 15 25
194A 75c. Scarlet cordia 20 30
195A $1 Shell-ginger 20 40
196A $3 Blue petrea 30 1·10
197A $5 Coral hibiscus 50 2·00
198A $10 Passion flower 80 3·50

1984. 1st Anniv of Independence of St. Kitts–Nevis. Multicoloured.

199 15c. Type **28** 10 10
200 55c. Alexander Hamilton's birthplace 10 10
201 $1.10 Local agricultural produce 20 40
202 $3 Nevis Peak and Pinney's Beach 50 1·00

1984. Leaders of the World. Automobiles (2nd series). As T **25**. The first in each pair shows technical drawings and the second paintings.

203 5c. black, blue and brown 10 10
204 5c. multicoloured 10 10
205 30c. black, turquoise and brown 15 15
206 30c. multicoloured 15 15
207 50c. black, drab and brown 15 15
208 50c. multicoloured 15 15
209 $3 black, brown and green 30 45
210 $3 multicoloured 30 45

DESIGNS: Nos. 203/4, Lagonda "Speed Model" touring car (1929); 205/6, Jaguar "E-Type" 4.2 litre (1967); 207/8, Volkswagen "Beetle" (1947); 209/10, Pierce Arrow "V12" (1932).

1984. Leaders of the World. Cricketers (1st series). As T **29**. The first in each pair shows a head portrait and the second the cricketer in action. Multicoloured.

211 5c. Type **29** 10 10
212 5c. C. P. Mead 10 10
213 25c. J. B. Statham 20 30
214 25c. J. B. Statham 20 30
215 55c. Sir Learie Constantine 30 40
216 55c. Sir Learie Constantine 30 40
217 $2.50 Sir Leonard Hutton 50 1·25
218 $2.50 Sir Leonard Hutton 50 1·25

See also Nos. 237/4.

1984. Leaders of the World. Railway Locomotives (2nd series). As T **21**. The first in each pair shows technical drawings and the second the locomotive at work.

219 5c. multicoloured 10 10
220 5c. multicoloured 10 10
221 10c. multicoloured 10 10
222 10c. multicoloured 10 10
223 60c. multicoloured 15 25
224 60c. multicoloured 15 25
225 $2 multicoloured 50 70
226 $2 multicoloured 50 70

DESIGNS: Nos. 219/20, Class EF81 electric locomotive, Japan (1968); 221/22, Class 5500 electric locomotive, France (1927); 223/4, Class 240P, France (1940); 225/6, "Hikari" express train, Japan (1964).

30 Fifer and Drummer from Honeybees Band

1984. Christmas. Local Music. Multicoloured.

227 15c. Type **30** 15 10
228 40c. Guitar and "barhow" players from Canary Birds Band 25 10
229 60c. Shell All Stars steel band 30 10
230 $3 Organ and choir, St. John's Church, Fig Tree 1·25 1·00

1984. Leaders of the World. British Monarchs (2nd series). As T **22**. Multicoloured.

231 5c. King John and Magna Carta 10 10
232 5c. Barons and King John 10 10
233 55c. King John 10 15
234 55c. Newark Castle 10 15
235 $2 Coat of arms 25 40
236 $2 King John (different) 25 40

1984. Leaders of the World. Cricketers (2nd series). As T **29**. The first in each pair listed shows a head portrait and the second the cricketer in action. Multicoloured.

237 5c. J. D. Love 10 10
238 5c. J. D. Love 10 10
239 15c. S. J. Dennis 10 15
240 15c. S. J. Dennis 10 15
241 55c. B. W. Luckhurst 15 20
242 55c. B. W. Luckhurst 15 20
243 $2.50 B. L. D'Oliveira 40 60
244 $2.50 B. L. D'Oliveira 40 60

1984. Tourism (2nd series). As T **23**. Multicoloured.

245 $1.20 Croney's Old Manor Hotel 15 25
246 $1.20 Montpelier Plantation Inn 15 25
247 $1.20 Nisbet's Plantation Inn 15 25
248 $1.20 Zetland Plantation Inn 15 25

1985. Leaders of the World. Automobiles (3rd series). As T **25**. The first in each pair shows technical drawings and the second paintings.

249 1c. black, green and light green 10 10
250 1c. multicoloured 10 10
251 5c. black, blue and light blue 10 10
252 5c. multicoloured 10 10
253 10c. black, green and light green 10 10
254 10c. multicoloured 10 10
255 50c. black, green and brown 10 10
256 50c. multicoloured 10 10
257 60c. black, green and blue 10 10
258 60c. multicoloured 10 10
259 75c. black, red and orange 10 10
260 75c. multicoloured 10 10
261 $2.50 black, green and blue 20 30
262 $2.50 multicoloured 20 30
263 $3 black, green and light green 20 30
264 $3 multicoloured 20 30

DESIGNS: Nos. 249/50, Delahaye "Type 35 Cabriolet" (1935); 251/2, Ferrari "Testa Rossa" (1958); 253/4, Voisin "Aerodyne" (1934); 255/6, Buick "Riviera" (1963); 257/8, Cooper "Climax" (1960); 259/60, Ford "999" (1904); 261/2, MG "M-Type Midget" (1930); 263/4, Rolls- Royce "Corniche" (1971).

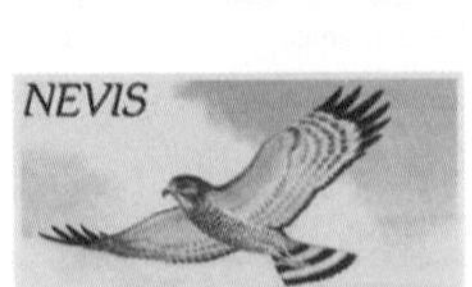

31 Broad-winged Hawk

1985. Local Hawks and Herons. Multicoloured.

265 20c. Type **31** 1·25 20
266 40c. Red-tailed hawk 1·40 30
267 60c. Little blue heron 1·40 40
268 $3 Great blue heron (white phase) 2·75 1·90

32 Eastern Bluebird

1985. Leaders of the World. Birth Bicentenary of John J. Audubon (ornithologist) (1st issue). Multicoloured.

269 5c. Type **32** 10 10
270 5c. Common cardinal 10 10
271 55c. Belted kingfisher 20 55
272 55c. Mangrove cuckoo 20 55
273 60c. Yellow warbler 20 55
274 60c. Cerulean warbler 20 55
275 $2 Burrowing owl 60 1·25
276 $2 Long-eared owl 60 1·25

See also Nos. 285/92.

1985. Leaders of the World. Railway Locomotives (3rd series). As T **21**. The first in each pair showing technical drawings and the second the locomotive at work.

277 1c. multicoloured 10 10
278 1c. multicoloured 10 10
279 60c. multicoloured 20 20
280 60c. multicoloured 20 20
281 90c. multicoloured 25 25
282 90c. multicoloured 25 25
283 $2 multicoloured 40 60
284 $2 multicoloured 40 60

DESIGNS: Nos. 277/8, Class "Wee Bogie", Great Britain (1882); 279/80, "Comet", Great Britain (1851); 281/2, Class 8H No. 6173, Great Britain (1908); 283/4, Class A No. 23, Great Britain (1866).

1985. Leaders of the World. Birth Bicentenary of John J. Audubon (ornithologist) (2nd issue). As T **32**. Multicoloured.

285 1c. Painted bunting 10 10
286 1c. Golden-crowned kinglet 10 10
287 40c. Common flicker 25 40
288 40c. Western tanager 25 40
289 60c. Varied thrush 25 45
290 60c. Evening grosbeak 25 45
291 $2.50 Blackburnian warbler 50 80
292 $2.50 Northern oriole 50 80

33 Guides and Guide Headquarters

1985. 75th Anniv of Girl Guide Movement. Multicoloured.

293 15c. Type **33** 10 10
294 60c. Girl Guide uniforms of 1910 and 1985 (vert) 15 25
295 $1 Lord and Lady Baden-Powell (vert) 20 40
296 $3 Princess Margaret in Guide uniform (vert) 50 1·25

1985. Leaders of the World. Railway Locomotives (4th series). As T **21**. The first in each pair shows technical drawings and the second the locomotive at work.

297 5c. multicoloured 10 10
298 5c. multicoloured 10 10
299 30c. multicoloured 10 15
300 30c. multicoloured 10 15
301 60c. multicoloured 10 20
302 60c. multicoloured 10 20
303 75c. multicoloured 10 25
304 75c. multicoloured 10 25
305 $1 multicoloured 10 25
306 $1 multicoloured 10 25
307 $2.50 multicoloured 20 60
308 $2.50 multicoloured 20 60

DESIGNS: Nos. 297/8, "Snowdon Ranger" (1878); 299/300, Large Belpaire locomotive, Great Britain (1904); 301/2, Class "County" No. 3821, Great Britain (1904); 303/4, "L'Outrance", France (1877); 305/6, Class PB-15, Australia (1899); 307/8, Class 64, Germany (1928).

34 The Queen Mother at Garter Ceremony

35 Isambard Kingdom Brunel

1985. Leaders of the World. Life and Times of Queen Elizabeth the Queen Mother. Various vertical portraits.

309 **34** 45c. multicoloured 10 15
310 – 45c. multicoloured 10 15
311 – 75c. multicoloured 10 20
312 – 75c. multicoloured 10 20
313 – $1.20 multicoloured 15 35
314 – $1.20 multicoloured 15 35
315 – $1.50 multicoloured 20 40
316 – $1.50 multicoloured 20 40

MS317 85 × 114 mm. $2 multicoloured; $2 multicoloured 50 1·40

Each value was issued in pairs showing a floral pattern across the bottom of the portraits which stops short of the left-hand edge on the first stamp and of the right-hand edge on the second.

1985. 150th Anniv of Great Western Railway. Designs showing railway engineers and their achievements. Multicoloured.

318 25c. Type **35** 15 35
319 25c. Royal Albert Bridge, 1859 15 35
320 50c. William Dean 20 45
321 50c. Locomotive "Lord of the Isles", 1895 20 45
322 $1 Locomotive "Lode Star", 1907 25 65
323 $1 G. J. Churchward 25 65

324 $2.50 Locomotive "Pendennis Castle", 1924 . . . . . . 35 80
325 $2.50 C. B. Collett 35 80
Nos. 318/19, 320/1, 322/3 and 324/5 were printed together se-tenant, each pair forming a composite design.

1985. Leaders of the World. Automobiles (4th series). As T **25**. The first in each pair shows technical drawings and the second paintings.
326 10c. black, blue and red . . . 10 10
327 10c. multicoloured 10 10
328 35c. black, turquoise and blue 10 25
329 35c. multicoloured 10 25
330 75c. black, green and brown 10 40
331 75c. multicoloured 10 40
332 $1.15 black, brown and green 15 45
333 $1.15 multicoloured 15 45
334 $1.50 black, blue and red . . 15 50
335 $1.50 multicoloured 15 50
336 $2 black, lilac and violet . . 20 60
337 $2 multicoloured 20 60
DESIGNS: Nos. 326/7, Sunbeam "Coupe de l'Auto" (1912); 328/9, Cisitalia "Pininfarina Coupe" (1948); 330/1, Porsche "928S" (1980); 332/3, MG "K3 Magnette" (1933); 334/5, Lincoln "Zephyr" (1937); 336/7, Pontiac 2 Door (1926).

1985. Royal Visit. Nos. 76/7, 83, 86, 92/3, 98/9 and 309/10 optd **CARIBBEAN ROYAL VISIT 1985** or surch also.
338 **16** 15c. multicoloured . . . . 75 1·25
339 – 30c. multicoloured (No. 92) 1·75 1·75
340 – 30c. multicoloured (No. 99) 75 1·25
341 – 40c. on 55c. mult (No. 86) 1·75 2·00
342 **34** 45c. multicoloured . . . . 1·50 3·00
343 – 45c. multicoloured (No. 310) . . . . 1·50 3·00
344 – 55c. multicoloured (No. 83) 1·50 1·25
345 – $1.50 on $5 multicoloured (No. 76) . . . . 2·25 2·75
346 – $1.50 on $5 multicoloured (No. 77) . . . . 13·00 17·00
347 – $2.50 mult (No. 93) . . . 2·25 3·50

36 St. Paul's Anglican Church, Charlestown

1985. Christmas. Churches of Nevis (1st series). Multicoloured.
348 10c. Type **36** 15 10
349 40c. St. Theresa Catholic Church, Charlestown . . . 35 30
350 60c. Methodist Church, Gingerland 40 50
351 $3 St. Thomas Anglican Church, Lowland . . . . 80 2·75
See also Nos. 462/5.

1986. Leaders of the World. Railway Locomotives (5th series). As T **21**. The first in each pair shows technical drawings and the second the locomotive at work.
352 30c. multicoloured 15 25
353 30c. multicoloured 15 25
354 75c. multicoloured 25 50
355 75c. multicoloured 25 50
356 $1.50 multicoloured 40 70
357 $1.50 multicoloured 40 70
358 $2 multicoloured 50 80
359 $2 multicoloured 50 80
DESIGNS: Nos. 352/3, "Stourbridge Lion", U.S.A. (1829); 354/5, EP-2 Bi-Polar electric locomotive, U.S.A. (1919); 356/7, Gas turbine No. 59, U.S.A. (1953); 358/9 Class FL9 diesel locomotive No. 2039, U.S.A. (1955).

1986. Leaders of the World. Automobiles (5th series). As T **25**. The first in each pair showing technical drawings and the second paintings.
360 10c. black, brown and green 10 10
361 10c. multicoloured 10 10
362 60c. black, orange and red 15 25
363 60c. multicoloured 15 25
364 75c. black, light brown and brown 15 25
365 75c. multicoloured 15 25
366 $1 black, light grey and grey 15 30
367 $1 multicoloured 15 30
368 $1.50 black, yellow and green 20 35
369 $1.50 multicoloured 20 35
370 $3 black, light blue and blue 30 65
371 $3 multicoloured 30 65
DESIGNS: Nos. 360/1, Adler "Trumpf" (1936); 362/3, Maserati "Tipo 250F" (1957); 364/5, Oldsmobile "Limited" (1910); 366/7, Jaguar "C-Type" (1951); 368/9, ERA "1.5L B Type" (1937); 370/1, Chevrolet "Corvette" (1953).

37 Supermarine Spitfire Prototype, 1936

1986. 50th Anniv of Spitfire (fighter aircraft). Multicoloured.
372 $1 Type **37** 20 50
373 $2.50 Supermarine Spitfire Mk 1A in Battle of Britain, 1940 . . . . 30 75
374 $3 Supermarine Spitfire Mk XII over convoy, 1944 30 75
375 $4 Supermarine Spitfire Mk XXIV, 1948 . . . . . 30 1·25
MS376 114 × 86 mm. $6 Supermarine Seafire Mk III on escort carrier H.M.S. "Hunter" 1·10 3·75

38 Head of Amerindian

39 Brazilian Player

1986. 500th Anniv (1992) of Discovery of America by Columbus (1st issue). Multicoloured.
377 75c. Type **38** . . . . 75 1·00
378 75c. Exchanging gifts for food from Amerindians . . 75 1·00
379 $1.75 Columbus's coat of arms . . . . 1·25 2·00
380 $1.75 Breadfruit plant . . . 1·25 2·00
381 $2.50 Columbus's fleet . . . 1·25 2·25
382 $2.50 Christopher Columbus 1·25 2·25
MS383 95 × 84 mm. $6 Christopher Columbus (different) . . . . . 6·00 9·50
The two designs of each value were printed together, se-tenant, each pair forming a composite design showing charts of Columbus's route in the background.
See also Nos. 546/54, 592/600, 678/84 and 685/6.

1986. 60th Birthday of Queen Elizabeth II. As T **117a** of Montserrat. Multicoloured.
384 5c. Queen Elizabeth in 1976 10 10
385 75c. Queen Elizabeth in 1953 15 25
386 $2 In Australia 20 60
387 $8 In Canberra, 1982 (vert) 75 2·00
MS388 85 × 115 mm. $10 Queen Elizabeth II . . . . 4·50 7·50

1986. World Cup Football Championship, Mexico. Multicoloured.
389 1c. Official World Cup mascot (horiz) 10 10
390 2c. Type **39** 10 10
391 5c. Danish player 10 10
392 10c. Brazilian player (different) 10 10
393 20c. Denmark v Spain . . . 20 20
394 30c. Paraguay v Chile 30 30
395 60c. Italy v West Germany 40 55
396 75c. Danish team (56 × 36 mm) 40 65
397 $1 Paraguayan team (56 × 36 mm) 50 70
398 $1.75 Brazilian team (56 × 36 mm) . . . . . . 60 1·25
399 $3 Italy v England . . . . . 75 1·90
400 $6 Italian team (56 × 36 mm) 1·10 3·00
MS401 Five sheets, each 85 × 115 mm. (a) $1.50 As No. 398. (b) $2 As No. 393. (c) $2 As No. 400. (d) $2.50 As No. 395. (e) $4 As No. 394 Set of 5 sheets 12·00 15·00

40 Clothing Machinist

1986. Local Industries. Multicoloured.
402 15c. Type **40** 20 15
403 40c. Carpentry/joinery workshop 45 30
404 $1.20 Agricultural produce market . . . . 1·25 1·50
405 $3 Fishing boats landing catch . . . . 2·50 3·25

1986. Royal Wedding. As T **118a** of Montserrat. Multicoloured.
406 60c. Prince Andrew in midshipman's uniform . . 15 25
407 60c. Miss Sarah Ferguson . . 15 25
408 $2 Prince Andrew on safari in Africa (horiz) 40 60
409 $2 Prince Andrew at the races (horiz) 40 60
MS410 115 × 85 mm. $10 Duke and Duchess of York on Palace balcony after wedding (horiz) 2·50 5·00
See also Nos. 454/7.

1986. Automobiles (6th series). As T **25**. The first in each pair showing technical drawings and the second paintings.
411 15c. multicoloured 10 10
412 15c. multicoloured 10 10
413 45c. black, light blue and blue 20 25
414 45c. multicoloured 20 25
415 60c. multicoloured 20 30
416 60c. multicoloured 20 30
417 $1 black, light green and green 25 40
418 $1 multicoloured 25 40
419 $1.75 black, lilac and deep lilac 30 50
420 $1.75 multicoloured 30 50
421 $3 multicoloured 50 90
422 $3 multicoloured 50 90
DESIGNS: Nos. 411/12, Riley "Brooklands Nine" (1930); 413/14, Alfa Romeo "GTA" (1966); 415/16, Pierce Arrow "Type 66" (1913); 417/18, Willys-Knight "66A" (1928); 419/20, Studebaker "Starliner" (1953); 421/2, Cunningham "V-8" (1919).

41 Gorgonia

41a Statue of Liberty and World Trade Centre, Manhattan

1986. Corals (2nd series). Multicoloured.
423 15c. Type **41** 25 15
424 60c. Fire coral 55 55
425 $2 Elkhorn coral . . . . . . 90 2·00
426 $3 Vase sponge and feather star . . . . 1·10 2·50

1986. Railway Locomotives (6th series). As T **21**. The first in each pair showing technical drawings and the second the locomotive at work.
427 15c. multicoloured 10 10
428 15c. multicoloured 10 10
429 45c. multicoloured 15 25
430 45c. multicoloured 15 25
431 60c. multicoloured 20 30
432 60c. multicoloured 20 30
433 75c. multicoloured 20 40
434 75c. multicoloured 20 40
435 $1 multicoloured 20 50
436 $1 multicoloured 20 50
437 $1.50 multicoloured 25 60
438 $1.50 multicoloured 25 60
439 $2 multicoloured 30 65
440 $2 multicoloured 30 65
441 $3 multicoloured 35 80
442 $3 multicoloured 35 80
DESIGNS: Nos. 427/8, Connor Single Class, Great Britain (1859); 429/30, Class P2 "Cock o' the North", Great Britain (1934); 431/2, Class 7000 electric locomotive, Japan (1926); 433/4, Class P3, Germany (1897); 435/6, "Dorchester", Canada (1836); 436/7, Class "Centennial" diesel locomotive, U.S.A. (1969); 439/40, "Lafayette", U.S.A. (1837); 441/2, Class C-16 No. 222, U.S.A. (1882).

1986. Centenary of Statue of Liberty. Multicoloured.
443 15c. Type **41a** 20 15
444 25c. Sailing ship passing statue 30 20
445 40c. Statue in scaffolding . . 30 25
446 60c. Statue (side view) and scaffolding 30 30
447 75c. Statue and regatta . . . 40 40
448 $1 Tall Ships parade passing statue (horiz) 40 45
449 $1.50 Head and arm of statue above scaffolding 40 60
450 $2 Ships with souvenir flags (horiz) 55 80
451 $2.50 Statue and New York waterfront 60 90
452 $3 Restoring statue . . . . . 80 1·25
MS453 Four sheets, each 85 × 115 mm. (a) $3.50 Statue at dusk. (b) $4 Head of Statue. (c) $4.50 Statue and lightning. (d) $5 Head and torch at sunset Set of 4 sheets . . . . 3·50 11·00

1986. Royal Wedding (2nd issue). Nos. 406/9 optd **Congratulations to T.R.H. The Duke & Duchess of York**.
454 60c. Prince Andrew in midshipman's uniform . . 15 40
455 60c. Miss Sarah Ferguson . . 15 40
456 $2 Prince Andrew on safari in Africa (horiz) . . . . . 40 1·00
457 $2 Prince Andrew at the races (horiz) . . . . 40 1·00

42 Dinghy sailing

1986. Sports. Multicoloured.
458 10c. Type **42** 20 10
459 25c. Netball 35 15
460 $2 Cricket . . . . 3·00 2·50
461 $3 Basketball . . . . 3·75 3·00

43 St. George's Anglican Church, Gingerland

44 Constitution Document, Quill and Inkwell

1986. Christmas. Churches of Nevis (2nd series). Multicoloured.
462 10c. Type **43** 15 10
463 40c. Trinity Methodist Church, Fountain 30 25
464 $1 Charlestown Methodist Church 60 65
465 $5 Wesleyan Holiness Church, Brown Hill . . . 2·75 3·75

1987. Bicentenary of U.S. Constitution and 230th Birth Anniv of Alexander Hamilton (U.S. statesman). Multicoloured.
466 15c. Type **44** 10 10
467 40c. Alexander Hamilton and Hamilton House 20 25
468 60c. Alexander Hamilton . . 25 35
469 $2 Washington and his Cabinet . . . . 90 1·25
MS470 70 × 82 mm. $5 Model ship "Hamilton" on float, 1788 . . 6·50 7·50

1987. Victory of "Stars and Stripes" in America's Cup Yachting Championship. No. 54 optd **America's Cup 1987 Winners 'Stars & Stripes'**.
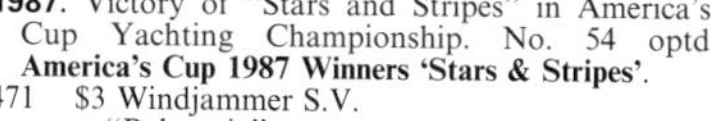
471 $3 Windjammer S.V. "Polynesia" . . . . 1·10 1·60

46 Fig Tree Church

1987. Bicentenary of Marriage of Horatio Nelson and Frances Nisbet. Multicoloured.
472 15c. Type **46** 15 10
473 60c. Frances Nisbet 40 30
474 $1 H.M.S. "Boreas" (frigate) 1·25 1·00
475 $3 Captain Horatio Nelson 2·50 3·25
MS476 102 × 82 mm. $3 As No. 473; $3 No. 475 . . . . 5·00 6·50

47 Queen Angelfish

1987. Coral Reef Fishes. Multicoloured.
477 60c. Type **47** 35 60
478 60c. Blue angelfish 35 60
479 $1 Stoplight parrotfish (male) 40 80
480 $1 Stoplight parrotfish (female) 40 80
481 $1.50 Red hind 45 90
482 $1.50 Rock hind 45 90
483 $2.50 Coney (bicoloured phase) . . . . 50 1·50
484 $2.50 Coney (red-brown phase) . . . . 50 1·50
Nos. 478, 480, 482 and 484 are inverted triangles.

48 "Panaeolus antillarum"

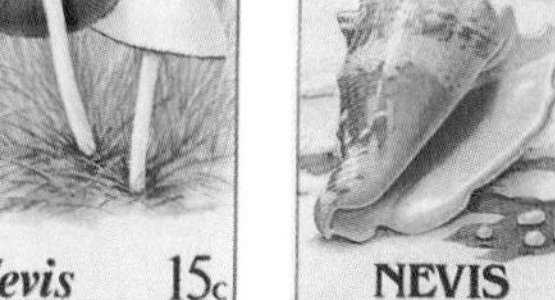

50 Hawk-wing Conch

49 Rag Doll

1987. Fungi (1st series). Multicoloured.
485 15c. Type **48** 80 30
486 50c. "Pycnoporus sanguineus" . . . . 1·50 80

487 $2 "Gymnopilus chrysopellus" . . . . . . 2·75 3·25
488 $3 "Cantharellus cinnabarinus" . . . . . . 3·25 4·25
See also Nos. 646/53.

1987. Christmas. Toys. Multicoloured.
489 10c. Type **49** 10 10
490 40c. Coconut boat 20 25
491 $1.20 Sandbox cart 55 60
492 $5 Two-wheeled cart . . . . 1·75 3·75

1988. Sea Shells and Pearls. Multicoloured.
493 15c. Type **50** 20 15
494 40c. Rooster-tail conch . . . 30 20
495 60c. Emperor helmet 50 40
496 $2 Queen or pink conch . . . 1·60 2·00
497 $3 King helmet . . . . . . 1·75 2·25

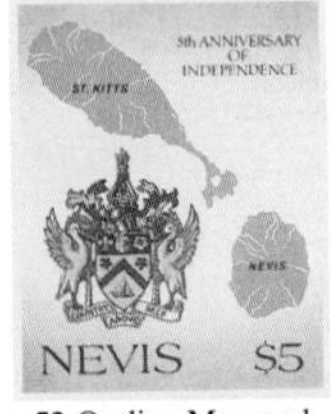

51 Visiting Pensioners at Christmas

52 Athlete on Starting Blocks

1988. 125th Anniv of International Red Cross. Multicoloured.
498 15c. Type **51** 10 10
499 40c. Teaching children first aid 15 20
500 60c. Providing wheelchairs for the disabled 25 35
501 $5 Helping cyclone victim . . 2·10 3·25

1988. Olympic Games, Seoul. Multicoloured.
502 10c. Type **52** 10 35
503 $1.20 At start . . . . [illegible] [illegible]
504 $2 During race . . . . . . 85 1·25
505 $3 At finish . . . . 1·25 1·50
MS506 137 × 80 mm. As Nos. 502/5, but each size 24 × 36 mm . . . 2·75 3·75
Nos. 502/5 were printed together, se-tenant, each strip forming a composite design showing an athlete from start to finish of race.

53 Outline Map and Arms of St. Kitts–Nevis

54 Poinsettia

1988. 5th Anniv of Independence.
507 **53** $5 multicoloured . . . . . 2·10 3·00

1988. 300th Anniv of Lloyd's of London. As T **167a** of Malawi. Multicoloured.
508 15c. House of Commons passing Lloyd's Bill, 1871 20 10
509 60c. "Cunard Countess" (liner) (horiz) . . . . . 1·10 65
510 $2.50 Space shuttle deploying satellite (horiz) . . . . 2·25 3·00
511 $3 "Viking Princess" (cargo liner) on fire, 1966 . . . . 2·25 3·00

1988. Christmas. Flowers. Multicoloured.
512 15c. Type **54** 10 10
513 40c. Tiger claws 15 20
514 60c. Sorrel flower 25 30
515 $1 Christmas candle 40 60
516 $5 Snow bush . . . . 1·60 3·50

55 British Fleet off St. Kitts

56 Cicada

1989. "Philexfrance 89" International Stamp Exhibition, Paris. Battle of Frigate Bay, 1782. Multicoloured.
517 50c. Type **55** . . . . 1·00 1·25
518 $1.20 Battle off Nevis . . . . 1·25 1·60
519 $2 British and French fleets exchanging broadsides . . 1·50 1·75
520 $3 French map of Nevis, 1764 . . . . 2·00 2·25
Nos. 517/19 were printed together, se-tenant, forming a composite design.

1989. "Sounds of the Night". Multicoloured.
521 10c. Type **56** 20 15
522 40c. Grasshopper 40 35
523 60c. Cricket 55 50
524 $5 Tree frog . . . . 3·75 5·50
MS525 135 × 81 mm. Nos. 521/4 5·50 7·00

1989. 20th Anniv of First Manned Landing on Moon. As T **51a** of Kiribati. Multicoloured.
526 15c. Vehicle Assembly Building, Kennedy Space Centre 15 10
527 40c. Crew of "Apollo 12" (30 × 30 mm) 20 20
528 $2 "Apollo 12" emblem (30 × 30 mm) . . . . . . 1·00 1·60
529 $3 "Apollo 12" astronaut on Moon . . . . 1·40 1·90
MS530 100 × 83 mm. $6 Aldrin undertaking lunar seismic experiment . . . . 2·50 3·50

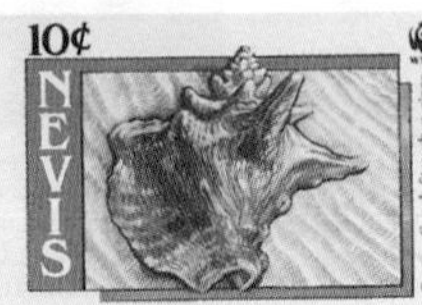

57 Queen or Pink Conch feeding

1990. Queen or Pink Conch. Multicoloured.
531 10c. Type **57** 60 30
532 40c. Queen or pink conch from front 90 40
533 60c. Side view of shell . . . 1·25 90
534 $1 Black and flare . . . . . 1·60 2·00
MS535 72 × 103 mm. $5 Underwater habitat . . . . 3·50 4·50

58 Wyon Medal Portrait

59

1990. 150th Anniv of the Penny Black.
536 **58** 15c. black and brown . . . 15 10
537 – 40c. black and green . . . 30 25
538 – 60c. black 45 55
539 – $4 black and blue . . . . 2·50 3·50
MS540 114 × 84 mm. $5 black, red and brown . . . . 4·00 5·00
DESIGNS: 40c. Engine-turned background; 60c. Heath's engraving of portrait; $4 Essay with inscriptions; $5 Penny Black.
No. **MS**540 also commemorates "Stamp World London 90" International Stamp Exhibition.

1990. 500th Anniv of Regular European Postal Services.
541 **59** 15c. brown 20 15
542 – 40c. green 35 25
543 – 60c. violet 55 65
544 – $4 blue . . . . 2·75 3·50
MS545 110 × 82 mm. $5 red, brown and grey . . . . 4·00 5·00
Nos. 541/5 commemorate the Thurn and Taxis postal service and the designs are loosely based on those of the initial 1852–58 series.

60 Sand Fiddler

1990. 500th Anniv (1992) of Discovery of America by Columbus (2nd issue). New World Natural History—Crabs. Multicoloured.
546 5c. Type **60** 10 20
547 15c. Great land crab 15 15
548 20c. Blue crab 15 15
549 40c. Stone crab 30 30
550 60c. Mountain crab 45 45
551 $2 Sargassum crab . . . . . 1·40 1·75
552 $3 Yellow box crab . . . . 1·75 2·25
553 $4 Spiny spider crab . . . . 2·25 3·00
MS554 Two sheets, each 101 × 70 mm. (a) $5 Sally Lightfoot. (b) $5 Wharf crab Set of 2 sheets . . . . 9·00 10·00

1990. 90th Birthday of Queen Elizabeth the Queen Mother. As T **198a** of Lesotho.
555 $2 black, mauve and buff . . 1·40 1·60
556 $2 black, mauve and buff . . 1·40 1·60
557 $2 black, mauve and buff . . 1·40 1·60
MS558 90 × 75 mm. $6 brown, mauve and black . . . . . . 3·50 4·25
DESIGNS: No. 555, Duchess of York with corgi; 556, Queen Elizabeth in Coronation robes, 1937; 557, Duchess of York in garden; **MS**558, Queen Elizabeth in Coronation robes, 1937 (different).

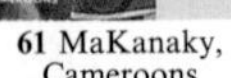

61 MaKanaky, Cameroons

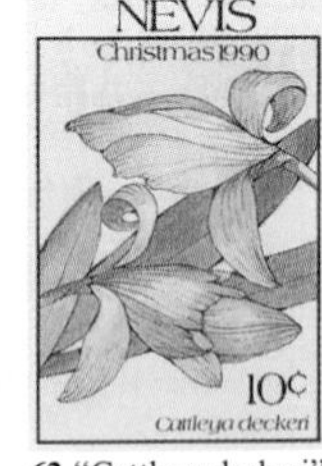

62 "Cattleya deckeri"

1990. World Cup Football Championship, Italy. Star Players. Multicoloured.
559 10c. Type **61** 40 10
560 25c. Chovanec, Czechoslovakia 45 15
561 $2.50 Robson, England . . . 2·75 3·25
562 $5 Voller, West Germany . . 3·75 5·50
MS563 Two sheets, each 90 × 75 mm. (a) $5 Maradona, Argentina. (b) $5 Gordillo, Spain Set of 2 sheets . . . . 6·75 8·00

1990. Christmas. Native Orchids. Mult.
564 10c. Type **62** 55 20
565 15c. "Epidendrum ciliare" . . 55 20
566 20c. "Epidendrum fragrans" 65 20
567 40c. "Epidendrum ibaguense" 85 25
568 60c. "Epidendrum latifolium" 1·10 50
569 $1.20 "Maxillaria conferta" 1·40 1·75
570 $2 "Epidendrum strobiliferum" . . . . . . 1·75 2·75
571 $3 "Brassavola cucullata" . . 2·00 3·00
MS572 102 × 71 mm. $5 "Rodriguezia lanceolata" . . . 7·00 8·00

1991. 350th Death Anniv of Rubens. As T **250** of Maldive Islands, showing details from "The Feast of Achelous". Multicoloured.
573 10c. Two jugs (vert) 55 15
574 40c. Woman at table (vert) 1·00 30
575 60c. Two servants with fruit (vert) . . . . 1·25 45
576 $4 Achelous (vert) . . . . . 3·25 5·50
MS577 101 × 71 mm. $5 "The Feast of Achelous" . . . . 4·50 5·50

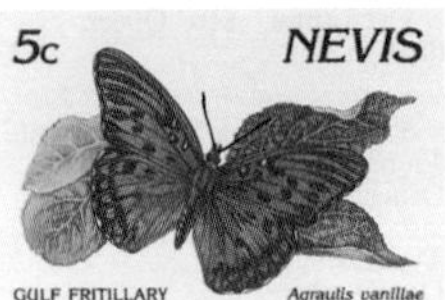

63 "Agraulis vanillae"

1991. Butterflies. Multicoloured.
578B 5c. Type **63** 20 50
579A 10c. "Historis odius" . . . 40 50
580B 15c. "Marpesia corinna" 20 20
581B 20c. "Anartia amathea" . . 30 30
582B 25c. "Junonia evarete" . . 30 30
583B 40c. "Heliconius charithonia" 40 30
584B 50c. "Marpesia petreus" 70 35
585A 60c. "Dione juno" 75 50
586B 75c. "Heliconius doris" . . 80 60
586cB 80c. As 60c. 80 60
587A $1 "Hypolimnas misippus" 90 80
588A $3 "Danaus plexippus" . . 2·00 2·75
589A $5 "Heliconius sara" . . . 2·75 4·00
590A $10 "Tithorea harmonia" 5·00 8·00
591A $20 "Dryas julia" . . . . 9·50 13·00

64 "Viking Mars Lander", 1976

1991. 500th Anniv of Discovery of America by Columbus (1992) (3rd issue). History of Exploration. Multicoloured.
592 15c. Type **64** 20 20
593 40c. "Apollo 11", 1969 . . . 30 25
594 60c. "Skylab", 1973 . . . . 45 45
595 75c. "Salyut 6", 1977 . . . . 55 55
596 $1 "Voyager 1", 1977 . . . . 65 65
597 $2 "Venera 7", 1970 . . . . 1·25 1·60
598 $4 "Gemini 4", 1965 . . . . 2·50 3·25
599 $5 "Luna 3", 1959 . . . . . 2·75 3·25
MS600 Two sheets, each 105 × 76 mm. (a) $6 Bow of "Santa Maria" (vert). (b) $6 Christopher Columbus (vert) Set of 2 sheets . . . . 8·00 9·00

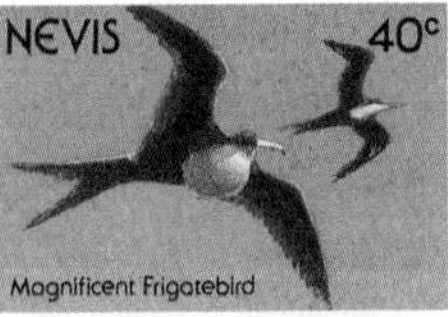

65 Magnificent Frigate Bird

1991. Island Birds. Multicoloured.
601 40c. Type **65** 70 65
602 40c. Roseate tern 70 65
603 40c. Red-tailed hawk 70 65
604 40c. Zenaida dove 70 65
605 40c. Bananaquit 70 65
606 40c. American kestrel 70 65
607 40c. Grey kingbird 70 65
608 40c. Prothonotary warbler . . 70 65
609 40c. Blue-hooded euphonia 70 65
610 40c. Antillean crested hummingbird 70 65
611 40c. White-tailed tropic bird 70 65
612 40c. Yellow-bellied sapsucker 70 65
613 40c. Green-throated carib . . 70 65
614 40c. Purple-throated carib . . 70 65
615 40c. Red-billed whistling duck ("Black-bellied tree-duck") 70 65
616 40c. Ringed kingfisher . . . 70 65
617 40c. Burrowing owl 70 65
618 40c. Ruddy turnstone 70 65
619 40c. Great blue heron 70 65
620 40c. Yellow-crowned night-heron 70 65
MS621 76 × 59 mm. $6 Great egret 10·00 11·00
Nos. 601/20 were printed together, se-tenant, forming a composite design.

1991. 65th Birthday of Queen Elizabeth II. As T **210** of Lesotho. Multicoloured.
622 15c. Queen Elizabeth at polo match with Prince Charles 40 20
623 40c. Queen and Prince Philip on Buckingham Palace balcony 50 35
624 $2 In carriage at Ascot, 1986 1·75 1·75
625 $4 Queen Elizabeth II at Windsor polo match, 1989 3·00 3·75
MS626 68 × 90 mm. $5 Queen Elizabeth and Prince Philip . . 4·25 5·00

1991. 10th Wedding Anniv of Prince and Princess of Wales. As T **210** of Lesotho. Multicoloured.
627 10c. Prince Charles and Princess Diana 60 20
628 50c. Prince of Wales and family 70 30
629 $1 Prince William and Prince Harry . . . . 1·00 1·00
630 $5 Prince and Princess of Wales . . . . 4·00 4·00
MS631 68 × 90 mm. $5 Prince and Princess of Wales in Hungary, and young princes at Christmas . . 6·00 6·00

1991. "Phila Nippon '91" International Stamp Exhibition, Tokyo. Japanese Railway Locomotives. As T **257** of Maldive Islands. Mult.
632 10c. Class C62 steam locomotive 70 30
633 15c. Class C56 steam locomotive (horiz) 80 30
634 40c. Class C55 streamlined steam locomotive (horiz) 1·25 50
635 60c. Class 1400 steam locomotive (horiz) . . . . 1·40 80
636 $1 Class 485 diesel rail car 1·60 1·00
637 $2 Class C61 steam locomotive . . . . 2·50 2·25
638 $3 Class 485 diesel train (horiz) . . . . 2·75 2·75
639 $4 Class 7000 electric train (horiz) . . . . 3·00 3·50
MS640 Two sheets, each 108 × 72 mm. (a) $5 Class D51 steam locomotive (horiz). (b) $5 "Hikari" express train (horiz) Set of 2 sheets . . . . 8·00 8·50

1991. Christmas. Drawings by Albrecht Durer. As T **211** of Lesotho.
641 10c. black and green 15 10
642 40c. black and orange . . . 30 25
643 60c. black and blue 35 30
644 $3 black and mauve . . . . 1·40 2·75
MS645 Two sheets, each 96 × 124 mm. (a) $6 black. (b) $6 black Set of 2 sheets . . . . . 5·50 6·25
DESIGNS: 10c. "Mary being Crowned by an Angel"; 40c. "Mary with the Pear"; 60c. "Mary in a Halo"; $3 "Mary with Crown of Stars and Sceptre"; $6 (**MS**645a) "The Holy Family" (detail); $6 (**MS**645b) "Mary at the Yard Gate" (detail).

66 "Marasmius haemtocephalus"

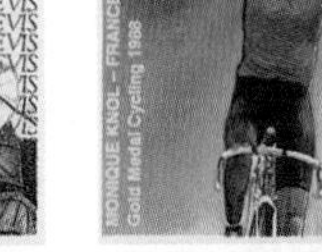

67 Monique Knol (cycling), Netherlands

1991. Fungi (2nd series). Multicoloured.
646 15c. Type **66** 30 20
647 40c. "Psilocybe cubensis" . . 40 30
648 60c. "Hygrocybe acutoconica" 50 40
649 75c. "Hygrocybe occidentalis" 60 60
650 $1 "Boletellus cubensis" . . . 70 70
651 $2 "Gymnopilus chrysopellus" . . . . . . 1·25 1·50

652 $4 "Cantharellus cinnabarinus" 2·25 2·75

653 $5 "Chlorophyllum molybdites" 2·25 2·75

MS654 Two sheets, each 70×58 mm. (a) $6 "Psilocybe cubensis", "Hygrocybe acutoconica" and "Boletellus cubensis" (horiz). (b) $6 "Hygrocybe occidentalis", "Marasmius haematocephalus" and "Gymnopilus chrysopellus" (horiz) Set of 2 sheets 9·00 9·50

1992. 40th Anniv of Queen Elizabeth II's Accession. As T **214** of Lesotho. Multicoloured.

655 10c. Charlestown from the sea 40 10

656 40c. Charlestown square 60 25

657 $1 Mountain scenery 1·00 60

658 $5 Early cottage 3·00 3·75

MS659 Two sheets, each 74×97 mm. (a) $6 Queen or pink conch on beach. (b) $6 Nevis sunset Set of 2 sheets 8·50 9·00

1992. Olympic Games, Barcelona. Gold Medal Winners of 1988. Multicoloured.

660 20c. Type **67** 75 30

661 25c. Roger Kingdom (hurdles), U.S.A. 50 30

662 50c. Yugoslavia (men's waterpolo) 75 50

663 80c. Anja Fichtel (foil), West Germany 90 70

664 $1 Said Aouita (mid-distance running), Morocco 1·00 80

665 $1.50 Yuri Sedykh (hammer throw), U.S.S.R. 1·25 1·40

666 $3 Shushunova (women's gymnastics), U.S.S.R. 2·25 2·75

667 $5 Valimir Artemov (men's gymnastics), U.S.S.R. 2·50 3·25

MS668 Two sheets, each 103×73 mm. (a) $6 Niam Suleymanoglu (weightlifting), Turkey. (b) $6 Florence Griffith-Joyner (women's 100 metres), U.S.A. Set of 2 sheets 5·50 7·00

No. 660 is inscribed "France" in error.

68 "Landscape" (Mariano Fortuny i Marsal)

69 Early Compass and Ship

1992. "Granada '92" International Stamp Exhibition, Spain. Spanish Paintings. Multicoloured.

669 20c. Type **68** 40 30

670 25c. "Dona Juana la Loca" (Francisco Pradilla Ortiz) (horiz) 40 30

671 50c. "Idyll" (Fortuny i Marsal) 60 50

672 80c. "Old Man Naked in the Sun" (Fortuny i Marsal) 80 70

673 $1 "The Painter's Children in the Japanese Salon" (detail) (Fortuny i Marsal) 90 80

674 $2 "The Painter's Children in the Japanese Salon" (different detail) (Fortuny i Marsal) 1·40 1·40

675 $3 "Still Life: Sea Bream and Oranges" (Luis Eugenio Melendez) (horiz) 2·25 2·75

676 $5 "Still Life: Box of Sweets, Pastry and Other Objects" (Melendez) 2·75 3·50

MS677 Two sheets, each 121×95 mm. (a) $6 "Bullfight" (Fortuny i Marsal) (111×86 mm). (b) $6 "Moroccans" (Fortuny i Marsal) (111×86 mm). Imperf Set of 2 sheets 5·50 6·50

1992. 500th Anniv of Discovery of America by Columbus (4th issue) and "World Columbian Stamp Expo '92", Chicago. Multicoloured.

678 20c. Type **69** 75 25

679 50c. Manatee and fleet 1·25 50

680 80c. Green turtle and "Santa Maria" 1·50 80

681 $1.50 "Santa Maria" and arms 2·25 1·75

682 $3 Queen Isabella of Spain and commission 2·50 3·25

683 $5 Pineapple and colonists 3·00 4·50

MS684 Two sheets, each 101×70 mm. (a) $6 British storm petrel and town (horiz). (b) $6 Peppers and carib canoe (horiz) Set of 2 sheets 10·00 12·00

1992. 500th Anniv of Discovery of America by Columbus (5th issue). Organization of East Caribbean States. As Nos. 911/12 of Montserrat. Multicoloured.

685 $1 Columbus meeting Amerindians 50 50

686 $2 Ships approaching island 1·25 1·40

1992. Postage Stamp Mega Event, New York. Sheet 100×70 mm, containing multicoloured design as T **219** of Lesotho.

MS687 $6 Empire State Building 4·50 5·00

70 Minnie Mouse

71 Care Bear and Butterfly

1992. Mickey's Portrait Gallery. Mult.

688 10c. Type **70** 50 20

689 15c. Mickey Mouse 50 20

690 40c. Donald Duck 70 30

691 80c. Mickey Mouse, 1930 90 70

692 $1 Daisy Duck 1·00 80

693 $2 Pluto 1·75 1·50

694 $4 Goofy 2·75 3·00

695 $5 Goofy, 1932 2·75 3·00

MS696 Two sheets. (a) 102×128 mm. $6 Mickey in armchair (horiz). (b) 128×102 mm. $6 Mickey and Minnie in airplane (horiz) Set of 2 sheets 10·00 11·00

1992. Christmas. Religious Paintings. As T **218** of Lesotho. Multicoloured.

697 20c. "The Virgin and Child between Two Saints" (Giovanni Bellini) 40 15

698 40c. "The Virgin and Child surrounded by Four Angels" (Master of the Castello Nativity) 55 25

699 50c. "Virgin and Child surrounded by Angels with St. Frediano and St. Augustine" (detail) (Filippo Lippi) 60 30

700 80c. "The Virgin and Child between St. Peter and St. Sebastian" (Bellini) 85 70

701 $1 "The Virgin and Child with St. Julian and St. Nicholas of Myra" (Lorenzo di Credi) 1·00 80

702 $2 "St. Bernardino and a Female Saint presenting a Donor to Virgin and Child" (Francesco Bissolo) 1·75 1·50

703 $4 "Madonna and Child with Four Cherubs" (ascr Barthel Bruyn) 2·75 3·50

704 $5 "The Virgin and Child" (Quentin Metsys) 3·00 3·50

MS705 Two sheets, each 76×102 mm. (a) $6 "Virgin and Child surrounded by Two Angels" (detail) (Perugino). (b) $6 "Madonna and Child with the Infant, St. John and Archangel Gabriel" (Sandro Botticelli) Set of 2 sheets 7·00 8·00

No. 699 is inscribed "Fillipo Lippi" in error.

1993. Ecology. Multicoloured.

706 80c. Type **71** 60 60

MS707 71×101 mm. $2 Care Bear on beach 2·25 2·50

1993. Bicentenary of the Louvre, Paris. As T **221** of Lesotho. Multicoloured.

708 $1 "The Card Cheat" (left detail) (La Tour) 85 85

709 $1 "The Card Cheat" (centre detail) (La Tour) 85 85

710 $1 "The Card Cheat" (right detail) (La Tour) 85 85

711 $1 "St. Joseph, the Carpenter" (La Tour) 85 85

712 $1 "St. Thomas" (La Tour) 85 85

713 $1 "Adoration of the Shepherds" (left detail) (La Tour) 85 85

714 $1 "Adoration of the Shepherds" (right detail) (La Tour) 85 85

715 $1 "Mary Magdalene with a Candle" (La Tour) 85 85

MS716 70×100 mm. $6 "Archangel Raphael leaving the Family of Tobius" (Rembrandt) (52×85 mm) 4·25 4·75

1993. 15th Death Anniv of Elvis Presley (singer). As T **280** of Maldive Islands. Multicoloured.

717 $1 Elvis Presley 1·10 85

718 $1 Elvis with guitar 1·10 85

719 $1 Elvis with microphone 1·10 85

72 Japanese Launch Vehicle H-11

73 "Plumeria rubra"

1993. Anniversaries and Events. Mult.

720 15c. Type **72** 60 30

721 50c. Airship "Hindenburg" on fire, 1937 (horiz) 1·00 65

722 75c. Konrad Adenauer and Charles de Gaulle (horiz) 65 65

723 80c. Red Cross emblem and map of Nevis (horiz) 1·25 80

724 80c. "Resolute" (yacht), 1920 1·25 80

725 80c. Nelson Museum and map of Nevis (horiz) 1·25 80

726 80c. St. Thomas's Church (horiz) 70 80

727 $1 Blue whale (horiz) 2·00 1·25

728 $3 Mozart 3·00 2·75

729 $3 Graph and U.N. emblems (horiz) 1·75 2·25

730 $3 Lions Club emblem 1·75 2·25

731 $5 Soviet "Energia" launch vehicle SL-17 3·25 3·75

732 $5 Lebaudy-Juillot airship No. 1 "La Jaune" (horiz) 3·25 3·75

733 $5 Adenauer and Pres. Kennedy (horiz) 3·25 3·75

MS734 Five sheets. (a) 104×71 mm. $6 Astronaut. (b) 104×71 mm. $6 Zeppelin LZ-5, 1909 (horiz). (c) 100×70 mm. $6 Konrad Adenauer (horiz). (d) 75×103 mm. $6 "America 3" (yacht), 1992 (horiz). (e) 98×66 mm. $6 Masked reveller from "Don Giovanni" (horiz) Set of 5 sheets 18·00 19·00

ANNIVERSARIES AND EVENTS—Nos. 720, 731, **MS**734a, International Space Year; 721, 732, **MS**734b, 75th death anniv of Count Ferdinand von Zeppelin (airship pioneer); 722, 733, **MS**734c, 25th death anniv of Konrad Adenauer (German statesman); 723, 50th anniv of St. Kitts–Nevis Red Cross; 724, **MS**734d, Americas Cup Yachting Championship; 725, Opening of Nelson Museum; 726, 150th anniv of Anglican Diocese of North-eastern Caribbean and Aruba; 727, Earth Summit '92, Rio; 728, **MS**734e, Death bicent of Mozart; 729, International Conference on Nutrition, Rome; 730, 75th anniv of International Association of Lions Clubs.

1993. West Indian Flowers. Multicoloured.

735 10c. Type **73** 70 30

736 25c. "Bougainvillea" 80 30

737 50c. "Allamanda cathartica" 1·00 50

738 80c. "Anthurium andraeanum" 1·40 70

739 $1 "Ixora coccinea" 1·60 75

740 $2 "Hibiscus rosa-sinensis" 2·50 2·25

741 $4 "Justicia brandegeeana" 3·75 4·75

742 $5 "Antigonon leptopus" 3·75 4·75

MS743 Two sheets, each 100×70 mm. (a) $6 "Lantana camara". (b) $6 "Petrea volubilis" Set of 2 sheets 7·50 8·50

74 Antillean Blue (male)

1993. Butterflies. Multicoloured.

744 10c. Type **74** 60 40

745 25c. Cuban crescentspot (female) 75 40

746 50c. Ruddy daggerwing 1·00 50

747 80c. Little yellow (male) 1·25 75

748 $1 Atala 1·25 90

749 $1.50 Orange-barred giant sulphur 2·00 2·25

750 $4 Tropic queen (male) 3·25 4·50

751 $5 Malachite 3·25 4·50

MS752 Two sheets, each 76×105 mm. (a) $6 Polydamus swallowtail (male). (b) $6 West Indian buckeye Set of 2 sheets 10·00 11·00

1993. 40th Anniv of Coronation. As T **224** of Lesotho.

753 10c. multicoloured 15 20

754 80c. brown and black 45 55

755 $2 multicoloured 1·10 1·40

756 $4 multicoloured 2·00 2·25

MS757 71×101 mm. $6 multicoloured 3·00 3·50

DESIGNS—38×47 mm: 10c. Queen Elizabeth II at Coronation (photograph by Cecil Beaton); 80c. Queen wearing Imperial State Crown; $2 Crowning of Queen Elizabeth II; $4 Queen and Prince Charles at polo match. 28½×42½ mm: $6 "Queen Elizabeth II, 1977" (detail) (Susan Crawford).

75 Flag and National Anthem

76 "Annunciation of Mary"

1993. 10th Anniv of Independence of St. Kitts–Nevis. Multicoloured.

758 25c. Type **75** 1·00 25

759 80c. Brown pelican and map of St. Kitts–Nevis 1·40 1·00

1993. World Cup Football Championship 1994, U.S.A. As T **278** of Maldive Islands. Mult.

760 10c. Imre Garaba (Hungary) and Michel Platini (France) (horiz) 60 30

761 25c. Diego Maradona (Argentina) and Giuseppe Bergomi (Italy) (horiz) 75 30

762 50c. Luis Fernandez (France) and Vasily Rats (Russia) (horiz) 95 45

763 80c. Victor Munez (Spain) (horiz) 1·40 65

764 $1 Preben Elkjaer (Denmark) and Andoni Goicoechea (Spain) (horiz) 1·60 85

765 $2 Elzo Coelho (Brazil) and Jean Tigana (France) (horiz) 2·50 2·25

766 $3 Pedro Troglio (Argentina) and Sergei Alejnikov (Russia) (horiz) 2·75 3·00

767 $5 Jan Karas (Poland) and Antonio Luiz Costa (Brazil) (horiz) 3·25 4·25

MS768 Two sheets. (a) 100×70 mm. $5 Belloumi (Algeria) (horiz). (b) 70×100 mm. $5 Trevor Steven (England) Set of 2 sheets 11·00 11·00

1993. Christmas. Religious Paintings by Durer. Black, yellow and red (Nos. 769/73 and 776) or multicoloured (others).

769 20c. Type **76** 50 15

770 40c. "The Nativity" (drawing) 70 30

771 50c. "Holy Family on a Grassy Bank" 80 30

772 80c. "The Presentation of Christ in the Temple" 1·00 55

773 $1 "Virgin in Glory on the Crescent" 1·25 70

774 $1.60 "The Nativity" (painting) 2·00 2·25

775 $3 "Madonna and Child" 2·50 3·25

776 $5 "The Presentation of Christ in the Temple" (detail) 3·25 4·75

MS777 Two sheets, each 105×130 mm. (a) $6 "Mary, Child and the Long-tailed Monkey" (detail) (Durer). (b) $6 "The Rest on the Flight into Egypt" (detail) (Jean-Honure Fragonard) (horiz) Set of 2 sheets 8·50 9·50

77 Mickey Mouse playing Basketball

1994. Sports and Pastimes. Walt Disney cartoon characters. Multicoloured (except No. **MS**786a).

778 10c. Type **77** 40 30

779 25c. Minnie Mouse sunbathing (vert) 50 20

780 50c. Mickey playing volleyball 70 40

781 80c. Minnie dancing (vert) . . 80 60
782 $1 Mickey playing football 1·00 70
783 $1.50 Minnie hula hooping (vert) . . . . 1·75 2·00
784 $4 Minnie skipping (vert) . . 2·75 3·50
785 $5 Mickey wrestling Big Pete 2·75 3·50
MS786 Two sheets. (a) 127 × 102 mm. $6 Mickey, Donald Duck and Goofy in tug of war (black, red and green). (b) 102 × 127 mm. $6 Mickey using Test your Strength machine Set of 2 sheets . . . . 9·00 10·00

1994. "Hong Kong '94" International Stamp Exhibition. No. **MS**752 optd with "HONG KONG '94" logo on sheet margins.
MS787 Two sheets, each 76 × 105 mm. (a) $6 Polydamas swallowtail (male). (b) $6 West Indian buckeye Set of 2 sheets 7·50 8·00

1994. Hummel Figurines. As T **256** of Maldive Islands. Multicoloured.
788 5c. Girl with umbrella . . . 15 40
789 25c. Boy holding beer mug and parsnips 45 15
790 50c. Girl sitting in tree . . . 65 35
791 80c. Boy in hat and scarf . . 85 60
792 $1 Boy with umbrella . . . . 1·00 70
793 $1.60 Girl with bird . . . . 1·75 1·75
794 $2 Boy on sledge . . . . . . 2·00 2·00
795 $5 Boy sitting in apple tree 2·75 3·75
MS796 Two sheets, each 94 × 125 mm. (a) Nos. 788 and 792/4. (b) Nos. 789/91 and 795 Set of 2 sheets . . . . 6·50 7·50

79 Beekeeper collecting Wild Nest

1994. Beekeeping. Multicoloured.
797 50c. Type **79** 65 30
798 80c. Beekeeping club 90 40
799 $1.60 Extracting honey from frames . . . . 1·75 1·75
800 $3 Keepers placing queen in hive . . . . 2·75 3·75
MS801 100 × 70 mm. $6 Queen and workers in hive and mechanical honey extractor . . . . 5·00 5·50

80 Blue Point Himalayan

1994. Persian Cats. Multicoloured.
802 80c. Type **80** 90 90
803 80c. Black and white Persian 90 90
804 80c. Cream Persian 90 90
805 80c. Red Persian 90 90
806 80c. Persian 90 90
807 80c. Persian black smoke . . 90 90
808 80c. Chocolate smoke Persian 90 90
809 80c. Black Persian 90 90
MS810 Two sheets, each 100 × 70 mm. (a) $6 Silver tabby Persian. (B) $6 Brown tabby Persian Set of 2 sheets . . . . 10·00 11·00

81 Black Coral

83 Symbol 1. Turtles and Cloud

82 Striped Burrfish

1994. Endangered Species. Black Coral.
811 **81** 25c. multicoloured 60 75
812 – 40c. multicoloured 70 80
813 – 50c. multicoloured 70 80
814 – 80c. multicoloured 80 90
DESIGNS: 40c. to 80c. Different forms of coral.

1994. Fishes. Multicoloured.
815 10c. Type **82** 50 50
816 50c. Flame-backed angelfish 55 55
817 50c. Reef bass 55 55
818 50c. Long-finned damselfish ("Honey Gregory") 55 55
819 50c. Saddle squirrelfish . . . 55 55
820 50c. Cobalt chromis 55 55
821 50c. Genie's neon goby . . . 55 55
822 50c. Slender-tailed cardinalfish 55 55
823 50c. Royal gramma 55 55
824 $1 Blue-striped grunt 75 75
825 $1.60 Blue angelfish . . . . 1·00 1·25
826 $3 Cocoa damselfish . . . . 1·50 1·75
MS827 Two sheets, each 100 × 70 mm. (a) $6 Blue marlin. (b) $6 Sailfish (vert) Set of 2 sheets 8·00 8·50
Nos. 816/23 were printed together, se-tenant, forming a composite design.
No. 824 is inscribed "BLUESRIPED GRUNT" in error.

1994. "Philakorea '94" International Stamp Exhibition, Seoul. Longevity symbols. Multicoloured.
828 50c. Type **83** 35 50
829 50c. Symbol 2. Manchurian cranes and bamboo 35 50
830 50c. Symbol 3. Deer and bamboo 35 50
831 50c. Symbol 4. Turtles and Sun 35 50
832 50c. Symbol 5. Manchurian cranes under tree 35 50
833 50c. Symbol 6. Deer and tree 35 50
834 50c. Symbol 7. Turtles and rock 35 50
835 50c. Symbol 8. Manchurian cranes above tree 35 50

84 Twin-roofed House with Veranda

1994. Island Architecture. Multicoloured.
836 25c. Type **84** 60 20
837 50c. Two-storey house with outside staircase 85 30
838 $1 Government Treasury . . 1·25 1·10
839 $5 Two-storey house with red roof . . . . 3·75 5·50
MS840 102 × 72 mm. $6 Raised bungalow with veranda . . . . 3·75 5·00

85 William Demas

1994. First Recipients of Order of Caribbean Community. Multicoloured.
841 25c. Type **85** 30 10
842 50c. Sir Shridath Ramphal 50 45
843 $1 Derek Walcott . . . . . 1·90 1·25

86 "The Virgin Mary as Queen of Heaven" (detail) (Jan Provost)

88 Rufous-breasted Hermit

87 Mickey and Minnie Mouse

1994. Christmas. Religious Paintings. Multicoloured.
844 20c. Type **86** 20 10
845 40c. "The Virgin Mary as Queen of Heaven" (different detail) (Provost) 35 25
846 50c. "The Virgin Mary as Queen of Heaven" (different detail) (Provost) 40 30
847 80c. "Adoration of the Magi" (detail) (Circle of Van der Goes) 60 40
848 $1 "Adoration of the Magi" (different detail) (Circle of Van der Goes) 70 50
849 $1.60 "Adoration of the Magi" (different detail) (Circle of Van der Goes) 1·25 1·50
850 $3 "Adoration of the Magi" (different detail) (Circle of Van der Goes) . . . . . . 2·00 2·50
851 $5 "The Virgin Mary as Queen of Heaven" (different detail) (Provost) 3·00 3·75
MS852 Two sheets, each 96 × 117 mm. (a) $5 "The Virgin Mary as Queen of Heaven" (different detail) (Provost). (b) $6 "Adoration of the Magi" (different detail) (Circle of Van der Goes) Set of 2 sheets . . . . . 8·00 8·50

1995. Disney Sweethearts (1st series). Walt Disney Cartoon Characters. Multicoloured.
853 10c. Type **87** 20 20
854 25c. Donald and Daisy Duck 35 20
855 50c. Pluto and Fifi 50 35
856 80c. Clarabelle Cow and Horace Horsecollar 70 50
857 $1 Pluto and Figaro 85 65
858 $1.50 Polly and Peter Penguin . . . . 1·25 1·50
859 $4 Prunella Pullet and Hick Rooster . . . . 2·50 3·25
860 $5 Jenny Wren and Cock Robin . . . . 2·50 3·25
MS861 Two sheets, each 133 × 107 mm. (a) $6 Daisy Duck (vert). (b) $6 Minnie Mouse (vert) Set of 2 sheets . . . . 8·00 8·50
See also Nos. 998/1007.

1995. Birds. Multicoloured.
862 50c. Type **88** 40 40
863 50c. Purple-throated carib . . 40 40
864 50c. Green mango 40 40
865 50c. Bahama woodstar . . . 40 40
866 50c. Hispaniolan emerald . . . 40 40
867 50c. Antillean crested hummingbird 40 40
868 50c. Green-throated carib . . 40 40
869 50c. Antillean mango 40 40
870 50c. Vervain hummingbird 40 40
871 50c. Jamaican mango 40 40
872 50c. Cuban emerald 40 40
873 50c. Blue-headed hummingbird 40 40
874 50c. Hooded merganser . . . 40 40
875 80c. Green-backed heron . . 65 50
876 $2 Double-crested cormorant 1·25 1·40
877 $3 Ruddy duck . . . . . . 1·50 1·75
MS878 Two sheets, each 100 × 70 mm. (a) $6 Black skimmer. (b) $6 Snowy plover Set of 2 sheets . . . . 7·50 8·00
No. 870 is inscribed "VERVIAN" in error.

89 Pointer

1995. Dogs. Multicoloured.
879 25c. Type **89** 30 20
880 50c. Old Danish pointer . . . 50 50
881 80c. Irish setter 65 65
882 80c. Weimaraner 65 65
883 80c. Gordon setter 65 65
884 80c. Brittany spaniel 65 65
885 80c. American cocker spaniel 65 65
886 80c. English cocker spaniel 65 65
887 80c. Labrador retriever . . . 65 65
888 80c. Golden retriever 65 65
889 80c. Flat-coated retriever . . 65 65
890 $1 German short-haired pointer 75 75
891 $2 English setter . . . . . . 1·40 1·40
MS892 Two sheets, each 72 × 58 mm. (a) $6 German shepherds. (b) $6 Bloodhounds Set of 2 sheets . . . . 7·50 8·00
"POINTER" is omitted from the inscription on No. 890. No. **MS**892a is incorrectly inscribed "SHEPHARD".

90 "Schulumbergera truncata"

92 Oriental and African People

91 Scouts backpacking

1995. Cacti. Multicoloured.
893 40c. Type **90** 30 20
894 50c. "Echinocereus pectinatus" 40 25
895 80c. "Mammillaria zeilmanniana alba" 65 40
896 $1.60 "Lobivia hertriehiana" 1·10 1·25
897 $2 "Hammatocactus setispinus" . . . . 1·40 1·50
898 $3 "Astrophytum myriostigma" . . . . . . 1·60 2·00
MS899 Two sheets, each 106 × 76 mm. (a) $6 "Opuntia robusta". (b) $6 "Rhipsalidopsis gaertneri" Set of 2 sheets . . . 7·00 7·50

1995. 18th World Scout Jamboree, Netherlands. Multicoloured.
900 $1 Type **91** . . . . 1·00 1·10
901 $2 Scouts building aerial rope way . . . . 1·50 1·75
902 $4 Scout map reading . . . . 2·00 2·25
MS903 101 × 71 mm. $6 Scout in canoe (vert) . . . . 3·50 4·00
Nos. 900/2 were printed together, se-tenant, forming a composite design.

1995. 50th Anniv of End of Second World War in Europe. As T **317** of Maldive Islands. Multicoloured.
904 $1.25 Clark Gable and aircraft . . . . 1·00 1·00
905 $1.25 Audie Murphy and machine-gunner . . . . . 1·00 1·00
906 $1.25 Glenn Miller playing trombone . . . . 1·00 1·00
907 $1.25 Joe Louis and infantry 1·00 1·00
908 $1.25 Jimmy Doolittle and U.S.S. "Hornet" (aircraft carrier) . . . . 1·00 1·00
909 $1.25 John Hersey and jungle patrol . . . . 1·00 1·00
910 $1.25 John F. Kennedy in patrol boat . . . . 1·00 1·00
911 $1.25 James Stewart and bombers . . . . 1·00 1·00
MS912 101 × 71 mm. $6 Jimmy Doolittle (vert) . . . . 3·00 3·50

1995. 50th Anniv of United Nations. Each lilac and black.
913 $1.25 Type **92** 55 80
914 $1.60 Asian people . . . . . 75 1·10
915 $3 American and European people . . . . 1·40 1·60
MS916 105 × 75 mm. $6 Pres. Nelson Mandela of South Africa . . . 2·75 3·50
Nos. 913/15 were printed together, se-tenant, forming a composite design.

1995. 50th Anniv of F.A.O. As T **92**. Multicoloured.
917 40c. Woman wearing yellow headdress 15 60
918 $2 Babies and emblem . . . 85 1·25
919 $3 Woman wearing blue headdress . . . . 1·25 1·60
MS920 105 × 80 mm. $6 Man carrying hoe . . . . 2·50 3·50
Nos. 917/19 were printed together, se-tenant, forming a composite design.
No. **MS**920 is inscribed "1945–1955" in error.

93 Rotary Emblem on Nevis Flag

1995. 90th Anniv of Rotary International. Multicoloured.
921 $5 Type **93** . . . . 2·50 3·25
MS922 95 × 66 mm. $6 Rotary emblem and beach . . . . . 3·00 3·75

1995. 95th Birthday of Queen Elizabeth the Queen Mother. As T **321** of Maldive Islands.
923 $1.50 brown, light brown and black . . . . 1·75 1·75
924 $1.50 multicoloured . . . . 1·75 1·75
925 $1.50 multicoloured . . . . 1·75 1·75
926 $1.50 multicoloured . . . . 1·75 1·75
MS927 102 × 127 mm. $6 multicoloured . . . . 6·00 6·00
DESIGNS: No. 923, Queen Elizabeth the Queen Mother (pastel drawing); 924, Wearing pink hat; 925, At desk (oil painting); 926, Wearing blue hat; **MS**927, Wearing tiara.
No. **MS**927 was also issued additionally inscribed "IN MEMORIAM 1900–2002" on margin.

1995. 50th Anniv of End of Second World War in the Pacific. United States Aircraft. As T **317** of Maldive Islands. Multicoloured.
928 $2 Grumman F4F Wildcat 1·40 1·40
929 $2 Chance Vought F4U-1A Corsair . . . . 1·40 1·40
930 $2 Vought SB2U Vindicator 1·40 1·40
931 $2 Grumman F6F Hellcat . . 1·40 1·40

932 $2 Douglas SDB Dauntless . . . 1·40 1·40
933 $2 Grumman TBF-1 Avenger . . . 1·40 1·40
MS934 108 × 76 mm. $6 Chance Vought F4U-1A Corsair on carrier flight deck . . . . . . 4·50 5·50

94 Emil von Behring (1901 Medicine)

1995. Centenary of Nobel Trust Fund. Past Prize Winners. Multicoloured.
935 $1.25 Type **94** 75 85
936 $1.25 Wilhelm Rontgen (1901 Physics) 75 85
937 $1.25 Paul Heyse (1910 Literature) 75 85
938 $1.25 Le Duc Tho (1973 Peace) 75 85
939 $1.25 Yasunari Kawabata (1968 Literature) 75 85
940 $1.25 Tsung-dao Lee (1957 Physics) 75 85
941 $1.25 Werner Heisenberg (1932 Physics) 75 85
942 $1.25 Johannes Stark (1919 Physics) 75 85
943 $1.25 Wilhelm Wien (1911 Physics) 75 85
MS944 101 × 71 mm. $6 Kenzaburo Oe (1994 Literature) . . . . . 3·25 3·75

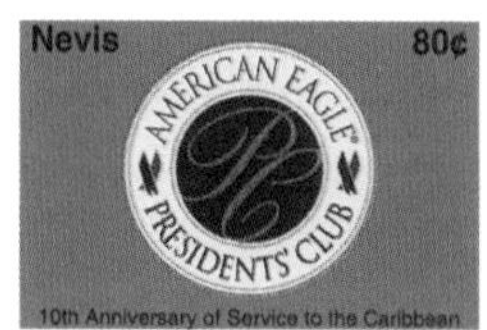

95 American Eagle Presidents' Club Logo

1995. 10th Anniv of American Eagle Air Services to the Caribbean. Sheet 70 × 100 mm, containing T **95** and similar horiz design. Multicoloured.
MS945 80c. Type **95**; $3 Aircraft over Nevis beach . . . . . . 2·40 2·50

96 Great Egrets

1995. Marine Life. Multicoloured.
946 50c. Type **96** 55 55
947 50c. 17th-century galleon . . 55 55
948 50c. Galleon and marlin . . 55 55
949 50c. Herring gulls 55 55
950 50c. Nassau groupers 55 55
951 50c. Spotted eagleray 55 55
952 50c. Leopard shark and hammerhead 55 55
953 50c. Hourglass dolphins . . . 55 55
954 50c. Spanish hogfish 55 55
955 50c. Jellyfish and seahorses 55 55
956 50c. Angelfish and buried treasure 55 55
957 50c. Hawksbill turtle 55 55
958 50c. Common octopus . . . 55 55
959 50c. Moray eel 55 55
960 50c. Queen angelfish and butterflyfish 55 55
961 50c. Ghost crab and sea star 55 55
MS962 Two sheets. (a) 106 × 76 mm. $5 Nassau grouper. (b) 76 × 106 mm. $5 Queen angelfish (vert) Set of 2 sheeets . . . . 7·00 7·00
No. **MS**962 also commemorates the "Singapore '95" International Stamp Exhibition.
Nos. 946/61 were printed together, se-tenant, forming a composite design.

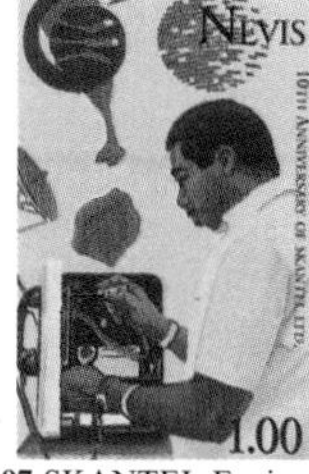

97 SKANTEL Engineer

1995. 10th Anniv of SKANTEL (telecommunications company). Multicoloured.
963 $1 Type **97** 60 50
964 $1.50 SKANTEL sign outside Nevis office . . . . 80 1·25
MS965 76 × 106 mm. $5 St. Kitts SKANTEL office (horiz) . . . 3·00 3·50

98 "Rucellai Madonna and Child" (detail) (Duccio)

1995. Christmas. Religious Paintings by Duccio di Buoninsegna. Multicoloured.
966 20c. Type **98** 20 15
967 50c. "Angel form the Rucellai Madonna" (detail) 40 25
968 80c. "Madonna and Child" (different) 60 40
969 $1 "Angel from the Annunciation" (detail) . . 75 60
970 $1.60 "Madonna and Child" (different) . . . . 1·25 1·50
971 $3 "Angel from the Rucellai Madonna" (different) . . . 1·90 2·75
MS972 Two sheets, each 102 × 127 mm. (a) $5 "Nativity with the Prophets Isaiah and Ezekiel" (detail). (b) $6 "The Crevole Madonna" (detail) Set of 2 sheets . . . . 6·50 7·50

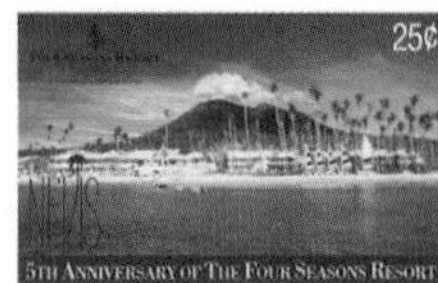

99 View of Nevis Four Seasons Resort

1996. 5th Anniv of Four Seasons Resort, Nevis. Multicoloured.
973 25c. Type **99** 15 20
974 50c. Catamarans, Pinney's Beach 25 30
975 80c. Robert Trent Jones II Golf Course 40 45
976 $2 Prime Minister Simeon Daniel laying foundation stone . . . . 1·00 1·40
MS977 76 × 106 mm. $6 Sunset over resort . . . . 3·00 3·50

100 Rat, Plant and Butterfly

1996. Chinese New Year ("Year of the Rat"). Multicoloured.
978 $1 Type **100** 50 60
979 $1 Rat with prickly plant . . 50 60
980 $1 Rat and bee 50 60
981 $1 Rat and dragonfly 50 60
MS982 74 × 104 mm. Nos. 978/81 2·25 2·50
MS983 74 × 104 mm. $3 Rat eating 2·00 2·25

101 Ancient Greek Boxers

1996. Olympic Games, Atlanta. Previous Medal Winners. Multicoloured.
984 25c. Type **101** 25 20
985 50c. Mark Spitz (U.S.A.) (Gold – swimming, 1972) 35 30
986 80c. Siegbert Horn (East Germany) (Gold – single kayak slalom, 1972) . . . 50 45
987 $1 Jim Thorpe on medal (U.S.A.), 1912 (vert) . . . 60 70
988 $1 Glenn Morris on medal (U.S.A.), 1936 (vert) . . . 60 70
989 $1 Bob Mathias on medal (U.S.A.), 1948 and 1952 (vert) 60 70
990 $1 Rafer Johnson on medal (U.S.A.), 1960 (vert) . . . 60 70
991 $1 Bill Toomey (U.S.A.), 1968 (vert) 60 70
992 $1 Nikolay Avilov (Russia), 1972 (vert) 60 70
993 $1 Bruce Jenner (U.S.A.), 1976 (vert) 60 70
994 $1 Daley Thompson (Great Britain), 1980 and 1984 (vert) 60 70
995 $1 Christian Schenk (East Germany), 1988 (vert) . . 60 70
996 $3 Olympic Stadium and Siegestor Arch, Munich (vert) . . . . 1·60 2·00
MS997 Two sheets, each 105 × 75 mm. (a) $5 Willi Holdorf (West Germany) (Gold – decathlon, 1964) (vert). (b) $5 Hans-Joachim Walde (West Germany) (Silver – decathlon, 1968) (vert) Set of 2 sheets . . 6·50 7·00

1996. Disney Sweethearts (2nd series). As T **87**. Walt Disney Cartoon Characters. Multicoloured.
998 $2 Pocahontas and John Smith . . . . 1·75 1·50
999 $2 Mowgli and the Girl . . 1·75 1·50
1000 $2 Belle and the Beast . . . 1·75 1·50
1001 $2 Cinderella and Prince Charming . . . . 1·75 1·50
1002 $2 Pinocchio and the Dutch Girl . . . . 1·75 1·50
1003 $2 Grace Martin and Henry Coy . . . . 1·75 1·50
1004 $2 Snow White and the Prince . . . . 1·75 1·50
1005 $2 Aladdin and Jasmine . . 1·75 1·50
1006 $2 Pecos Bill and Slue Foot Sue . . . . 1·75 1·50
MS1007 Two sheets, each 110 × 130 mm. (a) $6 Sleeping Beauty and Prince Phillip (vert). (b) $6 Ariel and Eric Set of 2 sheets . . . . 9·00 10·00

102 Qian Qing Gong, Peking

1996. "CHINA '96" 9th Asian International Stamp Exhibition, Peking. Peking Pagodas. Multicoloured.
1008 $1 Type **102** 50 60
1009 $1 Temple of Heaven . . . 50 60
1010 $1 Zhongnanhai 50 60
1011 $1 Da Zing Hall, Shehyang Palace 50 60
1012 $1 Temple of the Sleeping Buddha 50 60
1013 $1 Huang Qiong Yu, Altar of Heaven 50 60
1014 $1 The Grand Bell Temple 50 60
1015 $1 Imperial Palace 50 60
1016 $1 Pu Tuo Temple 50 60
MS1017 104 × 74 mm. $6 Summer Palace of Emperor Wan Yan-liang (vert) . . . . 3·00 3·50

1996. 70th Birthday of Queen Elizabeth II. As T **334** of Maldive Islands. Multicoloured.
1018 $2 Queen Elizabeth II . . . 1·25 1·40
1019 $2 Wearing evening dress 1·25 1·40
1020 $2 In purple hat and coat 1·25 1·40
MS1021 125 × 103 mm. $6 Taking the salute at Tropping the Colour 4·00 4·25

103 Children reading Book

1996. 50th Anniv of U.N.I.C.E.F. Multicoloured.
1022 25c. Type **103** 25 20
1023 50c. Doctor and child . . . 40 30
1024 $4 Children . . . . 2·50 3·25
MS1025 75 × 105 mm. $6 Young girl (vert) . . . . 3·00 3·50

104 Cave Paintings, Tassili n'Ajjer, Algeria

1996. 50th Anniv of U.N.E.S.C.O. Multicoloured.
1026 25c. Type **104** 35 20
1027 $2 Temple, Tikai National Park, Guatemala (vert) . . 1·10 1·40
1028 $3 Temple of Hera, Samos, Greece . . . . 1·60 2·00
MS1029 106 × 76 mm. $6 Pueblo, Taos, U.S.A. . . . . 3·00 3·50

105 American Academy of Ophthalmology Logo

1996. Centenary of American Academy of Ophthalmology.
1030 **105** $5 multicoloured . . . . 2·50 3·00

106 "Rothmannia longiflora"
107 Western Meadowlark on Decoration

1996. Flowers. Multicoloured.
1031 25c. Type **106** 25 20
1032 50c. "Gloriosa simplex" . . 35 30
1033 $1 "Monodora myristica" 60 70
1034 $1 Giraffe 60 70
1035 $1 "Adansonia digitata" . . 60 70
1036 $1 "Ansellia gigantea" . . . 60 70
1037 $1 "Geissorhiza rochensis" 60 70
1038 $1 "Arctotis venusta" . . . 60 70
1039 $1 "Gladiotus cardinalis" 60 70
1040 $1 "Eucomis bicolor" . . . 60 70
1041 $1 "Protea obtusifolia" . . 60 70
1042 $2 "Catharanthus roseus" 1·10 1·25
1043 $3 "Plumbago auriculata" 1·60 1·90
MS1044 75 × 105 mm. $5 "Strelitzia reginae" . . . . 2·50 3·00

1996. Christmas. Birds. Multicoloured.
1045 25c. Type **107** 30 20
1046 50c. Bird (incorrectly inscr as "American goldfinch") with decorations (horiz) 45 30
1047 80c. Santa Claus, sleigh and reindeer (horiz) 60 45
1048 $1 American goldfinch on stocking 70 55
1049 $1.60 Northern mockingbird ("Mockingbird") with snowman decoration . . . 1·00 1·10
1050 $5 Yellow-rumped cacique and bauble . . . . . . 2·75 3·50
MS1051 Two sheets. (a) 106 × 76 mm. $6 Blue and yellow macaw ("Macaw") (horiz). (b) 76 × 106 mm. $6 Vermilion flycatcher (horiz) Set of 2 sheets 6·00 6·75
No. 1048 is inscribed "WESTERN MEADOWLARK" and No. 1050 "YELLOW-RUMPED CAIEQUE", both in error.

108 Ox (from "Five Oxen" by Han Huang)

1997. Chinese New Year ("Year of the Ox"). T **108** and similar oxen from the painting by Han Huang. Sheet 230 × 93 mm.
MS1052 50c., 80c., $1.60, $2 multicoloured . . . . 3·25 3·50
The fifth ox appears on a small central label.

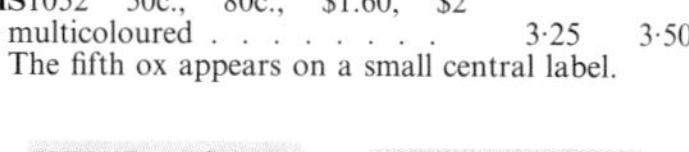

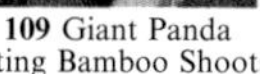

109 Giant Panda eating Bamboo Shoots
110 Elquemedo Willett

1997. "HONG KONG '97" International Stamp Exhibition. Giant Pandas. Multicoloured.
1053 $1.60 Type **109** . . . . . . 1·25 1·25
1054 $1.60 Head of panda . . . 1·25 1·25

1055 $1.60 Panda with new-born cub . . . . 1·25 1·25
1056 $1.60 Panda hanging from branch . . . . 1·25 1·25
1057 $1.60 Panda asleep on tree 1·25 1·25
1058 $1.60 Panda climbing trunk 1·25 1·25
MS1059 73 × 103 mm. $5 Panda with cub . . . . 2·50 3·00

1997. Nevis Cricketers. Multicoloured.
1060 25c. Type **110** 30 25
1061 80c. Stuart Williams 70 50
1062 $2 Keith Arthurton . . . . 1·25 1·50
MS1063 Two sheets, each 106 × 76 mm. (a) $5 Willett, Arthurton and Williams as part of the 1990 Nevis team (horiz). (b) $5 Williams and Arthurton as part of the 1994 West Indies team Set of 2 sheets . . . . 5·00 5·25

111 Crimson-speckled Moth

1997. Butterflies and Moths. Multicoloured.
1064 10c. Type **111** 15 20
1065 25c. Purple emperor 25 20
1066 50c. Regent skipper 35 30
1067 80c. Provence burnet moth 60 45
1068 $1 Common wall butterfly 60 70
1069 $1 Red-lined geometrid . . 60 70
1070 $1 Boisduval's autumnal moth 60 70
1071 $1 Blue pansy 60 70
1072 $1 Common clubtail 60 70
1073 $1 Tufted jungle king . . . 60 70
1074 $1 Lesser marbled fritillary 60 70
1075 $1 Peacock royal 60 70
1076 $1 Emperor gum moth . . . 60 70
1077 $1 Orange swallow-tailed moth 60 70
1078 $4 Cruiser butterfly . . . . 2·25 2·50
MS1079 Two sheets. (a) 103 × 73 mm. $5 Great purple. (b) 73 × 103 mm. $5 Jersey tiger moth Set of 2 sheets . . . . 5·00 5·75
No. 1073 is inscribed "TUFTED JUNGLE QUEEN" in error.

112 Boy with Two Pigeons

1997. 300th Anniv of Mother Goose Nursery Rhymes. Sheet 72 × 102 mm.
MS1080 **112** $5 multicoloured . . 2·50 3·00

113 Paul Harris and Literacy Class

1997. 50th Death Anniv of Paul Harris (founder of Rotary International). Multicoloured.
1081 $2 Type **113** . . . . 1·00 1·25
MS1082 78 × 108 mm. $5 Football coaching session, Chile . . . . 2·50 3·00

1997. Golden Wedding of Queen Elizabeth and Prince Philip. As T **350** of Maldive Islands. Multicoloured.
1083 $1 Queen Elizabeth II . . . 80 80
1084 $1 Royal Coat of Arms . . 80 80
1085 $1 Queen Elizabeth wearing red hat and coat with Prince Philip 80 80
1086 $1 Queen Elizabeth in blue coat and Prince Philip . . 80 80
1087 $1 Caernarvon Castle . . . 80 80
1088 $1 Prince Philip in R.A.F. uniform 80 80
MS1089 100 × 70 mm. $5 Queen Elizabeth at Coronation . . . 2·50 3·00

1997. "Pacific '97" International Stamp Exhibition, San Francisco. Death Centenary of Heinrich von Stephan. As T **351** of Maldive Islands.
1090 $1.60 green . . . . 90 1·10
1091 $1.60 brown . . . . 90 1·10
1092 $1.60 blue . . . . 90 1·10
MS1093 82 × 118 mm. $5 sepia 2·50 3·00
DESIGNS: No. 1090, Russian reindeer post, 1859; 1091, Von Stephan and Mercury; 1092, "City of Cairo" (paddle-steamer), Mississippi, 1800s; **MS**1093, Von Stephan and Bavarian postal messenger, 1640.

1997. Birth Bicentenary of Hiroshige (Japanese painter). "One Hundred Famous Views of Edo". As T **352** of Maldive Islands. Multicoloured.
1094 $1.60 "Scattered Pines, Tone River" . . . . 90 1·10
1095 $1.60 "Mouth of Nakagawa River" . . . . 90 1·10
1096 $1.60 "Niijuku Ferry" . . . 90 1·10

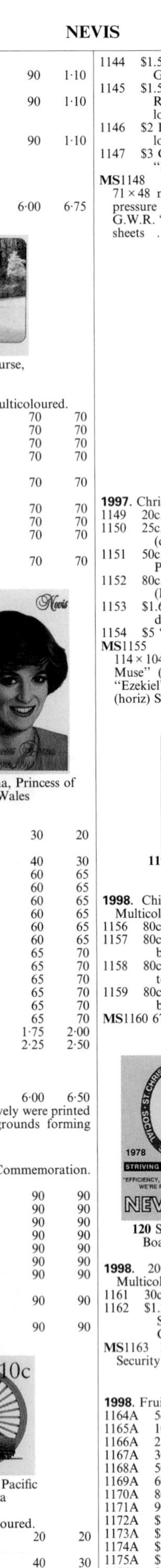

1097 $1.60 "Horie and Nekozane" . . . . 90 1·10
1098 $1.60 "Konodai and the Tone River" . . . . . . 90 1·10
1099 $1.60 "Maple Trees, Tekona Shrine and Bridge, Mama" . . . . 90 1·10
MS1100 Two sheets, each 102 × 127 mm. (a) $6 "Mitsumata Wakarenofuchi". (b) $6 "Moto-Hachiman Shrine, Sunamura" Set of 2 sheets . . . . 6·00 6·75

114 Augusta National Course, U.S.A.

1997. Golf Courses of the World. Multicoloured.
1101 $1 Type **114** 70 70
1102 $1 Cabo del Sol, Mexico . . 70 70
1103 $1 Cypress Point, U.S.A. . . 70 70
1104 $1 Lost City, South Africa 70 70
1105 $1 Moscow Country Club, Russia 70 70
1106 $1 New South Wales, Australia 70 70
1107 $1 Royal Montreal, Canada 70 70
1108 $1 St. Andrews, Scotland . . 70 70
1109 $1 Four Seasons Resort, Nevis 70 70

115 "Cantharellus cibarius" **116** Diana, Princess of Wales

1997. Fungi. Multicoloured.
1110 25c. Type **115** 30 20
1111 50c. "Stropharia aeruginosa" 40 30
1112 80c. "Suillus hiteus" 60 65
1113 80c. "Amanita muscaria" 60 65
1114 80c. "Lactarius rufus" . . . 60 65
1115 80c. "Amanita rubescens" 60 65
1116 80c. "Armillaria mellea" . . 60 65
1117 80c. "Russula sardonia" . . 60 65
1118 $1 "Boletus edulis" 65 70
1119 $1 "Pholiota lenta" 65 70
1120 $1 "Cortinarius bolaris" . . 65 70
1121 $1 "Coprinus picaceus" . . 65 70
1122 $1 "Amanita phalloides" . . 65 70
1123 $1 "Cystolepiota aspera" . . 65 70
1124 $3 "Lactarius turpis" . . . 1·75 2·00
1125 $4 "Entoloma clypeatum" 2·25 2·50
MS1126 Two sheets, each 98 × 68 mm. (a) $5 "Galerina mutabilis". (b) $5 "Gymnopilus junonius" Set of 2 sheets . . . . 6·00 6·50
Nos. 1112/17 and 1118/23 respectively were printed together, se-tenant, with the backgrounds forming composite designs.

1997. Diana, Princess of Wales Commemoration. Multicoloured.
1127 $1 Type **116** 90 90
1128 $1 Wearing white blouse . . 90 90
1129 $1 In wedding dress, 1981 90 90
1130 $1 Wearing turquoise blouse 90 90
1131 $1 Wearing tiara 90 90
1132 $1 Wearing blue blouse . . 90 90
1133 $1 Wearing pearl necklace 90 90
1134 $1 Wearing diamond drop earrings 90 90
1135 $1 Wearing sapphire necklace and earrings . . 90 90

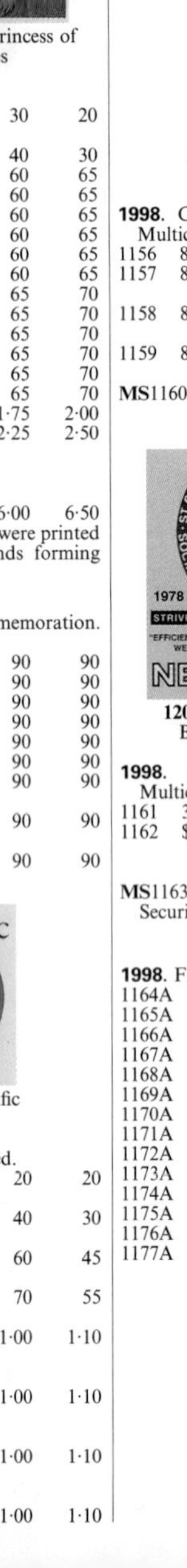

117 Victoria Govt Class S Pacific Locomotive, Australia

1997. Trains of the World. Multicoloured.
1136 10c. Type **117** 20 20
1137 50c. Express steam locomotive, Japan 40 30
1138 80c. L.M.S. steam-turbine locomotive, Great Britain 60 45
1139 $1 Electric locomotive, Switzerland 70 55
1140 $1.50 "Mikado" steam locomotive, Sudan . . . . 1·00 1·10
1141 $1.50 "Mohammed Ali el Kebir" steam locomotive, Egypt . . . . 1·00 1·10
1142 $1.50 Southern Region steam locomotive "Leatherhead" . . . . . 1·00 1·10
1143 $1.50 Great Southern Railway Drumm battery-powered railcar, Ireland 1·00 1·10
1144 $1.50 Pacific locomotive, Germany . . . . 1·00 1·10
1145 $1.50 Canton–Hankow Railway Pacific locomotive, China . . . . 1·00 1·10
1146 $2 L.M.S. high-pressure locomotive, Great Britain 1·40 1·50
1147 $3 Great Northern Railway "Kestrel", Ireland . . . . 1·75 1·90
MS1148 Two sheets, each 71 × 48 mm. (a) $5 L.M.S. high-pressure locomotive. (b) $5 G.W.R. "King George V" Set of 2 sheets . . . . 5·50 6·50

118 "Selection of Angels" (detail) (Durer)

1997. Christmas. Paintings. Multicoloured.
1149 20c. Type **118** 20 15
1150 25c. "Selection of Angels" (different detail) (Durer) 25 20
1151 50c. "Andromeda and Perseus" (Rubens) 40 30
1152 80c. "Harmony" (detail) (Raphael) 60 45
1153 $1.60 "Harmony" (different detail) (Raphael) . . . . 1·10 1·25
1154 $5 "Holy Trinity" (Raphael) 3·00 3·50
MS1155 Two sheets, each 114 × 104 mm. (a) $5 "Study Muse" (Raphael) (horiz). (b) $5 "Ezekiel's Vision" (Raphael) (horiz) Set of 2 sheets . . . . 5·00 5·75

119 Tiger (semi-circular character at top left)

1998. Chinese New Year ("Year of the Tiger"). Multicoloured.
1156 80c. Type **119** 40 45
1157 80c. Oblong character at bottom right 40 45
1158 80c. Circular character at top left 40 45
1159 80c. Square character at bottom right 40 45
MS1160 67 × 97 mm. $2 Tiger (vert) 95 1·00

120 Social Security Board Emblem **121** Soursop

1998. 20th Anniv of Social Security Board. Multicoloured.
1161 30c. Type **120** 15 20
1162 $1.20 Opening of Social Security building, Charlestown (horiz) . . . 55 60
MS1163 100 × 70 mm. $6 Social Security staff (59 × 39 mm) . . 3·00 3·25

1998. Fruits. Multicoloured.
1164A 5c. Type **121** 10 10
1165A 10c. Carambola 10 10
1166A 25c. Guava 10 15
1167A 30c. Papaya 15 20
1168A 50c. Mango 25 30
1169A 60c. Golden apple 30 35
1170A 80c. Pineapple 40 45
1171A 90c. Watermelon 45 50
1172A $1 Bananas 50 55
1173A $1.80 Orange 85 90
1174A $3 Honeydew . . . . . . 1·40 1·50
1175A $5 Cantelope . . . . . . 2·40 2·50
1176A $10 Pomegranate . . . . 4·75 5·00
1177A $20 Cashew . . . . 9·50 9·75

122 African Fish Eagle ("Fish Eagle")

1998. Endangered Species. Multicoloured.
1178 30c. Type **122** 15 20
1179 80c. Summer tanager at nest 40 45
1180 90c. Orang-Utan and young 45 50
1181 $1 Young chimpanzee . . . 50 55
1182 $1 Keel-billed toucan . . . 50 55
1183 $1 Chaco peccary 50 55
1184 $1 Spadefoot toad and insect 50 55
1185 $1 Howler monkey 50 55
1186 $1 Alaskan brown bear . . 50 55
1187 $1 Koala bears 50 55
1188 $1 Brown pelican 50 55
1189 $1 Iguana 50 55
1190 $1.20 Tiger cub 55 60
1191 $2 Cape pangolin . . . . . 95 1·00
1192 $3 Hoatzin . . . . 1·40 1·50
MS1193 Two sheets, each 69 × 99 mm. (a) $5 Young mandrill. (b) $5 Polar bear cub Set of 2 sheets . . . . 4·75 5·00
No. 1185 is inscribed "MOWLER MONKEY" and No. 1192 "MOATZIN", both in error.

123 Chaim Topol (Israeli actor)

1998. "Israel 98" International Stamp Exn, Tel-Aviv.
1194 **123** $1.60 multicoloured . . 75 80

124 Boeing 747 200B (U.S.A.)

1998. Aircraft. Multicoloured.
1195 10c. Type **124** 10 10
1196 90c. Cessna 185 Skywagon (U.S.A.) 45 50
1197 $1 Northrop B-2 A (U.S.A.) 50 55
1198 $1 Lockheed SR-71A (U.S.A.) 50 55
1199 $1 Beechcraft T-44A (U.S.A.) 50 55
1200 $1 Sukhoi Su-27UB (U.S.S.R.) 50 55
1201 $1 Hawker Siddeley Harrier GR. Mk1 (Great Britain) 50 55
1202 $1 Boeing E-3A Sentry (U.S.A.) 50 55
1203 $1 Convair B-36H (U.S.A.) 50 55
1204 $1 IAI KFIR C2 (Israel) . . 50 55
1205 $1.80 McDonnell Douglas DC-9 SO (U.S.A.) 85 90
1206 $5 Airbus A-300 B4 (U.S.A.) . . . . 2·40 2·50
MS1207 Two sheets, each 76 × 106 mm. (a) $5 Lockheed F-117A (U.S.A.) (56 × 42 mm). (b) $5 Concorde (Great Britain) (56 × 42 mm) Set of 2 sheets . . 4·75 5·00

125 Anniversary Logo

127 Prime Minister Kennedy Simmonds receiving Constitutional Instruments from Princess Margaret, 1983

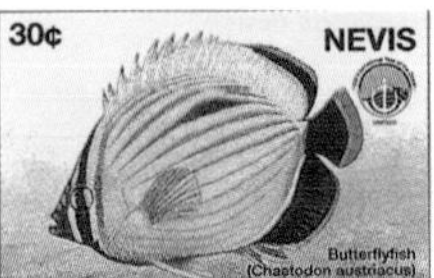

126 Butterflyfish

1998. 10th Anniv of "Voice of Nevis" Radio.
1208 **125** 20c. vio, lt vio & blk . . 10 15
1209 – 30c. multicoloured . . . 15 20
1210 – $1.20 multicoloured . . 55 60
MS1211 110 × 85 mm. $5 multicoloured . . . . 2·40 2·50
DESIGNS: 30c. Evered Herbert (Station Manager); $1.20, V.O.N. studio; $5 Merritt Herbert (Managing Director).

1998. International Year of the Ocean. Multicoloured.

No.	Description		
1212	30c. Type **126**	15	20
1213	80c. Bicolor cherub	40	45
1214	90c. Copperbanded butterfly-fish (vert)	45	50
1215	90c. Forcepsfish (vert)	45	50
1216	90c. Double-saddled butterfly-fish (vert)	45	50
1217	90c. Blue surgeonfish (vert)	45	50
1218	90c. Orbiculate batfish (vert)	45	50
1219	90c. Undulated triggerfish (vert)	45	50
1220	90c. Rock beauty (vert)	45	50
1221	90c. Flamefish (vert)	45	50
1222	90c. Queen angelfish (vert)	45	50
1223	$1 Pyjama cardinal fish	50	55
1224	$1 Wimplefish	50	55
1225	$1 Long-nosed filefish	50	55
1226	$1 Oriental sweetlips	50	55
1227	$1 Blue-spotted boxfish	50	55
1228	$1 Blue-stripe angelfish	50	55
1229	$1 Goldrim tang	50	55
1230	$1 Blue chromis	50	55
1231	$1 Common clownfish	50	55
1232	$1.20 Silver badgerfish	55	60
1233	$2 Asfur angelfish	95	1·00
MS1234	Two sheets. (a) 76×106 mm. $5 Red-faced batfish (vert). (b) 106×76 mm. $5 Longhorned cowfish (vert) Set of 2 sheets	4·75	5·00

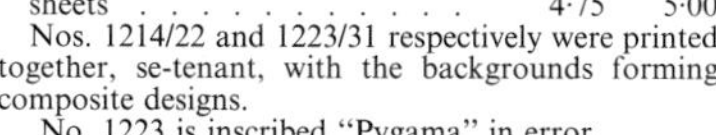

Nos. 1214/22 and 1223/31 respectively were printed together, se-tenant, with the backgrounds forming composite designs.

No. 1223 is inscribed "Pygama" in error.

1998. 15th Anniv of Independence.

No.	Description		
1235	**127** $1 multicoloured	50	55

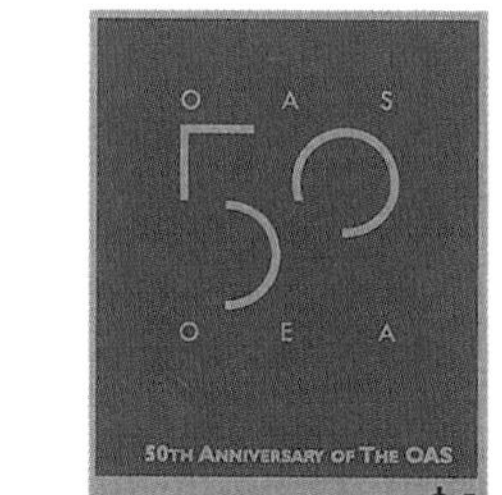

128 Stylized "50"

1998. 50th Anniv of Organization of American States.

No.	Description		
1236	**128** $1 blue, light blue and black	50	55

129 365 "California"

1998. Birth Centenary of Enzo Ferrari (car manufacturer). Multicoloured.

No.	Description		
1237	$2 Type **129**	1·40	1·40
1238	$2 Pininfarina's P6	1·40	1·40
1239	$2 250 LM	1·40	1·40
MS1240	104×70 mm. $5 212 "Export Spyder" (91×34 mm)	2·75	3·00

130 Scouts of Different Nationalities

1998. 19th World Scout Jamboree, Chile. Multicoloured.

No.	Description		
1241	$3 Type **130**	1·40	1·50
1242	$3 Scout and Gettysburg veterans, 1913	1·40	1·50
1243	$3 First black scout troop, Virginia, 1928	1·40	1·50

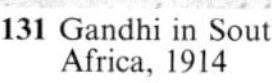

131 Gandhi in South Africa, 1914

133 Princess Diana

132 Panavia Tornado F3

1998. 50th Death Anniv of Mahatma Gandhi. Multicoloured.

No.	Description		
1244	$1 Type **131**	50	55
1245	$1 Gandhi in Downing Street, London	50	55

1998. 80th Anniv of Royal Air Force. Multicoloured.

No.	Description		
1246	$2 Type **132**	95	1·00
1247	$2 Panavia Tornado F3 firing Skyflash missile	95	1·00
1248	$2 Tristar Mk1 Tanker refuelling Tornado GR1	95	1·00
1249	$2 Panavia Tornado GR1 firing AIM-9L missile	95	1·00
MS1250	Two sheets, each 91×68 mm. (a) $5 Bristol F2B Fighter and two peregrine falcons (birds). (b) $5 Wessex helicopter and EF-2000 Eurofighter Set of 2 sheets	4·75	5·00

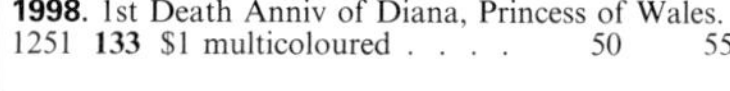

1998. 1st Death Anniv of Diana, Princess of Wales.

No.	Description		
1251	**133** $1 multicoloured	50	55

134 Kitten and Santa Claus Decoration

1998. Christmas. Multicoloured.

No.	Description		
1252	25c. Type **134**	10	15
1253	60c. Kitten playing with bauble	30	35
1254	80c. Kitten in Christmas stocking (vert)	40	45
1255	90c. Fox Terrier puppy and presents	45	50
1256	$1 Angel with swallows	50	55
1257	$3 Boy wearing Santa hat (vert)	1·40	1·50
MS1258	Two sheets. (a) 71×102 mm. $5 Two dogs. (b) 102×71 mm. $5 Family with dog (vert) Set of 2 sheets	4·75	5·00

135 Mickey Mouse

1998. 70th Birthday of Mickey Mouse. Walt Disney cartoon characters playing basketball. Mult.

No.	Description		
1259	$1 Type **135**	70	70
1260	$1 Donald Duck bouncing ball	70	70
1261	$1 Minnie Mouse in green kit	70	70
1262	$1 Goofy wearing purple	70	70
1263	$1 Huey in green baseball cap	70	70
1264	$1 Goofy and Mickey	70	70
1265	$1 Mickey bouncing ball	70	70
1266	$1 Huey, Dewey and Louie	70	70
1267	$1 Mickey, in purple, shooting ball	70	70
1268	$1 Goofy in yellow shorts and vest	70	70
1269	$1 Minnie in purple	70	70
1270	$1 Mickey in yellow vest and blue shorts	70	70
1271	$1 Minnie in yellow	70	70
1272	$1 Donald spinning ball on finger	70	70
1273	$1 Donald and Mickey	70	70
1274	$1 Dewey shooting for goal	70	70
MS1275	Four sheets. (a) 127×105 mm. $5 Minnie wearing purple bow (horiz). (b) 105×127 mm. $5 Minnie wearing green bow (horiz). (c) 105×127 mm. $6 Mickey in yellow vest (horiz). (d) 105×127 mm. $6 Mickey in purple vest (horiz) Set of 4 sheets	12·00	13·00

136 Black Silver Fox Rabbits

1999. Chinese New Year ("Year of the Rabbit"). Multicoloured.

No.	Description		
1276	$1.60 Type **136**	75	80
1277	$1.60 Dutch rabbits (brown with white "collar")	75	80
1278	$1.60 Dwarf rabbits (brown)	75	80
1279	$1.60 Netherlands Dwarf rabbits (white with brown markings)	75	80
MS1280	106×76 mm. $5 Dwarf albino rabbit and young (57×46 mm)	2·40	2·50

137 Laurent Blanc (France)

1999. Leading Players of 1998 World Cup Football Championship, France. Multicoloured.

No.	Description		
1281	$1 Type **137**	50	55
1282	$1 Dennis Bergkamp (Holland)	50	55
1283	$1 Davor Sukor (Croatia)	50	55
1284	$1 Ronaldo (Brazil)	50	55
1285	$1 Didier Deschamps (France)	50	55
1286	$1 Patrick Kluivert (Holland)	50	55
1287	$1 Rivaldo (Brazil)	50	55
1288	$1 Zinedine Zidane (France)	50	55
MS1289	121×96 mm. $5 Zinedine Zidane (France)	2·40	2·50

Nos. 1281/8 were printed together, se-tenant, with the backgrounds forming a composite design.

138 Kritosaurus

1999. "Australia '99" World Stamp Exhibition, Melbourne. Prehistoric Animals. Multicoloured.

No.	Description		
1290	30c. Type **138**	15	20
1291	60c. Oviraptor	30	35
1292	80c. Eustreptospondylus	40	45
1293	$1.20 Tenontosaurus	55	60
1294	$1.20 Edmontosaurus	55	60
1295	$1.20 Avimimus	55	60
1296	$1.20 Minmi	55	60
1297	$1.20 Segnosaurus	55	60
1298	$1.20 Kentrosaurus	55	60
1299	$1.20 Deinonychus	55	60
1300	$1.20 Saltasaurus	55	60
1301	$1.20 Compsoganthus	55	60
1302	$1.20 Hadrosaurus	55	60
1303	$1.20 Tuojiangosaurus	55	60
1304	$1.20 Euoplocephalus	55	60
1305	$1.20 Anchisaurus	55	60
1306	$2 Ouranosaurus	95	1·00
1307	$3 Muttaburrasaurus	1·40	1·50
MS1308	Two sheets, each 110×85 mm. (a) $5 Triceratops. (b) $5 Stegosaurus Set of 2 sheets	4·75	5·00

Nos. 1294/9 and 1300/5 respectively were printed together, se-tenant, with the backgrounds forming composite designs.

139 Emperor Haile Selassie of Ethiopia

1999. Millennium Series. Famous People of the Twentieth Century. World Leaders. Multicoloured.

No.	Description		
1309	90c. Type **139**	45	50
1310	90c. Haile Selassie and Ethiopian warriors (56×41 mm)	45	50
1311	90c. David Ben-Gurion, woman soldier and ancient Jewish prophet (56×41 mm)	45	50
1312	90c. David Ben-Gurion (Prime Minister of Israel)	45	50
1313	90c. President Franklin D. Roosevelt of U.S.A. and Mrs. Roosevelt	45	50
1314	90c. Franklin and Eleanor Roosevelt campaigning (56×41 mm)	45	50
1315	90c. Mao Tse-tung and the Long March, 1934 (56×41 mm)	45	50
1316	90c. Poster of Mao Tse-tung (founder of People's Republic of China)	45	50
MS1317	Two sheets. (a) 76×105 mm. $5 President Nelson Mandela of South Africa. (b) 105×76 mm. $5 Mahatma Gandhi (leader of Indian Independence movement) Set of 2 sheets	4·75	5·00

140 Malachite Kingfisher

1999. Birds. Multicoloured.

No.	Description		
1318	$1.60 Type **140**	75	80
1319	$1.60 Lilac-breasted roller	75	80
1320	$1.60 Swallow-tailed bee eater	75	80
1321	$1.60 Jay ("Eurasian Jay")	75	80
1322	$1.60 Black-collared apalis	75	80
1323	$1.60 Grey-backed camaroptera	75	80
1324	$1.60 Yellow warbler	75	80
1325	$1.60 Common yellowthroat	75	80
1326	$1.60 Painted bunting	75	80
1327	$1.60 Belted kingfisher	75	80
1328	$1.60 American kestrel	75	80
1329	$1.60 Northern oriole	75	80
MS1330	Two sheets, each 76×106 mm. (a) $5 Bananaquit. (b) $5 Groundscraper thrush (vert) Set of 2 sheets	4·75	5·00

141 "Phaius" hybrid

142 Miss Sophie Rhys-Jones and Prince Edward

1999. Orchids. Multicoloured.

No.	Description		
1331	20c. Type **141**	10	15
1332	25c. "Cuitlauzina pendula"	10	15
1333	50c. "Bletilla striata"	25	30
1334	80c. "Cymbidium" "Showgirl"	40	45
1335	$1 "Cattleya intermedia"	50	55
1336	$1 "Cattleya" "Sophia Martin"	50	55
1337	$1 "Phalaenopsis" "Little Hal"	50	55
1338	$1 "Laeliocattleya alisal" "Rodeo"	50	55
1339	$1 "Laelia lucasiana fournieri"	50	55
1340	$1 "Cymbidium" "Red Beauty"	50	55
1341	$1 "Sobralia" sp.	50	55
1342	$1 "Promenaea xanthina"	50	55
1343	$1 "Cattleya pumpernickel"	50	55
1344	$1 "Odontocidium artur elle"	50	55
1345	$1 "Neostylis lou sneary"	50	55
1346	$1 "Phalaenopsis aphrodite"	50	55
1347	$1 "Arkundina graminieolia"	50	55
1348	$1 "Cymbidium" "Hunter's Point"	50	55
1349	$1 "Rhynchostylis coelestis"	50	55
1350	$1 "Cymbidium" "Elf's Castle"	50	55
1351	$1.60 "Zygopetalum crinitium" (horiz)	75	80
1352	$3 "Dendrobium nobile" (horiz)	1·40	1·50
MS1353	Two sheets, each 106×81 mm. (a) $5 "Spathoglottis plicata" (horiz). (b) $5 "Arethusa bulbosa" Set of 2 sheets	4·75	5·00

1999. Royal Wedding. Multicoloured.

No.	Description		
1354	$2 Type **142**	95	1·00
1355	$2 Miss Sophie Rhys-Jones at Ascot	95	1·00
1356	$2 Miss Sophie Rhys-Jones smiling	95	1·00
1357	$2 Prince Edward smiling	95	1·00
1358	$2 Miss Sophie Rhys-Jones wearing black and white checked jacket	95	1·00
1359	$2 Prince Edward and Miss Sophie Rhys-Jones wearing sunglasses	95	1·00

1360 $2 Miss Sophie Rhys-Jones wearing black hat and jacket . . . . 95 1·00
1361 $2 Prince Edward wearing red-striped tie . . . . . . 95 1·00
MS1362 Two sheets, each 83 × 66 mm. (a) $5 Prince Edward and Miss Sophie Rhys-Jones smiling (horiz). (b) $5 Prince Edward kissing Miss Sophie Rhys-Jones (horiz) Set of 2 sheets . . 4·75 5·00

1999. "iBRA '99" International Stamp Exhibition, Nuremberg. As T **262** of Lesotho. Multicoloured.

1363 30c. "Beuth" (railway locomotive) and Baden 1851 1k. stamp 15 20
1364 80c. "Beuth" and Brunswick 1852 1sgr. stamp 40 45
1365 90c. "Kruzenshtern" (cadet barque) and Bergedorf 1861 ½s. and 1s. stamps 45 50
1366 $1 "Kruzenshtern" and Bremen 1855 3gr. stamp 50 55
MS1367 134 × 90 mm. $5 1912 First Bavarian air flight label . . . 2·40 2·50

1999. 150th Death Anniv of Katsushika Hokusai (Japanese artist). As T **263** of Lesotho. Mult.

1368 $1 "Women returning Home at Sunset" (women by lake) 50 55
1369 $1 "Blind Man" (without beard) 50 55
1370 $1 "Women returning Home at Sunset" (women descending hill) 50 55
1371 $1 "Young Man on a White Horse" 50 55
1372 $1 "Blind Man" (with beard) 50 55
1373 $1 "Peasant crossing a Bridge" 50 55
1374 $1.60 "Poppies" (one flower) 75 80
1375 $1.60 "Blind Man" (with beard) 75 80
1376 $1.60 "Poppies" (two flowers) 75 80
1377 $1.60 "Abe No Nakamaro gazing at the Moon from a Terrace" 75 80
1378 $1.60 "Blind Man" (without beard) 75 80
1379 $1.60 "Cranes on a Snowy Pine" 75 80
MS1380 Two sheets, each 74 × 103 mm. (a) $5 "Carp in a Waterfall". (b) $5 "Rider in the Snow" Set of 2 sheets . . . . 4·75 5·00

1999. "PhilexFrance '99" International Stamp Exhibition, Paris. Two sheets, each 106 × 81 mm, containing horiz designs as T **372** of Maldive Islands. Multicoloured.

MS1381 (a) $5 First Class carriage, 1837. (b) $5 "141.R" Mixed Traffic steam locomotive Set of 2 sheets . . . . 4·75 5·00

143 Steelband

1999. 25th Culturama Festival. Multicoloured.

1382 30c. Type **143** 15 20
1383 80c. Clowns 40 45
1384 $1.80 Masqueraders with band 85 90
1385 $5 Local string band . . . 2·40 2·50
MS1386 91 × 105 mm. $5 Carnival dancers (50 × 37 mm) . . . . . 2·40 2·50

1999. "Queen Elizabeth the Queen Mother's Century". As T **267** of Lesotho.

1387 $2 black and gold . . . . . 95 1·00
1388 $2 multicoloured . . . . . 95 1·00
1389 $2 black and gold . . . . . 95 1·00
1390 $2 multicoloured . . . . . 95 1·00
MS1391 153 × 157 mm. $6 multicoloured . . . . 3·00 3·25

DESIGNS: No. 1387, Lady Elizabeth Bowes-Lyon on Wedding Day, 1923; 1388, Duchess of York with Princess Elizabeth, 1926; 1389, King George VI and Queen Elizabeth during Second World War; 1390, Queen Mother in 1983. 37 × 49 mm: No. **MS**1391, Queen Mother in 1957.

No. **MS**1391 was also issued with the embossed gold coat of arms at bottom left replaced by the inscription "Good Health and Happiness to Her Majesty the Queen Mother on her 101st Birthday".

144 "The Adoration of the Magi" (Durer)

146 Boris Yeltsin (President of Russian Federation, 1991)

145 Flowers forming Top of Head

1999. Christmas. Religious Paintings. Multicoloured.

1392 30c. Type **144** 15 20
1393 90c. "Canigiani Holy Family" (Raphael) . . . 45 50
1394 $1.20 "The Nativity" (Durer) 55 60
1395 $1.80 "Madonna and Child surrounded by Angels" (Rubens) 85 90
1396 $3 "Madonna and Child surrounded by Saints" (Rubens) . . . . 1·40 1·50
MS1397 76 × 106 mm. $5 "Madonna and Child by a Window" (Durer) (horiz) . . . . 2·40 2·50

1999. Faces of the Millennium: Diana, Princess of Wales. Showing collage of miniature flower photographs. Multicoloured.

1398 $1 Type **145** (face value at left) 50 55
1399 $1 Top of head (face value at right) 50 55
1400 $1 Ear (face value at left) 50 55
1401 $1 Eye and temple (face value at right) 50 55
1402 $1 Cheek (face value at left) 50 55
1403 $1 Cheek (face value at right) 50 55
1404 $1 Blue background (face value at left) 50 55
1405 $1 Chin (face value at right) 50 55

Nos. 1398/1405 were printed together, se-tenant, and when viewed as a sheetlet, forms a portrait of Diana, Princess of Wales.

2000. New Millennium. People and Events of Eighteenth Century (1700–49). As T **268** of Lesotho. Multicoloured.

1406 30c. Jonathan Swift ("Gulliver's Travels", 1726) 15 20
1407 30c. Emperor Kangxi of China 15 20
1408 30c. Bartolommeo Cristofori (invention of piano, 1709) 15 20
1409 30c. Captain William Kidd hanging on gibbet, 1701 15 20
1410 30c. William Herschel (astronomer) 15 20
1411 30c. King George I of Great Britain, 1714 . . . . . . 15 20
1412 30c. Peter the Great of Russia (trade treaty with China, 1720) 15 20
1413 30c. "Death" (bubonic plague in Austria and Germany, 1711) 15 20
1414 30c. "Standing Woman" (Kaigetsudo Dohan (Japanese artist)) 15 20
1415 30c. Queen Anne of England, 1707 . . . . . 15 20
1416 30c. Anders Celcius (invention of centigrade thermometer, 1742) . . . 15 20
1417 30c. Vitus Bering (discovery of Alaska and Aleutian Islands, 1741) 15 20
1418 30c. Edmund Halley (calculation of Halley's Comet, 1705) 15 20
1419 30c. John Wesley (founder of Methodist Church, 1729) 15 20
1420 30c. Sir Isaac Newton (publication of "Optick Treatise", 1704) 15 20
1421 30c. Queen Anne (Act of Union between England and Scotland, 1707) (59 × 39 mm) 15 20
1422 30c. Johann Sebastian Bach (composition of "The Well-tempered Klavier", 1722) 15 20

No. 1418 is inscribed "cometis" in error.

2000. New Millennium. People and Events of Twentieth Century (1990–99). Multicoloured.

1423 50c. Type **146** 25 30
1424 50c. American soldiers and burning oil wells (Gulf War, 1991) 25 30
1425 50c. Soldiers (Bosnian Civil War, 1992) 25 30
1426 50c. Pres. Clinton, Yitzchak Rabin and Yasser Arafat (Oslo Accords, 1993) . . 25 30
1427 50c. Prime Ministers John Major and Albert Reynolds (Joint Declaration on Northern Ireland, 1993) 25 30
1428 50c. Frederik de Klerk and Nelson Mandela (end of Apartheid, South Africa, 1994) 25 30
1429 50c. Cal Ripkin (record number of consecutive baseball games, 1995) . . 25 30
1430 50c. Kobe from air (earthquake, 1995) . . . 25 30
1431 50c. Mummified Inca girl preserved in ice, 1995 . . 25 30
1432 50c. NASA's "Sojourner" on Mars, 1997 . . . . . 25 30
1433 50c. Dr. Ian Wilmat and cloned sheep, 1997 . . . 25 30
1434 50c. Death of Princess Diana, 1997 . . . . . . 25 30
1435 50c. Fireworks over Hong Kong on its return to China, 1997 . . . . . . 25 30
1436 50c. Mother with septuplets, 1998 . . . . 25 30
1437 50c. Guggenheim Museum, Bilbao, 1998 . . . . . . 25 30
1438 50c. "2000" and solar eclipse, 1999 (59 × 39 mm) 25 30
1439 50c. Pres. Clinton (impeachment in 1999) . . 25 30

No. 1423 incorrectly identifies his office as "Prime Minister".

147 Dragon

2000. Chinese New Year ("Year of the Dragon"). Multicoloured.

1440 $1.60 Type **147** 75 80
1441 $1.60 Dragon with open claws (face value bottom left) 75 80
1442 $1.60 Dragon holding sphere (face value bottom right) 75 80
1443 $1.60 Dragon looking up (face value bottom left) 75 80
MS1444 76 × 106 mm. $5 Dragon (37 × 50 mm) . . . . 2·40 2·50

148 Spotted Scat

2000. Tropical Fish. Showing fish in spotlight. Multicoloured.

1445 30c. Type **148** 15 20
1446 80c. Delta topsail platy ("Platy Variatus") 40 45
1447 90c. Emerald betta 45 50
1448 $1 Sail-finned tang 50 55
1449 $1 Black-capped basslet ("Black-capped Gramma") 50 55
1450 $1 Sail-finned snapper ("Majestic Snapper") . . 50 55
1451 $1 Purple fire goby 50 55
1452 $1 Clown triggerfish 50 55
1453 $1 Forceps butterflyfish ("Yellow Long-nose") . . 50 55
1454 $1 Clown wrasse 50 55
1455 $1 Yellow-headed jawfish . . 50 55
1456 $1 Oriental sweetlips 50 55
1457 $1 Royal gramma 50 55
1458 $1 Thread-finned butterflyfish 50 55
1459 $1 Yellow tang 50 55
1460 $1 Bicoloured angelfish . . 50 55
1461 $1 Catalina goby 50 55
1462 $1 Striped mimic blenny ("False Cleanerfish") . . 50 55
1463 $1 Powder-blue surgeonfish 50 55
1464 $4 Long-horned cowfish . . 1·90 2·00
MS1465 Two sheets, each 97 × 68 mm. (a) $5 Clown killifish. (b) $5 Twin-spotted wrasse ("Clown Coris") Set of 2 sheets 4·75 5·00

Nos. 1448/55 and 1456/63 were each printed together, se-tenant, the backgrounds forming composite designs.

149 Miniature Pinscher

2000. Dogs of the World. Multicoloured.

1466 10c. Type **149** 10 10
1467 20c. Pyrenean mountain dog 10 15
1468 30c. Welsh springer spaniel 15 20
1469 80c. Alaskan malamute . . 40 45
1470 90c. Beagle (horiz) 45 50
1471 90c. Bassett hound (horiz) 45 50
1472 90c. St. Bernard (horiz) . . 45 50
1473 90c. Rough collie (horiz) . . 45 50
1474 90c. Shih tzu (horiz) 45 50
1475 90c. American bulldog (horiz) 45 50
1476 $1 Irish red and white setter (horiz) 50 55
1477 $1 Dalmatian (horiz) . . . 50 55
1478 $1 Pomeranian (horiz) . . . 50 55
1479 $1 Chihuahua (horiz) . . . 50 55
1480 $1 English sheepdog (horiz) 50 55
1481 $1 Samoyed (horiz) 50 55
1482 $2 Bearded collie . . . . . 95 1·00
1483 $3 American cocker spaniel 1·40 1·50
MS1484 Two sheets. (a) 76 × 106 mm. $5 Leonberger dog. (b) 106 × 76 mm. $5 Longhaired miniature dachshund (horiz) Set of 2 sheets . . . . 4·75 5·00

2000. 18th Birthday of Prince William. As T **278** of Lesotho. Multicoloured.

1485 $1.60 Prince William shaking hands 75 80
1486 $1.60 Wearing ski outfit . . 75 80
1487 $1.60 At airport 75 80
1488 $1.60 Wearing blue shirt and jumper 75 80
MS1489 100 × 80 mm. $5 At official engagement (38 × 50 mm) . . . 2·40 2·50

150 "Mariner 9"

2000. "EXPO 2000" World Stamp Exhibition, Anaheim, U.S.A. Exploration of Mars. Multicoloured.

1490 $1.60 Type **150** 75 80
1491 $1.60 "Mars 3" 75 80
1492 $1.60 "Mariner 4" 75 80
1493 $1.60 "Planet B" 75 80
1494 $1.60 "Mars Express Lander" 75 80
1495 $1.60 "Mars Express" . . . 75 80
1496 $1.60 "Mars 4" 75 80
1497 $1.60 "Mars Water" 75 80
1498 $1.60 "Mars 1" 75 80
1499 $1.60 "Viking" 75 80
1500 $1.60 "Mariner 7" 75 80
1501 $1.60 "Mars Surveyor" . . . 75 80
MS1502 Two sheets, each 106 × 76 mm. (a) $5 "Mars Observer" (horiz). (b) $5 "Mars Climate Orbiter" Set of 2 sheets 4·75 5·00

Nos. 1490/5 and 1496/1501 were each printed together, se-tenant, with the backgrounds forming composite designs.

2000. 50th Anniv of Berlin Film Festival. As T **272** of Lesotho showing actors, directors and film scenes with awards. Multicoloured.

1503 $1.60 "Rani Radovi", 1969 75 80
1504 $1.60 Salvatore Giuliano (director), 1962 . . . . . 75 80
1505 $1.60 "Schonzeit fur Fuches", 1966 . . . . . 75 80
1506 $1.60 Shirley Maclaine (actress), 1971 . . . . . 75 80
1507 $1.60 Simone Signoret (actress), 1971 . . . . . 75 80
1508 $1.60 Tabejad Bijad (director), 1974 . . . . . 75 80
MS1509 97 × 103 mm. $5 "Komissar", 1988 . . . . . . 2·40 2·50

2000. 175th Anniv of Stockton and Darlington Line (first public railway). As T **273** of Lesotho. Multicoloured.

1510 $3 Locomotion No. 1, 1875, and George Stephenson 1·40 1·50
1511 $3 Original drawing of Richard Trevithick's locomotive, 1804 . . . . 1·40 1·50

2000. 250th Death Anniv of Johann Sebastian Bach (German composer). Sheet 76 × 88 mm, containing vert design as T **274** of Lesotho. Multicoloured.

MS1512 $5 Johann Sebastian Bach 2·40 2·50

151 Albert Einstein

2000. Election of Albert Einstein (mathematical physicist) as *Time Magazine* "Man of the Century". Showing portraits with photographs in background. Multicoloured.

1513 $2 Type **151** . . . . . . 95 1·00
1514 $2 Riding bicycle . . . . . 95 1·00
1515 $2 Standing on beach . . . 95 1·00

2000. Centenary of First Zeppelin Flight. As T **276** of Lesotho.

1516 $3 green, purple and black 1·40 1·50
1517 $3 green, purple and black 1·40 1·50
1518 $3 green, purple and black 1·40 1·50
MS1519 116 × 76 mm. $5 green, mauve and black . . . . . . 2·40 2·50

DESIGNS: (38 × 24 mm)—No. 1516, LZ-129 *Hindenburg*, 1929; 1517, LZ-1, 1900; 1518, LZ-11 *Viktoria Luise*. (50 × 37 mm)—No. **MS**1519, LZ-127 *Graf Zeppelin*, 1928.

No. 1516 is inscribed "Hindenberg" in error.

2000. Olympic Games, Sydney. As T **277** of Lesotho. Multicoloured.

1520	$2 Gisela Mauermeyer (discus), Berlin (1936)	95	1·00
1521	$2 Gymnast on uneven bars	95	1·00
1522	$2 Wembley Stadium, London (1948) and Union Jack	95	1·00
1523	$2 Ancient Greek horseman	95	1·00

2000. West Indies Cricket Tour and 100th Test Match at Lord's. As T **206** of Montserrat. Multicoloured.

1524	$2 Elquemeda Willett	95	1·00
1525	$3 Keith Arthurton	1·40	1·50
MS1526	121 × 104 mm. $5 Lord's Cricket Ground (horiz)	2·40	2·50

152 King Edward III of England

2000. Monarchs of the Millennium.

1527	**152** $1.60 black, stone and brown	75	80
1528	– $1.60 multicoloured	75	80
1529	– $1.60 multicoloured	75	80
1530	– $1.60 black, stone and brown	75	80
1531	– $1.60 black, stone and brown	75	80
1532	– $1.60 purple, stone and brown	75	80
MS1533	115 × 135 mm. $5 multicoloured	2·40	2·50

DESIGNS: No. 1528, Emperor Charles V (of Spain); 1529, King Joseph II of Hungary; 1530, Emperor Henry II of Germany; 1531, King Louis IV of France; 1532, King Ludwig II of Bavaria; **MS**1533, King Louis IX of France.

153 Member of The Angels

154 Bob Hope in Ranger Uniform, Vietnam

2000. Famous Girl Pop Groups. Multicoloured.

1534	90c. Type **153**	45	50
1535	90c. Member of The Angels with long hair	45	50
1536	90c. Member of The Angels with chin on hand	45	50
1537	90c. Member of The Dixie Cups (record at left)	45	50
1538	90c. Member of The Dixie Cups with shoulder-length hair	45	50
1539	90c. Member of The Dixie Cups with short hair and slide	45	50
1540	90c. Member of The Vandellas (record at left)	45	50
1541	90c. Member of The Vandellas ("Nevis" clear of hair)	45	50
1542	90c. Member of The Vandellas ("is" of "Nevis" on hair)	45	50

Each horizontal row depicts a different group with Nos. 1534/6 having green backgrounds, Nos. 1537/9 yellow and Nos. 1540/2 mauve.

2000. Bob Hope (American entertainer).

1543	**154** $1 black, grey and mauve	50	55
1544	– $1 Indian red, grey and mauve	50	55
1545	– $1 black, grey and mauve	50	55
1546	– $1 multicoloured	50	55
1547	– $1 black, grey and mauve	50	55
1548	– $1 multicoloured	50	55

DESIGNS: No. 1544, On stage with Sammy Davis Jnr.; 1545, With wife Dolores; 1546, Playing golf; 1547, Making radio broadcast; 1548, Visiting Great Wall of China.

155 David Copperfield

157 Beach Scene and Logo

156 Mike Wallace

2000. David Copperfield (conjurer).

1549	**155** $1.60 multicoloured	75	80

2000. Mike Wallace (television journalist). Sheet 120 × 112 mm.

MS1550	**156** $5 multicoloured	2·40	2·50

2000. 2nd Caribbean Beekeeping Congress. No. **MS**801 optd **2nd Caribbean Beekeeping Congress August 14–18, 2000** on top margin.

MS1551	100 × 70 mm. $6 Queen and workers in hive and mechanical honey extractor	3·00	3·25

2000. "Carifesta VII" Arts Festival. Multicoloured.

1552	30c. Type **157**	15	20
1553	90c. Carnival scenes	45	50
1554	$1.20 Stylized dancer with streamers	55	60

158 Golden Elegance Oriental Lily

2000. Caribbean Flowers. Multicoloured.

1555	30c. Type **158**	15	20
1556	80c. Frangipani	40	45
1557	90c. Star of the March	45	50
1558	90c. Tiger lily	45	50
1559	90c. Mont Blanc lily	45	50
1560	90c. Torch ginger	45	50
1561	90c. Cattleya orchid	45	50
1562	90c. St. John's wort	45	50
1563	$1 Culebra	50	55
1564	$1 Rubellum lily	50	55
1565	$1 Silver elegance oriental lily	50	55
1566	$1 Chinese hibiscus	50	55
1567	$1 Tiger lily (different)	50	55
1568	$1 Royal poincia	50	55
1569	$1.60 Epiphyte	75	80
1570	$1.60 Enchantment lily	75	80
1571	$1.60 Glory lily	75	80
1572	$1.60 Purple granadilla	75	80
1573	$1.60 Jacaranda	75	80
1574	$1.60 Shrimp plant	75	80
1575	$1.60 Garden zinnia	75	80
1576	$5 Rose elegance lily	2·40	2·50
MS1577	Two sheets. (a) 75 × 90 mm. $5 Bird of paradise (plant). (b) 90 × 75 mm. $5 Dahlia Set of 2 sheets	4·75	5·00

Nos. 1557/62, 1563/8 and 1569/74 were each printed together, se-tenant, with the backgrounds forming composite designs.

159 Aerial View of Resort

2000. Re-opening of Four Seasons Resort. Mult.

1578	30c. Type **159**	15	20
1579	30c. Palm trees on beach	15	20
1580	30c. Golf course	15	20
1581	30c. Couple at water's edge	15	20

160 "The Coronation of the Virgin" (Velazquez)

2000. Christmas. Religious Paintings. Multicoloured.

1582	30c. Type **160**	15	20
1583	80c. "The Immaculate Conception" (Velazquez)	40	45
1584	90c. "Madonna and Child" (Titian) (horiz)	45	50
1585	$1.20 "Madonna and Child with St. John the Baptist and St. Catherine" (Titian) (horiz)	55	60
MS1586	108 × 108 mm. $6 "Madonna and Child with St. Catherine" (Titian) (horiz)	3·00	3·25

Nos. 1584/5 are both inscribed "Titien" in error.

161 Snake coiled around Branch

2001. Chinese New Year. "Year of the Snake". Multicoloured.

1587	$1.60 Type **161**	75	80
1588	$1.60 Snake in tree	75	80
1589	$1.60 Snake on path	75	80
1590	$1.60 Snake by rocks	75	80
MS1591	70 × 100 mm. $5 Cobra at foot of cliff	2·40	2·50

162 Charlestown Methodist Church

2001. Leeward Islands District Methodist Church Conference. Multicoloured.

1592	50c. Type **162**	25	30
1593	50c. Jessups Methodist Church	25	30
1594	50c. Clifton Methodist Church	25	30
1595	50c. Trinity Methodist Church	25	30
1596	50c. Combermere Methodist Church	25	30
1597	50c. New River Methodist Church	25	30
1598	50c. Gingerland Methodist Church	25	30

163 Two Giraffes

2001. Wildlife from "The Garden of Eden". Multicoloured.

1599	$1.60 Type **163**	75	80
1600	$1.60 Rainbow boa constrictor	75	80
1601	$1.60 Suffolk sheep and mountain cottontail hare	75	80
1602	$1.60 Bluebuck antelope	75	80
1603	$1.60 Fox	75	80
1604	$1.60 Box turtle	75	80
1605	$1.60 Pileated woodpecker ("Red-crested Woodpecker") and unicorn	75	80
1606	$1.60 African elephant	75	80
1607	$1.60 Siberian tiger	75	80
1608	$1.60 Greater flamingo and Adam and Eve	75	80
1609	$1.60 Hippopotamus	75	80
1610	$1.60 Harlequin frog	75	80
MS1611	Four sheets, each 84 × 69 mm. (a) $5 Keel-billed toucan ("Toucan") (vert). (b) $5 American bald eagle. (c) $5 Koala bear (vert). (d) $5 Blue and yellow macaw (vert) Set of 4 sheets	9·50	9·75

Nos. 1599/1604 and 1605/10 were each printed together, se-tenant, with the backgrounds forming composite designs.

164 Zebra

2001. Butterflies of Nevis. Multicoloured.

1612	30c. Type **164**	15	20
1613	80c. Julia	40	45
1614	$1 Ruddy dagger	50	55
1615	$1 Common morpho	50	55
1616	$1 Banded king shoemaker	50	55
1617	$1 Figure of eight	50	55
1618	$1 Grecian shoemaker	50	55
1619	$1 Mosaic	50	55
1620	$1 White peacock	50	55
1621	$1 Hewitson's blue hairstreak	50	55
1622	$1 Tiger pierid	50	55
1623	$1 Gold drop helicopsis	50	55
1624	$1 Cramer's mesene	50	55
1625	$1 Red-banded pereute	50	55
1626	$1.60 Small flambeau	75	80
1627	$5 Purple mort bleu	2·40	2·50
MS1628	Two sheets, each 72 × 100 mm. (a) $5 Common mechanitis. (b) $5 Hewitson's pierella Set of 2 sheets	4·75	5·00

165 *Clavulinopsis corniculata*

2001. Caribbean Fungi. Multicoloured.

1629	20c. Type **165**	10	10
1630	25c. *Cantharellus cibarius*	10	15
1631	50c. *Chlorociboria aeruginascens*	25	30
1632	80c. *Auricularia auricula-judae*	40	45
1633	$1 *Entoloma incanum*	50	55
1634	$1 *Entoloma nitidum*	50	55
1635	$1 *Stropharia cyanea*	50	55
1636	$1 *Otidea onotica*	50	55
1637	$1 *Aleuria aurantia*	50	55
1638	$1 *Mitrula paludosa*	50	55
1639	$1 *Gyromitra esculenta*	50	55
1640	$1 *Helvella crispa*	50	55
1641	$1 *Morcella semilibera*	50	55
1642	$2 *Peziza vesiculosa*	95	1·00
1643	$3 *Mycena acicula*	1·40	1·50
MS1644	Two sheets, each 110 × 85 mm. (a) $5 *Russula sardonia*. (b) $5 *Omphalotus olearius* Set of 2 sheets	4·75	5·00

166 Early Life of Prince Shotoku

2001. "Philanippon 01" International Stamp Exhibition, Tokyo. Prince Shotoku Pictorial Scroll. Multicoloured.

1645	$2 Type **166**	95	1·00
1646	$2 With priests and nuns, and preaching	95	1·00
1647	$2 Subduing the Ezo	95	1·00
1648	$2 Playing with children	95	1·00
1649	$2 Passing through gate	95	1·00
1650	$2 Battle against Mononobe-no-Moriya	95	1·00
1651	$2 Yumedono Hall	95	1·00
1652	$2 Watching dog and deer	95	1·00

167 Prince Albert

168 Queen Elizabeth II wearing Blue Hat

2001. Death Centenary of Queen Victoria. Multicoloured.

1653	$1.20 Type **167**	55	60
1654	$1.20 Queen Victoria at accession	55	60
1655	$1.20 Queen Victoria as a young girl	55	60

1656 $1.20 Victoria Mary Louisa, Duchess of Kent (Queen Victoria's mother) 55 60
1657 $1.20 Queen Victoria in old age 55 60
1658 $1.20 Albert Edward, Prince of Wales as a boy 55 60
MS1659 97 × 70 mm. $5 Queen Victoria at accession . . . . . 2·40 2·50

2001. Queen Elizabeth II's 75th Birthday. Multicoloured.
1660 90c. Type **168** 45 50
1661 90c. Wearing tiara 45 50
1662 90c. Wearing yellow hat . . 45 50
1663 90c. Wearing grey hat . . . 45 50
1664 90c. Wearing red hat . . . 45 50
1665 90c. Bare-headed and wearing pearl necklace . . 45 50
MS1666 95 × 107 mm. $5 Wearing blue hat . . . . 2·40 2·50

169 Christmas Candle (flower)

171 Maracana Football Stadium, Brazil 1950

170 Flag of Antigua & Barbuda

2001. Christmas. Flowers. Multicoloured.
1667 30c. Type **169** 15 20
1668 90c. Poinsettia (horiz) . . . 45 50
1669 $1.20 Snowbush (horiz) . . 55 60
1670 $3 Tiger claw . . . . 1·40 1·50

2001. Flags of the Caribbean Community. Multicoloured.
1671 90c. Type **170** 45 50
1672 90c. Bahamas 45 50
1673 90c. Barbados 45 50
1674 90c. Belize 45 50
1675 90c. Dominica 45 50
1676 90c. Grenada 45 50
1677 90c. Guyana 45 50
1678 90c. Jamaica 45 50
1679 90c. Montserrat 45 50
1680 90c. St. Kitts & Nevis . . . 45 50
1681 90c. St. Lucia 45 50
1682 90c. Surinam 45 50
1683 90c. St. Vincent and the Grenadines 45 50
1684 90c. Trinidad & Tobago . . 45 50
No. 1675 shows the former flag of Dominica, superseded in 1990.

2001. World Cup Football Championship, Japan and Korea (2002). Multicoloured.
1685 $1.60 Type **171** 75 80
1686 $1.60 Ferenc Puskas (Hungary), Switzerland 1954 . . . . 75 80
1687 $1.60 Luiz Bellini (Brazil), Sweden 1958 . . . . . . 75 80
1688 $1.60 Mauro (Brazil), Chile 1962 . . . . 75 80
1689 $1.60 West German cap, England 1966 . . . . . . 75 80
1690 $1.60 Pennant, Mexico 1970 75 80
1691 $1.60 Passarella (Argentina), Argentina 1978 . . . . . 75 80
1692 $1.60 Dino Zoff (Italy), Spain 1982 . . . . 75 80
1693 $1.60 Azteca Stadium, Mexico 1986 . . . . . . 75 80
1694 $1.60 San Siro Stadium, Italy 1990 . . . . 75 80
1695 $1.60 Dennis Bergkamp (Holland), U.S.A. 1994 75 80
1696 $1.60 Stade de France, France 1998 . . . . . . 75 80
MS1697 Two sheets, each 88 × 75 mm. (a) $5 Detail of Jules Rimet Trophy, Uruguay 1930. (b) $5 Detail of World Cup Trophy, Japan/Korea 2002 Set of 2 sheets 4·75 5·00
Nos. 1685 and 1687 are inscribed "Morocana" and "Luis" respectively, both in error.

172 Queen Elizabeth and Duke of Edinburgh in reviewing Car

2002. Golden Jubilee. Multicoloured.
1698 $2 Type **172** . . . . 95 1·00
1699 $2 Prince Philip . . . . . . 95 1·00
1700 $2 Queen Elizabeth wearing yellow coat and hat . . . 95 1·00
1701 $2 Queen Elizabeth and horse at polo match . . . 95 1·00
MS1702 76 × 108 mm. $5 Queen Elizabeth with Prince Philip in naval uniform . . . . 2·40 2·50

173 Chestnut and White Horse

2002. Chinese New Year ("Year of the Horse"). Paintings by Ren Renfa. Multicoloured.
1703 $1.60 Type **173** 75 80
1704 $1.60 Bay horse 75 80
1705 $1.60 Brown horse 75 80
1706 $1.60 Dappled grey horse 75 80

174 Beechey's Bee

2002. Fauna. Multicoloured.
1707 $1.20 Type **174** 55 60
1708 $1.20 Banded king shoemaker butterfly . . . 55 60
1709 $1.20 Streaked sphinx caterpillar 55 60
1710 $1.20 Hercules beetle . . . 55 60
1711 $1.20 South American palm weevil 55 60
1712 $1.20 Giant katydid 55 60
1713 $1.60 Roseate spoonbill . . 75 80
1714 $1.60 White-tailed tropicbird 75 80
1715 $1.60 Ruby-throated tropicbird 75 80
1716 $1.60 Black skimmer . . . 75 80
1717 $1.60 Black-necked stilt . . 75 80
1718 $1.60 Mourning dove . . . 75 80
1719 $1.60 Sperm whale and calf 75 80
1720 $1.60 Killer whale 75 80
1721 $1.60 Minke whales 75 80
1722 $1.60 Fin whale 75 80
1723 $1.60 Blaineville's beaked whale 75 80
1724 $1.60 Pygmy sperm whale 75 80
MS1725 Three sheets, each 105 × 78 mm. (a) $5 Click beetle. (b) $5 Royal tern. (c) $5 Humpback whale (vert) . . . . 7·25 7·50
Nos. 1707/12 (insects), 1713/18 (birds) and 1719/24 (whales) were each printed together, se-tenant, with the backgrounds forming composite designs.

175 Mount Assiniboine, Canada

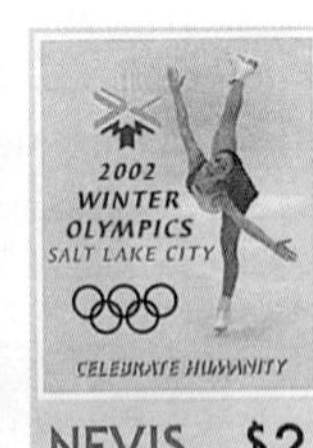

177 Women's Figure Skating

176 Horse-riders on Beach

2002. International Year of Mountains. Multicoloured.
1726 $2 Type **175** . . . . 95 1·00
1727 $2 Mount Atitlan, Guatemala . . . . 95 1·00
1728 $2 Mount Adams, U.S.A. 95 1·00
1729 $2 The Matterhorn, Switzerland . . . . 95 1·00
1730 $2 Mount Dhaulagiri, Nepal 95 1·00
1731 $2 Mount Chamlang, Nepal 95 1·00
MS1732 106 × 125 mm. $5 Mount Kvaenangen, Norway . . . . 2·40 2·50
Nos. 1727 and 1729 are inscribed "ATAILAN" and "MATTHERORN", both in error.

2002. Year of Eco Tourism. Multicoloured.
1733 $1.60 Type **176** 75 80
1734 $1.60 Windsurfing 75 80
1735 $1.60 Pinney's Beach . . . 75 80
1736 $1.60 Hikers by beach . . . 75 80
1737 $1.60 Robert T. Jones Golf Course 75 80
1738 $1.60 Scuba diver and fish 75 80
MS1739 115 × 90 mm. $5 Snorkel diver on reef . . . . 2·40 2·50

2002. Winter Olympic Games, Salt Lake City. Multicoloured.
1740 $2 Type **177** . . . . 95 1·00
1741 $2 Aerial skiing . . . . . . 95 1·00
MS1742 88 × 119 mm. Nos. 1740/1 1·90 2·00

178 Two Scout Canoes in Mist

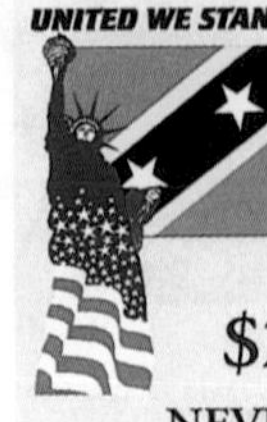

179 U.S. Flag as Statue of Liberty with Nevis Flag

2002. 20th World Scout Jamboree, Thailand. Multicoloured.
1743 $2 Type **178** . . . . 95 1·00
1744 $2 Canoe in jungle . . . . 95 1·00
1745 $2 Scout on rope-ladder . . 95 1·00
1746 $2 Scouts with inflatable boats . . . . 95 1·00
MS1747 105 × 125 mm. $5 Scout painting . . . . 2·40 2·50

2002. "United We Stand". Support for Victims of 11 September 2001 Terrorist Attacks.
1748 **179** $2 multicoloured . . . . 95 1·00

180 "Nevis Peak with Windmill" (Eva Wilkin)

2002. Art. Mmulticoloured (except Nos. 1750/1).
1749 $1.20 Type **180** 55 60
1750 $1.20 "Nevis Peak with ruined Windmill" (Eva Wilkin) (brown and black) 55 60
1751 $1.20 "Fig Tree Church" (Eva Wilkin) (brown and black) 55 60
1752 $1.20 "Nevis Peak with Blossom" (Eva Wilkin) 55 60
1753 $2 "Golden Pheasants and Loquat" (Kano Shoei) (30 × 80 mm) . . . . . . 95 1·00
1754 $2 "Flowers and Birds of the Four Seasons" (Winter) (Ikeda Koson) (30 × 80 mm) . . . . . . 95 1·00
1755 $2 "Pheasants and Azaleas" (Kano Shoei) (30 × 80 mm) . . . . . . 95 1·00
1756 $2 "Flowers and Birds of the Four Seasons" (Spring) (Ikeda Koson) (different) (30 × 80 mm) 95 1·00
1757 $3 "White Blossom" (Shikibu Terutada) (38 × 62 mm) . . . . . . 1·40 1·50
1758 $3 "Bird and Flowers" (Shikibu Terutada) (38 × 62 mm) . . . . . . 1·40 1·50
1759 $3 "Bird and Leaves" (Shikibu Terutada) (38 × 62 mm) . . . . . . 1·40 1·50
1760 $3 "Red and White Flowers" (Shikibu Terutada) (38 × 62 mm) 1·40 1·50
1761 $3 "Bird on Willow Tree" (Yosa Buson) (62 × 38 mm) . . . . . . 1·40 1·50
1762 $3 "Bird on Peach Tree" (Yosa Buson) (62 × 38 mm) . . . . . . 1·40 1·50
MS1763 Two sheets, each 105 × 105 mm. (a) $5 "Golden Pheasants among Rhododendrons" (Yamamoto Baiitsu) (38 × 62 mm). (b) $5 "Musk Cat and Camellias" (Uto Gyoshi) (62 × 38 mm) . . . . 4·75 5·00
Nos. 1757/62 were printed together, se-tenant, with the backgrounds forming a composite design.

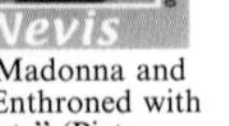

181 "Madonna and Child Enthroned with Saints" (Pietro Perugino)

182 Claudio Reyna (U.S.A.) and Torsten Frings (Germany)

2002. Christmas. Religious Art. Multicoloured.
1764 30c. Type **181** 15 20
1765 80c. "Adoration of the Magi" (Domenico Ghirlandaio) 40 45
1766 90c. "San Zaccaria Altarpiece" (Giovanni Bellini) 45 50
1767 $1.20 "Presentation at the Temple" (Bellini) 55 60
1768 $5 "Madonna and Child" (Simone Martini) . . . . 2·40 2·50
MS1769 102 × 76 mm. $6 "Maesa" (Martini) . . . . 3·00 3·25

2002. World Cup Football Championship, Japan and Korea. Multicoloured.
1770 $1.20 Type **182** 55 60
1771 $1.20 Michael Ballack (Germany) and Eddie Pope (U.S.A.) 55 60
1772 $1.20 Sebastian Kehl (Germany) and Brian McBride (U.S.A.) 55 60
1773 $1.20 Carlos Puyol (Spain) and Eul Yong Lee (South Korea) 55 60
1774 $1.20 Jin Cheul Choi (South Korea) and Gaizka Mendieta (Spain) 55 60
1775 $1.20 Juan Valeron (Spain) and Jin Cheul Choi (South Korea) 55 60
1776 $1.60 Emile Heskey (England) and Edmilson (Brazil) 55 60
1777 $1.60 Rivaldo (Brazil) and Sol Campbell (England) 55 60
1778 $1.60 Ronaldinho (Brazil) and Nicky Butt (England) 55 60
1779 $1.60 Ilhan Mansiz (Turkey) and Omar Daf (Senegal) 55 60
1780 $1.60 Hasan Sas (Turkey) and Pape Bouba Diop (Senegal) 55 50
1781 $1.60 Lamine Diata (Senegal) and Hakan Sukur (Turkey) 55 60
MS1782 Four sheets, each 82 × 82 mm. (a) $3 Sebastian Kehl (Germany); $3 Frankie Hejduk (U.S.A.). (b) $3 Hong Myung Bo (South Korea); $3 Gaizka Mendieta (Spain). (c) $3 David Beckham (England) and Roque Junior (Brazil); $3 Paul Scholes (England) and Rivaldo (Brazil). (d) $3 Alpay Ozalan (Turkey); $3 Khalilou Fadiga (Senegal) . . 11·50 12·00
No. 1780 is inscribed "Papa" in error.

183 Ram and Two Ewes

2003. Chinese New Year ("Year of the Ram").
1783 **183** $2 multicoloured . . . . 95 1·00

OFFICIAL STAMPS

1980. Nos. 40/49 optd **OFFICIAL**.
O 1 15c. Sugar cane being harvested 10 10
O 2 25c. Crafthouse (craft centre) 10 10
O 3 30c. "Europa" (liner) . . . 10 10
O 4 40c. Lobster and sea crab . . 15 15
O 5 45c. Royal St. Kitts Hotel and golf course 20 20
O 6 50c. Pinney's Beach, Nevis 15 20
O 7 55c. New runway at Golden Rock 15 20
O 8 $1 Picking cotton 15 25

O 9 $5 Brewery 45 55
O10 $10 Pineapples and peanuts 70 90

1981. Nos. 60/71 optd **OFFICIAL**.
O11 15c. New River Mill 10 10
O12 20c. Nelson Museum 10 10
O13 25c. St. James' Parish Church 10 15
O14 30c. Nevis Lane 15 15
O15 40c. Zetland Plantation . . . 15 20
O16 45c. Nisbet Plantation . . . 20 25
O17 50c. Pinney's Beach 20 25
O18 55c. Eva Wilkin's Studio . . 25 30
O19 $1 Nevis at dawn 30 30
O20 $2.50 Ruins of Fort Charles 40 50
O21 $5 Old Bath House 50 65
O22 $10 Beach at Nisbet's . . . 80 1·00

1983. Nos. 72/7 optd or surch **OFFICIAL**.
O23 45c. on $2 "Royal Sovereign" 10 15
O24 45c. on $2 Prince Charles and Lady Diana Spencer 20 25
O25 55c. "Royal Caroline" . . . 10 15
O26 55c. Prince Charles and Lady Diana Spencer . . . 25 25
O27 $1.10 on $5 "Britannia" . . 20 25
O28 $1.10 on $5 Prince Charles and Lady Diana Spencer 55 60

1985. Nos. 187/98 optd **OFFICIAL**.
O29 15c. Flamboyant 20 20
O30 20c. Eyelash orchid 30 30
O31 30c. Bougainvillea 30 40
O32 40c. Hibiscus sp 30 40
O33 50c. Night-blooming cereus 35 40
O34 55c. Yellow mahoe 35 45
O35 60c. Spider-lily 40 50
O36 75c. Scarlet cordia 45 55
O37 $1 Shell-ginger 60 60
O38 $3 Blue petrea . . . . . . 1·25 1·75
O39 $5 Coral hibiscus . . . . . 2·00 2·25
O40 $10 Passion flower . . . . . 3·00 2·50

1993. Nos. 578/91 optd **OFFICIAL**.
O41 5c. Type **63** 55 75
O42 10c. "Historis odius" 60 75
O43 15c. "Marpesia corinna" . . 70 60
O44 20c. "Anartia amathea" . . 70 40
O45 25c. "Junonia evarete" . . . 70 40
O46 40c. "Heliconius charithonia" 85 45
O47 50c. "Marpesia petreus" . . 85 45
O48 75c. "Heliconius doris" . . . 1·25 60
O49 80c. "Dione juno" . . . . . 1·25 50
O50 $1 "Hypolimnas misippus" 1·25 80
O51 $3 "Danaus plexippus" . . . 2·50 2·75
O52 $5 "Heliconius sara" . . . . 3·50 4·00
O53 $10 "Tithorea harmonia" . . 6·50 7·00
O54 $20 "Dryas julia" . . . . . 12·00 13·00

1999. Nos. 1166/77 optd **OFFICIAL**.
O55 25c. Guava 10 15
O56 30c. Papaya 15 20
O57 50c. Mango 25 30
O58 60c. Golden apple 30 35
O59 80c. Pineapple 40 45
O60 90c. Watermelon 45 50
O61 $1 Bananas 50 55
O62 $1.80 Orange 85 90
O63 $3 Honeydew . . . . 1·40 1·50
O64 $5 Cantaloupe . . . . . . 2·40 2·50
O65 $10 Pomegranate . . . . . 4·75 5·00
O66 $20 Cashew . . . . 9·50 9·75

NEW BRUNSWICK Pt. 1

An eastern province of the Dominion of Canada, whose stamps are now used.

1851. 12 pence = 1 shilling;
20 shilling = 1 pound.
1860. 100 cents = 1 dollar.

1 Royal Crown and Heraldic Flowers of the United Kingdom

1851.
2 **1** 3d. red £2000 £325
4 6d. yellow £4500 £700
5 1s. mauve £13000 £4000

2 Locomotive

3 Queen Victoria

1860.
8 **2** 1c. purple . . . . 35·00 35·00
10 **3** 2c. orange . . . . 18·00 18·00
13 – 5c. brown £4250
14 – 5c. green . . . . 16·00 13·00
17 – 10c. red . . . . 38·00 38·00
18 – 12½c. blue . . . . 50·00 40·00
19 – 17c. black . . . . 38·00 45·00

DESIGNS—VERT: 5c. brown, Charles Connell; 5c. green, 10c. Queen Victoria; 17c. King Edward VII when Prince of Wales. HORIZ: 12½c. Steamship.

NEW CALEDONIA Pt. 6

A French Overseas Territory in the S. Pacific, E. of Australia, consisting of New Caledonia and a number of smaller islands.

100 centimes = 1 franc.

1 Napoleon III

1860. Imperf.
1 **1** 10c. black £250

Nos. 5/30 are stamps of French Colonies optd or surch.

1881. "Peace and Commerce" type surch **N C E** and new value. Imperf.
5 H 05 on 40c. red on yellow . . 14·00 20·00
8a 5 on 40c. red on yellow . . 12·50 12·50
9 5 on 75c. red . . . . 35·00 35·00
6 25 on 35c. black on orange £200 £200
7 25 on 75c. red £275 £275

1886. "Peace and Commerce" (imperf) and "Commerce" types surch **N.C.E. 5c.**
10 J 5c. on 1f. green . . . . . . 17·00 19·00
11 H 5c. on 1f. green £7500 £8500

1891. "Peace and Commerce" (imperf) and "Commerce" types surch **N.-C.E. 10 c.** in ornamental frame.
13 H 10c. on 40c. red on yellow 26·00 22·00
14 J 10c. on 40c. red on yellow 12·50 13·50

1892. "Commerce" type surch **N.-C.E. 10 centimes** in ornamental frame.
15 J 10c. on 30c. brown on drab 10·50 11·00

1892. Optd **NLLE CALEDONIE**. (a) "Peace and Commerce" type. Imperf.
16 H 20c. red on green £250 £275
17 35c. black on orange . . . . 50·00 60·00
19 1f. green £200 £200

(b) "Commerce" type.
20 J 5c. green on green . . . . . 14·50 9·00
21 10c. black on lilac . . . . . £120 65·00
22 15c. blue . . . . 85·00 42·00
23 20c. red on green . . . . . £100 60·00
24 25c. brown on yellow . . . . 21·00 6·25
25 25c. black on pink . . . . . £100 10·00
26 30c. brown on drab . . . . 75·00 65·00
27 35c. black on orange £200 £150
29 75c. red on pink £190 £120
30 1f. green £120 £120

1892. "Tablet" key-type inscr "NLLE CALEDONIE ET DEPENDANCES".
31 D 1c. black and red on blue . . 30 15
32 2c. brown and blue on buff 40 55
33 4c. brown and blue on grey 1·10 3·50
55 5c. green and red . . . . . 2·75 25
34 10c. black and blue on lilac 4·00 2·75
56 10c. red and blue . . . . . 5·00 50
35 15c. blue and red . . . . . 16·00 1·40
57 15c. grey and red . . . . . 8·75 30
36 20c. red and blue on green 6·50 8·50
37 25c. black and red on pink 10·00 2·00
58 25c. blue and red . . . . . 10·50 4·50
38 30c. brown and blue on drab 10·00 8·50
39 40c. red and blue on yellow 16·00 9·25
40 50c. red and blue on pink 60·00 23·00
59 50c. brown and red on blue 35·00 85·00
60 50c. brown and blue on blue 38·00 42·00
41 75c. brown & red on orange 22·00 18·00
42 1f. green and red . . . . . 16·00 17·00

1892. Surch **N-C-E** in ornamental scroll and new value. (a) "Peace and Commerce" type. Imperf.
44 H 10 on 1f. green £4500 £3250

(b) "Commerce" type.
45 J 5 on 20c. red on green . . . 27·00 7·00
46 5 on 75c. red on pink . . . . 16·00 9·25
48 10 on 1f. green . . . . 13·00 8·00

1899. Stamps of 1892 surch (a) **N-C-E** in ornamental scroll and **5**.
50 D 5 on 2c. brown & bl on buff 10·00 12·50
51 5 on 4c. brown & bl on grey 1·25 3·25

(b) **N.C.E.** and **15** in circle.
52 D 15 on 30c. brown and blue on drab . . . . 2·50 5·00
53 15 on 75c. brown and red on orange . . . . 10·00 10·50
54 15 on 1f. green and red . . 32·00 25·00

1902. Surch **N.-C.E.** and value in figures.
61 D 5 on 30c. brown and blue on drab . . . . 3·50 7·75
62 15 on 40c. red and blue on yellow . . . . 3·50 7·00

1903. 50th Anniv of French Annexation. Optd **CINQUANTENAIRE 24 SEPTEMBRE 1853 1903** and eagle.
63 D 1c. black and red on blue . . 70 1·10
64 2c. brown and blue on buff 2·50 2·25
65 4c. brown and blue on grey 4·50 4·50
66 5c. green and red . . . . . 3·00 3·25
69 10c. black and blue on lilac 3·50 5·25
70 15c. grey and red . . . . . 9·25 4·50
71 20c. red and blue on green 15·00 12·00
72 25c. black and red on pink 17·00 17·00
73 30c. brown and blue on drab 26·00 21·00
74 40c. red and blue on yellow 38·00 21·00
75 50c. red and blue on pink 60·00 40·00
76 75c. brown & blue on orange . . . . 85·00 £110
77 1f. green and red £110 £100

1903. Nos. 64 etc further surch with value in figures within the jubilee opt.
78 D 1 on 2c. brown & bl on buff 60 75
79 2 on 4c. brown & bl on grey 2·50 3·00
80 4 on 5c. green and red . . . 90 2·50
82 10 on 15c. grey and red . . 45 1·00
83 15 on 20c. red and blue on green . . . . 50 2·50
84 20 on 25c. black and red on pink . . . . 2·75 4·00

15 Kagu

16

17 "President Felix Faure" (barque)

1905.
85 **15** 1c. black on green 25 30
86 2c. brown 25 25
87 4c. blue on orange 40 55
88 5c. green 40 55
112 5c. blue 25 35
113 10c. green 60 60
114 10c. red . . . . 1·25 70
90 15c. lilac 60 50
91 **16** 20c. brown 15 25
92 25c. blue on green . . . . 1·10 35
115 25c. red on yellow 35 20
93 30c. brown on orange . . . 30 1·60
116 30c. red . . . . 1·25 3·50
117 30c. orange . . . . 50 1·25
94 35c. black on yellow . . . 40 1·25
95 40c. red on green . . . . 1·60 2·25
96 45c. red . . . . 1·40 2·75
97 50c. red on orange . . . . 3·25 3·50
118 50c. blue . . . . 70 1·00
119 50c. grey 30 95
120 65c. blue . . . . 90 2·75
98 75c. olive . . . . 35 2·75
121 75c. blue . . . . 1·50 2·25
122 75c. violet . . . . 80 2·75
99 **17** 1f. blue on green . . . . 1·25 2·75
123 1f. blue . . . . 2·00 3·25
100 2f. red on blue . . . . . 3·50 3·75
101 5f. black on orange . . . . 8·50 9·25

1912. Stamps of 1892 surch.
102 D 05 on 15c. grey and red . . 45 1·50
103 05 on 20c. red and blue on green . . . . 25 1·75
104 05 on 30c. brown and blue on drab . . . . 25 2·50
105 10 on 40c. red and blue on yellow . . . . 75 1·60
106 10 on 50c. brown and blue on blue . . . . 1·60 2·25

1915. Surch **NCE 5** and red cross.
107 **15** 10c.+5c. red . . . . 1·25 1·90

1915. Surch **5c** and red cross.
109 **15** 10c.+5c. red . . . . 1·40 3·00
110 15c.+5c. lilac . . . . . . 20 2·75

1918. Surch **5 CENTIMES**.
111 **15** 5c. on 15c. lilac . . . . . 1·60 3·25

1922. Surch **0 05**.
124 **15** 0.05 on 15c. lilac 50 50

1924. Types **15/17** (some colours changed) surch.
125 **15** 25c. on 15c. lilac . . . . . 40 2·50
126 **17** 25c. on 2f. red on blue . . 55 2·25
127 25c. on 5f. black on orange 70 3·00
128 **16** 60 on 75c. green . . . . . 25 2·00
129 65 on 45c. purple . . . . 55 3·75
130 85 on 45c. purple . . . . 1·10 4·25
131 90 on 75c. red . . . . . . 25 3·00
132 **17** 1f.25 on 1f. blue . . . . . 45 3·25
133 1f.50 on 1f. blue on blue 80 3·50
134 3f. on 5f. mauve . . . . . 1·50 3·75
135 10f. on 5f. green on mauve 2·75 10·00
136 20f. on 5f. red on yellow 10·00 20·00

22 Pointe des Paletuviers

23 Chief's Hut

24 La Perouse, De Bougainville and "L'Astrolabe"

1928.
137 **22** 1c. blue and purple . . . . 10 1·90
138 2c. green and brown . . . 10 1·75
139 3c. blue and red . . . . . 15 2·50
140 4c. blue and orange . . . 15 2·25
141 5c. brown and blue . . . . 15 1·25
142 10c. brown and lilac . . . 20 60
143 15c. blue and brown . . . 20 50
144 20c. brown and red . . . . 20 1·40
145 25c. brown and green . . . 25 15
146 **23** 30c. deep green and green 20 1·25
147 35c. mauve and black . . . 50 20
148 40c. green and red . . . . 15 2·75
149 45c. red and blue . . . . 1·50 3·25
150 45c. green and deep green 2·50 3·00
151 50c. brown and mauve . . 25 25
152 55c. red and blue . . . . 2·50 1·10
153 60c. red and blue . . . . 20 2·75
154 65c. blue and brown . . . 35 1·25
155 70c. brown and mauve . . 1·75 3·00
156 75c. drab and blue . . . . 1·10 2·25
157 80c. green and purple . . . 1·50 2·50
158 85c. brown and green . . . 2·50 2·00
159 90c. pink and red . . . . 1·75 2·75
160 90c. red and brown . . . . 2·00 1·50
161 **24** 1f. pink and drab . . . . 5·50 1·60
162 1f. carmine and red . . . . 85 2·50
163 1f. green and red . . . . . 1·00 2·75
164 1f.10 brown and green . . 10·00 17·00
165 1f.25 green and brown . . 2·25 3·00
166 1f.25 carmine and red . . . 70 3·00
167 1f.40 red and blue . . . . 1·25 2·75
168 1f.50 light blue and blue 50 2·25
169 1f.60 brown and green . . 2·25 3·25
170 1f.75 orange and blue . . . 2·00 2·75
171 1f.75 blue and ultramarine 2·25 3·00
172 2f. brown and orange . . . 75 50
173 2f.25 blue and ultramarine 2·25 3·00
174 2f.50 brown . . . . 70 2·50
175 3f. brown and mauve . . . 70 2·25
176 5f. brown and blue . . . . 55 2·25
177 10f. brown & pur on pink 1·90 2·75
178 20f. brown & red on yellow 2·50 3·75

1931. "Colonial Exhibition" key-types.
179 E 40c. green and black . . . 5·25 6·00
180 F 50c. mauve and black . . . 5·25 6·00
181 G 90c. red and black . . . . 5·25 6·00
182 H 1f.50 blue and black . . . 5·25 5·00

1932. Paris–Noumea Flight. Optd with Couzinet 33 airplane and **PARIS-NOUMEA Verneilh-Deve-Munch 5 Avril 1932**.
183 **23** 40c. olive and red £350 £375
184 50c. brown and mauve . . £350 £375

1933. 1st Anniv of Paris–Noumea Flight. Optd **PARIS-NOUMEA Premiere liaison aerienne 5 Avril 1932** and Couzinet 33 airplane.
185 **22** 1c. blue and purple . . . . 8·00 12·00
186 2c. green and brown . . . 8·50 12·00

187 4c. blue and orange . . . 7·75 12·00
188 5c. brown and blue . . . . 7·50 12·00
189 10c. brown and lilac . . . 8·25 12·00
190 15c. blue and brown . . . 7·50 11·50
191 20c. brown and red . . . . 7·50 12·00
192 25c. brown and green . . . 8·50 12·00
193 **23** 30c. deep green and green 8·00 12·00
194 35c. mauve and black . . . 7·25 12·00
195 40c. green and red . . . . 8·50 9·75
196 45c. red and blue . . . . 7·75 12·00
197 50c. brown and mauve . . 7·00 12·00
198 70c. brown and mauve . . 8·00 14·00
199 75c. drab and blue . . . . 8·75 11·00
200 85c. brown and green . . . 8·00 11·00
201 90c. pink and red . . . . 8·00 11·50
202 **24** 1f. pink and drab . . . . 10·50 14·00
203 1f.25 green and brown . . 10·50 13·50
204 1f.50 light blue and blue 10·00 13·50
205 1f.75 orange and blue . . . 8·00 9·75
206 2f. brown and orange . . . 10·00 16·00
207 3f. brown and mauve . . . 10·00 15·00
208 5f. brown and blue . . . . 12·50 16·00
209 10f. brown & pur on pink 8·00 16·00
210 20f. brown & red on yellow 8·25 16·00

1937. International Exhibition, Paris. As Nos. 168/73 of St.-Pierre et Miquelon.
211 20c. violet . . . . 55 3·50
212 30c. green . . . . 70 3·50
213 40c. red . . . . 35 3·00
214 50c. brown and blue . . . . 3·00 4·00
215 90c. red . . . . 2·00 2·75
216 1f.50 blue . . . . 2·50 4·50
DESIGNS—HORIZ: 30c. Sailing ships; 40c. Berber, Negress and Annamite; 90c. France extends torch of civilization; 1f.50, Diane de Poitiers. VERT: 50c. Agriculture.

27 Breguet Saigon Flying Boat over Noumea

1938. Air.
217 **27** 65c. violet . . . . 50 3·25
218 4f.50 red . . . . 2·00 2·75
219 7f. green . . . . 35 2·50
220 9f. blue . . . . 3·00 4·00
221 20f. orange . . . . 2·00 2·75
222 50f. black . . . . 2·50 4·50

1938. Int Anti-cancer Fund. As T **22** of Mauritania.
223 1f.75+50c. blue . . . . . . 5·75 18·00

1939. New York World's Fair. As T **28** of Mauritania.
224 1f.25 red . . . . 65 3·50
225 2f.25 blue . . . . 70 2·00

1939. 150th Anniv of French Revolution. As T **29** of Mauritania.
226 45c.+25c. green and black (postage) . . . . 10·00 13·50
227 70c.+30c. brown and black 9·50 13·50
228 90c.+35c. orange and black 8·75 13·50
229 1f.25+1f. red and black . . . 10·00 13·50
230 2f.25+2f. blue and black . . 10·50 13·50
231 4f.50+4f. black and orange (air) . . . . 7·75 45·00

1941. Adherence to General de Gaulle. Optd **France Libre**.
232 **22** 1c. blue and purple . . . . 8·25 24·00
233 2c. green and brown . . . 10·50 23·00
234 3c. blue and red . . . . 8·50 23·00
235 4c. blue and orange . . . 8·00 23·00
236 5c. brown and blue . . . . 7·00 23·00
237 10c. brown and lilac . . . 7·50 32·00
238 15c. blue and brown . . . 20·00 32·00
239 20c. brown and red . . . . 15·00 22·00
240 25c. brown and green . . . 15·00 22·00
241 **23** 30c. deep green and green 14·00 22·00
242 35c. mauve and black . . . 14·50 22·00
243 40c. green and red . . . . 19·00 22·00
244 45c. green and deep green 18·00 24·00
245 50c. brown and mauve . . 15·00 24·00
246 55c. red and blue . . . . 19·00 30·00
247 60c. red and blue . . . . 15·00 24·00
248 65c. blue and brown . . . 21·00 30·00
249 70c. brown and mauve . . 15·00 30·00
250 75c. drab and blue . . . . 19·00 30·00
251 80c. green and purple . . . 19·00 24·00
252 85c. brown and green . . . 18·00 27·00
253 90c. pink and red . . . . 18·00 27·00
254 **24** 1f. carmine and red . . . . 17·00 27·00
255 1f.25 green and brown . . 14·50 27·00
256 1f.40 red and blue . . . . 14·50 27·00
257 1f.50 light blue and blue 17·00 27·00
258 1f.60 brown and green . . 17·00 27·00
259 1f.75 orange and blue . . . 19·00 27·00
260 2f. brown and orange . . . 21·00 27·00
261 2f.25 blue and ultramarine 17·00 27·00
262 2f.50 brown . . . . 22·00 30·00
263 3f. brown and mauve . . . 18·00 30·00
264 5f. brown and blue . . . . 18·00 30·00
265 10f. brown & pur on pink 20·00 36·00
266 20f. brown & red on yellow 21·00 40·00

29 Kagu

30 Fairey FC-1 Airliner

1942. Free French Issue. (a) Postage.
267 **29** 5c. brown . . . . 30 1·75
268 10c. blue . . . . 30 1·75
269 25c. green . . . . 30 1·25
270 30c. red . . . . 30 2·75
271 40c. green . . . . 35 1·50
272 80c. purple . . . . 30 1·50
273 1f. mauve 90 80
274 1f.50 red 75 35
275 2f. black . . . . 1·10 50
276 2f.50 blue . . . . 1·50 1·75
277 4f. violet . . . . 1·00 40
278 5f. yellow 50 85
279 10f. brown 50 60
280 20f. green . . . . 1·10 1·90

(b) Air.
281 **30** 1f. orange . . . . 25 2·25
282 1f.50 red . . . . 30 2·75
283 5f. purple . . . . 60 2·00
284 10f. black . . . . 65 2·75
285 25f. blue . . . . 60 1·90
286 50f. green . . . . 75 1·25
287 100f. red . . . . 1·40 2·25

1944. Mutual Aid and Red Cross Funds. As T **19b** of Oceanic Settlements.
288 5f.+20f. red . . . . 1·00 3·25

1945. Eboue. As T **20a** of Oceanic Settlements.
289 2f. black . . . . 40 2·50
290 25f. green . . . . 1·60 3·25

1945. Surch.
291 **29** 50c. on 5c. brown 45 50
292 60c. on 5c. brown . . . . 45 3·00
293 70c. on 5c. brown . . . . 65 3·00
294 1f.20 on 5c. brown . . . . 30 2·50
295 2f.40 on 25c. green . . . . 1·60 3·00
296 3f. on 25c. green . . . . . 1·40 2·00
297 4f.50 on 25c. green . . . . 1·40 2·75
298 15f. on 2f.50 blue . . . . 2·00 1·10

1946. Air. Victory. As T **20b** of Oceanic Settlements.
299 8f. blue . . . . 25 3·00

1946. Air. From Chad to the Rhine. As T **25a** of Madagascar.
300 **35** 5f. black . . . . 80 2·50
301 – 10f. red . . . . 55 2·50
302 – 15f. blue . . . . 55 3·50
303 – 20f. brown . . . . 75 3·50
304 – 25f. green . . . . 60 3·75
305 – 50f. purple . . . . 70 4·25
DESIGNS: 5f. Legionaries by Lake Chad; 10f. Battle of Koufra; 15f. Tank Battle, Mareth; 20f. Normandy Landings; 25f. Liberation of Paris; 50f. Liberation of Strasbourg.

36 Two Kagus

37 Sud Est Languedoc Airliners over Landscape

1948. (a) Postage.
306 **36** 10c. purple and yellow . . 20 2·75
307 30c. purple and green . . 20 2·75
308 40c. purple and brown . . 20 2·75
309 – 50c. purple and pink . . . 15 25
310 – 60c. brown and yellow . . 1·50 2·50
311 – 80c. green and light green 1·50 2·75
312 – 1f. violet and orange . . . 20 25
313 – 1f.20 brown and blue . . . 50 2·75
314 – 1f.50 blue and yellow . . . 40 1·25
315 – 2f. brown and green . . . 30 35
316 – 2f.40 red and purple . . . 70 2·75
317 – 3f. violet and orange . . . 2·50 75
318 – 4f. indigo and blue 75 25
319 – 5f. violet and red 75 30
320 – 6f. brown and yellow . . . 65 65
321 – 10f. blue and orange . . . 60 40
322 – 15f. red and blue 75 55
323 – 20f. violet and yellow . . . 75 60
324 – 25f. blue and orange . . . 1·75 95

(b) Air.
325 – 50f. purple and orange . . 2·50 3·75
326 **37** 100f. blue and green . . . 7·25 4·25
327 – 200f. brown and yellow . . 6·50 7·25
DESIGNS—As T **36**: HORIZ: 50c. to 80c. Ducos Sanatorium; 1f.50, Porcupine Is; 2f. to 4f. Nickel foundry; 5f. to 10f. "The Towers of Notre Dame" Rocks. VERT: 15f. to 25f. Chief's hut. As T **37**: HORIZ: Sud Est Languedoc airliner over- 50f. St. Vincent Bay; 200f. Noumea.

38 People of Five Races, Bomber and Globe

1949. Air. 75th Anniv of U.P.U.
328 **38** 10f. multicoloured . . . . 1·75 8·50

39 Doctor and Patient

40

1950. Colonial Welfare Fund.
329 **39** 10f.+2f. purple & brown 2·25 6·75

1952. Military Medal Centenary.
330 **40** 2f. red, yellow and green 3·00 5·25

41 Admiral D'Entrecasteaux

1953. French Administration Centenary. Inscr "1853 1953".
331 **41** 1f.50 lake and brown . . . 2·75 3·00
332 – 2f. blue and turquoise . . 1·90 1·50
333 – 6f. brown, blue and red . . 4·00 3·25
334 – 13f. blue and green . . . . 4·25 3·50
DESIGNS: 2f. Mgr. Douarre and church; 6f. Admiral D'Urville and map; 13f. Admiral Despointes and view.

42 Normandy Landings, 1944

1954. Air. 10th Anniv of Liberation.
335 **42** 3f. blue and deep blue . . 8·25 8·25

43 Towers of Notre-Dame (rocks)

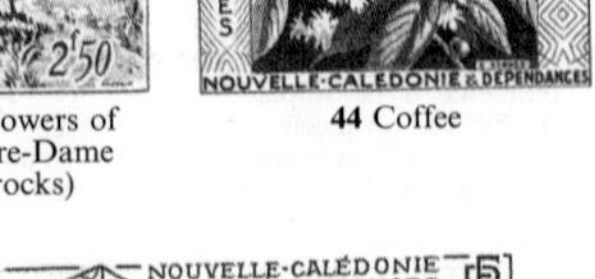
44 Coffee

45 Transporting Nickel

1955.
336 **43** 2f.50c. blue, green and sepia (postage) . . . . . 80 1·60
337 3f. blue, brown and green 3·00 3·25
338 **44** 9f. deep blue and blue . . 90 40
339 **45** 14f. blue and brown (air) 1·00 1·10

46 Dumbea Barrage

47 "Xanthostemon"

1956. Economic and Social Development Fund.
340 **46** 3f. green and blue 70 45

1958. Flowers.
341 **47** 4f. multicoloured . . . . . 1·25 1·40
342 – 15f. red, yellow and green 2·75 1·60
DESIGN: 15f. Hibiscus.

48 "Human Rights"

49 Zebra Lionfish

1958. 10th Anniv of Declaration of Human Rights.
343 **48** 7f. red and blue . . . . . 85 1·10

1959.
344 **49** 1f. brown and grey 45 25
345 – 2f. blue, purple and green 1·60 1·60
346 – 3f. red, blue and green . . 60 75
347 – 4f. purple, red and green 2·50 2·75
348 – 5f. bistre, blue and green 2·50 2·25
349 – 10f. multicoloured . . . . 1·25 40
350 – 26f. multicoloured . . . . 2·25 4·75
DESIGNS—HORIZ: 2f. Outrigger canoes racing; 3f. Harlequin tuskfish; 5f. Sail Rock, Noumea; 26f. Fluorescent corals. VERT: 4f. Fisherman with spear. 10f. Blue sea lizard and "Spirographe" (coral).

49a The Carved Rock, Bourail

1959. Air.
351 – 15f. green, brown and red 4·00 2·75
352 – 20f. brown and green . . 9·50 4·75
353 – 25f. black, blue and purple . . . . 9·50 3·75
354 – 50f. brown, green and blue . . . . 6·25 5·50
355 – 50f. brown, green and blue . . . . 7·75 4·00
356 – 100f. brown, green & blue 36·00 9·50
357 **49a** 200f. brown, green & blue 16·00 14·00
DESIGNS—HORIZ: 15f. Fisherman with net; 20f. New Caledonia nautilus; 25f. Underwater swimmer shooting bump-headed unicornfish; 50f. (No. 355), Isle of Pines; 100f. Corbeille de Yate. VERT: 50f. (No. 354), Yate barrage.

49b Napoleon III

49c Port-de-France, 1859

1960. Postal Centenary.
358 **15** 4f. red 75 90
359 – 5f. brown and lake . . . 65 1·50
360 – 9f. brown and turquoise 75 2·00
361 – 12f. black and blue . . . 70 2·50
362 **49b** 13f. blue . . . . 1·40 2·75
363 **49c** 19f. red, green & turquoise . . . . 1·75 1·75
364 – 33f. red, green and blue 2·25 3·25
DESIGNS—As Type **49c**: HORIZ: 5f. Girl operating cheque-writing machine; 12f. Telephone receiver and exchange building; 33f. As Type **49c** but without stamps in upper corners. VERT: 9f. Letter-box on tree.

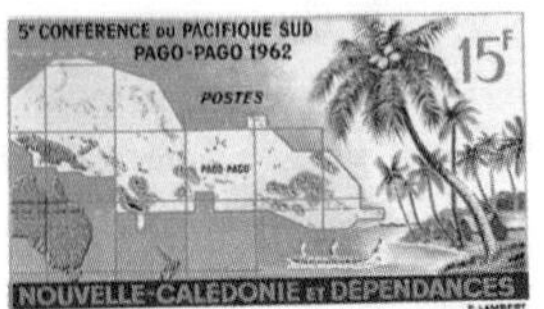
49d Map of Pacific and Palms

1962. 5th South Pacific Conference, Pago-Pago.
365 **49d** 15f. multicoloured . . . . 1·60 2·50

49e Map and Symbols of Meteorology

1962. 3rd Regional Assembly of World Meteorological Association, Noumea.
366 **49e** 50f. multicoloured . . . . 6·25 8·00

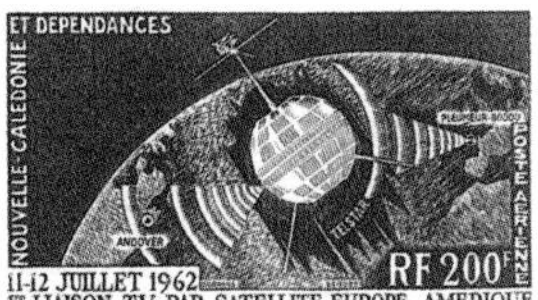

50 "Telstar" Satellite and part of Globe

1962. Air. 1st Transatlantic TV Satellite Link.
367 **50** 200f. turquoise, brown & bl . . . . 18·00 15·00

51 Emblem and Globe

1963. Freedom from Hunger.
368 **51** 17f. blue and purple . . . 2·25 2·50

52 Relay-running **53** Centenary Emblem

1963. 1st South Pacific Games, Suva, Fiji.
369 **52** 1f. red and green . . . . . 70 1·75
370 – 7f. brown and blue . . . . 1·00 2·00
371 – 10f. brown and green . . . 2·00 2·00
372 – 27f. blue and deep purple 4·50 4·00
DESIGNS: 7f. Tennis; 10f. Football; 27f. Throwing the javelin.

1963. Red Cross Centenary.
373 **53** 37f. red, grey and blue . . 6·75 6·75

54 Globe and Scales of Justice **54a** "Bikkia fritillarioides"

1963. 15th Anniv of Declaration of Human Rights.
374 **54** 50f. red and blue . . . . . 9·25 9·00

1964. Flowers. Multicoloured.
375 1f. "Freycinettia" . . . . . 1·50 1·60
376 2f. Type **54a** . . . . 55 1·90
377 3f. "Xanthostemon francii" 1·40 2·25
378 4f. "Psidiomyrtus locellatus" 2·75 1·75
379 5f. "Callistemon suberosum" 3·25 2·75
380 7f. "Montrouziera sphaeroidea" (horiz) . . . 5·75 3·00
381 10f. "Ixora collina" (horiz) 5·75 3·00
382 17f. "Deplanchea speciosa" 5·75 4·75

54b "Ascidies polycarpa" **54c** "Philately"

1964. Corals and Marine Animals from Noumea Aquarium.
383 **54b** 7f. red, brown and blue (postage) . . . . 1·75 2·50
384 – 10f. red and blue . . . . 2·50 2·50
385 – 17f. red, green and blue 5·50 2·25
388 – 13f. bistre, black and orange (air) . . . . . 4·25 2·75
389 – 15f. green, olive and blue 6·25 3·00
390 – 25f. blue and green . . . 10·50 5·75
386 – 27f. multicoloured . . . . 6·00 4·50
387 – 37f. multicoloured . . . . 10·00 6·75
DESIGNS—As T **54b**: VERT: 10f. "Alcyonium catalai" (coral). HORIZ: 17f. "Hymenocera elegans" (crab). 48 × 28 mm: 27f. Palette surgeonfish; 37f. "Phyllobranchus" (sea slug). 48 × 27 mm: 13f. Twin-spotted wrasse (young); 15f. Twin-spotted wrasse (subadult); 25f. Twin-spotted wrasse (adult).

1964. "PHILATEC 1964" Int Stamp Exn, Paris.
391 **54c** 40f. brown, green & violet 7·00 9·25

54d Houailou Mine

1964. Air. Nickel Production at Houailou.
392 **54d** 30f. multicoloured . . . . 4·25 4·25

54e Ancient Greek Wrestling

1964. Air. Olympic Games, Tokyo.
393 **54e** 10f. sepia, mauve & green 20·00 21·00

55 Weather Satellite **56** "Syncom" Communications Satellite, Telegraph Poles and Morse Key

1965. Air. World Meteorological Day.
394 **55** 9f. multicoloured . . . . . 4·50 3·75

1965. Air. Centenary of I.T.U.
395 **56** 40f. purple, brown and blue . . . . 10·00 11·50

56a De Gaulle's Appeal of 18 June 1940 **56b** Amedee Lighthouse

1965. 25th Anniv of New Caledonia's Adherence to the Free French.
396 **56a** 20f. black, red and blue 10·00 9·50

1965. Inauguration of Amedee Lighthouse.
397 **56b** 8f. bistre, blue and green 1·40 2·00

56c Rocket "Diamant"

1966. Air. Launching of 1st French Satellite.
398 **56c** 8f. lake, blue and turquoise . . . . 5·25 3·25
399 – 12f. lake, blue & turquoise 4·50 4·50
DESIGN: 12f. Satellite "A1".

56d Games Emblem

1966. Publicity for 2nd South Pacific Games, Noumea.
400 **56d** 8f. black, red and blue . . 1·75 2·25

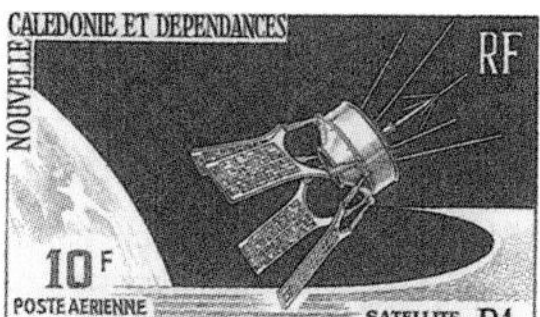

56e Satellite "D1"

1966. Air. Launching of Satellite "D1".
401 **56e** 10f. brown, blue and buff 2·00 2·50

57 Noumea, 1866 (after Lebreton)

1966. Air. Centenary of Renaming of Port-de-France as Noumea.
402 **57** 30f. slate, red and blue . . 5·00 5·00

58 Red-throated Parrot Finch **59** U.N.E.S.C.O. Allegory

1966. Birds. Multicoloured.
403 1f. Type **58** (postage) . . . . 3·00 2·50
404 1f. New Caledonian grass warbler . . . . 2·25 1·75
405 2f. New Caledonian whistler 2·75 1·75
406 3f. New Caledonian pigeon ("Notou") . . . . 4·00 2·75
407 3f. White-throated pigeon ("Collier blanc") . . . . . 3·00 2·25
408 4f. Kagu . . . . 3·00 2·25
409 5f. Horned parakeet . . . . 6·75 3·00
410 10f. Red-faced honeyeater . . 10·00 3·75
411 15f. New Caledonian friarbird . . . . 8·25 3·50
412 30f. Sacred kingfisher . . . . 11·50 6·50
413 27f. Horned parakeet (diff) (air) . . . . 6·75 4·25
414 37f. Scarlet honeyeater . . . 11·50 7·25
415 39f. Emerald dove . . . . . 14·50 5·00
416 50f. Cloven-feathered dove 19·00 19·00
417 100f. Whistling kite . . . . . 34·00 13·00
Nos. 413/14 are 26 × 45½ mm; Nos. 415/17 are 27½ × 48 mm.

1966. 20th Anniv of U.N.E.S.C.O.
418 **59** 16f. purple, ochre and green . . . . 2·75 2·50

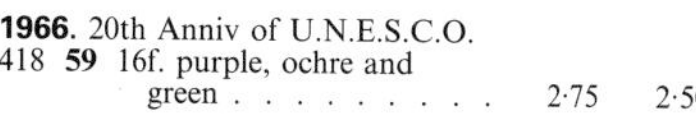

60 High Jumping

1966. South Pacific Games, Noumea.
419 **60** 17f. violet, green and lake 3·25 1·25
420 – 20f. green, purple and lake 4·75 2·75
421 – 40f. green, violet and lake 5·75 4·00
422 – 100f. purple, turq & lake 12·00 7·50
DESIGNS: 20f. Hurdling; 40f. Running; 100f. Swimming.

61 Lekine Cliffs

1967.
424 **61** 17f. grey, green and blue 2·50 1·25

62 Ocean Racing Yachts

1967. Air. 2nd Whangarei–Noumea Yacht Race.
425 **62** 25f. red, blue and green . . 7·25 5·00

63 Magenta Stadium

1967. Sport Centres. Multicoloured.
426 10f. Type **63** . . . . 2·75 2·00
427 20f. Ouen Toro swimming pool . . . . 4·00 1·60

64 New Caledonian Scenery

1967. International Tourist Year.
428 **64** 30f. multicoloured . . . . 5·75 3·50

65 19th-century Postman

1967. Stamp Day.
429 **65** 7f. red, green and turquoise 2·75 2·50

66 "Papilio montrouzieri"

1967. Butterflies and Moths.
430 **66** 7f. blue, black and green (postage) . . . . 3·00 2·50
431 – 9f. blue, brown and mauve 4·25 2·25
432 – 13f. violet, purple & brown 5·00 3·00
433 – 15f. yellow, purple and blue . . . . 8·25 4·00
434 – 19f. orange, brown and green (air) . . . . 7·25 3·25
435 – 29f. purple, red and blue 10·00 6·50
436 – 85f. brown, red and yellow 23·00 12·00
BUTTERFLIES—As T **66**: 9f. "Polyura clitarchus"; 13f. Common eggfly (male), and 15f. (female). 48 × 27 mm: 19f. Orange tiger; 29f. Silver-striped hawk moth; 85f. "Dellas elipsis".

67 Garnierite (mineral), Factory and Jules Garnier

1967. Air. Centenary of Garnierite Industry.
437 **67** 70f. multicoloured . . . . 9·75 7·50

67a Lifou Island

1967. Air.
438 **67a** 200f. multicoloured . . . 19·00 12·50

67b Skier and Snow-crystal

1967. Air. Winter Olympic Games, Grenoble.
439 **67b** 100f. brown, blue & green 18·00 12·50

68 Bouquet, Sun and W.H.O. Emblem

69 Human Rights Emblem

1968. 20th Anniv of W.H.O.
440 **68** 20f. blue, red and violet . . 3·00 2·00

1968. Human Rights Year.
441 **69** 12f. red, green and yellow 1·75 2·50

70 Ferrying Mail Van across Tontouta River

1968. Stamp Day.
442 **70** 9f. brown, blue and green 2·50 2·75

71 Geography Cone

72 Dancers

1968. Sea Shells.
443 – 1f. brn, grey & grn (postage) . . . . . . 2·25 2·00
444 – 1f. purple and violet . . . 2·00 2·00
445 – 2f. purple, red and blue . . 2·25 2·25
446 – 3f. brown and green . . . 2·25 1·90
447 – 5f. red, brown and violet 2·75 85
448 **71** 10f. brown, grey and blue 2·75 2·00
449 – 10f. yellow, brown and red 3·75 2·00
450 – 10f. black, brown & orange 3·25 2·25
451 – 15f. red, grey and green . . 6·00 3·00
452 – 21f. brown, sepia and green 6·50 2·75
453 – 22f. red, brown & blue (air) . . . . 6·25 3·25
454 – 25f. brown and red . . . . 4·00 3·50
455 – 33f. brown and blue . . . 8·00 4·50
456 – 34f. violet, brown & orange 7·75 3·50
457 – 39f. brown, grey and green 7·50 3·75
458 – 40f. black, brown and red 7·00 4·00
459 – 50f. red, purple and green 7·25 5·00
460 – 60f. brown and green . . . 16·00 8·00
461 – 70f. brown, grey and violet 17·00 8·00
462 – 100f. brown, black and blue . . . . 30·00 18·00
DESIGNS—VERT: 1f. (No. 443) Swan conch ("Strombus epidromis"); 1f. (No. 444) Scorpion conch ("Lambis scorpius"); 3f. Common spider conch; 10f. (No. 450) Variable conch ("Strombus variabilis"). 27×48 mm: 22f. Laciniate cone; 25f. Orange spider conch; 34f. Vomer conch; 50f. Chiragra spider conch. 36×22 mm: 2f. Snipe's-bill murex; 5f. Troschel's murex; 10f. (No. 449) Sieve cowrie; 15f. "Murex sp."; 21f. Mole cowrie. 48×27 mm: 33f. Eyed cowrie; 39f. Lienardi's cone; 40f. Cabrit's cone; 60f. All-red map cowrie; 70f. Scarlet cone; 100f. Adusta murex.

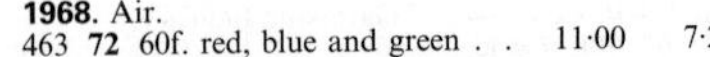

1968. Air.
463 **72** 60f. red, blue and green . . 11·00 7·25

73 Rally Car

1968. 2nd New Caledonian Motor Safari.
464 **73** 25f. blue, red and green . . 5·25 3·50

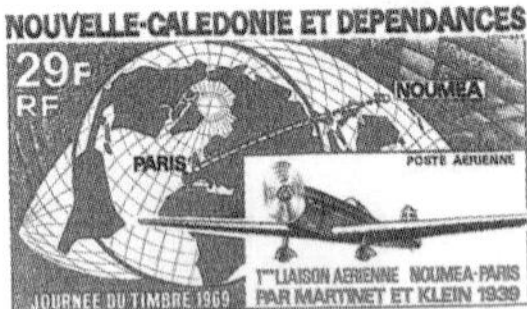

74 Caudron C-60 "Aiglon" and Route Map

1969. Air. Stamp Day. 30th Anniv of 1st Noumea–Paris Flight by Martinet and Klein.
465 **74** 29f. red, blue and violet . . 4·50 2·50

75 Concorde in Flight

1969. Air. 1st Flight of Concorde.
466 **75** 100f. green and light green 26·00 27·00

76 Cattle-dip

1969. Cattle-breeding in New Caledonia.
467 **76** 9f. brown, green and blue (postage) . . . . 2·50 2·25
468 – 25f. violet, brown and green . . . . 4·25 2·75
469 – 50f. purple, red & grn (air) 7·00 4·50
DESIGNS: 25f. Branding. LARGER 48×27 mm; 50f. Stockman with herd.

77 Judo

1969. 3rd South Pacific Games, Port Moresby, Papua New Guinea.
470 **77** 19f. purple, bl & red (post) 3·00 1·50
471 – 20f. black, red and green 4·00 2·75
472 – 30f. black and blue (air) . . 6·00 3·50
473 – 39f. brown, green and black . . . . 9·50 4·50
DESIGNS—HORIZ: 20f. Boxing; 30f. Diving (38×27 mm). VERT: 39f. Putting the shot (27×48 mm).

1969. Air. Birth Bicentenary of Napoleon Bonaparte. As T **114b** of Mauritania. Multicoloured.
474 40f. "Napoleon in Coronation Robes" (Gerard) (vert) . . . . . . 26·00 16·00

78 Douglas DC-4 over Outrigger Canoe

1969. Air. 20th Anniv of Regular Noumea–Paris Air Service.
475 **78** 50f. green, brown and blue 8·00 5·00

79 I.L.O. Building Geneva

1969. 50th Anniv of I.L.O.
476 **79** 12f. brown, violet & salmon . . . . 2·25 2·50

80 "French Wings around the World"

1970. Air. 10th Anniv of French "Around the World" Air Service.
477 **80** 200f. brown, blue and violet . . . . 26·00 10·50

81 New U.P.U. Building, Berne

1970. Inauguration of New U.P.U. Headquarters Building, Berne.
478 **81** 12f. red, grey and brown 2·75 2·25

82 Packet Steamer "Natal", 1883

1970. Stamp Day.
479 **82** 9f. black, green and blue 5·25 3·25

83 Cyclists on Map

1970. Air. 4th "Tour de Nouvelle Caledonie" Cycle Race.
480 **83** 40f. brown, blue & lt blue 6·25 4·00

84 Mt. Fuji and Japanese "Hikari" Express Train

1970. Air. "EXPO 70" World Fair, Osaka, Japan. Multicoloured.
481 20f. Type **84** . . . . 4·25 2·75
482 45f. "EXPO" emblem, map and Buddha . . . . 6·00 3·00

85 Racing Yachts

1971. Air. One Ton Cup Yacht Race Auckland, New Zealand.
483 **85** 20f. green, red and black 4·50 2·25

86 Steam Mail Train, Dumbea

1971. Stamp Day.
484 **86** 10f. black, green and red 4·00 2·75

87 Ocean Racing Yachts

1971. 3rd Whangarei–Noumea Ocean Yacht Race.
485 **87** 16f. turquoise, green and blue . . . . 5·25 3·25

88 Lieut.-Col. Broche and Theatre Map

1971. 30th Anniv of French Pacific Battalion's Participation in Second World War Mediterranean Campaign.
486 **88** 60f. multicoloured . . . . 8·75 6·00

89 Early Tape Machine

90 Weightlifting

1971. World Telecommunications Day.
487 **89** 19f. orange, purple and red 3·75 2·50

1971. 4th South Pacific Games, Papeete, French Polynesia.
488 **90** 11f. brown & red (postage) 2·75 2·75
489 – 23f. violet, red and blue . . 4·00 1·10
490 – 25f. green and red (air) . . 4·00 3·50
491 – 100f. blue, green and red 8·25 5·00
DESIGNS—VERT: 23f. Basketball. HORIZ: 48×27 mm: 25f. Pole-vaulting; 100f. Archery.

91 Port de Plaisance, Noumea

1971. Air.
492 **91** 200f. multicoloured . . . . 25·00 12·50

92 De Gaulle as President of French Republic, 1970

93 Publicity Leaflet showing De Havilland Gipsy Moth "Golden Eagle"

1971. 1st Death Anniv of General De Gaulle.
493 **92** 34f. black and purple . . . 8·50 3·75
494 – 100f. black and purple . . 17·00 10·00
DESIGN: 100f. De Gaulle in uniform, 1940.

1971. Air. 40th Anniv of 1st New Caledonia to Australia Flight.
495 **93** 90f. brown, blue and orange . . . . 13·00 7·25

94 Downhill Skiing

1972. Air. Winter Olympic Games, Sapporo, Japan.
496 **94** 50f. green, red and blue . . 4·50 4·25

95 St. Mark's Basilica, Venice

1972. Air. U.N.E.S.C.O. "Save Venice" Campaign.
497 **95** 20f. brown, green and blue 4·75 3·00

96 Commission Headquarters, Noumea

1972. Air. 25th Anniv of South Pacific Commission.
498 **96** 18f. multicoloured . . . . 3·00 2·50

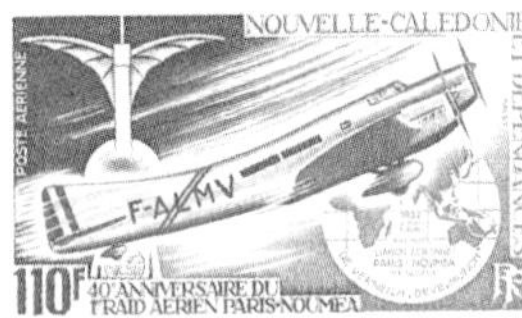

97 Couzinet 33 "Le Biarritz" and Noumea Monument

1972. Air. 40th Anniv of 1st Paris–Noumea Flight.
499 **97** 110f. black, purple & green 3·00 2·75

98 Pacific Island Dwelling

99 Goa Door-post

1972. Air. South Pacific Arts Festival, Fiji.
500 **98** 24f. brown, blue and orange . . . . 4·50 3·00

1972. Exhibits from Noumea Museum.
501 **99** 1f. red, green & grey (post) 1·75 1·75
502 – 2f. black, green & deep grn 1·60 1·75
503 – 5f. multicoloured . . . . . 2·25 2·00
504 – 12f. multicoloured . . . . 4·00 2·75
505 – 16f. multicoloured (air) . . 3·25 2·75
506 – 40f. multicoloured . . . . 5·00 3·00
DESIGNS: 2f. Carved wooden pillow; 5f. Monstrance; 12f. Tchamba mask; 16f. Ornamental arrowheads; 40f. Portico, chief's house.

100 Hurdling over "H" of "MUNICH"

1972. Air. Olympic Games, Munich.
507 **100** 72f. violet, purple and blue . . . . 11·00 6·25

101 New Head Post Office Building, Noumea

1972. Air.
508 **101** 23f. brown, blue and green . . . . 4·00 2·50

102 J.C.I. Emblem

1972. 10th Anniv of New Caledonia Junior Chamber of Commerce.
509 **102** 12f. multicoloured . . . . 2·75 2·50

103 Forest Scene

1973. Air. Landscapes of the East Coast. Multicoloured.
510 11f. Type **103** . . . . 2·75 2·25
511 18f. Beach and palms (vert) 4·25 2·75
512 21f. Waterfall and inlet (vert) 5·25 3·00
See also Nos. 534/6.

104 Moliere and Characters

1973. Air. 300th Death Anniv of Moliere (playwright).
513 **104** 50f. multicoloured . . . . 7·50 4·50

105 Tchamba Mask

1973.
514 **105** 12f. purple (postage) . . . 4·25 3·00
515 – 23f. blue (air) . . . . . . 9·25 7·00
DESIGN: 23f. Concorde in flight.

106 Liner "El Kantara" in Panama Canal

1973. 50th Anniv of Marseilles–Noumea Shipping Service via Panama Canal.
516 **106** 60f. black, brown & green 9·75 6·50

107 Globe and Allegory of Weather

1973. Air. Centenary of World Meteorological Organization.
517 **107** 80f. multicoloured . . . . 9·50 4·75

108 DC-10 in Flight

1973. Air. Inauguration of Noumea–Paris DC-10 Air Service.
518 **108** 100f. green, brown & blue 11·50 6·25

109 Common Egg Cowrie

1973. Marine Fauna from Noumea Aquarium. Multicoloured.
519 8f. Black-wedged butterflyfish (daylight) . . . . 2·75 2·25
520 14f. Black-wedged butterflyfish (nocturnal) . . 3·25 2·75
521 3f. Type **109** (air) . . . . . 2·25 2·00
522 32f. Orange-spotted surgeonfish (adult and young) . . . . 7·00 3·50
523 32f. Green-lined paper bubble ("Hydatina") . . . . . . 4·50 3·25
524 37f. Pacific partridge tun ("Dolium perdix") . . . . 6·00 3·25

111 Office Emblem

1973. 10th Anniv of Central Schools Co-operation Office.
532 **111** 20f. blue, yellow and green . . . . 2·75 2·50

112 New Caledonia Mail Coach, 1880

1973. Air. Stamp Day.
533 **112** 15f. multicoloured . . . . 3·50 2·00

1974. Air. Landscapes of the West Coast. As T **103**. Multicoloured.
534 8f. Beach and palms (vert) . . 2·50 2·25
535 22f. Trees and mountain . . 3·25 2·50
536 26f. Trees growing in sea . . 3·75 2·75

113 Centre Building

1974. Air. Opening of Scientific Studies Centre, Anse-Vata, Noumea.
537 **113** 50f. multicoloured . . . . 4·50 3·00

114 "Bird" embracing Flora

1974. Nature Conservation.
538 **114** 7f. multicoloured . . . . 1·90 1·90

115 18th-century French Sailor

1974. Air. Discovery and Reconnaissance of New Caledonia and Loyalty Islands.
539 – 20f. violet, red and blue 3·25 2·50
540 – 25f. green, brown and red 3·25 2·75
541 **115** 28f. brown, blue and green . . . . 3·25 2·75
542 – 30f. blue, brown and red 4·00 3·00
543 – 36f. red, brown and blue 6·25 3·75
DESIGNS—HORIZ: 20f. Captain Cook, H.M.S. "Endeavour" and map of Grand Terre island; 25f. La Perouse, "L'Astrolabe" and map of Grand Terre island (reconnaissance of west coast); 30f. Entrecasteaux, ship and map of Grand Terre island (reconnaissance of west coast); 36f. Dumont d'Urville, "L'Astrolabe" and map of Loyalty Islands.

116 "Telecommunications"

1974. Air. Centenary of U.P.U.
544 **116** 95f. orange, purple & grey 8·25 5·00

117 "Art"

1974. Air. "Arphila 75" International Stamp Exhibition, Paris (1975) (1st issue).
545 **117** 80f. multicoloured . . . . 6·00 4·00
See also No. 554.

118 Hotel Chateau-Royal

1974. Air. Inauguration of Hotel Chateau Royal, Noumea.
546 **118** 22f. multicoloured . . . . 3·00 3·25

118a Animal Skull, Burnt Tree and Flaming Landscape

1975. "Stop Bush Fires".
547 **118a** 20f. multicoloured . . . 1·90 2·25

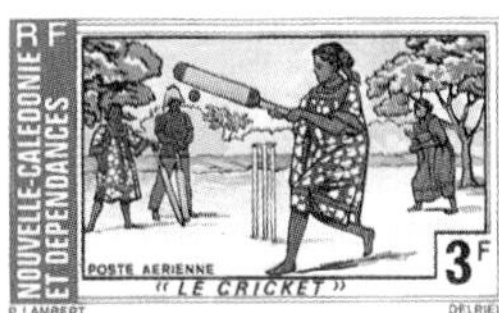

119 "Cricket"

1975. Air. Tourism. Multicoloured.
548 3f. Type **119** . . . . 2·25 2·00
549 25f. "Bougna" ceremony . . 3·25 2·25
550 31f. "Pilou" native dance . . 4·00 2·50

120 "Calanthe veratrifolia"

121 Global "Flower"

1975. New Caledonian Orchids. Multicoloured.
551 8f. Type **120** (postage) . . . 2·50 2·00
552 11f. "Lyperanthus gigas" . . 2·75 2·25
553 42f. "Eriaxis rigida" (air) . . 6·25 3·50

1975. Air. "Arphila 75" International Stamp Exhibition, Paris (2nd issue).
554 **121** 105f. purple, green & blue 9·50 5·00

122 Throwing the Discus

1975. Air. 5th South Pacific Games, Guam.
555 24f. Type **122** . . . . 3·25 2·50
556 50f. Volleyball . . . . 4·50 3·00

123 Festival Emblem
124 Birds in Flight

1975. "Melanesia 2000" Festival, Noumea.
557 **123** 12f. multicoloured . . . . 1·90 1·90

1975. 10th Anniv of Noumea Ornithological Society.
558 **124** 5f. multicoloured . . . . 2·10 1·90

125 Pres. Pompidou

127 Brown Booby

126 Concordes

1975. Pompidou Commemoration.
559 **125** 26f. grey and green . . . 3·00 2·50

1976. Air. First Commercial Flight of Concorde.
560 **126** 147f. blue and red . . . . 18·00 11·00

1976. Ocean Birds. Multicoloured.
561 1f. Type **127** . . . . 1·25 2·00
562 2f. Blue-faced booby . . . . 1·50 1·90
563 8f. Red-footed booby (vert) 2·75 2·50

128 Festival Emblem

1976. South Pacific Festival of Arts, Rotorua, New Zealand.
564 **128** 27f. multicoloured . . . . 3·00 2·50

129 Lion and Lions' Emblem

130 Early and Modern Telephones

1976. 15th Anniv of Lions Club, Noumea.
565 **129** 49f. multicoloured . . . . 5·00 3·50

1976. Air. Telephone Centenary.
566 **130** 36f. multicoloured . . . . 3·75 2·75

131 Capture of Penbosct

1976. Air. Bicent of American Revolution.
567 **131** 24f. purple and brown . . 3·00 2·75

132 Bandstand

1976. "Aspects of Old Noumea". Multicoloured.
568 25f. Type **132** . . . . 2·25 2·25
569 30f. Monumental fountain (vert) . . . . 2·50 3·25

133 Athletes

1976. Air. Olympic Games, Montreal.
570 **133** 33f. violet, red and purple 3·50 2·75

134 "Chick" with Magnifier

1976. Air. "Philately in Schools", Stamp Exhibition, Noumea.
571 **134** 42f. multicoloured . . . . 4·50 3·00

135 Dead Bird and Trees

1976. Nature Protection.
572 **135** 20f. multicoloured . . . . 2·25 2·25

136 South Pacific Heads

1976. 16th South Pacific Commission Conference.
573 **136** 20f. multicoloured . . . . 2·75 2·25

137 Old Town Hall, Noumea

1976. Air. Old and New Town Halls, Noumea. Mult.
574 75f. Type **137** . . . . 6·50 4·50
575 125f. New Town Hall . . . . 11·00 5·00

138 Water Carnival

1977. Air. Summer Festival, Noumea.
576 **138** 11f. multicoloured . . . . 1·50 1·90

139 "Pseudophyllanax imperialis" (cricket)

1977. Insects.
577 **139** 26f. emerald, green & brn 2·75 2·75
578 – 31f. brown, sepia & green 3·75 2·50
DESIGN: 31f. "Agrianome fairmairei" (long-horn beetle).

140 Miniature Roadway

1977. Air. Road Safety.
579 **140** 50f. multicoloured . . . . 4·25 2·75

141 Earth Station

1977. Earth Satellite Station, Noumea.
580 **141** 29f. multicoloured . . . . 2·75 2·25

142 "Phajus daenikeri"

1977. Orchids. Multicoloured.
581 22f. Type **142** . . . . 2·75 2·25
582 44f. "Dendrobium finetianum" . . . . 4·25 3·00

143 Mask and Palms

1977. La Perouse School Philatelic Exn.
583 **143** 35f. multicoloured . . . . 2·75 2·75

144 Trees

1977. Nature Protection.
584 **144** 20f. multicoloured . . . . 1·75 2·25

145 Palm Tree and Emblem

1977. French Junior Chambers of Commerce Congress.
585 **145** 200f. multicoloured . . . 12·00 9·00

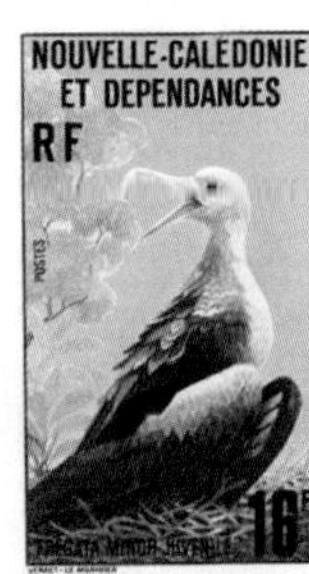

146 Young Bird

1977. Great Frigate Birds. Multicoloured.
586 16f. Type **146** (postage) . . . 1·50 2·25
587 42f. Adult male bird (horiz) (air) . . . . 4·50 3·50

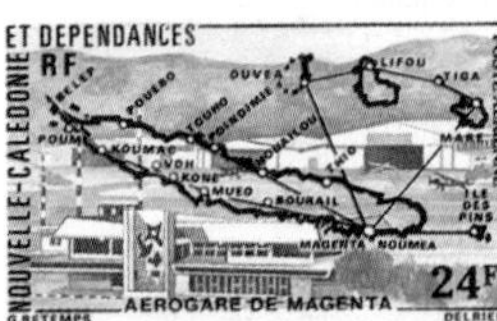

147 Magenta Airport and Map of Internal Air Network

1977. Air. Airports. Multicoloured.
588 24f. Type **147** . . . . 2·75 2·25
589 57f. La Tontout International Airport, Noumea . . . . . 4·50 3·25

1977. Air. 1st Commercial Flight of Concorde, Paris–New York. Optd **22.11.77 PARIS NEW-YORK**.
590 **126** 147f. blue and red . . . . 19·00 16·00

149 Horse and Foal

1977. 10th Anniv of S.E.C.C. (Horse-breeding Society).
591 **149** 5f. brown, green and blue 2·25 1·90

150 "Moselle Bay" (H. Didonna)

1977. Air. Views of Old Noumea (1st series).
592 **150** 41f. multicoloured . . . . 4·50 3·25
593 – 42f. purple and brown . . 4·50 3·25
DESIGN—49 × 27 mm: 42f. "Settlers Valley" (J. Kreber).

151 Black-naped Tern

1978. Ocean Birds. Multicoloured.
594 22f. Type **151** . . . . 2·00 2·25
595 40f. Sooty tern . . . . 4·00 3·25

152 "Araucaria montana" **153** "Halityle regularis"

1978. Flora. Multicoloured.
596 16f. Type **152** (postage) . . . 2·00 2·00
597 42f. "Amyema scandens" (horiz) (air) . . . . 3·75 2·50

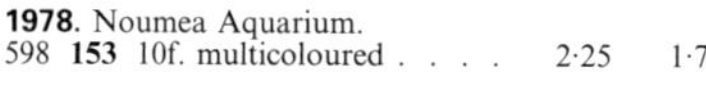

1978. Noumea Aquarium.
598 **153** 10f. multicoloured . . . . 2·25 1·75

154 Turtle

1978. Protection of the Turtle.
599 **154** 30f. multicoloured . . . . 2·50 2·50

155 New Caledonian Flying Fox

1978. Nature Protection.
600 **155** 20f. multicoloured . . . . 2·50 2·25

156 "Underwater Carnival"

1978. Air. Aubusson Tapestry.
601 **156** 105f. multicoloured . . . 6·75 4·00

157 Pastor Maurice Leenhardt

1978. Birth Centenary of Pastor Maurice Leenhardt.
602 **157** 37f. sepia, green & orange 3·00 2·75

158 Hare chasing "Stamp" Tortoise

1978. School Philately (1st series).
603 **158** 35f. multicoloured . . . . 4·00 3·00

159 Heads, Map, Magnifying Glass and Cone Shell

1978. Air. Thematic Philately at Bourail.
604 **159** 41f. multicoloured . . . . 3·25 2·75

160 Candles **161** Footballer and League Badge

1978. 3rd New Caledonian Old People's Day.
605 **160** 36f. multicoloured . . . . 2·50 2·25

1978. 50th Anniv of New Caledonian Football League.
606 **161** 26f. multicoloured . . . . 2·50 2·25

162 "Fauberg Blanchot" (after Lacouture)

1978. Air. Views of Old Noumea.
607 **162** 24f. multicoloured . . . . 2·00 2·25

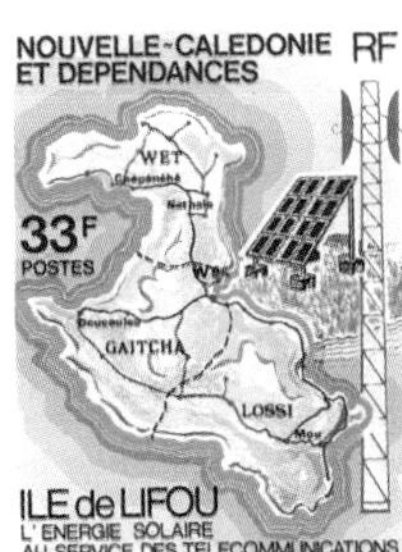

163 Map of Lifou, Solar Energy Panel and Transmitter Mast

1978. Telecommunications through Solar Energy.
608 **163** 33f. multicoloured . . . . 2·75 2·50

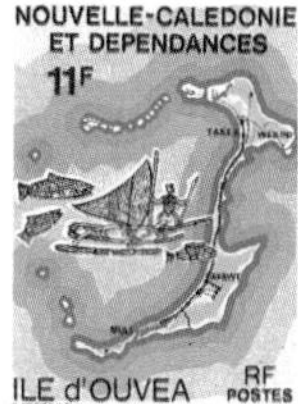

164 Petroglyph, Mere Region **165** Ouvea Island and Outrigger Canoe

1979. Archaeological Sites.
609 **164** 10f. red . . . . 1·90 1·25

1979. Islands. Multicoloured.
610 11f. Type **165** . . . . 2·25 1·75
611 31f. Mare Island and ornaments (horiz) . . . . 1·75 1·10
See also Nos. 629 and 649.

166 Satellite Orbit of Earth **167** 19th-century Barque and Modern Container Ship

1979. Air. 1st World Survey of Global Atmosphere.
612 **166** 53f. multicoloured . . . . 3·25 2·75

1979. Air. Centenary of Chamber of Commerce and Industry.
613 **167** 49f. mauve, blue & brown 3·25 2·50

168 Child's Drawing

1979. Air. International Year of the Child.
614 **168** 35f. multicoloured . . . . 3·25 2·50

169 House at Artillery Point

1979. Views of Old Noumea.
615 **169** 20f. multicoloured . . . . 2·25 1·75

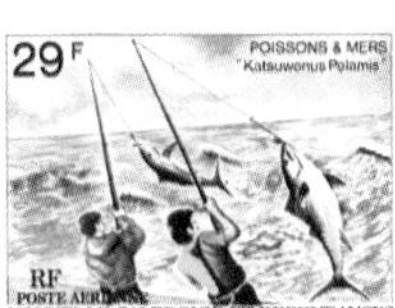

170 Skipjack Tuna

1979. Air. Sea Fishes (1st series). Multicoloured.
616 29f. Type **170** . . . . 2·75 2·25
617 30f. Black marlin . . . . . . 2·75 2·25
See also Nos. 632/3 and 647/8.

171 L. Tardy de Montravel (founder) and View of Port-de-France (Noumea)

1979. Air. 125th Anniv of Noumea.
618 **171** 75f. multicoloured . . . . 4·75 3·25

172 The Eel Queen (Kanaka legend) **173** Auguste Escoffier

1979. Air. Nature Protection.
619 **172** 42f. multicoloured . . . . 3·75 3·00

1979. Auguste Escoffier Hotel School.
620 **173** 24f. brown, green and turquoise . . . . 2·25 2·25

174 Games Emblem and Catamarans

1979. 6th South Pacific Games, Fiji.
621 **174** 16f. multicoloured . . . . 2·25 1·10

175 Children of Different Races, Map and Postmark

1979. Air. Youth Philately.
622 **175** 27f. multicoloured . . . . 2·25 2·00

176 Aerial View of Centre

1979. Air. Overseas Scientific and Technical Research Office (O.R.S.T.O.M.) Centre, Noumea.
623 **176** 25f. multicoloured . . . . 2·50 2·25

177 "Agathis ovata"

1979. Trees. Multicoloured.
624 5f. Type **177** . . . . 1·60 1·90
625 34f. "Cyathea intermedia" . . 2·50 2·25

178 Rodeo Riding

1979. Pouembout Rodeo.
626 **178** 12f. multicoloured . . . . 2·25 1·75

179 Hill, 1860 10c. Stamp and Post Office

1979. Air. Death Centenary of Sir Rowland Hill.
627 **179** 150f. black, brown & orge 7·75 4·50

180 "Bantamia merleti"

1980. Noumea Aquarium. Fluorescent Corals (1st issue).
628 **180** 23f. multicoloured . . . . 2·50 1·75
See also No. 646.

1980. Islands. As T **165**. Multicoloured.
629 23f. Map of Ile des Pins and ornaments (horiz) . . . . 1·90 1·25

181 Outrigger Canoe

1980. Air.
630 **181** 45f. blue, turq & indigo 2·75 2·25

182 Globe, Rotary Emblem, Map and Carving

1980. Air. 75th Anniv of Rotary International.
631 **182** 100f. multicoloured . . . 5·50 3·25

1980. Air. Sea Fishes (2nd series). As T **170**. Multicoloured.
632 34f. Angler holding dolphin (fish) . . . . 2·25 1·90
633 39f. Fishermen with sailfish (vert) . . . . 2·75 2·00

183 "Hibbertia virotii"

184 High Jumper, Magnifying Glass, Albums and Plimsoll

1980. Flowers. Multicoloured.
634 11f. Type **183** . . . . 1·60 85
635 12f. "Grevillea meisneri" . . 1·60 1·40

1980. School Philately.
636 **184** 30f. multicoloured . . . . 1·90 1·50

185 Scintex Super Emeraude Airplane and Map

1980. Air. Coral Sea Air Rally.
637 **185** 31f. blue, green and brown . . . . 2·00 1·90

186 Sailing Canoe

1980. Air. South Pacific Arts Festival, Port Moresby.
638 **186** 27f. multicoloured . . . . 1·90 1·75

187 Road Signs as Road-users

1980. Road Safety.
639 **187** 15f. multicoloured . . . . 1·60 1·10

188 "Parribacus caledonicus"

1980. Noumea Aquarium. Marine Animals (1st series). Multicoloured.
640 5f. Type **188** . . . . 1·00 30
641 8f. "Panulirus versicolor" . . 1·25 1·10
See also Nos. 668/9.

189 Kiwanis Emblem

1980. Air. 10th Anniv of Noumea Kiwanis Club.
642 **189** 50f. multicoloured . . . . 2·75 2·25

190 Sun, Tree and Solar Panel

1980. Nature Protection. Solar Energy.
643 **190** 23f. multicoloured . . . . 1·90 1·60

191 Old House, Poulou

1980. Air. Views of Old Noumea (4th series).
644 **191** 33f. multicoloured . . . . 1·90 1·75

192 Charles de Gaulle

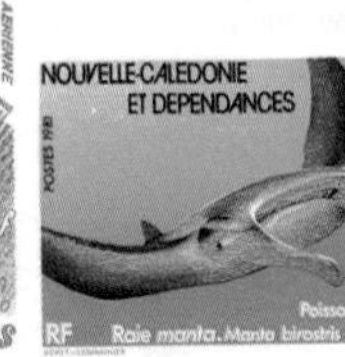

193 Manta Ray

1980. Air. 10th Death Anniv of Charles de Gaulle (French statesman).
645 **192** 120f. green, olive and blue 8·00 4·25

1981. Air. Noumea Aquarium. Fluorescent Corals (2nd series). As T **180**. Multicoloured.
646 60f. "Trachyphyllia geoffroyi" . . . . 3·00 2·00

1981. Sea Fishes (3rd series). Multicoloured.
647 23f. Type **193** . . . . 1·75 1·50
648 25f. Grey reef shark . . . . 1·75 1·50

1981. Islands. As T **165**. Multicoloured.
649 26f. Map of Belep Archipelago and diver (horiz) . . . . 1·75 1·40

194 "Xeronema moorei"

1981. Air. Flowers. Multicoloured.
650 38f. Type **194** . . . . 2·00 1·50
651 51f. "Geissois pruinosa" . . 2·00 1·75

195 Yuri Gagarin and "Vostok 1"

1981. Air. 20th Anniv of First Men in Space. Multicoloured.
652 64f. Type **195** . . . . 2·75 2·50
653 155f. Alan Shepard and "Freedom 7" . . . . . . 6·75 4·25

196 Liberation Cross, "Zealandia" (troopship) and Badge

1981. Air. 40th Anniv of Departure of Pacific Battalion for Middle East.
655 **196** 29f. multicoloured . . . . 2·75 1·75

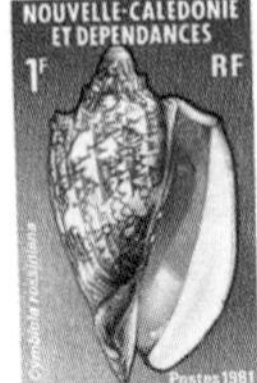

197 Rossini's Volute

198 Sail Corvette "Constantine"

1981. Shells. Multicoloured.
656 1f. Type **197** . . . . 95 1·00
657 2f. Clouded cone . . . . . . 90 1·10
658 13f. Stolid cowrie (horiz) . . 1·75 1·25

1981. Ships (1st series).
659 **198** 10f. blue, brown and red 1·50 1·25
660 – 25f. blue, brown and red 2·00 1·75
DESIGN: 25f. Paddle-gunboat "Le Phoque", 1853.
See also Nos. 680/1 and 725/6.

199 "Echinometra mathaei"

1981. Air. Water Plants. Multicoloured.
661 38f. Type **199** . . . . 1·90 1·60
662 51f. "Prionocidaris verticillata" . . . . 2·50 1·75

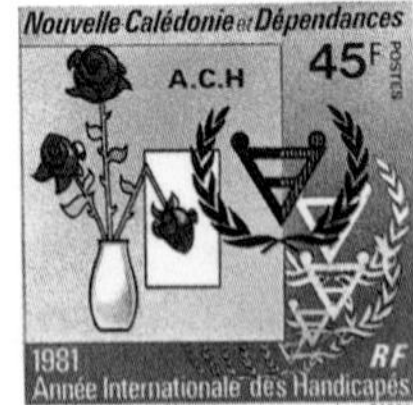

200 Broken-stemmed Rose and I.Y.D.P. Emblems

1981. International Year of Disabled Persons.
663 **200** 45f. multicoloured . . . . 2·75 1·90

201 25c. Surcharged Stamp of 1881

202 Latin Quarter

1981. Air. Stamp Day.
664 **201** 41f. multicoloured . . . . 2·25 1·75

1981. Air. Views of Old Noumea.
665 **202** 43f. multicoloured . . . . 2·25 1·75

203 Trees and Unicornfish

204 Victor Roffey and "Golden Eagle"

1981. Nature Protection.
666 **203** 28f. blue, green and brown . . . . 1·75 1·75

1981. Air. 50th Anniv of First New Caledonia–Australia Airmail Flight.
667 **204** 37f. black, violet and blue 2·00 1·60

1982. Noumea Aquarium. Marine Animals (2nd series). As T **188**. Multicoloured.
668 13f. "Calappa calappa" . . . 1·00 1·40
669 25f. "Etisus splendidus" . . . 1·50 90

205 "La Rousette"

1982. Air. New Caledonian Aircraft (1st series).
670 **205** 38f. brown, red and green 1·90 1·50
671 – 51f. brown, orange & grn 2·25 1·75
DESIGN: 51f. "Le Cagou".
See also Nos. 712/13.

206 Chalcantite, Ouegoa

1982. Rocks and Minerals (1st series). Multicoloured.
672 15f. Type **206** . . . . 1·90 1·25
673 30f. Anorthosite, Blue River 2·50 1·75
See also Nos. 688/9.

207 De Verneilh, Deve and Munch (air crew), Couzinet 33 "Le Biarritz" and Route Map

1982. Air. 50th Anniv of First Flight from Paris to Noumea.
674 **207** 250f. mauve, blue and black . . . . 9·75 5·00

208 Scout and Guide Badges and Map

1982. Air. 50th Anniv of New Caledonian Scout Movement.
675 **208** 40f. multicoloured . . . . 2·00 1·75

209 "The Rat and the Octopus" (Canaque legend)

1982. "Philexfrance 82" International Stamp Exhibition, Paris.
676 **209** 150f. blue, mauve and deep blue . . . . . . 5·25 4·00

210 Footballer, Mascot and Badge

1982. Air. World Cup Football Championship, Spain.
677 **210** 74f. multicoloured . . . . 3·00 1·75

211 Savanna Trees at Niaoulis **212** Islanders, Map and Kagu

1982. Flora. Multicoloured.
678 20f. Type **211** . . . . 1·75 1·40
679 29f. "Melaleuca quinquenervia" (horiz) . . 2·00 1·10

1982. Ships (2nd series). As T **198**.
680 44f. blue, purple and brown 1·90 1·75
681 59f. blue, light brown and brown . . . . 2·50 1·90
DESIGNS: 44f. Naval transport barque "Le Cher"; 59f. Sloop "Kersaint", 1902.

1982. Air. Overseas Week.
682 **212** 100f. brown, green & blue 2·50 2·25

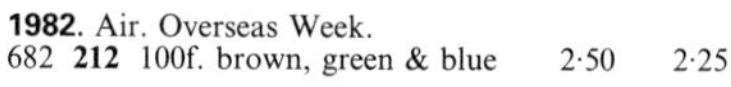

213 Ateou Tribal House **214** Grey's Fruit Dove

1982. Traditional Houses.
683 **213** 52f. multicoloured . . . . 2·75 2·00

1982. Birds. Multicoloured.
684 32f. Type **214** . . . . 1·75 1·75
685 35f. Rainbow lory . . . . . 1·75 1·75

215 Canoe

1982. Central Education Co-operation Office.
686 **215** 48f. multicoloured . . . . 2·50 1·75

216 Bernheim and Library

1982. Bernheim Library, Noumea.
687 **216** 36f. brown, purple & blk 1·90 1·50

1983. Air. Rocks and Minerals (2nd series). As T **206**. Multicoloured.
688 44f. Paya gypsum (vert) . . . 2·25 1·90
689 59f. Kone silica (vert) . . . . 2·75 2·00

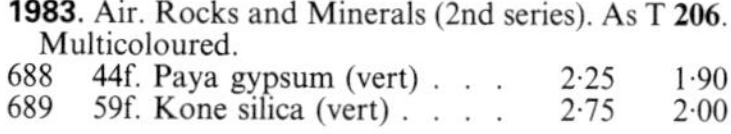

217 "Dendrobium oppositifolium"

1983. Orchids. Multicoloured.
690 10f. Type **217** . . . . 1·10 60
691 15f. "Dendrobium munificum" . . . . 1·25 1·00
692 29f. "Dendrobium fractiflexum" . . . . . . 1·75 90

218 W.C.Y. Emblem, Map of New Caledonia and Globe

1983. Air. World Communications Year.
693 **218** 170f. multicoloured . . . 6·25 3·75

219 "Crinum asiaticum"

1983. Flowers. Multicoloured.
694 1f. Type **219** 45 55
695 2f. "Xanthostemon aurantiacum" . . . . . . 45 1·00
696 4f. "Metrosideros demonstrans" (vert) . . . 45 55

220 Wall Telephone and Noumea Post Office, 1890

1983. 25th Anniv of Post and Telecommunications Office. Multicoloured.
697 30f. Type **220** . . . . 1·75 75
698 40f. Telephone and Noumea Post Office, 1936 . . . . . 1·90 1·25
699 50f. Push-button telephone and Noumea Post Office, 1972 . . . . 2·50 1·40

221 "Laticaudata laticaudata" **224** Volleyball

223 Bangkok Temples

1983. Noumea Aquarium. Sea Snakes. Multicoloured.
701 31f. Type **221** . . . . 1·75 1·25
702 33f. "Laticauda colubrina" 2·00 1·40

1983. Air. New Caledonian Aircraft (2nd series). As T **205**. Each red, mauve & brown.
712 46f. Mignet HM14 "Pou du Ciel" . . . . 2·00 1·75
713 61f. Caudron C-600 "Aiglon" 2·50 1·90

1983. Air. "Bangkok 1983" International Stamp Exhibition.
714 **223** 47f. multicoloured . . . . 2·00 1·90

1983. 7th South Pacific Games, Western Samoa.
715 **224** 16f. purple, blue and red 1·75 1·40

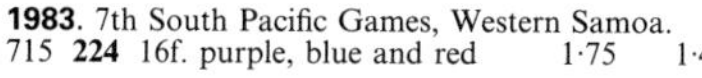

225 Oueholle

1983. Air.
716 **225** 76f. multicoloured . . . . 2·75 2·25

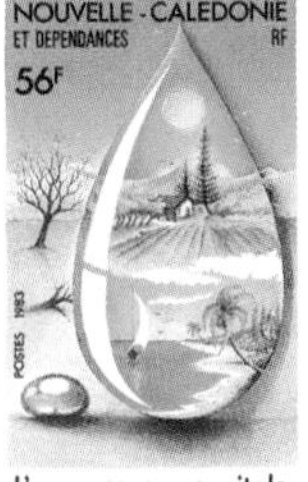

226 Desert and Water Drop showing Fertile Land **227** Barn Owl

1983. Water Resources.
717 **226** 56f. multicoloured . . . . 2·75 1·50

1983. Birds of Prey. Multicoloured.
718 34f. Type **227** . . . . 1·90 1·90
719 37f. Osprey . . . . 3·25 2·25

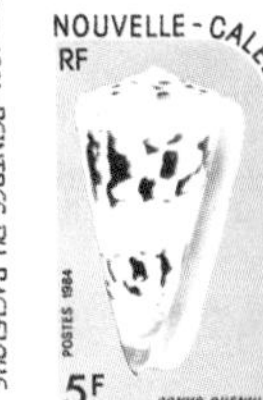

228 "Young Man on Beach" (R. Mascart) **229** "Conus chenui"

1983. Air. Paintings. Multicoloured.
720 100f. Type **228** . . . . 4·00 3·00
721 350f. "Man with Guitar" (P. Nielly) . . . . 13·00 6·25

1984. Sea Shells (1st series). Multicoloured.
722 5f. Type **229** . . . . 1·10 1·00
723 15f. Molucca cone . . . . . 1·25 1·00
724 20f. "Conus optimus" . . . 1·75 1·40
See also Nos. 761/2 and 810/11.

230 "St. Joseph" (freighter)

1984. Ships (3rd series). Each black, red and blue.
725 18f. Type **230** . . . . 1·60 1·40
726 31f. "Saint Antoine" (freighter) . . . . 1·75 1·40

231 Yellow-tailed Anemonefish

1984. Air. Noumea Aquarium. Fishes. Multicoloured.
727 46f. Type **231** . . . . 2·25 1·75
728 61f. Bicoloured angelfish . . 2·75 2·25

232 Arms of Noumea **233** "Araucaria columnaris"

1984.
729 **232** 35f. multicoloured . . . . 1·75 1·40

1984. Air. Trees. Multicoloured.
730 51f. Type **233** . . . . 2·50 1·75
731 67f. "Pritchardiopsis jeanneneyi" . . . . 2·50 1·90

234 Tourist Centres

1984. Nature Protection.
732 **234** 65f. multicoloured . . . . 2·75 1·90

235 Swimming

1984. Air. Olympic Games, Los Angeles. Multicoloured.
733 50f. Type **235** . . . . 2·50 2·00
734 83f. Windsurfing . . . . . . 3·00 2·50
735 200f. Marathon . . . . . . 7·75 5·50

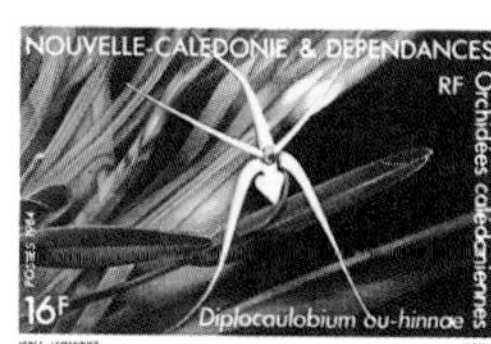

236 "Diplocaulobium ou-hinnae"

1984. Orchids. Multicoloured.
736 16f. Type **236** . . . . 1·60 1·40
737 38f. "Acianthus atepalus" . . 2·00 1·90

237 Royal Exhibition Hall, Melbourne

1984. Air. "Ausipex 84" International Stamp Exhibition, Melbourne.
738 **237** 150f. green, brown & mve 6·25 4·50

238 School and Arrow Sign-post **239** Anchor, Rope and Stars

1984. Centenary of Public Education.
740 **238** 59f. multicoloured . . . . 2·25 1·75

1984. Air. Armed Forces Day.
741 **239** 51f. multicoloured . . . . 2·00 1·75

240 "Women looking for Crabs" (Mme. Bonnet de Larbogne)

1984. Air. Art. Multicoloured.
742 120f. Type **240** . . . . 4·50 3·00
743 300f. "Cook discovering New Caledonia" (tapestry by Pilioko) . . . . 10·50 7·25

241 Kagu

1985.
744 **241** 1f. blue 45 45
745 2f. green 45 45
746 3f. orange 50 45
747 4f. green 50 45
748 5f. mauve 45 50
749 35f. red . . . . 1·00 70
750 38f. red 95 80
751 40f. red . . . . 1·25 60
For similar design but with "& DEPENDANCES" omitted, see Nos. 837/43.

1985. Sea Shells (2nd series). As T **229**. Multicoloured.
761 55f. Bubble cone . . . . . . 2·00 1·90
762 72f. Lambert's cone . . . . 2·75 2·25

243 Weather Station transmitting Forecast to Boeing 737 and Trawler

1985. World Meteorology Day.
763 **243** 17f. multicoloured . . . . 1·25 1·25

244 Map and Hands holding Red Cross

1985. International Medicines Campaign.
764 **244** 41f. multicoloured . . . . 2·00 1·40

245 Electronic Telephone Exchange

1985. Inaug of Electronic Telephone Equipment.
765 **245** 70f. multicoloured . . . . 2·75 1·90

246 Marguerite la Foa Suspension Bridge

1985. Protection of Heritage.
766 **246** 44f. brown, red and blue 2·00 1·60

247 Kagu with Magnifying Glass and Stamp

1985. "Le Cagou" Stamp Club.
767 **247** 220f. multicoloured . . . 6·00 4·50

248 Festival Emblem

1985. 4th Pacific Arts Festival, Papeete. Mult.
769 55f. Type **248** . . . . 2·50 90
770 75f. Girl blowing trumpet triton . . . . 2·75 2·25

249 Flowers, Barbed Wire and Starving Child

1985. International Youth Year.
771 **249** 59f. multicoloured . . . . 2·25 1·60

250 "Amedee Lighthouse" (M. Hosken)
251 Tree and Seedling

1985. Electrification of Amedee Lighthouse.
772 **250** 89f. multicoloured . . . . 3·25 2·25

1985. "Planting for the Future".
773 **251** 100f. multicoloured . . . 3·50 2·25

252 De Havilland Dragon Rapide and Route Map

1985. Air. 30th Anniv of First Regular Internal Air Service.
774 **252** 80f. multicoloured . . . . 2·75 2·25

253 Hands and U.N. Emblem

1985. 40th Anniv of U.N.O.
775 **253** 250f. multicoloured . . . 8·00 4·50

254 School, Map and "Nautilus"

1985. Air. Jules Garnier High School.
776 **254** 400f. multicoloured . . . 13·00 7·25

255 Purple Swamphen

1985. Birds. Multicoloured.
777 50f. Type **255** . . . . . . 1·50 1·75
778 60f. Island thrush . . . . . 1·75 2·00

256 Aircraft Tail Fins and Eiffel Tower

1986. Air. 30th Anniv of Scheduled Paris–Noumea Flights.
779 **256** 72f. multicoloured . . . . 2·75 2·00

257 Merlet Scorpionfish

1986. Noumea Aquarium. Multicoloured.
780 10f. Emperor angelfish . . . 75 1·10
781 17f. Type **257** . . . . 90 1·25

258 Kanumera Bay, Isle of Pines

1986. Landscapes (1st series). Multicoloured.
782 50f. Type **258** . . . . 2·00 1·60
783 55f. Inland village . . . . . 2·25 1·60
See also Nos. 795/6 and 864/5.

259 "Bavayia sauvagii"

1986. Geckos. Multicoloured.
784 20f. Type **259** . . . . 1·50 1·25
785 45f. "Rhacodactylus leachianus" . . . .

260 Players and Azteca Stadium

1986. World Cup Football Championship, Mexico.
786 **260** 60f. multicoloured . . . . 1·90 2·00

261 Vivarium, Nou Island

1986. Air. Protection of Heritage.
787 **261** 230f. deep brown, blue and brown . . . . . . 7·25 5·00

262 Pharmaceutical Equipment

1986. 120th Anniv of First Pharmacy.
788 **262** 80f. multicoloured . . . . 2·75 2·25

263 "Coelogynae licastioides"

1986. Orchids. Multicoloured.
789 44f. Type **263** . . . . 2·00 1·60
790 58f. "Calanthe langei" . . . 2·50 1·90

264 Black-backed Magpie

1986. "Stampex 86" National Stamp Exhibition, Adelaide.
791 **264** 110f. multicoloured . . . 3·25 3·75

265 Aerospatiale/Aeritalia ATR 42 over New Caledonia

1986. Air. Inaugural Flight of ATR 42.
792 **265** 18f. multicoloured . . . . 1·25 1·25

266 Emblem and 1860 Stamp
267 Arms of Mont Dore

1986. Air. "Stockholmia 86" International Stamp Exhibition.
793 **266** 108f. black, red and lilac 3·50 3·00

1986.
794 **267** 94f. multicoloured . . . . 3·25 2·25

1986. Landscapes (2nd series). As T **258**. Multicoloured.
795 40f. West coast (vert) . . . . 1·75 1·40
796 76f. South . . . . 2·75 2·00

268 Wild Flowers
269 Club Banner

1986. Association for Nature Protection.
797 **268** 73f. multicoloured . . . . 2·75 2·00

1986. 25th Anniv of Noumea Lions Club.
798 **269** 350f. multicoloured . . . 10·00 8·25

270 "Moret Bridge" (Alfred Sisley)

1986. Paintings. Multicoloured.
799 74f. Type **270** . . . . 2·75 2·00
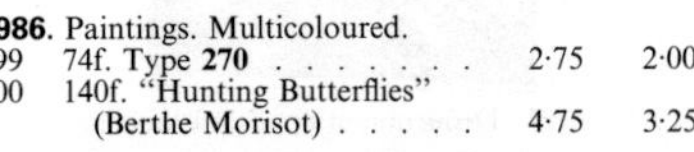
800 140f. "Hunting Butterflies" (Berthe Morisot) . . . . . 4·75 3·25

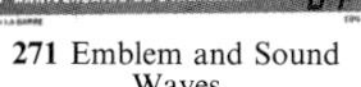

271 Emblem and Sound Waves

272 "Challenge France"

1987. Air. 25th Anniv of New Caledonia Amateur Radio Association.
801 **271** 64f. multicoloured . . . . 2·00 1·90

1987. America's Cup Yacht Race. Multicoloured.
802 30f. Type **272** . . . . 2·00 1·60
803 70f. "French Kiss" . . . . . 2·75 2·25

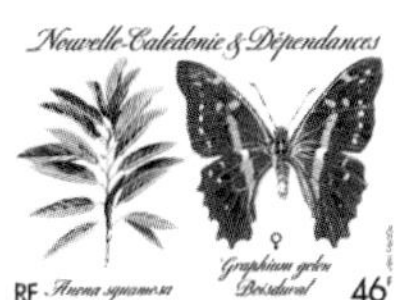

273 "Anona squamosa" and "Graphium gelon"

1987. Plants and Butterflies. Multicoloured.
804 46f. Type **273** . . . . 2·25 1·75
805 54f. "Abizzia granulosa" and "Polyura gamma" . . . . 2·50 1·90

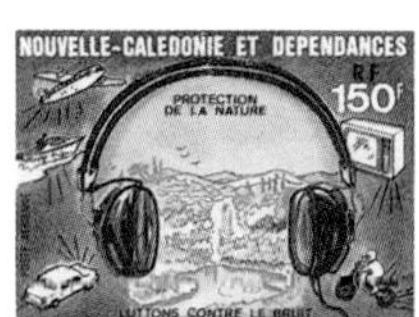

274 Peaceful Landscape, Earphones and Noisy Equipment

1987. Air. Nature Protection. Campaign against Noise.
806 **274** 150f. multicoloured . . . 5·25 3·00

275 Isle of Pines Canoe

1987. Canoes. Each brown, green and blue.
807 72f. Type **275** . . . . 2·50 2·00
808 90f. Ouvea canoe . . . . . 3·00 2·25

276 Town Hall

1987. New Town Hall, Mont Dore.
809 **276** 92f. multicoloured . . . . 3·25 2·25

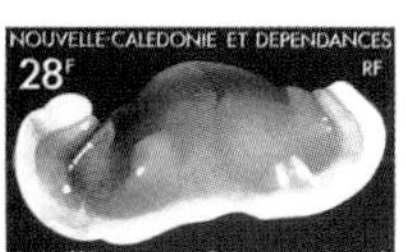

277 Money Cowrie

1987. Sea Shells (3rd series). Multicoloured.
810 28f. Type **277** . . . . 1·50 1·40
811 36f. Martin's cone . . . . . 1·90 1·60

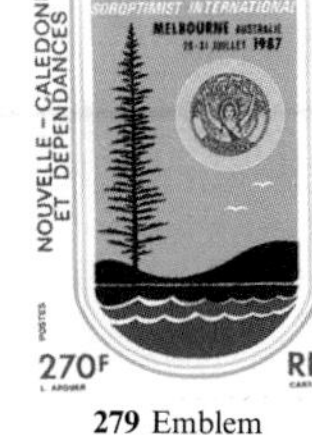

278 Games Emblem

279 Emblem

1987. 8th South Pacific Games. Noumea (1st issue).
812 **278** 40f. multicoloured . . . . 1·75 1·60
See also Nos. 819/21.

1987. 13th Soroptimists International Convention, Melbourne.
813 **279** 270f. multicoloured . . . 8·75 6·00

280 New Caledonia White-Eye

1987. Birds. Multicoloured.
814 18f. Type **280** . . . . 1·10 1·25
815 21f. Peregrine falcon (vert) 1·10 1·25

281 Flags on Globe

1987. 40th Anniv of South Pacific Commission.
816 **281** 200f. multicoloured . . . 6·75 4·00

282 Globe and Magnifying Glass on Map of New Caledonia

1987. Schools Philately.
817 **282** 15f. multicoloured . . . . 1·25 1·10

283 Cricketers

1987. Air. French Cricket Federation.
818 **283** 94f. multicoloured . . . . 3·25 2·50

284 Golf

1987. 8th South Pacific Games, Noumea (2nd issue). Multicoloured.
819 20f. Type **284** . . . . 1·25 1·10
820 30f. Rugby football . . . . . 1·60 1·25
821 100f. Long jumping . . . . 3·25 2·25

285 Arms of Dumbea

287 University

286 Route Map, "L'Astrolabe", "La Boussole" and La Perouse

1988. Air.
822 **285** 76f. multicoloured . . . . 2·75 2·00

1988. Bicentenary of Disappearance of La Perouse's Expedition.
823 **286** 36f. blue, brown and red 1·75 1·40

1988. French University of South Pacific, Noumea and Papeete.
824 **287** 400f. multicoloured . . . 12·50 8·25

288 Semicircle Angelfish

289 Mwaringou House, Canala

1988. Noumea Aquarium. Fishes. Multicoloured.
825 30f. Type **288** . . . . 1·60 1·40
826 46f. Sapphire sergeant major 2·00 1·60

1988. Traditional Huts. Each brown, green and blue.
827 19f. Type **289** . . . . 1·10 1·10
828 21f. Nathalo house, Lifou (horiz) . . . . 1·10 1·10

290 Anniversary Emblem

1988. 125th Anniv of International Red Cross.
829 **290** 300f. blue, green and red 10·50 6·00

291 "Ochrosia elliptica"

1988. Medicinal Plants. Multicoloured.
830 28f. Type **291** (postage) . . . 1·50 1·40
831 64f. "Rauvolfia sevenetii" (air) . . . . 2·50 1·90

292 "Gymnocrinus richeri"

1988.
832 **292** 51f. multicoloured . . . . 2·25 1·75

293 Furnished Room and Building Exterior

1988. Bourail Museum and Historical Association.
833 **293** 120f. multicoloured . . . 3·50 3·00

294 La Perouse sighting Phillip's Fleet in Botany Bay

1988. "Sydpex 88" Stamp Exhibition, Sydney. Multicoloured.
834 42f. Type **294** . . . . 2·00 1·75
835 42f. Phillip sighting "La Boussole" and "L'Astrolabe" . . . . . . 2·00 1·75

295 Kagu

297 Laboratory Assistant, Noumea Institute and Pasteur

296 Table Tennis

1988.
837 **295** 1f. blue 75 10
838 2f. green 80 30
839 3f. orange 75 30
840 4f. green 75 10
841 5f. mauve 75 30
842 28f. orange . . . . 1·10 55
843 40f. red . . . . 1·40 40

1988. Olympic Games, Seoul.
846 **296** 150f. multicoloured . . . 4·75 3·00

1988. Centenary of Pasteur Institute, Paris.
847 **297** 100f. red, black and blue 3·25 2·50

298 Georges Baudoux

1988. Writers.
848 **298** 72f. brown, green and purple (postage) . . . . 2·75 1·90
849 – 73f. brown, bl & blk (air) 2·75 2·00
DESIGN: 73f. Jean Mariotti.

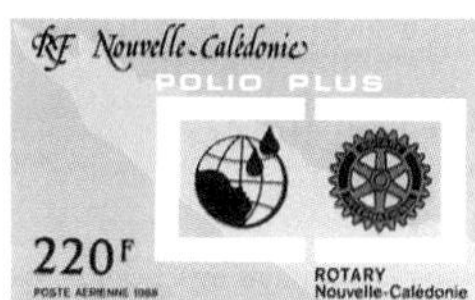

299 Map and Emblems

1988. Air. Rotary International Anti-Polio Campaign.
850 **299** 220f. multicoloured . . . 6·25 5·00

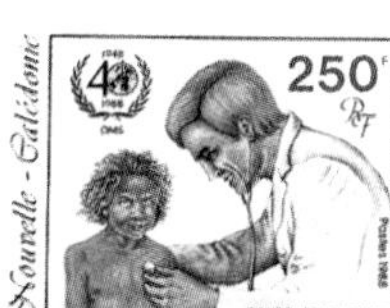

300 Doctor examining Child

1988. 40th Anniv of W.H.O.
851 **300** 250f. multicoloured . . . 8·00 4·50

301 "Terre des Hommes" (L. Bunckley)

1988. Paintings. Multicoloured.
852 54f. Type **301** . . . . 2·50 1·90
853 92f. "Latin Quarter" (Marik) 3·50 2·50

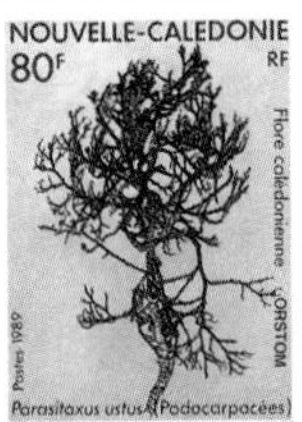

302 Arms of Koumac 303 "Parasitaxus ustus"

1989.
854 **302** 200f. multicoloured . . . 5·75 4·00

1989. Flowers. Multicoloured.
855 80f. Type **303** . . . . 2·50 2·00
856 90f. "Tristaniopsis guillainii" (horiz) . . . . 2·75 2·25

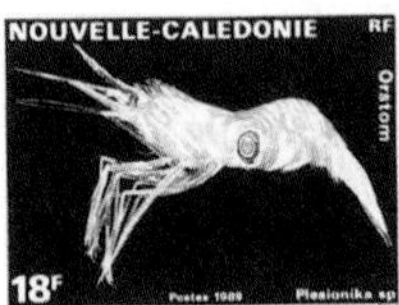

304 "Plesionika sp."

1989. Marine Life. Multicoloured.
857 18f. Type **304** . . . . 1·40 1·10
858 66f. Sail-backed scorpionfish 2·25 1·90
859 110f. Cristiate latiaxis . . . . 3·50 2·75

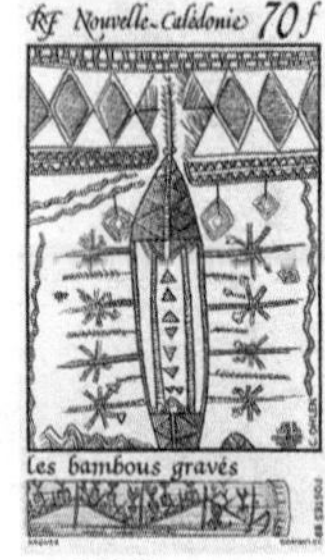

305 "Liberty" 306 Canoe and Diamond Decoration

1989. Bicentenary of French Revolution and "Philexfrance 89" International Stamp Exhibition, Paris. Multicoloured.
860 40f. Type **305** (postage) . . . 1·75 1·40
861 58f. "Equality" (air) . . . . 2·25 1·75
862 76f. "Fraternity" . . . . . . 2·75 2·00

1989. Landscapes (3rd series). As T **258**. Mult.
864 180f. Ouaieme ferry (post) . . 5·75 3·25
865 64f. "The Broody Hen" (rocky islet), Hienghene (air) . . . . 2·50 1·75

1989. Bamboo Decorations by C. Ohlen. Each black, bistre and orange.
866 70f. Type **306** (postage) . . . 2·75 1·90
867 44f. Animal design (air) . . . 1·75 1·60

307 "Hobie Cat 14" Yachts

1989. 10th World "Hobie Cat" Class Catamaran Championship, Noumea.
868 **307** 350f. multicoloured . . . 10·50 6·50

308 Book Title Pages and Society Members

1989. 20th Anniv of Historical Studies Society.
869 **308** 74f. black and brown . . 2·75 2·00

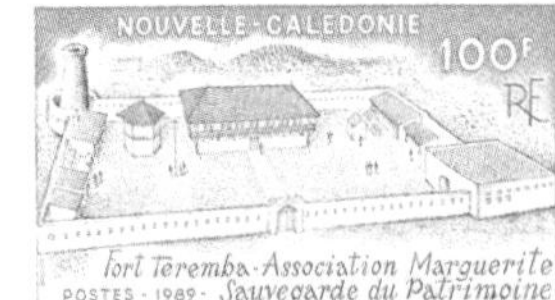

309 Fort Teremba

1989. Protection of Heritage.
870 **309** 100f. green, brown & blue 3·25 2·25

310 "Rochefort's Escape" (Edouard Manet)

1989. Paintings. Multicoloured.
871 130f. Type **310** . . . . 4·50 3·00
872 270f. "Self-portrait" (Gustave Courbet) . . . . 8·25 5·50

311 Fr. Patrick O'Reilly

1990. Writers.
873 **311** 170f. black and mauve . . 5·25 3·25

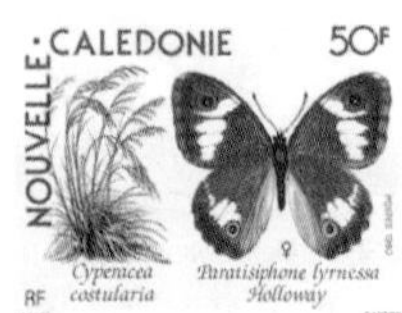

312 Grass and Female Butterfly

1990. "Cyperacea costularia" (grass) and "Paratisiphone lyrnessa" (butterfly). Multicoloured.
874 50f. Type **312** (postage) . . . 1·90 1·60
875 18f. Grass and female butterfly (different) (air) . . 1·10 1·10
876 94f. Grass and male butterfly 3·00 2·25

313 "Maize" Stem with Face 314 Exhibit

1990. Kanaka Money.
877 **313** 85f. olive, orange & green 3·00 1·90
878 – 140f. orange, black & grn 4·50 2·75
DESIGN: 140f. "Rope" stem with decorative end.

1990. Jade and Mother-of-pearl Exhibition.
879 **314** 230f. multicoloured . . . 7·25 4·50

315 Ocellate Nudibranch

1990. Noumea Aquarium. Sea Slugs. Multicoloured.
880 10f. Type **315** . . . . 75 1·00
881 42f. "Chromodoris kuniei" (vert) . . . . 1·60 1·40

316 Head of "David" (Michelangelo) and Footballers

1990. World Cup Football Championship, Italy.
882 **316** 240f. multicoloured . . . 7·00 4·25

317 De Gaulle 318 Neounda Site

1990. Air. 50th Anniv of De Gaulle's Call to Resist.
883 **317** 160f. multicoloured . . . 4·75 3·50

1990. Petroglyphs.
884 **318** 40f. brown, green and red (postage) . . . . 1·50 1·40
885 – 58f. black, brown and blue (air) . . . . 2·00 1·75
DESIGN—HORIZ: 58f. Kassducou site.

319 Map and Pacific International Meeting Centre

1990.
886 **319** 320f. multicoloured . . . 8·00 4·25

320 New Zealand Cemetery, Bourail 321 Kagu

1990. Air. "New Zealand 1990" International Stamp Exhibition, Auckland. Multicoloured.
887 80f. Type **320** . . . . 2·75 2·25
888 80f. Brigadier William Walter Dove . . . . 2·75 2·25

1990.
890 **321** 1f. blue 45 45
891 2f. green 45 45
892 3f. yellow 45 45
893 4f. green 45 45
894 5f. violet 45 45
895 9f. grey 50 50
896 12f. red 50 50
897 40f. mauve 75 75
898 50f. red 80 80
899 55f. red 85 85

The 5 and 55f. exist both perforated with ordinary gum and imperforate with self-adhesive gum.
For design with no value expressed see No. 994.

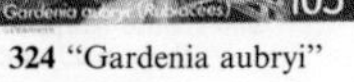

322 "Munidopsis sp" 324 "Gardenia aubryi"

323 Emblem

1990. Air. Deep Sea Animals. Multicoloured.
900 30f. Type **322** . . . . 1·10 1·25
901 60f. "Lyreidius tridentatus" 1·75 1·60

1990. Air. 30th South Pacific Conference, Noumea.
902 **323** 85f. multicoloured . . . . 2·25 2·00

1990. Flowers. Multicoloured.
903 105f. Type **324** . . . . 3·00 2·25
904 130f. "Hibbertia baudouinii" 3·50 2·75

325 De Gaulle

1990. Air. Birth Centenary of Charles de Gaulle (French statesman).
905 **325** 410f. blue . . . . 12·00 5·00

326 "Mont Dore, Mountain of Jade" (C. Degroiselle)

1990. Air. Pacific Painters. Multicoloured.
906 365f. Type **326** (postage) . . 10·00 6·00
907 110f. "The Celieres House" (M. Petron) (air) . . . . . 3·25 2·75

327 Fayawa-Ouvea Bay

1991. Air. Regional Landscapes. Multicoloured.
908 36f. Type **327** . . . . 1·60 1·40
909 90f. Coastline of Mare . . . 2·75 2·00

328 Louise Michel and Classroom

1991. Writers.
910 **328** 125f. mauve and blue . . 3·75 2·50
911 – 125f. blue and brown . . 3·75 2·50
DESIGN: No. 911, Charles B. Nething and photographer.

329 Houailou Hut 330 Northern Province

1991. Melanesian Huts. Multicoloured.
912 12f. Type **329** . . . . 1·10 1·00
913 35f. Hienghene hut . . . . . 1·50 1·25

1991. Provinces. Multicoloured.
914 45f. Type **330** . . . . 1·75 1·60
915 45f. Islands Province . . . . 1·75 1·60
916 45f. Southern Province . . . 1·75 1·60

331 "Dendrobium biflorum"

1991. Orchids. Multicoloured.
917 55f. Type **331** . . . . 2·00 1·60
918 70f. "Dendrobium closterium" . . . . 2·25 1·75

332 Japanese Pineconefish

1991. Fishes. Multicoloured.
919 60f. Type **332** . . . . 2·25 1·60
920 100f. Japanese bigeye . . . . 3·00 2·25

333 Research Equipment and Sites

1991. French Scientific Research Institute for Development and Co-operation.
921 **333** 170f. multicoloured . . . 5·00 2·75

334 Emblem

336 Emblems

335 Map and Dragon

1991. 9th South Pacific Games, Papua New Guinea.
922 **334** 170f. multicoloured . . . 5·00 2·75

1991. Centenary of Vietnamese Settlement in New Caledonia.
923 **335** 300f. multicoloured . . . 8·25 5·00

1991. 30th Anniv of Lions International in New Caledonia.
924 **336** 192f. multicoloured . . . 5·50 3·00

337 Map, "Camden" (missionary brig), Capt. Robert Clark Morgan and Trees

1991. 150th Anniv of Discovery of Sandalwood.
925 **337** 200f. blue, turquoise & grn . . . . 5·50 3·25

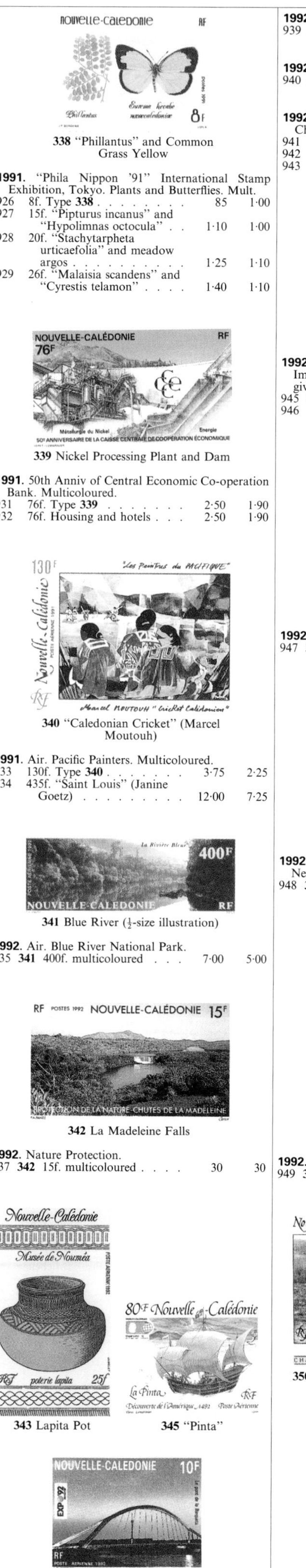

338 "Phillantus" and Common Grass Yellow

1991. "Phila Nippon '91" International Stamp Exhibition, Tokyo. Plants and Butterflies. Mult.
926 8f. Type **338** . . . . 85 1·00
927 15f. "Pipturus incanus" and "Hypolimnas octocula" . . 1·10 1·00
928 20f. "Stachytarpheta urticaefolia" and meadow argos . . . . 1·25 1·10
929 26f. "Malaisia scandens" and "Cyrestis telamon" . . . . 1·40 1·10

339 Nickel Processing Plant and Dam

1991. 50th Anniv of Central Economic Co-operation Bank. Multicoloured.
931 76f. Type **339** . . . . 2·50 1·90
932 76f. Housing and hotels . . . 2·50 1·90

340 "Caledonian Cricket" (Marcel Moutouh)

1991. Air. Pacific Painters. Multicoloured.
933 130f. Type **340** . . . . 3·75 2·25
934 435f. "Saint Louis" (Janine Goetz) . . . . 12·00 7·25

341 Blue River (½-size illustration)

1992. Air. Blue River National Park.
935 **341** 400f. multicoloured . . . 7·00 5·00

342 La Madeleine Falls

1992. Nature Protection.
937 **342** 15f. multicoloured 30 30

343 Lapita Pot

345 "Pinta"

344 Barqueta Bridge

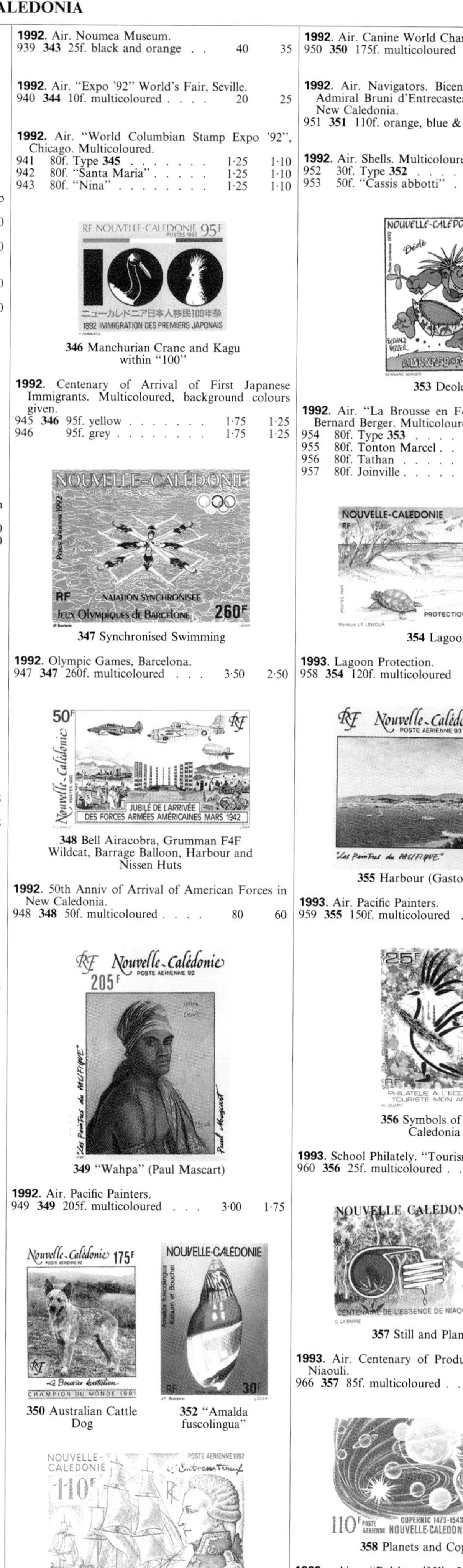

1992. Air. Noumea Museum.
939 **343** 25f. black and orange . . 40 35

1992. Air. "Expo '92" World's Fair, Seville.
940 **344** 10f. multicoloured 20 25

1992. Air. "World Columbian Stamp Expo '92", Chicago. Multicoloured.
941 80f. Type **345** . . . . 1·25 1·10
942 80f. "Santa Maria" . . . . . 1·25 1·10
943 80f. "Nina" . . . . 1·25 1·10

346 Manchurian Crane and Kagu within "100"

1992. Centenary of Arrival of First Japanese Immigrants. Multicoloured, background colours given.
945 **346** 95f. yellow . . . . 1·75 1·25
946 95f. grey . . . . 1·75 1·25

347 Synchronised Swimming

1992. Olympic Games, Barcelona.
947 **347** 260f. multicoloured . . . 3·50 2·50

348 Bell Airacobra, Grumman F4F Wildcat, Barrage Balloon, Harbour and Nissen Huts

1992. 50th Anniv of Arrival of American Forces in New Caledonia.
948 **348** 50f. multicoloured 80 60

349 "Wahpa" (Paul Mascart)

1992. Air. Pacific Painters.
949 **349** 205f. multicoloured . . . 3·00 1·75

350 Australian Cattle Dog

352 "Amalda fuscolingua"

351 Entrecasteaux and Fleet

1992. Air. Canine World Championships.
950 **350** 175f. multicoloured . . . 2·50 1·75

1992. Air. Navigators. Bicentenary of Landing of Admiral Bruni d'Entrecasteaux on West Coast of New Caledonia.
951 **351** 110f. orange, blue & green 1·75 1·10

1992. Air. Shells. Multicoloured.
952 30f. Type **352** 60 45
953 50f. "Cassis abbotti" 85 65

353 Deole

1992. Air. "La Brousse en Folie" (comic strip) by Bernard Berger. Multicoloured.
954 80f. Type **353** . . . . 1·25 85
955 80f. Tonton Marcel . . . . . 1·25 85
956 80f. Tathan . . . . 1·25 85
957 80f. Joinville . . . . 1·25 85

354 Lagoon

1993. Lagoon Protection.
958 **354** 120f. multicoloured . . . 2·40 1·60

355 Harbour (Gaston Roullet)

1993. Air. Pacific Painters.
959 **355** 150f. multicoloured . . . 2·25 1·50

356 Symbols of New Caledonia

1993. School Philately. "Tourism my Friend".
960 **356** 25f. multicoloured 45 35

357 Still and Plantation

1993. Air. Centenary of Production of Essence of Niaouli.
966 **357** 85f. multicoloured . . . . 1·25 90

358 Planets and Copernicus

1993. Air. "Polska '93" International Stamp Exhibition, Poznan. 450th Death Anniv of Nicolas Copernicus (astronomer).
967 **358** 110f. blue, turquoise & grey . . . . 1·60 1·00

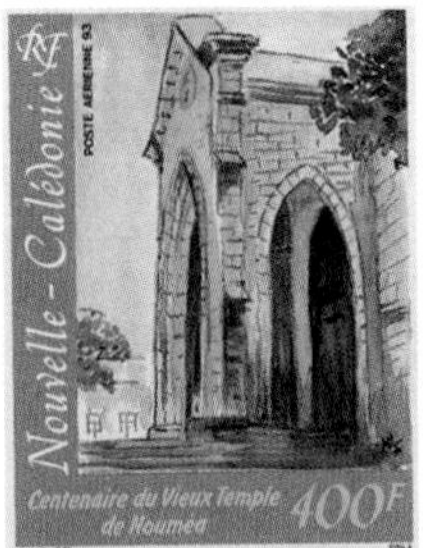
359 Noumea Temple

1993. Air. Centenary of First Protestant Church in Noumea.
968 **359** 400f. multicoloured . . . 6·00 4·00

1993. No. 898 surch **55F**.
969 **321** 55f. on 50f. red . . . . . 1·00 75

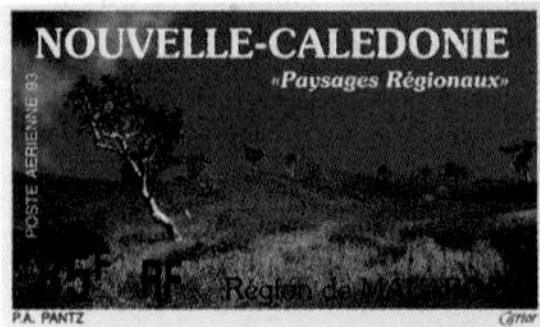
361 Malabou

1993. Air. Regional Landscapes.
970 **361** 85f. multicoloured . . . . 1·25 85

362 Locomotive and Bridge

1993. Air. Centenary of Little Train of Thio.
971 **362** 115f. red, green and lilac 1·75 1·10

363 Rochefort

364 "Megastylis paradoxa"

1993. Air. 80th Death Anniv of Henri Rochefort (journalist).
972 **363** 100f. multicoloured . . . 1·60 1·00

1993. Air. "Bangkok 1993" International Stamp Exhibition, Thailand. Multicoloured.
973 30f. Type **364** 70 40
974 30f. "Vanda coerulea" . . . 70 40

365 Route Map and Boeing 737-300/500

1993. Air. 10th Anniv of Air Cal (national airline).
976 **365** 85f. multicoloured . . . . 1·60 1·25

366 "Francois Arago" (cable ship)

1993. Air. Centenary of New Caledonia–Australia Telecommunications Cable.
977 **366** 200f. purple, blue & turq 4·00 2·40

367 "Oxypleurodon orbiculatus"

1993. Air. Deep-sea Life.
978 **367** 250f. multicoloured . . . 4·50 2·75

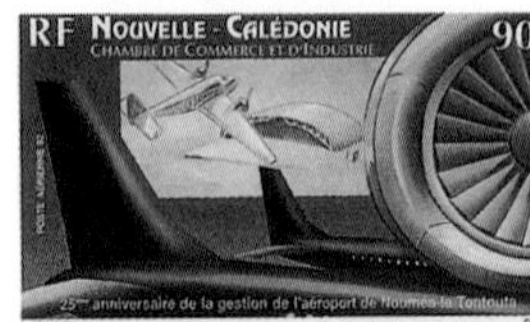
368 Aircraft, Engine and Hangar

1993. Air. 25th Anniv of Chamber of Commerce and Industry's Management of La Tontouta Airport, Noumea.
979 **368** 90f. multicoloured . . . . 1·75 1·10

369 First Christmas Mass, 1843 (stained glass window, Balade church)

1993. Air. Christmas.
980 **369** 120f. multicoloured . . . 2·10 1·40

370 Bourail

1993. Town Arms. Multicoloured.
981 70f. Type **370** . . . . 1·60 1·25
982 70f. Noumea . . . . 1·60 1·25
983 70f. Canala . . . . 1·60 1·25
984 70f. Kone . . . . 1·60 1·25
985 70f. Paita . . . . 2·75 1·40
986 70f. Dumbea . . . . 1·60 1·25
987 70f. Koumac . . . . 1·60 1·25
988 70f. Ponerihouen . . . . . . 1·60 1·25
989 70f. Kaamoo Hyehen . . . . 1·60 1·25
990 70f. Mont Dore . . . . . . 2·50 1·40
991 70f. Thio . . . . 1·60 1·25
992 70f. Kaala-Gomen . . . . . 1·60 1·25
993 70f. Touho . . . . 1·60 1·25

1994. No value expressed
994 **321** (60f.) red . . . . 1·10 40

371 Dog, Exhibition Emblem and Chinese Horoscope Signs (New Year)

1994. Air. "Hong Kong '94" International Stamp Exhibition.
995 **371** 60f. multicoloured . . . . 1·40 90

372 Airbus Industrie A340

1994. Air 1st Paris–Noumea Airbus Flight. Self-adhesive.
997 **372** 90f. multicoloured . . . . 2·10 1·40

1994. "Philexjeunes '94" Youth Stamp Exhibition, Grenoble. No. 960 optd **PHILEXJEUNES'94 GRENOBLE 22–24 AVRIL**.
998 **356** 25f. multicoloured 50 40

374 Photograph of Canala Post Office and Post Van

1994. 50th Anniv of Noumea–Canala Postal Service.
999 **374** 15f. brown, green and blue 50 40

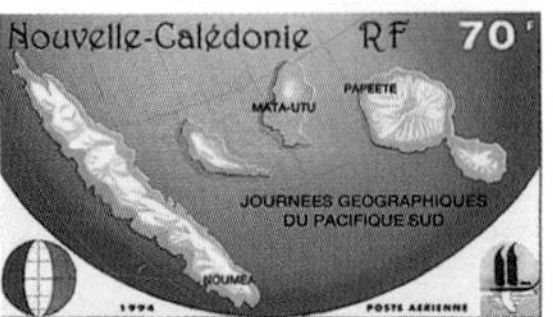
375 Pacific Islands on Globe

1994. Air. South Pacific Geographical Days.
1000 **375** 70f. multicoloured . . . 1·40 95

376 Post Office, 1859

1994. Postal Administration Head Offices. Mult.
1001 30f. Type **376** 60 50
1002 60f. Posts and Telecommunications Office, 1936 . . . . . . 1·40 80
1003 90f. Ministry of Posts and Telecommunications, 1967 1·90 1·40
1004 120f. Ministry of Posts and Telecommunications, 1993 2·50 1·75

377 "The Mask Wearer"

1994. Pacific Sculpture.
1005 **377** 60f. multicoloured . . . 1·40 70

378 "Legend of the Devil Fish" (Micheline Neporon)

1994. Air. Pacific Painters.
1006 **378** 120f. multicoloured . . . 2·25 1·50

379 "Chambeyronia macrocarpa"

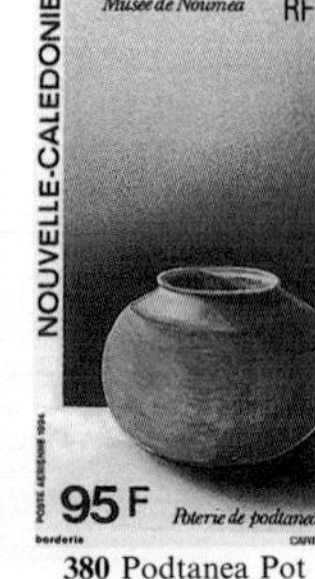
380 Podtanea Pot

1994.
1007 **379** 90f. multicoloured . . . 1·90 1·25

1994. Air. Noumea Museum.
1008 **380** 95f. multicoloured . . . 1·90 1·40

381 Trophy, U.S. Flag and Ball

1994. Air. World Cup Football Championship, U.S.A.
1009 **381** 105f. multicoloured . . . 2·00 1·60

1994. No. D707 with "Timbre Taxe" obliterated by black bar.
1010 D **222** 5f. multicoloured . . 10·00 2·50

382 Timor Deer

1994. Bourail Fair.
1011 **382** 150f. multicoloured . . . 3·00 1·75

383 Korean Family

1994. Air. "Philakorea 1994" International Stamp Exhibition, Seoul. (Int Year of the Family).
1012 **383** 60f. multicoloured . . . 1·25 75

384 "L'Atalante" (oceanographic research vessel)

1994. Air. ZoNeCo (evaluation programme of Economic Zone).
1014 **384** 120f. multicoloured . . . 2·40 1·75

385 "Nivose"

1994. Attachment of the "Nivose" (French surveillance frigate) to New Caledonia. Multicoloured.
1015 30f. Type **385** 70 50
1016 30f. Aircraft over frigate . . 70 50
1017 30f. Frigate moored at quay 70 50
1018 60f. Frigate and map of New Caledonia on parchment . . . . 1·40 90
1019 60f. Ship's bell . . . . . . 1·40 90
1020 60f. Frigate and sailor . . . 1·40 90

386 Driving Cattle

1994. Air. 1st European Stamp Salon, Flower Gardens, Paris. Multicoloured.
1021 90f. Aerial view of island . . 1·75 1·25
1022 90f. Type **386** . . . . 1·75 1·25

387 Paper Darts around Girl

1994. School Philately.
1023 **387** 30f. multicoloured . . . 60 40

388 Jaques Nervat

1994. Writers.
1024 **388** 175f. multicoloured . . . 3·50 2·00

389 Satellite transmitting to Globe and Computer Terminal

1994. Air. 50th Anniv of Overseas Scientific and Technical Research Office.
1025 **389** 95f. multicoloured . . . 2·25 1·40

390 Emblem and Temple

1994. Air. 125th Anniv of Freemasonary in New Caledonia.
1026 **390** 350f. multicoloured . . . 7·00 3·50

391 Thiebaghi Mine

1994. Air.
1027 **391** 90f. multicoloured . . . 1·90 1·25

392 Place des Cocotiers, Noumea

1994. Christmas.
1028 **392** 30f. multicoloured . . . 70 60

No. 1028 covers any one of five stamps which were issued together in horizontal se-tenant strips, the position of the bell, tree and monument differing on each stamp. The strip is stated to produce a three-dimensional image without use of a special viewer.

393 Globe and Newspapers

1994. 50th Anniv of "Le Monde" (newspaper).
1029 **393** 90f. multicoloured . . . 2·25 1·75

394 1988 100f. Pasteur Institute Stamp

1995. Death Centenary of Louis Pasteur (chemist).
1030 **394** 120f. multicoloured . . . 2·25 1·50

395 Pictorial Map

1995. Air. Tourism.
1031 **395** 90f. multicoloured . . . 1·90 1·25

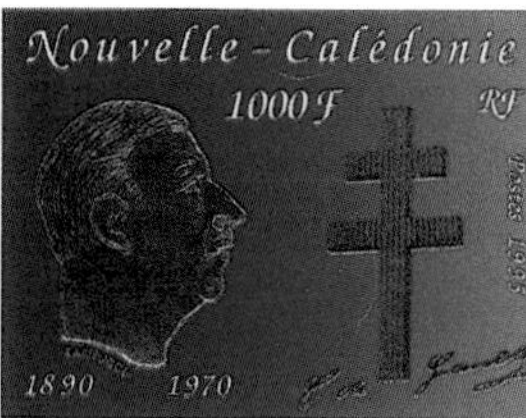

396 Profile of De Gaulle (Santucci) and Cross of Lorraine

1995. 25th Death Anniv of Charles de Gaulle (French President, 1959–69).
1032 **396** 1000f. deep blue, blue and gold . . . . . . 18·00 15·00

397 Emblem

1995. Pacific University Teachers' Training Institute.
1033 **397** 100f. multicoloured . . . 1·90 1·40

398 "Sylviornis neocaledoniae"

1995.
1034 **398** 60f. multicoloured . . . 1·60 1·25

399 Swimming, Cycling and Running

1995. Triathlon.
1035 **399** 60f. multicoloured . . . 1·40 90

400 Tent and Trees

1995. 50th Anniv of Pacific Franc.
1036 **400** 10f. multicoloured . . . 30 30

No. 1036 covers any one of four stamps which were issued together in horizontal se-tenant strips, the position of the central motif rotating slightly in a clockwise direction from the left to the right-hand stamp. The strip is stated to produce a three-dimensional image without use of a special viewer.

401 Bourbon Palace (Paris), Map of New Caledonia and Chamber

1995. 50th Anniversaries. Multicoloured.
1037 60f. Type **401** (first representation of New Caledonia at French National Assembly) . . . 1·40 70
1038 90f. National emblems, De Gaulle and Allied flags (end of Second World War) . . . . 1·90 1·25
1039 90f. U.N. Headquarters, New York (U.N.O.) . . . 1·90 1·25

402 "Sebertia acuminata"

1995.
1040 **402** 60f. multicoloured . . . 1·50 80

403 Common Noddy

1995. "Singapore'95" International Stamp Exhibition. Sea Birds. Multicoloured.
1041 5f. Type **403** 10 15
1042 10f. Silver gull 20 25
1043 20f. Roseate tern 40 45
1044 35f. Osprey 80 60
1045 65f. Red-footed booby . . . 1·25 1·25
1046 125f. Great frigate bird . . 2·25 1·75

404 Golf

1995. 10th South Pacific Games.
1048 **404** 90f. multicoloured . . . 1·75 1·40

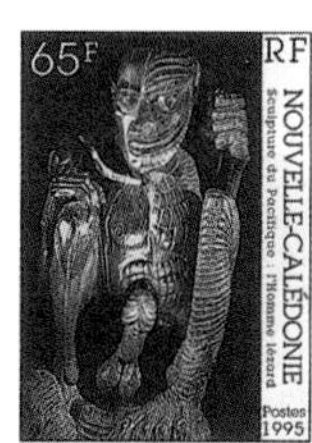

405 "The Lizard Man" (Dick Bone)

1995. Pacific Sculpture.
1049 **405** 65f. multicoloured . . . 1·25 90

406 Venue

1995. Air. 35th South Pacific Conference.
1050 **406** 500f. multicoloured . . . 8·00 5·50

407 Silhouette of Francis Carco

1995. Writers.
1051 **407** 95f. multicoloured . . . 1·75 1·40

408 Ouare

1995. Air. Kanak Dances. Multicoloured.
1052 95f. Type **408** . . . . 1·75 1·25
1053 100f. Pothe . . . . 1·75 1·25

409 Saw-headed Crocodilefish

1995. World of the Deep.
1054 **409** 100f. multicoloured . . . 2·00 1·40

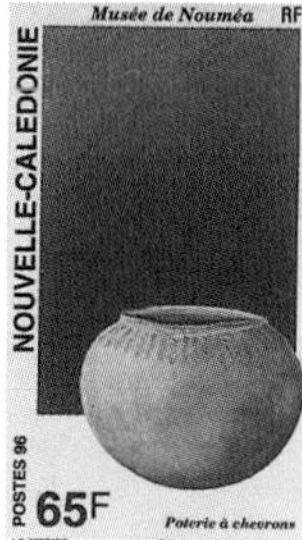

410 "Mekosuchus inexpectatus"

1996. Air.
1055 **410** 125f. multicoloured . . . 2·40 1·60

411 Vessel with decorated Rim

1996. Noumea Museum.
1056 **411** 65f. multicoloured . . . 1·25 90

412 "Captaincookia margaretae"

1996. Flowers. Multicoloured.
1057 65f. Type **412** . . . . 1·25 80
1058 95f. "Ixora cauliflora" . . . 1·75 1·25

413 Pirogue on Beach

1996. World Pirogue Championships, Noumea. Multicoloured.
1059 30f. Type **413** 60 40
1060 65f. Pirogue leaving shore 1·40 70
1061 95f. Double-hulled pirogue 1·75 1·10
1062 125f. Sports pirogue . . . . 2·25 1·90

Nos. 1059/62 were issued together, se-tenant, forming a composite design.

414 Red Batfish

1996. "China'96" International Stamp Exhibition, Peking. Deep Sea Life. Multicoloured.
1063 25f. Type **414** 50 40
1064 40f. "Perotrochus deforgesi" (slit shell) 70 50

1065 65f. "Mursia musorstomia" (crab) . . . . 1·25 80
1066 125f. Sea lily . . . . 2·50 1·60

415 "Sarcolchilus koghiensis"

1996. "Capex'96" International Stamp Exhibition, Toronto, Canada. Orchids. Multicoloured.
1067 5f. Type **415** 10 10
1068 10f. "Phaius robertsii" . . . 20 10
1069 25f. "Megastylis montana" 40 35
1070 65f. "Dendrobium macrophyllum" . . . . . 1·10 85
1071 95f. "Dendrobium virotii" 1·75 1·25
1072 125f. "Ephemerantha comata" . . . . 2·00 1·50

416 Indonesian Couple beneath Tree

417 Louis Brauquier

1996. Air. Centenary of Arrival of First Indonesian Immigrants.
1073 **416** 130f. multicoloured . . . 2·25 1·75

1996. Air. Writers.
1074 **417** 95f. multicoloured . . . 1·75 1·25

1996. 50th Anniv of U.N.I.C.E.F. No. 1023 optd **unicef** and emblem.
1075 **387** 30f. multicoloured . . . 60 50

419 Dish Aerial

1996. Air. Anniversaries. Multicoloured.
1076 95f. Type **419** (20th anniv of New Caledonia's first Earth Station) . . . . . 1·75 1·25
1077 125f. Guglielmo Marconi (inventor) and telegraph masts (centenary of radio-telegraphy) . . . . 2·40 1·25

420 Tribal Dance

1996. Air. 7th South Pacific Arts Festival.
1078 **420** 100f. multicoloured . . . 1·75 1·40

421 "The Woman" (Elija Trijikone)

1996. Sculptures of the Pacific.
1079 **421** 105f. multicoloured . . . 2·00 1·40

422 Ordination, St. Joseph's Cathedral,Noumea

1996. 50th Anniv of Ordination of First Priests in New Caledonia.
1080 **422** 160f. multicoloured . . . 3·00 2·00

423 "Man" (Paula Boi)

1996. Pacific Painters.
1081 **423** 200f. multicoloured . . . 3·50 2·50

424 Gaica Dance

1996.
1082 **424** 500f. multicoloured . . . 8·50 5·50

425 Great Reef

1996. Air. 50th Autumn Stamp Show, Paris. Multicoloured.
1083 95f. Type **425** . . . . 1·75 1·25
1084 95f. Mount Koghi . . . . . 1·75 1·25

426 Decorated Sandman

1996. Christmas.
1085 **426** 95f. multicoloured . . . 1·75 90

427 Horned Tortoises

1997. Air.
1086 **427** 95f. multicoloured . . . 1·75 1·40

428 Emblem

1997. Air. 50th Anniv of South Pacific Commission.
1087 **428** 100f. multicoloured . . . 1·75 1·25

429 Junk, Hong Kong, Ox and Flag

1997. Air. "Hong Kong '97" Stamp Exhibition. Year of the Ox.
1088 **429** 95f. multicoloured . . . 1·75 1·25

430 Mitterrand

1997. 1st Death Anniv of Francois Mitterrand (French President, 1981–95).
1090 **430** 1000f. multicoloured . . 16·00 12·00

431 Windmill ("Letters from My Windmill")

432 Lapita Pot with Geometric Pattern

1997. Death Centenary of Alphonse Daudet (writer). Multicoloured.
1091 65f. Type **431** . . . . 1·40 90
1092 65f. Boy sitting by wall ("The Little Thing") . . . 1·40 90
1093 65f. Hunter in jungle ("Tartarinde Tarascon") 1·40 90
1094 65f. Daudet at work . . . . 1·40 90

1997. Air. Melanesian Pottery in Noumea Museum. Multicoloured.
1096 95f. Type **432** . . . . 1·75 1·25
1097 95f. Lapita pot with "face" design . . . . 1·75 1·25

433 French Parliament Building and Lafleur

1997. Appointment of Henri Lafleur as First New Caledonian Senator in French Parliament.
1098 **433** 105f. multicoloured . . . 2·00 1·50

434 Cotton Harlequin Bug

1997. Insects. Multicoloured.
1099 65f. Type **434** . . . . 1·50 1·25
1100 65f. "Kanakia gigas" . . . 1·50 1·25
1101 65f. "Aenetus cohici" (moth) 1·50 1·25

435 Iekawe

1997. 5th Death Anniv of Jacques Ieneic Iekawe (first Melanesian Prefect).
1102 **435** 250f. multicoloured . . . 4·00 3·00

436 Consolidated Catalina Flying Boat and South Pacific Routes Map

1997. Air. 50th Anniv of Establishment by TRAPAS of First Commercial Air Routes in South Pacific. Multicoloured.
1103 95f. Type **436** . . . . 1·50 1·25
1104 95f. TRAPAS emblem, seaplane and New Caledonia domestic flight routes . . . . 1·50 1·25

437 Kagu

438 Cup and Harness Racing

1997.
1105 **437** 5f. violet 10 10
1107 30f. orange 50 40
1113 95f. blue . . . . 1·50 60
1114 100f. blue . . . . 1·00 80
No. 1114 also comes self-adhesive.
See also No. 1128.

1997. Equestrian Sports. Multicoloured.
1118 65f. Type **438** . . . . 1·25 80
1119 65f. Cup and horse racing 1·25 80

439 Port de France (engraving)

1997.
1120 **439** 95f. multicoloured . . . 1·50 1·00

440 "Marianne", Voter and Tiki

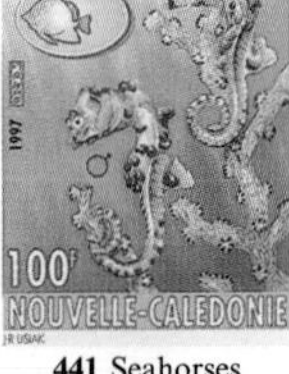

441 Seahorses

1997. 50th Anniv of First Elections of Melanesian Representatives to French Parliament.
1121 **440** 150f. multicoloured . . . 2·40 1·75

1997. 5th Indo-Pacific Fishes Conference.
1122 **441** 100f. multicoloured . . . 1·50 1·00

442 Hammerhead Shark Dance Mask (Ken Thaiday)

1997. Pacific Art and Culture. Multicoloured.
1123 100f. Type **442** . . . . . . 1·50 1·10
1124 100f. Painting of traditional Melanesian images by Yvette Bouquet . . . . . 1·50 1·10
1125 100f. "Doka" (figurines by Frank Haikiu) . . . . . 1·50 1·10

443 Father Christmas surfing to Earth

1997. Christmas. Multicoloured.
1126 95f. Type **443** . . . . 1·40 1·00
1127 100f. Dolphin with "Meilleurs Voeux" banner 1·40 1·00

1998. As Nos. 1107/13 but with no value expressed. Ordinary or self-adhesive gum.
1128 **437** (70f.) red . . . . 1·00 40

444 "Lentinus tuber-regium" **445** Mask from Northern Region

1998. Edible Mushrooms. Multicoloured.
1130 70f. Type **444** . . . . . . 1·00 80
1131 70f. "Morchella anteridiformis" . . . . . 1·00 80
1132 70f. "Volvaria bombycina" 1·00 80

1998. Territorial Museum. Multicoloured.
1133 105f. Type **445** . . . . . . 1·50 1·00
1134 110f. Section of door frame from Central Region . . . 1·50 1·00

446 Painting by Gauguin

1998. 150th Birth Anniv of Paul Gauguin (painter).
1135 **446** 405f. multicoloured . . . 5·00 3·75

447 Player

1998. World Cup Football Championship, France.
1136 **447** 100f. multicoloured . . . 1·40 95

448 "Mitimitia"

1998. Tjibaou Cultural Centre. Multicoloured.
1137 30f. Type **448** 40 30
1138 70f. Jean-Marie Tjibaou (politician) and Centre . . 90 70
1139 70f. Detail of a Centre building (Renzo Piano) (vert) 90 70
1140 105f. "Man Bird" (Mathias Kauage) (vert) . . . . . 1·40 95

449 Broken Chains and Slaves

1998. 150th Anniv of Abolition of Slavery.
1141 **449** 130f. brown, blue and purple . . . . 1·60 1·25

450 Dogs watching Postman delivering Letter

1998. Stamp Day.
1142 **450** 70f. multicoloured . . . 85 65

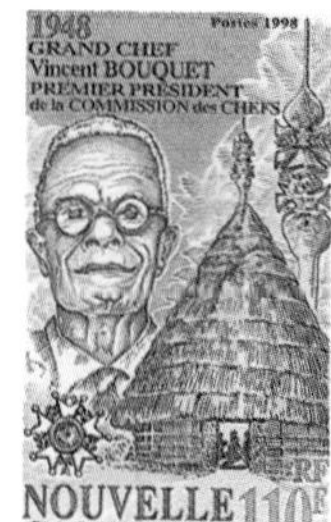

451 Vincent Bouquet

1998. 50th Anniv of Election of First President of Commission of Chiefs.
1143 **451** 110f. multicoloured . . . 1·40 95

452 Noumea Fantasia, 1903

1998. 100 Years of Arab Presence.
1144 **452** 80f. multicoloured . . . 95 70

453 Departure

1998. "Portugal 98" International Stamp Exhibition, Lisbon. 500th Anniv of Vasco da Gama's Voyage to India via Cape of Good Hope. Multicoloured.
1145 100f. Type **453** . . . . . . 1·40 95
1146 100f. Fleet at Cape of Good Hope . . . . 1·40 95
1147 100f. Vasco da Gama meeting Indian king . . . 1·40 95
1148 100f. Vasco da Gama in armorial shield flanked by plants . . . . 1·40 95

454 Kagu

455 Liberty Trees

1998. Endangered Species. The Kagu. Multicoloured.
1150 5f. Type **454** 10 10
1151 10f. Kagu by branch . . . 10 10
1152 15f. Two kagus 20 15
1153 70f. Two kagus, one with wings outspread 80 60

1998. 50th Anniv of Universal Declaration of Human Rights.
1154 **455** 70f. green, black and blue 85 65

456 "Prison, Nou Island" (engraving)

1998.
1155 **456** 155f. multicoloured . . . 1·90 1·40

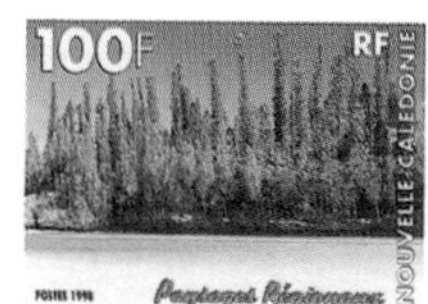

457 View of Island

1998. Regional Scenes. Multicoloured.
1156 100f. Type **457** . . . . . . 1·40 95
1157 100f. View of sea . . . . . 1·40 95

458 Switchboard, Post Van, Postman on Bicycle and Post Office (1958) **459** Marine Life forming Christmas Tree ("Merry Christmas")

1998. 40th Anniv of Posts and Telecommunications Office. Multicoloured.
1158 70f. Type **458** 75 55
1159 70f. Automatic service machine, woman with mobile phone, dish aerial, motor cycle courier and post office (1998) 75 55

1998. Greetings stamps. Multicoloured.
1160 100f. Type **459** . . . . . . 1·10 80
1161 100f. Treasure chest ("Best Wishes") . . . . 1·10 80
1162 100f. Fish ("Good Holiday") . . . . 1·10 80
1163 100f. Fishes and reefs ("Happy Birthday") . . . 1·10 80

460 Map, Memorial and "Monique"

1998. 20th Anniv of Erection of Memorial to the Victims of the "Monique" (inter-island freighter) Disaster.
1164 **460** 130f. multicoloured . . . 1·40 1·00

461 "Argiope aetherea"

1999. Spiders. Multicoloured.
1165 70f. Type **461** 75 55
1166 70f. "Latrodectus hasselti" 75 55
1167 70f. "Cyrtophora moluccensis" 75 55
1168 70f. "Barycheloides alluvviophilus" 75 55

462 Tooth

1999. Giant-toothed Shark.
1169 **462** 100f. multicoloured . . . 1·10 80

463 Athletics

1999. 11th South Pacific Games. Multicoloured.
1171 5f. Type **463** 10 10
1172 10f. Tennis 10 10
1173 30f. Karate 30 55
1174 70f. Baseball 75 55

464 Bwanjep **466** School Building and Computer

465 Scene from "Les Filles de la Neama" and Bloc

1999. Traditional Musical Instruments. Mult.
1175 30f. Type **464** 30 25
1176 70f. Bells 75 55
1177 100f. Flutes . . . . 1·10 80

1999. 29th Death Anniv of Paul Bloc (writer).
1178 **465** 105f. blue, green & purple . . . . 1·10 80

1999. 20th Anniv of Auguste Escoffier Commercial and Hotelier Professional School. Multicoloured.
1179 70f. Type **466** 75 55
1180 70f. School building and chef's hat 75 55

467 Unloading Supplies, Helicopters and Map

1999. Humanitarian Aid.
1181 **467** 135f. multicoloured . . . 1·40 1·00

468 10c. Napoleon III Stamp, 1860

1999. 140th Anniv (2000) of First New Caledonian Stamp and "Philexfrance 99" International Stamp Exhibition, Paris.
1182 **468** 70f. multicoloured . . . 75 55

469 Food Platter

1999. Hotels and Restaurants. Multicoloured.
1184 5f. Type **469** 10 10
1185 30f. Seafood platter 30 25

1186 70f. Hotel cabins by lake . . 75 55
1187 100f. Modern hotel and swimming pool . . . . . 1·00 80

470 Eiffel Tower, Lighthouse with 1949 and 1999 Aircraft

1999. Air. 50th Anniv of First Paris–Noumea Scheduled Flight.
1188 **470** 100f. multicoloured . . . 1·00 80

471 Paintings (½-size illustration)

1999.
1189 **471** 70f. multicoloured . . . 75 55

472 Aji Aboro (Kanak dance)

1999.
1190 **472** 70f. multicoloured . . . 75 55

473 Chateau Hagen

1999. Historic Monuments of South Province.
1191 **473** 155f. multicoloured . . . 1·60 1·10

474 Children protecting Tree

1999. Nature Protection: "Don't touch my Tree".
1192 **474** 30f. multicoloured . . . 30 25

475 Children around Tree

1999. Greetings Stamps. Multicoloured.
1193 100f. Type **475** ("Merry Christmas") . . . . . . 1·00 85
1194 100f. Children with flowers and star ("Best Wishes 2000") . . . . 1·00 85
1195 100f. Children and Year 2000 cake ("Happy Birthday") . . . . 1·00 85
1196 100f. Children looking in pram ("Congratulations") 1·00 85

476 Amedee Lighthouse

2000.
1197 **476** 100f. multicoloured . . . 1·00 80

477 *L'Emile Renouf* (four-masted steel barque)

2000. Centenary of Loss of *Emile Renouf* on Durand Reef, Insel Mare.
1198 **477** 135f. multicoloured . . . 1·40 1·00

478 Painted Shells (Gilles Subileau)

2000. Pacific Painters.
1199 **478** 155f. multicoloured . . . 1·60 1·10

480 Prawn

2000. Noumia Aquarium. Multicoloured.
1201 70f. Type **480** 75 55
1202 70f. Fluorescent corals . . . 75 55
1203 70f. Hump-headed wrasse (*Cheilinus undulatus*) . . . 75 55

481 Lockheed P-38 Lightning Fighter

2000. Air. Birth Centenary of Antoine de Saint-Exupery (writer and pilot).
1204 **481** 130f. multicoloured . . . 1·40 1·00

482 Aerial View

2000. Mangrove Swamp, Voh.
1205 **482** 100f. multicoloured . . . 1·00 80

483 Archery

2000. Olympic Games, Sydney. Multicoloured.
1206 10f. Type **483** 10 10
1207 30f. Boxing 30 35
1208 80f. Cycling 85 70
1209 100f. Fencing . . . . 1·00 80

484 Museum Exhibit

487 Henri Dunant (founder), Baby and Patients with Volunteers

485 Library Building and Lucien Bernheim

2000. Museum of New Caledonia. Multicoloured.
1210 90f. Type **484** 90 75
1211 105f. Museum exhibit . . . 1·10 85

2000. Bernheim Library, Noumea.
1212 **485** 500f. brown, blue and green . . . . 5·00 4·25

2000. Red Cross.
1214 **487** 100f. multicoloured . . . 1·00 80

488 Canoeist

2000. Regional Landscapes. Multicoloured.
1215 100f. Type **488** . . . . . . 1·00 80
1216 100f. Speedboat near island 1·00 80
1217 100f. Sunset and man on raft . . . . 1·00 80

489 Queen Hortense

490 Boy on Roller Skates (Kevyn Pamoiloun)

2000.
1218 **489** 110f. red, green and blue 1·10 85

2000. "Philately at School". Entries in Children's Painting Competition. Multicoloured.
1219 70f. Type **490** 75 55
1220 70f. People using airborne vehicles (Lise-Marie Samanich) 75 55
1221 70f. Aliens (Alexandre Mandin) 75 55

491 Kagu Parents ("Congratulations")

2000. Greetings Stamps. Multicoloured.
1222 100f. Type **491** . . . . . . 1·00 80
1223 100f. Kagu on deck chair ("Happy Holidays") . . . 1·00 80
1224 100f. Kagu with bunch of flowers ("Best Wishes") 1·00 80

492 The Nativity

2000. Christmas.
1225 **492** 100f. multicoloured . . . 1·00 80

493 Snakes

2001. Chinese New Year. Year of the Snake.
1226 **493** 100f. multicoloured . . . 1·00 80

494 *France II* (barque)

2001. Reconstruction of *France II* .
1228 **494** 110f. multicoloured . . . 1·10 90

495 Two Nautili

2001. Noumea Aquarium. The New Calendonia Nautilus. Multicoloured.
1229 100f. Type **495** . . . . . . 1·00 80
1230 100f. Section through nautilus . . . . 1·00 80
1231 100f. Two nautili (different) 1·00 80

496 New Caledonian Crow, Tools and Emblem

2001. Association for the Protection of New Caledonian Nature (ASNNC).
1232 **496** 70f. multicoloured . . . 70 60

497 Humpback Whale and Calf

2001. Operation Cetaces (marine mammal South Pacific study programme). Multicoloured.
1233 100f. Type **497** . . . . . . 1·00 80
1234 100f. Whales leaping . . . . 1·00 80

498 "Guards of Gaia" (statue) (I.Waia)

2001. Ko Neva 2000 Prize Winner.
1235 **498** 70f. multicoloured . . . 70 60

499 "Vision of Oceania" (J. Lebars)

2001.
1236 **499** 110f. multicoloured . . . 1·10 90

500 Profiles

2001. Year of Communication.
1237 **500** 265f. multicoloured . . . 2·75 2·25

501 Air International Caledonie Airbus A310-300

2001. Air. First Anniv of Noumea–Osaka Passenger Service.
1238 **501** 110f. multicoloured . . . 1·10 90

502 "The Solitary Boatman" (Marik)

2001. Pacific Painters.
1239 **502** 110f. multicoloured . . . 1·10 90

503 Observation Capsule on Coral Reef

2001.
1240 **503** 135f. multicoloured . . . 1·40 1·25

504 Qanono Church, Lifou

2001.
1241 **504** 500f. multicoloured . . . 5·00 4·00

505 Fernande Leriche (educator and author)

507 Kite Surfer

506 Cyclists

2001.
1242 **505** 155f. brown, red and blue . . . . 1·60 1·25

2001. 1st Olympic Gold Medal for New Caledonian Sportsman.
1243 **506** 265f. multicoloured . . . 2·75 2·25

2001.
1244 **507** 100f. multicoloured . . . 1·00 80

508 Children on Book

2001. School Philately.
1245 **508** 70f. multicoloured . . . 70 60

509 Easo

2001. Lifou Island. Multicoloured.
1246 100f. Type **509** . . . . . . 1·00 80
1247 100f. Jokin . . . . 1·00 80

510 Father Christmas

2001. Christmas. Multicoloured.
1248 100f. Type **510** . . . . . . 1·00 80
1249 100f. Bat with spotted wings and "Meilleurs Voeux" 1·00 80
1250 100f. Bat with party hat and red nose and "Vive la Fete" . . . . 1·00 80

511 Horse and Sea Horse

2002. Chinese New Year. Year of the Horse. Multicoloured.
1251 100f. Type **511** . . . . . . 1·25 1·00
MS1252 190 × 30 mm. 70f. Horse's head; 70f. Sea horse . . . . . 1·75 1·40

512 Two Flying Foxes

2002. St. Valentine's Day.
1253 **512** 100f. multicoloured . . . 1·25 1·00

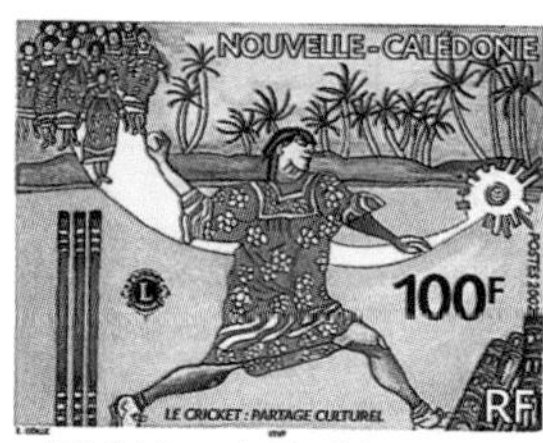

513 Cricketer in Traditional Dress

2002. Cricket.
1254 **513** 100f. multicoloured . . . 1·25 1·00

514 Ancient Axe

2002.
1255 **514** 505f. multicoloured . . . 6·00 5·00

515 Hobie 16 Catamaran

2002. Hobie 16 Catamaran World Championship.
1256 **515** 70f. multicoloured . . . 85 70

516 Loggerhead Turtle (*Caretta caretta*)

2002. Noumea Aquarium. Sheet 185 × 120 mm in shape of turtle containing T **516** and similar horiz designs. Multicoloured.
MS1257 30f. Type **516**; 30f. Green sea turtle (*Chelonia mydas*); 70f. Hawksbill turtle (*Eretmochelys imbricata*) (inscr "imbricat"); 70f. Leatherback sea turtle (*Dermochelys coriacea*) . . . . 2·40 2·00

517 Player

2002. World Cup Football Championship 2002, Japan and South Korea.
1258 **517** 100f. multicoloured . . . 1·25 1·00

518 Coffee Bean Plant

2002. Coffee Production. Multicoloured.
1259 70f. Type **518** 85 70
1260 70f. Coffee production process 85 70
1261 70f. Cafe and cup of coffee 85 70

519 *Alcmene* (French corvette)

2002. Exploration of Coast of New Caledonia by *Alcmene*.
1262 **519** 210f. multicoloured . . . 2·60 2·10

520 Emma Piffault (statue)

521 Circus School

2002. Emma Piffault Commemoration.
1263 **520** 10f. multicoloured . . . 15 10

2002.
1264 **521** 70f. multicoloured . . . 85 70

522 Telescope and Caillard

2002. 90th Birth Anniv of Edmond Caillard (astronomer).
1265 **522** 70f. multicoloured . . . 85 70

523 Face in Landscape, Couple, Ship and Birds

2002. Jean Mariotti (writer).
1266 **523** 70f. multicoloured . . . 85 70

524 Adult Sperm Whale and Calf

2002. New Caledonia–Norfolk Island Joint Issue. Operation Cetaces (marine mammal study). Multicoloured.
1267 100f. Type **524** 1·25 1·00
1268 100f. Sperm whale attacked by giant squid 1·25 1·00
Stamps of similar designs were issued by Norfolk Islands.

525 Coral Snake Musicians

2002. Christmas.
1269 **525** 100f. multicoloured 1·25 1·00

526 Central Mountain Chain

2002. International Year of Mountains. Litho.
1270 **526** 100f. multicoloured 1·25 1·00

527 Powder Store, Bourail Military Post (½-size illustration)

2002.
1271 **527** 1000f. multicoloured 11·00 9·50

528 "Life and Death" (Adrian Trohmae)

2002. Pacific Painters.
1272 **528** 100f. multicoloured 1·25 85

OFFICIAL STAMPS

O 49 Ancestor Pole
O 110 Carved Wooden Pillow (Noumea Museum)

1958. Inscr "OFFICIEL".
O344 **O 49** 1f. yellow 45 85
O345 3f. green 70 90
O346 4f. purple 85 60
O347 5f. blue 60 1·10
O348 9f. black 1·10 1·25
O349 A 10f. violet 2·75 90
O350 13f. green 1·50 2·50
O351 15f. blue 2·00 1·60
O352 24f. mauve 3·00 2·00
O353 26f. orange 1·90 4·00
O354 B 50f. green 2·00 4·00
O355 100f. brown 9·00 10·00
O356 200f. red 9·75 23·00
DESIGNS: A, B, Different idols.

1973.
O525 **O 110** 1f. green, blk & yell 1·90 1·75
O526 2f. red, black & grn 1·75 1·75
O527 3f. green, blk & brn 1·90 1·75
O528 4f. green, black & bl 1·90 1·75
O529 5f. green, blk & mve 2·00 1·75
O530 9f. green, black & bl 2·25 2·25
O531 10f. green, blk & orge 2·25 2·00
O532 11f. grn, blk & mve 2·00 1·75
O533 12f. green, blk & turq 2·25 2·25
O534 15f. green, blk & lt grn 2·00 1·75
O535 20f. green, blk & red 2·00 1·75
O536 23f. green, blk & red 2·25 2·25
O537 24f. green, blk & bl 2·00 2·00
O538 25f. green, blk & grey 2·25 2·25
O539 26f. green, blk & yell 2·25 2·00
O540 29f. red, black & grn 2·50 2·25
O541 31f. red, black & yell 2·25 2·25
O542 35f. red, black & yell 2·25 2·25
O543 36f. green, blk & mve 2·25 2·25
O544 38f. red, black & brn 2·25 2·25
O545 40f. red, black & bl 2·25 2·25
O546 42f. green, blk & brn 2·25 2·25
O547 50f. green, blk & bl 2·50 2·25
O548 58f. blue, blk & grn 2·75 2·25
O549 65f. red, black & mve 2·75 2·25
O550 76f. red, black & yell 3·25 2·50
O551 100f. green, blk & red 4·00 3·00
O552 200f. green, blk & yell 7·25 4·25

PARCEL POST STAMPS

1926. Optd **Colis Postaux** or surch also.
P137 **17** 50c. on 5f. green on mauve 35 3·25
P138 1f. blue 65 3·75
P139 2f. red on blue 1·00 4·25

1930. Optd **Colis Postaux**.
P179 **23** 50c. brown and mauve 60 3·00
P180 **24** 1f. pink and drab 60 3·50
P181 2f. brown and orange 80 4·00

POSTAGE DUE STAMPS

1903. Postage Due stamps of French Colonies optd **CINQUANTENAIRE 24 SEPTEMBRE 1853 1903** and eagle. Imperf.
D78 U 5c. blue 1·75 1·10
D79 10c. brown 7·00 6·25
D80 15c. green 19·00 4·00
D81 30c. red 12·50 11·50
D82 50c. purple 60·00 10·00
D83 60c. brown on buff £200 55·00
D84 1f. pink 27·00 10·00
D85 2f. brown £750 £800

D 18 Outrigger Canoe

D 25 Sambar Stag

D 38

1906.
D102 **D 18** 5c. blue on blue 15 45
D103 10c. brown on buff 40 2·75
D104 15c. green 45 2·25
D105 20c. black on yellow 50 1·60
D106 30c. red 55 2·50
D107 50c. blue on cream 90 3·25
D108 60c. green on blue 75 3·00
D109 1f. green on cream 95 3·75

1926. Surch.
D137 **D 18** 2f. on 1f. mauve 1·00 5·00
D138 3f. on 1f. brown 1·00 5·00

1928.
D179 **D 25** 2c. brown and blue 15 2·25
D180 4c. green and red 25 2·25
D181 5c. grey and orange 35 2·75
D182 10c. blue and mauve 20 1·00
D183 15c. red and olive 25 2·75
D184 20c. olive and red 1·50 3·25
D185 25c. blue and brown 25 3·00
D186 30c. olive and green 20 3·25
D187 50c. red and brown 2·00 3·75
D188 60c. red and mauve 3·00 3·50
D189 1f. green and blue 2·50 3·00
D190 2f. olive and red 3·50 3·25
D191 3f. brown and violet 3·00 4·50

1948.
D328 **D 38** 10c. mauve 15 2·50
D329 30c. brown 20 3·00
D330 50c. green 25 3·00
D331 1f. brown 25 3·00
D332 2f. red 60 3·00
D333 3f. brown 35 3·00
D334 4f. blue 60 3·00
D335 5f. red 50 3·25
D336 10f. green 1·00 3·50
D337 20f. blue 1·10 3·00

D 222 New Caledonian Flying Fox

1983.
D703 **D 223** 1f. multicoloured 10 10
D704 2f. multicoloured 10 10
D705 3f. multicoloured 10 10
D706 4f. multicoloured 20 20
D707 5f. multicoloured 20 20
D708 10f. multicoloured 20 20
D709 20f. multicoloured 40 40
D710 40f. multicoloured 80 80
D711 50f. multicoloured 90 90

NEWFOUNDLAND Pt. 1

An island off the east coast of Canada. A British Dominion merged since 1949 with Canada, whose stamps it now uses.

1857. 12 pence = 1 shilling;
20 shillings = 1 pound.
1866. 100 cents = 1 dollar.

1

2

3 Royal Crown and Heraldic Flowers of the United Kingdom

1857. Imperf.
1 **1** 1d. purple 95·00 £160
10 **2** 2d. red £325 £450
11 **3** 3d. green 75·00 £150
12 **2** 4d. red £2250 £800
13 **1** 5d. brown 90·00 £300
14 **2** 6d. red £2750 £600
7 6½d. red £2250 £2500
8 8d. red £250 £450
9 1s. red £13000 £4750
The frame design of Type **2** differs for each value.

1861. Imperf.
16 **1** 1d. brown £170 £300
17 **2** 2d. lake £170 £400
18 4d. lake 30·00 90·00
19 **1** 5d. brown 65·00 £300
20 **2** 6d. lake 22·00 £100
21 6½d. lake 70·00 £425
22 8d. lake 80·00 £550
23 1s. lake 38·00 £300

6 Codfish

7 Common Seal on Ice-floe

8 Prince Consort

9 Queen Victoria

10 Schooner

11 Queen Victoria

1866. Perf (2c. also roul).
31 **6** 2c. green 75·00 35·00
26 **7** 5c. brown £500 £170
32 **8** 10c. black £180 40·00
33 **9** 12c. brown 48·00 48·00
29 **10** 13c. orange 95·00 75·00
30 **11** 24c. blue 35·00 35·00

12 King Edward VII when Prince of Wales

14 Queen Victoria

1868. Perf or roul.
34 **12** 1c. purple 55·00 50·00
36 3c. orange £250 £100
42 3c. blue £275 4·25
38 **7** 5c. black £250 £110
43 5c. blue £180 3·50
39 **14** 6c. red 8·00 18·00

19 Newfoundland Dog

15 King Edward VII when Prince of Wales

16 Codfish

17

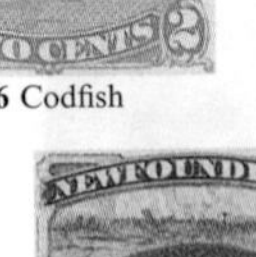
18 Common Seal on Ice-floe

20 Atlantic Brigantine

21 Queen Victoria

1880.
49 **19** ½c. red 11·00 7·50
59 ½c. black 9·50 5·00
44a **15** 1c. brown 26·00 9·00
50a 1c. green 6·00 3·25
46 **16** 2c. green 48·00 23·00
51 2c. orange 16·00 4·75
47 **17** 3c. blue 80·00 5·50
52 3c. brown 60·00 1·50
59a **18** 3c. blue 65·00 3·50
54 **20** 10c. black 50·00 55·00

1890.
55 **21** 3c. grey 28·00 1·75
This stamp on pink paper was stained by sea-water.

22 Queen Victoria

23 John Cabot

24 Cape Bonavista

25 Caribou-hunting

1897. 400th Anniv of Discovery of Newfoundland and 60th Year of Queen Victoria's Reign. Dated "1497 1897".
66 **22** 1c. green 2·50 6·00
67 **23** 2c. red 2·25 2·75
68 **24** 3c. blue 3·50 1·00
69 **25** 4c. olive 9·50 3·50
70 – 5c. violet 13·00 3·00
71 – 6c. brown 9·50 3·25
72 – 8c. orange 21·00 9·00
73 – 10c. brown 42·00 7·00
74 – 12c. blue 35·00 6·00
75 – 15c. red 20·00 18·00
76 – 24c. violet 25·00 20·00
77 – 30c. blue 45·00 65·00
78 – 35c. red 60·00 60·00
79 – 60c. black 17·00 12·00
DESIGNS—As Type **24**: 5c. Mining; 6c. Logging; 8c. Fishing; 10c. Cabot's ship, the "Matthew"; 15c. Seals; 24c. Salmon-fishing; 35c. Iceberg. As Type **23**: 12c. Willow/red grouse; 30c. Seal of the Colony; 60c. Henry VII.

1897. Surch **ONE CENT** and bar.
80 **21** 1c. on 3c. grey 48·00 21·00

39 Prince Edward, later Duke of Windsor

40 Queen Victoria

1897. Royal portraits.
83 **39** ½c. olive 2·25 1·50
84 **40** 1c. red 3·25 3·50

85a	–	1c. green	8·00	20
86	–	2c. orange	3·50	4·00
87	–	2c. red	15·00	40
88	–	3c. orange	18·00	30
89	–	4c. violet	24·00	4·50
90	–	5c. blue	40·00	3·00

DESIGNS: 2c. King Edward VII when Prince of Wales; 3c. Queen Alexandra when Princess of Wales; 4c. Queen Mary when Duchess of York; 5c. King George V when Duke of York.

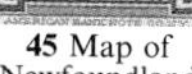

45 Map of Newfoundland **46** King James I

47 Arms of Colonisation Co. **49** "Endeavour" (immigrant ship), 1610

1908.

94	**45**	2c. lake	27·00	1·00

1910. Dated "1610 1910".

109	**46**	1c. green	1·25	30
107	**47**	2c. red	4·50	40
97	–	3c. olive	6·00	15·00
98	**49**	4c. violet	15·00	13·00
108	–	5c. blue	8·00	2·75
111	–	6c. purple	18·00	45·00
112	–	8c. bistre	48·00	70·00
102	–	9c. green	40·00	80·00
103	–	10c. grey	55·00	£100
115	–	12c. brown	60·00	60·00
105	–	15c. black	65·00	£100

DESIGNS—HORIZ: 5c. Cupids; 8c. Mosquito; 9c. Logging camp, Red Indian Lake; 10c. Paper mills, Grand Falls. VERT: 3c. John Guy; 6c. Sir Francis Bacon; 12c. King Edward VII; 15c. King George V. (Cupids and Mosquito are places).

57 Queen Mary **58** King George V

67 Seal of Newfoundland

1911. Coronation.

117	**57**	1c. green	8·00	30
118	**58**	2c. red	4·00	20
119	–	3c. brown	20·00	30·00
120	–	4c. purple	19·00	26·00
121	–	5c. blue	7·00	1·50
122	–	6c. grey	13·00	25·00
123	–	8c. blue	55·00	75·00
124	–	9c. blue	17·00	42·00
125	–	10c. green	28·00	40·00
126	–	12c. plum	24·00	45·00
127	**67**	15c. lake	19·00	45·00

PORTRAITS—VERT (As Type **57/8**): 3c. Duke of Windsor when Prince of Wales; 4c. King George VI when Prince Albert; 5c. Princess Mary, the Princess Royal; 6c. Duke of Gloucester when Prince Henry; 8c. Duke of Kent when Prince George; 9c. Prince John; 10c. Queen Alexandra; 12c. Duke of Connaught.

68 Caribou

1919. Newfoundland Contingent, 1914–18.

130	**68**	1c. green	3·75	20
131		2c. red	3·75	85
132		3c. brown	6·50	20
133		4c. mauve	6·00	70
134		5c. blue	8·00	1·25
135		6c. grey	6·00	38·00
136		8c. purple	11·00	42·00
137		10c. green	6·00	4·25
138		12c. orange	18·00	55·00
139		15c. blue	15·00	55·00
140		24c. brown	22·00	28·00
141		36c. olive	15·00	28·00

DESIGNS—Each inscr with the name of a different action: 1c. Suvla Bay; 3c. Gueudecourt; 4c. Beaumont Hamel; 6c. Monchy; 10c. Steenbeck; 15c. Langemarck; 24c. Cambrai; 36c. Combles. The 2, 5, 8 and 12c. are inscribed "Royal Naval Reserve-Ubique".

1919. Air. Hawker Flight. No. 132a optd **FIRST TRANS- ATLANTIC AIR POST April, 1919.**

142	**68**	3c. brown	£15000	£8000

1919. Air. Alcock and Brown Flight. Surch **Trans-Atlantic AIR POST, 1919. ONE DOLLAR.**

143	$1 on 15c. red (No. 75)	£110	£110

1920. Surch in words between bars.

144	2c. on 30c. blue (No. 77)	4·25	18·00
146	3c. on 15c. red (No. 75)	16·00	16·00
147	3c. on 35c. red (No. 78)	7·50	12·00

1921. Air. Optd **AIR MAIL to Halifax, N.S. 1921.**

148a	35c. red (No. 78)	80·00	80·00

73 Twin Hills, Tor's Cove **75** Statue of Fighting Newfoundlander, St. John's

1923.

149	**73**	1c. green	1·50	20
150	–	2c. red	75	10
151	**75**	3c. brown	1·00	10
152	–	4c. purple	1·00	30
153	–	5c. blue	2·25	1·75
154	–	6c. grey	3·75	8·50
155	–	8c. purple	5·00	3·50
156	–	9c. green	18·00	29·00
157	–	10c. violet	5·50	3·25
158	–	11c. olive	3·75	17·00
159	–	12c. lake	3·25	10·00
160	–	15c. blue	3·25	18·00
161	–	20c. brown	9·00	12·00
162	–	24c. brown	45·00	75·00

DESIGNS—HORIZ: 2c. South-west Arm, Trinity; 6c. Upper Steadies, Humber River; 8c. Quidi Vidi, near St. John's; 9c. Caribou crossing lake; 11c. Shell Bird Island; 12c. Mount Moriah, Bay of Islands; 20c. Placentia. VERT: 4c. Humber River; 5c. Coast at Trinity; 10c. Humber River Canon; 15c. Humber River, near Little Rapids; 24c. Topsail Falls.

1927. Air. Optd **Air Mail DE PINEDO 1927.**

163	60c. black (No. 79)	£25000	£7500

88 Newfoundland and Labrador **89** S.S. "Caribou"

90 King George V and Queen Mary **91** Duke of Windsor when Prince of Wales

1928. Publicity issue.

164	**88**	1c. green	2·25	1·25
180	**89**	2c. red	1·75	40
181	**90**	3c. brown	1·00	20
201	**91**	4c. mauve	2·00	1·25
183	–	5c. grey	7·00	3·00
184a	–	6c. blue	2·25	15·00
170	–	8c. brown	3·50	27·00
171	–	9c. green	9·00	22·00
185	–	10c. violet	4·25	3·50
173	–	12c. lake	2·00	20·00
174a	–	14c. purple	5·00	8·50
175	–	15c. blue	3·25	27·00
176a	–	20c. black	2·50	7·00
177	–	28c. green	28·00	48·00
178	–	30c. brown	6·00	17·00

DESIGNS—HORIZ: 5c. Express train; 6c. Newfoundland Hotel, St. John's; 8c. Heart's Content; 10c. War Memorial, St. John's; 15c. Vickers Vimy aircraft; 20c. Parliament House, St. John's. VERT: 9, 14c. Cabot Tower, St. John's; 12, 28c. G.P.O., St. John's; 30c. Grand Falls, Labrador.

1929. Surch **THREE CENTS.**

188	3c. on 6c. (No. 154)	1·00	5·00

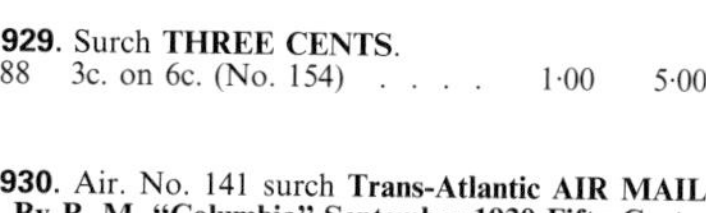

1930. Air. No. 141 surch **Trans-Atlantic AIR MAIL By B. M. "Columbia" September 1930 Fifty Cents.**

191	**68**	50c. on 36c. olive	£4750	£4250

103 Westland Limousine III and Dog-team

104 Vickers Vimy Biplane and early Sailing Packet

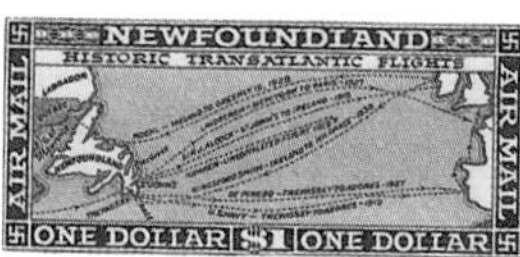

105 Routes of historic Trans-Atlantic Flights

1931. Air.

192	**103**	15c. brown	7·00	13·00
193	**104**	50c. green	32·00	55·00
194	**105**	$1 blue	50·00	95·00

107 Codfish **108** King George V

110 Duke of Windsor when Prince of Wales **111** Reindeer

112 Queen Elizabeth II when Princess **121** Corner Brook Paper Mills

1932.

209	**107**	1c. green	2·50	30
276		1c. grey	20	80
210	**108**	2c. red	1·50	20
223		2c. green	75	10
211	–	3c. brown	1·50	20
212	**110**	4c. lilac	5·50	2·00
224		4c. red	2·25	40
213	**111**	5c. purple	4·50	1·25
225c		5c. violet	70	30
214	**112**	6c. blue	4·00	14·00
226	–	7c. lake	2·75	3·75
282	**121**	8c. red	2·00	2·25
215	–	10c. brown	70	65
216	–	14c. black	4·25	5·50
217	–	15c. purple	1·25	2·00
218	–	20c. green	1·00	1·00
228	–	24c. blue	85	3·25
219	–	25c. grey	2·00	2·25
220	–	30c. blue	35·00	35·00
289	–	48c. brown	4·00	6·50

DESIGNS—VERT: 3c. Queen Mary; 7c. Queen Mother when Duchess of York. HORIZ: 10c. Salmon; 14c. Newfoundland dog; 15c. Harp seal; 20c. Cape Race; 24c. Loading iron ore, Bell Island; 25c. Sealing fleet; 30, 48c. Fishing fleet.

1932. Air. Surch **TRANS-ATLANTIC WEST TO EAST Per Dornier DO-X May, 1932. One Dollar and Fifty Cents.**

221	**105**	$1.50 on $1 blue	£200	£225

1933. Optd **L. & S. Post.** ("Land and Sea") between bars.

229	**103**	15c. brown	3·50	12·00

124 Put to Flight

1933. Air.

230	**124**	5c. brown	17·00	17·00
231	–	10c. yellow	13·00	30·00
232	–	30c. blue	32·00	42·00
233	–	60c. green	48·00	95·00
234	–	75c. brown	48·00	90·00

DESIGNS: 10c. Land of Heart's Delight; 30c. Spotting the herd; 60c. News from home; 75c. Labrador.

1933. Air. Balbo Trans-Atlantic Mass Formation Flight. No. 234 surch **1933 GEN. BALBO FLIGHT. $4.50.**

235	$4.50 on 75c. brown	£275	£325

130 Sir Humphrey Gilbert **131** Compton Castle, Devon

1933. 350th Anniv of Annexation. Dated "1583 1933".

236	**130**	1c. black	80	1·50
237	**131**	2c. green	1·25	70
238	–	3c. brown	2·00	1·25
239	–	4c. red	80	50
240	–	5c. violet	2·00	80
241	–	7c. blue	13·00	17·00
242	–	8c. orange	7·50	14·00
243	–	9c. blue	7·00	13·00
244	–	10c. brown	4·00	9·50
245	–	14c. black	14·00	30·00
246w	–	15c. red	7·50	19·00
247	–	20c. green	13·00	18·00
248	–	24c. purple	14·00	23·00
249	–	32c. black	7·00	50·00

DESIGNS—VERT: 3c. Gilbert coat of arms; 5c. Anchor token; 14c. Royal Arms; 15c. Gilbert in the "Squirrel"; 24c. Queen Elizabeth I; 32c. Gilbert's statue at Truro. HORIZ: 4c. Eton College; 7c. Gilbert commissioned by Elizabeth; 8c. Fleet leaving Plymouth, 1583; 9c. Arrival at St. John's; 10c. Annexation, 5 August, 1583; 20c. Map of Newfoundland.

1935. Silver Jubilee. As T **14a** of Kenya, Uganda and Tanganyika.

250	4c. red	1·00	1·75
251	5c. violet	1·25	2·00
252	7c. blue	1·75	7·00
253	24c. olive	5·00	11·00

1937. Coronation. As T **14b** of Kenya, Uganda and Tanganyika.

254	2c. green	1·00	2·50
255	4c. red	1·60	3·00
256	5c. purple	3·00	3·25

144 Atlantic Cod **155** King George VI

1937. Coronation.

257	**144**	1c. grey	3·00	30
258e	–	3c. brown	4·75	3·50
259	–	7c. blue	2·50	1·25
260	–	8c. red	1·75	3·25
261	–	10c. black	4·00	8·50
262	–	14c. black	1·40	2·75
263	–	15c. red	11·00	4·25
264f	–	20c. green	2·50	8·50
265	–	24c. blue	2·50	2·50
266	–	25c. black	2·75	1·75
267	–	48c. purple	8·50	5·50

DESIGNS: 3c. Map of Newfoundland; 7c. Rein-deer; 8c. Corner Brook Paper Mills; 10c. Atlantic salmon; 14c. Newfoundland dog; 15c. Harp seal; 20c. Cape Race; 24c. Bell Island; 25c. Sealing fleet; 48c. The Banks fishing fleet.

1938.

277	**155**	2c. green	30	50
278	–	3c. red	30	20
270	–	4c. blue	2·00	50
271	–	7c. blue	75	4·75

DESIGNS: 3c. Queen Mother; 4c. Queen Elizabeth II, aged 12; 7c. Queen Mary.

159 King George VI and Queen Elizabeth

1938. Royal Visit.
272 **159** 5c. blue . . . . 2·50 75

1939. Surch in figures and triangles.
273 **159** 2c. on 5c. blue . . . . . 2·25 50
274 4c. on 5c. blue . . . . . 1·50 90

161 Grenfell on the "Strathcona" (after painting by Gribble)

1941. 50th Anniv of Sir Wilfred Grenfell's Labrador Mission.
275 **161** 5c. blue 30 70

162 Memorial University College

1942.
290 **162** 30c. red . . . . 1·00 2·50

163 St. John's

165 Queen Elizabeth II when Princess

1943. Air.
291 **163** 7c. blue 50 80

1946. Surch **TWO CENTS**.
292 **162** 2c. on 30c. red 30 75

1947. 21st Birthday of Princess Elizabeth.
293 **165** 4c. blue 30 75

166 Cabot off Cape Bonavista

1947. 450th Anniv of Cabot's Discovery of Newfoundland.
294 **166** 5c. violet 20 80

POSTAGE DUE STAMPS

D 1

1939.
D1 **D 1** 1c. green . . . . 2·25 8·50
D2 2c. red . . . . 13·00 7·50
D3 3c. blue . . . . 5·00 22·00
D4 4c. orange . . . . 9·00 17·00
D5 5c. brown . . . . 5·50 26·00
D6 10c. purple . . . . 6·00 18·00

NEW GUINEA Pt. 1

Formerly a German Colony, part of the island of New Guinea. Occupied by Australian forces during the 1914–18 war and subsequently joined with Papua and administered by the Australian Commonwealth under trusteeship. After the Japanese defeat in 1945 Australian stamps were used until 1952 when the combined issue appeared for Papua and New Guinea (q.v.). The stamps overprinted "N.W. PACIFIC ISLANDS" were also used in Nauru and other ex-German islands.

12 pence = 1 shilling;
20 shillings = 1 pound.

1914. "Yacht" key-types of German New Guinea surch **G.R.I.** and value in English currency.
16 N 1d. on 3pf. brown . . . . . 45·00 55·00
17 1d. on 5pf. green . . . . . 18·00 30·00
18 2d. on 10pf. red . . . . . 24·00 40·00
19 2d. on 20pf. blue . . . . . 28·00 45·00
5 2½d. on 10pf. red . . . . . 65·00 £140
6 2½d. on 20pf. blue . . . . . 75·00 £150
22 3d. on 25pf. blk & red on yell £110 £150
23 3d. on 30pf. blk & orge on buff . . . . . 90·00 £130
24 4d. on 40pf. black and red £100 £160
25 5d. on 50pf. black & pur on buff £160 £190
26 8d. on 80pf. blk & red on rose £325 £400
12 O 1s on 1m. red £1500 £2000
13 2s. on 2m. blue £1700 £2500
14 3s. on 3m. black £3250 £4250
15 5s. on 5m. red and black . . £6500 £8500

Nos. 3/4 surch **1**.
31 N "1" on 2d. on 10pf. red . . £14000 £14000
32 "1" on 2d. on 20pf. blue . . £13000 £8500

4

1914. Registration labels with names of various towns surch **G.R.I. 3d.**
33 **4** 3d. black and red £180 £200

1914. "Yacht" key-types of German Marshall Islands surch **G.R.I.** and value in English currency.
50 N 1d. on 3pf. brown . . . . 50·00 85·00
51 1d. on 5pf. green . . . . 50·00 55·00
52 2d. on 10pf. red . . . . 17·00 26·00
53 2d. on 20pf. blue . . . . 18·00 30·00
64g 2½d. on 10pf. red £7000
64h 2½d. on 20pf. blue £10000
54 3d. on 25pf. black and red on yellow £275 £375
55 3d. on 30pf. black and orange on buff £300 £400
56 4d. on 40pf. black and red £100 £130
57 5d. on 50pf. black and purple on buff £140 £180
58 8d. on 80pf. black and red on rose £400 £500
59 O 1s. on 1m. red £1800 £3000
60 2s. on 2m. blue £1200 £2000
61 3s. on 3m. black £3250 £4750
62 5s. on 5m. red and black £6500 £8500

1915. Nos. 52 and 53 surch **1**.
63 N "1" on 2d. on 10pf. red . . £140 £170
64 "1" on 2d. on 20pf. blue . . £3000 £2250

1915. Stamps of Australia optd **N. W. PACIFIC ISLANDS**.
102 **3** ½d. green . . . . 1·50 3·50
103 1d. red . . . . 2·75 1·60
120 1d. violet . . . . 1·75 6·50
94 **1** 2d. grey . . . . 5·50 14·00
121 **3** 2d. orange . . . . 6·00 2·75
122 2d. red . . . . 9·00 3·75
74 **1** 2½d. blue . . . . 2·75 16·00
96 3d. olive . . . . 5·50 11·00
70 **3** 4d. orange . . . . 4·00 15·00
123 4d. violet . . . . 20·00 40·00
124 4d. blue . . . . 11·00 60·00
105 5d. brown . . . . 2·00 12·00
110 **1** 6d. blue . . . . 4·50 14·00
89 9d. violet . . . . 16·00 21·00
90 1s. green . . . . 11·00 24·00
115 2s. brown . . . . 21·00 38·00
116 5s. grey and yellow . . . . 60·00 65·00
84 10s. grey and pink £110 £160
99 £1 brown and blue £250 £400

1918. Nos. 105 and 90 surch **One Penny**.
100 **3** 1d. on 5d. brown . . . . . 90·00 80·00
101 **1** 1d. on 1s. green . . . . . 90·00 75·00

12 Native Village

14 Raggiana Bird of Paradise (Dates either side of value)

1925.
125 **12** ½d. orange . . . . 2·50 7·00
126 1d. green . . . . 2·50 5·50
126a 1½d. red . . . . 3·25 2·75
127 2d. red . . . . 2·50 4·50
128 3d. blue . . . . 4·50 4·00
129 4d. olive . . . . 13·00 21·00
130b 6d. brown . . . . 4·50 48·00
131 9d. purple . . . . 13·00 45·00
132 1s. green . . . . 15·00 27·00
133 2s. lake . . . . 30·00 48·00
134 5s. brown . . . . 48·00 65·00
135 10s. red £100 £180
136 £1 grey £190 £300

1931. Air. Optd with biplane and **AIR MAIL**.
137 **12** ½d. orange . . . . 1·50 6·00
138 1d. green . . . . 1·60 5·00
139 1½d. red . . . . 1·25 5·00
140 2d. red . . . . 1·25 7·00
141 3d. blue . . . . 1·75 13·00
142 4d. olive . . . . 1·25 9·00
143 6d. brown . . . . 1·75 14·00
144 9d. purple . . . . 3·00 17·00
145 1s. green . . . . 3·00 17·00
146 2s. lake . . . . 7·00 42·00
147 5s. brown . . . . 20·00 65·00
148 10s. red . . . . 75·00 £100
149 £1 grey £140 £250

1931. 10th Anniv of Australian Administration. Dated "1921–1931".
150 **14** 1d. green . . . . 4·00 1·50
151 1½d. red . . . . 5·00 10·00
152 2d. red . . . . 5·00 4·25
153 3d. blue . . . . 5·00 4·75
154 4d. olive . . . . 6·50 19·00
155 5d. green . . . . 5·00 19·00
156 6d. brown . . . . 5·00 19·00
157 9d. violet . . . . 8·50 19·00
158 1s. grey . . . . 6·00 15·00
159 2s. lake . . . . 10·00 29·00
160 5s. brown . . . . 42·00 55·00
161 10s. red . . . . 85·00 £130
162 £1 grey £190 £250

1931. Air. Optd with biplane and **AIR MAIL**.
163 **14** ½d. orange . . . . 3·25 3·25
164 1d. green . . . . 4·00 4·75
165 1½d. red . . . . 3·75 10·00
166 2d. red . . . . 3·75 3·00
167 3d. blue . . . . 6·00 6·50
168 4d. olive . . . . 6·00 6·00
169 5d. green . . . . 6·00 11·00
170 6d. brown . . . . 7·00 26·00
171 9d. violet . . . . 8·00 15·00
172 1s. grey . . . . 7·50 15·00
173 2s. lake . . . . 16·00 48·00
174 5s. brown . . . . 42·00 70·00
175 10s. red . . . . 60·00 £120
176 £1 grey £110 £250

1932. As T **14**, but without dates.
177 1d. green . . . . 1·75 20
178 1½d. red . . . . 1·75 11·00
179 2d. red . . . . 1·75 20
179a 2½d. green . . . . 6·50 20·00
180 3d. blue . . . . 2·25 80
180a 3½d. red . . . . 13·00 10·00
181 4d. olive . . . . 2·25 6·00
182 5d. green . . . . 2·25 70
183 6d. brown . . . . 3·75 3·25
184 9d. violet . . . . 9·50 22·00
185 1s. grey . . . . 4·50 10·00
186 2s. lake . . . . 4·00 17·00
187 5s. brown . . . . 27·00 45·00
188 10s. red . . . . 48·00 70·00
189 £1 grey . . . . 95·00 £100

1932. Air. T **14**, but without dates, optd with biplane and **AIR MAIL**.
190 ½d. orange . . . . 60 1·50
191 1d. green . . . . 1·25 1·50
192 1½d. mauve . . . . 1·75 7·50
193 2d. red . . . . 1·75 30
193a 2½d. green . . . . 6·00 2·50
194 3d. blue . . . . 3·25 3·00
194a 3½d. red . . . . 4·50 3·25
195 4d. olive . . . . 4·50 10·00
196 5d. green . . . . 7·00 7·50
197 6d. brown . . . . 4·50 15·00
198 9d. violet . . . . 6·00 9·00
199 1s. grey . . . . 6·00 9·00
200 2s. lake . . . . 10·00 45·00
201 5s. brown . . . . 48·00 55·00
202 10s. red . . . . 80·00 80·00
203 £1 grey . . . . 75·00 55·00

16 Bulolo Goldfields

18 King George VI

1935. Air.
204 **16** £2 violet £225 £130
205 £5 green £500 £375

1935. Silver Jubilee. Nos. 177 and 179 optd **HIS MAJESTY'S JUBILEE. 1910–1935**.
206 1d. green 75 50
207 2d. red . . . . 1·75 50

1937. Coronation.
208 **18** 2d. red 50 65
209 3d. blue . . . . 50 1·25
210 5d. green . . . . 50 1·25
211 1s. purple 50 65

1939. Air. As T **16** but inscr "AIR MAIL POSTAGE".
212 ½d. orange . . . . 3·75 7·00
213 1d. green . . . . 3·25 4·50
214 1½d. red . . . . 4·00 9·50
215 2d. red . . . . 8·00 3·50
216 3d. blue . . . . 12·00 18·00
217 4d. olive . . . . 13·00 8·50
218 5d. green . . . . 11·00 3·50
219 6d. brown . . . . 24·00 17·00
220 9d. violet . . . . 24·00 23·00
221 1s. green . . . . 24·00 18·00
222 2s. red . . . . 65·00 48·00
223 5s. brown . . . . £130 95·00
224 10s. pink £350 £225
225 £1 olive £100 £110

OFFICIAL STAMPS

1915. Nos. 16 and 17 optd **O. S.**
O1 N 1d on 3pf. brown . . . . . 26·00 75·00
O2 1d. on 3pf. green . . . . . 80·00 £140

1925. Optd **O S**.
O22 **12** 1d. green . . . . 1·00 4·50
O23 1½d. red . . . . 5·50 17·00
O24 2d. red . . . . 1·75 3·75
O25 3d. blue . . . . 3·50 7·25
O26 4d. olive . . . . 4·50 8·50
O27a 6d. brown . . . . 7·00 35·00
O28 9d. purple . . . . 4·00 35·00
O29 1s. green . . . . 5·50 35·00
O30 2s. lake . . . . 28·00 60·00

1931. Optd **O S**.
O31 **14** 1d. green . . . . 5·50 13·00
O32 1½d. red . . . . 6·50 12·00
O33 2d. red . . . . 10·00 7·00
O34 3d. blue . . . . 6·50 6·00
O35 4d. olive . . . . 5·50 8·50
O36 5d. green . . . . 10·00 12·00
O37 6d. brown . . . . 13·00 17·00
O38 9d. violet . . . . 16·00 28·00
O39 1s. grey . . . . 16·00 28·00
O40 2s. lake . . . . 40·00 70·00
O41 5s. brown £100 £170

1932. T **14**, but without dates, optd **O S**.
O42 1d. green . . . . 6·50 7·00
O43 1½d. red . . . . 7·50 12·00
O44 2d. red . . . . 7·50 3·25
O45 2½d. green . . . . 3·25 6·00
O46 3d. blue . . . . 7·50 24·00
O47 3½d. red . . . . 3·25 9·00
O48 4d. olive . . . . 7·50 18·00
O49 5d. green . . . . 6·50 18·00
O50 6d. brown . . . . 12·00 40·00
O51 9d. violet . . . . 11·00 40·00
O52 1s. grey . . . . 16·00 28·00
O53 2s. lake . . . . 35·00 75·00
O54 5s. brown £120 £170

For later issues see **PAPUA NEW GUINEA**.

NEW HEBRIDES Pt. 1

A group of islands in the Pacific Ocean, E. of Australia, under joint administration of Gt. Britain and France. The Condominium ended in 1980, when the New Hebrides became independent as the Republic of Vanuatu.

1908. 12 pence = 1 shilling;
20 shillings = 1 pound.
1938. 100 gold centimes = 1 gold franc.
1977. 100 centimes = 1 New Hebrides franc.

BRITISH ADMINISTRATION

1908. Stamps of Fiji optd. (a) **NEW HEBRIDES. CONDOMINIUM.** (with full points).
1a **23** ½d. green . . . . 40 7·00
2 1d. red 50 40
5 2d. purple and orange . . . 60 70
6 2½d. purple and blue on blue 60 70
7 5d. purple and green . . . . 80 2·00
8 6d. purple and red . . . . 70 1·25
3 1s. green and red . . . . . 19·00 3·75

(b) **NEW HEBRIDES CONDOMINIUM** (without full points).
10 **23** ½d. green . . . . 3·50 24·00
11 1d. red . . . . 10·00 8·50
12 2d. grey . . . . 60 3·00
13 2½d. blue . . . . 65 4·00
14 5d. purple and green . . . . 1·25 5·50
15 6d. purple and deep purple 1·00 5·00
16 1s. black and green . . . . 1·00 7·50

3 Weapons and Idols

1911.
18 **3** ½d. green . . . . 85 1·75
19 1d. red . . . . 3·75 2·00
20 2d. grey . . . . 8·00 4·00
21 2½d. blue . . . . 3·00 5·50
24 5d. green . . . . 4·50 7·00
25 6d. purple . . . . 3·00 5·00
26 1s. black on green . . . . 2·75 13·00
27 2s. purple on blue . . . . 21·00 22·00
28 5s. green on yellow . . . . 35·00 48·00

1920. Surch. (a) On T **3**.
40 **3** 1d. on ½d. green . . . . . 4·00 22·00
30 1d. on 5d. green . . . . . 7·00 60·00
31 1d. on 1s. black on green . . 1·25 13·00
32 1d. on 2s. purple on blue . . 1·00 10·00
33 1d. on 5s. green on yellow . . 1·00 10·00
41 3d. on 1d. red . . . . . . 4·00 11·00
42 5d. on 2½d. blue . . . . . 7·50 21·00

(b) On No. F16 of French New Hebrides.
34 **3** 2d. on 40c. red on yellow . . 1·00 17·00

5

1925.
43 **5** ½d. (5c.) black . . . . . . 1·25 11·00
44 1d. (10c.) green . . . . . . 1·00 11·00
45 2d. (20c.) grey . . . . . . 1·75 2·50
46 2½d. (25c.) brown . . . . . 1·00 13·00
47 5d. (50c.) blue . . . . . . 3·00 2·75
48 6d. (60c.) purple . . . . . 3·50 11·00
49 1s. (1f.25) black on green . . 3·25 19·00
50 2s. (2f.50) purple on blue . . 6·00 22·00
51 5s. (6f.25) green on yellow . . 6·00 25·00

6 Lopevi Islands and Outrigger Canoe

1938.

52 **6** 5c. green . . . . 2·50 3·75
53 10c. orange . . . . 1·25 1·75
54 15c. violet . . . . 3·50 3·75
55 20c. red . . . . 1·60 2·25
56 25c. brown . . . . 1·60 2·25
57 30c. blue . . . . 2·25 2·25
58 40c. olive . . . . 4·50 5·50
59 50c. purple . . . . 1·60 2·25
60 1f. red on green . . . . . . 4·00 8·00
61 2f. blue on green . . . . . . 30·00 17·00
62 5f. red on yellow . . . . . . 70·00 48·00
63 10f. violet on blue . . . . . £200 75·00

1949. U.P.U. As T **4d/g** of Pitcairn Islands.
64 10c. orange 30 60
65 15c. violet 30 60
66 30c. blue 30 60
67 50c. purple 40 60

7 Outrigger Sailing Canoes

1953.

68 **7** 5c. green 60 10
69 10c. red 60 10
70 15c. yellow 60 10
71 20c. blue 60 10
72 – 25c. olive 60 10
73 – 30c. brown 60 10
74 – 40c. sepia 60 10
75 – 50c. violet . . . . 1·00 10
76 – 1f. orange . . . . 5·00 70
77 – 2f. purple . . . . 5·00 8·00
78 – 5f. red . . . . 7·00 22·00
DESIGNS: 25c. to 50c. Native carving; 1f. to 5f. Two natives outside hut.

1953. Coronation. As T **4h** of Pitcairn Islands.
79 10c. black and red 60 50

10 "San Pedro y San Paulo" (Quiros) and Map

1956. 50th Anniv of Condominium. Inscr "1906 1956".
80 **10** 5c. green 15 10
81 10c. red 15 10
82 – 20c. blue 10 10
83 – 50c. lilac 15 15
DESIGN: 20, 50c. "Marianne", "Talking Drum" and "Britannia".

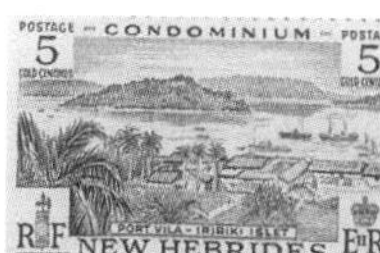

12 Port Villa; Iririki Islet

1957.

84 **12** 5c. green 40 85
85 10c. red 30 10
86 15c. yellow 50 85
87 20c. blue 40 10
88 – 25c. olive 45 10
89 – 30c. brown 45 10
90 – 40c. sepia 45 10
91 – 50c. violet 45 10
92 – 1f. orange . . . . 1·00 1·00
93 – 2f. mauve . . . . 4·00 3·00
94 – 5f. black . . . . 9·00 4·75
DESIGNS: 25c. to 50c. River scene and spear fisherman; 1f. to 5f. Woman drinking from coconut.

1963. Freedom from Hunger. As T **20a** of Pitcairn Islands.
95 60c. green 50 15

1963. Centenary of Red Cross. As T **20b** of Pitcairn Islands, but with British and French cyphers in place of the Queen's portrait.
96 15c. red and black 20 10
97 45c. red and blue 35 20

17 Cocoa Beans

1963.

98 – 5c. red, brown and blue . . 1·00 50
99 **17** 10c. brown, buff and green 15 10
100 – 15c. bistre, brown and violet 15 10
101 – 20c. black, green and blue 55 10
102 – 25c. violet, brown and red 50 70
103 – 30c. brown, bistre and violet 75 10
104 – 40c. red and blue . . . . 80 1·40
105 – 50c. green, yellow and blue 60 10
129 – 60c. red and blue 40 15
106 – 1f. red, black and green . 2·00 3·25
107 – 2f. black, purple and green 2·00 1·75
108 – 3f. multicoloured . . . . . 10·00 6·00
109 – 5f. blue, deep blue and black . . . . 10·00 21·00
DESIGNS: 5 c Exporting manganese, Forari; 15c. Copra; 20c. Fishing from Palikulo Point; 25c. Picasso triggerfish; 30c. New Caledonian nautilus shell; 40, 60c. Lionfish; 50c. Clown surgeonfish; 1f. Cardinal honeyeater (bird); 2f. Buff-bellied flycatcher; 3f. Thicket warbler; 5f. White-collared kingfisher.

1965. Centenary of I.T.U. As T **24a** of Pitcairn Islands, but with British and French cyphers in place of the Queen's portrait.
110 15c. red and drab 20 10
111 60c. blue and red 35 20

1965. I.C.Y. As T **24b** of Pitcairn Islands, but with British and French cyphers in place of the Queen's portrait.
112 5c. purple and turquoise . . 15 10
113 55c. green and lavender . . . 20 20

1966. Churchill Commemoration. As T **24c** of Pitcairn Islands, but with British and French cyphers in place of the Queen's portrait.
114 5c. blue 20 10
115 15c. green 40 10
116 25c. brown 50 10
117 30c. violet 50 10

1966. World Cup Football Championship. As T **25** of Pitcairn Islands, but with British and French cyphers in place of the Queen's portrait.
118 20c. multicoloured 30 15
119 40c. multicoloured 70 15

1966. Inauguration of W.H.O. Headquarters, Geneva. As T **24** of Montserrat, but with British and French cyphers in place of the Queen's portrait.
120 25c. black, green and blue . . 15 10
121 60c. black, purple and ochre 40 20

1966. 20th Anniv of U.N.E.S.C.O. As T **25b/d** of Pitcairn Islands, but with British and French cyphers in place of the Queen's portrait.
122 15c. multicoloured 25 10
123 30c. yellow, violet and olive 65 10
124 45c. black, purple and orange 75 15

36 The Coast Watchers

1967. 25th Anniv of Pacific War. Multicoloured.
125 15c. Type **36** 15 10
126 25c. Map of war zone, U.S. marine and Australian soldier 40 20
127 60c. H.M.A.S. "Canberra" (cruiser) 45 30
128 1f. Boeing B-17 "Flying Fortress" 45 60

40 Globe and Hemispheres

1968. Bicent of Bougainville's World Voyage.
130 **40** 15c. green, violet and red 15 10
131 – 25c. olive, purple and blue 30 10
132 – 60c. brown, purple & green 35 10
DESIGNS: 25c. Ships "La Boudeuse" and "L'Etoile", and map; 60c. Bougainville, ship's figure-head and bougainvillea flowers.

43 Concorde and Vapour Trails

1968. Anglo-French Concorde Project.
133 **43** 25c. blue, red and blue . . 35 20
134 – 60c. red, black and blue . . 40 25
DESIGN: 60c. Concorde in flight.

45 Kauri Pine

1969. Timber Industry.
135 **45** 20c. multicoloured 10 10

46 Cyphers, Flags and Relay Runner receiving Baton

1969. 3rd South Pacific Games, Port Moresby. Multicoloured.
136 25c. Type **46** 10 10
137 1f. Runner passing baton . . 20 20

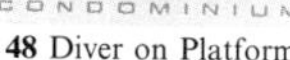

48 Diver on Platform

52 General Charles de Gaulle

51 U.P.U. Emblem and Headquarters Building

1969. Pentecost Island Land Divers. Mult.
138 15c. Type **48** 10 10
139 25c. Diver jumping 10 10
140 1f. Diver at end of fall . . . 20 20

1970. New U.P.U. Headquarters Building.
141 **51** 1f.05 slate, orange & purple 15 15

1970. 30th Anniv of New Hebrides' Declaration for the Free French Government.
142 **52** 65c. multicoloured 35 70
143 1f.10 multicoloured 45 70

1970. No. 101 surch **35**.
144 35c. on 20c. black, green and blue 30 30

54 "The Virgin and Child" (Bellini)

57 Kauri Pine, Cone and Arms of Royal Society

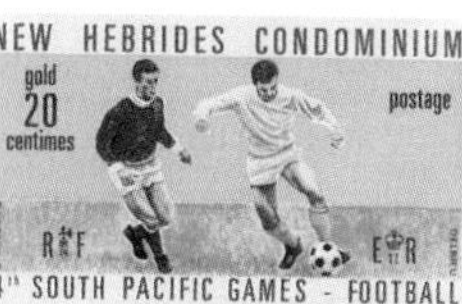

56 Football

1970. Christmas. Multicoloured.
145 15c. Type **54** 10 10
146 50c. "The Virgin and Child" (Cima) 20 20

1971. Death of General Charles de Gaulle. Nos. 142/3 optd **1890-1970 IN MEMORIAM 9-11-70**.
147 **52** 65c. multicoloured 15 10
148 1f.10 multicoloured 15 20

1971. 4th South Pacific Games, Papeete, French Polynesia.
149 20c. Type **56** 10 10
150 65c. Basketball (vert) 30 20

1971. Royal Society's Expedition to New Hebrides.
151 **57** 65c. multicoloured 20 15

58 "The Adoration of the Shepherds" (detail, Louis le Nain)

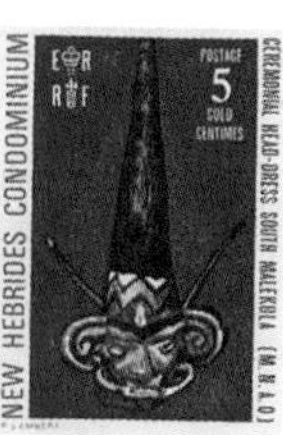

60 Ceremonial Headdress, South Malekula

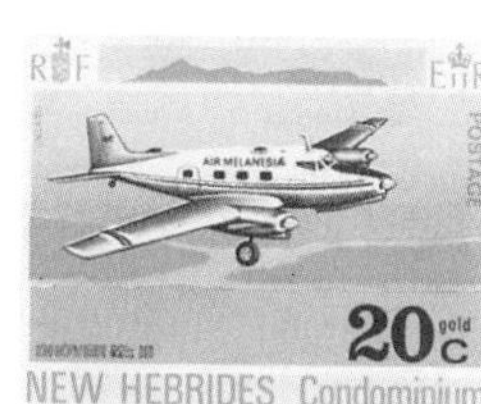

59 De Havilland Drover 3

1971. Christmas. Multicoloured.
152 25c. Type **58** 10 10
153 50c. "The Adoration of the Shepherds" (detail, Tintoretto) 30 60

1972. Aircraft. Multicoloured.
154 20c. Type **59** 30 15
155 25c. Short S25 Sandringham 4 flying boat 30 15
156 30c. De Havilland Dragon Rapide 30 15
157 65c. Sud Aviation SE 210 Caravelle . . . . 75 1·25

1972. Multicoloured.
158 5c. Type **60** 10 20
159 10c. Baker's pigeon 25 20
160 15c. Gong and carving, North Ambrym 15 20
161 20c. Red-headed parrot finch 40 25
162 25c. Graskoin's cowrie (shell) 40 25
163 30c. Red-lip olive (shell) . . 50 30
164 35c. Chestnut-bellied kingfisher 65 40
165 65c. Pretty conch (shell) . . . 75 60
166 1f. Gong (North Malekula) and carving (North Ambrym) . . . . 50 1·00
167 2f. Palm lorikeet . . . . . . 3·50 4·50
168 3f. Ceremonial headdress, South Malekula (different) 1·50 6·00
169 5f. Great green turban (shell) 4·00 13·00

61 "Adoration of the Kings" (Spranger)

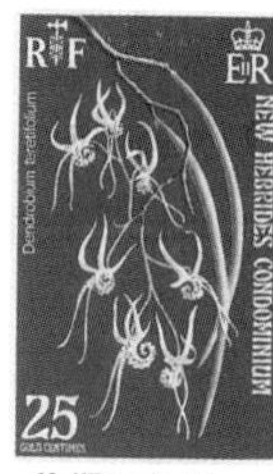

63 "Dendrobium teretifolium"

1972. Christmas. Multicoloured.
170 25c. Type **61** 10 10
171 70c. "The Virgin and Child in a Landscape" (Provoost) 20 20

1972. Royal Silver Wedding. As T **98** of Gibraltar, but with Royal and French cyphers in background.
172 35c. violet 15 10
173 65c. green 20 10

1973. Orchids. Multicoloured.
174 25c. Type **63** 25 10
175 30c. "Ephemerantha comata" 25 10
176 35c. "Spathoglottis petri" . . 30 10
177 65c. "Dendrobium mohlianum" 60 55

64 New Wharf at Vila

65 Wild Horses

1973. Opening of New Wharf at Villa. Mult.
178 25c. Type **64** 20 10
179 70c. As Type **64** but horiz . . 40 30

1973. Tanna Island. Multicoloured.
180 35c. Type **65** 30 15
181 70c. Yasur Volcano 55 20

66 Mother and Child

1973. Christmas. Multicoloured.
182 35c. Type **66** 10 10
183 70c. Lagoon scene 20 20

67 Pacific Pigeon

1974. Wild Life. Multicoloured.
184 25c. Type **67** 60 25
185 35c. "Lyssa curvata" (moth) 60 60
186 70c. Green sea turtle 60 70
187 1f.15 Grey-headed flying fox 80 1·50

1974. Royal Visit. Nos. 164 and 167 optd **ROYAL VISIT 1974**.
188 35c. multicoloured 40 10
189 2f. multicoloured 60 40

69 Old Post Office

1974. Inaug of New Post Office, Vila. Mult.
190 35c. Type **69** 15 50
191 70c. New Post Office 15 60

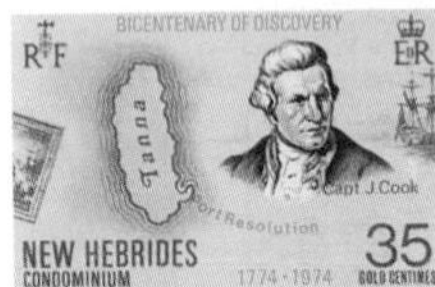

70 Capt. Cook and Map

1974. Bicent of Discovery. Multicoloured.
192 35c. Type **70** . . . . 1·25 2·00
193 35c. William Wales and beach landing . . . . . . 1·25 2·00
194 35c. William Hodges and island scene . . . . 1·25 2·00
195 1f.15 Capt. Cook, map and H.M.S. "Resolution" (59 × 34 mm) . . . . . . 2·50 3·50

71 U.P.U. Emblem and Letters

1974. Centenary of U.P.U.
196 **71** 70c. multicoloured 30 70

72 "Adoration of the Magi" (Velazquez)

74 Canoeing

73 Charolais Bull

1974. Christmas. Multicoloured.
197 35c. Type **72** 10 10
198 70c. "The Nativity" (Gerard van Honthorst) 20 20

1975.
199 **73** 10f. brown, green and blue 7·00 18·00

1975. World Scout Jamboree, Norway. Mult.
200 25c. Type **74** 15 10
201 35c. Preparing meal 15 10
202 1f. Map-reading 35 15
203 5f. Fishing . . . . 1·25 2·50

75 "Pitti Madonna" (Michelangelo)

77 Telephones of 1876 and 1976

76 Concorde in British Airways Livery

1975. Christmas. Michelangelo's Sculptures. Mult.
204 35c. Type **75** 10 10
205 70c. "Bruges Madonna" . . 15 10
206 2f.50 "Taddei Madonna" . . 70 50

1976. 1st Commercial Flight of Concorde.
207 **76** 5f. multicoloured . . . . . 5·00 5·00

1976. Centenary of Telephone. Multicoloured.
208 25c. Type **77** 15 10
209 70c. Alexander Graham Bell 30 10
210 1f.15 Satellite and Noumea Earth Station 50 50

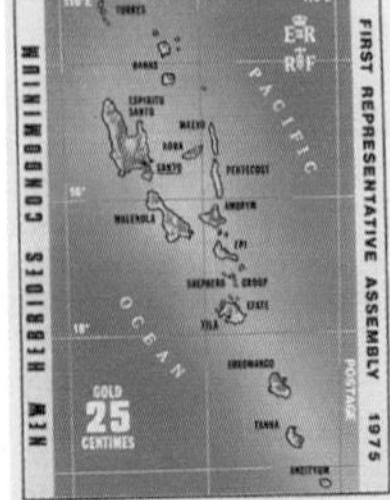

78 Map of the Islands

1976. Constitutional Changes. Multicoloured.
211 25c. Type **78** 40 15
212 1f. View of Santo (horiz) . . 75 60
213 2f. View of Vila (horiz) . . 1·10 2·00
Nos. 212/13 are smaller, 36 × 26 mm.

79 "The Flight into Egypt" (Lusitano)

80 Royal Visit, 1974

1976. Christmas. Multicoloured.
214 35c. Type **79** 10 10
215 70c. "Adoration of the Shepherds" 15 10
216 2f.50 "Adoration of the Magi" 45 50
Nos. 215/16 show retables by the Master of Santos-o-Novo.

1977. Silver Jubilee. Multicoloured.
217 35c. Type **80** 10 10
218 70c. Imperial State Crown . . 15 10
219 2f. The Blessing 30 65

1977. Currency change. Nos. 158/69 and 199 surch.
233 5f. on 5c. Type **60** 50 15
234 10f. on 10c. Baker's pigeon 50 15
222 15f. on 15c. Gong and carving . . . . 60 1·25
223 20f. on 20c. Red-headed parrot finch . . . . 1·25 55
224 25f. on 25c. Gaskoin's cowrie (shell) . . . . 1·75 1·75
225 30f. on 30c. Red-lip olive (shell) . . . . 1·75 80
226 35f. on 35c. Chestnut-bellied kingfisher . . . . 1·75 1·25
239 40f. on 65c. Pretty conch (shell) . . . . 1·50 55
228 50f. on 1f. Gong and carving 1·00 1·75
229 70f. on 2f. Palm lorikeet . . 5·00 75
230 100f. on 3f. Ceremonial headdress . . . . 1·00 3·75
231 200f. on 5f. Great green turban (shell) . . . . . 5·00 14·00
241 500f. on 10f. Type **73** . . . . 19·00 14·00

89 Island of Erromango and Kauri Pine

90 "Tempi Madonna" (Raphael)

1977. Islands. Multicoloured.
242 5f. Type **89** 30 10
243 10f. Territory map and copra-making 40 30
244 15f. Espiritu Santo and cattle 30 30
245 20f. Efate and Vila P.O. . . . 30 25
246 25f. Malekula and headdresses 40 40
247 30f. Aobe, Maewo and pigs' tusks 45 50
248 35f. Pentecost and land diver 50 65
249 40f. Tanna and John Frum Cross 70 60
250 50f. Shepherd Is. and canoe 1·00 40
251 70f. Banks Is. and dancers . . 1·75 3·50
252 100f. Ambrym and idols . . 1·75 90
253 200f. Aneityum and baskets 1·75 2·50
254 500f. Torres Is. and archer fisherman . . . . 4·00 7·50

1977. Christmas. Multicoloured.
255 10f. Type **90** 20 35
256 15f. "The Flight into Egypt" (Gerard David) 30 50
257 30f. "Virgin and Child" (Batoni) 40 85

91 Concorde over New York

1978. Concorde Commemoration.
258 10f. Type **91** . . . . 1·00 75
259 20f. Concorde over London 1·25 1·00
260 30f. Concorde over Washington . . . . 1·60 1·40
261 40f. Concorde over Paris . . 1·90 1·60

92 White Horse of Hanover

93 "Madonna and Child"

1978. 25th Anniv of Coronation.
262 **92** 40f. brown, blue and silver 15 30
263 – 40f. multicoloured 15 30
264 – 40f. brown, blue and silver 15 30
DESIGNS: No. 263, Queen Elizabeth II; 264, Gallic Cock.

1978. Christmas. Paintings by Durer. Mult.
265 10f. Type **93** 10 10
266 15f. "The Virgin and Child with St. Anne" 10 10
267 30f. "Madonna of the Siskin" 15 10
268 40f. "Madonna of the Pear" 20 15

1979. 1st Anniv of Internal Self-Government. Surch **166°E 11.1.79 FIRST ANNIVERSARY INTERNAL SELF-GOVERNMENT** and new value.
269 **78** 10f. on 25f. multicoloured (blue background) . . . 10 10
270 40f. on 25f. multicoloured (green background) . . . 20 20

95 1938 5c. Stamp and Sir Rowland Hill

96 Chubwan Mask

1979. Death Centenary of Sir Rowland Hill. Mult.
271 10f. Type **95** 10 10
272 20f. 1969 25c. Pentecost Island Land Divers commemorative 20 10
273 40f. 1925 2d. (20c.) 25 20
MS274 143 × 94 mm. Nos. 272 and F286 . . . . 75 90

1979. Arts Festival. Multicoloured.
275 5f. Type **96** 10 10
276 10f. Nal-Nal clubs and spears 10 10
277 20f. Ritual puppet 15 10
278 40f. Neqatmalow headdress 25 15

97 "Native Church" (Metas Masongo)

1979. Christmas and International Year of the Child. Children's Drawings. Multicoloured.
279 5f. Type **97** 10 10
280 10f. "Priest and Candles" (Herve Rutu) 10 10
281 20f. "Cross and Bible" (Mark Deards) (vert) 10 10
282 40f. "Green Candle and Santa Claus" (Dev Raj) (vert) 15 15

98 White-bellied Honeyeater

1980. Birds. Multicoloured.
283 10f. Type **98** 50 10
284 20f. Scarlet robin 70 10
285 30f. Yellow-fronted white-eye 90 45
286 40f. Fan-tailed cuckoo . . . 1·00 70

POSTAGE DUE STAMPS

1925. Optd **POSTAGE DUE.**
D1 **5** 1d. (10c.) green . . . . . . 30·00 1·00
D2 2d. (20c.) grey . . . . 35·00 1·00
D3 3d. (30c.) red . . . . 35·00 2·50
D4 5d. (50c.) blue . . . . 40·00 4·50
D5 10d. (1c.) red on blue . . . 45·00 5·50

1938. Optd **POSTAGE DUE.**
D 6 6 5c. green 24·00 35·00
D 7 10c. orange 24·00 35·00
D 8 20c. red 28·00 50·00
D 9 40c. olive 35·00 60·00
D10 1f. red on green 45·00 70·00

1953. Nos. 68/9, 71, 74 and 76 optd **POSTAGE DUE.**
D11 7 5c. green 4·00 12·00
D12 10c. red 1·75 9·00
D13 20c. blue 5·00 18·00
D14 – 40c. sepia (No. 74) 7·00 28·00
D15 – 1f. orange (No. 76) 4·50 28·00

1957. Optd **POSTAGE DUE.**
D16 12 5c. green 30 1·50
D17 10c. red 30 1·50
D18 20c. blue 75 1·75
D19 – 40c. sepia (No. 90) 1·00 2·50
D20 – 1f. orange (No. 92) 1·25 3·25

FRENCH ADMINISTRATION

1908. Stamps of New Caledonia optd **NOUVELLES HEBRIDES.**
F1 15 5c. green 4·50 4·50
F2 10c. red 5·50 3·50
F3 16 25c. blue on green 5·75 2·25
F4 50c. red on green 7·00 4·75
F5 17 1f. blue on green 17·00 20·00

1910. Nos. F1/5 further optd **CONDOMINIUM.**
F 6 15 5c. green 2·25 3·00
F 7 10c. red 2·25 1·25
F 8 16 25c. blue on green 2·25 3·75
F 9 50c. red on orange 6·50 9·75
F10 17 1f. blue on green 14·00 22·00

The following issues are as stamps of British Administration but are inscr "NOUVELLES HEBRIDES" except where otherwise stated.

1911.
F11 3 5c. green 1·00 2·75
F12 10c. red 50 75
F13 20c. grey 1·00 2·25
F25 25c. blue 1·25 5·50
F15 30c. brown on yellow 6·50 5·25
F16 40c. red on yellow 1·40 3·75
F17 50c. olive 2·00 3·75
F18 75c. orange 7·00 23·00
F19 1f. red on blue 2·50 3·00
F20 2f. violet 8·50 22·00
F21 5f. red on green 12·00 35·00

1920. Surch in figures.
F34 5c. on 40c. red on yellow (No. F16) 27·00 90·00
F32a 5c. on 50c. red on orange (No. F4) £425 £425
F33 5c. on 50c. red on orange (No. F9) 2·40 10·00
F38 10c. on 5c. green (No. F11) 1·00 4·50
F33a 10c. on 25c. blue on green (No. F8) 50 1·50
F35 20c. on 30c. brown on yellow (No. F26) 11·00 65·00
F39 30c. on 10c. red (No. F12) 1·00 2·50
F41 50c. on 25c. blue (No. F25) 2·50 23·00

1921. Stamp of New Hebrides (British) surch **10c.**
F37 10c. on 5d. green (No. 24) 11·00 50·00

1925.
F42 5 5c. (½d.) black 75 10·00
F43 10c. (1d.) green 1·00 9·00
F44 20c. (2d.) grey 1·75 2·75
F45 25c. (2½d.) brown 1·50 9·00
F46 30c. (3d.) red 1·50 7·00
F47 40c. (4d.) red on yellow 1·50 7·00
F48 50c. (5d.) blue 1·50 1·75
F49 75c. (7½d.) brown 1·50 12·00
F50 1f. (10d.) red on blue 1·50 2·50
F51 2f. (1s.8d.) violet 2·50 23·00
F52 5f. (4d.) red on green 3·50 23·00

1938.
F53 6 5c. green 1·90 4·50
F54 10c. orange 1·60 1·40
F55 15c. violet 1·25 3·25
F56 20c. red 1·60 2·75
F57 25c. brown 4·50 3·25
F58 30c. blue 4·00 3·50
F59 40c. olive 1·25 7·50
F60 50c. purple 1·25 2·25
F61 1f. red on green 1·75 4·25
F62 2f. blue on green 26·00 28·00
F63 5f. red on yellow 50·00 45·00
F64 10f. violet and blue £120 90·00

1941. Free French Issue. As last, optd **France Libre.**
F65 6 5c. green 2·00 23·00
F66 10c. orange 3·00 22·00
F67 15c. violet 5·00 35·00
F68 20c. red 16·00 30·00
F69 25c. brown 19·00 38·00
F70 30c. blue 19·00 32·00
F71 40c. olive 17·00 35·00
F72 50c. purple 17·00 32·00
F73 1f. red on green 18·00 32·00
F74 2f. blue on green 16·00 32·00
F75 5f. red on yellow 16·00 32·00
F76 10f. violet on blue 16·00 32·00

1949. 75th Anniv of U.P.U.
F77 10c. orange 2·25 4·75
F78 15c. violet 3·50 8·50
F79 30c. blue 5·00 11·00
F80 50c. purple 6·00 14·00

1953.
F81 7 5c. green 1·75 2·50
F82 10c. red 2·80 2·50
F83 15c. yellow 2·50 2·75
F84 20c. blue 2·50 2·50
F85 – 25c. olive 1·25 2·50
F86 – 30c. brown 1·25 2·75
F87 – 40c. sepia 1·75 2·75
F88 – 50c. violet 1·25 2·50
F89 – 1f. orange 8·50 7·00
F90 – 2f. purple 15·00 45·00
F91 – 5f. red 18·00 85·00

1956. 50th Anniv of Condominium.
F92 10 5c. green 1·00 2·00
F93 10c. red 1·00 2·25
F94 – 20c. blue 65 2·50
F95 – 50c. violet 1·00 2·50

1957.
F 96 12 5c. green 40 1·50
F 97 10c. red 1·25 2·00
F 98 15c. yellow 1·50 2·25
F 99 20c. blue 1·40 1·75
F100 – 25c. olive 1·25 1·50
F101 – 30c. brown 1·40 1·50
F102 – 40c. sepia 2·00 1·00
F103 – 50c. violet 2·00 1·40
F104 – 1f. orange 5·50 3·75
F105 – 2f. mauve 11·00 21·00
F106 – 5f. black 22·00 48·00

F 7 Emblem and Globe

1963. Freedom from Hunger.
F107 F 7 60c. green and brown 10·00 15·00

F 8 Centenary Emblem

F 9 "Syncom" Communications Satellite, Telegraph Poles and Morse Key

1963. Centenary of Red Cross.
F108 F 8 15c. red, grey and orange 7·25 8·25
F109 45c. red, grey and bistre 9·75 24·00

1963.
F110 – 5c. lake, brown and blue 55 65
F111 – 10c. brown, buff and green* 1·25 2·00
F112 – 10c. brown, buff and green 75 1·60
F113 18 15c. bistre, brown and violet 6·00 1·25
F114 – 20c. black, green and blue* 2·25 3·75
F115 – 20c. black, green and blue 1·50 1·60
F116 – 25c. violet, brown and red 70 1·10
F117 – 30c. brown, bistre and violet 7·50 1·25
F118 – 40c. red and blue 3·25 7·50
F119 – 50c. green, yellow and turquoise 8·50 1·60
F120 – 60c. red and blue 1·75 1·90
F121 – 1f. red, black and green 2·00 4·00
F122 – 2f. black, brown and olive 17·00 8·00
F123 – 3f. multicoloured* 10·50 26·00
F124 – 3f. multicoloured 7·00 11·00
F125 – 5f. blue, indigo and black 22·00 28·00

The stamps indicated by an asterisk have "RF" wrongly placed on the left.

1965. Centenary of I.T.U.
F126 F 9 15c. blue, green and brown 5·75 8·25
F127 60c. red, grey and green 11·00 27·00

1965. I.C.Y. As Nos. 112/13.
F128 5c. purple and turquoise 2·50 5·00
F129 55c. green and lavender 9·50 12·00

1966. Churchill Commem. As Nos. 114/17.
F130 5c. multicoloured 2·10 3·00
F131 15c. multicoloured 3·00 1·90
F132 25c. multicoloured 3·50 5·50
F133 30c. multicoloured 4·25 5·00

1966. World Cup Football Championship. As Nos. 118/19.
F134 20c. multicoloured 1·90 4·00
F135 40c. multicoloured 3·50 4·00

1966. Inauguration of W.H.O. Headquarters, Geneva. As Nos. 120/1.
F136 25c. black, green and blue 2·50 3·50
F137 60c. black, mauve and ochre 3·50 7·50

1966. 20th Anniv of U.N.E.S.C.O. As Nos. 122/4.
F138 15c. multicoloured 1·50 2·25
F139 30c. yellow, violet and olive 2·25 3·50
F140 45c. black, purple and orange 2·25 4·25

1967. 25th Anniv of Pacific War. As Nos. 125/8.
F141 15c. multicoloured 1·60 1·50
F142 25c. multicoloured 1·90 3·00
F143 60c. multicoloured 2·10 2·50
F144 1f. multicoloured 2·50 2·75

1968. Bicentenary of Bougainville's World Voyage. As Nos. 130/2.
F145 15c. green, violet and red 55 1·10
F146 25c. olive, purple and blue 65 1·25
F147 60c. brown, purple and green 1·10 1·50

1968. Anglo-French Concorde Project. As Nos. 133/4.
F148 25c. blue, red and violet 1·90 2·40
F149 60c. red, black and blue 2·25 4·25

1969. Timber Industry. As No. 135.
F150 20c. multicoloured 45 1·00

1969. 3rd South Pacific Games, Port Moresby, Papua New Guinea. As Nos. 136/7.
F151 25c. multicoloured 50 1·40
F152 1f. multicoloured 1·50 2·00

1969. Land Divers of Pentecost Island. As Nos. 138/40.
F153 15c. multicoloured 55 1·25
F154 25c. multicoloured 45 1·25
F155 1f. multicoloured 1·10 2·00

1970. Inauguration of New U.P.U. Headquarters Building, Berne. As No. 141.
F156 1f.05 slate, orange & purple 90 2·25

1970. New Hebrides' Declaration for the Free French Government. As Nos. 142/3.
F157 65c. multicoloured 1·50 2·00
F158 1f.10 multicoloured 1·75 2·25

1970. No. F115 surch **35.**
F159 35c. on 20c. black, green and blue 65 1·50

1970. Christmas. As Nos. 145/6.
F160 15c. multicoloured 25 1·00
F161 50c. multicoloured 45 1·25

1971. Death of General Charles de Gaulle. Nos. F157/8 optd **1890-1970 IN MEMORIAM 9-11-70.**
F162 65c. multicoloured 1·00 1·50
F163 1f.10 multicoloured 1·50 2·00

1971. 4th South Pacific Games, Papeete, French Polynesia. As Nos. 149/50.
F164 20c. multicoloured 75 1·00
F165 65c. multicoloured 1·00 1·50

1971. Royal Society Expedition to New Hebrides. As No. 151.
F166 65c. multicoloured 90 1·50

1971. Christmas. As Nos. 152/3.
F167 25c. multicoloured 50 75
F168 50c. multicoloured 60 1·25

1972. Aircraft. As Nos. 154/7.
F169 20c. multicoloured 1·00 1·60
F170 25c. multicoloured 1·00 1·60
F171 30c. multicoloured 1·10 1·60
F172 65c. multicoloured 2·75 5·00

1972. As Nos. 158/69.
F173 5c. multicoloured 85 1·40
F174 10c. multicoloured 1·90 1·75
F175 15c. multicoloured 90 1·25
F176 20c. multicoloured 2·50 1·50
F177 25c. multicoloured 1·90 1·60
F178 30c. multicoloured 1·90 1·50
F179 35c. multicoloured 3·00 1·50
F180 65c. multicoloured 2·40 2·00
F181 1f. multicoloured 2·40 2·75
F182 2f. multicoloured 15·00 13·50
F183 3f. multicoloured 7·50 17·00
F184 5f. multicoloured 10·00 30·00

1972. Christmas. As Nos. 170/1.
F185 25c. multicoloured 45 1·00
F186 70c. multicoloured 65 1·50

1972. Royal Silver Wedding. As Nos. 172/3.
F187 35c. multicoloured 50 50
F188 65c. multicoloured 60 1·25

1973. Orchids. As Nos. 174/7.
F189 25c. multicoloured 2·75 1·40
F190 30c. multicoloured 2·75 1·60
F191 35c. multicoloured 2·75 1·60
F192 65c. multicoloured 4·75 5·00

1973. Opening of New Wharf at Vila. As Nos. 178/9.
F193 25c. multicoloured 80 1·10
F194 70c. multicoloured 1·10 2·25

1973. Tanna Island. As Nos. 180/1.
F195 35c. multicoloured 2·25 2·25
F196 70c. multicoloured 3·25 3·25

1973. Christmas. As Nos. 182/3.
F197 35c. multicoloured 50 1·00
F198 70c. multicoloured 75 2·25

1974. Wild Life. As Nos. 184/7.
F199 25c. multicoloured 4·50 3·25
F200 35c. multicoloured 5·75 2·40
F201 70c. multicoloured 6·00 4·75
F202 1f.15 multicoloured 7·50 11·00

1974. Royal Visit of Queen Elizabeth II. Nos. F179 and F182 optd **VISITE ROYALE 1974.**
F203 35c. Chestnut-bellied kingfisher 3·00 90
F204 2f. Green palm lorikeet 6·50 8·25

1974. Inauguration of New Post Office, Vila. As Nos. 190/1.
F205 35c. multicoloured 1·00 2·00
F206 70c. multicoloured 1·00 2·00

1974. Bicent of Discovery. As Nos. 192/5.
F207 35c. multicoloured 5·00 5·75
F208 35c. multicoloured 5·00 5·75
F209 35c. multicoloured 5·00 5·75
F210 1f.15 multicoloured 9·50 12·00

1974. Centenary of U.P.U. As No. 196.
F210a 70c. blue, red and black 1·40 2·75

1974. Christmas. As Nos. 197/8.
F211 35c. multicoloured 40 75
F212 70f. multicoloured 60 1·25

1975. Charolais Bull. As No. 199.
F213 10f. brown, green and blue 30·00 45·00

1975. World Scout Jamboree, Norway. As Nos. 200/3.
F214 25c. multicoloured 70 50
F215 35c. multicoloured 75 60
F216 1f. multicoloured 1·25 1·25
F217 5f. multicoloured 6·50 10·00

1975. Christmas. As Nos. 204/6.
F218 35c. multicoloured 35 50
F219 70c. multicoloured 55 90
F220 2f.50 multicoloured 1·90 3·00

1976. 1st Commercial Flight of Concorde. As No. 207, but Concorde in Air France livery.
F221 5f. multicoloured 15·00 14·00

1976. Centenary of Telephone. As Nos. 208/10.
F222 25c. multicoloured 60 50
F223 70c. multicoloured 1·50 1·50
F224 1f.15 multicoloured 1·75 2·75

1976. Constitutional Changes. As Nos. 211/13.
F225 25c. multicoloured 60 50
F226 1f. multicoloured 1·50 1·25
F227 2f. multicoloured 2·50 2·75

1976. Christmas. Paintings. As Nos. 214/16.
F228 35c. multicoloured 30 30
F229 70c. multicoloured 50 50
F230 2f.50 multicoloured 1·75 3·00

1977. Silver Jubilee. As Nos. F217/9.
F231 35c. multicoloured 30 20
F232 70c. multicoloured 55 35
F233 2f. multicoloured 55 65

1977. Currency change. Nos. F173/84 and F213, surch.
F234 5f. on 5c. multicoloured 1·00 1·25
F235 10f. on 10c. multicoloured 2·50 1·25
F236 15f. on 15c. multicoloured 1·25 1·25
F237 20f. on 20c. multicoloured 3·00 1·50
F238 25f. on 25c. multicoloured 2·50 1·75
F239 30f. on 30c. multicoloured 2·50 2·25
F240 35f. on 35c. multicoloured 4·25 2·25
F241 40f. on 65c. multicoloured 3·25 3·00
F242 50f. on 1f. multicoloured 2·50 3·00
F243 70f. on 2f. multicoloured 7·50 4·00
F244 100f. on 3f. multicoloured 3·50 6·00
F245 200f. on 5f. multicoloured 13·00 25·00
F246 500f. on 10f. multicoloured 23·00 45·00

1977. Islands. As Nos. 242/54.
F256 5f. multicoloured 1·25 1·75
F257 10f. multicoloured 1·00 1·75
F258 15f. multicoloured 2·00 1·75
F259 20f. multicoloured 2·00 1·75
F260 25f. multicoloured 2·00 1·75
F261 30f. multicoloured 2·00 1·75
F262 35f. multicoloured 2·75 1·75
F263 40f. multicoloured 1·50 2·25
F264 50f. multicoloured 2·75 2·25
F265 70f. multicoloured 5·50 4·50
F266 100f. multicoloured 4·50 4·00
F267 200f. multicoloured 6·00 12·00
F268 500f. multicoloured 10·00 18·00

1977. Christmas. As Nos. 255/7.
F269 10f. multicoloured 30 30
F270 15f. multicoloured 50 50
F271 30f. multicoloured . . . . 80 1·40

1978. Concorde. As Nos. 258/61.
F272 10f. multicoloured . . . . 2·50 1·50
F273 20f. multicoloured . . . . 2·75 1·75
F274 30f. multicoloured . . . . 3·25 2·25
F275 40f. multicoloured . . . . 3·75 3·50

1978. Coronation. As Nos. 262/4.
F276 40f. brown, blue and silver 25 70
F277 40f. multicoloured 25 70
F278 40f. brown, blue and silver 25 70

1978. Christmas. As Nos. 265/8.
F279 10f. multicoloured 15 30
F280 15f. multicoloured 20 35
F281 30f. multicoloured 30 70
F282 40f. multicoloured 35 85

1979. Internal Self-Government. As T **37** surch **166°E PREMIER GOUVERNEMENT AUTONOME 11.1.78. 11.1.79** and new value.
F283 10f. on 25f. multicoloured (blue background) . . . 90 1·00
F284 40f. on 25f. multicoloured (green background) . . . 1·60 1·75

1979. Death Centenary of Sir Rowland Hill. As Nos. 271/3.
F285 10f. multicoloured 35 50
F286 20f. multicoloured 35 60
F287 40f. multicoloured . . . . 40 1·00

1979. Arts Festival. As Nos. 273/8.
F288 5f. multicoloured 30 50
F289 10f. multicoloured 30 50
F290 20f. multicoloured 40 70
F291 40f. multicoloured . . . . 60 1·10

1979. Christmas and International Year of the Child. As Nos. 279/82.
F292 5f. multicoloured 85 60
F293 10f. multicoloured . . . . 1·00 60
F294 20f. multicoloured . . . . 1·10 80
F295 40f. multicoloured . . . . 1·90 2·00

1980. Birds. As Nos. 283/6.
F296 10f. multicoloured . . . . 1·10 1·75
F297 20f. multicoloured . . . . 1·40 2·00
F298 30f. multicoloured . . . . 1·75 2·75
F299 40f. multicoloured . . . . 1·90 3·25

POSTAGE DUE STAMPS

1925. Nos. F32 etc, optd **CHIFFRE TAXE**.
FD53 **5** 10c. (1d.) green . . . . . 48·00 3·00
FD54 20c. (2d.) grey . . . . . 55·00 3·00
FD55 30c. (3d.) red . . . . . 55·00 3·00
FD56 50c. (5d.) blue . . . . . 45·00 3·00
FD57 1f. (10d.) red on blue . . 45·00 3·00

1938. Optd **CHIFFRE TAXE**.
FD65 **6** 5c. green . . . . 14·00 48·00
FD66 10c. orange . . . . 17·00 48·00
FD67 20c. red . . . . 23·00 50·00
FD68 40c. olive . . . . 48·00 £100
FD69 1f. red on green . . . . . 48·00 £120

1941. Free French Issue. As last optd **France Libre**.
FD77 **6** 5c. green . . . . 12·00 32·00
FD78 10c. orange . . . . 12·00 32·00
FD79 20c. red . . . . 12·00 32·00
FD80 40c. olive . . . . 16·00 32·00
FD81 1f. red on green . . . . . 15·00 32·00

1953. Optd **TIMBRE-TAXE**.
FD92 **7** 5c. green . . . . 7·50 19·00
FD93 10c. red . . . . 6·00 18·00
FD94 20c. blue . . . . 19·00 28·00
FD95 – 40c. sepia (No. F87) . . . 12·00 26·00
FD96 – 1f. orange (No. F89) . . . 17·00 48·00

1957. Optd **TIMBRE-TAXE**.
FD107 **12** 5c. green . . . . 90 9·00
FD108 10c. red . . . . 1·40 9·00
FD109 20c. blue . . . . 2·75 13·00
FD110 – 40c. sepia (No. F102) . . 6·50 26·00
FD111 – 1f. orange (No. F104) . . 5·50 32·00

For later issues see **VANUATU**.

NEW REPUBLIC Pt. 1

A Boer republic originally part of Zululand. It was incorporated with the South African Republic in 1888 and annexed to Natal in 1903.

12 pence = 1 shilling;
20 shillings = 1 pound.

1

1886. On yellow or blue paper.
1 **1** 1d. black . . . . † £3000
2 1d. violet . . . . 10·00 12·00
73 2d. violet . . . . 8·50 8·50
74 3d. violet . . . . 13·00 13·00
75 4d. violet . . . . 13·00 13·00
81 6d. violet . . . . 8·00 8·00
82 9d. violet . . . . 8·50 8·50
83 1s. violet . . . . 8·50 8·50
77 1s.6d. violet . . . . 14·00 14·00
85 2s. violet . . . . 18·00 16·00
86 2s.6d. violet . . . . 23·00 23·00
87 3s. violet . . . . 42·00 42·00
88 4s. violet . . . . 11·00 11·00
89 5s. violet . . . . 13·00 13·00
90 5s.6d. violet . . . . 12·00 12·00
91 7s.6d. violet . . . . 14·00 17·00
92 10s. violet . . . . 12·00 12·00
93 10s.6d. violet . . . . 16·00 16·00
44 12s. violet £300
23 13s. violet £400
94 £1 violet . . . . 45·00 45·00
25 30s. violet . . . . 95·00

Some stamps are found with Arms embossed in the paper, and others with the Arms and without a date above "ZUID-AFRIKA".

NEW SOUTH WALES Pt. 1

A S.E. state of the Australian Commonwealth, whose stamps it now uses.

12 pence = 1 shilling;
20 shillings = 1 pound.

1 Seal of the Colony **8**

1850. Imperf.
11 **1** 1d. red £2250 £275
25 2d. blue £1800 £130
42 3d. green £2500 £225

1851. Imperf.
47 **8** 1d. red £900 £110
83 1d. orange . . . . £200 18·00
86 2d. blue . . . . £140 8·50
87 3d. green . . . . £250 28·00
76 6d. brown £1600 £250
79 8d. yellow £3500 £600

16 **11**

1854. Imperf.
109 **16** 1d. red . . . . £160 22·00
112 2d. blue . . . . £140 9·00
115 3d. green . . . . £800 80·00
88 **11** 5d. green £1000 £600
90 6d. grey . . . . £400 35·00
96 6d. brown . . . . £450 35·00
98 8d. orange £3500 £850
100 1s. red . . . . £750 70·00

For these stamps perforated, see No. 134 etc.

24

1860. Perf.
195 **16** 1d. red . . . . 42·00 15·00
134 2d. blue . . . . 95·00 10·00
226e 3d. green . . . . 5·50 80
329 **11** 5d. green . . . . 7·50 1·25
143 6d. brown . . . . £275 45·00
165 6d. violet . . . . 60·00 4·75
218 8d. orange . . . . £110 17·00
168 1s. red . . . . 90·00 7·50
297c **24** 5s. purple . . . . 42·00 13·00

26 **28**

1862. Queen Victoria. Various frames.
207 **26** 1d. red . . . . 7·50 65
210 **28** 2d. blue . . . . 10·00 65
230c – 4d. brown . . . . 32·00 1·50
234 – 6d. lilac . . . . 48·00 1·25
310 – 10d. lilac . . . . 13·00 5·00
237 – 1s. black . . . . 22·00 3·00

1871. As No. 310, surch **NINEPENCE**.
236d 9d. on 10d. brown . . . . 8·00 6·50

42

1885.
238b **42** 5s. green and lilac . . . . £350 85·00
277b 10s. red and violet . . . £180 48·00
240a £1 red and lilac £2750

45 View of Sydney **46** Emu

52 Capt. Arthur Phillip, 1st Governor, and Lord Carrington, Governor in 1888

55 Allegorical Figure of Australia

1888. Cent of New South Wales.
253 **45** 1d. mauve . . . . 4·00 50
254 **46** 2d. blue . . . . 7·00 20
338 – 4d. brown . . . . 9·50 3·50
256 – 6d. red . . . . 21·00 3·50
297fb – 6d. green . . . . 22·00 9·00
342 – 6d. yellow . . . . 11·00 2·25
257 – 8d. purple . . . . 18·00 3·25
347 – 1s. brown . . . . 22·00 1·75
263 – 5s. violet . . . . £140 28·00
350b **52** 20s. blue . . . . £160 60·00

DESIGNS—As Type **45**: 4d. Capt. Cook; 6d. Queen Victoria and Arms; 8d. Superb lyrebird; 1s. Kangaroo. As Type **52**: 5s. Map of Australia.

1890.
265 **55** 2½d. blue . . . . 3·50 50

1891. Types as 1862, but new value and colours, surch in words.
266 **26** ½d. on 1d. grey . . . . . 3·00 3·75
267a – 7½d. on 6d. brown . . . 5·00 2·75
268d – 12½d. on 1s. red . . . . 11·00 9·00

58 **62**

63 **64**

66 Superb Lyrebird **67**

1892.
272 **58** ½d. grey . . . . 2·25 20
298 ½d. green . . . . 1·00 30
300 **62** 1d. red . . . . 1·25 10
335 **63** 2d. blue . . . . 2·00 10
296 **64** 2½d. violet . . . . 8·00 1·25
303 2½d. blue . . . . 3·25 70
352 **67** 9d. brown and blue . . . 9·00 1·50
349a **66** 2s.6d. green . . . . . . 30·00 18·00

60

1897. Diamond Jubilee and Hospital Charity.
280 **60** 1d. (1s.) green and brown 40·00 40·00
281 – 2½d. (2s.6d.) gold & blue £170 £170

DESIGN—VERT: 2½d. Two female figures.

OFFICIAL STAMPS

1879–92. Various issues optd **O S**.

A. Issues of 1854 to 1871
O20b **26** 1d. red . . . . 8·50 1·40
O21c **28** 2d. blue . . . . 8·00 1·00
O25c **16** 3d. green . . . . 5·00 3·50
O27a – 4d. brown (No. 230c) . . 13·00 3·50
O28 **11** 5d. green . . . . 13·00 15·00
O31 – 6d. lilac (No. 234) . . . 20·00 6·00
O32b **11** 8d. orange . . . . 22·00 10·00
O11 – 9d. on 10d. (No. 236d) £450
O18a – 10d. lilac (No. 310) . . . £160 £100
O33 – 1s. black (No. 237) . . . 25·00 7·50
O18 **24** 5s. purple . . . . £180 8·50

B. Fiscal stamps of 1885.
O37 **24** 10s. red and violet £1600 £650
O38 £1 red and violet £7000 £4500

C. Issue of 1888 (Nos. 253/346b).
O39 1d. mauve . . . . 2·50 50
O40 2d. blue . . . . 4·25 30
O41 4d. brown . . . . 11·00 3·50
O42 6d. red . . . . 8·50 5·00
O43 8d. purple . . . . 20·00 11·00
O44 1s. brown . . . . 19·00 3·75
O49a 5s. violet . . . . £170 70·00
O48 20s. blue £1700 £800

D. Issues of 1890 and 1892
O58a **58** ½d. grey . . . . 5·00 11·00
O55 **26** ½d. on 1d. grey . . . . 55·00 55·00
O54 **55** 2½d. blue . . . . 8·50 7·00
O56 – 7½d. on 6d. (No. 283) . . 35·00 38·00
O57 – 12½d. on 1s. (No. 284c) 60·00 70·00

POSTAGE DUE STAMPS

D 1

1891.
D 1 **D 1** ½d. green . . . . 3·75 3·00
D 2a 1d. green . . . . 7·00 1·25
D 3 2d. green . . . . 11·00 1·75
D 4 3d. green . . . . 20·00 4·00
D 5 4d. green . . . . 13·00 1·75
D 6 6d. green . . . . 23·00 4·75
D 7 8d. green . . . . 70·00 15·00
D 8 5s. green . . . . £120 42·00
D 9a 10s. green £200 £120
D10b 20s. green £250 £150

REGISTRATION STAMPS

15

1856.
102 **15** (6d.) red and blue (Imp) £800 £170
106 (6d.) orange and blue (Imp) £950 £180
127 (6d.) red and blue (Perf) 85·00 18·00
120 (6d.) orange and blue (Perf) . . . . £375 60·00

NEW ZEALAND Pt. 1

A group of islands in the south Pacific Ocean. A Commonwealth Dominion.

1855. 12 pence = 1 shilling;
20 shillings = 1 pound.
1967. 100 cents = 1 dollar.

1

3

1855. Imperf.
35 **1** 1d. red £375 £225
34 1d. orange £425 £190
39 2d. blue . . . . £300 70·00
40 3d. lilac £325 £130
43 6d. brown . . . . £750 90·00
45 1s. green £950 £250

1862. Perf.
110 **1** 1d. orange . . . . £120 28·00
132 1d. brown . . . . £110 32·00
114 2d. blue . . . . £120 18·00
133 2d. orange . . . . £100 25·00
117 3d. lilac . . . . 95·00 28·00
119 4d. red £2250 £250
120 4d. yellow . . . . £150 95·00
122 6d. brown . . . . £170 24·00
136 6d. blue . . . . £120 50·00
125 1s. green . . . . £150 85·00

1873.
151 **3** ½d. pink . . . . 9·50 1·25

5

6

7

8

9

10

11

1874. Inscr "POSTAGE".
180 **5** 1d. lilac . . . . 40·00 3·75
181 **6** 2d. red . . . . 42·00 2·25
154 **7** 3d. brown . . . . £100 55·00
182 **8** 4d. purple . . . . £140 42·00
183 **9** 6d. blue . . . . 80·00 10·00
184 **10** 1s. green . . . . £120 38·00
185 **11** 2s. red £325 £275
186 5s. grey £350 £275

13

16

19 F 4

1882. Inscr "POSTAGE & REVENUE".
236 **13** ½d. black . . . . 3·75 15
237 **10** 1d. red . . . . 3·75 10
238 **9** 2d. mauve . . . . 10·00 30
239 **16** 2½d. blue . . . . 45·00 3·75
198 **10** 3d. yellow . . . . 42·00 6·50
222 **6** 4d. green . . . . 50·00 4·00
200 **19** 5d. black . . . . 48·00 13·00
224b **8** 6d. brown . . . . 55·00 7·00
202 **9** 8d. blue . . . . 65·00 45·00
226 **7** 1s. brown . . . . 75·00 6·50

1882.
F 90 **F 4** 2s. blue . . . . 25·00 4·00
F 99 2s.6d. brown . . . . . 27·00 4·50
F100 3s. mauve . . . . . . 70·00 6·00
F102 5s. green . . . . . . 70·00 8·50
F 87 10s. brown . . . . . . £130 18·00
F 77 £1 red . . . . £170 50·00

The above are revenue stamps authorised for use as postage stamps as there were no other postage stamps available in these denominations. Other values in this and similar types were mainly used for revenue purposes.

23 Mount Cook or Aorangi

24 Lake Taupo and Mount Ruapehu

26 Lake Wakatipu and Mount Earnslaw

25 Pembroke Peak, Milford Sound

28 Sacred Huia Birds

29 White Terrace, Rotomahana

30 Otira Gorge and Mount Ruapehu

31 Brown Kiwi

32 Maori War Canoe

33 Pink Terrace, Rotomahana

34 Kea and Kaka

35 Milford Sound

1898.
246 **23** ½d. purple . . . . 5·50 1·00
302 ½d. green . . . . 5·50 60
247 **24** 1d. blue and brown . . . 4·50 30
248 **25** 2d. red . . . . 26·00 20
249 **26** 2½d. blue (A)* . . . . . 7·50 28·00
320 2½d. blue (B)* . . . . . 14·00 35·00
309 **28** 3d. brown . . . . 26·00 1·50
252 **29** 4d. red . . . . 13·00 17·00
311a **30** 5d. brown . . . . 25·00 5·00
254 **31** 6d. green . . . . 50·00 30·00
265 6d. red . . . . 35·00 4·00
325 **32** 8d. blue . . . . 27·00 11·00
326 **33** 9d. purple . . . . 27·00 8·00
268a **34** 1s. orange . . . . 50·00 4·00
328 **35** 2s. green . . . . 70·00 24·00
329 – 5s. red £170 £200

DESIGN—As Type **30**: 5s. Mount Cook.
*Type A of 2½d. is inscr "WAKITIPU", Type B "WAKATIPU".

40 Commemorative of the New Zealand Contingent in the South African War

1900.
274 **29** 1d. red . . . . 13·00 10
275b **40** 1½d. brown . . . . . . 9·50 4·00
319 **25** 2d. purple . . . . 5·50 1·75
322d **24** 4d. blue and brown . . . 4·00 2·50

The 1d., 2d. and 4d. are smaller than the illustrations of their respective types.

42

44 Maori Canoe "Te Arawa"

1901.
303 **42** 1d. red . . . . 3·00 10

1906. New Zealand Exhibition, Christchurch. Inscr "COMMEMORATIVE SERIES OF 1906".
370 **44** ½d. green . . . . 21·00 29·00
371 – 1d. red . . . . 16·00 16·00
372 – 3d. brown and blue . . . . 48·00 75·00
373 – 6d. red and green £170 £250

DESIGNS: 1d. Maori art; 3d. Landing of Cook; 6d. Annexation of New Zealand.

50

51 King Edward VII

53 Dominion

1907.
386 **50** 1d. red . . . . 22·00 1·50
383 **28** 3d. brown . . . . 35·00 15·00
376 **31** 6d. red . . . . 40·00 8·00
385 **34** 1s. orange . . . . £120 24·00

These are smaller in size than the 1898 and 1901 issues. Type **50** also differs from Type **42** in the corner ornaments.

1909.
387 **51** ½d. green . . . . 4·25 50
405 **53** 1d. red . . . . 1·75 10
388 **51** 2d. mauve . . . . 9·50 6·50
389 3d. brown . . . . 23·00 1·25
390a 4d. orange . . . . 6·00 6·50
391a 5d. brown . . . . 17·00 2·75
392 6d. red . . . . 40·00 1·25
393 8d. blue . . . . 10·00 1·25
394 1s. red . . . . 48·00 2·75

1913. Auckland Industrial Exhibition. Optd **AUCKLAND EXHIBITION, 1913.**
412 **51** ½d. green . . . . 13·00 48·00
413 **53** 1d. red . . . . 19·00 40·00
414 **51** 3d. brown £130 £250
415 6d. red £160 £275

62 King George V

1915.
446 **62** ½d. green . . . . 1·00 30
416 1½d. grey . . . . 3·00 1·75
438 1½d. brown . . . . 2·25 20
417a 2d. violet . . . . 7·00 35·00
439 2d. yellow . . . . 2·25 20
419 2½d. blue . . . . 3·25 5·00
449 3d. brown . . . . 7·50 65
421 4d. yellow . . . . 4·25 50·00
422e 4d. violet . . . . 7·00 50
423 4½d. green . . . . 12·00 23·00
424 5d. blue . . . . 6·50 1·00
425 6d. red . . . . 8·00 50
426 7½d. brown . . . . 10·00 23·00
427 8d. blue . . . . 11·00 50·00
428 8d. brown . . . . 18·00 1·50
429 9d. green . . . . 17·00 2·75
430c 1s. orange . . . . 14·00 50

1915. No. 446 optd **WAR STAMP** and stars.
452 **62** ½d. green . . . . 1·75 50

64 "Peace" and Lion

65 "Peace" and Lion

1920. Victory. Inscr "VICTORY" or dated "1914 1919" (6d.).
453 **64** ½d. green . . . . 3·00 2·50
454 **65** 1d. red . . . . 4·50 60
455 – 1½d. orange . . . . . . 3·00 50
456 – 3d. brown . . . . 12·00 14·00
457 – 6d. violet . . . . 13·00 17·00
458 – 1s. orange . . . . 20·00 48·00

DESIGNS—HORIZ (As Type **65**): 1½d. Maori chief. (As Type **64**): 3d. Lion; 1s. King George V. VERT (As Type **64**): 6d. "Peace" and "Progress".

1922. No. 453 surch **2d. 2d. TWOPENCE.**
459 **64** 2d. on ½d. green . . . . 3·50 1·40

69 New Zealand

70 Exhibition Buildings

1923. Restoration of Penny Postage.
460 **69** 1d. red . . . . 3·00 60

1925. Dunedin Exhibition.
463 **70** ½d. green on green . . . . 3·00 11·00
464 1d. red on rose . . . . . 3·50 5·50
465 4d. mauve on mauve . . . 30·00 70·00

71

73 Nurse

1926.
468 **71** 1d. red 75 20
469 – 2s. blue . . . . 50·00 22·00
470 – 3s. mauve . . . . 85·00 £140

The 2s. and 3s. are larger, 21 × 25 mm.

1929. Anti-T.B. Fund.
544 **73** 1d.+1d. red . . . . 11·00 18·00

1930. Inscr "HELP PROMOTE HEALTH".
545 **73** 1d.+1d. red . . . . 20·00 32·00

74 Smiling Boy

F 6 "Arms" Type

75 New Zealand Lake Scenery

1931. Health Stamps.
546 **74** 1d.+1d. red . . . . 75·00 75·00
547 2d.+1d. blue . . . . 75·00 60·00

1931. Air.
548 **75** 3d. brown . . . . 24·00 15·00
549 4d. purple . . . . 24·00 19·00
550 7d. orange . . . . 27·00 9·00

1931. Air. Surch **FIVE PENCE.**
551 **75** 5d. on 3d. green . . . . . 10·00 8·00

1931. Various frames.
F191 **F 6** 1s.3d. yellow . . . . . 9·00 1·75
F192 1s.3d. yellow and black 1·75 1·25
F193 2s.6d. brown . . . . . 8·50 60
F194 4s. red . . . . 15·00 1·00
F195 5s. green . . . . . . 18·00 1·00
F196 6s. red . . . . 32·00 3·25
F197 7s. blue . . . . 32·00 5·50
F198 7s.6d. grey . . . . . 60·00 50·00
F153 8s. violet . . . . . . 28·00 32·00
F154 9s. orange . . . . . . 30·00 29·00
F201 10s. red . . . . 30·00 2·25
F156 12s.6d. purple £140 £140
F202 15s. green . . . . . . 42·00 19·00
F203 £1 pink . . . . 28·00 3·75
F159 25s. blue £300 £400
F205w 30s. brown £225 £100
F161 35s. yellow £2500 £2750
F206 £2 violet . . . . . . 85·00 21·00
F207 £2 10s. red £250 £275
F208w £3 green . . . . . . £120 48·00
F165 £3 10s. red £1300 £1100
F210 £4 blue £140 £120
F167 £4 10s. grey £1000 £1100
F211w £5 blue . . . . £170 45·00

77 Hygeia Goddess of Health

78 The Path to Health

1932. Health Stamp.
552 **77** 1d.+1d. red . . . . 20·00 27·00

1933. Health Stamp.
553 **78** 1d.+1d. red . . . . 13·00 17·00

1934. Air. Optd **TRANS-TASMAN AIR MAIL "FAITH IN AUSTRALIA."**.
554 **75** 7d. blue . . . . 35·00 40·00

80 Crusader

1934. Health Stamp.
555 **80** 1d.+1d. red . . . . 11·00 17·00

81 Collared Grey Fantail

83 Maori Woman

86 Maori Girl

85 Mt. Cook

87 Mitre Peak

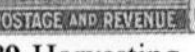
89 Harvesting

91 Maori Panel

93 Capt. Cook at Poverty Bay

1935.
556 **81** ½d. green . . . . 1·50 75
557 – 1d. red . . . . 1·75 60
558a **83** 1½d. brown . . . . . . 5·50 6·50
580 – 2d. orange 30 10
581c **85** 2½d. brown and grey . . 50 4·00
561 **86** 3d. brown . . . . . . 12·00 2·50
583d **87** 4d. black and brown . . 1·00 10
584c – 5d. blue . . . . 2·00 1·25
585c **89** 6d. red . . . . 1·25 10
586d – 8d. brown . . . . . . 3·75 70
631 **91** 9d. red and black . . . . 3·50 2·75
588 – 1s. green . . . . 2·50 60
589e **93** 2s. olive . . . . 6·50 1·50
590c – 3s. chocolate and brown 4·00 2·25
DESIGNS—As Type **81**: 1d. Brown kiwi; 2d. Maori carved house; 1s. Parson bird. As Type **87**: 8d. Tuatara lizard. As Type **85**: 5d. Swordfish; 3s. Mt. Egmont.

95 Bell Block Aerodrome

1935. Air.
570 **95** 1d. red . . . . 1·00 70
571 3d. violet . . . . 5·00 3·00
572 6d. blue . . . . 9·50 3·00

96 King George V and Queen Mary

1935. Silver Jubilee.
573 **96** ½d. green . . . . 75 1·00
574 1d. red . . . . 1·00 80
575 6d. orange . . . . 17·00 25·00

97 "The Key to Health"

99 N.Z. Soldier at Anzac Cove

1935. Health Stamp.
576 **97** 1d.+1d. red . . . . 2·50 2·75

1936. Charity. 21st Anniv of "Anzac" Landing at Gallipoli.
591 **99** ½d.+½d. green . . . . . . 60 1·75
592 1d.+1d. red . . . . 60 1·40

100 Wool

1936. Congress of British Empire Chambers of Commerce, Wellington. Inscr as in T **100**.
593 **100** ½d. green 30 30
594 – 1d. red (Butter) 30 20
595 – 2½d. blue (Sheep) . . . . 1·00 8·00
596 – 4d. violet (Apples) . . . . 80 5·50
597 – 6d. brown (Exports) . . . 2·25 4·50

105 Health Camp

1936. Health Stamp.
598 **105** 1d.+1d. red . . . . . . 1·75 3·75

106 King George VI and Queen Elizabeth

1937. Coronation.
599 **106** 1d. red 30 10
600 2½d. blue . . . . 80 2·25
601 6d. orange . . . . 1·10 2·00

107 Rock climbing

108 King George VI

1937. Health Stamp.
602 **107** 1d.+1d. red . . . . . . 2·50 3·50

1938.
603 **108** ½d. green . . . . 6·50 10
604 ½d. orange 20 30
605 1d. red . . . . 5·00 10
606 1d. green 20 10
607 1½d. brown . . . . . . 26·00 2·25
608 1½d. red 20 50
680 2d. orange 15 10
609 3d. blue 20 10
681 4d. purple 70 50
682 5d. grey 50 90
683 6d. red 50 10
684 8d. violet 65 50
685 9d. brown . . . . 1·75 50
686b – 1s. brown and red . . . 50 80
687 – 1s.3d. brown and blue 1·25 1·25
688 – 2s. orange and green . . 3·75 2·50
689 – 3s. brown and grey . . . 3·50 3·50
The shilling values are larger, 22 × 25½ mm, and "NEW ZEALAND" appears at the top.

109 Children playing

110 Beach Ball

1938. Health Stamp.
610 **109** 1d.+1d. red . . . . . . 5·50 2·75

1939. Health Stamps. Surch.
611 **110** 1d. on ½d.+½d. green . . 4·25 4·25
612 2d. on 1d.+1d. red . . . 4·25 4·25

1939. Surch in bold figures.
F212 F **6** 3/6 on 3s.6d. green . . . 20·00 7·00
F214 5/6 on 5s.6d. lilac . . . 48·00 18·00
F215 11/- on 11s. yellow . . . 75·00 48·00
F216 22/- on 22s. red £275 £130
F186 35/- on 35s. orange . . . £425 £225

112 "Endeavour", Chart of N.Z. and Captain Cook

1940. Centenary of Proclamation of British Sovereignty. Inscr "CENTENNIAL OF NEW ZEALAND 1840 1940".
613 – ½d. green 30 10
614 **112** 1d. brown and red . . . 2·75 10
615 – 1½d. blue and mauve . . 30 60
616 – 2d. green and brown . . 1·50 10
617 – 2½d. green and blue . . . 2·00 1·00
618 – 3d. purple and red . . . 3·75 1·00
619 – 4d. brown and red . . . 13·00 1·50
620 – 5d. blue and brown . . . 7·00 3·75
621 – 6d. green and violet . . . 11·00 1·25
622 – 7d. black and red . . . . 1·50 4·00
623 – 8d. black and red . . . . 11·00 3·00
624 – 9d. green and orange . . 7·50 2·00
625 – 1s. green and deep green 13·00 3·75
DESIGNS—HORIZ (as T **112**): ½d. Arrival of the Maoris, 1350; 1½d. British Monarchs; 2d. Abel Tasman with "Heemskerk" and chart; 3d. Landing of immigrants, 1840; 4d. Road, rail, ocean and air transport; 6d. "Dunedin" and "frozen mutton" sea route to London; 7, 8d. Maori council; 9d. Gold mining methods, 1861 and 1940. (25 × 21 mm): 5d. H.M.S. "Britomart" at Akaroa, 1840. VERT (21 × 25 mm): 2½d. Treaty of Waitangi. (As T **112**): 1s. Giant kauri tree.

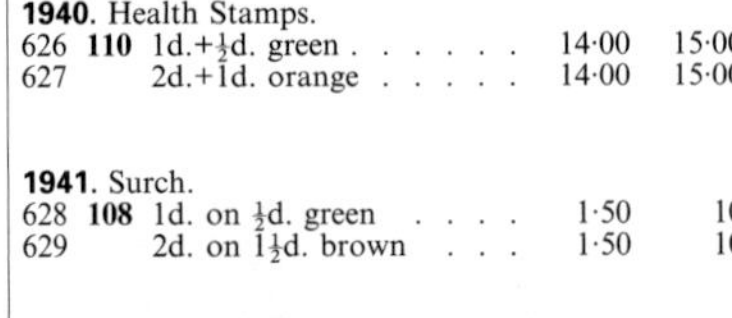

1940. Health Stamps.
626 **110** 1d.+½d. green . . . . . 14·00 15·00
627 2d.+1d. orange . . . . . 14·00 15·00

1941. Surch.
628 **108** 1d. on ½d. green . . . . 1·50 10
629 2d. on 1½d. brown . . . 1·50 10

1941. Health Stamps. Optd **1941**.
632 **110** 1d.+½d. green . . . . . 40 2·25
633 2d.+1d. orange . . . . . 40 2·25

125 Boy and Girl on Swing

1942. Health Stamps.
634 **125** 1d.+½d. green . . . . . 30 1·00
635 2d.+1d. orange . . . . . 30 1·00

126 Princess Margaret

1943. Health Stamps.
636 **126** 1d.+½d. green . . . . . 20 1·25
637 – 2d.+1d. brown 20 25
DESIGN: 2d. Queen Elizabeth II as Princess.

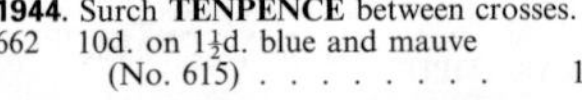

1944. Surch **TENPENCE** between crosses.
662 10d. on 1½d. blue and mauve (No. 615) 15 20

129 Queen Elizabeth II as Princess and Princess Margaret

130 Peter Pan Statue, Kensington Gardens

1944. Health Stamps.
663 **129** 1d.+½d. green 30 40
664 2d.+1d. blue 30 30

1945. Health Stamps.
665 **130** 1d.+½d. green and buff . . 15 20
666 2d.+1d. red and buff . . 15 20

131 Lake Matheson

132 King George VI and Parliament House, Wellington

133 St. Paul's Cathedral

139 "St. George" (Wellington College War Memorial window)

1946. Peace Issue.
667 **131** ½d. green and brown . . . 20 60
668 **132** 1d. green 10 10
669 **133** 1½d. red 10 40
670 – 2d. purple 15 10
671 – 3d. blue and grey 30 15
672 – 4d. green and orange . . 20 20
673 – 5d. green and blue . . . 40 60
674 – 6d. brown and red . . . 15 30
675 **139** 8d. black and red 15 20
676 – 9d. blue and black . . . 15 20
677 – 1s. grey 15 30
DESIGNS—As Type **132**: 2d. The Royal Family. As Type **131**: 3d. R.N.Z.A.F. badge and airplanes; 4d. Army badge, tank and plough; 5d. Navy badge, H.M.N.Z.S. "Achilles" (cruiser) and "Dominion Monarch" (liner); 6d. N.Z. coat of arms, foundry and farm; 9d. Southern Alps and Franz Josef Glacier. As T **139**: 1s. National Memorial campanile.

142 Soldier helping Child over Stile

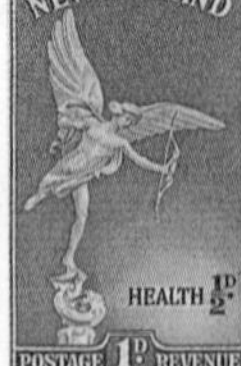
145 Statue of Eros

1946. Health Stamps.
678 **142** 1d.+½d. green and orange 15 15
679 2d.+1d. brown & orange 15 15

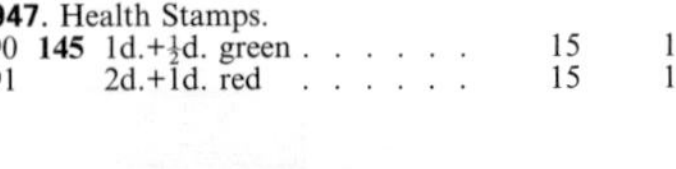

1947. Health Stamps.
690 **145** 1d.+½d. green 15 15
691 2d.+1d. red 15 15

146 Port Chalmers, 1848

1948. Centenary of Otago. Various designs inscr "CENTENNIAL OF OTAGO".
692 **146** 1d. blue and green . . . 20 30
693 – 2d. green and brown . . . 20 30
694 – 3d. purple 20 50
695 – 6d. black and red 20 50
DESIGNS—HORIZ: 2d. Cromwell, Otago; 6d. Otago University. VERT: 3d. First Church, Dunedin.

150 Boy sunbathing and Children playing **151** Nurse and Child

1948. Health Stamps.
696 **150** 1d.+½d. blue and green 15 15
697 2d.+1d. purple and red 15 15

1949. Health Stamps.
698 **151** 1d.+½d. green 25 20
699 2d.+1d. blue 25 20

1950. As Type F **6**, but without value, surch **1½d. POSTAGE.**
700 1½d. red 30 30
Type F **6** is illustrated next to Type **74**.

153 Queen Elizabeth II and Prince Charles **155** Cairn on Lyttleton Hills

1950. Health Stamps.
701 **153** 1d.+½d. green 20 15
702 2d.+1d. purple 20 15

1950. Centenary of Canterbury, N.Z.
703 – 1d. green and blue 30 50
704 **155** 2d. red and orange 30 50
705 – 3d. deep blue and blue 30 70
706 – 6d. brown and blue 40 70
707 – 1s. purple and blue 60 90
DESIGNS—VERT: 1d. Christchurch Cathedral; 3d. John Robert Godley. HORIZ: 6d. Canterbury University College; 1s. Aerial view of Timaru.

159 "Takapuna" class Yachts

1951. Health Stamps.
708 **159** 1½d.+½d. red and yellow 20 90
709 2d.+1d. green and yellow 20 20

160 Princess Anne **161** Prince Charles

1952. Health Stamps.
710 **160** 1½d.+½d. red 15 30
711 **161** 2d.+1d. brown 15 20

1952. Surch in figures.
712 **108** 1d. on ½d. orange 30 90
713 3d. on 1d. green 10 10

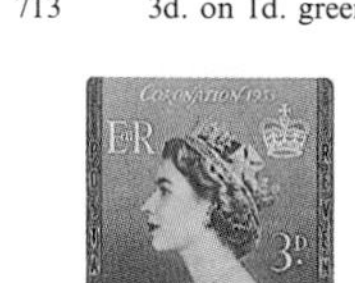

164 Queen Elizabeth II **166** Westminster Abbey

165 Coronation State Coach

1953. Coronation.
714 – 2d. blue 30 30
715 **164** 3d. brown 30 10
716 **165** 4d. red 1·25 2·50
717 **166** 8d. grey 80 1·60
718 – 1s.6d. purple and blue 2·00 2·75
DESIGNS—As Type **165**: 2d. Queen Elizabeth II and Buckingham Palace; 1s.6d. St. Edward's Crown and Royal Sceptre.

168 Girl Guides **169** Boy Scouts

1953. Health Stamps.
719 **168** 1½d.+½d. blue 15 10
720 **169** 2d.+1d. green 15 40

170 Queen Elizabeth II **171** Queen Elizabeth II and Duke of Edinburgh

1953. Royal Visit.
721 **170** 3d. purple 10 10
722 **171** 4d. blue 10 60

172 **173**

174 Queen Elizabeth II

1953. Small figures of value.
723 **172** ½d. black 15 30
724 1d. orange 15 10
725 1½d. red 20 10
726 2d. green 20 10
727 3d. red 20 10
728 4d. blue 40 50
729 6d. purple 70 1·40
730 8d. red 60 60
731 **173** 9d. brown and green 60 60
732 1s. black and red 65 10
733 1s.6d. black and blue 1·25 60
733c 1s.9d. black and orange 7·00 1·50
733d **174** 2s.6d. brown 18·00 8·00
734 3s. green 12·00 30
735 5s. red 17·00 4·25
736 10s. blue 40·00 18·00

175 Young Climber and Mts. Aspiring and Everest **176** Maori Mail-carrier

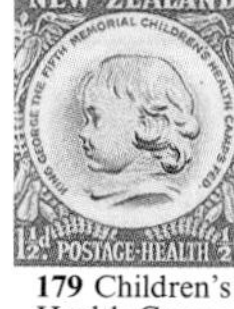

177 Queen Elizabeth II **179** Children's Health Camps Federation Emblem

1954. Health Stamps.
737 **175** 1½d.+½d. brown and violet 15 30
738 2d.+1d. brown and blue 15 30

1955. Centenary of First New Zealand Stamps. Inscr "1855–1955".
739 **176** 2d. brown and green 10 10
740 **177** 3d. red 10 10
741 – 4d. black and blue 60 80
DESIGN—HORIZ (As Type **176**): 4d. Douglas DC-3 airliner.

1955. Health Stamps.
742 **179** 1½d.+½d. brown and chestnut 10 40
743 2d.+1d. red and green 10 20
744 3d.+1d. brown and red 15 10

180 **183** Takahe

181 "The Whalers of Foveaux Strait"

1955. As 1953 but larger figures of value and stars omitted from lower right corner.
745 **180** 1d. orange 50 10
746 1½d. brown 60 60
747 2d. green 40 10
748b 3d. red 50 10
749 4d. blue 1·00 80
750 6d. purple 10·00 20
751 8d. brown 6·50 8·00

1956. Southland Centennial.
752 **181** 2d. green 30 15
753 – 3d. brown 10 10
754 **183** 8d. violet and red 1·25 1·75
DESIGN—As Type **181**: 3d. Allegory of farming.

184 Children picking Apples **185** New Zealand Lamb and Map

1956. Health Stamps.
755 **184** 1½d.+½d. brown 15 60
756 2d.+1d. green 15 50
757 3d.+1d. red 15 15

1957. 75th Anniv of First Export of N.Z. Lamb.
758 **185** 4d. blue 50 1·00
759 – 8d. red 75 1·25
DESIGN—HORIZ: 8d. Lamb, sailing ship "Dunedin" and "Port Brisbane" (refrigerated freighter).

187 Sir Truby King **188** Life-savers in Action

1957. 50th Anniv of Plunket Society.
760 **187** 3d. red 10 10

1957. Health Stamps.
761 **188** 2d.+1d. black and green 15 60
762 – 3d.+1d. blue and red 15 10
MS762b Two sheets, each 112 × 96 mm, with Nos. 761 and 762 in blocks of 6 (2 × 3) Per pair 9·00 23·00
DESIGN: 3d. Children on seashore.

1958. Surch.
763a **180** 2d. on 1½d. brown 15 10
808 2½d. on 3d. red 15 15

192 Boys' Brigade Bugler **193** Sir Charles Kingsford-Smith and Fokker F.IIa/3m Southern Cross

1958. Health Stamps.
764 – 2d.+1d. green 20 40
765 **192** 3d.+1d. blue 20 40
MS765a Two sheets, each 104 × 124 mm, with Nos. 764/5 in blocks of 6 (3 × 2) Per pair 7·00 16·00
DESIGN: 2d. Girls' Life Brigade cadet.

1958. 30th Anniv of 1st Air Crossing of Tasman Sea.
766 **193** 6d. blue 50 65

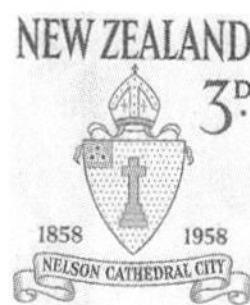

194 Seal of Nelson

1958. Centenary of City of Nelson.
767 **194** 3d. red 10 10

195 "Pania" Statue, Napier **196** Australian Gannets on Cape Kidnappers

1958. Centenary of Hawke's Bay Province.
768 **195** 2d. green 10 10
769 **196** 3d. blue 20 10
770 – 8d. brown 55 1·50
DESIGN—As Type **195**: 8d. Maori sheep-shearer.

197 "Kiwi", Jamboree Badge **198** Careening H.M.S. "Endeavour" at Ship Cove

1959. Pan-Pacific Scout Jamboree, Auckland.
771 **197** 3d. brown and red 30 10

1959. Centenary of Marlborough Province. Inscr as in T **198**.
772 **198** 2d. green 30 10
773 – 3d. blue 30 10
774 – 8d. brown 1·00 2·25
DESIGNS: 3d. Shipping wool, Wairau Bar, 1857; 8d. Salt industry, Grassmere.

201 Red Cross Flag

1959. Red Cross Commemoration.
775 **201** 3d.+1d. red and blue 20 10

202 Grey Teal **204** "The Explorer"

1959. Health Stamps.

776 **202** 2d.+1d. yellow, olive and red 50 65
777 – 3d.+1d. black, pink and blue 50 65
MS777c Two sheets, each 95×109 mm, with Nos. 776/7 in blocks of 6 (3×2) Per pair . . 8·00 21·00

DESIGN: 3d. New Zealand stilt.

1960. Centenary of Westland Province.

778 **204** 2d. green 20 10
779 – 3d. salmon 20 10
780 – 8d. black . . . . 70 3·00

DESIGNS: 3d. "The Gold Digger"; 8d. "The Pioneer Woman".

207 Manuka (Tea Tree)

215 Timber Industry

219 Taniwha (Maori Rock Drawing)

225 Sacred Kingfisher

1960.

781 **207** ½d. green and red . . . 10 10
782 – 1d. multicoloured . . . 10 10
783 – 2d. multicoloured . . . 10 10
784 – 2½d. multicoloured . . . 1·00 10
785 – 3d. multicoloured . . . 30 10
786 – 4d. multicoloured . . . 40 10
787 – 5d. multicoloured . . . 1·25 10
788 – 6d. lilac, green and turquoise 50 10
788d – 7d. red, green and yellow 50 1·40
789 – 8d. multicoloured . . . 40 10
790 – 9d. red and blue 40 10
791 **215** 1s. brown and green . . 30 10
792b – 1s.3d. red, sepia and blue . . . . 1·75 20
793 – 1s.6d. olive and brown 75 10
794 – 1s.9d. brown . . . . . 10·00 15
795 – 1s.9d. multicoloured . . 5·50 1·00
796 **219** 2s. black and buff . . . 2·50 10
797 – 2s.6d. yellow and brown 1·75 1·00
798 – 3s. sepia . . . . 23·00 75
799 – 3s. bistre, blue and green 3·25 1·75
800 – 5s. myrtle . . . . 3·00 80
801 – 10s. blue . . . . 5·50 3·25
802 – £1 mauve . . . . 12·00 6·00

DESIGNS—VERT (as Type **207**): 1d. Karaka; 2d. Kowhai Ngutu-kaka (Kaka Beak); 2½d. Titoki (plant); 3d. Kowhai; 4d. Puarangi (Hibiscus); 5d. Matua tikumu (Mountain daisy); 6d. Pikiarero (Clematis); 7d. Koromiko; 8d. Rata. (As T **215**): 1s.3d. Rainbow trout; 1s.6d. Tiki. (As T **219**): 5s. Sutherland Falls; £1 Potutu Geyser. HORIZ (as T **215**): 9d. National flag; 1s.9d. Aerial top-dressing. (As Type **219**): 2s.6d. Butter-making; 3s. Tongariro National Park and Chateau; 10s. Tasman Glacier.

1960. Health Stamps.

803 **225** 2d.+1d. sepia and blue . . 50 65
804 – 3d.+1d. purple & orange 50 65
MS804b Two sheets, each 95×107 mm, with Nos. 803/4 in blocks of 6 Per pair . . . . . 26·00 35·00

DESIGN: 3d. New Zealand pigeon.

227 "The Adoration of the Shepherds" (Rembrandt)

228 Great Egret

1960. Christmas.

805 **227** 2d. red & brown on cream 15 10

1961. Health Stamps.

806 **228** 2d.+1d. black and purple 50 65
807 – 3d.+1d. sepia and green 50 65
MS807a Two sheets, each 97×121 mm, with Nos. 806/7 in blocks of 6 (3×2) Per pair . . 26·00 28·00

DESIGN: 3d. New Zealand falcon.

232 "Adoration of the Magi" (Durer)

236 Tieke Saddleback

233 Morse Key and Port Hills, Lyttleton

1961. Christmas.

809 **232** 2½d. multicoloured . . . 10 10

1962. Telegraph Centenary.

810 **233** 3d. sepia and green . . . 10 10
811 – 8d. black and red 90 55

DESIGN: 8d. Modern teleprinter.

1962. Health Stamps.

812 – 2½d.+1d. multicoloured 50 65
813 **236** 3d.+1d. multicoloured . . 50 65
MS813b Two sheets, each 96×101 mm, with Nos. 812/13 in blocks of 6 (3×2) Per pair . . 45·00 50·00

DESIGN: 2½d. Red-fronted parakeet.

237 "Madonna in Prayer" (Sassoferrato)

238 Prince Andrew

1962. Christmas.

814 **237** 2½d. multicoloured . . . 10 10

1963. Health Stamps.

815 **238** 2½d.+1d. blue 30 70
816 – 3d.+1d. red 30 10
MS816a Two sheets, each 93×100 mm, with Nos. 815/16 in blocks of 6 (3×2) Per pair . . 23·00 35·00

DESIGN: 3d. Prince Andrew (different).

240 "The Holy Family" (Titian)

1963. Christmas.

817 **240** 2½d. multicoloured . . . 10 10

241 Steam Locomotive "Pilgrim" (1863) and Class DG Diesel Locomotive

1963. Centenary of New Zealand Railway. Inscr as in T **241**. Multicoloured.

818 3d. Type **241** 40 10
819 1s.9d. Diesel express and Mt. Ruapehu . . . . 1·50 1·50

243 "Commonwealth Cable"

1963. Opening of COMPAC (Trans-Pacific Telephone Cable).

820 **243** 8d. multicoloured . . . . 50 1·25

244 Road Map and Car Steering-wheel

1964. Road Safety Campaign.

821 **244** 3d. black, yellow and blue 30 10

245 Silver Gulls

1964. Health Stamps. Multicoloured.

822 2½d.+1d. Type **245** 40 50
823 3d.+1d. Little penguin . . . 40 50
MS823b Two sheets, each 171×84 mm, with Nos. 822/3 in blocks of 8 (4×2) Per pair . . 48·00 55·00

246 Rev. S. Marsden taking first Christian Service at Rangihoua Bay, 1814

1964. Christmas.

824 **246** 2½d. multicoloured . . . 10 10

1964. Surch **7D POSTAGE**.

825 F **6** 7d. on (–) red . . . . . . 50 1·50

248 Anzac Cove

1965. 50th Anniv of Gallipoli Landing.

826 **248** 4d. brown 10 10
827 – 5d. green and red 10 60

DESIGN: 5d. Anzac Cove and poppy.

249 I.T.U. Emblem and Symbols

250 Sir Winston Churchill

1965. Centenary of I.T.U.

828 **249** 9d. blue and brown . . . 55 35

1965. Churchill Commemoration.

829 **250** 7d. black, grey and blue 30 50

251 Wellington Provincial Council Building

252 Kaka

1965. Centenary of Government in Wellington.

830 **251** 4d. multicoloured 20 10

1965. Health Stamps. Multicoloured.

831 3d.+1d. Type **252** 40 50
832 4d.+1d. Collared grey fantail 40 50
MS832b Two sheets, each 100×109 mm, with Nos. 831/2 in blocks of 6 (3×2) Per pair . . 38·00 45·00

254 I.C.Y. Emblem

255 "The Two Trinities" (Murillo)

1965. International Co-operation Year.

833 **254** 4d. red and olive 20 10

1965. Christmas.

834 **255** 3d. multicoloured 10 10

256 Arms of New Zealand

1965. 11th Commonwealth Parliamentary Conf. Multicoloured.

835 4d. Type **256** 25 20
836 9d. Parliament House, Wellington, and Badge . . 65 1·25
837 2s. Wellington from Mt. Victoria . . . . 4·50 6·00

259 "Progress" Arrowhead

260 New Zealand Bell Bird

1966. 4th National Scout Jamboree, Trentham.

838 **259** 4d. gold and green . . . 15 10

1966. Health Stamps. Multicoloured.

839 3d.+1d. Type **260** 40 65
840 4d.+1d. Weka rail 40 65
MS841 Two sheets, each 107×91 mm. Nos. 839/40 in blocks of 6 (3×2) Per pair . . 22·00 48·00

262 "The Virgin with Child" (Maratta)

263 Queen Victoria and Queen Elizabeth II

1966. Christmas.

842 **262** 3d. multicoloured 10 10

1967. Centenary of New Zealand Post Office Savings Bank.

843 **263** 4d. black, gold and purple 10 10
844 – 9d. multicoloured 10 20

DESIGN: 9d. Half-sovereign of 1867 and commemorative dollar coin.

265 Manuka (Tea Tree)

268 Running with Ball

1967. Decimal Currency. Designs as earlier issues, but with values inscr in decimal currency as T **265**.

845 **265** ½c. blue, green and red 10 10
846 – 1c. mult (No. 782) . . 10 10
847 – 2c. mult (No. 783) . . 10 10
848 – 2½c. mult (No. 785) . . 10 10
849 – 3c. mult (No. 786) . . 10 10
850 – 4c. mult (No. 787) . . 30 10
851 – 5c. lilac, olive and green (No. 788) . . . 50 25
852 – 6c. mult (No. 788d) . . 50 60
853 – 7c. mult (No. 789) . . 60 60
854 – 8c. red and blue (No. 790) 60 30

855 **215** 10c. brown and green 60 30
856 – 15c. green and brown (No. 793) 1·75 1·00
857 **219** 20c. black and buff 1·25 10
858 – 25c. yellow and brown (No. 797) 1·50 2·00
859 – 30c. yellow, green and blue (No. 799) 1·50 25
860 – 50c. green (No. 800) 2·00 50
861 – $1 blue (No. 801) 9·00 70
862 – $2 mauve (No. 802) 4·00 6·00
F219a **F 6** $4 violet 2·50 1·50
F220a $6 green 3·00 3·00
F221a $8 blue 5·00 4·50
F222a $10 blue 6·00 3·75

For 15c. in different colours, see No. 874.

1967. Health Stamps. Rugby Football.
867 **268** 2½c.+1c. multicoloured 15 15
868 – 3c.+1c. multicoloured 15 15
MS869 Two sheets. (a) 76 × 130 mm (867). (b) 130 × 76 mm (868). Containing blocks of six Per pair 24·00 40·00

DESIGN—HORIZ: 3c. Positioning for place-kick.

271 Brown Trout **273** Forest and Timber

1967.
870 – 7c. multicoloured 1·50 90
871 **271** 7½c. multicoloured 50 70
872 – 8c. multicoloured 75 70
873 **273** 10c. multicoloured 50 10
874 – 15c. green, deep green and red (as No. 793) 1·00 1·00
875 – 18c. multicoloured 1·00 55
876 – 20c. multicoloured 1·00 20
877 – 25c. multicoloured 1·75 2·00
878 – 28c. multicoloured 60 10
879 – $2 black, ochre and blue (as No. 802) 13·00 13·00

DESIGNS: 7c. "Kaitia" (trawler) and catch; 8c. Apples and orchard; 18c. Sheep and the "Woolmark"; 20c. Consignments of beef and herd of cattle; 25c. Dairy farm, Mt. Egmont and butter consignment. VERT: 28c. Fox Glacier, Westland National Park.

No. 871 was originally issued to commemorate the introduction of the brown trout into New Zealand.

No. 874 is slightly larger than No. 793, measuring 21 × 25 mm, and the inscr and numerals differ in size.

278 "The Adoration of the Shepherds" (Poussin) **279** Mount Aspiring, Aurora Australis and Southern Cross

1967. Christmas.
880 **278** 2½c. multicoloured 10 10

1967. Cent of Royal Society of New Zealand.
881 **279** 4c. multicoloured 25 20
882 – 8c. multicoloured 25 80

DESIGN: 8c. Sir James Hector (founder).

281 Open Bible **282** Soldiers and Tank

1968. Centenary of Maori Bible.
883 **281** 3c. multicoloured 10 10

1968. New Zealand Armed Forces. Multicoloured.
884 4c. Type **282** 25 15
885 10c. Airmen, Fairey Firefly and English Electric Canberra aircraft 35 70
886 28c. Sailors and H.M.N.Z.S. "Achilles", 1939, and H.M.N.Z.S. "Waikato", 1968 50 2·25

285 Boy breasting Tape and Olympic Rings

1968. Health Stamps. Multicoloured.
887 2½c.+1c. Type **285** 20 15
888 3c.+1c. Girl swimming and Olympic rings 20 15
MS889 Two sheets, each 145 × 95 mm. Nos. 887/8 in blocks of 6 Per pair 16·00 42·00

287 Placing Votes in Ballot Box **288** Human Rights Emblem

1968. 75th Anniv of Universal Suffrage in New Zealand.
890 **287** 3c. ochre, green and blue 10 10

1968. Human Rights Year.
891 **288** 10c. red, yellow and green 10 30

289 "Adoration of the Holy Child" (G. van Honthorst)

1968. Christmas.
892 **289** 2½c. multicoloured 10 10

290 I.L.O. Emblem

1969. 50th Anniv of Int Labour Organization.
893 **290** 7c. black and red 15 30

291 Supreme Court Building, Auckland

1969. Centenary of New Zealand Law Society.
894 **291** 3c. multicoloured 10 10
895 – 10c. multicoloured 20 60
896 – 18c. multicoloured 30 1·25

DESIGNS—VERT: 10c. Law Society's coat of arms; 18c. "Justice" (from Memorial Window in University of Canterbury, Christchurch).

295 Student being conferred with Degree

1969. Centenary of Otago University. Mult.
897 3c. Otago University (vert) 10 10
898 10c. Type **295** 20 25

296 Boys playing Cricket

1969. Health Stamps.
899 **296** 2½c.+1c. multicoloured 40 65
900 – 3c.+1c. multicoloured 40 65
901 – 4c.+1c. brown and ultramarine 40 2·00
MS902 Two sheets, each 144 × 84 mm. Nos. 899/900 in blocks of 6 Per pair 16·00 48·00

DESIGNS—HORIZ: 3c. Girls playing cricket. VERT: 4c. Dr. Elizabeth Gunn (founder of first Children's Health Camp).

299 Oldest existing House in New Zealand, and Old Stone Mission Store, Kerikeri

1969. Early European Settlement in New Zealand, and 150th Anniv of Kerikeri. Multicoloured.
903 4c. Type **299** 20 25
904 6c. View of Bay of Islands 30 1·75

301 "The Nativity" (Federico Fiori Barocci) **306** Girl, Wheat Field and C.O.R.S.O. Emblem

302 Captain Cook, Transit of Venus and "Octant"

1969. Christmas.
905 **301** 2½c. multicoloured 10 10

1969. Bicentenary of Captain Cook's Landing in New Zealand.
906 **302** 4c. black, red and blue 75 35
907 – 6c. green, brown and black 1·00 2·50
908 – 18c. brown, green and black 1·75 2·50
909 – 28c. red, black and blue 2·75 4·00
MS910 109 × 90 mm. Nos. 906/9 18·00 35·00

DESIGNS: 6c. Sir Joseph Banks (naturalist) and outline of H.M.S. "Endeavour"; 18c. Dr. Daniel Solander (botanist) and his plant; 28c. Queen Elizabeth II and Cook's chart, 1769.

1969. 25th Anniv of C.O.R.S.O. (Council of Organizations for Relief Services Overseas). Multicoloured.
911 7c. Type **306** 35 1·10
912 8c. Mother feeding her child, dairy herd and C.O.R.S.O. emblem (horiz) 35 1·25

308 "Cardigan Bay" (champion trotter)

1970. Return of "Cardigan Bay" to New Zealand.
913 **308** 10c. multicoloured 30 30

309 "Vanessa gonerilla" (butterfly) **310** Queen Elizabeth II and New Zealand Coat of Arms

1970.
914 – ½c. multicoloured 10 20
915 **309** 1c. multicoloured 10 10
916 – 2c. multicoloured 10 10
917 – 2½c. multicoloured 30 20
918 – 3c. multicoloured 15 10
919 – 4c. multicoloured 15 10
920 – 5c. multicoloured 30 10
921 – 6c. black, green and red 30 65
922 – 7c. multicoloured 50 1·00
923 – 7½c. multicoloured 75 1·50
924 – 8c. multicoloured 50 1·00
925 **310** 10c. multicoloured 40 15
926 – 15c. black, flesh and brown 75 50
927 – 18c. green, brown & black 75 40
928 – 20c. black and brown 75 15
929 – 23c. multicoloured 60 30
930b – 25c. multicoloured 50 40
931 – 30c. multicoloured 50 15
932 – 50c. multicoloured 50 20
933 – $1 multicoloured 1·25 1·00
934 – $2 multicoloured 2·50 1·50

DESIGNS—VERT (as T **309**): ½c. "Lycaena salustius" (butterfly); 2c. "Argyrophenga antipodum" (butterfly); 2½c. "Nyctemera annulata (moth); 3c. "Detunda egregia" (moth); 4c. Charagia virescens" (moth); 5c. Scarlet wrasse ("Scarlet parrot fish"); 6c. Big-bellied sea horses; 7c. Leather-jacket (fish); 7½c. Intermediate halfbeak ("Garfish"); 8c. John Dory (fish). (As T **310**): 18c. Maori club; 25c. Hauraki Gulf Maritime Park; 30c. Mt. Cook National Park. HORIZ (as T **310**): 15c. Maori fish hook; 20c. Maori tattoo pattern; 23c. Egmont National Park; 50c. Abel Tasman National Park; $1 Geothermal power; $2 Agricultural technology.

311 Geyser Restaurant **312** U.N. H.Q. Building

1970. World Fair, Osaka. Multicoloured.
935 7c. Type **311** 20 75
936 8c. New Zealand Pavilion 20 75
937 18c. Bush Walk 40 75

1970. 25th Anniv of United Nations.
938 **312** 3c. multicoloured 10 10
939 – 10c. red and yellow 20 20

DESIGN: 10c. Tractor on horizon.

313 Soccer **314** "The Virgin adoring the Child" (Correggio)

1970. Health Stamps. Multicoloured.
940 2½c.+1c. Netball (vert) 25 65
941 3c.+1c. Type **313** 25 65
MS942 Two sheets. (a) 102 × 125 mm (940). (b) 125 × 102 mm (941). Containing blocks of six Per pair 18·00 45·00

1970. Christmas.
943 **314** 2½c. multicoloured 10 10
944 – 3c. multicoloured 10 10
945 – 10c. black, orange & silver 30 75

DESIGNS—VERT: 3c. Stained glass window, Invercargill Presbyterian Church "The Holy Family". HORIZ: 10c. Tower of Roman Catholic Church, Seckburn.

316 Chatham Islands Lily

1970. Chatham Islands. Multicoloured.
946 1c. Type **316** 10 35
947 2c. Shy albatross 30 40

317 Country Women's Institute Emblem

1971. 50th Annivs of Country Women's Institutes and Rotary International in New Zealand. Multicoloured.
948 4c. Type **317** 10 10
949 10c. Rotary emblem and map of New Zealand 20 50

318 "Rainbow II" (yacht)

1971. One Ton Cup Racing Trophy. Mult.
950 5c. Type **318** 25 25
951 8c. One Ton Cup 25 1·50

319 Civic Arms of Palmerston North

1971. City Centenaries. Multicoloured.
952 3c. Type **319** 10 10
953 4c. Arms of Auckland . . . 10 10
954 5c. Arms of Invercargill . . . 15 90

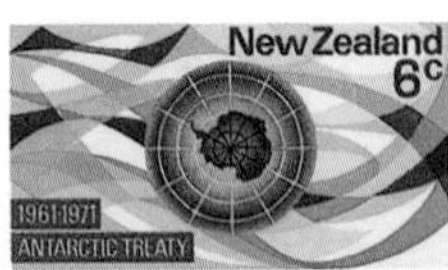

320 Antarctica on Globe

1971. 10th Anniv of Antarctic Treaty.
955 **320** 6c. multicoloured . . . . 1·00 1·50

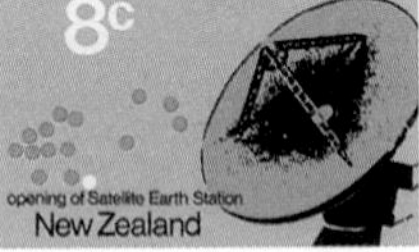

321 Child on Swing **323** Satellite-tracking Aerial

1971. 25th Anniv of U.N.I.C.E.F.
956 **321** 7c. multicoloured 50 80

1971. No. 917 surch **4c.**
957 4c. on 2½c. multicoloured . . 15 10

1971. Opening of Satellite Earth Station.
958 **323** 8c. black, grey and red . . 50 1·50
959 – 10c. black, green and violet . . . . 50 1·00
DESIGN: 10c. Satellite.

324 Girls playing Hockey

1971. Health Stamps. Multicoloured.
960 3c.+1c. Type **324** 45 65
961 4c.+1c. Boys playing hockey 45 65
962 5c.+1c. Dental health . . . . 1·10 2·00
MS963 Two sheets, each 122 × 96 mm. Nos. 960/1 in blocks of six Per pair . . . . 19·00 45·00

325 "Madonna bending over the Crib" (Maratta)

1971. Christmas. Multicoloured.
964 3c. Type **325** 10 10
965 4c. "The Annunciation" (stained-glass window) . . 10 10
966 10c. "The Three Kings" . . . 70 1·25
Nos. 965/6 are smaller, size 21½ × 38 mm.

326 "Tiffany" Rose **327** Lord Rutherford and Alpha Particles

1971. 1st World Rose Convention, Hamilton. Mult.
967 2c. Type **326** 15 30
968 5c. "Peace" 35 35
969 8c. "Chrysler Imperial" . . . 60 1·10

1971. Birth Centenary of Lord Rutherford (scientist). Multicoloured.
970 1c. Type **327** 20 50
971 7c. Lord Rutherford and formula . . . . 55 1·50

328 Benz (1895) **329** Coat of Arms of Wanganui

1972. International Vintage Car Rally. Mult.
972 3c. Type **328** 20 10
973 4c. Oldsmobile (1904) 20 10
974 5c. Ford "Model T" (1914) 20 10
975 6c. Cadillac Service car (1915) 25 45
976 8c. Chrysler (1924) . . . . . 55 1·90
977 10c. Austin "7" (1923) . . . 55 1·40

1972. Anniversaries.
978 **329** 3c. multicoloured 15 10
979 – 4c. orange, brown & black 15 10
980 – 5c. multicoloured 25 10
981 – 8c. multicoloured . . . . 40 1·10
982 – 10c. multicoloured . . . . 40 1·10
DESIGNS AND EVENTS—VERT: 3c. Type **329** (centenary of Wanganui Council); 5c. De Havilland D.H.89 Dragon Rapide and Boeing 737 (25th anniv of National Airways Corp); 8c. French frigate and Maori palisade (bicentenary of landing by Marion du Fresne). HORIZ: 4c. Postal Union symbol (10th anniv of Asian–Oceanic Postal Union); 10c. Stone cairn (150th anniv of New Zealand Methodist Church).

330 Black Scree Cotula **331** Boy playing Tennis

1972. Alpine Plants. Multicoloured.
983 4c. Type **330** 30 10
984 6c. North Island edelweiss . . 40 40
985 8c. Haast's buttercup 60 85
986 10c. Brown Mountain daisy 70 1·25

1972. Health Stamps.
987 **331** 3c.+1c. grey and brown 30 50
988 – 4c.+1c. brown, grey and yellow 30 50
MS989 Two sheets, each 107 × 123 mm. Nos. 987/8 in blocks of six Per pair . . . . 18·00 40·00
DESIGN: No. 988, Girl playing tennis.

332 "Madonna with Child" (Murillo) **333** Lake Waikaremoana

1972. Christmas. Multicoloured.
990 3c. Type **332** 10 10
991 5c. "The Last Supper" (stained-glass window, St. John's Church, Levin) 15 10
992 10c. Pohutukawa flower . . . 35 70

1972. Lake Scenes. Multicoloured.
993 6c. Type **333** . . . . 75 1·00
994 8c. Lake Hayes . . . . . . 85 1·00
995 18c. Lake Wakatipu . . . . 1·25 2·00
996 23c. Lake Rotomahana . . . 1·40 2·25

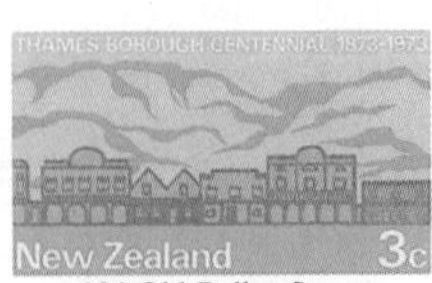

334 Old Pollen Street

1973. Commemorations.
997 **334** 3c. multicoloured 10 10
998 – 4c. multicoloured 15 10
999 – 5c. multicoloured 15 15
1000 – 6c. multicoloured 50 50
1001 – 8c. grey, blue and gold 35 50
1002 – 10c. multicoloured . . . 50 80

DESIGNS AND EVENTS: 3c. (centenary of Thames Borough); 4c. Coalmining and pasture (centenary of Westport Borough); 5c. Cloister (centenary of Canterbury University); 6c. Forest, birds and lake (50th anniv of Royal Forest and Bird Protection Society); 8c. Rowers (Success of N.Z. rowers in 1972 Olympics); 10c. Graph and people (25th anniv of E.C.A.F.E.).

335 Class W Locomotive

1973. New Zealand Steam Locomotives. Mult.
1003 3c. Type **335** 30 10
1004 4c. Class X 30 10
1005 5c. Class Ab 30 10
1006 10c. Class Ja No. 1274 . . . 1·75 1·40

336 "Maori Woman and Child" **337** Prince Edward

1973. Paintings by Frances Hodgkins. Mult.
1027 5c. Type **336** 30 15
1028 8c. "Hilltop" 40 75
1029 10c. "Barn in Picardy" . . . 60 90
1030 18c. "Self-portrait Still Life" 90 2·25

1973. Health Stamps.
1031 **337** 3c.+1c. green & brown 30 50
1032 4c.+1c. red and brown 30 50
MS1033 Two sheets, each 96 × 121 mm, with Nos. 1031/2 in blocks of 6 (3 × 2) Per pair . . 16·00 35·00

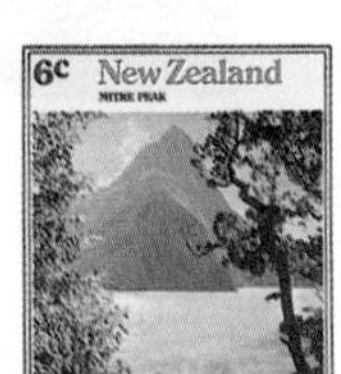

338 "Tempi Madonna" (Raphael) **339** Mitre Peak

1973. Christmas. Multicoloured.
1034 3c. Type **338** 10 10
1035 5c. "Three Kings" (stained-glass window, St. Theresa's Church, Auckland) 10 10
1036 10c. Family entering church 25 50

1973. Mountain Scenery. Multicoloured.
1037 6c. Type **339** 55 80
1038 8c. Mt. Ngauruhoe . . . . 65 1·00
1039 18c. Mt. Sefton (horiz) . . . 80 2·25
1040 23c. Burnett Range (horiz) 1·00 2·50

340 Hurdling **341** Queen Elizabeth II

1974. 10th British Commonwealth Games, Christchurch.
1041 **340** 4c. multicoloured 10 10
1042 – 5c. black and violet . . . 10 10
1043 – 10c. multicoloured . . . 20 15
1044 – 18c. multicoloured . . . 15 50
1045 – 23c. multicoloured . . . 20 70
DESIGNS: 5c. Ball-player (4th Paraplegic Games, Dunedin); 10c. Cycling; 18c. Rifle-shooting; 23c. Bowls.

1974. New Zealand Day. Sheet 131 × 74 mm, containing T **341** and similar horiz designs, size 37 × 20 mm. Multicoloured.
MS1046 4c. × 5 Treaty House, Waitangi; Signing Waitangi Treaty; Type **341**; Parliament Buildings extensions; Children in class . . . . 70 2·50

342 "Spirit of Napier" Fountain **344** Children, Cat and Dog

343 Boeing Seaplane, 1919

1974. Centenaries of Napier and U.P.U. Mult.
1047 4c. Type **342** 10 10
1048 5c. Clock Tower, Berne . . 20 30
1049 8c. U.P.U. Monument, Berne . . . . 55 1·60

1974. History of New Zealand Airmail Transport. Multicoloured.
1050 3c. Type **343** 25 10
1051 4c. Lockheed 10 Electra "Kauha", 1937 . . . . . 30 10
1052 5c. Bristol Type 170 Freighter Mk 31, 1958 . . 30 30
1053 23c. Short S.30 modified "G" Class flying boat "Aotearoa", 1940 . . . . 1·40 2·00

1974. Health Stamps.
1054 **344** 3c.+1c. multicoloured . . 20 50
1055 – 4c.+1c. multicoloured . . 25 50
1056 – 5c.+1c. multicoloured . . 1·00 1·50
MS1057 145 × 123 mm. No. 1055 in block of ten . . . . 21·00 38·00
Nos. 1055/6 are similar to Type **344**, showing children with pets.

345 "The Adoration of the Magi" (Konrad Witz) **346** Great Barrier Island

1974. Christmas. Multicoloured.
1058 3c. Type **345** 10 10
1059 5c. "The Angel Window" (stained glass window, Old St. Pauls Church, Wellington) 10 10
1060 10c. Madonna lily 30 90

1974. Offshore Islands. Multicoloured.
1061 6c. Type **346** 25 40
1062 8c. Stewart Island . . . . . 40 1·25
1063 18c. White Island . . . . . 50 1·25
1064 23c. The Brothers . . . . . 55 1·50

347 Crippled Child

1975. Anniversaries and Events. Multicoloured.
1065 3c. Type **347** 10 10
1066 5c. Farming family 10 10
1067 10c. I.W.Y. symbols 15 65
1068 18c. Medical School Building, Otago University . . . . 40 1·75
COMMEMORATIONS: 3c. 40th anniv of New Zealand Crippled Children Society; 5c. 50th anniv of Women's Division, Federated Farmers of New Zealand; 10c. International Women's Year; 18c. Centenary of Otago Medical School.

348 Scow "Lake Erie"

1975. Historic Sailing Ships.
1069 **348** 4c. black and red 30 10
1070 – 5c. black and blue . . . 30 10
1071 – 8c. black and yellow . . 40 60
1072 – 10c. black and yellow . . 45 60
1073 – 18c. black and brown . . 75 2·00
1074 – 23c. black and lilac . . . 85 2·00
SHIPS: 5c. Schooner "Herald"; 8c. Brigantine "New Zealander"; 10c. Topsail schooner "Jessie Kelly"; 18c. Barque "Tory"; 23c. Full-rigged clipper "Rangitiki".

349 Lake Sumner Forest Park

1975. Forest Park Scenes. Multicoloured.
1075 6c. Type **349** 30 60
1076 8c. North-west Nelson . . . 40 1·00
1077 18c. Kaweka . . . . 65 1·75
1078 23c. Coromandel . . . . . 90 1·75

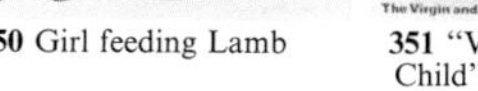
350 Girl feeding Lamb **351** "Virgin and Child" (Zanobi Machiavelli)

1975. Health Stamps. Multicoloured.
1079 3c.+1c. Type **350** 15 30
1080 4c.+1c. Boy with hen and chicks 15 30
1081 5c.+1c. Boy with duck and duckling . . . . 40 1·50
MS1082 123 × 146 mm. No. 1080 × 10 . . . . 15·00 38·00

1975. Christmas. Multicoloured.
1083 3c. Type **351** 10 10
1084 5c. "Cross in Landscape" (stained-glass window, Greendale Church) (horiz) 10 10
1085 10c. "I saw three ships" (carol) (horiz) 35 65

352 "Sterling Silver" **353** Queen Elizabeth II (photograph by W. Harrison)

353a Maripi (knife) **353b** Rainbow Abalone or Paua

1975. (a) Garden Roses. Multicoloured.
1086 1c. Type **352** 10 10
1087 2c. "Lilli Marlene" 10 20
1088 3c. "Queen Elizabeth" . . 60 10
1089 4c. "Super Star" 10 60
1090 5c. "Diamond Jubilee" . . 10 10
1091a 6c. "Cresset" . . . . . . 40 1·00
1092a 7c. "Michele Meilland" . . 40 10
1093a 8c. "Josephine Bruce" . . 30 10
1094 9c. "Iceberg" 30 60

(b) Type **353**.
1094ab 10c. multicoloured . . . 30 10

(c) Maori Artefacts.
1095 **353a** 11c. brown, yellow & black 30 80
1096 – 12c. brown, yellow & black 30 50
1097 – 13c. brown, mauve & black . . . . 40 1·00
1098 – 14c. brown, yellow & black 30 20
DESIGNS: 12c. Putorino (flute); 13c. Wahaika (club); 14c. Kotiate (club).

(d) Sea Shells. Multicoloured.
1099 20c. Type **353b** 15 20
1100 30c. Toheroa clam 25 50
1101 40c. Old woman or coarse dosinia 30 35
1102 50c. New Zealand or spiny murex 40 45
1103 $1 New Zealand scallop . . 70 1·00
1104 $2 Circular saw . . . . . . 1·00 1·75

(e) Building. Multicoloured.
1105 $5 "Beehive" (section of Parliamentary Buildings, Wellington) (22 × 26 mm) 2·00 1·50

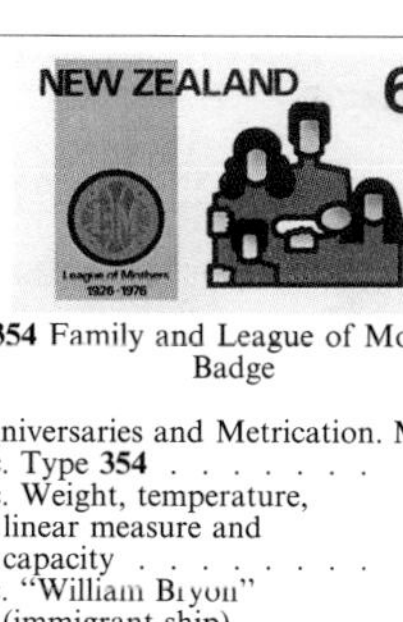

354 Family and League of Mothers Badge

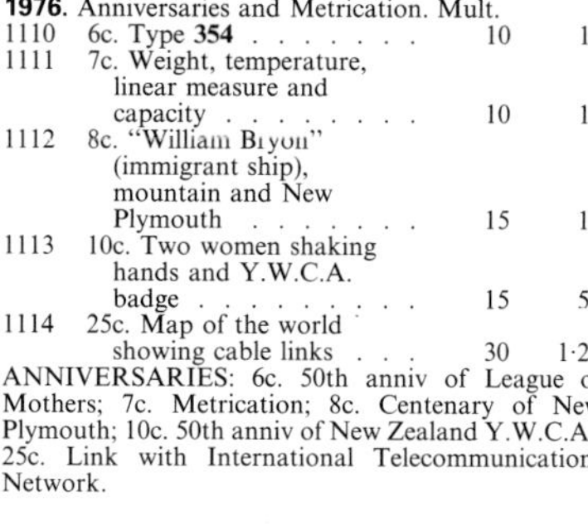
1976. Anniversaries and Metrication. Mult.
1110 6c. Type **354** 10 10
1111 7c. Weight, temperature, linear measure and capacity 10 10
1112 8c. "William Bryon" (immigrant ship), mountain and New Plymouth 15 10
1113 10c. Two women shaking hands and Y.W.C.A. badge 15 50
1114 25c. Map of the world showing cable links . . . 30 1·25
ANNIVERSARIES: 6c. 50th anniv of League of Mothers; 7c. Metrication; 8c. Centenary of New Plymouth; 10c. 50th anniv of New Zealand Y.W.C.A.; 25c. Link with International Telecommunications Network.

355 Gig

1976. Vintage Farm Transport. Multicoloured.
1115 6c. Type **355** 15 40
1116 7c. Thornycroft lorry . . . 15 10
1117 8c. Scandi wagon 30 15
1118 9c. Traction engine 20 40
1119 10c. Wool wagon 20 40
1120 25c. Cart . . . . 65 2·00

356 Purakaunui Falls **357** Boy and Pony

1976. Waterfalls. Multicoloured.
1121 10c. Type **356** 25 10
1122 14c. Marakopa Falls 40 95
1123 15c. Bridal Veil Falls . . . 45 1·10
1124 16c. Papakorito Falls . . . 55 1·25

1976. Health Stamps. Multicoloured.
1125 7c.+1c. Type **357** 20 30
1126 8c.+1c. Girl and calf 20 30
1127 10c.+1c. Girls and bird . . 40 90
MS1128 96 × 121 mm. Nos. 1125/7 × 2 . . . . 3·00 6·00

358 "Nativity" (Spanish carving) **359** Arms of Hamilton

1976. Christmas. Multicoloured.
1129 7c. Type **358** 15 10
1130 11c. "Resurrection" (stained-glass window, St. Joseph's Catholic Church, Grey Lynn) (horiz) 25 30
1131 18c. Angels (horiz) 40 90

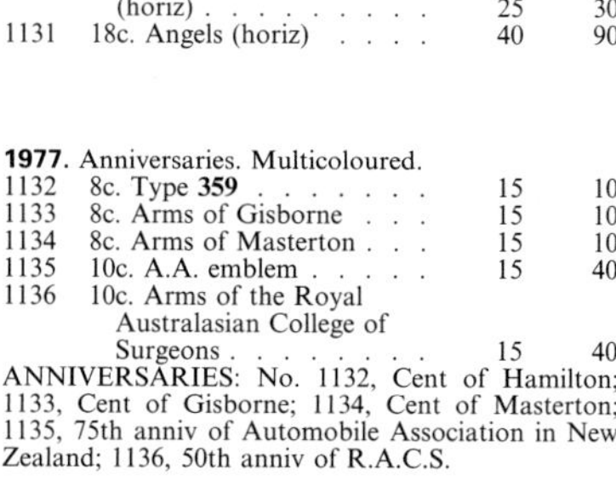
1977. Anniversaries. Multicoloured.
1132 8c. Type **359** 15 10
1133 8c. Arms of Gisborne . . . 15 10
1134 8c. Arms of Masterton . . . 15 10
1135 10c. A.A. emblem 15 40
1136 10c. Arms of the Royal Australasian College of Surgeons 15 40
ANNIVERSARIES: No. 1132, Cent of Hamilton; 1133, Cent of Gisborne; 1134, Cent of Masterton; 1135, 75th anniv of Automobile Association in New Zealand; 1136, 50th anniv of R.A.C.S.

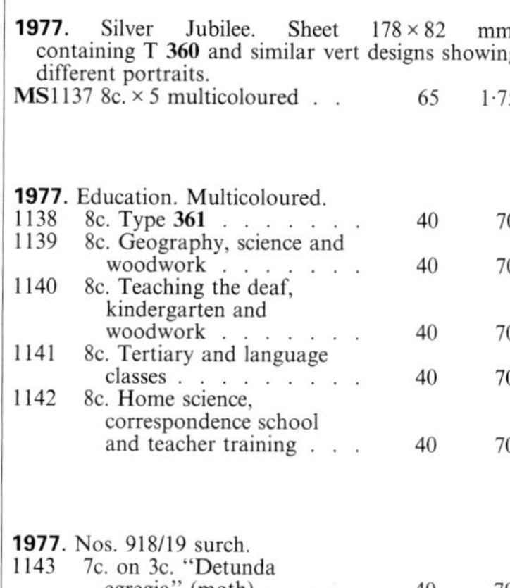

360 Queen Elizabeth II **361** Physical Education and Maori Culture

1977. Silver Jubilee. Sheet 178 × 82 mm, containing T **360** and similar vert designs showing different portraits.
MS1137 8c. × 5 multicoloured . . 65 1·75

1977. Education. Multicoloured.
1138 8c. Type **361** 40 70
1139 8c. Geography, science and woodwork 40 70
1140 8c. Teaching the deaf, kindergarten and woodwork 40 70
1141 8c. Tertiary and language classes 40 70
1142 8c. Home science, correspondence school and teacher training . . . 40 70

1977. Nos. 918/19 surch.
1143 7c. on 3c. "Detunda egregia" (moth) 40 70
1144 8c. on 4c. "Charagia virescens" (moth) 40 70

363 Karitane Beach

1977. Seascapes. Multicoloured.
1145 10c. Type **363** 15 10
1146 16c. Ocean Beach, Mount Maunganui 30 30
1147 18c. Piha Beach 30 30
1148 30c. Kaikoura Coast 35 40

364 Girl with Pigeon **365** "The Holy Family" (Correggio)

1977. Health Stamps. Multicoloured.
1149 7c.+2c. Type **364** 20 30
1150 8c.+2c. Boy with frog . . . 25 45
1151 10c.+2c. Girl with butterfly 45 1·00
MS1152 97 × 120 mm. Nos. 1149/51 × 2 . . . . 1·75 6·50
Stamps from No. **MS**1152 are without white border and together form a composite design.

1977. Christmas. Multicoloured.
1153 7c. Type **365** 15 10
1154 16c. "Madonna and Child" (stained-glass window, St. Michael's and All Angels, Dunedin) (vert) 25 25
1155 23c. "Partridge in a Pear Tree" (vert) . . . . . . 40 1·25

366 Merryweather Manual Pump, 1860

1977. Fire Fighting Appliances. Multicoloured.
1156 10c. Type **366** 15 10
1157 11c. 2-wheel hose, reel and ladder, 1880 . . . . . . 15 25
1158 12c. Shand Mason steam fire engine, 1873 . . . . 20 30
1159 23c. Chemical fire engine, 1888 . . . . 30 70

367 Town Clock and Coat of Arms, Ashburton **368** Students and Ivey Hall, Lincoln College

1978. Centenaries.
1160 **367** 10c. multicoloured . . . 15 10
1161 – 10c. multicoloured . . . 15 10
1162 – 12c. red, yellow and black 15 15
1163 – 20c. multicoloured . . . 20 30
DESIGNS—VERT: No. 1161, Mount Egmont (cent of Stratford); 1162, Early telephone (cent of telephone in New Zealand). HORIZ: No. 1163, Aerial view of Bay of Islands (cent of Bay of Islands County).

1978. Land Resources and Centenary of Lincoln College of Agriculture. Multicoloured.
1164 10c. Type **368** 15 10
1165 12c. Sheep grazing 15 30
1166 15c. Fertiliser ground spreading 15 30
1167 16c. Agricultural Field Days 15 40
1168 20c. Harvesting grain . . . 20 40
1169 30c. Dairy farming 30 90

369 **370** Maui Gas Drilling Platform

1978. Coil Stamps.
1170 **369** 1c. purple 10 65
1171 2c. orange 10 65
1172 5c. brown 10 65
1173 10c. blue 30 80

1978. Resources of the Sea. Multicoloured.
1174 12c. Type **370** 15 15
1175 15c. Trawler 15 20
1176 20c. Map of 200 mile fishing limit 20 30
1177 23c. Humpback whale and bottle-nosed dolphins . . 25 35
1178 35c. Kingfish, snapper, grouper and squid 40 60

371 First Health Charity Stamp **372** "The Holy Family" (El Greco)

1978. Health Stamps.
1179 **371** 10c.+2c. black, red and gold 30 35
1180 – 12c.+2c. multicoloured 30 40
MS1181 97 × 124 mm. Nos. 1179/80 × 3 . . . . . . 1·25 4·00
DESIGNS: 10c. Type **371** (50th anniv of Health Stamps); 12c. Heart Operation (National Heart Foundation).

1978. Christmas. Multicoloured.
1182 7c. Type **372** 10 10
1183 16c. All Saint's Church, Howick (horiz) 25 35
1184 23c. Beach scene (horiz) . . 30 50

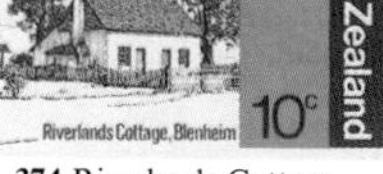

373 Sir Julius Vogel **374** Riverlands Cottage, Blenheim

1979. Statesmen. Designs each brown and drab.
1185 10c. Type **373** 25 50
1186 10c. Sir George Grey 25 50
1187 10c. Richard John Seddon 25 50

1979. Architecture (1st series).
1188 **374** 10c. black, light blue and blue 10 10
1189 – 12c. black, light green and green 15 25
1190 – 15c. black and grey 20 40
1191 – 20c. black, brown and sepia 25 40
DESIGNS: 12c. The Mission House, Waimate North; 15c. "The Elms", Tauranga; 20c. Provincial Council Buildings, Christchurch.
See also Nos. 1217/20 and 1262/5.

375 Whangaroa Harbour

1979. Small Harbours. Multicoloured.
1192 15c. Type **375** 15 10
1193 20c. Kawau Island 20 40
1194 23c. Akaroa Harbour (vert) 20 50
1195 35c. Picton Harbour (vert) 30 70

376 Children with Building Bricks

1979. International Year of the Child.
1196 **376** 10c. multicoloured 15 10

377 Two-spotted Chromis

1979. Health Stamps. Marine Life. Multicoloured.
1197 10c.+2c. Type **377** 30 60
1198 10c.+2c. Sea urchin 30 60
1199 12c.+2c. Red goatfish and underwater cameraman (vert) 30 60
MS1200 144 × 72 mm. Nos. 1197/9, each × 2 1·25 2·75

1979. Nos. 1091a/3a and 1094ab surch.
1201 4c. on 8c. "Josephine Bruce" 10 50
1202 14c. on 10c. Type **353** 30 10
1203 17c. on 6c. "Cresset" 30 1·00
1203a 20c. on 7c. "Michele Meilland" 30 10

379 "Madonna and Child" (sculpture, Ghiberti)

380 Chamber, House of Representatives

1979. Christmas. Multicoloured.
1204 10c. Type **379** 15 10
1205 25c. Christ Church, Russell 30 40
1206 35c. Pohutukawa (tree) 40 65

1979. 25th Commonwealth Parliamentary Conf, Wellington. Multicoloured.
1207 14c. Type **380** 15 10
1208 20c. Mace and Black Rod 20 30
1209 30c. "Beehive" wall hanging 30 75

381 1855 1d. Stamp

1980. Anniversaries and Events.
1210 **381** 14c. black, red and yellow 20 30
1211 – 14c. black, blue & yellow 20 30
1212 – 14c. black, green & yellow 20 30
1213 – 17c. multicoloured 20 30
1214 – 25c. multicoloured 25 35
1215 – 30c. multicoloured 25 40
MS1216 146 × 96 mm. Nos. 1210/12 (as horiz strip) (sold at 52c.) 1·00 4·00
DESIGNS: No. 1211, 1855 2d. stamp; 1212, 1855 1s. stamp (125th anniv of New Zealand stamps); 1213, Geyser, wood-carving and building (Centenary of Rotorua (town)); 1214, "Earina autumnalis" and "Thelymitra venosa" (International Orchid Conference, Auckland); 1215, Ploughing and Golden Plough Trophy (World Ploughing Championships, Christchurch).

382 Ewelme Cottage, Parnell

1980. Architecture (2nd series). Multicoloured.
1217 14c. Type **382** 15 10
1218 17c. Broadgreen, Nelson 15 25
1219 25c. Courthouse, Oamaru 20 35
1220 30c. Government Buildings, Wellington 25 40

383 Auckland Harbour

1980. Large Harbours. Multicoloured.
1221 25c. Type **383** 20 20
1222 30c. Wellington Harbour 25 30
1223 35c. Lyttelton Harbour 25 35
1224 50c. Port Chalmers 30 1·10

384 Surf-fishing

385 "Madonna and Child with Cherubim" (sculpture, Andrea della Robbia)

1980. Health Stamps. Fishing. Multicoloured.
1225 14c.+2c. Type **384** 30 85
1226 14c.+2c. Wharf-fishing 30 85
1227 17c.+2c. Spear-fishing 30 55
MS1228 148 × 75 mm. Nos. 1225/7, each × 2 1·60 3·25

1980. Christmas. Multicoloured.
1229 10c. Type **385** 15 10
1230 25c. St. Mary's Church, New Plymouth 25 25
1231 35c. Picnic scene 40 1·00

386 Te Heu Heu (chief)

387 Lt. Col. the Hon. W. H. A. Feilding and Borough of Feilding Crest (cent)

1980. Maori Personalities. Multicoloured.
1232 15c. Type **386** 10 10
1233 25c. Te Hau (chief) 15 20
1234 35c. Te Puea (princess) 20 10
1235 45c. Ngata (politician) 30 20
1236 60c. Te Ata-O-Tu (warrior) 35 25

1981. Commemorations.
1237 **387** 20c. multicoloured 20 20
1238 – 25c. orange and black 25 25
DESIGN AND COMMEMORATION: 25c. I.Y.D. emblem and cupped hands (International Year of the Disabled).

388 The Family at Play

389 Kaiauai River

1981. "Family Life". Multicoloured.
1239 20c. Type **388** 15 10
1240 25c. The family young and old 20 20
1241 30c. The family at home 20 35
1242 35c. The family at church 25 45

1981. River Scenes. Multicoloured.
1243 30c. Type **389** 20 25
1244 35c. Mangahao 20 30
1245 40c. Shotover (horiz) 25 40
1246 60c. Cleddau (horiz) 35 65

390 St. Paul's Cathedral

1981. Royal Wedding. Multicoloured.
1247 20c. Type **390** 30 30
1248 20c. Prince Charles and Lady Diana Spencer 30 30

391 Girl with Starfish

392 "Madonna suckling the Child" (painting, d'Oggiono)

1981. Health Stamps. Children playing by the Sea. Multicoloured.
1249 20c.+2c. Type **391** 25 65
1250 20c.+2c. Boy fishing 25 65
1251 25c.+2c. Children exploring rock pool 25 35
MS1252 100 × 125 mm. Nos. 1249/51, each × 2 1·25 3·00
Nos. 1249/50 were printed together, se-tenant, forming a composite design.
The stamps from No. **MS**1252 were printed together, se-tenant, in horizontal strips, each forming a composite design.

1981. Christmas. Multicoloured.
1253 14c. Type **392** 15 10
1254 30c. St. John's Church, Wakefield 20 25
1255 40c. Golden tainui (flower) 35 35

393 Tauranga Mission House

394 Map of New Zealand

1981. Commemorations. Multicoloured.
1256 20c. Type **393** 20 10
1257 20c. Water tower, Hawera 20 10
1258 25c. Cat 25 35
1259 30c. "Dunedin" (refrigerated sailing ship) 25 40
1260 35c. Scientific research equipment 25 45
COMMEMORATIONS: No. 1256, Centenary of Tauranga (town); 1257, Centenary of Hawera (town); 1258, Centenary of S.P.C.A. (Society for the Prevention of Cruelty to Animals in New Zealand); 1259, Centenary of frozen meat exports; 1260, International Year of Science.

1982.
1261 **394** 24c. green and blue 30 10

395 Alberton, Auckland

1982. Architecture (3rd series). Multicoloured.
1262 20c. Type **395** 15 15
1263 25c. Caccia Birch, Palmerston North 15 25
1264 30c. Railway station, Dunedin 40 30
1265 35c. Post Office, Ophir 25 40

396 Kaiteriteri Beach, Nelson (Summer)

1982. New Zealand Scenes. Multicoloured.
1266 35c. Type **396** 20 30
1267 40c. St. Omer Park, Queenstown (Autumn) 25 35
1268 45c. Mt. Ngauruhoe, Tongariro National Park (Winter) 25 40
1269 70c. Wairarapa farm (Spring) 40 60

397 Labrador

398 "Madonna with Child and Two Angels" (painting by Piero di Cosimo)

1982. Health Stamps. Dogs. Multicoloured.
1270 24c.+2c. Type **397** 80 1·00
1271 24c.+2c. Border collie 80 1·00
1272 30c.+2c. Cocker spaniel 80 1·00
MS1273 98 × 125 mm. Nos. 1270/2, each × 2 4·25 6·50

1982. Christmas. Multicoloured.
1274 18c. Type **398** 15 10
1275 35c. Rangiatea Maori Church, Otaki 25 30
1276 45c. Surf life-saving 40 40

399 Nephrite

399a Grapes

399b Kokako

400 Old Arts Building, Auckland University

1982. (a) Minerals. Multicoloured.
1277 1c. Type **399** 10 10
1278 2c. Agate 10 10
1279 3c. Iron pyrites 10 10
1280 4c. Amethyst 10 10
1281 5c. Carnelian 10 10
1282 9c. Native sulphur 20 10

(b) Fruits. Multicoloured.
1283 10c. Type **399a** 50 10
1284 20c. Citrus fruit 35 10
1285 30c. Nectarines 30 10
1286 40c. Apples 35 10
1287 50c. Kiwifruit 40 10

(c) Native Birds. Multicoloured.
1288 30c. Kakapo 60 25
1289 40c. Mountain ("Blue") duck 60 35
1290 45c. New Zealand falcon 1·25 35
1291 60c. New Zealand teal 2·25 1·00
1292 $1 Type **399b** 1·00 30
1293 $2 Chatham Island robin 1·00 50

1294	$3 Stitchbird	1·25	1·40
1295	$4 Saddleback	1·50	2·00
1296	$5 Takahe	3·50	3·00
1297	$10 Little spotted kiwi	5·00	6·00

1983. Commemorations. Multicoloured.

1303	24c. Salvation Army Centenary logo	20	10
1304	30c. Type **400**	20	40
1305	35c. Stylized kangaroo and kiwi	20	40
1306	40c. Rainbow trout	25	55
1307	45c. Satellite over Earth	25	55

COMMEMORATIONS: 24c. Salvation Army centenary; 30c. Auckland University centenary; 35c. Closer Economic Relationship agreement with Australia; 40c. Centenary of introduction of rainbow trout into New Zealand; 45c. World Communications Year.

401 Queen Elizabeth II

1983. Commonwealth Day. Multicoloured.

1308	24c. Type **401**	20	10
1309	35c. Maori rock drawing	30	50
1310	40c. Woolmark and woolscouring symbols	30	80
1311	45c. Coat of arms	30	80

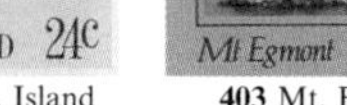

402 "Boats, Island Bay" (Rita Angus) **403** Mt. Egmont

1983. Paintings by Rita Angus. Multicoloured.

1312	24c. Type **402**	25	10
1313	30c. "Central Otago Landscape"	30	45
1314	35c. "Wanaka Landscape"	35	50
1315	45c. "Tree"	50	70

1983. Beautiful New Zealand. Multicoloured.

1316	35c. Type **403**	25	35
1317	40c. Cooks Bay	30	40
1318	45c. Lake Matheson (horiz)	30	45
1319	70c. Lake Alexandrina (horiz)	50	70

404 Tabby **405** "The Family of the Holy Oak Tree" (Raphael)

1983. Health Stamps. Cats. Multicoloured.

1320	24c.+2c. Type **404**	60	75
1321	24c.+2c. Siamese	60	75
1322	30c.+2c. Persian	85	1·00
MS1323	100 × 126 mm. Nos. 1320/2, each × 2	2·25	2·25

1983. Christmas. Multicoloured.

1324	18c. Type **405**	15	10
1325	35c. St. Patrick's Church, Greymouth	30	45
1326	45c. "The Glory of Christmas"	35	80

406 Geology

1984. Antarctic Research. Multicoloured.

1327	24c. Type **406**	35	10
1328	40c. Biology	45	40
1329	58c. Glaciology	60	1·50
1330	70c. Meteorology	70	85
MS1331	126 × 110 mm. Nos. 1327/30	1·90	3·50

407 "Mountaineer", Lake Wakatipu

1984. New Zealand Ferry Boats. Multicoloured.

1332	24c. Type **407**	20	10
1333	40c. "Waikana", Otago	25	45
1334	58c. "Britannia", Waitemata	30	1·40
1335	70c. "Wakatere", Firth of Thames	45	85

408 Mount Hutt

1984. Ski-slope Scenery. Multicoloured.

1336	35c. Type **408**	20	25
1337	40c. Coronet Park	25	30
1338	45c. Turoa	25	30
1339	70c. Whakapapa	40	75

409 Hamilton's Frog

1984. Amphibians and Reptiles. Multicoloured.

1340	24c. Type **409**	30	30
1341	24c. Great Barrier skink	30	30
1342	30c. Harlequin gecko	30	35
1343	58c. Otago skink	45	70
1344	70c. Gold-striped gecko	60	75

410 Clydesdales ploughing

1984. Health Stamps. Horses. Multicoloured.

1345	24c.+2c. Type **410**	50	75
1346	24c.+2c. Shetland ponies	50	75
1347	30c.+2c. Thoroughbreds	50	75
MS1348	148 × 75 mm. Nos. 1345/7, each × 2	1·60	2·50

411 "Adoration of the Shepherds" (Lorenzo di Credi)

1984. Christmas. Multicoloured.

1349	18c. Type **411**	15	10
1350	35c. Old St. Paul's, Wellington (vert)	30	30
1351	45c. "The Joy of Christmas" (vert)	40	70

412 Mounted Riflemen, South Africa, 1901

1984. New Zealand Military History. Mult.

1352	24c. Type **412**	25	10
1353	40c. Engineers, France, 1917	35	45
1354	58c. Tanks of 2nd N.Z. Divisional Cavalry, North Africa, 1942	50	1·50
1355	70c. Infantryman in jungle kit, and 25-pounder gun, Korea and South-East Asia, 1950–72	60	90
MS1356	122 × 106 mm. Nos. 1352/5	1·25	2·25

413 St. John Ambulance Badge

1985. Centenary of St. John Ambulance in New Zealand.

1357 **413**	24c. black, gold and red	20	15
1358	30c. black, silver and blue	25	45
1359	40c. black and grey	30	1·10

The colours of the badge depicted are those for Bailiffs and Dames Grand Cross (24c.), Knights and Dames of Grace (30c.) and Officer Brothers and Sisters (40c.).

414 Nelson Horse Tram, 1862

1985. Vintage Trams. Multicoloured.

1360	24c. Type **414**	40	10
1361	30c. Graham's Town steam tram, 1871	50	60
1362	35c. Dunedin cable car, 1881	50	70
1363	40c. Auckland electric tram, 1902	50	70
1364	45c. Wellington electric tram, 1904	60	90
1365	58c. Christchurch electric tram, 1905	70	1·75

415 Shotover Bridge **416** Queen Elizabeth II (from photo by Camera Press)

1985. Bridges of New Zealand. Multicoloured.

1366	35c. Type **415**	40	60
1367	40c. Alexandra Bridge	45	60
1368	45c. South Rangitikei Railway Bridge (vert)	50	1·25
1369	70c. Twin Bridges (vert)	60	1·25

1985. Multicoloured, background colours given.

1370 **416**	25c. red	50	10
1371	35c. blue	90	10

417 Princess of Wales and Prince William **418** The Holy Family in the Stable

1985. Health Stamps. Designs showing photographs by Lord Snowdon. Multicoloured.

1372	25c.+2c. Type **417**	90	1·25
1373	25c.+2c. Princess of Wales and Prince Henry	90	1·25
1374	35c.+2c. Prince and Princess of Wales with Princes William and Henry	90	1·25
MS1375	118 × 84 mm. Nos. 1372/4, each × 2	4·25	6·00

1985. Christmas. Multicoloured.

1376	18c. Type **418**	20	10
1377	40c. The shepherds	45	85
1378	50c. The angels	45	1·00

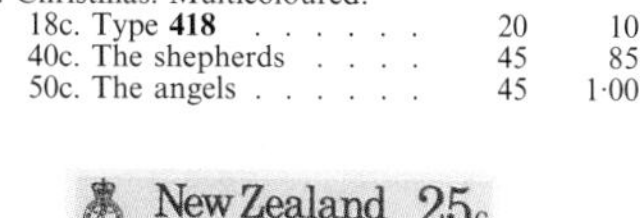

419 H.M.N.Z.S. "Philomel" (1914–47)

1985. New Zealand Naval History. Multicoloured.

1379	25c. Type **419**	70	15
1380	45c. H.M.N.Z.S. "Achilles" (1936–46)	1·10	1·40
1381	60c. H.M.N.Z.S. "Rotoiti" (1949–65)	1·40	2·00
1382	75c. H.M.N.Z.S. "Canterbury" (from 1971)	1·75	2·25
MS1383	124 × 108 mm. Nos. 1379/82	4·50	5·25

420 Police Computer Operator

1986. Centenary of New Zealand Police. Designs showing historical aspects above modern police activities. Multicoloured.

1384	25c. Type **420**	35	50
1385	25c. Detective and mobile control room	35	50
1386	25c. Policewoman and badge	35	50
1387	25c. Forensic scientist, patrol car and policeman with child	35	50
1388	25c. Police College, Porirua, "Lady Elizabeth II" (patrol boat) and dog handler	35	50

421 Indian "Power Plus" 1000cc Motor Cycle (1920)

1986. Vintage Motor Cycles. Multicoloured.

1389	35c. Type **421**	40	45
1390	45c. Norton "CS1" 500cc (1927)	45	65
1391	60c. B.S.A. "Sloper" 500cc (1930)	55	1·50
1392	75c. Triumph "Model H" 550cc (1915)	60	1·50

422 Tree of Life

1986. International Peace Year. Multicoloured.

1393	25c. Type **422**	30	30
1394	25c. Peace dove	30	30

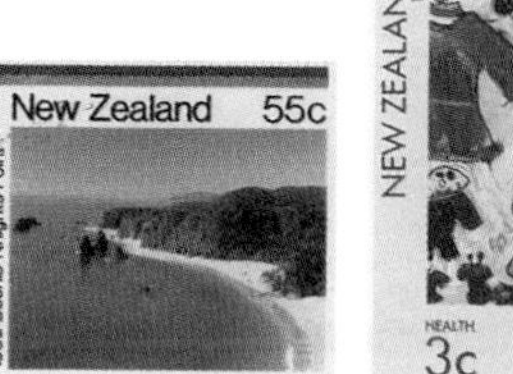

423 Knights Point **424** "Football" (Kylie Epapara)

1986. Coastal Scenery. Multicoloured.

1395	55c. Type **423**	55	65
1396	60c. Becks Bay	55	80
1397	65c. Doubtless Bay	60	1·25
1398	80c. Wainui Bay	75	1·25
MS1399	124 × 99 mm. No. 1398 (sold at $1.20)	1·40	1·25

1986. Health Stamps. Children's Paintings (1st series). Multicoloured.

1400	30c.+3c. Type **424**	40	65
1401	30c.+3c. "Children at Play" (Philip Kata)	40	65
1402	45c.+3c. "Children Skipping" (Mia Flannery) (horiz)	50	65
MS1403	144 × 81 mm. Nos. 1400/2, each × 2	2·25	2·25

See also Nos. 1433/5.

425 "A Partridge in a Pear Tree" **426** Conductor and Orchestra

1986. Christmas. "The Twelve Days of Christmas" (carol). Multicoloured.
1404 25c. Type **425** 20 10
1405 55c. "Two turtle doves" . . 45 55
1406 65c. "Three French hens" 50 1·00

1986. Music in New Zealand.
1407 **426** 30c. multicoloured . . . 25 10
1408 – 60c. black, blue & orange 45 70
1409 – 80c. multicoloured . . . 70 1·75
1410 – $1 multicoloured . . . . 80 1·25
DESIGNS: 60c. Cornet and brass band; 80c. Piper and Highland pipe band; $1 Guitar and country music group.

427 Jetboating **428** Southern Cross Cup

1987. Tourism. Multicoloured.
1411 60c. Type **427** 50 50
1412 70c. Sightseeing flights . . . 60 60
1413 80c. Camping 70 75
1414 85c. Windsurfing 70 85
1415 $1.05 Mountaineering . . . 90 1·10
1416 $1.30 River rafting . . . . 1·10 1·40

1987. Yachting Events. Designs showing yachts. Multicoloured.
1417 40c. Type **428** 35 15
1418 80c. Admiral's Cup 70 80
1419 $1.05 Kenwood Cup . . . . 85 1·25
1420 $1.30 America's Cup . . . 1·10 1·40

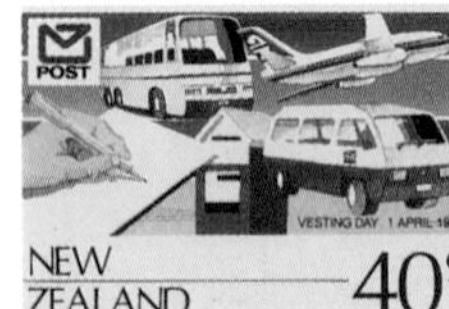

429 Hand writing Letter and Postal Transport

1987. New Zealand Post Ltd Vesting Day. Mult.
1421 40c. Type **429** . . . . . . 1·00 1·50
1422 40c. Posting letter, train and mailbox . . . . 1·00 1·50

430 Avro Type 626 and Wigram Airfield, 1937

1987. 50th Anniv of Royal New Zealand Air Force. Multicoloured.
1423 40c. Type **430** 65 15
1424 70c. Curtiss Kittyhawk I over World War II Pacific airstrip . . . . 90 1·75
1425 80c. Short S25 Sunderland flying boat and Pacific lagoon . . . . 1·00 1·75
1426 85c. Douglas A-4F Skyhawk and Mt. Ruapehu . . . . 1·10 1·60
MS1427 115 × 105 mm. Nos. 1423/6 5·00 6·00

431 Urewera National Park and Fern Leaf **432** "Kite Flying" (Lauren Baldwin)

1987. Centenary of National Parks Movement. Multicoloured.
1428 70c. Type **431** 70 55
1429 80c. Mt. Cook and buttercup 75 60
1430 85c. Fiordland and pineapple shrub 80 65
1431 $1.30 Tongariro and tussock 1·40 95
MS1432 123 × 99 mm. No. 1431 (sold at $1.70) . . . . 1·25 1·75

1987. Health Stamps. Children's Paintings (2nd series). Multicoloured.
1433 40c.+3c. Type **432** . . . . . 80 1·50
1434 40c.+3c. "Swimming" (Ineke Schoneveld) . . . . . . 80 1·50
1435 60c.+3c. "Horse Riding" (Aaron Tylee) (vert) . . . 1·25 1·50
MS1436 100 × 117 mm. Nos. 1433/5, each × 2 . . . . 5·00 7·00

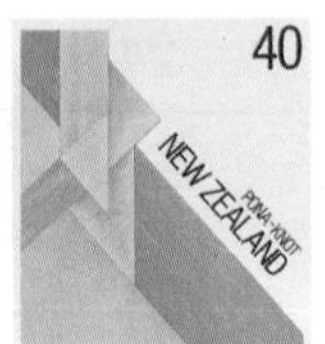

433 "Hark the Herald Angels Sing" **434** Knot ("Pona")

1987. Christmas. Multicoloured.
1437 35c. Type **433** 45 10
1438 70c. "Away in a Manger" 90 70
1439 85c. "We Three Kings of Orient Are" . . . . . . 1·10 85

1987. Maori Fibre-work. Multicoloured.
1440 40c. Type **434** 35 10
1441 60c. Binding ("Herehere") 45 55
1442 80c. Plait ("Whiri") . . . . 60 1·25
1443 85c. Cloak weaving ("Korowai") with flax fibre ("Whitau") . . . . 65 1·40

435 "Geothermal"

1988. Centenary of Electricity. Each shows radiating concentric circles representing energy generation.
1444 **435** 40c. multicoloured . . . 30 20
1445 – 60c. black, red and brown 40 45
1446 – 70c. multicoloured . . . 50 70
1447 – 80c. multicoloured . . . 55 60
DESIGNS: 60c. "Thermal"; 70c. "Gas"; 80c. "Hydro".

436 Queen Elizabeth II and 1882 Queen Victoria 1d. Stamp

1988. Centenary of Royal Philatelic Society of New Zealand. Multicoloured.
1448 40c. Type **436** 35 75
1449 40c. As Type **436**, but 1882 Queen Victoria 2d. . . . 35 75
MS1450 107 × 160 mm. $1 "Queen Victoria" (Chalon) (vert) . . . 3·00 3·50

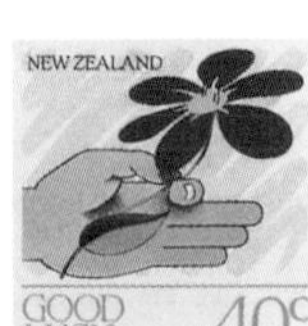

437 "Mangopare" **438** "Good Luck"

1988. Maori Rafter Paintings. Multicoloured.
1451 40c. Type **437** 40 45
1452 40c. "Koru" 40 45
1453 40c. "Raupunga" 40 45
1454 60c. "Koiri" 55 75

1988. Greetings Stamps. Multicoloured.
1455 40c. Type **438** 70 85
1456 40c. "Keeping in touch" . . 70 85
1457 40c. "Happy birthday" . . . 70 85
1458 40c. "Congratulations" (41 × 27 mm) 70 85
1459 40c. "Get well soon" (41 × 27 mm) 70 85

439 Paradise Shelduck **440** Milford Track

1988. Native Birds. Multicoloured.
1459a 5c. Sooty crake 10 30
1460 10c. Double-banded plover 10 30
1461 20c. Yellowhead 20 30
1462 30c. Grey-backed white-eye ("Silvereye") 30 30
1463 40c. Brown kiwi 35 40
1463b 45c. Rock wren 80 80
1464 50c. Sacred kingfisher . . . 50 50
1465 60c. Spotted cormorant ("Spotted shag") 50 55
1466 70c. Type **439** . . . . . . 70 1·00
1467 80c. Victoria penguin ("Fiordland Crested Penguin") . . . . 1·00 1·00
1467a 80c. New Zealand falcon 2·00 1·40
1468 90c. New Zealand robin 1·25 1·50
The 40 and 45c. also exist self-adhesive.

1988. Scenic Walking Trails. Multicoloured.
1469 70c. Type **440** 50 60
1470 80c. Heaphy Track 55 75
1471 85c. Copland Track 60 80
1472 $1.30 Routeburn Track . . 90 1·25
MS1473 124 × 99 mm. No. 1472 (sold at $1.70) . . . . 1·50 1·50

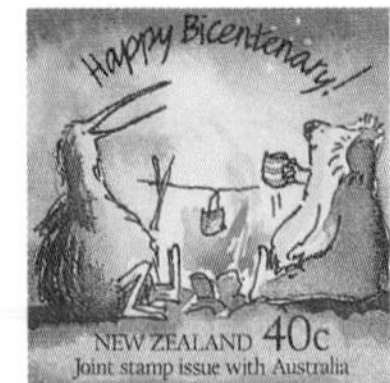

441 Kiwi and Koala at Campfire

1988. Bicentenary of Australian Settlement.
1474 **441** 40c. multicoloured . . . 40 35
A stamp in a similar design was also issued by Australia.

442 Swimming **443** "O Come All Ye Faithful"

1988. Health Stamps. Olympic Games, Seoul. Mult.
1475 40c.+3c. Type **442** 40 70
1476 60c.+3c. Athletics . . . . . 60 1·10
1477 70c.+3c. Canoeing . . . . . 70 1·10
1478 80c.+3c. Show-jumping . . 90 1·40
MS1479 120 × 90 mm. Nos. 1475/8 3·25 4·50

1988. Christmas. Carols. Designs showing illuminated verses. Multicoloured.
1480 35c. Type **443** 30 30
1481 70c. "Hark the Herald Angels Sing" 50 65
1482 80c. "Ding Dong Merrily on High" 50 85
1483 85c. "The First Nowell" . . 55 95

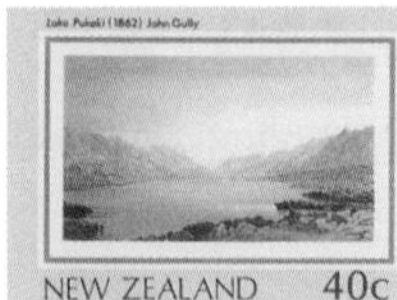

444 "Lake Pukaki" (John Gully)

1988. New Zealand Heritage (1st issue). "The Land". Designs showing 19th-century paintings. Multicoloured.
1484 40c. Type **444** 35 20
1485 60c. "On the Grass Plain below Lake Arthur" (William Fox) 45 45
1486 70c. "View of Auckland" (John Hoyte) 55 70
1487 80c. "Mt. Egmont from the Southward" (Charles Heaphy) 60 70
1488 $1.05 "Anakiwa, Queen Charlotte Sound" (John Kinder) . . . . 80 1·10
1489 $1.30 "White Terraces, Lake Rotomahana", (Charles Barraud) . . . . 95 1·40
See also Nos. 1505/10, 1524/9, 1541/6, 1548/53 and 1562/7.

445 Brown Kiwi

1988.
1490 **445** $1 green . . . . 2·00 3·25
1490b $1 red . . . . 2·00 2·75
1490c $1 blue . . . . 1·00 1·40
2090 $1 violet 75 80
2090a $1.10 gold 70 75
2090b £1.50 brown . . . . . 95 1·00
See also Nos. **MS**1745, **MS**1786 and **MS**2342.

446 Humpback Whale and Calf

1988. Whales. Multicoloured.
1491 60c. Type **446** 80 85
1492 70c. Killer whales . . . . . 1·00 1·10
1493 80c. Southern right whale 1·10 1·25
1494 85c. Blue whale . . . . . . 1·25 1·50
1495 $1.05 Southern bottlenose whale and calf . . . . . 1·50 2·00
1496 $1.30 Sperm whale . . . . 1·60 2·00
Although inscribed "ROSS DEPENDENCY" Nos. 1491/6 were available from post offices throughout New Zealand.

447 Clover **448** Katherine Mansfield

1989. Wild Flowers. Multicoloured.
1497 40c. Type **447** 40 20
1498 60c. Lotus 50 65
1499 70c. Montbretia . . . . . . 60 1·25
1500 80c. Wild ginger . . . . . 70 1·25

1989. New Zealand Authors. Multicoloured.
1501 40c. Type **448** 30 25
1502 60c. James K. Baxter . . . 40 50
1503 70c. Bruce Mason 50 70
1504 80c. Ngaio Marsh 55 70

449 Moriori Man and Map of Chatham Islands

1989. New Zealand Heritage (2nd issue). The People.
1505 **449** 40c. multicoloured . . . 45 25
1506 – 60c. brown, grey and deep brown 60 75
1507 – 70c. green, grey and deep green 65 90
1508 – 80c. blue, grey and deep blue 75 90
1509 – $1.05 grey, light grey and black . . . . . . 1·00 1·60
1510 – $1.30 red, grey and brown . . . . 1·25 2·00
DESIGNS: 60c. Gold prospector; 70c. Settler ploughing; 80c. Whaling; $1.05, Missionary preaching to Maoris; $1.30, Maori village.

450 White Pine (Kahikatea) **451** Duke and Duchess of York with Princess Beatrice

1989. Native Trees. Multicoloured.
1511 80c. Type **450** 75 80
1512 85c. Red pine (Rimu) . . . 80 85

1513 $1.05 Totara . . . . 1·00 1·10
1514 $1.30 Kauri . . . . 1·25 1·40
MS1515 102 × 125 mm. No. 1514 (sold at $1.80) . . . . 1·75 1·75

1989. Health Stamps. Multicoloured.
1516 40c.+3c. Type **451** . . . . . 80 1·50
1517 40c.+3c. Duchess of York with Princess Beatrice . . 80 1·50
1518 80c.+3c. Princess Beatrice 1·40 1·75
MS1519 120 × 89 mm. Nos. 1516/18, each × 2 . . . . 5·50 7·50

452 One Tree Hill, Auckland through Bedroom Window

1989. Christmas. Designs showing Star of Bethlehem. Multicoloured.
1520 35c. Type **452** 40 15
1521 65c. Shepherd and dog in mountain valley 75 70
1522 80c. Star over harbour . . . 95 1·10
1523 $1 Star over globe . . . . . 1·25 1·40

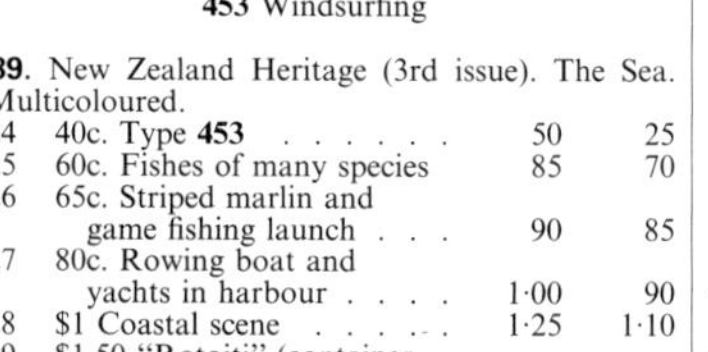

453 Windsurfing

1989. New Zealand Heritage (3rd issue). The Sea. Multicoloured.
1524 40c. Type **453** 50 25
1525 60c. Fishes of many species 85 70
1526 65c. Striped marlin and game fishing launch . . . 90 85
1527 80c. Rowing boat and yachts in harbour . . . . 1·00 90
1528 $1 Coastal scene . . . . . 1·25 1·10
1529 $1.50 "Rotoiti" (container ship) and tug . . . . . . 1·90 2·25

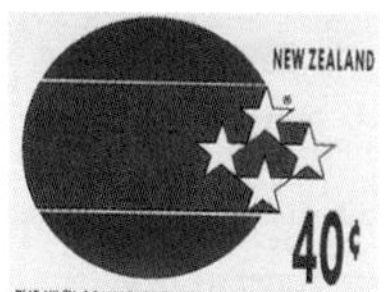

454 Games Logo

1989. 14th Commonwealth Games, Auckland. Mult.
1530 40c. Type **454** 40 35
1531 40c. Goldie (games kiwi mascot) 40 35
1532 40c. Gymnastics 40 35
1533 50c. Weightlifting 50 55
1534 65c. Swimming 65 70
1535 80c. Cycling 80 90
1536 $1 Lawn bowling . . . . . 1·00 1·25
1537 $1.80 Hurdling . . . . . . 1·75 1·90
MS1538 Two sheets, each 105 × 92 mm, with different margin designs. (a) Nos. 1530/1 (horiz pair). (b) Nos. 1530/1 (vert pair) Set of 2 sheets . . . . . 5·00 3·50

455 Short S.30 modified "G" Class Flying Boat "Aotearoa" and Boeing 747-200

1990. 50th Anniv of Air New Zealand.
1539 **455** 80c. multicoloured . . . 1·40 1·10

456 Chief Kawiti signing Treaty

458 *Thelymitra pulchella*

457 Maori Voyaging Canoe

1990. 150th Anniv of Treaty of Waitangi. Sheet 80 × 118 mm, containing T **456** and similar multicoloured design.
MS1540 40c. Type **456**; 40c. Chief Hone Heke (first signatory) and Lieut-Governor Hobson (horiz) 3·25 3·75

1990. New Zealand Heritage (4th issue). The Ships. Multicoloured.
1541 40c. Type **457** 60 25
1542 50c. H.M.S. "Endeavour" (Cook), 1769 . . . . . . 85 80
1543 60c. "Tory" (barque), 1839 95 1·00
1544 80c. "Crusader" (full-rigged immigrant ship), 1871 . . 1·40 1·50
1545 $1 "Edwin Fox" (full-rigged immigrant ship), 1873 . . 1·60 1·50
1546 $1.50 "Arawa" (steamer), 1884 . . . . 2·00 3·00

1990. "New Zealand 1990" International Stamp Exhibition, Auckland. Native Orchids. Sheet 179 × 80 mm, containing T **458** and similar vert designs. Multicoloured.
MS1547 40c. Type **458**; 40c. "Corybas macranthus"; 40c. "Dendrobium cunninghamii"; 40c. "Pterostylis banksii"; 80c. "Aporostylis bifolia" (sold at $4.90) . . . . 4·50 4·50
The stamps in No. **MS**1547 form a composite design.

459 Grace Neill (social reformer) and Maternity Hospital, Wellington

1990. New Zealand Heritage (5th issue). Famous New Zealanders. Multicoloured.
1548 40c. Type **459** 55 30
1549 50c. Jean Batten (pilot) and Percival P.3 Gull Six aircraft 65 85
1550 60c. Katherine Sheppard (suffragette) and 19th-century women . . . 85 1·50
1551 80c. Richard Pearse (inventor) and early flying machine . . . . 1·10 1·50
1552 $1 Lt.-Gen. Sir Bernard Freyberg and tank . . . 1·25 1·50
1553 $1.50 Peter Buck (politician) and Maori pattern . . . 1·50 2·50

460 Akaroa

461 Jack Lovelock (athlete) and Race

1990. 150th Anniv of European Settlements. Mult.
1554 80c. Type **460** 75 75
1555 $1 Wanganui 95 95
1556 $1.50 Wellington . . . . . 1·40 2·25
1557 $1.80 Takapuna Beach, Auckland . . . . 1·60 2·25
MS1558 125 × 100 mm. No. 1557 (sold at $2.30) . . . . 3·50 3·50

1990. Health Stamps. Sportsmen (1st series). Mult.
1559 40c.+5c. Type **461** 50 85
1560 80c.+5c. George Nepia (rugby player) and match 75 1·40
MS1561 115 × 96 mm. Nos. 1559/60, each × 2 . . . . 2·75 3·75
See also Nos. 1687/8.

462 Creation Legend of Rangi and Papa

1990. New Zealand Heritage (6th issue). The Maori. Multicoloured.
1562 40c. Type **462** 40 30
1563 50c. Pattern from Maori feather cloak 55 80
1564 60c. Maori women's choir 60 90
1565 80c. Maori facial tattoos . . 75 1·00
1566 $1 War canoe prow (detail) 90 1·25
1567 $1.50 Maori haka . . . . . 1·40 2·75

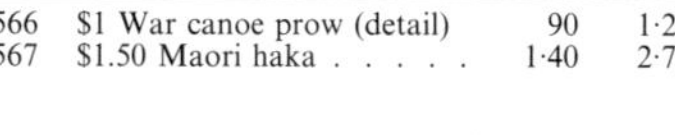

463 Queen Victoria

464 Angel

1990. 150th Anniv of the Penny Black. Sheet 169 × 70 mm, containing T **463** and similar vert designs.
MS1568 40c. × 6 blue (Type **463**, King Edward VII, King George V, King Edward VIII, King George VI, Queen Elizabeth II) 4·50 5·00

1990. Christmas.
1569 **464** 40c. purple, blue & brn 40 10
1570 – $1 purple, green & brown 80 50
1571 – $1.50 purple, red & brown . . . . 1·40 2·50
1572 – $1.80 purple, red & brown . . . . 1·60 2·50
DESIGNS: $1 to $1.80, Different angels.

465 Antarctic Petrel

466 Coopworth Ewe and Lambs

1990. Antarctic Birds. Multicoloured.
1573 40c. Type **465** 80 30
1574 50c. Wilson's storm petrel 90 75
1575 60c. Snow petrel . . . . . 1·10 1·25
1576 80c. Southern fulmar . . . 1·25 1·25
1577 $1 Bearded penguin ("Chinstrap Penguin") . . 1·40 1·25
1578 $1.50 Emperor penguin . . 1·60 3·00
Although inscribed "Ross Dependency" Nos. 1573/8 were available from post offices throughout New Zealand.

1991. New Zealand Farming and Agriculture. Sheep Breeds. Multicoloured.
1579 40c. Type **466** 40 20
1580 60c. Perendale 55 75
1581 80c. Corriedale 70 85
1582 $1 Drysdale 85 90
1583 $1.50 South Suffolk . . . . 1·25 2·50
1584 $1.80 Romney . . . . . . 1·50 2·50

467 Moriori, Royal Albatross, Nikau Palm and Artefacts

469 Tuatara on Rocks

468 Goal and Footballers

1991. Bicentenary of Discovery of Chatham Islands. Multicoloured.
1585 40c. Type **467** 75 50
1586 80c. Carvings, H.M.S. "Chatham", Moriori house of 1870, and Tommy Solomon . . . . 1·50 2·00

1991. Centenary of New Zealand Football Association. Multicoloured.
1587 80c. Type **468** . . . . . . 1·40 1·75
1588 80c. Five footballers and referee . . . . 1·40 1·75
Nos. 1587/8 were printed together, se-tenant, forming a composite design.

1991. Endangered Species. The Tuatara. Mult.
1590 40c. Type **469** 40 60
1591 40c. Tuatara in crevice . . . 40 60
1592 40c. Tuatara with foliage . . 40 60
1593 40c. Tuatara in dead leaves 40 60

470 Clown

471 Cat at Window

1991. "Happy Birthday". Multicoloured.
1594 40c. Type **470** 75 85
1595 40c. Balloons 75 85
1596 40c. Party hat 75 85
1597 40c. Birthday present (41 × 27 mm) 75 85
1598 40c. Birthday cake (41 × 27 mm) 75 85
1599 45c. Type **470** 75 85
1600 45c. As No. 1595 . . . . . 75 85
1601 45c. As No. 1596 . . . . . 75 85
1602 45c. As No. 1597 . . . . . 75 85
1603 45c. As No. 1598 . . . . . 75 85

1991. "Thinking of You". Multicoloured.
1604 40c. Type **471** 75 85
1605 40c. Cat playing with slippers 75 85
1606 40c. Cat with alarm clock 75 85
1607 40c. Cat in window (41 × 27 mm) 75 85
1608 40c. Cat at door (41 × 27 mm) 75 85
1609 45c. Type **471** 75 85
1610 45c. As No. 1605 . . . . . 75 85
1611 45c. As No. 1606 . . . . . 75 85
1612 45c. As No. 1607 . . . . . 75 85
1613 45c. As No. 1608 . . . . . 75 85

472 Punakaiki Rocks

1991. Scenic Landmarks. Multicoloured.
1614 40c. Type **472** 40 30
1615 50c. Moeraki Boulders . . . 55 55
1616 80c. Organ Pipes 85 85
1617 $1 Castle Hill 95 95
1618 $1.50 Te Kaukau Point . . 1·50 1·60
1619 $1.80 Ahuriri River Clay Cliffs . . . . 1·75 1·90

473 Dolphins Underwater

1991. Health Stamps. Hector's Dolphin. Mult.
1620 45c.+5c. Type **473** . . . . . 90 1·25
1621 80c.+5c. Dolphins leaping 1·25 2·00
MS1622 115 × 100 mm. Nos. 1620/1, each × 2 . . . . . 5·00 6·50

474 Children's Rugby

475 "Three Shepherds"

1991. World Cup Rugby Championship. Mult.
1623 80c. Type **474** . . . . . . 1·00 1·25
1624 $1 Women's rugby . . . . 1·10 95
1625 $1.50 Senior rugby . . . . 1·75 2·50
1626 $1.80 "All Blacks" (national team) . . . . 2·00 2·50
MS1627 113 × 90 mm. No. 1626 (sold at $2.40) . . . . 4·00 5·00

1991. Christmas. Multicoloured.
1628 45c. Type **475** 55 80
1629 45c. Two Kings on camels 55 80
1630 45c. Mary and Baby Jesus 55 80
1631 45c. King with gift 55 80
1632 65c. Star of Bethlehem . . . 70 80
1633 $1 Crown 85 95
1634 $1.50 Angel . . . . 1·40 2·25

476 "Dodonidia helmsii"

1991. Butterflies. Multicoloured.
1640 $1 Type **476** . . . . 1·75 80
1641 $2 "Zizina otis oxleyi" . . . 2·50 1·75
1642 $3 "Vanessa itea" . . . . . 3·00 3·00
1643 $4 "Lycaena salustius" . . . 2·25 2·40
1644 $5 "Bassaris gonerilla" . . . 2·75 3·00

479 Yacht "Kiwi Magic", 1987

1992. New Zealand Challenge for America's Cup. Multicoloured.
1655 45c. Type **479** 45 20
1656 80c. Yacht "New Zealand", 1988 . . . . 80 70
1657 $1 Yacht "America", 1851 95 85
1658 $1.50 "America's Cup" Class yacht, 1992 . . . . 1·60 1·60

480 "[illegible]"

1992. Great Voyages of Discovery. Mult.
1659 45c. Type **480** 55 25
1660 80c. "Zeehan" . . . . . . 90 1·10
1661 $1 "Santa Maria" . . . . . 1·25 1·10
1662 $1.50 "Pinta" and "Nina" 1·50 2·50
Nos. 1659/60 commemorate the 350th anniv of Tasman's discovery of New Zealand and Nos. 1661/2 the 500th anniv of discovery of America by Columbus.

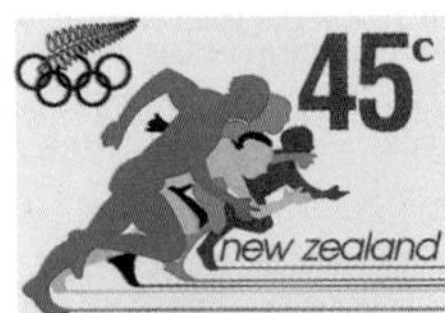

481 Sprinters

1992. Olympic Games, Barcelona (1st issue).
1663 **481** 45c. multicoloured . . . 50 50
See also Nos. 1670/3.

482 Weddell Seal and Pup

1992. Antarctic Seals. Multicoloured.
1664 45c. Type **482** 70 30
1665 50c. Crabeater seals swimming 80 60
1666 65c. Leopard seal and Adelie penguins . . . . . 1·00 1·25
1667 80c. Ross seal . . . . . . 1·25 1·25
1668 $1 Southern elephant seal and harem . . . . 1·40 1·25
1669 $1.80 Hooker's sea lion and pup . . . . 2·25 3·25
Although inscribed "ROSS DEPENDENCY" Nos. 1664/9 were available from post offices throughout New Zealand.

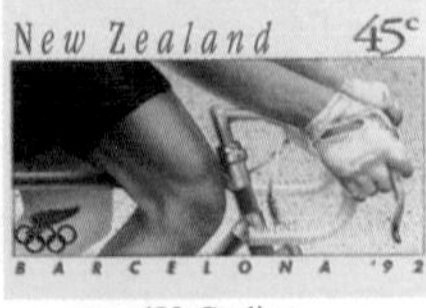

483 Cycling

1992. Olympic Games, Barcelona (2nd issue). Multicoloured.
1670 45c. Type **483** 65 35
1671 80c. Archery 90 70
1672 $1 Equestrian three-day eventing . . . . 1·00 85
1673 $1.50 Sailboarding . . . . 1·50 1·40
MS1674 125 × 100 mm. Nos. 1670/3 3·50 4·00

484 Ice Pinnacles, Franz Josef Glacier

1992. Glaciers. Multicoloured.
1675 45c. Type **484** 40 25
1676 50c. Tasman Glacier 50 45
1677 80c. Snowball Glacier, Marion Plateau 70 70
1678 $1 Brewster Glacier 85 85
1679 $1.50 Fox Glacier . . . . . 1·40 1·60
1680 $1.80 Franz Josef Glacier 1·50 1·60

485 "Grand Finale" Camellia

486 Tree and Hills

1992. Camellias. Multicoloured.
1681 45c. Type **485** 60 25
1682 50c. "Showa-No-Sakae" . . 70 60
1683 80c. "Sugar Dream" 90 80
1684 $1 "Night Rider" . . . . . 1·10 85
1685 $1.50 "E.G. Waterhouse" 1·50 2·75
1686 $1.80 "Dr. Clifford Parks" 1·75 3·00

1992. Health Stamps. Sportsmen (2nd series). As T **461**. Multicoloured.
1687 45c.+5c. Anthony Wilding (tennis player) and match 1·00 1·25
1688 80c.+5c. Stewie Dempster (cricketer) and batsman 1·00 1·50
MS1689 115 × 96 mm. Nos. 1687/8, each × 2 . . . . 4·50 [illegible]

1992. Landscapes. Multicoloured.
1690 45c. Type **486** 60 65
1691 45c. River and hills 60 65
1692 45c. Hills and mountain . . 60 65
1693 45c. Glacier 60 65
1694 45c. Hills and waterfall . . 60 65
1695 45c. Tree and beach 60 65
1696 45c. Estuary and cliffs . . . 60 65
1697 45c. Fjord 60 65
1698 45c. River delta 60 65
1699 45c. Ferns and beach . . . 60 65

487 Reindeer over Houses

488 1920s Fashions

1992. Christmas. Multicoloured.
1700 45c. Type **487** . . . . . . 90 1·00
1701 45c. Santa Claus on sleigh over houses . . . . . . 90 1·00
1702 45c. Christmas tree in window . . . . 90 1·00
1703 45c. Christmas wreath and children at window . . . 90 1·00
1704 65c. Candles and fireplace 1·10 90
1705 $1 Family going to church 1·40 1·00
1706 $1.50 Picnic under Pohutukawa tree . . . . 2·00 2·75

1992. New Zealand in the 1920s. Multicoloured.
1707 45c. Type **488** 50 20
1708 50c. Dr. Robert Jack and early radio announcer . . 55 65
1709 80c. "All Blacks" rugby player, 1924 . . . . . . 85 1·00
1710 $1 Swaggie and dog . . . . 95 1·00
1711 $1.50 Ford "Model A" car and young couple . . . . 1·75 2·25
1712 $1.80 Amateur aviators and biplane . . . . 2·00 2·75

489 "Old Charley" Toby Jug

490 Women's Fashions of the 1930s

1993. Royal Doulton Ceramics Exhibition, New Zealand. Multicoloured.
1713 45c. Type **489** 50 20
1714 50c. "Bunnykins" nursery plate 55 60
1715 80c. "Maori Art" tea set . . 85 85
1716 $1 "Ophelia" handpainted plate . . . . 1·00 90
1717 $1.50 "St. George" figurine 1·60 2·50
1718 $1.80 "Lambeth" salt-glazed stoneware vase . . . . . 1·90 2·50
MS1719 125 × 100 mm. No. 1718 1·60 2·50

1993. New Zealand in the 1930s. Multicoloured.
1720 45c. Type **490** 50 25
1721 50c. Unemployed protest march 55 75
1722 80c. "Phar Lap" (racehorse) 85 95
1723 $1 State housing project . . 1·00 1·00
1724 $1.50 Boys drinking free school milk . . . . 1·75 3·00
1725 $1.80 Cinema queue . . . . 1·90 2·75

491 Women signing Petition

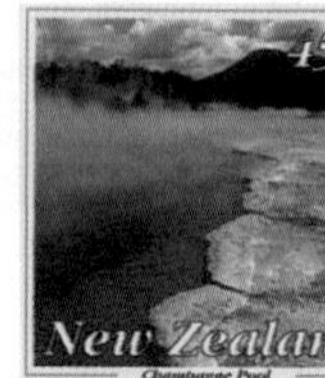

492 Champagne Pool

1993. Centenary of Women's Suffrage. Mult.
1726 45c. Type **491** 50 20
1727 80c. Aircraft propeller and woman on tractor . . . . 1·00 85
1728 $1 Housewife with children 1·00 95
1729 $1.50 Modern women . . . 1·60 2·00

1993. Thermal Wonders, Rotorua. Multicoloured.
1730 45c. Type **492** 60 25
1731 50c. Boiling mud 60 40
1732 80c. Emerald pool 85 70
1733 $1 Hakereteke Falls 95 80
1734 $1.50 [illegible] 1·50 1·75
1735 $1.80 Pohutu Geyser . . . 1·60 1·75
See also No. **MS**1770.

493 Yellow-eyed Penguin, Hector's Dolphin and New Zealand Fur Seal

1993. Endangered Species Conservation. Mult.
1736 45c. Type **493** 85 95
1737 45c. Taiko (bird), Mount Cook lily and mountain duck ("Blue Duck") . . . 85 95
1738 45c. Giant snail, rock wren and Hamilton's frog . . . 85 95
1739 45c. Kaka (bird), New Zealand pigeon and giant weta 85 95
1740 45c. Tusked weta (23 × 28 mm) 85 95

494 Boy with Puppy

495 Christmas Decorations (value at left)

1993. Health Stamps. Children's Pets. Mult.
1741 45c.+5c. Type **494** 60 90
1742 80c.+5c. Girl with kitten . . 90 1·50
MS1743 115 × 96 mm. Nos. 1741/2, each × 2 . . . . 2·75 4·25

1993. "Taipei '93" Asian International Stamp Exhibition, Taiwan. (a) No. **MS**1743 optd **TAIPEI '93** and emblem on sheet margin. Mult.
MS1744 Nos. 1741/2, each × 2 . . 12·00 13·00

(b) Sheet 125 × 100 mm, containing Nos. 1490/c.
MS1745 **445** $1 green, $1 blue, $1 red . . . . 5·00 5·00

1993. Christmas. Multicoloured.
1746 45c. Type **495** 60 85
1747 45c. Christmas decorations (value at right) 60 85
1748 45c. Sailboards, gifts and Christmas pudding (value at left) 60 85
1749 45c. Sailboards, gifts and Christmas pudding (value at right) 60 85
1750 $1 Sailboards, baubles and Christmas cracker . . . . 1·50 1·25
1751 $1.50 Sailboards, present and wreath . . . . 2·00 3·25

496 Rainbow Abalone or Paua

497 Sauropod

1993. Marine Life. Multicoloured.
1752 45c. Type **496** 95 95
1753 45c. Green mussels 95 95
1754 45c. Tarakihi 95 95
1755 45c. Salmon 95 95
1756 45c. Southern blue-finned tuna, yellow-finned tuna and kahawai 95 95
1757 45c. Rock lobster 95 95
1758 45c. Snapper 95 95
1759 45c. Grouper 95 95
1760 45c. Orange roughy 95 95
1761 45c. Squid, hoki and black oreo 95 95

1993. Prehistoric Animals. Multicoloured.
1762 45c. Type **497** 60 45
1763 45c. Carnosaur and sauropod (30 × 25 mm) . . 75 60
1764 80c. Pterosaur . . . . . . 1·10 85
1765 $1 Ankylosaur . . . . . . 1·25 95
1766 $1.20 Mauisaurus . . . . . 1·50 2·50
1767 $1.50 Carnosaur . . . . . 1·60 2·50
MS1768 125 × 100 mm. $1.50 No. 1767 . . . . 1·75 1·75

1993. "Bangkok '93" International Stamp Exhibition, Thailand. (a) No. **MS**1768 optd **BANGKOK '93** and emblem on sheet margin. Multicoloured.
MS1769 $1.50 No. 1767 . . . . 1·60 2·00

(b) Sheet 115 × 100 mm, containing No. 1735.
MS1770 $1.80 multicoloured . . 2·75 3·75

498 Soldiers, National Flag and Pyramids

499 Bungy Jumping

1993. New Zealand in the 1940s. Multicoloured.
1771 45c. Type **498** 80 25
1772 50c. Aerial crop spraying . . 85 60
1773 80c. Hydro-electric scheme 1·10 80
1774 $1 Marching majorettes . . 1·40 90
1775 $1.50 American troops . . . 1·90 2·00
1776 $1.80 Crowd celebrating victory . . . . 2·00 2·25

1994. Tourism. Multicoloured.
1777 45c. Type **499** 50 25
1778 45c. White water rafting (25 × 25 mm) 50 55
1779 80c. Trout fishing 70 70
1780 $1 Jet boating (horiz) . . . 80 80
1781 $1.50 Tramping . . . . . . 1·40 2·00
1782 $1.80 Heli-skiing . . . . . 1·90 2·00
See also No. **MS**1785.

500 "New Zealand Endeavour" (yacht)

503 Rock and Roll Dancers

501 Mt. Cook and New Zealand Symbols

1994. Round the World Yacht Race.
1783 **500** $1 multicoloured . . . . 1·40 1·60

1994.
1784 **501** $20 blue and gold . . . 13·00 13·50

1994. "Hong Kong '94" International Stamp Exhibition. Multicoloured.
MS1785 95 × 115 mm. $1.80 No. 1782 . . . . 3·50 3·50
MS1786 100 × 125 mm. $1 × 3 As Nos. 1490/c . . . . 4·50 4·50

1994. New Zealand in the 1950s. Multicoloured.
1787 45c. Type **503** 45 25
1788 80c. Sir Edmund Hillary on Mt. Everest 75 75
1789 $1 Aunt Daisy (radio personality) 85 85
1790 $1.20 Queen Elizabeth II during 1953 royal visit . . 1·25 1·25
1791 $1.50 Children playing with Opo the dolphin . . . . 1·60 2·00
1792 $1.80 Auckland Harbour Bridge . . . . 1·90 2·00

504 Mt. Cook and Mt. Cook Lily ("Winter")

1994. The Four Seasons. Multicoloured.
1793 45c. Type **504** 45 25
1794 70c. Lake Hawea and Kowhai ("Spring") . . . 65 65
1795 $1.50 Opononi Beach and Pohutukawa ("Summer") 1·40 1·60
1796 $1.80 Lake Pukaki and Puriri ("Autumn") . . . 1·75 1·75

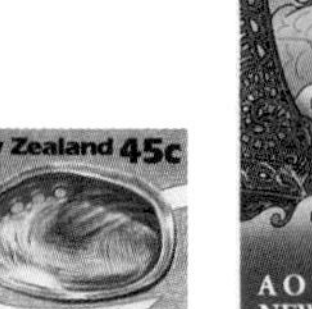

505 Rainbow Abalone or Paua Shell
506 Maui pulls up Te Ika

1994. New Zealand Life. Multicoloured.
1797 45c. Type **505** (25 × 20 mm) 40 45
1798 45c. Pavlova dessert (35 × 20 mm) 40 45
1799 45c. Hokey pokey ice cream (25 × 20 mm) 40 45
1800 45c. Fish and chips (35 × 20 mm) 40 45
1801 45c. Jandals (30 × 20 mm) 40 45
1802 45c. Bush shirt (25 × 30½ mm) 40 45
1803 45c. Buzzy Bee (toy) (35 × 30½ mm) 40 45
1804 45c. Gumboots and black singlet (25 × 30½ mm) . . 40 45
1805 45c. Rugby boots and ball (35 × 30½ mm) 40 45
1806 45c. Kiwifruit (30 × 30½ mm) 40 45
See also Nos. 2318/27.

1994. Maori Myths. Multicoloured.
1807 45c. Type **506** 50 25
1808 80c. Rona snatched up by Marama 85 85
1809 $1 Maui attacking Tuna . . 1·00 1·00
1810 $1.20 Tane separating Rangi and Papa . . . . 1·40 2·00
1811 $1.50 Matakauri slaying the Giant of Wakatipu . . . 1·50 2·00
1812 $1.80 Panenehu showing crayfish to Tangaroa . . 1·75 2·00

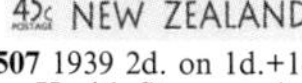

507 1939 2d. on 1d.+1d. Health Stamp and Children playing with Ball
508 Astronaut on Moon (hologram)

1994. Health Stamps. 75th Anniv of Children's Health Camps. Multicoloured.
1813 45c.+5c. Type **507** 50 80
1814 45c.+5c. 1949 1d.+½d. stamp and nurse holding child 50 80
1815 45c.+5c. 1969 4c.+1c. stamp and children reading . . . 50 80
1816 80c.+5c. 1931 2d.+1d. stamp and child in cap . . . . 75 1·00
MS1817 130 × 90 mm. Nos. 1813/16 2·00 3·25

1994. 25th Anniv of First Manned Moon Landing.
1818 **508** $1.50 multicoloured . . 2·00 2·25

509 "people reaching people"

1994. Self-adhesive.
1818ab **509** 40c. multicoloured . . 60 55
1819 45c. multicoloured . . 80 65

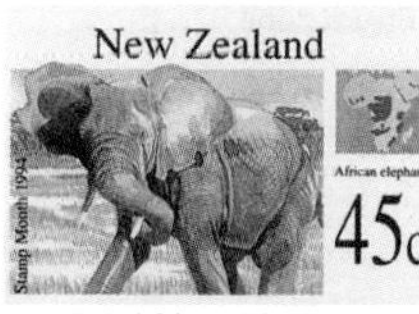

510 African Elephants

1994. Stamp Month. Wild Animals. Multicoloured.
1820 45c. Type **510** 80 80
1821 45c. White rhinoceros . . . 80 80
1822 45c. Lions 80 80
1823 45c. Common zebras . . . 80 80
1824 45c. Giraffe and calf 80 80
1825 45c. Siberian tiger 80 80
1826 45c. Hippopotamuses . . . 80 80
1827 45c. Spider monkey 80 80
1828 45c. Giant panda 80 80
1829 45c. Polar bear and cub . . 80 80

1994. "Philakorea '94" International Stamp Exhibition, Seoul. Multicoloured.
MS1830 125 × 100 mm. Nos. 1459a/65 . . . . 6·50 6·00
MS1831 125 × 100 mm. Nos. 1820, 1822, 1824/5 and 1828/9 . . . 3·75 4·50

511 Children with Crib
512 Batsman

1994. Christmas. Multicoloured.
1832 45c. Father Christmas and children (30 × 25 mm) . . 45 40
1833 45c. Type **511** 45 20
1834 70c. Man and toddler with crib 65 80
1835 80c. Three carol singers . . 70 85
1836 $1 Five carol singers 90 90
1837 $1.50 Children and candles 1·25 2·00
1838 $1.80 Parents with child . . 1·60 2·00
MS1839 125 × 100 mm. Nos. 1833/6 2·75 2·75

1994. Centenary of New Zealand Cricket Council.
(a) Horiz designs, each 30 × 25 mm. Multicoloured.
1840 45c. Bathers catching balls 55 70
1841 45c. Child on surf board at top 55 70
1842 45c. Young child with rubber ring at top 55 70
1843 45c. Man with beach ball at top 55 70
1844 45c. Woman with cricket bat at right 55 70
1845 45c. Boy in green cap with bat 55 70
1846 45c. Man in spotted shirt running 55 70
1847 45c. Woman in striped shorts with bat 55 70
1848 45c. Boy in wet suit with surf board at right . . . 55 70
1849 45c. Sunbather with newspaper at right . . . 55 70

(b) T **512** and similar vert designs. Multicoloured.
1850 45c. Type **512** 60 40
1851 80c. Bowler . . . . 1·00 80
1852 $1 Wicket keeper . . . . . 1·25 1·00
1853 $1.80 Fielder . . . . 2·00 1·75

1995. "POST X '95" Postal History Exhibition, Auckland. Sheet 130 × 90 mm, containing No. 1297 and a reproduction of No. 557 optd "SPECIMEN".
MS1854 $10 multicoloured . . . 17·00 17·00

513 Auckland

1995. New Zealand by Night. Multicoloured.
1855 45c. Type **513** 55 25
1856 80c. Wellington 85 65
1857 $1 Christchurch . . . . . 1·00 85
1858 $1.20 Dunedin . . . . . . 1·25 1·40
1859 $1.50 Rotorua . . . . . . 1·40 1·60
1860 $1.80 Queenstown . . . . . 1·60 1·60
See also No. **MS**1915.

514 The 15th Hole, Waitangi
515 New Zealand Pigeon and Nest

1995. New Zealand Golf Courses. Multicoloured.
1861 45c. Type **514** 65 30
1862 80c. The 6th hole, New Plymouth . . . . . . 1·00 90
1863 $1.20 The 9th hole, Rotorua 1·50 2·50
1864 $1.80 The 5th hole, Queenstown . . . . . . 2·40 3·00

1995. Environment. Multicoloured.
1865 45c. Type **515** 65 65
1866 45c. Planting sapling 65 65
1867 45c. Dolphins and whales 65 65
1868 45c. Thunderstorm 65 65
1869 45c. Backpackers 65 65
1870 45c. Animal pests 65 65
1871 45c. Noxious plants 65 65
1872 45c. Undersized fish and shellfish 65 65
1873 45c. Pollution from factories 65 65
1874 45c. Family at picnic site . . 65 65

516 Teacher with Guitar and Children
517 Map of Australasia and Asia

1995. Maori Language Year. Multicoloured.
1875 45c. Type **516** 50 20
1876 70c. Singing group 75 75
1877 80c. Mother and baby . . . 85 85
1878 $1 Women performing traditional welcome . . . 1·10 1·10
1879 $1.50 Grandfather reciting family genealogy . . . . 1·75 2·25
1880 $1.80 Tribal orator . . . . 2·00 2·25

1995. Meetings of Asian Development Bank Board of Governors and International Pacific Basin Economic Council, Auckland. Multicoloured.
1881 $1 Type **517** . . . . 1·25 1·00
1882 $1.50 Map of Australasia and Pacific . . . . 1·75 2·75

518 "Black Magic" (yacht)

1995. New Zealand's Victory in 1995 America's Cup.
1883 **518** 45c. multicoloured . . . 55 55

519 Boy on Skateboard

1995. Health Stamps. Children's Sports. Mult.
1884 45c.+5c. Type **519** . . . . 75 1·25
1885 80c.+5c. Girl on bicyle . . . 1·75 1·75
MS1886 130 × 90 mm. Nos. 1884/5, each × 2 . . . . 4·00 5·00

1995. "Stampex '95" National Stamp Exhibition, Wellington. No. **MS**1886 additionally inscr with "Stampex '95" and emblem on sheet margin. Mult.
MS1887 130 × 90 mm. Nos. 1884/5, each × 2 . . . . 5·50 6·50

520 Lion Red Cup and Players

1995. Centenary of Rugby League. Multicoloured.
1888 45c. Trans Tasman test match (30 × 25 mm) . . . 60 60
1889 45c. Type **520** 50 20
1890 $1 Children's rugby and mascot . . . . 1·25 1·10
1891 $1.50 George Smith, Albert Baskerville and early match . . . . 2·00 2·50
1892 $1.80 Courtney Goodwill Trophy and match against Great Britain . . . . . . 2·25 2·50
MS1893 125 × 100 mm. No. 1892 3·00 3·00

521 Sheep and Lamb
522 Archangel Gabriel

1995. Farmyard Animals. Multicoloured.
1894 40c. Type **521** 75 75
1895 40c. Deer 75 75
1896 40c. Mare and foal 75 75
1897 40c. Cow with calf 75 75
1898 40c. Goats and kid 75 75
1899 40c. Common turkey . . . 75 75
1900 40c. Ducks 75 75
1901 40c. Red junglefowl 75 75
1902 40c. Sow with piglets . . . 75 75
1903 40c. Border collie 75 75
1904 45c. As Type **521** 75 75
1905 45c. As No. 1895 . . . . . 75 75
1906 45c. As No. 1896 . . . . . 75 75
1907 45c. As No. 1897 . . . . . 75 75
1908 45c. As No. 1898 . . . . . 75 75
1909 45c. As No. 1899 . . . . . 75 75
1910 45c. As No. 1900 . . . . . 75 75
1911 45c. As No. 1901 . . . . . 75 75
1912 45c. As No. 1902 . . . . . 75 75
1913 45c. As No. 1903 . . . . . 75 75

1995. "Singapore '95" International Stamp Exhibition. Multicoloured.
MS1914 170 × 70 mm. Nos. 1909/13 3·25 4·00
MS1915 148 × 210 mm. Nos. 1855/60 9·50 10·00
No. **MS**1915 also includes the "JAKARTA '95" logo.

1995. Christmas. Stained Glass Windows from St. Mary's Anglican Church, Merivale (Nos. 1916/18), The Lady Chapel of St. Luke's Anglican Church, Christchurch (Nos. 1919/22) or St. John the Evangelist Church, Cheviot (No. 1923). Multicoloured. (a) As T **522**.
1916 40c. Type **522** 70 25
1917 45c. Type **522** 70 25
1918 70c. Virgin Mary . . . . . 1·00 90
1919 80c. Shepherds . . . . . . 1·10 1·00
1920 $1 Virgin and Child . . . . 1·40 1·10
1921 $1.50 Two Wise Men . . . 2·25 2·75
1922 $1.80 Wise Man kneeling . . 2·50 2·75

(b) Smaller design, 25 × 30 mm.
1923 40c. Angel with trumpet . . 60 50

523 Face and Nuclear Disarmament Symbol
524 Mt. Cook

1995. Nuclear Disarmament.
1924 **523** $1 multicoloured . . . . 1·00 1·00

1995. New Zealand Scenery. Multicoloured.
1925 5c. Type **524** 10 10
1926 10c. Champagne Pool . . 10 10
1927 20c. Cape Reinga 15 20
1928 30c. Mackenzie Country 20 25
1929 40c. Mitre Peak (vert) . . 25 30
1930 50c. Mt. Ngauruhoe . . . 30 35
1931 60c. Lake Wanaka (vert) 40 45
1932 70c. Giant kauri tree (vert) 45 50
1933 80c. Doubtful Sound (vert) 50 55
1934 90c. Waitomo Limestone Cave (vert) 60 65
1934a 90c. Rangitoto Island . . 60 65
1934b $1 Taiaroa Head (27 × 22 mm) 65 70
1934c $1.10 Kaikoura Coast (27 × 22 mm) 70 75
1934d $1.30 Lake Camp, South Canterbury (27 × 22 mm) 85 90

1934e $2 Great Barrier Island (27 × 22 mm) . . . . . 1·25 1·40
1934f $3 Cape Kidnappers (27 × 22 mm) . . . . . 1·90 2·00
1935 $10 Mt. Ruapehu (38 × 32 mm) . . . . . 7·00 7·25

For similar self-adhesive designs see Nos. 1984b/91b.

For miniature sheets containing some of these designs see Nos. **MS**1978, **MS**1998, **MS**2005, **MS**2328 and **MS**2401.

525 Dame Kiri te Kanawa (opera singer)

526 National Flags, Peace Dove and "50"

1995. Famous New Zealanders. Multicoloured.
1936 40c. Type **525** 75 40
1937 80c. Charles Upham, V.C. (war hero) . . . . 1·00 85
1938 $1 Barry Crump (author) . . 1·25 1·00
1939 $1.20 Sir Brian Barratt-Boyes (surgeon) . . . . . 1·75 1·25
1940 $1.50 Dame Whina Cooper (Maori leader) . . . . . 1·75 1·75
1941 $1.80 Sir Richard Hadlee (cricketer) . . . . 2·75 2·25

1995. 50th Anniv of United Nations.
1942 **526** $1.80 multicoloured . . 2·75 2·50

527 Fern and Globe

1995. Commonwealth Heads of Government Meeting, Auckland. Multicoloured.
1943 40c. Type **527** 75 40
1944 $1.80 Fern and New Zealand flag . . . . . . 3·50 2·75

528 "Kiwi"

1996. Famous Racehorses. Multicoloured.
1945 40c. Type **528** 55 25
1946 80c. "Rough Habit" 95 95
1947 $1 "Blossom Lady" . . . . 1·25 1·25
1948 $1.20 "Il Vicolo" . . . . . 1·60 1·60
1949 $1.50 "Horlicks" . . . . . 1·75 2·00
1950 $1.80 "Bonecrusher" . . . . 2·50 2·50
MS1951 Seven sheets, each 162 × 110 mm. (a) No. 1945. (b) No. 1946. (c) No. 1947. (d) No. 1948. (e) No. 1949. (f) No. 1950. (g) Nos. 1945/50 Set of 7 sheets . . . . 16·00 19·00

529 Kete (basket)

530 Southern Black-backed Gulls

1996. Maori Crafts. Multicoloured.
1952 40c. Type **529** 50 25
1953 80c. Head of Taiaha (spear) 90 90
1954 $1 Taniko (embroidery) . . 1·25 1·25
1955 $1.20 Pounamu (greenstone) 1·50 1·75
1956 $1.50 Hue (gourd) . . . . . 1·75 2·50
1957 $1.80 Korowai (feather cloak) . . . . 2·00 2·50
See also No. **MS**2049.

1996. Marine Life. Multicoloured. Self-adhesive or ordinary gum.
1958 40c. Type **530** 70 80
1959 40c. Children, sea cucumber and spiny starfish 70 80
1960 40c. Yacht, gull and common shrimps 70 80
1961 40c. Gaudy nudibranch . . 70 80
1962 40c. Large rock crab and clingfish 70 80
1963 40c. Snake skin chiton and red rock crab 70 80
1964 40c. Estuarine triplefin and cat's-eye shell 70 80
1965 40c. Cushion star and sea horses 70 80
1966 40c. Blue-eyed triplefin and Yaldwyn's triplefin . . . 70 80
1967 40c. Common octopus . . . 70 80

1996. "SOUTHPEX '96" Stamp Show, Invercargill. Sheet 100 × 215 mm, containing No. 1929 × 10.
MS1978 40c. × 10 multicoloured 5·50 5·50

531 Fire and Ambulance Services

532 Mt. Egmont, Taranaki

1996. Rescue Services. Multicoloured.
1979 40c. Type **531** 50 40
1980 80c. Civil Defence 90 90
1981 $1 Air-sea rescue . . . . . 1·10 1·10
1982 $1.50 Air ambulance and rescue helicopter . . . . 1·60 2·50
1983 $1.80 Mountain rescue and Red Cross . . . . 2·25 2·50

1996. New Zealand Scenery. Self-adhesive. Mult.
1984b 40c. Type **532** 25 30
1985 40c. Piercy Island, Bay of Islands 25 30
1986 40c. Tory Channel, Malborough Sounds . . 25 30
1987 40c. "Earnslaw" (ferry), Lake Wakatipu 25 30
1988 40c. Lake Matheson . . . 25 30
1989 40c. Fox Glacier 25 30
1990 80c. Doubtful Sound (as No. 1933) 50 55
1991 $1 Pohutukawa tree (33 × 22 mm) 70 70
1991b $1.10 Kaikoura Coast . . 70 75

533 Yellow-eyed Penguin

534 Baby in Car Seat

1996. Marine Wildlife. Multicoloured.
1992 40c. Type **533** 50 50
1993 80c. Royal albatross (horiz) 90 90
1994 $1 Great egret (horiz) . . . 1·10 1·10
1995 $1.20 Flukes of sperm whale (horiz) . . . . 1·40 1·60
1996 $1.50 Fur seals . . . . . . 1·60 2·00
1997 $1.80 Bottlenose dolphin . . 2·00 2·00
See also Nos. **MS**1999 and **MS**2037.

1996. "CHINA '96" 9th International Stamp Exhibition, Peking. Multicoloured.
MS1998 180 × 80 mm. Nos. 1926/8 and 1930 . . . . 1·75 2·00
MS1999 140 × 90 mm. Nos. 1994 and 1996 . . . . 2·75 3·00
No. **MS**1999 also shows designs as Nos. 1992/3, 1995 and 1997, but without face values.

1996. Health Stamps. Child Safety. Multicoloured. Self-adhesive (2003) or ordinary (others) gum.
2000 40c.+5c. Type **534** 50 75
2003 40c.+5c. Type **534** (21½ × 38 mm) 50 75
2001 80c.+5c. Child and adult on zebra crossing . . . . . 90 1·25
MS2002 130 × 90 mm. Nos. 2000/1, each × 2 . . . . 2·75 2·75
Stamps from No. **MS**2002 are slightly larger with "NEW ZEALAND" and the face values redrawn.

1996. "CAPEX '96" International Stamp Exhibition, Toronto. (a) No. **MS**2002 optd **CAPEX '96** and emblem on sheet margin. Mult.
MS2004 Nos. 2000/1, each × 2 . . 3·25 2·75

(b) Sheet 180 × 80 mm, containing Nos. 1931/4.
MS2005 $3 multicoloured . . . . 3·25 3·25

535 Violin

1996. 50th Anniv of New Zealand Symphony Orchestra. Multicoloured.
2006 40c. Type **535** 40 40
2007 80c. French horn . . . . . 1·00 1·50

536 Swimming

537 "Hinemoa"

1996. Centennial Olympic Games, Atlanta. Mult.
2008 40c. Type **536** 50 25
2009 80c. Cycling . . . . 1·25 1·00
2010 $1 Running . . . . 1·25 1·00
2011 $1.50 Rowing . . . . 1·75 3·00
2012 $1.80 Dinghy racing . . . . 2·00 3·00
MS2013 120 × 80 mm. Nos. 2008/12 6·00 6·50

1996. Centenary of New Zealand Cinema. Mult.
2014 40c. Type **537** 50 40
2015 80c. "Broken Barrier" . . . 1·00 1·00
2016 $1.50 "Goodbye Pork Pie" 1·75 2·50
2017 $1.80 "Once Were Warriors" . . . . 1·75 2·50

538 Danyon Loader (swimmer) and Blyth Tait (horseman)

539 Beehive Ballot Box

1996. New Zealand Olympic Gold Medal Winners, Atlanta.
2018 **538** 40c. multicoloured . . . 50 50

1996. New Zealand's First Mixed Member Proportional Representation Election.
2019 **539** 40c. black, red and yellow 50 50

540 King following Star

1996. Christmas. Multicoloured. (a) Size 35 × 35 mm.
2020 40c. Type **540** 50 20
2021 70c. Shepherd and Baby Jesus 80 80
2022 80c. Angel and shepherd . . 90 90
2023 $1 Mary, Joseph and Baby Jesus . . . . 1·25 1·00
2024 $1.50 Mary and Joseph with donkey . . . . 2·00 2·50
2025 $1.80 The Annunciation . . 2·00 2·25

(b) Size 30 × 24 mm. Self-adhesive.
2026 40c. Angels with trumpets 50 80
2027 40c. King with gift 70 50

541 Adzebill

1996. Extinct Birds. Multicoloured. (a) Size 40 × 28 mm.
2028 40c. Type **541** 60 40
2029 80c. South Island whekau ("Laughing Owl") . . . . 1·25 1·25
2030 $1 Piopio . . . . 1·25 1·10
2031 $1.20 Huia . . . . 1·50 1·75
2032 $1.50 Giant eagle . . . . . 1·75 2·50
2033 $1.80 Giant moa . . . . . 2·00 2·50
MS2034 105 × 92 mm. No. 2033 2·00 2·00

(b) Size 30 × 24 mm. Self-adhesive.
2035 40c. Stout-legged wren . . . 70 50

1996. "TAIPEI '96" 10th Asian International Stamp Exhibition, Taiwan. (a) No. **MS**2034 overprinted with "TAIPEI '96" logo on sheet margin. Multicoloured.
MS2036 105 × 92 mm. No. 2033 2·75 2·75

(b) Sheet 140 × 90 mm, containing Nos. 1993 and 1997. Multicoloured.
MS2037 Nos. 1993 and 1997 . . 2·75 2·75
No. **MS**2037 also shows designs as Nos. 1992 and 1994/6, but without face values.

542 Seymour Square, Blenheim

543 Holstein Friesian Cattle

1996. Scenic Gardens. Multicoloured.
2038 40c. Type **542** 50 25
2039 80c. Pukekura Park, New Plymouth . . . . 1·00 1·00
2040 $1 Wintergarden, Auckland 1·25 1·10
2041 $1.50 Botanic Garden, Christchurch . . . . . . 1·75 2·25
2042 $1.80 Marine Parade Gardens, Napier . . . . 1·90 2·25

1997. Cattle Breeds. Multicoloured.
2043 40c. Type **543** 70 40
2044 80c. Jersey . . . . 1·40 1·00
2045 $1 Simmental . . . . 1·60 1·00
2046 $1.20 Ayrshire . . . . . . 1·90 1·60
2047 $1.50 Angus . . . . 1·90 2·00
2048 $1.80 Hereford . . . . . . 2·25 2·00

1997. "HONG KONG '97" International Stamp Exhibition. Multicoloured.
MS2049 130 × 110 mm. Nos. 1952/3 and 1956 . . . . 3·00 3·00
MS2050 101 × 134 mm. Nos. 2044/5 and 2047 . . . . 3·50 3·50
No. **MS**2050 is also inscribed for the Chinese New Year ("Year of the Ox").

544 James Cook and Sextant

1997. Millennium Series (1st issue). Discoverers of New Zealand. Multicoloured.
2051 40c. Type **544** 80 45
2052 80c. Kupe and ocean-going canoe . . . . 1·00 90
2053 $1 Carved panel depicting Maui (vert) . . . . . . 1·25 1·00
2054 $1.20 Anchor and "St. Jean Baptiste" (Jean de Surville) (vert) . . . . . 1·75 1·60
2055 $1.50 Dumont d'Urville, crab and "Lastrolabe" . . 2·00 2·00
2056 $1.80 Abel Tasman and illustration from journal 2·00 2·00
See also Nos. 2140/5, 2216/21, 2239/44, 2304/9 and 2310.

545 Rippon Vineyard, Central Otago

1997. New Zealand Vineyards. Multicoloured.
2057 40c. Type **545** 60 25
2058 80c. Te Mata Estate, Hawke's Bay . . . . . . 1·00 90
2059 $1 Cloudy Bay Vineyard, Marlborough . . . . . . 1·25 1·00
2060 $1.20 Pegasus Bay Vineyard, Waipara . . . . 1·50 1·75
2061 $1.50 Milton Vineyard, Gisborne . . . . 1·75 2·50
2062 $1.80 Goldwater Estate, Waiheke Island . . . . . 1·90 2·50
MS2063 Seven sheets, each 150 × 110 mm. (a) No. 2057. (b) No. 2058. (c) No. 2059. (d) No. 2060. (e) No. 2061. (f) No. 2062. (g) Nos. 2057/62 Set of 7 sheets . . . . 13·00 14·00
See also No. **MS**2081.

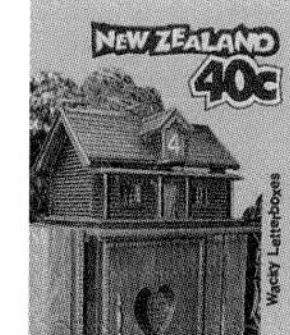

546 Cottage Letterbox

1997. Curious Letterboxes. Multicoloured. Self-adhesive.
2064 40c. Type **546** 50 50
2065 40c. Owl letterbox 50 50
2066 40c. Blue whale letterbox 50 50
2067 40c. "Kilroy is Back" letterbox 50 50
2068 40c. Nesting box letterbox 50 50
2069 40c. Piper letterbox 50 50
2070 40c. Diver's helmet letterbox 50 50
2071 40c. Aircraft letterbox 50 50
2072 40c. Water tap letterbox 50 50
2073 40c. Indian palace letterbox 50 50

547 "The Promised Land", 1948 (Colin McCahon)

1997. Contemporary Paintings by Colin McCahon. Multicoloured.
2074 40c. Type **547** 50 35
2075 $1 "Six Days in Nelson and Canterbury", 1950 1·10 90
2076 $1.50 "Northland Panels" (detail), 1958 1·75 2·25
2077 $1.80 "Moby Dick is sighted off Muriwai Beach", 1972 2·25 2·25

548 Carrier Pigeon (based on 1899 "Pigeon-gram" local stamp)

1997. Centenary of Great Barrier Island Pigeon Post.
2078 **548** 40c. red 50 70
2079 80c. blue 90 1·40
See also Nos. **MS**2080 and **MS**2122.

1997. "Pacific '97" International Stamp Exhibition, San Francisco. Multicoloured.
MS2080 137 × 120 mm. Nos. 2078/9, each × 2 2·50 2·50
MS2081 140 × 100 mm. Nos. 2057, 2059 and 2061 3·00 3·00
No. **MS**2080 is in a triangular format.

549 Rainbow Trout and Red Setter Fly

1997. Fly Fishing. Multicoloured.
2082 40c. Type **549** 40 35
2083 $1 Sea-run brown trout and grey ghost fly 90 90
2084 $1.50 Brook charr and twilight beauty fly 1·40 2·50
2085 $1.80 Brown trout and Hare and Cooper fly 1·60 2·50
See also No. **MS**2172.

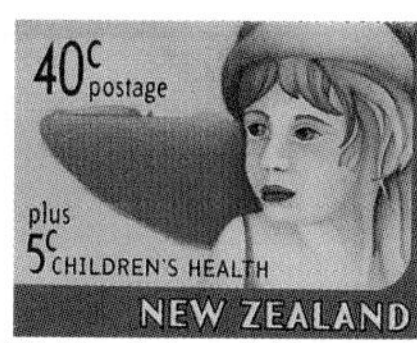

550 "Beach Scene" (Fern Petrie)

1997. Children's Health. Children's paintings. Mult.
(a) Ordinary gum.
2086 40c.+5c. Type **550** 45 75
2087 80c.+5c. "Horse-riding on the Waterfront" (Georgia Dumergue) 80 1·25
MS2088 130 × 90 mm. Nos. 2086/7 and 40c.+ 5c. As No. 2089 (25 × 36 mm) 1·75 1·75

(b) Self-adhesive.
2089 40c.+5c. "Picking Fruit" (Anita Pitcher) 60 60

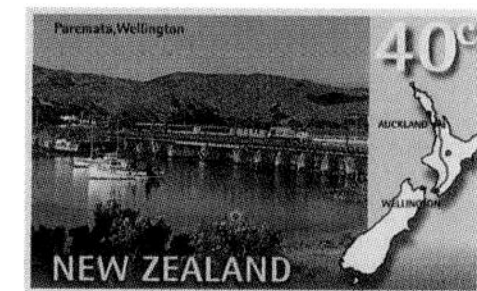

551 The "Overlander" at Paremata, Wellington

1997. Scenic Railway Services. Multicoloured.
2091 40c. Type **551** 50 35
2092 80c. The "Tranz Alpine" in the Southern Alps 90 80
2093 $1 The "Southener" at Canterbury 1·00 90
2094 $1.20 The "Coastal Pacific" on the Kaikoura Coast 1·40 2·00
2095 $1.50 The "Bay Express" at Central Hawke's Bay 1·60 2·25
2096 $1.80 The "Kaimai Express" at Tauranga Harbour 1·75 2·25
See also No. **MS**2173.

552 Samuel Marsden's "Active", Bay of Islands

553 Huhu Beetle

1997. Christmas. Multicoloured. (a) Ordinary gum.
2097 40c. Type **552** 45 20
2098 70c. Revd. Marsden preaching 75 65
2099 80c. Marsden and Maori chiefs 85 75
2100 $1 Maori family 1·00 90
2101 $1.50 Handshake and cross 1·60 2·00
2102 $1.80 Pohutukawa (flower) and Rangihoua Bay 1·75 2·00

(b) Smaller design, 29 × 24 mm. Self-adhesive.
2103 40c. Memorial cross, Pohutukawa and Bay of Islands 40 40

1997. Insects. Multicoloured. Self-adhesive.
2104 40c. Type **553** 50 50
2105 40c. Giant land snail 50 50
2106 40c. Giant weta 50 50
2107 40c. Giant dragonfly 50 50
2108 40c. Peripatus 50 50
2109 40c. Cicada 50 50
2110 40c. Puriri moth 50 50
2111 40c. Veined slug 50 50
2112 40c. Katipo 50 50
2113 40c. Flax weevil 50 50

554 "Rosa rugosa"

555 Queen Elizabeth II and Prince Philip

1997. New Zealand–China Joint Issue. Roses. Mult.
2114 40c. Type **554** 50 50
2115 40c. "Aotearoa" 50 50
MS2116 115 × 95 mm. 80c. Nos. 2114/15 1·00 1·00

1997. Golden Wedding of Queen Elizabeth and Prince Philip.
2117 **555** 40c. multicoloured 50 50

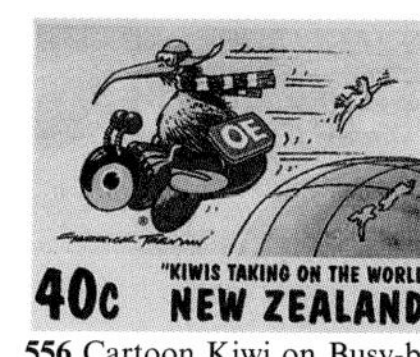

556 Cartoon Kiwi on Busy-bee

1997. New Zealand Cartoons. "Kiwis Taking on the World". Multicoloured.
2118 40c. Type **556** 60 25
2119 $1 "Let's have 'em for Breakfast" 1·10 80
2120 $1.50 Kiwi dinghy winning race 1·40 1·75
2121 $1.80 "CND" emblem cut in forest 1·75 1·75

1997. "Aupex '97" National Stamp Exhibtion, Auckland. Sheet 140 × 120 mm. Multicoloured.
MS2122 Nos. 2078/9, each × 2 2·10 2·10
No. **MS**2122 is in a triangular format.

1997. International Stamp and Coin Exhibition 1997, Shanghai. Sheet as No. **MS**2116, but redrawn to include "Issued by New Zealand Post to commemorate the International Stamp and Coin Expo. Shanghai, China. 19–23 November 1997" inscr in English and Chinese with additional die-stamped gold frame and logo.
MS2123 115 × 95 mm. Nos. 2114/15 70 70

557 Modern Dancer

1998. Performing Arts. Multicoloured.
2124 40c. Type **557** 50 25
2125 80c. Trombone player 85 75
2126 $1 Opera singer 1·50 85
2127 $1.20 Actor 1·50 1·50
2128 $1.50 Singer 1·75 2·50
2129 $1.80 Ballet dancer 2·25 2·50
MS2130 Seven sheets, each 150 × 110 mm. (a) No. 2124. (b) No. 2125. (c) No. 2126. (d) No. 2127. (e) No. 2128. (f) No. 2129. (g) Nos. 2124/9 Set of 7 sheets 15·00 18·00

558 Museum of New Zealand

1998. Opening of Museum of New Zealand, Wellington. Multicoloured.
2131 40c. Type **558** 30 35
2132 $1.80 Museum, spotted cormorant and silver gull 1·40 1·40

559 Domestic Cat

560 Maoris and Canoe

1998. Cats. Multicoloured.
2133 40c. Type **559** 40 35
2134 80c. Burmese 75 80
2135 $1 Birman 85 80
2136 $1.20 British blue 1·00 1·40
2137 $1.50 Persian 1·25 1·75
2138 $1.80 Siamese 1·75 2·00

1998. Chinese New Year ("Year of the Tiger"). Multicoloured.
MS2139 100 × 135 mm. Nos. 2133, 2135 and 2138 3·00 3·00

1998. Millennium Series (2nd issue). Immigrants. Multicoloured.
2140 40c. Type **560** 35 25
2141 80c. 19th-century European settlers and immigrant ship 75 65
2142 $1 Gold miners and mine 1·00 80
2143 $1.20 Post 1945 European migrants and liner 1·25 1·10
2144 $1.50 Pacific islanders and church 1·40 1·40
2145 $1.80 Asian migrant and jumbo jet 1·60 1·40

561 "With Great Respect to the Mehmetcik" Statue, Gallipoli

562 Mother and Son Hugging

1998. Joint Issue New Zealand–Turkey. Memorial Statues. Multicoloured.
2146 40c. Type **561** 30 35
2147 $1.80 "Mother with Children", National War Memorial, Wellington 1·25 1·40

1998. "Stay in Touch" Greetings Stamps. Mult. Self-adhesive.
2148 40c. Type **562** 25 30
2149 40c. Couple on beach 25 30
2150 40c. Boys striking hands 25 30
2151 40c. Grandmother and grandson 25 30
2152 40c. Young boys in pool (horiz) 25 30
2153 40c. "I'LL MISS YOU ... PLEASE WRITE" (horiz) 25 30
2154 40c. Symbolic couple and clouds (horiz) 25 30
2155 40c. Young couple kissing (horiz) 25 30
2156 40c. Couple sat on sofa (horiz) 25 30
2157 40c. Maoris rubbing noses (horiz) 25 30

563 Mount Cook or Aorangi

565 Girl wearing Lifejacket

564 "Wounded at Cassino"

1998. Centenary of 1898 Pictorial Stamps. Designs as T **23/26** and **28/35** with modern face values as T **563**.
2158 **563** 40c. brown 50 50
2159 **24** 40c. blue and brown 50 50
2160 **25** 40c. brown 50 50
2161 **28** 40c. brown 50 50
2162 **29** 40c. red 50 50
2163 **31** 40c. green 50 50
2164 **32** 40c. blue 50 50
2165 **34** 40c. orange 50 50
2166 **26** 80c. blue (inscr "LAKE WAKITIPU") (35 × 23 mm) 85 75
2167 80c. blue (inscr "LAKE WAKATIPU") (35 × 23 mm) 85 75
2168 **30** $1 brown (23 × 35 mm) 95 85
2169 **33** $1.20 brown (35 × 23 mm) 1·00 1·25
2170 **35** $1.50 green (35 × 23 mm) 1·25 1·50
2171 – $1.80 red (as No. 329) (23 × 35 mm) 1·40 1·50
See also Nos. **MS**2188 and **MS**2214.

1998. "Israel '98" World Stamp Exhibition, Tel Aviv. Multicoloured.
MS2172 112 × 90 mm. Nos. 2082 and 2085 2·50 2·75
MS2173 125 × 100 mm. Nos. 2092/3 and 2095 4·00 4·00

1998. Paintings by Peter McIntyre. Multicoloured.
2174 40c. Type **564** 35 30
2175 $1 "The Cliffs of Rangitikei" 85 75
2176 $1.50 "Maori Children, King Country" 1·25 1·40
2177 $1.80 "The Anglican Church, Kakahi" 1·40 1·50
See also No. **MS**2215.

1998. Children's Health. Water Safety. Mult. (a) Ordinary gum.
2178 40c.+5c. Type **565** 40 50
2179 80c.+5c. Boy learning to swim 60 75
MS2180 125 × 90 mm. Nos. 2178/9, each × 2 2·00 2·00

(b) Smaller design, 25 × 37 mm. Self-adhesive.
2181 40c.+5c. Type **565** 30 50

566 Sunrise near Cambridge

1998. Scenic Skies. Multicoloured.
2182 40c. Type **566** 40 20
2183 80c. Clouds over Lake Wanaka 75 65
2184 $1 Sunset over Mount Maunganui 85 75
2185 $1.20 Rain clouds over South Bay, Kaikoura . . 1·00 1·10
2186 $1.50 Sunset near Statue of Wairaka, Whakatane Harbour . . . . 1·40 1·25
2187 $1.80 Cloud formation above Lindis Pass . . . . 1·60 1·75
See also No. **MS**2245.

1998. "TARAPEX '98" National Stamp Exhibition, New Plymouth.
MS2188 90 × 80 mm. Nos. 2166/7 1·60 1·75

567 Virgin Mary and Christ Child

568 Lemon and Mineral Water Bottle, Paeroa

1998. Christmas. Multicoloured. (a) Ordinary gum.
2189 40c. Type **567** 35 15
2190 70c. Shepherds approaching the stable 55 55
2191 80c. Virgin Mary, Joseph and Christ Child 65 65
2192 $1 Magi with gift of gold 80 80
2193 $1.50 Three magi . . . . . 1·25 1·40
2194 $1.80 Angel and shepherds 1·40 1·50
(b) Smaller design, 24 × 29 mm. Self-adhesive.
2195 40c. Type **567** 35 30

1998. Town Icons. Multicoloured. Self-adhesive.
2196 40c. Type **568** 35 35
2197 40c. Carrot, Ohakune . . . 35 35
2198 40c. Brown Trout, Gore (25 × 36 mm) 35 35
2199 40c. Crayfish, Kaikoura (25 × 36 mm) 35 35
2200 40c. Sheep-shearer, Te Kuiti (25 × 36 mm) 35 35
2201 40c. "Pania of the Reef" (Maori legend), Napier (25 × 36 mm) 35 35
2202 40c. Paua Shell, Riverton (24 × 29 mm) 35 35
2203 40c. Kiwifruit, Te Puke (24 × 29 mm) 35 35
2204 40c. Border Collie, Lake Tekapo (24 × 29 mm) . . 35 35
2205 40c. "Big Cow", Hawera (24 × 29 mm) 35 35

569 Moonfish

571 "Fuchsia excorticata"

570 Wellington in 1841 and 1998

1998. International Year of the Ocean. Mult.
2206 40c. Type **569** 35 50
2207 40c. Mako shark 35 50
2208 40c. Yellowfin tuna 35 50
2209 40c. Giant squid 35 50
2210 80c. Striped marlin 60 70
2211 80c. Porcupine fish 60 70
2212 80c. Eagle ray 60 70
2213 80c. Sandager's wrasse . . . 60 70

Nos. 2206/9 and 2210/13 respectively were printed together, se-tenant, forming composite designs.
See also Nos. **MS**2246 and **MS**2277.

1998. "Italia '98" International Philatelic Exhibition, Milan. Multicoloured.
MS2214 90 × 80 mm. Nos. 2167 and 2170 . . . . 3·00 3·25
MS2215 112 × 90 mm. Nos. 2176/7 2·00 2·25

1998. Millennium Series (3rd issue). Urban Transformations. Multicoloured.
2216 40c. Type **570** 70 30
2217 80c. Auckland in 1852 and 1998 . . . . 95 55
2218 $1 Christchurch in 1851 and 1998 . . . . 1·10 70
2219 $1.20 Westport in 1919 and 1998 . . . . 1·40 1·25
2220 $1.50 Tauranga in 1880 and 1998 . . . . 1·60 1·50
2221 $1.80 Dunedin in 1862 and 1998 . . . . 1·75 1·60

1999. Flowering Trees of New Zealand. Mult.
2222 40c. Type **571** 40 20
2223 80c. "Solanum laciniatum" 65 55
2224 $1 "Sophora tetraptera" . . 75 70
2225 $1.20 "Carmichaelia stevensonii" . . . . . . 85 1·00
2226 $1.50 "Olearia angustifolia" 1·25 1·60
2227 $1.80 "Metrosideros umbellata" . . . . 1·40 1·60
See also No. **MS**2286.

572 Civic Theatre, Auckland

573 Labrador Puppy and Netherland Dwarf Rabbit

1999. Art Deco Architecture. Multicoloured.
2228 40c. Type **572** 50 20
2229 $1 Masonic Hotel, Napier 2·00 80
2230 $1.50 Medical and Dental Chambers, Hastings . . . 1·40 1·60
2231 $1.80 Buller County Chambers, Westport . . . 1·40 1·60

1999. Popular Pets. Multicoloured.
2232 40c. Type **573** 40 30
2233 80c. Netherland dwarf rabbit 80 55
2234 $1 Tabby kitten and Netherland dwarf rabbit 90 70
2235 $1.20 Lamb . . . . 1·25 1·25
2236 $1.50 Welsh pony . . . . . 1·40 1·50
2237 $1.80 Two budgerigars . . . 1·50 1·60
MS2238 100 × 135 mm. Nos. 2232/4 1·75 1·75
No. **MS**2238 also commemorates the Chinese New Year ("Year of the Rabbit").
See also No. **MS**2287.

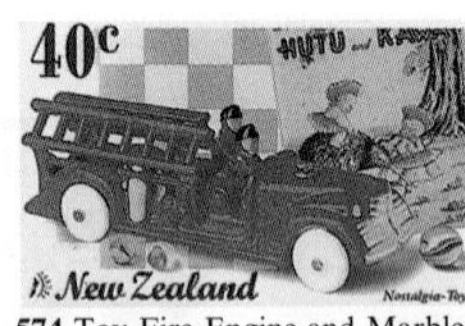

574 Toy Fire Engine and Marbles

1999. Millennium Series (4th issue). Nostalgia. Multicoloured.
2239 40c. Type **574** 40 30
2240 80c. Commemorative tin of biscuits and cereal packet 70 55
2241 $1 Tram, tickets and railway crockery 85 70
2242 $1.20 Radio and "Woman's Weekly" magazine . . . 1·00 1·25
2243 $1.50 Coins, postcards and stamps . . . . 1·25 1·40
2244 $1.80 Lawn mower and seed packets . . . . 1·40 1·60

1999. "Australia '99" World Stamp Exhibition, Melbourne. Multicoloured.
MS2245 130 × 70 mm. Nos. 2182 and 2187 . . . . 1·90 1·90
MS2246 130 × 90 mm. Nos. 2206/7 and 2210/11 . . . . 2·00 2·00

575 Hunter Building, Victoria University

576 Auckland Blues Player kicking Ball

1999. Centenary of Victoria University, Wellington.
2247 **575** 40c. multicoloured . . . 30 30

1999. New Zealand U-Bix Rugby Super 12 Championship. Multicoloured. Ordinary or self-adhesive gum.
2248 40c. Type **576** 40 40
2249 40c. Auckland Blues player being tackled 40 40
2250 40c. Chiefs player being tackled 40 40
2251 40c. Chiefs lineout jump . . 40 40
2252 40c. Wellington Hurricanes player being tackled . . . 40 40
2253 40c. Wellington Hurricanes player passing ball . . . 40 40
2254 40c. Canterbury Crusaders lineout jump 40 40
2255 40c. Canterbury Crusaders player kicking ball . . . 40 40
2256 40c. Otago Highlanders player diving for try . . . 40 40
2257 40c. Otago Highlanders player running with ball 40 40

577 "The Lake, Tuai"

1999. Paintings by Doris Lusk. Multicoloured.
2268 40c. Type **577** 35 30
2269 $1 "The Pumping Station" 80 70
2270 $1.50 "Arcade Awning, St. Mark's Square, Venice (2)" . . . . 1·10 1·25
2271 $1.80 "Tuam St. II" . . . . 1·25 1·40
See also No. **MS**2276.

578 "A Lion in the Meadow" (Margaret Mahy)

1999. Children's Health. Children's Books. Mult. (a) Ordinary gum.
2272 40c.+5c. Type **578** 55 55
2273 80c.+5c. "Greedy Cat" (Joy Cowley) 70 70
MS2274 130 × 90 mm. 40c. + 5c. Type **578**; 40c. + 5c. As No. 2275 (37 × 25 mm); 80c. + 5c. No. 2273 1·40 1·40
(b) Smaller design, 37 × 25 mm. Self-adhesive.
2275 40c.+5c. "Hairy Maclary's Bone" (Lynley Dodd) (37 × 25 mm) 50 50

1999. "PhilexFrance '99" International Stamp Exhibiton, Paris. Multicoloured.
MS2276 112 × 90 mm. Nos. 2268 and 2271 . . . . 1·75 1·75
MS2277 130 × 90 mm. Nos. 2208/9 and 2212/13 . . . . 2·00 2·00

579 "APEC"

1999. 10th Asia-Pacific Economic Co-operation Meeting, New Zealand.
2278 **579** 40c. multicoloured . . . 30 30

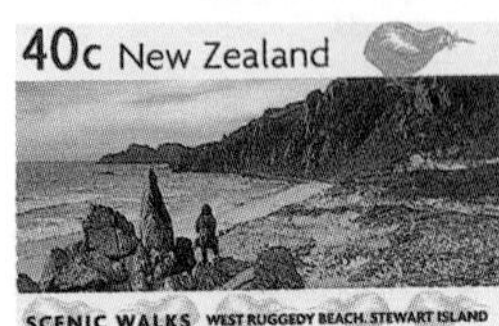

580 West Ruggedy Beach, Stewart Island

1999. Scenic Walks. Multicoloured.
2279 40c. Type **580** 35 30
2280 80c. Ice lake, Butler Valley, Westland 60 55
2281 $1 Tonga Bay, Abel Tasman National Park 75 70
2282 $1.20 East Matakitaki Valley, Nelson Lakes National Park 85 90
2283 $1.50 Great Barrier Island 1·10 1·25
2284 $1.80 Mt. Egmont, Taranaki 1·40 1·40
MS2285 Seven sheets, each 150 × 110 mm. (a) No. 2279. (b) No. 2280. (c) No. 2281. (d) No. 2282. (e) No. 2283. (f) No. 2284. (g) Nos. 2279/84 Set of 7 sheets . . . . 9·50 10·00
See also No. **MS**2295.

1999. "China '99" International Stamp Exhibition, Peking. Multicoloured.
MS2286 112 × 90 mm. Nos. 2222/3 1·00 1·00
MS2287 100 × 135 mm. Nos. 2232 and 2234 . . . . 1·00 1·00

581 Baby Jesus with Animals

1999. Christmas. Multicoloured. (a) Ordinary gum.
2288 40c. Type **581** 30 15
2289 80c. Virgin Mary praying 65 55
2290 $1.10 Mary and Joseph on way to Bethlehem 80 75
2291 $1.20 Angel playing harp . . 85 80
2292 $1.50 Three shepherds . . . 1·10 1·25
2293 $1.80 Three wise men with gifts . . . . 1·40 1·40
(b) Smaller design, 23 × 28 mm. Self-adhesive.
2294 40c. Type **581** 30 30

1999. "Palmpex '99" National Stamp Exhibition, Palmerston North. Sheet 130 × 90 mm, containing No. 2284. Multicoloured.
MS2295 $1.80, Mt. Egmont, Taranaki . . . . 1·40 1·40

582 "P" Class Dinghy

1999. Yachting. Multicoloured. (a) Size 28 × 39 mm. Ordinary gum.
2296 40c. Type **582** 35 15
2297 80c. Laser dinghy 60 55
2298 $1.10 18ft skiff 80 75
2299 $1.20 Hobie catamaran . . 85 80
2300 $1.50 Racing yacht . . . . 1·10 1·25
2301 $1.80 Cruising yacht . . . . 1·25 1·40
MS2302 125 × 100 mm. Nos. 2296/301 . . . . 4·50 5·00
(b) Size 23 × 28 mm. Self-adhesive.
2303 40c. Optimist dinghy 30 30

583 Group of Victorian Women (female suffrage, 1893)

1999. Millenium Series (5th issue). New Zealand Achievements. Multicoloured.
2304 40c. Type **583** 35 15
2305 80c. Richard Pearse's aircraft (powered flight, 1903) 60 55
2306 $1.10 Lord Rutherford (splitting the atom, 1919) 80 75
2307 $1.20 Boat on lake (invention of jet boat, 1953) 85 80
2308 $1.50 Sir Edmund Hillary (conquest of Everest, 1953) . . . . 1·10 1·25
2309 $1.80 Protesters and warship (nuclear free zone, 1987) 1·25 1·40

584 Sunrise and World Map

2000. Millennium Series (6th issue).
2310 **584** 40c. multicoloured . . . 65 30

585 Araiteuru (North Island sea guardian)

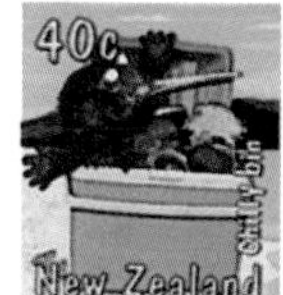

586 Chilly Bin (cool box)

2000. Chinese New Year ("Year of the Dragon"). Maori Spirits and Guardians. Multicoloured.
2311 40c. Type **585** 35 15
2312 80c. Kurangaituku (giant bird woman) 60 55
2313 $1.10 Te Hoata and Te Pupu (volcanic taniwha sisters) 80 75
2314 $1.20 Patupaiarehe (mountain fairy tribe) . . 85 80
2315 $1.50 Te Ngarara-huarau (giant first lizard) . . . . 1·10 1·25
2316 $1.80 Tuhirangi (South Island sea guardian) . . . 1·25 1·40
MS2317 125 × 90 mm. Nos. 2315/16 2·50 2·50

2000. New Zealand Life (2nd series). Each including a cartoon kiwi. Multicoloured. Self-adhesive.
2318 40c. Type **586** 35 35
2319 40c. Pipis (seafood delicacy) 35 35
2320 40c. "Lilo" 35 35
2321 40c. Chocolate fish 35 35
2322 40c. Bach or Crib (holiday home) 35 35
2323 40c. Barbeque 35 35
2324 40c. Ug (fur-lined) boots . . 35 35
2325 40c. Anzac biscuits 35 35
2326 40c. Hot dog 35 35
2327 40c. Meat pie 35 35

2000. "The Stamp Show 2000" International Stamp Exhibition, London. Sheet 110 × 80 mm, containing Nos. 1934b and 1934e/f. Multicoloured.
MS2328 $1 Taiaroa Head; $2 Great Barrier Island; $3 Cape kidnappers . . . . 4·00 4·50

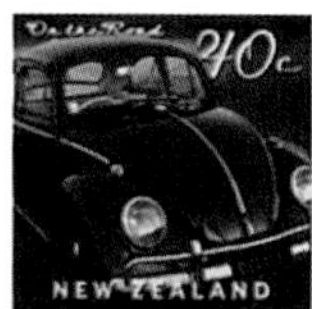

587 Volkswagen Beetle

2000. "On The Road". Motor Cars.
2329 **587** 40c. brown and black . . 35 30
2330 – 80c. blue and black . . . 60 55
2331 – $1.10 brown and black 80 80
2332 – $1.20 green and black . . 85 85
2333 – $1.50 brown and black 1·10 1·25
2334 – $1.80 lilac and black . . 1·25 1·40
MS2335 Seven sheets, each 150 × 110 mm. (a) No. 2329. (b) No. 2330. (c) No. 2331. (d) No. 2332. (e) No. 2333. (f) No. 2334. (g) Nos. 2329/34 Set of 7 sheets . . . . 11·00 12·00
DESIGNS: 80c. Ford Zephyr Mk I; $1.10, Morris Mini Mk II; $1.20, Holden HQ Kingswood; $1.50, Honda Civic; $1.80, Toyota Corolla.

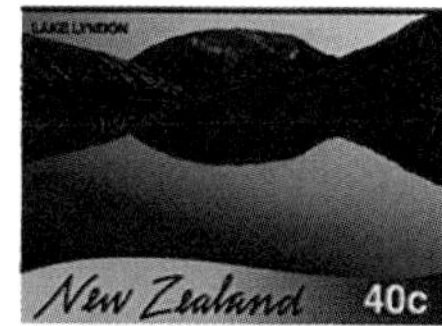

588 Lake Lyndon, Canterbury

2000. Scenic Reflections. Multicoloured.
2336 40c. Type **588** 50 30
2337 80c. Lion (cruising launch) on Lake Wakatipu . . . 85 55
2338 $1.10 Eruption of Mount Ruapehu . . . . 1·00 80
2339 $1.20 Rainbow Mountain Scenic Reserve, Rotorua 1·10 85
2340 $1.50 Tairua Harbour, Coromandel Peninsula . . 1·40 1·25
2341 $1.80 Lake Alexandrina . . 1·50 1·40
See also No. **MS**2368.

2000. "EXPO 2000" World Stamp Exhibition, Anaheim, U.S.A. Sheet 132 × 78 mm, containing Nos. 1490, 1490b/c and 2090/a.
MS2342 $1 red; $1 blue; $1 violet; $1 green; $1.10 gold . . . . . . 3·00 3·25

589 Lady Elizabeth Bowes-Lyon and Glamis Castle, 1907

2000. Queen Elizabeth the Queen Mother's 100th Birthday. Multicoloured.
2343 40c. Type **589** 60 30
2344 $1.10 Fishing in New Zealand, 1966 . . . . . 1·10 70
2345 $1.80 Holding bunch of daisies, 1997 . . . . . . 1·75 1·60
MS2346 115 × 60 mm. Nos. 2343/5 2·40 2·40

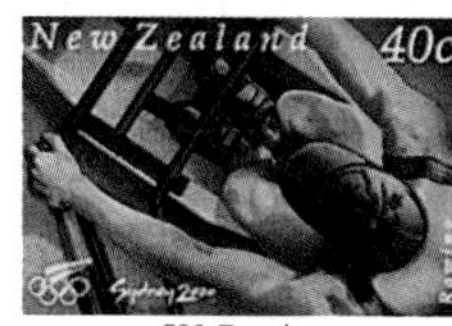

590 Rowing

2000. Olympic Games, Sydney, and other Sporting Events. Multicoloured.
2347 40c. Type **590** 35 30
2348 80c. Show jumping 65 55
2349 $1.10 Cycling 80 80
2350 $1.20 Triathlon 85 85
2351 $1.50 Bowling . . . . . . 1·10 1·25
2352 $1.80 Netball . . . . 1·25 1·40
Nos. 2351/2 omit the Olympic logo.

591 Virgin Mary and Baby Jesus

2000. Christmas. Multicoloured. (a) Ordinary gum.
2353 40c. Type **591** 35 30
2354 80c. Mary and Joseph on way to Bethlehem 60 55
2355 $1.10 Baby Jesus in manger 85 80
2356 $1.20 Archangel Gabriel . . 95 90
2357 $1.50 Shepherd with lamb 1·25 1·40
2358 $1.80 Three Wise Men . . . 1·40 1·60

(b) Self-adhesive. Size 30 × 25 mm.
2359 40c. Type **591** 25 30

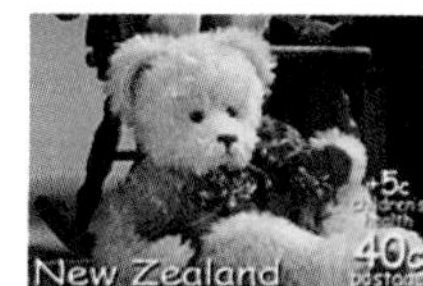

592 Geronimo (teddy bear)

2000. Children's Health. Teddy Bears and Dolls. Multicoloured. (a) Ordinary gum.
2360 40c.+5c. Type **592** 45 50
2361 80c.+5c. Antique French doll and wooden Schoenhut doll 70 80
2362 $1.10 Chad Valley bear . . 75 70
2363 $1.20 Poppy (doll) 80 80
2364 $1.50 Swanni (large bear) and Dear John (small bear) . . . . 90 1·25
2365 $1.80 Lia (doll) and bear . . 1·10 1·25
MS2366 100 × 60 mm. 40c. + 5c. Type **592**; 80c. + 5c. As No. 2361 1·00 1·00

(b) Self-adhesive. Size 29 × 24 mm.
2367 40c.+5c. Type **592** 35 40

2000. "CANPEX 2000" National Stamp Exhibition, Christchurch. Sheet 95 × 80 mm, containing Nos. 2336 and 2341. Multicoloured.
MS2368 40c. Type **588**; $1.80 Lake Alexandrina . . . . 1·40 1·50

593 Lesser Kestrel

2000. Threatened Birds. Multicoloured.
2369 40c. Type **593** 50 30
2370 40c. Yellow-fronted parakeet 50 30
2371 80c. New Zealand stilt ("Black Stilt") 70 55
2372 $1.10 Fernbird ("Stewart Island Fernbird") 75 70
2373 $1.20 Kakapo . . . . . . 90 1·00
2374 $1.50 Weka rail ("North Island Weka") . . . . . . 1·10 1·25
2375 $1.80 Brown kiwi ("Okarito Brown Kiwi") . . . . . 1·25 1·25
Nos. 2369 and 2375 form a joint issue with France. See also No. **MS**2393.

594 *Sonoma* (mail ship) at Quay

2001. Moving the Mail in the 20th Century.
2376 **594** 40c. purple and red . . . 30 35
2377 – 40c. green 30 35
2378 – 40c. agate 30 35
2379 – 40c. blue 30 35
2380 – 40c. brown 30 35
2381 – 40c. purple 30 35
2382 – 40c. black and cinnamon 30 35
2383 – 40c. multicoloured . . . 30 35
2384 – 40c. mauve 30 35
2385 – 40c. multicoloured . . . 30 35
DESIGNS: No. 2377, Stagecoach crossing river; 2378, Early postal lorry; 2379, Paddle steamer on River Wanganui; 2380, Railway T.P.O.; 2381, Loading mail through nose door of aircraft; 2382, Postwoman with bicycle; 2383, Loading lorry by fork-lift truck; 2384, Aircraft at night; 2385, Computer mouse.
See also No. **MS**2424.

595 Green Turtle

2001. Chinese New Year ("Year of the Snake"). Marine Reptiles. Multicoloured.
2386 40c. Type **595** 45 30
2387 80c. Leathery turtle 70 55
2388 90c. Loggerhead turtle . . . 75 60
2389 $1.30 Hawksbill turtle . . . 1·10 1·10
2390 $1.50 Banded sea-snake . . 1·25 1·25
2391 $2 Yellow-bellied sea-snake 1·40 1·40
MS2392 125 × 90 mm. Nos. 2390/1 2·10 2·25

2001. "Hong Kong 2001" Stamp Exhibition. Sheet 100 × 80 mm, containing Nos. 2374/5. Multicoloured.
MS2393 $1.50, North Island weka; $1.80, Okarito brown kiwi . . 1·90 2·00

596 Camellia

2001. Garden Flowers. Multicoloured.
2394 40c. Type **596** 30 25
2395 80c. Siberian iris 60 55
2396 90c. Daffodil 65 60
2397 $1.30 Chrysanthemum . . . 85 1·10
2398 $1.50 Sweet pea . . . . . . 90 1·25
2399 $2 Petunia . . . . 1·10 1·25
MS2400 95 × 125 mm. Nos. 2394/9 4·00 4·25

2001. Invercargill "Stamp Odyssey 2001" National Stamp Exhibition. Sheet 133 × 81 mm, containing Nos. 1934a/d. Multicoloured.
MS2401 90c. Rangitoto Island; $1 Taiaroa Head; $1.10, Kaikoura Coast; $1.30, Lake Camp, South Canterbury . . . . 2·50 2·75

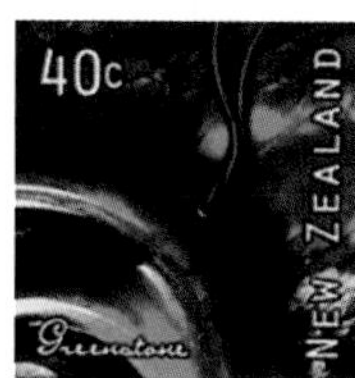

597 Greenstone Amulet

2001. Art from Nature. Multicoloured.
2402 40c. Type **597** 35 30
2403 80c. Oamaru stone sculpture 65 55
2404 90c. Paua ornament 70 60
2405 $1.30 Kauri ornament . . . 95 1·10
2406 $1.50 Flax basket . . . . . 1·10 1·25
2407 $2 Silver-dipped fern frond 1·25 1·25
Nos. 2402/7 were each printed in sheets of 25 (5 × 5) in which the stamps were included in four different orientations so that four blocks of 4 in each sheet showed the complete work of art.

598 Douglas DC-3

2001. Aircraft. Multicoloured.
2408 40c. Type **598** 35 30
2409 80c. Fletcher FU24 Topdresser 65 55
2410 90c. De Havilland DH82A Tiger Moth 70 60
2411 $1.30 Fokker FVIIb/3m Southern Cross . . . . . 90 1·10
2412 $1.50 De Havilland DH100 Vampire . . . . 1·00 1·25
2413 $2 Boeing & Westervelt seaplane . . . . 1·25 1·25

599 Parcel

2001. Greetings Stamps. Multicoloured.
2414 40c. Type **599** 25 30
2415 40c. Trumpet 25 30
2416 40c. Heart and ribbon . . . 25 30
2417 40c. Balloons 25 30
2418 40c. Flower 25 30
2419 90c. Photo frame 60 65
2420 90c. Fountain pen and letter 60 65
2421 90c. Candles on cake . . . 60 65
2422 90c. Star biscuits 60 65
2423 90c. Candle and flowers . . 60 65

2001. "Belgica 2001" International Stamp Exhibition, Brussels. Sheet 180 × 90 mm, containing Nos. 2376/85. Multicoloured.
MS2424 40c. × 10, Nos. 2376/85 3·00 3·50

600 Bungy Jumping, Queenstown

2001. Tourism Centenary. Multicoloured. (a) Size 38 × 32 mm. Ordinary gum.
2425 40c. Type **600** 25 30
2426 80c. Maori Canoe on Lake Rotoiti 45 50
2427 90c. Sightseeing from Mount Alfred 55 60
2428 $1.30 Fishing on Glenorchy river 75 80
2429 $1.50 Sea-kayaking in Abel Tasman National Park . . 85 90
2430 $2 Fiordland National Park 1·10 1·25

(b). Size 30 × 25 mm. Self-adhesive.
2431 40c. Type **600** 25 30
2432 90c. Sightseeing from Mount Alfred 55 60
2433 $1.50 Sea-kayaking in Abel Tasman National Park . . 85 90

2001. "Philanippon '01" International Stamp Exhibition, Tokyo. Sheet 90 × 82 mm, containing Nos. 2429/30. Multicoloured.
MS2434 $1.50 Sea-kayaking in Abel Tasman National Park; $2 Fiordland National Park . . . 2·25 2·40

601 Family cycling

2001. Children's Health. Cycling. Multicoloured. (a) Size 39 × 29 mm. Ordinary gum.
2435 40c. + 5c. Type **601** 25 30
2436 90c. + 5c. Mountain bike stunt 55 60
MS2437 Circular, 100 mm diameter. Nos. 2435/6 . . . . 1·00 1·10

(b) Size 29 × 231/2. Self-adhesive.
2438 40c. + 5c. Boy on bike . . . 25 30

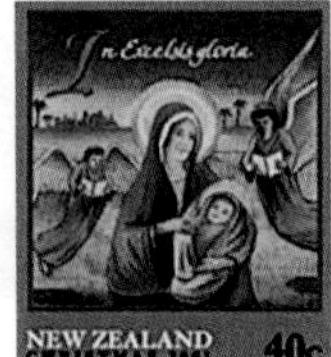

602 "When Christ was born of Mary free"

2001. Christmas. Carols. Multicoloured. (a) Size 29 × 34 mm. Ordinary gum.

2439 40c. Type **602** 30 30

2440 80c. "Away in a manger" . . 55 50

2441 90c. "Joy to the world" . . . 60 55

2442 $1.30 "Angels we have heard on high" 85 80

2443 $1.50 "O holy night" 95 90

2444 $2 "While shepherds watched" . . . . 1·25 1·25

(b) Size 21 × 26 mm. Self-adhesive.

2445 40c. Type **602** 35 30

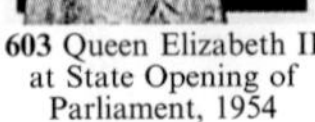

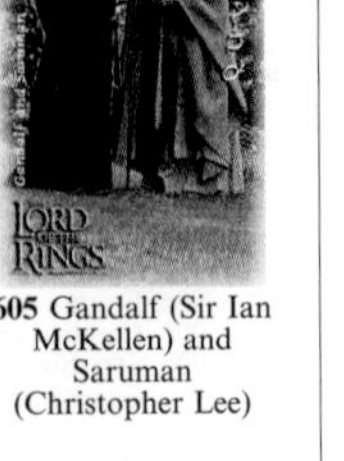

603 Queen Elizabeth II at State Opening of Parliament, 1954

605 Gandalf (Sir Ian McKellen) and Saruman (Christopher Lee)

604 Rockhopper Penguins

2001. Queen Elizabeth II's 75th Birthday. Multicoloured (except 40c.).

2446 40c. Type **603** (black and silver) 35 30

2447 80c. Queen Elizabeth II on walkabout, 1970 . . . . 55 50

2448 90c. Queen Elizabeth II wearing Maori cloak, 1977 . . . . 60 55

2449 $1.30 Queen Elizabeth II with bouquet, 1986 . . . 85 80

2450 $1.50 Queen Elizabeth II at Commonwealth Games, 1990 . . . . 95 90

2451 $2 Queen Elizabeth II, 1997 1·25 1·25

2001. New Zealand Penguins. Multicoloured.

2452 40c. Type **604** 40 30

2453 80c. Little penguin ("Little Blue Penguin") 60 50

2454 90c. Snares Island penguins ("Snares Crested Penguins") 65 55

2455 $1.30 Big-crested penguins ("Erect-crested Penguins") 90 80

2456 $1.50 Victoria penguins ("Fiordland Crested Penguins") . . . . 1·10 90

2457 $2 Yellow-eyed penguins . . 1·40 1·25

2001. Making of *The Lord of the Rings* Film Trilogy (1st issue): *The Fellowship of the Ring*. Multicoloured. (a) Designs 24 × 50 mm or 50 × 24 mm.

2458 40c. Type **605** 25 30

2459 80c. The Lady Galadriel (Cate Blanchett) 45 50

2460 90c. Sam Gamgee (Sean Austin) and Frodo Baggins (Elijah Wood) (horiz) 50 55

2461 $1.30 Guardian of Rivendell 75 80

2462 $1.50 Strider (Viggo Mortensen) 85 90

2463 $2 Boromir (Sean Bean) (horiz) . . . . 1·10 1·25

(b) Designs 26 × 37 mm or 37 × 26 mm. Self-adhesive.

2464 40c. Type **605** 25 30

2465 80c. The Lady Galadriel (Cate Blanchett) 45 50

2466 90c. Sam Gamgee (Sean Austin) and Frodo Baggins (Elijah Wood) (horiz) 50 55

2467 $1.30 Guardian of Rivendell 75 80

2468 $1.50 Strider (Viggo Mortensen) 85 90

2469 $2 Boromir (Sean Bean) (horiz) . . . . 1·10 1·25

See also No. **MS**2490.

606 "Christian Cullen" (harness racing)

2002. Chinese New Year ("Year of the Horse"). New Zealand Racehorses. Multicoloured.

2470 40c. Type **606** 30 30

2471 80c. "Lyell Creek" (harness racing) 50 50

2472 90c. "Yulestar" (harness racing) 55 55

2473 $1.30 "Sunline" 80 80

2474 $1.50 "Ethereal" 90 90

2475 $2 "Zabeel" . . . . 1·25 1·25

MS2476 127 × 90 mm. Nos. 2473/4 3·75 4·25

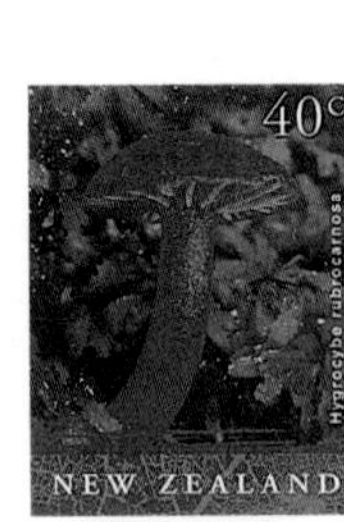

607 *Hygrocybe rubrocarnosa*

608 War Memorial Museum, Auckland

2002. Fungi. Multicoloured.

2477 40c. Type **607** 35 30

2478 80c. *Entoloma hochstetteri* 60 50

2479 90c. *Aseroe rubra* 65 55

2480 $1.30 *Hericium coralloides* 95 95

2481 $1.50 *Thaxterogaster porphyreus* . . . . 1·10 1·25

2482 $2 *Ramaria aureorhiza* . . . 1·40 1·50

MS2483 114 × 104 mm. Nos. 2477/82 5·00 5·00

2002. Architectural Heritage. Multicoloured.

2484 40c. Type **608** 35 30

2485 80c. Stone Store, Kerikeri (25 × 30 mm) 60 50

2486 90c. Arts Centre, Christchurch (50 × 30 mm) 65 55

2487 $1.30 Government Buildings, Wellington (50 × 30 mm) 95 80

2488 $1.50 Dunedin Railway Station (25 × 30 mm) . . 1·10 90

2489 $2 Sky Tower, Auckland . . 1·25 1·25

2002. "Northpex 2002" Stamp Exhibition. Sheet 130 × 95 mm, containing Nos. 2458, 2461 and 2463. Multicoloured.

MS2490 40c. Gandalf (Sir Ian Mckellen) and Saruman (Christopher Lee); $1.30 Guardian of Rivendell; $2 Boromir (Sean Bean) (horiz) . . . . 3·50 3·50

No. **MS**2490 was sold at face value.

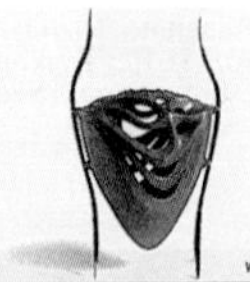

609 "Starfish Vessel" (wood sculpture) (Graeme Priddle)

2002. Artistic Crafts. Joint Issue with Sweden. Multicoloured.

2491 40c. Type **609** 35 30

2492 40c. Flax basket (Willa Rogers) (37 × 29 mm) . . 35 30

2493 80c. "Catch II" (clay bowl) (Raewyn Atkinson) . . . 55 50

2494 90c. "Vessel Form" (silver brooch) (Gavin Hitchings) 60 55

2495 $1.30 Glass towers from "Immigration" series (Emma Camden) 85 85

2496 $1.50 "Pacific Rim" (clay vessel) (Merilyn Wiseman) 95 1·10

2497 $2 Glass vase (Ola and Maria Höglund) (37 × 29 mm) . . . . . . 1·25 1·40

Nos. 2492 and 2497 are additionally inscribed "JOINT ISSUE WITH SWEDEN".

610 *Brodie* (Anna Poland, Cardinal McKeefry School) (National Winner)

2002. Children's Book Festival. Stamp Design Competition. Designs illustrating books. Multicoloured.

2498 40c. Type **610** 25 30

2499 40c. *The Last Whale* (Hee Su Kim, Glendowie Primary School) 25 30

2500 40c. *Scarface Claw* (Jayne Bruce, Rangiora Borough School) 25 30

2501 40c. *Which New Zealand Bird?* (Teigan Stafford-Bush, Ararimu School) . . 25 30

2502 40c. *Which New Zealand Bird?* (Hazel Gilbert, Gonville School) 25 30

2503 40c. *The Plight of the Penguin* (Gerard Mackle, Temuka High School) . . 25 30

2504 40c. *Scarface Claw* (Maria Rodgers, Salford School) 25 30

2505 40c. *Knocked for Six* (Paul Read, Ararimu School) 25 30

2506 40c. *Grandpa's Shorts* (Jessica Hitchings, Ashleigh Bree, Malyna Sengdara and Aniva Kini, Glendene Primary School) 25 30

2507 40c. *Which New Zealand Bird?* (Olivia Duncan, Takapuna Intermediate School) 25 30

MS2508 230 × 90 mm. Nos. 2498/507 2·50 2·75

611 Queen Elizabeth the Queen Mother, 1992

2002. Queen Elizabeth the Queen Mother Commemoration.

2509 **611** $2 multicoloured . . . . 1·25 1·40

612 Tongaporutu Cliffs, Taranaki

2002. Coastlines. Multicoloured. (a) Size 38 × 29 mm. Ordinary gum.

2510 40c. Type **612** 25 30

2511 80c. Lottin Point, East Cape 50 55

2512 90c. Curio Bay, Catlins . . 60 65

2513 $1.30 Kaikoura Coast . . . 85 90

2514 $1.50 Meybille Bay, West Coast . . . . 95 1·00

2515 $2 Papanui Point, Raglan 1·25 1·40

(b) Size 28 × 21 mm. Self-adhesive.

2516 40c. Type **612** 25 30

2517 90c. Curio Bay, Catlins . . 60 65

2518 $1.50 Meybille Bay, West Coast . . . . 95 1·00

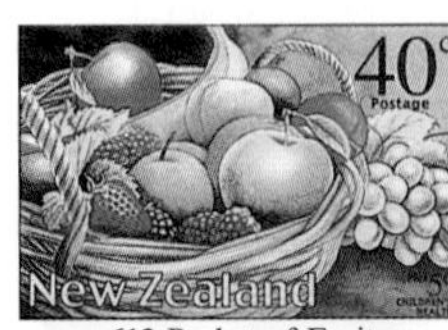

613 Basket of Fruit

2002. Children's Health. Healthy Eating. Multicoloured. (a) Ordinary gum.

2519 40c.+5c. Type **613** 30 35

2520 90c.+5c. Selection of vegetables 60 65

MS2521 90 × 75 mm. Nos. 2519/20 and as No. 2522 (22 × 26 mm) 1·25 1·40

(b) Self-adhesive.

2522 40c.+5c. Fruit and vegetables (22 × 26 mm) 30 35

2002. "Amphilex 2002" International Stamp Exhibition, Amsterdam. Sheet 130 × 95 mm, containing Nos. 2462/3. Multicoloured.

MS2523 $1.50 Strider (Viggo Mortensen); $2 Boromir (Sean Bean) (horiz) . . . . 95 1·00

No. **MS**2523 was sold at face value.

614 St. Werenfried, Tokaanu

2002. Christmas. Church Interiors. Multicoloured. (a) Size 35 × 35 mm. Ordinary gum.

2524 40c. Type **614** 25 30

2525 80c. St. David's, Christchurch 50 55

2526 90c. Orthodox Church of Transfiguration of Our Lord, Masterton 60 65

2527 $1.30 Cathedral of the Holy Spirit, Palmerston North 85 90

2528 $1.50 St. Paul's Cathedral, Wellington . . . . 95 1·00

2529 $2 Cathedral of the Blessed Sacrament, Christchurch 1·25 1·40

(b) Size 25 × 30 mm. Self-adhesive.

2530 40c. St. Werenfried, Tokaanu 25 30

615 *KZ 1* (racing yacht)

2002. Racing and Leisure Craft. Multicoloured.

2531 40c. Type **615** 25 30

2532 80c. *High 5* (ocean racing yacht) 50 55

2533 90c. *Gentle Spirit* (sports fishing and diving boat) 60 65

2534 $1.30 *North Star* (luxury motor cruiser) 85 90

2535 $1.50 *Ocean Runner* (powerboat) . . . . . . 95 1·00

2536 $2 *Salperton* (ocean-going yacht) . . . . 1·25 1·40

MS2537 140 × 80 mm. Nos. 2531/6 4·50 4·75

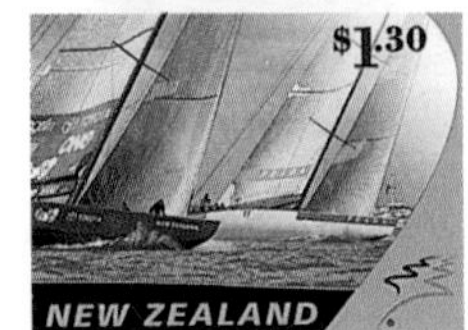

616 *Black Magic* (New Zealand) and *Luna Rossa* (Italy)

2002. America's Cup, 2003 (1st issue). Scenes from 2000 final, between New Zealand and Italy. Multicoloured.

2538 $1.30 Type **616** 85 90

2539 $1.50 Aerial view of race . . 95 1·00

2540 $2 Yachts turning . . . . . 1·25 1·40

MS2541 140 × 80 mm. Nos. 2538/40 3·00 3·25

See also Nos. 2562/5.

2002. "Stampshow 02" International Stamp Exhibition, Melbourne. No. **MS**2541 with "Stampshow 02" emblem and inscription on the margin. Multicoloured.

MS2542 140 × 80 mm. Nos. 2538/40 3·00 3·25

617 Green-roofed Holiday Cottage and Paua Shell

2002. Holiday Homes. Multicoloured.

2543 40c. Type **617** 25 30

2544 40c. Red-roofed cottage and sunflower 25 30

2545 40c. White-roofed cottage and life-belt 25 30

2546 40c. Cottage with orange door, boat and fishing fly 25 30

2547 40c. Blue-roofed cottage and fish 25 30

2548 40c. Cottage and caravan 25 30

618 "The Nativity" (15th-cent painting in style of Di Baldese)

2002. New Zealand–Vatican City Joint Issue.
2549 **618** $1.50 multicoloured . . 95 1·00

2002. Making of *The Lord of the Rings* Film Trilogy (2nd issue): The Two Towers. As T **605**. Multicoloured. (a) Designs 50 × 24 mm or 24 × 50 mm. Ordinary gum.
2550 40c. Aragorn (Viggo Mortenson) and Eowyn (Miranda Otto) (horiz) . . 25 30
2551 80c. Orc raider (horiz) . . . 50 55
2552 90c. Gandalf the White (Sir Ian McKellen) 60 65
2553 $1.30 Easterling warriors (horiz) 85 90
2554 $1.50 Frodo (Elijah Wood) 95 1·00
2555 $2 Eowyn, Shield Maiden of Rohan (Miranda Otto) (horiz) . . . . 1·25 1·40

(b) Designs 37 × 26 mm or 26 × 37 mm. Self-adhesive.
2556 40c. Strider (Viggo Mortenson) and Eowyn (Miranda Otto) (horiz) . . 25 30
2557 80c. Orc raider (horiz) . . . 50 55
2558 90c. Gandalf the White (Sir Ian McKellen) 60 65
2559 $1.30 Easterling warriors (horiz) 85 90
2560 $1.50 Frodo (Elijah Wood) 95 1·00
2561 $2 Eowyn, Shield Maiden of Rohan (Miranda Otto) (horiz) . . . . 1·25 1·40

2003. America's Cup (2nd issue). The Defence. As T **616**. Multicoloured.
2562 40c. Aerial view of Team New Zealand yacht . . . 25 30
2563 80c. Two Team New Zealand yachts 50 55
2564 90c. Team New Zealand yacht tacking 60 65
MS2565 140 × 80 mm. Nos. 2562/4 1·40 1·50

619 Shepherd with Flock in High Country

2003. Chinese New Year ("Year of the Sheep"). Sheep Farming. Multicoloured.
2566 40c. Type **619** 25 30
2567 90c. Mustering the sheep . . 50 55
2568 $1.30 Sheep in pen with sheep dog 85 90
2569 $1.50 Sheep shearing . . . 95 1·00
2570 $2 Sheep shearing (different) 1·25 1·40
MS2571 125 × 85 mm. Nos. 2568 and 2570 . . . . 2·10 2·25

620 Jon Trimmer in *Carmina Burana*

621 Officer, Forest Rangers, 1860s

2003. 50th Anniv of Royal New Zealand Ballet. Scenes from past productions. Multicoloured.
2572 40c. Type **620** 25 30
2573 90c. *Papillon* (horiz) 60 65
2574 $1.30 *Cinderella* 85 90
2575 $1.50 *FrENZy* . . . . . . 95 1·00
2576 $2 *Swan Lake* (horiz) . . . 1·25 1·40

2003. New Zealand Military Uniforms. Multicoloured.
2577 40c. Type **621** 25 30
2578 40c. Lieutenant, Napier Naval Artillery Volunteers, 1890s 25 30
2579 40c. Officer, 2nd Regt, North Canterbury Mounted Rifles, 1900–10 25 30
2580 40c. Mounted Trooper, New Zealand Mounted Rifles, South Africa 1899–1902 25 30
2581 40c. Staff Officer, New Zealand Division, France, 1918 . . . . 25 30
2582 40c. Petty Officer, Royal New Zealand Navy, 1914–18 . . . . 25 30
2583 40c. Rifleman, New Zealand Rifle Brigade, France, 1916–18 . . . . 25 30
2584 40c. Sergeant, New Zealand Engineers, 1939–45 . . . 25 30
2585 40c. Matron, Royal New Zealand Navy Hospital, 1940s 25 30
2586 40c. Private, New Zealand Women's Auxiliary Army Corps, Egypt, 1942 . . . 25 30
2587 40c. Pilot serving with R.A.F. Bomber Command, Europe, 1943 25 30
2588 40c. Fighter Pilot, No. 1 (Islands) Group, Royal New Zealand Air Force, Pacific, 1943 . . . . . . 25 30
2589 40c. Driver, Women's Auxiliary Air Force, 1943 25 30
2590 40c. Gunner, 16th Field Regt, Royal New Zealand Artillery, Korea, 1950–53 25 30
2591 40c. Acting Petty Officer, H.M.N.Z.S. *Tamaki*, 1957 25 30
2592 40c. Scouts, New Zealand Special Air Service, Malaya, 1955–57 . . . . 25 30
2593 40c. Canberra Pilot serving with R.A.F. Far East Command, Malaya, 1960 25 30
2594 40c. Infantrymen, 1st Bn, Royal New Zealand Infantry Regt, South Vietnam, 1960s 25 30
2595 40c. Infantryman, New Zealand Bn, UNTAET, East Timor, 2000 . . . . 25 30
2596 40c. Monitor, Peace Monitoring Group, Bougainville, 2001 . . . . 25 30

Nos. 2577/96 were printed together, se-tenant, with detailed descriptions of the designs printed on the reverse.

622 Ailsa Mountains

2003. New Zealand Landscapes. Each including the fern symbol after the country inscr. Multicoloured.
2597 50c. Type **622** 30 35
2598 $1 Coromandel 65 70
2599 $1.50 Arrowtown . . . . . 95 1·00
2600 $2 Tongariro National Park 1·25 1·40
2601 $5 Castlepoint Lighthouse 3·25 3·50

No. 2599 also comes self-adhesive.

EXPRESS DELIVERY STAMPS

E 1

1903.
E1 E **1** 6d. red and violet . . . . 38·00 23·00

E **2** Express Mail Delivery Van

1939.
E6 E **2** 6d. violet . . . . 1·50 1·75

LIFE INSURANCE DEPARTMENT

L 1

L **3** Castlepoint Lighthouse

1891.
L13 L **1** ½d. purple . . . . 55·00 3·25
L14 1d. blue . . . . 55·00 75
L15 2d. brown . . . . 75·00 3·50
L 4 3d. brown . . . . £160 20·00
L 5 6d. green . . . . £275 60·00
L 6 1s. pink £500 £120

1905. Similar type but "V.R." omitted.
L24 ½d. green . . . . 14·00 1·75
L22 1d. blue . . . . £160 30·00
L38 1d. red . . . . 3·25 2·00
L26 1½d. black . . . . 40·00 7·50
L27 1½d. brown . . . . 1·50 2·50
L21 2d. brown . . . . £1000 80·00
L28 2d. purple . . . . 48·00 27·00
L29 2d. yellow . . . . 5·50 2·00
L30 3d. brown . . . . 45·00 26·00
L35 3d. red . . . . 18·00 22·00
L41 6d. pink . . . . 13·00 35·00

1947. Lighthouses.
L42 L **3** ½d. green and orange . . 1·50 60
L43 – 1d. olive and blue . . . 1·50 1·00
L44 – 2d. blue and black . . . 80 80
L45 – 2½d. black and blue . . . 9·50 13·00
L46 – 3d. mauve and blue . . . 3·00 65
L47 – 4d. brown and orange . . 4·00 1·50
L48 – 6d. brown and blue . . . 3·75 2·25
L49 – 1s. brown and blue . . . 3·75 3·00

LIGHTHOUSES—HORIZ: 1d. Taiaroa; 2d. Cape Palliser; 6d. The Brothers. VERT: 2½d. Cape Campbell; 3d. Eddystone; 4d. Stephens Island; 1s. Cape Brett.

1967. Decimal currency. Stamps of 1947–65 surch.
L50a 1c. on 1d. (No. L43) . . . 1·00 4·25
L51 2c. on 2½d. (No. L45) . . . 9·50 14·00
L52 2½c. on 3d. (No. L46) . . . 1·50 4·50
L53 3c. on 4d. (No. L47) . . . 4·50 5·50
L54 5c. on 6d. (No. L48) . . . 75 6·00
L55a 10c. on 1s. (No. L49) . . . 75 4·00

L **13** Moeraki Point Lighthouse

1969.
L56 L **13** ½c. yellow, red and violet . . . . 65 1·75
L57 – 2½c. blue, green and buff 50 1·25
L58 – 3c. stone, yellow & brn 50 75
L59 – 4c. green, ochre and blue . . . . 50 1·00
L60 – 8c. multicoloured . . . 40 2·75
L61 – 10c. multicoloured . . . 40 2·75
L62 – 15c. multicoloured . . . 40 2·00

DESIGNS—HORIZ: 2½c. Puysegur Point Lighthouse; 4c. Cape Egmont Lighthouse. VERT: 3c. Baring Head Lighthouse; 8c. East Cape; 10c. Farewell Spit; 15c. Dog Island Lighthouse.

1978. No. L57 surch **25c.**
L63 25c. on 2½c. blue, green and buff . . . . 75 1·75

L 17

1981.
L64 L **17** 5c. multicoloured . . . 10 10
L65 10c. multicoloured . . . 10 10
L66 20c. multicoloured . . . 15 15
L67 30c. multicoloured . . . 25 25
L68 40c. multicoloured . . . 30 30
L69 50c. multicoloured . . . 30 35

OFFICIAL STAMPS

1891. Optd **O.P.S.O.**
O 1 **3** ½d. pink . . . . — £500
O 2 **13** ½d. black . . . . — £225
O13 **23** ½d. green . . . . — £225
O 4 **10** 1d. pink . . . . — £225
O19 **42** 1d. red . . . . — £250
O 6 **9** 2d. mauve . . . . — £375
O 8 **16** 2½d. blue . . . . — £275
O14 **26** 2½d. blue (A) . . . . . — £450
O21 2½d. blue (B) . . . . . — £325
O22 **28** 3d. brown . . . . — £450
O16 **24** 4d. blue and brown . . . — £425
O11 **19** 5d. black . . . . — £425
O17a **30** 5d. brown . . . . — £425
O12 **8** 6d. brown (No. 224b) . . — £600
O18 **32** 8d. blue . . . . — £550
O23 **34** 1s. red . . . . — £900
O24 **35** 2s. green . . . . — £1400

Optd **OFFICIAL.**

1907. Pictorials.
O59 **23** ½d. green . . . . 8·50 60
O61a **25** 2d. purple . . . . 8·50 1·60
O63 **28** 3d. brown . . . . 42·00 1·75
O64 **31** 6d. red . . . . £140 19·00
O65 **34** 1s. orange . . . . 85·00 15·00
O66 **35** 2s. green . . . . 70·00 75·00
O67 – 5s. red (No. 329) £150 £170

1907. "Universal" type.
O60b **42** 1d. red . . . . 9·50 50

1908.
O70 **50** 1d. red . . . . 65·00 2·50
O72 **31** 6d. red (No. 254) . . . . £130 35·00

1910. King Edward VII etc.
O73 **51** ½d. green . . . . 4·50 30
O78 **53** 1d. red . . . . 3·25 10
O74 **51** 3d. brown . . . . 14·00 80
O75 6d. red . . . . 19·00 5·00
O76 8d. blue . . . . 12·00 18·00
O77 1s. orange . . . . 48·00 15·00

1913. Queen Victoria.
O82 F **4** 2s. blue . . . . 48·00 45·00
O83 5s. green . . . . 75·00 90·00
O84 £1 red £550 £550

1915. King George V.
O 96 **62** ½d. green . . . . 1·50 10
O 90 1½d. grey . . . . 5·00 90
O 91 1½d. brown . . . . . . 5·00 30
O 98 2d. yellow . . . . 2·50 50
O 99 3d. brown . . . . 5·00 50
O101 4d. violet . . . . 14·00 3·75
O102 6d. red . . . . 5·00 75
O103 8d. brown . . . . 65·00 £150
O104 9d. green . . . . 40·00 38·00
O105b 1s. orange . . . . 7·00 2·00

1927. King George V.
O111 **71** 1d. red . . . . 2·00 20
O112 2s. blue . . . . 70·00 £100

1933. "Arms".
O113 F **6** 5s. green £250 £300

Optd **Official.**

1936. "Arms".
O133 F **6** 5s. green . . . . 40·00 6·00

1936. As 1935.
O120 **81** ½d. green . . . . 7·50 4·50
O115 – 1d. red (No. 557) . . . 3·50 1·25
O122 **83** 1½d. brown . . . . . . 20·00 4·75
O123 – 2d. orange (No. 580) . . 3·50 10
O124a **85** 2½d. brown and grey . . 14·00 21·00
O125 **86** 3d. brown . . . . . . 48·00 3·50
O126c **87** 4d. black and brown . . 4·50 1·00
O127c **89** 6d. red . . . . 10·00 30
O128a – 8d. brown (No. 586b) 8·50 16·00
O130 **91** 9d. red and black . . . 20·00 22·00
O131b – 1s. green (No. 588) . . 24·00 1·50
O132d **93** 2s. olive . . . . 42·00 7·50

1938. King George VI.
O134 **108** ½d. green . . . . . . 19·00 2·25
O135 ½d. orange . . . . . . 1·60 3·50
O136 1d. red . . . . 18·00 15
O137 1d. green . . . . 2·75 10
O138 1½d. brown . . . . . . 75·00 18·00
O139 1½d. red . . . . 9·00 5·50
O152 2d. orange . . . . . . 2·00 10
O140 3d. blue . . . . 2·75 10
O153 4d. purple . . . . . . 4·25 2·50
O154 6d. red . . . . 12·00 50
O155 8d. violet . . . . . . 8·00 6·50
O156 9d. brown . . . . . . 9·00 6·50
O157a – 1s. brown and red (No. 686b) . . . . . 8·50 9·00
O158 – 2s. orange and green (No. 688) . . . . . 26·00 16·00

1940. Centenary stamps.
O141 ½d. green . . . . 2·25 35
O142 1d. brown and red . . . . 4·75 10
O143 1½d. blue and mauve . . . 3·25 2·00
O144 2d. green and brown . . . 4·50 10
O145 2½d. green and blue . . . 4·50 2·75
O146 3d. purple and red . . . . 8·00 1·00
O147 4d. brown and red . . . . 40·00 1·50
O148 6d. green and violet . . . 25·00 1·50
O149 8d. black and red . . . . 30·00 17·00
O150 9d. olive and red . . . . 11·00 5·00
O151 1s. green . . . . 48·00 3·00

O **6** Queen Elizabeth II

1954.
O159 O **6** 1d. orange 75 40
O160 1½d. brown . . . . . . 3·75 5·00
O161 2d. green 50 40
O162 2½d. olive . . . . . . 3·50 1·50
O163 3d. red 70 10
O164 4d. blue . . . . 1·25 65
O165 9d. red . . . . 7·00 2·25
O166 1s. purple . . . . . . 1·00 10
O167 3s. slate . . . . 30·00 48·00

1959. Surch.
O169 O **6** 2½d. on 2d. green . . . 1·00 1·50
O168 6d. on 1½d. brown . . . 50 1·10

POSTAGE DUE STAMPS

D 1

D 2

1899.
D 9 D **1** ½d. red and green . . . 3·00 16·00
D10 1d. red and green . . . 11·00 1·75
D15 2d. red and green . . . 45·00 5·00
D12 3d. red and green . . . 13·00 3·50
D16 4d. red and green . . . 32·00 9·00
D 6 5d. red and green . . . 22·00 22·00
D 7 6d. red and green . . . 29·00 26·00
D 2 8d. red and green . . . 60·00 75·00
D 8 10d. red and green . . . 70·00 85·00
D 3 1s. red and green . . . 65·00 85·00
D 4 2s. red and green £120 £140

1902.
D18 D **2** ½d. red and green . . . 1·75 1·75
D30 1d. red and green . . . 3·75 80
D22a 2d. red and green . . . 5·50 1·75
D36 3d. red and green . . . 15·00 42·00

D 3

1939.

D41 **D 3** ½d. green 5·00 5·00
D42 1d. red 2·75 50
D46 2d. blue 8·00 1·40
D47aw 3d. brown 9·00 9·00

NICARAGUA Pt. 15

A republic of Central America, independent since 1821.

1862. 100 centavos = 1 peso (paper currency).
1912. 100 centavos de cordoba = 1 peso de cordoba (gold currency).
1925. 100 centavos = 1 cordoba.

2 Volcanoes

5

1862. Perf or roul.
13 **2** 1c. brown 1·50 75
4 2c. blue 2·25 75
14 5c. black 6·00 1·25
18 10c. red 2·25 1·40
19 25c. green 2·25 2·40

1882.
20 **5** 1c. green 15 20
21 2c. red 15 20
22 5c. blue 15 15
23 10c. violet 15 60
24 15c. yellow 30 1·50
25 20c. grey 50 3·00
26 50c. violet 70 6·00

6 Steam Locomotive and Telegraph Key

7

1890.
27 **6** 1c. brown 25 30
28 2c. red 25 30
29 5c. blue 25 20
30 10c. grey 25 25
31 20c. red 25 1·75
32 50c. violet 25 5·50
33 1p. brown 40 7·75
34 2p. green 40 10·00
35 5p. red 50 19·00
36 10p. orange 50 27·00

1891.
37 **7** 1c. brown 15 30
38 2c. red 15 30
39 5c. blue 15 25
40 10c. grey 15 35
41 20c. lake 15 1·75
42 50c. violet 15 3·00
43 1p. sepia 15 4·50
44 2p. green 15 5·00
45 5p. red 15 12·00
46 10p. orange 15 15·00

8 First Sight of the New World

1892. Discovery of America.
47 **8** 1c. brown 15 25
48 2c. red 15 25
49 5c. blue 15 20
50 10c. grey 15 25
51 20c. red 15 1·75
52 50c. violet 15 4·25
53 1p. brown 15 4·25
54 2p. green 15 5·00
55 5p. red 15 14·00
56 10p. orange 15 18·00

9 Volcanoes
10

1893.
57 **9** 1c. brown 15 25
58 2c. red 15 25
59 5c. blue 15 20
60 10c. grey 15 25
61 20c. brown 15 1·40
62 50c. violet 15 3·50
63 1p. brown 15 4·25
64 2p. green 15 5·00
65 5p. red 15 11·00
66 10p. orange 15 14·00

1894.
67 **10** 1c. brown 15 25
68 2c. red 15 25
69 5c. blue 15 20
70 10c. grey 15 25
71 20c. red 15 1·50
72 50c. violet 15 3·50
73 1p. brown 15 4·25
74 2p. green 15 7·50
75 5p. brown 15 9·00
76 10p. orange 15 12·00

11
12 Map of Nicaragua
13 Arms of Republic of Central America

1895.
77 **11** 1c. brown 15 20
78 2c. red 15 20
79 5c. blue 15 15
80 10c. grey 15 20
81 20c. red 15 70
82 50c. violet 15 3·00
83 1p. brown 15 4·50
84 2p. green 15 4·75
85 5p. red 15 9·25
86 10p. orange 15 14·50

1896. Date "1896".
90 **12** 1c. violet 15 75
91 2c. green 15 50
92 5c. red 15 35
93 10c. blue 30 65
94 20c. brown 1·75 3·50
95 50c. grey 35 4·75
96 1p. black 35 6·50
97 2p. red 35 9·00
98 5p. blue 35 9·00

1897. As T **12**, dated "1897".
99 **12** 1c. violet 25 35
100 2c. green 25 35
101 5c. red 25 20
102 10c. blue 3·75 65
103 20c. brown 1·50 2·25
104 50c. grey 5·25 5·75
105 1p. black 5·25 8·75
106 2p. red 11·50 11·00
107 5p. blue 11·50 25·00

1898.
108 **13** 1c. brown 20 20
109 2c. grey 20 20
110 4c. lake 20 30
122 5c. olive 15·00 15
112 10c. purple 8·75 40
113 15c. blue 25 1·00
114 20c. blue 6·00 1·00
115 50c. yellow 6·00 5·75
116 1p. blue 30 9·50
117 2p. brown 11·00 13·00
118 5p. orange 15·00 19·00

14

15 Mt. Momotombo

1899.
126 **14** 1c. green 10 25
127 2c. brown 10 25
128 4c. red 20 25
129 5c. blue 15 25
130 10c. orange 15 25
131 15c. brown 15 40
132 20c. green 20 70
133 50c. red 15 1·75
134 1p. orange 15 5·00
135 2p. violet 15 12·00
136 5p. blue 15 14·50

1900.
137 **15** 1c. red 35 10
138 2c. orange 65 15
139 3c. green 75 20
140 4c. olive 95 25
184 5c. red 1·50 45
185 5c. blue 1·50 45
142 6c. red 19·00 5·50
186 10c. mauve 1·50 45
144 15c. blue 10·00 35
145 20c. brown 9·00 30
146 50c. lake 9·00 1·60
147 1p. yellow 20·00 6·75
148 2p. red 8·00 75
149 5p. black 14·00 2·50

1901. Surch **1901** and value.
151 **15** 2c. on 1p. yellow 11·00 8·50
169 3c. on 6c. red 8·00 5·00
163 4c. on 6c. red 7·00 4·00
173 5c. on 1p. yellow 11·50 5·75
168 10c. on 2p. red 8·00 1·75
152 10c. on 5p. black 14·00 11·00
153 20c. on 2p. red 22·00 20·00
176 20c. on 5p. black 6·00 3·75

1901. Postage Due stamps of 1900 optd **1901 Correos**.
177 **D 16** 1c. red 60 30
178 2c. orange 45 30
179 5c. blue 55 45
180 10c. violet 55 45
181 20c. brown 75 1·00
182 30c. green 70 1·00
183 50c. lake 70 1·00

1902. Surch **1902** and value.
187 **15** 15c. on 2c. orange 4·00 1·50
188 30c. on 1c. red 1·50 4·25

27 Pres. Santos Zelaya

37 Arms

1903. 10th Anniv of Revolution against Sacaza and 1st election of Pres. Zelaya.
189 **27** 1c. black and green 25 45
190 2c. black and red 50 45
191 5c. black and blue 25 45
192 10c. black and orange 25 70
193 15c. black and lake 45 1·40
194 20c. black and violet 45 1·40
195 50c. black and olive 45 3·00
196 1p. black and brown 45 3·50

1904. Surch **15 Centavos**.
200 **15** 15c. on 10c. mauve 5·75 3·00

1904. Surch **Vale**, value and wavy lines.
203 **15** 5c. on 10c. mauve 1·90 50
204 15c. on 10c. mauve 60 40

1905. No. 186 surch **5 CENTS**.
205 **15** 5c. on 10c. mauve 75 50

1905.
206 **37** 1c. green 20 15
207 2c. red 20 15
208 3c. violet 25 20
280 3c. orange 25 15
209 4c. orange 25 20
281 4c. violet 25 15
282 5c. blue 25 15
211 6c. grey 45 30
283 6c. brown 1·75 1·10
212 10c. brown 55 20
284 10c. lake 60 10
213 15c. olive 55 25
285 15c. black 60 10
214 20c. lake 45 25
286 20c. olive 60 10
215 50c. orange 1·75 1·40
287 50c. green 70 35
216 1p. black 90 90
288 1p. yellow 70 35
217 2p. green 90 1·25
289 2p. red 70 35
218 5p. violet 1·00 1·50

1906. Surch **Vale** (or **VALE**) and value in one line.
292 **37** 2c. on 3c. orange 90 75
293 5c. on 20c. olive 30 25
247 10c. on 2c. red 1·10 45
223 10c. on 3c. violet 30 15
248 10c. on 4c. orange 1·25 55
291 10c. on 15c. black 30 25
250 10c. on 20c. lake 1·90 85
252 10c. on 50c. orange 1·40 45
234 10c. on 2p. green 12·00 7·00
235 10c. on 5p. violet 60·00 42·00
226 15c. on 1c. green 30 20
229 20c. on 2c. red 40 25
230 20c. on 5c. blue 45 35
236 35c. on 6c. grey 1·60 1·60
232 50c. on 6c. grey 45 35
238 1p. on 5p. violet 25·00 14·50

51

50

64

1908. Fiscal stamps as T **51** optd **CORREO–1908** or surch **VALE** and value also.
260 **51** 1c. on 5c. yellow 35 20
261 2c. on 5c. yellow 35 25
262 4c. on 5c. yellow 65 30
256 5c. yellow 45 35
257 10c. blue 35 20
263 15c. on 50c. green 45 30
264 35c. on 50c. green 2·50 65
258 1p. brown 20 1·40
259 2p. grey 20 1·50

1908. Fiscal stamps as T **50** optd **CORREOS–1908** or surch **VALE** and value also.
268 **50** 2c. orange 2·10 1·00
269 4c. on 2c. orange 1·00 65
270 5c. on 2c. orange 1·10 45
271 10c. on 2c. orange 1·10 25

1909. Surch **CORREOS–1909 VALE** and value.
273 **51** 1c. on 50c. green 2·25 95
274 2c. on 50c. green 4·00 1·75
275 4c. on 50c. green 4·00 1·75
276 5c. on 50c. green 2·25 1·10
277 10c. on 50c. green 65 40

1910. Surch **Vale** and value in two lines.
296 **37** 2c. on 3c. orange 65 35
300 2c. on 4c. violet 25 15
301 5c. on 20c. olive 25 15
302 10c. on 15c. black 30 15
303 10c. on 50c. green 20 15
299 10c. on 1p. yellow 65 35
305 10c. on 2p. red 45 35

1911. Surch **Correo 1911** (or **CORREOS 1911**) and value.
307 **51** 2c. on 5p. blue 25 30
312 5c. on 2p. grey 90 70
308 5c. on 10p. pink 55 30
309 10c. on 25c. lilac 30 20
310 10c. on 2p. grey 30 20
311 35c. on 1p. brown 30 25

1911. Surch **VALE POSTAL de 1911** and value.
313 **51** 5c. on 25c. lilac 90 70
314 5c. on 50c. green 3·00 3·00
315 5c. on 5p. blue 4·00 4·00
317 5c. on 50p. red 3·00 3·00
318 10c. on 50c. green 70 45

1911. Railway tickets as T **64**, with fiscal surch on the front, further surch for postal use. (a) Surch **vale CORREO DE 1911** and value on back.
319 **64** 2c. on 5c. on 2nd class blue 55 65
320 05c. on 5c. on 2nd class blue 30 40
321 10c. on 5c. on 2nd class blue 30 40
322 15c. on 10c. on 1st class red 40 50

(b) Surch **vale CORREO DE 1911** and value on front.
322c **64** 2c. on 5c. on 2nd class blue 8·00 8·00
322d 05c. on 5c. on 2nd class blue £170 £170
322e 10c. on 5c. on 2nd class blue 80·00 80·00
322f 15c. on 10c. on 1st class red 22·00 22·00

(c) Surch **CORREO** and value on front.
323 **64** 2c. on 10c. on 1st class red 80 80
324 20c. on 10c. on 1st class red 4·00 4·00
325 50c. on 10c. on 1st class red 7·50 7·50

(d) Surch **Correo Vale 1911** and value on front.
326 **64** 2c. on 10c. on 1st class red 15 15
328 5c. on 5c. on 2nd class blue 90 80
327 5c. on 10c. on 1st class red 20 1·25
330 10c. on 10c. on 1st class red 70 50

(e) Surch **Vale CORREO DE 1911** and value on back.
331 **64** 5c. on 10c. on 1st class red 18·00
332 10c. on 10c. on 1st class red 7·00

(f) Surch **CORREO Vale 10 cts. 1911** and bar obliterating **oficial** on front.
333 **64** 10c. on 10c. on 1st class red 1·25 1·00

70

71

1912.
337 **70** 1c. green 25 15
338 2c. red 25 15

339 3c. brown 25 15
340 4c. purple 25 15
341 5c. black and blue 25 15
342 6c. brown 25 70
343 10c. brown 25 15
344 15c. violet 25 15
345 20c. brown 25 15
346 25c. black and green 25 15
347 **71** 35c. brown and green 1·10 1·10
348 **70** 50c. blue 65 30
349 1p. orange 90 1·40
350 2p. green 90 1·75
351 5p. black 1·60 2·10

1913. Surch **Vale 15 cts Correos 1913**.
352 **71** 15c. on 35c. brown & green 30 20

1913. Surch **VALE 1913** and value in "centavos de cordoba". A. On stamps of 1912 issue.
353 **70** ½c. on 3c. brown 35 25
354 ½c. on 15c. violet 20 15
355 ½c. on 1p. orange 20 15
356 1c. on 3c. brown 55 45
357 1c. on 4c. purple 20 15
358 1c. on 50c. blue 20 15
359 1c. on 5p. black 20 15
360 2c. on 4c. purple 25 20
361 2c. on 20c. brown 2·25 2·75
362 2c. on 25c. black & green 25 15
363 **71** 2c. on 35c. brown & green 20 35
364 **70** 2c. on 50c. blue 20 90
365 2c. on 2p. green 15 15
366 3c. on 6c. brown 15 10
B. On Silver Currency stamps of 1912 (Locomotive type).
367 **Z 1** ½c. on 2c. red 3·25 2·50
368 1c. on 3c. brown 2·10 1·60
369 1c. on 4c. red 2·10 1·60
370 1c. on 6c. red 2·10 1·60
371 1c. on 20c. blue 2·10 1·60
372 1c. on 25c. black & green 2·10 1·60
384 2c. on 1c. green 25·00 19·00
373 2c. on 25c. black & green 11·25 8·50
374 5c. on 35c. black & green 2·10 1·60
375 5c. on 50c. olive 2·10 1·60
376 6c. on 1p. orange 2·10 1·60
377 10c. on 2p. brown 2·10 1·60
378 1p. on 5p. green 2·10 1·60

1914. No. 352 surch with new value and **Cordoba** and thick bar over old surch.
385 **71** ½c. on 15c. on 35c. 15 10
386 1c. on 15c. on 35c. 20 15

1914. Official stamps of 1913 surch with new value and thick bar through "OFICIAL".
387 **70** 1c. on 25c. blue 30 20
388 **71** 1c. on 35c. blue 30 20
389 **70** 1c. on 1p. blue 20 15
391 2c. on 50c. blue 30 15
392 2c. on 2p. blue 20 15
393 5c. on 5p. blue 20 15

79 National Palace, Managua
80 Leon Cathedral

1914. Various frames.
394 **79** ½c. blue 50 15
395 1c. green 50 15
396 **80** 2c. orange 50 15
397 **79** 3c. brown 80 25
398 **80** 4c. red 80 25
399 **79** 5c. grey 30 10
400 **80** 6c. sepia 5·25 3·25
401 10c. yellow 55 15
402 **79** 15c. violet 3·50 1·40
403 **80** 20c. grey 6·50 3·25
404 **79** 25c. orange 85 20
405 **80** 50c. blue 85 25
See also Nos. 465/72, 617/27 and 912/24.

1915. Surch **VALE 5 cts. de Cordoba 1915**.
406 **80** 5c. on 6c. sepia 1·10 35

1918. Stamps of 1914 surch **Vale centavos de cordoba**.
407 **80** ½c. on 6c. sepia 2·00 75
408 ½c. on 10c. yellow 1·40 25
409 **79** ½c. on 15c. violet 1·40 45
410 ½c. on 25c. orange 3·00 85
411 **80** ½c. on 50c. blue 1·40 25
440 1c. on 2c. orange 90 20
413 **79** 1c. on 3c. brown 1·50 25
414 **80** 1c. on 6c. sepia 7·00 2·10
415 1c. on 10c. yellow 13·00 4·75
416 **79** 1c. on 15c. violet 2·40 55
418 **80** 1c. on 20c. grey 1·40 25
420 **79** 1c. on 25c. orange 2·40 70
421 **80** 1c. on 50c. blue 7·75 2·25
422 2c. on 4c. red 1·75 25
423 2c. on 6c. sepia 13·00 4·75
424 2c. on 10c. yellow 13·00 2·50
425 2c. on 20c. grey 7·00 2·10
426 **79** 2c. on 25c. orange 3·00 30
427 **80** 5c. on 6c. sepia 5·00 2·50
428 **79** 5c. on 15c. violet 1·75 45

1919. Official stamps of 1915 surch **Vale centavo de cordoba** and with bar through "OFICIAL".
444 **80** ½c. on 2c. blue 30 15
445 ½c. on 4c. blue 70 15
446 **79** 1c. on 3c. blue 70 25
432 1c. on 25c. blue 1·10 20
433 **80** 2c. on 50c. blue 1·10 20
443a 10c. on 20c. blue 1·00 40

1921. Official stamps of 1913 optd **Particular** and wavy lines through "OFICIAL".
441 **70** 1c. blue 90 45
442 5c. blue 90 35

1921. No. 399 surch **Vale medio centavo**.
447 **79** ½c. on 5c. black 35 15

1921. Official stamp of 1915 optd **Particular R de C** and bars.
448 **79** 1c. blue 3·50 1·00

1921. Official stamps of 1915 surch **Vale un centavo R de C** and bars.
449 **79** 1c. on 5c. blue 95 35
450 **80** 1c. on 6c. blue 50 20
451 1c. on 10c. blue 65 20
452 **79** 1c. on 15c. blue 1·10 20

90
91 Jose C. del Valle

1921. Fiscal stamps as T **23** surch **R de C Vale** and new value.
453 **90** 1c. on 1c. red and black 10 10
454 1c. on 2c. green and black 10 10
455 1c. on 4c. orange and black 10 10
456 1c. on 15c. blue and black 10 10
No. 456 is inscr "TIMBRE TELEGRAFICO".

1921. Independence Centenary.
457 – ½c. black and blue 30 25
458 **91** 1c. black and green 30 25
459 – 2c. black and red 30 25
460 – 5c. black and violet 30 25
461 – 10c. black and orange 20 25
462 – 25c. black and yellow 30 25
463 – 50c. black and violet 30 25
DESIGNS: ½c. Arce; 2c. Larreinaga; 5c. F. Chamorro; 10c. Jerez; 25c. J. P. Chamorro; 50c. Dario.

1922. Surch **Vale un centavo R. de C.**
464 **80** 1c. on 10c. yellow 10 10

1922. As Nos. 394, etc, but colours changed.
465 **79** ½c. green 15 10
466 1c. violet 15 10
467 **80** 2c. red 15 10
468 **79** 3c. olive 25 15
469 **80** 6c. brown 15 15
470 **79** 15c. brown 25 15
471 **80** 20c. brown 35 15
472 1cor. brown 65 35
Nos. 465/72 are size 27 × 22¾ mm.
For later issues of these types, see Nos. 617/27 and 912/24.

1922. Optd **R. de C.**
473 **79** 1c. violet 10 10

1922. Independence issue of 1921 surch **R. de C. Vale un centavo**.
474 **91** 1c. on 1c. black and green 55 45
475 – 1c. on 5c. black and violet 55 55
476 – 1c. on 10c. black and orange 55 30
477 – 1c. on 25c. black and yellow 55 25
478 – 1c. on 50c. black and violet 25 20

94
99 F. Hernandez de Cordoba

1922. Surch **Nicaragua R. de C. Vale un cent.**
479 **94** 1c. yellow 10 10
480 1c. mauve 10 10
481 1c. blue 10 10

1922. Surch **Vale 0.01 de Cordoba** in two lines.
482 **80** 1c. on 10c. yellow 70 25
483 2c. on 10c. yellow 70 20

1923. Surch **Vale 2 centavos de cordoba** in three lines.
484 **79** 1c. on 5c. black 70 15
485 **80** 2c. on 10c. yellow 70 15

1923. Optd **Sello Postal**.
486 – ½c. black and blue (No. 457) 5·50 4·25
487 **91** 1c. black and green 1·40 70

1923. Independence issue of 1921 surch **R. de C. Vale un centavo de cordoba**.
488 1c. on 2c. black and red 30 30
489 1c. on 5c. black and violet 35 15
490 1c. on 10c. black and orange 15 15
491 1c. on 25c. black and yellow 25 25
492 1c. on 50c. black and violet 15 10

1923. Fiscal stamp optd **R. de C.**
493 **90** 1c. red and black 15 10

1924. Optd **R. de C. 1924** in two lines.
494 **79** 1c. violet 15 15

1924. 400th Anniv of Foundation of Leon and Granada.
495 **99** 1c. green 90 25
496 2c. red 90 25
497 5c. blue 65 25
498 10c. brown 65 45

1925. Optd **R. de C. 1925** in two lines.
499 **79** 1c. violet 15 10

1927. Optd **Resello 1927**.
525 **79** ½c. green 10 10
528 1c. violet (No. 466) 10 10
555 1c. violet (No. 473) 15 10
532 **80** 2c. red 15 10
533 **79** 3c. green 20 10
537 **80** 4c. red 9·50 8·00
539 **79** 5c. grey 55 20
542 **80** 6c. brown 7·75 6·50
543 10c. yellow 25 15
545 **79** 15c. brown 55 25
547 **80** 20c. brown 25 15
549 **79** 25c. orange 30 15
551 **80** 50c. blue 30 15
553 1cor. brown 35 15

1928. Optd **Resello 1928**.
559 **79** ½c. green 20 15
560 1c. violet 10 10
561 **80** 2c. red 15 10
562 **79** 3c. green 15 10
563 **80** 4c. red 15 10
564 **79** 5c. grey 15 10
565 **80** 6c. brown 15 10
566 10c. yellow 20 10
567 **79** 15c. brown 25 20
568 **80** 20c. brown 35 20
569 **79** 25c. orange 55 20
570 **80** 50c. blue 90 10
571 1cor. brown 75 25

1928. Optd **Correos 1928**.
574 **79** ½c. green 15 10
575 1c. violet 10 10
576 3c. olive 55 20
577 **80** 4c. red 25 10
578 **79** 5c. grey 20 10
579 **80** 6c. brown 30 15
580 10c. yellow 35 15
581 **79** 15c. brown 1·00 15
582 **80** 20c. brown 1·00 15
583 **79** 25c. orange 1·00 20
584 **80** 50c. blue 1·00 20
585 1cor. brown 3·00 1·50

1928. No. 577 surch **Vale 2 cts.**
586 **80** 2c. on 4c. red 90 25

1928. Fiscal stamp as T **90**, but inscr "TIMBRE TELEGRAFICO" and surch **Correos 1928 Vale** and new value.
587 **90** 1c. on 5c. blue and black 25 15
588 2c. on 5c. blue and black 25 15
589 3c. on 5c. blue and black 25 15

1928. Obligatory Tax. No. 587 additionally optd **R. de T.**
590 **90** 1c. on 5c. blue and black 45 10

1928. As Nos. 465/72 but colours changed.
591 **79** ½c. red 30 15
592 1c. orange 30 15
593 **80** 2c. green 30 15
594 **79** 3c. purple 30 20
595 **80** 4c. brown 30 20
596 **79** 5c. yellow 30 15
597 **80** 6c. blue 30 20
598 10c. blue 65 20
599 **79** 15c. red 85 35
600 **80** 20c. green 85 35
601 **79** 25c. purple 16·00 3·75
602 **80** 50c. brown 1·90 70
603 1cor. violet 3·75 1·75
See also Nos. 617/27 and 912/24.

106

1928.
604 **106** 1c. purple 20 10
647 1c. red 25 10
For 1c. green see No. 925.

1929. Optd **R. de C.**
605 **79** 1c. orange 10 10
628 1c. olive 15 10

1929. Optd **Correos 1929**.
606 **79** ½c. green 20 15

1929. Optd **Correos 1928**.
607 **99** 10c. brown 55 45

1929. Fiscal stamps as T **90**, but inscr "TIMBRE TELEGRAFICO". A. Surch **Correos 1929 R. de C. C$ 0.01** vert.
613 **90** 1c. on 5c. blue and black 10 15
B. Surch **Correos 1929** and value.
611 **90** 1c. on 10c. green and black 20 15
612 2c. on 5c. blue and black 20 10
C. Surch **Correos 1929** and value vert and **R. de C.** or **R. de T.** horiz.
608 **90** 1c. on 5c. blue and black (R. de T.) 20 15
609 2c. on 5c. blue and black (R. de T.) 15 15
610 2c. on 5c. blue and black (R. de C.) 13·00 70

1929. Air. Optd **Correo Aereo 1929. P.A.A.**
614 **79** 25c. sepia 1·40 1·40
615 25c. orange 1·00 1·00
616 25c. violet 90 70

1929. As Nos. 591/603 but colours changed.
617 **79** 1c. green 10 10
618 3c. blue 25 15
619 **80** 4c. blue 25 15
620 **79** 5c. brown 30 15
621 **80** 6c. drab 30 15
622 10c. brown 45 15
623 **79** 15c. red 65 20
624 **80** 20c. orange 80 25
625 **79** 25c. violet 20 10
626 **80** 50c. green 35 15
627 1cor. yellow 2·75 90
See also Nos. 912/24.

112 Mt. Momotombo

1929. Air.
629 **112** 15c. purple 25 10
630 20c. green 70 45
631 25c. olive 50 30
632 50c. sepia 80 45
633 1cor. red 1·10 55
See also Nos. 926/30.

1930. Air. Surch **Vale** and value.
634 **112** 15c. on 25c. olive 40 30
635 20c. on 25c. olive 60 45

114 G.P.O. Managua

1930. Opening of the G.P.O., Managua.
636 **114** ½c. sepia 80 60
637 1c. red 80 60
638 2c. orange 65 45
639 3c. orange 1·00 90
640 4c. yellow 1·00 90
641 5c. olive 1·60 1·10
642 6c. green 1·60 1·10
643 10c. black 1·60 1·00
644 25c. blue 3·25 2·40
645 50c. blue 5·25 3·50
646 1cor. violet 15·00 7·25

1931. Optd **1931** and thick bar obliterating old overprint "1928".
648 **99** 10c. brown (No. 607) 45 90

1931. No. 607 surch **C$ 0.02**.
649 **99** 2c. on 10c. brown 55 45

1931. Optd **1931** and thick bar.
650 **99** 2c. on 10c. brown (No. 498) 55 1·75

1931. Air. Nos. 614/16 surch **1931 Vale** and value.
651 **79** 15c. on 25c. sepia 90·00 90·00
652 15c. on 25c. orange 45·00 45·00
653 15c. on 25c. violet 9·00 9·00
654 20c. on 25c. violet 9·00 9·00

1931. Optd **1931**.
656 **79** ½c. green 35 10
657 1c. olive 35 10
665 1c. orange (No. 605) 10 10
658 **80** 2c. red 35 10
659 **79** 3c. blue 35 15

660 5c. yellow 2·10 1·40
661 5c. sepia 65 20
662 15c. orange 70 45
663 25c. sepia 9·00 3·75
664 25c. violet 3·50 1·50

1931. Air. Surch **1931** and value.
667 **80** 15c. on 25c. olive 4·75 4·75
668 15c. on 50c. sepia 36·00 36·00
669 15c. on 1cor. red 90·00 90·00
666 15c. on 20c. on 25c. olive (No. 635) 7·50 7·50

120 G.P.O. before and after the Earthquake

1932. G.P.O. Reconstruction Fund.
670 **120** ½c. green (postage) 90 90
671 1c. brown 1·25 1·25
672 2c. red 90 90
673 3c. blue 90 90
674 4c. blue 90 90
675 5c. brown 1·40 1·40
676 6c. brown 1·40 1·40
677 10c. brown 2·25 1·50
678 15c. red 3·50 2·25
679 20c. orange 2·10 2·10
680 25c. violet 2·25 2·25
681 50c. green 2·25 2·25
682 1cor. yellow 4·50 4·50
683 15c. mauve (air) 90 75
684 20c. green 1·10 1·10
685 25c. brown 5·50 5·50
686 50c. brown 7·00 7·00
687 1cor. red 10·50 10·50

1932. Air. Surch **Vale** and value.
688 **112** 30c. on 50c. sepia 1·40 1·40
689 35c. on 50c. sepia 1·40 1·40
690 40c. on 1cor. red 1·60 1·60
691 55c. on 1cor. red 1·60 1·60
For similar surcharges on these stamps in different colours see Nos. 791/4 and 931/4.

1932. Air. International Air Mail Week. Optd **Semana Correo Aereo Internacional 11–17 Septiembre 1932.**
692 **112** 15c. violet 40·00 40·00

1932. Air. Inauguration of Inland Airmail Service. Surch **Inauguracion Interior 12 Octubre 1932 Vale C$0.08.**
693 **112** 8c. on 1cor. red 13·00 13·00

1932. Air. Optd **Interior–1932** or surch **Vale** and value also.
705 **120** 25c. brown 4·75 4·75
706 32c. on 50c. brown 5·50 5·50
707 40c. on 1cor. red 4·25 4·25

1932. Air. Nos. 671, etc, optd **Correo Aereo Interior** in one line and **1932**, or surch **Vale** and value also.
694 **120** 1c. brown 12·00 12·00
695 2c. red 12·00 12·00
696 3c. blue 5·50 5·50
697 4c. blue 5·50 5·50
698 5c. brown 5·50 5·50
699 6c. brown 5·50 5·50
700 8c. on 10c. brown 5·25 5·25
701 16c. on 20c. orange 5·25 5·25
702 24c. on 25c. violet 5·25 5·25
703 50c. green 5·25 5·25
704 1cor. yellow 5·50 5·50

1932. Air. Surch **Correo Aereo Interior–1932** in two lines and **Vale** and value below.
710 **80** 1c. on 2c. red 40 40
711 **79** 2c. on 3c. blue 40 40
712 **80** 3c. on 4c. blue 40 40
713 **79** 4c. on 5c. sepia 40 40
714 **80** 5c. on 6c. brown 40 40
715 6c. on 10c. brown 40 40
716 **79** 8c. on 15c. orange 40 40
717 **80** 16c. on 20c. orange 40 40
718 **79** 24c. on 25c. violet 85 60
719 25c. on 25c. violet 85 60
720 **80** 32c. on 50c. green 85 75
721 40c. on 50c. green 95 85
722 50c. on 1cor. yellow 1·25 1·25
723 100c. on 1cor. yellow 2·50 2·50

127 Wharf, Port San Jorge

128 La Chocolata Cutting

1932. Opening of Rivas Railway.
726 **127** 1c. yellow (postage) 19·00
727 – 2c. red 19·00
728 – 5c. sepia 19·00
729 – 10c. brown 19·00
730 – 15c. yellow 19·00
731 **128** 15c. violet (air) 25·00
732 – 20c. green 25·00
733 – 25c. brown 25·00
734 – 50c. sepia 25·00
735 – 1cor. red 25·00
DESIGNS—HORIZ: 2c. El Nacascolo Halt; 5c. Rivas Station; 10c. San Juan del Sur; 15c. (No. 730), Arrival platform at Rivas; 20c. El Nacascolo; 25c. La Cuesta cutting; 50c. San Juan del Sur quay; 1cor. El Estero.

1932. Surch **Vale** and value in words.
736 **79** 1c. on 3c. blue 35 15
737 **80** 2c. on 4c. blue 30 15

130 Railway Construction

1932. Opening of Leon–Sauce Railway.
739 – 1c. yellow (postage) 19·00
740 – 2c. red 19·00
741 – 5c. sepia 19·00
742 **130** 10c. brown 19·00
743 – 15c. yellow 19·00
744 – 15c. violet (air) 25·00
745 – 20c. green 25·00
746 – 25c. brown 25·00
747 – 50c. sepia 25·00
748 – 1cor. red 25·00
DESIGNS—HORIZ: 1c. El Sauce; 2c., 15c. (No. 744), Bridge at Santa Lucia; 5c. Santa Lucia; 15c. (No. 743), Santa Lucia cutting; 20c. Santa Lucia River Halt; 25c. Malpaicillo Station; 50c. Railway panorama; 1cor. San Andres.

1933. Surch **Resello 1933 Vale** and value in words.
749 **79** 1c. on 3c. blue 20 15
750 1c. on 5c. sepia 20 15
751 **80** 2c. on 10c. brown 20 15

133 Flag of the Race

1933. 441st Anniv of Columbus' Departure from Palos. Roul.
753 **133** ½c. green (postage) 95 95
754 1c. green 80 80
755 2c. red 80 80
756 3c. red 80 80
757 4c. orange 80 80
758 5c. yellow 95 95
759 10c. brown 95 95
760 15c. brown 95 95
761 20c. blue 95 95
762 25c. blue 95 95
763 30c. violet 2·40 2·40
764 50c. purple 2·40 2·40
765 1cor. brown 2·40 2·40
766 1c. brown (air) 90 90
767 2c. purple 90 90
768 4c. violet 1·50 1·40
769 5c. blue 1·40 1·40
770 6c. blue 1·40 1·40
771 8c. brown 45 45
772 15c. brown 45 45
773 20c. yellow 1·40 1·40
774 25c. orange 1·40 1·40
775 50c. red 1·40 1·40
776 1cor. green 9·00 9·00

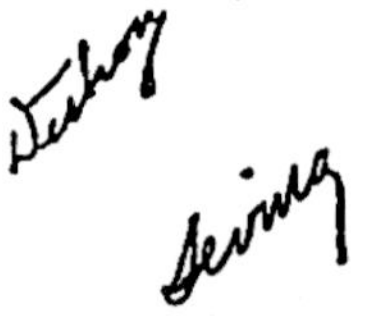

(**134**) (Facsimile signatures of R. E. Deshon, Minister of Transport and J. R. Sevilla, P.M.G.)

1933. Optd with T **134**.
777 **79** ½c. green 30 15
778 1c. green 15 10
779 **80** 2c. red 40 15
780 **79** 3c. blue 15 10
781 **80** 4c. blue 20 15
782 **79** 5c. brown 20 10
783 **80** 6c. drab 25 20
784 10c. brown 25 15
785 **79** 15c. red 30 20
786 **80** 20c. orange 40 30
787 **79** 25c. violet 45 25
788 **80** 50c. green 75 50
789 1cor. yellow 4·00 1·60

1933. No. 605 optd with T **134**.
790 **79** 1c. orange 25 15

1933. Air. Surch **Vale** and value.
791 **112** 30c. on 50c. orange 35 15
792 35c. on 50c. blue 45 20
793 40c. on 1cor. yellow 70 15
794 55c. on 1cor. green 70 30

135 Lake Xolotlan

1933. Air. International Airmail Week.
795 **135** 10c. brown 90 90
796 15c. violet 75 75
797 25c. red 85 85
798 50c. blue 90 90

(**136**)

1933. Air. Inland service. Colours changed. Surch as T **136** and optd with T **134**.
799 **80** 1c. on 2c. green 15 15
800 **79** 2c. on 3c. olive 15 15
801 **80** 3c. on 4c. red 15 15
802 **79** 4c. on 5c. blue 15 15
803 **80** 5c. on 6c. blue 15 15
804 6c. on 10c. sepia 15 10
805 **79** 8c. on 15c. brown 20 15
806 **80** 16c. on 20c. brown 20 15
807 **79** 24c. on 25c. red 15 15
808 25c. on 25c. orange 30 30
809 **80** 32c. on 50c. violet 30 25
810 40c. on 50c. green 40 25
811 50c. on 1cor. yellow 40 30
812 1cor. on 1cor. red 95 80

1933. Obligatory Tax. As No. 647 optd with T **134**. Colour changed.
813 **106** 1c. orange 25 15

1934. Air. Surch **Servicio Centroamericano Vale 10 centavos**.
814 **112** 10c. on 20c. green 35 35
815 10c. on 25c. olive 35 35
See also No. 872.

1935. Optd **Resello 1935**. (a) Nos. 778/9.
816 **79** 1c. green 10 10
817 **80** 2c. red 15 10
(b) No. 813 but without T **134** opt.
818 **106** 1c. orange 15 10

1935. No. 783 surch **Vale Medio Centavo**.
819 **80** ½c. on 6c. brown 35 15

1935. Optd with T **134** and **RESELLO – 1935** in a box.
820 **79** ½c. green 20 15
821 **80** ½c. on 6c. brown (No. 819) 15 10
822 **79** 1c. green 25 10
823 **80** 2c. red 55 10
824 2c. red (No. 817) 30 10
825 **79** 3c. blue 30 15
826 **80** 4c. blue 30 15
827 **79** 5c. brown 25 10
828 **80** 6c. drab 30 10
829 10c. brown 55 20
830 **79** 15c. red 15 10
831 **80** 20c. orange 90 25
832 **79** 25c. violet 30 15
833 **80** 50c. green 35 25
834 1cor. yellow 45 35

1935. Obligatory Tax. No. 605 optd with **RESELLO – 1935** in a box.
835 **79** 1c. orange 25·00

1935. Obligatory Tax. Optd **RESELLO – 1935** in a box. (a) No. 813 without T **134** opt.
836 **106** 1c. orange 25 15
(b) No. 818.
868 **106** 1c. orange 20 15

1935. Air. Nos. 799/812 optd with **RESELLO – 1935** in a box.
839 **80** 1c. on 2c. green 10 10
840 **79** 2c. on 3c. olive 20 20
879 **80** 3c. on 4c. red 15 15
880 **79** 4c. on 5c. blue 15 15
881 **80** 5c. on 6c. blue 15 15
882 6c. on 10c. sepia 15 15
883 **79** 8c. on 15c. brown 15 15
884 **80** 16c. on 20c. brown 15 15
847 **79** 24c. on 25c. red 35 30
848 25c. on 25c. orange 25 25
849 **80** 32c. on 50c. violet 20 20
850 40c. on 50c. green 30 25
851 50c. on 1cor. yellow 45 35
852 1cor. on 1cor. red 85 40

1935. Air. Optd with **RESELLO – 1935** in a box. (a) Nos. 629/33.
853 **112** 15c. purple 30 10
873 20c. green 40 30
855 25c. green 40 35
856 50c. sepia 40 35
857 1cor. red 65 35
(b) Nos. 791/4.
858 **112** 30c. on 50c. orange 40 35
859 35c. on 50c. blue 40 25
860 40c. on 1cor. yellow 40 35
861 55c. on 1cor. green 40 30
(c) Nos. 814/5.
862 **112** 10c. on 20c. green £300 £300
863 10c. on 25c. olive 60 50

1935. Optd with **RESELLO – 1935** in a box.
864 **79** ½c. green (No. 465) 15 10
865 1c. green (No. 617) 20 10
866 **80** 2c. red (No. 467) 55 10
867 **79** 3c. blue (No. 618) 20 15

1936. Surch **Resello 1936 Vale** and value.
869 **79** 1c. on 3c. blue (No. 618) 15 10
870 2c. on 5c. brown (No. 620) 15 10

1936. Air. Surch **Servicio Centroamericano Vale diez centavos** and **RESELLO – 1935** in a box.
871 **112** 10c. on 25c. olive 30 30

1936. Obligatory Tax. No. 818 optd **1936**.
874 **106** 1c. orange 50 20

1936. Obligatory Tax. No. 605 optd with T **134** and **1936**.
875 **79** 1c. orange 50 20

1936. Air. No. 622 optd **Correo Aereo Centro-Americano Resello 1936**.
876 **80** 10c. brown 20 20

1936. Air. Nos. 799/800 and 805 optd **Resello 1936**.
885 **80** 1c. on 2c. green 25 20
886 **79** 2c. on 3c. olive 10 10
887 8c. on 15c. brown 25 25

1936. Optd with or without T **37**, surch **1936 Vale** and value.
888 **79** ½c. on 15c. red 20 15
889 **80** 1c. on 4c. blue 25 15
890 **79** 1c. on 5c. brown 25 20
891 **80** 1c. on 6c. drab 45 20
892 **79** 1c. on 15c. red 25 20
893 **80** 1c. on 20c. orange 20 15
895 2c. on 10c. brown 30 20
896 **79** 2c. on 15c. red 60 50
897 **80** 2c. on 20c. orange 55 45
898 **79** 2c. on 25c. violet 35 20
900 **80** 2c. on 50c. green 35 25
901 2c. on 1cor. yellow 35 30
902 3c. on 4c. blue 40 30

1936. Optd **Resello 1936**.
903 **79** 3c. blue (No. 618) 35 25
904 5c. brown (No. 620) 30 15
905 **80** 10c. brown (No. 784) 30 20

1936. Air. Surch **1936 Vale and value**.
906 **112** 15c. on 50c. brown 30 25
907 15c. on 1cor. red 30 25

1936. Fiscal stamps surch **RECONSTRUCCION COMUNICACIONES 5 CENTAVOS DE CORDOBA** and further surch **Vale dos centavos Resello 1936**.
908 **90** 1c. on 5c. green 25 10
909 2c. on 5c. green 25 10

1936. Obligatory Tax. Fiscal stamps surch **RECONSTRUCCION COMUNICACIONES 5 CENTAVOS DE CORDOBA** and further surch. (a) **1936 R. de C. Vale Un Centavo**.
910 **90** 1c. on 5c. green 15 10
(b) **Vale un centavo R. de C. 1936**.
911 **90** 1c. on 5c. green 20 10

1937. Colours changed. Size 27 × 22¾ mm.
912 **79** ½c. black 15 10
913 1c. red 15 10

No.	Type	Description	Unused	Used
914	**80**	2c. blue	15	10
915	**79**	3c. brown	15	10
916	**80**	4c. yellow	20	10
917	**79**	5c. red	15	10
918	**80**	6c. violet	20	10
919		10c. green	20	10
920	**79**	15c. green	15	10
921	**80**	20c. brown	30	10
922	**79**	25c. orange	30	10
923	**80**	50c. brown	35	15
924		1cor. blue	40	25

1937. Obligatory Tax. Colour changed.

No.	Type	Description	Unused	Used
925	**106**	1c. green	15	10

1937. Air. Colours changed.

No.	Type	Description	Unused	Used
926	**112**	15c. orange	20	10
927		20c. red	20	15
928		25c. black	25	15
929		50c. violet	45	15
930		1cor. orange	65	15

1937. Air. Surch **Vale** and value. Colours changed.

No.	Type	Description	Unused	Used
931	**112**	30c. on 50c. red	30	10
932		35c. on 50c. olive	35	10
933		40c. on 1cor. green	35	15
934		55c. on 1cor. blue	35	30

1937. Air. Surch **Servicio Centroamericano Vale Diez Centavos**.

No.	Type	Description	Unused	Used
949	**112**	10c. on 1cor. red	30	15

1937. Air. No. 805 (without T **134**) optd **1937**.

No.	Type	Description	Unused	Used
950	**79**	8c. on 15c. brown	50	15

142 Baseball Player

1937. Obligatory Tax. For 1937 Central American Olympic Games. Optd with ball in red under "OLIMPICO".

No.	Type	Description	Unused	Used
951	**142**	1c. red	35	15
952		1c. yellow	35	15
953		1c. blue	35	15
953a		1c. green	35	15

1937. Nos. 799/809 optd **Habilitado 1937**.

No.	Type	Description	Unused	Used
954	**80**	1c. on 2c. green	10	10
955	**79**	2c. on 3c. olive	10	10
956	**80**	3c. on 4c. red	10	10
957	**79**	4c. on 5c. blue	10	10
958	**80**	5c. on 6c. blue	10	10
959		6c. on 10c. brown	10	10
960	**79**	8c. on 15c. brown	10	10
961	**80**	16c. on 20c. brown	20	20
962	**79**	24c. on 25c. red	20	20
963		25c. on 25c. orange	20	25
964	**80**	32c. on 50c. violet	20	25

144 Presidential Palace, Managua

1937. Air. Inland.

No.	Type	Description	Unused	Used
965	**144**	1c. red	15	10
966		2c. blue	15	10
967		3c. olive	15	10
968		4c. black	15	10
969		5c. purple	20	10
970		6c. brown	20	10
971		8c. violet	20	10
972		16c. orange	35	25
973		24c. yellow	20	15
974		25c. green	50	25

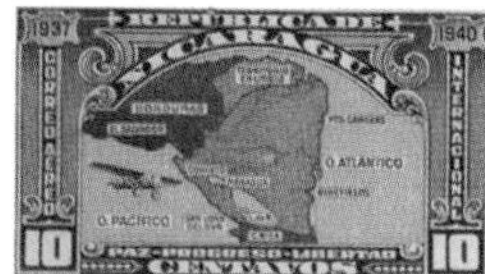

145 Nicaragua

1937. Air. Abroad.

No.	Type	Description	Unused	Used
975	**145**	10c. green	25	10
976		15c. blue	25	10
977		20c. yellow	30	25
978		25c. violet	30	25
979		30c. red	40	25
980		50c. orange	60	25
981		1cor. olive	65	45

146 Presidential Palace

1937. Air. Abroad. 150th Anniv of U.S. Constitution.

No.	Type	Description	Unused	Used
982	–	10c. blue and green	1·10	70
983	**146**	15c. blue and orange	1·10	70
984	–	20c. blue and red	80	65
985	–	25c. blue and brown	80	65
986	–	30c. blue and green	80	65
987	–	35c. blue and yellow	35	25
988	–	40c. blue and green	55	40
989	–	45c. blue and purple	55	40
990	–	50c. blue and mauve	55	40
991	–	55c. blue and green	2·25	1·25
992	–	75c. blue and green	55	30
993	–	1cor. red and blue	75	30

DESIGNS: 10c. Children's Park, Managua; 20c. S. America; 25c. C. America; 30c. N. America; 35c. Lake Tiscapa; 40c. Pan-American motor-road; 45c. Priniomi Park; 50c. Piedrecitas Park; 55c. San Juan del Sur; 75c Rio Tipitapa; 1cor. Granade landscape.

146b Diriangen

1937. Air. Day of the Race.

No.	Type	Description	Unused	Used
993a	**146b**	1c. green (inland)	15	10
993b		4c. lake	15	10
993c		5c. violet	25	15
993d		8c. blue	15	10
993e		10c. brown (abroad)	20	10
993f		15c. blue	20	10
993g		20c. pink	30	15

147 Letter Carrier

1937. 75th Anniv of Postal Administration.

No.	Type	Description	Unused	Used
994	**147**	½c. green	15	10
995	–	1c. mauve	15	10
996	–	2c. brown	15	10
997	–	3c. violet	65	20
998	–	5c. blue	65	20
999	–	7½c. red	2·50	75

DESIGNS: 1c. Mule transport; 2c. Diligence; 3c. Yacht; 5c. Packet steamer; 7½c. Steam mail train.

147a Gen. Tomas Martinez

1938. Air. 75th Anniv of Postal Administration.

No.	Type	Description	Unused	Used
999a	**147a**	1c. blk & orge (inland)	25	20
999b		5c. black and violet	25	20
999c		8c. black and blue	30	30
999d		16c. black and brown	40	35
999e	–	10c. blk & grn (abroad)	30	25
999f	–	15c. black and blue	40	35
999g	–	25c. black and violet	25	25
999h	–	50c. black and red	40	30

DESIGNS: 10c. to 50c. Gen. Anastasio Somoza.

1938. Surch **1938** and **Vale**, new value in words and **Centavos**.

No.	Type	Description	Unused	Used
1000	**79**	3c. on 25c. orange	10	10
1001	**80**	5c. on 50c. brown	10	10
1002		6c. on 1 cor. blue	15	15

149 Dario Park

150 Lake Managua

151 President Somoza

1939.

No.	Type	Description	Unused	Used
1003	**149**	1½c. green (postage)	10	10
1004		2c. red	10	10
1005		3c. blue	10	10
1006		6c. brown	10	10
1007		7½c. green	10	10
1008		10c. brown	15	10
1009		15c. orange	15	10
1010		25c. violet	15	15
1011		50c. green	30	20
1012		1cor. yellow	60	45
1013	**150**	2c. blue (air: inland)	15	15
1014		3c. olive	15	15
1015		8c. mauve	15	15
1016		16c. orange	25	15
1017		24c. yellow	25	15
1018		32c. green	35	15
1019		50c. red	40	15
1020	**151**	10c. brown (air: abroad)	15	10
1021		15c. blue	15	10
1022		20c. yellow	15	20
1023		25c. violet	15	15
1024		30c. red	20	20
1025		50c. orange	30	20
1026		1cor. olive	45	35

1939. Nos. 920/1. Surch **Vale un Centavo 1939**.

No.	Type	Description	Unused	Used
1027	**79**	1c. on 15c. green	10	10
1028	**80**	1c. on 20c. brown	10	10

153 Will Rogers and Managua Airport

1939. Air. Will Rogers Commemorative. Inscr "WILL ROGERS/1931/1939".

No.	Type	Description	Unused	Used
1029	**153**	1c. green	10	10
1030	–	2c. red	10	10
1031	–	3c. blue	10	10
1032	–	4c. blue	15	10
1033	–	5c. red	10	10

DESIGNS: 2c. Rogers at Managua; 3c. Rogers in P.A.A. hut; 4c. Rogers and U.S. Marines; 5c. Rogers and street in Managua.

156 Senate House and Pres. Somoza

1940. Air. President's Visit to U.S.A. (a) Inscr "AEREO INTERIOR".

No.	Type	Description	Unused	Used
1034	–	4c. brown	15	10
1035	**156**	8c. brown	10	10
1036	–	16c. green	15	10
1037	**156**	20c. mauve	30	15
1038	–	32c. red	20	20

(b) Inscr "CORREO AEREO INTERNACIONAL".

No.	Type	Description	Unused	Used
1039	–	25c. blue	20	15
1040	–	30c. black	20	10
1041	**156**	50c. red	25	40
1042	–	60c. green	30	35
1043	–	65c. brown	30	20
1044	–	90c. olive	40	35
1045	–	1cor. violet	60	30

DESIGNS: 4c., 16c., 25c., 30c., 65c., 90c. Pres. Somoza addressing Senate; 32c., 60c., 1cor. Portrait of Pres. Somoza between symbols of Nicaragua and New York World's Fair.

158 L. S. Rowe, Statue of Liberty and Union Flags

1940. Air. 50th Anniv of Pan-American Union.

No.	Type	Description	Unused	Used
1046	**158**	1cor.25 multicoloured	40	35

159 First Issue of Nicaragua and Sir Rowland Hill

1941. Air. Centenary of First Adhesive Postage stamps.

No.	Type	Description	Unused	Used
1047	**159**	2cor. brown	2·25	75
1048		3cor. blue	7·00	80
1049		5cor. red	20·00	2·10

1941. Surch **Servicio ordinario Vale Diez Centavos de Cordoba**.

No.	Type	Description	Unused	Used
1050	**153**	10c. on 1c. green	15	10

161 Rube Dario

1941. 25th Death Anniv of Ruben Dario (poet).

No.	Type	Description	Unused	Used
1051	**161**	10c. red (postage)	20	15
1052		20c. mauve (air)	25	15
1053		35c. green	30	20
1054		40c. orange	35	25
1055		60c. blue	40	35

1943. Surch **Servicio Ordinario Vale Diez Centavos**

No.	Type	Description	Unused	Used
1056	**153**	10c. on 1c. green	10	10

162 "V" for Victory

163 Red Cross

164 Red Cross Workers and Wounded

1943. Victory.

No.	Type	Description	Unused	Used
1057	**162**	10c. red and violet (postage)	10	10
1058		30c. red and brown	15	10
1059		40c. red and green (air)	15	10
1060		60c. red and blue	20	10

1944. Air. 80th Anniv of Int Red Cross Society.

No.	Type	Description	Unused	Used
1061	**163**	25c. red	40	15
1062	–	50c. bistre	65	35
1063	**164**	1cor. green	1·25	1·00

DESIGN—VERT: 50c. Two Hemispheres.

165 Columbus and Lighthouse

166 Columbus's Fleet and Lighthouse

1945. Honouring Columbus's Discovery of America and Erection of Columbus Lighthouse near Trujillo City, Dominican Republic.

No.	Type	Description	Unused	Used
1064	**165**	4c. black & green (postage)	15	10
1065		6c. black and orange	20	10
1066		8c. black and red	20	15
1067		10c. black and blue	30	15
1068	**166**	20c. grey and green (air)	60	20
1069		35c. black and red	95	25
1070		75c. pink and green	1·75	55
1071		90c. blue and red	2·00	85
1072		1cor. blue and black	2·25	50
1073		2cor.50 red and blue	6·00	2·50

168 Roosevelt as a Stamp Collector

1946. President Roosevelt Commemorative Inscr "HOMENAJE A ROOSEVELT".

No.	Type	Description	Unused	Used
1074	**168**	4c. green & black (postage)	15	15
1075	–	8c. violet and black	20	20
1076	–	10c. blue and black	30	25
1077	–	16c. red and black	40	30
1078	–	32c. brown and black	50	25
1079	–	50c. grey and black	50	25

1080 – 25c. orange & black (air) 20 10
1081 – 75c. red and black 25 20
1082 – 1cor. green and black 30 30
1083 – 3cor. violet and black 2·25 2·25
1084 – 5cor. blue and black 3·00 3·00
DESIGNS—portraying Roosevelt. HORIZ: 8c., 25c. with Churchill at the Atlantic Conference; 16c., 1cor. with Churchill, De Gaulle and Giraud at the Casablanca Conference; 32c., 3cor. with Churchill and Stalin at the Teheran Conference. VERT: 10c., 75c. Signing Declaration of War against Japan; 50c., 5cor. Head of Roosevelt

171 Managua Cathedral

172 G.P.O., Managua

1947. Managua Centenary. Frames in black.
1085 **171** 4c. red (postage) 10 10
1086 – 5c. blue 15 10
1087 – 6c. green 20 15
1088 – 10c. olive 20 15
1089 – 75c. brown 30 25

1090 – 5c. violet (air) 10 10
1091 **172** 20c. green 15 15
1092 – 35c. orange 15 15
1093 – 90c. purple 30 20
1094 – 1cor. brown 45 35
1095 – 2cor.50 purple 1·00 1·10
DESIGNS—POSTAGE (as Type **171**): 5c. Health Ministry; 6c. Municipal Building; 10c. College; 75c. G.P.O., Managua. AIR (as Type **172**): 5c. College; 35c. Health Ministry; 90c. National Bank; 1cor. Municipal Building; 2cor.50, National Palace.

173 San Cristobal Volcano

174 Ruben Dario Monument, Managua

1947. (a) Postage.
1096 **173** 2c. orange and black 10 10
1097 – 3c. violet and black 10 10
1098 – 4c. grey and black 10 10
1099 – 5c. red and black 20 10
1100 – 6c. green and black 15 10
1101 – 8c. brown and black 15 10
1102 – 10c. red and black 25 15
1103 – 20c. blue and black 1·10 25
1104 – 30c. purple and black 70 25
1105 – 50c. red and black 1·90 70
1106 – 1cor. brown and black 60 35
DESIGNS—as Type **173**: 3c. Lion on Ruben Dario's tomb, Leon Cathedral; 4c. Race stand; 5c. Soldiers' Monument; 6c. Sugar cane; 8c. Tropical fruits; 10c. Cotton; 20c. Horses; 30c. Coffee plant; 50c. Prize bullock; 1cor. Agricultural landscape.

(b) Air.
1107 **174** 5c. red and green 10 10
1108 – 6c. orange and black 10 10
1109 – 8c. brown and red 10 10
1110 – 10c. blue and brown 15 10
1111 – 20c. orange and blue 15 10
1112 – 25c. green and red 20 15
1113 – 35c. brown and black 30 15
1114 – 50c. black and violet 20 10
1115 – 1cor. red and black 45 25
1116 – 1cor.50 green and red 50 45
1117 – 5cor. red and brown 3·75 3·75
1118 – 10cor. brown and violet 3·00 3·00
1119 – 25cor. yellow and green 6·00 6·00
DESIGNS—As Type **174**: 6c. Baird's tapir; 8c. Highway and Lake Managua; 10c. Genizaro Dam; 20c. Ruben Dario Monument, Managua; 25c. Sulphur Lagoon, Nejapa; 35c. Managua Airport; 50c. Mouth of Rio Prinzapolka; 1cor. Thermal Baths, Tipitapa; 1cor.50, Rio Tipitapa; 5cor. Embassy building; 10cor. Girl carrying basket of fruit; 2cor. Franklin D. Roosevelt Monument, Managua.

175 Softball

176 Pole-vaulting

177 Tennis

178 National Stadium, Managua

1949. 10th World Amateur Baseball Championships. (a) Postage as T **175/6**.
1120 **175** 1c. brown 10 10
1121 – 2c. blue 50 15
1122 **176** 3c. green 25 10
1123 – 4c. purple 15 15
1124 – 5c. orange 40 15
1125 – 10c. green 40 15
1126 – 15c. red 50 15
1127 – 25c. blue 50 20
1128 – 35c. green 80 20
1129 – 40c. violet 1·75 30
1130 – 60c. black 1·40 35
1131 – 1cor. red 1·50 90
1132 – 2cor. purple 2·75 1·50
DESIGNS—VERT: 2c. Scout; 5c. Cycling; 25c. Boxing; 35c. Basketball. HORIZ: 4c. Diving; 10c. Stadium; 15c. Baseball; 40c. Yachting; 60c. Table tennis; 1cor. Football; 2cor. Tennis.

(b) Air as T **177**.
1133 **177** 1c. red 10 10
1134 – 2c. black 10 10
1135 – 3c. red 10 10
1136 – 4c. black 10 10
1137 – 5c. blue 35 15
1138 – 15c. green 65 10
1139 – 25c. purple 1·25 25
1140 – 30c. brown 1·00 25
1141 – 40c. violet 50 25
1142 – 75c. mauve 2·50 1·60
1143 – 1cor. blue 3·00 80
1144 – 2cor. olive 1·25 1·00
1145 – 5cor. green 2·10 2·10
DESIGNS—SQUARE: 2c. Football; 3c. Table tennis; 4c. Stadium; 5c. Yachting; 15c. Basketball; 25c. Boxing; 30c. Baseball; 40c. Cycling; 75c. Diving; 1cor. Pole-vaulting; 2cor. Scout; 5cor. Softball.

1949. Obligatory Tax stamps. Stadium Construction Fund.
1146 **178** 5c. blue 20 10
1146a 5c. red 20 10

179 Rowland Hill

180 Heinrich von Stephan

1950. 75th Anniv of U.P.U. Frames in black.
1147 **179** 20c. red (postage) 15 10
1148 – 25c. green 15 10
1149 – 75c. blue 50 50
1150 – 80c. green 30 25
1151 – 4cor. blue 85 80
DESIGNS—VERT: 25c. Portrait as Type **180**; 75c. Monument, Berne; 80c., 4cor. Obverse and reverse of Congress Medal.

1152 – 16c. red (air) 15 10
1153 **180** 20c. orange 15 10
1154 – 25c. black 15 15
1155 – 30c. red 25 10
1156 – 85c. green 55 50
1157 – 1cor.10 brown 50 35
1158 – 2cor.14 green 1·25 1·25
DESIGNS—HORIZ: 16c. Rowland Hill; 25, 30c. U.P.U. Offices, Berne; 85c. Monument, Berne; 1cor.10 and 2cor.14, Obverse and reverse of Congress Medal.

181 Queen Isabella and Columbus's Fleet

182 Isabella the Catholic

1952. 500th Birth Anniv of Isabella the Catholic.
1159 – 10c. mauve (postage) 10 10
1160 **181** 96c. blue 1·50 65
1161 – 98c. red 1·50 65
1162 – 1cor.20 brown 50 40
1163 **182** 1cor.76 purple 60 60

1164 2cor.30 red (air) 1·40 1·10
1165 – 2cor.80 orange 1·00 95
1166 – 3cor. green 4·25 1·75
1167 **181** 3cor.30 blue 4·25 2·00
1168 – 3cor.60 green 1·50 1·25
DESIGNS—VERT: 10c., 3cor.60, Queen facing right; 98c., 3cor. Queen and "Santa Maria"; 1cor.20, 2cor.80, Queen and Map of Americas.

183 O.D.E.C.A. Flag

1953. Foundation of Organization of Central American States.
1169 **183** 4c. blue (postage) 10 10
1170 – 5c. green 10 10
1171 – 6c. brown 10 10
1172 – 15c. olive 20 15
1173 – 50c. sepia 25 15

1174 – 20c. red (air) 10 10
1175 **183** 25c. blue 15 10
1176 – 30c. brown 15 15
1177 – 60c. green 25 20
1178 – 1cor. purple 35 45
DESIGNS: 5c., 1cor. Map of C. America; 6c., 20c. Hands holding O.D.E.C.A. arms; 15c., 30c. Five presidents of C. America; 50c., 60c. Charter and flags.

184 Pres. Solorzano

185 Pres. Arguello

1953. Presidential Series. Portraits in black. (a) Postage. As T **184**.
1179 **184** 4c. red 10 10
1180 – 6c. blue (D. M. Chamorro) 10 10
1181 – 8c. brown (Diaz) 10 10
1182 – 15c. red (Somoza) 15 10
1183 – 50c. green (E. Chamorro) 20 15

(b) Air. As T **185**.
1184 **185** 4c. red 10 10
1185 – 5c. orange (Moncada) 10 10
1186 – 20c. blue (J. B. Sacasa) 10 10
1187 – 25c. blue (Zelaya) 10 10
1188 – 30c. lake (Somoza) 10 10
1189 – 35c. green (Martinez) 20 20
1190 – 40c. plum (Guzman) 20 20
1191 – 45c. olive (Cuadra) 20 20
1192 – 50c. red (P. J. Chamorro) 35 25
1193 – 60c. blue (Zavala) 40 40
1194 – 85c. brown (Cardenas) 40 40
1195 – 1cor.10 purple (Carazo) 60 55
1196 – 1cor.20 bistre (R. Sacasa) 65 55

186 Sculptor and U.N. Emblem

1954. U.N.O. Inscr "HOMENAJE A LA ONU".
1197 **186** 3c. drab (postage) 10 10
1198 A 4c. green 15 10
1199 B 5c. green 20 10
1200 C 15c. green 55 20
1201 D 1cor. turquoise 45 40

1202 E 3c. red (air) 10 10
1203 F 4c. orange 10 10
1204 C 5c. red 15 10
1205 D 30c. pink 75 15
1206 B 2cor. red 80 70
1207 A 3cor. brown 1·50 1·00
1208 **186** 5cor. purple 1·75 1·40
DESIGNS: A, Detail from Nicaragua's coat of arms; B, Globe; C, Candle and Nicaragua's Charter; D, Flags of Nicaragua and U.N.; E, Torch; F, Trusting hands.

187 Capt. D. L. Ray

188 North American Sabre

1954. National Air Force. Frames in black. (a) Postage. Frames as T **187**.
1209 **187** 1c. black 10 10
1210 – 2c. black 10 10
1211 – 3c. myrtle 10 10
1212 – 4c. orange 15 10
1213 – 5c. green 20 10
1214 – 15c. turquoise 15 10
1215 – 1cor. violet 35 25

(b) Air. Frames as T **188**.
1216 – 10c. black 10 10
1217 **188** 15c. black 15 10
1218 – 20c. mauve 15 10
1219 – 25c. red 20 10
1220 – 30c. blue 10 10
1221 – 50c. blue 75 50
1222 – 1cor. green 65 35
DESIGNS—POSTAGE: 2c. North American Sabre; 3c. Douglas Boston; 4c. Consolidated Liberator; 5c. North American Texan trainer; 15c. Pres. Somoza; 1cor. Emblem. AIR: 10c. D. L. Ray; 20c. Emblem; 25c. Hangars; 30c. Pres. Somoza; 50c. North American Texan trainers; 1cor. Lockheed Lightning airplanes.

189 Rotary Slogans

190a

1955. 50th Anniv of Rotary International.
1223 **189** 15c. orange (postage) 10 10
1224 A 20c. olive 15 15
1225 B 35c. violet 15 15
1226 C 40c. red 15 15
1227 D 90c. black 30 25

1228 D 1c. red (air) 10 10
1229 A 2c. blue 10 10
1230 C 3c. green 10 10
1231 **189** 4c. violet 10 10
1232 B 5c. brown 10 10
1233 25c. turquoise 15 15
1234 **189** 30c. black 15 10
1235 C 45c. mauve 30 25
1236 A 50c. green 25 20
1237 D 1cor. blue 45 30
DESIGNS—VERT: A, Clasped hands; B, Rotarian and Nicaraguan flags; D, Paul P. Harris. HORIZ: C, World map and winged emblem.

1956. National Exhibition. Surch **Conmemoracion Exposicion Nacional Febrero 4-16, 1956** and value.
1238 5c. on 6c. brown (No. 1171) (postage) 10 10
1239 5c. on 6c. black & bl (No. 1180) 10 10
1240 5c. on 8c. brn & blk (No. 1101) 10 10
1241 15c. on 35c. violet (No. 1225) 15 10
1242 15c. on 80c. grn & blk (No. 1150) 15 10
1243 15c. on 90c. black (No. 1227) 15 10
1244 30c. on 35c. black and green (No. 1189) (air) 10 15
1245 30c. on 45c. blk & ol (No. 1191) 25 15
1246 30c. on 45c. mauve (No. 1235) 25 15
1247 2cor. on 5cor. purple (No. 1208) 50 35

1956. Obligatory Tax. Social Welfare Fund.
1247a **190a** 5c. blue 10 10

191 Gen. J. Dolores Estrada

192 President Somoza

1956. Cent of War of 1856. Inscr as in T **191**.
1248 – 5c. brown (postage) 10 10
1249 – 10c. lake 10 10
1250 – 15c. grey 10 10
1251 – 25c. red 15 15
1252 – 50c. purple 30 20

1253 **191** 30c. red (air) 10 10
1254 – 60c. brown 20 15
1255 – 1cor.50 green 20 35
1256 – 2cor.50 blue 30 30
1257 – 10cor. orange 1·90 1·75
DESIGNS—VERT: 5c. Gen. M. Jerez; 10c. Gen. F. Chamorro; 50c. Gen. J. D. Estrada; 1cor.50, E. Mangalo; 10cor. Commodore H. Paulding. HORIZ: 15c. Battle of San Jacinto; 25c. Granada in flames; 60c. Bas-relief; 2cor.50, Battle of Rivas.

1957. Air. National Mourning for Pres. G. A. Somoza. Various frames. Inscr as in T **192**. Centres in black.
1258 – 15c. black 10 10
1259 – 30c. blue 15 15
1260 **192** 2cor. violet 80 70
1261 – 3cor. olive 1·25 1·10
1262 – 5cor. sepia 1·90 1·90

193 Scout and Badge

194 Clasped Hands, Badge and Globe

1957. Birth Centenary of Lord Baden-Powell.
1263 **193** 10c. olive & vio (postage) 10 10
1264 – 15c. sepia and purple . . 15 15
1265 – 20c. brown and blue . . 15 15
1266 – 25c. brown and turquoise 15 15
1267 – 50c. olive and red . . . 35 35
1268 **194** 3c. olive and red (air) . . 15 15
1269 – 4c. blue and brown . . . 15 15
1270 – 5c. brown and green . . 15 15
1271 – 6c. drab and violet . . . 15 15
1272 – 8c. red and black 15 15
1273 – 30c. black and green . . 15 15
1274 – 40c. black and blue . . . 15 15
1275 – 75c. sepia and purple . . 35 35
1276 – 85c. grey and red . . . 40 40
1277 – 1cor. brown and green 40 40
DESIGNS—VERT: 4c. Scout badge; 5c., 15c. Wolf cub; 6c. Badge and flags; 8c. Badge and emblems of scouting 20c. Scout; 25., 1cor. Lord Baden-Powell; 30., 50c. Joseph A. Harrison; 75c. Rover Scout; 85c. Scout. HORIZ: 40c. Presentation to Pres. Somoza.

195 Pres. Luis Somoza

197 Archbishop of Managua

196 Managua Cathedral

1957. Election of Pres. Somoza. Portrait in brown.
(a) Postage. Oval frame.
1278 **195** 10c. red 10 10
1279 15c. blue 10 10
1280 35c. purple 10 10
1281 50c. brown 15 15
1282 75c. green 40 40
(b) Air. Rectangular frame.
1283 – 20c. blue 10 10
1284 – 25c. mauve 15 10
1285 – 30c. sepia 15 15
1286 – 40c. turquoise 15 15
1287 – 2cor. violet 95 95

1957. Churches and Priests. Centres in olive.
1288 **196** 5c. green (postage) . . . 10 10
1289 – 10c. purple 10 10
1290 **197** 15c. blue 10 10
1291 – 20c. sepia 15 10
1292 – 50c. green 20 15
1293 – 1cor. violet 30 30
1294 **197** 30c. green (air) 10 10
1295 **196** 60c. brown 15 15
1296 – 75c. blue 25 25
1297 – 90c. red 30 30
1298 – 1cor.50 turquoise 35 35
1299 – 2cor. purple 40 40
DESIGNS—HORIZ: As Type **196**: 20, 90c. Leon Cathedral; 50c., 1cor.50, La Merced, Granada Church. VERT: As Type **197**: 10, 75c. Bishop of Nicaragua; 1, 2cor. Father Mariano Dubon.

198 "Honduras" (freighter)

1957. Nicaraguan Merchant Marine Commemoration. Inscr as in T **198**.
1300 **198** 4c. black, blue and myrtle (postage) . . . 30 10
1301 – 5c. violet, blue and brown 30 10
1302 – 6c. black, blue and red 30 10
1303 – 10c. black, green and sepia 30 10
1304 – 15c. brown, blue and red 50 10
1305 – 50c. brown, blue and violet 60 20
1306 – 25c. purple, blue and ultramarine (air) . . . 60 20
1307 – 30c. grey, buff and brown 15 10
1308 – 50c. bistre, blue and violet 20 20
1309 – 60c. black, turquoise and purple 85 30
1310 – 1cor. black, blue and red 1·10 30
1311 – 2cor.50 brown, blue and black . . . . 2·25 1·25
DESIGNS: 5c. Gen. A. Somoza, founder of Mamenic (National) Shipping Line, and "Guatemala" (freighter); 6c. "Guatemala"; 10c. "Salvador" (freighter); 15c. Freighter between hemispheres; 25c. "Managua" (freighter); 30c. Ship's wheel and world map; 50c. (No. 1305), Hemispheres and ship; 50c. (No. 1308), Mamenic Shipping Line flag; 60c. "Costa Rica" (freighter); 1cor. "Nicarao" (freighter); 2cor.50, Map, freighter and flag.

199 Exhibition Emblem

1958. Air. Brussels International Exn. Inscr "EXPOSICION MUNDIAL DE BELGICA 1958".
1312 **199** 25c. black, yellow & green 10 10
1313 – 30c. multicoloured . . . 15 15
1314 – 45c. black, ochre and blue 15 15
1315 **199** 1cor. black, blue and dull purple 25 25
1316 – 2cor. multicoloured . . . 25 25
1317 – 10cor. sepia, purple and blue . . . . 1·40 1·00
DESIGNS: As Type **199**: 30c., 20cor. Arms of Nicaragua; 45c., 10cor. Nicaraguan pavilion.

200 Emblems of C. American Republics

1958. 17th Central American Lions Convention. Inscr as in T **200**. Emblems (5c., 60c.) multicoloured; Lions badge (others) in blue, red, yellow (or orange and buff).
1318 **200** 5c. blue (postage) . . . 10 10
1319 – 10c. blue and orange . . 10 10
1320 – 20c. blue and green . . . 10 10
1321 – 50c. blue and purple . . 15 15
1322 – 75c. blue and mauve . . 30 25
1323 – 1cor.50 blue, salmon and drab 45 45
1324 – 30c. blue and orange (air) 10 10
1325 **200** 60c. blue and pink . . . 20 15
1326 – 90c. blue 25 20
1327 – 1cor.25 blue and olive 35 30
1328 – 2cor. blue and green . . 60 50
1329 – 3cor. blue, red and violet 95 90
DESIGNS—HORIZ: 10c., 1cor.25, Melvin Jones; 20, 30c. Dr. T. A. Arias; 50, 90c. Edward G. Barry; 75c., 2cor. Lions emblem; 1cor.50, 3cor. Map of C. American Isthmus.

201 Arms of La Salle

202 U.N. Emblem

1958. Brothers of the Nicaraguan Christian Schools Commemoration. Inscr as in T **201**.
1330 **201** 5c. red, blue and yellow (postage) 10 10
1331 – 10c. sepia, blue and green 10 10
1332 – 15c. sepia, brown & bistre 10 10
1333 – 20c. black, red and bistre 10 10
1334 – 50c. sepia, orange & bis 15 15
1335 – 75c. sepia, turquoise & green 25 20
1336 – 1cor. black, violet & bis 40 30
1337 **201** 30c. blue, red & yellow (air) 10 10
1338 – 60c. sepia, purple & grey 25 20
1339 – 85c. black, red and blue 30 25
1340 – 90c. black, green & ochre 35 35
1341 – 1cor.25 black, red and ochre 50 45
1342 – 1cor.50 sepia, green and grey 60 55
1343 – 1cor.75 black, brn & bl 65 55
1344 – 2cor. sepia, green & grey 65 65
DESIGNS—HORIZ: 10, 60c. Managua Teachers Institute. VERT: 15, 85c. De La Salle (founder); 20, 90c. Brother Carlos; 50c., 1cor.50, Brother Antonio; 75c., 1cor.25, Brother Julio; 1cor., 1cor.75, Brother Argeo; 2cor. Brother Eugenio.

1958. Inauguration of U.N.E.S.C.O. Headquarters Building, Paris. Inscr as in T **202**.
1345 **202** 10c. blue & mauve (postage) 10 10
1346 – 15c. mauve and blue . . 10 10
1347 – 25c. brown and green . . 10 10
1348 – 40c. black and red . . . 15 15
1349 – 45c. mauve and blue . . 20 20
1350 **202** 50c. green and brown . . 25 25
1351 – 60c. blue and mauve (air) 25 15
1352 – 75c. brown and green . . 25 20
1353 – 90c. green and brown . . 30 25
1354 – 1cor. mauve and blue . . 40 30
1355 – 3cor. red and black . . . 60 60
1356 – 5cor. blue and mauve . . 1·00 85
DESIGNS—VERT: 15c. Aerial view of H.Q. 25, 45c. Facade composed of letters "UNESCO"; 40c. H.Q. and Eiffel Tower. In oval vignettes—60c. As 15c.; 75c., 5cor. As 25c.; 90c., 3cor. As 40c.; 1cor. As Type **202**.

203

204

1959. Obligatory Tax. Consular Fiscal stamps surch. Serial Nos. in red.
1357 **203** 5c. on 50c. blue 10 10
1358 **204** 5c. on 50c. blue 10 10

205

206 Cardinal Spellman with Pope John XXIII

207 Abraham Lincoln

1959. Obligatory Tax.
1359 **205** 5c. blue 15 10

1959. Cardinal Spellman Commemoration.
1360 **206** 5c. flesh & green (postage) 10 10
1361 A 10c. multicoloured . . . 10 10
1362 B 15c. red, black and green 10 10
1363 C 20c. yellow and blue . . 10 10
1364 D 25c. red and blue 10 10
1365 E 30c. blue, red & yell (air) 10 10
1366 **206** 35c. bronze and orange 10 10
1367 A 1cor. multicoloured . . . 30 30
1368 B 1cor.5 red and black . . 35 30
1369 C 1cor.50 yellow and blue 45 35
1370 D 2cor. blue, violet and red 55 45
1371 E 5cor. multicoloured . . . 75 55
DESIGNS—VERT: A, Cardinal's Arms; B, Cardinal; D, Cardinal wearing sash. HORIZ: C, Cardinal and Cross; E, Flags of Nicaragua, Vatican City and U.S.A.

1960. 150th Birth Anniv of Abraham Lincoln. Portrait in black.
1372 **207** 5c. red (postage) 10 10
1373 10c. green 10 10
1374 15c. orange 10 10
1375 1cor. purple 25 25
1376 2cor. blue 30 45
1377 30c. blue (air) 10 10
1378 35c. red 15 10
1379 70c. purple 20 20
1380 1cor.5 green 35 35
1381 1cor.50 violet 50 45
1382 – 5cor. ochre and black . . 55 55
DESIGN—HORIZ: 5cor. Scroll inscr "Dar al que necesite—A. Lincoln".

1960. Air. 10th Anniv of San Jose (Costa Rica) Philatelic Society. Optd **X Aniversario Club Filatelico S. J.—C. R.**
1383 2cor. red (No. 1206) 70 60
1384 2cor.50 blue (No. 1256) . . 75 75
1385 3cor. green (No. 1166) . . . 1·40 90

1960. Red Cross Fund for Chilean Earthquake Relief. Nos. 1372/82 optd **Resello** and Maltese Cross. Portrait in black.
1386 **207** 5c. red (postage) 10 10
1387 10c. green 10 10
1388 15c. orange 10 10
1389 1cor. purple 25 25
1390 2cor. blue 30 25
1391 30c. blue (air) 25 20
1392 35c. red 20 20
1393 70c. purple 25 25
1394 1cor.5 green 30 30
1395 1cor.50 violet 40 35
1396 – 5cor. ochre and black . . 1·00 1·00

210

1961. Air. World Refugee Year. Inscr "ANO MUNDIAL DEL REFUGIADO".
1397 – 2cor. multicoloured . . . 20 20
1398 **210** 5cor. ochre, blue & green 60 60
DESIGN: 2cor. Procession of refugees.

211 Pres. Roosevelt, Pres. Somoza and Officer

1961. Air. 20th Anniv of Nicaraguan Military Academy.
1399 **211** 20c. multicoloured . . . 10 10
1400 – 25c. red, blue and black 10 10
1401 – 30c. multicoloured . . . 10 10
1402 – 35c. multicoloured . . . 10 10
1403 – 40c. multicoloured . . . 10 10
1404 – 45c. black, flesh and red 15 15
1405 **211** 60c. multicoloured . . . 15 15
1406 – 70c. multicoloured . . . 20 20
1407 – 1cor.5 multicoloured . . 25 25
1408 – 1cor.50 multicoloured . . 35 35
1409 – 2cor. multicoloured . . . 50 50
1410 – 5cor. black, flesh & grey 70 60
DESIGNS—VERT: 25, 70c. Flags; 35c., 1cor.50, Standard bearers; 40c., 2cor. Pennant and emblem. HORIZ: 30c., 1cor.5 Group of officers; 45c., 5cor. Pres. Somoza and Director of Academy.

1961. Air. Consular Fiscal stamps as T **203/4** with serial Nos. in red, surch **Correo Aereo** and value.
1411 20c. on 50c. blue 15 10
1412 20c. on 1cor. olive 15 10
1413 20c. on 2cor. green 15 10
1414 20c. on 3cor. red 15 10
1415 20c. on 5cor. red 15 10
1416 20c. on 10cor. violet 15 10
1417 20c. on 20cor. brown . . . 15 10
1418 20c. on 50cor. brown . . . 15 10
1419 20c. on 100cor. lake 15 10

213 I.J.C. Emblem and Global Map of the Americas

1961. Air. Junior Chamber of Commerce Congress.
1420 2c. multicoloured 10 10
1421 3c. black and yellow 10 10
1422 4c. multicoloured 10 10
1423 5c. black and red 10 10
1424 6c. multicoloured 15 10
1425 10c. multicoloured 10 10
1426 15c. black, green and blue 10 10
1427 30c. black and blue 15 10
1428 35c. multicoloured 15 10
1429 70c. black, red and yellow 20 20
1430 1cor.5 multicoloured 35 30
1431 5cor. multicoloured 70 70
DESIGNS—HORIZ: 2c., 15c. Type **213**; 4c., 35c. "J.C.I." upon Globe. VERT: 3c., 30c. I.J.C. emblem; 5c., 70c. Scroll; 6c., 1cor.5, Handclasp; 10c., 5cor. Regional map of Nicaragua.

1961. Air. 1st Central American Philatelic Convention, San Salvador. Optd **Convencion Filatelica–Centro–America–Panama–San Salvador–27 Julio 1961.**
1432 **158** 1cor.25 multicoloured . . 25 25

215 R. Cabezas

1961. Air. Birth Centenary of Cabezas.
1433 **215** 20c. blue and orange . . 10 10
1434 – 40c. purple and blue . . 15 15
1435 – 45c. sepia and green . . 15 15
1436 – 70c. green and brown . . 25 20
1437 – 2cor. blue and pink . . . 60 40
1438 – 10cor. purple and turquoise . . . . . . 1·50 1·50
DESIGNS—HORIZ: 40c. Map and view of Cartago; 45c. 1884 newspaper; 70c. Assembly outside building; 2cor. Scroll; 10cor. Map and view of Masaya.

216 Official Gazettes

219 "Cattleya skinneri"

1961. Centenary of Regulation of Postal Rates.
1439 **216** 5c. brown and turquoise . . . 10 10
1440 – 10c. brown and green . . 10 10
1441 – 15c. brown and red . . . 10 10
DESIGNS: 10c. Envelopes and postmarks; 15c. Martinez and Somoza.

1961. Air. Dag Hammarskjold Commemoration. Nos. 1351/6 optd **Homenaje a Hammarskjold Sept. 18-1961.**
1442 60c. blue and mauve 30 30
1443 75c. brown and green . . . 35 35
1444 90c. green and brown . . . 45 45
1445 1cor. mauve and blue . . . 50 50
1446 3cor. red and black 80 80
1447 5cor. blue and mauve . . . 1·50 1·50

1962. Air. Surch **RESELLO C$ 1.00.**
1448 – 1cor. on 1cor.10 brown (No. 1157) 30 25
1449 **207** 1cor. on 1cor.5 black and green 30 25
See also Nos. 1498/1500a, 1569/70, 1608/14, 1669/76 and 1748/62.

1962. Obligatory Tax. Nicaraguan Orchids. Mult.
1450 5c. Type **219** 10 10
1451 5c. "Bletia roezlii" 10 10
1452 5c. "Sobralia pleiantha" . . . 10 10
1453 5c. "Lycaste macrophylla" . . 10 10
1454 5c. "Schomburgkia tibicinus" 10 10
1455 5c. "Maxillaria tenuifolia" . . 10 10
1456 5c. "Stanhopea ecornuta" . . 10 10
1457 5c. "Oncidium ascendens" and "O. cebolleta" . . . 10 10
1458 5c. "Cycnoches egertonianum" 10 10
1459 5c. "Hexisia bidentata" . . 10 10

220 U.N.E.S.C.O. "Audience"

222 Arms of Nueva Segovia

1962. Air. 15th Anniv of U.N.E.S.C.O.
1460 **220** 2cor. multicoloured . . . 15 15
1461 – 5cor. multicoloured . . . 80 80
DESIGN: 5cor. U.N. and U.N.E.S.C.O. emblems.

1962. Air. Malaria Eradication. Nos. 1425, 1428/31 optd with mosquito surrounded by **LUCHA CONTRA LA MALARIA.**
1462 – 10c. 35 30
1463 – 35c. 45 30
1464 – 70c. 60 45
1465 – 1cor.5 . . . . 80 65
1466 – 5cor. . . . . 1·00 1·25

1962. Urban and Provincial Arms. Arms mult; inscr black; background colours below.
1467 **222** 2c. mauve (postage) . . 10 10
1468 – 3c. blue 10 10
1469 – 4c. lilac 10 10
1470 – 5c. yellow 10 10
1471 – 6c. brown 10 10
1472 **222** 30c. red (air) 10 10
1473 – 50c. orange 15 10
1474 – 1cor. green 25 20
1475 – 2cor. grey 45 40
1476 – 5cor. blue 75 60
ARMS: 3c., 50c. Leon; 4c., 1cor. Managua; 5c., 2cor. Granada; 6c., 5cor. Rivas.

223 Liberty Bell

1963. Air. 150th Anniv of Independence.
1477 **223** 30c. drab, blue & black 15 10

224 Blessing

1963. Air. Death Tercentenary of St. Vincent de Paul and St. Louise de Marillac.
1478 – 60c. black and orange . . 15 10
1479 **224** 1cor. olive and orange . . 25 20
1480 – 2cor. black and red . . . 50 45
DESIGNS—VERT: 60c. "Comfort" (St. Louise and woman). HORIZ: 2cor. St. Vincent and St. Louise.

225 "Map Stamp"

226 Cross on Globe

1963. Air. Central American Philatelic Societies Federation Commemoration.
1481 **225** 1cor. blue and yellow . . 30 20

1963. Air. Ecumenical Council, Vatican City.
1482 **226** 20c. red and yellow . . . 15 10

227 Ears of Wheat

228 Boxing

1963. Air. Freedom from Hunger.
1483 **227** 10c. green and light green 10 10
1484 – 25c. sepia and yellow . . 15 10
DESIGN: 25c. Barren tree and campaign emblem.

1963. Air. Sports. Multicoloured.
1485 2c. Type **228** 10 10
1486 3c. Running 10 10
1487 4c. Underwater harpooning 10 10
1488 5c. Football 10 10
1489 6c. Baseball 15 10
1490 10c. Tennis 20 10
1491 15c. Cycling 20 10
1492 20c. Motor-cycling 20 10
1493 35c. Chess 30 15
1494 60c. Angling 45 20
1495 1cor. Table-tennis 55 35
1496 2cor. Basketball 75 55
1497 5cor. Golf . . . . 1·90 1·10

1964. Air. Surch **Resello or RESELLO** (1500a) and value.
1498 – 5c. on 6c. (No. 1424) 35 10
1499 – 10c. on 30c. (No. 1365) 45 15
1500 **207** 15c. on 30c. 70 20
1500a **201** 20c. on 30c. 15 10
See also Nos. 1448/9, 1569/70, 1608/14 and 1669/76.

1964. Optd **CORREOS.**
1501 5c. multicoloured (No. 1451) 10 10

231 Flags

232 "Alliance Emblem"

1964. Air. "Centro America".
1502 **231** 40c. multicoloured . . . 15 15

1964. Air. "Alliance for Progress". Multicoloured.
1503 5c. Type **232** 10 10
1504 10c. Red Cross post (horiz) 10 10
1505 15c. Highway (horiz) . . . 10 10
1506 20c. Ploughing (horiz) . . . 10 10
1507 25c. Housing (horiz) . . . 15 10
1508 30c. Presidents Somoza and Kennedy and Eugene Black (World Bank) (horiz) 15 10
1509 35c. School and adults (horiz) 20 15
1510 40c. Chimneys (horiz) . . . 25 15

233 Map of Member Countries

1964. Air. Central American "Common Market". Multicoloured.
1511 15c. Type **233** 10 10
1512 25c. Ears of wheat 10 10
1513 40c. Cogwheels 10 10
1514 50c. Heads of cattle 15 10

1964. Air. Olympic Games, Tokyo. Nos. 1485/7, 1489 and 1495/6 optd **OLIMPIADAS TOKYO - 1964.**
1515 2c. Type **108** 10 10
1516 3c. Running 10 10
1517 4c. Underwater harpooning 10 10
1518 6c. Baseball 10 10
1519 1cor. Table-tennis . . . . . 1·10 1·10
1520 2cor. Basketball . . . . . . 2·25 2·25

235 Rescue of Wounded Soldier

1965. Air. Red Cross Centenary. Multicoloured.
1521 20c. Type **235** 10 10
1522 25c. Blood transfusion . . . 15 10
1523 40c. Red Cross and snowbound town 15 15
1524 10cor. Red Cross and map of Nicaragua . . . . . . 1·50 1·50

236 Statuettes

1965. Air. Nicaraguan Antiquities. Multicoloured.
1525 5c. Type **236** 10 10
1526 10c. Totem 10 10
1527 15c. Carved dog (horiz) . . 10 10
1528 20c. Composition of "objets d'art" 10 10
1529 25c. Dish and vase (horiz) 10 10
1530 30c. Pestle and mortar . . . 10 10
1531 35c. Statuettes (different) (horiz) 10 10
1532 40c. Deity 15 10
1533 50c. Wine vessel and dish 15 10
1534 60c. Bowl and dish (horiz) 20 10
1535 1cor. Urn 45 15

237 Pres. Kennedy

238 A. Bello

1965. Air. Pres. Kennedy Commemorative.
1536 **237** 35c. black and green . . 15 10
1537 75c. black and mauve . . 25 15
1538 1cor.10 black and blue . . 35 25
1539 2cor. black and brown . . 90 55

1965. Air. Death Centenary of Andres Bello (poet and writer).
1540 **238** 10c. black and brown . . 10 10
1541 15c. black and blue . . 10 10
1542 45c. black and purple . . 15 10
1543 80c. black and green . . 20 15
1544 1cor. black and yellow . . 25 20
1545 2cor. black and grey . . 45 45

1965. 9th Central American Scout Camporee. Nos. 1450/9 optd with scout badge and **CAMPOREE SCOUT 1965.**
1546 5c. multicoloured 20 20
1547 5c. multicoloured 20 20
1548 5c. multicoloured 20 20
1549 5c. multicoloured 20 20
1550 5c. multicoloured 20 20
1551 5c. multicoloured 20 20
1552 5c. multicoloured 20 20
1553 5c. multicoloured 20 20
1554 5c. multicoloured 20 20
1555 5c. multicoloured 20 20

240 Sir Winston Churchill

241 Pope John XXIII

1966. Air. Churchill Commemorative.
1556 **240** 20c. mauve and black . . 10 10
1557 – 35c. green and black . . 15 10
1558 – 60c. ochre and black . . 15 15
1559 – 75c. red 20 20
1560 – 1cor. purple 30 25
1561 **240** 2cor. violet, lilac & black 60 55
1562 – 3cor. blue and black . . 65 60
DESIGNS—HORIZ: 35c., 1cor. Churchill broadcasting. VERT: 60c., 3cor. Churchill crossing the Rhine; 75c. Churchill in Hussars' uniform.

1966. Air. Closure of Vatican Ecumenical Council. Multicoloured.
1564 20c. Type **241** 10 10
1565 35c. Pope Paul VI 15 15
1566 1cor. Archbishop Gonzalez y Robleto 30 25
1567 2cor. St. Peter's, Rome . . . 30 25
1568 3cor. Papal arms 60 40

1967. Air. Nos. 1533/4 surch **RESELLO** and value.
1569 10c. on 50c. multicoloured 10 10
1570 15c. on 60c. multicoloured 10 10
See also Nos. 1448/9, 1498/1500a, 1608/14 and 1669/76.

243 Dario and Birthplace

1967. Air. Birth Centenary of Ruben Dario (poet). Designs showing Dario and view. Multicoloured.
1571 5c. Type **243** 10 10
1572 10c. Monument, Managua 10 10
1573 20c. Leon Cathedral (site of Dario's tomb) 10 10
1574 40c. Allegory of the centaurs 15 10
1575 75c. Allegory of the mute swans 30 20
1576 1cor. Roman triumphal march 25 20
1577 2cor. St. Francis and the wolf 45 40
1578 5cor. "Faith" opposing "Death" 65 60

244 "Megalura peleus"

1967. Air. Butterflies. Multicoloured.
1580 5c. "Heliconius petiveranus" (vert) 10 10
1581 10c. "Colaenis julia" (vert) 10 10
1582 15c. Type **244** 10 10
1583 20c. "Aneyluris jurgensii" 10 10
1584 25c. "Thecla regalis" . . . 10 10
1585 30c. "Doriana thia" (vert) 10 10
1586 35c. "Lymnias pixae" (vert) 15 10
1587 40c. "Metamorpho dido" 25 10
1588 50c. "Papilio arcas" (vert) 25 15
1589 60c. "Ananea cleomestra" 35 15
1590 1cor. "Victorina epaphaus" (vert) 60 30
1591 2cor. "Prepona demophon" 1·10 50

245 McDivitt and White

1967. Air. Space Flight of McDivitt and White. Multicoloured.
1592 5c. Type **245** 10 10
1593 10c. Astronauts and "Gemini 5" on launching pad 10 10
1594 15c. "Gemini 5" and White in Space 10 10
1595 20c. Recovery operation at sea 15 10

1596 35c. Type **245** 10 10
1597 40c. As 10c. 15 10
1598 75c. As 15c. 20 20
1599 1cor. As 20c. 35 25

246 National Flower of Costa Rica

1967. Air. 5th Year of Central American Economic Integration. Designs showing national flowers of Central American countries. Multicoloured.
1600 40c. Type **246** 15 10
1601 40c. Guatemala 15 10
1602 40c. Honduras 15 10
1603 40c. Nicaragua 15 10
1604 40c. El Salvador 15 10

247 Presidents Diaz and Somoza

1968. Air. Visit of Pres. Diaz of Mexico.
1605 – 20c. black 10 10
1606 **247** 40c. olive 20 10
1607 – 1cor. brown 35 20
DESIGNS—VERT: 20c. Pres. Somoza greeting Pres. Diaz; 1cor. Pres. Diaz of Mexico.

1968. Surch **RESELLO** and value.
1608 – 5c. on 6c. (No. 1180) (postage) 10 10
1609 – 5c. on 6c. (No. 1471) . . 10 10
1610 – 5c. on 6c. (No. 1424) (air) 10 10
1611 – 5c. on 6c. (No. 1489) . . 10 10
1612 **156** 5c. on 8c. (No. 1035) . . 10 10
1614 – 1cor. on 1cor.50 (No. 1369) 25 20
See also Nos. 1448/9, 1498/1500a, 1569/70 and 1669/76.

249 Mangoes

1968. Air. Nicaraguan Fruits. Multicoloured.
1615 5c. Type **249** 10 10
1616 10c. Pineapples 10 10
1617 15c. Oranges 10 10
1618 20c. Pawpaws 10 10
1619 30c. Bananas 10 10
1620 35c. Avocado pears 15 10
1621 50c. Water-melons 15 10
1622 75c. Cashews 25 15
1623 1cor. Sapodilla plums . . . 35 20
1624 2cor. Cocoa beans 45 20

250 "The Crucifixion" (Fra Angelico)

1968. Air. Religious Paintings. Multicoloured.
1625 10c. Type **250** 10 10
1626 15c. "The Last Judgement" (Michelangelo) (vert) . . 10 10
1627 35c. "The Beautiful Gardener" (Raphael) (vert) 15 15
1628 2cor. "The Spoliation of Christ" (El Greco) (vert) 45 30
1629 3cor. "The Conception" (Murillo) (vert) 60 45

1968. Air. Pope Paul's Visit to Bogota. Nos. 1625/8 optd **Visita de S. S. Paulo VI C. E. de Bogota 1968**.
1631 **250** 10c. multicoloured . . . 10 10
1632 – 15c. multicoloured . . . 10 10
1633 – 35c. multicoloured . . . 10 10
1634 – 2cor. multicoloured . . . 30 20

252 Basketball

1969. Air. Olympic Games, Mexico. Mult.
1635 10c. Type **252** 10 10
1636 15c. Fencing (horiz) 10 10
1637 20c. High-diving 10 10
1638 35c. Running 10 10
1639 50c. Hurdling (horiz) . . . 15 10
1640 75c. Weightlifting 20 15
1641 1cor. Boxing (horiz) 35 20
1642 2cor. Football 55 55

253 Midas Cichlid

1969. Air. Fishes. Multicoloured.
1644 10c. Type **253** 10 10
1645 15c. Moga cichlid 10 10
1646 20c. Common carp 20 10
1647 30c. Tropical gar 25 10
1648 35c. Swordfish 30 10
1649 50c. Big-mouthed sleeper . . 35 15
1650 75c. Atlantic tarpon 40 20
1651 1cor. Lake Nicaragua shark 60 25
1652 2cor. Sailfish 75 45
1653 3cor. Small-toothed sawfish 1·40 70

1969. Air. Various stamps surch **RESELLO** and value.
1655 10c. on 25c. (No. 1507) . . 10 10
1656 10c. on 25c. (No. 1512) . . 10 10
1657 15c. on 25c. (No. 1529) . . 10 10
1658 50c. on 70c. (No. 1379) . . 15 10

255 Scenery, Tower and Emblem

258 "Minerals"

1969. Air. "Hemisfair" (1968) Exhibition.
1659 **255** 30c. blue and red 10 10
1660 35c. purple and red . . . 10 10
1661 75c. red and blue 15 10
1662 1cor. purple and black 30 20
1663 2cor. purple and green 55 40

1969. Various stamps surch. (a) Optd **CORREO**.
1665 5c. (No. 1450) 10 10
1666 5c. (No. 1453) 10 10
1667 5c. (No. 1454) 10 10
1668 5c. (No. 1459) 10 10

(b) Optd **RESELLO** and surch.
1670 10c. on 30c. (No. 1324) . . 10 10
1671 10c. on 30c. (No. 1427) . . 10 10
1669 10c. on 25c. (No. 1529) . . 10 10
1672 10c. on 30c. (No. 1530) . . 10 10
1673 15c. on 35c. (No. 1531) . . 10 10
1674 20c. on 30c. (No. 1307) . . 10 10
1675 20c. on 30c. (No. 1401) . . 10 10
1676 20c. on 35c. (No. 1509) . . 10 10

1969. Air. Nicaraguan Products. Multicoloured.
1677 5c. Type **258** 10 10
1678 10c. "Fish" 10 10
1679 15c. "Bananas" 10 10
1680 20c. "Timber" 10 10
1681 35c. "Coffee" 10 10
1682 40c. "Sugar-cane" 15 10
1683 60c. "Cotton" 20 10
1684 75c. "Rice and Maize" . . . 20 15
1685 1cor. "Tobacco" 30 20
1686 2cor. "Meat" 35 25

1969. 50th Anniv of I.L.O. Obligatory tax stamps. Nos. 1450/9, optd **O.I.T. 1919-1969**.
1687 5c. multicoloured 10 10
1688 5c. multicoloured 10 10
1689 5c. multicoloured 10 10
1690 5c. multicoloured 10 10
1691 5c. multicoloured 10 10
1692 5c. multicoloured 10 10
1693 5c. multicoloured 10 10
1694 5c. multicoloured 10 10
1695 5c. multicoloured 10 10
1696 5c. multicoloured 10 10

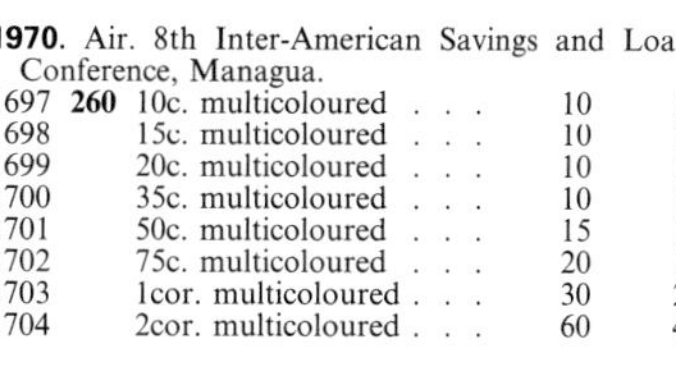

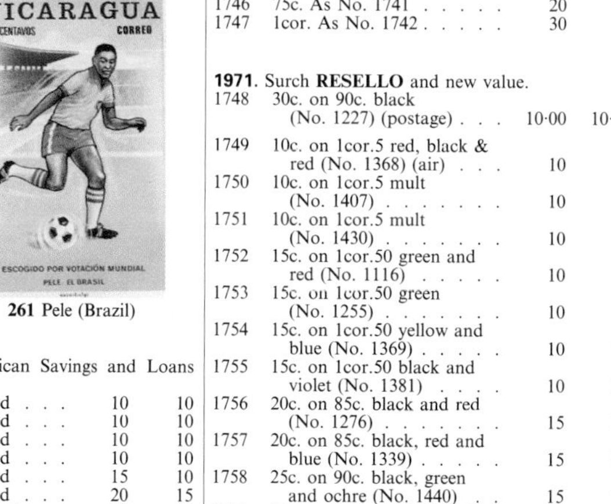
260 Girl carrying Tinaja

261 Pele (Brazil)

1970. Air. 8th Inter-American Savings and Loans Conference, Managua.
1697 **260** 10c. multicoloured . . . 10 10
1698 15c. multicoloured . . . 10 10
1699 20c. multicoloured . . . 10 10
1700 35c. multicoloured . . . 10 10
1701 50c. multicoloured . . . 15 10
1702 75c. multicoloured . . . 20 15
1703 1cor. multicoloured . . 30 20
1704 2cor. multicoloured . . . 60 40

1970. World Football "Hall of Fame" Poll-winners. Multicoloured.
1705 5c. Type **261** (postage) . . . 10 10
1706 10c. Puskas (Hungary) . . . 10 10
1707 15c. Matthews (England) . . 10 10
1708 40c. Di Stefano (Argentina) 10 10
1709 2cor. Facchetti (Italy) . . . 55 45
1710 3cor. Yashin (Russia) . . . 70 65
1711 5cor. Beckenbauer (West Germany) 70 90
1712 20c. Santos (Brazil) (air) . . 10 10
1713 80c. Wright (England) . . . 20 15
1714 1cor. Flags of 16 World Cup finalists 25 20
1715 4cor. Bozsik (Hungary) . . 90 75
1716 5cor. Charlton (England) . . 1·10 90

262 Torii (Gate)

263 Module and Astronauts on Moon

1970. Air. EXPO 70, World Fair, Osaka, Japan.
1717 **262** 25c. multicoloured . . . 10 10
1718 30c. multicoloured . . . 10 10
1719 35c. multicoloured . . . 10 10
1720 75c. multicoloured . . . 25 15
1721 1cor.50 multicoloured . . 35 30
1722 3cor. multicoloured . . . 45 35

1970. Air. "Apollo 11" Moon Landing (1969). Mult.
1724 35c. Type **263** 10 10
1725 40c. Module landing on Moon 10 10
1726 60c. Astronauts with U.S. flag 20 15
1727 75c. As 40c. 25 15
1728 1cor. As 60c. 35 20
1729 2cor. Type **263** 40 35

264 F. D. Roosevelt

265 "The Annunciation" (Grunewald)

1970. Air. 25th Death Anniv of Franklin D. Roosevelt.
1730 **264** 10c. black 10 10
1731 – 15c. brown and black . . 10 10
1732 – 20c. green and black . . 10 10
1733 **264** 35c. purple and black . . 10 10
1734 – 50c. brown 15 10
1735 **264** 75c. blue 20 15
1736 – 1cor. red 25 20
1737 – 2cor. black 30 35
PORTRAITS: 15c., 1cor. Roosevelt with stamp collection; 20c., 50c., 2cor. Roosevelt (full-face).

1970. Air. Christmas. Paintings. Multicoloured.
1738 10c. Type **265** 10 10
1739 10c. "The Nativity" (detail, El Greco) 10 10
1740 10c. "The Adoration of the Magi" (detail, Durer) . . 10 10
1741 10c. "Virgin and Child" (J. van Hemessen) 10 10
1742 10c. "The Holy Shepherd" (Portuguese School, 16th cent) 10 10
1743 15c. Type **265** 10 10
1744 20c. As No. 1739 . . . . . 10 10
1745 35c. As No. 1740 . . . . . 15 10
1746 75c. As No. 1741 . . . . . 20 15
1747 1cor. As No. 1742 . . . . . 30 20

1971. Surch **RESELLO** and new value.
1748 30c. on 90c. black (No. 1227) (postage) . . . 10·00 10·00
1749 10c. on 1cor.5 red, black & red (No. 1368) (air) . . . 10 10
1750 10c. on 1cor.5 mult (No. 1407) 10 10
1751 10c. on 1cor.5 mult (No. 1430) 10 10
1752 15c. on 1cor.50 green and red (No. 1116) 10 10
1753 15c. on 1cor.50 green (No. 1255) 10 10
1754 15c. on 1cor.50 yellow and blue (No. 1369) 10 10
1755 15c. on 1cor.50 black and violet (No. 1381) 10 10
1756 20c. on 85c. black and red (No. 1276) 15 10
1757 20c. on 85c. black, red and blue (No. 1339) 15 10
1758 25c. on 90c. black, green and ochre (No. 1440) . . 15 15
1759 30c. on 1cor.10 black and purple (No. 1195) 15 15
1760 40c. on 1cor.10 brown and black (No. 1157) 65 65
1761 40c. on 1cor.50 mult (No. 1408) 65 65
1762 1cor. on 1cor.10 black and blue (No. 1538) . . . . . 1·60 1·60

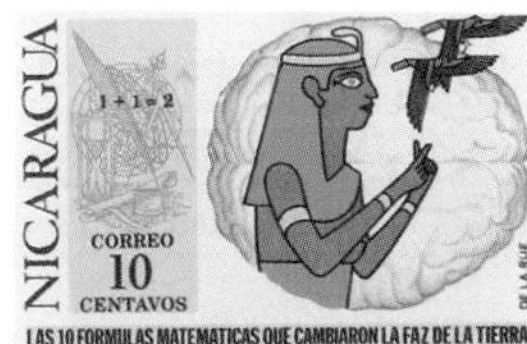

266 Basic Mathematical Equation

1971. Scientific Formulae. "The Ten Mathematical Equations that changed the Face of the Earth". Multicoloured.
1763 10c. Type **266** (postage) . . 10 10
1764 15c. Newton's Law 10 10
1765 20c. Einstein's Law 10 10
1766 1cor. Tsiolkovsky's Law . . 25 25
1767 2cor. Maxwell's Law . . . 90 75
1768 25c. Napier's Law (air) . . . 10 10
1769 30c. Pythagoras' Law . . . 10 10
1770 40c. Boltzmann's Law . . . 15 10
1771 1cor. Broglie's Law 30 20
1772 2cor. Archimedes' Law . . . 55 40

267 Peace Emblem

1971. "Is There a Formula for Peace?"
1773 **267** 10c. blue and black . . . 10 10
1774 15c. blue, black and violet 10 10
1775 20c. blue, black & brown 10 10
1776 40c. blue, black and green 10 10
1777 50c. blue, black & purple 15 10
1778 80c. blue, black and red 15 15
1779 1cor. blue, black & green 30 20
1780 2cor. blue, black & violet 55 35

268 Montezuma Oropendola

269 "Moses with the Tablets of the Law" (Rembrandt)

1971. Air. Nicaraguan Birds. Multicoloured.
1781 10c. Type **268** 45 20
1782 15c. Turquoise-browed motmot 45 20
1783 20c. White-throated magpie-jay 55 20
1784 25c. Scissor-tailed flycatcher 55 20
1785 30c. Spotted-breasted oriole (horiz) 70 20
1786 35c. Rufous-naped wren . . 85 20
1787 40c. Great kiskadee 85 20
1788 75c. Red-legged honeycreeper (horiz) . . . 1·50 40

1789 1cor. Great-tailed grackle (horiz) . . . . 1·75 50
1790 2cor. Belted kingfisher . . . 5·50 1·00

1971. "The Ten Commandments". Paintings. Multicoloured.
1791 10c. Type **269** (postage) . . 10 10
1792 15c. "Moses and the Burning Bush" (Botticelli) (1st Commandment) . . . 10 10
1793 20c. "Jepthah's Daughter" (Degas) (2nd Commandment) (horiz) 10 10
1794 30c. "St. Vincent Ferrer preaching in Verona" (Morone) (3rd Commandment) (horiz) 10 10
1795 35c. "Noah's Drunkenness" (Michelangelo) (4th Commandment) (horiz) 10 10
1796 40c. "Cain and Abel" (Trevisani) (5th Commandment) (horiz) 10 10
1797 50c. "Joseph accused by Potiphar's Wife" (Rembrandt) (6th Commandment) 10 10
1798 60c. "Isaac blessing Jacob" (Eeckhout) (7th Commandment) (horiz) 15 10
1799 75c. "Susannah and the Elders" (Rubens) (8th Commandment) (horiz) 25 20
1800 1cor. "Bathsheba after her Bath" (Rembrandt) (9th Commandment) (air) . . 25 20
1801 2cor. "Naboth's Vineyard" (Smetham) (10th Commandment) 40 35

270 U Thant and Pres. Somoza

1971. Air. 25th Anniv of U.N.O.
1802 **270** 10c. brown and red . . . 10 10
1803 15c. green and emerald 10 10
1804 20c. blue and light blue 10 10
1805 25c. red and purple . . . 10 10
1806 30c. brown and orange 10 10
1807 40c. green and grey . . . 15 10
1808 1cor. green and sage . . 25 20
1809 2cor. brown & light brown 30 35

1972. Olympic Games, Munich. Nos. 1709, 1711, 1713 and 1716 surch **OLIMPIADAS MUNICH 1972**, emblem and value or optd only (5cor.).
1810 40c. on 2cor. multicoloured (postage) 10 10
1811 50c. on 3cor. multicoloured 15 10
1812 20c. on 80c. mult (air) . . . 10 10
1813 60c. on 4cor. multicoloured 15 10
1814 5cor. multicoloured 65 65

272 Figurine and Apoyo Site on Map

1972. Air. Pre-Columbian Art. A. H. Heller's Pottery Discoveries. Multicoloured.
1815 10c. Type **272** 10 10
1816 15c. Cana Castilla 10 10
1817 20c. Catarina 10 10
1818 25c. Santa Helena 10 10
1819 30c. Mombacho 10 10
1820 35c. Tisma 10 10
1821 40c. El Menco 10 10
1822 50c. Los Placeres 15 10
1823 60c. Masaya 15 15
1824 80c. Granada 20 15
1825 1cor. Las Mercedes 30 20
1826 2cor. Nindiri 55 35

273 "Lord Peter Wimsey" (Dorothy Sayers)

1972. Air. 50th Anniv of International Criminal Police Organization (INTERPOL). Famous Fictional Detectives. Multicoloured.
1827 5c. Type **273** 10 10
1828 10c. "Philip Marlowe" (Raymond Chandler) . . 10 10
1829 15c. "Sam Spade" (D. Hammett) . . . . . 6·00 20
1830 20c. "Perry Mason" (Erle Stanley Gardner) 10 10
1831 25c. "Nero Wolfe" (Rex Stout) 10 10
1832 35c. "C. Auguste Dupin" (Edgar Allan Poe) 10 10
1833 40c. "Ellery Queen" (F. Dannay and M. Lee) 10 10
1834 50c. "Father Brown" (G. K. Chesterton) 10 10
1835 60c. "Charlie Chan" (Earl D. Biggers) 15 10
1836 80c. "Inspector Maigret" (Georges Simenon) . . . 25 15
1837 1cor. "Hercule Poirot" (Agatha Christie) 25 20
1838 2cor. "Sherlock Holmes" (A. Conan Doyle) 70 70

274 "The Shepherdess and her Brothers"

1972. Air. Christmas. Scenes from Legend of the Christmas Rose. Multicoloured.
1839 10c. Type **274** 10 10
1840 15c. Adoration of the Wise Men 10 10
1841 20c. Shepherdess crying . . 10 10
1842 35c. Angel appears to Shepherdess 10 10
1843 40c. Christmas Rose 10 10
1844 60c. Shepherdess thanks angel for roses 15 10
1845 80c. Shepherdess takes roses to Holy Child 15 15
1846 1cor. Holy Child receiving roses 20 15
1847 2cor. Nativity scene 45 35

275 Sir Walter Raleigh and Elizabethan Galleon

1973. Air. Causes of the American Revolution. Multicoloured.
1849 10c. Type **275** 40 10
1850 15c. Signing "Mayflower Compact" 10 10
1851 20c. Acquittal of Peter Zenger (vert) 10 10
1852 25c. Acclaiming American resistance (vert) 10 10
1853 30c. Revenue stamp (vert) 10 10
1854 35c. "Serpent" slogan— "Join or die" 10 10
1855 40c. Boston Massacre (vert) 10 10
1856 50c. Boston Tea-party . . . 10 10
1857 60c. Patrick Henry on trial (vert) 15 10
1858 75c. Battle of Bunker Hill 20 10
1859 80c. Declaration of Independence 20 15
1860 1cor. Liberty Bell 30 20
1861 2cor. US seal (vert) 90 60

1973. Nos. 1450/54, 1456 and 1458/9 optd **CORREO**.
1862 **219** 5c. multicoloured 25 10
1863 – 5c. multicoloured 25 10
1864 – 5c. multicoloured 25 10
1865 – 5c. multicoloured 25 10
1866 – 5c. multicoloured 25 10
1867 – 5c. multicoloured 25 10
1868 – 5c. multicoloured 25 10
1869 – 5c. multicoloured 25 10

277 Baseball, Player and Map

278 Givenchy, Paris

1973. Air. 20th International Baseball Championships, Managua (1972).
1870 **277** 15c. multicoloured . . . 10 10
1871 20c. multicoloured . . . 10 10
1872 40c. multicoloured . . . 10 10
1873 10cor. multicoloured . . 1·50 90

1973. World-famous Couturiers. Mannequins. Mult.
1875 1cor. Type **278** (postage) . . 25 20
1876 2cor. Hartnell, London . . . 40 40
1877 5cor. Balmain, Paris . . . . 1·00 90
1878 10c. Lourdes, Nicaragua (air) 10 10
1879 15c. Halston, New York . . 10 10
1880 20c. Pino Lancetti, Rome . . 10 10
1881 35c. Madame Gres, Paris . . 10 10

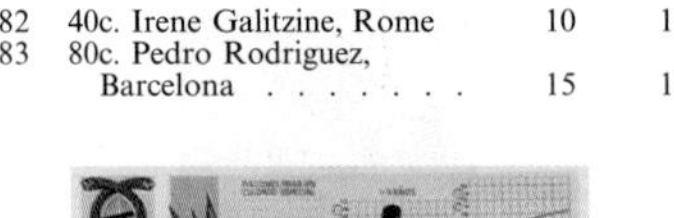
1882 40c. Irene Galitzine, Rome 10 10
1883 80c. Pedro Rodriguez, Barcelona 15 15

279 Diet Chart

1973. Air. Child Welfare. Multicoloured.
1885 5c.+5c. Type **279** 10 10
1886 10c.+5c. Senora Samoza with baby, and Children's Hospital 10 10
1887 15c.+5c. "Childbirth" . . . 10 10
1888 20c.+5c. "Immunization" . . 10 10
1889 30c.+5c. Water purification 10 10
1890 35c.+5c. As No. 1886 . . . 10 10
1891 50c.+10c. Alexander Fleming and "Antibiotics" 30 10
1892 60c.+15c. Malaria control 15 10
1893 70c.+10c. Laboratory analysis 15 15
1894 80c.+20c. Gastroenteritis . . 20 15
1895 1cor.+50c. As No. 1886 . . 30 25
1896 2cor. Pediatric surgery . . . 45 35

280 Virginia and Father

1973. Christmas. "Does Santa Claus exist?" (Virginia O'Hanlon's letter to American "Sun" newspaper). Multicoloured.
1897 2c. Type **280** (postage) . . . 10 10
1898 3c. Text of letter 10 10
1899 4c. Reading the reply . . . 10 10
1900 5c. Type **280** 10 10
1901 1[illegible] 10 10
1902 20c. As 4c. 10 10
1903 1cor. Type **280** (air) 20 15
1904 2cor. As 3c. 35 30
1905 4cor. As 4c. 75 65

281 Churchill making Speech, 1936

1974. Birth Cent of Sir Winston Churchill.
1907 **281** 2c. multicoloured (postage) 10 10
1908 – 3c. black, blue and brown 10 10
1909 – 4c. multicoloured 10 10
1910 – 5c. multicoloured 10 10
1911 – 10c. brown, green & blue 30 10
1912 – 5cor. multicoloured (air) 90 80
1913 – 6cor. black, brown & bl 1·00 90
DESIGNS: 3c. "The Four Churchills" (wartime cartoon); 4c. Candle, cigar and "Action" stickers; 5c. Churchill, Roosevelt and Stalin at Yalta; 10c. Churchill landing in Normandy, 1944; 5cor. Churchill giving "V" sign; 6cor. "Bulldog Churchill" (cartoon).

282 Presentation of World Cup to Uruguay, 1930

1974. World Cup Football Championship. Mult.
1915 1c. Type **282** (postage) . . . 10 10
1916 2c. Victorious Italian team, 1934 . . . . 10 10
1917 3c. Presentation of World Cup to Italy, 1938 . . . . 10 10
1918 4c. Uruguay's winning goal, 1950 . . . . 10 10
1919 5c. Victorious West Germany, 1954 . . . . . 10 10
1920 10c. Rejoicing Brazilian players, 1958 . . . . . . 10 10
1921 15c. Brazilian player holding World Cup, 1962 . . . . 10 10
1922 20c. Queen Elizabeth II presenting Cup to Bobby Moore, 1966 . . . . . . 10 10
1923 25c. Victorious Brazilian players, 1970 . . . . . . 10 10

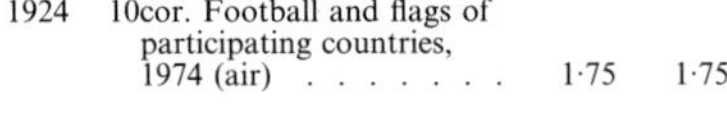
1924 10cor. Football and flags of participating countries, 1974 (air) . . . . 1·75 1·75

283 "Malachra sp."

284 Nicaraguan 7½c. Stamp of 1937

1974. Wild Flowers and Cacti. Multicoloured.
1926 2c. Type **283** (postage) . . . 10 10
1927 3c. "Paguira insignis" . . . 10 10
1928 4c. "Convolvulus sp." . . . 10 10
1929 5c. "Pereschia autumnalis" 10 10
1930 10c. "Ipomea tuberosa" . . 10 10
1931 15c. "Hibiscus elatus" . . . 10 10
1932 20c. "Plumeria acutifolia" 10 10
1933 1cor. "Centrosema sp." (air) 20 20
1934 3cor. "Hylocereus undatus" 60 55

1974. Centenary of U.P.U.
1935 **284** 2c. red, green & blk (postage) 10 20
1936 – 3c. blue, green and black 10 10
1937 – 4c. multicoloured 10 10
1938 – 5c. brown, mauve & blk 10 10
1939 – 10c. red, brown and black 10 10
1940 – 20c. green, blue and black 10 10
1941 – 40c. multicoloured (air) 10 10
1942 – 3cor. green, black & pink 50 40
1943 – 5cor. blue, black and lilac . . . . 1·00 80
DESIGNS—VERT: 3c. 5c. stamp of 1937; 5c. 2c. stamp of 1937; 10c. 1c. stamp of 1937; 20c. ½c. stamp of 1937; 40c. 10c. stamp of 1961; 5cor. 4cor. U.P.U. stamp of 1950. HORIZ: 4c. 10c. air stamp of 1934; 3cor. 85c. U.P.U. air stamp of 1950.

1974. Air. West Germany's Victory in World Cup Football Championship. No. 1924 optd **TRIUMFADOR ALEMANIA OCCIDENTAL**.
1945 10cor. multicoloured . . . . 1·75 1·60

286 Tamandua

1974. Nicaraguan Fauna. Multicoloured.
1947 1c. Type **286** (postage) . . . 10 10
1948 2c. Puma 10 10
1949 3c. Common raccoon . . . 10 10
1950 4c. Ocelot 10 10
1951 5c. Kinkajou 10 10
1952 10c. Coypu 10 10
1953 15c. Collared peccary . . . 15 10
1954 20c. Baird's tapir 15 10
1955 3cor. Red brocket (air) . . . 1·50 1·40
1956 5cor. Jaguar . . . . 2·40 2·00

287 "Prophet Zacharias"

1975. Christmas. 500th Birth Anniv of Michelangelo. Multicoloured.
1957 1c. Type **287** (postage) . . . 10 10
1958 2c. "Christ amongst the Jews" 10 10
1959 3c. "The Creation of Man" (horiz) 10 10
1960 4c. Interior of Sistine Chapel, Rome 10 10
1961 5c. "Moses" 10 10
1962 10c. "Mouscron Madonna" 10 10
1963 15c. "David" 10 10
1964 20c. "Doni Madonna" . . . 10 10
1965 40c. "Madonna of the Steps" (air) 10 10
1966 80c. "Pitti Madonna" . . . 15 15
1967 2cor. "Christ and Virgin Mary" 35 30
1968 5cor. "Michelangelo" (self-portrait) 75 75

288 Giovanni Martinelli ("Othello")

1975. Great Opera Singers. Multicoloured.

No.	Description	Mint	Used
1970	1c. Type **288** (postage)	10	10
1971	2c. Tito Gobbi ("Simone Boccanegra")	10	10
1972	3c. Lotte Lehmann ("Der Rosenkavalier")	10	10
1973	4c. Lauritz Melchior ("Parsifal")	10	10
1974	5c. Nellie Melba ("La Traviata")	10	10
1975	15c. Jussi Bjoerling ("La Boheme")	10	10
1976	20c. Birgit Nilsson ("Turandot")	10	10
1977	25c. Rosa Ponselle ("Norma") (air)	10	10
1978	35c. Guiseppe de Luca ("Rigoletto")	10	10
1979	40c. Joan Sutherland ("La Figlia del Reggimiento")	10	10
1980	50c. Enzio Pinza ("Don Giovanni")	10	10
1981	60c. Kirsten Flagstad ("Tristan and Isolde")	15	10
1982	80c. Maria Callas ("Tosca")	15	15
1983	2cor. Fyodor Chaliapin ("Boris Godunov")	60	35
1984	5cor. Enrico Caruso ("La Juive")	1·10	60

289 The First Station **290** "The Spirit of 76"

1975. Easter. The 14 Stations of the Cross.

No.	Description	Mint	Used
1986	**289** 1c. multicoloured (postage)	10	10
1987	– 2c. multicoloured	10	10
1988	– 3c. multicoloured	10	10
1989	– 4c. multicoloured	10	10
1990	– 5c. multicoloured	10	10
1991	– 15c. multicoloured	10	10
1992	– 20c. multicoloured	10	10
1993	– 25c. multicoloured	10	10
1994	– 35c. multicoloured	10	10
1995	– 40c. multicoloured (air)	10	10
1996	– 50c. multicoloured	10	10
1997	– 80c. multicoloured	15	15
1998	– 1cor. multicoloured	20	15
1999	– 5cor. multicoloured	80	65

DESIGNS: 2c. to 5cor. Different Stations of the Cross.

1975. Bicentenary of American Independence (1st series). Multicoloured.

No.	Description	Mint	Used
2000	1c. Type **290** (postage)	10	10
2001	2c. Pitt addressing Parliament	10	10
2002	3c. Paul Revere's Ride (horiz)	10	10
2003	4c. Demolishing statue of George III (horiz)	10	10
2004	5c. Boston Massacre	10	10
2005	10c. Tax stamp and George III 3d. coin (horiz)	10	10
2006	15c. Boston Tea Party (horiz)	10	10
2007	20c. Thomas Jefferson	10	10
2008	25c. Benjamin Franklin	10	10
2009	30c. Signing of Declaration of Independence (horiz)	10	10
2010	35c. Surrender of Cornwallis at Yorktown (horiz)	10	10
2011	40c. Washington's Farewell (horiz) (air)	10	10
2012	50c. Washington addressing Congress (horiz)	10	10
2013	2cor. Washington arriving for Presidential Inauguration (horiz)	70	30
2014	5cor. Statue of Liberty and flags	75	45

See also Nos. 2056/71.

291 Saluting the Flag

1975. "Nordjamb 75" World Scout Jamboree, Norway. Multicoloured.

No.	Description	Mint	Used
2016	1c. Type **291** (postage)	10	10
2017	2c. Scout canoe	10	10
2018	3c. Scouts shaking hands	10	10
2019	4c. Scout preparing meal	10	10
2020	5c. Entrance to Nicaraguan camp	10	10
2021	20c. Scouts meeting	10	10
2022	35c. Aerial view of camp (air)	10	10
2023	40c. Scouts making music	10	10
2024	1cor. Camp-fire	20	15
2025	10cor. Lord Baden-Powell	1·25	1·10

292 President Somoza

1975. President Somoza's New Term of Office, 1974–81.

No.	Description	Mint	Used
2027	**292** 20c. multicoloured (postage)	10	10
2028	40c. multicoloured	10	10
2029	1cor. multicoloured (air)	20	20
2030	10cor. multicoloured	1·25	1·10
2031	20cor. multicoloured	3·25	2·75

293 "Chess Players" (L. Carracci)

1975. Chess. Multicoloured.

No.	Description	Mint	Used
2032	1c. Type **293** (postage)	10	10
2033	2c. "Arabs playing Chess" (Delacroix)	10	10
2034	3c. "Cardinals playing Chess" (V. Marais-Milton)	10	10
2035	4c. "Duke Albrecht V of Bavaria and Anna of Austria at Chess" (H. Muelich) (vert)	10	10
2036	5c. "Chess game" (14th-century Persian manuscript)	10	10
2037	10c. "Origins of Chess" (India, 1602)	10	10
2038	15c. "Napoleon playing Chess in Schonbrunn Palace in 1809" (A. Uniechowski) (vert)	10	10
2039	20c. "The Chess Game in the House of Count Ingenheim" (J.E. Hummel)	10	10
2040	40c. "The Chess-players" (T. Eakins) (air)	10	10
2041	2cor. Fischer v Spassky match, Reykjavik, 1972	55	35
2042	5cor. "William Shakespeare and Ben Jonson playing Chess" (K. van Mander)	60	50

294 Choir of King's College, Cambridge

1975. Christmas. Famous Choirs. Multicoloured.

No.	Description	Mint	Used
2044	1c. Type **294** (postage)	10	10
2045	2c. Abbey Choir, Einsiedeln	10	10
2046	3c. Regensburg Cathedral choir	10	10
2047	4c. Vienna Boys' choir	10	10
2048	5c. Sistine Chapel choir	10	10
2049	15c. Westminster Cathedral choir	10	10
2050	20c. Mormon Tabernacle choir	10	10
2051	50c. School choir, Montserrat (air)	10	10
2052	1cor. St. Florian children's choir	20	15
2053	2cor. "Little Singers of the Wooden Cross" (vert)	45	35
2054	5cor. Pope with choristers of Pueri Cantores	60	50

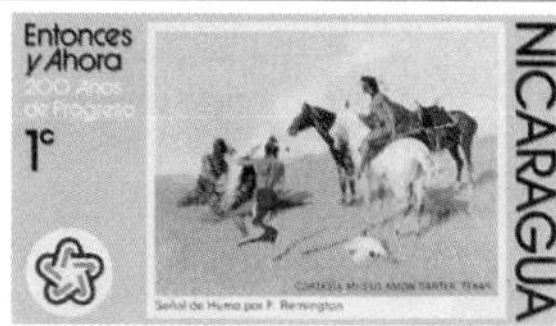

295 "The Smoke Signal" (F. Remington)

1976. Bicent of American Revolution (2nd series). "200 Years of Progress". Multicoloured.

No.	Description	Mint	Used
2056	1c. Type **295** (postage)	10	10
2057	1c. Houston Space Centre	10	10
2058	2c. Lighting candelabra, 1976	10	10
2059	2c. Edison's lamp and houses	10	10
2060	3c. "Agriculture 1776"	10	10
2061	3c. "Agriculture 1976"	10	10
2062	4c. Harvard College, 1776	10	10
2063	4c. Harvard University, 1976	10	10
2064	5c. Horse and carriage	15	10
2065	5c. Boeing 747-100 airliner	15	10
2066	80c. Philadelphia, 1776 (air)	25	15
2067	80c. Washington, 1976	25	15
2068	2cor.75 "Bonhomme Richard" (American frigate) (John Paul Jones's flagship) and H.M.S. "Seraphis" (frigate), Battle of Flamborough Head	1·50	70
2069	2cor.75 U.S.S. "Glenard Phipscomp" (nuclear submarine)	1·50	70
2070	4cor. Wagon train	90	70
2071	4cor. Amtrak gas turbine train, 1973	3·25	1·75

296 Italy, 1968

1976. Olympic Games, Victors in Rowing and Sculling. Multicoloured.

No.	Description	Mint	Used
2073	1c. Denmark 1964 (postage)	10	10
2074	2c. East Germany 1972	10	10
2075	3c. Type **296**	10	10
2076	4c. Great Britain 1936	10	10
2077	5c. France 1952 (vert)	10	10
2078	35c. U.S.A. 1920 (vert)	10	10
2079	55c. Russia 1956 (vert) (air)	20	10
2080	70c. New Zealand 1972 (vert)	20	15
2081	90c. New Zealand 1968	25	20
2082	20cor. U.S.A. 1956	2·75	2·50

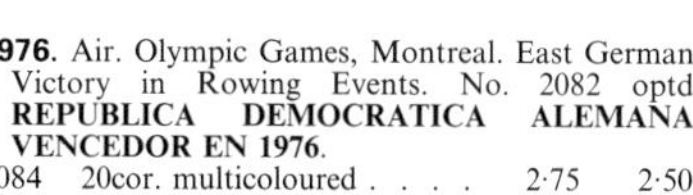

1976. Air. Olympic Games, Montreal. East German Victory in Rowing Events. No. 2082 optd **REPUBLICA DEMOCRATICA ALEMANA VENCEDOR EN 1976**.

No.	Description	Mint	Used
2084	20cor. multicoloured	2·75	2·50

299 Mauritius 1847 2d. "Post Office"

1976. Rare and Famous Stamps. Multicoloured.

No.	Description	Mint	Used
2087	1c. Type **299** (postage)	10	10
2088	2c. Western Australia 1854 "Inverted Mute Swan"	85	15
2089	3c. Mauritius 1847 1d. "Post Office"	10	10
2090	4c. Jamaica 1920 1s. inverted frame	10	10
2091	5c. U.S 1918 24c. inverted aircraft	10	10
2092	10c. Swiss 1845 Basel "Dove"	10	10
2093	25c. Canada 1959 Seaway inverted centre	10	10
2094	40c. Hawaiian 1851 2c. "Missionary" (air)	10	10
2095	1cor. G.B. 1840 "Penny Black"	20	20
2096	2cor. British Guiana 1850 1c. black on magenta	40	35
2097	5cor. Honduras 1925 airmail 25c. on 10c.	3·50	1·10
2098	10cor. Newfoundland 1919 "Hawker" airmail stamp	1·25	1·10

300 Olga Nunez de Saballos (Member of Parliament)

1977. Air. International Women's Year. Multicoloured.

No.	Description	Mint	Used
2100	35c. Type **300**	10	10
2101	1cor. Josefa Toledo de Aguerri (educator)	20	20
2102	10cor. Hope Portocarreo de Samoza (President's wife)	1·25	1·00

301 "Graf Zeppelin" in Hangar

1977. 75th Anniv of First Zeppelin Flight. Mult.

No.	Description	Mint	Used
2104	1c. Type **301** (postage)	10	10
2105	2c. "Graf Zeppelin" in flight	10	10
2106	3c. Giffard's steam-powered dirigible airship, 1852	15	10
2107	4c. "Graf Zeppelin" in mooring hangar	15	10
2108	5c. "Graf Zeppelin" on ground	15	10
2109	35c. Astra airship "Ville de Paris" (air)	35	15
2110	70c. "Schwaben"	40	20
2111	3cor. "Graf Zeppelin" over Lake Constance	1·00	65
2112	10cor. LZ-2 on Lake Constance	3·75	2·25

302 Lindbergh and Map

1977. 50th Anniv of Lindbergh's Transatlantic Flight. Multicoloured.

No.	Description	Mint	Used
2114	1c. Type **302** (postage)	10	10
2115	2c. Map and "Spirit of St. Louis"	10	10
2116	3c. Charles Lindbergh (vert)	10	10
2117	4c. "Spirit of St. Louis" crossing Atlantic	10	10
2118	5c. Charles Lindbergh standing by "Spirit of St. Louis"	10	10
2119	20c. Lindbergh, route and "Spirit of St. Louis"	20	15
2120	55c. Lindbergh landing in Nicaragua (1928) (air)	20	15
2121	80c. "Spirit of St. Louis" and route map	35	15
2122	2cor. "Spirit of St. Louis" flying along Nicaraguan coast	65	35
2123	10cor. Passing Momotombo (Nicaragua)	1·90	1·25

303 Christmas Festival

1977. Christmas. Scenes from Tchaikovsky's "Nutcracker" Suite. Multicoloured.

No.	Description	Mint	Used
2125	1c. Type **303**	10	10
2126	2c. Doll's dance	10	10
2127	3c. Clara and snowflakes	10	10
2128	4c. Snow fairy and prince	10	10
2129	5c. Snow fairies	10	10
2130	15c. Sugar fairy and prince	10	10
2131	40c. Waltz of the Flowers	10	10
2132	90c. Chinese dance	20	15
2133	1cor. Senora Bonbonierre	20	20
2134	10cor. Arabian dance	1·40	1·25

304 "Mr. and Mrs. Andrews". (Gainsborough)

1978. Paintings. Multicoloured.

No.	Description	Mint	Used
2136	1c. Type **304** (postage)	10	10
2137	2c. "Giovanna Bacelli" (Gainsborough)	10	10
2138	3c. "Blue Boy" (Gainsborough)	10	10
2139	4c. "Francis I" (Titian)	10	10
2140	5c. "Charles V at Battle of Muhlberg" (Titian)	10	10
2141	25c. "Sacred Love" (Titian)	10	10
2142	5cor. "Hippopotamus and Crocodile Hunt" (Rubens) (air)	60	50
2143	10cor. "Duke of Lerma on Horseback" (Rubens)	1·75	1·40

305 Gothic Portal with Rose Window, Small Basilica of St. Francis

1978. 750th Anniv of Canonisation of St. Francis of Assisi. Multicoloured.

2145 1c. Type **305** (postage) . . . 10 10
2146 2c. St. Francis preaching to birds 10 10
2147 3c. Painting of St. Francis 10 10
2148 4c. Franciscan genealogical tree 10 10
2149 5c. Portiuncola 10 10
2150 15c. Autographed blessing 10 10
2151 25c. Windows of Large Basilica 10 10
2152 80c. St. Francis and wolf (air) 15 10
2153 10cor. St. Francis . . . . . 1·60 1·50

306 Locomotive No. 6, 1921

1978. Centenary of Railway. Multicoloured.

2155 1c. Type **306** (postage) . . . 10 10
2156 2c. Lightweight cargo locomotive 10 10
2157 3c. Steam locomotive No. 10, 1909 . . . . . . 10 10
2158 4c. Baldwin steam locomotive No. 31, 1906 10 10
2159 5c. Baldwin steam locomotive No. 21, 1911 10 10
2160 15c. Presidential Pullman coach 15 10
2161 35c. Steam locomotive No. 33, 1907 (air) 20 15
2162 4cor. Baldwin steam locomotive No. 36, 1907 2·50 90
2163 10cor. Juniata steam locomotive, 1914, U.S.A. 6·25 2·25

307 Mongol Warriors ("Michael Strogoff")

1978. 150th Birth Anniv of Jules Verne. Mult.

2165 1c. Type **307** (postage) . . . 10 10
2166 2c. Sea scene ("The Mysterious Island") . . . 10 10
2167 3c. Sea monsters ("Journey to the Centre of the Earth") 10 10
2168 4c. Balloon and African elephant ("Five Weeks in a Balloon") 20 10
2169 90c. Submarine ("Twenty Thousand Leagues Under the Sea") (air) 75 20
2170 10cor. Balloon, Indian, steam locomotive and elephant ("Around the World in Eighty Days") 6·50 4·00

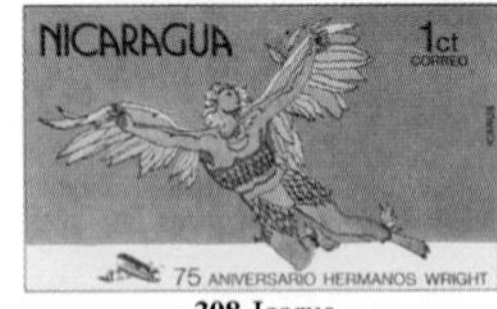

308 Icarus

1978. 75th Anniv of History of Aviation. First Powered Flight. Multicoloured.

2172 1c. Type **308** (postage) . . . 10 10
2173 2c. Montgolfier balloon (vert) 10 10
2174 3c. Wright Flyer I 10 10
2175 4c. Orville Wright in Wright Type A (vert) 10 10
2176 55c. Vought-Sikorsky VS-300 helicopter prototype (air) 30 10
2177 10cor. Space Shuttle . . . . 2·10 1·00

309 Ernst Ocwirk and Alfredo di Stefano

310 "St. Peter" (Goya)

1978. World Cup Football Championship, Argentina. Multicoloured.

2179 20c. Type **309** (postage) . . 10 10
2180 25c. Ralk Edstrom and Oswaldo Piazza 10 10
2181 50c. Franz Beckenbauer and Dennis Law (air) 10 10
2182 5cor. Dino Zoff and Pele . . 65 50

1978. Christmas. Multicoloured.

2184 10c. Type **310** (postage) . . 10 10
2185 15c. "St. Gregory" (Goya) 10 10
2186 3cor. "The Apostles John and Peter" (Durer) (air) 40 30
2187 10cor. "The Apostles Paul and Mark" (Durer) . . . 1·40 1·00

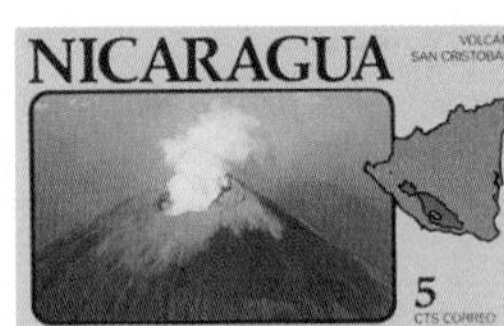

311 San Cristobal

1978. Volcanoes and Lakes. Multicoloured.

2189 5c. Type **311** (postage) . . . 10 10
2190 5c. Lake de Cosiguina . . . 10 10
2191 20c. Telica 10 10
2192 20c. Lake Jiloa 10 10
2193 35c. Cerro Negro (air) . . . 10 10
2194 35c. Lake Masaya 10 10
2195 90c. Momotombo 20 15
2196 90c. Lake Asososca 20 15
2197 1cor. Mombacho 20 15
2198 1cor. Lake Apoyo 20 15
2199 10cor. Concepcion . . . . 1·60 80
2200 10cor. Lake Tiscapa . . . . 1·60 80

312 General O'Higgins

1979. Air. Birth Bicentenary of Bernardo O'Higgins (liberation hero).

2201 **312** 20cor. multicoloured . . 3·75 1·90

313 Ginger Plant and Broad-tailed Hummingbird

1979. Air. Flowers. Multicoloured.

2202 50c. Type **313** 60 20
2203 55c. Orchids 10 10
2204 70c. Poinsettia 15 10
2205 80c. "Poro poro" 15 10
2206 2cor. "Morpho cypris" (butterfly) and Guayacan flowers 50 30
2207 4cor. Iris 45 30

314 Children with football

315 Indian Postal Runner

316 Einstein and Albert Schweitzer

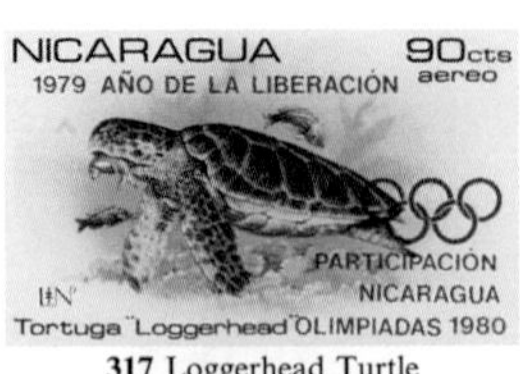

317 Loggerhead Turtle

1980. Year of Liberation (1979) and Nicaragua's Participation in Olympic Games. Unissued stamps overprinted. (a) International Year of the Child. Mult.

2208 20c. Children on roundabout (postage) . . 15 15
2209 90c. Type **314** (air) 65 65
2210 2cor. Children with stamp albums . . . . 1·50 1·50
2211 2cor.20 Children playing with toy steam train and aircraft . . . . 14·00 14·00
2212 10cor. Baseball . . . . . . 7·50 7·50

(b) Death Centenary of Sir Rowland Hill. Mult.

2214 20c. Type **315** (postage) . . 20 20
2215 35c. Pony express 40 40
2216 1cor. Pre-stamp letter (horiz) 1·10 1·10
2217 1cor.80 Sir Rowland Hill examining sheet of Penny Black stamps (air) . . . . 1·90 1·90
2218 2cor.20 Penny Blacks (horiz) 2·40 2·40
2219 5cor. Nicaraguan Zeppelin flight cover (horiz) . . . 5·50 5·50

(c) Birth Centenary of Albert Einstein (physicist). Multicoloured.

2221 5c. Type **316** (postage) . . . 15 15
2222 10c. Einstein and equation 25 25
2223 15c. Einstein and 1939 World Fair pavilion . . . 40 40
2224 20c. Einstein and Robert Oppenheimer 50 50
2225 25c. Einstein in Jerusalem 65 65
2226 1cor. Einstein and Nobel Prize medal (air) . . . . 2·50 2·50
2227 2cor.75 Einstein and space exploration . . . . 7·00 7·00
2228 10cor. Einstein and Mahatma Gandhi . . . . 15·00 15·00

(d) Endangered Turtles. Multicoloured.

2230 90c. Type **317** . . . . . . 1·00 80
2231 2cor. Leatherback turtle . . 2·25 1·75
2232 2cor.30 Ridley turtle . . . . 1·75 1·75
2233 10cor. Hawksbill turtle . . . 7·50 7·50

318 Rigoberto Lopez Perez and Crowds pulling down Statue

1980. 1st Anniv of the Revolution. Multicoloured.

2235 40c. Type **318** 10 10
2236 75c. Street barricade 10 10
2237 1cor. "Learn to Read" emblem (vert) 15 10
2238 1cor.25 German Pomares Ordonez and jungle fighters 20 15
2239 1cor.85 Victory celebrations (vert) 25 15
2240 2cor.50 Carlos Fonesca and camp-fire 35 35
2241 5cor. Gen. Augusto Sandino and flag (vert) 70 55

1980. Literacy Year. Unissued stamps optd **1980 ANO DE LA ALFABETIZACION**. (a) International Year of the Child. As Nos. 2208/12.

2243 – 20c. Children on roundabout (postage) 1·00 1·00
2244 **314** 90c. Children with football (air) . . . . . 1·00 1·00
2245 – 2cor. Children with stamp albums . . . . 1·00 1·00
2246 – 2cor.20 Children playing with toy steam train and airplane . . . . . 2·00 2·00
2247 – 10cor. Baseball . . . . 4·50 4·50

(b) Death Centenary of Sir Rowland Hill. Nos. 2214/16.

2249 **315** 20c. Indian postal runner 70 70
2250 – 35c. Pony express . . . 70 70
2251 – 1cor. Pre-stamp letter (horiz) 70 70

(c) Birth Centenary of Albert Einstein (physicist). As Nos. 2221/8.

2253 5c. Optd **"YURI GAGARIN/12/IV/1961/ LER HOMBRE EN EL ESPACIO"** (postage) . . 1·10 1·10
2254 10c. Optd **"LURABA 1981"** and space shuttle . . . . 1·10 1·10
2255 15c. Optd **"SPACE SHUTTLE"** and craft . . 1·10 1·10
2256 20c. Optd **ANO DE LA ALFABETIZACION** . . 1·10 1·10
2257 25c. Optd **"16/VII/1969/LER HOMBRE A LA LUNA"** and **"APOLLO XI"** . . . 1·10 1·10
2258 1cor. Optd As No. 2256 (air) . . . . 1·10 1·10
2259 2cor.75 Optd As No. 2256 1·10 1·10
2260 10cor.75 Optd **"LUNOJOD 1"** and vehicle . . . . . 1·10 1·10

(d) Air. Endangered Species. Turtles. As Nos. 2230/3. Multicoloured.

2262 **317** 90c. Loggerhead turtle 1·00 1·00
2263 – 2cor. Leatherback turtle 1·00 1·00
2264 – 2cor.20 Ridley turtle . . 1·00 1·00
2265 – 10cor. Hawksbill turtle 1·00 1·00

321 Footballer and El Molinon Stadium

1981. World Cup Football Championship, Spain. (1st issue). Venues. Multicoloured.

2268 5c. Type **321** 10 10
2269 20c. Sanchez Pizjuan, Seville 10 10
2270 25c. San Mames, Bilbao . . 10 10
2271 30c. Vincent Calderon, Madrid 10 10
2272 50c. R.C.D. Espanol, Barcelona 10 10
2273 4cor. New Stadium, Valladolid 55 35
2274 5cor. Balaidos, Vigo 55 35
2275 10cor. Santiago Bernabeu, Madrid . . . . 1·10 65

See also Nos. 2325/31.

322 Adult Education

1981. 2nd Anniv of Revolution. Multicoloured.

2277 50c. Type **322** (postage) . . 10 10
2278 2cor.10 Workers marching (air) 30 15
2279 3cor. Roadbuilding and container ship 65 30
2280 6cor. Medical services . . . 50 25

323 Allegory of Revolution

1981. 20th Anniv of Sandinista National Liberation Front. Multicoloured.

2281 50c. Type **323** (postage) . . 10 10
2282 4cor. Sandinista guerrilla (air) 25 10

324 Postman

1981. 12th Postal Union of the Americas and Spain Congress, Managua. Multicoloured.

2283 50c. Type **324** (postage) . . 10 10

2284 2cor.10 Pony Express (air) 30 15
2285 3cor. Postal Headquarters, Managua 45 25
2286 6cor. Government building, globe and flags of member countries 50 25

326 "Nymphaea capensis"

1981. Water Lilies. Multicoloured.
2288 50c. Type **326** (postage) 10 10
2289 1cor. "Nymphaea daubenyana" 15 10
2290 1cor.20 "Nymphaea Marliacea Chromat" 20 10
2291 1cor.80 "Nymphaea Dir. Geo. T. Moore" 25 15
2292 2cor. "Nymphaea lotus" 30 15
2293 2cor.50 "Nymphaea B.G. Berry" 35 20
2294 10cor. "Nymphaea Gladstoniana" (air) 60 40

328 Cardinal Tetra

1981. Tropical Fishes. Multicoloured.
2296 50c. Type **328** (postage) 15 10
2297 1cor. Guppy 30 20
2298 1cor.85 Striped headstander 50 30
2299 2cor.10 Skunk corydoras 65 35
2300 2cor.50 Black-finned pearlfish 75 40
2301 3cor.50 Long-finned killie (air) 1·10 65
2302 4cor. Red swordtail 1·25 80

330 Lineated Woodpecker

331 Satellite in Orbit

1981. Birds. Multicoloured.
2304 50c. Type **330** (postage) 35 15
2305 1cor.20 Keel-billed toucan (horiz) 70 25
2306 1cor.80 Finsch's conure (horiz) 80 35
2307 2cor. Scarlet macaw 1·10 40
2308 3cor. Slaty-tailed trogon (air) 1·25 50
2309 4cor. Violet sabrewing (horiz) 1·75 60
2310 6cor. Blue-crowned motmot 3·50 1·00

1981. Satellite Communications. Multicoloured.
2311 50c. Type **331** (postage) 10 10
2312 1cor. "Intelstat IVA" 15 10
2313 1cor.50 "Intelstat V" moving into orbit 20 15
2314 2cor. Rocket releasing "Intelstat V" 30 20
2315 3cor. Satellite and Space Shuttle (air) 45 25
2316 4cor. "Intelstat V" and world maps 55 30
2317 5cor. Tracking stations 70 45

332 Steam Locomotive at Lake Granada

1981. Locomotives. Multicoloured.
2318 50c. Type **332** (postage) 20 10
2319 1cor. Vulcan Iron Works steam locomotive No. 35, 1946 40 10
2320 1cor.20 Baldwin steam locomotive No. 21, 1911 (inscribed "Philadelphia Iron Works") 45 10
2321 1cor.80 Steam crane, 1909 70 10
2322 2cor. General Electric Model "U10B" diesel locomotive, 1960s 75 10
2323 2cor.50 German diesel railbus, 1954 (dated "1956") 90 15
2324 6cor. Japanese-built diesel railbus, 1967 (air) 2·40 35

333 Heading Ball

1982. World Cup Football Championship, Spain (2nd issue). Multicoloured.
2325 5c. Type **333** (postage) 10 10
2326 20c. Running with ball 10 10
2327 25c. Running with ball (different) 10 10
2328 2cor.50 Saving goal 35 20
2329 3cor.50 Goalkeeper diving for ball (horiz) 50 30
2330 4cor. Kicking ball (air) 55 35
2331 10cor. Tackle (horiz) 60 40

334 Cocker Spaniel

1982. Pedigree Dogs. Multicoloured.
2333 5c. Type **334** (postage) 10 10
2334 20c. Alsatian 10 10
2335 25c. English setter 10 10
2336 2cor.50 Brittany spaniel 35 20
2337 3cor. Boxer (air) 45 25
2338 3cor.50 Pointer 50 30
2339 6cor. Collie 60 30

335 Satellite Communications

1982. Air. I.T.U. Congress.
2340 **335** 25cor. multicoloured 2·10 1·50

336 "Dynamine myrrhina"

1982. Butterflies. Multicoloured.
2341 50c. Type **336** (postage) 20 10
2342 1cor.20 "Eunica alcmena" 40 10
2343 1cor.50 "Callizona acesta" 40 10
2344 2cor. "Adelpha leuceria" 60 20
2345 3cor. "Parides iphidamas" (air) 1·00 30
2346 3cor.50 "Consul hippona" 1·10 35
2347 4cor. "Morpho peleides" 1·25 40

337 Dog and Russian Rocket

1982. Space Exploration. Multicoloured.
2348 5c. Type **337** (postage) 10 10
2349 15c. Satellite (vert) 10 10
2350 50c. "Apollo–Soyuz" link 10 10
2351 1cor.50 Satellite 20 15
2352 2cor.50 Docking in space 35 20
2353 5cor. Russian space station (air) 45 20
2354 6cor. Space shuttle "Columbia" (vert) 60 30

338 Mailcoach

1982. Centenary of U.P.U. Membership. Mult.
2355 50c. Type **338** (postage) 10 10
2356 1cor.20 "Victoria" (packet steamer) 1·10 35
2357 3cor.50 Steam locomotive, 1953 (air) 2·75 25
2358 10cor. Boeing 727-100 airliner 1·50 1·10

339 Cyclists

1982. 14th Central American and Caribbean Games. Multicoloured.
2359 10c. Type **339** (postage) 10 10
2360 15c. Swimming (horiz) 10 10
2361 25c. Basketball 10 10
2362 50c. Weightlifting 10 10
2363 2cor.50 Handball (air) 35 20
2364 3cor. Boxing (horiz) 45 25
2365 9cor. Football (horiz) 75 45

341 Washington passing through Trenton

1982. 250th Birth Anniv of George Washington. Multicoloured.
2368 50c. Mount Vernon, Washington's house (39 × 49 mm) (postage) 10 10
2369 1cor. Washington signing the Constitution (horiz) 15 10
2370 2cor. Type **341** 30 20
2371 2cor.50 Washington crossing the Delaware (horiz) (air) 35 20
2372 3cor.50 Washington at Valley Forge (horiz) 50 30
2373 4cor. Washington at the Battle of Trenton 55 35
2374 6cor. Washington at Princeton 60 55

342 Carlos Fonseca, Dove and Flags

1982. 3rd Anniv of Revolution. Multicoloured.
2375 50c. Type **342** (postage) 10 10
2376 2cor.50 Ribbons forming dove (vert) (air) 35 20
2377 1cor. Augusto Sandino and dove (vert) 55 30
2378 6cor. Dove 60 55

343 "Vase of Flowers" (R. Penalba)

1982. Paintings. Multicoloured.
2379 25c. Type **343** (postage) 10 10
2380 50c. "El Gueguense" (M. Garcia) (horiz) 10 10
2381 1cor. "The Couple" (R. Perez) 15 10
2382 1cor.20 "Canales Valley" (A. Mejias) (horiz) 20 10
2383 1cor.85 "Portrait of Senora Castellon" (T. Jerez) 25 15
2384 2cor. "The Vendors" (L. Cerrato) 30 20
2385 9cor. "Sitting Woman" (A. Morales) (horiz) (air) 55 35

344 Lenin and Dimitrov, Moscow, 1921

1982. Birth Centenary of Georgi Dimitrov (Bulgarian statesman). Multicoloured.
2387 50c. Type **344** (postage) 10 10
2388 2cor.50 Dimitrov & Todor Yikov, Sofia, 1946 (air) 35 20
2389 4cor. Dimitrov and flag 55 35

345 Ausberto Narvaez

1982. 26th Anniv of State of Resistance Movement. Multicoloured.
2390 50c. Type **345** (postage) 10 10
2391 2cor.50 Cornelio Silva 35 20
2392 4cor. Rigoberto Lopez Perez (air) 55 35
2393 6cor. Edwin Castro 60 55

346 Old Ruins at Leon

1982. Tourism. Multicoloured.
2394 50c. Type **346** (postage) 10 10
2395 1cor. Ruben Dario Theatre and Park, Managua 15 10
2396 1cor.20 Independence Square, Granada 20 10
2397 1cor.80 Corn Island 25 15
2398 2cor. Carter Santiago Volcano, Masaya 30 20
2399 2cor.50 El Coyotepe Fortress, Masaya (air) 35 20
2400 3cor.50 Luis A. Velazquez Park, Managua 50 30

347 Karl Marx and View of Trier

1982. Death Centenary of Karl Marx. Mult.
2401 1cor. Type **347** (postage) 15 10
2402 4cor. Marx and grave in Highgate Cemetery (air) 55 35

348 Stacking Cane and Fruit

1982. World Food Day. Multicoloured.

2403	50c. Picking Fruit (horiz) . .	10	10
2404	1cor. Type **348**	15	10
2405	2cor. Cutting sugar cane (horiz)	30	20
2406	10cor. F.A.O. and P.A.N. emblems (horiz)	85	65

349 "Santa Maria"

1982. 490th Anniv of Discovery of America. Multicoloured.

2407	50c. Type **349** (postage) . .	65	20
2408	1cor. "Nina"	1·25	30
2409	1cor.50 "Pinta"	1·75	45
2410	2cor. Columbus and fleet . .	2·00	70
2411	2cor.50 Fleet and map of route (air)	2·00	70
2412	4cor. Arrival in America . .	55	35
2413	7cor. Death of Columbus	65	60

350 "Lobelia laxiflora"

351 "Micrurus lemniscatus"

1982. Woodland Flowers. Multicoloured.

2415	50c. Type **350** (postage) . .	10	10
2416	1cor.20 "Bombacopsis quinata"	20	10
2417	1cor.80 "Mimosa albida"	25	15
2418	2cor. "Epidendrum alatum"	30	20
2419	2cor.50 Passion flower "Passiflora foetida" wrongly inscr "Pasiflora" (air)	35	20
2420	3cor.50 "Clitoria sp." . . .	50	30
2421	5cor. "Russelia sarmentosa"	70	45

1982. Reptiles. Multicoloured.

2422	10c. Type **351** (postage) . .	10	10
2423	50c. Common iguana "Iguana iguana" (horiz)	10	10
2424	2cor. "Lachesis muta" (snake) (horiz)	30	20
2425	2cor.50 Hawksbill turtle "Eretmochelys imbricata" (horiz) (air)	35	20
2426	3cor. Boa constrictor "Constrictor constrictor"	45	25
2427	3cor.50 American crocodile "Crocodilus acutus" (horiz)	50	30
2428	5cor. Diamond-back rattlesnake "Sistrurus catenatus" (horiz)	70	45

352 Tele-cor Building, Managua

1982. Telecommunications Day. Multicoloured.

2429	1cor. Type **352** (postage) . .	15	10
2430	50c. Interior of radio transmission room (air)	10	10

353 Girl with Dove

1983. Air. Non-Aligned States Conference.

2431	**353**	4cor. multicoloured . . .	55	35

354 Jose Marti and Birthplace

1983. 130th Birth Anniv of Jose Marti (Cuban revolutionary).

2432	**354**	1cor. multicoloured . . .	15	10

355 Boxing

356 "Neomarica coerulea"

1983. Olympic Games, Los Angeles (1st issue). Multicoloured.

2433	50c. Type **355** (postage) . .	10	10
2434	1cor. Gymnastics	15	10
2435	1cor.50 Running	20	15
2436	2cor. Weightlifting	30	20
2437	4cor. Discus (air)	55	35
2438	5cor. Basketball	70	45
2439	6cor. Cycling	90	55

See also Nos. 2609/15.

1983. Flowers.

2441	**356**	1cor. blue	15	10
2442	–	1cor. violet	15	10
2443	–	1cor. mauve	15	10
2444	–	1cor. brown	15	10
2445	–	1cor. green	15	10
2446	–	1cor. blue	15	10
2447	–	1cor. green	15	10
2448	–	1cor. green	15	10
2449	–	1cor. mauve	15	10
2450	–	1cor. red	15	10
2451	–	1cor. grey	15	10
2452	–	1cor. yellow	15	10
2453	–	1cor. brown	15	10
2454	–	1cor. purple	15	10
2455	–	1cor. green	15	10
2456	–	1cor. black	15	10

DESIGNS: No. 2442, "Tabebula ochraceae"; 2443, "Laella sp"; 2444, "Plumeria rubra"; 2445, "Brassavola nodosa"; 2446, "Stachytarpheta indica"; 2447, "Cochiospermum sp"; 2448, "Malvaviscus arboreus"; 2449, "Telecoma stans"; 2450, "Hibiscus rosa-sinensis"; 2451, "Cattleya lueddemanniana"; 2452, "Tagetes erecta"; 2453, "Senecio sp"; 2454, "Sobralia macrantha"; 2455, "Thumbergia alata"; 2456, "Bixa orellana".

See also Nos. 2739/54, 2838/53 and 3087/3102.

357 Momotombo Geothermal Electrical Plant

1983. Air. Energy.

2457	**357**	2cor.50 multicoloured . .	35	20

358 Map of Nicaragua and Girl picking Coffee

1983. Papal Visit.

2458	–	50c. red, black and blue (postage)	10	10
2459	**358**	1cor. multicoloured . . .	15	10
2460	–	4cor. multicoloured (air)	55	35
2461	–	7cor. multicoloured . . .	1·00	60

DESIGNS: 50c. Demonstrating crowd; 4cor. Pres. Cordova Rivas and Pope John Paul II; 7cor. Pope outside Managua Cathedral.

359 "Xilophanes chiron"

1983. Moths. Multicoloured.

2463	15c. Type **359** (postage) . .	10	10
2464	50c. "Protoparce ochus" . .	15	10
2465	65c. "Pholus lasbruscae" . .	25	10
2466	1cor. "Amphypterus gannascus"	30	10
2467	1cor.50 "Pholus licaon" . .	40	15
2468	2cor. "Agrius cingulata" . .	60	25
2469	10cor. "Rothschildia jurulla" (vert) (air) . . .	3·25	95

360 La Recoleccion Church, Leon

1983. Monuments. Multicoloured.

2470	50c. Subtiava Church, Leon (horiz) (postage)	10	10
2471	1cor. La Inmaculada Castle, Rio San Juan (horiz) . .	15	10
2472	2cor. Type **360**	30	20
2473	4cor. Ruben Dario Monument, Managua (air)	55	35

361 Passenger Carriage

1983. Railway Wagons. Multicoloured.

2474	15c. Type **361** (postage) . .	10	10
2475	65c. Goods wagon No. 1034	25	10
2476	1cor. Tanker wagon No. 931	30	10
2477	1cor.50 Xolotlan hopper wagon	45	10
2478	4cor. Railcar (air)	1·25	35
2479	5cor. Tipper truck	1·50	40
2480	7cor. Railbus	2·25	60

362 Helping Earthquake Victim

1983. Red Cross. Multicoloured.

2481	50c. Aiding flood victims (horiz) (postage)	10	10
2482	1cor. Placing stretcher patient into ambulance (horiz)	15	10
2483	4cor. Type **362** (air)	55	35
2484	5cor. Doctor examining wounded soldier (horiz)	70	45

363 Raising Telephone Pole

1983. World Communications Year.

2485	**363**	1cor. multicoloured . . .	15	10

365 Basketball

1983. 9th Pan-American Games. Multicoloured.

2487	15c. Basketball (horiz) (postage)	10	10
2488	50c. Water polo (horiz) . .	10	10
2489	65c. Running (horiz)	15	10
2490	1cor. Type **365**	15	10
2491	2cor. Weightlifting	30	20
2492	7cor. Fencing (horiz) (air)	65	30
2493	8cor. Gymnastics (horiz) . .	70	40

367 Container Ship being Unloaded

1983. 4th Anniv of Revolution. Multicoloured.

2496	1cor. Type **367**	55	15
2497	2cor. Telcor building, Leon	30	20

368 Carlos Fonseca

369 Simon Bolivar on Horseback

1983. Founders of Sandinista National Liberation Front. Multicoloured.

2498	50c. Escobar, Navarro, Ubeda, Pomares and Ruiz (postage)	10	10
2499	1cor. Santos Lopez, Borge, Buitrago and Mayorga . .	15	10
2500	4cor. Type **368** (air)	55	35

1983. Birth Bicentenary of Simon Bolivar. Mult.

2501	50c. Bolivar and Sandinista guerrilla	10	10
2502	1cor. Type **369**	15	10

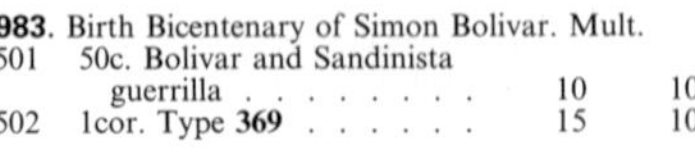

371 Movements of a Pawn

1983. Chess. Multicoloured.

2504	15c. Type **371** (postage) . .	10	10
2505	65c. Knight's movements . .	10	10
2506	1cor. Bishop's movements	15	10
2507	2cor. Rook's movements . .	30	20
2508	4cor. Queen's movements (air)	55	35
2509	5cor. King's movements . .	70	45
2510	7cor. Game in progress . .	75	60

372 Speed Skating

1983. Winter Olympic Games, Sarajevo (1984) (1st issue). Multicoloured.

2511	50c. Type **372** (postage)	10	10
2512	1cor. Slalom	15	10
2513	1cor.50 Luge	20	15
2514	2cor. Ski jumping	30	20
2515	4cor. Figure skating (air)	55	35
2516	5cor. Downhill skiing	70	45
2517	6cor. Biathlon	90	55

373 Soldiers with German Shepherd Dog — 374 "Madonna of the Chair"

1983. Armed Forces.

2519	**373** 4cor. multicoloured	55	35

1983. 500th Birth Anniv of Raphael. Multicoloured.

2520	50c. Type **374** (postage)	10	10
2521	1cor. "Esterhazy Madonna"	15	10
2522	1cor.50 "Sistine Madonna"	20	15
2523	2cor. "Madonna of the Linnet"	30	20
2524	4cor. "Madonna of the Meadow" (air)	55	35
2525	5cor. "Madonna of the Garden"	70	45
2526	6cor. "Adoration of the Kings"	90	55

375 Pottery Idol

1983. Archaeological Finds. Multicoloured.

2528	50c. Type **375** (postage)	10	10
2529	1cor. Pottery dish with ornamental lid	15	10
2530	2cor. Vase with snake design	30	20
2531	4cor. Pottery dish (air)	55	35

376 Metal being poured into Moulds

1983. Nationalization of Mines. Multicoloured.

2532	1cor. Type **376** (postage)	15	10
2533	4cor. Workers and mine (air)	55	35

377 Radio Operator and Sinking Liner

1983. "Fracap '83" Congress of Radio Amateurs of Central America and Panama. Multicoloured.

2534	1cor. Type **377**	70	15
2535	4cor. Congress emblem and town destroyed by earthquake	55	35

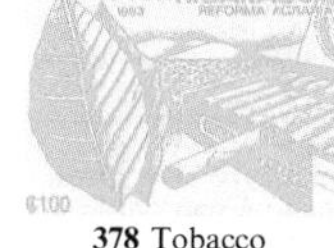

378 Tobacco

1983. Agrarian Reform.

2536	**378** 1cor. green	15	10
2537	– 2cor. orange	30	20
2538	– 4cor. brown	35	35
2539	– 5cor. blue	45	45
2540	– 6cor. lavender	55	55
2541	– 7cor. purple	60	60
2542	– 8cor. purple	70	65
2543	– 10cor. brown	90	90

DESIGNS: 2cor. Cotton; 4cor. Maize; 5cor. Sugar; 6cor. Cattle; 7cor. Rice; 8cor. Coffee; 10cor. Bananas.

See also Nos. 2755/62 and 2854/61.

379 Fire Engine with Ladder

1983. Fire Engines. Multicoloured.

2544	50c. Type **379** (postage)	10	10
2545	1cor. Water tanker	15	10
2546	6cor. Crew vehicle, 1930	90	55
2547	1cor.50 Pump with extension fire hoses (air)	20	15
2548	2cor. Pump with high-pressure tank	30	20
2548a	4cor. Water tanker	60	40
2549	5cor. Fire engine, 1910	70	45

380 Jose Marti and General Sandino

1983. Nicaragua–Cuba Solidarity. Multicoloured.

2550	1cor. Type **380** (postage)	15	10
2551	4cor. Teacher, doctor and welder (air)	55	35

381 "Adoration of the Shepherds" (Hugo van der Gaes) — 382 Anniversary Emblem

1983. Christmas. Multicoloured.

2552	50c. Type **381** (postage)	10	10
2553	1cor. "Adoration of the Kings" (Domenico Ghirlandaio)	15	10
2554	2cor. "Adoration of the Shepherds" (El Greco)	30	20
2555	7cor. "Adoration of the Kings" (Konrad von Soest) (air)	65	30

1984. Air. 25th Anniv of Cuban Revolution.

2557	**382** 4cor. red, blue and black	45	20
2558	– 6cor. multicoloured	55	30

DESIGN: 6cor. Fidel Castro and Che Guevara.

383 Bobsleigh

1984. Winter Olympic Games, Sarajevo. Mult.

2559	50c. Type **383** (postage)	10	10
2560	50c. Biathlon	10	10
2561	1cor. Slalom	20	15
2562	1cor. Speed skating	20	15
2563	4cor. Skiing (air)	45	45
2564	5cor. Ice-dancing	55	55
2565	10cor. Ski-jumping	90	60

384 Chinchilla

1984. Cats. Multicoloured.

2567	50c. Type **384** (postage)	10	10
2568	50c. Longhaired white	10	10
2569	1cor. Red tabby	20	15
2570	2cor. Tortoiseshell	35	20
2571	4cor. Burmese	70	45
2572	3cor. Siamese (air)	50	35
2573	7cor. Longhaired silver	70	35

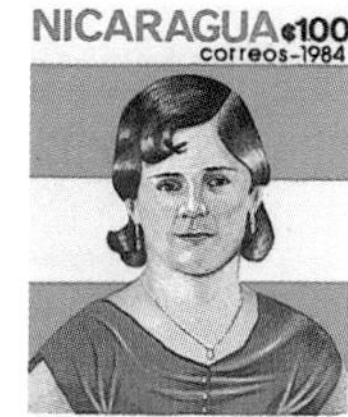

385 National Arms — 386 Blanca Arauz

1984. 50th Death Anniv of Augusto Sandino. Mult.

2574	1cor. Type **385** (postage)	20	15
2575	4cor. Augusto Sandino (air)	35	20

1984. International Women's Day.

2576	**386** 1cor. multicoloured	20	15

387 Sunflower — 388 "Soyuz"

1984. Agricultural Flowers. Multicoloured.

2577	50c. Type **387** (postage)	10	10
2578	50c. "Poinsettia pulcherrima"	10	10
2579	1cor. "Cassia alata"	20	15
2580	2cor. "Antigonon leptopus"	35	20
2581	3cor. "Bidens pilosa" (air)	50	35
2582	4cor. "Althaea rosea"	70	45
2583	5cor. "Rivea corymbosa"	85	55

1984. Space Anniversaries. Multicoloured.

2584	50c. Type **388** (15th anniv of "Soyuz 6", "7" and "8" flights) (postage)	10	10
2585	50c. "Soyuz" (different) (15th anniv of "Soyuz 6", "7" and "8" flights)	10	10
2586	1cor. "Apollo 11" approaching Moon (15th anniv of 1st manned landing)	20	15
2587	2cor. "Luna I" (25th anniv of 1st Moon satellite)	35	20
2588	3cor. "Luna II" (25th anniv of 1st Moon landing) (air)	50	35
2589	4cor. "Luna III" (25th anniv of 1st photographs of far side of Moon)	70	45
2590	9cor. Rocket (50th anniv of Korolev's book on space flight)	1·25	75

389 "Noli me Tangere" (detail) — 390 Daimler, 1886

1984. 450th Death Anniv of Correggio (artist). Multicoloured.

2591	50c. Type **389** (postage)	10	10
2592	50c. "Madonna of St. Jerome" (detail)	10	10
2593	1cor. "Allegory of Virtue"	20	15
2594	2cor. "Allegory of Pleasure"	35	20
2595	3cor. "Ganymedes" (detail) (air)	50	35
2596	5cor. "The Danae" (detail)	55	55
2597	8cor. "Leda and the Swan" (detail)	1·00	60

1984. 150th Birth Anniv of Gottlieb Daimler (automobile designer). Multicoloured.

2599	1cor. Type **390** (postage)	10	10
2600	1cor. Abadal, 1914 (horiz)	10	10
2601	2cor. Ford, 1903	1·50	45
2602	2cor. Renault, 1899	35	20
2603	3cor. Rolls Royce, 1910 (horiz) (air)	50	35
2604	4cor. Metallurgique, 1907 (horiz)	70	45
2605	7cor. Bugatti "Mod 40" (horiz)	75	50

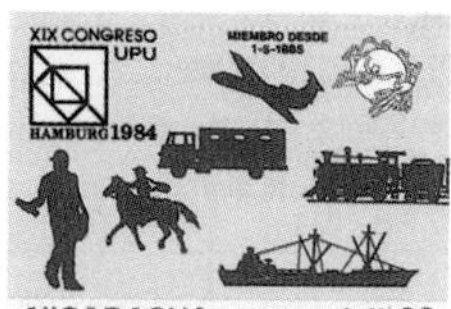

392 Mail Transport

1984. Air. 19th Universal Postal Union Congress Philatelic Salon, Hamburg.

2607	**392** 15cor. multicoloured	5·75	2·10

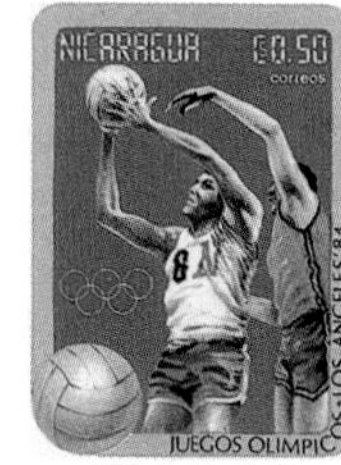

393 Basketball

1984. Olympic Games, Los Angeles (2nd issue). Multicoloured.

2609	50c. Type **393** (postage)	10	10
2610	50c. Volleyball	10	10
2611	1cor. Hockey	20	15
2612	2cor. Tennis (air)	35	20
2613	3cor. Football (horiz)	50	35
2614	4cor. Water polo (horiz)	70	45
2615	9cor. Soccer (horiz)	1·10	75

395 Rural Construction Site

1984. 5th Anniv of Revolution. Multicoloured.

2618	5c. Type **395** (postage)	10	10
2619	1cor. Diesel locomotive, Pacific–Atlantic line	1·50	30
2620	4cor. Ploughing with oxen and tractor (Agrarian reform) (air)	40	20
2621	7cor. State Council building	75	35

396 "Children defending Nature" (Pablo Herrera Berrios)

1984. U.N.E.S.C.O. Environmental Protection Campaign. Multicoloured.

2622	50c. Type **396** (postage)	10	10
2623	1cor. Living and dead forests	20	15
2624	2cor. Fisherman and dried river bed	35	20
2625	10cor. Hands holding plants (vert) (air)	85	75

397 Red Cross Airplane and Ambulance

1984. 50th Anniv of Nicaraguan Red Cross. Mult.

2626	1cor. Type **397** (postage)	30	15
2627	7cor. Battle of Solferino (125th anniv) (air)	90	45

399 Ventura Escalante and Dominican Republic Flag

1984. Baseball. Multicoloured.
2629 50c. Type **399** (postage) . . 10 10
2630 50c. Danial Herrera and Mexican flag 10 10
2631 1cor. Adalberto Herrera and Venezuelan flag 20 15
2632 1cor. Roberto Clemente and Nicaraguan flag 20 15
2633 3cor. Carlos Colas and Cuban flag (air) 30 35
2634 4cor. Stanley Cayasso and Argentinian flag 45 45
2635 5cor. Babe Ruth and U.S.A.. flag 55 55

400 Central American Tapir

1984. Wildlife Protection. Multicoloured.
2636 25c. Type **400** (postage) . . 10 10
2637 25c. Young tapir 10 10
2638 3cor. Close-up of tapir (air) 15 10
2639 4cor. Mother and young . . 20 15

401 Football in 1314

1985. World Cup Football Championship, Mexico (1986) (1st issue). Multicoloured.
2640 50c. Type **401** (postage) . . 10 10
2641 50c. Football in 1500 . . . 10 10
2642 1cor. Football in 1872 . . . 10 10
2643 1cor. Football in 1846 . . . 10 10
2644 2cor. Football in 1883 (air) 10 10
2645 4cor. Football in 1890 . . . 20 15
2646 6cor. Football in 1953 . . . 30 20
See also Nos. 2731/7 and 2812/18.

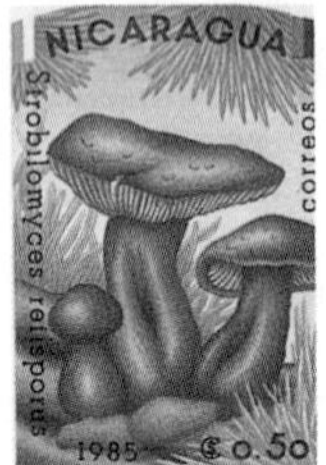

402 "Strobilomyces retisporus"

1985. Fungi. Multicoloured.
2648 50c. Type **402** (postage) . . 10 10
2649 50c. "Boletus calopus" . . . 10 10
2650 1cor. "Boletus luridus" . . 15 10
2651 1cor. "Xerocomus illudens" (air) 15 10
2652 4cor. "Gyrodon merulioides" 55 25
2653 5cor. "Tylopilus plumbeoviolaceus" . . . 65 30
2654 8cor. "Gyroporus castaneus" . . . . 1·10 40

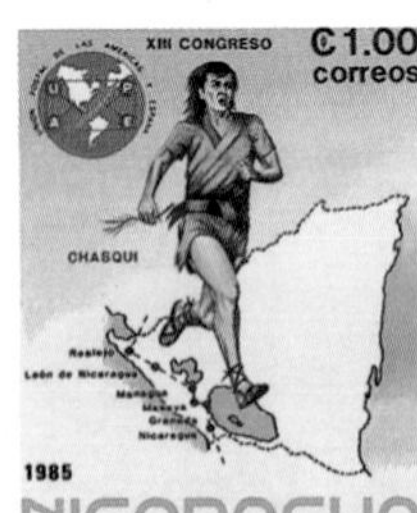

403 Postal Runner and Map

1985. 13th Postal Union of the Americas and Spain Congress. Multicoloured.
2655 1cor. Type **403** (postage) . . 10 10
2656 7cor. Casa Aviocar mail plane over map (air) . . . 45 20

406 Steam Locomotive, Oldenburg

1985. 150th Anniv of German Railway. Mult.
2659 1cor. Type **406** (postage) . . 20 10
2660 1cor. Electric locomotive, Prussia 20 10
2661 9cor. Steam locomotive No. 88, Prussia (air) . . . 75 15
2662 9cor. Double-deck tram . . 75 15
2663 15cor. Steam locomotive, Wurttemberg . . . . . . 1·10 25
2664 21cor. Steam locomotive, Germany . . . . 1·75 40

407 Douglas, 1928

1985. Centenary of Motor Cycle. Multicoloured.
2666 50c. Type **407** (postage) . . 10 10
2667 50c. FN, 1928 . . . . . . 10 10
2668 1cor. Puch, 1938 . . . . . 10 10
2669 2cor. Wanderer, 1939 (air) 10 10
2670 4cor. Honda, 1949 . . . . 10 10
2671 5cor. BMW, 1984 . . . . . 10 10
2672 7cor. Honda, 1984 . . . . 40 10

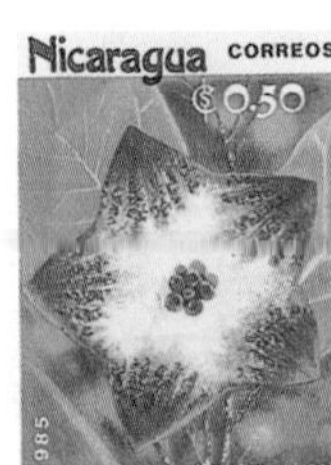

408 "Matelea quirosii" **409** "Capitulation of German Troops" (P. Krivonogov)

1985. Flowers. Multicoloured.
2673 50c. Type **408** (postage) . . 10 10
2674 50c. "Ipomea nil" 10 10
2675 1cor. "Lysichitum americanum" 10 10
2676 2cor. "Clusia sp." (air) . . . 10 10
2677 4cor. "Vanilla planifolia" . . 10 10
2678 7cor. "Stemmadenia obovata" 75 40

1985. 40th Anniv of End of World War II. Mult.
2679 9cor.50 Type **409** (postage) 1·00 50
2680 28cor. Woman behind barbed wire and Nuremberg trial (air) . . 3·00 1·50

410 Lenin and Red Flag **413** Common Pheasant

412 Victoria de Julio Sugar Factory

1985. 115th Birth Anniv of Lenin. Multicoloured.
2681 4cor. Type **410** 10 10
2682 21cor. Lenin addressing crowd 45 30

1985. Air. 6th Anniv of Revolution. Multicoloured.
2684 9cor. Type **412** 20 15
2685 9cor. Soldier and flag . . . 20 15

1985. Domestic Birds. Multicoloured.
2686 50c. Type **413** 25 20
2687 50c. Hen 50 10
2688 1cor. Helmeted guineafowl 35 20
2689 2cor. Swan goose 65 20
2690 6cor. Ocellated turkey . . . 2·10 35
2691 8cor. Duck . . . . 1·75 10

414 Luis A. Delgadillo **415** Zeledon

1985. International Music Year. Multicoloured.
2692 1cor. Type **414** (postage) . . 10 10
2693 1cor. Masked dancer with floral headdress 10 10
2694 9cor. Masked procession (air) 65 40
2695 9cor. Crowd outside church 65 40
2696 15cor. Masked dancer in brimmed hat . . . . . . 1·10 55
2697 21cor. Procession resting . . 1·50 75

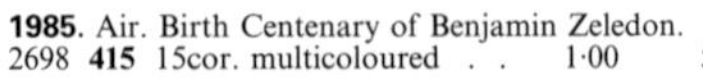

1985. Air. Birth Centenary of Benjamin Zeledon.
2698 **415** 15cor. multicoloured . . 1·00 55

416 Dunant and Lifeboat

1985. 75th Death Anniv of Henri Dunant (founder of Red Cross). Multicoloured.
2699 3cor. Type **416** 40 10
2700 15cor. Dunant and Ilyushin Il-86 and Tupolev Tu-154 aircraft . . . . 1·25 55

417 Fire Engine

1985. 6th Anniv of SINACOI Fire Service. Mult.
2701 1cor. Type **417** (postage) . . 10 10
2702 1cor. Fire station 10 10
2703 1cor. Engine with water jet 10 10
2704 3cor. Foam tender (air) . . 10 10
2705 9cor. Airport fire engine . . 50 15
2706 15cor. Engine at fire 85 45
2707 21cor. Fireman in protective clothing . . . . 1·10 75

418 Halley, Masaya Volcano and Comet

1985. Appearance of Halley's Comet. Mult.
2708 1cor. Type **418** (postage) . . 10 10
2709 3cor. Armillary sphere and 1910 trajectory 10 10
2710 3cor. "Venus" space probe and Tycho Brahe underground observatory 10 10
2711 9cor. Habermel's astrolabe and comet's path through solar system (air) 50 15
2712 15cor. Hale Telescope, Mt. Palomar, and Herschel's telescope 85 45
2713 21cor. Galileo's telescope and sections through telescopes of Newton, Cassegrain and Ritchey 1·25 60

419 Tapir eating

1985. Protected Animals. Baird's Tapir. Mult.
2714 1cor. Type **419** (postage) . . 10 10
2715 3cor. Tapir in water (air) . . 10 10
2716 5cor. Tapir in undergrowth 10 10
2717 9cor. Mother and calf . . . 20 15

420 "Rosa spinosissima"

1986. Wild Roses. Multicoloured.
2718 1cor. Type **420** 10 10
2719 1cor. Dog rose ("R. canina") 10 10
2720 3cor. "R. eglanteria" . . . 10 10
2721 5cor. "R. rubrifolia" 10 10
2722 9cor. "R. foetida" 20 15
2723 100cor. "R. rugosa" . . . . 2·00 1·10

421 Crimson Topaz **422** Footballer and Statue

1986. Birds. Multicoloured.
2724 1cor. Type **421** 10 10
2725 3cor. Orange-billed nightingale thrush 10 10
2726 3cor. Troupial 10 10
2727 5cor. Painted bunting . . . 20 15
2728 10cor. Frantzius's nightingale thrush 60 40
2729 21cor. Great horned owl . . 1·25 1·00
2730 75cor. Great kiskadee . . . 5·50 3·00

1986. World Cup Football Championship, Mexico (2nd issue). Multicoloured.
2731 1cor. Type **422** (postage) . . 10 10
2732 1cor. Footballer and sculptured head 10 10
2733 3cor. Footballer and water holder with man as stem (air) 10 10
2734 3cor. Footballer and sculpture 10 10
2735 5cor. Footballer and sculptured head (different) 10 10
2736 9cor. Footballer and sculpture (different) . . . 20 15
2737 100cor. Footballer and sculptured snake's head 3·00 1·50

1986. (a) Flowers. As Nos. 2441/56 but values changed.
2739 5cor. blue 10 10
2740 5cor. violet 10 10
2741 5cor. purple 10 10
2742 5cor. orange 10 10
2743 5cor. green 10 10
2744 5cor. blue 10 10
2745 5cor. green 10 10
2746 5cor. green 10 10
2747 5cor. mauve 10 10
2748 5cor. red 10 10
2749 5cor. grey 10 10
2750 5cor. orange 10 10
2751 5cor. brown 10 10
2752 5cor. brown 10 10
2753 5cor. green 10 10
2754 5cor. black 10 10
DESIGNS: No. 2739, Type **356**; 2740, "Tabebula ochraceae"; 2741, "Laelia sp"; 2742, Frangipani ("Plumeria rubra"); 2743, "Brassavola nodosa"; 2744, "Strachytarpheta indica"; 2745, "Cochlospermum sp"; 2746, "Malvaviscus arboreus"; 2747, "Tecoma stans"; 2748, Chinese hibiscus ("Hibiscus rosa-sinensis"); 2749, "Cattleya lueddemanniana"; 2750, African marigold ("Tagetes erecta"); 2751, "Senecio sp"; 2752, "Sobralia macrantha"; 2753, "Thumbergia alata"; 2754, "Bixa orellana".

(b) Agrarian Reform. As T **378**.
2755 1cor. brown 10 10
2756 9cor. violet 20 15
2757 15cor. purple 30 20
2758 21cor. red 45 30
2759 33cor. orange 65 45
2760 42cor. green 90 55
2761 50cor. brown . . . . 1·00 65
2762 100cor. blue . . . . 2·00 1·50
DESIGNS: 1cor. Type **378**; 9cor. Cotton; 15cor. Maize; 21cor. Sugar; 33cor. Cattle; 42cor. Rice; 50cor. Coffee; 100cor. Bananas.

423 Alfonso Cortes

1986. National Libraries. Latin American Writers. Multicoloured.
2763 1cor. Type **423** (postage) . . 10 10
2764 3cor. Azarias H. Pallais . . 10 10
2765 3cor. Salomon de la Selva 10 10
2766 5cor. Ruben Dario 10 10
2767 9cor. Pablo Neruda 10 10
2768 15cor. Alfonso Reyes (air) 45 25
2769 100cor. Pedro Henriquez Urena . . . . 3·00 1·50

424 Great Britain Penny Black and Nicaragua 1929 25c. Stamp

1986. Air. 125th Anniv of Nicaraguan Stamps. Designs showing G.B. Penny Black and Nicaragua stamps.
2770 **424** 30cor. multicoloured . . 90 45
2771 – 40cor. brown, black and grey . . . . 1·25 60
2772 – 50cor. red, black and grey . . . . 1·50 75
2773 – 100cor. blue, black and grey . . . . 3·00 1·50
DESIGNS: 40c. 1903 1p. stamp; 50c. 1892 5p. stamp; 1p. 1862 2c. stamp.

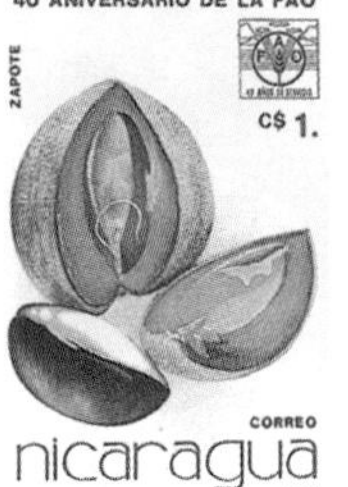

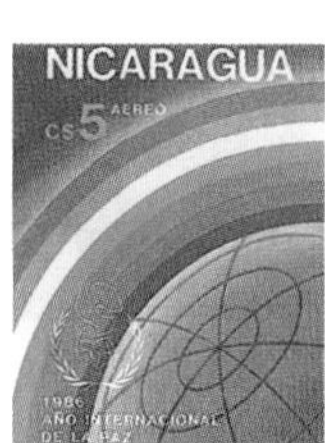

425 Sapodilla **426** Rainbow and Globe

1986. 40th Anniv of F.A.O. Multicoloured.
2774 1cor. Type **425** (postage) . . 10 10
2775 1cor. Maranon 10 10
2776 3cor. Tree-cactus 10 10
2777 3cor. Granadilla 10 10
2778 5cor. Custard-apple (air) . . 10 10
2779 21cor. Melocoton 65 35
2780 100cor. Mamey . . . . . . 3·00 1·50

1986. Air. International Peace Year. Multicoloured.
2781 5cor. Type **426** 10 10
2782 10cor. Dove and globe . . . 30 10

427 Lockheed L-1011 TriStar 500

1986. "Stockholmia 86" International Stamp Exhibition. Multicoloured.
2783 1cor. Type **427** (postage) . . 10 10
2784 1cor. Yakovlev Yak-40 . . 10 10
2785 3cor. B.A.C. One Eleven . . 10 10
2786 3cor. Boeing 747-100 . . . 10 10
2787 9cor. Airbus Industrie A300 (air) 30 10
2788 15cor. Tupolev Tu-154 . . . 45 10
2789 100cor. Concorde (vert) . . 3·00 1·50

428 "Pinta" and 16th-century Map

1986. 500th Anniv (1992) of Discovery of America by Columbus (1st issue). Multicoloured.
2791 1cor. Type **428** (postage) . . 80 30
2792 1cor. "Santa Maria" and "Nina" 80 30
2793 9cor. Juan de la Cosa (air) 30 10
2794 9cor. Christopher Columbus 30 10
2795 21cor. King and Queen of Spain 65 35
2796 100cor. Courtiers behind Columbus and Indians . . 3·00 1·50
The designs of the same value and Nos. 2795/6 were printed together in se-tenant pairs within their sheets, Nos. 2791/2 and 2795/6 forming composite designs.
See also Nos. 2903/8.

429 Fonseca and Flags

1986. Air. 25th Anniv of Sandinista Front and 10th Death Anniv of Carlos Fonseca (co-founder).
2798 **429** 15cor. multicoloured . . 10 10

430 Rhinoceros **431** "Theritas coronata"

1986. Air. Endangered Animals. Multicoloured.
2799 15cor. Type **430** 45 10
2800 15cor. Zebra 45 10
2801 25cor. Elephant 75 40
2802 25cor. Giraffe 75 40
2803 50cor. Tiger . . . . 1·50 75
2804 50cor. Mandrill . . . . . . 1·50 75

1986. Butterflies. Multicoloured.
2805 10cor. Type **431** (postage) 20 10
2806 15cor. "Salamis cacta" (air) 20 10
2807 15cor. "Charayes nitebis" 20 10
2808 15cor. "Papilio maacki" . . 20 10
2809 25cor. "Palaeochrysophonus hippothoe" 20 10
2810 25cor. "Euphaedro cyparissa" 20 10
2811 30cor. "Ritra aurea" . . . 20 10

432 Player and French Flag **433** Ernesto Mejia Sanchez

1986. Air. World Cup Football Championship, Mexico (3rd issue). Finalists. Multicoloured. Designs showing footballers and national flags.
2812 10cor. Type **432** 10 10
2813 10cor. Argentina 10 10
2814 10cor. West Germany . . . 10 10
2815 15cor. England 10 10
2816 15cor. Brazil 10 10
2817 25cor. Spain 10 10
2818 50cor. Belgium (horiz) . . . 10 10

1987. Ruben Dario Cultural Order of Independence. Multicoloured.
2820 10cor. Type **433** (postage) 10 10
2821 10cor. Fernando Gordillo 10 10
2822 10cor. Francisco Perez Estrada 10 10
2823 15cor. Order medal (air) . . 10 10
2824 30cor. Julio Cortazar . . . 20 20
2825 60cor. Enrique Fernandez Morales 35 25

434 Ice Hockey **435** Development

1987. Winter Olympic Games, Calgary (1988). Multicoloured.
2826 10cor. Type **434** (postage) 10 10
2827 10cor. Speed skating 10 10
2828 15cor. Downhill skiing (air) 10 10
2829 15cor. Figure skating . . . 10 10
2830 20cor. Shooting 15 10
2831 30cor. Slalom 20 10
2832 40cor. Ski jumping 25 10

1987. U.N.I.C.E.F. Child Survival Campaign. Multicoloured.
2834 10cor. Type **435** (postage) 10 10
2835 25cor. Vaccination (air) . . 75 40
2836 30cor. Oral rehydration therapy 90 45
2837 50cor. Breast-feeding . . . 1·50 75

1987. (a) Flowers. As Nos. 2441/56 and 2739/54 but values changed.
2838 10cor. blue 10 10
2839 10cor. violet 10 10
2840 10cor. purple 10 10
2841 10cor. red 10 10
2842 10cor. green 10 10
2843 10cor. blue 10 10
2844 10cor. green 10 10
2845 10cor. green 10 10
2846 10cor. mauve 10 10
2847 10cor. red 10 10
2848 10cor. green 10 10
2849 10cor. orange 10 10
2850 10cor. brown 10 10
2851 10cor. purple 10 10
2852 10cor. turquoise 10 10
2853 10cor. black 10 10
DESIGNS: No. 2838, Type **356**; 2839, "Tabebula ochraceae"; 2840, "Laelia sp"; 2841, Frangipani; 2842, "Brassavola nodosa"; 2843, "Stachytarpheta indica"; 2844, "Cochlospermum sp"; 2845, "Malvaviscus arboreus"; 2846, "Tecoma stans"; 2847, Chinese hibiscus; 2848, "Cattleya lueddermanniana"; 2849, African marigold; 2850, "Senecio sp"; 2851, "Sobralla macrantha"; 2852, "Thumbergia alata"; 2853, "Bixa orellana".

(b) Agrarian Reform. As T **378**. Dated "1987".
2854 10cor. brown 10 10
2855 10cor. violet 10 10
2856 15cor. purple 10 10
2857 25cor. red 15 10
2858 30cor. orange 20 10
2859 50cor. brown 30 20
2860 60cor. green 35 25
2861 100cor. blue 65 45
DESIGNS: No. 2854, Type **378**; 2855, Cotton; 2856, Maize; 2857, Sugar; 2858, Cattle; 2859, Coffee; 2860, Rice; 2861, Bananas.

436 Flags and Buildings **438** Tennis Player

437 "Mammuthus columbi"

1987. 77th Interparliamentary Conf, Managua.
2862 **436** 10cor. multicoloured . . 10 10

1987. Prehistoric Animals. Multicoloured.
2863 10cor. Type **437** (postage) 10 10
2864 10cor. Triceratops 10 10
2865 10cor. Dimetrodon 10 10
2866 15cor. Uintaterium (air) . . 10 10
2867 15cor. Dinichthys 10 10
2868 30cor. Pteranodon 60 35
2869 40cor. Tilosaurus 85 45

1987. "Capex 87" International Stamp Exhibition, Toronto.
2870 10cor. multicoloured (Type **438**) (postage) . . . 10 10
2871 10cor. mult 10 10
2872 15cor. mult (male player) (air) 45 10
2873 15cor. mult (female player) 45 10
2874 20cor. multicoloured 60 30
2875 30cor. multicoloured 60 45
2876 40cor. multicoloured 85 60
DESIGNS: Nos. 2871/6, Various tennis players.

439 Dobermann Pinscher **441** Levski

440 Modern Wooden Houses

1987. Dogs. Multicoloured.
2878 10cor. Type **439** (postage) 10 10
2879 10cor. Bull mastiff 10 10
2880 15cor. Japanese spaniel (air) 45 10
2881 15cor. Keeshond 45 10
2882 20cor. Chihuahua 60 30
2883 30cor. St. Bernard 90 45
2884 40cor. West Gotha spitz . . 85 60

1987. Air. International Year of Shelter for the Homeless. Multicoloured.
2885 20cor. Type **440** 15 10
2886 30cor. Modern brick-built houses 20 10

1987. Air. 150th Birth Anniv of Vasil Levski (revolutionary).
2887 **441** 30cor. multicoloured . . 20 10

442 "Opuntia acanthocarpa major"

1987. Cacti. Multicoloured.
2888 10cor. Type **442** (postage) 10 10
2889 10cor. "Lophocereus schottii" 10 10
2890 10cor. "Echinocereus engelmanii" 10 10
2891 20cor. Saguaros (air) . . . 60 30
2892 20cor. "Lemaireocereus thurberi" 60 30
2893 30cor. "Opuntia fulgida" . . 90 45
2894 50cor. "Opuntia ficus indica" . . . . 1·50 75

443 High Jumping

1987. 10th Pan-American Games, Indiana. Mult.
2895 10cor. Type **443** (postage) 10 10
2896 10cor. Handball 10 10
2897 15cor. Running (air) 45 10
2898 15cor. Gymnastics 45 10
2899 20cor. Baseball 60 30
2900 30cor. Synchronized swimming (vert) 90 45
2901 40cor. Weightlifting (vert) 1·25 60

445 "Cosmos"

1987. Cosmonautics Day. Multicoloured.
2904 10cor. Type **445** (postage) 10 10
2905 10cor. "Sputnik" 10 10
2906 15cor. "Proton" (air) . . . 45 10
2907 25cor. "Luna" 75 40
2908 25cor. "Meteor" 75 40
2909 30cor. "Electron" 90 45
2910 50cor. "Mars-1" . . . . . 1·50 75

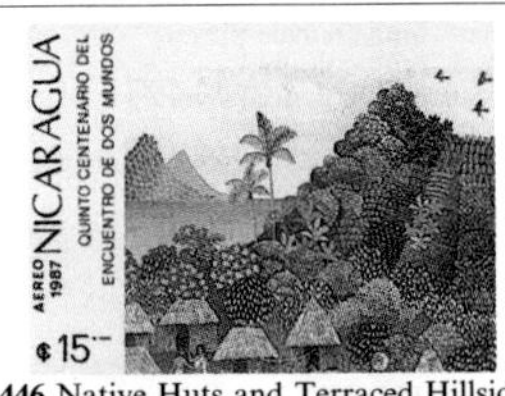

446 Native Huts and Terraced Hillside

1987. Air. 500th Anniv (1992) of Discovery of America by Columbus (2nd issue). Mult.

2911 15cor. Type **446** 45 20
2912 15cor. Columbus's fleet . . 90 30
2913 20cor. Spanish soldiers in native village 60 30
2914 30cor. Mounted soldiers killing natives 90 45
2915 40cor. Spanish people and houses . . . . 1·25 60
2916 50cor. Church and houses 1·50 75

447 Tropical Gar

1987. World Food Day. Fishes. Multicoloured.

2917 10cor. Type **447** (postage) 20 10
2918 10cor. Atlantic tarpon ("Tarpon atlanticus") . . 20 10
2919 10cor. Jaguar guapote ("Cichlasoma managuense") 20 10
2920 15cor. Banded astyanax ("Astyana fasciatus") (air) 90 45
2921 15cor. Midas cichlid ("Cichlasoma citrimellum") 90 45
2922 20cor. Wolf cichlid . . . . 1·25 65
2923 50cor. Lake Nicaragua shark . . . . 3·00 1·50

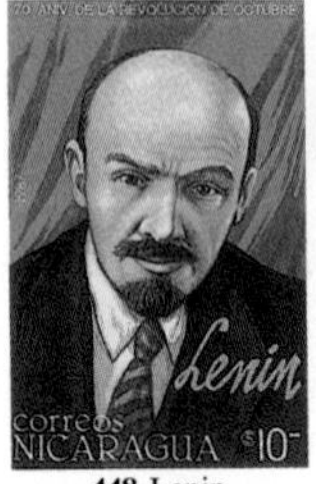

448 Lenin

449 "Nativity"

1987. 70th Anniv of Russian Revolution. Mult.

2924 10cor. Type **448** (postage) 10 10
2925 30cor. "Aurora" (cruiser) (horiz) (air) 50 15
2926 50cor. Russian arms 30 20

1987. Christmas. Details of Painting by L. Saenz. Multicoloured.

2927 10cor. Type **449** 10 10
2928 20cor. "Adoration of the Magi" 60 30
2929 25cor. "Adoration of the Magi" (close-up detail) . . 75 40
2930 50cor. "Nativity" (close-up detail) . . . . 1·50 75

1987. Surch.

2931 **435** 400cor. on 10cor. mult (postage) 30 15
2935 **440** 200cor. on 20cor. multicoloured (air) . . 15 10
2932 – 600cor. on 50cor. mult (No. 2837) 40 20
2933 – 1000cor. on 25cor. mult (No. 2835) 70 35
2936 – 3000cor. on 30cor. mult (No. 2886) . . . . . 2·10 1·00
2934 – 5000cor. on 30cor. mult (No. 2836) . . . . . 3·50 1·75

451 Cross-country Skiing

452 Flag around Globe

1988. Winter Olympic Games, Calgary. Mult.

2937 10cor. Type **451** 10 10
2938 10cor. Rifle-shooting (horiz) 10 10
2939 15cor. Ice hockey 45 10
2940 20cor. Ice skating 60 30
2941 25cor. Downhill skiing . . . 75 40
2942 30cor. Ski jumping (horiz) 90 45
2943 40cor. Slalom . . . . 1·25 60

1988. 10th Anniv of Nicaragua Journalists' Association. Multicoloured.

2945 1cor. Type **452** (postage) . . 10 10
2946 5cor. Churches of St. Francis Xavier, Sandino and Fatima, Managua, and speaker addressing journalists (42 × 27 mm) (air) . . . . 1·25 60

453 Basketball

1988. Olympic Games, Seoul. Multicoloured.

2947 10cor. Type **453** 10 10
2948 10cor. Gymnastics 10 10
2949 15cor. Volleyball 45 10
2950 20cor. Long jumping . . . 60 30
2951 25cor. Football 75 40
2952 30cor. Water polo 90 45
2953 40cor. Boxing . . . . . . 1·25 60

454 Brown Bear

1988. Mammals and their Young. Multicoloured.

2955 10c. Type **454** (postage) . . 10 10
2956 15c. Lion 10 10
2957 25c. Cocker spaniel 10 10
2958 50c. Wild boar 15 10
2959 4cor. Cheetah (air) 55 20
2960 7cor. Spotted hyena . . . . 1·00 40
2961 8cor. Red fox . . . . 1·25 50

455 Slide Tackle

1988. "Essen '88" International Stamp Fair and European Football Championship, Germany. Mult.

2963 50c. Type **455** (postage) . . 10 10
2964 1cor. Footballers 15 10
2965 2cor. Lining up shot (vert) (air) 30 10
2966 3cor. Challenging for ball (vert) 50 20
2967 4cor. Heading ball (vert) . . 65 25
2968 5cor. Tackling (vert) 80 30
2969 6cor. Opponent winning possession . . . . 1·00 40

456 Bell JetRanger III (½-size illustration)

1988. "Finlandia 88" International Stamp Exhibition, Helsinki. Helicopters. Multicoloured.

2971 4cor. Type **456** (postage) . . 15 10
2972 12cor. MBB-Kawasaki BK-117A-3 (air) 20 10
2973 16cor. Boeing-Vertol B-360 30 10
2974 20cor. Agusta A.109 MR11 40 10
2975 24cor. Sikorsky S-61N . . . 55 20
2976 28cor. Aerospatiale SA.365 Dauphin 2 . . . . 60 25
2977 56cor. Sikorsky S-76 Spirit 1·25 50

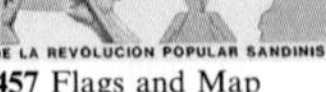

457 Flags and Map

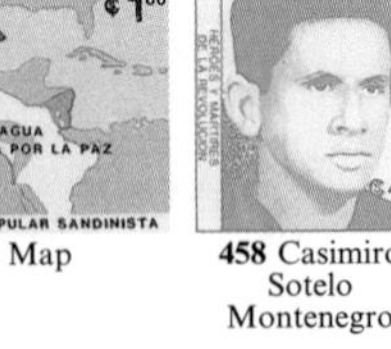

458 Casimiro Sotelo Montenegro

1988. 9th Anniv of Revolution. Multicoloured.

2979 1cor. Type **457** (postage) . . 20 10
2980 5cor. Landscape and hands releasing dove (air) . . . 80 30

1988. Revolutionaries.

2981 **458** 4cor. blue (postage) . . 15 10
2982 – 12cor. mauve (air) . . . 20 10
2983 – 16cor. green 30 10
2984 – 20cor. red 45 15
2985 – 24cor. brown 55 20
2986 – 28cor. violet 65 25
2987 – 50cor. red . . . . 1·25 45
2988 – 100cor. purple . . . . . 2·40 1·00

DESIGNS: 12cor. Ricardo Morales Aviles; 16cor. Silvio Mayorga Delgado; 20cor. Pedro Arauz Palacios; 24cor. Oscar A. Turcios Chavarrias; 28cor. Julio C. Buitrago Urroz; 50cor. Jose B. Escobar Perez; 100cor. Eduardo E. Contreras Escobar.

459 "Acacia baileyana"

460 West Indian Fighting Conch

1988. Flowers. Multicoloured.

2989 4cor. Type **459** (postage) . . 15 10
2990 12cor. "Anigozanthos manglesii" (air) 20 10
2991 16cor. "Telopia speciosissima" 30 10
2992 20cor. "Eucalyptus ficifolia" 45 15
2993 24cor. "Boronia heterophylla" 60 30
2994 28cor. "Callistemon speciosus" 70 35
2995 30cor. "Nymphaea caerulea" (horiz) 80 40
2996 50cor. "Clianthus formosus" 1·25 60

1988. Molluscs. Multicoloured.

2997 4cor. Type **460** (postage) . . 20 10
2998 12cor. Painted polymita (air) 30 10
2999 16cor. Giant sundial 40 10
3000 20cor. Japanese baking oyster 55 10
3001 24cor. Yoka star shell . . . 75 20
3002 28cor. Gawdy frog shell . . 80 25
3003 50cor. Mantled top . . . . 1·75 50

461 Zapotecan Funeral Urn

462 "Chrysina macropus"

1988. 500th Anniv (1992) of Discovery of America by Columbus (3rd issue). Multicoloured.

3004 4cor. Type **461** (postage) . . 15 10
3005 12cor. Mochican ceramic seated figure (air) 20 10
3006 16cor. Mochican ceramic head 30 10
3007 20cor. Tainan ceramic vessel 45 10
3008 28cor. Nazcan vessel (horiz) 65 20
3009 100cor. Incan ritual pipe (horiz) . . . . 2·40 1·00

1988. Beetles. Multicoloured.

3011 4cor. Type **462** (postage) . . 15 10
3012 12cor. "Plusiotis victoriana" (air) 20 10
3013 16cor. "Ceratotrupes bolivari" 30 10
3014 20cor. "Gymnetosoma stellata" 50 15
3015 24cor. "Euphoria lineoligera" 60 20
3016 28cor. "Euphoria candezei" 70 30
3017 50cor. "Sulcophanaeus chryseicollis" . . . . . . 1·25 50

463 Dario

1988. Air. Centenary of Publication of "Blue" by Ruben Dario.

3018 **463** 25cor. multicoloured . . 60 20

464 Simon Bolivar, Jose Marti, Gen. Sandino and Fidel Castro

1989. Air. 30th Anniv of Cuban Revolution.

3019 **464** 20cor. multicoloured . . 50 20

465 Pochomil Tourist Centre

1989. Tourism. Multicoloured.

3020 4cor. Type **465** (postage) . . 15 10
3021 12cor. Granada Tourist Centre (air) 45 15
3022 20cor. Olof Palme Convention Centre . . . 65 30
3023 24cor. Masaya Volcano National Park 55 20
3024 28cor. La Boquita Tourist Centre 70 25
3025 30cor. Xiloa Tourist Centre 75 30
3026 50cor. Managua Hotel . . . 1·25 60

466 Footballers

467 Downhill Skiing

1989. Air. World Cup Football Championship, Italy (1990).

3028 **466** 100cor. multicoloured . . 10 10
3029 – 200cor. multicoloured . . 10 10
3030 – 600cor. multicoloured . . 10 10
3031 – 1000cor. multicoloured 30 10
3032 – 2000cor. multicoloured 60 10
3033 – 3000cor. multicoloured 90 40
3034 – 5000cor. multicoloured 1·50 50

DESIGNS: 200cor. to 5000cor. Different footballers.

1989. Air. Winter Olympic Games, Albertville (1992) (1st issue). Multicoloured.

3036 50cor. Type **467** 10 10
3037 300cor. Ice hockey 10 10
3038 600cor. Ski jumping 10 10
3039 1000cor. Ice skating 30 10
3040 2000cor. Biathlon 60 10
3041 3000cor. Slalom 90 40
3042 5000cor. Skiing . . . . . . 1·50 50

See also Nos. 3184/90.

468 Water Polo

1989. Air. Olympic Games, Barcelona (1992). Mult.

3044 100cor. Type **468** 10 10
3045 200cor. Running 10 10
3046 600cor. Diving 10 10
3047 1000cor. Gymnastics 30 10
3048 2000cor. Weightlifting . . . 60 10

3049 3000cor. Volleyball 90 40
3050 5000cor. Wrestling . . . . 1·50 50
See also Nos. 3192/8.

469 Procession of States General at Versailles
470 American Darter

1989. "Philexfrance 89" International Stamp Exhibition, Paris, and Bicentenary of French Revolution. Multicoloured.
3052 50cor. Type **469** (postage) 15 10
3054 300cor. Oath of the Tennis Court (36 × 28 mm) (air) 10 10
3055 600cor. "The 14th of July" (29 × 40 mm) 10 10
3056 1000cor. Tree of Liberty (36 × 28 mm) 30 10
3057 2000cor. "Liberty guiding the People" (Eugene Delacroix) (29 × 40 mm) 60 10
3058 3000cor. Storming the Bastille (36 × 28 mm) . . 90 40
3059 5000cor. Lafayette taking oath (28 × 36 mm) . . . . 1·50 50

1989. Air. "Brasiliana 89" International Stamp Exhibition, Rio de Janeiro. Birds. Multicoloured.
3060 100cor. Type **470** 20 20
3061 200cor. Swallow-tailed kite 20 20
3062 600cor. Turquoise-browed motmot 25 20
3063 1000cor. Painted redstart . . 40 20
3064 2000cor. Great antshrike (horiz) 80 20
3065 3000cor. Northern royal flycatcher . . . . 1·10 90
3066 5000cor. White-flanked antwren (horiz) . . . . . 2·00 1·10

471 Anniversary Emblem
472 Animal-shaped Vessel

1989. Air. 10th Anniv of Revolution.
3068 **471** 300cor. multicoloured . . 10 10

1989. Air. America. Pre-Columbian Artefacts.
3070 **472** 2000cor. multicoloured 60 10

Currency Reform. 150000 (old) cordoba = 1 (new) cordoba
The following issues, denominated in the old currency, were distributed by agents but were not issued (each set consists of seven values and is dated "1990"):
"London 90" International Stamp Exn. Ships
World Cup Football Championship, Italy
Olympic Games, Barcelona (1992)
Fungi
Winter Olympic Games, Albertville (1992)

473 Little Spotted Kiwi

1991. "New Zealand 1990" International Stamp Exhibition, Auckland. Birds. Multicoloured.
3071 5c. Type **473** 15 10
3072 5c. Takahe 15 10
3073 10c. Red-fronted parakeet 20 15
3074 20c. Weka rail 45 25
3075 30c. Kagu (vert) 25 40
3076 60c. Kea . . . . 1·25 90
3077 70c. Kakapo . . . . 1·50 1·00

474 Jaguar

1991. 45th Anniv of Food and Agriculture Organization. Animals. Multicoloured.
3079 5c. Type **474** 10 10
3080 5c. Ocelot (vert) 10 10
3081 10c. Black-handed spider monkey (vert) 15 10
3082 20c. Baird's tapir 30 15
3083 30c. Nine-banded armadillo 45 20
3084 60c. Coyote 85 45
3085 70c. Two-toed sloth . . . . 1·00 50

475 Dr. Chamorro

476 Steam Locomotive, 1920s, Peru

1991. Dr. Pedro Joaquin Chamorro (campaigner for an independent Press).
3086 **475** 2cor.25 multicoloured . . 50 20

1991. Flowers. As T **356** but with currency inscribed in "oro".
3087 – 1cor. blue 25 10
3088 – 2cor. green 45 20
3089 – 3cor. brown 70 30
3090 – 4cor. purple 95 40
3091 – 5cor. red . . . . 1·10 45
3092 – 6cor. green . . . . . . 1·40 55
3093 **356** 7cor. blue . . . . 1·60 65
3094 – 8cor. green . . . . . . 1·90 75
3095 – 9cor. green . . . . . . 2·10 85
3096 – 10cor. violet . . . . . 2·25 90
3097 – 11cor. mauve . . . . . 2·50 1·00
3098 – 12cor. yellow . . . . . 2·75 1·10
3099 – 13cor. red . . . . . . 3·00 1·25
3100 – 14cor. green . . . . . 3·25 1·25
3101 – 15cor. mauve . . . . . 3·50 1·40
3102 – 16cor. black . . . . . 3·75 1·50
DESIGNS: 1cor. "Stachytarpheta indica"; 2cor. "Cochlospermum sp."; 3cor. "Senecio sp."; 4cor. "Sobralia macrantha"; 5cor. Frangipani; 6cor. "Brassavola nodosa"; 8cor. "Malvaviscus arboreus"; 9cor. "Cattleya lueddemanniana"; 10cor. "Tabebula ochraceae"; 11cor. "Laelia sp."; 12cor. African marigold; 13cor. Chinese hibiscus; 14cor. "Thumbergia alata"; 15cor. "Tecoma stans"; 16cor. "Bixa orellana".

1991. Steam Locomotives of South and Central America. Multicoloured.
3103 25c. Type **476** 30 10
3104 25c. Locomotive No. 508, 1917, Bolivia 30 10
3105 50c. Class N/O locomotive, 1910s, Argentina 50 10
3106 1cor.50 Locomotive, 1952, Chile 90 20
3107 2cor. Locomotive No. 61, 1944, Colombia . . . . . 1·25 25
3108 3cor. Locomotive No. 311, 1947, Brazil . . . . . . 2·00 35
3109 3cor.50 Locomotive No. 60, 1910, Paraguay . . . . . 2·25 45

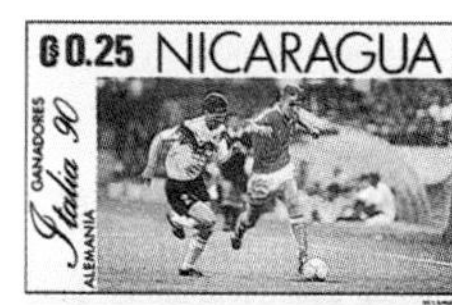

477 Match Scene (West Germany versus Netherlands)

1991. West Germany, Winners of World Cup Football Championship (1990). Multicoloured.
3111 25c. Type **477** 10 10
3112 25c. Match scene (West Germany versus Colombia) (vert) 10 10
3113 50c. West German players and referee 10 10
3114 1cor. West German players forming wall (vert) . . . 25 10
3115 1cor.50 Diego Maradona (Argentina) (vert) 35 15
3116 3cor. Argentinian players and Italian goalkeeper (vert) 70 30
3117 3cor.50 Italian players . . . 80 30

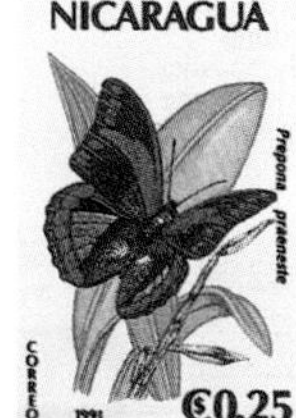

478 "Prepona praeneste"

1991. Butterflies. Multicoloured.
3119 25c. Type **478** 10 10
3120 25c. "Anartia fatima" . . . 10 10
3121 50c. "Eryphanis aesacus" . . 10 10
3122 1cor. "Heliconius melpomene" 25 10
3123 1cor.50 "Chlosyne janais" 35 15
3124 3cor. "Marpesia iole" . . . 70 30
3125 3cor.50 Rusty-tipped page 80 30

479 Dove and Cross

1991. 700th Anniv of Swiss Confederation.
3127 **479** 2cor.25 red, black and yellow 50 20

480 Yellow-headed Amazon

1991. "Rainforest is Life". Fauna. Multicoloured.
3128 2cor.25 Type **480** 50 20
3129 2cor.25 Keel-billed toucan 50 20
3130 2cor.25 Scarlet macaw . . . 50 20
3131 2cor.25 Resplendent quetzal 50 20
3132 2cor.25 Black-handed spider monkey 50 20
3133 2cor.25 White-throated capuchin 50 20
3134 2cor.25 Three-toed sloth . . 50 20
3135 2cor.25 Chestnut-headed oropendola 50 20
3136 2cor.25 Violet sabrewing . . 50 20
3137 2cor.25 Tamandua 50 20
3138 2cor.25 Jaguarundi 50 20
3139 2cor.25 Boa constrictor . . 50 20
3140 2cor.25 Common iguana . . 50 20
3141 2cor.25 Jaguar 50 20
3142 2cor.25 White-necked jacobin 50 20
3143 2cor.25 "Doxocopa clothilda" (butterfly) . . . 50 20
3144 2cor.25 "Dismorphia deione" (butterfly) 50 20
3145 2cor.25 Golden arrow-poison frog 50 20
3146 2cor.25 "Callithomia hezia" (butterfly) 50 20
3147 2cor.25 Chameleon 50 20
Nos. 3128/47 were issued together, se-tenant, forming a composite design.

481 "Isochilus major"

1991. Orchids. Multicoloured.
3148 25c. Type **481** 10 10
3149 25c. "Cycnoches ventricosum" 10 10
3150 50c. "Vanilla odorata" . . . 10 10
3151 1cor. "Helleriella nicaraguensis" 25 10
3152 1cor.50 "Barkeria spectabilis" 35 15
3153 3cor. "Maxillaria hedwigae" 70 30
3154 3cor.50 "Cattleya aurantiaca" 80 30

482 Concepcion Volcano

1991. America (1990).
3156 **482** 2cor.25 multicoloured . . 50 20

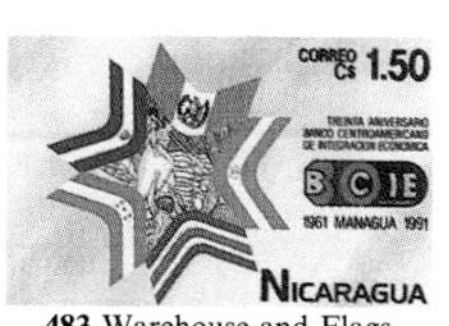

483 Warehouse and Flags

1991. 30th Anniv of Central American Bank of Economic Integration.
3157 **483** 1cor.50 multicoloured . . 35 15

484 "The One-eyed Man"

1991. Death Centenary (1990) of Vincent van Gogh (painter). Multicoloured.
3158 25c. Type **484** 10 10
3159 25c. "Head of Countrywoman with Bonnet" 10 10
3160 50c. "Self-portrait" 10 10
3161 1cor. "Vase with Carnations and other Flowers" . . . 25 10
3162 1cor.50 "Vase with Zinnias and Geraniums" 35 15
3163 3cor. "Portrait of Tanguy Father" 70 30
3164 3cor.50 "Portrait of a Man" (horiz) 80 30

485 Painting by Rafaela Herrera (1st-prize winner)

1991. National Children's Painting Competition.
3166 **485** 2cor.25 multicoloured . . 50 20

486 Golden Pavilion

1991. "Phila Nippon '91" International Stamp Exhibition, Tokyo. Multicoloured.
3167 25c. Type **486** 10 10
3168 50c. Himaji Castle 10 10
3169 1cor. Head of Bunraku doll 25 10
3170 1cor.50 Japanese cranes . . 35 15
3171 2cor.50 Phoenix pavilion . . 60 25
3172 3cor. "The Guardian" (statue) 70 30
3173 3cor.50 Kabuki actor . . . 80 30

487 Turquoise-browed Motmot
488 Columbus's Fleet

1992. Birds. Multicoloured.
3175 50c. Type **487** 15 10
3176 75c. Collared trogon 20 10
3177 1cor. Broad-billed motmot 25 10
3178 1cor.50 Wire-tailed manakin 40 15
3179 1cor.75 Paradise tanager (horiz) 45 20
3180 2cor.25 Resplendent quetzal 60 25
3181 2cor.25 Black-spotted bare-eye 60 25

1992. America (1991). Voyages of Discovery.
3183 **488** 2cor.25 multicoloured . . 35 15

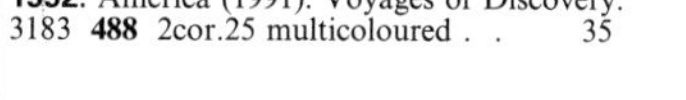

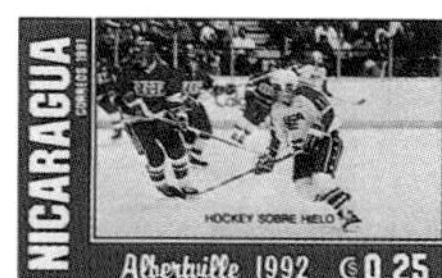

489 Ice Hockey

1992. Winter Olympic Games, Albertville (2nd issue). Multicoloured.
3184 25c. Type **489** 10 10
3185 25c. Four-man bobsleighing 10 10
3186 50c. Skiing (vert) 15 10
3187 1cor. Speed skating 25 10
3188 1cor.50 Cross-country skiing 40 15
3189 3cor. Double luge 75 30
3190 3cor.50 Ski jumping (vert) 90 35

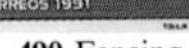

490 Fencing

491 Ceramic Vase with Face (Lorenza Pineda Co-operative)

1992. Olympic Games, Barcelona (2nd issue) Mult.

3192 25c. Type **490** 10 10
3193 25c. Throwing the javelin (horiz) 10 10
3194 50c. Basketball 15 10
3195 1cor.50 Running 40 15
3196 2cor. Long jumping 50 20
3197 3cor. Running 75 30
3198 3cor.50 Show jumping . . . 90 35

1992. Contemporary Arts and Crafts. Mult.

3200 25c. Type **491** 10 10
3201 25c. Ceramic spouted vessel (Jose Oritz) (horiz) . . . 10 10
3202 50c. Blue-patterned ceramic vase (Elio Gutierrez) . . . 15 10
3203 1cor. "Christ" (Jose de los Santos) 25 10
3204 1cor.50 "Family" (sculpture, Erasmo Moya) 40 15
3205 3cor. "Bird-fish" (Silvio Chavarria Co-operative) (horiz) 85 30
3206 3cor.50 Filigree ceramic vessel (Maria de los Angeles Bermudez) . . . 90 35

492 "Picnic Table with Three Objects" (Alejandro Arostegui)

493 Rivoli's Hummingbird

1992. Contemporary Paintings. Multicoloured.

3208 25c. Type **492** 10 10
3209 25c. "Prophetess of the New World" (Alberto Ycaza) 10 10
3210 50c. "Flames of Unknown Origin" (Bernard Dreyfus) (horiz) 15 10
3211 1cor.50 "Owl" (Orlando Sobalvarro) (horiz) . . . 40 15
3212 2cor. "Pegasus at Liberty" (Hugo Palma) (horiz) . . 50 20
3213 3cor. "Avocados" (Omar d'Leon) (horiz) 75 30
3214 3cor.50 "Gueguense" (Carlos Montenegro) . . 90 35

1992. 2nd U.N. Conference on Environment and Development, Rio de Janeiro. Tropical Forest Wildlife. Multicoloured.

3216 1cor.50 Type **493** 40 15
3217 1cor.50 Harpy eagle ("Aguila arpia") 40 15
3218 1cor.50 Orchid 40 15
3219 1cor.50 Keel-billed toucan and morpho butterfly . . 40 15
3220 1cor.50 Resplendent quetzal 40 15
3221 1cor.50 Guardabarranco . . 40 15
3222 1cor.50 Howler monkey ("Mono aullador") . . . 40 15
3223 1cor.50 Sloth ("Perezoso") 40 15
3224 1cor.50 Squirrel monkey ("Mono ardilla") 40 15
3225 1cor.50 Blue and yellow macaw ("Guacamaya") 40 15
3226 1cor.50 Emerald boa and scarlet tanager 40 15
3227 1cor.50 Poison-arrow frog 40 15
3228 1cor.50 Jaguar 40 15
3229 1cor.50 Anteater 40 15
3230 1cor.50 Ocelot 40 15
3231 1cor.50 Coati 40 15

Nos. 3216/31 were issued together, se-tenant, forming a composite design of a forest.

494 Fabretto with Children

1992. Father Fabretto, "Benefactor of Nicaraguan Children".

3232 **494** 2cor.25 multicoloured . . 60 25

495 "Nicaraguan Identity" (Claudia Gordillo)

1992. Winning Entry in Photography Competition.

3233 **495** 2cor.25 multicoloured . . 60 25

496 "The Indians of Nicaragua" (Milton Jose Cruz)

1992. Winning Entry in Children's Painting Competition.

3234 **496** 2cor.25 multicoloured . . 60 25

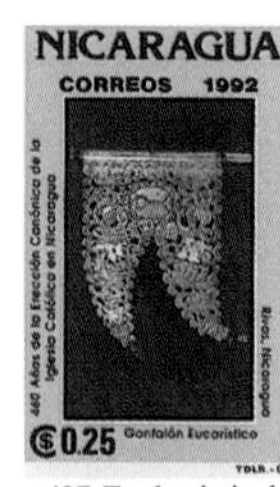

AMERICA
CORREOS
C$2.25
NICARAGUA

497 Eucharistical Banner

498 Rivas Cross, 1523

1993. 460th Anniv of Catholic Church in Nicaragua. Multicoloured.

3235 25c. Type **497** 10 10
3236 50c. "Shrine of the Immaculate Conception" 10 10
3237 1cor. 18th-century document 20 10
3238 1cor.50 16th-century baptismal font 30 10
3239 2cor. "The Immaculate Conception" 40 15
3240 2cor.25 Monsignor Diego Alvarez Osorio (1st Bishop of Leon) 50 20
3241 3cor. "Christ on the Cross" 65 25

1993. America (1992). 500th Anniv of Discovery of America by Columbus.

3242 **498** 2cor.25 multicoloured . . 50 20

499 Cathedral

1993. Inauguration of Cathedral of the Immaculate Conception of Mary, Managua. Multicoloured.

3243 3cor. Type **499** 65 25
3244 4cor. Cross, Virgin Mary and map of Nicaragua (2nd Provincial Council) 85 35

Nos. 3243/4 were issued together, se-tenant, forming a composite design.

500 Emblem and Voters queueing outside Poll Station

1993. 23rd General Assembly of Organization of American States.

3245 **500** 3cor. multicoloured . . . 85 45

501 Anniversary Emblem

1993. 90th Anniv of Pan-American Health Organization.

3246 **501** 3cor. multicoloured . . . 85 45

NICARAGUA
CORREOS 1993 Sonatina Alma Iris Perez 12 Años
C$3.00 PRIMER PREMIO DE PINTURA INFANTIL

502 "Sonatina" (Alma Iris Perez)

1993. Winning Entry in Children's Painting Competition.

3247 **502** 3cor. multicoloured . . . 85 45

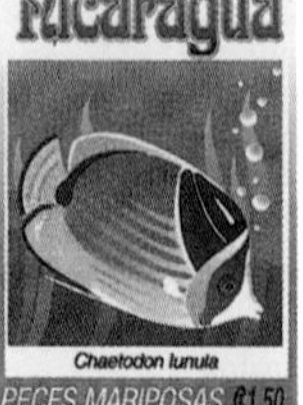

503 Racoon Buttterflyfish

1993. Butterflyfishes. Multicoloured.

3248 1cor.50 Type **503** 50 25
3249 1cor.50 Rainford's butterflyfish ("Chaetodon rainfordi") 50 25
3250 1cor.50 Mailed butterflyfish ("Chaetodon reticulatus") 50 25
3251 1cor.50 Thread-finned butterflyfish ("Chaetodon auriga") 50 25
3252 1cor.50 Pennant coralfish ("Heniochus acuminatus") 50 25
3253 1cor.50 Dark-banded butterflyfish ("Coradion fulvocinctus") 50 25
3254 1cor.50 Mirror butterflyfish ("Chaetodon speculum") 50 25
3255 1cor.50 Lined butterflyfish ("Chaetodon lineolatus") 50 25
3256 1cor.50 Bennett's butterflyfish ("Chaetodon bennetti") 50 25
3257 1cor.50 Black-backed butterflyfish ("Chaetodon melanotus") 50 25
3258 1cor.50 Golden butterflyfish ("Chaetodon aureus") . . 50 25
3259 1cor.50 Saddle butterflyfish ("Chaetodon ephippium") 50 25
3260 1cor.50 Pyramid butterflyfish ("Hemitaurichthys polylepis") 50 25
3261 1cor.50 Dotted butterflyfish ("Chaetodon semeion") 50 25
3262 1cor.50 Klein's butterflyfish ("Chaetodon kleinii") . . 50 25
3263 1cor.50 Copper-banded butterflyfish ("Chelmon rostratus") 50 25

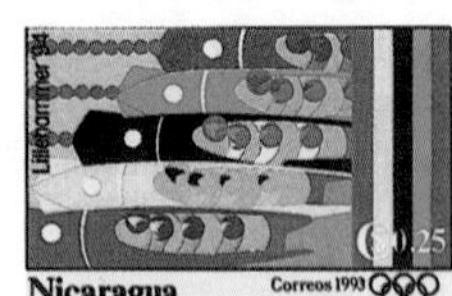

504 Four-man Bobsleigh

1993. Multicoloured. (a) Winter Olympic Games, Lillehammer, Norway (1994).

3264 25c. Type **504** 10 10
3265 25c. Skiing 10 10
3266 50c. Speed skating 15 10
3267 1cor.50 Ski jumping 45 20
3268 2cor. Women's figure skating 55 25
3269 3cor. Pairs' figure skating 85 45
3270 3cor.50 Shooting (biathlon) 1·00 45

(b) Olympic Games, Atlanta (1996).

3271 25c. Swimming 10 10
3272 25c. Diving 10 10
3273 50c. Long distance running 15 10
3274 1cor. Hurdling 30 15
3275 1cor.50 Gymnastics 45 20
3276 3cor. Throwing the javelin 85 45
3277 3cor.50 Sprinting . . . . . 1·00 50

505 "Bromeliaceae sp."

506 Tomas Brolin (Sweden)

1994. Tropical Forest Flora and Fauna. Mult.

3279 2cor. Type **505** 50 25
3280 2cor. Sparkling-tailed hummingbird ("Tilmatura dupontii") 50 25
3281 2cor. "Anolis biporcatus" (lizard) 50 25
3282 2cor. Lantern fly ("Fulgara laternaria") 50 25
3283 2cor. Sloth ("Bradypus sp.") 50 25
3284 2cor. Ornate hawk eagle ("Spizaetus ornatus") . . 50 25
3285 2cor. Lovely cotinga ("Cotinga amabilis") . . 50 25
3286 2cor. Schegel's lance-head snake ("Bothrops schlegelii") 50 25
3287 2cor. "Odontoglossum sp." (orchid) and bee 50 25
3288 2cor. Red-eyed tree frog ("Agalychnis callidryas") 50 25
3289 2cor. "Heliconius sapho" (butterfly) 50 25
3290 2cor. Passion flower ("Passiflora vitifolia") . . 50 25

Nos. 3279/90 were issued together, se-tenant, forming a composite design.

1994. World Cup Football Championship, U.S.A.. Players.

3292 50c. Type **506** 15 10
3293 1cor. Jan Karas (Poland) and Antonio Luiz Costa (Brazil) 30 15
3294 1cor. Maxime Bossis and Michel Platini (France) 30 15
3295 1cor.50 Harold Schumacher (Germany) 45 20
3296 2cor. Andoni Zubizarreta (Spain) 55 30
3297 2cor.50 Lothar Matthaeus (Germany) and Diego Maradona (Argentine Republic) 75 35
3298 3cor.50 Bryan Robson (England) and Carlos Santos (Portugal) . . . . 1·00 50

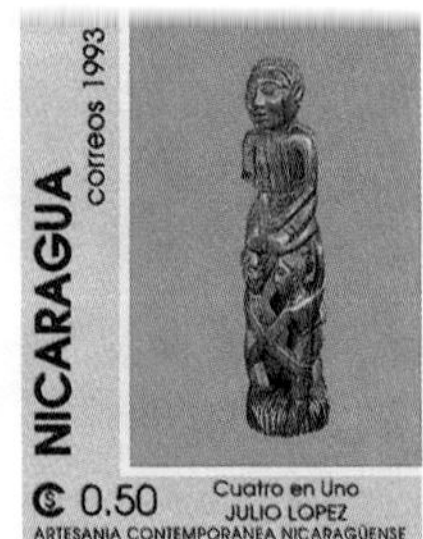

507 "Four in One" (Julio Lopez)

1994. Contemporary Arts. Multicoloured.

3300 50c. Rush mat (Rosalia Sevilla) (horiz) 15 10
3301 50c. Type **507** 15 10
3302 1cor. Ceramic church (Auxiliadora Bush) . . . 30 15
3303 1cor. Statuette of old woman (Indiana Robleto) 30 15
3304 2cor.50 "Santiago" (Jose de los Santos) 55 30
3305 3cor. "Gueguense" (Ines Gutierrez de Chong) . . . 85 45
3306 4cor. Ceramic hornet's nest (Elio Gutierrez) 95 45

508 "Callicore patelina"

1994. "Hong Kong '94" International Stamp Exhibition. Butterflies. Multicoloured.

3308 1cor.50 Type **508** 35 15
3309 1cor.50 "Chlosyne narva" 35 15
3310 1cor.50 Giant brimstone ("Anteos maerula") . . . 35 15
3311 1cor.50 Diadem ("Marpesia petreus") 35 15
3312 1cor.50 "Pierella helvetia" 35 15
3313 1cor.50 "Eurytides epidaus" 35 15
3314 1cor.50 Doris ("Heliconius doris") 35 15
3315 1cor.50 "Smyrna blomfildia" 35 15
3316 1cor.50 "Eueides lybia olympia" 35 15
3317 1cor.50 "Adelpha heraclea" 35 15
3318 1cor.50 "Heliconius hecale zuleika" 35 15
3319 1cor.50 "Parides montezuma" 35 15
3320 1cor.50 "Morpho polyphemus" 35 15
3321 1cor.50 "Eresia alsina" . . . 35 15
3322 1cor.50 "Prepona omphale octavia" 35 15
3323 1cor.50 "Morpho grenadensis" 35 15

509 "The Holy Family" (anonymous)

1994. Christmas (1993). Paintings. Multicoloured.
3324 1cor. Type **509** 25 15
3325 4cor. "Nativity" (Lezamon) 95 45

510 Sculpture

1994. Chontal Culture Statuary. Multicoloured, colour of frame given.
3326 **510** 50c. yellow 15 10
3327 – 50c. yellow 15 10
3328 – 1cor. emerald 30 15
3329 – 1cor. green 30 15
3330 – 2cor.50 blue 55 35
3331 – 3cor. blue 85 45
3332 – 4cor. green 95 45
DESIGNS: 50c. (No. 3327) to 4cor. Different sculptures.

511 "Virgin of Nicaragua" (Celia Lacayo)

1994. Contemporary Paintings. Multicoloured.
3334 50c. Type **511** 15 10
3335 50c. "Woman embroidering" (Guillermo Rivas Navas) 15 10
3336 1cor. "Couple dancing" (June Beer) 30 15
3337 1cor. "Song of Peace" (Alejandro Canales) . . . 30 15
3338 2cor.50 "Sapodilla Plums" (Genaro Lugo) (horiz) . . 55 30
3339 3cor. "Figure and Fragments" (Leonel Vanegas) 85 45
3340 4cor. "Eruption of Agua Volcano" (Asilia Guillen) (horiz) 95 45

512 Nicolas Copernicus and Satellite

1994. Astronomers. Mutlicoloured.
3342 1cor.50 Type **512** 35 15
3343 1cor.50 Tycho Brahe and astronomers 35 15
3344 1cor.50 Galileo Galilei and "Galileo" space probe . . 35 15
3345 1cor.50 Sir Isaac Newton and telescope 35 15
3346 1cor.50 Edmond Halley, space probe and Halley's Comet 35 15
3347 1cor.50 James Bradley and Greenwich Observatory 35 15
3348 1cor.50 William Herschel and telescope 35 15
3349 1cor.50 John Goodricke and Algol (star) 35 15
3350 1cor.50 Karl Friedrich Gauss and Gottingen Observatory 35 15
3351 1cor.50 Friedrich Bessel and 1838 star telescope . . . 35 15
3352 1cor.50 William Cranch Bond (wrongly inscr "Granch") and Harvard College Observatory . . . 35 15
3353 1cor.50 Sir George Airy and stellar disk 35 15
3354 1cor.50 Percival Lowell and Flagstaff Observatory, Arizona, U.S.A. 35 15
3355 1cor.50 George Hale (wrongly inscr "Halle") and solar spectroscope . . 35 15
3356 1cor.50 Edwin Hubble and Hubble telescope 35 15
3357 1cor.50 Gerard Kuiper and Miranda (Uranus moon) 35 15
Nos. 3342/57 were issued together, se-tenant, forming a composite design.

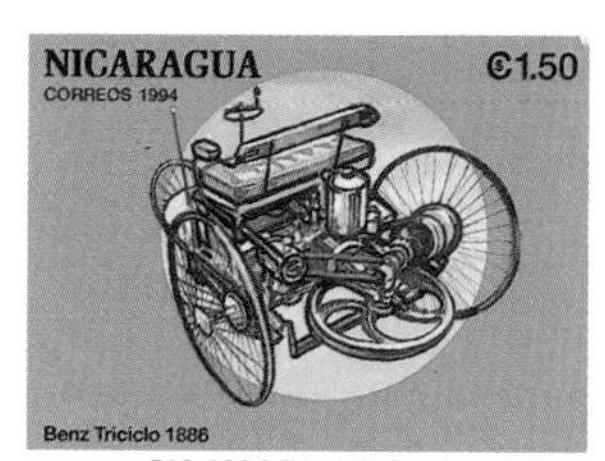

513 1886 Benz Tricycle

1994. Automobiles. Multicoloured.
3359 1cor.50 Type **513** 35 15
3360 1cor.50 1909 Benz Blitzen 35 15
3361 1cor.50 1923 Mercedes Benz 24/100/140 . . . . 35 15
3362 1cor.50 1928 Mercedes Benz SSK 35 15
3363 1cor.50 1934 Mercedes Benz 500K Cabriolet 35 15
3364 1cor.50 1949 Mercedes Benz 170S 35 15
3365 1cor.50 1954 Mercedes Benz W196 . . . . 35 15
3366 1cor.50 1954 Mercedes Benz 300SL 35 15
3367 1cor.50 1896 Ford Quadricycle 35 15
3368 1cor.50 1920 Ford taxi cab 35 15
3369 1cor.50 1928 Ford Roadster 35 15
3370 1cor.50 1932 Ford V-8 . . . 35 15
3371 1cor.50 1937 Ford V-8 78 35 15
3372 1cor.50 1939 Ford 91 Deluxe Tudor Sedan . . . 35 15
3373 1cor.50 1946 Ford V-8 Sedan Coupe 35 15
3374 1cor.50 1958 Ford Custom 300 . . . . 35 15

514 Hugo Eckener and Count Ferdinand von Zeppelin

1994. Zeppelin Airships. Multicoloured.
3376 1cor.50 Type **514** 35 15
3377 1cor.50 "Graf Zeppelin" over New York, 1928 . . 35 15
3378 1cor.50 "Graf Zeppelin" over Tokyo, 1929 . . . . 35 15
3379 1cor.50 "Graf Zeppelin" over Randolph Hearst's villa, 1929 . . . . 35 15
3380 1cor.50 Charles Lindbergh, Hugo Eckener and "Graf Zeppelin" at Lakehurst, 1929 . . . . 35 15
3381 1cor.50 "Graf Zeppelin" over St. Basil's Cathedral, Moscow (wrongly inscr "Santra Sofia") 35 15
3382 1cor.50 "Graf Zeppelin" over Paris, 1930 . . . . . 35 15
3383 1cor.50 "Graf Zeppelin" over Cairo, Egypt, 1931 35 15
3384 1cor.50 "Graf Zeppelin" over Arctic Sea 35 15
3385 1cor.50 "Graf Zeppelin" over Rio de Janeiro, 1932 35 15
3386 1cor.50 "Graf Zeppelin" over St. Paul's Cathedral, London, 1935 . . . . . 35 15
3387 1cor.50 "Graf Zeppelin" over St. Peter's Cathedral, Rome 35 15
3388 1cor.50 "Graf Zeppelin" over Swiss Alps 35 15
3389 1cor.50 "Graf Zeppelin over Brandenburg Gate, Berlin 35 15
3390 1cor.50 Hugo Eckener piloting "Graf Zeppelin" 35 15
3391 1cor.50 Captain Ernest Lehman, "Graf Zeppelin" and Dornier Do-X flying boat 35 15

515 Gabriel Horvilleur

1994. Nicaraguan Philatelists. Multicoloured.
3393 1cor. Type **515** 15 10
3394 3cor. Jose Cauadra 85 45
3395 4cor. Alfredo Pertz 95 45

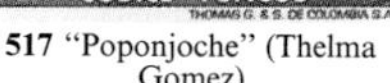

517 "Poponjoche" (Thelma Gomez)

518 Conference Emblem

1994. 1st Nicaraguan Tree Conference.
3397 **517** 4cor. multicoloured . . . 95 45

1994. 2nd International Conference on New and Restored Democracies, Managua.
3398 **518** 3cor. multicoloured . . . 55 55

519 Pulpit, Leon Cathedral

520 Mascot and Emblem

1994. Religious Art. Multicoloured.
3399 50c. Type **519** 15 10
3400 50c. "St. Anna" (porcelain figure), Chinandega Church 15 10
3401 1cor. "St. Joseph and Child" (porcelain figure), St. Peter's Church, Rivas 30 15
3402 1cor. "St. James", Jinotepe Church 30 15
3403 2cor.50 Gold chalice, Subtiava Temple, Leon 55 30
3404 3cor. Processional cross, Niquinohomo Church, Masaya 85 45
3405 4cor. "Lord of Miracles" (crucifix), Lord of Miracles Temple, Managua 95 45

1994. 32nd World Amateur Baseball Championship.
3407 **520** 4cor. multicoloured . . . 1·00 1·00

521 Mt. Sorak

1994. "Philakorea 1994" International Stamp Exhibition, Seoul. Views of South Korea. Mult.
3408 1cor.50 Type **521** 25 10
3409 1cor.50 Bronze Statue of Kim Yu-Shin 25 10
3410 1cor.50 Woedolgae (solitary rock) 25 10
3411 1cor.50 Stream, Mt. Hallasan, Cheju Island . . 25 10
3412 1cor.50 Mirukpong and Pisondae 25 10
3413 1cor.50 Ch'onbuldong Valley 25 10
3414 1cor.50 Bridge of the Seven Nymphs 25 10
3415 1cor.50 Piryong Waterfall 25 10

522 Piano on Stage

1994. 25th Anniv of Ruben Dario National Theatre, Managua.
3417 **522** 3cor. multicoloured . . . 55 20

523 Tyrannosaurus Rex

1994. Prehistoric Animals. Multicoloured.
3418 1cor.50 Type **523** 25 10
3419 1cor.50 Plateosaurus 25 10
3420 1cor.50 Pteranodon 25 10
3421 1cor.50 Camarasaurus . . . 25 10
3422 1cor.50 Euplocephalus . . . 25 10
3423 1cor.50 Sacuanjoche 25 10
3424 1cor.50 Deinonychus . . . 25 10
3425 1cor.50 Chasmosaurus . . . 25 10
3426 1cor.50 Dimorphodon . . . 25 10
3427 1cor.50 Ametriorhynchids 25 10
3428 1cor.50 Ichthyosaurus . . . 25 10
3429 1cor.50 Pterapsis and compsognathus 25 10
3430 1cor.50 Cephalopod 25 10
3431 1cor.50 Archelon 25 10
3432 1cor.50 Griphognatus and gyroptychius 25 10
3433 1cor.50 Plesiosaur and nautiloid 25 10
Nos. 3418/33 were issued together, se-tenant, forming a composite design.

524 Hawker Typhoon 1B

1994. 50th Anniv of D-Day. Multicoloured.
3434 3cor. Type **524** 55 20
3435 3cor. Douglas C-47 Skytrain transport dropping paratroops 55 20
3436 3cor. H.M.S. "Mauritius" (cruiser) bombarding Houlgate, Normandy . . 55 20
3437 3cor. Formation of Mulberry Harbours to transport supplies to beach 55 20
3438 3cor. British AVRE Churchill tank 55 20
3439 3cor. Tank landing craft . . 55 20

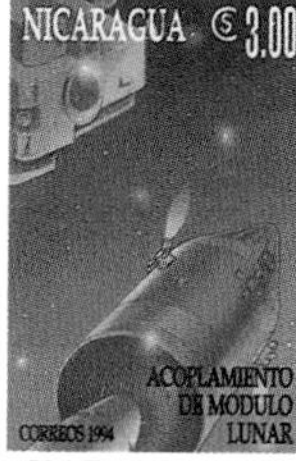

525 Renate Stecher (women's 200 m, 1972)

526 Detachment of Command module "Eagle"

1994. Centenary of International Olympic Committee. Gold Medal Winners. Multicoloured.
3440 3cor.50 Type **525** 60 25
3441 3cor.50 Cassius Clay (Muhammad Ali) (boxing, 1960) 60 25

1994. 25th Anniv of First Manned Moon Landing. Multicoloured.
3443 3cor. Type **526** 55 20
3444 3cor. Launch of "Saturn V", Cape Canaveral, Florida 55 20
3445 3cor. Command module orbiting Moon 55 20
3446 3cor. Footprint on Moon 55 20
3447 3cor. Primary space capsule separating 55 20
3448 3cor. Command module . . 55 20
3449 3cor. Lunar module landing on Moon 55 20
3450 3cor. Astronaut on Moon 55 20

527 "The Death Cart" (Erick Joanello Montoya)

1994. 1st Prize in Children's Painting Competition.
3452 **527** 4cor. multicoloured . . . 70 30

528 Black-crowned Night Heron

1994. Woodland Animals. Multicoloured.
3453 2cor. Type **528** 35 15
3454 2cor. Scarlet macaw ("Ara macao") 35 15
3455 2cor. Cattle egrets ("Bubulcus ibis") (wrongly inscr "Bulbulcus") 35 15
3456 2cor. American black vultures ("Coragyps atratus") 35 15
3457 2cor. Brazilian rainbow boa ("Epicrates cenchria") . . 35 15
3458 2cor. Red-legged honeycreepers ("Cyanerpes cyaneus") . . 35 15
3459 2cor. Plain chachalaca ("Ortalis vetula") 35 15
3460 2cor. Sloth ("Bradypus griseus") 35 15
3461 2cor. Jaguar ("Felis onca") 35 15
3462 2cor. American darter ("Anhinga anhinga") . . 35 15
3463 2cor. Baird's tapir ("Tapirus bairdi") 35 15
3464 2cor. Anteater ("Myrmecophaga jubata") 35 15
3465 2cor. Iguana ("Iguana iguana") 35 15
3466 2cor. Snapping turtle ("Chelydra serpentina") 35 15
3467 2cor. Red-billed whistling ducks ("Dendrocygna autumnalis") 35 15
3468 2cor. Ocelot ("Felis pardalis") 35 15

Nos. 3453/68 were issued together, se-tenant, forming a composite design.

529 "The Kid" (dir. Charlie Chaplin)

530 "Discovery of America"

1994. Centenary of Motion Pictures. Multicoloured.
3470 2cor. Type **529** 35 15
3471 2cor. "Citizen Kane" (dir. Orson Welles) 35 15
3472 2cor. "Lawrence of Arabia" (dir. David Lean) 35 15
3473 2cor. "Ivan the Terrible" (dir. Sergio Eisenstein) . . 35 15
3474 2cor. "Metropolis" (dir. Fritz Lang) 35 15
3475 2cor. "The Ten Commandments" (dir. Cecil B. De Mille) 35 15
3476 2cor. "Gandhi" (dir. Richard Attenborough) 35 15
3477 2cor. "Casablanca" (dir. Michael Curtiz) 35 15
3478 2cor. "Platoon" (dir. Oliver Stone) 35 15
3479 2cor. "The Godfather" (dir. Francis Ford Coppola) 35 15
3480 2cor. "2001: A Space Odyssey" (dir. Stanley Kubrick) 35 15
3481 2cor. "The Ocean Depths" (dir. Jean Renoir) 35 15

1994. 15th Death Anniv of Rodrigo Penalba (artist). Multicoloured.
3483 50c. Type **530** 10 10
3484 1cor. "Portrait of Mauricio" 20 10
3485 1cor.50 "Portrait of Franco" 25 10
3486 2cor. "Portrait of Mimi Hammer" 35 15
3487 2cor.50 "Seated Woman" 45 20
3488 3cor. "Still-life" (horiz) . . 55 20
3489 4cor. "Portrait of Maria Augusta" 70 30

531 Hen and Cock

1994. Endangered Species. The Highland Guan. Multicoloured.
3491 50c. Type **531** 10 10
3492 1cor. Cock 20 10
3493 2cor.50 Hen 45 20
3494 3cor. Cock and hen (different) 55 25

SILVER CURRENCY

The following were for use in all places on the Atlantic coast of Nicaragua where the silver currency was in use. This currency was worth about 50c. to the peso.

Earlier issues (overprints on Nicaraguan stamps) were also issued for Zelaya. These are listed in the Stanley Gibbons Part 15 (Central America) Catalogue.

G 1 Steam Locomotive

1912.
G 1 Z 1 1c. green . . . . 1·75 90
G 2 2c. red . . . . . 1·25 55
G 3 3c. brown . . . 1·75 85
G 4 4c. lake . . . . 1·75 70
G 5 5c. blue . . . . 1·75 70
G 6 6c. red . . . . . 9·75 5·00
G 7 10c. grey . . . . 1·75 70
G 8 15c. lilac . . . . 1·75 1·10
G 9 20c. blue . . . . 1·75 1·10
G10 25c. black and green . . . . 2·25 1·60
G11 35c. black and brown . . . . 3·25 1·90
G12 50c. green . . . 3·25 1·90
G13 1p. orange . . . 5·00 3·25
G14 2p. brown . . . 9·75 6·00
G15 5p. green . . . . 20·00 12·50

OFFICIAL STAMPS

Overprinted **FRANQUEO OFICIAL**.

1890. Stamps of 1890.
O37 **6** 1c. blue 30 60
O38 2c. blue 30 60
O39 5c. blue 30 70
O40 10c. blue 30 75
O41 20c. blue 35 90
O42 50c. blue . . . . 35 1·10
O43 1p. blue . . . . 40 1·75
O44 2p. blue . . . . 40 2·75
O45 5p. blue . . . . 45 6·00
O46 10p. blue . . . . 45 11·50

1891. Stamps of 1891.
O47 **7** 1c. green 15 40
O48 2c. green 15 40
O49 5c. green 15 40
O50 10c. green 15 40
O51 20c. green 15 70
O52 50c. green 15 75
O53 1p. green 15 90
O54 2p. green 15 90
O55 5p. green . . . . 15 2·25
O56 10p. green . . . . 15 3·50

1892. Stamps of 1892.
O57 **8** 1c. brown 15 30
O58 2c. brown 15 30
O59 5c. brown 15 30
O60 10c. brown 15 30
O61 20c. brown 15 50
O62 50c. brown 15 70
O63 1p. brown . . . . 15 1·10
O64 2p. brown . . . . 15 1·75
O65 5p. brown . . . . 15 2·75
O66 10p. brown . . . . 15 3·50

1893. Stamps of 1893.
O67 **9** 1c. black 15 30
O68 2c. black 15 30
O69 5c. black 15 30
O70 10c. black 15 30
O71 20c. black 15 50
O72 25c. black 15 65
O73 50c. black 15 70
O74 1p. black . . . . 15 1·00
O75 2p. black . . . . 15 1·25
O76 5p. black . . . . 15 2·75
O77 10p. black . . . . 15 3·50

1894. Stamps of 1894.
O78 **10** 1c. orange 15 30
O79 2c. orange 15 30
O80 5c. orange 15 30
O81 10c. orange 15 30
O82 20c. orange 15 30
O83 50c. orange 15 45
O84 1p. orange . . . . 15 1·00
O85 2p. orange . . . . 15 1·75
O86 5p. orange . . . . 15 3·50
O87 10p. orange . . . . . . 15 4·50

1895. Stamps of 1895.
O88 **11** 1c. green 15 30
O89 2c. green 15 30
O90 5c. green 15 30
O91 10c. green 15 30
O92 20c. green 15 50
O93 50c. green 15 80
O94 1p. green 15 80
O95 2p. green . . . . 15 1·25
O96 5p. green . . . . 15 1·90
O97 10p. green . . . . 15 2·40

1896. Stamps of 1896, dated "1896", optd **FRANQUEO OFICIAL** in oval frame.
O 99 **12** 1c. red . . . . 1·50 1·90
O100 2c. red . . . . 1·50 1·90
O101 5c. red . . . . 1·50 1·90
O102 10c. red . . . . 1·50 1·90
O103 20c. red . . . . 1·90 1·90
O104 50c. red . . . . 3·00 3·00
O105 1p. red . . . . 7·25 7·25
O106 2p. red . . . . 7·25 7·25
O107 5p. red . . . . 9·50 9·50

1896. Nos. D99/103 handstamped **Franqueo Oficial**.
O108 **D 13** 1c. orange . . . . . . — 4·25
O109 2c. orange . . . . . . — 4·25
O110 5c. orange . . . . . . — 3·00
O111 10c. orange . . . . . . — 3·00
O112 20c. orange . . . . . . — 3·00

1897. Stamps of 1897, dated "1897", optd **FRANQUEO OFICIAL** in oval frame.
O113 **12** 1c. red . . . . 2·00 2·00
O114 2c. red . . . . 2·00 2·00
O115 5c. red . . . . 2·00 2·00
O116 10c. red . . . . 1·90 2·10
O117 20c. red . . . . 1·90 2·40
O118 50c. red . . . . 3·00 3·00
O119 1p. red . . . . 8·25 8·25
O120 2p. red . . . . 9·75 9·75
O121 5p. red . . . . 15·00 15·00

1898. Stamps of 1898 optd **FRANQUEO OFICIAL** in oval frame.
O124 **13** 1c. red . . . . 2·00 2·00
O125 2c. red . . . . 2·00 2·00
O126 4c. red . . . . 2·00 2·00
O127 5c. red . . . . 1·50 1·50
O128 10c. red . . . . 2·40 2·40
O129 15c. red . . . . 3·75 3·75
O130 20c. red . . . . 3·75 3·75
O131 50c. red . . . . 5·00 5·00
O132 1p. red . . . . 6·50 6·50
O133 2p. red . . . . 6·50 6·50
O134 5p. red . . . . 6·50 6·50

1899. Stamps of 1899 optd **FRANQUEO OFICIAL** in scroll.
O137 **14** 1c. green 15 60
O138 2c. brown 15 60
O139 4c. red 15 60
O140 5c. blue 15 40
O141 10c. orange 15 60
O142 15c. brown . . . . 15 1·25
O143 20c. green . . . . 15 2·00
O144 50c. red . . . . 15 2·00
O145 1p. orange . . . . 15 6·00
O146 2p. violet . . . . 15 6·00
O147 5p. blue . . . . 15 9·00

O 16

O 38

1900.
O148 **O 16** 1c. purple 45 45
O149 2c. orange 35 35
O150 4c. olive 45 45
O151 5c. blue 90 30
O152 10c. violet 90 25
O153 20c. brown 65 25
O154 50c. lake 90 35
O155 1p. blue . . . . 2·10 1·50
O156 2p. orange . . . . . . 2·40 2·40
O157 5p. black . . . . . . 3·00 3·00

1903. Stamps of 1900 surch **OFICIAL** and value, with or without ornaments.
O197 **15** 1c. on 10c. mauve . . . 1·25 1·50
O198 2c. on 3c. green . . . . 1·50 1·90
O199 4c. on 3c. green . . . . 5·75 5·75
O200 4c. on 10c. mauve . . . 5·75 5·75
O201 5c. on 3c. green 70 70

1903. Surch.
O202 **O 16** 10c. on 20c. brown . . 15 15
O203 30c. on 20c. brown . . 15 15
O204 50c. on 20c. brown . . 35 25

1905.
O219 **O 38** 1c. green 20 20
O220 2c. red 20 20
O221 5c. blue 20 20
O222 10c. brown 20 20
O223 20c. orange 20 20
O224 50c. olive 20 20
O225 1p. lake 20 20
O226 2p. violet 20 20
O227 5p. black 20 20

1907. Surch **Vale 10 c**.
O239 **O 38** 10c. on 1c. green . . . 55 55
O241 10c. on 2c. red . . . . 15·00 11·50
O243 20c. on 2c. red . . . . 13·50 9·00
O245 50c. on 1c. green . . . 1·10 1·10
O247 50c. on 2c. red . . . . 13·50 6·50

1907. Surch **Vale 20 cts** or **Vale $1.00**.
O249 **O 38** 20c. on 1c. green . . . 70 70
O250 $1 on 2c. red . . . . 1·10 1·10
O251 $2 on 2c. red . . . . 1·10 1·10
O252 $3 on 2c. red . . . . 1·10 1·10
O253 $4 on 5c. blue . . . . 1·40 1·40

1907. No. 206 surch **OFICIAL** and value.
O256 **49** 10c. on 1c. green . . . . 9·00 7·75
O257 15c. on 1c. green . . . . 9·00 7·75
O258 20c. on 1c. green . . . . 9·00 7·75
O259 50c. on 1c. green . . . . 9·00 7·75
O260 1p. on 1c. green . . . . 8·25 7·75
O261 2p. on 1c. green . . . . 8·25 7·75

1907. Fiscal stamps as T **50** surch **10 cts. CORREOS 1907 OFICIAL 10 CTS**.
O262 **50** 10c. on 2c. orange . . . 10 10
O263 35c. on 1c. blue 10 10
O264 70c. on 1c. blue 10 10
O266 1p. on 2c. orange 10 15
O267 2p. on 2c. orange 10 15
O268 3p. on 5c. brown 10 15
O269 4p. on 5c. brown 15 15
O270 5p. on 5c. brown 15 15

1908. Stamp of 1905 surch **OFICIAL VALE** and value.
O271 **37** 10c. on 3c. violet . . . . 9·00 7·75
O272 15c. on 3c. violet . . . . 9·00 7·75
O273 20c. on 3c. violet . . . . 9·00 7·75
O274 35c. on 3c. violet . . . . 9·00 7·75
O275 50c. on 3c. violet . . . . 9·00 7·75

1908. Fiscal stamps as T **50** surch as last but dated 1908.
O276 **50** 10c. on 1c. blue 55 35
O277 10c. on 2c. orange . . . 75 30
O278 35c. on 1c. blue 55 35
O279 35c. on 2c. orange . . . 80 45
O280 50c. on 1c. blue 55 35
O281 50c. on 2c. orange . . . 80 45
O282 70c. on 2c. orange . . . 80 45
O283 1p. on 1c. blue . . . . . 23·00 23·00
O284 1p. on 2c. orange 80 45
O285 2p. on 1c. blue 65 55
O286 2p. on 2c. orange 80 45

1909. Stamps of 1905 optd **OFICIAL**.
O290 **37** 10c. lake 15 15
O291 15c. black 45 35
O292 20c. olive 70 55
O293 50c. green . . . . 1·10 70
O294 1p. yellow . . . . 1·25 90
O295 2p. red . . . . 1·75 1·40

1911. Stamps of 1905 optd **OFICIAL** and surch **Vale** and value.
O296 **37** 5c. on 3c. orange . . . . 3·75 3·75
O297 10c. on 4c. violet . . . . 3·00 3·00

1911. Railway tickets, surch **Timbre Fiscal Vale 10 ctvs.** further surch for official postal use. Printed in red. (a) Surch [illegible] front.
O334 **64** 10c. on 10c. on 1st class 5·25 4·50
O335 15c. on 10c. on 1st class 5·25 4·50
O336 20c. on 10c. on 1st class 5·25 4·50
O337 50c. on 10c. on 1st class 7·00 6·25
O338 $1 on 10c. on 1st class 8·00 11·00
O339 $2 on 10c. on 1st class 11·50 16·00

(b) Surch **CORREO OFICIAL** and new value on front.
O340 **64** 10c. on 10c. on 1st class 30·00 27·00
O341 15c. on 10c. on 1st class 30·00 27·00
O342 20c. on 10c. on 1st class 30·00 28·00
O343 50c. on 10c. on 1st class 27·00 24·00

(c) No. 322 surch on front **Correo Oficial Vale 1911** and new value and with **15 cts.** on back obliterated by heavy bar.
O344 **64** 5c. on 10c. on 1st class 10·00 9·50
O345 10c. on 10c. on 1st class 11·50 11·00
O346 15c. on 10c. on 1st class 13·00 12·00
O347 20c. on 10c. on 1st class 15·00 18·00
O348 50c. on 10c. on 1st class 17·00 16·00

(d) No. 322 surch on front **Correo Oficial 1912** and new value and with the whole surch on back obliterated.
O349 **64** 5c. on 10c. on 1st class 12·00 9·50
O350 10c. on 10c. on 1st class 12·00 9·50
O351 15c. on 10c. on 1st class 12·00 9·50
O352 20c. on 10c. on 1st class 12·00 9·50
O353 25c. on 10c. on 1st class 12·00 9·50
O354 50c. on 10c. on 1st class 12·00 9·50
O355 $1 on 10c. on 1st class 12·00 9·50

1913. Stamps of 1912 optd **OFICIAL**.
O356 **70** 1c. blue 10 10
O357 2c. blue 10 10
O358 3c. blue 10 10
O359 4c. blue 10 10
O360 5c. blue 10 10
O361 6c. blue 10 15
O362 10c. blue 10 15
O363 15c. blue 10 15
O364 20c. blue 15 20
O365 25c. blue 15 15
O366 **71** 35c. blue 20 20
O367 **70** 50c. blue . . . . 1·10 1·10
O368 1p. blue 25 25
O369 2p. blue 25 25
O370 5p. blue 35 35

1915. Optd **OFICIAL**.
O406 **79** 1c. blue 15 15
O407 **80** 2c. blue 15 15
O408 **79** 3c. blue 15 15
O409 **80** 4c. blue 15 15
O410 **79** 5c. blue 15 15
O411 **80** 6c. blue 15 15
O412 10c. blue 15 15
O413 **79** 15c. blue 15 15
O414 **80** 20c. blue 15 15
O415 **79** 25c. blue 25 25
O416 **80** 50c. blue 45 45

1925. Optd **Oficial** or **OFICIAL**.
O513 **79** ½c. green 10 10
O514 1c. violet 10 10
O515 **80** 2c. red 10 10
O516 **79** 3c. olive 10 10
O517 **80** 4c. red 10 10
O518 **79** 5c. black 10 10
O519 **80** 6c. brown 10 10
O520 10c. yellow 10 10
O521 **79** 15c. brown 10 10

O522	80	20c. brown	10	10
O523	79	25c. orange	40	40
O524	80	50c. blue	45	45

1929. Air. Official stamps of 1925 additionally optd **Correo Aereo**.

O618	79	25c. orange	35	35
O619	80	50c. blue	55	55

1931. Stamp of 1924 surch **OFICIAL C$ 0.05 Correos 1928**.

O651	99	5c. on 10c. brown	25	25

1931. No. 648 additionally surch **OFICIAL** and value.

O652	99	5c. on 10c. brown	25	25

1931. Stamps of 1914 optd **1931** (except 6c., 10c.), and also optd **OFICIAL**.

O670	79	1c. olive (No. 762)	20	20
O707	80	2c. red	6·50	6·50
O671	79	3c. blue	20	20
O672		5c. sepia	20	20
O673	80	6c. brown	25	25
O675		10c. brown	25	25
O674		10c. blue (No. 697)	1·10	1·10
O710	79	15c. orange	70	70
O711		25c. sepia	70	70
O712		25c. violet	1·75	1·75

1932. Air. Optd **Correo Aereo OFICIAL** only.

O688	79	15c. orange	45	45
O689	80	20c. orange	50	50
O690	79	25c. violet	50	50
O691	80	50c. green	60	60
O692		1cor. yellow	60	60

1932. Air. Optd **1931 Correo Aereo OFICIAL**.

O693	79	25c. sepia	25·00	25·00

1932. Optd **OFICIAL**.

O694	79	1c. olive	10	10
O695	80	2c. red	10	10
O696	79	3c. blue	15	10
O697	80	4c. blue	15	10
O698	79	5c. sepia	15	15
O699	80	6c. brown	20	10
O700		10c. brown	30	25
O701	79	15c. orange	40	25
O702	80	20c. orange	40	30
O703	79	25c. violet	1·25	50
O704	80	50c. green	15	15
O705		1cor. yellow	20	20

1933. 441st Anniv of Columbus's Departure from Palos. As T **133**, but inscr "CORREO OFICIAL". Roul.

O777		1c. yellow	60	60
O778		2c. yellow	60	60
O779		3c. brown	60	60
O780		4c. brown	60	60
O781		5c. brown	60	60
O782		6c. blue	75	75
O783		10c. violet	75	75
O784		15c. purple	75	75
O785		20c. green	75	75
O786		25c. green	1·75	1·75
O787		50c. red	2·25	2·25
O788		1cor. red	3·50	3·50

1933. Optd with T **134** and **OFICIAL**.

O814	79	1c. green	10	10
O815	80	2c. red	10	10
O816	79	3c. blue	10	10
O817	80	4c. blue	10	10
O818	79	5c. brown	10	10
O819	80	6c. grey	10	10
O820		10c. brown	10	10
O821	79	15c. red	15	15
O822	80	20c. orange	15	15
O823	79	25c. violet	15	15
O824	80	50c. green	25	25
O825		1cor. yellow	50	45

1933. Air. Optd with T **134** and **CORREO Aereo OFICIAL**.

O826	79	15c. violet	20	20
O827	80	20c. green	20	20
O828	79	25c. olive	20	20
O829	80	50c. green	35	35
O830		1cor. red	60	50

1935. Nos. O814/25 optd **RESELLO – 1935** in a box.

O864	79	1c. green	10	10
O865	80	2c. red	10	10
O866	79	3c. blue	10	10
O867	80	4c. blue	10	10
O868	79	5c. brown	10	10
O869	80	6c. grey	10	10
O870		10c. brown	10	10
O871	79	15c. red	15	15
O872	80	20c. orange	15	15
O873	79	25c. violet	15	15
O874	80	50c. green	20	20
O875		1cor. yellow	35	35

1935. Air. Nos. O826/30 optd **RESELLO – 1935** in a box.

O877	79	15c. violet	30	25
O878	80	20c. green	30	25
O879	79	25c. olive	30	30
O880	80	50c. green	90	90
O881		1cor. red	90	90

(O **141**)

O **151** Islets in the Great Lake

1937. Nos. 913, etc, optd with Type O **141**.

O935	79	1c. red	25	15
O936	80	2c. blue	25	15
O937	79	3c. brown	30	25
O938		5c. red	35	30
O939	80	10c. green	40	35
O940	79	15c. green	50	40
O941		25c. orange	60	45
O942	80	50c. brown	85	50
O943		1cor. blue	2·25	1·00

1937. Air. Nos. 926/30 optd with Type O **141**.

O944	112	15c. orange	50	35
O945		20c. red	50	35
O946		25c. black	50	45
O947		50c. violet	50	45
O948		1cor. orange	50	45

1939.

O1020	O 151	2c. red	15	15
O1021		3c. blue	15	15
O1022		6c. brown	15	15
O1023		7½c. green	15	15
O1024		10c. brown	15	15
O1025		15c. orange	15	15
O1026		25c. violet	30	30
O1027		50c. green	45	45

O **152** Pres. Somoza

1939. Air.

O1028	O 152	10c. brown	30	30
O1029		15c. blue	30	30
O1030		20c. yellow	30	30
O1031		25c. violet	30	30
O1032		30c. red	30	30
O1033		50c. orange	40	40
O1034		1cor. olive	75	75

O **175** Managua Airport

1947. Air.

O1120	O 175	5c. brown and black	15	10
O1121	–	10c. blue and black	15	15
O1122	–	15c. violet and black	15	10
O1123	–	20c. orange & black	20	10
O1124	–	25c. blue and black	15	15
O1125	–	50c. red and black	15	15
O1126	–	1cor. grey and black	40	35
O1127	–	2cor.50 brown and black	75	90

DESIGNS: 10c. Sulphur lagoon, Nejapa; 15c. Ruben Dario Monument, Managua; 20c. Baird's tapir; 25c. Genizaro Dam; 50c. Thermal baths, Tipitapa; 1cor. Highway and Lake Managua; 2cor.50, Franklin D. Roosevelt Monument, Managua.

O **181** U.P.U. Offices, Berne

1950. Air. 75th Anniv of U.P.U. Inscr as in Type O **181**. Frames in black.

O1159	–	5c. purple	10	10
O1160	–	10c. green	10	10
O1161	–	25c. purple	10	10
O1162	O 181	50c. orange	15	10
O1163	–	1cor. blue	35	30
O1164	–	2cor.60 black	2·10	1·75

DESIGNS—HORIZ: 5c. Rowland Hill; 10c. Heinrich von Stephan; 25c. Standehaus, Berne; 1cor. Monument, Berne; 2cor.60, Congress Medal.

1961. Air. Consular Fiscal stamps as T **203/4** with serial Nos. in red, surch **Oficial Aereo** and value.

O1448		10c. on 1cor. olive	10	10
O1449		15c. on 20cor. brown	10	10
O1450		20c. on 100cor. lake	10	10
O1451		25c. on 50c. blue	15	10
O1452		35c. on 50cor. brown	15	15
O1453		50c. on 3cor. red	15	15
O1454		1cor. on 2cor. green	25	20
O1455		2cor. on 5cor. red	25	45
O1456		5cor. on 10cor. violet	60	60

POSTAGE DUE STAMPS

D **13**

D **16**

1896.

D 99	D 13	1c. orange	45	1·10
D100		2c. orange	45	1·10
D101		5c. orange	45	1·10
D102		10c. orange	45	1·10
D103		20c. orange	45	1·10
D104		30c. orange	45	1·10
D105		50c. orange	45	1·40

1897.

D108	D 13	1c. violet	45	1·10
D109		2c. violet	45	1·10
D110		5c. violet	45	1·10
D111		10c. violet	45	1·10
D112		20c. violet	75	1·25
D113		30c. violet	45	90
D114		50c. violet	45	90

1898.

D124	D 13	1c. green	15	1·25
D125		2c. green	15	1·25
D126		5c. green	15	1·25
D127		10c. green	15	1·25
D128		20c. green	15	1·25
D129		30c. green	15	1·25
D130		50c. green	15	1·25

1899.

D137	D 13	1c. red	15	1·25
D138		2c. red	15	1·25
D139		5c. red	15	1·25
D140		10c. red	15	1·25
D141		20c. red	15	1·25
D142		50c. red	15	1·25

1900.

D146	D 16	1c. red	70	
D147		2c. orange	70	
D148		5c. blue	70	
D149		10c. violet	70	
D150		20c. brown	70	
D151		30c. green	1·40	
D152		50c. lake	1·40	

NIGER Pt. 6; Pt. 14

Area south of the Sahara. In 1920 was separated from Upper Senegal and Niger to form a separate colony. From 1944 to 1959 used the stamps of French West Africa.

In 1958 Niger became an autonomous republic within the French Community and on 3 August 1960 an independent republic.

100 centimes = 1 franc.

1921. Stamps of Upper Senegal and Niger optd **TERRITOIRE DU NIGER**.

1	7	1c. violet and purple	10	2·50
2		2c. purple and grey	10	2·25
3		4c. blue and black	15	2·50
4		5c. chocolate and brown	15	2·25
5		10c. green and light green	1·10	2·75
25		10c. pink on blue	10	2·25
6		15c. yellow and brown	50	2·00
7		20c. black and purple	40	2·25
8		25c. green and black	40	2·50
9		30c. carmine and red	1·75	3·00
26		30c. red and green	45	2·75
10		35c. violet and red	70	2·50
11		40c. red and grey	80	2·50
12		45c. brown and blue	35	3·00
13		50c. blue and ultramarine	1·50	2·75
27		50c. blue and grey	45	3·00
28		60c. red	35	2·75
14		75c. brown and yellow	60	3·50
15		1f. purple and brown	50	3·00
16		2f. blue and green	70	3·50
17		5f. black and violet	90	3·75

1922. Stamps of 1921 surch.

18	7	25c. on 15c. yellow & brown	50	3·00
19		25c. on 2f. blue and green	1·75	2·75
20		25c. on 5f. black and violet	1·40	2·75
21		60 on 75c. violet on pink	15	2·25
22		65 on 45c. brown and blue	1·60	3·75
23		85c. on 75c. brown & yellow	1·10	3·75
24		1f.25 on 1f. light blue & blue	55	3·25

3 Wells

5 Zinder Fort

4 Canoe on River Niger

1926.

29	3	1c. green and purple	10	1·25
30		2c. red and grey	10	2·50
31		3c. brown and mauve	10	2·75
32		4c. black and brown	20	2·75
33		5c. green and red	75	2·25
34		10c. green and blue	10	1·25
35		15c. light green and green	35	2·25
36		15c. red and lilac	10	2·25
37	4	20c. brown and blue	15	2·50
38		25c. pink and black	85	2·25
39		30c. light green and green	1·90	2·75
40		30c. mauve and yellow	75	2·50
41		35c. blue and red on blue	55	2·25
42		35c. green and deep green	1·40	2·75
43		40c. grey and purple	15	2·25
44		45c. mauve and yellow	1·10	3·00
45		45c. green and turquoise	1·10	3·25
46		50c. green and red on green	15	45
47		55c. brown and red	1·60	3·25
48		60c. brown and red	35	3·00
49		65c. red and green	1·25	2·75
50		70c. red and green	1·90	3·25
51		75c. mauve and green on pink	1·40	3·00
52		80c. green and purple	2·25	3·50
53		90c. red and carmine	1·10	3·25
54		90c. green and red	1·50	3·00
55	5	1f. green and red	4·50	7·00
56		1f. orange and red	1·60	1·25
57		1f. red and green	1·00	3·00
58		1f.10 green and brown	4·00	4·75
59		1f.25 red and green	1·25	2·25
60		1f.25 orange and red	2·00	3·00
61		1f.40 brown and mauve	2·00	3·00
62		1f.50 light blue and blue	1·60	2·00
63		1f.60 green and brown	2·00	3·25
64		1f.75 brown and mauve	1·90	3·75
65		1f.75 ultramarine and blue	1·75	3·25
66		2f. brown and orange	1·25	2·00
67		2f.25 ultramarine and blue	2·00	3·25
68		2f.50 brown	2·00	3·25
69		3f. grey and mauve	1·50	2·00
70		5f. black and purple on pink	90	2·50
71		10f. mauve and lilac	1·25	3·25
72		20f. orange and green	1·60	3·25

1931. "Colonial Exhibition" key types inscr "NIGER".

73	E	40c. green	2·25	2·25
74	F	50c. mauve	2·00	2·25
75	G	90c. red	2·50	2·75
76	H	1f.50 blue	2·50	2·75

1937. International Exhibition, Paris. As Nos. 71/6 of Mauritania.

77		20c. violet	45	3·00
78		30c. green	1·00	3·50
79		40c. red	75	3·00
80		50c. brown and agate	75	2·75
81		90c. red	85	3·25
82		1f.50 blue	55	2·75

1938. Int Anti-cancer Fund. As T **22** of Mauritania.

83		1f.75+50c. blue	6·75	21·00

1939. Caillé. As T **27** of Mauritania.

84		90c. orange	40	3·00
85		2f. violet	25	2·00
86		2f.25 blue	25	3·25

1939. New York World's Fair. As T **28** of Mauritania.

87		1f.25 red	1·75	3·25
88		2f.25 blue	45	3·00

1939. 150th Anniv of French Revolution. As T **29** of Mauritania.

89		45c.+25c. green and black	5·00	12·50
90		70c.+30c. brown and black	5·00	12·50
91		90c.+35c. orange and black	6·00	12·50
92		1f.25+1f. red and black	5·50	12·50
93		2f.25+2f. blue and black	6·25	12·50

1940. Air. As T **30** of Mauritania.

94		1f.90 blue	1·60	3·00
95		2f.90 red	95	3·00
96		4f.50 green	1·75	3·25
97		4f.90 olive	95	3·25
98		6f.90 orange	1·00	3·00

1941. National Defence Fund. Surch **SECOURS NATIONAL** and additional value.

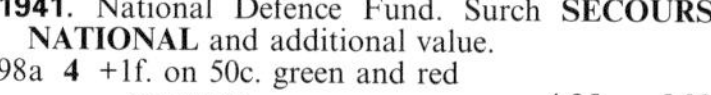

98a	4	+1f. on 50c. green and red on green	4·25	5·00
98b		+2f. on 80c. green & pur	6·25	7·00
98c	5	+2f. on 1f.50 lt blue & bl	9·00	10·50
98d		+3f. on 2f. brown & orge	8·50	10·50

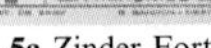

5a Zinder Fort **5c** "Vocation"

5b Weighing Baby

1942. Marshal Petain issue.
98e **5a** 1f. green . . . . 55 2·00
98f 2f.50 blue . . . . 10 2·00

1942. Air. Colonial Child Welfare Fund.
98g – 1f.50+3f.50 green . . . . 20 3·25
98h – 2f.+6f. brown . . . . . . 20 3·25
98i **5b** 3f.+9f. red . . . . 50 3·25
DESIGNS: 49 × 28 mm: 1f.50, Maternity Hospital, Dakar; 2f. Dispensary, Mopti.

1942. Air. Imperial Fortnight.
98j **5c** 1f.20+1f.80 blue and red . . 15 3·25

1942. Air. As T **32** of Mauritania but inscr "NIGER" at foot.
98k 50f. red and yellow . . . . . 1·75 3·50

7 Giraffes

8 Carmine Bee Eater

1959. Wild Animals and Birds. Inscr "PROTECTION DE LA FAUNE".
99 – 50c. turquoise, green and black (postage) . . . . . 1·40 1·75
100 – 1f. multicoloured 40 90
101 – 2f. multicoloured 40 90
102 – 5f. mauve, black and brown 50 65
103 – 7f. red, black and green . . 95 95
104 – 10f. multicoloured . . . . . 1·75 1·75
105 – 15f. sepia and turquoise . . 1·75 1·75
106 – 20f. black and violet . . . . 1·75 1·40
107 **7** 25f. multicoloured . . . . . 2·00 1·50
108 30f. brown, bistre and green 2·00 1·75
109 – 50f. blue and brown . . . . 3·50 1·75
110 – 60f. sepia and green . . . . 4·50 2·75
111 – 85f. brown and bistre . . . 4·75 2·50
112 – 100f. bistre and green . . . 6·25 2·75
113 **8** 200f. multicoloured (air) . . 20·00 7·00
114 – 500f. green, brown and blue 17·00 12·50
DESIGNS—As Type **7**: HORIZ: 50c., 10f. African manatee. VERT: 1, 2f. Crowned cranes; 5, 7f. Saddle-bill stork; 15, 20f. Barbary sheep; 50, 60f. Ostriches; 85, 100f. Lion. As Type **8**: VERT: 500f. Game animals.

1960. 10th Anniv of African Technical Co-operation Commission. As T **4** of Malagasy Republic.
115 25f. brown and ochre . . . . 1·75 2·25

9 Conseil de l'Entente Emblem **11** Pres. Diori Hamani

1960. 1st Anniv of Conseil de l'Entente.
116 **9** 25f. multicoloured . . . . . 1·25 2·25

1960. Independence. No. 112 surch **200 F Independance 3-8-60.**
117 200f. on 100f. bistre and green . . . . 9·00 9·00

1960.
118 **11** 25f. black and bistre . . . 35 25

12 U.N. Emblem and Niger Flag

1961. Air. 1st Anniv of Admission into U.N.
119 **12** 25f. red, green and orange 40 25
120 100f. green, red and emerald . . . . 1·40 90

1962. Air. "Air Afrique" Airline. As T **42** of Mauritania.
121 100f. violet, black and brown 1·50 75

1962. Malaria Eradication. As T **43** of Mauritania.
122 25f.+5f. brown 45 45

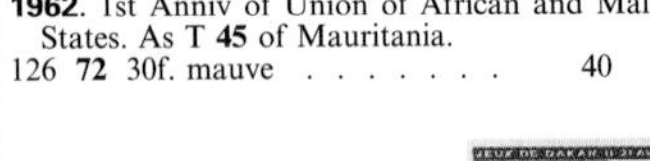
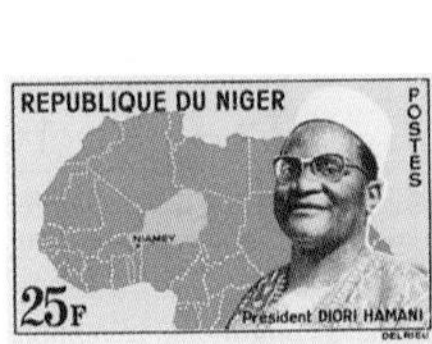

13 Athletics

1962. Abidjan Games, 1961. Multicoloured.
123 15f. Boxing and cycling (vert) 25 15
124 25f. Basketball and football (vert) 25 20
125 85f. Type **13** . . . . 1·10 55

1962. 1st Anniv of Union of African and Malagasy States. As T **45** of Mauritania.
126 **72** 30f. mauve 40 30

14 Pres. Hamani and Map **15** Running

1962. 4th Anniv of Republic.
127 **14** 25f. multicoloured 35 25

1963. Freedom from Hunger. As T **51** of Mauritania.
128 25f.+5f. purple, brn & olive 55 55

1963. Dakar Games.
129 – 15f. brown and blue . . . 25 15
130 **15** 25f. red and brown 35 20
131 – 45f. black and green . . . 70 40
DESIGNS—HORIZ: 15f. Swimming. VERT: 45f. Volleyball.

16 Agadez Mosque

1963. Air. 2nd Anniv of Admission to U.P.U. Multicoloured.
132 50f. Type **16** 75 40
133 85f. Gaya Bridge . . . . . . 1·25 60
134 100f. Presidential Palace, Niamey . . . . 1·25 70

17 Wood-carving

1963. Traditional Crafts. Multicoloured.
135 5f. Type **17** (postage) 15 15
136 10f. Skin-tanning (horiz) . . 20 15
137 25f. Goldsmith 40 20
138 30f. Mat-making (horiz) . . . 60 30
139 85f. Potter . . . . 1·40 80
140 100f. Canoe building (horiz) (47 × 27 mm) (air) . . . . 2·00 1·10

1963. Air. African and Malagasy Posts and Telecommunications Union. As T **56** of Mauritania.
141 85f. multicoloured 95 55

1963. Air. Red Cross Centenary. Optd with cross and **Centenaire de la Croix-Rouge** in red.
142 **12** 25f. red, green and orange 60 40
143 100f. green, red and emerald . . . . 1·40 85

19 Costume Museum

1963. Opening of Costume Museum, Niamey. Vert costume designs. Multicoloured.
144 15f. Berber woman 20 15
145 20f. Haussa woman 35 15
146 25f. Tuareg woman 45 20
147 30f. Tuareg man 55 20
148 60f. Djerma woman . . . . 1·25 50
149 85f. Type **19** . . . . 1·50 60

20 "Europafrique" **22** Man and Globe

21 Groundnut Cultivation

1963. Air. European–African Economic Convention.
150 **20** 50f. multicoloured . . . . 2·50 2·00

1963. Air. Groundnut Cultivation Campaign.
151 **21** 20f. blue, brown and green 35 20
152 – 45f. brown, blue and green 75 25
153 – 85f. multicoloured . . . . 1·40 65
154 – 100f. olive, brown and blue 1·50 90
DESIGNS: 45f. Camel transport; 85f. Fastening sacks; 100f. Dispatch of groundnuts by lorry.

1963. Air. 1st Anniv of "Air Afrique" and DC-8 Service Inauguration. As T **59** of Mauritania.
155 50f. multicoloured 70 45

1963. 15th Anniv of Declaration of Human Rights.
156 **22** 25f. blue, brown and green 45 25

23 "Telstar"

1964. Air. Space Telecommunications.
157 **23** 25f. olive and violet . . . 40 20
158 – 100f. green and purple . . 1·10 80
DESIGN: 100f. "Relay".

24 "Parkinsonia aculeata" **25** Statue, Abu Simbel

1964. Flowers. Multicoloured.
159 5f. Type **24** 60 30
160 10f. "Russelia equisetiformis" 50 30
161 15f. "Lantana camara" . . . 1·00 45
162 20f. "Agryeia nervosa" . . . 1·00 45
163 25f. "Luffa cylindrica" . . . 1·00 45
164 30f. "Hibiscus rosa-sinensis" 1·40 60
165 45f. "Plumierai rubra" . . . 2·00 1·25
166 50f. "Catharanthus roseus" 2·00 1·25
167 60f. "Caesalpinia pulcherrima" . . . . . . 3·50 1·50
Nos. 164/7 have "REPUBLIQUE DU NIGER" at the top and the value at bottom right.

1964. Air. Nubian Monuments Preservation.
168 **25** 25f. green and brown . . . 65 45
169 30f. brown and blue . . . 1·00 70
170 50f. blue and purple . . . 2·00 1·25

26 Globe and "Tiros" Satellite

1964. Air. World Meteorological Day.
171 **26** 50f. brown, blue and green 1·10 65

27 Sun Emblem and Solar Flares **28** Convoy of Lorries

1964. International Quiet Sun Years.
172 **27** 30f. red, violet and sepia 50 35

1964. O.M.N.E.S. (Nigerian Mobile Medical and Sanitary Organization) Commemoration.
173 **28** 25f. orange, olive and blue 40 20
174 – 30f. multicoloured 50 20
175 – 50f. multicoloured 80 30
176 – 60f. purple, orange & turq 90 35
DESIGNS: 30f. Tending children; 50f. Tending women; 60f. Open-air laboratory.

29 Rocket, Stars and Stamp Outline

1964. Air. "PHILATEC 1964" Int Stamp Exn, Paris.
177 **29** 50f. mauve and blue . . . 85 60

30 European, African and Symbols of Agriculture and Industry **31** Pres. Kennedy

1964. Air. 1st Anniv of European–African Economic Convention.
178 **30** 50f. multicoloured 65 40

1964. Air. Pres. Kennedy Commemoration.
179 **31** 100f. multicoloured . . . . 1·25 1·10

32 Water-polo

1964. Air. Olympic Games, Tokyo.
180 **32** 60f. brown, deep green and purple 60 50
181 – 85f. brown, blue and red 1·00 60
182 – 100f. blue, red and green 1·25 70
183 – 250f. blue, brown and green . . . . 2·50 1·75
DESIGNS—HORIZ: 85f. Relay-racing. VERT: 100f. Throwing the discus; 250f. Athlete holding Olympic Torch.

1964. French, African and Malagasy Co-operation. As T **68** of Mauritania.
184 50f. brown, orange and violet 65 40

33 Azawak Tuareg Encampment

1964. Native Villages. Multicoloured.
185 15f. Type **33** 20 20
186 20f. Songhai hut 25 20
187 25f. Wogo and Kourtey tents 30 20
188 30f. Djerma hut 40 25
189 60f. Sorkawa fishermen's encampment . . . . 1·00 30
190 85f. Hausa urban house . . . 1·25 50

34 Doctors and Patient and Microscope Slide
35 Abraham Lincoln

1964. Anti-leprosy Campaign.
191 **34** 50f. multicoloured 50 45

1965. Death Centenary of Abraham Lincoln.
192 **35** 50f. multicoloured 60 50

36 Instruction by "Radio-Vision"

1965. "Human Progress". Inscr as in T **36**.
193 **36** 20f. brown, yellow and blue 30 20
194 – 25f. sepia, brown and green 35 20
195 – 30f. purple, red and green 45 25
196 – 50f. purple, blue and brown 70 35
DESIGNS: 25f. Student; 30f. Adult class; 50f. Five tribesmen ("Alphabetization").

37 Ader's Telephone
38 Pope John XXIII

1965. I.T.U. Centenary.
197 **37** 25f. black, lake and green 50 25
198 – 30f. green, purple and red 60 30
199 – 50f. green, purple and red 1·00 50
DESIGNS: 30f. Wheatstone's telegraph; 50f. "Telautographe".

1965. Air. Pope John Commemoration.
200 **38** 100f. multicoloured . . . . 1·40 75

39 Hurdling

1965. 1st African Games, Brazzaville.
201 **39** 10f. purple, green & brown 20 15
202 – 15f. red, brown and grey 30 15
203 – 20f. purple, blue and green 40 20
204 – 30f. purple, green and lake 50 25
DESIGNS—VERT: 15f. Running; 30f. Long-jumping. HORIZ: 20f. Pole-vaulting.

40 "Capture of Cancer" (the Crab)
41 Sir Winston Churchill

1965. Air. Campaign against Cancer.
205 **40** 100f. brown, black & green 1·40 80

1965. Air. Churchill Commemoration.
206 **41** 100f. multicoloured . . . . 1·40 80

42 Interviewing

1965. Radio Club Promotion.
207 **42** 30f. brown, violet and green 30 15
208 – 45f. red, black and buff . . 45 25
209 – 50f. multicoloured 55 30
210 – 60f. purple, blue and ochre 60 40
DESIGNS—VERT: 45f. Recording; 50f. Listening to broadcast. HORIZ: 60f. Listeners' debate.

43 "Agricultural and Industrial Workers"
44 Fair Scene and Flags

1965. Air. International Co-operation Year.
211 **43** 50f. brown, black and bistre 70 35

1965. Air. International Fair, Niamey.
212 **44** 100f. multicoloured . . . . 1·10 70

45 Dr. Schweitzer and Diseased Hands

1966. Air. Schweitzer Commemoration.
213 **45** 50f. multicoloured 80 45

46 "Water Distribution and Control"

1966. Int Hydrological Decade Inauguration.
214 **46** 50f. blue, orange and violet 70 35

47 Weather Ship "France I"

1966. Air. 6th World Meteorological Day.
215 **47** 50f. green, purple and blue 1·50 70

48 White and "Gemini" Capsule

1966. Air. Cosmonauts.
216 **48** 50f. black, brown and green 75 40
217 – 50f. blue, violet and orange 75 40
DESIGN: No. 217, Leonov and "Voskhod" capsule.

49 Head-dress and Carvings

1966. World Festival of Negro Arts, Dakar.
218 **49** 30f. black, brown and green 45 25
219 – 50f. violet, brown and blue 60 35
220 – 60f. lake, violet and brown 70 40
221 – 100f. black, red and blue 1·25 70
DESIGNS: 50f. Carved figures and mosaics; 60f. Statuettes, drums and arch; 100f. Handicrafts and church.

50 "Diamant" Rocket and Gantry
52 Cogwheel Emblem and Hemispheres

51 Goalkeeper saving Ball

1966. Air. French Space Vehicles. Multicoloured designs each showing different satellites.
222 45f. Type **50** 70 40
223 60f. "A 1" (horiz) 80 45
224 90f. "FR 1" (horiz) . . . . . 1·00 50
225 100f. "D 1" (horiz) . . . . . 1·50 75

1966. World Cup Football Championship.
226 – 30f. red, brown and blue 55 25
227 **51** 50f. brown, blue and green 75 35
228 – 60f. blue, purple and bistre 85 50
DESIGNS—VERT: 30f. Player dribbling ball; 60f. Player kicking ball.

1966. Air. Europafrique.
229 **52** 50f. multicoloured 70 45

53 Parachutist

1966. 5th Anniv of National Armed Forces. Mult.
230 20f. Type **53** 35 15
231 30f. Soldiers with standard (vert) 45 20
232 45f. Armoured patrol vehicle (horiz) 70 30

1966. Air. Inauguration of DC-8F Air Services. As T **87** of Mauritania.
233 30f. olive, black and grey . . 60 25

54 Inoculating cattle

1966. Campaign for Prevention of Cattle Plague.
234 **54** 45f. black, brown and blue 1·00 50

55 "Voskhod 1"
56 U.N.E.S.C.O. "Tree"

1966. Air. Astronautics.
235 **55** 50f. blue, indigo and lake 65 35
236 – 100f. violet, blue and lake 1·25 75
DESIGN—HORIZ: 100f. "Gemini 6" and "7".

1966. 20th Anniv of U.N.E.S.C.O.
237 **56** 50f. multicoloured 70 25

57 Japanese Gate, Atomic Symbol and Cancer ("The Crab")
58 Furnace

1966. Air. International Cancer Congress, Tokyo.
238 **57** 100f. multicoloured . . . . 1·40 75

1966. Malbaza Cement Works.
239 **58** 10f. blue, orange and brown 15 10
240 – 20f. blue and green 30 15
241 – 30f. brown, grey and blue 45 20
242 – 50f. indigo, brown and blue 65 30
DESIGNS—HORIZ: 20f. Electrical power-house; 30f. Works and cement silos; 50f. Installation for handling raw materials.

59 Niamey Mosque

1967. Air.
243 **59** 100f. blue, green and grey 1·10 70

60 Durer (self-portrait)

1967. Air. Paintings. Multicoloured.
244 50f. Type **60** 80 60
245 100f. David (self-portrait) . . 1·50 90
246 250f. Delacroix (self-portrait) 3·00 2·00
See also Nos. 271/2 and 277/9.

61 Red-billed Hornbill **62** Bobsleigh Course, Villard-de-Lans

1967. Birds.
247 **61** 1f. bistre, red and green (postage) 25 20
248 – 2f. black, brown and green 25 20
249 – 30f. multicoloured . . . . 1·25 35
249a – 40f. purple, orange and green . . . . 1·40 60
250 – 45f. brown, green and blue . . . . 1·75 35
250a – 65f. yellow, brown & pur 2·00 80
251 – 70f. multicoloured . . . . 2·40 1·00
251a – 250f. blue, purple and green (48 × 27 mm) (air) 7·25 2·25
BIRDS: 2f. Lesser pied kingfishers; 30f. Common gonolek; 40f. Red bishop; 45f., 65f. Little masked weaver; 70f. Chestnut-bellied sandgrouse; 250f. Splendid glossy starlings.

1967. Grenoble—Winter Olympics Town (1968).
252 **62** 30f. brown, blue and green 40 25
253 – 45f. brown, blue and green 60 30
254 – 60f. brown, blue and green 80 50
255 – 90f. brown, blue and green 1·10 65
DESIGNS: 45f. Ski-jump, Autrans; 60f. Ski-jump, St. Nizier du Moucherotte; 90f. Slalom course, Chamrousse.

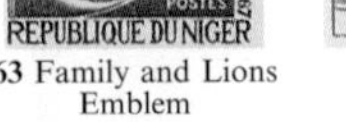

63 Family and Lions Emblem **64** Weather Ship

1967. 50th Anniv of Lions International.
256 **63** 50f. blue, red and green . . 60 35

1967. Air. World Meteorological Day.
257 **64** 50f. red, black and blue . . 1·50 70

65 View of World Fair

1967. Air. World Fair, Montreal.
258 **65** 100f. black, blue and purple . . . . 2·75 75

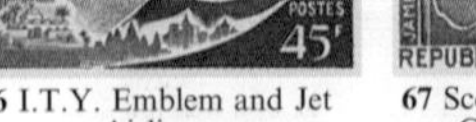

66 I.T.Y. Emblem and Jet Airliner **67** Scouts around Campfire

1967. International Tourist Year.
259 **66** 45f. violet, green and purple 45 35

1967. World Scout Jamboree, Idaho, U.S.A.
260 **67** 30f. brown, lake and blue 40 20
261 – 45f. blue, brown and orange 60 30
262 – 80f. lake, slate and bistre 1·25 50
DESIGNS—HORIZ: 45f. Jamboree emblem and scouts. VERT: 80f. Scout cooking meal.

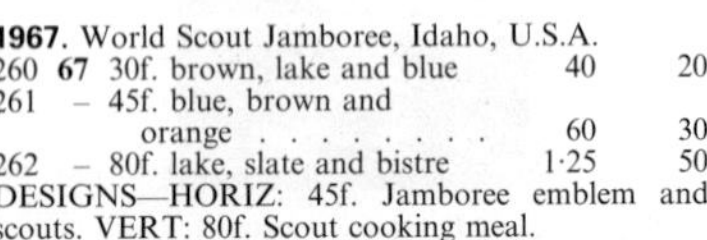

68 Audio-Visual Centre

1967. Air. National Audio-Visual Centre, Niamey.
263 **68** 100f. violet, blue and green 90 50

69 Carrying Patient **70** "Europafrique"

1967. Nigerian Red Cross.
264 **69** 45f. black, red and green 60 20
265 – 50f. black, red and green 75 25
266 – 60f. black, red and green 1·00 35
DESIGNS: 50f. Nurse with mother and child; 60f. Doctor giving injection.

1967. Europafrique.
267 **70** 50f. multicoloured 60 30

71 Dr. Konrad Adenauer **72** African Women

1967. Air. Adenauer Commemoration.
268 **71** 100f. brown and blue . . . 1·40 70

1967. Air. 5th Anniv of African and Malagasy Post and Telecommunications Union (U.A.M.P.T.). As T **101** of Mauritania.
270 100f. violet, green and red . . 1·10 60

1967. Air. Death Centenary of Jean Ingres (painter). Paintings by Ingres. As T **60**. Multicoloured.
271 100f. "Jesus among the Doctors" (horiz) . . . . . 1·60 1·00
272 150f. "Jesus restoring the Keys to St. Peter" (vert) 2·25 1·50

1967. U.N. Women's Rights Commission.
273 **72** 50f. brown, yellow and blue 60 35

1967. 5th Anniv of West African Monetary Union. As T **103** of Mauritania.
274 30f. green and purple 35 20

73 Nigerian Children

1967. Air. 21st Anniv of U.N.I.C.E.F.
275 **73** 100f. brown, blue and green . . . . 1·25 95

74 O.C.A.M. Emblem

1968. Air. O.C.A.M. Conference, Niamey.
276 **74** 100f. orange, green and blue . . . . 1·10 60

1968. Air. Paintings (self-portraits). As T **60**. Multicoloured.
277 50f. J.-B. Corot 70 40
278 150f. Goya . . . . 1·90 1·00
279 200f. Van Gogh . . . . . . 2·50 1·50

75 Allegory of Human Rights

1968. Human Rights Year.
280 **75** 50f. indigo, brown and blue 60 30

76 Breguet 27 Biplane over Lake

1968. Air. 35th Anniv of 1st France–Niger Airmail Service.
281 **76** 45f. blue, green and mauve 95 35
282 – 80f. slate, brown and blue 1·60 55
283 – 100f. black, green and blue 2·50 75
DESIGNS—Potez 25TOE biplane: 80f. On ground; 100f. In flight.

77 "Joyous Health"

1968. 20th Anniv of W.H.O.
284 **77** 50f. indigo, blue and brown 60 35

78 Cyclists of 1818 and 1968

1968. Air. 150th Anniv of Bicycle.
285 **78** 100f. green and red . . . . 1·50 70

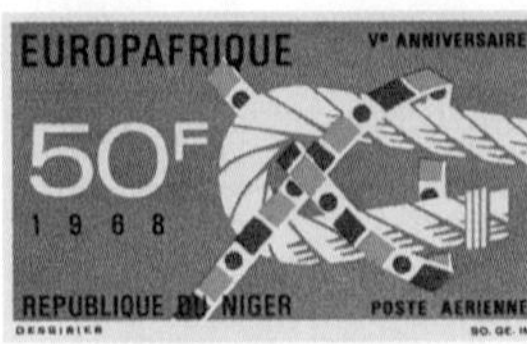

79 Beribboned Rope

1968. Air. 5th Anniv of Europafrique.
286 **79** 50f. multicoloured 65 40

80 Fencing

1968. Air. Olympic Games, Mexico.
287 **80** 50f. purple, violet and green 50 35
288 – 100f. black, purple and blue 85 50
289 – 150f. purple and orange . . 1·25 70
290 – 200f. blue, brown and green . . . . 1·75 1·25
DESIGNS—VERT: 100f. High-diving; 150f. Weight-lifting. HORIZ: 200f. Horse-jumping.

81 Woodland Kingfisher

1969. Birds. Dated "1968". Multicoloured.
292 5f. African grey hornbill (postage) 20 10
293 10f. Type **81** 30 15
294 15f. Senegal coucal 70 25
295 20f. Rose-ringed parakeets . . 85 45
296 25f. Abyssinian roller . . . . 1·10 60
297 50f. Cattle egret . . . . . . 1·60 85
298 100f. Violet starling (27 × 49 mm) (air) . . . . 3·50 1·75
See also Nos. 372/7, 567/8 and 714/15.

82 Mahatma Gandhi

1968. Air. "Apostles of Non-Violence".
299 **82** 100f. black and yellow . . 1·75 60
300 – 100f. black and turquoise 1·00 50
301 – 100f. black and grey . . . 1·00 50
302 – 100f. black and orange . . 1·00 50
PORTRAITS: No. 300, President Kennedy; No. 301, Martin Luther King; No. 302, Robert F. Kennedy.

1968. Air. "Philexafrique" Stamp Exhibition, Abidjan (Ivory Coast, 1969) (1st issue). As T **113a** of Mauritania. Multicoloured.
304 100f. "Pare, Minister of the Interior" (J. L. La Neuville) . . . . 1·60 1·60

83 Arms of the Republic

1968. Air. 10th Anniv of Republic.
305 **83** 100f. multicoloured . . . . 1·00 50

1969. Air. Napoleon Bonaparte. Birth Bicentenary. As T **114b** of Mauritania. Multicoloured.
306 50f. "Napoleon as First Consul" (Ingres) . . . . . 1·50 90
307 100f. "Napoleon visiting the plague victims of Jaffa" (Gros) . . . . 2·50 1·25
308 150f. "Napoleon Enthroned" (Ingres) . . . . 3·50 1·75
309 200f. "The French Campaign" (Meissonier) 5·00 2·50

1969. Air. "Philexafrique" Stamp Exhibition, Abidjan, Ivory Coast (2nd issue). As T **114a** of Mauritania.
310 50f. brown, blue and orange 1·25 1·00
DESIGN: 50f. Giraffes and stamp of 1926.

84 Boeing 707 over Rain-cloud and Anemometer

1969. Air. World Meteorological Day.
311 **84** 50f. black, blue and green 90 35

85 Workers supporting Globe

1969. 50th Anniv of I.L.O.
312 **85** 30f. red and green 40 20
313 50f. green and red 50 35

86 Panhard and Levassor (1909)

1969. Air. Veteran Motor Cars.
314 **86** 25f. green 45 20
315 – 45f. violet, blue and grey 55 25
316 – 50f. brown, ochre and grey 1·10 35
317 – 70f. purple, red and grey 1·50 45
318 – 100f. green, brown and grey . . . . 1·75 65
DESIGNS: 45f. De Dion Bouton 8 (1904); 50f. Opel "Doktor-wagen" (1909); 70f. Daimler (1910); 100f. Vermorel 12/16 (1912).

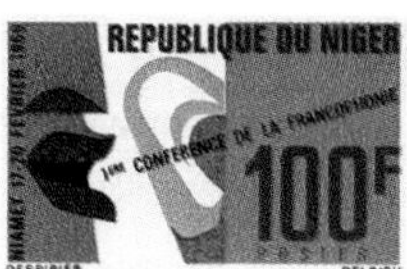

87 Mother and Child **88** Mouth and Ear

1969. 50th Anniv of League of Red Cross Societies.
319 **87** 45f. red, brown and blue 60 25
320 – 50f. red, grey and green . . 70 25
321 – 70f. red, brown and ochre 1·00 40
DESIGNS—VERT: 70f. Man with Red Cross parcel. HORIZ: 50f. Symbolic Figures, Globe and Red Crosses.

1969. 1st French Language Cultural Conf, Niamey.
322 **88** 100f. multicoloured . . . . 1·25 60

89 School Building

1969. National School of Administration.
323 **89** 30f. black, green and orange 30 20

1969. Air. 1st Man on the Moon. No. 114 optd **L'HOMME SUR LA LUNE JUILLET 1969 APOLLO 11** and moon module.
324 500f. green, brown and blue 6·50 6·50

91 "Apollo 8" and Rocket

1969. Air. Moon Flight of "Apollo 8". Embossed on gold foil.
325 **91** 1000f. gold . . . . 15·00 15·00

1969. 5th Anniv of African Development Bank. As T **122a** of Mauritania.
326 30f. brown, green and violet 35 15

92 Child and Toys

1969. Air. International Toy Fair, Nuremburg.
327 **92** 100f. blue, brown and green . . . . 2·75 75

93 Linked Squares

1969. Air. "Europafrique".
328 **93** 50f. yellow, black and violet 55 30

94 Trucks crossing Sahara

1969. Air. 45th Anniv of "Croisiere Noire" Trans-Africa Expedition.
329 **94** 50f. brown, violet & mauve 75 35
330 – 100f. violet, red and blue 1·50 65
331 – 150f. multicoloured . . . . 2·00 1·25
332 – 200f. green, indigo and blue . . . . 3·00 1·50
DESIGNS: 100f. Crossing the mountains; 150f. African children and expedition at Lake Victoria; 200f. Route Map, European greeting African and Citroen truck.

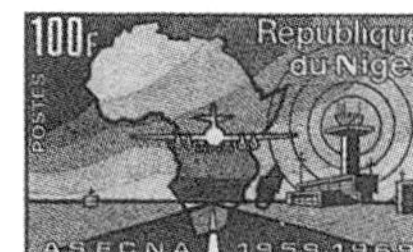

94a Aircraft, Map and Airport

1969. 10th Anniv of Aerial Navigation Security Agency for Africa and Madagascar (A.S.E.C.N.A.).
333 **94a** 100f. red . . . . 1·50 70

95 Classical Pavilion

1970. National Museum.
334 **95** 30f. blue, green and brown 30 15
335 – 45f. blue, green and brown 45 25
336 – 50f. blue, brown and green 50 25
337 – 70f. brown, blue and green 70 40
338 – 100f. brown, blue and green . . . . 1·10 60
DESIGNS: 45f. Temporary exhibition pavilion; 50f. Audio-visual pavilion; 70f. Local musical instruments gallery; 100f. Handicrafts pavilion.

96 Niger Village and Japanese Pagodas **97** Hypodermic "Gun" and Map

1970. Air. "EXPO 70" World Fair, Osaka, Japan (1st issue).
339 **96** 100f. multicoloured 90 45

1970. One Hundred Million Smallpox Vaccinations in West Africa.
340 **97** 50f. blue, purple and green 70 30

98 Education Symbols

1970. Air. International Education Year.
341 **98** 100f. slate, red and purple 1·00 45

99 Footballer

1970. World Cup Football Championship, Mexico.
342 **99** 40f. green, brown and purple 60 25
343 – 70f. purple, brown and blue . . . . 1·00 40
344 – 90f. red and black . . . . 1·25 60
DESIGNS: 70f. Football and Globe; 90f. Two footballers.

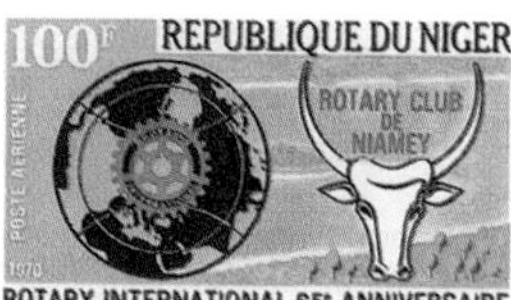

100 Rotary Emblems

1970. Air. 65th Anniv of Rotary International.
345 **100** 100f. multicoloured . . . 1·25 55

101 Bay of Naples and Niger Stamp

1970. Air. 10th "Europafrique" Stamp Exn, Naples.
346 **101** 100f. multicoloured . . . 1·00 60

102 Clement Ader's "Avion III" and Modern Airplane

1970. Air. Aviation Pioneers.
347 **102** 50f. grey, blue and red . . 70 25
348 – 100f. red, grey and blue 1·50 60
349 – 150f. lt brown, brn & grn 1·50 75
350 – 200f. red, bistre and violet 2·25 1·00
351 – 250f. violet, grey and red 3·50 1·40
DESIGNS: 100f. Joseph and Etienne Montgolfier balloon and rocket; 150f. Isaac Newton and gravity diagram; 200f. Galileo and rocket in planetary system; 250f. Leonardo da Vinci's drawing of a "flying machine" and Chanute's glider.

103 Cathode Ray Tube illuminating Books, Microscope and Globe

1970. Air. World Telecommunications Day.
352 **103** 100f. brown, green and red . . . . 1·25 50

1970. Inauguration of New U.P.U. Headquarters Building, Berne. As T **81** of New Caledonia.
353 30f. red, slate and brown . . 35 20
354 60f. violet, red and blue . . . 60 30

1970. Air. Safe Return of "Apollo 13". Nos. 348 and 350 optd **Solidarite Spatiale Apollo XIII 11-17 Avril 1970**.
355 100f. red, slate and blue . . 1·00 50
356 200f. red, bistre and violet . . 1·75 75

105 U.N. Emblem, Man, Woman and Doves

1970. Air. 25th Anniv of U.N.O.
357 **105** 100f. multicoloured . . . 1·00 50
358 150f. multicoloured . . . 1·50 75

106 Globe and Heads

1970. Air. International French Language Conference, Niamey. Die-stamped on gold foil.
359 **106** 250f. gold and blue . . . 2·50 2·50

107 European and African Women

1970. Air. "Europafrique".
360 **107** 50f. red and green 55 30

108 Japanese Girls and "EXPO 70" Skyline

1970. Air. "EXPO 70" World Fair, Osaka, Japan. (2nd issue).
361 **108** 100f. purple, orange & grn 90 40
362 – 150f. blue, brown & green 1·25 60
DESIGN: 150f. "No" actor and "EXPO 70" by night.

109 Gymnast on Parallel Bars **111** Beethoven, Keyboard and Manuscripts

1970. Air. World Gymnastic Championships, Ljubljiana.
363 **109** 50f. blue 50 30
364 – 100f. green . . . . 1·10 55
365 – 150f. purple . . . . . . 1·75 75
366 – 200f. red . . . . 2·00 95
GYMNASTS—HORIZ: 100f. Gymnast on vaulting-horse; 150f. Gymnast in mid-air. VERT: 200f. Gymnast on rings.

1970. Air. Moon Landing of "Luna 16". Nos. 349 and 351 surch **LUNA 16 – Sept. 1970 PREMIERS PRELEVEMENTS AUTOMATIQUES SUR LA LUNE** and value.
367 100f. on 150f. light brown, brown and green . . . . . 1·10 50
368 200f. on 250f. violet, grey and red . . . . 2·40 1·00

1970. Air. Birth Bicentenary of Beethoven. Mult.
369 100f. Type **111** . . . . 1·40 55
370 150f. Beethoven and allegory, "Hymn of Joy" . . . . . 2·25 85

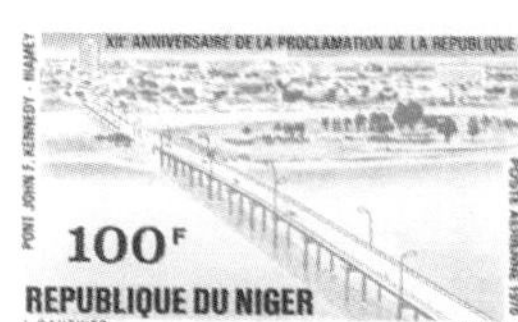

112 John F. Kennedy Bridge, Niamey

1970. Air. 12th Anniv of Republic.
371 **112** 100f. multicoloured . . . 1·10 45

1971. Birds. Designs similar to T **81**. Variously dated between 1970 and 1972. Multicoloured.
372 5f. African grey hornbill . . 65 30
373 10f. Woodland kingfisher . . 85 30
374 15f. Senegal coucal . . . . . 1·75 1·00
375 20f. Rose-ringed parakeet . . 2·10 1·00
376 35f. Broad-tailed paradise whydah . . . . 3·00 1·50
377 50f. Cattle egret . . . . . 3·75 2·75
The Latin inscription on No. 377 is incorrect, reading "Bulbucus ibis" instead of "Bubulcus ibis".
See also Nos. 714/15.

114 Pres. Nasser

1971. Air. Death of Pres. Gamal Nasser (Egyptian statesman). Multicoloured.
378 100f. Type **114** 75 40
379 200f. Nasser waving . . . . 1·50 75

115 Pres. De Gaulle

1971. Air. De Gaulle Commemoration. Embossed on gold foil.
380 **115** 1000f. gold . . . . 38·00 38·00

116 "MUNICH" and Olympic Rings

1971. Air. Publicity for 1972 Olympic Games, Munich.
381 **116** 150f. purple, blue & green 1·25 70

117 "Apollo 14" leaving Moon
118 Symbolic Masks

1971. Air. Moon Mission of "Apollo 14".
382 **117** 250f. green, orange & blue 2·25 1·25

1971. Air. Racial Equality Year.
383 **118** 100f. red, green and blue 90 40
384 – 200f. brown, green & blue 1·75 80
DESIGN: 200f. "Peoples" and clover-leaf emblem.

119 Niamey on World Map

1971. 1st Anniv of French-speaking Countries Co-operative Agency.
385 **119** 40f. multicoloured 50 25

120 African Telecommunications Map

1971. Air. Pan-African Telecommunications Network.
386 **120** 100f. multicoloured . . . 75 40

121 African Mask and Japanese Stamp

1971. Air. "PHILATOKYO 71" International Stamp Exhibition, Japan.
387 **121** 50f. olive, purple and green 65 30
388 – 100f. violet, red and green 1·10 45
DESIGN: 100f. Japanese scroll painting and Niger stamp.

122 "Longwood House, St. Helena" (C. Vernet)

1971. Air. 150th Anniv of Napoleon's Death. Paintings. Multicoloured.
389 150f. Type **122** . . . . 1·75 70
390 200f. "Napoleon's Body on his Camp-bed" (Marryat) 2·50 90

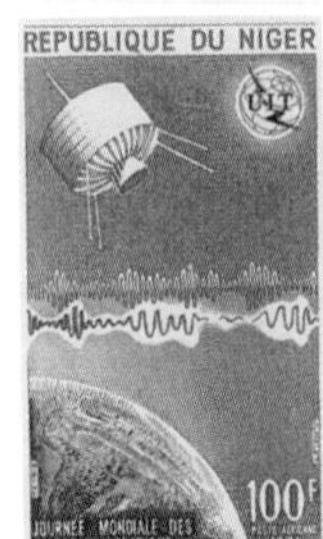

123 Satellite, Radio Waves, and Globe

1971. Air. World Telecommunications Day.
391 **123** 100f. multicoloured . . . 1·10 50

124 Pierre de Coubertin and Discus-throwers

1971. Air. 75th Anniv of Modern Olympic Games.
392 **124** 50f. red and blue 50 25
393 – 100f. multicoloured . . . 90 40
394 – 150f. blue and purple . . 1·40 65
DESIGNS—VERT: 100f. Male and female athletes holding torch. HORIZ: 150f. Start of race.

125 Scout Badges and Mount Fuji

1971. 13th World Scout Jamboree, Asagiri, Japan.
395 **125** 35f. red, purple and orange 40 20
396 – 40f. brown, plum and green 45 20
397 – 45f. green, red and blue 60 25
398 – 50f. green, violet and red 70 30
DESIGNS—VERT: 40f. Scouts and badge; 45f. Scouts converging on Japan. HORIZ: 50f. "Jamboree" in rope, and marquee.

126 "Apollo 15" on Moon

1971. Air. Moon Mission of "Apollo 15".
399 **126** 150f. blue, violet & brown 1·50 70

127 Linked Maps

1971. 2nd Anniv of Renewed "Europafrique" Convention, Niamey.
400 **127** 50f. multicoloured 60 30

128 Gouroumi (Hausa)
129 De Gaulle in Uniform

1971. Musical Instruments.
401 **128** 25f. brown, green and red 30 10
402 – 30f. brown, violet & green 35 15
403 – 35f. blue, green and purple 35 25
404 – 40f. brown, orange & grn 45 25
405 – 45f. ochre, brown and blue 55 35
406 – 50f. brown, red and black 95 45
DESIGNS: 30f. Molo (Djerma); 35f. Garaya (Hausa); 40f. Godjie (Djerma-Sonrai); 45f. Inzad (Tuareg); 50f. Kountigui (Sonrai).

1971. Air. 1st Death Anniv of Gen. Charles De Gaulle (French statesman).
407 **129** 250f. multicoloured . . . 5·00 4·00

1971. Air. 10th Anniv of African and Malagasy Posts and Telecommunications Union. As T **139a** of Mauritania. Multicoloured.
408 100f. U.A.M.P.T. H.Q. and rural scene 90 45

130 "Audience with Al Hariri" (Baghdad, 1237)

1971. Air. Moslem Miniatures. Multicoloured.
409 100f. Type **130** . . . . 1·00 45
410 150f. "Archangel Israfil" (Iraq, 14th-cent) (vert) . . 1·50 70
411 200f. "Horsemen" (Iraq, 1210) . . . . 2·25 1·25

131 Louis Armstrong
132 "Children of All Races"

1971. Air. Death of Louis Armstrong (American jazz musician). Multicoloured.
412 100f. Type **131** . . . . 1·50 55
413 150f. Armstrong playing trumpet . . . . 2·00 85

1971. 25th Anniv of U.N.I.C.E.F.
414 **132** 50f. multicoloured 60 45

133 "Adoration of the Magi" (Di Bartolo)

1971. Air. Christmas. Paintings. Multicoloured.
415 100f. Type **133** . . . . 1·00 45
416 150f. "The Nativity" (D. Ghirlandaio) (vert) . . 1·50 70
417 200f. "Adoration of the Shepherds" (Perugino) . . 2·00 1·00

134 Presidents Pompidou and Hamani

1972. Air. Visit of Pres. Pompidou of France.
418 **134** 250f. multicoloured . . . 4·75 3·50

135 Ski "Gate" and Cherry Blossom

1972. Air. Winter Olympic Games, Sapporo, Japan.
419 **135** 100f. violet, red and green 90 40
420 – 150f. red, purple and violet . . . . 1·25 70
DESIGN—HORIZ: 150f. Snow crystals and Olympic flame.

1972. Air. U.N.E.S.C.O. "Save Venice" Campaign. As T **127** of Mali.
422 50f. multicoloured (vert) . . 50 25
423 100f. multicoloured (vert) . . 1·00 45
424 150f. multicoloured (vert) . . 1·50 70
425 200f. multicoloured . . . . . 2·00 1·00
DESIGNS: Nos. 422/5 depict various details of Guardi's painting, "The Masked Ball".

136 Johannes Brahms and Music
137 Saluting Hand

1972. Air. 75th Death Anniv of Johannes Brahms (composer).
426 **136** 100f. green, myrtle and red . . . . 1·50 55

1972. Air. Int Scout Seminar, Cotonou, Dahomey.
427 **137** 150f. violet, blue & orange . . . . 1·50 60

138 Star Symbol and Open Book

1972. International Book Year.
428 **138** 35f. purple and green . . 35 20
429 – 40f. blue and lake . . . . 1·40 35
DESIGN: 40f. Boy reading, 16th-century galleon and early aircraft.

139 Heart Operation

1972. Air. World Heart Month.
430 **139** 100f. brown and red . . . 1·50 55

140 Bleriot XI crossing the Channel, 1909

1972. Air. Milestones in Aviation History.
431 **140** 50f. brown, blue and lake 1·10 50
432 – 75f. grey, brown and blue 1·75 60
433 – 100f. ultramarine, blue and purple . . . . . . 3·25 1·40
DESIGNS: 75f. Lindbergh crossing the Atlantic in "Spirit of St. Louis"; 100f. First flight of Concorde, 1969.

141 Satellite and Universe

1972. Air. World Telecommunications Day.
434 **141** 100f. brown, purple & red 1·10 45

142 Boxing

1972. Air. Olympic Games, Munich. Sports and Munich Buildings.
435 **142** 50f. brown and blue . . . 50 20
436 – 100f. brown and green . . 75 40
437 – 150f. brown and red . . . 1·25 60
438 – 200f. brown and mauve 1·75 85
DESIGNS—VERT: 100f. Long-jumping; 150f. Football. HORIZ: 200f. Running.

143 A. G. Bell and Telephone

1972. Air. 50th Death Anniv of Alexander Graham Bell (inventor of telephone).
440 **143** 100f. blue, purple and red 1·10 55

144 "Europe on Africa" Map

1972. Air. "Europafrique" Co-operation.
441 **144** 50f. red, green and blue 50 25

145 Herdsman and Cattle **146** Lottery Wheel

1972. Medicinal Salt-ponds at In-Gall. Multicoloured.
442 35f. Type **145** 50 25
443 40f. Cattle in salt-pond . . . 60 25

1972. 6th Anniv of National Lottery.
444 **146** 35f. multicoloured 35 25

147 Postal Runner

1972. Air. U.P.U. Day. Postal Transport.
445 **147** 50f. brown, green and lake 60 25
446 – 100f. green, blue and lake 90 45
447 – 150f. green, violet and lake . . . . 1·75 70
DESIGNS: 100f. Rural mail van; 150f. Loading Fokker Friendship mail plane.

1972. 10th Anniv of West African Monetary Union. As T **149** of Mauritania.
448 40f. grey, violet and brown 40 25

1972. Air. Gold Medal Winners. Munich Olympic Games. Nos. 435/8 optd with events and names, etc.
449 **142** 50f. brown and blue . . . 50 20
450 – 100f. brown and green . . 85 40
451 – 150f. brown and red . . . 1·40 60
452 – 200f. brown and mauve 1·75 80
OVERPRINTS: 50f. **WELTER CORREA MEDAILLE D'OR**; 100f. **TRIPLE SAUT SANEIEV MEDAILLE D'OR**; 150f. **FOOTBALL POLOGNE MEDAILLE D'OR**; 200f. **MARATHON SHORTER MEDAILLE D'OR**.

148 "The Raven and the Fox"

1972. Air. Fables of Jean de la Fontaine.
453 **148** 25f. black, brown & green 1·10 40
454 – 50f. brown, green & purple 60 25
455 – 75f. brown, green & brown . . . . 1·00 45
DESIGNS: 50f. "The Lion and the Rat"; 75f. "The Monkey and the Leopard".

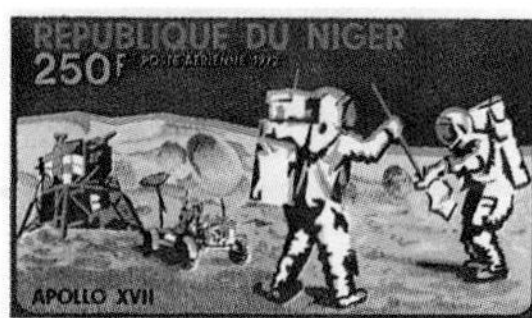

149 Astronauts on Moon

1972. Air. Moon Flight of "Apollo 17".
456 **149** 250f. multicoloured . . . 2·75 1·25

150 Dromedary Race

1972. Niger Sports.
457 **150** 35f. purple, red and blue 75 40
458 – 40f. lake, brown and green . . . . 1·00 60
DESIGN: 40f. Horse race.

151 Pole Vaulting **153** Knight and Pawn

152 "Young Athlete"

1973. 2nd African Games, Lagos, Nigeria. Mult.
459 35f. Type **151** 30 25
460 40f. Basketball 35 25
461 45f. Boxing 45 25
462 75f. Football 70 45

1973. Air. Antique Art Treasures.
463 **152** 50f. red 50 25
464 – 100f. violet . . . . 1·00 40
DESIGN: 100f. "Head of Hermes".

1973. World Chess Championships, Reykjavik, Iceland.
465 **153** 100f. green, blue and red 2·50 1·00

154 "Abutilon pannosum" **155** Interpol Badge

1973. Rare African Flowers. Multicoloured.
466 30f. Type **154** 70 30
467 45f. "Crotalaria barkae" . . 80 30
468 60f. "Dichrostachys cinerea" 1·40 45
469 80f. "Caralluma decaisneana" 1·60 55

1973. 50th Anniv of International Criminal Police Organization (Interpol).
470 **155** 50f. multicoloured 85 30

156 Scout with Radio

1973. Air. Scouting in Niger.
471 **156** 25f. brown, green and red 25 20
472 – 50f. brown, green and red 55 25
473 – 100f. brown, green and red . . . . 1·25 50
474 – 150f. brown, green and red . . . . 2·25 90
DESIGNS: 50f. First aid; 100f. Care of animals; 150f. Care of the environment.

157 Hansen and Microscope **158** Nurse tending Child

1973. Centenary of Dr. Hansen's Discovery of Leprosy Bacillus.
475 **157** 50f. brown, green and blue 85 35

1973. 25th Anniv of W.H.O.
476 **158** 50f. brown, red and blue 65 25

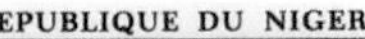

159 "The Crucifixion" (Hugo van der Goes)

1973. Air. Easter. Paintings. Multicoloured.
477 50f. Type **159** 55 25
478 100f. "The Deposition" (Cima de Conegliano) (horiz) . . . . 1·10 50
479 150f. "Pieta" (Bellini) (horiz) 1·60 65

160 Douglas DC-8 and Mail Van

1973. Air. Stamp Day.
480 **160** 100f. brown, red and green . . . . 1·50 55

161 W.M.O. Emblem and "Weather Conditions"

1973. Air. Centenary of W.M.O.
481 **161** 100f. brown, red and green . . . . 1·10 45

REPUBLIQUE DU NIGER

150F

POSTE AERIENNE

162 "Crouching Lioness" (Delacroix)

1973. Air. Paintings by Delacroix. Multicoloured.
482 150f. Type **162** . . . . 2·00 1·00
483 200f. "Tigress and Cub" . . 3·25 1·50

163 Crocodile

1973. Wild Animals from "Park W".
484 **163** 25f. multicoloured 45 20
485 – 35f. grey, gold and black 75 30
486 – 40f. multicoloured 75 30
487 – 80f. multicoloured . . . . 1·25 50
DESIGNS: 35f. African elephant; 40f. Hippopotamus; 80f. Warthog.

164 Eclipse over Mountain

1973. Total Eclipse of the Sun.
488 **164** 40f. violet 60 30

1973. Air. 24th International Scouting Congress, Nairobi, Kenya. Nos. 473/4 optd **24 Conference Mondiale du Scoutisme NAIROBI 1973**.
489 100f. brown, green and red 1·00 40
490 150f. brown, green and red 2·00 90

166 Palomino

1973. Horse-breeding. Multicoloured.
491 50f. Type **166** 90 30
492 75f. French trotter . . . . . 1·40 40
493 80f. English thoroughbred . . 1·50 55
494 100f. Arab thoroughbred . . 2·00 65

1973. Pan-African Drought Relief. African Solidarity. No. 436 surch **SECHERESSE SOLIDARITE AFRICAINE** and value.
495 **145** 100f. on 35f. multicoloured . . . . . 1·40 1·00

168 Rudolf Diesel and Oil Engine

1973. 60th Death Anniv of Rudolf Diesel (engineer).
496 **168** 25f. blue, purple and grey 80 45
497 – 50f. grey, green and blue 1·40 65
498 – 75f. blue, black and mauve . . . . 2·10 1·00
499 – 125f. blue, red and green 3·50 1·25
DESIGNS: 50f. Series "BB 100" diesel locomotive; 75f. Type "060-DB1" diesel locomotive, France; 125f. Diesel locomotive No. 72004, France.

1973. African and Malagasy Posts and Telecommunications Union. As T **155a** of Mauritania.
500 100f. red, green and brown 75 30

168a African Mask and Old Town Hall, Brussels
171 "Apollo"

169 T.V. Set and Class

1973. Air. African Fortnight, Brussels.
501 **168a** 100f. purple, blue and red . . . . 1·00 50

1973. Schools Television Service.
502 **169** 50f. black, red and blue 60 30

1973. 3rd International French Language and Culture Conf, Liege. No. 385 optd **3e CONFERENCE DE LA FRANCOPHONIE LIEGE OCTOBRE 1973**.
503 **110** 40f. multicoloured 50 25

1973. Classical Sculptures.
504 **171** 50f. green and brown . . 60 30
505 – 50f. black and brown . . 60 30
506 – 50f. brown and red . . . 60 30
507 – 50f. purple and red . . . 60 30
DESIGNS: No. 505, "Atlas"; No. 506, "Hercules"; No. 507, "Venus".

172 Bees and Honeycomb

1973. World Savings Day.
508 **172** 40f. brown, red and blue 45 25

173 "Food for the World"

1973. Air. 10th Anniv of World Food Programme.
509 **173** 50f. violet, red and blue 60 30

174 Copernicus and "Sputnik 1"
175 Pres. John Kennedy

1973. Air. 500th Birth Anniv of Copernicus (astonomer).
510 **174** 150f. brown, blue and red 1·40 70

1973. Air. 10th Death Anniv of U.S. President Kennedy.
511 **175** 100f. multicoloured . . . 1·00 50

176 Kounta Songhai Blanket
178 Lenin

177 Barges on River Niger

1973. Niger Textiles. Multicoloured.
513 35f. Type **176** 50 30
514 40f. Tcherka Snghai blanket (horiz) 70 40

1974. Air. 1st Anniv of Ascent of Niger by "Fleet of Hope".
515 **177** 50f. blue, green and red 75 35
516 – 75f. purple, blue and green . . . . 1·00 45
DESIGN: 75f. "Barban Maza" (tug) and barge.

1974. Air. 50th Death Anniv of Lenin.
517 **178** 50c. brown 50 30

179 Slalom Skiing

1974. Air. 50th Anniv of Winter Olympic Games.
518 **179** 200f. red, brown and blue 2·50 1·00

180 Newly-born Baby

1974. World Population Year.
519 **180** 50f. multicoloured 50 25

181 Footballers and "Global" Ball

1974. Air. World Cup Football Championship, West Germany.
520 **181** 75f. violet, black & brown 65 35
521 – 150f. brown, green & turq 1·40 55
522 – 200f. blue, orange & green 1·75 1·00
DESIGNS: 150, 200f. Football scenes similar to Type **181**.

182 "The Crucifixion" (Grunewald)

1974. Air. Easter. Paintings. Multicoloured.
524 50f. Type **182** 50 25
525 75f. "Avignon Pieta" (attributed to E. Quarton) 75 35
526 125f. "The Entombment" (G. Isenmann) . . . . . . 1·25 65

183 Class 230K Locomotive, 1948, France and Locomotive No. 5511, 1938, U.S.A.

1974. Famous Railway Locomotives of the Steam Era.
527 **183** 50f. green, black and violet . . . . 1·25 40
528 – 75f. green, black & brown 1·90 55
529 – 100f. multicoloured . . . 2·50 85
530 – 150f. brown, black and red . . . . 3·75 1·25
DESIGNS: 75f. Class 21 locomotive, 1893, France; 100f. Locomotive, 1866, U.S.A. and "Mallard", Great Britain; 150f. Marc Seguin locomotive, 1829, France and Stephenson's "Rocket", 1829.

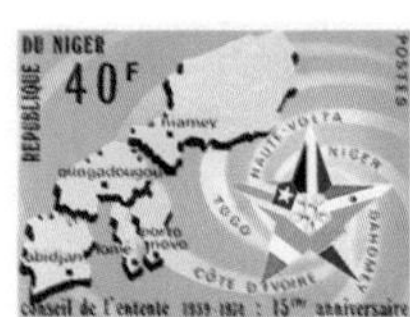
184 Map of Member Countries

1974. 15th Anniv of Conseil de l'Entente.
531 **184** 40f. multicoloured 40 20

185 Knights

1974. Air. 21st Chess Olympiad, Nice.
532 **185** 50f. brown, blue & indigo 1·25 65
533 – 75f. purple, brown & green . . . . 1·75 75
DESIGN: 75f. Kings.

186 Marconi and "Elettra" (steam yacht)

1974. Birth Centenary of Guglielmo Marconi (radio pioneer).
534 **186** 50f. blue, brown & mauve 50 30

187 Astronaut on Palm of Hand

1974. Air. 5th Anniv of 1st Landing on Moon.
535 **187** 150f. brown, blue & indigo . . . . 1·25 60

188 Tree on Palm of Hand
190 Camel Saddle

189 "The Rhinoceros" (Longhi)

1974. National Tree Week.
536 **188** 35f. turquoise, grn & brn 40 30

1974. Air. Europafrique.
537 **189** 250f. multicoloured . . . 5·00 3·00

1974. Handicrafts.
538 **190** 40f. red, blue and brown 45 20
539 – 50f. blue, red and brown 55 30
DESIGN: 50f. Statuettes of horses.

192 Frederic Chopin

1974. 125th Death Anniv of Frederic Chopin.
541 **192** 100f. black, red and blue 1·50 55

1974. Beethoven's Ninth Symphony Commemoration. As T **192**.
542 100f. lilac, blue and indigo 1·50 55
DESIGN: 100f. Beethoven.

193 European Woman and Douglas DC-8 Airliners
194 "Skylab" over Africa

1974. Air. Centenary of U.P.U.
543 **193** 50f. turquoise, grn & pur 50 25
544 – 100f. blue, mauve & ultram . . . . 2·25 75

545 – 150f. brown, blue & indigo . . . . 1·50 80
546 – 200f. brown, orange & red 1·60 1·25
DESIGNS: 100f. Japanese woman and electric locomotives; 150f. American Indian woman and liner; 200f. African woman and road vehicles.

1974. Air. "Skylab" Space Laboratory.
547 **194** 100f. violet, brown & blue 1·00 45

195 Don-don Drum

197 "Virgin and Child" (Correggio)

196 Tree and Compass Rose

1974.
548 **195** 60f. purple, green and red 90 45

1974. 1st Death Anniv of Tenere Tree (desert landmark).
549 **196** 50f. brown, blue and ochre . . . . 2·00 1·00

1974. Air. Christmas. Multicoloured.
550 100f. Type **197** . . . . 1·00 35
551 150f. "Virgin and Child, and St. Hilary" (F. Lippi) . . . 1·50 55
552 200f. "Virgin and Child" (Murillo) . . . . 2·00 95

198 "Apollo" Spacecraft

1975. Air. "Apollo–Soyuz" Space Test Project.
553 **198** 50f. green, red and blue 50 25
554 – 100f. grey, red and blue 80 40
555 – 150f. purple, plum & blue 1·25 60
DESIGNS: 100f. "Apollo" and "Soyuz" docked; 150f. "Soyuz" spacecraft.

199 European and African Women

1975. Air. Europafrique.
556 **199** 250f. brown, purple & red 2·25 1·75

200 Communications Satellite and Weather Map

1975. World Meteorological Day.
557 **200** 40f. red, black and blue 40 20

201 "Christ in the Garden of Olives" (Delacroix)

1975. Air. Easter. Multicoloured.
558 75f. Type **201** 65 35
559 125f. "The Crucifixion" (El Greco) (vert) . . . . . . 1·10 50
560 150f. "The Resurrection" (Limousin) (vert) . . . . . 1·25 75

202 Lt-Col. S. Kountche, Head of State

1975. Air. 1st Anniv of Military Coup.
561 **202** 100f. multicoloured . . . 1·00 50

203 "City of Truro", 1903, Great Britain

1975. Famous Locomotives. Multicoloured.
562 50f. Type **203** . . . . 1·25 35
563 75f. Class 05 steam locomotive No. 003, 1937, Germany . . . . 1·60 50
564 100f. "General", 1855, U.S.A. (dated "1863") . . . . . . 2·50 75
565 125f. Series BB 15000 electric locomotive, 1971, France 3·00 90

1975. Birds. As Nos. 296 and 298, but dated "1975". Multicoloured.
567 25f. Abyssinian roller (postage) . . . . 1·25 35
568 100f. Violet starlings (air) . . 3·25 90

205 "Zabira" Leather Bag

1975. Niger Handicrafts. Multicoloured.
569 35f. Type **205** 30 20
570 40f. Chequered rug 45 25
571 45f. Flower pot 50 30
572 60f. Gourd 75 35

206 African Woman and Child

1975. International Women's Year.
573 **206** 50f. blue, brown and red 75 50

207 Dr. Schweitzer and Lambarene Hospital

1975. Birth Centenary of Dr. Albert Schweitzer.
574 **207** 100f. brown, green & black . . . . 1·00 55

208 Peugeot, 1892

1975. Early Motor-cars.
575 **208** 50f. blue and mauve . . . 60 30
576 – 75f. purple and blue . . . 1·00 40
577 – 100f. mauve and green . . 1·40 60
578 – 125f. green and red . . . 1·50 70
DESIGNS: 75f. Daimler, 1895; 100f. Fiat, 1899; 125f. Cadillac, 1903.

209 Tree and Sun

1975. National Tree Week.
579 **209** 40f. green, orange and red 40 25

210 Boxing

1975. Traditional Sports.
580 **210** 35f. brown, orange & black 35 20
581 – 40f. brown, green & black 40 20
582 – 45f. brown, blue and black 50 25
583 – 50f. brown, red and black 55 30
DESIGNS—VERT: 40f. Boxing; 50f. Wrestling. HORIZ: 45f. Wrestling.

211 Leontini Tetradrachme

1975. Ancient Coins.
584 **211** 50f. grey, blue and red . . 60 20
585 – 75f. grey, blue and mauve 85 30
586 – 100f. grey, orange and blue . . . . 1·25 40
587 – 125f. grey, purple & green 1·50 60
COINS: 75f. Athens tetradrachme; 100f. Himer diadrachme; 125f. Gela tetradrachme.

212 Putting the Shot

1975. Air. "Pre-Olympic Year". Olympic Games, Montreal (1976).
588 **212** 150f. brown and red . . . 1·10 55
589 – 200f. red, chestnut and brown . . . . 1·50 85
DESIGN: 200f. Gymnastics.

213 Starving Family

1975. Pan-African Drought Relief.
590 **213** 40f. blue, brown & orange 55 30
591 – 45f. brown and blue . . . 1·10 50
592 – 60f. blue, green and orange . . . . 1·00 40
DESIGNS: 45f. Animal skeletons; 60f. Truck bringing supplies.

214 Trading Canoe crossing R. Niger

1975. Tourism. Multicoloured.
593 40f. Type **214** 50 25
594 45f. Boubon Camp entrance 55 25
595 50f. Boubon Camp view . . 60 35

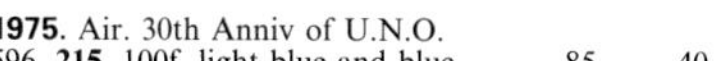

215 U.N. Emblem and Peace Dove

1975. Air. 30th Anniv of U.N.O.
596 **215** 100f. light blue and blue 85 40

216 "Virgin of Seville" (Murillo)

1975. Air. Christmas. Multicoloured.
597 50f. Type **216** 50 35
598 75f. "Adoration of the Shepherds" (Tintoretto) (horiz) 75 45
599 125f. "Virgin with Angels" (Master of Burgo d'Osma) 1·25 75

1975. Air. "Apollo–Soyuz" Space Link. Nos. 533/5 optd **JONCTION 17 Juillet 1975**.
600 **198** 50f. green, red and blue 50 25
601 – 100f. grey, red and blue 75 45
602 – 150f. purple, plum & blue 1·25 75

218 "Ashak"

1976. Literacy Campaign. Multicoloured.
603 25f. Type **218** 15 10
604 30f. "Kaska" 20 15
605 40f. "Iccee" 25 15
606 50f. "Tuuri-nya" 30 20
607 60f. "Lekki" 35 25

219 Ice Hockey

1976. Winter Olympic Games, Innsbruck, Austria. Multicoloured.
608 40f. Type **219** (postage) . . . 35 20
609 50f. Tobogganing 40 20
610 150f. Ski-jumping . . . . . 1·25 50
611 200f. Figure-skating (air) . . 1·50 75
612 300f. Cross-country skiing . . 2·00 1·00

220 Early Telephone and Satellite

1976. Telephone Centenary.
614 **220** 100f. orange, blue & green 85 50

221 Baby and Ambulance

1976. World Health Day.
615 **221** 50f. red, brown and purple 50 25

222 Washington crossing the Delaware (after Leutze)

1976. Bicentenary of American Revolution. Mult.
616 40f. Type **222** (postage) . . . 30 15
617 50f. First soldiers of the Revolution 40 20
618 150f. Joseph Warren – martyr of Bunker Hill (air) . . . . 1·10 35
619 200f. John Paul Jones aboard the "Bonhomme Richard" 1·50 60
620 300f. Molly Pitcher – heroine of Monmouth . . . . . . 2·00 90

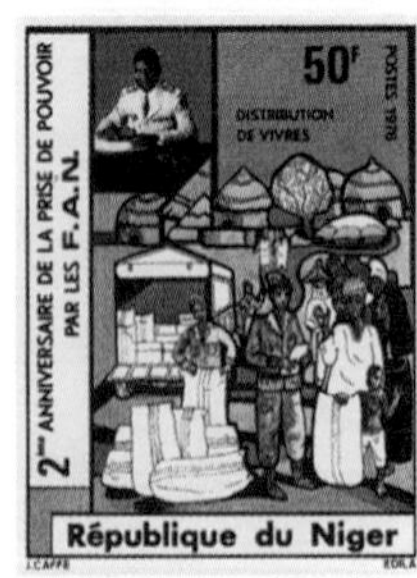

223 Distribution of Provisions

1976. 2nd Anniv of Military Coup. Multicoloured.
622 50f. Type **223** 35 25
623 100f. Soldiers with bulldozer (horiz) . . . . 1·10 45

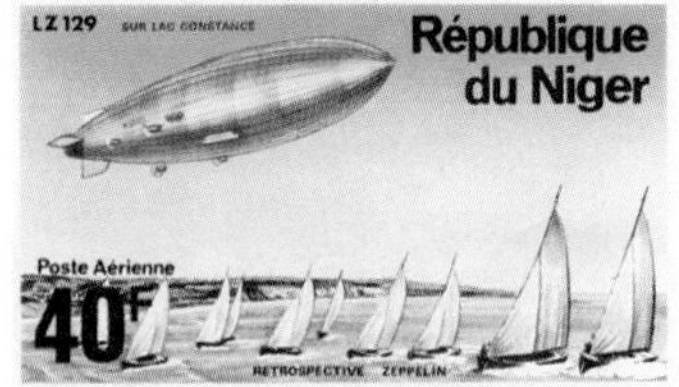

224 "Hindenburg" crossing Lake Constance

1976. Air. 75th Anniv of Zeppelin Airships. Multicoloured.
624 40f. Type **224** 40 15
625 50f. LZ-3 over Wurzberg . . 50 25
626 150f. L-9 over Friedrichshafen . . . . . . 1·40 55
627 200f. LZ-2 over Rothenburg (vert) . . . . 1·75 70
628 300f. "Graf Zeppelin II" over Essen . . . . 4·25 90

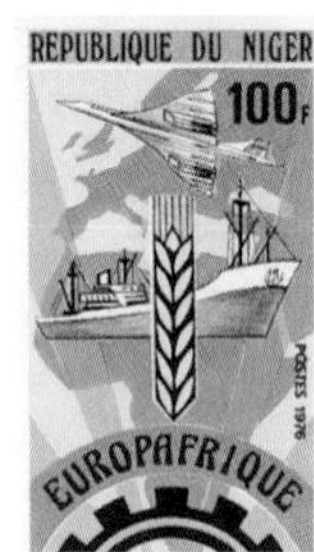

225 "Europafrique" Symbols

1976. "Europafrique".
630 **225** 100f. multicoloured . . . 1·40 50

226 Plant Cultivation

1976. Communal Works. Multicoloured.
631 25f. Type **226** 15 10
632 30f. Harvesting rice 20 15

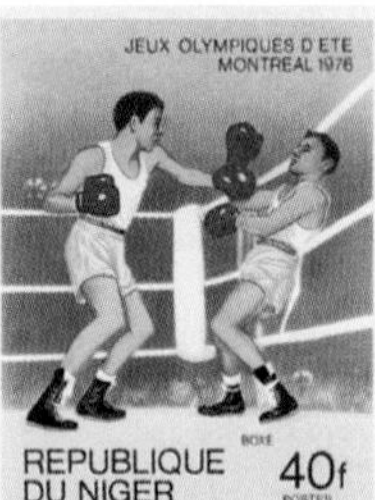

227 Boxing

1976. Olympic Games, Montreal. Multicoloured.
633 40f. Type **227** 25 15
634 50f. Basketball 40 20
635 60f. Football 45 25
636 80f. Cycling (horiz) 60 20
637 100f. Judo (horiz) 70 30

228 Motobecane "125"

1976. Motorcycles.
639 **228** 50f. violet, brown & turq 60 25
640 – 75f. green, red & turquoise 85 35
641 – 100f. brown, orange & pur . . . . 1·25 50
642 – 125f. slate, olive and black . . . . 1·50 75
DESIGNS: 75f. Norton "Challenge"; 100f. B.M.W. "903"; 125f. Kawasaki "1000".

229 Cultivation Map

1976. Operation "Sahel Vert". Multicoloured.
643 40f. Type **229** 30 15
644 45f. Tending plants (vert) . . 35 20
645 60f. Planting sapling (vert) . . 55 30

1976. International Literacy Day. Nos. 603/7 optd **JOURNEE INTERNATIONALE DE L'ALPHABETISATION**.
646 **218** 25f. multicoloured 15 15
647 – 30f. multicoloured 15 15
648 – 40f. multicoloured 20 15
649 – 50f. multicoloured 25 20
650 – 60f. multicoloured 30 20

231 Basket Making

1976. Niger Women's Association. Multicoloured.
651 40f. Type **231** 35 20
652 45f. Hairdressing (horiz) . . 40 25
653 50f. Making pottery 50 35

232 Wall Paintings

1976. "Archaeology". Multicoloured.
654 40f. Type **232** 45 25
655 50f. Neolithic statuettes . . . 30 25
656 60f. Dinosaur skeleton . . . 90 35

233 "The Nativity" (Rubens)

1976. Air. Christmas. Multicoloured.
657 50f. Type **233** 50 25
658 100f. "Holy Night" (Correggio) . . . . 1·10 45
659 150f. "Adoration of the Magi" (David) (horiz) . . 1·50 90

234 Benin Ivory Mask

1977. 2nd World Festival of Negro-African Arts, Lagos.
660 **234** 40f. brown 40 20
661 – 50f. blue 60 30
DESIGNS—HORIZ: 50f. Nigerian stick dance.

235 Students in Class

236 Examining Patient

1977. Alphabetization Campaign.
662 **235** 40f. multicoloured 30 15
663 50f. multicoloured 40 20
664 60f. multicoloured 60 20

1977. Village Health. Multicoloured.
665 40f. Type **236** 50 20
666 50f. Examining baby 60 30

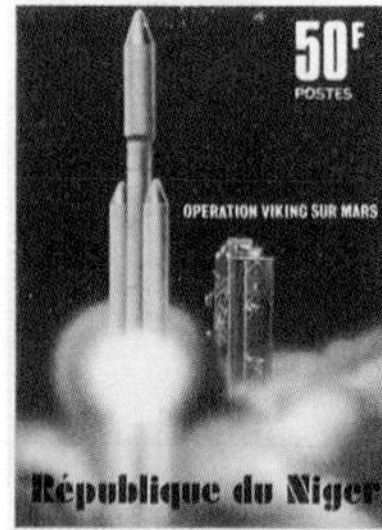

237 Rocket Launch

1977. "Viking" Space Mission. Multicoloured.
667 50f. Type **237** (postage) . . . 45 15
668 80f. "Viking" approaching Mars (horiz) 65 20
669 100f. "Viking" on Mars (horiz) (air) 65 25
670 150f. Parachute descent . . . 1·00 30
671 200f. Rocket in flight . . . . 1·40 45

238 Marabou Stork

1977. Fauna Protection.
673 **238** 80f. sepia, bistre and red 2·00 80
674 – 90f. brown and turquoise 1·25 60
DESIGN: 90f. Bushbuck.

239 Satellite and Weather Symbols

1977. World Meteorological Day.
675 **239** 100f. blue, black & turq 1·00 50

240 Gymnastic Exercise

1977. 2nd Youth Festival, Tahoua. Multicoloured.
676 40f. Type **240** 35 20
677 50f. High jumping 40 25
678 80f. Choral ensemble 70 35

241 Red Cross and Children playing

1977. World Health Day. Child Immunization Campaign.
679 **241** 80f. red, mauve and orange 75 35

242 Fly, Dagger, and W.H.O. Emblem in Eye

1977. Fight against Onchocerciasis (blindness caused by worm infestation).
680 **242** 100f. blue, grey and red . . . 1·40 55

243 Guirka Tahoua Dance

1977. "Popular Arts and Traditions". Multicoloured.
681 40f. Type **243** 45 25
682 50f. Maifilafili Gaya 50 20
683 80f. Naguihinayan Loga . . 80 45

244 Four Cavalrymen

1977. Chiefs' Traditional Cavalry. Multicoloured.
684 40f. Type **244** 55 25
685 50f. Chieftain at head of cavalry 65 30
686 60f. Chieftain and cavalry . . 90 45

245 Planting Crops

1977. "Operation Green Sahel" (recovery of desert).
687 **245** 40f. multicoloured 50 25

246 Albert John Luthuli (Peace, 1960)

1977. Nobel Prize Winners. Multicoloured.
688 50f. Type **246** 30 15
689 80f. Maurice Maeterlinck (Literature, 1911) 55 20
690 100f. Allan L. Hodgkin (Medicine, 1963) 70 25
691 150f. Albert Camus (Literature, 1957) . . . . 1·00 35
692 200f. Paul Ehrlich (Medicine, 1908) . . . . 1·50 40

247 Mao Tse-tung

1977. 1st Death Anniv of Mao Tse-tung (Chinese leader).
694 **247** 100f. black and red . . . 80 50

248 Vittorio Pozzo (Italy)

1977. World Football Cup Elimination Rounds. Multicoloured.
695 40f. Type **248** 30 10
696 50f. Vincente Feola, Spain . . 35 15
697 80f. Aymore Moreira, Portugal 50 20
698 100f. Sir Alf Ramsey, England 75 25
699 200f. Helmut Schon, West Germany . . . . 1·40 45

249 Horse's Head and Parthenon

1977. U.N.E.S.C.O. Commemoration.
701 **249** 100f. blue, red and pale blue . . . . 1·25 60

250 Carrying Water **252** Paul Follereau and Leper

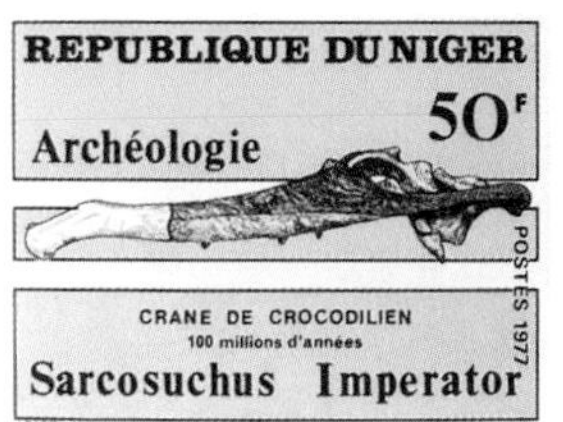

251 Crocodile Skull

1977. Women's Work. Multicoloured.
702 40f. Type **250** 35 30
703 50f. Pounding maize 40 25

1977. Archaeology. Multicoloured.
704 50f. Type **251** 60 40
705 80f. Neolithic tools 90 60

1978. 25th Anniv of World Leprosy Day.
706 **252** 40f. red, blue and orange 30 15
707 – 50f. black, red and orange 40 20
DESIGN—HORIZ: 50f. Follereau and two lepers.

253 "The Assumption"

1978. 400th Birth Anniv of Peter Paul Rubens. Paintings. Multicoloured.
708 50f. Type **253** 30 15
709 70f. "The Artist and his Friends" (horiz) 40 20
710 100f. "History of Maria de Medici" 70 25
711 150f. "Alathea Talbot" . . . 1·10 35
712 200f. "Portrait of the Marquise de Spinola" . . . 1·50 40

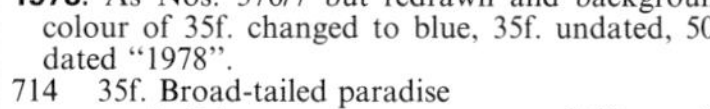

1978. As Nos. 376/7 but redrawn and background colour of 35f. changed to blue, 35f. undated, 50f. dated "1978".
714 35f. Broad-tailed paradise whydah . . . . 1·50 75
715 50f. Cattle egret . . . . . . 2·50 95
The 50f. is still wrongly inscribed "Balbucus".

254 Putting the Shot

1978. National Schools and University Sports Championships. Multicoloured.
716 40f. Type **254** 20 15
717 50f. Volleyball 30 20
718 60f. Long-jumping 35 20
719 100f. Throwing the javelin . . 55 35

255 Nurse assisting Patient

1978. Niger Red Cross.
720 **255** 40f. multicoloured 30 20

256 Station and Dish Aerial

1978. Goudel Earth Receiving Station.
721 **256** 100f. multicoloured . . . 65 40

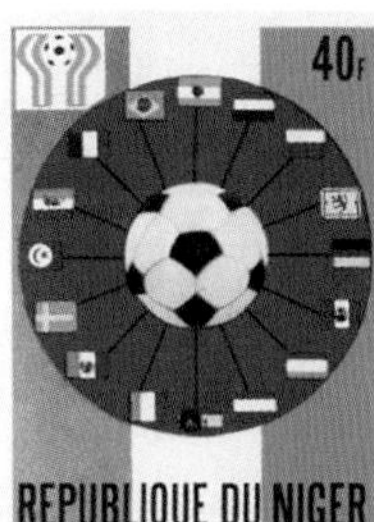

257 Football and Flags of Competing Nations

1978. World Cup Football Championship, Argentina. Multicoloured.
722 40f. Type **257** 25 10
723 50f. Football in net 35 15
724 100f. Globe and goal 75 25
725 200f. Tackling (horiz) . . . . 1·40 55

258 "Fireworks"

1978. Air. 3rd African Games, Algiers. Multicoloured.
727 40f. Type **258** 25 20
728 150f. Olympic rings emblem 1·00 60

259 Niamey Post Office

1978. Niamey Post Office. Multicoloured.
729 40f. Type **259** 25 15
730 60f. Niamey Post Office (different) 35 25

260 Aerial View of Water-works

1978. Goudel Water-works.
731 **260** 100f. multicoloured . . . 55 40

261 R.T.N. Emblem

1978. Air. 20th Anniv of Niger Broadcasting.
732 **261** 150f. multicoloured . . . 90 60

262 Golden Eagle and Oldenburg 2g. Stamp of 1859

1978. Air. "Philexafrique" Stamp Exhibition, Libreville, Gabon (1st issue) and Int Stamp Fair, Essen, West Germany. Multicoloured.
733 100f. Type **262** . . . . 2·50 1·25
734 100f. Giraffes and Niger 1959 2f. stamp . . . . 2·50 1·25
See also Nos. 769/70.

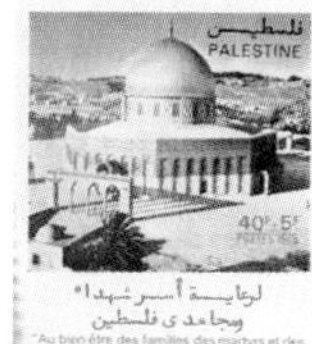

263 Giraffe **265** Dome of the Rock, Jerusalem

1978. Endangered Animals. Multicoloured.
735 40f. Type **263** 45 25
736 50f. Ostrich 85 25
737 70f. Cheetah 75 35
738 150f. Scimitar oryx (horiz) . . 1·50 75
739 200f. Addax (horiz) . . . . . 2·00 95
740 300f. Hartebeest (horiz) . . . 2·50 1·25

1978. World Cup Football Championship Finalists. Nos. 695/9 optd.
741 **248** 40f. multicoloured 30 20
742 – 50f. multicoloured 40 20
743 – 80f. multicoloured 55 25
744 – 100f. multicoloured . . . 65 40
745 – 200f. multicoloured . . . 1·40 75
OVERPRINTS: 40f. **EQUIPE QUATRIEME: ITALIE**; 50f. **EQUIPE TROISIEME: BRESIL**; 80f. **EQUIPE SECONDE: PAYS BAS**; 100f. **EQUIPE VAINQUEUR: ARGENTINE**. 200 f; **ARGENTINE - PAYS BAS 3 - 1**.

1978. Palestinian Welfare.
747 **265** 40f.+5f. multicoloured . . 40 30

266 Laying Foundation Stone, and View of University

1978. Air. Islamic University of Niger.
748 **266** 100f. multicoloured . . . 60 40

267 Tinguizi **268** "The Homecoming" (Daumier)

1978. Musicians. Multicoloured.
749 100f. Type **267** 75 40
750 100f. Chetima Ganga (horiz) 75 40
751 100f. Dan Gourmou 75 40

1979. Paintings. Multicoloured.
752 50f. Type **268** 50 20
753 100f. "Virgin in Prayer" (Durer) 60 20
754 150f. "Virgin and Child" (Durer) 90 30
755 200f. "Virgin and Child" (Durer) (different) . . . . 1·25 40

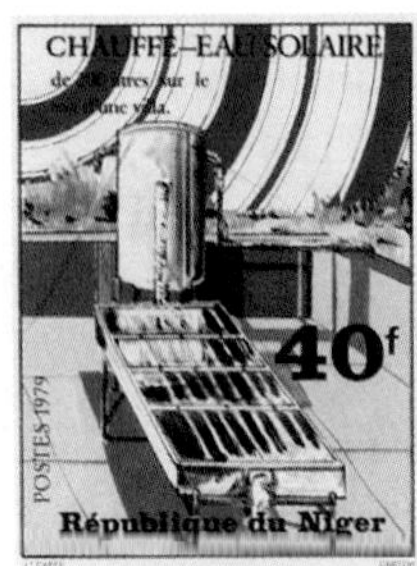

269 Feeder Tanks

1979. Solar Energy. Multicoloured.
757 40f. Type **269** 30 20
758 50f. Solar panels on house roofs (horiz) 40 25

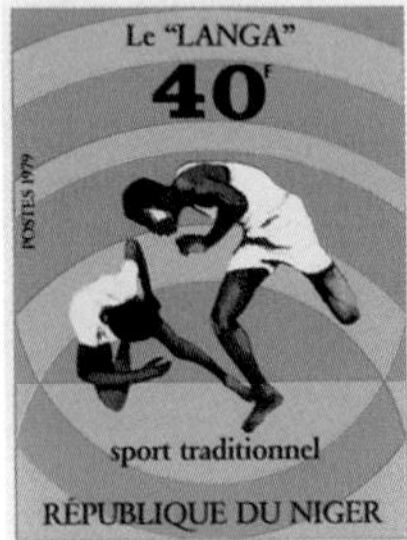

270 Langha Contestants

1979. Traditional Sports. Multicoloured.
759 40f. Type **270** 25 15
760 50f. Langha contestants clasping hands 35 20

271 Children with Building Bricks

1979. International Year of the Child. Multicoloured.
761 40f. Type **271** 25 15
762 100f. Children with book . . 60 25
763 150f. Children with model airplane . . . . 1·25 45

272 Rowland Hill, Peugeot Mail Van and French "Ceres" Stamp of 1849

1979. Death Centenary of Sir Rowland Hill. Mult.
764 40f. Type **272** 25 15
765 100f. Canoes and Austrian newspaper stamp, 1851 . . 60 25
766 150f. "DC-3" aircraft & U.S. "Lincoln" stamp, 1869 . . 1·10 35
767 200f. Advanced Passenger Train (APT), Great Britain and Canada 7½d. stamp, 1857 . . . . 2·25 40

273 Zabira Decorated Bag and Niger 45f. Stamp, 1965

1979. "Philexafrique 2" Exhibition, Gabon (2nd issue).
769 **273** 50f. multicoloured 65 40
770 – 150f. blue, red and carmine . . . . 1·60 1·10
DESIGN: 150f. Talking Heads, world map, satellite and U.P.U. emblem.

274 Alcock and Brown Statue and Vickers Vimy Aircraft

1979. 60th Anniv of First Transatlantic Flight.
771 **274** 100f. multicoloured . . . 1·00 35

275 Djermakoye Palace

1979. Historic Monuments.
772 **275** 100f. multicoloured . . . 55 40

276 Bororos in Festive Headdress

1979. Annual Bororo Festival. Multicoloured.
773 45f. Type **276** 30 20
774 60f. Bororo women in traditional costume (vert) 35 25

277 Boxing

1979. Pre-Olympic Year.
775 **277** 45f. multicoloured 30 15
776 – 100f. multicoloured . . . 55 25
777 – 150f. multicoloured . . . 85 35
778 – 250f. multicoloured . . . 1·25 45
DESIGNS: 100f. to 250f. Various boxing scenes.

278 Class of Learner-drivers

1979. Driving School.
780 **278** 45f. multicoloured 30 20

279 Douglas DC-10 over Map of Niger

1979. Air. 20th Anniv of ASECNA (African Air Safety Organization).
781 **279** 150f. multicoloured . . . 1·10 60

1979. "Apollo 11" Moon Landing. Nos. 667/8, 670/1 optd **alunissage apollo XI juillet 1969** and lunar module.
782 50f. Type **237** (postage) . . . 30 20
783 80f. "Viking" approaching Mars (horiz) 50 35
784 150f. Parachute descent (air) 90 60
785 200f. Rocket in flight . . . . 1·25 80

281 Four-man Bobsleigh

1979. Winter Olympic Games, Lake Placid (1980). Multicoloured.
787 40f. Type **281** 25 15
788 60f. Downhill skiing 35 15
789 100f. Speed skating 60 25
790 150f. Two-man bobsleigh . . 90 35
791 200f. Figure skating . . . . 1·10 45

282 Le Gaweye Hotel

1980. Air.
793 **282** 100f. multicoloured . . . 60 40

283 Sultan and Court

1980. Sultan of Zinder's Court. Multicoloured.
794 45f. Type **283** 30 20
795 60f. Sultan and court (different) 40 20

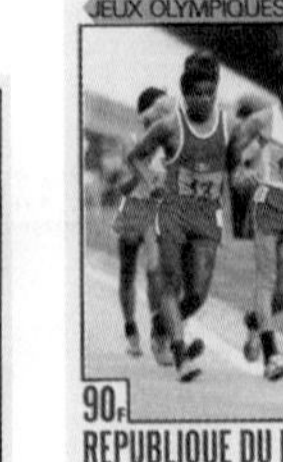

284 Chain Smoker and Athlete **285** Walking

1980. World Health Day. Anti-smoking Campaign.
796 **284** 100f. multicoloured . . . 65 40

1980. Olympic Games, Moscow. Multicoloured.
797 60f. Throwing the javelin . . 35 15
798 90f. Type **285** 50 20
799 100f. High jump (horiz) . . . 55 25
800 300f. Running (horiz) . . . . 1·50 55

1980. Winter Olympic Games Medal Winners. Nos. 787/91 optd.
802 **281** 40f. **VAINQUEUR R.D.A.** 25 15
803 – 60f. **VAINQUEUR STENMARK SUEDE** 30 20
804 – 100f. **VAINQUEUR HEIDEN Etats-Unis** . . 60 30
805 – 150f. **VAINQUEURS SCHERER-BENZ Suisse** 90 45
806 – 200f. **VAINQUEUR COUSINS Grande Bretagne** . . . . 1·25 65

287 Village Scene

1980. Health Year.
808 **287** 150f. multicoloured . . . 75 50

288 Class 150 (first locomotive in Japan, 1871)

1980. Steam Locomotives. Multicoloured.
809 45f. Type **288** 80 10
810 60f. "Fred Merril", 1848, U.S.A. . . . . 1·10 10
811 90f. Series 61, 1934, Germany 1·75 20
812 100f. Type P2, 1900, Prussia 2·25 20
813 130f. "Aigle", 1846, France 3·25 30

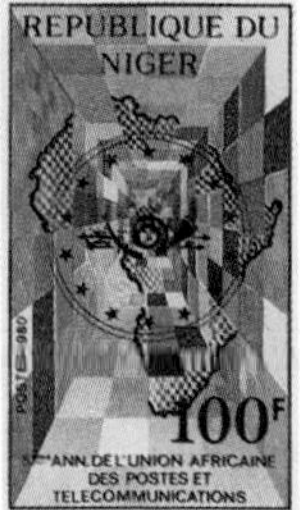

289 Steve Biko and Map of Africa **292** U.A.P.T. Emblem

291 Footballer

1980. 4th Death Anniv of Steve Biko (South African Anti-apartheid Worker).
815 **289** 150f. multicoloured . . . 80 60

1980. Olympic Medal Winners. Nos. 787/800 optd.
816 **285** 60f. **KULA (URSS)** . . . 35 15
817 – 90f. **DAMILANO (IT)** . . 55 25
818 – 100f. **WZSOLA (POL)** 60 30
819 – 300f. **YIFTER (ETH)** . . 1·60 90

1980. World Cup Football Championship, Spain (1982). Various designs showing Football.
821 **291** 45f. multicoloured 25 15
822 – 60f. multicoloured 30 15
823 – 90f. multicoloured 55 20
824 – 100f. multicoloured . . . 60 25
825 – 130f. multicoloured . . . 80 30

1980. 5th Anniv of African Posts and Telecommunications Union.
827 **292** 100f. multicoloured . . . 55 40

293 Earthenware Statuettes

1981. Kareygorou Culture Terracotta Statuettes. Multicoloured.
828 45f. Type **293** 25 20
829 60f. Head (vert) 35 20
830 90f. Head (different) (vert) . . 50 30
831 150f. Three heads 90 50

294 "Self-portrait"

1981. Paintings by Rembrandt. Multicoloured.

832	60f. Type **294**	40	15
833	90f. "Portrait of Hendrickje at the Window"	60	20
834	100f. "Portrait of an Old Man"	65	25
835	130f. "Maria Trip"	90	35
836	200f. "Self-portrait" (different)	1·25	45
837	400f. "Portrait of Saskia"	2·25	1·00

295 Ostrich

1981. Animals. Multicoloured.

839	10f. Type **295**	55	25
840	20f. Scimitar oryx	25	15
841	25f. Addra gazelle	20	15
842	30f. Arabian bustard	95	45
843	60f. Giraffe	50	20
844	150f. Addax	1·00	45

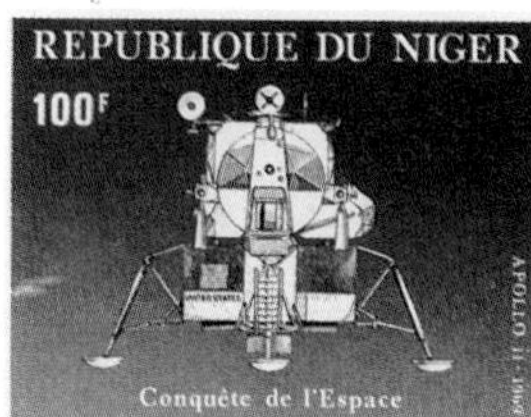
296 "Apollo 11"

1981. Air. Conquest of Space. Multicoloured.

845	100f. Type **296**	60	25
846	150f. Boeing 747 SCA carrying space shuttle	1·00	40
847	200f. Rocket carrying space shuttle	1·25	40
848	300f. Space shuttle flying over planet	3·00	1·00

297 Tanks

1981. 7th Anniv of Military Coup.

849 **297**	100f. multicoloured	1·00	40

298 Disabled Archer

1981. International Year of Disabled People.

850 **298**	50f. dp brown, red & brown	50	20
851 –	100f. brown, red and green	75	40

DESIGN: 100f. Disabled draughtsman.

299 Ballet Mahalba

1981. Ballet Mahalba. Multicoloured.

852	100f. Type **299**	70	35
853	100f. Ballet Mahalba (different)	70	35

300 "Portrait of Olga in an Armchair"

1981. Air. Birth Centenary of Pablo Picasso (artist). Multicoloured.

854	60f. Type **300**	40	20
855	90f. "The Family of Acrobats"	55	25
856	120f. "The Three Musicians"	70	35
857	200f. "Paul on a Donkey"	1·10	55
858	400f. "Young Girl drawing in an Interior" (horiz)	2·40	1·25

301 Mosque and Ka'aba

1981. 15th Centenary of Hejira.

859 **301**	100f. multicoloured	60	35

302 Carriage

1981. British Royal Wedding.

860 **302**	150f. multicoloured	60	35
861 –	200f. multicoloured	1·00	55
862 –	300f. multicoloured	1·25	1·00

DESIGNS: 200f., 300f. Similar designs showing carriages.

303 Sir Alexander Fleming

1981. Birth Centenary of Sir Alexander Fleming (discoverer of Penicillin).

864 **303**	150f. blue, brown and green	1·50	60

304 Pen-nibs, Envelope, Flower and U.P.U. Emblem

1981. International Letter Writing Week.

865 **304**	65f. on 45f. blue and red	40	20
866 –	85f. on 60f. blue, orange and black	50	30

DESIGN: 85f. Quill, hand holding pen and U.P.U. emblem.

305 Crops, Cattle and Fish

1981. World Food Day.

867 **305**	100f. multicoloured	1·00	35

306 Tackling

1981. World Cup Football Championship, Spain (1982). Multicoloured.

868	40f. Type **306**	25	20
869	65f. Goalkeeper fighting for ball	40	30
870	85f. Passing ball	55	35
871	150f. Running with ball	1·00	60
872	300f. Jumping for ball	2·25	1·10

307 Peugeot, 1912

1981. 75th Anniv of French Grand Prix Motor Race. Multicoloured.

874	20f. Type **307**	25	15
875	40f. Bugatti, 1924	35	20
876	65f. Lotus-Climax, 1962	55	30
877	85f. Georges Boillot	75	35
878	150f. Phil Hill	1·10	60

308 "Madonna and Child" (Botticelli)

309 Children watering Plants

1981. Christmas. Various Madonna and Child Paintings by named artists. Multicoloured.

880	100f. Type **308**	60	40
881	200f. Botticini	1·25	75
882	300f. Botticini (different)	2·00	1·10

1982. School Gardens. Multicoloured.

883	65f. Type **309**	50	30
884	85f. Tending plants and examining produce	60	35

310 Arturo Toscanini (conductor, 25th death anniv)

1982. Celebrities' Anniversaries. Multicoloured.

885	120f. Type **310**	1·00	45
886	140f. "Fruits on a Table" (Manet, 150th birth anniv) (horiz)	80	55
887	200f. "L'Estaque" (Braque, birth centenary) (horiz)	1·25	60
888	300f. George Washington (250th birth anniv)	2·00	90
889	400f. Goethe (poet, 150th death anniv)	2·50	1·25
890	500f. Princess of Wales (21st birthday)	2·75	1·50

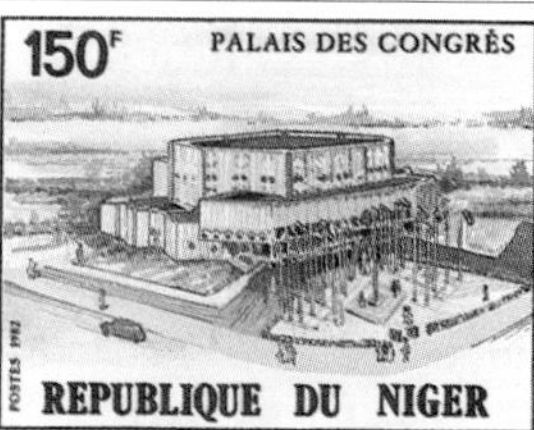
311 Palace of Congresses

1982. Palace of Congresses.

892 **311**	150f. multicoloured	90	60

312 Martial Arts

1982. 7th Youth Festival, Agadez. Multicoloured.

893	65f. Type **312**	40	30
894	100f. Traditional wrestling	60	40

313 Planting a Tree

315 Map of Africa showing Member States

314 Scouts in Pirogue

1982. National Re-afforestation Campaign. Multicoloured.

895	150f. Type **313**	1·00	60
896	200f. Forest and desert	1·25	75

1982. 75th Anniv of Boy Scout Movement. Mult.

897	65f. Type **314**	55	30
898	85f. Scouts in inflatable dinghy	65	30
899	130f. Scouts in canoe	1·25	45
900	200f. Scouts on raft	1·75	60

1982. Economic Community of West African States.

902 **315**	200f. yellow, black and blue	1·25	75

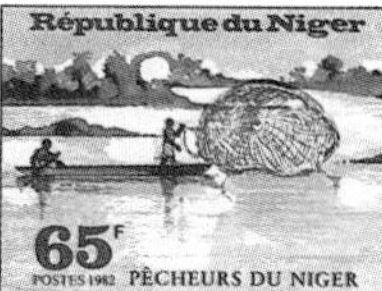
316 Casting Net

1982. Niger Fishermen. Multicoloured.

903	65f. Type **316**	85	30
904	85f. Net fishing	70	40

1982. Birth of Prince William of Wales. Nos. 860/2 optd **NAISSANCE ROYALE 1982**.

905 **302**	150f. multicoloured	75	60
906 –	200f. multicoloured	1·00	75
907 –	300f. multicoloured	1·40	1·10

318 Hands reaching towards Mosque

1982. 13th Islamic Foreign Ministers Meeting, Niamey.

909 **318**	100f. multicoloured	60	40

319 "Flautist"

1982. Norman Rockwell Paintings. Multicoloured.

910	65f. Type **319**	40	25
911	85f. "Clerk"	50	25
912	110f. "Teacher and Pupil"	70	35
913	150f. "Girl Shopper"	90	50

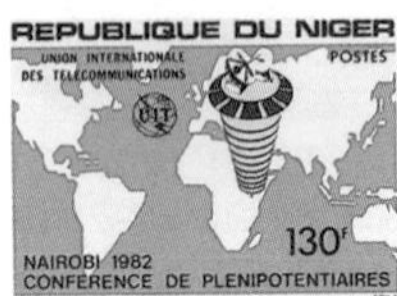

320 World Map and Satellite

1982. I.T.U. Delegates' Conference, Nairobi.

914	**320**	130f. blue, light blue and black	1·00	50

1982. World Cup Football Championship Winners. Nos. 868/72 optd.

915	40f. Type **306**	25	20
916	65f. Goalkeeper fighting for ball	40	30
917	85f. Passing ball	45	25
918	150f. Running with ball	90	50
919	300f. Jumping for ball	1·75	1·10

OVERPRINTS: 40f. **1966 VAINQUEUR GRANDE - BRETAGNE**; 65f. **"1970 VAINQUEUR BRESIL"**; 85f. **"1974 VAINQUEUR ALLEMAGNE (RFA)"**; 150f. **"1978 VAINQUEUR ARGENTINE"**; 300f. **"1982 VAINQUEUR ITALIE"**.

322 Laboratory Workers with Microscopes

1982. Laboratory Work. Multicoloured.

921	65f. Type **322**	60	40
922	115f. Laboratory workers	80	50

323 "Adoration of the Kings"

1982. Air. Christmas. Paintings by Rubens. Multicoloured.

923	200f. Type **323**	1·25	50
924	300f. "Mystic Marriage of St. Catherine"	2·00	75
925	400f. "Virgin and Child"	2·50	1·00

324 Montgolfier Balloon

1983. Air. Bicent of Manned Flight. Mult.

926	65f. Type **324**	45	15
927	85f. Charles's hydrogen balloon	60	20
928	200f. Goodyear Aerospace airship (horiz)	1·25	60
929	250f. Farman H.F.III biplane (horiz)	1·50	70
930	300f. Concorde	3·00	1·40
931	500f. "Apollo 11" spacecraft	3·00	1·40

No. 928 is wrongly inscribed "Zeppelin".

325 Harvesting Rice

326 E.C.A. Anniversary Emblem

1983. Self-sufficiency in Food. Multicoloured.

932	65f. Type **325**	60	30
933	85f. Planting rice	80	40

1983. 25th Anniv of Economic Commission for Africa.

934	**326**	120f. multicoloured	75	40
935		200f. multicoloured	1·25	70

327 "The Miraculous Draught of Fishes"

1983. 500th Birth Anniv of Raphael. Multicoloured.

936	65f. Type **327**	50	20
937	85f. "Grand Ducal Madonna" (vert)	50	20
938	100f. "The Deliverance of St. Peter"	60	25
939	150f. "Sistine Madonna" (vert)	1·00	45
940	200f. "The Fall on the Way to Calvary" (vert)	1·10	60
941	300f. "The Entombment"	1·75	80
942	400f. "The Transfiguration" (vert)	2·25	1·10
943	500f. "St. Michael fighting the Dragon" (vert)	3·00	1·40

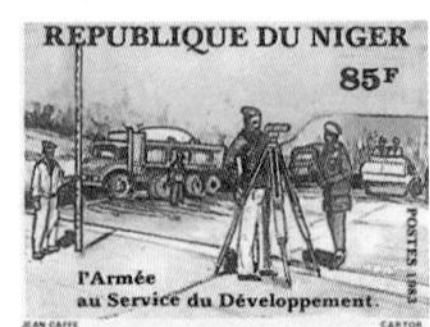

328 Surveying

1983. The Army in the Service of Development. Multicoloured.

944	85f. Type **328**	60	25
945	150f. Road building	1·00	50

329 Palace of Justice

1983. Palace of Justice, Agadez.

946	**329**	65f. multicoloured	40	20

330 Javelin

1983. Air. Olympic Games, Los Angeles. Mult.

947	85f. Type **330**	50	20
948	200f. Shotput	1·10	60
949	250f. Throwing the hammer (vert)	1·50	70
950	300f. Discus	1·75	80

331 Rural Post Vehicle

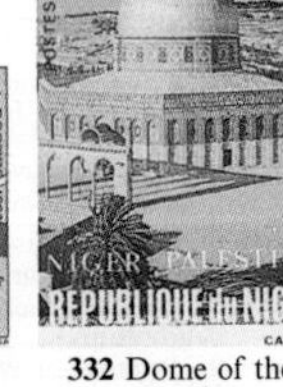

332 Dome of the Rock

1983. Rural Post Service. Multicoloured.

952	65f. Type **331**	50	20
953	100f. Post vehicle and map	75	30

1983. Palestine.

954	**332**	65f. multicoloured	65	20

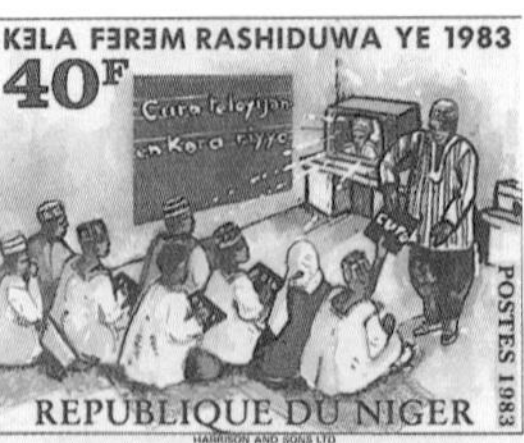

333 Class watching Television

1983. International Literacy Day. Multicoloured.

955	40f. Type **333**	25	15
956	65f. Teacher at blackboard (vert)	40	25
957	85f. Learning weights (vert)	55	30
958	100f. Outdoor class	60	35
959	150f. Woman reading magazine (vert)	1·00	50

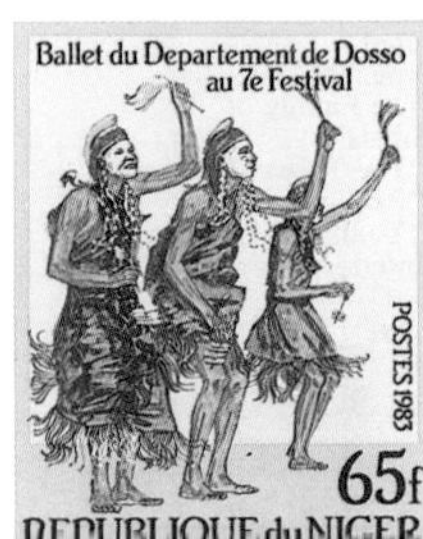

334 Three Dancers

1983. 7th Dosso Dance Festival. Multicoloured.

960	65f. Type **334**	50	25
961	85f. Four dancers	60	35
962	120f. Two dancers	90	50

335 Post Van

1983. World Communications Year. Multicoloured.

963	80f. Type **335**	60	40
964	120f. Sorting letters	80	40
965	150f. W.C.Y. emblem (vert)	1·00	50

336 Television Antenna and Solar Panel

1983. Solar Energy in the Service of Television. Multicoloured.

966	85f. Type **336**	60	30
967	130f. Land-rover and solar panel	90	45

337 "Hypolimnas misippus"

1983. Butterflies. Multicoloured.

968	75f. Type **337**	70	35
969	120f. "Papilio demodocus"	1·10	50
970	250f. "Vanessa antiopa"	2·00	90
971	350f. "Charexes jasius"	2·75	1·40
972	500f. "Danaus chrisippus"	4·50	1·75

338 "Virgin and Child with Angels"

339 Samariya Emblem

1983. Air. Christmas. Paintings by Botticelli. Multicoloured.

973	120f. Type **338**	75	40
974	350f. "Adoration of the Magi" (horiz)	2·25	1·00
975	500f. "Virgin of the Pomegranate"	3·00	1·25

1984. Samariya.

976	**339**	80f. black, orange & green	50	30

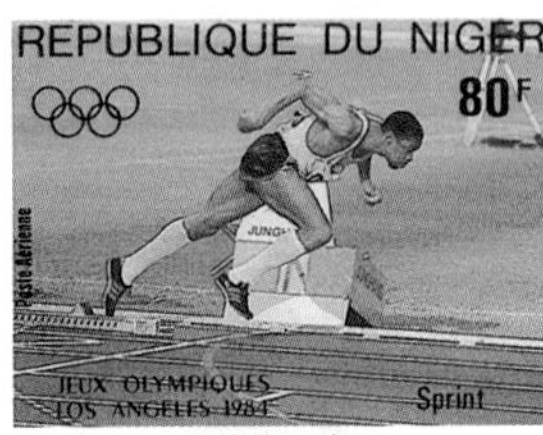

340 Running

1984. Air. Olympic Games, Los Angeles. Mult.

977	80f. Type **340**	40	20
978	120f. Pole vault	60	30
979	140f. High jump	80	30
980	200f. Triple jump (vert)	1·25	45
981	350f. Long jump (vert)	2·00	1·00

341 Boubon's Tetra

1984. Fish.

983	**341**	120f. multicoloured	2·75	80

342 Obstacle Course

1984. Military Pentathlon. Multicoloured.

984	120f. Type **342**	80	40
985	140f. Shooting	95	50

343 Radio Station

1984. New Radio Station.

986	**343**	120f. multicoloured	85	40

344 Flags, Agriculture and Symbols of Unity and Growth

1984. 25th Anniv of Council of Unity.

987	**344**	65f. multicoloured	40	25
988		85f. multicoloured	50	40

345 "Paris" (early steamer)

1984. Ships. Multicoloured.

989 80f. Type **345** 75 30
990 120f. "Jacques Coeur" (full-rigged ship) 85 40
991 150f. "Bosphorus" (full-rigged ship) . . . . 1·40 50
992 300f. "Comet" (full-rigged ship) . . . . 2·50 1·10

346 Daimler

1984. Motor Cars. Multicoloured.

993 100f. Type **346** 75 30
994 140f. Renault . . . . 1·10 45
995 250f. Delage "D 8" . . . . . 1·75 70
996 400f. Maybach "Zeppelin" 2·75 90

347 "Rickmer Rickmers" (full-rigged ship)

1984. Universal Postal Union Congress, Hamburg.

997 **347** 300f. blue, brown and green . . . . 2·75 1·75

348 Cattle

1984. Ayerou Market. Multicoloured.

998 80f. Type **348** 60 40
999 120f. View of market . . . . 1·00 60

349 Viper

1984.

1000 **349** 80f. multicoloured . . . 75 40

350 Carl Lewis (100 and 200 m)

1984. Air. Olympic Games Medal Winners. Multicoloured.

1001 80f. Type **350** 50 20
1002 120f. J. Cruz (800 m) . . . 70 40
1003 140f. A. Cova (10,000 m) . . 80 45
1004 300f. Al Joyner (Triple jump) . . . . 1·75 90

351 Emblem

1984. 10th Anniv of Economic Community of West Africa.

1006 **351** 80f. multicoloured . . . 50 30

352 Emblem and Extract from General Kountche's Speech

1984. United Nations Disarmament Decennials.

1007 **352** 400f. black and green . . 2·50 1·75
1008 500f. black and blue . . 3·00 1·75

353 Football

1984. Air. Preliminary Rounds of World Cup Football Championship, Mexico.

1009 **353** 150f. multicoloured . . . 1·00 45
1010 – 250f. multicoloured . . . 1·75 80
1011 – 450f. multicoloured . . . 2·50 1·25
1012 – 500f. multicoloured . . . 3·00 1·75

DESIGNS: 250 to 500f. Footballing scenes.

354 "The Visitation" (Ghirlandaio)

1984. Air. Christmas. Multicoloured.

1013 100f. Type **354** 60 30
1014 200f. "Virgin and Child" (Master of Saint Verdiana) . . . . 1·25 65
1015 400f. "Virgin and Child" (J. Koning) . . . . 2·50 1·25

1984. Drought Relief. Nos. 895/6 optd **Aide au Sahel 84**.

1016 150f. multicoloured . . . . 1·00 80
1017 200f. multicoloured . . . . 1·25 1·10

356 Organization Emblem

1985. 10th Anniv of World Tourism Organization.

1018 **356** 100f. black, orange and green 70 40

357 Breast-feeding Baby

360 Profile and Emblem

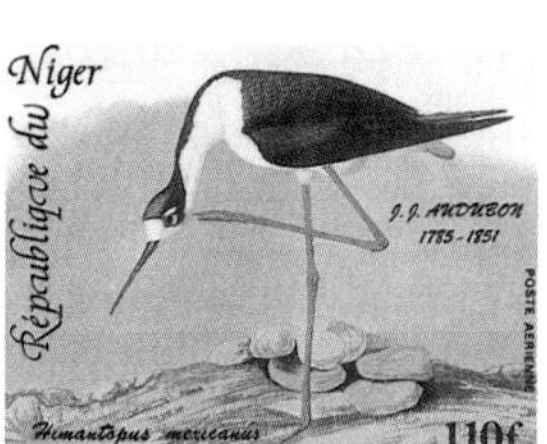

358 Black-necked Stilt

1985. Infant Survival Campaign. Multicoloured.

1019 85f. Type **357** 70 30
1020 110f. Feeding baby and changing nappy 90 40

1985. Air. Birth Centenary of John J. Audubon (ornithologist). Multicoloured.

1021 110f. Type **358** . . . . . . 1·10 45
1022 140f. Greater flamingo (vert) 1·50 65
1023 200f. Atlantic puffin . . . . 2·25 95
1024 350f. Arctic tern (vert) . . . 4·25 1·25

1985. 15th Anniv of Technical and Cultural Co-operation Agency.

1026 **360** 110f. brown, red & violet 65 40

361 Dancers

1985. 8th Niamey Festival. Multicoloured.

1027 85f. Type **361** 60 40
1028 110f. Four dancers (vert) . . 70 50
1029 150f. Dancers (different) . . 1·00 65

362 Wolf ("White Fang") and Jack London

1985. International Youth Year. Multicoloured.

1030 85f. Type **362** 60 25
1031 105f. Woman with lion and Joseph Kessel 75 30
1032 250f. Capt. Ahab harpooning white whale ("Moby Dick") . . . . . 1·75 90
1033 450f. Mowgli on elephant ("Jungle Book") . . . . 2·75 1·50

363 Two Children on Leaf

1985. "Philexafrique" Stamp Exhibition, Lome, Togo (1st issue). Multicoloured.

1034 200f. Type **363** . . . . . . 1·25 1·00
1035 200f. Mining . . . . 1·25 1·00

See also Nos. 1064/5.

364 "Hugo with his Son Francois" (A. de Chatillon)

1985. Death Centenary of Victor Hugo (writer).

1036 **364** 500f. multicoloured . . . 3·00 1·75

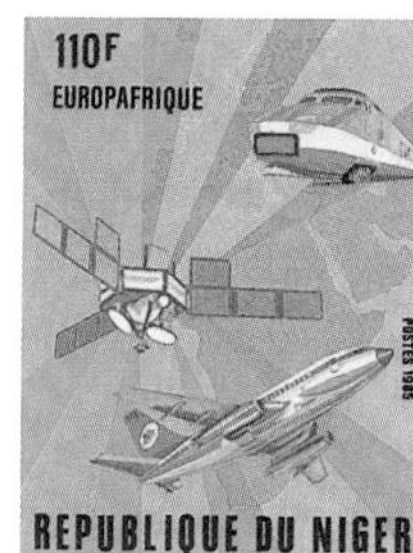

365 French Turbotrain TGV 001, Satellite and Boeing 737 on Map

1985. Europafrique.

1037 **365** 110f. multicoloured . . . 2·75 55

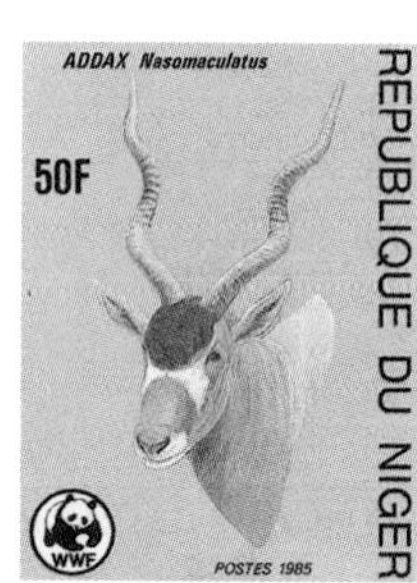

366 Addax

1985. Endangered Animals. Multicoloured.

1038 50f. Type **366** 40 15
1039 60f. Addax (different) (horiz) 45 25
1040 85f. Two scimitar oryxes (horiz) 55 25
1041 110f. Oryx 75 35

367 "Oedaleus sp" on Millet

368 Cross of Agadez

1985. Vegetation Protection. Multicoloured.

1042 85f. Type **367** 55 20
1043 110f. "Dysdercus volkeri" (beetle) 75 35
1044 150f. Fungi attacking sorghum and millet (horiz) . . . . 2·50 60
1045 210f. Sudan golden sparrows in tree . . . . 2·10 85
1046 390f. Red-billed queleas in tree . . . . 4·25 2·10

1985.

1047 **368** 85f. green 45 15
1048 – 110f. brown 55 15

DESIGN: 110f. Girl carrying water jar on head.

369 Arms, Flags and Agriculture

1985. 25th Anniv of Independence.

1049 **369** 110f. multicoloured . . . 70 40

370 Baobab

373 "Boletus"

371 Man watching Race

1985. Protected Trees. Multicoloured.
1050 110f. Type **370** 80 50
1051 210f. "Acacia albida" . . . 1·40 1·00
1052 390f. Baobab (different) . . 3·00 1·60

1985. Niamey–Bamako Powerboat Race. Mult.
1053 110f. Type **371** 70 45
1054 150f. Helicopter and powerboat . . . . 1·60 85
1055 250f. Powerboat and map 1·75 1·25

1985. "Trees for Niger". As Nos. 1050/2 but new values and optd **DES ARBRES POUR LE NIGER**.
1056 **370** 30f. multicoloured . . . 25 20
1057 – 85f. multicoloured . . . 55 40
1058 – 110f. multicoloured . . . 70 55

1985. Fungi. Multicoloured.
1059 85f. Type **373** . . . . 1·40 30
1060 110f. "Hypholoma fasciculare" . . . . . . 2·10 45
1061 200f. "Coprinus comatus" 3·00 1·10
1062 300f. "Agaricus arvensis" (horiz) . . . . 4·50 1·50
1063 400f. "Geastrum fimbriatum" (horiz) . . . 5·75 2·10

374 First Village Water Pump

1985. "Philexafrique" Stamp Exhibition, Lome, Togo (2nd issue). Multicoloured.
1064 250f. Type **374** . . . . . . 1·75 1·25
1065 250f. Handicapped youths playing dili (traditional game) . . . . 1·75 1·25

375 "Saving Ant" and Savings Bank Emblem

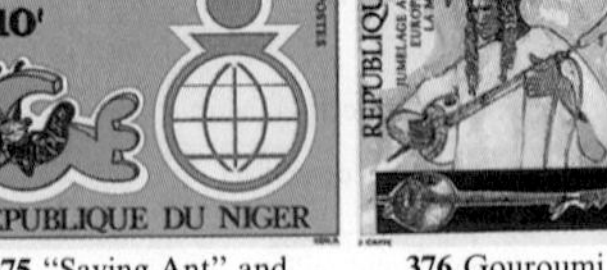

376 Gouroumi

1985. World Savings Day.
1066 **375** 210f. multicoloured . . . 1·40 85

1985. Musical Instruments. Multicoloured.
1067 150f. Type **376** . . . . . . 1·10 60
1068 210f. Gassou (drums) (horiz) 1·60 1·00
1069 390f. Algaita (flute) . . . . 2·75 1·50

377 "The Immaculate Conception"

379 National Identity Card

378 Comet over Paris, 1910

1985. Air. Christmas. Paintings by Murillo. Mult.
1071 110f. "Madonna of the Rosary" 65 35
1072 250f. Type **377** . . . . . . 1·75 90
1073 390f. "Virgin of Seville" . . 2·50 1·25

1985. Air. Appearance of Halley's Comet. Multicoloured.
1074 110f. Type **378** 70 35
1075 130f. Comet over New York 85 40
1076 200f. "Giotto" satellite . . . 1·50 70
1077 300f. "Vega" satellite . . . 2·25 1·00
1078 390f. "Planet A" space probe . . . . 2·50 1·25

1986. Civil Statutes Reform. Each black, green and orange.
1079 85f. Type **379** 65 30
1080 110f. Civil registration emblem 75 40

380 Road Signs

381 Oumarou Ganda (film producer)

1986. Road Safety Campaign.
1081 **380** 85f. black, yellow and red 75 30
1082 – 110f. black, red and green . . . . 1·00 40
DESIGN: 110f. Speed limit sign, road and speedometer ("Watch your speed").

1986. Honoured Artists. Multicoloured.
1083 60f. Type **381** 35 20
1084 85f. Idi na Dadaou 50 30
1085 100f. Dan Gourmou 60 40
1086 130f. Koungoui (comedian) 80 45

382 Martin Luther King

384 Statue and F. A. Bartholdi

383 Footballer and 1970 40f. Stamp

1986. Air. 18th Death Anniv of Martin Luther King (human rights activist).
1087 **382** 500f. multicoloured . . . 3·25 1·90

1986. Air. World Cup Football Championship, Mexico. Multicoloured.
1088 130f. Type **383** . . . . . . 1·00 30
1089 210f. Footballer and 1970 70f. stamp . . . . 1·25 45
1090 390f. Footballer and 1970 90f. stamp . . . . 2·75 1·00
1091 400f. Footballer and Mexican figure on "stamp" . . . . 2·75 1·00

1986. Air. Centenary of Statue of Liberty.
1093 **384** 300f. multicoloured . . . 2·25 1·10

385 Truck

1986. "Trucks of Hope". Multicoloured.
1094 85f. Type **385** 75 30
1095 110f. Mother and baby (vert) . . . . 1·00 40

386 Nelson Mandela and Walter Sisulu

387 Food Co-operatives

1986. International Solidarity with S. African and Namibian Political Prisoners Day. Multicoloured.
1096 200f. Type **386** . . . . . . 1·50 80
1097 300f. Nelson Mandela . . . 2·25 1·00

1986. 40th Anniv of F.A.O. Multicoloured.
1098 50f. Type **387** 30 20
1099 60f. Anti-desertification campaign 35 25
1100 85f. Irrigation 50 35
1101 100f. Rebuilding herds of livestock 60 40
1102 110f. Reafforestation . . . 75 45

388 Trees and Woman with Cooking Pots

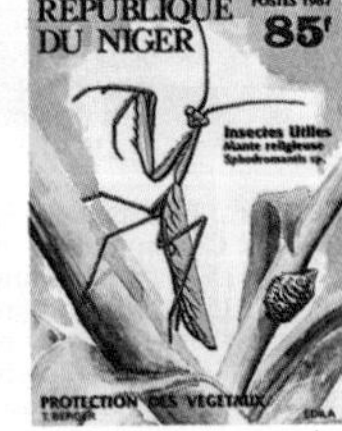

389 "Sphodromantis sp."

1987. "For a Green Niger". Multicoloured.
1103 85f. Type **388** 55 30
1104 110f. Trees, woman and cooking pots (different) 70 40

1987. Protection of Vegetation. Useful Insects. Multicoloured.
1105 85f. Type **389** 40 40
1106 110f. "Delta sp." 85 50
1107 120f. "Cicindela sp." . . . 95 65

390 Transmitter, Map and Woman using Telephone

1987. Liptako–Gourma Telecommunications Network.
1108 **390** 110f. multicoloured . . . 80 50

391 Morse Key and Operator, 19th-century

1987. 150th Anniv of Morse Telegraph. Mult.
1109 120f. Type **391** 75 40
1110 200f. Samuel Morse (inventor) (vert) . . . . . 1·25 70
1111 350f. Morse transmitter and receiver . . . . 2·25 1·25

392 Tennis Player

1987. Olympic Games, Seoul (1988). Multicoloured.
1112 85f. Type **392** 50 40
1113 110f. Pole vaulter 70 40
1114 250f. Footballer . . . . . . 1·50 90

393 Ice Hockey

1987. Winter Olympic Games, Calgary (1988) (1st issue). Multicoloured.
1116 85f. Type **393** 60 35
1117 110f. Speed skating 70 35
1118 250f. Figure skating (pairs) 1·75 90
See also Nos. 1146/9.

394 Long-distance Running

1987. African Games, Nairobi. Multicoloured.
1120 85f. Type **394** 50 35
1121 110f. High jumping 60 35
1122 200f. Hurdling . . . . . . 1·25 70
1123 400f. Javelin throwing . . . 2·50 1·40

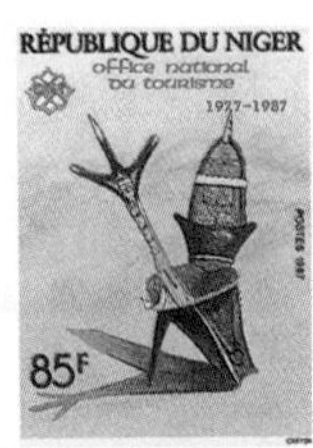

395 Chief's Stool, Sceptre and Crown

1987. 10th Anniv of National Tourism Office. Multicoloured.
1124 85f. Type **395** 50 35
1125 110f. Nomad, caravan and sceptre handle 60 35
1126 120f. Houses 70 40
1127 200f. Bridge over River Niger . . . . 1·25 70

396 Yaama Mosque at Dawn

1987. Aga Khan Prize.
1128 **396** 85f. multicoloured . . . 50 35
1129 – 110f. multicoloured . . . 60 35
1130 – 250f. multicoloured . . . 1·50 90
DESIGNS: 110, 250f. Yaama mosque at various times of the day.

397 Court Building

398 "Holy Family of the Sheep" (Raphael)

1987. Appeal Court, Niamey. Multicoloured.

1131 85f. Type **397** 50 30

1132 110f. Front entrance 60 35

1133 140f. Side view 90 55

1987. Christmas.

1134 **398** 110f. multicoloured . . . 65 40

399 Water Drainage

1988. Health Care. Multicoloured.

1136 85f. Type **399** 70 40

1137 110f. Modern sanitation . . 80 40

1138 165f. Refuse collection . . . 1·25 65

400 Singer and Band

402 New Great Market, Niamey

1988. Award of Dan-Gourmou Music Prize.

1139 **400** 85f. multicoloured . . . 80 50

1988. Winter Olympic Games Winners. Nos. 1116/18 optd.

1140 85f. **Medaille d'or URSS** . . 50 35

1141 110f. **Medaille d'or 5.000-10.00**

1988.

1143 **402** 85f. multicoloured . . . 60 40

403 Mother and Child

1988. U.N.I.C.E.F. Child Vaccination Campaign and 40th Anniv of W.H.O. Multicoloured.

1144 85f. Type **403** 70 40

1145 110f. Doctor and villagers 90 50

404 Kayak

405 Emblem

1988. Air. Olympic Games, Seoul (2nd issue) and 125th Birth Anniv of Pierre de Coubertin (founder of modern Olympic Games). Multicoloured.

1146 85f. Type **404** 50 20

1147 165f. Rowing (horiz) . . . 90 50

1148 200f. Two-man kayak (horiz) . . . . 1·25 70

1149 600f. One-man kayak . . . 3·50 2·00

1988. 25th Anniv of Organization of African Unity.

1151 **405** 85f. multicoloured . . . 50 30

406 Team working

407 Anniversary Emblem

1988. Dune Stabilization.

1152 **406** 85f. multicoloured . . . 60 40

1988. 125th Anniv of International Red Cross.

1153 **407** 85f. multicoloured . . . 60 30

1154 110f. multicoloured . . . 80 40

409 Emblem

410 Couple, Globe and Laboratory Worker

1989. Niger Press Agency.

1159 **409** 85f. black, orange & grn 45 30

1989. Campaign against AIDS.

1160 **410** 85f. multicoloured . . . 55 30

1161 110f. multicoloured . . . 85 40

411 Radar, Tanker and Signals

412 General Ali Seybou (Pres.)

1989. 30th Anniv of International Maritime Organization.

1162 **411** 100f. multicoloured . . . 1·75 75

1163 120f. multicoloured . . . 2·10 1·00

1989. 15th Anniv of Military Coup. Mult.

1164 85f. Type **412** 45 25

1165 110f. Soldiers erecting flag 65 35

413 Eiffel Tower

1989. "Philexfrance 89" International Stamp Exhibition, Paris. Multicoloured.

1166 100f. Type **413** 60 40

1167 200f. Flags on stamps . . . 1·25 65

414 "Planting a Tree of Liberty"

1989. Bicentenary of French Revolution.

1168 **414** 250f. multicoloured . . . 1·50 1·00

415 Telephone Dial, Radio Mast, Map and Stamp

417 Emblem

416 "Apollo 11" Launch

1989. 30th Anniv of West African Posts and Telecommunications Association.

1169 **415** 85f. multicoloured . . . 45 30

1989. Air. 20th Anniv of First Manned Landing on Moon. Multicoloured.

1170 200f. Type **416** . . . . . . 1·25 65

1171 300f. Crew . . . . 2·00 1·00

1172 350f. Astronaut and module on lunar surface . . . . 2·25 1·25

1173 400f. Astronaut and U.S. flag on lunar surface . . . 2·50 1·25

1989. 25th Anniv of African Development Bank.

1174 **417** 100f. multicoloured . . . 60 30

418 Before and After Attack, and "Schistocerca gregaria"

1989. Locusts.

1175 **418** 85f. multicoloured . . . 50 30

419 Auguste Lumiere and 1st Cine Performance, 1895

1989. 35th Death Anniv of Auguste Lumiere and 125th Birth Anniv of Louis Lumiere (photo-graphy pioneers). Multicoloured.

1176 150f. Type **419** 90 55

1177 250f. Louis Lumiere and first cine-camera, 1894 . . 1·50 85

1178 400f. Lumiere brothers and first colour cine-camera, 1920 . . . . 2·50 1·25

420 Tractor, Map and Pump

1989. 30th Anniv of Agriculture Development Council.

1179 **420** 75f. multicoloured . . . 45 30

421 Zinder Regional Museum

422 "Russelia equisetiformis"

1989. Multicoloured.

1180 85f. Type **421** 45 30

1182 165f. Temet dunes 90 60

1989. Flowers. Multicoloured.

1183 10f. Type **422** 15 10

1184 20f. "Argyreia nervosa" . . 15 10

1185 30f. "Hibiscus rosa-sinensis" 20 10

1186 50f. "Catharanthus roseus" 35 20

1187 100f. "Cymothoe sangaris" (horiz) 75 35

423 Emblem

424 Adults learning Alphabet

1990. 10th Anniv of Pan-African Postal Union.

1188 **423** 120f. multicoloured . . . 70 40

1990. International Literacy Year. Multicoloured.

1189 85f. Type **424** 45 25

1190 110f. Adults learning arithmetic 65 35

425 Emblem

427 Leland and Child

426 Footballers and Florence

1990. 20th Anniv of Islamic Conference Organization.

1191 **425** 85f. multicoloured . . . 50 30

1990. Air. World Cup Football Championship, Italy. Multicoloured.

1192 130f. Type **426** . . . . . . 1·00 40

1193 210f. Footballers and Verona . . . . 1·40 75

1194 500f. Footballers and Bari 3·25 1·75

1195 600f. Footballers and Rome 3·75 2·00

1990. Mickey Leland (American Congressman) Commemoration.

1196 **427** 300f. multicoloured . . . 1·75 1·00

1197 500f. multicoloured . . . 3·00 1·75

428 Emblem

429 Flags and Envelopes on Map

1990. 1st Anniv of National Movement for the Development Society.

1198 **428** 85f. multicoloured . . . 50 30

1990. 20th Anniv of Multinational Postal Training School, Abidjan.

1199 **429** 85f. multicoloured . . . 65 30

430 Gymnastics

1990. Olympic Games, Barcelona (1992). Mult.

1200 85f. Type **430** 40 25

1201 110f. Hurdling 60 35

1202 250f. Running . . . . . . 1·50 90

1203 400f. Show jumping . . . . 2·75 1·40

1204 500f. Long jumping . . . . 3·00 1·75

431 Arms, Map and Flag

432 Emblem

1990. 30th Anniv of Independence.

1206 **431** 85f. multicoloured . . . 45 30

1207 110f. multicoloured . . . 65 40

1990. 40th Anniv of United Nations Development Programme.

1208 **432** 100f. multicoloured . . . 50 30

433 The Blusher

434 Christopher Columbus and "Santa Maria"

1991. Butterflies and Fungi. Multicoloured.
1209 85f. Type **433** (postage) . . 1·00 30
1210 110f. "Graphium pylades" (female) 75 25
1211 200f. "Pseudacraea hostilia" 1·25 55
1212 250f. Cracked green russula 2·50 1·10
1213 400f. "Boletus impolitus" (air) . . . . 3·75 1·60
1214 500f. "Precis octavia" . . . 2·75 1·25

1991. 540th Birth of Christopher Columbus. Mult.
1216 85f. Type **434** (postage) . . 70 25
1217 110f. 15th-century Portuguese caravel . . . 1·00 30
1218 200f. 16th-century four-masted caravel . . . . 1·60 65
1219 250f. "Estremadura" (Spanish caravel), 1511 . . 2·00 85
1220 400f. "Vija" (Portuguese caravel), 1600 (air) . . . 3·25 1·10
1221 500f. "Pinta" . . . . 3·50 1·50

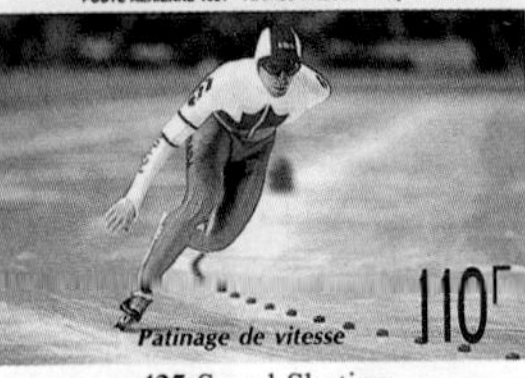

435 Speed Skating

1991. Winter Olympic Games, Albertville (1992). Multicoloured.
1223 110f. Type **435** 60 25
1224 300f. Ice-hockey . . . . . 1·25 80
1225 500f. Women's downhill skiing . . . . 2·50 1·25
1226 600f. Two-man luge . . . . 2·75 1·25

436 Flag and Boy holding Stone

437 Hairstyle

1991. Palestinian "Intifada" Movement.
1227 **436** 110f. multicoloured . . . 75 30

1991. Traditional Hairstyles. Multicoloured.
1228 85f. Type **437** 20 10
1229 110f. Netted hairstyle . . . 25 15
1230 165f. Braided hairstyle . . . 40 20
1231 200f. Plaited hairstyle . . . 45 25

438 Boubon Market

1991. African Tourism Year. Multicoloured.
1232 85f. Type **438** 20 10
1233 110f. Timia waterfalls (vert) 25 15
1234 130f. Ruins at Assode . . . 30 15
1235 200f. Tourism Year emblem (vert) 45 25

439 Anatoly Karpov and Gary Kasparov

1991. Anniversaries and Events. Multicoloured.
1236 85f. Type **439** (World Chess Championship) (postage) 20 10
1237 110f. Ayrton Senna and Alain Prost (World Formula 1 motor racing championship) 25 15
1238 200f. Reading of Declaration of Human Rights and Comte de Mirabeau (bicentenary of French Revolution) . . . 45 25
1239 250f. Dwight D. Eisenhower, Winston Churchill and Field-Marshal Montgomery (50th anniv of America's entry into Second World War) . . . . 3·50 85
1240 400f. Charles de Gaulle and Konrad Adenauer (28th anniv of Franco-German Co-operation Agreement) (air) 95 55
1241 500f. Helmut Kohl and Brandenburg Gate (2nd anniv of German reunification) . . . . . . 1·10 60

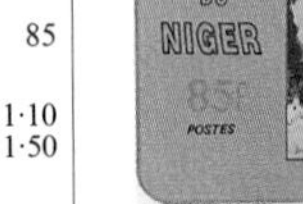
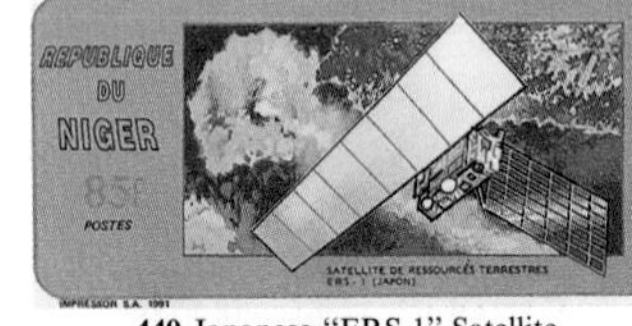

440 Japanese "ERS-1" Satellite

1991. Satellites and Transport. Multicoloured.
1243 85f. Type **440** (postage) . . 20 10
1244 110f. Japanese satellite observing Aurora Borealis 25 15
1245 200f. Louis Favre and "BB 415" diesel locomotive . . 2·50 45
1246 250f. "BB-BB 301" diesel locomotive . . . . 3·00 55
1247 400f. "DD 302" diesel locomotive (air) . . . . . 4·50 70
1248 500f. Lockheed Stealth fighter-bomber and Concorde . . . . 1·10 60

441 Crowd and Emblem on Map

443 Couple adding Final Piece to Globe Jigsaw

442 Timberless House

1991. National Conference (to determine new constitution).
1250 **441** 85f. multicoloured . . . 20 10

1992.
1251 **442** 85f. multicoloured . . . 20 10

1992. World Population Day. Multicoloured.
1252 85f. Type **443** 20 10
1253 110f. Children flying globe kite (after Robert Parker) 25 15

444 Columbus and Fleet

1992. 500th Anniv of Discovery of America by Columbus.
1254 **444** 250f. multicoloured . . . 60 35

445 Zaleye

1992. 2nd Death Anniv of Hadjia Haqua Issa (Zaleye) (singer).
1255 **445** 150f. multicoloured . . . 35 20

446 Conference Emblem

447 College Emblem

1992. International Nutrition Conference, Rome.
1256 **446** 145f. multicoloured . . . 35 20
1257 350f. multicoloured . . . 80 45

1993. 30th Anniv of African Meteorology and Civil Aviation College.
1258 **447** 110f. blue, black & green 25 15

448 Girl planting Sapling

1993. Anti-desertification Campaign.
1259 **448** 85f. multicoloured . . . 20 10
1260 165f. multicoloured . . . 40 20

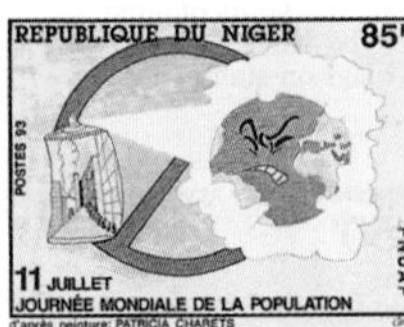

449 Aerosol spraying Globe (Patricia Charets)

1993. World Population Day. Children's Drawings. Multicoloured.
1261 85f. Type **449** 20 10
1262 110f. Tree and person with globe as head looking at high-rise tower blocks (Mathieu Chevrault) . . . 25 15

450 Jerusalem

1993. "Jerusalem, Holy City".
1268 **450** 110f. multicoloured . . . 30 15

451 People of Different Races

1994. Award of Nobel Peace Prize to Nelson Mandela and F. W. de Klerk (South African statesmen).
1269 **451** 270f. multicoloured . . . 70 40

OFFICIAL STAMPS

O **13** Djerma Women

1962. Figures of value in black.
O121 O **13** 1f. violet 10 10
O122 2f. green 10 10
O123 5f. blue 15 10
O124 10f. red 15 10
O125 20f. blue 20 15
O126 25f. orange 25 20
O127 30f. blue 30 25
O128 35f. green 35 30
O129 40f. brown 35 35
O130 50f. slate 40 40
O131 60f. turquoise 50 45
O132 85f. turquoise 70 40
O133 100f. purple 85 40
O134 200f. blue . . . . . . 1·50 80

1988. As Type O 13, but figures of value in same colour as remainder of design.
O1155 O **13** 5f. blue 10 10
O1156 10f. red 10 10
O1157 15f. yellow 10 10
O1158 20f. blue 20 10
O1159 45f. orange 25 20
O1160 50f. green 30 20

POSTAGE DUE STAMPS

1921. Postage Due stamps of Upper Senegal and Niger "Figure" key-type optd **TERRITOIRE DU NIGER**.
D18 M 5c. green . . . . 15 2·75
D19 10c. red . . . . 15 2·75
D20 15c. grey . . . . 20 2·75
D21 20c. brown . . . . 20 1·25
D22 30c. blue . . . . 30 3·00
D23 50c. black . . . . 60 3·00
D24 60c. orange . . . . 20 3·50
D25 1f. violet . . . . 30 2·50

D **6** Zinder Fort

1927.
D73 D **6** 2c. red and blue . . . . 10 2·75
D74 4c. black and orange . . 10 2·50
D75 5c. violet and yellow . . 15 2·50
D76 10c. violet and red . . . 15 2·00
D77 15c. orange and green 15 2·50
D78 20c. sepia and red . . . 20 1·90
D79 25c. sepia and black . . 35 2·25
D80 30c. grey and violet . . . 45 2·75
D81 50c. red on green . . . . 60 3·25
D82 60c. orange & lilac on bl 45 3·25
D83 1f. violet & blue on blue 55 2·75
D84 2f. mauve and red . . . 1·90 3·25
D85 3f. blue and brown . . . 2·00 3·75

D **13** Cross of Agadez

1962.
D123 D **13** 50c. green 10 10
D124 1f. violet 10 10
D125 2f. myrtle 10 10
D126 A 3f. mauve 10 10
D127 5f. green 15 15
D128 10f. orange 15 15
D129 B 15f. blue 15 15
D130 20f. red 20 20
D131 50f. brown 40 40
DESIGNS: A, Cross of Iferouane; B, Cross of Tahoua.

D **450** Cross of Iferouane

1993.

D1263 D **450** 5f. multicoloured . . 10 10
D1264 10f. orange and black 10 10
D1265 – 15f. multicoloured 10 10
D1266 – 20f. mve, yell & blk 10 10
D1267 – 50f. multicoloured 10 10
DESIGN: 15 to 50f. Cross of Tahoua.

NIGER COAST PROTECTORATE

Pt. 1

A district on the west coast of Africa. In 1900 became part of Southern Nigeria.

12 pence = 1 shilling;
20 pence = 1 pound.

1892. Stamps of Gt. Britain (Queen Victoria) optd **BRITISH PROTECTORATE OIL RIVERS**.
1 **71** ½d. red . . . . 9·50 6·50
2 **57** 1d. lilac . . . . 5·50 7·00
3 **73** 2d. green and red . . . . . 22·00 8·00
4 **74** 2½d. purple and blue . . . . 6·50 2·25
5 **78** 5d. purple and blue . . . . . 8·00 6·50
6 **82** 1s. green . . . . 55·00 75·00

1893. Half of No. 2 surch ½**d**.
7 **57** ½d. on half of 1d. lilac . . . £150 £140

1893. Nos. 1 to 6 surch in words (½d., 1s.) or figures (others).
20 **73** ½d. on 2d. green and red . . £300 £225
21 **74** ½d. on 2½d. purple on blue £275 £180
37 **73** 1s. on 2d. green and red . . £400 £350
40 5s. on 2d. green and red . . £9000 £10000
41 **78** 10s. on 5d. purple and blue £6000 £8000
42 **82** 20s. on 1s. green £70000

13

14

1893. Various frames with "OIL RIVERS" barred out and "NIGER COAST" above.
45 **13** ½d. red . . . . 4·00 3·75
46 1d. blue . . . . 6·00 3·25
47d 2d. green . . . . 19·00 13·00
48 2½d. red . . . . 8·50 3·50
49b 5d. lilac . . . . 14·00 13·00
50 1s. black . . . . 14·00 12·00

1894. Various frames.
66 **14** ½d. green . . . . 3·50 1·50
67 1d. red . . . . 4·50 1·50
68 2d. red . . . . 1·75 1·75
69 2½d. blue . . . . 7·50 2·00
55 5d. purple . . . . 6·00 5·50
71 6d. brown . . . . 7·00 6·50
56a 1s. black . . . . 40·00 7·00
73b 2s.6d. brown . . . . . . 22·00 80·00
74b 10s. violet . . . . 80·00 £160

1894. Surch with large figures.
58 ½ on half 1d. (No. 46) £700 £275
59 1 on half 2d. (No. 2) £1500 £300

1894. No. 67 bisected and surch.
64 **14** ½d. on half of 1d. red . . . £1900 £375

1894. Surch **ONE HALF PENNY** and bars.
65 **14** ½d. on 2½d. blue £350 £225

NIGERIA

Pt. 1

A former British colony on the west coast of Africa, comprising the territories of Northern and Southern Nigeria and Lagos. Attained full independence within the British Commonwealth in 1960 and became a Federal Republic in 1963.

The Eastern Region (known as Biafra (q.v)) seceded in 1967, remaining independent until overrun by Federal Nigerian troops during January 1970.

1914. 12 pence = 1 shilling;
20 shillings = 1 pound.
1973. 100 kobo = 1 naira.

1

1914.

15 **1** ½d. green . . . . 1·25 40
16 1d. red . . . . 3·25 30
17 1½d. orange . . . . 4·25 15
18 2d. grey . . . . 1·50 4·75
20 2d. brown . . . . 1·25 15
21 2½d. blue . . . . 1·00 6·00
5a 3d. purple on yellow . . . . 1·50 2·75
22 3d. violet . . . . 5·00 3·25
23 3d. blue . . . . 6·00 1·50
24 4d. black and red on yellow 65 55
25a 6d. purple . . . . 7·00 8·00
26 1s. black on green . . . . . 1·25 2·00
9 2s.6d. black and red on blue 16·00 6·50
10 5s. green and red on yellow 13·00 50·00
11d 10s. green and red on green 35·00 £100
12a £1 purple and black on red £160 £190

1935. Silver Jubilee. As T **14a** of Kenya, Uganda and Tanganyika.
30 1½d. blue and grey . . . . . 80 1·00
31 2d. green and blue . . . . . 1·50 1·00
32 3d. brown and blue . . . . . 3·00 12·00
33 1s. grey and purple . . . . . 3·00 28·00

3 Apapa Wharf

5 Victoria–Buea Road

1936.

34 **3** ½d. green . . . . 1·50 1·40
35 – 1d. red 50 40
36 – 1½d. brown . . . . 2·00 40
37 – 2d. black 50 80
38 – 3d. blue . . . . 2·00 1·50
39 – 4d. brown . . . . 2·00 2·00
40 – 6d. violet 50 60
41 – 1s. green . . . . 1·75 4·75
42 **5** 2s.6d. black and blue . . . . 3·75 22·00
43 – 5s. black and green . . . . . 6·50 27·00
44 – 10s. black and grey . . . . . 48·00 70·00
45 – £1 black and orange . . . . 75·00 £150
DESIGNS—VERT: 1d. Cocoa; 1½d. Tin dredger; 2d. Timber industry; 3d. Fishing village; 4d. Cotton ginnery; 6d. Habe minaret; 1s. Fulani cattle. HORIZ: 5s. Oil palms; 10s. River Niger at Jebba; £1 Canoe pulling.

1937. Coronation. As T **14b** of Kenya, Uganda and Tanganyika.
46 1d. red . . . . 50 2·25
47 1½d. brown . . . . 1·40 2·50
48 3d. blue . . . . 1·40 2·50

15 King George VI

1938.

49 **15** ½d. green 10 10
50a 1d. red 75 30
50b 1d. lilac 10 20
51a 1½d. brown 10 10
52 2d. black . . . . 10 1·00
52ab 2d. red 10 50
52b 2½d. orange 10 80
53 3d. blue 10 10
53b 3d. black 15 50
54 4d. orange . . . . 48·00 2·75
54a 4d. blue . . . . 15 1·75
55 6d. violet 40 10
56a 1s. olive 30 10
57 1s.3d. blue 90 30
58c – 2s.6d. black and blue . . 2·00 4·00
59b – 5s. black and orange . . 6·50 3·00
DESIGNS: 2s.6d., 5s. As Nos. 42 and 44 but with portrait of King George VI.

1946. Victory. As T **4a** of Pitcairn Islands.
60 1½d. brown 35 10
61 4d. blue . . . . 35 1·75

1948. Royal Silver Wedding. As T **4b/c** of Pitcairn Islands.
62 1d. mauve 35 30
63 5s. orange . . . . 5·00 9·00

1949. U.P.U. As T **4d/g** of Pitcairn Islands.
64 1d. purple 15 20
65 3d. blue . . . . 1·00 2·75
66 6d. purple . . . . 30 2·75
67 1s. olive . . . . 50 2·00

1953. Coronation. As T **4h** of Pitcairn Islands.
68 1½d. black and green 40 10

18 Old Manilla Currency

26 Victoria Harbour

29 New and Old Lagos

1953.

69 **18** ½d. black and orange . . 15 30
70 – 1d. black and bronze . . 20 10
71 – 1½d. turquoise 50 40
72 – 2d. black and ochre . . . 4·00 30
72cb – 2d. slate . . . . 3·50 40
73 – 3d. black and purple . . . 55 10
74 – 4d. black and blue . . . 2·50 20
75 – 6d. brown and black . . . 30 10
76 – 1s. black and purple . . . 40 10
77 **26** 2s.6d. black and green . . 6·00 50
78 – 5s. black and red . . . . 3·50 1·40
79 – 10s. black and brown . . 13·00 2·50
80 **29** £1 black and violet . . . 23·00 7·50
DESIGNS—HORIZ (As Type **18**): 1d. Bornu horsemen; 1½d. "Groundnuts"; 2d. "Tin"; 3d. Jebba Bridge and R. Niger; 4d. "Cocoa"; 1s. "Timber". (As Type **26**): 5s. "Palm oil"; 10s. "Hides and skins". VERT (As Type **18**): 6d. Ife bronze.

1956. Royal Visit. No. 72 optd **ROYAL VISIT 1956**.
81 2d. black and ochre 40 30

31 Victoria Harbour

1958. Centenary of Victoria, S. Cameroons.
82 **31** 3d. black and purple 20 30

32 Lugard Hall

1959. Attainment of Self-government. Northern Region of Nigeria.
83 **32** 3d. black and purple 15 10
84 – 1s. black and green 55 60
DESIGN: 1s. Kano Mosque.

35 Legislative Building

1960. Independence Commemoration.
85 **35** 1d. black and red 10 10
86 – 3d. black and blue 15 10
87 – 6d. green and brown 20 20
88 – 1s.3d. blue and yellow . . . 40 20
DESIGNS—As Type **35**: 3d. African paddling canoe; 6d. Federal Supreme Court. LARGER (40 × 24 mm): 1s.3d. Dove, torch and map.

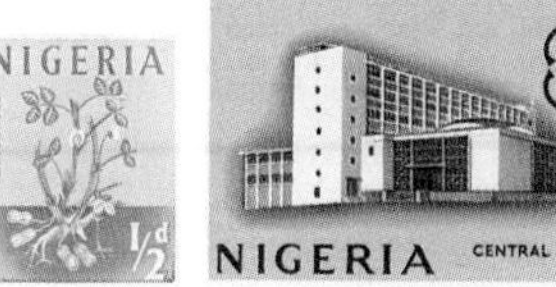

39 Groundnuts **48** Central Bank

1961.

89 **39** ½d. green 10 50
90 – 1d. violet 80 10
91 – 1½d. red . . . . 80 1·75
92 – 2d. blue 30 10
93 – 3d. green 40 10
94 – 4d. blue . . . . 40 1·50
95 – 6d. yellow and black . . . 80 10
96 – 1s. green . . . . 4·50 10
97 – 1s.3d. orange . . . . . . 1·25 10
98 **48** 2s.6d. black and yellow . . 2·75 15
99 – 5s. black and green . . . . 65 1·00
100 – 10s. black and blue . . . . 3·00 3·75
101 – £1 black and red . . . . . 11·00 13·00
DESIGNS—VERT (as Type **39**): 1d. Coal mining; 1½d. Adult education; 2d, Pottery; 3d. Oyo carver; 4d. Weaving; 6d. Benin mask; 1s. Yellow casqued hornbill; 1s.3d. Camel train. HORIZ (as Type **48**: 5s. Nigeria Museum; 10s. Kano airport; £1 Lagos railway station.

52 Globe and Diesel-electric Locomotive

1961. Admission into U.P.U. Inscr as in T **52**.
102 **52** 1d. orange and blue . . . 30 10
103 – 3d. olive and black 30 10
104 – 1s.3d. blue and red 80 20
105 – 2s.6d. green and blue . . . 85 2·00
DESIGNS: 3d. Globe and mail van; 1s.3d. Globe and Bristol 175 Britannia aircraft; 2s.6d. Globe and liner.

56 Coat of Arms

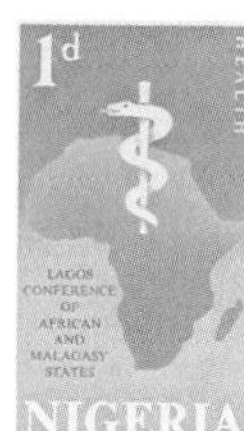

61 "Health"

1961. 1st Anniv of Independence.
106 **56** 3d. multicoloured 10 10
107 – 4d. green and orange . . . 20 10
108 – 6d. green 30 10
109 – 1s.3d. grey and blue . . . 35 10
110 – 2s.6d. green and blue . . . 40 2·00
DESIGNS—HORIZ: 4d. Natural resources map; 6d. Nigerian eagle; 1s 3d. Eagles in flight; 2s.6d. Nigerians and flag.

1962. Lagos Conf of African and Malagasy States.
111 **61** 1d. bistre 10 10
112 – 3d. purple 10 10
113 – 6d. green 15 10
114 – 1s. brown 20 10
115 – 1s.3d. blue 25 20
DESIGNS: Map and emblems symbolising Culture (3d.); Commerce (6d.); Communications (1s.); Co-operation (1s.3d.).

66 Malaria Eradication Emblem and Parasites

1962. Malaria Eradication.
116 **66** 3d. green and red 15 10
117 – 6d. blue and purple 20 10
118 – 1s.3d. mauve and blue . . 20 10
119 – 2s.6d. blue and brown . . 30 90
DESIGNS (embodying emblem): 6d. Insecticide-spraying; 1s.3d. Aerial spraying; 2s.6d. Mother, child and microscope.

70 National Monument

1962. 2nd Anniv of Independence.
120 **70** 3d. green and blue 10 10
121 – 5s. red, green and violet . . 1·00 1·00
DESIGN—VERT: 5s. Benin bronze.

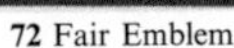

72 Fair Emblem — **76** "Arrival of Delegates"

1962. International Trade Fair, Lagos.
122 **72** 1d. red and olive 10 10
123 – 6d. black and red 15 10
124 – 1s. black and brown . . . 15 10
125 – 2s.6d. yellow and blue . . 60 20
DESIGNS—HORIZ: 6d. "Cogwheels of Industry"; 1s. "Cornucopia of Industry"; 2s.6d. Oilwells and tanker.

1962. 8th Commonwealth Parliamentary Conference, Lagos.
126 **76** 2½d. blue 15 70
127 – 4d. blue and rose 15 30
128 – 1s.3d. sepia and yellow . . 20 20
DESIGNS—HORIZ: 4d. National Hall. VERT: 1s.3d. Mace as Palm Tree.

80 Tractor and Maize — **81** Mercury Capsule and Kano Tracking Station

1963. Freedom from Hunger.
129 – 3d. olive . . . . 1·00 20
130 **80** 6d. mauve . . . . 1·50 20
DESIGN—VERT: 3d. Herdsman.

1963. "Peaceful Use of Outer Space".
131 **81** 6d. blue and green 25 10
132 – 1s.3d. black and turquoise 35 20
DESIGN: 1s.3d. Satellite and Lagos Harbour.

83 Scouts shaking Hands

1963. 11th World Scout Jamboree. Marathon.
133 **83** 3d. red and bronze 30 20
134 – 1s. black and red 95 80
MS134a 93 × 95 mm. Nos. 133/4 1·75 1·75
DESIGN: 1s. Campfire.

85 Emblem and First Aid Team — **88** President Azikiwe and State House

1963. Centenary of Red Cross.
135 **85** 3d. red and blue 40 10
136 – 6d. red and green 60 10
137 – 1s.3d. red and sepia . . . 80 70
MS137a 102 × 102 mm. No. 137 (block of four) . . . . . . 8·50 11·00
DESIGNS: 6d. Emblem and "Hospital Services"; 1s.3d. Patient and emblem.

1963. Republic Day.
138 **88** 3d. olive and green 10 10
139 – 1s.3d. brown and sepia . . 10 10
140 – 2s.6d. turquoise and blue 15 15
The buildings on the 1s.3d. and the 2s.6d. are the Federal Supreme Court and the Parliament Building respectively.

90 "Freedom of worship" — **93** Queen Nefertari

1963. 15th Anniv of Declaration of Human Rights.
141 – 3d. red 10 10
142 **90** 6d. green 15 10
143 – 1s.3d. blue 30 10
144 – 2s.6d. purple 45 30
DESIGNS—HORIZ: 3d. (Inscr "1948–1963"), Charter and broken whip. VERT: 1s.3d. "Freedom from Want"; 2s.6d. "Freedom of Speech".

1964. Nubian Monuments Preservation.
145 **93** 6d. olive and green 50 10
146 – 2s.6d. brown, olive & green 1·75 2·25
DESIGN: 2s.6d. Rameses II.

95 President Kennedy — **98** President Azikiwe

1964. Pres. Kennedy Memorial Issue.
147 **95** 1s.3d. lilac and black . . . 30 15
148 – 2s.6d. multicoloured . . . 40 65
149 – 5s. multicoloured . . . . . 70 1·75
MS149a 154 × 135 mm. No. 149 (block of four). Imperf . . . . 7·00 12·00
DESIGNS: 2s.6d. Kennedy and flags; 5s. Kennedy (U.S. coin head) and flags.

1964. 1st Anniv of Republic.
150 **98** 3d. brown 10 10
151 – 1s.3d. green 35 10
152 – 2s.6d. green 70 90
DESIGNS—25 × 42 mm: 1s.3d. Herbert Macaulay; 2s.6d. King Jaja of Opobo.

101 Boxing Gloves

1964. Olympic Games, Tokyo.
153 **101** 3d. sepia and green . . . 45 10
154 – 6d. green and blue . . . 60 10
155 – 1s.3d. sepia and olive . . 1·00 15
156 – 2s.6d. sepia and brown . . 1·75 3·75
MS156a 102 × 102 mm. No. 156 (block of four). Imperf . . . 3·00 4·25
DESIGNS—HORIZ: 6d. High-jumping. VERT: 1s.3d. Running. TRIANGULAR (60 × 30 mm): 2s.6d. Hurdling.

105 Scouts on Hill-top — **109** "Telstar"

1965. 50th Anniv of Nigerian Scout Movement.
157 **105** 1d. brown 10 10
158 – 3d. red, black and green 15 10
159 – 6d. red, sepia and green 25 20
160 – 1s.3d. brown, yellow and deep green 40 85
MS160a 76 × 104 mm. No. 160 (block of four). Imperf . . . . 5·00 8·50
DESIGNS: 3d. Scout badge on shield; 6d. Scout badges; 1s.3d. Chief Scout and Nigerian scout.

1965. International Quiet Sun Years.
161 **109** 6d. violet and turquoise 15 15
162 – 1s.3d. green and lilac . . 15 15
DESIGN: 1s.3d. Solar satellite.

111 Native Tom-tom and Modern Telephone

1965. Centenary of I.T.U.
163 **111** 3d. black, red and brown 20 10
164 – 1s.3d. black, green & blue 2·00 1·00
165 – 5s. multicoloured . . . . 5·00 7·00
DESIGNS—VERT: 1s.3d. Microwave aerial. HORIZ: 5s. Telecommunications satellite and part of globe.

114 I.C.Y. Emblem and Diesel-hydraulic Locomotive

1965. International Co-operation Year.
166 **114** 3d. green, red and orange 3·00 20
167 – 1s. black, blue and lemon 3·00 40
168 – 2s.6d. green, blue & yellow . . . . 9·00 7·00
DESIGNS: 1s. Students and Lagos Teaching Hospital; 2s.6d. Kainji (Niger) Dam.

117 Carved Frieze

1965. 2nd Anniv of Republic.
169 **117** 3d. black, red and yellow 10 10
170 – 1s.3d. brown, green & blue 25 10
171 – 5s. brown, sepia and green . . . . 60 1·25
DESIGNS—VERT: 1s.3d. Stone Images at Ikom; 5s. Tada bronze.

121 African Elephants

1965.
172 – ½d. multicoloured . . . 80 2·50
173 **121** 1d. multicoloured . . . 50 15
174 – 1½d. multicoloured . . . 7·50 8·00
222 – 2d. multicoloured . . . 2·25 90
176 – 3d. multicoloured . . . 1·25 30
177a – 4d. multicoloured . . . 30 10
225 – 6d. multicoloured . . . 2·25 20
179 – 9d. blue and red . . . . 3·00 60
227 – 1s. multicoloured . . . . 2·50 20
181 – 1s.3d. multicoloured . . 8·50 1·50
182 **227** 2s.6d. light brown, buff and brown . . . . . 75 1·75
183 – 5s. chestnut, yellow and brown . . . . 1·75 3·00
184 – 10s. multicoloured . . . 6·50 3·25
185 – £1 multicoloured . . . . 16·00 9·00
DESIGNS—VERT (as T **121**): ½d. Lion and cubs; 6d. Saddle-bill stork. (26½ × 46mm): 10s. Hippopotamus. HORIZ (as T **121**): 1½d. Splendid sunbird; 2d. Village weaver and red-headed malimbe; 3d. Cheetah; 4d. Leopards; 9d. Grey parrots. (46 × 26½ mm): 1s. Blue-breasted kingfishers; 1s.3d. Crowned cranes; 2s.6d. Kobs; 5s. Giraffes; £1 African buffalo.
The 1d., 3d., 4d., 1s., 1s.3d., 2s.6d., 5s. and £1 exist optd **F.G.N.** (Federal Government of Nigeria) twice in black. They were prepared in November 1968 as official stamps, but the scheme was abandoned. Some stamps held at a Head Post Office were sold in error and passed through the post. The Director of Posts then decided to put limited supplies on sale, but they had no postal validity.

1966. Commonwealth Prime Ministers' Meeting, Lagos. Optd **COMMONWEALTH P. M. MEETING 11. JAN. 1966.**
186 **48** 2s.6d. black and yellow . . 30 30

135 Y.W.C.A. Emblem and H.Q., Lagos

1966. Diamond Jubilee of Nigerian Y.W.C.A.
187 **135** 4d. multicoloured 15 10
188 9d. multicoloured 15 60

137 Telephone Handset and Linesman

1966. 3rd Anniv of Republic.
189 – 4d. green 10 10
190 **137** 1s.6d. black, brown & violet 30 50
191 – 2s.6d. multicoloured . . . 1·00 2·25
DESIGNS—VERT: 4d. Dove and flag. HORIZ: 2s.6d. North Channel Bridge over River Niger, Jebba.

139 "Education, Science and Culture"

1966. 20th Anniv of U.N.E.S.C.O.
192 **139** 4d. black, lake and orange 40 10
193 1s.6d. black, lake & turq 1·75 2·50
194 2s.6d. black, lake and pink . . . . 2·75 5·00

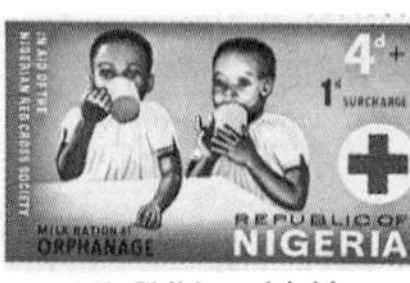

140 Children drinking

1966. Nigerian Red Cross.
195 **140** 4d.+1d. black, vio & red 30 30
196 – 1s.6d.+3d. multicoloured 55 3·75
197 – 2s.6d.+3d. multicoloured 65 4·25
DESIGNS—VERT: 1s.6d. Tending patient. HORIZ: 2s.6d. Tending casualties and badge.

143 Surveying

1967. Int Hydrological Decade. Mult.
198 4d. Type **143** 10 10
199 2s.6d. Water gauge on dam (vert) . . . . 25 1·50

145 Globe and Weather Satellite

1967. World Meteorological Day.
200 **145** 4d. mauve and blue . . . 15 10
201 – 1s.6d. black, yellow & blue 65 90
DESIGN: 1s.6d. Passing storm and sun.

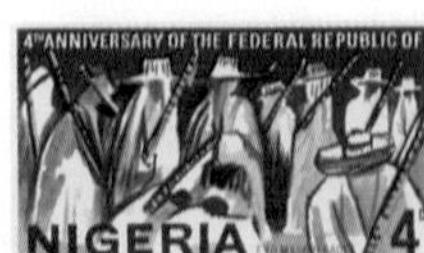

147 Eyo Masqueraders

1967. 4th Anniv of Republic. Multicoloured.
202 4d. Type **147** 15 10
203 1s.6d. Crowds watching acrobat . . . . 50 1·50
204 2s.6d. Stilt dancer (vert) . . . 75 3·25

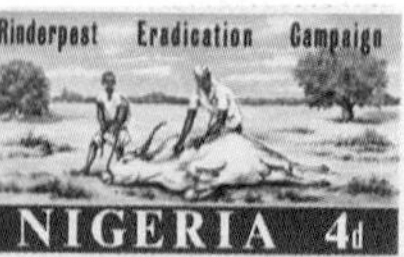

150 Tending Sick Animal

1967. Rinderpest Eradication Campaign.
205 **150** 4d. multicoloured 15 10
206 1s.6d. multicoloured . . . 55 1·50

151 Smallpox Vaccination

1968. 20th Anniv of W.H.O.
207 **151** 4d. mauve and black . . 15 10
208 – 1s.6d. orange, lemon & blk . . . . 55 1·00
DESIGN: 1s.6d. African and mosquito.

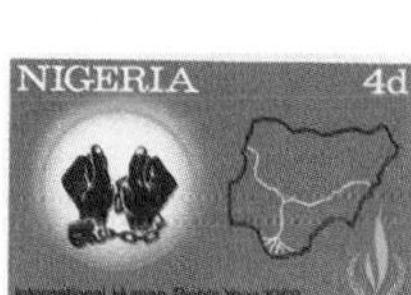
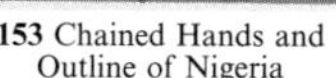

153 Chained Hands and Outline of Nigeria

155 Hand grasping at Doves of Freedom

1968. Human Rights Year.
209 **153** 4d. blue, black and yellow 10 10
210 – 1s.6d. green, red and black . . . . 20 1·00
DESIGN—VERT: 1s.6d. Nigerian flag and Human Rights emblem.

1968. 5th Anniv of Federal Republic.
211 **155** 4d. multicoloured 10 10
212 1s.6d. multicoloured . . . 20 60

156 Map of Nigeria and Olympic Rings

1968. Olympic Games, Mexico.
213 **156** 4d. black, green and red 20 10
214 – 1s.6d. multicoloured . . . 80 20
DESIGN: 1s.6d. Nigerian athletes, flag and Olympic rings.

158 G.P.O., Lagos

1969. Inauguration of Philatelic Service.
215 **158** 4d. black and green . . . 10 10
216 1s.6d. black and blue . . 20 20

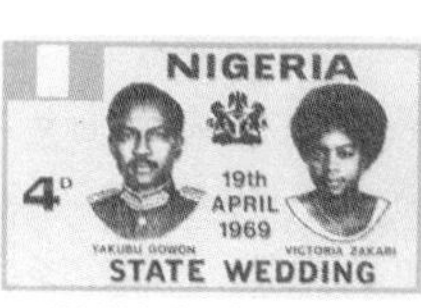

159 Yakubu Gowon and Victoria Zakari

160 Bank Emblem and "5th Anniversary"

1969. Wedding of General Gowon.
217 **159** 4d. brown and green . . . 10 10
218 1s.6d. black and green . . 65 20

1969. 5th Anniv of African Development Bank.
233 **160** 4d. orange, black and blue 10 10
234 – 1s.6d. yellow, black and purple . . . . 20 1·00
DESIGN: 1s.6d. Bank emblem and rays.

162 I.L.O. Emblem

1969. 50th Anniv of I.L.O.
235 **162** 4d. black and violet . . . 10 10
236 – 1s.6d. green and black . . 75 1·50
DESIGN: 1s.6d. World map and I.L.O. emblem.

164 Olumo Rock

1969. International Year of African Tourism.
237 **164** 4d. multicoloured 15 10
238 – 1s. black and green . . . 20 10
239 – 1s.6d. multicoloured . . . 1·25 50
DESIGNS—VERT: 1s. Traditional musicians; 1s.6d. Assob Falls.

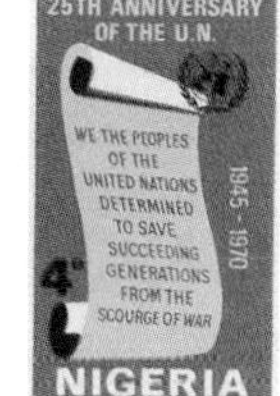

167 Symbolic Tree

169 Scroll

168 U.P.U. Headquarters Building

1970. "Stamp of Destiny". End of Civil War.
240 **167** 4d. gold, blue and black 10 10
241 – 1s. multicoloured 10 10
242 – 1s.6d. green and black . . 15 10
243 – 2s. multicoloured 20 20
DESIGNS—VERT: 1s. Symbolic wheel; 1s.6d. United Nigerians supporting map. HORIZ: 2s. Symbolic torch.

1970. New U.P.U. Headquarters Building.
244 **168** 4d. violet and yellow . . 10 10
245 1s.6d. blue and indigo . . 40 20

1970. 25th Anniv of United Nations.
246 **169** 4d. brown, buff and black 10 10
247 – 1s.6d. blue, brown & gold 30 20
DESIGN: 1s.6d. U.N. Building.

170 Oil Rig

172 Ibibio Face Mask

171 Children and Globe

1970. 10th Anniv of Independence.
248 2d. Type **170** 25 10
249 4d. University graduate . . . 15 10
250 6d. Durbar horsemen 30 10
251 9d. Servicemen raising flag 40 10
252 1s. Footballer 40 10
253 1s.6d. Parliament building . . 40 40
254 2s. Kainji Dam 70 90
255 2s.6d. Agricultural produce 70 1·00

1971. Racial Equality Year. Multicoloured.
256 4d. Type **171** 10 10
257 1s. Black and white men uprooting "Racism" (vert) 10 10
258 1s.6d. "The World in Black and White" (vert) 15 70
259 2s. Black and white men united . . . . 15 1·25

1971. Antiquities of Nigeria.
260 **172** 4d. black and blue . . . 10 10
261 – 1s.3d. brown and ochre 15 30
262 – 1s.9d. green, brown & yell 20 1·25
DESIGNS: 1s.3d. Benin bronze; 1s.9d. Ife bronze.

173 Children and Symbol

174 Mast and Dish Aerial

1971. 25th Anniv of U.N.I.C.E.F.
263 **173** 4d. multicoloured 10 10
264 – 1s.3d. orange, red & brn 15 40
265 – 1s.9d. turquoise and deep turquoise . . . . 15 1·00
DESIGNS: Each with U.N.I.C.E.F. symbol: 1s.3d. Mother and child; 1s.9d. Mother carrying child.

1971. Opening of Nigerian Earth Satellite Station.
266 **174** 4d. multicoloured 15 10
267 – 1s.3d. green, blue & black 25 50
268 – 1s.9d. brown, orange & blk . . . . 25 1·00
269 – 3s. mauve, black and purple . . . . 45 2·00
DESIGNS: Nos. 267/9 as Type **174**, but showing different views of the Satellite Station.

175 Trade Fair Emblem

177 Nok Style Terracotta Head

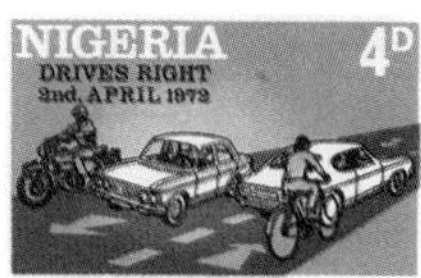

176 Traffic

1972. All-Africa Trade Fair.
270 **175** 4d. multicoloured 10 10
271 – 1s.3d. lilac, yellow & gold 15 35
272 – 1s.9d. yellow, orange & blk . . . . 15 1·40
DESIGNS—HORIZ: 1s.3d. Map of Africa with pointers to Nairobi. VERT: 1s.9d. Africa on globe.

1972. Change to Driving on the Right.
273 **176** 4d. orange, brown & black 50 10
274 – 1s.3d. multicoloured . . . 1·25 70
275 – 1s.9d. multicoloured . . . 1·25 1·25
276 – 3s. multicoloured . . . . 1·75 3·00
DESIGNS: 1s.3d. Roundabout; 1s.9d. Highway; 3s. Road junction.

1972. All-Nigeria Arts Festival. Multicoloured.
277 4d. Type **177** 10 10
278 1s.3d. Bronze pot from Igbo-Ukwu 25 60
279 1s.9d. Bone harpoon (horiz) 30 1·75

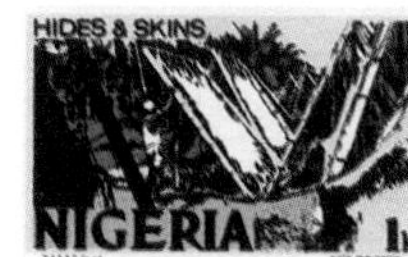

178 Hides and Skins

1973.
290 **178** 1k. multicoloured . . . 10 20
281 – 2k. multicoloured . . . 35 10
292 – 3k. multicoloured . . . 15 10
282a – 5k. multicoloured . . . 50 10
294 – 7k. multicoloured . . . 30 1·25
295 – 8k. multicoloured . . . 40 10
344 – 10k. multicoloured . . . 1·00 20
297 – 12k. black, green and blue . . . . 30 2·75
298 – 15k. multicoloured . . . 30 60
299 – 18k. multicoloured . . . 50 30
300 – 20k. multicoloured . . . 65 30
301 – 25k. multicoloured . . . 85 45
302 – 30k. black, yellow & blue . . . . 40 1·50
303 – 35k. multicoloured . . . 6·00 4·75
288a – 50k. multicoloured . . . 50 90
305 – 1n. multicoloured . . . 50 75
306 – 2n. multicoloured . . . 75 2·00
DESIGNS—HORIZ: 2k. Natural gas tanks; 3k. Cement works; 5k. Cattle-ranching; 7k. Timber mill; 8k. Oil refinery; 10k. Cheetahs, Yankari Game Reserve; 12k. New Civic Building; 15k. Sugar-cane harvesting; 20k. Vaccine production; 25k. Modern wharf; 35k. Textile machinery; 1n. Eko Bridge; 2n. Teaching Hospital, Lagos. VERT: 18k. Palm oil production; 30k. Argungu Fishing Festival; 50k. Pottery.

179 Athlete

1973. 2nd All-African Games, Lagos.
307 **179** 5k. lilac, blue and black 15 10
308 – 12k. multicoloured . . . 20 50
309 – 18k. multicoloured . . . 45 1·00
310 – 25k. multicoloured . . . 50 1·50
DESIGNS—HORIZ: 12k. Football; 18k. Table tennis. VERT: 25k. National stadium.

180 All-Africa House, Addis Ababa

1973. 10th Anniv of O.A.U. Multicoloured.
311 5k. Type **180** 10 10
312 18k. O.A.U. flag (vert) . . . 30 40
313 30k. O.A.U. emblem and symbolic flight of ten stairs (vert) 50 80

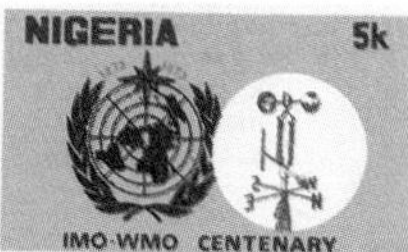

181 Dr. Hansen

182 W.M.O. Emblem and Weather-vane

1973. Cent of Discovery of Leprosy Bacillus.
314 **181** 5k.+2k. brown, pink and black 30 85

1973. Centenary of I.M.O./W.M.O.
315 **182** 5k. multicoloured 30 10
316 30k. multicoloured . . . 1·50 2·25

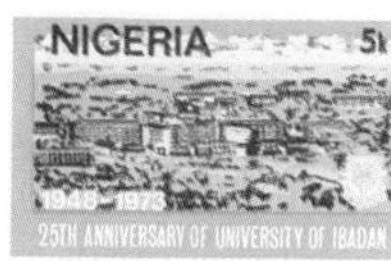

183 University Complex

1973. 25th Anniv of Ibadan University. Multicoloured.
317 5k. Type **183** 10 10
318 12k. Students' population growth (vert) 15 20
319 18k. Tower and students . . 25 35
320 30k. Teaching Hospital . . . 35 65

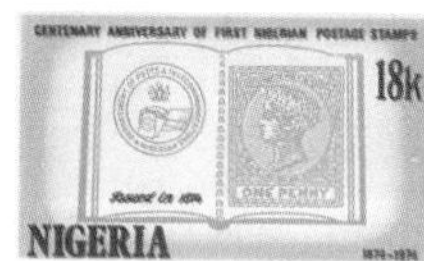

184 Lagos 1d. Stamp of 1874

1974. Stamp Centenary.
321 – 5k. green, orange & black 15 10
322 – 12k. multicoloured . . . 30 40
323 **184** 18k. green, mauve & black 50 70
324 – 30k. multicoloured . . . 1·50 2·00
DESIGNS: 5k. Graph of mail traffic growth; 12k. Northern Nigeria £25 stamp of 1904; 30k. Forms of mail transport.

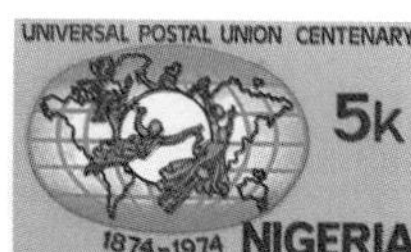

185 U.P.U. Emblem on Globe

1974. Centenary of U.P.U.
325 **185** 5k. blue, orange and black 15 10
326 – 18k. multicoloured . . . 2·00 60
327 – 30k. brown, green & black . . . . 1·75 1·75
DESIGNS: 18k. World transport map; 30k. U.P.U. emblem and letters.

186 Starving and Well-fed Children

187 Telex Network and Teleprinter

1974. Freedom from Hunger Campaign.
328 **186** 5k. green, buff and black 10 10
329 – 12k. multicoloured . . . 30 50
330 – 30k. multicoloured . . . 80 1·75
DESIGNS—HORIZ: 12k. Poultry battery. VERT: 30k. Water-hoist.

1975. Inauguration of Telex Network.
331 **187** 5k. black, orange & green 10 10
332 – 12k. black, yellow & brn 20 20

333 – 18k. multicoloured . . . 30 30
334 – 30k. multicoloured . . . 50 50
DESIGNS: 12, 18, 30k. are as Type **187** but with the motifs arranged differently.

188 Queen Amina of Zaria

190 Alexander Graham Bell

1975. International Women's Year.
335 **188** 5k. green, yellow and blue 35 10
336 18k. purple, blue & mauve . . . . 1·00 80
337 30k. multicoloured . . . 1·25 1·60

1976. Centenary of Telephone.
355 **190** 5k. multicoloured 10 10
356 – 18k. multicoloured . . . 40 55
357 – 25k. blue, light blue and brown . . . . 70 1·00
DESIGNS—HORIZ: 18k. Gong and modern telephone system. VERT: 25k. Telephones, 1876 and 1976.

191 Child writing

1976. Launching of Universal Primary Education.
358 **191** 5k. yellow, violet & mauve 10 10
359 – 18k. multicoloured . . . 45 60
360 – 25k. multicoloured . . . 70 1·00
DESIGNS—VERT: 18k. Children entering school; 25k. Children in class.

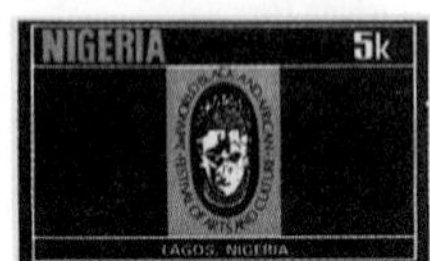

192 Festival Emblem

1976. 2nd World Black and African Festival of Arts and Culture, Nigeria.
361 **192** 5k. gold and brown . . . 35 10
362 – 10k. brown, yellow & blk 35 40
363 – 12k. multicoloured . . . 80 70
364 – 18k. yellow, brown & blk 90 90
365 – 30k. red and black . . . 1·00 1·50
DESIGNS: 10k. National Arts Theatre; 12k. African hair-styles; 18k. Musical instruments; 30k. "Nigerian arts and crafts".

193 General Murtala Muhammed and Map of Nigeria

194 Scouts saluting

1977. 1st Death Anniv of General Muhammed (Head of State). Multicoloured.
366 5k. Type **193** 10 10
367 18k. General in dress uniform (vert) 20 35
368 30k. General in battle dress (vert) 30 70

1977. 1st All-African Scout Jamboree, Jos, Nigeria. Multicoloured.
369 5k. Type **194** 15 10
370 18k. Scouts cleaning street (horiz) 60 70
371 25k. Scouts working on farm (horiz) . . . . 70 1·25
372 30k. Jamboree emblem and map of Africa (horiz) . . . 80 2·00

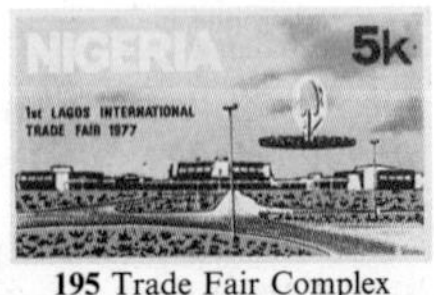

195 Trade Fair Complex

1977. 1st Lagos Int Trade Fair.
373 **195** 5k. black, blue and green 10 10
374 – 18k. black, blue and purple 20 25
375 – 30k. multicoloured . . . 30 45
DESIGNS: 18k. Globe and Trade Fair emblem; 30k. Weaving and basketry.

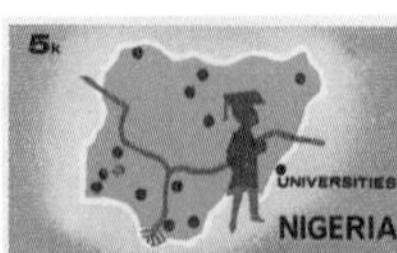

196 Map showing Nigerian Universities

1978. Global Conference on Technical Co-operation between Developing Countries, Buenos Aires.
376 **196** 5k. multicoloured 10 10
377 – 12k. multicoloured . . . 15 15
378 – 18k. multicoloured . . . 25 25
379 – 30k. yellow, violet & black 45 60
DESIGNS: 12k. Map of West African highways and telecommunications; 18k. Technologists undergoing training; 30k. World map.

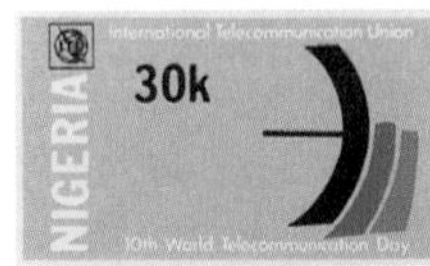

197 Microwave Antenna

1978. 10th World Telecommunications Day.
380 **197** 30k. multicoloured . . . 50 60

198 Students on "Operation Feed the Nation"

1978. "Operation Feed the Nation" Campaign. Multicoloured.
381 5k. Type **198** 10 10
382 18k. Family backyard farm 20 20
383 30k. Plantain farm (vert) . . 35 60

199 Mother with Infected Child

1978. Global Eradication of Smallpox.
384 **199** 5k. black, brown and lilac 15 10
385 – 12k. multicoloured . . . 25 35
386 – 18k. black, brown & yell 40 50
387 – 30k. black, silver and pink 55 95
DESIGNS—HORIZ: 12k. Doctor and infected child; 18k. Group of children being vaccinated. VERT: 30k. Syringe.

200 Nok Terracotta Human Figure, Bwari (900 B.C.–100 A.D.)

201 Anti-Apartheid Emblem

1978. Antiquities.
388 **200** 5k. black, blue and red 10 10
389 – 12k. multicoloured . . . 15 10
390 – 18k. black, blue and red 20 15
391 – 30k. multicoloured . . . 25 20
DESIGNS—HORIZ: 12k. Igbo-Ukwu bronze snail shell, Igbo Isaiah (9th-century A.D.). VERT: 18k. Ife bronze statue of a king (12th–15th century A.D.); 30k. Benin bronze equestrian figure (about 1700 A.D.).

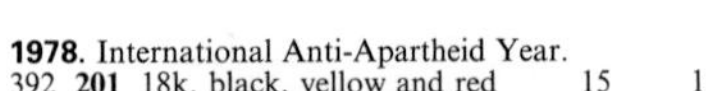

1978. International Anti-Apartheid Year.
392 **201** 18k. black, yellow and red 15 15

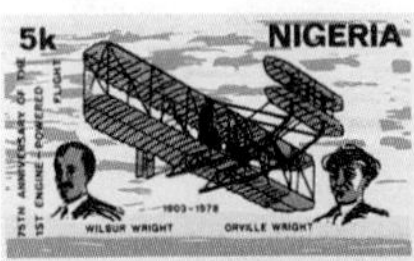

202 Wright Brothers and Wright Type A

1978. 75th Anniv of Powered Flight.
393 **202** 5k. multicoloured 20 10
394 – 18k. black, blue and light blue 60 20
DESIGN: 18k. Nigerian Air Force formation.

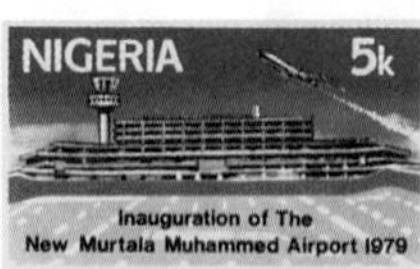

203 Murtala Muhammed Airport

1979. Opening of Murtala Muhammed Airport.
395 **203** 5k. black, grey and blue 40 30

204 Child with Stamp Album

1979. 10th Anniv of National Philatelic Service.
396 **204** 5k. multicoloured 10 20

205 Mother and Child

1979. International Year of the Child. Multicoloured.
397 5k. Type **205** 10 10
398 18k. Children studying . . . 35 30
399 25k. Children playing (vert) 40 50

206 Trainee Teacher making Audio Visual Aid Materials

207 Necom House

1979. 50th Anniv of International Bureau of Education. Multicoloured.
400 10k. Type **206** 10 10
401 30k. Adult education class . . 25 30

1979. 50th Anniv of Consultative Committee of International Radio.
402 **207** 10k. multicoloured . . . 15 20

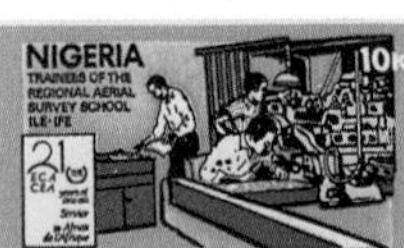

208 Trainees of the Regional Air Survey School, Ile-Ife

1979. 21st Anniv of Economic Commission for Africa.
403 **208** 10k. multicoloured . . . 20 20

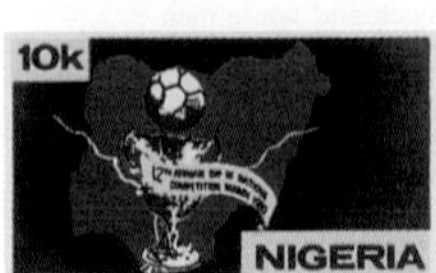

209 Football Cup and Map of Nigeria

1980. African Cup of Nations Football Competition, Nigeria. Multicoloured.
404 10k. Type **209** 20 10
405 30k. Footballer (vert) 60 50

210 Wrestling

1980. Olympic Games, Moscow.
406 **210** 10k. multicoloured . . . 10 10
407 – 20k. black and green . . 10 10
408 – 30k. black, orange & blue 15 15
409 – 45k. multicoloured . . . 20 20
DESIGNS—VERT: 20k. Long jump; 45k. Netball. HORIZ: 30k. Swimming.

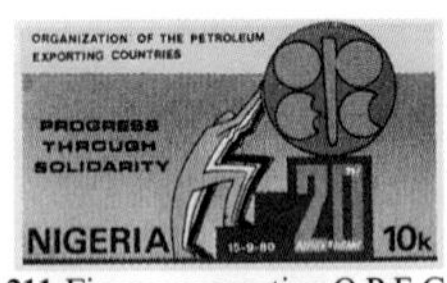

211 Figures supporting O.P.E.C. Emblem

1980. 20th Anniv of O.P.E.C. (Organization of Petroleum Exporting Countries).
410 **211** 10k. black, blue and yellow 15 10
411 – 45k. black, blue and mauve 70 60
DESIGN—VERT: 45k. O.P.E.C. emblem and globe.

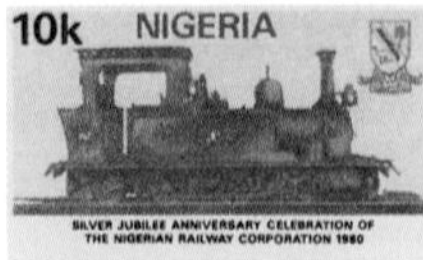

212 Tank Locomotive No. 2, Wushishi Tramway

1980. 25th Anniv of Nigerian Railway Corporation. Multicoloured.
412 10k. Type **212** 75 10
413 20k. Loading goods train . . 1·00 85
414 30k. Freight train . . . . . 1·40 1·25

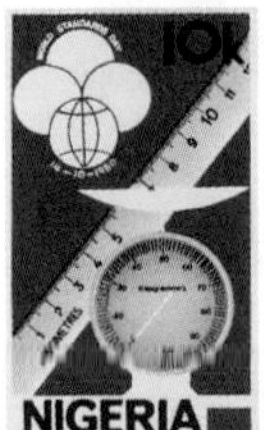

213 Metric Scales

215 Disabled Woman sweeping

214 "Communication" Symbols and Map of West Africa

1980. World Standards Day.
415 **213** 10k. red and black . . . 10 10
416 – 30k. multicoloured . . . 35 40
DESIGN—HORIZ: 30k. Quality control.

1980. 5th Anniv of Economic Community of West African States.
417 **214** 10k. black, orange & olive 10 10
418 – 25k. black, green and red 30 10
419 – 30k. black, yellow & brn 20 15
420 – 45k. black, turquoise & bl 25 25
DESIGNS: 25k. "Transport"; 30k. "Agriculture"; 45k. "Industry".

1981. International Year for Disabled Persons.
421 **215** 10k. multicoloured . . . 20 10
422 – 30k. black, brown and blue 65 65
DESIGN: 30k. Disabled man filming.

216 President launching "Green Revolution" (food production campaign)

1981. World Food Day.
423 **216** 10k. multicoloured . . . 10 10
424 – 25k. black, yellow & green 20 50
425 – 30k. multicoloured . . . 25 55
426 – 45k. black, brown & yell 45 85
DESIGNS—VERT: 25k. Food crops; 30k. Harvesting tomatoes. HORIZ: 45k. Pig farming.

217 Rioting in Soweto

1981. Anti-Apartheid Movement.
427 **217** 30k. multicoloured . . . 35 55
428 – 45k. black, red and green 50 1·25
DESIGN—VERT: 45k. "Police brutality".

218 "Preservation of Wildlife"

1982. 75th Anniv of Boy Scout Movement. Multicoloured.
429 30k. Type **218** 50 55
430 45k. Lord Baden-Powell taking salute 75 95

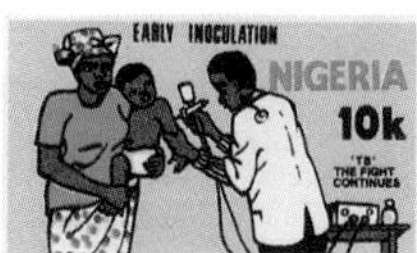

219 Early Inoculation

1982. Centenary of Robert Koch's Discovery of Tubercle Bacillus.
431 **219** 10k. multicoloured . . . 20 15
432 – 30k. black, brown and green 50 65
433 – 45k. black, brown and green . . . . 80 1·40
DESIGNS—HORIZ: 30k. Technician and microscope. VERT: 45k. Patient being X-rayed.

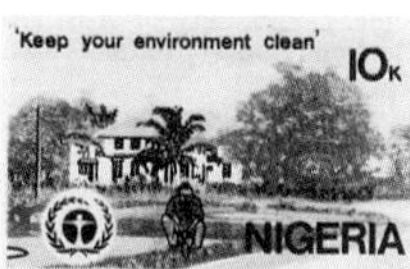

220 "Keep Your Environment Clean"

1982. 10th Anniv of U.N. Conference on Human Environment.
434 **220** 10k. multicoloured . . . 10 10
435 – 20k. orange, grey and black 20 40
436 – 30k. multicoloured . . . 35 60
437 – 45k. multicoloured . . . 55 85
DESIGNS: 20k. "Check air pollution"; 30k. "Preserve natural environment"; 45k. "Reafforestation concerns all".

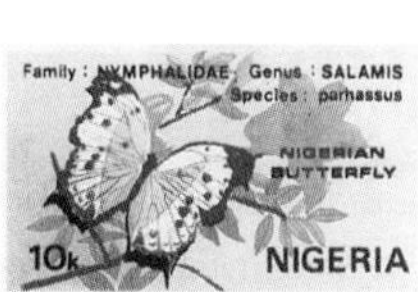

221 "Salamis parhassus" **222** Carving of "Male and Female Twins"

1982. Nigerian Butterflies. Multicoloured.
438 10k. Type **221** 15 10
439 20k. "Iterus zalmoxis" . . . 30 30
440 30k. "Cymothoe beckeri" . . 40 40
441 45k. "Papilio hesperus" . . . 70 70

1982. 25th Anniv of National Museum. Multicoloured.
442 10k. Type **222** 10 10
443 20k. Royal bronze leopard (horiz) 20 35
444 30k. Soapstone seated figure 35 90
445 45k. Wooden helmet mask 50 1·75

223 Three Generations

1983. Family Day. Multicoloured.
446 10k. Type **223** 15 10
447 30k. Parents with three children (vert) 50 65

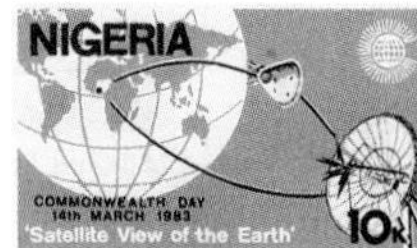

224 Satellite View of Globe

1983. Commonwealth Day.
448 **224** 10k. brown and black . . 10 10
449 – 25k. multicoloured . . . 20 30
450 – 30k. black, purple and grey 55 35
451 – 45k. multicoloured . . . 35 45
DESIGNS—HORIZ: 25k. National Assembly Buildings. VERT: 30k. Drilling for oil; 45k. Athletics.

225 Corps Members on Building Project **226** Postman on Bicycle

1983. 10th Anniv of National Youth Service Corps. Multicoloured.
452 10k. Type **225** 15 10
453 25k. On the assault-course (vert) 30 30
454 30k. Corps members on parade 40 40

1983. World Communications Year. Multicoloured.
455 10k. Type **226** 15 10
456 25k. Newspaper kiosk (horiz) 30 40
457 30k. Town crier blowing elephant tusk (horiz) . . . 35 70
458 45k. T.V. newsreader (horiz) 45 1·00

227 Pink Shrimp

1983. World Fishery Resources.
459 **227** 10k. red, blue and black 15 10
460 – 25k. multicoloured . . . 30 40
461 – 30k. multicoloured . . . 30 45
462 – 45k. multicoloured . . . 40 70
DESIGNS: 25k. Long-necked croaker; 30k. Barracuda; 45k. Fishing techniques.

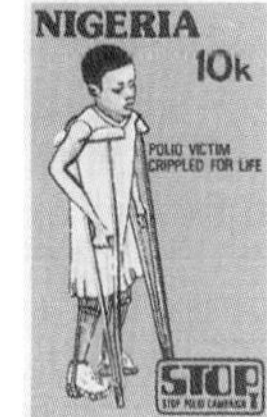

228 On Parade **229** Crippled Child

1983. Centenary of Boys' Brigade and 75th Anniv of Founding in Nigeria. Multicoloured.
463 10k. Type **228** 40 10
464 30k. Members working on cassava plantation (horiz) 1·50 1·50
465 45k. Skill training (horiz) . . 2·25 2·75

1984. Stop Polio Campaign.
466 **229** 10k. blue, black and brown 20 15
467 – 25k. orange, black & yell 40 75
468 – 30k. red, black and brown 60 1·10
DESIGNS—HORIZ: 25k. Child receiving vaccine. VERT: 30k. Healthy child.

230 Waterbuck **232** Boxing

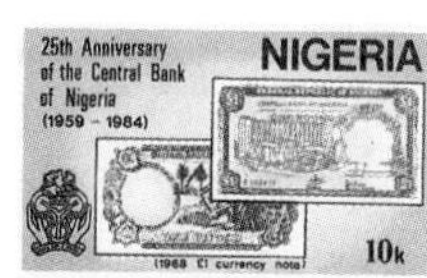

231 Obverse and Reverse of 1969 £1 Note

1984. Nigerian Wildlife.
469 **230** 10k. green, brown & black 15 10
470 – 25k. multicoloured . . . 30 50
471 – 30k. brown, black & green 40 90
472 – 45k. blue, orange & black 45 1·50
DESIGNS—HORIZ: 25k. Hartebeest; 30k. African buffalo. VERT: 45k. Diademed monkey.

1984. 25th Anniv of Nigerian Central Bank.
473 **231** 10k. multicoloured . . . 20 10
474 – 25k. brown, black & green 45 50
475 – 30k. red, black and green 55 60
DESIGNS: 25k. Central Bank; 30k. Obverse and reverse of 1959 £5 note.

1984. Olympic Games, Los Angeles. Mult.
476 10k. Type **232** 15 10
477 25k. Discus-throwing 35 50
478 30k. Weightlifting 40 60
479 45k. Cycling 60 90

233 Irrigation Project, Lesotho **234** Pin-tailed Whydah

1984. 20th Anniv of African Development Bank.
480 **233** 10k. multicoloured . . . 15 10
481 – 25k. multicoloured . . . 30 50
482 – 30k. black, yellow and blue 35 60
483 – 45k. black, brown and blue . . . . 1·75 90
DESIGNS—HORIZ: 25k. Bomi Hills Road, Liberia; 30k. School building project, Seychelles; 45k. Coal mining, Niger.

1984. Rare Birds. Multicoloured.
484 10k. Type **234** 75 20
485 25k. Spur-winged plover . . 1·50 70
486 30k. Red bishop . . . . . . 1·50 1·75
487 45k. Double-spurred francolin 1·75 2·50

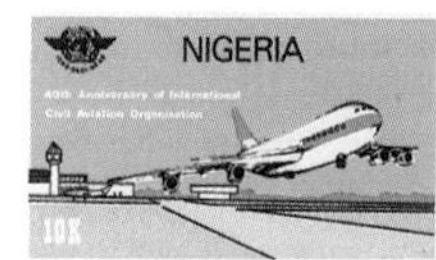

235 Boeing 747 Airliner taking-off

1984. 40th Anniv of International Civil Aviation Organization. Multicoloured.
488 10k. Type **235** 40 10
489 45k. Boeing 707 airliner circling globe . . . . . . 1·50 2·25

236 Office Workers and Clocks ("Punctuality")

1985. "War against Indiscipline". Mult.
490 20k. Type **236** 30 35
491 50k. Cross over hands passing banknotes ("Discourage Bribery") . . 55 75

237 Footballers receiving Flag from Major-General Buhari **239** Globe and O.P.E.C. Emblem

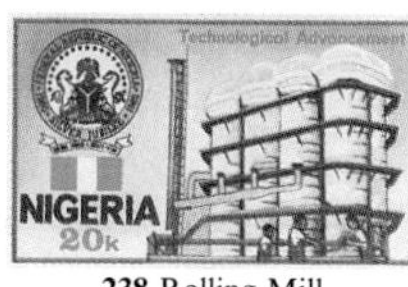

238 Rolling Mill

1985. International Youth Year. Mult.
492 20k. Type **237** 30 20
493 50k. Girls of different tribes with flag (vert) 55 70
494 55k. Members of youth organizations with flags (vert) 55 80

1985. 25th Anniv of Independence. Mult.
495 20k. Type **238** 25 10
496 50k. Map of Nigeria 40 45
497 55k. Remembrance Arcade 40 50
498 60k. Eleme, first Nigerian oil refinery . . . . 1·00 1·25
MS499 101 × 101 mm. Nos. 495/8 5·00 6·50

1985. 25th Anniv of Organization of Petroleum Exporting Countries.
500 **239** 20k. blue and red 75 35
501 – 50k. black and blue . . . 1·50 75
DESIGN—HORIZ: 50k. World map and O.P.E.C. emblem.

240 Waterfall **241** Map of Nigeria and National Flag

1985. World Tourism Day. Multicoloured.
502 20k. Type **240** 35 10
503 50k. Pottery, carved heads and map of Nigeria (horiz) 45 50
504 55k. Calabash carvings and Nigerian flag 45 50
505 60k. Leather work 45 55

1985. 40th Anniv of United Nations Organization and 25th Anniv of Nigerian Membership.
506 **241** 20k. black, green and blue 20 10
507 – 50k. black, blue and red 35 75
508 – 55k. black, blue and red 35 85
DESIGNS—HORIZ: 50k. United Nations Building, New York; 55k. United Nations logo.

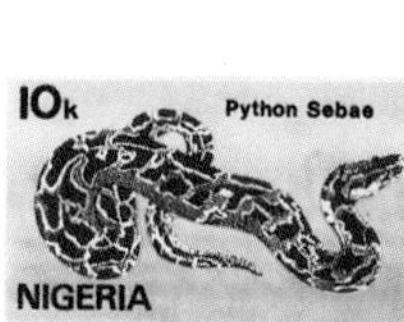

242 Rock Python **243** Social Worker with Children

1986. African Reptiles.
509 **242** 10k. multicoloured . . . 30 10
510 – 20k. black, brown and blue 50 90
511 – 25k. multicoloured . . . 50 1·00
512 – 30k. multicoloured . . . 50 1·00
DESIGNS: 20k. Long snouted crocodile; 25k. Gopher tortoise; 30k. Chameleon.

1986. Nigerian Life. Multicoloured.
513 1k. Type **243** 10 10
514 2k. Volkswagen motor assembly line (horiz) . . 10 10
515 5k. Modern housing estate (horiz) 10 10
516 10k. Harvesting oil palm fruit 10 10
517 15k. Unloading freighter (horiz) 15 10
518 20k. "Tecoma stans" (flower) 15 10
519 25k. Hospital ward (horiz) 15 10
519a 30k. Birom dancers (horiz) 15 10
520 35k. Telephonists operating switchboard (horiz) . . . 15 10
521 40k. Nkpokiti dancers . . 15 10
522 45k. Hibiscus (horiz) . . . 15 10
523a 50k. Post Office counter (horiz) 15 10
524 1n. Stone quarry (horiz) 15 15
525a 2n. Students in laboratory (horiz) 15 15
525ba 10n. Lekki Beach (horiz) 20 15
525c 20n. Ancient wall, Kano (horiz) . . . . 4·50 1·75
525d 50n. Rock bridge (horiz) 4·00 3·50
525e 100n. Ekpe masquerader 2·50 3·25
525f 500n. National Theatre (horiz) . . . . 8·00 8·50

244 Emblem and Globe

1986. International Peace Year. Mult.
526 10k. Type **244** 20 10
527 20k. Hands of five races holding globe . . . . . . 60 1·50

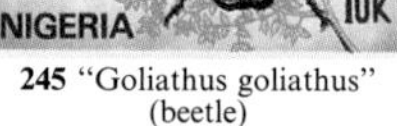

245 "Goliathus goliathus" (beetle) **246** Oral Rehydration Therapy

1986. Nigerian Insects. Multicoloured.
528 10k. Type **245** 30 10
529 20k. "Vespa vulgaris" (wasp) 40 40

530 25k. "Acheta domestica" (cricket) 45 90
531 30k. "Anthrenus verbasci" (beetle) . . . . 55 1·50
MS532 119 × 101 mm. Nos. 528/31 4·50 6·50

1986. 40th Anniv of U.N.I.C.E.F.
533 **246** 10k. multicoloured . . . 30 10
534 – 20k. black, brown & yell 40 40
535 – 25k. multicoloured . . . 45 70
536 – 30k. multicoloured . . . 55 1·00
DESIGNS: 20k. Immunization; 25k. Breast-feeding; 30k. Mother and child.

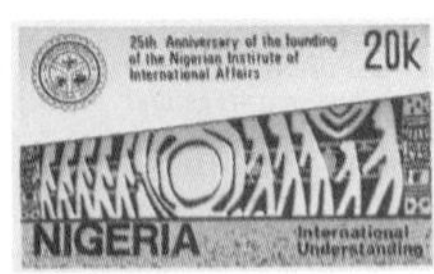

247 Stylized Figures on Wall ("International Understanding")

1986. 25th Anniv of Nigerian Institute of International Affairs.
537 **247** 20k. black, blue and green 50 50
538 – 30k. multicoloured . . . 75 1·25
DESIGN—VERT: 30k. "Knowledge" (bronze sculpture).

248 Freshwater Clam

1987. Shells.
539 **248** 10k. multicoloured . . . 65 10
540 – 20k. black, brown and pink . . . . 1·00 1·75
541 – 25k. multicoloured . . . 1·00 2·00
542 – 30k. multicoloured . . . 1·25 2·50
DESIGNS: 20k. Periwinkle; 25k. Bloody cockle (inscr "BLODDY COCKLE"); 30k. Mangrove oyster.

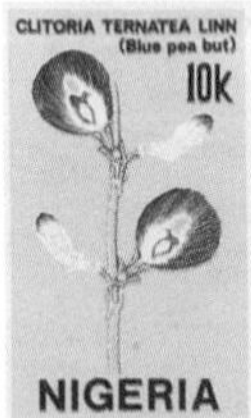

249 "Clitoria ternatea"

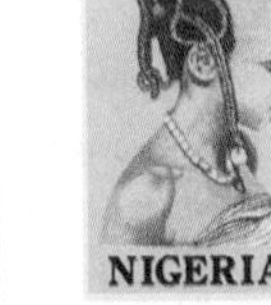

250 Doka Hairstyle

1987. Nigerian Flowers.
543 **249** 10k. multicoloured . . . 10 10
544 – 20k. brown, yellow and green 15 25
545 – 25k. multicoloured . . . 15 45
546 – 30k. multicoloured . . . 20 1·00
DESIGNS: 20k. "Hibiscus tiliaceus"; 25k. "Acanthus montanus"; 30k. "Combretum racemosum".

1987. Women's Hairstyles.
547 **250** 10k. black, brown and grey 10 10
548 – 20k. multicoloured . . . 15 25
549 – 25k. black, brown and red 20 55
550 – 30k. multicoloured . . . 20 1·00
DESIGNS: 20k. Eting; 25k. Agogo; 30k. Goto.

251 Family sheltering under Tree

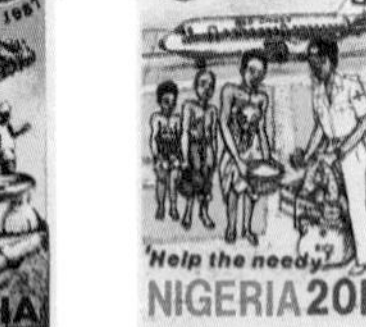

252 Red Cross Worker distributing Food

1987. International Year of Shelter for the Homeless. Multicoloured.
551 20k. Type **251** 15 15
552 30k. Family and modern house 15 90

1988. 125th Anniv of International Red Cross. Multicoloured.
553 20k. Type **252** 65 30
554 30k. Carrying patient to ambulance . . . . 65 1·75

253 Doctor vaccinating Baby

254 O.A.U. Logo

1988. 40th Anniv of W.H.O. Multicoloured.
555 10k. Type **253** 25 10
556 20k. W.H.O. logo and outline map of Nigeria 60 60
557 30k. Doctor and patients at mobile clinic 60 60

1988. 25th Anniv of Organization of African Unity.
558 **254** 10k. brown, green & orge 15 15
559 – 20k. multicoloured . . . 15 15
DESIGN: 20k. Four Africans supporting map of Africa.

255 Pink Shrimp

1988. Shrimps.
560 **255** 10k. multicoloured . . . 20 10
561 – 20k. black and green . . 25 15
562 – 25k. black, red and brown 25 25
563 – 30k. orange, brown & blk 30 60
MS564 120 × 101 mm. Nos. 560/3 1·50 2·00
DESIGNS: 20k. Tiger shrimp; 25k. Deepwater roseshrimp; 30k. Estuarine prawn.

256 Weightlifting

1988. Olympic Games, Seoul. Multicoloured.
565 10k. Type **256** 25 10
566 20k. Boxing 35 35
567 30k. Athletics (vert) 50 65

257 Banknote Production Line (½-size illustration)

1988. 25th Anniv of Nigerian Security Printing and Minting Co. Ltd.
568 **257** 10k. multicoloured . . . 10 10
569 – 20k. black, silver and green 20 20
570 – 25k. multicoloured . . . 30 30
571 – 30k. multicoloured . . . 50 50
DESIGNS—HORIZ (As T **257**): 20k. Coin production line. VERT (37 × 44 mm): 25k. Montage of products; 30k. Anniversary logos.

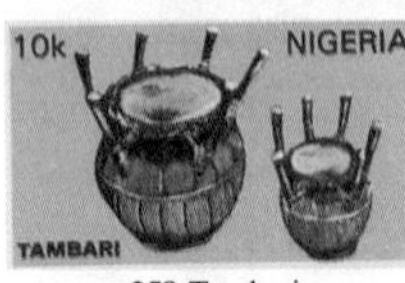

258 Tambari

1989. Nigerian Musical Instruments.
572 **258** 10k. multicoloured . . . 10 10
573 – 20k. multicoloured . . . 20 20
574 – 25k. brown, green & black 30 30
575 – 30k. brown and black . . 50 50
DESIGNS: 20k. Kundung; 25k. Ibid; 30k. Dundun.

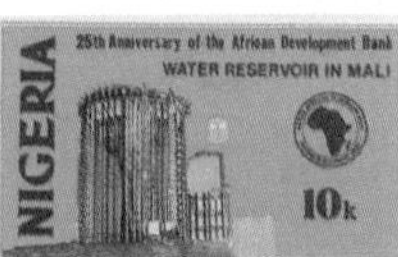

259 Construction of Water Towers, Mali

1989. 25th Anniv of African Development Bank. Multicoloured.
576 10k. Type **259** 10 10
577 20k. Paddy field, Gambia . . 15 15
578 25k. Bank Headquarters, Abidjan, Ivory Coast . . . 25 25
579 30k. Anniversary logo (vert) 35 35

260 Lighting Campfire

1989. 70th Anniv of Nigerian Girl Guides Association. Multicoloured.
580 10k. Type **260** 30 10
581 20k. Guide on rope bridge (vert) 70 60

261 Etubom Costume

262 Dove with Letter and Map of Africa

1989. Traditional Costumes. Multicoloured.
582 10k. Type **261** 15 10
583 20k. Fulfulde 25 25
584 25k. Aso-Ofi 35 75
585 30k. Fuska Kura . . . . . . 45 1·25

1990. 10th Anniv of Pan African Postal Union. Multicoloured.
586 10k. Type **262** 25 10
587 20k. Parcel and map of Africa 50 50

263 Oil Lamps

1990. Nigerian Pottery.
588 **263** 10k. black, brown & violet 10 10
589 – 20k. black, brown & violet 20 20
590 – 25k. brown and violet . . 25 25
591 – 30k. multicoloured . . . 35 35
MS592 120 × 100 mm. Nos. 588/91 80 90
DESIGNS: 20k. Water pots; 25k. Musical pots; 50k. Water jugs.

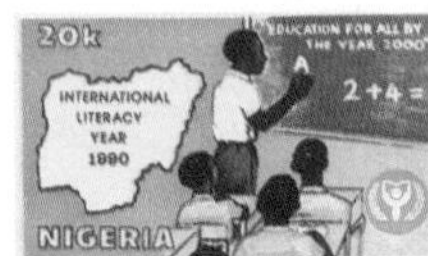

264 Teacher and Class

1990. International Literacy Year.
593 **264** 20k. multicoloured . . . 20 10
594 – 30k. brown, blue & yellow 30 30
DESIGN: 30k. Globe and book.

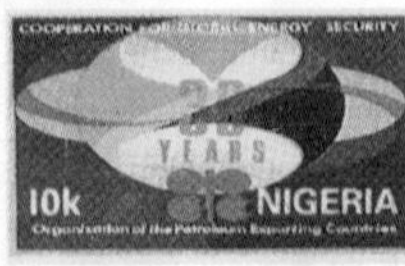

265 Globe and OPEC Logo

1990. 30th Anniv of the Organization of Petroleum Exporting Countries. Multicoloured.
595 10k. Type **265** 10 10
596 20k. Logo and flags of member countries (vert) . . 20 20
597 25k. World map and logo . . 25 25
598 30k. Logo within inscription "Co-operation for Global Energy Security" (vert) . . 35 35

266 Grey Parrot

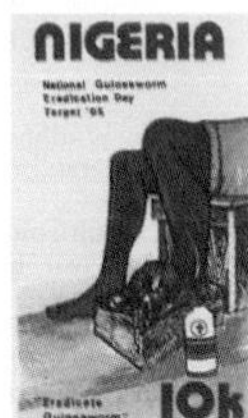

267 Eradication Treatment

1990. Wildlife. Multicoloured.
599 20k. Type **266** 20 10
600 30k. Roan antelope 20 10

601 1n.50 Grey-necked bald crow ("Rockfowl") 60 80
602 2n.50 Mountain gorilla . . . 85 1·25
MS603 118 × 119 mm. Nos. 599/602 1·75 2·25

1991. National Guineaworm Eradication Day. Multicoloured.
604 10k. Type **267** 15 10
605 20k. Women collecting water from river (horiz) 25 25
606 30k. Boiling pot of water . . 25 25

268 Hand holding Torch (Progress)

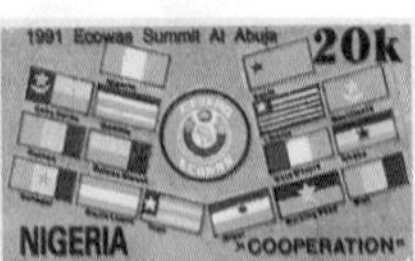

269 National Flags

1991. Organization of African Unity Heads of State and Governments Meeting, Abuja. Each showing outline map of Africa. Multicoloured.
607 20k. Type **268** 15 10
608 30k. Cogwheel (Unity) . . . 20 25
609 50k. O.A.U. flag (Freedom) 20 45

1991. Economic Community of West African States Summit Meeting, Abuja. Multicoloured.
610 20k. Type **269** 15 10
611 50k. Map showing member states 30 45

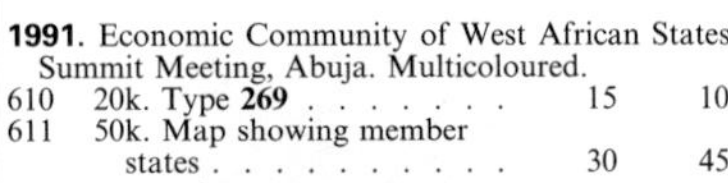

270 Electric Catfish

1991. Nigerian Fishes. Multicoloured.
612 10k. Type **270** 15 10
613 20k. Nile perch 25 25
614 30k. Nile mouthbrooder ("Talapia") 35 35
615 50k. Sharp-toothed catfish . . 50 55
MS616 121 × 104 mm. Nos. 612/15 2·00 2·50

271 Telecom '91 Emblem

1991. "Telecom '91" 6th World Telecommunication Exhibition, Geneva.
617 **271** 20k. black, green and violet 30 10
618 – 50k. multicoloured . . . 40 30
DESIGN—VERT: 50k. Emblem and patchwork.

272 Boxing

1992. Olympic Games, Barcelona (1st issue). Multicoloured.
619 50k. Type **272** 15 15
620 1n. Nigerian athlete winning race 25 25
621 1n.50 Table tennis 35 35
622 2n. Taekwondo 45 45
MS623 120 × 117 mm. Nos. 619/22 1·75 2·00
See also No. 624.

273 Football

274 Blood Pressure Gauge

1992. Olympic Games, Barcelona (2nd issue).
624 **273** 1n.50 multicoloured . . . 50 50

1992. World Health Day. Multicoloured.
625 50k. Type **274** 15 15
626 1n. World Health Day '92 emblem 20 20
627 1n.50 Heart and lungs . . . 30 30
628 2n. Interior of heart 45 45
MS629 123 × 111 mm. Nos. 625/8 1·10 1·25

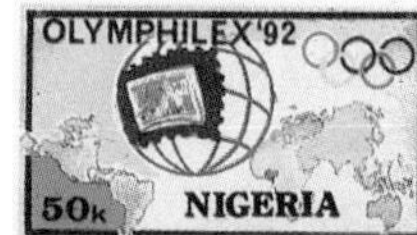

275 Map of World and Stamp on Globe

1992. "Olymphilex '92" Olympic Stamp Exhibition, Barcelona. Multicoloured.
630 50k. Type **275** 20 10
631 1n.50 Examining stamps . . 40 40
MS632 120 × 109 mm. Nos. 630/1 1·60 1·75

276 Gathering Plantain Fruit **277** Centre Emblem

1992. 25th Anniv of International Institute of Tropical Agriculture.
633 **276** 50k. multicoloured . . . 10 10
634 – 1n. multicoloured 15 15
635 – 1n.50 black, brown & grn 20 20
636 – 2n. multicoloured 25 25
MS637 121 × 118 mm. Nos. 633/6 1·25 1·50
DESIGNS—VERT: 1n.50, Harvesting cassava tubers; 2n. Stacking yams. HORIZ: 1n. Tropical foods.

1992. Commissioning of Maryam Babangida National Centre for Women's Development.
638 **277** 50k. gold, emerald and green 10 10
639 – 1n. multicoloured 15 15
640 – 1n.50 multicoloured . . . 20 20
641 – 2n. multicoloured 30 30
DESIGNS—VERT: 1n. Women working in fields; 2n. Woman at loom. HORIZ: 1n.50, Maryam Babangida National Centre.
All examples of No. 641 are without a "NIGERIA" inscription.

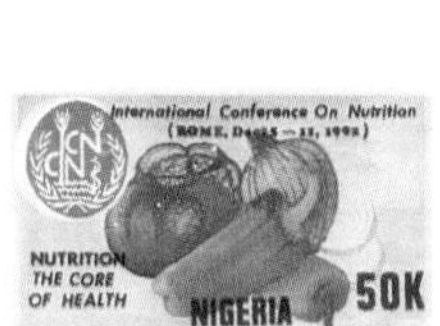

278 Healthy Food and Emblem **279** Sabada Dance

1992. International Conference on Nutrition, Rome. Multicoloured.
642 50k. Type **278** 10 10
643 1n. Child eating 15 15
644 1n.50 Fruit (vert) 20 20
645 2n. Vegetables 25 25
MS646 120 × 100 mm. Nos. 642/5 1·50 1·75

1992. Traditional Dances. Multicoloured.
647 50k. Type **279** 10 10
648 1n. Sato 15 15
649 1n.50 Asian Ubo Ikpa . . . 20 20
650 2n. Dundun 25 25
MS651 126 × 107 mm. Nos. 647/50 1·50 1·75

280 African Elephant

1993. Wildlife. Multicoloured.
652 1n.50 Type **280** . . . . . . 1·00 30
653 5n. Stanley crane (vert) . . . 1·25 40
654 20n. Roan antelope . . . . . 1·75 1·00
655 30n. Lion . . . . 2·00 1·25

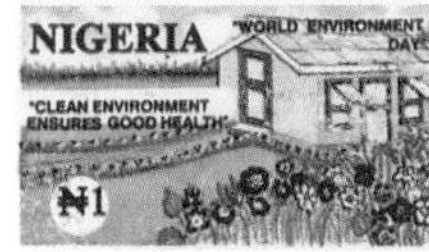

281 Suburban Garden

1993. World Environment Day. Multicoloured.
656 1n. Type **281** 10 10
657 1n.50 Water pollution 15 10
658 5n. Forest road 50 60
659 10n. Rural house . . . . . . 90 1·25

282 Oni Figure **283** "Bulbophyllum distans"

1993. 50th Anniv of National Museums and Monuments Commission. Multicoloured.
660 1n. Type **282** 10 10
661 1n.50 Bronze head of Queen Mother 10 10
662 5n. Bronze pendant (horiz) 30 50
663 10n. Nok head . . . . 70 1·00

1993. Orchids. Multicoloured.
664 1n. Type **283** 10 10
665 1n.50 "Eulophia cristata" . . 15 10
666 5n. "Eulophia horsfalli" . . . 45 55
667 10n. "Eulophia quartiniana" 1·00 1·25
MS668 103 × 121 mm. Nos. 664/7 1·75 2·00

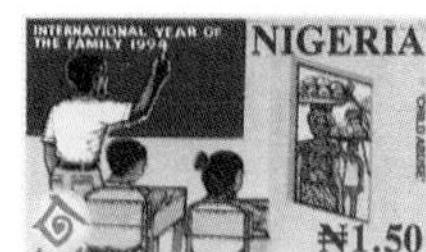

284 Children in Classroom and Adults carrying Food

1994. International Year of the Family. Mult.
669 1n.50 Type **284** 10 10
670 10n. Market . . . . 1·00 1·50

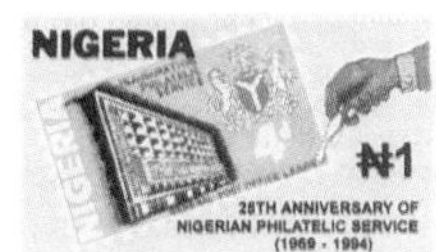

285 Hand with Tweezers holding 1969 4d. Philatelic Service Stamp

1994. 25th Anniv of Nat Philatelic Service. Mult.
671 1n. Type **285** 10 10
672 1n.50 Philatelic Bureau . . . 15 10
673 5n. Stamps forming map of Nigeria 45 60
674 10n. Philatelic counter . . . 1·00 1·40

286 "I Love Stamps"

1994. 120th Anniv of First Postage Stamps in Nigeria. Multicoloured.
675 1n. Type **286** 10 10
676 1n.50 "I Collect Stamps" . . 15 15
677 5n. 19th-century means of communication 45 60
678 10n. Lagos stamp of 1874 . . 1·00 1·40

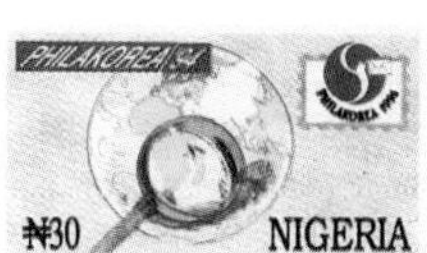

287 Magnifying Glass over Globe

1994. "Philakorea '94" International Stamp Exhibition, Seoul.
679 **287** 30n. multicoloured . . . 1·75 2·40
MS680 127 × 115 mm. **287** 30n. multicoloured . . . . 2·25 4·00

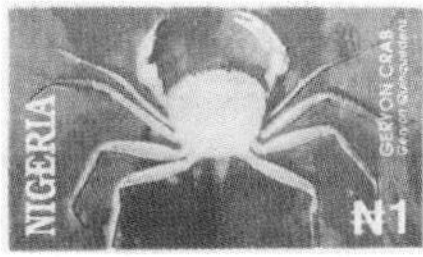

288 Geryon Crab

1994. Crabs. Multicoloured.
681 1n. Type **288** 10 10
682 1n.50 Spider crab 10 10
683 5n. Red spider crab 45 55
684 10n. Geryon maritae crab . . 90 1·25

289 Sewage Works **290** Letterbox

1994. 30th Anniv of African Development Bank. Multicoloured.
685 1n.50 Type **289** 15 10
686 30n. Development Bank emblem and flowers . . . 1·75 2·40

1995. 10th Anniv of Nigerian Post and Telecommunication Corporations. Multicoloured.
687 1n. Type **290** 10 10
688 1n.50 Letter showing "1 JAN 1985" postmark (horiz) . . 10 10
689 5n. Nipost and Nitel emblems (horiz) 30 45
690 10n. Mobile telephones . . . 60 1·00

291 Woman preparing Food **292** "Candlestick" Telephone

1995. Family Support Programme. Multicoloured.
691 1n. Type **291** 10 10
692 1n.50 Mother teaching children 10 10
693 5n. Family meal 30 45
694 10n. Agricultural workers and tractor 60 90

1995. Cent of First Telephone in Nigeria. Mult.
695 1n.50 Type **292** 10 10
696 10n. Early equipment . . . . 60 1·00

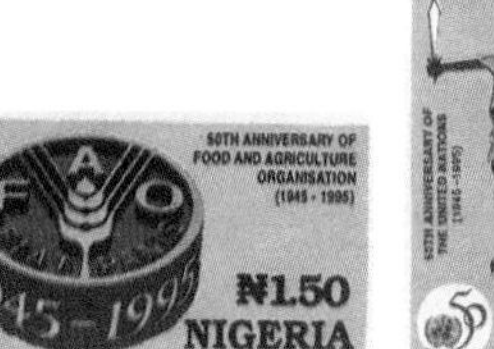

293 F.A.O. Emblem **294** "Justice" and 50th Anniversary Emblem

1995. 50th Anniv of F.A.O. Multicoloured.
697 1n.50 Type **293** 10 10
698 30n. Fishing canoes . . . . 1·90 2·25

1995. 50th Anniv of United Nations. Multicoloured.
699 1n. Type **294** 10 10
700 1n.50 Toxic waste (horiz) . . 10 10
701 5n. Tourist hut (horiz) . . . 30 40
702 10n. Nigerian armoured car on U.N. duty (horiz) . . . 90 1·40

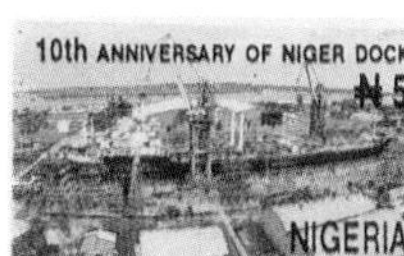

295 Container Ship in Dock

1996. 10th Anniv of Niger Dock. Multicoloured.
703 5n. Type **295** 35 30
704 10n. "Badagri" (tourist launch) on crane 65 60
705 20n. Shipping at dock . . . 1·00 1·50
706 30n. "Odoragushin" (ferry) 1·50 2·50

296 Scientist and Crops

1996. 21st Anniv of E.C.O.W.A.S. (Economic Community of West African States). Multicoloured.
707 5n. Type **296** 30 30
708 30n. Queue at border crossing . . . . 1·50 2·25

297 Judo **298** Nigerian Flag and Exhibition Emblem

1996. Olympic Games, Atlanta. Multicoloured.
709 5n. Type **297** 35 30
710 10n. Tennis 80 60
711 20n. Relay race . . . . . . 1·00 1·50
712 30n. Football . . . . 1·50 2·25

1996. "ISTANBUL '96" International Stamp Exhibition.
713 **298** 30n. mauve, green and black . . . . 1·50 2·25

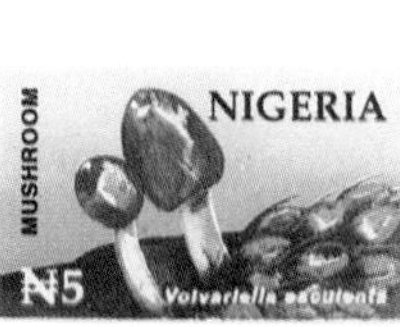

299 "Volvariella esculenta" **300** Boy with Toys

1996. Fungi. Multicoloured.
714 5n. Type **299** 45 30
715 10n. "Lentinus subnudus" . . 90 60
716 20n. "Tricholoma lobayensis" 1·25 1·50
717 30n. "Pleurotus tuber-regium" . . . . 1·50 2·25

1996. 50th Anniv of U.N.I.C.E.F. Multicoloured.
718 5n. Type **300** 30 30
719 30n. Girl reading book (horiz) . . . . 1·50 2·25

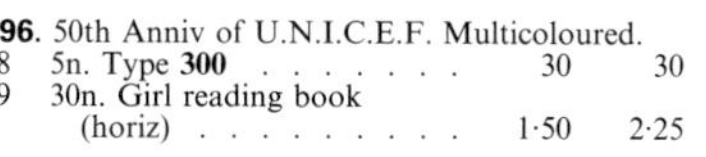
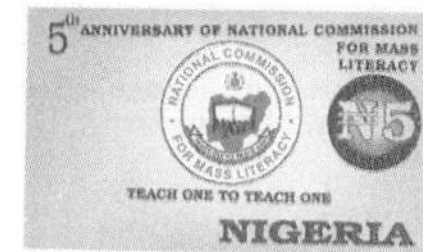

301 Literacy Logo

1996. 5th Anniv of Mass Literacy Commission.
720 **301** 5n. emerald, green and black 30 30
721 – 30n. emerald, green and black . . . . 1·50 2·25
DESIGN: 30n. Hands holding book and literacy logo.

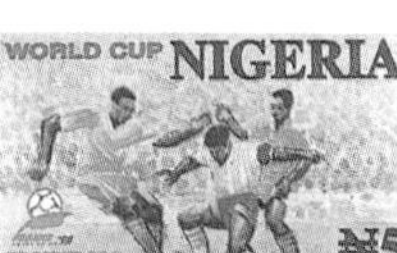

302 Three Footballers

1998. World Cup Football Championship, France. Multicoloured.
722 5n. Type **302** 25 30
723 10n. Player with ball (vert) 55 60
724 20n. Player receiving ball (vert) . . . . 1·10 1·25
725 30n. Two opposing players 1·60 2·00

303 University Tower and Complex

1998. 50th Anniv of Ibadan University. Mult.
726 5n. Type **303** 25 30
727 30n. Anniversary logo and University crest . . . . . 1·60 2·25

304 Ship and Logo

1998. 8th Anniv of Economic Community of West African States Military Arm (ECOMOG). Multicoloured.
728 5n. Type **304** 25 30
729 30n. Logo and original member states . . . . . . 1·25 1·75
730 50n. Current member states 2·25 3·00

305 Caged Steam Locomotive

1999. Centenary of Nigerian Railway Corporation. Multicoloured.
731 5n. Type **305** 25 30
732 10n. Iddo Terminus 55 60
733 20n. Diesel locomotive No. 2131 . . . . 1·10 1·25
734 30n. Passenger train pulling into station . . . . 1·60 2·00

306 Football and Globe

1999. 11th World Youth Football Championship, Nigeria. Multicoloured.
735 5n.+5n. Type **306** 15 30
736 10n.+5n. Player throwing ball 20 35
737 20n.+5n. Player scoring goal 35 50
738 30n.+5n. Map of Nigeria showing venues 50 70
739 40n.+5n. World Youth Football Championship logo 60 80
740 50n.+5n. Player being tackled 75 95
MS741 120 × 115 mm. Nos. 735/40 2·50 2·75

307 Sea Life and F.E.P.A. Emblem **308** Nicon Emblem

1999. 10th Anniv of Federal Environmental Protection Agency. Multicoloured.
742 5n. Type **307** 25 30
743 10n. Forest 55 60
744 20n. Monkeys . . . . 1·25 1·10
745 30n. Villagers and wildlife . . 2·00 2·25

1999. 30th Anniv of Nicon Insurance Corporation. Multicoloured.
746 5n. Type **308** 25 30
747 30n. Emblem and Nicon Building (horiz) . . . . . 1·00 1·50

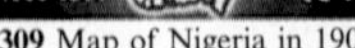

309 Map of Nigeria in 1900 **310** Sunshine Hour Recorder

2000. New Millennium (1st Issue). Multicoloured.
748 10n. Type **309** 20 15
749 20n. Map of Nigeria in 1914 45 35
750 30n. Coat of arms 50 60
751 40n. Map of Nigeria in 1996 75 90
See also Nos. 786/9.

2000. 50th Anniv of World Meteorological Organization.
752 **310** 10n. multicoloured . . . 15 15
753 – 30n. brown and blue . . . 55 75
DESIGN—HORIZ: 30n. Meteorological station.

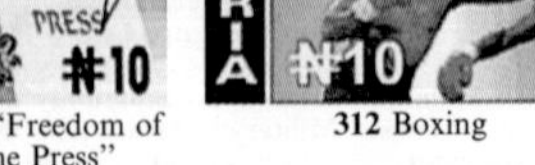

311 "Freedom of the Press" **312** Boxing

2000. Return to Democracy. Multicoloured.
754 10n. Type **311** 10 15
755 20n. "Justice for All" (horiz) 25 30
756 30n. Parliamentary Mace . . 35 50
757 40n. President Olusegun Obasanjo 50 70
MS758 99 × 109 mm. Nos. 754/7 1·10 1·40

2000. Olympic Games, Sydney. Multicoloured.
759 10n. Type **312** 10 15
760 20n. Weightlifting 25 30
761 30n. Women's football . . . 35 50
762 40n. Men's football 50 65
MS763 136 × 118 mm. Nos. 759/62 1·10 1·40

313 Obafemi Awolowo **314** Hug Plum

2000. 40th Anniv of Nigeria's Independence.
764 **313** 10n. black, emerald and green 10 15
765 – 20n. black, emerald and green 25 30
766 – 30n. black, emerald and green 35 40
767 – 40n. multicoloured . . . 80 70
768 – 50n. multicoloured . . . 95 1·00
DESIGNS—VERT: 20n. Abubakar Tafawa Balewa; 30n. Nnamdi Azikiwe. HORIZ: 40n. Liquified gas station; 50n. Container ships.

2001. Fruits. Multicoloured.
769 20n. Type **314** 30 30
770 30n. White star apple . . . 40 40
771 40n. African breadfruit . . . 60 65
772 50n. Akee apple 70 80

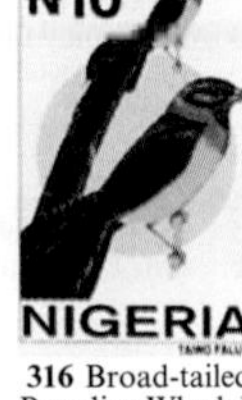

315 *Daily Times* Headquarters, Lagos **316** Broad-tailed Paradise Whydah

2001. 75th Anniv of *The Daily Times of Nigeria*. Multicoloured.
773 20n. Type **315** 25 30
774 30n. First issue of *Nigerian Daily Times*, 1926 . . . . 35 40
775 40n. *Daily Times* printing works, Lagos 50 55
776 50n. *Daily Times* masthead, 1947 . . . . 60 65

2001. Wildlife. Multicoloured.
777 10n. Type **316** 10 15
778 15n. Fire-bellied woodpecker 15 20
779 20n. Grant's zebra (horiz) . . 20 25
780 25n. Aardvark (horiz) 25 30
781 30n. Preuss's guenon (monkey) 30 35
782 40n. Great ground pangolin (horiz) 40 45
783 50n. Pygmy chimpanzee (*Pan paniscus*) (horiz) 45 50
784 100n. Red-eared guenon (monkey) . . . . 95 1·00

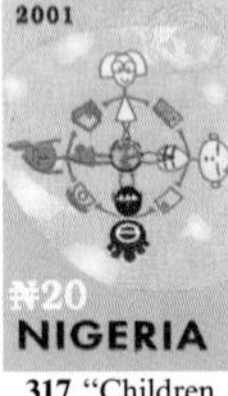

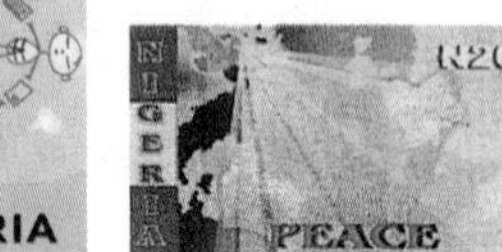

317 "Children encircling Globe" (Urska Golob) **318** Map of Nigeria and Dove

2001. U.N. Year of Dialogue among Civilisations.
785 **317** 20n. multicoloured . . . 25 30

2002. New Millennium (2nd issue). Multicoloured.
786 20n. Type **318** 30 30
787 30n. Globe and satellite dish 40 40
788 40n. Handshake across flag in shape of Nigeria 70 65
789 50n. Two overlapping hearts 70 80

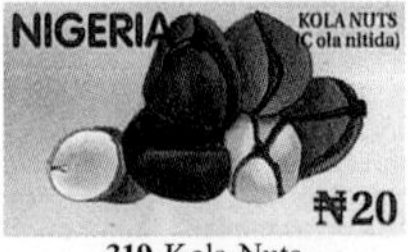

319 Kola Nuts

2002. Cash Crops. Multicoloured.
790 20n. Type **319** 20 25
791 30n. Oil palm 30 35
792 40n. Cassava 40 45
793 50n. Maize (vert) 45 50

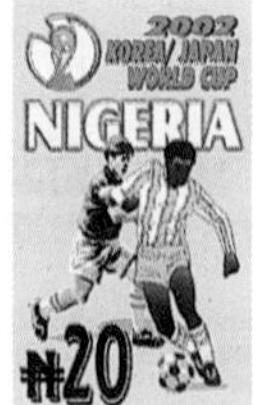

320 Nigerian Player dribbling Ball

2002. World Cup Football Championship, Japan and Korea. Multicoloured.
794 20n. Type **320** 20 25
795 30n. Footballs around Globe 30 35
796 40n. Footballer's legs and World Cup Trophy (horiz) 40 45
797 50n. World Cup Trophy . . 45 50

POSTAGE DUE STAMPS

D 1

1959.
D1 **D 1** 1d. orange . . . . 15 1·00
D2 2d. orange . . . . 20 1·00
D3 3d. orange . . . . 25 1·50
D4 6d. orange . . . . 25 5·00
D5 1s. black . . . . 50 6·50

1961.
D 6 **D 1** 1d. red 15 40
D 7 2d. blue 20 45
D 8 3d. green 25 60
D 9 6d. yellow . . . . 30 1·40
D10 1s. blue . . . . 50 2·25

1973. As Type **D 1**.
D11 2k. red 10 10
D12 3k. blue 10 10
D13 5k. yellow 10 10
D14 10k. green 10 10

NIUAFO'OU Pt. 1

A remote island, part of the Kingdom of Tonga, with local autonomy.

100 seniti = 1 pa'anga.

1 Map of Niuafo'ou **2a** SPIA De Havilland D.H.C. 6 Turin Otter 300

1983.
1 **1** 1s. stone, black and red . . . 30 90
2 2s. stone, black and green . . 30 90
3 3s. stone, black and blue . . 30 90
4 3s. stone, black and brown 30 90
5 5s. stone, black and purple 40 90
6 6s. stone, black and blue . . 40 90
7 9s. stone, black and green . . 40 90
8 10s. stone, black and blue . . 40 90
9 13s. stone, black and green 65 90
10 15s. stone, black and brown 70 1·25
11 20s. stone, black and blue . . 75 1·25
12 29s. stone, black and purple 1·00 80
13 32s. stone, black and green 1·00 90
14 47s. stone, black and red . . 1·40 1·40

1983. No. 820 of Tonga optd **NIUAFO'OU KINGDOM OF TONGA** or surch also.
15 1p. on 2p. green and black . . 2·50 3·50
16 2p. green . . . . 3·50 5·00

1983. Inauguration of Niuafo'ou Airport.
17 **2a** 29s. multicoloured . . . . . 1·25 1·00
18 1p. multicoloured . . . . . 3·00 3·25

1983. As T **1**, but without value, surch.
19 3s. stone, black and blue . . . 30 50
20 5s. stone, black and blue . . . 30 50
21 32s. stone, black and blue . . 1·75 1·25
22 2p. stone, black and blue . . . 8·50 10·00

4 Eruption of Niuafo'ou

1983. 25th Anniv of Re-settlement. Mult.
23 5s. Type **4** 40 30
24 29s. Lava flow . . . . 1·00 1·00
25 32s. Islanders fleeing to safety 1·10 1·00
26 1p.50 Evacuation by canoe . . 3·50 5·00

5 Purple Swamphen **6** Green Turtle

1983. Birds of Niuafo'ou.
27 **5** 1s. black and mauve . . . . 1·00 1·25
28 – 2s. black and blue . . . . . 1·00 1·25
29 – 3s. black and green . . . . . 1·00 1·25
30 – 5s. black and yellow . . . . 1·25 1·25
31 – 6s. black and orange . . . . 1·50 1·60
32 – 9s. multicoloured . . . . . . 1·75 1·25
33 – 10s. multicoloured . . . . . 1·75 2·00
34 – 13s. multicoloured . . . . . 2·25 1·60
35 – 15s. multicoloured . . . . . 2·25 2·50
36 – 20s. multicoloured . . . . . 2·50 2·75
37 – 29s. multicoloured . . . . . 2·75 1·50
38 – 32s. multicoloured . . . . . 2·75 1·60
39 – 47s. multicoloured . . . . . 3·25 2·25
40 – 1p. multicoloured . . . . . 6·00 8·50
41 – 2p. multicoloured . . . . . 8·00 12·00
DESIGNS—VERT (22 × 29 mm): 2s. White collared kingfisher; 3s. Red-headed parrot finch; 5s. Buff-banded rail ("Banded Rail"); 6s. Polynesian scrub hen ("Niuafo'ou megapode"); 9s. Green honeyeater; 10s. Purple swamphen (different). (22 × 36 mm): 29s. Red-headed parrot finch (different); 32s. White collared kingfisher (different). (29 × 42 mm): 1p. As 10s. HORIZ (29 × 22 mm): 13s. Buff-banded rail ("Banded Rail") (different): 15s. Polynesian scrub hen (different). (36 × 22 mm): 20s. As 13s.; 47s. As 15s. (42 × 29 mm): 2p. As 15s.

1984. Wildlife and Nature Reserve. Mult.
42 29s. Type **6** 70 70
43 32s. Insular flying fox (vert) 70 70
44 47s. Humpback whale . . . . 2·50 1·75
45 1p.50 Polynesian scrub hen ("Niuafo'ou megapode") (vert) . . . . 4·50 7·00

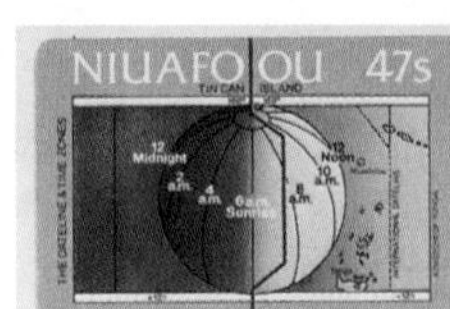

7 Diagram of Time Zones

1984. Cent of International Dateline. Mult.
46 47s. Type **7** 60 50
47 2p. Location map showing Niuafo'ou . . . . 1·90 3·25

8 Australia 1913 £2 Kangaroo Definitive **9** Dutch Brass Band entertaining Tongans

1984. "Ausipex" International Stamp Exhibition, Melbourne. Multicoloured.
48 32s. Type **8** 75 60
49 1p.50 Niuafo'ou 1983 10s. map definitive . . . . . . 2·25 3·00
MS50 90 × 100 mm. As Nos. 48/9, but without exhibition logo and with face value at foot . . . . 1·75 2·50

1985. 400th Birth Anniv of Jacob Le Maire (discoverer of Niuafo'ou).
51 **9** 13s. brown, yellow & orange 25 40
52 – 32s. brown, yellow and blue 55 60
53 – 47s. brown, yellow and green 75 80
54 – 1p.50 brown, cinnamon and yellow . . . . 2·25 3·00
MS55 90 × 90 mm. 1p.50 brown, light brown and blue. Imperf 1·50 2·00
DESIGNS: 32s. Tongans preparing kava; 47s. Tongan canoes and outriggers; 1p.50, "Eendracht" at anchor off Tafahi Island.

10 "Ysabel", 1902

1985. Mail Ships. Multicoloured.
56B 9s. Type **10** 35 55
57A 13s. "Tofua I", 1908 . . . . 70 55
58B 47s. "Mariposa", 1934 . . . 1·10 1·60
59B 1p.50 "Matua", 1936 . . . . 2·50 4·00

11 Preparing to fire Rocket

1985. Niuafo'ou Rocket Mails. Multicoloured.
60B 32s. Type **11** . . . . 1·00 80
61A 42s. Rocket in flight . . . . 1·25 1·00
62B 57s. Ship's crew watching rocket's descent . . . . . 1·60 1·40
63A 1p.50 Islanders reading mail 3·50 4·50

12 Halley's Comet, 684 A.D.

1986. Appearance of Halley's Comet. Multicoloured.
64 42s. Type **12** . . . . 5·00 3·00
65 42s. Halley's Comet, 1066, from Bayeux Tapestry . . . 5·00 3·00
66 42s. Edmond Halley . . . . . 5·00 3·00
67 42s. Halley's Comet, 1910 . . 5·00 3·00
68 42s. Halley's Comet, 1986 . . 5·00 3·00
69 57s. Type **12** . . . . 5·00 3·50
70 57s. As No. 65 . . . . 5·00 3·50
71 57s. As No. 66 . . . . 5·00 3·50
72 57s. As No. 67 . . . . 5·00 3·50
73 57s. As No. 68 . . . . 5·00 3·50

Nos. 64/8 and 69/73 were printed together, se-tenant, forming composite designs.

1986. Nos. 32/9 surch.
74 4s. on 9s. Green honeyeater 85 2·00
75 4s. on 10s. Purple swamphen 85 2·00
76 42s. on 13s. Buff-banded rail ("Banded Rail") . . . . . 2·75 2·00
77 42s. on 15s. Polynesian scrub hen . . . . 2·75 2·00
78 57s. on 29s. Red-headed parrot finch . . . . 3·25 2·25
79 57s. on 32s. White-collared kingfisher . . . . 3·25 2·25
80 2p.50 on 20s. Buff-banded rail ("Banded Rail") . . . . . 9·00 11·00
81 2p.50 on 47s. Polynesian scrub hen . . . . 9·00 11·00

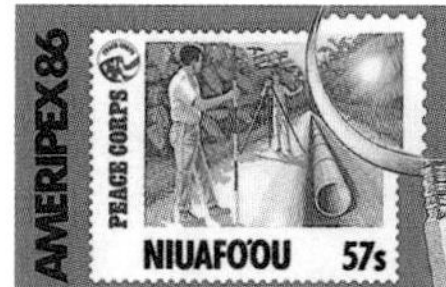

13a Peace Corps Surveyor and Pipeline

1986. "Ameripex '86" International Stamp Exhibition, Chicago. 25th Anniv of United States Peace Corps. Multicoloured.
82 57s. Type **13a** . . . . 1·25 1·25
83 1p.50 Inspecting crops . . . . 2·25 3·00
MS84 90 × 90 mm. Nos. 82/3, magnifying glass and tweezers. Imperf . . . . 3·75 5·00

14 Swimmers with Mail

1986. Centenary of First Tonga Stamps. Designs showing Niuafo'ou mail transport. Multicoloured.
85 42s. Type **14** 90 90
86 57s. Collecting tin can mail . . 1·10 1·10
87 1p. Ship firing mail rocket . . 2·00 2·50
88 2p.50 "Collecting the Mails" (detail) (C. Mayger) . . . . 3·50 4·75
MS89 135 × 80 mm. No. 88 . . . 5·00 7·00

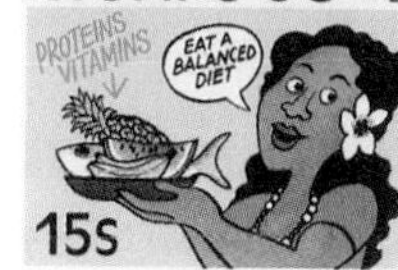

15 Woman with Nourishing Foods ("Eat a balanced diet")

1987. Red Cross. Preventive Medicine. Mult.
90 15s. Type **15** 60 60
91 42s. Nurse with baby ("Give them post-natal care") . . . 1·60 1·60
92 1p. Man with insecticide ("Insects spread disease") 2·50 3·25
93 2p.50 Boxer ("Say no to alcohol, drugs, tobacco") . . 4·00 5·50

16 Hammerhead

1987. Sharks. Multicoloured.
94 29s. Type **16** . . . . 2·00 1·75
95 32s. Tiger shark . . . . 2·00 1·75
96 47s. Grey nurse shark . . . . 2·50 2·25
97 1p. Great white shark . . . . 4·00 6·00
MS98 90 × 90 mm. 2p. Shark and fishes . . . . 11·00 12·00

17 Capt. E. C. Musick and Sikorsky S.42A Flying Boat "Samoan Clipper"

1987. Air Pioneers of the South Pacific. Multicoloured.
99 42s. Type **17** . . . . 1·75 1·40
100 57s. Capt. J. W. Burgess and Short S. 30 modified "G" Class flying boat "Aotearoa" . . . . 2·00 1·75
101 1p.50 Sir Charles Kingsford Smith and Fokker F.VIIa/3m "Southern Cross" . . . 3·00 3·75
102 2p. Amelia Earhart and Lockheed 10E Electra . . 3·50 4·50

18 Polynesian Scrub Hen and 1983 1s. Map Definitive

1988. 5th Annivs of First Niuafo'ou Postage Stamp (42, 57s.) and Niuafo'ou Airport Inauguration (1, 2p.). Multicoloured.
103 42s. Type **18** . . . . 1·00 75
104 57s. As Type **18**, but with stamp at left . . . . 1·00 95
105 1p. Concorde and 1983 Airport Inauguration 29s. stamp . . . . 3·75 3·25
106 2p. As 1p. but with stamp at left . . . . 4·25 4·00

19 Sailing Ship and Ship's Boat

20 Audubon's Shearwaters and Blowholes, Houma, Tonga

1988. Bicentenary of Australian Settlement. Sheet 115 × 110 mm containing T **19** and similar vert designs. Multicoloured.
MS107 42s. Type **19**; 42s. Aborigines; 42s. Early settlement; 42s. Marine and convicts; 42s. Sheep station; 42s. Mounted stockman; 42s. Kangaroos and early Trans Continental locomotive; 42s. Kangaroos and train carriages; 42s. Flying Doctor aircraft; 42s. Cricket match; 42s. Wicket and Sydney skyline; 42s. Fielders and Sydney Harbour Bridge . . . . 32·00 32·00

Each horizontal strip of 4 within No. **MS**107 shows a composite design.

1988. Islands of Polynesia. Multicoloured.
108 42s. Type **20** . . . . 1·50 95
109 57s. Brown kiwi at Akaroa Harbour, New Zealand . . 2·25 1·40
110 90s. Red-tailed tropic birds at Rainmaker Mountain, Samoa . . . . 2·50 2·50
111 2p.50 Laysan albatross at Kapoho Volcano, Hawaii 4·75 6·00

21 Sextant

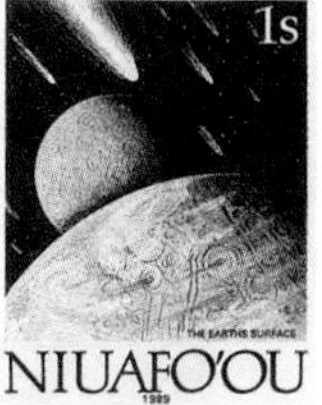

23 Formation of Earth's Surface

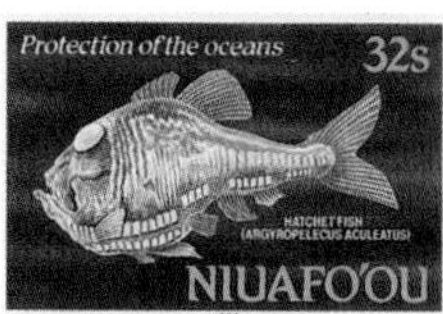

22 Spiny Hatchetfish

1989. Bicentenary of Mutiny on the Bounty. Sheet 115 × 110 mm containing T **21** and similar vert designs. Multicoloured.
MS112 42s. Type **21**; 42s. Capt. Bligh; 42s. Lieutenant, 1787; 42s. Midshipman, 1787; 42s. Tahitian woman and contemporary newspaper; 42s. Breadfruit plant; 42s. Pistol and extract from "Mutiny on the Bounty"; 42s. Book illustration of Bligh cast adrift; 42s. Profile of Tahitian woman and extract from contemporary newspaper; 42s. Signatures of "Bounty officers"; 42s. Fletcher Christian; 42s. Tombstone of John Adams, Pitcairn Island . . . . 13·00 14·00

1989. Fishes of the Deep. Multicoloured.
113 32s. Type **22** . . . . 85 1·00
114 42s. Snipe eel . . . . 1·00 1·00
115 57s. Viperfish . . . . 1·25 1·50
116 1p.50 Football anglerfish . . 3·00 4·00

1989. The Evolution of the Earth. Multicoloured.
(a) Size 27 × 35½ mm.
117 1s. Type **23** 30 50
118 2s. Cross-section of Earth's crust 30 50
119 5s. Volcano 40 50
120 10s. Cross-section of Earth during cooling 40 50
120a 13s. Gem stones 50 40
121 15s. Sea 40 40
122 20s. Mountains 40 40
123 32s. River gorge 50 35
124 42s. Early plant life, Silurian era 65 45
124a 45s. Early marine life . . . 65 65
125 50s. Fossils and Cambrian lifeforms 75 55
126 57s. Carboniferous forest and coal seams 75 55
126a 60s. Dinosaurs feeding . . . 80 70
126b 80s. Tyrannosaurus and triceratops fighting . . . 1·00 1·00

(b) Size 25½ × 40 mm.
127 1p. Dragonfly and amphibians, Carboniferous era . . . . 1·25 1·25
128 1p.50 Dinosaurs, Jurassic era . . . . 2·00 2·25
129 2p. Archaeopteryx and mammals, Jurassic era . . 2·00 2·25
130 5p. Human family and domesticated dog, Pleistocene era . . . . . 4·00 5·00
130a 10p. Mammoth and sabre-tooth tiger . . . . 7·00 8·50

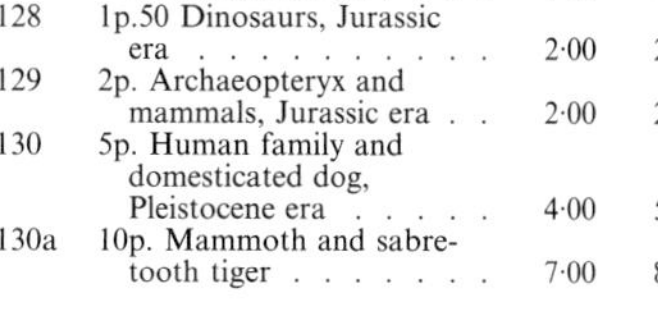

24 Astronaut on Moon and Newspaper Headline

1989. "World Stamp Expo '89" International Stamp Exhibition, Washington.
131 **24** 57s. multicoloured . . . . 1·75 1·25

1989. 20th Universal Postal Union Congress, Washington. Miniature sheet, 185 × 150 mm, containing designs as Nos. 117/20, 121/4, 125/6 and 127/30, but wuth U.P.U. emblem at top right and some new values.
MS132 32s. × 5 (as Nos. 117/20, 121); 42s. × 5 (as Nos. 122/4, 125/6); 57s. × 5 (as Nos. 127/30, 131) . . . . 20·00 22·00

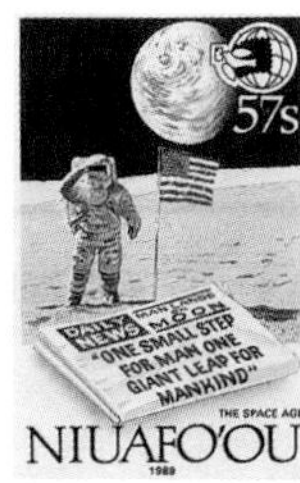

25 Lake Vai Lahi

1990. Niuafo'ou Crater Lake. Multicoloured.
133 42s. Type **25** . . . . 70 1·00
134 42s. Islands in centre of lake 70 1·00
135 42s. South-west end of lake and islet . . . . 70 1·00
136 1p. Type **25** . . . . 1·40 1·60
137 1p. As No. 134 . . . . . . 1·40 1·60
138 1p. As No. 135 . . . . . . 1·40 1·60

Nos. 133/8 were printed together in se-tenant strips of each value, forming a composite design.

26 Penny Black and Tin Can Mail Service

1990. 150th Anniv of the Penny Black. Mult.
139 42s. Type **26** . . . . 1·25 1·00
140 57s. U.S.A. 1847 10c. stamp 1·40 1·25
141 75s. Western Australia 1854 1d. stamp . . . . 1·60 2·00
142 2p.50 Mafeking Siege 1900 1d. stamp . . . . 5·00 6·00

27 Humpback Whale surfacing

1990. Polynesian Whaling. Multicoloured.
143 15s. Type **27** . . . . 1·75 1·60
144 42s. Whale diving under canoe . . . . 2·25 1·90
145 57s. Tail of Blue whale . . . 2·50 1·90
146 2p. Old man and pair of whales . . . . 6·50 7·50
MS147 120 × 93 mm. 1p. Pair of whales (38 × 30 mm) . . . . . 10·00 11·00

27a Agriculture and Fisheries

1990. 40th Anniv of U.N. Development Programme. Multicoloured.
148 57s. Type **27a** . . . . 90 1·40
149 57s. Education . . . . 90 1·40
150 2p.50 Healthcare . . . . . . 3·25 4·00
151 2p.50 Communications . . . 3·25 4·00

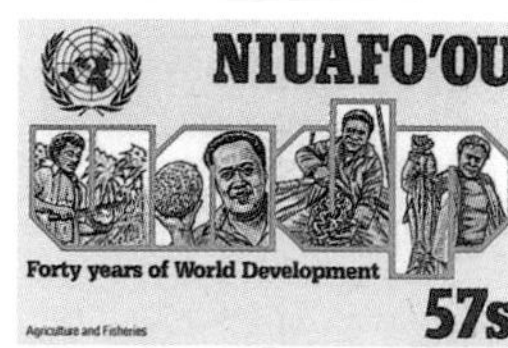

28 H.M.S. "Bounty"

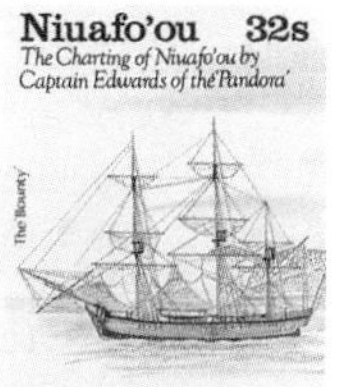

30 Longhorned Beetle Grub

1991. Bicentenary of Charting of Niuafo'ou. Multicoloured.
152 32s. Type **28** . . . . 1·25 1·75
153 42s. Chart of "Pandora's" course . . . . 1·40 1·75

154 57s. H.M.S. "Pandora" (frigate) . . . . 1·75 1·75
MS155 120×93 mm. 2p. Capt. Edwards of the "Pandora"; 3p. Capt. Bligh of the "Bounty" 11·00 12·00

1991. Ornithological and Scientific Expedition to Niuafo'ou. No. **MS**147 surch **1991 ORNITHOLOGICAL AND SCIENTIFIC EXPEDITION T $1.**
MS156 120×93 mm. 1p. on 1p. multicoloured . . . . 2·75 3·50

1991. Longhorned Beetle. Multicoloured.
157 42s. Type **30** . . . . 80 1·00
158 57s. Adult beetle . . . . . . 90 1·00
159 1p.50 Grub burrowing . . . 2·75 3·25
160 2p.50 Adult on tree trunk . . 4·00 4·50

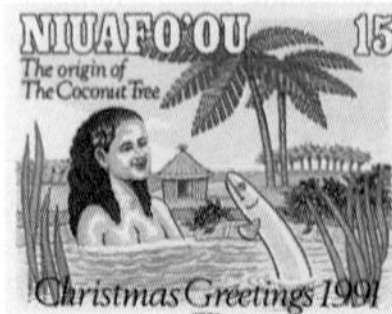

31 Heina meeting the Eel

1991. Christmas. The Legend of the Coconut Tree. Multicoloured.
161 15s. Type **31** 35 60
162 42s. Heina crying over the eel's grave . . . . 90 1·00
MS163 96×113 mm. 15s. Type **31**; 42s. No. 162; 1p.50, Heina's son collecting coconuts; 3p. Milk flowing from coconut . . . . 9·00 10·00

31a Columbus

1992. 500th Anniv of Discovery of America by Columbus. Sheet 119×109 mm. containing vert designs as T **31a**. Multicoloured.
MS164 57s. Columbus; 57s. Queen Isabella and King Ferdinand; 57s. Columbus being blessed by Abbot of Palos; 57s. 15th-century compass; 57s. Wooden traverse, windrose and the "Nina"; 57s. Bow of "Santa Maria"; 57s. Stern of "Santa Maria"; 57s. The "Pinta"; 57s. Crew erecting cross; 57s. Sailors and Indians; 57s. Columbus reporting to King and Queen; 57s. Coat of Arms . . 17·00 18·00

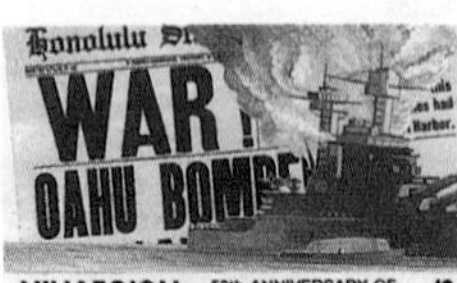

31b American Battleship Ablaze, Pearl Harbor

1992. 50th Anniv of War in the Pacific. Multicoloured.
165 42s. Type **31b** . . . . 1·10 1·25
166 42s. Destroyed American Douglas B-18 Bolo aircraft, Hawaii . . . . 1·10 1·25
167 42s. Newspaper and Japanese Mitsubishi A6M Zero-Sen fighter . . . . 1·10 1·25
168 42s. Pres. Roosevelt signing Declaration of War . . . . 1·10 1·25
169 42s. Japanese T95 light tank and Gen. MacArthur . . . 1·10 1·25
170 42s. Douglas SBD Dauntless dive bomber and Admiral Nimitz . . . . 1·10 1·25
171 42s. Bren gun and Gen. Sir Thomas Blamey . . . . . 1·10 1·25
172 42s. Australian mortar crew, Kokoda . . . . 1·10 1·25
173 42s. U.S.S. "Mississippi" in action and Maj. Gen. Julian C. Smith . . . . . 1·10 1·25
174 42s. U.S.S. "Enterprise" (aircraft carrier) . . . . . 1·10 1·25
175 42s. American marine and Maj. Gen. Curtis Lemay 1·10 1·25
176 42s. Boeing B-29 Superfortress bomber and Japanese surrender, Tokyo Bay . . . . 1·10 1·25
Nos. 165/76 were printed together, se-tenant, forming a composite design.

31c King Taufa'ahau Tupou IV and Queen Halaevalu During Coronation

1992. 25th Anniv of the Coronation of King Tupou IV.
177 **31c** 45s. multicoloured 75 75
178 – 80s. multicoloured . . . . 1·50 1·75
179 – 80s. black and brown . . 1·50 1·75
180 – 80s. multicoloured . . . . 1·50 1·75
181 – 2p. multicoloured . . . . 2·50 3·00
DESIGNS—(34×23 mm): No. 177, Type **31c**. (48×35 mm): No. 178, King Tupou IV and Tongan national anthem; 179, Extract from Investiture ceremony; 180, Tongan choir; 181, As 45s.
Nos. 177/81 show the King's first name incorrectly spelt as "Tauf'ahau".

32 Male and Female Scrub Hens searching for Food

1992. Endangered Species. Polynesian Scrub Hen. Multicoloured.
182 45s. Type **32** . . . . 1·00 1·25
183 60s. Female guarding egg . . 1·25 1·40
184 80s. Chick . . . . 1·60 1·75
185 1p.50 Head of male . . . . 2·75 3·50

33 1983 2s. Map Definitive and 1993 60s. Dinosaur Definitive

1993. 10th Anniv of First Niuafo'ou Stamp. Multicoloured.
186 60s. Type **33** . . . . 1·00 1·10
187 80s. 1983 5s. definitive and 1993 80s. dinosaurs definitive . . . . 1·25 1·40

34 De Havilland Twin Otter 200/300 of South Pacific Island Airways

34a King Tupou IV and "Pangai" (patrol boat)

1993. 10th Anniv of First Flight to Niuafo'ou. Multicoloured.
188 1p. Type **34** . . . . 1·50 2·00
189 2p.50 De Havilland Twin Otter 200/300 of Friendly Islands Airways . . . . . 3·50 4·50

1993. 75th Birthday of King Taufa'ahau Tupou IV. Multicoloured.
190 45s. Type **34a** 55 65
191 80s. King Tupou IV and musical instruments (38½×51 mm) . . . . . . 1·25 1·75
192 80s. King Tupou IV and sporting events (38½×51 mm) . . . . . . 1·25 1·75
193 80s. King Tupou IV with De Havilland Twin Otter 200/300 airplane and telecommunications . . . . 1·25 1·75
194 2p. As 45s. but larger (38½×51 mm) . . . . . . 2·75 3·25

35 Blue-crowned Lorikeets

35a "Crater Lake Megapode and Volcano" (Paea Puletau)

1993. Natural History of Lake Vai Lahi. Multicoloured.
195 60s. Type **35** . . . . 1·00 1·25
196 60s. White-tailed tropic bird and reef heron . . . . . . 1·00 1·25
197 60s. Black admiral (butterfly) and Niuafo'ou coconut beetle . . . . 1·00 1·25
198 60s. Niuafo'ou dragonfly, pacific black ducks and Niuafo'ou moths . . . . . 1·00 1·25
199 60s. Niuafo'ou megapode . . 1·00 1·25
Nos. 195/9 were printed together, se-tenant, forming a composite design.

1993. Children's Painting Competition Winners.
200 **35a** 10s. multicoloured 50 80
201 – 10s. black and grey . . . 50 80
202 – 1p. multicoloured . . . . 3·25 3·50
203 – 1p. multicoloured . . . . 3·25 3·50
DESIGNS: Nos. 200 and 202, Type **35a**; Nos. 201 and 203, "Ofato Beetle Grubs of Niuafo'ou" (Peni Finau).

36 "Scarabaeidea"

1994. Beetles. Multicoloured.
204 60s. Type **36** . . . . 85 1·00
205 80s. "Coccinellidea" . . . . 1·10 1·40
206 1p.50 "Cerambycidea" . . . 2·00 2·50
207 2p.50 "Pentatomidae" . . . 3·75 4·25

37 Stern of H.M.S. "Bounty"

38 Blue-crowned Lory and Lava Flows

1994. Sailing Ships. Multicoloured.
208 80s. Type **37** . . . . 1·75 2·25
209 80s. Bow of H.M.S. "Bounty" . . . . 1·75 2·25
210 80s. H.M.S. "Pandora" (frigate) . . . . 1·75 2·25
211 80s. Whaling ship . . . . . 1·75 2·25
212 80s. Trading schooner . . . 1·75 2·25

1994. Volcanic Eruptions on Niuafo'ou. Multicoloured.
213 80s. Type **38** . . . . 1·25 1·75
214 80s. Pacific ducks over lava flows . . . . 1·25 1·75
215 80s. Megapodes and palm trees . . . . 1·25 1·75
216 80s. White-tailed tropic birds and inhabitants . . . . . 1·25 1·75
217 80s. Reef heron and evacuation, 1946 . . . . . 1·25 1·75
Nos. 213/17 were printed together, se-tenant, forming a composite design.

1995. Visit South Pacific Year '95. Save the Whales. Nos. 143/6 surch **SAVE THE WHALES VISIT SOUTH PACIFIC YEAR '95**, emblem and value.
218 60s. on 42s. Whale diving under canoe . . . . 2·00 1·75
219 80s. on 15s. Type **27** . . . . 2·25 2·25
220 80s. on 57s. Tail of blue whale . . . . 2·25 2·25
221 2p. on 2p. Old man and pair of whales . . . . 4·25 4·50
MS222 120×93 mm. 1p.50 on 1p. Pair of whales (38×30 mm) . . 3·25 4·00

39a American Marine

1995. 50th Anniv of End of World War II in the Pacific.
223 **39a** 60s. yellow, black and blue . . . . 1·25 1·50
224 – 60s. yellow, black and blue . . . . 1·25 1·50
225 – 60s. yellow, black and blue . . . . 1·25 1·50
226 – 60s. yellow, black and blue . . . . 1·25 1·50
227 – 60s. yellow, black and blue . . . . 1·25 1·50
228 **39a** 80s. yellow, black and red 1·25 1·50
229 – 80s. yellow, black and red 1·25 1·50
230 – 80s. yellow, black and red 1·25 1·50
231 – 80s. yellow, black and red 1·25 1·50
232 – 80s. yellow, black and red 1·25 1·50
DESIGNS: Nos. 224 and 229, Marine firing and side of tank; 225 and 230, Tank; 226 and 231, Marines leaving landing craft; 227 and 232, Beach assault and palm trees.
Nos. 223/32 were printed together, se-tenant, forming two composite designs.

39b Dinosaurs Feeding

1995. "Singapore '95" International Stamp Exhibitions. Designs showing exhibition emblem. Multicoloured.
233 45s. Type **39b** (as No. 126a) 1·00 1·50
234 60s. Tyrannosaurus fighting Triceratops (as No. 126b) 1·00 1·50
MS235 110×70 mm. 2p. Plesiosaurus . . . . 2·50 3·25

39c Great Wall of China (½-size illustration)

1995. Beijing International Coin and Stamp Show '95. Sheet 143×87 mm.
MS236 **39c** 1p.40 multicoloured 2·00 2·50

39d St. Paul's Cathedral and Searchlights

1995. 50th Anniv of United Nations and End of Second World War.
237 **39d** 60s. multicoloured . . . . 1·00 1·50
238 – 60s. black and blue . . . 1·00 1·50
239 – 60s. multicoloured . . . . 1·00 1·50
240 – 80s. multicoloured . . . . 1·25 1·50
241 – 80s. blue and black . . . 1·25 1·50
242 – 80s. multicoloured . . . . 1·25 1·50
DESIGNS—HORIZ: No. 239, Concorde; 240, Allied prisoners of war and Burma Railway; 242, Mt. Fuji and express train. VERT—25×35 mm: Nos. 238 and 241, U.N. anniversary emblem.

40 Charles Ramsay and Swimmers with Poles

1996. Tin Can Mail Pioneers. Multicoloured.
243 45s. Type **40** 90 90
244 60s. Charles Ramsay and encounter with shark . . . 1·25 1·25
245 1p. Walter Quensell and transferring mail from canoes to ship . . . . . . 2·00 2·00
246 3p. Walter Quensell and Tin Can Mail cancellations . . 6·00 6·50

40a Cave Painting, Lake Village and Hunter

1996. 13th Congress of International Union of Prehistoric and Protohistoric Sciences, Forli, Italy. Multicoloured.
247 1p. Type **40a** . . . . 2·25 2·25
248 1p. Egyptians with Pyramid, Greek temple, and Romans with Colosseum . . . . . 2·25 2·25

40b Dolls, Model Truck and Counting Balls — **41** Island and Two Canoes

1996. 50th Anniv of U.N.I.C.E.F. Children's Toys. Multicoloured.
249 80s. Type **40b** . . . . 1·75 2·00
250 80s. Teddy bear, tricycle and model car . . . . 1·75 2·00
251 80s. Book, model helicopter, pedal car and roller skates 1·75 2·00
Nos. 249/51 were printed together, se-tenant, forming a composite design.

1996. 50th Anniv of Evacuation of Niuafo'ou. Multicoloured.
252 45s. Type **41** . . . . 85 1·10
253 45s. Erupting volcano and canoes . . . . 85 1·10
254 45s. End of island, volcanic cloud and canoe . . . . . 85 1·10
255 45s. Family and livestock in outrigger canoe . . . . . 85 1·10
256 45s. Islanders reaching "Matua" (inter-island freighter) . . . . 85 1·10
257 60s. Type **41** . . . . 95 1·10
258 60s. As No. 253 . . . . . . 95 1·10
259 60s. As No. 254 . . . . . . 95 1·10
260 60s. As No. 255 . . . . . . 95 1·10
261 60s. As No. 256 . . . . . . 95 1·10
Nos. 252/6 and 257/61 respectively were printed together, se-tenant, forming the same composite design.

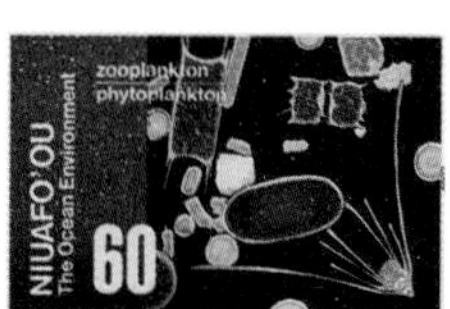

42 Plankton

1997. The Ocean Environment.
262 **42** 60s. multicoloured . . . . 1·00 1·00
263 – 80s. multicoloured . . . . 1·25 1·25
264 – 1p.50 multicoloured . . . 2·25 2·50
265 – 2p.50 multicoloured . . . 3·00 3·50
DESIGNS: 80s. to 2p.50, Different plankton.

42a Black-naped Tern

1997. "Pacific '97" International Stamp Exhibition, San Francisco. Sheet 85 × 110 mm.
MS266 **42a** 2p. multicoloured . . 2·75 3·25

42b King and Queen on Wedding Day

1997. King and Queen of Tonga's Golden Wedding and 30th Anniv of Coronation. Multicoloured.
267 80s. Type **42b** . . . . 1·50 1·75
268 80s. King Tupou in Coronation robes . . . . 1·50 1·75
MS269 82 × 70 mm. 5p. King Tupou with pages (horiz) . . . . . . 7·00 7·50

43 Blue-crowned Lory Nestlings — **43a** King Taufa'ahau Tupou IV

1998. Endangered Species. Blue-crowned Lory. Multicoloured.
270 10s. Type **43** . . . . 1·25 1·25
271 55s. Feeding on flowers . . . 2·50 1·25
272 80s. Perched on branch . . . 3·00 2·00
273 3p. Pair on branch . . . . . 6·50 7·00
MS274 160 × 112 mm. Nos. 270/3 × 2 24·00 24·00

1998. Diana, Princess of Wales Commemoration. Sheet, 145 × 70 mm, containing vert designs as T **91** of Kiribati. Multicoloured.
MS275 10s. Princess Diana in tartan jacket, 1987; 80s. Wearing white dress, 1992; 1p. Wearing check jacket, 1993; 2p.50, Wearing black jacket (sold at 4p.40+50s. charity premium) . . . . 5·50 6·00

1998. 80th Birthday of King Taufa'ahau Tupou IV.
276 **43a** 2p.70 multicoloured . . . 2·50 3·00

43b Tiger and Top Left Quarter of Clock Face

1998. Chinese New Year ("Year of the Tiger"). Sheet, 126 × 85 mm, containing horiz designs as T **43b**, each showing tiger and quarter segment of clock face. Multicoloured.
MS277 55s. Type **43b**; 80s. Top right quarter; 1p. Bottom left quarter; 1p. Bottom right quarter . . . 3·75 4·25
No. **MS**277 also includes "SINGPEX '98" Stamp Exhibition, Singapore emblem on the sheet margin.

43c "Amphiprion melanopus"

1998. International Year of the Ocean. Multicoloured.
278 10s. Type **43c** 40 50
279 55s. "Amphiprion perideraion" 80 90
280 80s. "Amphiprion chrysopterus" . . . . . . 1·00 1·10

43d Angel playing lute (inscr in Tongan)

1998. Christmas. Multicoloured.
281 20s. Type **43d** 70 55
282 55s. Angel playing violin (inscr in English) . . . . . 1·10 60
283 1p. Children and bells (inscr in Tongan) . . . . . . 1·60 1·75
284 1p.60 Children and candles (inscr in English) . . . . . 2·25 3·00

43e Rabbit on Hind Legs

1999. Chinese New Year ("Year of the Rabbit"). Sheet 126 × 85 mm, containing horiz designs as T **43e**, showing rabbits and segments of flower (each red, yellow and grey).
MS285 10s. Type **43e**; 55s. Rabbit facing left; 80s. Rabbit facing right; 1p. Two rabbits . . . . 2·50 3·00

44 "Eendracht" (Le Maire)

1999. Early Explorers. Multicoloured.
286 80s. Type **44** . . . . 1·75 1·00
287 2p.70 Tongiaki (outrigger canoe) . . . . 2·75 3·50
MS288 120 × 72 mm. Nos. 286/7 5·50 6·00
No. **MS**288 also includes the "Australia '99" emblem on the sheet margin.

44a "Cananga odorata"

1999. Fragrant Flowers. Multicoloured.
289 55s. Type **44a** 75 60
290 80s. "Gardenia tannaensis" (vert) . . . . 1·00 80
291 1p. "Coleus amboinicus" (vert) . . . . 1·40 1·40
292 2p.50 "Hernandia moerenhoutiana" . . . . . 2·75 3·50

45 Dove over Tafahi Island

2000. New Millennium. Sheet, 120 × 80 mm, containing T **45** and similar vert design. Multicoloured.
MS293 1p. Type **45**; 2p.50, Kalia (traditional canoe) passing island 2·75 3·25

45a Dragon in the Sky

2000. Chinese New Year ("Year of the Dragon"). Sheet, 126 × 85 mm, containing horiz designs as T **46a**. Multicoloured.
MS294 10s. Type **45a**; 55s. Dragon in the sky (facing left); 80s. Sea dragon (facing right); 1p. Sea dragon (facing left) . . . . . 2·25 2·75

45b Queen Elizabeth the Queen Mother — **46** Tongan Couple

2000. "The Stamp Show 2000" International Stamp Exhibition, London. Queen Elizabeth the Queen Mother's 100th Birthday. Sheet, 105 × 71 mm, containing designs as T **45b**.
MS295 1p.50, Type **45b**; 2p.50, Queen Salote Tupou III of Tonga 3·50 4·00

2000. "EXPO 2000" World Stamp Exhibition, Anaheim, U.S.A. Space Communications. Sheet, 120 × 90 mm, containing T **46** and similar vert designs. Multicoloured.
MS296 10s. Type **46**; 2p.50, Telecom dish aerial; 2p.70, "Intelsat" satelite . . . . 4·50 5·50

47 *Jamides bochus* (butterfly)

2000. Butterflies. Multicoloured.
297 55s. Type **47** 85 70
298 80s. *Hypolimnas bolina* . . . 1·10 90
299 1p. *Eurema hecabe aprica* . . 1·40 1·40
300 2p.70 *Danaus plexippus* . . . 2·50 3·00

48 Snake

2001. Chinese New Year ("Year of the Snake") and "Hong Kong 2001" Stamp Exhibition. Sheet, 125 × 87 mm, containing horiz designs as T **48** showing decorative snakes.
MS301 10s. multicoloured; 55s. multicoloured; 80s. multicoloured; 1p. multicoloured . . . . . . 1·75 1·90

49 Seale's Flying Fish

2001. Fishes. Multicoloured.
302 80s. Type **49** . . . . 1·10 80
303 1p. Swordfish . . . . 1·40 1·40
304 2p.50 Skipjack tuna . . . . 2·50 3·00
MS305 121 × 92 mm. Nos. 302/4 3·25 3·50

50 Pawpaw

2001. Tropical Fruit. Sheet, 120 × 67 mm, containing T **50** and similar vert designs. Multicoloured.
MS306 55s. Type **50**; 80s. Limes; 1p. Mango; 2p.50, Bananas . . . 3·75 4·25

51 Barn Owl in Flight

2001. Barn Owls. Multicoloured.
307 10s. Type **51** 30 50
308 55s. Adult feeding young in nest 75 55
309 2p.50 Adult and fledglings in nest . . . . 2·25 2·50
310 2p.70 Barn owl in palm tree 2·25 2·50
MS311 170 × 75 mm. Nos. 307/10 5·00 5·50

51a Queen Elizabeth with Princess Elizabeth, Coronation, 1937

2002. Golden Jubilee. Sheet 162 × 95 mm, containing designs as T **51a**.
MS312 15s. brown, violet and gold; 90s. multicoloured; 1p.20, multicoloured; 1p.40, multicoloured; 2p.25, multicoloured . . . . 6·00 6·50
DESIGNS—HORIZ (as Type **51a**): 15s. Type **51a**; 90s. Queen Elizabeth in lilac outfit; 1p.20, Princess Elizabeth in garden; 1p.40, Queen Elizabeth in red hat and coat. VERT (38 × 51 mm): 2p.25, Queen Elizabeth after Annigoni.

51b Two Horses with Foal

2002. Chinese New Year ("Year of the Horse"). Sheet, 126 × 89 mm, containing vert designs as T **51b**. Multicoloured.
MS313 65s. Two horses with foal; 80s. Horse drinking from river; 1p. Horse standing in river; 2p.50 Horse and foal on river bank 4·50 5·00

52 Polynesian Scrub Fowl with Eggs

2002. Polynesian Scrub Fowl. Multicoloured.
314 15s. Type **52** 30 50
315 70s. Two birds on rocks . . 90 90
316 90s. Polynesian scrub fowl by tree (vert) . . . . 1·10 1·10
317 2p.50 Two birds in undergrowth (vert) . . . . 2·25 2·50
MS318 72 × 95 mm. Nos. 316/17 3·50 4·00

53 Octopus (*Octopus vulgaris*)

2002. Cephalopods. Multicoloured.
319 80s. Type **53** 60 65
320 1p. Squid (*Sepioteuthis lessoniana*) 70 75
321 2p.50 Nautilus (*Nautilus belauensis*) . . . . 1·75 1·90
MS322 120 × 83 mm. Nos. 319/21 3·00 3·25

54 CASA C-212 Aviocar

2002. Mail Planes. Sheet, 140 × 80 mm, containing T **54** and similar horiz designs. Multicoloured.
MS323 80s. Type **54**; 1p.40 Britten-Norman Islander; 2p.50 DHC 6-300 Twin Otter . . . . . . 3·25 3·50

NIUE Pt. 1

One of the Cook Is. group in the S. Pacific. A dependency of New Zealand, the island achieved local self-government in 1974.

1902. 12 pence = 1 shilling;
20 shillings = 1 pound.
1967. 100 cents = 1 dollar.

1902. T **42** of New Zealand optd **NIUE** only.
1 **42** 1d. red £300 £300

Stamps of New Zealand surch **NIUE.** and value in native language.

1902. Pictorials of 1898 etc.
8 **23** ½d. green . . . . 1·00 1·00
9 **42** 1d. red . . . . 60 1·00
2 **26** 2½d. blue (B) . . . . . . 1·25 4·00
13 **28** 3d. brown . . . . 9·50 5·00
14 **31** 6d. red . . . . 12·00 11·00
16 **34** 1s. orange . . . . 35·00 35·00

1911. King Edward VII stamps.
17 **51** ½d. green 50 50
18 6d. red . . . . 2·00 7·00
19 1s. orange . . . . 6·50 45·00

1917. Dominion and King George V stamps.
21 **53** 1d. red . . . . 11·00 5·50
22 **62** 3d. brown . . . . 42·00 80·00

1917. Stamps of New Zealand (King George V, etc) optd **NIUE.** only.
23 **62** ½d. green . . . . 70 2·50
24 **53** 1d. red . . . . 10·00 8·50
25 **62** 1½d. grey . . . . 1·00 2·25
26 1½d. brown . . . . 70 4·25
28a 2½d. blue . . . . 1·25 5·00
29a 3d. brown . . . . 1·25 1·50
30a 6d. red . . . . 4·75 23·00
31a 1s. orange . . . . 5·50 24·00

1918. Stamps of New Zealand optd **NIUE.**
33 F **4** 2s. blue . . . . 16·00 32·00
34 2s.6d. brown . . . . . . 21·00 48·00
35 5s. green . . . . 25·00 50·00
36 10s. red . . . . 95·00 £130
37 £1 red £140 £190

1920. Pictorial types as Cook Islands (1920), but inscr "NIUE".
38 **9** ½d. black and green . . . . 3·75 3·75
45 – 1d. black and red . . . . . 1·75 1·00
40 – 1½d. black and red . . . . . 2·50 8·00
46 – 2½d. black and blue . . . . 4·25 11·00
41 – 3d. black and blue . . . . . 75 14·00
47 **7** 4d. black and violet . . . . 7·00 20·00
42 – 6d. brown and green . . . . 1·75 18·00
43 – 1s. black and brown . . . . 1·75 18·00

1927. Admiral type of New Zealand optd **NIUE.**
49 **71** 2s. blue . . . . 18·00 32·00

1931. No. 40 surch **TWO PENCE**.
50 2d. on 1½d. black and red . . 2·25 1·00

1931. Stamps of New Zealand (Arms types) optd **NIUE.**
83 F **6** 2s.6d. brown . . . . . . 3·50 11·00
84 5s. green . . . . 7·50 11·00
53 10s. red . . . . 35·00 £100
86 £1 pink . . . . 42·00 60·00

1932. Pictorial stamps as Cook Islands (1932) but inscr additionally "NIUE".
89 **20** ½d. black and green . . . . 50 2·25
90 – 1d. black and red . . . . . 50 1·50
64 **22** 2d. black and brown . . . . 50 1·25
92 – 2½d. black and blue . . . . 60 1·25
66 – 4d. black and blue . . . . 1·75 3·50
67 – 6d. black and orange . . . 70 75
61 – 1s. black and violet . . . . 2·25 5·00

1935. Silver Jubilee. As Nos. 63, 92 and 67, with colours changed, optd **SILVER JUBILEE OF KING GEORGE V. 1910-1935.**
69 1d. red . . . . 60 3·50
70 2½d. blue . . . . 3·25 7·00
71 6d. green and orange . . . . . 3·25 6·00

1937. Coronation. New Zealand stamps optd **NIUE.**
72 **106** 1d. red 30 10
73 2½d. blue . . . . 40 1·00
74 6d. orange 40 20

1938. As 1938 issue of Cook Islands, but inscr "NIUE COOK ISLANDS".
95 **29** 1s. black and violet . . . . 1·25 85
96 **30** 2s. black and brown . . . . 8·50 3·00
97 – 3s. blue and green . . . . . 15·00 7·00

1940. As No. 132 of Cook Islands but inscr "NIUE COOK ISLANDS".
78 **32** 3d. on 1½d. black and purple 60 20

1946. Peace. New Zealand stamps optd **NIUE** (twice on 2d.).
98 **132** 1d. green 30 10
99 – 2d. purple (No. 670) . . . 30 10
100 – 6d. brown & red (No. 674) 30 55
101 **139** 8d. black and red 40 55

18 Map of Niue

19 H.M.S. "Resolution"

1950.
113 **18** ½d. orange and blue . . . 10 50
114 **19** 1d. brown and green . . . 2·25 1·75
115 – 2d. black and red . . . . 1·00 90
116 – 3d. blue and violet 10 15
117 – 4d. olive and purple . . . 10 15
118 – 6d. green and orange . . . 60 1·00
119 – 9d. orange and brown . . 10 90
120 – 1s. purple and black . . . 10 15
121 – 2s. brown and green . . . 1·25 4·00
122 – 3s. blue and black . . . . 4·50 4·00
DESIGNS—HORIZ: 2d. Alofi landing; 3d. Native hut; 4d. Arch at Hikutavake; 6d. Alofi bay; 1s. Cave, Makefu. VERT: 9d. Spearing fish; 2s. Bananas; 3s. Matapa Chasm.

1953. Coronation. As Types of New Zealand but inscr "NIUE".
123 **164** 3d. brown 65 40
124 **168** 6d. grey 95 40

26

27 "Pua"

1967. Decimal Currency. (a) Nos. 113/22 surch.
125 **17** ½c. on ½d. 10 10
126 **18** 1c. on 1d. . . . . 1·10 15
127 – 2c. on 2d. 10 10
128 – 2½c. on 3d. 10 10
129 – 3c. on 4d. 10 10
130 – 5c. on 6d. 10 10
131 – 8c. on 9d. 10 10
132 – 10c. on 1s. 10 10
133 – 20c. on 2s. . . . . 35 1·00
134 – 30c. on 3s. . . . . 65 1·50

(b) Arms type of New Zealand without value, surch as in T **26**.
135 **26** 25c. brown 30 55
136 50c. green 70 80
137 $1 mauve . . . . 45 1·25
138 $2 pink . . . . 50 2·00

1967. Christmas. As T **278** of New Zealand but inscr "NIUE".
139 2½c. multicoloured 10 10

1969. Christmas. As No. 905 of New Zealand but inscr "NIUE".
140 2½c. multicoloured 10 10

1969. Flowers. Multicoloured; frame colours given.
141 **27** ½c. green 10 10
142 – 1c. red 10 10
143 – 2c. olive 10 10
144 – 2½c. brown 10 10
145 – 3c. blue 10 10
146 – 5c. red 10 10
147 – 8c. violet 10 10
148 – 10c. yellow 10 10
149 – 20c. blue . . . . 35 1·25
150 – 30c. green . . . . 1·10 1·75
DESIGNS: 1c. "Golden Shower"; 2c. Flamboyant; 2½c. Frangipani; 3c. Niue crocus; 5c. Hibiscus; 8c. "Passion Fruit"; 10c. "Kampui"; 20c. Queen Elizabeth II (after Anthony Buckley); 30c. Tapeu orchid.
For 20c. design as 5c. see No. 801.

37 Kalahimu

1970. Indigenous Edible Crabs. Mult.
151 3c. Type **37** 10 10
152 5c. Kalavi 10 10
153 30c. Unga 30 25

1970. Christmas. As T **314** of New Zealand, but inscr "NIUE".
154 2½c. multicoloured 10 10

38 Outrigger Canoe, and Fokker F.27 Friendship over Jungle

1970. Opening of Niue Airport. Multicoloured.
155 3c. Type **38** 10 20
156 5c. "Tofua II" (cargo liner) and Fokker F.27 Friendship over harbour 15 20
157 8c. Fokker F.27 Friendship over airport 15 30

39 Spotted Triller

1971. Birds. Multicoloured.
158 5c. Type **39** 15 35
159 10c. Purple-capped fruit dove 40 20
160 20c. Blue-crowned lory . . . 60 20

1971. Christmas. As T **325** of New Zealand, but inscr "Niue".
161 3c. multicoloured 10 10

40 Niuean Boy

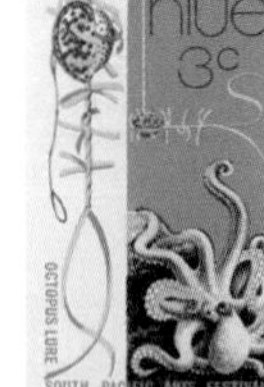

41 Octopus Lure

1971. Niuean Portraits. Multicoloured.
162 4c. Type **40** 10 10
163 6c. Girl with garland 10 20
164 9c. Man 10 40
165 14c. Woman with garland . . 15 80

1972. South Pacific Arts Festival, Fiji. Multicoloured.
166 3c. Type **41** 10 10
167 5c. War weapons 15 15
168 10c. Sika throwing (horiz) . . 20 15
169 25c. Vivi dance (horiz) . . . 30 25

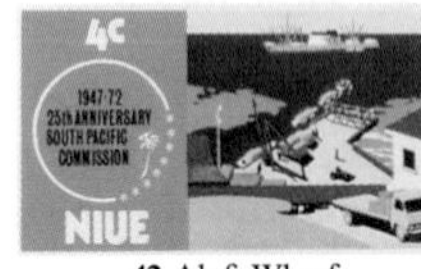

42 Alofi Wharf

1972. 25th Anniv of South Pacific Commission. Multicoloured.
170 4c. Type **42** 10 10
171 5c. Medical services 15 10
172 6c. Schoolchildren 15 10
173 18c. Dairy cattle 25 20

1972. Christmas. As T **332** of New Zealand, but inscr "NIUE".
174 3c. multicoloured 10 10

43 Silver Sweeper

1973. Fishes. Multicoloured.
175 8c. Type **43** 25 25
176 10c. Peacock hind ("Loi") . . 25 30
177 15c. Yellow-edged lyretail ("Malau") 30 40
178 20c. Ruby snapper ("Palu") 30 45

44 "Large Flower Piece" (Jan Brueghel)

46 King Fataaiki

45 Capt. Cook and Bowsprit

1973. Christmas. Flower studies by the artists listed. Multicoloured.
179 4c. Type **44** 10 10
180 5c. Bollongier 10 10
181 10c. Ruysch 20 20

1974. Bicent of Capt. Cook's Visit. Mult.
182 2c. Type **45** 20 20
183 3c. Niue landing place . . . 20 20
184 8c. Map of Niue 20 30
185 20c. Ensign of 1774 and Administration Building . . 30 65

1974. Self-government. Multicoloured.
186 4c. Type **46** 10 15
187 8c. Annexation Ceremony, 1900 . . . . 10 15
188 10c. Legislative Assembly Chambers (horiz) 10 15
189 20c. Village meeting (horiz) 15 25

47 Decorated Bicycles **48** Children going to Church

1974. Christmas. Multicoloured.
190 3c. Type **47** 10 10
191 10c. Decorated motorcycle 10 10
192 20c. Motor transport to church 20 30

1975. Christmas. Multicoloured.
193 4c. Type **48** 10 10
194 5c. Child with balloons on bicycle 10 10
195 10c. Balloons and gifts on tree 20 20

49 Hotel Buildings

1975. Opening of Tourist Hotel. Mult.
196 8c. Type **49** 10 10
197 20c. Ground-plan and buildings 20 20

50 Preparing Ground for Taro

1976. Food Gathering. Multicoloured.
198 1c. Type **50** 10 10
199 2c. Planting taro 10 10
200 3c. Banana gathering 10 10
201 4c. Harvesting taro 10 10
202 5c. Gathering shellfish . . . 30 10
203 10c. Reef fishing 10 10
204 20c. Luku gathering 15 15
205 50c. Canoe fishing 20 60
206 $1 Coconut husking 25 80
207 $2 Uga gathering . . . . . 45 1·40
See also Nos. 249/58 and 264/73.

51 Water

1976. Utilities. Multicoloured.
208 10c. Type **51** 10 10
209 15c. Telecommunications . . 15 15
210 20c. Power 15 15

52 Christmas Tree, Alofi

1976. Christmas. Multicoloured.
211 9c. Type **52** 15 15
212 15c. Church service, Avatele 15 15

53 Queen Elizabeth II and Westminster Abbey

1977. Silver Jubilee. Multicoloured.
213 $1 Type **53** 60 50
214 $2 Coronation regalia 80 75
MS215 72 × 104 mm. Nos. 213/14 1·10 1·60
Stamps from the miniature sheet have a blue border.

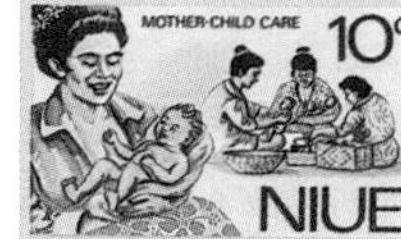

54 Child Care

1977. Personal Services. Multicoloured.
216 10c. Type **54** 15 10
217 15c. School dental clinic . . . 20 20
218 20c. Care of the aged 20 20

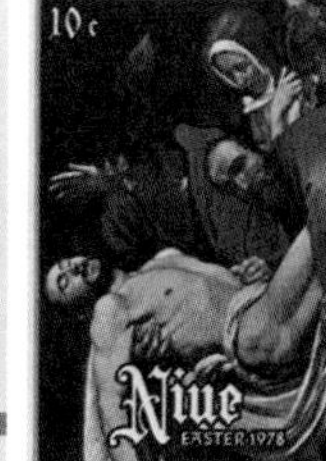

55 "The Annunciation" **58** "The Deposition of Christ" (Caravaggio)

57 "An Island View in Atooi"

1977. Christmas. Paintings by Rubens. Multicoloured.
219 10c. Type **55** 20 10
220 12c. "Adoration of the Magi" 20 15
221 20c. "Virgin in a Garland" 35 40
222 35c. "The Holy Family" . . 55 90
MS223 82 × 129 mm. Nos. 219/22 1·10 1·25

1977. Nos. 198/207, 214, 216 and 218 surch.
224 12c. on 1c. Type **50** 25 25
225 16c. on 2c. Planting taro . . 30 30
226 20c. on 3c. Banana gathering 30 40
227 35c. on 4c. Harvesting taro 30 45
228 40c. on 5c. Gathering shellfish 30 50
229 60c. on 20c. Luku gathering 30 55
230 70c. on $1 Coconut husking 30 55
231 85c. on $2 Uga gathering . . 30 60
232 $1.10 on 10c. Type **22** . . . 30 60
233 $2.60 on 20c. Care of the aged 50 70
234 $3.20 on $2 Coronation regalia 60 80

1978. Bicent of Discovery of Hawaii. Paintings by John Webber. Multicoloured.
235 12c. Type **57** 85 40
236 16c. "A View of Karakaooa, in Owhyhee" 95 50
237 20c. "An Offering before Capt. Cook in the Sandwich Islands" . . . . 1·00 60
238 30c. "Tereoboo, King of Owhyhee bringing presents to Capt. Cook" . . . . . 1·10 70
239 35c. "A Canoe in the Sandwich Islands, the rowers masked" . . . . . 1·25 80
MS240 121 × 121 mm. Nos. 235/9 4·75 2·75

1978. Easter. Paintings from the Vatican Galleries. Multicoloured.
241 10c. Type **58** 20 10
242 20c. "The Burial of Christ" (Bellini) 40 25
MS243 102 × 68 mm. Nos. 241/2 1·00 1·00

1978. Easter. Children's Charity. Designs as Nos. 241/2 in separate miniature sheets 64 × 78 mm, each with a face value of 70c.+5c.
MS244 As Nos. 241/2 Set of 2 sheets 1·00 2·00

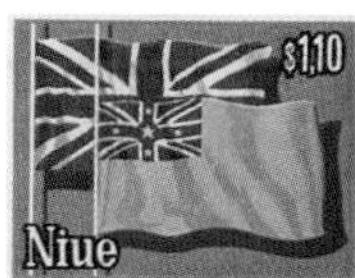

59 Flags of Niue and U.K.

1978. 25th Anniv of Coronation. Mult.
245 $1.10 Type **59** 60 90
246 $1.10 Coronation portrait by Cecil Beaton 60 90
247 $1.10 Queen's personal flag for New Zealand 60 90
MS248 87 × 98 mm. Nos. 245/7 with white borders . . . . 2·50 1·50

1978. Designs as Nos. 198/207 but margin colours changed and silver frame.
249 12c. Type **50** 20 20
250 16c. Planting taro 20 20
251 30c. Banana gathering . . . 30 25
252 35c. Harvesting taro 30 30
253 40c. Gathering shellfish . . . 40 40
254 60c. Reef fishing 40 35

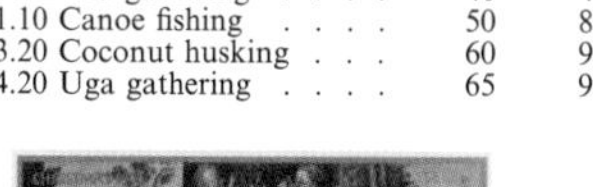

255 75c. Luku gathering 40 40
256 $1.10 Canoe fishing 50 80
257 $3.20 Coconut husking . . . 60 90
258 $4.20 Uga gathering 65 95

60 "Festival of the Rosary"

1978. Christmas. 450th Death Anniv of Durer. Multicoloured.
259 20c. Type **60** 40 20
260 30c. "The Nativity" 50 30
261 35c. "Adoration of the Magi" 60 35
MS262 143 × 82 mm. Nos. 259/61 1·50 2·00

1978. Christmas. Children's Charity. Designs as Nos. 259/61 in separate miniature sheets 74 × 66 mm., each with a face value of 60c.+5c.
MS263 As Nos. 259/61 Set of 3 sheets . . . . 1·00 2·00

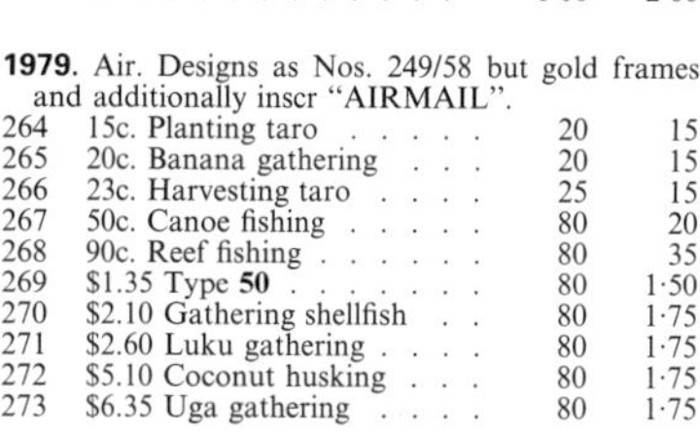

1979. Air. Designs as Nos. 249/58 but gold frames and additionally inscr "AIRMAIL".
264 15c. Planting taro 20 15
265 20c. Banana gathering . . . 20 15
266 23c. Harvesting taro 25 15
267 50c. Canoe fishing 80 20
268 90c. Reef fishing 80 35
269 $1.35 Type **50** . . . . 80 1·50
270 $2.10 Gathering shellfish . . 80 1·75
271 $2.60 Luku gathering . . . . 80 1·75
272 $5.10 Coconut husking . . . 80 1·75
273 $6.35 Uga gathering . . . . 80 1·75

61 "Pieta" (Gregorio Fernandez)

1979. Easter. Paintings. Multicoloured.
274 30c. Type **61** 30 25
275 35c. "Burial of Christ" (Pedro Roldan) 35 25
MS276 82 × 82 mm. Nos. 274/5 1·00 1·00

1979. Easter. Children's Charity. Designs as Nos. 274/5 in separate miniature sheets 86 × 69 mm., each with a face value of 70c.+5c.
MS277 As Nos. 274/5 Set of 2 sheets 1·10 1·75

62 "The Nurse and Child" (Franz Hals) **63** Penny Black Stamp

1979. International Year of the Child. Details of Paintings. Multicoloured.
278 16c. Type **62** 20 15
279 20c. "Child of the Duke of Osuna" (Goya) 20 20
280 30c. "Daughter of Robert Strozzi" (Titian) 35 35
281 35c. "Children eating Fruit" (Murillo) 45 40
MS282 80 × 115 mm. Nos. 278/81 1·25 2·25

1979. International Year of the Child. Children's Charity. Designs as Nos. 278/81 in separate miniature sheets 99 × 119 mm, each with a face value of 70c.+5c.
MS283 As Nos. 278/81 Set of 4 sheets . . . . 1·00 1·50

1979. Death Cent of Sir Rowland Hill. Mult.
284 20c. Type **63** 15 15
285 20c. Sir Rowland Hill and original Bath mail coach 15 15
286 30c. Basel 1845 2½r. stamp 15 20
287 30c. Sir Rowland Hill and Alpine village coach . . . 15 20
288 35c. U.S.A. 1847 5c. stamp 20 20
289 35c. Sir Rowland Hill and "Washington" (first transatlantic U.S.A. mail vessel) 20 20
290 50c. France 1849 20c. stamp 25 20
291 50c. Sir Rowland Hill and French Post Office railway van, 1849 . . . . 25 20
292 60c. Bavaria 1849 1k. stamp 25 20
293 60c. Sir Rowland Hill and Bavarian coach with mail 25 20
MS294 143 × 149 mm. Nos. 284/93 2·50 3·00
The two versions of each value were issued se-tenant within the sheet, forming composite designs.

64 Cook's Landing at Botany Bay

1979. Death Bicentenary of Captain Cook. Multicoloured.
295 20c. Type **64** 55 30
296 30c. Cook's men during a landing on Erromanga . . 75 40
297 35c. H.M.S. "Resolution" and H.M.S. "Discovery" in Queen Charlotte's Sound 85 45
298 75c. Death of Captain Cook, Hawaii . . . . 1·50 70
MS299 104 × 80 mm. Nos. 295/8 3·75 2·50

65 Launch of "Apollo 11" **66** "Virgin of Tortosa" (P. Serra)

1979. 10th Anniv of First Manned Moon Landing. Multicoloured.
300 30c. Type **65** 35 20
301 35c. Lunar module on Moon 45 25
302 60c. Sikorsky Sea King helicopter, recovery ship and command module after splashdown 90 40
MS303 120 × 82 mm. Nos. 300/2 1·25 1·60
Stamps from No. **MS**303 have the inscription in gold on a blue panel.

1979. Christmas. Paintings. Multicoloured.
304 20c. Type **66** 10 10
305 25c. "Virgin with Milk" (R. di Mur) 15 15
306 30c. "Virgin and Child" (S. di G. Sassetta) 20 20
307 50c. "Virgin and Child" (J. Huguet) 25 25
MS308 95 × 113 mm. Nos. 304/7 75 1·25

1979. Christmas Children's Charity. Designs as Nos. 304/7 in separate miniature sheets, 49 × 84 mm, each with a face value of 85c.+5c.
MS309 As Nos. 304/7 Set of 4 sheets 1·00 2·00

1980. Hurricane Relief. Surch **HURRICANE RELIEF Plus 2c**. (a) On Nos. 284/93 **HURRICANE RELIEF** spread over each se-tenant pair.
310 **63** 20c.+2c. multicoloured . . 20 40
311 – 20c.+2c. multicoloured (No. 285) 20 40
312 – 30c.+2c. multicoloured (No. 286) 25 45
313 – 30c.+2c. multicoloured (No. 287) 25 45
314 – 35c.+2c. multicoloured (No. 288) 30 50
315 – 35c.+2c. multicoloured (No. 289) 30 50
316 – 50c.+2c. multicoloured (No. 290) 35 65
317 – 50c.+2c. multicoloured (No. 291) 35 65
318 – 60c.+2c. multicoloured (No. 292) 35 70
319 – 60c.+2c. multicoloured (No. 293) 35 70

(b) On Nos. 295/8.
320 **64** 20c.+2c. multicoloured . . 40 50
321 – 30c.+2c. multicoloured . . 40 60
322 – 35c.+2c. multicoloured . . 40 65
323 – 75c.+2c. multicoloured . . 70 1·10

(c) On Nos. 300/2.
324 **65** 30c.+2c. multicoloured . . 25 40
325 – 35c.+2c. multicoloured . . 25 45
326 – 60c.+2c. multicoloured . . 50 75

(d) On Nos. 304/7.
327 **66** 20c.+2c. multicoloured . . 20 35
328 – 25c.+2c. multicoloured . . 20 40
329 – 30c.+2c. multicoloured . . 20 45
330 – 50c.+2c. multicoloured . . 30 70

68 "Pieta" (Bellini)

1980. Easter. "Pieta". Paintings. Mult.
331 25c. Type **68** 20 15
332 30c. Botticelli 25 20

333 35c. A. van Dyck 25 20
MS334 75 × 104 mm. As Nos. 331/3, but each with additional premium of **+ 2c.** 55 90

The premiums on No. **MS**334 were used to support Hurricane Relief.

1980. Easter. Hurricane Relief. Designs as Nos. 331/3 in separate miniature sheets, 75 × 52 mm, each with a face value of 85c.+5c.
MS335 As Nos. 331/3 Set of 3 sheets 1·00 1·50

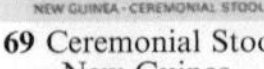

69 Ceremonial Stool, New Guinea

72 Queen Elizabeth the Queen Mother

1980. South Pacific Festival of Arts, New Guinea. Multicoloured.
336 20c. Type **69** 10 10
337 20c. Ku-Tagwa plaque, New Guinea 10 10
338 20c. Suspension hook, New Guinea 10 10
339 20c. Ancestral board, New Guinea 10 10
340 25c. Platform post, New Hebrides 10 10
341 25c. Canoe ornament, New Ireland 10 10
342 25c. Carved figure, Admiralty Islands 10 10
343 25c. Female with child, Admiralty Islands 10 10
344 30c. The God A'a, Rurutu (Austral Islands) 15 15
345 30c. Statue of Tangaroa, Cook Islands 15 15
346 30c. Ivory pendant, Tonga 15 15
347 30c. Tapa (Hiapo) cloth, Niue 15 15
348 35c. Feather box (Waka), New Zealand 15 15
349 35c. Hei-Tiki amulet, New Zealand 15 15
350 35c. House post, New Zealand 15 15
351 35c. Feather image of god Ku, Hawaii 15 15
MS352 Four sheets, each 86 × 124 mm. (a) Nos. 336, 340, 344, 348; (b) Nos. 337, 341, 345, 349; (c) Nos. 338, 342, 346, 350; (d) Nos. 339, 343, 347, 351. Each stamp with an additional premium of 2c. Set of 4 sheets . . . . . 1·50 2·00

1980. "Zeapex '80" International Stamp Exhibition, Auckland. Nos. 284/93 optd (A) **ZEAPEX'80 AUCKLAND** or (B) **NEW ZEALAND STAMP EXHIBITION** and emblem.
353 **63** 20c. multicoloured (A) . . 25 15
354 – 20c. multicoloured (B) . . 25 15
355 – 30c. multicoloured (A) . . 25 15
356 – 30c. multicoloured (B) . . 25 15
357 – 35c. multicoloured (A) . . 25 15
358 – 35c. multicoloured (B) . . 25 15
359 – 50c. multicoloured (A) . . 30 20
360 – 50c. multicoloured (B) . . 30 20
361 – 60c. multicoloured (A) . . 30 20
362 – 60c. multicoloured (B) . . 30 20
MS363 143 × 149 mm. Nos. 353/62, each additionally surcharged **+ 2c.** 3·50 2·75

1980. 80th Birthday of The Queen Mother.
364 **72** $1.10 multicoloured . . . 80 1·50
MS365 55 × 80 mm. **72** $3 multicoloured . . . . 1·00 1·75

73 100 m Dash

74 "The Virgin and Child"

1980. Olympic Games, Moscow.
366 **73** 20c. multicoloured 20 15
367 – 20c. multicoloured 20 15
368 – 25c. multicoloured 20 20
369 – 25c. multicoloured 20 20
370 – 30c. multicoloured 25 20
371 – 30c. multicoloured 25 20
372 – 35c. multicoloured 25 25
373 – 35c. multicoloured 25 25
MS374 119 × 128 mm. Nos. 366/73, each stamp including premium of 2c. . . . . 1·00 1·00

DESIGNS: No. 367, Allen Wells, Great Britain (winner 100 m dash); 368, 400 m freestyle 369, Ines Diers (winner, D.D.R.); 370, Soling Class; 371, Winner, Denmark; 372, Football; 373, Winner, Czechoslovakia.

Nos. 366/7, 368/9, 370/1 and 372/3 were printed se-tenant in pairs each pair forming a composite design. On the 25c. and 35c. stamps the face value is at right on the first design and at left on the second in each pair. For the 30c. No. 370 has a yacht with a green sail at left and No. 371 a yacht with a red sail.

1980. Christmas.
375 **74** 20c. multicoloured 15 15
376 – 25c. multicoloured 15 15
377 – 30c. multicoloured 20 20
378 – 35c. multicoloured 20 20
MS379 87 × 112 mm. Nos. 375/8 85 1·25

DESIGNS: 25c. to 35c. Various Virgin and Child paintings by Andrea del Sarto.

1980. Christmas. Children's Charity. Designs as Nos. 375/8 in separate miniature sheets 62 × 84 mm, each with a face value of 80c.+5c.
MS380 As Nos. 375/8 Set of 4 sheets 1·25 1·75

75 "Phalaenopsis sp."

77 Prince Charles

76 "Jesus Defiled" (El Greco)

1981. Flowers (1st series). Multicoloured.
381 2c. Type **75** 10 10
382 2c. Moth orchid 10 10
383 5c. "Euphorbia pulcherrima" 10 10
384 5c. Poinsettia 10 10
385 10c. "Thunbergia alata" . . 10 10
386 10c. Black-eyed Susan . . 10 10
387 15c. "Cochlospermum hibiscoides" 15 15
388 15c. Buttercup tree 15 15
389 20c. "Begonia sp." 20 20
390 20c. Begonia 20 20
391 25c. "Plumeria sp." 25 25
392 25c. Frangipani 25 25
393 30c. "Strelitzia reginae" . . . 30 30
394 30c. Bird of Paradise . . . 30 30
395 35c. "Hibiscus syriacus" . . . 30 30
396 35c. Rose of Sharon . . . 30 30
397 40c. "Nymphaea sp." 35 35
398 40c. Water lily 35 35
399 50c. "Tibouchina sp." . . . 45 45
400 50c. Princess flower 45 45
401 60c. "Nelumbo sp." 55 55
402 60c. Lotus 55 55
403 80c. "Hybrid hibiscus" . . . 75 75
404 80c. Yellow hibiscus 75 75
405 $1 Golden shower tree ("cassia fistula") . . . . . 1·25 1·00
406 $2 "Orchid var" . . . . . . 4·00 2·50
407 $3 "Orchid sp." . . . . . . 4·50 3·50
408 $4 "Euphorbia pulcherrima poinsettia" . . . . . . 3·50 4·00
409 $6 "Hybrid hibiscus" . . . . 5·00 6·00
410 $10 Scarlet hibiscus ("hibiscus rosa-sinensis") . . . . 8·50 9·00

Nos. 405/10 are larger, 47 × 35 mm.
See also Nos. 527/36.

1981. Easter. Details of Paintings. Mult.
425 35c. Type **76** 40 30
426 50c. "Pieta" (Fernando Gallego) 60 50
427 60c. "The Supper of Emmaus" (Jacopo de Pontormo) 65 55
MS428 69 × 111 mm. As Nos. 425/7, but each with charity premium of 2c. . . . . 1·00 1·75

1981. Easter. Children's Charity. Designs as Nos. 425/7 in separate miniature sheets 78 × 86 mm, each with a face value of 80c.+5c.
MS429 As Nos. 425/7 Set of 3 sheets 1·00 2·00

1981. Royal Wedding. Multicoloured.
430 75c. Type **77** 25 60
431 95c. Lady Diana Spencer . . 30 70
432 $1.20 Prince Charles and Lady Diana Spencer . . . 30 80
MS433 78 × 85 mm. Nos. 430/2 2·00 2·50

78 Footballer Silhouettes

1981. World Cup Football Championship, Spain (1982).
434 **78** 30c. green, gold and blue 20 20
435 – 30c. green, gold and blue 20 20
436 – 30c. green, gold and blue 20 20
437 – 35c. blue, gold and orange 20 20
438 – 35c. blue, gold and orange 20 20
439 – 35c. blue, gold and orange 20 20
440 – 40c. orange, gold and green 20 20
441 – 40c. orange, gold and green 20 20
442 – 40c. orange, gold and green 20 20
MS443 162 × 122 mm. 30c.+3c., 35c.+3c., 40c.+3c. (each × 3). As Nos. 434/42 . . . . 1·60 2·00

DESIGNS—Various footballer silhouettes: 435, gold figure 3rd from left; 436, gold figure 4th from left; 437, gold figure 3rd from left; 438, gold figure 4th from left; 439, gold figure 2nd from left; 440, gold figure 3rd from left displaying close control; 441, gold figure 2nd from left; 442, gold figure 3rd from left, heading.

1982. International Year for Disabled Persons. Nos. 430/2 surch **+5c**.
444 75c.+5c. Type **77** 50 85
445 95c.+5c. Lady Diana Spencer 60 1·00
446 $1.20+5c. Prince Charles and Lady Diana . . . . 60 1·25
MS447 78 × 85 mm. As Nos. 444/6, with each surcharged **+ 10c.** . . 1·75 4·50

80 "The Holy Family with Angels" (detail)

81 Prince of Wales

1981. Christmas. 375th Birth Anniv of Rembrandt. Multicoloured.
448 20c. Type **80** 65 45
449 35c. "Presentation in the Temple" 85 55
450 50c. "Virgin and Child in Temple" . . . . 95 1·10
451 60c. "The Holy Family" . . . 1·25 1·50
MS452 79 × 112 mm. Nos. 448/51 3·25 3·75

1982. Christmas. Children's Charity. Designs as Nos. 448/51 in separate miniature sheets 66 × 80 mm, each with a face value of 80c.+5c.
MS453 As Nos. 448/51 Set of 4 sheets . . . . 2·00 2·50

1982. 21st Birthday of Princess of Wales. Multicoloured.
454 50c. Type **81** 40 55
455 $1.25 Prince and Princess of Wales 60 90
456 $2.50 Princess of Wales . . . 1·50 1·40
MS457 81 × 101 mm. Nos. 454/6 4·75 3·50

The stamps from No. **MS**457 are without white borders.

1982. Birth of Prince William of Wales (1st issue). Nos. 430/3 optd.
458 75c. Type **77** . . . . 1·50 2·00
459 75c. Type **77** . . . . 1·50 2·00
460 95c. Lady Diana Spencer . . 2·50 2·50
461 95c. Lady Diana Spencer . . 2·50 2·50
462 $1.20 Prince Charles and Lady Diana Spencer . . . 2·50 2·75
463 $1.20 Prince Charles and Lady Diana Spencer . . . 2·50 2·75
MS464 78 × 85 mm. Nos. 430/2 6·00 6·00

OVERPRINTS: Nos. 458, 460 and 462 **COMMEMORATING THE ROYAL BIRTH 21 JUNE 1982**; 459, 461 and 463 **BIRTH OF PRINCE WILLIAM OF WALES 21 JUNE 1982**; **MS**464 **PRINCE WILLIAM OF WALES 21 JUNE 1982**.

1982. Birth of Prince William of Wales (2nd issue). As Nos. 454/6, but with changed inscriptions. Multicoloured.
465 50c. Type **81** 50 65
466 $1.25 Prince and Princess of Wales . . . . 1·00 1·25
467 $2.50 Princess of Wales . . . 3·75 3·00
MS468 81 × 101 mm. As Nos. 465/7 7·00 5·50

83 Infant

1982. Christmas. Paintings of Infants by Bronzion, Murillo and Boucher.
469 **83** 40c. multicoloured . . . . 1·50 80
470 – 52c. multicoloured . . . . 1·60 95
471 – 83c. multicoloured . . . . 2·50 2·50
472 – $1.05 multicoloured . . . 2·75 2·75
MS473 110 × 76 mm. Designs as Nos. 469/72 (each 31 × 27 mm), but without portrait of Princess and Prince William . . . . . 5·00 2·75

84 Prince and Princess of Wales with Prince William

86 Scouts signalling

85 Prime Minister Robert Rex

1982. Christmas. Children's Charity. Sheet 72 × 58 mm.
MS474 **84** 80c.+5c. multicoloured 1·50 1·50

1983. Commonwealth Day. Multicoloured.
475 70c. Type **85** 50 55
476 70c. H.M.S. "Resolution" and H.M.S. "Adventure" off Niue, 1774 . . . . . . 50 55
477 70c. Passion flower 50 55
478 70c. Limes 50 55

1983. 75th Anniv of Boy Scout Movement and 125th Birth Anniv of Lord Baden-Powell. Multicoloured.
479 40c. Type **86** 35 40
480 50c. Planting sapling 45 50
481 83c. Map-reading 85 90
MS482 137 × 90 mm. As Nos. 479/81, but each with premium of 3c. . . . . 1·25 1·75

1983. 15th World Scout Jamboree, Alberta, Canada. Nos. 479/81 optd **XV WORLD JAMBOREE CANADA**.
483 40c. Type **86** 35 40
484 50c. Planting sapling 45 50
485 83c. Map-reading 85 90
MS486 137 × 90 mm. As Nos. 483/5, but each with premium of 3c. 1·60 1·75

88 Black Right Whale

1983. Protect the Whales. Multicoloured.
487 12c. Type **88** 75 65
488 25c. Fin whale 95 80
489 35c. Sei whale . . . . 1·50 1·25
490 40c. Blue whale . . . . . . 1·75 1·50
491 58c. Bowhead whale . . . . 1·90 1·60
492 70c. Sperm whale . . . . . 2·25 1·75
493 83c. Humpback whale . . . . 2·50 2·25
494 $1.05 Minke whale . . . . . 3·00 2·50
495 $2.50 Grey whale . . . . . 4·25 4·00

89 Montgolfier Balloon, 1783

1983. Bicentenary of Manned Flight. Mult.
496 25c. Type **89**(postage) 50 25
497 40c. Wright Brothers Flyer I, 1903 . . . . 1·25 45
498 58c. Airship "Graf Zeppelin", 1928 . . . . 1·40 60
499 70c. Boeing 247, 1933 . . . 1·60 85
500 83c. "Apollo 8", 1968 . . . 1·60 1·00
501 $1.05 Space shuttle "Columbia", 1982 . . . . 1·90 1·40
MS502 118 × 130 mm. Nos. 496/501 (air) . . . . 3·00 3·25

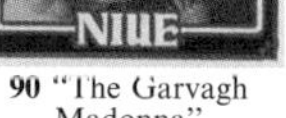

90 "The Garvagh Madonna" **91** Morse Key Transmitter

1983. Christmas. 500th Birth Anniv of Raphael. Multicoloured.
503 30c. Type **90** 75 40
504 40c. "Madonna of the Granduca" 80 45
505 58c. "Madonna of the Goldfish" . . . . 1·10 60
506 70c. "The Holy Family of Francis I" . . . . 1·25 70
507 83c. "The Holy Family with Saints" . . . . 1·40 80
MS508 120 × 114 mm. As Nos. 503/7 but each with a premium of 3c. 3·25 2·75

1983. Various stamps surch. (a) Nos. 393/4, 399/404 and 407.
509 52c. on 30c. "Strelitzia reginae" 70 45
510 52c. on 30c. Bird of paradise 70 45
511 58c. on 50c. "Tibouchina sp." 70 55
512 58c. on 50c. Princess flower 70 55
513 70c. on 60c. "Nelumbo sp." 85 60
514 70c. on 60c. Lotus 85 60
515 83c. on 80c. "Hybrid hibiscus" . . . . 1·00 75
516 83c. on 80c. Yellow hibiscus 1·00 75
517 $3.70 on $3 "Orchid sp." . . 6·00 3·25
(b) Nos. 431/2 and 455/6.
518 $1.10 on 95c. Lady Diana Spencer . . . . 2·50 2·25
519 $1.10 on $1.25 Prince and Princess of Wales . . . . 1·50 2·00
520 $2.60 on $1.20 Prince Charles and Lady Diana . . . . 3·00 3·50
521 $2.60 on $2.50 Princess of Wales . . . . 2·75 3·25

1983. Christmas. 500th Birth Anniv of Raphael. Children's Charity. Designs as Nos. 503/7 in separate miniature sheets, 65 × 80 mm, each with face value of 85c.+5c.
MS522 As Nos. 503/7 Set of 5 sheets 3·50 3·25

1984. World Communications Year. Multicoloured.
523 40c. Type **91** 30 35
524 52c. Wall-mounted phone . . 40 45
525 83c. Communications satellite 60 65
MS526 114 × 90 mm. Nos. 523/5 1·10 1·50

92 "Phalaenopsis sp." **93** Discus throwing

1984. Flowers (2nd series). Multicoloured.
527 12c. Type **92** 25 15
528 25c. "Euphorbia pulcherrima" 35 20
529 30c. "Cochlospermum hibiscoides" 40 25
530 35c. "Begonia sp." 40 25
531 40c. "Plumeria sp." 50 30
532 52c. "Strelitzia reginae" . . . 65 40
533 58c. "Hibiscus syriacus" . . . 70 45
534 70c. "Tibouchina sp." . . . 1·00 60
535 83c. "Nelumbo sp." . . . . 1·10 70
536 $1.05 "Hybrid hibiscus" . . . 1·25 85
537 $1.75 "Cassia fistula" . . . . 2·00 1·50
538 $2.30 "Orchid var" . . . . 4·50 2·00
539 $3.90 "Orchid sp." . . . . 6·00 4·00
540 $5 "Euphorbia pulcherrima poinsettia" . . . . . . 5·00 4·50
541 $6.60 "Hybrid hibiscus" . . . 6·00 6·00
542 $8.30 "Hibiscus rosa-sinensis" 8·00 7·00
Nos. 537/42 are larger, 39 × 31 mm.

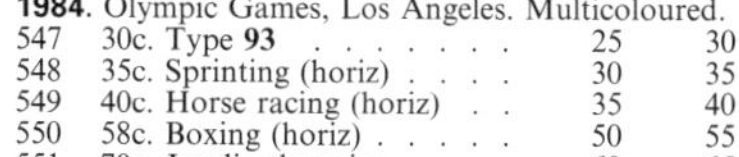

1984. Olympic Games, Los Angeles. Multicoloured.
547 30c. Type **93** 25 30
548 35c. Sprinting (horiz) 30 35
549 40c. Horse racing (horiz) . . 35 40
550 58c. Boxing (horiz) 50 55
551 70c. Javelin-throwing 60 65

94 Koala **98** "The Nativity" (A. Vaccaro)

96 Niue National Flag and Premier Sir Robert Rex

1984. "Ausipex" International Stamp Exhibition, Melbourne. (a) Designs showing Koala Bears.
552 **94** 25c. multicoloured (postage) 70 50
553 – 35c. multicoloured 80 55
554 – 40c. multicoloured 90 60
555 – 58c. multicoloured . . . . 1·00 85
556 – 70c. multicoloured . . . . 1·25 1·00
(b) Vert designs showing Kangaroos.
557 – 83c. multicoloured (air) . . 1·50 1·25
558 – $1.05 multicoloured . . . . 1·75 1·60
559 – $2.50 multicoloured . . . . 3·00 4·00
MS560 110 × 64 mm. $1.75 Wallaby; $1.75 Koala bear . . . . . . 4·00 4·00
See also Nos. **MS**566/7.

1984. Olympic Gold Medal Winners, Los Angeles. Nos. 547/51 optd.
561 30c. Type **93** 55 30
562 35c. Sprinting 60 35
563 40c. Horse racing 65 35
564 58c. Boxing 70 50
565 70c. Javelin-throwing 75 60
OPTS: 30c. **Discus Throw Rolf Danneberg Germany**; 35c. **1,500 Metres Sebastian Coe Great Britain**; 40c. **Equestrian Mark Todd New Zealand**; 58c. **Boxing Tyrell Biggs United States**; 70c. **Javelin Throw Arto Haerkoenen Finland**.

1984. "Ausipex" International Stamp Exhibition, Melbourne (2nd issue). Designs as Nos. 552/60 in miniature sheets of six or four. Multicoloured.
MS566 109 × 105 mm. Nos. 552/6 and $1.75 Koala bear (as No. **MS**560) . . . . 6·00 4·75
MS567 80 × 105 mm. Nos. 557/9 and $1.75 Wallaby (as No. **MS**560) 6·00 4·75

1984. 10th Anniv of Self-government. Mult.
568 40c. Type **96** . . . . . . 1·00 50
569 58c. Map of Niue and Premier Rex . . . . . . 1·00 60
570 70c. Premier Rex receiving proclamation of self-government . . . . . . 1·00 70
MS571 110 × 83 mm. Nos. 568/70 2·00 2·00
MS572 100 × 74 mm. $2.50 As 70c. (50 × 30 mm) . . . . 2·00 2·00

1984. Birth of Prince Henry. Nos. 430 and 454 surch **$2 Prince Henry 15. 9. 84**.
573 $2 on 50c. Type **81** . . . . 2·50 2·75
574 $2 on 75c. Type **77** . . . . 2·50 2·75

1984. Christmas. Multicoloured.
575 40c. Type **98** 60 35
576 58c. "Virgin with Fly" (anon, 16th-century) 75 50
577 70c. "The Adoration of the Shepherds" (B. Murillo) . . 85 60
578 80c. "Flight into Egypt" (B. Murillo) 95 70
MS579 115 × 111 mm. As Nos. 575/8 but each stamp with a 5c. premium 2·50 2·25
MS580 Four sheets, each 66 × 98 mm. As Nos. 575/8, but each stamp 30 × 42 mm. with a face value of 95c.+10c. Set of 4 sheets . . . . 3·75 3·00

99 House Wren

1985. Birth Bicentenary of John J. Audubon (ornithologist). Multicoloured.
581 40c. Type **99** . . . . . . 2·75 1·00
582 70c. Veery . . . . 3·00 1·60
583 83c. Grasshopper sparrow . . 3·25 2·00
584 $1.50 Henslow's sparrow . . 3·50 2·25
585 $2.50 Vesper sparrow . . . . 5·00 4·25
MS586 Five sheets, each 54 × 60 mm. As Nos. 581/5 but each stamp 34 × 26 mm with a face value of $1.75 and without the commemorative inscription Set of 5 sheets . . . . 13·00 8·50

100 The Queen Mother in Garter Robes

1985. Life and Times of Queen Elizabeth the Queen Mother. Multicoloured.
587 70c. Type **100** . . . . . . 1·25 1·25
588 $1.15 In open carriage with the Queen . . . . 1·40 1·40
589 $1.50 With Prince Charles during 80th birthday celebrations . . . . . . 1·50 1·50
MS590 70 × 70 mm. $3 At her desk in Clarence House (38 × 35 mm) 5·50 2·50
See also No. **MS**627.

1985. South Pacific Mini Games, Rarotonga. Nos. 547/8 and 550/1 surch **MINI SOUTH PACIFIC GAMES, RAROTONGA** and emblem.
591 52c. on 70c. Javelin throwing 40 55
592 83c. on 58c. Boxing 65 80
593 95c. on 35c. Sprinting . . . 75 90
594 $2 on 30c. Type **93** . . . . 1·50 2·00

1985. Pacific Islands Conference, Rarotonga. Nos. 475/8 optd **PACIFIC ISLANDS CONFERENCE, RAROTONGA** and emblem.
595 70c. Type **85** 55 75
596 70c. "Resolution" and "Adventure" off Niue, 1774 . . . . 55 75
597 70c. Passion flower 55 75
598 70c. Limes 55 75
Nos. 595 also shows an overprinted amendment to the caption which now reads **Premier Sir Robert Rex K.B.E.**

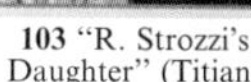

103 "R. Strozzi's Daughter" (Titian) **104** "Virgin and Child"

1985. International Youth Year. Mult.
599 58c. Type **103** . . . . . . 1·75 90
600 70c. "The Fifer" (E. Manet) 2·00 1·00
601 $1.15 "Portrait of a Young Girl" (Renoir) . . . . . 2·75 1·90
602 $1.50 "Portrait of M. Berard" (Renoir) . . . 3·00 2·50
MS603 Four sheets, each 63 × 79 mm. As Nos. 599/602 but each with a face value of $1.75+10c. Set of 4 sheets . . . 13·00 11·00

1985. Christmas. Details of Paintings by Correggio. Multicoloured.
604 58c. Type **104** . . . . . . 1·50 85
605 85c. "Adoration of the Magi" 1·75 1·40
606 $1.05 "Virgin with Child and St. John" . . . . 2·25 2·50
607 $1.45 "Virgin and Child with St. Catherine" . . . . . 2·75 3·50
MS608 83 × 123 mm. As Nos. 604/7 but each stamp with a face value of 60c.+10c. . . . . 3·00 2·75
MS609 Four sheets, each 80 × 90 mm. 65c. Type **104**; 95c. As No. 605; $1.20, As No. 606; $1.75, As No. 607 (each stamp 49 × 59 mm). Imperf Set of 4 sheets . . . . 4·00 4·00

105 "The Constellations" (detail)

1986. Appearance of Halley's Comet. Designs showing details from ceiling painting "The Constellations" by Giovanni de Vecchi. Nos. 611/13 show different spacecraft at top left. Multicoloured.
610 60c. Type **105** 50 50
611 75c. "Vega" spacecraft . . . 65 65
612 $1.10 "Planet A" spacecraft 90 90
613 $1.50 "Giotto" spacecraft . . 1·25 1·25
MS614 125 × 91 mm. As Nos. 610/13 but each stamp with a face value of 95c. . . . . 4·75 4·25
Stamps from No. **MS**614 are without borders.

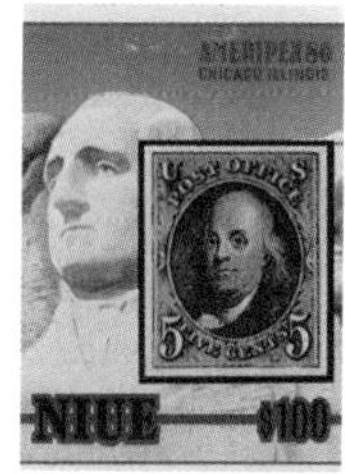

106 Queen Elizabeth II and Prince Philip **107** U.S.A. 1847 Franklin 5c. Stamp and Washington Sculpture, Mt. Rushmore, U.S.A.

1986. 60th Birthday of Queen Elizabeth II. Multicoloured.
615 $1.10 Type **106** . . . . . . 80 1·00
616 $1.50 Queen and Prince Philip at Balmoral . . . . 1·00 1·25
617 $2 Queen at Buckingham Palace . . . . 1·50 1·75
MS618 110 × 70 mm. As Nos. 615/17, but each stamp with a face value of 75c. . . . . . 2·75 3·25
MS619 58 × 89 mm. $3 Queen and Prince Philip at Windsor Castle 3·50 4·25

1986. "Ameripex '86" International Stamp Exhibition, Chicago. Multicoloured.
620 $1 Type **107** . . . . 3·25 3·25
621 $1 Flags of Niue and U.S.A. and Mt. Rushmore sculptures . . . . 3·25 3·25
Nos. 620/1 were printed together, se-tenant, forming a composite design.

108 "Statue under Construction, Paris, 1883" (Victor Dargaud)

1986. Centenary of Statue of Liberty. Multicoloured.
622 $1 Type **108** . . . . 2·00 2·00
623 $2.50 "Unveiling of Statue of Liberty" (Edmund Morand) . . . . 2·75 3·50
MS624 107 × 73 mm. As Nos. 622/3, but each stamp with a face value of $1.25 . . . . 2·50 3·00
See also No. **MS**648

109 Prince Andrew, Miss Sarah Ferguson and Westminster Abbey

1986. Royal Wedding.
625 **109** $2.50 multicoloured . . . 3·25 3·50
MS626 106 × 68 mm. $5 Prince Andrew and Miss sarah Ferguson (43 × 30 mm) . . . . 7·50 8·00

1986. 86th Birthday of Queen Elizabeth the Queen Mother. Nos. 587/9 in miniature sheet, 109 × 83 mm.
MS627 Nos. 587/9 . . . . 11·00 11·00

110 Great Egret **111** "Virgin and Child" (Perugino)

1986. "Stampex '86" Stamp Exhibition, Adelaide. Australian Birds. Multicoloured.
628 40c. Type **110** . . . . 2·75 1·75
629 60c. Painted finch (horiz) . . 3·00 2·00
630 75c. Australian king parrot 3·25 2·25
631 80c. Variegated wren (horiz) 3·50 2·50
632 $1 Peregrine falcon . . . . . 4·00 2·75
633 $1.65 Azure kingfisher (horiz) 5·50 4·00
634 $2.20 Budgerigars . . . . . 6·00 6·00
635 $4.25 Emu (horiz) . . . . . 7·50 7·50

1986. Christmas. Paintings from Vatican Museum. Multicoloured.
636 80c. Type **111** . . . . 2·00 1·75
637 $1.15 "Virgin of St. N. dei Frari" (Titian) . . . . . . 2·25 2·00
638 $1.80 "Virgin with Milk" (Lorenzo di Credi) . . . . 3·25 3·50
639 $2.60 "Madonna of Foligno" (Raphael) . . . . 4·00 5·00
MS640 87 × 110 mm. As Nos. 636/9, but each stamp with a face value of $1.50 . . . . 8·50 6·00
MS641 70 × 100 mm. $7.50 As No. 639, but 27 × 43 mm . . . 8·00 9·00

1986. Visit of Pope John Paul II to South Pacific. Nos. 636/9 surch **CHRISTMAS VISIT TO SOUTH PACIFIC OF POPE JOHN PAUL II NOVEMBER 21 24 1986**.
642 80c.+10c. Type **111** . . . . . 3·00 2·50
643 $1.15+10c. "Virgin of St. N. dei Frari" (Titian) . . . . 3·50 3·00
644 $1.80+10c. "Virgin with Milk" (Lorenzo di Credi) 4·75 4·00
645 $2.60+10c. "Madonna of Foligno" (Raphael) . . . . 6·00 5·00
MS646 87 × 110 mm. As Nos. 642/5, but each stamp with a face value of $1.50+10c. . . . . 14·00 11·00
MS647 70 × 100 mm. $7.50+50c. As No. 645, but 27 × 43 mm . . . 14·00 11·0

112a Sailing Ship under Brooklyn Bridge

1987. Centenary of Statue of Liberty (1986) (2nd issue). Two sheets, each 122 × 122 mm, containing T **112a** and similar multicoloured designs.
MS648 Two sheets. (a) 75c. Type **112a**; 75c. Restoring Statue's flame; 75c. Steam-cleaning Statue's torch; 75c. "Esmerelda" (children cadet barquentine) off Manhattan; 75c. Cadet barque at dusk. (b) 75c. Statue of Liberty at night (vert); 75c. Statue at night (side view) (vert); 75c. Cleaning Statue's crown (vert); 75c. Statue at night (rear view) (vert); 75c. Cleaning a finial (vert) Set of 2 sheets . . 7·00 8·00

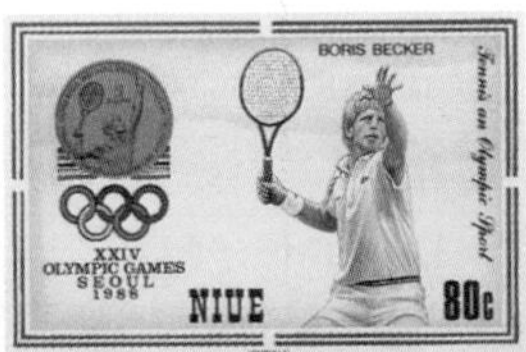

113 Boris Becker, Olympic Rings and Commemorative Coin

1987. Olympic Games, Seoul (1988). Tennis (1st issue). Designs showing Boris Becker in play.
649 **113** 80c. multicoloured . . . . 2·75 2·00
650 – $1.15 multicoloured . . . 3·00 2·25
651 – $1.40 multicoloured . . . 3·25 2·50
652 – $1.80 multicoloured . . . 4·00 3·25

1987. Olympic Games, Seoul (1988). Tennis (2nd issue). As T **113** but showing Steffi Graf.
653 85c. multicoloured . . . . . 2·75 1·75
654 $1.05 multicoloured . . . . 3·00 2·00
655 $1.30 multicoloured . . . . 3·25 2·25
656 $1.75 multicoloured . . . . 3·50 2·75

1987. Royal Ruby Wedding. Nos. 616/17 surch **40TH WEDDING ANNIV. 4.85**.
657 $4.85 on $1.50 Queen and Prince Philip at Balmoral 4·75 4·50
658 $4.85 on $2 Queen at Buckingham Palace . . . . 4·75 4·50

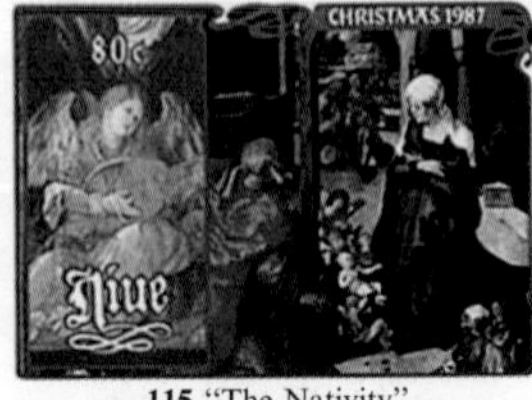

115 "The Nativity"

1987. Christmas. Religious Paintings by Durer. Multicoloured.
659 80c. Type **115** . . . . 1·50 1·25
660 $1.05 "Adoration of the Magi" . . . . 1·75 1·75
661 $2.80 "Celebration of the Rosary" . . . . 3·25 3·75
MS662 100 × 140 mm. As Nos. 659/61, but each size 48 × 37 mm with a face value of $1.30 . . . . 6·50 4·50
MS663 90 × 80 mm. $7.50 As No. 661, but size 51 × 33 mm 7·50 7·00
Nos. 659/61 each include detail of an angel with lute as in T **115**.
Stamps from the miniature sheets are without this feature.

116 Franz Beckenbauer in Action

1988. West German Football Victories. Mult.
664 20c. Type **116** 70 70
665 40c. German "All Star" team in action 90 90
666 60c. Bayern Munich team with European Cup, 1974 1·10 1·10
667 80c. World Cup match, England, 1966 . . . . . . 1·40 1·40
668 $1.05 World Cup match, Mexico, 1970 . . . . . . 1·60 1·60
669 $1.30 Beckenbauer with pennant, 1974 . . . . . . 2·00 2·00
670 $1.80 Beckenbauer and European Cup, 1974 . . . 2·25 2·25

1988. Steffi Graf's Tennis Victories. Nos. 653/6 optd.
671 85c. mult (optd **Australia 24 Jan 88 French Open 4 June 88**) . . . . 2·25 1·50
672 $1.05 multicoloured (optd **Wimbledon 2 July 88 U S Open 10 Sept. 88**) . . . . 2·75 1·75
673 $1.30 multicoloured (optd **Women's Tennis Grand Slam: 10 September 88**) . . 2·75 1·90
674 $1.75 mult (optd **Seoul Olympic Games Gold Medal Winner**) . . . . . . 2·75 2·10

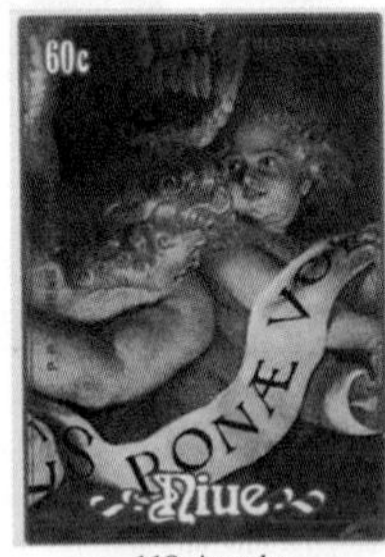

118 Angels

1988. Christmas. Details from "The Adoration of the Shepherds" by Rubens. Multicoloured.
675 60c. Type **118** . . . . 1·75 1·50
676 80c. Shepherds . . . . 2·00 1·75
677 $1.05 Virgin Mary . . . . . 2·75 2·50
678 $1.30 Holy Child . . . . . . 3·50 3·00
MS679 83 × 103 mm. $7.20 The Nativity (38 × 49 mm) . . . . 6·00 7·50

119 Astronaut and "Apollo 11" Emblem

1989. 20th Anniv of First Manned Landing on Moon. Multicoloured.
680 $1.50 Type **119** . . . . . . 4·00 4·00
681 $1.50 Earth and Moon . . . 4·00 4·00
682 $1.50 Astronaut and "Apollo 11" emblem . . . 4·00 4·00
MS683 160 × 64 mm. As Nos. 680/2, but each stamp with a face value of $1.15 . . . . 5·00 5·00

120 Priests

1989. Christmas. Details from "Presentation in the Temple" by Rembrandt. Multicoloured.
684 70c. Type **120** . . . . 2·75 2·50
685 80c. Virgin and Christ Child in Simeon's arms . . . . . 2·75 2·50
686 $1.05 Joseph . . . . 3·25 3·00
687 $1.30 Simeon and Christ Child . . . . 3·75 3·50
MS688 84 × 110 mm. $7.20 "Presentation in the Temple" (39 × 49 mm) . . . . 10·50 11·00

121 Fritz Walter

1990. World Cup Football Championship, Italy. German Footballers. Multicoloured.
689 80c. Type **121** . . . . 2·50 2·50
690 $1.15 Franz Beckenbauer . . 2·75 2·75
691 $1.40 Uwe Seeler . . . . . . 3·00 3·00
692 $1.80 German team emblem and signatures of former captains . . . . 4·00 4·00

122 "Merchant Maarten Looten" (Rembrandt)

123 Queen Elizabeth the Queen Mother

1990. 150th Anniv of the Penny Black. Rembrandt Paintings. Multicoloured.
693 80c. Type **122** . . . . 3·00 2·25
694 $1.05 "Rembrandt's Son Titus with Pen in Hand" 3·25 2·75
695 $1.30 "The Shipbuilder and his Wife" . . . . 3·50 3·00
696 $1.80 "Bathsheba with King David's Letter" . . . . . 3·75 3·25
MS697 82 × 143 mm. As Nos. 693/6, but each with a face value of $1.50 7·50 7·50

1990. 90th Birthday of Queen Elizabeth the Queen Mother.
698 **123** $1.25 multicoloured . . . 4·25 3·75
MS699 84 × 64 mm. **123** $7 multicoloured . . . . 13·00 11·00

124 "Adoration of the Magi" (Dirk Bouts)

129 "The Virgin and Child with Sts. Jerome and Dominic" (Lippi)

1990. Christmas. Religious Paintings. Mult.
700 70c. Type **124** . . . . 2·75 2·50
701 80c. "Holy Family" (Fra Bartolommeo) . . . . . . 3·00 2·75
702 $1.05 "Nativity" (Memling) 3·25 3·25
703 $1.30 "Adoration of the Kings" (Bruegel the Elder) 4·25 4·25
MS704 100 × 135 mm. $7.20 "Virgin and Child Enthroned" (detail, Cosimo Tura) . . . . 11·00 12·00

1990. "Birdpex '90" Stamp Exhibition, Christchurch, New Zealand. No. 410 optd **Birdpex '90** and logo.
705 $10 Scarlet hibiscus . . . . . 12·00 13·00

1991. 65th Birthday of Queen Elizabeth II. No. 409 optd **SIXTY FIFTH BIRTHDAY QUEEN ELIZABETH II**.
706 $6 "Hybrid hibiscus" . . . . 11·00 12·00

1991. 10th Wedding Anniv of Prince and Princess of Wales. Nos. 430/2 optd **TENTH ANNIVERSARY**.
707A 75c. Type **77** . . . . 2·00 1·75
708A 95c. Lady Diana Spencer 3·00 2·75
709A $1.20 Prince Charles and Lady Diana . . . . . . 3·00 2·75

1991. Christmas. Religious Paintings. Mult.
710 20c. Type **129** . . . . 1·00 85
711 50c. "The Isenheim Altarpiece" (M. Grunewald) . . . . . 2·00 1·75
712 $1 "The Nativity" (G. Pittoni) . . . . 3·00 3·00
713 $2 "Adoration of the Kings" (J. Brueghel the Elder) . . 4·00 4·50
MS714 79 × 104 mm. $7 "Adoration of the Sheperds" (G. Reni) . . 10·00 12·00

130 Buff-banded Rail

1992. Birds. Multicoloured.
718 20c. Type **130** . . . . 1·00 80
719 50c. Red-tailed tropic bird . . 1·50 1·10
720 70c. Purple swamphen . . . 2·00 1·25
721 $1 Pacific pigeon . . . . . . 2·50 1·75
722 $1.50 White-collared kingfisher . . . . 2·00 2·25
723 $2 Blue-crowned lory . . . . 2·25 2·50
724 $3 Purple-capped fruit dove 2·50 3·00
726 $5 Barn owl . . . . 5·50 5·50
727 $7 Longtailed koel ("Cockoo") (48½ × 35 mm) 5·50 7·50
728 $10 Reef heron (48½ × 35 mm) . . . . . . 7·50 9·50
729 $15 Spotted triller ("Polynesian Triller") (48½ × 35 mm) . . . . . . 11·00 14·00

131 Columbus before King Ferdinand and Queen Isabella

1992. 500th Anniv of Discovery of America by Columbus. Multicoloured.
731 $2 Type **131** . . . . 3·25 3·00
732 $3 Fleet of Columbus . . . . 5·50 5·00
733 $5 Claiming the New World for Spain . . . . 6·75 6·00

132 Tennis and $10 Commemorative Coin

1992. Olympic Games, Barcelona. Mult.
734 $2.50 Type **132** . . . . . . 5·50 5·00
735 $2.50 Olympic flame and national flags . . . . . . 5·50 5·00
736 $2.50 Gymnastics and different $10 coin . . . . 5·50 5·00
MS737 152 × 87 mm. $5 Water polo 10·00 11·00

1992. 6th Festival of Pacific Arts, Rarotonga. Nos. 336/51 surch **$1**.
738 $1 on 20c. Type **69** . . . . . 1·00 1·00
739 $1 on 20c. Ku-Tagwa plaque, New Guinea . . . . 1·00 1·00
740 $1 on 20c. Suspension hook, New Guinea . . . . . . 1·00 1·00
741 $1 on 20c. Ancestral board, New Guinea . . . . . . 1·00 1·00
742 $1 on 25c. Platform post, New Hebrides . . . . . . 1·00 1·00

743 $1 on 25c. Canoe ornament, New Ireland . . . . 1·00 1·00
744 $1 on 25c. Carved figure, Admiralty Islands . . . . 1·00 1·00
745 $1 on 25c. Female with child, Admiralty Islands . . . . 1·00 1·00
746 $1 on 30c. The God A'a, Rurutu, Austral Islands . . 1·00 1·00
747 $1 on 30c. Statue of Tangaroa, Cook Islands . . 1·00 1·00
748 $1 on 30c. Ivory pendant, Tonga . . . . 1·00 1·00
749 $1 on 30c. Tapa (Hiapo) cloth, Niue . . . . 1·00 1·00
750 $1 on 35c. Feather box (Waka), New Zealand . . 1·00 1·00
751 $1 on 35c. Hei-Tiki amulet, New Zealand . . . . . . 1·00 1·00
752 $1 on 35c. House post, New Zealand . . . . 1·00 1·00
753 $1 on 35c. Feather image of god Ku, Hawaii . . . . . 1·00 1·00

134 "St. Catherine's Mystic Marriage" (detail) (Memling)

135 Queen on Official Visit

1992. Christmas.
754 **134** 20c. multicoloured . . . . 1·00 75
755 – 50c. multicoloured . . . . 1·75 1·50
756 – $1 multicoloured . . . . 2·50 2·50
757 – $2 multicoloured . . . . 3·50 4·50
MS758 87 × 101 mm. $7 multicoloured (as 50c., but larger (36 × 47 mm) . . . . . . 10·00 11·00
DESIGNS: 50c., $1, $2 Different details from "St. Catherine's Mystic Marriage" by Hans Memling.

1992. 40th Anniv of Queen Elizabeth II's Accession. Multicoloured.
759 70c. Type **135** . . . . 2·00 1·75
760 $1 Queen in green evening dress . . . . 2·50 2·25
761 $1.50 Queen in white embroidered evening dress 3·00 2·75
762 $2 Queen with bouquet . . . 3·50 3·25

136 Rough-toothed Dolphin

1993. Endangered Species. South Pacific Dolphins. Multicoloured.
763 20c. Type **136** . . . . . . 1·25 90
764 50c. Fraser's dolphin . . . . . 2·00 1·60
765 75c. Pantropical spotted dolphin . . . . 2·50 2·75
766 $1 Risso's dolphin . . . . . 3·00 3·50

1993. Premier Sir Robert Rex Commemoration. Nos. 568/70 optd **1909 IN MEMORIAM 1992 SIR ROBERT R REX K.B.E.** or surch also.
767 40c. Type **96** . . . . 2·25 2·25
768 58c. Map of Niue and Premier Rex . . . . 2·25 2·25
769 70c. Premier Rex receiving proclamation of self-government . . . . 2·25 2·25
770 $1 on 40c. Type **96** . . . . . 2·50 2·50
771 $1 on 58c. Map of Niue and Premier Rex . . . . 2·50 2·50
772 $1 on 70c. Premier Rex receiving proclamation of self-government . . . . . 2·50 2·50

138 Queen Elizabeth II in Coronation Robes and St. Edward's Crown

1993. 40th Anniv of Coronation.
773 **138** $5 multicoloured . . . . 10·00 10·00

139 "Virgin of the Rosary" (detail) (Guido Reni)

1993. Christmas.
774 **139** 20c. multicoloured 85 75
775 – 70c. multicoloured . . . . 2·00 1·25
776 – $1 multicoloured . . . . 2·25 1·50
777 – $1. 50 multicoloured . . . 3·00 3·50
778 – $3 multicoloured (32 × 47 mm) . . . . . 4·75 6·50
DESIGNS: 70c. to $3 Different details of "Virgin of the Rosary" (Reni).

140 World Cup and Globe with Flags of U.S.A. and Previous Winners

1994. World Cup Football Championship, U.S.A.
779 **140** $4 multicoloured . . . . 6·50 7·50

141 "Apollo 11" and Astronaut on Moon

1994. 25th Anniv of First Manned Moon Landing. Multicoloured.
780 $2.50 Type **141** . . . . . . 6·00 6·00
781 $2.50 Astronaut and flag . . 6·00 6·00
782 $2.50 Astronaut and equipment . . . . 6·00 6·00

142 "The Adoration of the Kings" (Jan Gossaert)

1994. Christmas. Religious Paintings. Multicoloured.
783 70c. Type **142** . . . . 1·00 1·25
784 70c. "Madonna and Child with Sts. John and Catherine" (Titian) . . . . 1·00 1·25
785 70c. "The Holy Family and Shepherd" (Titian) . . . . 1·00 1·25
786 70c. "The Virgin and Child with Saints" (Gerard David) . . . . 1·00 1·25
787 $1 "The Adoration of the Shepherds" (cherubs detail) (Poussin) . . . . 1·25 1·50
788 $1 "The Adoration of the Shepherds" (Holy Family detail) (Poussin) . . . . . 1·25 1·50
789 $1 "Madonna and Child with Sts. Joseph and John" (Sebastiano) . . . . 1·25 1·50
790 $1 "The Adoration of the Kings" (Veronese) . . . . 1·25 1·50

143 Long John Silver and Jim Hawkins ("Treasure Island")

145 Tapeu Orchid

1994. Death Centenary of Robert Louis Stevenson (author). Multicoloured.
791 $1.75 Type **143** . . . . . . 3·25 3·00
792 $1.75 Transformation of Dr. Jekyll ("Dr. Jekyll and Mr. Hyde") . . . . 3·25 3·00
793 $1.75 Attack on David Balfour ("Kidnapped") . . 3·25 3·00
794 $1.75 Robert Louis Stevenson, tomb and inscription . . . . 3·25 3·00

1996. Nos. 720 and 722 surch.
795 50c. on 70c. Purple swamphen . . . . 6·00 3·50
796 $1 on $1.50 White-collared kingfisher . . . . 7·00 5·50

1996. Flowers. Multicoloured.
797 70c. Type **145** 80 80
798 $1 Frangipani . . . . 1·00 1·00
799 $1.20 "Golden Shower" . . . 1·40 1·75
800 $1.50 "Pua" . . . . 1·90 2·50

1996. Redrawn design as No. 146.
801 20c. red and green . . . . . 1·75 1·25

146 "Jackfish" (yacht)

1996. Sailing Ships. Multicoloured.
802 70c. Type **146** . . . . 1·10 1·10
803 $1 "Jennifer" (yacht) . . . . 1·60 1·60
804 $1.20 "Mikeva" (yacht) . . . 1·90 2·00
805 $2 "Eye of the Wind" (cadet brig) . . . . 2·50 3·00

147 "Desert Star" (ketch)

149 Ox

148 "Acropora gemmifera"

1996. "Taipei '96" International Philatelic Exhibition, Taiwan. Sheet 90 × 80 mm.
MS806 **147** $1.50 multicoloured 2·00 2·50

1996. Corals. Multicoloured.
807 20c. Type **148** 15 20
808 50c. "Acropora nobilis" . . . 30 35
809 70c. "Goniopora lobata" . . 45 50
810 $1 "Sylaster sp." 65 70
811 $1.20 "Alveopora catalai" . . 75 80
812 $1.50 "Fungia scutaria" . . . 95 1·00
813 $2 "Porites solida" . . . . . 1·25 1·40
814 $3 "Millepora sp." . . . . . 1·90 2·00
815 $4 "Pocillopora eydouxi" . . 2·50 2·75
816 $5 "Platygyra pini" . . . . . 3·25 3·50

1997. "HONG KONG '97" International Stamp Exhibition. Chinese New Year ("Year of the Ox"). Sheet 120 × 90 mm.
MS817 **149** $1.50 multicoloured 1·50 2·25

150 Steps to Lagoon

1997. Island Scenes. Multicoloured.
818 $1 Type **150** . . . . 1·25 1·50
819 $1 Islands in lagoon . . . . 1·25 1·50
820 $1 Beach with rocks in foreground . . . . 1·25 1·50
821 $1 Over-hanging rock on beach . . . . 1·25 1·50
Nos. 818/21 were printed together, se-tenant, forming a composite design.

151 Humpback Whale

1997. Whales (1st series). Multicoloured.
822 20c. Type **151** 50 45
823 $1 Humpback whale and calf (vert) . . . . 1·25 1·25
824 $1.50 Humpback whale surfacing (vert) . . . . . 1·75 2·00
MS825 120 × 90 mm. Nos. 822/4 3·00 3·50
No. **MS**825 shows the "Pacific '97" International Stamp Exhibition, San Francisco, emblem on the margin.
See also Nos. 827/9.

152 Niue 1902 Ovpt on New Zealand 1d.

153 Niue 1918–29 Overprint on New Zealand £1

1997. "Aupex '97" Stamp Exhibition, Auckland (1st issue). Sheet 136 × 90 mm.
MS826 **152** $2+20c. multicoloured 2·10 2·50

1997. Whales (2nd series). As T **151**. Multicoloured.
827 50c. Killer whale (vert) . . . 85 85
828 70c. Minke whale (vert) . . . 1·00 1·00
829 $1.20 Sperm whale (vert) . . 1·25 1·25

1997. "Aupex '97" Stamp Exhibition, Auckland (2nd issue). Sheet 90 × 135 mm.
MS830 **153** $2+20c. multicoloured 1·90 2·50

154 Floral Display in Woven Basket

1997. Christmas. Floral Displays. Multicoloured.
831 20c. Type **154** 45 40
832 50c. Display in white pot . . 70 60
833 70c. Display in white basket 90 90
834 $1 Display in purple vase . . 1·25 1·50

1998. Diana, Princess of Wales Commemoration. Sheet 145 × 70 mm, containing vert designs as T **91** of Kiribati. Multicoloured.
MS835 20c. Wearing white jacket, 1992; 50c. Wearing pearl-drop earrings, 1988; $1 In raincoat, 1990; $2 With Mother Theresa, 1992 (sold at $3.70+50c. charity premium) . . . . 3·00 3·50

155 Divers and Turtle

1998. Diving. Multicoloured.
836 20c. Type **155** 45 45
837 70c. Diver exploring coral reef 75 75
838 $1 Exploring underwater chasm (vert) 90 90
839 $1.20 Divers and coral fronds 1·10 1·25
840 $1.50 Divers in cave . . . . 1·40 1·75

157 Pacific Black Duck

1998. Coastal Birds (1st series). Multicoloured.
841 20c. Type **157** 60 40
842 70c. White tern ("Fairy Tern") . . . . 1·00 75
843 $1 Great frigate bird (vert) 1·00 1·00
844 $1.20 Pacific golden plover ("Lesser Golden Plover") 1·25 1·40
845 $2 Common noddy ("Brown Noddy") . . . . 1·75 2·00
See also Nos. 875/8.

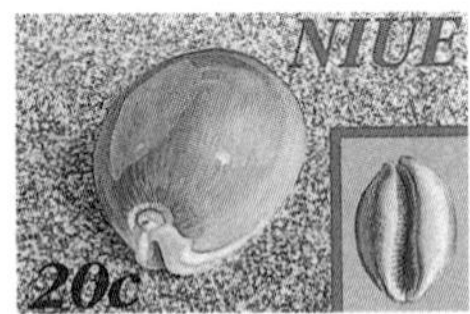

158 Golden Cowrie

1998. Shells. Multicoloured.
846 20c. Type **158** 40 30
847 70c. Cowrie shell 75 65
848 $1 Spider conch . . . . . . 1·00 1·00
849 $5 Helmet shell . . . . . . 5·00 6·50

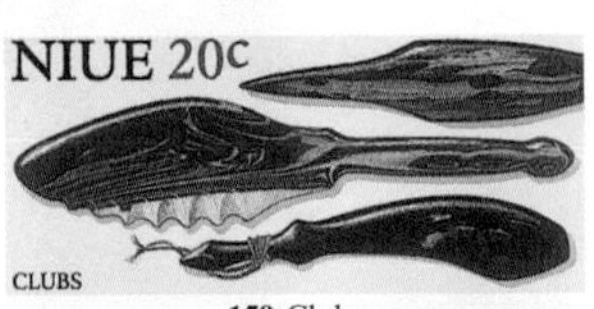

159 Clubs

1998. Ancient Weapons. Multicoloured.
850 20c. Type **159** 40 30
851 $1.20 Three spears (59 × 24 mm) . . . . . . 1·00 1·00
852 $1.50 Five spears (59 × 24 mm) . . . . . . 1·25 1·60
853 $2 Throwing stones . . . . . 1·50 2·00

160 Outrigger Canoe (first migration of Niue Fekai)

1999. "Australia '99" World Stamp Exhibition, Melbourne. Maritime History. Each blue.
854 70c. Type **160** 70 60
855 $1 H.M.S. "Resolution" (Cook) . . . . 1·25 1·00
856 $1.20 "John Williams" (missionary sailing ship) . . 1·40 1·60
857 $1.50 Captain James Cook 1·60 2·00

161 "Risbecia tryoni"

1999. Endangered Species. Nudibranchs. Mult.
858 20c. Type **161** 45 40
859 $1 "Chromodoris lochi" . . 1·10 1·00
860 $1.20 "Chromodoris elizabethina" . . . . . . 1·25 1·40
861 $1.50 "Chromodoris bullocki" . . . . 1·50 2·00
MS862 190 × 105 mm. Nos. 858/61 × 2 . . . . 6·50 8·00

162 Togo Chasm

1999. Scenic Views. Multicoloured.
863 $1 Type **162** . . . . 1·10 1·00
864 $1.20 Matapa Chasm . . . . 1·25 1·25
865 $1.50 Tufukia (horiz) . . . . 1·50 2·00
866 $2 Talava Arches (horiz) . . 1·75 2·25

163 Shallow Baskets

1999. Woven Baskets. Multicoloured.
867 20c. Type **163** 70 90
868 70c. Tray and bowl . . . . . 80 1·10
869 $1 Tall basket and deep bowls (44 × 34 mm) . . . . 1·00 1·40
870 $3 Tall basket and shallow bowls (44 × 34 mm) . . . . 2·10 2·50

164 Children, Yachts and Forest

1999. 25th Anniv of Self-Government. Sheet, 120 × 74 mm, containing T **164** and similar horiz design. Multicoloured.
MS871 20c. Type **164**; $5 Scuba diver, young child and sunset 3·75 4·50

165 Family and Man in Canoe

1999. New Millennium. Multicoloured.
872 20c. Type **165** . . . . 90 1·10
873 70c. People pointing up . . . 1·40 1·75
874 $4 Diver and man in traditional dress . . . . . 2·50 3·00
Nos. 872/4 were printed together, se-tenant, with the backgrounds forming a composite design.

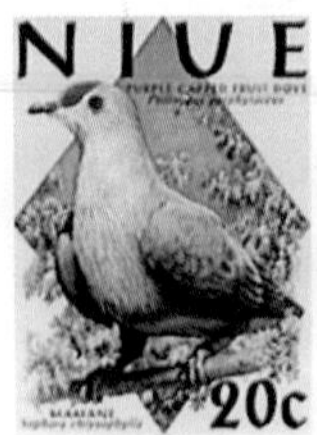

166 Purple-capped Fruit Dove

167 Queen Elizabeth the Queen Mother

2000. Coastal Birds (2nd series). Multicoloured.
875 20c. Type **166** 45 40
876 $1 Purple swamphen . . . . 1·00 90
877 $1.20 Barn owl . . . . . . 1·40 1·40
878 $2 Blue-crowned lory . . . . 1·75 2·00

2000. 100th Birthday of Queen Elizabeth the Queen Mother and 18th Birthday of Prince William. Multicoloured.
879 $1.50 Type **167** . . . . . . 1·75 1·75
880 $3 Queen Elizabeth the Queen Mother and Prince William (horiz) . . . . . 2·50 3·00

168 Pole Vault

2000. Olympic Games, Sydney. Multicoloured.
881 50c. Type **168** 60 45
882 70c. Diving 75 65
883 $1 Hurdling . . . . 1·10 1·10
884 $3 Gymnastics . . . . 2·25 3·00

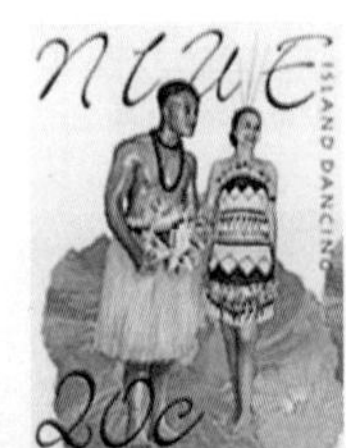

169 Couple in Traditional Costumes

2000. Island Dances. Multicoloured.
885 20c. Type **169** 45 70
886 70c. Woman in red costume 80 1·10
887 $1.50 Woman in white costume . . . . 1·25 1·40
888 $3 Child in costume made of leaves . . . . 1·75 1·90
Nos. 885/8 were printed together, se-tenant, with the backgrounds forming a composite design of flowers.

170 New Zealand Overprinted 1d. of 1902

2001. Centenary of First Niue Stamps. Multicoloured.
889 70c. Type **170** 75 75
890 $3 New Zealand overprinted £1 stamp of 1918–29 . . . 2·00 2·75

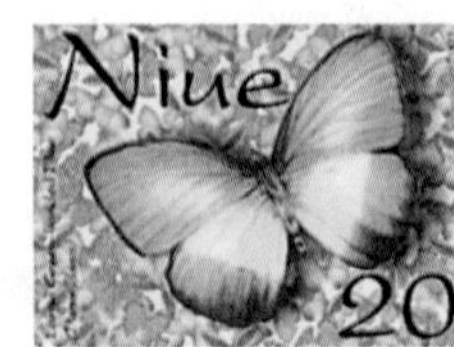

171 Large Green-banded Blue

2001. Butterflies. Multicoloured.
891 20c. Type **171** 40 35
892 70c. Leafwing 80 70
893 $1.50 Cairns birdwing . . . 1·25 1·40
894 $2 Meadow argus . . . . . 1·50 1·75

172 Green Turtle

2001. Turtles. Multicoloured.
895 50c. Type **172** 60 60
896 $1 Hawksbill turtle . . . . . 1·00 1·00
897 $3 Green turtle on beach . . 2·50 2·75

173 Coconut Crab emerging from Sea

2001. Coconut Crabs. Multicoloured.
898 20c. Type **173** 30 30
899 70c. Crab on beach with coconut palms 80 70
900 $1.50 Crab climbing coconut palm . . . . 1·25 1·40
901 $3 Crab with coconut . . . . 2·50 2·75

174 Government Offices

2001. Centenary of Annexation to New Zealand. Multicoloured.
902 $1.50 Type **174** . . . . . . 1·25 1·40
903 $2 New Zealand Commissioner and Niue Chief . . . . 1·50 1·75

175 Three Wise Men

2001. Christmas. Multicoloured.
904 20c. Type **175** 25 20
905 70c. Dove 70 55
906 $1 Angel 90 90
907 $2 Star . . . . 1·50 1·75

OFFICIAL STAMPS

1985. Nos. 409/10 and 527/42 optd **O.H.M.S.**
O 1 12c. Type **92** 35 30
O 2 25c. "Euphorbia pulcherrima" 40 35
O 3 30c. "Cochlospermum hibiscoides" 45 35
O 4 35c. "Begonia sp." 50 40
O 5 40c. "Plumeria sp." 50 45
O 6 52c. "Strelitzia reginae" . . 60 50
O 7 58c. "Hibiscus syriacus" . . 60 55
O 8 70c. "Tibouchina sp." . . . 75 70
O 9 83c. "Nelumbo sp." 90 80
O10 $1.05 "Hybrid hibiscus" . . 1·25 1·00
O11 $1.75 "Cassia fistula" . . . 1·75 1·75
O12 $2.30 Orchid var. . . . . . 5·50 2·75
O13 $3.90 Orchid sp. . . . . . . 6·00 4·25
O14 $4 "Euphorbia pulcherrima poinsettia" . . . . 5·50 6·00
O15 $5 "Euphorbia pulcherrima poinsettia" . . . . 5·50 6·00
O16 $6 "Hybrid hibiscus" . . . . 8·00 9·00
O17 $6.60 "Hybrid hibiscus" . . 8·00 9·00
O18 $8.30 "Hibiscus rosa-sinensis" . . . . 9·00 10·00
O19 $10 Scarlet hibiscus . . . . 10·00 11·00

1993. Nos. 718/29 optd **O.H.M.S.**
O20 20c. Type **130** . . . . 1·50 1·25
O21 50c. Red-tailed tropic bird 2·00 1·50
O22 70c. Purple swamphen . . . 2·50 1·75
O23 $1 Pacific pigeon . . . . . 2·75 1·75
O24 $1.50 White-collared kingfisher . . . . 3·50 2·75
O25 $2 Blue-crowned lory . . . 3·75 3·25
O26 $3 Crimson-crowned fruit dove . . . . 2·75 3·50
O27 $5 Barn owl . . . . 8·50 6·50
O28 $7 Longtailed cuckoo ($48\frac{1}{2}$ × 35 mm) . . . . . . 6·50 8·50
O29 $10 Eastern reef heron ($48\frac{1}{2}$ × 35 mm) . . . . . . 7·50 10·00
O30 $15 Spotted triller ("Polynesian Triller") ($48\frac{1}{2}$ × 35 mm) . . . . . . 16·00 17·00

NORFOLK ISLAND Pt. 1

A small island East of New South Wales, administered by Australia until 1960 when local government was established.

1947. 12 pence = 1 shilling; 20 shillings = 1 pound.
1966. 100 cents = $1 Australian.

1 Ball Bay

1947.
1 **1** $\frac{1}{2}$d. orange 85 60
2 1d. violet 50 60
3 $1\frac{1}{2}$d. green 50 70
4 2d. violet 55 40
5 $2\frac{1}{2}$d. red 80 30
6 3d. brown 70 70
6a 3d. green . . . . 16·00 7·50
7 4d. red . . . . 1·75 40
8 $5\frac{1}{2}$d. blue 70 30
9 6d. brown 70 30
10 9d. pink . . . . 1·25 40
11 1s. green 70 40
12 2s. brown . . . . 1·00 1·00
12a 2s. blue . . . . 24·00 8·00

12 "Hibiscus insularis"

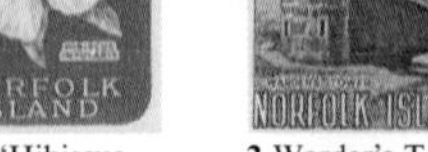

2 Warder's Tower

4 Old Stores (Crankmill)

17 Queen Elizabeth II (after Annigoni) and Cereus

22 Red-tailed Tropic Bird

1953.

24	**12**	1d. green	15	10
25	–	2d. red and green	20	10
26	–	3d. green	70	15
13	**2**	3½d. red	1·00	90
27	–	5d. purple	55	20
14	–	6½d. green	2·25	3·25
15	**4**	7½d. blue	1·50	3·00
28	–	8d. red	80	50
16	–	8½d. brown	1·75	4·75
29	**17**	9d. blue	80	45
17	–	10d. violet	1·00	75
30	–	10d. brown and violet	1·50	1·00
31	–	1s.1d. red	80	35
32	–	2s. brown	6·00	1·00
33	–	2s.5d. violet	1·00	40
34	–	2s.8d. brown and green	2·75	55
18	–	5s. brown	38·00	8·00
35	–	5s. brown and green	4·50	75
36	**22**	10s. green	35·00	32·00

DESIGNS—VERT: 2d. "Lagunaria patersonii"; 5d. Lantana; 8d. Red hibiscus; 8½d. Barracks entrance; 10d. Salt house; 1s.1d. Fringed hibiscus; 2s. Solander's petrel; 2s.5d. Passion-flower; 2s.8d. Rose apple. HORIZ: 3d. White tern; 6½d. Airfield; 5s. Bloody Bridge.

For Nos. 25 and 28 with face values in decimal currency see Nos. 600/1.

8 Norfolk Is. Seal and Pitcairners Landing

1956. Cent of Landing of Pitcairners on Norfolk Is.

19	**8**	3d. green	75	40
20		2s. violet	1·00	75

1958. Surch.

21	**4**	7d. on 7½d. blue	75	1·00
22	–	8d. on 8½d. brown (No. 16)	75	1·00

1959. 150th Anniv of Australian P.O. No. 331 of Australia surch **NORFOLK ISLAND 5D**.

23	**143**	5d. on 4d. slate	35	30

1960. As Nos. 13 and 14/15 but colours changed and surch.

37	**2**	1s.1d. on 3½d. blue	2·75	1·50
38		2s.5d. on 6½d. turquoise	3·25	1·25
39	**4**	2s.8d. on 7½d. sepia	8·00	5·50

26 Queen Elizabeth II and Map

1960. Introduction of Local Government.

40	**26**	2s.8d. purple	7·00	6·50

27 Open Bible and Candle

29 Stripey

28 Open Prayer Book and Text

1960. Christmas.

41	**27**	5d. mauve	60	50

1961. Christmas.

42	**28**	5d. blue	30	60

1962. Fishes.

43	**29**	6d. sepia, yellow and green	60	25
44	–	11d. orange, brown and blue	1·00	80
45	–	1s. blue, pink and olive	60	25
46	–	1s.3d. blue, brown and green	1·00	1·75
47	–	1s.6d. sepia, violet and blue	1·50	80
48	–	2s.3d. multicoloured	3·00	80

DESIGNS: 11d. Gold-mouthed emperor; 1s. Surge wrasse ("Po'ov"); 1s.3d. Seachub ("Dreamfish"); 1s.6d. Giant grouper; 2s.3d. White trevally.

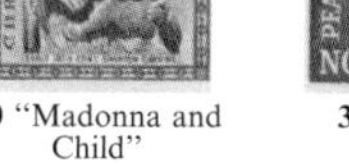

30 "Madonna and Child"

31 "Peace on Earth ..."

1962. Christmas.

49	**30**	5d. blue	45	80

1963. Christmas.

50	**31**	5d. red	40	70

32 Overlooking Kingston

33 Norfolk Pine

1964. Multicoloured.

51		5d. Type **32**	60	60
52		8d. Kingston	1·00	1·50
53		9d. The Arches (Bumboras)	1·75	30
54		10d. Slaughter Bay	1·75	30

1964. 50th Anniv of Norfolk Island as Australian Territory.

55	**33**	5d. black, red and orange	40	15
56		8d. black, red and green	40	1·10

34 Child looking at Nativity Scene

35 Nativity Scene

1964. Christmas.

57	**34**	5d. multicoloured	30	40

1965. 50th Anniv of Gallipoli Landing. As T **22** of Nauru, but slightly larger (22 × 34½ mm).

58		5d. brown, black and green	15	10

1965. Christmas.

59	**35**	5d. multicoloured	15	10

38 "Hibiscus insularis"

39 Headstone Bridge

1966. Decimal Currency. As earlier issue but with values in cents and dollars. Surch in black on silver tablets obliterating old value as in T **38**.

60	**38**	1c. on 1d.	20	10
61	–	2c. on 2d. (No. 25)	20	10
62	–	3c. on 3d. (No. 26)	50	90
63	–	4c. on 5d. (No. 27)	25	10
64	–	5c. on 8d. (No. 28)	30	10
65	–	10c. on 10d. (No. 30)	1·00	15
66	–	15c. on 1s.1d. (No. 31)	50	50
67	–	20c. on 2s. (No. 32)	2·75	2·75
68	–	25c. on 2s.5d. (No. 33)	1·00	40
69	–	30c. on 2s.8d. (No. 34)	1·00	50
70	–	50c. on 5s. (No. 35)	3·00	75
71a	**22**	$1 on 10s.	2·75	2·50

1966. Multicoloured.

72		7c. Type **39**	40	15
73		9c. Cemetery Road	40	15

41 St. Barnabas' Chapel (interior)

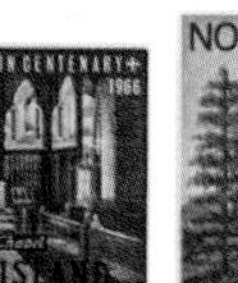

43 Star over Philip Island

1966. Centenary of Melanesian Mission. Mult.

74		4c. Type **41**	10	10
75		25c. St. Barnabas' Chapel (exterior)	20	20

1966. Christmas.

76	**43**	4c. multicoloured	10	10

44 H.M.S. "Resolution", 1774

1967. Multicoloured.

77		1c. Type **44**	10	10
78		2c. "La Boussole" and "L'Astrolabe", 1788	15	10
79		3c. H.M.S. "Supply" (brig), 1788	15	10
80		4c. H.M.S. "Sirius" (frigate), 1790	50	10
81		5c. "Norfolk" (sloop), 1798	20	10
82		7c. H.M.S. "Mermaid" (survey cutter), 1825	20	10
83		9c. "Lady Franklin" (full-rigged ship), 1853	20	10
84		10c. "Morayshire" (full-rigged transport), 1856	20	50
85		15c. "Southern Cross" (missionary ship), 1866	50	30
86		20c. "Pitcairn" (missionary schooner), 1891	60	40
87		25c. "Black Billy" (Norfolk Island whaleboat), 1895	1·50	75
88		30c. "Iris" (cable ship), 1907	1·50	2·00
89		50c. "Resolution" (schooner), 1926	4·75	3·50
90		$1 "Morinda" (freighter), 1931	5·50	3·50

45 Lions Badge and 50 Stars

47 Queen Elizabeth II

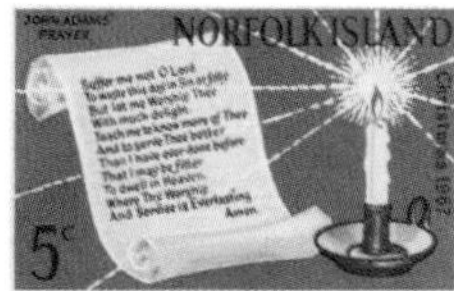

46 Prayer of John Adams and Candle

1967. 50th Anniv of Lions International.

91	**45**	4c. black, green and yellow	10	10

1967. Christmas.

92	**46**	5c. black, olive and red	10	10

1968.

93	**47**	3c. black, brown and red	10	10
94		4c. black, brown and green	10	10
95		5c. black, brown and violet	10	10
95a		6c. black, brown and lake	30	60

59 Avro Type 691 Lancastrian and Douglas DC-4 Aircraft

1968. 21st Anniv of QANTAS Air Service, Sydney–Norfolk Island.

96	**59**	5c. black, red and blue	15	10
97		7c. brown, red and turquoise	15	10

60 Bethlehem Star and Flowers

61 Captain Cook, Quadrant and Chart of Pacific Ocean

1968. Christmas.

98	**60**	5c. multicoloured	10	10

1969. Captain Cook Bicentenary (1st issue). Observation of the transit of Venus across the Sun from Tahiti.

99	**61**	10c. multicoloured	10	10

See also Nos. 118/19, 129, 152/5, 200/2 and 213/14.

62 Van Diemen's Land, Norfolk Island and Sailing Cutter

63 "The Nativity" (carved mother-of-pearl plaque)

1969. 125th Anniv of Annexation of Norfolk Island to Van Diemen's Land.

100	**62**	5c. multicoloured	10	10
101		30c. multicoloured	50	1·00

1969. Christmas.

102	**63**	5c. multicoloured	10	10

64 New Zealand Grey Flyeater

1970. Birds. Multicoloured.

103		1c. Scarlet robin (vert)	30	10
104		2c. Golden whistler (vert)	30	20
105		3c. Type **64**	30	10
106		4c. Long-tailed koels	60	10
107		5c. Red-fronted parakeet (vert)	1·50	60
108		7c. Long-tailed triller (vert)	45	10
109		9c. Island thrush	70	10
110		10c. Boobook owl (vert)	1·75	2·50
111		15c. Norfolk Island pigeon (vert)	1·50	65
112		20c. White-chested white-eye	8·00	3·25
113		25c. Norfolk Island parrots (vert)	2·50	40
114		30c. Collared grey fantail	8·00	1·75
115		45c. Norfolk Island starlings	2·25	80
116		50c. Crimson rosella (vert)	2·50	1·75
117		$1 Sacred kingfisher	10·00	10·00

65 Cook and Map of Australia

1970. Captain Cook Bicentenary (2nd issue). Discovery of Australia's East Coast. Mult.

118		5c. Type **65**	15	10
119		20c. H.M.S. "Endeavour" and aborigine	40	10

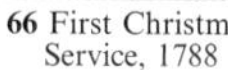

66 First Christmas Service, 1788

68 Rose Window, St. Barnabas Chapel, Kingston

67 Bishop Patteson, and Martyrdom of St. Stephen

1970. Christmas.

120	**66**	5c. multicoloured	10	10

1971. Death Cent of Bishop Patteson. Multicoloured.

121		6c. Type **67**	10	35
122		6c. Bible, Martyrdom of St. Stephen and knotted palm-frond	10	35
123		10c. Bishop Patteson and stained glass	10	35
124		10c. Cross and Bishop's Arms	10	35

1971. Christmas.

125	**68**	6c. multicoloured	10	10

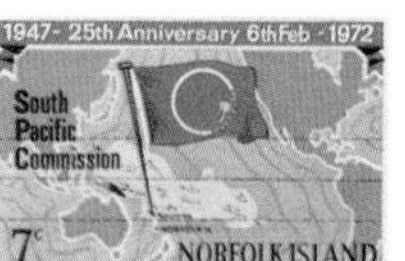

69 Map and Flag

1972. 25th Anniv of South Pacific Commission.

126	**69**	7c. multicoloured	15	20

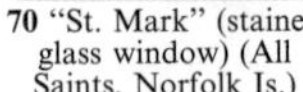

70 "St. Mark" (stained glass window) (All Saints, Norfolk Is.)

71 Cross and Pines (stained-glass window, All Saints Church)

1972. Christmas.
127 **70** 7c. multicoloured 10 10

1972. Cent of First Pitcairner-built Church.
128 **71** 12c. multicoloured 10 10

72 H.M.S. "Resolution" in the Antarctic

1973. Capt. Cook Bicentenary (3rd issue). Crossing of the Antarctic Circle.
129 **72** 35c. multicoloured . . . . 2·50 2·25

73 Child and Christmas Tree

1973. Christmas. Multicoloured.
130 7c. Type **73** 20 10
131 12c. Type **73** 25 10
132 35c. Fir trees and star . . . 70 90

74 Protestant Clergyman's Quarters

1973. Historic Buildings. Multicoloured.
133 1c. Type **74** 10 10
134 2c. Royal Engineers' Office 10 10
135 3c. Double Quarters for Free Overseers . . . . 25 1·00
136 4c. Guard House 20 20
137 5c. Entrance to Pentagonal Gaol 25 15
138 7c. Pentagonal Gaol 35 35
139 8c. Prisoners' Barracks . . . 1·25 2·25
140 10c. Officers' Quarters, New Military Barracks 50 55
141 12c. New Military Barracks 50 30
142 14c. Beach Stores 50 70
143 15c. The Magazine . . . . . 1·25 50
144 20c. Entrance, Old Military Barracks . . . . 50 1·00
145 25c. Old Military Barracks 1·25 1·50
146 30c. Old Stores (Crankmill) 50 60
147 50c. Commissariat Stores . . 50 2·00
148 $1 Government House . . . 1·00 4·00

75 Royal Couple and Map

1974. Royal Visit.
149 **75** 7c. multicoloured 40 20
150 25c. multicoloured 70 80

76 Chichester's De Havilland Gipsy Moth Seaplane "Madame Elijah"

1974. 1st Aircraft Landing on Norfolk Island.
151 **76** 14c. multicoloured 75 70

77 "Captain Cook" (engraving by J. Basire)

78 Nativity Scene (pearl-shell pew carving)

1974. Capt. Cook Bicentenary (4th issue). Discovery of Norfolk Is. Multicoloured.
152 7c. Type **77** 65 65
153 10c. H.M.S. "Resolution" (H. Roberts) . . . . 1·25 1·25
154 14c. Norfolk Island pine . . 1·00 1·50
155 25c. "Norfolk Island flax" (G. Raper) . . . . 1·00 2·00

1974. Christmas.
156 **78** 7c. multicoloured 15 10
157 30c. multicoloured 60 75

79 Norfolk Pine

1974. Centenary of Universal Postal Union. Multicoloured. Imperf. Self-adhesive.
158 10c. Type **79** 35 50
159 15c. Offshore islands 45 55
160 35c. Crimson rosella and sacred kingfisher 85 85
161 40c. Pacific map 85 95
MS162 106 × 101 mm. Map of Norfolk Is. cut-to-shape with reduced size replicas of Nos. 158/61 . . . . 20·00 24·00

80 H.M.S. "Mermaid" (survey cutter)

1975. 150th Anniv of Second Settlement. Multicoloured.
163 10c. Type **80** . . . . 40 1·10
164 35c. Kingston, 1835 (from painting by T. Seller) . . . 60 1·25

81 Star on Norfolk Island Pine

82 Memorial Cross

1975. Christmas.
165 **81** 10c. multicoloured 15 10
166 15c. multicoloured 20 10
167 35c. multicoloured 30 35

1975. Cent of St. Barnabas Chapel. Mult.
168 30c. Type **82** 20 15
169 60c. Laying foundation stone, and Chapel in 1975 . . . . 40 40

83 Launching of "Resolution"

1975. 50th Anniv of Launching of "Resolution" (schooner). Multicoloured.
170 25c. Type **83** 25 40
171 45c. "Resolution" at sea . . 40 70

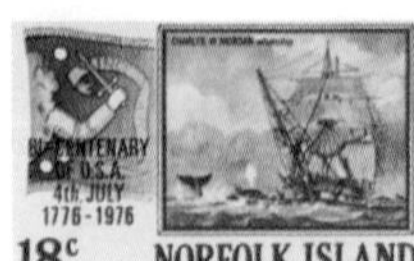

84 Whaleship "Charles W. Morgan"

1976. Bicent of American Revolution. Mult.
172 18c. Type **84** 25 35
173 25c. Thanksgiving Service . . 25 35
174 40c. Boeing B-17 Flying Fortress over Norfolk Island 40 85
175 45c. California quail 50 85

85 Antarctic Tern and Sun

86 "Vanessa ita"

1976. Christmas.
176 **85** 18c. multicoloured 30 15
177 25c. multicoloured 55 20
178 45c. multicoloured 90 50

1977. Butterflies and Moths. Multicoloured.
179 1c. Type **86** 10 40
180 2c. "Utetheisa pulchelloides" 10 40
181 3c. "Agathia asterias" . . . 10 20
182 4c. "Cynthia kershawi" . . . 10 25
183 5c. "Leucania loreyimima" 15 1·10
184 10c. "Hypolimnas bolina" . . 30 1·10
185 15c. "Pyrrhorachis pyrrhogona" 30 30
186 16c. "Austrocarea iocephala" 30 30
187 17c. "Pseudocoremia christiani" 35 30
188 18c. "Cleora idiocrossa" . . 35 30
189 19c. "Simplicia caeneusalis" 35 30
190 20c. "Austrocidaria ralstonae" 40 30
191 30c. "Hippotion scrofa" . . . 50 60
192 40c. "Papilio amynthor (ilioneus)" 50 40
193 50c. "Tiracola plagiata" . . . 50 75
194 $1 "Precis villida" 60 75
195 $2 "Cepora perimale" . . . 75 1·40

87 Queen's View, Kingston

1977. Silver Jubilee.
196 **87** 25c. multicoloured 35 30

88 Hibiscus Flowers and Oil Lamp

89 Captain Cook (from a portrait by Nathaniel Dance)

1977. Christmas.
197 **88** 18c. multicoloured 15 10
198 25c. multicoloured 15 10
199 45c. multicoloured 30 35

1978. Capt. Cook Bicentenary (5th issue). Discovery of Hawaii. Multicoloured.
200 18c. Type **89** 30 20
201 25c. Discovery of northern Hawaiian islands 30 30
202 80c. British flag against island background 60 70

90 Guide Flag and Globe

1978. 50th Anniv of Girl Guides. Multicoloured. Imperf. Self-adhesive.
203 18c. Type **90** 25 45
204 25c. Trefoil and scarf badge 30 55
205 35c. Trefoil and Queen Elizabeth 45 75
206 45c. Trefoil and Lady Baden-Powell 55 75

91 St. Edward's Crown

1978. 25th Anniv of Coronation. Mult.
207 25c. Type **91** 15 15
208 70c. Coronation regalia . . . 40 45

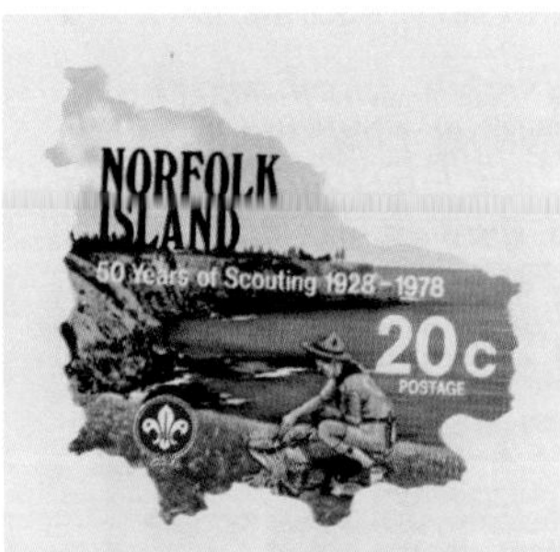

92 View of Duncombe Bay with Scout at Camp Fire

1978. 50th Anniv of Boy Scout Movement. Multicoloured. Imperf. Self-adhesive.
209 20c. Type **92** 30 45
210 25c. View from Kingston and emblem 35 55
211 35c. View of Anson Bay and Link Badge 50 90
212 45c. Sunset scene and Lord Baden-Powell 55 95

93 Chart showing Route of Arctic Voyage

1978. Captain Cook Bicentenary (6th issue). Northern-most Voyages. Multicoloured.
213 25c. Type **93** 30 30
214 90c. "H.M.S. "Resolution" and H.M.S. "Discovery" in Pack Ice" (Webber) . . . 80 80

94 Poinsettia and Bible

95 Cook and Village of Staithes near Marton

1978. Christmas. Multicoloured.
215 20c. Type **94** 15 10
216 30c. Native oak and bible . . 20 15
217 55c. Hibiscus and bible . . . 30 30

1978. 250th Birth Anniv of Captain Cook. Multicoloured.
218 20c. Type **95** 30 25
219 80c. Cook and Whitby Harbour . . . . 70 1·25

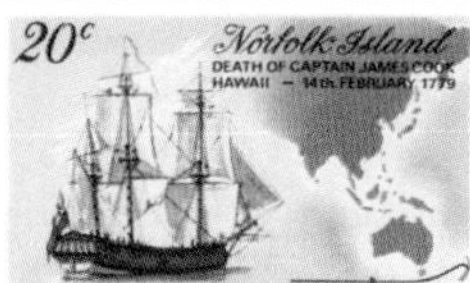

96 H.M.S. "Resolution"

1979. Death Bicent of Captain Cook. Mult.
220 20c. Type **96** 25 30
221 20c. Cook (statue) 25 30
222 40c. Cook's death 30 50
223 40c. Cook's death (different) 30 50
Nos. 220/1 were issued se-tenant, in horizontal pairs throughout the sheet, forming a composite design. A chart of Cook's last voyage is shown in the background. Nos. 222/3 were also issued se-tenant, the horizontal pair forming a composite design taken from an aquatint by John Clevely.

97 Assembly Building

1979. First Norfolk Island Legislative Assembly.
224 **97** $1 multicoloured 50 50

98 Tasmania 1853 1d. Stamp and Sir Rowland Hill

1979. Death Centenary of Sir Rowland Hill.
225 **98** 20c. blue and brown . . . 20 10
226 – 30c. red and grey 25 15
227 – 55c. violet and indigo . . . 40 30
MS228 142 × 91 mm. No. 227 . . 55 1·25
DESIGNS: 30c. Great Britain 1841 1d. red; 55c. 1947 "Ball Bay" 1d. stamp.

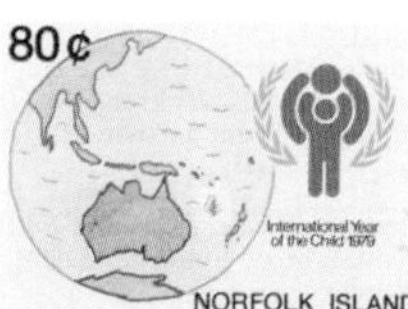

99 I.Y.C. Emblem and Map of Pacific showing Norfolk Island as Pine Tree

1979. International Year of the Child.
229 **99** 80c. multicoloured 40 45

100 Emily Bay

1979. Christmas.
230 **100** 15c. multicoloured 15 15
231 – 20c. multicoloured 15 15
232 – 30c. multicoloured 15 15
MS233 152 × 83 mm. Nos. 230/2 1·00 1·75
DESIGNS: 20, 30c. Different scenes.
Nos. 230/2 were printed together, se-tenant, forming a composite design.

101 Lions International Emblem

1980. Lions Convention.
234 **101** 50c. multicoloured 35 30

102 Rotary International Emblem

1980. 75th Anniv of Rotary International.
235 **102** 50c. multicoloured 35 30

103 De Havilland Gipsy Moth Seaplane "Madame Elijah"

1980. Airplanes. Multicoloured.
236 1c. Hawker Siddeley H.S.748 15 20
237 2c. Type **103** 15 20
238 3c. Curtis P-40E Kittyhawk I 15 20
239 4c. Chance Vought F4U-1 Corsair 15 30
240 5c. Grumman TBF Avenger 15 30
241 15c. Douglas SBD-5 Dauntless 30 30
242 20c. Cessna 172D Skyhawk 30 30
243 25c. Lockheed 414 Hudson 30 35
244 30c. Lockheed PV-1 Ventura 40 1·75
245 40c. Avro Type 685 York . . 50 55
246 50c. Douglas DC-3 . . . . . 65 65
247 60c. Avro Type 691 Lancastrian 75 75
248 80c. Douglas DC-4 . . . . . 1·00 1·00
249 $1 Beech 200 Super King Air 1·25 1·00
250 $2 Fokker F.27 Friendship 2·50 2·75
251 $5 Lockheed C-130 Hercules 4·00 2·00

104 Queen Elizabeth the Queen Mother

1980. 80th Birthday of The Queen Mother.
252 **104** 22c. multicoloured 20 20
253 60c. multicoloured 35 40

105 Red-tailed Tropic Birds

1980. Christmas. Birds. Multicoloured.
254 15c. Type **105** 30 25
255 22c. White terns 30 25
256 35c. White-capped noddys . . 30 25
257 60c. White terns (different) 40 45

106 "Morayshire" and View of Norfolk Island

1981. 125th Anniv of Pitcairn Islanders' Migration to Norfolk Island. Multicoloured.
258 5c. Type **106** 15 15
259 35c. Islanders arriving ashore 40 30
260 60c. View of new settlement 60 45
MS261 183 × 127 mm. Nos. 258/60 1·50 2·25

107 Wedding Bouquet from Norfolk Island

1981. Royal Wedding. Multicoloured.
262 35c. Type **107** 15 15
263 55c. Prince Charles at horse trials 25 25
264 60c. Prince Charles and Lady Diana Spencer 25 35

108 Uniting Church in Australia

1981. Christmas. Churches. Multicoloured.
265 18c. Type **108** 10 10
266 24c. Seventh Day Adventist Church 15 15
267 30c. Church of the Sacred Heart 15 20
268 $1 St. Barnabas Chapel . . . 35 70

109 Pair of White-chested White-Eyes

1981. White-chested White-Eye ("Silvereye"). Mult.
269 35c. Type **109** 35 40
270 35c. Bird on nest 35 40
271 35c. Bird with egg 35 40
272 35c. Parents with chicks . . . 35 40
273 35c. Fledgelings 35 40

110 Aerial view of Philip Island

1982. Philip and Nepean Islands. Mult.
274 24c. Type **110** 20 20
275 24c. Close-up view of Philip Island landscape 20 20
276 24c. Gecko ("Phyllodactylus guentheri"), Philip Island 20 20
277 24c. Sooty tern, Philip Island 20 20
278 24c. Philip Island hibiscus ("hibiscus insularis") . . . 20 20
279 35c. Aerial view of Nepean Island 25 25
280 35c. Close-up view of Nepean Island landscape 25 25
281 35c. Gecko ("phyllodactylus guentheri"), Nepean Island 25 25
282 35c. Blue-faced boobies, Nepean Island 25 25
283 35c. "Carpobrotus glaucescens" (flower), Nepean Island 25 25

111 Sperm Whale

1982. Whales.
284 **111** 24c. multicoloured 60 35
285 – 55c. multicoloured . . . . 1·10 95
286 – 80c. black, mauve & stone 1·40 2·00
DESIGNS: 55c. Black right whale; 80c. Humpback whale.

112 "Diocet", Wrecked 20 April 1873

1982. Shipwrecks. Multicoloured.
287 24c. H.M.S. "Sirius", wrecked 19 March 1790 . . 50 50
288 27c. Type **112** 50 50
289 35c. "Friendship", wrecked 17 May 1835 . . . . . . 90 80
290 40c. "Mary Hamilton", wrecked 6 May 1873 . . . 90 1·25
291 55c. "Fairlie", wrecked 14 February 1840 . . . . 1·25 1·25
292 65c. "Warrigal", wrecked 18 March 1918 . . . . . 1·25 1·75

113 R.N.Z.A.F. Lockheed 414 Hudson dropping Christmas Supplies, 1942

1982. Christmas. 40th Anniv of First Supply-plane Landings on Norfolk Island (Christmas Day 1942). Multicoloured.
293 27c. Type **113** 65 35
294 40c. R.N.Z.A.F. Lockheed 414 Hudson landing Christmas supplies 1942 . . 85 65
295 75c. Christmas, 1942 . . . . 1·00 1·40

114 50th (Queen's Own) Regiment

115 "Panaeolus papilionaceus"

1982. Military Uniforms. Multicoloured.
296 27c. Type **114** 25 35
297 40c. 58th (Rutlandshire) Regiment 30 75
298 55c. 80th (Staffordshire Volunteers) Battalion Company 35 95
299 65c. 11th (North Devonshire) Regiment . . . . 40 1·25

1983. Fungi. Multicoloured.
300 27c. Type **115** 30 35
301 40c. "Coprinus domesticus" 40 50
302 55c. "Marasmius niveus" . . 45 70
303 65c. "Cymatoderma elegans var lamellatum" 50 85

116 Beechcraft 18

1983. Bicentenary of Manned Flight. Mult.
304 10c. Type **116** 15 15
305 27c. Fokker F.28 Fellowship 25 35
306 45c. French military Douglas C-54 . . . . 40 60
307 75c. Sikorsky S-61N helicopter 60 95
MS308 105 × 100 mm. Nos. 304/7 1·75 2·75

117 St. Matthew

119 Popwood

118 Cable Ship "Chantik"

1983. Christmas. 150th Birth Anniv of Sir Edward Burne-Jones.
309 5c. Type **117** 10 10
310 24c. St. Mark 20 30
311 30c. Jesus Christ 25 40
312 45c. St. Luke 35 55
313 85c. St. John . . . . 55 1·10
DESIGNS: showing stained glass windows from St. Barnabas Chapel, Norfolk Island.

1983. World Communications Year. ANZCAN Cable. Multicoloured.
314 30c. Type **118** 25 40
315 45c. "Chantik" during in-shore operations 30 55
316 75c. Cable ship "Mercury" 40 95
317 85c. Diagram of cable route 40 1·10

1984. Flowers. Multicoloured.
318 1c. Type **119** 30 70
319 2c. Strand morning glory . . 40 70

320 3c. Native phreatia 45 70
321 4c. Philip Island wisteria . . 45 70
322 5c. Norfolk Island palm . . . 70 70
323 10c. Evergreen 50 70
324 15c. Bastard oak 60 70
325 20c. Devil's guts 60 70
326 25c. White oak 60 80
327 30c. Ti . . . . 60 1·00
328 35c. Philip Island hibiscus . . 60 1·00
329 40c. Native wisteria . . . . 60 1·25
330 50c. Native jasmine . . . . . 70 1·25
331 $1 Norfolk Island hibiscus . . 70 1·75
332 $3 Native oberonia . . . . . 1·10 4·00
333 $5 Norfolk Island pine . . . 1·50 4·50

120 Morwong

1984. Reef Fishes. Multicoloured.
334 30c. Type **120** 40 45
335 45c. Black-spotted goatfish 40 65
336 75c. Surgeonfish . . . . . . 50 1·10
337 85c. Three-striped butterflyfish . . . . 65 1·40

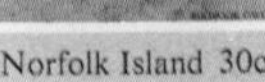

121 Owl with Eggs

123 Font, Kingston Methodist Church

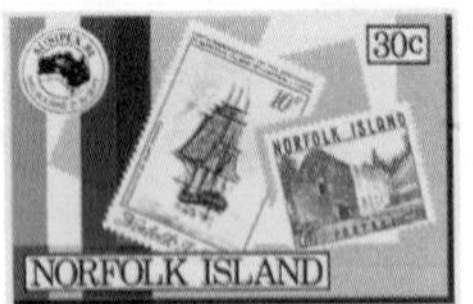

122 1953 7½d. and 1974 Cook Bicent 10c. Stamps

1984. Boobook Owl. Multicoloured.
338 30c. Type **121** 75 85
339 30c. Fledgeling 75 85
340 30c. Young owl on stump . . 75 85
341 30c. Adult on branch 75 85
342 30c. Owl in flight 75 85

1984. "Ausipex" International Stamp Exhibition, Melbourne. Multicoloured.
343 30c. Type **122** 30 35
344 45c. John Buffett commemorative postal stationery envelope 50 75
345 75c. Design from Presentation Pack for 1982 Military Uniforms issue . . 90 1·75
MS346 151 × 93 mm. Nos. 343/5 4·00 4·50

1984. Christmas. Centenary of Methodist Church on Norfolk Island. Multicoloured.
347 5c. Type **123** 10 25
348 24c. Church service in Old Barracks, Kingston, late 1800s 25 40
349 30c. The Revd. & Mrs. A. H. Phelps and sailing ship . . 35 45
350 45c. The Revd. A. H. Phelps and First Congregational Church, Chester, U.S.A. 40 65
351 85c. Interior of Kingston Methodist Church . . . . 80 1·40

124 The Revd. Nobbs teaching Pitcairn Islanders

126 The Queen Mother (from photo by Norman Parkinson)

125 "Fanny Fisher"

1984. Death Centenary of Revd. George Hunn Nobbs (leader of Pitcairn community). Multicoloured.
352 30c. Type **124** 25 45
353 45c. The Revd. Nobbs with sick islander 30 65
354 75c. Baptising baby . . . . . 45 1·10
355 85c. Presented to Queen Victoria, 1852 . . . . . . 55 1·40

1985. 19th-Century Whaling Ships (1st series). Multicoloured.
356 5c. Type **125** 30 50
357 33c. "Costa Rica Packet" . . 60 55
358 50c. "Splendid" . . . . . . 1·00 1·50
359 90c. "Onward" . . . . . . 1·25 2·25
See also Nos. 360/3.

1985. 19th-Century Whaling Ships (2nd series). As T **125**. Multicoloured.
360 15c. "Waterwitch" 60 70
361 20c. "Canton" 70 80
362 60c. "Aladdin" . . . . . . 1·25 1·75
363 80c. "California" . . . . . . 1·40 2·25

1985. Life and Times of Queen Elizabeth the Queen Mother. Multicoloured.
364 5c. The Queen Mother (from photo by Dorothy Wilding) 10 10
365 33c. With Princess Anne at Trooping the Colour . . . 25 25
366 50c. Type **126** 40 55
367 90c. With Prince Henry at his christening (from photo by Lord Snowdon) . . . . . 60 1·00
MS368 91 × 73 mm. $1 With Princess Anne at Ascot Races . . . . . 1·50 1·50

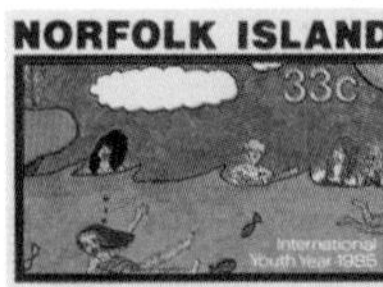

127 "Swimming"

1985. International Youth Year Children's Paintings. Multicoloured.
369 33c. Type **127** 40 40
370 50c. "A Walk in the Country" 70 85

128 Prize-winning Cow and Owner

1985. 125th Anniv of Royal Norfolk Island Agricultural and Horticultural Show. Mult.
371 80c. Type **128** 75 80
372 90c. Show exhibits 85 90
MS373 132 × 85 mm. Nos. 371/2 1·75 2·50

129 Shepherds with Flock

131 "Giotto" Spacecraft

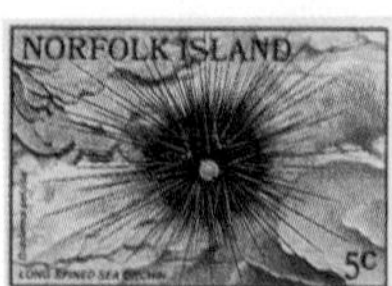

130 Long-spined Sea Urchin

1985. Christmas. Multicoloured.
374 27c. Type **129** 40 30
375 33c. Mary and Joseph with donkey 50 40
376 50c. The Three Wise Men . . 80 65
377 90c. The Nativity . . . . . 1·25 1·25

1986. Marine Life. Multicoloured.
378 5c. Type **130** 10 10
379 33c. Blue starfish 30 35
380 55c. Southern eagle ray . . . 50 85
381 75c. Snowflake moray . . . . 70 1·25
MS382 100 × 95 mm. Nos. 378/81 3·00 4·00

1986. Appearance of Halley's Comet. Mult.
383 $1 Type **131** . . . . 75 1·50
384 $1 Halley's Comet . . . . . 75 1·50
Nos. 383/4 were printed together, se-tenant, forming a composite design.

132 Isaac Robinson (U.S. Consul 1887–1908)

133 Princess Elizabeth and Dog

1986. "Ameripex '86" International Stamp Exhibition, Chicago. Multicoloured.
385 33c. Type **132** 30 35
386 50c. Ford "Model T" (first vehicle on island) (horiz) 50 50
387 80c. Statue of Liberty 55 80
MS388 125 × 100 mm. Nos. 385/7 1·50 2·25
No. 387 also commemorates the Centenary of the Statue of Liberty.

1986. 60th Birthday of Queen Elizabeth II. Multicoloured.
389 5c. Type **133** 10 10
390 33c. Queen Elizabeth II . . . 40 35
391 80c. Opening Norfolk Island Golf Club . . . . 1·60 1·40
392 90c. With Duke of Edinburgh in carriage . . . . 1·25 1·60

134 Stylized Dove and Norfolk Island

135 British Convicts, 1787

1986. Christmas.
393 **134** 30c. multicoloured 25 30
394 40c. multicoloured 30 45
395 $1 multicoloured . . . . 70 1·50

1986. Bicentenary (1988) of Norfolk Island Settlement (1st issue). Governor Phillip's Commission. Multicoloured.
396 36c. Type **135** 80 35
397 55c. Judge passing sentence of transportation . . . . . . 1·50 85
398 90c. Governor Phillip meeting Home Secretary (inscr "Home Society") . . . . . 2·50 3·50
399 90c. As No. 398, but correctly inscr "Home Secretary" . . . . 2·25 3·25
400 $1 Captain Arthur Phillip . . 2·50 2·50
See also Nos. 401/4, 421/4, 433/5, 436/7 and 438/43.

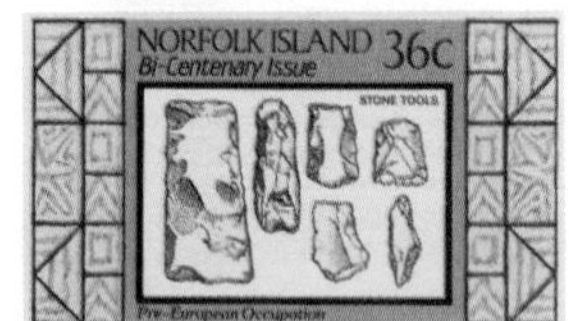

136 Stone Tools

1986. Bicentenary (1988) of Norfolk Island Settlement (2nd issue). Pre-European Occupation. Multicoloured.
401 36c. Type **136** 50 85
402 36c. Bananas and taro . . . 50 85
403 36c. Polynesian outrigger canoe 50 85
404 36c. Maori chief 50 85

137 Philip Island from Point Ross

138 Male Red-fronted Parakeet

1987. Norfolk Island Scenes. Multicoloured.
405 1c. Cockpit Creek Bridge . . 50 1·25
406 2c. Cemetery Bay Beach . . 50 1·25
407 3c. Island guesthouse . . . . 50 1·25
408 5c. Type **137** 30 75
409 15c. Cattle in pasture . . . . 80 1·75
410 30c. Rock fishing . . . . . . 30 1·00
411 37c. Old Pitcairner-style house . . . . 1·40 1·75
412 40c. Shopping centre . . . . 35 1·25
413 50c. Emily Bay . . . . . . 45 1·25
414 60c. Bloody Bridge . . . . . 2·00 2·75
415 80c. Pitcairner-style shop . . 1·75 2·50
416 90c. Government House . . . 1·25 2·00
417 $1 Melanesian Memorial Chapel . . . . 1·00 1·75
418 $2 Convict Settlement, Kingston . . . . 1·75 3·50
419 $3 Ball Bay . . . . 2·75 6·00
420 $5 Northern cliffs . . . . . 3·75 8·50

1987. Bicentenary of Norfolk Island Settlement (1988) (3rd issue). The First Fleet. As T **135**. Multicoloured.
421 5c. Loading supplies, Deptford 50 75
422 55c. Fleet leaving Spithead 1·75 2·25
423 55c. H.M.S. "Sirius" leaving Spithead . . . . 1·75 2·25
424 $1 Female convicts below decks . . . . 2·25 3·00
Nos. 422/3 were printed together, se-tenant, forming a composite design.

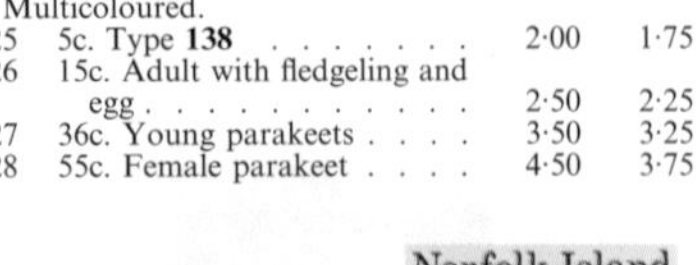

1987. Red-fronted Parakeet ("Green Parrot"). Multicoloured.
425 5c. Type **138** . . . . 2·00 1·75
426 15c. Adult with fledgeling and egg . . . . 2·50 2·25
427 36c. Young parakeets . . . . 3·50 3·25
428 55c. Female parakeet . . . . 4·50 3·75

139 Christmas Tree and Restored Garrison Barracks

140 Airliner, Container Ship and Sydney Harbour Bridge

1987. Christmas. Multicoloured.
429 30c. Type **139** 30 30
430 42c. Children opening presents 45 55
431 58c. Father Christmas with children . . . . 60 1·00
432 63c. Children's party . . . . 70 1·25

1987. Bicentenary of Norfolk Island Settlement (1988) (4th issue). Visit of La Perouse (navigator). As T **135**. Multicoloured.
433 37c. La Perouse with King Louis XVI 95 55
434 90c. "L'Astrolabe" and "La Boussole" off Norfolk Island . . . . 2·75 3·00
435 $1 "L'Astrolabe" wrecked in Solomon Islands . . . . . 2·75 3·00

1988. Bicentenary of Norfolk Island Settlement (5th issue). Arrival of First Fleet at Sydney. As T **135**. Multicoloured.
436 37c. Ship's cutter approaching Port Jackson 1·50 75
437 $1 Landing at Sydney Cove 3·00 3·50

1988. Bicentenary of Norfolk Island Settlement (6th issue). Foundation of First Settlement. As T **135**. Multicoloured.
438 5c. Lt. Philip Gidley King . . 20 50
439 37c. Raising the flag, March 1788 . . . . 85 75
440 55c. King exploring . . . . 1·75 1·50
441 70c. Landing at Sydney Bay, Norfolk Island . . . . . 2·00 2·50
442 90c. H.M.S. "Supply" (brig) 2·25 2·75
443 $1 Sydney Bay settlement, 1788 . . . . 2·25 2·75

1988. "Sydpex '88" National Stamp Exhibition, Sydney. Multicoloured.
444 37c. Type **140** . . . . 95 1·25
445 37c. Exhibition label under magnifying glass (horiz) . . 95 1·25
446 37c. Telephone and dish aerial . . . . 95 1·25
MS447 118 × 84 mm. Nos. 444/6 4·50 5·00

141 Flowers and Decorations

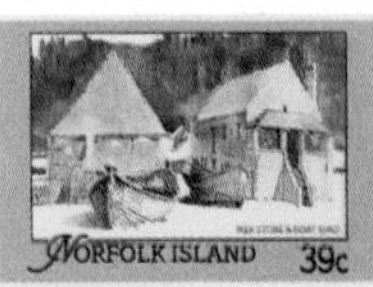

142 Pier Store and Boat Shed

1988. Christmas. Multicoloured.
448 30c. Type **141** 50 40
449 42c. Flowers 70 70
450 58c. Fishes and beach 85 95
451 63c. Norfolk Island . . . . . 95 1·25

1988. Restored Buildings from the Convict Era. Multicoloured.
452 39c. Type **142** 45 40
453 55c. Royal Engineers Building 60 60
454 90c. Old Military Barracks 1·00 1·60
455 $1 Commissariat Store and New Military Barracks . . 1·10 1·60

143 "Lamprima aenea"

1989. Endemic Insects. Multicoloured.
456 39c. Type **143** 65 40
457 55c. "Insulascirtus nythos" 90 75
458 90c. "Caedicia araucariae" 1·40 2·25
459 $1 "Thrincophora aridela" 1·60 2·25

144 H.M.S. "Bounty" off Tasmania

1989. Bicentenary of the Mutiny on the "Bounty". Multicoloured.
460 5c. Type **144** 60 60
461 39c. Mutineers and Polynesian women, Pitcairn Island . . . . 1·75 1·25
462 55c. Lake Windermere, Cumbria (Christian's home county) . . . . 2·25 2·25
463 $1.10 "Mutineers casting Bligh adrift" (Robert Dodd) . . . . 3·50 4·50
MS464 110 × 85 mm. 39c. No. 461; 90c. Isle of Man 1989 Mutiny 35p., No. 414; $1 Pitcairn Islands 1989 Settlement Bicent 90c., No. 345 . . . . 6·00 7·00

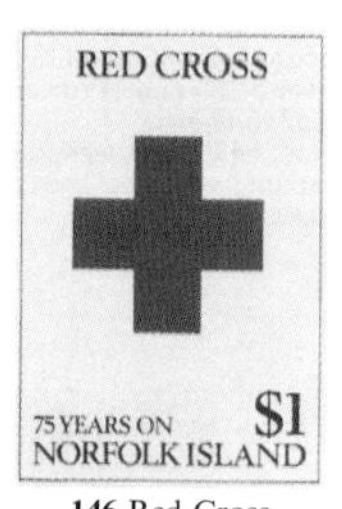

145 Norfolk Island Flag
146 Red Cross

1989. 10th Anniv of Internal Self-government. Multicoloured.
465 41c. Type **145** 90 55
466 55c. Old ballot box 95 65
467 $1 Norfolk Island Act, 1979 1·75 2·00
468 $1.10 Island crest . . . . . 1·75 2·75

1989. 75th Anniv of Red Cross on Norfolk Island.
469 **146** $1 red and blue . . . . . 3·00 3·25

147 "Gethsemane"

1989. Christmas. Designs showing opening lines of hymns and local scenes. Multicoloured.
470 36c. Type **147** 90 40
471 60c. "In the Sweet Bye and Bye" . . . . 1·75 2·00
472 75c. "Let the Lower Lights be Burning" . . . . 2·25 3·00
473 80c. "The Beautiful Stream" 2·25 3·00

148 John Royle (first announcer)
149 H.M.S. "Bounty" on fire, Pitcairn Island, 1790

1989. 50th Anniv of Radio Australia. Designs each showing Kingston buildings. Mult.
474 41c. Type **148** 95 65
475 65c. Radio waves linking Australia and Norfolk Island . . . . 1·75 2·50
476 $1.10 Anniversary kookaburra logo . . . . . 2·75 4·25

1990. History of the Norfolk Islanders (1st series). Settlement on Pitcairn Island. Mult.
477 70c. Type **149** . . . . 2·50 3·00
478 $1.10 Arms of Norfolk Island 2·75 3·50
See also Nos. 503/4 and 516/17.

150 H.M.S. "Sirius" striking Reef

1990. Bicentenary of Wreck of H.M.S. "Sirius". Multicoloured.
479 41c. Type **150** . . . . 1·75 2·00
480 41c. H.M.S. "Sirius" failing to clear bay . . . . 1·75 2·00
481 65c. Divers at work on wreck 2·50 3·00
482 $1 Recovered artifacts and chart of site . . . . 2·75 3·25
Nos. 479/80 were printed together, se-tenant, forming a composite design.

151 Unloading Lighter, Kingston
152 "Ile de Lumiere" (freighter)

1990. Ships.
483 **151** 5c. brown 20 50
484 10c. brown 20 50
485 – 45c. multicoloured . . . . 1·00 60
486 – 50c. multicoloured . . . . 1·00 1·00
487 – 65c. multicoloured . . . . 1·00 1·25
488 **152** 70c. multicoloured . . . . 1·00 1·25
489 – 75c. multicoloured . . . . 2·00 2·00
490 – 80c. multicoloured . . . . 2·00 2·25
491 – 90c. multicoloured . . . . 2·00 2·25
492 – $1 multicoloured . . . . 2·00 2·00
493 – $2 multicoloured . . . . 2·25 3·50
494 – $5 multicoloured . . . . 5·00 7·00
DESIGNS—As T **152**: 45c. "La Dunkerquoise" (French patrol vessel); 50c. "Dmitri Mendeleev" (Russian research vessel); 65c. "Pacific Rover" (tanker); 75c. "Norfolk Trader" (freighter); 80c. "Roseville" (transport); 90c. "Kalia" (container ship); $1 "Bounty" (replica); $2 H.M.A.S. "Success" (supply ship); $5 H.M.A.S. "Whyalla" (patrol vessel).

153 Santa on House Roof
154 William Charles Wentworth

1990. Christmas. Multicoloured.
499 38c. Type **153** 75 45
500 43c. Santa at Kingston Post Office 80 50
501 65c. Santa over Sydney Bay, Kingston (horiz) . . . . . 1·75 2·25
502 85c. Santa on Officers' Quarters (horiz) . . . . . 2·00 2·75

1990. History of the Norfolk Islanders (2nd series). The First Generation.
503 **154** 70c. brown and cinnamon 1·25 1·50
504 – $1.20 brown and cinnamon . . . . . . 2·00 2·50
DESIGN: $1.20, Thursday October Christian.

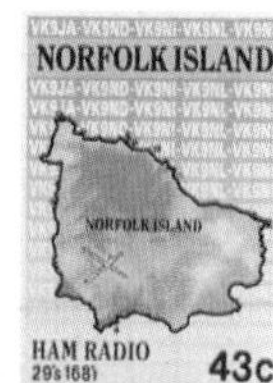

155 Adult Robin and Chicks in Nest
156 Map of Norfolk Island

1990. "Birdpex '90" Stamp Exhibition, Christchurch, New Zealand. Scarlet Robin. Multicoloured.
505 65c. Type **155** . . . . 1·25 1·50
506 $1 Hen on branch . . . . . 1·75 2·00
507 $1.20 Cock on branch . . . 1·75 2·25
MS508 70 × 90 mm. $1 Hen; $1 Cock and hen . . . . 4·50 4·75
Each inscribed "Norfolk Island Robin".

1991. Ham Radio Network. Multicoloured.
509 43c. Type **156** . . . . 1·25 70
510 $1 Globe showing Norfolk Island . . . . 2·75 3·00
511 $1.20 Map of south-west Pacific . . . . 2·75 4·00

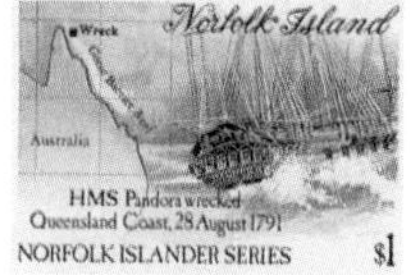

157 Display in "Sirius" Museum
158 H.M.S. "Pandora" wrecked on Great Barrier Reef (1791)

1991. Norfolk Island Museums. Mult.
512 43c. Type **157** 90 65
513 70c. 19th-century sitting room, House Museum (horiz) . . . . 1·75 2·50
514 $1 Carronade, "Sirius" Museum (horiz) . . . . . 2·50 3·25
515 $1.20 Reconstructed jug and beaker, Archaeological Museum . . . . 2·50 3·75

1991. History of the Norfolk Islanders (3rd series). Search for the "Bounty". Multicoloured.
516 $1 Type **158** . . . . 2·75 2·50
517 $1.20 H.M.S. "Pandora" leaving bay . . . . 2·75 3·00

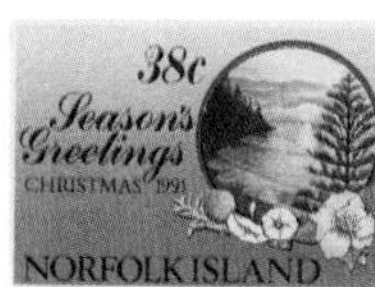

159 Hibiscus and Island Scene

1991. Christmas.
518 **159** 38c. multicoloured 90 45
519 43c. multicoloured . . . . 1·00 55
520 65c. multicoloured . . . . 1·50 2·00
521 85c. multicoloured . . . . 1·75 2·50

160 Tank and Soldier in Jungle
161 Coat of Arms

1991. 50th Anniv of Outbreak of Pacific War. Multicoloured.
522 43c. Type **160** . . . . 1·25 65
523 70c. Boeing B-17 Flying Fortress on jungle airstrip 2·25 2·75
524 $1 Warships . . . . 2·75 3·50

1992. 500th Anniv of Discovery of America by Columbus. Multicoloured.
525 45c. Type **161** 85 55
526 $1.05 "Santa Maria" . . . . 2·00 2·75
527 $1.20 Columbus and globe 2·50 3·25

162 Deployment Map
163 Norfolk Pines above Ball Bay

1992. 50th Anniv of Battle of the Coral Sea. Multicoloured.
528 45c. Type **162** . . . . 1·25 60
529 70c. H.M.A.S. "Australia" (cruiser) . . . . 2·00 2·50
530 $1.05 U.S.S. "Yorktown" (aircraft carrier) . . . . . 2·75 3·50

1992. 50th Anniv of Battle of Midway. As T **162**. Multicoloured.
531 45c. Battle area . . . . . . 1·25 60
532 70c. Consolidated PBY-5 Catalina flying boat over task force . . . . 2·00 2·50
533 $1.05 Douglas SBD Dauntless dive bomber and "Akagi" (Japanese aircraft carrier) burning . . . . . 2·75 3·50

1992. 50th Anniv of Battle of Guadalcanal. As T **162**. Multicoloured.
534 45c. American troops landing (horiz) . . . . 1·25 60
535 70c. Machine-gun crew (horiz) . . . . 2·00 2·50
536 $1.05 Map of Pacific with Japanese and American flags (horiz) . . . . 2·75 3·50

1992. Christmas. Multicoloured.
537 40c. Type **163** 70 40
538 45c. Headstone Creek 75 45
539 75c. South side of Ball Bay 1·50 2·25
540 $1.20 Rocky Point Reserve 2·00 3·00

164 Boat Shed and Flaghouses, Kingston

1993. Tourism. Historic Kingston. Mult.
541 45c. Type **164** . . . . 80 1·00
542 45c. Old Military Barracks 80 1·00
543 45c. All Saints Church . . . 80 1·00
544 45c. Officers' Quarters . . . 80 1·00
545 45c. Quality Row . . . . . 80 1·00
Nos. 541/5 were printed together, se-tenant, forming a composite design.

165 Fire Engine

1993. Emergency Services. Multicoloured.
546 45c. Type **165** . . . . 1·00 60
547 70c. Cliff rescue squad . . . 1·10 1·75
548 75c. Ambulance . . . . . . 1·40 1·90
549 $1.20 Police car . . . . . . 2·50 3·00

166 Blue Sea Lizard ("Glaucus atlanticus")

1993. Nudibranchs. Multicoloured.
550 45c. Type **166** 80 55
551 45c. Ocellate nudibranch ("Phyllidia ocellata") . . . 80 55
552 75c. "Bornella sp." . . . . . 1·50 1·75
553 85c. "Glossodoris rubroannolata" . . . . . 1·75 2·25
554 95c. "Halgerda willeyi" . . . 2·00 2·50
555 $1.05 "Ceratosoma amoena" 2·00 3·00

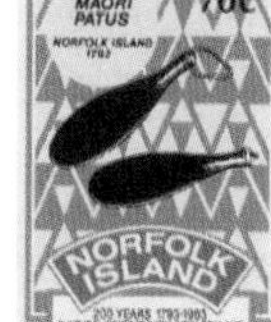

167 Christmas Wreath
168 Maori Stone Clubs

1993. Christmas.
556 **167** 40c. multicoloured 60 50
557 45c. multicoloured 60 50
558 75c. multicoloured . . . . 1·00 1·50
559 $1.20 multicoloured . . . 1·90 2·75

1993. Bicentenary of Contact with New Zealand. Multicoloured.
560 70c. Type **168** . . . . 1·25 1·50
561 $1.20 First Maori map of New Zealand, 1793 . . . . 2·00 2·75

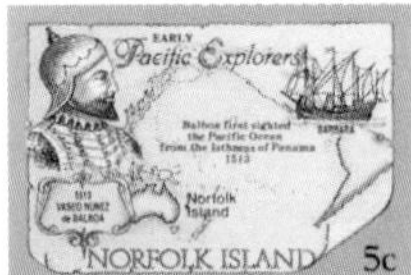

169 Alvaro de Saavedra, Route Map and "Florida"

1994. Pacific Explorers. Multicoloured.
562 5c. Vasco Nunez de Balboa, map and "Barbara" . . . 55 65
563 10c. Ferdinand Magellan, map and "Vitoria" 70 65
564 20c. Juan Sebastian del Cano, map and "Vitoria" . . . . 1·00 85
565 50c. Type **169** . . . . 1·00 1·00
566 70c. Ruy Lopez de Villalobos, map and "San Juan" . . . . 1·25 1·25
567 75c. Miguel Lopez de Legaspi, map and "San Lesmes" . . . . 1·25 1·25
568 80c. Sir Francis Drake, map and "Golden Hind" . . . 1·25 1·25
569 85c. Alvaro de Mendana, map and "Santiago" . . . 1·25 1·25
570 90c. Pedro Fernandes de Quiros, map and "San Pedro y Pablo" . . . . . 1·25 1·25
571 $1 Luis Baez de Torres, map and "San Pedrico" . . . . 1·40 1·40
572 $2 Abel Tasman, map and "Heemskerk" . . . . . . 2·00 2·50
573 $5 William Dampier, map and "Cygnet" . . . . . . 4·25 5·50
MS574 100 × 80 mm. $1.20 "Golden Hind" (Drake) (32 × 52 mm) 2·75 2·75

170 Sooty Tern

171 House and Star

1994. Sea Birds. Multicoloured.
575 45c. Type **170** . . . . 95 1·10
576 45c. Red-tailed tropic bird . . 95 1·10
577 45c. Australian gannet . . . 95 1·10
578 45c. Wedge-tailed shearwater 95 1·10
579 45c. Masked booby . . . . . 95 1·10
Nos. 575/9 were printed together, se-tenant, forming a composite design.

1994. Christmas. Multicoloured. Self-adhesive.
580 45c. Type **171** 80 55
581 75c. Figures from stained-glass windows . . . . . . 1·50 2·00
582 $1.20 Rainbow and "The Church of God" (missionary sailing ship) . . 2·50 3·00

172 Chevrolet, 1926

1995. Vintage Motor Vehicles. Multicoloured.
583 45c. Type **172** 75 55
584 75c. Ford Model "A", 1928 1·25 1·75
585 $1.05 Ford Model "A A/C", 1929 . . . . 1·60 2·00
586 $1.20 Ford Model "A", 1930 1·75 2·25

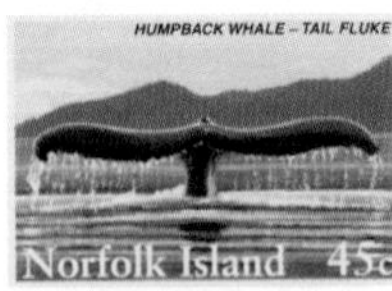

173 Tail Flukes of Humpback Whale

1995. Humpback Whale Conservation. Multicoloured.
587 45c. Type **173** . . . . 1·00 55
588 75c. Mother and calf . . . . 1·50 2·00
589 $1.05 Whale breaching (vert) 1·75 2·50
MS590 107 × 84 mm. $1.20 Humpback whale (29 × 49 mm) 2·50 2·75

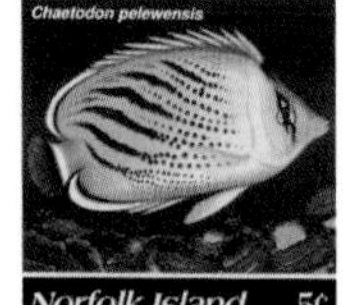

174 Dot-and-Dash Butterflyfish

1995. Butterflyfishes. Multicoloured.
591 5c. Type **174** 30 75
592 45c. Blue-spotted butterflyfish 85 50
593 $1.20 Three-belted butterflyfish . . . . 2·25 2·75
594 $1.50 Three-finned butterflyfish . . . . 2·50 3·25

1995. "JAKARTA '95" Stamp Exhibition, Indonesia. No. **MS**590 optd "Selamat Hari Merdeka" and emblem on sheet margin in gold.
MS595 107 × 84 mm. $1.20 Humpback whale . . . . . . 1·75 2·50

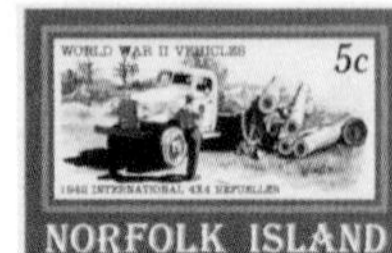

175 International 4 × 4 Refueller, 1942

1995. Second World War Vehicles. Multicoloured.
596 5c. Type **175** 30 75
597 45c. Ford Sedan, 1942 . . . 75 45
598 $1.20 Ford 3 ton tipper, 1942 2·00 2·50
599 $2 D8 caterpillar with scraper 3·00 4·00

1995. Flower designs as 1960 issues, but with face values in decimal currency.
600 5c. pink and green (as No. 25) 15 20
601 5c. red (as No. 28) 15 20

176 Servicing Fighter

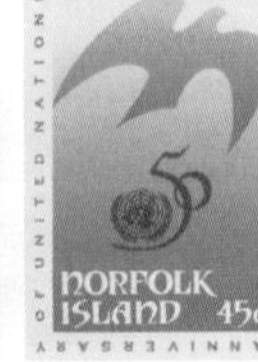

177 Peace Dove and Anniversary Emblem

1995. 50th Anniv of End of Second World War in the Pacific. Multicoloured.
602 5c. Type **176** 40 50
603 45c. Sgt. Tom Derrick, VC (vert) 70 45
604 75c. Gen. Douglas MacArthur (vert) . . . . 1·25 1·50
605 $1.05 Girls celebrating victory 1·75 2·00
606 $10 Pacific War medals (50 × 30 mm) . . . . . . 16·00 19·00
The $10 also includes the "Singapore '95" International stamp exhibition logo.

1995. Christmas. 50th Anniv of United Nations. Each including U.N. anniversary emblem.
607 **177** 45c. gold and blue 60 45
608 – 75c. gold and violet . . . 1·00 1·25
609 – $1.05 gold and red . . . 1·40 2·00
610 – $1.20 gold and green . . . 1·60 2·25
DESIGNS: 75c. Star of Bethlehem; $1.05, Symbolic candles on cake; $1.20, Olive branch.

178 Skink on Bank

1996. Endangered Species. Skinks and Geckos. Multicoloured.
611 5c. Type **178** 55 75
612 5c. Gecko on branch 55 75
613 45c. Skink facing right . . . 70 75
614 45c. Gecko on flower 70 75

179 Sopwith Pup Biplane and Emblem

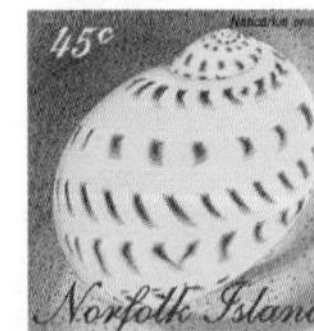

181 "Naticarlus oncus"

1996. 75th Anniv of Royal Australian Air Force. Aircraft. Multicoloured.
615 45c. Type **179** 60 60
616 45c. Wirraway fighter 60 60
617 75c. F-111C jet fighter . . . 1·00 1·40
618 85c. F/A-18 Hornet jet fighter 1·10 1·50

180 Rat

1996. Chinese New Year ("Year of the Rat"). Sheet 100 × 75 mm.
MS619 **180** $1 black, red and brown 1·50 2·25

1996. Shells. Multicoloured.
620 45c. Type **181** 70 85
621 45c. "Janthina janthina" . . 70 85
622 45c. "Cypraea caputserpentis" 70 85
623 45c. "Argonauta nodosa" . . 70 85

182 Shopping

183 The Nativity

1996. Tourism. Multicoloured.
624 45c. Type **182** 50 50
625 [illegible]ting Bounty Day 1·00 1·00
626 $2.50 Horse riding . . . . . 3·75 4·50
627 $3.70 Unloading lighter . . . 4·50 5·75

1996. Christmas. Multicoloured.
628 45c. Type **183** 50 50
629 45c. Star and boat sheds . . 50 50
630 75c. Star, bungalow and ox 90 1·50
631 85c. Star, fruit, flowers and ox . . . . 1·10 1·75

184 Coat of Arms

185 Calf

1997.
632 **184** 5c. blue and yellow . . . 20 30
633 – 5c. brown 20 30
DESIGN: No. 633, Great Seal of Norfolk Island.

1997. Beef Cattle. Sheet 67 × 67 mm.
MS634 **185** $1.20 multicoloured 2·00 2·50

1997. "HONG KONG '97" International Stamp Exhibition. As No. **MS**634, but with exhibition emblem on sheet margin.
MS635 67 × 67 mm. **185** $1.20 multicoloured . . . . 2·25 3·00

186 "Cepora perimale"

1997. Butterflies. Multicoloured.
636 75c. Type **186** . . . . 1·00 1·00
637 90c. "Danaus chrysippus" . . 1·25 1·60
638 $1 "Danaus hamata" . . . . 1·40 1·60
639 $1.20 "Danaus plexippus" . . 1·50 2·25

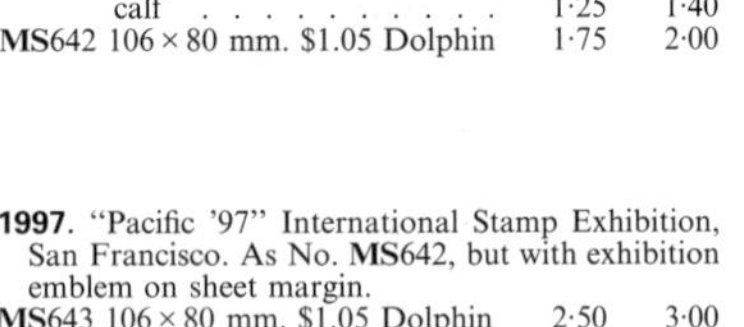

187 Dusky Dolphins

1997. Dolphins. Multicoloured.
640 45c. Type **187** 75 60
641 75c. Common dolphin and calf . . . . 1·25 1·40
MS642 106 × 80 mm. $1.05 Dolphin 1·75 2·00

1997. "Pacific '97" International Stamp Exhibition, San Francisco. As No. **MS**642, but with exhibition emblem on sheet margin.
MS643 106 × 80 mm. $1.05 Dolphin 2·50 3·00

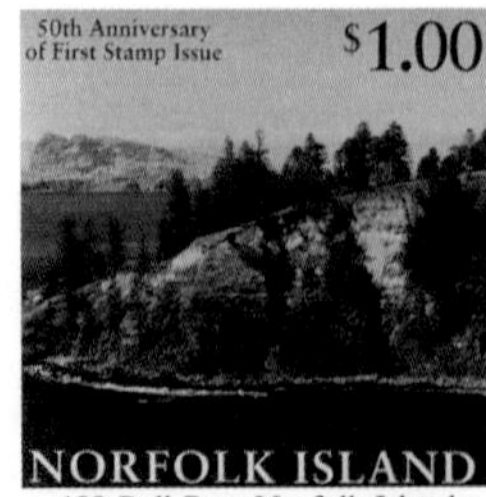

188 Ball Bay, Norfolk Island

1997. 50th Anniv of Norfolk Island Stamps. Multicoloured.
644 $1 Type **188** . . . . 1·25 1·75
645 $1.50 1947 2d. stamp . . . . 1·25 1·75
646 $8 Ball Bay and 1947 2s. bistre stamp (90 × 45 mm) 7·50 11·00

1997. Golden Wedding of Queen Elizabeth and Prince Philip. As T **87** of Kiribati. Multicoloured.
647 20c. Queen Elizabeth 40 50
648 25c. Prince Philip in carriage-driving trials 40 50
649 25c. Prince Philip 40 50
650 50c. Queen in phaeton at Trooping the Colour . . . 70 80
MS651 110 × 70 mm. $1.50 Queen Elizabeth and Prince Philip in landau (horiz) . . . . 1·75 2·25
Nos. 647/8 and 649/50 were each printed together, se-tenant, with the backgrounds forming composite designs.

189 Royal Yacht "Britannia" leaving Hong Kong

1997. Return of Hong Kong to China. Sheet 126 × 91 mm.
MS652 **189** 45c. multicoloured 1·00 1·50
No. **MS**652 is inscribed "Brittania" in error.

190 Christmas Tree

191 Oriental Pearl T.V. Tower, Shanghai

1997. Annual Festivals. Multicoloured.
653 45c. Type **190** 60 45
654 75c. Fireworks (New Year's Eve) . . . . 90 1·25
655 $1.20 Rose (Valentine's Day) 1·40 1·75

1997. "Shanghai '97" International Stamp and Coin Exhibition, shanghai. Sheet 103 × 138 mm.
MS656 **191** 45c. multicoloured 1·00 1·50

192 Tiger Mask

1998. Chinese New Year ("Year of the Tiger"). Sheet 75 × 95 mm.
MS657 **192** 45c. multicoloured . . . 1·00 1·50

193 "Pepper"

194 Entrance to Pentagonal Gaol

1998. Cats. Multicoloured.
658 45c. Type **193** 65 65
659 45c. "Tabitha" at window . . 65 65
660 75c. "Midnight" . . . . . . 85 1·00
661 $1.20 "Rainbow" with flower pot . . . . 1·25 1·50

1998.
662 **194** 5c. black and blue 15 25
663 – 5c. black and green . . . 15 25
DESIGN: No. 663, Ruined First Settlement cottage.

1998. Diana, Princess of Wales Commemoration. As T **91** of Kiribati.
664 45c. Princess Diana with bouquet, 1991 . . . . . . 50 50
MS665 145 × 70 mm. 45c. Wearing blue and white dress, 1989; 45c. Wearing pearl earrings, 1990; 45c. No. 664; 45c. Wearing striped dress (sold at $1.80+45c. charity premium) . . . . 1·60 2·00

195 Tweed Trousers

196 Hammer Throwing

1998. Reef Fishes. Multicoloured.
666 10c. Type **195** 25 30
667 20c. Conspicuous angelfish 45 45
668 30c. Moon wrasse 50 50
669 45c. Wide-striped clownfish 65 50
670 50c. Racoon butterflyfish . . 70 70
671 70c. Artooti (juvenile) 85 85
672 75c. Splendid hawkfish . . . 90 90
673 85c. Scorpion fish . . . . . 1·00 1·10
674 90c. Orange fairy basslet . . 1·00 1·10
675 $1 Sweetlips . . . . 1·10 1·10
676 $3 Moorish idol . . . . . . 2·50 3·25
677 $4 Gold-ribbon soapfish . . 3·00 4·00
MS678 110 × 85 mm. $1.20 Shark (29 × 39 mm) . . . . 1·25 1·50
Nos. 672 and 675 are incorrectly inscribed "Splendid Hawkefish" and "Sweetlip".

1998. 16th Commonwealth Games, Kuala Lumpur.
679 **196** 75c. red and black . . . . 85 1·00
680 – 95c. violet and black . . . 1·00 1·25
681 – $1.05 mauve and black . . 1·10 1·40
MS682 80 × 100 mm. 85c. green and black . . . . 1·00 1·50
DESIGNS—HORIZ: 95c. Trap shooting. VERT: 85c. Flag bearer; $1.05, Lawn bowls.

197 "Norfolk" (sloop)

1998. Bicentenary of the Circumnavigation of Tasmania by George Bass and Matthew Flinders.
683 **197** 45c. multicoloured . . . . 1·25 85
MS684 101 × 69 mm. **197** $1.20 multicoloured . . . . 2·00 2·25

198 Blue whale

1998. Whales of the Southern Oceans (joint issue with Namibia and South Africa). Sheet 103 × 70 mm.
MS685 **198** $1.50 multicoloured 1·90 2·25

199 "Peace on Earth"

1998. Christmas. Multicoloured.
686 45c. Type **199** 45 50
687 75c. "Joy to the World" . . 70 80
688 $1.05 "A Season of Love" . . 1·00 1·50
689 $1.20 "Light of the World" 1·00 1·50

200 Short S.23 Sandringham (flying boat)

201 Soft Toy Rabbit

1999. Aircraft. Each red and green.
690 5c. Type **200** 25 30
691 5c. DC-4 "Norfolk Trader" 25 30

1999. Chinese New Year ("Year of the Rabbit"). Sheet 80 × 100 mm.
MS692 **201** 95c. multicoloured 1·00 1·50

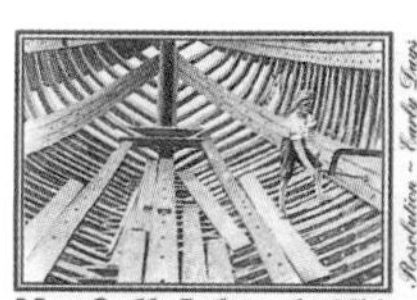

202 Hull of "Resolution" under Construction

1999. "Australia '99" International Stamp Exhibition, Melbourne. Schooner "Resolution". Multicoloured.
693 45c. Type **202** . . . . 1·00 1·00
694 45c. After being launched . . 1·00 1·00
695 45c. In Emily Bay . . . . . 1·00 1·00
696 45c. Off Cascade . . . . . . 1·00 1·00
697 45c. Alongside at Auckland 1·00 1·00

203 Pacific Black Duck

204 Solander's Petrel in Flight

1999. "iBRA '99" International Stamp Exhibition, nuremburg. Sheet 80 × 100 mm.
MS698 **203** $2.50 multicoloured 3·25 3·75

1999. Endangered Species. Solander's Petrel ("Providence Petrel"). Multicoloured.
699 75c. Type **204** . . . . . . 1·40 1·00
700 $1.05 Head of Solander's petrel (horiz) . . . . . . 1·50 1·40
701 $1.20 Adult and fledgling (horiz) . . . . 1·50 1·60
MS702 130 × 90 mm. $4.50 Solander's petrel in flight (35 × 51 mm) . . . . 6·50 6·50
See also No. MS738.

205 "Cecile Brunner" Rose

206 Pottery

1999. Roses. Multicoloured.
703 45c. Type **205** 50 40
704 75c. Green rose 75 90
705 $1.05 "David Buffett" rose 1·00 1·50
MS706 60 × 81 mm. $1.20 "A Country Woman" Rose . . . 1·10 1·40
No. MS706 also commemorates the 50th anniversary of the Country Women's Association on Norfolk Island.

1999. "China '99" International Stamp Exhibition, Beijing. No. MS692 with "China '99" logo optd on the margin in red.
MS707 80 × 100 mm. 95c. Type **201** 1·00 1·25

1999. Handicrafts of Norfolk Island. Multicoloured.
708 45c. Type **206** 50 50
709 45c. Woodcarving 50 50
710 75c. Quilting 75 90
711 $1.05 Basket-weaving . . . . 1·00 1·50

1999. "Queen Elizabeth the Queen Mother's Century". As T **267** of Lesotho. Multicoloured (except $1.20).
712 45c. Inspecting bomb damage, Buckingham Palace, 1940 . . . . . . 60 60
713 45c. At Abergeldy Castle sale of work, 1955 . . . . . . 60 60
714 75c. Queen Mother, Queen Elizabeth and Prince William, 1994 . . . . . . 85 85
715 $1.20 Inspecting the King's Regiment (black) . . . . . 1·40 1·60
MS716 145 × 70 mm. $3 Queen Elizabeth, 1937, and Amy Johnson's flight to Australia, 1930 3·00 3·25

207 Bishop George Augustus Selwyn

1999. Christmas. 150th Anniv of Melanesian Mission. Multicoloured (except 75c.).
717 45c. Type **207** 80 90
718 45c. Bishop John Coleridge Patteson 80 90
719 75c. "150 YEARS MELANESIAN MISSION" (black) . . . . 90 1·00
720 $1.05 Stained-glass windows 1·00 1·40
721 $1.20 "Southern Cross" (missionary ship) and religious symbols . . . . . 1·00 1·40
Nos. 717/21 were printed together, se-tenant, with the backgrounds forming a composite design.

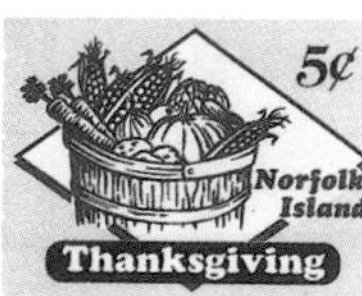

208 Basket of Food (Thanksgiving)

2000. Festivals.
722 **208** 5c. black and blue 15 25
723 – 5c. black and blue 15 25
DESIGN: No. 723, Musician playing guitar (Country Music Festival).

209 Dragon

2000. Chinese New Year ("Year of the Dragon"). Sheet 106 × 86 mm.
MS724 **209** $2 multicoloured . . 1·75 2·00

210 Domestic Goose

2000. Ducks and Geese. Multicoloured.
725 45c. Type **210** 55 50
726 75c. Pacific black duck . . . 1·00 1·00
727 $1.05 Mallard drake . . . . 1·25 1·50
728 $1.20 Aylesbury duck . . . . 1·25 1·50

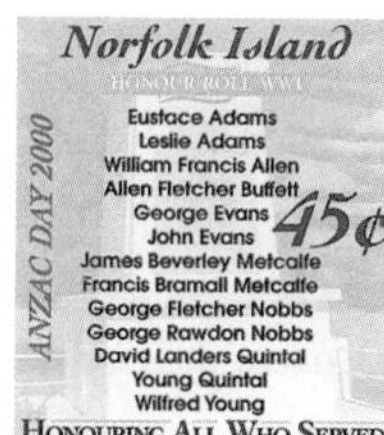

211 Honour Roll for First World War

2000. Anzac Day. Multicoloured.
729 45c. Type **211** 60 50
730 75c. Honour rolls for Second World War and Korea . . 80 1·10

212 Young Boy, Shipwright and Whaleboat

2000. "Whaler Project 2000". Two sheets, each 96 × 76 mm, containing T **212**. Multicoloured.
MS731 **212** $4 multicoloured . . . 4·00 4·50
MS732 $4 mult ("THE STAMP SHOW 2000" and Crown Agents logos added in gold) Imperf . . 3·50 4·00

213 Captain William Bligh and Bounty

2000. "Bounty" Day. Multicoloured.
733 45c. Type **213** 70 55
734 75c. Fletcher Christian and Tahiti . . . . 90 1·10

214 Turtle

215 Malcolm Champion (Olympic Gold Medal Winner, Stockholm, 1912)

2000. 8th Festival of Pacific Arts, New Caledonia. Multicoloured. (a) Size 24 × 29 mm. Self-adhesive.
735 45c. Urn and swat 50 50

(b) Sheet 130 × 70 mm.
MS736 75c. Type **214**; $1.05 Traditional mosaic; $1.20 Mask and spearhead; $2 Decorated utensils . . . . 4·00 4·50

2000. "Olymphilex 2000" International Stamp Exhibition, Sydney. Sheet 120 × 70 mm.
MS737 **215** $3 multicoloured . . 2·75 3·00

2000. "Canpex 2000" National Stamp Exhibition, Christchurch, New Zealand. Sheet 120 × 90 mm.
MS738 $2.40 No. 701 × 2 . . . . 2·25 2·50

216 Sun over Pines

2000. Christmas. Multicoloured.
739 45c. Type **216** 70 45
740 75c. Candle over pines . . . 1·00 80
741 $1.05 Moon over pines . . . 1·25 1·25
742 $1.20 Star over pines . . . . 1·50 1·50

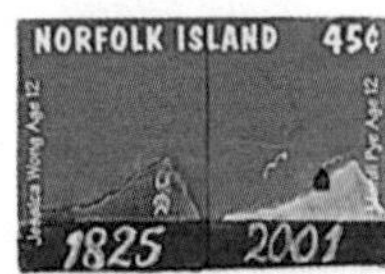

217 "Norfolk Island in 1825 and 2001" (Jessica Wong and Mardi Pye)

2000. New Millennium. Children's drawings. Mult.
743 45c. Type **217** 70 70
744 45c. "Seabirds over Norfolk Island" (Roxanne Spreag) 70 70
745 75c. "Trees and Clothes" (Tara Grube) . . . . . . 1·10 1·10
746 75c. "Underwater Scene" (Thomas Greenwood) . . . 1·10 1·10

218 Red-fronted Parakeet ("Green Parrot")

219 Purple Swamphen

2001. Green Parrot.
747 **218** 5c. red and green 10 10

2001. Chinese New Year "Year of the Snake" and International Stamp Exhibition, Hong Kong.
748 **219** 45c. multicoloured . . . . 1·00 75
MS749 110 × 70 mm. $2.30 Norfolk Island eel and purple swamphen (as Type **219**, but without country inscr and face value). Imperf 1·90 2·25

220 "Old Clothes"

222 Woman and Child in Victorian Dress

223 *Jasminium simplicifolium*

2001. Perfume from Norfolk Island. Multicoloured.
761 4c. Type **223** 10 10
762 75c. Girl's face in perfume bottle 55 60
763 $1.05 Girl and roses 75 90
764 $1.20 Taylor's Road, Norfolk Island . . . . 85 1·00
765 $1.50 Couple shopping for perfume . . . . 1·10 1·40
MS766 145 × 98 mm. $3 Girl and perfume bottle ("NORFOLK ISLAND" in two lines) (60 × 72 mm) . . . . 2·40 2·75
MS767 145 × 98 mm. $3 As No. **MS**766, but with "NORFOLK ISLAND" in one line across the top of the sheet and face value at bottom right . . . . 3·25 3·50
Nos. 761/5 were printed on paper impregnated with the Jasmine fragrance.
No. **MS**767 was issued imperf.

224 Whaleboat

226 Miamiti (cartoon owl) holding Island Flag

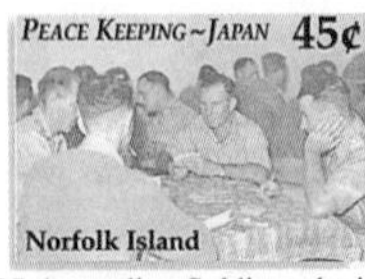

225 Australian Soldiers playing Cards

2001. Local Boats. Multicoloured.
768 45c. Type **224** 40 35
769 $1 Motor launch 80 90
770 $1 Family rowing boat (horiz) 80 90
771 $1.50 Sailing cutter (horiz) . . 1·25 1·40
No. 768 also comes self-adhesive.

2001. Centenary of Australian Army. B.C.O.F. Japan.
773 **225** 45c. brown and blue . . . 45 50
774 – 45c. brown and blue . . . 45 50
775 – $1 brown and green . . . 90 1·00
776 – $1 brown and green . . . 90 1·00
DESIGNS: No. 774, Christmas float; 775, Birthday cake; 776, Australian military policeman directing traffic.

2001. 6th South Pacific Mini Games (1st issue).
777 **226** 10c. brown and green . . 20 25
See also Nos. 794/5.

227 Strawberry Guava
228 Sacred Kingfisher

2001. Christmas. Island Plants. Each incorporating carol music. Multicoloured.
778 45c. Type **227** 45 45
779 45c. Poinsettia 45 45
780 $1 Christmas croton 80 90
781 $1 Hibiscus 80 90
782 $1.50 Indian shot . . . . . 1·25 1·50
No. 779 is inscribed "Pointsettia" in error.

2002. "Nuffka" (Sacred Kingfisher).
783 **228** 10c. deep blue and blue 20 25

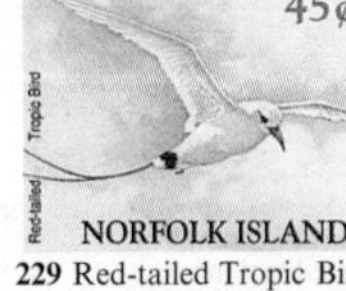

229 Red-tailed Tropic Bird

221 Satellite over China

2001. Centenary of Australian Federation. Cartoons from *The Bulletin Magazine*. Multicoloured.
750 45c. Type **220** 55 65
751 45c. "Tower of Babel" . . . 55 65
752 45c. "The Political Garotters" 55 65
753 45c. "Promises, Promises!" 55 65
754 45c. "The Gout of Federation" 55 65
755 45c. "The Federal Spirit" . . 55 65
756 75c. "Australia Faces the Dawn" 70 80
757 $1.05 "The Federal Capital Question" . . . . 90 1·25
758 $1.20 "The Imperial Fowl-Yard" . . . . 1·00 1·40

2001. Invercargill "Stamp Odyssey 2001" National Stamp Exhibition, New Zealand. Sheet, 136 × 105 mm, containing T **221** and similar vert designs. Multicoloured.
MS759 75c. Type **221**; 75c. Satellite over Pacific; 75c. Satellite over Australia . . . . 2·50 2·75

2001. Bounty Day.
760 **222** 5c. black and green . . . 10 10

2002. Cliff Ecology. Multicoloured.
784 45c. Type **229** 50 40
785 $1 White oak blossom . . . 80 90
786 $1 White oak tree 80 90
787 $1.50 Eagle ray . . . . . . 1·25 1·60

2002. Golden Jubilee. As T **211** of Pitcairn Islands.
788 45c. black, red and gold . . . 45 35
789 75c. multicoloured 70 70
790 $1 black, red and gold . . . 80 85
791 $1.50 multicoloured . . . . 1·25 1·40
MS792 162 × 95 mm. Nos. 788/91 and $3 multicoloured . . . . . 6·00 6·50
DESIGNS:—HORIZ:45c. Elizabeth, Duchess of York with Princesses Elizabeth and Margaret, 1930; 75c. Queen Elizabeth in multicoloured hat, 1977; $1 Queen Elizabeth wearing Imperial State Crown, Coronation 1953; $1.50, Queen Elizabeth at Windsor Horse Show, 2000. VERT (38 × 51 mm)— $3 Queen Elizabeth after Annigoni.
Designs as Nos. 788/91 in No. **MS**792 omit the gold frame around each stamp and the "Golden Jubilee 1952-2002" inscription.

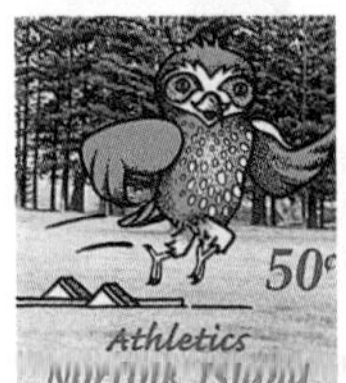

230 Derelict Steam Engine

2002. Restoration of Yeaman's Mill Steam Engine.
793 **230** $4.50 multicoloured . . . 3·25 3·75

231 Miamiti (cartoon owl) running

232 Lawn Bowls Player

2002. 6th South Pacific Mini Games (2nd issue). Multicoloured.
794 50c. Type **231** 35 40
795 $1.50 Miamiti playing tennis 1·10 1·25

2002. Bounty Bowls Tournament.
796 **232** 10c. black and green . . . 10 10

233 *Streblorrhiza speciosa*

234 Running

2002. Phillip Island Flowers. Multicoloured.
797 10c. Type **233** 10 10
798 20c. *Plumbago zeylanica* . . . 15 20
799 30c. *Canavalia rosea* 20 25
800 40c. *Ipomea pes-caprae* . . . 20 25
801 45c. *Hibiscus insularis* 30 35
802 50c. *Solanum laciniatum* . . . 35 40
803 95c. *Phormium tenax* 70 75
804 $1 *Lobelia anceps* 70 75
805 $1.50 *Carpobrotus glaucescens* 1·10 1·25
806 $2 *Abutilon julianae* . . . . . 1·40 1·50
807 $3 *Wollastonia biflora* . . . . 2·10 2·25
808 $5 *Oxalis corniculata* . . . . 3·50 3·75
No. 797 is inscribed "specioca" in error.

2002. 17th Commonwealth Games, Manchester. Multicoloured.
809 10c. Type **234** 10 10
810 45c. Cycling (horiz) 30 35
811 $1 Lawn bowls 70 75
812 $1.50 Shooting (horiz) . . . 1·10 1·25

235 Adult Sperm Whale and Calf

2002. Norfolk Island--New Caledonia Joint Issue. Operation Cetaces (marine mammal study). Multicoloured.
813 $1 Type **235** 70 75
814 $1 Sperm whale attacked by giant squid 70 75
A similar set was issued by New Caledonia.

236 White Tern incubating Egg

2002. Christmas. White Tern. Multicoloured.
815 45c. Type **236** 30 35
816 45c. White tern chick 30 35
817 $1 Two White terns in flight 70 75
818 $1.50 White tern landing . . 1·10 1·25

NORTH BORNEO Pt. 1

A territory in the north of the Island of Borneo in the China Sea, formerly under the administration of the British North Borneo Company. A Crown Colony since 1946. Joined Malaysia in 1963 and renamed Sabah in 1964.

100 cents = 1 dollar (Malayan).

1

1883. "POSTAGE NORTH BORNEO" at top.
8 **1** ½c. mauve . . . . 95·00 £180
9 1c. orange £180 £325
10 2c. brown . . . . 25·00 24·00
11 4c. pink . . . . 17·00 50·00
12 8c. green . . . . 19·00 50·00
13 10c. blue . . . . 28·00 50·00

1883. Surch **8 Cents.** vert.
2 **1** 8c. on 2c. brown £950 £650

1883. Surch **EIGHT CENTS**.
3 **1** 8c. on 2c. brown £450 £190

Where there are three price columns, prices in the second column are for postally used stamps and those in the third column are for stamps cancelled with black bars.

4

5

1883. Inscr "NORTH BORNEO".
4 **4** 50c. violet . . . . . . £120 – 24·00
5 **5** $1 red . . . . £110 – 11·00
For these designs with "BRITISH" in place of value in words at top, see Nos. 46/7.

1886. Optd **and Revenue**.
14 **1** ½c. mauve £110 £190
15 10c. blue £160 £190

1886. Surch in words and figures.
18 **1** 3c. on 4c. pink . . . . 90·00 £110
19 5c. on 8c. green . . . . . . 95·00 £110

9

10

13

19

1886. Inscr "BRITISH NORTH BORNEO".
22 **9** ½c. red . . . . . 3·00 13·00
24 1c. orange . . . . . 2·00 8·00
25 2c. brown . . . . . 2·00 8·50

No.	Type	Description			
26		4c. pink	3·00	9·50	
27		8c. green	10·00	18·00	
28		10c. blue	7·00	25·00	
45	10	25c. blue	55·00	80·00	75
46	–	50c. violet	80·00	£130	75
47	–	$1 red	27·00	£110	75
48	13	$2 green	£130	£180	1·50
49	19	$5 purple	£170	£180	8·50
50	–	$10 brown	£225	£300	12·00

DESIGNS: 50c. As Type 4; $1, As Type 5. $10 As Type 19 but with different frame.

14

1888. Inscr "POSTAGE & REVENUE".

No.	Type	Description			
36b	14	½c. red	1·50	4·00	60
37		1c. orange	2·00	4·00	50
38b		2c. brown	3·50	13·00	50
39		3c. violet	2·50	11·00	50
40		4c. pink	5·50	30·00	50
41		5c. grey	2·75	20·00	50
42		6c. red	8·00	20·00	50
43a		8c. green	19·00	24·00	50
44b		10c. blue	6·50	20·00	50

1890. Surch in words.

No.	Type	Description		
51	10	2c. on 25c. blue	70·00	90·00
52		8c. on 25c. blue	95·00	£110

1891. Surch in figures and words.

No.	Type	Description		
63	14	1c. on 4c. pink	22·00	14·00
64		1c. on 5c. grey	7·00	6·00
54	9	6c. on 8c. green	£7500	£4000
55	14	6c. on 8c. green	20·00	10·00
56	9	6c. on 10c. blue	60·00	20·00
57	14	6c. on 10c. blue	£140	26·00
65	10	8c. on 25c. blue	£140	£160

24 Dyak Chief

25 Sambar Stag ("Cervus unicolor")

26 Sago Palm

27 Great Argus Pheasant

28 Arms of the Company

29 Malay Prau

30 Estuarine Crocodile

31 Mt. Kinabalu

32 Arms of the Company with Supporters

1894.

No.	Type	Description			
66	24	1c. black and bistre	1·25	9·50	50
69	25	2c. black and red	5·50	4·75	50
70	26	3c. green and mauve	2·75	8·50	50
72	27	5c. black and red	14·00	11·00	60
73a	28	6c. black and brown	4·50	18·00	60
74	29	8c. black and lilac	6·50	11·00	60
75a	30	12c. black and blue	28·00	80·00	2·50
78	31	18c. black and green	27·00	50·00	2·00
79	32	24c. blue and red	23·00	75·00	2·00

1894. As Nos. 47, etc, but inscr "THE STATE OF NORTH BORNEO".

No.	Type	Description			
81		25c. blue	9·00	30·00	1·00
82		50c. violet	20·00	60·00	1·75
83		$1 red	12·00	24·00	1·25
84		$2 green	20·00	75·00	2·25
85b		$5 purple	£180	£250	7·50
86		$10 brown	£225	£300	14·00

1895. No. 83 surch in figures and words.

No.	Type	Description			
87		4 cents on $1 red	6·00	1·50	50
88		10 cents on $1 red	18·00	1·75	50
89		20 cents on $1 red	40·00	17·00	50
90		30 cents on $1 red	28·00	27·00	50
91		40 cents on $1 red	28·00	48·00	50

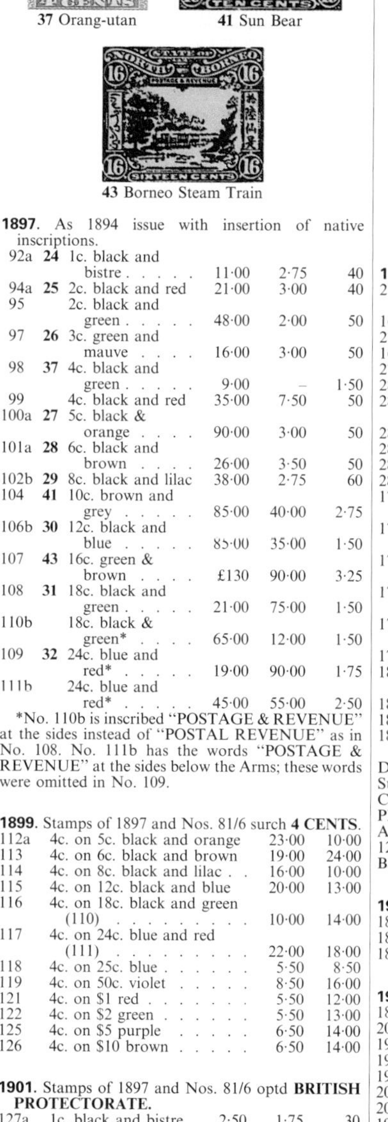

37 Orang-utan

41 Sun Bear

43 Borneo Steam Train

1897. As 1894 issue with insertion of native inscriptions.

No.	Type	Description			
92a	24	1c. black and bistre	11·00	2·75	40
94a	25	2c. black and red	21·00	3·00	40
95		2c. black and green	48·00	2·00	50
97	26	3c. green and mauve	16·00	3·00	50
98	37	4c. black and green	9·00	–	1·50
99		4c. black and red	35·00	7·50	50
100a	27	5c. black & orange	90·00	3·00	50
101a	28	6c. black and brown	26·00	3·50	50
102b	29	8c. black and lilac	38·00	2·75	60
104	41	10c. brown and grey	85·00	40·00	2·75
106b	30	12c. black and blue	85·00	35·00	1·50
107	43	16c. green & brown	£130	90·00	3·25
108	31	18c. black and green	21·00	75·00	1·50
110b		18c. black & green*	65·00	12·00	1·50
109	32	24c. blue and red*	19·00	90·00	1·75
111b		24c. blue and red*	45·00	55·00	2·50

*No. 110b is inscribed "POSTAGE & REVENUE" at the sides instead of "POSTAL REVENUE" as in No. 108. No. 111b has the words "POSTAGE & REVENUE" at the sides below the Arms; these words were omitted in No. 109.

1899. Stamps of 1897 and Nos. 81/6 surch **4 CENTS**.

No.	Type	Description		
112a		4c. on 5c. black and orange	23·00	10·00
113		4c. on 6c. black and brown	19·00	24·00
114		4c. on 8c. black and lilac	16·00	10·00
115		4c. on 12c. black and blue	20·00	13·00
116		4c. on 18c. black and green (110)	10·00	14·00
117		4c. on 24c. blue and red (111)	22·00	18·00
118		4c. on 25c. blue	5·50	8·50
119		4c. on 50c. violet	8·50	16·00
121		4c. on $1 red	5·50	12·00
122		4c. on $2 green	5·50	13·00
125		4c. on $5 purple	6·50	14·00
126		4c. on $10 brown	6·50	14·00

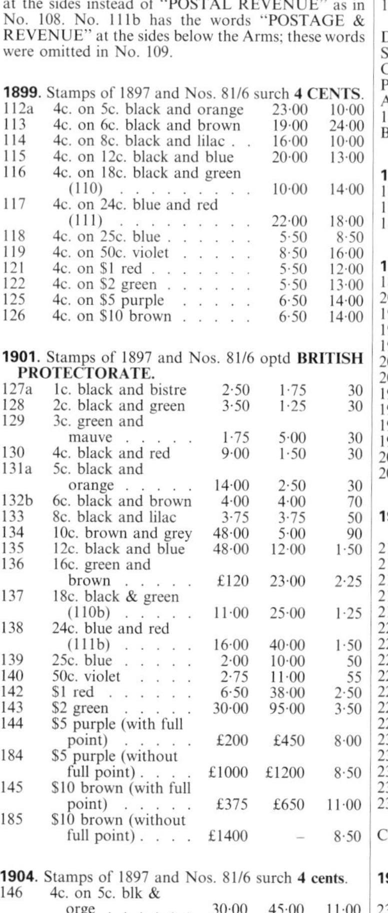

1901. Stamps of 1897 and Nos. 81/6 optd **BRITISH PROTECTORATE**.

No.	Type	Description			
127a		1c. black and bistre	2·50	1·75	30
128		2c. black and green	3·50	1·25	30
129		3c. green and mauve	1·75	5·00	30
130		4c. black and red	9·00	1·50	30
131a		5c. black and orange	14·00	2·50	30
132b		6c. black and brown	4·00	4·00	70
133		8c. black and lilac	3·75	3·75	50
134		10c. brown and grey	48·00	5·00	90
135		12c. black and blue	48·00	12·00	1·50
136		16c. green and brown	£120	23·00	2·25
137		18c. black & green (110b)	11·00	25·00	1·25
138		24c. blue and red (111b)	16·00	40·00	1·50
139		25c. blue	2·00	10·00	50
140		50c. violet	2·75	11·00	55
142		$1 red	6·50	38·00	2·50
143		$2 green	30·00	95·00	3·50
144		$5 purple (with full point)	£200	£450	8·00
184		$5 purple (without full point)	£1000	£1200	8·50
145		$10 brown (with full point)	£375	£650	11·00
185		$10 brown (without full point)	£1400	–	8·50

1904. Stamps of 1897 and Nos. 81/6 surch **4 cents**.

No.	Type	Description			
146		4c. on 5c. blk & orge	30·00	45·00	11·00
147		4c. on 6c. black & brn	7·00	21·00	11·00
148		4c. on 8c. blk & lilac	13·00	26·00	11·00
149		4c. on 12c. black & bl	25·00	40·00	11·00
150		4c. on 18c. black and green (110b)	14·00	38·00	11·00
151a		4c. on 24c. bl & red (111b)	17·00	48·00	11·00
152		4c. on 25c. blue	4·00	25·00	11·00
153		4c. on 50c. violet	4·50	38·00	11·00
154		4c. on $1 red	6·00	48·00	11·00
155		4c. on $2 green	6·00	48·00	11·00
156		4c. on $5 purple	12·00	48·00	11·00
157		4c. on $10 brown	12·00	48·00	11·00

51 Malayan Tapir

52 Traveller's Tree

64

(68)

1909. No. 177 is surch **20 CENTS**.

No.	Type	Description			
277	51	1c. black and brown	1·00	70	–
160	52	2c. black and green	1·00	70	30
278		2c. black and red	85	60	–
162	–	3c. black and red	2·75	2·50	40
279	–	3c. black and green	3·00	75	–
280	–	4c. black and red	50	10	–
281	–	5c. black and brown	4·75	2·75	–
282	–	6c. black and green	5·50	90	–
283	–	8c. black and red	3·25	50	–
284	–	10c. black and blue	3·75	90	–
285	–	12c. black and blue	21·00	80	–
174	–	16c. black and brown	26·00	7·00	1·00
175	–	18c. black and green	90·00	32·00	1·00
177	–	20c. on 18c. blk & grn	7·00	1·00	30
176	–	24c. black and green	28·00	3·50	1·25
178	64	25c. black and green	9·50	4·50	2·00
179	–	50c. black and blue	9·50	4·25	2·25
180	–	$1 black and brown	17·00	4·00	2·50
181	–	$2 black and lilac	60·00	17·00	4·50
182	–	$5 black and red	90·00	£110	30·00
183	–	$10 black and orange	£325	£375	65·00

DESIGNS—As T **51**: 3c. Jesselton railway station; 4c. Sultan of Sulu, his staff and W. C. Cowie, first Chairman of the Company; 5c. Asiatic elephant; 8c. Ploughing with buffalo; 24c. Dwarf cassowary. As T **52**: 6c. Sumatran rhinoceros; 10c. Wild boar; 12c. Palm cockatoo; 16 c Rhinoceros hornbill; 18 c Banteng. As T **64** but Arms with supporters: $5, $10.

1916. Stamps of 1909 surch.

No.	Type	Description		
186		2c. on 3c. black and red	23·00	15·00
187		4c. on 6c. black and olive	18·00	17·00
188		10c. on 12c. black and blue	50·00	60·00

1916. Nos. 277 etc, optd with T **68**.

No.	Type	Description		
189		1c. black and brown	7·50	35·00
203		2c. black and green	27·00	50·00
191		3c. black and red	27·00	48·00
192		4c. black and red	5·50	32·00
193		5c. black and brown	32·00	55·00
206		6c. black and green	45·00	65·00
207		8c. black and red	25·00	55·00
196		10c. black and blue	40·00	70·00
197		12c. black and blue	85·00	90·00
198		16c. black and brown	90·00	90·00
199		20c. on 18c. black and green	35·00	85·00
200		24c. black and mauve	95·00	£100
201		25c. black and green	£300	£375

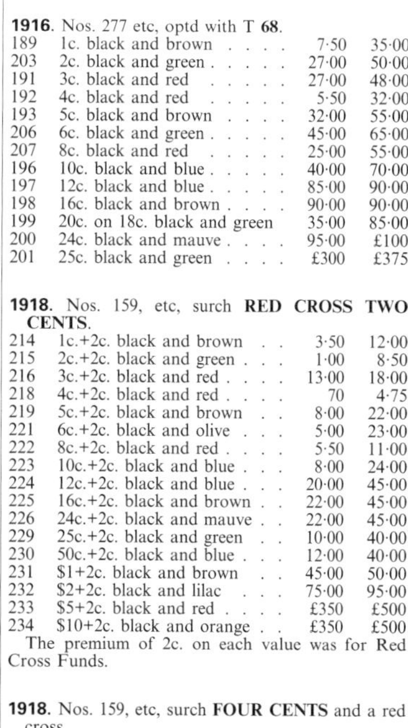

1918. Nos. 159, etc, surch **RED CROSS TWO CENTS**.

No.	Type	Description		
214		1c.+2c. black and brown	3·50	12·00
215		2c.+2c. black and green	1·00	8·50
216		3c.+2c. black and red	13·00	18·00
218		4c.+2c. black and red	70	4·75
219		5c.+2c. black and brown	8·00	22·00
221		6c.+2c. black and olive	5·00	23·00
222		8c.+2c. black and red	5·50	11·00
223		10c.+2c. black and blue	8·00	24·00
224		12c.+2c. black and blue	20·00	45·00
225		16c.+2c. black and brown	22·00	45·00
226		24c.+2c. black and mauve	22·00	45·00
229		25c.+2c. black and green	10·00	40·00
230		50c.+2c. black and blue	12·00	40·00
231		$1+2c. black and brown	45·00	50·00
232		$2+2c. black and lilac	75·00	95·00
233		$5+2c. black and red	£350	£500
234		$10+2c. black and orange	£350	£500

The premium of 2c. on each value was for Red Cross Funds.

1918. Nos. 159, etc, surch **FOUR CENTS** and a red cross.

No.	Type	Description		
235		1c.+4c. black and brown	60	5·00
236		2c.+4c. black and green	65	8·00
237		3c.+4c. black and red	1·00	3·75
238		4c.+4c. black and red	40	4·75
239		5c.+4c. black and brown	2·00	22·00
240		6c.+4c. black and olive	1·90	12·00
241		8c.+4c. black and red	1·25	9·50
242		10c.+4c. black and blue	3·75	12·00
243		12c.+4c. black and blue	14·00	14·00
244		16c.+4c. black and brown	8·00	16·00
245		24c.+4c. black and mauve	11·00	20·00
246		25c.+4c. black and green	6·00	50·00
248		50c.+4c. black and blue	15·00	45·00
249		$1+4c. black and brown	15·00	60·00
250		$2+4 c black and lilac	48·00	80·00
251		$5+4c. black and red	£275	£400
252		$10+4c. black and orange	£275	£400

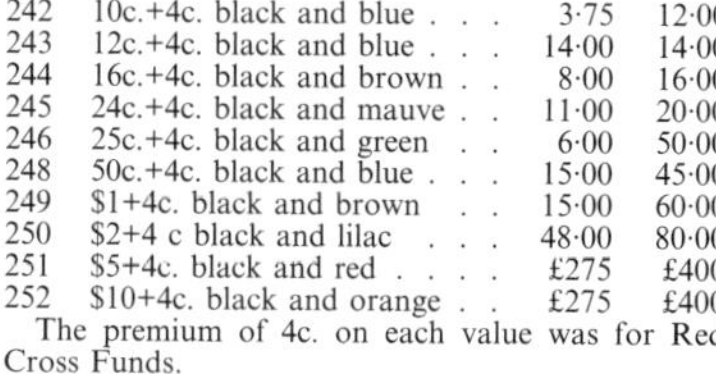

The premium of 4c. on each value was for Red Cross Funds.

1922. Nos. 159, etc, optd **MALAYA-BORNEO EXHIBITION 1922.**

No.	Type	Description		
253		1c. black and brown	11·00	55·00
255		2c. black and green	2·00	20·00
256		3c. black and red	13·00	50·00
257		4c. black and red	2·00	35·00
258		5c. black and brown	9·00	50·00
260		6c. black and green	8·00	55·00
262		8c. black and red	6·00	48·00
263		10c. black and blue	10·00	50·00
265		12c. black and blue	6·50	21·00
267		16c. black and brown	17·00	55·00
268		20c. on 18c. black and green	17·00	70·00
270		24c. black and mauve	30·00	55·00
274		25c. black and green	6·00	50·00
275		50c. black and blue	9·00	50·00

1923. No. 280 surch **THREE CENTS** and bars.

No.	Type	Description		
276	–	3c. on 4c. black and red	1·25	6·00

73 Head of a Murut

76 Mount Kinabalu

1931. 50th Anniv of North Borneo Company.

No.	Type	Description		
295	73	3c. black and green	1·25	80
296	–	6c. black and orange	16·00	3·25
297	–	10c. black and red	4·25	13·00
298	76	12c. black and blue	4·75	8·00
299	–	25c. black and violet	38·00	35·00
300	–	$1 black and green	27·00	£100
301	–	$2 black and brown	48·00	£110
302	–	$5 black and purple	£150	£400

DESIGNS—VERT: 6c. Orang-utan; 10c. Dyak warrior; $1, $2, $5 Arms. HORIZ: 25c. Clouded leopard.

81 Buffalo Transport

82 Palm Cockatoo

1939.

No.	Type	Description		
303	81	1c. green and brown	2·75	1·50
304	82	2c. purple and blue	5·00	1·50
305	–	3c. blue and green	3·50	2·00
306	–	4c. green and violet	6·00	50
307	–	6c. blue and red	5·50	7·00
308	–	8c. red	9·00	1·50
309	–	10c. violet and green	38·00	6·00
310	–	12c. green and blue	26·00	5·50
311	–	15c. green and brown	22·00	7·50
312	–	20c. violet and blue	12·00	3·75
313	–	25c. green and brown	18·00	10·00
314	–	50c. brown and violet	20·00	8·00
315	–	$1 brown and red	75·00	19·00
316	–	$2 violet and olive	£110	95·00
317	–	$5 blue	£300	£200

DESIGNS—VERT: 3c. Native; 4c. Proboscis monkey; 6c. Mounted Bajaus; 10c. Orang-utan; 15c. Dyak; $1, $2 Arms. HORIZ: 8c. Map of Eastern Archipelago; 12c. Murut with blow-pipe; 20c. River scene; 25c. Native boat; 50c. Mt. Kinabalu; $5 Arms with supporters.

1941. Optd **WAR TAX**.

No.	Type	Description		
318	81	1c. green and brown	1·50	3·25
319	82	2c. purple and blue	6·00	3·75

1945. British Military Administration. Stamps of 1939 optd **BMA**.

No.	Type	Description		
320	81	1c. green and brown	6·00	2·00
321	82	2c. purple and blue	14·00	2·00
322	–	3c. blue and green	1·25	1·25
323	–	4c. green and violet	16·00	16·00
324	–	6c. blue and red	1·25	1·00
325	–	8c. red	3·00	75
326	–	10c. violet and green	3·00	40
327	–	12c. green and blue	6·00	2·75
328	–	15c. green and brown	1·50	1·00
329	–	20c. violet and blue	4·25	1·25
330	–	25c. green and brown	6·50	1·50
331	–	50c. brown and violet	3·00	1·75
332	–	$1 brown and red	48·00	38·00
333	–	$2 violet and olive	45·00	32·00
334	–	$5 blue	19·00	14·00

1947. Stamps of 1939 optd with Crown over GR monogram and bars obliterating "THE STATE OF" and "BRITISH PROTECTORATE".

No.	Type	Description		
335	81	1c. green and brown	15	1·00
336	82	2c. purple and blue	1·75	90
337	–	3c. blue and green	15	90
338	–	4c. green and violet	70	90

339	–	6c. blue and red	25	20
340	–	8c. red	30	20
341	–	10c. violet and green	1·50	40
342	–	12c. green and blue	2·00	2·75
343	–	15c. green and brown	2·25	30
344	–	20c. violet and blue	2·25	85
345	–	25c. green and brown	2·50	50
346	–	50c. brown and violet	2·25	85
347	–	$1 brown and red	4·75	1·75
348	–	$2 violet and olive	12·00	17·00
349	–	$5 blue	21·00	17·00

1948. Silver Wedding. As T **4b/c** of Pitcairn Islands.

350	8c. red	30	80
351	$10 mauve	22·00	35·00

1949. U.P.U. As T **4d/g** of Pitcairn Islands.

352	8c. red	50	30
353	10c. brown	3·00	1·00
354	30c. brown	1·00	1·75
355	55c. blue	1·00	2·50

100 Mt. Kinabalu

102 Coconut Grove

1950.

356	**100**	1c. brown	15	1·00
357	–	2c. blue	15	50
358	**102**	3c. green	15	15
359	–	4c. purple	15	10
360	–	5c. violet	15	10
361	–	8c. red	75	85
362	–	10c. purple	1·25	15
363	–	15c. blue	2·00	65
364	–	20c. brown	1·25	10
365	–	30c. buff	3·50	20
366	–	50c. red ("JESSLETON")	85	3·00
366a	–	50c. red ("JESSELTON")	6·50	2·00
367	–	$1 orange	3·75	1·00
368	–	$2 green	4·75	13·00
369	–	$5 green	15·00	20·00
370	–	$10 blue	40·00	50·00

DESIGNS—VERT: 4c. Hemp drying; 5c. Cattle at Kota Belud; 30c. Suluk river canoe; 50c. Clock tower, Jesselton; $1 Bajau horsemen. HORIZ: 2c. Musician; 8c. Map; 10c. Log pond; 15c. Malay prau, Sandakan; 20c. Bajau chief; $2 Murut with blowpipe; $5 Net fishing; $10, King George VI and arms.

1953. Coronation. As T **4h** of Pitcairn Islands.

371	10c. black and red	1·25	60

1954. As 1950 but with portrait of Queen Elizabeth II.

372		1c. brown	10	30
373		2c. blue	60	15
374		3c. green	1·00	2·00
375		4c. purple	75	20
376		5c. violet	75	10
377		8c. red	60	30
378		10c. purple	30	10
379		15c. blue	1·00	10
380		20c. brown	30	15
381		30c. buff	2·00	20
382		50c. red (No. 366a)	5·00	20
383		$1 orange	6·50	20
384		$2 green	12·00	1·25
385		$5 green	10·00	25·00
386		$10 blue	24·00	35·00

117 Malay Prau

1956. 75th Anniv of Foundation of British North Borneo Co. Inscr "CHARTER 1ST NOVEMBER 1881".

387	–	10c. black and red	1·00	40
388	**117**	15c. black and brown	30	30
389	–	35c. black and green	30	1·50
390	–	$1 black and slate	65	2·50

DESIGNS—HORIZ: 10c. Borneo Railway, 1902; 35c. Mt. Kinabalu. VERT: $1 Arms of Chartered Company.

120 Sambar Stag

1961.

391	**120**	1c. green and red	20	10
392	–	4c. olive and orange	20	90
393	–	5c. sepia and violet	30	10
394	–	6c. black and turquoise	50	40
395	–	10c. green and red	50	10
396	–	12c. brown and myrtle	30	10
397	–	20c. turquoise and blue	3·50	10
398	–	25c. black and red	80	90
399	–	30c. sepia and olive	70	20
400	–	35c. slate and brown	1·75	90
401	–	50c. green and bistre	1·75	20
402	–	75c. blue and purple	8·00	90
403	–	$1 brown and green	13·00	80
404	–	$2 brown and slate	30·00	3·00
405	–	$5 green and purple	38·00	17·00
406	–	$10 red and blue	27·00	30·00

DESIGNS—HORIZ: 4c. Sun bear; 5c. Clouded leopard; 6c. Dusun woman with gong; 10c. Map of Borneo; 12c. Banteng; 20c. Butterfly orchid; 25c. Sumatran rhinoceros; 30c. Murut with blow-pipe; 35c. Mt. Kinabalu; 50c. Dusun and buffalo transport; 75c. Bajau horseman. VERT: $1 Orang-utan; $2 Rhinoceros hornbill; $5 Crested wood partridge; $10 Arms of N. Borneo.

1963. Freedom from Hunger. As T **20a** of Pitcairn Islands.

407	12c. blue	1·50	75

POSTAGE DUE STAMPS

Overprinted **POSTAGE DUE**.

1895. Issue of 1894.

D 2	**25**	2c. black and red	15·00	23·00	2·00
D 3	**26**	3c. green & mve	5·50	16·00	1·00
D 5	**27**	5c. black and red	55·00	25·00	3·00
D 6a	**28**	6c. black & brn	13·00	45·00	2·50
D 7	**29**	8c. black and lilac	45·00	48·00	2·75
D 8b	**30**	12c. black & blue	70·00	50·00	2·50
D10	**31**	18c. black & grn	70·00	60·00	4·00
D11b	**32**	24c. blue and red	26·00	55·00	4·00

1897. Issue of 1897.

D12	**25**	2c. black and red	8·50	9·00	1·50
D13		2c. black & green	45·00	†	70
D14	**26**	3c. green & mve	17·00	†	50
D16a		4c. black and red	38·00	†	50
D17a	**27**	5c. black & orge	20·00	42·00	1·75
D18	**28**	6c. black & brn	5·00	29·00	70
D20	**29**	8c. black & lilac	6·00	†	50
D21a	**30**	12c. black & blue	90·00	†	4·00
D22	**31**	18c. black and green (No. 108)	†	†	£600
D23		18c. black and green (No. 110b)	48·00	†	4·00
D24	**32**	24c. blue and red (No. 109)	–	†	£300
D25		24c. blue and red (No. 111b)	22·00	†	2·25

1902. Issue of 1901.

D37	1c. black and bistre	–	†	28·00
D38	2c. black and green	12·00	3·75	30
D39	3c. green and mauve	4·75	3·25	30
D40	4c. black and red	10·00	6·50	30
D41	5c. black and orange	22·00	4·50	30
D42	6c. black and brown	15·00	11·00	40
D43	8c. black and lilac	20·00	4·25	40
D45	10c. brown and grey	75·00	17·00	1·40
D46	12c. black and blue	23·00	14·00	1·75
D47	16c. green & brown	40·00	19·00	1·75
D48	18c. black and green	9·00	19·00	1·50
D49	24c. blue and red	11·00	23·00	1·75

1919. Issue of 1909.

D52	2c. black and green	11·00	75·00
D66	2c. black and red	50	1·75
D67	3c. black and green	6·50	24·00
D55	4c. black and red	1·00	1·25
D57	5c. black and brown	8·50	20·00
D70	6c. black and olive	4·75	2·75
D62	8c. black and red	1·50	1·50
D63	10c. black and blue	13·00	19·00
D64	12c. black and blue	50·00	45·00
D65a	16c. black and brown	18·00	50·00

POSTAGE DUE

D 2 Crest of the Company

1939.

D85	**D 2**	2c. brown	6·50	70·00
D86		4c. red	6·50	95·00
D87		6c. violet	22·00	£120
D88		8c. green	23·00	£200
D89		10c. blue	48·00	£350

For later issues see **SABAH**.

JAPANESE OCCUPATION

1942. Stamps of North Borneo optd as T **1** of Japanese Occupation of Brunei. (a) Issue of 1939.

J 1	**81**	1c. green and brown	£150	£225
J 2	**82**	2c. purple and blue	£160	£225
J 3	–	3c. blue and green	£130	£225
J 4a	–	4c. green and violet	50·00	£120
J 5	–	6c. blue and red	£130	£250
J 6	–	8c. red	£160	£190
J 7	–	10c. violet and green	£150	£250
J 8	–	12c. green and blue	£170	£400
J 9	–	15c. green and brown	£160	£400
J10	–	20c. violet and blue	£190	£450
J11	–	25c. green and brown	£190	£450
J12	–	50c. brown and violet	£275	£500
J13	–	$1 brown and red	£275	£650
J14	–	$2 violet and olive	£425	£850
J15	–	$5 blue	£500	£900

(b) War Tax Issue of 1941.

J16	**81**	1c. green and brown	£475	£275
J17	**82**	2c. purple and blue	£1100	£425

2 Mt. Kinabalu

3 Borneo Scene

1943.

J18	**2**	4c. red	16·00	38·00
J19	**3**	8c. blue	14·00	38·00

大日本
帝國郵便
北ボルネオ

(**4**) ("Imperial Japanese Postal Service, North Borneo")

大日本
帝國郵便
貳弗

(**5**) ("Imperial Japanese Postal Service, North Borneo")

1944. Optd with T **4**. (a) On stamps of North Borneo.

J20	**81**	1c. green and brown	5·00	12·00
J21	**82**	2c. purple and blue	7·50	9·00
J22	–	3c. blue and green	4·50	9·00
J23	–	4c. green and violet	7·00	14·00
J24	–	6c. blue and red	5·00	6·50
J25	–	8c. red	7·00	17·00
J26	–	10c. violet and green	8·50	13·00
J27	–	12c. green and blue	9·00	13·00
J28	–	15c. green and brown	9·00	16·00
J29	–	20c. violet and blue	21·00	45·00
J30	–	25c. green and brown	21·00	45·00
J31	–	50c. brown and violet	65·00	£120
J32	–	$1 brown and red	90·00	£150

(b) On stamps of Japanese Occupation of North Borneo.

J21a	2c. purple and blue (J2)	£425	
J22a	3c. blue and green (J3)	£425	
J25a	8c. red (J6)	£425	
J26b	10c. violet and green (J7)	£190	£375
J27a	12c. green and blue (J8)	£425	
J28a	15c. green and brown (J9)	£425	

1944. No. J1 surch with T **5**.

J33	**81**	$2 on 1c. green and brown	£4500	£3750

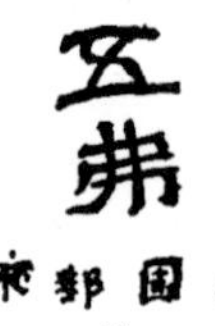

(**6**)

1944. No. 315 of North Borneo surch with T **6**.

J34		$5 on $1 brown and red	£4000	£2750

1944. Stamps of Japan optd as bottom line in T **4**.

J35	**126**	1s. brown	8·00	19·00
J36	**84**	2s. red	7·00	16·00
J37	–	3s. green (No. 319)	6·50	19·00
J38	**129**	4s. green	9·00	17·00
J39	–	5s. red (No. 396)	9·00	20·00
J40	–	6s. orange (No. 322)	9·50	21·00
J41	–	8s. violet (No. 324)	6·50	21·00
J42	–	10s. red (No. 399)	7·00	21·00
J43	–	15s. blue (No. 401)	9·00	21·00
J44	–	20s. blue (No. 328)	90·00	90·00
J45	–	25s. brown (No. 329)	55·00	70·00
J46	–	30s. blue (No. 330)	£160	95·00
J47	–	50s. olive and brown (No. 331)	60·00	65·00
J48	–	1y. brown (No. 332)	60·00	90·00

NORTH GERMAN CONFEDERATION Pt. 7

The North German Confederation was set up on 1 January 1868, and comprised the postal services of Bremen, Brunswick, Hamburg Lubeck, Mecklenburg (both), Oldenburg, Prussia (including Hanover, Schleswig-Holstein with Bergedorf and Thurn and Taxis) and Saxony.

The North German Confederation joined the German Reichspost on 4 May 1871, and the stamps of Germany were brought into use on 1 January 1872.

Northern District: 30 groschen = 1 thaler.
Southern District: 60 kreuzer = 1 gulden.

1

3

1868. Roul or perf. (a) Northern District.

19	**1**	¼g. mauve	17·00	11·00
22		⅓g. green	4·75	1·20
23		½g. orange	4·75	1·20
25		1g. red	4·25	40
27		2g. blue	7·50	85
29		5g. bistre	8·75	7·00

(b) Southern District.

30	–	1k. green	13·00	8·25
13	–	2k. orange	55·00	32·00
33	–	3k. red	7·50	1·70
36	–	7k. blue	11·00	7·50
18	–	18k. bistre	37·00	50·00

The 1k. to 18k. have the figures in an oval.

1869. Perf.

38	**3**	10g. grey	£325	65·00
39	–	30g. blue	£250	£130

The frame of the 30g. is rectangular.

OFFICIAL STAMPS

O 5

1870. (a) Northern District.

O40	**O 5**	¼g. black and brown	24·00	48·00
O41		⅓g. black and brown	11·00	22·00
O42		½g. black and brown	2·75	3·50
O43		1g. black and brown	2·75	55
O44		2g. black and brown	7·50	4·75

(b) Southern District.

O45	1k. black and grey	29·00	£275
O46	2k. black and grey	70·00	£900
O47	3k. black and grey	26·00	48·00
O48	7k. black and grey	39·00	£275

NORTH INGERMANLAND Pt. 10

Stamps issued during temporary independence of this Russian territory, which adjoins Finland.

100 pennia = 1 mark.

1 18th-century Arms of Ingermanland

4 Gathering Crops

1920.

1	**1**	5p. green	2·25	4·25
2		10p. red	2·25	4·25
3		25p. brown	2·25	4·25
4		50p. blue	2·25	4·25
5		1m. black and red	26·00	45·00
6		5m. black and purple	£100	£160
7		10m. black and brown	£180	£250

1920. Inscr as in T **2**.

8	–	10p. blue and green	3·00	7·50
9	–	30p. green and brown	3·00	7·50
10	–	50p. brown and blue	3·00	7·50
11	–	80p. grey and red	3·00	7·50
12	**4**	1m. grey and red	14·00	40·00
13	–	5m. red and violet	8·00	19·00
14	–	10m. violet and brown	7·75	19·00

DESIGNS—VERT: 10p. Arms; 30p. Reaper; 50p. Ploughing; 80p. Milking. HORIZ: 5m. Burning church; 10m. Zither players.

NORTH WEST RUSSIA Pt. 10

Issues made for use by the various Anti-bolshevist Armies during the Russian Civil War, 1918–20.

100 kopeks = 1 rouble.

NORTHERN ARMY

1 "OKCA" = Osobiy Korpus Severnoy Armiy—(trans "Special Corps, Northern Army")

1919. As T **1** inscr "OKCA".

1	**1**	5k. purple	10	40
2		10k. blue	10	40
3		15k. yellow	10	40
4		20k. red	10	40
5		50k. green	10	40

NORTH-WESTERN ARMY

Сѣв. Зап.
Армія

(**2**)

1919. Arms types of Russia optd as T **2**. Imperf or perf.

6 **22** 2k. green . . . . 3·00 7·50
16 3k. red . . . . 3·00 7·50
7 5k. lilac . . . . 3·00 7·50
8 **23** 10k. blue . . . . 4·50 10·00
9 **10** 15k. blue and brown . . . . 4·00 7·50
10 **14** 20k. red and blue . . . . 5·00 8·50
11 **10** 20k. on 14k. red and blue £250
12 25k. violet and green . . . 8·00 12·00
13 **14** 50k. green and purple . . . 8·00 12·00
14 **15** 1r. orange & brown on brn 16·00 24·00
17 **11** 3r.50 green and red . . . . 32·00 45·00
18 **22** 5r. blue on green . . . . 24·00 32·00
19 **11** 7r. pink and green . . . . 90·00 £160
15 **20** 10r. grey and red on yellow 60·00 85·00

1919. No. 7 surch.

20 **22** 10k. on 5k. lilac . . . . . 4·00 7·50

WESTERN ARMY

1919. Stamps of Latvia optd with Cross of Lorraine in circle with plain background. Imperf. (a) Postage stamps.

21 **1** 3k. lilac . . . . 30·00 40·00
22 5k. red . . . . 30·00 40·00
23 10k. blue £110 £190
24 20k. orange . . . . 30·00 40·00
25 25k. grey . . . . 30·00 40·00
26 35k. brown . . . . 30·00 40·00
27 50k. violet . . . . 30·00 40·00
28 75k. green . . . . 30·00 55·00

(b) Liberation of Riga issue.

29 **4** 5k. red . . . . 25·00 45·00
30 15k. green . . . . 15·00 35·00
31 35k. brown . . . . 15·00 35·00

1919. Stamps of Latvia optd with Cross of Lorraine in circle with burele background and characters **3. A** (= "Z. A."). Imperf. (a) Postage stamps.

32 **1** 3k. lilac . . . . 4·00 8·00
33 5k. red . . . . 4·00 8·00
34 10k. blue . . . . 90·00 £170
35 20k. orange . . . . 8·00 16·00
36 25k. grey . . . . 22·00 45·00
37 35k. brown . . . . 14·00 24·00
38 50k. violet . . . . 14·00 24·00
39 75k. green . . . . 14·00 24·00

(b) Liberation of Riga issue.

40 **4** 5k. red . . . . 2·75 6·50
41 15k. green . . . . 2·75 6·50
42 35k. brown . . . . 2·75 6·50

1919. Arms type of Russia surch with Cross of Lorraine in ornamental frame and **LP** with value in curved frame. Imperf or perf.

43 **22** 10k. on 2k. green . . . . . 4·50 6·00
54 20k. on 3k. red . . . . . . 4·00 7·50
44 **23** 30k. on 4k. red . . . . . . 4·50 7·00
45 **22** 40k. on 5k. lilac . . . . . 4·50 7·00
46 **23** 50k. on 10k. blue . . . . . 4·50 6·00
47 **10** 70k. on 15k. blue and brown . . . . 4·50 6·00
48 **14** 90k. on 20k. red and blue 6·00 8·00
49 **10** 1r. on 25k. violet and green 4·50 6·00
50 1r.50 on 35k. green & brown . . . . 35·00 55·00
51 **14** 2r. on 50k. green and purple 6·00 10·00
52 **10** 4r. on 70k. red and brown 16·00 24·00
53 **15** 6r. on 1r. orange, brown on brown . . . . 16·00 25·00
56 **11** 10r. on 3r.50 green & pur 40·00 48·00

NORTHERN NIGERIA Pt. 1

A British protectorate on the west coast of Africa. In 1914 incorporated into Nigeria.

12 pence = 1 shilling;
20 shillings = 1 pound.

1 5

1900.

1 **1** ½d. mauve and green . . . . 2·75 12·00
2 1d. mauve and red . . . . 3·50 3·75
3 2d. mauve and yellow . . . . 12·00 40·00
4 2½d. mauve and blue . . . . 9·00 38·00
5 5d. mauve and brown . . . . 21·00 42·00
6 6d. mauve and violet . . . . 18·00 28·00
7 1s. green and black . . . . 24·00 65·00
8 2s.6d. green and blue . . . . 95·00 £400
9 10s. green and brown £225 £550

1902. As T **1**, but portrait of King Edward VII.

10 ½d. purple and green . . . . 2·00 1·00
11 1d. purple and red . . . . 2·25 75
12 2d. purple and yellow . . . . 2·00 3·00
13 2½d. purple and blue . . . . 1·50 8·50
14 5d. purple and brown . . . . 2·50 5·00
15 6d. purple and violet . . . . 6·50 4·50
16 1s. green and black . . . . 3·50 6·00
17 2s.6d. green and blue . . . . 8·00 42·00
18 10s. green and brown . . . . 48·00 55·00

1910. As last. New colours etc.

28 ½d. green . . . . 2·00 1·25
29 1d. red . . . . 2·00 1·25
30 2d. grey . . . . 4·25 2·25
31 2½d. blue . . . . 2·25 7·00
32 3d. purple on yellow . . . . 3·50 75
34 5d. purple and green . . . . 4·00 11·00
35a 6d. purple . . . . 5·00 6·00
36 1s. black and green . . . . . 2·25 75
37 2s.6d. black and red on blue 10·00 28·00
38 5s. green and red on yellow 23·00 75·00
39 10s. green and red on green 42·00 48·00

1912.

40 **5** ½d. green . . . . 1·50 60
41 1d. red . . . . 1·50 60
42 2d. grey . . . . 3·00 7·00
43 3d. purple on yellow . . . . 2·25 1·25
44 4d. black and red on yellow 1·25 2·25
45 5d. purple and olive . . . . 4·00 9·00
46 6d. purple and violet . . . . 4·00 4·25
47 9d. purple and red . . . . . 2·00 12·00
48 1s. black on green . . . . . 4·50 2·25
49 2s.6d. black and red on blue 7·00 38·00
50 5s. green and red on yellow 20·00 80·00
51 10s. green and red on green 38·00 48·00
52 £1 purple and black on red £170 £110

NORTHERN RHODESIA Pt. 1

A British territory in central Africa, north of the Zambesi. From 1954 to 1963 part of the central African Federation and using the stamps of Rhodesia and Nyasaland (q.v.). A new constitution was introduced on 3 January 1964, with internal self-government and independence came on 24 October 1964 when the country was renamed Zambia (q.v.).

12 pence = 1 shilling;
20 shillings = 1 pound.

1

1925. The shilling values are larger and the view is in first colour.

1 **1** ½d. green . . . . 1·75 80
2 1d. brown . . . . 1·75 10
3 1½d. red . . . . 1·75 30
4 2d. orange . . . . 2·00 10
5 3d. blue . . . . 2·00 1·25
6 4d. violet . . . . 4·00 50
7 6d. grey . . . . 4·25 40
8 8d. purple . . . . 3·75 42·00
9 10d. olive . . . . 4·25 38·00
10 1s. orange and black . . . . 3·75 1·75
11 2s. brown and blue . . . . 14·00 22·00
12 2s.6d. black and green . . . 15·00 7·50
13 3s. violet and blue . . . . 23·00 19·00
14 5s. grey and violet . . . . 30·00 17·00
15 7s.6d. purple and black . . . £100 £150
16 10s. green and black . . . . 70·00 70·00
17 20s. red and purple £150 £170

1935. Silver Jubilee. As T **10a** of Gambia.

18 1d. blue and olive . . . . . 80 1·50
19 2d. green and blue . . . . . 80 1·50
20 3d. brown and blue . . . . . 2·50 5·50
21 6d. grey and purple . . . . . 3·75 1·50

1937. Coronation. As T **10b** of Gambia.

22 1½d. red 30 35
23 2d. brown 40 35
24 3d. blue . . . . 60 1·25

1938. As 1925, but with portrait of King George VI facing right and "POSTAGE & REVENUE" omitted.

25 ½d. green 10 10
26 ½d. brown . . . . 50 1·00
27 1d. brown 10 10
28 1d. green . . . . 60 1·25
29 1½d. red . . . . 45·00 60
30 1½d. orange 30 10
31 2d. brown . . . . 45·00 1·50
32 2d. red 30 30
33 2d. purple . . . . 45 1·25
34 3d. blue 30 10
35 3d. red . . . . 50 2·50
36 4d. violet 30 40
37 4½d. blue . . . . 40 5·50
38 6d. grey 30 10
39 9d. violet . . . . 40 3·75
40 1s. orange and black . . . . 3·00 50
41 2s.6d. black and green . . . 7·00 3·00
42 3s. violet and blue . . . . 13·00 7·00
43 5s. grey and violet . . . . 12·00 7·50
44 10s. green and black . . . . 14·00 12·00
45 20s. red and purple . . . . 38·00 48·00

1946. Victory. As T **4a** of Pitcairn Islands.

46 1½d. orange 10 20
47 2d. red 10 50

1948. Silver Wedding. As T **4b/c** of Pitcairn Islands.

48 1½d. orange 30 10
49 20s. red . . . . 42·00 45·00

1949. U.P.U. As T **4d/g** of Pitcairn Islands.

50 2d. red 20 30
51 3d. blue . . . . 1·50 1·50
52 6d. grey . . . . 55 1·50
53 1s. orange . . . . 55 1·00

5 Cecil Rhodes and Victoria Falls

1953. Birth Centenary of Cecil Rhodes.

54 **5** ½d. brown 50 75
55 1d. green 40 75
56 2d. mauve 40 20
57 4½d. blue . . . . 40 3·25
58 1s. orange and black . . . . 75 4·50

6 Arms of the Rhodesias and Nyasaland

9 Arms

1953. Rhodes Centenary Exhibition.

59 **6** 6d. violet . . . . 60 1·00

1953. Coronation. As T **4h** of Pitcairn Islands.

60 1½d. black and orange 60 20

1953. As 1938 but with portrait of Queen Elizabeth II facing left.

61 ½d. brown 65 10
62 1d. green 65 10
63 1½d. orange . . . . 1·00 10
64 2d. purple . . . . 1·00 10
65 3d. red 70 10
66 4d. violet . . . . 1·25 1·75
67 4½d. blue . . . . 1·25 4·25
68 6d. grey . . . . 1·25 10
69 9d. violet . . . . 80 4·25
70 1s. orange and black 70 10
71 2s.6d. black and green . . . 7·00 3·50
72 5s. grey and purple . . . . . 7·00 12·00
73 10s. green and black . . . . 7·00 24·00
74 20s. red and purple . . . . . 21·00 27·00

1963. Arms black, gold and blue; portrait and inscriptions black; background colours given.

75 **9** ½d. violet . . . . 40 1·00
76 1d. blue 70 10
77 2d. brown 30 10
78 3d. yellow 20 10
79 4d. green 30 30
80 6d. green 30 10
81 9d. bistre . . . . 30 1·40
82 1s. purple 30 10
83 1s.3d. purple . . . . 1·75 10
84 2s. orange . . . . 1·75 3·00
85 2s.6d. purple . . . . 1·75 1·50
86 5s. mauve . . . . 6·50 6·50
87 10s. mauve . . . . 7·50 15·00
88 20s. blue . . . . 8·00 17·00

Nos. 84/88 are larger (27 × 23 mm).

POSTAGE DUE STAMPS

D 1 D 2

1929.

D1 **D 1** 1d. black . . . . 2·50 2·50
D2 2d. black . . . . 3·00 3·00
D3 3d. black . . . . 3·00 26·00
D4 4d. black . . . . 9·50 30·00

1963.

D 5 **D 2** 1d. orange . . . . 90 4·25
D 6 2d. blue . . . . 90 4·00
D 7 3d. lake . . . . 1·00 4·75
D 8 4d. blue . . . . 1·00 7·50
D 9 6d. purple . . . . 5·50 8·50
D10 1s. green . . . . 6·50 21·00

For later issues see **ZAMBIA**.

NORWAY Pt. 11

In 1814 Denmark ceded Norway to Sweden, from 1814 to 1905 the King of Sweden was also King of Norway after which Norway was an independent Kingdom.

1855. 120 skilling = 1 speciedaler.
1877. 100 ore = 1 krone.

1

3 King Oscar I

1855. Imperf.

1 **1** 4s. blue . . . . £4000 75·00

1856. Perf.

4 **3** 2s. yellow . . . . £500 75·00
6 3s. lilac . . . . £250 42·00
7 4s. blue . . . . £225 6·50
11 8s. red . . . . £950 18·00

4 5

1863.

12 **4** 2s. yellow £550 £100
13 3s. lilac £425 £250
16 4s. blue . . . . £150 5·25
17 8s. pink . . . . £600 28·00
18 24s. brown . . . . 55·00 70·00

1867.

21 **5** 1s. black . . . . 60·00 29·00
23 2s. buff . . . . 26·00 26·00
26 3s. lilac . . . . £250 55·00
27 4s. blue . . . . 60·00 4·75
29 8s. red . . . . £300 21·00

6

10 With background shading

A

1872. Value in "Skilling".

33 **6** 1s. green . . . . 11·00 18·00
36 2s. blue . . . . 12·00 34·00
39 3s. red . . . . 55·00 5·75
42 4s. mauve . . . . 21·00 31·00
44 6s. brown . . . . £300 29·00
45 7s. brown . . . . 32·00 33·00

1877. Letters without serifs as Type A. Value in "ore".

47 **10** 1ore brown . . . . 4·75 3·75
83 2ore brown . . . . 4·75 4·25
84c 3ore orange . . . . 36·00 2·10
52 5ore blue . . . . 19·00 7·25
85d 5ore green . . . . 21·00 80
86a 10ore red . . . . 43·00 75
55 12ore green . . . . 75·00 10·50
75b 12ore brown . . . . 13·00 8·00
76 20ore brown . . . . 85·00 12·00
87 20ore blue . . . . 45·00 1·40
88 25ore mauve . . . . 43·00 6·75
61 35ore green . . . . 19·00 6·25
62 50ore purple . . . . 35·00 5·75
63 60ore blue . . . . 30·00 9·25

9 King Oscar II

1878.

68 **9** 1k. green and light green . . 32·00 5·50
69 1k.50 blue and ultramarine 65·00 24·00
70 2k. brown and pink . . . . 46·00 15·00

1888. Surch **2 ore**.

89a **6** 2ore on 12ore brown . . . 2·00 2·20

D

1893. Letters with serifs as Type D.

133 **10** 1ore drab 70 40
134 2ore brown 45 30
135 3ore orange 60 30
136 5ore green . . . . 6·75 20
529 5ore purple 20 15
138 7ore green 85 25
139 10ore red . . . . 6·50 15
140 10ore green . . . . 10·50 40
529a 10ore grey 20 15
141 12ore violet 80 90
530 15ore brown 35 20
143 15ore blue 60 30
144 20ore blue . . . . 9·50 20
530a 20ore green 20 15
146 25ore mauve . . . . 60·00 25
147 25ore red . . . . 9·50 50
531 25ore blue 15 15
148 30ore grey . . . . 16·00 35
149 30ore blue . . . . 7·50 3·00
119 35ore green . . . . 15·00 4·50
150 35ore brown . . . . 22·00 30
151 40ore green . . . . 11·00 35

152 40ore blue . . . . 32·00 30
531b 50ore purple 10 10
154 60ore blue . . . . 38·00 55
531c 60ore orange 10 10
531d 70ore orange 20 20
531e 80ore brown 20 15
531f 90ore brown 25 25
See also Nos. 279 etc and 1100/3.

1905. Surch.
122 **5** 1k. on 2s. buff . . . . . . 55·00 27·00
123 1k.50 on 2s. buff . . . . . 80·00 55·00
124 2k. on 2s. buff . . . . . . 95·00 47·00

1906. Surch.
162 **10** 5ore on 25ore mauve . . . 70 50
125 **6** 15ore on 4s. mauve . . . . 5·50 3·25
126 30ore on 7s. brown . . . . 12·00 6·00

15 King Haakon VII

16 King Haakon VII

1907.
127 **15** 1k. green . . . . 48·00 25·00
128 1¼k. blue . . . . 70·00 65·00
129 2k. red . . . . 95·00 90·00

1910.
155a **16** 1k. green 70 15
156 1¼k. blue . . . . 2·30 40
157 2k. red . . . . 3·00 55
158 5k. violet . . . . 4·75 3·50

17 Constitutional Assembly (after O. Wergeland)

19

1914. Centenary of Independence.
159 **17** 5ore green . . . . 1·90 40
160 10ore red . . . . 4·25 55
161 20ore blue . . . . 11·00 5·00

1922.
163 **19** 10ore green . . . . 15·00 45
164 20ore purple . . . . 24·00 20
165 25ore red . . . . 30·00 60
166 45ore blue . . . . 2·75 70

20 **21** **22**

1925. Air. Amundsen's Polar Flight.
167 **20** 2ore brown . . . . 2·00 1·80
168 3ore orange . . . . 3·75 3·00
169 5ore mauve . . . . 7·00 5·75
170 10ore green . . . . 9·50 10·50
171 15ore blue . . . . 9·50 11·50
172 20ore mauve . . . . . . 12·50 16·00
173 25ore red . . . . 3·50 3·50

1925. Annexation of Spitzbergen.
183 **21** 10ore green . . . . 6·25 6·75
184 15ore blue . . . . 6·25 3·75
185 20ore purple . . . . 6·25 1·10
186 45ore blue . . . . 7·25 4·75

1926. Size 16 × 19½ mm.
187 **22** 10ore green 85 15
187a 14ore orange . . . . . . 1·00 1·70
188 15ore brown . . . . . . 1·00 20
189 20ore purple . . . . . . 38·00 14·50
189a 20ore red . . . . 1·30 15
190 25ore red . . . . 14·00 1·60
190a 25ore brown . . . . . . 1·70 20
190b 30ore blue . . . . 1·90 25
191 35ore brown . . . . . . 85·00 20
191a 35ore violet . . . . . . 3·25 15
192 40ore blue . . . . 7·25 95
193 40ore grey . . . . 2·50 15
194 50ore pink . . . . 2·75 20
195 60ore blue . . . . 3·00 20
For stamps as Type **22** but size 17 × 21 mm, see Nos. 284, etc.

1927. Surcharged with new value and bar.
196 **22** 20ore on 25ore red . . . . 4·75 1·00
197 **19** 30ore on 45ore blue . . . 13·50 1·10
198 **21** 30ore on 45ore blue . . . 5·50 3·25

24 Akershus Castle

25 Ibsen

28 Abel

1927. Air.
199a **24** 45ore blue (with frame-lines) . . . . 7·25 1·80
323 45ore blue (without frame-lines) . . . . . 1·20 30

1928. Ibsen Centenary.
200 **25** 10ore green . . . . 7·75 1·40
201 15ore brown . . . . 3·25 1·80
202 20ore red . . . . 3·75 40
203 30ore blue . . . . 4·25 2·10

1929. Postage Due stamps optd **Post Frimerke** (204/6 and 211) or **POST** and thick bar (others).
204 D **12** 1ore brown 40 60
205 4ore mauve (No. D96a) 40 35
206 10ore green . . . . . . 1·80 1·90
207 15ore brown . . . . . 3·25 2·75
208 20ore purple . . . . . 1·40 45
209 40ore blue . . . . . . 3·75 60
210 50ore purple . . . . . 7·75 6·50
211 100ore yellow . . . . . 3·00 1·90
212 200ore violet . . . . . 4·50 2·50

1929. Death Cent of N. H. Abel (mathematician).
213 **28** 10ore green . . . . 4·25 60
214 15ore brown . . . . 3·25 1·20
215 20ore red . . . . 1·10 25
216 30ore blue . . . . 2·25 1·30

1929. Surch **14 ORE 14**.
217 **5** 14ore on 2s. buff . . . . . 1·70 3·00

30 St. Olaf (sculpture, Brunlanes Church)

31 Nidaros Trondhjem Cathedral

32 Death of St. Olaf (after P. N. Arbo)

1930. 9th Death Centenary of St. Olaf.
219 **30** 10ore green . . . . 8·50 30
220 **31** 15ore sepia and brown . . 1·10 45
221 **30** 20ore red . . . . 1·40 35
222 **32** 30ore blue . . . . 6·75 1·80

33 North Cape and "Bergensfjord" (liner)

1930. Norwegian Tourist Association Fund. Size 35½ × 21½ mm.
223 **33** 15ore+25ore brown . . . . 1·70 2·30
224 20ore+25ore red . . . . . 21·00 22·00
225 30ore+25ore blue . . . . 55·00 50·00
For smaller stamps in this design see Nos. 349/51, 442/66 and 464/6.

34 Radium Hospital

1931. Radium Hospital Fund.
226 **34** 20ore+10ore red . . . . . 9·50 3·75

35 Bjornson

36 L. Holberg

1932. Birth Cent of Bjornstjerne Bjornson (writer).
227 **35** 10ore green . . . . 9·75 45
228 15ore brown 95 90
229 20ore red . . . . 1·80 30
230 30ore blue . . . . 2·75 1·60

1934. 250th Birth Anniv of Holberg (writer).
231 **36** 10ore green . . . . 3·25 25
232 15ore brown 60 50
233 20ore red . . . . 14·50 20
234 30ore blue . . . . 2·75 1·50

37 Dr. Nansen

38 No background shading

38b King Haakon VII

1935. Nansen Refugee Fund.
235 **37** 10ore+10ore green . . . . 2·10 2·00
236 15ore+10ore brown . . . . 7·25 7·25
237 20ore+10ore red . . . . . 1·20 1·00
238 30ore+10ore blue . . . . 7·50 7·00
See also Nos. 275/8.

1937.
279 **38** 1ore green 80 45
280 2ore brown 45 55
281 3ore orange 70 65
282 5ore mauve 40 15
283 7ore green 60 20
413 10ore grey 45 15
285 12ore violet . . . . 75 1·20
414 15ore green . . . . 1·20 40
415 15ore brown 30 15
416 20ore brown . . . . 2·75 1·50
417 20ore green 30 15

1937. As T **22**, but size 17 × 21 mm.
284 **22** 10ore green 45 15
286 14ore orange . . . . . . 1·80 2·40
287 15ore green . . . . . . 1·70 20
288a 20ore red 35 15
289 25ore brown . . . . . . 1·90 20
289a 25ore red 95 15
290 30ore blue . . . . 2·20 20
290a 30ore grey . . . . 6·25 25
291 35ore violet . . . . . . 2·20 20
292 40ore grey . . . . 3·50 20
292a 40ore blue . . . . 3·25 20
293 50ore purple . . . . . . 2·10 30
293a 55ore orange . . . . . . 17·00 20
294 60ore blue . . . . 3·75 20
294a 80ore brown . . . . . . 17·00 15

1937.
255 **38b** 1k. green 10 20
256 1k.50 blue . . . . 70 1·50
257 2k. red . . . . 60 3·75
258 5k. purple . . . . 6·00 22·00

39 Reindeer

41 Joelster in Sunnfjord

1938. Tourist Propaganda.
262 **39** 15ore brown . . . . 1·00 55
263 – 20ore red 90 25
264 **41** 30ore blue . . . . 1·00 75
DESIGN—As T **39** but VERT: 20ore, Stave Church, Borgund.

42 Queen Maud

43 Lion Rampant

44 Dr. Nansen

1939. Queen Maud Children's Fund.
267 **42** 10ore+5ore green . . . . 45 3·75
268 15ore+5ore brown . . . . 45 3·75
269 20ore+5ore red . . . . . 45 3·00
270 30ore+5ore blue . . . . 45 3·75

1940.
271 **43** 1k. green 80 15
272 1¼k. blue . . . . 1·70 30
273 2k. red . . . . 2·50 85
274 5k. purple . . . . 3·75 3·50
See also Nos. 318/21.

1940. National Relief Fund.
275 **44** 10ore+10ore green . . . . 1·50 2·40
276 15ore+10ore brown . . . . 1·50 3·00
277 20ore+10ore red 45 80
278 30ore+10ore blue . . . . 95 1·60

46 Femboring (fishing boat) and Iceberg

47 Colin Archer (founder) and Lifeboat "Colin Archer"

1941. Haalogaland Exhibition and Fishermen's Families Relief Fund.
295 **46** 15ore+10ore blue . . . . 1·10 2·50

1941. 50th Anniv of National Lifeboat Institution.
296 **47** 10ore+10ore green . . . . 80 1·10
297 15ore+10ore brown . . . . 1·10 1·80
298 – 20ore+10ore red . . . . . 1·00 55
299 – 30ore+10ore blue . . . . 2·30 4·25
DESIGN—VERT: 20ore, 30ore, "Osloskoyta" (lifeboat).

48 Soldier and Flags

51 Oslo University

1941. Norwegian Legion Support Fund.
300 **48** 20ore+80ore red . . . . . 29·00 42·00

1941. Stamps of 1937 optd **V** (= Victory).
301B **38** 1ore green . . . . 35 2·50
302B 2ore brown . . . . 35 3·75
303B 3ore orange . . . . 35 3·00
304B 5ore mauve 35 30
305A 7ore green . . . . 75 2·75
306B **22** 10ore green 35 25
307B **38** 12ore violet . . . . 70 12·00
308A **22** 14ore orange . . . . . . 1·30 8·75
309A 15ore green . . . . 60 1·10
310B 20ore red 25 25
311B 25ore brown 50 45
312B 30ore blue . . . . 1·20 1·80
313A 35ore violet . . . . 1·50 85
314B 40ore grey 85 50
315B 50ore purple . . . . . . 1·20 1·90
316A 60ore blue . . . . 1·90 1·40
317B **43** 1k. green . . . . 1·50 45
318B 1¼k. blue . . . . 3·25 10·50
319B 2k. red . . . . 10·50 34·00
320B 5k. purple . . . . 18·00 75·00

1941. As No. 413, but with "V" incorporated in the design.
321 10ore green . . . . 80 8·25

1941. Centenary of Foundation of Oslo University Building.
322 **51** 1k. green . . . . 24·00 32·00

52 Queen Ragnhild's Dream

53 Stiklestad Battlefield

1941. 700th Death Anniv of Snorre Sturlason (historian).
324 **52** 10ore green 25 15
325 – 15ore brown 30 50
326 – 20ore red 25 15
327 – 30ore blue . . . . 1·40 1·80
328 – 50ore violet . . . . 1·00 1·30
329 **53** 60ore blue . . . . 1·00 1·40
DESIGNS (illustrations from "Sagas of Kings")—As T **53**: 15ore Einar Tambarskjelve at Battle of Svolder; 30ore King Olav II sails to his wedding; 50ore Svipdag's men enter Hall of the Seven Kings. As T **52**: 20ore Snorre Sturlason.

55 Vidkun Quisling

1942. (a) Without opt.
330 **55** 20ore+30ore red . . . . . 4·00 13·50

(b) Optd **1-2-1942**.
331 **55** 20ore+30ore red . . . . . 4·00 13·50
See also No. 336.

56 Rikard Nordraak

57 Embarkation of the Viking Fleet

1942. Birth Centenary of Rikard Nordraak (composer).
332 **56** 10ore green . . . . 1·10 1·40
333 **57** 15ore brown . . . . 1·10 1·70
334 **56** 20ore red . . . . 1·10 1·40
335 – 30ore blue . . . . 1·10 1·40
DESIGN—As Type **57**: 30ore Mountains across sea and two lines of the National Anthem.

1942. War Orphans' Relief Fund. As T **55** but inscr "RIKSTINGET 1942".
336 20ore+30ore red . . . . . . 45 3·25

58 J. H. Wessel

59 Reproduction of Types **55** and **1**

1942. Birth Bicentenary of Wessel (poet).
337 **58** 15ore brown 10 20
338 20ore red 10 20

1942. Inaug of European Postal Union, Vienna.
339 **59** 20ore red 15 45
340 30ore blue . . . . 15 1·00

60 "Sleipner" (Destroyer)

61 Edvard Grieg

1943.
341 **60** 5ore purple 20 15
342 – 7ore green 30 30
343 **60** 10ore green 20 10
344 – 15ore green 60 65
345 – 20ore red 20 20
346 – 30ore blue 80 90
347 – 40ore green 65 80
348 – 60ore blue 70 85
DESIGNS: 7ore, 30ore Merchant ships in convoy; 15ore Airman; 20ore "Vi Vil Vinne" (We will win) written on the highway; 40ore Soldiers on skis; 60ore King Haakon VII.

For use on correspondence posted at sea on Norwegian merchant ships and (in certain circumstances) from Norwegian camps in Gt. Britain during the German Occupation of Norway. After liberation all values were put on sale in Norway.

1943. Norwegian Tourist Association Fund. As T **33**, but reduced to 27 × 21 mm.
349 **33** 15ore+25ore brown 65 80
350 20ore+25ore red . . . . . 80 1·50
351 30ore+25ore blue . . . . 1·20 1·50

1943. Birth Centenary of Grieg (composer).
352 **61** 10ore green 20 25
353 20ore red 20 25
354 40ore green 20 25
355 60ore blue 20 25

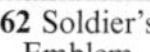
62 Soldier's Emblem

63 Fishing Station

1943. Soldiers' Relief Fund.
356 **62** 20ore+30ore red . . . . . 40 3·00

1943. Winter Relief Fund.
357 **63** 10ore+10ore green . . . . 75 2·20
358 – 20ore+10ore red . . . . . 70 2·50
359 – 40ore+10ore grey . . . . 70 2·50
DESIGNS: 20ore Mountain scenery; 40ore Winter landscape.

64 Sinking of "Baroy" (freighter)

65 Gran's Bleriot XI "Nordsjoen"

1944. Shipwrecked Mariners' Relief Fund.
360 **64** 10ore+10ore green . . . . 65 3·25
361 – 15ore+10ore brown . . . . 65 3·25
362 – 20ore+10ore red . . . . . 65 3·25
DESIGNS—HORIZ: 15ore "Sanct Svithun" (cargo liner) attacked by Bristol Type 142 Blenheim Mk IV airplane. VERT: 20ore Sinking of "Irma" (freighter).

1944. 30th Anniv of First North Sea Flight, by Tryggve Gran.
363 **65** 40ore blue . . . . 55 1·20

66 Girl Spinning

67 Arms

68 Henrik Wergeland

1944. Winter Relief Fund. Inscr as in T **66**.
364 **66** 5ore+10ore mauve . . . . 55 1·80
365 – 10ore+10ore green . . . . 55 1·80
366 – 15ore+10ore purple . . . . 55 1·80
367 – 20ore+10ore red . . . . . 55 1·80
DESIGNS: 10ore Ploughing; 15ore Tree felling; 20ore Mother and children.

1945.
368 **67** 1½k. blue . . . . 1·70 45

1945. Death Centenary of Wergeland (poet).
369 **68** 10ore green 15 25
370 15ore brown 40 70
371 20ore red 10 20

69 Red Cross Sister

70 Folklore Museum Emblem

1945. Red Cross Relief Fund and Norwegian Red Cross Jubilee.
372 **69** 20ore+10ore red 35 40

1945. 50th Anniv of National Folklore Museum.
373 **70** 10ore green 35 25
374 20ore red 35 25

71 Crown Prince Olav

72 "R.N.A.F."

1946. National Relief Fund.
375 **71** 10ore+10ore green 35 35
376 15ore+10ore brown 35 35
377 20ore+10ore red 35 35
378 30ore+10ore blue . . . . 90 1·20

1946. Honouring Norwegian Air Force trained in Canada.
379 **72** 15ore red 45 75

73 King Haakon VII

74 Fridtjof Nansen, Roald Amundsen and "Fram"

1946.
380 **73** 1k. green . . . . 1·10 15
381 1½k. blue . . . . 3·00 15
382 2k. brown . . . . 20·00 15
383 5k. violet . . . . 13·50 50

1947. Tercentenary of Norwegian Post Office.
384 – 5ore mauve 30 15
385 – 10ore green 30 15
386 – 15ore brown 60 15
387 – 25ore red 50 15
388 – 30ore grey 75 15
389 – 40ore blue . . . . 1·80 25
390 – 45ore violet . . . . 1·50 55
391 – 50ore brown . . . . 2·20 35
392 **74** 55ore orange . . . . . . 3·25 25
393 – 60ore grey . . . . 2·75 1·10
394 – 80ore brown . . . . 3·00 40
DESIGNS: 5ore Hannibal Schested (founder of postal service) and Akershus Castle; 10ore "Postal-peasant"; 15ore Admiral Tordenskiold and 18th-century warship; 25ore Christian M. Falsen; 30ore Cleng Peerson and "Restaurationen" (emigrant sloop), 1825; 40ore "Constitutionen" (paddle-steamer), 1827; 45ore First Norwegian locomotive "Caroline"; 50ore Svend Foyn and "Spes et Fides" (whale catcher); 60ore Coronation of King Haakon and Queen Maud in Nidaros Cathedral; 80ore King Haakon and Oslo Town Hall.

75 Petter Dass

76 King Haakon VII

1947. Birth Tercentenary of Petter Dass (poet).
395 **75** 25ore red 60 60

1947. 75th Birthday of King Haakon VII.
396 **76** 25ore orange 45 55

77 Axel Heiberg

80 A. L. Kielland

1948. 50th Anniv of Norwegian Forestry Society and Birth Centenary of Axel Heiberg (founder).
397 **77** 25ore red 55 35
398 80ore brown . . . . 1·30 30

1948. Red Cross. Surch **25+5** and bars.
399 **69** 25+5 ore on 20+10 ore red 50 65

1949. Nos. 288a and 292a surch.
400 **22** 25ore on 20ore red 30 15
401 45ore on 40ore blue . . . 1·80 50

1949. Birth Centenary of Alexander L. Kielland (author).
402 **80** 25ore red 85 20
403 40ore blue 85 45
404 80ore brown . . . . 1·40 65

81 Symbolising Universe

82 Pigeons and Globe

1949. 75th Anniv of U.P.U.
405 **81** 10ore green and purple . . 45 45
406 **82** 25ore red 25 20
407 – 40ore blue 25 45
DESIGN—37 × 21 mm: 40ore Dove, globe and signpost.

84 King Harald Haardraade and Oslo Town Hall

85 Child with Flowers

1950. 900th Anniv of Founding of Oslo.
408 **84** 15ore green 45 55
409 25ore red 35 20
410 45ore blue 45 55

1950. Infantile Paralysis Fund.
411 **85** 25ore+5ore red 35 65
412 45ore+5ore blue . . . . . 3·50 3·75

87 King Haakon VII

88 Arne Garborg (after O. Rusti)

1950.
418 **87** 25ore red 50 15
419 25ore grey . . . . 11·00 20
419a 25ore green 65 15
420 30ore grey . . . . 5·25 60
421 30ore red 50 15
422a 35ore red . . . . 3·00 15
422b 40ore purple . . . . 1·10 25
423 45ore blue . . . . 95 1·50
424 50ore brown . . . . 1·50 15
425 55ore orange . . . . 1·60 95
426 55ore blue . . . . 1·00 45
427 60ore blue . . . . 7·75 15
427a 65ore blue 70 25
427b 70ore brown . . . . 8·50 25
428 75ore purple . . . . 1·50 25
429 80ore brown . . . . 1·60 25
430 90ore orange 95 25

1951. Birth Centenary of Garborg (author).
431 **88** 25ore red 35 30
432 45ore blue . . . . 1·50 2·10
433 80ore brown . . . . 2·10 1·70
"NOREG" on the stamps was the spelling advocated by Arne Garborg.

89 Ice Skater

92 King Haakon VII

1951. 6th Winter Olympic Games. Inscr "OSLO 1952".
434 **89** 15ore+5ore green . . . . 1·80 2·50
435 – 30ore+10ore red . . . . . 1·80 2·50
436 – 55ore+20ore blue . . . . 6·00 9·00
DESIGNS—As T **89**: 30ore Ski jumping. 38 × 21 mm: 55ore Winter landscape.

1951. Surch in figures.
440 **38** 20ore on 15ore green . . . 45 20
437 **87** 30ore on 25ore red 50 15

1952. 80th Birthday of King Haakon.
438 **92** 30ore scarlet and red . . . 25 20
439 55ore blue and grey . . . 70 75

94 "Supplication"

95 Medieval Sculpture

1953. Anti-cancer Fund.
441 **94** 30ore+10ore red and cream 1·00 1·30

1953. Norwegian Tourist Association Fund. As T **33** but smaller 27½ × 21 mm.
442 **33** 20ore+10ore green . . . . 5·50 7·25
464 25ore+10ore green . . . . 2·50 3·50
443 30ore+15ore red . . . . . 5·50 7·25
465 35ore+15ore red . . . . . 3·50 4·75
444 55ore+25ore blue . . . . 10·00 11·00
466 65ore+25ore blue . . . . 2·50 3·00

1953. 8th Cent of Archbishopric of Nidaros.
445 **95** 30ore red 50 45

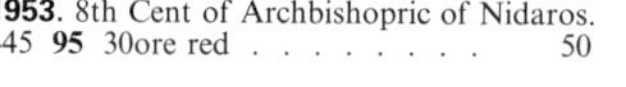

96 Stephenson Locomotive on Hoved Railway, 1854, and Horse-drawn Sledge

97 C. T. Nielsen (first Director)

1954. Centenary of Norwegian Railways.
446 **96** 20ore green 45 25
447 – 30ore red 45 20
448 – 55ore blue . . . . 1·10 1·00
DESIGNS: 30ore Diesel-hydraulic express train; 55ore Alfred Andersen (engine driver) in locomotive cab.

1954. Centenary of Telegraph Service.

449	97	20ore black and green . .	15	25
450	–	30ore red	15	20
451	–	55ore blue	80	75

DESIGNS: 30ore Radio masts at Tryvannshogda; 55ore Telegraph lineman on skis.

98 "Posthorn" Type Stamp

100 King Haakon and Queen Maud

1955. Norwegian Stamp Centenary.

452	–	20ore blue and green . . .	15	25
453	98	30ore deep red and red . .	15	10
454	–	55ore blue and grey . . .	35	50

DESIGNS: 20ore Norway's first stamp; 55ore "Lion" type stamp.

1955. Stamp Cent and Int Stamp Exn, Oslo. Nos. 452/4 with circular opt **OSLO NORWEX**.

455	–	20ore blue and green . . .	6·75	8·25
456	98	30ore deep red and red . .	6·75	8·25
457	–	55ore blue and grey . . .	6·75	8·25

Nos. 455/7 were only on sale at the Exhibition P.O. at face plus 1k. entrance fee.

1955. Golden Jubilee of King Haakon.

458	100	30ore red	25	20
459		55ore blue	35	45

101 Crown Princess Martha

101a Whooper Swans

1956. Crown Princess Martha Memorial Fund.

460	101	35ore+10ore red	50	65
461		65ore+10ore blue	2·10	2·20

1956. Northern Countries' Day.

462	101a	35ore red	35	40
463		65ore blue	35	55

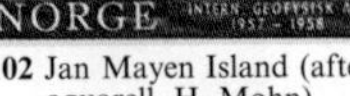

102 Jan Mayen Island (after aquarell, H. Mohn)

103 Map of Spitzbergen

1957. Int Geophysical Year. Inscr "INTERN. GEOFYSISK AR 1957–1958".

467	102	25ore green	60	35
468	103	35ore red and grey . . .	60	20
469	–	65ore green and blue . .	70	50

DESIGN—VERT: 65ore Map of Antarctica showing Queen Maud Land.

104 King Haakon VII

1957. 85th Birthday of King Haakon.

470	104	35ore red	15	20
471		65ore blue	50	60

105 King Olav V

106 King Olav V

1958.

472	105	25ore green	60	15
473		30ore violet	95	20
474		35ore red	45	25
474a		35ore green	2·00	15
475		40ore red	45	20
475a		40ore grey	2·20	1·10
476		45ore red	50	15
477		50ore brown	3·75	15
478		50ore red	4·00	15
479		55ore grey	1·10	80
480		60ore violet	2·75	80
481		65ore blue	95	40
482		80ore brown	4·50	55
483		85ore brown	1·00	25
484		90ore orange	50	15
485	106	1k. green	45	30
486		1k.50 blue	1·80	15
487		2k. red	1·30	40
488		5k. purple	23·00	15
489		10k. orange	3·25	15

107 Asbjorn Kloster (founder)

108 Society's Centenary Medal

1959. Cent of Norwegian Temperance Movement.

490	107	45ore brown	30	25

1959. 150th Anniv of Royal Norwegian Agricultural Society.

491	108	45ore brown and red . .	30	40
492		90ore grey and blue . . .	1·20	1·50

109 Sower

110 White Anemone

1959. Centenary of Norwegian Royal College of Agriculture.

493	109	45ore black and brown	45	40
494	–	90ore black and blue . .	85	90

DESIGN—VERT: 90ore Ears of corn.

1960. Tuberculosis Relief Funds.

495	110	45ore+10ore yellow, green and red	1·60	1·70
496	–	90ore+10ore mult	3·00	5·00

DESIGN: 90ore Blue anemone.

111 Society's Original Seal

112 Refugee Mother and Child

1960. Bicentenary of Royal Norwegian Society of Scientists.

497	111	45ore red on grey	35	35
498		90ore blue on grey . . .	1·00	1·20

1960. World Refugee Year.

499	112	45ore+25ore black and pink	2·40	3·50
500		90ore+25ore blk & bl . .	5·50	7·00

113 Viking Longship

1960. Norwegian Ships.

501	113	20ore black and grey . .	90	65
502	–	25ore black and green . .	80	65
503	–	45ore black and red . . .	80	50
504	–	55ore black and brown	1·90	2·00
505	–	90ore black and blue . .	1·60	1·40

SHIPS: 25ore Hanse kogge; 45ore "Skomvaer" (barque); 55ore "Dalfon" (tanker); 90ore "Bergensfjord" (liner).

113a Conference Emblem

113b Douglas DC-8

1960. Europa.

506	113a	90ore blue	45	45

1961. 10th Anniv of Scandinavian Airlines System (SAS).

507	113b	90ore blue	35	55

114 Throwing the Javelin

1961. Centenary of Norwegian Sport.

508	114	20ore brown	40	45
509	–	25ore green	40	55
510	–	45ore red	40	20
511	–	90ore mauve	2·30	85

DESIGNS: 25ore Ice skating; 45ore Ski jumping; 90ore Yachting.

115 Haakonshallen Barracks and Rosencrantz Tower

1961. 700th Anniv of Haakonshallen, Bergen.

512	115	45ore black and red . . .	35	20
513		1k. black and green . . .	35	35

116 Oslo University

1961. 150th Anniv of Oslo University.

514	116	45ore red	20	20
515		1k.50 blue	30	35

117 Nansen

119 Frederic Passy and Henri Dunant (winners in 1901)

118 Amundsen, "Fram" and Dog-team

1961. Birth Centenary of Fridtjof Nansen (polar explorer).

516	117	45ore black and red . . .	25	20
517		90ore black and blue . .	50	50

1961. 50th Anniv of Amundsen's Arrival at South Pole.

518	118	45ore red and grey . . .	35	30
519	–	90ore deep blue and blue	65	85

DESIGN: 90ore Amundsen's party and tent at South Pole.

1961. Nobel Peace Prize.

520	119	45ore red	35	20
521		1k. green	45	35

120 Prof. V. Bjerknes

1962. Birth Centenary of Prof. Vilhelm Bjerknes (physicist).

522	120	45ore black and red . . .	30	20
523		1k.50 black and blue . .	55	35

121 Etrich/Rumpler Taube Monoplane "Start"

1962. 50th Anniv of Norwegian Aviation.

524	121	1k.50 brown and blue . .	95	45

122 Branch of Fir, and Cone

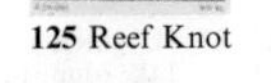

125 Reef Knot

123 Europa "Tree"

1962. Cent of State Forestry Administration.

525	122	45ore grey, black and red	60	45
526		1k. grey, black and green	3·00	25

1962. Europa.

527	123	50ore red	35	20
528		90ore blue	55	95

1962.

531g	–	25ore green	70	15
532	–	30ore drab	2·50	2·40
532a	–	30ore green	25	25
533	125	35ore green	20	15
533a	–	40ore red	95	30
534	–	40ore green	20	15
534a	–	45ore green	30	50
535	125	50ore red	2·10	15
535a		50ore grey	20	15
536	–	55ore brown	35	55
536a	125	60ore green	4·50	15
537		60ore red	60	30
537b	–	65ore violet	75	30
538	125	65ore red	35	15
538a		70ore brown	20	15
539	–	75ore green	20	15
539a	–	80ore purple	1·50	1·40
539b	–	80ore brown	30	15
540	–	85ore brown	30	25
540a	–	85ore buff	30	25
540b	–	90ore blue	30	20
541	–	100ore violet	30	15
541a	–	100ore red	30	15
542	–	110ore red	30	15
542a	–	115ore brown	45	35
543	–	120ore blue	40	25
543a	–	125ore red	30	15
544	–	140ore blue	40	25
544a	–	750ore brown	1·20	15

DESIGNS: 25, 40, 90, 100 (2), 110, 120, 125ore, Runic drawings; 30, 45, 55, 75, 85ore, Ear of wheat and Atlantic cod; 65 (537b), 80, 140ore, "Stave" (wooden) church and "Aurora Borealis"; 115ore Fragment of Urnes stave-church; 750ore Sigurd Farnesbane (the Dragon killer) and Regin (the blacksmith), portal from Hylestad stave-church.

126 Camilla Collett

127 Boatload of Wheat

1963. 150th Birth Anniv of Camilla Collett (author).

545	126	50ore red	20	30
546		90ore blue	55	1·70

1963. Freedom from Hunger.

547	127	25ore bistre	35	40
548		35ore green	45	60
549	–	50ore red	35	30
550	–	90ore blue	1·00	1·10

DESIGN—37½ × 21 mm: 50, 90ore Birds carrying food on cloth.

128 River Mail Boat

1963. Tercentenary of Southern-Northern Norwegian Postal Services.

551	128	50ore red	1·10	50
552	–	90ore blue	2·10	2·00

DESIGN: 90ore Femboring (Northern sailing vessel).

129 Ivar Aasen

130 "Co-operation"

1963. 150th Birth Anniv of Ivar Aasen (philologist).

553	129	50ore red and grey . . .	35	20
554		90ore blue and grey . . .	80	75

The note after No. 433 re "NOREG" also applies here.

1963. Europa.

555	130	50ore orange and purple	50	20
556		90ore green and blue . .	1·50	1·50

131 "Herringbone" Pattern

1963. 150th Anniv of Norwegian Textile Industry.
557 **131** 25ore green and bistre . . 55 55
558 35ore ultramarine and blue 65 75
559 50ore purple and red . . 55 45

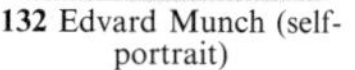
132 Edvard Munch (self-portrait) 133 Eilert Sundt (founder)

1963. Birth Centenary of Edvard Munch (painter and engraver).
560 **132** 25ore black 30 25
561 – 35ore green 30 25
562 – 50ore brown 30 15
563 – 90ore blue and indigo . . 65 65
DESIGNS (woodcuts)—HORIZ: 35ore "Fecundity"; 50ore "The Solitaries". VERT: 90ore "The Girls on the Bridge".

1964. Centenary of Oslo Workers' Society.
564 **133** 25ore green 40 40
565 – 50ore purple 40 25
DESIGN: 50ore Beehive emblem of O.W.S.

134 C. M. Guldberg and P. Waage (chemists)

1964. Centenary of Law of Mass Action.
566 **134** 35ore green 55 45
567 55ore stone . . . . 1·30 1·20

135 Eidsvoll Manor

1964. 150th Anniv of Norwegian Constitution.
568 **135** 50ore grey and red . . . 35 30
569 – 90ore black and blue . . 80 95
DESIGN: 90ore Storting (Parliament House), Oslo.

On 1 June 1964 a stamp depicting the U.N. refugee emblem and inscr "PORTO BETALT ... LYKKEBREVET 1964" was put on sale. It had a franking value of 50ore but was sold for 2k.50, the balance being for the Refugee Fund. In addition, each stamp bore a serial number representing participation in a lottery which took place in September. The stamp was on sale until 15 July and had validity until 10 August.

136 Harbour Scene 137 Europa "Flower"

1964. Cent of Norwegian Seamen's Mission.
570 **136** 25ore green and yellow 50 50
571 90ore blue and cream . . 1·20 1·40

1964. Europa.
572 **137** 90ore deep blue and blue 1·70 1·70

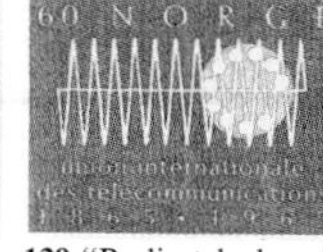
138 H. Anker and O. Arvesen (founders) 139 "Radio-telephone"

1964. Cent of Norwegian Folk High Schools.
573 **138** 50ore pink 55 30
574 90ore blue . . . . 1·90 1·90

The note after No. 433 re "NOREG" also applies here.

1965. Centenary of I.T.U.
575 **139** 60ore purple 55 25
576 – 90ore grey . . . . 1·00 1·00
DESIGN: 90ore "T.V. transmission".

140 Dove of Peace and Broken Chain

1965. 20th Anniv of Liberation.
577 **140** 30ore+10ore brown, green and sepia 25 30
578 – 60ore+10ore blue and red 25 30
DESIGN: 60ore Norwegian flags.

141 Mountain Landscapes

1965. Centenary of Norwegian Red Cross.
579 **141** 60ore brown and red . . 35 25
580 – 90ore blue and red . . . 2·50 2·10
DESIGN: 90ore Coastal view.

142 Europa "Sprig" 144 Rondane Mountains (after H. Sohlberg)

143 St. Sunniva and Bergen Buildings

1965. Europa.
581 **142** 60ore red 50 30
582 90ore blue . . . . 1·10 1·10

1965. Bicentenary of Harmonien Philharmonic Society.
583 – 30ore black and green . . 45 25
584 **143** 90ore black and blue . . 90 95
DESIGN—VERT: 30ore St. Sunniva.

1965. Rondane National Park.
585 **144** 1k.50 blue . . . . 1·00 25

145 "Rodoy Skier" (rock carving) 146 "The Bible"

1966. World Skiing Championships, Oslo. Inscr "VM OSLO 1966".
586 **145** 40ore brown 45 85
587 – 55ore green . . . . . . 1·20 1·20
588 – 60ore brown 45 25
589 – 90ore blue . . . . . . 85 1·10
DESIGNS—HORIZ: 55ore Ski jumper; 60ore Cross-country skier. VERT: 90ore Holmenkollen ski jumping tower, Oslo.

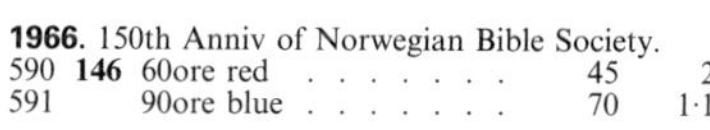

1966. 150th Anniv of Norwegian Bible Society.
590 **146** 60ore red 45 25
591 90ore blue . . . . . . 70 1·10

147 Guilloche Pattern 148 J. Sverdrup (after C. Krohg)

1966. 150th Anniv of Bank of Norway.
592 **147** 30ore green 45 40
593 – 60ore red (Bank building) 30 15
No. 593 is size $27\frac{1}{2}\times21$ mm.

1966. 150th Birth Anniv of Johan Sverdrup (statesman).
594 **148** 30ore green 35 25
595 60ore purple 30 25

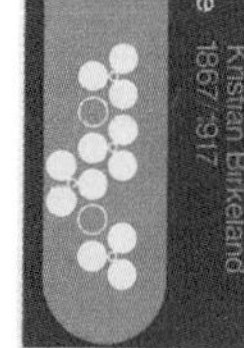
149 Europa "Ship" 150 Molecules in Test-tube

1966. Europa.
596 **149** 60ore red 50 25
597 90ore blue . . . . 1·10 95

1966. Birth Centenaries of S. Eyde (industrialist) (1966) and K. Birkeland (scientist) (1967), founders of Norwegian Nitrogen Industry.
598 **150** 40ore blue and light blue 1·20 1·10
599 – 55ore mauve and red . . 1·60 1·40
DESIGN: 55ore Ear of wheat and conical flask.

151 E.F.T.A. Emblem 152 "Owl" and Three Swords

1967. European Free Trade Association.
600 **151** 60ore red 40 20
601 90ore blue . . . . 1·30 1·40

1967. 150th Anniv of Higher Military Training.
602 **152** 60ore brown 50 40
603 90ore green . . . . . . 1·60 1·60

153 Cogwheels 154 Johanne Dybwad

1967. Europa.
604 **153** 60ore deep plum, plum and purple 35 20
605 90ore deep violet, violet and blue . . . . . . 1·00 1·10

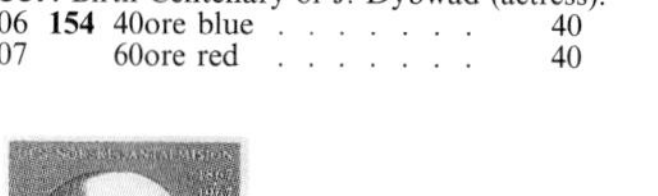

1967. Birth Centenary of J. Dybwad (actress).
606 **154** 40ore blue 40 30
607 60ore red 40 10

155 I. Skrefsrud (missionary and founder) 156 Climbers on Mountain-top

1967. Centenary of Norwegian Santal Mission.
608 **155** 60ore brown 40 20
609 – 90ore blue 90 75
DESIGN—HORIZ: 90ore Ebenezer Church, Benagaria, Santal, India.

1968. Centenary of Norwegian Mountain Touring Association.
610 **156** 40ore brown 75 75
611 – 60ore red 75 25
612 – 90ore blue . . . . 1·40 1·10
DESIGNS: 60ore Mountain cairn and scenery; 90ore Glitretind peak.

157 "The Blacksmiths" 158 Vinje

1968. Norwegian Handicrafts.
613 **157** 65ore brown, black & red 45 25
614 90ore brown, black & blue . . . . 95 1·10

1968. 150th Birth Anniv of Aasmund Vinje (poet).
615 **158** 50ore brown 35 40
616 65ore red 35 15
See note below No. 433.

159 Cross and Heart 160 Cathinka Guldberg (first deaconess)

1968. Centenary of Norwegian Lutheran Home Mission Society.
617 **159** 40ore red and green . . . 2·40 2·40
618 65ore red and violet . . . 50 15

1968. Centenary of Deaconess House, Oslo.
619 **160** 50ore blue 40 30
620 65ore red 40 20

161 K. P. Arnoldson and F. Bajer

1968. Nobel Peace Prize Winners of 1908.
621 **161** 65ore brown 40 25
622 90ore blue 75 75

161a Viking Ships (from old Swedish coin)

1969. 50th Anniv of Northern Countries' Union.
623 **161a** 65ore red 45 20
624 90ore blue 75 80

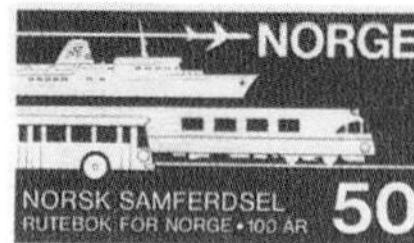
162 Transport

1969. Centenary of "Rutebok for Norge" ("Communications of Norway") and Road Safety Campaign.
625 **162** 50ore green 30 50
626 – 65ore red and green . . . 20 25
DESIGN: 65ore Pedestrian-crossing.

163 Colonnade

1969. Europa.
627 **163** 65ore black and red . . . 75 20
628 90ore black and blue . . 45 95

164 J. Hjort and Atlantic Cod Eggs

1969. Birth Centenary of Professor Johan Hjort (fisheries pioneer).
629 **164** 40ore brown and blue . . 75 60
630 – 90ore blue and green . . 2·40 1·20
DESIGN: 90ore Hjort and polyp.

165 Traena Islands

1969.
631 **165** 3k.50 black 70 20

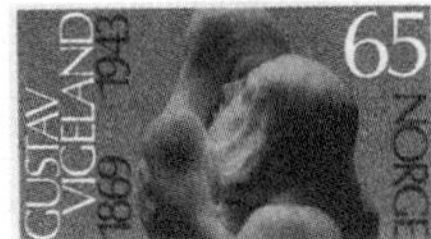

166 King Olav V **167** "Mother and Child"

1969.
632 **166** 1k. green 30 15
633 1k.50 blue 45 15
634 2k. red 45 15
635 5k. blue 95 15
636 10k. brown . . . . . . 2·75 15
637 20k. brown . . . . . . 2·50 15
637a 50k. green . . . . 9·75 40

1969. Birth Centenary of Gustav Vigeland (sculptor).
638 **167** 65ore black and red . . . 25 20
639 – 90ore black and blue . . 75 85
DESIGN: 90ore "Family" (sculpture).

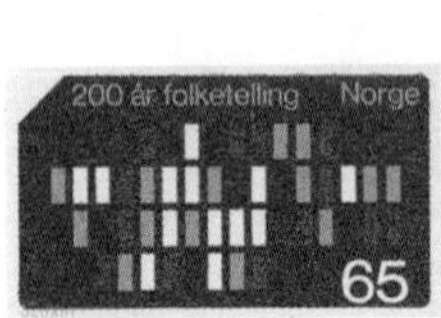

168 Punched Cards **169** Queen Maud

1969. Bicentenary of 1st National Census. Mult.
640 65ore Type **168** 25 20
641 90ore "People" (diagram) . . 75 85

1969. Birth Centenary of Queen Maud.
642 **169** 65ore purple 25 10
643 90ore blue 75 75

170 Wolf ("Canis lupus") **171** "V" Symbol

1970. Nature Conservation Year.
644 **170** 40ore brown and blue . . 75 80
645 – 60ore grey and brown . . 75 1·50
646 – 70ore brown and blue . . 1·00 45
647 – 100ore brown and blue 2·30 1·00
DESIGNS—VERT: 60ore Pale pasque flower ("Pulsatilla vernalis"); 70ore Voringsfossen Falls. HORIZ: 100ore White-tailed sea eagle ("Haliaeetus albicilla").

1970. 25th Anniv of Liberation.
648 **171** 70ore red and violet . . . 1·20 40
649 – 100ore blue and green . . 1·20 1·10
DESIGN—HORIZ: 100ore Merchant ships in convoy.

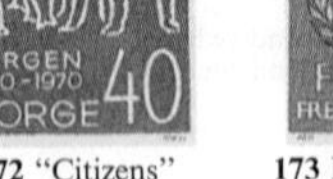

172 "Citizens" **173** Hands reaching for Globe

1970. 900th Anniv of Bergen.
650 **172** 40ore green 95 80
651 – 70ore purple . . . . . . 1·70 40
652 – 1k. blue . . . . 1·30 1·50
DESIGNS: 70ore "City between the Mountains"; 1k. "Ships".

1970. 25th Anniv of United Nations.
653 **173** 70ore red . . . . 1·80 45
654 100ore green . . . . . . 1·20 1·20

174 G. O. Sars **175** Ball-game

1970. Norwegian Zoologists.
655 **174** 40ore brown 75 95
656 – 50ore lilac 85 70
657 – 70ore brown . . . . . . 1·00 25
658 – 100ore blue . . . . . . 1·00 1·00
ZOOLOGISTS: 50ore Hans Strom; 70ore J. E. Gunnerus; 100ore Michael Sars.

1970. Centenary of Central School of Gymnastics, Oslo.
659 **175** 50ore brown and blue . . 50 40
660 – 70ore brown and red . . 75 10
DESIGN—HORIZ: 70ore "Leapfrog" exercise.

176 Tonsberg's Seal c. 1340

1971. 1100th Anniv of Tonsberg.
661 **176** 70ore red 50 20
662 100ore blue 75 70

177 Parliament House, Oslo

1971. Centenary of Introduction of Annual Parliamentary Sessions.
663 **177** 70ore lilac and red . . . 40 30
664 100ore green and blue . . 75 65

178 "Helping Hand"

1971. "Help for Refugees".
665 **178** 50ore green and black . . 45 60
666 70ore red and black . . . 30 75

179 "Hauge addressing Followers" (A. Tidemand)

1971. Birth Centenary of Hans Nielson Hauge (church reformer).
667 **179** 60ore black 45 35
668 70ore brown 30 25

180 Bishop welcoming Worshippers

1971. 900th Anniv of Oslo Bishopric.
669 – 70ore black and red . . . 35 20
670 **180** 1k. black and blue . . . 1·00 95
DESIGN—VERT: 70ore Masons building first church.

181 Roald Amundsen and Treaty Emblem

1971. 10th Anniv of Antarctic Treaty.
671 **181** 100ore red and blue . . . 1·30 1·30

182 "The Preacher and the King" **184** 3s. "Posthorn" Stamp

183 Anniversary Symbol

1971. Norwegian Folk Tales. Drawings by Erik Werenskiold.
672 – 40ore black and green . . 30 20
673 **182** 50ore black and blue . . 35 15
674 – 70ore black and purple . . 45 20
DESIGNS—VERT: 40ore "The Farmer and the Woman"; 70ore "The Troll and the Girl".

1972. 150th Anniv of Norwegian Savings Banks.
675 **183** 80ore gold and red . . . 45 20
676 1k.20 gold and blue . . . 45 65

1972. Centenary of Norwegian "Posthorn" Stamps.
677 **184** 80ore red and brown . . 35 9·00
678 1k. blue and violet . . . 55 45

185 Alstad "Picture" Stone (detail) **186** King Haakon VII

1972. 1100th Anniv of Norway's Unification. Relics.
680 **185** 50ore green 55 60
681 – 60ore brown 80 85
682 – 80ore red . . . . 1·10 35
683 – 1k.20 blue 35 95
DESIGNS: 60ore Portal, Hemsedal Church (detail); 80ore Figurehead of Oseberg Viking ship; 1k.20, Sword-hilt (Lodingen).

1972. Birth Centenary of King Haakon VII.
684 **186** 80ore red . . . . 1·00 25
685 1k.20 blue . . . . 75 1·00

187 "Joy" (Ingrid Ekrem) **189** "Maud"

1972. "Youth and Leisure".
686 **187** 80ore mauve 45 20
687 – 1k.20 blue . . . . 75 1·20
DESIGN: 1k.20, "Solidarity" (Ole Instefjord).

1972. "Interjunex 1972" Stamp Exhibition, Oslo. Nos. 686/7 optd **INTERJUNEX 72**.
688 **187** 80ore mauve . . . . . . 1·90 2·40
689 – 1k.20 blue . . . . 1·90 2·40

1972. Norwegian Polar Ships.
690 **189** 60ore olive and green . . 1·10 75
691 – 80ore red and black . . . 1·20 30
692 – 1k.20 blue and red . . . 1·20 1·10
DESIGNS: 80ore "Fram" (Amundsen and Nansen's ship); 1k.20, "Gjoa".

190 "Little Man" **191** Dr. Hansen and Bacillus Diagram

1972. Norwegian Folk Tales. Drawings of Trolls by Th. Kittelsen.
693 **190** 50ore black and green . . 30 20
694 – 60ore black and blue . . 45 35
695 – 80ore black and pink . . 30 15
TROLLS: 60ore "The troll who wonders how old he is"; 80ore "Princess riding on a bear".

1973. Centenary of Hansen's Identification of Leprosy Bacillus.
696 **191** 1k. red and blue 45 20
697 – 1k.40 blue and red . . . 65 95
DESIGN: 1k.40, As Type **191** but bacillus as seen in modern microscope.

192 Europa "Posthorn" **193** King Olav V

192a "The Nordic House", Reykjavik

1973. Europa.
698 **192** 1k. red, scarlet and carmine . . . . 1·10 25
699 1k.40 emerald, green and blue . . . . 1·10 1·10

1973. Nordic Countries' Postal Co-operation.
700 **192a** 1k. multicoloured . . . 35 15
701 1k.40 multicoloured . . 35 85

1973. King Olav's 70th Birthday.
702 **193** 1k. brown and purple . . 45 20
703 1k.40 brown and blue . . 45 75

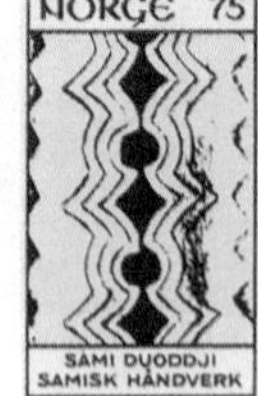

194 J. Aall **195** Bone Carving

1973. Birth Centenary of Jacob Aall (industrialist).
704 **194** 1k. purple 30 20
705 1k.40 blue 30 65

1973. Lapp Handicrafts.
706 **195** 75ore brown and cream 25 30
707 – 1k. red and cream 35 15
708 – 1k.40 black and blue . . 40 65
DESIGNS: 1k. Detail of weaving; 1k.40, Detail of tin-ware.

196 Yellow Wood Violet **197** Land Surveying

1973. Mountain Flowers. Multicoloured.
709 65ore Type **196** 15 20
710 70ore Rock speedwell 20 60
711 1k. Mountain heath 20 15

1973. Bicent of Norwegian Geographical Society.
712 **197** 1k. red 25 15
713 – 1k.40 blue 45 70
DESIGN: 1k.40, Old map of Hestbraepiggene (mountain range).

198 Lindesnes **199** "Bridal Procession on Hardanger Fjord" (A. Tidemand and H. Gude)

1974. Norwegian Capes.
714 **198** 1k. green 45 25
715 – 1k.40 blue . . . . 1·00 1·00
DESIGN: 1k.40, North Cape.

1974. Norwegian Paintings. Multicoloured.
716 1k. Type **199** 30 15
717 1k.40 "Stugunoset from Filefjell" (J. Dahl) 35 65

200 Gulating Law Manuscript, 1325 **201** Trees and Saw Blade

1974. 700th Anniv of King Magnus Lagaboter National Legislation.
718 **200** 1k. red and brown . . . 30 15
719 – 1k.40 blue and brown . . 50 70
DESIGN: 1k.40, King Magnus Lagaboter (sculpture in Stavanger Cathedral).

1974. Industrial Accident Prevention.
720 **201** 85ore green, deep green and emerald . . . . . 1·00 1·50
721 – 1k. carmine, red and orange 75 30
DESIGN: 1k. Flower and cogwheel.

202 J. H. L. Vogt **203** Buildings of the World

1974. Norwegian Geologists.
722 **202** 65ore brown and green 25 25
723 – 85ore brown and purple 70 1·00
724 – 1k. brown and orange 50 20
725 – 1k.40 brown and blue 75 80
DESIGNS: 85ore V. M. Goldschmidt; 1k. Th. Kjerulf; 1k.40, W. C. Brogger.

1974. Centenary of Universal Postal Union.
726 **203** 1k. brown and green 45 20
727 – 1k.40 blue and brown 50 65
DESIGN: 1k.40, People of the World.

204 Detail of Chest of Drawers **205** Woman Skier, 1900

1974. Norwegian Folk Art. Rose Painting. Mult.
728 85ore Type **204** 45 50
729 1k. Detail of cupboard 25 15

1975. Norwegian Skiing.
730 **205** 1k. red and green 50 25
731 – 1k.40 blue and brown 50 65
DESIGN: 1k.40, Skier making telemark turn.

206 "Three Women with Ivies" Gate, Vigeland Park, Oslo **207** Nusfjord Fishing Harbour, Lofoten Islands

1975. International Women's Year.
732 **206** 1k.25 violet and purple 30 15
733 1k.40 ultramarine and blue 30 70

1975. European Architectural Heritage Year.
734 **207** 1k. green 30 45
735 – 1k.25 red 25 15
736 – 1k.40 blue 30 60
DESIGNS: 1k.25, Old Stavanger; 1k.40, Roros.

208 Norwegian 1k. Coin, 1875 (Monetary Convention)

1975. Cent of Monetary and Metre Conventions.
737 **208** 1k.25 red 20 20
738 – 1k.40 blue 40 55
DESIGN: 1k.40, O. J. Broch (original Director of the International Bureau of Weights and Measures) (Metre Convention).

209 Camping and Emblem

1975. World Scout Jamboree, Lillehammer. Mult.
739 1k.25 Type **209** 25 20
740 1k.40 Skiing and emblem 45 75

210 Colonist's Peat House

1975. 150th Anniv of First Emigrations to America.
741 **210** 1k.25 brown 45 20
742 – 1k.40 blue 45 55
DESIGNS: 1k.40, C. Peerson and extract from letter to America, 1874.

211 "Templet" (Temple Mountain), Tempelfjord, Spitzbergen **212** "Television Screen" (T. E. Johnsen)

1975. 50th Anniv of Norwegian Administration of Spitzbergen.
743 **211** 1k. grey 30 45
744 – 1k.25 purple 30 10
745 – 1k.40 blue 80 1·20
DESIGNS: 1k.25, Miners leaving pit; 1k.40, Polar bear.

1975. 50th Anniv of Norwegian Broadcasting System. Multicoloured.
746 1k.25 Type **212** 15 20
747 1k.40 Telecommunications antenna (N. Davidsen) (vert) 25 50

213 "The Annunciation"

1975. Paintings from "Altaket" (wooden vault) of "Al" Stave Church, Hallingdal.
748 80ore Type **213** 20 20
749 1k. "The Visitation" 20 25
750 1k.25 "The Nativity" (30 × 38 mm) 20 10
751 1k.40 "The Adoration" (30 × 38 mm) 45 55

214 "Halling" (folk dance) **215** Silver Sugar Caster, Stavanger, 1770

1976. Norwegian Folk Dances. Multicoloured.
752 80ore Type **214** 30 50
753 1k. "Springar" 30 25
754 1k.25 "Gangar" 30 10

1976. Centenary of Oslo Museum of Applied Art.
755 **215** 1k.25 brown, red and pink 20 20
756 – 1k.40 lilac, blue and azure 35 65
DESIGN: 1k.40, Goblet, Nostetangen Glass-works, 1770.

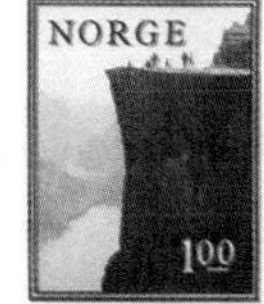

216 Bishop's "Mitre" Bowl, 1760 **217** "The Pulpit", Lyse Fjord

1976. Europa. Early Products of Herrebo Potteries, Halden.
757 **216** 1k.25 red and mauve 30 20
758 – 1k.40 ultramarine & blue 50 65
DESIGN: 1k.40, Decorative plate, 1760.

1976. Norwegian Scenery. Multicoloured.
759 1k. Type **217** 30 45
760 1k.25 Peak of Gulleplet ("The Golden Apple"), Balestrand, Sognefjord 45 25

218 Social Development Graph **219** Olav Duun and Cairn, Dun Mountain, Joa Island, Namsen Fjord

1976. Cent of Norwegian Central Bureau of Statistics.
761 **218** 1k.25 red 40 15
762 – 2k. blue 45 35
DESIGN: 2k. National productivity graph.

1976. Birth Centenary of Olav Duun (novelist).
763 **219** 1k.25 multicoloured 40 25
764 1k.40 multicoloured 45 80

220 "Slindebirkin" (T. Fearnley) **221** Details of "April"

1976. Norwegian Paintings. Multicoloured.
765 1k.25 Type **220** 45 20
766 1k.40 "Gamle Furutraer" (L. Hertervig) 55 65

1976. Tapestry from Baldishol Stave Church. Mult.
767 80ore Type **221** 25 20
768 1k. Detail of "May" 25 25
769 1k.25 "April" and "May" section of tapestry (48 × 30 mm) 25 15

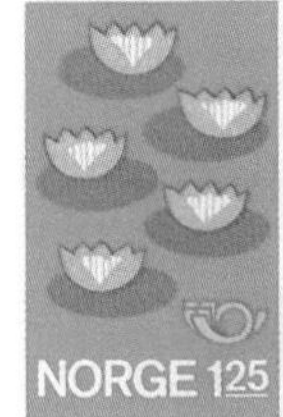

222 Five Water-lilies **223** Akershus Castle, Oslo

1977. Nordic Countries Co-operation in Nature Conservation and Environment Protection.
770 **222** 1k.25 multicoloured 30 15
771 1k.40 multicoloured 30 65

1977.
772 – 1k. green 25 20
773 – 1k.10 purple 25 20
774 **223** 1k.25 red 20 15
775 – 1k.30 brown 30 15
776 – 1k.40 lilac 25 20
777 – 1k.50 red 30 15
778 – 1k.70 green 40 40
779 – 1k.75 green 35 15
780 – 1k.80 blue 45 35
781 – 2k. red 45 15
782 – 2k.20 blue 45 40
783 – 2k.25 violet 45 35
784 – 2k.50 red 45 15
785 – 2k.75 red 50 60
786 – 3k. blue 50 25
787 – 3k.50 violet 60 25
DESIGNS—HORIZ: 1k. Austraat Manor; 1k.10, Trondenes Church, Harstad; 1k.30, Steinviksholm Fortress, Asen Fjord; 1k.40, Ruins of Hamar Cathedral; 2k.20, Tromsdalen Church; 2k.50, Loghouse, Breiland; 2k.75, Damsgard Palace, Laksevag, near Bergen; 3k. Ruins of Selje Monastery; 3k.50, Lindesnes lighthouse. VERT: 1k.50, Stavanger Cathedral; 1k.70, Rosenkrantz Tower, Bergen; 1k.75, Seamen's commemoration hall, Stavern; 1k.80, Torungen lighthouses, Arendal; 2k. Tofte royal estate, Dovre; 2k.25, Oscarshall (royal residence), Oslofjord.

224 Hamnoy, Lofoten Islands **225** Spruce

1977. Europa. Multicoloured.
795 1k.25 Type **224** 50 25
796 1k.80 Huldrefossen, Nordfjord (vert) 50 55

1977. Norwegian Trees.
797 **225** 1k. green 25 25
798 – 1k.25 brown 25 20
799 – 1k.80 black 35 45
DESIGNS: 1k.25, Fir; 1k.80, Birch.
See note below No. 433.

226 "Constitutionen" (paddle-steamer) at Arendal

1977. Norwegian Coastal Routes.
800 **226** 1k. brown 20 20
801 – 1k.25 red 30 25
802 – 1k.30 green 90 85
803 – 1k.80 blue 45 40
DESIGNS: 1k.25, "Vesteraalen" (coaster) off Bodo; 1k.30, "Kong Haakon" and "Dronningen" at Stavanger, 1893 (ferries); 1k.80, "Nordstjernen" and "Harald Jarl" (ferries).

227 "From the Herring Fishery" (after photo by S. A. Borretzen)

1977. Fishing Industry.
804 **227** 1k.25 brown on orange 20 20
805 – 1k.80 blue on blue 30 60
DESIGN: 1k.80, Saithe and fish hooks.
See note below No. 433.

228 "Saturday Evening" (H. Egedius)

1977. Norwegian Paintings. Multicoloured.
806 1k.25 Type **228** 30 20
807 1k.80 "Forest Lake in Lower Telemark" (A. Cappelen) 40 65

229 "David with the Bells" **230** "Peer and the Buck Reindeer" (after drawing by P. Krohg for "Peer Gynt")

1977. Miniatures from the Bible of Aslak Bolt. Mult.
808 80ore Type **229** 20 15
809 1k. "Singing Friars" 20 30
810 1k.25 "The Holy Virgin with the Child" (34 × 27 mm) 20 25

1978. 150th Birth Anniv of Henrik Ibsen (dramatist).
811 **230** 1k.25 black and stone 25 25
812 – 1k.80 multicoloured 35 50
DESIGN: 1k.80, Ibsen (after E. Werenskiold).

231 Heddal Stave Church, Telemark **232** Lenangstindene and Jaegervasstindene, Troms

1978. Europa.
813 **231** 1k.25 brown and orange 40 20
814 – 1k.80 green and blue 75 65
DESIGN: 1k.80, Borgund stave church, Sogn.

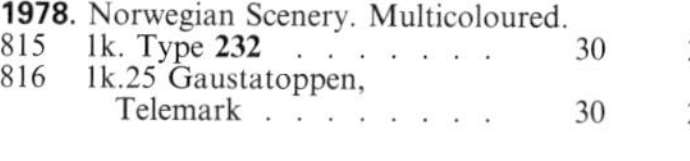

1978. Norwegian Scenery. Multicoloured.
815 1k. Type **232** 30 25
816 1k.25 Gaustatoppen, Telemark 30 25

233 King Olav in Sailing-boat

1978. 75th Birthday of King Olav V.
817 **233** 1k.25 brown 30 30
818 – 1k.80 violet 30 40
DESIGN—VERT: 1k.80, King Olav delivering royal speech at opening of Parliament.

234 Amundsen's Polar Flight Stamp of 1925

1978. "Norwex 80" International Stamp Exhibition.
819 **234** 1k.25 green and grey 40 60
820 1k.25 blue and grey 40 60
821 – 1k.25 green and grey 40 60
822 – 1k.25 blue and grey 40 60
823 **234** 1k.25 purple and grey 40 60
824 1k.25 red and grey 40 60

825 – 1k.25 purple and grey . . 40 60
826 – 1k.25 blue and grey . . . 40 60
DESIGNS: Nos. 821/2, 825/6, Annexation of Spitzbergen stamp of 1925.
On Nos. 819/26 each design incorporates a different value of the 1925 issues.

235 Willow Pipe Player **236** Wooden Doll, c. 1830

1978. Musical Instruments.
827 **235** 1k. green 20 20
828 – 1k.25 red 30 20
829 – 1k.80 blue 45 45
830 – 7k.50 grey . . . . 1·20 25
831 – 15k. brown . . . . 2·50 25
DESIGNS: 1k.25, Norwegian violin; 1k.80, Norwegian zither; 7k.50, Ram's horn; 15k. Jew's harp.
See note below No. 433.

1978. Christmas. Antique Toys from Norwegian Folk Museum. Multicoloured.
835 80ore Type **236** 20 20
836 1k. Toy town, 1896/7 . . . . 20 30
837 1k.25 Wooden horse from Torpo, Hallingdal 20 15

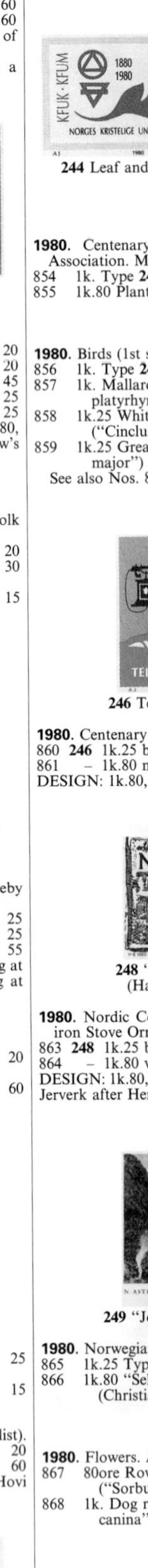

237 Ski Jumping at Huseby, 1879 **238** "Portrait of Girl" (M. Stoltenberg)

1979. Centenary of Skiing Competitions at Huseby and Holmenkollen.
838 **237** 1k. green 30 25
839 – 1k.25 red 30 25
840 – 1k.80 blue 25 55
DESIGNS: 1k.25, Crown Prince Olav ski jumping at Holmenkollen, 1922; 1k.80, Cross-country skiing at Holmenkollen, 1976.

1979. International Year of the Child. Mult.
841 1k.25 Type **238** 25 20
842 1k.80 "Portrait of Boy" (H. C. F. Hosenfelder) . . 35 60

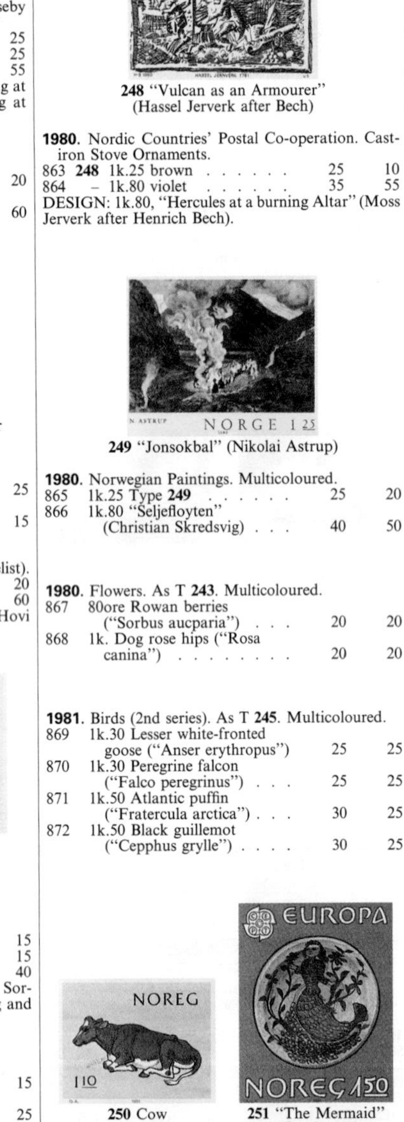

239 Road to Briksdal Glacier **240** Falkberget (after Harald Dal)

1979. Norwegian Scenery. Multicoloured.
843 1k. Type **239** 30 25
844 1k.25 Skjernoysund, near Mandal 30 15

1979. Birth Centenary of Johan Falkberget (novelist).
845 **240** 1k.25 brown 30 20
846 – 1k.80 blue 40 60
DESIGN: 1k.80, "Ann-Magritt and the Hovi Bullock" (statue by Kristofer Leirdal).

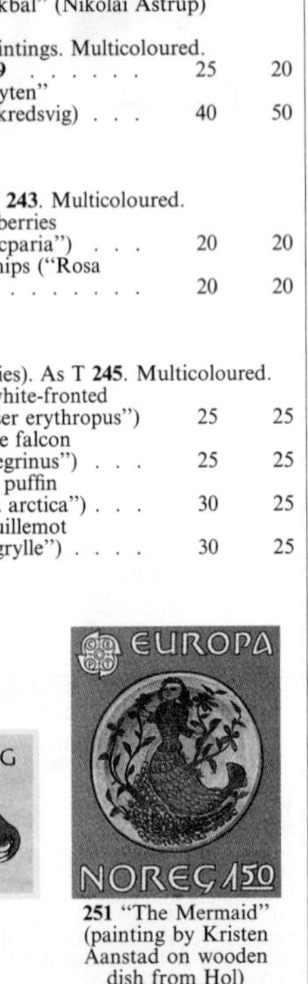

242 Steam Train on Kylling Bridge, Verma, Romsdal **243** Glacier Buttercup ("Ranunculus glacialis")

1979. Norwegian Engineering.
848 **242** 1k.25 black and brown . . 30 15
849 – 2k. black and blue . . . 30 15
850 – 10k. brown and bistre . . 1·60 40
DESIGNS: 2k. Vessingsjo Dam, Nea, Sor-Trondelag; 10k. Statfjord A offshore oil drilling and production platform.

1979. Flowers. Multicoloured.
851 80ore Type **243** 25 15
852 1k. Alpine cinquefoil ("Potentilla crantzii") . . . 20 25
853 1k.25 Purple saxifrage ("Saxifraga oppositifolia") 20 15
See also Nos. 867/8.

244 Leaf and Emblems **245** Oystercatcher Chick ("Haematopus ostralegus")

1980. Centenary of Norwegian Christian Youth Association. Multicoloured.
854 1k. Type **244** 25 25
855 1k.80 Plant and emblems . . 35 50

1980. Birds (1st series). Multicoloured.
856 1k. Type **245** 20 25
857 1k. Mallard chick ("Anas platyrhynchos") 20 25
858 1k.25 White-throated dipper ("Cinclus cinclus") 25 15
859 1k.25 Great tit ("Parus major") 25 15
See also Nos. 869/72, 894/5 and 914/15.

246 Telephone and Dish Aerial

1980. Centenary of Norwegian Telephone Service.
860 **246** 1k.25 brown, purple & bl 25 25
861 – 1k.80 multicoloured . . . 35 45
DESIGN: 1k.80, Erecting a telephone pole.

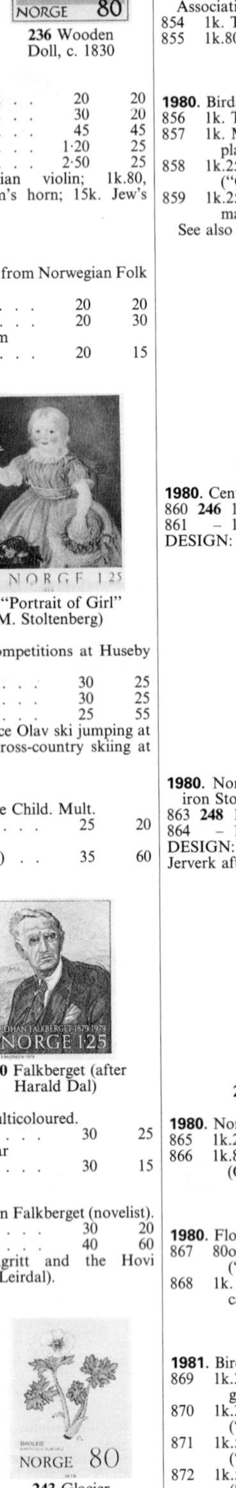

248 "Vulcan as an Armourer" (Hassel Jerverk after Bech)

1980. Nordic Countries' Postal Co-operation. Cast-iron Stove Ornaments.
863 **248** 1k.25 brown 25 10
864 – 1k.80 violet 35 55
DESIGN: 1k.80, "Hercules at a burning Altar" (Moss Jerverk after Henrich Bech).

249 "Jonsokbal" (Nikolai Astrup)

1980. Norwegian Paintings. Multicoloured.
865 1k.25 Type **249** 25 20
866 1k.80 "Seljefloyten" (Christian Skredsvig) . . . 40 50

1980. Flowers. As T **243**. Multicoloured.
867 80ore Rowan berries ("Sorbus aucparia") . . . 20 20
868 1k. Dog rose hips ("Rosa canina") 20 20

1981. Birds (2nd series). As T **245**. Multicoloured.
869 1k.30 Lesser white-fronted goose ("Anser erythropus") 25 25
870 1k.30 Peregrine falcon ("Falco peregrinus") . . . 25 25
871 1k.50 Atlantic puffin ("Fratercula arctica") . . . 30 25
872 1k.50 Black guillemot ("Cepphus grylle") 30 25

250 Cow **251** "The Mermaid" (painting by Kristen Aanstad on wooden dish from Hol)

1981. Centenary of Norwegian Milk Producers' National Association. Multicoloured.
873 1k.10 Type **250** 30 25
874 1k.50 Goat 30 15
See note below No. 433.

1981. Europa. Multicoloured.
875 1k.50 Type **251** 40 20
876 2k.20 "The Proposal" (painting by Ola Hansson on box from Nes) 60 55
See note below No. 433.

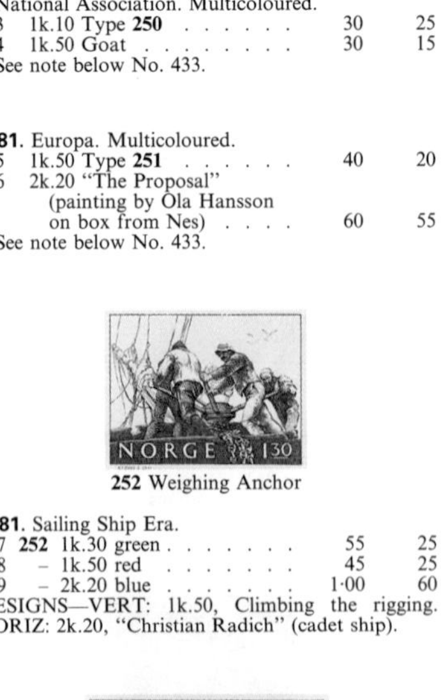

252 Weighing Anchor

1981. Sailing Ship Era.
877 **252** 1k.30 green 55 25
878 – 1k.50 red 45 25
879 – 2k.20 blue . . . . 1·00 60
DESIGNS—VERT: 1k.50, Climbing the rigging. HORIZ: 2k.20, "Christian Radich" (cadet ship).

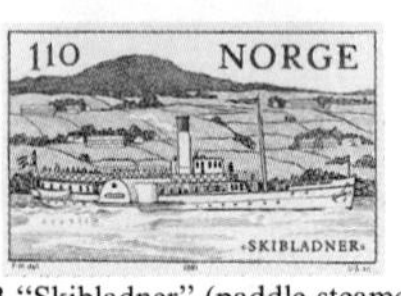

253 "Skibladner" (paddle-steamer)

1981. Norwegian Lake Shipping.
880 **253** 1k.10 brown 45 20
881 – 1k.30 green 45 35
882 – 1k.50 red 45 20
883 – 2k.30 blue 90 45
DESIGNS: 1k.30, "Victoria" (ferry); 1k.50, "Faemund II" (ferry); 2k.30, "Storegut" (train ferry).

254 Handicapped People as Part of Community

1981. International Year of Disabled Persons.
884 **254** 1k.50 pink, red and blue 30 25
885 – 2k.20 blue, deep blue and red 45 50
DESIGN: 2k.20, Handicapped and non-handicapped people walking together.

255 "Interior in Blue" (Harriet Backer)

1981. Norwegian Paintings. Multicoloured.
886 1k.50 Type **255** 30 25
887 1k.70 "Peat Moor on Jaeren" (Kitty Lange Kielland) . . 45 50

256 Hajalmar Branting and Christian Lange

1981. Nobel Peace Prize Winners of 1921.
888 **256** 5k. black 90 25

257 "One of the Magi" (detail from Skjak tapestry, 1625) **258** Ski Sticks

1981. Tapestries. Multicoloured.
889 1k.10 Type **257** 20 15
890 1k.30 "Adoration of Christ" (detail, Skjak tapestry, 1625) 20 35
891 1k.50 "Marriage in Cana" (pillow slip from Storen, 18th century) (29 × 36 mm) 20 15

1982. World Ski Championships, Oslo.
892 **258** 2k. red and blue 45 25
893 – 3k. blue and red 50 40
DESIGN: 3k. Skis.

1982. Birds (3rd series). As T **245**. Multicoloured.
894 2k. Bluethroat ("Luscinia svecica") 35 15
895 2k. European robin ("Erithacus rubecula") . . 35 15

259 Nurse **260** King Haakon VII disembarking from "Heimdal" after Election, 1905

1982. Anti-tuberculosis Campaign. Mult.
896 2k. Type **259** 45 15
897 3k. Microscope 50 45
See note below No. 433.

1982. Europa.
898 **260** 2k. brown 95 25
899 – 3k. blue . . . . 1·10 50
DESIGN: 3k. Crown Prince Olav greeting King Haakon VII after liberation, 1945.

261 "Girls from Telemark" (Erik Werenskiold)

1982. Norwegian Paintings. Multicoloured.
900 1k.75 Type **261** 40 40
901 2k. "Tone Veli by Fence" (Henrik Sorenson) (vert) 40 25
See note below No. 433.

262 Consecration Ceremony, Nidaros Cathedral, Trondheim

1982. 25th Anniv of King Olav V's Reign.
902 **262** 3k. violet 50 55

263 "Bjornstjerne Bjornson on Balcony at Aulestad" (Erik Werenskiold)

1982. Writers' Birth Anniversaries. Multicoloured.
903 1k.75 Type **263** (150th anniv) 45 25
904 2k. "Sigrid Undset" (after A. C. Svarstad) (birth centenary) 45 25

264 Construction of Letter "A" **265** Fridtjof Nansen

1982. Centenary of Graphical Union of Norway.
905 **264** 2k. yellow, green and black . . . 45 25
906 – 3k. multicoloured . . . 50 45
DESIGN: 3k. Offset litho printing rollers.

1982. 1922 Nobel Peace Prize Winner.
907 **265** 3k. blue . . . 50 40
See note below No. 433.

266 "Christmas Tradition" (Adolf Tidemand)

267 Buhund (farm dog)

1982. Christmas.
908 **266** 1k.75 multicoloured . . . 35 15

1983. Norwegian Dogs. Multicoloured.
909 2k. Type **267** . . . 45 35
910 2k.50 Elkhound . . . 45 15
911 3k.50 Lundehund (puffin hunter) . . . 45 60
See note below No. 433.

268 Mountain Scenery

269 Edvard Grieg with Concerto in A minor

1983. Nordic Countries' Postal Co-operation. "Visit the North". Multicoloured.
912 2k.50 Type **268** . . . 45 15
913 3k.50 Fjord scenery . . . 60 55

1983. Birds (4th series). As T **245**. Mult.
914 2k.50 Barnacle goose ("Branta leucopsis") . . . 45 15
915 2k.50 Little auk ("Alle alle") . . . 45 15

1983. Europa.
916 **269** 2k.50 red . . . 1·00 25
917 – 3k.50 blue and green . . . 1·00 75
DESIGN—VERT: 3k.50, Statue of Niels Henrik Abel (mathematician) by Gustav Vigeland.

270 Arrows forming Posthorn

1983. World Communications Year. Multicoloured.
918 2k.50 Type **270** . . . 45 20
919 3k.50 Arrows circling globe . . . 60 60

271 King Olav V and Royal Birch, Molde

1983. 80th Birthday of King Olav V.
920 **271** 5k. green . . . 1·00 25

272 Lie

273 Northern Femboring

1983. 150th Birth Anniv of Jonas Lie (author).
921 **272** 2k.50 red . . . 45 25

1983. North Norwegian Ships.
922 **273** 2k. blue and brown . . . 45 35
923 – 3k. brown and blue . . . 50 50
DESIGNS: 3k. Northern jekt.
See note below No. 433.

274 "The Sleigh Ride" (Axel Ender)

275 Post Office Counter

1983. Christmas. Multicoloured.
924 2k. Type **274** . . . 45 25
925 2k.50 "The Guests are arriving" (Gustav Wendel) . . . 45 15

1984. Postal Work. Multicoloured.
926 2k. Type **275** . . . 35 25
927 2k.50 Postal sorting . . . 45 25
928 3k.50 Postal delivery . . . 60 50

276 Freshwater Fishing

277 Magnetic Meridians and Parallels

1984. Sport Fishing.
929 **276** 2k.50 red . . . 30 10
930 – 3k. green . . . 35 40
931 – 3k.50 blue . . . 90 45
DESIGNS: 3k. Atlantic salmon fishing; 3k.50, Sea fishing.

1984. Birth Bicentenary of Christopher Hansteen (astronomer and geophysicist).
932 **277** 3k.50 blue . . . 60 45
933 – 5k. red . . . 1·00 40
DESIGN—VERT: 5k. Portrait of Hansteen by Johan Gorbitz.

278 Bridge

279 Vegetables, Fruit and Herbs

1984. Europa. 25th Anniv of European Post and Telecommunications Conference.
934 **278** 2k.50 multicoloured . . . 75 15
935 3k.50 multicoloured . . . 95 55

1984. Centenary of Norwegian Horticultural Society. Multicoloured.
936 2k. Type **279** . . . 25 30
937 2k.50 Rose and garland of flowers . . . 50 15

280 Honey Bees

281 Holberg (after J. M. Bernigeroth)

1984. Centenaries of Norwegian Beekeeping Society and Norwegian Poultry-breeding Society. Mult.
938 2k.50 Type **280** . . . 45 15
939 2k.50 Leghorn cock . . . 45 15
See note below No. 433.

1984. 300th Birth Anniv of Ludvig Holberg (writer).
940 **281** 2k.50 red . . . 45 25

282 Children reading

284 Karius and Baktus (tooth decay bacteria)

283 Entering Parliamentary Chamber, 2 July 1884

1984. 150th Anniv of "Norsk Penning-Magazin" (1st weekly magazine in Norway).
941 **282** 2k.50 purple, blue and red 45 15
942 – 3k.50 orange and violet 60 45
DESIGN: 3k.50, 1st edition of "Norsk Penning-Magazin".

1984. Cent of Norwegian Parliament.
943 **283** 7k.50 brown . . . 1·50 70

1984. Characters from Stories by Thorbjorn Egner. Multicoloured.
944 2k. Type **284** . . . 60 20
945 2k. The tree shrew playing guitar . . . 60 20
946 2k.50 Kasper, Jesper and Jonatan (Rovers) in Kardemomme Town . . . 65 15
947 2k.50 Chief Constable Bastian . . . 65 15

285 Mount Sagbladet (Saw Blade)

1985. Antarctic Mountains. Multicoloured.
948 2k.50 Type **285** . . . 50 10
949 3k.50 Mount Hoggestabben (Chopping Block) . . . 65 70

286 Return of Crown Prince Olav, 1945

1985. 40th Anniv of Liberation.
950 **286** 3k.50 red and blue . . . 60 50

287 Kongsten Fort

1985. 300th Anniv of Kongsten Fort.
951 **287** 2k.50 multicoloured . . . 45 15

288 Bronze Cannon, 1596

289 "Boy and Girl" (detail)

1985. Artillery Anniversaries. Multicoloured.
952 3k. Type **288** (300th anniv of Artillery) . . . 50 50
953 4k. Cannon on sledge carriage, 1758 (bicentenary of Artillery Officers Training School) . . . 70 40

1985. International Youth Year. Sculptures in Vigeland Park, Oslo. Multicoloured.
954 2k. Type **289** . . . 35 25
955 3k.50 Bronze fountain (detail) 70 55
See note below No. 433.

290 Torgeir Augundsson (fiddler)

291 Workers at Glomfjord

1985. Europa. Music Year.
956 **290** 2k.50 red . . . 75 20
957 – 3k.50 blue . . . 90 50
DESIGN: 3k.50, Ole Bull (composer and violinist).

1985. Centenary of Electricity in Norway.
958 **291** 2k.50 red and scarlet . . . 45 15
959 – 4k. blue and green . . . 70 35
DESIGN: 4k. Men working on overhead cable.

293 Carl Deichman on Book Cover

294 Wreath

1985. Bicentenary of Public Libraries.
961 **293** 2k.50 sepia and brown . . . 50 15
962 – 10k. green . . . 1·90 50
DESIGN—HORIZ: 10k. Library interior.

1985. Christmas. Multicoloured.
963 2k. Type **294** . . . 60 25
964 2k.50 Northern bullfinches . . . 60 15

295 "Berghavn" (dredger)

296 Sun

1985. 250th Anniv of Port Authorities and Bicentenary of Hydrography in Norway.
965 **295** 2k.50 purple, orange & bl 55 5·00
966 – 5k blue, green and brown 75 45
DESIGN: 5k. Sextant and detail of chart No. 1 of Lt. F.C. Grove showing Trondheim sealane, 1791.

1986.
967 **296** 2k.10 orange and brown 45 15
968 – 2k.30 green and blue . . . 45 15
970 – 2k.70 pink and red . . . 60 20
971 – 4k. blue and green . . . 85 15
DESIGNS: 2k.30, Atlantic cod and herring; 2k.70, Flowers; 4k. Star ornaments.

297 Marksman in Prone Position

1986. World Biathlon Championships. Mult.
977 2k.50 Type **297** . . . 70 10
978 3k.50 Marksman standing to take aim . . . 55 55

298 Industry and Countryside

299 Stone Cutter

1986. Europa. Multicoloured.
979 2k.50 Type **298** . . . 60 20
980 3k.50 Dead and living forest, mountains and butterflies . . . 1·00 70

1986. Centenary of Norwegian Craftsmen's Federation.
981 **299** 2k.50 lake and red . . . 45 15
982 – 7k. blue and red . . . 1·10 60
DESIGN: 7k. Carpenter.

300 Moss

1986. Nordic Countries' Postal Co-operation. Twinned Towns. Multicoloured.
983 2k.50 Type **300** . . . 50 15
984 4k. Alesund . . . 60 40
See note below No. 433.

301 Hans Polson Egede (missionary) and Map

303 "Olav Kyrre founds Diocese in Nidaros"

1986. Birth Anniversaries.
985 **301** 2k.10 brown and red . . 45 50
986 – 2k.50 red, green and blue 50 15
987 – 3k. brown and red . . . 50 40
988 – 4k. purple and lilac . . . 70 40
DESIGNS: 2k.10, Type **301** (300th anniv); 2k.50, Herman Wildenvey (poet) and poem carved in wall at Stavern (centenary); 3k. Tore Ojasaeter (poet) and old cupboard from Skjak (centenary); 4k. Engebret Soot (engineer) and lock gates, Orje (centenary).
See note below No. 433.

1986. Christmas. Stained Glass Windows by Gabriel Kielland in Nidaros Cathedral, Trondheim. Multicoloured.
990 2k.10 Type **303** 50 20
991 2k.50 "The King and the Peasant at Sul" 50 15

304 Doves

305 Numeral

1986. International Peace Year.
992 **304** 15k. red, blue and green 3·25 60

1987.
993 **305** 3k.50 yellow, red and blue 60 50
994 4k.50 blue, yellow & green 75 40

306 Wooden Building

1987. Europa. Multicoloured.
1000 2k.70 Type **306** 75 15
1001 4k.50 Building of glass and stone . . . . 1·30 40

307 The Final Vote

309 Funnel-shaped Chanterelle ("Cantharellus tubaeformis")

1987. 150th Anniv of Laws on Local Councils (granting local autonomy).
1002 **307** 12k. green . . . . 2·40 50

1987. Fungi (1st series). Multicoloured.
1004 2k.70 Type **309** 45 15
1005 2k.70 The gypsy ("Rozites caperata") 45 15
See also Nos. 1040/1 and 1052/3.

310 Bjornstad Farm from Vaga

1987. Centenary of Sandvig Collections, Maihaugen.
1006 **310** 2k.70 sepia and brown 50 15
1007 – 3k.50 purple and blue . 60 50
DESIGN: 3k.50, "Horse and Rider" (wooden carving, Christen Erlandsen Listad).

311 Valevag Churchyard

1987. Birth Centenary of Fartein Valen (composer).
1008 **311** 2k.30 blue and green . . 45 40
1009 – 4k.50 brown 90 25
DESIGN—VERT: 4k.50, Fartein Valen.
See note below No. 433.

312 "Storm at Sea" (Christian Krohg)

1987. Paintings. Multicoloured.
1010 2k.70 Type **312** 50 15
1011 5k. "The Farm" (Gerhard Munthe) . . . . 1·00 40

314 Cat with Children making Decorations

1987. Christmas. Multicoloured.
1013 2k.30 Type **314** 50 40
1014 2k.70 Dog with children making gingersnaps . . . 50 15

315 Dales Pony

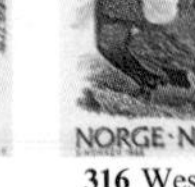

316 Western Capercaillie

1987. Native Ponies.
1015 **315** 2k.30 deep brown, green and brown 45 50
1016 – 2k.70 buff, brown & blue 50 20
1017 – 4k.50 brown, red and blue 70 40
DESIGNS: 2k.70, Fjord pony; 4k.50, Nordland pony.
See note below No. 433.

1988. Wildlife.
1018 – 2k.60 deep brown, brown and green . . . 50 20
1019 **316** 2k.90 black, brn & grn 50 15
1020 – 3k. brown, grey and green 50 15
1021 – 3k.20 ultramarine, green and blue 50 15
1022 – 3k.80 brown, blue & blk 60 15
1023 – 4k. brown, red and green 70 15
1024 – 4k.50 brown, green & bl 75 25
1025 – 5k.50 brown, grey & grn 95 25
1026 – 6k.40 brown, blk & grn 1·10 35
DESIGNS: 2k.60, Fox; 3k. Stoat; 3k.20, Mute swan; 3k.80, Reindeer; 4k. Eurasian red squirrel; 4k.50, Beaver; 5k.50, Lynx; 6k.40, Tengmalm's owl.

317 Band

1988. Centenary of Salvation Army in Norway. Multicoloured.
1035 2k.90 Type **317** 50 15
1036 4k.80 Othilie Tonning (early social worker) and Army nurse 85 55

318 Building Fortress

1988. Military Anniversaries.
1037 **318** 2k.50 green 45 25
1038 – 2k.90 brown 50 15
1039 – 4k.60 blue 75 45
DESIGNS: 2k.50, Type **318** (300th anniv of Defence Construction Service); 2k.90, Corps members in action (centenary of Army Signals corps); 4k.60, Making pontoon bridge (centenary of Engineer Corps).

1988. Fungi (2nd series). As T **309**. Mult.
1040 2k.90 Wood blewits ("Lepista nuda") 50 15
1041 2k.90 "Lactarius deterrimus" 50 15

319 Globe

320 King Olav V

1988. European Campaign for Interdependence and Solidarity of North and South.
1042 **319** 25k. multicoloured . . . 5·25 75

1988. 85th Birthday of King Olav V.
1043 **320** 2k.90 multicoloured . . 50 15

321 "Prinds Gustav" (paddle-steamer)

322 King Christian IV

1988. Europa. Transport and Communications.
1045 **321** 2k.90 black, red and blue 85 15
1046 – 3k.80 blue, red & yellow 1·30 75
DESIGN: 3k.80, Heroybrua Bridge.

1988. 400th Anniv of Christian IV's Accession to Danish and Norwegian Thrones.
1047 **322** 2k.50 black, stone & vio 60 20
1048 – 10k. multicoloured . . . 1·75 40
DESIGN: 10k. 1628 silver coin and extract from decree on mining in Norway.

324 Ludvig with Ski Stick

325 Start and Finish of Race

1988. Christmas. Multicoloured.
1050 2k.90 Type **324** 55 15
1051 2k.90 Ludvig reading letter 55 15

1989. Fungi (3rd series). As T **309**. Multicoloured.
1052 3k. Chanterelle ("Cantharellus cibarius") 50 15
1053 3k. Butter mushroom ("Suillus luteus") 50 15

1989. World Cross-country Championship, Stavanger.
1054 **325** 5k. multicoloured . . . 90 35

326 Vardo

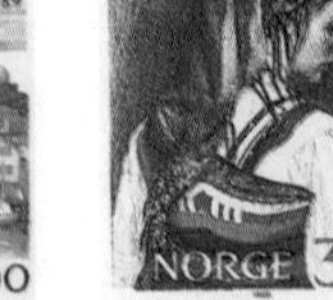

327 Setesdal Woman

1989. Town Bicentenaries.
1055 **326** 3k. blue, red & light blue 50 15
1056 – 4k. purple, blue & orange 60 50
DESIGN: 4k. Hammerfest.

1989. Nordic Countries' Postal Co-operation. Traditional Costumes. Multicoloured.
1057 3k. Type **327** 50 25
1058 4k. Kautokeino man 85 55

328 Children making Snowman

329 Rooster and Cover of 1804 First Reader

1989. Europa. Children's Games. Multicoloured.
1059 3k.70 Type **328** . . . . . 1·00 60
1060 5k. Cat's cradle . . . . . . 1·50 70
See note below No. 433.

1989. 250th Anniv of Primary Schools.
1061 **329** 2k.60 multicoloured . . 50 45
1062 – 3k. brown 50 15
DESIGN: 3k. Pocket calculator and child writing.

332 Arnulf Overland (poet, centenary)

333 Star Decoration

1989. Writers' Birth Anniversaries.
1065 **332** 3k. red and blue 50 15
1066 – 25k. blue, orange & green . . . . 4·50 75
DESIGN: 25k. Hanna Winsnes (pseudonym Hugo Schwartz) (bicentenary).

1989. Christmas. Tree Decorations. Mult.
1067 3k. Type **333** 50 15
1068 3k. Bauble 50 15

334 Larvik Manor

335 Emblem

1989. Manor Houses.
1069 **334** 3k. brown 50 15
1070 – 3k. green 50 15
DESIGN: No. 1070, Rosendal Barony.

1990. Winter Cities Events, Tromso.
1071 **335** 5k. multicoloured . . . 90 35

336 Common Spotted Orchid ("Dactylorhiza fuchsii")

337 Merchant Navy, Airforce, Home Guard, "Moses" (coastal gun) and Haakon VII's Monogram

1990. Orchids (1st series). Multicoloured.
1072 3k.20 Type **336** 50 15
1073 3k.20 Dark red helleborine ("Epipactis atrorubens") 50 15
See also Nos. 1141/2.

1990. 50th Anniv of Norway's Entry into Second World War. Multicoloured.
1074 3k.20 Type **337** 50 15
1075 4k. Second Battle of Narvik, 1940 . . . . 70 50

339 Trondheim Post Office

340 "Tordenskiold" (from print by J. W. Tegner after Balthazar Denner)

1990. Europa. Post Office Buildings. Mult.
1077 3k.20 Type **339** 85 25
1078 4k. Longyearbyen Post Office . . . . 1·30 50

1990. 300th Birth Anniv of Admiral Tordenskiold (Peter Wessel). Multicoloured.
1079 3k.20 Type **340** 50 15
1080 5k. Tordenskiold's coat-of-arms 75 40

341 Svendsen

343 "Children and Snowman" (Ragni Engstrom Nilsen)

1990. 150th Birth Anniv of Johan Svendsen (composer and conductor).

1081	**341**	2k.70 black and red . .	50	40
1082	–	15k. brown and yellow	2·50	45

DESIGN: 15k. Svendsen Monument (Stinius Fredriksen), Oslo.

1990. Christmas. Children's Prize-winning Drawings. Multicoloured.

1084	3k.20 Type **343**	55	15
1085	3k.20 "Christmas Church" (Jorgen Ingier)	55	15

344 Nobel Medal and Soderblom

1990. 60th Anniv of Award of Nobel Peace Prize to Nathan Soderblom, Archbishop of Uppsala.

1086	**344**	30k. brown, blue and red	5·75	70

345 Plan and Elevation of Container Ship and Propeller

1991. Centenaries of Federation of Engineering Industries (1989) and Union of Iron and Metal Workers.

1087	**345**	5k. multicoloured . . .	85	60

346 Satellite transmitting to Tromso

1991. Europa. Europe in Space. Mult.

1088	3k.20 Type **346**	85	25
1089	4k. Rocket leaving Andoya rocket range	1·20	40

See note below No. 433.

347 Christiansholm Fortress (late 17th- century)

348 Fountain, Vigeland Park, Oslo

1991. 350th Anniv of Kristiansand. Each black, blue and red.

1090	3k.20 Type **347**	60	25
1091	5k.50 Present day view of Christiansholm Fortress	95	30

1991. Nordic Countries' Postal Co-operation. Tourism. Multicoloured.

1092	3k.20 Type **348**	60	15
1093	4k. Globe, North Cape Plateau	95	65

349 "Skomvaer III" (lifeboat)

352 Posthorn

1991. Centenary of Norwegian Society for Sea Rescue.

1094	**349**	3k.20 brown, black & grn	50	25
1095	–	27k. brown, grey & purple	5·50	85

DESIGN—VERT: 27k. "Colin Archer" (first lifeboat).

1991.

1098	**352**	1k. black and orange . .	30	15
1099		2k. red and green . . .	45	25
1100		3k. green and blue . . .	50	15
1101		4k. red and orange . . .	70	15
1102		5k. blue and green . . .	90	25
1103		6k. red and green . . .	1·00	25
1104		7k. blue and brown . . .	1·30	25
1105		8k. green and purple . .	1·40	40
1106		9k. brown and blue . . .	1·60	35

353 Guisers with Goat Head

1991. Christmas. Guising. Multicoloured.

1120	3k.20 Type **353**	55	25
1121	3k.20 Guisers with lantern	55	25

354 Queen Sonja

355 King Harald

356 King Harald

1992.

1122	**354**	2k.80 lake, purple & red	50	25
1123		3k. green, deep green and turquoise	50	15
1124	**355**	3k.30 blue, ultramarine and light blue	60	15
1125		3k.50 black and grey . .	60	15
1127		4k.50 deep red and red	75	50
1128		5k.50 brown, sepia & blk	95	25
1129		5k.60 orange, red and vermilion	1·00	25
1131		6k.50 emerald, green and turquoise	1·10	55
1132		6k.60 maroon, purple and brown	1·10	25
1133		7k.50 violet, lilac and purple	50	65
1134		8k.50 chestnut, deep brown and brown . .	60	60
1135	**356**	10k. green	1·75	25
1438		20k. violet	3·25	1·30
1138		30k. blue	4·75	50
1139		50k. green	9·50	1·30

1992. Orchids (2nd series). As T **336**. Mult.

1141	3k.30 Lady's slipper orchid ("Cypripedium calceolus")	60	25
1142	3k.30 Fly orchid ("Ophrys insectifera")	60	25

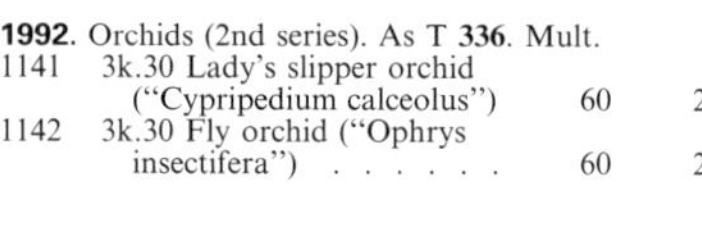

358 "Restaurationen" (emigrant sloop)

1992. Europa. 500th Anniv of Discovery of America by Columbus. Transatlantic Ships. Multicoloured.

1144	3k.30 Type **358**	95	25
1145	4k.20 "Stavangerfjord" (liner) and American skyline	1·40	45

See note below No. 433.

359 Norwegian Pavilion, Rainbow and Ship

360 Molde

1992. "Expo '92" World's Fair, Seville. Mult.

1146	3k.30 Type **359**	60	25
1147	5k.20 Mountains, rainbow, fish and oil rig	95	45

1992. 250th Anniversaries of Molde and Kristiansund.

1148	**360**	3k.30 blue, green & brn	50	25
1149	–	3k.30 blue, brown & lt bl	60	25

DESIGN: No. 1149, Kristiansund.

361 Banners and Lillehammer Buildings

363 Gnomes below Pillar Box

1992. Winter Olympic Games, Lillehammer (1994) (1st issue). Multicoloured.

1150	3k.30 Type **361**	60	25
1151	4k.20 Flags	70	50

See also Nos. 1169/70 and 1175/80.

1992. Christmas. Christmas card designs by Otto Moe. Multicoloured.

1153	3k.30 Type **363**	55	25
1154	3k.30 Gnome posting letter	55	25

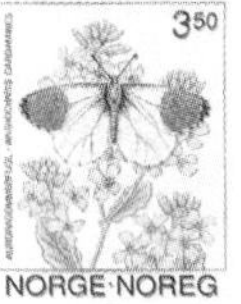

364 Orange-tip ("Anthocaris cardamines")

366 Grieg

1993. Butterflies (1st series). Multicoloured.

1155	3k.50 Type **364**	60	25
1156	3k.50 Small tortoiseshell ("Aglais urticae")	60	25

See also Nos. 1173/4.

1993. 150th Birth Anniv of Edvard Grieg (composer). Multicoloured.

1158	3k.50 Type **366**	60	25
1159	5k.50 "Spring"	95	40

367 Two-man Kayak on Lake

368 Richard With (founder) and "Vesteraalen"

1993. Nordic Countries' Postal Co-operation. Tourist Activities. Multicoloured.

1160	4k. Type **367**	70	25
1161	4k.50 White-water rafting	90	40

1993. Centenary of Express Coaster Service.

1162	**368**	3k.50 blue, violet and red	60	25
1163	–	4k.50 multicoloured . .	90	45

DESIGN: 4k.50, "Kong Harald".

369 Handball

370 Johann Castberg (politician)

1993. Sports Events. Multicoloured.

1164	3k.50 Type **369** (Women's World Championship, Norway)	60	25
1165	5k.50 Cycling (World Championships, Oslo and Hamar)	95	40

1993. Centenary of Workforce Protection Legislation.

1166	**370**	3k.50 brown and blue . .	60	25
1167	–	12k. blue and brown . .	2·25	55

DESIGN: 12k. Betzy Kjelsberg (first woman factory inspector).

372 Torch Bearer on Skis

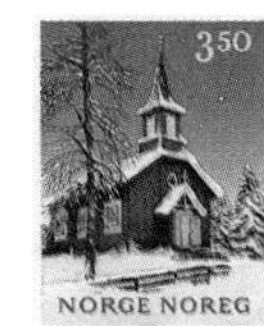

373 Store Mangen Chapel

1993. Winter Olympic Games, Lillehammer (1994) (2nd issue). Morgedal–Lillehammer Torch Relay. Multicoloured.

1169	3k.50 Type **372**	60	25
1170	3k.50 Lillehammer	60	25

Nos. 1169/70 were issued together, se-tenant, forming a composite design.

1993. Christmas. Multicoloured.

1171	3k.50 Type **373**	60	25
1172	3k.50 Stamnes church, Sandnessjoen	60	25

1994. Butterflies (2nd series). As T **364**. Mult.

1173	3k.50 Northern clouded yellow ("Colias hecla")	60	25
1174	3k.50 Freya's fritillary ("Clossiana freija") . . .	60	25

374 Flags

375 Cross-country Skiing

1994. Winter Olympic Games, Lillehammer (3rd issue). Multicoloured.

1175	3k.50 Type **374**	80	30
1176	3k.50 Flags (different) . . .	80	30
1177	3k.50 Lillehammer (church) and rings	80	30
1178	3k.50 Lillehammer (ski jump) and rings	80	30
1179	4k.50 Flags of European countries	75	50
1180	5k.50 Flags of non-European countries . . .	95	40

Nos. 1175/8 were issued together, se-tenant, forming a composite design.

1994. Paralympic Games, Lillehammer. Mult.

1181	4k.50 Type **375**	1·10	50
1182	5k.50 Downhill skiing . . .	1·00	45

376 King Christian VII's Signature and Seal

1994. Bicentenary of Tromso.

1183	**376**	3k.50 red, bistre & brn	60	25
1184	–	4k.50 blue, yellow and light blue	75	55

DESIGN: 4k.50, Tromsdalen church.

377 Mount Floy Incline Railway Cars, Bergen

1994. Tourism. Multicoloured.

1185	4k. Type **377**	70	40
1186	4k.50 "Svolvaer Goat" (rock formation), Lofoten . . .	85	55
1187	5k.50 Beacon, World's End, Tjome	95	35

378 Osterdal Farm Buildings

1994. Cent of Norwegian Folk Museum, Bygdoy.

1188	**378**	3k. multicoloured . . .	50	40
1189	–	3k.50 blue, yellow and purple	60	25

DESIGN: 3k.50, Horse-drawn sleigh, 1750 (Torsten Hoff).

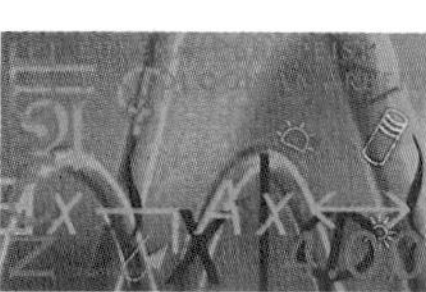
379 Technological Symbols and Formula ("Glass Flasks")

1994. EUREKA (European technology co-operation organization) Conference of Ministers, Lillehammer. Multicoloured.

1190	4k. Type **379**	60	45
1191	4k.50 Technological symbols ("Electronic Chips") . . .	85	45

380 Electric Tram and Street Plan of Oslo, 1894 — **382** Sledge

1994. Centenary of Electric Trams. Multicoloured.

1192 3k.50 Type **380** 60 25
1193 12k. Articulated tram and Oslo route map . . . . . 3·50 85

1994. Christmas.

1195 **382** 3k.50 red and black . . 60 25
1196 – 3k.50 ultramarine, blue and black 60 25

DESIGN: No. 1196, Kick-sledge.

383 Cowberry ("Vaccinium vitis-idaea") — **384** Swan Pharmacy, Bergen

1995. Wild Berries (1st Series). Multicoloured.

1197 3k.50 Type **383** 60 25
1198 3k.50 Bilberry ("Vaccinium myrtillus") 60 25

See also Nos. 1224/5.

1995. 400th Anniv of Norwegian Pharmacies. Multicoloured.

1199 3k.50 Type **384** 60 25
1200 25k. Scales, pestle and mortar and ingredients . . 5·25 1·90

385 German Commander saluting Terje Rollem (Home Guard commander)

1995. 50th Anniv of Liberation of Norway.

1201 **385** 3k.50 silver, green and black 60 25
1202 – 4k.50 silver, blue and black 90 70
1203 – 5k.50 silver, red and black 95 40

DESIGNS: 4k.50, King Haakon VII and family returning to Norway; 5k.50, Children waving Norwegian flags.

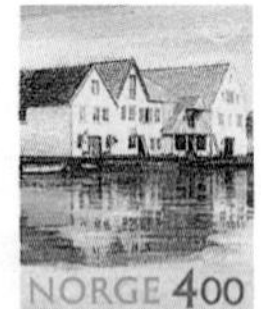

386 Old Moster Church — **387** Skudeneshavn

1995. Millenary of Christianity in Norway. Multicoloured.

1204 3k.50 Type **386** 60 25
1205 15k. Slettebakken Church, Bergen . . . . 3·00 1·20

1995. Nordic Countries' Postal Co-operation. Tourism. Multicoloured.

1206 4k. Type **387** 70 55
1207 4k.50 Hole in the Hat (coastal rock formation) 85 55

388 Flagstad as Isolde — **389** Disputants in Conflict

1995. Birth Centenary of Kirsten Flagstad (opera singer). Multicoloured.

1208 3k.50 Type **388** 60 25
1209 5k.50 Flagstad in scene from "Lohengrin" (Wagner) . . 95 40

1995. Bicentenary of Conciliation Boards. Multicoloured.

1210 7k. Type **389** . . . . . . 1·25 70
1211 12k. Disputants in conciliation with mediator 60 85

390 Letter and Vice-regent Hannibal Sehested (founder)

1995. 350th Anniv (1997) of Norwegian Postal Service (1st issue). Multicoloured.

1212 3k.50 Type **390** (letter post, 1647) 80 55
1213 3k.50 Wax seal (registered post, 1745) 80 55
1214 3k.50 Postmarks (1845) . . 80 55
1215 3k.50 Banknotes, coins and money orders (transfer of funds, 1883) 80 55
1216 3k.50 Editions of "Norska Intelligenz-Sedler" and "Arkiv" (newspapers and magazines, 1660) 80 55
1217 3k.50 Address label, cancellations and "Constitutionen" (paddle-steamer) (parcel post, 1827) 80 55
1218 3k.50 Stamps (1855) 80 55
1219 3k.50 Savings book (Post Office Savings Bank, 1950) 80 55

The dates are those of the introduction of the various services.

See also Nos. 1237/44 and 1283/90.

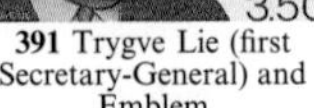

391 Trygve Lie (first Secretary-General) and Emblem — **392** Woolly Hat

1995. 50th Anniv of U.N.O. Multicoloured.

1220 3k.50 Type **391** 60 25
1221 5k.50 Relief worker, water pump and emblem . . . 95 40

1995. Christmas. Multicoloured.

1222 3k.50 Type **392** 60 25
1223 3k.50 Mitten 65 25

1996. Wild Berries (2nd series). As T **383**. Multicoloured.

1224 3k.50 Wild strawberries ("Fragaria vesca") 60 25
1225 3k.50 Cloudberries ("Rubus chamaemorus") 60 25

393 Advent Bay — **394** Cross-country Skier (Hakon Paulsen)

1996. Svalbard Islands. Multicoloured.

1226 10k. Type **393** . . . . . . 1·90 70
1227 20k. Polar bear . . . . . . 4·25 1·40

1996. Centenary of Modern Olympic Games. Children's Drawings. Multicoloured.

1228 3k.50 Type **394** 60 25
1229 5k.50 Athlete (Emil Tanem) 95 40

395 Besseggen — **396** Steam Train, Urskog-Holand Line

1996. Tourism. U.N.E.S.C.O. World Heritage Sites. Multicoloured.

1230 4k. Type **395** 70 50
1231 4k.50 Stave church, Urnes 75 50
1232 5k.50 Rock carvings, Alta 95 40

See also Nos. 1291/3.

1996. Railway Centenaries. Multicoloured.

1233 3k. Type **396** 50 35
1234 4k.50 Steam train, Setesdal line 90 60

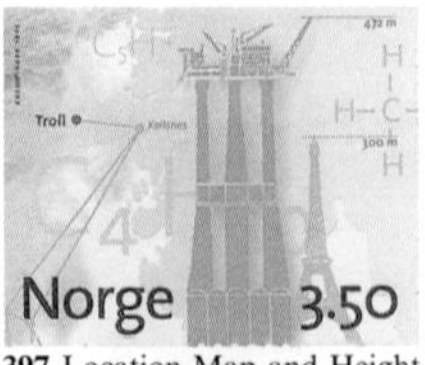

397 Location Map and Height Indicator

1996. Natural Gas Production at Troll, near Bergen. Multicoloured.

1235 3k.50 Type **397** 60 30
1236 25k. Planned route map of pipelines to Europe for next 200 years . . . . . 4·75 1·90

398 Postal Courier crossing Mountains

1996. 350th Anniv (1997) of Postal Service (2nd issue). Multicoloured.

1237 3k.50 Type **398** 75 65
1238 3k.50 "Framnaes" (fjord steamer) 75 65
1239 3k.50 Postal truck in Oslo 75 65
1240 3k.50 Taking mail on board "Ternen" (seaplane) on Jonsvatn Lake, Trondheim 75 65
1241 3k.50 Loading mail train at East Station, Oslo 75 65
1242 3k.50 Rural postman at Mago farm, Nittedal . . . 75 65
1243 3k.50 Serving customer, Elverum post office . . . 75 65
1244 3k.50 Computer, letters and globe 75 65

399 Leif Juster, Sean Connery, Liv Ullmann and Olsen Gang

1996. Centenary of Motion Pictures. Multicoloured.

1245 3k.50 Type **399** 60 25
1246 5k.50 Wenche Foss, Jack Fjeldstad, Marilyn Monroe, blood and gun 95 40
1247 7k. Charlie Chaplin in "Modern Times", Ottar Gladvedt, Laurel and Hardy and Marlene Dietrich . . . . 1·25 65

400 Left Detail of Embroidery — **401** Skram

1996. Christmas. Embroidery Details from Telemark Folk Costume. Multicoloured.

1248 3k.50 Type **400** 60 25
1249 3k.50 Right detail 60 25

Nos. 1248/9 were issued together, se-tenant, forming a composite design.

1996. 150th Birth Anniv of Amalie Skram (writer).

1250 **401** 3k.50 red 60 40
1251 – 15k. violet and red . . . 3·50 1·20

DESIGN: 15k. Scene from dramatisation of "People of Hellemyr".

402 Posthorn — **403** Coltsfoot

1997. Multicoloured, colour of oval given.

1252 **402** 10ore red 10 15
1253 20ore blue 10 15
1254 30ore orange 10 15
1255 40ore black 10 20
1256 50ore green 10 20

1997. Flowers. Multicoloured.

1259 3k.20 Red clover 50 25
1260 3k.40 Marsh marigold . . 50 20
1261 3k.60 Red campion 65 25
1262 3k.70 Type **403** 65 20
1263 3k.80 Wild pansy 70 30
1264 4k. Wood anemone . . . 70 25
1265 4k.30 Lily of the valley . . 70 35
1266 4k.50 White clover 75 25
1267 5k. Harebell 75 25
1268a 5k.40 Oeder's lousewort . . 70 25
1269 5k.50 Hepatica 95 45
1270 6k. Ox-eye daisy 70 40
1271 7k. Yellow wood violet . . 75 60
1272 7k.50 Pale pasque flower 95 35
1273a 8k. White water-lily . . . 1·50 40
1274 13k. Purple saxifrage . . . 2·20 60
1275a 14k. Globe flower . . . . 2·50 80
1276b 25k. Melancholy thistle . . 2·20 1·40

404 Bumble Bee — **405** Ski Jumping

1997. Insects (1st series). Multicoloured.

1277 3k.70 Type **404** 60 25
1278 3k.70 Ladybird 60 25

See also Nos. 1306/7.

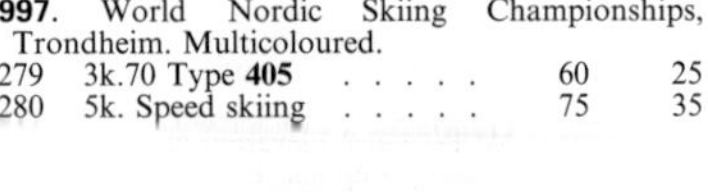

1997. World Nordic Skiing Championships, Trondheim. Multicoloured.

1279 3k.70 Type **405** 60 25
1280 5k. Speed skiing 75 35

406 King Harald (photo by Erik Johansen)

1997. 60th Birthdays of King Harald and Queen Sonja. Multicoloured.

1281 3k.70 Type **406** 60 25
1282 3k.70 Queen Sonja and King Harald (photo by Knut Falch) (horiz) . . . 60 25

407 Hammer, Plumb Line and Hook (post-war reconstruction)

1997. 350th Anniv of Postal Service (3rd issue). Post-war History. Multicoloured.

1283 3k.70 Type **407** 70 75
1284 3k.70 "Kon Tiki" (replica of balsa raft) (Thor Heyerdahl's expedition from Peru to Polynesia, 1947) 70 75
1285 3k.70 Grouse feather (official bird of Rondane National Park (first National Park, 1962)) . . 70 75
1286 3k.70 Hands of man and woman (Welfare State (introduction of National Insurance, 1967)) 70 75
1287 3k.70 Drilling platform, Ekofisk oil field (discovery of oil in Norwegian sector of North Sea, 1969) . . . 70 75
1288 3k.70 Grete Waitz (first women's world Marathon champion, 1983) 70 75
1289 3k.70 Askoy Bridge, 1992 (communications) 70 75
1290 3k.70 Crown Prince Haakon Magnus lighting Olympic flame (Winter Olympic Games, Lillehammer, 1994) 70 75

1997. Tourism. As T **395**. Multicoloured.

1291 4k.30 Roros 70 90
1292 5k. Faerder Lighthouse . . 75 60
1293 6k. Nusfjord . . . . 1·20 45

408 University, Cathedral, Statue of King Olav, City Gate and Broadcasting Tower

409 Gerhardsen and Storting (Parliament House)

1997. Millenary of Trondheim. Multicoloured.
1294 3k.70 Type **408** 60 25
1295 12k. Trees, mine, King Olav, pilgrims, burning buildings and harbour . . 2·00 1·20

1997. Birth Centenary of Einar Gerhardsen (Prime Minister 1945–51, 1955–63 and 1963–65).
1296 **409** 3k.70 black, stone and red 60 25
1297 – 25k. black, flesh and green . . . . 4·00 1·90
DESIGN: 25k. Gerhardsen, mountain, factory and electricity pylon.

410 Thematic Subjects

411 Harald Saeverud (composer)

1997. Inauguration of National Junior Stamp Club. Multicoloured.
1298 3k.70 Type **410** 60 25
1299 3k.70 Thematic subjects including fish and tiger . . 60 25

1997. Birth Centenaries.
1300 **411** 10k. blue . . . . 1·60 95
1301 – 15k. green . . . . 2·75 1·40
DESIGN: 15k. Tarjei Vesaas (writer).

412 Dass in Rowing Boat

1997. 350th Birth Anniv of Petter Dass (priest and poet). Multicoloured.
1302 **412** 3k.20 blue and brown . . 60 45
1303 – 3k.70 green, blue and brown 60 25
DESIGN: 3k.70, Dass and Alstahaug Church.

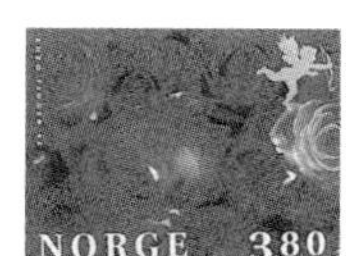

413 Golden Calendar Stick Symbols against Candle Flames

414 Roses

1997. Christmas. Multicoloured. Self-adhesive.
1304 3k.70 Type **413** 60 40
1305 3k.70 Silver calendar stick symbols against night sky 60 40

1998. Insects (2nd series). As T **404**. Multicoloured.
1306 3k.80 Dragonfly 60 25
1307 3k.80 Grasshopper 60 25

1998. St. Valentine's Day. Self-adhesive.
1308 **414** 3k.80 multicoloured . . 75 35

415 "Hornelen" (passenger and mail steamer)

416 Holmenkollen Ski Jump, Oslo

1998. Nordic Countries' Postal Co-operation. Ships.
1309 **415** 3k.80 blue and green . . 60 25
1310 – 4k.50 green and blue . . 75 65
DESIGN: No. 1310, "Kommandoren" (passenger catamaran).

1998. Tourist Sights. Multicoloured.
1311 3k.80 Type **416** 60 40
1312 4k.50 Fisherman, Alesund Harbour 75 90
1313 5k.50 Mt Hamaroyskaftet 95 95

417 Egersund Harbour

1998. Bicentenary of Egersund.
1314 **417** 3k.80 blue and pink . . 30 35
1315 – 6k. blue and mauve . . 1·00 45
DESIGN: No. 1315, Egersund ceramics.

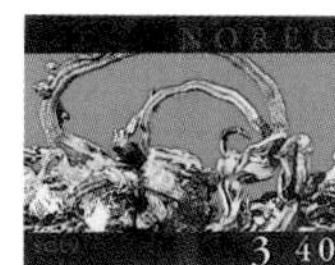

418 Silver

1998. Minerals. Multicoloured.
1316 3k.40 Type **418** 60 40
1317 5k.20 Cobalt 95 55

419 "Water Rider" (Frans Widerberg)

1998. Contemporary Art. Multicoloured.
1318 6k. Type **419** . . . . . . 1·00 65
1319 7k.50 "Red Moon" (carpet, Synnove Anker Aurdal) 1·20 80
1320 13k. "King Haakon VII" (sculpture, Nils Aas) . . . 2·20 1·50

420 Hopscotch

1998. Children's Games (1st series). Multicoloured.
1321 3k.80 Type **420** 60 25
1322 5k.50 Throwing coins at a stick 95 80
See also Nos 1355/6.

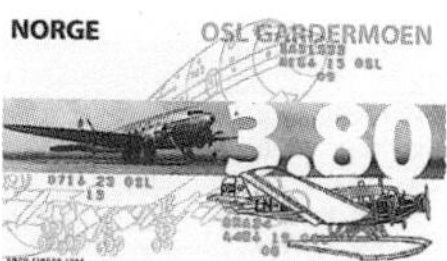

421 Boeing 747, Douglas DC-3 and Junkers Ju 52 Airliners

1998. Inauguration of Oslo Airport, Gardermoen. Multicoloured.
1323 3k.80 Type **421** 45 25
1324 6k. Boeing 737 airliner and map of former approaches to Gardermoen Airport 1·00 60
1325 24k. Terminal building, control tower and wings drawn by Leonardo da Vinci . . . . 3·75 2·10

422 Main Entrance and Guard

1998. 150th Anniv of Royal Palace, Oslo.
1326 **422** 3k.40 purple 60 50
1327 – 3k.80 blue, pink and yellow 70 25
DESIGN: 3k.80, Main front of palace.

423 Music Score

424 Cheese Slicer (Thor Bjorklund)

1998. Christmas. Multicoloured. Self-adhesive.
1328 3k.80 Type **423** (red background) 65 25
1329 3k.80 Music score (blue background) 65 25

1999. Norwegian Inventions. Self-adhesive.
1330 **424** 3k.60 black and blue . . 60 30
1331 – 4k. black and red . . . 70 30
1332 – 4k.20 black and green 70 25
DESIGNS: 4k. Paper clip (Johan Vaaler); 4k.20 Aerosol can (Erik Rotheim).

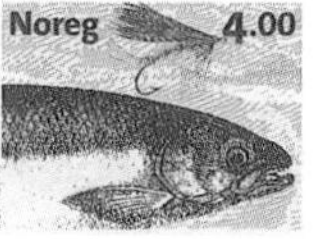

425 Salmon and Fly

1999. Fishes and Fishing Flies. Multicoloured. Self-adhesive.
1333 4k. Type **425** 70 25
1334 4k. Cod and fly 70 30

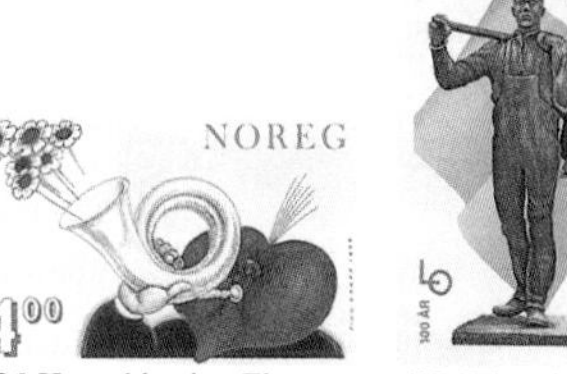

426 Heart blowing Flowers out of Posthorn

427 "The Pioneer" (statue, Per Palle Storm)

1999. St. Valentine's Day.
1335 **426** 4k. multicoloured . . . 70 40

1999. Centenary of Norwegian Confederation of Trade Unions.
1336 **427** 4k. multicoloured . . . 70 25

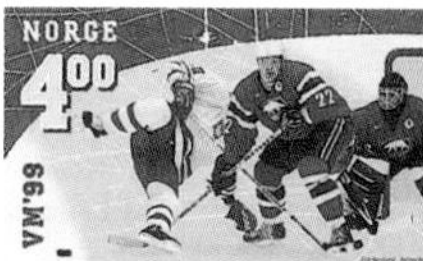

428 Poland v Norway, Class B Championship, 1998

1999. World Ice Hockey Championships, Norway. Multicoloured.
1337 4k. Type **428** 70 65
1338 7k. Switzerland v Sweden, Class A Championship, 1998 . . . . 1·20 65

429 Mute Swans

1999. Tourism. Multicoloured.
1339 4k. Type **429** 70 65
1340 5k. Hamar Cathedral . . . 75 45
1341 6k. Sami man from Troms 1·00 35

430 Emigration

1999. "Norway 2000" (1st issue). Norwegian History. Multicoloured.
1342 4k. Type **430** 70 55
1343 6k. King Olav and Bible (conversion to Christianity, 11th century) 1·00 95
1344 14k. Medal of King Christian IV and quarry workers (union of Norway and Denmark) 2·30 1·90
1345 26k. Oslo at Beier Bridge, 1850s (industrialization) 4·25 90

431 Horse Ferry, Amli, East Agder, 1900

1999. "Norway 2000" (2nd issue). Photographs of Everyday Life. Multicoloured.
1346 4k. Type **431** . . . . . . 65 16·00
1347 4k. Men hewing rock during construction of Valdres railway line, 1900 . . . . 65 16·00
1348 4k. Taxi driver Aarseth Odd filling up car with petrol, Kleive, 1930 . . . . . . 65 16·00
1349 4k. Dairymaid Mathea Isaksen milking cow, Karmoy, 1930 . . . . . 65 16·00
1350 4k. Haymakers, Hemsedal, 1943 . . . . 65 16·00
1351 4k. Cross-country skier Dagfinn Knutsen, 1932 65 16·00
1352 4k. "Bolgen" (coastal fishing boat), Varanger Fjord, 1977 . . . . 65 16·00
1353 4k. Boy Jon Andre Koch holding football, 1981 . . 65 16·00

432 Skateboarding

434 Family bringing in Logs

433 Wenche Foss and Per Haugen in "An Ideal Husband" (Oscar Wilde)

1999. Children's Games (2nd series). Multicoloured.
1355 4k. Type **432** 70 75
1356 6k. Inline skating . . . . . 1·00 60

1999. Centenary of National Theatre.
1357 **433** 3k.60 purple and orange 60 60
1358 – 4k. ultramarine and blue 70 50
DESIGN: 4k. Toralv Maurstad and Tore Segelcke in "Per Gynt" (Henrik Ibsen).

1999. Christmas. Multicoloured. Self-adhesive.
1359 4k. Type **434** 70 50
1360 4k. Family sitting by window 70 30

435 "Sunset" (Sverre Simonsen)

1999. Year 2000. Winning entries in photographic competition. Multicoloured. Self-adhesive.
1361 4k. Type **435** 75 45
1362 4k. "Winter Nights" (Poul Christensen) 75 40

436 Eye within Heart

2000. St. Valentine's Day.
1363 **436** 4k. multicoloured . . . 70 30

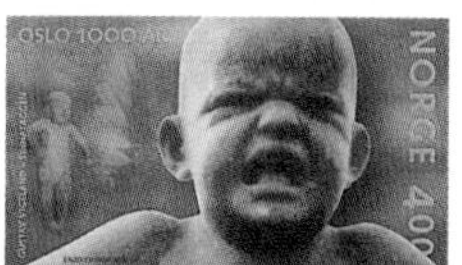

437 "Angry Child" (statue, Gustav Vigeland)

2000. Millenary of Oslo City. Multicoloured.
1364 4k. Type **437** 70 70
1365 6k. Christian IV statue . . . 1·00 95
1366 8k. City Hall and clock face 1·50 2·20
1367 27k. Oslo Stock Exchange and Mercury (statue) . . 4·75 1·30

438 Golden Eagle

2000. Endangered Species. Multicoloured.

1368 5k. Type **438** 95 80
1369 6k. European moose . . . . 1·00 60
1370 7k. Sperm whale . . . . . 1·30 40

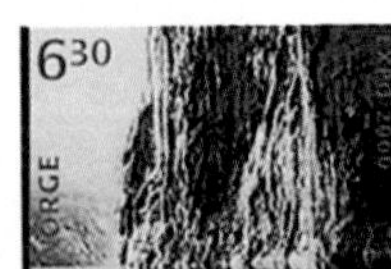

439 "Power and Energy"

2000. "EXPO 2000" World's Fair, Hanover, Germany. Paintings by Marianne Heske. Mult.

1371 4k.20 "The Quiet Room" 70 45
1372 6k.30 Type **439** . . . . . 1·10 60

440 Cadets, 1750 **441** Mackerel

2000. 250th Anniv of Royal Norwegian Military Academy.

1373 **440** 3k.60 multicoloured . . 60 80
1374 – 8k. blue, yellow and red 1·50 45

DESIGN: 8k. Cadets, 2000.

2000. Fishes. Multicoloured. Self-adhesive.

1375 4k.20 Type **441** . . . . . 1·10 25
1376 4k.20 Herring . . . . 1·10 25

442 Spaceman (May-Therese Vorland) **443** "Monument to Log Drivers" (sculpture, Trygve M. Barstad)

2000. "Stampin the Future". Winning Entries in Children's International Painting Competition. Multicoloured.

1377 4k.20 Type **442** 70 30
1378 6k.30 Rocket and Earth (Jann Fredrik Ronning) 1·10 50

2000. Millennium of Skien City. Multicoloured.

1379 4k.20 Type **443** 70 40
1380 15k. Skien Church . . . . 2·50 1·60

444 Laestadius, Lifelong Saxifrage and Laestadius Poppy **445** Nils og Blamann with Goat and Cart

2000. Birth Bicentenary of Lars Levi Laestadius (clergyman and botanist).

1381 **444** 5k. multicoloured . . . 75 65

2000. Cartoon Characters. Multicoloured. Self-adhesive.

1382 4k.20 Type **445** 75 25
1383 4k.20 Soldier No. 91 Stomperud and birds . . 75 30

446 Woven Altar Piece, Hamaroy Church

2000. Altar Pieces. Multicoloured.

1384 3k.60 Type **446** 60 55
1385 4k.20 Ski Church 75 40

2000.

1388 **352** 1k. multicoloured . . . 30 35
1389 2k. multicoloured . . . 45 25
1389a 5k. multicoloured . . . 85 40
1390 6k. multicoloured . . . 1·00 55
1392 9k. multicoloured . . . 1·50 60

447 Sekel Rose **448** Place Mat

2001. Roses (1st series). Multicoloured. Self-adhesive.

1395 4k.50 Type **447** 75 70
1396 4k.50 Namdal rose 75 55

See also Nos 1418/19 and 1491/2.

2001. Crafts (1st series). Multicoloured. Self-adhesive.

1397 4k. Type **448** 70 25
1398 4k.50 Pot with lid 85 35
1399 7k. Bunad (woven cloth) . . 1·20 55

See also Nos. 1415/17.

449 Aase Bye

2001. Thespians (1st series).

1400 **449** 4k. black and brown . . 70 30
1401 – 4k.50 black and blue . . 85 25
1402 – 5k.50 black and brown 95 60
1403 – 7k. black and purple . . 1·20 60
1404 – 8k. black and grey . . . 1·50 70

DESIGNS: 4k.50, Per Aabel; 5k.50, Alfred Maurstad; 7k. Lillebil Ibsen; 8k. Tore Segelcke.

See also Nos 1410/14 and 1450/4.

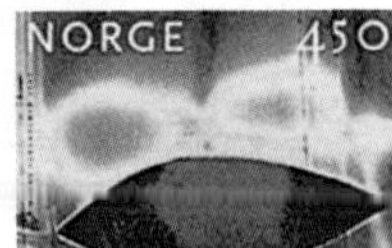

450 "Ties that Bind" (Magne Furuholmen)

2001. St. Valentine's Day.

1405 **450** 4k.50 multicoloured . . 75 25

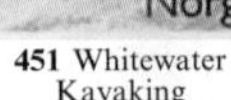

451 Whitewater Kayaking **453** Lalla Carlsen

452 Tuba Player

2001. Sports. Multicoloured. Self-adhesive.

1406 4k.50 Type **451** 85 40
1407 7k. Rock climbing . . . . . 1·20 1·00

2001. Centenary of School Bands. Multicoloured.

1408 4k.50 Type **452** 85 40
1409 9k. Majorette . . . . 1·50 1·10

2001. Thespians (2nd series). Multicoloured.

1410 5k. Type **453** 75 50
1411 5k.50 Leif Juster 95 40
1412 7k. Kari Diesen . . . . . . 1·20 90
1413 9k. Arvid Nilssen . . . . . 1·50 80
1414 10k. Einar Rose . . . . . . 1·70 85

2001. Crafts (2nd series). As T **449**. Multicoloured.

1415 5k. Wooden drinking vessel 95 40
1416 6k.50 Crocheted doll's clothing . . . . 1·20 80
1417 8k.50 Knitted woollen hat 1·50 1·10

454 Rose "Heidekonigin" **456** Kittens

455 Old Bank of Norway

2001. Roses (2nd series). Multicoloured. Self-adhesive.

1418 5k.50 Type **454** . . . . . . 1·00 35
1419 5k.50 Rose "Old Master" 1·00 35

Nos. 1418/19 are impregnated with the scent of roses.

2001. Norwegian Architecture. Multicoloured.

1420 5k.50 Type **455** 95 35
1421 8k.50 Ivar Aasen Centre . . 1·50 75

2001. Pets. Multicoloured.

1422 5k.50 Type **456** . . . . . . 1·00 45
1423 7k.50 Goat . . . . 1·40 70

457 Aung San Suu Kyi (Burmese opposition leader), 1991

2001. Centenary of Nobel Prizes. Peace Prize Winners (Nos.1424/5 and 1427). Multicoloured.

1424 5k.50 Type **457** . . . . . . 1·10 40
1425 5k.50 Nelson Mandela (South African President), 1993 . . . . 1·10 40
1426 7k. Alfred Nobel (Prize Fund founder) . . . . . 1·40 65
1427 7k. Henry Dunant (founder of Red Cross), 1901 . . . 1·40 65
1428 9k. Fridtjof Nansen (Norwegian organizer for League of Nations refugee relief), 1922 . . . . . . 1·90 80
1429 9k. Mikhail Gorbachev (Soviet President), 1990 1·40 80
1430 10k. Martin Luther King (Civil Rights leader), 1964 1·40 95
1431 10k. Rigoberta Menchu Tum (Guatemalan Civil Rights leader), 1992 . . . 1·30 1·00

Dates are those on which the Prize was awarded.

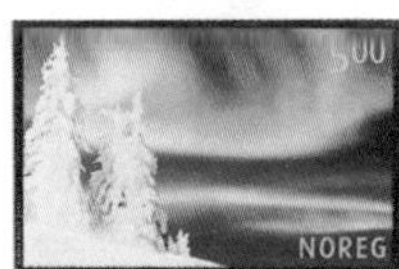

458 Snow-covered Trees and Lights

2001. Northern Lights. Multicoloured.

1433 5k. Type **458** 95 45
1434 5k.50 Lights and reindeer 1·00 50

459 Gingerbread Man **460** Tordis Maurstad

2001. Christmas. Multicoloured. Self-adhesive.

1435 5k.50 Type **459** . . . . . . 1·10 40
1436 5k.50 Gingerbread house . . 1·10 40

2002. Thespians (3rd series). Showing caricatures by Arne Roar Lund.

1450 **460** 5k. black and lilac . . . 85 40
1451 – 5k.50 black and grey . . 95 40
1452 – 7k. black and green . . 1·20 50
1453 – 9k. black and green . . 1·50 60
1454 – 10k. black and brown . . 1·70 70

DESIGNS: 5k.50 Rolf Just Nilsen; 7k. Lars Tvinde; 9k. Henry Gleditsch; 10k. Norma Balean.

461 Boys tackling **462** Scene from "Askeladden and the Good Helpers"

2002. Centenary of Norwegian Football Association (1st issue). Multicoloured. Self-adhesive.

1455 5k.50 Type **461** 90 40
1456 5k.50 German referee Peter Hertel and player 90 40
1457 5k.50 Girls tackling 90 40
1458 5k.50 Boy kicking ball . . . 90 40

See also Nos. 1469/**MS**1475.

2002. Fairytale Characters. Multicoloured. Self-adhesive.

1459 5k.50 Type **462** 90 40
1460 9k. Giant troll (drawing by Theodor Kittelsen) . . . 1·50 60

463 "Monument to Whaling"

2002. Nordic Countries' Postal Co-operation. Modern Art. Sculptures. Multicoloured.

1461 7k.50 Type **463** . . . . 1·30 50
1462 8k.50 "Throw" (Kåre Groven) . . . . 1·40 55

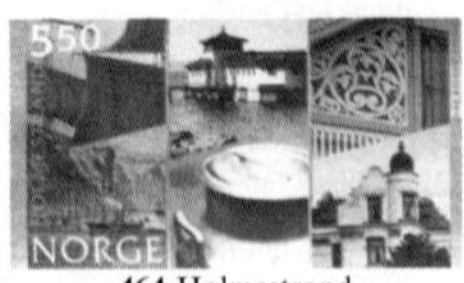

464 Holmestrand

2002. City Charter Anniversaries. Multicoloured.

1463 5k.50 Type **464** (300th anniv) 90 40
1464 5k.50 Kongsberg (200th anniv) 90 40

465 Abel

2002. Birth Bicentenary of Niels Henrik Abel (mathematician). Multicoloured.

1465 5k.50 Type **465** 90 40
1466 22k. Mathematical rosette 3·75 2·25

466 Johan Borgen **468** Clown on Tightrope

467 Norwegian Team (Olympic Games, Berlin, 1936)

2002. Writers' Birth Centenaries. Portraits by Nils Aas.

1467 **466** 11k. yellow and green . . 1·80 75
1468 – 20k. green and blue . . 3·50 2·00

DESIGN: 20k. Nordahl Grieg.

2002. Centenary of Norwegian Football Association (2nd issue). Multicoloured.

1469 5k. Type **467** 85 35
1470 5k.50 No. 9 player and Brazil No. 4 player (World Cup, France, 1998) 90 35
1471 5k.50 Norway and U. S. A. women players (Olympic Games, Sydney, 2000)) . . 90 35
1472 7k. Player capturing ball from Sweden No. 11 player (Norway--Sweden, 1960) . . . . 1·20 45
1473 9k. Player with chevron sleeves (Norway–England, 1981) . . . . 1·50 60
1474 10k. Winning team members (Rosenborg–Milan (Champions League, 1996)) . . . . 1·70 65

MS1475 140 × 127 mm. Nos. 1469/74 7·00 7·00

2002. Europa. Circus. Multicoloured.

1476 5k.50 Type **468** 90 35
1477 8k.50 Elephant, horse and chimpanzee . . . . 1·40 55

2002. "Nordia 2002" Nordic Stamp Exhibition, Kristiansand. Nos. 1465/6 surch **NORDIC 2002**.

1478 5k.50 multicoloured 90 35
1479 22k. multicoloured . . . . 3·75 2·20

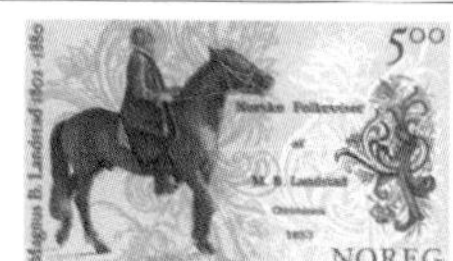

470 Landstad on Horseback and Frontispiece of "Norske Folkeviser"

2002. Birth Bicentenary of Magnus Brostrup Landstad (folk-song collector and hymn writer). Multicoloured.

1480 5k. Type **470** 85 35
1481 5k.50 Landstad and frontispiece of Kirkefalmebog 90 35

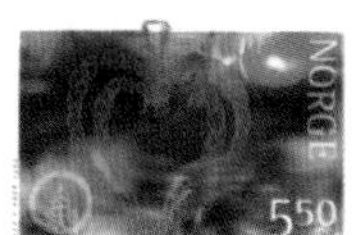

471 Straw Heart-shaped Decoration

2002. Christmas. Multicoloured. Self-adhesive.

1482 5k.50 Type **471** 90 35
1483 5k.50 Paper star-shaped decoration 90 35

472 "Nordmandens Krone" (Kare Espolin Johnson)

2003. Graphic Art. Multicoloured.

1484 5k. Type **472** 85 35
1485 8k.50 "Bla Hester" (Else Hagen) . . . . 1·40 55
1486 9k. "Dirigent og Solist" (Niclas Gulbrandsen) . . 1·50 60
1487 11k. "Olympia" (Svein Strand) . . . . 1·80 75
1488 22k. "Still Life XVII" (Rigmor Hansen) . . . . 3·75 2·20

473 Heart

2002. St. Valentine.

1489 **473** 5k.50 multicoloured . . 90 35

474 Doudji Knife Handle (Havard Larsen)

475 Rose "Grand Prix"

2003. Crafts. Coil stamp. Self-adhesive.

1490 **474** 5k.50 multicoloured . . 90 35

2003. Roses (3rd series). Multicoloured. Self-adhesive.

1491 5k.50 Type **475** 90 35
1492 5k.50 Rose "Champagne" 90 35

OFFICIAL STAMPS

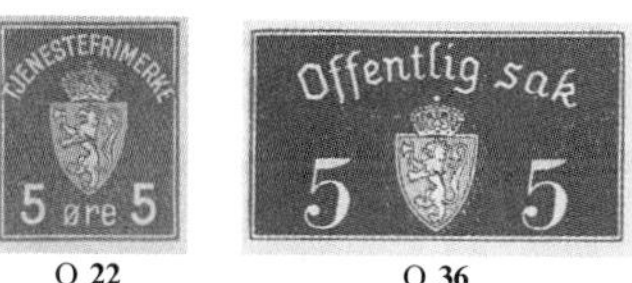

O 22 O 36

1925.

O187 O **22** 5ore mauve 70 65
O188 10ore green 35 20
O189 15ore blue . . . . . 1·50 1·70
O190 20ore purple 40 20
O191 30ore grey . . . . . 2·00 3·25
O192 40ore blue . . . . . 1·00 1·00
O193 60ore blue . . . . . 3·50 3·75

1929. Surch **2 2**.

O219 O **22** 2ore on 5ore mauve 40 60

1933.

O231 O **36** 2ore brown . . . . . 55 1·10
O243 5ore purple . . . . . 75 1·10
O233 7ore orange . . . . . 4·25 4·50
O245 10ore green 60 30
O235 15ore green 65 45
O247 20ore red 75 30
O237 25ore brown 50 50
O238 30ore blue 65 50
O248 35ore violet 60 40
O249 40ore grey 90 50
O250 60ore blue 90 80
O241 70ore brown . . . . . 1·10 1·70
O242 100ore blue . . . . . 1·25 1·50

O 39 O 58 Quisling Emblem

1937.

O267 O **39** 5ore mauve 25 25
O268 7ore orange 40 60
O269 10ore green 25 20
O270 15ore brown 25 20
O271 20ore red 25 20
O260 25ore brown 95 65
O273 25ore red 25 20
O261 30ore blue 70 60
O275 30ore grey 80 40
O276 35ore purple 40 25
O277 40ore grey 40 25
O278 40ore blue . . . . . . 2·75 25
O279 50ore lilac 60 20
O280 60ore blue 45 20
O281 100ore blue . . . . . 1·10 35
O282 200ore orange . . . . 1·40 30

1942.

O336 O **58** 5ore mauve . . . . . 70 1·30
O337 7ore orange . . . . . 70 1·30
O338 10ore green 20 25
O339 15ore brown . . . . . 1·40 9·25
O340 20ore red 20 25
O341 25ore brown . . . . . 2·50 13·50
O342 30ore blue . . . . . . 2·10 12·00
O343 35ore purple . . . . . 2·10 7·25
O344 40ore grey 35 30
O345 60ore blue . . . . . . 1·90 6·75
O346 1k. blue . . . . 2·10 9·50

1949. Surch **25** and bar.

O402 O **39** 25ore on 20ore red . . 30 30

O 89 O 99

1951.

O434 O **89** 5ore mauve 60 20
O435 10ore grey 60 10
O436 15ore brown 75 35
O437 30ore red 60 10
O438 35ore brown 90 45
O439 60ore blue 90 25
O440 100ore violet . . . . . 2·10 35

1955.

O458 O **99** 5ore purple 20 15
O459 10ore grey 20 15
O460 15ore brown . . . . . 45 1·30
O461 20ore green 50 15
O736 25ore green 20 20
O463 30ore red . . . . . . 1·40 55
O464 30ore green . . . . . 1·25 20
O465 35ore red 45 15
O466 40ore lilac 60 15
O467 40ore green 30 75
O468 45ore red . . . . . . 1·00 15
O469 50ore brown . . . . . 1·60 25
O470 50ore red 95 25
O471 50ore blue 45 25
O738 50ore grey 20 25
O739 60ore blue . . . . . . 85 3·50
O473 60ore red 50 15
O475 65ore red 75 30
O476 70ore brown . . . . . 3·00 65
O477 70ore red 20 20
O478 75ore purple . . . . . 9·00 9·00
O479 75ore green 60 55
O481 80ore brown 55 20
O741 80ore red 30 15
O482 85ore brown . . . . . 60 1·60
O483 90ore orange 70 15
O484 1k. violet 70 15
O485 1k. red 20 15
O486 1k.10 red 60 55
O744 1k.25 red 60 15
O745 1k.30 purple . . . . . 95 1·20
O746 1k.50 red 45 15
O747 1k.75 green . . . . . 1·00 1·00
O748 2k. green 50 15
O749 2k. red 60 15
O750 3k. violet 85 45
O488 5k. violet . . . . . . 9·75 6·00
O752 5k. blue 70 25

POSTAGE DUE STAMPS

D 12

1889. Inscr "at betale" and "PORTOMAERKE".

D95 D **12** 1ore green 70 75
D96a 4ore mauve 95 45
D97 10ore red . . . . . . 5·25 40
D98 15ore brown . . . . . 5·00 60
D99 20ore blue . . . . . 5·50 35
D94 50ore purple . . . . . 3·00 1·30

1922. Inscr "a betale" and "PORTOMERKE".

D162 D **12** 4ore purple . . . . . 4·75 6·50
D163 10ore green . . . . . 3·50 1·10
D164 20ore purple . . . . . 5·25 3·00
D165 40ore blue . . . . . 10·50 60
D166 100ore yellow . . . . 38·00 6·75
D167 200ore violet . . . . 46·00 16·00

NOSSI-BE Pt. 6

An island north-west of Madagascar, declared a French protectorate in 1840. In 1901 it became part of Madagascar and Dependencies.

100 centimes = 1 franc.

1889. Stamp of French Colonies, "Peace and Commerce" type, surch.

8 H 25c. on 40c. red on yellow . . £1600 £550

1889. Stamps of French Colonies, "Commerce" type, surch.

4 J 5c. on 10c. black on lilac . . . £1900 £550
2 5c. on 20c. red on green . . . £2250 £750
6 15 on 20c. red on green . . . £1900 £550
7 25 on 30c. brown on drab . . £1600 £450
9 25 on 40c. red on yellow . . . £1600 £450

1890. Stamps of French Colonies, "Commerce" type, surch. (a) **N S B 0 25**.

10 J 0 25 on 20c. red on green . . £275 £200
11 0 25 on 75c. red on pink . . £275 £200
12 0 25 on 1f. green £275 £200

(b) **N S B 25 c**.

13 J 25c. on 20c. red on green . . £275 £200
14 25c. on 75c. red on pink . . £250 £200
15 25c. on 1f. green £250 £200

(c) **N S B 25** in frame.

16 J 25 on 20c. red on green . . . £650 £450
17 25 on 75c. red on pink . . . £650 £450
18 25 on 1f. green £650 £450

1893. Stamps of French Colonies, "Commerce" type, surch **NOSSI-BE** and bar over value in figures.

36 J 25 on 20c. red on green . . . 29·00 26·00
37 50 on 10c. black on lilac . . 35·00 26·00
38 75 on 15c. blue £170 £140
39 1f. on 5c. green . . . . . . 75·00 60·00

1893. Stamps of French Colonies, "Commerce" type, optd **Nossi Be**.

40a J 10c. black on lilac . . . . . 16·00 6·50
41 15c. blue . . . . 16·00 15·00
42 20c. red on green . . . . . 75·00 44·00

1894. "Tablet" key-type inscr "NOSSI-BE" in red (1, 5, 15, 25, 75c., 1f.) or blue (others).

44 D 1c. black on blue . . . . . 1·10 90
45 2c. brown on buff . . . . . 1·25 1·75
46 4c. brown on grey . . . . . 2·00 2·50
47 5c. green on green . . . . . 2·00 1·75
48 10c. black on lilac . . . . . 2·50 2·75
49 15c. blue . . . . 7·75 3·00
50 20c. red on green . . . . . 7·50 5·00
51 25c. black on pink . . . . . 8·75 6·75
52 30c. brown on drab . . . . 9·25 7·75
53 40c. red on yellow . . . . . 12·50 10·00
54 50c. red on pink . . . . . . 8·25 7·00
55 75c. brown on orange . . . 29·00 11·50
56 1f. green . . . . 12·00 18·00

POSTAGE DUE STAMPS

1891. Stamps of French Colonies, "Commerce" type, surch **NOSSI-BE chiffre-taxe A PERCEVOIR** and value.

D19 J 0.20 on 1c. black on blue £225 £160
D20 0.30 on 2c. brown on buff £225 £160
D21 0.35 on 4c. brown on grey £250 £180
D22 0.35 on 20c. red on green £275 £180
D23 0.50 on 30c. brn on drab 65·00 55·00
D24 1f. on 35c. black on orge £150 £100

1891. Stamps of French Colonies, "Commerce" type, surch **Nossi-Be A PERCEVOIR** and value.

D25 J 5c. on 20c. red on green . . £120 £120
D26 10c. on 15c. blue on blue £130 £130
D33 0.10 on 5c. green . . . . 16·00 11·00
D27 15c. on 10c. black on lilac 90·00 90·00
D34 0.15 on 20c. red on green 18·00 20·00
D28 25c. on 5c. green on green 90·00 90·00
D35 0.25 on 75c. red on pink . . £375 £350

NOVA SCOTIA Pt. 1

An eastern province of the Dominion of Canada, whose stamps it now uses.

Currency: As Canada.

1 2 Emblem of the United Kingdom

1853. Imperf.

1 **1** 1d. brown £2000 £400
4 **2** 3d. blue £750 £140
5 6d. green £4000 £450
8 1s. purple £14000 £2750

3 4

1860. Perf.

9 **3** 1c. black . . . . 3·50 12·00
20 2c. purple . . . . 3·50 14·00
13 5c. blue . . . . £350 17·00
26 **4** 8½c. green . . . . 17·00 40·00
28 10c. red . . . . 4·00 24·00
17 12½c. black . . . . 27·00 26·00

NYASALAND PROTECTORATE Pt. 1

A British Protectorate in central Africa. Formerly known as British Central Africa. From 1954 to 1963 part of the Central African Federation using the stamps of Rhodesia and Nyasaland (q.v.). From July 1964 independent within the Commonwealth under its new name of Malawi.

12 pence = 1 shilling;
20 shillings = 1 pound.

1891. Stamps of Rhodesia optd **B.C.A.**

1 **1** 1d. black . . . . 4·50 4·50
2 2d. green and red . . . . . 4·50 4·00
3 4d. brown and black . . . . 4·75 5·00
5 6d. blue . . . . 7·50 8·00
6 8d. red and blue . . . . . 14·00 28·00
7 1s. brown . . . . 15·00 11·00
8 2s. red . . . . 26·00 50·00
9 2s.6d. purple . . . . 65·00 85·00
10 3s. brown and green . . . . 65·00 65·00
11 4s. black and red . . . . . 60·00 85·00
12 5s. yellow . . . . 70·00 75·00
13 10s. green £140 £190
14 – £1 blue £650 £550
15 – £2 red £850
16 – £5 olive £1400
17 – £10 brown £3250

1892. Stamps of Rhodesia surch **B.C.A.** and value in words.

18 **1** 3s. on 4s. black and red . . . £325 £325
19 4s. on 5s. yellow . . . . . . 70·00 85·00

1895. No. 2 surch **ONE PENNY.** and bar.

20 **1** 1d. on 2d. green and red . . 8·00 29·00

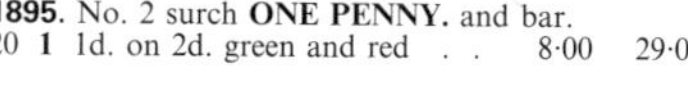

5 Arms of the Protectorate 7 Arms of the Protectorate

1895. The 2s.6d. and higher values are larger.

32 **5** 1d. black . . . . 3·25 4·75
33 2d. black and green . . . . 15·00 5·00
34 4d. black and orange . . . . 22·00 17·00
35 6d. black and blue . . . . . 25·00 13·00
36 1s. black and red . . . . . 25·00 14·00
37 2s.6d. black and mauve . . . £130 £130
38 3s. black and yellow . . . . 95·00 55·00
39 5s. black and olive £140 £180
29 £1 black and orange £900 £375
40 £1 black and blue £800 £475
30 £10 black and orange £4250 £3750
31 £25 black and green £7500

1897. The 2s.6d. and higher values are larger.

43 **7** 1d. black and blue . . . . . 3·25 1·25
57d 1d. purple and red . . . . 2·50 50
44 2d. black and yellow . . . . 2·00 2·00
45 4d. black and red . . . . . 6·50 1·50
57e 4d. purple and olive . . . . 8·50 11·00
46 6d. black and green . . . . 45·00 4·25
58 6d. purple and brown . . . 3·75 3·00

47 1s. black and purple 11·00 7·00
48 2s.6d. black and blue 48·00 42·00
49 3s. black and green £190 £225
50 4s. black and red 70·00 80·00
50a 10s. black and olive £130 £140
51 £1 black and purple £275 £160
52 £10 black and yellow £4500 £1700

1897. No. 49 surch **ONE PENNY**.
53 **7** 1d. on 3s. black and green 6·00 9·50

10 **11**

1898.
56a **10** 1d. red and blue (imperf) £2000 £150
57 1d. red and blue (perf) £2250 19·00

1903. The 2s.6d. and higher values are larger.
59 **11** 1d. grey and red 7·00 1·75
60 2d. purple 3·50 1·00
61 4d. green and black 2·50 9·00
62 6d. grey and brown 3·25 2·00
62b 1s. grey and blue 3·50 10·00
63 2s.6d. green 48·00 75·00
64 4s. purple 60·00 75·00
65 10s. green and black £110 £190
66 £1 grey and red £250 £180
67 £10 grey and blue £4250 £3250

13 **14**

1908.
73 **13** ½d. green 1·75 2·00
74 1d. red 4·00 1·00
75 3d. purple on yellow 1·50 4·25
76 4d. black and red on yellow 1·50 1·50
77 6d. purple 3·75 11·00
72 1s. black on green 2·75 9·50
78 **14** 2s.6d. black and red on blue 48·00 85·00
79 4s. red and black 80·00 £120
80 10s. green and red on green £120 £225
81 £1 purple and black on red £450 £550
82 £10 purple and blue £7000 £4750

1913. As 1908, but portrait of King George V.
100 ½d. green 1·50 50
101 1d. red 2·25 50
102 1½d. orange 3·25 17·00
103 2d. grey 1·00 50
89 2½d. blue 2·25 7·00
90 3d. purple on yellow 4·50 4·50
91 4d. black and red on yellow 2·00 2·50
107 6d. purple 3·00 3·25
93a 1s. black on green 5·50 1·50
109 2s. purple and blue on blue 15·00 12·00
94 2s.6d. black and red on blue 11·00 12·00
111 4s. red and black 19·00 26·00
112 5s. green and red on yellow 38·00 75·00
96 10s. green and red on green 80·00 £100
98 £1 purple and black on red £170 £140
99e £10 purple and blue £2750 £1700

17 King George V and Symbol of the Protectorate

1934.
114 **17** ½d. green 75 1·25
115 1d. brown 75 75
116 1½d. red 75 3·00
117 2d. grey 80 1·25
118 3d. blue 2·50 1·75
119 4d. mauve 2·50 3·50
120 6d. violet 2·50 50
121 9d. olive 6·00 9·00
122 1s. black and orange 8·50 14·00

1935. Silver Jubilee. As T **14a** of Kenya, Uganda and Tanganyika.
123 1d. blue and grey 1·00 2·00
124 2d. green and blue 1·00 1·25
125 3d. brown and blue 7·00 16·00
126 1s. grey and purple 16·00 40·00

1937. Coronation. As T **14b** of Kenya, Uganda and Tanganyika.
127 ½d. green 30 75
128 1d. brown 50 65
129 2d. grey 50 1·75

1938. As T **17** but with head of King George VI and "POSTAGE REVENUE" omitted.
130 ½d. green 30 1·50
130a ½d. brown 10 1·75
131 1d. brown 2·25 30
131a 1d. green 30 75
132 1½d. red 4·25 4·50
132a 1½d. grey 30 4·75
133 2d. grey 7·00 1·25
133a 2d. red 30 1·75
134 3d. blue 60 50
135 4d. mauve 2·50 1·25
136 6d. violet 2·50 1·25
137 9d. olive 2·50 2·50
138 1s. black and orange 3·25 1·50

1938. As T **14** but with head of King George VI facing right.
139 2s. purple and blue on blue 10·00 10·00
140 2s.6d. black and red on blue 12·00 12·00
141 5s. green and red on yellow 42·00 19·00
142 10s. green and red on green 50·00 40·00
143 £1 purple and black on red 32·00 27·00

20 Lake Nyasa

21 King's African Rifles

1945.
144 **20** ½d. black and brown 50 10
145 **21** 1d. black and green 20 70
160 – 1d. brown and green 30 20
146 – 1½d. black and grey 30 50
147 – 2d. black and red 1·00 70
148 – 3d. black and blue 20 30
149 – 4d. black and red 1·50 70
150 – 6d. black and violet 1·50 80
151 **20** 9d. black and olive 1·50 2·75
152 – 1s. blue and green 1·25 20
153 – 2s. green and purple 4·00 4·50
154 – 2s.6d. green and blue 7·50 4·50
155 – 5s. purple and blue 4·50 6·00
156 – 10s. red and green 13·00 13·00
157 – 20s. red and black 17·00 26·00
DESIGNS—HORIZ: 1½d., 6d. Tea estate; 2d., 1s., 10s. Map of Nyasaland; 4d., 2s.6d. Tobacco; 5s., 20s. Badge of Nyasaland. VERT: 1d. (No. 160), Leopard and sunrise; 3d., 2s. Fishing village.

1946. Victory. As T **4a** of Pitcairn Islands.
158 1d. green 10 20
159 2d. red 30 10

1948. Silver Wedding. As T **4b/c** of Pitcairn Islands.
161 1d. green 15 10
162 10s. mauve 15·00 26·00

1949. U.P.U. As T **4d/g** of Pitcairn Islands.
163 1d. green 30 20
164 3d. blue 2·00 2·75
165 6d. purple 50 50
166 1s. blue 30 50

27 Arms in 1891 and 1951

1951. Diamond Jubilee of Protectorate.
167 **27** 2d. black and red 1·25 1·50
168 3d. black and blue 1·25 1·50
169 6d. black and violet 1·25 2·00
170 5s. black and blue 3·75 7·00

1953. Rhodes Centenary Exhibition. As T **6** of Northern Rhodesia.
171 6d. violet 30 30

1953. Coronation. As T **4h** of Pitcairn Islands.
172 2d. black and orange 60 70

29 Grading Cotton

1953. As 1945 but with portrait of Queen Elizabeth II as in T **29**. Designs as for corresponding values except where stated.
173 **20** ½d. black and brown 10 1·25
174 – 1d. brn & grn (as No. 160) 65 30
175 – 1½d. black and grey 20 1·90
176a – 2d. black and orange 30 30
177 **29** 2½d. green and black 20 50
178 – 3d. black and red (as 4d.) 30 20
179 – 4½d. black and blue (as 3d.) 30 40
180a – 6d. black and violet 2·00 1·00
181 **20** 9d. black and olive 80 2·50
182 – 1s. blue and green 2·25 50
183 – 2s. green and red 2·00 3·25
184 – 2s.6d. green and blue 3·25 4·75
185 – 5s. purple and blue 7·00 4·75
186 – 10s. red and green 4·50 17·00
187 – 20s. red and black 16·00 24·00

30

32 Mother and Child

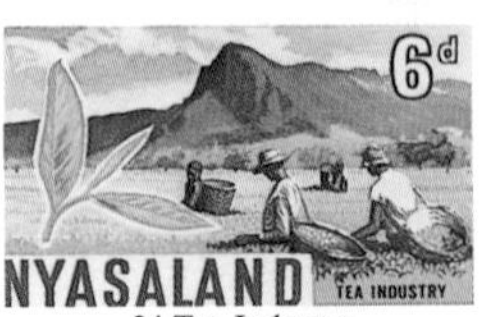

34 Tea Industry

1963. Revenue stamps optd **POSTAGE** as in T **30** or surch also.
188 **30** ½d. on 1d. blue 30 30
189 1d. green 30 10
190 2d. red 30 30
191 3d. blue 30 10
192 6d. purple 30 10
193 9d. on 1s. red 40 25
194 1s. purple 45 10
195 2s.6d. black 1·25 2·00
196 5s. brown 3·25 1·50
197 10s. olive 4·50 7·00
198 £1 violet 5·00 7·00

1964.
199 **31** ½d. violet 10 30
200 – 1d. black and green 10 10
201 – 2d. brown 10 10
202 – 3d. brown, green and bistre 10 10
203 – 4d. blue and yellow 20 30
204 **34** 6d. purple, green and blue 60 50
205 – 1s. brown, blue and yellow 15 10
206 – 1s.3d. bronze and brown 3·00 10
207 – 2s.6d. brown and blue 3·00 50
208 – 5s. blue, green, yellow & blk 1·50 1·25
209 – 10s. green, salmon and black 2·50 3·00
210 – £1 brown and yellow 7·00 8·00
DESIGNS—HORIZ (as Type **32**): 1d. Chambo (fish); 2d. Zebu bull; 3d. Groundnuts; 4d. Fishing. (As Type **34**): 1s. Timber; 1s.3d. Turkish tobacco industry; 2s.6d. Cotton industry; 5s. Monkey Bay, Lake Nyasa; 10s. Forestry, Afzelia. VERT (as Type **34**): £1 Nyala.

POSTAGE DUE STAMPS

1950. As Type **D 1** of Gold Coast, but inscr "NYASALAND".
D1 1d. red 3·75 22·00
D2 2d. blue 10·00 22·00
D3 3d. green 10·00 6·00
D4 4d. purple 18·00 40·00
D5 6d. orange 25·00 £110

For later issues see **MALAWI**.

NYASSA COMPANY Pt. 9

In 1894 Portugal granted a charter to the Nyassa Company to administer an area in the Northern part of Mozambique, including the right to issue its own stamps. The lease was terminated in 1929 and the administration was transferred to Mozambique whose stamps were used there.

1898. 1000 reis = 1 milreis.
1913. 100 centavos = 1 escudo.

1898. "Figures" and "Newspaper" key-types inscr "MOCAMBIQUE" optd **NYASSA**.
1 **V** 2½r. brown 85 85
2 **R** 5r. orange 85 85
3 10r. mauve 85 85
4 15r. brown 85 85
5 20r. lilac 85 85
6 25r. green 85 85
7 50r. blue 85 85
8 75r. pink 1·25 1·00
9 80r. green 1·25 1·00
10 100r. brown on buff 1·25 1·00
11 150r. red on pink 2·75 2·75
12 200r. blue on blue 1·90 1·90
13 300r. blue on brown 1·90 1·90

1898. "King Carlos" key-type inscr "MOCAMBIQUE" optd **NYASSA**.
14 **S** 2½r. grey 60 50
15 5r. red 60 50
16 10r. green 60 50
17 15r. brown 85 60
18 20r. lilac 85 60
19 25r. green 85 60
20 50r. blue 85 60
21 75r. pink 85 60
22 80r. mauve 1·00 85
23 100r. blue on blue 1·00 85
24 150r. brown on yellow 1·00 85
25 200r. purple on pink 1·00 85
26 300r. blue on pink 1·00 85

2 Giraffe **3** Dromedaries

1901.
27 **2** 2½r. brown and black 1·10 60
28 5r. violet and black 1·10 60
29 10r. green and black 1·10 60
30 15r. brown and black 1·10 60
31 20r. red and black 1·10 60
32 25r. orange and black 1·10 60
33 50r. blue and black 1·10 60
34 **3** 75r. red and black 1·40 60
35 80r. bistre and black 1·40 60
36 100r. brown and black 1·40 1·10
37 150r. brown and black 1·40 1·10
38 200r. green and black 1·40 1·10
39 300r. green and black 1·40 1·10

1903. (a) Surch in figures and words.
40 **3** 65r. on 80r. mauve and black 1·10 75
41 115r. on 150r. brown & black 1·10 75
42 130r. on 300r. green & black 1·10 75

(b) Optd **PROVISORIO**.
43 **2** 15r. brown and black 1·10 85
44 25r. orange and black 1·10 85

1910. Optd **PROVISORIO** and surch in figures and words.
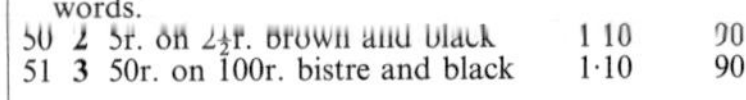
50 **2** 5r. on 2½r. brown and black 1·10 90
51 **3** 50r. on 100r. bistre and black 1·10 90

9 Dromedaries

12 Vasco de Gama's Flagship "Sao Gabriel"

1911. Optd **REPUBLICA**.
53 **9** 2½r. violet and black 90 40
54 5r. black 90 40
55 10r. green and black 90 40
56 – 20r. red and black 90 40
57 – 25r. brown and black 90 40
58 – 50r. blue and black 90 40
59 – 75r. brown and black 90 40
60 – 100r. brown & black on green 90 60
61 – 200r. green & black on orge 1·10 85
62 **12** 300r. black on blue 2·75 1·50
63 400r. brown and black 3·00 1·60
64 500r. violet and green 3·75 2·25
DESIGNS—HORIZ: 20, 25, 50r. Common zebra. VERT: 75, 100, 200r. Giraffe.

1918. Surch **REPUBLICA** and value in figures.
(a) Stamps of 1901.
65 **2** ¼c. on 2½c. brown and black 22·00 13·00
66 ½c. on 5r. violet and black 22·00 13·00
67 1c. on 10r. green and black 22·00 13·00
68 1½c. on 15r. brown and black 1·00 50
69 2c. on 20r. red and black 60 50
70 3½c. on 25r. orange and black 60 50
71 5c. on 50r. blue and black 60 50
72 **3** 7½c. on 75r. red and black 60 50
73 8c. on 80r. mauve and black 60 50
74 10c. on 100r. bistre and black 60 50
75 15c. on 150r. brown & black 1·00 90
76 20c. on 200r. green and black 80 90
77 30c. on 300r. green and black 1·50 1·25

(b) Nos. 43/4 and 40/2.
78 **2** 1½c. on 15r. brown and black 2·00 1·50
79 3½c. on 25r. orange and black 70 50
80 **3** 40c. on 65r. on 80r. 4·50 4·50
81 50c. on 115r. on 150r. 1·25 1·00
82 1c. on 130r. on 300r. 1·25 1·00

1921. Stamps of 1911 surch in figures and words.
83 **9** ¼c. on 2½r. violet and black 60 60
85 ½c. on 5r. black 60 60
86 1c. on 10r. green and black 60 60
87 **12** 1½c. on 300r. black on blue 60 60
88 – 2c. on 20r. red and black 60 60
89 – 2½c. on 25r. brown and black 60 60

90	**12**	3c. on 400r. brown & black	60	60
91	–	5c. on 50r. blue and black	60	60
92	–	7½c. on 75r. brown & black	60	60
93	–	10c. on 100r. brown and black on green	60	60
94	**12**	12c. on 500r. violet & green	60	60
95	–	20c. on 200r. green and black on orange	60	60

16 Giraffe

19 Common Zebra

1921.

96	**16**	¼c. purple	40	30
97		½c. blue	40	30
98		1c. black and green	40	30
99		1½c. orange and black	40	30
100	–	2c. black and red	40	30
101	–	2½c. green and black	40	30
102	–	4c. red and black	40	30
103	–	5c. black and blue	40	30
104	–	6c. violet and black	40	30
123	–	7½c. brown and black	70	30
124	–	8c. green and black	70	30
125	–	10c. brown and black	70	30
126	–	15c. red and black	70	30
127	–	20c. blue and black	80	40
110	**19**	30c. brown and black	2·25	40
111		40c. blue and black	1·75	40
112		50c. green and black	65	40
113		1e. brown and black	85	40
114	–	2e. black and brown	2·00	1·25
115	–	5e. brown and blue	1·60	1·10

DESIGNS—As Type **16**: 2c. to 6c. Vasco da Gama; 7½c. to 20c. Vasco da Gama's flagship "Sao Gabriel". As Type **19**: 2, 5e. Native dhow.

CHARITY TAX STAMPS

The notes under this heading in Portugal also apply here.

1925. Marquis de Pombal Commem. Nos. C327/9 of Mozambique optd **NYASSA**.

C141	C **22**	15c. brown	3·75	3·75
C142	–	15c. brown	3·75	3·75
C143	C **25**	15c. brown	3·75	3·75

POSTAGE DUE STAMPS

D **21** "Sao Gabriel"

1924.

D132	–	½c. green	1·75	1·50
D133	–	1c. blue	1·75	1·50
D134	–	2c. red	1·75	1·50
D135	–	3c. red	1·75	1·50
D136	D **21**	5c. brown	2·75	2·25
D137		6c. brown	2·75	2·25
D138		10c. purple	2·75	2·25
D139	–	20c. red	1·75	1·50
D140	–	50c. purple	1·75	1·50

DESIGNS: ½c., 1c. Giraffe; 2c., 3c. Common zebra; 20c., 50c. Vasco da Gama.

1925. De Pombal stamps of Mozambique, Nos. D327/9, optd **NYASSA**.

D144	C **22**	30c. brown	5·00	5·00
D145	–	30c. brown	5·00	5·00
D146	C **25**	30c. brown	5·00	5·00

OBOCK — Pt. 6

A port and district on the Somali Coast. During 1894 the administration was moved to Djibouti, the capital of French Somali Coast, and the Obock post office was closed.

1892. Stamps of French Colonies, "Commerce" type, optd **OBOCK**.

1	J	1c. black on blue	29·00	26·00
2		2c. brown on buff	32·00	29·00
12		4c. brown on grey	17·00	17·00
13		5c. green on green	17·00	17·00
14		10c. black on lilac	19·00	18·00
15		15c. blue	19·00	18·00
16		20c. red on green	38·00	29·00
17		25c. black on pink	16·00	14·50
8		35c. black on orange	£275	£275
18		40c. red on buff	48·00	38·00
19		75c. red on pink	£225	£160
20		1f. green	55·00	50·00

1892. Nos. 14, 15, 17 and 20 surch.

39	J	1 on 25c. black on red	9·00	11·00
40		2 on 10c. black on lilac	55·00	38·00
41		2 on 15c. blue	9·00	16·00
42		4 on 15c. blue	10·00	17·00
43		4 on 25c. black on red	17·00	16·00
44		5 on 25c. black on red	27·00	20·00
45		20 on 10c. black on lilac	65·00	60·00
46		30 on 10c. black on lilac	75·00	70·00
47		35 on 25c. black on red	70·00	55·00
48		75 on 1f. olive	75·00	75·00
49		5f. on 1f. olive	£550	£475

1892. "Tablet" key-type inscr "OBOCK" in red (1, 5, 15, 25, 75c., 1f.) or blue (others).

50	D	1c. black on blue	2·75	3·75
51		2c. brown on buff	1·10	1·90
52		4c. brown on grey	1·60	1·75
53		5c. green on green	3·50	4·25
54		10c. black on lilac	6·00	5·25
55		15c. blue	12·00	7·25
56		20c. red on green	22·00	21·00
57		25c. black on pink	20·00	20·00
58		30c. brown on drab	19·00	11·00
59		40c. red on yellow	18·00	10·50
60		50c. red on pink	20·00	13·00
61		75c. brown on orange	25·00	13·00
62		1f. green	32·00	32·00

5

1893.

63	**5**	2f. grey	55·00	55·00
64		5f. red	£120	£110

The 5f. stamp is larger than the 2f.

6

7

1894.

65	**6**	1c. black and red	35	55
66		2c. red and green	1·90	1·50
67		4c. red and orange	95	1·10
68		5c. green and brown	1·60	75
69		10c. black and green	5·25	4·00
70		15c. blue and red	3·00	1·25
71		20c. orange and purple	6·00	1·40
72		25c. black and blue	8·25	3·00
73		30c. yellow and green	25·00	11·00
74		40c. orange and green	11·50	7·50
75		50c. red and blue	8·50	6·75
76		75c. lilac and orange	9·50	7·00
77		1f. olive and purple	8·25	9·00
78	**7**	2f. orange and lilac	£110	£110
79		5f. red and blue	90·00	80·00
80		10f. lake and red	£120	£110
81		25f. blue and brown	£600	£575
82		50f. green and lake	£650	£650

Length of sides of Type **7**: 2f. 37 mm; 5f. 42 mm; 10f. 46 mm; 25, 50f. 49 mm.

POSTAGE DUE STAMPS

1892. Postage Due stamps of French Colonies optd **OBOCK**.

D25	U	1c. black	38·00	45·00
D26		2c. black	32·00	35·00
D27		3c. black	38·00	38·00
D28		4c. black	23·00	27·00
D29		5c. black	13·00	10·50
D30		10c. black	28·00	28·00
D31		15c. black	18·00	17·00
D32		20c. black	22·00	23·00
D33		30c. black	26·00	27·00
D34		40c. black	48·00	45·00
D35		60c. black	60·00	60·00
D36		1f. brown	£150	£150
D37		2f. brown	£160	£160
D38		5f. brown	£325	£325

For later issues see **DJIBOUTI**.

OCEANIC SETTLEMENTS — Pt. 6

Scattered French islands in the E. Pacific Ocean, including Tahiti and the Marquesas.

In 1957 the Oceanic Settlements were renamed French Polynesia.

1892. "Tablet" key-type.

1	D	1c. black and red on blue	70	50
2		2c. brown and blue on buff	90	1·10
3		4c. brown and blue on grey	1·50	1·25
14		5c. green and red	1·10	55
5		10c. black and blue on lilac	21·00	8·50
15		10c. red and blue	80	55
6		15c. blue and red	15·00	7·25
16		15c. grey and red	1·75	3·25
7		20c. red and blue on green	6·75	9·00
8		25c. black and red on pink	38·00	12·50
17		25c. blue and red	8·00	3·00
9		30c. brown and blue on drab	15·00	11·50
18		35c. black and red on yellow	3·00	3·75
10		40c. red and blue on yellow	90·00	80·00
19		45c. black and red on green	2·75	4·25
11		50c. red and blue on pink	4·25	5·75
20		50c. brown and red on blue	£170	£150
12		75c. brown and red on orange	8·75	10·00
13		1f. green and red	15·00	14·00

2 Tahitian Woman

3 Kanakas

4 Valley of Fautaua

1913.

21	**2**	1c. brown and violet	20	45
22		2c. grey and brown	20	1·25
23		4c. blue and orange	30	1·50
24		5c. light green and green	1·25	1·90
46		5c. black and blue	65	2·25
25		10c. orange and red	2·25	2·00
47		10c. light green and green	2·00	2·50
48		10c. purple and red on blue	1·90	2·50
25a		15c. black and orange	2·00	2·25
26		20c. violet and black	65	3·00
49		20c. green	1·90	3·00
50		20c. brown and red	1·90	2·50
27	**3**	25c. blue and ultramarine	2·50	1·50
51		25c. red and violet	50	2·00
28		30c. brown and grey	3·50	4·25
52		30c. red and carmine	2·00	3·75
53		30c. red and black	1·60	2·75
54		30c. green and blue	2·50	3·50
29		35c. red and green	1·40	2·75
30		40c. green and black	1·90	2·75
31		45c. red and orange	1·60	2·75
32		50c. black and brown	10·50	12·00
55		50c. blue and ultramarine	1·60	3·00
56		50c. blue and grey	1·25	2·00
57		60c. black and green	1·25	3·00
58		65c. mauve and brown	3·50	3·75
33		75c. violet and purple	2·25	3·00
59		90c. mauve and red	10·50	18·00
34	**4**	1f. black and red	2·75	2·50
60		1f.10 brown and mauve	2·25	3·25
61		1f.40 violet and brown	4·25	4·75
62		1f.50 light blue and blue	13·00	9·75
35		2f. green and brown	4·75	4·75
36		5f. blue and violet		

1915. "Tablet" key-type optd **E F O 1915** and bar.

37	D	10c. red	95	3·00

1915. Red Cross. No. 37 surch **5c** and red cross.

38	D	10c.+5c. red	10·50	24·00

1915. Red Cross. Surch **5c** and red cross.

41	**2**	10c.+5c. orange and red	3·00	3·25

1916. Surch.

42	**2**	10c. on 15c. black and orange	35	3·00
67	**4**	25c. on 2f. green and brown	90	3·25
68		25c. on 5f. blue and violet	60	3·25
63	**3**	60 on 75c. brown and blue	20	2·50
64	**4**	65 on 1f. brown and blue	1·10	3·50
65		85 on 1f. brown and blue	1·50	3·50
66	**3**	90 on 75c. mauve and red	2·25	3·50
69	**4**	1f.25 on 1f. ultramarine & bl	50	3·00
70		1f.50 on 1f. light blue & blue	1·75	3·00
71		20f. on 5f. mauve and red	10·00	24·00

1921. Surch **1921** and new value.

43	**2**	05 on 2c. grey and brown	26·00	26·00
44	**3**	10 on 45c. red and orange	28·00	28·00
45	**2**	25 on 15c. black and orange	5·50	3·25

1924. Surch **45c. 1924.**

72	**2**	45c. on 10c. orange and red	2·75	3·75

1926. Surch in words.

73	**4**	3f. on 5f. blue and grey	75	3·50
74		10f. on 5f. black and green	4·00	5·75

13 Papetoia Bay

1929.

75	**13**	3f. sepia and green	5·00	7·00
76		5f. sepia and blue	6·00	12·50
77		10f. sepia and red	13·00	45·00
78		20f. sepia and mauve	30·00	38·00

1931. "International Colonial Exhibition", Paris, key-types.

79	E	40c. black and green	5·25	6·50
80	F	50c. black and mauve	6·25	7·50
81	G	90c. black and red	5·75	7·75
82	H	1f.50 black and blue	6·25	7·25

14 Spearing Fish

15 Tahitian Girl

16 Native Gods

1934.

83	**14**	1c. black	15	2·25
84		2c. red	15	2·50
85		3c. blue	15	3·00
86		4c. orange	15	3·00
87		5c. mauve	35	3·00
88		10c. brown	15	3·00
89		15c. green	20	3·00
90		20c. red	15	2·75
91	**15**	25c. blue	1·25	2·50
92		30c. green	95	3·25
93		30c. orange	30	3·00
94	**16**	35c. green	2·75	4·50
95	**15**	40c. mauve	50	3·00
96		45c. red	8·25	11·00
97		45c. green	1·10	3·25
98		50c. violet	65	1·60
99		55c. blue	4·75	6·75
100		60c. black	50	3·00
101		65c. brown	3·75	4·25
102		70c. pink	1·60	3·50
103		75c. olive	7·50	9·75
104		80c. purple	1·10	3·50
105		90c. red	1·00	3·00
106	**16**	1f. brown	1·50	2·75
107		1f.25 purple	9·25	10·00
108		1f.25 red	1·50	3·00
109		1f.40 orange	1·50	3·00
110		1f.50 blue	1·50	2·00
111		1f.60 violet	1·50	3·00
112		1f.75 green	7·00	5·75
113		2f. red	80	3·50
114		2f.25 blue	1·10	3·50
115		2f.50 black	1·60	3·50
116		3f. orange	85	3·50
117		5f. mauve	1·75	3·50
118		10f. green	2·00	4·75
119		20f. brown	2·25	5·00

17 Flying Boat

1934. Air.

120	**17**	5f. green	1·50	3·00

1937. International Exhibition, Paris. As Nos. 168/73 of St.-Pierre et Miquelon.

121		20c. violet	1·40	3·75
122		30c. green	80	3·75

123 40c. red . . . . 65 3·25
124 50c. brown . . . . 70 3·00
125 90c. red . . . . 65 4·25
126 1f.50 blue . . . . 1·10 6·50

17a Pierre and Marie Curie

1938. International Anti-cancer Fund.
127 **17a** 1f.75+50c. blue . . . . . 6·75 22·00

17b

1939. New York World's Fair.
128 **17b** 1f.25 red . . . . 80 3·75
129 2f.25 blue . . . . 1·10 3·25

17c Storming the Bastille

1939. 150th Anniv of French Revolution.
130 **17c** 45c.+25c. green and black (postage) . . . . . . 9·25 22·00
131 70c.+30c. brown & black 11·50 22·00
132 90c.+35c. orange & black 10·50 22·00
133 1f.25+1f. red and black 15·00 22·00
134 2f.25+2f. blue and black 13·00 22·00
135 5f.+4f. black & orge (air) 29·00 45·00

1941. Adherence to General de Gaulle. Optd **FRANCE LIBRE**. (a) Nos. 75/8.
136 **13** 3f. brown and green . . . 1·60 4·25
137 5f. brown and blue . . . . 1·60 8·50
138 10f. brown and red . . . . 6·00 15·00
139 20f. brown and mauve . . 42·00 85·00

(b) Nos. 106 and 115/19.
140 **16** 1f. brown . . . . 1·25 6·75
141 2f.50 black . . . . 1·25 8·50
142 3f. red . . . . 2·00 8·50
143 5f. mauve . . . . 3·50 8·50
144 10f. green . . . . 22·00 55·00
145 20f. brown . . . . 21·00 55·00

(c) Air stamp of 1934.
146 **17** 5f. green . . . . 2·25 3·50

19 Polynesian Travelling Canoe

19a Airplane

1942. Free French Issue. (a) Postage.
147 **19** 5c. brown . . . . 15 2·75
148 10c. blue . . . . 15 2·75
149 25c. green . . . . 60 2·75
150 30c. red . . . . 15 2·75
151 40c. green . . . . 15 2·75
152 80c. purple . . . . 15 2·75
153 1f. mauve 75 75
154 1f.50 red . . . . 1·00 2·75
155 2f. black . . . . 1·00 1·75
156 2f.50 blue . . . . 1·10 3·25
157 4f. violet . . . . 85 3·00
158 5f. yellow . . . . 80 3·25
159 10f. brown . . . . 1·75 3·50
160 20f. green . . . . 1·60 3·00

(b) Air. As T **19a**.
161 1f. orange . . . . 1·10 2·50
162 1f.50 red . . . . 1·10 2·50
163 5f. purple . . . . 1·50 3·25
164 10f. black . . . . 1·60 3·75
165 25f. blue . . . . 2·50 4·25
166 50f. green . . . . 3·00 4·25
167 100f. red . . . . 2·75 4·25

19b

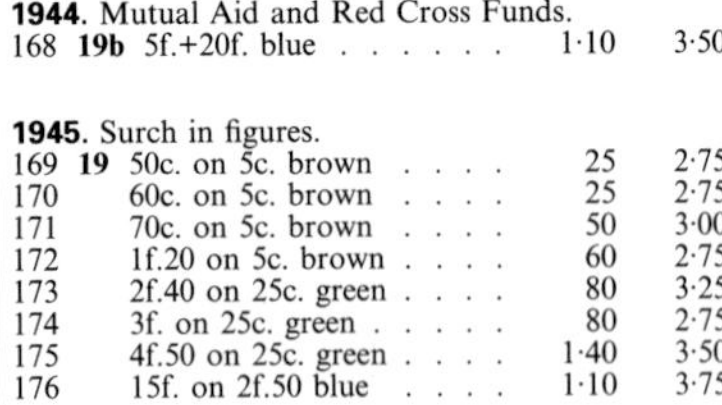

1944. Mutual Aid and Red Cross Funds.
168 **19b** 5f.+20f. blue . . . . . . 1·10 3·50

1945. Surch in figures.
169 **19** 50c. on 5c. brown . . . . 25 2·75
170 60c. on 5c. brown . . . . 25 2·75
171 70c. on 5c. brown . . . . 50 3·00
172 1f.20 on 5c. brown . . . . 60 2·75
173 2f.40 on 25c. green . . . . 80 3·25
174 3f. on 25c. green . . . . . 80 2·75
175 4f.50 on 25c. green . . . . 1·40 3·50
176 15f. on 2f.50 blue . . . . 1·10 3·75

20a Felix Eboue

1945. Eboue.
177 **20a** 2f. black . . . . 15 3·00
178 25f. green . . . . 1·60 3·75

20b "Victory"

1946. Air. Victory.
179 **20b** 8f. green . . . . 35 3·75

20c Legionaries by Lake Chad

1946. Air. From Chad to the Rhine.
180 **20c** 5f. red . . . . 1·25 4·00
181 – 10f. brown . . . . 55 4·00
182 – 15f. green . . . . 1·25 4·00
183 – 20f. red . . . . 1·60 4·00
184 – 25f. purple . . . . 1·25 5·00
185 – 50f. black . . . . 1·50 5·50
DESIGNS: 10f. Battle of Koufa; 15f. Tank Battle, Mareth; 20f. Normandy Landings; 25f. Liberation of Paris; 50f. Liberation of Strasbourg.

21 Moorea Coastline

22 Tahitian Girl

23 Wandering Albatross over Moorea

1948. (a) Postage as T **21/22**.
186 **21** 10c. brown 15 35
187 30c. green 15 40
188 40c. blue . . . . 15 2·25
189 – 50c. lake . . . . 50 2·50
190 – 60c. olive . . . . 65 3·00
191 – 80c. blue . . . . 75 3·00
192 – 1f. lake . . . . 2·25 95
193 – 1f.20 blue . . . . 2·25 3·00
194 – 1f.50 blue . . . . 90 1·60
195 **22** 2f. brown . . . . 2·75 75
196 2f.40 lake . . . . 2·75 3·25
197 3f. violet . . . . 7·75 90
198 4f. blue . . . . 2·25 85
199 – 5f. brown . . . . 2·75 55
200 – 6f. blue . . . . 3·00 65
201 – 9f. brown, black and red 3·50 5·00
202 – 10f. olive . . . . 3·75 65
203 – 15f. red . . . . 5·00 1·50
204 – 20f. blue . . . . 5·75 95
205 – 25f. brown . . . . 5·25 1·90

(b) Air. As T **23**.
206 – 13f. light blue and deep blue . . . . 3·50 2·25
207 **23** 50f. lake . . . . 25·00 14·00
208 – 100f. violet . . . . 17·00 11·00
209 – 200f. blue . . . . 48·00 18·00

DESIGNS: As T **22**: 50c. to 80c. Kanaka fisherman; 9f. Bora-Bora girl; 1f. to 1f.50, Faa village; 5 , 6 , 10f. Bora-Bora and Pandanus pine; 15f. to 25f. Polynesian girls. As T **23**: 13f. Pahia Peak and palms; 100f. Airplane over Moorea; 200f. Wandering albatross over Maupiti Island.

24a People of Five Races, Aircraft and Globe

1949. Air. 75th Anniv of U.P.U.
210 **24a** 10f. blue . . . . 5·00 20·00

24b Doctor and Patient

1950. Colonial Welfare.
211 **24b** 10f.+2f. green and blue 5·25 7·00

24c

25 "Nafea" (after Gauguin)

1952. Centenary of Military Medals.
212 **24c** 3f. violet, yellow and green . . . . 7·25 11·00

1953. Air. 50th Death Anniv of Gauguin (painter).
213 **25** 14f. sepia, red and turquoise . . . . 36·00 65·00

25a Normandy Landings, 1944

1954. Air. 10th Anniv of Liberation.
214 **25a** 3f. green and turquoise 5·75 6·00

26 Schooner in Dry Dock, Papeete

1956. Economic and Social Development Fund.
215 **26** 3f. turquoise . . . . 85 1·10

POSTAGE DUE STAMPS

1926. Postage Due stamps of France surch **Etabts Francais de l'Oceanie 2 francs a percevoir** (No. D80) or optd **Etablissements Francais de l'Oceanie** (others).
D73 **D 11** 5c. blue . . . . 25 2·75
D74 10c. brown . . . . . . 25 2·25
D75 20c. olive . . . . . . 35 3·00
D76 30c. red . . . . 50 3·00
D77 40c. red . . . . 1·10 4·25
D78 60c. green . . . . . . 95 4·25
D79 1f. red on yellow . . . 80 4·25
D80 2f. on 1f. red . . . . . 1·10 4·75
D81 3f. mauve . . . . 4·00 13·50

D 14 Fautaua Falls

D 24

1929.
D82 **D 14** 5c. brown and blue . . 20 2·50
D83 10c. green and orange 15 2·75
D84 30c. red and brown . . 40 3·00
D85 50c. brown and green 65 2·75
D86 60c. green and violet . . 2·00 5·00
D87 – 1f. mauve and blue . . 1·75 4·00
D88 – 2f. brown and red . . . 1·25 3·50
D89 – 3f. green and blue . . . 75 3·50
DESIGN: 1 to 3f. Polynesian man.

1948.
D210 **D 24** 10c. green . . . . . . 15 1·00
D211 30c. brown . . . . . 15 2·75
D212 50c. red . . . . 20 2·75
D213 1f. blue . . . . 35 2·75
D214 2f. green . . . . . . 75 3·25
D215 3f. red . . . . 1·25 3·50
D216 4f. violet . . . . . . 1·00 3·50
D217 5f. mauve . . . . . . 1·40 4·25
D218 10f. blue . . . . . . 2·50 5·50
D219 20f. lake . . . . . . 2·50 7·00

For later issues see **FRENCH POLYNESIA**.

OLDENBURG Pt. 7

A former Grand Duchy in North Germany. In 1867 it joined the North German Federation.

72 grote = 1 thaler.

1

2

3

1852. Imperf.
1 **1** $\frac{1}{3}$sgr. black on green £1100 £1100
2 $\frac{1}{30}$th. black on blue . . . . . . £325 22·00
5 $\frac{1}{15}$th. black on red . . . . . . £700 75·00
8 $\frac{1}{10}$th. black on yellow . . . . . £700 75·00

1859. Imperf.
17 **2** $\frac{1}{4}$g. yellow £275 £3250
10 $\frac{1}{3}$g. black on green £2250 £2750
19 $\frac{1}{3}$g. green £400 £750
21 $\frac{1}{2}$g. brown £375 £450
11 1g. black on blue . . . . . £650 36·00
23 1g. blue £200 £140
15 2g. black on red £800 £550
26 2g. red £400 £400
16 3g. black on yellow £800 £550
28 3g. yellow £400 £400

1862. Roul.
30 **3** $\frac{1}{3}$g. green £180 £180
32 $\frac{1}{2}$g. orange . . . . £180 90·00
42 1g. red . . . . 9·00 45·00
36 2g. blue . . . . £180 45·00
39 3g. bistre . . . . £180 45·00

OMAN (SULTANATE) Pt. 19

In January 1971, the independent Sultanate of Muscat and Oman was renamed Sultanate of Oman.

NOTE. Labels inscribed "State of Oman" or "Oman Imamate State" are said to have been issued by a rebel administration under the Imam of Oman. There is no convincing evidence that these labels had any postal use within Oman and they are therefore omitted. They can be found, however, used on covers which appear to emanate from Amman and Baghdad.

1971. 1000 baizas = 1 rial saidi.
1972. 1000 baizas = 1 rial omani.

1971. Nos. 110/21 of Muscat and Oman optd **SULTANATE of OMAN** in English and Arabic.
122 **12** 5b. purple 10 10
142 10b. brown 20 10
124 20b. brown 40 25
125 A 25b. black and violet . . . 50 25
126 30b. black and blue . . . 70 40
127 40b. black and orange . . 95 50
128 **14** 50b. mauve and blue . . . 1·25 65
129 B 75b. green and brown . . . 1·60 90
130 C 100b. blue and orange . . 1·90 1·25
131 $\frac{1}{4}$r. brown and green . . . 6·25 3·75
132 E $\frac{1}{2}$r. violet and red . . . . 12·50 6·25
133 F 1r. red and violet . . . . . 24·00 14·00

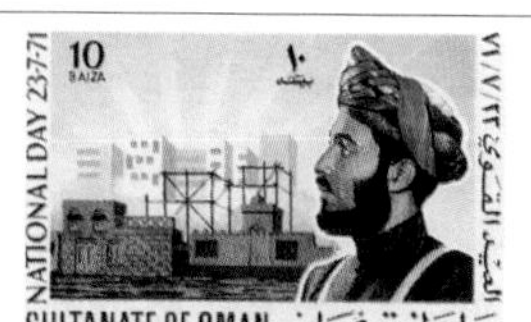

19 Sultan Qabus and Buildings ("Land Development")

1971. National Day. Multicoloured.
134 10b. Type **19** 35 25
135 40b. Sultan in military uniform and Omanis ("Freedom") 95 65
136 50b. Doctors and patients ("Health Services") . . . . 1·25 1·00
137 100b. Children at school ("Education") . . . . . . 2·50 1·90

1971. No. 94 of Muscat and Oman surch **SULTANATE of OMAN 5** in English and Arabic.
138 5b. on 3b. purple . . . . . 20·00 8·25

21 Child in Class

1971. 25th Anniv of U.N.I.C.E.F.
139 **21** 50b.+25b. multicoloured 2·50 2·50

22 Book Year Emblem

1972. International Book Year.
140 **22** 25b. multicoloured . . . . 3·25 1·25

سلطنة عمان

25 B ٢٥ ب

(24)

1972. Nos. 102 of Muscat and Oman and 127 of Oman optd with T **24**.
144 25b. on 1r. blue and orange 21·00 13·00
145 25b. on 40b. black and orange . . . . 21·00 13·00

26 Matrah, 1809

1972.
158 **26** 5b. multicoloured 20 10
147 10b. multicoloured 20 10
148 20b. multicoloured 30 10
149 25b. multicoloured 30 10
150 – 30b. multicoloured 45 25
151 – 40b. multicoloured 55 30
152 – 50b. multicoloured 70 45
153 – 75b. multicoloured . . . . 1·00 55
154 – 100b. multicoloured . . . 1·40 85
155 – ¼r. multicoloured . . . . . 3·50 1·40
156 – ½r. multicoloured . . . . . 6·75 3·50
157 – 1r. multicoloured . . . . . 15·50 6·50
DESIGNS—26 × 21 mm: 30b. to 75b. Shinas, 1809. 42 × 25 mm: 100b. to 1r. Muscat, 1809.

29 Government Buildings

1973. Opening of Ministerial Complex.
170 **29** 25b. multicoloured 45 35
171 100b. multicoloured . . . 1·90 1·25

30 Oman Crafts (dhow building)

1973. National Day. Multicoloured.
172 15b. Type **30** 40 25
173 50b. Seeb International Airport . . . . 2·25 1·25
174 65b. Dhow and tanker . . . 2·25 1·25
175 100b. "Ship of the Desert" (camel) . . . . 3·25 1·90

31 Aerial View of Port

1974. Inauguration of Port Qabus.
176 **31** 100b. multicoloured . . . 2·75 2·00

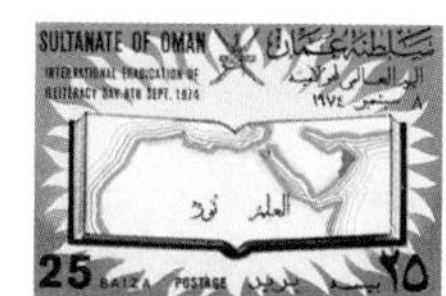

32 Map on Open Book

1974. Illiteracy Eradication Campaign. Mult.
177 25b. Type **32** 60 30
178 100b. Hands reaching for open book (vert) . . . . . 2·40 1·60

33 Sultan Qabus bin Said and Emblems

1974. Centenary of U.P.U.
179 **33** 100b. multicoloured . . . 1·75 1·25

34 Arab Scribe

1975. "Eradicate Illiteracy".
180 **34** 25b. multicoloured . . . . 3·50 95

35 New Harbour, Mina Raysoot

1975. National Day. Multicoloured.
181 30b. Type **35** 25 25
182 50b. Stadium and map . . . 65 40
183 75b. Water desalination plant 65 65
184 100b. Television station . . . 1·00 75
185 150b. Satellite Earth station and map . . . . 1·25 1·25
186 250b. Telecommunications symbols and map . . . . 2·50 2·00

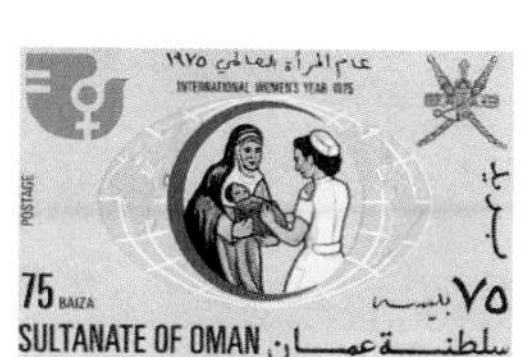

36 Arab Woman and Child with Nurse

1975. International Women's Year. Mult.
187 75b. Type **36** 70 65
188 150b. Mother and children (vert) . . . . 1·25 1·25

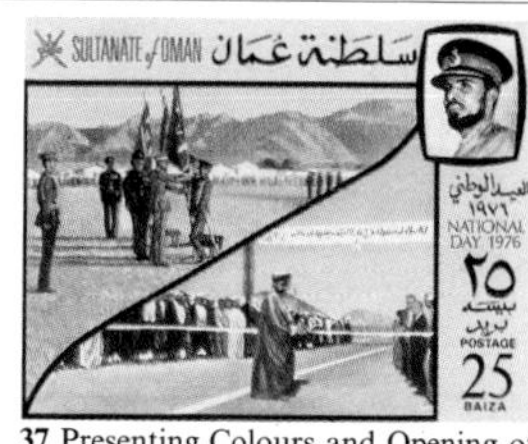

37 Presenting Colours and Opening of Seeb–Nizwa Highway

1976. National Day. Multicoloured.
201 25b. Type **37** 25 20
202 40b. Parachutists and harvesting 90 45
203 75b. Agusta-Bell AB-212 helicopters and Victory Day procession . . . . . 1·75 90
204 150b. Road construction and Salalah T.V. Station . . . 2·00 1·50

38 Great Bath, Moenjodaro

1977. "Save Moenjodaro" Campaign.
205 **38** 125b. multicoloured . . . 2·25 1·90

39 A.P.U. Emblem **40** Coffee Pots

1977. 25th Anniv of Arab Postal Union.
206 **39** 30b. multicoloured 65 40
207 75b. multicoloured . . . . 1·90 1·10

1977. National Day. Multicoloured.
208 40b. Type **40** 60 40
209 75b. Earthenware pots . . . 1·10 50
210 100b. Khor Rori inscriptions 1·25 75
211 150b. Silver jewellery . . . . 2·25 1·25

1978. Surch in English and Arabic.
212 40b. on 150b. mult (No. 185) 12·00 12·00
213 50b. on 150b. mult (No. 188) 15·00 15·00
214 75b. on 250b. mult (No. 186) 24·00 24·00

42 Mount Arafat, Pilgrims and Kaaba

1978. Pilgrimage to Mecca.
215 **42** 40b. multicoloured . . . . 1·75 1·40

43 Jalali Fort

1978. National Day. Forts. Multicoloured.
216 20b. Type **43** 25 20
217 25b. Nizwa Fort 30 25
218 40b. Rostaq Fort 70 40
219 50b. Sohar Fort 80 50
220 75b. Bahla Fort . . . . . . 1·00 80
221 100b. Jibrin Fort . . . . . . 1·50 1·00

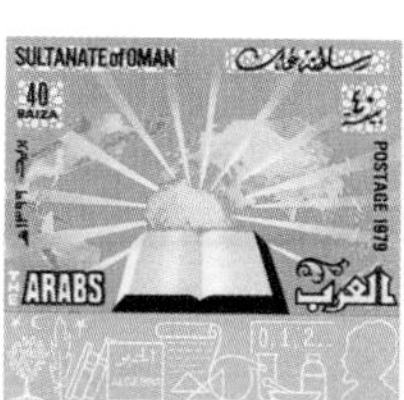

44 World Map, Koran and Symbols of Arab Achievements

1979. The Arabs.
222 **44** 40b. multicoloured 45 40
223 100b. multicoloured . . . 1·60 1·25

45 Child on Swing

1979. International Year of the Child.
224 **45** 40b. multicoloured . . . . 1·90 1·50

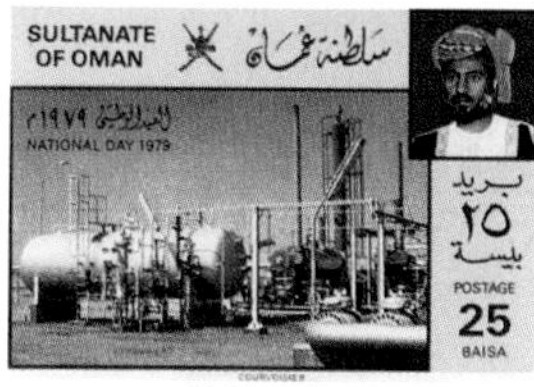

46 Gas Plant

1979. National Day. Multicoloured.
225 25b. Type **46** 95 45
226 75b. Dhow and modern trawler . . . . 2·25 1·50

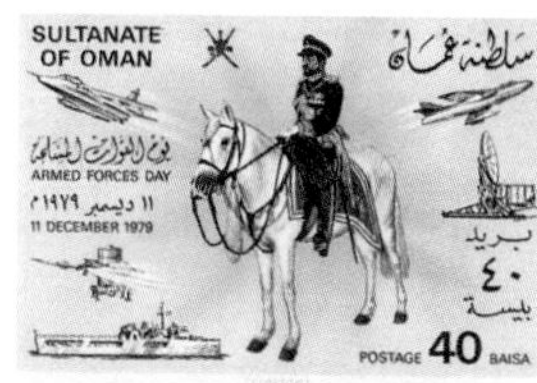

47 Sultan Qabus on Horseback

1979. Armed Forces Day. Multicoloured.
227 40b. Type **47** . . . . 2·25 75
228 100b. Soldier . . . . 3·00 1·90

48 Mosque, Mecca

1980. 1400th Anniv of Hegira. Multicoloured.
229 50b. Type **48** 60 50
230 150b. Mosque and Kaaba . . 2·25 1·60

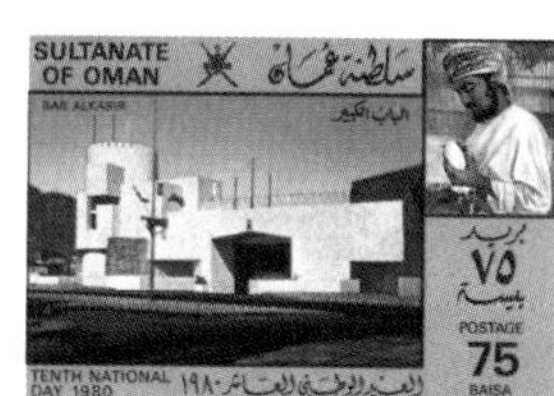

49 Bab Alkabir

1980. National Day. Multicoloured.
231 75b. Type **49** 55 50
232 100b. Corniche 90 80
233 250b. Polo match . . . . . 2·50 2·25
234 500b. Omani women . . . . 4·25 4·00

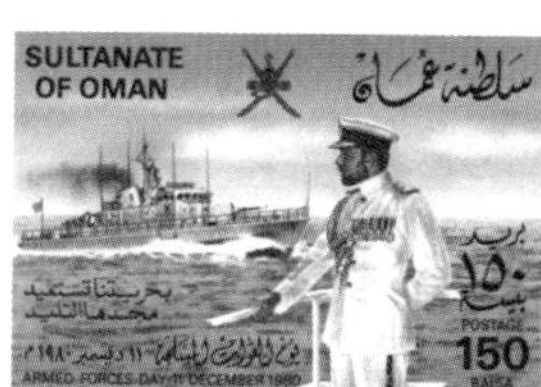

50 Sultan and Naval Patrol Boat

1980. Armed Forces Day. Multicoloured.
235 150b. Type **50** . . . . 1·60 1·50
236 750b. Sultan and mounted soldiers . . . . 7·00 7·00

51 Policewoman helping Children across Road

1981. National Police Day. Multicoloured.
237 50b. Type **51** 70 50
238 100b. Police bandsmen . . . 1·25 1·00
239 150b. Mounted police . . . . 1·75 1·50
240 ½r. Police headquarters . . . 5·50 4·75

1981. Nos. 231, 234 and 235/6 surch **POSTAGE** and new value in English and Arabic.
241 **50** 20b. on 150b. multicoloured 50 30
242 – 30b. on 750b. multicoloured 75 40
243 **49** 50b. on 75b. multicoloured 1·25 75
244 – 100b. on 500b. multicoloured . . . . . 2·75 1·75

53 Sultan's Crest

1981. Welfare of Blind.
245 **53** 10b. black, blue and red 40 25

54 Palm Tree, Fishes and Wheat

1981. World Food Day.
246 **54** 50b. multicoloured . . . . 2·00 1·25

55 Pilgrims at Prayer

1981. Pilgrimage to Mecca.
247 **55** 50b. multicoloured . . . . 1·60 75

56 Al Razha

1981. National Day. Multicoloured.
248 160b. Type **56** . . . . 1·50 1·50
249 300b. Sultan Qabus bin Said 2·50 2·50

57 Muscat Port, 1981

1981. Retracing the Voyage of Sinbad. Mult.
250 50b. Type **57** 50 50
251 100b. The "Sohar" (replica of medieval dhow) . . . 1·25 1·25
252 130b. Map showing route of voyage . . . . 1·60 1·60
253 200b. Muscat Harbour, 1650 2·25 2·25

58 Parachute-drop

1981. Armed Forces Day. Multicoloured.
255 100b. Type **58** . . . . 1·40 85
256 400b. Missile-armed corvettes 4·75 4·75

59 Police Launch

1982. National Police Day. Multicoloured.
257 50b. Type **59** . . . . 1·75 70
258 100b. Royal Oman Police Band at Cardiff . . . . . 1·60 1·10

60 "Nerium mascatense"

1982. Flora and Fauna. Multicoloured.
259 5b. Type **60** 10 10
260 10b. "Dionysia mira" 10 10
261 20b. "Teucrium mascatense" 15 10
262 25b. "Geranium mascatense" 15 15
263 30b. "Cymatium boschi" (horiz) 25 20
264 40b. Eloise's acteon (horiz) 25 20
265 50b. Teulere's cowrie (horiz) 30 25
266 75b. Lovely cowrie (horiz) . . 45 40
267 100b. Arabian chukar (25 × 33 mm) . . . . . . 1·90 1·25
268 ¼r. Hoopoe (25 × 33 mm) . . 5·00 4·50
269 ½r. Arabian tahr (25 × 39 mm) . . . . . . 4·25 3·75
270 1r. Arabian oryx (25 × 39 mm) . . . . . . 8·00 7·50
Nos. 259/62 show flowers, Nos. 263/6 shells, Nos. 267/8 birds and Nos. 269/70 animals.

61 Palm Tree

1982. Arab Palm Tree Day. Multicoloured.
271 40b. Type **61** 90 50
272 100b. Palm tree and nuts . . 2·10 1·25

62 I.T.U. Emblem

1982. I.T.U. Delegates Conference, Nairobi.
273 **62** 100b. multicoloured . . . 2·00 1·25

63 Emblem and Cups

1982. Municipalities Week.
274 **63** 40b. multicoloured . . . . 1·50 70

64 State Consultative Council Inaugural Session

1982. National Day. Multicoloured.
275 40b. Type **64** 50 45
276 100b. Petroleum refinery . . 1·75 1·25

65 Sultan meeting Troops

1982. Armed Forces Day. Multicoloured.
277 50b. Type **65** 75 50
278 100b. Mounted army band 2·00 1·25

66 Police Motorcyclist and Headquarters

1983. National Police Day.
279 **66** 50b. multicoloured . . . . 1·60 1·00

67 Satellite, W.C.Y. Emblem and Dish Aerial

1983. World Communications Year.
280 **67** 50b. multicoloured . . . . 1·60 1·00

68 Bee Hives

1983. Bee-keeping. Multicoloured.
281 50b. Type **68** . . . . 1·25 1·00
282 50b. Bee collecting nectar . . 1·25 1·00
Nos. 281/2 were issued together, se-tenant, each pair forming a composite design.

69 Pilgrims at Mudhalfa

1983. Pilgrimage to Mecca.
283 **69** 40b. multicoloured . . . . 1·90 1·00

70 Emblem, Map and Sultan

1983. Omani Youth Year.
284 **70** 50b. multicoloured . . . . 1·40 70

71 Sohar Copper Mine

1983. National Day. Multicoloured.
285 50b. Type **71** 90 50
286 100b. Sultan Qabus University and foundation stone . . . . 1·50 1·00

72 Machine Gun Post

1983. Armed Forces Day.
287 **72** 100b. multicoloured . . . 2·25 1·25

73 Police Cadets Parade

1984. National Police Day.
288 **73** 100b. multicoloured . . . 1·90 1·25

74 Footballers and Cup

1984. 7th Arabian Gulf Cup Football Tournament. Multicoloured.
289 40b. Type **74** 60 40
290 50b. Emblem and pictograms of footballers 1·00 65

75 Stoning the Devil

1984. Pilgrimage to Mecca.
291 **75** 50b. multicoloured . . . . 1·60 90

76 New Central Post Office and Automatic Sorting Machine

1984. National Day. Multicoloured.
292 130b. Type **76** . . . . 1·25 1·10
293 160b. Map of Oman with telecommunications symbols . . . . 1·90 1·75

77 Scouts reading Map

1984. 16th Arab Scouts Conference, Muscat. Multicoloured.
294 50b. Scouts pegging tent . . 45 40
295 50b. Type **77** 45 40
296 130b. Scouts assembled round flag . . . . 1·25 1·10
297 130b. Scout, cub, guide, brownie and scout leaders 1·25 1·10

78 Sultan, Jet Fighters and "Al Munassir" (landing craft)

1984. Armed Forces Day.
298 **78** 100b. multicoloured . . . 1·50 1·25

79 Bell 214ST Helicopter lifting Man from "Al-Ward" (tanker)

1985. National Police Day.
299 **79** 100b. multicoloured . . . 3·25 1·40

80 Al-Khaif Mosque and Tent, Mina

1985. Pilgrimage to Mecca.
300 **80** 50b. multicoloured . . . . 1·00 50

81 I.Y.Y. Emblem and Youth holding Olive Branches

1985. International Youth Year. Mult.
301 50b. Type **81** 50 50
302 100b. Emblem and young people at various activities 90 90

82 Palace before and after Restoration

1985. Restoration of Jabrin Palace. Mult.
303 100b. Type **82** 75 70
304 250b. Restored ceiling . . . 2·75 2·50

83 Drummers

1985. International Omani Traditional Music Symposium.
305 **83** 50b. multicoloured . . . . 1·00 55

84 Scenes of Child Care and Emblem

1985. U.N.I.C.E.F. Child Health Campaign.
306 **84** 50b. multicoloured . . . . 1·00 55

85 Flags around Map of Gulf

1985. 6th Supreme Council Session of Gulf Co-operation Council, Muscat. Multicoloured.
307 40b. Type **85** 60 50
308 50b. Portraits of rulers of Council member countries 80 60

86 Sultan Qabus University and Students

1985. National Day. Multicoloured.
309 20b. Type **86** 20 15
310 50b. Tractor and oxen ploughing field 45 40
311 100b. Port Qabus cement factory and Oman Chamber of Commerce . . 90 80
312 200b. Road bridge, Douglas DC-10 airliner and communications centre . . 2·25 1·50
313 250b. Portrait of Sultan Qabus (vert) . . . . 1·75 1·60

87 Military Exercise at Sea

1985. Armed Forces Day.
314 **87** 100b. multicoloured . . . 1·50 1·00

88 Red-tailed Butterflyfish

1985. Marine Life. Multicoloured.
315 20b. Type **88** 50 20
316 50b. Black-finned melon butterflyfish 90 55
317 100b. Gardiner's butterflyfish 1·60 1·10
318 150b. Narrow-barred Spanish mackerel . . . . 2·50 2·25
319 200b. Lobster (horiz) . . . . 1·60 1·50

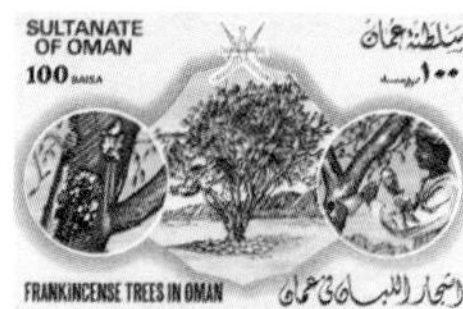

89 Frankincense Tree

1985. Frankincense Production.
320 **89** 100b. multicoloured . . . 60 50
321 3r. multicoloured . . . . . 20·00 14·00

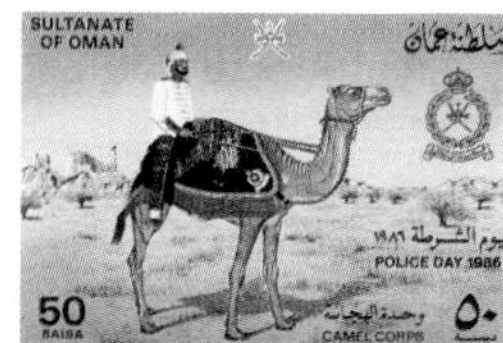

90 Camel Corps Member

1986. National Police Day.
322 **90** 50b. multicoloured 95 65

91 Cadet Barquentine "Shabab Oman", 1986

1986. Participation of "Shabab Oman" in Statue of Liberty Centenary Celebrations. Multicoloured.
323 50b. "Sultana" (full-rigged sailing ship), 1840 . . . . 70 50
324 100b. Type **91** . . . . 1·50 1·10

92 Crowd around Holy Kaaba

1986. Pilgrimage to Mecca.
326 **92** 50b. multicoloured 85 40

93 Scouts erecting Tent

1986. 17th Arab Scout Camp, Salalah. Multicoloured.
327 50b. Type **93** 55 35
328 100b. Scouts making survey 1·10 65

94 Sports Complex

1986. Inauguration of Sultan Qabus Sports Complex.
329 **94** 100b. multicoloured . . . 1·10 75

95 Mother and Baby, Emblem and Tank on Globe

1986. International Peace Year.
330 **95** 130b. multicoloured . . . 1·25 90

96 Al-Sahwa Tower

1986. National Day. Multicoloured.
331 50b. Type **96** 50 30
332 100b. Sultan Qabus University (inauguration) 1·10 65
333 130b. 1966 stamps and F.D.C. cancellation (20th anniv of first Oman stamp issue) (57 × 27 mm) . . . . 1·40 95

97 Camel Corps

1987. National Police Day.
334 **97** 50b. multicoloured 85 60

98 Family

1987. Arabian Gulf Social Work Week.
335 **98** 50b. multicoloured 85 45

99 Aqueduct

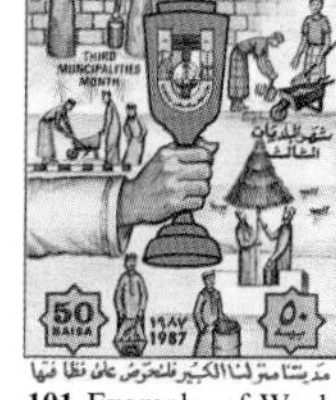

101 Examples of Work and Hand holding Cup

100 Crowd around Holy Kaaba

1987. International Environment Day. Mult.
336 50b. Greater flamingoes . . . 2·10 80
337 130b. Type **99** . . . . 1·25 80

1987. Pilgrimage to Mecca. Multicoloured.
338 50b. Type **100** 60 50
339 50b. Al-Khaif Mosque and tents, Mina 60 50
340 50b. Stoning the Devil . . . 60 50
341 50b. Pilgrims at Mudhalfa . . 60 50
342 50b. Pilgrims at prayer . . . 60 50
343 50b. Mount Arafat, pilgrims and Kaaba 60 50

1987. 3rd Municipalities Month.
344 **101** 50b. multicoloured . . . 75 50

102 Marine Science and Fisheries Centre

1987. National Day. Multicoloured.
345 50b. Type **102** 65 35
346 130b. Royal Hospital . . . . 1·10 85

103 Radio Operators

1987. 15th Anniv of Royal Omani Amateur Radio Society.
347 **103** 130b. multicoloured . . . 95 80

104 Weaver

1988. Traditional Crafts. Multicoloured.
348 50b. Type **104** 35 30
349 100b. Potter 60 50
350 150b. Halwa maker 85 75
351 200b. Silversmith . . . . . . 1·00 85

105 Show Jumping **106** Emblem

1988. Olympic Games, Seoul. Multicoloured.
353 100b. Type **105** 55 50
354 100b. Hockey 55 50
355 100b. Football 55 50
356 100b. Running 55 50
357 100b. Swimming 55 50
358 100b. Shooting 55 50

1988. 40th Anniv of W.H.O. "Health for All".
360 **106** 100b. multicoloured . . . 75 65

107 Tending Land and Crops

1988. National Day. Agriculture Year. Mult.
361 100b. Type **107** 70 70
362 100b. Livestock 70 70

108 Dhahira Region (woman's)

1989. Costumes. Multicoloured.
363 30b. Type **108** 15 10
364 40b. Eastern region (woman's) 20 15
365 50b. Batinah region (woman's) 25 20
366 100b. Interior region (woman's) 55 45
367 130b. Southern region (woman's) 70 60
368 150b. Muscat region (woman's) 80 70
369 200b. Dhahira region (man's) 1·10 95
370 ¼r. Eastern region (man's) . . 1·40 1·25
371 ½r. Southern region (man's) 2·75 2·40
372 1r. Muscat region (man's) . . 5·25 4·50

109 Fishing

1989. National Day. Agriculture Year. Mult.
375 100b. Type **109** . . . . . . 1·00 70
376 100b. Agriculture 65 55

110 Flags and Omani State Arms

1989. 10th Supreme Council Session of Arab Co-operation Council, Muscat. Multicoloured.
377 50b. Type **110** 30 25
378 50b. Council emblem and Sultan Qabus 30 25

111 Emblem and Map

1990. 5th Anniv (1989) of Gulf Investment Corporation.
379 **111** 50b. multicoloured . . . 30 25
380 130b. multicoloured . . . 80 70

112 Emblem and Douglas DC-10 Airliner

113 Map

1990. 40th Anniv of Gulf Air.
381 **112** 80b. multicoloured . . . 50 45

1990. Omani Ophiolite Symposium, Muscat.
382 **113** 80b. multicoloured . . . 60 50
383 150b. multicoloured . . . 1·25 1·10

114 Ahmed bin Na'aman al-Ka'aby (envoy), "Sultana" and Said bin Sultan al-Busaidi

1990. 150th Anniv of First Omani Envoy's Journey to U.S.A.
384 **114** 200b. multicoloured . . . 1·25 1·10

115 Sultan Qabus Rose

1990. 20th Anniv of Sultan Qabus's Accession.
385 **115** 200b. multicoloured . . . 1·25 1·10

116 National Day Emblem

1990. National Day.
386 **116** 100b. red and green on gold foil 60 50
387 – 200b. green and red on gold foil . . . . 1·25 1·10
DESIGN: 200b. Sultan Qabus.

117 Donor and Recipient

1991. Blood Donation.
389 **117** 50b. multicoloured . . . 35 30
390 200b. multicoloured . . . 1·50 1·25

118 Industrial Emblems

1991. National Day and Industry Year. Mult.
391 100b. Type **118** 70 60
392 200b. Sultan Qabus . . . . . 1·25 1·10

119 Weapons, Military Transport and Sultan Qabus

1991. Armed Forces Day.
394 **119** 100b. multicoloured . . . 90 60

120 Interior of Museum and National Flags

121 Satellite Picture of Asia

1992. Inaug of Omani-French Museum, Muscat.
395 **120** 100b. multicoloured . . . 65 55

1992. World Meteorological Day.
397 **121** 220b. multicoloured . . . 1·40 1·25

122 Emblem and Hands

123 Emblem and Hands protecting Handicapped Child

1992. World Environment Day.
398 **122** 100b. multicoloured . . . 65 55

1992. Welfare of Handicapped Children.
399 **123** 70b. multicoloured . . . 50 45

124 Sultan Qabus and Books

1992. Publication of Sultan Qabus "Encyclopedia of Arab Names".
400 **124** 100b. multicoloured . . . 60 50

125 Sultan Qabus, Factories and Industry Year Emblem

1992. National Day. Multicoloured.
401 100b. Type **125** 60 50
402 200b. Sultan Qabus and Majlis As'shura (Consultative Council) emblem . . . . 1·25 1·10

126 Mounted Policemen and Sultan Qabus

1993. National Police Day.
403 **126** 80b. multicoloured . . . 50 45

127 Census Emblem

1993. Population, Housing and Establishments Census.
404 **127** 100b. multicoloured . . . 55 50

128 Frigate and Sultan Qabus presenting Colours

1993. Navy Day.
405 **128** 100b. multicoloured . . . 75 55

129 Youth Year Emblem

1993. National Day and Youth Year. Multi.
406 100b. Type **129** 55 50
407 200b. Sultan Qabus . . . . . 1·10 95

130 Scout Headquarters and Emblem

1993. 61st Anniv of Scouting in Oman (408) and 10th Anniv of Sultan Qabus as Chief Scout (409). Multicoloured.
408 100b. Type **130** 35 30
409 100b. Scout camp and Sultan Qabus 35 30
Nos. 408/9 were issued together, se-tenant, forming a composite design.

131 Sei Whale and School of Dolphins

1993. Whales and Dolphins in Omani Waters. Multicoloured.
410 100b. Type **131** 55 45
411 100b. Sperm whale and dolphins 55 45
Nos. 410/11 were issued together, se-tenant, forming a composite design.

132 Water Drops and Falaj (ancient water system)

133 Municipality Building

1994. World Water Day.
413 **132** 50b. multicoloured . . . 30 25

1994. 70th Anniv of Muscat Municipality.
414 **133** 50b. multicoloured . . . 30 25

134 Centenary Emblem and Sports Pictograms

1994. Centenary of International Olympic Committee.
415 **134** 100b. multicoloured . . . 55 50

135 Emblem

1994. National Day. Multicoloured.
416 50b. Type **135** 15 10
417 50b. Sultan Qabus 15 10

136 Airplane and Emblem

1994. 50th Anniv of I.C.A.O.
418 **136** 100b. multicoloured . . . 30 25

137 Arms

139 Emblem and National Colours

138 Meeting

1994. 250th Anniv of Al-Busaid Dynasty. Multicoloured.
419 50b. Type **137** dated "1744–1775" 15 10
420 50b. Type **137** dated "1775–1779" 15 10
421 50b. Type **137** dated "1779–1792" 15 10
422 50b. Type **137** dated "1792–1804" 15 10
423 50b. Type **137** dated "1804–1807" 15 10
424 50b. Said bin Sultan (1807–1856) 15 10
425 50b. Type **137** dated "1856–1866" 15 10
426 50b. Type **137** dated "1866–1868" 15 10
427 50b. Type **137** dated "1868–1871" 15 10
428 50b. Turki bin Said (1871–1888) 15 10
429 50b. Feisal bin Turki (1888–1913) 15 10
430 50b. Taimur bin Feisal (1913–1932) 15 10
431 50b. Arms, Sultan Qabus and family tree 15 10
432 50b. Said bin Taimur (1932–1970) 15 10
433 50b. Sultan Qabus (1970–) 15 10

1995. Open Parliament.
435 **138** 50b. multicoloured . . . 15 10

1995. 50th Anniv of Arab League.
436 **139** 100b. multicoloured . . . 30 25

140 Anniversary Emblem

1995. 50th Anniv of U.N.O.
437 **140** 100b. multicoloured . . . 30 25

141 Sultan Qabus in Robes

1995. National Day. Multicoloured.
438 50b. Type **141** 15 10
439 100b. Sultan Qabus in military uniform 30 25

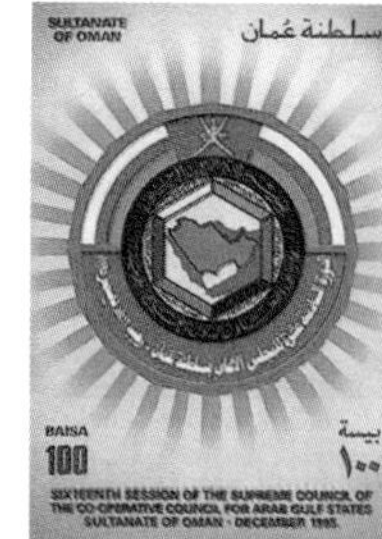
142 Council Emblem

1995. 16th Supreme Council Session of Gulf Co-operation Council, Oman. Multicoloured.
441 100b. Type **142** 30 25
442 200b. Sultan Qabus, members' flags and map 65 55

143 Ash'shashah

1996. Omani Sailing Vessels. Multicoloured.
443 50b. Type **143** 20 10
444 100b. Al-Battil 35 25
445 200b. Al-Boum 70 55
446 250b. Al-Badan 85 65
447 350b. As'sanbuq . . . . . . 1·25 90
448 450b. Al-Galbout . . . . . 1·50 1·10
449 650b. Al-Baghlah . . . . . 2·40 1·75
450 1r. Al-Ghanjah . . . . . . 3·50 2·75

144 Emblem, Poppy Head, Skull-like Face smoking Cigarette and Syringe

1996. United Nations Decade against Drug Abuse.
451 **144** 100b. multicoloured . . . 30 25

145 Shooting

1996. Olympic Games, Atlanta. Multicoloured.
452 100b. Type **145** 30 25
453 100b. Swimming 30 25
454 100b. Cycling 30 25
455 100b. Running 30 25
Nos. 452/5 were issued together, se-tenant, forming a composite design.

146 Tournament Emblem and Flags of Participating Countries

1996. 13th Arabian Gulf Cup Football Championship.
456 **146** 100b. multicoloured . . . 30 25

147 Sultan Qabus and Sur (left detail)

1996. National Day. Multicoloured.
457 50b. Type **147** 15 10
458 50b. Sultan Qabus and Sur (right detail) 15 10
Nos. 457/8 were issued together, se-tenant, forming a composite design.

148 Mother with Children

1996. 50th Anniv of U.N.I.C.E.F.
459 **148** 100b. multicoloured . . . 30 25

149 Nakl Fort

1997. Tourism. Multicoloured.
460 100b. Type **149** 30 25
461 100b. Wadi Tanuf (waterfall in centre of stamp) 30 25
462 100b. Fort on Muthrah Corniche 30 25
463 100b. Wadi Dayqah Dam . . 30 25
464 100b. Bahla fort (overlooking tree-covered plain) 30 25
465 100b. Wadi Darbut waterfall (near top of stamp) 30 25

150 Sultan Qabus and Dhofar Waterfalls

1997. National Day. Multicoloured.
466 100b. Type **150** 30 25
467 100b. Sultan Qabus seated by waterfalls 30 25

151 Guide Activities

1997. 25th Anniv of Oman Girl Guides.
468 **151** 100b. multicoloured . . . 30 25

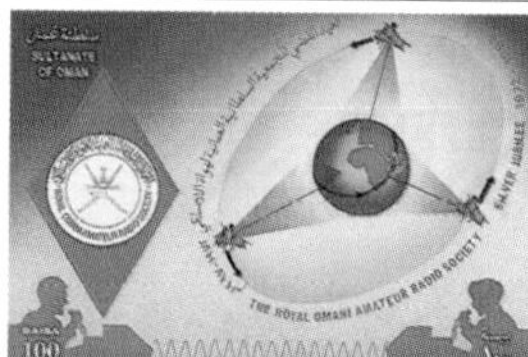
152 Society and Anniversary Emblems

1997. 25th Anniv of Royal Omani Amateur Radio Society.
469 **152** 100b. multicoloured . . . 30 25

153 Dagger and Sheath

1998. Al-Khanjar Assaidi. Multicoloured, background colours given.
470 **153** 50b. green 15 10
471 50b. red 15 10
471a 80b. yellow 20 15
472 100b. violet 30 25
473 200b. brown 65 55

154 Car, Traffic Lights, Hand and Police Motor Cycle

1998. Gulf Co-operation Council Traffic Week.
474 **154** 100b. multicoloured . . . 30 25

155 Sohar Fort

1998. Tourism. Multicoloured.
475 100b. Type **155** 30 25
476 100b. Wadi Shab 30 25
477 100b. Nizwa town 30 25
478 100b. Eid celebration (religious holiday) 30 25
479 100b. View of river 30 25
480 100b. Three young girls by an aqueduct 30 25

156 Exhibition Emblem

1998. 4th Arab Gulf Countries Stamp Exhibition, Muscat.
481 **156** 50b. multicoloured . . . 15 10

157 U.P.U. Emblem and Doves

1998. World Stamp Day.
482 **157** 100b. multicoloured . . . 30 25

158 Year Emblem

1998. National Day. Year of the Private Sector. Multicoloured.

483	100b. Sultan Qabus	30	25
484	100b. Type **158**	30	25

159 Map and Container Ship at Quayside

1998. Inauguration of Salalah Port Container Terminal.

486 **159**	50b. multicoloured	15	10

160 Sultan Qabus, Dove and Olive Branch

1998. International Peace Award.

487 **160**	500b. multicoloured	1·60	1·40

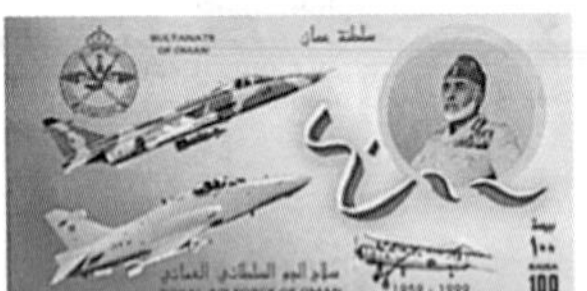

161 Military Aircraft and Sultan Qabus

1999. 40th Anniv of Royal Air Force of Oman.

488 **161**	100b. multicoloured	35	30

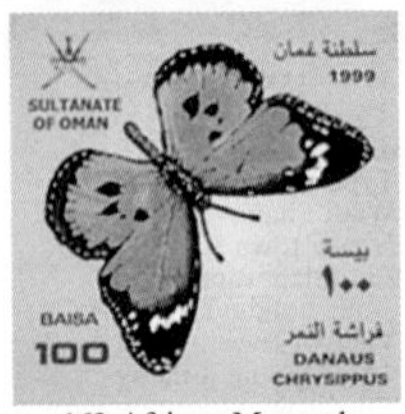

162 African Monarch

1999. Butterflies. Multicoloured.

489	100b. Type **162**	35	30
490	100b. Chequered swallowtail (*Papilio demoleus*)	35	30
491	100b. Blue pansy (*Precis orithya*)	35	30
492	100b. Yellow pansy (*Precis hierta*)	35	30

163 Longbarbel Goatfish

1999. Marine Life. Multicoloured.

494	100b. Type **163**	35	30
495	100b. Red-eyed round herring (*Etrumeus teres*)	35	30
496	100b. Brown-spotted grouper (*Epinephelus chlorostigma*)	35	30
497	100b. Blue-spotted emperor (*Lethrinus lentjan*)	35	30
498	100b. Blood snapper (*Lutjanus erythropterus*)	35	30
499	100b. Wahoo (*Acanthocybium solandri*)	35	30
500	100b. Long-tailed tuna (*Thunnus tonggol*)	35	30
501	100b. Crimson jobfish (*Pristipomoides filamentosus*)	35	30
502	100b. Yellow-finned tuna (*Thunnus albacares*)	35	30
503	100b. Cultured shrimp (*Penaeus indicus*)	35	30
504	100b. Pharaoh cuttlefish (*Sepia pharaonis*)	35	30
505	100b. Tropical rock lobster (*Panulirus homarus*)	35	30

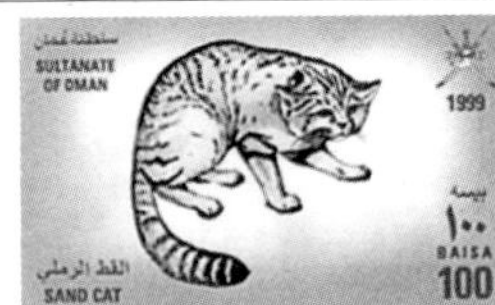

164 Sand Cat

1999. Wildlife. Multicoloured.

506	100b. Type **164**	35	30
507	100b. Genet	35	30
508	100b. Leopard	35	30
509	100b. Sand fox	35	30
510	100b. Caracal lynx	35	30
511	100b. Hyena	35	30

165 Globe and Emblem

1999. 125th Anniv of Universal Postal Union.

513 **165**	200b. multicoloured	70	60

166 Sultan Qabus and Musicians

1999. National Day. Multicoloured.

514	100b. Type **166**	35	30
515	100b. Sultan Qabus and horsemen	35	30

Nos. 514/15 were issued together, se-tenant, forming a composite design.

168 Water Droplet and Dried Earth

2000. World Water Week.

517 **168**	100b. multicoloured	35	25

169 Emblem, Airplane and Silhouette of Bird

2000. 50th Anniv of Gulf Air.

518 **169**	100b. multicoloured	35	25

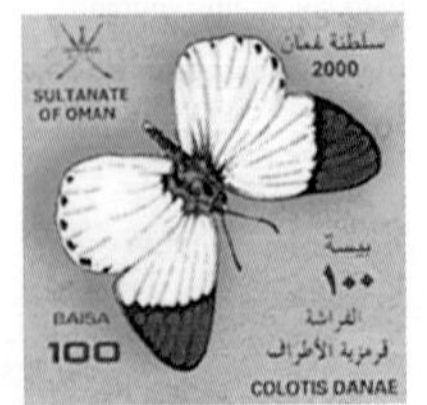

170 Crimson-tip Butterfly (*Colotis danae*)

2000. Butterflies. Multicoloured.

519	100b. Type **170**	35	25
520	100b. *Anaphaeis aurota*	35	25
521	100b. *Tarucus rosaceus*	35	25
522	100b. Long-tailed blue (*Lampides boeticus*)	35	25

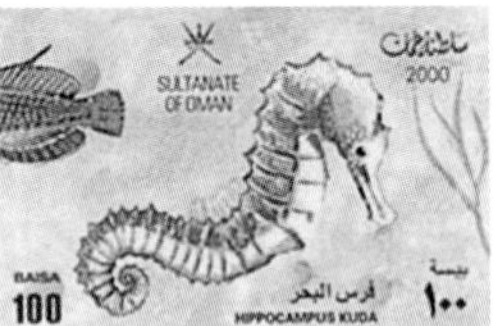

171 Yellow Seahorse (*Hippocampus kuda*)

2000. Marine Life. Multicoloured.

524	100b. Type **171**	35	25
525	100b. Yellow boxfish (*Ostracion cubicus*)	35	25
526	100b. Japanese pineconefish (*Monocentris japonica*)	35	25
527	100b. Broad-barred lionfish (*Pterois antennata*)	35	25
528	100b. *Rhinecanthus assasi*	35	25
529	100b. Blue-spotted stingray (*Taeniura lymma*)	35	25

172 Arabian Tahr

2000. Mammals. Multicoloured.

531	100b. Type **172**	35	25
532	100b. Nubian ibex	35	25
533	100b. Arabian oryx	35	25
534	100b. Arabian gazelle	35	25

173 Emblem

2000. Olympic Games, Sydney. Multicoloured.

536	100b. Type **173**	35	25
537	100b. Running	35	25
538	100b. Swimming	35	25
539	100b. Rifle-shooting	35	25

174 Sultan Qabus

2000. National Day. Multicoloured.

541	100b. Type **174**	35	25
542	100b. Sitting	35	25
543	100b. Wearing uniform including red beret	35	25
544	100b. Wearing (white) naval uniform	35	25
545	100b. Anniversary emblem	35	25
546	100b. Wearing (beige) police uniform	35	25

175 Egret and Sea Birds

2001. Environment Day. Sheet 83 × 46 mm.

MS548 175	200b. multicoloured	60	60

176 Dagger and Sheath

177 Child and Tank

2001. Al-Khanjar A'suri. Multicoloured, background colours given. (a) Size 24 × 27 mm.

549 **176**	50b. red	15	10
550	80b. yellow	25	20

(b) Size 26 × 34 mm.

551 **176**	100b. blue	30	25
552	200b. white	60	45
MS553	80 × 100 mm. Nos. 549/552	1·25	1·25

2001. Al Aqsa Uprising. Sheet 105 × 100 mm.

MS554 177	100b. multicoloured	30	30

ORANGE FREE STATE (ORANGE RIVER COLONY) Pt. 1

British possession 1848–54. Independent 1854–99. Annexed by Great Britain, 1900. Later a province of the Union of South Africa.

12 pence = 1 shilling;
20 shillings = 1 pound.

1

38 King Edward VII, Springbok and Gnu

1869.

48 **1**	½d. brown	1·75	50
84	½d. yellow	2·00	35
2	1d. brown	10·00	45
68	1d. purple	2·75	30
50	2d. mauve	11·00	30
51	3d. blue	2·25	2·00
19	4d. blue	4·00	2·50
7	6d. red	9·50	2·00
9	1s. orange	30·00	1·50
87	1s. brown	17·00	1·50
20	5s. green	9·00	11·00

1877. Surch in figures.

75 **1**	½d. on 3d. blue	5·00	2·75
36	½d. on 5s. green	13·00	3·75
54	1d. on 3d. blue	4·00	60
57	1d. on 4d. blue	24·00	4·25
22	1d. on 5s. green	50·00	18·00
53	2d. on 3d. blue	29·00	2·00
67	2½d. on 3d. blue	11·00	70
83	2½d. on 3d. blue	4·75	80
40	3d. on 4d. blue	28·00	16·00
12	4d. on 6d. red	£180	25·00

1896. Surch **Halve Penny.**

77 **1**	½d. on 3d. blue	65	50

1900. Surch **V.R.I.** and value in figures.

112 **1**	½d. on ½d. orange	30	20
113	1d. on 1d. purple	30	20
114	2d. on 2d. mauve	1·00	30
104	2½d. on 3d. blue (No. 83)	12·00	9·50
117	3d. on 3d. blue	50	30
118	4d. on 4d. blue	1·75	2·50
108	6d. on 6d. red	35·00	35·00
120	6d. on 6d. blue	70	40

121 1s. on 1s. brown 3·50 45
122 5s. on 5s. green 6·50 8·50

1900. Stamps of Cape of Good Hope optd **ORANGE RIVER COLONY.**
133 17 ½d. green 30 10
134 1d. red 75 10
135 6 2½d. blue 85 35

1902. No. 120 surch **4d** and bar.
136 1 4d. on 6d. blue 1·50 75

1902. Surch **E. R. I. 6d.**
137 1 6d. on 6d. blue 3·25 9·00

1902. No. 20 surch **One Shilling** and star.
138 1 1s. on 5s. green 7·00 11·00

1903.
139 38 ½d. green 8·00 1·25
140 1d. red 4·25 10
141 2d. brown 4·50 80
142 2½d. blue 1·60 50
143 3d. mauve 7·00 90
150 4d. red and green 4·50 2·25
145 6d. red and mauve 7·50 1·00
146 1s. red and brown 26·00 1·75
147 5s. blue and brown 75·00 22·00

MILITARY FRANK STAMP

M 1

1899.
M1 M 1 (–) black on yellow 13·00 45·00

POLICE FRANK STAMPS

PF 1 PF 2

1896.
PF2 PF 1 (–) black £140 £170

1899.
PF3 PF 2 (–) black on yellow £130 £130

ORCHHA Pt. 1

A state of Central India. Now uses Indian stamps.

12 pies = 1 anna; 16 annas = 1 rupee.

1 2

1913. Imperf.
1 1 ¼a. green 30·00 85·00
2 1a. red 19·00

1914. Imperf.
3a 2 ¼a. blue 40 3·50
4 ½a. green 55 4·50
5c 1a. red 2·50 5·00
6 2a. brown 4·50 22·00
7b 4a. yellow 8·00 27·00

3 Maharaja Vir Singh II 5 Maharaja Vir Singh II

1935.
8b 3 ¼a. purple and grey 35 2·25
9 ½a. grey and green 50 1·50
10 ¾a. mauve and green 50 1·60
11 – 1a. green and brown 50 1·50
12 3 1¼a. grey and mauve 45 1·50
13 1½a. brown and red 45 1·50
14 2a. blue and orange 45 1·50
15 2½a. brown and orange 65 1·60
16 3a. blue and mauve 65 1·60
17 4a. purple and green 65 3·50
18 6a. black and buff 70 3·50
19 8a. brown and purple 2·00 4·25
20 12a. green and purple 1·00 4·25
21 12a. blue and purple 25·00 60·00
22 1r. brown and green 80 5·00
24 2r. brown and yellow 2·75 13·00
25 3r. black and blue 1·50 13·00
26 4r. black and brown 2·75 15·00
27 5r. blue and purple 3·00 16·00
28 – 10r. green and red 7·00 23·00
29 – 15r. black and green 12·00 50·00
30 – 25r. orange and blue 16·00 60·00
DESIGN: 1a., 10r. to 25r. As Type 3, but inscr "POSTAGE & REVENUE". There are two different versions of the portrait for the 1r. value.

1939.
31 5 ¼a. brown 3·50 60·00
32 ½a. green 3·75 48·00
33 ¾a. blue 3·75 80·00
34 1a. red 3·75 16·00
35 1¼a. blue 3·75 80·00
36 1½a. mauve 4·00 95·00
37 2a. red 3·75 60·00
38 2½a. green 3·75 £175
39 3a. violet 5·00 90·00
40 4a. slate 6·50 24·00
41 8a. mauve 10·00 £170
42 – 1r. green 18·00
43 – 2r. violet 38·00 £450
44 – 5r. orange £110
45 – 10r. green £425
46 – 15r. lilac £8500
47 – 25r. purple £6000
The rupee values are larger (25 × 30 mm) and have different frame.

PAHANG Pt. 1

A state of the Federation of Malaya, incorporated in Malaysia in 1963.

100 cents = 1 dollar (Straits or Malayan).

1889. Nos. 52/3 and 63 of Straits Settlements optd **PAHANG.**
4a 2c. red 4·25 8·00
2 8c. orange £1700 £1400
3 10c. grey £225 £250

1891. No. 68 of Straits Settlements surch **PAHANG Two CENTS.**
7 2c. on 24c. green £140 £150

9 Tiger 10 Tiger

1891.
11 9 1c. green 4·00 3·25
12 2c. red 4·50 3·25
13 5c. blue 10·00 40·00

1895.
14 10 3c. purple and red 6·00 2·75
15 4c. purple and red 17·00 12·00
16 5c. purple and yellow 23 00 21·00

1897. No. 13 divided, and each half surch.
18 9 2c. on half of 5c. blue £1300 £375
18d 3c. on half of 5c. blue £1300 £375

1898. Stamps of Perak optd **Pahang.**
19 44 10c. purple and orange 17·00 25·00
20 25c. green and red 85·00 £150
21 50c. purple and black £325 £350
22 50c. green and black £200 £250
23 45 $1 green £325 £375
24 $5 green and blue £1000 £1300

1898. Stamp of Perak surch **Pahang Four cents.**
25 44 4c. on 8c. purple and blue 3·25 5·50

1899. No. 16 surch **Four cents.**
28 10 4c. on 5c. purple and yellow 14·00 55·00

15 Sultan Sir Abu Bakar 16 Sultan Sir Abu Bakar

1935.
29 15 1c. black 15 40
30 2c. green 70 50
31 3c. green 15·00 15·00
32 4c. orange 50 50
33 5c. brown 60 10
34 6c. red 11·00 1·75
35 8c. grey 60 10
36 8c. red 2·00 48·00
37 10c. purple 60 10
38 12c. blue 1·50 1·25
39 15c. blue 10·00 50·00
40 25c. purple and red 80 1·50
41 30c. purple and orange 80 1·10
42 40c. red and purple 75 2·00
43 50c. black on green 2·75 1·50
44 $1 black and red on blue 2·00 8·00
45 $2 green and red 18·00 27·00
46 $5 green and red on green 7·00 55·00

1948. Silver Wedding. As T **4b/c** of Pitcairn Islands.
47 10c. violet 15 60
48 $5 green 23·00 40·00

1949. U.P.U. As T **4d/g** of Pitcairn Islands.
49 10c. purple 30 20
50 15c. blue 90 1·10
51 25c. orange 35 1·10
52 50c. black 70 2·00

1950.
53 16 1c. black 10 10
54 2c. orange 20 10
55 3c. green 30 80
56 4c. brown 80 10
57a 5c. purple 50 15
58 6c. grey 30 30
59 8c. red 50 1·50
60 8c. green 85 75
61 10c. mauve 25 10
62 12c. red 85 1·25
63 15c. blue 75 10
64 20c. black and green 50 2·75
65 20c. blue 1·00 10
66 25c. purple and orange 50 10
67 30c. red and purple 1·25 35
68 35c. red and purple 60 25
69 40c. red and purple 1·50 7·50
70 50c. black and blue 1·50 10
71 $1 blue and purple 2·75 2·75
72 $2 green and red 13·00 21·00
73 $5 green and brown 55·00 65·00

1953. Coronation. As T **4h** of Pitcairn Islands.
74 10c. black and purple 1·00 10

1957. As Nos. 92/102 of Kedah but inset portrait of Sultan Sir Abu Bakar.
75 1c. black 10 10
76 2c. red 10 10
77 4c. sepia 10 10
78 5c. lake 10 10
79 8c. green 1·00 2·25
80 10c. sepia 85 10
81 10c. purple 3·00 30
82 20c. blue 2·00 20
83 50c. black and blue 30 75
84 $1 blue and purple 5·50 2·00
85 $2 green and red 3·50 9·00
86 $5 brown and green 9·50 15·00

17 "Vanda hookeriana"

1965. As Nos. 115/21 of Kedah but with inset portrait of Sultan Sir Abu Bakar as in T **17**.
87 17 1c. multicoloured 10 1·00
88 – 2c. multicoloured 10 1·00
89 – 5c. multicoloured 15 10
90 – 6c. multicoloured 30 1·00
91 – 10c. multicoloured 20 10
92 15c. multicoloured 1·00 10
93 – 20c. multicoloured 1·60 40
The higher values used in Pahang were Nos. 20/7 of Malaysia (National Issue).

18 "Precis orithya" 19 Sultan Haji Ahmad Shah

1971. Butterflies. As Nos. 124/30 of Kedah, but with portrait of Sultan Sir Abu Bakar as in T **18**.
96 – 1c. multicoloured 20 1·75
97 – 2c. multicoloured 40 1·75
98 – 5c. multicoloured 75 50
99 – 6c. multicoloured 1·50 2·00
100 – 10c. multicoloured 90 30
101 18 15c. multicoloured 1·60 10
102 – 20c. multicoloured 1·75 50
The higher values in use with this issue were Nos. 64/71 of Malaysia (National Issues).

1975. Installation of the Sultan.
103 19 10c. green, lilac and gold 50 1·10
104 15c. black, yellow and green 60 10
105 50c. black, blue and green 1·75 4·00

1977. As Nos. 97/8, 100/102 but with portrait of Sultan Haji Ahmad Shah.
106 – 2c. multicoloured 55·00 50·00
107 – 5c. multicoloured 60 1·00
108 – 10c. multicoloured 85 65
109 18 15c. multicoloured 85 30
110 – 20c. multicoloured 4·00 1·75

20 "Rhododendron scortechinii" 21 Rice

1979. Flowers. As Nos. 135/41 of Kedah but with portrait of Sultan Haji Ahmad Shah as in T **20**.
111 1c. "Rafflesia hasseltii" 10 75
112 2c. "Pterocarpus indicus" 10 75
113 5c. "Lagerstroemia speciosa" 10 30
114 10c. "Durio zibethinus" 15 10
115 15c. "Hibiscus rosa-sinensis" 15 10
116 20c. Type **20** 20 10
117 25c. "Etlingera elatior" (inscr "Phaeomeria speciosa") 40 40

1986. As Nos. 152/8 of Kedah but with portrait of Sultan Ahmad Shah as in T **21**.
125 1c. Coffee 10 10
126 2c. Coconuts 10 10
127 5c. Cocoa 10 10
128 10c. Black pepper 10 10
129 15c. Rubber 10 10
130 20c. Oil palm 10 10
131 30c. Type **21** 10 15

PAKHOI Pt. 17

An Indo-Chinese Post Office in China, closed in 1922.

1903. Stamps of Indo-China, "Tablet" key-type, surch **PACKHOI** and value in Chinese.
1 D 1c. black and red on blue 9·25 10·00
2 2c. brown and blue on buff 4·75 5·25
3 4c. brown and blue on grey 5·25 5·00
4 5c. green and red 2·75 4·00
5 10c. red and blue 1·75 4·50
6 15c. grey and red 3·50 5·50
7 20c. red and blue on green 8·50 11·00
8 25c. blue and red 5·50 8·50
9 25c. black and red on pink 6·50 9·50
10 30c. brown and blue on drab 15·00 13·00
11 40c. red and blue on yellow 55·00 55·00
12 50c. red and blue on pink £275 £275
13 50c. brown and red on blue 80·00 65·00
14 75c. brown and red on orange 70·00 65·00
15 1f. green and red 75·00 65·00
16 5f. mauve and blue on lilac £110 £110

1906. Stamps of Indo-China surch **PAK-HOI** and value in Chinese.
17 8 1c. green 2·50 2·75
18 2c. red on yellow 2·25 2·25
19 4c. mauve on blue 2·50 2·50
20 5c. green 3·00 1·90
21 10c. red 2·75 2·50
22 15c. brown on blue 6·25 6·50
23 20c. red on green 3·75 3·75
24 25c. blue 3·50 3·75
25 30c. brown on cream 4·50 4·00
26 35c. black on yellow 4·00 4·00
27 40c. black on grey 3·75 4·25
28 50c. olive on green 8·00 6·50
29 D 75c. brown on orange 60·00 60·00
30 8 1f. green 26·00 26·00
31 2f. brown on yellow 45·00 42·00
32 D 5f. mauve on lilac £100 £110
33 8 10f. red on green £110 £110

1908. Stamps of Indo-China (Native types) surch **PAKHOI** and value in Chinese.
34 10 1c. black and brown 1·50 1·00
35 2c. black and brown 1·00 1·25
36 4c. black and blue 1·00 1·50
37 5c. black and green 1·40 1·75
38 10c. black and red 1·75 3·25
39 15c. black and violet 2·50 3·25
40 11 20c. black and violet 2·50 2·75
41 25c. black and blue 2·75 3·50
42 30c. black and brown 3·25 4·25
43 35c. black and green 3·25 4·25
44 40c. black and brown 3·00 4·25
45 50c. black and red 3·75 4·25
46 12 75c. black and orange 6·25 6·25
47 – 1f. black and red 8·00 8·00
48 – 2f. black and green 17·00 18·00
49 – 5f. black and blue 80·00 £100
50 – 10f. black and violet £110 £110

1919. As last, surch in addition in figures and words.
51 10 ⅖c. on 1c. black and green 50 2·75
52 ⅘c. on 2c. black and brown 1·25 3·00
53 1⅗c. on 4c. black and blue 1·50 2·75
54 2c. on 5c. black and green 2·00 3·25
55 4c. on 10c. black and red 3·75 4·00
56 6c. on 15c. black and violet 3·00 3·00
57 11 8c. on 20c. black and violet 4·25 4·25
58 10c. on 25c. black and blue 4·50 4·25
59 12c. on 30c. black & brown 3·00 3·25
60 14c. on 35c. black and green 2·50 3·00
61 16c. on 40c. black & brown 3·50 3·75
62 20c. on 50c. black and red 2·75 3·25
63 12 30c. on 75c. black & orange 3·50 4·00
64 – 40c. on 1f. black and red 12·50 12·50
65 – 80c. on 2f. black and green 5·25 5·25
66 – 2pi. on 5f. black and blue 12·00 14·00
67 – 4pi. on 10f. black and violet 24·00 29·00

PAKISTAN Pt. 1

A Dominion created in 1947 from territory with predominantly Moslem population in Eastern and Western India. Became an independent Islamic Republic within the British Commonwealth in 1956. The eastern provinces declared their independence in 1971 and are now known as Bangladesh.

On 30 January 1972 Pakistan left the Commonwealth but rejoined on 1 October 1989.

1947. 12 pies = 1 anna;
16 annas = 1 rupee.
1961. 100 paisa = 1 rupee.

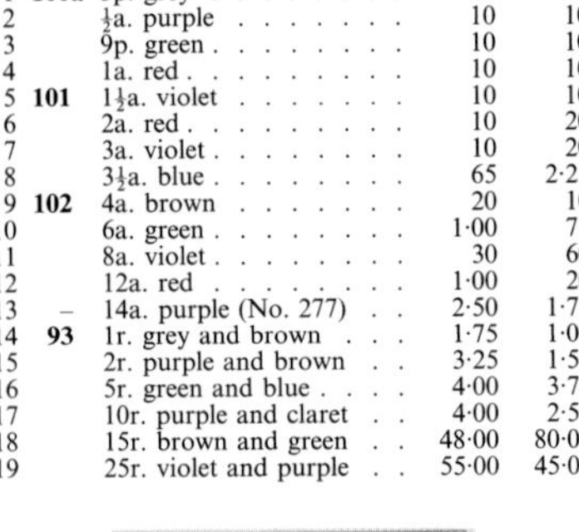

1947. King George VI stamps of India optd **PAKISTAN**.
1 **100a** 3p. grey 10 10
2 ½a. purple 10 10
3 9p. green 10 10
4 1a. red 10 10
5 **101** 1½a. violet 10 10
6 2a. red 10 20
7 3a. violet 10 20
8 3½a. blue . . . . 65 2·25
9 **102** 4a. brown 20 10
10 6a. green . . . . 1·00 75
11 8a. violet 30 60
12 12a. red . . . . 1·00 20
13 – 14a. purple (No. 277) . . 2·50 1·75
14 **93** 1r. grey and brown . . . 1·75 1·00
15 2r. purple and brown . . . 3·25 1·50
16 5r. green and blue . . . . 4·00 3·75
17 10r. purple and claret . . 4·00 2·50
18 15r. brown and green . . 48·00 80·00
19 25r. violet and purple . . 55·00 45·00

3 Constituent Assembly Building, Karachi

1948. Independence.
20 **3** 1½a. blue 80 60
21 – 2½a. green 80 10
22 – 3a. brown 80 30
23 – 1r. red 80 60
DESIGNS—HORIZ: 2½a. Entrance to Karachi Airport; 3a. Gateway to Lahore Fort. VERT: 1r. Crescent and Stars in foliated frame.

7 Scales of Justice

9 Lloyds Barrage

12 Salimullah Hostel, Dacca University

13 Khyber Pass

1948. Designs with crescent moon pointing to right.
24 **7** 3p. red 10 10
25 6p. violet 50 10
26 9p. green 50 10
27 – 1a. blue 10 50
28 – 1½a. green 10 10
29 – 2a. red 80 50
30 **9** 2½a. green . . . . 2·75 6·50
31 – 3a. green . . . . 7·50 1·00
32 **9** 3½a. blue . . . . 3·50 5·50
33 4a. brown 50 10
34 – 6a. blue 50 50
35 – 8a. black 50 60
36 – 10a. red . . . . 4·75 7·00
37 – 12a. red . . . . 6·50 1·00
38 **12** 1r. blue . . . . 5·50 10
39 2r. brown . . . . 20·00 60
40a 5r. red . . . . 11·00 20
41b **13** 10r. mauve . . . . 18·00 1·00
42 15r. green . . . . 18·00 13·00
210b 25r. violet . . . . 3·00 4·00
DESIGNS—VERT (as Type **7**): 1a., 1½a., 2a. Star and Crescent; 6a., 8a., 12a. Karachi Port Trust. HORIZ (as Type **12**): 3a., 10a. Karachi Airport.

1949. As 1948 but with crescent moon pointing to left.
44a – 1a. blue . . . . 3·50 10
45a – 1½a. green . . . . 3·00 10
46a – 2a. red . . . . 3·50 10
47 – 3a. green . . . . 11·00 75
48 – 6a. blue . . . . 9·00 1·00
49 – 8a. black . . . . 6·00 1·25
50 – 10a. red . . . . 17·00 1·75
51 – 12a. red . . . . 20·00 30

16

1949. 1st Death Anniv of Mohammed Ali Jinnah.
52 **16** 1½a. brown . . . . 1·75 1·10
53 3a. green . . . . 1·75 1·10
54 – 10a. black . . . . 5·50 7·00
DESIGN: 10a. inscription reads "QUAID-I-AZAM MOHAMMAD ALI JINNAH" etc.

17 Pottery

1951. 4th Anniv of Independence.
55 **17** 2½a. red . . . . 1·50 1·00
56 – 3a. purple 65 10
57 **17** 3½a. blue (A) . . . . . . 1·00 3·50
57a – 3½a. blue (B) . . . . . . 3·25 4·50
58 – 4a. green 65 10
59 – 6a. orange 75 10
60 – 8a. sepia . . . . 4·50 20
61 – 10a. violet . . . . 1·75 1·00
62 – 12a. slate . . . . 1·75 10
DESIGNS—VERT: 3, 12a. Airplane and hour-glass; 4, 6a. Saracenic leaf pattern. HORIZ: 8, 10a. Archway and lamp.
(A) has Arabic fraction on left as in Type **17**, (B) has it on right.
For similar 3½a. see No. 88.

21 "Scinde Dawk" Stamp and Ancient and Modern Transport

1952. Cent of "Scinde Dawk" Issue of India.
63 **21** 3a. green on olive 75 85
64 12a. brown on salmon . . . 1·00 15

22 Kaghan Valley

24 Tea Plantation, East Pakistan

1954. 7th Anniv of Independence.
65 **22** 6p. violet 10 10
66 – 9p. blue . . . . 3·25 1·75
67 – 1a. red 10 10
68 – 1½a. red 10 10
69 **24** 14a. myrtle 80 10
70 – 1r. green . . . . 11·00 10
71 – 2r. orange . . . . 2·75 10
DESIGNS—HORIZ (as Type **22**): 9p. Mountains, Gilgit; 1a. Badshahi Mosque, Lahore. (As Type **24**): 1r. Cotton plants, West Pakistan; 2r. Jute fields and river, East Pakistan. VERT (as Type **22**): 1½a. Mausoleum of Emperor Jehangir, Lahore.

29 View of K2

1954. Conquest of K2 (Mount Godwin-Austen).
72 **29** 2a. violet 30 30

30 Karnaphuli Paper Mill, East Bengal

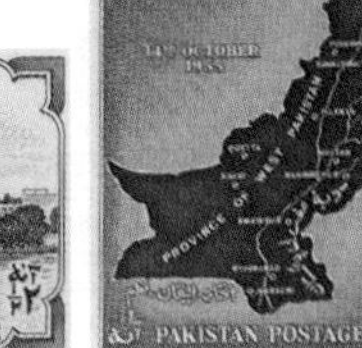

35 Map of West Pakistan

1955. 8th Anniv of Independence.
73 **30** 2½a. red (A) . . . . 50 1·40
73a – 2½a. red (B) . . . . 30 1·40
74 – 6a. blue . . . . 1·00 10
75 – 8a. violet . . . . 3·75 10
76 – 12a. red and orange . . . 4·00 10
DESIGNS: 6a. Textile mill, W. Pakistan; 8a. Jute mill, E. Pakistan; 12a. Main Sui gas plant.
(A) has Arabic fraction on left as in Type **30**, (B) has it on right.
For similar 2½a. see No. 87.

1955. 10th Anniv of U.N. Nos. 68 and 76 optd **TENTH ANNIVERSARY UNITED NATIONS 24.10.55.**
77 1½a. red . . . . 1·50 5·00
78 12a. red and orange . . . . . 50 3·50

1955. West Pakistan Unity.
79 **35** 1½a. green . . . . 25 1·00
80 2a. brown 40 10
81 12a. red . . . . 1·00 50

36 Constituent Assembly Building, Karachi

1956. Republic Day.
82 **36** 2a. green 80 10

37

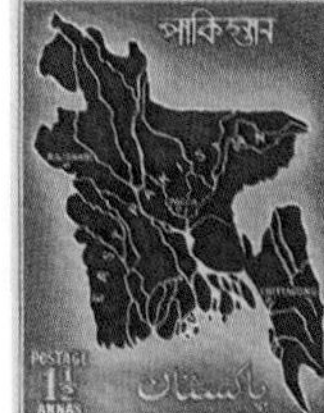

38 Map of East Pakistan

1956. 9th Anniv of Independence.
83 **37** 2a. red 65 10

1956. 1st Session of National Assembly of Pakistan at Dacca.
84 **38** 1½a. green . . . . 40 1·25
85 2a. brown 40 10
86 12a. red . . . . 40 1·10

41 Orange Tree

42 Pakistani Flag

1957. 1st Anniv of Republic.
87 – 2½a. red 20 10
88 – 3½a. blue 30 10
89 **41** 10r. green and orange . . . 80 20
DESIGNS: 2½a. as Type **30** without value in Arabic at right; 3½a. as Type **17** without value in Arabic at right.

1957. Centenary of Struggle for Independence (Indian Mutiny).
90 **42** 1½a. green 50 10
91 12a. blue . . . . 1·25 10

43 Pakistani Industries

1957. 10th Anniv of Independence.
92 **43** 1½a. blue 20 30
93 4a. salmon . . . . 45 1·25
94 12a. mauve 45 50

1958. 2nd Anniv of Republic. As T **41**.
209 15r. red and purple . . . . . 2·00 2·75
DESIGN: 15r. Coconut tree.

45

1958. 20th Death Anniv of Mohammed Iqbal (poet).
96 **45** 1½a. olive and black 55 40
97 2a. brown and black 55 10
98 14a. turquoise and black . . 90 10

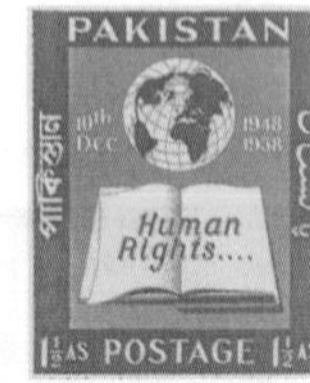

46 U.N. Charter and Globe

1958. 10th Anniv of Declaration of Human Rights.
99 **46** 1½a. turquoise 10 10
100 14a. sepia 45 10

1958. Scout Jamboree. Optd **PAKISTAN BOY SCOUT 2nd NATIONAL JAMBOREE CHITTAGONG Dec. 58-Jan. 59.**
101 **22** 6p. violet 20 10
102 – 8a. violet (No. 75) 40 10

1959. Revolution Day. No. 74 optd **REVOLUTION DAY Oct. 27, 1959.**
103 6a. blue 80 10

49 "Centenary of An Idea"

50 Armed Forces Badge

1959. Red Cross Commemoration.
104 **49** 2a. red and green 30 10
105 10a. red and blue 55 10

1960. Armed Forces Day.
106 **50** 2a. red, blue and green . . 50 10
107 14a. red and blue . . . . 1·00 10

51 Map of Pakistan

1960.
108 **51** 6p. purple 40 10
109 2a. red 60 10
110 8a. green . . . . 1·25 10
111 1r. blue . . . . 2·00 10

52 "Uprooted Tree"

55 "Land Reforms, Rehabilitation and Reconstruction"

53 Punjab Agricultural College

1960. World Refugee Year.

112	52	2a. red	20	10
113		10a. green	30	10

1960. Golden Jubilee of Punjab Agricultural College, Lyallpur.

114	53	2a. blue and red	10	10
115	–	8a. green and violet	20	10

DESIGN: 8a. College arms.

1960. Revolution Day.

116	55	2a. green, pink and brown	10	10
117		14a. green, yellow and blue	50	60

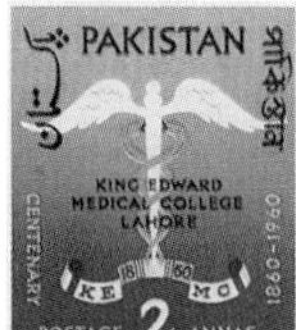

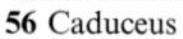
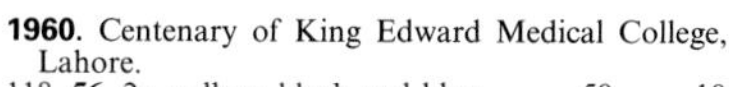

56 Caduceus **57** "Economic Co-operation"

1960. Centenary of King Edward Medical College, Lahore.

118	56	2a. yellow, black and blue	50	10
119	–	14a. green, black and red	1·75	90

1960. Int Chamber of Commerce C.A.F.E.A. Meeting, Karachi.

120	57	14a. brown	50	10

58 Zam-Zama Gun, Lahore ("Kim's Gun" after Rudyard Kipling)

1960. 3rd Pakistan Boy Scouts' National Jamboree, Lahore.

121	58	2a. red, yellow and green	80	10

1961. Surch in "PAISA".

122	–	1p. on 1½a. red (No. 68)	30	10
123	7	2p. on 3p. red	10	10
124	51	3p. on 6p. purple	15	10
125	–	7p. on 1a. red (No. 67)	30	10
126	51	13p. on 2a. red	30	10
127	37	13p. on 2a. red	30	10

See also Nos. 262/4.

60 Khyber Pass

61 Shalimar Gardens, Lahore **62** Chota Sona Masjid (gateway)

1961.

170	60	1p. violet	10	10
132		2p. red	80	10
133		3p. purple	50	10
173		5p. blue	10	10
135		7p. green	1·75	10
175	61	10p. brown	10	10
176		13p. violet	10	10
176a		15p. purple	20	10
176b		20p. green	30	10
138		25p. blue	4·75	10
178		40p. purple	15	30
179		50p. green	15	10
141		75p. red	40	50
142		90p. green	70	50
204	62	1r. red	30	10
144		1r.25 violet	75	80
206		2r. orange	55	15
207		5r. green	5·00	65

1961. Lahore Stamp Exn. No. 110 optd **LAHORE STAMP EXHIBITION 1961** and emblem.

145	51	8a. green	90	1·50

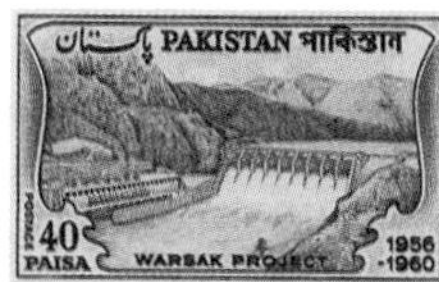

64 Warsak Dam and Power Station

1961. Completion of Warsak Hydro-electric Project.

146	64	40p. black and blue	60	10

65 Narcissus

1961. Child Welfare Week.

147	65	13p. turquoise	50	10
148		90p. mauve	1·25	20

66 Ten Roses **67** Police Crest and "Traffic Control"

1961. Co-operative Day.

149	66	13p. red and green	40	10
150		90p. red and blue	85	60

1961. Police Centenary.

151	67	13p. silver, black and blue	50	10
152		40p. silver, black and red	1·00	20

68 Locomotive "Eagle", 1861

1961. Railway Centenary.

153	68	13p. green, black and yellow	75	80
154	–	50p. yellow, black and green	1·00	1·25

DESIGN: 50p. Diesel locomotive No. 20 and tracks forming "1961".

1962. 1st Karachi–Dacca Jet Flight. No. 87 surch with Boeing 720B airliner and **FIRST JET FLIGHT KARACHI–DACCA 13 Paisa**.

155		13p. on 2½a. red	1·50	1·00

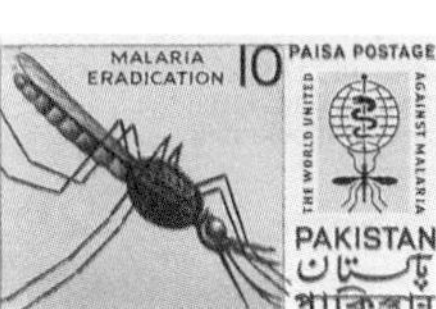

71 "Anopheles sp." (mosquito)

1962. Malaria Eradication.

156	71	10p. black, yellow and red	35	10
157	–	13p. black, lemon and red	35	10

DESIGN: 13p. Mosquito pierced by blade.

73 Pakistan Map and Jasmine

1962. New Constitution.

158	73	40p. green, turquoise & grey	70	10

74 Football

1962. Sports.

159	74	7p. black and blue	10	10
160	–	13p. black and green	60	1·00
161	–	25p. black and purple	20	10
162	–	40p. black and brown	2·00	2·50

DESIGNS: 13p. Hockey; 25p. Squash; 40p. Cricket.

78 Marble Fruit Dish and Bahawalpuri Clay Flask

1962. Small Industries.

163	78	7p. lake	10	10
164	–	13p. green	2·50	2·25
165	–	25p. violet	10	10
166	–	40p. green	10	10
167	–	50p. red	10	10

DESIGNS: 13p. Sports equipment; 25p. Camelskin lamp and brassware; 40p. Wooden powder-bowl and basket-work; 50p. Inlaid cigarette-box and brassware.

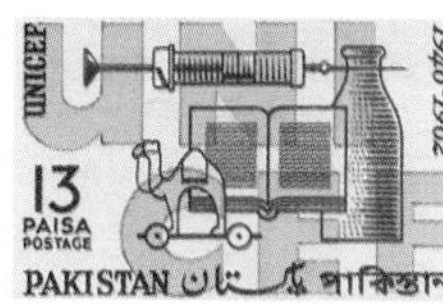

83 "Child Welfare"

1962. 16th Anniv of U.N.I.C.E.F.

168	83	13p. black, blue and purple	35	10
169		40p. black, yellow and blue	35	10

1963. Pakistan U.N. Force in West Irian. Optd **U.N. FORCE W. IRIAN**.

182	61	13p. violet	10	50

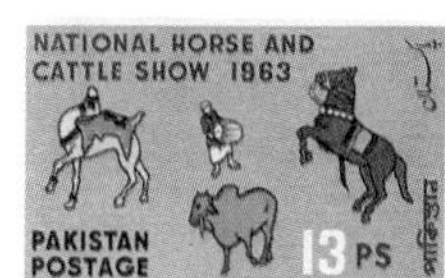

85 "Dancing" Horse, Camel and Bull

1963. National Horse and Cattle Show.

183	85	13p. blue, sepia and pink	10	10

86 Wheat and Tractor

1963. Freedom from Hunger.

184	86	13p. brown	2·00	10
185	–	50p. bistre	3·50	55

DESIGN: 50p. Lifting rice.

1963. 2nd International Stamp Exhibition, Dacca. Surch **13 PAISA INTERNATIONAL DACCA STAMP EXHIBITION 1963**.

186	51	13p. on 2a. red	50	10

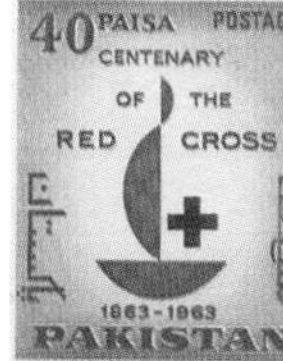

89 Centenary Emblem

1963. Centenary of Red Cross.

187	89	40p. red and olive	2·00	15

90 Paharpur

1963. Archaeological Series.

188	90	7p. blue	45	10
189	–	13p. sepia	45	10
190	–	40p. red	80	10
191	–	50p. violet	85	10

DESIGNS—VERT: 13p. Moenjodaro. HORIZ: 40p. Taxila; 50p. Mainamati.

1963. Centenary of Pakistan Public Works Department. Surch **100 YEARS OF P.W.D. OCTOBER, 1963 13**.

192	60	13p. on 3p. purple	10	10

95 Ataturk's Mausoleum

1963. 25th Death Anniv of Kemal Ataturk.

193	95	50p. red	50	10

96 Globe and U.N.E.S.C.O. Emblem

1963. 15th Anniv of Declaration of Human Rights.

194	96	50p. brown, red and blue	40	10

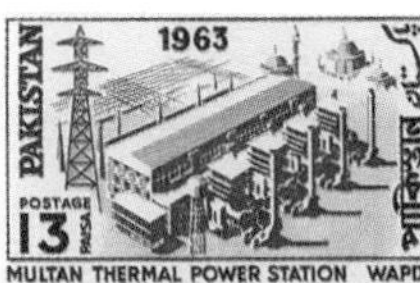

97 Thermal Power Installations

1963. Completion of Multan Thermal Power Station.

195	97	13p. blue	10	10

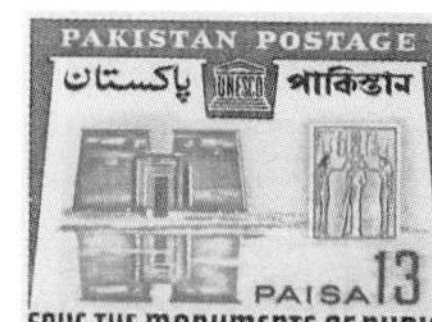

99 Temple of Thot, Queen Nefertari and Maids

1964. Nubian Monuments Preservation.

211	99	13p. blue and red	30	10
212	–	50p. purple and black	70	10

DESIGN: 50p. Temple of Abu Simbel.

101 "Unisphere" and Pakistan Pavilion

1964. New York World's Fair.

213	101	13p. blue	10	10
214	–	1r.25 blue and orange	40	20

DESIGN—VERT. 1r.25, Pakistan Pavilion on "Unisphere".

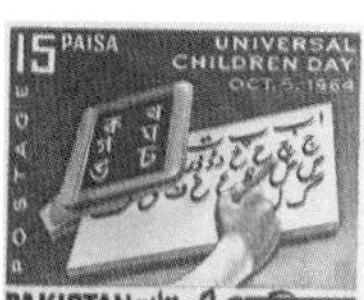

103 Shah Abdul Latif's Mausoleum **106** Bengali and Urdu Alphabets

104 Mausoleum of Quaid-i-Azam

1964. Death Bicentenary of Shah Abdul Latif of Bhit.

215	103	50p. blue and red	80	10

1964. 16th Death Anniv of Mohammed Ali Jinnah (Quaid-i-Azam).

216	104	15p. green	75	10
217	–	50p. green	2·00	10

DESIGN: 50p. As Type **104**, but 26½ × 31½ mm.

1964. Universal Children's Day.

218	106	15p. brown	10	10

107 University Building

1964. 1st Convocation of the West Pakistan University of Engineering and Technology, Lahore.
219 **107** 15p. brown 10 10

108 "Help the Blind"

1965. Blind Welfare.
220 **108** 15p. blue and yellow . . . 20 10

109 I.T.U. Emblem and Symbols

1965. Centenary of I.T.U.
221 **109** 15p. purple . . . . 1·50 30

110 I.C.Y. Emblem

1965. International Co-operation Year.
222 **110** 15p. black and blue . . . 50 15
223 50p. green and yellow . . 1·25 40

111 "Co-operation"

1965. 1st Anniv of Regional Development Co-operation Pact. Multicoloured.
224 15p. Type **111** 20 10
225 50p. Globe and flags of Turkey, Iran and Pakistan ($54\frac{3}{4}\times30\frac{3}{4}$ mm) . . . . . 1·10 10

113 Soldier and Tanks

1965. Pakistan Armed Forces. Multicoloured.
226 7p. Type **113** 75 30
227 15p. Naval Officer and "Tughril" (destroyer) . . . 1·50 10
228 50p. Pilot and Lockheed F-104C Starfighters . . . . 2·50 30

116 Army, Navy and Air Force Crests

1966. Armed Forces Day.
229 **116** 15p. blue, green and buff 75 10

117 Atomic Reactor, Islamabad

119 Children

118 Bank Crest

1966. Inauguration of Pakistan's 1st Atomic Reactor.
230 **117** 15p. black 10 10

1966. Silver Jubilee of Habib Bank.
231 **118** 15p. green, orange & sepia 10 10

1966. Universal Children's Day.
232 **119** 15p. black, red and yellow 10 10

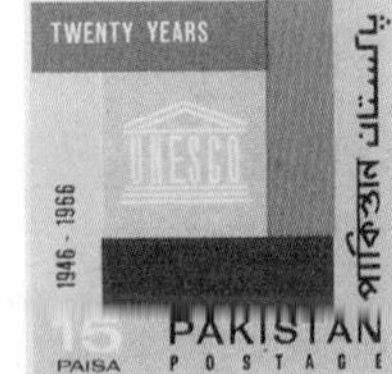

120 U.N.E.S.C.O. Emblem

1966. 20th Anniversary of U.N.E.S.C.O.
233 **120** 15p. multicoloured . . . 2·75 30

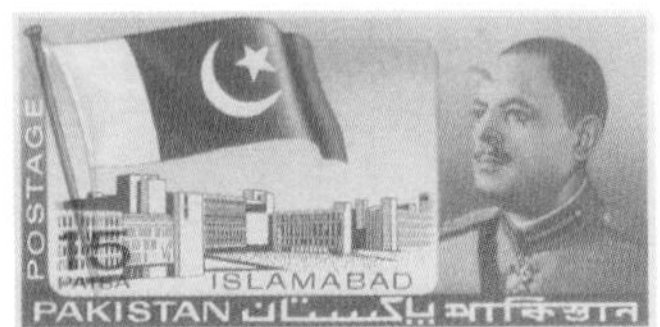

121 Flag, Secretariat Building and President Ayub

1966. Islamabad (new capital).
234 **121** 15p. multicoloured . . . 25 10
235 50p. multicoloured . . . 60 10

122 Avicenna

123 Mohammed Ali Jinnah

1966. Foundation of Health and Tibbi Research Institute.
236 **122** 15p. green and salmon . . 40 10

1966. 90th Birth Anniv of Mohammed Ali Jinnah.
237 **123** 15p. black, orange & blue 15 10
238 – 50p. black, purple and blue 35 10
DESIGN: 50p. Same portrait as 15p. but different frame.

124 Tourist Year Emblem

1967. International Tourist Year.
239 **124** 15p. black, blue and brown 10 10

125 Emblem of Pakistan T.B. Association

126 Scout Salute and Badge

1967. Tuberculosis Eradication Campaign.
240 **125** 15p. red, sepia and brown 10 10

1967. 4th National Scout Jamboree.
241 **126** 15p. brown and purple . . 15 10

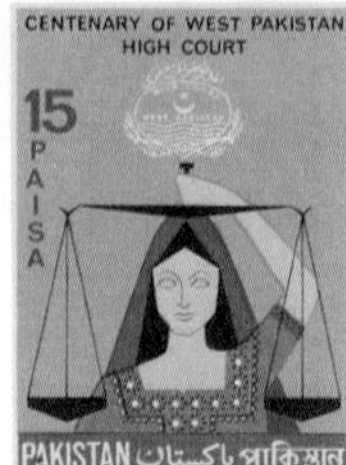

127 "Justice"

1967. Cent of West Pakistan High Court.
242 **127** 15p. multicoloured . . . 10 10

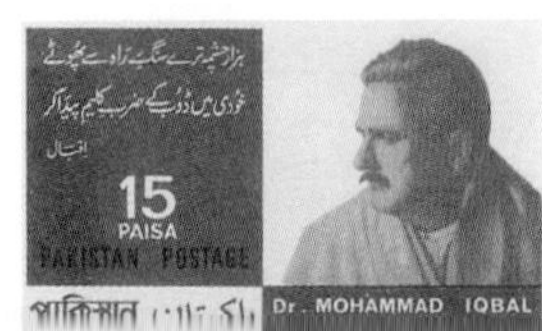

128 Dr. Mohammed Iqbal (philosopher)

1967. Iqbal Commemoration.
243 **128** 15p. sepia and red 15 10
244 1r. sepia and green . . . 35 10

129 Hilal-i-Isteqlal Flag

1967. Award of Hilal-i-Isteqlal (for Valour) to Lahore, Sialkot and Sargodha.
245 **129** 15p. multicoloured . . . 10 10

130 "20th Anniversary"

1967. 20th Anniv of Independence.
246 **130** 15p. red and green . . . 10 10

131 "Rice Exports"

1967. Pakistan Exports. Multicoloured.
247 10p. Type **131** 10 15
248 15p. Cotton plant, yarn and textiles (vert) (27 × 45 mm) 10 10
249 50p. Raw jute, bale and bags (vert) (27 × 45 mm) 20 15

134 Clay Toys

1967. Universal Children's Day.
250 **134** 15p. multicoloured . . . 10 10

135 Shah and Empress of Iran and Gulistan Palace, Teheran

1967. Coronation of Shah Mohammed Riza Pahlavi and Empress Farah of Iran.
251 **135** 50p. purple, blue and ochre 70 10

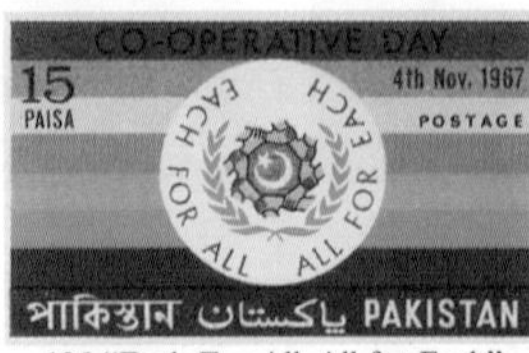

136 "Each For All–All for Each"

1967. Co-operative Day.
252 **136** 15p. multicoloured . . . 10 10

137 Mangla Dam

1967. Indus Basin Project.
253 **137** 15p. multicoloured . . . 10 10

138 Crab pierced by Sword

139 Human Rights Emblem

1967. The Fight Against Cancer.
254 **138** 15p. red and black . . . 70 10

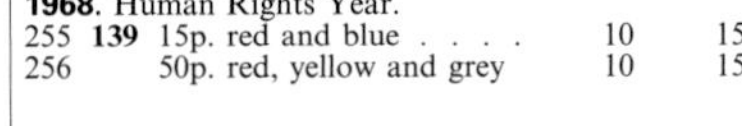

1968. Human Rights Year.
255 **139** 15p. red and blue 10 15
256 50p. red, yellow and grey 10 15

140 Agricultural University, Mymensingh

1968. First Convocation of East Pakistan Agricultural University.
257 **140** 15p. multicoloured . . . 10 10

141 W.H.O. Emblem

1968. 20th Anniv of W.H.O.
258 **141** 15p. orange and red . . . 10 15
259 50p. orange and blue . . 10 15

142 Kazi Nazrul Islam (poet, composer and patriot)

1968. Nazrul Islam Commemoration.
260 **142** 15p. sepia and yellow . . 35 15
261 50p. sepia and red 65 15

1968. Nos. 56, 74 and 61 surch.
262 4p. on 3a. purple . . . . . . 1·00 1·50
263 4p. on 6a. blue . . . . . . 1·25 1·50
264 60p. on 10a. violet 75 35

144 Children running with Hoops

1968. Universal Children's Day.
265 **144** 15p. multicoloured . . . 10 10

145 National Assembly

1968. "A Decade of Development".
266 **145** 10p. multicoloured . . . 10 10
267 – 15p. multicoloured . . . 10 10
268 – 50p. multicoloured . . . 2·00 20
269 – 60p. blue, purple and red 50 35
DESIGNS: 15p. Industry and Agriculture; 50p. Army, Navy and Air Force; 60p. Minaret and atomic reactor plant.

149 Chittagong Steel Mill

1969. Pakistan's First Steel Mill, Chittagong.
270 **149** 15p. grey, blue and olive 10 10

150 "Family"

1969. Family Planning.
271 **150** 15p. purple and blue . . . 10 10

151 Olympic Gold Medal and Hockey Player

1969. Olympic Hockey Champions.
272 **151** 15p. multicoloured . . . 75 50
273 1r. multicoloured . . . . 2·25 1·00

152 Mirza Ghalib and Lines of Verse

1969. Death Centenary of Mirza Ghalib (poet).
274 **152** 15p. multicoloured . . . 20 15
275 50p. multicoloured . . . 50 15
The lines of verse on No. 275 are different from those in Type **152**.

153 Dacca Railway Station

1969. 1st Anniv of New Dacca Railway Station.
276 **153** 15p. multicoloured . . . 30 10

154 I.L.O. Emblem and "1919–1969"

1969. 50th Anniv of I.L.O.
277 **154** 15p. buff and green . . . 10 10
278 50p. brown and red . . . 40 10

155 "Ladyon Balcony" (18th-cent Mogul)

1969. 5th Anniv of Regional Co-operation for Development. Miniatures. Multicoloured.
279 20p. Type **155** 15 10
280 50p. "Kneeling Servant" (17th-cent Persian) 15 10
281 1r. "Suleiman the Magnificent holding Audience" (16th-cent Turkish) 20 10

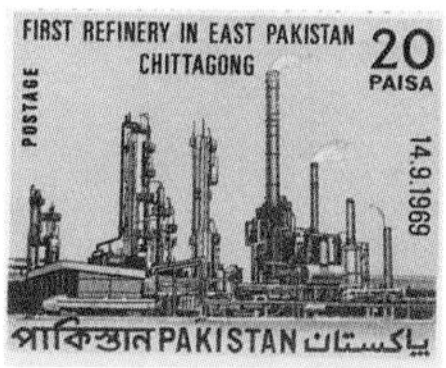

158 Eastern Refinery, Chittagong

1969. 1st East Pakistan Oil Refinery.
282 **158** 20p. multicoloured . . . 10 10

159 Children playing outside "School"

1969. Universal Children's Day.
283 **159** 20p. multicoloured . . . 10 10

160 Japanese Doll and P.I.A. Air Routes

1969. Inauguration of P.I.A. Pearl Route, Dacca–Tokyo.
284 **160** 20p. multicoloured . . . 40 10
285 50p. multicoloured . . . 60 40

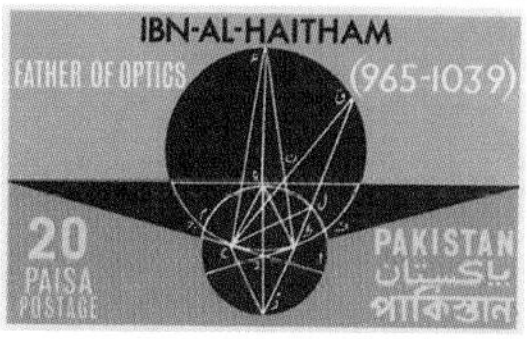

161 "Reflection of Light" Diagram

1969. Millenary Commemorative of Ibn-al-Haitham (physicist).
286 **161** 20p. black, yellow and blue 10 10

162 Vickers Vimy and Karachi Airport

1969. 50th Anniv of 1st England–Australia Flight.
287 **162** 50p. multicoloured . . . 70 35

163 Flags, Sun Tower and Expo Site Plan

1970. "Expo-70" World Fair, Osaka.
288 **163** 50p. multicoloured . . . 20 30

164 New U.P.U. H.Q. Building

1970. New U.P.U. Headquarters Building.
289 **164** 20p. multicoloured . . . 15 10
290 50p. multicoloured . . . 25 25

165 U.N. H.Q. Building

1970. 25th Anniv of United Nations. Mult.
291 20p. Type **165** 10 10
292 50p. U.N. emblem 15 20

167 I.E.Y. Emblem, Book and Pen

1970. International Education Year.
293 **167** 20p. multicoloured . . . 10 10
294 50p. multicoloured . . . 20 20

168 Saiful Malook Lake (Pakistan)

1970. 6th Anniv of Regional Co-operation for Development. Multicoloured.
295 20p. Type **168** 15 10
296 50p. Seeyo-Se-Pol Bridge, Esfahan (Iran) 20 10
297 1r. View from Fethiye (Turkey) 20 15

171 Asian Productivity Symbol

1970. Asian Productivity Year.
298 **171** 50p. multicoloured . . . 20 20

172 Dr. Maria Montessori

1970. Birth Centenary of Dr. Maria Montessori (educationist).
299 **172** 20p. multicoloured . . . 15 10
300 50p. multicoloured . . . 15 30

173 Tractor and Fertilizer Factory

1970. 10th Near East F.A.O. Regional Conference, Islamabad.
301 **173** 20p. green and brown . . 15 20

174 Children and Open Book

175 Pakistan Flag and Text

1970. Universal Children's Day.
302 **174** 20p. multicoloured . . . 15 10

1970. Elections for National Assembly.
303 **175** 20p. green and violet . . 15 10

1970. Elections for Provincial Assemblies. As No. 303 but inscr "PROVINCIAL ASSEMBLIES".
304 **175** 20p. green and red . . . 15 10

176 Conference Crest and burning Al-Aqsa Mosque

1970. Conference of Islamic Foreign Ministers, Karachi.
305 **176** 20p. multicoloured . . . 15 15

177 Coastal Embankments

1971. East Pakistan Coastal Embankments Project.
306 **177** 20p. multicoloured . . . 15 15

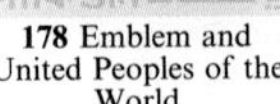

178 Emblem and United Peoples of the World

180 Chaharbagh School (Iran)

179 Maple Leaf Cement Factory, Daudkhel

1971. Racial Equality Year.

307	178	20p. multicoloured . . .	10	15
308		50p. multicoloured . . .	20	45

1971. 20th Anniv of Colombo Plan.

309	179	20p. brown, black & violet	10	10

1971. 7th Anniv of Regional Co-operation for Development. Multicoloured.

310	10p. Selimiye Mosque (Turkey) (horiz)	10	15
311	20p. Badshahi Mosque, Lahore (horiz)	20	25
312	50p. Type **180**	30	35

181 Electric Train and Boy with Toy Train

1971. Universal Children's Day.

313	181	20p. multicoloured . . .	1·75	50

182 Horseman and Symbols

1971. 2500th Anniv of Persian Monarchy.

314	182	10p. multicoloured . . .	20	30
315		20p. multicoloured . . .	30	40
316		50p. multicoloured . . .	40	75

183 Hockey-player and Trophy

1971. World Cup Hockey Tournament, Barcelona.

317	183	20p. multicoloured . . .	1·75	65

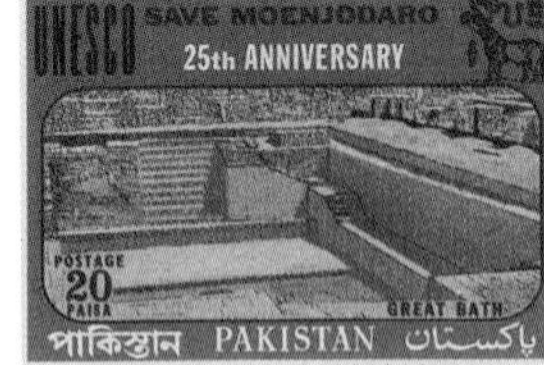

184 Great Bath, Moenjodaro

1971. 25th Anniv of U.N.E.S.C.O. and Campaign to save the Moenjodaro Excavations.

318	184	20p. multicoloured . . .	20	30

185 U.N.I.C.E.F. Symbol

1971. 25th Anniv of U.N.I.C.E.F.

319	185	50p. multicoloured . . .	30	60

186 King Hussein and Jordanian Flag

1971. 50th Anniv of Hashemite Kingdom of Jordan.

320	186	20p. multicoloured . . .	15	20

187 Badge of Hockey Federation and Trophy

1971. Hockey Championships Victory.

321	187	20p. multicoloured . . .	2·50	90

188 Reading Class

1972. International Book Year.

322	188	20p. multicoloured . . .	20	30

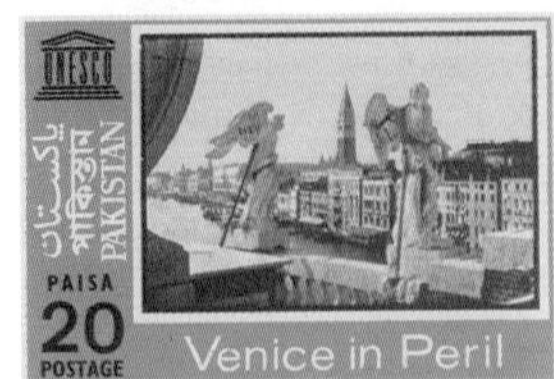

189 View of Venice

1972. U.N.E.S.C.O. Campaign to Save Venice.

323	189	20p. multicoloured . . .	30	30

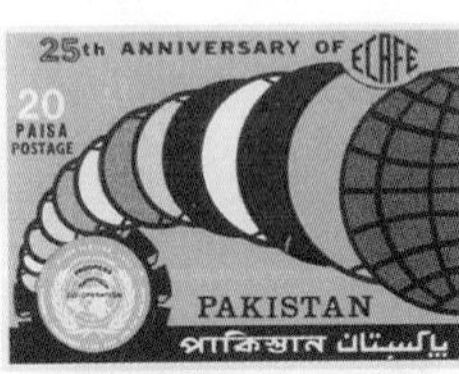

190 E.C.A.F.E. Emblem and Discs

1972. 25th Anniv of E.C.A.F.E.

324	190	20p. multicoloured . . .	15	30

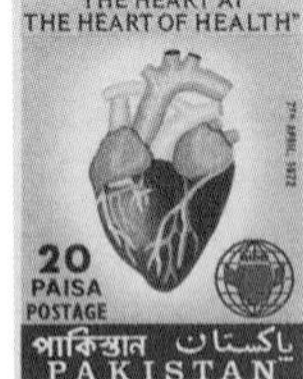

191 Human Heart

192 "Only One Earth"

1972. World Health Day.

325	191	20p. multicoloured . . .	20	30

1972. U.N. Conference on the Human Environment, Stockholm.

326	192	20p. multicoloured . . .	20	30

193 "Fisherman" (Cevat Dereli)

194 Mohammed Ali Jinnah and Tower

1972. 8th Anniv of Regional Co-operation for Development. Multicoloured.

327	10p. Type **193**	20	20
328	20p. "Iranian Woman" (Behzad)	35	25
329	50p. "Will and Power" (A. R. Chughtai)	55	70

1972. 25th Anniv of Independence. Mult.

330	10p. Type **194**	10	10
331	20p. "Land Reform" (74 × 23½)	15	25
332	20p. "Labour Reform" (74 × 23½)	15	25
333	20p. "Education Policy" (74 × 23½)	15	25
334	20p. "Health Policy" (74 × 23½)	15	25
335	60p. National Assembly Building (46 × 28 mm) . .	25	35

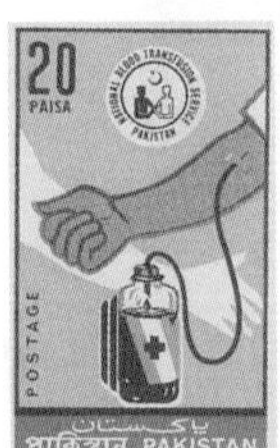

195 Donating Blood

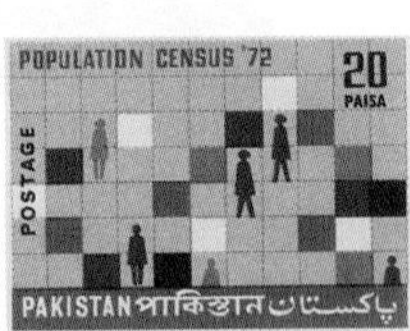

196 People and Squares

1972. National Blood Transfusion Service.

336	195	20p. multicoloured . . .	20	30

1972. Centenary of Population Census.

337	196	20p. multicoloured . . .	20	20

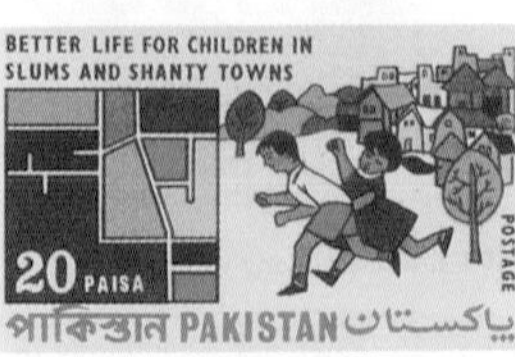

197 Children from Slums

1972. Universal Children's Day.

338	197	20p. multicoloured . . .	20	30

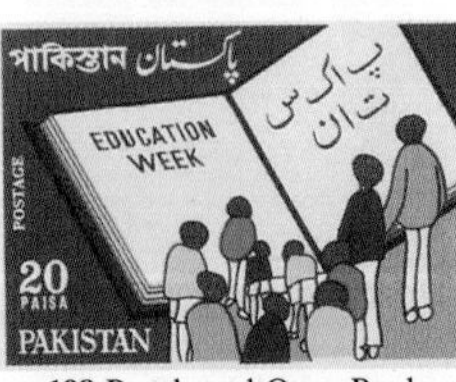

198 People and Open Book

1972. Education Week.

339	198	20p. multicoloured . . .	20	30

199 Nuclear Power Plant

1972. Inauguration of Karachi Nuclear Power Plant.

340	199	20p. multicoloured . . .	20	30

200 Copernicus in Observatory

1973. 500th Birth Anniv of Nicholas Copernicus (astronomer).

341	200	20p. multicoloured . . .	20	30

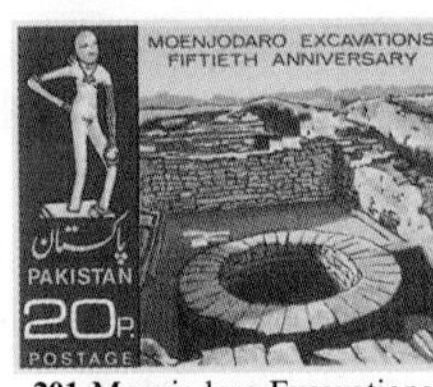

201 Moenjodaro Excavations

1973. 50th Anniv of Moenjodaro Excavations.

342	201	20p. multicoloured . . .	20	30

202 Elements of Meteorology

1973. Centenary of I.M.O./W.M.O.

343	202	20p. multicoloured . . .	30	40

203 Prisoners-of-war

1973. Prisoners-of-war in India.

344	203	1r.25 multicoloured . . .	1·50	2·25

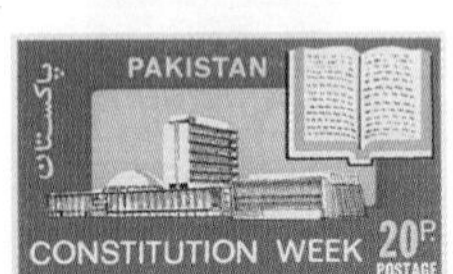

204 National Assembly Building and Constitution Book

1973. Constitution Week.

345	204	20p. multicoloured . . .	60	50

205 Badge and State Bank Building

1973. 25th Anniv of Pakistan State Bank.

346	205	20p. multicoloured . . .	15	30
347		1r. multicoloured	30	50

206 Lut Desert Excavations (Iran)

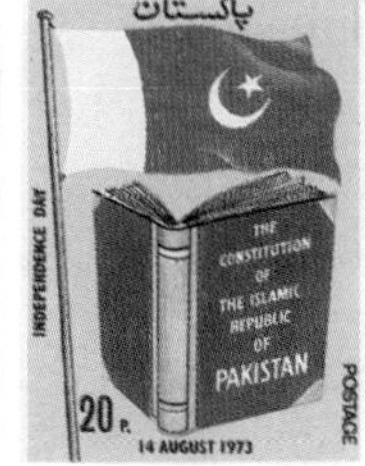

207 Constitution Book and Flag

1973. 9th Anniv of Regional Co-operation for Development. Multicoloured.

348 20p. Type **206** 30 20
349 60p. Main Street, Moenjodaro (Pakistan) . . 55 50
350 1r.25 Mausoleum of Antiochus I (Turkey) . . . 75 1·25

1973. Independence Day and Enforcement of the Constitution.

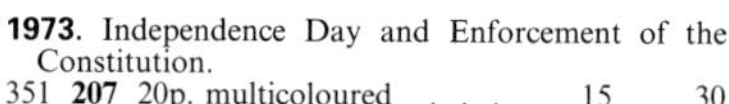

351 **207** 20p. multicoloured . . . 15 30

208 Mohammed Ali Jinnah (Quaid-i-Azam)

1973. 25th Death Anniv of Mohammed Ali Jinnah.

352 **208** 20p. green, yellow & black 15 30

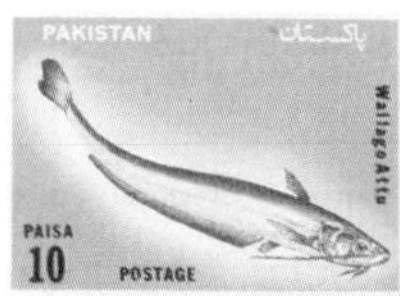

209 Wallago

1973. Fishes. Multicoloured.

353 10p. Type **209** . . . . 1·10 1·10
354 20p. Rohu . . . . 1·25 1·25
355 60p. Mozambique mouthbrooder . . . . . . 1·40 1·40
356 1r. Catla . . . . 1·40 1·40

210 Children's Education

1973. Universal Children's Day.

357 **210** 20p. multicoloured . . . 15 40

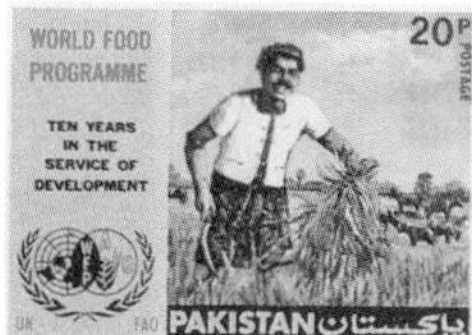

211 Harvesting

1973. 10th Anniv of World Food Programme.

358 **211** 20p. multicoloured . . . 60 40

212 Ankara and Kemal Ataturk

1973. 50th Anniv of Turkish Republic.

359 **212** 50p. multicoloured . . . 45 35

213 Boy Scout

214 "Basic Necessities"

1973. National Silver Jubilee Jamboree.

360 **213** 20p. multicoloured . . . 1·75 50

1973. 25th Anniv of Declaration of Human Rights.

361 **214** 20p. multicoloured . . . 30 40

215 Al-Biruni and Nandana Hill

1973. Al-Biruni Millennium Congress.

362 **215** 20p. multicoloured . . . 40 20
363 1r.25 multicoloured . . . 1·10 75

216 Dr. Hansen, Microscope and Bacillus

218 Conference Emblem

217 Family and Emblem

1973. Centenary of Hansen's Discovery of Leprosy Bacillus.

364 **216** 20p. multicoloured . . . 1·00 70

1974. World Population Year.

365 **217** 20p. multicoloured . . . 10 10
366 1r.25 multicoloured . . . 30 40

1974. Islamic Summit Conference, Lahore. Multicoloured.

367 20p. Type **218** 10 10
368 65p. Emblem on "Sun" (42 × 30 mm) 25 60
MS369 102 × 102 mm. Nos. 367/8. Imperf . . . . 1·50 4·75

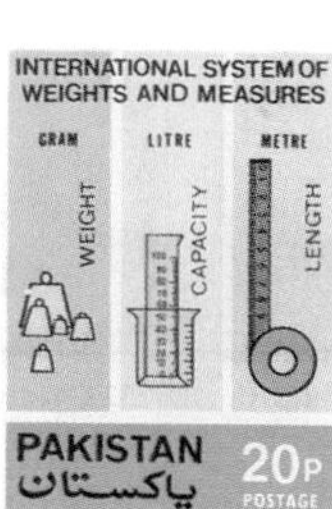

219 Units of Weight and Measurement

1974. Adoption of Int Weights and Measures System.

370 **219** 20p. multicoloured . . . 15 25

220 "Chand Chauthai" Carpet, Pakistan

1974. 10th Anniversary of Regional Co-operation for Development. Multicoloured.

371 20p. Type **220** 20 15
372 60p. Persian carpet, 16th-century 40 55
373 1r.25 Anatolian carpet, 15th-century . . . . 65 1·25

221 Hands protecting Sapling

222 Torch and Map

1974. Tree Planting Day.

374 **221** 20p. multicoloured . . . 50 50

1974. Namibia Day.

375 **222** 60p. multicoloured . . . 35 60

223 Highway Map

1974. Shahrah-e-Pakistan (Pakistan Highway).

376 **223** 20p. multicoloured . . . 1·00 70

224 Boy at Desk

225 U.P.U. Emblem

1974. Universal Children's Day.

377 **224** 20p. multicoloured . . . 30 40

1974. Centenary of U.P.U. Multicoloured.

378 20p. Type **225** 20 20
379 2r.25 U.P.U. emblem, Boeing 707 and mail-wagon (30 × 41 mm) . . . . . . 55 1·40
MS380 100 × 101 mm. Nos. 378/9. Imperf . . . . 1·25 5·00

226 Liaquat Ali Khan

227 Dr. Mohammed Iqbal (poet and philosopher)

1974. Liaquat Ali Khan (First Prime Minister of Pakistan).

381 **226** 20p. black and red . . . 30 40

1974. Birth Centenary of Dr. Iqbal (1977) (1st issue).

382 **227** 20p. multicoloured . . . 30 40
See also Nos. 399, 433 and 445/9.

228 Dr. Schweitzer and River Scene

1975. Birth Centenary of Dr. Albert Schweitzer.

383 **228** 2r.25 multicoloured . . . 3·75 3·25

229 Tourism Year Symbol

1975. South East Asia Tourism Year.

384 **229** 2r.25 multicoloured . . . 55 80

230 Assembly Hall, Flags and Prime Minister Bhutto

1975. 1st Anniv of Islamic Summit Conference, Lahore.

385 **230** 20p. multicoloured . . . 35 35
386 1r. multicoloured . . . . 75 1·40

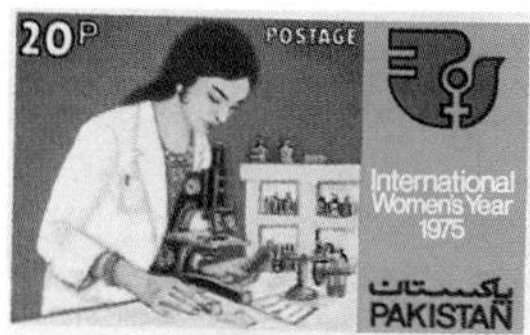

231 "Scientific Research"

1975. International Women's Year. Mult.

387 20p. Type **231** 20 25
388 2r.25 Girl teaching woman ("Adult Education") . . . 1·10 2·00

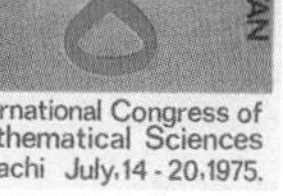

232 "Globe" and Algebraic Symbol

233 Pakistani Camel-skin Vase

1975. International Congress of Mathematical Sciences, Karachi.

389 **232** 20p. multicoloured . . . 50 50

1975. 11th Anniv of Regional Co-operation for Development. Multicoloured.

390 20p. Type **233** 25 30
391 60p. Iranian tile (horiz) . . . 50 1·00
392 1r.25 Turkish porcelain vase 75 1·50

234 Sapling and Dead Trees

235 Black Partridge

1975. Tree Planting Year.

393 **234** 20p. multicoloured . . . 35 40

1975. Wildlife Protection (1st series).
394 **235** 20p. multicoloured . . . 1·25 35
395 2r.25 multicoloured . . . 4·00 4·75
See also Nos. 400/1, 411/12, 417/18, 493/6, 560, 572/3, 581/2, 599, 600, 605, 621/2, 691, 702, 752, 780/3, 853 and 1027.

236 "Today's Girls" **238** Dr. Mohammed Iqbal

237 Hazrat Amir Khusrau, Sitar and Tabla ($\frac{1}{2}$-size illustration)

1975. Universal Children's Day.
396 **236** 20p. multicoloured . . . 30 40

1975. 700th Birth Anniv of Hazrat Amir Khusrau (poet and musician).
397 **237** 20p. multicoloured . . . 20 50
398 2r.25 multicoloured . . . 80 1·75

1975. Birth Cent (1977) of Dr. Iqbal (2nd issue).
399 **238** 20p. multicoloured . . . 30 40

239 Urial (wild sheep) **241** Dome and Minaret of the Rauza-e-Mubarak

240 Moenjodaro Remains

1975. Wildlife Protection (2nd series).
400 **239** 20p. multicoloured . . . 30 30
401 3r. multicoloured . . . . 1·75 3·25

1976. "Save Moenjodaro" (1st issue). Multicoloured.
402 10p. Type **240** 65 75
403 20p. Remains of houses . . . 75 85
404 65p. The Citadel 75 85
405 3r. Well inside a house . . . 75 85
406 4r. The "Great Bath" 85 95
See also Nos. 414 and 430.

1976. International Congress on Seerat.
407 **241** 20p. multicoloured . . . 15 20
408 3r. multicoloured 55 90

242 Alexander Graham Bell and Dial

1976. Telephone Centenary.
409 **242** 3r. multicoloured . . . . 1·25 2·00

243 College Arms within "Sun"

1976. Cent of National College of Arts, Lahore.
410 **243** 20p. multicoloured . . . 30 50

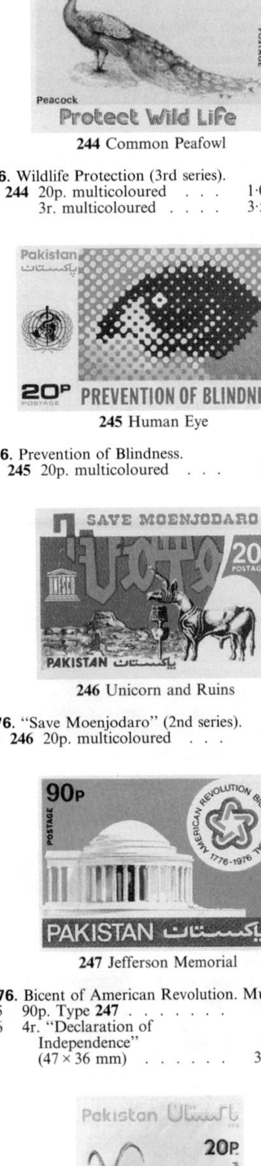

244 Common Peafowl

1976. Wildlife Protection (3rd series).
411 **244** 20p. multicoloured . . . 1·00 35
412 3r. multicoloured . . . . 3·50 4·50

245 Human Eye

1976. Prevention of Blindness.
413 **245** 20p. multicoloured . . . 85 70

246 Unicorn and Ruins

1976. "Save Moenjodaro" (2nd series).
414 **246** 20p. multicoloured . . . 30 40

247 Jefferson Memorial

1976. Bicent of American Revolution. Mult.
415 90p. Type **247** 75 60
416 4r. "Declaration of Independence" (47 × 36 mm) . . . . . . 3·00 5·00

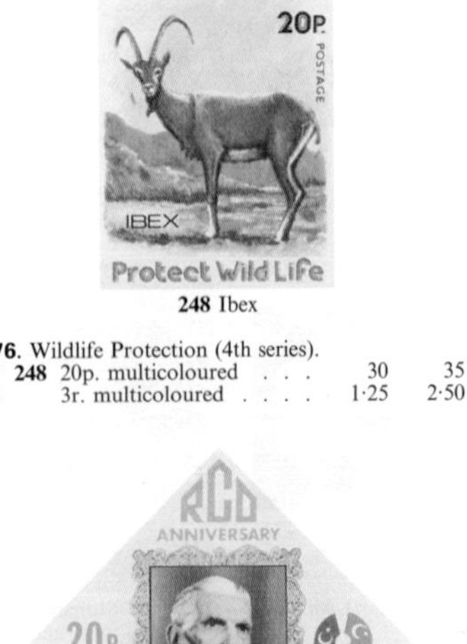

248 Ibex

1976. Wildlife Protection (4th series).
417 **248** 20p. multicoloured . . . 30 35
418 3r. multicoloured . . . . 1·25 2·50

249 Mohammed Ali Jinnah

1976. 12th Anniv of Regional Co-operation for Development. Multicoloured.
419 20p. Type **249** 65 90
420 65p. Reza Shah the Great (Iran) 65 90
421 90p. Kemal Ataturk (Turkey) 65 90

250 Urdu Text **251** Mohammed Ali Jinnah and Wazir Mansion

1976. Birth Cent of Mohammed Ali Jinnah (1st issue). (a) Type **250**.
422 **250** 5p. black, blue and yellow 20 25
423 10p. black, yellow & pur 20 25
424 15p. black and blue . . . 20 25
425 1r. black, yellow and blue 30 30

(b) Type **251**. Background Buildings given. Mult.
426 20p. Type **251** 20 25
427 40p. Sind Madressah 20 25
428 50p. Minar Qarardad-e-Pakistan 20 25
429 3r. Mausoleum 45 50
See also No. 436.

252 Dancing-girl, Ruins and King Priest

1976. "Save Moenjodaro" (3rd series).
430 **252** 65p. multicoloured . . . 35 80

253 U.N. Racial Discrimination Emblem

1976. U.N. Decade to Combat Racial Discrimination.
431 **253** 65p. multicoloured . . . 30 60

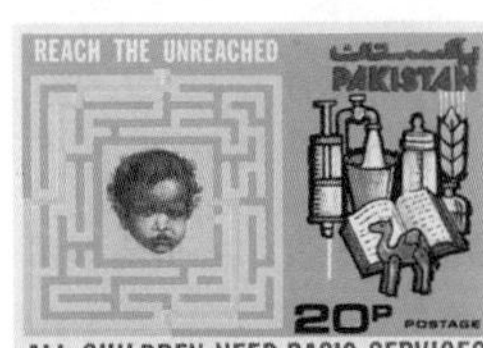

254 Child in Maze and Basic Services

1976. Universal Children's Day.
432 **254** 20p. multicoloured . . . 30 40

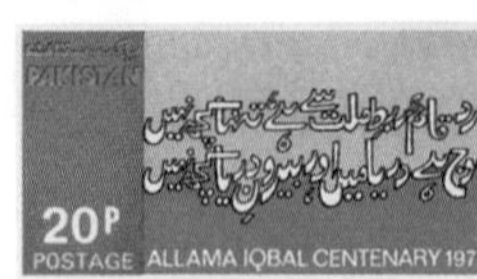

255 Verse from "Allama Iqbal"

1976. Birth Centenary (1977) of Dr. Iqbal (3rd issue).
433 **255** 20p. multicoloured . . . 15 30

256 Mohammed Ali Jinnah giving Scout Salute **257** Children Reading

1976. Quaid-i-Azam Centenary Jamboree.
434 **256** 20p. multicoloured . . . 75 40

1976. Children's Literature.
435 **257** 20p. multicoloured . . . 40 40

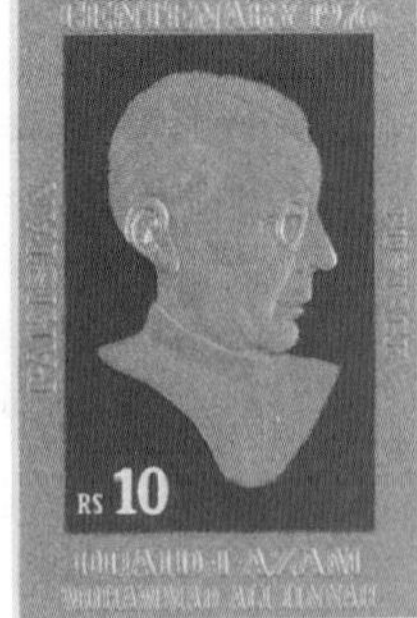

258 Mohammed Ali Jinnah

1976. Birth Centenary of Mohammed Ali Jinnah (2nd issue).
436 **258** 10r. green and gold . . . 2·50 3·50

259 Rural Family **261** Forest

260 Turkish Vase, 1800 B.C.

1977. Social Welfare and Rural Development Year.
437 **259** 20p. multicoloured . . . 25 10

1977. 13th Anniv of Regional Co-operation for Development.
438 **260** 20p. orange, blue & black 35 10
439 – 65p. multicoloured . . . 55 40
440 – 90p. multicoloured . . . 80 1·50
DESIGNS: 60p. Pakistani toy bullock cart from Moenjodaro; 90p. Pitcher with spout from Sialk Hill, Iran.

1977. National Tree Plantation Campaign.
441 **261** 20p. multicoloured . . . 20 30

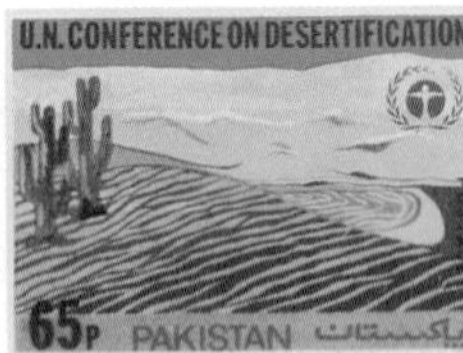

262 Desert Scene

1977. U.N. Conference on Desertification, Nairobi.
442 **262** 65p. multicoloured . . . 75 30

263 "Water for Children of the World" **265** Iqbal and Spirit of the Poet Roomi (from painting by Behzad)

264 Aga Khan III

1977. Universal Children's Day.
443 **263** 50p. multicoloured . . . 40 30

1977. Birth Centenary of Aga Khan III.
444 **264** 2r. multicoloured . . . . 55 1·00

1977. Birth Centenary of Dr. Mohammed Iqbal (4th issue). Multicoloured.

445	20p. Type **265**	40	50
446	65p. Iqbal looking at Jamaluddin Afghani and Saeed Haleem Pasha at prayer (Behzad)	40	50
447	1r.25 Urdu verse	45	55
448	2r.25 Persian verse	50	65
449	3r. Iqbal	55	75

266 The Holy "Khana-Kaaba" (House of God, Mecca)

1977. Haj (pilgrimage to Mecca).
450 **266** 65p. multicoloured . . . 30 30

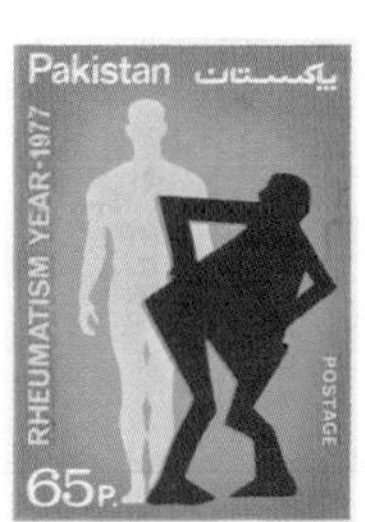

267 Rheumatic Patient and Healthy Man

268 Woman in Costume of Rawalpindi-Islamabad

1977. World Rheumatism Year.
451 **267** 65p. blue, black and yellow 30 20

1978. Indonesia–Pakistan Economic and Cultural Co-operation Organization.
452 **268** 75p. multicoloured . . . 30 20

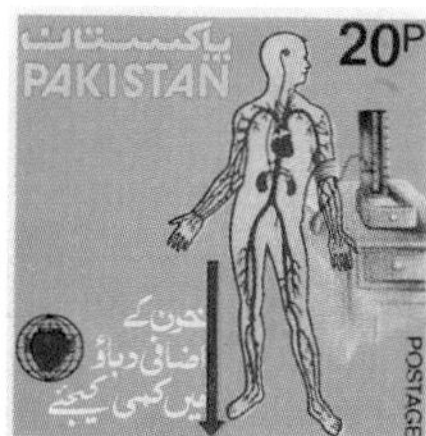

269 Human Body and Sphygmomanometer

1978. World Hypertension Month.

453	**269**	20p. multicoloured . . .	15	10
454	–	2r. multicoloured	60	90

The 2r. value is as Type **269** but has the words "Down with high blood pressure" instead of the Urdu inscription at bottom left.

270 Henri Dunant

1978. 150th Birth Anniv of Henri Dunant (founder of the Red Cross).
455 **270** 1r. multicoloured . . . . 1·00 20

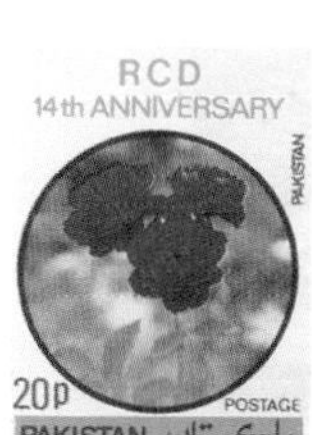

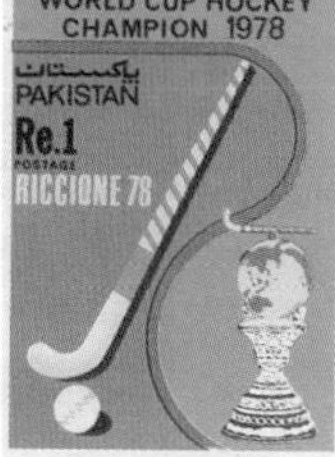

271 Red Roses (Pakistan)

272 "Pakistan, World Cup Hockey Champions"

1978. 14th Anniv of Regional Co-operation for Development. Roses. Multicoloured.

456	20p. Type **271**	35	20
457	90p. Pink roses (Iran)	50	20
458	2r. Yellow rose (Turkey) . .	75	25

1978. "Riccione '78" International Stamp Fair. Multicoloured.

459	1r. Type **272**	1·25	25
460	2r. Fountain at Piazza Turismo	50	35

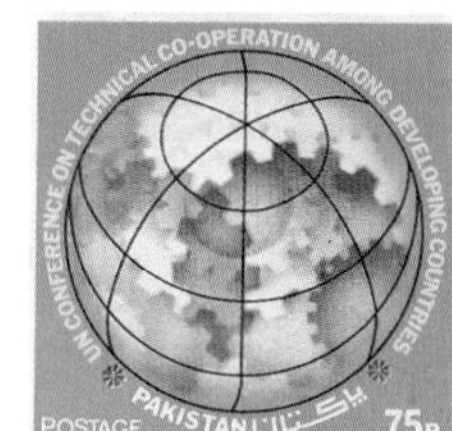

273 Cogwheels within Globe Symbol

1978. U.N. Technical Co-operation amongst Developing Countries Conference.
461 **273** 75p. multicoloured . . . 15 10

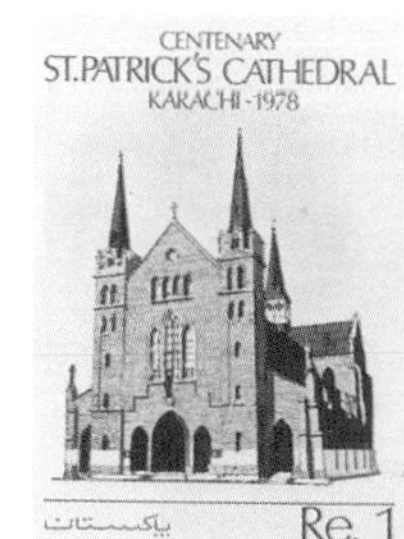

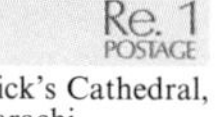

274 St. Patrick's Cathedral, Karachi

275 Minar-i-Qarardad-e-Pakistan

1978. Centenary of St. Patrick's Cathedral, Karachi. Multicoloured.

462	1r. Type **274**	10	10
463	2r. Stained glass window . .	25	25

1978.

464	**275**	2p. green	10	10
465		3p. black	10	10
466		5p. blue	10	10
467	–	10p. blue and turquoise	10	10
468	–	20p. green	60	10
469	–	25p. green and mauve	1·00	10
470	–	40p. blue and mauve . .	10	10
471	–	50p. lilac and green . .	30	10
472	–	60p. black	10	10
473b	–	75p. red	70	10
474	–	90p. mauve and blue . .	30	10
475	–	1r. green	20	10
476	–	1r.50 orange	20	10
477	–	2r. red	20	10
478	–	3r. blue	20	10
479	–	4r. black	20	10
480	–	5r. brown	20	10

DESIGNS—HORIZ (25 × 20 mm): 10p. to 90p. Tractor. VERT (21 × 25 mm): 1r. to 5r. Mausoleum of Ibrahim Khan Makli, Thatta.

277 Emblem and "United Races" Symbol

278 Maulana Mohammad Ali Jauhar

1978. International Anti-Apartheid Year.
481 **277** 1r. multicoloured 15 15

1978. Birth Centenary of Maulana Mohammad Ali Jauhar (patriot).
482 **278** 50p. multicoloured . . . 50 20

279 Panavia MRCA Tornado, De Havilland Dragon Rapide and Wright Flyer I

1978. 75th Anniv of Powered Flight. Mult.

483	65p. Type **279**	1·00	1·75
484	1r. McDonnell Douglas Phantom II, Lockheed Tristar 500 and Wright Flyer I	1·10	1·75
485	2r. North American X-15, Tupolev Tu-104 and Wright Flyer I	1·25	2·00
486	2r.25 Mikoyan Gurevich MiG-15, Concorde and Wright Flyer I	1·25	2·25

280 "Holy Koran illuminating Globe" and Raudha-e-Mubarak (mausoleum)

1979. "12th Rabi-ul-Awwal" (Prophet Mohammed's birthday).
487 **280** 20p. multicoloured . . . 40 15

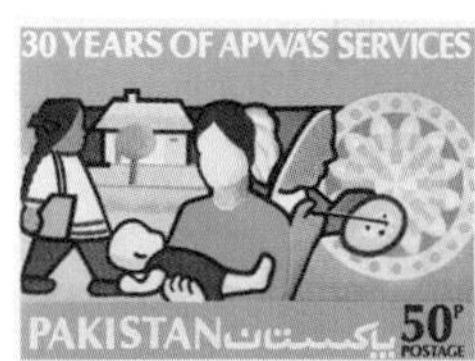

281 "Aspects of A.P.W.A."

1979. 30th Anniv of A.P.W.A. (All Pakistan Women's Association).
488 **281** 50p. multicoloured . . . 60 15

282 Tippu Sultan Shaheed of Mysore

1979. Pioneers of Freedom (1st series). Multicoloured.

490	10r. Type **282**	75	1·40
491	15r. Sir Syed Ahmad Khan	1·00	2·00
492	25r. Altaf Hussain Hali . . .	1·50	2·25

See also Nos. 757, 801/27, 838/46, 870/2, 904/6, 921/8, 961/2, 1007, 1019/20 and 1075/7.

283 Himalayan Monal Pheasant

1979. Wildlife Protection (5th series). Pheasants. Multicoloured.

493	20p. Type **283**	1·25	60
494	25p. Kalij pheasant	1·25	80
495	40p. Koklass pheasant . . .	1·60	1·75
496	1r. Cheer pheasant	3·00	2·00

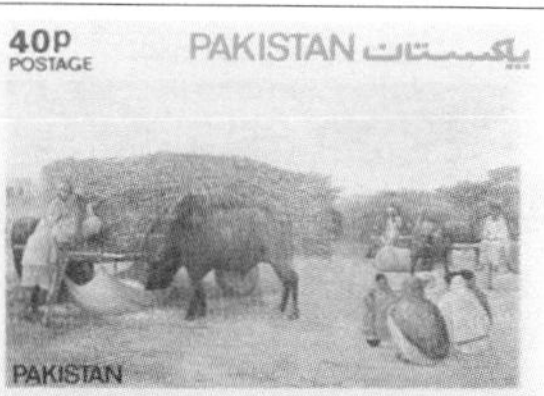

284 "Pakistan Village Scene" (Ustad Bakhsh)

1979. 15th Anniv of Regional Co-operation for Development. Multicoloured.

497	40p. Type **284**	20	25
498	75p. "Iranian Goldsmith" (Kamal al Molk)	20	25
499	1r.60 "Turkish Harvest" (Namik Ismail)	25	30

285 Guj Embroidered Shirt (detail)

1979. Handicrafts (1st series). Multicoloured.

500	40p. Type **285**	20	20
501	1r. Enamel inlaid brass plate	25	25
502	1r.50 Baskets	30	30
503	2r. Chain-stitch embroidered rug (detail)	40	40

See also Nos. 578/9, 595/6 and 625/8.

286 Children playing on Climbing-frame

1979. S.O.S. Children's Village, Lahore.
504 **286** 50p. multicoloured . . . 40 40

287 "Island" (Z. Maloof)

1979. International Year of the Child. Children's Paintings. Multicoloured.

505	40p. Type **287**	15	15
506	75p. "Playground" (R. Akbar)	25	25
507	1r. "Fairground" (M. Azam)	25	25
508	1r.50 "Hockey Match" (M. Tayyab)	30	30
MS509	79 × 64 mm. 2r. "Child looking at Faces in the Sky" (M. Mumtaz) (vert). Imperf . .	1·00	2·00

288 Warrior attacking Crab

289 Pakistan Customs Emblem

1979. "Fight Against Cancer".
510 **288** 40p. black, yellow and purple 70 70

1979. Centenary of Pakistan Customs Service.
511 **289** 1r. multicoloured 30 30

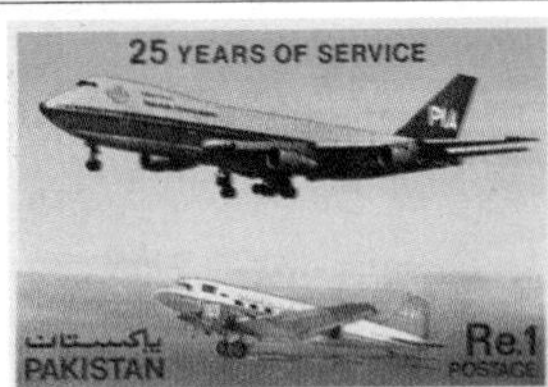

290 Boeing 747-200 and Douglas DC-3 Airliners

1980. 25th Anniv of Pakistan International Air Lines.
512 **290** 1r. multicoloured . . . . 1·75 90

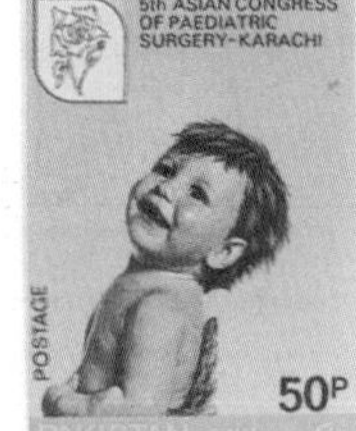

291 Islamic Pattern **292** Young Child

1980.
513 **291** 10p. green and yellow . . 10 10
514 15p. deep green and green 10 10
515 25p. violet and red . . . 10 50
516 35p. red and green . . . 10 50
517 – 40p. red and brown . . . 15 10
518 – 50p. violet and green . . 10 50
519 – 80p. green and black . . 15 50
The 40 to 80p. values also show different Islamic patterns, the 40p. being horizontal and the remainder vertical.

1980. 5th Asian Congress of Paediatric Surgery, Karachi.
530 **292** 50p. multicoloured . . . 75 1·50

293 Conference Emblem

1980. 11th Islamic Conference of Foreign Ministers, Islamabad.
531 **293** 1r. multicoloured 65 50

294 Karachi Port (½-size illustration)

1980. Centenary of Karachi Port Authority.
532 **294** 1r. multicoloured . . . . 1·75 1·40

1980. "Riccione 80" International Stamp Exhibition. Nos. 505/8 optd **RICCIONE 80**.
533 **287** 40p. multicoloured . . . 30 80
534 – 75p. multicoloured . . . 40 90
535 – 1r. multicoloured 45 90
536 – 1r.50 multicoloured . . . 60 1·10

296 College Emblem with Old and New Buildings

1980. 75th Anniv of Command and Staff College, Quetta.
537 **296** 1r. multicoloured 20 15

1980. World Tourism Conference, Manila. No. 496 optd **WORLD TOURISM CONFERENCE MANILA 80**.
538 1r. Cheer pheasant . . . . . 1·00 30

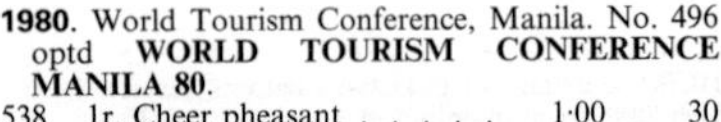

298 Birth Centenary Emblem

1980. Birth Cent of Hafiz Mahmood Shairani.
539 **298** 40p. multicoloured . . . 30 1·00

299 Shalimar Gardens, Lahore

1980. Aga Khan Award for Architecture.
540 **299** 2r. multicoloured . . . . 40 1·50

300 Rising Sun

1980. 1400th Anniv of Hegira (1st issue). Multicoloured.
541 40p. Type **300** 10 10
542 2r. Ka'aba and symbols of Moslem achievement (33 × 33 mm) 25 45
543 3r. Holy Koran illuminating the World (30 × 54 mm) . . 30 80
MS544 106 × 84 mm. 4r. Candles. Imperf . . . . 45 1·00
See also No. 549

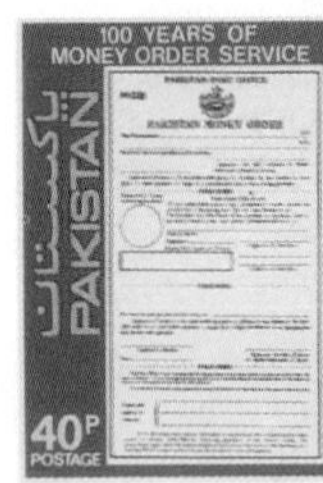

301 Money Order Form **302** Postcards encircling Globe

1980. Centenary of Money Order Service.
545 **301** 40p. multicoloured . . . 20 60

1980. Centenary of Postcard Service.
546 **302** 40p. multicoloured . . . 20 60

303 Heinrich von Stephan and U.P.U. Emblem

1981. 150th Birth Anniv of Heinrich von Stephan (U.P.U. founder).
547 **303** 1r. multicoloured 30 20

304 Aircraft and Airmail Letters

1981. 50th Anniv of Airmail Service.
548 **304** 1r. multicoloured 60 20

305 Mecca

1981. 1400th Anniv of Hegira (2nd issue).
549 **305** 40p. multicoloured . . . 20 60

306 Conference Emblem and Afghan Refugees

1981. Islamic Summit Conference (1st issue). Multicoloured.
550 40p. Type **306** 30 10
551 40p. Conference emblem encircled by flags and Afghan refugees (28 × 58 mm) 30 10
552 1r. Type **306** 50 10
553 1r. As No. 551 . . . . 50 10
554 2r. Conference emblem and map showing Afghanistan (48 × 32 mm) 65 50

307 Conference Emblem

1981. Islamic Summit Conference (2nd issue). Multicoloured.
555 40p. Type **307** 10 15
556 40p. Conference emblem and flags (28 × 46 mm) 10 15
557 85p. Type **307** 20 40
558 85p. As No. 556 . . . . . . 20 40

308 Kemal Ataturk

1981. Birth Centenary of Kemal Ataturk (Turkish statesman).
559 **308** 1r. multicoloured 50 15

309 Green Turtle

1981. Wildlife Protection (6th series).
560 **309** 40p. multicoloured . . . 1·25 40

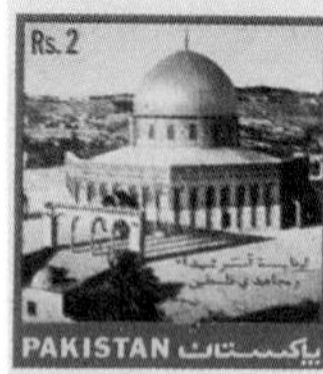

310 Dome of the Rock

1981. Palestinian Welfare.
561 **310** 2r. multicoloured 35 35

311 Malubiting West

1981. Mountain Peaks (1st series). Karakoram Range. Multicoloured.
562 40p. Type **311** 40 40
563 40p. Malubiting West (24 × 31 mm) 40 40
564 1r. Haramosh 55 75
565 1r. Haramosh (24 × 31 mm) 55 75
566 1r.50 K6 . . . . 70 1·00
567 1r.50 K6 (24 × 31 mm) . . . 70 1·00
568 2r. K2, Broad Peak, Gasherbrum 4 and Gasherbrum 2 . . . . . . 70 1·40
569 2r. K2 (24 × 31 mm) . . . . 70 1·40
See also Nos. 674/5.

312 Pakistan Steel "Furnace No. 1"

1981. 1st Firing of Pakistan Steel "Furnace No. 1", Karachi.
570 **312** 40p. multicoloured . . . 20 10
571 2r. multicoloured . . . . 60 1·50

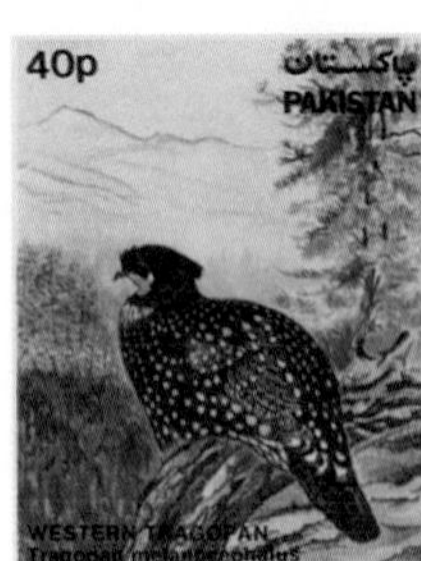

313 Western Tragopan

1981. Wildlife Protection (7th series).
572 **313** 40p. multicoloured . . . 2·00 75
573 – 2r. multicoloured . . . . 4·00 4·25
DESIGN: 2r. As Type **313** but with background showing a winter view.

314 Disabled People and I.Y.D.P. Emblem

1981. International Year for Disabled Persons.
574 **314** 40p. multicoloured . . . 30 50
575 2r. multicoloured . . . . 1·10 1·75

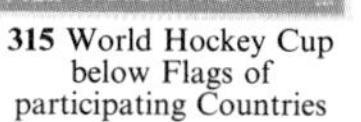

315 World Hockey Cup below Flags of participating Countries

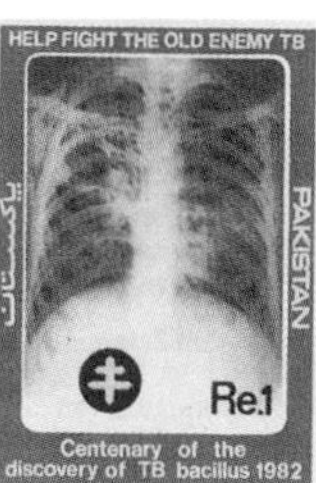

317 Chest X-Ray of Infected Person

316 Camel Skin Lamp

1982. Pakistan—World Cup Hockey Champions. Multicoloured.
576 1r. Type **315** . . . . 2·00 1·50
577 1r. World Hockey Cup above flags of participating countries . . . . 2·00 1·50

1982. Handicrafts (2nd series). Multicoloured.
578 1r. Type **316** 70 80
579 1r. Hala pottery 70 80
See also Nos. 595/6.

1982. Centenary of Robert Koch's Discovery of Tubercle Bacillus.
580 **317** 1r. multicoloured . . . . 1·25 1·25

318 Indus Dolphin

1982. Wildlife Protection (8th series).
581 **318** 40p. multicoloured . . . 1·50 1·00
582 – 1r. multicoloured . . . . 3·00 2·25
DESIGN: 1r. As Type **318** but with design reversed.

319 "Apollo–Soyuz" Link-up, 1975

1982. Peaceful Use of Outer Space.
583 **319** 1r. multicoloured . . . . 2·00 1·25

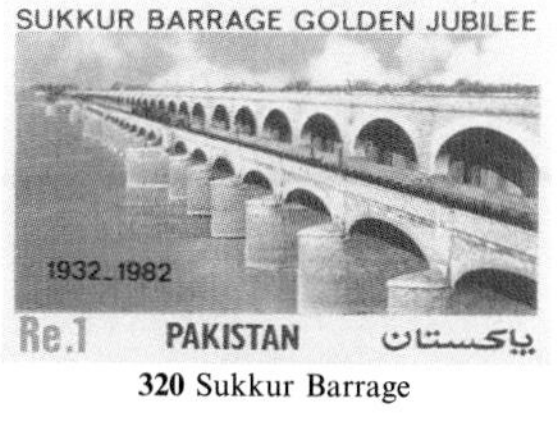

320 Sukkur Barrage

1982. 50th Anniv of Sukkur Barrage.
584 **320** 1r. multicoloured 30 30

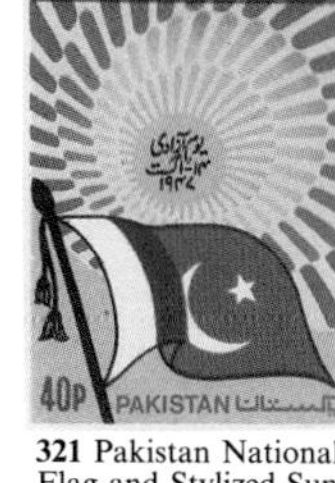

321 Pakistan National Flag and Stylized Sun

324 Scout Emblem and Tents

323 Arabic Inscription and University Emblem (⅔-size illustration)

1982. Independence Day. Multicoloured.
585 40p. Type **321** 15 30
586 85p. Map of Pakistan and stylized torch 35 95

1982. "Riccione '82" Stamp Exhibition. No. 584 optd **RICCIONE-82**.
587 **320** 1r. multicoloured 20 20

1982. Centenary of the Punjab University.
588 **323** 40p. multicoloured . . . 75 50

1983. 75th Anniv of Boy Scout Movement.
589 **324** 2r. multicoloured 50 50

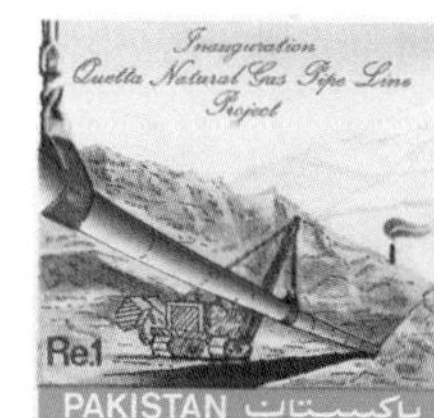
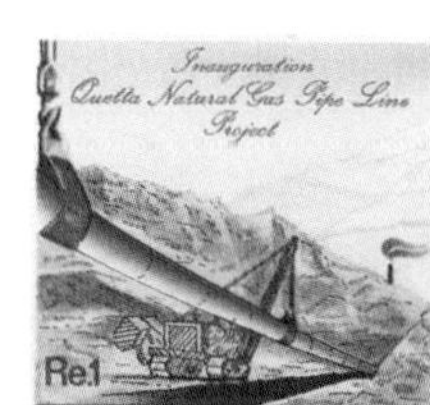

325 Laying Pipeline

1983. Inaug of Quetta Natural Gas Pipeline Project.
590 **325** 1r. multicoloured 30 30

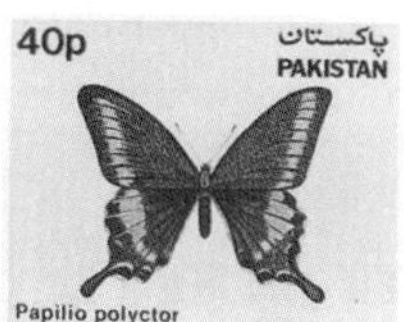

326 "Papilio polyctor"

1983. Butterflies. Multicoloured.
591 40p. Type **326** . . . . 1·25 20
592 50p. "Atrophaneura aristolochiae" . . . . . . 1·50 20
593 60p. "Danaus chrysippus" . . 1·75 60
594 1r.50 "Papilio demoleus" . . 2·50 2·25

1983. Handicrafts (3rd series). As T **316**. Multicoloured.
595 1r. Five flower motif needlework, Sind 15 15
596 1r. Straw mats 15 15

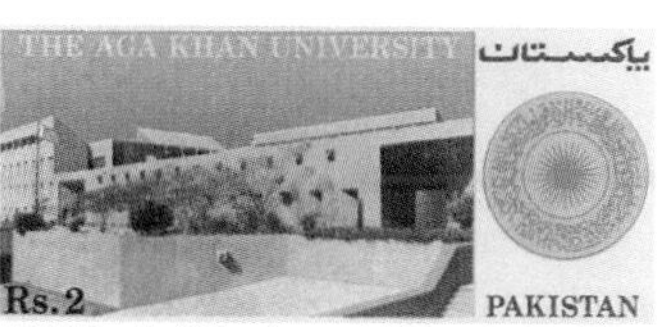

327 School of Nursing and University Emblem

1983. Presentation of Charter to Aga Khan University, Karachi.
597 **327** 2r. multicoloured . . . . 1·00 1·40

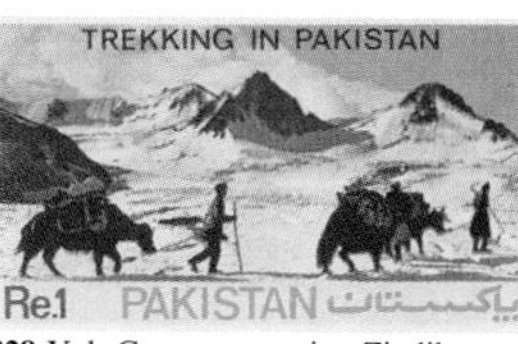
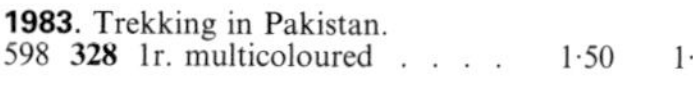

328 Yak Caravan crossing Zindiharam-Darkot Pass, Hindu Kush

1983. Trekking in Pakistan.
598 **328** 1r. multicoloured . . . . 1·50 1·25

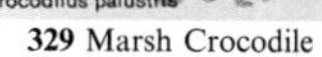

329 Marsh Crocodile

331 Floral Design

330 Goitred Gazelle

1983. Wildlife Protection (9th series).
599 **329** 3r. multicoloured . . . . 3·50 2·00

1983. Wildlife Protection (10th series).
600 **330** 1r. multicoloured . . . . 2·50 2·00

1983. 36th Anniv of Independence. Mult.
601 60p. Type **331** 10 10
602 4r. Hand holding flaming torch 40 45

332 Traditional Weaving, Pakistan

1983. Indonesian–Pakistan Economic and Cultural Co-operation Organization, 1969–1983. Mult.
603 2r. Type **332** 20 25
604 2r. Traditional weaving, Indonesia 20 25

333 "Siberian Cranes" (Great White Cranes) (Sir Peter Scott)

1983. Wildlife Protection (11th series).
605 **333** 3r. multicoloured . . . . 3·00 3·25

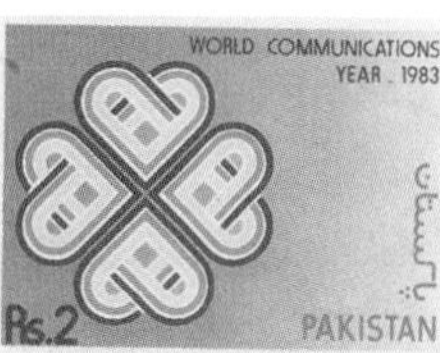

334 W.C.Y. Emblem

1983. World Communications Year. Multicoloured.
606 2r. Type **334** 20 25
607 3r. W.C.Y. emblem (different) (33 × 33 mm) 30 35

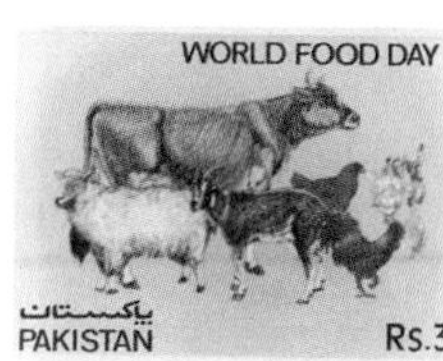

335 Farm Animals

1983. World Food Day. Multicoloured.
608 3r. Type **335** . . . . 1·50 1·75
609 3r. Fruit . . . . 1·50 1·75
610 3r. Crops . . . . 1·50 1·75
611 3r. Sea food . . . . 1·50 1·75

336 Agriculture Produce and Fertilizer Factory

337 Lahore, 1852

1983. National Fertilizer Corporation.
612 **336** 60p. multicoloured . . . 15 30

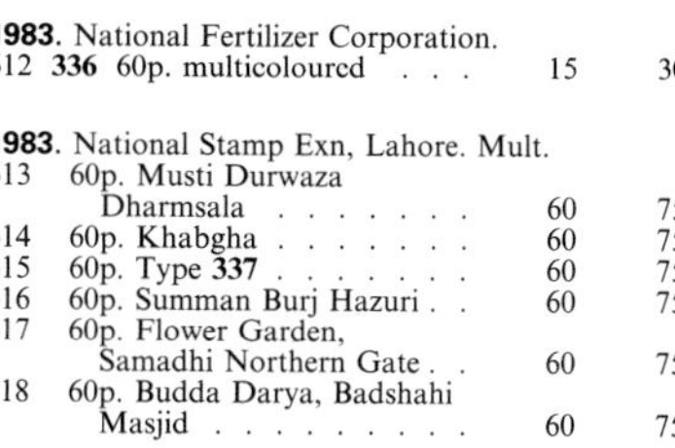

1983. National Stamp Exn, Lahore. Mult.
613 60p. Musti Durwaza Dharmsala 60 75
614 60p. Khabgha 60 75
615 60p. Type **337** 60 75
616 60p. Summan Burj Hazuri . . 60 75
617 60p. Flower Garden, Samadhi Northern Gate . . 60 75
618 60p. Budda Darya, Badshahi Masjid 60 75

338 Winner of "Enterprise" Event

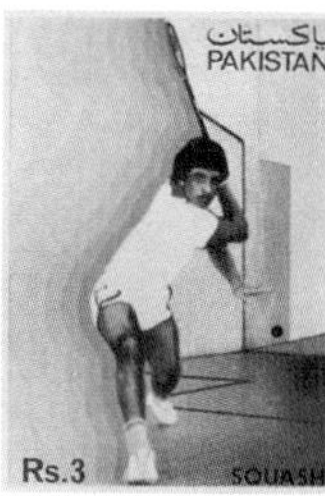

340 Jahangir Khan (World Squash Champion)

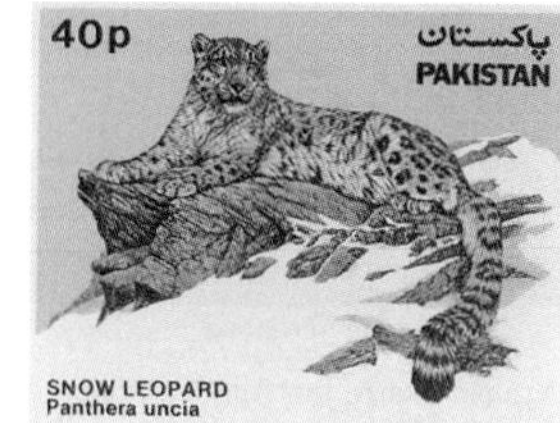

339 Snow Leopard

1983. Yachting Champions, Asian Games, Delhi. Multicoloured.
619 60p. Type **338** . . . . 1·75 1·75
620 60p. Winner of "OK" Dinghy event . . . . . . 1·75 1·75

1984. Wildlife Protection (12th series).
621 **339** 40p. multicoloured . . . 1·75 90
622 1r.60 multicoloured . . . 4·75 6·00

1984. Squash.
623 **340** 3r. multicoloured . . . . 2·25 1·75

341 P.I.A. Boeing 707 Airliner

1984. 20th Anniv of Pakistan International Airways Service to China.
624 **341** 3r. multicoloured . . . . 5·00 5·00

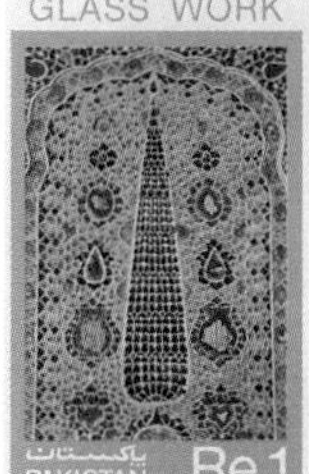

342 Glass-work

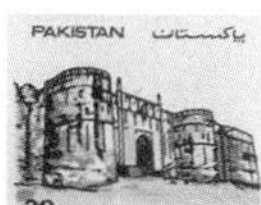

343 Attock Fort

1984. Handicrafts (4th series). Multicoloured, frame colours given.
625 **342** 1r. blue 25 15
626 – 1r. red 25 15
627 – 1r. green 25 15
628 – 1r. violet 25 15
DESIGNS: showing glass-work in Sheesh Mahal, Lahore Fort. Nos. 627/8 are horizontal designs.

1984. Forts.

No.	Type	Description	Unused	Used
629	–	5p. black and purple . . .	20	30
630	–	10p. black and red . . .	20	10
631	–	15p. violet and brown . .	60	10
632	343	20p. black and violet . .	50	10
633	–	50p. brown and red . . .	1·10	10
634	–	60p. light brown & brown	80	10
635	–	70p. blue	1·10	10
636	–	80p. brown and red . . .	1·10	10

DESIGNS: 5p. Kot Diji Fort; 10p. Rohtas Fort; 15p. Bala Hissar Fort; 50p. Hyderabad Fort; 60p. Lahore Fort; 70p. Sibi Fort; 80p. Ranikot Fort.

344 Shah Rukn i Alam's Tomb, Multan

1984. Aga Khan Award for Architecture.
647 **344** 60p. multicoloured . . . 1·75 2·00

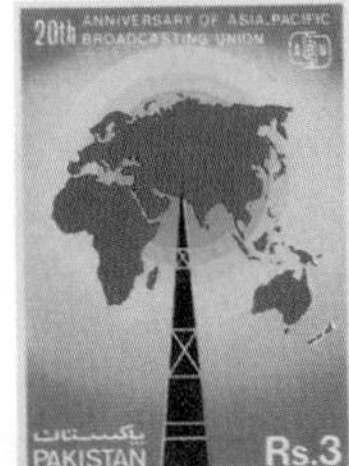

345 Radio Mast and Map of World

1984. 20th Anniv of Asia–Pacific Broadcasting Union.
648 **345** 3r. multicoloured 80 60

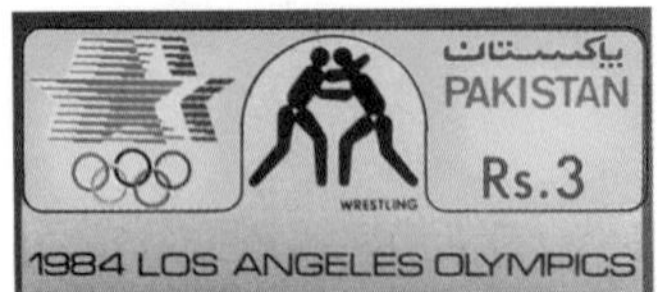

346 Wrestling

1984. Olympic Games, Los Angeles. Mult.

No.	Description	Unused	Used
649	3r. Type **346**	1·25	1·50
650	3r. Boxing	1·25	1·50
651	3r. Athletics	1·25	1·50
652	3r. Hockey	1·25	1·50
653	3r. Yachting	1·25	1·50

347 Jasmine (National flower) and Inscription

1984. Independence Day. Multicoloured.

No.	Description	Unused	Used
654	60p. Type **347**	10	10
655	4r. Symbolic torch	45	50

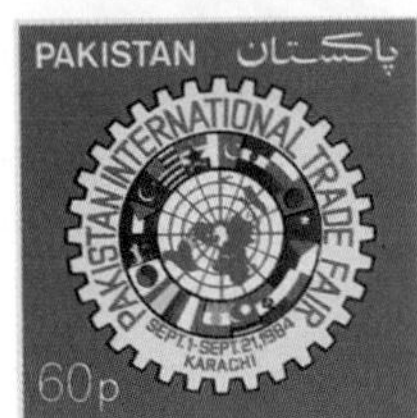

348 Gearwheel Emblem and Flags of Participating Nations

1984. Pakistan International Trade Fair.
656 **348** 60p. multicoloured . . . 1·00 30

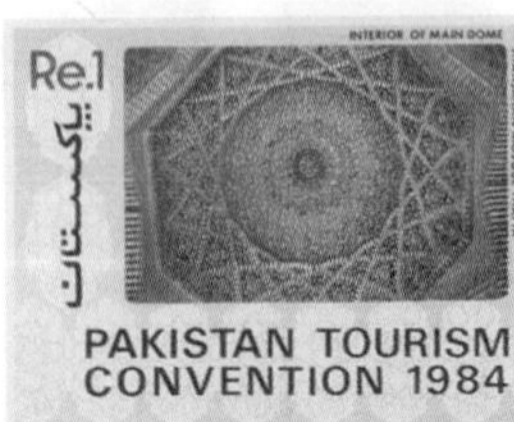

349 Interior of Main Dome

1984. Tourism Convention, Shahjahan Mosque, Thatta. Multicoloured.

No.	Description	Unused	Used
657	1r. Type **349**	50	60
658	1r. Brick and glazed tile work	50	60
659	1r. Gateway	50	60
660	1r. Symmetrical archways . .	50	60
661	1r. Interior of a dome . . .	50	60

350 Bank Emblem in Floral Pattern

1984. 25th Anniv of United Bank Ltd.
662 **350** 60p. multicoloured . . . 80 80

351 Conference Emblem

1984. 20th United Nations Conference of Trade and Development.
663 **351** 60p. multicoloured . . . 80 40

352 Postal Life Insurance Emblem within Hands

353 Bull (wall painting)

1984. Centenary of Postal Life Insurance. Multicoloured.

No.	Description	Unused	Used
664	60p. Type **352**	60	15
665	1r. "100" and Postal Life Insurance emblem	80	15

1984. U.N.E.S.C.O. Save Moenjadoro Campaign. Multicoloured.

No.	Description	Unused	Used
666	2r. Type **353**	1·40	1·00
667	2r. Bull (seal)	1·40	1·00

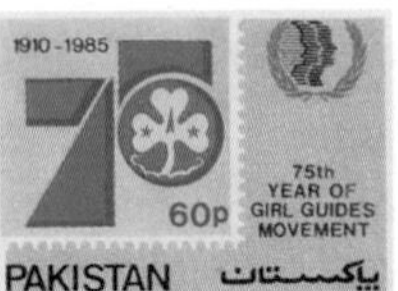

354 International Youth Year Emblem and "75"

1985. 75th Anniv of Girl Guide Movement.
668 **354** 60p. multicoloured . . . 3·00 1·50

355 Smelting Ore

1985. Inauguration of Pakistan Steel Corporation. Multicoloured.

No.	Description	Unused	Used
669	60p. Type **355**	65	25
670	1r. Pouring molten steel from ladle (28 × 46 mm)	1·10	25

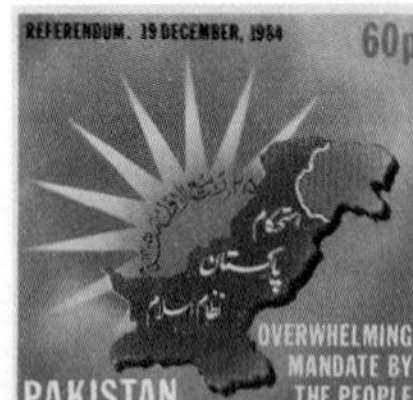

356 Map of Pakistan and Rays of Sun

1985. Presidential Referendum of 19 December 1984.
671 **356** 60p. multicoloured . . . 1·50 55

357 Ballot Box and Voting Paper

1985. March Elections. Multicoloured.

No.	Description	Unused	Used
672	1r. Type **357**	65	15
673	1r. Minar-e-Qarardad-e-Pakistan Tower, and word "Democracy" (31 × 43 mm)	65	15

1985. Mountain Peaks (2nd series). As T **311**. Multicoloured.

No.	Description	Unused	Used
674	40p. Rakaposhi (Karakoram Range)	1·75	75
675	2r. Nangaparbat (Western Himalayas)	3·75	5·00

358 Trophy and Medals from Olympic Games 1984, Asia Cup 1985 and World Cup 1982

1985. Pakistan Hockey Team "Grand Slam" Success.
676 **358** 1r. multicoloured . . . . 2·50 2·00

359 King Edward Medical College

1985. 125th Anniv of King Edward Medical College, Lahore.
677 **359** 3r. multicoloured . . . . 1·75 85

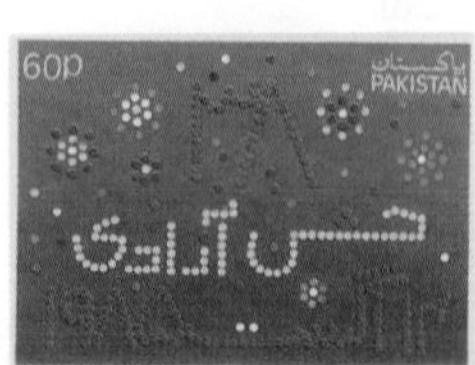

360 Illuminated Inscription in Urdu

1985. Independence Day. Multicoloured.

No.	Description	Unused	Used
678	60p. Type **360**	40	50
679	60p. Illuminated "XXXVIII" (inscr in English)	40	50

361 Sind Madressah-tul-Islam, Karachi

1985. Centenary of Sind Madressah-tul-Islam (theological college), Karachi.
680 **361** 2r. multicoloured . . . . 1·75 85

362 Jamia Masjid Mosque by Day

1985. Inauguration of New Jamia Masjid Mosque, Karachi. Multicoloured.

No.	Description	Unused	Used
681	1r. Type **362**	90	50
682	1r. Jamia Masjid illuminated at night	90	50

363 Lawrence College, Murree

1985. 125th Anniv of Lawrence College, Murree.
683 **363** 3r. multicoloured . . . . 2·00 85

364 United Nations Building, New York

1985. 40th Anniv of United Nations Organization. Multicoloured.

No.	Description	Unused	Used
684	1r. Type **364**	30	15
685	2r. U.N. Building and emblem	40	35

365 Tents and Jamboree Emblem

1985. 10th National Scout Jamboree.
686 **365** 60p. multicoloured . . . 2·25 2·25

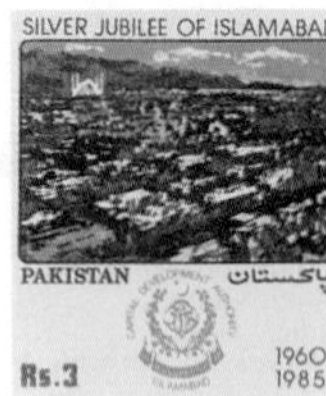

366 Islamabad

1985. 25th Anniv of Islamabad.
687 **366** 3r. multicoloured . . . . 2·25 65

367 Map of S.A.A.R.C. Countries and National Flags

1985. 1st Summit Meeting of South Asian Association for Regional Co-operation, Dhaka, Bangladesh. Multicoloured.

No.	Description	Unused	Used
688	1r. Type **367**	1·50	4·00
689	2r. National flags (39 × 39 mm)	75	2·00

368 Globe and Peace Dove

1985. 25th Anniv of U.N. General Assembly's Declaration on Independence for Colonial Territories.
690 **368** 60p. multicoloured . . . 1·00 60

369 Peregrine Falcon

1986. Wildlife Protection (13th series). Peregrine Falcon.
691 **369** 1r.50 multicoloured . . . 4·25 4·25

370 A.D.B.P. Building, Islamabad

1986. 25th Anniv of Agricultural Development Bank of Pakistan.
692 **370** 60p. multicoloured . . . 1·50 50

371 Government S.E. College

1986. Centenary of Government Sadiq Egerton College, Bahawalpur.
693 **371** 1r. multicoloured . . . . 2·50 50

372 Emblem and Bar Graph

373 "1947 1986"

1986. 25th Anniv of Asian Productivity Organization.
694 **372** 1r. multicoloured . . . . 2·50 30

1986. 39th Anniv of Independence. Multicoloured.
695 80p. Type **373** . . . . 1·25 25
696 1r. Illuminated inscription in Urdu . . . . 1·25 25

374 Open Air Class

375 Mother and Child

1986. International Literacy Day.
697 **374** 1r. multicoloured . . . . 1·50 30

1986. U.N.I.C.E.F. Child Survival Campaign.
698 **375** 80p. multicoloured . . . 1·75 65

376 Aitchison College

1986. Centenary of Aitchison College, Lahore.
699 **376** 2r.50 multicoloured . . . 1·25 60

377 Two Doves carrying Olive Branches

378 Table Tennis Players

1986. International Peace Year.
700 **377** 4r. multicoloured 50 65

1986. 4th Asian Cup Table Tennis Tournament, Karachi.
701 **378** 2r. multicoloured . . . . 2·00 85

379 Argali

1986. Wildlife Protection (14th series). Argali.
702 **379** 2r. multicoloured . . . . 3·00 3·00

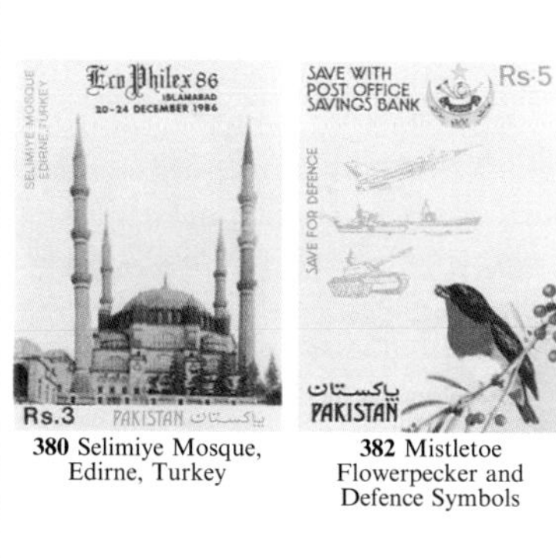

380 Selimiye Mosque, Edirne, Turkey

382 Mistletoe Flowerpecker and Defence Symbols

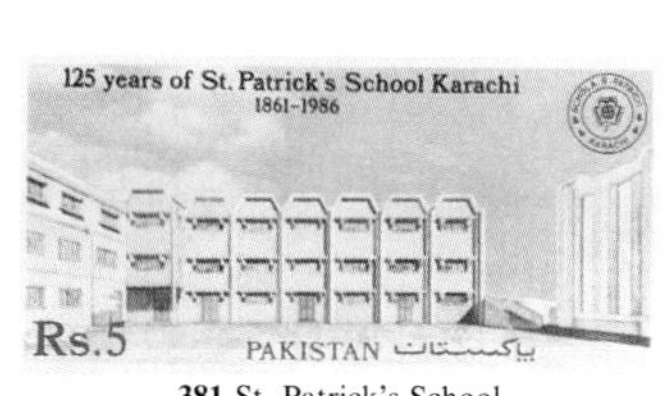

381 St. Patrick's School

1986. "Ecophilex '86" International Stamp Exhibition, Islamabad. Multicoloured.
703 3r. Type **380** . . . . 1·40 1·60
704 3r. Gawhar Shad Mosque, Mashhad, Iran . . . . . . 1·40 1·60
705 3r. Grand Mosque, Bhong, Pakistan . . . . 1·40 1·60

1987. 125th Anniv of St. Patrick's School, Karachi.
706 **381** 5r. multicoloured . . . . 2·00 1·25

1987. Post Office Savings Bank Week. Multicoloured.
707 5r. Type **382** . . . . 1·10 1·00
708 5r. Spotted pardalote and laboratory apparatus . . . 1·10 1·00
709 5r. Black-throated blue warbler and agriculture symbols . . . . 1·10 1·00
710 5r. Red-capped manakin and industrial skyline . . . . . 1·10 1·00

383 New Parliament House, Islamabad

1987. Inauguration of New Parliament House, Islamabad.
711 **383** 3r. multicoloured 50 50

384 Opium Poppies and Flames

1987. Campaign Against Drug Abuse.
712 **384** 1r. multicoloured 55 20

385 Flag and National Anthem Score

1987. 40th Anniv of Independence. Mult.
713 80p. Type **385** . . . . 1·00 20
714 3r. Text of speech by Mohammed Ali Jinnah, Minar-e-Qardad-e-Pakistan Tower and arms . . . . . 1·50 30

386 Hawker Tempest Mk II

1987. Air Force Day. Military Aircraft. Mult.
715 3r. Type **386** . . . . 1·25 1·25
716 3r. Hawker Fury . . . . . . 1·25 1·25
717 3r. Supermarine Attacker . . 1·25 1·25
718 3r. North American F-86 Sabre . . . . 1·25 1·25
719 3r. Lockheed F-104C Starfighter . . . . 1·25 1·25
720 3r. Lockheed C-130 Hercules 1·25 1·25
721 3r. Shenyang/Tianjin F-6 . . 1·25 1·25
722 3r. Dassault Mirage III . . . 1·25 1·25
723 3r. North American A-5A Vigilante . . . . 1·25 1·25
724 3r. General Dynamics F-16 Fighting Falcon . . . . . 1·25 1·25

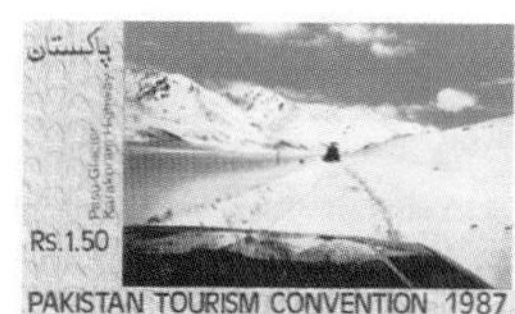

387 Pasu Glacier

1987. Pakistan Tourism Convention. Views along Karakoram Highway. Multicoloured.
725 1r.50 Type **387** 60 40
726 1r.50 Apricot trees 60 40
727 1r.50 Karakoram Highway 60 40
728 1r.50 View from Khunjerab Pass 60 40

388 Shah Abdul Latif Bhitai Mausoleum

1987. Shah Abdul Latif Bhitai (poet) Commem.
729 **388** 80p. multicoloured . . . 20 20

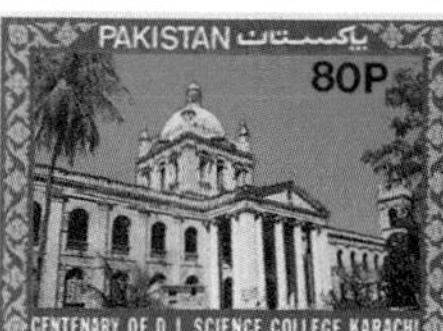

389 D. J. Sind Science College, Karachi

1987. Centenary of D. J. Sind Science College, Karachi.
730 **389** 80p. multicoloured . . . 20 20

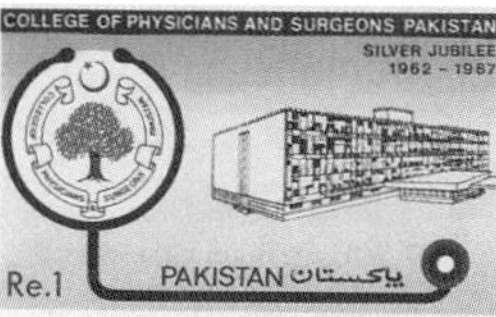

390 College Building

1987. 25th Anniv of College of Physicians and Surgeons.
731 **390** 1r. multicoloured . . . . 1·00 20

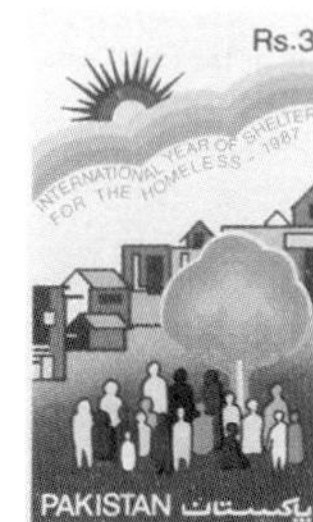

391 Homeless People, Houses and Rising Sun

1987. International Year of Shelter for the Homeless.
732 **391** 3r. multicoloured 50 50

392 Cathedral Church of the Resurrection, Lahore

1987. Centenary of Cathedral Church of the Resurrection, Lahore.
733 **392** 3r. multicoloured 50 50

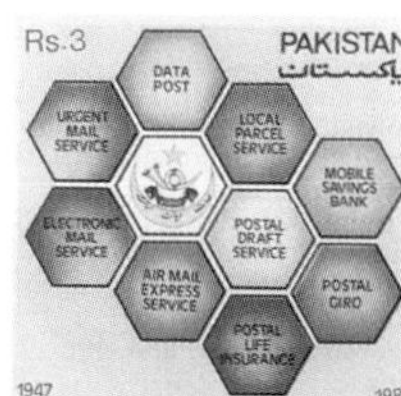

393 Honeycomb and Arms

1987. 40th Anniv of Pakistan Post Office.
734 **393** 3r. multicoloured 50 50

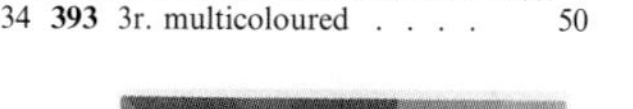

394 Corporation Emblem

1987. Radio Pakistan's New Programme Schedules.
735 **394** 80p. multicoloured . . . 15 15

395 Jamshed Nusserwanjee Mehta and Karachi Municipal Corporation Building

1988. Birth Centenary (1986) of Jamshed Nusserwanjee Mehta (former President of Karachi Municipal Corporation).
736 **395** 3r. multicoloured 50 50

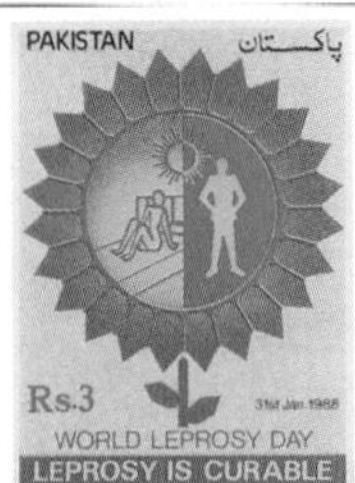

396 Leprosy Symbols within Flower

398 Globe

397 W.H.O. Building, Geneva

1988. World Leprosy Day.
737 **396** 3r. multicoloured 75 50

1988. 40th Anniv of W.H.O.
738 **397** 4r. multicoloured 60 50

1988. 125th Anniv of Int Red Cross and Crescent.
739 **398** 3r. multicoloured 50 50

399 Crescent, Leaf Pattern and Archway

1988. Independence Day.
740 **399** 80p. multicoloured . . . 10 10
741 4r. multicoloured 45 50

400 Field Events

1988. Olympic Games, Seoul. Multicoloured.
742 10r. Type **400** . . . . 1·10 1·10
743 10r. Track events . . . . . . 1·10 1·10
744 10r. Jumping and pole vaulting . . . . 1·10 1·10
745 10r. Gymnastics . . . . . . 1·10 1·10
746 10r. Table tennis, tennis, hockey and baseball . . . 1·10 1·10
747 10r. Volleyball, football, basketball and handball . . 1·10 1·10
748 10r. Wrestling, judo, boxing and weightlifting . . . . . 1·10 1·10
749 10r. Shooting, fencing and archery . . . . 1·10 1·10
750 10r. Water sports . . . . . 1·10 1·10
751 10r. Equestrian events and cycling . . . . 1·10 1·10

401 Markhor

1988. Wildlife Protection (15th series).
752 **401** 2r. multicoloured 50 50

402 Islamia College, Peshawar

1988. 75th Anniv of Islamia College, Peshawar.
753 **402** 3r. multicoloured 50 50

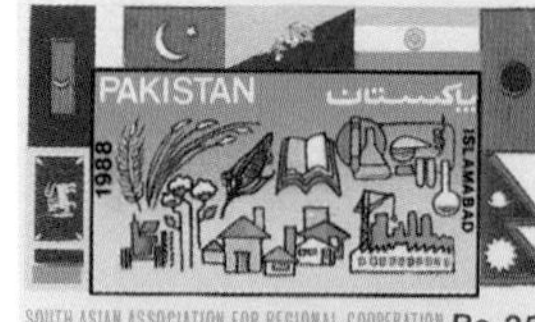

403 Symbols of Agriculture, Industry and Education with National Flags

1988. South Asian Association for Regional Co-operation 4th Summit Meeting, Islamabad. Multicoloured.
754 25r. Type **403** . . . . 1·50 1·50
755 50r. National flags on globe and symbols of communications (33 × 33 mm) . . . . . . 3·25 3·25
756 75r. Stamps from member countries (52 × 29 mm) . . 4·50 4·50

1989. Pioneers of Freedom (2nd series). As T **282**. Multicoloured.
757 3r. Maulana Hasrat Mohani 30 30

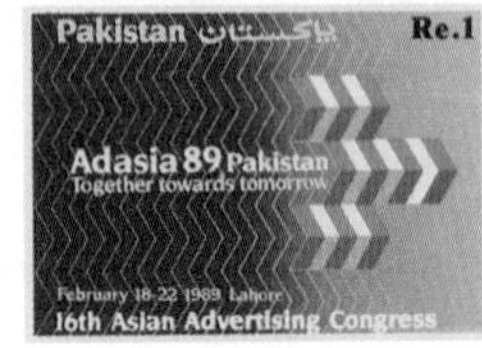

404 Logo

1989. "Adasia 89" 16th Asian Advertising Congress, Lahore.
758 **404** 1r. multicoloured ("Pakistan" in yellow) 1·10 1·25
759 1r. multicoloured ("Pakistan" in blue) . . 1·10 1·25
760 1r. multicoloured ("Pakistan" in white) 1·10 1·25

405 Zulfikar Ali Bhutto

1989. 10th Death Anniv of Zulfikar Ali Bhutto (statesman). Multicoloured.
761 1r. Type **405** 15 10
762 2r. Zulfikar Ali Bhutto (different) 20 20

406 "Daphne" Class Submarine

1989. 25 Years of Pakistan Navy Submarine Operations. Multicoloured.
763 1r. Type **406** . . . . 1·10 1·25
764 1r. "Fleet Snorkel" class submarine . . . . 1·10 1·25
765 1r. "Agosta" class submarine 1·10 1·25

407 "The Oath of the Tennis Court" (David)

1989. Bicentenary of French Revolution.
766 **407** 7r. multicoloured . . . . 1·75 90

408 Pitcher, c. 2200 B.C.

1989. Archaeological Artefacts. Terracotta pottery from Baluchistan Province. Mult.
767 1r. Type **408** 20 20
768 1r. Jar, c. 2300 B.C. 20 20
769 1r. Vase, c. 3600 B.C. 20 20
770 1r. Jar, c. 2600 B.C. 20 20

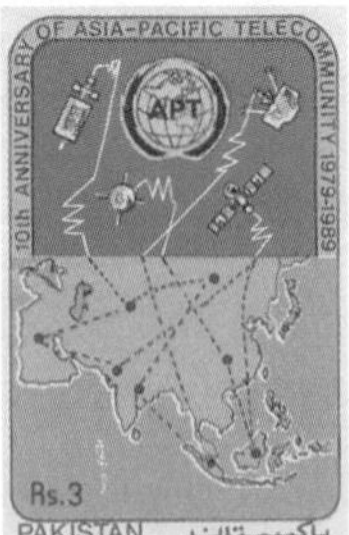

409 Satellites and Map of Asian Telecommunications Network

1989. 10th Anniv of Asia–Pacific Telecommunity.
771 **409** 3r. multicoloured 50 50

410 Container Ship at Wharf

1989. Construction of Integrated Container Terminal, Port Qasim.
772 **410** 6r. multicoloured . . . . 3·00 3·75

411 Mohammed Ali Jinnah

412 Mausoleum of Shah Abdul Latif Bhitai

1989.
773 **411** 1r. multicoloured 60 10
774 1r.50 multicoloured . . . 70 30
775 2r. multicoloured 80 30
776 3r. multicoloured . . . . 1·00 50
777 4r. multicoloured . . . . 1·25 60
778 5r. multicoloured . . . . 1·25 60

1989. 300th Birth Anniv of Shah Abdul Latif Bhitai (poet).
779 **412** 2r. multicoloured 50 50

413 Asiatic Black Bear

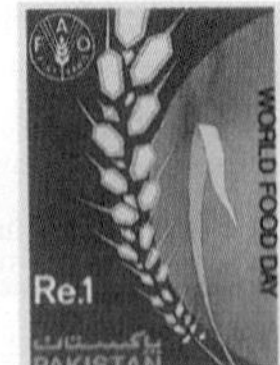

414 Ear of Wheat encircling Globe

1989. Wildlife Protection (16th series). Asiatic Black Bear. Multicoloured.
780 4r. Type **413** . . . . 90 1·10
781 4r. Bear among boulders . . 90 1·10
782 4r. Standing on rock . . . . 90 1·10
783 4r. Sitting by trees . . . . . 90 1·10

1989. World Food Day.
784 **414** 1r. multicoloured 35 35

415 Games Emblem and Flags of Member Countries

1989. 4th South Asian Sports Federation Games, Islamabad.
785 **415** 1r. multicoloured 35 35

416 Patchwork Kamblee (cloth) entering Gate of Heaven

1989. 800th Birth Anniv of Baba Farid (Muslim spiritual leader).
786 **416** 3r. multicoloured 30 30

417 Pakistan Television Logo

1989. 25th Anniv of Television Broadcasting in Pakistan.
787 **417** 3r. multicoloured 30 30

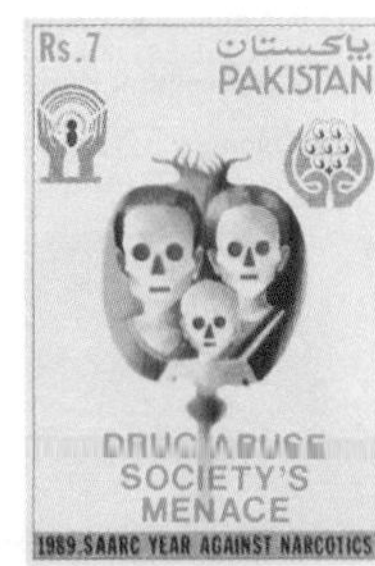

418 Family of Drug Addicts in Poppy Bud

1989. South Asian Association for Regional Co-operation Anti-Drugs Campaign.
788 **418** 7r. multicoloured . . . . 2·25 1·40

419 Murray College, Sialkot

1989. Centenary of Murray College, Sialkot.
789 **419** 6r. multicoloured . . . . 75 1·00

420 Government College, Lahore

1989. 125th Anniv of Government College, Lahore.
790 **420** 6r. multicoloured . . . . 50 1·00

421 Fields, Electricity Pylons and Rural Buildings

1989. 10th Anniv of Centre for Asia and Pacific Integrated Rural Development.
791 **421** 3r. multicoloured 55 75

422 Emblem and Islamic Patterns

1990. 20th Anniv of Organization of the Islamic Conference.
792 **422** 1r. multicoloured . . . . 1·00 20

423 Hockey Match

1990. 7th World Hockey Cup, Lahore.
793 **423** 2r. multicoloured . . . . 4·50 4·25

424 Mohammed Iqbal addressing Crowd and Liaquat Ali Khan taking Oath

1990. 50th Anniv of Passing of Pakistan Resolution. Multicoloured.
794 1r. Type **424** . . . . 80 1·00
795 1r. Maulana Mohammad Ali Jauhar and Mohammed Ali Jinnah with banner . . . . 80 1·00
796 1r. Women with Pakistan flag, and Mohammed Ali Jinnah taking Governor-General's oath, 1947 . . . 80 1·00
797 7r. Minar-i-Qarardad-e-Pakistan Monument and Resolution in Urdu and English (86 × 42 mm) . . . 2·25 2·75
Nos. 794/6 were printed together, se-tenant, forming a composite design.

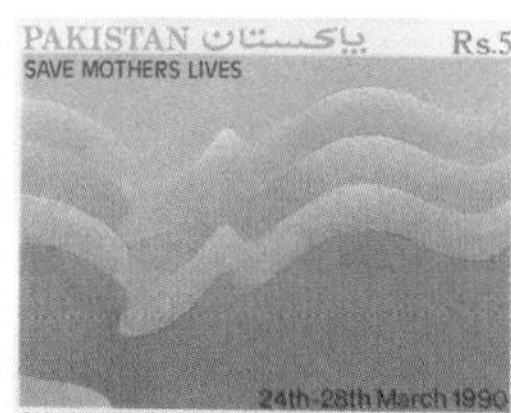

425 Pregnant Woman resting

1990. "Safe Motherhood" South Asia Conference, Lahore.
798 **425** 5r. multicoloured . . . . 75 1·00

426 "Decorated Verse by Ghalib" (Shakir Ali)

1990. Painters of Pakistan (1st series). Shakir Ali.
799 **426** 1r. multicoloured . . . . 2·00 1·00
See also Nos. 856/7.

427 Satellite in Night Sky

1990. Launch of "Badr I" Satellite.
800 **427** 3r. multicoloured . . . . 3·50 3·25

428 Allama Mohammed Iqbal

1990. Pioneers of Freedom (3rd series). Each brown and green.
801 1r. Type **428** 35 35
802 1r. Mohammed Ali Jinnah 35 35
803 1r. Sir Syed Ahmad Khan . . 35 35
804 1r. Nawab Salimullah 35 35
805 1r. Mohtarma Fatima Jinnah 35 35
806 1r. Aga Khan III 35 35
807 1r. Nawab Mohammad Ismail Khan 35 35
808 1r. Hussain Shaheed Suhrawardy 35 35
809 1r. Syed Ameer Ali 35 35
810 1r. Nawab Bahadur Yar Jung 35 35
811 1r. Khawaja Nazimuddin . . 35 35
812 1r. Maulana Obaidullah Sindhi 35 35
813 1r. Sahibzada Abdul Qaiyum Khan 35 35
814 1r. Begum Jahanara Shah Nawaz 35 35
815 1r. Sir Ghulam Hussain Hidayatullah 35 35
816 1r. Qazi Mohammad Isa . . 35 35
817 1r. Sir M. Shahnawaz Khan Mamdot 35 35
818 1r. Pir Sahib of Manki Sharif 35 35
819 1r. Liaquat Ali Khan 35 35
820 1r. Maulvi A. K. Fazl-ul-Haq 35 35
821 1r. Allama Shabbir Ahmad Usmani 35 35
822 1r. Sadar Abdur Rab Nishtar 35 35
823 1r. Bi Amma 35 35
824 1r. Sir Abdullah Haroon . . 35 35
825 1r. Chaudhry Rahmat Ali . . 35 35
826 1r. Raja Sahib of Mahmudabad 35 35
827 1r. Hassanally Effendi . . . 35 35
See also Nos. 838/46, 870/2, 904/6, 921/8, 961/2, 1007, 1019/20 and 1075/7.

429 Cultural Aspects of Indonesia and Pakistan

1990. Indonesia–Pakistan Economic and Cultural Co-operation Organization.
828 **429** 7r. multicoloured . . . . 2·00 1·75

430 Globe, Open Book and Pen

1990. International Literacy Year.
829 **430** 3r. multicoloured . . . . 1·00 1·50

431 College Crests **432** Children and Globe

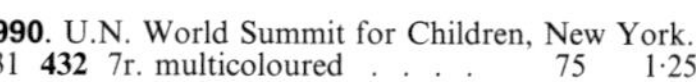

1990. Joint Meeting between Royal College of Physicians, Edinburgh, and College of Physicians and Surgeons, Pakistan.
830 **431** 2r. multicoloured 60 60

1990. U.N. World Summit for Children, New York.
831 **432** 7r. multicoloured . . . . 75 1·25

433 Girl within Members' Flags

1990. South Asian Association for Regional Co-operation Year of Girl Child.
832 **433** 2r. multicoloured 70 75

434 Paper passing over Rollers **435** Civil Defence Worker protecting Islamabad

1990. 25th Anniv of Security Papers Limited.
833 **434** 3r. multicoloured . . . . 2·00 1·50

1991. International Civil Defence Day.
834 **435** 7r. multicoloured . . . . 1·25 1·50

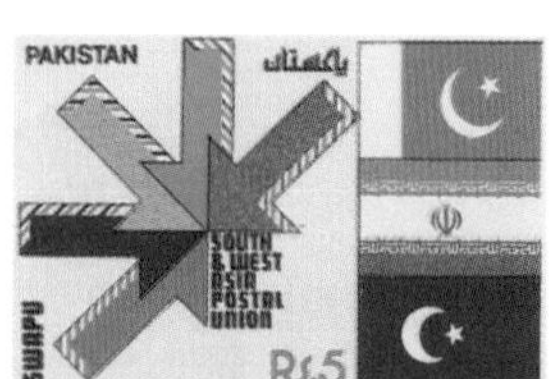

436 Logo and Flags of Member Countries

1991. South and West Asia Postal Union Commemoration.
835 **436** 5r. multicoloured . . . . 1·60 1·90

437 Globe and Figures

1991. World Population Day.
836 **437** 10r. multicoloured . . . . 1·90 2·50

438 Mentally Handicapped Athlete **439** Habib Bank Headquarters and Emblem

1991. Pakistan Participation in Special Olympic Games.
837 **438** 7r. multicoloured . . . . 1·75 2·25

1991. Pioneers of Freedom (4th series). As T **428**. Each brown and green.
838 1r. Maulana Zafar Ali Khan 55 60
839 1r. Maulana Mohamed Ali Jauhar 55 60
840 1r. Chaudhry Khaliquzzaman 55 60
841 1r. Hameed Nizami 55 60
842 1r. Begum Ra'ana Liaquat Ali Khan 55 60
843 1r. Mirza Abol Hassan Ispahani 55 60
844 1r. Raja Ghazanfar Ali Khan 55 60
845 1r. Malik Barkat Ali 55 60
846 1r. Mir Jaffer Khan Jamali 55 60

1991. 50th Anniv of Habib Bank.
847 **439** 1r. multicoloured . . . . 1·00 10
848 5r. multicoloured . . . . 3·00 3·50

440 St. Joesph's Convent School

1991. 130th Anniv (1992) of St. Joesph's Convent School, Karachi.
849 **440** 5r. multicoloured . . . . 3·25 3·50

441 Emperor Sher Shah Suri **443** Houbara Bustard

442 Jinnah Antarctic Research Station

1991. Emperor Sher Shah Suri (founder of road network) Commemoration.
850 **441** 5r. multicoloured . . . . 1·50 2·00
MS851 92 × 80 mm. 7r. Emperor on horseback and portrait as Type **441**. Imperf . . . . . . 1·40 2·25

1991. Pakistan Scientific Expedition to Antarctica.
852 **442** 7r. multicoloured . . . . 2·50 2·25

1991. Wildlife Protection (17th series).
853 **443** 7r. multicoloured . . . . 2·00 2·25

444 Mosque

1991. 300th Death Anniv of Hazrat Sultan Bahoo.
854 **444** 7r. multicoloured . . . . 1·25 1·75

445 Development Symbols and Map of Asia

1991. 25th Anniv of Asian Development Bank.
855 **445** 7r. multicoloured . . . . 2·50 2·50

1991. Painters of Pakistan (2nd series). As T **426**. Multicoloured.
856 1r. "Procession" (Haji Muhammad Sharif) . . . . 1·75 1·50
857 1r. "Women harvesting" (Ustad Allah Bux) . . . . 1·75 1·50

446 American Express Travellers Cheques of 1891 and 1991 (⅔-size illustration)

1991. Centenary of American Express Travellers Cheques.
858 **446** 7r. multicoloured . . . . 1·75 2·50

447 Flag, Banknote and Banking Equipment

1992. 1st Anniv of Muslim Commercial Bank Privatization. Multicoloured.

859 1r. Type **447** 10 10

860 7r. Flag with industrial and commercial scenes 45 70

448 Imran Khan (team captain) and Trophy

1992. Pakistan's Victory in World Cricket Championship. Multicoloured.

861 2r. Type **448** 70 70

862 5r. Trophy and national flags (horiz) . . . . 1·50 1·50

863 7r. Pakistani flag, trophy and symbolic cricket ball . . . 1·75 1·75

449 "Rehber-1" Rocket and Satellite View of Earth

1992. International Space Year. Mult.

864 1r. Type **449** 20 10

865 2r. Satellite orbiting Earth and logo 30 40

450 Surgical Instruments

1992. Industries. Multicoloured.

866 10r. Type **450** . . . . 90 1·10

867 15r. Leather goods . . . . . 1·10 1·50

868 25r. Sports equipment . . . 2·00 2·50

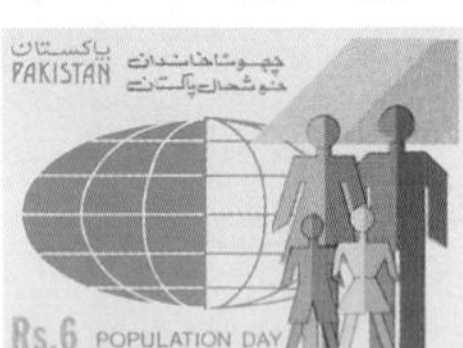

451 Globe and Symbolic Family

1992. Population Day.

869 **451** 6r. multicoloured . . . . 80 1·10

1992. Pioneers of Freedom (5th series). As T **428**. Each brown and green.

870 1r. Syed Suleman Nadvi . . 1·10 1·10

871 1r. Nawab Iftikhar Hussain Khan Mamdot . . . . . . 1·10 1·10

872 1r. Maulana Muhammad Shibli Naumani . . . . . 1·10 1·10

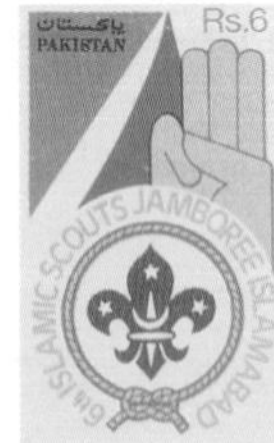

452 Scout Badge and Salute

1992. 6th Islamic Scout Jamboree and 4th Islamic Scouts Conference. Multicoloured.

873 6r. Type **452** 50 75

874 6r. Conference centre and scout salute 50 75

453 College Building

1992. Centenary of Islamia College, Lahore.

875 **453** 3r. multicoloured 50 60

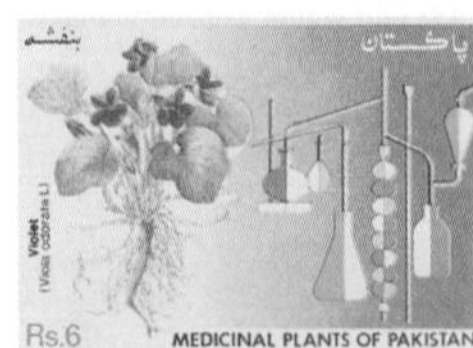

454 "Viola odorata" (flower) and Symbolic Drug Manufacture

1992. Medicinal Plants (1st series).

876 **454** 6r. multicoloured . . . . 2·00 1·75

See also Nos. 903, 946, 1010, 1026, 1037, 1099, 1123, 1142 and 1159.

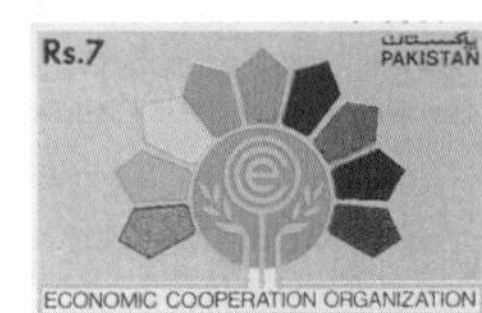

455 Emblem

1992. Extraordinary Ministerial Council Session of Economic Co-operation Organization, Islamabad.

877 **455** 7r. multicoloured . . . . 1·00 1·75

456 Emblems and Field **457** Alhambra Palace, Granada, Spain

1992. International Conference on Nutrition, Rome.

878 **456** 7r. multicoloured . . . . 70 1·10

1992. Cultural Heritage of Muslim Granada.

879 **457** 7r. multicoloured . . . . 70 1·10

458 Mallard **459** Baluchistan Costume

Four different versions of designs as T **458**:

Type A. "Rs.5" at right with rainbow 8 mm beneath "P" of "PAKISTAN"

Type B. "Rs.5" at right with rainbow 2 mm beneath "P"

Type C. "Rs.5" at left with rainbow 2 mm beneath "N" of "PAKISTAN"

Type D. "Rs.5" at left with rainbow 8 mm beneath "N"

1992. Water Birds. Multicoloured.

880 5r. Type **458** (A) 60 70

881 5r. Type **458** (B) 60 70

882 5r. Type **458** (C) 60 70

883 5r. Type **458** (D) 60 70

884 5r. Greylag goose (A) 60 70

885 5r. As No. 884 (B) 60 70

886 5r. As No. 884 (C) 60 70

887 5r. As No. 884 (D) 60 70

888 5r. Gadwall (A) 60 70

889 5r. As No. 888 (B) 60 70

890 5r. As No. 888 (C) 60 70

891 5r. As No. 888 (D) 60 70

892 5r. Common shelduck (A) . . 60 70

893 5r. As No. 892 (B) 60 70

894 5r. As No. 892 (C) 60 70

895 5r. As No. 892 (D) 60 70

Nos. 880/95 were printed together, se-tenant, each horizontal row having a composite design of a rainbow.

1993. Women's Traditional Costumes. Multicoloured.

896 6r. Type **459** . . . . 1·25 1·50

897 6r. Punjab . . . . 1·25 1·50

898 6r. Sindh . . . . 1·25 1·50

899 6r. North-west Frontier Province . . . . 1·25 1·50

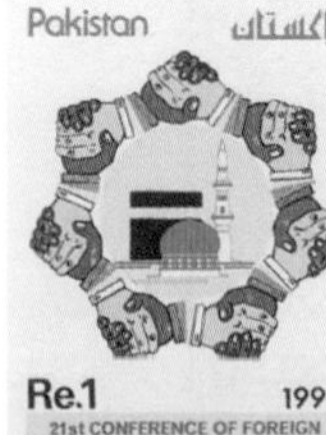

460 Clasped Hands and Islamic Symbols **461** I.T.U. Emblem

1993. 21st Conference of Islamic Foreign Ministers, Karachi.

900 **460** 1r. multicoloured 65 10

901 6r. multicoloured . . . . 1·50 2·00

1993. 25th Anniv of World Telecommunication Day.

902 **461** 1r. multicoloured . . . . 1·00 30

1993. Medicinal Plants (2nd issue). As T **454**. Multicoloured.

903 6r. Fennel and symbolic drug manufacture . . . . 2·50 2·25

1993. Pioneers of Freedom (6th series). As T **428**. Each brown and red.

904 1r. Ghulam Mohammad Bhurgri . . . . 1·00 1·00

905 1r. Ahmed Yar Khan . . . . 1·00 1·00

906 1r. Mohammad Pir Sahib Zakori Sharif . . . . . . 1·00 1·00

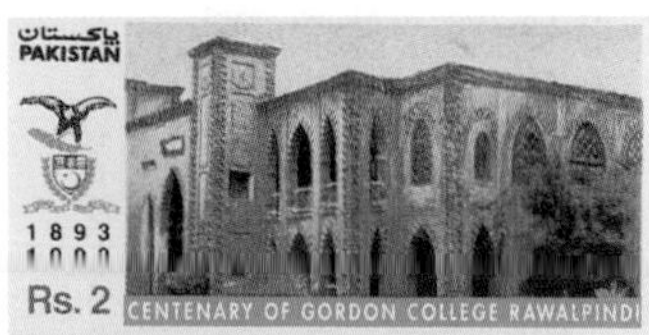

462 College Building and Arms

1993. Centenary of Gordon College, Rawalpindi.

907 **462** 2r. multicoloured . . . . 1·25 1·25

463 Juniper Forest

1993. Campaign to Save the Juniper Forest, Ziarat.

907a **463** 1r. multicoloured . . . . 1·00 30

908 7r. multicoloured . . . . 2·75 2·75

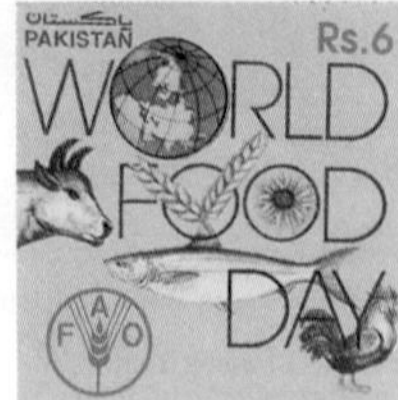

464 Globe, Produce and Emblem

1993. World Food Day.

909 **464** 6r. multicoloured . . . . 80 1·00

465 Burn Hall Institution, Abbottabad **466** Peace Dove carrying Letter and National Flags

1993. 50th Anniv of Burn Hall Institutions.

910 **465** 7r. multicoloured . . . . 2·00 2·25

1993. South and West Asia Postal Union Commemoration.

911 **466** 7r. multicoloured . . . . 2·00 2·25

467 Congress Emblem **468** Wazir Mansion (birthplace)

1993. Pakistan College of Physicians and Surgeons International Medical Congress.

912 **467** 1r. multicoloured . . . . 1·25 30

1993. 45th Death Anniv of Mohammed Ali Jinnah.

913 **468** 1r. multicoloured 60 30

469 Emblem and National Flag

1994. 75th Anniv of I.L.O.

914 **469** 7r. multicoloured . . . . 1·75 1·75

470 Ratan Jot (flower)

1994. Ratification of International Biological Diversity Convention. Multicoloured.

915 6r. Type **470** 35 50

916 6r. Wetlands habitat 35 50

917 6r. Golden mahseer ("Tor puttitora") (fish) 35 50

918 6r. Brown bear 35 50

471 Silhouette of Family and Emblem

1994. International Year of the Family.

919 **471** 7r. multicoloured 50 50

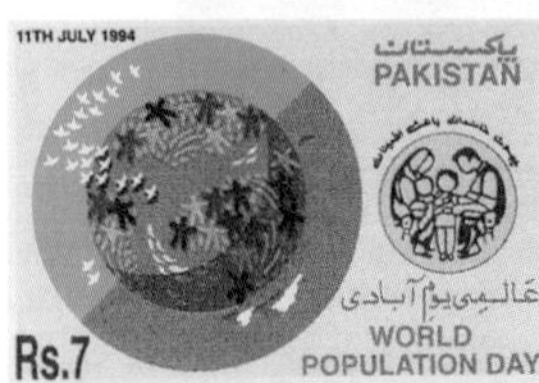

472 Symbolic Globe and Logo

1994. World Population Day.

920 **472** 7r. multicoloured 50 50

1994. Pioneers of Freedom (7th series). As T **428**. Each brown and green.

921 1r. Nawab Mohsin-Ul-Mulk 20 25

922 1r. Sir Shahnawaz Bhutto . . 20 25

923 1r. Nawab Viqar-Ul-Mulk . . 20 25

924 1r. Pir Ilahi Bux 20 25

925 1r. Sheikh Abdul Qadir . . . 20 25

926 1r. Dr. Sir Ziauddin Ahmed 20 25

927 1r. Jam Mir Ghulam Qadir Khan 20 25

928 1r. Sardar Aurangzeb Khan 20 25

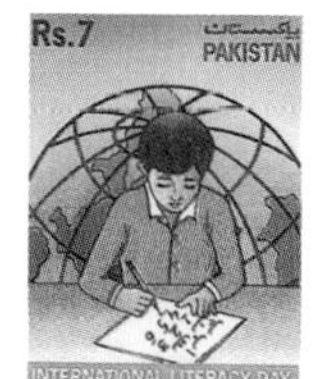

473 Hala Pottery, Pakistan

474 Boy writing and Globe

1994. Indonesia–Pakistan Economic and Cultural Co-operation Organization. Multicoloured.
929 10r. Type **473** . . . . 1·25 1·40
930 10r. Lombok pottery, Indonesia . . . . 1·25 1·40

1994. International Literacy Day.
931 **474** 7r. multicoloured 50 50

475 Mohammed Ali Jinnah and Floral Pattern

1994.
932 **475** 1r. multicoloured 20 10
933 2r. multicoloured 25 10
934 3r. multicoloured 30 10
935 4r. multicoloured 30 10
936 5r. multicoloured 30 15
937 7r. multicoloured 30 20
938 10r. multicoloured 20 25
939 12r. multicoloured 25 30
940 15r. multicoloured 35 40
941 20r. multicoloured 45 50
942 25r. multicoloured 55 60
943 30r. multicoloured 65 70

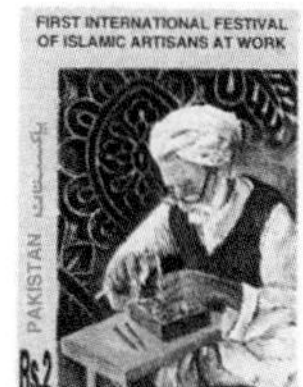

476 Gateway and Emblem

477 Engraver

1994. 2nd South Asian Association for Regional Co-operation and 12th National Scout Jamborees, Quetta.
944 **476** 7r. multicoloured 60 75

1994. 1st Int Festival of Islamic Artisans at Work.
945 **477** 2r. multicoloured 75 50

478 Henbane

479 Abu-I Kasim Firdausi (poet)

1994. Medicinal Plants (3rd issue).
946 **478** 6r. multicoloured 65 70

1994. Millenary of "Shah Namah" (poem).
947 **479** 1r. multicoloured 15 15

480 Museum Building

1994. Centenary of Lahore Museum.
948 **480** 4r. multicoloured 50 60

481 World Cup Trophies for 1971, 1978, 1982 and 1994

1994. Victory of Pakistan in World Cup Hockey Championship.
949 **481** 5r. multicoloured 65 75

482 Tourist Attractions

1995. 20th Anniv of World Tourism Organization.
950 **482** 4r. multicoloured 50 60

483 Khan Khushal of Khattak and Army

1995. Khan Khushal of Khattak (poet) Commemoration.
951 **483** 7r. multicoloured . . . . 1·00 1·00

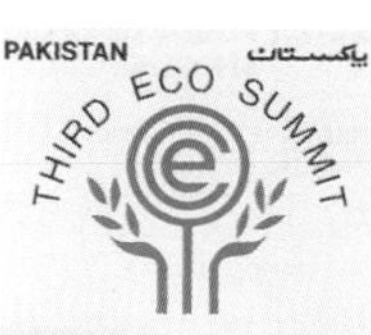

484 E.C.O. Emblem

1995. 3rd Economic Co-operation Organization Summit, Islamabad.
952 **484** 6r. multicoloured 75 85

485 Common Indian Krait

1995. Snakes. Multicoloured.
953 6r. Type **485** 70 85
954 6r. Indian cobra 70 85
955 6r. Indian python 70 85
956 6r. Russell's viper 70 85

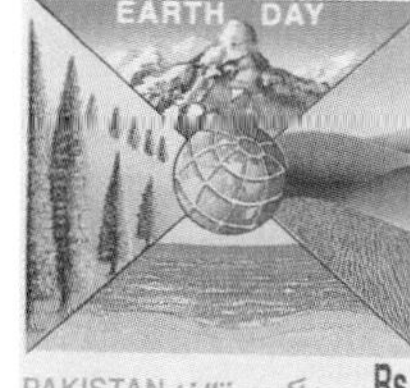

486 Globe and Environments

1995. Earth Day.
957 **486** 6r. multicoloured 55 65

487 Victoria Carriage, Karachi

1995. Traditional Transport.
958 **487** 5r. multicoloured 50 60

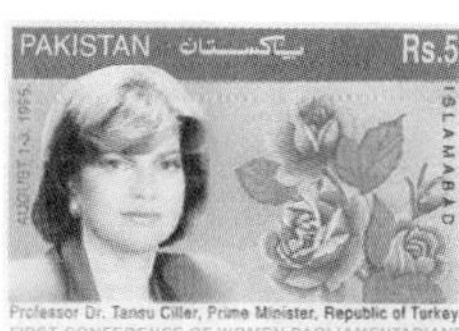

488 Prime Minister Tansu Ciller of Turkey and Rose

1995. 1st Muslim Women Parliamentarians' Conference, Islamabad. Multicoloured.
959 5r. Type **488** 80 90
960 5r. Prime Minister Benazir Bhutto and jasmine 80 90

1995. Pioneers of Freedom (8th series). As T **428**. Each brown and green.
961 1r. Maulana Shaukat Ali . . 50 40
962 1r. Chaudhry Ghulam Abbas 50 40

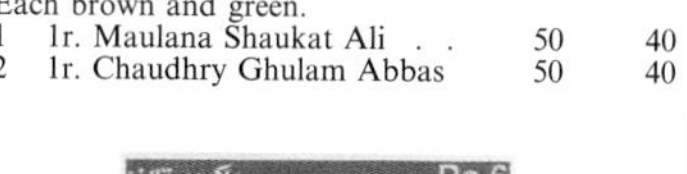

489 Oil Sardine

1995. Fishes. Multicoloured.
963 6r. Type **489** 70 75
964 6r. Mozambique mouthbrooder ("Tilapia") 70 75
965 6r. Brown trout 70 75
966 6r. Rohu 70 75

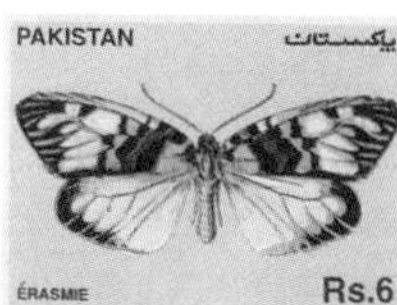

490 "Erasmia pulchella"

1995. Butterflies. Multicoloured.
967 6r. Type **490** 50 70
968 6r. "Callicore astarte" (inscr "Catogramme") 50 70
969 6r. "Ixias pyrene" 50 70
970 6r. "Heliconius" 50 70

491 Major Raja Aziz Bhatti Shaheed and Medal

1995. Defence Day.
971 **491** 1r.25 multicoloured . . . 1·25 70

492 Presentation Convent School, Rawalpindi

1995. Centenary of Presentation Convent School, Rawalpindi.
972 **492** 1r.25 multicoloured . . . 85 70

493 Women Soldiers, Golfer and Scientist

494 "Louis Pasteur in Laboratory" (Edelfelt)

1995. 4th World Conference on Women, Peking. Multicoloured.
973 1r.25 Type **493** 30 30
974 1r.25 Women graduates, journalist, computer operator and technicians 30 30
975 1r.25 Sewing machinist and women at traditional crafts 30 30
976 1r.25 Army officer and women at traditional tasks 30 30

1995. Death Centenary of Louis Pasteur (chemist).
977 **494** 5r. multicoloured 65 75

495

496 Liaquat Ali Khan

1995.
978 **495** 5p. blue, orange and brown 10 10
979 15p. orange, violet and brown 15 10
980 25p. blue, mauve and purple 20 10
981 75p. green, brown and deep brown 40 10

1995. Birth Centenary (1995) of Liaquat Ali Khan (statesman).
987 **496** 1r.25 multicoloured . . . 30 20

497 Village and Irrigated Fields

1995. 50th Anniv of F.A.O.
988 **497** 1r.25 multicoloured . . . 30 20

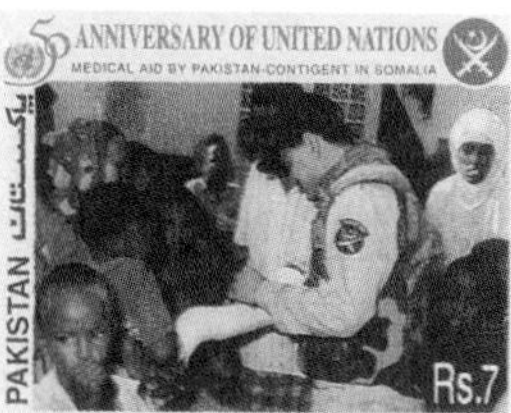

498 Pakistani Soldier treating Somali Refugees

1995. 50th Anniv of United Nations.
989 **498** 7r. multicoloured 50 70

499 Education Emblem

500 Hand holding Book, Eye and Pen Nib

1995. 80th Anniv (1993) of Kinnaird College for Women, Lahore.
990 **499** 1r.25 multicoloured . . . 30 20

1995. International Conference of Writers and Intellectuals, Islamabad.
991 **500** 1r.25 multicoloured . . . 30 20

501 Children holding Hands and S.A.A.R.C. Logo

502 Jet Skier

1995. 10th Anniv of South Asian Association for Regional Co-operation.
992 **501** 1r.25 multicoloured . . . 30 20

1995. National Water Sports Gala, Karachi. Multicoloured.
993 1r.25 Type **502** 25 30
994 1r.25 Local punts 25 30
995 1r.25 Sailboard 25 30
996 1r.25 Water skier 25 30

503 Mortar Board and Books

1995. 20th Anniv of Allama Iqbal Open University.
997 **503** 1r.25 multicoloured . . . 30 20

504 Balochistan Quetta University Building

1995. 25th Anniv of Balochistan Quetta University.
998 **504** 1r.25 multicoloured . . . 30 20

505 Zulfikar Ali Bhutto, Flag and Crowd

1996. 17th Death Anniv of Zulfikar Ali Bhutto (former Prime Minister). Multicoloured.
999 1r.25 Type **505** 75 20
1000 4r. Zulfikar Ali Bhutto and flag (53 × 31 mm) . . . . 2·00 1·75
MS1001 118 × 74 mm. 8r. Zulfikar Ali Bhutto and crowd. Imperf 1·40 1·40

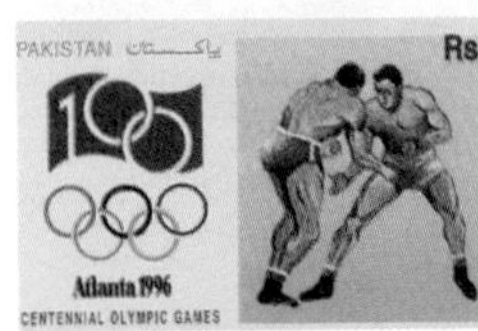

506 Wrestling

1996. Olympic Games, Atlanta. Multicoloured.
1002 5r. Type **506** 50 60
1003 5r. Boxing 50 60
1004 5r. Pierre de Coubertin . . . 50 60
1005 5r. Hockey 50 60
MS1006 112 × 100 mm. 25r. Designs as Nos. 1002/5, but without face values. Imperf . . . . 2·00 2·25

1996. Pioneers of Freedom (9th series). Allama Abdullah Yousuf Ali. As T **428**.
1007 1r. brown and green 20 10

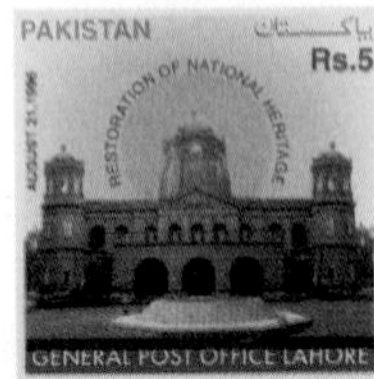

507 G.P.O. Building, Lahore

1996. Restoration of G.P.O. Building, Lahore.
1008 **507** 5r. multicoloured 35 50

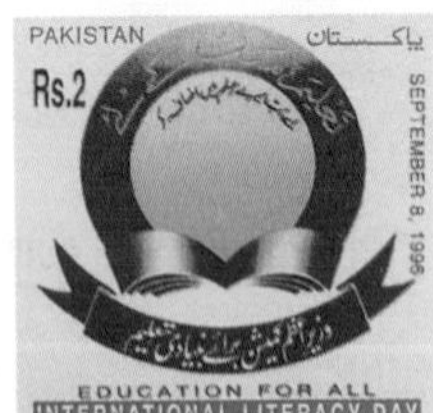

508 Symbolic Open Book and Text

1996. International Literacy Day.
1009 **508** 2r. multicoloured 30 20

509 Yarrow

510 Faiz Ahmed Faiz

1996. Medicinal Plants (4th series).
1010 **509** 3r. multicoloured 60 70

1997. 86th Birth Anniv of Faiz Ahmed Faiz (poet).
1011 **510** 3r. multicoloured 35 35

511 Golden Jubilee and O.I.C. Emblems

512 Amir Timur

1997. Special Summit Conference of Organization of Islamic Countries commemorating 50th anniv of Pakistan.
1012 **511** 2r. multicoloured 25 25

1997. 660th Birth Anniv of Timur (founder of Timurid Empire).
1013 **512** 3r. multicoloured 35 35

513 Jalal-al-din Moulana Rumi

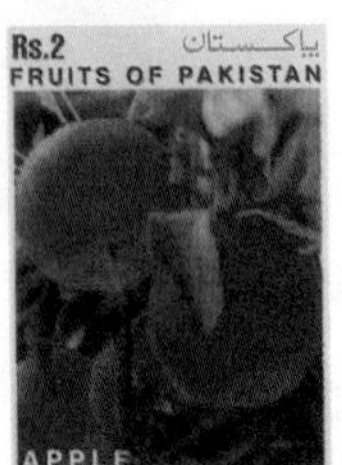

514 Apple

1997. Pakistan–Iran Joint Issue.
1014 3r. Type **513** 30 35
1015 3r. Allama Mohammad Iqbal (poet) 30 35

1997. Fruit.
1016 **514** 2r. multicoloured 25 25

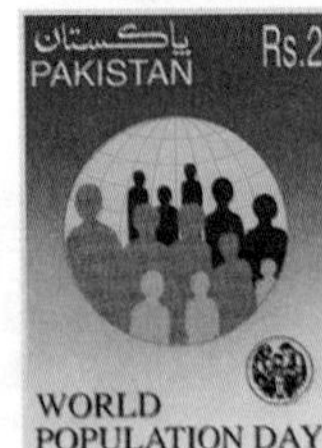

515 People on Globe

1997. World Population Day.
1017 **515** 2r. multicoloured 25 25

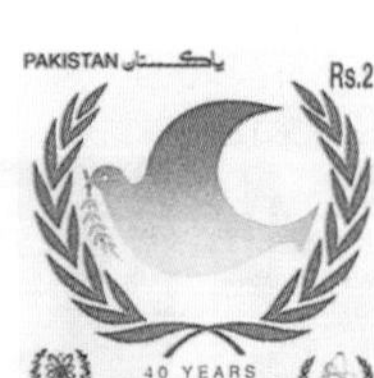

516 Stylized Dove of Peace

1997. 40th Anniv of Co-operation between International Atomic Energy Agency and Pakistan Atomic Energy Corporation.
1018 **516** 2r. multicoloured 25 25

1997. Pioneers of Freedom (10th series). As T **428**. Each brown and green.
1019 1r. Mohammad Ayub Khuhro 30 30
1020 1r. Begum Salma Tassaduq Hussain 30 30

517 Mohammed Ali Jinnah

1997. 50th Anniv of Independence. Multicoloured.
1021 3r. Type **517** 10 10
1022 3r. Allama Mohammad Iqbal 10 10
1023 3r. Mohtarma Fatima Jinnah 10 10
1024 3r. Liaquat Ali Khan . . . 10 10

518 College Building

1997. 75th Anniv of Lahore College for Women.
1025 **518** 3r. multicoloured 70 60

519 Garlic

1997. Medicinal Plants (5th series).
1026 **519** 2r. multicoloured 40 30

520 Himalayan Monal Pheasant

521 Globe and Cracked Ozone Layer

1997. Wildlife Protection (18th series).
1027 **520** 2r. multicoloured . . . . 1·00 60

1997. Save Ozone Layer Campaign.
1028 **521** 3r. multicoloured 85 65

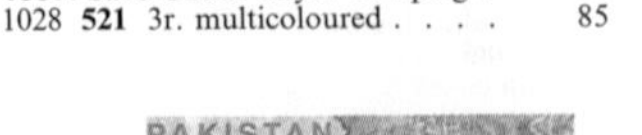
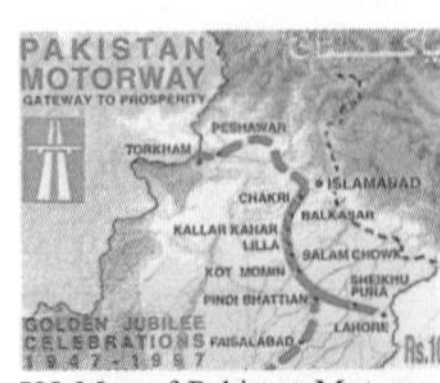

522 Map of Pakistan Motorway Project

1997. Pakistan Motorway Project.
1029 **522** 10r. multicoloured . . . 20 25
MS1030 117 × 97 mm. No. 1029 (sold at 15r.) . . . . 2·25 2·50

523 Emblem and Disabled People

1997. International Day for the Disabled.
1031 **523** 4r. multicoloured 10 10

524 Karachi Grammar School

1997. 150th Anniv of Karachi Grammar School.
1032 **524** 2r. multicoloured 70 40

525 Mirza Ghalib

1998. Birth Bicentenary (1997) of Mirza Ghalib (poet).
1033 **525** 2r. multicoloured 10 10
No. 1033 is inscr "DEATH ANNIVERSARY".

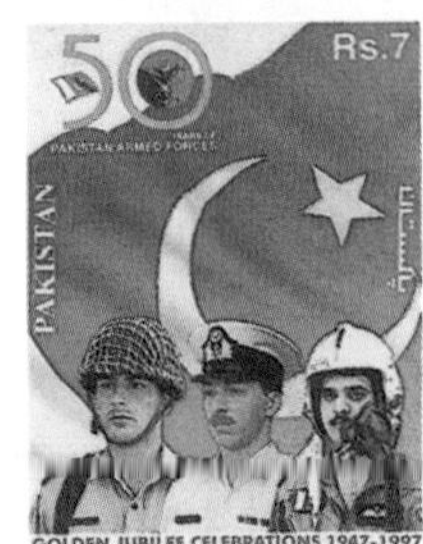

526 Servicemen, Pakistan Flag and "50"

1998. 50th Anniv (1997) of Armed Forces.
1034 **526** 7r. multicoloured 15 20

527 Sir Syed Ahmed Khan

1998. Death Centenary of Sir Syed Ahmed Khan (social reformer).
1035 **527** 7r. brown, green & stone 15 20

528 Olympic Torch and Sports

1998. 27th National Games, Peshawar.
1036 **528** 7r. multicoloured 15 20

529 Thornapple

1998. Medicinal Plants (6th series).
1037 **529** 2r. multicoloured 10 10

530 Silver Jubilee Emblem

531 Mohammed Ali Jinnah

1998. 25th Anniv of Senate.
1038 **530** 2r. multicoloured 10 10
1039 5r. multicoloured 10 15

1998.
1039a **531** 1r. red and black . . . 10 10
1040 2r. blue and red 10 10
1041 3r. green and brown . . 10 10
1042 4r. purple and orange 10 10
1043 5r. brown and green . . 10 15
1044 6r. green and blue . . . 15 20
1045 7r. red and violet . . . 15 20

532 College Building

1998. Cent of Government College, Faisalabad.
1046 **532** 5r. multicoloured 10 15

533 "Mohammed Ali Jinnah" (S. Akhtar)

1998. 50th Death Anniv of Mohammed Ali Jinnah.
1047 **533** 15r. multicoloured . . . 35 40
MS1048 72 × 100 mm. **533** 15r. multicoloured (sold at 20r.) . . 1·50 1·75

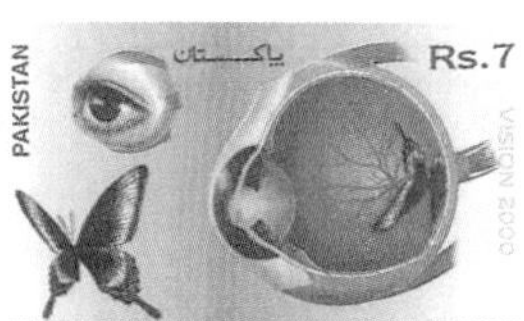

534 Cross-section of Eye

1998. 21st International Ophthalmology Congress, Islamabad.
1049 **534** 7r. multicoloured 15 20

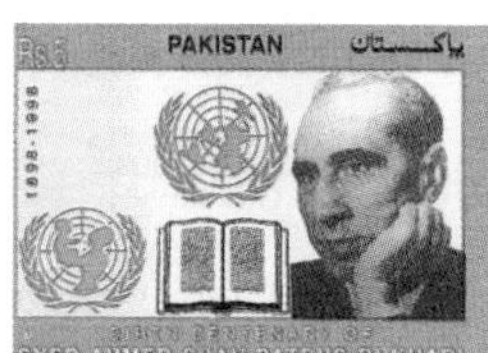

535 United Nations Emblems and Bukhari

1998. Birth Centenary of Syed Ahmed Shah Patrus Bukhari.
1050 **535** 5r. multicoloured 10 15

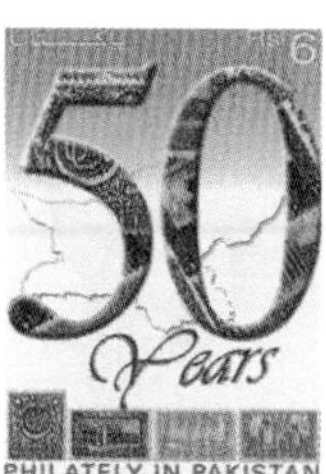

536 Map, "50 years" and Stamps

538 Dr. Abdus Salam

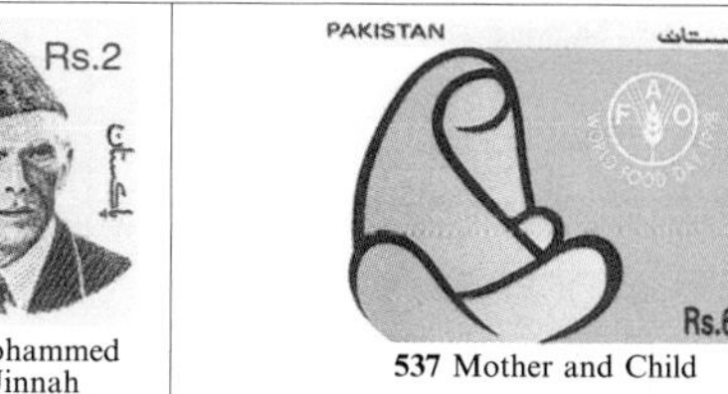

537 Mother and Child

1998. 50th Anniv of Philately in Pakistan.
1051 **536** 6r. multicoloured 15 20

1998. World Food Day.
1052 **537** 6r. multicoloured 15 20

1998. Scientists of Pakistan (1st series). Dr. Abdus Salam.
1053 **538** 2r. multicoloured 10 10
See also No. 1068.

539 Satellite Dish Aerial

1998. "Better Pakistan" Development Plan. Mult.
1054 2r. Type **539** 10 10
1055 2r. Combine harvester . . . 10 10
1056 2r. Airliner 10 10
1057 2r. Children and doctor . . 10 10

540 Globe and Human Rights Emblem

1998. 50th Anniv of Universal Declaration of Human Rights.
1058 **540** 6r. multicoloured 15 20

541 Pakistani Woman carrying Water Pot

1998. 50th Anniv of U.N.I.C.E.F. in Pakistan. Multicoloured.
1059 2r. Type **541** 10 10
1060 2r. Woman reading 10 10
1061 2r. Woman with goitre . . . 10 10
1062 2r. Young boy receiving oral vaccine 10 10

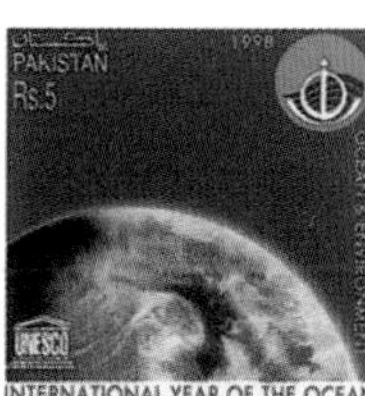

542 Earth seen from Space

1998. International Year of the Ocean.
1063 **542** 5r. multicoloured 10 15

543 Marchers and Route Map

1998. Qaumi Parcham March, Khyber to Chaghi.
1064 **543** 2r. multicoloured 10 10

544 Centenary Logo

545 Dr. Salimuz Zaman Siddiqui

1999. Centenary of Saudi Dynasty of Saudi Arabia. Multicoloured.
1065 2r. Type **544** 10 10
1066 15r. As Type **544**, but with mosaic pattern in corners 35 40
MS1067 73 × 100 mm. 15r. No. 1066 (sold at 20r.) . . . . 1·50 1·75

1999. Scientists of Pakistan (2nd series). Dr. Salimuz Zaman Siddiqui.
1068 **545** 5r. multicoloured 10 15

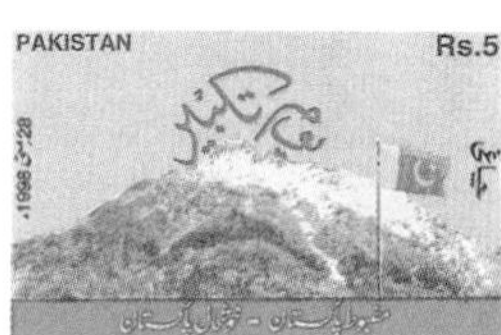

546 Mountains and Pakistan Flag

1999. "Atoms for Peace".
1069 **546** 5r. multicoloured 10 15

547 Plan and View of Mosque

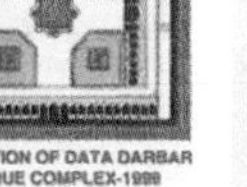

548 Fasting Buddha Statue (drapery on left knee)

1999. Completion of Data Darbar Mosque Complex, Lahore.
1070 **547** 7r. multicoloured 15 20

1999. Archaeological Heritage. Multicoloured.
1071 7r. Type **548** 15 20
1072 7r. Fasting Buddha (drapery on right knee) 15 20
MS1073 107 × 90 mm. Nos. 1071/2 (sold at 25r.) . . . . 1·75 2·00
No. **MS**1073 includes the "China '99" International Stamp Exhibition, Beijing, logo on the margin.

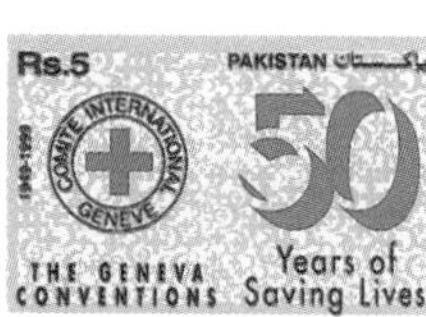

549 Red Cross International Committee Emblem and "50"

1999. 50th Anniv of Geneva Conventions.
1074 **549** 5r. red and black 10 15

1999. Pioneers of Freedom (11th series). As T **428**. Each brown and green.
1075 2r. Maulana Abdul Hamid Badayuni 10 10
1076 2r. Chaudhry Muhammad Ali 10 10
1077 2r. Sir Adamjee Haji Dawood 10 10

550 Ustad Nusrat Fateh Ali Khan

1999. Ustad Nusrat Fateh Ali Khan (musician) Commemoration.
1078 **550** 2r. multicoloured 10 10

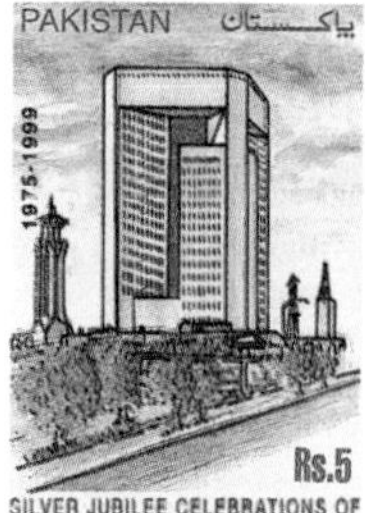

551 Islamic Development Bank Building

552 Crowd celebrating

1999. 25th Anniv of Islamic Development Bank.
1079 **551** 5r. multicoloured 10 15

1999. 50th Anniv of People's Republic of China. Multicoloured.
1080 2r. Type **552** 10 10
1081 15r. Bust of Mao Tse-tung (Chinese leader) and emblem (horiz) 35 40

553 "Enterprise" Sailing Dinghy

554 "Optimist" Sailing Dinghies

1999. 9th Asian Sailing Championship. Sailing Craft. Multicoloured.
1082 2r. Type **553** 10 10
1083 2r. "470" dinghy 10 10
1084 2r. "Optimist" dinghy . . . 10 10
1085 2r. "Laser" dinghy 10 10
1086 2r. "Mistral" sailboard . . . 10 10

1999. 10th Asian "Optimist" Sailing Championship.
1087 **554** 2r. multicoloured 10 10

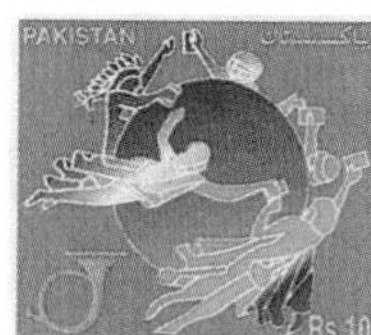

555 U.P.U. Emblem

1999. 125th Anniv of Universal Postal Union.
1088 **555** 10r. multicoloured . . . 20 25

556 Hakim Mohammed Said

557 National Bank of Pakistan Building

1999. 1st Death Anniv of Hakim Mohammed Said.
1089 **556** 5r. multicoloured 10 15

1999. 50th Anniv of National Bank of Pakistan.
1090 **557** 5r. multicoloured 10 15

558 Evolution of the "Shell" Emblem

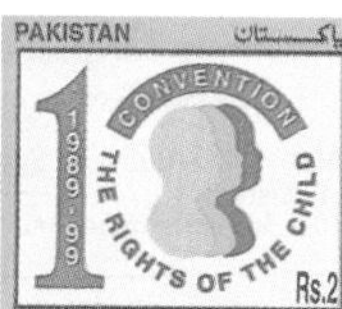

559 Profiles of Children in "10"

1999. Centenary of Shell in Pakistan.
1091 **558** 4r. multicoloured 10 10

1999. 10th Anniv of United Nations Rights of the Child Convention.
1092 **559** 2r. emerald, green and red 10 10

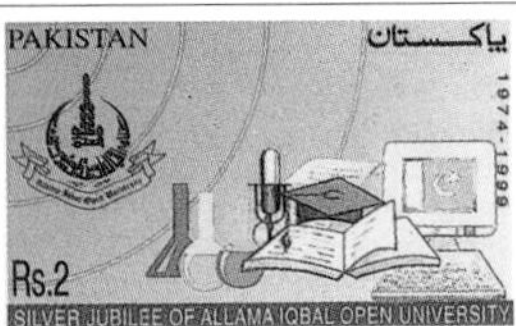

560 Science Equipment, Books and Computer

1999. 25th Anniv of Allama Iqbal Open University. Multicoloured.
1093 2r. Type **560** 10 10
1094 3r. Scholastic symbols as Type **560** 10 10
1095 5r. Map of Pakistan 10 15

561 Josh Malihabadi

1999. Birth Centenary of Josh Malihabadi (poet).
1096 **561** 5r. multicoloured 10 15

562 Dr. Afzal Qadri and Locusts

1999. 25th Death Anniv of Dr. Afzal Qadri (scientist).
1097 **562** 3r. multicoloured 10 10

563 Ghulam Bari Aleeg **564** Plantain

1999. 50th Death Anniv of Ghulam Bari Aleeg (writer).
1098 **563** 5r. multicoloured 10 15

1999. Medicinal Plants (7th series).
1099 **564** 5r. multicoloured 10 15

565 Mosque (½-size illustration)

1999. Eid-ul-Fitr Greetings.
1100 **565** 2r. multicoloured 10 10
1101 15r. multicoloured . . . 35 40

566 Woman and Young Boy

2000. 25th Anniv of S.O.S. Children's Villages in Pakistan.
1102 **566** 2r. multicoloured 10 10

567 Racing Cyclists

2000. Centenary of International Cycling Union.
1103 **567** 2r. multicoloured 10 10

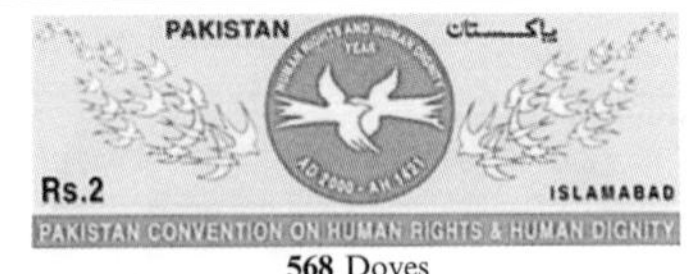

568 Doves

2000. Pakistan Convention on Human Rights and Human Dignity.
1104 **568** 2r. multicoloured 10 10

569 College Building

2000. Centenary of Edwardes College, Peshawar.
1105 **569** 2r. multicoloured 10 10

570 Mahomed Ali Habib

2000. Mahomed Ali Habib (founder of Habib Bank Ltd) Commemoration.
1106 **570** 2r. multicoloured 10 10

571 Emblems and Symbols

2000. 50th Anniv of Institute of Cost and Management Accountants. Multicoloured.
1107 2r. Type **571** 10 10
1108 15r. Emblems, graph, keyboard and globe . . . 35 40

572 Ahmed Jaffer

2000. 10th Death Anniv of Ahmed Jaffer (prominent businessman).
1109 **572** 10r. multicoloured . . . 20 25

573 "Sarfaroshaane Tehreeke Pakistan" (detail)

2000. "Sarfaroshaane Tehreeke Pakistan" (painting). Showing different details. Multicoloured.
1110 5r. Type **573** 10 15
1111 5r. Bullock carts with tree in foreground 10 15
1112 5r. Bullock carts and crowd carrying Pakistan flag . . 10 15
1113 5r. Unloading bullock cart 10 15

574 Captain Muhammad Sarwar

2000. Defence Day. Showing winners of Nishan-e-Haider medal. Multicoloured.
1114 5r. Type **574** 10 15
1115 5r. Major Tufail Muhammad 10 15
See also No. 1173/4.

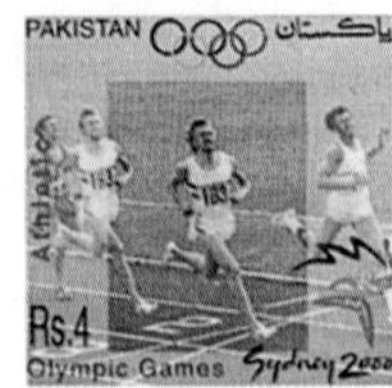

575 Athletics

2000. Olympic Games, Sydney. Multicoloured.
1116 4r. Type **575** 10 10
1117 4r. Hockey 10 10
1118 4r. Weightlifting 10 10
1119 4r. Cycling 10 10

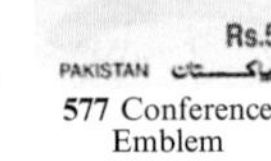

576 Emblem and Building **577** Conference Emblem

2000. 125th Anniv of National College of Arts, Lahore.
1120 **576** 5r. multicoloured 10 15

2000. "Creating the Future" Business Conference.
1121 **577** 5r. multicoloured 10 15

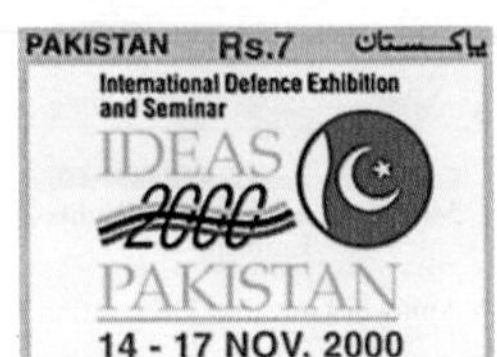

578 Exhibition Emblem

2000. "Ideas 2000" International Defence Exhibition and Seminar.
1122 **578** 7r. multicoloured 15 20

579 Liquorice

2000. Medicinal Plants (8th series).
1123 **579** 2r. multicoloured 10 10

580 Crippled Child and Rotary Emblem

2000. "A World Without Polio" Campaign.
1124 **580** 2r. multicoloured 10 10

581 Refugee Family and Emblems

2000. 50th Anniv of United Nations High Commissioner for Refugees.
1125 **581** 2r. multicoloured 10 10

582 Hafeez Jalandhri

2001. Birth Centenary of Hafeez Jalandhri (poet).
1126 **582** 2r. multicoloured 10 10

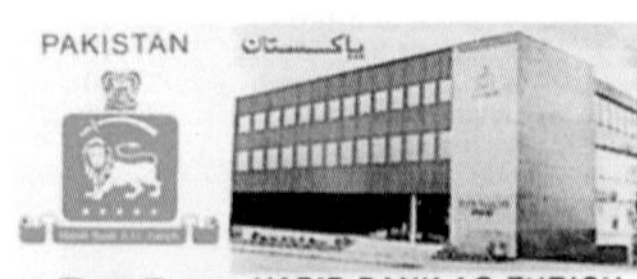

583 Habib Bank AG Zurich Head Office

2001. Habib Bank AG Zurich Commemoration.
1127 **583** 5r. multicoloured 10 15

584 Chashma Nuclear Power Station

2001. Opening of Chashma Nuclear Power Station.
1128 **584** 4r. multicoloured 10 10

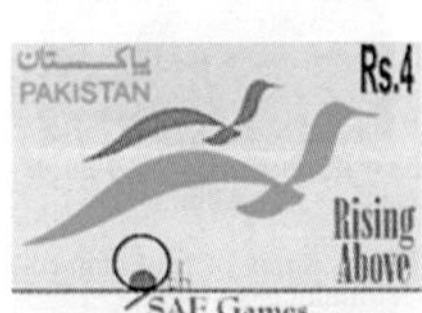

585 S.A.F. Games Emblem

2001. 9th S.A.F. Games, Islamabad.
1129 **585** 4r. multicoloured (blue background) 10 10
1130 4r. multicoloured (pink background) 10 10

586 "Ma Gu's Birthday Offering"

2001. 50th Anniv of Pakistan–China Friendship. Multicoloured.
1131 4r. Type **586** 10 10
1132 4r. "Two Pakistani Women drawing Water" 10 10
1133 4r. Girls in traditional Yugur and Hunza costumes 10 10
No. 1131 is inscribed "BIRTTHDAY" in error.

587 Mohammad Ali Jinnah

589 Khawaja Ghulam Farid

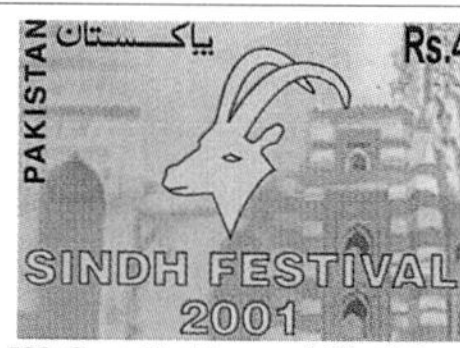

588 Goat Emblem and Traditional Architecture

2001. 125th Birth Anniv of Mohammad Ali Jinnah ("Quaid-e-Azam") (1st issue).
1134 **587** 4r. multicoloured 10 10
See also Nos. 1152/6.

2001. Defence Day. As T **574** showing winners of Nishan-e-Haider medal. Multicoloured.
1135 4r. Major Shabbir Sharif Shaheed 10 10
1136 4r. Major Mohammad Akram Shaheed 10 10

2001. Sindh Festival, Karachi.
1137 **588** 4r. yellow, black and green 10 10

2001. Death Centenary of Khawaja Ghulam Farid (poet).
1138 **589** 5r. multicoloured 10 15

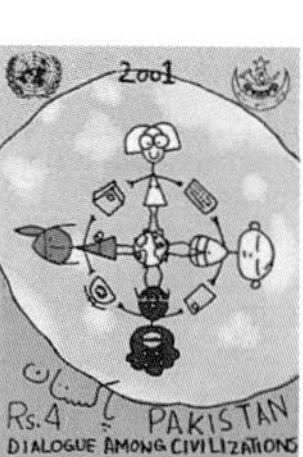
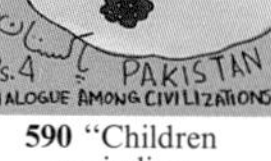

590 "Children encircling Globe" (Urska Golob)

591 Syed Imitaz Ali Taj

2001. U.N. Year of Dialogue among Civilizations.
1139 **590** 4r. multicoloured 10 10

2001. Syed Imitiaz Ali Taj (writer) Commemoration.
1140 **591** 5r. multicoloured 10 15

592 Pres. Saparmurat Niyazov of Turkmenistan

593 Peppermint

2001. 10th Anniv of Turkmenistan Independence.
1141 **592** 5r. multicoloured 10 15

2001. Medicinal Plants (9th series).
1142 **593** 4r. multicoloured 10 10

594 Convent of Jesus and Mary, Lahore

2001. 125th Anniv of Convent of Jesus and Mary, Lahore.
1143 **594** 4r. multicoloured 10 10

595 Dr. Ishtiaq Husain Qureshi

596 Blue Throat

2001. 20th Death Anniv of Dr. Ishtiaq Husain Qureshi (historian).
1144 **595** 4r. multicoloured 10 10

2001. Birds. Multicoloured.
1145 4r. Type **596** 10 10
1146 4r. Hoopoe 10 10
1147 4r. Pin-tailed sandgrouse . . 10 10
1148 4r. Magpie robin 10 10

597 Handshake beneath Flags of U.A.E. and Pakistan

598 Nishtar Medical College, Multan

2001. 30th Anniv of Diplomatic Relations between Pakistan and United Arab Emirates. Multicoloured.
1149 5r. Type **597** 10 15
1150 30r. Pres. Sheikh Zayed bin Sultan Al Nahyan of U.A.E. and Mohammed Ali Jinnah (horiz) . . . . 1·50 1·75

2001. 50th Anniv of Nishtar Medical College, Multan.
1151 **598** 5r. multicoloured 10 15

599 Mohammad Ali Jinnah taking Oath as Governor General, 1947

600 Troops and Ordnance

2001. 125th Birth Anniv of Mohammad Ali Jinnah ("Quaid-e-Azam") (2nd issue). Multicoloured.
1152 4r. Type **599** 10 10
1153 4r. Opening State Bank, Karachi, 1948 . . . . . 10 10
1154 4r. Taking salute, Peshawar, 1948 . . . . 10 10
1155 4r. Inspecting guard of honour, 1948 (55 × 27 mm) 10 10
1156 4r. With anti-aircraft gun crew, 1948 (55 × 27 mm) 10 10

2001. 50th Anniv of Pakistan Ordnance Factories.
1157 **600** 4r. multicoloured 10 10

601 Samandar Khan Samandar

2002. Samandar Khan Samandar (poet) Commemoration.
1158 **601** 5r. multicoloured 10 15

602 Hyssop

2002. Medicinal Plants (10th series).
1159 **602** 5r. multicoloured 10 15

603 Statues of Buddha

2002. 50th Anniv of Diplomatic Relations between Pakistan and Japan.
1160 **603** 5r. multicoloured 10 15

604 Pakistan and Kyrgyzstan Flags

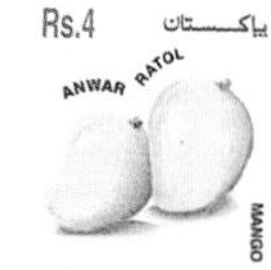

605 Anwar Ratol Mangoes

2002. 10th Anniv of Diplomatic Relations between Pakistan and Kyrgyzstan.
1161 **604** 5r. multicoloured 10 15

2002. Fruits of Pakistan. Mangoes. Multicoloured.
1162 4r. Type **605** 10 10
1163 4r. Dusehri mangoes 10 10
1164 4r. Chaunsa mangoes . . . 10 10
1165 4r. Sindhri mango 10 10

606 Begum Noor us Sabah

607 Children with Animals and Pakistan Flag

2002. 55th Independence Day Celebrations. Political Figures. Multicoloured.
1166 4r. Type **606** 10 10
1167 4r. I. Chundrigar 10 10
1168 4r. Habib Ibrahim Rahimtoola 10 10
1169 4r. Qazi Mureed Ahmed . . 10 10

2002. World Summit on Sustainable Development, Johannesburg. Multicoloured.
1170 4r. Type **607** 10 10
1171 4r. Mountain and cartoon character (37 × 37 mm) . . 10 10

608 Mohammad Aly Rangoonwala (politician/ philanthropist)

2002. Mohammad Aly Rangoonwala Commem.
1172 **608** 4r. multicoloured 10 10

2002. Defence Day. As T **574** showing winners of Nishan-e-Haider medal. Multicoloured.
1173 4r. Lance Naik Muhammad Mahfuz Shaheed 10 10
1174 4r. Sawar Muhammad Hussain Shaheed 10 10

609 Muhammad Iqbal in Academic Gown

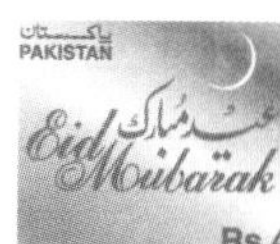

610 "Eid Mubarak"

2002. 125th Birth Anniv of Muhammad Iqbal (writer). Multicoloured.
1174 4r. Type **609** 10 10
1175 4r. Muhammad Iqbal in library 10 10

2002. Eid-ul-Fitr Festival.
1176 **610** 4r. multicoloured 10 10

611 Hakim Muhammad Hassan Qarshi and Plants

2002. Hakim Muhammad Hassan Qarshi (pioneer of Tibb homeopathic medicine) Commemoration.
1177 **611** 4r. multicoloured 10 10

OFFICIAL STAMPS

1947. King George VI Official stamps of India optd **PAKISTAN**.
O 1 O **20** 3p. slate . . . . 1·50 50
O 2 ½a. purple 30 10
O 3 9p. green . . . . 4·75 2·50
O 4 1a. red 30 10
O 5 1½a. violet 30 10
O 6 2a. orange 30 10
O 7 2½a. violet . . . . . . 7·00 8·00
O 8 4a. brown . . . . . . 1·25 50
O 9 8a. violet . . . . . . 1·75 1·25
O10 **93** 1r. slate and brown (No. O138) . . . . . 80 1·25
O11 2r. purple and brown (No. O139) . . . . . 4·00 3·50
O12 5r. green and blue (No. O140) . . . . 17·00 30·00
O13 10r. purple and red (No. O141) . . . . . 48·00 90·00

1948. Optd **SERVICE**. Crescent moon pointing to right.
O14 **7** 3p. red 10 10
O15 6p. violet 10 10
O37 9p. green 10 10
O17 – 1a. blue . . . . 3·75 10
O18 – 1½a. green . . . . . . 3·50 10
O19 – 2a. red . . . . 1·50 10
O20 – 3a. green . . . . 26·00 7·50
O21 **9** 4a. brown . . . . . . 1·00 10
O22 – 8a. black . . . . 2·00 8·50
O23 **12** 1r. blue . . . . 1·00 10
O42 2r. brown . . . . 4·25 20
O61 5r. red . . . . 7·50 15
O26 **13** 10r. mauve . . . . 14·00 42·00

1949. Optd **SERVICE**. Crescent moon pointing to left.
O38 – 1a. blue 10 10
O39 – 1½a. green 10 10
O40 – 2a. red 15 10
O30 – 3a. green . . . . 25·00 5·00
O31 – 8a. black . . . . 38·00 16·00

1951. 4th Anniv of Independence. As Nos. 56, 58 and 60 but inscr "SERVICE" instead of "PAKISTAN POSTAGE".
O32 3a. purple . . . . 6·50 9·00
O33 4a. green . . . . 1·75 10
O34 8a. sepia . . . . 7·50 3·50

1954. 7th Anniv of Independence. Nos. 65/71 optd **SERVICE**.
O53 6p. violet 10 10
O54 9p. blue 10 10
O55 1a. red 10 10
O56 1½a. red 10 10
O57 14a. myrtle . . . . 50 4·00
O58 1r. green 50 10
O51 2r. orange . . . . 1·75 15

1955. 8th Anniv of Independence. Nos. 74/5 optd **SERVICE**.
O63 6a. blue 15 10
O64 8a. violet 15 10

1959. 9th Anniv of Independence. Optd **SERVICE**.
O65 **37** 2a. red 10 10

1961. 1st Anniv of Republic. Optd **SERVICE**.
O62 **41** 10r. green and orange . . 7·00 8·50

1961. Optd **SERVICE**.
O66 **51** 8a. green 20 10
O67 1r. blue 20 10

1961. New currency. Provisional stamps. Nos. 122 etc. optd **SERVICE**.
O68 – 1p. on 1½a. red 10 10
O69 **7** 2p. on 3p. red 10 10
O70 **51** 3p. on 6p. purple 10 10
O71 – 7p. on 1a. red 10 10
O72 **51** 13p. on 2a. red 10 10
O73 **37** 13p. on 2a. red 10 10

1961. Definitive issue optd **SERVICE**.
O 74 **60** 1p. violet 10 10
O 75 2p. red 10 10
O 79 3p. purple 10 10
O 94 5p. blue 10 10
O 81 7p. green 10 10
O 82 **61** 10p. brown 10 10
O 83 13p. violet 10 10
O 98 15p. purple . . . . 10 1·50
O 99 20p. green 10 40
O100 25p. blue . . . . 8·50 2·75
O 85 40p. purple 10 10
O102 50p. turquoise 10 15
O 87 75p. red 20 10
O104 90p. green . . . . 4·50 4·00
O 88 **62** 1r. red 35 10
O 89 2r. orange . . . . 1·50 20
O 90 5r. green . . . . 4·25 7·00

1979. Optd **SERVICE**.
O109 **275** 2p. green 10 10
O110 – 3p. black 10 10
O111 – 5p. blue 10 10
O112 **275** 10p. blue and turquoise 10 10
O113 – 20p. green (No. 468) . . 10 10
O114 – 25p. green and mauve (No. 489) 10 10
O115 – 40p. blue and mauve (No. 470) 30 10
O116 – 50p. lilac and green (No. 471) 10 10
O117 – 60p. black (No. 472) . . 1·00 10
O118 – 75p. red (No. 473) . . . 1·00 10
O119 – 1r. green (No. 475) . . 2·25 10
O120 – 1r.50 orange (No. 476) 20 20
O121 – 2r. red (No. 477) . . . 20 10
O122 – 3r. blue (No. 478) . . . 30 30
O123 – 4r. black (No. 479) . . 2·50 50
O124 – 5r. brown (No. 480) . . 2·50 50

1980. As Nos. 513/19 but inscr "SERVICE".
O125 **291** 10p. green and yellow 1·00 10
O126 15p. deep green & green 1·00 10
O127 25p. violet and red . . . 15 50
O128 35p. red and green . . . 20 60
O129 – 40p. red and brown . . 1·00 10
O130 – 50p. red and green . . . 20 30
O131 – 80p. green and black . . 30 1·25

1984. Nos. 629/30 and 632/6 optd **SERVICE**.
O132 – 5p. black and purple . . 10 40
O133 – 10p. black and red . . . 10 30
O135 **343** 20p. black and violet . . 20 30
O136 – 50p. brown and red . . 30 30
O137 – 60p. lt brown & brown 35 40
O138 – 70p. blue 40 50
O139 – 80p. brown and red . . 45 50

1989. No. 773 optd **SERVICE**.
O140 **411** 1r. multicoloured . . . 3·50 85

O 7 State Bank of Pakistan Building, Islamabad

1990.
O141 **O 7** 1r. red and green . . . 10 10
O142 2r. red and pink 10 10
O143 3r. red and blue 10 10
O144 4r. red and brown . . . 10 10
O145 5r. red and purple . . . 10 15
O146 10r. red and brown . . 20 25

PALAU Pt. 22

Formerly part of the United States Trust Territory of the Pacific Islands, Palau became an autonomous republic on 1 January 1981. Until 1983 it continued to use United States stamps.

Palau became an independent republic on 1 October 1994.

100 cents = 1 dollar.

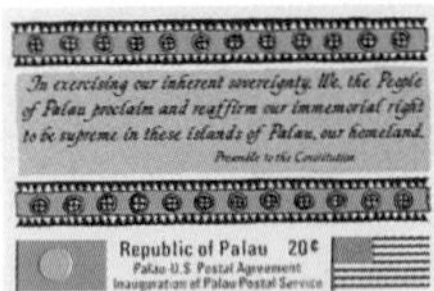

1 Preamble to Constitution

1983. Inaug of Postal Independence. Mult.
1 20c. Type **1** 60 45
2 20c. Natives hunting (design from Koror meeting house) 60 45
3 20c. Preamble to Constitution (different) 60 45
4 20c. Three fishes (design from Koror meeting house) 60 45

2 Palau Fruit Dove

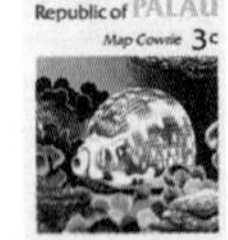

3 Map Cowrie

1983. Birds. Multicoloured.
5 20c. Type **2** 85 85
6 20c. Morning bird 85 85
7 20c. Palau white-eye (inscr "Giant White-eye") 85 85
8 20c. Palau fantail 85 85

1983. Marine Life. Multicoloured.
9 1c. Sea fan 10 10
10 3c. Type **3** 10 10
11 5c. Jellyfish 15 10
12 10c. Hawksbill turtle 20 10
13 13c. Giant clam 25 15
14 14c. Trumpet triton 30 25
15 20c. Parrotfish 40 25
16 22c. Indo-Pacific hump-headed ("Bumphead") parrotfish 40 30
17 25c. Soft coral and damselfishes 40 30
17a 28c. Chambered nautilus . . 55 40
18 30c. Dappled sea cucumber 55 40
18a 33c. Sea anemone and anemonefishes ("Clownfish") 55 40
19 37c. Sea urchin 75 40
19a 39c. Green sea turtle 75 60
19b 44c. Sailfish 85 70
20 50c. Starfish . . . . 1·00 60
21 $1 Common squid . . . . . 1·75 1·00
22 $2 Dugong . . . . 3·25 2·25
23 $5 Pink sponge . . . . . . 7·50 5·50
24 $10 Spinner dolphin . . . . 12·50 11·00

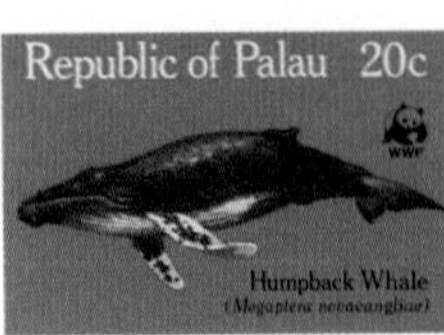

4 Humpback Whale

1983. World Wildlife Fund. Whales. Mult.
25 20c. Type **4** 70 45
26 20c. Blue whale 70 45
27 20c. Fin whale 70 45
28 20c. Sperm whale 70 45

5 "Spear fishing at New Moon"

6 King Abba Thulle

1983. Christmas. Paintings by Charlie Gibbons. Mult.
29 20c. Type **5** 55 35
30 20c. "Taro Gardening" . . . 55 35
31 20c. "First Child Ceremony" 55 35
32 20c. "Traditional Feast at the Bai" 55 35
33 20c. "Spear Fishing from Red Canoe" 55 35

1983. Bicentenary of Captain Henry Wilson's Voyage to Palau.
34 **6** 20c. brown, blue & deep blue 55 35
35 – 20c. brown, blue & deep blue 55 35
36 – 20c. brown, blue & deep blue 55 35
37 – 20c. brown, blue & deep blue 55 35
38 – 20c. brown, blue & deep blue 55 35
39 – 20c. brown, blue & deep blue 55 35
40 – 20c. brown, blue & deep blue 55 35
41 – 20c. brown, blue & deep blue 55 35

DESIGNS—VERT: No. 37, Ludec (King Abba Thulle's wife); 38, Capt. Henry Wilson; 41, Prince Lee Boo. HORIZ: (47 × 20 mm): 35, Mooring in Koror; 36, Village scene in Pelew Islands; 39, Approaching Pelew; 40, Englishman's camp on Ulong.

7 Trumpet Triton

1984. Sea Shells (1st series). Multicoloured.
42 20c. Type **7** 50 40
43 20c. Horned helmet 50 40
44 20c. Giant clam 50 40
45 20c. Laciniate conch 50 40
46 20c. Royal oak ("cloak") scallop 50 40
47 20c. Trumpet triton (different) 50 40
48 20c. Horned helmet (different) 50 40
49 20c. Giant clam (different) . . 50 40
50 20c. Laciniate conch (different) 50 40
51 20c. Royal oak ("cloak") scallop (different) 50 40

Nos. 43/6 have mauve backgrounds, Nos. 48/51 blue backgrounds.

See also Nos. 145/9, 194/8, 231/5, 256/60 and 515/19.

8 White-tailed Tropic Bird

1984. Air. Birds. Multicoloured.
52 40c. Type **8** . . . . 1·25 1·10
53 40c. White tern (inscr "Fairy Tern") . . . . 1·25 1·10
54 40c. White-capped noddy (inscr "Black Noddy") . . . 1·25 1·10
55 40c. Black-naped tern . . . . 1·25 1·10

9 "Oroolong" (Wilson's schooner)

1984. 19th Universal Postal Union Congress Philatelic Salon, Hamburg. Multicoloured.
56 40c. Type **9** . . . . 1·00 75
57 40c. Missionary ship "Duff" 1·00 75
58 40c. German expeditionary steamer "Peiho" . . . . . 1·00 75
59 40c. German gunboat "Albatros" . . . . 1·00 75

10 Spear Fishing

1984. "Ausipex 84" International Stamp Exhibition, Melbourne. Fishing. Multicoloured.
60 20c. Type **10** 55 35
61 20c. Kite fishing 55 35
62 20c. Underwater spear fishing 55 35
63 20c. Net fishing 55 35

11 Mountain Apple

1984. Christmas. Multicoloured.
64 20c. Type **11** 50 35
65 20c. Beach morning glory . . 50 35
66 20c. Turmeric 50 35
67 20c. Plumeria 50 35

12 Chick

1985. Birth Bicentenary of John J. Audubon (ornithologist). Designs showing Audubon's Shearwater. Multicoloured.
68 22c. Type **12** (postage) 80 80
69 22c. Head of shearwater . . . 80 80
70 22c. Shearwater flying 80 80
71 22c. Shearwater on lake . . . 80 80
72 44c. "Audubon's Shearwater" (Audubon) (air) . . . . . . 1·50 1·50

13 Borotong (cargo canoe)

1985. Traditional Canoes and Rafts. Multicoloured.
73 22c. Type **13** 70 45
74 22c. Kabeki (war canoe) . . . 70 45
75 22c. Olechutel (bamboo raft) 70 45
76 22c. Kaeb (racing/sailing canoe) 70 45

14 Boy with Guitar

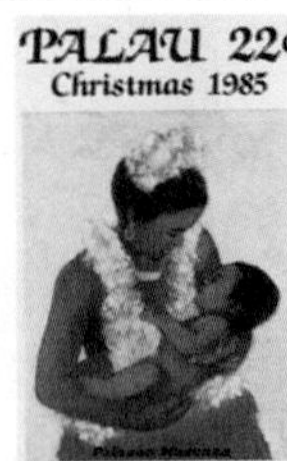

16 Mother cuddling Child

15 Raising German Flag at Palau, 1885, and German 1880 20pf. Stamp

1985. International Youth Year. Multicoloured.
77 44c. Type **14** 75 60
78 44c. Boy with fishing rod . . . 75 60
79 44c. Boy with baseball bat . . 75 60
80 44c. Boy with spade 75 60

Nos. 77/80 were issued together se-tenant, each block forming a composite design showing a ring of children of different races.

1985. Air. Centenary of Vatican Treaty (granting German trading privileges in Caroline Islands). Multicoloured.
81 44c. Type **15** 90 75
82 44c. Early German trading post, Angaur, and Marshall Islands 1899 5pf. overprinted stamp 90 75
83 44c. Abai (village meeting house) and Caroline Islands 1901 3m. yacht stamp . . . 90 75
84 44c. "Cormoran" (German cruiser), 1914, and Caroline Islands 1901 40pf. yacht stamp 90 75

1985. Christmas. Multicoloured.
85 14c. Mother with child on lap 35 15
86 22c. Type **16** 55 30
87 33c. Mother supporting child in arms 85 50
88 44c. Mother lifting child in air 1·00 70

17 Consolidated Catalina Amphibian over Natural Bridge

1985. Air. 50th Anniv of First Trans-Pacific Airmail Flight. Multicoloured.
89 44c. Type **17** . . . . 1·00 65
90 44c. Douglas DC-6B approaching Airai–Koror Passage . . . . 1·00 65
91 44c. Grumman Albatross flying boat over Airai Village . . . . 1·00 65
92 44c. Douglas DC-4 landing at Airai . . . . 1·00 65

18 Comet and Kaeb, 1758

1985. Appearance of Halley's Comet. Multicoloured.
94 44c. Type **18** 85 60
95 44c. Comet and U.S.S. "Vincennes", 1835 . . . . . 85 60
96 44c. Comet and "Scharnhorst" (German cruiser), 1910 . . . 85 60
97 44c. Comet and tourist cabin cruiser, 1986 . . . . 85 60

19 Micronesian Flycatchers

1986. Songbirds. Multicoloured.
98 44c. Type **19** ("Mangrove Flycatchers") 1·10 1·10
99 44c. Cardinal honeyeaters 1·10 1·10
100 44c. Blue-faced parrot finches 1·10 1·10
101 44c. Grey-brown white-eye ("Dusky White-eye") and bridled white eye 1·10 1·10

20 Spear Fisherman

1986. "Ameripex '86" International Stamp Exhibition, Chicago. Sea and Reef World. Multicoloured.
102 14c. Type **20** 90 55
103 14c. Olechutel (native raft) 90 55
104 14c. Kaebs (sailing canoes) 90 55
105 14c. Rock islands and sailfish 90 55
106 14c. Inter-island ferry and two-winged flyingfishes 90 55
107 14c. Bonefishes 90 55
108 14c. Jacks 90 55
109 14c. Japanese mackerel 90 55
110 14c. Sailfishes 90 55
111 14c. Barracuda 90 55
112 14c. Undulate triggerfishes 90 55
113 14c. Dolphin (fish) 90 55
114 14c. Spear fisherman with grouper 90 55
115 14c. Manta ray 90 55
116 14c. Striped marlin 90 55
117 14c. Black-striped parrotfishes 90 55
118 14c. Red-breasted wrasse 90 55
119 14c. Malabar blood snappers 90 55
120 14c. Malabar blood snapper and clupeid ("Herring") school 90 55
121 14c. Dugongs 90 55
122 14c. Powder-blue surgeonfishes 90 55
123 14c. Spotted eagle ray 90 55
124 14c. Hawksbill turtle 90 55
125 14c. Needlefishes 90 55
126 14c. Tuna 90 55
127 14c. Octopus 90 55
128 14c. Anemonefishes ("Clownfish") 90 55
129 14c. Squid 90 55
130 14c. Groupers 90 55
131 14c. Moorish idols 90 55
132 14c. Queen conch and starfish 90 55
133 14c. Diadem soldierfishes 90 55
134 14c. Starfish and stingrays 90 55
135 14c. Lionfish 90 55
136 14c. Emperor angelfishes 90 55
137 14c. Saddle butterflyfishes 90 55
138 14c. Spiny lobster 90 55
139 14c. Mangrove crab 90 55
140 14c. Giant clam ("Tridacna gigas") 90 55
141 14c. Moray 90 55

Nos. 102/41 are each inscribed on the back (over the gum) with the name of the subject featured on the stamp.

Nos. 102/41 were printed together, se-tenant, forming a composite design.

21 Presidential Seal

1986. Air. Haruo I. Remeliik (first President) Commemoration. Multicoloured.
142 44c. Type **21** 90 60
143 44c. Kabeki (war canoe) passing under Koror–Babeldaob Bridge 90 60
144 44c. Presidents Reagan and Remeliik 90 60

1986. Sea Shells (2nd series). As T **7**. Multicoloured.
145 22c. Commercial trochus 55 40
146 22c. Marble cone 55 40
147 22c. Fluted giant clam 55 40
148 22c. Bullmouth helmet 55 40
149 22c. Golden cowrie 55 40

23 Crab inhabiting Soldier's rusting Helmet

1986. International Peace Year. Multicoloured.
150 22c. Type **23** (postage) 50 40
151 22c. Marine life inhabiting airplane 50 40
152 22c. Rusting tank behind girl 50 40
153 22c. Abandoned assault landing craft, Airai 65 65
154 22c. Statue of Liberty, New York (centenary) (air) 75 70

24 Gecko

1986. Reptiles. Multicoloured.
155 22c. Type **24** 60 45
156 22c. Emerald tree skink 60 45
157 22c. Estuarine crocodile 60 45
158 22c. Leatherback turtle 60 45

25 Girl with Guitar and Boy leading Child on Goat

26 Tailed Jay on Soursop

1986. Christmas. Multicoloured.
159 22c. Type **25** 35 25
160 22c. Boys singing and girl carrying flowers 35 25
161 22c. Mother holding baby 35 25
162 22c. Children carrying baskets of fruit 35 25
163 22c. Girl with white terns 45 45

Nos. 159/63 were issued together, se-tenant, forming a composite design.

1987. Butterflies (1st series). Multicoloured.
164 44c. Type **26** 95 75
165 44c. Common mormon on sweet orange 95 75
166 44c. Common eggfly on swamp cabbage 95 75
167 44c. Oleander butterfly on fig 95 75

See also Nos. 223/6.

27 Bat flying

1987. Air. Palau Fruit Bat. Multicoloured.
168 44c. Type **27** 90 70
169 44c. Bat hanging from branch 90 70
170 44c. Bat feeding 90 70
171 44c. Head of bat 90 70

28 "Ixora casei"

31 "The President shall be the chief executive ..."

29 Babeldaob

1987. Flowers. Multicoloured.
172 1c. Type **28** 10 10
173 3c. "Lumnitzera littorea" 10 10
174 5c. "Sonneratia alba" 10 10
175 10c. Woody vine 15 10
176 14c. "Bikkia palauensis" 20 10
177 15c. "Limophila aromatica" 20 10
178 22c. "Bruguiera gymnorhiza" 30 20
179 25c. "Fragraea ksid" 30 20
180 36c. "Ophiorrhiza palauensis" 45 35
181 39c. "Cerbera manghas" 60 40
182 44c. "Samadera indica" 65 45
183 45c. "Maesa canfieldiae" 55 45
184 50c. "Dolichandrone spathacea" 80 55
185 $1 "Barringtonia racemosa" 1·50 1·10
186 $2 "Nepenthes mirabilis" 2·50 2·00
187 $5 Orchid 6·00 4·50
188 $10 Bouquet of mixed flowers 12·00 9·00

1987. "Capex '87" International Stamp Exhibition, Toronto. Multicoloured.
190 22c. Type **29** 40 30
191 22c. Floating Garden Islands 40 30
192 22c. Rock Island 40 30
193 22c. Koror 40 30

1987. Sea Shells (3rd series). As T **7**. Multicoloured.
194 22c. Black-striped triton 50 35
195 22c. Tapestry turban 50 35
196 22c. Adusta murex 50 35
197 22c. Little fox mitre 50 35
198 22c. Cardinal mitre 50 35

1987. Bicentenary of United States of America Constitution. Multicoloured.
199 14c. Type **31** 25 20
200 14c. Palau and U.S. Presidents' seals (24 × 37 mm) 25 20
201 14c. "The executive power shall be vested ..." 25 20
202 22c. "The legislative power of Palau ..." 35 25
203 22c. Palau Olbiil Era Kelulau and U.S. Senate seals (24 × 37 mm) 35 25
204 22c. "All legislative powers herein granted ..." 35 25
205 44c. "The judicial power of Palau ..." 70 60
206 44c. Palau and U.S. Supreme Court seals (24 × 37 mm) 70 60
207 44c. "The judicial power of the United States ..." 70 60

The three designs of the same value were printed together in se-tenant strips, the top stamp of each strip bearing extracts from the Palau Constitution and the bottom stamp extracts from the U.S. Constitution.

32 Japanese Mobile Post Office and 1937 Japan ½s. Stamp

1987. Links with Japan. Multicoloured.
208 14c. Type **32** 30 25
209 22c. Phosphate mine and Japan 1942 5s. stamp 50 40
210 33c. Douglas DC-2 flying over Badrulchau monuments and Japan 1937 2s.+2s. stamp 65 50
211 44c. Japanese Post Office, Koror, and Japan 1927 10s. stamp 90 65

33 Huts, White Tern and Outrigger Canoes

34 Snapping Shrimp and Watchman Goby

1987. Christmas. Multicoloured.
213 22c. Type **33** 65 65
214 22c. Flying white tern carrying twig 65 65
215 22c. Holy Family in kaeb 65 65
216 22c. Angel and kaeb 65 65
217 22c. Outrigger canoes and hut 65 65

Nos. 213/17 were issued together, se-tenant, forming a composite design; each stamp bears a verse of the carol "I Saw Three Ships".

1987. 25th Anniv of World Ecology Movement. Multicoloured.
218 22c. Type **34** 50 40
219 22c. Mauve vase sponge and sponge crab 50 40
220 22c. Lemon ("Pope's") damselfish and blue-streaked cleaner wrasse 50 40
221 22c. Clown anemonefishes and sea anemone 50 40
222 22c. Four-coloured nudibranch and banded coral shrimp 50 40

1988. Butterflies (2nd series). As T **26**.
223 44c. Orange tiger on "Tournefotia argentia" 65 55
224 44c. Swallowtail on "Citrus reticulata" 65 55
225 44c. Lemon migrant on "Crataeva speciosa" 65 55
226 44c. "Appias ada" (wrongly inscr "Colias philodice") on "Crataeva speciosa" 65 55

35 Whimbrel

39 Angel Violinist and Singing Cherubs

37 Baseball

1988. Ground-dwelling Birds. Multicoloured.
227 44c. Type **35** 1·10 1·10
228 44c. Chinese little bittern ("Yellow Bittern") 1·10 1·10
229 44c. Nankeen ("Rufous Night Heron") 1·10 1·10
230 44c. Buff-banded rail ("Banded Rail") 1·10 1·10

1988. Sea Shells (4th series). As T **7**. Mult.
231 25c. Striped engina 45 35
232 25c. Ivory cone 45 35
233 25c. Plaited mitre 45 35
234 25c. Episcopal mitre 45 35
235 25c. Isabelle cowrie 45 35

1988. Olympic Games, Seoul. Multicoloured.
237 25c.+5c. Type **37** 40 35
238 25c.+5c. Running 40 35
239 45c.+5c. Diving 70 55
240 45c.+5c. Swimming 70 55

1988. Christmas. Multicoloured.
242 25c. Type **39** 40 30
243 25c. Angels and children singing 40 30
244 25c. Children adoring child 55 55
245 25c. Angels and birds flying 55 55
246 25c. Running children and angels playing trumpets 40 30

Nos. 242/6 were issued together, se-tenant, forming a composite design.

41 Nicobar Pigeon

43 Robin-redbreast Triton

42 False Chanterelle

1989. Endangered Birds. Multicoloured.
248 45c. Type **41** 1·10 1·10
249 45c. Palau ground dove 1·10 1·10
250 45c. Marianas scrub hen 1·10 1·10
251 45c. Palau scops owl 1·10 1·10

1989. Fungi. Multicoloured.
252 45c. Type **42** (inscr "Gilled Auricularia) 90 60
253 45c. Black fellows' bread ("Rock mushroom") 90 60
254 45c. Chicken mushroom ("Polyporous") 90 60
255 45c. Veiled stinkhorn 90 60

1989. Sea Shells (5th series). Multicoloured.
256 25c. Type **43** 50 45
257 25c. Hebrew cone 50 45
258 25c. Tadpole triton 50 45
259 25c. Lettered cone 50 45
260 25c. Rugose mitre 50 45

44 Cessna 207 Stationair 7 **46** Jettison of Third Stage

1989. Air. Aircraft. Multicoloured.

261	36c. Type **44**	50	40
262	39c. Embraer Bandeirante airliner	60	50
264	45c. Boeing 727 jetliner	70	60

No. 261 is wrongly inscribed "Skywagon".

1989. 20th Anniv of First Manned Landing on Moon. Multicoloured.

267	25c. Type **46**	35	25
268	25c. Command Module adjusting position	35	25
269	25c. Lunar Excursion Module "Eagle" docking	35	25
270	25c. Space module docking	35	25
271	25c. Propulsion for entry into lunar orbit	35	25
272	25c. Third stage burn	35	25
273	25c. Command Module orbiting Moon	35	25
274	25c. Command Module and part of "Eagle"	35	25
275	25c. Upper part of "Eagle" on Moon	35	25
276	25c. Descent of "Eagle"	35	25
277	25c. Nose of rocket	35	25
278	25c. Reflection in Edwin "Buzz" Aldrin's visor	35	25
279	25c. Neil Armstrong and flag on Moon	35	25
280	25c. Footprints and astronaut's oxygen tank	35	25
281	25c. Upper part of astronaut descending ladder	35	25
282	25c. Launch tower and body of rocket	35	25
283	25c. Survival equipment on Aldrin's space suit	35	25
284	25c. Blast off from lunar surface	35	25
285	25c. View of Earth and astronaut's legs	35	25
286	25c. Leg on ladder	35	25
287	25c. Lift off	35	25
288	25c. Spectators at launch	35	25
289	25c. Capsule parachuting into Pacific	35	25
290	25c. Re-entry	35	25
291	25c. Space Module jettison	35	25
292	$2.40 "Buzz" Aldrin on Moon (photo by Neil Armstrong) (34 × 47 mm)	3·50	2·50

Nos. 267/91 were issued together, se-tenant, forming a composite design.

47 Girl as Astronaut **48** Bridled Tern

1989. Year of the Young Reader. Multicoloured.

293	25c. Type **47**	35	25
294	25c. Boy riding dolphin	40	40
295	25c. Cheshire Cat in tree	40	40
296	25c. Mother Goose	40	40
297	25c. Baseball player	35	25
298	25c. Girl reading	35	25
299	25c. Boy reading	35	25
300	25c. Mother reading to child	35	25
301	25c. Girl holding flowers listening to story	35	25
302	25c. Boy in baseball strip	35	25

1989. "World Stamp Expo '89" International Stamp Exhibition, Washington D.C. Stilt Mangrove. Multicoloured.

303	25c. Type **48**	50	50
304	25c. Lemon migrant (inscr "Sulphur Butterfly")	50	50
305	25c. Micronesian flycatcher ("Mangrove Flycatcher")	50	50
306	25c. White-collared kingfisher	50	50
307	25c. Fruit bat	50	50
308	25c. Estuarine crocodile	50	50
309	25c. Nankeen ("Rufous Night Heron")	50	50
310	25c. Stilt mangrove	50	50
311	25c. Bird's nest fern	50	50
312	25c. Beach hibiscus tree	50	50
313	25c. Common eggfly (butterfly)	50	50
314	25c. Dog-faced watersnake	45	35
315	25c. Mangrove jingle shell	45	35
316	25c. Palau bark cricket	45	35
317	25c. Periwinkle and mangrove oyster	45	35
318	25c. Jellyfish	45	35
319	25c. Flat-headed grey ("Striped") mullet	45	35
320	25c. Mussels, sea anemones and algae	45	35
321	25c. Pajama cardinalfish	45	35
322	25c. Black-tailed snappers	45	35

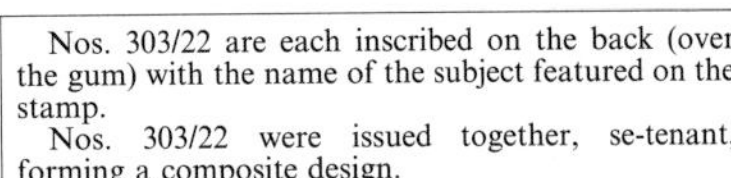

Nos. 303/22 are each inscribed on the back (over the gum) with the name of the subject featured on the stamp.

Nos. 303/22 were issued together, se-tenant, forming a composite design.

49 Angels, Sooty Tern and Audubon's Shearwater **50** Pink Coral

1989. Christmas. Carol of the Birds. Mult.

323	25c. Type **49**	55	55
324	25c. Palau fruit dove and angel	55	55
325	25c. Madonna and child, cherub and birds	55	55
326	25c. Angel, blue-faced parrot finch, Micronesian flycatcher and cardinal honeyeater	55	55
327	25c. Angel, Micronesian flycatcher and black-headed gulls	55	55

Nos. 323/7 were printed together, se-tenant, forming a composite design.

1990. Soft Corals. Multicoloured.

328	25c. Type **50**	50	35
329	25c. Mauve coral	50	35
330	25c. Yellow coral	50	35
331	25c. Orange coral	50	35

See also Nos. 392/5.

51 Siberian Rubythroat

1990. Forest Birds. Multicoloured.

332	45c. Type **51**	75	75
333	45c. Palau bush warbler	75	75
334	45c. Micronesian starling	75	75
335	45c. Common cicdabird ("Cicadabird")	75	75

52 Prince Lee Boo, Capt. Henry Wilson and H.M.S. "Victory"

1990. "Stamp World London 90" International Stamp Exhibition. Prince Lee Boo's Visit to England, 1784, and 150th Anniv of the Penny Black. Multicoloured.

336	25c. Type **52**	40	25
337	25c. St. James's Palace	40	25
338	25c. Rotherhithe Docks	40	25
339	25c. Oroolong House, Devon (Capt. Wilson's home)	40	25
340	25c. Vincenzo Lunardi's balloon	40	25
341	25c. St. Paul's Cathedral	40	25
342	25c. Prince Lee Boo's grave	40	25
343	25c. St. Mary's Church, Rotherhithe	40	25
344	25c. Memorial tablet to Prince Lee Boo	40	25

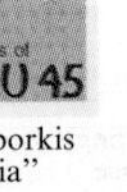

53 "Corymborkis veratrifolia" **55** White Tern, Pacific Golden Plover and Sanderling

54 Plane Butterfly on Beach Sunflower

1990. "Expo 90" International Garden and Greenery Exposition, Osaka. Orchids. Multicoloured.

346	45c. Type **53**	60	40
347	45c. "Malaxis setipes"	60	40
348	45c. "Dipodium freycinetianum"	60	40
349	45c. "Bulbophyllum micronesiacum"	60	40
350	45c. "Vanda teres"	60	40

1990. Butterflies. Multicoloured.

351	45c. Type **54**	70	55
352	45c. Painted lady on coral tree	70	55
353	45c. "Euploea nemertes" on sorcerer's flower	70	55
354	45c. Meadow argus (inscr "Buckeye") on beach pea	70	55

1990. Lagoon Life. Multicoloured.

355	25c. Type **55**	50	50
356	25c. Bidekill fisherman	35	25
357	25c. Yacht and insular halfbeaks	35	25
358	25c. Palauan kaebs	35	25
359	25c. White-tailed tropic bird	50	50
360	25c. Spotted eagle ray	35	25
361	25c. Great barracudas	35	25
362	25c. Reef needlefish	35	25
363	25c. Reef needlefish and black-finned reef ("Reef Blacktip") shark	35	25
364	25c. Hawksbill turtle	35	25
365	25c. Six-feelered threadfins and octopus	35	25
366	25c. Narrow-banded batfish and six-feelered threadfins	35	25
367	25c. Lionfish and six-feelered threadfins	35	25
368	25c. Snowflake moray and six-feelered threadfins	35	25
369	25c. Inflated and uninflated porcupinefishes and six-feelered threadfins	35	25
370	25c. Regal angelfish, blue-streaked cleaner wrasse, blue sea star and corals	35	25
371	25c. Clown triggerfish and spotted garden eels	35	25
372	25c. Anthias and spotted garden eels	35	25
373	25c. Sail-finned snapper ("Bluelined sea bream"), blue-green chromis, blue ("Sapphire") damselfish and spotted garden eel	35	25
374	25c. Masked ("Orange-spine") unicornfish and ribbon-striped ("White-tipped") soldierfish	35	25
375	25c. Slatepencil sea urchin and leopard sea cucumber	35	25
376	25c. Pacific partridge tun (shell)	35	25
377	25c. Mandarin fish and spotted garden eel	35	25
378	25c. Tiger cowrie	35	25
379	25c. Feather starfish and orange-finned anemonefish	35	25

Nos. 355/79 were printed together, se-tenant, forming a composite design.

56 "Delphin", 1890, and Card

1990. Pacifica. Mail Transport. Multicoloured.

380	45c. Type **56**	65	45
381	45c. Right-hand half of card flown on 1951 inaugural U.S. civilian airmail flight and forklift unloading mail from Boeing 727	65	45

Nos. 380/1 were issued together, se-tenant, forming a composite design.

57 Girls singing and Boy with Butterfly

1990. Christmas. Multicoloured.

382	25c. Type **57**	45	45
383	25c. White terns perching on girl's songbook	45	45
384	25c. Girl singing and boys playing flute and guitar	45	45
385	25c. Couple with baby	30	20
386	25c. Three girls singing	30	20

58 Consolidated B-24S Liberator Bombers over Peleliu

1990. 46th Anniv of U.S. Action in Palau Islands during Second World War.

387	45c. Type **58**	65	50
388	45c. Landing craft firing rocket barrage	65	50
389	45c. 1st Marine division attacking Peleliu	65	50
390	45c. U.S. Infantryman and Palauan children	65	50

1991. Hard Corals. As T **50**.

392	30c. Staghorn coral	40	30
393	30c. Velvet leather coral	40	30
394	30c. Van Gogh's cypress coral	40	30
395	30c. Violet lace coral	40	30

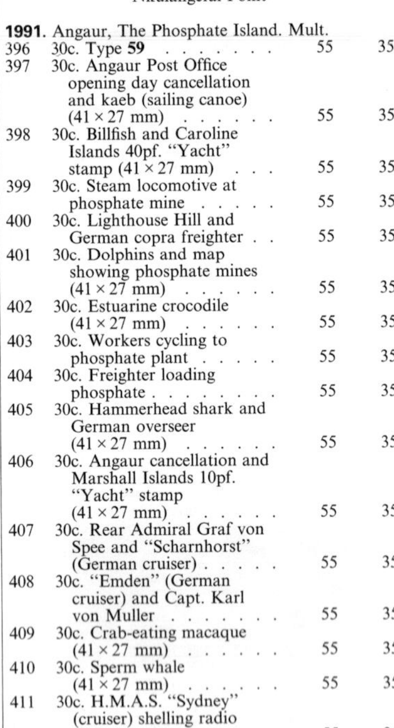

59 Statue of Virgin Mary, Nkulangelul Point

1991. Angaur, The Phosphate Island. Mult.

396	30c. Type **59**	55	35
397	30c. Angaur Post Office opening day cancellation and kaeb (sailing canoe) (41 × 27 mm)	55	35
398	30c. Billfish and Caroline Islands 40pf. "Yacht" stamp (41 × 27 mm)	55	35
399	30c. Steam locomotive at phosphate mine	55	35
400	30c. Lighthouse Hill and German copra freighter	55	35
401	30c. Dolphins and map showing phosphate mines (41 × 27 mm)	55	35
402	30c. Estuarine crocodile (41 × 27 mm)	55	35
403	30c. Workers cycling to phosphate plant	55	35
404	30c. Freighter loading phosphate	55	35
405	30c. Hammerhead shark and German overseer (41 × 27 mm)	55	35
406	30c. Angaur cancellation and Marshall Islands 10pf. "Yacht" stamp (41 × 27 mm)	55	35
407	30c. Rear Admiral Graf von Spee and "Scharnhorst" (German cruiser)	55	35
408	30c. "Emden" (German cruiser) and Capt. Karl von Muller	55	35
409	30c. Crab-eating macaque (41 × 27 mm)	55	35
410	30c. Sperm whale (41 × 27 mm)	55	35
411	30c. H.M.A.S. "Sydney" (cruiser) shelling radio tower	55	35

Nos. 396/411 were issued together, se-tenant, with the centre block of eight stamps forming a composite design of a map of the island.

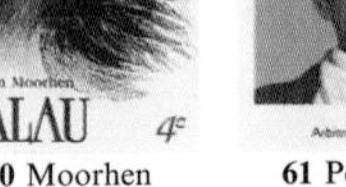

60 Moorhen **61** Pope Leo XIII and 19th-century Spanish and German Flags

1991. Birds. Multicoloured.

412	1c. Palau bush warbler	15	15
413	4c. Type **60**	15	15
414	6c. Buff-banded rail ("Banded Rail")	15	15
415	19c. Palau fantail	30	20
416	20c. Micronesian flycatcher ("Mangrove Flycatcher")	30	20
417	23c. Purple swamphen	35	30
418	29c. Palau fruit dove	45	40
419	35c. Crested tern	50	40
420	40c. Reef herons (inscr "Pacific Reef-Heron")	60	55
421	45c. Micronesian pigeon	65	60
422	50c. Great frigate bird	70	60
423	52c. Little pied cormorant	75	70

424 75c. Jungle nightjar . . . . . 1·10 1·10
425 95c. Cattle egret . . . . . . 1·40 1·25
426 $1.34 Sulphur-crested cockatoo . . . . 2·00 1·75
427 $2 Blue-faced parrot finch . . 3·00 2·75
428 $5 Eclectus parrots . . . . . 7·00 7·00
429 $10 Palau bush warblers feeding chicks (51 × 28 mm) 13·50 13·50

1991. Centenary of Christianity in Palau Islands. Multicoloured.
432 29c. Type **61** 40 30
433 29c. Ibedul Ilengelekei and Church of the Sacred Heart, Koror, 1920 . . . . 40 30
434 29c. Marino de la Hoz, Emilio Villar and Elias Fernandez (Jesuit priests executed in Second World War) 40 30
435 29c. Centenary emblem and Fr. Edwin G. McManus (compiler of Palauan–English dictionary) 40 30
436 29c. Present Church of the Sacred Heart, Koror . . . 40 30
437 29c. Pope John Paul II and Palau and Vatican flags . . 40 30

62 Pacific White-sided Dolphin

1991. Pacific Marine Life. Multicoloured.
438 29c. Type **62** 45 30
439 29c. Common dolphin . . . 45 30
440 29c. Rough-toothed dolphin 45 30
441 29c. Bottle-nosed dolphin . . 45 30
442 29c. Common (inscr "Harbor") porpoise . . . 45 30
443 29c. Head and body of killer whale 45 30
444 29c. Tail of killer whale, spinner dolphin and yellow-finned tuna 45 30
445 29c. Dall's porpoise 45 30
446 29c. Finless porpoise 45 30
447 29c. Map of Palau Islands and bottle-nosed dolphin 45 30
448 29c. Dusky dolphin 45 30
449 29c. Southern right whale dolphin 45 30
450 29c. Striped dolphin 45 30
451 29c. Fraser's dolphin 45 30
452 29c. Peale's dolphin 45 30
453 29c. Spectacled porpoise . . 45 30
454 29c. Spotted dolphin 45 30
455 29c. Hourglass dolphin . . . 45 30
456 29c. Risso's dolphin 45 30
457 29c. Hector's dolphin 45 30

63 McDonnell Douglas Wild Weasel Fighters

1991. Operation Desert Storm (liberation of Kuwait). Multicoloured.
458 20c. Type **63** 35 30
459 20c. Lockheed Stealth fighter-bomber 35 30
460 20c. Hughes Apache helicopter 35 30
461 20c. "M-109 TOW" missile on "M998 HMMWV" vehicle 35 30
462 20c. President Bush of U.S.A. 35 30
463 20c. M2 "Bradley" tank . . 35 30
464 20c. U.S.S. "Ranger" (aircraft carrier) 35 30
465 20c. "Pegasus" (patrol boat) 35 30
466 20c. U.S.S. "Wisconsin" (battleship) 35 30
467 $2.90 Sun, dove and yellow ribbon . . . . 3·25 2·75

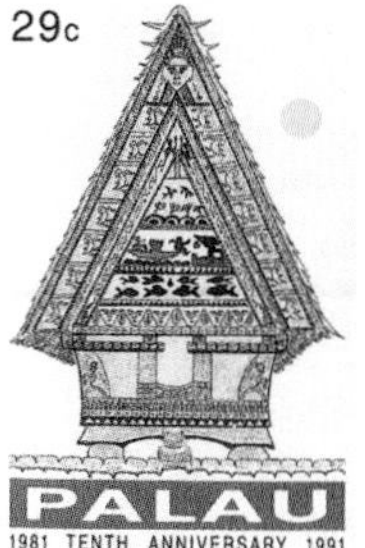

64 Bai Gable

66 "Silent Night, Holy Night!"

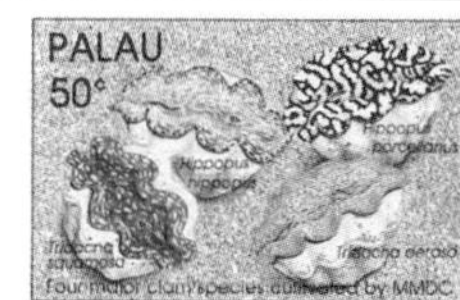

65 Bear's-paw Clam, China Clam, Fluted Giant Clam and "Tridacna derasa"

1991. 10th Anniv of Republic of Palau and Palau–Pacific Women's Conference, Koror. Bai (community building) Decorations. Mult. Imperf (self-adhesive) (50c.), perf (others).
469 29c. Type **64** (postage) . . . 40 30
470 29c. Interior of bai (left side) (32 × 48 mm) 40 30
471 29c. Interior of bai (right side) (32 × 48 mm) 40 30
472 29c. God of construction . . 40 30
473 29c. Bubuu (spider) (value at left) (30 × 23 mm) 40 30
474 29c. Delerrok, the money bird (facing right) (31 × 23 mm) 40 30
475 29c. Delerrok (facing left) (31 × 23 mm) 40 30
476 29c. Bubuu (value at right) (30 × 23 mm) 40 30
477 50c. Bai gable (as in Type **64**) (24 × 51 mm) (air) 65 45
Nos. 469/76 were issued together, se-tenant, Nos. 470/1 forming a composite design.

1991. Conservation and Cultivation of Giant Clams. Multicoloured.
478 50c. Type **65** 70 50
479 50c. Symbiotic relationship between giant clam and "Symbiodinium microadriaticum" 70 50
480 50c. Hatchery 70 50
481 50c. Diver measuring clams in sea-bed nursery 70 50
482 50c. Micronesian Mariculture Demonstration Center, Koror (108 × 16 mm) . . . 70 50

1991. Christmas. Multicoloured.
483 29c. Type **66** 40 30
484 29c. "All is calm, all is bright;" 40 30
485 29c. "Round yon virgin mother and child!" 40 30
486 29c. "Holy Infant, so tender and mild," 40 30
487 29c. "Sleep in heavenly peace." 40 30
Nos. 483/7 were issued together, se-tenant, forming a composite design.

67 Flag, Islands and Children

1991. 25th Anniv of Presence of United States Peace Corps in Palau. Children's paintings.
488 29c. Type **67** 40 30
489 29c. Volunteers arriving by airplane 40 30
490 29c. Health care 40 30
491 29c. Fishing 40 30
492 29c. Agriculture 40 30
493 29c. Education 40 30

68 "Zuiho Maru" (commercial trochus shell breeding and marine research)

1991. "Phila Nippon '91" International Stamp Exhibition, Tokyo. Japanese Heritage in Palau. Multicoloured.
494 29c. Type **68** 55 55
495 29c. Man carving story board (traditional arts) 40 30
496 29c. Tending pineapple crop (agricultural training) . . . 55 55
497 29c. Klidm (stone carving), Koror (archaeological research) 40 30
498 29c. Teaching carpentry and building design 40 30
499 29c. Kawasaki "Mavis" flying boat (air transport) 40 30

69 Mitsubishi Zero-Sen attacking Shipping at Pearl Harbor

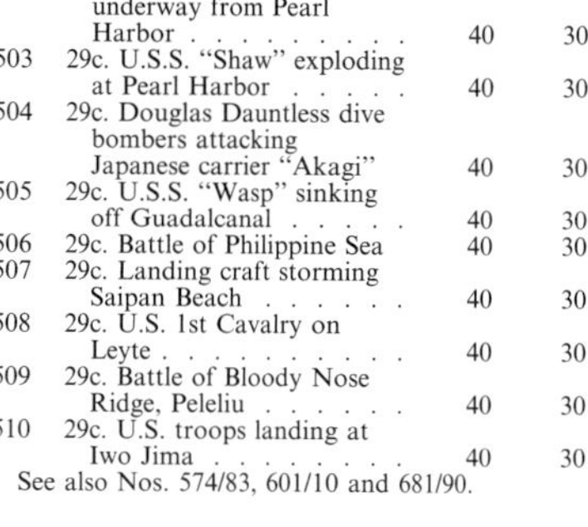

70 "Troides criton"

1991. Pacific Theatre in Second World War (1st issue). Multicoloured.
501 29c. Type **69** 40 30
502 29c. U.S.S. "Nevada" underway from Pearl Harbor 40 30
503 29c. U.S.S. "Shaw" exploding at Pearl Harbor 40 30
504 29c. Douglas Dauntless dive bombers attacking Japanese carrier "Akagi" 40 30
505 29c. U.S.S. "Wasp" sinking off Guadalcanal 40 30
506 29c. Battle of Philippine Sea 40 30
507 29c. Landing craft storming Saipan Beach 40 30
508 29c. U.S. 1st Cavalry on Leyte 40 30
509 29c. Battle of Bloody Nose Ridge, Peleliu 40 30
510 29c. U.S. troops landing at Iwo Jima 40 30
See also Nos. 574/83, 601/10 and 681/90.

1992. Butterflies. Multicoloured.
511 50c. Type **70** 65 45
512 50c. "Alcides zodiaca" . . . 65 45
513 50c. "Papilio poboroi" . . . 65 45
514 50c. "Vindula arsinoe" . . . 65 45

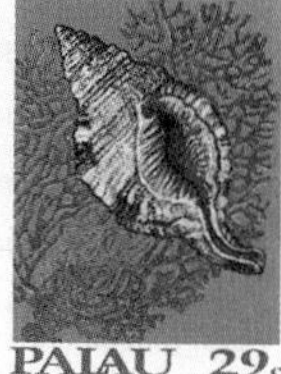

71 Common Hairy Triton

73 "And darkness was upon the face of the deep ..."

72 Christopher Columbus

1992. Sea Shells (6th series). Multicoloured.
515 29c. Type **71** 50 35
516 29c. Eglantine cowrie 50 35
517 29c. Sulcate swamp cerith . . 50 35
518 29c. Black-spined murex . . 50 35
519 29c. Black-mouth moon . . . 50 35

1992. Age of Discovery from Columbus to Drake. Multicoloured.
520 29c. Type **72** 45 30
521 29c. Ferdinand Magellan . . 45 30
522 29c. Sir Francis Drake . . . 45 30
523 29c. Cloud blowing northerly wind 45 30
524 29c. Compass rose 45 30
525 29c. Dolphin and "Golden Hind" (Drake's ship) . . . 45 30
526 29c. Corn cobs and "Santa Maria" (Columbus's ship) 45 30
527 29c. Mythical fishes 45 30
528 29c. Betel palm, cloves and black pepper 55 55
529 29c. "Vitoria" (Magellan's ship), Palau Islands, Audubon's shearwater and crested tern 55 55
530 29c. White-tailed tropic bird, bicoloured parrotfish, pineapple and potatoes . . 45 30
531 29c. Compass 45 30
532 29c. Mythical sea monster . . 45 30
533 29c. Paddles and astrolabe . . 45 30
534 29c. Parallel ruler, divider and Inca gold treasure . . 45 30
535 29c. Backstaff 45 30
536 29c. Cloud blowing southerly wind 45 30
537 29c. Amerigo Vespucci . . . 45 30
538 29c. Francisco Pizarro . . . 45 30
539 29c. Vasco Nunez de Balboa 45 30
With the exception of Nos. 523 and 536 each stamp is inscribed on the back (over the gum) with the name of the subject featured on the stamp.

Nos. 520/39 were issued together, se-tenant, the backgrounds forming a composite design of the hemispheres.

1992. 2nd U.N. Conference on Environment and Development, Rio de Janeiro. The Creation of the World from the Book of Genesis, Chapter 1. Multicoloured.
540 29c. Type **73** 40 30
541 29c. Sunlight 40 30
542 29c. "Let there be a firmament in the midst of the waters, ..." 40 30
543 29c. Sky and clouds 40 30
544 29c. "Let the waters under the heaven ..." 40 30
545 29c. Tree 40 30
546 29c. Waves and sunlight (no inscr) 40 30
547 29c. Waves and sunlight ("... and it was good.") 40 30
548 29c. Waves and clouds (no inscr) 40 30
549 29c. Waves and clouds ("... and it was so.") 40 30
550 29c. Plants on river bank (no inscr) 40 30
551 29c. Plants on river bank ("... and it was good.") 40 30
552 29c. "Let there be lights in the firmament ..." 40 30
553 29c. Comet, planet and clouds 40 30
554 29c. "Let the waters bring forth abundantly the moving creature ..." . . . 50 50
555 29c. Great frigate bird and red-tailed tropic bird flying and collared lory on branch 50 50
556 29c. "Let the earth bring forth the living creature after his kind ..." 40 30
557 29c. Woman, man and rainbow 40 30
558 29c. Mountains ("... and it was good.") 40 30
559 29c. Sun and hills 40 30
560 29c. Killer whale and fishes 40 30
561 29c. Fishes ("... and it was good.") 40 30
562 29c. Elephants and squirrel 40 30
563 29c. Orchard and cat ("... and it was very good.") . . 40 30
Nos. 540/63 were issued together, se-tenant, forming six composite designs each covering four stamps.

75 Presley and Dove

1992. 15th Death Anniv of Elvis Presley (entertainer). Multicoloured.
565 29c. Type **75** 55 40
566 29c. Presley and dove's wing 55 40
567 29c. Presley in yellow cape 55 40
568 29c. Presley in white and red shirt (¾ face) 55 40
569 29c. Presley singing into microphone 55 40
570 29c. Presley crying 55 40
571 29c. Presley in red shirt (¾ face) 55 40
572 29c. Presley in purple shirt (full face) 55 40
573 29c. Presley (left profile) . . . 55 40

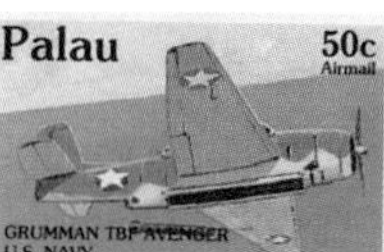

76 Grumman Avenger

1992. Air. Pacific Theatre in Second World War (2nd issue). Aircraft. Multicoloured.
574 50c. Type **76** 75 50
575 50c. Curtiss P-40C of the Flying Tigers fighters . . . 75 50
576 50c. Mitsubishi Zero-Sen fighter 75 50
577 50c. Hawker Hurricane Mk I fighter 75 50
578 50c. Consolidated Catalina flying boat 75 50
579 50c. Curtiss Hawk 75 fighter 75 50
580 50c. Boeing Flying Fortress bomber 75 50
581 50c. Brewster Buffalo fighter 75 50
582 50c. Vickers Supermarine Walrus flying boat 75 50
583 50c. Curtiss Kittyhawk I fighter 75 50

77 "Thus Every Beast"

1992. Christmas. "The Friendly Beasts" (carol). Multicoloured.
584 29c. Type **77** 40 30
585 29c. "By Some Good Spell" 40 30
586 29c. "In the Stable Dark was Glad to Tell" 55 55
587 29c. "Of the Gift He Gave Emanuel" (angel on donkey) 40 30
588 29c. "The Gift He Gave Emanuel" (Palau fruit doves) 55 55

78 Dugong

1993. Animals. Multicoloured.
589 50c. Type **78** 75 50
590 50c. Blue-faced booby ("Masked Booby") 95 95
591 50c. Crab-eating macaque . . 75 50
592 50c. New Guinea crocodile 75 50

79 Giant Deepwater Crab

1993. Seafood. Multicoloured.
593 29c. Type **79** 45 30
594 29c. Scarlet shrimp 45 30
595 29c. Smooth nylon shrimp . . 45 30
596 29c. Armed nylon shrimp . . 45 30

80 Oceanic White-tipped Shark

1993. Sharks. Multicoloured.
597 50c. Type **80** 75 50
598 50c. Great hammerhead . . . 75 50
599 50c. Zebra ("Leopard") shark 75 50
600 50c. Black-finned reef shark 75 50

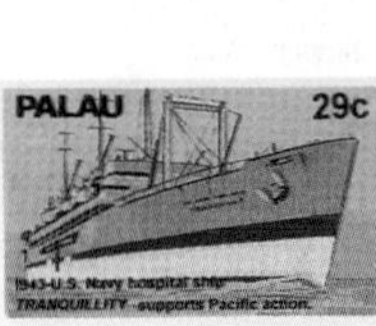

81 U.S.S. "Tranquility" (hospital ship)

82 Girl with Goat

1993. Pacific Theatre in Second World War (3rd issue). Multicoloured.
601 29c. Capture of Guadalcanal 40 30
602 29c. Type **81** 40 30
603 29c. New Guineans drilling 40 30
604 29c. Americans land in New Georgia 40 30
605 29c. U.S.S. "California" (battleship) 40 30
606 29c. Douglas Dauntless dive bombers over Wake Island 40 30
607 29c. Flame-throwers on Tarawa 40 30
608 29c. American advance on Makin 40 30
609 29c. North American B-25 Mitchells bomb Simpson Harbour, Rabaul 40 30
610 29c. Aerial bombardment of Kwajalein 40 30

1992. Christmas. Multicoloured.
611 29c. Type **82** 70 70
612 29c. Children with garlands and goats 70 70
613 29c. Father Christmas . . . 40 30
614 29c. Musicians and singer . . 70 70
615 29c. Family carrying food . . 40 30

83 Pterosaur

85 Flukes of Whale's Tail

84 "After Child-birth Ceremony" (Charlie Gibbons)

1993. Monsters of the Pacific. Multicoloured.
616 29c. Type **83** 50 40
617 29c. Outrigger canoe 50 40
618 29c. Head of plesiosaur . . . 50 40
619 29c. Pterosaur and neck of plesiosaur 50 40
620 29c. Pterosaur (flying towards left) 50 40
621 29c. Giant crab 50 40
622 29c. Tentacles of squid and two requiem sharks 50 40
623 29c. Hammerhead shark, tentacle of squid and neck of plesiosaur 50 40
624 29c. Head of lake serpent . . 50 40
625 29c. Hammerhead shark and neck of serpent 50 40
626 29c. Squid ("Kraken") . . . 50 40
[illegible] squid and body of plesiosaur 50 40
628 29c. Three barracudas and body of plesiosaur 50 40
629 29c. Angelfishes and serpent's claw 50 40
630 29c. Octopus and body of serpent 50 40
631 29c. Nautilus and body of plesiosaur 50 40
632 29c. Moorish idols (two striped fishes) 50 40
633 29c. Lionfish 50 40
634 29c. Squid 50 40
635 29c. Requiem shark and body of kronosaur 50 40
636 29c. Zebra shark and sea-bed 50 40
637 29c. Squid and sea-bed . . . 50 40
638 29c. Giant nautilus and tail of serpent 50 40
639 29c. Head of kronosaur . . . 50 40
640 29c. Lionfish, body of kronosaur and sea-bed . . 50 40
Nos. 616/40 were issued together, se-tenant, forming a composite design.

1993. International Year of Indigenous Peoples. Multicoloured.
641 29c. Type **84** 75 60
642 29c. "Village in Early Palau" (Charlie Gibbons) 75 60

1993. Jonah and The Whale. Multicoloured.
644 29c. Type **85** 50 40
645 29c. Bird and part of fluke 50 40
646 29c. Two birds 50 40
647 29c. Kaeb (canoe) 50 40
648 29c. Sun, birds and dolphin 50 40
649 29c. Shark and whale's tail 50 40
650 29c. Shoal of brown fishes and part of whale 50 40
651 29c. Hammerhead shark, shark's tail and fishes . . . 50 40
652 29c. Dolphin (fish) and shark's head 50 40
653 29c. Dolphin and fishes . . . 50 40
654 29c. Scombroid and other fishes and part of whale . . 50 40
655 29c. Two turtles swimming across whale's body . . . 50 40
656 29c. Shoal of pink fishes and whale's back 50 40
657 29c. Spotted eagle ray, manta ray and top of whale's head 50 40
658 29c. Two groupers and shoal of small brown fishes . . . 50 40
659 29c. Jellyfish and wrasse (blue fish) 50 40
660 29c. Wrasse, other fishes and whale's dorsal fin 50 40
661 29c. Whale's eye and corner of mouth 50 40
662 29c. Opened mouth 50 40
663 29c. Jonah 50 40
664 29c. Convict tang (yellow and black striped fish) and brain corals on sea bed . . 50 40
665 29c. Hump-headed bannerfishes and sea anenome 50 40
666 29c. Undulate triggerfish (blue-striped) and corals on sea bed 50 40
667 29c. Brown and red striped fish, corals and part of whale's jaw 50 40
668 29c. Two groupers (spotted) on sea bed 50 40
Nos. 644/68 were issued together, se-tenant, forming a composite design.

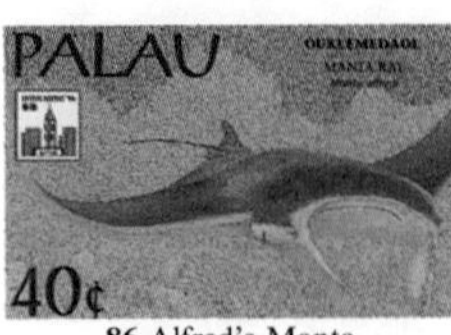

86 Alfred's Manta

1994. "Hong Kong '94" International Stamp Exhibition. Rays. Multicoloured.
669 40c. Type **86** 55 40
670 40c. Spotted eagle ray . . . 55 40
671 40c. Coachwhip stingray . . 55 40
672 40c. Black-spotted stingray 55 40

87 Crocodile's Head

1994. The Estuarine Crocodile. Multicoloured.
673 20c. Type **87** 40 30
674 20c. Hatchling and eggs . . . 40 30
675 20c. Crocodile swimming underwater 40 30
676 20c. Crocodile half-submerged 40 30

88 Red-footed Booby

1994. Sea Birds. Multicoloured.
677 50c. Type **88** . . . . 1·25 1·25
678 50c. Great frigate bird . . . 1·25 1·25
679 50c. Brown booby . . . . . 1·25 1·25
680 50c. Little pied cormorant . . 1·25 1·25

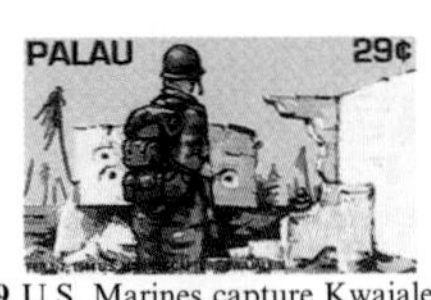

89 U.S. Marines capture Kwajalein

1994. Pacific Theatre in Second World War (4th issue). Multicoloured.
681 29c. Type **89** 40 30
682 29c. Aerial bombardment of Japanese airbase, Truk . . 40 30
683 29c. U.S.S. 284 "Tullibee" (submarine) (Operation Desecrate) 40 30
684 29c. Landing craft storming Saipan beach 40 30
685 29c. Shooting down Japanese Mitsubishi Zero-Sen bombers, Mariana Islands (Turkey Shoot) 40 30
686 29c. Liberated civilians, Guam 40 30
687 29c. U.S. troops taking Peleliu 40 30
688 29c. Securing Angaur 40 30
689 29c. General Douglas MacArthur 40 30
690 29c. U.S. Army memorial . . 40 30

90 Allied Warships

1994. 50th Anniv of D-day (Allied Landings in Normandy). Multicoloured.
691 50c. C-47 transport aircraft dropping paratroopers . . 65 45
692 50c. Type **90** 65 45
693 50c. Troops disembarking from landing craft 65 45
694 50c. Tanks coming ashore . . 65 45
695 50c. Sherman tank crossing minefield 65 45
696 50c. Aircraft attacking German positions 65 45
697 50c. Gliders dropping paratroops behind lines . . 65 45
698 50c. Pegasus Bridge 65 45
699 50c. Allied forces pushing inland 65 45
700 50c. Beach at end of 6 June 1944 . . . . 65 45

91 Baron Pierre de Coubertin (founder of modern games)

1994. Centenary of International Olympic Committee. Multicoloured.
701 **91** 29c. multicoloured 40 30

92 Top of "Saturn V" Rocket and Command and Lunar Modules joined

93 Sail-finned Goby

1994. 25th Anniv of First Manned Moon Landing. Multicoloured.
703 29c. Type **92** 50 40
704 29c. Lunar module preparing to land (side view) 50 40
705 29c. Lunar module leaving surface (top view) 50 40
706 29c. Command module (view of circular end) 50 40
707 29c. Earth viewed from Moon 50 40
708 29c. "Saturn V" third stage 50 40
709 29c. Neil Armstrong descending ladder to lunar surface 50 40
710 29c. Footprint in lunar surface 50 40
711 29c. Alan Shepard and lunar module on Moon 50 40
712 29c. Command module separating from service module 50 40
713 29c. "Saturn V" second stage (rocket inscr "USA USA") 50 40
714 29c. Rear view of "Apollo 17" astronaut at Splitrock Valley of Taurus-Littrow 50 40
715 29c. Lunar module reflected in visor of Edwin Aldrin 50 40
716 29c. James Irwin and David Scott raising flag on "Apollo 15" mission . . . 50 40
717 29c. Command module descending with parachutes deployed 50 40
718 29c. "Saturn V" lifting off from Kennedy Space Center 50 40
719 29c. "Apollo 17" astronaut Harrison Schmitt collecting lunar surface samples with shovel 50 40
720 29c. "Apollo 16" astronaut John Young and lunar rover vehicle 50 40
721 29c. "Apollo 12" astronaut Charles Conrad collecting samples with machine . . . 50 40
722 29c. Command module after splashdown 50 40
Nos. 703/22 were issued together, se-tenant, forming a composite design.

1994. "Philakorea 1994" International Stamp Exhibition, Seoul. Philatelic Fantasies. Designs showing named animal with various postal items. Multicoloured.
723 29c. Type **93** (postage) . . . 45 35
724 29c. Black-saddled ("Sharpnose") puffers . . . 45 35
725 29c. Lightning butterflyfish 45 35
726 29c. Clown anemonefish . . 45 35
727 29c. Parrotfish 45 35
728 29c. Narrow-banded batfish 45 35
729 29c. Clown triggerfish 45 35
730 29c. Twin-spotted wrasse . . 45 35
731 40c. Palau fruit bat 55 45
732 40c. Crocodile 55 45
733 40c. Dugong 55 45
734 40c. Banded sea snake . . . 55 45
735 40c. Bottle-nosed dolphin . . 55 45
736 40c. Hawksbill turtle 55 45
737 40c. Common octopus . . . 55 45
738 40c. Manta ray 55 45
739 50c. Palau fantail and chicks (air) . . . . 1·00 1·00
740 50c. Banded crake . . . . . 1·00 1·00
741 50c. Grey-rumped ("Island") swiftlets . . . . 1·00 1·00
742 50c. Micronesian kingfisher 1·00 1·00
743 50c. Red-footed booby . . . 1·00 1·00
744 50c. Great frigate bird . . . 1·00 1·00
745 50c. Palau scops owl . . . . 1·00 1·00
746 50c. Palau fruit dove . . . . 1·00 1·00

95 Micronesian Monument (Henrik Starcke), U.N. Headquarters

97 Tebruchel in Mother's Arms

96 Mickey and Minnie Mouse at Airport

1994. Attainment of Independence. Multicoloured.

748 29c. Type **95** 45 35
749 29c. Presidential seal 45 35
750 29c. Pres. Kuniwo Nakamura of Palau and Pres. William Clinton of United States shaking hands (56 × 41 mm) 45 35
751 29c. Palau and United States flags 45 35
752 29c. Score of "Belau Er Kid" (national anthem) 45 35

Nos. 748/52 were issued together, se-tenant, forming a composite design.

1994. Tourism. Walt Disney cartoon characters. Multicoloured.

753 29c. Type **96** 50 40
754 29c. Goofy on way to hotel 50 40
755 29c. Donald Duck on beach 50 40
756 29c. Minnie Mouse and Daisy Duck learning Ngloik (dance) 50 40
757 29c. Mickey and Minnie rafting to natural bridge 50 40
758 29c. Uncle Scrooge finding stone money in Babeldaob Jungle 50 40
759 29c. Goofy and napoleon wrasse after collision . . . 50 40
760 29c. Minnie visiting clam garden 50 40
761 29c. Grandma Duck weaving basket 50 40

1994. International Year of the Family. Illustrating story of Tebruchel. Multicoloured.

763 20c. Type **97** 25 15
764 20c. Tebruchel's father (kneeling on beach) 25 15
765 20c. Tebruchel as youth . . . 25 15
766 20c. Tebruchel's wife (standing on beach) 25 15
767 20c. Tebruchel with catch of fish 25 15
768 20c. Tebruchel's pregnant wife sitting in house . . . 25 15
769 20c. Tebruchel's aged mother in dilapidated house . . . 25 15
770 20c. Tebruchel's aged father (standing) 25 15
771 20c. Tebruchel holding first child 25 15
772 20c. Tebruchel's wife (sitting on beach mat) 25 15
773 20c. Tebruchel with aged mother 25 15
774 20c. Tebruchel's father (sitting cross-legged) and wife holding child 25 15

Nos. 763/74 were issued together, se-tenant, forming a composite design.

98 Wise Men and Cherubs

99 Bora Milutinovic (coach)

1994. Christmas. "O Little Town of Bethlehem" (carol). Multicoloured.

775 29c. Type **98** 45 35
776 29c. Angel, shepherds with sheep and cherub 45 35
777 29c. Angels and Madonna and Child 40 40
778 29c. Angels, Bethlehem and shepherd with sheep . . . 45 35
779 29c. Cherubs and Palau fruit doves 40 40

Nos. 775/9 were issued together, se-tenant, forming a composite design.

1994. World Cup Football Championship, U.S.A. Multicoloured.

780 29c. Type **99** 45 35
781 29c. Cle Kooiman 45 35
782 29c. Ernie Stewart 45 35
783 29c. Claudio Reyna 45 35
784 29c. Thomas Dooley 45 35
785 29c. Alexi Lalas 45 35
786 29c. Dominic Kinnear . . . 45 35
787 29c. Frank Klopas 45 35
788 29c. Paul Caligiuri 45 35
789 29c. Marcelo Balboa 45 35
790 29c. Cobi Jones 45 35
791 29c. U.S.A. flag and World Cup trophy 45 35
792 29c. Tony Meola 45 35
793 29c. John Doyle 45 35
794 29c. Eric Wynalda 45 35
795 29c. Roy Wegerle 45 35
796 29c. Fernando Clavijo . . . 45 35
797 29c. Hugo Perez 45 35
798 29c. John Harkes 45 35
799 29c. Mike Lapper 45 35
800 29c. Mike Sorber 45 35
801 29c. Brad Friedel 45 35
802 29c. Tab Ramos 45 35
803 29c. Joe-Max Moore 45 35
804 50c. Babeto (Brazil) 70 50
805 50c. Romario (Brazil) 70 50
806 50c. Franco Baresi (Italy) . . 70 50
807 50c. Roberto Baggio (Italy) 70 50
808 50c. Andoni Zubizarreta (Spain) 70 50
809 50c. Oleg Salenko (Russia) 70 50
810 50c. Gheorghe Hagi (Rumania) 70 50
811 50c. Dennis Bergkamp (Netherlands) 70 50
812 50c. Hristo Stoichkov (Bulgaria) 70 50
813 50c. Tomas Brolin (Sweden) 70 50
814 50c. Lothar Matthaus (Germany) 70 50
815 50c. Arrigo Sacchi (Italy coach), Carlos Alberto Parreira (Brazil coach), flags and World Cup trophy 70 50

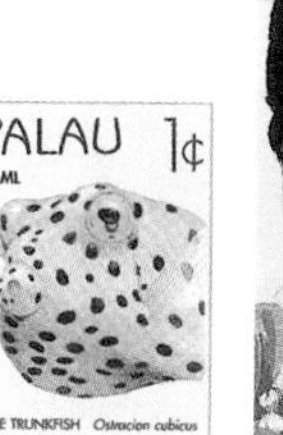

100 Yellow Boxfish ("Cube Trunkfish")

101 Presley

1995. Fishes. Multicoloured.

816 1c. Type **100** 10 10
817 2c. Lionfish 10 10
818 3c. Scarlet-finned ("Long-jawed") squirrelfish . . . 10 10
819 4c. Harlequin ("Longnose") filefish 10 10
820 5c. Ornate butterflyfish . . . 10 10
821 10c. Yellow seahorse 15 10
822 20c. Magenta dottyback (22 × 30 mm) 25 15
836 20c. Magenta dottyback (17½ × 21 mm) 25 15
823 32c. Reef lizardfish (22 × 30 mm) 40 30
837 32c. Reef lizardfish (17½ × 21 mm) 40 30
824 50c. Multibarred goatfish . . 65 45
825 55c. Barred blenny 70 50
826 $1 Fingerprint pufferfish . . 1·25 90
827 $2 Long-nosed hawkfish . . 2·50 1·75
828 $3 Mandarin fish . . . . . . 3·25 2·75
829 $5 Palette ("Blue") surgeonfish . . . . 6·50 4·75
830 $10 Coral hind (47 × 30 mm) 13·00 9·50

1995. 60th Birth Anniv of Elvis Presley (entertainer). Multicoloured.

838 32c. Type **101** 55 45
839 32c. Presley wearing white shirt and blue jacket . . . 55 45
840 32c. Presley with microphone and flower 55 45
841 32c. Presley wearing blue shirt and jumper 55 45
842 32c. Presley with rose 55 45
843 32c. Presley with brown hair wearing white shirt 55 45
844 32c. Presley wearing blue open-necked shirt 55 45
845 32c. Presley (in green shirt) singing 55 45
846 32c. Presley as boy (with fair hair) 55 45

102 Grey-rumped ("Palau") Swiftlets

1995. Air. Birds. Multicoloured.

847 50c. Type **102** . . . . 1·25 1·25
848 50c. Barn swallows . . . . . 1·25 1·25
849 50c. Jungle nightjar . . . . . 1·25 1·25
850 50c. White-breasted wood swallow . . . . 1·25 1·25

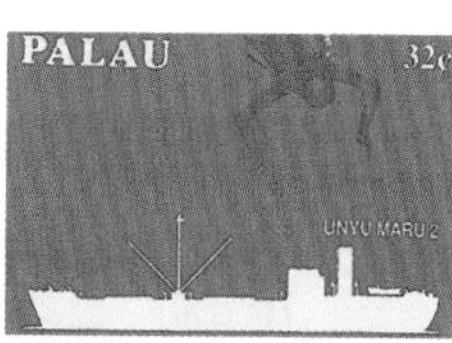

103 "Unyu Maru 2" (tanker)

1995. Japanese Fleet Sunk off Rock Islands (1944). Multicoloured.

851 32c. Type **103** 45 35
852 32c. "Wakatake" (destroyer) 45 35
853 32c. "Teshio Maru" (freighter) 45 35
854 32c. "Raizan Maru" (freighter) 45 35
855 32c. "Chuyo Maru" (freighter) 45 35
856 32c. "Shinsei Maru" (No. 18 freighter) 45 35
857 32c. "Urakami Maru" (freighter) 45 35
858 32c. "Ose Maru" (tanker) . . 45 35
859 32c. "Iro" (tanker) 45 35
860 32c. "Shosei Maru" (freighter) 45 35
861 32c. Patrol Boat 31 . . . . . 45 35
862 32c. "Kibi Maru" (freighter) 45 35
863 32c. "Amatsu Maru" (tanker) 45 35
864 32c. "Gozan Maru" (freighter) 45 35
865 32c. "Matuei Maru" (freighter) 45 35
866 32c. "Nagisan Maru" (freighter) 45 35
867 32c. "Akashi" (repair ship) 45 35
868 32c. "Kamikazi Maru" (freighter) 45 35

Nos. 851/68 were issued together, se-tenant, forming a composite design.

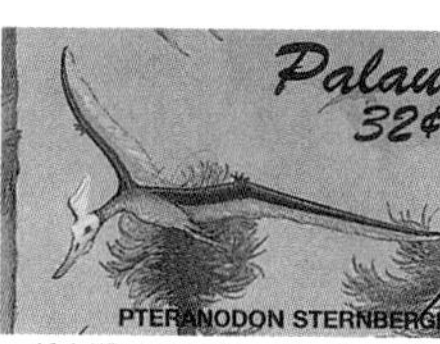

104 "Pteranodon sternbergi"

1995. 25th Anniv of Earth Day. Prehistoric Winged Animals. Multicoloured.

869 32c. Type **104** 45 35
870 32c. "Pteranodon ingens" . . 45 35
871 32c. Pterodactyls 45 35
872 32c. Dorygnathus 45 35
873 32c. Dimorphodon 45 35
874 32c. Nyctosaurus 45 35
875 32c. "Pterodactylus kochi" . . 45 35
876 32c. Ornithodesmus 45 35
877 32c. "Diatryma" sp. 65 65
878 32c. Archaeopteryx 65 65
879 32c. Campylognathoides . . 45 35
880 32c. Gallodactylus 45 35
881 32c. Batrachognathus 45 35
882 32c. Scaphognathus 45 35
883 32c. Peteinosaurus 45 35
884 32c. "Ichthyornis" sp. . . . 65 65
885 32c. Ctenochasma 45 35
886 32c. Rhamphorhynchus . . . 45 35

Nos. 869/86 were issued together, se-tenant, forming a composite design.

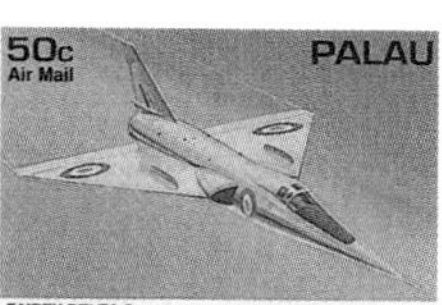

105 Fairey Delta 2

1995. Research and Experimental Jet-propelled Aircraft. Multicoloured.

887 50c. Type **105** 70 50
888 50c. B-70 Valkyrie 70 50
889 50c. Douglas X-3 Stiletto . . 70 50
890 50c. Northrop/Nasa HL-10 70 50
891 50c. Bell XS-1 . . . . 70 50
892 50c. Tupolev Tu-144 . . . . 70 50
893 50c. Bell X-1 . . . . 70 50
894 50c. Boulton Paul P.111 . . . 70 50
895 50c. EWR VJ 101C 70 50
896 50c. Handley Page HP-115 70 50
897 50c. Rolls Royce TMR "Flying Bedstead" 70 50
898 50c. North American X-15 70 50

106 Scuba Gear

1995. Submersibles. Multicoloured.

900 32c. Type **106** 45 35
901 32c. Cousteau midget submarine "Denise" . . . 45 35
902 32c. Jim suit 45 35
903 32c. Beaver IV 45 35
904 32c. "Ben Franklin" 45 35
905 32c. U.S.S. "Nautilus" (submarine) 45 35
906 32c. Deep Rover 45 35
907 32c. Beebe bathysphere . . . 45 35
908 32c. "Deep Star IV" 45 35
909 32c. U.S. Navy Deep Submergence Rescue Vehicle 45 35
910 32c. "Aluminaut" (aluminium submarine) 45 35
911 32c. "Nautile" 45 35
912 32c. "Cyana" 45 35
913 32c. French Navy (F.N.R.S.) bathyscaphe 45 35
914 32c. Woods Hole Oceanographic Institute's "Alvin" 45 35
915 32c. "Mir I" (research submarine) 45 35
916 32c. "Archimede" (bathyscaphe) 45 35
917 32c. "Trieste" (bathyscaphe) 45 35

Nos. 900/917 were issued together, se-tenant, forming a composite design.

107 Dolphins, Diver and Pufferfish

1995. "Singapore'95" International Stamp Exhibition. Marine Life. Multicoloured.

918 32c. Type **107** 45 35
919 32c. Turtle and diver 45 35
920 32c. Grouper, anemonefish and crab on sea-bed (emblem on right) 45 35
921 32c. Parrotfish, lionfish and angelfish (emblem on left) 45 35

108 Dove in Helmet (Peace)

1995. 50th Annivs of U.N.O. and F.A.O. Mult.

922 60c. Type **108** 85 65
923 60c. Ibedul Gibbons (Palau chief) in flame (human rights) 85 65
924 60c. Palau atlas in open book (education) 85 65
925 60c. Bananas in tractor (agriculture) 85 65

Nos. 922/5 were issued together, se-tenant, the centre of each block forming a composite design of the U.N. emblem.

109 Palau Fruit Doves

1995. 1st Anniv of Independence. Each showing Palau national flag. Multicoloured.

927 20c. Type **109** 30 20
928 20c. Rock Islands 30 20
929 20c. Map of Palau islands . . 30 20
930 20c. Orchid and hibiscus . . 30 20
931 32c. Raccoon butterflyfish, soldierfish and conch shell 45 35

110 "Preparing Tin-Fish" (William Draper)

1995. 50th Anniv of the End of Second World War. Multicoloured.

932 32c. Type **110** 45 35
933 32c. "Hellcat's Take-off into Palau's Rising Sun" (Draper) 45 35
934 32c. "Dauntless Dive Bombers over Malakal Harbor" (Draper) 45 35
935 32c. "Planes Return from Palau" (Draper) 45 35
936 32c. "Communion Before Battle" (Draper) 45 35
937 32c. "The Landing" (Draper) 45 35
938 32c. "First Task Ashore" (Draper) 45 35
939 32c. "Fire Fighters save Flak-torn Pilot" (Draper) 45 35
940 32c. "Young Marine Headed for Peleliu" (Tom Lea) 45 35
941 32c. "Peleliu" (Lea) 45 35
942 32c. "Last Rites" (Lea) 45 35
943 32c. "The Thousand Yard Stare" (Lea) 45 35
944 60c. "Admiral Chester W. Nimitz" (Albert Murray) (vert) 85 65
945 60c. "Admiral William F. Halsey" (Murray) (vert) 85 65
946 60c. "Admiral Raymond A. Spruance" (Murray) (vert) 85 65
947 60c. "Vice-Admiral Marc A. Mitscher" (Murray) (vert) 85 65
948 60c. "General Holland M. Smith" (Murray) (vert) 85 65

111 Angel with Animals

1995. Christmas. "We Three Kings of Orient Are" (carol). Multicoloured.

950 32c. Type **111** 45 35
951 32c. Two wise men 45 35
952 32c. Shepherd at crib 45 35
953 32c. Wise man and shepherd 45 35
954 32c. Children with goat 45 35

Nos. 950/4 were issued together, se-tenant, forming a composite design.

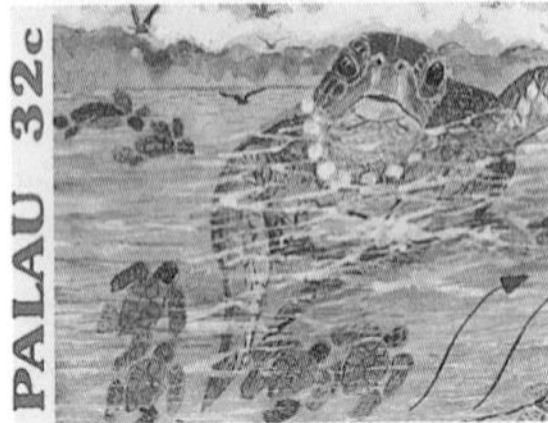

112 Mother and Young in Feeding Area

1995. Year of the Sea Turtle. Multicoloured.

955 32c. Type **112** 45 35
956 32c. Young adult females meeting males 45 35
957 32c. Sun, cockerel in tree and mating area 45 35
958 32c. Woman and hatchlings 45 35
959 32c. Couple and nesting area 45 35
960 32c. House and female swimming to lay eggs 45 35

Nos. 955/60 were issued together, se-tenant, forming a composite design of the turtle's life cycle.

113 Lennon

114 Rats leading Procession

1995. 15th Death Anniv of John Lennon (entertainer).

961 **113** 32c. multicoloured 45 35

1996. Chinese New Year. Year of the Rat. Multicoloured.

962 10c. Type **114** 20 10
963 10c. Three rats playing instruments 20 10
964 10c. Rats playing tuba and banging drum 20 10
965 10c. Family of rats outside house 20 10

Nos. 962/5 were issued together, se-tenant, forming a composite design of a procession.

115 Girls

1996. 50th Anniv of U.N.I.C.E.F. Each showing three children. Multicoloured.

967 32c. Type **115** 45 35
968 32c. Girl in centre wearing lei around neck 45 35
969 32c. Girl in centre wearing headscarf 45 35
970 32c. Boy in centre and girls holding bunches of grass 45 35

Nos. 967/70 were issued together, se-tenant, forming a composite design of the children around a globe and the U.N.I.C.E.F. emblem.

116 Basslet and Vermiculate Parrotfish ("P")

1996. Underwater Wonders. Illuminated letters spelling out PALAU. Multicoloured.

971 32c. Type **116** 50 40
972 32c. Yellow-striped cardinalfish ("A") 50 40
973 32c. Pair of atoll butterflyfish ("L") 50 40
974 32c. Starry moray and slate-pencil sea urchin ("A") 50 40
975 32c. Blue-streaked cleaner wrasse and coral hind ("Grouper") ("U") 50 40

117 Ferdinand Magellan and "Vitoria"

1996. "CAPEX'96" International Stamp Exhibition, Toronto, Canada. Circumnavigators. Multicoloured.

976 32c. Type **117** (postage) 50 40
977 32c. Charles Wilkes and U.S.S. "Vincennes" (sail frigate) 50 40
978 32c. Joshua Slocum and "Spray" (yacht) 50 40
979 32c. Ben Carlin and "Half-Safe" (amphibian) 50 40
980 32c. Edward Beach and U.S.S. "Triton" (submarine) 50 40
981 32c. Naomi James and "Express Crusader" (yacht) 50 40
982 32c. Sir Ranulf Fiennes and snow vehicle 50 40
983 32c. Rick Hansen and wheelchair 50 40
984 32c. Robin Knox-Johnson and "Enza New Zealand" (catamaran) 50 40
986 60c. Lowell Smith and Douglas world cruiser seaplanes (air) 85 60
987 60c. Ernst Lehmann and "Graf Zeppelin" (dirigible airship) 85 60
988 60c. Wiley Post and Lockheed Vega "Winnie Mae" 85 60
989 60c. Yuri Gagarin and "Vostok I" (spaceship) 85 60
990 60c. Jerrie Mock and Cessna 180 "Spirit of Columbus" 85 60
991 60c. H. Ross Perot jnr. and Bell LongRanger III helicopter "Spirit of Texas" 85 60
992 60c. Brooke Knapp and Gulfstream III "The American Dream" 85 60
993 60c. Jeana Yeager and Dick Rutan and "Voyager" 85 60
994 60c. Fred Lasby and Piper Commanche 85 60

118 Simba, Nala and Timon ("The Lion King")

1996. Disney Sweethearts. Multicoloured.

995 1c. Type **118** 10 10
996 2c. Georgette, Tito and Oliver ("Oliver & Company") 10 10
997 3c. Duchess, O'Malley and Marie ("The Aristocats") 10 10
998 4c. Bianca, Jake and Polly ("The Rescuers Down Under") 10 10
999 5c. Tod, Vixey and Copper ("The Fox and the Hound") 10 10
1000 6c. Thumper, Flower and their Sweethearts ("Bambi") 10 10
1001 60c. As No. 995 85 60
1002 60c. Bernard, Bianca and Mr. Chairman ("The Rescuers") 85 60
1003 60c. As No. 996 85 60
1004 60c. As No. 997 85 60
1005 60c. As No. 998 85 60
1006 60c. As No. 999 [illegible] [illegible]
1007 60c. Robin Hood, Maid Marian and Alan-a-Dale ("Robin Hood") 85 60
1008 60c. As No. 1000 85 60
1009 60c. Pongo, Perdita and the Puppies ("101 Dalmatians") 85 60

119 Hakeem Olajuwan (basketball)

1996. Centenary of Modern Olympic Games and Olympic Games, Atlanta. Multicoloured.

1011 32c. Type **119** 45 35
1012 32c. Pat McCormick (gymnastics) 45 35
1013 32c. Jim Thorpe (pentathlon and decathlon) 45 35
1014 32c. Jesse Owens (athletics) 45 35
1015 32c. Tatyana Gutsu (gymnastics) 45 35
1016 32c. Michael Jordan (basketball) 45 35
1017 32c. Fu Mingxia (diving) 45 35
1018 32c. Robert Zmelik (decathlon) 45 35
1019 32c. Ivan Pedroso (long jumping) 45 35
1020 32c. Nadia Comaneci (gymnastics) 45 35
1021 32c. Jackie Joyner-Kersee (long jumping) 45 35
1022 32c. Michael Johnson (running) 45 35
1023 32c. Kristin Otto (swimming) 45 35
1024 32c. Vitai Scherbo (gymnastics) 45 35
1025 32c. Johnny Weissmuller (swimming) 45 35
1026 32c. Babe Didrikson (track and field athlete) 45 35
1027 32c. Eddie Tolan (track athlete) 45 35
1028 32c. Krisztina Egerszegi (swimming) 45 35
1029 32c. Sawao Kato (gymnastics) 45 35
1030 32c. Aleksandr Popov (swimming) 45 35
1031 40c. Fanny Blankers-Koen (track and field athlete) (vert) 65 50
1032 40c. Bob Mathias (decathlon) (vert) 65 50
1033 60c. Torchbearer entering Wembley Stadium, 1948 65 50
1034 60c. Entrance to Olympia Stadium, Athens, and flags 65 50

Nos. 1011/30 were issued together, se-tenant, forming a composite design of the athletes and Olympic rings.

120 The Creation

1996. 3000th Anniv of Jerusalem. Illustrations by Guy Rowe from "In Our Image: Character Studies from the Old Testament". Mult.

1035 20c. Type **120** 30 20
1036 20c. Adam and Eve 30 20
1037 20c. Noah and his Wife 30 20
1038 20c. Abraham 30 20
1039 20c. Jacob's Blessing 30 20
1040 20c. Jacob becomes Israel 30 20
1041 20c. Joseph and his Brethren 30 20
1042 20c. Moses and Burning Bush 30 20
1043 20c. Moses and the Tablets 30 20
1044 20c. Balaam 30 20
1045 20c. Joshua 30 20
1046 20c. Gideon 30 20
1047 20c. Jephthah 30 20
1048 20c. Samson 30 20
1049 20c. Ruth and Naomi 30 20
1050 20c. Saul anointed 30 20
1051 20c. Saul denounced 30 20
1052 20c. David and Jonathan 30 20
1053 20c. David and Nathan 30 20
1054 20c. David mourns 30 20
1055 20c. Solomon praying 30 20
1056 20c. Solomon judging 30 20
1057 20c. Elijah 30 20
1058 20c. Elisha 30 20
1059 20c. Job 30 20
1060 20c. Isaiah 30 20
1061 20c. Jeremiah 30 20
1062 20c. Ezekiel 30 20
1063 20c. Nebuchadnezzar's Dream 30 20
1064 20c. Amos 30 20

121 Nankeen Night Heron

1996. Birds over Palau Lagoon. Multicoloured.

1065 50c. Eclectus parrot (female) ("Iakkotsiang") 70 55
1066 50c. Type **121** 70 55
1067 50c. Micronesian pigeon ("Belochel") 70 55
1068 50c. Eclectus parrot (male) ("Iakkotsiang") 70 55
1069 50c. White tern ("Sechosech") 70 55
1070 50c. Common noddy ("Mechadelbedaoch") 70 55
1071 50c. Nicobar pigeon ("Laib") 70 55
1072 50c. Chinese little bittern ("Cheloteachel") 70 55
1073 50c. Little pied cormorant ("Deroech") 70 55
1074 50c. Black-naped tern ("Kerkirs") 70 55
1075 50c. White-tailed tropic bird ("Dudek") 70 55
1076 50c. Sulphur-crested cockatoo ("Iakkotsiang") (white bird) 70 55
1077 50c. White-capped noddy ("Bedaoch") 70 55
1078 50c. Bridled tern ("Bedebedchakl") 70 55
1079 50c. Reef heron (grey) ("Sechou") 70 55
1080 50c. Grey-tailed tattler ("Kekereielderariik") 70 55
1081 50c. Reef heron (white) ("Sechou") 70 55
1082 50c. Audubon's shearwater ("Ochaieu") 70 55
1083 50c. Black-headed gull ("Oltirakladial") 70 55
1084 50c. Ruddy turnstone ("Omechederiibabad") 70 55

Nos. 1065/84 were issued together, se-tenant, forming a composite design.

122 Lockheed U-2

1996. Spy Planes. Multicoloured.

1085 40c. Type **122** 55 40
1086 40c. General Dynamics EF-111A 55 40
1087 40c. Lockheed YF-12A 55 40
1088 40c. Lockheed SR-71 55 40
1089 40c. Teledyne Ryan Tier II Plus 55 40

1090 40c. Lockheed XST 55 40
1091 40c. Lockheed ER-2 . . . . 55 40
1092 40c. Lockheed F-117A Nighthawk 55 40
1093 40c. Lockheed EC-130E . . 55 40
1094 40c. Ryan Firebee 55 40
1095 40c. Lockheed Martin/ Boeing Darkstar 55 40
1096 40c. Boeing E-3A Sentry . . 55 40

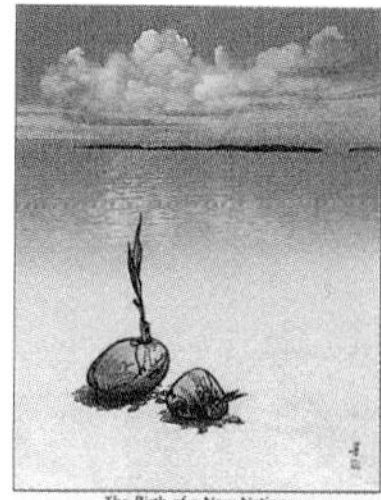

123 "The Birth of a New Nation"

1996. 2nd Anniv of Independence. Illustrations from "Kirie" by Koh Sekiguchi. Multicoloured.
1098 20c. Type **123** 30 20
1099 20c. "In the Blue Shade of Trees" 30 20

124 Pandanus

1996. Christmas. "O Tannenbaum" (carol). Decorated Trees. Multicoloured.
1100 32c. Type **124** 45 35
1101 32c. Mangrove 45 35
1102 32c. Norfolk Island pine . . 45 35
1103 32c. Papaya 45 35
1104 32c. Casuarina 45 35
Nos. 1100/4 were issued together, se-tenant, forming a composite design.

125 "Viking I" in Orbit (½-size illustration)

1996. Space Missions to Mars. Multicoloured.
1105 32c. Type **125** 45 35
1106 32c. "Viking I" emblem (top half) 45 35
1107 32c. "Mars Lander" firing de-orbit engines 45 35
1108 32c. "Viking I" emblem (bottom half) 45 35
1109 32c. Phobos (Martian moon) 45 35
1110 32c. "Mars Lander" entering Martian atmosphere 45 35
1111 32c. "Mariner 9" (first mission, 1971) 45 35
1112 32c. Parachute opens for landing and heat shield jettisons 45 35
1113 32c. Projected U.S./Russian manned spacecraft, 21st century (top half) 45 35
1114 32c. "Lander" descent engines firing 45 35
1115 32c. Projected U.S./Russian spacecraft (bottom half) 45 35
1116 32c. "Viking I Lander" on Martian surface, 1976 . . 45 35
Nos. 1105/16 were issued together, se-tenant, forming several composite designs.

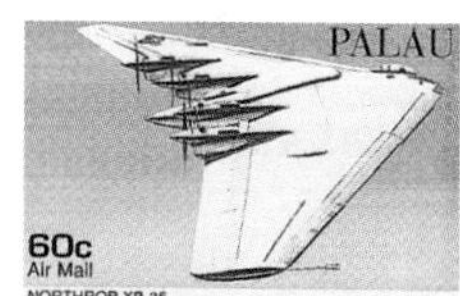

126 Northrop XB-35 Bomber

1996. Oddities of the Air. Aircraft Designs. Multicoloured.
1118 60c. Type **126** 85 65
1119 60c. Leduc O.21 . . . . . 85 65
1120 60c. Convair Model 118 flying car 85 65
1121 60c. Blohm und Voss BV 141 . . . . 85 65
1122 60c. Vought V-173 . . . . 85 65
1123 60c. McDonnell XF-85 Goblin 85 65
1124 60c. North American F-82B Twin Mustang fighter . . 85 65
1125 60c. Lockheed XFV-1 vertical take-off fighter . . 85 65
1126 60c. Northrop XP-79B . . . 85 65
1127 60c. Saunders Roe SR/A1 flying boat fighter 85 65
1128 60c. "Caspian Sea Monster" hovercraft 85 65
1129 60c. Grumman X-29 demonstrator 85 65

129 Pemphis

130 "Apollo 15" Command Module splashing-down

1997. "Hong Kong '97" Stamp Exhibition. Flowers. Multicoloured.
1133 1c. Type **129** 10 10
1134 2c. Sea lettuce 10 10
1135 3c. Tropical almond 10 10
1136 4c. Guettarda 10 10
1137 5c. Pacific coral bean . . . 10 10
1138 32c. Black mangrove . . . 45 35
1139 32c. Cordia 45 35
1140 32c. Lantern tree 45 35
1141 32c. Palau rock-island flower 45 35
1142 50c. Fish-poison tree 65 50
1143 50c. Indian mulberry . . . 65 50
1144 50c. Pacific poison-apple . . 65 50
1145 50c. "Ailanthus" sp. 65 50
1146 $3 Sea hibiscus (73 × 48 mm) 3·75 2·75

1997. Bicentenary of the Parachute. Multicoloured.
1147 32c. Type **130** (postage) . . 45 35
1148 32c. Skydiving team in formation (40 × 23 mm) 45 35
1149 32c. Cargo drop from airplane 45 35
1150 32c. Parasailing (40 × 23 mm) 45 35
1151 32c. Parachutist falling to earth 45 35
1152 32c. Parachute demonstration team (40 × 23 mm) 45 35
1153 32c. Parachutist falling into sea 45 35
1154 32c. Drag-racing car (40 × 23mm) 45 35
1156 60c. Parachuting demonstration (air) . . . 85 65
1157 60c. "The Blue Flame" (world land-speed record attempt) (40 × 23 mm) . . 85 65
1158 60c. Atmospheric Re-entry Demonstrator (capsule with three canopies) . . . 85 65
1159 60c. Spies parachuting behind enemy lines during Second World War (40 × 23 mm) 85 65
1160 60c. Andre Jacques Garnerin's first successful parachute descent (from balloon), 1797 . . . . . 85 65
1161 60c. C-130E airplane demonstrating Low Altitude Parachute Extraction System (airplane and capsule with four canopies) (40 × 23 mm) 85 65
1162 60c. U.S. Army parachutist flying parafoil 85 65
1163 60c. Parachute (one canopy) slowing high performance airplane (40 × 23mm) . . 85 65

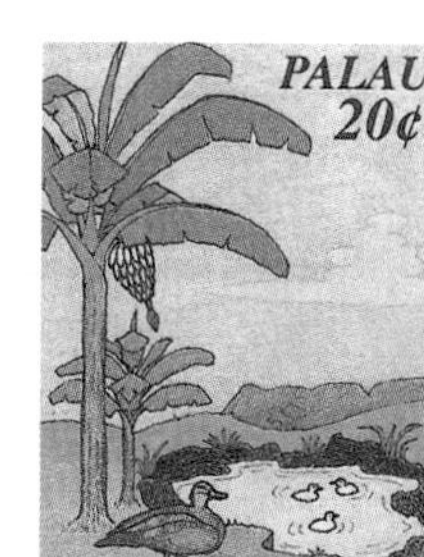

131 Pacific Black Duck beneath Banana Tree

1997. Palau's Avian Environment. Multicoloured.
1164 20c. Type **131** 30 20
1165 20c. Pair of red junglefowl beneath calamondin (clustered orange fruits) 30 20
1166 20c. Nicobar pigeon in parinari tree (single orange fruits) 30 20
1167 20c. Cardinal honeyeater in wax apple tree (clustered brown fruits) 30 20
1168 20c. Purple swamphen and Chinese little bittern amid taro plants 30 20

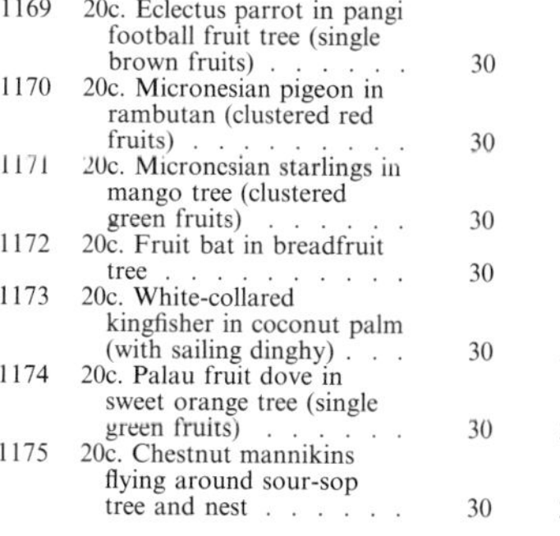
1169 20c. Eclectus parrot in pangi football fruit tree (single brown fruits) 30 20
1170 20c. Micronesian pigeon in rambutan (clustered red fruits) 30 20
1171 20c. Micronesian starlings in mango tree (clustered green fruits) 30 20
1172 20c. Fruit bat in breadfruit tree 30 20
1173 20c. White-collared kingfisher in coconut palm (with sailing dinghy) . . . 30 20
1174 20c. Palau fruit dove in sweet orange tree (single green fruits) 30 20
1175 20c. Chestnut mannikins flying around sour-sop tree and nest 30 20

132 Himeji Temple, Japan

1997. 50th Anniv of U.N.E.S.C.O. Multicoloured.
1176 32c. Type **132** 45 35
1177 32c. Kyoto, Japan 45 35
1178 32c. Pagoda roofs, Himeji Temple (white inscr at left) 45 35
1179 32c. Garden, Himeji Temple 45 35
1180 32c. Path and doorway, Himeji Temple 45 35
1181 32c. Pagoda roofs, Himeji Temple (white inscr at right) 45 35
1182 32c. Roof ridge and decoration, Himeji Temple 45 35
1183 32c. Inscribed post and veranda, Himeji Temple 45 35
1184 60c. Ceiling, Augustusburg Castle, Germany (horiz) 85 65
1185 60c. Augustusburg Castle (horiz) 85 65
1186 60c. Falkenlust Castle, Germany (horiz) 85 65
1187 60c. Roman ruins, Trier, Germany (horiz) 85 65
1188 60c. House, Trier (horiz) . . 85 65

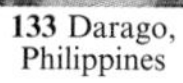
133 Darago, Philippines

134 "Swallows and Peach Blossoms under a Full Moon"

1997. "Pacific 97" International Stamp Exhibition, San Francisco. Volcano Goddesses of the Pacific. Multicoloured.
1190 32c. Type **133** 45 35
1191 32c. Fuji, Japan 45 35
1192 32c. Pele, Hawaii 45 35
1193 32c. Pare and Hutu, Polynesia 45 35
1194 32c. Dzalarhons, Haida tribe, North America . . 45 35
1195 32c. Chuginadak, Aleutian Islands, Alaska 45 35

1997. Birth Bicentenary of Ando Hiroshige (Japanese painter). Multicoloured.
1196 32c. Type **134** 55 45
1197 32c. "Parrot on a Flowering Branch" 55 45
1198 32c. "Crane and Rising Sun" 55 45
1199 32c. "Cock, Unbrella and Morning Glories" 55 45
1200 32c. "Titmouse hanging Head Downward on a Camellia Branch" 55 45

135 Bai (community building)

1997. 3rd Anniv of Independence.
1202 **135** 32c. multicoloured . . . 45 35

136 "Albatross" (U.S.A.)

1997. Oceanic Research. Research Vessels. Multicoloured.
1203 32c. Type **136** 45 35
1204 32c. "Mabahiss" (Egypt) . . 45 35
1205 32c. "Atlantis II" (U.S.A.) 45 35
1206 32c. Hans Hass's "Xarifa" (schooner) 45 35
1207 32c. "Meteor" (Germany) 45 35
1208 32c. "Egabras III" (U.S.A.) 45 35
1209 32c. "Discoverer" (U.S.A.) 45 35
1210 32c. "Kaiyo" (Japan) . . . 45 35
1211 32c. "Ocean Defender" (Great Britain) 45 35

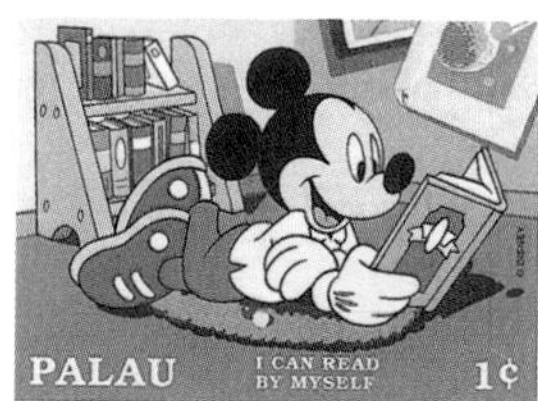

137 "I Can Read by Myself"

1997. Literacy Campaign. Walt Disney cartoon characters. Multicoloured.
1213 1c. Type **137** 10 10
1214 2c. "Start Them Young" . . 10 10
1215 3c. "Share your Knowledge" 10 10
1216 4c. "The insatiable Reader" 10 10
1217 5c. "Reading is the ultimate Luxury" 10 10
1218 10c. "Real Men read" . . . 10 10
1219 32c. "Exercise your Right to Read" 45 35
1220 32c. As No. 1217 . . . . . 45 35
1221 32c. As No. 1215 . . . . . 45 35
1222 32c. As No. 1214 . . . . . 45 35
1223 32c. "Reading is fundamental" 45 35
1224 32c. As No. 1216 . . . . . 45 35
1225 32c. "Reading Time is Anytime" 45 35
1226 32c. As No. 1218 . . . . . 45 35
1227 32c. Type **137** 45 35

138 Boy and Girl

139 Diana, Princess of Wales

1997. Christmas. "Some Children See Him" (carol). Multicoloured.
1229 32c. Type **138** 45 35
1230 32c. Asian boy and white girl 45 35
1231 32c. Madonna and Child behind boy and girl . . . 45 35
1232 32c. White girl and Oriental children 45 35
1233 32c. Asian boy and Palauan girl 45 35
Nos. 1229/33 were issued together, se-tenant, forming a composite design.

1997. Diana, Princess of Wales Commemoration.
1234 **139** 60c. multicoloured . . . 85 65

141 Nucleus of Galaxy M100

1998. Hubble Space Telescope. Multicoloured.

1236 32c. Type **141** 45 35
1237 32c. Top of Hubble telescope 45 35
1238 32c. Astronaut on robot arm 45 35
1239 32c. Astronaut fixing new camera to telescope . . . 45 35
1240 32c. Astronaut in cargo space of shuttle "Endeavour" 45 35
1241 32c. Hubble released after repair 45 35

142 Mother Teresa

1998. Mother Teresa (founder of Missionaries of Charity) Commemoration. Portraits of Mother Teresa. Multicoloured.

1243 60c. Type **142** 85 65
1244 60c. Facing right 85 65
1245 60c. Wearing cross 85 65
1246 60c. Wearing cardigan . . . 85 65

143 Ladybird Remotely Operated Vehicle, Japan

1998. International Year of the Ocean. Deep-sea Robots. Multicoloured.

1247 32c. Type **143** 45 35
1248 32c. Slocum Glider 45 35
1249 32c. "Hornet" 45 35
1250 32c. "Scorpio" 45 35
1251 32c. "Odyssey" Autonomous Underwater Vehicle 45 35
1252 32c. Jamstec Survey System launcher, Japan 45 35
1253 32c. "Scarab II" (servicer of undersea telephone cables) 45 35
1254 32c. U.S. Navy torpedo finder 45 35
1255 32c. Jamstec Survey System vehicle, Japan 45 35
1256 32c. Cetus tether for undersea cables 45 35
1257 32c. Deep-sea remotely operated vehicle 45 35
1258 32c. Abe (autonomous benthic explorer) 45 35
1259 32c. OBSS 45 35
1260 32c. Remote controlled vehicle 225G "Swimming Eyeball" (for inspection of undersea oil rigs) 45 35
1261 32c. Japanese Underwater Remotely Operated Vehicle 45 35
1262 32c. Benthos remotely piloted vehicle 45 35
1263 32c. Curv III (cable-controlled underwater research vehicle) 45 35
1264 32c. "Smartie", Great Britain 45 35

1998. "Israel 98" International Stamp Exhibition, Tel Aviv. Nos. 1035/64 optd with emblem.

1266 20c. multicoloured 35 20
1267 20c. multicoloured 35 20
1268 20c. multicoloured 35 20
1269 20c. multicoloured 35 20
1270 20c. multicoloured 35 20
1271 20c. multicoloured 35 20
1272 20c. multicoloured 35 20
1273 20c. multicoloured 35 20
1274 20c. multicoloured 35 20
1275 20c. multicoloured 35 20
1276 20c. multicoloured 35 20
1277 20c. multicoloured 35 20
1278 20c. multicoloured 35 20
1279 20c. multicoloured 35 20
1280 20c. multicoloured 35 20
1281 20c. multicoloured 35 20
1282 20c. multicoloured 35 20
1283 20c. multicoloured 35 20
1284 20c. multicoloured 35 20
1285 20c. multicoloured 35 20
1286 20c. multicoloured 35 20
1287 20c. multicoloured 35 20
1288 20c. multicoloured 35 20
1289 20c. multicoloured 35 20
1290 20c. multicoloured 35 20
1291 20c. multicoloured 35 20
1292 20c. multicoloured 35 20
1293 20c. multicoloured 35 20
1294 20c. multicoloured 35 20
1295 20c. multicoloured 35 20

145 Hut

146 Footballer

1998. The Legend of Orachel. Multicoloured.

1296 40c. Type **145** 55 45
1297 40c. Outrigger canoes moored by hut 55 45
1298 40c. Hut and man in canoe 55 45
1299 40c. Bird in tree 55 45
1300 40c. Front half of three-man canoe 55 45
1301 40c. Rear half of canoe and head of snake 55 45
1302 40c. Crocodile, fishes and coral 55 45
1303 40c. Shark and fishes . . . 55 45
1304 40c. Turtle, jellyfish and body of snake 55 45
1305 40c. Underwater bai (community building) . . 55 45
1306 40c. Orachel swimming underwater and fishes . . 55 45
1307 40c. Coral, fishes and seaweed 55 45

1998. World Cup Football Championship, France. Multicoloured.

1308 50c. Type **146** 70 55
1309 50c. Player in blue and white striped shirt 70 55
1310 50c. Player in green shirt and white shorts 70 55
1311 50c. Player in white shirt and blue shorts 70 55
1312 50c. Player in green shirt and black shorts 70 55
1313 50c. Player in red short-sleeved shirt 70 55
1314 50c. Player in yellow shirt and blue shorts 70 55
1315 50c. Player in red long-sleeved shirt 70 55

147 Scuba Fishing

1998. 4th Micronesian Islands Games, Palau. Multicoloured.

1317 32c. Type **147** 45 35
1318 32c. Spear throwing 45 35
1319 32c. Swimming 45 35
1320 32c. Coconut throwing . . . 45 35
1321 32c. Games emblem 45 35
1322 32c. Coconut tree climbimg 45 35
1323 32c. Canoe racing 45 35
1324 32c. Coconut husking . . . 45 35
1325 32c. Diving 45 35

148 Rudolph and other Reindeer

1998. Christmas. "Rudolph the Red Nosed Reindeer" (carol). Multicoloured.

1326 32c. Type **148** 45 35
1327 32c. Two reindeer and girl in yellow dress 45 35
1328 32c. Two reindeer, boy and girl 45 35
1329 32c. Two reindeer, girl in long pink dress and star 45 35
1330 32c. Father Christmas and sleigh 45 35

Nos. 1326/30 were issued together, se-tenant, forming a composite design.

149 Princess Dot (ant)

1998. "A Bug's Life" (computer animated film). Multicoloured.

1331 20c. Type **149** 30 20
1332 20c. Heimlich (caterpillar), Francis (ladybird) and Slim (stick insect) 30 20
1333 20c. Hopper (grasshopper) 30 20
1334 20c. Princess Atta (ant) . . 30 20
1335 32c. Princess Atta and Flick (ant) in boat 45 35
1336 32c. Princess Atta and Flick sitting on heart 45 35
1337 32c. Flick with Princess Atta sitting on leaf 45 35
1338 32c. Flick handing Princess Atta a flower 45 35
1339 50c. Butterfly, Heimlich, Francis and other bugs (horiz) 70 55
1340 50c. Slim, Francis and Heimlich (horiz) 70 55
1341 50c. Manny (praying mantis) (horiz) 70 55
1342 50c. Francis (horiz) 70 55
1343 60c. Slim and Flick juggling 85 65
1344 60c. Francis on cycle, Heimlich and Slim . . . 85 65
1345 60c. Manny hynotizing Flick 85 65
1346 60c. Manny, Rosie (spider) and other bugs 85 65

150 Group Photograph of Astronauts, 1962

1999. John Glenn's Return to Space. Multicoloured.

1348 60c. Type **150** 75 55
1349 60c. Glenn in space helmet (looking straight ahead) 75 55
1350 60c. Group photograph of five astronauts 75 55
1351 60c. Glenn in space helmet (head turned to left) . . . 75 55
1352 60c. Glenn in civilian suit 75 55
1353 60c. Glenn in space helmet (eyes looking right) . . . 75 55
1354 60c. Glenn with Pres. John Kennedy 75 55
1355 60c. Glenn in space suit (bare-headed) ("John Glenn, 1962") 75 55
1356 60c. Glenn (head raised) . .
1357 60c. "Discovery" (space shuttle) on launch pad . . 75 55
1358 60c. Glenn and two fellow astronauts with three NASA employees 75 55
1359 60c. Glenn (wearing glasses and looking straight ahead) 75 55
1360 60c. "Discovery" in hangar 75 55
1361 60c. Glenn in space suit (bare-headed) ("John Glenn") 75 55
1362 60c. Glenn (wearing glasses and looking down) . . . 75 55
1363 60c. Glenn in space suit and inner helmet 75 55

151 Rachel Carson (naturalist)

1999. Environmental Heroes of the 20th Century. Multicoloured.

1365 33c. Type **151** 40 30
1366 33c. Ding Darling (President of U.S. National Wildlife Federation, 1936) 40 30
1367 33c. David Brower 40 30
1368 33c. Jacques Cousteau (oceanologist) 40 30
1369 33c. Roger Tory Peterson (ornithologist) 40 30
1370 33c. Prince Philip, Duke of Edinburgh (President of World Wide Fund for Nature) 40 30
1371 33c. Joseph Wood Krutch 40 30
1372 33c. Aldo Leopold 40 30
1373 33c. Dian Fossey (zoologist) (wrongly inscr "Diane") 40 30
1374 33c. Al Gore 40 30
1375 33c. Sir David Attenborough (naturalist and broadcaster) 40 30
1376 33c. Paul MacCready (aeronautical engineer) (wrongly inscr "McCready") 40 30
1377 33c. Sting 40 30
1378 33c. Paul Winter 40 30
1379 33c. Ian MacHarg 40 30
1380 33c. Denis Hayes 40 30

152 "Soyuz" Spacecraft

153 Haruo Remeliik

1999. "Mir" Space Station. Multicoloured.

1381 33c. Type **152** 40 30
1382 33c. "Specktr" science module 40 30
1383 33c. Rear of space shuttle 40 30
1384 33c. "Kuant 2" scientific and air lock module . . . 40 30
1385 33c. "Kristall" technological module 40 30
1386 33c. Front of "Atlantis" (space shuttle) and docking module 40 30

1999. Multicoloured.

1388 1c. Type **153** 10 10
1389 2c. Lazarus Salii 10 10
1390 20c. Charlie Gibbons . . . 25 20
1391 22c. Admiral Raymond Spruance 30 25
1392 33c. Pres. Kuniwo Nakamura 40 30
1393 50c. Admiral William Halsey 65 50
1394 55c. Colonel Lewis Puller 70 55
1395 60c. Franklin Roosevelt (U.S. President, 1933–45) 75 55
1396 77c. Harry Truman (U.S. President, 1945–53) . . . 95 70
1400 $3.20 Jimmy Carter (U.S. President, 1977–81) . . . 4·00 3·00

154 Leatherback Turtle

1999. Endangered Reptiles and Amphibians. Multicoloured.

1405 33c. Type **154** 40 30
1406 33c. Kemp's Ridley turtle 40 30
1407 33c. Green turtles 40 30
1408 33c. Marine iguana 40 30
1409 33c. Table Mountain ghost frog 40 30
1410 33c. Spiny turtle 40 30
1411 33c. Hewitt's ghost frog . . 40 30
1412 33c. Geometric tortoise . . 40 30
1413 33c. Limestone salamander 40 30
1414 33c. Desert rain frog 40 30
1415 33c. Cape plantanna 40 30
1416 33c. Long-toed tree frog . . 40 30

155 Caroline Islands 1901 5 and 20pf. Stamps and Golsdorf Steam Railway Locomotive

1999. "iBRA '99" International Stamp Exhibition, Nuremberg, Germany. Multicoloured.

1418 55c. Type **155** 70 55
1419 55c. Caroline Islands 1901 5m. yacht stamp and carriage of Leipzig–Dresden Railway 70 55

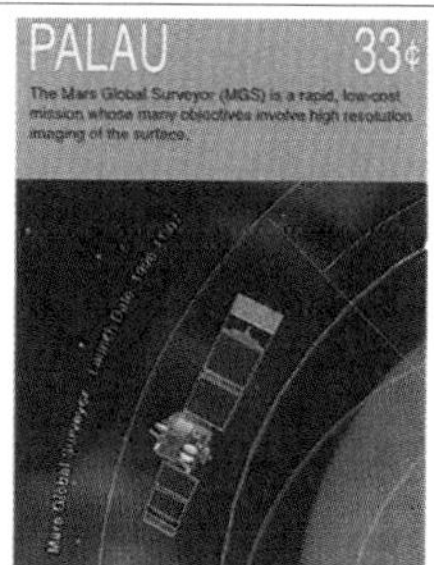

156 "Mars Global Surveyor" in Orbit

1999. Space Missions to Mars. Multicoloured.

1421 33c. Type **156** 40 30
1422 33c. "Mars Climate" Orbiter 40 30
1423 33c. "Mars Polar" Lander 40 30
1424 33c. "Deep Space 2" 40 30
1425 33c. "Mars Surveyor 2001" Orbiter 40 30
1426 33c. "Mars Surveyor 2001" Lander 40 30

Nos. 1421/6 were issued together, se-tenant, forming a composite design.

157 "Banza natida"

1999. Earth Day. Pacific Insects. Multicoloured.

1428 33c. Type **157** 40 30
1429 33c. "Drosophila heteroneura" (fruit-fly) . . 40 30
1430 33c. "Nesomicromus lagus" 40 30
1431 33c. "Megalagrian leptodemus" 40 30
1432 33c. "Pseudopsectra cookeorum" 40 30
1433 33c. "Ampheida neocaledonia" 40 30
1434 33c. "Pseudopsectra swezeyi" 40 30
1435 33c. "Deinacrida heteracantha" 40 30
1436 33c. Beech forest butterfly 40 30
1437 33c. Hercules moth 40 30
1438 33c. Striped sphinx moth . . 40 30
1439 33c. Tussock butterfly . . . 40 30
1440 33c. Weevil 40 30
1441 33c. Bush cricket 40 30
1442 33c. Longhorn beetle . . . 40 30
1443 33c. "Abathrus bicolor" . . 40 30
1444 33c. "Stylogymnusa subantartica" 40 30
1445 33c. Moth butterfly 40 30
1446 33c. "Paraconosoma naviculare" 40 30
1447 33c. Cairn's birdwing ("Ornithoptera priamus") 40 30

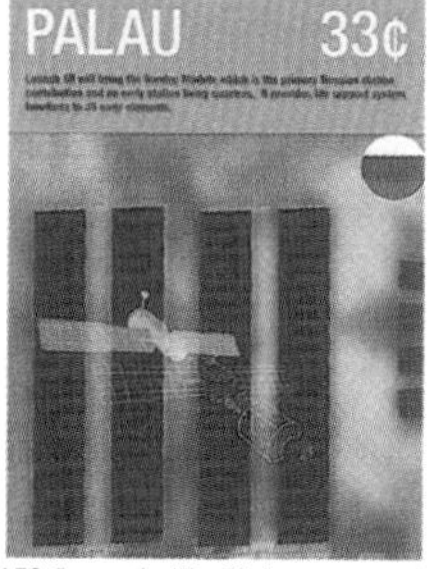

158 Launch 1R (living quarters)

1999. International Space Station, 1998–2004. Multicoloured.

1448 33c. Type **158** 40 30
1449 33c. Launch 14A (final solar arrays) 40 30
1450 33c. Launch 8A (mechanical arm) 40 30
1451 33c. Launch 1J (Japanese experiment module) . . . 40 30
1452 33c. Launch 1E (Colombus Orbital Facility laboratory) 40 30
1453 33c. Launch 16A (habitation module) 40 30

159 William Gibson

161 Queen Mother and Attendants

160 "Women Divers"

1999. The Information Age: Visionaries in the Twentieth Century. Multicoloured.

1455 33c. Type **159** 40 30
1456 33c. Danny Hillis 40 30
1457 33c. Steve Wozntak 40 30
1458 33c. Steve Jobs 40 30
1459 33c. Nolan Bushnell 40 30
1460 33c. John Warnock 40 30
1461 33c. Ken Thompson 40 30
1462 33c. Al Shugart 40 30
1463 33c. Rand and Robyn Miller 40 30
1464 33c. Nicolas Negroponte . . 40 30
1465 33c. Bill Gates 40 30
1466 33c. Arthur C. Clarke . . . 40 30
1467 33c. Marshall McLuhan . . 40 30
1468 33c. Thomas Watson Jr . . 40 30
1469 33c. Gordon Moore 40 30
1470 33c. James Gosling 40 30
1471 33c. Sabeer Bhatia and Jack Smith 40 30
1472 33c. Esther Dyson 40 30
1473 33c. Jerry Young and David Filo 40 30
1474 33c. Jeff Bezos 40 30
1475 33c. Bob Kahn 40 30
1476 33c. Jaron Lanier 40 30
1477 33c. Andy Grove 40 30
1478 33c. Jim Clark 40 30
1479 33c. Bob Metcalfe 40 30

1999. 150th Death Anniv of Katsushika Hokusai (Japanese artist). Multicoloured.

1480 33c. Type **160** 40 30
1481 33c. "Bull and Parasol" . . 40 30
1482 33c. Drawing of bare-breasted woman 40 30
1483 33c. Drawing of fully-clothed woman (sitting) 40 30
1484 33c. "Japanese Spaniel" . . 40 30
1485 33c. "Porter in Landscape" 40 30
1486 33c. "Bacchanalian Revelry" (musician in bottom right corner) 40 30
1487 33c. "Bacchanalian Revelry" (different) 40 30
1488 33c. Drawing of woman (crouching) 40 30
1489 33c. Drawing of woman (reclining on floor) . . . 40 30
1490 33c. "Ox-herd" (ox) 40 30
1491 33c. "Ox-herd" (man on bridge) 40 30

1999. "Queen Elizabeth the Queen Mother's Century".

1493 **161** 60c. black and gold . . . 75 55
1494 – 60c. black and gold . . . 75 55
1495 – 60c. multicoloured . . . 75 55
1496 – 60c. multicoloured . . . 75 55

DESIGNS: No. 1494, Queen Mother with corgi; 1495, Queen Mother in pink coat and hat; 1496, Queen Mother in yellow evening dress and tiara.

162 Launch of Rocket

1999. 30th Anniv of First Manned Moon Landing. Multicoloured.

1498 33c. Type **162** 40 30
1499 33c. Spacecraft above Earth and Moon's surface . . . 40 30
1500 33c. Astronaut descending ladder 40 30
1501 33c. Distant view of rocket launch 40 30
1502 33c. Astronaut planting flag on Moon 40 30
1503 33c. "Apollo 11" crew members 40 30

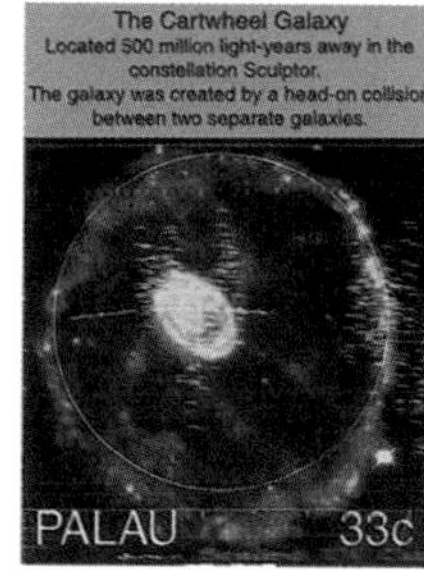

163 Cartwheel Galaxy

1999. Images from Space: Hubble Telescope. Multicoloured.

1505 33c. Type **163** 40 30
1506 33c. Stingray Nebula . . . 40 30
1507 33c. Planetary Nebula NGC 3918 . . . . 40 30
1508 33c. Cat's Eye Nebula . . . 40 30
1509 33c. Galaxy NGC 7742 . . 40 30
1510 33c. Eight-burst Nebula . . 40 30

164 Calves and Chickens

165 "Keep Safe"

1999. Christmas. "Puer Nobis" (carol). Mult.

1512 20c. Type **164** 25 20
1513 20c. Donkey, geese and rabbit 25 20
1514 20c. Child Jesus, cats and lambs 25 20
1515 20c. Geese, goat and sheep 25 20
1516 20c. Donkey and cockerel 25 20

Nos. 1512/16 were issued together, se-tenant, forming a composite design.

1999. "How to Love Your Dog". Multicoloured.

1517 33c. Type **165** 40 30
1518 33c. Girl with puppies (Show affection) 40 30
1519 33c. Dog asleep (A place of one's own) 40 30
1520 33c. Girl with Scottish terrier (Communicate) . . 40 30
1521 33c. Dog eating (Good food) 40 30
1522 33c. Vet examining dog (Annual check-up) 40 30
1523 33c. Girl with prone dog (Teach rules) 40 30
1524 33c. Dog with disc (Exercise and play) 40 30
1525 33c. Dog with basket (Let him help) 40 30
1526 33c. Dog with heart on collar (Unconditional love) 40 30

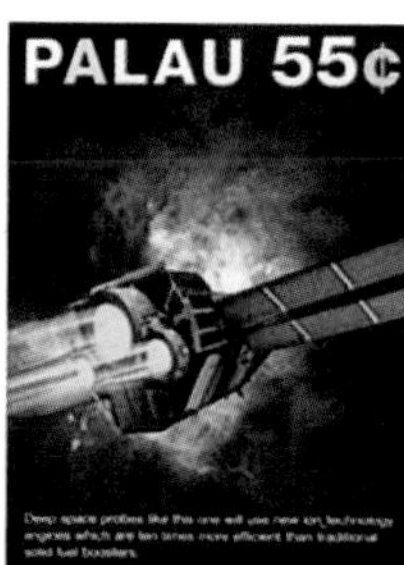

166 Deep Space Probe

2000. Projected Space Probes. Multicoloured.

1528 55c. Type **166** 80 50
1529 55c. Piggy back probe . . . 80 50
1530 55c. Deep space telescope probe 80 50
1531 55c. Space probe on course to rendezvous with comet 80 50
1532 55c. Yellow space probe orbiting planet 80 50
1533 55c. Deep space probe with advanced onboard artificial intelligence . . . 80 50

167 Native Brazilian Indians, 1800

168 Lech Walesa and Shipyard Workers

2000. New Millennium (1st series). The Nineteenth Century 1800–1850. Multicoloured.

1535 20c. Type **167** 30 20
1536 20c. Broken manacles (Haiti slave revolt, 1800) 30 20
1537 20c. Napolcon I (assumption of title of Emperor of France, 1804) 30 20
1538 20c. Shaka (Zulu leader) . . 30 20
1539 20c. Monster (publication of *Frankenstein* (novel) by Mary Shelley, 1818) . . . 30 20
1540 20c. Simon Bolivar (revolutionary) 30 20
1541 20c. Camera (development of photography) 30 20
1542 20c. Dripping tap (introduction of water purification system, 1829) 30 20
1543 20c. Steam locomotive (inauguration in Great Britain of first passenger-carrying railway, 1830) . . 30 20
1544 20c. Discovery of electromagnetic induction by Michael Faraday, 1831 30 20
1545 20c. First use of anaesthesia in surgery by Crawford Williamson Long, 1842 30 20
1546 20c. Morse key (transmission of first message by Samuel Morse, 1844) 30 20
1547 20c. Poster (first convention on Women's Rights, Seneca Falls, U.S.A., 1848) 30 20
1548 20c. Karl Marx (publication of the *Communist Manifesto*), 1848 . . . . 30 20
1549 20c. Charles Darwin's (naturalist) voyage on *Beagle* (56 × 36 mm) . . . 30 20
1550 20c. Revolution in Germany, 1848 . . . . . 30 20
1551 20c. Commencement of Taiping Rebellion, China, 1850 . . . . 30 20

There are a number of errors in the stamp inscriptions and descriptions.

See also Nos. 1552/68, 1691/1702 and 1741/57.

2000. New Millennium (2nd series). The Twentieth Century 1980–1989. Multicoloured.

1552 20c. Type **168** (foundation of Solidarity (trade union), 1980) 30 20
1553 20c. First photographic image taken by *Voyager I* of Saturn, 1980 . . . . . 30 20
1554 20c. Election of Ronald Reagan as President of the United States of America, 1980 . . . . . 30 20
1555 20c. A.I.D.S. virus (identification of A.I.D.S.) 30 20
1556 20c. Marriage of Prince Charles and Lady Diana Spencer, 1981 . . . . . . 30 20
1557 20c. Production of the compact disc, 1983 . . . 30 20
1558 20c. Leak of poisonous gas from insecticide plant, Bhopal, India, 1984 . . . 30 20
1559 20c. Inauguration of Pai's Pyramid, 1984 . . . . . 30 20
1560 20c. Mikhail Gorbachev elected Secretary General of the Soviet Communist Party, 1985 . . . . 30 20
1561 20c. Explosion at the Chernobyl nuclear power plant, 1986 . . . . 30 20
1562 20c. Explosion of space shuttle *Challenger*, 1986 30 20
1563 20c. Klaus Barbie, ((former chief of German Gestapo in France) sentenced to life imprisonment), 1987 30 20
1564 20c. Salman Rushdie (author) (publication of *The Satanic Verses*, 1988) 30 20
1565 20c. Election of Benazir Bhutto as Prime Minister of Pakistan, 1988 . . . . 30 20
1566 20c. Tiananmen Square (student demonstrations, 1989) 30 20
1567 20c. Demonstrators breaching Berlin Wall, 1989 (59 × 39 mm) 30 20
1568 20c. Development of the World Wide Web 30 20

170 Bill Clinton (1992–2000) **171** Australopithecine (Southern Ape species, Africa)

2000. Former United States Presidents.
1570 **170** $1 black and brown . . 1·40 85
1571 – $2 black and blue . . . 2·75 1·60
1572 – $3 black and mauve . . 4·25 2·50
1574 – $5 black and brown . . 7·00 4·25
1575 – $11.75 black and brown (40 × 23 mm) . . . . 17·00 10·00
DESIGNS: $2 Ronald Reagan (1980–88); $3 Gerald Ford (1974–76); $5 George Bush (1988–92); $11.75 John F. Kennedy (1960–63).

2000. Pre-historic Discoveries of the 20th-Century. Multicoloured.
1580 20c. Type **171** 25 15
1581 20c. Australopithecine skull 25 15
1582 20c. Homo habilis using hand axe 25 15
1583 20c. Hand-axe 25 15
1584 20c. Homo habilis skull . . 25 15
1585 20c. Australo pithecine skeleton "Lucy" 25 15
1586 20c. Archaic Homo sapien skull 25 15
1587 20c. Diapithicine skull . . . 25 15
1588 20c. Homo erectus family 25 15
1589 20c. Wood hut 25 15
1590 20c. Australopithecine ethopis skull 25 15
1591 20c. Homo sapien 25 15
1592 20c. Homo sapien skull . . 25 15
1593 20c. Discovery of Taung Baby, 1924 . . . . 25 15
1594 20c. Homo erectus skull . . 25 15
1595 20c. Louis Leaky (archaeologist) 25 15
1596 20c. Neanderthal skull . . . 25 15
1597 20c. Neanderthal man . . . 25 15
1598 20c. Development of the fully bipedal foot 25 15
1599 20c. Raymond Dart (discoverer of Taung Baby) 25 15

172 Tennis Player

2000. Olympic Games, Sydney. Multicoloured.
1600 33c. Type **172** 40 25
1601 33c. Shot put 40 25
1602 33c. Greek flag and stadium 40 25
1603 33c. Ancient Olympic athletes 40 25

173 Re-usable Launch Vehicle

2000. Projected Unmanned Craft and Space Exploration. Multicoloured.
1604 33c. Type **173** 40 25
1605 33c. Single stage vertical take-off craft 40 25
1606 33c. Robotic rocket plane 40 25
1607 33c. Single-stage craft . . . 40 25
1608 33c. Fully-automated deep-space exploration craft . . 40 25
1609 33c. Magnetohydrodynamics-powered launch craft . . 40 25
MS1610 Four sheets, each 100 × 135 mm. (a) $2 Spacecraft taking-off (privately funded launch craft); (b) $2 Emergency crew return craft using parachutes (horiz); (c) $2 Interplanetary space craft (horiz); (d) $2 Space shuttle leaving space station . . . . . 5·50 5·50

174 Banded Crake (*Rallina eurizonoides*)

2000. Birds. Multicoloured.
1611 20c. Type **174** 25 15
1612 20c. Micronesian kingfisher (*Halcyon cinnamomina*) . . 25 15
1613 20c. Little pied cormorant (*Phalacrocorax melanoleucos*) 25 15
1614 20c. Eastern reef heron (*Egretta sacra*) 25 15
1615 20c. Nicobar pigeon (*Caloenas nicobarica*) . . 25 15
1616 20c. Rufous night heron (*Nycticorax caledonicus*) 25 15
1617 33c. Palau ground dove (*Gallicolumba canifrons*) 40 25
1618 33c. Palau scops owl (*Pyrroglaux podargina*) . . 40 25
1619 33c. Mangrove flycatcher (*Cyornis rufigastra*) (wrongly inscr "Pyrrboglaux podargina") 40 25
1620 33c. Palau bushwarbler (*Cettia annae*) 40 25
1621 33c. Palau fantail (*Rhipidura lepida*) 40 25
1622 33c. Morning bird (*Celluricincla tenebrosa*) 40 25
MS1623 Two sheets, each 76 × 126 mm. (a) $2 Palau whiteeye (*Megazosterops palauensis*) (horiz); (b) $2 Palau fruitdove (*Ptilinopus pelewensis*) (horiz) . . . . 4·75 4·75
No. 1611 is inscribed "Slatey-legged Crake" and No. 1614 "Pacific reef egret" both in error. There are also several errors in the Latin names.

175 Booker T. Washington (educationist)

2000. 20th-Century Personalities. Multicoloured.
1624 33c. Type **175** 40 25
1625 33c. Buckmeister Fuller (inventor and designer) . . 40 25
1626 33c. Marie Curie (physicist) 40 25
1627 33c. Walt Disney (animator and producer) 40 25
1629 33c. Franklin D. Roosevelt (32nd United States President) 40 25
1629 33c. Henry Ford (car manufacturer) 40 25
1630 33c. Betty Friedan (author and feminist leader) . . . 40 25
1631 33c. Sigmund Freud (founder of psychoanalysis) 40 25
1632 33c. Mahatma Ghandi (Indian leader) 40 25
1633 33c. Mikhail Gorbachev (Soviet President) 40 25
1633 33c. Stephan Hawkings (theoretical physicist) . . . 40 25
1635 33c. Martin Luther King Jr. (civil rights leader) . . . 40 25
1636 33c. Toni Morrison (writer) 40 25
1637 33c. Georgia O'Keeffe (artist) 40 25
1638 33c. Rosa Parks (civil rights activist) 40 25
1639 33c. Carl Sagan (astronomer) 40 25
1640 33c. Jonas Salk (immunologist) 40 25
1641 33c. Sally Ride (astronaut and astrophysicist) . . . 40 25
1642 33c. Nikola Tesla (electrical engineer and physicist) . . 40 25
1643 33c. Wilbur and Orville Wright (aviation pioneer) 40 25

176 Reef Bass (*Pseudogramma gregoryi*)

2000. Marine Life of the Atlantic and Pacific Oceans. Multicoloured.
1644 20c. Type **176** 25 15
1645 20c. Great white shark (*Carcharodon carcharias*) 25 15
1646 20c. Sharptail eel (*Myrichthys breviceps*) . . 25 15
1647 20c. Sailfish (*Istiophorus platypterus*) 25 15
1648 20c. Southern stingray (*Dasyatis americana*) . . . 25 15
1649 20c. Ocean triggerfish (*Canthidermis sufflamen*) 25 15
1650 55c. Scalloped hammerhead (*Sphyrna lewini*) (vert) . . 65 40
1651 55c. White-tipped reef shark (*Triaenodon obesus*) (vert) 65 40
1652 55c. Moon jellyfish (*Aurelia aurita*) (vert) 65 40
1653 55c. Lionfish (*Pterois volitans*) (vert) 65 40
1654 55c. Seahorse (*Hippocampus abdominalis*) (vert) 65 40
1655 55c. Spotted eagle ray (*Aetobatus narinari*) (vert) 65 40
MS1656 Two sheets, each 110 × 85 mm. (a) $2 Short bigeye (*Pristigenys alta*) (vert); (b) $2 Gaff-topsail catfish (*Bagre marinus*) (vert) . . . . 4·75 4·75

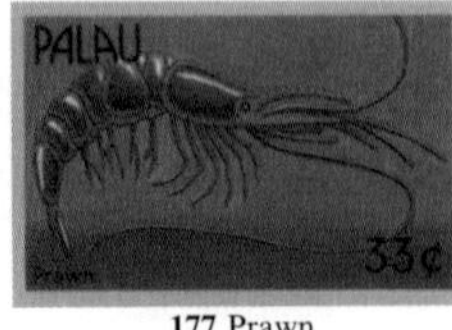

177 Prawn

2000. Marine Life. Multicoloured.
1657 33c. Type **177** 40 25
1658 33c. Deep sea angler 40 25
1659 33c. Rooster fish 40 25
1660 33c. Grenadier 40 25
1661 33c. *Platyberix opalescens* 40 25
1662 33c. Lantern fish 40 25
1663 33c. Emperor angelfish . . . 40 25
1664 33c. Nautilus 40 25
1665 33c. Moorish idol 40 25
1666 33c. Seahorse 40 25
1667 33c. Clown triggerfish . . . 40 25
1668 33c. Clown fish 40 25
MS1669 Two sheets, each 106 × 75 mm. (a) $2 Giant squid; (b) $2 Manta ray . . . . . . 4·75 4·75

178 James Watson (co-discoverer of structure of D.N.A.)

2000. Advances in Science and Medicine. Multicoloured.
1670 33c. Type **178** 40 25
1671 33c. Har Gobing Khorana and Robert Holley (work on genetic code) 40 25
1672 33c. Hamilton Smith and Werner Arber (discovered restriction enzymes) . . . 40 25
1673 33c. Centrifugation machine and D.N.A. double helix 40 25
1674 33c. Richard Roberts (discovered R.N.A. splicing and split genes) 40 25
1675 33c. Maurice Wilkins (co-discoverer of structure of D.N.A.) 40 25
1676 33c. D.N.A. double helix . . 40 25
1677 33c. Frederick Sanger and Walter Gilbert (developed methods for determining nucleotide sequences for D.N.A. molecules) . . . 40 25
1678 33c. Kary Mullis (discovered polymerase chain reaction) 40 25
1679 33c. D.N.A. double helix and frogs (mapping location of genes) 40 25
1680 33c. Francis Crick (co-discoverer of structure of D.N.A.) 40 25
1681 33c. Marshall Nirenberg (work on genetic code) . . 40 25
1682 33c. Daniel Nathans (discovered restriction enzymes) 40 25
1683 33c. Harold Varmus and Michael Bishop (identified several genes involved in cancer) 40 25
1684 33c. Phillip Sharp (discovered polymerase chain reaction) 40 25
1685 33c. Sheep (cloning sheep to produce Dolly, 1997) . . 40 25
1686 33c. D.N.A. being separated by electrophoresis 40 25
1687 33c. Paul Berg (first developed methods for cloning genes, 1980) . . . 40 25
1688 33c. Michael Smith and D.N.A. (discovered polymerase chain reaction) 40 25
1689 33c. D.N.A. and deer (human genome project) 40 25
MS1690 Two sheets, each 97 × 117 mm. (a) $2 Dolly (cloned sheep) (37 × 50 mm). (b) $2 D.N.A. and deer (37 × 50 mm) 4·75 4·75

179 Hourglass and Map of South East Asia

2000. New Millennium (3rd series). Multicoloured.
1691 20c. Type **179** 25 15
1692 20c. Hourglass and map of North America 25 15
1693 20c. Hourglass and map of Europe 25 15
1694 20c. Hourglass and map of Australia 25 15
1695 20c. Hourglass and map of South America 25 15
1696 20c. Hourglass and map of Africa 25 15
1697 55c. Clock face and clouds (vert) 35 20
1698 55c. Clock face and building faade (vert) 35 20
1699 55c. Clock face and coastline (vert) 35 20
1700 55c. Clock face and farm buildings (vert) 35 20
1701 55c. Clock face and forest (vert) 35 20
1702 55c. Clock face and desert (vert) 35 20

180 American Bald Eagle **181** Rhamphorhynchus

2000. Endangered Species. Multicoloured.
1703 33c. Type **180** 40 25
1704 33c. Small whorled pogonia 40 25
1705 33c. Arctic peregrine falcon 40 25
1706 33c. Golden lion tamarin . . 40 25
1707 33c. American alligator . . 40 25
1708 33c. Brown pelican 40 25
1709 33c. Aleutian Canada goose 40 25
1710 33c. Western grey kangaroo 40 25
1711 33c. Palau scops owl 40 25
1712 33c. Jocotoco antpitta . . . 40 25
1713 33c. Orchid 40 25
1714 33c. Red lechwe 40 25
MS1715 Two sheets, each 120 × 92 mm. (a) $2 Lahontan cutthroat trout (horiz); (b) $2 Leopard . . . . 4·75 4·75

2000. Dinosaurs. Multicoloured.
1716 33c. Type **181** 40 25
1717 33c. Ceratosaurus 40 25
1718 33c. Apatosaurus 40 25
1719 33c. Stegosaurus 40 25
1720 33c. Archaeopteryx 40 25
1721 33c. Allosaurus 40 25
1722 33c. Parasaurolophus . . . 40 25
1723 33c. Pteranodonrus 40 25
1724 33c. Tyrannosaurus 40 25
1725 33c. Triceratops 40 25
1726 33c. Ankylosaurus 40 25
1727 33c. Velociraptor 40 25
MS1728 Two sheets, each 94 × 71 mm. (a) $2 Jurassic landscape; (b) $2 Cretaceous landscape . . . . 4·75 4·75
Nos. 1716/21 and 1722/7 were each issued together, se-tenant, forming a composite design.

182 Lebaudy–Juillot Airship Le Jaune

2000. Centenary of First Zeppelin Flight and Airship Development. Multicoloured.
1729 55c. Type **182** 40 25
1730 55c. Forlanini airship *Leonardo DaVinci* 40 25
1731 55c. Thomas Baldwin's airship U.S. Military No. 1, 1908 . . . . . . 40 25
1732 55c. Astra-Torres 1 . . . . 40 25
1733 55c. Rear of Astra-Torres 1 and Parseval PL VII . . . 40 25
1734 55c. Rear of Parseval PL VII and Lebaudy airship *Liberte* **MS**1735 Two sheets, each 110 × 85 mm. (a) $2 Santos-Dumont airship Ballon No. 9 La Badaleuse; (b) $2 Santos-Dumont Ballon No. 6 circling Eiffel Tower . . . 4·75 4·75
Nos. 1729/34 were issued together, se-tenant, forming a composite design.

183 Duke and Duchess of York

184 Viking Diver attacking Danish Ship

2000. 100th Birthday of Queen Elizabeth the Queen Mother. Multicoloured.
1736 55c. Type **183** 40 25
1737 55c. As Duchess of York wearing cloche hat . . . 40 25
1738 55c. Wearing green floral hat 40 25
1739 55c. Wearing blue hat . . . 40 25
MS1740 99×84 mm. $2 Wearing yellow coat and hat . . . . . 1·25 1·25

2000. New Millennium (4th series). Development of Diving Equipment. Multicoloured.
1741 33c. Type **184** 40 25
1742 33c. Issa (12th-century Arab diver) 40 25
1743 33c.15 th-century salvage diver using breathing tube 40 25
1744 33c. 17 th-century diver wearing leather suit and carrying halberd 40 25
1745 33c. Edmund Halley's wooden diving bell, 1690 40 25
1746 33c. David Bushnell's diving bell Turtle, 1776 . . . . 40 25
1747 33c. Diver wearing suit and Siebe helmet,1819 . . . . 40 25
1748 33c. *Hunley* (Confederate submarine) 40 25
1749 33c. Argonaut (first underwater salvage vehicle), 1899 . . . . . . 40 25
1750 33c. John Williamson's underwater filming vehicle photosphere, 1914 . . . . 40 25
1751 33c. Diver wearing brass helmet, weighted boots, with air supply and safety lines (circa 1930) 40 25
1752 33c. William Beebe and Otis Barton's bathysphere, 1934 . . . . 40 25
1753 33c. Coelacanth (prehistoric fish previously thought extinct) 40 25
1754 33c. Italian divers on chariot planting explosive charges on ship hull during World War II 40 25
1755 33c. *Trieste* (bathyscaphe) (record dive by Jaques Picard and Lt. Don Walsh, 1960) 40 25
1756 33c. *Alvin* (submersible) surveying thermal vents in Galapagos Rift (1977) (60×40 mm) 40 25
1757 33c. Sylvia Earle wearing Jim Suit, 1979 . . . . . 40 25

PALESTINE Pt. 1

A territory at the extreme east of the Mediterranean Sea, captured from the Turks by Great Britain in 1917 and under Military Occupation until 1920. It was a British Mandate of the League of Nations from 1923 to May 1948 when the State of Israel was proclaimed.

1918. 10 milliemes = 1 piastre.
1927. 1,000 mills = £P1.

1 (2)

1918.
3 **1** 1p. blue . . . . 2·00 2·00

1918. Surch with T **2**.
4 **1** 5m. on 1p. blue . . . . 3·75 2·75

3 "E.E.F." = Egyptian Expeditionary Force

فلسطين
PALESTINE
פלשתינה א״י
(4)

1918.
5 **3** 1m. brown 30 40
6 2m. green 30 45
7 3m. brown 35 35
8 4m. red 35 40
9 5m. orange . . . . 1·50 30
10 1p. blue 35 30
11 2p. olive . . . . 1·00 60
12 5p. purple . . . . 1·75 2·25
13 9p. ochre . . . . 3·50 4·50
14 10p. blue . . . . 2·75 3·00
15 20p. grey . . . . 11·00 16·00
Nos. 1/15 were also valid in Transjordan, Cilicia, Lebanon and Syria.

1920. Optd with T **4**.
71 **3** 1m. brown 75 30
61 2m. green . . . . 1·25 30
72 2m. yellow . . . . 1·00 30
62 3m. brown . . . . 1·50 30
73 3m. blue . . . . 1·25 15
74 4m. red . . . . 1·25 20
75 5m. orange . . . . 1·50 30
76 6m. green . . . . 1·50 30
77 7m. brown . . . . 1·50 30
78 8m. red . . . . 1·50 30
79 1p. grey . . . . 1·75 30
65 1p. blue . . . . 1·75 35
80 13m. blue . . . . 1·50 15
66 2p. olive . . . . 2·25 40
82 5p. purple . . . . 4·75 1·25
87 9p. ochre . . . . 9·00 9·00
88 10p. blue . . . . 7·50 2·50
26 20p. grey . . . . 24·00 42·00
89 20p. violet . . . . 9·00 5·50

9 Rachel's Tomb

10 Dome of the Rock

11 Citadel, Jerusalem

12 Sea of Galilee

1927.
90 **9** 2m. blue 65 10
91 3m. green 75 10
92 **10** 4m. red . . . . 4·00 1·25
104 4m. purple . . . . . . 1·00 10
93 **11** 5m. orange . . . . . . 1·50 10
94a **10** 6m. green 75 20
95 **11** 7m. red . . . . 4·75 60
105 7m. violet 60 10
96 **10** 8m. brown . . . . . . 12·00 6·00
106 8m. red . . . . 1·25 20
97 **9** 10m. grey 65 10
98 **10** 13m. blue . . . . . . 5·00 30
107 13m. brown . . . . . . 1·00 10
108a 15m. blue . . . . . . 2·00 40
99 **11** 20m. olive . . . . . . 1·50 15
100 **12** 50m. purple . . . . . . 1·50 30
101 90m. bistre . . . . . . 55·00 60·00
102 100m. blue . . . . . . 2·25 70
103b 200m. violet . . . . . 7·00 3·50
109 250m. brown . . . . . 4·00 1·75
110 500m. red . . . . . . 4·50 3·00
111 £P1 black . . . . . . 6·00 3·50

POSTAGE DUE STAMPS

D 1

D 2

1920.
D1 **D 1** 1m. brown . . . . . . 15·00 25·00
D2 2m. green . . . . . . 10·00 10·00
D3 4m. red . . . . 10·00 10·00
D4 8m. mauve . . . . . . 7·00 7·00
D5 13m. blue . . . . . . 6·00 6·00

1924.
D 6 **D 2** 1m. brown . . . . . 90 2·00
D 7 2m. yellow . . . . . 2·25 1·75
D 8 4m. green . . . . . 2·00 1·25
D 9 8m. red . . . . . . 3·00 90
D10 13m. blue . . . . . 2·75 2·50
D11 5p. violet . . . . . 8·50 1·75

1928. As Type D **2**, but inscr "MIL" instead of "MILLIEME".
D12 **D 2** 1m. brown 50 85
D13 2m. yellow . . . . . . 1·00 60
D14 4m. green . . . . . . 1·25 1·60
D15 6m. brown . . . . . . 15·00 5·00
D16 8m. red . . . . 1·75 90
D17 10m. grey . . . . . . 1·25 60
D18 13m. blue . . . . . . 1·75 1·75
D19 20m. olive . . . . . . 1·75 1·25
D20 50m. violet . . . . . . 2·50 1·25

PANAMA Pt. 15

Country situated on the C. American isthmus. Formerly a State or Department of Colombia, Panama was proclaimed an independent republic in 1903.

1878. 100 centavos = 1 peso.
1906. 100 centesimos = 1 balboa.

1 Coat of Arms

3 Map

1878. Imperf. The 50c. is larger.
1 **1** 5c. green . . . . 15·00 13·50
2 10c. blue . . . . 38·00 35·00
3 20c. red . . . . 24·00 21·00
4 50c. yellow . . . . 9·75

1887. Perf.
5 **3** 1c. black on green 50 65
6 2c. black on pink . . . . . 1·25 1·00
7 5c. black on blue 90 35
7a 5c. black on grey . . . . . 1·50 45
8 10c. black on yellow 90 45
9 20c. black on lilac 90 45
10 50c. brown . . . . 1·50 75

5 Map of Panama

38 Map of Panama

1892.
12a **5** 1c. green 15 15
12b 2c. red 20 20
12c 5c. blue 90 45
12d 10c. orange 20 20
12e 20c. violet 25 25
12f 50c. brown 30 25
12g 1p. lake . . . . 3·75 2·40

1894. Surch **HABILITADO 1894** and value.
13 **5** 1c. on 2c. red 35 35
15 **3** 5c. on 20c. black on lilac . . 1·50 1·00
18 10c. on 50c. brown . . . . . 1·90 1·90

1903. Optd **REPUBLICA DE PANAMA**.
70 **5** 1c. green . . . . 1·25 75
36 2c. red 55 55
37 5c. blue . . . . 1·25 55
38 10c. orange . . . . 1·25 1·25
39 20c. violet . . . . 2·40 2·40
75 **3** 50c. brown . . . . 14·00 14·00
40 **5** 50c. brown . . . . 6·00 4·25
41 1p. lake . . . . 29·00 24·00

1903. Optd **PANAMA** twice.
53 **5** 1c. green 25 25
54 2c. red 25 25
55 5c. blue 30 30
56 10c. orange 30 30
64 20c. violet 90 90
65 50c. brown . . . . 1·50 1·50
66 1p. lake . . . . 3·50 2·75

1904. Optd **Republica de Panama**.
94 **5** 1c. green 35 35
97 2c. red 45 45
98 5c. blue 45 45
99 10c. orange 45 45
100 20c. violet 45 45
103 **3** 50c. brown . . . . 1·75 1·75
104 **5** 1p. lake . . . . 9·50 8·25

1905.
151 **38** ½c. orange 55 45
136 1c. green 55 40
137 2c. red 70 55

1906. Surch **PANAMA** twice and new value and thick bar.
138 **5** 1c. on 20c. violet 25 25
139 2c. on 50c. brown 25 25
140 5c. on 1p. lake 55 45

41 Panamanian Flag

42 Vasco Nunez de Balboa

43 F. de Cordoba

44 Arms of Panama

45 J. Arosemena

46 M. J. Hurtado

47 J. de Obaldia

1906.
142 **41** ½c. multicoloured 40 35
143 **42** 1c. black and green 40 35
144 **43** 2c. black and red 55 35
145 **44** 2½c. red 55 35
146 **45** 5c. black and blue . . . . 1·00 35
147 **46** 8c. black and purple . . . 55 40
148 **47** 10c. black and violet . . . 55 35
149 – 25c. black and brown . . . 1·50 60
150 – 50c. black . . . . 3·75 2·10
DESIGNS: 25c. Tomas Herrera; 50c. Jose de Fabrega.

48 Balboa

49 De Cordoba

50 Arms

51 Arosemena

52 Hurtado

53 Obaldia

1909.
152 **48** 1c. black and green 65 50
153 **49** 2c. black and red 65 30
154 **50** 2½c. red 90 30
155 **51** 5c. black and blue . . . . 1·10 30
156 **52** 8c. black and purple . . . 4·25 2·50
157 **53** 10c. black and purple . . . 2·10 1·10

56 Balboa viewing Pacific Ocean

57 Balboa reaches the Pacific

1913. 400th Anniv of Discovery of Pacific Ocean.
160 **56** 2½c. yellow and green . . . 45 40

1915. Panama Exhibition and Opening of Canal.
161 – ½c. black and olive 45 35
162 – 1c. black and green 55 35
163 **57** 2c. black and red 65 35
164 – 2½c. black and red 65 35
165 – 3c. black and violet . . . . 1·00 35
166 – 5c. black and blue . . . . 2·50 50
167 – 10c. black and orange . . 1·50 50
168 – 20c. black and brown . . . 7·25 2·40
DESIGNS: ½c. Chorrera Falls; 1c. Relief Map of Panama Canal; 2½c. Cathedral ruins, Old Panama; 3c. Palace of Arts, National Exhibition; 5c. Gatun Locks; 10c. Culebra Cut; 20c. Archway, S. Domingo Monastery.

62 Balboa Docks

1918. Views of Panama Canal.
178 – 12c. black and violet . . . 20·00 5·50
179 – 15c. black and blue . . . . 12·00 2·75
180 – 24c. black and brown . . . 35·00 9·00

181 **62** 50c. black and orange . . 42·00 20·00
182 – 1b. black and violet . . . 45·00 22·00
DESIGNS: 12c. "Panama" (cargo liner) in Gaillard Cut, north; 15c. "Panama" in Gaillard Cut, south; 24c. "Cristobal" (cargo liner) in Gatun Locks; 1b. "Nereus" (U.S. Navy collier) in Pedro Miguel Locks.

1919. 400th Anniv of Founding of City of Panama. No. 164 surch **1519 1919 2 CENTESIMOS 2.**
183 2c. on 2½c. black and red . . 45 45

64 Arms of Panama **65** Vallarino

68 Bolivar's Speech **70** Hurtado

1921. Independence Centenary. Dated "1821 1921".
184 **64** ½c. orange 55 30
185 **65** 1c. green 55 25
186 – 2c. red ("Land Gate", Panama City) 70 30
187 **65** 2½c. red (Bolivar) 95 75
188 – 3c. violet (Cervantes statue) 95 75
189 **68** 5c. blue 90 45
190 **65** 8c. olive (Carlos Ycaza) . . 3·50 2·10
191 – 10c. violet (Government House 1821–1921) . . . 2·40 85
192 – 15c. blue (Balboa statue) 3·00 1·25
193 – 20c. brown (Los Santos Church) . . . . 5·00 2·40
194 **65** 24c. sepia (Herrera) . . . 5·00 3·00
195 – 50c. black (Fabrega) . . . 8·75 4·50

1921. Birth Centenary of Manuel Jose Hurtado (writer).
196 **70** 2c. green 55 35

1923. No. 164 surch **1923 2 CENTESIMOS 2.**
197 2c. on 2½c. black and red . . 35 35

72

73 Simon Bolivar

74 Statue of Bolivar

75 Congress Hall, Panama

1924.
198 **72** ½c. orange 20 10
199 1c. green 20 10
200 2c. red 25 10
201 5c. blue 35 15
202 10c. violet 40 20
203 12c. olive 45 35
204 15c. blue 55 45
205 24c. brown . . . . 2·25 65
206 50c. orange . . . . 3·75 90
207 1b. black . . . . 5·50 2·25

1926. Bolivar Congress.
208 **73** ½c. orange 35 15
209 1c. green 35 15
210 2c. red 40 25
211 4c. grey 40 25
212 5c. blue 65 40
213 **74** 8c. purple 75 65
214 10c. violet 60 60
215 12c. olive 90 90
216 15c. blue . . . . 1·25 1·10
217 20c. brown . . . . 2·40 1·25
218 **75** 24c. slate . . . . 3·00 1·50
219 50c. black . . . . 7·00 3·50

78 "Spirit of St. Louis" over Map

1928. Lindbergh's Flying Tour.
222 – 2c. red on rose 55 35
223 **78** 5c. blue on green 75 55
DESIGN—VERT: 2c. "Spirit of St. Louis" over Old Panama with opt **HOMENAJE A LINDBERGH.**

1928. 25th Anniv of Independence. Optd **1903 NOV 3 BRE 1928.**
224 **70** 2c. green 30 20

1929. Air. No. E226 surch with Fokker Universal airplane and **CORREO AEREO 25 25 VEINTICINCO CENTESIMOS.**
225 E **81** 25c. on 10c. orange . . . 1·10 90

1929. Air. Nos. E226/7 optd **CORREO AEREO** or additionally surch with new value in **CENTESIMOS.**
238 E **81** 5c. on 10c. orange . . . 55 55
228 10c. orange 55 55
268 10c. on 20c. brown . . . 90 55
229 15c. on 10c. orange . . . 55 55
269 20c. brown 90 55
230 25c. on 20c. brown . . . 1·25 1·10

83

87

1930. Air.
231 **83** 5c. blue 20 10
232 5c. orange 35 10
233 7c. red 35 10
234 8c. black 35 10
235 15c. green 45 10
236 20c. red 50 10
237 25c. blue 55 55

1930. No. 182 optd with airplane and **CORREO AEREO.**
239 1b. black and violet . . . . 20·00 16·00

1930. Air.
244 **87** 5c. blue 20 10
245 10c. orange 35 25
246 30c. violet . . . . 6·75 4·00
247 50c. red . . . . 1·25 35
248 1b. black . . . . 6·75 4·25

1930. Bolivar's Death Centenary. Surch **1830 - 1930 17 DE DICIEMBRE UN CENTESIMO.**
249 **73** 1c. on 4c. grey 25 20

89 Seaplane over Old Panama

92 Manuel Amador Guerrero

1931. Air. Opening of service between Panama City and western provinces.
250 **89** 5c. blue . . . . 1·00 90

1932. Optd **HABILITADA** or surch also.
251 **64** ½c. orange (postage) . . . 35 20
252 **73** ½c. orange 20 20
253 1c. green 25 20
270 **68** 1c. on 5c. blue 45 35
254 **73** 2c. red 20 20
255 5c. blue 45 30
256 – 10c. violet (No. 191) . . . 70 35
258 **74** 10c. on 12c. olive 75 40
259 10c. on 15c. blue 70 35
257 20c. brown . . . . 1·00 1·10
260 **83** 20c. on 25c. blue (air) . . . 4·00 55

1932. Birth Centenary of Dr. Guerrero (first president of republic).
261 **92** 2c. red 45 20

95 National Institute

1934. 25th Anniv of National Institute.
262 – 1c. green 55 55
263 – 2c. red 55 55
264 – 5c. blue 75 60
265 **95** 10c. brown . . . . 2·10 1·00
266 – 12c. green . . . . 3·50 1·50
267 – 15c. blue . . . . 4·75 1·75
DESIGNS—VERT: 1c. J. D. de Obaldia; 2c. E. A. Morales; 5c. Sphinx and Quotation from Emerson. HORIZ: 12c. J. A. Facio; 15c. P. Arosemena.

(**98**)

100 Urraca Monument

99 Custom House Ruins, Portobelo

1936. Birth Centenary of Pablo Arosemena. (a) Postage. Surch as T **98**, but without **CORREO AEREO.**
271 **72** 2c. on 24c. brown 55 45

(b) Air. Surch with T **98.**
272 **72** 5c. on 50c. orange 60 50

1936. 4th Spanish-American Postal Congress (1st issue). Inscr "IV CONGRESO POSTAL AMERICO-ESPANOL".
273 **99** ½c. orange (postage) . . . 40 25
274 – 1c. green 40 25
275 – 2c. red 40 25
276 – 5c. blue 45 30
277 – 10c. violet 75 45
278 – 15c. blue 75 60
279 – 20c. red . . . . 95 1·00
280 – 25c. brown . . . . 1·50 1·40
281 – 50c. orange . . . . 8·50 2·75
282 – 1b. black . . . . 9·00 7·00
DESIGNS: 1c. "Panama" (Old tree); 2c. "La Pollera" (woman in costume); 5c. Bolivar; 10c. Ruins of Old Panama Cathedral; 15c. Garcia y Santos; 20c. Madden Dam; 25c. Columbus; 50c. "Resolute" (liner) in Gaillard Cut; 1b. Panama Cathedral.

283 **100** 5c. blue (air) 70 40
284 – 10c. orange 90 65
285 – 20c. red . . . . 1·25 1·00
286 – 30c. violet . . . . 2·10 1·90
287 – 50c. red . . . . 30·00 18·00
288 – 1b. black . . . . 9·00 6·50
DESIGNS—HORIZ: 10c. "Man's Genius Uniting the Oceans"; 20c. Panama; 50c. San Pedro Miguel Locks; 1b. Courts of Justice. VERT: 30c. Balboa Monument.

1937. 4th Spanish-American Postal Congress (2nd issue). Nos. 273/88 optd **UPU.**
289 **99** ½c. orange (postage) . . . 35 20
290 – 1c. green 45 20
291 – 2c. red 45 20
292 – 5c. blue 45 30
293 – 10c. violet 75 45
294 – 15c. blue . . . . 4·75 2·40
295 – 20c. red . . . . 1·10 1·10
296 – 25c. brown . . . . 1·75 90
297 – 50c. orange . . . . 7·00 4·25
298 – 1b. black . . . . 8·75 7·50
299 **99** 5c. blue (air) 45 45
300 – 10c. orange 70 55
301 – 20c. red 95 75
302 – 30c. violet . . . . 3·50 2·40
303 – 50c. red . . . . 25·00 20·00
304 – 1b. black . . . . 11·50 9·50

1937. Optd **1937-38.**
305 **73** ½c. orange 50 45
306 **65** 1c. green 30 25
307 **73** 1c. green 30 25
308 **70** 2c. green 35 25
309 **73** 2c. red 35 30

1937. Surch **1937-38** and value.
310 **73** 2c. on 4c. grey 45 30
311 **78** 2c. on 8c. olive 45 30
312 **74** 2c. on 8c. purple 45 30
313 2c. on 10c. violet 45 30
314 2c. on 12c. olive 45 30
315 – 2c. on 15c. blue (No. 192) 45 30
316 **65** 2c. on 24c. sepia 45 30
317 2c. on 50c. black 45 30

1937. Air. Optd **CORREO AEREO** or surch also.
318 **73** 5c. blue 45 45
319 **74** 5c. on 15c. blue 45 45
320 5c. on 20c. brown 45 45
321 **75** 5c. on 24c. slate 45 45
322 **62** 5c. on 1b. black and violet 6·75 3·75
323 – 10c. on 10c. violet (No. 191) . . . . . . 1·40 90
324 **75** 10c. on 50c. black . . . . 1·40 90

105 Fire-Engine

106 Firemen's Monument

107 Fire-Brigade Badge

1937. 50th Anniv of Fire Brigade.
325 – ½c. orange (postage) . . . 45 25
326 – 1c. green 45 25
327 – 2c. red 45 30
328 **105** 5c. blue 65 30
329 **106** 10c. violet . . . . 1·10 65
330 – 12c. green . . . . 1·50 1·10
331 **107** 5c. blue (air) 55 35
332 – 10c. orange 70 45
333 – 20c. red 90 55
DESIGNS—VERT: ½c. R. Arango; 1c. J. A. Guizado; 10c. (No. 332), F. Arosemena; 12c. D. H. Brandon; 20c. J. G. Duque. HORIZ: 2c. House on fire.

108 Basketball Player

111 Old Panama Cathedral and Statue of Liberty

1938. Air. Central American and Caribbean Olympic Games.
334 **108** 1c. red 80 30
335 – 2c. green (Baseball player) (horiz) 80 15
336 – 7c. grey (Swimmer) (horiz) 1·10 35
337 – 8c. brown (Boxers) (horiz) 1·10 35
338 – 15c. blue (Footballer) . . 2·60 1·10

1938. Opening of Aguadulce Normal School, Santiago. Optd **NORMAL DE SANTIAGO JUNIO 5 1938** or surch also.
340 **72** 2c. red (postage) 30 25
341 **87** 7c. on 30c. violet (air) . . 45 45
342 **83** 8c. on 15c. green 45 45

1938. 150th Anniv of U.S. Constitution. Flags in red, white and blue.
343 **111** 1c. black and green (postage) 45 20
344 2c. black and red 55 25
345 5c. black and blue 60 45
346 12c. black and olive . . . 1·10 65
347 15c. black and blue . . . 1·40 75
348 7c. black and grey (air) 50 30
349 8c. black and blue 70 30
350 15c. black and brown . . 90 70
351 50c. black and orange . . 12·00 9·00
352 1b. black . . . . 12·00 9·00
Nos. 343/7 are without the Douglas DC-3 airliner.

112 Pierre and Marie Curie

1939. Obligatory Tax. Cancer Research Fund. Dated "1939".
353 **112** 1c. red 55 15
354 1c. green 55 15
355 1c. orange 55 15
356 1c. blue 55 15

113 Gatun Locks

1939. 25th Anniv of Opening of Panama Canal.
357 **113** ½c. yellow (postage) . . . 2·10 2·10
358 – 1c. green . . . . 2·25 1·75
359 – 2c. red 55 15
360 – 5c. blue . . . . 1·75 20
361 – 10c. violet . . . . 5·50 90
362 – 12c. olive 75 55
363 – 15c. blue 75 70

364 – 50c. orange 1·75 1·25
365 – 1b. brown 3·50 2·25
DESIGNS: 1c. "Santa Elena" (liner) in Pedro Miguel Locks; 2c. Allegory of canal construction; 5c. "Rangitata" (liner) in Culebra Cut; 10c. Panama canal ferry; 12c. Aerial view; 15c. Gen. Gorgas; 50c. M. A. Guerrero; 1b. Woodrow Wilson.

366 – 1c. red (air) 35 10
367 – 2c. green 35 15
368 – 5c. blue 55 20
369 – 10c. violet 70 25
370 – 15c. blue 95 35
371 – 20c. red 2·50 95
372 – 50c. brown 3·00 90
373 – 1b. black 6·00 4·00
PORTRAITS: 1c. B. Porras; 2c. Wm. H. Taft; 5c. P. J. Sosa; 10c. L. B. Wise; 15c. A. Reclus; 20c. Gen. Goethals; 50c. F. de Lesseps; 1b. Theodore Roosevelt.

115 Flags of American Republics
120a "Liberty"

1940. Air. 50th Anniv of Pan-American Union.
374 **115** 15c. blue 45 30

1940. Air. No. 370 surch **55**.
375 5c. on 15c. blue 25 25

No. 363 surch **AEREO SIETE**.
376 7c. on 15c. blue 40 30

No. 371 surch **SIETE**.
377 7c. on 20c. red 40 30

No. 374 surch **8–8**.
378 **115** 8c. on 15c. blue 40 30

1941. Obligatory Tax. Cancer Research Fund. Optd **LUCHA CONTRA EL CANCER**.
379 **72** 1c. green 1·40 1·10

1941. Enactment of New Constitution. (a) Postage. Optd **CONSTITUCION 1941**.
380 **72** ½c. orange 35 20
381 1c. green 35 20
382 2c. red 35 25
383 5c. blue 45 20
384 10c. violet 65 45
385 15c. blue 1·00 65
386 50c. orange 5·50 2·50
387 1b. black 13·00 4·50

(b) Air. Surch **CONSTITUCION 1941 AEREO** and value in figures.
388 E **81** 7c. on 10c. orange 65 65
389 **72** 15c. on 24c. brown 2·25 1·50

(c) Air. Optd **CONSTITUCION 1941**.
390 **83** 20c. red 3·25 2·25
391 **87** 50c. red 7·50 4·25
392 1b. black 17·00 9·00

1941. Obligatory Tax. Cancer Research Fund. Dated "1940".
393 **112** 1c. red 45 10
394 1c. green 45 10
395 1c. orange 45 10
396 1c. blue 45 10

1942. Telegraph stamps as T **120a** optd or surch. (a) Optd **CORREOS 1942** and (No. 397) surch **2c**.
397 2c. on 5c. blue 70 55
398 10c. violet 90 70

(b) Air. Optd **CORREO AEREO 1942**.
399 20c. brown 1·75 1·50

123 Flags of Panama and Costa Rica

1942. 1st Anniv of Revised Frontier Agreement between Panama and Costa Rica.
400 **123** 2c. red (postage) 30 25
401 15c. green (air) 60 15

1942. Obligatory Tax. Cancer Research Fund. Dated "1942".
402 **112** 1c. violet 45 15

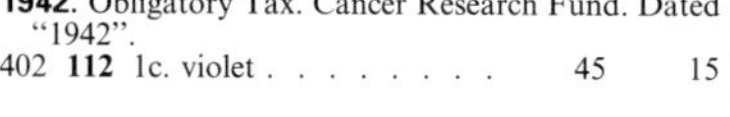

127 Balboa reaches Pacific

129 J. D. Arosemena Normal School
131 A. G. Melendez

1942. (a) Postage stamps.
403 – ½c. red, blue and violet 10 10
404 – ½c. blue, orange and red 15 10
405 – 1c. green 10 10
406 – 1c. red 10 10
407 – 2c. red ("ACARRERO") 20 10
408 – 2c. red ("ACARREO") 45 10
409 – 2c. black and red 15 10
410 **127** 5c. black and blue 20 10
411 – 5c. blue 30 10
412 – 10c. orange and red 45 20
413 – 10c. orange and purple 35 20
414 – 15c. black and blue 35 55
415 – 15c. black 35 20
416 – 50c. black and red 85 60
417 – 1b. black 1·75 70
DESIGNS—VERT: ½c. National flag; 1c. Farm girl; 10c. Golden Altar, Church of St. Jose; 50c. San Blas Indian woman and child. HORIZ: 2c. Oxen drawing sugar cart; 15c. St. Thomas's Hospital; 1b. National highway.

(b) Air.
418 – 2c. red 45 10
419 – 7c. red 55 20
420 – 8c. black and brown 20 10
421 – 10c. black and blue 20 15
422 – 15c. violet 30 10
423 – 15c. grey 35 15
424 **129** 20c. brown 35 10
425 20c. green 35 20
426 – 50c. green 1·25 45
427 – 50c. red 3·50 2·60
428 – 50c. blue 60 40
429 – 1b. orange, yellow and black 1·40 65
DESIGNS—HORIZ: 2c., 7c. Black marlin; 8c., 10c. Gate of Glory, Portobelo; 15c. Taboga Is; 50c. Fire Brigade H.Q., Panama City; 1b. Idol (Golden Beast).

1943. Obligatory Tax. Cancer Research Fund. Dated "1943".
433 **112** 1c. green 45 15
434 1c. red 45 15
435 1c. orange 45 15
436 1c. blue 45 15

1943. Air.
437 **131** 3b. grey 5·50 5·50
438 – 5b. blue (T. Lefevre) 8·50 7·00

1945. Obligatory Tax. Cancer Research Fund. Dated "1945".
439 **112** 1c. red 45 20
440 1c. green 45 20
441 1c. orange 45 20
442 1c. blue 45 20

1946. Obligatory Tax. Cancer Research Fund. Surch **CANCER B/. 0.01 1947**.
443 **72** 1c. on ½c. orange 55 15
444 1c. on 1c. green 55 15
445 – 1c. on ½c. red, blue and violet (No. 403) 45 10
446 **72** 1c. on 12c. olive 45 15
447 1c. on 24c. brown 45 15

1947. Air. Surch **AEREO 1947** and value.
448 – 5c. on 7c. red (No. 419) 20 20
449 **83** 5c. on 8c. black 20 20
450 – 5c. on 8c. black and brown (No. 420) 20 20
451 **83** 10c. on 15c. green 55 35
452 – 10c. on 15c. violet (422) 30 25

134 Flag of Panama

135 National Theatre

1947. 2nd Anniv of National Constitutional Assembly.
453 **134** 2c. red, deep red and blue (postage) 15 10
454 – 5c. blue 20 20
455 **135** 8c. violet (air) 45 30
DESIGN—As Type **134**: 5c. Arms of Panama.

1947. Cancer Research Fund. Dated "1947".
456 **112** 1c. red 45 10
457 1c. green 45 10
458 1c. orange 45 10
459 1c. blue 45 10

1947. Surch **HABILITADA CORREOS** and value.
460 **83** ½c. on 8c. black 10 10
461 – ½c. on 8c. black and brown (No. 420) 10 10
462 1c. on 7c. red (No. 419) 15 15
463 **135** 2c. on 8c. violet 20 15

1947. Surch **Habilitada CORREOS B/. 0.50**.
464 **72** 50c. on 24c. brown 65 65

138 J. A. Arango

1948. Air. Honouring members of the Revolutionary Junta of 1903.
465 – 3c. black and blue 35 25
466 **138** 5c. black and brown 35 25
467 – 10c. black and orange 35 25
468 – 15c. black and red 35 55
469 – 20c. black and red 40 40
470 – 50c. black 3·75 1·60
471 – 1b. black and green 3·00 2·75
472 – 2b. black and yellow 7·00 6·00
PORTRAITS—HORIZ: 3c. M. A. Guerrero; 10c. F. Boyd; 15c. R. Arias. VERT: 20c. M. Espinosa; 50c. Carlos Arosemena (engineer); 1b. N. de Obarrio; 2b. T. Arias.

140 Firemen's Monument

1948. 50th Anniv of Colon Fire Brigade.
473 **140** 5c. black and red 20 15
474 – 10c. black and orange 35 20
475 – 20c. black and blue 70 40
476 – 25c. black and brown 70 55
477 – 50c. black and violet 90 55
478 – 1b. black and green 1·50 90
DESIGNS—HORIZ: 10c. Fire engine; 20c. Fire hose; 25c. Fire Brigade Headquarters. VERT: 50c. Commander Walker; 1b. First Fire Brigade Commander.

142 F. D. Roosevelt and J. D. Arosemena

144 Roosevelt Monument, Panama

1948. Air. Homage to F. D. Roosevelt.
479 **142** 5c. black and red 20 15
480 – 10c. orange 30 30
481 **144** 20c. green 35 35
482 – 50c. black and blue 40 35
483 – 1b. black 90 75
DESIGNS—HORIZ: 10c. Woman with palm symbolizing "Four Freedoms"; 50c. Map of Panama Canal. VERT: 1b. Portrait of Roosevelt.

147 Cervantes

148 Monument to Cervantes

1948. 400th Birth Anniv of Cervantes.
484 **147** 2c. black and red (postage) 30 15
485 **148** 5c. black and blue (air) 20 10
486 – 10c. black and mauve 35 30
DESIGN—HORIZ: 10c. Don Quixote and Sancho Panza (inscr as Type **148**).

1949. Air. Jose Gabriel Duque (philanthropist). Birth Centenary. No. 486 optd **"CENTENARIO DE JOSE GABRIEL DUQUE" "18 de Enero de 1949"**.
487 10c. black and mauve 40 40

1949. Obligatory Tax. Cancer Research Fund. Surch **LUCHA CONTRA EL CANCER** and value.
488 **142** 1c. on 5c. black and red 35 10
489 – 1c. on 10c. orange (No. 480) 35 10

1949. Incorporation of Chiriqui Province Cent. Stamps of 1930 and 1942 optd **1849 1949 CHIRIQUI CENTENARIO**. (a) On postage stamps as No. 407. (i) Without surcharge.
491 – 2c. red 20 10

(ii) Surch **1 UN CENTESIMO 1** also.
490 – 1c. on 2c. red 20 10

(b) Air.
492 – 2c. red (No. 418) 20 20
493 **83** 5c. blue 30 30
494 – 15c. grey (No. 423) 40 40
495 – 50c. red (No. 427) 1·75 1·75

1949. 75th Anniv of U.P.U. Stamps of 1930 and 1942/3 optd **1874 1949 U.P.U.** No. 625 is also surch **B/0.25**.
496 – 1c. green (No. 405) (postage) 20 10
497 – 2c. red (No. 407) 30 15
498 **127** 5c. blue 45 25
499 – 2c. red (No. 418) (air) 20 20
500 **83** 5c. orange 55 35
501 – 10c. black and blue (No. 421) 20 20
502 **131** 25c. on 3b. grey 30 30
503 – 50c. red (No. 427) 1·60 1·60

1949. Cancer Research Fund. Dated "1949".
504 **112** 1c. brown 45 10

153 Father Xavier

154 St. Xavier University

1949. Bicentenary of Founding of St. Xavier University.
505 **153** 2c. black and red (postage) 25 15
506 **154** 5c. black and blue (air) 35 15

155 Dr. Carlos J. Finlay

156 "Aedes aegypti"

1950. Dr. Finlay (medical research worker).
507 **155** 2c. black and red (postage) 35 15
508 **156** 5c. black and blue (air) 85 40

1950. Death Centenary of San Martin. Optd **CENTENARIO del General** (or **Gral.**) **Jose de San Martin 17 de Agosto de 1950** or surch also. The 50c. is optd **AEREO** as well.
509 – 1c. green (No. 405) (postage) 15 10
510 – 2c. on ½c. blue, orange and red (No. 404) 20 10
511 **127** 5c. black and blue 25 20
512 – 2c. red (No. 418) (air) 35 30
513 **83** 5c. orange 35 35
514 – 10c. black & blue (No. 421) 55 45
515 **83** 25c. blue 90 70
516 – 50c. black & violet (No. 477) 1·40 1·00

158 Badge

159 Stadium

1950. Obligatory Tax. Physical Culture Fund. Dated "1950".
517 – 1c. black and red 70 20
518 **158** 1c. black and blue 70 20
519 **159** 1c. black and green . . . 70 20
520 – 1c. black and orange . . 70 20
521 – 1c. black and violet . . . 70 20
DESIGNS—VERT: No. 520, as Type **159** but medallion changed and incorporating four "F"s; 521, Discus thrower. HORIZ: No. 517, as Type **159** but front of stadium.

1951. Birth Tercentenary of Jean-Baptiste de La Salle (educational reformer). Optd **Tercer Centenario del Natalicio de San Juan Baptista de La Salle. 1651-1951.**
522 2c. black and red (No. 409) 15 15
523 5c. blue (No. 411) 25 15

1952. Air. Surch **AEREO 1952** and value.
524 2c. on 10c. black and blue (No. 421) 20 15
525 5c. on 10c. black and blue (No. 421) 25 10
526 1b. on 5b. blue (No. 438) . . 23·00 23·00

1952. Surch **1952** and figure of value.
527 1c. on ½c. (No. 404) 15 10
Air. Optd **AEREO** also.
528 5c. on 2c. (No. 408) 15 10
529 25c. on 10c. (No. 413) . . . 70 65

164 Isabella the Catholic

167 Masthead of "La Estrella"

1952. 500th Birth Anniv of Isabella the Catholic.
530 **164** 1c. black & grn (postage) 10 10
531 2c. black and red 15 10
532 5c. black and blue 20 15
533 10c. black and violet . . . 25 20
534 4c. black and orange (air) 10 10
535 5c. black and olive . . . 15 10
536 10c. black and buff . . . 35 30
537 25c. black and slate . . . 55 35
538 50c. black and brown . . 75 45
539 1b. black . . . . 3·00 3·00

1953. Surch **B/.0.01 1953.**
540 1c. on 10c. (No. 413) 10 10
541 1c. on 15c. black (No. 415) 15 10

1953. Air. No. 421 surch **5 1953.**
542 5c. on 10c. black and blue . . 35 10

1953. Air. Centenary of "La Estrella de Panama", Newspaper.
543 **167** 5c. red 20 15
544 10c. blue 25 25

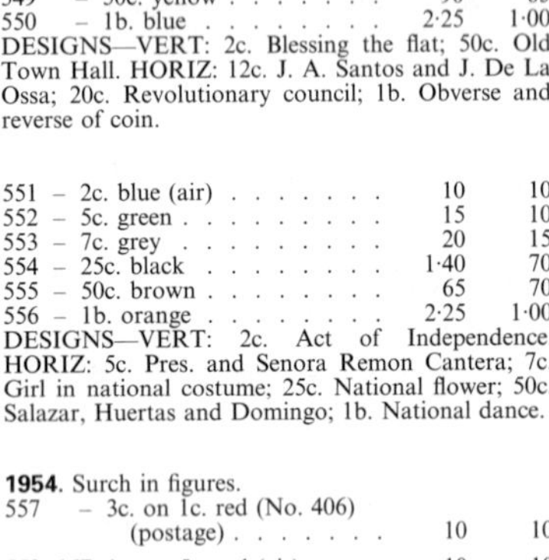

168 Pres. and Senora Amador Guerrero

1953. 50th Anniv of Panama Republic.
545 – 2c. violet (postage) . . . 15 10
546 **168** 5c. orange 20 10
547 – 12c. purple 35 15
548 – 20c. indigo . . . . 2·25 45
549 – 50c. yellow 90 65
550 – 1b. blue . . . . 2·25 1·00
DESIGNS—VERT: 2c. Blessing the flat; 50c. Old Town Hall. HORIZ: 12c. J. A. Santos and J. De La Ossa; 20c. Revolutionary council; 1b. Obverse and reverse of coin.

551 – 2c. blue (air) 10 10
552 – 5c. green 15 10
553 – 7c. grey 20 15
554 – 25c. black . . . . 1·40 70
555 – 50c. brown 65 70
556 – 1b. orange . . . . 2·25 1·00
DESIGNS—VERT: 2c. Act of Independence. HORIZ: 5c. Pres. and Senora Remon Cantera; 7c. Girl in national costume; 25c. National flower; 50c. Salazar, Huertas and Domingo; 1b. National dance.

1954. Surch in figures.
557 – 3c. on 1c. red (No. 406) (postage) 10 10
558 **167** 1c. on 5c. red (air) . . . 10 10
559 1c. on 10c. blue 10 10

170 Gen. Herrera at Conference Table

1954. Death Centenary of Gen. Herrera.
560 – 3c. violet (postage) . . . 20 10
561 **170** 6c. green (air) 15 10
562 – 1b. black and red . . . . 2·25 2·10
DESIGNS—VERT: 3c. Equestrian statue. HORIZ: 1b. Cavalry charge.

171 Rotary Emblem and Map

1955. Air. 50th Anniv of Rotary International.
563 **171** 6c. violet 15 10
564 21c. red 55 35
565 1b. black . . . . 3·50 1·90

172 Tocumen Airport

173 President Remon Cantera

1955.
566 **172** ½c. brown 10 10

1955. National Mourning for Pres. Remon Cantera.
567 **173** 3c. black & pur (postage) 15 10
568 6c. black and violet (air) 20 15

174 V. de la Guardia y Azala and M. Chiaria

175 F. de Lesseps

1955. Centenary of Cocle Province.
569 **174** 5c. violet 20 10

1955. 150th Birth Anniv of De Lesseps (engineer).
570 **175** 3c. lake on pink (postage) 30 10
571 – 25c. blue on blue . . . . 4·25 2·50
572 – 50c. violet on lilac 90 60
573 – 5c. myrtle on green (air) 20 10
574 – 1b. black and mauve . . 3·00 1·75
DESIGNS—VERT: 5c. P. J. Sosa; 50c. T. Roosevelt. HORIZ: 25c. First excavations for Panama Canal; 1b. "Ancon I" (first ship to pass through canal) and De Lesseps.

1955. Air. No. 564 surch.
575 **171** 15c. on 21c. red 45 35

177 Pres. Eisenhower (United States)

178 Bolivar Statue

1956. Air. Pan-American Congress, Panama and 30th Anniv of First Congress.
576 – 6c. black and blue 30 20
577 – 6c. black and bistre . . . 30 20
578 – 6c. black and green . . . 30 20
579 – 6c. sepia and green . . . 30 20
580 – 6c. green and yellow . . . 30 20
581 – 6c. green and violet . . . 30 20
582 – 6c. blue and lilac 30 20
583 – 6c. green and purple . . . 30 20
584 – 6c. blue and olive 30 20
585 – 6c. sepia and yellow . . . 30 20
586 – 6c. blue and sepia 30 20
587 – 6c. green and mauve . . . 30 20
588 – 6c. sepia and red 30 20
589 – 6c. green and blue 30 20
590 – 6c. sepia and blue 30 20
591 – 6c. black and orange . . . 30 20
592 – 6c. sepia and grey 30 20
593 – 6c. black and pink . . . 30 20
594 **177** 6c. blue and red 70 35
595 – 6c. blue and grey 30 20
596 – 6c. green and brown . . . 30 20
597 **178** 20c. grey 40 55
598 – 50c. green 75 75
599 – 1b. sepia . . . . 1·50 95
PRESIDENTIAL PORTRAITS as Type **177**: No. 576, Argentina; 577, Bolivia; 578, Brazil; 579, Chile; 580, Colombia; 581, Costa Rica; 582, Cuba; 583, Dominican Republic; 584, Ecuador; 585, Guatemala; 586, Haiti; 587, Honduras; 588, Mexico; 589, Nicaragua; 590, Panama; 591, Paraguay; 592, Peru; 593, Salvador; 595, Uruguay; 596, Venezuela. As Type **178**—HORIZ: No. 598, Bolivar Hall. VERT: No. 599, Bolivar Medallion.

179 Arms of Panama City

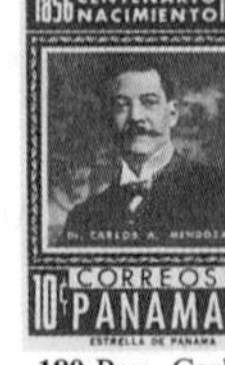

180 Pres. Carlos A. Mendoza

1956. 6th Inter-American Congress of Municipalities, Panama City.
600 **179** 3c. green (postage) . . . 15 10
601 – 25c. red (air) 55 35
602 – 50c. black 65 55
DESIGNS: 25c. Stone bridge, Old Panama; 50c. Town Hall, Panama.

1956. Birth Centenary of Pres. Carlos A. Mendoza.
604 **180** 10c. green and red 20 15

182 Dr. Belisario Porras

1956. Birth Centenary of Dr. Porras.
605 – 15c. grey (postage) . . . 45 20
606 **182** 25c. blue and red 65 45
607 – 5c. green (air) 10 10
608 – 15c. red 30 25
DESIGNS—HORIZ: 15c. (No. 605), National Archives; 15c. (No. 608), St. Thomas's Hospital. VERT: 5c. Porras Monument.

183 Isthmus Highway

185 Manuel E. Batista

1957. 7th Pan-American Highway Congress.
609 **183** 3c. green (postage) . . . 15 10
610 – 10c. black (air) 20 15
611 – 20c. black and blue . . . 35 35
612 – 1b. green . . . . 1·75 1·75
DESIGNS—VERT: 10c. Highway under construction; 20c. Darien Forest; 1b. Map of Pan-American Highway.

1957. Air. Surch **1957 x 10c x**.
614 **173** 10c. on 6c. black & violet 20 20

1957. Birth Centenary of Manuel Espinosa Batista (independence leader).
615 **185** 5c. blue and green 15 10

186 Portobelo Castle

189 U.N. Emblem

1957. Air. Buildings. Centres in black.
616 **186** 10c. grey 25 15
617 – 10c. purple 25 15
618 – 10c. violet 25 15
619 – 10c. grey and green . . . 25 15
620 – 10c. blue 25 15
621 – 10c. brown 25 15
622 – 10c. orange 25 15
623 – 10c. light blue 25 15
624 – 1b. red . . . . 2·10 95
DESIGNS—HORIZ: No. 617, San Jeronimo Castle; 618, Portobelo Customs-house; 619, Panama Hotel; 620, Pres. Remon Cantera Stadium; 621, Palace of Justice; 622, Treasury; 623, San Lorenzo Castle. VERT: No. 624, Jose Remon Clinics.

1957. Surch **1957** and value.
625 **172** 1c. on ½c. brown 10 10
626 3c. on ½c. brown 10 10

1958. Air. Surch **1958** and value.
627 **170** 5c. on 6c. green 20 10

1958. Air. 10th Anniv of U.N.O.
628 **189** 10c. green 20 10
629 21c. blue 45 35
630 50c. orange 45 45
631 – 1b. red, blue and grey . . 1·75 1·40
DESIGN: 1b. Flags of Panama and United Nations.

1958. No. 547 surch **3c 1958.**
633 3c. on 12c. purple 10 10

191 Flags Emblem

192 Brazilian Pavilion

1958. 10th Anniv of Organization of American States. Emblem (T **191**) multicoloured within yellow and black circular band; background colours given below.
634 **191** 1c. grey (postage) 10 10
635 2c. green 10 10
636 3c. red 15 10
637 7c. blue 25 10
638 5c. blue (air) 15 10
639 10c. red 20 15
640 – 50c. black, yellow and grey 35 35
641 **191** 1b. black . . . . 1·75 1·40
DESIGN—VERT: 50c. Headquarters building.

1958. Brussels International Exhbition.
642 **192** 1c. green & yellow (postage) 10 10
643 – 3c. green and blue 15 10
644 – 5c. slate and brown . . . 15 10
645 – 10c. brown and blue . . . 20 20
646 – 15c. violet and grey (air) 35 35
647 – 50c. brown and slate . . . 60 60
648 – 1b. turquoise and lilac . . 1·25 1·25
DESIGNS—PAVILIONS: As Type **192**: 3c. Argentina; 5c. Venezuela; 10c. Great Britain; 15c. Vatican City; 50c. United States; 1b. Belgium.

193 Pope Pius XII

194 Children on Farm

1959. Pope Pius XII Commemoration.
650 **193** 3c. brown (postage) . . . 15 10
651 – 5c. violet (air) 15 15
652 – 30c. mauve 30 25
653 – 50c. grey 75 60
PORTRAITS (Pope Pius XII): 5c. when Cardinal; 30c. wearing Papal tiara; 50c. enthroned.

1959. Obligatory Tax. Youth Rehabilitation Institute. Size 35 × 24 mm.
655 **194** 1c. grey and red 15 10

195 U.N. Headquarters, New York

197 J. A. Facio

1959. 10th Anniv of Declaration of Human Rights.
656 **195** 3c. olive & brown (postage) 10 10
657 – 15c. green and orange . . 35 25
658 – 5c. blue and green (air) 15 10
659 – 10c. brown and grey . . . 20 15
660 – 20c. slate and brown . . . 35 35
661 – 50c. blue and green . . . 60 60
662 **195** 1b. blue and red . . . . 1·40 1·25

DESIGNS: 5c., 15c. Family looking towards light; 10c., 20c. U.N. emblem and torch; 50c. U.N. flag.

1959. 8th Latin-American Economic Commission Congress. Nos. 656/61 optd **8A REUNION C.E.P.A.L. MAYO 1959** or surch also.
663 **195** 3c. olive and brown (postage) 10 10
664 – 15c. green and orange . . 35 20
665 – 5c. blue and green (air) 10 10
666 – 10c. brown and grey . . . 25 15
667 – 20c. slate and brown . . . 45 35
668 – 1b. on 50c. blue and green 1·60 1·60

1959. 50th Anniv of National Institute.
670 – 3c. red (postage) 10 10
671 – 13c. green 30 15
672 – 21c. blue 40 30
673 **197** 5c. black (air) 10 10
674 – 10c. black 20 10
DESIGNS—VERT: 3c. E. A. Morales (founder); 10c. Ernesto de la Guardia, Nr; 13c. A. Bravo. HORIZ: 21c. National Institute building.

1959. Obligatory Tax. Youth Rehabilitation Institute. As No. 655, but colours changed and inscr "1959".
675 **194** 1c. green and black . . . 10 10
676 1c. blue and black 10 10
See also No. 690.

198 Football **200** Administration Building

1959. 3rd Pan-American Games, Chicago. Inscr "III JUEGOS DEPORTIVOS PANAMERICANOS".
677 **198** 1c. green & grey (postage) 10 10
678 – 3c. brown and blue . . . 15 10
679 – 20c. brown and green . . 50 45
680 – 5c. brown and black (air) 15 10
681 – 10c. brown and grey . . . 25 20
682 – 50c. brown and blue . . . 45 40
DESIGNS: 3c. Swimming; 5c. Boxing; 10c. Baseball; 20c. Hurdling; 50c. Basketball.

1960. Air. World Refugee Year. Nos. 554/6 optd **NACIONES UNIDAS ANO MUNDIAL REFUGIADOS. 1959–1960.**
683 25c. black 35 35
684 50c. brown 70 55
685 1b. orange . . . . 1·50 1·10

1960. Air. 25th Anniv of National University.
686 **200** 10c. green 15 15
687 – 21c. blue 30 20
688 – 25c. blue 50 35
689 – 30c. black 55 40
DESIGNS: 21c. Faculty of Science; 25c. Faculty of Medicine; 30c. Statue of Dr. Octavio Mendez Pereira (first rector) and Faculty of Law.

1960. Obligatory Tax. Youth Rehabilitation Institute. As No. 655 but smaller (32 × 22 mm) and inscr "1960".
690 **194** 1c. grey and red 10 10

202 Fencing **204** "Population"

1960. Olympic Games.
691 **202** 3c. purple & violet (postage) 10 10
692 – 5c. green and turquoise 20 10
693 – 5c. red and orange (air) 10 10
694 – 10c. black and bistre . . . 20 15
695 – 25c. deep blue and blue 45 40
696 – 50c. black and brown . . 60 45
DESIGNS—VERT: 5c. (No. 692), Football; (No. 693), Basketball; 25c. Javelin-throwing; 50c. Runner with Olympic Flame. HORIZ: 10c. Cycling.

1960. Air. 6th National Census (5c.) and Central American Census.
698 **204** 5c. black 10 10
699 – 10c. brown 20 15
DESIGN: 10c. Two heads and map.

205 Boeing 707 Airliner

1960. Air.
700 **205** 5c. blue 15 10
701 10c. green 40 20
702 20c. brown 85 40

206 Pastoral Scene

1961. Agricultural Census (16th April).
703 **206** 3c. turquoise 10 10

207 Helen Keller School

1961. 25th Anniv of Lions Club.
705 – 3c. blue (postage) 10 10
706 **207** 5c. black (air) 10 10
707 – 10c. green 20 10
708 – 21c. blue, red and yellow 40 30
DESIGNS: 3c. Nino Hospital; 10c. Children's Colony, Verano; 21c. Lions emblem, arms and slogan.

1961. Air. Obligatory Tax. Youth Rehabilitation Fund. Surch **1 c "Rehabilitacion de Menores"**.
709 – 1c. on 10c. black and bistre (No. 694) 10 10
710 **205** 1c. on 10c. green 10 10

1961. Air. Surch **HABILITAD. en** and value.
712 **200** 1c. on 10c. green 10 10
713 – 1b. on 25c. blue and blue (No. 695) . . . . . . 1·25 1·25

210 Flags of Costa Rica and Panama

1961. Meeting of Presidents of Costa Rica and Panama.
715 **210** 3c. red and blue (postage) 15 10
716 – 1b. black and gold (air) 1·25 75
DESIGN: 1b. Pres. Chiari of Panama and Pres. Echandi of Costa Rica.

211 Girl using Sewing-machine **212** Campaign Emblem

1961. Obligatory Tax. Youth Rehabilitation Fund.
717 **211** 1c. violet 10 10
718 1c. yellow 10 10
719 1c. green 10 10
720 1c. blue 10 10
721 1c. purple 10 10
722 – 1c. mauve 10 10
723 – 1c. grey 10 10
724 – 1c. blue 10 10
725 – 1c. orange 10 10
726 – 1c. red 10 10
DESIGN: Nos. 722/6, Boy sawing wood.

1961. Air. Malaria Eradication.
727 **212** 5c.+5c. red 60 30
728 10c.+10c. blue 60 30
729 15c.+15c. green 60 30

213 Dag Hammarskjold **214** Arms of Panama

1961. Air. Death of Dag Hammarskjold.
730 **213** 10c. black and grey . . . 20 15

1962. Air. (a) Surch **Vale B/.0.15**.
731 **200** 15c. on 10c. green 30 20
(b) No. 810 surch **XX** over old value and **VALE B/ .1.00**.
732 – 1b. on 25c. deep blue and blue . . . . 1·25 75

1962. 3rd Central American Inter-Municipal Co-operation Assembly.
733 **214** 3c. red, yellow and blue (postage) 10 10
734 – 5c. black and blue (air) 20 10
DESIGN—HORIZ: 5c. City Hall, Colon.

215 Mercury on Cogwheel **217** Social Security Hospital

1962. 1st Industrial Census.
735 **215** 3c. red 10 10

1962. Surch **VALE** and value with old value obliterated.
736 **212** 10c. on 5c.+5c. red . . . 90 45
737 20c. on 10c.+10c. blue . . 1·50 90

1962. Opening of Social Security Hospital, Panama City.
738 **217** 3c. black and red 10 10

218 Colon Cathedral **221** Col. Glenn and Capsule "Friendship 7"

220 Thatcher Ferry Bridge nearing Completion

1962. "Freedom of Worship". Inscr "LIBERTAD DE CULTOS". Centres in black.
739 – 1c. red and blue (postage) 10 10
740 – 2c. red and cream 10 10
741 – 3c. blue and cream . . . 10 10
742 – 5c. red and green 10 10
743 – 10c. green and cream . . 20 15
744 – 10c. mauve and blue . . . 20 15
745 – 15c. blue and green . . . 30 20
746 **218** 20c. red and pink 35 25
747 – 25c. green and pink . . . 45 35
748 – 50c. blue and pink . . . 60 55
749 – 1b. violet and cream . . . 1·75 1·40
DESIGNS—HORIZ: 1c. San Francisco de Veraguas Church; 3c. David Cathedral; 25c. Orthodox Greek Temple; 1b. Colon Protestant Church. VERT: 2c. Panama Old Cathedral; 5c. Nata Church; 10c. Don Bosco Temple; 15c. Virgin of Carmen Church; 50c. Panama Cathedral.

750 – 5c. violet and flesh (air) . . 10 10
751 – 7c. light mauve and mauve 15 10
752 – 8c. violet and blue 15 10
753 – 10c. violet and salmon . . . 20 10
754 – 10c. green and purple . . . 20 20
755 – 15c. red and orange 25 20
756 – 21c. sepia and blue 35 30
757 – 25c. blue and pink 45 35
758 – 30c. mauve and blue 50 45
759 – 50c. purple and green . . . 70 70
760 – 1b. blue and salmon . . . . 1·25 1·10
DESIGNS—HORIZ: 5c. Cristo Rey Church; 7c. San Miguel Church; 21c. Canal Zone Synagogue; 25c. Panama Synagogue; 50c. Canal Zone Protestant Church. VERT: 8c. Santuario Church; 10c. Los Santos Church; 15c. Santa Ana Church; 30c. San Francisco Church; 1b. Canal Zone Catholic Church.

1962. Air. 9th Central American and Caribbean Games, Jamaica. Nos. 693 and 695 optd **"IX JUEGOS C.A. Y DEL CARIBE KINGSTON - 1962"** or surch also.
762 5c. red and orange 15 15
764 10c. on 25c. deep blue & blue 55 50
765 15c. on 25c. deep blue & blue 40 35
766 20c. on 25c. deep blue & blue 45 45
763 25c. deep blue and blue . . . 55 50

1962. Opening of Thatcher Ferry Bridge, Canal Zone.
767 **220** 3c. black and red (postage) 10 10
768 – 10c. black and blue (air) 20 15
DESIGN: 10c. Completed bridge.

1962. Air. Col. Glenn's Space Flight.
769 **221** 5c. red 10 10
770 – 10c. yellow 20 20
771 – 31c. blue 45 40
772 – 50c. green 65 65
DESIGNS—HORIZ: "Friendship": 10c. Over Earth; 31c. In space. VERT: 50c. Col. Glenn.

222 U.P.A.E. Emblem **225** F.A.O. Emblem

223 Water Exercise

1963. Air. 50th Anniv of Postal Union of Americas and Spain.
774 **222** 10c. multicoloured 20 15

1963. 75th Anniv of Panama Fire Brigade.
775 **223** 1c. black & green (postage) 10 10
776 – 3c. black and blue 10 10
777 – 5c. black and red 10 10
778 – 10c. black and orange (air) 15 15
779 – 15c. black and purple . . 20 20
780 – 21c. blue, gold and red . . 50 45
DESIGNS: 3c. Brigade officers; 5c. Brigade president and advisory council; 10c. "China" pump in action, 1887; 15c. "Cable 14" station and fire-engine; 21c. Fire Brigade badge.

1963. Air. Red Cross Cent (1st issue). Nos. 769/71 surch with red cross **1863 1963** and premium.
781 **215** 5c.+5c. red . . . . 1·40 1·40
782 – 10c.+10c. yellow . . . . 2·75 2·75
783 – 31c.+15c. blue . . . . . 2·75 2·75
See also No. 797.

1963. Air. Freedom from Hunger.
784 **225** 10c. red and green 20 20
785 15c. red and blue 30 25

1963. Air. 22nd Central American Lions Convention. Optd **"XXII Convencion Leonistica Centroamericana Panama, 18-21 Abril 1963"**.
786 **207** 5c. black 10 10

1963. Air. Surch **HABILITADO Vale B./0.04**.
789 **200** 4c. in 10c. green 10 10

1963. Air. Nos. 743 and 769 optd **AEREO** vert.
790 10c. green and cream 20 15
791 20c. brown and green 30 25

1963. Air. Freedom of the Press. No. 693 optd **LIBERTAD DE PRENSA 20-VIII-63**.
792 5c. red and orange 10 10

1963. Air. Visit of U.S. Astronauts to Panama. Optd **"Visita Astronautas Glenn-Schirra Sheppard Cooper a Panama"** or surch also.
793 **221** 5c. red . . . . 2·50 2·50
794 10c. on 5c. red . . . . . 3·25 3·25

1963. Air. Surch **HABILITADO 10c.**
796 **221** 10c. on 5c. red . . . . . 5·50 5·50

1963. Air. Red Cross Centenary (2nd issue). No. 781 surch **"Centenario Cruz Roja Internacional 10c"** with premium obliterated.
797 **221** 10c. on 5c.+5c. red . . . 6·00 6·00

1963. Surch **VALE** and value.
798 **217** 4c. on 3c. black and red (postage) 15 10
799 – 4c. on 3c. black, blue and cream (No. 741) . . . 15 10
800 **220** 4c. on 3c. black and red 15 10
801 – 4c. on 3c. black and blue (No. 776) 15 10
802 **182** 10c. on 25c. blue and red 35 15
803 – 10c. on 25c. blue (No. 688) (air) 20 15

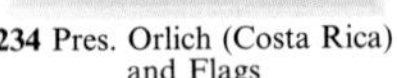

234 Pres. Orlich (Costa Rica) and Flags

236 Vasco Nunez de Balboa

235 Innsbruck

1963. Presidential Reunion, San Jose (Costa Rica). Multicoloured. Presidents and flags of their countries.
804 1c. Type **234** (postage) . . . 10 10
805 2c. Somoza (Nicaragua) . . . 15 15
806 3c. Villeda (Honduras) . . . 20 15
807 4c. Chiari (Panama) 25 20

808 5c. Rivera (El Salvador) (air) 30 30
809 10c. Ydigoras (Guatemala) 55 45
810 21c. Kennedy (U.S.A.) . . . 1·60 1·40

1963. Winter Olympic Games, Innsbruck.
811 ½c. red and blue (postage) . . 10 10
812 1c. red, brown and turquoise 10 10
813 3c. red and blue 25 15
814 4c. red, brown and green . . 35 20

815 5c. red, brown and mauve (air) 45 25
816 15c. red, brown and blue . . 1·10 90
817 21c. red, brown and myrtle 2·25 1·90
818 31c. red, brown and blue . . 3·00 2·25
DESIGNS: ½c. (expressed "B/0.005"), 3c. Type **235**; 1, 4c. Speed-skating; 5c. to 31c. Skiing (slalom).

1964. 450th Anniv of Discovery of Pacific Ocean.
820 **236** 4c. green on flesh (postage) 10 10
821 10c. violet on pink (air) 20 20

237 Boy Scout

238 St. Paul's Cathedral, London

1964. Obligatory Tax for Youth Rehabilitation Institute.
822 **237** 1c. red 10 10
823 1c. grey 10 10
824 1c. light blue 10 10
825 1c. olive 10 10
826 1c. violet 10 10
827 – 1c. brown 10 10
828 – 1c. orange 10 10
829 – 1c. turquoise 10 10
830 – 1c. violet 10 10
831 – 1c. yellow 10 10
DESIGN: Nos. 827/31, Girl guide.

1964. Air. Ecumenical Council, Vatican City (1st issue). Cathedrals. Centres in black.
832 21c. red (Type **238**) 55 35
833 21c. blue (Kassa, Hungary) 55 35
834 21c. green (Milan) 55 35
835 21c. black (St. John's, Poland) 55 35
836 21c. brown (St. Stephen's, Vienna) 55 35
837 21c. brown (Notre Dame, Paris) 55 35
838 21c. violet (Moscow) 55 35
839 21c. violet (Lima) 55 35
840 21c. red (Stockholm) 55 35
841 21c. mauve (Cologne) 55 35
842 21c. bistre (New Delhi) . . . 55 35
843 21c. deep turquoise (Basel) 55 35
844 21c. green (Toledo) 55 35
845 21c. red (Metropolitan, Athens) 55 35
846 21c. olive (St. Patrick's, New York) 55 35
847 21c. green (Lisbon) 55 35
848 21c. turquoise (Sofia) 55 35
849 21c. deep brown (New Church, Delft, Netherlands) 55 35
850 21c. deep sepia (St. George's Patriarchal Church, Istanbul) 55 35
851 21c. blue (Basilica, Guadalupe, Mexico) . . . 55 35
852 1b. blue (Panama) . . . . . 1·75 1·75
853 2b. green (St. Peter's, Rome) 3·00 3·00
See also Nos. 882, etc.

1964. As Nos. 749 and 760 but colours changed and optd **HABILITADA**.
855 1b. black, red & blue (postage) . . . . 1·75 1·60
856 1b. black, green & yellow (air) . . . . 1·75 1·25

1964. Air. No. 756 surch **VALE B/. 0.50**.
857 50c. on 21c. black, sepia and blue 65 40

241 Discus-thrower

1964. Olympic Games, Tokyo.
858 ½c. ("B/0.005") purple, red, brown and green (postage) 10 10
859 1c. multicoloured 10 10

860 5c. black, red and olive (air) 35 25
861 10c. black, red and yellow . . 70 45
862 21c. multicoloured . . . . . 1·40 90
863 50c. multicoloured . . . . . 2·75 1·75
DESIGNS: ½c. Type **241**; 1c. Runner with Olympic Flame; 5c. to 50c. Olympic Stadium, Tokyo, and Mt. Fuji.

1964. Air. Nos. 692 and 742 surch **Aereo B/.0.10**.
865 10c. on 5c. green and turquoise 20 15
866 10c. on 5c. black, red and green 20 15

243 Space Vehicles (Project "Apollo")

1964. Space Exploration. Multicoloured.
867 ½c. ("B/0.005") Type **243** (postage) 10 10
868 1c. Rocket and capsule (Project "Gemini") 10 10

869 5c. W. M. Schirra (air) . . . 20 20
870 10c. L. G. Cooper 30 30
871 21c. Schirra's capsule 75 75
872 50c. Cooper's capsule . . . . 3·25 3·00

1964. No. 687 surch **Correos B/. 0.10**.
874 10c. on 21c. blue 15 15

245 Water-skiing

1964. Aquatic Sports. Multicoloured.
875 ½c. ("B/0.005") Type **245** (postage) 10 10
876 1c. Underwater swimming . . 10 10

877 5c. Fishing (air) 20 10
878 10c. Sailing (vert) . . . . . 1·50 60
879 21c. Speedboat racing . . . . 2·75 1·50
880 31c. Water polo at Olympic Games, 1964 . . . . . . 3·50 1·75

1964. Air. Ecumenical Council, Vatican City (2nd issue). Stamps of 1st issue optd **1964**. Centres in black.
882 21c. red (No. 832) 70 50
883 21c. green (No. 834) 70 50
884 21c. olive (No. 836) 70 50
885 21c. deep sepia (No. 850) . . 70 50
886 1b. blue (No. 852) . . . . . 2·75 2·00
887 2b. green (No. 853) . . . . . 5·50 4·50

247 General View

248 Eleanor Roosevelt

1964. Air. New York's World Fair.
889 **247** 5c. black and yellow . . . 30 25
890 – 10c. black and red 75 60
891 – 15c. black and green . . . 1·25 80
892 – 21c. black and blue . . . 1·90 1·50
DESIGNS: 10c., 15c. Fair pavilions (different); 21c. Unisphere.

1964. Mrs. Eleanor Roosevelt Commemoration.
894 **248** 4c. black and red on yellow (postage) 15 10
895 20c. black and green on buff (air) 50 45

249 Dag Hammarskjold

250 Pope John XXIII

1964. Air. U.N. Day.
897 **249** 21c. black and blue . . . 70 50
898 – 21c. blue and black . . . 70 50
DESIGN: No. 898, U.N. Emblem.

1964. Air. Pope John Commemoration.
900 **250** 21c. black and bistre . . . 70 50
901 – 21c. mult (Papal Arms) 70 50

251 Slalom Skiing Medals

1964. Winter Olympic Winners' Medals. Medals in gold, silver and bronze.
903 **251** ½c. ("B/0.005") turquoise (postage) 10 10
904 – 1c. deep blue 10 10
905 – 2c. brown 20 15
906 – 3c. mauve 25 15
907 – 4c. lake 35 20

908 – 5c. violet (air) 45 25
909 – 6c. blue 55 30
910 – 7c. violet 65 35
911 – 10c. green 90 50
912 – 21c. red . . . . 1·40 95
913 – 31c. blue . . . . 2·50 1·40
DESIGNS—Medals for: 1c., 7c. Speed-skating; 2c., 21c. Bobsleighing; 3c., 10c. Figure-skating; 4c. Ski-jumping; 5c., 6c., 31c. Cross-country skiing. Values in the same design show different medal-winners and country names.

252 Red-billed Toucan

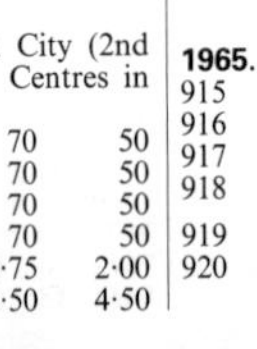

1965. Birds. Multicoloured.
915 1c. Type **252** (postage) . . . 65 10
916 2c. Scarlet macaw 65 10
917 3c. Woodpecker sp. . . . . . 1·00 15
918 4c. Blue-grey tanager (horiz) 1·00 25

919 5c. Troupial (horiz) (air) . . . 1·25 40
920 10c. Crimson-backed tanager (horiz) . . . . 2·60 55

253 Red Snapper

1965. Marine Life. Multicoloured.
921 1c. Type **253** (postage) . . . 10 10
922 2c. Dolphin (fish) 10 10

923 8c. Shrimp (air) 20 15
924 12c. Smooth hammerhead . . 60 25
925 13c. Sailfish 65 30
926 25c. Lined seahorse (vert) . . 80 35

254 Double Daisy and Emblem

1966. Air. 50th Anniv of Junior Chamber of Commerce. Flowers. Multicoloured: background colour given.
927 **254** 30c. mauve 55 45
928 – 30c. flesh (Hibiscus) . . . 55 45
929 – 30c. olive (Mauve orchid) 55 45
930 – 40c. green (Water lily) . . 60 55
931 – 40c. blue (Gladiolus) . . . 60 55
932 – 40c. pink (White orchid) 60 55
Each design incorporates the Junior Chamber of Commerce Emblem.

1966. Surch. (a) Postage.
933 13c. on 25c. (No. 747) . . . 30 20

(b) Air.
934 3c. on 5c. (No. 680) 10 10
935 13c. on 25c. (No. 695) . . . 30 25

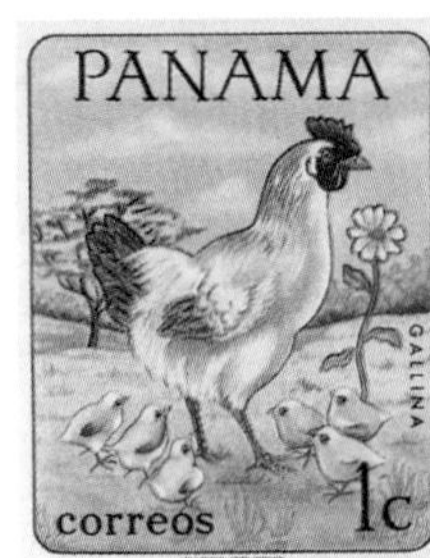

256 Chicken

1967. Domestic Animals. Multicoloured.
936 1c. Type **256** (postage) . . . 10 10
937 3c. Cockerel 10 10
938 5c. Pig (horiz) 10 10
939 8c. Cow (horiz) 15 10

940 10c. Pekingese dog (air) . . . 25 20
941 13c. Zebu (horiz) 30 20
942 30c. Cat 60 50
943 40c. Horse (horiz) 75 60

257 American Darter

1967. Wild Birds. Multicoloured.
944 ½c. Type **257** 70 15
945 1c. Resplendent quetzal . . . 70 15
946 3c. Turquoise-browed motmot 90 20
947 4c. Red-necked aracari (horiz) . . . . 1·00 30
948 5c. Chestnut-fronted macaw 1·40 30
949 13c. Belted kingfisher . . . . 5·00 1·40

258 "Deer" (F. Marc)

1967. Wild Animals. Paintings. Multicoloured.
950 1c. Type **258** (postage) . . . 10 10
951 3c. "Cougar" (F. Marc) (vert) 10 10
952 5c. "Monkeys" (F. Marc) . . 10 10
953 8c. "Fox" (F. Marc) 20 10
954 10c. "St. Jerome and the Lion" (Durer) (vert) (air) 20 15
955 13c. "The Hare" (Durer) (vert) 30 20
956 20c. "Lady with the Ermine" (Da Vinci) (vert) 45 25
957 30c. "The Hunt" (Delacroix) 65 45

259 Map of Panama and People

1969. National Population Census.
958 **259** 5c. blue 10 10
959 – 10c. purple 20 15
DESIGN—VERT: 10c. People and map of the Americas.

260 Cogwheel

1969. 50th Anniv of Rotary Int in Panama.
960 **260** 13c. black, yellow and blue 20 20

261 Cornucopia and Map

1969. 1st Anniv of 11 October Revolution.
961 **261** 10c. multicoloured 20 10

262 Tower and Map

1969.
962 **262** 3c. black and orange . . 10 10
963 – 5c. green 10 10
964 – 8c. brown 20 15
965 – 13c. black and green . . . 25 15
966 – 20c. brown 35 25
967 – 21c. yellow 35 25
968 – 25c. green 45 30
969 – 30c. black 50 45
970 – 34c. brown 55 45
971 – 38c. blue 60 45
972 – 40c. yellow 65 45
973 – 50c. black and purple . . 85 65
974 – 59c. purple . . . . 1·00 60
DESIGNS—HORIZ: 5c. Peasants; 13c. Hotel Continental; 25c. Del Rey Bridge; 34c. Panama Cathedral; 38c. Municipal Palace; 40c. French Plaza; 50c. Thatcher Ferry Bridge; 59c. National Theatre. VERT: 8c. Nata Church; 20c. Virgin of Carmen Church; 21c. Altar, San Jose Church; 30c. Dr. Arosemena statue.

263 Discus-thrower and Stadium

1970. 11th Central American and Caribbean Games, Panama (1st series).
975 **263** 1c. multicoloured (postage) 10 10
976 2c. multicoloured 10 10
977 3c. multicoloured 10 10
978 5c. multicoloured 10 10
979 10c. multicoloured 20 15
980 13c. multicoloured 25 15
981 – 13c. multicoloured 25 15
982 **263** 25c. multicoloured 45 35
983 30c. multicoloured 55 45
984 – 13c. multicoloured (air) 1·00 25
985 – 30c. multicoloured 60 45
DESIGNS—VERT: No. 981, "Flor del Espirited Santo" (flowers); 985, Indian girl. HORIZ: No. 984, Thatcher Ferry Bridge and palm.
See also Nos. 986/94.

264 J. D. Arosemena and Stadium

1970. Air. 11th Central American and Caribbean Games, Panama (2nd series). Multicoloured.
986 1c. Type **264** 10 10
987 2c. Type **264** 10 10
988 3c. Type **264** 10 10
989 5c. Type **264** 10 10
990 13c. Basketball 20 15
991 13c. New Gymnasium . . . 20 15
992 13c. Revolution Stadium . . 20 15
993 13c. Panamanian couple in festive costume 20 15
994 30c. Eternal Flame and stadium 45 35

265 A. Tapia and M. Sosa (first comptrollers)

1971. 40th Anniv of Panamanian Comptroller-General's Office. Multicoloured.
996 3c. Comptroller-General's Building (1970) (vert) . . . 10 10
997 5c. Type **265** 10 10
998 8c. Comptroller-General's emblem (vert) 15 10
999 13c. Comptroller-General's Building (1955–70) 30 15

266 "Man and Alligator"

267 Map of Panama on I.E.Y. Emblem

1971. Indian Handicrafts.
1000 **266** 8c. multicoloured 20 15

1971. International Education Year.
1001 **267** 1b. multicoloured . . . 1·50 1·50

268 Astronaut on Moon

269 Panama Pavilion

1971. Air. "Apollo 11" and "Apollo 12" Moon Missions. Multicoloured.
1002 13c. Type **268** 35 25
1003 13c. "Apollo 12" astronauts 35 25

1971. Air. "EXPO 70" World Fair, Osaka, Japan.
1004 **269** 10c. multicoloured . . . 15 15

270 Conference Text and Emblem

1971. 9th Inter-American Loan and Savings Association Conference, Panama City.
1005 **270** 25c. multicoloured . . . 60 35

271 Panama Flag

1971. Air. American Tourist Year. Multicoloured.
1006 5c. Type **271** 10 10
1007 13c. Map of Panama and Western Hemisphere . . . 30 20

272 New U.P.U. H.Q. Building

1971. Inauguration of New U.P.U. Headquarters Building, Berne. Multicoloured.
1008 8c. Type **272** 20 10
1009 30c. U.P.U. Monument, Berne (vert) 60 35

273 Cow and Pig

1971. 3rd Agricultural Census.
1010 **273** 3c. multicoloured 10 10

274 Map and "4S" Emblem

1971. "4S" Programme for Rural Youth.
1011 **274** 2c. multicoloured 10 10

275 Gandhi

276 Central American Flags

1971. Air. Birth Centenary (1969) of Mahatma Gandhi.
1012 **275** 10c. multicoloured . . . 20 15

1971. Air. 150th Anniv of Central American States' Independence from Spain.
1013 **276** 13c. multicoloured . . . 30 20

277 Early Panama Stamp

278 Altar, Nata Church

1971. Air. 2nd National, Philatelic and Numismatic Exhibition, Panama.
1014 **277** 8c. blue, black and red 20 15

1972. Air. 450th Anniv of Nata Church.
1015 **278** 40c. multicoloured . . . 50 45

279 Telecommunications Emblem

1972. Air. World Telecommunications Day.
1016 **279** 13c. black, blue & lt blue 20 15

280 "Apollo 14" Badge

1972. Air. Moon Flight of "Apollo 14".
1017 **280** 13c. multicoloured . . . 60 25

281 Children on See-saw

1972. 25th Anniv (1971) of U.N.I.C.E.F. Mult.
1018 1c. Type **281** (postage) . . . 10 10
1019 5c. Boy sitting by kerb (vert) (air) 10 10
1020 8c. Indian mother and child (vert) 15 10
1021 50c. U.N.I.C.E.F. emblem (vert) 70 45

282 Tropical Fruits

1972. Tourist Publicity. Multicoloured.
1023 1c. Type **282** (postage) . . . 10 10
1024 2c. "Isle of Night" 10 10
1025 3c. Carnival float (vert) . . 10 10
1026 5c. San Blas textile (air) . . 10 10
1027 8c. Chaquira (beaded collar) 20 10
1028 25c. Ruined fort, Portobelo 35 30

283 Map and Flags

284 Baseball Players

1973. Obligatory Tax. Panama City Post Office Building Fund. 7th Bolivar Games.
1030 **283** 1c. black 10 10

1973. Air. 7th Bolivar Games.
1031 **284** 8c. red and yellow . . . 15 10
1032 – 10c. black and blue . . . 20 15
1033 – 13c. multicoloured . . . 30 20
1034 – 25c. black, red and green 55 30
1035 – 50c. multicoloured . . . 1·25 55
1036 – 1b. multicoloured . . . 2·50 1·10
DESIGNS—VERT: 10c. Basketball; 13c. Flaming torch. HORIZ: 25c. Boxing; 50c. Panama map and flag, Games emblem and Bolivar; 1b. Games' medals.

1973. U.N. Security Council Meeting, Panama City. Various stamps surch **O.N.U.** in laurel leaf, **CONSEJO DE SEGURIDAD 15 - 21 Marzo 1973** and value.
1037 8c. on 59c. (No. 974) (postage) 10 10
1038 10c. on 1b. (No. 1001) . . . 15 15
1039 13c. on 30c. (No. 969) . . . 20 15
1040 13c. on 40c. (No. 1015) (air) 25 15

286 Farming Co-operative

1973. Obligatory Tax. Post Office Building Fund.
1041 **286** 1c. green and red 10 10
1042 – 1c. grey and red 10 10
1043 – 1c. yellow and red . . . 10 10
1044 – 1c. orange and red . . . 10 10
1045 – 1c. blue and red 10 10
DESIGNS: No. 1042, Silver coins; 1043, V. Lorenzo; 1044, Cacique Urraca; 1045, Post Office building.
See also Nos. 1061/2.

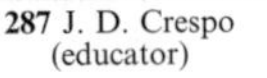

287 J. D. Crespo (educator)

290 Women's upraised Hands

1973. Famous Panamanians. Multicoloured.
1046 3c. Type **287** (postage) . . . 10 10
1047 5c. Isabel Obaldia (educator) (air) 10 10
1048 8c. N. V. Jaen (educator) . . 20 15
1049 10c. "Forest Scene" (Roberto Lewis, painter) 20 15
1050 13c. R. Miro (poet) 35 20
1051 13c. "Portrait of a Lady" (M. E. Amador, painter) 35 20
1052 20c. "Self-Portrait" (Isaac Benitez, painter) 55 20
1053 21c. M. A. Guerrero (statesman) 55 25
1054 25c. Dr. B. Porras (statesman) 55 30
1055 30c. J. D. Arosemena (statesman) 70 35
1056 34c. Dr. O. M. Pereira (writer) 90 45
1057 38c. Dr. R. J. Alfaro (writer) . . . . 1·10 50

1973. Air. 50th Anniv of Isabel Obaldia Professional School. Nos. 1047, 1054 and 1056 optd **1923 1973 Godas de Oro Escuela Profesional Isabel Herrera Obaldia** and EP emblem.
1058 5c. multicoloured 15 10
1059 25c. multicoloured 55 30
1060 34c. multicoloured 60 55

1974. Obligatory Tax. Post Office Building Fund. As Nos. 1044/5.
1061 1c. orange 10 10
1062 2c. blue 10 10

1974. Surch **VALE** and value.
1063 5c. on 30c. black (No. 969) (postage) 10 10
1064 10c. on 34c. brown (No. 970) 15 10
1065 13c. on 21c. yellow (No. 967) 20 15
1066 1c. on 25c. multicoloured (No. 1028) (air) 10 10
1067 3c. on 20c. mult (No. 1052) 10 10
1068 8c. on 38c. mult (No. 1057) 15 10
1069 10c. on 34c. mult (No. 1056) 15 15
1070 13c. on 21c. mult (No. 1053) 20 15

1975. Air. International Women's Year.
1071 **290** 17c. multicoloured . . . 45 20

291 Bayano Dam

1975. Air. 7th Anniv of October 1968 Revolution.
1073 **291** 17c. black, brown & blue 20 15
1074 – 27c. blue and green . . . 30 25
1075 – 33c. multicoloured . . . 1·10 30
DESIGNS—VERT: 27c. Victoria sugar plant, Veraguas, and sugar cane. HORIZ: 33c. Tocumen International Airport.

1975. Obligatory Tax. Various stamps surch **VALE PRO EDIFICIO** and value.
1076 – 1c. on 30c. black (No. 969) (postage) . . 10 10
1077 – 1c. on 40c. yellow (No. 972) 10 10
1078 – 1c. on 50c. black and purple (No. 973) . . . 10 10
1079 – 1c. on 30c. mult (No. 1009) 10 10
1080 **282** 1c. on 1c. multicoloured 10 10
1081 – 1c. on 2c. multicoloured (No. 1024) 10 10
1082 **278** 1c. on 40c. mult (air) . . 10 10
1083 – 1c. on 25c. mult (No. 1028) 10 10
1084 – 1c. on 25c. mult (No. 1052) 10 10
1085 – 1c. on 20c. mult (No. 1054) 10 10
1086 – 1c. on 30c. mult (No. 1055) 10 10

1975. Obligatory Tax. Post Office Building Fund. As No. 1045.
1087 1c. red 10 10

294 Bolivar and Thatcher Ferry Bridge

1976. 150th Anniv of Panama Congress (1st issue). Multicoloured.
1088 6c. Type **294** (postage) . . . 10 10
1089 23c. Bolivar Statue (air) . . 30 25
1090 35c. Bolivar Hall, Panama City (horiz) 50 30
1091 41c. Bolivar and flag . . . 60 40

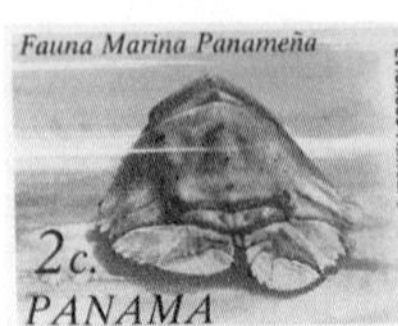

295 "Evibacus princeps"

1976. Marine Fauna. Multicoloured.
1092 2c. Type **295** (postage) . . . 10 10
1093 3c. "Ptitosarcus sinuosus" (vert) 10 10
1094 4c. "Acanthaster planci" . . 10 10
1095 7c. "Oreaster reticulatus" . . 10 10
1096 17c. Porcupinefish (vert) (air) 60 20
1097 27c. "Pocillopora damicornis" 40 25

296 "Simon Bolivar"

1976. 150th Anniv of Panama Congress (2nd issue). Designs showing details of Bolivar Monument or flags of Latin-American countries. Multicoloured.
1099 20c. Type **296** 30 20
1100 20c. Argentina 30 20
1101 20c. Bolivia 30 20
1102 20c. Brazil 30 20
1103 20c. Chile 30 20
1104 20c. "Battle scene" 30 20
1105 20c. Colombia 30 20
1106 20c. Costa Rica 30 20
1107 20c. Cuba 30 20
1108 20c. Ecuador 30 20
1109 20c. El Salvador 30 20
1110 20c. Guatemala 30 20
1111 20c. Guyana 30 20
1112 20c. Haiti 30 20
1113 20c. "Congress assembly" . . 30 20
1114 20c. "Liberated people" . . 30 20
1115 20c. Honduras 30 20
1116 20c. Jamaica 30 20
1117 20c. Mexico 30 20
1118 20c. Nicaragua 30 20
1119 20c. Panama 30 20
1120 20c. Paraguay 30 20
1121 20c. Peru 30 20
1122 20c. Dominican Republic . . 30 20
1123 20c. "Bolivar and standard-bearer" 30 20
1124 20c. Surinam 30 20
1125 20c. Trinidad and Tobago . . 30 20
1126 20c. Uruguay 30 20
1127 20c. Venezuela 30 20
1128 20c. "Indian Delegation" . . 30 20

297 Nicanor Villalaz (designer of Panama Arms)

298 National Lottery Building, Panama City

1976. Villalaz Commemoration.
1130 **297** 5c. blue 10 10

1976. "Progressive Panama".
1131 **298** 6c. multicoloured 10 10

299 Cerro Colorado, Copper Mine

1976. Air.
1132 **299** 23c. multicoloured . . . 30 20

300 Contadora Island

1977. Tourism.
1133 **300** 3c. multicoloured 10 10

301 Secretary-General of Pan-American Union, A. Orfila

1978. Signing of Panama–U.S.A. Treaty. Mult.
1134 3c. Type **301** 10 10
1135 23c. Treaty signing scene (horiz) 30 25
1136 40c. President Carter . . . 55 30
1137 50c. Gen. O. Torrijos of Panama 70 50
Nos. 1134 and 1136/7 were issued together se-tenant in horizontal stamps of three showing Treaty signing as No. 1135.

302 Signing Ratification of Panama Canal Treaty

1978. Ratification of Panama Canal Treaty.
1138 **302** 3c. multicoloured 10 10
1139 – 5c. multicoloured 10 10
1140 – 35c. multicoloured . . . 50 25
1141 – 41c. multicoloured . . . 60 30
DESIGNS: 5, 35, 41c. As Type **302**, but with the design of the Ratification Ceremony spread over the three stamps, issued as a se-tenant strip in the order 5c. (29 × 39 mm), 41c. (44 × 39 mm), 35c. (29 × 39 mm).

303 Colon Harbour and Warehouses

1978. 30th Anniv of Colon Free Zone.
1142 **303** 6c. multicoloured 10 10

304 Children's Home and Melvin Jones

1978. Birth Centenary of Melvin Jones (founder of Lions International).
1143 **304** 50c. multicoloured . . . 70 55

305 Pres. Torrijos, "Flavia" (liner) and Children

1979. Return of Canal Zone. Multicoloured.
1144 3c. Type **305** . . . . 1·25 55
1145 23c. Presidents Torrijos and Carter, liner and flags of Panama and U.S.A. . . . 50 25

306 "75" and Bank Emblem

1979. 75th Anniv of National Bank.
1146 **306** 6c. black, red and blue 10 10

307 Rotary Emblem

308 Children inside Heart

1979. 75th Anniv of Rotary International.
1147 **307** 17c. blue and yellow . . 25 20

1979. International Year of the Child.
1148 **308** 50c. multicoloured . . . 70 45

309 U.P.U. Emblem and Globe

310 Colon Station

1979. 18th Universal Postal Union Congress, Rio de Janeiro.
1149 **309** 35c. multicoloured . . . 50 30

1980. Centenary of Trans-Panamanian Railway.
1150 **310** 1c. purple and lilac . . . 20 35

311 Postal Headquarters, Balboa (inauguration)

318 Boys in Children's Village

1980. Anniversaries and Events.
1151 **311** 3c. multicoloured 10 10
1152 – 6c. multicoloured 10 10
1153 – 17c. multicoloured . . . 25 20
1154 – 23c. multicoloured . . . 30 20
1155 – 35c. blue, black and red 50 30
1156 – 41c. pink and black . . 60 40
1157 – 50c. multicoloured . . . 70 45
DESIGNS—HORIZ: 17c. Map of Central America and flags (census of the Americas); 23c. Tourism and Convention Centre (opening); 35c. Bank emblem (Inter-American Development Bank, 25th anniv); 41c. F. de Lesseps (Panama Canal cent); 50c. Olympic Stadium, Moscow (Olympic Games). VERT: 6c. National flag (return of Canal Zone).

1980. Olympic Games, Lake Placid and Moscow. (a) Optd **1980 LAKE PLACID MOSCU** and venue emblems.
1158 20c. (No. 1099) 80 80
1159 20c. (1101) 80 80
1162 20c. (1103) 80 80
1164 20c. (1105) 80 80
1166 20c. (1107) 80 80
1168 20c. (1109) 80 80
1170 20c. (1111) 80 80
1172 20c. (1113) 80 80
1174 20c. (1115) 80 80
1176 20c. (1117) 80 80
1178 20c. (1119) 80 80
1180 20c. (1121) 80 80
1182 20c. (1123) 80 80

1184 20c. (1125) 80 80
1186 20c. (1127) 80 80

(b) Optd with Lake Placid Olympic emblems and medals total of country indicated.
1159 20c. "**ALEMANIA D.**" (1101) 80 80
1161 20c. "**AUSTRIA**" (1102) . . 80 80
1163 20c. "**SUECIA**" (1104) . . . 80 80
1165 20c. "**U.R.S.S.**" (1106) . . . 80 80
1167 20c. "**ALEMANIA F.**" (1108) 80 80
1169 20c. "**ITALIA**" (1110) . . . 80 80
1171 20c. "**U.S.A.**" (1112) 80 80
1173 20c. "**SUIZA**" (1114) . . . 80 80
1175 20c. "**CANADA/GRAN BRETANA**" (1116) . . . 80 80
1177 20c. "**NORUEGA**" (1118) 80 80
1179 20c. "**LICHTENSTEIN**" (1120) 80 80
1181 20c. "**HUNGRIA/ BULGARIA**" (1122) . . . 80 80
1183 20c. "**FINLANDIA**" (1124) 80 80
1185 20c. "**HOLANDA**" (1126) 80 80
1187 20c. "**CHECOS- LOVAQUIA/FRANCIA**" (1128) 80 80

Nos. 1158, etc, occur on 1st, 3rd and 5th rows and Nos. 1159, etc, occur on the others.

(c) Lake Placid and Moscow and venue with Olympic rings.
1188 20c. (No. 1099) 80 80
1190 20c. (1101) 80 80
1192 20c. (1103) 80 80
1194 20c. (1105) 80 80
1196 20c. (1107) 80 80
1198 20c. (1109) 80 80
1200 20c. (1111) 80 80
1202 20c. (1113) 80 80
1204 20c. (1115) 80 80
1206 20c. (1117) 80 80
1208 20c. (1119) 80 80
1210 20c. (1121) 80 80
1212 20c. (1123) 80 80
1214 20c. (1125) 80 80
1216 20c. (1127) 80 80

(d) Optd with country names as indicated.
1189 20c. "**RUSIA/ALEMANIA D.**" (1101) 80 80
1191 20c. "**SUECIA/ FINLANDIA**" (1102) . . 80 80
1193 20c. "**GRECIA/BELGICA/ INDIA**" (1104) 80 80
1195 20c. "**BULGARIA/CUBA**" (1106) 80 80
1197 20c. "**CHECOS- LOVAQUIA/ YUGOSLAVIA**" (1108) 80 80
1199 20c. "**ZIMBAWE/COREA DEL NORTE/ MONGOLIA**" (1110) . . 80 80
1201 20c. "**ITALIA/HUNGRIA**" (1112) 80 80
1203 20c. "**AUSTRALIA/ DINAMARCA**" (1114) . . 80 80
1205 20c. "**TANZANIA/ MEXICO/HOLANDA**" (1116) 80 80
1207 20c. "**RUMANIA/ FRANCIA**" (1118) . . . 80 80
1209 20c. "**BRASIL/ETIOPIA**" (1120) 80 80
1211 20c. "**IRLANDA/UGANDA/ VENEZUELA**" (1122) . . 80 80
1213 20c. "**GRAN BRETANA/ POLONIA**" (1124) . . . 80 80
1215 20c. "**SUIZA/ESPANA/ AUSTRIA**" (1126) . . . 80 80
1217 20c. "**JAMAICA/LIBANO/ GUYANA**" (1128) 80 80

Nos. 1188, etc, occur on 1st, 3rd and 5th rows and Nos. 1189, etc, on the others.

1980. Medal Winners at Winter Olympic Games, Lake Placid. (a) Optd with 1980, medals and venue emblems.
1219 20c. 1980 medals and venue and emblems (No. 1099) 80 80
1221 20c. As No. 1219 (1101) . . 80 80
1223 20c. As No. 1219 (1103) . . 80 80
1225 20c. As No. 1219 (1105) . . 80 80
1227 20c. As No. 1219 (1107) . . 80 80
1229 20c. As No. 1219 (1109) . . 80 80
1231 20c. As No. 1219 (1111) . . 80 80
1233 20c. As No. 1219 (1113) . . 80 80
1235 20c. As No. 1219 (1115) . . 80 80
1237 20c. As No. 1219 (1117) . . 80 80
1239 20c. As No. 1219 (1119) . . 80 80
1241 20c. As No. 1219 (1121) . . 80 80
1243 20c. As No. 1219 (1123) . . 80 80
1245 20c. As No. 1219 (1125) . . 80 80
1247 20c. As No. 1219 (1127) . . 80 80

(b) Optd with 1980 medals and venue emblems and Olympic torch and country indicated.
1220 20c. "**ALEMANIA D.**" (1100) 80 80
1222 20c. "**AUSTRIA**" (1102) . . 80 80
1224 20c. "**SUECIA**" (1104) . . . 80 80
1226 20c. "**U.R.S.S.**" (1106) . . . 80 80
1228 20c. "**ALEMANIA F.**" (1108) 80 80
1230 20c. "**ITALIA**" (1110) . . . 80 80
1232 20c. "**U.S.A.**" (1112) 80 80
1234 20c. "**SUIZA**" (1114) . . . 80 80
1236 20c. "**CANADA/GRAN BRETANA**" (1116) . . . 80 80
1238 20c. "**NORUEGA**" (1118) 80 80
1240 20c. "**LICHTENSTEIN**" (1120) 80 80
1242 20c. "**HUNGRIA/ BULGARIA**" (1122) . . . 80 80
1244 20c. "**FINLANDIA**" (1124) 80 80
1246 20c. "**HOLANDA**" (1126) 80 80
1248 20c. "**CHECOS- LOVAQUIA/FRANCIA**" (1128) 80 80

Nos. 1219, etc, occur on 1st, 3rd and 5th rows and Nos. 1220, etc, on the others.

1980. World Cup Football Championship, Argentina (1978) and Spain (1980). Optd with: A. Football cup emblems. B. "**ESPAMER 80**" and "Argentina '78" emblems and inscriptions "**ESPANA '82/ CAMPEONATO/MUNDIAL DE FUTBOL**". C. World Cup Trophy and "**ESPANA '82.**". D. "**ESPANA 82/Football/Argentina '78/BESPAMER '80 MADRID**". E. FIFA globes emblem and "**ESPANA '82/ARGENTINAA '78/ESPANA '82**". F. With ball and inscription as for B.
1249 20c. No. 1099 (A, C, E) . . 80 80
1250 20c. No. 1100 (B, D, F) . . 80 80
1251 20c. No. 1101 (A, C, E) . . 80 80
1252 20c. No. 1102 (B, D, F) . . 80 80
1253 20c. No. 1103 (A, C, E) . . 80 80
1254 20c. No. 1104 (B, D, F) . . 80 80
1255 20c. No. 1105 (A, C, E) . . 80 80
1256 20c. No. 1106 (B, D, F) . . 80 80
1257 20c. No. 1107 (A, C, E) . . 80 80
1258 20c. No. 1108 (B, D, F) . . 80 80
1259 20c. No. 1109 (A, C, E) . . 80 80
1260 20c. No. 1110 (B, D, F) . . 80 80
1261 20c. No. 1111 (A, C, E) . . 80 80
1262 20c. No. 1112 (B, D, F) . . 80 80
1263 20c. No. 1113 (A, C, E) . . 80 80
1264 20c. No. 1114 (B, D, F) . . 80 80
1265 20c. No. 1115 (A, C, E) . . 80 80
1266 20c. No. 1116 (B, D, F) . . 80 80
1267 20c. No. 1117 (A, C, E) . . 80 80
1268 20c. No. 1118 (B, D, F) . . 80 80
1269 20c. No. 1119 (A, C, E) . . 80 80
1270 20c. No. 1120 (B, D, F) . . 80 80
1271 20c. No. 1121 (A, C, E) . . 80 80
1272 20c. No. 1122 (B, D, F) . . 80 80
1273 20c. No. 1123 (A, C, E) . . 80 80
1274 20c. No. 1124 (B, D, F) . . 80 80
1275 20c. No. 1125 (A, C, E) . . 80 80
1276 20c. No. 1126 (B, D, F) . . 80 80
1277 20c. No. 1127 (A, C, E) . . 80 80
1278 20c. No. 1128 (B, D, F) . . 80 80

1980. Obligatory Tax. Children's Village. Mult.
1280 2c. Type **318** 10 10
1281 2c. Boy with chicks 10 10
1282 2c. Working in the fields . . 10 10
1283 2c. Boys with pig 10 10

319 Jean Baptiste de la Salle and Map showing La Salle Schools

320 Louis Braille

1981. Education in Panama by the Christian Schools.
1285 **319** 17c. blue, black and red 25 20

1981. International Year of Disabled People.
1286 **320** 23c. multicoloured . . . 30 20

321 Statue of the Virgin

1981. 150th Anniv of Apparition of Miraculous Virgin to St. Catharine Laboure.
1287 **321** 35c. multicoloured . . . 50 35

322 Crimson-backed Tanager

1981. Birds. Multicoloured.
1288 3c. Type **322** 55 10
1289 6c. Chestnut-fronted macaw (vert) 70 15
1290 41c. Violet sabrewing (vert) 2·75 1·00
1291 50c. Keel-billed toucan . . . 3·75 1·25

323 "Boy feeding Donkey" (Ricardo Morales)

324 Banner

1981. Obligatory Tax. Christmas. Children's Village. Multicoloured.
1292 2c. Type **323** 10 10
1293 2c. "Nativity" (Enrique Daniel Austin) 10 10
1294 2c. "Bird in Tree" (Jorge Gonzalez) 10 10
1295 2c. "Church" (Eric Belgrane) 10 10

1981. National Reaffirmation.
1297 **324** 3c. multicoloured 10 10

325 General Herrera

326 Ricardo J. Alfaro

1982. 1st Death Anniv of General Omar Torrijos Herrera. Multicoloured.
1298 5c. Aerial view of Panama (postage) 10 10
1299 6c. Colecito army camp . . 10 10
1300 17c. Bayano river barrage 25 20
1301 50c. Felipillo engineering works 70 45
1302 23c. Type **325** (air) 35 25
1303 35c. Security Council reunion 50 30
1304 41c. Gen. Omar Torrijos airport . . . . 1·25 45

1982. Birth Cent of Ricardo J. Alfaro (statesman).
1306 **326** 3c. black, mauve and blue (postage) 10 10
1307 – 17c. black and mauve (air) 25 15
1308 – 23c. multicoloured . . . 30 20

DESIGNS: 17c. Profile of Alfaro wearing spectacles (as humanist); 23c. Portrait of Alfaro (as lawyer).

328 Pig Farming

329 Pele (Brazilian footballer)

1982. Obligatory Tax. Christmas. Children's Village. Multicoloured.
1309 2c. Type **328** 10 10
1310 2c. Gardening 10 10
1311 2c. Metalwork (horiz) . . . 10 10
1312 2c. Bee-keeping (horiz) . . . 10 10

1982. World Cup Football Championship, Spain. Multicoloured.
1314 50c. Italian team (horiz) (postage) 70 45
1315 23c. Football emblem and map of Panama (air) . . 30 20
1316 35c. Type **329** 50 30
1317 41c. World Cup Trophy . . 60 35

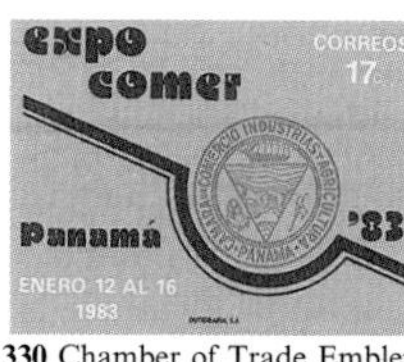

330 Chamber of Trade Emblem

1983. "Expo Comer" Chamber of Trade Exhibition.
1319 **330** 17c. lt blue, blue, & gold 25 15

331 Dr. Nicolas Solano

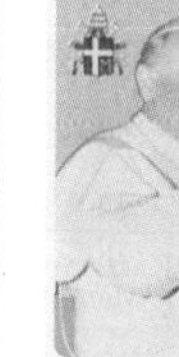

332 Pope John Paul II giving Blessing

1983. Air. Birth Centenary (1982) of Dr. Nicolas Solano (anti-tuberculosis pioneer).
1320 **331** 23c. brown 35 20

1983. Papal Visit. Multicoloured.
1321 6c. Type **332** (postage) . . . 10 10
1322 17c. Pope John Paul II . . . 25 15
1323 35c. Pope and map of Panama (air) 50 30

333 Map of Americas and Sunburst

334 Simon Bolivar

1983. 24th Assembly of Inter-American Development Bank Governors.
1324 **333** 50c. light blue, blue and gold 70 45

1983. Birth Bicentenary of Simon Bolivar.
1325 **334** 50c. multicoloured . . . 70 45

335 Postal Union of the Americas and Spain Emblem

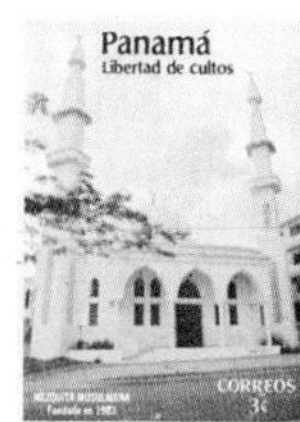

336 Moslem Mosque

1983. World Communications Day. Mult.
1327 30c. Type **335** 45 25
1328 40c. W.C.Y. emblem 60 40
1329 50c. Universal Postal Union emblem 70 45
1330 60c. "Flying Dove" (Alfredo Sinclair) 85 55

1983. Freedom of Worship. Multicoloured.
1332 3c. Type **336** 10 10
1333 5c. Bahal temple 10 10
1334 6c. Church of St. Francis of the Mountains, Veraguas 10 10
1335 17c. Shevet Ahim synagogue 25 15

337 "The Annunciation" (Dagoberto Moran)

338 Ricardo Miro (writer)

1983. Obligatory Tax. Christmas. Children's Village. Multicoloured.
1336 2c. Type **337** 10 10
1337 2c. Church and houses (Leonidas Molinar) (vert) 10 10
1338 2c. Bethlehem and star (Colon Olmedo Zambrano) (vert) 10 10
1339 2c. Flight into Egypt (Hector Ulises Velasquez) (vert) 10 10

1983. Famous Panamanians. Multicoloured.
1341 1c. Type **338** 10 10
1342 3c. Richard Newman (educationalist) 10 10
1343 5c. Cristobal Rodriguez (politician) 10 10
1344 6c. Alcibiades Arosemena (politician) 10 10
1345 35c. Cirilo Martinez (educationalist) 50 30

339 "Rural Architecture" (Juan Manuel Cedero)

1983. Paintings. Multicoloured.
1346 1c. Type **339** 10 10
1347 1c. "Large Nude" (Manuel Chong Neto) 10 10
1348 3c. "On another Occasion" (Spiros Vamvas) 10 10
1349 6c. "Punta Chame" (Guillermo Trujillo) . . . 10 10
1350 28c. "Neon Light" (Alfredo Sinclair) 30 20
1351 35c. "The Prophet" (Alfredo Sinclair) (vert) 50 30
1352 41c. "Highland Girls" (Al Sprague) (vert) 60 40
1353 1b. "One Morning" (Ignacio Mallol Pibernat) . . . . 1·40 75

340 Tonosi Double Jug

1984. Archaeological Finds. Multicoloured.
1354 30c. Type **340** 35 10
1355 40c. Dish on stand 60 20
1356 50c. Jug decorated with human face (vert) 70 25
1357 60c. Waisted bowl (vert) . . 85 35

341 Boxing

1984. Olympic Games, Los Angeles. Mult.
1359 19c. Type **341** 35 25
1360 19c. Baseball 35 25
1361 19c. Basketball (vert) . . . 35 25
1362 19c. Swimming (vert) . . . 35 25

342 Roberto Duran

1984. Roberto Duran (boxer) Commem.
1363 **342** 26c. multicoloured . . . 45 30

343 Shooting

1984. Olympic Games, Los Angeles (2nd series). Multicoloured.
1364 6c. Type **343** (postage) . . . 15 10
1366 30c. Weightlifting (air) . . . 50 30
1367 37c. Wrestling 65 45
1368 1b. Long jump . . . . . . 1·25 90

344 "Pensive Woman" (Manuel Chong Neto)

1984. Paintings. Multicoloured.
1369 1c. Type **344** 10 10
1370 3c. "The Child" (Alfredo Sinclair) (horiz) 10 10
1371 6c. "A Day in the Life of Rumalda" (Brooke Alfaro) (horiz) 15 10
1372 30c. "Highlanders" (Al Sprague) 50 10
1373 37c. "Ballet Interval" (Roberto Sprague) (horiz) 65 15
1374 44c. "Wood on Chame Head" (Guillermo Trujillo) (horiz) 75 25
1375 50c. "La Plaza Azul" (Juan Manuel Cedeno) (horiz) 60 25
1376 1b. "Ira" (Spiros Vamvas) (horiz) . . . . 1·25 90

345 Map, Pres. Torrijos Herrera and Liner in Canal Lock

1984. 5th Anniv of Canal Zone Postal Sovereignty.
1377 **345** 19c. multicoloured . . . 1·10 1·10

346 Emblem as Seedling **347** Boy

1984. Air. World Food Day.
1378 **346** 30c. red, green and blue 50 45

1984. Obligatory Tax. Christmas. Children's Village. Multicoloured.
1379 2c. Type **347** 10 10
1380 2c. Boy in tee-shirt 10 10
1381 2c. Boy in checked shirt . . 10 10
1382 2c. Cub scout 10 10

348 American Manatee

1984. Animals. Each in black.
1384 3c. Type **348** (postage) . . . 10 10
1385 30c. "Tayra" (air) 60 25
1386 44c. Jaguarundi 85 40
1387 50c. White-lipped peccary 90 40

349 Copper One Centesimo Coins, 1935

1985. Coins. Multicoloured.
1389 3c. Type **349** (postage) . . . 10 10
1390 3c. Silver ten centesimo coins, 1904 . . . . 10 10
1391 3c. Silver five centesimo coins, 1916 . . . . 10 10
1392 30c. Silver 50 centesimo coins, 1904 (air) 50 30
1393 37c. Silver half balboa coins, 1962 . . . . 65 45
1394 44c. Silver balboa coins, 1953 . . . . 75 50

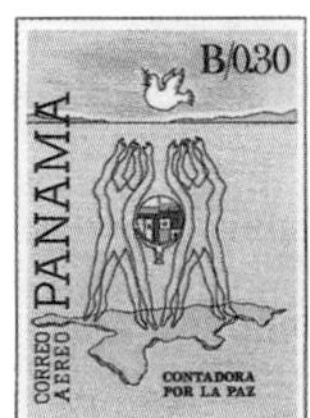

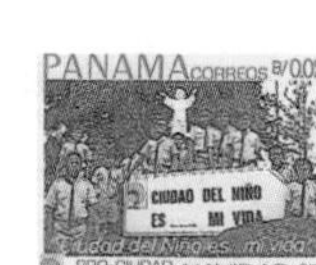

350 Figures on Map reaching for Dove **352** Scouts with Statue of Christ

351 Tanker in Dock

1985. Contadora Peace Movement.
1395 **350** 10c. multicoloured . . . 15 10
1396 20c. multicoloured . . . 30 20
1397 30c. multicoloured . . . 40 25

1985. 70th Anniv of Panama Canal.
1399 **351** 19c. multicoloured . . . 2·75 90

1985. Obligatory Tax. Christmas. Children's Village. Multicoloured.
1400 2c. Type **352** 10 10
1401 2c. Children holding cards spelling "Feliz Navidad" 10 10
1402 2c. Children holding balloons 10 10
1403 2c. Group of cub scouts . . 10 10

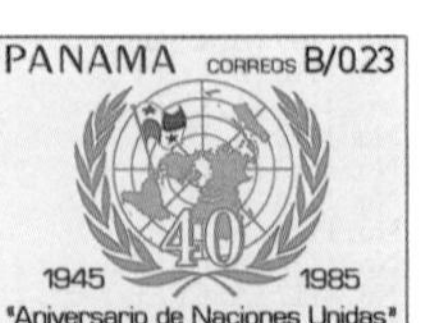

353 "40" on Emblem

1986. 40th Anniv (1985) of U.N.O.
1405 **353** 23c. multicoloured . . . 30 20

354 Boys in Cab of Crane

1986. International Youth Year (1985).
1406 **354** 30c. multicoloured . . . 40 25

355 "Awaiting Her Turn" (Al Sprague)

1986. Paintings. Multicoloured.
1407 3c. Type **355** 10 10
1408 5c. "Aerobics" (Guillermo Trujillo) (horiz) 10 10
1409 19c. "House of Cardboard" (Eduardo Augustine) . . 30 20
1410 30c. "Tierra Gate" (Juan Manuel Cedeno) (horiz) 40 25
1411 36c. "Supper for Three" (Brood Alfaro) 50 30
1412 42c. "Tenderness" (Alfredo Sinclair) 60 40
1413 50c. "Lady of Character" (Manuel Chong Neto) . . 70 45
1414 60c. "Calla Lilies No. 1" (Maigualida de Diaz) (horiz) 80 55

356 Atlapa Convention Centre

1986. Miss Universe Contest. Multicoloured.
1415 23c. Type **356** 30 20
1416 60c. Emblem 80 55

357 Comet and Globe **358** Angels

1986. Appearance of Halley's Comet.
1417 **357** 23c. multicoloured . . . 25 15
1418 – 30c. blue, brown and yellow 35 25
DESIGN: 30c. Panama la Vieja Cathedral tower.

1986. Obligatory Tax. 20th Anniv of Children's Village. Children's drawings. Multicoloured.
1420 2c. Type **358** 10 10
1421 2c. Cupids 10 10
1422 2c. Indians 10 10
1423 2c. Angels (different) . . . 10 10

359 Basketball **360** Argentina Player

1986. 15th Central American and Caribbean Games, Santiago. Multicoloured.
1425 20c. Type **359** 20 10
1426 23c. Sports 25 15

1986. World Cup Football Championship, Mexico. Multicoloured.
1427 23c. Type **360** 25 15
1428 30c. West Germany player 35 25
1429 37c. West Germany and Argentina players 45 30

361 Crib **362** Dove and Globe

1986. Christmas. Multicoloured.
1431 23c. Type **361** 25 15
1432 36c. Tree and presents . . . 40 25
1433 42c. As No. 1432 . . . . . 45 30

1986. International Peace Year. Multicoloured.
1434 8c. Type **362** 10 10
1435 19c. Profiles and emblem . . 20 10

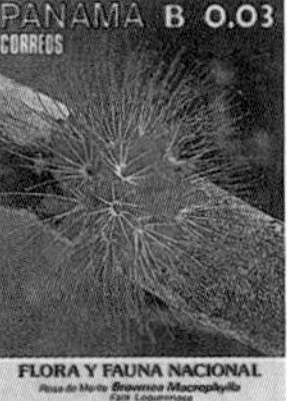

363 Mask **365** Mountain Rose

364 Headquarters Building

1987. Tropical Carnival. Multicoloured.
1436 20c. Type **363** 20 10
1437 35c. Sun with eye mask . . 40 25

1987. 50th Anniv (1985) of Panama Lions Club.
1439 **364** 37c. multicoloured . . . 45 30

1987. Flowers and Birds. Multicoloured.
1440 3c. Type **365** 10 10
1441 5c. Blue-grey tanager (horiz) 40 10
1442 8c. Golden cup 10 10
1443 15c. Tropical kingbird (horiz) 80 25
1444 19c. "Barleria micans" (flower) 20 10
1445 23c. Brown pelican (horiz) 1·10 40
1446 30c. "Cordia dentata" (flower) 35 25
1447 36c. Rufous pigeon (horiz) 1·50 65

366 Octavio Menendez Pereira (founder) and Anniversary Monument

1987. 50th Anniv (1986) of Panama University.
1448 **366** 19c. multicoloured . . . 20 10

367 Emblem in "40"

1987. 40th Anniv (1985) of F.A.O.
1449 **367** 10c. brown, yellow and black 10 10
1450 45c. brown, green and black 50 30

368 Heinrich Schutz **369** Development Projects

1987. Composers and 7th Anniv (1986) of National Theatre.
1451 **368** 19c. multicoloured . . . 20 10
1452 – 30c. green, mauve & brown 35 25
1453 – 37c. brown, blue and deep blue 45 30
1454 – 60c. green, yellow & black 70 45
DESIGNS—HORIZ: 30c. National Theatre. VERT: 37c. Johann Sebastian Bach; 60c. Georg Friedrich Handel.

1987. 25th Anniv (1986) of Inter-American Development Bank.
1455 **369** 23c. multicoloured . . . 25 15

370 Horse-drawn Fire Pump, 1887, and Modern Appliance **372** "Adoration of the Magi" (Albrecht Nentz)

371 Wrestling

1987. Centenary of Fire Service. Multicoloured.
1456 25c. Type **370** 30 20
1457 35c. Fireman carrying boy 40 25

1987. 10th Pan-American Games, Indianapolis. Mult.
1458 15c. Type **371** 20 10
1459 25c. Tennis (vert) 25 15
1460 30c. Swimming 35 25
1461 41c. Basketball (vert) . . . 45 30
1462 60c. Cycling (vert) 70 45

1987. Christmas. Multicoloured.
1464 22c. Type **372** 25 15
1465 35c. "The Virgin adored by Angels" (Matthias Grunewald) 40 25
1466 37c. "Virgin and Child" (Konrad Witz) 45 30

373 Distressed Family and Poor Housing **374** Heart falling into Crack

1987. International Year of Shelter for the Homeless. Multicoloured.
1467 45c. Type **373** 50 30
1468 50c. Happy family and stylized modern housing 50 30

1988. Anti-drugs Campaign.
1469 **374** 10c. red and orange . . 10 10
1470 17c. red and green . . . 20 10
1471 25c. red and blue 30 20

375 Hands and Sapling **376** Breastfeeding

1988. Reafforestation Campaign.
1472 **375** 35c. deep green and green 40 25
1473 40c. red and purple . . . 45 30
1474 45c. brown and bistre . . 50 30

1988. U.N.I.C.E.F. Infant Survival Campaign. Mult.
1475 20c. Type **376** 25 15
1476 31c. Vaccination 35 25
1477 45c. Children playing by lake (vert) 50 30

377 Rock Beauty and Cuban Hogfish

1988. Fishes. Multicoloured.
1478 7c. Type **377** 15 10
1479 35c. French angelfish . . . 65 30
1480 60c. Black-barred soldierfish 1·10 55
1481 1b. Spotted drum . . . . . 2·00 1·25

378 Emblem and Clasped Hands **379** "Virgin with Donors"

1988. 75th Anniv of Girl Guide Movement.
1482 **378** 35c. multicoloured . . . 35 25

1988. Christmas. Anonymous Paintings from Museum of Colonial Religious Art. Mult.
1483 17c. Type **379** (postage) . . 20 10
1484 45c. "Virgin of the Rosary with St. Dominic" 50 30
1485 35c. "St. Joseph with the Child" (air) 35 25

380 Athletes and Silver Medal (Brazil)

1989. Seoul Olympic Games Medals. Mult.
1486 17c. Type **380** (postage) . . 20 10
1487 25c. Wrestlers and gold medal (Hungary) 30 20
1488 60c. Weightlifter and gold medal (Turkey) 70 45
1490 35c. Boxers and bronze medal (Colombia) (air) . . 35 25

381 St. John Bosco **382** Anniversary Emblem

1989. Death Centenary of St. John Bosco (founder of Salesian Brothers). Multicoloured.
1491 10c. Type **381** 15 10
1492 20c. Menor Basilica and St. John with people . . . 25 15

1989. 125th Anniv of Red Cross Movement.
1493 **382** 40c. black and red . . . 50 30
1494 – 1b. multicoloured . . . 1·50 90
DESIGN: 1b. Red Cross workers putting patient in ambulance.

383 "Ancon I" (first ship through Canal)

1989. Air. 75th Anniv of Panama Canal.
1495 **383** 35c. red, black and yellow . . . . 2·25 80
1496 – 60c. multicoloured . . . 3·25 1·25
DESIGN: 60c. Modern tanker.

384 Barriles Ceremonial Statue

1989. America. Pre-Columbian Artefacts. Mult.
1497 20c. Type **384** 25 15
1498 35c. Ceramic vase 45 30

385 "March of the Women on Versailles" (engraving)

1989. Bicent of French Revolution. Mult.
1499 25c. Type **385** (postage) . . 30 20
1500 35c. "Storming the Bastille" (air) 45 30
1501 45c. Birds 55 35

386 "Holy Family"

1989. Christmas. Multicoloured.
1502 17c. Type **386** 20 10
1503 35c. 1988 crib in Cathedral 45 30
1504 45c. "Nativity" 55 35
The 17 and 45c. show children's paintings.

387 "Byrsonima crassifolia"

1990. Fruit. Multicoloured.
1505 20c. Type **387** 20 10
1506 35c. "Bactris gasipaes" . . . 40 25
1507 40c. "Anacardium occidentale" 40 25

388 Sinan

1990. 88th Birthday of Rogelio Sinan (writer).
1508 **388** 23c. brown and blue . . 25 15

389 Pond Turtle

1990. Reptiles. Multicoloured.
1509 35c. Type **389** 40 25
1510 45c. Olive loggerhead turtle 50 35
1511 60c. Red-footed tortoise . . 65 40

390 Carrying Goods on Yoke (after Oviedo)

1990. America.
1512 **390** 20c. brown, light brown and gold 20 10
1513 – 35c. multicoloured . . . 70 50
DESIGN—VERT: 35c. Warrior wearing gold chest ornament and armbands.

391 Dr. Guillermo Patterson, jun., "Father of Chemistry" **393** St. Ignatius

392 In Sight of Land

1990. Chemistry in Panama.
1514 **391** 25c. black and turquoise 25 15
1515 – 35c. multicoloured . . . 40 25
1516 – 45c. multicoloured . . . 50 35
DESIGNS: 35c. Evaporation experiment; 45c. Books and laboratory equipment.

1991. America. 490th Anniv of Discovery of Panama Isthmus by Rodrigo Bastidas.
1517 **392** 35c. multicoloured . . . 50 35

1991. 450th Anniv of Society of Jesus and 500th Birth Anniv of St. Ignatius de Loyola (founder).
1518 **393** 20c. multicoloured . . . 30 20

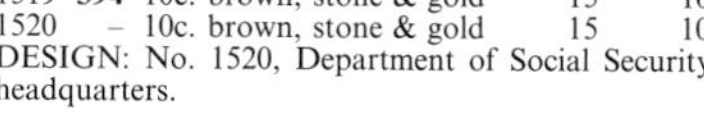

394 Declaration of Women's Right to Vote

1991. 50th Anniv of First Presidency of Dr. Arnulfo Arias Madrid.
1519 **394** 10c. brown, stone & gold 15 10
1520 – 10c. brown, stone & gold 15 10
DESIGN: No. 1520, Department of Social Security headquarters.

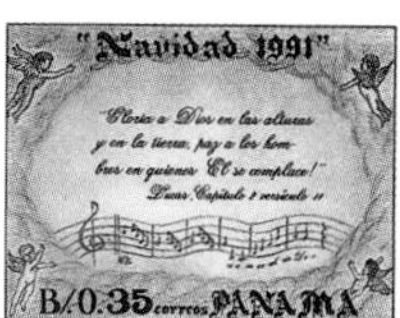

395 "Glory to God ..." (Luke 2: 14) and Score of "Gloria in Excelsis"

1991. Christmas. Multicoloured.
1521 35c. Type **395** 50 35
1522 35c. Nativity 50 35

396 Adoration of the Kings

1992. Epiphany.
1523 **396** 10c. multicoloured . . . 15 10

397 Family and Housing Estate

1992. "New Lives" Housing Project.
1524 **397** 5c. multicoloured 10 10

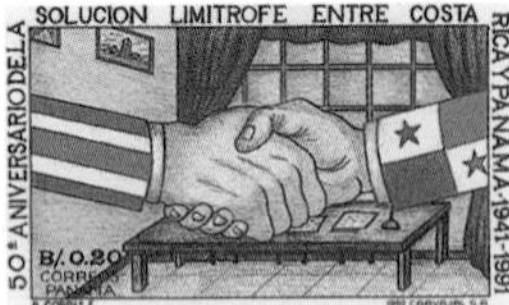

398 Costa Rican and Panamanian shaking Hands

1992. 50th Anniv (1991) of Border Agreement with Costa Rica. Multicoloured.
1525 20c. Type **398** 30 20
1526 40c. Map showing Costa Rica and Panama 55 35
1527 50c. Presidents Calderon and Arias and national flags 70 45

399 Pollutants and Hole over Antarctic

1992. "Save the Ozone Layer".
1528 **399** 40c. multicoloured . . . 55 35

400 Exhibition Emblem

1992. "Expocomer 92" 10th International Trade Exhibition, Panama City.
1529 **400** 10c. multicoloured . . . 15 10

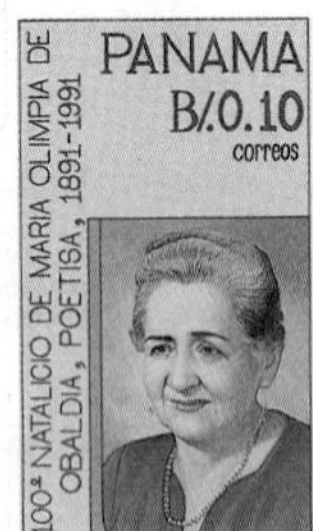

401 Portrait **402** Maria Olimpia de Obaldia

1992. 1st Death Anniv of Dame Margot Fonteyn (ballet dancer). Portraits by Pietro Annigoni. Multicoloured.
1530 35c. Type **401** 50 35
1531 45c. On stage 60 40

1992. Birth Centenary of Maria Olimpia de Obaldia (poet).
1532 **402** 10c. multicoloured . . . 15 10

403 Athletics Events and Map of Spain

1992. Olympic Games, Barcelona.
1533 **403** 10c. multicoloured . . . 15 10

404 Paca

1992. Endangered Animals.
1534 **404** 5c. brown, stone & black 10 10
1535 – 10c. black, brn & stone 25 25
1536 – 15c. brown, blk & stone 20 15
1537 – 20c. multicoloured . . . 30 20
DESIGNS: 10c. Harpy eagle; 15c. Jaguar; 20c. Iguana.

405 Zion Baptist Church, Bocas del Toro

1992. Centenary of Baptist Church in Panama.
1538 **405** 20c. multicoloured . . . 30 20

406 Columbus's Fleet

1992. America. 500th Anniv of Discovery of America by Columbus. Multicoloured.
1539 20c. Type **406** 45 30
1540 35c. Columbus planting flag 75 50

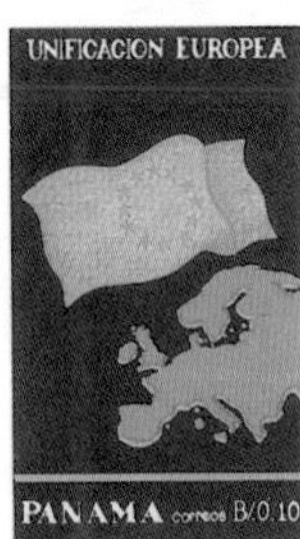

407 Flag and Map of Europe **408** Mascot

1992. European Single Market.
1541 **407** 10c. multicoloured . . . 15 10

1992. "Expo '92" World's Fair, Seville.
1542 **408** 10c. multicoloured . . . 15 10

409 Occupations

1992. American Workers' Health Year.
1543 **409** 15c. multicoloured . . . 20 15

410 Angel and Shepherds

1992. Christmas. Multicoloured.
1544 20c. Type **410** 30 20
1545 35c. Mary and Joseph arriving at Bethlehem . . 50 35

411 Jesus lighting up the Americas

1993. 500th Anniv (1992) of Evangelization of the American Continent.
1546 **411** 10c. multicoloured . . . 15 10

412 Woman on Crutches and Wheelchair-bound Man

1993. National Day of Disabled Persons.
1547 **412** 5c. multicoloured 10 10

413 Herrera (bust)

1993. 32nd Death Anniv of Dr. Jose de la Cruz Herrera (essayist).
1548 **413** 5c. multicoloured 10 10

414 Nutritious Foods and Emblems

1993. International Nutrition Conference, Rome.
1549 **414** 10c. multicoloured . . . 15 10

415 Caravel and Columbus in Portobelo Harbour

1994. 490th Anniv (1992) of Columbus's Fourth Voyage and Exploration of the Panama Isthmus.
1550 **415** 50c. multicoloured . . . 65 45

416 Panama Flag and Greek Motifs **418** Chinese Family and House

1995. 50th Anniv of Greek Community in Panama.
1551 **416** 20c. multicoloured . . . 25 15

1995. Various stamps surch.
1553 – 20c. on 23c. multicoloured (1459) 25 15
1554 **373** 25c. on 45c. multicoloured 30 20
1555 – 30c. on 45c. multicoloured (1510) 40 25
1556 **375** 35c. on 45c. brown and bistre 45 30
1557 – 35c. on 45c. multicoloured (1477) 45 30
1558 – 40c. on 41c. multicoloured (1461) 50 35
1559 – 50c. on 60c. multicoloured (1511) 65 45
1560 – 1b. on 50c. multicoloured (1480) 1·25 85

1996. Chinese Presence in Panama. 142nd Anniv of Arrival of First Chinese Immigrants.
1561 **418** 60c. multicoloured . . . 75 50

419 The King's Bridge from the North (16th century)

1996. 475th Anniv (1994) of Founding by the Spanish of Panama City. Multicoloured.
1563 15c. Type **419** 20 15
1564 20c. City arms, 1521 (vert) 25 15
1565 25c. Plan of first cathedral 30 20
1566 35c. Present-day ruins of Cathedral of the Assumption of Our Lady 45 30

420 "60", Campus and Emblem

1996. 60th Anniv of Panama University.
1567 **420** 40c. multicoloured . . . 50 35

421 Anniversary Emblem

1996. 75th Anniv of Panama Chapter of Rotary International.
1568 **421** 5b. multicoloured . . . 6·25 4·25

422 Great Tinamou

1996. America (1993). Endangered Species.
1569 **422** 20c. multicoloured . . . 25 15

423 Northern Coati

1996. Mammals. Multicoloured.
1570 25c. Type **423** 30 20
1571 25c. Collared anteater ("Tamandua mexicana") 30 20
1572 25c. Two-toed anteater ("Cyclopes didactylus") 30 20
1573 25c. Puma 30 20

424 De Lesseps **425** "50" and Emblem

1996. Death Centenary of Ferdinand, Vicomte de Lesseps (builder of Suez Canal).
1574 **424** 35c. multicoloured . . . 45 30

1996. 50th Anniv of U.N.O.
1575 **425** 45c. multicoloured . . . 55 35

426 Emblem and Motto **427** Bello

1996. 25th Anniv (1993) of Panama Chapter of Kiwanis International.
1576 **426** 40c. multicoloured . . . 50 35

1996. 25th Anniv (1995) of Andres Bello Covenant for Education, Science, Technology and Culture.
1577 **427** 35c. multicoloured . . . 45 30

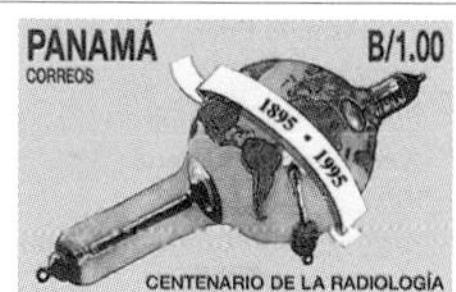

428 World Map on X-ray Equipment

1996. Centenary of Discovery of X-rays by Wilhelm Rontgen.
1578 **428** 1b. multicoloured . . . 1·25 85

429 Madonna and Child

1996. Christmas.
1579 **429** 35c. multicoloured . . . 45 30

430 Diesel Train and Panama Canal

1996. America (1994). Postal Transport.
1580 **430** 30c. multicoloured . . . 35 25

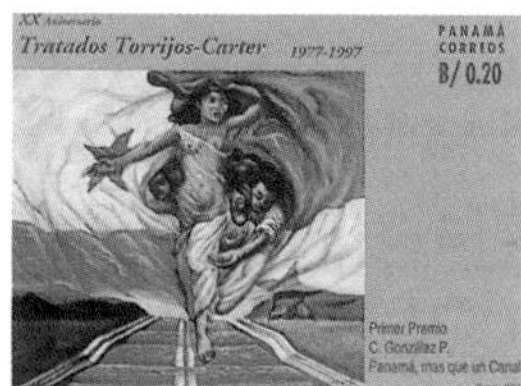

431 "Panama, More than a Canal" (C. Gonzalez)

1997. 20th Anniv of Torrijos–Carter Treaty (transferring Control of Canal Zone to Panama in Year 2000). Multicoloured.
1581 20c. Type **431** 25 15
1582 30c. "A Curtain of Our Flag" (A. Siever) (vert) 35 25
1583 45c. "Perpetual Steps" (R. Martinez) 55 35
1584 50c. Kurt Waldheim (U.N. Secretary-General), President Carter of U.S.A. and President Torrijos of Panama at signing ceremony 60 40

432 Pedro Miguel Locks

1997. World Congress on Panama Canal. Mult.
1586 45c. Type **432** 55 35
1587 45c. Miraflores Locks . . . 55 35

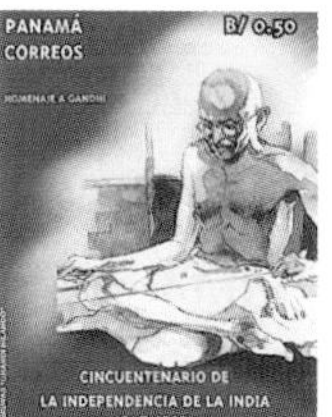

433 "Gandhi Spinning" (P. Biswas)

435 Mary and Joseph searching for Lodgings

434 Crocodile on Rock

1997. 50th Anniv of Independence of India.
1589 **433** 50c. multicoloured . . . 60 40

1997. The American Crocodile. Multicoloured.
1590 25c. Type **434** 30 20
1591 25c. Looking across water 30 20
1592 25c. Two crocodiles 30 20
1593 25c. Head with mouth open 30 20

1997. Christmas.
1594 **435** 35c. multicoloured . . . 45 30

436 Fire Engines from 1941 and 1948

1997. Centenary of Colon City Fire Brigade.
1595 **436** 20c. multicoloured . . . 25 15

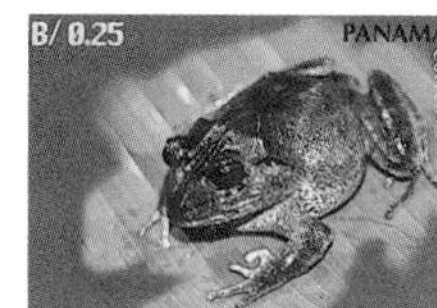

437 "Eleutherodactylus biporcatus" (robber frog)

1997. Frogs. Multicoloured.
1596 25c. Type **437** 30 20
1597 25c. "Hyla colymba" (tree frog) 30 20
1598 25c. "Hyla rufitela" (tree frog) 30 20
1599 25c. "Nelsonephryne aterrima" 30 20

438 Women wearing Polleras

1997. America (1996). Traditional Costumes.
1600 **438** 20c. multicoloured . . . 25 15

439 Arosemena

440 Emblem

1997. Death Centenary of Justo Arosemena (President, 1855–56).
1601 **439** 40c. multicoloured . . . 50 35

1997. 85th Anniv of Colon Chamber of Commerce, Agriculture and Industry.
1602 **440** 1b. multicoloured . . . 1·25 85

441 Douglas DC-3

1997. 50th Anniv of Panamanian Aviation Company. Multicoloured.
1603 35c. Type **441** 45 30
1604 35c. Martin 4-0-4 . . . . . 45 30
1605 35c. Avro HS-748 . . . . . 45 30
1606 35c. Lockheed L-168 Electra 45 30
1607 35c. Boeing 727-100 . . . . 45 30
1608 35c. Boeing 737-200 Advanced 45 30

442 Wailing Wall

444 Central Avenue, San Felipe

443 Building Facade and Emblem

1997. 3000th Anniv of Jerusalem. Multicoloured.
1609 20c. Type **442** 25 15
1610 25c. Service in the Basilica of the Holy Sepulchre . . 30 20
1611 60c. Dome of the Rock . . 75 50

1998. 50th Anniv of Organization of American States.
1613 **443** 40c. multicoloured . . . 10 10

1998. Tourism. Multicoloured.
1614 10c. Type **444** 10 10
1615 20c. Tourists in rainforest 25 15
1616 25c. Gatun Locks, Panama Canal (horiz) 30 20
1617 35c. Panama City (horiz) . . 45 30
1618 40c. San Jeronimo Fort, San Felipe de Portobelo (horiz) 50 30
1619 45c. Rubber raft, River Chagres (horiz) 55 35
1620 60c. Beach, Dog's Island, Kuna Yala (horiz) 75 50

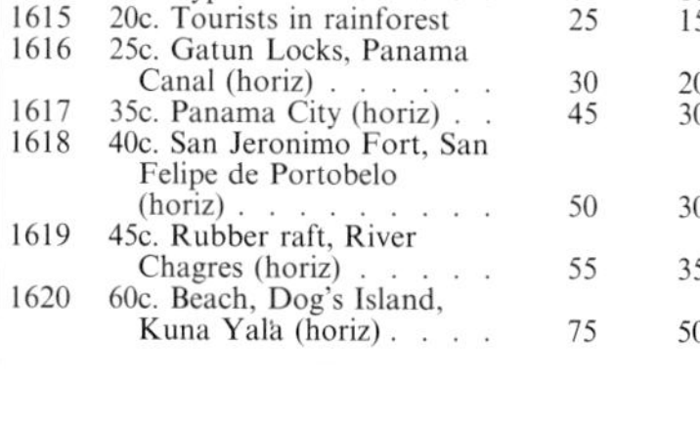

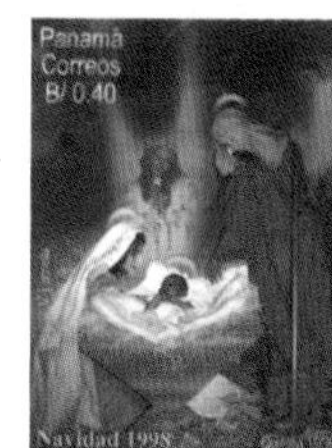

445 Nativity

2000. Christmas.
1621 **445** 40c. multicoloured . . . 45 25

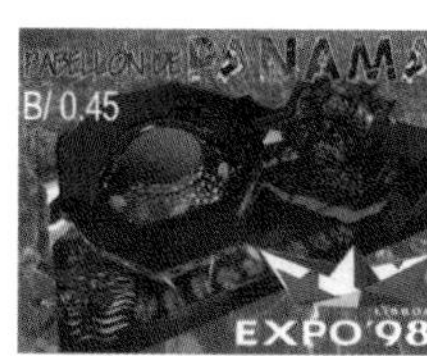

446 Pavilion

2000. "World Expo'98" World's Fair, Lisbon, Portugal.
1622 **446** 45c. multicoloured . . . 50 30

447 Harpy Eagle

2000. The Harpy Eagle. Entries in painting competition by named artist.
1623 **447** 20c. black and green . . 25 15
1624 – 20c. multicoloured . . . 25 15
1625 – 20c. multicoloured . . . 25 15
1626 – 20c. multicoloured . . . 25 15
DESIGNS: No. 1624, J. JimEnez; 1625, S. Castro; 1626, J. Ramos.

448 Emblem

2000. 40th Anniv of Business Executives' Association.
1627 **448** 50c. multicoloured . . . 60 35

449 Emblem

2000. 50th Anniv of Colon Free Trade Zone.
1628 **449** 15c. multicoloured . . . 20 15

450 Emblem

2000. 50th Anniv of Universal Declaration of Human Rights.
1629 **450** 15c. multicoloured . . . 20 15

451 *Platyphora haroldi*

2000. Beetles. Multicoloured.
1630 30c. Type **451** 35 20
1631 30c. *Stilodes leoparda* . . . 35 20
1632 30c. *Stilodes fuscolineata* . . 35 20
1633 30c. *Platyphora boucardi* . . 35 20

452 Cruise Ship

2000. Return of Control of Panama Canal to Panama (1999). Multicoloured.
1634 20c. Type **452** 25 15
1635 35c. Cruise ship at lock gate 40 25
1636 40c. View down canal . . . 45 25
1637 45c. Cruise ship passing through lock 50 30

453 Constructing Canal

2000. 85th Anniv of Panama Canal. Multicoloured.
1638 40c. Type **453** 45 25
1639 40c. Construction of canal (different) 45 25
MS1640 106 × 56 mm. 1b.50 View of canal at early stage of construction 1·75 1·75

454 Crowd and Madrid wearing surgical mask

2001. Birth Centenary of Dr. Arnulfo Arias Madrid.
1641 **454** 20c. black and brown . . 25 15
1642 – 20c. black and sepia . . 25 15
1643 – 30c. multicoloured . . . 35 20
1644 – 30c. multicoloured . . . 35 20
DESIGNS: No. 1642, Crowd and Madrid holding glasses; 1643, Flag, building faade and Madrid; 1644, Crowd and Madrid.
Nos. 1641/25 and 1643/4 respectively were each issued together, se-tenant, forming a composite design.

455 Baby Jesus

2001. Year 2000.
1645 **455** 20c. multicoloured . . . 25 15

456 Crowned Globe, Rainbow and Birds

2001. "Dreaming of the Future". Winning Entries in Stamp Design Competition. Multicoloured.
1646 20c. Type **456** 25 15
1647 20c. Globe in flower (L. Guerra) 25 15
MS1648 105 x 54 mm. 75c. Tree, birds, globe and children (J. Aguilar) (horiz); 75c. Blue birds holding ribbons, globe and children holding hands (S. Sitton) (horiz) 90 90

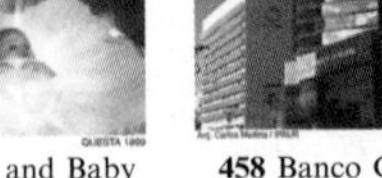
457 Angel and Baby Jesus
458 Banco General Tower (Carlos Medina)

2001. Christmas.
1649 **457** 35c. multicoloured . . . 40 25

2001. Architecture of 1990s. Multicoloured.
1650 35c. Type **458** 40 25
1651 35c. Los Delfines condominium (Edwin Brown) 40 25
MS1652 104 × 54 mm. 75c. Circular building (Ricardo Moreno and Jesus Santamaria) (horiz); 75c. Building with three gables (Ricardo Moreno and Jesus Santamaria) (horiz) . . . . . 1·75 1·75

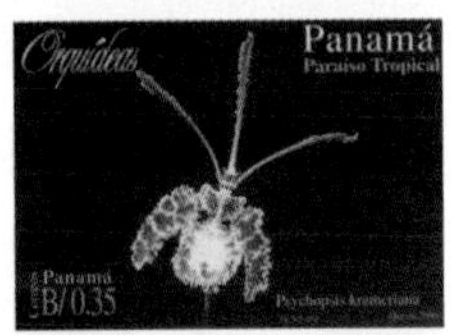
459 *Psychopsis krameriana*

2001. Orchids. Multicoloured.
1653 35c. Type **459** 40 25
1654 35c. *Cattleya dowiana* . . . 40 25
MS1655 104 × 54 mm. 75c. *Peristeria elata*; 75c. *Miltoniopsis roezlii* 1·75 1·75

460 1878 50c. Sovereign State and 1904 1c. Republic of Panama Stamps

2001. 18th U. P. A. E. P. Congress, Panama.
1656 **460** 5b. multicoloured . . . 6·00 6·00

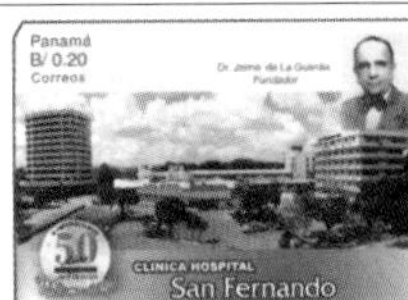

461 Hospital Buildings and Dr Jaime de la Guardia (founder)

2001. 50th Anniv of San Fernando Clinical Hospital.
1657 **461** 20c. multicoloured . . . 25 15

ACKNOWLEDGEMENT OF RECEIPT STAMPS

1898. Handstamped **A. R. COLON COLOMBIA**.
AR24 **5** 5c. blue . . . . 4·50 3·75
AR25 10c. orange . . . . 8·00 8·00

1902. Handstamped **AR** in circle.
AR32 **5** 5c. blue . . . . 3·00 3·00
AR33 10c. orange . . . . 6·00 6·00

1903. No. AR169 of Colombia handstamped **AR** in circle.
AR34 AR **60** 5c. red . . . . . . 11·00 11·00

AR 37

1904.
AR135 AR **37** 5c. blue 90 90

1916. Optd **A.R.**
AR177 **50** 2½c. red 90 90

EXPRESS LETTER STAMPS

1926. Optd **EXPRESO**.
E220 **57** 10c. black and orange . . 4·25 2·10
E221 20c. black and brown . . 5·50 2·10

E **81** Cyclist Messenger

1929.
E226 E **81** 10c. orange 90 70
E227 20c. brown . . . . . . 1·75 1·10

INSURANCE STAMPS

1942. Surch **SEGURO POSTAL HABILITADO** and value.
IN430 5c. on 1b. black (No. 373) 45 35
IN431 10c. on 1b. brown (No. 365) 70 55
IN432 25c. on 50c. brown (No. 372) . . . . 1·25 1·25

POSTAGE DUE STAMPS

D **58** San Geronimo Castle Gate, Portobelo

1915.
D169 D **58** 1c. brown . . . . . . 1·90 30
D170 – 2c. brown . . . . . . 2·75 25
D171 – 4c. brown . . . . . . 3·75 55
D172 – 10c. brown . . . . . 2·75 1·10
DESIGNS—VERT: 2c. Statue of Columbus. HORIZ: 4c. House of Deputies. VERT: 10c. Pedro J. Sosa.
No. D169 is wrongly inscr "CASTILLO DE SAN LORENZO CHAGRES".

D 86

1930.
D240 D **86** 1c. green 70 25
D241 2c. red 70 20
D242 4c. blue 75 30
D243 10c. violet 75 40

REGISTRATION STAMPS

R 4

1888.
R12 R **4** 10c. black on grey . . . 6·00 4·00

1897. Handstamped **R COLON** in circle.
R22 **5** 10c. orange . . . . 4·25 4·00

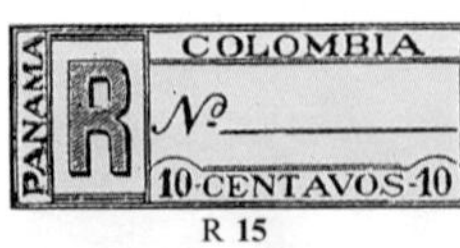

R 15

1900.
R29 R **15** 10c. black on blue . . . 2·50 2·10
R30 10c. red . . . . 18·00 15·00

1902. No. R30 surch by hand.
R31 R **15** 20c. on 10c. red . . . . 15·00 12·00

1903. Type R **85** of Colombia optd **REPUBLICA DE PANAMA**.
R42 20c. red on blue . . . . . . 27·00
R43 20c. blue on blue . . . . . 27·00

1903. Nos. R42/3 surch.
R46 10c. on 20c. red on blue . . 50·00 50·00
R47 10c. on 20c. blue on blue . . 50·00 50·00

1904. Optd **PANAMA**.
R60 **5** 10c. orange . . . . 2·10 2·10

1904. Type R **6** of Colombia surch **Panama 10** and bar.
R67 10c. on 20c. red on blue . . 38·00 35·00
R68 10c. on 20c. blue on blue . . 38·00 35·00

1904. Type R **85** of Colombia optd **Republica de Panama**.
R106 20c. red on blue . . . . . 5·00 5·00

R 35

1904.
R133 R **35** 10c. green 70 30

1916. Stamps of Panama surch **R 5 cts**.
R175 **46** 5c. on 8c. black & purple 2·10 1·40
R176 **52** 5c. on 8c. black & purple 2·10 50

TOO LATE STAMPS

1903. Too Late stamp of Colombia optd **REPUBLICA DE PANAMA**.
L44 L **86** 5c. violet on red . . . . 7·50 5·50

L 36

1904.
L134 L **36** 2½c. red 70 40

1910. Typewritten optd **Retardo**.
L158 **50** 2½c. red . . . . 75·00 75·00

1910. Optd **RETARDO**.
L159 **50** 2½c. red . . . . 38·00 30·00

1916. Surch **RETARDO UN CENTESIMO**.
L174 **38** 1c. on ½c. orange . . . . 15·00 12·00

APPENDIX

The following stamps have either been issued in excess of postal needs or have not been available to the public in reasonable quantities at face value. Such stamps may later be given full listing if there is evidence of regular postal use.

1964.

Satellites. Postage ½, 1c.; Air 5, 10, 21, 50c.

1965.

Tokyo Olympic Games Medal Winners. Postage ½, 1, 2, 3, 4c.; Air 5, 6, 7, 10, 21, 31c.

Space Research. Postage ½, 1, 2, 3c.; Air 5, 10, 11, 31c.

400th Birth Anniv of Galileo. Air 10, 21c.

Peaceful Uses of Atomic Energy. Postage ½, 1, 4c.; Air 6, 10, 21c.

Nobel Prize Medals. Air 10, 21c.

Pres. John Kennedy. Postage ½, 1c.; Air 10+5c., 21+10c., 31+15c.

1966.

Pope Paul's Visit to U.N. in New York. Postage ½, 1c.; Air 5, 10, 21, 31c.

Famous Men. Postage ½c.; Air 10, 31c.

Famous Paintings. Postage ½c.; Air 10, 31c.

World Cup Football Championship. Postage ½, ½c.; Air 10, 10, 21, 21c.

Italian Space Research. Postage ½, 1c.; Air 5, 10, 21c.

Centenary of I.T.U. Air 31c.

World Cup Winners. Optd on 1966 World Cup Issue. Postage ½, ½c.; Air 10, 10, 21, 21c.

Religious Paintings. Postage ½, 1, 2, 3c.; Air 21, 21c.

Churchill and Space Research. Postage ½c.; Air 10, 31c.

3rd Death Anniv of Pres. John Kennedy. Postage ½, 1c.; Air 10, 31c.

Jules Verne and Space Research. Postage ½, 1c.; Air 5, 10, 21, 31c.

1967.

Religious Paintings. Postage ½, 1c.; Air 5, 10, 21, 31c.

Mexico Olympics. Postage ½, 1c.; Air 5, 10, 21, 31c.

Famous Paintings. Postage 5c. × 3; Air 21c. × 3.

Goya's Paintings. Postage 2, 3, 4c.; Air 5, 8, 10, 13, 21c.

1968.

Religious Paintings. Postage 1, 1, 3c.; Air 4, 21, 21c.

Mexican President's Visit. Air 50c., 1b.

Winter Olympic Games, Grenoble. Postage ½, 1c.; Air 5, 10, 21, 31c.

Butterflies. Postage ½, 1, 3, 4c.; Air 5, 13c.

Ship Paintings. Postage ½, 1, 3, 4c.; Air 5, 13c.

Fishes. Postage ½, 1, 3, 4c.; Air 5, 13c.

Winter Olympic Medal Winners. Postage 1, 2, 3, 4, 5, 6, 8c.; Air 13, 30c.

Paintings of Musicians. Postage 5, 10, 15, 20, 25, 30c.

Satellite Transmissions from Panama T.V. (a) Olympic Games, Mexico. Optd on 1964 Satellites issue. Postage ½c.; Air 50c. (b) Pope Paul's Visit to Latin America. Postage ½c.; Air 21c. (c) Panama Satellite Transmissions. Inauguration. (i) optd on Space Research issue of 1965. Postage 5c.; Air 31c. (ii) optd on Churchill and Space Research issue of 1966. Postage ½c.; Air 10c.

Hunting Paintings. Postage 1, 3, 5, 10c.; Air 13, 30c.

Horses and Jockeys. Postage 5, 10, 15, 20, 25, 30c.

Mexico Olympics. Postage 1, 2, 3, 4, 5, 6, 8c.; Air 13, 30c.

1969.

1st International Philatelic and Numismatic Exhibition. Optd on 1968 Issue of Mexican President's Visit. Air 50c., 1b.

Telecommunications Satellites. Air 5, 10, 15, 20, 25, 30c.

Provisionals. Surch "Decreto No. 112 (de 6 de marzo de 1969)" and new values on No. 781 and 10c.+5c. and 21c.+10c. of 1965 Issue of 3rd Death Anniv of Pres. John Kennedy. Air 5c. on 5c.+5c., 5c. on 10c.+5c., 10c. on 21c.+10c.

Pope Paul VI Visit to Latin America. Religious Paintings. Postage 1, 2, 3, 4, 5c.; Air 6, 7, 8, 10c.

PAPAL STATES Pt. 8

Parts of Italy under Papal rule till 1870 when they became part of the Kingdom of Italy.

1852. 100 bajocchi = 1 scudo.
1866. 100 centesimi = 1 lira.

1

2

1852. Papal insignia as in T **1** and **2** in various shapes and frames. Imperf.
2 ½b. black on grey . . . . . £425 42·00
5 ½b. black on lilac . . . . . 35·00 £120
10 1b. black on green . . . . . 46·00 55·00
11 2b. black on green . . . . . £130 11·00
14 2b. black on white . . . . . 8·50 50·00
15 3b. black on brown . . . . . 60·00 26·00
16 3b. black on yellow . . . . . 23·00 £160
17 4b. black on brown . . . . . £4500 65·00
19 4b. black on yellow . . . . . £120 34·00
20 5b. black on pink . . . . . . £150 7·50
22 6b. black on lilac £850 £190
23 6b. black on grey . . . . . . £550 48·00
25 7b. black on blue . . . . . . £850 60·00
26 8b. black on white . . . . . £400 32·00

27	50b. blue	£12000	£1500
29	1s. pink	£3000	£3000

1867. Same types. Imperf.

30	2c. black on green	£110	£200
32	3c. black on grey	£1800	£2250
33	5c. black on blue	£130	£170
34	10c. black on red	£850	55·00
35	20c. black on red	£120	75·00
36	40c. black on yellow	£140	£170
37	80c. black on pink	£140	£450

1868. Same types. Perf.

42	2c. black on green	8·00	60·00
43	3c. black on grey	35·00	£3000
45	5c. black on blue	9·75	38·00
46	10c. black on orange	2·75	11·00
49	20c. black on mauve	3·75	30·00
50	20c. black on red	2·20	13·00
52	40c. black on yellow	5·50	85·00
55	80c. black on pink	25·00	£325

PAPUA Pt. 1

(Formerly **BRITISH NEW GUINEA**)

The eastern portion of the island of New Guinea, to the North of Australia, a territory of the Commonwealth of Australia, now combined with New Guinea. Australian stamps were used after the Japanese defeat in 1945 until the combined issue appeared in 1952.

12 pence = 1 shilling;
20 shilling = 1 pound.

1 Lakatoi (native canoe) with Hanuabada Village in Background

6

1901.

9	1	½d. black and green	7·50	3·75
10		1d. black and red	3·50	2·00
11		2d. black and violet	9·50	4·00
12		2½d. black and blue	11·00	12·00
13		4d. black and brown	32·00	50·00
6		6d. black and green	45·00	35·00
7		1s. black and orange	60·00	65·00
8		2s.6d. black and brown	£550	£500

1906. Optd **Papua**.

38	1	½d. black and green	8·00	10·00
39		1d. black and red	3·50	5·00
40		2d. black and violet	4·50	2·25
24		2½d. black and blue	3·75	15·00
42		4d. black and brown	26·00	48·00
43		6d. black and green	28·00	42·00
19		1s. black and orange	20·00	38·00
37		2s.6d. black and brown	32·00	48·00

1907.

66	6	½d. black and green	1·60	3·75
94		1d. black and red	1·40	1·25
68		2d. black and purple	3·50	5·50
51a		2½d. black and blue	5·50	6·50
63		4d. black and brown	4·75	9·00
80		6d. black and green	7·50	7·50
81		1s. black and orange	5·50	19·00
82		2s.6d. black and brown	35·00	45·00

1911.

84a	6	½d. green	50	2·25
85		1d. red	70	75
86		2d. mauve	70	75
87		2½d. blue	4·75	8·50
88		4d. olive	2·25	11·00
89		6d. brown	3·75	5·00
90		1s. yellow	9·00	15·00
91		2s.6d. red	32·00	38·00

1916.

93	6	½d. green and olive	80	1·00
95		1½d. blue and brown	1·50	80
96		2d. purple and red	1·75	75
97		2½d. green and blue	4·75	12·00
98		3d. black and turquoise	1·50	1·75
99		4d. brown and orange	2·50	5·00
100		5d. grey and brown	4·25	16·00
101		6d. purple	3·25	9·50
127		9d. lilac and violet	4·50	30·00
102		1s. brown and olive	3·50	7·00
128		1s.3d. lilac and blue	7·50	32·00
103		2s.6d. red and pink	19·00	40·00
104		5s. black and green	42·00	48·00
105		10s. green and blue	£140	£160

1917. Surch **ONE PENNY**.

106a	6	1d. on ½d. green	1·00	1·25
107		1d. on 2d. mauve	12·00	15·00
108		1d. on 2½d. blue	1·25	3·75
109		1d. on 4d. green	1·75	4·50
110		1d. on 6d. brown	8·00	17·00
111		1d. on 2s.6d. red	1·50	6·00

1929. Air. Optd **AIR MAIL**.

114	6	3d. black and turquoise	1·00	7·00

(11)

1930. Air. Optd with T **11**.

118	6	3d. black and turquoise	1·00	6·00
119		6d. purple	7·00	10·00
120		1s. brown and olive	4·25	15·00

1931. Surch in words or figures and words.

122	6	2d. on 1½d. blue and brown	1·00	2·00
125		5d. on 1s. brown and olive	1·00	1·75
126		9d. on 2s.6d. red and pink	5·50	8·50
123		1s.3d. on 5d. black and green	4·25	9·00

15 Motuan Girl

18 Raggiana Bird of Paradise

20 Native Mother and Child

1932.

130	15	½d. black and orange	1·50	3·25
131	–	1d. black and green	1·75	60
132	–	1½d. black and red	1·50	8·00
133	18	2d. red	11·00	30
134	–	3d. black and blue	3·25	6·50
135	20	4d. olive	5·50	9·50
136	–	5d. black and green	3·00	3·00
137	–	6d. brown	7·50	5·50
138	–	9d. black and violet	10·00	21·00
139	–	1s. green	4·00	8·50
140	–	1s.3d. black and purple	15·00	25·00
141	–	2s. black and green	15·00	23·00
142	–	2s.6d. black and mauve	25·00	38·00
143	–	5s. black and brown	55·00	55·00
144	–	10s. violet	85·00	85·00
145	–	£1 black and grey	£180	£150

DESIGNS—VERT (as T **15**): 1d. Chieftain's son; 1½d. Tree houses; 3d. Papuan dandy; 5d. Masked dancer; 9d. Shooting fish; 1s. Ceremonial platform; 1s.3d. Lakatoi; 2s. Papuan art; 2s.6d. Pottery-making; 5d. Native policeman; £1 Delta house. VERT (as T **18**): 6d. Papuan mother. HORIZ: (as T **20**): 10s. Lighting fire.

31 Hoisting the Union Jack

35 King George VI

1934. 50th Anniv of Declaration of British Protectorate. Inscr "1884 1834".

146	31	1d. green	1·00	3·50
147	–	2d. red	1·75	3·00
148	31	3d. blue	1·75	3·00
149	–	5d. purple	11·00	13·00

DESIGN: 2d., 5d. Scene on H.M.S. "Nelson".

1935. Silver Jubilee. Optd **HIS MAJESTY'S JUBILEE 1910 1935 (1910 – 1935** on 2d.).

150	–	1d. black & green (No. 131)	75	3·00
151	18	2d. red	2·00	3·00
152	–	3d. black and blue (No. 134)	1·75	3·00
153	–	5d. black & green (No. 136)	2·50	3·00

1937. Coronation.

154	35	1d. green	45	15
155		2d. red	45	65
156		3d. blue	45	85
157		5d. purple	45	1·40

36 Port Moresby

1938. Air. 50th Anniv of Declaration of British Possession.

158	36	2d. red	3·75	2·25
159		3d. blue	3·75	2·25
160		5d. green	3·75	3·25
161		8d. red	8·00	14·00
162		1s. mauve	22·00	15·00

37 Natives poling Rafts

1939. Air.

163	37	2d. red	3·00	3·75
164		3d. blue	3·00	7·50
165		5d. green	3·00	1·50
166		8d. red	8·00	2·50
167		1s. mauve	10·00	7·00
168		1s.6d. olive	30·00	32·00

OFFICIAL STAMPS

1931. Optd **O S**.

O55	6	½d. green and olive	2·00	4·75
O56a		1d. black and red	4·00	7·50
O57		1½d. blue and brown	1·60	12·00
O58		2d. brown and purple	3·75	9·00
O59		3d. black and turquoise	2·50	22·00
O60		4d. brown and orange	2·50	18·00
O61		5d. grey and brown	6·00	38·00
O62		6d. purple and red	4·00	8·50
O63		9d. lilac and violet	30·00	48·00
O64		1s. brown and olive	9·00	30·00
O65		1s.3d. lilac and blue	30·00	48·00
O66		2s.6d. red and pink	40·00	85·00

PAPUA NEW GUINEA Pt. 1

Combined territory on the island of New Guinea administered by Australia under trusteeship. Self-government was established during 1973.

1952. 12 pence = 1 shilling;
20 shillings = 1 pound.
1966. 100 cents = $1 Australian.
1975. 100 toea = 1 kina.

1 Matschie's Tree Kangaroo

7 Kiriwina Chief House

1952.

1	1	½d. green	30	10
2	–	1d. brown	20	10
3	–	2d. blue	35	10
4	–	2½d. orange	3·00	50
5	–	3d. myrtle	50	10
6	–	3½d. red	50	10
6a	–	3½d. black	6·00	90
18	–	4d. red	75	10
19	–	5d. green	75	10
7	7	6½d. purple	1·25	10
20	–	7d. green	5·50	10
8	–	7½d. blue	2·50	1·00
21	–	8d. blue	75	1·50
9	–	9d. brown	2·75	40
10	–	1s. green	1·75	10
11	–	1s.6d. myrtle	5·00	60
22	–	1s.7d. brown	11·00	6·50
12	–	2s. blue	3·00	10
23	–	2s.5d. red	2·50	1·75
13	–	2s.6d. purple	3·00	40
24	–	5s. red and olive	9·00	1·00
14	–	10s. slate	32·00	13·00
15	–	£1 brown	32·00	13·00

DESIGNS—VERT (as T **1**): 1d. Buka head-dresses; 2d. Native youth; 2½d. Greater bird of paradise; 3d. Native policeman; 3½d. Papuan head-dress; 4d., 5d. Cacao plant. (As T **7**): 7½d. Kiriwina Yam house; 1s.6d. Rubber tapping; 2s. Sepik dancing masks; 5s. Coffee beans; £1 Papuan shooting fish. HORIZ (as T **7**): 7, 8d. Klinki plymill; 9d. Copra making; 1s. Lakatoi; 1s.7d., 2s.5d. Cattle; 2s.6d. Native shepherd and flock; 10s. Map of Papua and New Guinea.

1957. Nos. 4, 1 and 10 surch.

16	–	4d. on 2½d. orange	1·25	10
25	1	5d. on ½d. green	75	10
17	–	7d. on 1s. green	40	10

23 Council Chamber, Port Moresby

1961. Reconstitution of Legislative Council.

26	23	5d. green and yellow	1·00	25
27		2s.3d. green and salmon	3·00	1·50

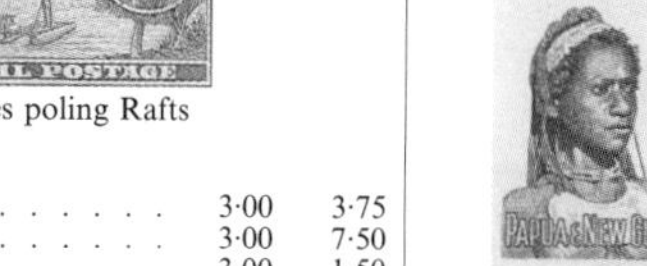

24 Female, Goroka, New Guinea

26 Female Dancer

39 Waterfront, Port Moresby

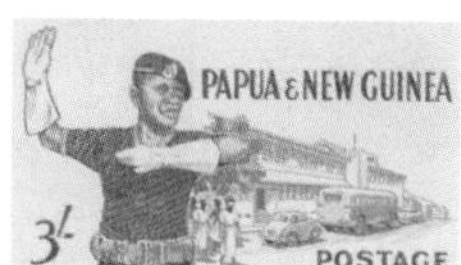

28 Traffic Policeman

1961.

28	24	1d. lake	90	10
29	–	3d. blue	30	10
47	39	8d. green	30	15
30	26	1s. green	2·00	15
31	–	2s. purple	45	15
48	–	2s.3d. blue	30	30
32	28	3s. green	1·25	1·75

DESIGNS—As Type **24**: 3d. Tribal elder, Tari, Papua. As Type **39**: 2s.3d. Piaggio P-166B Portofino aircraft landing at Tapini. As Type **26**: 2s. Male dancer.

29 Campaign Emblem

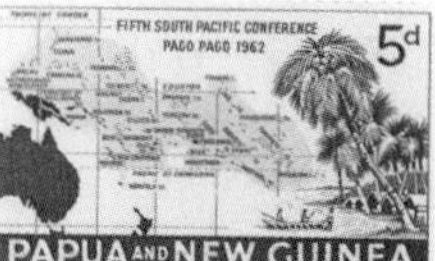

30 Map of South Pacific

1962. Malaria Eradication.

33	29	5d. lake and blue	30	15
34		1s. red and brown	50	25
35		2s. black and green	60	70

1962. 5th South Pacific Conference, Pago Pago.

36	30	5d. red and green	50	15
37		1s.6d. violet and yellow	75	70
38		2s.6d. green and blue	75	1·40

31 Throwing the Javelin

1962. 7th British Empire and Commonwealth Games, Perth.

39	31	5d. brown and blue	20	10
40	–	5d. brown and orange	20	10
41	–	2s.3d. brown and green	70	75

SPORTS—As T **31**: No. 40, High jump. 32 × 23 mm: No. 41, Runners.

34 Raggiana Bird of Paradise

37 Queen Elizabeth II

36 Rabaul

1963.

42	34	5d. yellow, brown and sepia	1·00	10
43	–	6d. red, brown and grey	60	1·25

44 **36** 10s. multicoloured 12·00 7·00
45 **37** £1 brown, gold and green 2·00 1·75
DESIGN—As Type **34**: 6d. Common phalanger.

38 Centenary Emblem

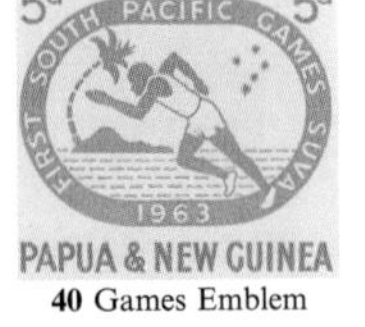
40 Games Emblem

1963. Centenary of Red Cross.
46 **38** 5d. red, grey and green 60 10

1963. 1st South Pacific Games, Suva.
49 **40** 5d. brown 10 10
50 1s. green 30 40

41 Watam Head

45 Casting Vote

1964. Native Artefacts. Multicoloured.
51 11d. Type **41** 25 10
52 2s.5d. Watam head (different) 30 1·50
53 2s.6d. Bosmun head 30 10
54 5s. Medina head 35 15

1964. Common Roll Elections.
55 **45** 5d. brown and drab 10 10
56 2s.3d. brown and blue 20 25

46 "Health Centres"

50 Striped Gardener Bowerbird

1964. Health Services.
57 **46** 5d. violet 10 10
58 – 8d. green 10 10
59 – 1s. blue 15 10
60 – 1s.2d. red 20 35
DESIGNS: 8d. "School health"; 1s. "Infant child and maternal health"; 1s.2d. "Medical training".

1964. Multicoloured.
61 1d. Type **50** 40 10
62 3d. Adelbert bowerbird 50 10
63 5d. Blue bird of paradise 55 10
64 6d. Lawes's parotia 75 10
65 8d. Black-billed sicklebill 1·00 20
66 1s. Emperor of Germany bird of paradise 1·00 10
67 2s. Brown sicklebill 75 30
68 2s.3d. Lesser bird of paradise 75 85
69 3s. Magnificent bird of paradise 75 1·25
70 5s. Twelve-wired bird of paradise 9·00 1·50
71 10s. Magnificent riflebird 4·50 9·00
Nos. 66/71 are larger, $25\frac{1}{2} \times 36\frac{1}{2}$ mm.

61 Canoe Prow

1965. Sepik Canoe Prows in Port Moresby Museum.
72 **61** 4d. multicoloured 50 10
73 – 1s.2d. multicoloured 1·50 1·75
74 – 1s.6d. multicoloured 50 10
75 – 4s. multicoloured 50 50
Each show different carved prows as Type **61**.

61a "Simpson and his Donkey"

1965. 50th Anniv of Gallipoli Landing.
76 **61a** 2s.3d. brown, black & green 20 10

65 Urban Plan and Native House

69 "Papilio ulysses"

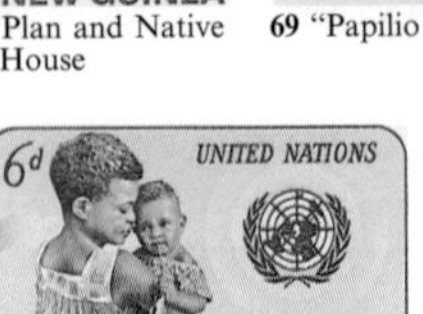
66 Mother and Child

1965. 6th South Pacific Conference, Lae.
77 **65** 6d. multicoloured 10 10
78 – 1s. multicoloured 10 10
No. 78 is similar to Type **65** but with the plan on the right and the house on the left. Also "URBANISATION" reads downwards.

1965. 20th Anniv of U.N.O.
79 **66** 6d. sepia, blue and turquoise 10 10
80 – 1s. brown, blue and violet 10 10
81 – 2s. blue, green and olive 10 10
DESIGNS—VERT: 1s. Globe and U.N. emblem; 2s. U.N. emblem and globes.

1966. Decimal Currency. Butterflies. Mult.
82 1c. Type **69** 40 80
83 3c. "Cyrestis acilia" 40 80
84 4c. "Graphium weiskei" 40 80
85 5c. "Terinos alurgis" 40 10
86 10c. "Ornithoptera priamus" (horiz) 50 30
86a 12c. "Euploea callithoe" (horiz) 2·50 2·25
87 15c. "Papilio euchenor" (horiz) 1·50 80
88 20c. "Parthenos sylvia" (horiz) 50 25
89 25c. "Delias aruna" (horiz) 70 1·25
90 50c. "Apaturina erminea" (horiz) 10·00 1·25
91 $1 "Doleschallia dascylus" (horiz) 4·00 1·75
92 $2 "Ornithoptera paradisea" (horiz) 6·00 8·50

80 "Molala Harai"

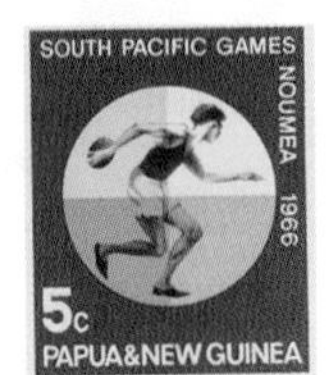
84 Throwing the Discus

1966. Folklore. Elema Art (1st series).
93 **80** 2c. black and red 10 10
94 – 7c. black, yellow and blue 10 30
95 – 30c. black, red and green 15 15
96 – 60c. black, red and yellow 40 50
DESIGNS: 7c. "Marai"; 30c. "Meavea Kivovia"; 60c. "Toivita Tapaivita".

1966. South Pacific Games, Noumea. Mult.
97 5c. Type **84** 10 10
98 10c. Football 15 10
99 20c. Tennis 20 40

87 "Mucuna novoguineensis"

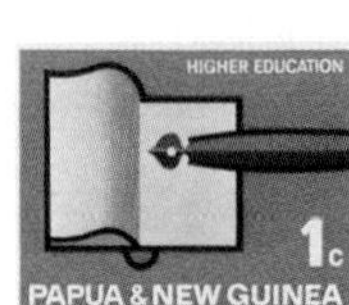
91 "Fine Arts"

1966. Flowers. Multicoloured.
100 5c. Type **87** 15 10
101 10c. "Tecomanthe dendrophila" 15 10
102 20c. "Rhododendron macgregoriae" 20 10
103 60c. "Rhododendron konori" 50 1·40

1967. Higher Education. Multicoloured.
104 1c. Type **91** 10 10
105 3c. "Surveying" 10 10
106 4c. "Civil Engineering" 10 10
107 5c. "Science" 10 10
108 20c. "Law" 10 10

96 "Sagra speciosa"

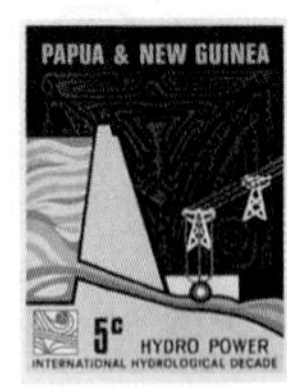
100 Laloki River

1967. Fauna Conservation (Beetles). Mult.
109 5c. Type **96** 15 10
110 10c. "Eupholus schoenherri" 15 10
111 20c. "Sphingnotus albertisi" 25 10
112 25c. "Cyphogastra albertisi" 25 10

1967. Laloki River Hydro-electric Scheme, and "New Industries". Multicoloured.
113 5c. Type **100** 10 10
114 10c. Pyrethrum 10 10
115 20c. Tea plant 15 10
116 25c. Type **100** 15 10

103 Air Attack at Milne Bay

107 Papuan Lory

1967. 25th Anniv of Pacific War. Multicoloured.
117 2c. Type **103** 10 50
118 5c. Kokoda Trail (vert) 10 10
119 20c. The Coast watchers 25 10
120 50c. Battle of the Coral Sea 80 70

1967. Christmas. Territory Parrots. Mult.
121 5c. Type **107** 20 10
122 7c. Pesquet's parrot 25 90
123 20c. Dusky lory 30 10
124 25c. Edward's fig parrot 35 10

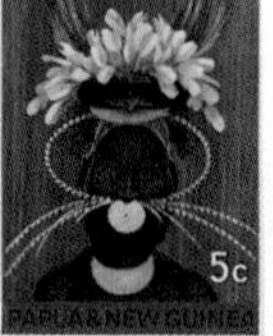
111 Chimbu Head-dress

115 "Hyla thesaurensis"

1968. "National Heritage". Designs showing different Head-dresses. Multicoloured.
125 5c. Type **111** 10 10
126 10c. Southern Highlands (horiz) 15 10
127 20c. Western Highlands (horiz) 15 10
128 60c. Chimbu (different) 40 45

1968. Fauna Conservation (Frogs). Mult.
129 5c. Type **115** 15 50
130 10c. "Hyla iris" 15 10
131 15c. "Ceratobatrachus guentheri" 15 10
132 20c. "Nyctimystes narinosa" 20 50

119 Human Rights Emblem and Papuan Head-dress (abstract)

1968. Human Rights Year. Multicoloured.
133 5c. Type **119** 10 20
134 10c. Human Rights in the World (abstract) 10 10

121 Leadership (abstract)

1968. Universal Suffrage. Multicoloured.
135 20c. Type **121** 15 20
136 25c. Leadership of the Community (abstract) 15 30

123 Common Egg Cowrie

1968. Sea Shells. Multicoloured.
137 1c. Type **123** 10 10
138 3c. Laciniate conch 30 1·00
139 4c. Lithograph cone 20 1·00
140 5c. Marbled cone 25 10
141 7c. Episcopal mitre 35 10
142 10c. "Cymbiola rutila ruckeri" 45 10
143 12c. Checkerboard bonnet 1·25 1·75
144 15c. Scorpion conch 60 1·00
145 20c. Fluted giant clam or scale tridacna 70 10
146 25c. Camp pitar venus 70 70
147 30c. Ramose murex 70 1·00
148 40c. Chambered or pearly nautilus 75 1·00
149 60c. Trumpet triton 70 60
150 $1 Manus green papuina 1·00 75
151 $2 Glory of the sea cone 13·00 4·00

138 Tito Myth

142 "Fireball" Class Dinghy

1969. Folklore. Elema Art (2nd series).
152 **138** 5c. black, yellow and red 10 50
153 – 5c. black, yellow and red 10 50
154 – 10c. black, grey and red 15 50
155 – 10c. black, grey and red 15 50
DESIGNS: No. 153, Iko Myth; 154, Luvuapo Myth; 155, Miro Myth.

1969. 3rd South Pacific Games, Port Moresby.
156 **142** 5c. black 10 25
157 – 10c. violet 10 10
158 – 20c. green 15 20
DESIGNS—HORIZ: 10c. Swimming pool, Boroko; 20c. Games arena, Konedobu.

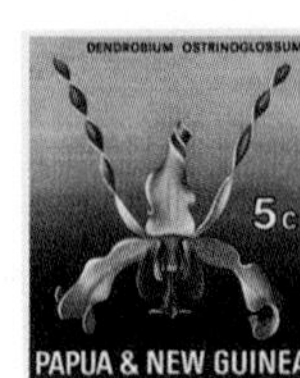
145 "Dendrobium ostrinoglossum"

149 Bird of Paradise

1969. Flora Conservation (Orchids). Multicoloured.
159 5c. Type **145** 25 10
160 10c. "Dendrobium lawesii" 30 70
161 20c. "Dendrobium pseudofrigidum" 35 90
162 30c. "Dendrobium conanthum" 40 70

1969.
162a **149** 2c. blue, black and red 10 65
163 5c. green, brown & orge 10 10

150 Native Potter

151 Tareko

1969. 50th Anniv of I.L.O.
164 **150** 5c. multicoloured 10 10

1969. Musical Instruments.
165 **151** 5c. multicoloured 10 10
166 – 10c. black, green & yellow 10 10
167 – 25c. black, yellow & brown 15 15
168 – 30c. multicoloured 25 15
DESIGNS: 10c. Garamut; 25c. Iviliko; 30c. Kundu.

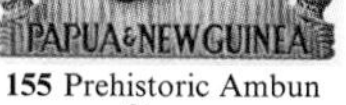

155 Prehistoric Ambun Stone

159 King of Saxony Bird of Paradise

1970. "National Heritage". Multicoloured.
169 5c. Type **155** 10 10
170 10c. Masawa canoe of Kula Circuit 10 10
171 25c. Torres' map, 1606 . . . 40 15
172 30c. H.M.S. "Basilisk" (paddle-sloop), 1873 . . . 65 25

1970. Fauna Conservation. Birds of Paradise. Mult.
173 5c. Type **159** 80 15
174 10c. King bird of paradise . . 80 60
175 15c. Raggiana bird of paradise . . . . 1·25 1·00
176 25c. Sickle-crested bird of paradise . . . . 1·50 70

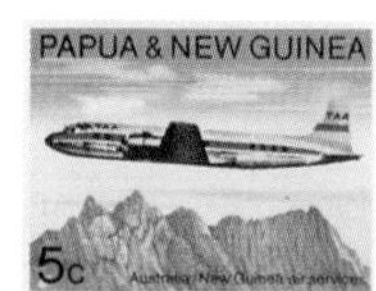

163 Douglas DC-6B and Mt. Wilhelm

1970. Australian and New Guinea Air Services. Multicoloured.
177 5c. Type **163** 25 30
178 5c. Lockheed Electra and Mt. Yule 25 30
179 5c. Boeing 727-100 and Mt. Giluwe 25 30
180 5c. Fokker Friendship and Manam Island 25 30
181 25c. Douglas DC-3 and Matupi Volcano 35 40
182 30c. Boeing 707 and Hombrom's Bluff 35 60

169 N. Miklouho-Maclay (scientist) and Effigy

1970. 42nd A.N.Z.A.A.S. Congress, Port Moresby. Multicoloured.
183 5c. Type **169** 10 10
184 10c. B. Malinowski (anthropologist) and native hut 20 10
185 15c. T. Salvadori (ornithologist) and double-wattled cassowary 90 25
186 20c. F. R. R. Schlechter (botanist) and flower . . . 60 25
A.N.Z.A.A.S. = Australian–New Zealand Association for the Advancement of Science.

170 Wogeo Island Food Bowl

171 Eastern Highlands Dwelling

1970. Native Artefacts. Multicoloured.
187 5c. Type **170** 10 10
188 10c. Lime pot 20 10
189 15c. Albom sago storage pot 20 10
190 30c. Manus island bowl (horiz) 25 30

1971. Native Dwellings. Multicoloured.
191 5c. Type **171** 10 10
192 7c. Milne Bay stilt dwelling 15 90
193 10c. Purari Delta dwelling . . 15 10
194 40c. Sepik dwelling 25 90

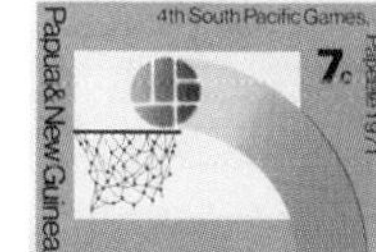

172 Spotted Phalanger

173 "Basketball"

1971. Fauna Conservation. Multicoloured.
195 5c. Type **172** 30 10
196 10c. Long-fingered possum 35 10
197 15c. Feather-tailed possum 50 80
198 25c. Long-tailed echidna . . 70 80
199 30c. Ornate tree kangaroo (horiz) 70 50

1971. 4th South Pacific Games, Papeete. Mult.
200 7c. Type **173** 10 10
201 14c. "Sailing" 15 20
202 21c. "Boxing" 15 30
203 28c. "Athletics" 15 40

174 Bartering Fish for Vegetables

175 Sia Dancer

1971. Primary Industries. Multicoloured.
204 7c. Type **174** 10 10
205 9c. Man stacking yams . . . 15 30
206 14c. Vegetable market . . . 25 10
207 30c. Highlanders cultivating garden 45 65

1971. Native Dancers. Multicoloured.
208 7c. Type **175** 20 10
209 9c. Urasena dancer 25 20
210 20c. Siassi Tubuan dancers (horiz) 60 75
211 28c. Sia dancers (horiz) . . . 80 90

176 Papuan Flag over Australian Flag

1971. Constitutional Development.
212 **176** 7c. multicoloured 30 10
213 – 7c. multicoloured 30 10
DESIGN: No. 213, Crest of Papua New Guinea and Australian coat of arms.

177 Map of Papua New Guinea and Flag of South Pacific Commission

1972. 25th Anniv of South Pacific Commission.
214 **177** 15c. multicoloured 45 55
215 – 15c. multicoloured 45 55
DESIGN: No. 215, Man's face and flag of the Commission.

178 Turtle

1972. Fauna Conservation (Reptiles). Mult.
216 7c. Type **178** 40 10
217 14c. Rainforest dragon . . . 65 1·25
218 21c. Green python . . . . . 65 1·50
219 30c. Salvador's monitor . . . 80 1·25

179 Curtiss MF-6 Seagull and "Eureka" (schooner)

1972. 50th Anniv of Aviation. Multicoloured.
220 7c. Type **179** 40 10
221 14c. De Havilland D.H.37 and native porters . . . . 70 1·25
222 20c. Junkers G.31 and gold dredger . . . . 95 1·25
223 25c. Junkers F-13 and mission church . . . . . . 95 1·25

180 New National Flag

181 Rev. Copland King

1972. National Day. Multicoloured.
224 7c. Type **180** 20 10
225 10c. Native drum 25 25
226 30c. Trumpet triton 45 50

1972. Christmas. Missionaries. Multicoloured.
227 7c. Type **181** 25 40
228 7c. Rev. Dr. Flierl 25 40
229 7c. Bishop Verjus 25 40
230 7c. Pastor Ruatoka 25 40

182 Mt. Tomavatur Station

183 Queen Carola's Parotia

1973. Completion of Telecommunications Project, 1968–72. Multicoloured.
231 7c. Type **182** 15 20
232 7c. Mt. Kerigomma Station 15 20
233 7c. Sattelburg Station 15 20
234 7c. Wideru Station 15 20
235 9c. Teleprinter 15 20
236 30c. Network map 35 50
Nos. 235/6 are larger, 36 × 26 mm.

1973. Birds of Paradise. Multicoloured.
237 7c. Type **183** . . . . 1·00 35
238 14c. Goldie's bird of paradise 2·25 1·00
239 21c. Ribbon-tailed bird of paradise . . . . 2·50 1·50
240 28c. Princess Stephanie's bird of paradise . . . . 3·00 2·00
Nos. 239/40 are size 18 × 49 mm.

184 Wood Carver

1973. Multicoloured.
241 1c. Type **184** 10 10
242 3c. Wig-makers 40 10
243 5c. Mt. Bagana 55 10
244 6c. Pig exchange . . . . . . 80 1·50
245 7c. Coastal village 20 10
246 8c. Arawe mother 35 30
247 9c. Fire dancers 20 20
248 10c. Tifalmin hunter 55 10
249 14c. Crocodile hunters . . . 45 70
250 15c. Mt. Elimbari 50 30
251 20c. Canoe-racing, Manus . . 70 40
252 21c. Making sago . . . . . 40 1·00
253 25c. Council House 40 45
254 28c. Menyamya bowmen . . 40 1·00
255 30c. Shark-snaring 40 50
256 40c. Fishing canoes, Madang 40 40
257 60c. Tapa cloth-making . . . 55 50
258 $1 Asaro Mudmen . . . . . 55 1·10
259 $2 Enga "Sing Sing" . . . . 1·75 6·00

185 Stamps of German New Guinea, 1897

1973. 75th Anniv of Papua New Guinea Stamps.
260 **185** 1c. multicoloured 10 15
261 – 6c. indigo, blue and silver 15 30
262 – 7c. multicoloured 15 30
263 – 9c. multicoloured 15 30
264 – 25c. orange and gold . . . 30 80
265 – 30c. plum and silver . . . 30 90

DESIGNS—As Type **185**: 6c. 2 mark stamp of German New Guinea, 1900; 7c. Surcharged registration label of New Guinea, 1914. 46 × 35 mm: 9c. Papuan 1s. stamp, 1901. 45 × 38 mm: 25c. ½d. stamp of New Guinea, 1925; 30c. Papuan 10s. stamp, 1932.

186 Native Carved Heads

187 Queen Elizabeth II (from photo by Karsh)

1973. Self-government.
266 **186** 7c. multicoloured 30 15
267 10c. multicoloured 50 65

1974. Royal Visit.
268 **187** 7c. multicoloured 25 15
269 30c. multicoloured . . . . 75 1·50

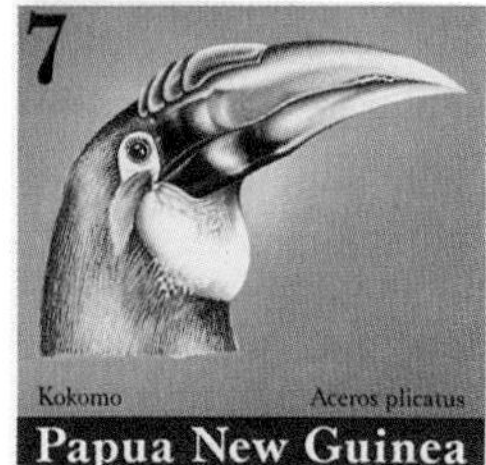

188 Blyth's Hornbill

1974. Birds' Heads. Multicoloured.
270 7c. Type **188** . . . . 1·25 70
271 10c. Double-wattled cassowary (33 × 49 mm) . . 2·00 3·25
272 30c. New Guinea harpy eagle 4·00 8·50

189 "Dendrobium bracteosum"

191 1-toea Coin

190 Motu Lakatoi

1974. Flora Conservation. Multicoloured.
273 7c. Type **189** 30 10
274 10c. "D. anosmum" 40 60
275 20c. "D. smillieae" . . . . . 50 1·40
276 30c. "D. insigne" . . . . . 60 1·75

1974. National Heritage. Canoes. Multicoloured.
277 7c. Type **190** 30 10
278 10c. Tami two-master morobe 30 55
279 25c. Aramia racing canoe . . 60 3·00
280 30c. Buka Island canoe . . . 60 1·00

1975. New Coinage. Multicoloured.
281 1t. Type **191** 10 30
282 7t. New 2t. and 5t. coins . . 25 10
283 10t. New 10t. coin 25 30
284 20t. New 20t. coin 40 80
285 1k. New 1k. coin . . . . . . 1·25 4·50
SIZES: 10, 20t. As Type **191**; 7t., 1k. 45 × 26 mm.

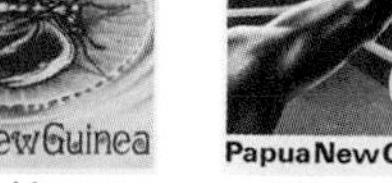

192 "Ornithoptera alexandrae"

193 Boxing

1975. Fauna Conservation (Birdwing Butterflies). Multicoloured.
286 7t. Type **192** 40 10
287 10t. "O. victoriae" 50 65
288 30t. "O. allottei" . . . . . 80 2·00
289 40t. "O. chimaera" . . . . . 1·25 3·50

1975. 5th South Pacific Games, Guam. Mult.
290 7t. Type **193** 10 10
291 20t. Running 15 30
292 25t. Basketball 30 45
293 30t. Swimming 30 50

194 Map and National Flag

1975. Independence. Multicoloured.
294 7t. Type **194** 20 10
295 30t. Map and National emblem 40 65
MS296 116 × 58 mm. Nos. 294/5 1·10 1·75

195 M.V. "Bulolo"

1976. Ships of the 1930s. Multicoloured.
297 7t. Type **195** 25 10
298 15t. M.V. "Macdhui" 35 30
299 25t. M.V. "Malaita" 40 65
300 60t. S.S. "Montoro" . . . . 70 2·50

196 Rorovana Carvings

1976. Bougainville Art. Multicoloured.
301 7t. Type **196** 10 10
302 20t. Upe hats 20 35
303 25t. Kapkaps . . . . 25 1·00
304 30t. Canoe paddles 30 80

197 Rabaul House

1976. Native Dwellings. Multicoloured.
305 7t. Type **197** 10 10
306 15t. Aramia house 15 20
307 30t. Telefomin house 25 60
308 40t. Tapini house . . . . . 25 1·50

198 Landscouts

1976. 50th Annivs of Survey Flight and Scouting in Papua New Guinea. Multicoloured.
309 7t. Type **198** 20 10
310 10t. De Havilland D.H.50A seaplane 20 20
311 15t. Seascouts 30 40
312 60t. De Havilland D.H.50A seaplane on water . . . . 80 3·00

199 Father Ross and New Guinea Highlands

1976. William Ross Commemoration.
313 **199** 7t. multicoloured 40 15

1976. Fauna Conservation (Tropical Fish). Mult.
314 5t. Type **200** 30 10
315 15t. Emperor angelfish . . . 45 45
316 30t. Six-blotched hind 70 80
317 40t. Thread-finned butterflyfish . . . . 80 1·10

201 Man from Kundiawa

202 Headdress, Wasara Tribe

1977. Headdresses. Multicoloured.
318 1t. Type **201** 10 10
319 5t. Masked dancer, Abelam area of Maprik 10 10
320 10t. Headdress from Koiari 20 15
321 15t. Woman with face paint, Hanuabada 25 20
322 20t. Orokaiva dancer 40 30
323 25t. Haus Tambaran dancer, Abelam area of Maprik . . 30 30
324 30t. Asaro Valley headdress 30 35
325 35t. Singsing costume, Garaina 30 45
326 40t. Waghi Valley headdress 30 35
327 50t. Trobriand Island dancer 40 60
328 1k. Type **202** . . . . 50 1·50
329 2k. Headdress, Meko tribe 75 3·00
SIZES: 1, 5, 20t. 25 × 31 mm; 35, 40t. 23 × 38 mm; 1k. 28 × 35 mm; 2k. 33 × 23 mm; others 26 × 26 mm.

203 National Flag and Queen Elizabeth II

1977. Silver Jubilee. Multicoloured.
330 7t. Type **203** 20 10
331 15t. The Queen and national emblem 25 35
332 35t. The Queen and map of P.N.G. 40 70

204 White-breasted Ground Pigeon

1977. Fauna Conservation (Birds). Mult.
333 5t. Type **204** 35 10
334 7t. Victoria crowned pigeon 35 10
335 15t. Pheasant pigeon 65 65
336 30t. Orange-fronted fruit dove . . . . 80 1·10
337 50t. Banded imperial pigeon 1·25 3·50

205 Guides and Gold Badge

206 Kari Marupi Myth

1977. 50th Anniv of Guiding in Papua New Guinea. Multicoloured.
338 7t. Type **205** 20 10
339 15t. Guides mapping 25 20
340 30t. Guides washing 40 50
341 35t. Guides cooking 40 60

1977. Folklore. Elema Art (3rd series).
342 **206** 7t. multicoloured 15 10
343 – 20t. multicoloured 35 35
344 – 30t. red, blue and black 40 75
345 – 35t. red, yellow and black 40 75
DESIGNS: 20t. Savoripi clan myth; 30t. Oa-Laea myth; 35t. Oa-Iriarapo myth.

1978. Fauna Conservation (Skinks). Mult.
346 10t. Type **207** 20 10
347 15t. Green tree skink 25 25
348 35t. Crocodile skink 30 70
349 40t. New Guinea blue-tongued skink 45 85

208 "Roboastra arika"

1978. Sea Slugs. Multicoloured.
350 10t. Type **208** 20 10
351 15t. "Chromodoris fidelis" . . 25 30
352 35t. "Flabellina macassarana" 45 85
353 40t. "Chromodoris marginata" . . . . 50 1·00

209 Present Day Royal Papua New Guinea Constabulary

1978. History of Royal Papua New Guinea Constabulary. Uniformed Police and Constabulary Badges. Multicoloured.
354 10t. Type **209** 20 10
355 15t. Mandated New Guinea Constabulary, 1921–41 . . 25 15
356 20t. British New Guinea Armed Constabulary 1890–1906 . . . . 25 40
357 25t. German New Guinea Police, 1899–1914 . . . . 30 45
358 30t. Royal Papua and New Guinea Constabulary, 1906–64 . . . . 30 60

210 Ocarina

211 East New Britain Canoe Prow

1979. Musical Instruments. Mult.
359 7t. Type **210** 10 10
360 20t. Musical bow (horiz) . . 20 20
361 28t. Launut 25 30
362 35t. Nose flute (horiz) . . . 30 45

1979. Traditional Canoe Prows and Paddles. Mult.
363 14t. Type **211** 20 15
364 21t. Sepik war canoe 30 25
365 25t. Trobriand Island canoe 30 30
366 40t. Milne Bay canoe 40 60

212 Katudababila (waist belt)

213 "Aenetus cyanochlora"

1979. Traditional Currency. Multicoloured.
367 7t. Type **212** 10 10
368 15t. Doga (chest ornament) 20 30
369 25t. Mwali (armshell) 35 55
370 35t. Soulava (necklace) . . . 45 75

1979. Fauna Conservation. Moths. Multicoloured.
371 7t. Type **213** 20 10
372 15t. "Celerina vulgaris" . . . 30 35
373 20t. "Alcidis aurora" (vert) 30 75
374 25t. "Phyllodes conspicillator" . . . . . 35 1·00
375 30t. "Lyssa patroclus" (vert) 40 1·00

214 "The Right to Affection and Love"

216 Detail from Betrothal Ceremony Mural, Minj District, Western Highlands Province

215 "Post Office Service"

1979. International Year of the Child. Mult.
376 7t. Type **214** 10 10
377 15t. "The right to adequate nutrition and medical care" 15 15
378 30t. "The right to play" . . . 20 20
379 60t. "The right to a free education" 45 60

1980. Admission to U.P.U. (1979). Multicoloured.
380 7t. Type **215** 10 10
381 25t. "Wartime mail" 25 25
382 35t. "U.P.U. emblem 35 40
383 40t. "Early postal services" 40 50

1980. South Pacific Festival of Arts.
384 **216** 20t. yellow, orange & blk 15 35
385 – 20t. mult (two figures, left-hand in black and yellow; right-hand in black, yellow and red) 15 35
386 – 20t. mult (two figures, left-hand in black and orange; right-hand in black) 15 35
387 – 20t. mult (two figures, one behind the other) . . . 15 35
388 – 20t. mult (one figure) . . 15 35
DESIGNS: Nos. 385/8, further details of Betrothal Ceremony.
Nos. 384/8 were issued together in horizontal se-tenant strips of five within the sheet, forming a composite design.

217 Family being Interviewed

1980. National Census. Multicoloured.
389 7t. Type **217** 10 10
390 15t. Population symbol . . . 15 15
391 40t. Papua New Guinea map 30 40
392 50t. Heads symbolizing population growth 35 50

218 Donating Blood

1980. Red Cross Blood Bank. Multicoloured.
393 7t. Type **218** 15 10
394 15t. Receiving transfusion . . 20 20
395 30t. Map of Papua New Guinea showing blood transfusion centres 25 25
396 60t. Blood and its components 40 60

219 Dugong

1980. Mammals. Multicoloured.
397 7t. Type **219** 10 10
398 30t. New Guinea marsupial cat (vert) 30 45
399 35t. Tube-nosed bat (vert) . . 30 45
400 45t. Rufescent bandicoot . . 40 55

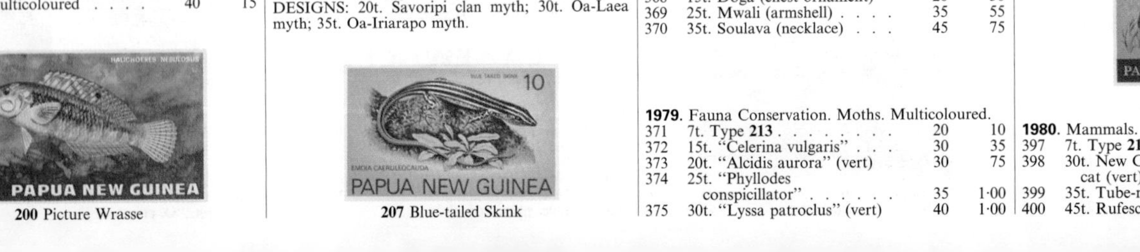
200 Picture Wrasse

207 Blue-tailed Skink

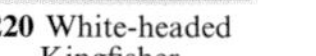

220 White-headed Kingfisher   **221** Native Mask

1981. Kingfishers. Multicoloured.
401 3t. Type **220** 25 60
402 7t. Forest kingfisher 25 10
403 20t. Sacred kingfisher 30 50
404 25t. White-tailed kingfisher (26 × 46 mm) 30 85
405 60t. Blue-winged kookaburra 60 3·00

1981.
406 **221** 2t. violet and orange . . . 10 20
407 – 5t. red and green 10 20
DESIGN: 5t. Hibiscus flower.

222 Mortar Team

1981. Defence Force. Multicoloured.
408 7t. Type **222** 15 10
409 15t. Douglas DC-3 and aircrew 25 25
410 40t. "Aitape" (patrol boat) and seamen 35 65
411 50t. Medical team examining children 35 75

223 M.A.F. (Missionary Aviation Fellowship) Cessna Super Skywagon

1981. "Mission Aviation". Multicoloured.
412 10t. Type **223** 20 10
413 15t. Catholic mission British Aircraft Swallow "St. Paulus" 25 15
414 20t. S.I.L. (Summer Institute of Linguistics) Hiller 12E helicopter 25 25
415 30t. Lutheran mission Junkers F-13 . . . . . . 35 40
416 35t. S.D.A. (Seventh Day Adventist Church) Piper PA-23 Aztec 35 55

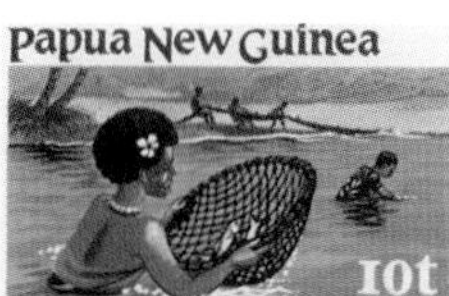

224 Scoop Net Fishing

1981. Fishing. Multicoloured.
417 10t. Type **224** 15 10
418 15t. Kite fishing 20 30
419 30t. Rod fishing 30 50
420 60t. Scissor net fishing . . . 55 85

225 Buhler's Papuina

1981. Land Snail Shells. Multicoloured.
421 5t. Type **225** 10 10
422 15t. Yellow naninia 20 25
423 20t. Adonis papuina and Hermoine papuina 20 35
424 30t. Hinde's papuina and New Pommeranian papuina 30 50
425 40t. "Papuina strabo" . . . 40 80

226 Lord Baden-Powell and Flag-raising Ceremony

1981. 75th Anniv of Boy Scout Movement. Mult.
426 15t. Type **226** 20 15
427 25t. Scout leader and camp 20 30
428 35t. Scout and hut building 20 45
429 50t. Percy Chaterton and Scouts administering first aid 30 75

227 Yangoru and Boiken Bowls, East Sepik

1981. Native Pottery. Multicoloured.
430 10t. Type **227** 10 10
431 20t. Utu cooking pot and small Gumalu pot, Madang 20 30
432 40t. Wanigela pots, Northern (37 × 23 mm) 40 55
433 50t. Ramu Valley pots, Madang (37 × 23 mm) . . 45 80

228 "Eat Healthy Foods"

1982. Food and Nutrition. Multicoloured.
434 10t. Type **228** 10 10
435 15t. Protein foods 20 30
436 30t. Protective foods 40 55
437 40t. Energy foods 45 70

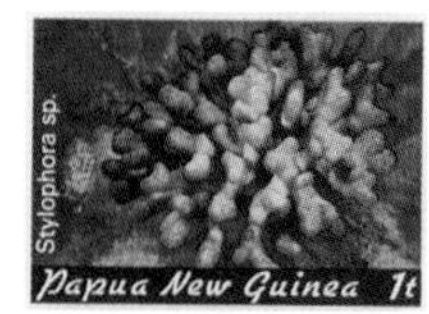

229 "Stylophora sp."

1982. Multicoloured.
438 1t. Type **229** 10 20
439 3t. "Dendrophyllia sp." (vert) 60 1·00
440 5t. "Acropora humilis" . . . 15 10
441 10t. "Dendronephthya sp." (vert) 80 60
442 12t. As 10t. . . . . 3·50 5·50
443 15t. "Distichopora sp." . . . 20 20
444 20t. "Isis sp" (vert) 90 25
445 25t. "Acropora sp." (vert) . . 50 50
446 30t. "Dendronephthya sp." (different) (vert) . . . . . 1·25 90
447 35t. "Stylaster elegans" (vert) 1·25 50
448 40t. "Antipathes sp." (vert) 1·25 1·25
449 45t. "Turbinarea sp." (vert) 2·00 1·00
450 1k. "Xenia sp." . . . . 1·00 85
451 3k. "Distichopora sp." (vert) 2·75 3·50
452 5k. Raggiana bird of paradise (33 × 33 mm) . . . . . . 7·00 9·00

230 Missionaries landing on Beach   **231** Athletics

1982. Centenary of Catholic Church in Papua New Guinea. Mural on Wall of Nordup Catholic Church, East New Britain. Multicoloured.
457 10t. Type **230** 20 50
458 10t. Missionaries talking to natives 20 50
459 10t. Natives with slings and spears ready to attack . . 20 50
Nos. 457/9 were issued together, se-tenant, forming a composite design.

1982. Commonwealth Games and "Anpex 82" Stamp Exhibition, Brisbane. Multicoloured.
460 10t. Type **231** 15 10
461 15t. Boxing 20 25
462 45t. Rifle-shooting 40 70
463 50t. Bowls 45 75

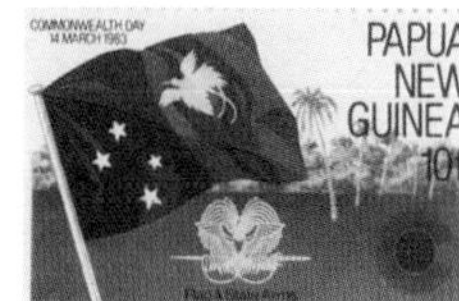

232 National Flag

1983. Commonwealth Day. Multicoloured.
464 10t. Type **232** 15 10
465 15t. Basket-weaving and cabbage-picking 20 30
466 20t. Crane hoisting roll of material 25 35
467 50t. Lorries and ships 60 75

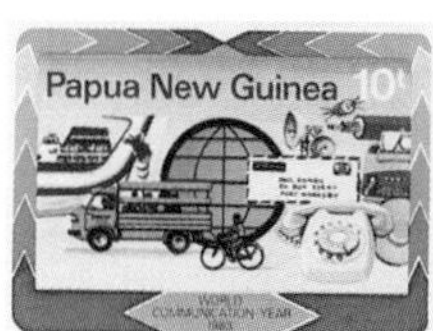

233 Transport Communications

1983. World Communications Year. Multicoloured.
468 10t. Type **233** 30 10
469 25t. "Postal service" 50 25
470 30t. "Telephone service" . . 55 30
471 60t. "Transport service" . . . 1·10 90

234 "Chelonia depressa"

1984. Turtles. Multicoloured.
472 5t. Type **234** 20 10
473 10t. "Chelonia mydas" . . . 25 10
474 15t. "Eretmochelys imbricata" 30 30
475 20t. "Lepidochelys olivacea" 40 35
476 25t. " Caretta caretta" . . . 45 50
477 40t. "Dermochelys coriacea" 60 75

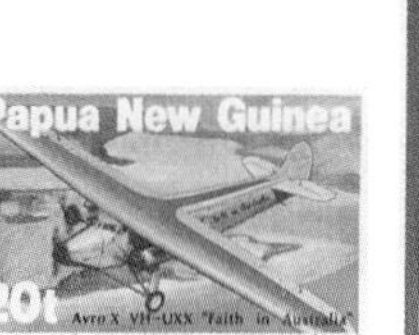

235 Avro Type 618 Ten "Faith in Australia"   **237** Ceremonial Shield and Club, Central Province

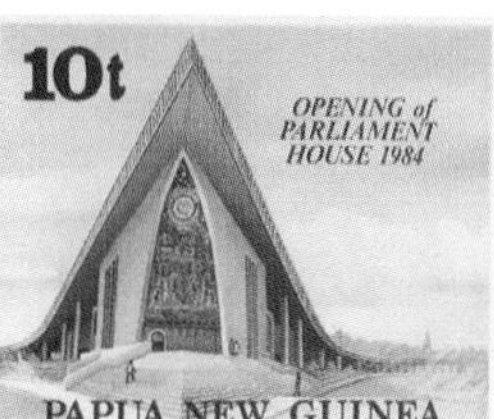

236 Parliament House

1984. 50th Anniv of First Airmail Australia–Papua New Guinea. Multicoloured.
478 20t. Type **235** 40 30
479 25t. De Havilland Dragon Express "Carmania" . . . 40 45
480 40t. Westland Widgeon . . . 50 80
481 60t. Consolidated PBY-5 Catalina flying boat . . . 70 1·25

1984. Opening of New Parliament House.
482 **236** 10t. multicoloured 30 30

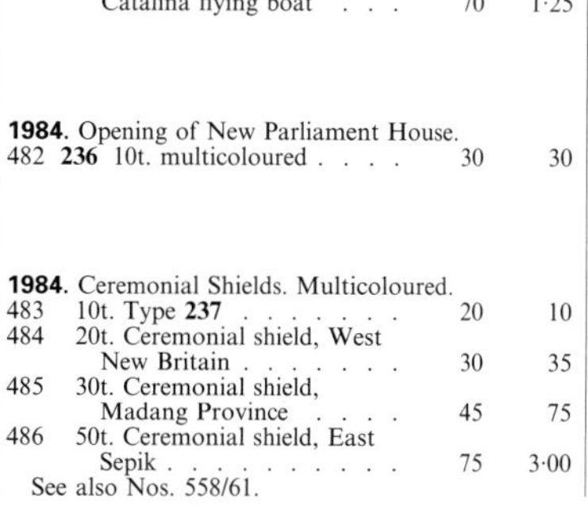

1984. Ceremonial Shields. Multicoloured.
483 10t. Type **237** 20 10
484 20t. Ceremonial shield, West New Britain 30 35
485 30t. Ceremonial shield, Madang Province 45 75
486 50t. Ceremonial shield, East Sepik . . . . 75 3·00
See also Nos. 558/61.

238 H.M.S. "Nelson" at Port Moresby, 1884   **239** Fergusson Island

1984. Centenary of Protectorate Proclamations for British New Guinea and German New Guinea. Multicoloured.
487 10t. Type **238** 35 55
488 10t. Papua New Guinea flag and Port Moresby, 1984 35 55
489 45t. Papua New Guinea flag and Rabaul, 1984 . . . . 50 1·90
490 45t. German warship "Elizabeth" at Rabaul, 1884 . . . . 50 1·90
Nos. 487/8 and 489/90 were issued in se-tenant pairs, each pair forming a composite picture.

1985. Tourist Scenes. Multicoloured.
491 10t. Type **239** 25 10
492 25t. Sepik River 50 60
493 40t. Chimbu Gorge (horiz) 75 1·40
494 60t. Dali Beach, Vanimo (horiz) . . . . 1·25 1·90

1985. No. 408 surch **12t.**
495 **222** 12t. on 7t. multicoloured 60 75

241 Dubu Platform, Central Province   **242** Head of New Britain Collared Sparrow Hawk

1985. Ceremonial Structures. Multicoloured.
496 15t. Type **241** 35 15
497 20t. Tamuniai house, West New Britain 50 50
498 30t. Traditional yam tower, Trobriand Island 65 80
499 60t. Huli grave, Tari . . . . 1·00 1·75

1985. Birds of Prey. Multicoloured.
500 12t. Type **242** . . . . 70 1·50
501 12t. New Britain collared sparrow hawk in flight . . 70 1·50
502 30t. Doria's goshawk . . . . 1·00 1·75
503 30t. Doria's goshawk in flight 1·00 1·75
504 60t. Long-tailed honey buzzard . . . . 1·50 2·25
505 60t. Long-tailed honey buzzard in flight . . . . . 1·50 2·25

243 National Flag and Parliament House   **244** Early Postcard, Aerogramme, Inkwell and Spectacles

1985. 10th Anniv of Independence.
506 **243** 12t. multicoloured 60 85

1985. Centenary of Papua New Guinea Post Office. Multicoloured.
507 12t. Type **244** 45 10
508 30t. Queensland 1897 1d. die with proof and modern press printing stamps . . . 1·10 1·00
509 40t. Newspaper of 1885 announcing shipping service and loading mail into aircraft . . . . 1·75 2·25
510 60t. Friedrich-Wilhelmshafen postmark of 1892 and Port Moresby F.D.C. postmark of 9 October 1985 . . . . 2·00 3·75
MS511 As Nos. 507/10, but designs continue on sheet margins . . 6·00 7·00

245 Figure with Eagle

246 Valentine or Prince Cowrie

1985. Nombowai Wood Carvings. Mult.
512 12t. Type **245** 50 10
513 30t. Figure with clam shell 1·25 75
514 60t. Figure with dolphin . . 2·00 3·00
515 80t. Figure of woman with cockerel . . . . 2·50 5·00

1986. Sea Shells. Multicoloured.
516 15t. Type **246** 75 15
517 35t. Bulow's olive . . . . . 1·60 1·40
518 45t. Parkinson's olive . . . . 2·00 2·25
519 70t. Golden cowrie . . . . . 2·50 5·75

246a Princess Elizabeth in A.T.S. Uniform, 1945

1986. 60th Birthday of Queen Elizabeth II. Mult.
520 15t. Type **246a** 15 15
521 35t. Silver Wedding Anniversary photograph (by Patrick Lichfield), Balmoral, 1972 . . . . . . [illegible] 10
522 50t. Queen inspecting guard of honour, Port Moresby, 1982 . . . . 40 85
523 60t. On board Royal Yacht "Britannia", Papua New Guinea, 1982 . . . . 65 1·00
524 70t. At Crown Agents' Head Office, London, 1983 . . . 40 1·25

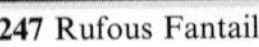
247 Rufous Fantail

248 Martin Luther nailing Theses to Cathedral Door, Wittenberg and Modern Lutheran Pastor

1986. "Ameripex '86" International Stamp Exhibition, Chicago. Small Birds (1st series). Multicoloured.
525 15t. Type **247** 90 30
526 35t. Streaked berry pecker . . 1·75 1·25
527 45t. Red-breasted pitta . . . 1·90 1·25
528 70t. Olive-yellow robin (vert) 2·50 6·00
See also Nos. 597/601.

1986. Centenary of Lutheran Church in Papua New Guinea. Multicoloured.
529 15t. Type **248** 75 15
530 70t. Early church, Finschhafen, and modern Martin Luther Chapel, Lae Seminary . . . . 2·25 3·50

249 "Dendrobium vexillarius"

250 Maprik Dancer

1986. Orchids. Multicoloured.
531 15t. Type **249** 95 20
532 35t. "Dendrobium lineale" 2·00 75
533 45t. "Dendrobium johnsoniae" . . . . 2·00 1·10
534 70t. "Dendrobium cuthbertsonii" . . . . . . 2·75 5·50

1986. Papua New Guinea Dancers. Multicoloured.
535 15t. Type **250** 75 15
536 35t. Kiriwina . . . . 1·50 80
537 45t. Kundiawa . . . . 1·60 95
538 70t. Fasu . . . . 2·75 4·25

251 White-bonnet Anemonefish

1987. Anemonefish. Multicoloured.
539 17t. Type **251** 70 25
540 30t. Orange-finned anemonefish . . . . 1·40 1·10
541 35t. Fire anemonefish ("Tomato clownfish") . . . 1·50 1·40
542 70t. Spine-cheeked anemonefish . . . . 2·50 6·00

252 "Roebuck" (Dampier), 1700

1987. Ships. Multicoloured.
543 1t. "La Boudeuse" (De Bougainville, 1768) . . . . 50 1·00
544 5t. Type **252** . . . . 70 1·50
545 10t. H.M.S. "Swallow" (Philip Carteret), 1767 . . 1·00 1·50
546 15t. H.M.S. "Fly" (Blackwood), 1845 . . . . 1·50 1·00
547 17t. As 15t. . . . . 1·50 75
548 20t. H.M.S. "Rattlesnake" (Owen Stanley), 1849 . . . 1·50 1·00
549 20t. "Vitiaz" (Maclay), 1871 1·75 2·50
550 35t. "San Pedrico" (Torres) and zabra, 1606 . . . . . 70 1·00
551 40t. "L'Astrolabe" (D'Urville), 1827 . . . . . 2·00 2·50
552 45t. "Neva" (D. Albertis), 1876 . . . . 75 1·25
553 60t. Spanish galleon (Jorge de Meneses), 1526 . . . . . . 2·50 3·50
554 70t. "Eendracht" (Schouten and Le Maire), 1616 . . . 1·75 2·75
555 1k. H.M.S. "Blanche" (Simpson), 1872 . . . . . 2·50 3·00
556 2k. "Merrie England" (steamer), 1889 . . . . . 3·25 3·00
557 3k. "Samoa" (German colonial steamer), 1884 . . . 4·00 6·00
For some of these designs redrawn for "Australia '99" World Stamp Exhibition see Nos. 857/60.

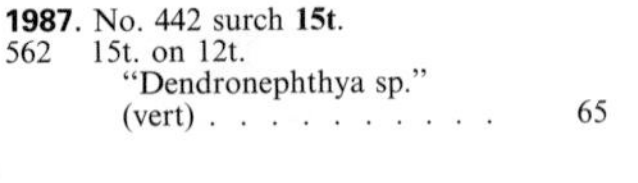

1987. War Shields. As T **237**. Multicoloured.
558 15t. Gulf Province 20 25
559 35t. East Sepik 45 50
560 45t. Madang Province . . . 55 60
561 70t. Telefomin 85 90

1987. No. 442 surch **15t**.
562 15t. on 12t. "Dendronephthya sp." (vert) 65 65

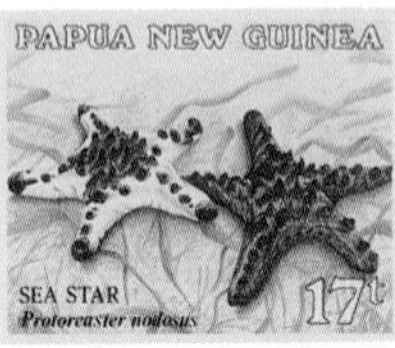
254 "Protoreaster nodosus"

1987. Starfish. Multicoloured.
563 17t. Type **254** 55 25
564 35t. "Gomophia egeriae" . . 1·10 70
565 45t. "Choriaster granulatus" 1·25 80
566 70t. "Neoferdina ocellata" . . 1·75 3·50

255 Cessna Stationair 6 taking off, Rabaraba

1987. Aircraft in Papua New Guinea. Mult.
567 15t. Type **255** 80 25
568 35t. Britten Norman Islander over Hombrum Bluff . . . 1·50 90
569 45t. De Havilland Twin Otter 100 over Highlands . . . 1·50 1·00
570 70t. Fokker F.28 Fellowship over Madang . . . . . . 2·50 5·75

256 Pre-Independence Policeman on Traffic Duty and Present-day Motorcycle Patrol

1988. Centenary of Royal Papua New Guinea Constabulary. Multicoloured.
571 17t. Type **256** 45 25
572 35t. British New Guinea Armed Constabulary, 1890, and Governor W. MacGregor 80 50
573 45t. Police badges 90 65
574 70t. German New Guinea Police, 1888, and Dr. A Hahl (founder) . . . . . . 1·50 1·75

257 Lakatoi (canoe) and Sydney Opera House

1988. "Sydpex '88" Nat Stamp Exn, Sydney.
575 **257** 35t. multicoloured . . . . 80 1·25

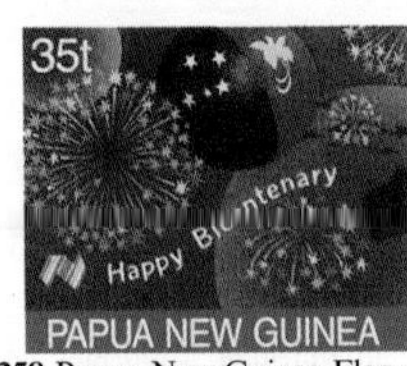
258 Papua New Guinea Flag on Globe and Fireworks

1988. Bicent of Australian Settlement. Mult.
576 35t. Type **258** . . . . 1·00 1·40
577 35t. Australian flag on globe and fireworks . . . . . . 1·00 1·40
MS578 90 × 50 mm. Nos. 576/7 1·50 1·75
Nos. 576/7 were printed together, se-tenant, forming a composite design.

259 Male and Female Butterflies in Courtship

1988. Endangered Species. "Ornithoptera alexandrae" (butterfly). Multicoloured.
579 5t. Type **259** . . . . 1·00 1·25
580 17t. Female laying eggs and mature larva (vert) . . . . 2·00 40
581 25t. Male emerging from pupa (vert) . . . . 2·75 3·50
582 35t. Male feeding . . . . . 3·25 3·50

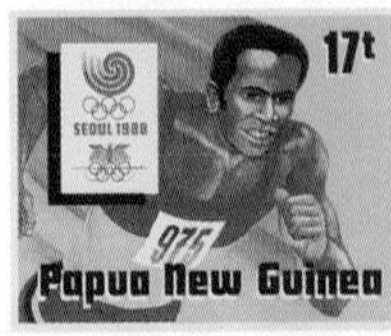
260 Athletics

1988. Olympic Games, Seoul. Multicoloured.
583 17t. Type **260** 30 30
584 45t. Weightlifting 70 70

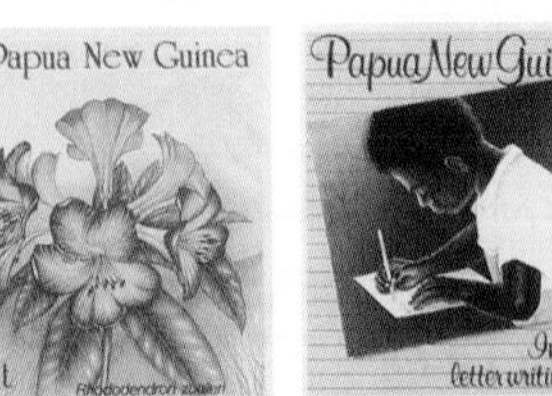
261 "Rhododendron zoelleri"

263 Writing Letter

1989. Rhododendrons. Multicoloured.
585 3t. Type **261** 10 10
586 20t. "Rhododendron cruttwellii" 50 30
587 60t. "Rhododendron superbum" . . . . 1·25 1·50
588 70t. "Rhododendron christianae" . . . . 1·50 1·75

1989. Int Letter Writing Week. Multicoloured.
589 20t. Type **263** 30 30
590 35t. Stamping letter 55 50
591 60t. Posting letter . . . . . 90 1·10
592 70t. Reading letter . . . . . 1·10 1·40

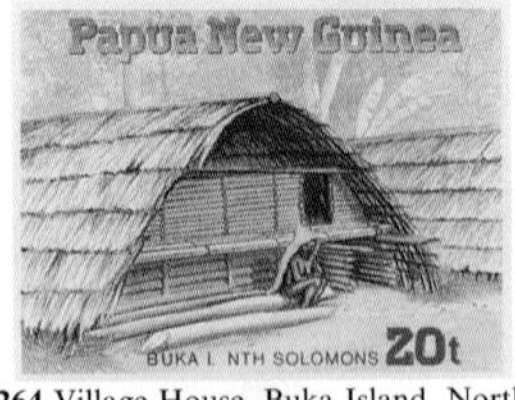
264 Village House, Buka Island, North Solomons

1989. Traditional Dwellings. Multicoloured.
593 20t. Type **264** 40 35
594 35t. Tree house, Koiari, Central Province 70 60
595 60t. Longhouse, Lauan, New Ireland . . . . 1·25 1·40
596 70t. Decorated house, Basilaki, Milne Bay . . . 1·50 1·60

265 Tit Berrypecker (female)

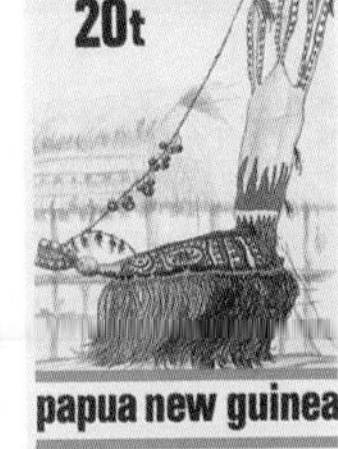
266 Motu Motu Dancer, Gulf Province

1989. Small Birds (2nd issue). Multicoloured.
597 20t. Type **265** . . . . 1·00 1·00
598 20t. Tit berrypecker (male) 1·00 1·00
599 35t. Blue-capped babbler . . 1·50 80
600 45t. Black-throated robin . . 1·50 1·00
601 70t. Large mountain sericornis . . . . 2·25 2·50

1989. No. 539 surch **20t**.
602 20t. on 17t. Type **251** 60 70

1989. Traditional Dancers. Multicoloured.
603 20t. Type **266** 65 35
604 35t. Baining, East New Britain . . . . 1·10 90
605 60t. Vailala River, Gulf Province . . . . 2·00 2·25
606 70t. Timbunke, East Sepik Province . . . . 2·00 2·50

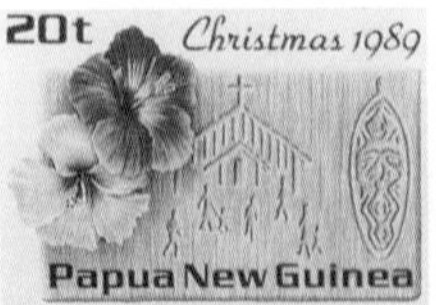
267 Hibiscus, People going to Church and Gope Board

1989. Christmas. Designs showing flowers and carved panels. Multicoloured.
607 20t. Type **267** 40 35
608 35t. Rhododendron, Virgin and Child and mask . . . 60 60
609 60t. D'Albertis creeper, Christmas candle and war shield . . . . 1·25 1·60
610 70t. Pacific frangipani, peace dove and flute mask . . . 1·40 1·90

268 Guni Falls

270 Gwa Pupi Dance Mask

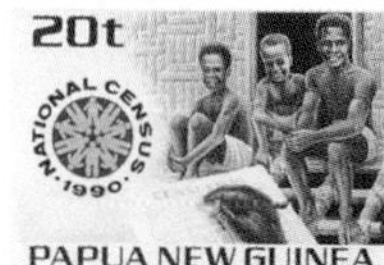

269 Boys and Census Form

1990. Waterfalls. Multicoloured.
611 20t. Type **268** 60 35
612 35t. Rouna Falls 85 75
613 60t. Ambua Falls . . . . . . 1·40 1·50
614 70t. Wawoi Falls . . . . . . 1·60 1·75

1990. National Census. Multicoloured.
615 20t. Type **269** 40 30
616 70t. Family and census form 1·50 2·25

1990. Gogodala Dance Masks. Multicoloured.
617 20t. Type **270** 80 30
618 35t. Tauga paiyale . . . . . 1·25 70
619 60t. A: ga . . . . 2·00 3·00
620 70t. Owala . . . . 2·00 3·50

271 Sepik and Maori Kororu Masks

1990. "New Zealand 1990" International Stamp Exhibition, Auckland.
621 **271** 35t. multicoloured . . . . 75 1·00

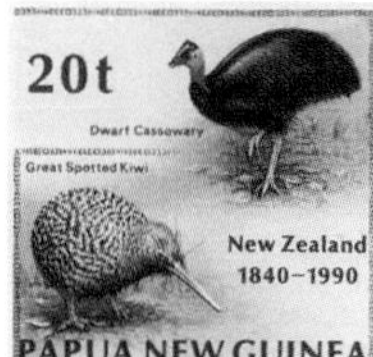

272 Dwarf Cassowary and Great Spotted Kiwi

1990. 150th Anniv of Treaty of Waitangi. Mult.
622 20t. Type **272** . . . . 1·25 50
623 35t. Double-wattled cassowary and brown kiwi 1·50 1·50

273 Whimbrel

1990. Migratory Birds. Multicoloured.
624 20t. Type **273** 85 40
625 35t. Sharp-tailed sandpiper 1·25 80
626 60t. Ruddy turnstone . . . . 2·25 3·25
627 70t. Terek sandpiper . . . . 2·50 3·25

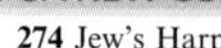

274 Jew's Harp

276 Magnificent Riflebird

275 Weigman's Papuina

1990. Musical Instruments. Multicoloured.
628 20t. Type **274** 60 30
629 35t. Musical bow 90 50
630 60t. Wantoat drum . . . . . 1·75 2·25
631 70t. Gogodala rattle . . . . 1·75 2·50

1991. Land Shells. Multicoloured.
632 21t. Type **275** 65 30
633 40t. "Papuina globula" and "Papuina azonata" . . . . 1·00 85
634 50t. "Planispira deaniana" . . 1·40 1·60
635 80t. Chance's papuina and golden-mouth papuina . . 2·00 2·75

1991. Birds of Paradise. Multicoloured. (a) Face values shown as "t" or "K".
636 1t. Type **276** 15 40
637 5t. Loria's bird of paradise 20 40
638 10t. Sickle-crested bird of paradise 20 40
639 20t. Wahnes' parotia 50 30
640 21t. Crinkle-collared manucode . . . . 1·25 30
641 30t. Goldie's bird of paradise 30 40
642 40t. Wattle-billed bird of paradise 50 50
643 45t. King bird of paradise . . 4·50 80
644 50t. Short-tailed paradigalla bird of paradise 50 55
645 60t. Queen Carola's parotia 7·00 2·75
646 90t. Emperor of Germany bird of paradise . . . . . 7·50 4·00
647 1k. Magnificent bird of paradise . . . . 1·75 1·75
648 2k. Superb bird of paradise 1·90 2·00
649 5k. Trumpet bird . . . . . . 3·00 6·50
650 10k. Lesser bird of paradise (32 × 32 mm) . . . . . . 6·50 10·00

(b) Face values shown as "T".
650a 21t. Crinkle-collared manucode 90 40
650b 45t. King bird of paradise 2·00 1·00
650c 60t. Queen Carola's parotia 2·25 2·25
650d 90t. Emperor of Germany bird of paradise . . . . . 2·75 3·50

For designs as Nos. 642, 644 and 647/8 but without "1992 BIRD OF PARADISE" at foot, see Nos. 704/7.

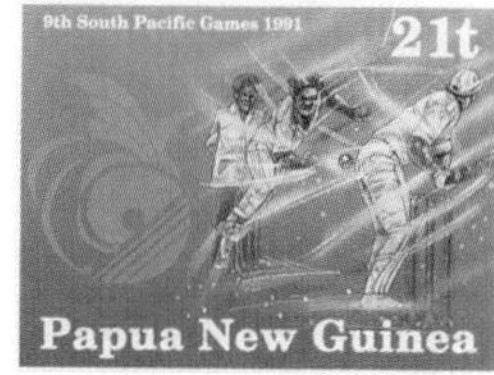

277 Cricket

1991. 9th South Pacific Games. Multicoloured.
651 21t. Type **277** . . . . 1·75 40
652 40t. Athletics . . . . 1·50 1·00
653 50t. Baseball . . . . 1·75 2·25
654 80t. Rugby Union . . . . . 2·75 4·00

278 Cathedral of St. Peter and St. Paul, Dogura

1991. Cent of Anglican Church in Papua New Guinea. Multicoloured.
655 21t. Type **278** 70 30
656 40t. Missionaries landing, 1891, and Kaieta shrine . . 1·40 1·40
657 80t. First church and Modawa tree . . . . . . 2·25 3·50

279 Rambusto Headdress, Manus Province

281 Canoe Prow Shield, Bamu

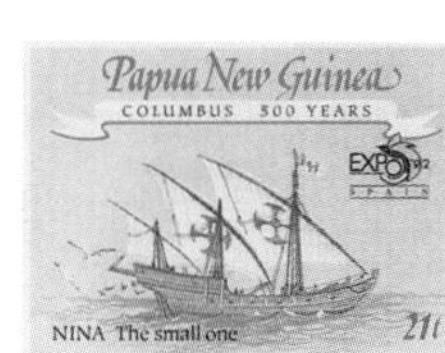

280 "Nina"

1991. Tribal Headdresses. Multicoloured.
658 21t. Type **279** 60 30
659 40t. Marawaka, Eastern Highlands . . . . 1·10 1·40
660 50t. Tufi, Oro Province . . . 1·25 2·00
661 80t. Sina Sina, Simbu Province . . . . 2·00 4·00

1992. 500th Anniv of Discovery of America by Columbus and "EXPO '92" World's Fair, Seville. Multicoloured.
662 21t. Type **280** 60 30
663 45t. "Pinta" . . . . 1·25 1·00
664 60t. "Santa Maria" . . . . . 1·75 2·00
665 90t. Christopher Columbus and ships . . . . 2·25 3·50

1992. "World Columbian Stamp Expo '92", Chicago. Sheet, 110 × 80 mm, containing Nos. 664/5.
MS666 60t. "Santa Maria"; 90t. Christopher Columbus and ships (sold at 1k. 70) . . . . 4·25 5·50

1992. Papuan Gulf Artifacts. Multicoloured.
667 21t. Type **281** 40 30
668 45t. Skull rack, Kerewa . . . 85 75
669 60t. Ancestral figure, Era River . . . . 1·25 1·50
670 90t. Gope (spirit) board, Urama . . . . 1·60 2·75

282 Papuan Infantryman

283 "Hibiscus tiliaceus"

1992. 50th Anniv of Second World War Campaigns in Papua New Guinea. Multicoloured.
671 21t. Type **282** 60 30
672 45t. Australian militiaman . . 1·25 90
673 60t. Japanese infantryman . . 1·75 2·25
674 90t. American infantryman 2·50 3·75

1992. Flowering Trees. Multicoloured.
675 21t. Type **283** 65 30
676 45t. "Castanospermum australe" . . . . 1·50 1·00
677 60t. "Cordia subcordata" . . 2·50 2·75
678 90t. "Acacia auriculiformis" 2·75 4·00

284 Three-striped Dasyure

1993. Mammals. Multicoloured.
679 21t. Type **284** 40 30
680 45t. Striped bandicoot . . . 90 80
681 60t. Dusky black-eared giant rat . . . . 1·25 1·50
682 90t. Painted ringtail possum 1·75 2·75

285 Rufous Wren Warbler

1993. Small Birds. Multicoloured.
683 21t. Type **285** 45 30
684 45t. Superb pitta 90 80
685 60t. Mottled whistler . . . . 1·25 1·50
686 90t. Slaty-chinned longbill . . 1·60 2·75

1993. "Taipei '93" Asian Int Stamp Exn, Taiwan. Nos. 683/6 optd **TAIPEI'93** and emblem.
687 21t. Type **285** 75 30
688 45t. Superb pitta . . . . . . 1·40 80
689 60t. Mottled whistler . . . . 1·60 2·50
690 90t. Slaty-chinned longbill . . 2·00 3·25

287 Thread-finned Rainbowfish

1993. Freshwater Fishes. Multicoloured.
691 21t. Type **287** 60 30
692 45t. Peacock gudgeon . . . . 1·25 80
693 60t. Northern rainbowfish . . 1·60 2·25
694 90t. Popondetta blue-eye . . 2·25 3·75

288 Blue Bird of Paradise

1993. "Bangkok '93" Asian International Stamp Exhibition, Thailand. Sheet 100 × 65 mm.
MS695 **288** 2k. multicoloured . . 6·00 7·50

289 Douglas DC-3

1993. 20th Anniv of Air Niugini. Multicoloured.
696 21t. Type **289** 75 25
697 45t. Fokker F.27 Friendship 1·75 70
698 60t. De Havilland D.H.C.7 Dash Seven . . . . 2·00 2·25
699 90t. Airbus Industrie A310 2·75 4·00

290 Girl holding Matschie's Tree Kangaroo

292 Hagen Axe, Western Highlands

1994. Matschie's (Huon Gulf) Tree Kangaroo. Mult.
700 21t. Type **290** 35 25
701 45t. Adult male 90 60
702 60t. Female with young in pouch . . . . 1·25 1·75
703 90t. Adolescent on ground 1·90 3·00

1994. "Hong Kong '94 International Stamp Exhibition. Designs as Nos. 642, 644 and 647/8, but without "1992 BIRD OF PARADISE" at foot. Multicoloured.
704 40t. Yellow-breasted bird of paradise . . . . 85 1·25
705 50t. Short-tailed paradigalla bird of paradise . . . . . 1·25 1·50
706 1k. Magnificent bird of paradise . . . . 2·00 2·75
707 2k. Superb bird of paradise 3·00 3·50

1994. Nos. 541 and 551 surch.
708 21t. on 35t. Fire anemonefish 7·00 50
709 1k.20 on 40t. "L'Astrolabe" (D'Urville) . . . . 1·50 1·50

1994. Artifacts. Multicoloured.
710 1t. Type **292** 10 50
711 2t. Telefomin shield, West Sepik 10 50
712 20t. Head mask, Gulf Province 80 30
713 21t. Kanganaman stool, East Sepik 30 10
714 45t. Trobriand lime gourd, Milne Bay 50 25
715 60t. Yuat River flute stopper, East Sepik . . . . 1·00 30
716 90t. Tami Island dish, Morobe 60 40
717 1k. Kundu (drum), Ramu River estuary . . . . . 3·00 2·25
723 5k. Gogodala dance mask, Western Province . . . . 1·60 1·75
724 10k. Malanggan mask, New Ireland . . . . 3·25 3·50

293 Ford Model "T", 1920

1994. Historical Cars. Multicoloured.
725 21t. Type **293** 35 25
726 45t. Chevrolet "490", 1915 90 60
727 60t. Austin "7", 1931 . . . . 1·25 1·75
728 90t. Willys jeep, 1942 . . . . 1·90 3·00

294 Grizzled Tree Kangaroo

298 Peter To Rot

297 "Daphnis hypothous pallescens"

1994. "Phila Korea '94" International Stamp Exhibition, Seoul. Tree Kangaroos. Sheet 106×70 mm, containing T **294** and similar vert design. Multicoloured.
MS729 90t. Type **294**; 1k.20, Doria's tree kangaroo 65 70

1994. Surch.
730 – 5t. on 35t. mult (No. 604) 1·00 75
731 – 5t. on 35t. mult (No. 629) 14·00 10·00
732 **271** 10t. on 35t. mult . . . . 22·00 5·50
733 – 10t. on 35t. mult (No. 623) . . . . . . 10·00 3·50
734 – 21t. on 80t. mult (No. 635) . . . . . . 40·00 75
735 – 50t. on 35t. mult (No. 612) . . . . . . 27·00 13·00
736 – 50t. on 35t. mult (No. 618) . . . . . . 90·00 18·00
737 – 65t. on 70t. mult (No. 542) . . . . . . 2·00 1·40
738 – 65t. on 70t. mult (No. 616) . . . . . . 2·00 1·40
739 – 1k. on 70t. mult (No. 614) 17·00 5·00
740 – 1k. on 70t. mult (No. 620) 2·00 3·00

1994. Moths. Multicoloured.
741 21t. Type **297** 35 25
742 45t. "Tanaorhinus unipuncta" 80 65
743 60t. "Neodiphthera sciron" 1·10 1·50
744 90t. "Parotis marginata" . . 1·60 2·25

1995. Beatification of Peter To Rot (catechist) and Visit of Pope John Paul II. Multicoloured.
745 21t. Type **298** 10 10
746 1k. on 90t. Pope John Paul II 30 35
No. 746 was not issued without surcharge.

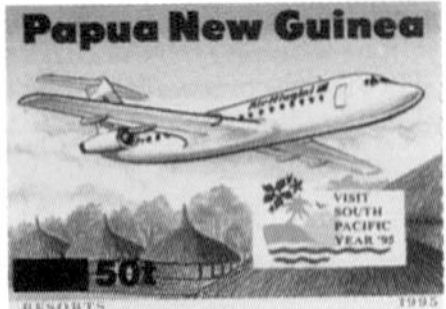

299 Airliner over Holiday Village

1995. Tourism. Multicoloured.
747 21t. "Melanesian Discoverer" (cruise ship) and launch . . 10 10
748 21t. Tourist taking photo of traditional mask 10 10
749 50t. on 45t. Type **299** 15 20
750 50t. on 45t. Holiday homes 15 20
751 65t. on 60t. Tourists and guide crossing river 20 25
752 65t. on 60t. White water rafting 20 25
753 1k. on 90t. Scuba diver and "Chertan" (launch) 30 35
754 1k. on 90t. Divers and wreck of aircraft 30 35
Nos. 749/54 were not issued without surcharge.

1995. Nos. 643, 646, 650b, 650d and 692/4 surch **21t**.
755 21t. on 45t. King bird of paradise (643) . . . . . . 1·50 1·00
757 21t. on 45t. King bird of paradise (650b) . . . . . 4·75 3·00
759 21t. on 45t. Peacock gudgeon 55 40
760 21t. on 60t. Northern rainbowfish . . . . 1·50 2·00
756 21t. on 90t. Emperor of Germany bird of paradise (646) . . . . 1·50 1·00
758 21t. on 90t. Emperor of Germany bird of paradise (650d) . . . . 6·00 1·00
761 21t. on 90t. Popondetta blue-eye 55 60

302 "Lentinus umbrinus"

302a "Lentinus umbrinus"

1995. Fungi. Multicoloured.
762 25t. Type **302** 45 30
765a 25t. Type **302a** 35 35
763 50t. "Amanita hemibapha" 80 80
764 65t. "Boletellus emodensis" 95 1·25
765 1k. "Ramaria zippellii" . . 1·60 2·25
On Type **302a** the fungi illustration is larger, 26×32 mm instead of 27×30½ mm, face value and inscriptions are in a different type and there is no imprint date at foot.

303 Anniversary Emblem and Map of Papua New Guinea

1995. 20th Anniv of Independence. Multicoloured.
766 21t. Type **303** 30 25
767 50t. Emblem and lines on graph 70 80
768 1k. As 50t. . . . . 1·40 2·00

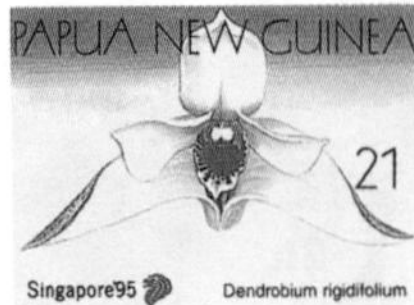

304 "Dendrobium rigidifolium"

1995. "Singapore '95" International Stamp Exhibition. Orchids. Sheet 150×95 mm, containing T **304** and similar horiz designs. Multicoloured.
MS769 21t. Type **304**; 45t. "Dendrobium convolutum"; 60t. "Dendrobium spectabile"; 90t. "Dendrobium tapiniense" (sold at 3k.) . . . . 95 1·00

305 Pig

1995. Chinese New Year ("Year of the Pig"). Sheet 150×95 mm.
MS770 **305** 3k. multicoloured . . 95 1·00
No. **MS**770 is inscribed "BEIJING '95" on the sheet margin.

306 Volcanic Eruption, Tavarvur

1995. 1st Anniv of Volcanic Eruption, Rabaul.
771 **306** 2k. multicoloured 65 70

307 "Zosimus aeneus"

1995. Crabs. Multicoloured.
772 21t. Type **307** 40 25
773 50t. "Cardisoma carnifex" . . 75 60
774 65t. "Uca tetragonon" . . . 90 1·25
775 1k. "Eriphia sebana" . . . . 1·25 2·00

308 Pesquet's Parrot

309 "Lagriomorpha indigacea"

1996. Parrots. Multicoloured.
776 25t. Type **308** 85 30
777 50t. Rainbow lory . . . . . 1·40 65
778 65t. Green-winged king parrot . . . . 1·60 1·40
779 1k. Red-winged parrot . . . 1·75 2·50

1996. Beetles. Multicoloured.
780 25t. Type **309** 10 15
781 50t. "Eupholus geoffroyi" . . 15 20
782 65t. "Promechus pulcher" . . 20 25
783 1k. "Callistola pulchra" . . . 30 35

310 Guang Zhou Zhong Shang Memorial Hall

1996. "China '96" 9th Asian International Stamp Exhibition, Peking. Sheet 105×70 mm.
MS784 **310** 70t. multicoloured . . 20 25

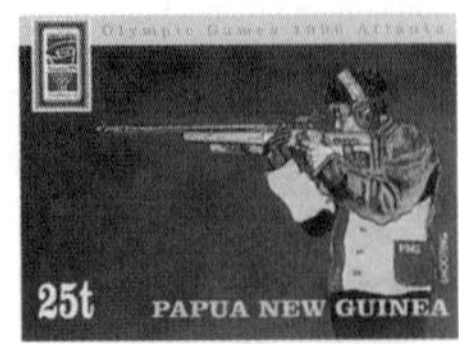

311 Rifle-shooting

1996. Olympic Games, Atlanta. Multicoloured.
785 25t. Type **311** 10 15
786 50t. Athletics 15 20
787 65t. Weightlifting 20 25
788 1k. Boxing 30 35

312 Air Traffic Controller

1996. Centenary of Radio. Multicoloured.
789 25t. Type **312** 10 15
790 50t. Radio disc-jockey . . . 15 20
791 65t. Dish aerials 20 25
792 1k. Early radio transmitter 30 35

313 Dr. Sun Yat-sen

1996. "TAIPEI '96" 10th Asian International Stamp Exhibition, Taiwan. Sheet 105×70 mm, containing T **313** and similar vert design. Multicoloured.
MS793 65t. Type **313**; 65t. Dr. John Guise (former speaker of Papua New Guinea House of Assembly) 40 45

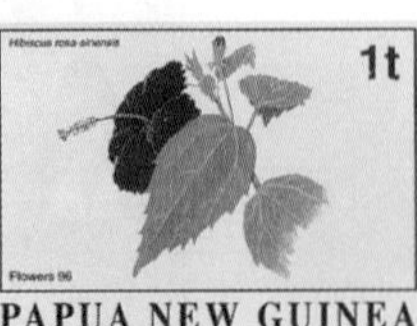

314 "Hibiscus rosa-sinensis"

1996. Flowers. Multicoloured.
794 1t. Type **314** 10 10
795 5t. "Bougainvillea spectabilis" 10 10
796 10t. "Thunbergia fragrans" (vert) 10 10
797 20t. "Caesalpinia pulcherrima" (vert) 10 10
798 25t. "Hoya sp." (vert) . . . 10 15
799 30t. "Heliconia spp." (vert) 10 15
800 50t. "Amomum goliathensis" (vert) 15 20
801 65t. "Plumeria rubra" . . . 20 25
802 1k. "Mucuna novoguineensis" 30 35

315 Ox and National Flag

1997. "HONG KONG '97" International Stamp Exhibition. Sheet 130×90 mm.
MS808 **315** 1k.50 multicoloured 45 50

316 Gogodala Canoe Prow

1997. Canoe Prows. Multicoloured.
809 25t. Type **316** 10 15
810 50t. East New Britain 15 20
811 65t. Trobriand Island 20 25
812 1k. Walomo 30 35

1997. Golden Wedding of Queen Elizabeth and Prince Philip. As T **87** of Kiribati. Multicoloured.
813 25t. Prince Philip on polo pony, 1972 . . . . 10 15
814 25t. Queen Elizabeth at Windsor Polo Club 10 15
815 50t. Prince Philip carriage-driving, 1995 . . . . . . 15 20
816 50t. Queen Elizabeth and Prince Edward on horseback 15 20
817 1k. Prince Philip waving and Peter and Zara Phillips on horseback 30 35
818 1k. Queen Elizabeth waving and Prince Harry on horseback 30 35
MS819 105×71 mm. 2k. Queen Elizabeth and Prince Philip in landau (horiz) 65 70
Nos. 813/14, 815/16 and 818/19 respectively were printed together, se-tenant, with the backgrounds forming composite designs.

317 Air Niugini Airliner over Osaka

1997. Inaugural Air Niugini Port moresby to Osaka Flight. Sheet 110×80 mm.
MS820 **317** 3k. multicoloured . . 95 1·00

318 "Pocillopora woodjonesi"

1997. Pacific Year of the Coral Reef. Corals. Mult.
821 25t. Type **318** 10 15
822 50t. "Subergorgia mollis" . . 15 20
823 65t. "Oxypora glabra" . . . 20 25
824 1k. "Turbinaria reinformis" 30 35

319 Greater Sooty Owl

1998. Birds. Multicoloured.
825 25t. Type **319** 40 20
826 50t. Wattled brush turkey . . 60 45
827 65t. New Guinea grey-headed goshawk 70 90
828 1k. Forest bittern . . . . . 1·10 1·75

1998. Diana, Princess of Wales Commemoration. Sheet, 145×70 mm, containing vert designs as T **91** or Kiribati. Multicoloured.
MS829 1k., Wearing pink jacket, 1992; 1k. Wearing purple dress; 1988; 1k. wearing tartan jacket, 1990; 1k. Carrying bouquets, 1990 (sold at 4k.+50t. charity premium) 1·40 1·50

320 Mother Teresa and Child

1998. Mother Teresa Commemoration. Mult.

830 65t. Type **320** 20 25
831 1k. Mother Teresa 30 35

1998. No. 774 surch **25t.**

832 25t. on 65t. "Uca tetragonon" 10 15

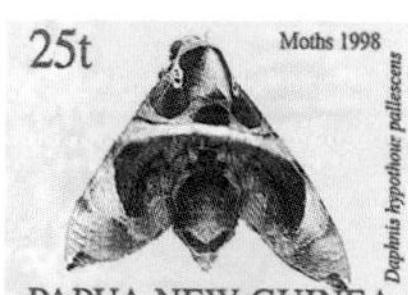

322 "Daphnis hypothous pallescens"

1998. Moths. Multicoloured.

833 25t. Type **322** 10 15
834 50t. "Theretra polistratus" . . 15 20
835 65t. "Psilogramma casurina" . 20 25
836 1k. "Meganoton hyloicoides" . 30 35

323 "Coelogyne fragrans" **324** Weightlifting

1998. Orchids. Multicoloured.

837 25t. Type **323** 10 15
838 50t. "Den cuthbertsonii" . . 15 20
839 65t. "Den vexillarius "var" retroflexum" 20 25
840 1k. "Den finisterrae" 30 35

1998. 16th Commonwealth Games, Kuala Lumpur, Malaysia. Multicoloured.

841 25t. Type **324** 10 15
842 50t. Lawn bowls 15 20
843 65t. Rugby Union 20 25
844 1k. Squash 30 35

325 Double Kayak

1998. Sea Kayaking World Cup, Manus Island. Multicoloured.

845 25t. Type **325** 10 15
846 50t. Running 15 20
847 65t. Traditional canoe and modern kayak 20 25
848 1k. Single kayak and stylized bird of paradise 30 35

326 The Holy Child

1998. Christmas. Multicoloured.

849 25t. Type **326** 10 15
850 50t. Mother breast-feeding baby 15 20
851 65t. Holy Child and tribal elders 20 25
852 1k. Map of Papua New Guinea and festive bell . . 30 35

1999. "Australia '99" World Stamp Exhibition, Melbourne. Designs as Nos. 543, 552 and 556/7, showing ships, redrawn to include exhibition emblem at top right and with some face values changed. Multicoloured.

853 25t. "La Boudeuse" (De Bougainville) (as No. 543) 10 15
854 50t. "Neva" (D'Albertis) (as No. 552) 15 20
855 65t. "Merrie England" (steamer) (as No. 556) . . 20 25
856 1k. "Samoa" (German colonial steamer) (as No. 557) 30 35
MS857 165 × 110 mm. 5t. H.M.S. "Rattlesnake" (Owen Stanley) (as No. 548); 10t. H.M.S. "Swallow" (Philip Carteret) (as No. 545); 15t. "Roebuck" (Dampier) (as No. 544); 20t. H.M.S. "Blanche" (SImpson) (as No. 55); 30t. "Vitaz" (Maclay) (as No. 549); 40t. "San Pedrico" (Torres) and zabra (as No. 550); 60t. Spanish galleon (Jorge de Meneses) (as No. 553); 1k.20, "L' Astrolabe" (D' Urville) (as No. 551) . . . 95 1·00

No. 855 is inscribed "Merrir England" in error. Of the designs in No. **MS**857 the 5t. is inscribed "Simpson Blanche 1872", 10t. "Carterel", 15t. "Dampien", 40t. "eabra" and 60t. "Menesis", all in error.

327 German New Guinea 1900 Yacht Type 2m. Stamp

1999. "iBRA '99" International Stamp Exhibition, Nuremberg. Multicoloured.

858 1k. Type **327** 30 35
859 1k. German New Guinea 1897 3pf. and 5pf. optd on Germany 30 35

328 Father Jules Chevalier

1999. "PhilexFrance '99" International Stamp Exhibition, Paris. Famous Frenchmen. Mult.

860 25t. Type **327** 10 15
861 50t. Bishop Alain-Marie . . . 15 20
862 65t. Joseph-Antoine d'Entrecasteaux (explorer) 20 25
863 1k. Louis de Bougainville (explorer) 30 35

329 Hiri Claypot and Traditional Dancer

1999. Hiri Moale Festival. Multicoloured (except No. **MS**686).

864 25t. Type **329** 10 15
865 50t. Three dancers 15 20
866 65t. Hiri Lagatoi (trading canoe) and dancer 20 25
867 1k. Hiri Sorcerer and dancer 30 35
MS868 140 × 64mm. 1k. Hiri Sorcerer (deep blue and blue); 1k. Hiri Claypot (deep purple and blue); 1k. Hiri Lagatoi (green and blue) . . . . 95 1·00

330 Lap-top Computer, Globe and Watch

1999. New Millennium. Modern Technology. Each showing Globe. Multicoloured.

869 25t. Type **330** 10 15
870 50t. Globe within concentric circles 15 20
871 65t. Compact disc, web site and man using computer 20 25
872 1k. Keyboard, dish aerial and solar eclipse 30 35

331 *Turbo petholatus*

2000. Sea Shells. Multicoloured.

873 25t. Type **331** 10 15
874 50t. *Charonia tritonis* 15 20
875 65t. *Cassis cornuta* 20 25
876 1k. *Ovula ovum* 30 35

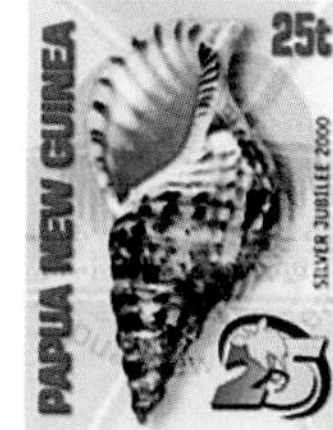

332 Rabbit **333** Shell

2000. Chinese New Year ("Year of the Rabbit") (1999). Sheet, 145 × 70mm, containing T **332** and similar vert designs. Multicoloured.

MS877 65t. Type **332**; 65t. Light brown rabbit running; 65t. White rabbit grinning; 65t. Pink rabbit hiding behind grass knoll . . . 85 90

2000. 25th Anniv of Independence. Multicoloured.

878 25t. Type **333** 10 15
879 50t. Raggiana bird of Paradise 15 20
880 65t. Ornament 20 25
881 1k. Red bird of Paradise perched on spear and drums 75 85
MS882 145 × 75 mm. Nos. 878/81 75 95

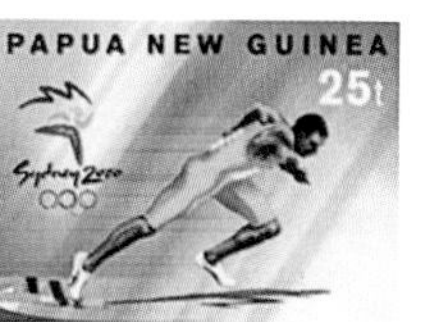

334 Athletics

2000. Olympic Games, Sydney. Multicoloured.

883 25t. Type **334** 10 15
884 50t. Swimming 15 20
885 65t. Boxing 20 25
886 1k. Weightlifting 30 35
MS887 80 × 90 mm. 3k. Runner with Olympic Torch (34 × 45 mm) (sold at 3k.50) . . . . 1·10 1·25

No. **MS**887 includes the "Olymphilex 2000" stamp exhibition logo on the sheet margin.

335 Queen Mother in Yellow Coat and Hat

2000. Queen Elizabeth the Queen Mother's 100th Birthday. Multicoloured.

888 25t. Type **335** 10 15
889 50t. Queen Mother with bouquet of roses 15 20
890 65t. Queen Mother in green coat 20 25
891 1k. Lady Elizabeth Bowes-Lyon 30 35

336 Comb-crested Jacana

2001. Water Birds. Multicoloured.

892 35t. Type **336** 10 15
893 70t. Masked lapwing 20 25
894 90t. Australian white ibis . . 30 35
895 1k.40 Black-tailed godwit . . 45 50

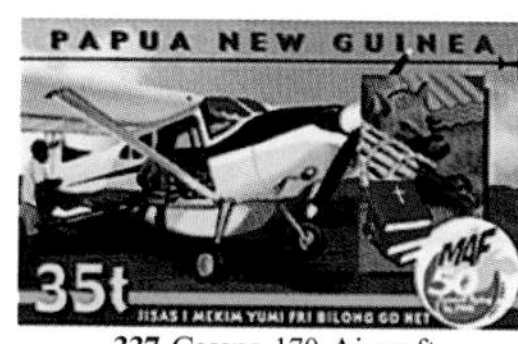

337 Cessna 170 Aircraft

2001. 50th Anniv of Mission Aviation Fellowship. Multicoloured.

896 35t. Type **337** 10 15
897 70t. Auster Autocar 20 25
898 90t. Cessna 260 . . . . . . 30 35
899 1k.40 Twin Otter 45 50

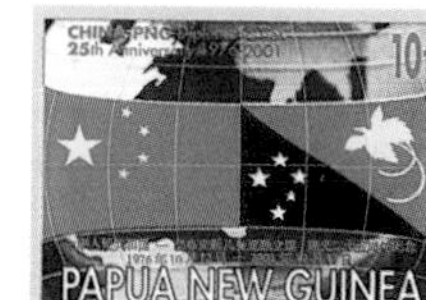

338 Flags of China and Papua New Guinea

2001. 25th Anniv of Diplomatic Relations between Papua New Guinea and China. Multicoloured.

900 10t. Type **338** 10 10
901 50t. Dragon and bird of paradise 15 20
902 2k. Tian An Men (Gate of Heavenly Peace), Beijing, and Parliament House, Port Moresby 65 70

2001. Nos. 745, 862, 866, 871 and 883 surch.

903 50t. on 21t. Type **248** 15 20
904 50t. on 25t. Type **334** 15 20
905 50t. on 65t. Compact disc, web site and man using computer 15 20
906 2k.65 on 65t. Joseph-Antoine d'Entrecasteaux 85 90
907 2k.65 on 65t. Hiri Lagatoi (trading canoe) and dancer 85 90

341 Flag of Enga Province

2001. Provincial Flags. Multicoloured.

908 10t. Type **341** 10 10
909 15t. Simbu Province 10 10
910 20t. Manus Province 10 10
911 50t. Central Province 15 20
912 2k. New Ireland Province . . 65 70
913 5k. Sandaun Province . . . . 1·60 1·75

2002. Golden Jubilee. As T **211** of St. Helena.

914 1k.25 multicoloured 35 40
915 1k.45 multicoloured 45 50
916 2k. black, brown and gold . . 65 70
917 2k.65 multicoloured 85 90
MS918 162 × 95 mm. Nos. 914/17 and 5k. multicoloured . . . . 4·00 4·25

DESIGNS–HORIZ:1k.25, Queen Elizabeth with Princesses Elizabeth and Margaret, 1941; 1k.45, Queen Elizabeth in evening dress, 1975; 2k. Princess Elizabeth, Duke of Edinburgh and children, 1951; 2k.65, Queen Elizabeth at Henley-on-Thames. VERT (38 × 51 mm)--5k. Queen Elizabeth after Annigoni.

Designs as Nos. 914/17 in No. **MS**918 omit the gold frame around each stamp and the "Golden Jubilee 1952–2002" inscription.

342 Lakotoi (trading canoe) and Hanuabada Village

2002. Centenary of First Papuan Stamps (2001).

919 **342** 5t. black and mauve . . . 10 10
920 15t. black and brown . . 10 10
921 20t. black and blue . . . 10 10
922 1k.25 black and brown . . 35 40
923 1k.45 black and green . . 45 50
924 10k. black and orange . . 3·25 3·50
MS925 127 × 99 mm. Nos. 919/24 4·25 4·50

The design of Type **342** is adapted from that of the first Papua issue of 1901.

343 Queen Elizabeth with Princess Elizabeth in South Africa

2002. Queen Elizabeth the Queen Mother Commemoration. Multicoloured (No. 929) or black and blue (others).

926 2k. Type **343** 65 70
927 2k. Queen Elizabeth with Princess Elizabeth at Balmoral, 1951 . . . . . 65 70
928 2k. Queen Mother at Sandown races, 2001 (26 × 30 mm) 65 70
929 2k. Queen Mother with Irish Guards, 1988 (41 × 30 mm) 65 70
930 2k. Queen Mother at the Derby, 1988 (26 × 30 mm) 65 70

931	2k. Queen Mother at Ascot races, 1966	65	70
932	2k. King George VI with Queen Elizabeth at Balmoral, 1951	65	70
MS933	Two sheets, each 65 × 101 mm. (a) 3k. Queen Mother at Lord Linley's wedding, 1993; 3k. At Aintree racecourse, 1991 (wearing brooch). (b) 3k. Lady Elizabeth Bowes-Lyon as a young girl; Queen Mother on Remembrance Day, 1988 (each 26 × 40 mm)	2·25	2·50

POSTAGE DUE STAMPS

1960. Stamps of 1952 surch **POSTAL CHARGES** and value.

D2	1d. on 6½d. purple	3·25	5·50
D3	3d. on ½d. green	3·50	2·50
D1	6d. on 7½d. blue (A)	£800	£425
D4	6d. on 7½d. blue (B)	27·00	9·00
D5	1s.3d. on 3½d. black	4·00	3·00
D6	3s. on 2½d. orange	14·00	5·50

In (A) value and "POSTAGE" is obliterated by a solid circle and a series of "IX's" but these are omitted in (B).

D 3

1960.

D 7	D 3	1d. orange	65	75
D 8		3d. brown	70	75
D 9		6d. blue	75	40
D10		9d. red	75	1·75
D11		1s. green	75	50
D12		1s.3d. violet	1·00	2·00
D13		1s.6d. blue	4·00	6·00
D14		3s. yellow	2·50	75

PARAGUAY Pt. 20

A republic in the centre of S. America, independent since 1811.

1870. 8 reales = 1 peso.
1878. 100 centavos = 1 peso.
1944. 100 centimos = 1 guarani.

1 7

1870. Various frames. Values in "reales". Imperf.
1 1 1r. red . . . 4·00 2·25
3 2r. blue . . . 55·00 32·00
4 3r. black . . . 90·00 55·00

1878. Handstamped with large **5**. Imperf.
5 1 5c. on 1r. red . . . 40·00 26·00
9 5c. on 2r. blue . . . £140 75·00
13 5c. on 3r. black . . . £110 70·00

1879. Prepared for use but not issued (wrong currency). Values in "reales". Perf.
14 7 5r. orange . . . 40
15 10r. brown . . . 50

1879. Values in "centavos". Perf.
16 7 5c. brown . . . 1·10 70
17 10c. green . . . 1·60 95

1881. Handstamped with large figures.
18 7 1 on 10c. green . . . 8·00 4·75
19 2 on 10c. green . . . 8·00 4·75

1881. As T **1** (various frames), but value in "centavos". Perf.
20 1 1c. blue . . . 40 40
21a 2c. red . . . 30 40
22 4c. brown . . . 40 50

1884. No. 1 handstamped with large **1**. Imperf.
23 1 1c. on 1r. red . . . 2·40 1·40

13 24

1884. Perf.
24 13 1c. green . . . 30 15
25 2c. red . . . 40 15
26 5c. blue . . . 40 15

1887.
32 24 1c. green . . . 15 15
33a 2c. red . . . 15 15
34 5c. blue . . . 30 20
35 7c. brown . . . 30 25
36 10c. mauve . . . 45 30
37 15c. orange . . . 45 30
38 20c. pink . . . 45 30
50 40c. blue . . . 2·00 70
51 60c. orange . . . 95 30
52 80c. blue . . . 80 30
53 1p. green . . . 85 30

25 27 C. Rivarola

1889. Imperf or perf.
40 25 15c. purple . . . 1·60 95

1892.
42 27 1 CENTAVOS grey . . . 15 10
54 1 CENTAVO grey . . . 15 10
43 – 2c. green . . . 15 10
44 – 4c. red . . . 10 10
57 – 5c. purple . . . 15 10
46 – 10c. violet . . . 30 25
47 – 14c. brown . . . 55 30
48 – 20c. red . . . 95 30
49 – 30c. green . . . 1·25 30
84 – 1p. blue . . . 40 25
PORTRAITS: 2c. S. Jovellano; 4c. J. Bautista Gil; 5c. H. Uriarte; 10c. C. Barreiro; 14c. Gen. B. Caballero; 20c. Gen. P. Escobar; 30c. J. Gonzales; 1p. J. B. Egusquisa.

1892. 400th Anniv of Discovery of America. No. 46 optd **1492 12 DE OCTUBRE 1892** in oval.
41 10c. violet . . . 5·75 1·50

1895. Surch **PROVISORIO 5**.
59 24 5c. on 7c. brown . . . 30 30

30 39

1896. Telegraph stamps as T **30** surch **CORREOS 5 CENTAVOS** in oval.
60 30 5c. on 2c. brown, blk & grey . . . 45 20
61 5c. on 4c. orange, blk & grey . . . 45 20

1898. Surch **Provisorio 10 Centavos**.
63 24 10c. on 15c. orange . . . 35 35
62 10c. on 40c. blue . . . 25 25

1900. Telegraph stamps as T **30** surch with figures of value twice and bar.
64 30 5c. on 30c. green, blk & grey . . . 1·60 70
65 10c. on 50c. lilac, blk & grey . . . 3·50 1·50

1900.
76 39 1c. green . . . 10 10
67 2c. grey . . . 10 10
73 2c. pink . . . 20 15
68 3c. brown . . . 10 10
78 4c. blue . . . 15 10
69 5c. green . . . 10 10
74 5c. brown . . . 20 10
79 5c. lilac . . . 25 10
80 8c. brown . . . 20 15
71 10c. red . . . 20 15
72 24c. blue . . . 45 20
82 28c. orange . . . 25 35
83 40c. blue . . . 25 10

1902. Surch **Habilitado en** and new values.
88 – 1c. on 14c. brown (No. 47) . . . 30 20
91 – 1c. on 1p. blue (No. 84) . . . 20 15
86 39 5c. on 8c. brown (No. 80) . . . 35 20
87 5c. on 28c. orange (No. 82) . . . 20 30
89 24 5c. on 60c. orange (No. 51) . . . 20 25
90 5c. on 80c. blue (No. 52) . . . 30 25
85 39 20c. on 24c. blue (No. 72) . . . 35 20

46 47

1903.
92 46 1c. grey . . . 20 15
93 2c. green . . . 25 20
94a 5c. blue . . . 25 10
95 10c. brown . . . 45 20
96 20c. red . . . 45 25
97 30c. blue . . . 50 25
98 60c. violet . . . 1·25 55

1903.
99 47 1c. green . . . 15 10
100 2c. orange . . . 15 10
101 5c. blue . . . 20 15
102 10c. violet . . . 30 20
103 20c. green . . . 50 25
104 30c. blue . . . 90 30
105 60c. brown . . . 95 35

48 50

51 National Palace, Asuncion

1904.
106 48 10c. blue . . . 35 20

1904. End of successful Revolt against Govt. (begun in August). Surch **PAZ 12 Dic. 1904.30 centavos.**
107 48 30c. on 10c. blue . . . 50 35

1905.
108 50 1c. orange . . . 15 10
109 1c. red . . . 15 10
110 1c. blue . . . 15 10
112 2c. green . . . 40·00
113 2c. red . . . 15 10
114 5c. blue . . . 15 10
116 5c. yellow . . . 15 10
117 10c. brown . . . 15 10
118 10c. green . . . 15 10
119 10c. blue . . . 15 10
120 20c. lilac . . . 45 35
121 20c. brown . . . 45 35
122 20c. green . . . 35 20
123 30c. blue . . . 45 20
124 30c. grey . . . 45 20
125 30c. lilac . . . 50 35
126 60c. brown . . . 35 25
128 60c. pink . . . 4·00 1·40
129 51 1p. black and red . . . 1·75 80
130 1p. black and brown . . . 65 35
131 1p. black and green . . . 35 35
132 2p. black and blue . . . 35 25
133 2p. black and red . . . 35 25
134 2p. black and brown . . . 40 30
135 5p. black and red . . . 90 35
136 5p. black and blue . . . 90 35
137 5p. black and green . . . 90 35
138 10p. black and brown . . . 80 35
139 10p. black and blue . . . 80 35
141 20p. black and green . . . 2·25 1·25
142 20p. black and yellow . . . 2·25 1·25
143 20p. black and purple . . . 2·25 1·25

1907. Surch **Habilitado en** and value and bars.
159 50 5c. on 1c. blue . . . 10 10
160 5c. on 2c. red . . . 15 10
145 5c. on 2c. green . . . 40 25
172 39 5c. on 28c. orange . . . 1·60 60
173 5c. on 40c. blue . . . 30 25
163 50 5c. on 60c. brown . . . 15 10
162 5c. on 60c. pink . . . 20 15
175 20c. on 1c. blue . . . 20 15
180 24 20c. on 2c. red . . . 4·00 2·10
177 50 20c. on 2c. red . . . 6·75 3·50
178 20c. on 30c. blue . . . 2·00 1·10
179 20c. on 30c. lilac . . . 30 30

1907. Official stamps surch **Habilitado en**, value and bars. Where not otherwise stated, the design is as T **50** but with "OFICIAL" below the lion.
164 – 5c. on 10c. green . . . 30 20
149 – 5c. on 10c. brown . . . 30 20
150 – 5c. on 10c. lilac . . . 30 20
181 24 5c. on 15c. orange (No. O63) . . . 3·00 2·40
182 5c. on 20c. pink (No. O64) . . . 45·00 32·00
166 – 5c. on 20c. brown . . . 30 25
151 – 5c. on 20c. green . . . 30 20
167 – 5c. on 20c. pink . . . 30 25
152 – 5c. on 20c. lilac . . . 30 20
157 46 5c. on 30c. blue (No. O104) . . . 95 85
154 – 5c. on 30c. blue . . . 50 50
169 – 5c. on 30c. yellow . . . 10 10
168 – 5c. on 30c. grey . . . 20 15
183 24 5c. on 50c. grey (No. O65) . . . 21·00 15·00
158 46 5c. on 60c. violet (No. O105) . . . 35 25
155 – 5c. on 60c. brown . . . 20 15
171 – 5c. on 60c. blue . . . 20 10
184 24 20c. on 5c. blue (No. O60) . . . 1·90 1·50
174 46 20c. on 5c. blue (No. O101) . . . 1·90 1·50

1907. Official stamps, as T **50** and **51** with "OFICIAL" added, optd **Habilitado** and one bar.
146 5c. grey . . . 30 20
148 5c. blue . . . 25 15
185 1p. black and orange . . . 35 35
186 1p. black and red . . . 30 25

1907. Official stamps, as T **51** with "OFICIAL" added, surch **Habilitado 1908 UN CENTAVO** and bar.
188 1c. on 1p. black and red . . . 20 20
189 1c. on 1p. black and brown . . . 1·00 50

1908. Optd **1908**.
190 50 1c. green . . . 10 10
191 5c. yellow . . . 10 10
192 10c. brown . . . 10 10
193 20c. orange . . . 10 10
194 30c. red . . . 40 30
195 60c. mauve . . . 30 30
196 51 1p. blue . . . 15 15

1909. Optd **1909**.
197 50 1c. blue . . . 10 10
198 1c. red . . . 10 10
199 5c. green . . . 10 10
200 5c. orange . . . 10 10
201 10c. red . . . 20 15
202 10c. brown . . . 20 15
203 20c. lilac . . . 20 20
204 20c. yellow . . . 10 10
205 30c. brown . . . 45 30
206 30c. blue . . . 45 30

62 63 65

1910.
207 62 1c. brown . . . 10 10
208 5c. lilac . . . 10 10
209 5c. green . . . 10 10
210 5c. blue . . . 10 10
211 10c. green . . . 10 10
212 10c. violet . . . 10 10
213 10c. red . . . 10 10
214 20c. red . . . 10 10
215 50c. red . . . 45 20
216 75c. blue . . . 15 10

1911. No. 216 perf diagonally and each half used as 20c.
217 62 20c. (½ of 75c.) blue . . . 15 10

1911. Independence Centenary.
218 63 1c. black and olive . . . 10 10
219 2c. black and blue . . . 10 10
220 5c. black and red . . . 20 10
221 10c. brown and blue . . . 30 15
222 20c. blue and olive . . . 30 15
223 50c. blue and lilac . . . 45 30
224 75c. purple and olive . . . 45 30

1912. Surch **Habilitada en VEINTE** and thin bar.
225 62 20c. on 50c. red . . . 10 10

1913.
226 65 1c. black . . . 10 10
227 2c. orange . . . 10 10
228 5c. mauve . . . 10 10
229 10c. green . . . 10 10
230 20c. red . . . 10 10
231 40c. red . . . 10 10
232 75c. blue . . . 10 10
233 80c. yellow . . . 10 10
234 1p. blue . . . 10 10
235 1p.25 blue . . . 30 10
236 3p. green . . . 30 10

1918. No. D242 surch **HABILITADO EN 0.05 1918** and bar.
237 5c. on 40c. brown . . . 10 10

1918. Nos. D239/42 optd **HABILITADO 1918**.
238 5c. brown . . . 10 10
239 10c. brown . . . 10 10
240 20c. brown . . . 10 10
241 40c. brown . . . 15 10

1918. Surch **HABILITADO EN 0.30 1918** and bar.
242 65 30c. on 40c. red . . . 10 10

1920. Surch **HABILITADO en**, value and **1920**.
243 65 50c. on 80c. yellow . . . 15 10
244 1p.75 on 3p. green . . . 60 50

1920. Nos. D243/4 optd **HABILITADO 1920** or surch also.
245 1p. brown . . . 20 10
246 1p. on 1p.50 brown . . . 35 10

72 Parliament House, Asuncion

1920. Jubilee of Constitution.
247 72 50c. black and red . . . 30 20
248 1p. black and blue . . . 50 40
249 1p.75 black and blue . . . 20 15
250 3p. black and yellow . . . 75 25

1920. Surch **50**.
251 65 50 on 75c. blue . . . 45 10

1921. Surch **50** and two bars.
252 62 50 on 75c. blue . . . 10 10
253 65 50 on 75c. blue . . . 25 10

75

1922.
254 75 50c. blue and red . . . 10 10
255 1p. brown and blue . . . 10 10

Between 1922 and 1936 many regular postage stamps were overprinted **C** (= Campana—country), these being used at post offices outside Asuncion but not for mail sent abroad. The prices quoted are for whichever is the cheapest.

77 Starting-point of Conspirators 80 Map

1922. Independence.
256 77 1p. blue . . . 20 10
258 1p. blue and red . . . 30 10
259 1p. grey and purple . . . 30 10
260 1p. grey and orange . . . 30 10
257 5p. purple . . . 30 25

261 5p. brown and blue 30 25
262 5p. black and green 30 25
263 5p. blue and red 30 25

1924. Surch **Habilitado en**, value and **1924**.
265 **65** 50c. on 75c. blue 10 10
266 $1 on 1p.25 blue 10 10
267 – $1 on 1p.50 brown (No. D244) 10 10

1924.
268 **80** 1p. blue 10 10
269 2p. red 15 10
270 4p. blue 30 10

81 Gen. Jose E. Diaz

82 Columbus

1925.
271 **81** 50c. red 10 10
272 1p. blue 10 10
273 1p. green 10 10

1925.
274 **82** 1p. blue 15 10

1926. Surch **Habilitado en** and new value.
275 **62** 1c. on 5c. blue 10 10
276 $0.02 on 5c. blue 10 10
277 **65** 7c. on 40c. red 10 10
278 15c. on 75c. blue 10 10
279 **50** $0.50 on 60c. purple (No. 195) 10 10
280 – $0.50 on 75c. blue (No. O243) 10 10
281 – $1.50 on 1p.50 brown (No. D244) 15 10
282 **80** $1.50 on 4p. blue 10 10

86

87 P. J. Caballero

88 Paraguay

89 Cassel Tower, Asuncion

90 Columbus

92 Arms of De Salazarde Espinosa, founder of Asuncion

1927.
283 **86** 1c. red 10 10
284 2c. orange 10 10
285 7c. lilac 10 10
286 7c. green 10 10
287 10c. green 10 10
288 10c. red 10 10
290 10c. blue 10 10
291 20c. blue 10 10
292 20c. purple 10 10
293 20c. violet 10 10
294 20c. pink 10 10
295 50c. blue 10 10
296 50c. red 10 10
323 50c. orange 10 10
326 50c. green 10 10
299 50c. mauve 10 10
300 50c. pink 10 10
301 70c. blue 10 10
328 **87** 1p. green 10 10
329 1p. red 10 10
330 1p. purple 10 10
331 1p. blue 10 10
304 1p. orange 10 10
332 1p. violet 10 10
333 **88** 1p.50 brown 10 10
334 1p.50 lilac 10 10
307 1p.50 pink 10 10
335 1p.50 blue 10 10
308 – 2p.50 bistre 10 10
337 – 2p.50 violet 10 10
338 – 3p. grey 10 10
310 – 3p. red 10 10
311 – 3p. violet 10 10
312 **89** 5p. brown 25 20
340 5p. violet 10 10
314 5p. orange 10 10
315 **90** 10p. red 35 35
317 10p. blue 35 35
318 **88** 20p. red 1·60 85
319 20p. green 1·60 85
320 20p. purple 1·60 85
DESIGNS—As Type **87**: 2p.50, Fulgencio Yegros; 3p. V. Ignacio Yturbe.

1928. Foundation of Asuncion, 1537.
342 **92** 10p. purple 95 70

93 Pres. Hayes of U.S.A. and Villa Hayes

1928. 50th Anniv of Hayes's Decision to award Northern Chaco to Paraguay.
343 **93** 10p. brown 3·75 1·40
344 10p. grey 3·75 1·40

1929. Air. Surch **Correo Aereo Habilitado en** and value.
357 **86** $0.95 on 7c. lilac 20 20
358 $1.90 on 20c. blue 20 20
345 – $2.85 on 5c. purple (No. O239) 95 70
348 – $3.40 on 3p. grey (No. 338) 1·90 85
359 **80** $3.40 on 4p. blue 30 30
360 $4.75 on 4p. blue 55 30
346 – $5.65 on 10c. green (No. O240) 35 45
361 – $6.80 on 3p. grey (No. 338) 35 35
349 **80** $6.80 on 4p. blue 1·90 85
347 – $11.30 on 50c. red (No. O242) 60 50
350 **89** $17 on 5p. brown (A) 1·90 85
362 $17 on 5p. brown (B) 1·50 1·10
On No. 350 (A) the surcharge is in four lines, and on No. 362 (B) it is in three lines.

95

1929. Air.
352 **95** 2.85p. green 35 30
353 – 5.65p. brown 60 30
354 – 5.65p. red 40 35
355 – 11.30p. purple 70 55
356 – 11.30p. blue 35 35
DESIGNS: 5.65p. Carrier pigeon; 11.30p. Stylized airplane.

1930. Air. Optd **CORREO AEREO** or surch also in words.
363 **86** 5c. on 10c. green 10 10
364 5c. on 70c. blue 10 10
365 10c. green 10 10
366 20c. blue 20 20
367 **87** 20c. on 1p. red 30 30
368 **86** 40c. on 50c. orange 15 10
369 **87** 1p. green 35 35
370 – 3p. grey (No. 338) 35 35
371 **90** 6p. on 10p. red 60 50
372 **88** 10p. on 20p. red 5·50 3·25
373 10p. on 20p. purple 6·50 4·75

101

103

1930. Air.
374 **101** 95c. blue on blue 40 35
375 95c. red on pink 40 35
376 – 1p.90 purple on blue 40 35
377 – 1p.90 red on pink 40 35
378 **103** 6p.80 black on blue 40 35
379 6p.80 green on pink 45 40
DESIGN: 1p.90, Asuncion Cathedral.

104 Declaration of Independence

105

1930. Air. Independence Day.
380 **104** 2p.85 blue 40 35
381 3p.40 green 35 25
382 4p.75 purple 35 25

1930. Red Cross Fund.
383 **105** 1p.50+50c. blue 1·10 70
384 1p.50+50c. red 1·10 70
385 1p.50+50c. lilac 1·10 70

106 Portraits of Archbishop Bogarin

1930. Consecration of Archbishop Bogarin.
386 **106** 1p.50 blue 1·10 60
387 1p.50 red 1·10 60
388 1p.50 violet 1·10 60

1930. Surch **Habilitado en CINCO**.
389 **86** 5c. on 7c. green 10 10

108 Planned Agricultural College at Ypacarai

1931. Agricultural College Fund.
390 **108** 1p.50+50c. blue on red 30 30

109 Arms of Paraguay

1931. 60th Anniv of First Paraguay Postage Stamps.
391 **109** 10p. brown 30 25
392 10p. red on blue 35 25
393 10p. blue on red 35 25
395 10p. grey 50 20
396 10p. blue 20 20

110 Gunboat "Paraguay"

1931. Air. 60th Anniv of Constitution and Arrival of new Gunboats.
397 **110** 1p. red 25 20
398 1p. blue 25 20
399 2p. orange 30 25
400 2p. brown 30 25
401 3p. green 65 40
402 3p. blue 65 45
403 3p. red 60 40
404 6p. green 75 60
405 6p. mauve 95 65
406 6p. blue 70 50
407 10p. red 2·00 1·40
408 10p. green 2·50 1·90
409 10p. blue 1·40 1·00
410 10p. brown 2·25 1·60
411 10p. pink 2·00 1·40

1931. As T **110**.
412 – 1p.50 violet 95 35
413 – 1p.50 blue 15 10
DESIGN: Gunboat "Humaita".
No. 413 is optd with large **C**.

112 War Memorial

113 Orange Tree and Yerba Mate

114 Yerba Mate

115 Palms

116 Yellow-headed Caracara

1931. Air.
414 **112** 5c. blue 15 10
415 5c. green 15 10
416 5c. red 20 10
417 5c. purple 15 10
418 **113** 10c. violet 10 10
419 10c. red 10 10
420 10c. brown 10 10
421 10c. blue 10 10
422 **114** 20c. red 15 10
423 20c. blue 20 10
424 20c. green 20 15
425 20c. brown 15 10
426 **115** 40c. green 20 10
426a 40c. blue 15 10
426b 40c. red 20 10
427 **116** 80c. blue 35 30
428 80c. green 35 20
428a 80c. red 25 20

1931. Air. Optd with airship "Graf Zeppelin" and **Correo Aereo "Graf Zeppelin"** or surch also.
429 **80** 3p. on 4p. blue 7·75 6·25
430 4p. blue 7·75 6·25

118 Farm Colony

1931. 50th Anniv of Foundation of San Bernardino.
431 **118** 1p. green 35 20
432 1p. red 10 10

1931. New Year. Optd **FELIZ ANO NUEVO 1932**.
433 **106** 1p.50 blue 60 60
434 1p.50 red 60 60

120 "Graf Zeppelin"

1932. Air.
435 **120** 4p. blue 1·40 1·75
436 8p. red 2·40 2·00
437 12p. green 1·90 1·75
438 16p. purple 3·75 3·00
439 20p. brown 4·00 3·75

121 Red Cross H.Q.

122 (Trans: "Has been, is and will be")

1932. Red Cross Fund.
440 **121** 50c.+50c. pink 25 25

1932. Chaco Boundary Dispute.
441 **122** 1p. purple 20 10
442 1p.50 pink 10 10
443 1p.50 brown 10 10
444 1p.50 green 10 10
445 1p.50 blue 10 10
Nos. 443/5 are optd with a large **C**.

1932. New Year. Surch **CORREOS FELIZ ANO NUEVO 1933** and value.
446 **120** 50c. on 4p. blue 35 30
447 1p. on 8p. red 35 30
448 1p.50 on 12p. green 35 30
449 2p. on 16p. purple 35 30
450 5p. on 20p. brown 1·25 75

124 "Graf Zeppelin" over Paraguay

125 "Graf Zeppelin" over Atlantic

1933. Air. "Graf Zeppelin" issue.
451 **124** 4p.50 blue . . . . 1·25 75
452 9p. red . . . . 2·50 1·90
453 13p.50 green . . . . . . 2·50 1·90
454 **125** 22p.50 brown . . . . . . 6·00 4·50
455 45p. violet . . . . 8·25 6·75

126 Columbus's Fleet

1933. 441st Anniv of Departure of Columbus from Palos. Maltese Crosses in violet.
456 **126** 10c. olive and red 45 15
457 20c. blue and lake 45 15
458 50c. red and green 75 35
459 1p. brown and blue . . . 60 40
460 1p.50 green and blue . . 60 40
461 2p. green and sepia . . . 1·75 70
462 5p. lake and olive . . . . 3·75 1·40
463 10p. sepia and blue . . . 3·75 1·40

127 G.P.O., Asuncion

1934. Air.
464 **127** 33p.75 blue . . . . 1·60 95
468 33p.75 red . . . . 1·60 95
466 33p.75 green . . . . . . 1·40 85
467 33p.75 brown . . . . . . 1·40 85

1934. Air. Optd **1934**.
469 **124** 4p.50 blue . . . . 1·75 1·75
470 9p. red . . . . 2·25 2·25
471 13p.50 green . . . . . . 6·50 6·50
472 **125** 22p.50 brown . . . . . . 5·25 5·25
473 45p. violet . . . . 11·00 11·00

1935. Air. Optd **1935**.
474 **124** 4p.50 red . . . . 2·25 2·25
475 9p. green . . . . 3·25 3·25
476 13p.50 brown . . . . . . 9·25 9·25
477 **125** 22p.50 purple . . . . . . 8·75 8·75
478 45p. blue . . . . 23·00 23·00

131 Tobacco Plant

1935. Air.
479 **131** 17p. brown . . . . 3·75 3·00
480 17p. red . . . . 6·75 5·00
481 17p. blue . . . . 4·25 3·50
482 17p. green . . . . 2·10 1·75

132 Church of the Incarnation

1935. Air.
483 **132** 102p. red . . . . 5·00 3·75
485 102p. blue . . . . 2·50 1·90
486 102p. brown . . . . . . 2·50 1·90
487 102p. violet . . . . . . 1·10 80
487a 102p. orange . . . . . 1·10 85

1937. Air. Surch **Habilitado en** and value in figures.
488 **127** $24 on 33p.75 blue . . . 40 50
489 **132** $65 on 102p. grey . . . 1·25 95
490 $84 on 102p. green . . . 1·25 95

134 Arms of Asuncion

135 Monstrance

1937. 4th Centenary of Asuncion (1st issue).
491 **134** 50c. purple and violet . . 10 10
492 1p. green and bistre . . . 10 10
493 3p. blue and red 10 10
494 10p. yellow and red . . . 15 10
495 20p. grey and blue . . . 20 20

1937. 1st National Eucharistic Congress.
496 **135** 1p. red, yellow and blue 10 10
497 3p. red, yellow and blue 10 10
498 10p. red, yellow and blue 15 10

136 Oratory of the Virgin of Asuncion

137 Asuncion

1938. 4th Centenary of Asuncion (2nd issue).
499 **136** 5p. olive 25 10
500 5p. red 35 10
501 11p. brown 25 10

1939. Air.
502 **137** 3p.40 blue 75 45
503 3p.40 green 75 45
504 3p.40 brown 75 45

138 J. E. Diaz

1939. Reburial in National Pantheon of Ashes of C. A. Lopez and J. E. Diaz.
505 **138** 2p. brown and blue . . . 25 15
506 – 2p. brown and blue . . . 25 15
DESIGN—VERT: No. 506, C. A. Lopez.

139 Pres. Caballero and Senator Decoud

1939. 50th Anniv of Asuncion University.
507 – 50c. blk & orge (postage) 10 10
508 – 1p. black and blue . . . 15 10
509 – 2p. black and red 25 10
510 **139** 5p. black and blue . . . 35 20
511 28p. black and red (air) 4·75 3·75
512 90p. black and green . . 8·00 6·50
DESIGN: Nos. 507/9, Pres. Escobar and Dr. Zubizarreta.

140 Coats of Arms

141 Pres. Baldomir and Flags of Paraguay and Uruguay

1939. Chaco Boundary Peace Conference, Buenos Aires (1st issue).
513 **140** 50c. blue (postage) . . . 15 10
514 **141** 1p. olive 15 10
515 A 2p. green 20 10
516 B 3p. brown 35 25
517 C 5p. orange 25 20
518 D 6p. violet 40 30
519 E 10p. brown 50 35
520 F 1p. brown (air) 10 10
521 **140** 3p. blue 10 10
522 E 5p. olive 10 15
523 D 10p. violet 15 15
524 C 30p. orange 25 15
525 B 50p. brown 15 25
526 A 100p. green 60 25
527 **141** 200p. green . . . . 2·75 1·75
528 – 500p. black . . . . . . 13·00 10·50
DESIGNS (flag on right is that of country named): A, Benavides (Peru); B, Eagle (USA); C, Alessandri (Chile); D, Vargas (Brazil); E, Ortiz (Argentina); F, Figure of "Peace" (Bolivia); 500p. (30 × 40 mm), Map of Chaco frontiers.
See also Nos. 536/43.

143 Arms of New York 144 Asuncion–New York Air Route

1939. New York World's Fair.
529 **143** 5p. red (postage) 20 15
530 10p. blue 40 30
531 11p. green 25 45
532 22p. grey 35 30
533 **144** 30p. brown (air) . . . . 3·25 2·40
534 80p. orange . . . . . . 4·25 3·00
535 90p. violet . . . . 7·00 5·50

145 Soldier

147 Waterfall

1940. Chaco Boundary Peace Conference, Buenos Aires (2nd issue). Inscr "PAZ DEL CHACO".
536 **145** 50c. orange 15 10
537 – 1p. purple 15 15
538 – 3p. green 25 20
539 – 5p. brown 10 25
540 – 10p. mauve 35 20
541 – 20p. blue 30 25
542 – 50p. green . . . . 1·10 35
543 **147** 100p. black . . . . 2·50 1·60
DESIGNS: As Type **145**: VERT: 1p. Water-carrier; 5p. Ploughing with oxen. HORIZ: 3p. Cattle Farming. As Type **147**: VERT: 10p. Fishing in the Paraguay River. HORIZ: 20p. Bullock-cart; 50p. Cattle-grazing.

148 Western Hemisphere

149 Reproduction of Paraguay No. 1

1940. 50th Anniv of Pan-American Union.
544 **148** 50c. orange (postage) . . 10 10
545 1p. green 10 10
546 5p. blue 25 10
547 10p. brown 30 30
548 20p. red (air) 35 25
549 70p. blue 35 30
550 100p. green 80 65
551 500p. violet . . . . . . 2·75 1·40

1940. Cent of First Adhesive Postage Stamps. Inscr "CENTENARIO DEL SELLO POSTAL 1940".
552 **149** 1p. purple and green . . . 65 35
553 – 5p. brown and green . . . 85 45
554 – 6p. blue and brown . . . 1·75 50
555 – 10p. black and red . . . 1·90 60
DESIGNS: 5p. Sir Rowland Hill; 6p., 10p. Early Paraguayan stamps.

1940. National Mourning for Pres. Estigarribia. Surch **7-IX-40/DUELO NACIONAL/5 PESOS** in black border.
556 **145** 5p. on 50c. orange . . . 25 25

152 Dr. Francia

154 Our Lady of Asuncion

1940. Death Centenary of Dr. Francia (dictator).
557 **152** 50c. red 15 10
558 – 50c. purple 15 10
559 **152** 1p. green 15 10
560 – 5p. blue 15 10
PORTRAIT: Nos. 558 and 560, Dr. Francia seated in library.

1941. Visit of President Vargas of Brazil. Optd **Visita al Paraguay Agosto de 1941**.
560a 6p. violet (No. 518) 25 25

1941. Mothers' Fund.
561 **154** 7p.+3p. brown 35 25
562 7p.+3p. violet 35 25
563 7p.+3p. red 35 25
564 7p.+3p. blue 35 25

1942. Nos. 520/2 optd **Habilitado** and bar(s).
565 – 1p. brown 15 10
566 **140** 3p. blue 20 10
567 – 5p. olive 25 10

156 Arms of Paraguay

158 Irala's Vision

1942.
568 **156** 1p. green 10 10
569 1p. orange 10 10
570 7p. blue 10 10
571 7p. brown 10 10
For other values as Type **156** see Nos. 631, etc.

1942. 4th Centenary of Asuncion.
572 – 2p. green (postage) . . . 75 40
573 **158** 5p. red 75 40
574 – 7p. blue 75 35
575 – 20p. purple (air) 95 30
576 **158** 70p. brown . . . . 2·40 1·25
577 – 500p. olive . . . . 7·25 5·25
DESIGNS—VERT: 2p., 20p. Indian hailing ships; 7p., 500p. Irala's Arms.

160 Columbus sighting America

161 Pres. Morinigo and Symbols of Progress

1943. 450th Anniv of Discovery of America by Columbus.
578 **160** 50c. violet 25 20
579 1p. brown 20 10
580 5p. green 65 20
581 7p. blue 35 10

1943. Three Year Plan.
582 **161** 7p. blue 10 10

NOTE: From No. 583 onwards, the currency having been changed, the letter "c" in the value description indicates "centimos" instead of "centavos".

1944. St. Juan Earthquake Fund. Surch **U.P.A.E. Adhesion victimas San Juan y Pueblo Argentino centimos** and bar.
583 E 10c. on 10p. brown (No. 519) 40 25

1944. No. 311 surch **Habilitado en un centimo**.
584 1c. on 3p. violet 10 10

1944. Surch **1944/5 Centimos 5**.
585 **160** 5c. on 7p. blue 15 10
586 **161** 5c. on 7p. blue 15 10

164 Primitive Indian Postmen

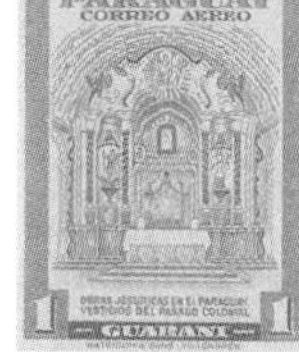
181 Jesuit Relics of Colonial Paraguay

1944.
587 **164** 1c. black (postage) . . . 10 10
588 – 2c. brown 15 10
589 – 5c. olive . . . . 3·25 80
590 – 7c. blue 15 20
591 – 10c. green . . . . 1·50 45
592 – 15c. blue 40 25

No.	Type	Description	Mint	Used
593	–	50c. black	35	35
594	–	1g. red	70	40

DESIGNS—HORIZ: 2c. Ruins of Humaita Church; 7c. Marshal Francisco S. Lopez; 1g. Ytororo Heroes' Monument. VERT: 5c. First Paraguayan railway locomotive; 10c. "Tacuary" (paddle-steamer); 15c. Port of Asuncion; 50c. Meeting place of Independence conspirators.

No.	Type	Description	Mint	Used
595	–	1c. blue (air)	20	15
596	–	2c. green	10	10
597	–	3c. purple	80	20
598	–	5c. green	20	10
599	–	10c. violet	20	15
600	–	20c. brown	4·00	1·60
601	–	30c. blue	25	25
602	–	40c. olive	15	15
603	–	70c. red	25	20
604	181	1g. orange	90	40
605	–	2g. brown	2·25	55
606	–	5g. brown	5·50	2·75
607	–	10g. blue	13·00	9·75

DESIGNS—HORIZ: 1c. Port of Asuncion; 2c. First telegraphic apparatus in S. America; 3c. Paddle-steamer "Tacuary"; 5c. Meeting place of Independence Conspirators; 10c. Antequera Monument; 20c. First Paraguayan railway locomotive; 40c. Government House. VERT: 30c. Ytororo Heroes' Monument; 70c. As Type **164** but vert: 2g. Ruins of Humaita Church; 5g. Oratory of the Virgin; 10g. Marshal Francisco S. Lopez.

See also Nos. 640/51.

1945. No. 590 surch with figure **5** over ornaments deleting old value.

No.	Type	Description	Mint	Used
608		5c. on 7c. blue	10	10

186 Clasped Hands and Flags

1945. President Morinigo's Goodwill Visits. Designs of different sizes inscr "CONFRATERNIDAD" between crossed flags of Paraguay and another American country, mentioned in brackets. (a) Postage.

No.	Type	Description	Mint	Used
609	186	1c. green (Panama)	10	10
610		3c. red (Venezuela)	10	10
611		5c. grey (Ecuador)	10	10
612		2g. brown (Peru)	1·50	90

(b) Air.

No.	Type	Description	Mint	Used
613		20c. orange (Colombia)	10	30
614		40c. olive (Bolivia)	10	25
615		70c. red (Mexico)	40	40
616		1g. blue (Chile)	50	50
617		2g. violet (Brazil)	75	75
618		5g. green (Argentina)	2·25	2·25
619		10g. brown (U.S.A.)	6·50	6·50

The 5 and 10g. are larger, 32 × 28 and 33½ × 30 mm respectively.

1945. Surch **1945 5 Centimos 5**.

No.	Type	Description	Mint	Used
620	160	5c. on 7p. blue	50	20
621	161	5c. on 7p. blue	50	20
622	–	5c. on 7p. blue (No. 590)	50	20

1945. Surch **1945** and value.

No.	Type	Description	Mint	Used
623	154	2c. on 7p.+3p. brown	10	10
624		2c. on 7p.+3p. violet	10	10
625		2c. on 7p.+3p. red	10	10
626		2c. on 7p.+3p. blue	10	10
627		5c. on 7p.+3p. brown	20	10
628		5c. on 7p.+3p. violet	20	10
629		5c. on 7p.+3p. red	20	10
630		5c. on 7p.+3p. blue	20	10

1946. As T **156** but inscr "U.P.U." at foot.

No.	Type	Description	Mint	Used
631	156	5c. grey	10	10
631a		5c. pink	10	10
631b		5c. brown	10	10
686		10c. blue	10	10
687		10c. pink	10	10
631c		30c. green	10	10
631d		30c. brown	10	10
775		45c. green	10	10
631e		50c. mauve	10	10
776		50c. purple	10	10
858		70c. brown	10	10
777		90c. blue	10	10
778		1g. violet	10	10
860		1g.50 mauve	10	10
814		2g. ochre	10	10
780		2g.20 mauve	10	10
781		3g. brown	10	10
782		4g.20 green	10	10
862		4g.50 blue	15	10
816		5g. red	10	10
689		10g. orange	20	30
784		10g. green	20	15
818		12g.45 green	20	10
819		15g. orange	25	15
786		20g. blue	40	30
820		30g. bistre	20	30
812		50g. brown	30	25
821		100g. blue	90	50

See also Nos. 1037/49.

1946. Surch **1946 5 Centimos 5**.

No.	Type	Description	Mint	Used
632	154	5c. on 7p.+3p. brown	25	35
633		5c. on 7p.+3p. violet	25	35
634		5c. on 7p.+3p. red	25	35
635		5c. on 7p.+3p. blue	25	35

1946. Air. Surch **1946 5 Centimos 5**.

No.	Type	Description	Mint	Used
636		5c. on 20c. brown (No. 600)	5·50	5·75
637		5c. on 30c. blue (No. 601)	30	30
638		5c. on 40c. olive (No. 602)	30	30
639		5c. on 70c. red (No. 603)	30	30

1946. As Nos. 587/607 but colours changed and some designs smaller.

No.	Type	Description	Mint	Used
640	–	1c. red (postage)	20	15
641	–	2c. violet	10	10
642	164	5c. blue	10	10
643	–	10c. orange	10	10
644	–	15c. olive	15	15
645	181	50c. green	50	30
646	–	1g. blue	95	30

DESIGNS—VERT: 1c. Paddle-steamer "Tacuary"; 1g. Meeting place of Independence Conspirators. HORIZ: 2c. First telegraphic apparatus in S. America; 10c. Antequera Monument; 15c. Ytororo Heroes' Monument.

No.	Type	Description	Mint	Used
647	–	10c. red (air)	10	10
648	–	20c. green	80	20
649	–	1g. brown	25	25
650	–	5g. purple	2·25	1·40
651	–	10g. red	7·25	4·00

DESIGNS—VERT: 10c. Ruins of Humaita Church. HORIZ: 20c. Port of Asuncion; 1g. Govt. House; 5g. Marshal Francisco S. Lopez; 10g. Oratory of the Virgin.

189 Marshal Francisco Lopez **190** Archbishop of Paraguay

1947. Various frames.

No.	Type	Description	Mint	Used
652	189	1c. violet (postage)	10	10
653		2c. red	10	10
654		5c. green	10	10
655		15c. blue	10	10
656		50c. green	40	40
657		32c. red (air)	10	10
658		64c. brown	25	25
659		1g. blue	40	40
660		5g. purple and blue	1·60	60
661		10g. green and red	2·75	95

1947. 50th Anniv of Archbishopric of Paraguay.

No.	Type	Description	Mint	Used
662	190	2c. grey (postage)	10	10
663	–	5c. red	10	10
664	–	10c. black	10	10
665	–	15c. green	25	15
666	–	20c. black (air)	10	10
667	–	30c. grey	10	10
668	–	40c. mauve	15	10
669	190	70c. red	25	25
670	–	1g. lake	30	30
671	–	2g. red	95	40
672	190	5g. slate and red	1·60	70
673	–	10g. brown and green	3·75	1·75

DESIGNS: 5, 20c., 10g. Episcopal Arms; 10, 30c, 1g. Sacred Heart Monument; 15, 40c., 2g. Vision of projected monument.

194 Torchbearer **195** C. A. Lopez, J. N. Gonzalez and "Paraguari" (freighter)

1948. Honouring the "Barefeet" (political party). Badge in red and blue.

No.	Type	Description	Mint	Used
674	194	5c. red (postage)	10	10
675		15c. orange	15	10
676		69c. green (air)	40	40
677		5g. blue	3·25	1·50

1948. Centenary of Paraguay's Merchant Fleet. Centres in black, red and blue.

No.	Type	Description	Mint	Used
678	195	2c. orange	15	10
679		5c. blue	20	10
680		10c. black	25	10
681		15c. violet	40	10
682		50c. green	60	20
683		1g. red	90	25

1949. Air. National Mourning for Archbishop of Paraguay. Surch **DUELO NACIONAL 5 CENTIMOS 5**.

No.	Type	Description	Mint	Used
684	190	5c. on 70c. red	15	15

1949. Air. Aid to Victims of Ecuadorean Earthquake. No. 667 surch **AYUDA AL ECUADOR 5 + 5** and two crosses.

No.	Type	Description	Mint	Used
685		5c.+5c. on 30c. slate	10	10

198 "Postal Communications" **199** President Roosevelt

1950. Air. 75th Anniv of U.P.U.

No.	Type	Description	Mint	Used
691	198	20c. violet and green	1·50	1·60
692		30c. brown and purple	45	50
693		50c. green and grey	50	50
694		1g. brown and blue	50	50
695		5g. black and red	1·50	1·60

1950. Air. Honouring F. D. Roosevelt. Flags in red and blue.

No.	Type	Description	Mint	Used
696	199	20c. orange	10	10
697		30c. black	10	10
698		50c. purple	15	10
699		1g. green	25	25
700		5g. blue	30	30

1951. 1st Economic Congress of Paraguay. Surch **PRIMER CONGRESO DE ENTIDADES ECONOMICAS DEL PARAGUAY 18–IV–1951** and shield over a block of four stamps.

No.	Type	Description	Mint	Used
700a	156	5c. pink	20	10
700b		10c. blue	35	25
700c		30c. green	50	40

Prices are for single stamps. Prices for blocks of four, four times single prices.

200 Columbus Lighthouse

201 Urn

1952. Columbus Memorial Lighthouse.

No.	Type	Description	Mint	Used
701	200	2c. brown (postage)	10	10
702		5c. blue	10	10
703		10c. pink	10	10
704		15c. blue	10	10
705		20c. purple	10	10
706		50c. orange	15	10
707		1g. green	25	25
708	201	10c. blue (air)	10	10
709		20c. green	10	10
710		30c. purple	10	10
711		40c. pink	10	10
712		50c. bistre	10	10
713		1g. blue	15	10
714		2g. orange	25	20
715		5g. lake	25	40

202 Isabella the Catholic

1952. Air. 500th Birth Anniv of Isabella the Catholic.

No.	Type	Description	Mint	Used
716	202	1g. blue	10	10
717		2g. brown	20	20
718		5g. green	40	40
719		10g. purple	40	40

203 S. Pettirossi (aviator) **204** San Roque Church, Asuncion

1954. Pettirossi Commemoration.

No.	Type	Description	Mint	Used
720	203	5c. blue (postage)	10	10
721		20c. red	10	10
722		50c. purple	10	10
723		60c. violet	15	10
724		40c. brown (air)	10	10
725		55c. green	10	10
726		80c. blue	10	10
727		1g.30 grey	35	35

1954. Air. San Roque Church Centenary.

No.	Type	Description	Mint	Used
728	204	20c. red	10	10
729		30c. purple	10	10
730		50c. blue	10	10
731		1g. purple and brown	10	10
732		1g. black and brown	10	10
733		1g. green and brown	10	10
734		1g. orange and brown	10	10
735		5g. yellow and brown	20	20
736		5g. olive and brown	20	20
737		5g. violet and brown	20	20
738		5g. buff and brown	20	20

205 Marshal Lopez, C. A. Lopez and Gen. Caballero

1954. National Heroes.

No.	Type	Description	Mint	Used
739	205	5c. violet (postage)	10	10
740		20c. blue	10	10
741		50c. mauve	10	10
742		1g. brown	10	10
743		2g. green	15	10
744		5g. violet (air)	20	15
745		10g. olive	35	35
746		20g. grey	35	30
747		50g. pink	1·60	1·25
748		100g. blue	5·50	4·50

206 Presidents Stroessner and Peron

1955. Visit of President Peron. Flags in red and blue.

No.	Type	Description	Mint	Used
749	206	5c. brown & buff (postage)	10	10
750		10c. lake and buff	10	10
751		50c. grey	10	10
752		1g.30 lilac and buff	10	10
753		2g.20 blue and buff	20	10
754		60c. olive and buff (air)	10	10
755		2g. green	10	10
756		3g. red	20	10
757		4g.10 mauve and buff	30	20

207 Trinidad Campanile

1955. Sacerdotal Silver Jubilee of Mgr. Rodriguez.

No.	Type	Description	Mint	Used
758	207	5c. brown (postage)	10	10
759	–	20c. brown	10	10
760	–	50c. brown	10	10
761	–	2g.50 green	10	10
762	–	5g. brown	15	10
763	–	15g. green	30	20
764	–	25g. green	35	35
765	207	2g. blue (air)	10	10
766	–	3g. green	10	10
767	–	4g. green	10	10
768	–	6g. brown	10	10
769	–	10g. red	20	10
770	–	20g. brown	30	10
771	–	30g. green	95	70
772	–	50g. blue	2·40	1·60

DESIGNS—HORIZ: 20c., 3g. Cloisters in Trinidad; 5, 10g. San Cosme Portico; 15, 20g. Church of Jesus. VERT: 50c., 4g. Cornice in Santa Maria; 2g.50, 6g. Santa Rosa Tower; 25, 30g. Niche in Trinidad; 50g. Trinidad Sacristy.

208 Angel and Marching Soldiers **209** Soldier and Flags

1957. Chaco Heroes. Inscr "HOMENAJE A LOS HEROES DEL CHACO". Flags in red, white and blue.

No.	Type	Description	Mint	Used
787	208	5c. green (postage)	10	10
788		10c. red	10	10
789		15c. blue	10	10
790		20c. purple	10	10
791		25c. black	10	10
792	–	30c. blue	10	10
793	–	40c. black	10	10
794	–	50c. lake	10	10
795	–	1g. turquoise	10	10
796	–	1g.30 blue	10	10

797 – 1g.50 purple 10 10
798 – 2g. green 10 10

799 **209** 10c. blue (air) 10 10
800 15c. purple 10 10
801 20c. red 10 10
802 25c. blue 10 10
803 50c. turquoise 10 10
804 1g. red 10 10
805 – 1g.30 purple 10 10
806 – 1g.50 blue 10 10
807 – 2g. green 10 10
808 – 4g.10 vermilion and red 10 10
809 – 5g. black 10 10
810 – 10g. turquoise 15 15
811 – 25g. blue 40 15

DESIGNS—HORIZ: Nos. 792/8, Man, woman and flags; 805/11, "Paraguay" and kneeling soldier.

212 R. Gonzalez and St. Ignatius

213 President Stroessner

1958. 4th Centenary of St. Ignatius of Loyola.
822 **212** 50c. green 10 10
823 – 50c. brown 10 10
824 – 1g.50 violet 10 10
825 – 3g. blue 10 10
826 **212** 6g.25 red 15 10

DESIGNS—VERT: 50c. brown; 3g. Statue of St. Ignatius. HORIZ: 1g.50, Jesuit Fathers' house, Antigua.

See also Nos. 1074/81.

1958. Re-election of Pres. Stroessner. Portrait in black.
827 **213** 10c. red (postage) 10 10
828 15c. violet 10 10
829 25c. green 10 10
830 30c. lake 10 10
831 50c. mauve 10 10
832 75c. blue 10 10
833 5g. turquoise 10 10
834 10g. brown 10 15

835 12g. mauve (air) 40 35
836 18g. orange 25 40
837 23g. brown 65 40
838 36g. green 65 40
839 50g. olive 80 50
840 65g. grey . . . . 1·25 75

1959. Nos. 758/72 surch with star enclosed by palm leaves and value.
841 1g.50 on 5c. ochre (postage) 10 10
842 1g.50 on 20c. brown 10 10
843 1g.50 on 50c. purple 10 10
844 3g. on 2g.50 olive 10 10
845 6g.25 on 5g. brown 10 10
846 20g. on 15g. turquoise . . . 35 35
847 30g. on 25g. green 50 50

848 4g. on 2g. blue (air) 10 10
849 12g.45 on 3g. olive 25 20
850 18g.15 on 6g. brown 35 30
851 23g.40 on 10g. red 25 35
852 34g.80 on 20g. bistre . . . 40 50
853 36g. on 4g. green 40 30
854 43g.95 on 30g. green . . . 75 60
855 100g. on 50g. blue . . . . 1·90 1·10

215 U.N. Emblem

216 U.N. Emblem and Map of Paraguay

1959. Air. Visit of U.N. Secretary-General.
856 **215** 5g. blue and orange . . . 75 30

1959. Air. U.N. Day.
857 **216** 12g.45 orange and blue 25 20

217 Football

218 "Uprooted Tree"

1960. Olympic Games, Rome. Inscr "1960".
863 **217** 30c. red & green (postage) 10 10
864 50c. purple and blue . . . 10 10
865 75c. green and orange . . 10 10
866 1g.50 violet and green . . 10 10

867 – 12g.45 blue and red (air) 25 25
868 – 18g.15 green and purple 35 35
869 – 36g. red and green . . . 80 30

DESIGN—AIR: Basketball.

1960. World Refugee Year (1st issue).
870 **218** 25c. pink and green (postage) 10 10
871 50c. green and red 10 10
872 70c. brown and mauve . . 30 25
873 1g.50 blue and deep blue 30 30
874 3g. grey and brown . . . 65 35

875 – 4g. pink and green (air) 95 70
876 – 12g.45 green and blue . . 1·90 1·25
877 – 18g.15 orange and red . . 2·75 2·00
878 – 23g.40 blue and red . . . 3·50 2·75

DESIGN—AIR. As Type **218** but with "ANO MUNDIAL" inscr below tree.

See also Nos. 971/7.

219 U.N. Emblem

220 U.N. Emblem and Flags

1960. "Human Rights". Inscr "DERECHOS HUMANOS".
879 **219** 1g. red and blue (postage) 10 10
880 – 3g. orange and blue . . . 10 10
881 – 6g. orange and green . . 10 10
882 – 20g. yellow and red . . . 15 15

883 **219** 40g. blue and red (air) . . 30 30
884 – 60g. red and green . . . 75 65
885 – 100g. red and blue . . . 1·40 95

DESIGNS: 3g., 6g. Hand holding scales; 6g. Hands breaking chain; 20g., 100g. "Freedom flame".

1960. U.N. Day. Flags and inscr in blue and red.
886 **220** 30c. blue (postage) . . . 10 10
887 75c. yellow 10 10
888 90c. mauve 10 10

889 3g. orange (air) 10 10
890 4g. green 10 10

221 Bridge with Arms of Brazil and Paraguay

222 Timber Truck

1961. Inauguration of International Bridge between Brazil and Paraguay.
891 **221** 15c. green (postage) . . . 10 10
892 30c. blue 10 10
893 50c. orange 10 10
894 75c. blue 10 10
895 1g. violet 10 10

896 – 3g. red (air) 15 10
897 – 12g.45 lake 30 25
898 – 18g.15 green 35 30
899 – 36g. blue 75 25

DESIGN—HORIZ: Nos. 896/9, Aerial view of bridge.

1961. Paraguayan Progress. Inscr "PARAGUAY EN MARCHA".
900 **222** 25c. red & green (postage) 10 10
901 – 90c. yellow and blue . . . 10 10
902 – 1g. red and orange . . . 10 10
903 – 2g. green and pink . . . 10 10
904 – 5g. violet and green . . . 15 10

905 **222** 12g.45 blue and buff (air) 40 25
906 – 18g.15 violet and buff . . 55 35
907 – 22g. blue and orange . . 30 40
908 – 36g. yellow, green and blue 60 50

DESIGNS: 90c., 2g., 18g.15, Motorized timber barge; 1, 5, 22g. Radio mast; 36g. Boeing 707 jetliner.

223 P. J. Caballero, J. G. R. de Francia and F. Yegros

224 "Chaco Peace"

1961. 150th Anniv of Independence. (a) 1st issue.
909 **223** 30c. green (postage) . . . 10 10
910 50c. mauve 10 10
911 90c. violet 10 10
912 1g.50 blue 10 10
913 3g. bistre 10 10
914 4g. blue 10 10
915 5g. brown 10 10

916 – 12g.45 red (air) 20 15
917 – 18g.15 blue 30 25
918 – 23g.40 green 40 30
919 – 30g. violet 45 35
920 – 36g. red 65 50
921 – 44g. brown 70 35

DESIGN: Nos. 916/21, Declaration of Independence.

(b) 2nd issue. Inscr "PAZ DEL CHACO".
922 **224** 25c. red (postage) 10 10
923 30c. green 10 10
924 50c. brown 10 10
925 1g. violet 10 10
926 2g. blue 10 10

927 – 3g. blue (air) 20 15
928 – 4g. purple 20 20
929 – 100g. green . . . . . . 1·40 1·00

DESIGN: Nos. 927/9, Clasped hands.

225 Puma

226 Arms of Paraguay

(c) 3rd issue.
930 **225** 75c. violet (postage) . . . 10 10
931 1g.50 brown 10 10
932 4g.50 green 15 10
933 10g. blue 25 20

934 – 12g.45 purple (air) 90 40
935 – 18g.15 blue . . . . 1·25 75
936 – 34g.80 brown . . . . . . 2·25 1·25

DESIGN: Nos. 934/6, Brazilian tapir.

(d) 4th issue.
937 **226** 15c. blue (postage) . . . 10 10
938 25c. red 10 10
939 75c. green 10 10
940 1g. red 10 10

941 3g. brown (air) 10 10
942 12g.45 mauve 25 25
943 36g. turquoise 65 30

The air stamps have a background pattern of horiz lines.

227 Grand Hotel, Guarani

(e) 5th issue.
944 **227** 50c. grey (postage) . . . 10 10
945 1g. green 10 10
946 4g.50 violet 10 10

947 – 3g. brown (air) 10 10
948 – 4g. blue 10 10
949 – 18g.15 orange 40 35
950 – 36g. red 30 50

The air stamps are similar to Type **227** but inscr "HOTEL GUARANI" in upper left corner. See also Nos. 978/85 and 997/1011.

228 Racquet, Net and Balls

1961. 28th South American Tennis Championships, Asuncion (1st issue). Centres multicoloured; border colours given.
951 **228** 35c. pink (postage) . . . 10 10
952 75c. yellow 10 10
953 1g.50 blue 10 10
954 2g.25 turquoise 10 10
955 4g. grey 15 10

956 12g.45 orange (air) . . . 90 40
957 20g. orange . . . . 1·40 40
958 50g. orange . . . . 2·25 75

See also Nos. 978/85.

229

1961. "Europa".
959 **229** 50c. red, blue and mauve 10 10
960 75c. red, blue and green 10 10
961 1g. red, blue and brown 10 10
962 1g.50 red, blue & lt blue 10 10
963 4g.50 red, blue and yellow 20 20

230 Comm. Alan Shepard and Solar System

231

1961. Commander Shepard's Space Flight.
964 – 10c. brown and blue (postage) 10 10
965 – 25c. mauve and blue . . . 10 10
966 – 50c. orange and blue . . 10 10
967 – 75c. green and blue . . . 10 10

968 **230** 18g.15 blue and green (air) . . . . 4·00 3·00
969 36g. blue and orange . . 4·00 3·00
970 50g. blue and mauve . . . 5·50 3·50

DESIGN—HORIZ: Nos. 964/7, Comm. Shepard.

1961. World Refugee Year (2nd issue).
971 **231** 10c. deep blue and blue (postage) 10 10
972 25c. purple and orange . . 10 10
973 50c. mauve and pink . . 10 10
974 75c. blue and green . . . 10 10

975 – 18g.15 red and brown (air) 55 25
976 – 36g. green and red . . . 1·25 55
977 – 50g. orange and green . . 1·50 1·10

Nos. 975/7 have a different background and frame.

232 Tennis-player

233 Scout Bugler

1962. 150th Anniv of Independence (6th issue) and 28th South American Tennis Championships, Asuncion (2nd issue).
978 **232** 35c. blue (postage) . . . 10 10
979 75c. violet 10 10
980 1g.50 brown 10 10
981 2g.25 green 10 10

982 – 4g. red (air) 10 10
983 – 12g.45 purple 60 30
984 – 20g. turquoise 80 25
985 – 50g. brown . . . . 1·60 40

Nos. 982/5 show tennis-player using backhand stroke.

1962. Boy Scouts Commemoration.
986 **233** 10c. green & pur (postage) 10 10
987 20c. green and red 10 10
988 25c. green and brown . . 10 10
989 30c. green and emerald 10 10
990 50c. green and blue . . . 10 10

991 – 12g.45 mauve & blue (air) 50 40
992 – 36g. mauve and green . . 1·50 90
993 – 50g. mauve and yellow . . 1·90 90

DESIGN: Nos. 991/3, Lord Baden-Powell.

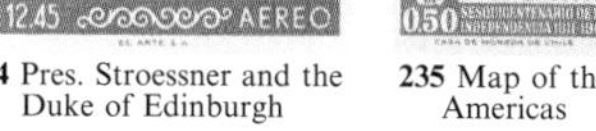

234 Pres. Stroessner and the Duke of Edinburgh

235 Map of the Americas

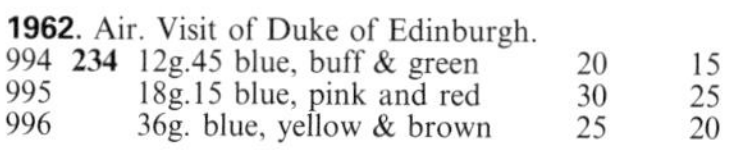

1962. Air. Visit of Duke of Edinburgh.
994 **234** 12g.45 blue, buff & green 20 15
995 18g.15 blue, pink and red 30 25
996 36g. blue, yellow & brown 25 20

1962. 150th Anniv of Independence (7th issue) and Day of the Americas.
997 **235** 50c. orange (postage) . . 10 10
998 75c. blue 10 10
999 1g. violet 10 10
1000 1g.50 green 10 10
1001 4g.50 red 10 10

1002 – 20g. mauve (air) 30 20
1003 – 50g. orange 70 50

DESIGN: 20g., 50g. Hands supporting Globe.

236 U.N. Emblem

238 Football Stadium

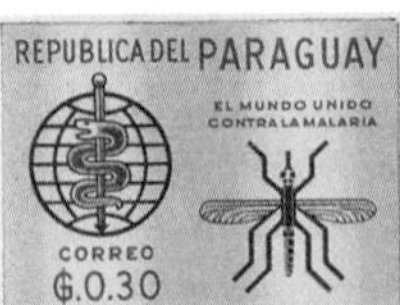
237 Mosquito and W.H.O. Emblem

1962. 150th Anniv of Independence (8th issue).
1004 **236** 50c. brown (postage) 10 10
1005 75c. purple 10 10
1006 1g. blue 10 10
1007 2g. brown 10 10
1008 – 12g.45 violet (air) 35 35
1009 – 18g.15 green 25 25
1010 – 23g.40 red 35 35
1011 – 30g. red 80 65
DESIGN: Nos. 1008/11, U.N. Headquarters, New York.

1962. Malaria Eradication.
1012 **237** 30c. black, blue and pink (postage) 10 10
1013 50c. black, green & bistre 10 10
1014 – 75c. black, bistre and red 10 10
1015 – 1g. black, bistre and green 10 10
1016 – 1g.50 black, bistre & brown 10 10
1017 **237** 3g. black, red & blue (air) 10 10
1018 4g. black, red and green 10 10
1019 – 12g.45 black, grn & brn 25 10
1020 – 18g.15 black, red and purple 90 55
1021 – 36g. black, blue and red 1·25 85
DESIGN: Nos. 1014/16, 1019/21, Mosquito on U.N. emblem, and microscope.

1962. World Cup Football Championship, Chile.
1022 **238** 15c. brown & yell (postage) 10 10
1023 25c. brown and green 10 10
1024 30c. brown and violet 10 10
1025 40c. brown and orange 10 10
1026 50c. brown and green 10 10
1027 – 12g.45 black, red and violet (air) 1·10 25
1028 – 18g.15 black, brn & vio 90 45
1029 – 36g. black, grey & brown 2·00 80
DESIGN—HORIZ: Nos. 1027/9, Footballers and Globe.

239 "Lago Ypoa" (freighter)

1962. Paraguayan Merchant Marine Commem.
1030 **239** 30c. brown (postage) 15 10
1031 – 90c. blue 20 10
1032 – 1g.50 purple 25 10
1033 – 2g. green 35 15
1034 – 4g.20 blue 50 20
1035 – 12g.45 red (air) 30 15
1036 – 44g. blue 30 45
DESIGNS—HORIZ: 90c. Freighter; 1g.50, "Olympo" (freighter); 2g. Freighter (diff); 4g.20, "Rio Apa" (freighter). VERT: 12g.45, 44g. Ship's wheel.

1962. As Nos. 631, etc, but with taller figures of value.
1037 **156** 50c. blue 10 10
1038 70c. lilac 10 10
1039 1g.50 violet 10 10
1040 3g. blue 10 10
1041 4g.50 brown 10 10
1042 5g. mauve 10 10
1043 10g. mauve 20 10
1044 12g.45 blue 20 10
1045 15g.45 red 25 10
1046 18g.15 purple 10 15
1047 20g. brown 10 15
1048 50g. brown 25 30
1049 100g. grey 90 30

241 Gen. A. Stroessner

242 Popes Paul VI, John XXIII and St. Peter's

1963. Re-election of Pres. Stroessner to Third Term of Office.
1050 **241** 50c. brown and drab (postage) 10 10
1051 75c. brown and pink 10 10
1052 1g.50 brown and mauve 10 10
1053 3g. brown and green 10 10
1054 12g.45 red and pink (air) 25 20
1055 18g.15 green and pink 65 30
1056 36g. violet and pink 85 40

1964. Popes Paul VI and John XXIII.
1057 **242** 1g.50 yellow and red (postage) 10 10
1058 3g. green and red 10 10
1059 4g. brown and red 10 10
1060 – 12g.45 olive & grn (air) 35 20
1061 – 18g.15 green and violet 45 30
1062 – 36g. green and blue 1·25 60
DESIGNS: Nos. 1060/2, Cathedral, Asuncion.

243 Arms of Paraguay and France

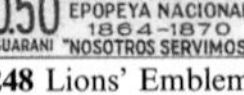
245 Map of the Americas

1964. Visit of French President.
1063 **243** 1g.50 brown (postage) 10 10
1064 – 3g. blue 40 10
1065 **243** 4g. grey 10 10
1066 – 12g.45 violet (air) 25 20
1067 **243** 18g.15 green 70 30
1068 – 36g. red 1·25 60
DESIGNS: 3, 12g.45, 36g. Presidents Stroessner and De Gaulle.

1965. 6th Reunion of the Board of Governors of the Inter-American Development Bank. Optd **Centenario de la Epopeya Nacional 1,864–1,870** as in T **245**.
1069 **245** 1g.50 green (postage) 10 10
1070 3g. pink 10 10
1071 4g. blue 10 10
1072 12g.45 brown (air) 20 10
1073 36g. violet 65 45
The overprint refers to the National Epic of 1864–70, the war with Argentina, Brazil and Uruguay and this inscription occurs on many other issues from 1965 onwards.
Nos. 1069/73 without the overprint were not authorized.

246 R. Gonzalez and St. Ignatius

247 Ruben Dario

1966. 350th Anniv of Founding of San Ignacio Guazu Monastery.
1074 **246** 15c. blue (postage) 10 10
1075 25c. blue 10 10
1076 75c. blue 10 10
1077 90c. blue 10 10
1078 – 3g. brown (air) 10 10
1079 – 12g.45 brown 10 10
1080 – 18g.15 brown 20 10
1081 – 23g.40 brown 35 25
DESIGNS: Nos. 1078/81, Jesuit Fathers' house, Antigua.
For similar stamps with different inscriptions, see Nos. 822, 824 and 826.

1966. 50th Death Anniv of Ruben Dario (poet).
1082 **247** 50c. blue 10 10
1083 70c. brown 10 10
1084 1g.50 lake 10 10
1085 3g. violet 10 10
1086 4g. turquoise 10 10
1087 5g. black 10 10
1088 – 12g.45 blue (air) 10 10
1089 – 18g.15 violet 10 10
1090 – 23g.40 brown 35 10
1091 – 36g. green 65 25
1092 – 50g. red 75 25
DESIGNS: Nos. 1088/92, Open book inscr "Paraguay de Fuego ..." by Dario.

248 Lions' Emblem on Globe

249 W.H.O. Emblem

1967. 50th Anniv of Lions International.
1093 **248** 50c. violet (postage) 10 10
1094 70c. blue 10 10
1095 – 1g.50 blue 10 10
1096 – 3g. brown 10 10
1097 – 4g. blue 10 10
1098 – 5g. brown 10 10
1099 – 12g.45 brown (air) 10 10
1100 – 18g.15 violet 15 10
1101 – 23g.40 purple 20 10
1102 – 36g. blue 25 25
1103 – 50g. red 25 25
DESIGNS—VERT: 1g.50, 3g. M. Jones; 4, 5g. Lions headquarters, Chicago. HORIZ: 12g.45, 18g.15, Library–"Education"; 23g.40, 36g., 50g. Medical laboratory–"Health".

1968. 20th Anniv of W.H.O.
1104 **249** 3g. turquoise (postage) 10 10
1105 4g. purple 10 10
1106 5g. brown 10 10
1107 10g. violet 10 10
1108 – 36g. brown (air) 40 25
1109 – 50g. red 45 30
1110 – 100g. blue 60 35
DESIGN—VERT: Nos. 1108/10, W.H.O. emblem on scroll.

250

251

1969. World Friendship Week.
1111 **250** 50c. red 10 10
1112 70c. blue 10 10
1113 1g.50 brown 10 10
1114 3g. mauve 10 10
1115 4g. green 10 10
1116 5g. violet 10 10
1117 10g. purple 20 10

1969. Air. Campaign for Houses for Teachers.
1118 **251** 36g. blue 40 20
1119 50g. brown 75 30
1120 100g. red 1·40 50

252 Pres. Lopez

253 Paraguay 2r. Stamp of 1870

1970. Death Centenary of Pres. F. Solano Lopez.
1121 **252** 1g. brown (postage) 10 10
1122 2g. violet 10 10
1123 3g. pink 10 10
1124 4g. red 10 10
1125 5g. blue 10 10
1126 10g. green 10 10
1127 15g. blue (air) 10 10
1128 20g. brown 20 10
1129 30g. green 55 20
1130 40g. purple 60 25

1970. Centenary of First Paraguayan Stamps.
1131 **253** 1g. red (postage) 10 10
1132 A 2g. blue 10 10
1133 B 3g. brown 10 10
1134 **253** 5g. violet 10 10
1135 A 10g. lilac 20 10
1136 B 15g. purple (air) 65 25
1137 **253** 30g. green 80 50
1138 A 36g. red 90 30
DESIGNS: First Paraguay stamps. A, 1r.; B, 3r.

254 Teacher and Pupil

255 UNICEF Emblem

1971. International Education Year–UNESCO.
1139 **254** 3g. blue (postage) 10 10
1140 5g. lilac 10 10
1141 10g. green 10 10
1142 20g. red (air) 20 10
1143 25g. mauve 25 15
1144 30g. brown 25 20
1145 50g. green 40 35

1972. 25th Anniv of UNICEF.
1146 **255** 1g. brown (postage) 10 10
1147 2g. blue 10 10
1148 3g. red 10 10
1149 4g. purple 10 10
1150 5g. green 10 10
1151 10g. purple 10 10
1152 20g. blue (air) 20 10
1153 25g. green 25 15
1154 30g. brown 25 20

256 Acaray Dam

1972. Tourist Year of the Americas.
1155 **256** 1g. brown (postage) 10 10
1156 – 2g. brown 10 10
1157 – 3g. blue 10 10
1158 – 5g. red 10 10
1159 – 10g. green 10 10
1160 – 20g. red (air) 25 10
1161 – 25g. grey 30 15
1162 – 50g. lilac 1·40 45
1163 – 100g. mauve 80 40
DESIGNS: 2g. Statue of Lopez; 3g. Friendship Bridge; 5g. Rio Tebicuary Bridge; 10g. Grand Hotel, Guarani; 20g. Motor coach; 25g. Social Service Institute Hospital; 50g. Liner "Presidente Stroessner"; 100g. Lockheed Electra airliner.

257 O.E.A. Emblem

1973. 25th Anniv of Organization of American States (O.E.A.).
1164 **257** 1g. mult (postage) 10 10
1165 2g. multicoloured 10 10
1166 3g. multicoloured 10 10
1167 4g. multicoloured 10 10
1168 5g. multicoloured 10 10
1169 10g. multicoloured 10 10
1170 20g. multicoloured (air) 20 10
1171 25g. multicoloured 30 15
1172 50g. multicoloured 25 35
1173 100g. multicoloured 1·00 40

258 Exhibition Emblem

1973. International Industrial Exhibition, Paraguay.
1174 **258** 1g. brown (postage) 10 10
1175 2g. red 10 10
1176 3g. blue 10 10
1177 4g. green 10 10
1178 5g. lilac 10 10
1179 20g. mauve (air) 20 10
1180 25g. red 25 10

259 Carrier Pigeon with Letter

1975. Centenary of U.P.U.
1181 **259** 1g. violet & blk (postage) 10 10
1182 2g. red and black 10 10
1183 3g. blue and black 10 10
1184 5g. blue and black 10 10
1185 10g. purple and black 10 10
1186 20g. brown & black (air) 25 15
1187 25g. green and black 30 20

260 Institute Buildings

1976. Inauguration (1974) of Institute of Higher Education.

1188	**260**	5g. violet, red and black (postage)	10	10
1189		10g. blue, red and black	10	10
1190		30g. brn, red & blk (air)	25	15

261 Rotary Emblem

1976. 70th Anniv of Rotary International.

1191	**261**	3g. blue, bistre and black (postage)	10	10
1192		4g. blue, bistre and mauve	10	10
1193		25g. blue, bistre and green (air)	30	15

262 Woman and I.W.Y. Emblem

1976. International Women's Year.

1194	**262**	1g. brown & blue (postage)	10	10
1195		2g. brown and red	10	10
1196		20g. brown & green (air)	25	10

263 Black Palms

1977. Flowering Plants and Trees. Multicoloured.

1197	2g. Type **263** (postage)	10	10
1198	3g. Mburucuya flowers	10	10
1199	20g. Marsh rose (tree) (air)	35	25

264 Nanduti Lace

1977. Multicoloured.

1200	1g. Type **264** (postage)	10	10
1201	5g. Nanduti weaver	10	10
1202	25g. Lady holding jar (air)	40	25

265 F. S. Lopez

1977. 150th Birth Anniv of Marshal Francisco Solano Lopez.

1203	**265**	10g. brown (postage)	10	10
1204		50g. blue (air)	40	50
1205		100g. green	75	60

266 General Bernardino Caballero National College

1978. Cent of National College of Asuncion.

1206	**266**	3g. red (postage)	10	10
1207		4g. blue	10	10
1208		5g. violet	10	10
1209		20g. brown (air)	20	15
1210		25g. purple	25	20
1211		30g. green	35	25

267 Marshal Jose F. Estigarribia, Trumpeter and Flag

268 Congress Emblem

1978. "Salon de Bronce" Commemoration.

1212	**267**	3g. purple, blue and red (postage)	10	10
1213		5g. violet, blue and red	10	10
1214		10g. grey, blue and red	10	10
1215		20g. green, bl & red (air)	25	15
1216		25g. violet, blue and red	30	20
1217		30g. purple, blue and red	35	25

1979. 22nd Latin American Tourism Congress, Asuncion.

1218	**268**	10g. black, blue and red (postage)	10	10
1219		50g. black, blue and red (air)	30	40

269 Spanish Colonial House, Pilar

1980. Bicentenary of Pilar City.

1220	**269**	5g. mult (postage)	10	10
1221		25g. multicoloured (air)	30	20

270 Boeing 707

1980. Inauguration of Paraguayan Airlines Boeing 707 Service.

1222	**270**	20g. mult (postage)	30	10
1223		100g. multicoloured (air)	1·40	70

271 Seminary, Communion Cup and Bible

1981. Air. Centenary of Metropolitan Seminary, Asuncion.

1224	**271**	5g. blue	10	10
1225		10g. brown	10	10
1226		25g. green	30	20
1227		50g. black	60	40

272 U.P.U. Monument, Berne

1981. Centenary of Admission to U.P.U.

1228	**272**	5g. red and black (postage)	10	10
1229		10g. mauve and black	10	10
1230		20g. green and black (air)	50	15
1231		25g. red and black	60	20
1232		50g. blue and black	60	40

273 St. Maria Mazzarello

275 Sun and Map of Americas

274 Stroessner and Bridge over River Itaipua

1981. Air. Death Centenary of Mother Maria Mazzarello (founder of Daughters of Mary).

1233	**273**	20g. green and black	50	15
1234		25g. red and black	60	20
1235		50g. violet and black	60	40

1983. 25th Anniv of President Stroessner City.

1236	**274**	3g. green, blue & blk (postage)	10	10
1237		5g. red, blue and black	10	10
1238		10g. violet, blue and black	10	10
1239		20g. grey, blue & blk (air)	25	15
1240		25g. purple, blue & black	30	20
1241		50g. blue, grey and black	30	40

1985. Air. 25th Anniv of Inter-American Development Bank.

1242	**275**	3g. orange, yellow & pink	10	10
1243		5g. orange, yellow & mauve	10	10
1244		10g. orange, yellow & mauve	10	10
1245		50g. orange, yellow & brown	10	10
1246		65g. orange, yellow & bl	15	10
1247		95g. orange, yellow & green	20	15

276 U.N. Emblem

277 1886 1c. Stamp

1986. Air. 40th Anniv of U.N.O.

1248	**276**	5g. blue and brown	10	10
1249		10g. blue and grey	10	10
1250		50g. blue and black	10	10

1986. Centenary of First Official Stamp.

1251	**277**	5g. deep blue, brown and blue (postage)	10	10
1252		15g. deep blue, brown and blue	10	10
1253		40g. deep blue, brown and blue	10	10
1254	–	65g. blue, green and red (air)	15	15
1255	–	100g. blue, green and red	50	25
1256	–	150g. blue, green and red	70	40

DESIGNS: 65, 100, 150g. 1886 7c. stamp.

278 Integration of the Nations Monument, Colmena

1986. Air. 50th Anniv of Japanese Immigration. Multicoloured.

1257	5g. La Colmena vineyards (horiz)	10	10
1258	10g. Flowers of cherry tree and lapacho (horiz)	10	10
1259	20g. Type **278**	10	10

279 Caballero, Stroessner and Road

1987. Centenary of National Republican Association (Colorado Party).

1260	**279**	5g. multicoloured (postage)	10	10
1261		10g. multicoloured	10	10
1262		25g. multicoloured	10	10
1263	–	150g. multicoloured (air)	25	40
1264	–	170g. multicoloured	55	20
1265	–	200g. multicoloured	60	25

DESIGN: 150 to 200g. Gen. Bernardino Caballero (President 1881–86 and founder of party), Pres. Alfredo Stroessner and electrification of countryside.

280 Emblem of Visit

281 Silver Mate

1988. Visit of Pope John Paul II.

1266	**280**	10g. blue and black (postage)	10	10
1267		20g. blue and black	10	10
1268		50g. blue and black	15	10
1269	–	100g. multicoloured (air)	55	20
1270	–	120g. multicoloured	65	25
1271	–	150g. multicoloured	80	35

DESIGN—HORIZ: 100 to 150g. Pope and Caacupe Basilica.

1988. Air. Centenary of New Germany Colony. Multicoloured.

1272	90g. Type **281**	25	10
1273	105g. Mate ("Ilex paraguayensis") plantation	30	20
1274	120g. As No. 1273	35	25

1988. Air. 75th Anniv of Paraguay Philatelic Centre. No. 1249 optd * **75o ANIVERSARIO DE FUNDACION CENTRO FILATELICO DEL PARAGUAY 15 JUNIO-1913 - 1988.**

1275	**276**	10g. blue and grey	10	10

283 Pres. Stroessner and Government Palace

1988. Air. Re-election of President Stroessner.

1276 **283** 200g. multicoloured . . 55 25
1277 500g. multicoloured . . 1·40 90
1278 1000g. multicoloured . . 2·75 1·50

1989. "Parafil 89" Stamp Exhibition. Nos. 1268 and 1270 optd **PARAFIL 89**.

1279 **280** 50g. blue and black (postage) 15 10
1280 – 120g. multicoloured (air) 35 25

285 Green-winged Macaw

1989. Birds. Multicoloured.

1281 50g. Type **285** (postage) . . 20 20
1282 100g. Brazilian merganser (horiz) (air) 20 20
1283 300g. Greater rhea (horiz) 60 60
1284 500g. Toco toucan (horiz) 95 95
1285 1000g. Bare-faced curassow (horiz) . . . . 2·10 2·10
1286 2000g. Wagler's macaw and blue and yellow macaw 4·00 4·00

286 Anniversary Emblem

1990. Centenary of Organization of American States. Multicoloured.

1287 50g. Type **286** 10 10
1288 100g. Organization and anniversary emblems (vert) 10 10
1289 200g. Map of Paraguay . . 45 15

287 Basket **288** Flags on Map

1990. America. Pre-Columbian Life. Mult.

1290 150g. Type **287** (postage) . . 15 10
1291 500g. Guarani post (air) . . 1·10 95

1990. Postal Union of the Americas and Spain Colloquium. Multicoloured.

1292 200g. Type **288** 20 15
1293 250g. First Paraguay stamp 25 15
1294 350g. Paraguay 1990 America first day cover (horiz) 35 25

289 Planned Building

1990. Centenary of National University. Mult.

1295 300g. Type **289** 70 55
1296 400g. Present building . . . 95 75
1297 600g. Old building . . . . 1·40 1·10

290 Guarambare Church

1990. Franciscan Churches. Multicoloured.

1298 50g. Type **290** 10 10
1299 100g. Yaguaron Church . . 25 20
1300 200g. Ita Church 45 35

1991. Visit of King and Queen of Spain. Nos. 1290/1 optd **Vista de sus Majestades Los Reyes de Espana 22-24 Octubre 1990.**

1301 **287** 150g. mult (postage) . . 15 10
1302 – 500g. multicoloured (air) 1·10 95

292 "Human Rights" (Hugo Pistilli)

1991. 40th Anniv of United Nations Development Programme. Multicoloured.

1303 50g. Type **292** 10 10
1304 100g. "United Nations" (sculpture, Hermann Guggiari) 10 20
1305 150f. First Miguel de Cervantes prize, awarded to Augusto Roa Bastos, 1989 . . . . 15 10

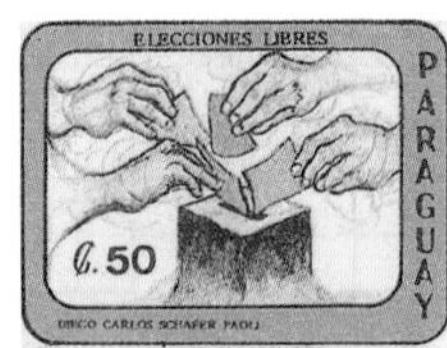

294 Hands and Ballot Box (free elections)

1991. Democracy. Multicoloured.

1308 50g. Type **294** (postage) . . 10 10
1309 100g. Sun (State and Catholic Church) (vert) 10 10
1310 200g. Arrows and male and female symbols (human rights) (vert) 55 10
1311 300g. Dove and flag (freedom of the press) (vert) (air) 50 20
1312 500g. Woman and child welcoming man (return of exiles) 70 25
1313 3000g. Crowd with banners (democracy) . . . . . . 4·75 2·75

295 Julio Manuel Morales (gynaecologist)

1991. Medical Professors.

1314 **295** 50g. mult (postage) . . . 10 10
1315 – 100g. multicoloured . . 10 10
1316 – 200g. multicoloured . . 50 10
1317 – 300g. brown, black & green 70 20
1318 – 350g. brown, black and green (air) 75 20
1319 – 500g. multicoloured . . 1·10 50

DESIGNS: 100g. Carlos Gatti (surgeon); 200g. Gustavo Gonzalez (symptomatologist); 300g. Juan Max Boettner (physician and musician); 350g. Juan Boggino (pathologist); 500g. Andres Barbero (founder of Paraguayan Red Cross).

1991. "Espamer '91" Spain–Latin America Stamp Exhibition, Buenos Aires. Nos. 1298/1300 optd **ESPAMER 91 BUENOS AIRES 5 14 Jul** and Conquistador in oval.

1323 50g. multicoloured 10 10
1324 100g. multicoloured 10 10
1325 200g. multicoloured 60 10

298 Ruy Diaz de Guzman (historian)

1991. Writers and Musicians. Multicoloured.

1326 50g. Type **298** (postage) . . 10 10
1327 100g. Maria Talavera (war chronicler) (vert) 10 10
1328 150g. Augusto Roa Bastos (writer and 1989 winner of Miguel de Cervantes Prize) (vert) 40 10
1329 200g. Jose Asuncion Flores (composer of "La Guarania") (vert) (air) . . 45 10
1330 250g. Felix Perez Cardozo (harpist and composer) . . 65 40
1331 300g. Juan Carlos Moreno Gonzalez (composer) . . 85 45

299 Battle of Tavare

1991. America. Voyages of Discovery. Mult.

1332 100g. Type **299** (postage) . . 10 10
1333 300g. Arrival of Domingo Martinez de Irala in Paraguay (air) 75 50

300 "Compass of Life" (Alfredo Moraes)

1991. Paintings. Multicoloured.

1334 50g. Type **300** (postage) . . 10 10
1335 100g. "Callejon Illuminated" (Michael Burt) 35 10
1336 150g. "Arete" (Lucy Yegros) 45 10
1337 200g. "Itinerants" (Hugo Bogado Barrios) (air) . . 50 10
1338 250g. "Travellers without a Ship" (Bernardo Ismachoviez) 65 15
1339 300g. "Guarani" (Lotte Schulz) 75 50

301 Chaco Peccary

1992. Endangered Mammals. Multicoloured.

1340 50g. Type **301** 10 10
1341 100g. Ocelot (horiz) 10 10
1342 150g. Brazilian tapir 35 10
1343 200g. Maned wolf 40 10

302 Geometric Design, Franciscan Church, Caazapa

1992. 500th Anniv of Discovery of America by Columbus (1st series). Church Roof Tiles. Mult.

1344 50g. Type **302** 10 10
1345 100g. Church, Jesuit church, Trinidad 10 10
1346 150g. Missionary ship, Jesuit church, Trinidad 50 10
1347 200g. Plant, Franciscan church, Caazapa 50 10

See also Nos. 1367/71.

1992. "Granada '92" International Thematic Stamp Exhibition. Nos. 1344/7 optd **GRANADA '92** and emblem.

1348 50g. multicoloured 10 10
1349 100g. multicoloured 10 10
1350 150g. multicoloured 40 10
1351 200g. multicoloured 50 10

304 Malcolm L. Norment (founder) and Emblem

1992. 68th Anniv of Paraguay Leprosy Foundation. Multicoloured.

1352 50g. Type **304** 10 10
1353 250g. Gerhard Hansen (discoverer of leprosy bacillus) 50 15

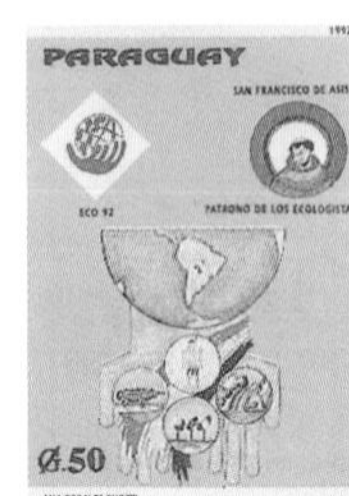

305 Southern Hemisphere and Ecology Symbols on Hands

1992. 2nd United Nations Conference on Environment and Development, Rio de Janeiro. Multicoloured.

1354 50g. Type **305** 10 10
1355 100g. Butterfly and chimneys emitting smoke 10 10
1356 250g. Tree and map of South America on globe 45 15

306 Factories and Cotton (economy)

1992. National Population and Housing Census. Multicoloured.

1357 50g. Type **306** 10 10
1358 200g. Houses (vert) 15 10
1359 250g. Numbers and stylized people (population) (vert) 20 15
1360 300g. Abacus (education) . . 50 20

307 Football

1992. Olympic Games, Barcelona. Multicoloured.

1361 50g. Type **307** 10 10
1362 100g. Tennis 10 10
1363 150g. Running 10 10
1364 200g. Swimming (horiz) . . 15 10
1365 250g. Judo 20 15
1366 350g. Fencing (horiz) . . . 50 20

308 Brother Luis Bolanos

1992. 500th Anniv of Discovery of America by Columbus (2nd series). Evangelists. Mult.

1367 50g. Type **308** (translator of Catechism into Guarani and founder of Guarani Christian settlements) . . 10 10
1368 100g. Brother Juan de San Bernardo (Franciscan and first Paraguayan martyr) 10 10
1369 150g. St. Roque Gonzalez de Santa Cruz (Jesuit missionary and first Paraguayan saint) 10 10

1370 200g. Fr. Amancio Gonzalez (founder of Melodia settlement) 15 10
1371 250g. Mgr. Juan Sinforiano Bogarin (first Archbishop of Asuncion) (vert) . . . 45 15

309 Fleet approaching Shore

1992. America. 500th Anniv of Discovery of America by Columbus. Multicoloured.
1372 150g. Type **309** (postage) . . 30 10
1373 350g. Christopher Columbus (vert) (air) 50 20

1992. 30th Anniv of United Nations Information Centre in Paraguay. Nos. 1354/6 optd **NACIONES UNIDAS 1992 - 30 ANOS CENTRO INFORMACION OUN EN PARAGUAY.**
1374 50g. multicoloured 10 10
1375 100g. multicoloured 10 10
1376 250g. multicoloured 45 15

1992. Christmas. Nos. 1367/9 optd **Navidad 92.**
1377 50g. multicoloured 10 10
1378 100g. multicoloured 10 10
1379 150g. multicoloured 35 10

1992. "Parafil 92" Paraguay–Argentina Stamp Exhibition, Buenos Aires. Nos. 1372/3 optd **PARAFIL 92.**
1380 150g. multicoloured (postage) 35 10
1381 350g. multicoloured (air) . . 50 20

313 Planting and Hoeing

1992. 50th Anniv of Pan-American Agricultural Institute. Multicoloured.
1382 50g. Type **313** 10 10
1383 100g. Test tubes 10 10
1384 200g. Cotton plant in cupped hands 15 10
1385 250g. Cattle and maize plant 45 15

314 Yolanda Bado de Artecona

1992. Centenary of Paraguayan Writers' College. Multicoloured.
1386 50g. Type **314** 10 10
1387 100g. Jose Ramon Silva . . 10 10
1388 150g. Abelardo Brugada Valpy 10 10
1389 200g. Tomas Varela 15 10
1390 250g. Jose Livio Lezcano . . 45 15
1391 300g. Francisco I. Fernandez 50 20

315 Members' Flags and Map of South America **316** Orange Flowers (Gilda Hellmers)

1993. 1st Anniv (1992) of Treaty of Asuncion forming Mercosur (common market of Argentina, Brazil, Paraguay and Uruguay). Multicoloured.
1392 50g. Type **315** 10 10
1393 350g. Flags encircling globe showing map of South America 65 20

1993. 50th Anniv of St. Isabel Leprosy Association. Flower paintings by artists named. Multicoloured.
1394 50g. Type **316** 10 10
1395 200g. Luis Alberto Balmelli 15 10

1396 250g. Lili del Monico . . . 20 15
1397 350g. Brunilde Guggiari . . 50 20

317 Goethe (after J. Lips) and Manuscript of Poem

1993. Centenary of Goethe College.
1398 **317** 50g. brown, black & blue 10 10
1399 – 200g. multicoloured . . 40 10
DESIGN: 200g. Goethe (after J. Tischbein).

1993. "Brasiliana 93" International Stamp Exhibition, Rio de Janeiro. Nos. 1398/9 optd **BRASILIANA 93.**
1400 50g. brown, black and blue 10 10
1401 200g. multicoloured 15 10

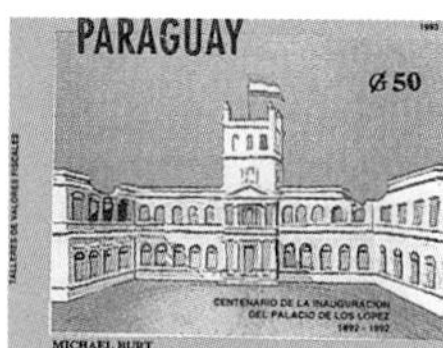

319 Palace (Michael Burt)

1993. Centenary (1992) of Los Lopez (Government) Palace, Asuncion. Paintings of palace by artists named. Multicolured.
1402 50g. Type **319** 10 10
1403 100g. Esperanza Gill 10 10
1404 200g. Emili Aparici 15 10
1405 250g. Hugo Bogado Barrios (vert) 15 10

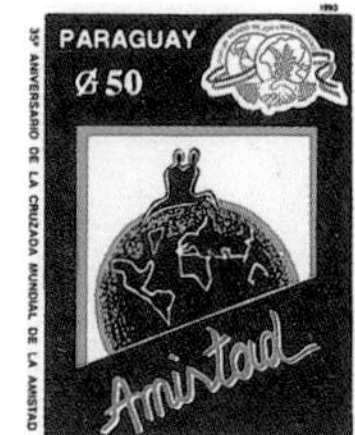

320 Couple sitting on Globe and Emblem

1993. 35th Anniv of World Friendship Crusade.
1406 **320** 50g. black, blue and mauve 10 10
1407 – 100g. multicoloured . . 10 10
1408 – 200g. multicoloured . . 15 10
1409 – 250g. multicoloured . . 15 10
DESIGNS: 100g. Dr. Ramon Artemio Bracho (founder), map of Americas and emblem; 200g. Children and sun emerging from cloud; 250g. Couple hugging and emblem.

1993. Inauguration of President Juan Carlos Wasmosy. Nos. 1402/5 optd **TRANSMISION DEL MANDO PRESIDENCIAL GRAL. ANDRES RODRIGUEZ ING. JUAN C. WASMOSY 15 DE AGOSTO 1993.**
1410 50g. multicoloured 10 10
1411 100g. multicoloured 10 10
1412 200g. multicoloured 15 10
1413 250g. multicoloured 15 10

322 "Church of the Incarnation" (Juan Guerra Gaja)

1993. Centenary of Church of the Incarnation. Paintings. Multicoloured.
1414 50g. Type **322** 10 10
1415 350g. "Church of the Incarnation" (Hector Blas Ruiz) (horiz) 25 20

323 Bush Dog

1993. America. Endangered Animals. Mult.
1416 250g. Type **323** (postage) . . 40 10
1417 50g. Great anteater (air) . . 10 10

1993. 80th Anniv of World Food Programme. Nos. 1383/4 optd **'30 ANOS DEL PROGRAMA MUNDIAL DE ALIMENTOS'** and emblem.
1418 100g. multicoloured 10 10
1419 200g. multicoloured 15 10

325 Children Carol-singing

1993. Christmas. Multicoloured.
1420 50g. Type **325** 10 10
1421 250g. Wise men following star 15 10

326 Boy and Girl Scouts

1993. 80th Anniv of Paraguay Scouts Association. Multicoloured.
1422 50g. Type **326** 10 10
1423 100g. Boy scouts in camp 10 10
1424 200g. Lord Robert Baden-Powell (founder of Scouting movement) . . . 15 10
1425 250g. Girl scout with flag 15 10

327 Cecilio Baez

1994. Centenary of First Graduation of Lawyers from National University, Asuncion.
1426 **327** 50g. red and crimson . . 10 10
1427 – 100g. yellow and orange 10 10
1428 – 250g. yellow and green 15 10
1429 – 500g. blue and deep blue 30 20
DESIGNS—VERT: 100g. Benigno Riquelme. HORIZ: 250g. Emeterio Gonzalez; 500g. J. Gaspar Villamayor.

328 Basketball **329** Penalty Kick

1994. 50th Anniv of Phoenix Sports Association. Multicoloured.
1430 50g. Type **328** 10 10
1431 200g. Football 15 10
1432 250g. Pedro Andres Garcia Arias (founder) and tennis (horiz) 15 10

1994. World Cup Football Championship, U.S.A. Multicoloured.
1433 250g. Type **329** 15 10
1434 500g. Tackle 55 20
1435 1000g. Dribbling ball past opponent . . . . 1·10 75

330 Runner

1994. Centenary of International Olympic Committee. Multicoloured.
1436 350g. Type **330** 25 20
1437 400g. Athlete lighting Olympic Flame 55 20

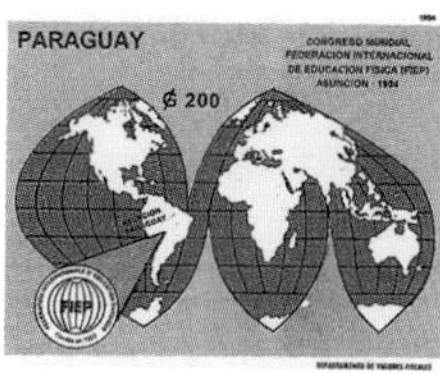

331 World Map and Emblem

1994. World Congress of International Federation for Physical Education, Asuncion. Multicoloured.
1438 200g. Type **331** 15 10
1439 1000g. Family exercising and flag (vert) . . . . . 1·25 80

1994. Brazil, Winners of World Cup Football Championship. Nos. 1433/5 optd **BRASIL Campeon Mundial de Futbol Estados Unidos '94.**
1440 250g. multicoloured 40 10
1441 500g. multicoloured 80 50
1442 1000g. multicoloured . . . 1·60 95

1994. 25th Anniv of First Manned Moon Landing. No. 1407 optd **25 Anos, Conquista de la Luna por el hombre 1969 - 1994.**
1443 100g. multicoloured 10 10

334 Barrios

1994. 50th Death Anniv of Agustin Pio Barrios Mangore (guitarist). Multicoloured.
1444 250g. Type **334** 15 10
1445 500g. Barrios wearing casual clothes and a hat 65 20

335 Police Commandant, 1913

1994. 151st Anniv of Police Force. Multicoloured.
1446 50g. Type **335** 10 10
1447 250g. Carlos Bernardino Cacabelos (first Commissioner) and Pedro Nolasco Fernandez (first Chief of Asuncion Police Dept) 15 10

336 Maguari Stork

1994. "Parafil 94" Stamp Exhibition. Birds. Mult.
1448 100g. Type **336** 35 35
1449 150g. Yellow-billed cardinal 35 35
1450 400g. Green kingfisher (vert) 2·00 75
1451 500g. Jabiru (vert) . . . . . 2·25 75

337 Nicolas Copernicus and Eclipse

1994. Total Eclipse of the Sun, November 1994. Astronomers. Multicoloured.
1452 50g. Type **337** 10 10
1453 200g. Johannes Kepler and sun dial, St. Cosmas and Damian Jesuit settlement 15 10

338 Steam Locomotive

1994. America. Postal Transport. Multicoloured.
1454 100g. Type **338** . . . . . . 1·00 60
1455 1000g. Express mail motor cycle . . . . 1·25 80

339 Mother and Child

1994. International Year of the Family. Details of paintings by Olga Blinder. Multicoloured.
1456 50g. Type **339** 10 10
1457 250g. Mother and children 15 10

340 Holy Family and Angels

1994. Christmas. Ceramic Figures. Multicoloured.
1458 150g. Type **340** 10 10
1459 700g. Holy Family (vert) . . 80 55

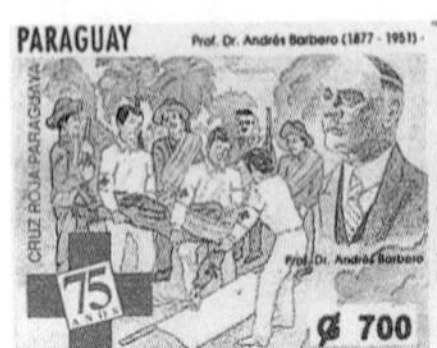

341 Red Cross Workers and Dr. Andres Barbero (founder)

1994. 75th Anniv of Paraguay Red Cross. Mult.
1460 150g. Scouts, anniversary emblem and Henri Dunant (founder of International Red Cross) 10 10
1461 700g. Type **341** 80 55

342 Sculpture by Herman Guggiari and Pope John Paul II

1994. 90th Anniv of San Jose College. Mult.
1462 200g. Type **342** 15 10
1463 250g. College entrance and Pope John Paul II 15 10

343 Pasteur and Hospital Facade

1995. Paraguayan Red Cross. Death Centenary of Louis Pasteur (chemist) and Centenary of Clinical Hospital.
1464 **343** 1000g. multicoloured . . 1·10 75

344 Couple

1995. Anti-AIDS Campaign. Multicoloured.
1465 500g. Type **344** 60 20
1466 1000g. Sad and happy blood droplets . . . . 1·00 50

345 Jug and Loaf

1995. 50th Anniv of F.A.O. Paintings by Hernan Miranda. Multicoloured.
1467 950g. Type **345** . . . . . . 1·00 75
1468 2000g. Melon and leaf . . . 2·10 1·40

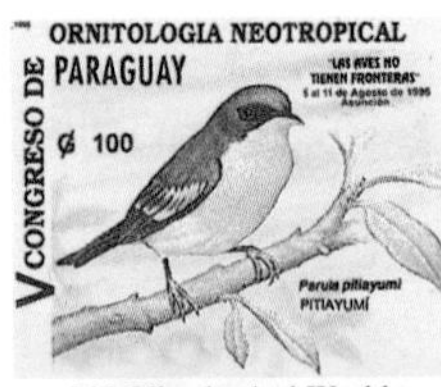

346 Olive-backed Warbler

1995. 5th Neo-tropical Ornithological Congress, Asuncion. Multicoloured.
1469 100g. Type **346** 10 10
1470 200g. Swallow-tailed manakin 15 10
1471 600g. Troupial 65 30
1472 1000g. Hooded siskin . . . 1·00 75

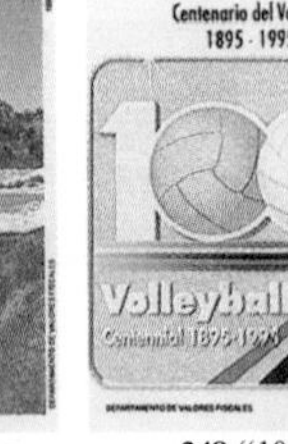

347 River Monday Rapids

348 "100"

1995. 5th International Town, Ecology and Tourism Symposium. Multicoloured.
1473 1150g. Type **347** . . . . . 1·25 85
1474 1300g. Aregua railway station . . . . 4·50 2·75

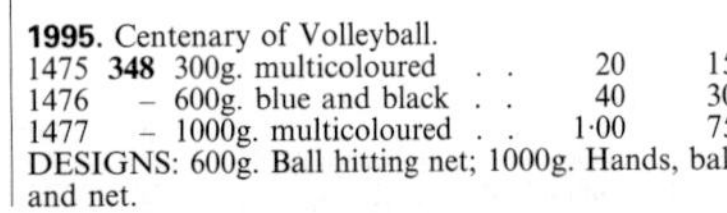

1995. Centenary of Volleyball.
1475 **348** 300g. multicoloured . . 20 15
1476 – 600g. blue and black . . 40 30
1477 – 1000g. multicoloured . . 1·00 75
DESIGNS: 600g. Ball hitting net; 1000g. Hands, ball and net.

349 Macizo, Acahay

1995. America. Environmental Protection. Mult.
1478 950g. Type **349** 85 45
1479 2000g. Tinfunque Reserve, Chaco (vert) . . . . . . 1·60 1·00

350 Anniversary Emblem

1995. 50th Anniv of U.N.O. Multicoloured.
1480 200g. Type **350** 15 10
1481 3000g. Stylized figures supporting emblem . . . 3·25 2·00

351 Couple holding Star

1995. Christmas. Multicoloured.
1482 200g. Type **351** 15 10
1483 1000g. Crib 95 50

352 Marti and "Hedychium coronarium"

1995. Birth Cent of Jose Marti (revolutionary). Multicoloured.
1484 200g. Type **352** 10 10
1485 1000g. Marti, Cuban national flag and "Hedychium coronarium" (horiz) . . . . 1·10 50

353 "Railway Station" (Asuncion)

1996. 25th Latin American and Caribbean Forum of Lions International. Paintings by Esperanza Gill. Multicoloured.
1486 200g. Type **353** 10 10
1487 1000g. "Viola House" . . . 1·10 70

354 "Cattleya nobilior"

1996. Orchids. Multicoloured.
1488 100g. Type **354** 10 10
1489 200g. "Oncidium varicosum" 10 10
1490 1000g. "Oncidium jonesianum" (vert) . . . 1·00 45
1491 1150g. "Sophronitis cernua" 1·10 55

355 Emblems and Gymnast on "Stamp"

1996. Centenary of Modern Olympic Games and Olympic Games, Atlanta. Multicoloured.
1492 500g. Type **355** 30 20
1493 1000g. Emblems and runner on "stamp" 60 45

356 Bosco, Monks and Boys

1996. Centenary of Salesian Brothers in Paraguay. Multicoloured.
1494 200g. Type **356** 10 10
1495 300g. Madonna and Child, Pope John Paul II and St. John Bosco (vert) . . 15 10
1496 1000g. St. John Bosco (founder) and map . . . 40 20

357 Family Outing (Silvia Cacares Baez)

1996. 50th Anniv of UNICEF. Multicoloured.
1497 1000g. Type **357** 50 30
1498 1300g. Families (Cinthia Perez Alderete) 65 40

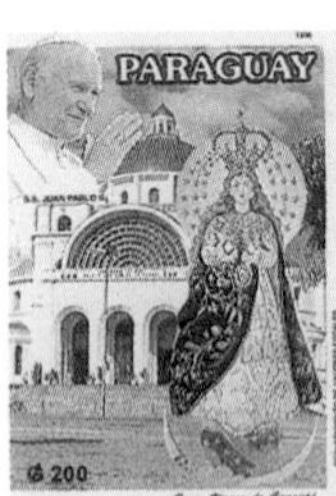

358 Pope John Paul II, Caacupe Cathedral and Virgin

359 Woman

1996. Our Lady of Caacupe. Multicoloured.
1499 200g. Type **358** 10 10
1500 1300g. Pope John Paul II, floodlit cathedral and Virgin (horiz) 65 40

1996. America. Traditional Costumes. Mult.
1501 500g. Type **359** 25 20
1502 1000g. Couple 50 30

360 Boxes and Food

1996. International Year for Eradication of Poverty. Multicoloured.
1503 1000g. Type **360** 50 30
1504 1150g. Boy with boxes and food (vert) 55 30

361 Mother and Baby

362 "Eryphanis automedon"

1996. Christmas. Multicoloured.
1505 200g. Type **361** 10 10
1506 1000g. Mother with smiling child 50 30

1997. Butterflies. Multicoloured.
1507 200g. Type **362** 10 10
1508 500g. "Dryadula phaetusa" 25 15
1509 1000g. "Vanessa myrinna" 50 30
1510 1150g. Rare tiger 55 30

363 First Government Palace (legislative building)

1997. Buildings. Multicoloured.
1511 200g. Type **363** 10 10
1512 1000g. Patri Palace (postal headquarters) 50 30

364 Crucifix, Piribebuy

1997. Year of Jesus Christ.
1513 **364** 1000g. multicoloured . . 50 30

365 Summit Emblem

1997. 11th Group of Rio Summit Meeting, Asuncion.
1514 **365** 1000g. multicoloured . . 40 20

366 Cactus

1997. "The Changing Climate—Everyone's Concern". Plants. Multicoloured.
1515 300g. Type **366** 15 10
1516 500g. "Bromelia balansae" (vert) 20 10
1517 1000g. "Monvillea kroenlaini" 40 20

367 Tiger Cat

1997. 1st Mercosur (South American Common Market), Chile and Bolivia Stamp Exhibition, Asuncion. Mammals. Multicoloured.
1518 200g. Type **367** 10 10
1519 1000g. Black howler monkey (vert) 40 20
1520 1150g. Paca 50 30

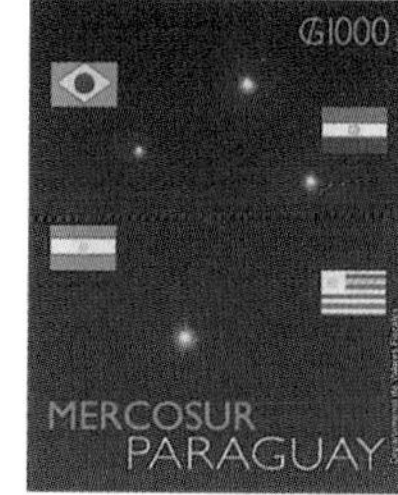

368 Members' Flags and Southern Cross

1997. 6th Anniv of Mercosur (South American Common Market).
1521 **368** 1000g. multicoloured . . 40 20

369 Postman and Letters circling Globe

370 Neri Kennedy (javelin)

1997. America. The Postman. Multicoloured.
1522 1000g. Type **369** 40 20
1523 1150g. Weather and terrain aspects of postal delivery and postman (horiz) . . . 50 30

1997. 50th Anniv of National Sports Council. Multicoloured.
1524 200g. Type **370** 10 10
1525 1000g. Ramon Milciades Gimenez Gaona (discus) 40 20

1997. "Mevifil '97" First International Exhibition of Philatelic Audio-visual and Computer Systems, Buenos Aires, Argentina. Nos. 1446/7 optd **MEVIFIL '97**.
1526 50g. multicoloured 10 10
1527 250g. multicoloured 10 10

372 Mother and Child (Olga Blinder)

373 Boy

1997. Christmas. Multicoloured.
1528 200g. Type **372** 10 10
1529 1000g. Mother and child (Hernan Miranda) 40 20

1997. "Children of the World with AIDS". Children's Paintings. Multicoloured.
1530 500g. Type **373** 20 10
1531 1000g. Girl 40 20

374 Drinking Vessel and Emblem forming "70"

375 Julio Cesar Romero (1986 World Cup team member)

1997. 70th Anniv of Asuncion Rotary Club.
1532 **374** 1150g. multicoloured . . 50 30

1998. World Cup Football Championship, France. Multicoloured.
1533 200g. Type **375** 10 10
1534 500g. Carlos Gamarra (World Cup team member) tackling opponent 20 10
1535 1000g. World Cup team (horiz) 40 20

376 Silver Tetra

1998. Fishes. Multicoloured.
1536 200g. Type **376** 10 10
1537 300g. Spotted sorubim . . . 15 10
1538 500g. Dorado 20 10
1539 1000g. Pira jagua 40 20

377 Painting by Carlos Colombino

378 Cep

1998. Paintings by artists named. Multicoloured.
1540 200g. Type **377** 10 10
1541 300g. Felix Toranzos . . . 15 10
1542 400g. Edith Gimenez . . . 15 10
1543 1000g. Ricardo Migliorisi (horiz) 40 20

1998. Fungi. Multicoloured.
1544 400g. Type **378** 15 10
1545 600g. Parasol mushroom . . 25 15
1546 1000g. Collared earthstar . . 40 20

379 Carlos Lopez's House, Botanical and Zoological Gardens, Asuncion

1998. 50th Anniv of Organization of American States. Multicoloured.
1547 500g. Type **379** 20 10
1548 1000g. Villa Palmerola, Aregua 40 20

380 Door of Sanctuary, Caazapa Church

1998. 400th Anniv of Ordination of First Paraguayan Priests by Brother Hernando de Trejo y Sanabria. Multicoloured.
1549 400g. Type **380** 15 10
1550 1700g. Statue of St. Francis of Assisi, Atyra Church (horiz) 70 40

381 "Acacia caven"

1998. Flowers. Multicoloured.
1551 100g. Type **381** 10 10
1552 600g. "Cordia trichotoma" 25 15
1553 1900g. "Glandularia" sp. . . 80 45

382 Ruins of the Mission of Jesus, Itapua

1998. Mercosur (South American Common Market) Heritage Sites.
1554 **382** 5000g. multicoloured . . 2·10 1·25

383 Serafina Davalos (first female lawyer in Paraguay) and National College

1998. America. Famous Women. Multicoloured.
1555 1600g. Type **383** 60 35
1556 1700g. Adela Speratti (first director) and Teachers' Training College 65 35

384 Abstract (Carlos Colombino)

1998. 50th Anniv of Universal Declaration of Human Rights. Multicoloured.
1557 500g. Type **384** 20 10
1558 1000g. Man on crutches (after Joel Filartiga) . . . 40 20

385 Crib

1998. Christmas. Multicoloured.
1559 300g. Type **385** 10 10
1560 1600g. Crib (different) (vert) 60 35

386 Coral Cobra

1999. Reptiles. Multicoloured.
1561 100g. Type **386** 10 10
1562 300g. Ground lizard 10 10
1563 1600g. Red-footed tortoise 65 35
1564 1700g. Paraguay caiman . . 70 40

1999. "Chaco Peace 99" Stamp Exhibition, Paraguay and Bolivia. No. 1542 optd **1era. Exposicion Filatelica Paraguayo-Boliviana PAZ DEL CHACO 99**.
1565 400g. multicoloured 15 10

388 Painting by Ignacio Nunes Soler

1999. Paintings. Showing paintings by named artists.
1566 500g. Type **388** 20 10
1567 1600g. Modesto Delgado Rodas 65 35
1568 1700g. Jaime Bestard . . . 70 40

389 Carlos Humberto Parades being tackled

1999. American Cup Football Championship, Paraguay. Multicoloured.
1569 300g. Type **389** 10 10
1570 500g. South American Football Federation Building, Luque, Paraguay (horiz) 20 10
1571 1900g. Feliciano Caceres Stadium, Luque (horiz) 75 45

390 Toucan

1999. 50th Anniv of S.O.S. Children's Villages. Multicoloured.
1572 1700g. Type **390** 70 40
1573 1900g. Toucan (different) (vert) 75 45

391 Government Palace

1999. Assassination of Dr. Luis Marua Argana (Vice-president, 1998–99). Multicoloured.
1574 100g. Type **391** 10 10
1575 500g. Dr. Argana (vert) . . 20 10
1576 1500g. Crowd before National Congress building 60 35

392 *Cochlospermum regium*

1999. Medicinal Plants. Multicoloured.
1577 600g. Type **392** 25 10
1578 700g. *Borago officinalis* . . . 30 15
1579 1700g. *Passiflora cincinnata* 70 40

393 "The Man who carries the Storm"

1999. America. A New Millennium without Arms. Showing paintings by Ricardo Migliorisi. Mult.
1580 1500g. Type **393** 60 35
1581 3000g. "The Man who dominates the Storm" (vert) . . . . 1·25 75

394 "Couple" (Olga Blinder)

1999. International Year of the Elderly. Mult.
1582 1000g. Type **394** 40 20
1583 1900g. "Old Woman" (Marma de los Reyes Omella Herrero) (vert) . . 75 45

395 "Mother and Child" (Manuel Viedma)

1999. Christmas. Multicoloured.
1584 300g. Type **395** 10 10
1585 1600g. "Nativity" (Federico Ordinana) 65 35

396 *Tabebuia impetiginosa*

1999. Centenary of Pedro Juan Caballero City. Multicoloured.
1586 1000g. Type **396** 40 20
1587 1600g. *Tabebuia pulcherrima* (vert) 65 35

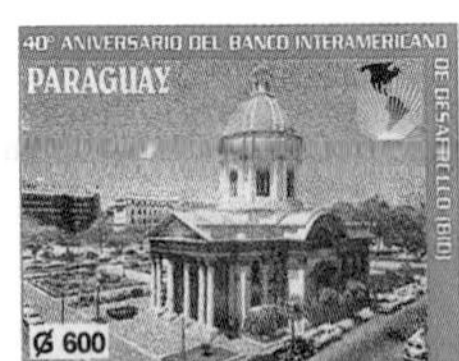

397 Oratory of the Virgin Our Lady of the Assumption and National Mausoleum

1999. 40th Anniv of Inter-American Development Bank. Multicoloured.
1588 600g. Type **397** 25 15
1589 700g. Government Palace 30 15

398 Carmen Casco de Lara Castro and "Conjunction" (bronze sculpture, Domingo Rivarola)

2000. International Women's Day. Carmen Casco de Lara Castro (founder of National Commission for Human Rights). Multicoloured.
1590 400g. Type **398** 15 10
1591 2000g. Carmen Casco de Lara Castro and "Violation" (bronze sculpture, Gustavo Beckelman) 80 45

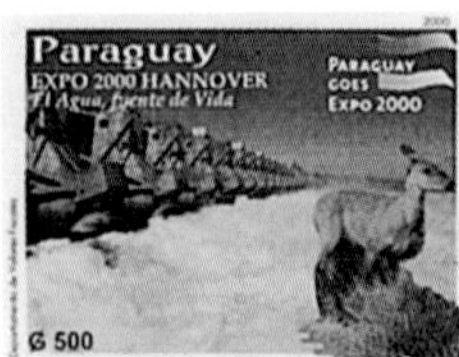

399 Hydroelectric Dam, Yacyreta, and Marsh Deer

2000. "EXPO 2000" World's Fair, Hanover, Germany. Showing bi-lateral development projects. Multicoloured.
1592 500g. Type **399** (Paraguay–Argentine Republic) . . . 20 10
1593 2500g. Hydroelectric dam, Itaipu and Brazilian tapir (Paraguay–Brazil) . . . . 1·00 60

400 Students and Pope John Paul II

2000. Centenary of the Daughters of Maria Auxiliadora College. Multicoloured.
1594 600g. Type **400** 25 15
1595 2000g. College building . . 80 45

401 Footballers chasing Ball

2000. Olympic Games, Sydney. Multicoloured.
1596 2500g. Type **401** 70 40
1597 3000g. Francisco Rojas Soto (athlete), Munich Olympics, 1972 (horiz) . . 85 50

402 Adult Hands protecting Child (Nahuel Moreno Lezcano)

2000. 10th Anniv of United Nations Convention on the Rights of the Child. Multicoloured.
1598 1500g. Type **402** 45 25
1599 1700g. Hand prints (Claudia Alessandro Irala Chavez) (horiz) 50 30

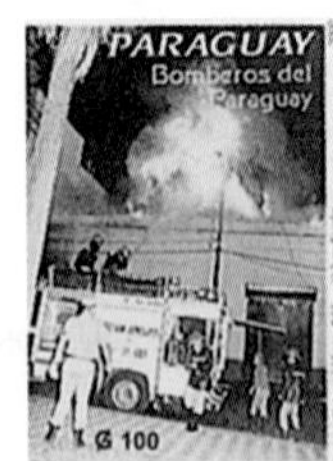

403 Firemen attending to Fire

2000. 95th Anniv of Fire Service. Multicoloured.
1600 100g. Type **403** 10 10
1601 200g. Badge and fireman wearing 1905 dress uniform 10 10
1602 1500g. Firemen attending fire (horiz) 45 25
1603 1600g. Firemen using hose (horiz) 45 25

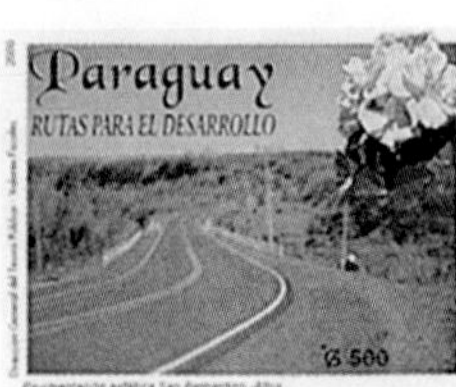

404 Stretch of Road from San Bernardino to Altos

2000. Road Development Scheme. Multicoloured.
1604 500g. Type **404** 15 10
1605 3000g. Gaspar Rodriguez de Francia motorway 85 50

405 Signpost and Emblem

2000. America. AIDS Awareness Campaign. Mult.
1606 1500g. Type **405** 45 25
1607 2500g. Ribbon emblem on noughts and crosses grid 70 40

406 "Love and Peace" (metal sculpture, Hugo Pistilli)

2000. International Year of Culture and Peace. Multicoloured.
1608 500g. Type **406** 15 10
1609 2000g. "For Peace" (metal sculpture, Herman Guggiari) 60 35

407 "Holy Family" (metal sculpture, Hugo Pistilli)

2000. Christmas. Multicoloured.
1610 100g. Type **407** 10 10
1611 500g. Poem, pen and Jose Luis Appleyard (poet and writer) 15 10
1612 2000g. Nativity (crib firgures) (horiz) 65 35

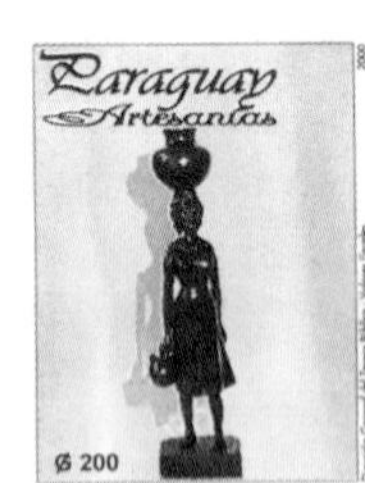

408 Country Woman (sculpture, Behage)

2000. Art. Multicoloured.
1613 200g. Type **408** 10 10
1614 1500g. Drinking vessels (Quintin Velazquez) (horiz) 45 25
1615 2000g. Silver orchid brooch (Quirino Torres) 65 35

409 Flores

2000. 30th Birth Anniv (2002) of Jose Asuncion Flores (musician). Multicoloured.
1616 100g. Type **409** 10 10
1617 1500g. Violin 45 25
1618 2500g. Trombone 70 40

OFFICIAL STAMPS

O 14

O 19

O 20

O 37

1886. Various types as O **14**, O **19** and O **20** optd **OFICIAL**. (a) Imperf.

O32		1c. orange	3·50	2·25
O33		2c. violet	3·50	2·25
O34		5c. orange	3·50	2·25
O35		7c. green	3·50	2·25
O36		10c. brown	3·50	2·25
O37		15c. blue	8·50	11·00
O38		20c. lake	3·50	2·25
		(b) New colours. Perf.		
O39		1c. green	80	65
O40		2c. red	80	65
O41		5c. blue	80	65
O42		7c. orange	80	65
O43		10c. lake	80	65
O44		15c. brown	15·00	9·00
O45		20c. blue	80	65

1889. Stamp of 1889 surch **OFICIAL** and value. Perf.

O47	**25**	1 on 15c. purple	1·60	75
O48		2 on 10c. purple	1·60	75

1889. Stamp of 1889 surch **OFICIAL** and value. Imperf.

O49	**25**	3 on 15c. purple	1·60	75
O50		5 on 15c. brown	1·60	75

1890. Stamps of 1887 optd **OFICIAL** or **Oficial**.

O58	**24**	1c. green	10	10
O59		2c. red	15	10
O60		5c. blue	15	10
O61		7c. brown	1·40	75
O55		10c. mauve	20	15
O63		15c. orange	20	15
O64		20c. pink	25	15
O65		50c. grey	15	15
O86		1p. green	10	10

1901.

O73	O **37**	1c. blue	30	30
O74		2c. red	10	10
O75		4c. brown	10	10
O76		5c. green	10	10
O77		8c. brown	10	10
O78		10c. red	10	10
O79		20c. blue	20	15

1903. Stamps of 1903, optd **OFICIAL**.

O 99	**46**	1c. grey	10	10
O100		2c. green	10	10
O101		5c. blue	15	10
O102		10c. brown	10	10
O103		20c. red	10	10
O104		30c. blue	10	10
O105		60c. violet	20	20

1904. As T **50**, but inscr "OFICIAL".

O106		1c. green	20	10
O107		1c. olive	30	10
O108		1c. orange	35	15
O109		1c. red	30	20
O110		2c. orange	20	10
O111		2c. green	20	10
O112		2c. red	60	40
O113		2c. grey	50	30
O114		5c. blue	25	20
O116		5c. grey	1·10	75
O117		10c. lilac	15	10
O118		20c. lilac	50	30

1913. As T **65**, but inscr "OFICIAL".

O237		1c. grey	10	10
O238		2c. orange	10	10
O239		5c. purple	10	10
O240		10c. green	10	10
O241		20c. red	10	10
O242		50c. red	10	10
O243		75c. blue	10	10
O244		1p. blue	10	10
O245		2p. yellow	20	20

1935. Optd **OFICIAL**.

O474	**86**	10c. blue	10	10
O475		50c. mauve	10	10
O476	**87**	1p. orange	10	10
O477	**122**	1p.50 green	10	10
O478	–	2p.50 violet (No. 337)	10	10

1940. 50th Anniv of Asuncion University. As T **139**, inscr "SERVICIO OFICIAL", but portraits of Pres. Escobar and Dr. Zubizarreta.

O513		50c. black and red	10	10
O514		1p. black and red	10	10
O515		2p. black and blue	10	10
O516		5p. black and blue	10	10
O517		10p. black and blue	10	10
O518		50p. black and orange	40	10

POSTAGE DUE STAMPS

D 48

1904.

D106	D **48**	2c. green	30	30
D107		4c. green	30	30
D108		10c. green	30	30
D109		20c. green	30	30

1913. As T **65**, but inscr "DEFICIENTE".

D237		1c. brown	10	10
D238		2c. brown	10	10
D239		5c. brown	10	10
D240		10c. brown	10	10
D241		20c. brown	10	10
D242		40c. brown	10	10
D243		1p. brown	10	10
D244		1p.50 brown	10	10

APPENDIX

The following stamps have either been issued in excess of postal needs or have not been available to the public in reasonable quantities at face value. Such stamps may later be given full listing if there is evidence of regular postal use.

1962.

Manned Spacecraft. Postage 15, 25, 30, 40, 50c.; Air 12g.45, 18g.15, 36g.

Previous Olympic Games (1st series). Vert designs. Postage 15, 25, 30, 40, 50c.; Air 12g.45, 18g.15, 36g.

Vatican Council. Postage 50, 70c., 1g.50, 2, 3g.; Air 5, 10g., 12g.45, 18g.15, 23g.40, 36g.

Europa. Postage 4g.; Air 36g.

Solar System. Postage 10, 20, 25, 30, 50c.; Air 12g.45, 36g., 50g.

1963.

Previous Olympic Games (2nd series). Horiz designs. Postage 15, 25, 30, 40, 50c.; Air 12g.45, 18g.15, 36g.

Satellites and Space Flights. Vert designs. Postage 10, 20, 25, 30, 50c.; Air 12g.45, 36, 50g.

Previous Winter Olympic Games. Postage 10, 20, 25, 30, 50c.; Air 12g.45, 36, 50g.

Freedom from Hunger. Postage 10, 25, 50, 75c.; Air 18g.15, 36, 50g.

"Mercury" Space Flights. Postage 15, 25, 30, 40, 50c.; Air 12g.45, 18g.15, 50g.

Winter Olympic Games. Postage 15, 25, 30, 40, 50c.; Air 12g.45, 18g.15, 50g.

1964.

Tokyo Olympic Games. Postage 15, 25, 30, 40, 50c.; Air 12g.45, 18g.15, 50g.

Red Cross Centenary. Postage 10, 25, 30, 50c.; Air 18g.15, 36, 50g.

"Gemini", "Telstar" and "Apollo" Projects. Postage 15, 25, 30, 40, 50c.; Air 12g.45, 18g.15, 50g.

Spacecraft Developments. Postage 15, 25, 30, 40, 50c.; Air 12g.45, 18g.15, 50g.

United Nations. Postage 15, 25, 30, 40, 50c.; Air 12g.45, 18g.15, 50g.

American Space Research. Postage 10, 15, 20, 30, 40c.; Air 12g.45+6g., 18g.15+9g., 20g.+20g.

Eucharistic Conference. Postage 20g.+10g., 30g.+15g., 50g.+25g., 100g.+50g.

Pope John Memorial Issue. Postage 20g.+10g., 30g.+15g., 50g.+25g., 100g.+50g.

1965.

Scouts. Postage 10, 15, 20, 30, 50c.; Air 12g.45, 18g.15, 36g.

Tokyo Olympic Games Medals. Postage 15, 25, 30, 40, 50c.; Air 12g.45, 18g.15, 50g.

Famous Scientists. Postage 10, 15, 20, 30, 40c.; Air 12g.45+6g., 18g.15+9g., 20g.+20g.

Orchids and Trees. Postage 20, 30, 90c., 1g.50, 4g.50.; Air 3, 4, 66g.

Kennedy and Churchill. Postage 15, 25, 30, 40, 50c.; Air 12g.45, 18g.15, 50g.

I.T.U. Centenary. Postage 10, 15, 20, 30, 40c.; Air 12g.45+6g., 18g.15+9g., 20g.+10g.

Pope Paul VI. Visit to United Nations. Postage 10, 15, 20, 30, 50c.; Air 12g.45, 18g.15, 36g.

1966.

"Gemini" Space Project. Postage 15, 25, 30, 40, 50c.; Air 12g.45, 18g.15, 50g.

Events of 1965. Postage 10, 15, 20, 30, 50c.; Air 12g.45, 18g.15, 36g.

Mexico Olympic Games. Postage 10, 15, 20, 30, 50c.; Air 12g.45, 18g.15, 36g.

German Space Research. Postage 10, 15, 20, 30, 50c.; Air 12g.45, 18g.15, 36g.

Famous Writers. Postage 10, 15, 20, 30, 50c.; Air 12g.45, 18g.15, 36g.

Italian Space Research. Postage 10, 15, 20, 30, 50c.; Air 12g.45, 18g.15, 36g.

Moon Missions. Postage 10, 15, 20, 30, 50c.; Air 12g.45, 18g.15, 36g.

Sports Commemorative Issue. Postage 10, 15, 20, 30, 50c.; Air 12g.45, 18g.15, 36g.

3rd Death Anniv of Pres. John Kennedy. Postage 10, 15, 20, 30, 50c.; Air 12g.45, 18g.15, 36g.

Famous Paintings. Postage 10, 15, 20, 30, 50c.; Air 12g.45, 18g.15, 36g.

1967.

Religious Paintings. Postage 10, 15, 20, 30, 50c.; Air 12g.45, 18g.15, 36g.

16th-century. Religious Paintings. Postage 10, 15, 20, 30, 50c.; Air 12g.45, 18g.15, 36g.

Impressionist Paintings. Postage 10, 15, 20, 30, 50c.; Air 12g.45, 18g.15, 36g.

European Paintings of 17th and 18th Cent. Postage 10, 15, 20, 25, 30, 50c.; Air 12g.45, 18g.15, 36g.

Birth Anniv of Pres. John Kennedy. Postage 10, 15, 20, 25, 30, 50c.; Air 12g.45, 18g.15, 36g.

Sculpture. Postage 10, 15, 20, 25, 30, 50c.; Air 12g.45, 18g.15, 50g.

Mexico Olympic Games. Archaeological Relics. Postage 10, 15, 20, 25, 30, 50c.; Air 12g.45, 18g.15, 36g.

1968.

Religious Paintings. Postage 10, 15, 20, 25, 30, 50c.; Air 12g.45, 18g.15, 36g.

Winter Olympic Games, Grenoble. Paintings. Postage 10, 15, 20, 25, 30, 50c.; Air 12g.45, 18g.15, 36g.

Paraguayan Stamps from 1870–1970. Postage 10, 15, 20, 25, 30, 50c.; Air 12g.45, 18g.15, 36g.

Mexico Olympic Games, Paintings of Children. Postage 10, 15, 20, 25, 30, 50c.; Air 12g.45, 18g.15, 36g. (Sailing ship and Olympic Rings).

Visit of Pope Paul VI to Eucharistic Congress. Religious Paintings. Postage 10, 15, 20, 25, 30, 50c.; Air 12g.45, 18g.15, 36g.

Important Events of 1968. Postage 10, 15, 20, 25, 30, 50c.; Air 12g.45, 18g.15, 50g.

1969.

Gold Medal Winners of 1968 Mexico Olympic Games. Postage 10, 15, 20, 25, 30, 50c.; Air 12g.45, 18g.15, 50g.

Int. Projects in Outer Space. Postage 10, 15, 20, 25, 30, 50c.; Air 12g.45, 18g.15, 50g.

Latin American Wildlife. Postage 10, 10, 15, 15, 20, 20, 25, 25, 30, 30, 50, 50, 75, 75 c; Air 12g.45 × 2, 18g.15 × 2.

Gold Medal Winners in Olympic Football, 1900–1968. Postage 10, 15, 20, 25, 30, 50, 75c.; Air 12g.45, 18g.15.

Paraguayan Football Champions, 1930–1966. Postage 10, 15, 20, 25, 30, 50, 75c.; Air 12g.45, 18g.15.

Paintings by Goya. Postage 10, 15, 20, 25, 30, 50, 75c.; Air 12g.45, 18g.15.

Christmas. Religious Paintings. Postage 10, 15, 20, 25, 30, 50, 75c.; Air 12g.45, 18g.15.

1970.

Moon Walk. Postage 10, 15, 20, 25, 30, 50, 75c.; Air 12g.45, 18g.15.

Easter. Paintings. Postage 10, 15, 20, 25, 30, 50, 75c.; Air 12g.45, 18g.15.

Munich Olympic Games. Postage 10, 15, 20, 25, 30, 50, 75c.; Air 12g.45, 18g.15.

Paintings from the Pinakothek Museum in Munich. Postage 10, 15, 20, 25, 30, 50, 75c.; Air 12g.45, 18g.15.

"Apollo" Space Programme. Postage 10, 15, 20, 25, 30, 50, 75c.; Air 12g.45, 18g.15.

Space Projects in the Future. Postage 10, 15, 20, 25, 30, 50, 75c.; Air 12g.45, 18g.15.

"Expo 70" World Fair, Osaka, Japan. Japanese Paintings. Postage 10, 15, 20, 25, 30, 50, 75c.; Air 12g.45, 18g.15, 50g.

Flower Paintings. Postage 10, 15, 20, 25, 30, 50, 75c.; Air 12g.45, 18g.15, 50g.

Paintings from Prado Museum, Madrid. Postage 10, 15, 20, 25, 30, 50, 75c.; Air 12g.45, 18g.15, 50g.

Paintings by Durer. Postage 10, 15, 20, 25, 30, 50, 75c.; Air 12g.45, 18g.15, 50g.

1971.

Christmas 1970/71. Religious Paintings. Postage 10, 15, 20, 25, 30, 50, 75c.; Air 12g.45, 18g.15, 50g.

Munich Olympic Games, 1972. Postage 10, 15, 20, 25, 30, 50, 75c.; Air 12g.45, 18g.15, 50g.

Paintings of Horses and Horsemen. Postage 10, 15, 20, 25, 30, 50, 75c.; Air 12g.45, 18g.15, 50g.

Famous Paintings from the Louvre, Paris. Postage 10, 15, 20, 25, 30, 50, 75c.; Air 12g.45, 18g.15, 50g.

Paintings in the National Museum, Asuncion. Postage 10, 15, 20, 25, 30, 50, 75c.; Air 12g.45, 18g.15, 50g.

Hunting Paintings. Postage 10, 15, 20, 25, 30, 50, 75c.; Air 12g.45, 18g.15, 50g.

Philatokyo '71, Stamp Exhibition, Tokyo. Japanese Paintings. Postage 10, 15, 20, 25, 30, 50, 75c.; Air 12g.45, 18g.15, 50g.

Winter Olympic Games, Sapporo, 1972. Japanese Paintings. Postage 10, 15, 20, 25, 30, 50, 75c.; Air 12g.45, 18g.15, 50g.

150th Death Anniv of Napoleon. Paintings. Postage 10, 15, 20, 25, 30, 50, 75c.; Air 12g.45, 18g.15, 50g.

Famous Paintings from the Dahlem Museum, Berlin. Postage 10, 15, 20, 25, 30, 50, 75c.; Air 12g.45, 18g.15, 50g.

1972.

Locomotives (1st series). Postage 10, 15, 20, 25, 30, 50, 75c.; Air 12g.45, 18g.15, 50g.

Winter Olympic Games, Sapporo. Postage 10, 15, 20, 25, 30, 50, 75c.; Air 12g.45, 18g.15, 50g.

Racing Cars. Postage 10, 15, 20, 25, 30, 50, 75c.; Air 12g.45, 18g.15, 50g.

Famous Sailing Ships. Postage 10, 15, 20, 25, 30, 50, 75c.; Air 12g.45, 18g.15, 50g.

Famous Paintings from the Vienna Museum. Postage 10, 15, 20, 25, 30, 50, 75c.; Air 12g.45, 18g.15, 50g.

Famous Paintings from the Asuncion Museum. Postage 10, 15, 20, 25, 30, 50, 75c.; Air 12g.45, 18g.15, 50g.

Visit of the Argentine President to Paraguay. Postage 10, 15, 20, 25, 30, 50, 75c.; Air 12g.45, 18g.15.

Visit of President of Paraguay to Japan. Postage 10, 15, 20, 25, 30, 50, 75c.; Air 12g.45, 18g.15.

Paintings of Animals and Birds. Postage 10, 15, 20, 25, 30, 50, 75c.; Air 12g.45, 18g.15.

Locomotives (2nd series). Postage 10, 15, 20, 25, 30, 50, 75c.; Air 12g.45, 18g.15.

South American Fauna. Postage 10, 15, 20, 25, 30, 50, 75c.; Air 12g.45, 18g.15.

1973.

Famous Paintings from the Florence Museum. Postage 10, 15, 20, 25, 30, 50, 75c.; Air 5, 10, 20g.

South American Butterflies. Postage 10, 15, 20, 25, 30, 50, 75c.; Air 5, 10, 20g.

Cats. Postage 10, 15, 20, 25, 30, 50, 75c.; Air 5, 10, 20g.

Portraits of Women. Postage 10, 15, 20, 25, 30, 50, 75c.; Air 5, 10, 20g.

World Cup Football Championship, West Germany (1974) (1st issue). Postage 10, 15, 20, 25, 30, 50, 75c.; Air 5, 10, 20g.

Paintings of Women. Postage 10, 15, 20, 25, 30, 50, 75c.; Air 5, 10, 20g.

Birds. Postage 10, 15, 20, 25, 30, 50, 75c.; Air 5, 10, 20g.

"Apollo" Moon Missions and Future Space Projects. Postage 10, 15, 20, 25, 30, 50, 75c.; Air 5, 10, 20g.

Visit of Pres. Stroessner to Europe and Morocco. Air 5, 10, 25, 50, 150g.

Folk Costume. Postage 25, 50, 75c., 1g., 1g.50, 1g.75, 2g.25.

Flowers. Postage 10, 20, 25, 30, 40, 50, 75c.

1974.

World Cup Football Championship, West Germany (2nd issue). Air 5, 10, 20g.

Roses. Postage 10, 15, 20, 25, 30, 50, 75c.

Famous Paintings from the Gulbenkian Museum, New York. Postage 10, 15, 20, 25, 30, 50, 75 c; Air 5, 10, 20g.

U.P.U. Centenary. Postage 10, 15, 20, 25, 30, 50, 75c.; Air 5, 10, 20g.

Famous Masterpieces. Postage 10, 15, 20, 25, 30, 50, 75c.; Air 5, 10, 20g.

Visit of Pres. Stroessner to France. Air 100g.

World Cup Football Championship, West Germany (3rd issue). Air 4, 5, 10g.

Ships. Postage 5, 10, 15, 20, 25, 35, 40, 50c.

Events of 1974. Air 4g. (U.P.U.), 5g. (President of Chile's visit), 10g. (President Stroessner's visit to South Africa).

Centenary of U.P.U. Air 4, 5, 10, 20g.

1975.

Paintings. Postage 5, 10, 15, 20, 25, 35, 40, 50c.

Christmas (1974). Postage 5, 10, 15, 20, 25, 35, 40, 50c.

"Expo '75" Okinawa, Japan. Air 4, 5, 10g.

Paintings from National Gallery, London. Postage 5, 10, 15, 20, 25, 35, 40, 50c.

Dogs. Postage 5, 10, 15, 20, 25, 35, 40, 50c.

South American Fauna. Postage 5, 10, 15, 20, 25, 35, 40, 50c.

"Espana '75". Air 4, 5, 10g.

500th Birth Anniv of Michelangelo. Postage 5, 10, 15, 20, 25, 35, 40, 50c.; Air 4, 5, 10g.

Winter Olympic Games, Innsbruck (1976). Postage 1, 2, 3, 4, 5g.; Air 10, 15, 20g.

Olympic Games, Montreal (1976). Gold borders. Postage 1, 2, 3, 4, 5g.; Air 10, 15, 20g.

Various Commemorations. Air 4g. (Zeppelin), 5g. (1978 World Cup), 10g. (Nordposta Exhibition).

Bicent (1976) of American Revolution (1st issue). Paintings of Sailing Ships. Postage 5, 10, 15, 20, 25, 35, 40, 50c.

Bicent (1976) of American Revolution (2nd issue). Paintings. Postage 5, 10, 15, 20, 25, 35, 40, 50c.

Bicent (1976) of American Revolution (3rd issue). Lunar Rover and American Cars. Air 4, 5, 10g.

Various Commemorations. Air 4g. (Concorde), 5g. (Lufthansa), 10g. ("Exfilmo" and "Espamer" Stamp Exhibitions).

Paintings by Spanish Artists. Postage 1, 2, 3, 4, 5g.; Air 10, 15, 20g.

1976.

Holy Year. Air 4, 5, 10g.

Cats. Postage 5, 10, 15, 20, 25, 35, 40, 50c.

Railway Locomotives (3rd series). Postage 1, 2, 3, 4, 5g.; Air 10, 15, 20g.

Butterflies. Postage 5, 10, 15, 20, 25, 35, 40, 50c.

Domestic Animals. Postage 1, 2, 3, 4, 5g.; Air 10, 15, 20g.

Bicent of American Revolution (4th issue) and U.S. Postal Service. Postage 1, 2, 3, 4, 5g.; Air 10, 15, 20g.

"Paintings and Planets". Postage 1, 2, 3, 4, 5g.; Air 10, 15, 20g.

Ship Paintings. Postage 1, 2, 3, 4, 5g.; Air 10, 15, 20g.

German Ship Paintings (1st issue). Postage 1, 2, 3, 4, 5g.; Air 10, 15, 20g.

Bicentenary of American Revolution (5th issue). Paintings of Cowboys and Indians. Postage 1, 2, 3, 4, 5g.; Air 10, 15, 20g.

Gold Medal Winners. Olympic Games, Montreal. Postage 1, 2, 3, 4, 5g.; Air 10, 15, 20g.

Paintings by Titian. Postage 1, 2, 3, 4, 5g.; Air 10, 15, 20g.

History of the Olympics. Postage 1, 2, 3, 4, 5g.; Air 10, 15, 20g.

1977.

Paintings by Rubens (1st issue). Postage 1, 2, 3, 4, 5g.; Air 10, 15, 20g.

Bicent of American Revolution (6th issue). Astronautics. Postage 1, 2, 3, 4, 5g.; Air 10, 15, 20g.

"Luposta 77" Stamp Exn. Zeppelin and National Costumes. Postage 1, 2, 3, 4, 5g.; Air 10, 15, 20g.

History of Aviation. Postage 1, 2, 3, 4, 5g.; Air 10, 15, 20g.

Paintings. Postage 1, 2, 3, 4, 5g.; Air 10, 15, 20g.

German Ship Paintings (2nd issue). Postage 1, 2, 3, 4, 5g.; Air 10, 15, 20g.

Nobel Prize-winners for Literature. Postage 1, 2, 3, 4, 5g.; Air 10, 15, 20g.

History of World Cup (1st issue). Postage 1, 2, 3, 4, 5g.; Air 10, 15, 20g.

History of World Cup (2nd issue). Postage 1, 2, 3, 4, 5g.; Air 10, 15, 20g.

1978.

Paintings by Rubens (2nd issue). Postage 1, 2, 3, 4, 5g.; Air 10, 15, 20g.

Chess Olympiad, Buenos Aires. Paintings of Chess Games. Postage 1, 2, 3, 4, 5g.; Air 10, 15, 20g.

Paintings by Jordaens. Postage 3, 4, 5, 6, 7, 8, 20g.; Air 10, 25g.

450th Death Anniv of Durer (1st issue). Postage 3, 4, 5, 6, 7, 8, 20g.; Air 10, 25g.

Paintings by Goya. Postage 3, 4, 5, 6, 7, 8, 20g.; Air 10, 25g.

Astronautics of the Future. Postage 3, 4, 5, 6, 7, 8, 20g.; Air 10, 25g.

Racing Cars. Postage 3, 4, 5, 6, 7, 8, 20g.; Air 10, 25g.

Paintings by Rubens (3rd issue). Postage 3, 4, 5, 6, 7, 8, 20g.; Air 10, 25g.

25th Anniv of Queen Elizabeth's Coronation (reproduction of stamps). Postage 3, 4, 5, 6, 7, 8, 20g.; Air 10, 25g.

Paintings and Stamp Exhibition Emblems. Postage 3, 4, 5, 6, 7, 8, 20g.; Air 10, 25g.

Various Commemorations. Air 75g. (Satellite Earth Station), 500g. (Coat of Arms), 1000g. (Pres. Stroessner).

International Year of the Child (1st issue). Snow White and the Seven Dwarfs. Postage 3, 4, 5, 6, 7, 8, 20g.; Air 10, 25g.

Military Uniforms. Postage 3, 4, 5, 6, 7, 8, 20g.; Air 10, 25g.

1979.

World Cup Football Championship, Argentina. Postage 3, 4, 5, 6, 7, 8, 20g.; Air 10, 25g.

Christmas (1978). Paintings of Madonnas. Postage 3, 4, 5, 6, 7, 8, 20g.; Air 10, 25g.

History of Aviation. Postage 3, 4, 5, 6, 7, 8, 20g.; Air 10, 25g.

450th Death Anniv of Durer (2nd issue). Postage 3, 4, 5, 6, 7, 8, 20g.; Air 10, 25g.

Death Centenary of Sir Rowland Hill (1st issue). Reproduction of Stamps. Postage 3, 4, 5, 6, 7, 8, 20g.; Air 10, 25g.

International Year of the Child (2nd issue). Cinderella. Postage 3, 4, 5, 6, 7, 8, 20g.; Air 10, 25g.

Winter Olympic Games, Lake Placid (1980). Postage 3, 4, 5, 6, 7, 8, 20g.; Air 10, 25g.

Sailing Ships. Postage 3, 4, 5, 6, 7, 8, 20g.; Air 10, 25g.

International Year of the Child (3rd issue). Cats. Postage 3, 4, 5, 6, 7, 8, 20g.; Air 10, 25g.

International Year of the Child (4th issue). Little Red Riding Hood. Postage 3, 4, 5, 6, 7, 8, 20g.; Air 10, 25g.

Olympic Games, Moscow (1980). Greek Athletes. Postage 3, 4, 5, 6, 7, 8, 20g.; Air 10, 25g.

Centenary of Electric Locomotives. Postage 3, 4, 5, 6, 7, 8, 20g.; Air 10, 25g.

1980.

Death Centenary of Sir Rowland Hill (2nd issue). Military Aircraft. Postage 3, 4, 5, 6, 7, 8, 20 g; Air 10, 25g.

Death Centenary of Sir Rowland Hill (3rd issue). Stamps. Postage 3, 4, 5, 6, 7, 8, 20g.; Air 10, 25g.

Winter Olympic Games Medal Winners (1st issue). Postage 3, 4, 5, 6, 7, 8, 20g.; Air 10, 25g.

Composers. Scenes from Ballets. Postage 3, 4, 5, 6, 7, 8, 20g.; Air 20, 25g.

International Year of the Child (1979) (5th issue). Christmas. Postage 3, 4, 5, 6, 7, 8, 20g.; Air 10, 25g.

Exhibitions. Paintings of Ships. Postage 3, 4, 5, 6, 7, 8, 20g.; Air 10, 25g.

World Cup Football Championship, Spain (1982) (1st issue). Postage 3, 4, 5, 6, 7, 8, 20g.; Air 10, 25g.

World Chess Championship, Merano. Postage 3, 4, 5, 6, 7, 8, 20g.; Air 10, 25g.

1981.

Winter Olympic Games Medal Winners (2nd issue). Postage 25, 50c., 1, 2, 3, 4, 5g.; Air 5, 10, 30g.

International Year of the Child (1979) (6th issue). Children and Flowers. Postage 10, 25, 50, 100, 200, 300, 400g.; Air 75, 500, 1000g.

"WIPA 1981" International Stamp Exhibition, Vienna. 1980 Composers stamp optd. Postage 4g.; Air 10g.

Wedding of Prince of Wales (1st issue). Postage 25, 50c., 1, 2, 3, 4, 5g.; Air 5, 10, 30g.

Costumes and Treaty of Itaipu. Postage 10, 25, 50, 100, 200, 300, 400g.

Paintings by Rubens. Postage 25, 50c., 1, 2, 3, 4, 5g.

Anniversaries and Events. Air 5g. (250th birth anniv of George Washington), 10g. (80th birthday of Queen Mother), 30g. ("Philatokyo '81").

Flight of Space Shuttle. Air 5, 10, 30g.

Birth Bicentenary of Ingres. Postage 25, 50c., 1, 2, 3, 4, 5g.

World Cup Football Championship, Spain (1982) (2nd issue). Air 5, 10, 30g.

Birth Centenary of Picasso. Postage 25, 50c., 1, 2, 3, 4, 5g.

"Philatelia '81" International Stamp Exhibition, Frankfurt. Picasso stamps optd. Postage 25, 50c., 1, 2, 3, 4g.

"Espamer '81" International Stamp Exhibition. Picasso stamps optd. Postage 25, 50c., 1, 2, 3, 4g.

Wedding of Prince of Wales (2nd issue). Postage 25, 50c., 1, 2, 3, 4, 5g.; Air 5, 10, 30g.

International Year of the Child (1979) (7th issue). Christmas. Postage 25, 50c., 1, 2, 3, 4, 5g.

Christmas. Paintings. Air 5, 10, 30g.

1982.

International Year of the Child (1979) (8th issue). Puss in Boots. Postage 25, 50c., 1, 2, 3, 4, 5g.

World Cup Football Championship, Spain (3rd issue). Air 5, 10, 30g.

75th Anniv of Boy Scout Movement and 125th Birth Anniv of Lord-Baden Powell (founder). Postage 25, 50c., 1, 2, 3, 4, 5g.; Air 5, 10, 30g.

"Essen 82" International Stamp Exhibition, 1981 International Year of the Child (7th issue) Christmas stamps optd. Postage 25, 50c., 1, 2, 3, 4g.

Cats. Postage 25, 50c., 1, 2, 3, 4, 5g.

Chess paintings. Air 5, 10, 30g.

"Philexfrance 82" International Stamp Exhibition. 1981 Ingres stamps optd. Postage 25, 50c., 1, 2, 3g.

World Cup Football Championship, Spain (4th issue). Postage 25, 50c., 1, 2, 3, 4, 5g.; Air 5, 10, 30g.

"Philatelia 82" International Stamp Exhibition, Hanover. 1982 Cats issue optd. Postage 25, 50c., 1, 2, 3, 4, 5g.

500th Birth Anniv of Raphael (1st issue). Postage 25, 50c., 1, 2, 3, 4, 5g.

500th Birth Anniv of Raphael (2nd issue) and Christmas (1st issue). Postage 25, 50c., 1, 2, 3, 4, 5g.

World Cup Football Championship Results. Air 5, 10, 30g.

Christmas (2nd issue). Paintings by Rubens. Air 5, 10, 30g.

Paintings by Durer. Life of Christ. Postage 25, 50c., 1, 2, 3, 4, 5g.

500th Birth Anniv of Raphael (3rd issue) and Christmas (3rd issue). Air 5, 10, 30g.

1983.

Third International Railways Congress, Malaga (1982). Postage 25, 50c., 1, 2, 3, 4, 5g.

Racing Cars. Postage 25, 50c., 1, 2, 3, 4, 5g.

Paintings by Rembrandt. Air 5, 10, 30g.

German Astronautics. Air 5, 10, 30g.

Winter Olympic Games, Sarajevo (1984). Postage 25, 50c., 1, 2, 3, 4, 5g.

Bicentenary of Manned Flight. Air 5, 10, 30g.

Pope John Paul II. Postage 25, 50c., 1, 2, 3, 4, 5g.

Olympic Games, Los Angeles (1984). Air 5, 10, 30g.

Veteran Cars. Postage 25, 50c., 1, 2, 3, 4, 5g.; Air 5, 10, 30g.

"Brasiliana '83" International Stamp Exhibition and 52nd F.I.P. Congress (1st issue). 1982 World Cup (4th issue) stamps optd. Postage 25, 50c., 1, 2, 3, 4g.

"Brasiliana '83" International Stamp Exhibition and 52nd F.I.P. Congress (2nd issue). 1982 Raphael/ Christmas stamps optd. Postage 25, 50c., 1, 2, 3, 4g.

Aircraft Carriers. Postage 25, 50c., 1, 2, 3, 4, 5g.

South American Flowers. Air 5, 10, 30g.

South American Birds. Postage 25, 50c., 1, 2, 3, 4, 5g.

25th Anniv of International Maritime Organization. Air 5, 10, 30g.

"Philatelia '83" International Stamp Exhibition, Dusseldorf. 1983 International Railway Congress stamps optd. Postage 25, 50c., 1, 2, 3, 4g.

"Exfivia - 83" International Stamp Exn, Bolivia. 1982 Durer paintings optd. Postage 25, 50c., 1, 2, 3, 4g.

Flowers, Postage 10, 25g.; Chaco soldier, Postage 50g.; Dams, Postage 75g; Air 100g.; President, Air 200g.

1984.

Bicent of Manned Flight. Postage 25, 50c., 1, 2, 3, 4, 5g.

World Communications Year. Air 5, 10, 30g.

Dogs. Postage 25, 50c., 1, 2, 3, 4, 5g.

Olympic Games, Los Angeles. Air 5, 10, 30g.

Animals. Postage 10, 25, 50, 75g.

1983 Anniversaries. Air 100g. (birth bicentenary of Bolivar), 200g. (76th anniv of boy scout movement).

Christmas (1983) and New Year. Postage 25, 50c., 1, 2, 3, 4, 5g.

Winter Olympic Games, Sarajevo. Air 5, 10, 30g.

Troubador Knights. Postage 25, 50c., 1, 2, 3, 4, 5g.

World Cup Football Championship, Spain (1982) and Mexico (1986). Air 5, 10, 30g.

International Stamp Fair, Essen. 1983 Racing Cars stamps optd. Postage 25, 50c., 1, 2, 3, 4g.

Extinct Animals. Postage 25, 50c., 1, 2, 3, 4, 5g.

60th Anniv of International Chess Federation. Air 5, 10, 30g.

19th Universal Postal Union Congress Stamp Exhibition, Hamburg (1st issue) Sailing Ships. Postage 25, 50c., 1, 2, 3, 4, 5g.

19th Universal Postal Union Congress Stamp Exhibition, Hamburg (2nd issue). Troubadour Knights stamp optd. Postage 5g.

Leaders of the World. British Railway Locomotives. Postage 25, 50c., 1, 2, 3, 4, 5g.

50th Anniv of First Lufthansa Europe–South America Direct Mail Flight. Air 5, 10, 30g.

30th Anniv of Presidency of Alfredo Stroessner. Dam stamp optd. Air 100g.

"Ausipex 84" International Stamp Exhibition, Melbourne. 1974 U.P.U. Centenary stamps optd. Postage 10, 15, 20, 25, 30, 50, 75c.

"Phila Korea 1984" International Stamp Exhibition, Seoul. Olympic Games, Los Angeles, and Extinct Animals stamps optd. Postage 5g.; Air 30g.

German National Football Championship and Sindelfingen Stamp Bourse. 1974 World Cup stamps (1st issue) optd. Postage 10, 15, 20, 25, 30, 50, 75c.

Cats. Postage 25, 50c., 1, 2, 3, 4, 5g.

Winter Olympic Games Medal Winners. Air 5, 10, 30g.

Centenary of Motor Cycle. Air 5, 10, 30g.

1985.

Olympic Games Medal Winners. Postage 25, 50c., 1, 2, 3, 4, 5g.

Christmas (1984). Costumes. Air 5, 10, 30g.

Fungi. Postage 25, 50c., 1, 2, 3, 4, 5g.

Participation of Paraguay in Preliminary Rounds of World Cup Football Championship. Air 5, 10, 30g.

"Interpex 1985" and "Stampex 1985" Stamp Exhibitions. 1981 Queen Mother's Birthday stamp optd. Postage 10g. × 2.

International Federation of Aero-Philatelic Societies Congress, Stuttgart. 1984 Lufthansa Europe–South America Mail Flight stamp optd. Air 10g.

Paraguayan Animals and Extinct Animals. Postage 25, 50c., 1, 2, 3, 4, 5g.

"Olymphilex 85" Olympic Stamps Exhibition, Lausanne. 1984 Winter Olympics Games Medal Winners stamp optd. Postage 10g.

"Israphil 85" International Stamp Exhibition, Tel Aviv. 1982 Boy Scout Movement stamp optd. Postage 5g.

Music Year. Air 5, 10, 30g.

Birth Bicentenary of John J. Audubon (ornithologist). Birds. Postage 25, 50c., 1, 2, 3, 4, 5g.

Railway Locomotives. Air 5, 10, 30g.

"Italia '85" International Stamp Exhibition, Rome (1st issue). 1983 Pope John Paul II stamp optd. Postage 5g.

50th Anniv of Chaco Peace (1st issue). 1972 Visit of Argentine President stamp optd. Postage 30c.

"Mophila 85" Stamp Exhibition, Hamburg. 1984 U.P.U. Congress Stamp Exhibition (1st issue) stamp optd. Postage 5g.

"Lupo 85" Stamp Exhibition, Lucerne. 1984 Bicentenary of Manned Flight stamp optd. Postage 5g.

"Expo 85" World's Fair, Tsukuba. 1981 "Philatokyo '81" stamp optd. Air 30g.

International Youth Year. Mark Twain. Postage 25, 50c., 1, 2, 3, 4, 5g.

75th Death Anniv of Henri Dunant (founder of Red Cross). Air 5, 10, 30g.

150th Anniv of German Railways (1st issue). Postage 25, 50c., 1, 2, 3, 4, 5g.

International Chess Federation Congress, Graz. Air 5, 10, 30g.

50th Anniv of Chaco Peace (2nd issue) and Government Achievements. Postage 10, 25, 50, 75g.; Air 100, 200g.

Paintings by Rubens. Postage 25, 50c., 1, 2, 3, 4, 5g.

Explorers and their Ships. Air 5, 10, 30g.

"Italia '85" International Stamp Exhibition, Rome (2nd issue). Paintings. Air 5, 10, 30g.

1986.

Paintings by Titian. Postage 25, 50c., 1, 2, 3, 4, 5g.

International Stamp Fair, Essen. 1985 German Railways stamps optd. Postage 25, 50c., 1, 2, 3, 4g.

Fungi. Postage 25, 50c., 1, 2, 3, 4, 5g.

"Ameripex '86" International Stamp Exhibition, Chicago. Air 5, 10, 30g.

Lawn Tennis (1st issue). Inscriptions in black or red. Air 5, 10, 30g.

Centenary of Motor Car. Postage 25, 50c., 1, 2, 3, 4, 5g.

Appearance of Halley's Comet. Air 5, 10, 30g.

Qualification of Paraguay for World Cup Football Championship Final Rounds, Mexico (1st issue). Postage 25, 50c., 1, 2, 3, 4, 5g.

Tenth Pan-American Games, Indianapolis (1987). 1985 Olympic Games Medal Winners stamp optd. Postage 5g.

Maybach Cars. Postage 25, 50c., 1, 2, 3, 4, 5g.

Freight Trains. Air 5, 10, 30g.

Qualification of Paraguay for World Cup Football Championship Final Rounds (2nd issue). Air 5, 10, 30g.

Winter Olympic Games, Calgary (1988) (1st issue). 1983 Winter Olympic Games stamp optd. Postage 5g.

Centenary of Statue of Liberty. Postage 25, 50c., 1, 2, 3, 4, 5g.

Dogs. Postage 25, 50c., 1, 2, 3, 4, 5g.

150th Anniv of German Railways (2nd issue). Air 5, 10, 30g.

Lawn Tennis (2nd issue). Postage 25, 50c., 1, 2, 3, 4, 5g.

Visit of Prince Hitachi of Japan. 1972 Visit of President of Paraguay to Japan stamps optd. Postage 10, 15, 20, 25, 30, 50, 75c.

International Peace Year. Paintings by Rubens. Air 5, 10, 30g.

Olympic Games, Seoul (1988) (1st issue). Postage 25, 50c., 1, 2, 3, 4, 5g.

27th Chess Olympiad, Dubai. 1982 Chess Paintings stamp optd. Air 10g.

1987.

World Cup Football Championship, Mexico (1986) and Italy (1990). Air 5, 10, 20, 25, 30g.

12th Spanish American Stamp and Coin Exhibition, Madrid, and 500th Anniv of Discovery of America by Columbus. 1975 South American Fauna and 1983 25th Anniv of I.M.O. stamps optd. Postage 15, 20, 25, 35, 40g.; Air 10g.

Tennis as Olympic Sport. 1986 Lawn Tennis (1st issue) stamps optd. Air 10, 30g.

Olympic Games, Barcelona (1992). 1985 Olympic Games Medal Winners stamps optd. Postage 25, 50c., 1, 2, 3, 4g.

"Olymphilex '87" Olympic Stamps Exhibition, Rome. 1985 Olympic Games Medal Winners stamp optd. Postage 5g.

Cats. Postage 1, 2, 3, 5, 60g.

Paintings by Rubens (1st issue). Postage 1, 2, 3, 5, 60g.

Saloon Cars. Air 5, 10, 20, 25, 30g.

National Topics. Postage 10g. (steel plant), 25g. (Franciscan monk), 50g. (400th anniv of Ita and Yaguaron), 75g. (450th Anniv of Asuncion); Air 100g. (airliner), 200g. (Pres. Stroessner).

"Capex 87" International Stamp Exhibition, Toronto. Cats stamps optd. Postage 1, 2, 3, 5g.

500th Anniv of Discovery of America by Columbus. Postage 1, 2, 3, 5, 60g.

Winter Olympic Games, Calgary (1988) (2nd issue). Air 5, 10, 20, 25, 30g.

Centenary of Colorado Party. National Topics and 1978 Pres. Stroessner stamps optd. Air 200, 1000g.

750th Anniv of Berlin (1st issue) and "Luposta '87" Air Stamps Exhibition, Berlin. Postage 1, 2, 3, 5, 60g.

Olympic Games, Seoul (1988) (2nd issue). Air 5, 10, 20, 25, 30g.

Rally Cars. Postage 1, 2, 3, 5, 60g.

"Exfivia 87" Stamp Exhibition, Bolivia. National Topics stamps optd. Postage 75g.; Air 100g.

"Olymphilex '88" Olympic Stamps Exhibition, Seoul. 1986 Olympic Games, Seoul (1st issue) stamps optd. Postage 2, 3, 4, 5g.

"Philatelia '87" International Stamp Exhibition, Cologne. 1986 Lawn Tennis (2nd issue) stamps optd. Postage 25, 50c., 1, 2, 3, 4g.

Italy–Argentina Match at Zurich to Launch 1990 World Cup Football Championship, Italy. 1986

Paraguay Qualification (2nd issue) stamps optd. Air 10, 30g.

"Exfilna '87" Stamp Exhibition, Gerona. 1986 Olympic Games, Seoul (1st issue) stamps optd. Postage 25, 50c.

Spanish Ships. Postage 1, 2, 3, 5, 60g.

Paintings by Rubens (2nd issue). Air 5, 10, 20, 25, 30g.

Christmas. Air 5, 10, 20, 25, 30g.

Winter Olympic Games, Calgary (1988) (3rd issue). Postage 1, 2, 3, 5, 60g.

1988.

150th Anniv of Austrian Railways. Air 5, 10, 20, 25, 30g.

"Aeropex 88" Air Stamps Exhibition, Adelaide, 1987. 750th Anniv of Berlin and "Luposta '87" stamps optd. Postage 1, 2, 3, 5g.

"Olympex" Stamp Exhibition, Calgary. 1987 Winter Olympic Games (3rd issue) stamps optd. Postage 1, 2, 3g.

Olympic Games, Seoul (3rd issue). Equestrian Events. Postage 1, 2, 3, 5, 60g.

Space Projects. Air 5, 10, 20, 25, 30g.

750th Anniv of Berlin (2nd issue). Paintings. Postage 1, 2, 3, 5, 60g.

Visit of Pope John Paul II. Postage 1, 2, 3, 5, 60g.

"Lupo Wien 88" Stamp Exhibition, Vienna. 1987 National Topics stamp optd. Air 100g.

World Wildlife Fund. Extinct Animals. Postage 1, 2, 3, 5g.

Paintings in West Berlin State Museum. Air 5, 10, 20, 25, 30g.

Bicentenary of Australian Settlement. 1981 Wedding of Prince of Wales (1st issue) optd. Postage 25, 50c., 1, 2g.

History of World Cup Football Championship (1st issue). Air 5, 10, 20, 25, 30g.

New Presidential Period, 1988–1993. 1985 Chaco Peace and Government Achievements issue optd. Postage 10, 25, 50, 75g.; Air 100, 200g.

Olympic Games, Seoul (4th issue). Lawn Tennis and Medal. Postage 1, 2, 3, 5, 60g.

Calgary Winter Olympics Gold Medal Winners. Air 5, 10, 20, 25, 30g.

History of World Cup Football Championship (2nd issue). Air 5, 10, 20, 25, 30g.

"Prenfil '88" International Philatelic Press Exhibition, Buenos Aires. "Ameripex '86" stamp optd. Air 30g.

"Philexfrance 89" International Stamp Exhibition, Paris. 1985 Explorers stamp optd. Air 30g.

PARMA — Pt. 8

A former Grand Duchy of N. Italy, united with Sardinia in 1860 and now part of Italy.

100 centesimi = 1 lira.

1 Bourbon "fleur-de-lis" — 2 — 3

1852. Imperf.

2	**1**	5c. black on yellow	42·00	85·00
11		5c. yellow	£5000	£600
4		10c. black	70·00	95·00
5		15c. black on pink	£1900	42·00
13		15c. red	£6000	£130
7		25c. black on purple	£9500	£140
14		25c. brown		£275
9		40c. black on blue	£1700	£225

1857. Imperf.

17	**2**	15c. red	£200	£325
19		25c. purple	£375	£150
20		40c. blue	46·00	£400

1859. Imperf.

28	**3**	5c. green	£1900	£3250
29		10c. brown	£700	£350
32		20c. blue	£1000	£160
33		40c. red	£475	£7000
35		80c. yellow	£6000	

NEWSPAPER STAMPS

1853. As T **3**. Imperf.

N1	**3**	6c. black on pink	£1100	£250
N3		9c. black on blue	70·00	95·00

PATIALA — Pt. 1

A "convention" state in the Punjab, India.

12 pies = 1 anna;
16 annas = 1 rupee.

1884. Stamps of India (Queen Victoria) with curved opt **PUTTIALLA STATE** vert.

1	**23**	½a. turquoise	3·25	3·25
2	–	1a. purple	45·00	48·00
3	–	2a. blue	11·00	11·00
4	–	4a. green (No. 96)	65·00	65·00
5	–	8a. mauve	£325	£800
6	–	1r. grey (No. 101)	£130	£450

1885. Stamps of India (Queen Victoria) optd **PUTTIALLA STATE** horiz.

7	**23**	½a. turquoise	2·00	30
11	–	1a. purple	50	30
8	–	2a. blue	3·75	1·60
9	–	4a. green (No. 96)	3·00	2·75
12	–	8a. mauve	15·00	35·00
10	–	1r. grey (No. 101)	9·50	60·00

Stamps of India optd **PATIALA STATE**.

1891. Queen Victoria.

32	**40**	3p. red	10	10
13	**23**	½a. turquoise (No. 84)	30	10
33	–	½a. green (No. 114)	70	30
14	–	9p. red	75	1·50
15	–	1a. purple	1·25	30
34	–	1a. red	2·25	80
17	–	1a.6p. brown	1·00	70
18	–	2a. blue	1·25	30
20	–	3a. orange	1·75	50
22	–	4a. green (No. 96)	2·00	60
23	–	6a. brown (No. 80)	2·25	10·00
26	–	8a. mauve	1·75	10·00
27	–	12a. purple on red	1·75	11·00
28	**37**	1r. green and red	4·00	40·00
29	**38**	2r. red and orange	£110	£650
30		3r. brown and green	£150	£700
31		5r. blue and violet	£190	£750

1903. King Edward VII.

36	3p. grey	30	10
37	½a. green (No. 122)	1·00	15
38	1a. red (No. 123)	30	10
39	2a. lilac	1·10	65
40	3a. orange	1·00	35
41	4a. olive	2·75	1·00
42	6a. bistre	3·00	7·00
43	8a. mauve	3·50	1·50
44	12a. purple on red	5·50	20·00
45	1r. green and red	3·00	3·50

1912. King Edward VII. Inscr "INDIA POSTAGE & REVENUE".

46	½a. green (No. 149)	30	20
47	1a. red (No. 150)	1·50	75

1912. King George V. Optd in two lines.

48	**55**	3p. grey	25	10
49	**56**	½a. green	60	20
50	**57**	1a. red	1·25	20
61		1a. brown	2·75	40
51	**58**	1½d. brown (A)	30	55
52	**59**	2a. purple	75	60
53	**62**	3a. orange	1·75	75
62		3a. blue	3·00	6·50
54	**63**	4a. olive	2·75	2·25
55	**64**	6a. ochre	1·10	3·00
56	**65**	8a. mauve	2·25	1·25
57	**66**	12a. red	3·25	7·50
58	**67**	1r. brown and green	5·50	11·00
59		2r. red and brown	12·00	£140
60		5r. blue and violet	27·00	£140

1928. King George V. Optd in one line.

63	**55**	3p. grey	1·50	10
64	**56**	½a. green	25	10
75	**79**	½a. green	75	30
65	**80**	9p. green	1·25	60
66	**57**	1a. brown	75	25
76	**81**	1a. brown	1·10	20
67	**82**	1a.3p. mauve	2·75	15
77	**59**	2a. red	40	1·25
68	**70**	2a. lilac	1·50	35
69	**61**	2a.6p. orange	4·00	1·40
70	**62**	3a. blue	2·50	1·25
78		3a. red	5·50	6·50
71	**71**	4a. green	3·00	1·00
79	**63**	4a. olive	1·50	1·60
72	**65**	8a. mauve	4·50	2·25
73	**66**	1r. brown and green	6·50	7·00
74w		2r. red and orange	9·00	48·00

1937. King George VI. Optd in one line.

80	**91**	3p. grey	30·00	35
81		½a. brown	9·00	40
82		9p. green	3·50	90
83		1a. red	2·50	20
84	**92**	2a. red	1·50	7·00
85	–	2a.6p. violet	4·25	15·00
86	–	3a. green	3·50	6·50
87	–	3a.6p. blue	4·75	19·00
88	–	4a. brown	21·00	12·00
89	–	6a. green	21·00	42·00
90	–	8a. violet	21·00	30·00
91	–	12a. red	22·00	48·00
92	**93**	1r. grey and brown	22·00	38·00
93		2r. purple and brown	24·00	85·00
94		5r. green and blue	30·00	£180
95		10r. purple and red	45·00	£300
96		15r. brown and green	90·00	£450
97		25r. grey and purple	£120	£500

1943. King George VI. Optd **PATIALA** only.

(a) Issue of 1938.

98	**94**	3p. grey	9·50	1·50
99		½a. brown	6·50	1·00
100		9p. green	£170	4·25
101		1a. red	21·00	1·40
102	**93**	1r. grey and brown	11·00	75·00

(b) Issue of 1940.

103	**92**	3p. grey	2·75	15
104		½a. mauve	2·75	15
105		9p. green	1·00	15
106		1a. red	1·00	10
107	**101**	1a.3p. bistre	1·60	2·50
108		1½a. violet	11·00	2·50
109		2a. red	8·50	35
110		3a. violet	7·50	1·75
111		3½a. blue	18·00	27·00
112	**102**	4a. brown	7·00	2·50
113		6a. green	3·00	20·00
114		8a. violet	3·00	10·00
115		12a. purple	12·00	60·00

OFFICIAL STAMPS
Overprinted **SERVICE**.

1884. Nos. 1 to 3 (Queen Victoria).

O1	**23**	½a. turquoise	10·00	30
O2	–	1a. purple	75	10
O3	–	2a. blue	£4250	£110

1885. Nos. 7, 11 and 8 (Queen Victoria).

O4	**23**	½a. turquoise	60	20
O5	–	1a. purple	50	10
O7	–	2a. blue	50	20

1891. Nos. 13 to 28 and No. 10 (Queen Victoria).

O 8	**23**	½a. turquoise (No. 13)	30	10
O 9	–	1a. purple	4·25	10
O20	–	1a. red	30	10
O10a	–	2a. blue	3·25	1·75
O12	–	3a. orange	75	2·00
O13a	–	4a. green	85	20
O15	–	6a. brown	1·25	35
O16a	–	8a. mauve	1·75	1·10
O18	–	12a. purple on red	75	50
O19	–	1r. grey	1·25	65
O21	**37**	1r. green and red	5·50	9·00

1903. Nos. 36 to 45 (King Edward VII).

O22	3p. grey	30	10
O24	½a. green	30	10
O25	1a. red	40	10
O26a	2a. lilac	40	10
O28	3a. brown	3·00	2·25
O29	4a. olive	1·25	20
O30	8a. mauve	1·00	75
O32	1r. green and red	1·25	70

1907. Nos. 46/7 (King Edward VII). Inscr "INDIA POSTAGE & REVENUE".

O33	½a. green	40	20
O34	1a. red	40	10

1913. Official stamps of India (King George V). Optd **PATIALA STATE** in two lines.

O35	**55**	3p. grey	10	20
O36	**56**	½a. green	10	10
O37	**57**	1a. red	10	10
O38		1a. brown	6·50	1·00
O39	**59**	2a. mauve	60	40
O40	**63**	4a. olive	50	30
O41	**64**	6a. bistre	1·25	2·00
O42	**65**	8a. mauve	55	70
O43	**67**	1r. brown and green	1·40	1·40
O44		2r. red and brown	15·00	40·00
O45		5r. blue and violet	9·00	20·00

1927. Postage stamps of India (King George V) optd **PATIALA STATE SERVICE** in two lines.

O47	**55**	3p. grey	10	10
O48	**56**	½a. green	75	55
O58	**79**	½a. green	10	10
O49	**57**	1a. brown	15	10
O59	**81**	1a. brown	30	30
O50	**82**	1a.3p. mauve	40	10
O51	**70**	2a. purple	20	30
O52		2a. red	30	35
O60	**59**	2a. red	15	30
O53w	**61**	2½a. orange	60	80
O54	**71**	4a. green	50	30
O62	**63**	4a. olive	1·75	75
O55	**65**	8a. purple	1·00	65
O56w	**66**	1r. brown and green	2·75	2·50
O57		2r. red and orange	9·50	32·00

1938. Postage stamps of India (King George VI) optd **PATIALA STATE SERVICE**.

O63	**91**	½a. brown	75	20
O64		9p. green	13·00	55·00
O65		1a. red	75	20
O66	**93**	1r. grey and brown	1·00	5·00
O67		2r. purple and green	4·50	5·00
O68		5r. green and blue	15·00	50·00

1939. Surch **1A SERVICE 1A**.

O70	**82**	1a. on 1¼a. mauve	7·00	2·25

1940. Official stamps of India optd **PATIALA**.

O71	**O 20**	3p. grey	1·00	10
O72		½a. brown	4·50	10
O73		½a. purple	50	10
O74		9p. green	50	40
O75		1a. red	2·00	10
O76		1a.3p. bistre	1·00	25
O77		1½a. violet	4·50	75
O78		2a. orange	7·00	30
O79		2½a. violet	2·50	75
O80		4a. brown	1·40	2·00
O81		8a. violet	2·75	5·00

1940. Postage stamps of India (King George VI) optd **PATIALA SERVICE**.

O82	**93**	1r. slate and brown	5·00	8·50
O83		2r. purple and brown	12·00	50·00
O84		5r. green and blue	20·00	75·00

PENANG — Pt. 1

A British Settlement which became a state of the Federation of Malaya, incorporated in Malaysia in 1963.

100 cents = 1 dollar (Straits or Malayan).

1948. Silver Wedding. As T **4b/c** of Pitcairn Islands.

1	10c. violet	30	20
2	$5 brown	30·00	28·00

1949. As Nos. 278/92 of Straits Settlement.

3	1c. black	20	10
4	2c. orange	85	10
5	3c. green	20	75
6	4c. brown	20	10
7	5c. purple	1·75	2·50
8	6c. grey	30	20
9	8c. red	60	3·00
10	8c. green	1·25	1·50
11	10c. mauve	20	10
12	12c. red	1·75	4·00
13	15c. blue	50	30
14	20c. black and green	50	1·00
15	20c. blue	55	1·00
16	25c. purple and orange	1·50	20
17	35c. red and purple	1·00	1·00
18	40c. red and purple	1·25	10·00
19	50c. black and blue	2·00	20
20	$1 blue and purple	16·00	1·75
21	$2 green and red	21·00	1·75
22	$3 green and brown	48·00	3·00

1949. U.P.U. As T **4d/g** of of Pitcairn Islands.

23	10c. purple	20	10
24	15c. blue	1·75	2·25
25	25c. orange	45	2·25
26	30c. black	1·50	3·25

1953. Coronation. As T **4h** of Pitcairn Islands.

27	10c. black and purple	1·25	10

1954. As T **1** of Malacca, but inscr "PENANG".

28	1c. black	10	70
29	2c. orange	50	30
30	4c. brown	70	10
31	5c. mauve	2·00	3·00
32	6c. grey	15	80
33	8c. green	20	3·25
34	10c. purple	20	10
35	12c. red	30	3·25
36	20c. blue	50	10
37	25c. purple and orange	30	10
38	30c. red and purple	30	10
39	35c. red and purple	70	60
40	50c. black and blue	50	10
41	$1 blue and purple	2·25	20
42	$2 green and red	9·00	3·50
43	$5 green and brown	45·00	3·50

1957. As Nos. 92/102 of Kedah, but inset portrait of Queen Elizabeth II.

44	1c. black	10	1·00
45	2c. red	10	1·00
46	4c. sepia	10	10
47	5c. lake	10	30
48	8c. green	1·25	2·00
49	10c. brown	30	10
50	20c. blue	60	40
51	50c. black and blue	50	60
52	$1 blue and purple	5·50	75
53	$2 green and red	16·00	11·00
54	$5 brown and green	19·00	11·00

1 Copra

1960. As Nos. 44/54, but with inset Arms of Penang as in T **1**.

55	1c. black	10	1·40
56	2c. red	10	1·40
57	4c. brown	10	10
58	5c. lake	10	10
59	8c. green	2·75	4·25
60	10c. purple	30	10
61	20c. blue	40	10
62	50c. black and blue	30	20
63	$1 blue and purple	4·25	1·50
64	$2 green and red	4·25	5·50
65	$5 brown and green	10·00	8·00

2 "Vanda hookeriana"

1965. As Nos. 115/21 of Kedah, but with Arms of Penang inset and inscr "PULAU PINANG" as in T **2**.

66	**2**	1c. multicoloured	10	1·00
67	–	2c. multicoloured	10	1·00
68	–	5c. multicoloured	20	10
69	–	6c. multicoloured	30	1·00
70	–	10c. multicoloured	20	10
71	–	15c. multicoloured	1·00	10
72	–	20c. multicoloured	1·60	30

The higher values used in Penang were Nos. 20/7 of Malaysia (National Issues).

3 "Valeria valeria"

1971. Butterflies. As Nos. 124/30 of Kedah but with Arms of Penang inset and inscr "pulau pinang" as in T 3.

No.	Type	Description	Mint	Used
75	–	1c. multicoloured	40	1·75
76	–	2c. multicoloured	70	1·75
77	–	5c. multicoloured	1·50	40
78	–	6c. multicoloured	1·50	1·75
79	–	10c. multicoloured	1·50	15
80	–	15c. multicoloured	1·50	10
81	3	20c. multicoloured	1·75	60

The higher values in use with this issue were Nos. 64/71 of Malaysia (National Issues).

4 "Etlingera elatior" (inscr "Phaeomeria speciosa")

5 Cocoa

1979. Flowers. As Nos. 135/41 of Kedah, but with Arms of Penang and inscr "pulau pinaug" as in T 4.

No.	Description	Mint	Used
86	1c. "Rafflesia hasseltii"	10	75
87	2c. "Pterocarpus indicus"	10	75
88	5c. "Lagerstroemia speciosa"	10	25
89	10c. "Durio zibethinus"	15	10
90	15c. "Hibiscus rosa-sinensis"	15	10
91	20c. "Rhododendron scortechinii"	20	10
92	25c. Type 4	40	30

1986. As Nos. 152/8 of Kedah but with Arms of Penang and inscr "PULAU PINANG" as in T 5.

No.	Description	Mint	Used
100	1c. Coffee	10	10
101	2c. Coconuts	10	10
102	5c. Type 5	10	10
103	10c. Black pepper	10	10
104	15c. Rubber	10	10
105	20c. Oil palm	10	10
106	30c. Rice	10	15

PENRHYN ISLAND Pt. 1

One of the Cook Islands in the South Pacific. A dependency of New Zealand. Used Cook Islands stamps until 1973 when further issues for use in the Northern group of the Cook Islands issues appeared.

A. NEW ZEALAND DEPENDENCY

1902. Stamps of New Zealand (Pictorials) surch **PENRHYN ISLAND.** and value in native language.

No.	Type	Description	Mint	Used
4	23	½d. green	80	5·50
10	42	1d. red	1·25	3·75
1	26	2½d. blue (No. 249)	2·75	8·00
14	28	3d. brown	10·00	21·00
15	31	6d. red	15·00	35·00
16a	34	1s. orange	42·00	48·00

1914. Stamps of New Zealand (King Edward VII) surch **PENRHYN ISLAND.** and value in native language.

No.	Type	Description	Mint	Used
19	51	½d. green	8·00	8·00
22		6d. red	23·00	70·00
23		1s. orange	42·00	95·00

1917. Stamps of New Zealand (King George V) optd **PENRHYN ISLAND.**

No.	Type	Description	Mint	Used
28	62	½d. green	1·00	2·00
29		1½d. grey	6·50	17·00
30		1½d. brown	60	17·00
24a		2½d. blue	2·00	6·50
31		3d. brown	3·50	20·00
26a		6d. red	5·00	18·00
27a		1s. orange	12·00	32·00

1920. Pictorial types as Cook Islands (1920), but inscr "PENRHYN".

No.	Type	Description	Mint	Used
32	9	½d. black and green	1·00	16·00
33	–	1d. black and red	1·50	15·00
34	–	1½d. black and violet	6·50	19·00
40	–	2½d. brown and black	3·50	27·00
35	–	3d. black and red	2·50	8·50
36	–	6d. brown and red	3·25	20·00
37	–	1s. black and blue	10·00	26·00

B. PART OF COOK ISLANDS

1973. Nos. 228/9, 231, 233/6, 239/40 and 243/5 of Cook Is. optd **PENRHYN NORTHERN** or **PENRHYN** ($1, 2).

No.	Description	Mint	Used
41B	1c. multicoloured	10	10
42B	2c. multicoloured	10	10
43B	3c. multicoloured	20	10
44B	4c. multicoloured	10	10
45B	5c. multicoloured	10	10
46B	6c. multicoloured	15	30
47B	8c. multicoloured	20	40
48B	15c. multicoloured	30	50
49B	20c. multicoloured	1·50	80
50B	50c. multicoloured	50	1·75
51B	$1 multicoloured	50	2·00
52B	$2 multicoloured	50	2·25

1973. Nos. 450/2 of Cook Is. optd **PENRHYN NORTHERN.**

No.	Type	Description	Mint	Used
53	138	25c. multicoloured	30	20
54	–	30c. multicoloured	30	20
55	–	50c. multicoloured	30	20

10 "Ostracion sp."

1974. Fishes. Multicoloured.

No.	Description	Mint	Used
56	½c. Type 10	50	75
57	1c. "Monodactylus argenteus"	70	75
58	2c. "Pomacanthus imperator"	80	75
59	3c. "Chelmon rostratus"	80	50
60	4c. "Chaetodon ornatissimus"	80	50
61	5c. "Chaetodon melanotus"	80	50
62	8c. "Chaetodon raffessi"	80	50
63	10c. "Chaetodon ephippium"	85	50
64	20c. "Pygoplites diacanthus"	1·75	50
65	25c. "Heniochus acuminatus"	1·75	50
66	60c. "Plectorhynchus chaetodonoides"	2·50	90
67	$1 "Balistipus undulatus"	3·25	1·25
68	$2 Bird's-eye view of Penrhyn	3·50	12·00
69	$5 Satellite view of Australasia	3·50	5·00

Nos. 68/9 are size 63 × 25 mm.

11 Penrhyn Stamps of 1902

13 Churchill giving "V" sign

12 "Adoration of the Kings" (Memling)

1974. Cent of Universal Postal Union. Mult.

No.	Description	Mint	Used
70	25c. Type 11	20	45
71	50c. Stamps of 1920	35	55

1974. Christmas. Multicoloured.

No.	Description	Mint	Used
72	5c. Type 12	20	30
73	10c. "Adoration of the Shepherds" (Hugo van der Goes)	25	30
74	25c. "Adoration of the Magi" (Rubens)	40	45
75	30c. "The Holy Family" (Borgianni)	45	65

1974. Birth Cent of Sir Winston Churchill.

No.	Type	Description	Mint	Used
76	13	30c. brown and gold	35	85
77	–	50c. green and gold	45	90

DESIGN: 50c. Full-face portrait.

1975. "Apollo–Soyuz" Space Project. Optd **KIA ORANA ASTRONAUTS** and emblem.

No.	Description	Mint	Used
78	$5 Satellite view of Australasia	1·75	2·50

15 "Virgin and Child" (Bouts)

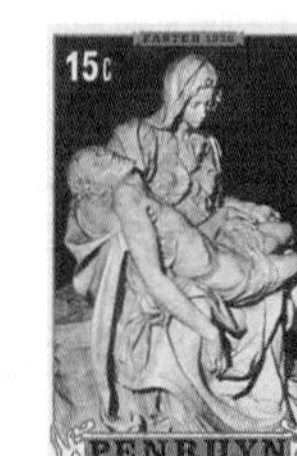

16 "Pieta"

1975. Christmas. Paintings of the "Virgin and Child" by artists given below. Multicoloured.

No.	Description	Mint	Used
79	7c. Type 15	40	10
80	15c. Leonardo da Vinci	70	20
81	35c. Raphael	1·10	35

1976. Easter. 500th Birth Anniv of Michelangelo.

No.	Type	Description	Mint	Used
82	16	15c. brown and gold	25	15
83	–	20c. lilac and gold	30	15
84	–	35c. green and gold	40	20
MS85		112 × 72 mm. Nos. 82/4	85	1·25

DESIGNS: Nos. 83/4 show different views of the "Pieta".

17 "Washington crossing the Delaware" (E. Leutze)

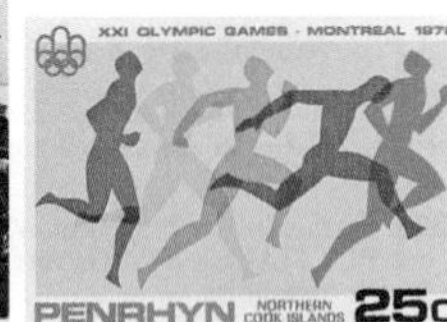

18 Running

1976. Bicentenary of American Revolution.

No.	Type	Description	Mint	Used
86	17	30c. multicoloured	30	15
87	–	30c. multicoloured	30	15
88	–	30c. multicoloured	30	15
89	–	50c. multicoloured	40	20
90	–	50c. multicoloured	40	20
91	–	50c. multicoloured	40	20
MS92		103 × 103 mm. Nos. 86/91	1·50	1·50

DESIGNS: Nos. 86/88, "Washington crossing the Delaware" (E. Leutze); Nos. 89/91, "The Spirit of '76" (A. M. Willard).

Nos. 86/88 and 89/91 were each printed together, se-tenant, forming a composite design of the complete painting. Type 17 shows the left-hand stamp of the 30c. design.

1976. Olympic Games, Montreal. Multicoloured.

No.	Description	Mint	Used
93	25c. Type 18	25	15
94	30c. Long jumping	30	15
95	75c. Throwing the javelin	55	25
MS96	86 × 128 mm. Nos. 93/5	1·10	2·00

19 "The Flight into Egypt"

1976. Christmas. Durer Engravings.

No.	Type	Description	Mint	Used
97	19	7c. black and silver	15	10
98	–	15c. blue and silver	25	15
99	–	35c. violet and silver	35	25

DESIGNS: 15c. "Adoration of the Magi"; 35c. "The Nativity".

20 The Queen in Coronation Robes

1977. Silver Jubilee. Multicoloured.

No.	Description	Mint	Used
100	50c. Type 20	25	60
101	$1 The Queen and Prince Philip	35	65
102	$2 Queen Elizabeth II	50	80
MS103	128 × 87 mm. Nos. 100/2	1·00	1·50

Stamps from the miniature sheet have silver borders.

21 "The Annunciation"

1977. Christmas. Illustrations by J. S. von Carolsfeld.

No.	Type	Description	Mint	Used
104	21	7c. brown, purple and gold	40	15
105	–	15c. red, purple and gold	60	15
106	–	35c. deep green, green and gold	1·00	30

DESIGNS: 15c. "The Announcement to the Shepherds"; 35c. "The Nativity".

22 Iiwi

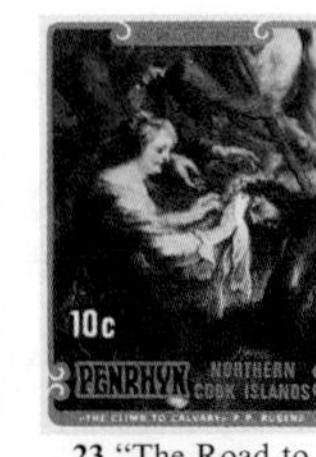

23 "The Road to Calvary"

1978. Bicentenary of Discovery of Hawaii. Birds and Artefacts. Multicoloured.

No.	Description	Mint	Used
107	20c. Type 22	80	30
108	20c. Elgin cloak	80	30
109	30c. Apapane	90	40
110	30c. Feather image of a god	90	40
111	35c. Moorhen	90	45
112	35c. Feather cape, helmet and staff	90	45
113	75c. Hawaii O-o	1·50	80
114	75c. Feather image and cloak	1·50	80
MS115	Two sheets, each 78 × 119 mm. containing. (a) Nos. 107, 109, 111, 113. (b) Nos. 108, 110, 112, 114	5·00	7·00

1978. Easter. 400th Birth Anniv of Rubens. Multicoloured.

No.	Description	Mint	Used
116	10c. Type 23	20	10
117	15c. "Christ on the Cross"	25	15
118	35c. "Christ with Straw"	45	25
MS119	87 × 138 mm. Nos. 116/18	1·00	1·60

Stamps from No. **MS**119 are slightly larger (28 × 36 mm).

1978. Easter. Children's Charity. Designs as Nos. 116/18 in separate miniature sheets, 49 × 68 mm, each with a face value of 60c.+5c.

No.	Description	Mint	Used
MS120	As Nos. 116/18. Set of 3 sheets	90	1·50

24 Royal Coat of Arms

25 "Madonna of the Pear"

1978. 25th Anniv of Coronation.

No.	Type	Description	Mint	Used
121	24	90c. black, gold and mauve	30	60
122	–	90c. multicoloured	30	60
123	–	90c. black, gold and green	30	60
MS124		75 × 122 mm. Nos. 121/3	1·10	2·00

DESIGNS: No. 122, Queen Elizabeth II; No. 123, New Zealand coat of arms.

1978. Christmas. 450th Death Anniv of Albrecht Durer. Multicoloured.

No.	Description	Mint	Used
125	30c. Type 25	65	30
126	35c. "The Virgin and Child with St. Anne" (Durer)	65	30
MS127	101 × 60 mm. Nos. 125/6	1·00	1·25

26 Sir Rowland Hill and G.B. Penny Black Stamp

27 Max and Moritz

1979. Death Centenary of Sir Rowland Hill. Mult.

No.	Description	Mint	Used
128	75c. Type 26	40	55
129	75c. 1974 U.P.U. Centenary 25c. and 50c. commemoratives	40	55
130	90c. Sir Rowland Hill	45	70
131	90c. 1978 Coronation Anniversary 90c. commemorative	45	70
MS132	116 × 58 mm. Nos. 128/31	1·25	1·50

Stamps from No. **MS**132 have cream backgrounds.

1979. International Year of the Child. Illustrations from "Max and Moritz" stories by Wilhelm Busch. Multicoloured.

No.	Description	Mint	Used
133	12c. Type 27	15	15
134	12c. Max and Moritz looking down chimney	15	15
135	12c. Max and Moritz making off with food	15	15
136	12c. Cook about to beat dog	15	15
137	15c. Max sawing through bridge	20	15
138	15c. Pursuer approaching bridge	20	15
139	15c. Collapse of bridge	20	15
140	15c. Pursuer in river	20	15
141	20c. Baker locking shop	20	20
142	20c. Max and Moritz emerge from hiding	20	20
143	20c. Max and Moritz falling in dough	20	20
144	20c. Max and Moritz made into buns	20	20

28 "Christ carrying Cross" (Book of Ferdinand II)

29 "Queen Elizabeth, 1937" (Sir Gerald Kelly)

1980. Easter. Scenes from 15th-cent Prayer Books. Multicoloured.
145 12c. Type **28** 15 20
146 20c. "The Crucifixion" (William Vrelant, Book of Duke of Burgundy) 20 25
147 35c. "Descent from the Cross" (Book of Ferdinand II) 30 45
MS148 111 × 65 mm. Nos. 145/7 55 1·00
Stamps from No. **MS**148 have cream borders.

1980. Easter. Children's Charity. Designs as Nos. 145/7 in separate miniature sheets 54 × 85 mm, each with a face value of 70c.+5c.
MS149 As Nos. 145/7. Set of 3 sheets 75 1·00

1980. 80th Birthday of The Queen Mother.
150 **29** $1 multicoloured . . . . . 1·25 1·25
MS151 55 × 84 mm. **29** $2.50 multicoloured . . . . 1·60 1·60

30 Falk Hoffman, East Germany (platform diving) (gold)

31 "The Virgin of Counsellors" (Luis Dalmau)

1980. Olympic Medal Winners. Multicoloured.
152 10c. Type **30** 25 10
153 10c. Martina Jaschke, East Germany (platform diving) 25 10
154 20c. Tomi Polkolainen, Finland (archery) 30 15
155 20c. Kete Losaberidse, U.S.S.R. (archery) 30 15
156 30c. Czechoslovakia (football) 35 20
157 30c. East Germany (football) 35 20
158 50c. Barbel Wockel, East Germany (200 m) 45 30
159 50c. Pietro Mennea, Italy (200 m) 45 30
MS160 150 × 106 mm. Nos. 152/9 1·40 1·75
Stamps from No. **MS**160 have gold borders.

1980. Christmas. Mult.
161 20c. Type **31** 15 15
162 35c. "Virgin and Child" (Serra brothers) 20 20
163 50c. "The Virgin of Albocacer" (Master of the Porciuncula) 30 30
MS164 135 × 75 mm. Nos. 161/3 1·50 1·50

1980. Christmas. Children's Charity. Design as Nos. 161/3 in separate miniature sheets, 54 × 77 mm, each with a face value of 70c.+5c.
MS165 As Nos. 161/3. Set of 3 sheets 1·50 1·50

32 Amatasi

33 "Jesus at the Grove" (Veronese)

1981. Sailing Craft and Ships (1st series). Mult.
166 1c. Type **32** 20 15
167 1c. Ndrua (canoe) 20 15
168 1c. Waka (canoe) 20 15
169 1c. Tongiaki (canoe) 20 15
170 3c. Va'a Teu'ua (canoe) . . . 40 15
171 3c. "Vitoria" (Del Cano's ship) 40 15
172 3c. "Golden Hind" (Drake's ship) 40 15
173 3c. "La Boudeuse" (Bougainville's ship) . . . 40 15
174 4c. H.M.S. "Bounty" 50 15
175 4c. "L'Astrolabe" (Dumont d'Urville's ship) 50 15
176 4c. "Star of India" (full-rigged ship) 50 15
177 4c. "Great Republic" (clipper) 50 15
178 6c. "Balcutha" (clipper) . . . 50 20
179 6c. "Coonatto" (clipper) . . 50 20
180 6c. "Antiope" (clipper) . . . 50 20
181 6c. "Taeping" (clipper) . . . 50 20
182 10c. "Preussen" (full rigged ship) 50 75
183 10c. "Pamir" (barque) . . . 50 75
184 10c. "Cap Hornier" (full-rigged ship) 50 75
185 10c. "Patriarch" (clipper) . . 50 75
186 15c. Type **32** 50 85
187 15c. As No. 167 . . . . . . 50 85
188 15c. As No. 168 . . . . . . 50 85
189 15c. As No. 169 . . . . . . 50 85
190 20c. As No. 170 . . . . . . 50 85
191 20c. As No. 171 . . . . . . 50 85
192 20c. As No. 172 . . . . . . 50 85
193 20c. As No. 173 . . . . . . 50 85
194 30c. As No. 174 . . . . . . 50 95
195 30c. As No. 175 . . . . . . 50 95
196 30c. As No. 176 . . . . . . 50 95
197 30c. As No. 177 . . . . . . 50 95
198 50c. As No. 178 . . . . . . 1·00 1·75
199 50c. As No. 179 . . . . . . 1·00 1·75
200 50c. As No. 180 . . . . . . 1·00 1·75
201 50c. As No. 181 . . . . . . 1·00 1·75
202 $1 As No. 182 . . . . 2·50 1·50
203 $1 As No. 183 . . . . 2·50 1·50
204 $1 As No. 184 . . . . 2·50 1·50
205 $1 As No. 185 . . . . 2·50 1·50
206 $2 "Cutty Sark" (clipper) . . 4·50 3·25
207 $4 "Mermerus" (clipper) . . 9·00 5·00
208 $6 H.M.S. "Resolution" and H.M.S. "Discovery" (Cook's ships) . . . . . . 15·00 12·00
Nos. 186/201 are 41 × 35 mm, Nos. 202/5 41 × 25 mm and Nos. 206/8 47 × 33 mm in size.
Nos. 181 and 201 are wrongly inscribed "TEAPING".
See also Nos. 337/55.

1981. Easter. Paintings. Multicoloured.
218 30c. Type **33** 40 20
219 40c. "Christ with Crown of Thorns" (Titian) 55 25
220 50c. "Pieta" (Van Dyck) . . 60 30
MS221 110 × 68 mm. Nos. 218/20 2·75 2·00

1981. Easter. Children's Charity. Designs as Nos. 218/20 in separate miniature sheets 70 × 86 mm, each with a face value of 70c.+5c.
MS222 As Nos. 218/20. Set of 3 sheets . . . . 1·50 1·50

34 Prince Charles as Young Child

35 Footballers

1981. Royal Wedding. Multicoloured.
223 40c. Type **34** 15 35
224 50c. Prince Charles as schoolboy 15 40
225 60c. Prince Charles as young man 20 40
226 70c. Prince Charles in ceremonial Naval uniform 20 45
227 80c. Prince Charles as Colonel-in-Chief, Royal Regiment of Wales 20 45
MS228 99 × 89 mm. Nos. 223/7 90 2·00

1981. International Year for Disabled Persons. Nos. 223/7 surch **+5c**.
229 **34** 40c.+5c. multicoloured . . 15 50
230 – 50c.+5c. multicoloured . . 15 55
231 – 60c.+5c. multicoloured . . 20 55
232 – 70c.+5c. multicoloured . . 20 60
233 – 80c.+5c. multicoloured . . 20 65
MS234 99 × 89 mm. As Nos. 229/33, but 10c. premium on each stamp 80 2·50

1981. World Cup Football Championship, Spain (1982). Multicoloured.
235 15c. Type **35** 20 15
236 15c. Footballer wearing orange jersey with black and mauve stripes 20 15
237 15c. Player in blue jersey . . 20 15
238 35c. Player in blue jersey . . 30 25
239 35c. Player in red jersey . . . 30 25
240 35c. Player in yellow jersey with green stripes 30 25
241 50c. Player in orange jersey 40 35
242 50c. Player in mauve jersey 40 35
243 50c. Player in black jersey . . 40 35
MS244 113 × 151 mm. As Nos. 235/43, but each stamp with a premium of 3c. . . . . . . 4·75 2·75

36 "The Virgin on a Crescent"

37 Lady Diana Spencer as Baby

1981. Christmas. Engravings by Durer.
245 **36** 30c. violet, purple and stone . . . . 90 1·00
246 – 40c. violet, purple and stone . . . . 1·25 1·40
247 – 50c. violet, purple and stone . . . . 1·50 1·75
MS248 134 × 75 mm. As Nos. 245/7, but each stamp with a premium of 2c. . . . . 2·25 2·25
MS249 Designs as Nos. 245/7 in separate miniature sheets, 58 × 85 mm, each with a face value of 70c.+5c. Set of 3 sheets . . 1·75 1·75
DESIGNS: 40c. "The Virgin at the Fence"; 50c. "The Holy Virgin and Child".

1982. 21st Birthday of Princess of Wales. Multicoloured.
250 30c. Type **37** 30 30
251 50c. As young child 40 45
252 70c. As schoolgirl 60 60
253 80c. As teenager 70 80
254 $1.40 As a young lady . . . 1·10 1·25
MS255 87 × 110 mm. Nos. 250/4 6·00 3·50

1982. Birth of Prince William of Wales (1st issue). Nos. 223/7 optd **BIRTH OF PRINCE WILLIAM OF WALES 21 JUNE 1982**.
256 40c. Type **34** 30 35
257 50c. Prince Charles as schoolboy 40 45
258 60c. Prince Charles as young man 45 55
259 70c. Prince Charles in ceremonial Naval uniform 50 60
260 80c. Prince Charles as Colonel-in-Chief, Royal Regiment of Wales 50 65
MS261 99 × 89 mm. Nos. 256/60 6·00 7·00

1982. Birth of Prince William of Wales (2nd issue). As Nos. 250/5 but with changed inscriptions. Multicoloured.
262 30c. As Type **37** (A) 60 55
263 30c. As Type **37** (B) 60 55
264 50c. As No. 251 (A) 70 65
265 50c. As No. 251 (B) 70 65
266 70c. As No. 252 (A) 90 80
267 70c. As No. 252 (B) 90 80
268 80c. As No. 253 (A) 95 85
269 80c. As No. 253 (B) 95 85
270 $1.40 As No. 254 (A) . . . . 1·40 1·25
271 $1.40 As No. 254 (B) . . . . 1·40 1·25
MS272 88 × 109 mm. As No. **MS**255 (c) . . . . 4·75 3·25
INSCR: A. "21 JUNE 1982. BIRTH OF PRINCE WILLIAM OF WALES"; B. "COMMEMORATING THE BIRTH OF PRINCE WILLIAM OF WALES"; C. "21 JUNE 1982. ROYAL BIRTH PRINCE WILLIAM OF WALES".

39 "Virgin and Child" (detail, Joos Van Cleve)

40 Red Coral

1982. Christmas. Details from Renaissance Paintings of "Virgin and Child". Multicoloured.
273 25c. Type **39** 30 40
274 48c. "Virgin and Child" (Filippino Lippi) 45 55
275 60c. "Virgin and Child" (Cima da Conegliano) . . 60 70
MS276 134 × 73 mm. As Nos. 273/5 but each with 2c. charity premium 1·00 2·00

1982. Christmas. Children's Charity. Designs as Nos. 273/5, but without frames, in separate miniature sheets, 60 × 85 mm, each with a face value of 70c.+5c.
MS277 As Nos. 273/5. Set of 3 sheets 1·25 1·60

1983. Commonwealth Day. Multicoloured.
278 60c. Type **40** 40 45
279 60c. Aerial view of Penrhyn atoll 40 45
280 60c. Eleanor Roosevelt on Penrhyn during Second World War 40 45
281 60c. Map of South Pacific . . 40 45

41 Scout Emblem and Blue Tropical Flower

1983. 75th Anniv of Boy Scout Movement. Multicoloured.
282 36c. Type **41** . . . . 1·50 65
283 48c. Emblem and pink flower 1·75 75
284 60c. Emblem and orange flower . . . . 1·75 1·00
MS285 86 × 46 mm. $2 As 48c., but with elements of design reversed 1·75 3·00

1983. 15th World Scout Jamboree, Alberta, Canada. Nos. 282/4 optd **XV WORLD JAMBOREE CANADA 1983**.
286 36c. Type **41** . . . . 1·25 40
287 48c. Emblem and pink flower 1·50 55
288 60c. Emblem and orange flower . . . . 1·60 75
MS289 86 × 46 mm. $2 As 48c., but with elements of design reversed 1·75 3·50

43 School of Sperm Whales

1983. Whale Conservation. Multicoloured.
290 8c. Type **43** . . . . 1·00 70
291 15c. Harpooner preparing to strike . . . . 1·40 95
292 35c. Whale attacking boat . . 2·00 1·40
293 60c. Dead whales marked with flags . . . . 3·00 2·00
294 $1 Dead whales on slipway 3·75 3·00

44 "Mercury" (cable ship)

1983. World Communications Year. Multicoloured.
295 36c. Type **44** 80 35
296 48c. Men watching cable being laid 85 45
297 60c. "Mercury" (different) . . 1·10 60
MS298 115 × 90 mm. As Nos. 295/7 but each with charity premium of 3c. . . . . 1·50 1·60
On No. **MS**298 the values are printed in black and have been transposed with the World Communications Year logo.

1983. Various stamps surch. (a) Nos. 182/5, 190/7 and 206.
299 18c. on 10c. "Preussen" . . . 75 30
300 18c. on 10c. "Pamir" 75 30
301 18c. on 10c. "Cap Hornier" 75 30
302 18c. on 10c. "Patriarch" . . 75 30
303 36c. on 20c. Va'a Teu'ua . . 1·00 45
304 36c. on 20c. "Vitoria" . . . 1·00 45
305 36c. on 20c. "Golden Hind" 1·00 45
306 36c. on 20c. "La Boudeuse" 1·00 45
307 36c. on 30c. H.M.S. "Bounty" . . . . 1·00 45
308 36c. on 30c. "L'Astrolabe" 1·00 45
309 36c. on 30c. "Star of India" 1·00 45
310 36c. on 30c. "Great Republic" . . . . 1·00 45
311 $1.20 on $2 "Cutty Sark" . . 4·00 1·60

(b) Nos. 252/3.
312 72c. on 70c. Princess Diana as schoolgirl . . . . 4·00 1·50
313 96c. on 80c. Princess Diana as teenager . . . . 4·00 1·75

1983. Nos. 225/6, 268/9, 253 and 208 surch.
314 48c. on 60c. Prince Charles as young man . . . . 3·75 1·75
315 72c. on 70c. Prince Charles in ceremonial Naval uniform 4·25 1·90
316 96c. on 80c. As No. 253 (inscr "21 JUNE 1982 ...") 3·00 1·10
317 96c. on 80c. As No. 253 (inscr "COMMEMORATING ...") . . . . 2·00 1·10
318 $1.20 on $4.40 As young lady 3·50 1·60
319 $5.60 on $6 H.M.S. "Resolution" and "Discovery" . . . . 18·00 10·00

45 George Cayley's Airship Design, 1837

1983. Bicentenary of Manned Flight. Mult. A. Inscr "NORTHERN COOK ISLANDS".
320A 36c. Type **45** . . . . 1·00 80
321A 48c. Dupuy de Lome's man-powered airship, 1872 . . . . 1·25 90
322A 60c. Santos Dumont's airship "Ballon No. 6", 1901 . . . . 1·50 1·25
323A 96c. Lebaudy-Juillot's airship, No. 1 "La Jaune", 1902 . . . . . . 2·25 1·75
324A $1.32 Airship LZ-127 "Graf Zeppelin", 1929 . . . . 3·00 2·50
MS325A 113 × 138 mm. Nos. 320A/4A . . . . 6·50 11·00

B. Corrected spelling optd in black on silver over original inscription.
320B 36c. Type **45** 35 30
321B 48c. Dupuy de Lome's man-powered airship, 1872 . . 40 45
322B 60c. Santos Dumont's airship "Ballon No. 6", 1901 . . . . 45 50
323B 96c. Lebaudy-Juillot's airship No. 1 "La Jaune", 1902 . . . . 75 80
324B $1.32 Airship LZ-127 "Graf Zeppelin", 1929 . . . . 1·00 1·10
MS325B 113 × 138 mm. Nos. 320B/4B . . . . 2·25 4·25

46 "Madonna in the Meadow" **47** Waka

1983. Christmas. 500th Birth Anniv of Raphael. Multicoloured.
326 36c. Type **46** 60 40
327 42c. "Tempi Madonna" . . . 60 40
328 48c. "The Smaller Cowper Madonna" 80 50
329 60c. "Madonna della Tenda" 95 60
MS330 87 × 115 mm. As Nos. 326/9 but each with a charity premium of 3c. . . . . 3·00 2·50

1983. Nos. 266/7, 227 and 270 surch.
331 72c. on 70c. As No. 252 (inscr "21 JUNE 1982 ...") 1·75 80
332 72c. on 70c. As No. 252 (inscr "COMMEMORATING ...") . . . . 1·00 60
333 96c. on 80c. Prince Charles as Colonel-in-Chief, Royal Regiment of Wales . . . . 1·75 65
334 $1.20 on $1.40 As No. 254 (inscr "21 JUNE 1982 ...") 2·00 70
335 $1.20 on $1.40 As No. 254 (inscr "COMMEMORATING ...") . . . . 1·50 65

1983. Christmas. 500th Birth Anniv of Raphael. Children's Charity. Designs as Nos. 326/9 in separate miniature sheets, 65 × 84 mm, each with a face value of 75c.+5c.
MS336 As Nos. 326/9. Set of 4 sheets 2·00 3·00

1984. Sailing Craft and Ships (2nd series). Multicoloured.
337 2c. Type **47** 70 70
338 4c. Amatasi 70 70
339 5c. Ndrua 70 70
340 8c. Tongiaki 70 70
341 10c. "Vitoria" 70 60
342 18c. "Golden Hind" . . . . 1·00 70
343 20c. "La Boudeuse" 70 70
344 30c. H.M.S. "Bounty" . . . 1·00 70
345 36c. "L'Astrolabe" 70 70
346 48c. "Great Republic" . . . 70 70
347 50c. "Star of India" 70 70
348 60c. "Coonatto" 70 70
349 72c. "Antiope" 70 70
350 80c. "Balcutha" 70 70
351 96c. "Cap Hornier" 85 85
352 $1.20 "Pamir" . . . . 2·50 1·40
353 $3 "Mermerus" (41 × 31 mm) 5·00 3·00
354 $5 "Cutty Sark" (41 × 31 mm) . . . . . . 5·50 5·00
355 $9.60 H.M.S. "Resolution" and H.M.S. "Discovery" (41 × 31 mm) . . . . . . 17·00 16·00

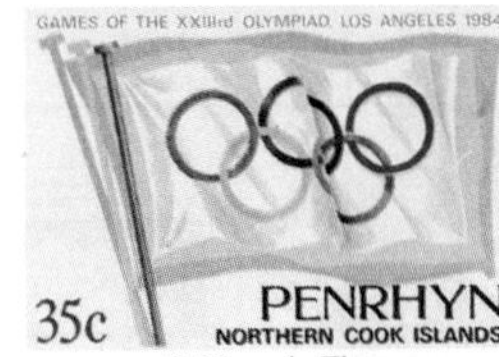

48 Olympic Flag

1984. Olympic Games, Los Angeles. Mult.
356 35c. Type **48** 30 35
357 60c. Olympic torch and flags 50 55
358 $1.80 Ancient athletes and Coliseum . . . . 1·50 1·60
MS359 103 × 86 mm. As Nos. 356/8 but each with a charity premium of 5c. . . . . 2·40 2·50

49 Penrhyn Stamps of 1978, 1979 and 1981

1984. "Ausipex" International Stamp Exhibition, Melbourne. Multicoloured.
360 60c. Type **49** 50 75
361 $1.20 Location map of Penrhyn . . . . 1·00 1·25
MS362 90 × 90 mm. As Nos. 360/1, but each with a face value of 96c. 1·75 2·00

1984. Birth of Prince Harry. Nos. 223/4 and 250/1 surch **$2 Birth of Prince Harry 15 Sept. 1984**.
363 $2 on 30c. Type **37** . . . . . 1·60 1·50
364 $2 on 40c. Type **34** . . . . . 1·75 1·75
365 $2 on 50c. Prince Charles as schoolboy . . . . 1·75 1·75
366 $2 on 50c. Lady Diana as young child 1·60 1·50

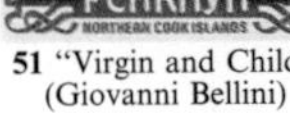

51 "Virgin and Child" (Giovanni Bellini) **53** Lady Elizabeth Bowes-Lyon, 1921

52 Harlequin Duck

1984. Christmas. Paintings of the Virgin and Child by different artists. Multicoloured.
367 36c. Type **51** 60 35
368 48c. Lorenzo di Credi 75 45
369 60c. Palma the Older 80 50
370 96c. Raphael . . . . 1·00 80
MS371 93 × 118 mm. As Nos. 367/70, but each with a charity premium of 5c. . . . . 2·50 3·00

1984. Christmas. Children's Charity. Designs as Nos. 367/70, but without frames, in separate miniature sheets 67 × 81 mm, each with a face value of 96c.+10c.
MS372 As Nos. 367/70. Set of 4 sheets . . . . 3·00 3·50

1985. Birth Bicentenary of John J. Audubon (ornithologist). Multicoloured.
373 20c. Type **52** . . . . 2·00 1·75
374 55c. Sage grouse . . . . . . 2·75 2·75
375 65c. Solitary sandpiper . . . 3·00 3·00
376 75c. Dunlin . . . . 3·25 3·50
MS377 Four sheets, each 70 × 53 mm. As Nos. 373/6, but each with a face value of 95c. 8·50 6·50
Nos. 373/6 show original paintings.

1985. Life and Times of Queen Elizabeth the Queen Mother. Each violet, silver and yellow.
378 75c. Type **53** 40 65
379 95c. With baby Princess Elizabeth, 1926 . . . . . 50 80
380 $1.20 Coronation Day, 1937 65 1·00
381 $2.80 On her 70th birthday 1·25 2·00
MS382 66 × 90 mm. $5 The Queen Mother . . . . 2·40 3·25
See also No. **MS**403.

54 "The House in the Wood"

1985. International Youth Year. Birth Centenary of Jacob Grimm (folklorist). Multicoloured.
383 75c. Type **54** . . . . 2·50 2·25
384 95c. "Snow-White and Rose-Red" . . . . 2·75 2·50
385 $1.15 "The Goose Girl" . . . 3·00 2·75

55 "The Annunciation"

1985. Christmas. Paintings by Murillo. Mult.
386 75c. Type **55** . . . . 1·25 1·25
387 $1.15 "Adoration of the Shepherds" . . . . 1·75 1·75
388 $1.80 "The Holy Family" . . 2·50 2·50
MS389 66 × 131 mm. As Nos. 386/8, but each with a face value of 95c. 2·75 3·00
MS390 Three sheets, each 66 × 72 mm. As Nos. 386/8, but with face values of $1.20, $1.45 and $2.75. Set of 3 sheets . . . 4·50 4·75

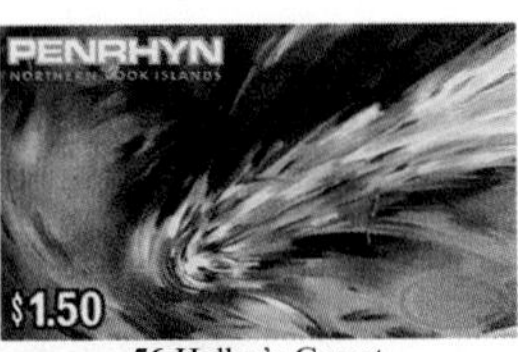

56 Halley's Comet

1986. Appearance of Halley's Comet. Design showing details of the painting "Fire and Ice" by Camille Rendal. Multicoloured.
391 $1.50 Type **56** . . . . 2·00 1·50
392 $1.50 Stylized "Giotto" spacecraft . . . . 2·00 1·50
MS393 108 × 43 mm. $3 As Nos. 391/2 (104 × 39 mm). Imperf 2·25 2·50
Nos. 391/2 were printed together, forming a composite design of the complete painting.

57 Princess Elizabeth aged Three, 1929, and Bouquet

1986. 60th Birthday of Queen Elizabeth II. Multicoloured.
394 95c. Type **57** . . . . 1·50 80
395 $1.45 Profile of Queen Elizabeth and St. Edward's Crown . . . . 2·00 1·25
396 $2.50 Queen Elizabeth aged three and in profile with Imperial State Crown (56 × 30 mm) . . . . . . 2·50 2·00

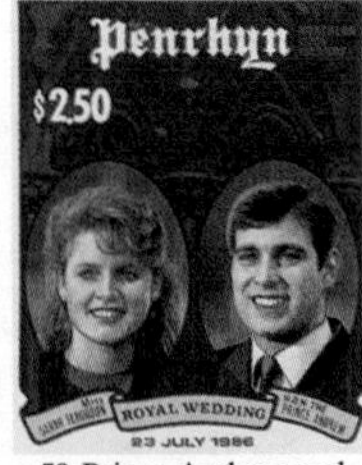

58 Statue of Liberty under Construction, Paris **59** Prince Andrew and Miss Sarah Ferguson

1986. Centenary of Statue of Liberty. Each black, gold and green.
397 95c. Type **58** 65 70
398 $1.75 Erection of Statue, New York . . . . 1·10 1·25
399 $3 Artist's impression of Statue, 1876 . . . . 2·10 2·25
See also No. **MS**412.

1986. Royal Wedding. Multicoloured.
400 $2.50 Type **59** . . . . 3·50 3·50
401 $3.50 Profiles of Prince Andrew and Miss Sarah Ferguson . . . . 4·00 4·00

1986. "Stampex '86" Stamp Exhibition, Adelaide. No. **MS**362 surch **$2** in black on gold.
MS402 $2 on 96c. × 2 . . . . . 6·00 7·00
The "Stampex '86" exhibition emblem is overprinted on the sheet margin.

1986. 86th Birthday of Queen Elizabeth the Queen Mother. Nos. 378/81 in miniature sheet, 90 × 120 mm.
MS403 Nos. 378/81 . . . . . . 12·00 9·50

61 "Adoration of the Shepherds" **65** "The Garvagh Madonna"

1986. Christmas. Engravings by Rembrandt. Each brown, ochre and gold.
404 65c. Type **61** . . . . 1·75 1·75
405 $1.75 "Virgin and Child" . . 3·00 3·00
406 $2.50 "The Holy Family" . . 4·25 4·25
MS407 120 × 87 mm. As Nos. 404/6, but each size 31 × 39 mm with a face value of $1.50 . . . . . . 11·00 9·00

1986. Visit of Pope John Paul II to **South Pacific**. Nos. 404/6 surch **SOUTH PACIFIC VISIT 21 TO 24 NOVEMBER 1986 +10c**.
408 65c.+10c. Type **61** . . . . 3·00 2·00
409 $1.75+10c. "Virgin and Child" . . . . 4·50 3·50
410 $2.50+10c. "The Holy Family" . . . . 5·50 4·00
MS411 120 × 87 mm. As Nos. 408/10, but each size 31 × 39 mm with a face value of $1.50+10c. . . . . 13·00 9·00

1987. Centenary of Statue of Liberty (1986) (2nd issue). Two sheets, each 122 × 122 mm, containing multicoloured designs as T **112a** of Niue.
MS412 Two sheets. (a) 65c. Head and torch of Statue; 65c. Torch at sunset; 65c. Restoration workers with flag; 65c. Statue and Manhattan skyline; 65c. Workers and scaffolding. (b) 65c. Workers on Statue crown (horiz); 65c. Aerial view of Ellis Island (horiz); 65c. Ellis Island Immigration Centre (horiz); 65c. View from Statue to Ellis Island and Manhattan (horiz); 65c. Restoration workers (horiz). Set of 2 sheets . . . . 7·50 11·00

1987. Royal Ruby Wedding. Nos. 68/9 optd **Fortieth Royal Wedding Anniversary 1947–87**.
413 $2 Birds-eye view of Penrhyn 2·00 2·25
414 $5 Satellite view of Australasia . . . . 3·50 4·25

1987. Christmas. Religious Paintings by Raphael. Multicoloured.
415 95c. Type **65** . . . . 1·50 1·50
416 $1.60 "The Alba Madonna" 2·00 2·00
417 $2.25 "The Madonna of the Fish" . . . . 3·00 3·00
MS418 91 × 126 mm. As Nos. 415/17, but each with a face value of $1.15 . . . . 11·00 12·00
MS419 70 × 86 mm. $4.80 As No. 417, but size 36 × 39 mm. 12·00 12·00

66 Athletics

1988. Olympic Games, Seoul. Multicoloured.
420 55c. Type **66** 75 65
421 95c. Pole vaulting (vert) . . . 1·25 1·00

422 $1.25 Shot putting . . . . . 1·50 1·40
423 $1.50 Lawn tennis (vert) . . 2·50 1·75
MS424 110 × 70 mm. As Nos. 421 and 423, but each with a face value of $2.50 . . . . 4·00 5·00

1988. Olympic Gold Medal Winners, Seoul. Nos. 420/3 optd.
425 55c. Type **66** (optd **CARL LEWIS UNITED STATES 100 METERS**) 80 60
426 95c. Pole vaulting (optd **LOUISE RITTER UNITED STATES HIGH JUMP**) . . . . 1·25 90
427 $1.25 Shot putting (optd **ULF TIMMERMANN EAST GERMANY SHOT-PUT**) 1·50 1·25
428 $1.50 Lawn tennis (optd **STEFFI GRAF WEST GERMANY WOMEN'S TENNIS**) . . . . 4·00 1·75
MS429 110 × 70 mm. $2.50 As No. 421 (optd **JACKIE JOYNER-KERSEE United States Heptathlon**); $2.50 As No. 423 (optd **STEFFI GRAF West Germany Women's Tennis MILOSLAV MECIR Czechoslovakia Men's Tennis**) 5·00 5·50

67 "Virgin and Child"

69 Virgin Mary

68 Neil Armstrong stepping onto Moon

1988. Christmas. Designs showing different "Virgin and Child" paintings by Titian.
430 **67** 70c. multicoloured 90 90
431 – 85c. multicoloured . . . . 1·00 1·00
432 – 95c. multicoloured . . . . 1·25 1·25
433 – $1.25 multicoloured . . . 1·50 1·50
MS434 100 × 80 mm. $6.40 As type **67**, but diamond-shaped (57 × 57 mm) . . . . 6·00 7·00

1989. 20th Anniv of First Manned Moon Landing. Multicoloured.
435 55c. Type **68** . . . . 1·40 70
436 75c. Astronaut on Moon carrying equipment . . . . 1·60 85
437 95c. Conducting experiment on Moon . . . . 1·90 1·10
438 $1.25 Crew of "Apollo 11" 2·25 1·40
439 $1.75 Crew inside "Apollo 11" . . . . 2·40 1·90

1989. Christmas. Details from "The Nativity" by Durer. Multicoloured.
440 55c. Type **69** 80 80
441 70c. Christ Child and cherubs 90 90
442 85c. Joseph . . . . 1·25 1·25
443 $1.25 Three women . . . . . 1·60 1·60
MS444 88 × 95 mm. $6.40 "The Nativity" (31 × 50 mm) . . . . 6·50 7·50

70 Queen Elizabeth the Queen Mother

1990. 90th Birthday of Queen Elizabeth the Queen Mother.
445 **70** $2.25 multicoloured . . . 2·50 2·50
MS446 85 × 73 mm. **70** $7.50 multicoloured . . . . 12·00 12·00

71 "Adoration of the Magi" (Veronese)

1990. Christmas. Religious Paintings. Multicoloured.
447 55c. Type **71** . . . . 1·00 1·00
448 70c. "Virgin and Child" (Quentin Metsys) . . . . . 1·40 1·40
449 85c. "Virgin and Child Jesus" (Hugo van der Goes) . . . 1·60 1·60
450 $1.50 "Adoration of the Kings" (Jan Gossaert) . . 2·50 2·50
MS451 108 × 132 mm. $6.40 "Virgin and Child with Saints, Francis, John the Baptist, Zenobius and Lucy" (Domenico Veneziano) 8·00 9·00

1990. "Birdpex '90" Stamp Exhibition, Christchurch, New Zealand. Nos. 373/6 surch **Birdpex '90** and emblem.
452 $1.50 on 20c. Type **52** . . . 1·90 2·25
453 $1.50 on 55c. Sage grouse . . 1·90 2·25
454 $1.50 on 65c. Solitary sandpiper . . . . 1·90 2·25
455 $1.50 on 75c. Dunlin . . . . 1·90 2·25

1991. 65th Birthday of Queen Elizabeth II. No. 208 optd **COMMEMORATING 65th BIRTHDAY OF H.M. QUEEN ELIZABETH II.**
456 $6 H.M.S. "Resolution" and "Discovery", 1776–80 . . . 12·00 13·00

74 "The Virgin and Child with Saints" (G. David)

1991. Christmas. Religious Paintings. Multicoloured.
457 55c. Type **74** . . . . 1·00 1·00
458 85c. "Nativity" (Tintoretto) 1·50 1·50
459 $1.15 "Mystic Nativity" (Botticelli) . . . . 1·75 1·75
460 $1.85 "Adoration of the Shepherds" (B. Murillo) . . 2·75 3·25
MS461 79 × 103 mm. $6.40 "The Madonna of the Chair" (Raphael) (vert) . . . . 11·00 11·00

74a Running

1992. Olympic Games, Barcelona. Multicoloured.
462 75c. Type **74a** . . . . 1·60 1·60
463 95c. Boxing . . . . 1·75 1·75
464 $1.15 Swimming . . . . . . 2·00 2·00
465 $1.50 Wrestling . . . . . . 2·25 2·25

75 Marquesan Canoe

1992. 6th Festival of Pacific Arts, Rarotonga. Multicoloured.
466 $1.15 Type **75** . . . . 1·60 1·60
467 $1.75 Tangaroa statue from Rarotonga . . . . 2·00 2·00
468 $1.95 Manihiki canoe . . . . 2·25 2·25

1992. Royal Visit by Prince Edward. Nos. 466/8 optd **ROYAL VISIT.**
469 $1.15 Type **75** . . . . 2·25 2·00
470 $1.75 Tangaroa statue from Rarotonga . . . . 3·00 2·75
471 $1.95 Manihiki canoe . . . . 3·75 3·50

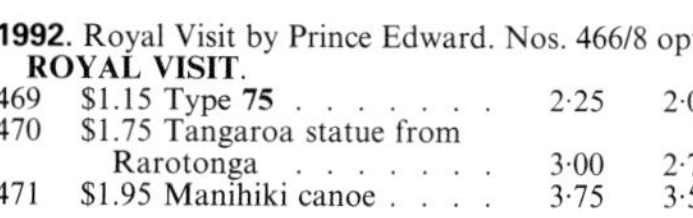

76 "Virgin with Child and Saints" (Borgognone)

1992. Christmas. Religious Paintings by Ambrogio Borgognone. Multicoloured.
472 55c. Type **76** 75 75
473 85c. "Virgin on Throne" . . 1·10 1·10
474 $1.05 "Virgin on Carpet" . . 1·40 1·40
475 $1.85 "Virgin of the Milk" 2·25 2·25
MS476 101 × 86 mm. $6.40 As 55c., but larger (36 × 46 mm) . . . . 7·00 8·00

77 Vincente Pinzon and "Nina"

1992. 500th Anniv of Discovery of America by Columbus. Multicoloured.
477 $1.15 Type **77** . . . . 2·00 2·00
478 $1.35 Martin Pinzon and "Pinta" . . . . 2·25 2·25
479 $1.75 Christopher Columbus and "Santa Maria" . . . . 3·00 3·00

78 Queen Elizabeth II in 1953

80 "Virgin on Throne with Child" (detail) (Tura)

79 Bull-mouth Helmet

1993. 40th Anniv of Coronation.
480 **78** $6 multicoloured . . . . . 6·50 8·50

1993. Marine Life. Multicoloured.
481 5c. Type **79** 10 10
482 10c. Daisy coral 10 10
483 15c. Hydroid coral 10 15
484 20c. Feather-star 15 20
485 25c. Sea star 15 20
486 30c. Varicose nudibranch . . 20 25
487 50c. Smooth sea star 30 35
488 70c. Black-lip pearl oyster . . 45 50
489 80c. Four-coloured nudibranch 50 55
490 85c. Prickly sea cucumber . . 55 60
491 90c. Organ pipe coral 60 65
492 $1 Blue sea lizard 65 70
493 $2 Textile cone shell . . . . 1·25 1·40
494 $3 Starfish . . . . 1·90 2·00
495 $5 As $3 . . . . 3·25 3·50
496 $8 As $3 . . . . 5·00 5·25
497 $10 As $3 . . . . 7·00 7·25
Nos. 494/7 are larger, 47 × 34 mm, and include a portrait of Queen Elizabeth II at top right.

1993. Christmas.
499 **80** 55c. multicoloured . . . . 1·00 1·00
500 – 85c. multicoloured . . . . 1·50 1·50
501 – $1.05 multicoloured . . . 1·75 1·75
502 – $1.95 multicoloured . . . 2·75 3·00
503 – $4.50 mult (32 × 47 mm) 6·00 7·00
DESIGNS: 80c. to $4.50, Different details from "Virgin on Throne with Child" (Cosme Tura).

81 Neil Armstrong stepping onto Moon

1994. 25th Anniv of First Manned Moon Landing.
504 **81** $3.25 multicoloured . . . 7·50 8·00

82 "The Virgin and Child with Sts. Paul and Jerome" (Vivarini)

84 Queen Elizabeth the Queen Mother at Remembrance Day Ceremony

83 Battleship Row burning, Pearl Harbor

1994. Christmas. Religious Paintings. Multicoloured.
505 90c. Type **82** . . . . 1·10 1·25
506 90c. "The Virgin and Child with St. John" (Luini) . . 1·10 1·25
507 90c. "The Virgin and Child with Sts. Jerome and Dominic" (Lippi) . . . . 1·10 1·25
508 90c. "Adoration of the Shepherds" (Murillo) . . . 1·10 1·25
509 $1 "Adoration of the Kings" (detail of angels) (Reni) . . 1·10 1·25
510 $1 "Madonna and Child with the Infant Baptist" (Raphael) . . . . 1·10 1·25
511 $1 "Adoration of the Kings" (detail of manger) (Reni) 1·10 1·25
512 $1 "Virgin and Child" (Borgognone) . . . . . . 1·10 1·25

1995. 50th Anniv of End of Second World War. Multicoloured.
513 $3.75 Type **83** . . . . 7·50 7·50
514 $3.75 Boeing B-25 Superfortress "Enola Gay" over Hiroshima . . . . . 7·50 7·50

1995. 95th Birthday of Queen Elizabeth the Queen Mother.
515 **84** $4.50 multicoloured . . . 8·00 8·50

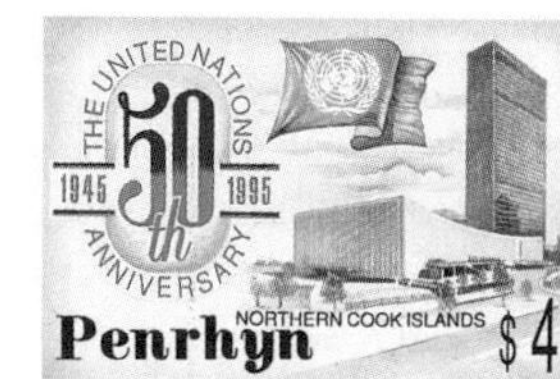

85 Anniversary Emblem, United Nations Flag and Headquarters

1995. 50th Anniv of United Nations.
516 **85** $4 multicoloured . . . . . 4·00 5·50

86 Loggerhead Turtle

1995. Year of the Sea Turtle. Multicoloured.
517 $1.15 Type **86** . . . . . . 1·75 2·00
518 $1.15 Hawksbill turtle . . . 1·75 2·00
519 $1.65 Olive ridley turtle . . . 2·25 2·50
520 $1.65 Green turtle . . . . . 2·25 2·50

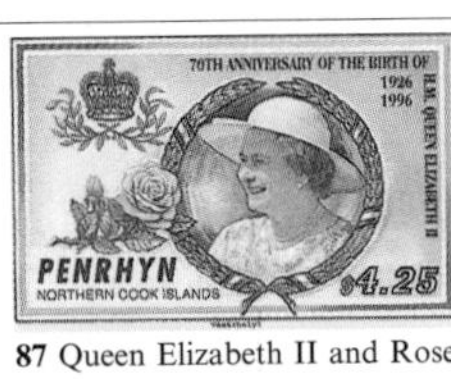

87 Queen Elizabeth II and Rose

1996. 70th Birthday of Queen Elizabeth.
521 **87** $4.25 multicoloured . . . 5·00 6·50

88 Olympic Flame, National Flags and Sports

1996. Centenary of Modern Olympic Games.
522 **88** $5 multicoloured . . . . . 6·50 8·00

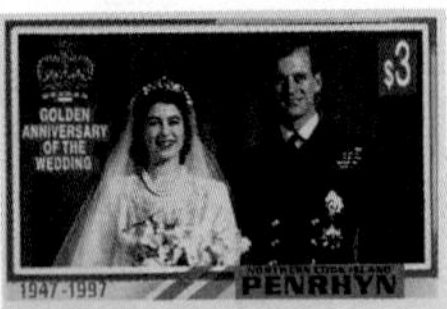

89 Royal Wedding, 1947

1997. Golden Wedding of Queen Elizabeth and Prince Philip.
523 **89** $3 multicoloured . . . . . 3·75 3·75
MS524 42×28 mm. **89** $4 multicoloured . . . . 4·00 5·00

90 Diana, Princess of Wales with Sons

90a King George VI and Queen Elizabeth on Wedding Day

1998. Diana, Princess of Wales Commemoration.
525 **90** $1.50 multicoloured . . . 1·50 1·75
MS526 70×100 mm. **90** $3.75 multicoloured . . . . 6·50 6·50

1998. Children's Charities. No. **MS**526 surch **+$1 CHILDREN'S CHARITIES.**
MS527 70×100 mm. **90** $3.75+$1 multicoloured . . . . 3·50 4·25

1999. New Millennium. Nos. 466/8 optd **KIA ORANA THIRD MILLENNIUM.**
528 $1.15 Type **75** . . . . 1·25 1·25
529 $1.75 Tangaroa statue from Rarotonga . . . . 1·60 1·60
530 $1.95 Manihiki canoe . . . . 1·75 1·75

2000. Queen Elizabeth the Queen Mother's 100th Birthday.
531 **90a** $2.50 purple and brown 2·25 2·40
532 – $2.50 brown . . . . . . 2·25 2·40
533 – $2.50 green and brown . . 2·25 2·40
534 – $2.50 blue and brown . . 2·25 2·40
MS535 72×100 mm. $10 multicoloured . . . . 7·50 8·50
DESIGNS: No. 532, Queen Elizabeth with young Princess Elizabeth; 533, Royal Family in 1930; 534, Queen Elizabeth with Princesses Elizabeth and Margaret; **MS**535, Queen Elizabeth wearing blue gown.

90b Ancient Greek Javelin-throwers

2000. Olympic Games, Sydney. Multicoloured.
536 $2.75 Type **90b** . . . . . . 2·40 2·50
537 $2.75 Modern javelin-thrower 2·40 2·50
538 $2.75 Ancient Greek discus-thrower . . . . 2·40 2·50
539 $2.75 Modern discus-thrower 2·40 2·50
MS540 90×99 mm. $3.50 Cook Islands Olympic Torch Relay runner in traditional costume (vert) . . . . 3·00 3·50

91 Ocean Sunfish

2003. Endangered Species. Ocean Sunfish.
541 **91** 80c. multicoloured 50 55
542 — 90c. multicoloured 60 65
543 — $1.15 multicoloured . . . 75 80
544 — $1.95 multicoloured . . . 1·25 1·40
DESIGNS: 90c. to $1.95, Ocean sunfish.

OFFICIAL STAMPS

1978. Optd or surch **O.H.M.S.**
O 1 1c. multicoloured (No. 57) 15 10
O 2 2c. multicoloured (No. 58) 15 10
O 3 3c. multicoloured (No. 59) 25 10
O 4 4c. multicoloured (No. 60) 25 10
O 5 5c. multicoloured (No. 61) 30 10
O 6 8c. multicoloured (No. 62) 35 15
O 7 10c. multicoloured (No. 63) 40 15
O 8 15c. on 60c. mult (No. 66) 45 25
O 9 18c. on 60c. mult (No. 66) 50 25
O10 20c. multicoloured (No. 64) 50 25
O11 25c. multicoloured (No. 65) 55 30
O12 30c. on 60c. mult (No. 66) 55 35
O13 50c. multicoloured (No. 89) 1·10 55
O14 50c. multicoloured (No. 90) 1·10 55
O15 50c. multicoloured (No. 91) 1·10 55
O16 $1 multicoloured (No. 101) 1·75 45
O17 $2 multicoloured (No. 102) 3·00 50

1985. Nos. 206/8, 278/81, 337/47 and 349/55 optd **O.H.M.S.** or surch also.
O18 2c. Type **47** 60 70
O19 4c. Amatasi 60 70
O20 5c. Ndrua 60 70
O21 8c. Tongiaki 60 70
O22 10c. "Vitoria" 60 70
O23 18c. "Golden Hind" . . . . 1·75 90
O24 20c. "La Boudeuse" . . . . 1·50 90
O25 30c. H.M.S. "Bounty" . . . 2·50 1·00
O26 40c. on 36c. "L'Astrolabe" 1·50 90
O27 50c. "Star of India" . . . . 1·50 90
O28 55c. on 48c. "Great Republic" . . . . 1·50 90
O39 65c. on 60c. Type **40** . . . . 80 1·00
O40 65c. on 60c. Aerial view of Penrhyn atoll . . . . . . 80 1·00
O41 65c. on 60c. Eleanor Roosevelt on Penrhyn during Second World War 80 1·00
O42 65c. on 60c. Map of South Pacific . . . . 80 1·00
O29 75c. on 72c. "Antiope" . . . 2·25 1·40
O30 75c. on 96c. "Cap Hornier" 2·25 1·40
O31 80c. "Balcutha" . . . . . . 2·25 1·40
O32 $1.20 "Pamir" . . . . . . 2·50 1·60
O33 $2 "Cutty Sark" . . . . . . 5·00 3·25
O34 $3 "Mermerus" . . . . . . 4·00 3·50
O35 $4 "Mermerus" . . . . . . 5·00 4·75
O36 $5 "Cutty Sark" . . . . . . 7·00 6·00
O37 $6 H.M.S. "Resolution" and H.M.S. "Discovery" . . . 8·50 7·50
O38 $9.60 H.M.S. "Resolution" and H.M.S. "Discovery" 12·00 11·00

1998. Nos. 481/93 optd **O.H.M.S.**
O43 5c. Type **79** 10 10
O44 10c. Daisy coral 10 10
O45 15c. Hydroid coral 10 15
O46 20c. Feather-star 15 20
O47 25c. Sea star 15 20
O48 30c. Varicose nudibranch . . 20 25
O49 50c. Smooth sea star 30 35
O50 70c. Black-lip pearl oyster 45 50
O51 80c. Four-coloured nudibranch 50 55
O52 85c. Prickly sea cucumber . . 55 60
O53 90c. Organ pipe coral . . . 60 65
O54 $1 Blue sea lizard 65 70
O55 $2 Textile cone shell . . . . 1·25 1·40

PERAK Pt. 1

A state of the Federation of Malaya, incorporated in Malaysia in 1963.

100 cents = 1 dollar (Straits or Malayan).

Stamps of Straits Settlement optd or surch.

1878. No. 11 optd with crescent and star and **P** in oval.
1 2c. brown £1300 £950

1880. Optd **PERAK.**
10 **9** 2c. brown . . . . 19·00 45·00
17 2c. red . . . . 2·50 1·75

1883. Surch **2 CENTS PERAK.**
16 2c. on 4c. red £550 £250

1886. No. 63a surch **ONE CENT PERAK.**
(a) Without full point.
30 1c. on 2c. red . . . . 38·00 50·00

(b) With final full point.
26 1c. on 2c. red . . . . 60·00 80·00

1886. No. 63a surch **1 CENT PERAK.**
28 1c. on 2c. red £110 £120

1886. No. 63a surch **One CENT PERAK.**
33b 1c. on 2c. red . . . . 2·00 2·00

1889. No. 17 surch **ONE CENT** (with full point).
41 1c. on 2c. red £200 £130

1891. Surch **PERAK One CENT.**
57 1c. on 2c. red . . . . 1·50 6·00
43 1c. on 6c. lilac . . . . 42·00 25·00

1891. Surch **PERAK Two CENTS.**
48 2c. on 24c. green . . . . . . 13·00 9·00

42 Tiger

44 Tiger

45 Elephants

1892.
61 **42** 1c. green . . . . 2·25 15
62 2c. red . . . . 1·75 30
63 2c. orange . . . . 50 3·25
64 5c. blue . . . . 3·25 7·50

1895. Surch **3 CENTS.**
65 **42** 3c. red . . . . 2·50 2·00

1895.
66 **44** 1c. purple and green . . . . 2·00 50
67 2c. purple and brown . . . 2·00 50
68 3c. purple and red . . . . . 2·25 40
69 4c. purple and red . . . . . 10·00 4·75
70 5c. purple and yellow . . . 3·50 55
71 8c. purple and blue . . . . 45·00 65
72 10c. purple and orange . . . 12·00 50
73 25c. green and red . . . . £130 12·00
74 50c. purple and black . . . 45·00 29·00
75 50c. green and black . . . £160 £150
76 **45** $1 green £150 £160
77 $2 green and red £250 £275
78 $3 green and yellow £300 £350
79 $5 green and blue £500 £475
80 $25 green and orange . . . £7000 £2500

1900. Surch in words.
81 **44** 1c. on 2c. purple and brown 50 2·25
82 1c. on 4c. purple and red . . 75 9·50
83 1c. on 5c. purple and yellow 1·50 10·00
84 3c. on 8c. purple and blue 3·50 8·00
85 3c. on 50c. green and black 2·00 5·50
86 **45** 3c. on $1 green . . . . . . 55·00 £140
87 3c. on $2 green and red . . 28·00 85·00

52 Sultan Yussuf 'Izzuddin Shah

53 Sultan Idris Shah

50 Sultan Iskandar

51 Sultan Iskandar

1935.
88 **50** 1c. black 75 10
89 2c. green 75 10
90 4c. orange . . . . 1·00 10
91 5c. brown 50 10
92 6c. red . . . . 11·00 4·25
93 8c. grey 75 10
94 10c. purple 65 15
95 12c. blue . . . . 1·50 1·00
96 25c. purple and red . . . . 1·50 1·00
97 30c. purple and orange . . . 2·00 1·50
98 40c. red and purple . . . . 3·75 4·50
99 50c. black on green . . . . 4·00 1·25
100 $1 black and red on blue 2·50 1·25
101 $2 green and red . . . . . 18·00 8·50
102 $5 green and red on green 80·00 35·00

1938.
103 **51** 1c. black . . . . 8·00 10
104 2c. green . . . . 3·75 10
105 2c. orange . . . . 3·00 6·00
106a 3c. green . . . . 2·50 4·25
107 4c. orange . . . . 38·00 10
108 5c. brown . . . . 5·50 10
109 6c. red . . . . 27·00 10
110 8c. grey . . . . 24·00 10
111 8c. red . . . . 1·00 65·00
112 10c. purple . . . . 25·00 10
113 12c. blue . . . . 20·00 1·00
114 15c. blue . . . . 3·50 13·00
115 25c. purple and red . . . 60·00 3·25
116 30c. purple and orange . . 9·50 2·25
117 40c. red and purple . . . 50·00 2·00
118 50c. black on green . . . 30·00 75
119 $1 black and red on blue £130 16·00
120 $2 green and red . . . . £140 60·00
121 $5 green and red on green £200 £275

1948. Silver Wedding. As T **4b/c** of Pitcairn Islands.
122 10c. violet 15 10
123 $5 green . . . . 21·00 27·00

1949. U.P.U. As T **4d/g** of Pitcairn Islands.
124 10c. purple 15 10
125 15c. blue . . . . 1·50 1·75
126 25c. orange . . . . 30 1·50
127 50c. black . . . . 1·25 3·50

1950.
128 **52** 1c. black 10 10
129 2c. orange 20 10
130 3c. green . . . . 2·50 10
131 4c. brown 50 10
132 5c. purple . . . . 50 1·75
133 6c. grey 30 10
134 8c. red . . . . 65 1·75
135 8c. green . . . . 1·00 85
136 10c. purple 20 10
137 12c. red . . . . 1·00 3·50
138 15c. blue 75 10
139 20c. black and green . . . 75 50
140 20c. blue 75 10
141 25c. purple and orange . . 50 10
142 30c. red and purple . . . . 1·50 20
143 35c. red and purple . . . . 1·00 25
144 40c. red and purple . . . . 2·25 5·00
145 50c. black and blue . . . . 2·25 10
146 $1 blue and purple . . . . 7·00 85
147 $2 green and red . . . . . 13·00 6·00
148 $5 green and brown . . . 38·00 12·00

1953. Coronation. As T **4h** of Pitcairn Islands.
149 10c. black and purple . . . . 1·50 10

1957. As Nos. 92/102 of Kedah, but portrait of Sultan Yussuf Izzuddin Shah.
150 1c. black 10 20
151 2c. orange 30 80
152 4c. brown 10 10
153 5c. lake 10 10
154 8c. green . . . . 2·00 3·25
155 10c. sepia . . . . 1·00 10
156 10c. purple . . . . 2·75 10
157 20c. blue . . . . 1·75 10
158a 50c. black and blue 40 10
159 $1 blue and purple . . . . 6·00 30
160a $2 green and red . . . . . 3·25 2·00
161a $5 brown and green . . . . 8·00 7·00

1963. Installation of Sultan of Perak.
162 **53** 10c. multicoloured 10 10

54 "Vanda hookeriana"

1965. As Nos. 115/21 of Kedah, but with inset portrait of Sultan Idris as in T **54**.
163 **54** 1c. multicoloured 10 50
164 – 2c. multicoloured 10 50
165 – 5c. multicoloured 10 10
166 – 6c. multicoloured 15 30
167 – 10c. multicoloured 15 10
168 – 15c. multicoloured 80 10
169 – 20c. multicoloured . . . . 1·25 10
The higher values used in Perak were Nos. 20/7 of Malaysia (National Issues).

55 "Delias ninus"

1971. Butterflies. As Nos. 124/30 of Kedah, but with portrait of Sultan Idris as In T **55**.

172 **55** 1c. multicoloured . . . . . 40 1·75
173 – 2c. multicoloured . . . . . 1·00 1·75
174 – 5c. multicoloured . . . . . 1·25 10
175 – 6c. multicoloured . . . . . 1·25 1·75
176 – 10c. multicoloured . . . . 1·25 10
177 – 15c. multicoloured . . . . 1·00 10
178 – 20c. multicoloured . . . . 1·75 30

The higher values in use with this issue were Nos. 64/71 of Malaysia (National Issues).

56 "Rafflesia hasseltii" **57** Coffee

1979. Flowers. As Nos. 135/41 of Kedah but with portrait of Sultan Idris as in T **56**.

184 1c. Type **56** 10 65
185 2c. "Pterocarpus indicus" . . 10 65
186 5c. "Lagerstroemia speciosa" 10 10
187 10c. "Durio zibethinus" . . . 15 10
188 15c. "Hibiscus rosa-sinensis" 15 10
189 20c. "Rhododendron scortechinii" 20 10
190 25c. "Etlingera elatior" (inscr"Phaeomeria speciosa") 40 10

1986. As Nos. 152/8 of Kedah but with portrait of Sultan Azlan Shah as in T **57**.

198 1c. Type **57** 10 10
199 2c. Coconuts 10 10
200 5c. Cocoa 10 10
201 10c. Black pepper 10 10
202 15c. Rubber 10 10
203 20c. Oil palm 10 10
204 30c. Rice 10 15

OFFICIAL STAMPS

1889. Stamps of Straits Settlements optd **P.G.S.**

O1 **30** 2c. red . . . . 3·25 4·50
O2 4c. brown . . . . 10·00 19·00
O3 6c. lilac . . . . 22·00 42·00
O4 8c. orange . . . . 28·00 65·00
O5 **38** 10c. grey . . . . 75·00 75·00
O6 **30** 12c. blue £190 £225
O7 12c. purple £225 £300
O9 24c. green £170 £190

1894. No. 64 optd **Service**.

O10 **30** 5c. blue . . . . 65·00 1·00

1895. No. 70 optd **Service**.

O11 **31** 5c. purple and yellow . . 2·00 50

PERLIS Pt. 1

A state of the Federation of Malaya, incorporated in Malaysia in 1963.

100 cents = 1 dollar (Straits or Malayan).

1948. Silver Wedding. As T **4b/c** of Pitcairn Islands.

1 10c. violet . . . . 30 2·50
2 $5 brown . . . . 29·00 42·00

1949. U.P.U. As T **4d/g** of Pitcairn Islands.

3 10c. purple . . . . 30 1·25
4 15c. blue . . . . 1·25 3·00
5 25c. orange . . . . 45 2·00
6 50c. black . . . . 1·00 3·75

1 Raja Syed Putra **2** "Vanda hookeriana"

1951.

7 **1** 1c. black . . . . 20 1·00
8 2c. orange 75 50
9 3c. green . . . . 1·50 2·75
10 4c. brown . . . . 1·25 30
11 5c. purple . . . . 50 3·00
12 6c. grey . . . . 1·50 1·25
13 8c. red . . . . 2·25 4·75
14 8c. green . . . . 75 3·00
15 10c. purple 50 30
16 12c. red . . . . 75 2·50
17 15c. blue . . . . 3·50 3·75
18 20c. black and green . . . . 2·00 6·00
19 20c. blue . . . . 1·00 70
20 25c. purple and orange . . . 1·75 1·75
21 30c. red and purple . . . . 1·75 8·50
22 35c. red and purple . . . . 75 4·00
23 40c. red and purple . . . . 2·75 17·00
24 50c. black and blue . . . . 3·75 4·25
25 $1 blue and purple . . . . 7·50 19·00
26 $2 green and red . . . . . 14·00 29·00
27 $5 green and brown . . . . 50·00 75·00

1953. Coronation. As T **4h** of Pitcairn Islands.

28 10c. black and purple . . . . 1·00 2·75

1957. As Nos. 92/102 of Kedah, but inset portrait of Raja Syed Putra.

29 1c. black 10 30
30 2c. red 10 30
31 4c. brown 10 30
32 5c. lake 10 10
33 8c. green . . . . 2·00 1·75
34 10c. brown . . . . 1·00 2·00
35 10c. purple . . . . 4·00 3·00
36 20c. blue . . . . 1·75 3·00
37 50c. black and blue . . . . 50 3·25
38 $1 blue and purple . . . . 6·00 9·50
39 $2 green and red . . . . . 6·00 7·50
40 $5 brown and green . . . . 9·50 10·00

1965. As Nos. 115/21 of Kedah, but with inset portrait of Tunku Bendahara Abu Bakar as in T **2**.

41 **2** 1c. multicoloured 10 75
42 – 2c. multicoloured . . . . . 10 1·25
43 – 5c. multicoloured 15 30
44 – 6c. multicoloured . . . . . 65 1·25
45 – 10c. multicoloured 65 30
46 – 15c. multicoloured . . . . 1·00 35
47 – 20c. multicoloured . . . . 1·00 1·50

The higher values used in Perlis were Nos. 20/7 of Malaysia (National Issues).

3 "Danaus melanippus" **4** Raja Syed Putra

1971. Butterflies. As Nos. 124/30 of Kedah, but with portrait of Raja Syed Putra as in T **3**.

48 – 1c. multicoloured . . . . . 20 1·25
49 **3** 2c. multicoloured . . . . . 40 2·00
50 – 5c. multicoloured . . . . . 1·25 1·00
51 – 6c. multicoloured . . . . . 1·25 2·50
52 – 10c. multicolored . . . . . 1·25 1·00
53 – 15c. multicoloured . . . . 1·25 40
54 – 20c. multicoloured . . . . 1·25 2·00

The higher values in use with this issue were Nos. 64/71 of Malaysia (National Issues).

1971. 25th Anniv of Installation of Raja Syed Putra.

56 **4** 10c. multicoloured . . . . . 30 2·00
57 15c. multicoloured 30 60
58 50c. multicoloured . . . . . 80 3·75

5 "Pterocarpus indicus" **6** Coconuts

1979. Flowers. As Nos. 135/41 of Kedah, but with portrait of Raja Syed Putra as in T **5**.

59 1c. "Rafflesia hasseltii" . . . 10 90
60 2c. Type **5** 10 90
61 5c. "Lagerstroemia speciosa" 10 90
62 10c. "Durio zibethinus" . . . 15 25
63 15c. "Hibiscus rosa-sinensis" 15 10
64 20c. "Rhododendron scortechinii" 20 10
65 25c. "Etlingera elatior" (inscr "Phaeomeria speciosa") . . 40 75

1986. As Nos. 152/8 of Kedah, but with portrait of Raja Syed Putra as in T **6**.

73 1c. Coffee 10 10
74 2c. Type **6** 10 10
75 5c. Cocoa 10 10
76 10c. Black pepper 10 10
77 15c. Rubber 10 10
78 20c. Oil palm 10 10
79 30c. Rice 10 15

7 Raja Syed Putra and Aspects of Perlis

1995. 50th Anniv of Raja Syed Putra's Accession. Multicoloured.

80 30c. Type **7** 50 30
81 $1 Raja Syed Putra and Palace 1·50 2·50

PERU Pt. 20

A republic on the N.W. coast of S. America independent since 1821.

1857. 8 reales = 1 peso.
1858. 100 centavos = 10 dineros = 5 pesetas = 1 peso.
1874. 100 centavos = 1 sol.
1985. 100 centimos = 1 inti.
1991. 100 centimos = 1 sol.

7 **8**

1858. T **7** and similar designs with flags below arms. Imperf.

8 **7** 1d. blue . . . . 75·00 5·00
13 1 peseta red . . . . 90·00 11·00
5 ½ peso yellow £1300 £225

1862. Various frames. Imperf.

14 **8** 1d. red . . . . 10·00 1·75
20 1d. green . . . . 10·00 2·10
16 1 peseta, brown . . . . . 55·00 17·00
22 1 peseta, yellow . . . . . 70·00 21·00

10 Vicuna **13** **14**

1866. Various frames. Perf.

17 **10** 5c. green . . . . 5·00 60
18 – 10c. red . . . . 5·00 1·10
19 – 20c. brown . . . . 17·00 3·50

See also No. 316.

1871. 20th Anniv of First Railway in Peru (Callao–Lima–Chorillos). Imperf.

21a **13** 5c. red . . . . £110 28·00

1873. Roul by imperf.

23 **14** 2c. blue . . . . 25·00 £200

15 Sun-god **16**

20 **21**

1874. Various frames. Perf.

24 **15** 1c. orange 40 40
25a **16** 2c. violet 40 40
26 5c. blue 70 25
27 10c. green 15 15
28 20c. red . . . . 1·60 40
29 **20** 50c. green . . . . 7·50 2·10
30 **21** 1s. pink . . . . 1·25 1·25

For further stamps in these types, see Nos. 278, 279/84 and 314/5.

(24) **(27)** Arms of Chile

1880. Optd with T **24**.

36 **15** 1c. green 40 40
37 **16** 2c. red . . . . 1·10 45
39 5c. blue . . . . 1·60 70
40 **20** 50c. green . . . . 23·00 14·50
41 **21** 1s. red . . . . 80·00 38·00

1881. Optd as T **24**, but inscr "LIMA" at foot instead of "PERU".

42 **15** 1c. green 95 30
43 **16** 2c. red . . . . 15·00 7·50
44 5c. blue . . . . 1·75 45
286 10c. green 40 50
45 **20** 50c. green £375 £200
46 **21** 1s. red . . . . 85·00 45·00

1881. Optd with T **27**.

57 **15** 1c. orange 60 85
58 **16** 2c. violet . . . . 60 3·50
59 2c. red . . . . 1·90 16·00
60 5c. blue . . . . 55·00 60·00
61 10c. green . . . . 1·50 2·00
62 20c. red £100 £100

(28) **(28a)**

1882. Optd with T **27** and **28**.

63 **15** 1c. green 80 65
64 **16** 5c. blue . . . . 1·10 65
66 **20** 50c. red . . . . 2·25 1·60
67 **21** 1s. blue . . . . 4·75 3·75

1883. Optd with T **28** only.

200 **15** 1c. green . . . . 1·60 1·00
201 **16** 2c. red . . . . 1·40 3·25
202 5c. blue . . . . 2·25 1·60
203 **20** 50c. pink . . . . 65·00
204 **21** 1s. blue . . . . 30·00

1883. Handstamped with T **28a** only.

206 **15** 1c. orange . . . . 1·00 65
210 **16** 5c. blue . . . . 8·50 4·25
211 10c. green 95 65
216 **20** 50c. green . . . . 7·50 3·00
220 **21** 1s. red . . . . 11·50 5·00

1883. Optd with T **24** and **28a**, the inscription in oval reading "PERU".

223 **20** 50c. green . . . . £100 50·00
225 **21** 1s. red . . . . £120 75·00

1883. Optd with T **24** and **28a**, the inscription in oval reading "LIMA".

227 **15** 1c. green . . . . 4·50 3·25
228 **16** 2c. red . . . . 4·50 3·25
232 5c. blue . . . . 7·75 5·00
234 **20** 50c. green . . . . £120 75·00
236 **21** 1s. red £160 £100

1883. Optd with T **28** and **28a**.

238 **15** 1c. green . . . . 1·25 65
241 **16** 2c. red . . . . 1·25 60
246 5c. blue . . . . 1·40 65

1884. Optd **CORREOS LIMA** and sun.

277 **16** 5c. blue 75 25

1886. Re-issue of 1866 and 1874 types.

278 **15** 1c. violet 60 20
314 1c. red 30 20
279 **16** 2c. green 85 10
315 2c. blue 25 20
280 5c. orange 70 10
316 **10** 5c. lake . . . . 1·60 35
281 **16** 10c. black 50 10
317 – 10c. orange (Llamas) . . . 1·10 25
282 **16** 20c. blue . . . . 5·25 35
318 – 20c. blue (Llamas) . . . . 7·50 1·10
283 **20** 50c. red . . . . 1·90 35
284 **21** 1s. brown . . . . 1·50 35

(71 Pres. R. M. Bermudez) **73**

1894. Optd with T **71**.

294 **15** 1c. orange 75 25
295 1c. green 45 20
296c **16** 2c. violet 45 15
297 2c. red 50 20
298 5c. blue . . . . 2·75 1·50
299 10c. green 50 20
300 **20** 50c. green . . . . 1·60 1·00

1894. Optd with T **28** and **71**.

301 **16** 2c. red 45 20
302 5c. blue . . . . 1·10 30
303 **20** 50c. red . . . . 38·00 25·00
304 **21** 1s. blue . . . . 95·00 75·00

1895. Installation of Pres. Nicolas de Pierola.

328 **73** 1c. violet . . . . 1·75 75
329 2c. green . . . . 1·75 75
330 5c. yellow . . . . 1·75 75
331 10c. blue . . . . 1·75 75
332 – 20c. orange . . . . 1·90 80
333 – 50c. blue . . . . 10·50 3·75
334 – 1s. lake . . . . 42·00 21·00

Nos. 332/4 are larger (30 × 36 mm) and the central device is in a frame of laurel.

See also Nos. 352/4.

75 Atahualpa

76 Pizarro

77 General de la Mar

1896.
335 **75** 1c. blue 55 15
336 1c. green 55 10
337 2c. blue 60 15
338 2c. red 60 10
341 **76** 5c. blue 85 10
340 5c. green 85 10
342 10c. yellow . . . . 1·40 20
343 10c. black . . . . 1·40 10
344 20c. orange . . . . 2·75 25
345 **77** 50c. red . . . . 5·25 50
346 1s. red . . . . 7·00 85
347 2s. lake . . . . 3·00 65

1897. No. D31 optd **FRANQUEO**.
348 D **22** 1c. brown 50 25

82 Suspension Bridge at Paucartambo

83 Pres. D. Nicolas de Pierola

1897. Opening of New Postal Building. Dated "1897".
349 **82** 1c. blue 80 30
350 – 2c. brown 80 25
351 **83** 5c. red . . . . 1·25 30
DESIGN: 2c. G.P.O. Lima.

1899. As Nos. 328/34, but vert inscr replaced by pearl ornaments.
352 **73** 22c. green 30 15
353 – 5s. red . . . . 1·90 1·40
354 – 10s. green £425 £275

84 President Eduardo Lopez de Romana

85 Admiral Grau

1900.
357 **84** 22c. black and green . . . 10·00 70

1901. Advent of the Twentieth Century.
358 **85** 1c. black and green . . . . 1·10 25
359 – 2c. black and red . . . . 1·10 25
360 – 5c. black and lilac . . . . 1·25 25
PORTRAITS: 2c. Col. Bolognesi; 5c. Pres. Romana.

90 Municipal Board of Health Building

1905.
361 **90** 12c. black and blue . . . . 1·25 25

1907. Surch.
362 **90** 1c. on 12c. black and blue 25 20
363 2c. on 12c. black and blue 50 35

97 Bolognesi Monument

98 Admiral Grau

99 Llama

101 Exhibition Buildings

103 G.P.O., Lima

107 Columbus

1907.
364 **97** 1c. black and green . . . 25 15
365 **98** 2c. purple and red 25 15
366 **99** 4c. olive . . . . 5·00 60
367 – 5c. black and blue 40 10
368 **101** 10c. black and brown . . 1·00 25
369 – 20c. black and green . . . 19·00 90
370 **103** 50c. black . . . . 21·00 95
371 – 1s. green and violet . . . £100 2·10
372 – 2s. black and blue . . . . £100 85·00
DESIGNS—VERT: As Type **98**: 5c. Statue of Bolivar. (24×33 mm): 2c. Columbus Monument. HORIZ: As Type **101**: 20c. Medical School, Lima. (33×24 mm): 1s. Grandstand, Santa Beatrice Racecourse, Lima.

1909. Portraits.
373 – 1c. grey (Manco Capac) 15 15
374 **107** 2c. green 15 15
375 – 4c. red (Pizarro) 40 15
376 – 5c. purple (San Martin) 15 10
377 – 10c. blue (Bolivar) 55 15
378 – 12c. blue (de la Mar) . . 85 25
379 – 20c. brown (Castilla) . . 90 40
380 – 50c. orange (Grau) . . . 5·50 30
381 – 1s. black and lake (Bolognesi) . . . . . . 9·50 30
See also Nos. 406/13, 431/5, 439/40 and 484/9.

1913. Surch **UNION POSTAL 8 Cts. Sud Americana** in oval.
382 **90** 8c. on 12c. black and blue 55 20

1915. As 1896, 1905 and 1907, surch **1915** and value.
383 **75** 1c. on 1c. green . . . . . 13·50 10·00
384 **97** 1c. on 1c. black and green 70 50
385 **98** 1c. on 2c. purple and red 1·00 85
386 **76** 1c. on 10c. black 85 60
387 **99** 1c. on 4c. green . . . . . 2·00 1·75
388 **101** 1c. on 10c. black & brown 35 20
389 2c. on 10c. black & brown 80·00 65·00
390 **90** 2c. on 12c. black and blue 65 50
391 – 2c. on 20c. black and green (No. 369) . . . . 11·50 10·00
392 **103** 2c. on 50c. black . . . . 3·00 3·00

1916. Surch **VALE**, value and **1916**.
393 1c. on 12c. blue (378) 15 15
394 1c. on 20c. brown (379) . . . 15 15
395 1c. on 50c. orange (380) . . . 15 15
396 2c. on 4c. red (375) 15 15
397 10c. on 1s. black & lake (381) 40 25

1916. Official stamps of 1909 optd **FRANQUEO 1916** or surch **VALE 2 Cts** also.
398 O **108** 1c. red 15 15
399 2c. on 50c. olive . . . 15 15
400 10c. brown 20 15

1916. Postage Due stamps of 1909 surch **FRANQUEO VALE 2 Cts. 1916**.
401 D **109** 2c. on 1c. brown . . . 40 40
402 2c. on 5c. brown . . . 15 15
403 2c. on 10c. brown . . . 15 15
404 2c. on 50c. brown . . . 15 15

1917. Surch **Un Centavo**.
405 1c. on 4c. (No. 375) 20 15

1918. Portraits as T **107**.
406 1c. black & orge (San Martin) 10 10
407 2c. black and green (Bolivar) 15 10
408 4c. black and red (Galvez) . . 25 10
409 5c. black and blue (Pardo) 15 10
410 8c. black and brown (Grau) 90 25
411 10c. black and blue (Bolognesi) 35 10
412 12c. black and lilac (Castilla) 1·10 15
413 20c. black and green (Caceres) . . . . 1·50 15

126 Columbus at Salamanca University

129 A. B. Leguia

1918.
414 **126** 50c. black and brown . . 4·25 35
415a – 1s. black and green . . 13·00 50
416 – 2s. black and blue . . . 22·00 55
DESIGNS: 1s. Funeral of Atahualpa; 2s. Battle of Arica.

1920. New Constitution.
417 **129** 5c. black and blue 15 15
418 5c. black and brown . . . 15 15

130 San Martin

131 Oath of Independence

132 Admiral Cochrane

137 J. Olaya

1921. Centenary of Independence.
419 **130** 1c. brown (San Martin) 25 15
420 2c. green (Arenales) . . . 25 15
421 4c. red (Las Heras) . . . 85 50
422 **131** 5c. brown 35 15
423 **132** 7c. violet 70 35
424 **130** 10c. blue (Guisse) 70 35
425 12c. black (Vidal) . . . . 2·75 40
426 20c. black and red (Leguia) . . . . 2·75 70
427 50c. violet and purple (S. Martin Monument) 7·75 2·00
428 **131** 1s. green and red (San Martin and Leguia) . . 11·00 3·00

1923. Surch **CINCO Centavos 1923**.
429 5c. on 8c. black & brn (No. 410) 40 20

1924. Surch **CUATRO Centavos 1924**.
430 4c. on 5c. (No. 409) 25 15

1924. Portraits as T **107**. Size 18½ × 23 mm.
431 2c. olive (Rivadeneyra) . . . 10 10
432 4c. green (Melgar) 10 10
433 8c. black (Iturregui) . . . . 1·60 90
434 10c. red (A. B. Leguia) . . . 15 10
435 15c. blue (De La Mar) 50 15
439 1s. brown (De Saco) . . . . 7·50 85
440 2s. blue (J. Leguia) . . . . . 19·00 4·25

1924. Monuments.
436 **137** 20c. blue 95 10
437 20c. yellow . . . . 1·25 15
438 – 50c. purple (Bellido) . . . 4·25 35
See also Nos. 484/9.

139 Simon Bolivar

140

1924. Cent of Battle of Ayacucho. Portraits of Bolivar.
441 – 2c. olive 35 10
442 **139** 4c. green 65 10
443 5c. black . . . . 1·25 10
444 **140** 10c. red 70 10
445 – 20c. blue . . . . 1·40 15
446 – 50c. lilac . . . . 4·00 50
447 – 1s. brown . . . . 10·00 2·00
448 – 2s. blue . . . . 21·00 8·25

1925. Surch **DOS Centavos 1925**.
449 **137** 2c. on 20c. blue . . . . . 1·25 50

1925. Optd**Plebiscito**.
450 10c. red (No. 434) 70 70

143 The Rock of Arica

1925. Obligatory Tax. Tacna–Arica Plebiscite.
451 **143** 2c. orange . . . . 1·50 40
452 5c. blue . . . . 2·50 50
453 5c. red . . . . 1·90 40
454 5c. green . . . . 2·25 60
455 – 10c. brown . . . . 3·00 60
456 – 50c. green . . . . 16·00 7·50
DESIGNS—HORIZ: 39×30 mm: 10c. Soldiers with colours. VERT: 27×33 mm: 50c. Bolognesi Statue.

146 The Rock of Arica

1927. Obligatory Tax. Figures of value not encircled.
457 **146** 2c. orange . . . . 2·25 50
458 2c. brown . . . . 2·75 50
459 2c. blue . . . . 2·50 50
460 2c. violet . . . . 1·75 50
461 **146** 2c. green . . . . 1·25 50
462 20c. red . . . . 6·00 1·50

1927. Air. Optd **Servicio Aereo**.
463 **9** 50c. purple (No. 438) . . . 32·00 20·00

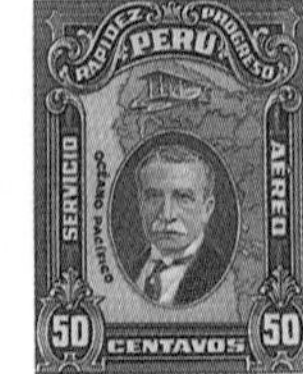
148 Pres. A. B. Leguia

149 The Rock of Arica

1927. Air.
464 **148** 50c. green 70 35

1928. Obligatory Tax. Plebiscite Fund.
465 **149** 2c. mauve 60 20

1929. Surch **Habilitada 2 Cts. 1929**.
466 – 2c. on 8c. (No. 410) . . . 50 50
468 **137** 15c. on 20c. (No. 437) . . 70 70

1929. Surch **Habilitada 2 centavos 1929**.
467 2c. on 8c. (No. 410) 70 70

1930. Optd **Habilitada Franqueo**.
469 **149** 2c. mauve 85 85

1930. Surch **Habilitada 2 Cts. 1930**.
470 **137** 2c. on 20c. yellow 25 25

1930. Surch **Habilitada Franqueo 2 Cts. 1930**.
471 **148** 2c. on 50c. green 25 25

156 Arms of Peru

157 Lima Cathedral

1930. 6th (inscribed "seventh") Pan-American Child Congress.
472 **156** 2c. green 60 55
473 **157** 5c. red . . . . 2·00 1·00
474 – 10c. blue . . . . 1·25 85
475 – 50c. brown . . . . 17·00 10·00
DESIGNS—HORIZ: 10c. G.P.O., Lima. VERT: 50c. Madonna and Child.

1930. Fall of Leguia Govt. No. 434 optd with Arms of Peru or surch with new value in four corners also.
477 2c. on 10c. red 10 10
478 4c. on 10c. red 20 20
479 10c. red 15 10
476 15c. on 10c. red 20 15

159 Simon Bolivar

161 Pizarro

162 The Old Stone Bridge, Lima

1930. Death Centenary of Bolivar.
480 **159** 2c. brown 35 20
481 4c. red 70 30
482 10c. green 35 25
483 15c. grey 70 50

1930. As T **107** and **137** but smaller, 18 × 22 mm.
484 – 2c. olive (Rivadeneyra) . . 15 10
485 – 4c. green (Melgar) 15 10
486 – 15c. blue (De la Mar) . . 50 10
487 **137** 20c. yellow (Olaya) . . . 1·00 20
488 – 50c. purple (Bellido) . . . 1·25 25
489 – 1s. brown (De Saco) . . . 1·60 35

1931. Obligatory Tax. Unemployment Fund. Surch **Habilitada Pro Desocupados 2 Cts.**
490 **159** 2c. on 4c. red 70 35
491 2c. on 10c. green 50 35
492 2c. on 15c. grey 50 35

1931. 1st Peruvian Philatelic Exhibition.
493 **161** 2c. slate . . . . 1·90 1·10
494 4c. brown . . . . 1·90 1·10
495 **162** 10c. red . . . . 1·90 1·10
496 10c. green and mauve . . 1·90 1·10
497 **161** 15c. green . . . . 1·90 1·10
498 **162** 15c. red and grey . . . . 1·90 1·10
499 15c. blue and orange . . 1·90 1·10

163 Manco Capac

164 Oil Well

170

1931.
500 **163** 2c. olive 20 10
501 **164** 4c. green 40 30
502 – 10c. orange 85 10
503 – 15c. blue . . . . 1·50 25
504 – 20c. yellow . . . . 6·00 40
505 – 50c. lilac . . . . 5·00 40
506 – 1s. brown . . . . 11·00 85
DESIGNS—VERT: 10c. Sugar Plantation; 15c. Cotton Plantation; 50c. Copper Mines. 1s. Llamas. HORIZ: 20c. Guano Islands.

1931. Obligatory Tax. Unemployment Fund.
507 **170** 2c. green 10 10
508 2c. red 10 10

171 Arms of Piura

172 Parakas

1932. 4th Centenary of Piura.
509 **171** 10c. blue (postage) . . . 5·50 5·00
510 15c. violet . . . . 5·50 5·00
511 50c. red (air) . . . . . . 18·00 16·00

1932. 400th Anniv of Spanish Conquest of Peru. Native designs.
512 **172** 10c. purple (22 × 19½ mm) 15 10
513 – 15c. lake (25 × 19½ mm) 35 10
514 – 50c. brown (19½ × 22 mm) 75 15
DESIGNS: 15c. Chimu; 50c. Inca.

175 Arequipa and El Misti

176 Pres. Sanchez Cerro

1932. 1st Anniv of Constitutional Government.
515 **175** 2c. blue 15 10
527 2c. black 15 10
528 2c. green 15 10
516 4c. brown 15 10
529 4c. orange 15 10
517 **176** 10c. red . . . . 15·00 8·25
530 – 10c. red 50 10
518 – 15c. blue 35 10
531 – 15c. mauve 35 10
519 – 20c. lake 50 10
532 – 20c. violet 50 15
520 – 50c. green 70 15
521 – 1s. orange . . . . 5·50 35
533 – 1s. brown . . . . 6·25 40
DESIGNS—VERT: 10c. (No. 530), Statue of Liberty; 15c. to 1s. Bolivar Monument, Lima.

178 Blacksmith

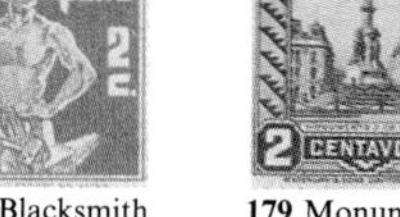
179 Monument of 2nd May to Battle of Callao

1932. Obligatory Tax. Unemployment Fund.
522 **178** 2c. grey 10 10
523 2c. violet 10 10

1933. Obligatory Tax. Unemployment Fund.
524 **179** 2c. violet 15 10
525 2c. orange 15 10
526 2c. purple 15 10

181 Hawker Hart Bomber

184 F. Pizarro

185 Coronation of Huascar

186 The Inca

1934. Air.
534 **181** 2s. blue . . . . 4·50 35
535 5s. brown . . . . 9·50 70

1934. Obligatory Tax. Unemployment Fund. Optd **Pro-Desocupados**. (a) In one line.
536 **176** 2c. green 10 10
585 – 2c. purple (No. 537) . . . 10 10

(b) In two lines.
566 – 2c. purple (No. 537) 10 10

1934.
537 – 2c. purple 10 10
538 – 4c. green 15 10
539 **184** 10c. red 15 10
540 15c. blue 50 10
541 **185** 20c. blue . . . . 1·00 15
542 50c. brown . . . . 1·00 15
543 **186** 1s. violet . . . . 2·75 35
DESIGNS: 2, 4c. show the scene depicted in Type **189**.

187 Lake of the Marvellous Cure

188 Grapes

1935. Tercentenary of Founding of Ica.
544 – 4c. black 65 65
545 **187** 5c. red 65 65
546 **188** 10c. mauve . . . . 3·75 1·40
547 **187** 20c. green . . . . 1·60 1·00
548 – 35c. red . . . . 7·50 3·50
549 – 50c. brown and orange . . 5·00 3·50
550 – 1s. red and violet . . . . 14·50 8·25
DESIGNS—HORIZ: 4c. City of Ica; 50c. Don Diego Lopez and King Philip IV of Spain. VERT: 35c. Cotton blossom; 1s. Supreme God of the Nazcas.

189 Pizarro and "The Thirteen"

192 Funeral of Atahualpa

1935. 4th Centenary of Founding of Lima.
551 **189** 2c. brown (postage) . . . 35 20
552 – 4c. violet 50 35
553 – 10c. red 50 20
554 – 15c. blue 85 40
555 **189** 20c. grey . . . . 1·40 50
556 – 50c. green . . . . 1·90 1·25
557 – 1s. blue . . . . 4·00 2·40
558 – 2s. brown . . . . 11·00 6·75
DESIGNS—HORIZ: 4c. Lima Cathedral. VERT: 10c., 50c. Miss L. S. de Canevaro; 15c., 2s. Pizarro; 1s. The "Tapada" (a veiled woman).

559 **192** 5c. green (air) 35 20
560 – 35c. brown 75 35
561 – 50c. yellow . . . . 1·25 70
562 – 1s. purple . . . . 1·75 75
563 – 2s. orange . . . . 1·75 1·50
564 **192** 5s. purple . . . . 7·75 4·25
565 **189** 10s. blue . . . . 30·00 20·00
DESIGNS—HORIZ: 35c. Airplane near San Cristobal Hill; 50c., 1s. Airplane over Avenue of Barefoot Friars. VERT: 2s. Palace of Torre Tagle.

207 "San Cristobal" (caravel)

1936. Callao Centenary.
567 **207** 2c. black (postage) . . . 1·25 20
568 – 4c. green 45 15
569 – 5c. brown 45 15
570 – 10c. blue 45 20
571 – 15c. green . . . . 2·00 25
572 – 20c. brown 45 25
573 – 50c. lilac . . . . 1·25 45
574 – 1s. olive . . . . 23·00 1·60
575 – 2s. purple . . . . 15·00 5·00
576 – 5s. red . . . . 21·00 12·00
577 – 10s. brown and red . . . 45·00 30·00

578 – 35c. slate (air) . . . . . 8·00 4·00
DESIGNS—HORIZ: 4c. La Punta Naval College; 5c. Independence Square, Callao; 10c. Aerial view of Callao; 15c. "Reina del Pacifico" (liner) in Callao Docks and Custom House; 20c. Plan of Callao, 1746; 35c. "La Callao" (locomotive); 1s. Gunboat "Sacramento"; 10s. Real Felipe Fortifications. VERT: 50c. D. Jose de la Mar; 2s. Don Jose de Velasco; 5s. Fort Maipo and miniature portraits of Galvez and Nunez.

1936. Obligatory Tax. St. Rosa de Lima Cathedral Construction Fund. Optd **"Ley 8310"**.
579 **179** 2c. purple 10 10

1936. Surch **Habilitado** and value in figures and words.
580 – 2c. on 4c. green (No. 538) (postage) 10 10
581 **185** 10c. on 20c. blue 15 15
582 **186** 10c. on 1s. violet 20 20
583 **181** 5c. on 2s. blue (air) . . . 35 15
584 25c. on 5s. brown 70 25

211 Guanay Cormorants

217 Mail Steamer "Inca" on Lake Titicaca

1936.
586 **211** 2c. brown (postage) . . . 1·40 25
616 2c. green . . . . 1·75 25
587 – 4c. brown 50 25
617 – 4c. black 25 15
618 – 10c. red 10 10
619 – 15c. blue 50 25
590 – 20c. black 70 15
620 – 20c. brown 25 15
591 – 50c. yellow . . . . 2·10 50
621 – 50c. grey 70 15
592 – 1s. purple . . . . 4·25 70
622 – 1s. blue . . . . 1·40 35
593 – 2s. blue . . . . 9·00 2·00
623 – 2s. violet . . . . 3·00 35
594 – 5s. blue . . . . 9·00 3·00
595 – 10s. brown and violet . . 50·00 19·00
DESIGNS—VERT: 4c. Oil well; 10c. Inca postal runner; 1s. G.P.O., Lima; 2s. M. de Amat y Junyent; 5s. J. A. de Pando y Riva; 10s. J. D. Condemarin. HORIZ: 15c. Paseo de la Republica, Lima; 20c. Municipal Palace and Natural History Museum; 50c. University of San Marcos, Lima..

596 – 5c. green (air) 25 10
625 **217** 15c. blue 90 15
598 – 20c. grey 90 15
626 – 20c. green 85 15
627 – 25c. red 40 10
628 – 30c. brown 80 15
600 – 35c. brown . . . . 1·60 1·40
601 – 50c. yellow 75 45
629 – 50c. red . . . . 1·10 30
630 – 70c. green . . . . 1·25 50
603 – 80c. black . . . . 14·00 7·00
631 – 80c. green . . . . 4·50 1·00
604 – 1s. blue . . . . 9·00 1·50
632 – 1s. brown . . . . 6·00 60
605 – 1s. 50 brown . . . . . . 9·00 5·50
633 – 1s. 50 orange . . . . . 5·50 40
606 – 2s. blue . . . . 15·00 6·50
634 – 2s. green . . . . 11·00 70
607 – 5s. green . . . . 20·00 3·25
608 – 10s. brown and red . . . £100 65·00
DESIGNS—HORIZ: 5c. La Mar Park; 20c. Native recorder player and llama; 30c. Chuquibambilla ram; 25, 35c. J. Chavez; 50c. Mining Area; 70c. Ford "Tin Goose" airplane over La Punta; 1s. Steam train at La Cima; 1s.50, Aerodrome at Las Palmas, Lima. 2s. Douglas DC-2 mail plane; 5s. Valley of R. Inambari. VERT: 80c. Infiernillo Canyon, Andes; 10s. St. Rosa de Lima

223 St. Rosa de Lima

1937. Obligatory Tax. St. Rosa de Lima Construction Fund.
609 **223** 2c. red 15 10

1937. Surch **Habilit.** and value in figures and words.
(a) Postage.
610 1s. on 2s. blue (593) . . . . 3·25 3·25

(b) Air.
611 15c. on 30c. brown (599) . . 45 40
612 15c. on 35c. brown (600) . . 45 25
613 15c. on 70c. green (630) . . . 3·50 2·25
614 25c. on 80c. black (603) . . . 7·50 6·00
615 1s. on 2s. blue (606) . . . . 5·50 3·00

225 Bielovucic over Lima

226 Jorge Chavez

1937. Air. Pan-American Aviation Conference.
635 **225** 10c. violet 40 10
636 **226** 15c. green 50 10
637 – 25c. brown 40 10
638 – 1s. black . . . . 1·90 1·00
DESIGNS—As T **225**: 25c. Limatambo Airport; 1s. Peruvian air routes.

229 "Protection" (by John Q. A. Ward)

230 Children's Holiday Camp

1938. Obligatory Tax. Unemployment Fund.
757c **229** 2c. brown 10 10

1938. Designs as T **230**.
693 **230** 2c. green 10 10
694 – 4c. brown 10 10
642 – 10c. red 20 10
696 – 15c. blue 10 10
727 – 15c. turquoise 10 10
644 – 20c. purple 15 10
740 – 20c. violet 10 10
698 – 50c. blue 15 10
741 – 50c. brown 15 10
699 – 1s. purple 85 10
742 – 1s. brown 25 10
700 – 2s. green . . . . 2·50 10
731 – 2s. blue 55 10
701 – 5s. brown and violet . . . 5·75 35
732 – 5s. purple and blue . . . 75 35
702 – 10s. blue and black . . . 10·00 50
733 – 10s. black and green . . . 2·50 70
DESIGNS—VERT: 4c. Chavin pottery; 10c. Automobile roads in Andes; 20c. (2) Industrial Bank of Peru; 1s. (2) Portrait of Toribio de Luzuriaga; 5s. (2) Chavin Idol. HORIZ: 15c. (2) Archaeological Museum, Lima; 50c. (2) Labourers' homes at Lima; 2s. (2) Fig Tree; 10s. (2) Mt. Huascaran.

240 Monument on Junin Plains

248 Seal of City of Lima

1938. Air. As T **240**.
650 – 5c. brown 15 10
743 – 5c. green 10 10
651 **240** 15c. brown 15 10
652 – 20c. red 40 10
653 – 25c. green 20 10
654 – 30c. orange 20 10
735 – 30c. red 15 10
655 – 50c. green 35 30
656 – 70c. grey 50 25

736 – 70c. blue 30 10
657 – 80c. green 60 10
737 – 80c. red 55 15
658 – 1s. green . . . . 5·00 2·75
705 – 1s.50 violet 45 35
738 – 1s.50 purple 45 30
660 – 2s. red and blue . . . . . 1·60 50
661 – 5s. purple . . . . 10·50 1·10
662 – 10s. blue and green . . . 55·00 27·00
DESIGNS—VERT: 20c. Rear-Admiral M. Villar; 70c. (No. 656, 736), Infiernillo Canyon; 2s. Stele from Chavin Temple. HORIZ: 5c. People's restaurant, Callao; 25c. View of Tarma; 30c. Ica River irrigation system; 50c. Port of Iquitos; 80c. Mountain roadway; 1s. Plaza San Martin, Lima; 1s.50, Nat. Radio Station, San Miguel; 5s. Ministry of Public Works; 10s. Heroe's Crypt, Lima.

1938. 8th Pan-American Congress, Lima.
663 – 10c. grey (postage) . . . 50 20
664 **248** 15c. gold, blue, red & blk 85 25
665 – 1s. brown . . . . 1·90 85
DESIGNS (39 × 32½ mm): 10c. Palace and Square, 1864; 1s. Palace, 1938.

666 – 25c. blue (air) 55 50
667 – 1s.50 lake . . . . 1·90 1·25
668 – 2s. black 90 45
DESIGNS—VERT: 26 × 37 mm: 25c. Torre Tagle Palace. HORIZ: 39 × 32½ mm: 1s.50, National Congress Building, Lima; 2s. Congress Presidents, Ferreyros, Paz Soldan and Arenas.

1940. No. 642 surch **Habilitada 5 cts**.
669 5c. on 10c. red 15 10

251 National Broadcasting Station

1941. Optd **FRANQUEO POSTAL**.
670 **251** 50c. yellow . . . . 1·60 15
671 1s. violet . . . . 1·60 20
672 2s. green . . . . 3·25 50
673 5s. brown . . . . 19·00 5·50
674 10s. mauve . . . . 29·00 4·75

1942. Air. No. 653 surch **Habilit 0.15**.
675 15c. on 25c. green 85 10

253 Map of S. America showing R. Amazon
254 Francisco de Orellana

255 Francisco Pizarro
257 Samuel Morse

1943. 400th Anniv of Discovery of R. Amazon.
676 – 2c. red 10 10
677 **254** 4c. grey 15 10
678 **255** 10c. brown 20 10
679 **253** 15c. blue 50 20
680 – 20c. olive 20 15
681 – 25c. orange . . . . 2·00 35
682 **254** 30c. red 35 20
683 **253** 50c. green 35 40
685 – 70c. violet . . . . 2·50 70
686 – 80c. blue . . . . 2·50 70
687 – 1s. brown . . . . 4·75 70
688 **255** 5s. black . . . . 9·50 4·00
DESIGNS—As Type **254**: 2, 70c. Portraits of G. Pizarro and Orellana in medallion; 20, 80c. G. Pizarro. As Type **253**: 25c., 1s. Orellana's Discovery of the R. Amazon.

1943. Surch with Arms of Peru (as Nos. 483, etc) above **10 CTVS**.
689 10c. on 10c. red (No. 642) . . 15 10

1944. Centenary of Invention of Telegraphy.
691 **257** 15c. blue 15 15
692 30c. brown 50 20

1946. Surch **Habilitada S/o 0.20**.
706 20c. on 1s. purple (No. 699) 25 10

259

261

1947. 1st National Tourist Congress, Lima. Unissued designs inscr "V Congreso Pan Americano de Carreteras 1944" optd **Habilitada I Congreso Nac. de Turismo Lima–1947**.
707 **259** 15c. black and red 25 15
708 – 1s. brown 35 20
709 – 1s.35 green 35 25
710 **261** 3s. blue 85 50
711 – 5s. green . . . . 2·10 1·25
DESIGNS—VERT: 1s. Mountain road; 1s.35, Forest road. HORIZ: 5s. Road and house.

1947. Air. 1st Peruvian Int Airways Lima–New York Flight. Optd with PIA badge and **PRIMER VUELO LIMA - NUEVA YORK**.
712 5c. brown (No. 650) 10 10
713 50c. green (No. 655) 15 10

263 Basketball Players

1948. Air. Olympic Games.
714 – 1s. blue . . . . 3·75 2·25
715 **263** 2s. brown . . . . 5·75 3·00
716 – 5s. green . . . . 11·50 5·00
717 – 10s. yellow . . . . 15·00 6·50
DESIGNS: 1s. Map showing air route from Peru to Great Britain; 5s. Discus thrower; 10s. Rifleman.
No. 714 is inscr "AEREO" and Nos. 715/17 are optd **AEREO**.
The above stamps exist overprinted **MELBOURNE 1956** but were only valid for postage on one day.

1948. Air. Nos. 653, 736 and 657 surch **Habilitada S/o.** and value.
722 5c. on 25c. green 10 10
723 10c. on 25c. green 30 10
718 10c. on 70c. blue 65 20
719 15c. on 70c. blue 30 10
720 20c. on 70c. blue 30 10
724 30c. on 80c. green 90 15
721 55c. on 70c. blue 30 10

263a
263b

1949. Anti-tuberculosis Fund. Surch **Decreto Ley No. 18** and value.
724a **263a** 3c. on 4c. blue 55 10
724b **263b** 3c. in 10c. blue 55 10

264 Statue of Admiral Grau
264a "Education"

1949.
726 **264** 10c. blue and green . . . 10 10

1950. Obligatory Tax. National Education Fund.
851 **264a** 3c. lake (16½ × 21 mm) 10 10
897 3c. lake (18 × 21½ mm) 15 10

265 Park, Lima

1951. Air. 75th Anniv of U.P.U. Unissued stamps inscr "VI CONGRESO DE LA UNION POSTAL DE LAS AMREICAS Y ESPANA-1949" optd **U.P.U. 1874–1949**.
745 **265** 5c. green 10 10
746 – 30c. red and black 15 10
747 – 55c. green 15 10
748 – 95c. turquoise 20 15
749 – 1s.50 red 30 25
750 – 2s. blue 35 30
751 – 5s. red . . . . 3·00 2·10
752 – 10s. violet . . . . 4·75 3·00
753 – 20s. blue and brown . . . 8·50 5·00
DESIGNS: 30c. Peruvian flag; 55c. Huancayo Hotel; 95c. Ancash Mtns; 1s.50, Arequipa Hotel; 2s. Coaling Jetty; 5s. Town Hall, Miraflores; 10s. Congressional Palace; 20s. Pan-American flags.

1951. Air Surch **HABILITADA S/o. 0.25**.
754 25c. on 30c. red (No. 735) . . 15 10

1951. Surch **HABILITADA S/.** and figures.
755 1c. on 2c. (No. 693) 10 10
756 5c. on 15c. (No. 727) 10 10
757 10c. on 15c. (No. 727) . . . 10 10

268 Obrero Hospital, Lima

1951. 5th Pan-American Highways Congress. Unissued "VI CONGRESO DE LA UNION POSTAL" ... optd **V Congreso Panamericano de Carreteras 1951**.
758 – 2c. green 10 10
759 **268** 4c. red 10 10
760 – 15c. grey 15 10
761 – 20c. brown 10 10
762 – 50c. purple 15 10
763 – 1s. blue 20 10
764 – 2s. blue 30 10
765 – 5s. red . . . . 1·50 1·00
766 – 10s. brown . . . . 3·25 85
DESIGNS—HORIZ: 2c. Aguas Promenade; 50c. Archiepiscopal Palace, Lima; 1s. National Judicial Palace; 2s. Municipal Palace; 5s. Lake Llanganuco, Ancash. VERT: 15c. Inca postal runner; 20c. Old P.O., Lima; 10s. Machu-Picchu ruins.

269 Father Tomas de San Martin and Capt. J. de Aliaga

1951. Air. 4th Cent of S. Marcos University.
767 **269** 30c. black 10 10
768 – 40c. blue 15 10
769 – 50c. mauve 20 10
770 – 1s.20 green 30 15
771 – 2s. grey 35 15
772 – 5s. multicoloured . . . . 1·50 20
DESIGNS: 40c. San Marcos University; 50c. Santo Domingo Convent; 1s.20, P. de Peralto Barnuevo, Father Tomas de San Martin and Jose Baquijano; 2s. Toribio Rodriguez, Jose Hipolito Unanue and Jose Cayetano Heredia; 5s. University Arms in 1571 and 1735.

270 Engineer's School

1952. (a) Postage.
774 – 2c. purple 10 10
775 – 5c. green 30 10
776 – 10c. green 30 10
777 – 15c. grey 25 15
777a – 15c. brown . . . . 1·25 50
829 – 20c. brown 20 10
779 **270** 25c. red 15 10
779a 25c. green 30 10
780 – 30c. blue 10 10
780a – 30c. red 15 10
830 – 30c. mauve 15 10
924 – 50c. green 10 10
831 – 50c. purple 15 10
782 – 1s. brown 30 10
782a – 1s. blue 30 10
783 – 2s. turquoise 40 10
783a – 2s. grey 55 15

DESIGNS—As Type **270**: HORIZ: 2c. Hotel, Tacna; 5c. Tuna fishing boat and indigenous fish; 10c. View of Matarani; 15c. Steam train; 30c. Public Health and Social Assistance. VERT: 20c. Vicuna. Larger (35 × 25 mm): HORIZ: 50c. Inca maize terraces; 1s. Inca ruins, Paramonga Fort; 2s. Agriculture Monument, Lima.

(b) Air.
784 – 40c. green 65 10
785 – 75c. brown . . . . 1·10 25
834 – 80c. red 50 10
786 – 1s.25 blue 25 10
787 – 1s.50 red 20 10
788 – 2s.20 blue 65 15
789 – 3s. brown 75 25
835 – 3s. green 50 30
836 – 3s.80 orange 85 35
790 – 5s. brown 50 15
791 – 10s. brown . . . . 1·50 35
838 – 10s. red . . . . 1·00 45
DESIGNS—As Type **270**. HORIZ: 40c. Gunboat "Maranon"; 1s.50, Housing Complex. VERT: 75c., 80c. Colony of Guanay cormorants. Larger (25 × 25 mm.): HORIZ: 1s.25, Corpac-Limatambo Airport; 2s.20, 3s.80, Inca Observatory, Cuzco; 5s. Garcilaso (portrait). VERT: 3s. Tobacco plant, leaves and cigarettes; 10s. Manco Capac Monument (25 × 37 mm).
See also Nos. 867, etc.

271 Isabella the Catholic

272 "Santa Maria", "Pinta" and "Nina"
273

1953. Air. 500th Birth Anniv of Isabella the Catholic.
792 **271** 40c. red 20 10
793 **272** 1s.25 green . . . . . . 2·25 50
794 **271** 2s.15 purple 35 25
795 **272** 2s.20 black . . . . . . 4·25 75

1954. Obligatory Tax. National Marian Eucharistic Congress Fund. Roul.
796 **273** 5c. blue and red 25 10

274 Gen. M. Perez Jimenez
275 Arms of Lima and Bordeaux

1956. Visit of President of Venezuela.
797 **274** 25c. brown 10 10

1957. Air. Exhibition of French Products, Lima.
798 **275** 40c. lake, blue and green 10 10
799 – 50c. black, brown & green 15 10
800 – 1s.25 deep blue, green and blue . . . . 1·75 35
801 – 2s.20 brown and blue . . 40 30
DESIGNS—HORIZ: 50c. Eiffel Tower and Lima Cathedral; 1s.25, Admiral Dupetit-Thouars and frigate "La Victorieuse"; 2s.20, Exhibition building, Pres. Prado and Pres. Coty.

276 1857 Stamp
277 Carlos Paz Soldan (founder)

1957. Air. Centenary of First Peruvian Postage Stamp.
802 – 5c. black and grey 10 10
803 **276** 10c. turquoise and mauve 10 10
804 – 15c. brown and green . . 10 10
805 – 25c. blue and yellow . . . 10 10
806 – 30c. brown and chocolate 10 10
807 – 40c. ochre and black . . . 15 10
808 – 1s.25 brown and blue . . 35 25

809 – 2s.20 red and blue 50 30
810 – 5s. red and mauve . . . . 1·25 1·00
811 – 10s. violet and green . . . 3·25 2·00
DESIGNS: 5c. Pre-stamp Postmarks; 15c. 1857 2r. stamp; 25c. 1d. 1858; 30c. 1p. 1858 stamp; 40c. ½ peso 1858 stamp; 1s.25, J. Davila Condemarin, Director of Posts, 1857; 2s.20, Pres. Ramon Castilla; 5s. Pres. D. M. Prado; 10s. Various Peruvian stamps in shield.

1958. Air. Centenary of Lima–Callao Telegraph Service.
812 **277** 40c. brown and red . . . 10 10
813 – 1s. green 15 10
814 – 1s.25 blue and purple . . 25 15
DESIGNS—VERT: 1s. Marshal Ramon Castilla. HORIZ: 1s.25, Pres. D. M. Prado and view of Callao.
No. 814 also commemorates the political centenary of the Province of Callao.

278 Flags of France and Peru
279 Father Martin de Porras Velasquez

1958. Air. "Treasures of Peru" Exhibition, Paris.
815 **278** 50c. red, blue & deep blue 10 10
816 – 65c. multicoloured 10 10
817 – 1s.50 brown, purple & bl 25 10
818 – 2s.50 purple, turq & grn 45 20
DESIGNS—HORIZ: 65c. Lima Cathedral and girl in national costume; 1s.50, Caballero and ancient palace. VERT: 2s.50, Natural resources map of Peru.

1958. Air. Birth Centenary of D. A. Carrion Garcia (patriot).
819 **279** 60c. multicoloured 10 10
820 – 1s.20 multicoloured . . . 15 10
821 – 1s.50 multicoloured . . . 25 10
822 – 2s.20 black 30 20
DESIGNS—VERT: 1s.20, D. A. Carrion Garcia. 1s.50, J. H. Unanue Pavon. HORIZ: 2s.20, First Royal School of Medicine (now Ministry of Government Police, Posts and Telecommunications).

280 Gen. Alvarez Thomas
281 Association Emblems

1958. Air. Death Centenary of Gen. Thomas.
823 **280** 1s.10 purple, red & bistre 20 15
824 1s.20 black, red and bistre 25 15

1958. Air. 150th Anniv of Advocates' College, Lima. Emblems in bistre and blue.
825 **281** 80c. green 10 10
826 1s.10 red 15 10
827 1s.20 blue 15 10
828 1s.50 purple 20 10

282 Piura Arms and Congress Emblem
283

1960. Obligatory Tax. 6th National Eucharistic Congress Fund.
839 **282** 10c. multicoloured . . . 20 10
839a 10c. blue and red 20 10

1960. Air. World Refugee Year.
840 **283** 80c. multicoloured 30 30
841 4s.30 multicoloured . . . 50 50

284 Sea Bird bearing Map
285 Congress Emblem

1960. Air. International Pacific Fair, Lima.
842 **284** 1s. multicoloured 40 15

1960. 6th National Eucharistic Congress, Piura.
843 **285** 50c. red, black and blue 15 10
844 – 1s. multicoloured (Eucharistic symbols) 25 10

286 1659 Coin

1961. Air. 1st National Numismatic Exhibition, Lima.
845 – 1s. grey and brown . . . 20 10
846 **286** 2s. grey and blue 25 15
DESIGNS: 1s. 1659 coin.

287 "Amazonas"

1961. Air. Centenary of World Tour of Cadet Sailing Ship "Amazonas".
847 **287** 50c. green and brown . . 35 10
848 80c. red and purple . . . 50 10
849 1s. black and green . . . 70 15

288 Globe, Moon and Stars
289 Olympic Torch

1961. Air. I.G.Y.
850 **288** 1s. multicoloured 15 15

1961. Air. Olympic Games, 1960.
852 **289** 5c. blue and black 40 35
853 10s. red and black 95 60

290 "Balloon"
291 Fair Emblem

1961. Christmas and New Year.
854 **290** 20c. blue 30 10

1961. Air. 2nd International Pacific Fair, Lima.
855 **291** 1s. multicoloured 20 15

292 Symbol of Eucharist
293 Sculptures "Cahuide" and "Cuauhtemoc"

1962. Obligatory Tax. 7th National Eucharistic Congress Fund. Roul.
857 **292** 10c. blue and yellow . . . 10 10

1962. Air. Peruvian Art Treasures Exhibition, Mexico 1960. Flags red and green.
859 **293** 1s. red 15 10
860 – 2s. turquoise 25 15
861 – 3s. brown 30 15
DESIGNS: 2s. Tupac-Amaru and Hidalgo; 3s. Presidents Prado and Lopez.

294 Frontier Maps

1962. Air. 20th Anniv of Ecuador–Peru Border Agreement.
862 **294** 1s.30 black & red on grey 25 15
863 1s.50 multicoloured . . . 25 15
864 2s.50 multicoloured . . . 30 30

295 The Cedar, Pomabamba
296 "Man"

1962. Centenary of Pomabamba and Pallasca Ancash.
865 **295** 1s. green and red (postage) 35 15
866 – 1s. black and grey (air) 10 10
DESIGN: No. 866, Agriculture, mining, etc, Pallasca Ancash (31½ × 22 mm.).

1962. As Nos. 774/91 but colours and some designs changed and new values. (a) Postage.
867 20c. purple 20 10
921 20c. red 10 10
922 30c. blue (as No. 776) . . . 10 10
923 40c. orange (as No. 784) . . 60 10
871 60c. black (as No. 774) . . 25 10
925 1s. red 10 10

(b) Air.
873 1s.30 ochre (as No. 785) . . 60 20
874 1s.50 purple 35 10
875 1s.80 blue (as No. 777) . . . 1·25 40
876 2s. green 40 15
926 2s.60 green (as No. 783) . . 30 15
877 3s. purple 40 15
927 3s.60 purple (as No. 789) . . 45 20
878 4s.30 orange 80 30
928 4s.60 orange (as No. 788) . . 35 25
879 5s. green 80 35
880 10s. blue . . . . 1·60 40

1963. Air. Chavin Excavations Fund. Pottery.
881 – 1s.+50c. grey and pink . . 15 15
882 – 1s.50+1s. grey and blue 15 15
883 – 3s.+2s.50 grey & green . . 50 50
884 **296** 4s.30+3s. grey and green 85 65
885 – 6s.+4s. grey and olive . . 1·25 85
FIGURES—HORIZ: 1s. "Griffin"; 1s.50, "Eagle"; 3s. "Cat". VERT: 6s. "Deity".

297 Campaign and Industrial Emblems

1963. Freedom from Hunger.
886 **297** 1s. bistre and red (postage) 15 10
887 4s.30 bistre and green (air) 40 40

298 Henri Dunant and Centenary Emblem

1964. Air. Red Cross Centenary.
888 **298** 1s.30+70c. multicoloured 25 25
889 4s.30+1s.70 multicoloured 55 55

299 Chavez and Wing
300 Alliance Emblem

1964. Air. 50th Anniv of Jorge Chavez's Trans-Alpine Flight.
890 **299** 5s. blue, purple and brn 75 35

1964. "Alliance for Progress". Emblem black, green and blue.
891 **300** 40c. black & yell (postage) 10 10
892 – 1s.30 black & mauve (air) 15 10
893 **300** 3s. black and blue 30 25
DESIGN—HORIZ: 1s.30, As Type **300**, but with inscription at right.

301 Fair Poster
302 Net, Flag and Globe

1965. Air. 3rd International Pacific Fair, Lima.
894 **301** 1s. multicoloured 10 10

1965. Air. Women's World Basketball Championships, Lima.
895 **302** 1s.30 violet and red . . . 30 15
896 4s.30 bistre and red . . . 45 30

303 St. Martin de Porras (anonymous)
304 Fair Emblem

1965. Air. Canonization of St. Martin de Porras (1962). Paintings. Multicoloured.
898 1s.30 Type **303** 15 10
899 1s.80 "St. Martin and the Miracle of the Animals" (after painting by Camino Brent) 25 10
900 4s.30 "St. Martin and the Angels" (after painting by Fausto Conti) 50 25
Porras is wrongly spelt "Porres" on the stamps.

1965. 4th International Pacific Fair, Lima.
901 **304** 1s.50 multicoloured . . . 15 10
902 2s.50 multicoloured . . . 20 10
903 3s.50 multicoloured . . . 30 20

305 Father Christmas and Postmarked Envelope
312 2nd May Monument and Battle Scene

1965. Christmas.
904 **305** 20c. black and red 15 10
905 50c. black and green . . . 20 10
906 1s. black and blue 30 10
The above stamps were valid for postage only on November 2nd. They were subsequently used as postal employees' charity labels.

1966. Obligatory Tax. Journalists' Fund. (a) Surch **HABILITADO "Fondo del Periodista Peruano" Ley 16078 S/o. 0.10.**
907 **264a** 10c. on 3c. (No. 897) . . 65 10
(b) Surch **Habilitado "Fondo del Periodista Peruano" Ley 16078 S/. 0.10.**
909 **264a** 10c. on 3c. (No. 897) . . 25 10

1966. Obligatory Tax. Journalists' Fund. No. 857 optd **Periodista Peruano LEY 16078**.
910 **292** 10c. blue and yellow . . . 10 10

1966. Nos. 757c, 851 and 897 surch **XX Habilitado S/. 0.10.**
911 **229** 10c. on 2c. brown . . . 10 10
912 **264a** 10c. on 3c. lake (No. 897) 10 10
912b 10c. on 3c. lake (No. 851) . . . . . 2·00 70

1966. Air. Centenary of Battle of Callao. Mult.
913 1s.90 Type **312** 30 20
914 3s.60 Monument and sculpture 45 30
915 4s.60 Monument and Jose Galvez 50 40

313 Funerary Mask

1966. Gold Objects of Chimu Culture. Multicoloured.
916 1s.90+90c. Type **313** 35 35
917 2s.60+1s.30 Ceremonial knife (vert) 40 40
918 3s.60+1s.80 Ceremonial urn 90 90
919 4s.60+2s.30 Goblet (vert) . . 1·25 1·25
920 20s.+10s. Ear-ring . . . . . 4·75 4·75

314 Civil Guard Emblem

1966. Air. Civil Guard Centenary Multicoloured.
929 90c. Type **314** 10 10
930 1s.90 Emblem and activities of Civil Guard 20 10

315 Map and Mountains

1966. Opening of Huinco Hydro-electric Scheme.
931 **315** 70c. black, deep blue and blue (postage) 10 10
932 1s.90 black, blue and violet (air) 20 15

316 Globe

1967. Air. Peruvian Photographic Exhibition, Lima.
933 – 2s.60 red and black . . . 25 15
934 – 3s.60 black and blue . . . 35 25
935 **316** 4s.60 multicoloured . . . 40 30
DESIGNS: 2s.60, "Sun" carving; 3s.60, Map of Peru within spiral.

317 Symbol of Construction

1967. Six-year Construction Plan.
936 **317** 90c. black, gold and mauve (postage) . . . 10 10
937 1s.90 black, gold and ochre (air) 15 15

318 "St. Rosa" (from painting by A. Medoro) **319** Vicuna within Figure "5"

1967. Air. 350th Death Anniv of St. Rosa of Lima. Designs showing portraits of St. Rosa by artists given below. Multicoloured.
938 1s.90 Type **318** 30 15
939 2s.60 C. Maratta 40 15
940 3s.60 Anon., Cusquena School 55 25

1967. 5th International Pacific Fair, Lima.
941 **319** 1s. black, green and gold (postage) 10 10
942 1s. purple, black and gold (air) 10 10

320 Pen-nib made of Newspaper **321** Wall Reliefs (fishes)

1967. Obligatory Tax. Journalists' Fund.
943 **320** 10c. black and red 10 10

1967. Obligatory Tax. Chan-Chan Excavation Fund.
944 **321** 20c. black and blue . . . 10 10
945 – 20c. black and mauve . . 10 10
946 – 20c. black and brown . . 10 10
947 – 20c. multicoloured 10 10
948 – 20c. multicoloured 10 10
949 – 20c. black and green . . . 10 10
DESIGNS: No. 945, Ornamental pattern; No. 946, Carved "bird"; No. 947, Temple on hillside; No. 948, Corner of Temple; No. 949, Ornamental pattern (birds).

322 Lions' Emblem **323** Nazca Jug

1967. Air. 50th Anniv of Lions International.
950 **322** 1s.60 violet, blue and grey 15 10

1968. Air. Ceramic Treasures of Nazca Culture. Designs showing painted pottery jugs. Mult.
951 1s.90 Type **323** 15 15
952 2s.60 Falcon 20 15
953 3s.60 Round jug decorated with bird 25 20
954 4s.60 Two-headed snake . . 30 25
955 5s.60 Sea Bird 40 35

324 Alligator **325** "Antarqui" (Airline Symbol)

1968. Gold Sculptures of Mochica Culture. Mult.
956 1s.90 Type **324** 15 10
957 2s.60 Bird (vert) 15 10
958 3s.60 Lizard 25 15
959 4s.60 Bird (vert) 30 15
960 5s.60 Jaguar 35 20

1968. Air. 12th Anniv of APSA (Peruvian Airlines).
961 **325** 3s.60 multicoloured . . . 30 15
962 – 5s.60 brown, black & red 45 20
DESIGN: 5s.60, Alpaca and stylized Boeing 747.

326 Human Rights Emblem **327** "The Discus-thrower"

1968. Air. Human Rights Year.
963 **326** 6s.50 red, green & brown 25 20

1968. Air. Olympic Games, Mexico.
964 **327** 2s.30 brown, blue & yell 15 10
965 3s.50 blue, red and green 20 15
966 5s. black, blue and pink 25 15
967 6s.50 purple, brown & bl 35 20
968 8s. blue, mauve and lilac 40 25
969 9s. violet, green and orange 45 30

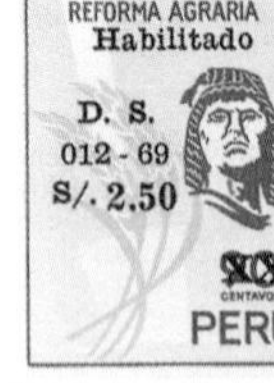

328 **331** Indian's Head and Wheat

1968. Obligatory Tax. Unissued stamps surch as in T **328**.
970 **328** 20c. on 50c. violet, orange and black 40 40
971 20c. on 1s. blue, orange and black 40 40

1968. Obligatory Tax. Journalists' Fund. No. 897 surch **Habilitado Fondo Periodista Peruano Ley 17050 S/.** and value.
972 **264a** 20c. on 3c. lake 10 10

1968. Christmas. No. 900 surch **PRO NAVIDAD Veinte Centavos R.S. 5-11-68.**
973 20c. on 4s.30 multicoloured 25 20

1969. Unissued Agrarian Reform stamps, surch as in T **331**. Multicoloured.
974 2s.50 on 90c. Type **331** (postage) 15 10
975 3s. on 90c. Man digging . . 15 15
976 4s. on 90c. As No. 975 . . . 25 15
977 5s.50 on 1s.90 Corn-cob and hand scattering cobs (air) 30 15
978 6s.50 on 1s.90 As No. 977 . . 40 20

333 First Peruvian Coin (obverse and reverse)

1969. Air. 400th Anniv of 1st Peruvian Coinage.
979 **333** 5s. black, grey and yellow 25 15
980 5s. black, grey and green 25 15

334 Worker holding Flag and Oil Derrick

1969. Nationalization of International Petroleum Company's Oilfields and Refinery (9 October 1968).
981 **334** 2s.50 multicoloured . . . 15 10
982 3s. multicoloured 20 10
983 4s. multicoloured 25 15
984 5s.50 multicoloured . . . 30 20

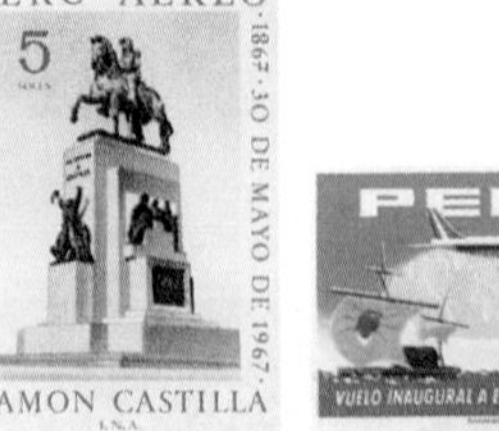

335 Castilla Monument **336** Boeing 707, Globe and "Kon Tiki" (replica of balsa raft)

1969. Air. Death Centenary of President Ramon Castilla.
985 **335** 5s. blue and green 30 15
986 – 10s. brown and purple . . 70 30
DESIGN—(21 × 37 mm): 10s. President Castilla.

1969. 1st A.P.S.A. (Peruvian Airlines) Flight to Europe.
987 **336** 2s.50 mult (postage) . . . 20 10
988 3s. multicoloured (air) . . 30 10
989 4s. multicoloured 40 10
990 5s.50 multicoloured . . . 50 15
991 6s.50 multicoloured . . . 60 25

337 Dish Aerial, Satellite and Globe

1969. Air. Inauguration of Lurin Satellite Telecommunications Station, Lima.
992 **337** 20s. multicoloured . . . . 1·50 60

338 Captain Jose A. Quinones Gonzales (military aviator)

1969. Quinones Gonzales Commemoration.
994 **338** 20s. mult (postage) . . . 1·50 70
995 20s. multicoloured (air) 1·50 45

339 W.H.O. Emblem

1969. Air. 20th Anniv (1968) of W.H.O.
996 **339** 5s. multicoloured 15 15
997 6s.50 multicoloured . . . 20 15

340 Peasant breaking Chains **341** Arms of the Inca Garcilaso de la Vega (historian)

1969. Agrarian Reform Decree.
998 **340** 2s.50 deep blue, blue and red (postage) 10 10
999 3s. purple, lilac and black (air) 10 10
1000 4s. brown and light brown 15 10

1969. Air. Garcilaso de la Vega Commemoration.
1001 **341** 2s.40 black, silver & grn 10 10
1002 – 3s.50 black, buff and blue 15 10
1003 – 5s. multicoloured 20 15
DESIGNS: 3s.50, Title page, "Commentarios Reales", Lisbon, 1609; 5s. Inca Garcilaso de la Vega.

342 Admiral Grau and Ironclad Warship "Huascar"

1969. Navy Day.
1005 **342** 50s. multicoloured . . . 4·50 2·50

343 "6" and Fair Flags

1969. 6th International Pacific Fair, Lima.
1006 **343** 2s.50 mult (postage) . . 10 10
1007 3s. multicoloured (air) 15 10
1008 4s. multicoloured 15 10

344 Father Christmas and Greetings Card

345 Col. F. Bolognesi and Soldier

1969. Christmas.
1009 **344** 20c. black and red . . . 10 10
1010 20c. black and orange 10 10
1011 20c. black and brown . . 10 10

1969. Army Day.
1012 **345** 1s.20 black, gold and blue (postage) 10 10
1013 50s. black, gold and brown (air) . . . . . 3·00 1·10

346 Arms of Amazonas

1970. Air. 150th Anniv (1971) of Republic (1st issue).
1014 **346** 10s. multicoloured . . . 35 30
See also Nos. 1066/70, 1076/80 and 1081/90.

347 I.L.O. Emblem on Map

1970. Air. 50th Anniv of I.L.O.
1015 **347** 3s. deep blue and blue 15 10

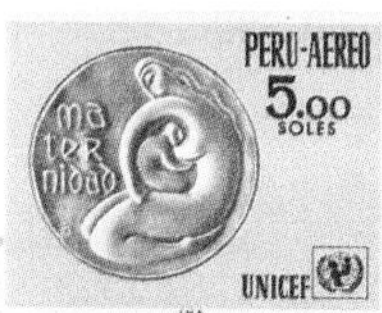

348 "Motherhood"

1970. Air. 24th Anniv of UNICEF.
1016 **348** 5s. black and yellow . . 25 15
1017 6s.50 black and pink . . 35 20

349 "Puma" Jug

350 Ministry Building

1970. Vicus Culture. Ceramic Art. Multicoloured.
1018 2s.50 Type **349** (postage) . . 15 10
1019 3s. Squatting warrior (statuette) (air) 20 15
1020 4s. Animal jug 25 15
1021 5s.50 Twin jugs 30 20
1022 6s.50 Woman with jug (statuette) 40 25

1970. Ministry of Transport and Communications.
1023 **350** 40c. black and purple . . 10 10
1024 40c. black and yellow . . 10 10
1025 40c. black and grey . . . 10 10
1026 40c. black and red . . . 10 10
1027 40c. black and brown . . 10 10

351 Peruvian Anchovy

352 Telephone and Skyline

1970. Fishes. Multicoloured.
1028 2s.50 Type **351** (postage) . . 35 10
1029 2s.50 Chilean hake 35 10
1030 3s. Swordfish (air) 40 15
1031 3s. Yellow-finned tuna . . . 40 15
1032 5s.50 Atlantic wolffish . . . 1·00 25

1970. Air. Nationalization of Lima Telephone Service.
1033 **352** 5s. multicoloured 30 15
1034 10s. multicoloured . . . 55 25

353 "Soldier and Farmer"

354 U.N. Headquarters and Dove

1970. Unity of Armed Forces and People.
1035 **353** 2s.50 mult (postage) . . 15 10
1036 3s. multicoloured (air) 25 10
1037 5s.50 multicoloured . . . 35 15

1970. Air. 25th Anniv of U.N.O.
1038 **354** 3s. blue and light blue 15 10

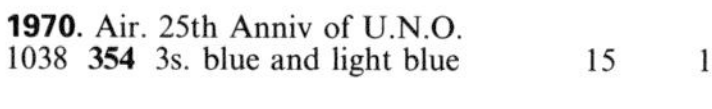

355 Rotary Emblem

1970. Air. 50th Anniv of Lima Rotary Club.
1039 **355** 10s. gold, red and black 75 25

356 Military Parade (Army Staff College, Chorrillos)

1970. Military, Naval and Air Force Academies. Multicoloured.
1040 2s.50 Type **356** 35 20
1041 2s.50 Parade, Naval Academy, La Punta . . . 35 20
1042 2s.50 Parade, Air Force Officer Training School, Las Palmas 35 20

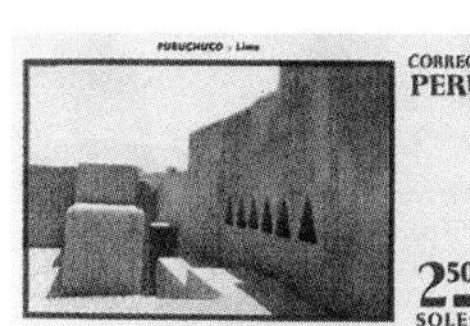

357 Puruchuco, Lima

1970. Tourism. Multicoloured.
1043 2s.50 Type **357** (postage) . . 15 10
1044 3s. Chan-Chan-Trujillo, La Libertad (air) 15 10
1045 4s. Sacsayhuaman, Cuzco (vert) 25 10
1046 5s.50 Lake Titicaca, Pomata, Puno (vert) 30 15
1047 10s. Machu-Picchu, Cuzco (vert) 60 30

358 Festival Procession

1970. Air. October Festival, Lima. Multicoloured.
1049 3s. Type **358** 15 10
1050 4s. "The Cock-fight" (T. Nunez Ureta) 25 10
1051 5s.50 Altar, Nazarenas Shrine (vert) 30 20
1052 6s.50 "The Procession" (J. Vinatea Reinoso) . . . 35 25
1053 8s. "The Procession" (Jose Sabogal) (vert) 50 20

359 "The Nativity" (Cuzco School)

1970. Christmas. Paintings by Unknown Artists. Multicoloured.
1054 1s.20 Type **359** 30 25
1055 1s.50 "The Adoration of the Magi" (Cuzquena School) 10 10
1056 1s.80 "The Adoration of the Shepherds" (Peruvian School) 10 10

360 "Close Embrace" (petroglyph)

1971. Air. "Gratitude for World Help in Earthquake of May 1970".
1057 **360** 4s. olive, black and red 25 15
1058 5s.50 blue, flesh and red 35 15
1059 6s.50 grey, blue and red 40 20

361 "St. Rosa de Lima" (F. Laso)

1971. 300th Anniv of Canonization of St. Rosa de Lima.
1060 **361** 2s.50 multicoloured . . . 15 10

362 Tiahuanaco Fabric

1971. Ancient Peruvian Textiles.
1061 **362** 1s.20 mult (postage) . . 15 10
1062 – 2s.50 multicoloured . . . 25 10
1063 – 3s. multicoloured (air) 30 10
1064 – 4s. pink, green & dp grn 40 10
1065 – 5s.50 multicoloured . . . 55 15
DESIGNS—HORIZ: 2s.50, Chancay fabric; 4s. Chancay lace. VERT: 3s. Chancay tapestry; 5s.50, Paracas fabric.

363 M. Garcia Pumacahua

364 Violet Amberjack (Nazca Culture)

1971. 150th Anniv of Independence (2nd issue). National Heroes.
1066 **363** 1s.20 blk & red (postage) 10 10
1067 – 2s.50 black and blue . . 15 10
1068 – 3s. black and mauve (air) 15 10
1069 – 4s. black and green . . . 15 10
1070 – 5s.50 black and brown 25 15
DESIGNS: 2s.50, F. Antonio de Zela; 3s. T. Rodriguez de Mendoza; 4s. J. P. Viscardo y Guzman; 5s.50, J. G. Condorcanqui, Tupac Amani.
See also Nos. 1076/80 and Nos. 1081/90.

1971. "Traditional Fisheries of Peru". Piscatorial Ceramics. Multicoloured.
1071 1s.50 Type **364** (postage) . . 25 10
1072 3s.50 Pacific bonito (Chimu Inca) (air) 55 15
1073 4s. Peruvian anchovy (Mochica) 75 20
1074 5s.50 Chilian hake (Chimu) 1·10 35
1075 8s.50 Peruvian menhaden (Nazca) . . . . 1·75 60

1971. 150th Anniv of Independence. National Heroes (3rd issue). As T **363**. Multicoloured.
1076 1s.20 M. Melgar (postage) 10 10
1077 2s.50 J. Baquijano y Carrillo 15 10
1078 3s. J. de la Riva Aguero (air) 15 10
1079 4s. H. Unanue 15 10
1080 5s.50 F. J. de Luna Pizarro 25 15

366 Liberation Expedition Monument

367 R. Palma (author and poet)

1971. 150th Anniv of Independence (4th issue). As T **366**. Multicoloured.
1081 1s.50 M. Bastidas (postage) 10 10
1082 2s. J. F. Sanchez Carrion . . 10 10
1083 2s.50 M. J. Guise 15 10
1084 3s. F. Vidal (air) 15 10
1085 3s.50 J. de San Martin . . . 15 15
1086 4s.50 Type **366** 20 15
1087 6s. "Surrender of the 'Numancia Battalion'" (horiz) (42 × 35 mm) . . . 30 15
1088 7s.50 Alvarez de Arenales Monument (horiz) (42 × 39 mm) 35 20
1089 9s. Monument to Founders of the Republic, Lima (horiz) (42 × 39 mm) . . . 40 20
1090 10s. "Proclamation of Independence" (horiz) (46 × 35 mm) 50 20

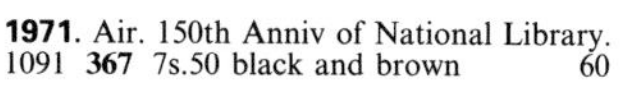

1971. Air. 150th Anniv of National Library.
1091 **367** 7s.50 black and brown 60 25

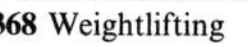
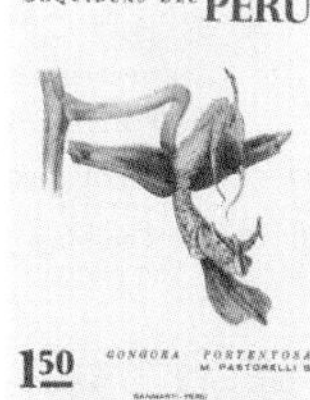

368 Weightlifting

369 "Gongora portentosa"

1971. Air. 25th World Weightlifting Championships, Huampani, Lima.
1092 **368** 7s.50 black and blue . . 60 25

1971. Peruvian Flora (1st series). Orchids. Mult.
1093 1s.50 Type **369** 25 10
1094 2s. "Odontoglossum cristatum" 30 10
1095 2s.50 "Mormolyca peruviana" 35 10

1096 3s. "Trichocentrum pulchrum" 45 15
1097 3s.50 "Oncidium sanderae" 35 20
See also Nos. 1170/4 and 1206/10.

370 Family and Flag 371 Schooner "Sacramento" of 1821

1971. Air. 3rd Anniv of October 3rd Revolution.
1098 **370** 7s.50 black, red and blue 50 30

1971. Air. 150th Anniv of Peruvian Navy and "Order of the Peruvian Sun".
1100 **371** 7s.50 blue and light blue 1·50 30
1101 – 7s.50 multicoloured . . . 50 25
DESIGN: No. 1101, Order of the Peruvian Sun.

372 "Development and Liberation" (detail)

1971. 2nd Ministerial Meeting of "The 77" Group.
1102 **372** 1s.20 multicoloured (postage) 10 10
1103 – 3s.50 multicoloured . . . 25 10
1104 – 50s. multicoloured (air) 3·00 1·50
DESIGNS—As Type **372**: 3s.50, 50s. Detail from the painting "Development and Liberation".

373 "Plaza de Armas, 1843" (J. Rugendas)

1971. "Exfilima" Stamp Exhibition, Lima.
1105 **373** 3s. black and green . . . 30 10
1106 – 3s.50 black and pink . . 40 15
DESIGN: 3s.50, "Plaza de Armas, 1971" (C. Zeiter).

374 Fair Emblem 375 Army Crest

1971. Air. 7th International Pacific Fair, Lima.
1107 **374** 4s.50 multicoloured . . . 20 15

1971. 150th Anniv of Peruvian Army.
1108 **375** 8s.50 multicoloured . . . 60 20

376 "The Flight into Egypt"

1971. Christmas. Multicoloured.
1109 1s.80 Type **376** 20 10
1110 2s.50 "The Magi" 25 10
1111 3s. "The Nativity" 35 10

377 "Fishermen" (J. Ugarte Elespuru) 378 Chimu Idol

1971. Social Reforms. Paintings. Mulicoloured
1112 3s.50 Type **377** 45 10
1113 4s. "Threshing Grain in Cajamarca" (Camilo Blas) 45 10
1114 6s. "Hand-spinning Huanca Native Women" (J. Sabogal) 60 15

1972. Peruvian Antiquities. Multicoloured.
1115 3s.90 Type **378** 35 15
1116 4s. Chimu statuette 35 15
1117 4s.50 Lambayeque idol . . . 45 15
1118 5s.40 Mochica collar 55 15
1119 6s. Lambayeque "spider" pendant 60 15

379 Peruvian Bigeye

1972. Peruvian Fishes. Multicoloured.
1120 1s.20 Type **379** (postage) . . 30 10
1121 1s.50 Common guadana . . 30 15
1122 2s.50 Jack mackerel 55 20
1123 3s. Diabolico (air) 65 20
1124 5s.50 Galapagos hogfish . . 1·25 35

380 "Peruvian Family" (T. Nunez Ureta)

1972. Air. Education Reforms.
1125 **380** 6s.50 multicoloured . . . 35 20

381 Mochica Warrior 382 White-tailed Trogon

1972. Peruvian Art (1st series). Mochica Ceramics. Multicoloured.
1126 1s.20 Type **381** 15 10
1127 1s.50 Warrior's head 15 10
1128 2s. Kneeling deer 25 10
1129 2s.50 Warrior's head (different) 35 10
1130 3s. Kneeling warrior 40 15
See also Nos. 1180/4.

1972. Air. Peruvian Birds. Multicoloured.
1131 2s. Type **382** . . . . 1·50 20
1132 2s.50 Amazonian umbrellabird . . . . . . 1·75 20
1133 3s. Andean cock of the rock 2·00 25
1134 6s.50 Red-billed toucan . . 3·75 45
1135 8s.50 Blue-crowned motmot 4·75 55

383 "The Harvest" (July) 384 "Quipu" on Map

1972. 400th Anniv of G. Poma de Ayala's "Inca Chronicles". Woodcuts.
1136 **383** 2s.50 black and red . . . 35 10
1137 – 3s. black and green . . . 60 10
1138 – 2s.50 black and pink . . 30 10
1139 – 3s. black and blue . . . 50 10
1140 – 2s.50 black and orange 50 10
1141 – 3s. black and lilac . . . 50 10
1142 – 2s.50 black and brown 35 10
1143 – 3s. black and green . . . 50 10
1144 – 2s.50 black and blue . . 35 10
1145 – 3s. black and orange . . 50 10
1146 – 2s.50 black and mauve 35 10
1147 – 3s. black and yellow . . 50 10

DESIGNS: No. 1137, "Land Purification" (August); No. 1138, "Sowing" (September); No. 1139, "Invocation of the Rains" (October); No. 1140, "Irrigation" (November); No. 1141, "Rite of the Nobility" (December); No. 1142, "Maize Cultivation Rights" (January); No. 1143, "Ripening of the Maize" (February); No. 1144, "Birds in the Maize" (March); No. 1145, "Children as camp-guards" (April); No. 1146, "Gathering the harvest" (May); No. 1147, "Removing the harvest" (June).

1972. Air. "Exfibra 72" Stamp Exn, Rio de Janeiro.
1148 **384** 5s. multicoloured 25 15

385 "The Messenger" 386 Catacaos Woman

1972. Air. Olympic Games, Munich.
1149 **385** 8s. multicoloured 55 20

1972. Air. Provincial Costumes (1st series). Mult.
1150 2s. Tupe girl 15 10
1151 3s.50 Type **386** 30 10
1152 4s. Conibo Indian 40 10
1153 4s.50 Agricultural worker playing "quena" and drum 40 15
1154 5s. "Moche" (Trujillo) girl 40 15
1155 6s.50 Ocongate (Cuzco) man and woman 55 40
1156 8s. "Chucupana" (Ayacucho) girl 60 50
1157 8s.50 "Cotuncha" (Junin) girl 70 55
1158 10s. "Pandilla" dancer . . . 60 60
See also Nos. 1248/9.

387 Ruins of Chavin (Ancash)

1972. Air. 25th Death Anniv Julio C. Tello (archaeologist). Multicoloured.
1159 1s.50 "Stone of the 12 Angles", Cuzco (vert) . . 15 10
1160 3s.50 Type **387** 30 10
1161 4s. Burial-tower, Sillustani (Puno) (vert) 30 10
1162 5s. Gateway, Chavin (Ancash) 45 15
1163 8s. "Wall of the 3 Windows", Machu Picchu (Cuzco) 55 25

388 "Territorial Waters"

1972. 4th Anniv of Armed Forces Revolution. Mult.
1164 2s. Agricultural Workers ("Agrarian Reform") (vert) 10 10
1165 2s.50 Type **388** 50 10
1166 3s. Oil rigs ("Nationalization of Petroleum Industry") (vert) 20 10

389 "The Holy Family" (wood-carving) 390 "Ipomoea purpurea"

1972. Christmas. Multicoloured.
1167 1s.50 Type **389** 15 10
1168 2s. "The Holy Family" (carved Huamanga stone) (horiz) 15 10
1169 2s.50 "The Holy Family" (carved Huamanga stone) 20 10

1972. Peruvian Flora (2nd series). Multicoloured.
1170 1s.50 Type **390** 15 10
1171 2s.50 "Amaryllis ferreyrae" 20 10
1172 3s. "Liabum excelsum" . . 30 10
1173 3s.50 "Bletia catenulata" . . 55 10
1174 5s. "Cantua buxifolia cantuta" 35 20

391 Inca Poncho 392 Mochica Cameo and Cups

1973. Air. Ancient Inca Textiles.
1175 **391** 2s. multicoloured 15 10
1176 – 3s.50 multicoloured . . . 25 10
1177 – 4s. multicoloured 25 10
1178 – 5s. multicoloured 30 12
1179 – 8s. multicoloured 55 25
DESIGNS: Nos. 1176/9, similar to T **391**.

1973. Air. Peruvian Art (2nd series). Jewelled Antiquities. Multicoloured.
1180 1s.50 Type **392** 10 10
1181 2s.50 Gold-plated arms and hands (Lambayeque) . . 15 10
1182 4s. Bronze effigy (Mochica) 25 10
1183 5s. Gold pendants (Nazca) 30 15
1184 8s. Gold cat (Mochica) . . . 60 25

393 [illegible] 394 "The [illegible]" (J. Sabogal)

1973. Air. Fauna Protection (1st series). Mult.
1185 2s.50 Lesser rhea . . . . . 1·00 30
1186 3s.50 Giant otter 45 10
1187 4s. Type **393** 40 20
1188 5s. Vicuna 60 15
1189 6s. Chilian flamingo . . . . 2·25 40
1190 8s. Spectacled bear 70 25
1191 8s.50 Bush dog (horiz) . . . 60 25
1192 10s. Short-tailed chinchilla (horiz) 75 30
See also Nos. 1245/6.

1973. Air. Peruvian Paintings. Multicoloured.
1193 1s.50 Type **394** 10 10
1194 8s. "Yananacu Bridge" (E. C. Brent) (horiz) . . . 30 15
1195 8s.50 "Portrait of a Lady" (D. Hernandez) 35 15
1196 10s. "Peruvian Birds" (T. N. Ureta) . . . . 1·25 40
1197 20s. "The Potter" (F. Laso) 1·10 40
1198 50s. "Reed Boats" (J. V. Reinoso) (horiz) . . . . . 3·50 1·50

395 Basketball Net and Map

1973. Air. 1st World Basketball Festival.
1199 **395** 5s. green 35 10
1200 20s. purple . . . . . . 1·40 40

396 "Spanish Mayor on Horseback" 398 Fair Emblem (poster)

1973. 170th Birth Anniv of Pancho Fierro (painter). Multicoloured.
1201 1s.50 Type **396** 10 10
1202 2s. "Peasants" 15 10
1203 2s.50 "Father Abregu" . . . 20 10
1204 3s.50 "Dancers" 30 10
1205 4s.50 "Esteban Arredondo on horseback" 45 20

1973. Air. Peruvian Flora (3rd series). Orchids. As T **390**. Multicoloured.
1206 1s.50 "Lycaste reichenbachii" 20 10
1207 2s.50 "Masdevallia amabilis" 30 10

1208 3s. "Sigmatostalix peruviana" 40 10

1209 3s.50 "Porrogossum peruvianum" 40 10

1210 8s. "Oncidium incarum" 60 25

1973. Air. 8th International Pacific Fair, Lima.

1211 **398** 8s. red, black and grey 60 20

399 Symbol of Flight

1973. Air. 50th Anniv of Air Force Officers' School.

1212 **399** 8s.50 multicoloured 60 15

400 "The Presentation of the Child"

1973. Christmas. Paintings of the Cuzco School. Multicoloured.

1213 1s.50 Type **400** 10 10

1214 2s. "The Holy Family" (vert) 15 10

1215 2s.50 "The Adoration of the Kings" 15 10

401 Freighter "Ilo"

1973. Air. National Development. Multicoloured.

1216 1s.50 Type **401** 75 20

1217 2s.50 Trawlers 85 20

1218 8s. B.A.C. One Eleven 200 airliner and seagull 1·00 25

402 House of the Mulberry Tree, Arequipa

1974. Air. "Landscapes and Cities". Mult.

1219 1s.50 Type **402** 10 10

1220 2s.50 El Misti (peak), Arequipa 15 10

1221 5s. Giant puya, Cordillera Blanca, Ancash (vert) 30 15

1222 6s. Huascaran (peak), Cordillera Blanca, Ancash 35 15

1223 8s. Lake Querococha, Cordillera Blanca, Ancash 55 20

403 Peruvian 2c. Stamp of 1873

405 Church of San Jeronimo, Cuzco

404 Room of the Three Windows, Machu Picchu

1974. Stamp Day and 25th Anniv of Peruvian Philatelic Association.

1224 **403** 6s. blue and grey 40 15

1974. Air. Archaeological Discoveries. Mult.

(a) Cuzco Relics.

1225 3s. Type **404** 15 10

1226 5s. Baths of Tampumacchay 25 15

1227 10s. "Kencco" 45 25

(b) Dr. Tello's Discoveries at Chavin de Huantar. Stone carvings.

1228 3s. Mythological jaguar (vert) 15 10

1229 5s. Rodent ("Vizcacha") (vert) 25 15

1230 10s. Chavin warrior (vert) 45 25

1974. Air. Architectural Treasures. Multicoloured.

1231 1s.50 Type **405** 10 10

1232 3s.50 Cathedral of Santa Catalina, Cajamarca 20 10

1233 5s. Church of San Pedro, Zepita, Puno (horiz) 25 10

1234 6s. Cuzco Cathedral 30 15

1235 8s.50 Wall of the Coricancha, Cuzco 80 20

406 "Colombia" Bridge, Tarapoto–Juanjui Highway

1974. "Structural Changes". Multicoloured.

1236 2s. Type **406** 15 10

1237 8s. Tayacaja hydro-electric scheme 40 20

1238 10s. Tablachaca dam 50 25

407 "Battle of Junin" (F. Yanez)

1974. 150th Anniv of Battle of Junin.

1239 **407** 1s.50 mult (postage) 10 10

1240 2s.50 multicoloured 10 10

1241 6s. multicoloured (air) 30 10

408 "Battle of Ayacucho" (F. Yanez)

1974. 150th Anniv of Battle of Ayacucho.

1242 **408** 2s. mult (postage) 10 10

1243 3s. multicoloured 15 10

1244 7s.50 multicoloured (air) 45 15

1974. Air. Fauna Protection (2nd series). As T **393**. Multicoloured.

1245 8s. Red uakari 50 15

1246 20s. As 8s. 85 50

409 Chimu Gold Mask

1974. Air. 8th World Mining Congress, Lima.

1247 **409** 8s. multicoloured 45 15

1974. Air. Provincial Costumes (2nd series). As T **386**. Multicoloured.

1248 5s. Horseman in "chalan" (Cajamarca) 35 15

1249 8s.50 As 5s. 60 15

410 Pedro Paulet and Spacecraft

1974. Air. Centenary of U.P.U. and Birth Centenary of Pedro E. Paulet (aviation scientist).

1250 **410** 8s. violet and blue 40 15

411 Copper Smelter, La Oroya

1974. Expropriation of Cerro de Pasco Mining Complex.

1251 **411** 1s.50 blue and deep blue 10 10

1252 3s. red and brown 15 10

1253 4s.50 green and grey 25 15

412 "Capitulation of Ayacucho" (D. Hernandez)

1974. Air. 150th Anniv of Spanish Forces' Capitulation at Ayacucho.

1254 **412** 3s.50 multicoloured 20 10

1255 8s.50 multicoloured 60 20

1256 10s. multicoloured 80 25

413 "Madonna and Child"

415 Map and Civic Centre, Lima

414 "Andean Landscape" (T. Nunez Ureta)

1974. Christmas. Paintings of the Cuzco Shool. Multicoloured.

1257 1s.50 Type **413** (postage) 10 10

1258 6s.50 "Holy Family" (air) 30 15

1974. Air. Andean Pact Communications Ministers' Meeting, Cali, Colombia.

1259 **414** 6s.50 multicoloured 35 15

1975. Air. 2nd General Conference of U.N. Organization for Industrial Development.

1260 **415** 6s. black, red and grey 25 15

1975. Air. Various stamps surch.

1261 – 1s.50 on 3s.60 purple (No. 927) 10 10

1262 – 2s. on 2s.60 green (No. 926) 15 10

1263 – 2s. on 3s.60 purple (No. 927) 15 10

1263a – 2s. on 3s.60 black and blue (No. 934) 10 10

1264 – 2s. on 4s.30 orange (No. 878) 10 10

1265 – 2s. on 4s.30 multicoloured (No. 900) 15 10

1266 – 2s. on 4s.60 orange (No. 928) 10 10

1267 – 2s.50 on 4s.60 orange (No. 928) 25 10

1268 – 3s. on 2s.60 green (No. 926) 15 10

1294 – 3s.50 on 4s.60 orange (No. 928) 20 10

1269 – 4s. on 2s.60 green (No. 926) 20 10

1270 – 4s. on 3s.60 purple (No. 927) 20 10

1271 – 4s. on 4s.60 orange (No. 928) 15 10

1295 – 4s.50 on 3s.80 orange (No. 836) 20 10

1272 – 5s. on 3s.60 purple (No. 927) 20 10

1273 – 5s. on 3s.80 orange (No. 836) 35 10

1296 – 5s. on 4s.30 orange (No. 878) 30 10

1297 – 6c. on 4s.60 orange (No. 928) 40 15

1277 **316** 6s. on 4s.60 multicoloured (No. 935) 45 10

1278 – 7s. on 4s.30 orange (No. 878) 40 15

1279 – 7s.50 on 3s.60 purple (No. 927) 50 15

1280 – 8s. on 3s.60 purple (No. 927) 50 15

1281 **271** 10s. on 2s.15 purple (No. 794) 40 25

1298 – 10s. on 2s.60 green (No. 926) 60 20

1282 – 10s. on 3s.60 purple (No. 927) 60 25

1283 – 10s. on 3s.60 multicoloured (No. 940) 50 25

1284 – 10s. on 4s.30 orange (No. 878) 25 25

1285 – 10s. on 4s.60 orange (No. 928) 60 25

1286 – 20s. on 3s.60 purple (No. 927) 40 15

1287 – 24s. on 3s.60 multicoloured (No. 953) 1·40 45

1288 – 28s. on 4s.60 multicoloured (No. 954) 1·50 55

1289 – 32s. on 5s.60 multicoloured (No. 955) 1·50 65

1290 – 50s. on 2s.60 green (No. 926) 2·75 1·00

1299 – 50s. on 3s.60 purple (No. 927) 2·25 1·50

1292 – 100s. on 3s.80 orange (No. 836) 3·50 1·50

417 Lima on World Map

1975. Air. Conference of Non-aligned Countries' Foreign Ministers, Lima.

1311 **417** 6s.50 multicoloured 40 15

418 Maria Parado de Bellido

1975. "Year of Peruvian Women" and International Women's Year. Multicoloured.

1312 1s.50 Type **418** 15 10

1313 2s. Micaela Bastidas (vert) 15 10

1314 2s.50 Juana Alarco de Dammert 20 10

1315 3s. I.W.Y. emblem (vert) 35 10

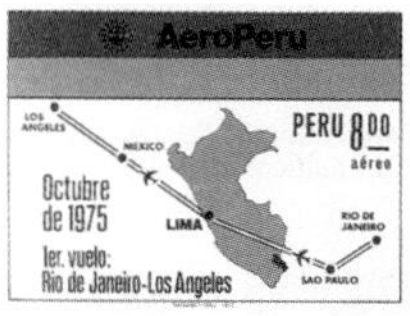

419 Route Map of Flight

1975. Air. 1st "Aero Peru" Flight, Rio de Janeiro–Lima–Los Angeles.

1316 **419** 8s. multicoloured 60 15

420 San Juan Macias

421 Fair Poster

1975. Canonization of St. Juan Macias.

1317 **420** 5s. multicoloured 30 10

1975. Air. 9th International Pacific Fair, Lima.

1318 **421** 6s. red, brown and black 50 15

422 Col. F. Bolognesi

423 "Nativity"

1975. Air. 159th Birth Anniv of Colonel Francisco Bolognesi.

1319 **422** 20s. multicoloured 1·25 35

1976. Air. Christmas (1975).

1320 **423** 6s. multicoloured 35 15

424 Louis Braille

1976. 150th Anniv of Braille System for Blind.
1321 **424** 4s.50 red, black and grey . . . 30 10

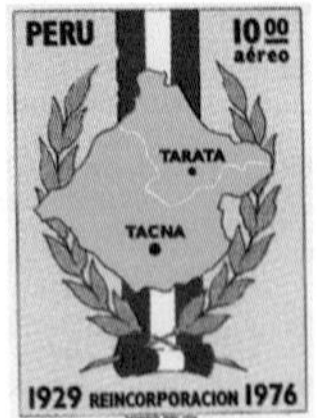

426 Inca Postal Runner 427 Map on Riband

1976. Air. 11th UPAE Congress, Lima.
1322 **426** 5s. black, brown and red 50 10

1976. Air. Reincorporation of Tacna.
1323 **427** 10s. multicoloured . . . 30 15

428 Peruvian Flag

1976. 1st Anniv of Second Phase of Revolution.
1324 **428** 5s. red, black and grey 15 10

429 Police Badge

1976. Air. 54th Anniv of Peruvian Special Police.
1325 **429** 20s. multicoloured . . . 1·00 40

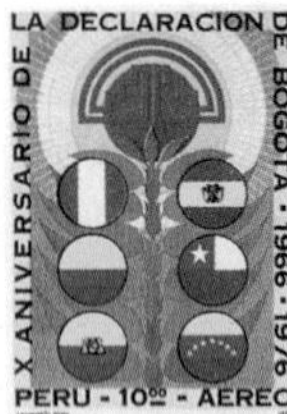

430 "Tree of Badges" 431 Chairman Pal Losonczi

1976. Air. 10th Anniv of Bogota Declaration.
1326 **430** 10s. multicoloured . . . 30 20

1976. Air. Visit of Hungarian Head of State.
1327 **431** 7s. black and blue . . . 40 15

432 "St. Francis of Assisi" (El Greco) 434 "Nativity"

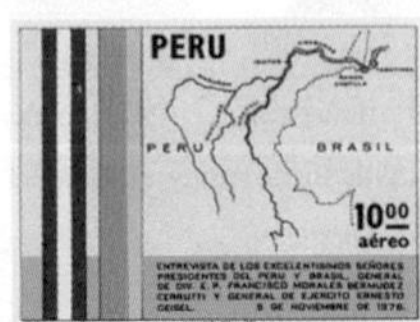

433 Map and National Colours

1976. 750th Death Anniv of St. Francis of Assisi.
1328 **432** 5s. brown and gold . . . 35 10

1976. Air. Meeting of Presidents of Peru and Brazil.
1329 **433** 10s. multicoloured . . . 30 20

1976. Christmas.
1330 **434** 4s. multicoloured 30 10

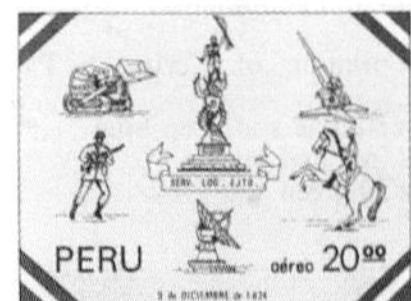

435 Military Monument and Symbols

1977. Air. Army Day.
1331 **435** 20s. black, buff and red 40 40

436 Map and Scroll

1977. Air. Visit of Peruvian President to Venezuela.
1332 **436** 12s. multicoloured . . . 60 25

437 Printed Circuit

1977. Air. World Telecommunications Day.
1333 **437** 20s. red, black and silver 1·10 40

438 Inca Postal Runner 439 Petrochemical Plant, Map and Tanker

1977.
1334 **438** 6s. black and turquoise (postage) 40 15
1335 8s. black and red 40 15
1336 10s. black and blue . . . 55 25
1337 12s. black and green . . 55 35
1338 24s. black and red (air) 1·00 50
1339 28s. black and blue . . . 1·10 50
1340 32s. black and brown . . 1·50 70

1977. Air. Bayovar Petrochemical Complex.
1341 **439** 14s. multicoloured . . . 1·50 30

440 Arms of Arequipa 441 President Videla

1977. Air. "Gold of Peru" Exhibition, Arequipa.
1342 **440** 10s. multicoloured . . . 20 10

1977. Air. Visit of President Videla of Argentina.
1343 **441** 36s. multicoloured . . . 75 25

1977. Various stamps surch **FRANQUEO** and new value.
1344 **325** 6s. on 3s.60 multicoloured 40 15
1345 8s. on 3s.60 multicoloured 45 15
1346 – 10s. on 5s.60 brown, black and red (No. 962) 50 25
1347 **305** 10s. on 50c. black & grn 30 10
1348 20s. on 20c. black and red 50 20
1349 30s. on 1s. black and blue 70 35

444 Fair Emblem and Flags 445 Republican Guard Badge

1977. 10th International Pacific Fair.
1350 **444** 10s. multicoloured . . . 20 10

1977. 58th Anniv of Republican Guard.
1351 **445** 12s. multicoloured . . . 25 15

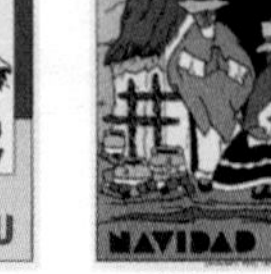

446 Admiral Miguel Grau 447 "The Holy Family"

1977. Air. Navy Day.
1352 **446** 28s. multicoloured . . . 35 25

1977. Christmas. Multicoloured.
1353 8s. Type **447** (postage) . . . 10 10
1354 20s. "The Adoration of the Shepherds" (air) 50 20

448 Open Book of Flags 449 Inca Head

1978. Air. 8th Meeting of Education Ministers.
1355 **448** 30s. multicoloured . . . 40 25

1978.
1356 **449** 6s. green (postage) . . . 10 10
1357 10s. red 15 10
1358 16s. brown 20 20
1359 24s. mauve (air) 30 25
1360 30s. pink 40 30
1361 65s. blue 90 70
1362 95s. blue . . . . 1·50 1·00

450 Emblem and Flags of West Germany, Argentina, Austria and Brazil

1978. World Cup Football Championship, Argentina (1st issue). Multicoloured.
1367 10s. Type **450** 20 10
1368 10s. Emblem and flags of Hungary, Iran, Italy and Mexico 20 10
1369 10s. Emblem and flags of Scotland, Spain, France and Netherlands 20 10
1370 10s. Emblem and flags of Peru, Poland, Sweden and Tunisia 20 10
See also Nos. 1412/15.

451 Microwave Antenna

1978. Air. 10th World Telecommunications Day.
1371 **451** 50s. grey, deep blue and blue 75 50

1978. Various stamps surch **Habilitado Dif.-Porte** and value (Nos. 1372/4), **Habilitado R.D. No. 0118** and value (Nos. 1377/8, 1381, 1384, 1390) or with value only (others).
1372 **229** 2s. on 2c. brown (postage) 10 10
1373 **229** 4s. on 2c. brown 10 10
1374 5s. on 2c. brown 10 10
1375 **313** 20s. on 1s.90+90c. multicoloured 75 60
1376 – 30s. on 2s.60+1s.30 multicoloured (No. 917) 60 60
1377 **229** 35s. on 2c. brown . . . . 1·25 20
1378 50s. on 2c. brown . . . 4·00 60
1379 – 55s. on 3s.60+1s.80 multicoloured (No. 918) . . . . . . 1·10 55
1380 – 65s. on 4s.60+2s.30 multicoloured (No. 919) . . . . . . 1·75 1·10
1381 – 80s. on 5s.60 mult (No. 960) . . . . . . 1·40 40
1382 – 85s. on 20s.+10s. multicoloured (No. 920) . . . . . . 2·00 1·25
1383 – 25s. on 4s.60 mult (No. 954) (air) 20 15
1384 **316** 34s. on 4s.60 mult . . . 50 15
1385 **302** 40s. on 4s.30 bistre and red 50 20
1386 **449** 45s. on 28s. green . . . 45 25
1387 – 70s. on 2s.60 green (No. 926) . . . . . . 2·75 40
1388 **449** 75s. on 28s. green . . . 75 40
1389 – 105s. on 5s.60 mult (No. 955) . . . . . . 1·00 85
1390 – 110s. on 3s.60 purple (No. 927) . . . . . . 1·90 60
1391 – 265s. on 4s.30 mult (No. 900) . . . . . . 4·00 1·50
The 28s. value as Type **449** was not issued without a surcharge.

1978. Surch **SOBRE TASA OFICIAL** and value.
1400 **229** 3s. on 2s. brown 10 10
1401 6s. on 2c. brown 15 10

456 San Martin 457 Elmer Faucett and Stinson-Faucett F-19 and Boeing 727-200 Aircraft

1978. Air. Birth Bicentenary of General Jose de San Martin.
1410 **456** 30s. multicoloured . . . 40 30

1978. 50th Anniv of Faucett Aviation.
1411 **457** 40s. multicoloured . . . 50 30

1978. World Cup Football Championship, Argentina (2nd issue). Multicoloured.
1412 16s. As Type **450** 15 10
1413 16s. As No. 1368 . . . . . 15 10
1414 16s. As No. 1369 . . . . . 15 10
1415 16s. As No. 1370 . . . . . 15 10

458 Nazca Bowl 459 Peruvian Nativity

1978.
1416 **458** 16s. blue 15 10
1417 20s. green 15 10
1418 25s. green 20 15
1419 35s. red 35 15
1420 45s. brown 40 25
1421 50s. black 50 25
1422 55s. mauve 50 25
1423 70s. mauve 60 35
1424 75s. blue 55 40
1425 80s. brown 55 40
1426 200s. violet . . . . . . 1·90 1·50

1978. Christmas.
1436 **459** 16s. multicoloured . . . 15 10

460 Ministry of Education, Lima **461** Queen Sophia and King Juan Carlos

1979. National Education.
1437 **460** 16s. multicoloured . . . 15 10

1979. Air. Visit of King and Queen of Spain.
1438 **461** 75s. multicoloured . . . 60 25

462 Red Cross Emblem

1979. Centenary of Peruvian Red Cross Society.
1439 **462** 16s. multicoloured . . . 10 10

463 "Naval Battle of Iquique" (E. Velarde)

1979. Pacific War Centenary. Multicoloured.
1440 14s. Type **463** 40 10
1441 25s. "Col. Jose Joaquin Inclan" (vert) 30 15
1442 25s. "Arica Blockade-runner, the Corvette "Union" 60 15
1443 25s. "Heroes of Angamos" 60 15
1444 25s. "Lt. Col. Pedro Ruiz Gallo" (vert) 30 15
1445 85s. "Marshal Andres H. Caceres" (vert) 45 40
1446 100s. "Battle of Angamos" (T. Castillo) . . . . . . 1·75 60
1447 100s. "Battle of Tarapaca" 55 45
1448 115s. "Admiral Miguel Grau" (vert) . . . . . . 1·40 50
1449 200s. "Bolognesi's Reply" (Leppiani) . . . . 1·25 90
1450 200s. "Col. Francisco Bolognesi" (vert) . . . . 1·60 1·10
1451 200s. "Col. Alfonso Ugarte" (Morizani) . . . . 1·60 1·10

A similar 200s. value, showing the Crypt of the Fallen was on sale for a very limited period only.

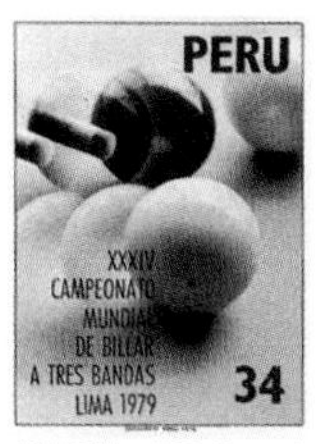

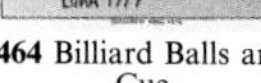

464 Billiard Balls and Cue **465** Arms of Cuzco

1979. 34th World Billiards Championship, Lima.
1456 **464** 34s. multicoloured . . . 30 15

1979. Inca Sun Festival, Cuzco.
1457 **465** 50s. multicoloured . . . 35 20

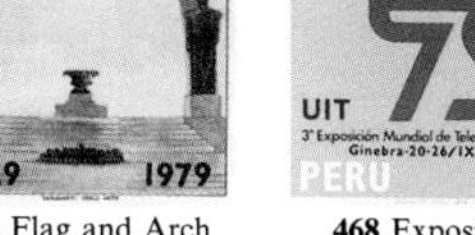

466 Flag and Arch **468** Exposition Emblem

1979. 50th Anniv of Reincorporation of Tacna into Peru.
1458 **466** 16s. multicoloured . . . 15 10

1979. Surch in figures only.
1459 **229** 7s. on 2c. brown 10 10
1460 9s. on 2c. brown 10 10
1461 15s. on 2c. brown . . . 15 10

1979. 3rd World Telecommunications Exhibition, Geneva.
1467 **468** 15s. orange, blue and grey 10 10

469 Caduceus

1979. Int Stomatology Congress, Lima, and 50th Anniv of Peruvian Academy of Stomatology.
1468 **469** 25s. gold, black & turq 20 15

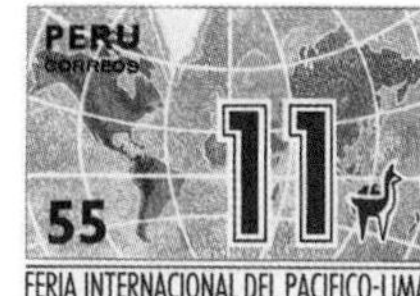

470 Fair Emblem on World Map

1979. 11th International Pacific Fair.
1469 **470** 55s. multicoloured . . . 40 30

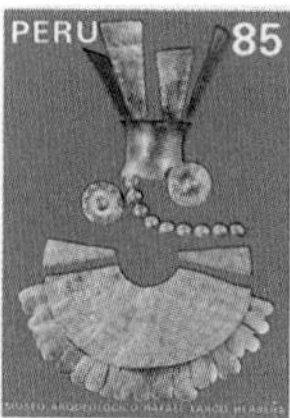

471 Regalia of Chimu Chief (Imperial period) **472** Angel with Lute

1979. Rafael Larco Herrera Museum of Archaeology.
1470 **471** 85s. multicoloured . . . 60 40

1980. Christmas.
1471 **472** 25s. multicoloured . . . 20 10

1980. Various stamps surch.
1472 **466** 20s. on 16s. multicoloured (postage) 15 10
1473 **463** 25s. on 14s. multicoloured 30 15
1474 **464** 65s. on 34s. multicoloured 45 35
1475 **458** 80s. on 70s. mauve . . . 55 40
1476 **449** 35s. on 24s. mauve (air) 25 15
1477 **438** 45s. on 32s. black and brown 30 20

474 "Respect and Comply with the Constitution" **475** Ceramic Vase (Chimu Culture)

1980. Citizens' Duties.
1478 **474** 15s. turquoise 10 10
1479 – 20s. red 15 10
1480 – 25s. blue 20 15
1481 – 30s. mauve 20 15
1482 – 35s. black 25 20
1483 – 45s. green 30 25
1484 – 50s. brown 35 25

INSCRIPTIONS: 20s. "Honour your country and protect your interests"; 25s. "Comply with the elective process"; 30s. "Comply with your military service"; 35s. "Pay your taxes"; 45s. "Work and contribute to national progress"; 50s. "Respect the rights of others".

1980. Rafael Larco Herrera Archaeological Museum.
1485 **475** 35s. multicoloured . . . 25 20

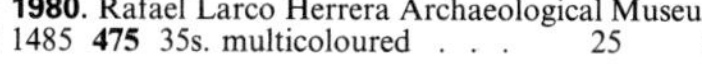

476 "Liberty" and Map of Peru **478** Rebellion Memorial, Cuzco (Joaquin Ugarte)

477 Machu Picchu

1980. Return to Democracy.
1486 **476** 25s. black, buff and red 20 15
1487 – 35s. black and red . . . 25 20
DESIGN: 35s. Handshake.

1980. World Tourism Conference, Manila.
1488 **477** 25s. multicoloured . . . 20 15

1980. Bicentenary of Tupac Amaru Rebellion.
1489 **478** 25s. multicoloured . . . 20 15
See also No. 1503.

479 Nativity

1980. Christmas.
1490 **479** 15s. multicoloured . . . 10 10

480 Bolivar and Flags **482** Presidential Badge of Office, Laurel Leaves and Open Book

1981. 150th Death Anniv of Simon Bolivar.
1491 **480** 40s. multicoloured . . . 30 20

1981. Various stamps surch.
1492 – 25s. on 35s. black and red (No. 1487) 20 15
1493 **482** 40s. on 25s. multicoloured 30 20
1494 **458** 85s. on 200s. violet . . . 60 45
1495 – 100s. on 115s. mult (No. 1448) 95 50
1496 **482** 130s. on 25s. mult . . . 95 40
1497 140s. on 25s. mult . . . 1·10 50

1981. Re-establishment of Constitutional Government.
1498 **482** 25s. multicoloured . . . 20 15

483 Stone Head, Pallasca

1981.
1499 **483** 30s. violet 20 15
1500 – 40s. blue 30 20
1501 – 100s. mauve 70 45
1502 – 140s. green 95 60

DESIGNS—VERT: 40s. Stone head, Huamachuco; 100s. Stone head (Chavin culture). HORIZ: 140s. Stone puma head (Chavin culture).

484 Tupac Amaru and Micaela Bastidas (sculptures by Miguel Boca Rossi)

1981. Bicentenary of Revolution of Tupac Amaru and Micaela Bastidas.
1503 **484** 60s. multicoloured . . . 40 30

485 Post Box, 1859 **486** Map of Peru and I.Y.D.P. Emblem

1981. 50th Anniv of Postal and Philatelic Museum, Lima.
1504 **485** 130s. multicoloured . . . 95 60

1981. International Year of Disabled Persons.
1505 **486** 100s. violet, mauve and gold 70 45

487 Victor Raul Haya de la Torre (President of Constitutional Assembly) **490** Inca Messenger (drawing by Guaman Ponce de Ayala)

1981. Constitution.
1506 **487** 30s. violet and grey . . . 20 15

1981. No. 801 surch.
1507 30s. on 2s.20 brown & blue 20 15
1508 40s. on 2s.20 brown & blue 30 20

1981. 12th International Pacific Fair. No. 801 surch with **12 Feria Internacional del Pacifico 1981 140**.
1509 140s. on 2s.20 brown & blue 95 70

1981. Christmas.
1510 **490** 30s. black and mauve . . 20 10
1511 40s. black and red . . . 35 10
1512 130s. black and green . . 75 35
1513 140s. black and blue . . 90 40
1514 200s. black and brown 1·25 60

1982. Various stamps surch **Habilitado Franq. Postal** and value (Nos. 1520/1) or with value only (others).
1515 **229** 10s. on 2c. brown (postage) 15 10
1516 — 10s. on 10c. red (No. 642) 10 10
1517 **292** 40s. on 10c. blue and yellow 15 10
1518 **273** 70s. on 5c. blue and red 35 20
1519 **264a** 80s. on 3c. lake . . . 30 15
1520 D **109** 80s. on 10c. green . . 30 15
1521 O **108** 80s. on 10c. brown 30 15
1522 **292** 100s. on 10c. blue and yellow 40 20
1523 — 140s. on 50c. brown, yellow and red . . 50 25
1524 — 140s. on 1s. mult . . 50 25
1525 **264a** 150s. on 3c. lake . . 40 20
1526 180s. on 3c. lake . . 55 30
1527 200s. on 3c. lake . . 70 40
1528 **273** 280s. on 5c. blue and red 85 55
1529 — 40s. on 1s.25 blue and purple (No. 814) (air) . . 30 15
1530 — 100s. on 2s.20 (No. 801) brown and blue 40 20
1531 — 240s. on 1s.25 blue and purple (No. 814) . . . . 1·25 85

Nos. 1523/4 are surcharged on labels for the Seventh Eucharistic Congress which previously had no postal validity.

493 Inca Pot

494 Jorge Basadre (after Oscar Lopez Aliaga)

1982. Indian Ceramics.

1532 **493** 40s. orange 30 15
1533 80s. lilac 50 25
1534 – 80s. red 60 25
1535 **493** 180s. green . . . . . . 1·25 70
1536 – 240s. blue . . . . 1·25 60
1537 – 280s. violet . . . . . . 1·40 70

DESIGNS: 80s., (No. 1534), 240, 280s. Nazca fish ceramic.

1982. Jorge Basadre (historian) Commemoration.

1538 **494** 100s. black and green . . 25 20

495 Julio C. Tello (bust, Victoria Macho)

1982. Birth Centenary of Julio C. Tello (archaeologist).

1539 **495** 200s. green and blue . . 45 30

496 Championship Emblem

497 Disabled Person in Wheelchair

1982. 9th World Women's Volleyball Championship, Peru.

1540 **496** 80s. red and black . . . 20 15

1982. Rights for the Disabled Year.

1541 **497** 200s. blue and red . . . 50 30

498 Andres A. Caceres Medallion

1982. Centenary of Brena Campaign.

1542 **498** 70s. brown and grey . . 20 15

499 Footballers

500 Congress Emblem

1982. World Cup Football Championship, Spain.

1543 **499** 80s. multicoloured . . . 20 15

1982. 16th Int Latin Notaries Congress, Lima.

1544 **500** 500s. black, gold and red 1·10 50

501 Bull (clay jar)

502 Pedro Vilcapaza

1982. Handicrafts Year.

1545 **501** 200s. red, brown and black 50 30

1982. Death Bicentenary of Pedro Vilcapaza (Indian leader).

1546 **502** 240s. brown and black 35 35

503 Jose Davila Condemarin (after J. Y. Pastor)

504 "Nativity" (Hilario Mendivil)

1982. Death Centenary of Jose Davila Condemarin (Director General of Posts).

1547 **503** 150s. black and blue . . 40 25

1982. Christmas.

1548 **504** 280s. multicoloured . . . 40 30

505 Centre Emblem and Hand holding Potatoes

1982. 10th Anniv of International Potato Centre.

1549 **505** 240s. brown and grey . . 35 35

506 Arms of Piura

1982. 450th Anniv of San Miguel de Piura.

1550 **506** 280s. multicoloured . . . 40 40

507 Microscope

1982. Centenary of Discovery of Tubercule Bacillus.

1551 **507** 240s. green 35 35

508 "St. Theresa of Avila" (Jose Espinoza de los Monteros)

1983. 400th Death Anniv of St. Theresa of Avila.

1552 **508** 100s. multicoloured . . . 25 15

509 Civil Defence Badge and Interlocked Hands

1983. 10th Anniv of Civil Defence System.

1553 **509** 100s. blue, orange & blk 25 15

510 Silver Shoe

1983. "Peru, Land of Silver".

1554 **510** 250s. silver, black & blue 55 35

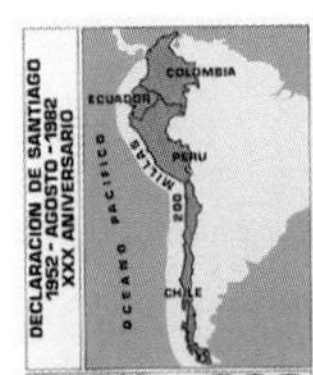

511 Map of Signatories and 200 Mile Zone

513 "75"

512 Boeing 747-200

1983. 30th Anniv of Santiago Declaration.

1555 **511** 280s. brown, blue & black 40 40

1983. 25th Anniv of Lima–Bogota Airmail Service.

1556 **512** 150s. multicoloured . . . 60 25

1983. 75th Anniv of Lima and Callao State Lotteries.

1557 **513** 100s. blue and purple . . 20 15

514 Cruiser "Almirante Grau"

1983. Peruvian Navy. Multicoloured.

1558 150s. Type **514** 95 25
1559 350s. Submarine "Ferre" . . 1·50 55

1983. Various stamps surch.

1560 **493** 100s. on 40s. orange . . 20 15
1561 **498** 100s. on 70s. brown and grey 20 15
1562 **496** 100s. on 80s. red and black 20 15
1563 **502** 100s. on 240s. brown and black 20 15
1564 **505** 100s. on 240s. ochre, deep brown and brown 20 15
1565 **507** 100s. on 240s. green . . 20 15
1566 **506** 150s. on 280s. mult . . . 30 15
1567 **511** 150s. on 280s. brown, blue and black 30 15
1568 **504** 200s. on 280s. mult . . . 40 25
1569 **493** 300s. on 180s. green . . 55 35
1570 400s. on 180s. green . . 75 50
1571 **499** 500s. on 80s. mult . . . 95 65

516 Simon Bolivar

517 "Virgin and Child" (Cuzquena School)

1983. Birth Bicentenary of Simon Bolivar.

1572 **516** 100s. blue and black . . 20 15

1983. Christmas.

1573 **517** 100s. multicoloured . . . 20 10

518 Fair Emblem

520 Leoncio Prado

519 W.C.Y. Emblem

1983. 14th International Pacific Fair.

1574 **518** 350s. multicoloured . . . 40 15

1984. World Communications Year.

1575 **519** 700s. multicoloured . . . 75 30

1984. Death Centenary (1983) of Colonel Leoncio Prado.

1576 **520** 150s. bistre and brown 15 10

521 Container Ship "Presidente Jose Pardo" at Wharf

1984. Peruvian Industry.

1577 **521** 250s. purple 65 20
1578 – 300s. blue 90 25

DESIGN: 300s. "Presidente Jose Pardo" (container ship).

522 Ricardo Palma

523 Pistol Shooting

1984. 150th Birth Anniv (1983) of Ricardo Palma (writer).

1579 **522** 200s. violet 15 10

1984. Olympic Games, Los Angeles.

1580 **523** 500s. mauve and black 45 25
1581 – 750s. red and black . . . 60 30

DESIGN: 750s. Hurdling.

524 Arms of Callao

525 Water Jar

1984. Town Arms.

1582 **524** 350s. grey 25 15
1583 – 400s. brown 55 25
1584 – 500s. brown 65 30

DESIGNS: 400s. Cajamarca; 500s. Ayacucho.

1984. Wari Ceramics (1st series).

1585 **525** 100s. brown 10 10
1586 – 150s. brown 15 10
1587 – 200s. brown 20 10

DESIGNS: 150s. Llama; 200s. Vase.

See also Nos. 1616/18.

526 Hendee's Woolly Monkeys

1984. Fauna.

1588 **526** 1000s. multicoloured . . 75 40

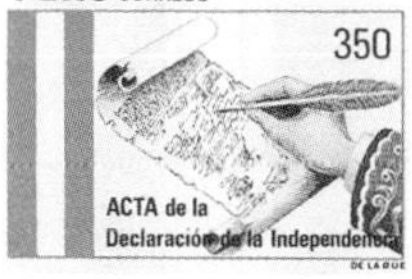

527 Signing Declaration of Independence

1984. Declaration of Independence.
1589 **527** 350s. black, brown & red . . . 25 15

528 General Post Office, Lima — 529 "Canna edulis"

1984. Postal Services.
1590 **528** 50s. olive 10 10

1984. Flora.
1591 **529** 700s. multicoloured . . . 45 25

530 Grau (after Pablo Muniz) — 531 Hipolito Unanue

1984. 150th Anniv of Admiral Miguel Grau. Mult.
1592 600s. Type 35 20
1593 600s. Battle of Angamos (45×35 mm) . . . 85 30
1594 600s. Grau's seat, National Congress 35 20
1595 600s. "Battle of Iquique" (Guillermo Spier) (45×35 mm) 85 30

1984. 150th Death Anniv (1983) of Hipolito Unanue (founder of School of Medicine).
1596 **531** 50s. green 10 10

532 Destroyer "Almirante Guise"

1984. Peruvian Navy.
1597 **532** 250s. blue 35 20
1598 – 400s. turquoise and blue . . 75 25
DESIGN: 400s. River gunboat "America".

533 "The Adoration of the Shepherds" — 534 Belaunde

1984. Christmas.
1599 **533** 1000s. multicoloured . . 40 15

1984. Birth Centenary (1983) of Victor Andres Belaunde (diplomat).
1600 **534** 100s. purple 15 10

535 Street in Cuzco — 536 Fair Emblem

1984. 450th Anniv of Founding of Cuzco by the Spanish.
1601 **535** 1000s. multicoloured . . 40 25

1984. 15th International Pacific Fair, Lima.
1602 **536** 1000s. blue and red . . . 40 25

537 "Foundation of Lima" (Francisco Gonzalez Gamarra) — 538 Pope John Paul II

1985. 450th Anniv of Lima.
1603 **537** 1500s. multicoloured . . 55 30

1985. Papal Visit.
1604 **538** 2000s. multicoloured . . 45 35

539 Dish Aerial, Huancayo — 540 Jose Carlos Mariategui

1985. 15th Anniv (1984) of Entel Peru (National Telecommunications Enterprise).
1605 **539** 1100s. multicoloured . . 25 15

1985. 60th Death Anniv (1984) of Jose Carlos Mariategui (writer).
1606 **540** 800s. red 20 15

541 Emblem

1985. 25th Meeting of American Airforces Co-operation System.
1607 **541** 400s. multicoloured . . . 15 10

542 Captain Quinones

1985. 44th Death Anniv of Jose Abelardo Quinones Gonzales (airforce captain).
1608 **542** 1000s. multicoloured . . 25 15

543 Arms of Huancavelica — 544 Globe and Emblem

1985.
1609 **543** 700s. orange 15 15
See also Nos. 1628/9.

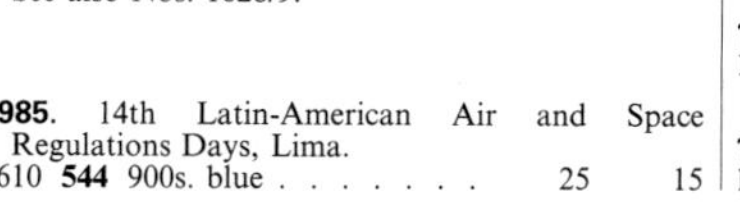

1985. 14th Latin-American Air and Space Regulations Days, Lima.
1610 **544** 900s. blue 25 15

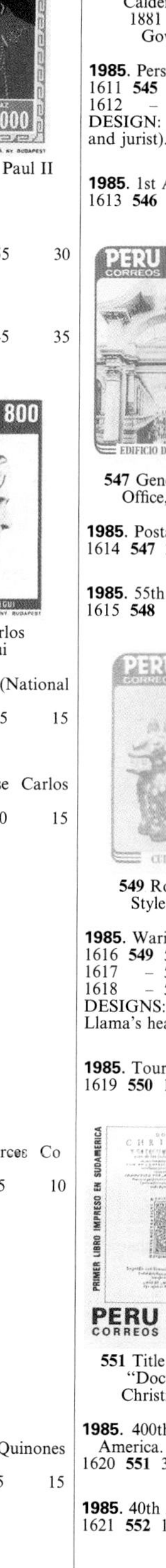

545 Francisco Garcia Calderon (head of 1881 Provisional Government) — 546 Cross, Flag and Map

1985. Personalities.
1611 **545** 500s. green 20 10
1612 – 800s. green 35 15
DESIGN: 800s. Oscar Miro Quesada (philosopher and jurist).

1985. 1st Anniv of Constitucion City.
1613 **546** 300s. multicoloured . . . 15 10

547 General Post Office, Lima — 548 Society Emblem, Satellite and Radio Equipment

1985. Postal Services.
1614 **547** 200s. grey 10 10

1985. 55th Anniv of Peruvian Radio Club.
1615 **548** 1300s. blue and orange 35 20

549 Robles Moqo Style Cat Vase — 550 St. Francis's Monastery, Lima

1985. Wari Ceramics (2nd series).
1616 **549** 500s. brown 15 10
1617 – 500s. brown 15 10
1618 – 500s. brown 15 10
DESIGNS: No. 1617, Cat, Huaura style; No. 1618, Llama's head, Robles Moqo Style.

1985. Tourism Day.
1619 **550** 1300s. multicoloured . . 30 15

551 Title Page of "Doctrina Christiana" — 552 Emblem and Curtiss "Jenny" Airplane

1985. 400th Anniv of First Book printed in South America.
1620 **551** 300s. black and stone . . 15 10

1985. 40th Anniv of I.C.A.O.
1621 **552** 1100s. black, blue and red 40 15

553 Humboldt Penguin — 554 "Virgin and Child" (Cuzquena School)

1985. Fauna.
1622 **553** 1500s. multicoloured . . 2·10 20

1985. Christmas.
1623 **554** 2i.50 multicoloured . . . 20 10

555 Postman lifting Child — 556 Cesar Vallejo

1985. Postal Workers' Christmas and Children's Restaurant Funds.
1624 **555** 2i.50 multicoloured . . . 30 20

1986. Poets.
1625 **556** 800s. blue 20 10
1626 – 800s. brown 20 10
DESIGN: No. 1626, Jose Santos Chocano.

557 Arms

1986. 450th Anniv of Trujillo.
1627 **557** 3i. multicoloured 30 15

1986. Town Arms. As T **543**.
1628 700s. blue 15 10
1629 900s. brown 25 15
DESIGNS: 700s. Huanuco; 900s. Puno.

558 Stone Carving of Fish — 559 "Hymenocallis amancaes"

1986. Restoration of Chan-Chan.
1630 **558** 50c. multicoloured . . . 15 10

1986. Flora.
1631 **559** 1100s. multicoloured . . 25 15

560 Alpaca and Textiles — 561 St. Rosa de Lima (Daniel Hernandez)

1986. Peruvian Industry.
1632 **560** 1100s. multicoloured . . 25 15

1986. 400th Birth Anniv of St. Rosa de Lima.
1633 **561** 7i. multicoloured 95 40

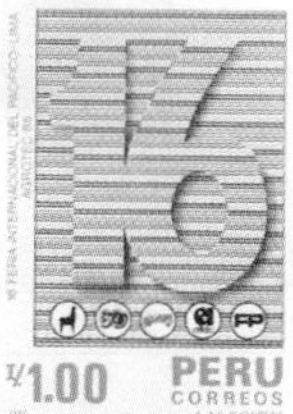

562 Daniel Alcides Carrion — 563 Emblems and "16"

1986. Death Centenary (1985) of Daniel Alcides Carrion.
1634 **562** 50c. brown 10 10

1986. 16th International Pacific Fair, Lima.
1635 **563** 1i. multicoloured 10 10

564 Woman Handspinning and Boy in Reed Canoe

1986. International Youth Year.
1636 **564** 3i.50 multicoloured . . . 65 20

565 Pedro Vilcapaza **567** Fernando and Justo Albujar Fayaque and Manuel Guarniz

566 U.N. Building, New York

1986. 205th Anniv of Vilcapaza Rebellion.
1637 **565** 50c. brown 10 10

1986. 40th Anniv (1985) of U.N.O.
1638 **566** 3i.50 multicoloured . . . 30 20

1986. National Heroes.
1639 **567** 50c. brown 10 10

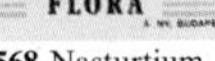

568 Nasturtium **570** Tinta Costumes, Canchis Province

569 Submarine "Casma (R-1)", 1926

1986. Flora.
1640 **568** 80c. multicoloured . . . 10 10

1986. Peruvian Navy. Each blue.
1641 1i.50 Type **569** 80 20
1642 2i.50 Submarine "Abtao", 1954 . . . . 1·40 35

1986. Costumes.
1643 **570** 3i. multicoloured 30 20

571 Sacsayhuaman Fort, Cuzco

1986. Tourism Day (1st issue).
1644 **571** 4i. multicoloured 40 30
See also No. 1654.

572 La Tomilla Water Treatment Plant

1986. 25th Anniv of Inter-American Development Bank.
1645 **572** 1i. multicoloured 10 10

573 "Datura candida" **575** Chavez, Bleriot XI and Simplon Range

574 Pope John Paul and Sister Ana

1986. Flora.
1646 **573** 80c. multicoloured . . . 10 10

1986. Beatification of Sister Ana of the Angels Monteagudo.
1647 **574** 6i. multicoloured 90 45

1986. 75th Anniv of Trans-Alpine Flight by Jorge Chavez Dartnell.
1648 **575** 5i. multicoloured . . . . 1·00 35

576 Emblem **577** "Martyrs of Uchuraccay"

1986. National Vaccination Days.
1649 **576** 50c. blue 10 10

1986. Peruvian Journalists' Fund.
1650 **577** 1i.50 black and blue . . 15 10

578 "Canis nudus" **579** Brigantine "Gamarra"

1986. Fauna.
1651 **578** 2i. multicoloured 20 15

1986. Navy Day.
1652 **579** 1i. blue and light blue 75 25
1653 – 1i. blue and red 75 25
DESIGN: No. 1653, Battleship "Manco Capac".

580 Intihuatana Cuzco

1986. Tourism Day (2nd issue).
1654 **580** 4i. multicoloured 40 30

581 Institute Building

1986. 35th Anniv (1985) of Institute of Higher Military Studies.
1655 **581** 1i. multicoloured 15 10

582 Children **583** White-winged Guan

1986. Postal Workers' Christmas and Children's Restaurant Funds.
1656 **582** 2i.50 black and brown 30 20

1986. Fauna.
1657 **583** 2i. multicoloured . . . . 2·00 40

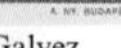

584 Galvez **585** "St. Joseph and Child" (Cuzquena School)

1986. Birth Centenary (1985) of Jose Galvez Barrenechea (poet).
1658 **584** 50c. brown 10 10

1986. Christmas.
1659 **585** 5i. multicoloured 75 30

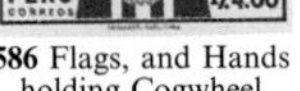

586 Flags, and Hands holding Cogwheel **587** Shipibo Costumes

1986. 25th Anniv of "Senati" (National Industrial Training Organization).
1660 **586** 4i. multicoloured 40 30

1987. Christmas.
1661 **587** 3i. multicoloured 30 25

588 Harvesting Mashua **590** Santos

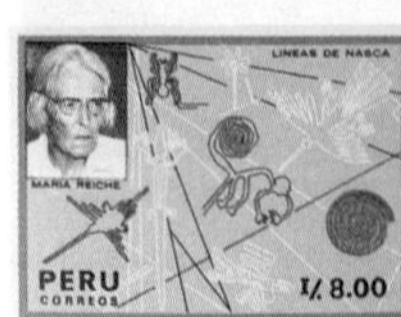

589 Dr. Reiche and Diagram of Nazca Lines

1987. World Food Day.
1662 **588** 50c. multicoloured . . . 10 10

1987. Dr. Maria Reiche (Nazca Lines researcher).
1663 **589** 8i. multicoloured 80 60

1987. Mariano Santos (Hero of War of the Pacific).
1664 **590** 50c. violet 10 10

591 Show Jumping

1987. 50th Anniv of Peruvian Horse Club.
1665 **591** 3i. multicoloured 30 25

592 Salaverry **593** Colca Canyon

1987. 150th Death Anniv (1986) of General Felipe Santiago Salaverry (President, 1835–36).
1666 **592** 2i. multicoloured 20 15

1987. "Arequipa 87" National Stamp Exhibition.
1667 **593** 6i. multicoloured 50 30

594 1857 1 & 2r. Stamps **595** Arguedas

1987. "Amifil 87" National Stamp Exhibition, Lima.
1668 **594** 1i. brown, blue and grey 10 10

1987. 75th Birth Anniv (1986) of Jose Maria Arguedas (writer).
1669 **595** 50c. brown 10 10

596 Carving, Emblem and Nasturtium

1987. Centenary of Arequipa Chamber of Commerce and Industry.
1670 **596** 2i. multicoloured 20 15

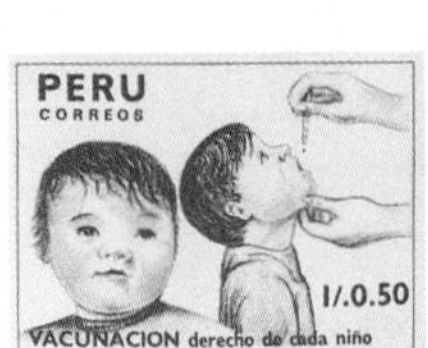

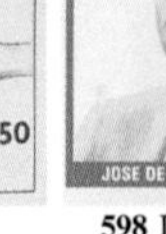

597 Vaccinating Child **598** De la Riva Aguero

1987. Child Vaccination Campaign.
1671 **597** 50c. red 10 10

1987. Birth Centenary (1985) of Jose de la Riva Aguero (historian).
1672 **598** 80c. brown 10 10

599 Porras Barrenechea **600** Footballers

1987. 90th Birth Anniv of Raul Porras Barrenechea (historian).
1673 **599** 80c. brown 10 10

1987. World Cup Football Championship, Mexico (1986).
1674 **600** 4i. multicoloured 20 15

601 Stone Carving of Man

1987. Restoration of Chan-Chan.
1675 **601** 50c. multicoloured . . . 10 10

602 Comet and "Giotto" Space Probe

1987. Appearance of Halley's Comet (1986).
1676 **602** 4i. multicoloured 45 15

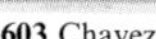

603 Chavez **604** Osambela Palace

1987. Birth Centenary of Jorge Chavez Dartnell (aviator).
1677 **603** 2i. brown, ochre and gold 10 10

1987. 450th Birth Anniv of Lima.
1678 **604** 2i.50 multicoloured . . . 15 10

605 Machu Picchu

1987. 75th Anniv (1986) of Discovery of Machu Picchu.
1679 **605** 9i. multicoloured 40 30

606 St. Francis's Church

1987. Cajamarca, American Historical and Cultural Site.
1680 **606** 2i. multicoloured 10 10

607 National Team, Emblem and Olympic Rings

1988. 50th Anniv (1986) of First Peruvian Participation in Olympic Games (at Berlin).
1681 **607** 1i.50 multicoloured . . . 10 10

608 Children

1988. 150th Anniv of Ministry of Education.
1682 **608** 1i. multicoloured 10 10

609 Statue and Pope

1988. Coronation of Virgin of Evangelization, Lima.
1683 **609** 10i. multicoloured . . . 40 30

610 Emblems **611** Postman and Lima Cathedral

1988. Rotary International Anti-Polio Campaign.
1684 **610** 2i. blue, gold and red . . 10 10

1988. Postal Workers' Christmas and Children's Restaurant Funds.
1685 **611** 9i. blue 30 20

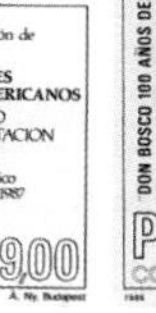

612 Flags **613** St. John Bosco

1988. 1st Meeting of Eight Latin American Presidents of Contadora and Lima Groups, Acapulco, Mexico.
1686 **612** 9i. multicoloured 30 20

1988. Death Centenary of St. John Bosco (founder of Salesian Brothers).
1687 **613** 5i. multicoloured 20 15

614 Supply Ship "Humboldt" and Globe

1988. 1st Peruvian Scientific Expedition to Antarctica.
1688 **614** 7i. multicoloured 90 20

615 Clay Wall

1988. Restoration of Chan-Chan.
1689 **615** 4i. brown and black . . 15 10

616 Vallejo (after Picasso) **617** Journalists at Work

1988. 50th Death Anniv of Cesar Vallejo (poet).
1690 **616** 25i. black, yellow & brn 50 40

1988. Peruvian Journalists' Fund.
1691 **617** 4i. blue and brown . . . 10 10

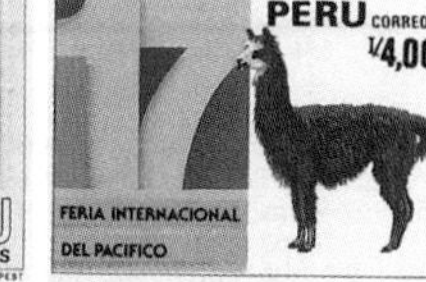

618 1908 2s. Columbus Monument Stamp **619** "17" and Guanaco

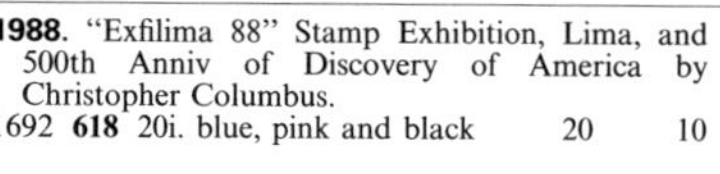

1988. "Exfilima 88" Stamp Exhibition, Lima, and 500th Anniv of Discovery of America by Christopher Columbus.
1692 **618** 20i. blue, pink and black 20 10

1988. 17th International Pacific Fair, Lima.
1693 **619** 4i. multicoloured 10 10

620 "Village Band" **621** Dogs

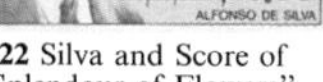
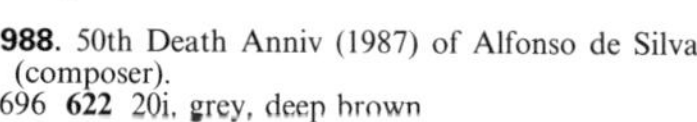

1988. Birth Centenary of Jose Sabogal (painter).
1694 **620** 12i. multicoloured . . . 15 10

1988. "Canino '88" International Dog Show, Lima.
1695 **621** 20i. multicoloured . . . 20 10

622 Silva and Score of "Splendour of Flowers" **623** Pope

1988. 50th Death Anniv (1987) of Alfonso de Silva (composer).
1696 **622** 20i. grey, deep brown and brown 20 10

1988. 2nd Visit of Pope John Paul II.
1697 **623** 50i. multicoloured . . . 35 25

624 Volleyball **625** Volleyball

1988. Olympic Games, Seoul.
1698 **624** 25i. multicoloured . . . 20 10

1988. Postal Workers' Christmas and Children's Restaurant Funds. Unissued stamp surch as in T **625**.
1699 **625** 95i. on 300s. black and red 60 50

626 Ceramic Vase **627** Map

1988. Chavin Culture. Unissued stamps surch as in T **626**.
1700 **626** 40i. on 100s. red 30 20
1701 80i. on 10s. black . . . 25 15

1989. Forest Boundary Road. Unissued stamp surch as in T **627**.
1702 **627** 70i. on 80s. green, black and blue 40 30

628 Arm **629** Huari Weaving

1989. Laws of the Indies. Unissued stamp surch as in T **628**.
1703 **628** 230i. on 300s. brown . . 60 15

1989. Centenary of Credit Bank of Peru.
1704 **629** 500i. multicoloured . . . 85 20

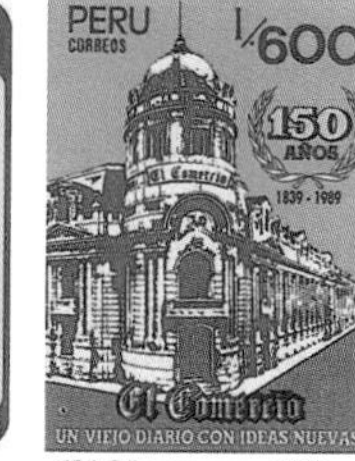

630 Special Postal Services Emblem **631** Newspaper Offices

1989. Postal Services.
1705 **630** 50i. blue and green . . . 10 10
1706 – 100i. red and pink . . . 10 10
DESIGN: 100i. National Express Post emblem.

1989. 150th Anniv of "El Comercio" (newspaper).
1707 **631** 600i. multicoloured . . . 50 10

632 Garcilaso de la Vega

1989. 450th Birth Anniv of Garcilaso de la Vega (writer).
1708 **632** 300i. multicoloured . . . 10 10

633 Emblem

1989. Express Mail Service.
1709 **633** 100i. red, blue and orange 10 10

634 Dr. Luis Loli Roca (founder of Journalists' Federation)

1989. Peruvian Journalists' Fund.
1710 **634** 100i. blue, deep blue and black 10 10

635 Relief of Birds

1989. Restoration of Chan-Chan.
1711 **635** 400i. multicoloured . . . 35 10

636 Old Map of South America

1989. Centenary of Lima Geographical Society.
1712 **636** 600i. multicoloured . . . 1·40 20

637 Painting

1989. 132nd Anniv of Society of Founders of Independence.

1713 **637** 300i. multicoloured . . . 10 10

638 Lake Huacachina

1989. 3rd Meeting of Latin American Presidents of Contadora and Lima Groups, Ica.

1714 **638** 1300i. multicoloured . . 1·10 60

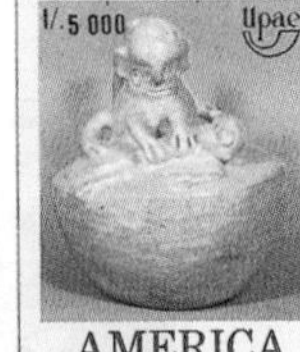

639 Children buying Stamps for Commemorative Envelopes

641 Vessel with Figure of Doctor examining Patient

640 "Corryocactus huincoensis"

1989. Postal Workers' Christmas and Children's Restaurant Funds.

1715 **639** 1200i. multicoloured . . 30 20

1989. Cacti. Multicoloured.

1716 500i. Type **640** 15 10
1717 500i. "Haagocereus clavispinus" (vert) 15 10
1718 500i. "Loxanthocereus acanthurus" 15 10
1719 500i. "Matucana cereoides" (vert) 15 10
1720 500i. "Trichocereus peruvianus" (vert) 15 10

1989. America. Pre-Columbian Ceramics. Mult.

1721 5000i. Type **641** . . . . . . 1·60 1·00
1722 5000i. Vessel with figure of surgeon performing cranial operation . . . . 1·60 1·00

642 Bethlehem Church

1990. Cajamarca, American Historical and Cultural Site.

1723 **642** 600i. multicoloured . . . 15 10

643 Climber in Andes

644 Pope and Virgin of Evangelization

1990. Huascaran National Park. Multicoloured.

1724 900i. Type **643** 20 15
1725 900i. Llanganuco Lake (horiz) 20 15
1726 1000i. "Puya raimondi" (plant) 25 20
1727 1000i. Snow-covered mountain peak (horiz) . . 25 20
1728 1100i. Huascaran Mountain (horiz) 30 25
1729 1100i. Andean condor over mountain slopes (horiz) 50 30

1990. 2nd Visit of Pope John Paul II.

1730 **644** 1250i. multicoloured . . 30 25

645 "Agrias beata" (female)

1990. Butterflies. Multicoloured.

1731 1000i. Type **645** 35 25
1732 1000i. "Agrias beata" (male) 35 25
1733 1000i. "Agrias amydon" (female) 35 25
1734 1000i. "Agrias sardanapalus" (female) . . 35 25
1735 1000i. "Agrias sardanapalus" (male) . . 35 25

646 Victor Raul Haya de la Torre (President of Constituent Assembly)

647 Emblem

1990. 10th Anniv of Political Constitution.

1736 **646** 2100i. multicoloured . . 45 10

1990. 40th Anniv of Peruvian Philatelic Association.

1737 **647** 300i. brown, blk & cream 60 20

648 Globe and Exhibition Emblem

1990. "Prenfil '88" International Philatelic Literature Exhibition, Buenos Aires.

1738 **648** 300i. multicoloured . . . 10 10

649 "Republic" (Antoine-Jean Gros)

1990. Bicentenary of French Revolution. Paintings. Multicoloured.

1739 2000i. Type **649** 40 10
1740 2000i. "Storming the Bastille" (Hubert Robert) 40 10
1741 2000i. "Lafayette at the Festival of the Republic" (anon) 40 10
1742 2000i. "Jean Jacques Rousseau and Symbols of the Revolution" (E. Jeaurat) 40 10

650 "Founding Arequipa" (Teodoro Nunez Ureta)

1990. 450th Anniv of Arequipa.

1743 **650** 50000i. multicoloured . . 10 10

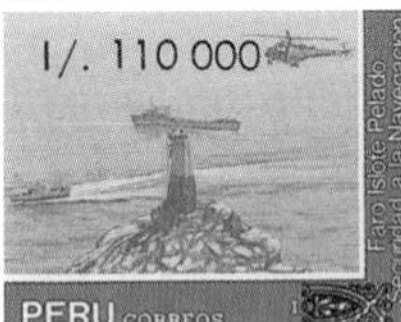

651 Pelado Island Lighthouse

1990. Peruvian Navy. Unissued stamps, each light blue and blue, surch as in T **651**.

1744 110000i. on 200i. Type **651** 1·25 25
1745 230000i. on 400i. "Morona" (hospital ship) . . . . . 3·00 50

652 Games Mascot

653 1857 1r. Stamp and Container Ship

1990. 4th South American Games (1st issue). Multicoloured.

1746 110000i. Type **652** 25 20
1747 280000i. Shooting . . . . . 1·10 60
1748 290000i. Athletics (horiz) . . 1·25 65
1749 300000i. Football . . . . . 1·25 65

See also Nos. 1753/6.

1990. 150th Anniv of Pacific Steam Navigation Company. Multicoloured. Self-adhesive.

1750 250000i. Type **653** . . . . . 1·90 75
1751 350000i. 1857 2r. stamp and container ship 2·75 1·00

654 Postal Van

1990. Postal Workers' Christmas and Children's Restaurant Funds.

1752 **654** 310000i. multicoloured 1·25 70

1991. 4th South American Games (2nd issue). As T **652**. Multicoloured.

1753 560000i. Swimming . . . . 1·90 1·10
1754 580000i. Show jumping (vert) . . . . 2·00 1·25
1755 600000i. Yachting (vert) . . 3·00 1·40
1756 620000i. Tennis (vert) . . . 2·10 1·40

655 Maria Jesus Castaneda de Pardo

1991. Red Cross. Unissued stamp surch.

1757 **655** 0.15i/m. on 2500i. red . . 50 25

Note. "i/m" on No. 1757 onwards indicates face value in million intis.

656 Adelie Penguins, Scientist and Station

1991. 2nd Peruvian Scientific Expedition to Antarctica. Unissued stamps surch. Multicoloured.

1758 0.40i/m. on 50000i. Type **656** . . . . 3·00 80
1759 0.45i/m. on 80000i. Station and Pomarine skua . . . 3·50 1·00
1760 0.50i/m. on 100000i. Whale, map and station . . . . 1·60 10

657 "Siphoonandra elliptica" (plant No. 1 in University herbarium)

658 "Virgin of the Milk"

1991. 300th Anniv of National University of St. Anthony Abad del Cusco. Multicoloured.

1761 10c. Type **657** 15 10
1762 20c. Bishop Manuel de Mollinedo y Angulo (first Chancellor) 50 20
1763 1s. University arms . . . . 2·50 1·00

1991. Postal Workers' Christmas and Children's Restaurant Funds. Paintings by unknown artists. Multicoloured.

1764 70c. Type **658** . . . . . . 1·25 50
1765 70c. "Divine Shepherdess" 1·25 50

659 Lake

1991. America (1990). The Natural World. Mult.

1766 0.50i/m. Type **659** 90 40
1767 0.50i/m. Waterfall (vert) . . 90 40

660 Sir Rowland Hill and Penny Black

1992. 150th Anniv (1990) of the Penny Black.

1768 **660** 0.40i/m. black, grey & bl 70 35

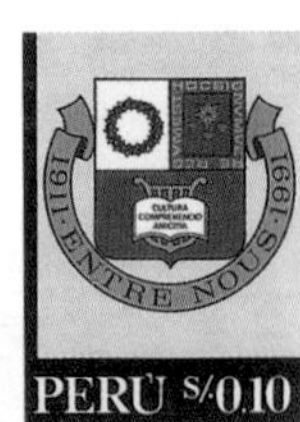

661 Arms and College

662 Arms

1992. 150th Anniv (1990) of Our Lady of Guadalupe College.

1769 **661** 0.30i/m. multicoloured 55 10

1992. 80th Anniv (1991) of Entre Nous Society, Lima (literature society for women).

1770 **662** 10c. multicoloured . . . 10 10

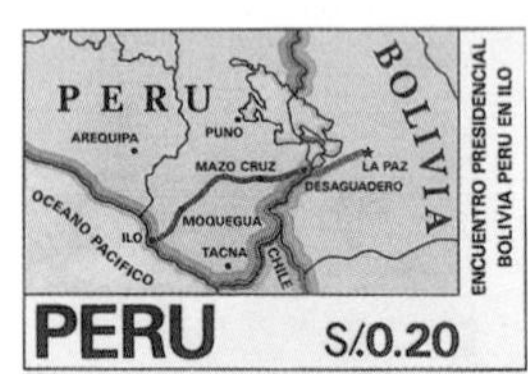

663 Map

1992. Bolivia–Peru Presidential Meeting, Ilo.

1771 **663** 20c. multicoloured . . . 15 10

664 Tacaynamo Idol

665 Raimondi

1992. Restoration of Chan-Chan.
1772 **664** 0.15i/m. multicoloured 10 10
See note below No. 1757.

1992. Death Centenary of Jose Antonio Raimondi (naturalist).
1773 **665** 0.30i/m. multicoloured 25 20
See note below No. 1757.

666 First Issue

668 1568 Eight Silver Reales Coin

667 Melgar

1992. Bicentenary (1990) of "Diario de Lima" (newspaper).
1774 **666** 35c. black and yellow 35 15

1992. Birth Bicentenary (1990) of Mariano Melgar (poet).
1775 **667** 60c. multicoloured 50 25

1992. 1st Peruvian Coinage.
1776 **668** 70c. multicoloured 1·00 35

669 Emblem

1992. 75th Anniv of Catholic University of Peru.
1777 **669** 90c. black and stone 1·25 35

670 Emblem

672 "Virgin of the Spindle" (painting, Santa Clara Monastery, Cuzco)

1992. 90th Anniv of Pan-American Health Organization. Self-adhesive. Imperf.
1778 **670** 3s. multicoloured 3·25 1·10

1992. Various stamps surch.
1779 – 40c. on 500i. multicoloured (1717) 30 15
1780 – 40c. on 500i. multicoloured (1718) 30 15
1781 – 40c. on 500i. multicoloured (1719) 30 15
1782 – 40c. on 500i. multicoloured (1720) 30 15
1783 **493** 50c. on 180s. green 40 20
1784 **648** 50c. on 300i. mult 40 20
1785 **645** 50c. on 1000i. mult 40 20
1786 – 50c. on 1000i. mult (1732) 40 20
1787 – 50c. on 1000i. mult (1733) 40 20
1788 – 50c. on 1000i. mult (1734) 40 20
1789 – 50c. on 1000i. mult (1735) 40 20
1790 **647** 1s. on 300i. brown, black and cream 3·00 90
1791 **644** 1s. on 1250i. mult 1·60 80
1792 **638** 1s. on 1300i. mult 2·10 1·00

1993. Self-adhesive. Imperf.
1793 **672** 80c. multicoloured 65 30

673 Gold Figures

1993. Sican Culture (1st series). Multicoloured. Self-adhesive. Imperf.
1794 2s. Type **673** 2·75 80
1795 5s. Gold foil figure (vert) 5·00 2·00
See also Nos. 1814/15.

674 Incan Gold Decoration and Crucifix on Chancay Robe

1993. 500th Anniv of Evangelization of Peru.
1796 **674** 1s. multicoloured 1·25 65

675 "The Marinera" (Monica Rojas)

676 "Madonna and Child" (statue)

1993. Paintings of Traditional Scenes. Multicoloured. Self-adhesive. Imperf.
1797 1s.50 Type **675** 1·50 60
1798 1s.50 "Fruit Sellers" (Angel Chavez) 1·50 60

1993. Centenary (1991) of Salesian Brothers in Peru. Self-adhesive. Imperf.
1799 **676** 70c. multicoloured 95 25

677 Francisco Pizarro and Spanish Galleon

1993. America (1991). Voyages of Discovery. Multicoloured.
1800 90c. Type **677** 1·25 30
1801 1s. Spanish galleon and route map of Pizarros' second voyage 1·50 40
Nos. 1800/1 were issued together, se-tenant, forming a composite design.

678 Gold Mask

1993. Jewels from Funerary Chamber of "Senor of Sipan" (1st series).
1802 **678** 50c. multicoloured 55 15
See also Nos. 1830/1.

679 Escriva

680 Cherry Blossom and Nazca Lines Hummingbird

1993. 1st Anniv of Beatification of Josemaria Escriva (founder of Opus Dei). Self-adhesive. Imperf.
1803 **679** 30c. multicoloured 45 10

1993. 120th Anniv of Diplomatic Relations and Peace, Friendship, Commerce and Navigation Treaty with Japan. Multicoloured.
1804 1s.50 Type **680** 1·75 45
1805 1s.70 Peruvian and Japanese children and Mts. Huascaran (Peru) and Fuji (Japan) 1·90 55

681 Sea Lions

682 Delgado

1993. Stamp Exhibitions. Multicoloured.
1806 90c. Type **681** ("Amifil '93" National Stamp Exhibition, Lima) 1·10 25
1807 1s. Blue and yellow macaw ("Brasiliana '93" International Stamp Exhibition, Rio de Janeiro) (vert) 2·00 80

1993. Birth Centenary of Dr. Honorio Delgado (psychiatrist and neurologist). Self-adhesive. Imperf.
1808 **682** 50c. brown 30 15

683 Morales Macedo

684 "The Sling" (Quechua Indians)

1993. Birth Centenary of Rosalia de Lavalle de Morales Macedo (founder of Society for Protection of Children and of Christian Co-operation Bank). Self-adhesive. Imperf.
1809 **683** 80c. orange 80 25

1993. Ethnic Groups (1st series). Statuettes by Felipe Lettersten. Multicoloured. Self-adhesive. Imperf.
1810 2s. Type **684** 1·60 60
1811 3s.50 "Fire" (Orejon Indians) 3·25 1·50
See also Nos. 1850/1.

685 "20" on Stamp

686 "Virgin of Loreta"

1993. 20th International Pacific Fair.
1812 **685** 1s.50 multicoloured 1·40 70

1993. Christmas.
1813 **686** 1s. multicoloured 1·00 55

687 Artefacts from Tomb, Poma

688 Ceramic Figure

1993. Sican Culture (2nd series). Multicoloured. Self-adhesive. Imperf.
1814 2s.50 Type **687** 2·25 1·10
1815 4s. Gold mask 4·00 2·00

1993. Chancay Culture. Multicoloured. Self-adhesive. Imperf.
1816 10s. Type **688** 9·25 4·50
1817 20s. Textile pattern (horiz) 19·00 9·50

689 "With AIDS There is No Tomorrow"

690 Computer Graphics

1993. International AIDS Day.
1818 **689** 1s.50 multicoloured 1·40 70

1994. 25th Anniv of National Council for Science and Technology. Self-adhesive. Imperf.
1819 **690** 1s. multicoloured 1·40 25

691 "The Bridge" (woodcut from "New Chronicle and Good Government" by Poma de Ayala)

692 Engraved Mate Dish

1994. Self-adhesive. Imperf.
1820 **691** 20c. blue 35 10
1821 40c. orange 55 10
1822 50c. violet 70 15
For similar design see Nos. 1827/9.

1994. Multicoloured. Self-adhesive. Imperf.
1823 1s.50 Type **692** 2·00 40
1824 1s.50 Engraved silver and mate vessel (vert) 2·00 40
1825 3s. Figure of bull from Pucara 3·75 85
1826 3s. Glazed plate decorated with fishes 3·75 85

693 "The Bridge" (Poma de Ayala)

694 Gold Trinkets

1994.
1827 **693** 30c. brown 45 10
1828 40c. black 60 10
1829 50c. red 70 15

1994. Jewels from Funerary Chamber of Senor de Sipan (2nd series). Multicoloured.
1830 3s. Type **694** 3·75 85
1831 5s. Gold mask (vert) 6·50 1·25

695 El Brujo

1994. Archaeology. El Brujo Complex, Trujillo.
1832 **695** 70c. multicoloured 75 20

696 "Baby Emmanuel" (Cuzco sculpture)

697 Brazilian Player

1995. Christmas (1994). Multicoloured.
1833 1s.80 Type **696** 1·40 50
1834 2s. "Nativity" (Huamanga ceramic) 1·50 55

1995. World Cup Football Championship, U.S.A. (1994). Multicoloured.
1835 60c. Type **697** 35 15
1836 4s.80 Mascot, pitch and flags 3·50 1·50

698 Jauja–Huancayo Road

1995. 25th Anniv (1994) of Ministry of Transport, Communications, Housing and Construction.
1837 **698** 20c. multicoloured 10 10

699 Mochican Pot (Rafael Larco Herrera Museum of Archaeology)

700 Juan Parra del Reigo (poet) (after David Alfaro)

1995. Museum Exhibits. Multicoloured.
1838 40c. Type **699** 20 10
1839 80c. Mochican gold and gemstone ornament of man with slingshot (Rafael Larco Herrera Museum of Archaeology, Lima) 70 20
1840 90c. Vessel in shape of beheaded man (National Museum) 80 25

1995. Writers' Birth Centenaries (1994). Mult.
1841 90c. Type **700** 75 50
1842 90c. Jose Carlos Mariategui 75 50

701 Church

702 Violoncello and Music Stand

1995. 350th Anniv (1993) of Carmelite Monastery, Lima.
1843 **701** 70c. multicoloured . . . 70 20

1995. Musical Instruments. Multicoloured.
1844 20c. Type **702** 10 10
1845 40c. Andean drum 45 10

703 Steam-powered Fire Engine

1995. Volunteer Firemen. Multicoloured.
1846 50c. Type **703** 55 10
1847 90c. Modern fire engine . . 95 25

704 Union Club and Plaza de Armas

1995. World Heritage Site. Lima. Multicoloured.
1848 90c. Type **704** 95 25
1849 1s. Cloisters of Dominican Monastery . . . . 1·10 25

705 "Bora Child"

1995. Ethnic Groups (2nd series). Statuettes by Felipe Lettersten. Multicoloured.
1850 1s. Type **705** . . . . 1·10 25
1851 1s.80 "Aguaruna Man" . . 1·90 50

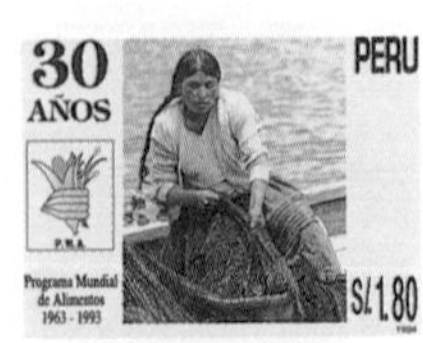

706 Woman fishing

1995. 30th Anniv (1993) of World Food Programme.
1852 **706** 1s.80 multicoloured . . . 1·90 50

707 Potato Plant

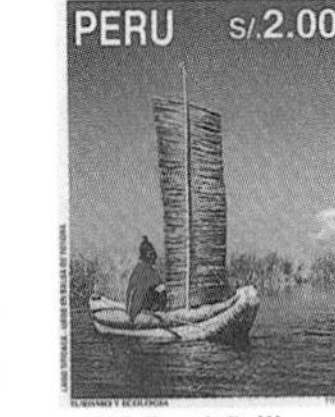

708 Reed Sailing Canoe

1995. The Potato. Multicoloured.
1853 1s.80 Type **707** . . . . . . 1·90 50
1854 2s. Mochican ceramic of potato tubers . . . . . . 2·10 55

1995. Tourism and Ecology. Lake Titicaca.
1855 **708** 2s. multicoloured . . . . 2·25 75

709 Great Horned Owl

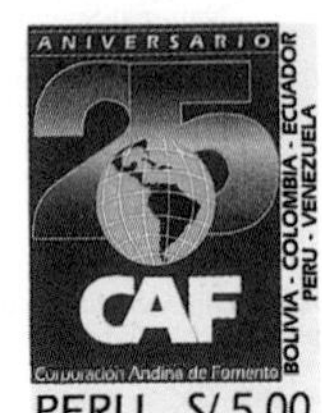

710 Anniversary Emblem

1995. Endangered Animals. Multicoloured.
1856 1s. Type **709** . . . . 1·25 25
1857 1s.80 Jaguar on branch (horiz) . . . . 1·90 50

1995. 25th Anniv of Andean Development Corporation.
1858 **710** 5s. multicoloured . . . . 5·00 1·25

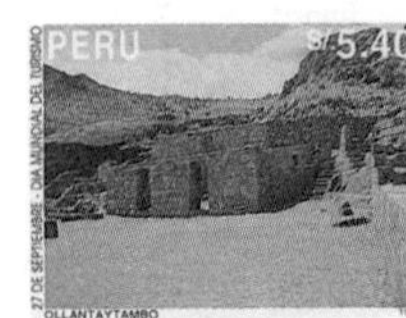

711 Ollantaytambo

1995. World Tourism Day.
1859 **711** 5s.40 multicoloured . . . 5·25 1·50

712 Ancient Letterbox, Head Post Office

1995. World Post Day.
1860 **712** 1s.80 multicoloured . . . 1·75 50

713 Columbus landing on Beach

1995. America (1992 and 1993). Multicoloured.
1861 1s.50 Type **713** (500th anniv of discovery of America) 1·50 40
1862 1s.70 Guanaco (vert) . . . 1·75 60

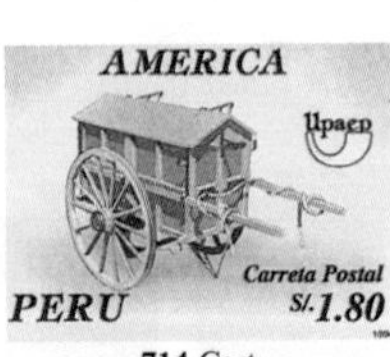

714 Cart

1995. America (1994). Postal Transport. Mult.
1863 1s.80 Type **714** . . . . . . 1·75 60
1864 2s. Post vans . . . . 2·00 55

715 Lima Cathedral (rear entrance)

1995. Doorways. Multicoloured.
1865 30c. Type **715** 40 10
1866 70c. St. Francis's Church (side entrance) 75 20

716 Peruvian Delegation, San Francisco Conference, 1945

1995. 50th Anniv of U.N.O.
1867 **716** 90c. multicoloured . . . 95 25

717 Ceramic Church (National Culture Museum)

718 Lady Olave Baden-Powell (Girl Guides)

1995. Museum Exhibits. Multicoloured.
1868 20c. Type **717** 10 10
1869 20c. "St. John the Apostle" (figurine) (Riva Aguero Institute Museum of Popular Art) 10 10
1870 40c. "Allegory of Asia" (alabaster figurine) (National Culture Museum) 45 10
1871 50c. "Archangel Moro" (figurine) (Riva Aguero Institute Museum of Popular Art) 50 10

1995. Scouting. Multicoloured.
1872 80c. Type **718** 85 20
1873 1s. Lord Robert Baden Powell (founder of Boy Scouts) 90 25

Nos. 1872/3 were issued together, se-tenant, forming a composite design.

719 "Festejo"

720 Stream in Sub-tropical Forest

1995. Folk Dances. Multicoloured.
1874 1s.80 Type **719** . . . . . . 1·75 50
1875 2s. "Marinera Limena" (horiz) . . . . 1·90 55

1995. Manu National Park, Madre de Dios. Multicoloured.
1876 50c. Type **720** 55 10
1877 90c. American chamaeleon (horiz) 95 25

721 Toma de Huinco

722 St. Toribio de Mogrovejo (Archbishop of Lima)

1995. Electricity and Development. Multicoloured.
1878 20c. Type **721** 10 10
1879 40c. Antacoto Lake 45 10

1995. Saints. Multicoloured.
1880 90c. Type **722** 90 25
1881 1s. St. Francisco Solano (missionary) 95 25

723 Cultivating Crops

1996. 50th Anniv (1995) of F.A.O.
1882 **723** 60c. multicoloured . . . 55 15

724 Crib

1996. Christmas (1995). Porcelain Figures. Multicoloured.
1883 30c. Type **724** 15 10
1884 70c. Three Wise Men (horiz) 70 15

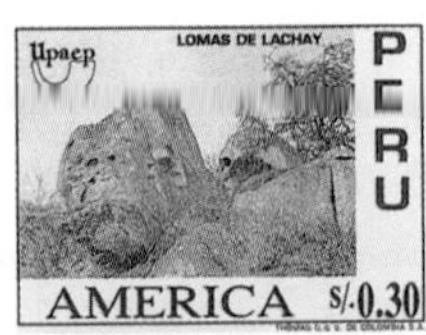

725 Lachay National Park

1996. America (1995). Environmental Protection. Multicoloured.
1885 30c. Type **725** 15 10
1886 70c. Black caiman 70 15

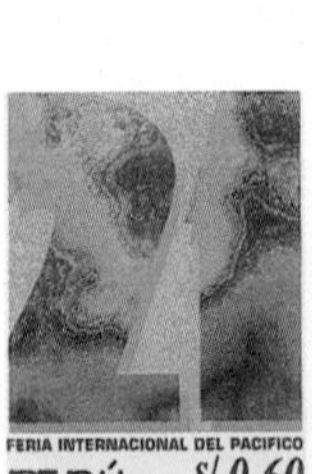

726 "21"

727 Rifle Shooting

1996. 21st International Pacific Fair, Lima.
1887 **726** 60c. multicoloured . . . 60 15

1996. Olympic Games, Barcelona (1992). Multicoloured.
1888 40c. Type **727** 45 10
1889 40c. Tennis 45 10
1890 60c. Swimming 55 15
1891 60c. Weightlifting 55 15

Nos. 1888/91 were issued together, se-tenant, forming a composite design of the sports around the games emblem.

728 Archaeological Find from Sipan

1996. "Expo'92" World's Fair, Seville.
1892 **728** 1s.50 multicoloured . . . 1·40 35

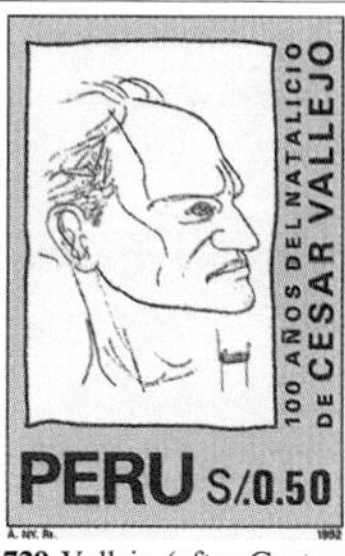

729 Vallejo (after Gaston Garreu)

1996. Birth Centenary of Cesar Vallejo (writer).
1893 **729** 50c. black 50 10

730 Avenue of the Descalzos

1996. UNESCO World Heritage Site. Lima.
1894 **730** 30c. brown and stone . . 15 10

731 "Kon Tiki" (replica of balsa raft)

1997. 50th Anniv of Thor Heyerdahl's "Kon Tiki" Expedition (voyage from Peru to Tuamoto Island, South Pacific).
1895 **731** 3s.30 multicoloured . . . 1·90 70

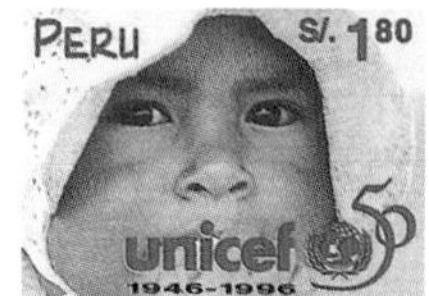

732 Child 733 Owl

1997. 50th Anniv (1996) of UNICEF.
1896 **732** 1s.80 multicoloured . . . 1·50 40

1997. Mochica Culture.
1897 **733** 20c. green 10 10
1898 – 30c. violet 15 10
1899 – 50c. black 45 10
1900 – 1s. orange 75 20
1901 – 1s.30 red . . . . 1·10 25
1902 – 1s.50 brown . . . . . . 1·25 30
DESIGNS—Vessels in shape of: 30c. Crayfish; 50c. Cormorant; 1s. Monkeys; 1s.30, Duck; 1s.50, Jaguar.
See also Nos. 1942/6.

734 Shooting

1997. Olympic Games, Atlanta, U.S.A. (1996). Multicoloured.
1903 2s.70 Type **734** . . . . . . 1·25 60
1904 2s.70 Volleyball . . . . . . 1·25 60
1905 2s.70 Boxing . . . . 1·25 60
1906 2s.70 Football . . . . 1·25 60

735 White-bellied Caique 736 Scout Badge and Tents

1997. 25th Anniv of Peru Biology College.
1907 **735** 5s. multicoloured . . . . 2·50 1·10

1997. 90th Anniv of Boy Scout Movement.
1908 **736** 6s.80 multicoloured . . . 3·25 1·50

737 Man on Reed Raft

1997. 8th International Anti-corruption Conference, Lima.
1909 **737** 2s.70 multicoloured . . . 1·50 60

738 Emblem

1997. 10th Anniv of Montreal Protocol (on reduction of use of chlorofluorocarbons).
1910 **738** 6s.80 multicoloured . . . 3·25 1·50

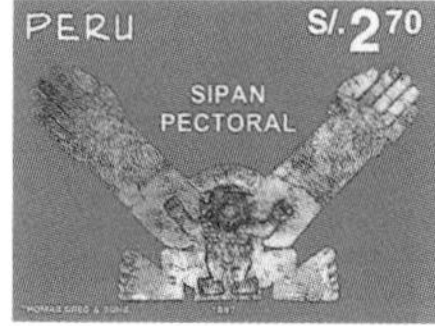

739 Pectoral

1997. Funerary Chamber of "Senor of Sipan". Multicoloured.
1911 2s.70 Type **739** . . . . . . 2·10 50
1912 3s.30 Ear-cap (vert) . . . . 2·75 60

740 Von Stephan 741 Shipibo Woman

1997. Death Centenary of Heinrich von Stephan (founder of U.P.U.).
1914 **740** 10s. multicoloured . . . 8·00 1·75

1997. America (1996). Traditional Costumes. Multicoloured.
1915 2s.70 Type **741** . . . . . . 2·25 50
1916 2s.70 Shipibo man . . . . 2·25 50

742 Inca Messenger 743 Castilla

1997. America. The Postman. Multicoloured.
1917 2s.70 Type **742** . . . . . . 2·25 50
1918 2s.70 Modern postman . . . 2·25 50

1997. Birth Bicentenary of Ramon Castilla (President, 1845–51 and 1855–62).
1919 **743** 1s.80 multicoloured . . . 1·50 30

744 Tennis 745 River Kingfisher

1997. 13th Bolivarian Games, Arequipa. Mult.
1920 2s.70 Type **744** . . . . . . 2·25 50
1921 2s.70 Football . . . . . . 2·25 50
1922 2s.70 Basketball . . . . . . 2·25 50
1923 2s.70 Volleyball . . . . . . 2·25 50
Nos. 1920/3 were issued together, se-tenant, containing a composite design of a ball in the centre.

1997. Manu National Park. Birds. Multicoloured.
1924 3s.30 Type **745** . . . . . . 2·75 60
1925 3s.30 Green woodpecker . . 2·75 60
1926 3s.30 Red crossbill . . . . 2·75 60
1927 3s.30 Eagle . . . . 2·75 60
1928 3s.30 Jabiru . . . . 2·75 60
1929 3s.30 Cuban screech owl . . 2·75 60

746 Concentric Circles over Map 747 Map and Krill

1997. 30th Anniv of Treaty of Tlatelolco (banning nuclear weapons in Latin America and the Caribbean).
1930 **746** 20s. multicoloured . . . 16·00 3·50

1997. 8th Peruvian Scientific Expedition to Antarctica.
1931 **747** 6s. multicoloured . . . . 5·00 1·00

748 Holy Family 749 Map, Emblem and Unanue

1997. Christmas.
1932 **748** 2s.70 multicoloured . . . 2·10 50

1997. 25th Anniv (1996) of Hipolito Unanue Agreement (health co-operation in Andes region).
1933 **749** 1s. multicoloured 80 15

751 Facade 753 Map and Emblem

752 School and Cadets

1997. Cent of Posts and Telegraph Headquarters.
1935 **751** 1s. multicoloured 80 15

1998. Centenary of Chorrillos Military School.
1936 **752** 2s.70 multicoloured . . . 2·10 50

1998. 50th Anniv of Organization of American States.
1937 **753** 2s.70 multicoloured . . . 2·10 50

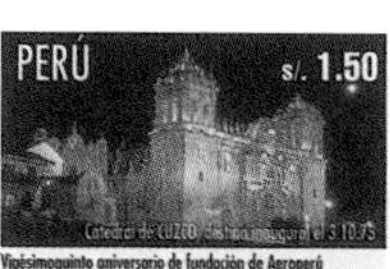

754 Cuzco Cathedral

1998. 25th Anniv of Aeroperu. Multicoloured.
1938 1s.50 Type **754** . . . . . . 1·25 25
1939 2s.70 Airbus Industrie A320 jetliner . . . . 2·25 50

755 "Paso Horse" (Enrique Arambur Ferreyros) 756 Lima Cathedral

1998. 50th Anniv of National Association of Breeders and Owners of Paso Horses.
1940 **755** 2s.70 violet . . . . . . 2·00 50

1998. Centenary of Restoration of Lima Cathedral.
1941 **756** 2s.70 red, yellow and black . . . . 2·00 50

1998. Mochica Culture. As Nos. 1897 and 1899/1902 but values and/or colours changed.
1942 1s. blue 80 15
1943 1s.30 purple . . . . 1·00 20
1944 1s.50 blue . . . . 1·25 25
1945 2s.70 bistre . . . . 2·10 50
1946 3s.30 black . . . . 2·50 60
DESIGNS: 1s.30, Type **733**; 1s.50, Jaguar; 2s.70, Cormorant; 3s.30, Duck.

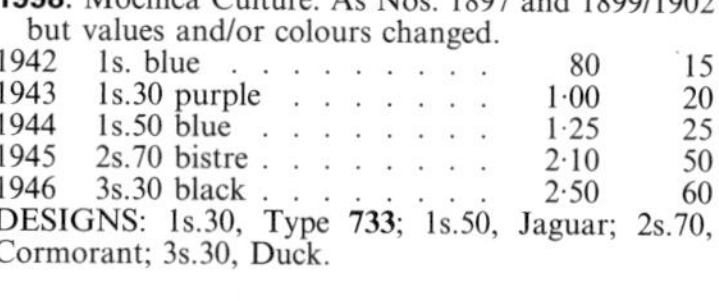

757 Ceremony, Sacsayhuaman, Cuzco 758 Goalkeeper

1998. "Inti-Raymi" Inca Festival.
1947 **757** 5s. multicoloured . . . . 3·50 85

1998. World Cup Football Championship, France. Multicoloured.
1948 2s.70 Type **758** . . . . . . 2·00 50
1949 3s.30 Two players . . . . . 2·50 60
Nos. 1948/9 were issued together, se-tenant, forming a composite design.

759 Lloque Yupanqui

1998. Inca Chiefs (1st issue). Multicoloured.
1951 2s.70 Type **759** 95 45
1952 2s.70 Sinchi Roca 95 45
1953 9s.70 Mancoc Capau . . . 3·50 1·75
See also Nos. 2008/11.

761 Fishermen (Moche sculpture) and Emblem

1998. International Year of the Ocean.
1955 **761** 6s.80 multicoloured . . . 4·50 1·25

762 Bars of Music and Conductor's Hands 763 Mother Teresa and Baby

1998. 60th Anniv of National Symphony Orchestra.
1956 **762** 2s.70 multicoloured . . . 95 45

1998. 1st Death Anniv of Mother Teresa (founder of Missionaries of Charity).
1957 **763** 2s.70 multicoloured . . . 95 45

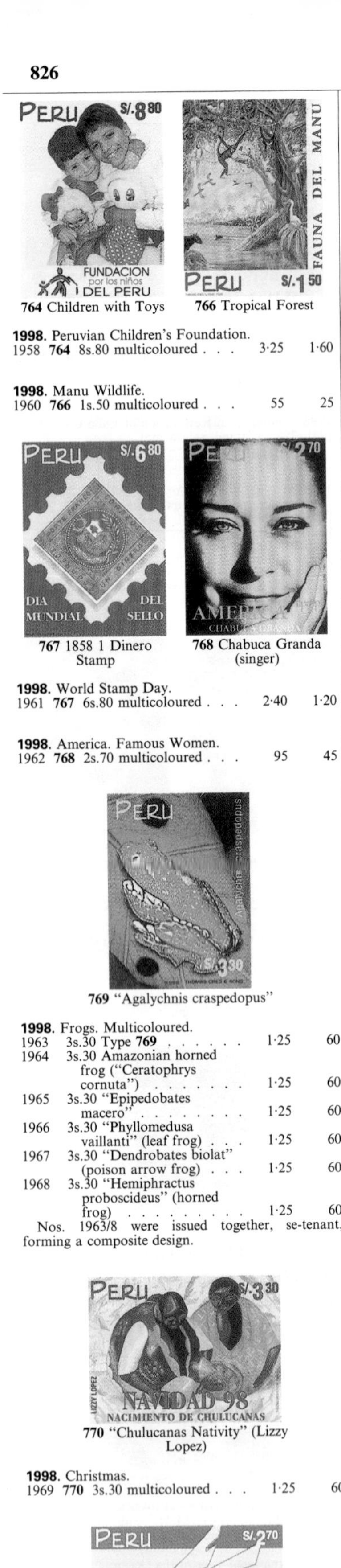

764 Children with Toys **766** Tropical Forest

1998. Peruvian Children's Foundation.
1958 **764** 8s.80 multicoloured . . . 3·25 1·60

1998. Manu Wildlife.
1960 **766** 1s.50 multicoloured . . . 55 25

767 1858 1 Dinero Stamp **768** Chabuca Granda (singer)

1998. World Stamp Day.
1961 **767** 6s.80 multicoloured . . . 2·40 1·20

1998. America. Famous Women.
1962 **768** 2s.70 multicoloured . . . 95 45

769 "Agalychnis craspedopus"

1998. Frogs. Multicoloured.
1963 3s.30 Type **769** . . . . . . 1·25 60
1964 3s.30 Amazonian horned frog ("Ceratophrys cornuta") . . . . 1·25 60
1965 3s.30 "Epipedobates macero" . . . . 1·25 60
1966 3s.30 "Phyllomedusa vaillanti" (leaf frog) . . . 1·25 60
1967 3s.30 "Dendrobates biolat" (poison arrow frog) . . . 1·25 60
1968 3s.30 "Hemiphractus proboscideus" (horned frog) . . . . 1·25 60
Nos. 1963/8 were issued together, se-tenant, forming a composite design.

770 "Chulucanas Nativity" (Lizzy Lopez)

1998. Christmas.
1969 **770** 3s.30 multicoloured . . . 1·25 60

771 Dove and Flags of Peru, Ecuador and Guarantor Countries

1998. Signing of Peru–Ecuador Peace Agreement, Brasilia.
1970 **771** 2s.70 multicoloured . . . 95 45

772 Children on Hillside

1998. 50th Anniv of Universal Declaration of Human Rights.
1971 **772** 5s. multicoloured . . . . 1·75 85

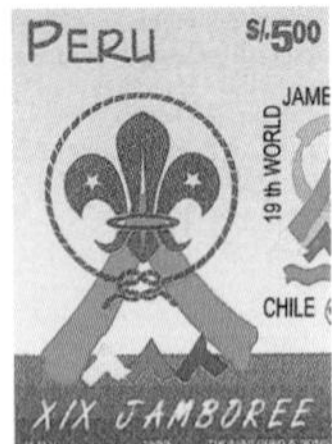

773 Scout Badge and Tents

1999. 19th World Scout Jamboree, Chile. Multicoloured.
1972 5s. Type **773** . . . . 1·75 85
1973 5s. Emblem and tents . . . 1·75 85

774 Emblem

1999. 50th Anniv of Peruvian Philatelic Association.
1974 **774** 2s.70 multicoloured . . . 95 45

775 "Evening Walk"

1999. 120th Death Anniv of Pancho Fierro (artist). Multicoloured.
1975 2s.70 Type **775** 95 45
1976 3s.30 "The Sound of the Devil" . . . . 1·25 60

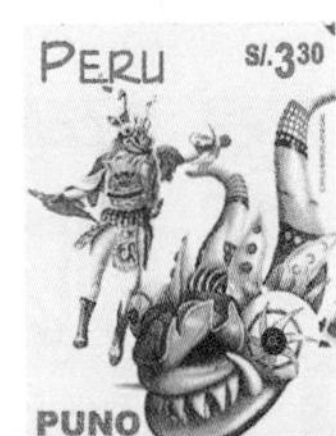

776 Dancer and Detail from Costume

1999. "Puno" (traditional dance).
1977 **776** 3s.30 multicoloured . . . 1·25 60

1999. Mochica Culture. As Nos. 1943/46 but values and or colours changed.
1978 1s. red 35 15
1979 1s.50 blue 55 25
1980 1s.80 brown 65 30
1981 2s. orange 70 35
DESIGNS: Vessels in shape of—1s. Jaguar; 1s.50, Duck; 1s.80, Type **733**; 2s. Cormorant.

777 Inca blowing Conch Shell

1999. 25th Anniv of Peruvian Folklore Centre (CENDAF).
1982 **777** 1s.80 multicoloured . . . 65 30

778 Malinowski and Train crossing Bridge

1999. Death Centenary of Ernest Malinowski (designer of iron bridge between Lima and La Oroya).
1983 **778** 5s. multicoloured . . . . 1·75 85

779 Sick and Healthy Hearts with Smiling Face

1999. Child Heart Care.
1984 **779** 2s.70 multicoloured . . . 95 45

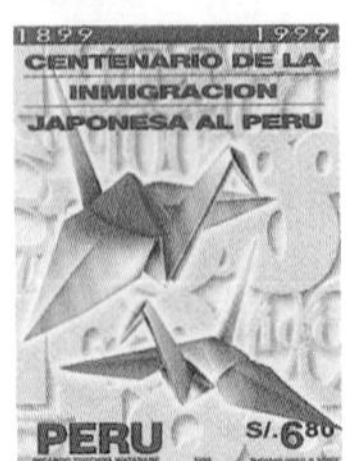

780 Origami Birds

1999. Centenary of Japanese Immigration.
1985 **780** 6s.80 multicoloured . . . 2·40 1·25

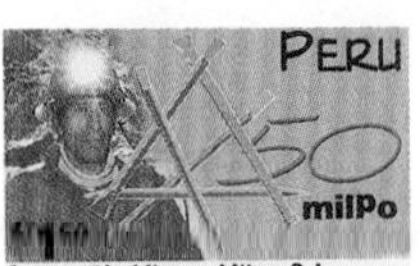

781 Miner and Crowbars

1999. 50th Anniv of Milpo S.A. Mining Company.
1986 **781** 1s.50 multicoloured . . . 55 25

782 Wildlife

1999. Flora and Fauna.
1987 **782** 5s. multicoloured . . . . 1·75 1·00
MS1988 79 × 98 mm. 10s. Jaguar, Manu National Park (horiz) 3·50 3·30

1999. Nos. 1888/91 surch.
1989 1s. on 40c. Rifle shooting 35 20
1990 1s. on 40c. Tennis 35 20
1991 1s. on 60c. Swimming . . . 35 20
1992 1s. on 60c. Weightlifting . . 35 20
1993 1s.50 on 40c. Rifle shooting 35 20
1994 1s.50 on 40c. Tennis 35 20
1995 1s.50 on 60c. Swimming . . 35 20
1996 1s.50 on 60c. Weightlifting 35 20
1997 2s.70 on 40c. Rifle shooting 35 20
1998 2s.70 on 40c. Tennis 35 20
1999 2s.70 on 60c. Swimming . . 35 20
2000 2s.70 on 60c. Weightlifting 35 20
2001 3s.30 on 40c. Rifle shooting 35 20
2002 3s.30 on 40c. Tennis 35 20
2003 3s.30 on 60c. Swimming . . 35 20
2004 3s.30 on 60c. Weightlifting 35 20

1999. No. 1894 surch.
2005 2s.40 on 30c. brown and ochre 80 45

785 Penguin and Antarctic Vessel

1999. 40th Anniv of Antarctic Treaty.
2006 **785** 6s.80 multicoloured . . . 2·40 1·40

786 Bird

1999. Nazca Lines. Sheet 98 × 79 mm.
MS2007 **786** 10s. multicoloured 3·50 3 .50

1999. Inca Chiefs (2nd issue). As T **759**. Multicoloured.
2008 3s.30 Maita Capac 80 45
2009 3s.30 Inca Roca 80 45
2010 3s.30 Capac Yupanqui . . . 80 45
2011 3s.30 Yahuar Huaca 80 45

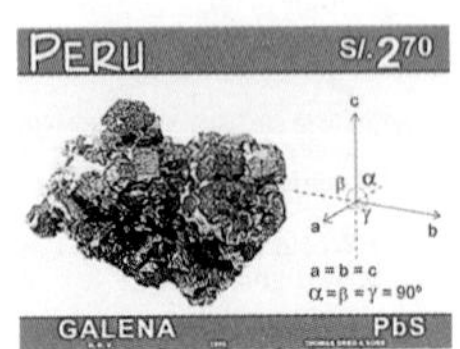

787 Galena

1999. Minerals. Multicoloured.
2012 2s.70 Type **787** 95 55
2013 3s.30 Scheelita . . . . . . 1·10 65
2014 5s. Virgotrigonia peterseni 1·75 1·00

788 Virgin of Carmen

1999.
2015 **788** 3s.30 multicoloured . . . 1·10 65

789 Building

1999. St. Catalina Monastery, Arequipa.
2016 **789** 2s.70 multicoloured . . . 95 35

790 Emblem and Dragon

1999. 150th Anniv of Chinese Immigration to Peru.
2017 **790** 1s.50 red and black . . . 55 35

791 Taking Pulse

1999. 25th Anniv of Peruvian Medical Society.
2018 **791** 1s.50 multicoloured . . . 55 35

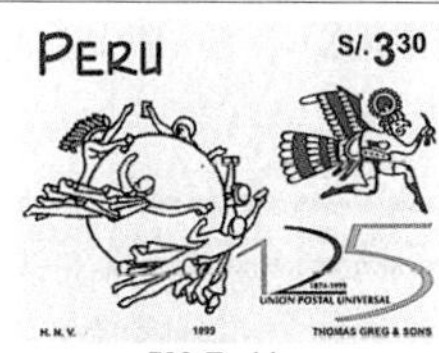

792 Emblem

1999. 125th Anniv of Universal Postal Union.
2019 **792** 3s.30 multicoloured . . . 1·10 65

793 Sunflower growing out of Gun

1999. America. A New Millennium without Arms. Multicoloured.
2020 2s.70 Type **793** 95 55
2021 3s.30 Man emerging from Globe (horiz) . . . . . . 1·10 65

794 Woman with Fumigator

1999. Seor de los Milagros Festival, Lima. Multicoloured.
2022 1s. Type **794** 35 20
2023 1s.50 Procession 55 30

795 Young Child and Emblem

1999. 40th Anniv of Inter-American Development Bank.
2024 **795** 1s.50 multicoloured . . . 55 30

796 *Pterourus zagreus chrysomelus*

1999. Butterflies. Multicoloured.
2025 3s.30 Type **796** . . . . . . 1·10 65
2026 3s.30 *Asterope buckleyi* . . . 1·10 65
2027 3s.30 *Parides chabrias* . . . 1·10 65
2028 3s.30 *Mimoides pausanias* . . 1·10 65
2029 3s.30 *Nessaea obrina* . . . . 1·10 65
2030 3s.30 *Pterourus zagreus zagreus* . . . . 1·10 65

797 Map of Cunhuime Sur Sub-sector

1999. 1st Anniv of Peru–Ecuador Border Peace Agreement. Multicoloured.
2031 1s. Type **797** 35 20
2032 1s. Map of Lagartococha-Gueppi sector 35 20
2033 1s. Map of Cusumasa Bumbuiza-Yaupi Santiago sub-sector (horiz) 35 20

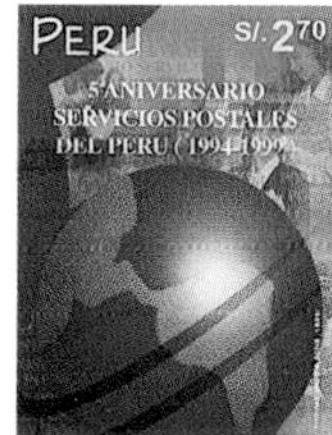

798 Globe

1999. 5th Anniv of Serpost S.A. (Peruvian postal services).
2034 **798** 2s.70 multicoloured . . . 95 55

799 Virgin of Belen

1999. Christmas.
2035 **799** 2s.70 multicoloured . . . 95 55

800 Mujica and Factory

1999. Birth Centenary of Ricardo Bentin Mujica (industrialist).
2036 **800** 2s.70 multicoloured . . . 95 55

801 Flags encircling Globe

2000. New Millennium. Sheet 79 × 99 mm.
MS2037 **801** 10s. multicoloured 3·50 3·50

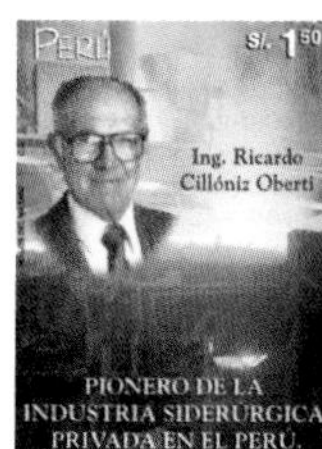

802 Oberti and Foundry

2000. Ricardo Cilloniz Oberti (founder of Peruvian steel industry).
2038 **802** 1s.50 multicoloured . . . 55 30

803 Llamas

2000. Michell Group (Peruvian alpaca exporters). Multicoloured.
2039 1s.50 Type **803** 55 30
2040 1s.50 Llamas (different) . . 55 30
Nos. 2039/40 were issued together, se-tenant, forming a composite design.

804 Power Station

2000. 25th Anniv of Peruvian Institute of Nuclear Energy (I.P.E.N.).
2041 **804** 4s. multicoloured . . . . 1·40 80

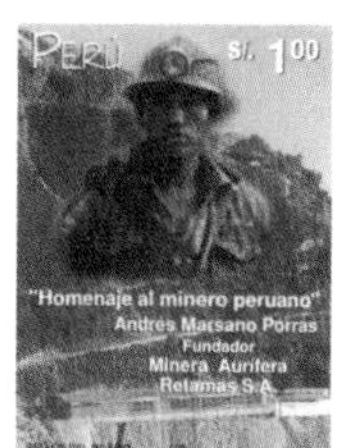

805 Miner

2000. Mining Industry. Multicoloured.
2042 1s. Type **805** 35 20
2043 1s. View of mine 35 20
Nos. 2042/3 were issued together, se-tenant, forming a composite design.

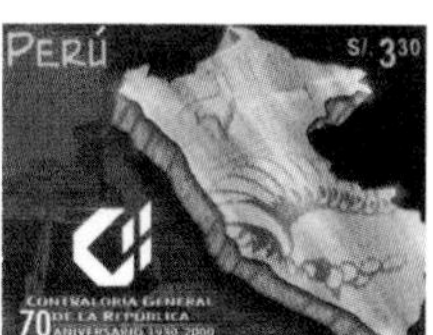

806 Stylized Outline of Peru

2000. 70th Anniv of Comptroller General of Republic.
2044 **806** 3s.30 multicoloured . . . 1·10 65

807 Field and Emilio Guimoye Hernandez

2000. Poblete Agriculture Group.
2045 **807** 1s.50 multicoloured . . . 55 30

808 Pupils carrying Flags

2000. National School Sports Games.
2046 **808** 1s.80 multicoloured . . . 60 35

809 Machu Picchu

2000. World Heritage Sites.
2047 **809** 1s.30 multicoloured . . . 45 25

810 Emblem

2000. Campaign Against Domestic Violence.
2048 **810** 3s.80 multicoloured . . . 1·25 75

811 Emblem

2000. Year
2049 **811** 3s.20 multicoloured . . . 1·10 65

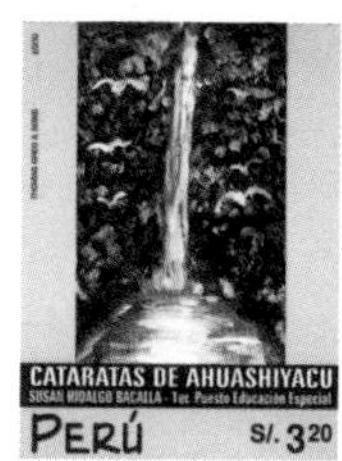

812 "Cataratas de Ahuashiyacu" (Susan Hidalgo Bacalla)

2000. Winning Entries in Students' Painting Competition. Multicoloured.
2050 3s.20 Type **812** . . . . . . 1·10 65
2051 3s.20 "Laguna Yarinacocha" (Mari Trini Ramos Vargas) (horiz) . . 1·10 65
2052 3s.80 "La Campina Arequipena" (Anibal Lajo Yanez) (horiz) . . . . . 1·25 75

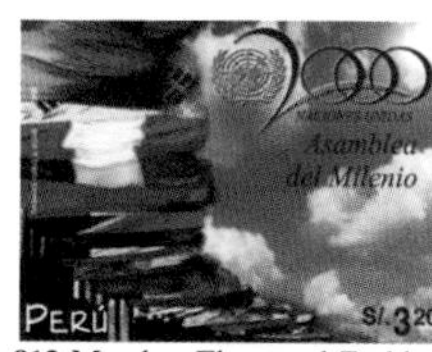

813 Member Flags and Emblem

2000. United Nations Millennium Summit, New York, U.S.A.
2053 **813** 3s.20 multicoloured . . . 1·10 65

814 San Martín

2000. 150th Death Anniv of General Jose de San Martin.
2054 **814** 3s.80 multicoloured . . . 1·25 75

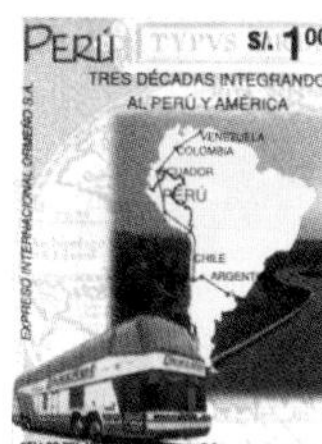

815 Bus, Map of South America and Road

2000. 30th Anniv of Peru-North America Bus Route. Multicoloured.
2055 1s. Type **815** 35 20
2056 2s.70 Bus, map of North America and road 95 55
Nos. 2055/6 were issued together, se-tenant, forming a composite design.

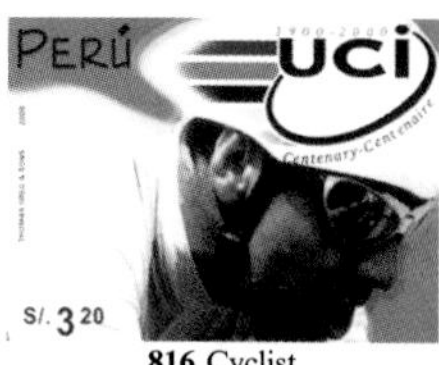

816 Cyclist

2000. Centenary of International Cycling Union.
2057 **816** 3s.20 multicoloured . . . 1·10 65

817 Sun Dial

2000. 50th Anniv of World Meteorological Organization.
2058 **817** 1s.50 multicoloured . . . 55 30

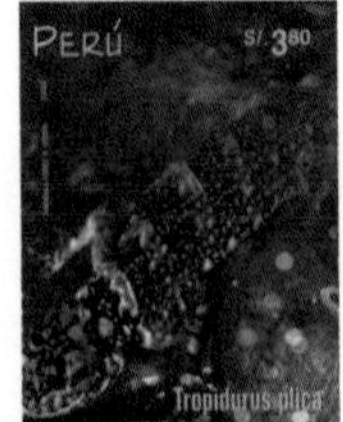

818 Western Leaf Lizard (*Tropidurus plica*)

2000. Lizards. Multicoloured.
2059 3s.80 Type **818** . . . . . . 1·25 75
2060 3s.80 Haitian ameiva (*Ameiva ameiva*) . . . . 1·25 75
2061 3s.80 Two-lined skink (*Mabouya bistriata*) . . . 1·25 75
2062 3s.80 *Neusticurus ecpleopus* 1·25 75
2063 3s.80 Blue-lipped forest anole (*Anolis fuscoauratus*) 1·25 75
2064 3s.80 Horned wood lizard (*Enyalioides palpebralis*) 1·25 75
Nos. 2059/64 were issued together, se-tenant, forming a composite design.

819 *Matucana madisoniorum*

2000. Cacti.
2065 **819** 3s.80 multicoloured . . . 1·25 75

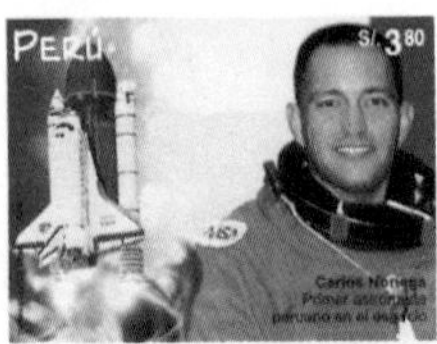

820 Noriega and Space Shuttle

2000. Carlos Noriega (first Peruvian astronaut).
2066 **820** 3s.80 multicoloured . . . 1·25 75

821 De Mendoza and Library

2000. 250th Birth Anniv Toribio Rodríguez de Mendoza.
2067 **821** 3s.20 multicoloured . . . 1·10 65

822 Symbols of Ucayali

2000. Centenary of Ucayali Province.
2068 **822** 3s.20 multicoloured . . . 1·10 65

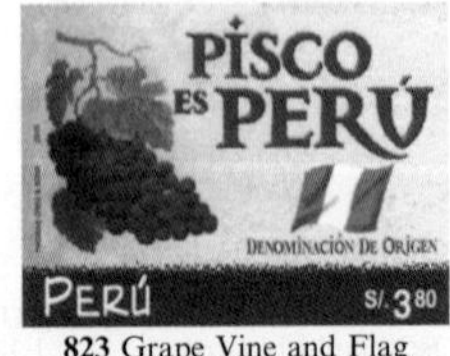

823 Grape Vine and Flag

2000. Wines of Peru.
2069 **823** 3s.80 multicoloured . . . 1·25 75

824 Flags on Watch Parts

2000. 20th Anniv of ALADI (Latin-American integration association).
2070 **824** 10s.20 multicoloured . . 3·30 3·50

825 Emblem

2000. 50th Anniv of Federation of Journalists.
2071 **825** 1s.50 multicoloured . . . 55 30

EXPRESS LETTER STAMPS

1908. Optd **EXPRESO**.
E373 **76** 10c. black . . . . . . 17·00 12·50
E382 – 10c. blue (No. 377) . . 21·00 11·50
E383 **101** 10c. black and brown 11·50 10·00

OFFICIAL STAMPS

1890. Stamps of 1866 optd **GOBIERNO** in frame.
O287 **15** 1c. violet . . . . 1·10 1·10
O324 1c. red . . . . 7·00 7·00
O288 **16** 2c. green . . . . . . 1·10 1·10
O325 2c. blue . . . . 7·00 7·00
O289 5c. orange . . . . . . 1·60 1·60
O326 **10** 5c. lake . . . . 5·50 5·50
O290 **16** 10c. black 85 45
O291 20c. blue . . . . 2·50 1·60
O327 20c. blue (as T **10**) . . . 5·50 5·50
O292 **20** 50c. red . . . . 3·50 1·75
O293 **21** 1s. brown . . . . 4·25 3·75

1894. Stamps of 1894 (with "Head" optd) optd **GOBIERNO** in frame.
O305 **15** 1c. orange (No. 294) . . 19·00 19·00
O306 1c. green (No. 295) . . . 1·10 1·10
O307 **16** 2c. violet (No. 296) . . . 1·10 1·10
O308 2c. red (No. 297) 90 90
O309 5c. blue (No. 298) . . . 8·50 7·50
O310 10c. green (No. 299) . . 3·00 3·00
O311 **20** 50c. green (No. 300) . . 4·25 4·25

1894. Stamps of 1894 (with "Head" and "Horseshoe" optd) optd **GOBIERNO** in frame.
O312 **16** 2c. red (No. 301) . . . . 1·60 1·60
O313 5c. blue (No. 302) . . . 1·60 1·60

1896. Stamps of 1896 optd **GOBIERNO**.
O348 **75** 1c. blue 10 10
O349 **76** 10c. yellow . . . . . . 1·00 25
O350 10c. black 10 10
O351 **77** 50c. red 25 20

O 108

1909.
O382 **108** 1c. red 10 10
O572 10c. brown 40 30
O385 10c. purple 15 10
O573 50c. green 35 20

1935. Optd **Servicio Oficial**.
O567 **184** 10c. red 10 10

PARCEL POST STAMPS

P 79

1895. Different frames.
P348 **79** 1c. purple . . . . 1·90 1·60
P349 2c. brown . . . . 2·10 1·90
P350 5c. blue . . . . 8·50 5·50
P351 10c. brown . . . . 11·50 8·25
P352 20c. pink . . . . 14·50 12·00
P353 50c. green . . . . 38·00 32·00

1903. Surch in words.
P361 **79** 1c. on 20c. pink . . . . 12·50 10·00
P362 1c. on 50c. green . . . . 12·50 10·00
P363 5c. on 10c. brown . . . . 75·00 60·00

POSTAGE DUE STAMPS

D 22

D 23

D 109

1874.
D31 D **22** 1c. brown 10 10
D32 D **23** 5c. red 30 15
D33 10c. orange 30 15
D34 20c. blue 50 30
D35 50c. brown . . . . . . 10·00 3·00

1881. Optd with T **24** ("LIMA" at foot instead of "PERU").
D47 D **22** 1c. brown . . . . . . 3·00 2·00
D48 D **23** 5c. red . . . . 5·50 5·00
D49 10c. orange . . . . . . 5·50 5·50
D50 20c. blue . . . . 21·00 17·00
D51 50c. brown . . . . . . 45·00 42·00

1881. Optd **LIMA CORREOS** in double-lined circle.
D52 D **22** 1c. brown . . . . . . 4·25 4·25
[illegible] 5·50 5·00
D54 10c. orange . . . . . . 6·75 5·50
D55 20c. blue . . . . 21·00 17·00
D56 50c. brown . . . . . . 65·00 55·00

1883. Optd with T **24** (inscr "LIMA" instead of "PERU") and also with T **28a**.
D247 D **22** 1c. brown . . . . . . 4·25 3·00
D250 D **23** 5c. red . . . . 6·25 5·75
D253 10c. orange . . . . . 6·25 5·75
D256 20c. blue £400 £375
D258 50c. brown . . . . . 55·00 45·00

1884. Optd with T **28a** only.
D259 D **22** 1c. brown 40 40
D262 D **23** 5c. red 30 20
D267 10c. orange 35 25
D269 20c. blue . . . . . . 1·00 35
D271 50c. brown . . . . . 3·00 75

1894. Optd **LIMA CORREOS** in double-lined circle and with T **28a**.
D275 D **22** 1c. brown . . . . . . 10·50 9·25

1896. Optd **DEFICIT**.
D348 D **22** 1c. brown (D31) . . . 15 15
D349 D **23** 5c. red (D32) 20 15
D350 10c. orange (D33) . . 55 15
D351 20c. blue (D34) . . . 70 20
D352 **20** 50c. red (283) 60 20
D353 **21** 1s. brown (284) . . . 85 35

1899. As T **73**, but inscr "DEFICIT" instead of "FRANQUEO".
D355 5s. green . . . . 1·40 4·25
D356 10s. brown £800 £800

1902. Surch **DEFICIT** and value in words.
D361 1c. on 10s. (D356) 85 50
D362 5c. on 10s. (354) 50 40

1902. Surch **DEFICIT** and value in words.
D363 **23** 1c. on 20c. (D34) 60 40
D364 5c. on 20c. (D34) . . . . 1·50 1·00

1909.
D382 **109** 1c. brown 35 15
D419 1c. purple 15 15
D420 2c. purple 15 15
D570 2c. brown 15 15
D383 5c. brown 35 15
D421 5c. purple 25 20
D384 10c. brown 40 15
D422 10c. purple 40 15
D571 10c. green 40 15
D385 50c. brown 60 20
D423 50c. purple . . . . . . 1·40 50
D424 1s. purple . . . . . . 10·00 3·00
D425 2s. purple . . . . . . 19·00 6·75

1935. Optd **Deficit**.
D568 – 2c. purple (No. 537) . . 40 40
D569 **184** 10c. red 50 40

PHILIPPINES Pt. 9; Pt. 22; Pt. 21

A group of islands in the China Sea, E. of Asia, ceded by Spain to the United States after the war of 1898. Under Japanese Occupation from 1941 until 1945. An independent Republic since 1946.

1854. 20 cuartos = 1 real; 8 reales = 1 peso plata fuerte.
1864. 100 centimos = 1 peso plata fuerte.
1871. 100 centimos = 1 escudo (= $\frac{1}{2}$ peso).
1872. 100 centimos = 1 peseta (= $\frac{1}{5}$ peso).
1876. 1000 milesimas = 100 centavos or centimos = 1 peso.
1899. 100 cents = 1 dollar.
1906. 100 centavos = 1 peso.
1962. 100 sentimos = 1 piso.

SPANISH ADMINISTRATION

1 Queen Isabella II

4 Queen Isabella II

5 Queen Isabella II

1854. Imperf.
1 **1** 5c. red £1200 £180
3 10c. red £400 £120
5 1r. blue £450 £130
7a 2r. green £650 £120
On the 1r. the inscriptions are reversed.

1859. Imperf.
13 **4** 5c. red . . . . 10·00 4·00
14 10c. pink . . . . 10·00 12·00

1861. Larger lettering. Imperf.
17 **5** 5c. red . . . . 23·00 7·50

7

8

1863. Imperf.
19 **7** 5c. red . . . . 9·00 3·75
20 10c. red . . . . 27·00 28·00
21 1r. mauve £500 £325
22 2r. blue £400 £275

1863. Imperf.
25 **8** 1r. green . . . . £100 38·00

1864. As T **14** of Spain, but value in "centimos de peso". Imperf.
26 $3\frac{1}{8}$c. black on buff . . . . . . 2·50 1·40
27 $6\frac{2}{8}$c. green on pink . . . . . . 2·50 70
28 $12\frac{4}{8}$c. blue on pink . . . . . . 5·00 70
29 25c. red on pink . . . . . . 10·00 4·00
30 25c. red on white . . . . . . 7·00 2·00

1868. Optd **HABILITADO POR LA NACION**.
(a) On 1854 to 1863 issues of Philippines.
41 **7** 5c. red . . . . 42·00 27·00
53 **4** 10c. pink . . . . 85·00 45·00
36 **8** 1r. green . . . . 42·00 12·00
42 **7** 1r. mauve £425 £275
52 **1** 1r. blue £2000 £1000
43 **7** 2r. blue £400 £180
(b) On 1864 issues of Philippines.
31 $3\frac{1}{8}$c. black on buff . . . . . . 15·00 3·00
32 $6\frac{2}{8}$c. green on pink . . . . . . 15·00 3·00
33 $12\frac{4}{8}$c. blue on pink . . . . . . 40·00 18·00
34 25c. red . . . . 18·00 10·00
(c) On Nos. 10/11a of Cuba (as T **8** of Philippines).
44 1r. green . . . . £130 60·00
45 2r. red . . . . £170 65·00

12

13 King Amadeo

1871.
37 **12** 5c. blue . . . . 42·00 4·50
38 10c. green . . . . 6·00 3·75
39 20c. brown . . . . 48·00 26·00
40 40c. red . . . . 65·00 14·00

1872.
46 **13** 12c. pink . . . . 9·50 3·50
47 16c. blue . . . . 95·00 25·00
48a 25c. grey . . . . 7·50 3·50
49 62c. mauve . . . . 23·00 6·50
50a 1p.25 brown . . . . 42·00 20·00

14

1874.

54	**14**	12c. grey	11·00	3·25
55		25c. blue	3·75	1·40
56		62c. pink	32·00	3·25
57		1p.25 brown	£160	48·00

15

16

1875. With rosettes each side of "FILIPINAS".

58	**15**	2c. pink	1·50	50
59		2c. blue	£140	65·00
60		6c. orange	7·50	1·75
61		10c. blue	2·00	45
62		12c. mauve	2·10	45
63		20c. brown	9·50	2·25
64		25c. green	7·50	45

1878. Without rosettes.

65	**16**	25m. black	1·90	30
66		25m. green	45·00	21·00
67		50m. purple	22·00	8·50
68a		(62½m.) 0.0625 lilac	40·00	13·00
69		100m. red	75·00	32·00
70		100m. green	7·00	2·00
71		125m. blue	3·50	30
72		200m. pink	23·00	4·75
74		250m. brown	8·50	2·00

1877. Surch **HABILITADO 12 CS. PTA.** in frame.

75	**15**	12c. on 2c. pink	65·00	22·00
76	**16**	12c. on 25m. black	65·00	22·00

1879. Surch **CONVENIO UNIVERSAL DE CORREOS HABILITADO** and value in figures and words.

78	**16**	2c. on 25m. green	35·00	7·50
79		8c. on 100m. red	28·00	5·50

1880. "Alfonso XII" key-type inscr "FILIPINAS".

97	X	1c. green	30	10
82a		2c. red	60	1·25
83		2½c. brown	6·00	1·25
95		2$\frac{4}{8}$		
99		50m. bistre	30	15
85		5c. grey	60	1·25
100		6c. brown	8·00	1·25
87		6$\frac{2}{8}$c. green	4·75	7·50
88		8c. brown	27·00	14·00
89a		10c. brown	2·50	1·25
90		10c. purple	5·00	10·00
91		10c. green	£300	£180
92		12$\frac{4}{8}$c. pink	1·25	1·25
93		20c. brown	2·50	1·25
94		25c. brown	3·25	1·25

1881. "Alfonso XII" key-type inscr "FILIPINAS" with various circular surcharges. (a) **HABILITADO U. POSTAL** and value.

111	X	1c. on 2$\frac{4}{8}$c. blue	60	40
102		10c. on 2$\frac{4}{8}$c. blue	6·00	1·25

(b) **HABILITADO CORREOS 2 CENTS. DE PESO.**

101	X	2c. on 2½c. brown	3·00	1·15

(c) **HABILITADO PA. U. POSTAL 8 CMOS.**

106	X	8c. on 2c. red	6·00	1·40

(d) **HABILITADO PA. CORREOS DE** and value.

107	X	10c. cuartos on 2c. red	3·50	1·40
112		16 cuartos on 2$\frac{4}{8}$c. blue	8·50	2·00
103		20c. on 8c. brown	8·25	2·50
113		1r. on 2c. red	5·50	2·00
109		1r. on 5c. lilac	5·00	2·25
110		1r. on 8c. brown	9·50	3·00
105		2r. on 2$\frac{4}{8}$c. blue	5·00	1·40

25

29

30

31

34

1881. Fiscal and telegraph stamps. (a) with circular surch **HABILITADO CORREOS, HABILITADO PARA CORREOS, HABILITADO PA. U. POSTAL** or **HABILITADO PA. CORREOS** and value in figures and words.

115	**25**	2c. on 10 cuartos bistre	21·00	13·50
129	**29**	2c. on 200m. green	4·75	2·25
116	**25**	2$\frac{4}{8}$c. on 10 cuartos bistre	3·00	65
117		2$\frac{4}{8}$c. on 2r. blue	£150	65·00
124		6$\frac{2}{8}$c. on 12$\frac{4}{8}$c. lilac	4·75	2·75
118		8c. on 2r. blue	8·50	2·25
119		8c. on 10c. brown	£170	£130
123		16 cmos. on 2r. blue	5·75	2·40
137	**31**	20c. on 150m. blue	25·00	21·00
134		20c. on 250m. blue	95·00	80·00
127	**25**	1r. on 10 cuartos bistre	10·00	3·50
121		1r. on 12$\frac{4}{8}$c. lilac	7·00	3·00
130	**29**	1r. on 200m. green	55·00	35·00
131		1r. on 1 peso green	28·00	13·50
132	**30**	1r. on 10 pesetas bistre	40·00	21·00
133	**31**	2r. on 250m. blue	9·00	3·00

(b) With two circular surcharges as above, showing two different values.

128	**25**	8c. on 2r. on 2r. blue	20·00	12·00
136	**31**	1r. on 20c. on 250m. blue	9·00	4·50

(c) Optd **HABILITADO PARA CORREOS** in straight lines.

122	**25**	10 cuartos bistre	£150	65·00
126		1r. green	85·00	65·00

1887. Various stamps with oval surch **UNION GRAL. POSTAL HABILITADO** (No. 142) or **HABILITADO PARA COMMUNICACIONES** and new value. (a) "Alfonso XII" key-type inscr "FILIPINAS".

138	X	2$\frac{4}{8}$c. on 1c. green	1·90	1·00
139		2$\frac{4}{8}$c. on 5c. lilac	1·25	50
140		2$\frac{4}{8}$c. on 50m. bistre	1·75	1·10
141		2$\frac{4}{8}$c. on 10c. green	1·25	65
142		8c. on 2$\frac{4}{8}$c. blue	75	40

(b) "Alfonso XII" key-type inscr "FILIPAS-IMPRESOS".

143	X	2$\frac{4}{8}$c. on $\frac{1}{8}$c. green	40	15

(c) Fiscal and telegraph stamps.

144	**29**	2$\frac{4}{8}$c. on 200m. green	3·50	1·25
145		2$\frac{4}{8}$c. on 20c. brown	10·00	4·75
146	**34**	2$\frac{4}{8}$c. on 1c. bistre	75	50

1889. Various stamps with oval surch **RECARGO DE CONSUMOS HABILITADO** and new value. (a) "Alfonso XII" key-type inscr "FILIPINAS".

147	X	2$\frac{4}{8}$c. on 1c. green	15	15
148		2$\frac{4}{8}$c. on 2c. red	10	10
149		2$\frac{4}{8}$c. on 2$\frac{4}{8}$c. blue	10	10
150		2$\frac{4}{8}$c. on 5c. lilac	10	10
151		2$\frac{4}{8}$c. on 50m. bistre	10	10
152		2$\frac{4}{8}$c. on 12$\frac{4}{8}$c. pink	60	60

(b) "Alfonso XII" key-type inscr "FILIPAS-IMPRESOS".

160	X	2$\frac{4}{8}$c. on $\frac{1}{8}$c. green	15	15

(c) Fiscal and telegraph stamps.

153	**34**	2$\frac{4}{8}$c. on 1c. bistre	30	30
154		2$\frac{4}{8}$c. on 2c. red	30	30
155		2$\frac{4}{8}$c. on 2$\frac{4}{8}$c. brown	10	10
156		2$\frac{4}{8}$c. on 5c. blue	10	10
157		2$\frac{4}{8}$c. on 10c. green	10	10
158		2$\frac{4}{8}$c. on 10c. mauve	60	65
159		2$\frac{4}{8}$c.on 20c. mauve	20	20
161	–	17$\frac{4}{8}$c. on 5p. green		70·00

No. 161 is a fiscal stamp inscribed "DERECHO JUDICIAL" with a central motif as T **43** of Spain.

1890. "Baby" key-type inscr "FILIPINAS".

176	Y	1c. violet	40	15
188		1c. red	13·00	6·50
197		1c. green	1·75	60
162		2c. red	10	10
177		2c. violet	10	10
190		2c. brown	10	10
198		2c. blue	25	25
163		2$\frac{4}{8}$c. blue	40	10
178		2$\frac{4}{8}$c. grey	15	10
165		5c. blue	30	10
163		5c. green	40	10
199		5c. brown	7·50	3·25
181		6c. purple	20	10
192		6c. red	1·40	70
166		8c. green	20	10
182		8c. blue	40	20
193		8c. red	65	20
167		10c. green	1·40	20
172		10c. pink	50	10
202		10c. brown	20	10
173		12$\frac{4}{8}$c. green	15	10
184		12$\frac{4}{8}$c. orange	50	10
185		15c. brown	50	20
195		15c. red	1·60	70
203		15c. green	1·75	1·75
169		20c. red	55·00	29·00
186		20c. brown	1·50	25
196		20c. purple	13·00	6·50
204		20c. orange	3·75	1·75
170		25c. brown	4·25	75
175		25c. blue	1·50	15
205		40c. purple	18·00	5·00
206		80c. red	26·00	14·50

1897. Surch **HABILITADO CORREOS PARA** 1897 and value in frame. (a) "Baby" key-type inscr "FILIPINAS".

212	Y	5c. on 5c. green	3·00	2·00
208		15c. on 15c. red	3·00	2·00
213		15c. on 15c. brown	3·50	2·00
209		20c. on 20c. purple	15·00	8·00
214		20c. on 20c. brown	5·00	3·50
210		20c. on 25c. brown	10·00	8·00

(b) "Alfonso XII" key-type inscr "FILIPINAS".

215	X	5c. on 5c. lilac	4·00	2·25

1898. "Curly Head" key-type inscr "FILIPNAS 1898 y 99".

217	Z	1m. brown	15	15
218		2m. brown	15	15
219		3m. brown	15	15
220		4m. brown	6·00	1·25
221		5m. brown	15	15
222		1c. purple	15	15
223		2c. green	15	15
224		3c. brown	15	15
225		4c. orange	12·00	7·50
226		5c. red	15	15
227		6c. blue	75	45
228		8c. brown	35	15
229		10c. red	1·25	75
230		15c. grey	1·25	65
231		20c. purple	1·25	90
232		40c. lilac	75	60
233		60c. black	3·25	2·25
234		80c. brown	4·00	2·25
235		1p. green	9·50	9·25
236		2p. blue	22·00	12·00

STAMPS FOR PRINTED MATTER

1886. "Alfonso XII" key-type inscr "FILIPAS-IMPRESOS".

P138	X	1m. red	20	10
P139		$\frac{1}{8}$c. green	20	10
P140		2m. blue	20	10
P141		5m. brown	20	10

1890. "Baby" key-type inscr "FILIPAS-IMPRESOS".

P171	Y	1m. purple	10	10
P172		$\frac{1}{8}$c. purple	10	10
P173		2m. purple	10	10
P174		5m. purple	10	10

1892. "Baby" key-type inscr "FILIPAS-IMPRESOS".

P192	Y	1m. green	1·40	40
P193		$\frac{1}{8}$c. green	80	15
P194		2m. green	2·00	40
P191		5m. green	£190	40·00

1894. "Baby" key-type inscr "FILIPAS-IMPRESOS".

P197	Y	1m. grey	20	20
P198		$\frac{1}{8}$c. brown	20	20
P199		2m. grey	20	20
P200		5m. grey	20	20

1896. "Baby" key-type inscr "FILIPAS-IMPRESOS".

P205	Y	1m. blue	25	15
P206		$\frac{1}{8}$c. blue	75	60
P207		2m. brown	25	15
P208		5m. blue	2·25	1·40

UNITED STATES ADMINISTRATION

1899. United States stamps of 1894 (No. 267 etc) optd **PHILIPPINES**.

252	–	1c. green	2·50	65
253	–	2c. red	1·25	50
255	–	3c. violet	4·00	1·60
256	–	4c. brown	17·00	4·75
257	–	5c. blue	4·00	1·00
258	–	6c. purple	20·00	6·00
259	–	8c. brown	22·00	6·00
260	–	10c. brown	14·00	3·00
262	–	15c. green	25·00	6·50
263	**83**	50c. orange	90·00	30·00
264	–	$1 black	£325	£190
266	–	$2 blue	£400	£200
267	–	$5 green	£700	£550

1903. United States stamps of 1902 optd **PHILIPPINES**.

268	**103**	1c. green	3·00	30
269	**104**	2c. red	5·00	1·25
270	**105**	3c. violet	55·00	11·00
271a	**106**	4c. brown	60·00	16·00
272	**107**	5c. blue	8·50	70
273	**108**	6c. lake	65·00	18·00
274	**109**	8c. violet	28·00	10·00
275	**110**	10c. brown	16·00	1·90
276	**111**	13c. purple	23·00	13·00
277	**112**	15c. olive	42·00	10·00
278	**113**	50c. orange	£100	28·00
279	**114**	$1 black	£350	£200
280	**115**	$2 blue	£600	£375
281	**116**	$5 green	£750	£700

1904. United States stamp of 1903 optd **PHILIPPINES**.

282a	**117**	2c. red	4·25	1·60

45 Rizal **46** Arms of Manila

1906. Various portraits as T **45** and T **46**.

337	**45**	2c. green	10	10
338	–	4c. red (McKinley)	10	10
339	–	6c. violet (Magellan)	30	10
340	–	8c. brown (Legaspi)	25	10
341	–	10c. blue (Lawton)	20	10
288	–	12c. red (Lincoln)	4·00	1·75
342	–	12c. orange (Lincoln)	45	15
289	–	16c. black (Sampson)	3·00	15
298	–	16c. green (Sampson)	2·00	10
344	–	16c. olive (Dewey)	1·00	15
290	–	20c. brown (Washington)	3·25	20
345	–	20c. yellow (Washington)	35	10
291	–	26c. brown (Carriedo)	4·50	1·75
346	–	26c. green (Carriedo)	65	30
292	–	30c. green (Franklin)	3·75	1·10
313	–	30c. blue (Franklin)	2·75	35
347	–	30c. grey (Franklin)	45	10
293	**46**	1p. orange	18·00	5·00
363a		1p. violet	3·50	3·50
294		2p. black	23·00	1·00
364		2p. brown	8·00	8·00
350		4p. blue	20·00	25
351		10p. green	42·00	4·50

Nos. 288, 289, 298, 290, 291, 292, 313, 293 and 294 exist perf only, the other values perf or imperf.

1926. Air. Madrid–Manila Flight. Stamps as last, optd **AIR MAIL 1926 MADRID-MANILA** and aeroplane propeller.

368	**45**	2c. green	5·50	3·25
369		4c. red	7·00	3·75
370	–	6c. violet	32·00	8·00
371	–	8c. brown	32·00	9·50
372	–	10c. blue	32·00	9·50
373	–	12c. orange	32·00	14·00
374	–	16c. green (Sampson)	£1200	£1000
375	–	16c. olive (Dewey)	38·00	13·50
376	–	20c. yellow	38·00	13·50
377	–	26c. green	38·00	13·50
378	–	30c. grey	38·00	13·50
383	**46**	1p. violet	£120	75·00
379		2p. brown	£325	£180
380		4p. blue	£475	£275
381		10p. green	£750	£450

49 Legislative Palace

1926. Inauguration of Legislative Palace.

384	**49**	2c. black and green	40	25
385		4c. black and red	40	30
386		16c. black and olive	60	50
387		18c. black and brown	70	45
388		20c. black and orange	90	80
389		24c. black and grey	75	50
390		1p. black and mauve	40·00	24·00

1928. Air. London–Orient Flight by British Squadron of Seaplanes. Stamps of 1906 optd **L.O.F.** (= London Orient Flight), **1928** and Fairey IIID seaplane.

402	**45**	2c. green	35	20
403	–	4c. red	40	30
404	–	6c. violet	2·40	1·60
405	–	8c. brown	2·40	2·00
406	–	10c. blue	2·40	2·00
407	–	12c. orange	4·00	2·40
408	–	16c. olive (Dewey)	3·75	2·40
409	–	20c. yellow	4·00	2·40
410	–	26c. green	7·50	5·50
411	–	30c. grey	7·50	5·50
412	**46**	1p. violet	32·00	32·00

54 Mayon Volcano

57 Vernal Falls, Yosemite National Park, California, wrongly inscr "PAGSANJAN FALLS"

1932.

424	**54**	2c. green	35	15
425	–	4c. red	30	20
426	–	12c. orange	75	40
427	**57**	18c. red	16·00	7·00
428	–	20c. yellow	55	45
429	–	24c. violet	80	55
430	–	32c. brown	80	65

DESIGNS—HORIZ: 4c. Post Office, Manila; 12c. Freighters at Pier No. 7, Manila Bay; 20c. Rice plantation; 24c. Rice terraces; 32c. Baguio Zigzag.

1932. No. 350 surch in words in double circle.

431	**46**	1p. on 4p. blue	1·50	30
432		2p. on 4p. blue	2·75	55

1932. Air. Nos. 424/30 optd with Dornier Do-J flying boat "Gronland Wal" and **ROUND-THE-WORLD FLIGHT VON GRONAU 1932**.

433		2c. green	30	30
434		4c. red	30	30
435		12c. orange	40	40
436		18c. red	2·75	2·50
437		20c. yellow	1·40	1·25
438		24c. violet	1·40	1·25
439		32c. brown	1·40	1·25

1933. Air. Stamps of 1906 optd **F. REIN MADRID-MANILA FLIGHT-1933** under propeller.

440	**45**	2c. green	30	30
441	–	4c. red	35	35
442	–	6c. violet	60	60
443	–	8c. brown	1·60	1·25
444	–	10c. blue	1·40	90
445	–	12c. orange	1·25	90
446	–	16c. olive (Dewey)	1·25	90
447	–	20c. orange	1·25	90
448	–	26c. green	1·60	1·10
449	–	30c. grey	2·00	1·25

1933. Air. Nos. 337 and 425/30 optd with **AIR MAIL** on wings of airplane.

450		2c. green	40	30
451		4c. red	15	10
452		12c. orange	25	10
453		20c. yellow	25	15
454		24c. violet	35	15
455		32c. brown	40	25

66 Baseball

1934. 10th Far Eastern Championship Games.
456 **66** 2c. brown . . . . 1·25 60
457 – 6c. blue 25 15
458 – 16c. purple 50 40
DESIGNS—VERT: 6c. Tennis; 16c. Basketball.

69 Dr. J. Rizal **72** Pearl Fishing

1935. Designs as T **69/70** in various sizes (sizes in millimetres).
459 2c. red (19 × 22) 10 10
460 4c. green (34 × 22) 10 10
461 6c. brown (22½ × 28) 15 10
462 8c. violet (34 × 22) 20 15
463 10c. red (34 × 22) 30 15
464 12c. black (34 × 22) 25 20
465 16c. blue (34 × 22) 35 15
466 20c. bistre (19 × 22) 25 10
467 26c. blue (34 × 22) 40 20
468 30c. red (34 × 22) 40 30
469 1p. black and orange (37 × 27) . . . . 2·40 90
470 2p. black and brown (37 × 27) 4·25 1·25
471 4p. black and blue (37 × 27) 4·00 2·50
472 5p. black and green (27 × 37) 9·50 1·75
DESIGNS: 4c. Woman, Carabao and Rice-stalks; 6c. Filipino girl; 10c. Fort Santiago; 12c. Salt springs; 16c. Magellan's landing; 20c. "Juan de la Cruz"; 26c. Rice terraces; 30c. Blood Compact; 1p. Barasoain Church; 2p. Battle of Manila Bay; 4p. Montalban Gorge; 5p. George Washington (after painting by John Faed).

COMMONWEALTH OF THE PHILIPPINES

83 "Temples of Human Progress"

1935. Inauguration of Commonwealth of the Philippines.
483 **83** 2c. red 15 15
484 6c. violet 20 15
485 16c. blue 20 15
486 36c. green 40 25
487 50c. brown 60 50

1935. Air. "China Clipper" Trans-Pacific Air Mail Flight. Optd **P.I. U.S. INITIAL FLIGHT December-1935** and Martin M-130 flying boat.
488 10c. red (No. 463) 25 20
489 30c. red (No. 468) 40 35

85 J. Rizal y Mercado **89** Manuel L. Quezon

1936. 75th Birth Anniv of Rizal.
490 **85** 2c. yellow 10 15
491 6c. blue 15 15
492 36c. brown 45 40

1936. Air. Manila–Madrid Flight by Arnaiz and Calvo. Stamps of 1906 surch **MANILA-MADRID ARNACAL FLIGHT–1936** and value.
493 **45** 2c. on 4c. red 10 10
494 6c. on 12c. orange 15 10
495 16c. on 26c. green 20 15

1936. Stamps of 1935 (Nos. 459/72) optd **COMMON-WEALTH** (2c., 6c., 20c.) or **COMMONWEALTH** (others).
496 2c. red 10 10
497 4c. green 50 40
526 6c. brown 10 10
527 8c. violet 10 10
528 10c. red 10 10
529 12c. black 10 10
530 16c. blue 20 10
531 20c. bistre 20 10
532 26c. blue 30 20
505 30c. red 30 15
534 1p. black and orange 50 15
535 2p. black and brown . . . . 2·50 75
508 4p. black and blue . . . . . 17·00 2·50
509 5p. black and green . . . . 2·40 1·25

1936. 1st Anniv of Autonomous Government.
510 **89** 2c. brown 10 10
511 6c. green 10 10
512 12c. blue 15 15

90 Philippine Is **92** Arms of Manila

1937. 33rd International Eucharistic Congress.
513 **90** 2c. green 10 10
514 6c. brown 15 10
515 12c. blue 20 10
516 20c. orange 25 10
517 36c. violet 35 30
518 50c. red 45 25

1937.
522 **92** 10p. grey . . . . 3·50 1·50
523 20p. brown . . . . 1·75 1·10

1939. Air. 1st Manila Air Mail Exhibition. Surch **FIRST AIR MAIL EXHIBITION Feb 17 to 19, 1939** and value.
548a – 8c. on 26c. green (346) . . 60 35
549 **92** 1p. on 10p. grey . . . . 3·00 2·40

1939. 1st National Foreign Trade Week. Surch **FIRST FOREIGN TRADE WEEK MAY 21-27, 1939** and value.
551 – 2c. on 4c. green (460) . . 10 10
552a **45** 6c. on 26c. green (346) . . 20 15
553 **92** 50c. on 20p. brown . . . 90 85

101 Triumphal Arch **102** Malacanan Palace

103 Pres. Quezon taking Oath of Office

1939. 4th Anniv of National Independence.
554 **101** 2c. green 10 10
555 6c. red 15 10
556 12c. blue 20 10
557 **102** 2c. green 10 10
558 6c. orange 15 10
559 12c. red 20 10
560 **103** 2c. orange 10 10
561 6c. green 15 10
562 12c. violet 30 15

104 Jose Rizal **105** Filipino Vinta and Boeing 314 Flying Boat

1941.
563 **104** 2c. green 10 10
623 – 2c. brown 10 10
In No. 623 the head faces to the right.

1941. Air.
566 **105** 8c. red 90 80
567 20c. blue . . . . 1·10 50
568 60c. green . . . . 1·60 85
569 1p. sepia 80 55

For Japanese Occupation issues of 1941–45 see **JAPANESE OCCUPATION OF PHILIPPINE ISLANDS.**

1945. Victory issue. Nos. 496, 525/31, 505, 534 and 522/3 optd **VICTORY**.
610 2c. red 10 10
611 4c. green 10 10
612 6c. brown 15 10
613 8c. violet 20 15
614 10c. red 20 10
615 12c. black 25 15
616 16c. blue 40 15
617 20c. bistre 40 10
618 30c. red 70 50
619 1p. black and orange . . . . 1·40 30
620 10p. grey . . . . 40·00 14·00
621 20p. brown . . . . 35·00 16·00

INDEPENDENT REPUBLIC

111 "Independence" **113** Bonifacio Monument

1946. Proclamation of Independence.
625 **111** 2c. red 30 30
626 6c. green 45 30
627 12c. blue 70 45

1946. Optd **PHILIPPINES 50TH ANNIVERSARY MARTYRDOM OF RIZAL 1896–1946.**
628 **104** 2c. brown (No. 623) . . . 30 20

1947.
629 – 4c. brown 15 10
630 **113** 10c. red 20 10
631 – 12c. blue 25 10
632 – 16c. grey . . . . 1·50 90
633 – 20c. brown 45 15
634 – 50c. green . . . . 1·10 75
635 – 1p. violet . . . . 2·25 55
DESIGNS—VERT: 4c. Rizal Monument; 50c., 1p. Avenue of Palm Trees. HORIZ: 12c. Jones Bridge; 16c. Santa Lucia Gate; 20c. Mayon Volcano.

115 Manuel L. Quezon **117** Presidents Quezon and Roosevelt

116 Pres. Roxas taking Oath of Office

1947.
636 **115** 1c. green 15 10

1947. 1st Anniv of Independence.
638 **116** 4c. red 20 15
639 6c. green 25 25
640 16c. purple 70 40

1947. Air.
641 **117** 6c. green 60 35
642 40c. orange . . . . 1·10 75
643 80c. blue . . . . 2·75 2·10

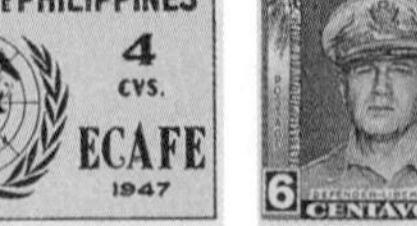
119 United Nations Emblem **121** General MacArthur

1947. Conference of Economic Commission for Asia and Far East, Baguio. Imperf or perf.
648 **119** 4c. red and pink 75 60
649 6c. violet and light violet 1·00 75
650 12c. blue and light blue 1·25 85

1948. 3rd Anniv of Liberation.
652 **121** 4c. violet 25 20
653 6c. red 50 30
654 16c. blue 90 45

122 Threshing Rice **125** Dr. Jose Rizal

1948. United Nations Food and Agriculture Organization Conference, Baguio.
655 **122** 2c. green & yell (postage) 50 25
656 6c. brown and stone . . . 60 30
657 18c. blue and light blue 1·60 90
658 40c. red and pink (air) . . 8·50 4·00

1948.
662 **125** 2c. green 15 10

126 Pres. Manuel Roxas **127** Scout and Badge

1948. President Roxas Mourning Issue.
663 **126** 2c. black 15 10
664 4c. black 25 10

1948. 25th Anniv of Philippine Boy Scouts. Perf or imperf.
665 **127** 2c. green and brown . . . 40 20
666 4c. pink and brown . . . 60 40

128 Sampaguita, National Flower

1948. Flower Day.
667 **128** 3c. green and black . . . 35 30

130 Santos, Tavera and Kalaw

131 "Doctrina Christiana" (first book published in Philippines)

1949. Library Rebuilding Fund.
671 **130** 4c.+2c. brown 75 50
672 **131** 6c.+4c. violet . . . . . 2·10 1·50
673 – 18c.+7c. blue . . . . . . 3·25 2·40
DESIGN—VERT: 18c. Title page of Rizal's "Noli Me Tangere".

132 U.P.U. Monument, Berne

1949. 75th Anniv of U.P.U.
674 **132** 4c. green 20 10
675 6c. violet 20 10
676 18c. blue 55 25

133 General del Pilar at Tirad Pass **134** Globe

1949. 50th Death Anniv of Gen. Gregorio del Pilar.
678 **133** 2c. brown 15 15
679 4c. green 35 30

1950. 5th International Congress of Junior Chamber of Commerce.
680 **134** 2c. violet (postage) . . . 15 10
681 6c. green 25 10
682 18c. blue 40 20
683 30c. orange (air) 90 20
684 50c. red . . . . 1·75 25

135 Red Lauan Trees

136 Franklin D. Roosevelt

1950. 15th Anniv of Forestry Service.
685 **135** 2c. green 20 10
686 4c. violet 45 15

1950. 25th Anniv of Philatelic Association.
687 **136** 4c. brown 20 10
688 6c. pink 25 20
689 18c. blue 60 30

137 Lions Emblem

138 President Quirino taking Oath of Office

1950. "Lions" International Convention, Manila.
691 **137** 2c. orange (postage) . . . 60 20
692 4c. lilac 70 30
693 30c. green (air) 80 25
694 50c. blue 90 40

1950. Pres. Quirino's Inauguration.
696 **138** 2c. red 10 10
697 4c. purple 15 10
698 6c. green 25 15

1950. Surch **ONE CENTAVO**.
699 **125** 1c. on 2c. green 15 10

140 Dove and Map

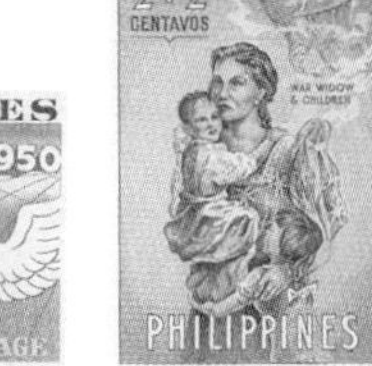
141 War Widow and Children

1950. Baguio Conference.
701 **140** 5c. green 30 25
702 6c. red 30 25
703 18c. blue 70 50

1950. Aid to War Victims.
704 **141** 2c.+2c. red 10 10
705 – 4c.+4c. violet 15 15
DESIGN: 4c. Disabled veteran.

142 Arms of Manila

143 Soldier and Peasants

1950. As T **142**. Various arms and frames. (a) Arms inscr "MANILA".
706 5c. violet 60 20
707 6c. grey 45 15
708 18c. blue 60 20

(b) Arms inscr "CEBU".
709 5c. red 60 20
710 6c. brown 45 15
711 18c. violet 60 20

(c) Arms inscr "ZAMBOANGA".
712 5c. green 60 20
713 6c. brown 45 15
714 18c. blue 60 20

(d) Arms inscr "ILOILO".
715 5c. green 60 20
716 6c. violet 45 15
717 18c. blue 60 20

1951. Guarding Peaceful Labour. Perf or imperf.
718 **143** 5c. green 65 10
719 6c. purple 30 15
720 18c. blue 30 20

144 Philippines Flag and U.N. Emblem

145 Statue of Liberty

1951. U.N. Day.
721 **144** 5c. red 75 20
722 6c. green 35 20
723 18c. blue 45 30

1951. Human Rights Day.
724 **145** 5c. green 75 25
725 6c. orange 40 25
726 18c. blue 55 35

146 Schoolchildren

147 M. L. Quezon

1952. 50th Anniv of Philippine Educational System.
727 **146** 5c. orange 50 25

1952. Portraits.
728 **147** 1c. brown 10 10
729 – 2c. black (J. Abad Santos) 10 10
730 – 3c. red (A. Mabini) . . . 10 10
731 – 5c. red (M. H. del Pilar) 10 10
732 – 10c. blue (Father J. Burgos) 15 10
733 – 20c. red (Lapu-Lapu) . . 30 10
734 – 25c. green (Gen. A. Luna) 45 10
735 – 50c. red (C. Arellano) . . 55 10
736 – 60c. red (A. Bonifacio) . . 70 25
737 – 2p. violet (G. L. Jaena) 1·90 50

149 Aurora A. Quezon

1952. Fruit Tree Memorial Fund.
742 **149** 5c.+1c. blue 15 15
743 6c.+2c. pink 40 40
See also No. 925.

150 Milkfish and Map of Oceania

1952. Indo-Pacific Fisheries Council.
744 **150** 5c. brown . . . . 1·50 65
745 6c. blue . . . . 1·00 50

151 "A Letter from Rizal"

1952. Pan-Asiatic Philatelic Exhibition, Manila.
746 **151** 5c. blue (postage) 60 15
747 6c. brown 40 20
748 30c. red (air) . . . . . . 1·25 50

152 Wright Park, Baguio City

153 F. Baltazar (poet)

1952. 3rd Lions District Convention.
749 **152** 5c. red 45 20
750 6c. green 65 30

1953. National Language Week.
751 **153** 5c. bistre 50 20

154 "Gateway to the East"

155 Pres. Quirino and Pres. Sukarno

1953. International Fair, Manila.
752 **154** 5c. turquoise 30 15
753 6c. red 35 15

1953. Visit of President to Indonesia. Flags in yellow, blue and red.
754 **155** 5c. blue, yellow and black 30 10
755 6c. green, yellow and black 15 10

156 Doctor examining patient

1953. 50th Anniv of Philippines Medical Association.
756 **156** 5c. mauve 40 20
757 6c. blue 35 20

1954. Optd **FIRST NATIONAL BOY SCOUTS JAMBOREE APRIL 23-30, 1954** or surch also.
758 5c. red (No. 731) . . . . . . 1·00 40
759 18c. on 50c. green (No. 634) 1·50 75

158 Stamp of 1854, Magellan and Manila P.O.

1954. Stamp Centenary. Central stamp in orange.
760 **158** 5c. violet (postage) . . . 25 15
761 18c. blue 50 35
762 30c. green . . . . 1·50 1·00
763 10c. brown (air) . . . . . 1·25 50
764 20c. green . . . . 2·25 75
765 50c. red . . . . 6·25 2·00

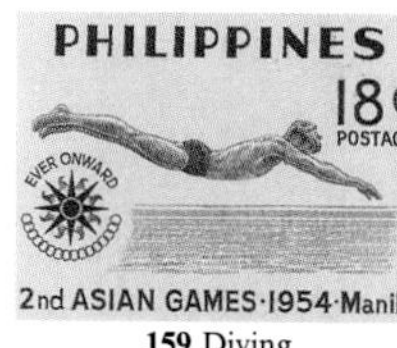
159 Diving

1954. 2nd Asian Games, Manila.
766 – 5c. blue on blue (Discus) 1·40 50
767 **159** 18c. green on green . . . 45 25
768 – 30c. red on pink (Boxing) 1·10 85

1954. Surch **MANILA CONFERENCE OF 1954** and value.
769 **113** 5c. on 10c. red 55 30
770 – 18c. on 20c. brown (No. 633) 40 30

161 "Independence"

162 "The Immaculate Conception" (Murillo)

1954. Independence Commemoration.
771 **161** 5c. red 65 10
772 18c. blue 45 25

1954. Marian Year.
773 **162** 5c. blue 30 10

163 Mayon Volcano and Filipino Vinta

1955. 50th Anniv of Rotary International.
774 **163** 5c. blue (postage) 25 10
775 18c. red 50 20
776 50c. green (air) . . . . . 2·00 50

164 "Labour"

165 Pres. Magsaysay

1955. Labour-Management Congress, Manila.
777 **164** 5c. brown . . . . 2·75 1·10

1955. 9th Anniv of Republic.
778 **165** 5c. blue 25 10
779 20c. red 70 25
780 30c. green 70 25

166 Lt. J. Gozar

1955. Air. Air Force Heroes.
781 **166** 20c. violet . . . . 1·10 15
782 – 30c. red (Lt. C. F. Basa) 50 15
783 **166** 50c. green 80 15
784 – 70c. blue (Lt. C. F. Basa) 75 30

167 Liberty Well

1956. Artesian Wells for Rural Areas.
785 **167** 5c. violet 35 15
786 20c. green 70 25

1956. 5th Conference of World Confederation of Organizations of the Teaching Profession. No. 731 optd **WCOTP CONFERENCE MANILA**.
787 5c. red 25 20

169 Nurse and War Victims

170 Monument (landing marker) in Leyte

1956. 50th Anniv of Philippines Red Cross.
788 **169** 5c. violet and red 25 20
789 20c. brown and red . . . 75 35

1956. Liberation Commem. Perf or imperf.
790 **170** 5c. red 25 15

171 St. Thomas's University

172 Statue of the Sacred Heart

1956. University of St. Thomas.
791 **171** 5c. brown and red 25 25
792 60c. brown and mauve . . 1·25 75

1956. 2nd National Eucharistic Congress and Centenary of the Feast of the Sacred Heart.
793 **172** 5c. green 25 15
794 20c. pink 85 50

1956. Surch **5 5**.
795 5c. on 6c. brown (No. 710) 20 10
796 5c. on 6c. brown (No. 713) 20 10
797 5c. on 6c. violet (No. 716) . . 20 10

174 Girl Guide, Badge and Camp

175 Pres. Ramon Magsaysay

1957. Girl Guides' Pacific World Camp, Quezon City, and Birth Centenary of Lord Baden-Powell. Perf or imperf.
798 **174** 5c. blue 45 30

1957. Death of Pres. Magsaysay.
799 **175** 5c. black 15 10

176 Sergio Osmena (Speaker) and First Philippine Assembly

1957. 50th Anniv of First Philippine Assembly.
800 **176** 5c. green 15 15

177 "The Spoliarium" after Juan Luna

1957. Birth Centenary of Juan Luna (painter).
801 **177** 5c. red 15 10

1957. Inauguration of President C. P. Garcia and Vice-President D. Macapagal. Nos. 732/3 surch **GARCIA-MACAPAGAL INAUGURATION DEC. 30, 1957** and value.
802 5c. on 10c. blue 20 10
803 10c. on 20c. red 30 15

179 University of the Philippines

1958. Golden Jubilee of University of the Philippines.
804 **179** 5c. red 20 10

180 Pres. Garcia

1958. 12th Anniv of Republic.
805 **180** 5c. multicoloured 15 10
806 20c. multicoloured 30 15

181 Main Hospital Building, Quezon Institute

1958. Obligatory Tax. T.B. Relief Fund.
807 **181** 5c.+5c. green and red . . 10 10
808 10c.+5c. violet and red . . 20 10

182 The Immaculate Conception and Manila Cathedral

1958. Inauguration of Manila Cathedral.
809 **182** 5c. multicoloured 20 10

1959. Surch **One Centavo**.
810 1c. on 5c. red (No. 731) . . . 15 10

1959. 14th Anniv of Liberation. Nos. 704/5 surch.
812 **141** 1c. on 2c.+2c. red 10 10
813 – 6c. on 4c.+4c. violet . . . 20 10

186 Philippines Flag

187 Bulacan Seal

1959. Adoption of Philippine Constitution.
814 **186** 6c. red, blue and yellow 15 10
815 20c. red, blue and yellow 25 15

1959. Provincial Seals. (a) Bulacan Seal and 60th Anniv of Malolos Constitution.
816 **187** 6c. green 10 10
817 20c. red 20 10

(b) Capiz Seal and 11th Death Anniv of Pres. Roxas.
818 6c. brown 10 10
819 25c. violet 20 10

The shield within the Capiz seal bears the inset portrait of Pres. Roxas.

(c) Bacolod Seal.
820 6c. green 75 40
821 10c. purple . . . . 1·25 65

188 Scout at Campfire

1959. 10th World Scout Jamboree, Manila.
822 **188** 6c.+4c. red on yellow (postage) 25 20
823 6c.+4c. red 25 20
824 – 25c.+5c. blue on yellow 40 25
825 – 25c.+5c. blue 40 25

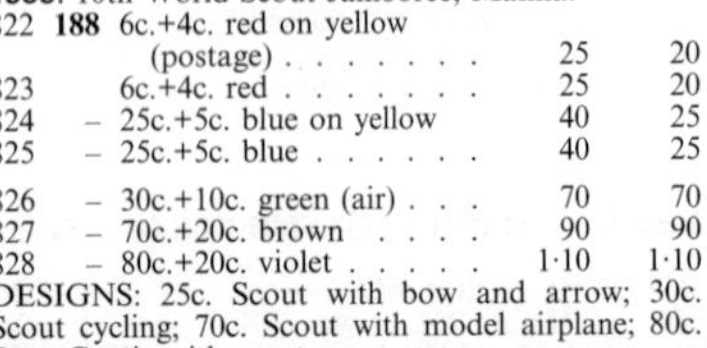

826 – 30c.+10c. green (air) . . . 70 70
827 – 70c.+20c. brown 90 90
828 – 80c.+20c. violet . . . . . 1·10 1·10

DESIGNS: 25c. Scout with bow and arrow; 30c. Scout cycling; 70c. Scout with model airplane; 80c. Pres. Garcia with scout.

190 Bohol Sanatorium

1959. Obligatory Tax. T.B. Relief Fund. Nos. 807/8 surch **HELP FIGHT T B** with Cross of Lorraine and value and new design (T **190**).
830 **181** 3c.+5c. on 5c.+5c. . . . 15 10
831 6c.+5c. on 10c.+5c. . . . 15 10
832 **190** 6c.+5c. green and red . . 15 10
833 25c.+5c. blue and red . . 25 15

191 Pagoda and Gardens at Camp John Hay

1959. 50th Anniv of Baguio.
834 **191** 6c. green 10 10
835 25c. red 30 20

1959. U.N. Day. Surch **6c UNITED NATIONS DAY**.
836 **132** 6c. on 18c. blue 15 10

193 Maria Cristina Falls

196 Dr. Jose Rizal

195

1959. World Tourist Conference, Manila.
837 **193** 6c. green and violet . . . 15 15
838 30c. green and brown . . 35 20

1959. No. 629 surch **One** and bars.
839 1c. on 4c. brown 15 10

1959. Centenary of Manila Athenaeum (school).
840 **195** 6c. blue 10 10
841 30c. red 30 20

1959.
842 **196** 6c. blue 15 10

197 Book of the Constitution

1960. 25th Anniv of Philippines Constitution.
844 **197** 6c. brn & gold (postage) 15 10
845 30c. blue and silver (air) 30 20

198 Congress Building

1960. 5th Anniv of Manila Pact.
846 **198** 6c. green 10 10
847 25c. orange 30 20

199 Sunset, Manila Bay

1960. World Refugee Year.
848 **199** 6c. multicoloured 25 15
849 25c. multicoloured 60 30

200 North American F-86 Sabre and Boeing P-12 Fighters

1960. Air. 25th Anniv of Philippine Air Force.
850 **200** 10c. red 30 15
851 20c. blue 55 35

1960. Surch.
852 **134** 1c. on 18c. blue 10 10
853 **161** 5c. on 18c. blue 25 20
854 **163** 5c. on 18c. red 30 15
855 **158** 10c. on 18c. orange & blue 25 15
856 **140** 10c. on 18c. blue 25 20

202 Lorraine Cross

204 Pres. Quezon

1960. 50th Anniv of Philippine Tuberculosis Society. Lorraine Cross and wreath in red and gold.
857 **202** 5c. green 15 10
858 6c. blue 15 10

1960. Obligatory Tax. T.B. Relief Fund. Surch **6+5 HELP PREVENT TB**.
859 **181** 6c.+5c. on 5c.+5c. green and red 20 15

1960.
860 **204** 1c. green 15 10

205 Basketball

1960. Olympic Games.
861 **205** 6c. brown & grn (postage) 15 10
862 – 10c. brown and purple . . 20 15
863 – 30c. brown and orange (air) 30 20
864 – 70c. purple and blue . . . 70 50

DESIGNS: 10c. Running; 30c. Rifle-shooting; 70c. Swimming.

206 Presidents Eisenhower and Garcia

1960. Visit of President Eisenhower.
865 **206** 6c. multicoloured 10 10
866 20c. multicoloured 25 15

207 "Mercury" and Globe

1961. Manila Postal Conference.
867 **207** 6c. multicoloured (postage) 15 10
868 30c. multicoloured (air) 25 15

1961. Surch **20 20**.
869 20c. on 25c. green (No. 734) 25 15

1961. 2nd National Scout Jamboree, Zamboanga. Nos. 822/5 surch **2nd National Boy Scout Jamboree Pasonanca Park** and value.
870 10c. on 6c.+4c. red on yellow 15 15
871 10c. on 6c.+4c. red 40 25
872 30c. on 25c.+5c. blue on yellow 30 15
873 30c. on 25c.+5c. blue 50 30

210 La Salle College

1961. 50th Anniv of La Salle College.
874 **210** 6c. multicoloured 15 10
875 10c. multicoloured 15 10

211 Rizal when Student, School and University Buildings

1961. Birth Centenary of Dr. Jose Rizal.
876 **211** 5c. multicoloured 10 10
877 – 6c. multicoloured 10 10
878 – 10c. brown and green . . 20 10
879 – 20c. turquoise and brown 30 15
880 – 30c. multicoloured 45 20
DESIGNS: 6c. Rizal and birthplace at Calamba, Laguna; 10c. Rizal, mother and father; 20c. Rizal extolling Luna and Hidalgo at Madrid; 30c. Rizal's execution.

1961. 15th Anniv of Republic. Optd **IKA 15 KAARAWAN Republika ng Pilipinas Hulyo 4, 1961.**
881 **198** 6c. green 25 25
882 25c. orange 40 40

213 Roxas Memorial T.B. Pavilion

1961. Obligatory Tax. T.B. Relief Fund.
883 **213** 6c.+5c. brown and red . . 20 15

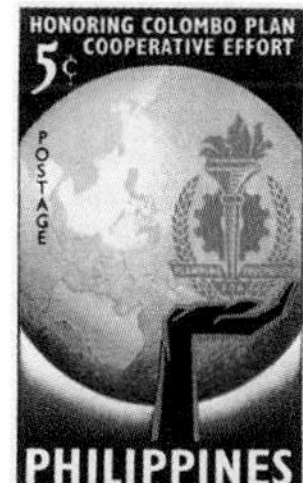

214 Globe, Plan Emblem and Supporting Hand

1961. 7th Anniv of Admission of Philippines to Colombo Plan.
884 **214** 5c. multicoloured 15 10
885 6c. multicoloured 15 10

1961. Philippine Amateur Athletic Federation's Golden Jubilee. Surch with P.A.A.F. monogram and **6c PAAF GOLDEN JUBILEE 1911 1961**.
886 **200** 6c. on 10c. red 25 20

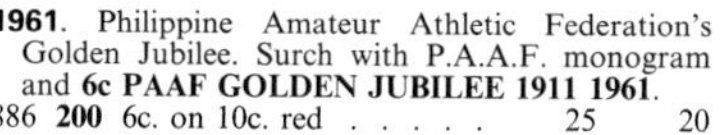

216 Typist

1961. Government Employees' Association.
887 **216** 6c. violet and brown . . . 15 10
888 10c. blue and brown . . . 25 15

1961. Inauguration of Pres. Macapagal and Vice-Pres. Pelaez. Surch **MACAPAGAL-PELAEZ DEC. 30, 1961 INAUGURATION 6c.**
889 6c. on 25c. violet (No. 819) 15 10

1962. Cross obliterated by Arms and surch **6s**.
890 **181** 6c. on 5c.+5c. green and red 15 15

220 Waling-Waling

221 A. Mabini (statesman)

1962. Orchids. Multicoloured.
892 5c. Type **220** 10 10
893 6c. White Mariposa 15 10
894 10c. "Dendrobium sanderii" 20 15
895 20c. Sanggumay 45 20

1962. New Currency.
896 – 1s. brown 10 10
897 **221** 3s. red 10 10
898 – 5s. red 10 10
899 – 6s. brown 10 10
900 – 6s. blue 10 10
901 – 10s. purple 10 10
902 – 20s. blue 10 10
903 – 30s. red 15 15
904 – 50s. violet 15 10
905 – 70s. blue 35 15
906 – 1p. green 40 15
907 – 1p. orange 40 15
PORTRAITS: 1s. M. L. Quezon; 5s. M. H. del Pilar; 6s. (2) J. Rizal (different); 10s. Father J. Burgos; 20s. Lapu-Lapu; 30s. Rajah Soliman; 50s. C. Arellano; 70s. S. Osmena; 1p. (No. 906) E. Jacinto; 1p. (No. 907) J. M. Panganiban.

225 Pres. Macapagal taking Oath

1962. Independence Day.
915 **225** 6s. multicoloured 10 10
916 10s. multicoloured 10 10
917 30s. multicoloured 20 15

226 Valdes Memorial T.B. Pavilion

1962. Obligatory Tax Stamps. T.B. Relief Fund. Cross in red.
918 **226** 6s.+5s. purple 10 10
919 30s.+5s. blue 15 10
920 70s.+5s. blue 40 15

227 Lake Taal

1962. Malaria Eradication.
921 **227** 6s. multicoloured 15 15
922 10s. multicoloured 20 15
923 70s. multicoloured 50 35

1962. Bicentenary of Diego Silang Revolt. No. 734 surch **1762 1962 BICENTENNIAL Diego Silang Revolt 20.**
924 20s. on 25c. green 25 10

1962. No. 742 with premium obliterated.
925 **149** 5c. blue 15 10

230 Dr. Rizal playing Chess

1962. Rizal Foundation Fund.
926 **230** 6s.+4s. green and mauve 15 10
927 – 30s.+5s. blue and purple 30 15
DESIGN: 30s. Dr. Rizal fencing.

1963. Surch.
928 **221** 1s. on 3s. red 15 10
929 – 5s. on 6s. brown (No. 899) 15 10

1963. Diego Silang Bicentenary Art and Philatelic Exhibition, G.P.O., Manila. No. 737 surch **1763 1963 DIEGO SILANG BICENTENNIAL ARPHEX** and value.
930 6c. on 2p. violet 10 10
931 20c. on 2p. violet 15 10
932 70c. on 2p. violet 30 15

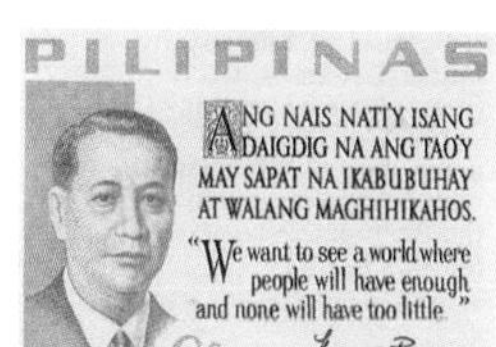

233 "We want to see ..." (Pres. Roxas)

1963. Presidential Sayings (1st issue).
933 **233** 6s. blue and black 15 10
934 30s. brown and black . . 30 15
See also Nos. 959/60, 981/2, 1015/16, 1034/5, 1055/6, 1148/9 and 1292/3.

234 Lorraine Cross on Map

1963. Obligatory Tax. T.B. Relief Fund. Cross in red.
935 **234** 6s.+5s. pink and violet . . 15 10
936 10s.+5s. pink and green 15 15
937 50s.+5s. pink & brown . . 30 20

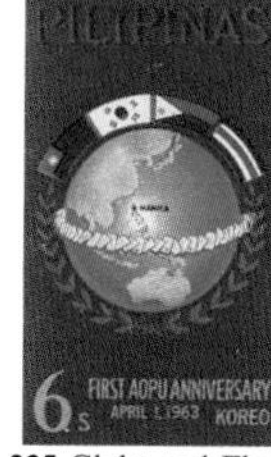

235 Globe and Flags

236 Centenary Emblem

1963. 1st Anniv of Asian-Oceanic Postal Union.
938 **235** 6s. multicoloured 15 15
939 20s. multicoloured 20 15

1963. Red Cross Centenary. Cross in red.
940 **236** 5s. grey and violet 15 10
941 6s. grey and blue 15 10
942 20s. grey and green . . . 30 15

237 Tinikling (dance)

1963. Folk Dances. Multicoloured.
943 5s. Type **237** 15 10
944 6s. Pandanggo sa Ilaw . . . 15 10
945 10s. Itik-Itik 15 10
946 20s. Singkil 35 10

238 Pres. Macapagal and Philippine Family

1963. President's Social-Economic Programme.
947 **238** 5s. multicoloured 10 10
948 6s. multicoloured 10 10
949 20s. multicoloured 20 10

239 Presidents' Meeting

1963. Visit of President Mateos of Mexico.
950 **239** 6s. multicoloured 25 10
951 30s. multicoloured 40 10

240 Bonifacio and Flag

1963. Birth Cent of Andres Bonifacio (patriot).
952 **240** 5s. multicoloured 15 10
953 6s. multicoloured 15 10
954 25s. multicoloured 30 20

241 Harvester

242 Bamboo Organ, Catholic Church, Las Pinas

1963. Freedom from Hunger.
956 **241** 6s. multicoloured (postage) 10 10
957 30s. multicoloured (air) 25 15
958 50s. multicoloured 40 15

1963. Presidential Sayings (2nd issue). As T **233** but with portrait and saying changed.
959 6s. black and violet 15 10
960 30s. black and green 35 15
PORTRAIT AND SAYING: Pres. Magsaysay, "I believe ...".

1964. Las Pinas Organ Commemoration.
961 **242** 5s. multicoloured 15 10
962 6s. multicoloured 15 10
963 20s. multicoloured 40 25

243 A. Mabini (patriot)

245 S.E.A.T.O. Emblems and Flags

244 Negros Oriental T.B. Pavilion

1964. Birth Centenary of A. Mabini.
964 **243** 6s. gold and violet 15 10
965 10s. gold and brown . . . 15 15
966 30s. gold and green . . . 25 15

1964. Obligatory Tax. T.B. Relief Fund. Cross in red.
967 **244** 5s.+5s. purple 15 10
968 6s.+5s. blue 10 10
969 30s.+5s. brown 15 15
970 70s.+5s. green 30 20

1964. 10th Anniv of S.E.A.T.O.
971 **245** 6s. multicoloured 10 10
972 10s. multicoloured 10 10
973 25s. multicoloured 20 15

246 President signing the Land Reform Code

247 Basketball

1964. Agricultural Land Reform Code. President and inscr at foot in brown, red and sepia.
974 **246** 3s. green (postage) . . . 10 10
975 6s. blue 10 10
976 30s. brown (air) 20 15

1964. Olympic Games, Tokyo. Sport in brown. Perf or imperf.
977 **247** 6s. blue and gold 10 10
978 – 10s. pink and gold . . . 15 10
979 – 20s. yellow and gold . . . 25 15
980 – 30s. green and gold . . . 40 15
SPORTS: 10s. Relay-racing, 20s. Hurdling; 30s. Football.

1965. Presidential Sayings (3rd issue). As T **233** but with portrait and saying changed.
981 6s. black and green 10 10
982 30s. black and purple 35 15
PORTRAIT AND SAYING: Pres. Quirino, "So live ...".

248 Presidents Luebke and Macapagal

1965. Visit of President of German Federal Republic.
983 **248** 6s. multicoloured 10 10
984 10s. multicoloured 10 10
985 25s. multicoloured 10 10

249 Meteorological Emblems

250 Pres. Kennedy

1965. Cent of Philippines Meteorological Services.
986 **249** 6s. multicoloured 10 10
987 20s. multicoloured 10 10
988 50s. multicoloured 25 15

1965. John F. Kennedy (U.S. President) Commemoration.
989 **250** 6s. multicoloured 10 10
990 10s. multicoloured 10 10
991 30s. multicoloured 20 10

251 King Bhumibol and Queen Sirikit, Pres. Macapagal and Wife

1965. Visit of King and Queen of Thailand.
992 **251** 2s. multicoloured 10 10
993 6s. multicoloured 10 10
994 30s. multicoloured 20 10

252 Princess Beatrix and Mrs. Macapagal

1965. Visit of Princess Beatrix of the Netherlands.
995 **252** 2s. multicoloured 10 10
996 6s. multicoloured 10 10
997 10s. multicoloured 15 10

1965. Obligatory Tax. T.B. Relief Fund. Surch.
998 **244** 1s.+5s. on 6s.+5s. . . . 15 10
999 3s.+5s. on 6s.+5s. . . . 20 15

254 Hand holding Cross and Rosary

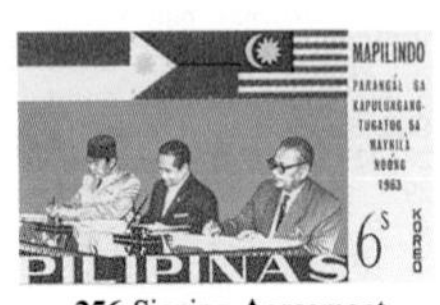
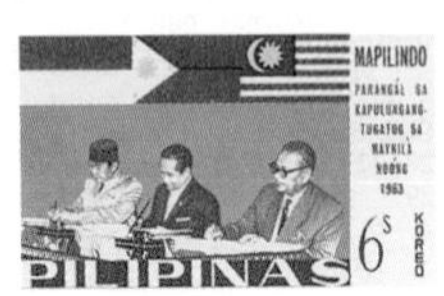

256 Signing Agreement

1965. 400th Anniv of Philippines Christianisation. Multicoloured.
1000 3s. Type **254** (postage) . . . 15 10
1001 6s. Legaspi-Urdaneta, monument 15 10
1002 30s. Baptism of Filipinos by Father Urdaneta, Cebu (horiz) (48 × 27 mm) (air) 30 15
1003 70s. "Way of the Cross"–ocean map of Christian voyagers' route, Spain to the Philippines (horiz) (48 × 27 mm) . . . . 1·00 30

1965. "MAPILINDO" Conference, Manila.
1005 **256** 6s. blue, red and yellow 10 10
1006 10s. multicoloured . . . 10 10
1007 25s. multicoloured . . . 25 15
The above stamps depict Pres. Sukarno of Indonesia, former Pres. Macapagal of the Philippines and Prime Minister Tunku Abdul Rahman of Malaysia.

257 Cyclists and Globe

259 Dr. A. Regidor

1965. 2nd Asian Cycling Championships, Philippines.
1008 **257** 6s. multicoloured 10 10
1009 10s. multicoloured . . . 20 15
1010 25s. multicoloured . . . 40 15

1965. Inauguration of Pres. Marcos and Vice-Pres. Lopez. Nos. 926/7 surch **MARCOS-LOPEZ INAUGURATION DEC. 30, 1965** and value.
1011 **230** 10s. on 6s.+4s. 15 10
1012 – 30s. on 30s.+5s. 35 15

1966. Regidor (patriot) Commemoration.
1013 **259** 6s. blue 10 10
1014 30s. brown 20 10

1966. Presidential Sayings (4th issue). As T **233** but with portrait and saying changed.
1015 6s. black and red 15 10
1016 30s. black and blue 35 15
PORTRAIT AND SAYING: Pres. Aguinaldo, "Have faith ...".

1966. Campaign Against Smuggling. No. 900 optd **HELP ME STOP SMUGGLING Pres. MARCOS**.
1017 6s. blue 10 10

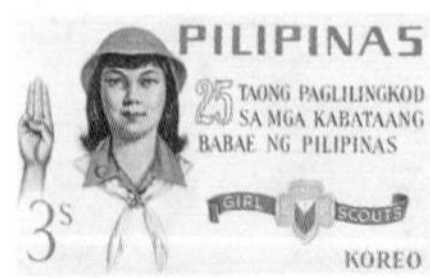

261 Girl Scout

1966. Silver Jubilee of Philippines Girl Scouts.
1018 **261** 3s. multicoloured 10 10
1019 6s. multicoloured 15 10
1020 20s. multicoloured . . . 20 15

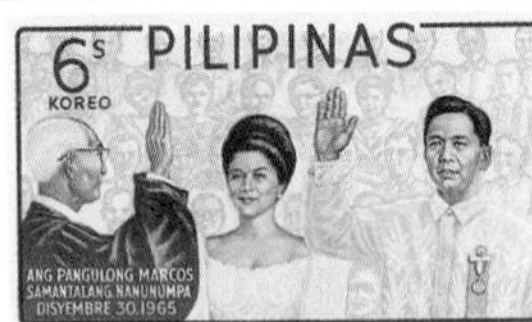

262 Pres. Marcos taking Oath

1966. Inauguration (1965) of Pres. Marcos.
1021 **262** 6s. multicoloured 10 10
1022 20s. multicoloured . . . 15 15
1023 30s. multicoloured . . . 25 25

263 Manila Seal and Historical Scenes

1966. Introduction of New Seal for Manila.
1024 **263** 6s. multicoloured 15 15
1025 30s. multicoloured . . . 25 15

264 Bank Facade and 1 peso Coin

1966. 50th Anniv of Philippines National Bank. Mult.
1026 6s. Type **264** 10 10
1027 10s. Old and new bank buildings 15 10

266 Bank Building

1966. 60th Anniv of Postal Savings Bank.
1029 **266** 6s. violet, yellow & green 10 10
1030 10s. red, yellow and green 15 10
1031 20s. blue, yellow & green 20 15

1966. Manila Summit Conference. Nos. 1021 and 1023 optd **MANILA SUMMIT CONFERENCE 1966 7 NATIONS** and emblem.
1032 **262** 6s. multicoloured 10 10
1033 30s. multicoloured . . . 30 15

1966. Presidential Sayings (5th issue). As T **233** but with portrait and saying changed.
1034 6s. black and brown 10 10
1035 30s. black and blue 35 15
PORTRAIT AND SAYING: Pres. Laurel; "No one can love the Filipinos better ...".

1967. 50th Anniv of Lions International. Nos. 977/80 optd with Lions emblem and **50th ANNIVERSARY LIONS INTERNATIONAL 1967**.Imperf.
1036 **247** 6c. blue and gold 10 10
1037 – 10c. pink and gold . . . 15 10
1038 – 20c. yellow and gold . . 25 20
1039 – 30c. green and gold . . . 40 20

269 "Succour" (after painting by F. Amorsolo)

1967. 25th Anniv of Battle of Bataan.
1040 **269** 5s. multicoloured 15 10
1041 20s. multicoloured . . . 25 15
1042 2p. multicoloured . . . 90 30

1967. Nos. 900 and 975 surch.
1043 – 4s. on 6s. blue 15 10
1044 **246** 5s. on 6s. blue 15 10

271 Stork-billed Kingfisher

1967. Obligatory Tax. T.B. Relief Fund. Birds. Multicoloured.
1045 1s.+5s. Type **271** 10 10
1046 5s.+5s. Rufous hornbill . . 25 20
1047 10s.+5s. Philippine eagle . . 55 35
1048 30s.+5s. Great-billed parrot 90 65
See also Nos. 1113/16.

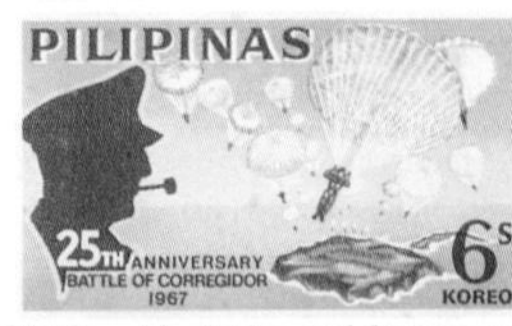

272 Gen. MacArthur and Paratroopers landing on Corregidor

1967. 25th Anniv of Battle of Corregidor.
1049 **272** 6s. multicoloured 10 10
1050 5p. multicoloured . . . 3·50 2·00

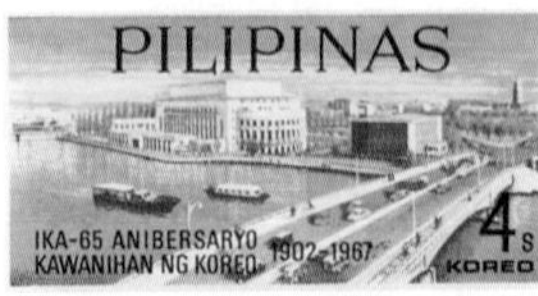

273 Bureau of Posts Building, Manila

1967. 65th Anniv of Philippines Bureau of Posts.
1051 **273** 4s. multicoloured 20 10
1052 20s. multicoloured . . . 30 15
1053 50s. multicoloured . . . 55 20

274 Escaping from Eruption

1967. Obligatory Tax. Taal Volcano Eruption (1965) (1st issue).
1054 **274** 70s. multicoloured . . . 70 30
For compulsory use on foreign air mail where the rate exceeds 70s. in aid of Taal Volcano Rehabilitation Committee.
See also No. 1071.

1967. Presidential Sayings (6th issue). As T **233** but with portrait and saying changed.
1055 10s. black and blue 15 10
1056 30s. black and violet 30 15
PORTRAIT AND SAYING: Pres. Quezon. "Social justice is far more beneficial ...".

275 "The Holy Family" (Filipino version)

1967. Christmas.
1057 **275** 10s. multicoloured . . . 10 10
1058 40s. multicoloured . . . 40 20

276 Pagoda, Pres. Marcos and Chiang Kai-shek

1967. China–Philippines Friendship.
1059 **276** 5s. multicoloured 10 10
1060 – 10s. multicoloured . . . 20 15
1061 – 20s. multicoloured . . . 45 15
DESIGNS (with portraits of Pres. Marcos and Chiang Kai-shek): 10s. Gateway, Chinese Garden, Rizal Park, Luneta; 20s. Chinese Garden, Rizal Park, Luneta.

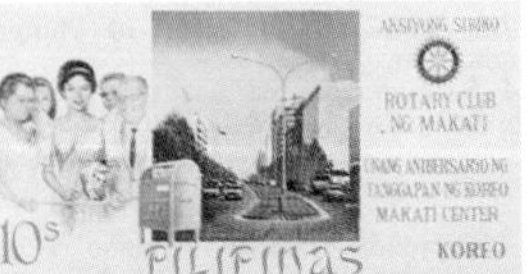

277 Ayala Avenue, Manila, Inaugural Ceremony and Rotary Badge

1968. 1st Anniv of Makati Centre Post Office, Manila.
1062 **277** 10s. multicoloured . . . 10 10
1063 20s. multicoloured . . . 15 10
1064 40s. multicoloured . . . 35 15

1968. Surch.
1065 – 5s. on 6s. (No. 981) . . 15 10
1066 – 5s. on 6s. (No. 1034) . . 15 10
1067 **244** 10s. on 6s.+5s. 20 10

280 Calderon, Barasoain Church and Constitution

1968. Birth Centenary of Felipe G. Calderon (lawyer and author of Malolos Constitution).
1068 **280** 10s. multicoloured . . . 10 10
1069 40s. multicoloured . . . 20 10
1070 75s. multicoloured . . . 40 25

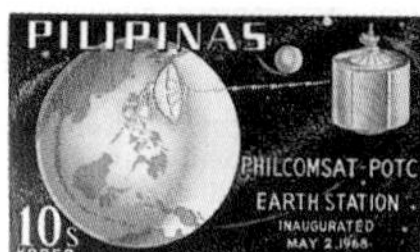
281 Eruption **282** "Philcomsat", Earth Station and Globe

1968. Taal Volcano Eruption (1965) (2nd issue).
1071 **281** 70s. multicoloured . . . 40 20

Two issues were prepared by an American Agency under a contract signed with the Philippine postal authority but at the last moment this contract was cancelled by the Philippine Government. In the meanwhile the stamps had been on sale in the U.S.A. but they were never issued in the Philippines and they had no postal validity.

They comprise a set for the Mexican Olympic Games in the values 1, 2, 3 and 15s. postage and 50, 75s., 1, 2p. airmail and a set in memory of J. F. Kennedy and Robert Kennedy in the values 1, 2, 3s. postage and 5, 10p. airmail.

1968. Inauguration of "Philcomsat"–POTC Earth Station, Tanay, Rizal, Luzon.
1072 **282** 10s. multicoloured . . . 10 15
1073 40s. multicoloured . . . 30 15
1074 75s. multicoloured . . . 60 20

283 "Tobacco Production" (mural)

1968. Philippines Tobacco Industry.
1075 **283** 10s. multicoloured . . . 10 10
1076 40s. multicoloured . . . 15 10
1077 70s. multicoloured . . . 35 20

284 "Kudyapi"

1968. St. Cecilia's Day. Musical Instruments. Mult.
1078 10s. Type **284** 15 10
1079 20s. "Ludag" 15 15
1080 30s. "Kulintangan" 35 20
1081 50s. "Subing" 50 25

285 Concordia College **286** Children singing Carols

1968. Centenary of Concordia Women's College.
1082 **285** 10s. multicoloured . . . 10 10
1083 20s. multicoloured . . . 15 10
1084 70s. multicoloured . . . 50 25

1968. Christmas.
1085 **286** 10s. multicoloured . . . 10 10
1086 40s. multicoloured . . . 20 10
1087 75s. multicoloured . . . 60 30

287 Philippine Tarsier

1969. Philippines Fauna. Multicoloured.
1088 2s. Type **287** 15 15
1089 10s. Tamarau 15 15
1090 20s. Water buffalo 25 20
1091 75s. Greater Malay chevrotain . . . . 1·25 50

288 President Aguinaldo and Cavite Building

1969. Birth Centenary of President Amilio Aguinaldo.
1092 **288** 10s. multicoloured . . . 10 10
1093 40s. multicoloured . . . 20 10
1094 70s. multicoloured . . . 35 15

289 Rotary Emblem and "Bastion of San Andres"

1969. 50th Anniv of Manila Rotary Club.
1095 **289** 10s. mult (postage) . . . 10 10
1096 40s. multicoloured (air) 25 10
1097 75s. multicoloured . . . 50 20

290 Senator C. M. Recto **292** Jose Rizal College

1969. Recto Commemoration.
1098 **290** 10s. purple 15 10

1969. Philatelic Week. No. 1051 optd **PHILATELIC WEEK NOV. 24-30, 1968**.
1099 **273** 4s. multicoloured 25 10

1969. 50th Anniv of Jose Rizal College, Mandaluyong, Rizal.
1100 **292** 10s. multicoloured . . . 10 10
1101 40s. multicoloured . . . 20 10
1102 50s. multicoloured . . . 30 15

1969. 4th National Boy Scout Jamboree, Palayan City. No. 1019 surch **4th NATIONAL BOY SCOUT JAMBOREE PALAYAN CITY–MAY, 1969 5s.**
1103 5s. on 6s. multicoloured . . 20 15

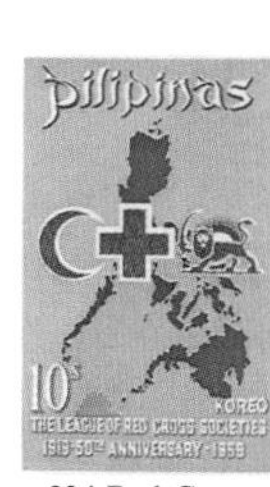

294 Red Cross Emblems and Map **295** Pres. and Mrs. Marcos harvesting Rice

1969. 50th Anniv of League of Red Cross Societies.
1104 **294** 10s. red, blue and grey 10 10
1105 40s. red, blue and cobalt 25 15
1106 75s. red, brown and buff 40 25

1969. "Rice for Progress".
1107 **295** 10s. multicoloured . . . 10 10
1108 40s. multicoloured . . . 25 15
1109 75s. multicoloured . . . 40 25

296 "The Holy Child of Leyte" (statue)

1969. 80th Anniv of Return of the "Holy Child of Leyte" to Tacloban.
1110 **296** 5s. mult (postage) . . . 10 10
1111 10s. multicoloured . . . 15 10
1112 40s. multicoloured (air) 45 20

1969. Obligatory Tax. T.B. Relief Fund. Birds as T **271**.
1113 1s.+5s. Common gold-backed woodpecker . . . 10 10
1114 5s.+5s. Philippine trogon . . 25 15
1115 10s.+5s. Johnstone's (inscr "Mt. Apo") lorikeet . . . 55 35
1116 40s.+5s. Scarlet (inscr "Johnstone's") minivet . . 85 50

297 Bank Building

1969. Inauguration of Philippines Development Bank, Makati, Rizal.
1117 **297** 10s. black, blue and green 20 10
1118 40s. black, purple and green . . . . 1·25 40
1119 75s. black, brown & grn 1·75 90

298 "Philippine Birdwing"

1969. Philippine Butterflies. Multicoloured.
1120 10s. Type **298** 25 15
1121 20s. Tailed jay 50 20
1122 30s. Red Helen 55 30
1123 40s. Birdwing 80 45

299 Children of the World

1969. 15th Anniv of Universal Children's Day.
1124 **299** 10s. multicoloured . . . 10 10
1125 20s. multicoloured . . . 10 10
1126 30s. multicoloured . . . 25 15

300 Memorial and Outline of Landing **303** Melchora Aquino

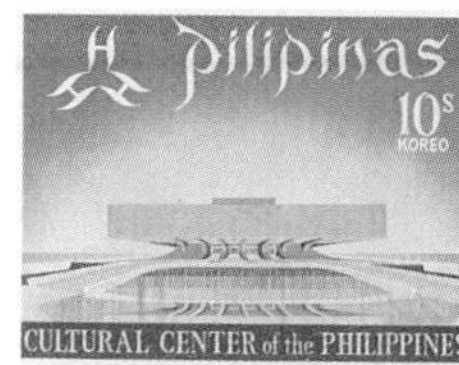
301 Cultural Centre

1969. 25th Anniv of U.S. Forces' Landing on Leyte.
1127 **300** 5s. multicoloured 10 10
1128 10s. multicoloured . . . 15 15
1129 40s. multicoloured . . . 40 20

1969. Cultural Centre, Manila.
1130 **301** 10s. blue 10 10
1131 30s. purple 30 15

1969. Philatelic Week. Nos. 943/6 (Folk Dances) optd **1969 PHILATELIC WEEK** or surch also.
1132 5s. multicoloured 20 15
1133 5s. on 6s. multicoloured . . 20 15
1134 10s. multicoloured 30 20
1135 10s. on 20s. multicoloured 40 20

1969. 50th Death Anniv of Melchora Aquino, "Tandang Sora" (Grand Old Woman of the Revolution).
1136 **303** 10s. multicoloured . . . 10 10
1137 20s. multicoloured . . . 15 10
1138 30s. multicoloured . . . 30 15

1969. 2nd-term Inaug of President Marcos. Surch **PASINAYA, IKA-2 PANUNUNGKULAN PANGULONG FERDINAND E. MARCOS DISYEMBRE 30, 1969.**
1139 **262** 5s. on 6s. multicoloured 20 10

305 Ladle and Steel Mills

1970. Iligan Integrated Steel Mills.
1140 **305** 10s. multicoloured . . . 35 10
1141 20s. multicoloured . . . 90 30
1142 30s. multicoloured . . . 1·40 45

1970. Nos. 900, 962 and 964 surch.
1143 – 4s. on 6s. blue 20 10
1144 **242** 5s. on 6s. multicoloured 20 10
1145 **243** 5s. on 6s. multicoloured 20 10

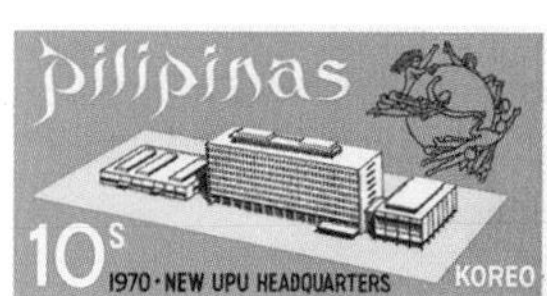
307 New U.P.U. Headquarters Building

1970. New U.P.U. Headquarters Building, Berne.
1146 **307** 10s. ultramarine, yellow and blue 10 10
1147 30s. blue, yellow and green 25 15

1970. Presidential Sayings (7th issue). As T **233** but with portrait and saying changed.
1148 10s. black and purple . . . 10 10
1149 40s. black and green 35 15
PORTRAIT AND SAYING: Pres. Osmena, "Ante todo el bien de nuestro pueblo" ("The well-being of our nation comes above all").

308 Dona Julia V. de Ortigas and T.B. Society Headquarters

1970. Obligatory Tax. T.B. Relief Fund.
1150 **308** 1s.+5s. multicoloured . . 15 10
1151 5s.+5s. multicoloured . . 20 10
1152 30s.+5s. multicoloured 60 25
1153 70s.+5s. multicoloured 85 35

309 I.C.S.W. Emblem

1970. 15th Int Conference on Social Welfare.
1154 **309** 10s. multicoloured . . . 10 10
1155 20s. multicoloured . . . 15 10
1156 30s. multicoloured . . . 20 15

310 "Crab" (after sculpture by A. Calder)

1970. "Fight Cancer" Campaign.
1157 **310** 10s. multicoloured . . . 10 10
1158 40s. multicoloured . . . 20 10
1159 50s. multicoloured . . . 30 15

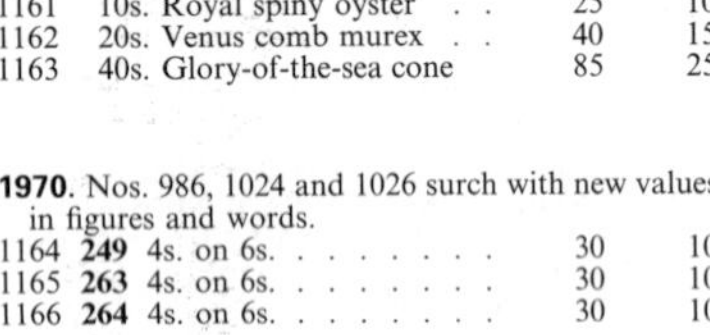

311 Scaled Tridacna

1970. Sea Shells. Multicoloured.
1160 5s. Type **311** 10 10
1161 10s. Royal spiny oyster . . 25 10
1162 20s. Venus comb murex . . 40 15
1163 40s. Glory-of-the-sea cone 85 25

1970. Nos. 986, 1024 and 1026 surch with new values in figures and words.
1164 **249** 4s. on 6s. 30 10
1165 **263** 4s. on 6s. 30 10
1166 **264** 4s. on 6s. 30 10

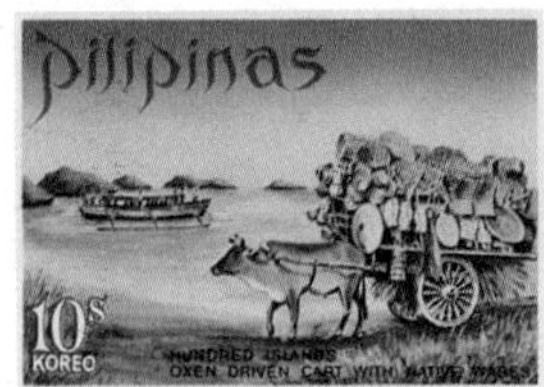

313 The "Hundred Islands" and Ox-cart

1970. Tourism (1st series). Multicoloured.
1167 10s. Type **313** 15 15
1168 20s. Tree-house, Pasonanca Park, Zamboanga City . . 20 15
1169 30s. "Filipino" (statue) and sugar plantation, Negros Island 30 25
1170 2p. Calesa (horse-carriage) and Miagao Church, Iloilo . . . . 1·90 75
See also Nos. 1186/9, 1192/5 and 1196/9.

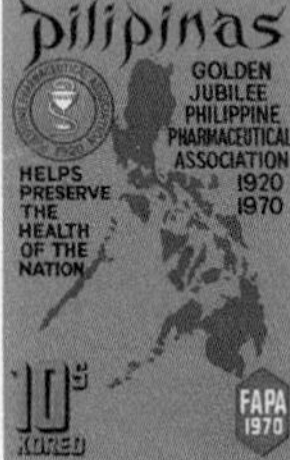

314 Map of the Philippines

318 Mariano Ponce

317 Pope Paul VI and Map

1970. Golden Jubilee of Philippine Pharmaceutical Association.
1171 **314** 10s. multicoloured . . . 15 10
1172 50s. multicoloured . . . 40 15

1970. U.P.U./A.O.P.U. Regional Seminar, Manila. No. 938 surch **UPU-AOPU REGIONAL SEMINAR NOV. 23 - DEC. 5, 1970 TEN 10s**.
1173 **235** 10s. on 6s. multicoloured 25 15

1970. Philatelic Week. No. 977 surch **1970 PHILATELIC WEEK 10s TEN**.
1174 **247** 10s. on 6s. brown, blue and gold 20 10

1970. Pope Paul's Visit to the Philippines.
1175 **317** 10s. mult (postage) . . . 15 10
1176 30s. multicoloured . . . 35 10
1177 40s. multicoloured (air) 45 15

1970.
1178 **318** 10s. red 15 10
1179 – 15s. brown 15 10
1180 – 40s. red 30 10
1181 – 1p. blue 60 15
DESIGNS: 15s. Josefa Llanes Escoda; 40s. Gen. Miguel Malvar; 1p. Julian Felipe.

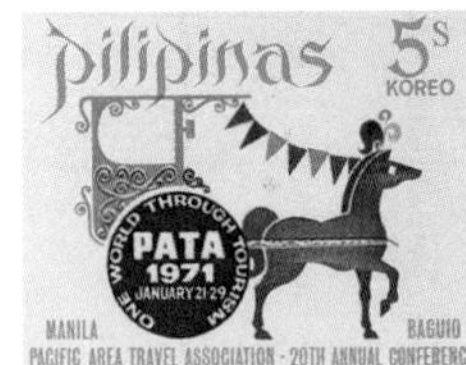

320 "PATA" Horse and Carriage

1971. 20th PATA Conference and Workshop, Manila.
1183 **320** 5s. multicoloured 10 10
1184 10s. multicoloured . . . 15 15
1185 70s. multicoloured . . . 50 25

1971. Tourism (2nd series). Views as T **313**. Multicoloured.
1186 10s. Nayong Pilipino resort 20 10
1187 20s. Fish farm, Iloilo . . . 30 15
1188 30s. Pagsanjan Falls 50 20
1189 5p. Watch-tower, Punta Cruz . . . . 2·10 1·10

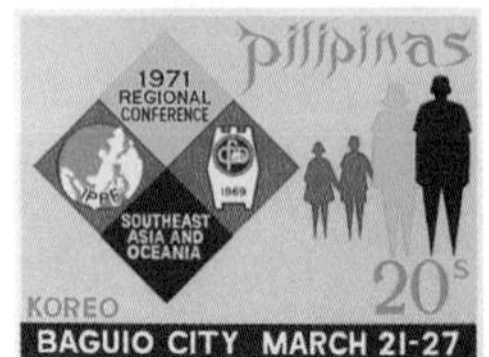

321 Emblem and Family

1971. Regional Conference of International Planned Parenthood Federation for South-East Asia and Oceania.
1190 **321** 20s. multicoloured . . . 10 10
1191 40s. multicoloured . . . 20 10

1971. Tourism (3rd series). As T **313**. Mult.
1192 10s. Aguinaldo pearl farm 20 10
1193 20s. Coral-diving, Davao . . 35 15
1194 40s. Taluksengay Mosque 55 20
1195 1p. Ifugao woman and Banaue rice-terraces . . . 1·00 30

1971. Tourism (4th series). As T **313**. Mult.
1196 10s. Cannon and Filipino vintas, Fort del Pilar . . 20 10
1197 30s. Magellan's Cross, Cebu City 25 15
1198 50s. "Big Jar", Calamba, Laguna (Rizal's birthplace) 50 25
1199 70s. Mayon Volcano and diesel train . . . . 2·50 65

1971. Surch **FIVE 5s**.
1200 **264** 5s. on 6s. multicoloured 30 10

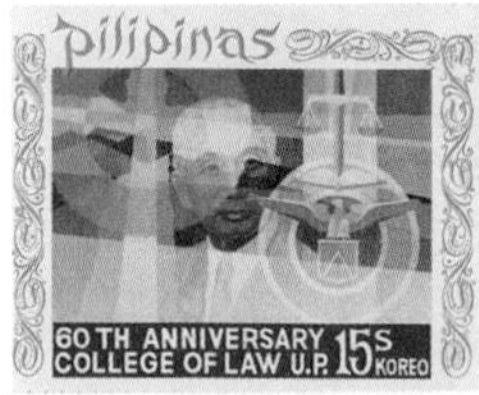

323 G. A. Malcolm (founder) and Law Symbols

1971. 60th Anniv of Philippines College of Law.
1201 **323** 15s. mult (postage) . . . 15 15
1202 1p. multicoloured (air) 45 30

324 Commemorative Seal

1971. 400th Anniv of Manila.
1203 **324** 10s. multicoloured (postage) 15 10
1204 1p. multicoloured (air) 50 20

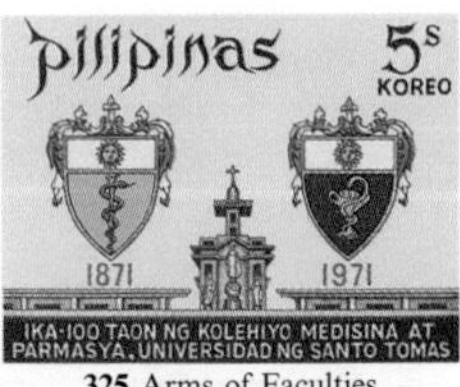

325 Arms of Faculties

1971. Centenaries of Faculties of Medicine and Surgery, and of Pharmacy, Santo Tomas University.
1205 **325** 5s. mult (postage) . . . 15 10
1206 2p. multicoloured (air) 75 30

1971. University Presidents' World Congress, Manila. Surch **MANILA MCMLXX1 CONGRESS OF UNIVERSITY PRESIDENTS 5s FIVE** and emblem.
1207 **266** 5s. on 6s. violet, yellow and green 15 10

327 "Our Lady of Guia"

1971. 400th Anniv of "Our Lady of Guia", Ermita, Manila.
1208 **327** 10s. multicoloured . . . 20 10
1209 75s. multicoloured . . . 70 25

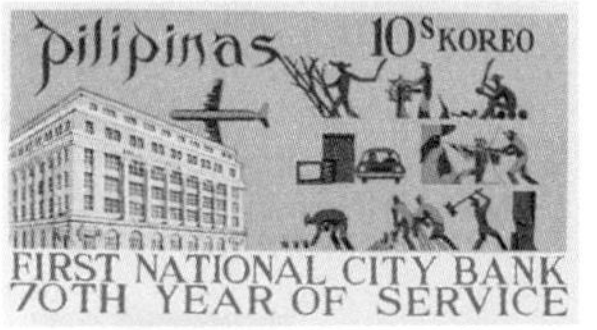

328 Bank and "Customers"

1971. 70th Anniv of First National City Bank.
1210 **328** 10s. multicoloured . . . 15 10
1211 30s. multicoloured . . . 20 10
1212 1p. multicoloured . . . 40 25

1971. Surch in figure and word.
1213 **259** 4s. on 6s. blue 15 10
1214 5s. on 6s. blue 15 10

1971. Philatelic Week. Surch **1971 - PHILATELIC WEEK 5s FIVE**.
1215 **266** 5s. on 6s. violet, yellow and green 20 10

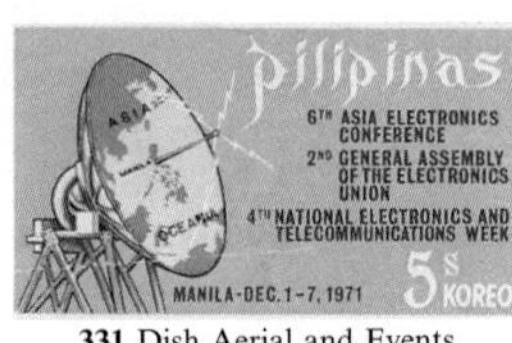

331 Dish Aerial and Events

1972. 6th Asian Electronics Conference, Manila (1971) and Related Events.
1216 **331** 5s. multicoloured 10 10
1217 40s. multicoloured . . . 25 15

332 Fathers Burgos, Gomez and Zamora

1972. Centenary of Martyrdom of Fathers Burgos, Gomez and Zamora.
1218 **332** 5s. multicoloured 15 10
1219 60s. multicoloured . . . 50 25

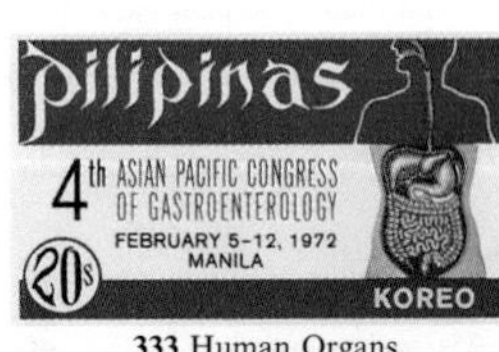

333 Human Organs

1972. 4th Asian–Pacific Gastro-enterological Congress, Manila.
1220 **333** 20s. mult (postage) . . . 15 10
1221 40s. multicoloured (air) 30 10

1972. Surch **5s FIVE**.
1222 **263** 5s. on 6s. multicoloured 45 10

1972. No. O914 with optd **G.O.** obliterated by bars.
1223 50s. violet 50 25

1972. Surch.
1224 **245** 10s. on 6s. multicoloured 30 10
1225 **251** 10s. on 6s. multicoloured 30 10
1226 – 10s. on 6s. black and red (No. 1015) 30 10

336 Memorial Gardens, Manila

1972. Tourism. "Visit Asean Lands" Campaign.
1227 **336** 5s. multicoloured 15 10
1228 50s. multicoloured . . . 25 15
1229 60s. multicoloured . . . 50 20

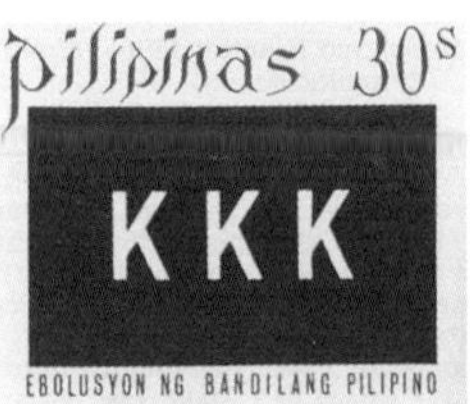

337 "KKK" Flag

1972. Evolution of Philippines' Flag.
1230 **337** 30s. red and blue 55 25
1231 – 30s. red and blue 55 25
1232 – 30s. red and blue 55 25
1233 – 30s. black and blue . . . 55 25
1234 – 30s. red and blue 55 25
1235 – 30s. red and blue 55 25
1236 – 30s. red and blue 55 25
1237 – 30s. red and blue 55 25
1238 – 30s. black, red and blue 55 25
1239 – 30s. yellow, red and blue 55 25
FLAGS: No. 1231, Three "K"s in pyramid; No. 1232, Single "K"; No. 1233, "K", skull and crossbones; No. 1234, Three "K"s and sun in triangle; No. 1235, Sun and three "K"s; No. 1236, Ancient Tagalog "K" within sun; No. 1237, Face in sun; No. 1238, Tricolor; No. 1239, Present national flag—sun and stars within triangle, two stripes.

338 Mabol, Santol and Papaya

1972. Obligatory Tax. T.B. Relief Fund. Fruits. Mult.
1240 1s.+5s. Type **338** 15 10
1241 10s.+5s. Bananas, balimbang and mangosteen 25 15
1242 40s.+5s. Guava, mango, duhat and susongkalabac 50 20
1243 1p.+5s. Orange, pineapple, lanzones and sirhuelas . . 90 40

339 Bridled Parrotfish

1972. Fishes. Multicoloured.
1244 5s. Type **339** (postage) . . . 10 10
1245 10s. Klein's butterflyfish . . 20 10
1246 20s. Moorish idol 40 15
1247 50s. Two-spined angelfish (air) . . . . 1·25 40

340 Bank Headquarters

1972. 25th Anniv of Philippines Development Bank.
1248 **340** 10s. multicoloured . . . 10 10
1249 20s. multicoloured . . . 15 10
1250 60s. multicoloured . . . 30 15

341 Pope Paul VI

1972. 1st Anniv of Pope Paul's Visit to Philippines.
1251 **341** 10s. mult (postage) . . . 10 10
1252 50s. multicoloured . . . 40 20
1253 60s. multicoloured (air) 50 25

1972. Various stamps surch.
1254 **240** 10s. on 6s. (No. 953) . . 30 10
1255 – 10s. on 6s. (No. 959) . . 30 10
1256 **250** 10s. on 6s. (No. 989) . . 30 10

343 "La Barca de Aqueronte" (Hidalgo)

1972. 25th Anniv of Stamps and Philatelic Division, Philippines Bureau of Posts. Filipino Paintings. Multicoloured.
1257 5s. Type **343** 10 10
1258 10s. "Afternoon Meal of the Rice Workers" (Amorsolo) 20 10
1259 30s. "Espana y Filipinas" (Luna) (27 × 60 mm) . . . 40 15
1260 70s. "The Song of Maria Clara" (Amorsolo) . . . 70 35

344 Lamp, Emblem and Nurse

1972. 50th Anniv of Philippine Nurses Assn.
1261 **344** 5s. multicoloured 10 10
1262 10s. multicoloured . . . 10 10
1263 70s. multicoloured . . . 40 25

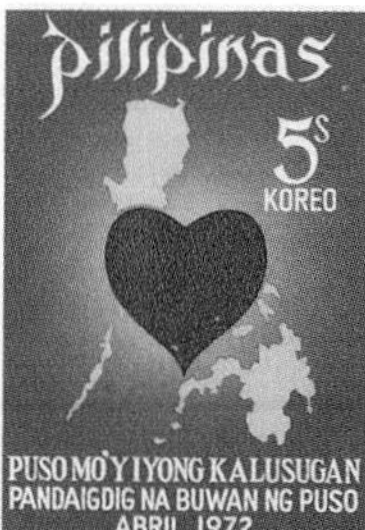

345 Heart on Map

1972. World Heart Month.
1264 **345** 5s. red, green and violet 10 10
1265 10s. red, green and blue 10 10
1266 30s. red, blue and green 25 20

346 "The First Mass" (C. V. Francisco)

1972. 450th Anniv of 1st Mass in Limasawa (1971).
1267 **346** 10s. mult (postage) . . . 10 10
1268 60s. multicoloured (air) 40 20

1972. Asia-Pacific Scout Conference, Manila. Various stamps surch **ASIA PACIFIC SCOUT CONFERENCE NOV, 1972** and value.
1269 **233** 10s. on 6s. (No. 933) . . 25 10
1270 **240** 10s. on 6s. (No. 953) . . 25 10
1271 – 10s. on 6s. (No. 981) . . 25 10

348 Olympic Emblems and Torch

1972. Olympic Games, Munich.
1272 **348** 5s. multicoloured 10 10
1273 10s. multicoloured . . . 15 10
1274 70s. multicoloured . . . 70 40

1972. Philatelic Week. Nos. 950 and 983 surch **1972 PHILATELIC WEEK TEN 10s.**
1275 **239** 10s. on 6s. multicoloured 25 10
1276 **248** 10s. on 6s. multicoloured 25 10

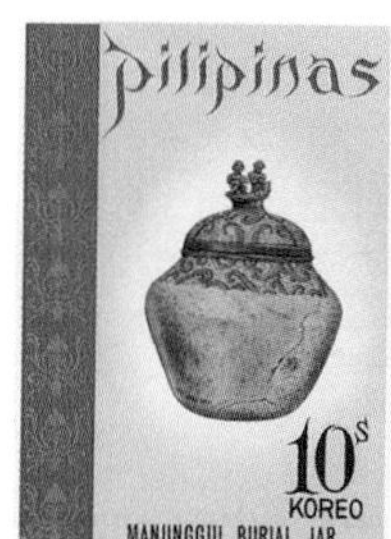

350 Manunggul Burial Jar

1972. Philippine Archaeological Discoveries. Multicoloured.
1277 10s. Type **350** 20 10
1278 10s. Ritual earthenware vessel 20 10
1279 10s. Metal pot 20 10
1280 10s. Earthenware vessel . . 20 10

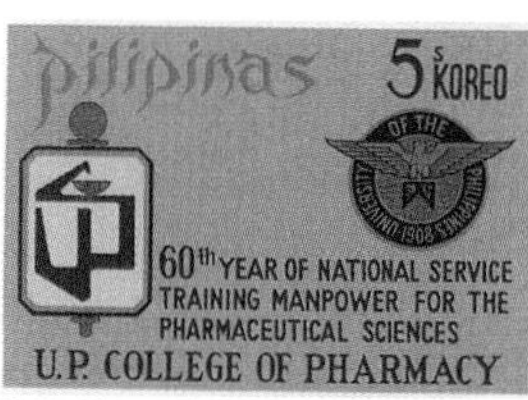

351 Emblems of Pharmacy and University of the Philippines

1972. 60th Anniv of National Training for Pharmaceutical Sciences, University of the Philippines.
1281 **351** 5s. multicoloured 10 10
1282 10s. multicoloured . . . 10 10
1283 30s. multicoloured . . . 25 15

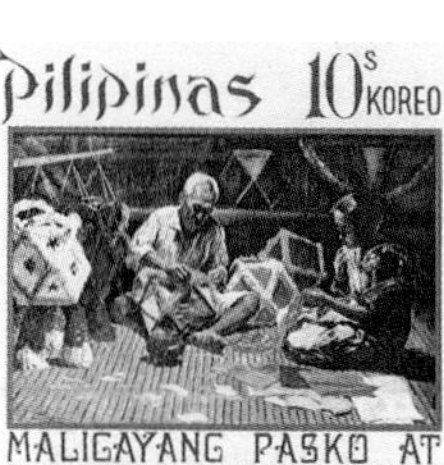

352 "The Lantern-makers" (J. Pineda)

1972. Christmas.
1284 **352** 10s. multicoloured . . . 10 10
1285 30s. multicoloured . . . 25 15
1286 50s. multicoloured . . . 55 20

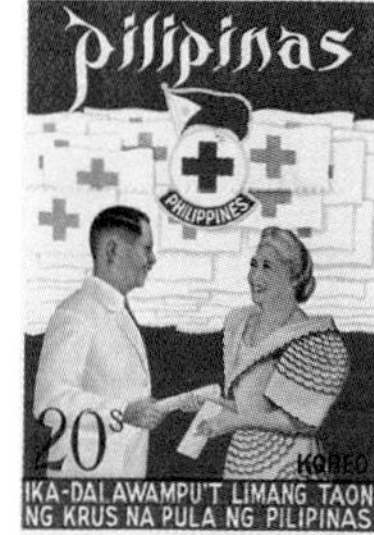

353 President Roxas and Wife

1972. 25th Anniv of Philippines Red Cross.
1287 **353** 5s. multicoloured 10 10
1288 20s. multicoloured . . . 15 10
1289 30s. multicoloured . . . 25 15

1973. Nos. 948 and 1005 surch **10s.**
1290 **238** 10s. on 6s. multicoloured 20 10
1291 **256** 10s. on 6s. blue. red and yellow 20 10

1973. Presidential Sayings (8th issue). As **T 233** but with portrait and saying changed.
1292 10s. black and bistre 15 10
1293 30s. black and mauve . . . 35 15
PORTRAIT AND SAYING: 10s., 30s. Pres. Garcia, "I would rather be right than successful".

355 University Building

1973. 60th Anniv of St. Louis University, Baguio City.
1294 **355** 5s. multicoloured 10 10
1295 10s. multicoloured . . . 10 10
1296 75s. multicoloured . . . 40 20

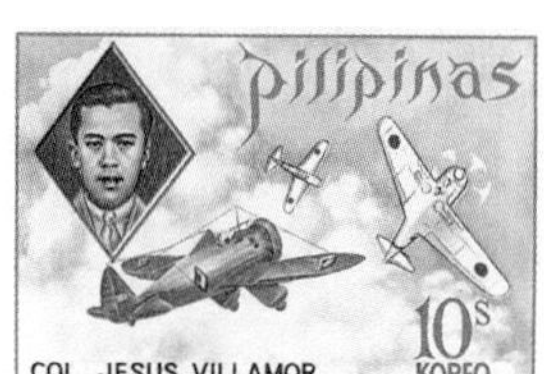

356 Col. J. Villamor and Air Battle

1973. Villamor Commemoration.
1297 **356** 10s. multicoloured . . . 15 10
1298 2p. multicoloured . . . 1·40 80

1973. Various stamps surch.
1299 **252** 5s. on 6s. multicoloured 35 20
1300 **266** 5s. on 6s. violet, yellow and green 35 15
1301 **318** 15s. on 10s. red (No. O1182) 25 10

359 Actor and Stage Performance

1973. 1st "Third-World" Theatre Festival, Manila.
1302 **359** 5s. multicoloured 10 10
1303 10s. multicoloured . . . 10 10
1304 50s. multicoloured . . . 25 10
1305 70s. multicoloured . . . 45 15

1973. President Marcos's Anti-smuggling Campaign. No. 1017 surch **5s.**
1306 5s. on 6s. blue 25 10

1973. 10th Death Anniv of John F. Kennedy. No. 989 surch **5s.**
1307 5s. on 6s. multicoloured . . 25 10

1973. Compulsory Tax Stamps. T.B. Relief Fund. Nos. 1241/2 surch.
1308 15s.+5s. on 10s.+5s. mult 15 10
1309 60s.+5s. on 40s.+5s. mult 50 20

363 Proclamation Scenes

1973. 75th Anniv of Philippine Independence.
1310 **363** 15s. multicoloured . . . 10 10
1311 45s. multicoloured . . . 25 10
1312 90s. multicoloured . . . 45 20

364 M. Agoncillo (maker of first national flag)

365 Imelda Marcos

1973. Perf or imperf.
1313 – 15s. violet 15 10
1314 **364** 60s. brown 45 10
1315 – 90s. blue 45 10
1316 – 1p.10 blue 40 10
1317 – 1p.50 red 75 15
1318 – 1p.50 brown 80 20
1319 – 1p.80 green 70 30
1320 – 5p. blue . . . . 2·50 75
DESIGNS: 15s. Gabriela Silang (revolutionary); 90s. Teodoro Yangco (businessman); 1p.10, Pio Valenzuela (physician); 1p.50 (No. 1317), Pedro Paterno (revolutionary); 1p.50 (No. 1318), Teodora Alonso (mother of Jose Rizal); 1p.80, E. Evangelista (revolutionary); 5p. F. M. Guerrero (writer).
For similar designs see Nos. 1455/8.

1973. Projects Inaugurated by Sra Imelda Marcos.
1321 **365** 15s. multicoloured . . . 10 10
1322 50s. multicoloured . . . 30 10
1323 60s. multicoloured . . . 35 15

366 Malakanyang Palace

1973. Presidential Palace, Manila.
1324 **366** 15s. mult (postage) . . 10 10
1325 50s. multicoloured . . . 30 15
1326 60s. multicoloured (air) 50 15

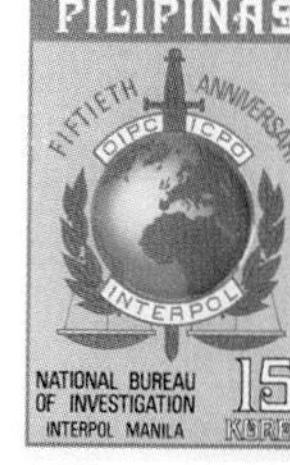

367 Interpol Emblem **368** Scouting Activities

1973. 50th Anniv of International Criminal Police Organization (Interpol).
1327 **367** 15s. multicoloured . . . 15 10
1328 65s. multicoloured . . . 25 15

1973. Golden Jubilee of Philippine Boy Scouts. Perf or imperf.
1329 **368** 15s. bistre and green . . 15 10
1330 – 65s. blue and yellow . . 25 15
DESIGN: 65s. Scouts reading brochure.

369 Bank Emblem, Urban and Agricultural Landscapes

1974. 25th Anniv of Central Bank of the Philippines. Multicoloured.
1331 15s. Type **369** 45 25
1332 60s. Bank building, 1949 25 10
1333 1p.50 Bank complex, 1974 60 25

370 "Maria Clara" Costume
373 Map of South-East Asia

1974. Centenary of U.P.U. Philippine Costumes. Multicoloured.
1334 15s. Type **370** 15 10
1335 60s. "Balintawak" 35 15
1336 80s. "Malong" 50 20

1974. Philatelic Week (1973). No. 1303 surch **1973 PHILATELIC WEEK 15s**.
1337 **359** 15s. on 10s. multicoloured 25 10

1974. 25th Anniv of Philippine "Lionism". Nos. 1297 and 1180 surch **PHILIPPINE LIONISM 1949-1974 15s** and Lions emblem.
1338 **356** 15s. on 10s. multicoloured 20 10
1339 – 45s. on 40s. red 40 20

1974. Asian Paediatrics Congress, Manila. Perf or imperf.
1340 **373** 30s. red and blue 15 10
1341 1p. red and green 50 20

374 Gen. Valdes and Hospital

1974. Obligatory Tax. T.B. Relief Fund. Perf or imperf.
1342 **374** 15s.+5s. green and red 20 10
1343 1p.10+5s. blue and red 40 15

1974. Nos. 974, 1024 and 1026 surch.
1344 **246** 5s. on 3s. green 25 10
1345 **263** 5s. on 6s. multicoloured 35 10
1346 **264** 5s. on 6s. multicoloured 55 10

378 W.P.Y. Emblem

1974. World Population Year. Perf or imperf.
1347 **378** 5s. black and orange 10 10
1348 2p. blue and green 1·00 40

379 Red Feather Emblem

1974. 25th Anniv of Community Chest Movement in the Philippines. Perf or imperf.
1349 **379** 15s. red and blue 10 10
1350 40s. red and green 15 10
1351 45s. red and brown 25 15

381 Sultan Mohammad Kudarat, Map, Malayan Prau and Order

1975. Sultan Kudarat of Mindanao Commem.
1352 **381** 15s. multicoloured 15 10

382 Association Emblem
383 Rafael Palma

1975. 25th Anniv of Philippine Mental Health Association. Perf or imperf.
1353 **382** 45s. green and orange 20 10
1354 1p. green and purple 45 15

1975. Birth Centenary of Rafael Palma (educationalist and statesman). Perf or imperf (15s.), perf (30s.).
1355 **383** 15s. green 15 10
1436 30s. brown 15 10

384 Heart Centre Emblem

1975. Inauguration of Philippine Heart Centre for Asia, Quezon City. Perf or imperf.
1356 **384** 15s. red and blue 20 10
1357 50s. red and green 40 20

385 Cadet in Full Dress, and Academy Building

1975. 70th Anniv of Philippine Military Academy.
1358 **385** 15s. multicoloured 15 10
1359 45s. multicoloured 30 15

387/9, 392/4 "Helping the Disabled"

1975. 25th Anniv (1974) of Philippines Orthopaedic Association. Perf or imperf.
1360 – 45s. green (inscr at left and top) 20 15
1361 **387** 45s. green 20 15
1362 **388** 45s. green 20 15
1363 **389** 45s. green 20 15
1364 – 45s. green (inscr at top and right) 20 15
1365 – 45s. green (inscr at left and bottom) 20 15
1366 **392** 45s. green 20 15
1367 **393** 45s. green 20 15
1368 **394** 45s. green 20 15
1369 – 45s. green (inscr at bottom and right) 20 15
DESIGNS—23 × 30 mm: Nos. 1360, 1364/5, 1369, Details of corners of the mural.
Nos. 1360/9 were issued together, se-tenant, forming a composite design.

1975. Nos. 1153 and 1342/3 surch.
1370 **374** 5s. on 15s.+5s. green and red 20 10
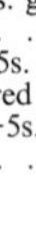
1371 **308** 60s. on 70s.+5s. multicoloured 35 15
1372 **374** 1p. on 1p.10+5s. blue and red 50 25

397 Planting Sapling

398 Jade Vine

1975. Forest Conservation. Multicoloured.
1373 45s. Type **397** 20 10
1374 45s. Sapling and tree-trunks 20 10

1975.
1375 **398** 15s. multicoloured 15 10

399 Imelda Marcos and I.W.Y. Emblem
400 Commission Badge

1975. International Women's Year. Perf or imperf.
1376 **399** 15s. black, blue & dp blue 15 10
1377 80s. black, blue and pink 45 20

1975. 75th Anniv of Civil Service Commission. Perf or imperf.
1378 **400** 15s. multicoloured 15 15
1379 50s. multicoloured 40 15

401 Angat River Barrage

1975. 25th Anniv of International Irrigation and Drainage Commission. Perf or imperf.
1380 **401** 40s. blue and orange 15 10
1381 1p.50 blue and mauve 50 25

402 "Welcome to Manila"
403 N. Romualdez (legislator and writer)

1975. Centenary of Hong Kong and Shanghai Banking Corporation's Service in the Philippines.
1382 **402** 1p.50 multicoloured 1·75 35

1975. Birth Centenaries. Perf or imperf.
1383 **403** 60s. lilac 30 10
1384 – 90s. mauve 40 15
DESIGN: 90s. General G. del Pilar.

405 Boeing 747-100 Airliner and Martin M-130 Flying Boat

1975. 40th Anniv of First Trans-Pacific China Clipper Airmail Flight. San Francisco–Manila.
1385 **405** 60s. multicoloured 45 20
1386 1p.50 multicoloured 1·25 55

1975. Airmail Exn. Nos. 1314 and 1318 optd **AIRMAIL EXHIBITION NOV 22-DEC 9**.
1387 **364** 60s. brown 30 20
1388 – 1p.50 brown 70 55

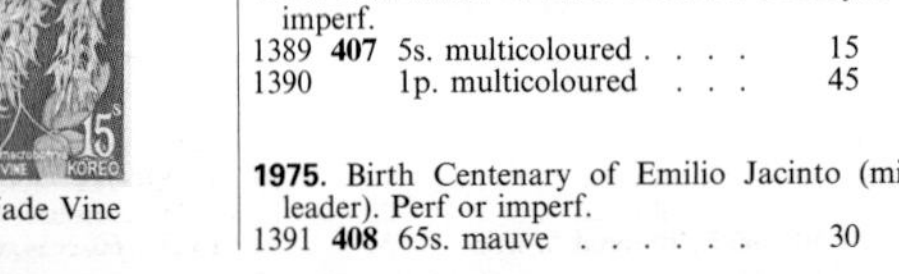
407 APO Emblem
408 E. Jacinto

1975. 25th Anniv of APO Philatelic Society. Perf or imperf.
1389 **407** 5s. multicoloured 15 10
1390 1p. multicoloured 45 20

1975. Birth Centenary of Emilio Jacinto (military leader). Perf or imperf.
1391 **408** 65s. mauve 30 10

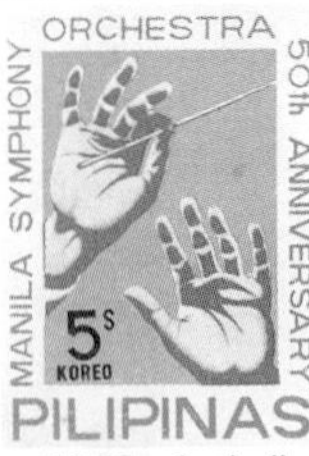

409 San Agustin Church
410 "Conducting" Hands

1975. Holy Year. Churches. Perf or imperf.
1392 **409** 20s. blue 20 10
1393 – 30s. black and yellow 20 10
1394 – 45s. red, pink and black 35 15
1395 – 60s. bistre, yellow & black 50 20
DESIGNS—HORIZ: 30s. Morong Church; 45s. Taal Basilica. VERT: 60s. San Sebastian Church.

1976. 50th Anniv of Manila Symphony Orchestra.
1396 **410** 5s. multicoloured 10 10
1397 50s. multicoloured 35 15

411 Douglas DC-3 and DC-10

1976. 30th Anniv of Philippines Airlines (PAL).
1398 **411** 60s. multicoloured 40 15
1399 1p.50 multicoloured 1·25 55

412 Felipe Agoncillo (statesman)
413 University Building

1976. Felipe Agoncillo Commemoration.
1400 **412** 1p.60 black 60 15

1976. 75th Anniv of National University.
1401 **413** 45s. multicoloured 20 10
1402 60s. multicoloured 45 10

414 "Foresight Prevents Blindness"
415 Emblem on Book

1976. World Health Day.
1403 **414** 15s. multicoloured 25 10

1976. 75th Anniv of National Archives.
1404 **415** 1p.50 multicoloured 70 20

416 College Emblem and University Tower

1976. 50th Anniv of Colleges of Education and Science, Saint Thomas's University.
1405 **416** 15s. multicoloured 15 10
1406 50s. multicoloured 35 10

417 College Building

1976. 50th Anniv of Maryknoll College.
1407 **417** 15s. multicoloured . . . 15 10
1408 1p.50 multicoloured . . 65 20

1976. Olympic Games, Montreal. Surch **15s Montreal 1976 21st OLYMPICS, CANADA** and emblem.
1409 **348** 15s. on 10s. mult 30 10

419 Constabulary Headquarters, Manila

1976. 75th Anniv of Philippine Constabulary. Perf or imperf.
1410 **419** 15s. multicoloured . . . 15 10
1411 60s. multicoloured . . . 45 15

420 Land and Aerial Surveying

1976. 75th Anniv of Lands Bureau.
1412 **420** 80s. multicoloured . . . 75 20

422 Badges of Banking Organizations

1976. International Monetary Fund and World Bank Joint Board of Governors Annual Meeting, Manila.
1414 **422** 60s. multicoloured . . . 15 10
1415 1p.50 multicoloured . . 65 30

423 Virgin of Antipolo

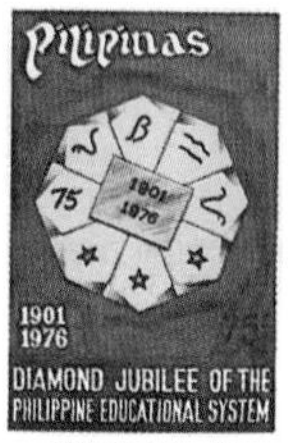

426 Facets of Education

425 "Going to Church"

1976. 350th Anniv of "Virgin of Antipolo".
1416 **423** 30s. multicoloured . . . 15 10
1417 90s. multicoloured . . . 45 15

1976. Philatelic Week. Surch **1976 PHILATELIC WEEK 30s.**
1418 **355** 30s. on 10s. mult 25 10

1976. Christmas.
1419 **425** 15s. multicoloured . . . 15 10
1420 30s. multicoloured . . . 30 10

1976. 75th Anniv of Philippine Educational System.
1421 **426** 30s. multicoloured . . . 15 10
1422 75s. multicoloured . . . 30 10

1977. Surch.
1423 1p.20 on 1p.10 blue (No. 1316) 55 20
1424 3p. on 5p. blue (No. 1320) 1·50 40

428 Jose Rizal

429 Flags, Map and Emblem

1977. Famous Filipinos. Multicoloured.
1425 30s. Type **428** 20 10
1426 2p.30 Dr. Galicano Apacible 65 15

1977. 15th Anniv of Asian–Oceanic Postal Union.
1427 **429** 50s. multicoloured . . . 20 10
1428 1p.50 multicoloured . . 70 15

430 Worker and Cogwheels

431 Commission Emblem

1977. 10th Anniv of Asian Development Bank.
1429 **430** 90s. multicoloured . . . 35 15
1430 2p.30 multicoloured . . 90 25

1977. National Rural Credit Commission.
1431 **431** 30s. multicoloured . . . 15 10

433 Solicitor-General's Emblem

1977. 75th Anniv of Office of Solicitor-General.
1433 **433** 1p.65 multicoloured . . 60 15

434 Conference Emblem

1977. World Law Conference, Manila.
1434 **434** 2p.20 multicoloured . . 80 15

435 A.S.E.A.N. Emblem

1977. 10th Anniv of Association of South East Asian Nationals (A.S.E.A.N.).
1435 **435** 1p.50 multicoloured . . 80 15

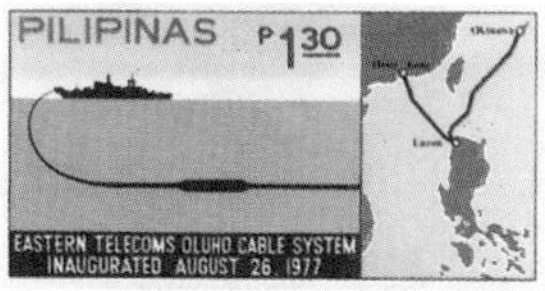

436 Cable Ship "Mercury" and Map

1977. Inauguration of OLUHO Cable (Okinawa–Luzon–Hong Kong).
1437 **436** 1p.30 multicoloured . . 75 20

437 President Marcos

1977. 60th Birthday of President Marcos.
1438 **437** 30s. multicoloured . . . 15 10
1439 2p.30 multicoloured . . 75 20

438 People raising Flag

439 Bishop Gregorio Aglipay (founder)

1977. 5th Anniv of "New Society".
1440 **438** 30s. multicoloured . . . 20 10
1441 2p.30 multicoloured . . 70 20

1977. 75th Anniv of Aglipayan Church.
1442 **439** 30s. multicoloured . . . 15 10
1443 90s. multicoloured . . . 60 15

441 Fokker F.7 Trimotor "General New" and World Map

1977. 50th Anniv of 1st Pan-Am International Air Service.
1445 **441** 2p.30 multicoloured . . 1·40 30

442 Eight-pointed Star and Children

445 University Badge

444 Scouts and Map of Philippines

1977. Christmas.
1446 **442** 30s. multicoloured . . . 20 10
1447 45s. multicoloured . . . 30 10

1977. Philatelic Week. Surch **90s 1977 PHILATELIC WEEK.**
1448 **407** 90s. on 1p. multicoloured 45 15

1977. National Scout Jamboree.
1449 **444** 30s. multicoloured . . . 25 10

1978. 50th Anniv of Far Eastern University.
1450 **445** 30s. multicoloured . . . 15 10

446 Sipa Player

1978. "Sipa" (Filipino ball game).
1451 **446** 5s. multicoloured 10 10
1452 – 10s. multicoloured . . . 10 10
1453 – 40s. multicoloured . . . 20 10
1454 – 75s. multicoloured . . . 40 15
DESIGNS: Nos. 1452/4, Different players.
Nos. 1451/4 were issued together, se-tenant, forming a composite design.

447 Jose Rizal

448 Arms of Meycauayan

1978.
1455 **447** 30s. blue 20 10
1456 – 30s. mauve 20 10
1457 – 90s. green 60 10
1458 – 1p.20 red 45 10
DESIGNS: No. 1456, Rajah Kalantiaw (Panay chief); 1457, Lope K. Santos ("Father of Filipino grammar"); 1458, Gregoria de Jesus (patriot).

1978. 400th Anniv of Meycauayan.
1459 **448** 1p.05 multicoloured . . 45 15

449 Horse-drawn Mail Cart

1978. "CAPEX 78" International Stamp Exhibition, Toronto. Multicoloured.
1460 2p.50 Type **449** . . . . . . 1·00 65
1461 5p. Filipino vinta (sailing canoe) . . . . 2·75 2·00

450 Andres Bonifacio Monument (Guillermo Tolentino)

1978. Andres Bonifacio Monument.
1463 **450** 30s. multicoloured . . . 20 10

451 Knight, Rook and Globe

1978. World Chess Championship, Baguio City.
1464 **451** 30s. red and violet . . . 25 10
1465 2p. red and violet . . . 75 20

452 Miner

1978. 75th Anniv of Benguet Consolidated Mining Company.
1466 **452** 2p.30 multicoloured . . 3·00 1·00

453 Pres. Quezon

455 Pres. Osmena

454 Law Association and Conference Emblems

1978. Birth Centenary of Manuel L. Quezon (former President).
1467 **453** 30s. multicoloured . . . 15 10
1468 1p. multicoloured . . . 55 15

1978. 58th Int Law Association Conf, Manila.
1469 **454** 2p.30 multicoloured . . 85 20

1978. Birth Centenary of Sergio Osmena (former President).
1470 **455** 30s. multicoloured . . . 20 10
1471 1p. multicoloured . . . 55 15

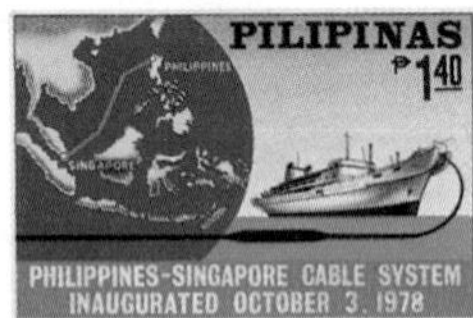

456 Map of Cable Route and Cable Ship "Mercury"

1978. Inauguration of Philippines–Singapore Submarine Cable.
1472 **456** 1p.40 multicoloured . . 90 25

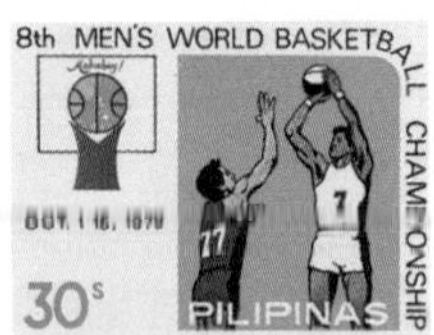

457 Basketball

1978. 8th Men's World Basketball Championship, Manila.
1473 **457** 30s. multicoloured . . . 15 10
1474 2p.30 multicoloured . . 95 25

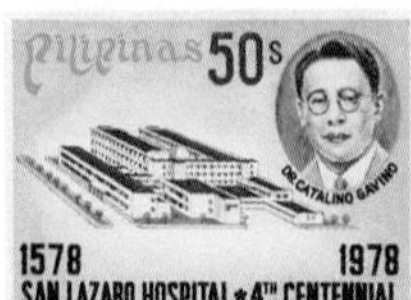

458 Dr. Catalino Gavino and Hospital

1978. 400th Anniv of San Lazaro Hospital.
1475 **458** 50s. multicoloured . . . 30 10
1476 90s. multicoloured . . . 45 15

459 Nurse vaccinating Child
461 Man on Telephone, Map and Satellite

1978. Global Eradication of Smallpox.
1477 **459** 30s. multicoloured . . . 15 10
1478 1p.50 multicoloured . . 95 25

1978. Philatelic Week. No. 1391 surch **1978 PHILATELIC WEEK 60s**.
1479 **408** 60s. on 65s. mauve . . . 40 10

1978. 50th Anniv of Philippine Long Distance Telephone Company. Multicoloured.
1480 30s. Type **461** 20 10
1481 2p. Woman on telephone and globe 90 45
Nos. 1480/1 were issued together, se-tenant, forming a composite design.

462 Family travelling in Ox-drawn Cart

1978. Decade of the Filipino Child.
1482 **462** 30s. multicoloured . . . 15 10
1483 1p.35 multicoloured . . 60 15

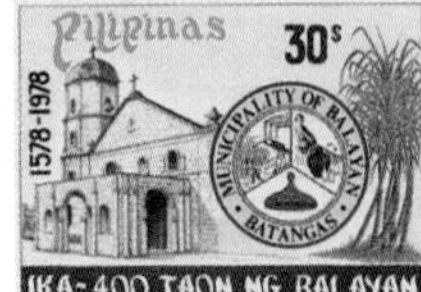

463 Spanish Colonial Church and Arms

1978. 400th Anniv of Agoo Town.
1484 **463** 30s. multicoloured . . . 20 10
1485 45s. multicoloured . . . 25 10

464 Church and Arms

1978. 400th Anniv of Balayan Town.
1486 **464** 30s. multicoloured . . . 15 10
1487 90s. multicoloured . . . 40 10

465 Dr. Sison
466 Family and Houses

1978. Dr. Honoria Acosta Sison (first Filipino woman physician) Commemoration.
1488 **465** 30s. multicoloured . . . 15 10

1978. 30th Anniv of Declaration of Human Rights.
1489 **466** 30s. multicoloured . . . 15 10
1490 3p. multicoloured . . . 1·25 35

467 Melon butterflyfish

1978. Fishes. Multicoloured.
1491 30s. Type **467** 15 10
1492 1p.20 Black triggerfish . . . 75 20
1493 2p.20 Picasso triggerfish . . 1·25 45
1494 2p.30 Copper-banded butterflyfish . . . . . . 1·25 60
1495 5p. Atoll butterflyfish ("Chaetodon mertensi") 3·00 1·25
1496 5p. Yellow-faced butterflyfish ("Euxiphipops xanthometapon") . . . . 3·00 1·25

468 Carlos P. Romulo

1979. 80th Anniv of Carlos P. Romulo (1st Asian President of U.N. General Assembly).
1497 **468** 30s. multicoloured . . . 10 10
1498 2p. multicoloured . . . 90 20

469 Cogwheel (Rotary Emblem)
470 Rosa Sevilla de Alvero

1979. 60th Anniv of Manila Rotary Club.
1499 **469** 30s. multicoloured . . . 15 10
1500 2p.30 multicoloured . . 95 25

1979. Birth Centenary of Rosa Sevilla de Alvero (writer and educator).
1501 **470** 30s. mauve 15 10

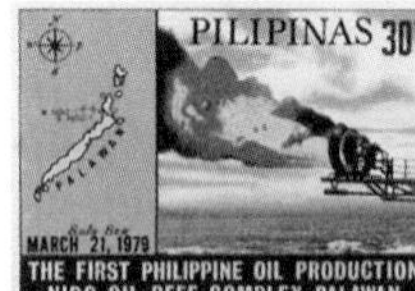

471 Burning-off Gas and Map

1979. 1st Oil Production. Nido Complex, Palawan.
1502 **471** 30s. multicoloured . . . 35 10
1503 45s. multicoloured . . . 55 15

472 Merrill's Fruit Dove

1979. Birds. Multicoloured.
1504 30s. Type **472** 55 20
1505 1p.20 Brown tit-babbler . . 1·00 30
1506 2p.20 Mindoro zone-tailed (inscr "Imperial") pigeon 1·90 65
1507 2p.30 Steere's pitta . . . . 2·00 65
1508 5p. Koch's pitta and red-breasted pitta . . . . . . 3·75 1·40
1509 5p. Great eared nightjar . . 3·75 1·40

473 Association Emblem

1979. 25th Anniv of Association of Special Libraries of the Philippines.
1510 **473** 30s. green, black & yell 10 10
1511 75s. green, black & yell 25 10
1512 1p. green, black & orange 60 25

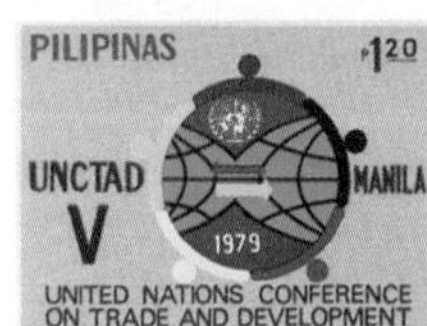

474 Conference Emblem

1979. 5th U.N. Conference on Trade and Development, Manila.
1513 **474** 1p.20 multicoloured . . 35 15
1514 2p.30 multicoloured . . 90 35

475 Malay Civet

1979. Animals. Multicoloured.
1515 30s. Type **475** 15 10
1516 1p.20 Crab-eating macaque 75 20
1517 2p.20 Javan pig . . . . . . 1·25 30
1518 2p.30 Leopard cat . . . . . 1·25 30
1519 5p. Oriental small-clawed otter . . . . 3·00 60
1520 5p. Malayan pangolin . . . 3·00 60

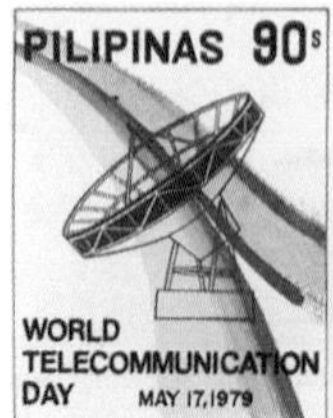

476 Dish Aerial

1979. World Telecommunications Day. Mult.
1521 90s. Type **476** 50 10
1522 1p.30 Hemispheres 60 15

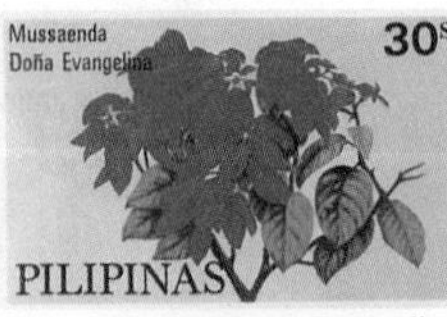

477 Mussaenda "Dona Evangelina"

1979. Cultivated Mussaendas. Multicoloured.
1523 30s. Type **477** 15 10
1524 1p.20 "Dona Esperanza" . . 75 15
1525 2p.20 "Dona Hilaria" . . . 1·25 30
1526 2p.30 "Dona Aurora" . . . 1·25 30
1527 5p. "Gining Imelda" . . . 3·00 60
1528 5p. "Dona Trining" . . . . 3·00 60

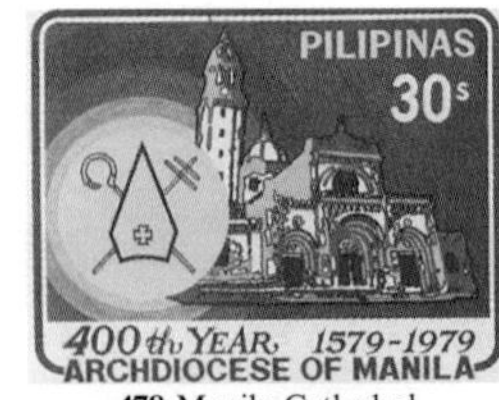

478 Manila Cathedral

1979. 400th Anniv of Archdiocese of Manila.
1529 **478** 30s. multicoloured . . . 15 10
1530 75s. multicoloured . . . 35 10
1531 90s. multicoloured . . . 45 15

479 "Bagong Lakas" (patrol boat)

1979. Philippine Navy Foundation Day.
1532 **479** 30s. multicoloured . . . 25 10
1533 45s. multicoloured . . . 35 15

1979. Air. 1st Scout Philatelic Exhibition and 25th Anniv of 1st National Jamboree. Surch **1ST SCOUT PHILATELIC EXHIBITION JULY 4.14, 1979 QUEZON CITY AIRMAIL 90s**.
1534 **188** 90s. on 6c.+4c. red on yellow 60 30

481 Drug Addict breaking Manacles

1979. "Fight Drug Abuse" Campaign.
1536 **481** 30s. multicoloured . . . 10 10
1537 90s. multicoloured . . . 35 15
1538 1p.05 multicoloured . . 40 20

482 Afghan Hound

1979. Cats and Dogs. Multicoloured.
1539 30s. Type **482** 20 10
1540 90s. Tabby cats 65 15
1541 1p.20 Dobermann pinscher 85 25
1542 2p.20 Siamese cats . . . . 1·50 40
1543 2p.30 German shepherd dog 1·60 50
1544 5p. Chinchilla cats . . . . 3·25 60

483 Children flying Kites

1979. International Year of the Child. Paintings by Rod Dayao. Multicoloured.
1545 15s. Type **483** 10 10
1546 20s. Boys fighting with catapults 20 10
1547 25s. Girls dressing-up . . . 20 10
1548 1p.20 Boy playing policeman 55 15

484 Hands holding Emblems

1979. 80th Anniv of Methodism in the Philippines.
1549 **484** 30s. multicoloured . . . 15 10
1550 1p.35 multicoloured . . 45 15

485 Anniversary Medal and 1868 Coin

1979. 50th Anniv of Philippine Numismatic and Antiquarian Society.
1551 **485** 30s. multicoloured . . . 15 10

486 Concorde over Manila and Paris

1979. 25th Anniv of Air France Service to the Philippines. Multicoloured.
1552 1p.05 Type **486** 60 30
1553 2p.20 Concorde over monument . . . . 1·40 55

1979. Philatelic Week. Surch **1979 PHILATELIC WEEK 90s.**
1554 **412** 90s. on 1p.60 black . . . 40 15

488 "35" and I.A.T.A. Emblem

1979. 35th Annual General Meeting of International Air Transport Association, Manila.
1555 **488** 75s. multicoloured . . . 35 15
1556 2p.30 multicoloured . . 90 25

489 Bureau of Local Government Emblem

490 Christmas Greetings

1979. Local Government Year.
1557 **489** 30s. multicoloured . . . 15 10
1558 45s. multicoloured . . . 20 10

1979. Christmas. Multicoloured.
1559 30s. Type **490** 15 10
1560 90s. Stars 40 10

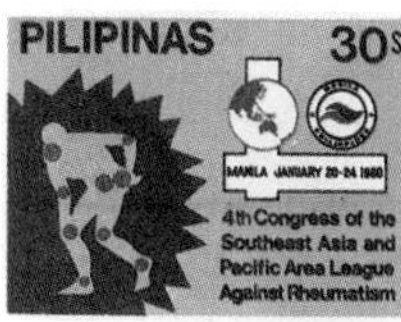

491 Rheumatism Victim

1980. 4th Congress of Southeast Asia and Pacific Area League Against Rheumatism, Manila.
1561 **491** 30s. multicoloured . . . 25 10
1562 90s. multicoloured . . . 70 25

492 Birthplace and MacArthur Memorial Foundation

1980. Birth Centenary of General Douglas MacArthur (U.S. Army Chief of Staff). Mult.
1563 30s. Type **492** 15 10
1564 75s. General MacArthur . . 35 15
1565 2p.30 Hat, pipe and glasses 1·10 45

493 Columbus and Emblem

495 Tirona, Benitez and University

494 Soldiers and Academy Emblem

1980. 75th Anniv of Knights of Columbus Organization in Philippines.
1567 **493** 30s. multicoloured . . . 20 10
1568 1p.35 multicoloured . . 75 20

1980. 75th Anniv of Philippine Military Academy.
1569 **494** 30s. multicoloured . . . 20 10
1570 1p.20 multicoloured . . 65 20

1980. 60th Anniv of Philippine Women's University.
1571 **495** 30s. multicoloured . . . 20 10
1572 1p.05 multicoloured . . 55 15

496 Boats and Burning City

1980. 75th Anniv of Rotary International. Details of painting by Carlos Francisco. Multicoloured.
1573 30s. Type **496** 20 10
1574 30s. Priest with cross, swordsmen and soldier . . 20 10
1575 30s. "K K K" flag and group around table . . . 20 10
1576 30s. Man in midst of spearmen and civilian scenes 20 10
1577 30s. Reading the Constitution, soliders and U.S. and Philippine flags 20 10
1578 2p.30 Type **496** 75 35
1579 2p.30 As No. 1574 . . . . 75 35
1580 2p.30 As No. 1575 . . . . 75 35
1581 2p.30 As No. 1576 . . . . 75 35
1582 2p.30 As No. 1577 . . . . 75 35

Nos. 1573/7 and 1578/82 were issued together in se-tenant strips of five, each strip forming a composite design.

497 Mosque and Koran

498 Hand stubbing out Cigarette

1980. 600th Anniv of Islam in the Philippines.
1583 **497** 30s. multicoloured . . . 20 10
1584 1p.30 multicoloured . . 65 20

1980. World Health Day. Anti-smoking Campaign.
1585 **498** 30s. multicoloured . . . 15 10
1586 75s. multicoloured . . . 75 20

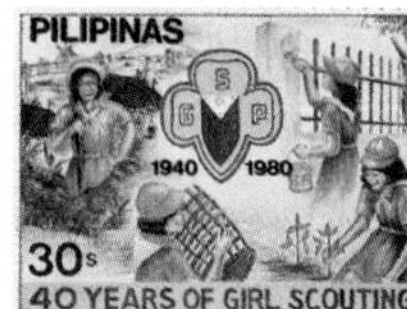

499 Scouting Activities and Badge

1980. 40th Anniv of Girl Scouting in the Philippines.
1587 **499** 30s. multicoloured . . . 25 10
1588 2p. multicoloured . . . 70 25

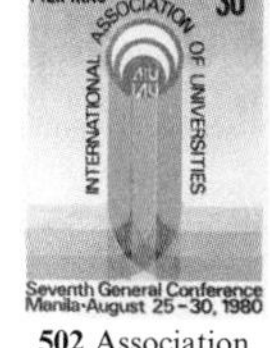

500 Jeepney

502 Association Emblem

1980. Philippine Jeepneys (decorated jeeps). Multicoloured.
1589 30s. Type **500** 20 10
1590 1p.20 Side view of Jeepney 70 30

1980. 82nd Anniv of Independence. Surch **PHILIPPINE INDEPENDENCE 82ND ANNIVERSARY 1898 1980.**
1591 **412** 1p.35 on 1p.60 black . . 60 20
1592 1p.50 on 1p.80 green (No. 1319) 80 30

1980. 7th General Conference of International Association of Universities, Manila.
1593 **502** 30s. multicoloured . . . 15 10
1594 2p.30 multicoloured . . 95 30

503 Map and Emblems

504 Filipinos and Emblem

1980. 46th Congress of International Federation of Library Associations and Institutions, Manila.
1595 **503** 30s. green and black . . 15 10
1596 75s. blue and black . . 25 10
1597 2p.30 red and black . . 85 20

1980. 5th Anniv of Kabataang Barangay (national council charged with building the "New Society").
1598 **504** 30s. multicoloured . . . 20 10
1599 40s. multicoloured . . . 25 10
1600 1p. multicoloured . . . 55 20

1980. Nos. 1433, 1501, 1536, 1557 and 1559 surch.
1601 **470** 40s. on 30s. mauve . . . 35 10
1602 **481** 40s. on 30s. multicoloured 60 10
1603 **489** 40s. on 30s. multicoloured 35 10
1604 **490** 40s. on 30s. multicoloured 35 10
1605 **433** 2p. on 1p.65 mult . . . 1·10 25

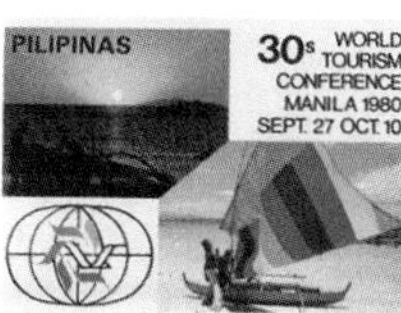

506 Sunset, Filipino Vinta and Conference Emblem

1980. World Tourism Conference, Manila.
1606 **506** 30s. multicoloured . . . 30 10
1607 2p.30 multicoloured . . 1·75 60

507 Magnifying Glass and Stamps

508 U.N. Headquarters and Philippines Flag

1980. Postage Stamp Day.
1608 **507** 40s. multicoloured . . . 25 10
1609 1p. multicoloured . . . 60 15
1610 2p. multicoloured . . . 1·25 25

1980. 35th Anniv of U.N.O.
1611 40s. Type **508** 25 10
1612 3p.20 U.N. Headquarters and U.N. and Philippines flags . . . . 1·50 45

509 Alabaster Murex

510 Interpol Emblem on Globe

1980. Shells. Multicoloured.
1613 40s. Type **509** 25 10
1614 60s. Giant frog shell 35 15
1615 1p.20 Zambo's murex . . . 65 15
1616 2p. Pallid carrier shell . . . 1·25 25

1980. 49th General Assembly of Interpol, Manila.
1617 **510** 40s. multicoloured . . . 20 10
1618 1p. multicoloured . . . 40 15
1619 3p.20 multicoloured . . 1·00 35

511 University and Faculty Emblems

513 Christmas Tree and Presents

1980. 75th Anniv of Central Philippine University. Multicoloured, background colour given.
1620 **511** 40s. blue 20 10
1621 3p.20 green . . . . . . 1·40 50

1980. Philatelic Week. No. 1377 surch **1980 PHILATELIC WEEK P1.20.**
1622 **399** 1p.20 on 80s. black, blue and pink 75 20

1980. Christmas.
1623 **513** 40s. multicoloured . . . 30 10

1981. Various stamps surch.
1624 **244** 10s. on 6s.+5s. blue . . 35 10
1625 **462** 10s. on 30s. mult . . . 30 10
1626 **408** 40s. on 65s. mauve . . . 35 10
1627 **458** 40s. on 90s. mult . . . 80 15
1628 **481** 40s. on 90s. mult . . . 40 10
1629 – 40s. on 90s. mult (No. 1560) 65 15
1630 **448** 40s. on 1p.05 mult . . . 35 10
1631 **462** 40s. on 1p.35 mult . . . 35 10
1632 **399** 85s. on 80s. black, blue and pink 75 20
1633 **408** 1p. on 65s. mauve . . . 75 20
1634 **401** 1p. on 1p.50 blue and mauve 80 10
1635 **422** 1p. on 1p.50 mult . . . 75 20
1636 – 1p.20 on 1p.50 brown (No. 1318) . . . . . 1·10 20
1637 **433** 1p.20 on 1p.65 mult . . 1·10 20
1638 – 1p.20 on 1p.80 green (No. 1319) 80 20
1639 **401** 2p. on 1p.50 blue and mauve . . . . 1·60 25
1640 **434** 3p.20 on 2p.20 mult . . 2·25 45

1981. 30th Anniv of APO Philatelic Society. Surch **NOV. 30, 1980 APO PHILATELIC SOCIETY PEARL JUBILEE 40s.**
1641 **455** 40s. on 30s. mult 25 10

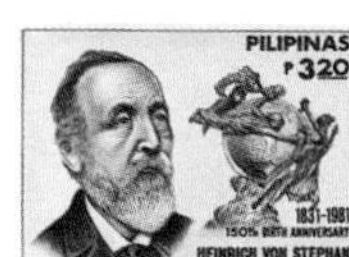

516 Von Stephan and U.P.U. Emblem

1981. 150th Birth Anniv of Heinrich von Stephan (founder of U.P.U.).
1642 **516** 3p.20 multicoloured . . 1·75 60

1981. Girl Scouts Camp. No. 1589 surch **GSP RJASIA-PACIFIC REGIONAL CAMP PHILIPPINES DECEMBER 23, 1980 40s.**
1643 **500** 40s. on 30s. mult 90 15

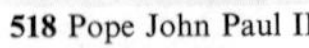

518 Pope John Paul II **519** Parliamentary Debate

1981. Papal Visit. Multicoloured.
1644 90s. Type **518** 40 15
1645 1p.20 Pope and cardinals . . 50 20
1646 2p.30 Pope blessing crowd (horiz) . . . . 1·10 30
1647 3p. Pope and Manila Cathedral (horiz) . . . . 1·60 50

1981. Interparliamentary Union Meeting, Manila.
1649 **519** 2p. multicoloured . . . 80 30
1650 3p.20 multicoloured . . 1·25 45

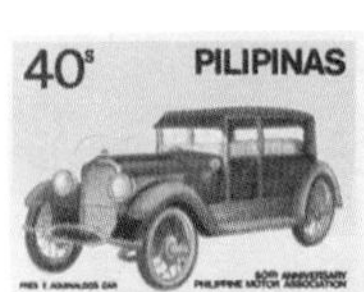

520 Monument **521** President Aguinaldo's Car

1981. Jose Rizal Monument, Luneta Park.
1651 **520** 40s. black, yellow & brn 20 10

1981. 50th Anniv of Philippine Motor Association. Multicoloured.
1652 40s. Type **521** 30 10
1653 40s. 1930 model car 30 10
1654 40s. 1937 model car 30 10
1655 40s. 1937 model car (different) 30 10

522 Bubble Coral

1981. Corals. Multicoloured.
1656 40s. Type **522** 25 10
1657 40s. Branching corals . . . 25 10
1658 40s. Brain coral 25 10
1659 40s. Table coral 60 15

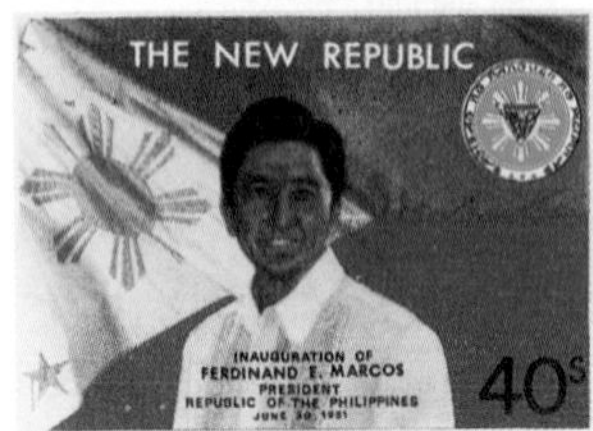

523 President Marcos and Flag

1981. Inauguration of President Marcos. Perf or imperf.
1660 **523** 40s. multicoloured . . . 25 10

524 St. Ignatius de Loyola (founder)

1981. 400th Anniv of Jesuits in the Philippines. Mult.
1662 40s. Type **524** 25 10
1663 40s. Dr. Jose P. Rizal and Intramuros Ateneo . . . 25 10
1664 40s. Father Frederico Faura (director) and Manila Observatory 25 10
1665 40s. Father Saturnino Urios (missionary) and map of Mindanao 25 10

525 F. R. Castro **526** Pres. Ramon Magsaysay

1981. Chief Justice Fred Ruiz Castro.
1667 **525** 40s. multicoloured . . . 20 10

1981.
1668 – 1p. brown and black . . 50 10
1669 **526** 1p.20 brown and black 50 10
1670 – 2p. purple and black . . 80 15
DESIGNS: 1p. General Gregorio del Pilar; 2p. Ambrosio R. Bautista.
See also Nos. 1699/1704, 1807 etc and 2031/3.

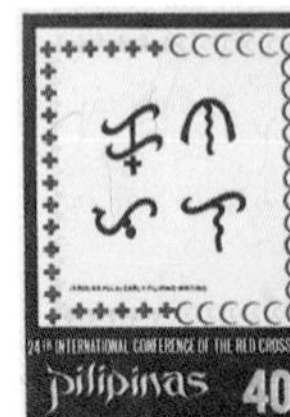

527 Man in Wheelchair **528** Early Filipino Writing

1981. International Year of Disabled Persons.
1671 **527** 40s. multicoloured . . . 25 10
1672 3p.20 multicoloured . . 1·50 40

1981. 24th International Red Cross Conference.
1673 **528** 40s. black, red and bistre 20 10
1674 2p. black and red . . . . 1·10 25
1675 3p.20 black, red and mauve . . . . 1·50 50

529 Isabel II Gate, Manila

1981.
1676 **529** 40s. black 20 10

530 Concert in Park

1981. Opening of Concert at Park 200.
1677 **530** 40s. multicoloured . . . 25 10

1981. Philatelic Week. No. 1435 surch **P120 1981 PHILATELIC WEEK**.
1678 **435** 1p.20 on 1p.50 mult . . 90 20

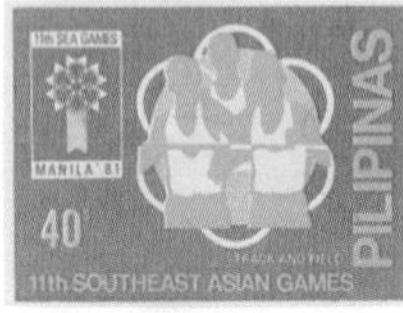

532 Running

1981. 11th South-east Asian Games, Manila.
1679 **532** 40s. yellow, green & brn 25 10
1680 – 1p. multicoloured . . . 50 10
1681 – 2p. multicoloured . . . 1·00 25
1682 – 2p.30 multicoloured . . 1·25 40
1683 – 2p.80 multicoloured . . 1·50 50
1684 – 3p.20 violet and blue . . 1·75 60
DESIGNS: 1p. Cycling; 2p. President Marcos and Juan Antonio Samaranch (president of International Olympic Committee); 2p.30, Football; 2p.80, Shooting; 3p.20, Bowling.

533 Manila Film Centre

1982. Manila International Film Festival. Mult.
1685 40s. Type **533** 25 10
1686 2p. Front view of trophy . . 1·00 20
1687 3p.20 Side view of trophy 1·50 50

534 Carriedo Fountain

1982. Centenary of Manila Metropolitan Waterworks and Sewerage System.
1688 **534** 40s. blue 25 10
1689 1p.20 brown 65 15

535 Lord Baden-Powell (founder) **537** President Marcos presenting Sword of Honour

536 Embroidered Banner

1982. 75th Anniv of Boy Scout Movement. Mult.
1690 40s. Type **535** 25 10
1691 2p. Scout . . . . 1·40 25

1982. 25th Anniv of Children's Museum and Library Inc. Multicoloured.
1692 40s. Type **536** 25 10
1693 1p.20 Children playing . . . 65 20

1982. Military Academy.
1694 **537** 40s. multicoloured . . . 25 10
1695 1p. multicoloured . . . 50 20

538 Soldier and Memorial

1982. Bataan Day. Multicoloured.
1696 40s. Type **538** 25 10
1697 2p. Doves and rifle . . . . 1·10 20

1982. Portraits. As T **526**.
1699 40s. blue 25 10
1700 1p. red 55 10
1701 1p.20 brown 65 35
1702 2p. mauve . . . . 1·25 50
1703 2p.30 purple . . . . 1·40 55
1704 3p.20 blue . . . . 1·50 95
DESIGNS: 40s. Isabelo de los Reyes (founder of first workers' union); 1p. Aurora Aragon Quezon (social worker and former First Lady); 1p.20, Francisco Dagohoy; 2p. Juan Sumulong (politician); 2p.30, Professor Nicanor Abelardo (composer); 3p.20, General Vicente Lim.
For these designs in other values, see Nos. 1811/15.

539 Worker with Tower Award

1982. Tower Awards (for best "Blue Collar" Workers). Multicoloured.
1705 40s. Type **539** (inscr "MANGGAGAWA") 25 10
1705d 40s. Type **539** (inscr "MANGAGAWA") . . 60 10
1706 1p.20 Cogwheel and tower award (inscr "MANGGAGAWA") 65 20
1706b 1p.20 As No. 1706 but inscr "Mangagawa" . . 1·25 20

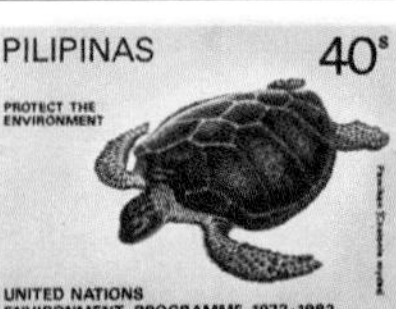

PILIPINAS 40s
PROTECT THE ENVIRONMENT
UNITED NATIONS
ENVIRONMENT PROGRAMME 1972-1982

541 Green Turtle

1982. 10th Anniv of United Nations Environment Programme. Multicoloured.
1707 40s. Type **541** 25 10
1708 3p.20 Philippine eagle . . . 3·50 1·25

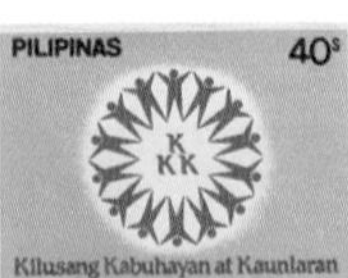

542 K.K.K. Emblem

1982. Inauguration of Kilusang Kabuhayan at Kaunlaran (national livelihood movement).
1709 **542** 40s. green, light green and black 15 10
1816 60s. green, light green and black 20 10
1817 60s. green, red and black 20 15

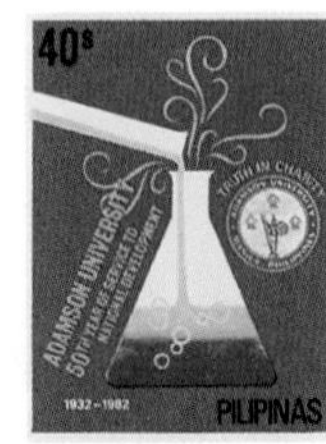

543 Chemistry Apparatus and Emblem

1982. 50th Anniv of Adamson University.
1710 **543** 40s. multicoloured . . . 25 10
1711 1p.20 multicoloured . . 65 20

544 Dr. Fernando G. Calderon and Emblems

1982. 75th Anniv of College of Medicine, University of the Philippines.
1712 **544** 40s. multicoloured . . . 25 10
1713 3p.20 multicoloured . . 1·50 50

545 President Marcos **546** Hands supporting Family

1982. 65th Birthday of President Ferdinand Marcos.
1714 **545** 40s. multicoloured . . . 25 10
1715 3p.20 multicoloured . . 1·50 40

1982. 25th Anniv of Social Security System.
1717 **546** 40s. black, orange & blue 20 10
1718 1p.20 black, orange and green 65 15

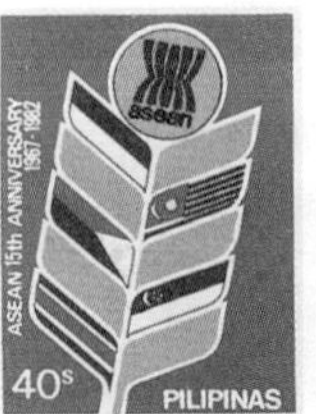

547 Emblem and Flags forming Ear of Wheat

1982. 15th Anniv of Association of South East Asian Nations.
1719 **547** 40s. multicoloured . . . 30 10

548 St. Theresa of Avila

1982. 400th Death Anniv of St. Theresa of Avila. Multicoloured.
1720 40s. Type **548** 25 10
1721 1p.20 St. Theresa and map of Europe, Africa and Asia 50 15
1722 2p. As 1p.20 . . . . 1·00 25

549 St. Isabel College

1982. 350th Anniv of St. Isabel College.
1723 **549** 40s. multicoloured . . . 25 10
1724 1p. multicoloured . . . 65 20

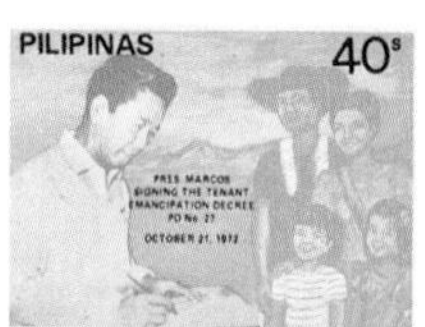

550 President Marcos signing Decree and Tenant Family

1982. 10th Anniv of Tenant Emancipation Decree.
1725a **550** 40s. green, brown and black (37 × 27 mm) 30 10
1726 40s. green, brown and black (32 × 22½ mm) 25 10

551 "Reading Tree"

1982. Literacy Campaign.
1727 **551** 40s. multicoloured . . . 20 10
1728 2p.30 multicoloured . . 1·00 25

552 Helmeted Heads

1982. 43rd World Congress of Skal Clubs, Manila.
1729 40s. Type **552** 25 10
1730 2p. Head in feathered head-dress . . . . 1·40 25

553 Dancers with Parasols

1982. 25th Anniv of Bayanihan Folk Arts Centre. Multicoloured.
1731 40s. Type **553** 35 10
1732 2p.80 Dancers (different) . . 1·50 30

554 Dr. Robert Koch and Bacillus

1982. Cent of Discovery of Tubercule Bacillus.
1733 **554** 40s. red, blue and black 25 10
1734 2p.80 multicoloured . . 1·60 50

555 Father Christmas in Sleigh

1982. Christmas.
1735 **555** 40s. multicoloured . . . 60 10
1736 1p. multicoloured . . . 1·75 20

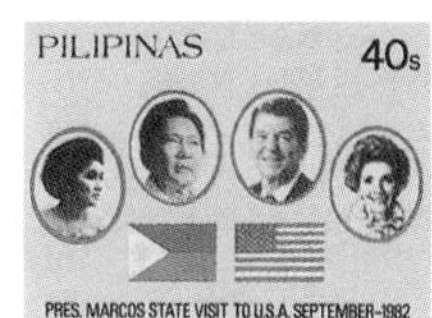

556 Presidential Couples and Flags

1982. State Visit of Pres. Marcos to United States.
1737 **556** 40s. multicoloured . . . 20 10
1738 3p.20 multicoloured . . 1·40 45

557 Woman with Sewing Machine

559 Eulogio Rodriguez

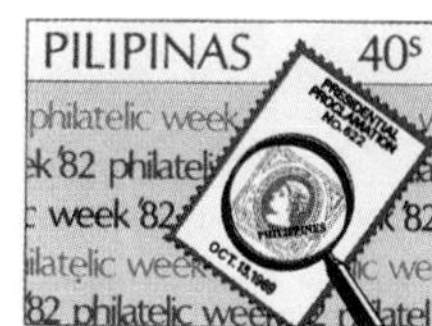

558 Stamp and Magnifying Glass

1982. U.N. World Assembly on Ageing.
1740a **557** 1p.20 green and orange 85 15
1741a – 2p. pink and blue . . . 1·10 20
DESIGN: 2p. Man with carpentry tools.

1983. Philatelic Week.
1742 **558** 40s. multicoloured . . . 20 10
1743 1p. multicoloured . . . 60 15

1983. Birth Centenary of Eulogio Rodriguez (former President of Senate).
1744a **559** 40s. multicoloured . . . 25 10
1745 1p.20 multicoloured . . 65 15

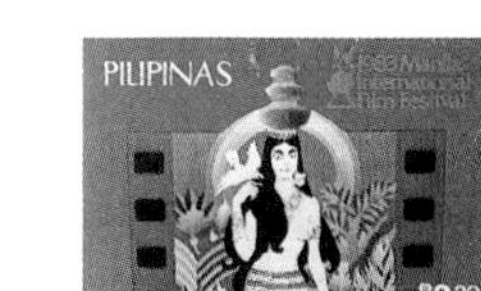

560 Symbolic Figure and Film Frame

1983. Manila International Film Festival.
1746a **560** 40s. multicoloured . . . 25 10
1747a 3p.20 multicoloured . . 1·50 30

561 Monument

1983. 2nd Anniv of Beatification of Lorenzo Ruiz.
1748 **561** 40s. yellow, red and black 25 10
1749 1p.20 multicoloured . . 70 15

562 Early Printing Press

1983. 390th Anniv of First Local Printing Press.
1750 **562** 40s. green and black . . 25 10

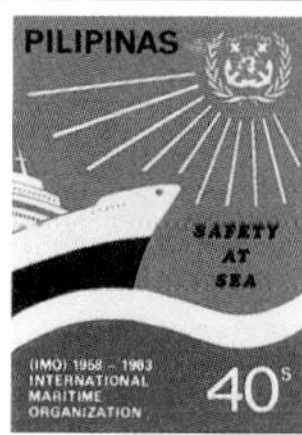

563 Emblem and Ship

1983. 25th Anniv of International Maritime Organization.
1751 **563** 40s. red, black and blue 25 10

1983. 7th National Scout Jamboree. No. 1709 optd **7TH BSP NATIONAL JAMBOREE 1983**.
1752 **542** 40s. green, light green and black 25 10

1983. Nos. 1360/9 surch **40s**.
1753 – 40s. on 45c. green . . . 35 10
1754 **387** 40s. on 45c. green . . . 35 10
1755 **388** 40s. on 45c. green . . . 35 10
1756 **389** 40s. on 45c. green . . . 35 10
1757 – 40s. on 45c. green . . . 35 10
1758 – 40s. on 45c. green . . . 35 10
1759 **392** 40s. on 45c. green . . . 35 10
1760 **393** 40s. on 45c. green . . . 35 10
1761 **394** 40s. on 45c. green . . . 35 10
1762 – 40s. on 45c. green . . . 35 10

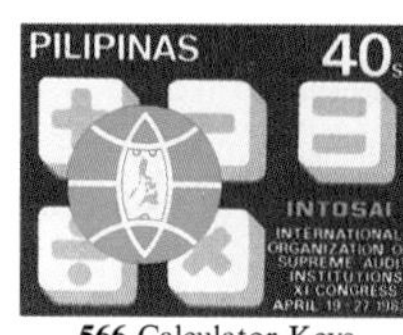

566 Calculator Keys

1983. 11th International Organization of Supreme Audit Institutions Congress.
1763 **566** 40s. blue, light blue and silver 25 10
1764 – 2p.80 multicoloured . . 1·25 40
DESIGN: 2p.80, Congress emblem.

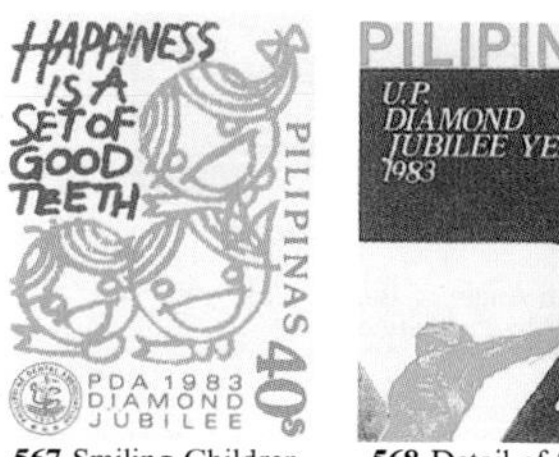

567 Smiling Children **568** Detail of Statue

1983. 75th Anniv of Philippine Dental Association.
1766 **567** 40s. green, mauve & brn 25 10

1983. 75th Anniv of University of the Philippines.
1767 **568** 40s. brown and green . . 20 10
1768 – 1p.20 multicoloured . . 60 15
DESIGN: 1p.20, Statue and diamond.

569 Yasuhiro Nakasone and Pres. Marcos

1983. Visit of Japanese Prime Minister.
1769 **569** 40s. multicoloured . . . 25 10

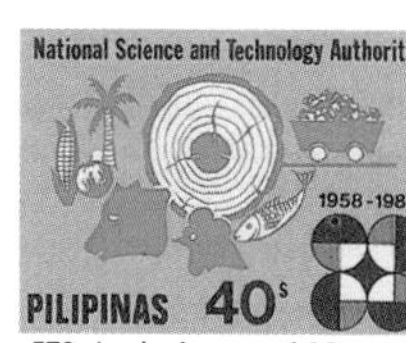

570 Agriculture and Natural Resources

1983. 25th Anniv of National Science and Technology Authority. Multicoloured.
1770 40s. Type **570** 70 30
1771 40s. Heart, medical products and food (Health and nutrition) 30 10
1772 40s. Industrial complex and air (Industry and energy) 45 15
1773 40s. House, scientific equipment and book (Sciences and social science) 30 10

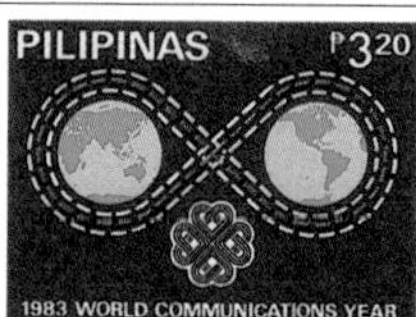

571 Globes and W.C.Y. Emblem

1983. World Communication Year.
1774 **571** 3p.20 multicoloured . . 1·50 50

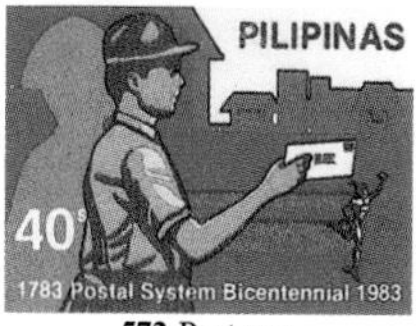

572 Postman

1983. Bicent of Philippine Postal System.
1775 **572** 40s. multicoloured . . . 25 10

573 Woman with Tambourine

575 Woman casting Vote

574 University Activities

1983. Christmas. Multicoloured.
1776 40s. Type **573** 30 10
1777 40s. Man turning spit (left side) 30 10
1778 40s. Pig on spit 30 10
1779 40s. Man turning spit (right side) 30 10
1780 40s. Man with guitar . . . 30 10
Nos. 1776/80 were issued together, se-tenant, forming a composite design.

1983. 50th Anniv of Xavier University.
1782 **574** 40s. multicoloured . . . 25 10
1783 60s. multicoloured . . . 50 10

1983. 50th Anniv of Female Suffrage.
1784 **575** 40s. multicoloured . . . 25 10
1785 60s. multicoloured . . . 50 10

576 Workers

578 Red-vented Cockatoo

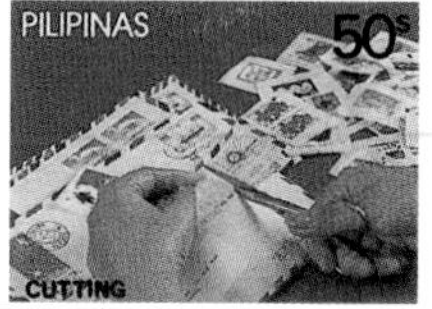

577 Cutting Stamp from Envelope

1983. 50th Anniv of Ministry of Labour and Employment.
1786 **576** 40s. multicoloured . . . 25 10
1787 60s. multicoloured . . . 50 10

1983. Philatelic Week. Multicoloured.
1788 50s. Type **577** 45 20
1789 50s. Sorting stamps 45 20
1790 50s. Soaking stamps 45 20
1791 50s. Hinging stamp 45 20
1792 50s. Mounting stamp in album 45 20

1984. Parrots. Multicoloured.
1793 40s. Type **578** 20 15
1794 2p.30 Guaiabero 80 40
1795 2p.80 Mountain racket-tailed parrot . . . . . . 1·00 40
1796 3p.20 Great-billed parrot . . 1·25 50

1797 3p.60 Muller's parrot . . . 1·50 50
1798 5p. Philippine hanging parrot . . . . 2·10 80

579 Princess Tarhata Kiram
580 Nun and Congregation

1984. 5th Death Anniv of Princess Tarhata Kiram.
1799 **579** 3p. deep green, green and red . . . . 1·00 15

1984. 300th Anniv of Religious Congregation of the Virgin Mary.
1800 **580** 40s. multicoloured . . . 30 10
1801 60s. multicoloured . . . 60 10

581 Dona Concha Felix de Calderon
583 Manila

1984. Birth Centenary of Dona Concha Felix de Calderon.
1802 **581** 60s. green and black . . 40 10
1803 3p.60 green and red . . 1·00 15

1984. Various stamps surch.
1804 **545** 60s. on 40s. multicoloured 20 10
1805 **558** 60s. on 40s. multicoloured 20 10
1806 – 3p.60 on 3p.20 blue (No. 1704) . . . . . 1·60 45

1984. As Nos. 1700/4 but values changed, and new designs as T **526**.
1807 60s. brown and black . . . 30 10
1808 60s. violet and black 35 10
1809 60s. black 40 10
1913 60s. blue 20 10
1889 60s. brown 20 10
1914 60s. red 15 10
1811 1p.80 blue 80 15
1812 2p.40 purple . . . . 1·00 15
1813 3p. brown . . . . 1·50 15
1814 3p.60 red . . . . 1·25 15
1815 4p.20 purple . . . . 1·75 30
DESIGNS: No. 1807, General Artemio Ricarte; 1808, Teodoro M. Kalaw (politician); 1809, Carlos P. Garcia (4th President); 1913, Quintin Paredes (senator); 1889, Dr. Deogracias V. Villadolid; 1914, Santiago Fonacier (former Senator and army chaplain); 1811, General Vicente Lim; 1812, Professor Nicanor Abelardo; 1813, Francisco Dagohoy; 1814, Aurora Aragon Quezon; 1815, Juan Sumulong.

1984. 150th Anniv of Ayala Corporation.
1818 **583** 70s. multicoloured . . . 30 10
1819 3p.60 multicoloured . . 1·25 30

584 "Lady of the Most Holy Rosary with St. Dominic" (C. Francisco)

1984. "Espana 84" International Stamp Exhibition, Madrid. Multicoloured.
1820 2p.50 Type **584** 65 20
1821 5p. "Spoliarum" (Juan Luna) . . . . 1·40 50

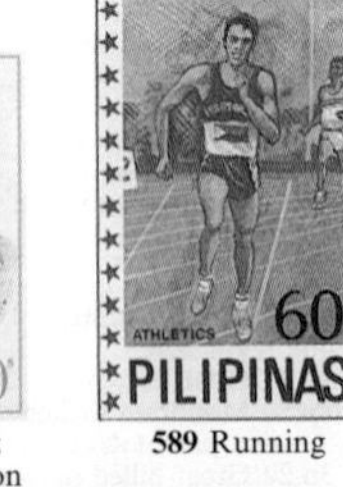

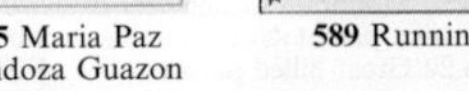

585 Maria Paz Mendoza Guazon
589 Running

586 "Adolias amlana"

1984. Birth Centenary of Dr. Maria Paz Mendoza Guazon.
1823 **585** 60s. red and blue 55 10
1824 65s. red, black and blue 45 20

1984. Butterflies. Multicoloured.
1825 60s. Type **586** 35 10
1826 2p.40 "Papilio daedalus" . . 70 15
1827 3p. "Prothoe franckii semperi" 95 25
1828 3p.60 Philippine birdwing 1·00 30
1829 4p.20 Lurcher . . . . . . 1·40 35
1830 5p. "Chilasa idaeoides" . . 1·75 35

1984. National Children's Book Day. Stamp from miniature sheet ("The Monkey and the Turtle") surch **7-17-84 NATIONAL CHILDREN'S BOOK DAY 20**. Perf or imperf.
1831 7p.20 on 7p.50 multicoloured . . . . . . 13·00 9·25

1984. 420th Anniv of Philippine–Mexican Friendship. Stamp from miniature sheet (Virgin of Manila) surch **420TH PHIL-MEXICAN FRIENDSHIP 8-3-84 20**. Perf or imperf.
1832 7p.20 on 7p.50 multicoloured . . . . . . 13·00 9·25

1984. Olympic Games, Los Angeles. Multicoloured.
1833 60s. Type **589** 25 10
1834 2p.40 Boxing 60 20
1835 6p. Swimming . . . . . . 1·25 25
1836 7p.20 Windsurfing . . . . . 1·60 40
1837 8p.40 Cycling . . . . 1·75 45
1838 20p. Running (woman athlete) . . . . 4·00 75

590 The Mansion

1984. 75th Anniv of Baguio City.
1840 **590** 1p.20 multicoloured . . 75 15

1984. 300th Anniv of Our Lady of Holy Rosary Parish. Stamp from miniature sheet ("Lady of the Most Holy Rosary") surch **9-1-84 300TH YR O.L. HOLY ROSARY PARISH 20**. Perf or imperf.
1841 7p.20 on 7p.50 multicoloured . . . . . . 13·00 9·25

592 Electric Train on Viaduct

1984. Light Railway Transit.
1842 **592** 1p.20 multicoloured . . 75 15

593 Australian and Philippine Stamps and Koalas

1984. "Ausipex 84" International Stamp Exhibition, Melbourne.
1843 **593** 3p. multicoloured . . . 1·00 25
1844 3p.60 multicoloured . . 1·25 30

1984. National Museum Week. Stamp from miniature sheet (as No. 1821) surch **NATIONAL MUSEUM WEEK 10-5-84 20**. Perf or imperf.
1846 7p.20 on 7p.50 multicoloured . . . . . . 13·00 9·25

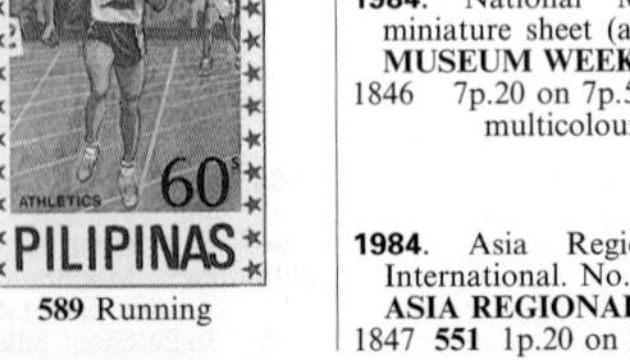

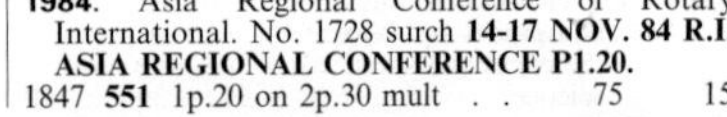

1984. Asia Regional Conference of Rotary International. No. 1728 surch **14-17 NOV. 84 R.I. ASIA REGIONAL CONFERENCE P1.20.**
1847 **551** 1p.20 on 2p.30 mult . . 75 15

596 Gold Award

1984. Philatelic Week. Gold Award at "Ausipex 84" to Mario Que. Multicoloured.
1848 1p.20 Type **596** 45 15
1849 3p. Page of Que's exhibit . . 1·10 30

597 Caracao

1984. Water Transport. Multicoloured.
1850 60s. Type **597** 25 10
1851 1p.20 Chinese junk 55 20
1852 6p. Spanish galleon . . . . 1·50 25
1853 7p.20 Casco (Filipino cargo prau) . . . . 1·90 40
1854 8p.40 Early paddle-steamer 2·10 45
1855 20p. Modern liner . . . . . 4·50 75

599 Anniversary Emblem

1984. 125th Anniv of Ateneo de Manila University.
1857 **599** 60s. blue and gold . . . 30 10
1858 1p.20 blue and silver . . 60 15

600 Virgin and Child
602 Abstract

601 Manila–Dagupan Steam Locomotive, 1892

1984. Christmas. Multicoloured.
1859 60s. Type **600** 45 10
1860 1p.20 Holy Family 90 25

1984. Rail Transport. Multicoloured.
1861 60s. Type **601** 25 10
1862 1p.20 Light Rail Transit eletric train, 1984 . . . . 55 20
1863 6p. Bicol express, 1955 . . . 1·50 25
1864 7p.20 Electric tram, 1905 . . 1·90 40
1865 8p.40 Diesel commuter railcar, 1972 . . . . . . 2·10 45
1866 20p. Horse tram, 1898 . . . 4·50 75

1984. 10th Anniv of Philippine Jaycees' Ten Outstanding Young Men Awards. Abstracts by Raul Isidro. Multicoloured.

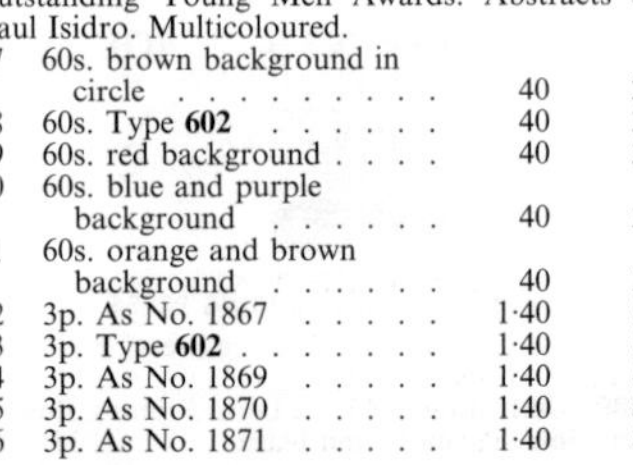

1867 60s. brown background in circle 40 20
1868 60s. Type **602** 40 20
1869 60s. red background 40 20
1870 60s. blue and purple background 40 20
1871 60s. orange and brown background 40 20
1872 3p. As No. 1867 . . . . . 1·40 80
1873 3p. Type **602** . . . . . . 1·40 80
1874 3p. As No. 1869 . . . . . 1·40 80
1875 3p. As No. 1870 . . . . . 1·40 80
1876 3p. As No. 1871 . . . . . 1·40 80

603 Tobacco Plant and Dried Leaf

1985. 25th Anniv of Philippine Virginia Tobacco Administration.
1877 **603** 60s. multicoloured . . . 20 10
1878 3p. multicoloured . . . 1·00 30

1985. Philatelic Week, 1984. Nos. 1848/9 optd **Philatelic Week 1984**.
1879 **596** 1p.20 multicoloured . . 40 15
1880 – 3p. multicoloured . . . 85 35

605 National Research Council Emblem

1985. 5th Pacific Science Association Congress.
1881 **605** 60s. black, blue and light blue 20 10
1882 1p.20 black, blue and orange 55 10

606 "Carmona retusa"

1985. Medicinal Plants. Multicoloured.
1883a 60s. Type **606** 25 10
1884 1p.20 "Orthosiphon aristatus" 50 15
1885 2p.40 "Vitex negundo" . . 80 30
1886 3p. "Aloe barbadensis" . . 90 35
1887 3p.60 "Quisqualis indica" 1·00 45
1888 4p.20 "Blumea balsamifera" . . . . . . 1·25 45

607 "Early Bird" Satellite

1985. 20th Anniv of International Telecommunications Satellite Organization.
1896 **607** 60s. multicoloured . . . 20 10
1897 3p. multicoloured . . . 1·25 25

608 Piebalds

1985. Horses. Multicoloured.
1898 60s. Type **608** 25 10
1899 1p.20 Palominos 55 20
1900 6p. Bays . . . . 1·50 25
1901 7p.20 Browns . . . . 1·90 40
1902 8p.40 Greys . . . . 2·10 45
1903 20p. Chestnuts . . . . . . 4·50 75

609 Emblem

1985. 25th Anniv of National Tax Research Centre.
1905 **609** 60s. multicoloured . . . 20 10

610 Transplanting Rice

1985. 25th Anniv of International Rice Research Institute, Los Baños. Multicoloured.

1906 60s. Type **610** 20 10

1907 3p. Paddy fields . . . . . . 1·25 30

611 Image of Holy Child of Cebu

1985. 420th Anniv of Filipino–Spanish Treaty. Mult.

1908 1p.20 Type **611** 30 15

1909 3p.60 Rajah Tupas and Miguel Lopez de Lagazpi signing treaty 95 20

613 Early Anti-TB Label

1985. 75th Anniv of Philippine Tuberculosis Society. Multicoloured.

1911 60s. Screening for TB, laboratory work, health education and inoculation 15 10

1912 1p.20 Type **613** 25 15

1985. 45th Anniv of Girl Scout Charter. No. 1409 surch **45th ANNIVERSARY GIRL SCOUT CHARTER**, emblem and new value.

1917 **348** 2p.40 on 15s. on 10s. multicoloured 95 30

1918 4p.20 on 15s. on 10s. multicoloured . . . . 1·25 40

1919 7p.20 on 15s. on 10s. multicoloured . . . . 2·40 75

616 "Our Lady of Fatima" **617** Family planting Tree

1985. Marian Year. 2000th Birth Anniversary of Virgin Mary. Multicoloured.

1920 1p.20 Type **616** 80 25

1921 2p.40 "Our Lady of Beaterio" (Juan Bueno Silva) . . . . 1·25 40

1922 3p. "Our Lady of Penafrancia" . . . . . . 1·50 50

1923 3p.60 "Our Lady of Guadalupe" . . . . . . 2·00 80

1985. Tree Week. International Year of the Forest.

1924 **617** 1p.20 multicoloured . . 60 15

618 Battle of Bessang Pass **619** Vicente Orestes Romualdez

1985. 40th Anniv of Bessang Pass Campaign.

1925 **618** 1p.20 multicoloured . . 75 15

1985. Birth Centenary of Vicente Orestes Romualdez (lawyer).

1926a **619** 60s. blue 20 10

1927a 2p. mauve 80 20

620 Fishing

1985. International Youth Year. Children's Paintings. Multicoloured.

1928 2p.40 Type **620** 65 15

1929 3p.60 Picnic 75 30

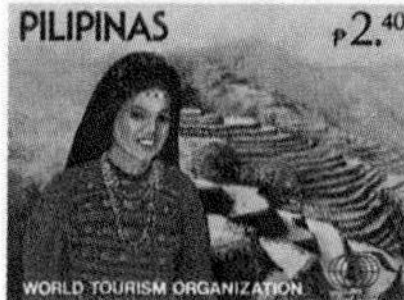

621 Banawe Rice Terraces

1985. World Tourism Organization Congress, Sofia, Bulgaria.

1930 **621** 2p.40 multicoloured . . 1·10 30

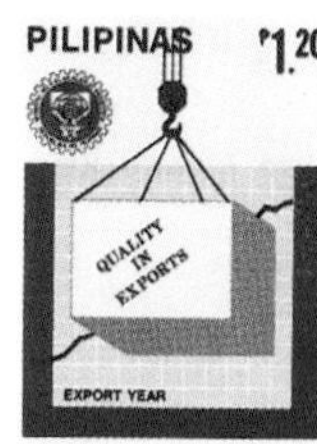

622 Export Graph and Crane lifting Crate **624** Emblem and Dove with Olive Branch

1985. Export Promotion Year.

1931 **622** 1p.20 multicoloured . . 60 15

1985. No. 1815 surch **P360**.

1932 3p.60 on 4p.20 purple . . . 2·25 55

1985. 40th Anniv of U.N.O.

1933 **624** 3p.60 multicoloured . . 1·50 50

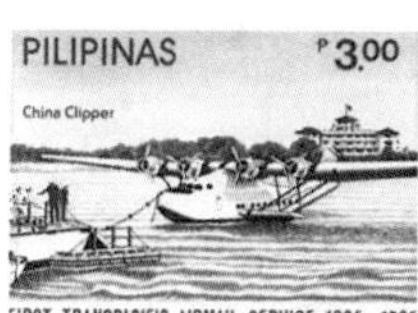

625 Martin M-130 Flying Boat "China Clipper"

1985. 50th Anniv of First Trans-Pacific Commercial Flight (San Francisco–Manila). Multicoloured.

1934 3p. Type **625** . . . . 1·00 30

1935 3p.60 Route map, "China Clipper" and anniversary emblem . . . . 1·50 40

1985. Philatelic Week. Nos. 1863/4 surch **PHILATELIC WEEK 1985**, No. 1937 further optd **AIRMAIL**.

1936 60s. on 6p. mult (postage) 25 15

1937 3p. on 7p.20 mult (air) . . . 1·25 45

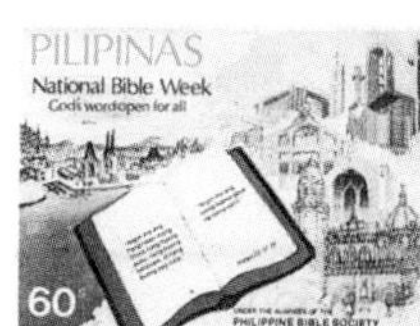

627 Bible and Churches

1985. National Bible Week.

1938 **627** 60s. multicoloured . . . 30 10

1939 3p. multicoloured . . . 1·25 40

628 Panuluyan (enactment of search for an inn)

1985. Christmas. Multicoloured.

1940 60s. Type **628** 25 10

1941 3p. Pagdalaw (nativity) . . 1·75 50

629 Justice holding Scales **630** Rizal and "Noli Me Tangere"

1986. 75th Anniv of College of Law.

1942 **629** 60s. mauve and black . . 25 10

1943 3p. green, purple & black . . . . 1·00 40

See also No. 2009.

1986. Centenary of Publication of "Noli Me Tangere" (Jose Rizal's first book).

1944 **630** 60s. violet 20 10

1945 – 1p.20 green 70 10

1946 – 3p.60 brown 85 10

DESIGNS: 1p.20, 3p.60, Rizal, "To the Flowers of Heidelberg" (poem) and Heidelberg University.

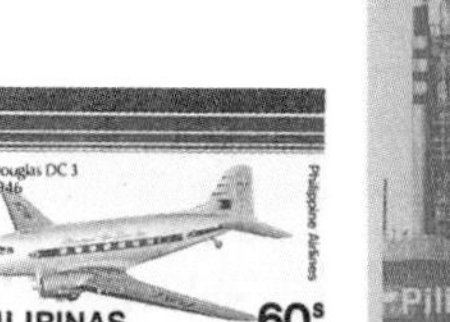

631 Douglas DC-3, 1946 **632** Oil Refinery, Manila Bay

1986. 45th Anniv of Philippine Airlines. Each red, black and blue.

1947 60s. Type **631** 20 10

1948 60s. Douglas DC-4 Skymaster, 1946 . . . . 20 10

1949 60s. Douglas DC-6, 1948 . . 20 10

1950 60s. Vickers Viscount 784, 1957 . . . . 20 10

1951 2p.40 Fokker F.27 Friendship, 1960 . . . . 80 35

1952 2p.40 Douglas DC-8-50, 1962 . . . . 80 35

1953 2p.40 B.A.C. One Eleven 500, 1964 . . . . . . 80 35

1954 2p.40 Douglas DC-10-30, 1974 . . . . 80 35

1955 3p.60 Beech 18, 1941 . . . 1·10 55

1956 3p.60 Boeing 747-200, 1980 1·10 55

See also No. 2013.

1986. 25th Anniv of Bataan Refinery Corporation.

1957 **632** 60s. silver and green . . 25 10

1958 – 3p. silver and blue . . . 1·00 35

DESIGN—HORIZ: 3p. Refinery (different).

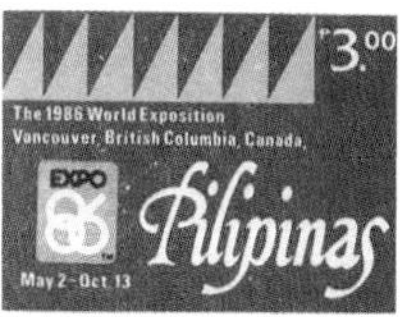

633 Emblem

1986. "Expo 86" World's Fair, Vancouver.

1959 **633** 60s. multicoloured . . . 25 10

1960 3p. multicoloured . . . 1·00 25

634 Emblem and Industrial and Agricultural Symbols

1986. 25th Anniv of Asian Productivity Organization.

1961 **634** 60s. black, green & orge 25 10

1962 3p. black, green & orange . . . . 1·25 30

1963 3p. brown (30 × 22 mm) 65 10

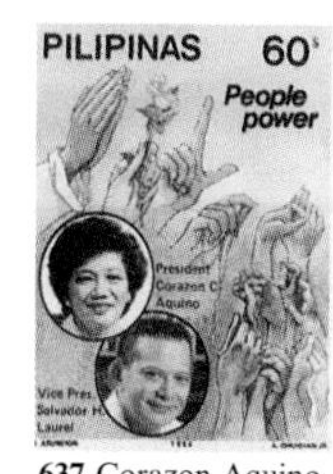

635 1906 2c. Stamp **637** Corazon Aquino, Salvador Laurel and Hands

1986. "Ameripex 86" Int Stamp Exhibition, Chicago.

1964 **635** 60s. green, black & yellow 25 10

1965 – 3p. bistre, black and green . . . . 1·25 30

DESIGN: 3p. 1935 20c. stamp.

See also No. 2006.

1986. "People Power". Multicoloured.

1966 60s. Type **637** 10 10

1967 1p.20 Radio antennae, helicopter and people . . 40 10

1968 2p.40 Religious procession 75 15

1969 3p. Crowds around soldiers in tanks 75 25

638 Monument and Paco and Taft Schools

1986. 75th Anniv of First La Salle School in Philippines.

1971 **638** 60s. black, lilac and green 25 10

1972 – 2p.40 black, blue & grn 65 15

1973 – 3p. black, yellow & green . . . . 1·10 25

DESIGNS: 2p.40, St. Miguel Febres Cordero and Paco School; 3p. St. Benilde and Taft school; 7p.20, Founding brothers of Paco school.

639 Aquino praying **640** "Vanda sanderiana"

1986. 3rd Death Anniv of Benigno S. Aquino, jun.

1975 – 60s. green 25 10

1976 **639** 2p. multicoloured . . . 65 15

1977 – 3p.60 multicoloured . . 1·10 25

DESIGNS—27 × 36 mm (as T **526**): 60s. Aquino. HORIZ (as T **639**): 3p.60, Aquino (different).

See also No. 2007.

1986. Orchids. Multicoloured.

1979 60s. Type **640** 30 10

1980 1p.20 "Epigeneium lyonii" 90 15

1981 2p.40 "Paphiopedilum philippinense" . . . . . 1·60 30

1982 3p. "Amesiella philippinense" . . . . . 1·90 45

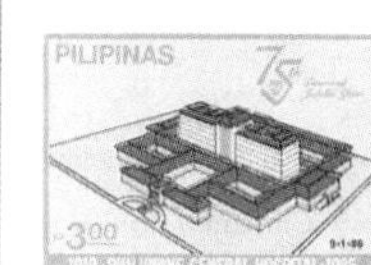

641 "Christ carrying the Cross" **642** Hospital

1986. 400th Anniv of Quiapo District.

1983 **641** 60s. red, black and mauve 25 10

1984 – 3p.60 blue, black & grn 1·50 40

DESIGN—HORIZ: 3p.60, Quiapo Church.

1986. 75th Anniv of Philippine General Hospital.

1985 **642** 60s. multicoloured . . . 20 10

1986 3p. multicoloured . . . 1·00 20

2012 5p. brown . . . . 1·25 15

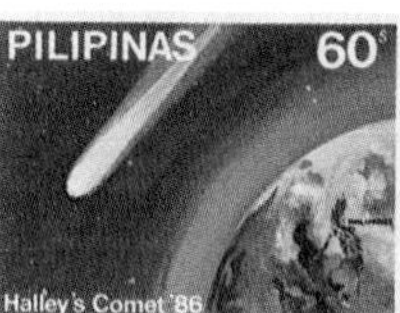

643 Comet and Earth

1986. Appearance of Halley's Comet. Multicoloured.

1987 60s. Type **643** 25 10

1988 2p.40 Comet, Moon and Earth . . . . 1·10 20

644 Handshake

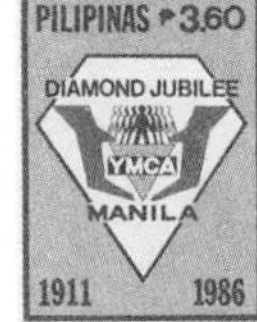

645 Emblem

1986. 74th International Dental Federation Congress, Manila. Multicoloured.

1989		60s. Type **644**	25	10
1990		3p. Jeepney, Manila	1·10	20

See also Nos. 2008 and 2011.

1986. 75th Anniv of Manila Young Men's Christian Association.

1991	**645**	2p. blue	80	15
1992		3p.60 red	1·60	25
2058		4p. blue	1·00	10

646 Old and New Buildings

1986. 85th Anniv of Philippine Normal College.

1993	–	60s. multicoloured	30	10
1994	**646**	3p.60 yellow, brown & bl	1·50	30

DESIGN: 60s. Old and new buildings (different).

647 Butterfly and Beetles

1986. Philatelic Week and International Peace Year.

1995	**647**	60s. multicoloured	55	10
1996	–	1p. blue and black	1·10	20
1997	–	3p. multicoloured	1·60	40

DESIGNS—VERT: 1p. Peace Year emblem. HORIZ: 3p. Dragonflies.

648 Mother and Child

651 Emblem

650 Manila Hotel, 1912

1986. Christmas. Multicoloured.

1998		60s. Type **648**	25	10
1999		60s. Couple with child and cow	25	10
2000		60s. Mother and child with doves	25	10
2001		1p. Mother and child receiving gifts (horiz)	35	10
2002		1p. Mother and child beneath arch (horiz)	35	10
2003		1p. Madonna and shepherd adoring child (horiz)	35	10
2004		1p. Shepherds and animals around child in manger (horiz)	35	10

1987. No. 1944 surch **P100**.

2005	**630**	1p. on 60s. violet	25	10

1987. As previous issues but smaller, 22 × 30 mm, 30 × 22 mm or 32 × 22 mm (5p.50), and values and colours changed.

2006	–	75s. green (As No. 1965)	25	10
2007	–	1p. blue (As No. 1975)	25	10
2008	**644**	3p.25 green	75	20
2009	**629**	3p.50 brown	1·00	25
2011	–	4p.75 green (As No. 1990)	1·25	20
2013	–	5p.50 blue (As No. 1956)	1·50	25

1987. 75th Anniv of Manila Hotel.

2014	**650**	1p. bistre and black	25	10
2015	–	4p. multicoloured	1·00	15
2016	–	4p.75 multicoloured	1·40	25
2017	–	5p.50 multicoloured	1·75	45

DESIGNS: 4p. Hotel; 4p.75, Lobby; 5p.50, Staff in ante-lobby.

1987. 50th Anniv of International Eucharistic Congress, Manila. Multicoloured.

2018		75s. Type **651**	25	10
2019		1p. Emblem (different) (horiz)	35	10

652 Pres. Cory Aquino taking Oath

1987. Ratification of New Constitution.

2020	**652**	1p. multicoloured	25	15
2021	–	5p.50 blue and brown	1·25	30
2060	–	5p.50 green and brown (22 × 31 mm)	1·10	20

DESIGN: 5p.50, Constitution on open book and dove.

653 Dr. Jose P. Laurel (founder) and Tower

1987. 35th Anniv of Lyceum.

2022	**653**	1p. multicoloured	30	10
2023		2p. multicoloured	70	15

654 City Seal, Man with Philippine Eagle and Woman with Fruit

1987. 50th Anniv of Davao City.

2024	**654**	1p. multicoloured	20	15

655 Salary and Policy Loans

656 Emblem and People in Hand

1987. 50th Anniv of Government Service Insurance System. Multicoloured.

2025		1p. Type **655**	25	10
2026		1p.25 Disability and medicare	40	10
2027		2p. Retirement benefits	70	15
2028		3p.50 Survivorship benefits	95	25

1987. 50th Anniv of Salvation Army in Philippines.

2029	**656**	1p. multicoloured	60	10

657 Woman, Ballot Box and Map

659 Man with Outstretched Arm

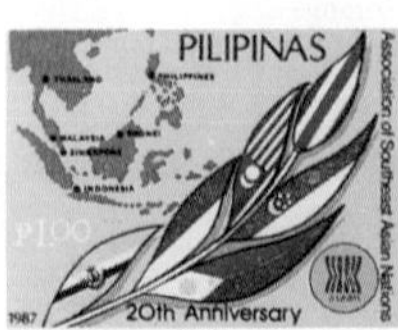

658 Map and Flags as Leaves

1987. 50th Anniv of League of Women Voters.

2030	**657**	1p. blue and mauve	30	10

1987. As T **526**.

2031		1p. green	25	10
2032		1p. blue	25	10
2033		1p. red	25	10
2034		1p. purple and red	20	10

DESIGNS: No. 2031, Gen. Vicente Lukban; 2032, Wenceslao Q. Vinzons; 2033, Brigadier-General Mateo M. Capinpin; 2034, Jesus Balmori.

1987. 20th Anniv of Association of South-East Asian Nations.

2035	**658**	1p. multicoloured	45	10

1987. Exports.

2036	**659**	1p. multicoloured	20	10
2037	–	2p. green, yellow & brn	45	10
2059	–	4p.75 blue and black	95	10

DESIGN: 2p., 4p.75, Man, cogwheel and factory.

660 Nuns, People and Crucifix within Flaming Heart

661 Statue and Stained Glass Window

1967. 125th Anniv of Daughters of Charity in the Philippines.

2038	**660**	1p. blue, red and black	35	10

1987. Canonization of Blessed Lorenzo Ruiz de Manila (first Filipino saint). Multicoloured.

2039		1p. Type **661**	40	15
2040		5p.50 Lorenzo Ruiz praying before execution	1·60	35

1987. No. 2012 surch **P4.75**.

2042	**642**	4p.75 on 5p. brown	1·10	20

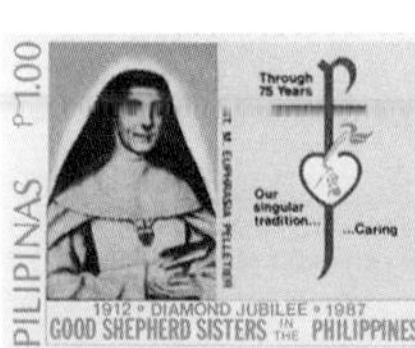

663 Nun and Emblem

1987. 75th Anniv of Good Shepherd Sisters in Philippines.

2043	**663**	1p. multicoloured	75	15

664 Founders

1987. 50th Anniv of Philippines Boy Scouts.

2044	**664**	1p. multicoloured	35	10

665 Family with Stamp Album

1987. 50th Anniv of Philippine Philatelic Club.

2045	**665**	1p. multicoloured	35	10

666 Monks, Church and Wrecked Galleon

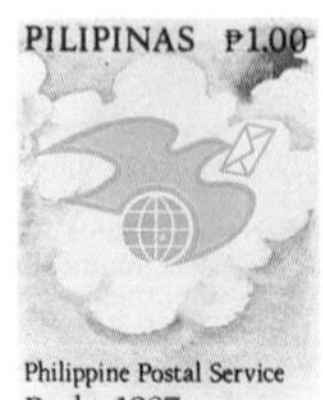

668 Dove with Letter

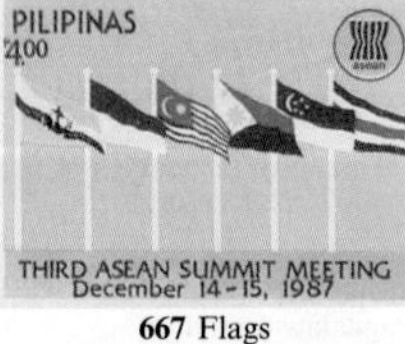

667 Flags

1987. 400th Anniv of Dominican Order in Philippines.

2046	**666**	1p. black, blue and orange	25	15
2047	–	4p.75 multicoloured	1·10	20
2048	–	5p.50 multicoloured	1·60	25

DESIGNS: 4p.75, J. A. Jeronimo Guerrero, Diego de Sta. Maria and Letran Dominican college; 5p.50, Pope and monks.

1987. 3rd Association of South-east Asian Nations Summit Meeting.

2049	**667**	4p. multicoloured	1·50	20

1987. Christmas. Multicoloured.

2050		1p. Type **668**	40	15
2051		1p. People and star decoration	40	15
2052		4p. Crowd going to church	1·25	20
2053		4p.75 Mother and children exchanging gifts	1·40	20
2054		5p.50 Children and bamboo cannons	1·75	25
2055		8p. Children at table bearing festive fare	2·25	40
2056		9p.50 Woman at table	2·50	45
2057		11p. Woman having Christmas meal	3·00	50

669 Emblem, Headquarters and Dr. Rizal

1987. 75th Anniv of Grand Lodge of Philippine Masons.

2061	**669**	1p. multicoloured	45	10

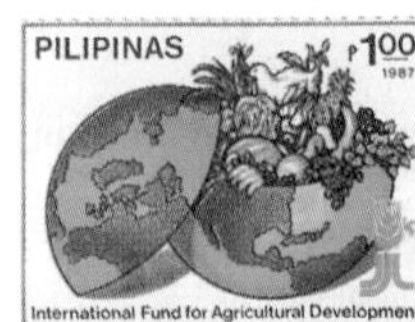

670 Foodstuffs in Split Globe

1987. 40th Anniv of U.N.O. Multicoloured.

2062		1p. Type **670** (International Fund for Agricultural Development)	25	10
2063		1p. Means of transport and communications (Asian and Pacific Transport and Communications Decade)	25	10
2064		1p. People and hands holding houses (International Year of Shelter for the Homeless)	25	10
2065		1p. Happy children playing musical instruments (World Health Day: UNICEF child vaccination campaign)	25	10

671 Official Seals and Gavel

1988. Opening Session of 1987 Congress. Mult.

2066		1p. Type **671**	25	10
2067		5p.50 Congress in session and gavel (horiz)	1·75	35

672 Children and Bosco

1988. Death Centenary of St. John Bosco (founder of Salesian Brothers).

2068	**672**	1p. multicoloured	20	10
2069		5p.50 multicoloured	1·50	30

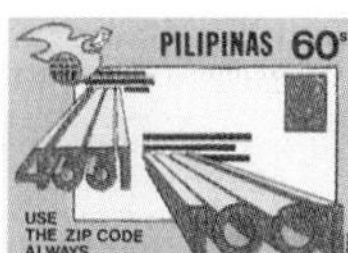

673 Emblem
675 Envelope with Coded Addresses

1988. Buy Philippine-Made Movement Month.
2070 **673** 1p. multicoloured . . . 25 10

1988. Various stamps surch **P 3.00**.
2071 – 3p. on 3p.60 brown (No. 1946) 85 25
2072 **645** 3p. on 3p.60 red 85 25
2073 – 3p. on 3p.60 mult (No. 1977) 90 25
2074 – 3p. on 3p.60 blue, black and green (No. 1984) 1·10 25
2075 **646** 3p. on 3p.60 yellow, brown and blue . . . 1·10 25

1988. Postal Codes.
2076 **675** 60s. multicoloured . . . 20 10
2077 1p. multicoloured . . . 25 10

676 "Vesbius purpureus" (soldier bug)
677 Solar Eclipse

1988. Insect Predators. Multicoloured.
2078 1p. Type **676** 25 10
2079 5p.50 "Campsomeris aurulenta" (dagger wasp) 1·25 25

1988.
2080 **677** 1p. multicoloured . . . 35 10
2081 5p.50 multicoloured . . 1·40 25

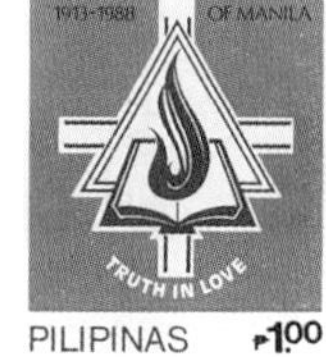

678 Teodoro
679 Emblem

1988. 101st Birth Anniv of Toribio Teodoro (industrialist).
2082 **678** 1p. cinnamon, brn & red 20 10
2083 1p.20 blue, brown & red 25 10

1988. 75th Anniv of College of Holy Spirit.
2084 **679** 1p. brown, gold & black 25 10
2085 – 4p. brown, green & black . . . . 1·00 20
DESIGN: 4p. Arnold Janssen (founder) and Sister Edelwina (director, 1920–47).

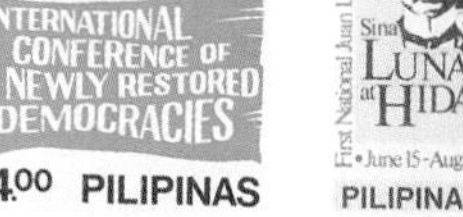

680 Emblem
681 Luna and Hidalgo

1988. Newly Restored Democracies International Conference.
2086 **680** 4p. blue, ultram & blk 1·25 20

1988. National Juan Luna and Felix Resurreccion Hidalgo Memorial Exhibition.
2087 **681** 1p. black, yellow & brn 25 10
2088 5p.50 black, cinnamon and brown . . . . . 1·00 20

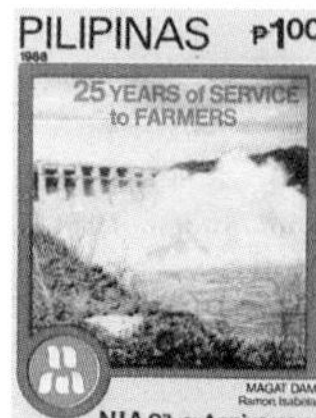

682 Magat Dam, Ramon, Isabela

1988. 25th Anniv of National Irrigation Administration.
2089 **682** 1p. multicoloured . . . 25 10
2090 5p.50 multicoloured . . 1·25 25

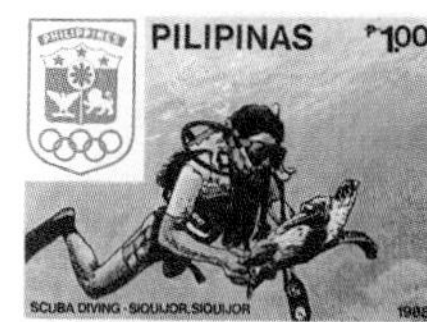

683 Scuba Diving, Siquijor

1988. Olympic Games, Seoul (1st issue). Multicoloured. Perf or imperf.
2091 1p. Type **683** 25 10
2092 1p.20 Big game fishing, Aparri, Cagayan 40 15
2093 4p. Yachting, Manila Central . . . . 1·00 20
2094 5p.50 Mountain climbing, Mt. Apo, Davao . . . . 1·10 20
2095 8p. Golfing, Cebu City . . . 1·60 25
2096 11p. Cycling (Tour of Mindanao), Marawi City 2·25 55
See also Nos. 2113/18.

684 Headquarters, Plaza Santa Cruz, Manila
686 Balagtas

1988. Banking Anniversaries. Multicoloured.
2097 1p. Type **684** (50th anniv of Philippine International Commercial Bank) . . . 25 10
2098 1p. Family looking at factory and countryside (25th anniv of Land Bank) 25 10
2099 5p.50 Type **684** . . . . . . 1·25 25
2100 5p.50 As No. 2098 . . . . 1·25 25

1988. Various stamps surch.
2101 1p.90 on 2p.40 mult (No. 1968) 60 15
2102 1p.90 on 2p.40 black, blue and green (No. 1972) . . . 60 25
2103 1p.90 on 2p.40 mult (No. 1981) 60 15
2104 1p.90 on 2p.40 mult (No. 1988) 60 15

1988. Birth Bicentenary of Francisco Balagtas Baltasco (writer). Each green, brown and yellow.
2105 1p. Type **686** 20 10
2106 1p. As Type **686** but details reversed 20 10

687 Hospital
688 Brown Mushroom

1988. 50th Anniv of Quezon Institute (tuberculosis hospital).
2107 **687** 1p. multicoloured . . . 25 10
2108 5p.50 multicoloured . . 1·50 35

1988. Fungi. Multicoloured.
2109 60s. Type **688** 20 10
2110 1p. Rat's ear fungus 40 15
2111 2p. Abalone mushroom . . 65 25
2112 4p. Straw mushroom . . . 1·40 45

689 Archery
691 Red Cross Work

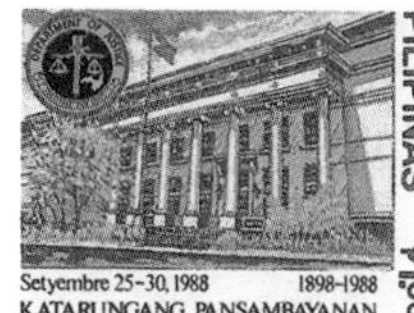

690 Department of Justice

1988. Olympic Games, Seoul (2nd issue). Multicoloured. Perf or imperf.
2113 1p. Type **689** 25 10
2114 1p.20 Tennis 25 10
2115 4p. Boxing . . . . 1·00 15
2116 5p.50 Athletics . . . . . . 1·25 15
2117 8p. Swimming . . . . . . 1·60 20
2118 11p. Cycling . . . . 2·25 55

1988. Law and Justice Week.
2120 **690** 1p. multicoloured . . . 20 10

1988. 125th Anniv of Red Cross.
2121 **691** 1p. multicoloured . . . 25 10
2122 5p.50 multicoloured . . 1·50 35

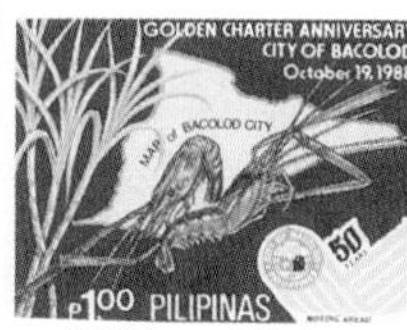

692 Girl and Boy
693 Map and Shrimps

1988. 50th Anniv of Christian Children's Fund.
2123 **692** 1p. multicoloured . . . 20 10

1988. 50th Anniv of Bacolod City Charter.
2124 **693** 1p. multicoloured . . . 25 10

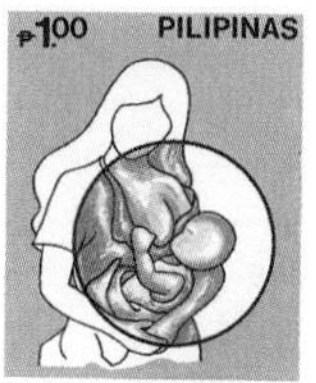

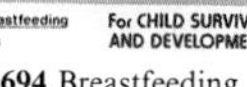

694 Breastfeeding
695 A. Aragon Quezon

1988. Child Survival Campaign. Multicoloured.
2125 1p. Type **694** 25 10
2126 1p. Growth monitoring . . 25 10
2127 1p. Immunization 25 10
2128 1p. Oral rehydration 25 10
2129 1p. Access for the disabled (U.N. Decade of Disabled Persons) 25 10

1988. Birth Centenary of Aurora Aragon Quezon.
2130 **695** 1p. multicoloured . . . 20 10
2131 5p.50 multicoloured . . 1·25 25

696 Post Office
697 Sampaloc Branch Transmitter

1988. Philatelic Week. Multicoloured.
2132 1p. Type **696** (inscr "1938") 20 15
2132b 1p. Type **696** (inscr "1988") 35 15
2133 1p. Stamp counter 20 15
2134 1p. Fern and stamp displays 20 15
2135 1p. People looking at stamp displays 20 15

1988. 10 Years of Technological Improvements by Philippine Long Distance Telephone Company.
2136 **697** 1p. multicoloured . . . 25 10

698 Clasped Hands and Dove
699 Crowd with Banners

1988. Christmas. Multicoloured.
2137 75s. Type **698** 20 10
2138 1p. Children making decorations (horiz) . . . 20 10
2139 2p. Man carrying decorations on yoke (horiz) 50 15
2140 3p.50 Christmas tree 75 15
2141 4p.75 Candle and stars . . . 1·00 20
2142 5p.50 Reflection of star forming heart (horiz) . . 1·25 25

1988. Commission on Human Rights (2143) and 40th Anniv of Universal Declaration of Human Rights (2144). Multicoloured.
2143 1p. Type **699** 25 10
2144 1p. Doves escaping from cage 25 10

700 Church, 1776
701 Statue and School

1988. 400th Anniv of Malate. Multicoloured.
2145 1p. Type **700** 20 10
2146 1p. Our Lady of Remedies Church anniversary emblem and statue of Virgin (Eduardo Castrillo) 20 10
2147 1p. Church, 1880 . . . . . 20 10
2148 1p. Church, 1988 . . . . . 20 10

1988. 50th Anniv of University of Santo Tomas Graduate School.
2149 **701** 1p. multicoloured . . . 25 10

702 Order's Activities
703 Miguel Ver (first leader)

1989. 50th Anniv of Oblates of Mary Immaculate.
2150 **702** 1p. multicoloured . . . 25 10

1989. 47th Anniv of Recognition of Hunters ROTC Guerrilla Unit (formed by Military Academy and University students). Mult.
2151 1p. Type **703** 15 10
2152 1p. Eleuterio Adevoso (leader after Ver's death) 15 10

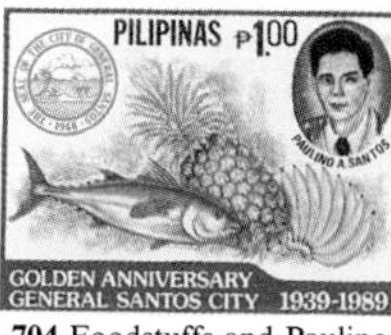

704 Foodstuffs and Paulino Santos
705 Sinulog

1989. 50th Anniv of General Santos City.
2153 **704** 1p. multicoloured . . . 30 10

1989. "Fiesta Islands '89" (1st series). Mult.
2154 4p.75 Type **705** 80 15
2155 5p.50 Cenaculo (Lenten festival) 85 30
2156 6p.25 Iloilo Paraw Regatta 1·00 20
See also Nos. 2169/71, 2177/9, 2194/6 and 2210.

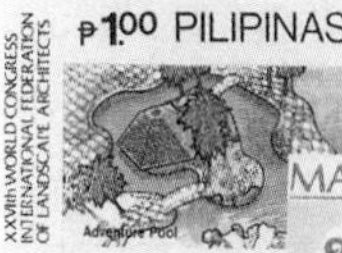

706 Tomas Mapua
707 Adventure Pool

1989. Birth Centenaries. Multicoloured.
2157 1p. Type **706** 25 10
2158 1p. Camilo Osias 25 10
2159 1p. Dr. Olivia Salamanca 25 10
2160 1p. Dr. Francisco Santiago 25 10
2161 1p. Leandro Fernandez . . 25 10

1989. 26th International Federation of Landscape Architects World Congress, Manila. Mult.
2162 1p. Type **707** 20 10
2163 1p. Paco Park 20 10
2164 1p. Street improvements in Malacanang area 20 10
2165 1p. Erosion control on upland farm 20 10

708 Palawan Peacock- Pheasant
709 Entrance and Statue of Justice

1989. Environment Month. Multicoloured.
2166 1p. Type **708** 20 10
2167 1p. Palawan bear cat . . . 15 10

1989. Supreme Court.
2168 **709** 1p. multicoloured . . . 25 10

1989. "Fiesta Islands '89" (2nd series). As T **705**. Multicoloured.
2169 60s. Turumba 10 10
2170 75s. Pahiyas 15 10
2171 3p.50 Independence Day . . 65 15

710 Birds, Quill, "Noli Me Tangere" and Flags

1989. Bicentenary of French Revolution and Decade of Philippine Nationalism.
2172 **710** 1p. multicoloured . . . 25 10
2173 5p.50 multicoloured . . 1·25 25

711 Graph
713 Monument, Flag, Civilian and Soldier

1989. National Science and Technology Week. Multicoloured.
2174 1p. Type **711** 15 10
2175 1p. "Man" (Leonardo da Vinci) and emblem of Philippine Science High School) 15 10

1989. New Constitution stamp of 1987 surch **P4 75**.
2176 4p.75 on 5p.50 green and brown (2060) 70 15

1989. "Fiesta Island 89" (3rd series). As T **705**.
2177 1p. Pagoda Sa Wawa (carnival float) 30 10
2178 4p.75 Cagayan de Oro Fiesta 60 15
2179 5p.50 Penafrancia Festival 80 20

1989. 50th Anniv of National Defence Department.
2180 **713** 1p. multicoloured . . . 25 10

714 Map and Satellite
715 Annunciation

1989. 10th Anniv of Asia–Pacific Telecommunity.
2181 **714** 1p. multicoloured . . . 50 15

1989. Christmas. Multicoloured.
2182 60s. Type **715** 15 10
2183 75s. Mary and Elizabeth . . 20 10
2184 1p. Mary and Joseph travelling to Bethlehem 25 10
2185 2p. Search for an inn . . . 50 15
2186 4p. Magi and star 70 15
2187 4p.75 Adoration of shepherds . . . . 1·00 25

716 Lighthouse, Liner and Lifebelt

1989. International Maritime Organization.
2188 **716** 1p. multicoloured . . . 50 15

717 Spanish Philippines 1854 5c. and Revolutionary Govt 1898 2c. Stamps

1989. "World Stamp Expo '89" International Stamp Exhibition, Washington D.C. Multicoloured.
2189 1p. Type **717** 15 10
2190 4p. U.S. Administration 1899 50c. and Commonwealth 1935 6c. stamps 70 20
2191 5p.50 Japanese Occupation 1942 2c. and Republic 1946 6c. stamps 80 25

718 Teacher using Stamp as Teaching Aid

1989. Philatelic Week. Philately in the Classroom. Multicoloured.
2192 1p. Type **718** 20 10
2193 1p. Children working with stamps 20 10

1989. "Fiesta Islands '89" (4th series). As T **705**.
2194 1p. Masked festival, Negros 15 10
2195 4p.75 Grand Canao, Baguio 75 15
2196 5p.50 Fireworks 85 20

719 Heart

1990. 11th World Cardiology Congress, Manila.
2197 **719** 5p.50 red, blue and black 75 15

720 Glasses of Beer

1990. Centenary of San Miguel Brewery.
2198 **720** 1p. multicoloured . . . 15 10
2199 5p.50 multicoloured . . 85 20

721 Houses and Family

1990. Population and Housing Census. Multicoloured, colours of houses given.
2200 **721** 1p. blue 20 10
2201 1p. pink 20 10

722 Scouts
723 Claro Recto (politician)

1990. 50th Anniv of Philippine Girl Scouts.
2202 **722** 1p. multicoloured . . . 20 10
2203 1p.20 multicoloured . . 20 10

1990. Birth Centenaries. Multicoloured.
2204 1p. Type **723** 15 10
2205 1p. Manuel Bernabe (poet) 15 10
2206 1p. Guillermo Tolentino (sculptor) 15 10
2207 1p. Elpidio Quirino (President 1948–53) . . . 15 10
2208 1p. Dr. Bienvenido Gonzalez (University President, 1937–51) . . . 15 10

724 Badge and Globe

1990. 50th Anniv of Legion of Mary.
2209 **724** 1p. multicoloured . . . 25 10

1990. "Fiesta Islands '89" (5th series). As No. 2179 but new value.
2210 4p. multicoloured . . . . . 1·50 20

725 Torch

1990. 20th Anniv of Asian–Pacific Postal Training Centre.
2211 **725** 1p. multicoloured . . . 20 10
2212 4p. multicoloured . . . 80 20

726 Catechism Class
727 Waling Waling Flowers

1990. National Catechetical Year.
2213 **726** 1p. multicoloured . . . 15 10
2214 3p.50 multicoloured . . 60 15

1990. 29th Orient and South-East Asian Lions Forum, Manila. Multicoloured.
2215 1p. Type **727** 30 10
2216 4p. Sampaguita flowers . . 1·10 20

728 Areas for Improvement

1990. 40th Anniv of United Nations Development Programme.
2217 **728** 1p. multicoloured . . . 15 10
2218 5p.50 multicoloured . . 90 25

729 Letters of Alphabet

1990. International Literacy Year.
2219 **729** 1p. green, orange & black 15 10
2220 5p.50 green, yellow & blk 90 25

730 "Laughter" (A. Magsaysay-Ho)

1990. Philatelic Week. Multicoloured.
2221 1p. "Family" (F. Amorsolo) (horiz) 25 10
2222 4p.75 "The Builders" (V. Edades) . . . . . . 1·10 25
2223 5p.50 Type **730** . . . . . . 1·25 35

731 Star

1990. Christmas. Multicoloured.
2224 1p. Type **731** 20 10
2225 1p. Stars within stars (blue background) 20 10
2226 1p. Red and white star . . . 20 10
2227 1p. Gold and red star (green background) 20 10
2228 5p.50 Geometric star (Paskuhan Village, San Fernando) . . . . 1·25 45

732 Figures

1990. International White Cane Safety Day.
2229 **732** 1p. black, yellow and blue 20 10

733 La Solidaridad in 1990 and 1890 and Statue of Rizal

1990. Centenary of Publication of "Filipinas Dentro de Cien Anos" by Jose Rizal.
2230 **733** 1p. multicoloured . . . 20 10

734 Crowd before Figure of Christ
735 Tailplane and Stewardess

1991. 2nd Plenary Council of the Philippines.
2231 **734** 1p. multicoloured . . . 20 10

1991. 50th Anniv of Philippine Airlines.
2232 **735** 1p. mult (postage) . . . 15 10
2233 5p.50 multicoloured (air) 85 20

736 Gardenia
737 Sheepshank

1991. Flowers. Multicoloured.
2234 60s. Type **736** 15 10
2235 75s. Yellow bell 15 10
2475 1p. Yellow bell 15 10
2236 1p. Yellow plumeria 20 10
2237 1p. Red plumeria 20 10
2238 1p. Pink plumeria 20 10
2239 1p. White plumeria 20 10
2240 1p.20 Nerium 30 10
2241 3p.25 Ylang-ylang 80 15
2242 4p. Pink ixora 75 15
2243 4p. White ixora 75 15
2244 4p. Yellow ixora 75 15
2245 4p. Red ixora 75 15
2246 4p.75 Orange bougainvillea 90 20
2247 4p.75 Purple bougainvillea 90 20
2248 4p.75 White bougainvillea 90 20
2249 4p.75 Red bougainvillea . . 90 20
2250 5p. Canna 90 20
2251 5p.50 Red hibiscus . . . 1·00 25
2252 5p.50 Yellow hibiscus . . . 1·00 25
2253 5p.50 White hibiscus . . . . 1·00 25
2254 5p.50 Pink hibiscus . . . . 1·00 25
See also Nos. 2322/41.

1991. 12th Asia–Pacific and 9th National Boy Scouts Jamboree. Multicoloured.
2255 1p. Reef knot 20 10
2256 4p. Type **737** 55 10
2257 4p.75 Granny knot 60 20

738 Jorge Vargas

739 "Antipolo" (Carlos Francisco) and Score

1991. Birth Centenaries. Multicoloured.
2259 1p. Type **738** 15 10
2260 1p. Ricardo Paras 15 10
2261 1p. Jose Laurel 15 10
2262 1p. Vicente Fabella 15 10
2263 1p. Maximo Kalaw 15 10

1991. 400th Anniv of Antipolo.
2264 **739** 1p. multicoloured . . . 25 10

740 Philippine Eagle

1991. Endangered Species. The Philippine Eagle. Multicoloured.
2265 1p. Type **740** 60 55
2266 4p.75 Eagle on branch . . . 1·75 1·10
2267 5p.50 Eagle in flight . . . . 3·25 2·00
2268 8p. Eagle feeding chick . . 3·75 2·40

741 Emblem

1991. Centenary of Founding of Society of Lawyers (from 1904 Philippine Bar Association).
2269 **741** 1p. multicoloured . . . 20 10

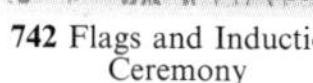

742 Flags and Induction Ceremony

743 First Regular Division Emblem

1991. 50th Anniv of Induction of Philippine Reservists into United States Army Forces in the Far East. Background colours given where necessary in brackets.
2270 **742** 1p. multicoloured . . . 20 10
2272 **743** 2p. red, black and yellow 40 15
2273 – 2p. multicoloured (yellow) (2nd Regular) 40 15
2274 – 2p. multicoloured (yellow) (11th) 40 15
2275 – 2p. blue, yellow and black (yellow) (21st) 40 15
2276 **743** 2p. red and black . . . 40 15
2277 – 2p. black, blue and red (2nd Regular) 40 15
2278 – 2p. multicoloured (white) (11th) 40 15
2279 – 2p. blue, yellow and black (white) (21st) . . 40 15
2280 – 2p. multicoloured (yellow) (31st) 40 15
2281 – 2p. multicoloured (yellow) (41st) 40 15
2282 – 2p. multicoloured (yellow) (51st) 40 15
2283 – 2p. multicoloured (yellow) (61st) 40 15
2284 – 2p. red, blue and black (31st) 40 15
2285 – 2p. multicoloured (white) (41st) 40 15
2286 – 2p. blue, black and red (51st) 40 15
2287 – 2p. multicoloured (white) (61st) 40 15
2288 – 2p. multicoloured (yellow) (71st) 40 15
2289 – 2p. multicoloured (yellow) (81st) 40 15
2290 – 2p. multicoloured (yellow) (91st) 40 15
2291 – 2p. multicoloured (yellow) (101st) . . . 40 15
2292 – 2p. multicoloured (white) (71st) 40 15
2293 – 2p. multicoloured (white) (81st) 40 15
2294 – 2p. multicoloured (white) (91st) 40 15
2295 – 2p. multicoloured (white) (101st) 40 15
2296 – 2p. blue, black and yellow (Bataan Force) 40 15
2297 – 2p. yellow, red and black (yellow) (Philippine) 40 15
2298 – 2p. multicoloured (yellow) (Air Corps) 40 15
2299 – 2p. black, blue and yellow (Offshore Patrol) 40 15
2300 – 2p. blue and black (Bataan Force) . . . 40 15
2301 – 2p. yellow, red and black (white) (Philippine) . . 40 15
2302 – 2p. multicoloured (white) (Air Corps) 40 15
2303 – 2p. black and blue (Offshore Patrol) . . . 40 15
Nos. 2272/2303 (all as T **743**) show divisional emblems.

744 Basilio

745 St. John of the Cross

1991. Centenary of Publication of "El Filibusterismo" by Jose Rizal. Characters from the novel. Each red, blue and black.
2304 1p. Type **744** 20 10
2305 1p. Simoun 20 10
2306 1p. Father Florentino . . . 20 10
2307 1p. Juli 20 10

1991. 400th Death Anniv of St. John of the Cross.
2308 **745** 1p. multicoloured . . . 25 10

746 Faces (Children's Fund)

1991. United Nations Agencies.
2310 **746** 1p. multicoloured . . . 15 10
2311 – 4p. multicoloured . . . 55 15
2312 – 5p.50 black, red and blue 75 25
DESIGNS: 4p. Hands supporting boatload of people (High Commissioner for Refugees); 5p.50, 1951 15c. and 1954 3c. U.N. stamps (40th anniv of Postal Administration).

747 "Bayanihan" (Carlos "Botong" Francisco)

1991. Philatelic Week. Multicoloured.
2313 2p. Type **747** 30 10
2314 7p. "Sari-Sari Vendor" (Mauro Malang Santos) 95 20
2315 8p. "Give Us This Day" (Vicente Manansala) . . . 1·10 25

748 Gymnastics

1991. 16th South-East Asian Games, Manila. Multicoloured.
2316 2p. Type **748** 20 10
2317 2p. Gymnastics (emblem at bottom) 20 10
2318 6p. Arnis (martial arts) (emblem at left) (vert) . . 65 20
2319 6p. Arnis (emblem at right) (vert) 65 20
Designs of the same value were issued together, se-tenant, each pair forming a composite design.

1991. Flowers. As T **736**. Multicoloured.
2322 1p.50 Type **736** 25 10
2323 2p. Yellow plumeria 35 10
2324 2p. Red plumeria 35 10
2325 2p. Pink plumeria 35 10
2326 2p. White plumeria 35 10
2327 3p. Nerium 50 10
2328 5p. Ylang-ylang 80 15
2329 6p. Pink ixora . . . . . . 1·00 15
2330 6p. White ixora . . . . . . 1·00 15
2331 6p. Yellow ixora . . . . . 1·00 15
2332 6p. Red ixora . . . . 1·00 15
2333 7p. Orange bougainvillea . . 1·10 20
2334 7p. Purple bougainvillea . . 1·10 20
2335 7p. White bougainvillea . . 1·10 20
2336 7p. Red bougainvillea . . . 1·10 20
2337 8p. Red hibiscus . . . . . 1·25 25
2338 8p. Yellow hibiscus . . . . 1·25 25
2339 8p. White hibiscus . . . . 1·25 25
2340 8p. Pink hibiscus . . . . . 1·25 25
2341 10p. Canna . . . . 1·60 30

750 Church

751 Player

1991. Christmas. Children's Paintings. Mult.
2342 2p. Type **750** 30 10
2343 6p. Christmas present . . . 80 15
2344 7p. Santa Claus and tree . . 1·00 15
2345 8p. Christmas tree and star 1·25 25

1991. Centenary of Basketball. Multicoloured.
2346 2p. Type **751** 50 10
2347 6p. Basketball player and map (issue of first basketball stamp, 1934) (horiz) . . . . 1·25 15
2348 7p. Girls playing basketball (introduction of basketball in Philippines, 1904) (horiz) . . . . 1·50 25
2349 8p. Players . . . . 1·75 30

752 Monkey firing Cannon

1991. New Year. Year of the Monkey.
2351 **752** 2p. multicoloured . . . 75 15
2352 6p. multicoloured . . . 2·25 30

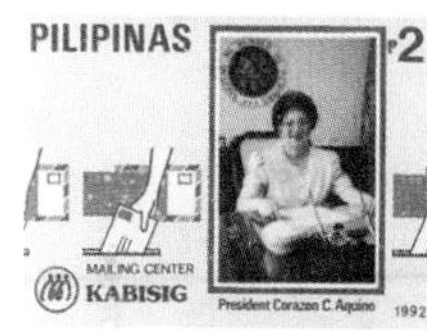

753 Pres. Aquino and Mailing Centre Emblem

1992. Kabisig Community Projects Organization. Multicoloured.
2353 2p. Type **753** 25 10
2354 6p. Housing 75 15
2355 7p. Livestock 95 15
2356 8p. Handicrafts . . . . . . 1·10 25

754 "Curcuma longa"

1992. Asian Medicinal Plants Symposium, Los Banos, Laguna. Multicoloured.
2357 2p. Type **754** 45 10
2358 6p. "Centella asiatica" . . . 95 15
2359 7p. "Cassia alata" . . . . . 1·10 20
2360 8p. "Ervatamia pandacaqui" 1·40 25

755 "Mahal Kita", Envelopes and Map

1992. Greetings Stamps. Multicoloured.
2361 2p. Type **755** 25 10
2362 2p. As No. 2361 but inscr "I Love You" 25 10
2363 6p. Heart and doves ("Mahal Kita") 70 15
2364 6p. As No. 2363 but inscr "I Love You" 70 15
2365 7p. Basket of flowers ("Mahal Kita") 85 20
2366 7p. As No. 2365 but inscr "I Love You" 85 20
2367 8p. Cupid ("Mahal Kita") 1·75 25
2368 8p. As No. 2367 but inscr "I Love You" . . . . 1·75 25

756 Philippine Pavilion and Couple Dancing

757 "Our Lady of the Sun" (icon)

1992. "Expo '92" World's Fair, Seville. Mult.
2369 2p. Type **756** 25 10
2370 8p. Pavilion, preacher and conquistador holding globe . . . . 1·00 20

1992. 300th Anniv of Apparition of Our Lady of the Sun at Gate, Vaga Cavite.
2372 **757** 2p. multicoloured . . . 25 10
2373 8p. multicoloured . . . 1·00 20

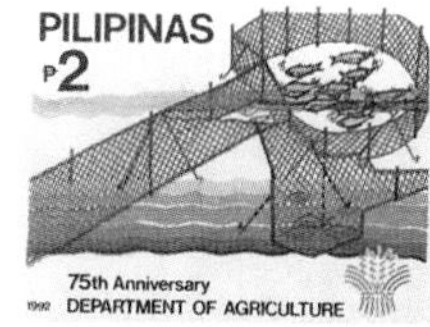

758 Fish Farming

1992. 75th Anniv of Department of Agriculture. Multicoloured.
2374 2p. Type **758** 40 15
2375 2p. Pig farming 20 15
2376 2p. Sowing seeds 20 15

759 Race Horses and Emblem

760 Manuel Roxas (President, 1946–48)

1992. 125th Anniv of Manila Jockey Club.
2377 **759** 2p. multicoloured . . . 30 15

1992. Birth Centenaries. Multicoloured.
2379 2p. Type **760** 20 10
2380 2p. Natividad Almeda-Lopez (judge) 20 10
2381 2p. Roman Ozaeta (judge) 20 10
2382 2p. Engracia Cruz-Reyes (women's rights campaigner and environmentalist) 20 10
2383 2p. Fernando Amorsolo (artist) 20 10

761 Queen, Bishop and 1978 30s. Stamp

1992. 30th Chess Olympiad, Manila. Mult.
2384 2p. Type **761** 35 10
2385 6p. King, queen and 1962 6s.+4s. stamp 90 25

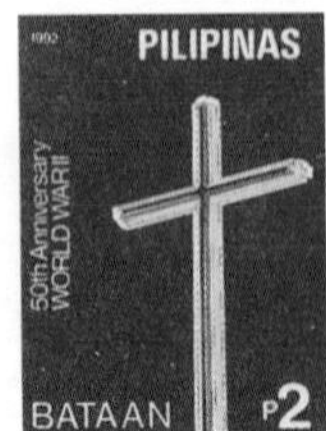

762 Bataan Cross

1992. 50th Anniv of Pacific Theatre in Second World War. Multicoloured.
2387 2p. Type **762** 25 10
2388 6p. Map inside "W" 85 15
2389 8p. Corregidor eternal flame 1·00 20

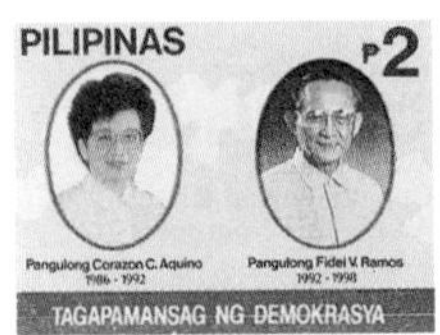

763 President Aquino and President-elect Ramos

1992. Election of Fidel Ramos to Presidency.
2391 **763** 2p. multicoloured . . . 25 10

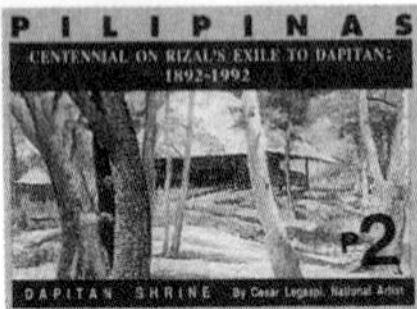

764 "Dapitan Shrine" (Cesar Legaspi)

1992. Centenary of Dr. Jose Rizal's Exile to Dapitan. Multicoloured.
2392 2p. Type **764** 30 15
2393 2p. Portrait (after Juan Luna) (vert) 30 15

765 "Spirit of ASEAN" (Visit Asean Year)

766 Member of the Katipunan

1992. 25th Anniv of Association of South-East Asian Nations. Multicoloured.
2394 2p. Type **765** 20 10
2395 2p. "ASEAN Sea" (25th Ministerial Meeting and Postal Ministers' Conf) 20 10
2396 6p. Type **765** 60 15
2397 6p. As No. 2395 . . . . . 60 15

1992. Centenary of Katipunan ("KKK") (revolutionary organization). Multicoloured.
2398 2p. Type **766** 40 10
2399 2p. Revolutionaries 40 10
2400 2p. Plotting (horiz) 40 10
2401 2p. Attacking (horiz) . . . 40 10

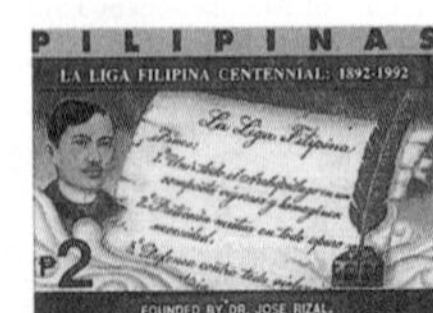

767 Dr. Jose Rizal, Text and Quill

1992. Centenary of La Liga Filipina.
2402 **767** 2p. multicoloured . . . 30 10

768 Swimming

1992. Olympic Games, Barcelona. Multicoloured.
2403 2p. Type **768** 20 10
2404 7p. Boxing 80 20
2405 8p. Hurdling . . . . 1·00 25

769 School, Emblem and Students

1992. Centenaries. Multicoloured.
2407 2p. Type **769** (Sisters of the Assumption in the Philippines) 25 15
2408 2p. San Sebastian's Basilica, Manila (centenary (1991) of blessing of fifth construction) (vert) . . . 25 15

770 Masonic Symbols

1992. Centenary of Nilad Lodge (first Filipino Masonic Lodge).
2409 **770** 2p. black and green . . 25 10
2410 – 6p. multicoloured . . . 85 15
2411 – 8p. multicoloured . . . 1·00 20
DESIGNS: 6p. Antonio Luna and symbols; 8p. Marcelo del Pilar ("Father of Philippine Masonry") and symbols.

771 Ramos taking Oath

1992. Swearing in of President Fidel Ramos. Mult.
2412 2p. Type **771** 25 10
2413 8p. President taking oath in front of flag . . . . . . 1·00 20

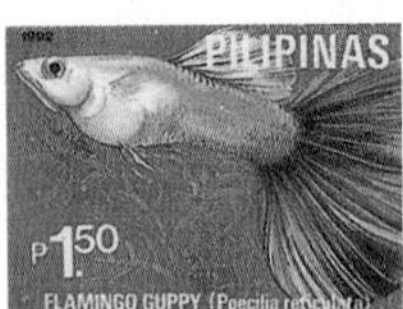

772 Flamingo Guppy

1992. Freshwater Aquarium Fishes (1st series). Multicoloured.
2414 1p.50 Type **772** 20 15
2415 1p.50 Neon tuxedo guppy 20 15
2416 1p.50 King cobra guppy . . 20 15
2417 1p.50 Red-tailed guppy . . 20 15
2418 1p.50 Tiger lace-tailed guppy 20 15
2419 2p. Pearl-scaled goldfish . . 35 20
2420 2p. Red-capped goldfish . . 35 20
2421 2p. Lion-headed goldfish . . 35 20
2422 2p. Black moor goldfish . . 35 20
2423 2p. Bubble-eyed goldfish . . 35 20
2424 4p. Delta topsail platy ("Variatus") 70 40
2425 4p. Orange-spotted hi-fin platy 70 40
2426 4p. Red lyre-tailed swordtail 70 40
2427 4p. Bleeding heart hi-fin platy 70 40
See also Nos. 2543/56.

774 Couple

1992. Greetings Stamps. "Happy Birthday". Multicoloured.
2430 2p. Type **774** 25 10
2431 6p. Type **774** 85 10
2432 7p. Balloons and candles on birthday cake . . . . . . 1·00 15
2433 8p. As No. 2432 . . . . . 1·25 20

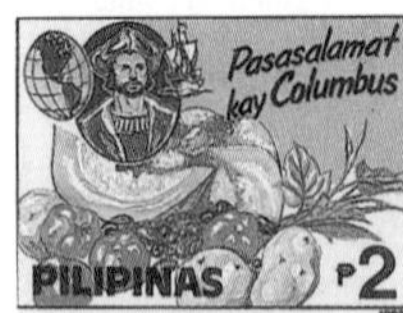

775 Melon, Beans, Tomatoes and Potatoes

1992. 500th Anniv of Discovery of America by Columbus. Multicoloured.
2434 2p. Type **775** 35 15
2435 6p. Maize and sweet potatoes . . . . 1·40 20
2436 8p. Pineapple, cashews, avocado and water melon 1·60 30

777 Figures around World Map

1992. International Nutrition Conference, Rome.
2438 **777** 2p. multicoloured . . . 20 10

778 Mother and Child

780 Family and Canoe

1992. Christmas.
2439 **778** 2p. multicoloured . . . 25 10
2440 – 6p. multicoloured . . . 85 10
2441 – 7p. multicoloured . . . 95 15
2442 – 8p. multicoloured . . . 1·25 20
DESIGNS: 6p. to 8p. Various designs showing mothers and children.

1992. Anti-drugs Campaign. Multicoloured.
2444 2p. Type **780** 20 10
2445 8p. Man carrying paddle, children and canoe . . . 1·00 20

781 Damaged Trees

782 Red Junglefowl

1992. Mt. Pinatubo Fund (for victims of volcanic eruption). Multicoloured.
2446 25s. Type **781** 10 10
2447 1p. Mt. Pinatubo erupting 20 10
2448 1p. Cattle in ash-covered field 20 10
2449 1p. Refugee settlement . . . 20 10
2450 1p. People shovelling ash . . 20 10

1992. New Year. Year of the Cock. Mult.
2451 2p. Type **782** 25 20
2452 6p. Maranao Sarimanok (mythical bird) 80 15

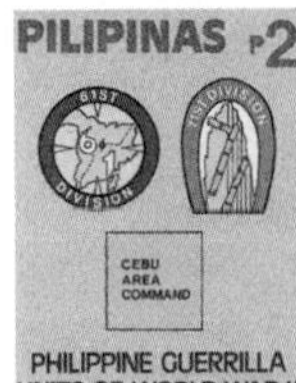

784 Badges of 61st and 71st Divisions, Cebu Area Command

785 "Family" (Cesar Legaspi) (family ties)

1992. Philippine Guerrilla Units of Second World War (1st series). Multicoloured.
2455 2p. Type **784** 45 15
2456 2p. Vinzon's Guerrillas and badges of 48th Chinese Guerrilla Squadron and 101st Division 45 15
2457 2p. Anderson's Command, Luzon Guerrilla Army Forces and badge of Bulacan Military Area . . 45 15
2458 2p. President Quezon's Own Guerrillas and badges of Marking's Fil-American Troops and Hunters ROTC Guerrillas 45 15
See also Nos. 2594/7, 2712/15 and 2809/12.

1992. Philatelic Week. Multicoloured.
2459 2p. Type **785** 25 10
2460 6p. "Pounding Rice" (Nena Saguil) (hard work and industry) 75 15
2461 7p. "Fish Vendors" (Romeo Tabuena) (flexibility and adaptability) 75 25

786 Black Shama

1992. Endangered Birds. Multicoloured. (a) As T **786**.
2462 2p. Type **786** 30 25
2463 2p. Blue-headed fantail . . . 30 25
2464 2p. Mindoro zone-tailed (inscr "Imperial") pigeon 30 25
2465 2p. Sulu hornbill 30 25
2466 2p. Red-vented (inscr "Philippine") cockatoo . . 30 25

(b) Size 29 × 39 mm.
2467 2p. Philippine trogon . . . 30 25
2468 2p. Rufous hornbill 30 25
2469 2p. White-bellied black woodpecker 30 25
2470 2p. Spotted wood kingfisher 30 25

(c) Size 36 × 26½ mm.
2471 2p. Brahminy kite 30 25
2472 2p. Philippine falconet . . . 30 25
2473 2p. Reef heron 30 25
2474 2p. Philippine duck (inscr "Mallard") 30 25

787 Flower (Jasmine)

788 Flower (Jasmine)

1993. National Symbols. Multicoloured. (a) As T **787**. "Pilipinas" in brown at top.
2476 1p. Type **787** 15 10
2571 2p. Flag 20 10
2478 6p. Leaf (palm) 70 10
2479 7p. Costume 90 15
2480 8p. Fruit (mango) . . . . . 1·00 20

(b) As T **788**. "Pilipinas" in red at foot.
2481 60s. Tree 10 10
2512 1p. Flag 10 10
2513 1p. House 10 10
2514 1p. Costume 10 10
2515 1p. As No. 2481 . . . . . 10 10
2516 1p. Type **788** 10 10
2517 1p. Fruit 10 10
2518 1p. Leaf 10 10
2519 1p. Fish (milkfish) 15 10
2520 1p. Animal (water buffalo) 10 10
2521 1p. Bird (Philippine trogons) 10 10
2482 1p.50 As No. 2519 . . . . 15 10
2565 2p. Hero (Dr. Jose Rizal) 15 10
2566 2p. As No. 2513 . . . . . 15 10
2567 2p. As No. 2514 . . . . . 15 10
2568 2p. Dance ("Tinikling") . . 15 10
2569 2p. Sport (Sipa) 15 10
2570 2p. As No. 2521 . . . . . 30 20
2572 2p. As No. 2520 . . . . . 15 10
2573 2p. Type **788** 15 10
2574 2p. As No. 2481 . . . . . 15 10
2575 2p. As No. 2517 . . . . . 15 10
2576 2p. As No. 2518 . . . . . 15 10
2577 2p. As No. 2519 . . . . . 25 10
2578 2p. As No. 2512 . . . . . 15 10
2644 3p. As No. 2520 . . . . . 30 10
2645 5p. As No. 2521 . . . . . 65 40
2646 6p. As No. 2518 . . . . . 55 15
2647 7p. As No. 2514 . . . . . 60 15
2486 8p. As No. 2517 . . . . . 70 15
2649 10p. As No. 2513 . . . . . 90 15
See also Nos. 2781/94, 2822/44, 2980/5 and 2991.

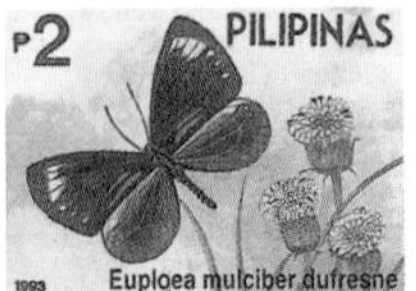

789 "Euploea mulciber dufresne"

1993. Butterflies. Multicoloured. (a) As T **789**.
2488 2p. Type **789** 25 10
2489 2p. "Cheritra orpheus" . . 25 10
2490 2p. "Delias henningia" . . . 25 10

2491 2p. "Mycalesis ita" 25 10
2492 2p. "Delias diaphana" . . . 25 10

(b) Size 28 × 35 mm.
2493 2p. "Papilio rumanzobia" 25 10
2494 2p. "Papilio palinurus" . . 25 10
2495 2p. "Trogonoptera trojana" 25 10
2496 2p. Tailed jay ("Graphium agamemnon") 25 10

Nos. 2488/92 were issued together, se-tenant, forming a composite design.

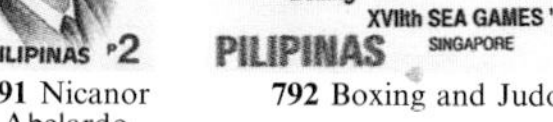

791 Nicanor Abelardo

792 Boxing and Judo

1993. Birth Centenaries. Multicoloured.
2499 2p. Type **791** 20 10
2500 2p. Pilar Hidalgo-Lim . . . 20 10
2501 2p. Manuel Viola Gallego . . 20 10
2502 2p. Maria Ylagan-Orosa . . 20 10
2503 2p. Eulogio B. Rodriguez 20 10

1993. 17th South-East Asian Games, Singapore. Multicoloured.
2504 2p. Weightlifting, archery, fencing and shooting (79 × 29 mm) 20 10
2505 2p. Type **792** 20 10
2506 2p. Athletics, cycling, gymnastics and golf (79 × 29 mm) 20 10
2507 6p. Table tennis, football, volleyball and badminton (79 × 29 mm) 50 15
2508 6p. Billiards and bowling . . 50 15
2509 6p. Swimming, water polo, yachting and diving (79 × 29 mm) 50 15

794 "Spathoglottis chrysantha"

1993. Orchids. Multicoloured.
2522 2p. Type **794** 20 10
2523 2p. "Arachnis longicaulis" 20 10
2524 2p. "Phalaenopsis mariae" 20 10
2525 2p. "Coelogyne marmorata" 20 10
2526 2p. "Dendrobium sanderae" 20 10
2527 3p. "Dendrobium serratilabium" 30 10
2528 3p. "Phalaenopsis equestris" 30 10
2529 3p. "Vanda merrillii" . . . 30 10
2530 3p. "Vanda luzonica" . . . 30 10
2531 3p. "Grammatophyllum martae" 30 10

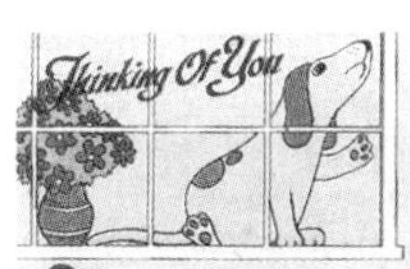

796 Dog in Window ("Thinking of You")

1993. Greetings Stamps. Multicoloured.
2534 2p. Type **796** 15 10
2535 2p. As No. 2534 but inscr "Naaalala Kita" 15 10
2536 6p. Dog looking at clock ("Thinking of You") . . 70 15
2537 6p. As No. 2536 but inscr "Naaalala Kita" 70 15
2538 7p. Dog looking at calendar ("Thinking of You") . . 70 15
2539 7p. As No. 2538 but inscr "Naaalala Kita" 70 15
2540 8p. Dog with pair of slippers ("Thinking of You") 90 20
2541 8p. As No. 2540 but inscr "Naaalala Kita" 90 20

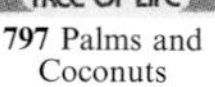
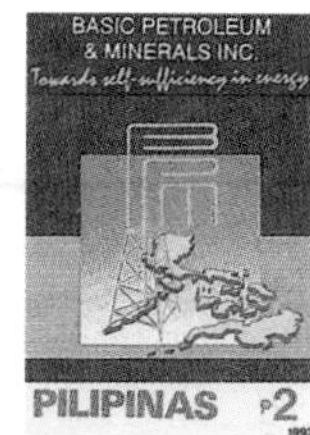

797 Palms and Coconuts

799 Map and Emblem

798 Albino Ryukin Goldfish

1993. "Tree of Life".
2542 **797** 2p. multicoloured . . . 20 10

1993. Freshwater Aquarium Fishes (2nd series). Multicoloured. (a) As T **798**.
2543 2p. Type **798** 35 15
2544 2p. Black oranda goldfish 35 15
2545 2p. Lion-headed goldfish . . 35 15
2546 2p. Celestial goldfish 35 15
2547 2p. Pompon goldfish 35 15
2548 2p. Paradise fish 35 15
2549 2p. Pearl gourami 35 15
2550 2p. Red-tailed black shark (carp) 35 15
2551 2p. Tiger barb 35 15
2552 2p. Cardinal tetra 35 15

(b) Size 29 × 39 mm.
2553 2p. Pearl-scaled freshwater angelfish 35 15
2554 2p. Zebra freshwater angelfish 35 15
2555 2p. Marble freshwater angelfish 35 15
2556 2p. Black freshwater angelfish 35 15

1993. Basic Petroleum and Minerals Inc. "Towards Self-sufficiency in Energy".
2558 **799** 2p. multicoloured . . . 15 10

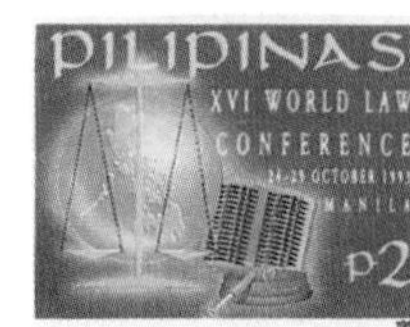

801 Globe, Scales, Book and Gavel

1993. 16th Int Law Conference, Manila. Mult.
2560 2p. Type **801** 20 10
2561 6p. Globe, scales, gavel and conference emblem on flag of Philippines (vert) . . . 60 15
2562 7p. Woman holding scales, conference building and globe 75 15
2563 8p. Fisherman pulling in nets and emblem (vert) . . 90 20

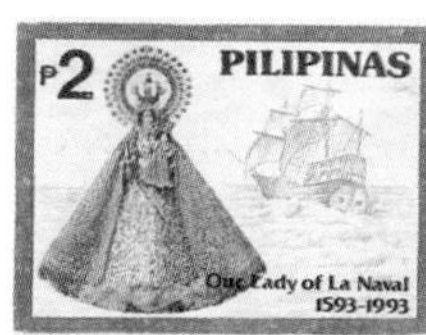

802 Our Lady of La Naval (statue) and Galleon

1993. 400th Anniv of Our Lady of La Naval.
2564 **802** 2p. multicoloured . . . 30 10

803 Woman and Terraced Hillside

1993. International Year of Indigenous Peoples. Women in traditional costumes. Multicoloured.
2579 2p. Type **803** 20 10
2580 6p. Woman, plantation and mountain 70 15
2581 7p. Woman and mosque . . 90 20
2582 8p. Woman and Filipino vintas (sail canoes) . . . 1·25 30

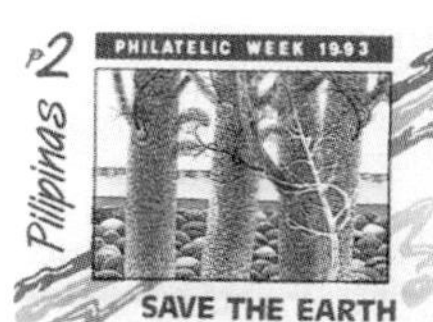

804 Trees

1993. Philatelic Week. "Save the Earth". Mult.
2583 2p. Type **804** 20 10
2584 6p. Marine flora and fauna 70 15
2585 7p. Dove and irrigation system 90 60
2586 8p. Effects of industrial pollution . . . . 1·40 70

805 1949 6c.+4c. Stamp and Symbols

806 Moon-buggy and Society Emblem

1993. 400th Anniv of Publication of "Doctrina Christiana" (first book published in Philippines).
2587 **805** 2p. multicoloured . . . 25 10

1993. 50th Anniv of Filipino Inventors Society. Multicoloured.
2588 2p. Type **806** 25 10
2589 2p. Rice-harvesting machine 25 10

Nos. 2588/9 were issued together, se-tenant, forming a composite design.

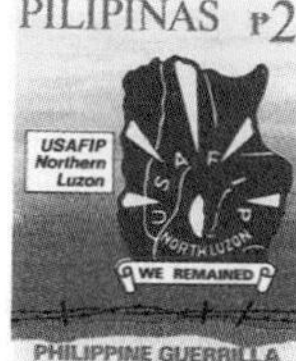

807 Holy Family

808 Northern Luzon

1993. Christmas. Multicoloured.
2590 2p. Type **807** 25 10
2591 6p. Church goers 65 15
2592 7p. Cattle and baskets of food 75 15
2593 8p. Carol-singers 85 20

1993. Philippine Guerrilla Units of Second World War (2nd series). Multicoloured.
2594 2p. Type **808** 20 10
2595 2p. Bohol Area Command 20 10
2596 2p. Leyte Area Command 20 10
2597 2p. Palawan Special Battalion and Sulu Area Command 20 10

809 Dove over City (peace and order)

1993. "Philippines 2000" (development plan). Multicoloured.
2598 2p. Type **809** 25 10
2599 6p. Means of transport and communications 90 35
2600 7p. Offices, roads and factories (infrastructure and industry) 75 15
2601 8p. People from different walks of life (people empowerment) 85 20

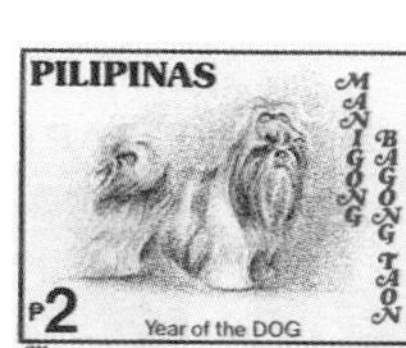

810 Shih Tzu

1993. New Year. Year of the Dog. Multicoloured.
2603 2p. Type **810** 25 10
2604 6p. Chow 75 15

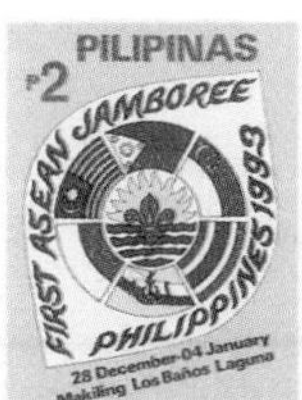

811 Jamboree Emblem and Flags

1993. 1st Association of South-East Asian Nations Scout Jamboree, Makiling. Multicoloured.
2606 2p. Type **811** 20 10
2607 6p. Scout at camp-site, flags and emblem 65 15

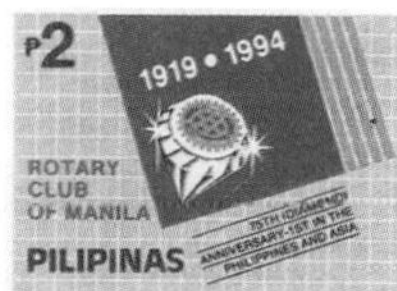

812 Club Emblem on Diamond

1994. 75th Anniv of Manila Rotary Club.
2609 **812** 2p. multicoloured . . . 20 10

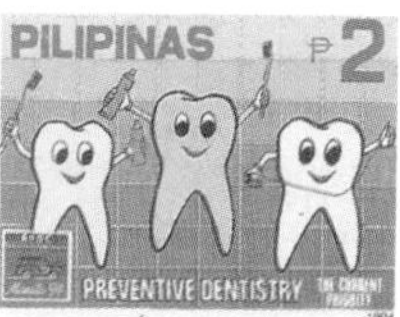

813 Teeth and Dental Hygiene Products

1994. 17th Asian–Pacific Dental Congress, Manila. Multicoloured.
2610 2p. Type **813** 20 10
2611 6p. Teeth, flags of participating countries and teeth over globe with Philippines circled (vert) 65 15

814 "Acropora micropthalma"

1994. Corals. Multicoloured.
2612 2p. Type **814** 20 10
2613 2p. "Seriatopora hystrix" . . 20 10
2614 2p. "Acropora latistella" . . 20 10
2615 2p. "Millepora tenella" . . 20 10
2616 2p. "Millepora tenella" (different) 20 10
2617 2p. "Pachyseris valenciennesi" 20 10
2618 2p. "Pavona decussata" . . 20 10
2619 2p. "Galaxea fascicularis" 20 10
2620 2p. "Acropora formosa" . . 20 10
2621 2p. "Acropora humilis" . . 20 10
2622 2p. "Isis sp." (vert) 20 10
2623 2p. "Plexaura sp." (vert) . . 20 10
2624 2p. "Dendronepthya sp." (vert) 20 10
2625 2p. "Heteroxenia sp." (vert) 20 10

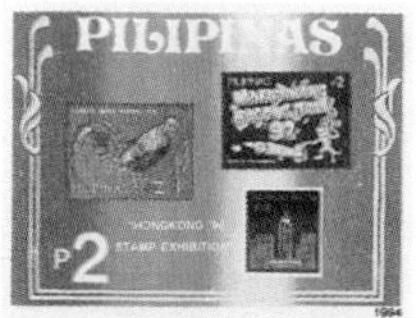

815 New Year Stamps of 1991 and 1992 bearing Exhibition Emblem

1994. "Hong Kong '94" Stamp Exhibition. Multicoloured.
2627 2p. Type **815** 25 30
2628 6p. 1993 New Year stamps 45 15

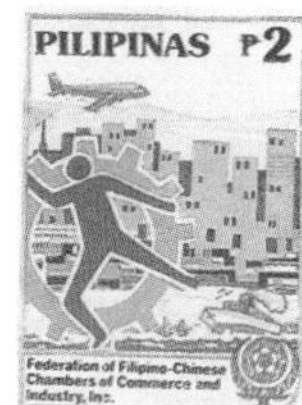

816 Class of 1944 Emblem

817 Airplane over Harbour, Man and Cogwheel and Emblem

1994. 50th Anniv of Philippine Military Academy Class of 1944.
2630 **816** 2p. multicoloured . . . 15 10

1994. Federation of Filipino–Chinese Chambers of Commerce and Industry.
2632 **817** 2p. multicoloured . . . 30 10

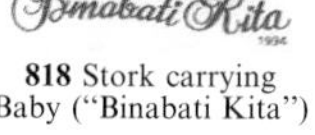
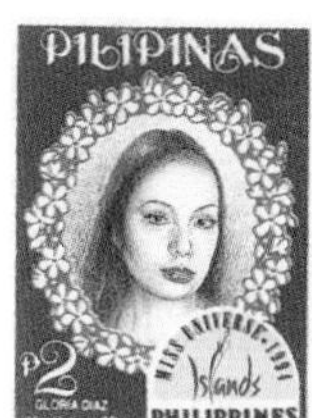

818 Stork carrying Baby ("Binabati Kita")

819 Gloria Diaz (Miss Universe 1969)

1994. Greetings Stamps. Multicoloured.

2633	2p. Type **818**	10	10
2634	2p. As No. 2633 but inscr "Congratulations"	10	10
2635	2p. Bouquet ("Binabati Kita")	10	10
2636	2p. As No. 2635 but inscr "Congratulations"	10	10
2637	2p. Mortar board, scroll and books ("Binabati Kita")	10	10
2638	2p. As No. 2637 but inscr "Congratulations"	10	10
2639	2p. Bouquet, doves and heads inside heart ("Binabati Kita")	10	10
2640	2p. As No. 2639 but inscr "Congratulations"	10	10

1994. Miss Universe Beauty Contest. Multicoloured.

2653	2p. Type **819**	10	10
2654	2p. Margie Moran (Miss Universe 1973)	10	10
2655	6p. Crown	30	15
2656	7p. Contestant	35	15

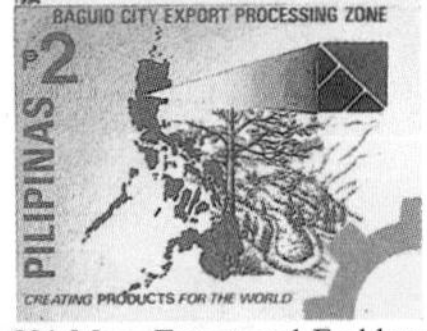

820 Antonio Molina (composer)

821 Map, Forest and Emblem (Baguio City)

1994. Birth Centenaries. Multicoloured.

2658	2p. Type **820**	10	10
2659	2p. Jose Yulo (Secretary of Justice)	10	10
2660	2p. Josefa Jara-Martinez (social worker)	10	10
2661	2p. Nicanor Reyes (accountant)	10	10
2662	2p. Sabino Padilla (judge)	10	10

1994. Export Processing Zones. Multicoloured.

2664	2p. Type **821**	10	10
2665	2p. Cross on hilltop (Bataan)	10	10
2666	2p. Octagonal building (Mactan)	10	10
2667	2p. Aguinaldo Shrine (Cavite)	10	10
2668	7p. Map and products	35	15
2669	8p. Globe and products	45	15

Nos. 2264/7 and 2668/9 repectively were issued together, se-tenant, forming composite designs.

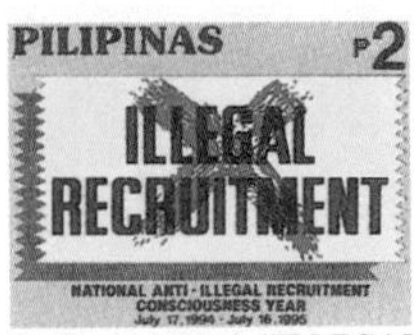

822 Cross through "ILLEGAL RECRUITMENT"

1994. Anti-illegal Recruitment Campaign.

2670	**822**	2p. multicoloured	10	10

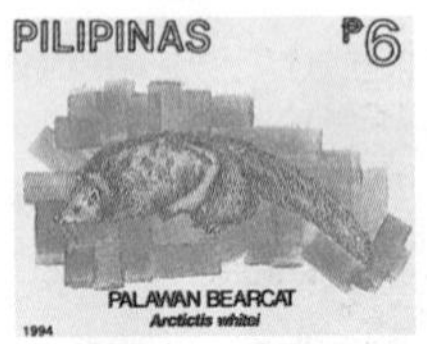

823 Palawan Bearcat

1994. Mammals. Multicoloured.

2671	6p. Type **823**	35	15
2672	6p. Philippine tarsier	35	15
2673	6p. Malayan pangolin (inscr "Scaly Anteater")	35	15
2674	6p. Indonesian ("Palawan") porcupine	35	15

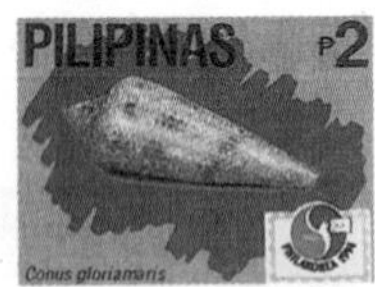

824 Glory of the Sea Cone ("Conus gloriamaris")

1994. "Philakorea 1994" International Stamp Exhibition, Seoul. Shells. Multicoloured.

2676	2p. Type **824**	10	10
2677	2p. Striate cone ("Conus striatus")	10	10
2678	2p. Geography cone ("Conus geographus")	10	10
2679	2p. Textile cone ("Conus textile")	10	10

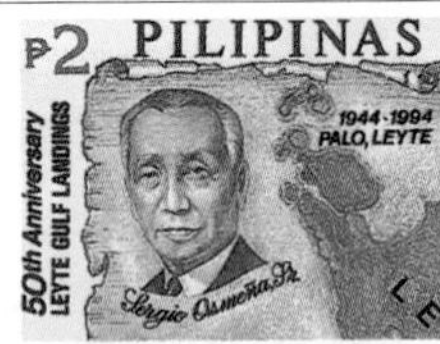

825 Sergio Osmena, Snr.

1994. 50th Anniv of Leyte Gulf Landings. Multicoloured.

2682	2p. Type **825**	10	10
2683	2p. Soldiers landing at Palo	10	10
2684	2p. "Peace – A Better World" emblem	10	10
2685	2p. Carlos Romulo	10	10

Nos. 2682/5 were issued together, se-tenant, forming a composite design.

826 Family (International Year of the Family)

1994. Anniversaries and Event. Multicoloured.

2686	2p. Type **826**	10	10
2687	6p. Workers (75th anniv of I.L.O.)	45	10
2688	7p. Aircraft and symbols of flight (50th anniv of I.C.A.O.)	55	15

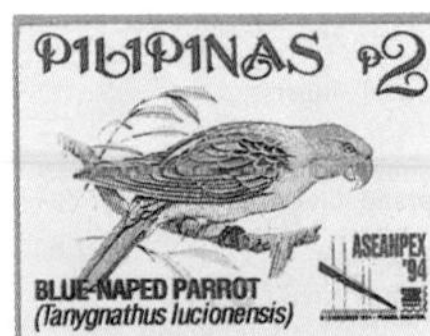

827 Blue-naped Parrot

1994. "Aseanpex '94" Stamp Exhibition, Penang, Malaysia. Birds. Muilticoloured.

2689	2p. Type **827**	35	20
2690	2p. Luzon bleeding heart ("Bleeding Heart Pigeon")	35	20
2691	2p. Palawan peacock-pheasant	35	20
2692	2p. Koch's pitta	35	20

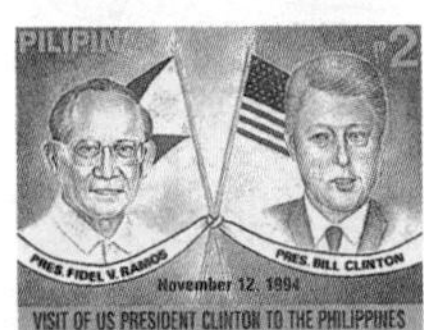

828 Presidents Fidel Ramos and W. Clinton

1994. Visit of United States President William Clinton to Philippines.

2694	**828**	2p. multicoloured	10	10
2695		8p. multicoloured	45	15

829 Convention Emblem

830 "Soteranna Puson y Quintos de Ventenilla" (Dionisio de Castro)

1994. Association of South-East Asian Nations Eastern Business Convention, Davao City.

2696	**829**	2p. multicoloured	10	10
2697		6p. multicoloured	35	15

1994. Philatelic Week. Portraits. Multicoloured.

2698	2p. Type **830**	10	10
2699	6p. "Quintina Castor de Sadie" (Simon Flores y de la Rosa)	30	10
2700	7p. "Portrait of the Artist's Mother" (Felix Hidalgo y Padilla)	35	15
2701	8p. "Una Bulaquena" (Juan Luna y Novicio)	40	15

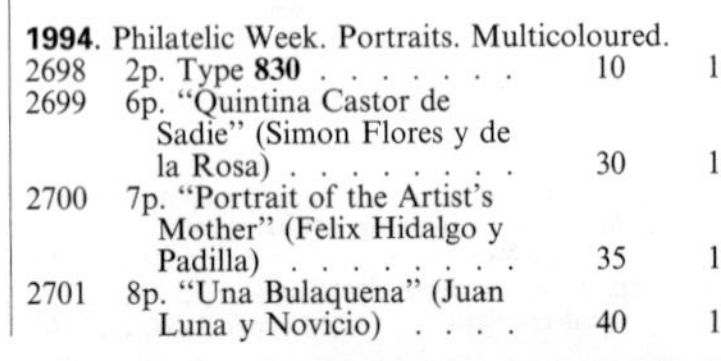

831 Wreath

1994. Christmas. Multicoloured.

2703	2p. Type **831**	10	10
2704	6p. Angels	30	10
2705	7p. Bells	35	15
2706	8p. Christmas basket	40	15

832 Piggy Bank

1994. New Year. Year of the Pig. Multicoloured.

2707	2p. Type **832**	15	10
2708	6p. Pig couple	40	15

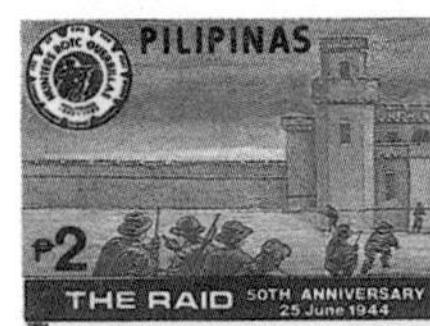

833 Raid on Prison

1994. 50th Anniversaries of Raid by Hunters ROTC Guerrillas on Psew Bilibi Prison and of Mass Escape by Inmates. Multicoloured.

2710	2p. Type **833**	10	10
2711	2p. Inmates fleeing	10	10

Nos. 2710/11 were issued together, se-tenant, forming a composite design.

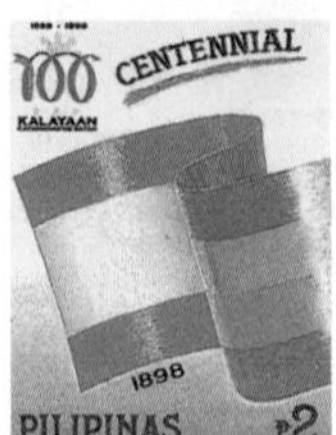

834 East Central Luzon Guerrilla Area

835 Ribbon on Globe

1994. Philippine Guerrilla Units of Second World War (3rd series). Multicoloured.

2712	2p. Type **834**	10	10
2713	2p. Mindoro Provincial Battalion and Marinduque Guerrilla Force	10	10
2714	2p. Zambales Military District and Masbate Guerrilla Regiment	10	10
2715	2p. Samar Area Command	10	10

1994. National AIDS Awareness Campaign.

2716	**835**	2p. multicoloured	10	10

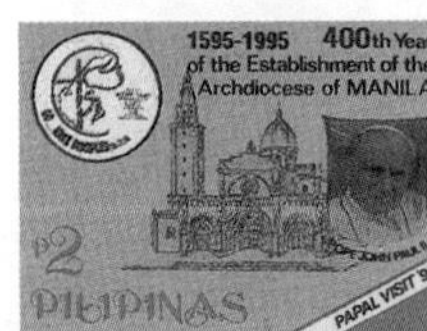

836 Flag

1994. Centenary of Declaration of Philippine Independence. Multicoloured.

2717	2p. Type **836**	10	10
2718	2p. Present state flag	10	10
2719	2p. Anniversary emblem	10	10

Nos. 2717/19 were issued together, se-tenant, forming a composite design.

837 Pope John Paul II and Manila Cathedral

1995. Papal Visit. Multicoloured.

2720	2p. Type **837** (400th anniv of Manila Archdiocese)	10	10
2721	2p. Pope and Cebu Cathedral (400th anniv of Diocese)	10	10
2722	2p. Pope and Caceres Cathedral (400th anniv of Diocese)	10	10
2723	2p. Pope and Nueva Segovia Cathedral (400th anniv of Diocese)	10	10
2724	2p. Pope, globe and Pope's arms	10	10
2725	6p. Pope and Federation of Asian Bishops emblem (6th Conference, Manila)	30	15
2726	8p. Pope, youths and emblem (10th World Youth Day)	40	20

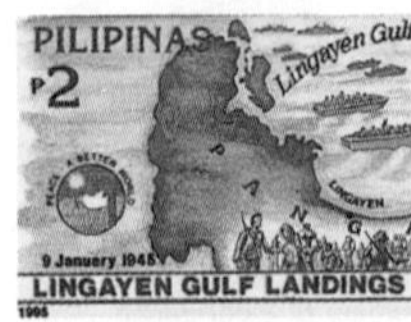

839 Landing Craft and Map

1995. 50th Anniv of Lingayen Gulf Landings. Multicoloured.

2729	2p. Type **839**	30	10
2730	2p. Map and emblems of 6th, 37th, 40th and 43rd army divisions	30	10

Nos. 2729/30 were issued together, se-tenant, forming a composite design.

840 Monument (Peter de Guzman) and Ruins of Intramuros ($\frac{1}{2}$-size illustration)

1995. 50th Anniv of Battle for the Liberation of Manila. Multicoloured.

2731	2p. Type **840**	10	10
2732	8p. Monument and ruins of Legislative Building and Department of Agriculture	40	20

841 Diokno

1995. 8th Death Anniv of Jose Diokno (politician).

2733	**841**	2p. multicoloured	10	10

842 Anniversary Emblem and Ethnic Groups

1995. 75th Anniv of International School, Manila. Multicoloured.

2734	2p. Type **842**	10	10
2735	8p. Globe and cut-outs of children	40	20

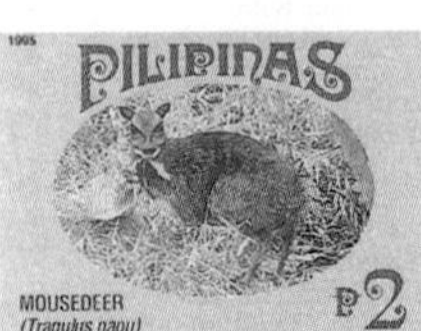

843 Greater Malay Mouse Deer

1995. Mammals. Multicoloured.

2736	2p. Type **843**	10	10
2737	2p. Tamarau	10	10
2738	2p. Visayan warty pig	10	10
2739	2p. Palm civet	10	10

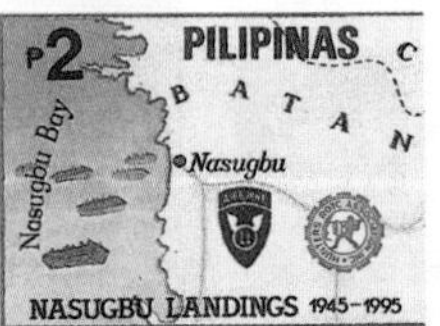

844 Nasugbu Landings

1995. 50th Anniversaries. Multicoloured.
2741 2p. Type **844** 30 10
2742 2p. Tagaytay Landings . . . 10 10
2743 2p. Battle of Nichols Airbase and Fort McKinley 10 10
Nos. 2741/2 were issued together, se-tenant, forming a composite design.

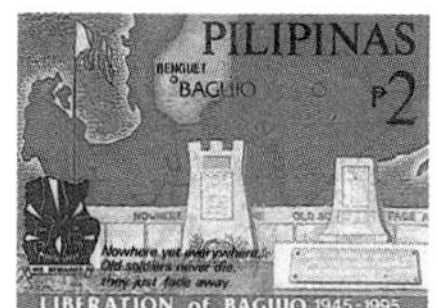

845 Memorial

1995. 50th Anniv of Liberation of Baguio.
2744 **845** 2p. multicoloured . . . 10 10

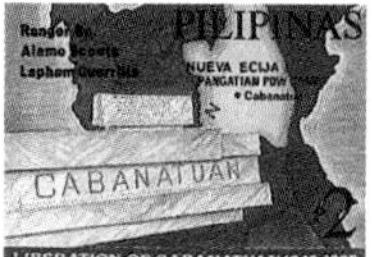

846 Cabanatuan Camp **847** Victorio Edades (artist)

1995. 50th Anniv of Liberation of Internment and Prisoner of War Camps. Multicoloured.
2745 2p. Type **846** 10 10
2746 2p. Entrance to U.S.T. camp 10 10
2747 2p. Los Banos camp 10 10
Nos. 2746/7 are wrongly inscribed "Interment".

1995. Birth Centenaries. Multicoloured.
2748 2p. Type **847** 10 10
2749 2p. Jovita Fuentes (opera singer) 10 10
2750 2p. Candido Africa (medical researcher) 10 10
2751 2p. Asuncion Arriola-Perez (politician) 10 10
2752 2p. Eduardo Quisumbing (botanist) 10 10

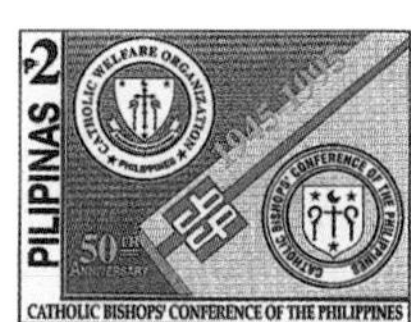

848 Emblems and Bible

1995. 50th Anniv of Philippine Catholic Bishops' Conference, Manila.
2754 **848** 2p. multicoloured . . . 10 10

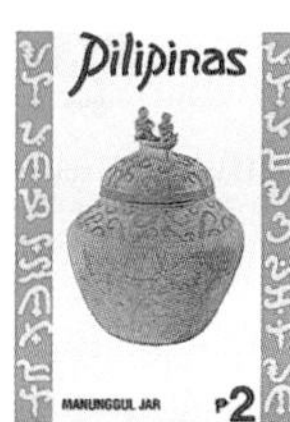

849 Ferrer **850** Neolithic Burial Jar, Manunggul

1995. 8th Death Anniv of Jaime Ferrer (administrator).
2755 **849** 2p. multicoloured . . . 10 10

1995. Archaeology. Multicoloured.
2756 2p. Type **850** 10 10
2757 2p. Iron age secondary burial jar, Ayub Cave, Mindanao 10 10
2758 2p. Iron age secondary burial jar (different), Ayub Cave 10 10
2759 2p. Neolithic ritual drinking vessel, Leta-Leta Cave, Palawan 10 10

852 Right Hand supporting Wildlife

1995. Association of South-East Asian Nations Environment Year. Multicoloured.
2762 2p. Type **852** 10 10
2763 2p. Left hand supporting wildlife 10 10
Nos. 2762/3 were issued together, se-tenant, forming a composite design.

853 Anniversary Emblem, Buildings and Trolley

1995. 50th Anniv of Mercury Drug Corporation.
2765 **853** 2p. multicoloured . . . 10 10

854 Parish Church

1995. 400th Anniv of Parish of Saint Louis Bishop, Lucban.
2766 **854** 2p. multicoloured . . . 10 10

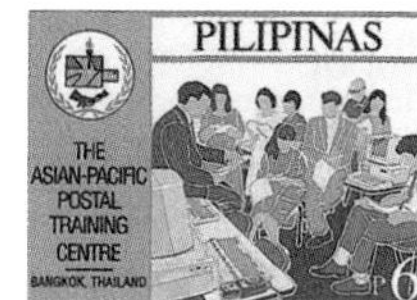

855 Instructor and Pupils

1995. 25th Anniv of Asian-Pacific Postal Training Centre, Bangkok.
2768 **855** 6p. multicoloured . . . 30 15

856 Crops and Child drinking from Well **857** Carlos Romulo

1995. 50th Anniv of F.A.O.
2769 **856** 8p. multicoloured . . . 40 20

1995. 50th Anniv of U.N.O. Multicoloured.
2770 2p. Jose Bengzon (inscr "Cesar Bengzon") 10 10
2771 2p. Rafael Salas (Assistant Secretary General) 10 10
2772 2p. Salvador Lopez (Secretary) 10 10
2773 2p. Jose Ingles (Under-secretary) 10 10
2775 2p. Type **857** 10 10
No. 2770 depicts Jose Bengzon in error for his brother Cesar.

858 Anniversary Emblem **859** Eclipse

1995. 50th Anniv of Manila Overseas Press Club.
2779 **858** 2p. multicoloured . . . 10 10

1995. Total Solar Eclipse.
2780 **859** 2p. multicoloured . . . 10 10

860 Flag **861** "Two Igorot Women" (Victorio Edades)

1995. National Symbols. With blue barcode at top. "Pilipinas" in red. Variously dated. Multicoloured.
2781 2p. Flag ("Pilipinas" at top) 10 10
2782 2p. Hero (Jose Rizal) . . . 10 10
2783 2p. House 10 10
2784 2p. Costume 10 10
2785 2p. Dance 10 10
2786 2p. Sport 10 10
2787 2p. Bird (Philippine eagle) 10 10
2788 2p. Type **860** 10 10
2789 2p. Animal (water buffalo) 10 10
2790 2p. Flower (jasmine) 10 10
2791 2p. Tree 10 10
2792 2p. Fruit (mango) 10 10
2793 2p. Leaf (palm) 10 10
2794 2p. Fish (milkfish) 15 10
For designs with barcode but "Pilipinas" in blue, see Nos. 2822/44.

1995. National Stamp Collecting Month (1st issue). Paintings by Filipino artists. Multicoloured.
2795 2p. Type **861** 10 10
2796 6p. "Serenade" (Carlos Francisco) 30 10
2797 7p. "Tuba Drinkers" (Vicente Manansala) . . . 35 15
2798 8p. "Genesis" (Hernando Ocampo) 40 15

862 Tambourine **863** Abacus and Anniversary Emblem

1995. Christmas. Musical instruments and Lines from Carols. Multicoloured.
2800 2p. Type **862** 10 10
2801 6p. Maracas 30 10
2802 7p. Guitar 35 15
2803 8p. Drum 40 15

1995. 50th Anniv of Sycip Gorres Velayo & Co. (accountants).
2804 **863** 2p. multicoloured . . . 10 10

865 Rat and Fireworks

1995. New Year. Year of the Rat. Multicoloured.
2806 2p. Type **865** 10 10
2807 6p. Model of rat 35 15

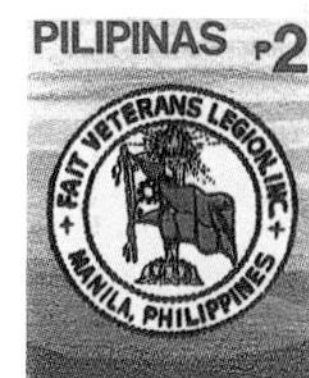

866 Badge of Fil-American Irregular Troops Veterans Legion

1995. Philippine Guerrilla Units of Second World War (4th series). Multicoloured.
2809 2p. Type **866** 10 10
2810 2p. Badge of Bicol Brigade Veterans 10 10
2811 2p. Map of Fil-American Guerrilla forces (Cavite) and Hukbalahap unit (Pampanga) 10 10
2812 2p. Map of South Tarlac military district and Northwest Pampanga . . 10 10

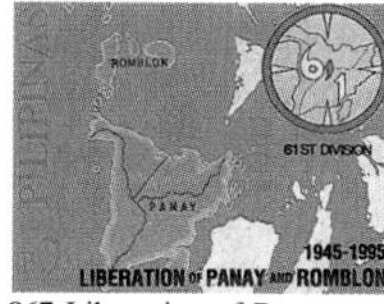

867 Liberation of Panay and Romblon

1995. 50th Anniversaries. Multicoloured.
2813 2p. Type **867** 10 10
2814 2p. Liberation of Cebu . . . 10 10
2815 2p. Battle of Ipo Dam . . . 10 10
2816 2p. Battle of Bessang Pass 10 10
2817 2p. Surrender of General Yamashita 10 10

868 Jose Rizal **870** "Treating Patient" (Manuel Baldemor)

1995. Centenary of Declaration of Philippine Independence Revolutionaries. Multicoloured.
2818 2p. Type **868** 10 10
2819 2p. Andres Bonifacio . . . 10 10
2820 2p. Apolinario Mabini . . . 10 10

1996. National Symbols. As T **860**, with blue barcode at top. "Pilipinas" in blue. Variously dated. Multicoloured.
2822 1p. Flower (jasmine) . . . 10 10
2823 1p.50 Fish (milkfish) . . . 15 10
2823a 2p. Flower (jasmine) . . . 10 10
2824 3p. Animal (water buffalo) 15 10
2825 4p. Flag ("Pilipinas" at top) 20 10
2826 4p. Hero (Jose Rizal) . . . 20 10
2827 4p. House 20 10
2828 4p. Costume 20 10
2829 4p. Dance 20 10
2830 4p. Sport 20 10
2831 4p. Bird (Philippine eagle) 20 10
2832 4p. Type **860** 20 10
2833 4p. Animal (head of water buffalo) (dated "1995") 20 10
2834 4p. Flower (jasmine) . . . 20 10
2835 4p. Tree 20 10
2836 4p. Fruit (mango) 20 10
2837 4p. Leaf (palm) 20 10
2838 4p. Fish (milkfish) 35 10
2839 4p. Animal (water buffalo) (dated "1996") 20 10
2840 5p. Bird (Philippine eagle) 25 15
2841 6p. Leaf (palm) 20 10
2842 7p. Costume 30 10
2843 8p. Fruit (mango) 35 10
2844 10p. House 45 10

1996. 23rd International Congress of Internal Medicine, Manila.
2856 **870** 2p. multicoloured . . . 10 10

871 Walled City of Intramuros

1996. Centenary of Sun Life of Canada (insurance company). Multicoloured.
2857 2p. Type **871** 10 10
2858 8p. Manila Bay sunset . . . 35 10

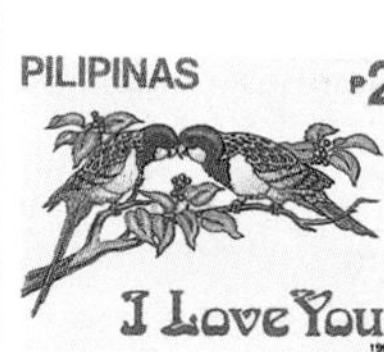

872 Pair of Eastern Rosella (birds) on Branch ("I Love You") **873** University Building and Map of Islands on Grid

1996. Greetings Stamps. Multicoloured.
2859 2p. Type **872** 10 10
2860 2p. Eastern rosella (birds) ("Happy Valentine") . . 10 10
2861 6p. Cupid holding banner ("I Love You") 25 10
2862 6p. Cupid holding banner ("Happy Valentine") . . 25 10
2863 7p. Box of chocolates ("I Love You") 30 15
2864 7p. Box of chocolates ("Happy Valentine") . . 30 15
2865 8p. Butterfly and roses ("I Love You") 35 15
2866 8p. Butterfly and roses ("Happy Valentine") . . 35 15
Nos. 2861/2 were issued together, se-tenant, forming a composite design.

1996. 50th Anniv of Gregorio Araneta University Foundation.
2867 **873** 2p. multicoloured . . . 10 10

874 Hospital

1996. 50th Anniv of Santo Tomas University Hospital.
2868 **874** 2p. multicoloured . . . 10 10

875 Racoon Butterflyfish

1996. Fishes (1st series). Multicoloured.
2869 4p. Type **875** 40 20
2870 4p. Clown triggerfish . . . 40 20
2871 4p. Regal angelfish 40 20
2872 4p. Mandarin fish 40 20
2873 4p. Emperor angelfish . . . 40 20
2874 4p. Japan surgeonfish ("Powder Brown Tang") 40 20
2875 4p. Blue-girdled ("Majestic") angelfish 40 20
2876 4p. Palette surgeonfish ("Blue tang") 40 20
2877 4p. Moorish idol 40 20
2878 4p. Yellow-tailed ("Two-banded") anemonefish . . 40 20
See also Nos. 2885/94.

877 Francisco Ortigas

1996.
2882 **877** 4p. multicoloured . . . 20 10

878 Mother Francisca and Convent

1996. 300th Anniv of Dominican Sisters of St. Catherine of Siena.
2883 **878** 4p. multicoloured . . . 20 10

879 Nuclear Reactor **(880)**

1996. Centenary of Discovery of Radioactivity by Antoine Henri Becquerel.
2884 **879** 4p. multicoloured . . . 20 10

1996. Fishes (2nd series). As T **875**. Multicoloured.
2885 4p. Spotted boxfish 40 20
2886 4p. Saddle ("Saddleback") butterflyfish 40 20
2887 4p. Sail-finned tang 40 20
2888 4p. Harlequin tuskfish . . . 40 20
2889 4p. Clown wrasse 40 20
2890 4p. Yellow-faced ("Blue-faced") angelfish 40 20
2891 4p. Long-horned cowfish . . 40 20
2892 4p. Queen angelfish 40 20
2893 4p. Forceps ("Long-nosed") butterflyfish 40 20
2894 4p. Yellow tang 40 20

1996. 10th Anniv of Young Philatelists' Society. Nos. 2471/4 optd with T **880**.
2897 2p. multicoloured 10 10
2898 2p. multicoloured 10 10
2899 2p. multicoloured 10 10
2900 2p. multicoloured 10 10

881 Carlos Garcia (President, 1957–61)

882 Satellite, Dish Aerial, Cock and Map

1996. Birth Centenaries. Multicoloured.
2901 4p. Type **881** 15 10
2902 4p. Casimiro del Rosario (physicist) 15 10
2903 4p. Geronima Pecson (first woman senator) 15 10
2904 4p. Cesar Bengson (member of International Court of Justice) 15 10
2905 4p. Jose Corazon de Jesus (writer) 15 10

1996. 50th Anniv of ABS-CBN Broadcasting Services in Philippines. Multicoloured.
2907 4p. Type **882** 20 10
2908 8p. Cock, satellite and hemispheres 35 15

883 "M" and Heart

1996. "Convention City Manila".
2909 **883** 4p. multicoloured . . . 20 10

884 Cojuangco

1996. Birth Centenary of Jose Cojuangco (entrepreneur and Corazon Aquino's father).
2910 **884** 4p. multicoloured . . . 20 10

885 Brass Helmet and Top Hat

1996. 50th Anniv of Republic Day. Philippine–American Friendship Day. Multicoloured.
2911 4p. Type **885** 20 10
2912 8p. Philippine eagle and American bald eagle . . . 40 15

886 Boxing

1996. Centenary of Modern Olympic Games. Mult.
2914 4p. Type **886** 20 10
2915 6p. Athletics 30 10
2916 7p. Swimming 35 15
2917 8p. Equestrian 40 15

887 "Alma Mater" (statue, Guillermo Tolentino) and Manila Campus (after Florentino Concepcion)

1996. 50th Anniv of University of the East, Manila and Kalookan City.
2919 **887** 4p. multicoloured . . . 20 10

888 "Dendrobium anosmum"

1996. Orchids. Multicoloured.
2920 4p. Type **888** 20 10
2921 4p. "Phalaenopsis equestris-alba" 20 10
2922 4p. "Aerides lawrenceae" . . 20 10
2923 4p. "Vanda javierii" 20 10
2924 4p. "Renanthera philippinensis" 20 10
2925 4p. "Dendrobium schuetzei" 20 10
2926 4p. "Dendrobium taurinum" 20 10
2927 4p. "Vanda lamellata" . . . 20 10

889 Emblem and Globe

1996. 6th Asia–Pacific International Trade Fair, Manila.
2929 **889** 4p. multicoloured . . . 20 10

890 Children's Activities

891 Fran's Fantasy "Aiea"

1996. 50th Anniv of UNICEF. Multicoloured.
2930 4p. Type **890** 20 10
2931 4p. Windmills, factories, generator, boy with radio and children laughing . . 20 10
2932 4p. Mother holding "sun" baby and children gardening 20 10
2933 4p. Wind blowing toy windmills, boy with electrical fan and children playing 20 10

1996. "Taipeh 96" Asian Stamp Exhibition. Orchids. Multicoloured.
2935 4p. Type **891** 10 10
2936 4p. Malvarosa Green Goddess "Nani" 10 10
2937 4p. Ports of Paradise "Emerald Isle" 10 10
2938 4p. Mem. Conrada Perez "Nani" 10 10
2939 4p. Pokai Tangerine "Lea" 10 10
2940 4p. Mem. Roselyn Reisman "Diana" 10 10
2941 4p. C. Moscombe x Toshie Aoki 10 10
2942 4p. Mem. Benigno Aquino "Flying Aces" 10 10

892 Communications

893 Philippine Nativity (Gilbert Miraflor)

1996. 4th Asia–Pacific Economic Co-operation Summit Conference, Subic. Multicoloured.
2944 4p. Type **892** 20 10
2945 6p. Open hands reaching towards sun (horiz) . . . 25 10
2946 7p. Grass and buildings (horiz) 30 10
2947 8p. Members' flags lining path leading to emblem, city and sun 35 15

1996. Christmas. Stamp design competition winning entries. Multicoloured.
2948 4p. Type **893** 20 10
2949 6p. Church (Stephanie Miljares) (horiz) 25 10
2950 7p. Carol singer with guitars (Mark Sales) (horiz) . . . 30 10
2951 8p. Carol singers and statue of buffalo (Lecester Glaraga) 35 15

894 Perez

1996. Birth Centenary of Eugenio Perez (politician).
2952 **894** 4p. multicoloured . . . 20 10

895 Carabao

1996. New Year. Year of the Ox. Multicoloured.
2953 4p. Type **895** 20 10
2954 6p. Tamaraw 30 15

896 Rizal aged 14

897 Father Mariano Gomez

1996. "Aseanpex '96" Association of South-East Asian Nations Stamp Exhibition, Manila. Death Centenary of Dr. Jose Rizal (1st issue). Mult.
2956 4p. Type **896** 20 10
2957 4p. Rizal aged 18 . . . . . 20 10
2958 4p. Rizal aged 25 . . . . . 20 10
2959 4p. Rizal aged 31 . . . . . 20 10
2960 4p. Title page of "Noli Me Tangere" (first novel) . . 20 10
2961 4p. Gomburza and associates 20 10
2962 4p. "Oyang Dapitana" (sculpture by Rizal) . . . 20 10
2963 4p. Bust by Rizal of Ricardo Carnicero (commandant of Dapitan) 20 10
2964 4p. Rizal's house at Calamba (horiz) 20 10
2965 4p. University of Santo Tomas, Manila (horiz) . . 20 10
2966 4p. Hotel de Oriente, Manila (horiz) 20 10
2967 4p. Dapitan during Rizal's exile (horiz) 20 10
2968 4p. Central University, Madrid (horiz) 20 10
2969 4p. British Museum, London (horiz) 20 10
2970 4p. Botanical Garden, Madrid (horiz) 20 10
2971 4p. Heidelberg, Germany (horiz) 20 10
See also No. 2976.

1996. Centenary of Declaration of Philippine Independence. Execution of Secularist Priests, 1872. Multicoloured.
2973 4p. Type **897** 20 10
2974 4p. Father Jose Burgos . . 20 10
2975 4p. Father Jacinto Zamora 20 10

898 Rizal (poster)

1996. Death Centenary of Dr. Jose Rizal (2nd issue).
2976 **898** 4p. multicoloured . . . 20 10

899 Soldier, Dove and National Colours

1997. Centenary of Philippine Army.
2978 **899** 4p. multicoloured . . . 20 10

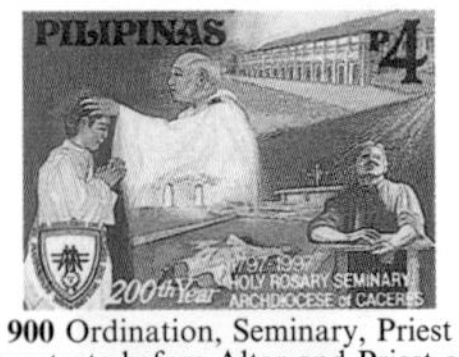

900 Ordination, Seminary, Priest prostrate before Altar and Priest at Devotions

1997. Bicentenary of Holy Rosary Seminary, Naga City.
2979 **900** 4p. multicoloured . . . 15 10

1997. National Symbols. As T **788** (no bar code). "Pilipinas" in blue. Multicoloured.
2980 1p. Flower (jasmine) 10 10
2981 5p. Bird (Philippine eagle) 15 10
2982 6p. Leaf (palm) 20 10
2983 7p. Costume 20 10
2984 8p. Fruit (mango) 25 10
2985 10p. House 30 10

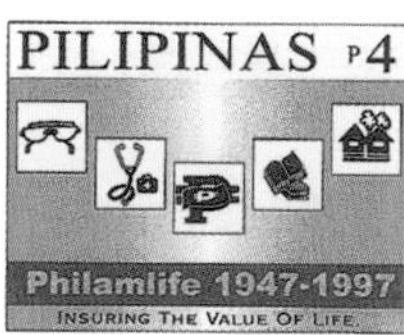

901 Volunteers attending Patient

1997. 50th Anniv of Philippine National Red Cross.
2986 **901** 4p. multicoloured . . . 15 10

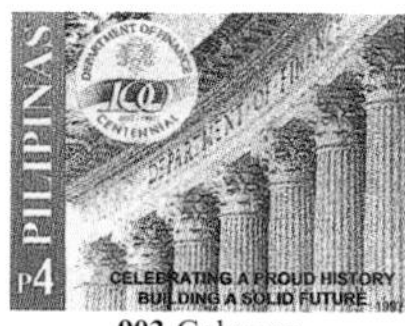

902 Insurance Services

1997. 50th Anniv of Philippine American Life Insurance Company.
2987 **902** 4p. multicoloured . . . 15 10

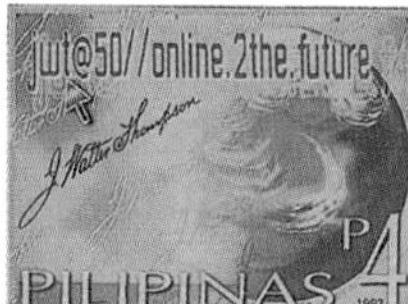

903 Columns

1997. Centenary of Department of Finance.
2988 **903** 4p. multicoloured . . . 15 10

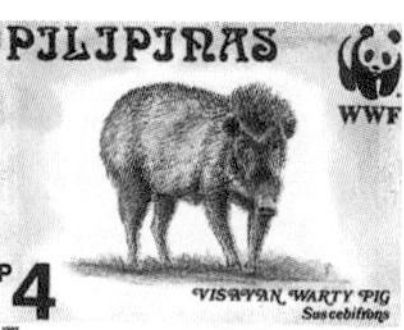

904 Signatures and Globe

1997. 50th Anniv of J. Walter Thompson (Philippines) Inc. (advertising agency).
2989 **904** 4p. multicoloured . . . 15 10

1997. National Symbol. As T **860** (with bar code). "Pilipinas" in black at foot. Multicoloured.
2991 4p. Gem (South Sea pearls) 15 10

906 Visayan Warty Pig

1997. Endangered Animals. Multicoloured.
2992 4p. Type **906** 15 10
2993 4p. Sow and young Visayan warty pig 15 10
2994 4p. Visayan spotted deer buck 15 10
2995 4p. Roe and young Visayan spotted deer 15 10

907 Founding Signatories

1997. 30th Anniv of Association of South-East Asian Nations. Multicoloured.
2996 4p. Type **907** 15 10
2997 4p. Flags of founding member nations 15 10
2998 6p. Members' flags as figures forming circle around ASEAN emblem 20 10
2999 6p. Members' flags encircling globe 20 10

908 Symbols of Education and Law, University Building and Graduate

1997. 50th Anniv of Manuel L. Quezon University.
3000 **908** 4p. multicoloured . . . 15 10

909 Assembly Emblem **910** Isabelo Abaya

1997. 2nd World Scout Parliamentary Union General Assembly, Manila.
3001 **909** 4p. multicoloured . . . 15 10

1997. Battle of Candon. Multicoloured.
3002 4p. Type **910** 15 10
3003 6p. Abaya rallying revolutionaries (horiz) . . 20 10

911 Roberto Regala (diplomat and lawyer) **912** St. Theresa

1997. Birth Centenaries. Multicoloured.
3004 4p. Type **911** 15 10
3005 4p. Doroteo Espiritu (dentist) 15 10
3006 4p. Elisa Ochoa (nurse, first Congresswoman and 1930s' national tennis champion) 15 10
3007 4p. Mariano Marcos (politician) 15 10
3008 4p. Jose Romero (politician) 15 10

1997. Death Centenary of St. Theresa of Lisieux.
3009 **912** 6p. multicoloured . . . 20 10

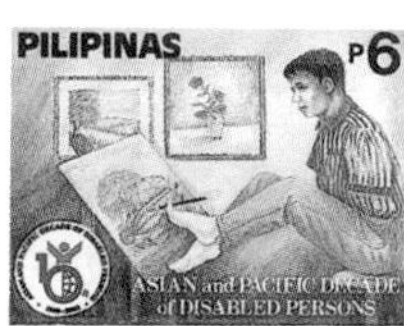

913 "Homage to the Heroes of Bessang Pass" (Hernando Ruiz Ocampo)

1997. 50th Anniv of Stamp and Philatelic Division. Modern Art. Multicoloured.
3011 4p. Type **913** 15 10
3012 6p. "Jardin III" (Fernando Zobel) 20 10
3013 7p. "Abstraction" (Nena Saguil) (vert) 20 10
3014 8p. "House of Life" (Jose Joya) (vert) 30 10

914 Man Painting with Feet

1997. Asian and Pacific Decade of Disabled Persons.
3016 **914** 6p. multicoloured . . . 20 10

915 Bonifacio writing

1997. Centenary of Declaration of Philippine Independence. Statues of Andres Bonifacio. Multicoloured.
3017 4p. Type **915** 15 10
3018 4p. Bonifacio holding flag 15 10
3019 4p. Bonifacio holding sword 15 10

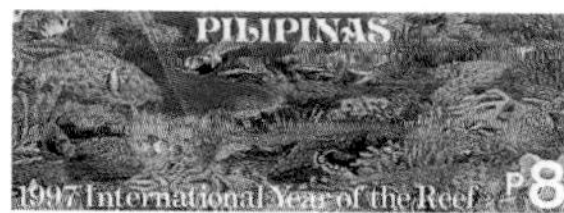

916 Von Stephan

1997. Death Centenary of Heinrich von Stephan (founder of U.P.U.).
3020 **916** 4p. multicoloured . . . 15 10

917 Underwater Scene (½-size illustration)

1997. International Year of the Reef.
3021 **917** 8p. multicoloured . . . 25 10

918 "Adoration of the Magi" **920** "Dalagang Bukid" (Fernando Amorsolo)

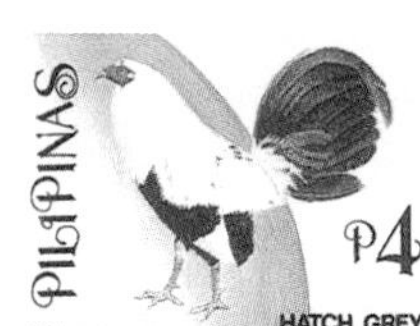
919 Tiger

1997. Christmas. Stained Glass Windows. Mult.
3023 4p. Type **918** 15 10
3024 6p. Mary, Jesus and Wise Men 20 10
3025 7p. Mary on donkey and Nativity 20 10
3026 8p. "Nativity" 25 10

1997. New Year. Year of the Tiger. Multicoloured.
3027 4p. Type **919** 15 10
3028 6p. Head of tiger and tiger climbing rockface 20 10

1997. Stamp Collecting Month. Paintings. Multicoloured.
3030 4p. Type **920** 15 10
3031 6p. "Bagong Taon" (Arturo Luz) 20 10
3032 7p. "Jeepneys" (Vicente Manansala) (horiz) . . . 20 10
3033 8p. "Encounter of the 'Nuestra Senora de Cavadonga' and the 'Centurion' " (Alfredo Carmelo) (horiz) 25 10

921 Hatch Grey

1997. Gamecocks. Multicoloured.
3035 4p. Type **921** 15 10
3036 4p. Spangled roundhead . . 15 10
3037 4p. Racey mug 15 10
3038 4p. Silver grey 15 10
3039 4p. Grey (vert) 15 10
3040 4p. Kelso (vert) 15 10
3041 4p. Bruner roundhead (vert) 15 10
3042 4p. Democrat (vert) 15 10

922 Philippine Eagle

1997. National Symbols. Multicoloured.
3044 20p. Type **922** 65 25
3045 30p. Philippine eagle (different) 95 35
3046 50p. Philippine eagle (different) . . . . 1·60 60

923 Flag and Stars

1998. 50th Anniv of Art Association of the Philippines. Multicoloured.
3047 4p. Type **923** 15 10
3048 4p. Hand clasping paintbrushes 15 10

924 Mother Philippines, Club Building and Emblem **925** Marie Eugenie

1998. Centenary of Club Filipino (social club).
3049 **924** 4p. multicoloured . . . 15 10

1998. Death Centenary of Blessed Marie Eugenie (founder of the Sisters of the Assumption).
3050 **925** 4p. multicoloured . . . 15 10

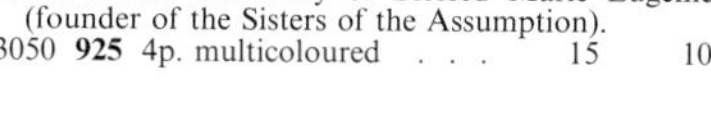 

926 Philippine and United States Flags **927** Emilio Jacinto

1998. 50th Anniv of Fulbright (student exchange) Program.
3051 **926** 4p. multicoloured . . . 15 10

1998. Heroes of the Revolution. Multicoloured. White backgrounds. Blue barcode at foot.
3052 2p. Type **927** 10 10
3054 4p. Melchora Aquino . . . 15 10
3055 4p. Jose Rizal 15 10
3056 5p. Antonio Luna 15 10
3057 8p. Marcelo del Pilar . . . 25 10
3058 10p. Gregorio del Pilar . . . 30 10
3059 11p. Andres Bonifacio . . . 35 10
3060 13p. Apolinario Mabini . . . 40 15
3061 15p. Emilio Aguinaldo . . . 50 20
3062 18p. Juan Luna 55 20
See also Nos. 3179/88 and 3189/98.

928 Mt. Apo, Bagobo Woman, Orchids and Fruit **929** School and Emblem

1998. 50th Anniv of Apo View Hotel, Davao City.
3070 **928** 4p. multicoloured . . . 15 10

1998. 75th Anniv of Philippine Cultural High School.
3071 **929** 4p. multicoloured . . . 15 10

930 Old and Present School Buildings

1998. 75th Anniv of Victorino Mapa High School, San Rafael.
3072 **930** 4p. multicoloured . . . 15 10

931 Lighthouse, Warship and Past and Present Uniforms

1998. Centenary of Philippine Navy.
3073 **931** 4p. multicoloured . . . 30 10

932 University and Igorot Dancer

1998. 50th Anniv of University of Baguio.
3074 **932** 4p. multicoloured 15 10

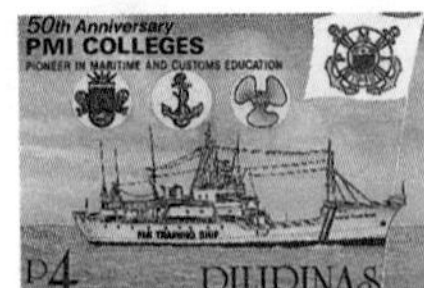

933 Training Ship and Emblem

1998. 50th Anniv of Philippine Maritime Institute.
3075 **933** 4p. multicoloured 30 10

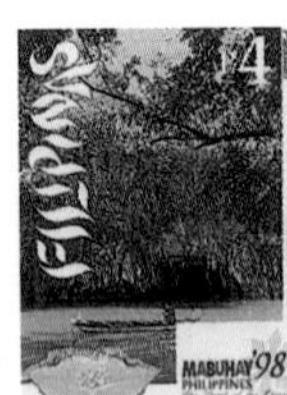

934 Forest, Palawan

1998. "EXPO '98" World's Fair, Lisbon. Mult.
3076 4p. Type **934** 15 10
3077 15p. Filipino vinta (sail canoe), Zamboanga (horiz) 65 50

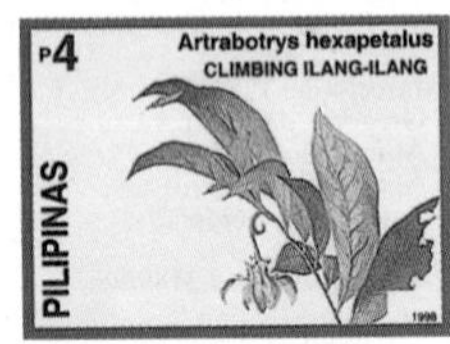

935 Climbing Ilang-ilang

1998. "Florikultura'98" International Garden Festival, San Fernando, Pampanga. Illustrations from "Flowers of the Philippines" by Manuel Blanco. Multicoloured.
3079 4p. Type **935** 10 10
3080 4p. "Hibiscus rosa-sinensis" 10 10
3081 4p. "Nerium oleander" 10 10
3082 4p. Arabian jasmine ("Jasminum sambac") 10 10
3083 4p. "Gardenia jasminoides" (vert) 10 10
3084 4p. Flame-of-the-forest ("Ixora coccinea") (vert) 10 10
3085 4p. Indian coral bean ("Erythrina indica") (vert) 10 10
3086 4p. "Abelmoschus moschatus" (vert) 10 10

936 City and Clark International Airport (½-size illustration)

1998. Clark Special Economic Zone.
3088 **936** 15p. multicoloured 45 35

937 Manila Galleon

1998. Centenary of Declaration of Philippine Independence. Philippines–Mexico–Spain Friendship. Multicoloured.
3089 15p. Type **937** 65 50
3090 15p. Philippine woman with flag, Legaspi-Urdaneta Monument and galleon 65 50
3091 15p. Spanish and Philippine flags, Cebu Basilica (after M. Miguel) and "Holy Child" (statuette) 65 50

938 "Spoliarium" (Juan Luna)
939 Andres Soriano (accountant)

1998. Centenary of Declaration of Philippine Independence. Multicoloured.
3093 4p. Type **938** 10 10
3094 8p. General Emilio Aguinaldo introducing Philippine national flag at Cavite 25 20
3095 16p. Execution of Jose Rizal, 1896 50 40
3096 16p. Andres Bonifacio and Katipunan monument 50 40
3097 20p. Barasoain Church (venue of first Philippine Congress, 1898) 60 45

1998. Birth Centenaries. Multicoloured.
3098 4p. Type **939** 10 10
3099 4p. Tomas Fonacier (Univeristy dean and historian) 10 10
3100 4p. Josefa Escoda (founder of Filipino Girl Scouts and social reformer) 10 10
3101 4p. Lorenzo Tanada (politician) 10 10
3102 4p. Lazaro Francisco (writer) 10 10

940 Melchora Aquino

1998. Centenary of Declaration of Philippine Independence Women Revolutionaries. Mult.
3103 4p. Type **940** 10 10
3104 4p. Nazaria Lagos 10 10
3105 4p. Agueda Kahabagan 10 10

1998. Centenary of Declaration of Philippine Independence. Nos. 2644 (1993), 2825/32 and 2834/9 optd **1898 1998 KALAYAAN** and emblem.
3107 3p. Animal (head of water buffalo) 10 10
3108 4p. Flag ("Pilipinas" at top) 10 10
3109 4p. Hero (Jose Rizal) 10 10
3110 4p. House 10 10
3111 4p. Costume 10 10
3112 4p. Dance 10 10
3113 4p. Sport 10 10
3114 4p. Bird (Philippine eagle) 10 10
3115 4p. Type **860** 10 10
3116 4p. Flower (jasmine) 10 10
3117 4p. Tree 10 10
3118 4p. Fruit (mango) 10 10
3119 4p. Leaf (palm) 10 10
3120 4p. Fish 10 10
3121 4p. Animal (water buffalo) 10 10

942 River Pasig

1998. River Pasig Environmental Campaign.
3122 **942** 4p. multicoloured 15 10

943 Bottle-nosed ("Bottlenose") Dolphin

1998. Marine Mammals. Multicoloured.
3123 4p. Type **943** 10 10
3124 4p. Humpback whale 10 10
3125 4p. Fraser's dolphin 10 10
3126 4p. Melon-headed whale 10 10
3127 4p. Minke whale 10 10
3128 4p. Striped dolphin 10 10
3129 4p. Sperm whale 10 10
3130 4p. Pygmy killer whale 10 10
3131 4p. Cuvier's beaked whale 10 10
3132 4p. Killer whale 10 10
3133 4p. Bottle-nosed ("Bottlenose") dolphin (different) 10 10
3134 4p. Spinner dolphin ("Long-snouted spinner dolphin") 10 10
3135 4p. Risso's dolphin 10 10
3136 4p. Finless porpoise 10 10
3137 4p. Pygmy sperm whale 10 10
3138 4p. Pantropical spotted dolphin 10 10
3139 4p. False killer whale 10 10
3140 4p. Blainville's beaked whale 10 10
3141 4p. Rough-toothed dolphin 10 10
3142 4p. Bryde's whale 10 10

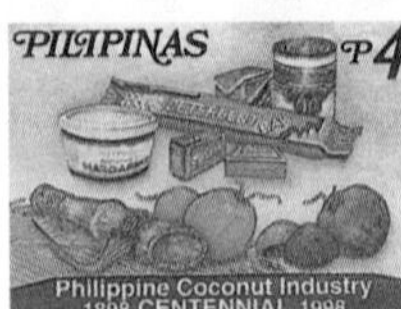

944 Coconuts and Products

1998. Centenary of Philippine Coconut Industry.
3144 **944** 4p. multicoloured 10 10

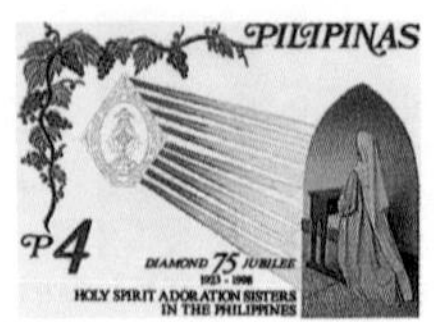

945 Grapes, Emblem and Nun

1998. 75th Anniv of Holy Spirit Adoration Sisters in the Philippines.
3145 **945** 4p. multicoloured 10 10

946 Child posting Letter
947 Holly Wreath

1998. Centenary of Postal Service. Multicoloured.
3146 6p. Type **946** 20 15
3147 6p. Globe and handshake 20 15
3148 6p. Philippine stamps, globe, airplane, galleon and building 20 15
3149 6p. Flags, dove and letters floating down to girl 20 15

1998. Christmas. Multicoloured.
3151 6p. Type **947** 20 15
3152 11p. Star wreath 35 25
3153 13p. Flower wreath 40 30
3154 15p. Bell wreath 45 35

949 Person gagged with Barbed Wire

1998. 50th Anniv of Universal Declaration of Human Rights.
3156 **949** 4p. multicoloured 10 10

950 Papal Mitre

1998. Shells. Multicoloured.
3157 4p. Type **950** 10 10
3158 4p. "Vexillum citrinum" 10 10
3159 4p. "Rugose mitre" ("Vexillum rugosum") 10 10
3160 4p. "Volema carinifera" 10 10
3161 4p. "Teramachia dalli" 10 10
3162 4p. "Nassarius vitiensis" 10 10
3163 4p. "Cymbiola imperialis" 10 10
3164 4p. "Cymbiola aulica" 10 10

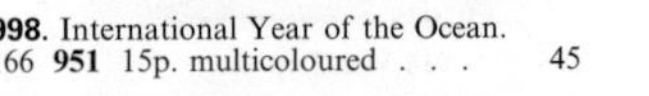

951 Sea Creatures (½-size illustration)

1998. International Year of the Ocean.
3166 **951** 15p. multicoloured 45 35

952 Taking Oath

1998. Inauguration of President Joseph Ejercito Estrada. Multicoloured.
3168 6p. Type **952** 20 15
3169 15p. Inaugural speech 45 35

953 Rabbit

1998. New Year. Year of the Rabbit. Multicoloured.
3170 4p. Type **953** 10 10
3171 11p. Two rabbits 35 25

954 "Dyesebel"

1998. National Stamp Collecting Month. Film Posters.
3173 **954** 6p. blue and black 20 15
3174 – 11p. brown and black 35 25
3175 – 13p. mauve and black 40 30
3176 – 15p. green and black 45 35
DESIGNS: 11p. "Ang Sawa sa Lumang Simboryo"; 13p. "Prinsipe Amante"; 15p. "Anak Da Lita".

1998. Heroes of the Revolution. As Nos. 3052/62. Multicoloured. Blue barcode at foot. (a) Yellow backgrounds.
3179 6p. Type **927** 20 15
3180 6p. Melchora Aquino 20 15
3181 6p. Jose Rizal 20 15
3182 6p. Antonio Luna 20 15
3183 6p. Marcelo del Pilar 20 15
3184 6p. Gregorio del Pilar 20 15
3185 6p. Andres Bonifacio 20 15
3186 6p. Apolinario Mabini 20 15
3187 6p. Emilio Aguinaldo 20 15
3188 6p. Juan Luna 20 15

(b) Green backgrounds.
3189 15p. Type **927** 45 35
3190 15p. Melchora Aquino 45 35
3191 15p. Jose Rizal 45 35
3192 15p. Antonio Luna 45 35
3193 15p. Marcelo del Pilar 45 35
3194 15p. Gregorio del Pilar 45 35
3195 15p. Andres Bonifacio 45 35
3196 15p. Apolinario Mabini 45 35
3197 15p. Emilio Aguinaldo 45 35
3198 15p. Juan Luna 45 35

(c) Pink background.
3229 5p. Jose Rizal 15 10

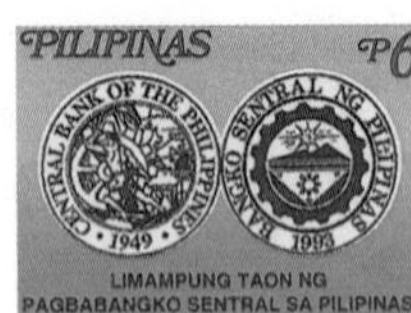

956 Old and New Bank Emblems

1999. 50th Anniv of Central Bank of the Philippines.
3199 **956** 6p. multicoloured 20 15

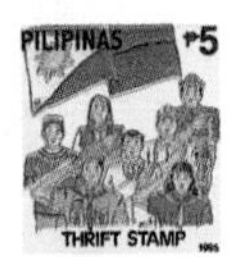

957 Anniversary Emblem
958 Scouts and Guides

1999. Centenary of Declaration of Philippine Independence. Multicoloured.
3200 6p. Type **957** 20 15
3201 6p. General Emilio Aguinaldo's house (site of declaration, June 1898) 20 15
3202 6p. Malolos Congress, Barasoain Church, Bulacan (ratification by regions of declaration, September 1898) 20 15

3203 6p. House in Western Negros (uprising of 5 November 1898) 20 15
3204 6p. Cry of Santa Barbara, Iloilo (inauguration of government, 17 November 1898) 20 15
3205 6p. Cebu City (Victory over Colonial Forces of Spain, December 1898) 20 15
3206 6p. Philippine flag and emblem (declaration in Butaan City of sovereignty over Mindanao, 17 January 1899) 20 15
3207 6p. Facade of Church (Ratification of Constitution, 22 January 1899) 20 15
3208 6p. Carnival procession, Malolos (Inauguration of Republic, 23 January 1899) 20 15
3209 6p. Barosoain Church and anniversary emblem . . . 20 15

1999.

3210 5p. Type **958** 15 10
3211 5p. Children gardening . . . 15 10

Nos. 3210/11 were originally issued as Savings Bank stamps in 1995, but were authorized for postal use from 16 January 1999.

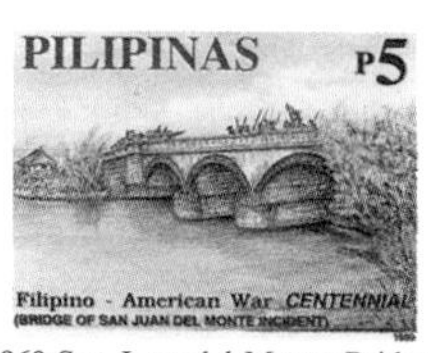

959 Cruise Liner

1999. Centenary of Department of Transportation and Communication. Multicoloured.
3212 6p. Type **959** 20 15
3213 6p. Airplane 20 15
3214 6p. Air traffic control tower 20 15
3215 6p. Satellite dish aerial and bus 20 15

Nos. 3212/15 were issued together, se-tenant, forming a composite design.

960 San Juan del Monte Bridge

1999. Centenary of American–Filipino War.
3217 **960** 5p. multicoloured . . . 15 10

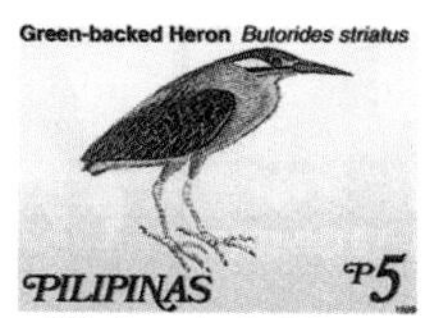

961 General Emilio Aguinaldo and Academy Arms

1999. Centenary (1998) of Philippine Military Academy.
3218 **961** 5p. multicoloured . . . 15 10

962 Green-backed Heron

1999. Birds. Multicoloured.
3219 5p. Type **962** 15 10
3220 5p. Common tern 15 10
3221 5p. Greater crested tern . . 15 10
3222 5p. Ruddy Turnstone . . . 15 10
3223 5p. Black-winged stilt . . . 15 10
3224 5p. Asiatic Dowitcher . . . 15 10
3225 5p. Whimbrel 15 10
3226 5p. Reef heron 15 10

963 Man holding Crutches

1999. 50th Anniv of Philippine Orthopaedic Association.
3230 **963** 5p. multicoloured . . . 15 10

964 Francisco Ortigas and Emblem

1999. 50th Anniv of Manila Lions Club
3231 **964** 5p. multicoloured . . . 15 10

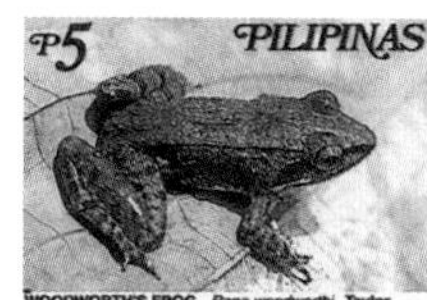

965 Entrance to Garden

1999. La Union Botanical Garden, San Fernando.
3232 5p. Type **965** 15 10
3233 5p. Kiosk 15 10

Nos. 3232/3 were issued together, se-tenant, forming a composite design.

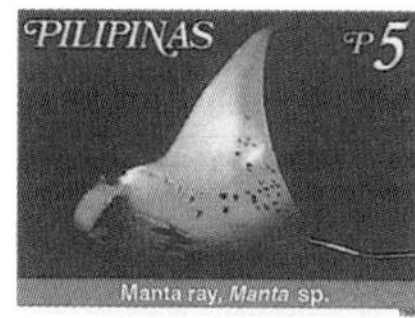

966 Gliding Tree Frog

1999. Frogs. Multicoloured.
3234 5p. Type **966** 15 10
3235 5p. Common forest frog . . 15 10
3236 5p. Woodworth's frog . . . 15 10
3237 5p. Giant Philippine frog . . 15 10

967 Manta Ray

1999. Marine Life. Multicoloured.
3239 5p. Type **967** 15 10
3240 5p. Painted rock lobster . . 15 10
3241 5p. Sea squirt 15 10
3242 5p. Banded sea snake . . . 15 10

968 Nakpil

1999. Birth Centenary of Juan Nakpil (architect).
3244 **968** 5p. multicoloured . . . 15 10

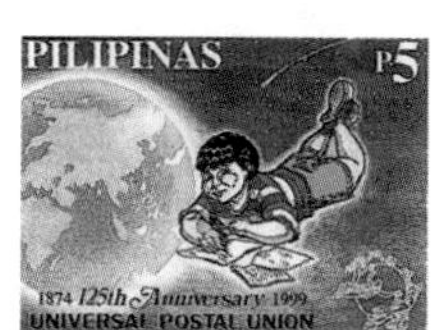

969 Child writing Letter and Globe

1999. 125th Anniv of Universal Postal Union. Multicoloured.
3245 5p. Type **969** 15 10
3246 15p. Girl with stamp album 65 50

970 Waling-Waling and Cattleya "Queen Sirikit"

971 Child writing

1999. 50 Years of Philippines–Thailand Diplomatic Relations. Multicoloured.
3247 5p. Type **970** 15 10
3248 11p. As Type **970** but with flowers transposed 35 25

1999. 150th Anniv of Mongol Pencils.
3249 **971** 5p. multicoloured . . . 15 10

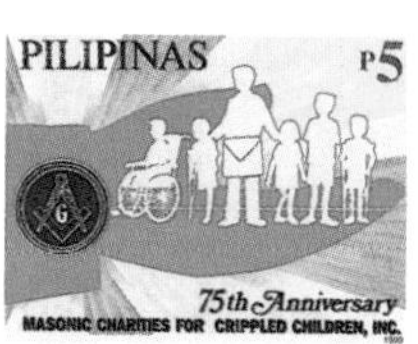

972 Emblem and Handicapped Children

1999. 75th Anniv of Masonic Charities for Handicapped Children.
3250 **972** 5p. multicoloured . . . 15 10

973 Sampaguita and Rose of Sharon

975 Dove, Fishes, Bread and Quotation from Isaiah

974 Teachers, Nurses and Machinists

1999. 50 Years of Philippines–South Korea Diplomatic Relations. Multicoloured.
3251 5p. Type **973** 15 10
3252 11p. As Type **973** but with flowers transposed 35 25

1999. 50th Anniv of Community Chest Foundation.
3253 **974** 5p. multicoloured . . . 15 10

1999. Centenary of Philippine Bible Society.
3254 **975** 5p. multicoloured . . . 15 10

976 Score, Jose Palma (lyricist) and Julian Felipe (composer)

1999. Centenary of National Anthem.
3255 **976** 5p. multicoloured . . . 15 10

977 St. Francis of Assisi and Parish Church

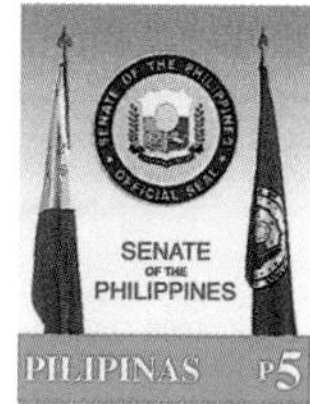

979 Flags and Official Seal

1999. 400th Anniv of St. Francis of Assisi Parish, Sariaya, Quezon.
3256 **977** 5p. multicoloured . . . 15 10

1999. The Senate.
3258 **979** 5p. multicoloured . . . 15 10

980 New Business, Arts and Sciences Faculty Building

1999. 60th Anniv of Chiang Kai Shek College, Manila.
3259 **980** 5p. multicoloured . . . 15 10

981 School Building

1999. 50th Anniv of Tanza National High School.
3260 **981** 5p. multicoloured . . . 15 10

982 St. Agustin Church, Paoay (World Heritage Day)

1999. United Nations Day. Multicoloured.
3261 5p. Type **982** 15 10
3262 11p. Elderly couple (International Year of the Older Person) 35 25
3263 15p. "Rizal Learns the Alphabet and Prayers from his Mother" (Miguel Galvez) (World Teachers' Day) 45 35

983 Angel

984 Tamaraw and Polar Bear

1999. Christmas. Multicoloured.
3264 5p. Type **983** 15 10
3265 11p. Angel holding star . . 35 25
3266 13p. Angel holding ribbon 40 30
3267 15p. Angel holding flowers 45 35

1999. 50 Years of Philippines–Canada Diplomatic Relations. Multicoloured.
3269 5p. Type **984** 15 10
3270 15p. As Type **984** but with animals transposed . . . 45 35

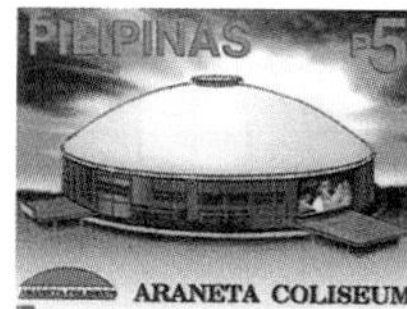

985 Coliseum

1999. Renovation of Araneta Coliseum.
3271 **985** 5p. multicoloured . . . 15 10

986 Sunrise

987 "Kristo" (Arturo Luz)

1999. 3rd Informal Summit of Association of South-east Asian Nations, Manila.
3272 **986** 5p. multicoloured . . . 15 10
3273 11p. multicoloured . . . 35 25

1999. National Stamp Collecting Month. Modern Sculptures. Multicoloured.
3274 5p. Type **987** 15 10
3275 11p. "Homage to Dodgie Laurel" (J. Elizalde Navarro) 35 25
3276 13p. "Hilojan" (Napoleon Abueva) 40 30
3277 15p. "Mother and Child" (Napoleon Abueva) . . . 45 35

988 Dragon

1999. New Year. Year of the Dragon. Multicoloured.
3279 5p. Type **988** 15 10
3280 15p. Dragon amongst clouds 45 35

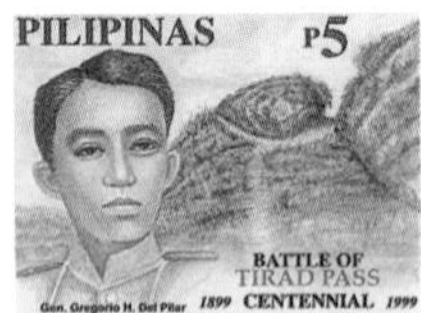

989 Gen. Gregorio H. del Pilar

1999. Centenary of the Battle of Tirad Pass.
3282 **989** 5p. multicoloured . . . 15 10

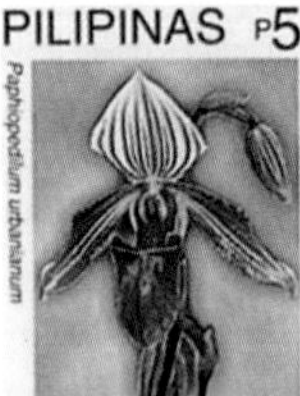

990 *Paphiopedilum urbanianum*

1999. Orchids. Multicoloured.
3283 5p. Type **990** 15 10
3284 5p. *Phalaenopsis schilleriana* 15 10
3285 5p. *Dendrobium amethystoglossum* 15 10
3286 5p. *Paphiopedilum barbatum* 15 10

991 General Licerio Geronimo

1999. Centenary of Battle of San Mateo.
3288 **991** 5p. multicoloured . . . 15 10

992 Crowds around Soldiers in Tanks

1999. New Millennium (1st series). "People Power". Multicoloured.
3289 5p. Type **992** 15 10
3290 5p. Radio antennae, helicopters and people . . 15 10
3291 5p. Religious procession . . 15 10

Nos. 3289/91 were issued together, se-tenant, forming a composite design.

See also Nos. 3311/13, 3357/9 and 3394/6.

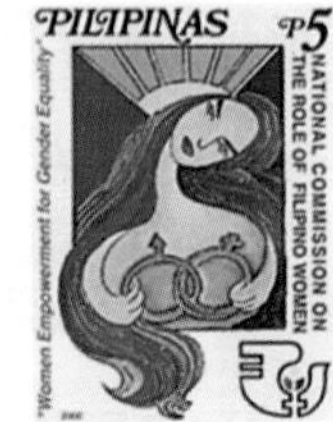

993 Woman holding Gender Signs

2000. 25th Anniv of National Commission on Role of Filipino Women.
3292 **993** 5p. multicoloured . . . 15 10

994 Newspaper Headline and Headquarters

995 Manuel Roxas (1946–48)

2000. Centenary of the Manila Bulletin (newspaper).
3293 **994** 5p. multicoloured . . . 15 10

2000. Presidential Office. Multicoloured.
3294 5p. Type **995** 15 10
3295 5p. Elpidio Quirino (1948–53) 15 10

996 Golfer, Sailing Boat and Swimmers

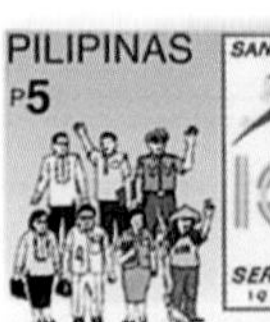

997 Joseph Ejercito Estrada (1998–2000)

2000. 150th Anniv of La Union Province. Mult.
3296 5p. Type **996** 15 10
3297 5p. Tractor, building and worker 15 10
3298 5p. Government building . . 15 10
3299 5p. Airplane, bus, satellite dish, workers and bus . . 15 10

2000. Presidential Office. Multicoloured.
3300 5p. Presidential seal (face value at top left) 15 10
3301 5p. Type **997** 15 10
3302 5p. Fidel V. Ramos (1992–98) 15 10
3303 5p. Corazon C. Aquino (1986–92) 15 10
3304 5p. Ferdinand E. Marcos (1965–86) 15 10
3305 5p. Diosdado Macapagal (1961–65) 15 10
3306 5p. Carlos P. Garcia (1957–61) 15 10
3307 5p. Ramon Magsaysay (1953–57) 15 10
3308 5p. Elpidio Quirino (1948–53) 15 10
3309 5p. Manuel Roxas (1946–48) 15 10

998 Workers and Emblem

2000. Centenary of the Civil Service Commission.
3310 **998** 5p. multicoloured . . . 15 10

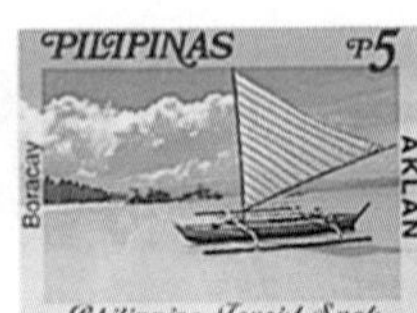

999 Golden Garuda, Palawan

2000. New Millennium (2nd series). Artefacts. Mult.
3311 5p. Type **999** 15 10
3312 5p. Sunrise at Pusan Point, Davao Oriental 15 10
3313 5p. Golden Tara, Agusan 15 10

1000 Outrigger Canoe, Boracay Island

2000. Tourist Sites. Multicoloured.
3314 5p. Type **1000** 15 10
3315 5p. Chocolate Hills, Bohol 15 10
3316 5p. El Nido Forest, Palawan 15 10
3317 5p. Vigan House, Ilocos Sur 15 10

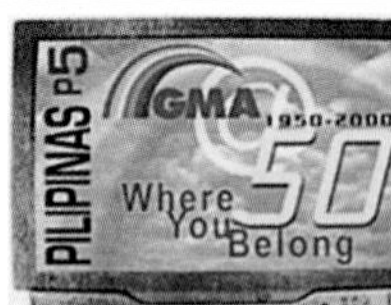

1001 Great Wall of China and Chinese Phoenix

2000. 25th Anniv of Diplomatic Relations with Republic of China. Multicoloured.
3319 5p. Type **1001** 15 10
3320 11p. Banaue rice terraces and Philippine Sarimanok 30 20

1002 Television and Emblem

2000. 50th Anniv of GMA Television and Radio Network.
3322 **1002** 5p. multicoloured . . . 15 10

1003 Church Building

1004 Carlos P. Garcia

2000. 400th Anniv of St. Thomas de Aquinas Parish, Mangaldan.
3323 **1003** 5p. multicoloured . . . 15 10

2000. Presidential Office. Multicoloured.
3324 10p. Type **1004** 25 20
3325 10p. Ramon Magsaysay . . 25 20
3326 11p. Ferdinand E. Marcos 30 20
3327 11p. Diosdado Macapagal 30 20
3328 13p. Corazon C. Aquino . . 35 25
3329 13p. Fidel V. Ramos . . . 35 25
3330 15p. Joseph Ejercito Estrada 40 30
3331 15p. Presidential seal (face value at top right) 40 30

1005 Memorial and Map

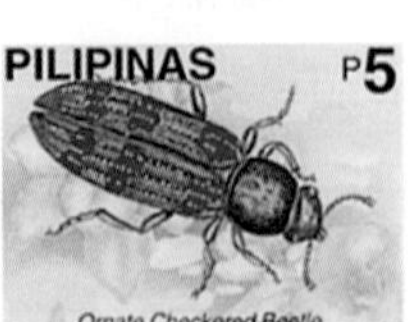

1006 Joseph Ejercito Estrada

2000. Battle Centenaries. Multicoloured.
3332 5p. Type **1005** (Battle of Pulang Lupa) 15 10
3333 5p. Memorial and soldiers (Battle of Mabitac) . . . 15 10
3334 5p. Sun and soldiers (Battles of Cagayan, Agusan Hill and Makahambus Hill) (vert) 15 10
3335 5p. Map, memorial and bamboo signalling device (Battle of Paye) (vert) . . 15 10

2000. Presidential Office. Multicoloured.
3336 5p. Presidential seal 15 10
3337 5p. Type **1006** 15 10
3338 5p. Fidel V. Ramos 15 10
3339 5p. Corazon C. Aquino . . . 15 10
3340 5p. Ferdinand E. Marcos . . 15 10
3341 5p. Diosdado Macapagal . . 15 10
3342 5p. Carlos P. Garcia 15 10
3343 5p. Ramon Magsaysay . . . 15 10
3344 5p. Elpidio Quirino 15 10
3345 5p. Manuel Roxas 15 10

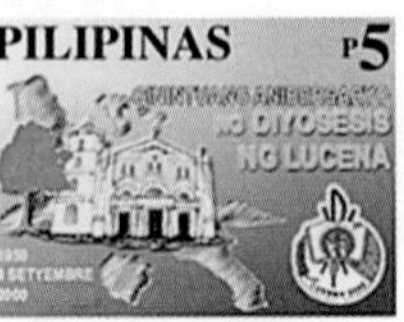

1007 Ornate Chequered Beetle

2000. Insects. Multicoloured.
3346 5p. Type **1007** 15 10
3347 5p. Sharpshooter bug . . . 15 10
3348 5p. Milkweed bug 15 10
3349 5p. Spotted cucumber beetle 15 10
3350 5p. Green June beetle . . . 15 10
3351 5p. Convergent ladybird beetle 15 10
3352 5p. Eastern hercules beetle 15 10
3353 5p. Harlequin cabbage bug 15 10

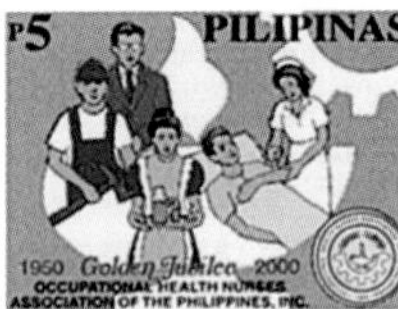

1008 St. Ferdinand Cathedral, Map and Emblem

2000. 50th Anniv of Lucena Diocese.
3355 **1008** 5p. multicoloured . . . 15 10

1009 Nurses and Patients

2000. 50th Anniv of Occupational Health Nurses' Association.
3356 **1009** 5p. multicoloured . . . 15 10

1010 Balanghai

2000. New Millennium (3rd series). Traditional Sea Craft. Multicoloured.
3357 5p. Type **1010** 15 10
3358 5p. Vinta 15 10
3359 5p. Caracoa 15 10

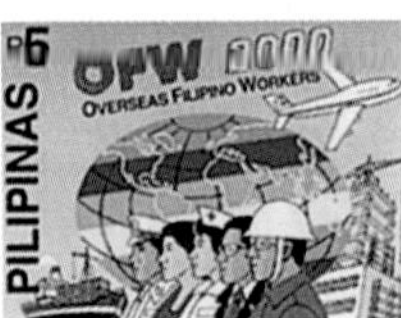

1011 Jars, Bank Note, Circuit Board, Computer Mouse and Emblem

2000. 50th Anniv of Equitable PCI Bank.
3360 **1011** 5p. multicoloured . . . 15 10

1012 Ship, Globe, Airplane and Workers

2000. Year of Overseas Filipino Workers.
3361 **1012** 5p. multicoloured . . . 15 10

1013 Pedro Poveda (founder), Buildings and Emblem

2000. 50th Anniv of the Teresian Association (international lay preacher association) in the Philippines.
3362 **1013** 5p. multicoloured . . . 15 10

1014 Congress in Session

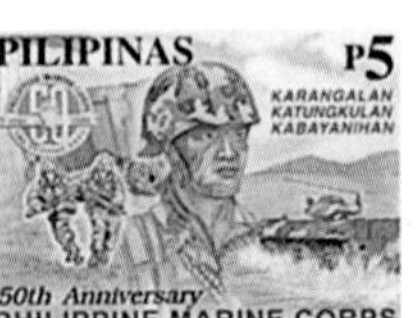

1016 Running

1015 Soldiers, Tank and Emblem

2000. House of Representatives.
3363 **1014** 5p. multicoloured . . . 15 10

2000. 50th Anniv of Philippine Marine Corps.
3364 **1015** 5p. multicoloured . . . 15 10

2000. Olympic Games, Sydney. Multicoloured.
3365 5p. Type **1016** 15 10
3366 5p. Archery 15 10
3367 5p. Rifle shooting 15 10
3368 5p. Diving 15 10

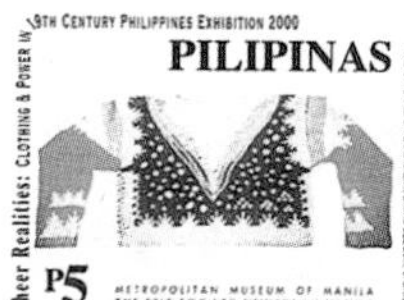

1017 Boy, Envelopes and Statue of Postman (½-size illustration)

2000. Postal Service. Sheet 100 × 60 mm.
MS3370 **1017** 15p. multicoloured . . . 35 35

1018 B'laan Woman's Blouse, Davao del Sur

2000. "Sheer Realities: Clothing and Power in 19th-century Philippines" Exhibition, Manila. Multicoloured.
3371 5p. Type **1018** 10 10
3372 5p. T'boli T'nalak abaca cloth, South Cotabato . . 10 10
3373 5p. Kalinga/Gaddang cotton loincloth, Cordilleras (vert) 10 10
3374 5p. Portrait of Leticia Jimenez (anon) (vert) . . 10 10
MS3375 101 × 70 mm. 5p. Portrait of Teodora Devera Ygnacio (Justiniano Asuncion); 15p. Tawsug silk sash, Sulu Archipelago 45 45

1019 Angel cradling Sunflowers

1021 1955 5c. Labour Management Congress Stamp

2000. Christmas. Multicoloured.
3376 5p. Type **1019** 10 10
3377 5p. As No. 3376 but inscribed "CHRISTMAS JUBILEUM" 10 10
3378 11p. Angel with basket of fruit and swag of leaves 25 10
3379 13p. Angel with basket of fruit on shoulder 30 15
3380 15p. Angel with garland of flowers 35 15

2000. No. 1977 surch **P5.00**.
3381 5p on 3p.60 multicoloured . . 10 10

2000. 50th Anniv of Amateur Philatelists Organization Philatelic Society. Multicoloured.
3382 5p. Type **1021** 10 10
3383 5p. 1957 5c. Juan Luna birth centenary stamp (horiz) 10 10
3384 5p. 1962 5c. orchid stamp 10 10
3385 5p. 1962 6 + 4c. Rizal Foundation Fund stamp (horiz) 10 10

1022 "Portrait of an Unknown Lady" (Juan Novicio Luna)

2000. Modern Art. Multicoloured.
3386 5p. Type **1022** 10 10
3387 11p. "Nude" (Jose Joya) (horiz) 25 10
3388 13p. "Lotus Odalisque" (Rodolfo Paras-Perez) (horiz) 30 15
3389 15p. "Untitled (Nude)" (Fernando Amorsolo) (horiz) 35 15
MS3390 100 x 80 mm. 15p. "The Memorial" (Cesar Legaspi) (79 × 29 mm) 35 15

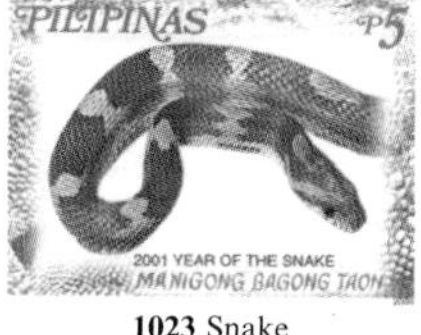

1023 Snake

2000. New Year. Year of the Snake. Multicoloured.
3391 5p. Type **1023** 10 10
3392 11p. Snake 25 10
MS3393 98 × 88 mm. Nos. 3391/2 Perf or imperf 35 15

1024 Ships in Port (Trade and Industry)

2000. New Millennium (4th series). Multicoloured.
3394 5p. Type **1024** 10 10
3395 5p. Pupils and teacher (Education and Knowledge) 10 10
3396 5p. Globe, satellite, family using computer and woman using telephone (Communications and Technology) 10 10

1025 Pesos Fuertes (1st Philippines Banknote)

2001. 150th Anniv of Philippines Bank.
3397 **1025** 5p. multicoloured . . . 10 10

1026 Eagle

2001. "Hong Kong 2001" International Stamp Exhibition. Flora and Fauna. Multicoloured.
3398 5p. Type **1026** 10 10
3399 5p. Philippine tarsier 10 10
3400 5p. "Talisman Cove" (flower) 10 10
3401 5p. Turtle 10 10
3402 5p. Tamaraw 10 10
MS3403 Five sheets, each 80 × 71 mm. (a) 11p. As Type **1026**. (b) 11p As No. 3399. (c) 11p. As No. 3400. (d) 11p. As No. 3401. (e) 11p. As No. 3402 1·25 1·25

PILIPINAS P5
General PACIANO RIZAL
150th Birth Anniversary 1851-2001

1027 Rizal

2001. 150th Birth Anniv of General Paciano Rizal.
3404 **1027** 5p. multicoloured . . . 10 10

1028 Facade

2001. Centenary of San Beda College.
3405 **1028** 5p. multicoloured . . . 10 10

1029 High Altar, St. Peter's Basilica, Rome

1030 Presidential Seal

2001. 50th Anniv of Diplomatic Relations with Vatican City. Multicoloured.
3406 5p. Type **1029** 10 10
3407 15p. High altar, San Agustin Church, Manila 35 15
MS3408 90 × 71 mm. 15p. Adam; 15p. God 65 65
The two stamps in No. **MS**3408 form the composite design of "Creation of Adam" (Michaelangelo).

2001. Multicoloured, background colour given.
3409 **1030** 5p. yellow 10 10
3413 15p. blue 35 15

PILIPINAS P5
Our Lady of Manaoag
1926 Diamond Jubilee 2001
Canonical Coronation

1031 Our Lady of Manaoag

1032 Pres. Macapagal-Arroyo taking Presidential Oath

2001. 75th Anniv of Canonical Coronation of Our Lady of the Rosary of Manaoag.
3414 **1031** 5p. multicoloured . . . 10 10

2001. President Gloria Macapagal-Arroyo. Multicoloured.
3415 5p. Type **1032** 10 10
3416 5p. Pres. Macapagal-Arroyo waving 10 10

1033 Sydney Opera House and Philippines Cultural Centre

2001. Philippine-Australia Diplomatic Relations. Multicoloured.
3417 5p. Type **1033** 10 10
3418 13p. As Type **1033** but with subjects transposed . . . 30 15
MS3419 96 × 60 mm. 13p. Philippines Cultural Centre and Sydney Opera House (79 × 29 mm) 30 15

1034 Philippine Normal University

2001. University Centenaries. Multicoloured.
3420 5p. Type **1034** 10 10
3421 5p. Facade of Silliman University 10 10

1035 Scales of Justice and Court Building

2001. Centenary of Supreme Court.
3422 **1035** 5p. multicoloured . . . 10 10

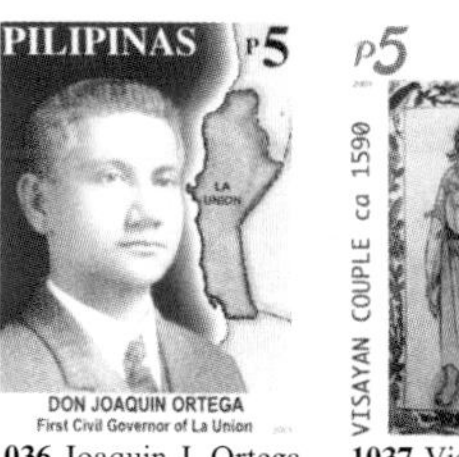

1036 Joaquin J. Ortega

1037 Visayan Couple

2001. Anniversaries. Multicoloured.
3423 5p. Type 1**036** (centenary of appointment as first Civil Governor of the Province of La Union) 10 10
3424 5p. Eugenio H. Lopez (businessman, birth centenary) 10 10

2001. "PHILANIPPON '01" International Stamp Exhibition, Japan. Boxer Codex (manuscript depicting Philippine lifestyle during first century of Spanish contact). Multicoloured.
3425 5p. Type **1037** 10 10
3426 5p. Tagalog couple 10 10
3427 5p. Moros of Luzon (man wearing red tunic) 10 10
3428 5p. Moros of Luzon (woman wearing blue dress) 10 10
MS3429 82 × 107 mm. 5p. Tattooed Pintados; 5p. Pintados wearing costumes; 5p. Cagayan woman; 5p. Zambal 45 45

1038 Teachers and Thomas (transport)

2001. Centenary of Arrival of American Teachers. Multicoloured.
3430 5p. Type **1038** 10 10
3431 15p. Pupils and school building 35 15

1039 Emblem

2001. Centenary of Technology University, Manila.
3432 **1039** 5p. multicoloured . . . 10 10

1040 Museum Artefacts

2001. Centenary of National Museum.
3433 **1040** 5p. multicoloured . . . 10 10

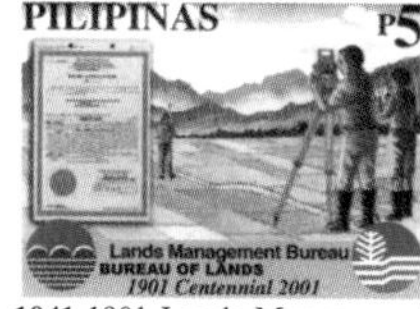

1041 1901 Lands Management Charter, Modern Surveyors and Emblems

2001. Centenary of Lands Management Bureau.
3434 **1041** 5p. multicoloured . . . 10 10

OFFICIAL STAMPS

1926. Commemorative issue of 1926 optd **OFFICIAL**.
O391 **49** 2c. black and green . . . 1·50 80
O392 4c. black and red . . . . 1·50 80
O393 18c. black and brown . . . 5·50 3·25
O394 20c. black and orange . . 4·50 1·50

1931. Stamps of 1906 optd **O.B.**
O413 2c. green (No. 337) 10 10
O414 4c. red (No. 338) 10 10
O415 6c. violet (No. 339) 10 10
O416 8c. brown (No. 340) . . . 10 10
O417 10c. blue (No. 341) 55 10
O418 12c. orange (No. 342) . . . 30 15
O419 16c. olive (No. 344) 30 10
O420 20c. orange (No. 345) . . . 40 10
O421 26c. green (No. 346) . . . 50 40
O422 30c. grey (No. 347) 40 30

1935. Nos. 459/68 optd **O.B.**
O473 2c. red 10 10
O474 4c. green 10 10
O475 6c. brown 10 10
O476 8c. violet 15 15
O477 10c. red 15 10
O478 12c. black 20 15
O479 16c. blue 40 15
O480 20c. bistre 20 15
O481 26c. blue 40 35
O482 30c. red 45 40

1936. Stamps of 1935 Nos. 459/68 optd **O. B. COMMON-WEALTH** (2, 6, 20c.) or **O. B. COMMONWEALTH** (others).
O538 2c. red 10 10
O539 4c. green 10 10
O540 6c. brown 15 10
O541 8c. violet 15 10
O542 10c. red 15 10
O543 12c. black 15 15
O544 16c. blue 40 10
O545 20c. bistre 40 40

O546 26c. blue 45 45
O547 30c. red 45 45

1941. Nos. 563 and 623 optd **O. B.**
O565 **104** 2c. green 10 10
O624 – 2c. brown 10 10

1948. Various stamps optd **O.B.**
O738 **147** 1c. brown 10 10
O668 **125** 2c. green 15 10
O659 – 4c. brown (No. 629) . . 15 10
O739 – 5c. red (No. 731) . . . 10 10
O843 – 6c. blue (No. 842) . . . 15 10
O660 **113** 10c. red 20 10
O740 – 10c. blue (No. 732) . . 15 10
O661 – 16c. grey (No. 632) . . 1·10 35
O669 – 20c. brown (No. 633) 30 10
O741 – 20c. red (No. 733) . . . 25 10
O670 – 50c. green (No. 634) . . 40 15

1950. Surch **ONE CENTAVO.**
O700 **125** 1c. on 2c. green (No. O668) 15 10

1959. No. 810 optd **O B.**
O811 1c. on 5c. red 10 10

1962. Nos. 898/904 optd **G. O.**
O908 5s. red 10 10
O909 6s. brown 10 10
O910 6s. blue 10 10
O911 10s. purple 10 10
O912 20s. blue 10 10
O913 30s. red 10 10
O914 50s. violet 15 10

1970. Optd **G.O.**
O1182 **318** 10s. red 10 10

OFFICIAL SPECIAL DELIVERY STAMP

1931. No. E353b optd **O.B.**
EO423 E **47** 20c. violet 50 35

POSTAGE DUE STAMPS

1899. Postage Due stamps of United States of 1894 optd **PHILIPPINES**.
D268 D **87** 1c. red . . . . 3·75 1·00
D269 2c. red . . . . 4·00 90
D270 3c. red . . . . 13·00 4·50
D271 5c. red . . . . 10·50 1·75
D272 10c. red . . . . 14·00 4·00
D273 30c. red . . . . £180 75·00
D274 50c. red . . . . £140 70·00

D **51** Post Office Clerk

D **118**

1928.
D395 D **51** 4c. red 15 15
D396 6c. red 25 25
D397 8c. red 25 25
D398 10c. red 25 25
D399 12c. red 25 25
D400 16c. red 30 30
D401 20c. red 25 25

1937. Surch **3 CVOS. 3**.
D521 D **51** 3c. on 4c. red 20 15

1947.
D644 D **118** 3c. red 10 10
D645 4c. blue 10 10
D646 6c. green 20 10
D647 10c. orange 25 15

SPECIAL DELIVERY STAMPS

1901. Special Delivery stamp of United States of 1888 optd **PHILIPPINES**.
E268 **46** 10c. blue (No. E283) . . 85·00 80·00

1907. Special Delivery stamp of United States optd **PHILIPPINES**.
E298 E **117** 10c. blue £1500

E **47** Messenger running

1919. Perf (E353), perf or imperf (E353b).
E353 E **47** 20c. blue 45 20
E353b 20c. violet 45 15

1939. Optd **COMMONWEALTH**. Perf.
E550 E **47** 20c. violet 30 20

1945. Optd **VICTORY**.
E622 E **47** 20c. violet (No. E550) 50 50

E **120** Cyclist Messenger and Post Office

1947.
E651 E **120** 20c. purple 25 10

E **219** G.P.O., Manila

E891 E **219** 20c. mauve 25 10

PITCAIRN ISLANDS Pt. 1

An island group in the Pacific Ocean, nearly midway between Australia and America.

1940. 12 pence = 1 shilling;
20 shillings = 1 pound.
1967. 100 cents = 1 New Zealand dollar.

4 Lt. Bligh and the "Bounty"

1940.
1 – ½d. orange and green 40 60
2 – 1d. mauve and magenta . . . 55 70
3 – 1½d. grey and red 55 50
4 **4** 2d. green and brown . . . . 1·75 1·40
5 – 3d. green and blue . . . . . 1·25 1·40
5b – 4d. black and green . . . . 15·00 10·00
6 – 6d. brown and blue . . . . . 5·00 1·50
6a – 8d. green and mauve . . . . 16·00 7·00
7 – 1s. violet and grey . . . . . 3·00 1·75
8 – 2s.6d. green and brown . . . 8·00 3·75
DESIGNS—HORIZ: ½d. Oranges; 1d. Fletcher Christian, crew and Pitcairn Is.; 1½d. John Adams and house; 3d. Map of Pitcairn Is. and Pacific; 4d. Bounty Bible; 6d. H.M.S. "Bounty"; 8d. School, 1949; 1s. Christian and Pitcairn Is.; 2s.6d. Christian, crew and Pitcairn coast.

4a Houses of Parliament, London

1946. Victory.
9 **4a** 2d. brown 60 15
10 3d. blue 60 15

4b King George VI and Queen Elizabeth

4c King George VI and Queen Elizabeth

1949. Silver Wedding.
11 **4b** 1½d. red . . . . 2·00 1·00
12 **4c** 10s. mauve . . . . 35·00 50·00

4d Hermes, Globe and Forms of Transport

4e Hemispheres, Jet-powered Vickers Viking Airliner and Steamer

4f Hermes and Globe

4g U.P.U. Monument

1949. U.P.U.
13 **4d** 2½d. brown . . . . 1·00 4·25
14 **4e** 3d. blue . . . . 8·00 4·25
15 **4f** 6d. green . . . . 4·00 4·25
16 **4g** 1s. purple . . . . 4·00 4·00

4h Queen Elizabeth II

1953. Coronation.
17 **4h** 4d. black and green . . . . 2·00 3·50

12 Handicrafts: Bird Model

1957.
33 – ½d. green and mauve . . . 65 60
19 – 1d. black and green . . . 3·50 1·75
20 – 2d. brown and blue . . . 1·25 60
21 **12** 2½d. brown and pink . . . 50 40
22 – 3d. green and blue . . . 80 40
23 – 4d. red and blue (I) . . . 90 40
23a – 4d. red and blue (II) . . . 5·00 1·50
24 **12** 6d. buff and blue . . . . 1·50 55
25 – 8d. green and red 60 40
26 – 1s. black and brown . . . 2·25 40
27 – 2s. green and orange . . . 14·00 10·00
28 – 2s.6d. blue and red . . . . 23·00 9·00
DESIGNS—HORIZ: ½d. "Cordyline terminalis"; 3d. Bounty Bay; 4d. Pitcairn School; 6d. Map of Pacific; 8d. Inland scene; 1s. Model of the "Bounty"; 2s.6d. Launching new whaleboat. VERT: 1d. Map of Pitcairn; 2d. John Adams and "Bounty" Bible; 2s. Island wheelbarrow.

The 4d. Type I is inscr "PITCAIRN SCHOOL"; Type II is inscr "SCHOOL TEACHER'S HOUSE".

20 Pitcairn Island and Simon Young

1961. Cent of Return of Pitcairn Islanders.
29 **20** 3d. black and yellow 50 45
30 – 6d. brown and blue . . . . 1·00 75
31 – 1s. orange and green . . . . 1·00 75
DESIGNS: 6d. Maps of Norfolk and Pitcairn Islands; 1s. Migrant brigantine "Mary Ann".

20a Protein Foods

1963. Freedom from Hunger.
32 **20a** 2s.6d. blue . . . . 7·50 3·00

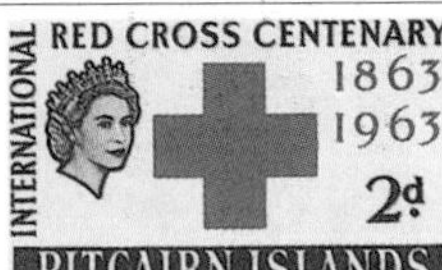

20b Red Cross Emblem

1963. Cent of Red Cross.
34 **20b** 2d. red and black . . . . 1·50 1·00
35 2s.6d. red and blue . . . . 3·50 4·00

23 Pitcairn Is. Longboat

24 Queen Elizabeth II (after Anthony Buckley)

1964. Multicoloured.
36 ½d. Type **23** 10 30
37 1d. H.M.S. "Bounty" 30 30
38 2d. "Out from Bounty Bay" 30 30
39 3d. Great frigate bird 75 30
40 4d. White tern 75 30
41 6d. Pitcairn warbler 75 30
42 8d. Red-footed booby 75 30
43 10d. Red-tailed tropic birds . . 60 30
44 1s. Henderson Island crake . . 60 30
45 1s.6d. Stephen's lory . . . . . 4·50 1·25
46 2s.6d. Murphy's petrel . . . . . 4·00 1·50
47 4s. Henderson Island fruit dove . . . . 6·00 1·75
48 8s. Type **24** . . . . 2·75 1·75

24a I.T.U. Emblem

1965. Centenary of I.T.U.
49 **24a** 1d. mauve and brown . . . 1·00 40
50 2s.6d. turquoise and blue 5·00 3·50

24b I.C.Y. Emblem

1965. International Co-operation Year.
51 **24b** 1d. purple and turquoise 1·00 40
52 2s.6d. green and lavender 4·00 3·00

24c Sir Winston Churchill and St. Paul's Cathedral in Wartime

1966. Churchill Commemoration.
53 **24c** 2d. blue . . . . 1·25 85
54 3d. green . . . . 3·75 1·00
55 6d. brown . . . . 4·00 1·75
56 1s. violet . . . . 5·50 2·50

25 Footballer's Legs, Ball and Jules Rimet Cup

1966. World Cup Football Championship.
57 **25** 4d. multicoloured . . . . . 1·25 1·00
58 2s.6d. multicoloured . . . . 2·50 1·75

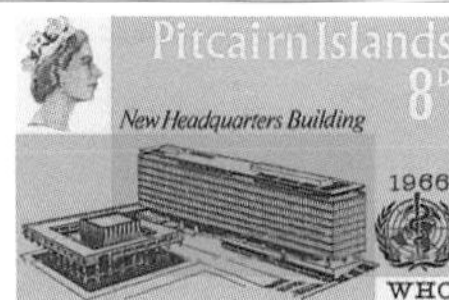

25a W.H.O. Building.

1966. Inauguration of W.H.O. Headquarters, Geneva.
59 **25a** 8d. black, green and blue . . . 4·00 3·25
60 1s.6d. black, purple and ochre . . . 5·50 3·75

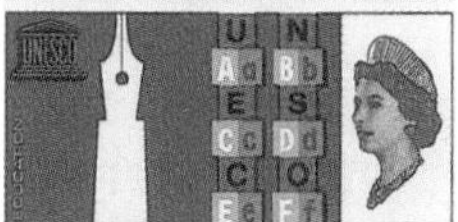

25b "Education"

25c "Science"

25d "Culture"

1966. 20th Anniv of UNESCO.
61 **25b** ½d. multicoloured . . . 20 75
62 **25c** 10d. yellow, violet and olive . . . 3·25 2·75
63 **25d** 2s. black, purple and orange . . . 6·00 4·25

36 Mangarevan Canoe, c. 1325

1967. Bicentenary of Discovery of Pitcairn Islands'. Multicoloured.
64 ½d. Type **36** . . . 10 20
65 1d. P. F. de Quiros and "San Pedro y San Pablo", 1606 . . . 20 20
66 8d. "San Pedro y San Pablo" and "Los Tres Reyes", 1606 . . . 25 20
67 1s. Carteret and H.M.S. "Swallow", 1767 . . . 25 25
68 1s.6d. "Hercules", 1819 . . . 25 25

1967. Decimal Currency. Nos. 36/48 surch with "Bounty" anchor and value.
69 **23** ½c. on ½d. multicoloured . . 10 10
70 – 1c. on 1d. multicoloured . . 30 1·00
71 – 2c. on 2d. multicoloured . . 25 1·00
72 – 2½c. on 3d. multicoloured . . 25 1·00
73 – 3c. on 4d. multicoloured . . 25 20
74 – 5c. on 6d. multicoloured . . 30 1·00
75 – 10c. on 8d. multicoloured . . 30 30
76 – 15c. on 10d. multicoloured . . 1·25 40
77 – 20c. on 1s. multicoloured . . 1·25 55
78 – 25c. on 1s.6d. multicoloured . . 1·75 1·25
79 – 30c. on 2s.6d. multicoloured . . 2·25 1·25
80 – 40c. on 4s. multicoloured . . 2·50 1·25
81 **24** 45c. on 8s. multicoloured . . 2·00 1·50

42 Bligh and "Bounty's" Launch

1967. 150th Death Anniv of Admiral Bligh.
82 **42** 1c. black, ultramarine & blue . . . 10 10
83 – 8c. black, yellow and mauve . . 25 65
84 – 20c. black, brown and buff . . 25 70
DESIGNS: 8c. Bligh and followers cast adrift; 20c. Bligh's tomb.

45 Human Rights Emblem

1968. International Human Rights Year.
85 **45** 1c. multicoloured . . . 10 10
86 2c. multicoloured . . . 10 10
87 25c. multicoloured . . . 35 35

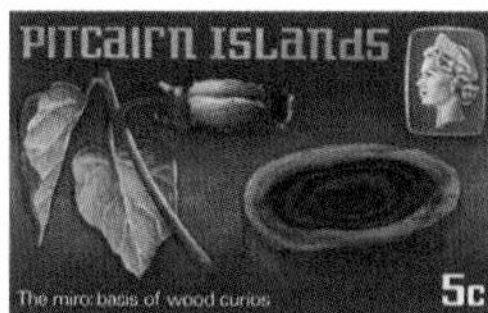

46 Moro Wood and Flower

1968. Handicrafts (1st series).
88 **46** 5c. multicoloured . . . 20 30
89 – 10c. green, brown and orange . . . 20 40
90 – 15c. violet, brown & salmon . . 25 40
91 – 20c. multicoloured . . . 25 45
DESIGNS—HORIZ: 10c. flying fish model. VERT: 15c. "Hand" vases; 20c. Woven baskets.
See also Nos. 207/10.

50 Microscope and Slides

1968. 20th Anniv of World Health Organization.
92 **50** 2c. black, turquoise and blue . . 10 20
93 – 20c. black, orange and purple . . . 40 50
DESIGN: 20c. Hypodermic syringe and jars of tablets.

52 Pitcairn Island

64b Queen Elizabeth II

65 Lantana

1969. Multicoloured.
94 1c. Type **52** . . . 1·50 70
95 2c. Captain Bligh and "Bounty" chronometer . . . 25 15
96 3c. "Bounty" anchor (vert) . . 25 15
97 4c. Plans and drawing of "Bounty" . . . 1·50 15
98 5c. Breadfruit containers and plant . . . 60 15
99 6c. Bounty Bay . . . 30 20
100 8c. Pitcairn longboat . . . 1·50 20
101 10c. Ship landing point . . . 2·50 85
102 15c. Fletcher Christian's Cave . . . 1·50 50
103 20c. Thursday October Christian's house . . . 60 40
104 25c. "Flying fox" cable system (vert) . . . 70 40
105 30c. Radio Station, Taro Ground . . . 55 45
106 40c. "Bounty" Bible . . . 75 60
106a 50c. Pitcairn Coat-of-Arms . . 2·00 11·00
106b $1 Type **64b** . . . 7·00 17·00

1970. Flowers. Multicoloured.
107 1c. Type **65** . . . 20 50
108 2c. "Indian Shot" . . . 25 65
109 5c. Pulau . . . 35 75
110 25c. Wild gladiolus . . . 80 2·00

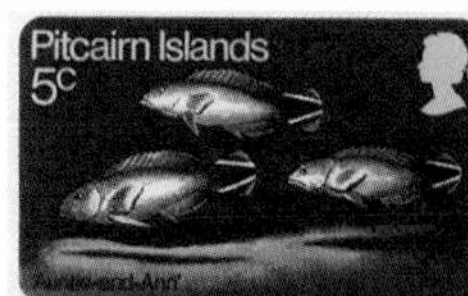

69 Band-tailed Hind

1970. Fishes. Multicoloured.
111 5c. Type **69** . . . 2·75 70
112 10c. High-finned rudderfish . 2·75 85
113 15c. Elwyn's wrasse . . . 3·25 1·00
114 20c. Yellow wrasse ("Whistling daughter") . . 3·50 1·25

1971. Royal Visit. No. 101 optd **ROYAL VISIT 1971**.
115 10c. multicoloured . . . 1·00 1·50

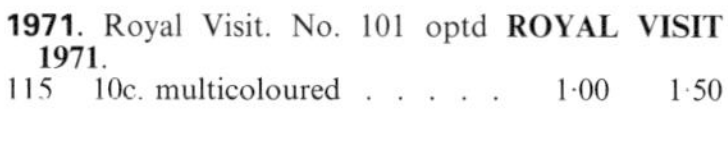

71 Polynesian Rock Carvings

1971. Polynesian Pitcairn. Multicoloured.
116 5c. Type **71** . . . 1·25 75
117 10c. Polynesian artefacts (horiz) . . . 1·50 1·00
118 15c. Polynesian stone fish-hook (horiz) . . . 1·50 1·00
119 20c. Polynesian stone deity 1·75 1·25

72 Commission Flag

74 Rose-apple

73 Red-tailed Tropic Birds and Longboat

1972. 25th Anniv of South Pacific Commission. Multicoloured.
120 4c. Type **72** . . . 50 70
121 8c. Young and elderly (Health) . . . 50 70
122 18c. Junior school (Education) . . . 60 90
123 20c. Goods store (Economy) 80 1·60

1972. Royal Silver Wedding. Multicoloured, background colour given.
124 **73** 4c. green . . . 30 60
125 20c. blue . . . 45 90

1973. Flowers. Multicoloured.
126 4c. Type **74** . . . 1·00 55
127 8c. Mountain-apple . . . 1·25 75
128 15c. "Lata" . . . 1·50 1·00
129 20c. "Dorcas-flower" . . . 1·50 1·25
130 35c. Guava . . . 1·50 1·75

74a Princess Anne and Captain Mark Phillips

1973. Royal Wedding. Multicoloured, background colours given.
131 **74a** 10c. mauve . . . 20 15
132 25c. green . . . 25 30

75 Obelisk Vertagus and Episcopal Mitre Shells

1974. Shells. Multicoloured.
147 4c. Type **75** . . . 65 80
148 10c. Turtle dove-shell . . . 75 1·00
149 18c. Indo-Pacific limpet, fringed false limpet and "Siphonaria normalis" . . 80 1·40
150 50c. "Ctena divergen" . . . 1·25 2·00
MS151 130×121 mm. Nos. 147/50 4·25 14·00

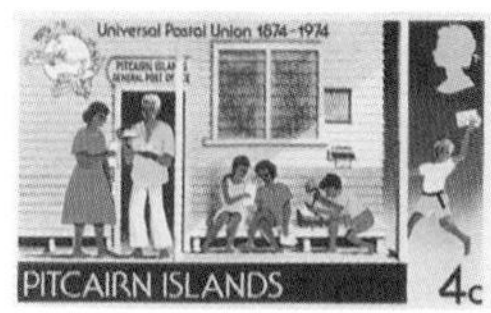

76 Island Post Office

1974. Centenary of U.P.U.
152 **76** 4c. multicoloured . . . 20 35
153 – 20c. purple, brown & black 25 60
154 – 35c. multicoloured . . . 35 70
DESIGNS: 20c. Pre-stamp letter, 1922; 35c. Mailship and Pitcairn longboat.

77 Churchill and Text "Lift up your Hearts ..."

1974. Birth Cent of Sir Winston Churchill.
155 **77** 20c. olive, green and grey 30 65
156 – 35c. brown, green and grey 40 75
DESIGN: 35c. Text "Give us the tools ...".

78 H.M.S. "Seringapatam" (frigate), 1830

1975. Mailboats. Multicoloured.
157 4c. Type **78** . . . 35 60
158 10c. "Pitcairn" (missionary schooner), 1890 . . . 40 85
159 18c. "Athenic" (liner), 1904 45 1·40
160 50c. "Gothic" (liner), 1948 80 2·25
MS161 145×110mm. Nos. 157/60 11·00 16·00

79 "Polistes jadwigae" (wasp)

1975. Pitcairn Insects. Multicoloured.
162 4c. Type **79** . . . 35 45
163 6c. "Euconocephalus sp." (grasshopper) . . . 35 55
164 10c. "Anomis flavia" and "Chasmina tibialis" (moth) 40 70
165 15c. "Pantala flavescens" (skimmer) . . . 50 1·25
166 20c. "Gnathothlibus erotus" (banana moth) . . . 60 1·50

80 Fletcher Christian

81 Chair of Homage

1976. Bicent of American Revolution. Mult.
167 5c. Type **80** . . . 20 65
168 10c. H.M.S. "Bounty" . . . 25 80
169 30c. George Washington . . 25 95
170 50c. "Mayflower", 1620 . . . 35 1·50

1977. Silver Jubilee. Multicoloured.
171 8c. Prince Philip's visit, 1971 . . 10 15
172 20c. Type **81** 20 25
173 50c. Enthronement 40 50

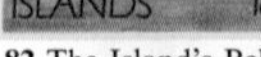

82 The Island's Bell **84** Coronation Ceremony

83 Building a "Bounty" Model

1977. Multicoloured.
174 1c. Type **82** 10 50
175 2c. Building a longboat (horiz) 10 50
176 5c. Landing cargo (horiz) 15 50
177 6c. Sorting supplies (horiz) 15 50
178 9c. Cleaning wahoo (fish) 15 50
179 10c. Cultivation (horiz) . . 15 50
179a 15c. Sugar Mill (horiz) . . . 75 1·00
180 20c. Grating coconut and bananas (horiz) 15 50
181 35c. The Island church (horiz) 15 70
182 50c. Fetching miro logs, Henderson Is. (horiz) . . 20 80
182b 70c. Burning obsolete stamp issues . . . . 75 1·25
183 $1 Prince Philip, Bounty Bay and Royal Yacht "Britannia" (horiz) . . . 40 1·10
184 $2 Queen Elizabeth II (photograph by Reginald Davis) . . . . 50 1·75

1978. "Bounty" Day. Multicoloured.
185 6c. Type **83** 20 20
186 20c. The model at sea . . . 25 25
187 35c. Burning the model . . . 35 35
MS188 166 × 122 mm. Nos. 185/7 6·00 9·50

1978. 25th Anniv of Coronation. Sheet 94 × 78 mm.
MS189 **84** $1.20 multicoloured 80 1·75

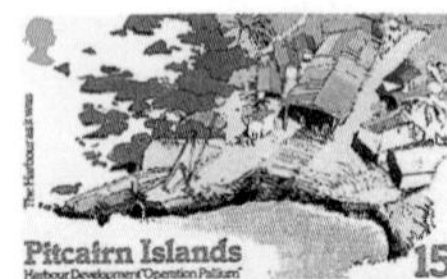

85 Harbour before Development

1978. "Operation Pallium" (Harbour Development Project). Multicoloured.
190 15c. Type **85** 30 50
191 20c. Unloading R.F.A. "Sir Geraint" 40 60
192 30c. Work on the jetty . . . 45 70
193 35c. Harbour after development 50 80

86 John Adams and Diary Extract

1979. 150th Death Anniv of John Adams ("Bounty" mutineer). Multicoloured.
194 35c. Type **86** 30 70
195 70c. John Adams' grave and diary extract 45 90

87 Pitcairn's Island sketched from H.M.S. "Amphitrite"

1979. 19th-century Engravings.
196 **87** 6c. black, brown and stone 15 20
197 – 9c. black, violet & lt violet 15 25
198 – 20c. black, green and yellow 15 40
199 – 70c. black, scarlet and red 50 1·00
DESIGNS: 9c. Bounty Bay and Village of Pitcairn; 20c. Lookout Ridge; 70c. Church and School House.

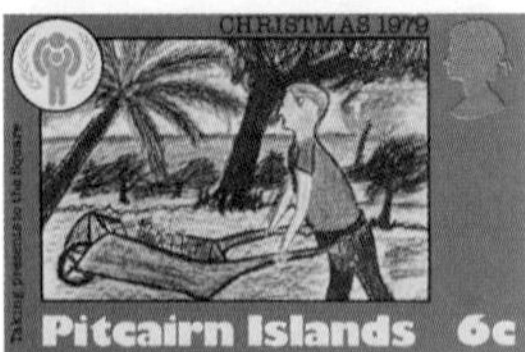

88 Taking Presents to the Square

1979. Christmas. Int Year of the Child. Mult.
200 6c. Type **88** 10 20
201 9c. Decorating trees with presents 10 25
202 20c. Chosen men distributing gifts 20 40
203 35c. Carrying presents home 25 50
MS204 198 × 73 mm. Nos. 200/3 75 1·40

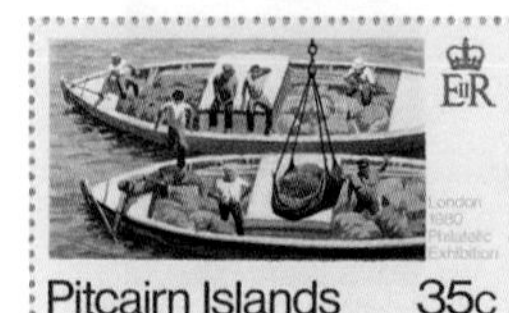

89 Loading Mail from Supply Ship to Longboats

1980. "London 1980" International Stamp Exhibition. Sheet 120 × 135 mm containing T **89** and similar horiz designs. Multicoloured.
MS205 35c. Type **89**; 35c. Mail being conveyed by "Flying Fox" (hoisting mechanism) to the Edge; 35c. Tractor transporting mail from the Edge to Adamstown; 35c. Mail being off-loaded at Post Office . . . . 75 1·50

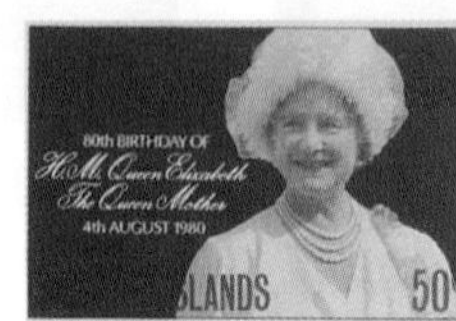

90 Queen Elizabeth the Queen Mother at Henley Regatta

1980. 80th Birthday of The Queen Mother.
206 **90** 50c. multicoloured 40 70

1980. Handicrafts (2nd series). As T **46**. Multicoloured.
207 9c. Turtles (wood carvings) 10 10
208 20c. Pitcairn wheelbarrow (wood carving) 10 15
209 35c. Gamet (wood carving) (vert) 15 25
210 40c. Woven bonnet and fan (vert) 15 25

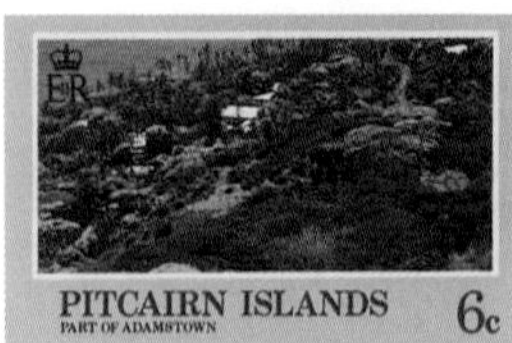

91 Part of Adamstown

1981. Landscapes. Multicoloured.
211 6c. Type **91** 10 10
212 9c. Big George 10 15
213 20c. Christian's Cave, Gannets Ridge 15 20
214 35c. Radio Station from Pawala Valley Ridge . . . 20 30
215 70c. Tatrimoa 30 45

92 Islanders preparing for Departure

1981. 125th Anniv of Pitcairn Islanders' Migration to Norfolk Island. Multicoloured.
216 9c. Type **92** 20 30
217 35c. View of Pitcairn Island from "Morayshire" 35 50
218 70c. "Morayshire" 55 90

93 Prince Charles as Colonel-in-Chief, Cheshire Regiment **95** Pitcairn Islands Coat of Arms

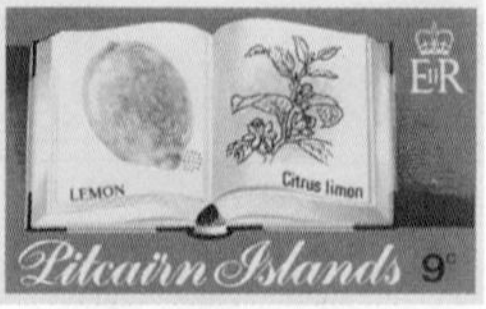

94 Lemon

1981. Royal Wedding. Multicoloured.
219 20c. Wedding bouquet from Pitcairn Islands 20 20
220 35c. Type **93** 25 20
221 $1.20 Prince Charles and Lady Diana Spencer . . . 75 60

1982. Fruit. Multicoloured.
222 9c. Type **94** 10 10
223 20c. Pomegranate 15 20
224 35c. Avocado 20 30
225 70c. Pawpaw 40 65

1982. 21st Birthday of Princess of Wales. Multicoloured.
226 6c. Type **95** 10 20
227 9c. Princess at Royal Opera House, Covent Garden, December 1981 . . . . . 45 20
228 70c. Balcony Kiss 70 60
229 $1.20 Formal portrait . . . . 1·50 80

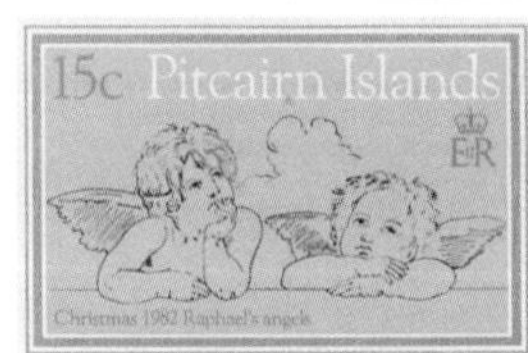

96 Raphael's Angels

1982. Christmas. Raphael's Angels.
230 **96** 15c. black, silver and pink 20 20
231 – 20c. black, silver and yellow 20 20
232 – 50c. brown, silver and stone 30 30
233 – $1 black, silver and blue 40 40
DESIGNS: 20c. to $1 Different details, the 50c. and $1 being vertical.

97 Radio Operator

1983. Commonwealth Day. Multicoloured.
234 6c. Type **97** 10 10
235 9c. Postal clerk 10 10
236 70c. Fisherman 35 65
237 $1.20 Artist . . . . 60 1·10

98 "Topaz" sights Smoke on Pitcairn

1983. 175th Anniv of Folger's Discovery of the Settlers. Multicoloured.
238 6c. Type **98** 30 20
239 20c. Three islanders approach the "Topaz" 35 30
240 70c. Capt. Mayhew Folger welcomed by John Adams 60 75
241 $1.20 Folger presented with "Bounty" chronometer . . 75 1·10

99 Hattie-Tree

1983. Trees of Pitcairn Islands (1st series). Multicoloured.
242 35c. Type **99** 25 55
243 35c. Leaves from Hattie-Tree 25 55
244 70c. Pandanus 40 90
245 70c. Pandanus and basket weaving 40 90
See also Nos. 304/7.

100 Atava wrasse

1984. Fishes. Multicoloured.
246 1c. Type **100** 20 30
247 4c. Black-eared wrasse . . . 30 35
248 6c. Long-finned parrotfish . . 30 35
249 9c. Yellow-edged lyretail . . 30 35
250 10c. Black-eared angelfish . . 30 40
251 15c. Emery's damselfish . . . 30 40
252 20c. Smith's butterflyfish . . 40 50
253 35c. Crosshatched triggerfish 50 60
254 50c. Yellow damselfish . . . 50 75
255 70c. Pitcairn angelfish 70 95
312 90c. As 9c. . . . . 3·75 4·50
256 $1 Easter Island soldierfish 70 1·25
257 $1.20 Long-finned anthias . . 75 2·00
258 $2 White trevally . . . . . . 1·25 2·50
313 $3 Wakanoura moray . . . . 5·00 7·00

101 "Southern Cross"

1984. Night Sky.
259 **101** 15c. blue, lilac and gold 20 20
260 – 20c. blue, green and gold 30 30
261 – 70c. blue, brown and gold 75 75
262 – $1 blue, light blue and gold . . . . 1·00 1·00
DESIGNS: 20c. "Southern Fish"; 70c. "Lesser Dog"; $1 "The Virgin".

102 Aluminium Longboat

1984. "Ausipex" International Stamp Exhibition, Melbourne. Sheet 134 × 86 mm containing T **102** and similar horiz design. Multicoloured.
MS263 50c. Type **102**; $2 Traditional-style wooden longboat 1·50 2·00

103 "H.M.S. "Portland" standing off Bounty Bay" (J. Linton Palmer) **104** The Queen Mother with the Queen and Princess Margaret, 1980

1985. 19th-century Paintings (1st series). Mult.
264 6c. Type **103** 30 20
265 9c. "Christian's Look Out" (J. Linton Palmer) 30 20
266 35c. "The Golden Age" (J. Linton Palmer) 65 50
267 $2 "A View of the Village, 1825" (William Smyth) (48 × 31 mm) . . . . . . 1·75 1·60
See also Nos. 308/11.

1985. Life and Times of Queen Elizabeth the Queen Mother. Multicoloured.
268 6c. Receiving the Freedom of Dundee, 1964 . . . . . . 10 20
269 35c. Type **104** 30 55
270 70c. The Queen Mother in 1983 . . . . 50 80
271 $1.20 With Prince Henry at his christening (from photo by Lord Snowdon) . . . . 70 1·00
MS272 91 × 73 mm. $2 In coach at Ascot Races . . . . 2·50 2·00

105 "Act 6" (container ship)

1985. Ships (1st issue). Multicoloured.
273 50c. Type **105** . . . . 95 1·75
274 50c. "Columbus Louisiana" (container ship) . . . . . 95 1·75
275 50c. "Essi Gina" (tanker) (48 × 35 mm) . . . . . . 95 1·75
276 50c. "Stolt Spirit" tanker (48 × 35 mm) . . . . . . 95 1·75
See also Nos. 296/9.

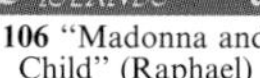

106 "Madonna and Child" (Raphael)

107a Prince Andrew and Miss Sarah Ferguson

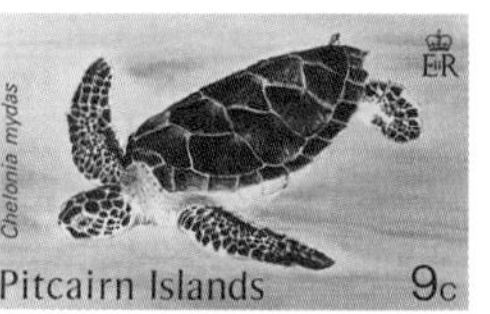

107 Green Turtle

1985. Christmas. Designs showing "Madonna and Child" paintings. Multicoloured.
277 6c. Type **106** 60 50
278 9c. Krause (after Raphael) . . 60 50
279 35c. Andreas Mayer . . . . 1·00 70
280 $2 Unknown Austrian master 2·75 3·50

1986. Turtles. Multicoloured.
281 9c. Type **107** . . . . 1·00 90
282 20c. Green turtle and Pitcairn Island . . . . 1·60 1·25
283 70c. Hawksbill turtle . . . . 3·00 3·75
284 $1.20 Hawksbill turtle and Pitcairn Island . . . . . . 3·50 4·25

1986. 60th Birthday of Queen Elizabeth II. As T **246b** of Papua New Guinea.
285 6c. Princess Elizabeth at Royal Lodge, Windsor, 1946 . . . . 15 15
286 9c. Wedding of Princess Anne, 1973 . . . . 15 15
287 20c. At Order of St. Michael and St. George service, St. Paul's Cathedral, 1961 25 30
288 $1.20 At Electrical Engineering Concert, Royal Festival Hall, 1971 . . . . 60 1·25
289 $2 At Crown Agents Head Office, London 1983 . . . 75 1·75

1986. Royal Wedding. Multicoloured.
290 20c. Type **107a** 50 50
291 $1.20 Prince Andrew aboard "Bluenose II" off Halifax, Canada, 1985 . . . . . . 1·60 2·25

108 John I. Tay (pioneer missionary) and First Church

110 *Bounty* (replica)

109 Pitcairn Island Home

1986. Centenary of Seventh-Day Adventist Church on Pitcairn. Multicoloured.
292 6c. Type **108** 50 50
293 20c. "Pitcairn" (missionary schooner) and second church (1907) . . . . . . 1·25 1·00
294 35c. Baptism at Down Isaac and third church (1945) . . 1·75 1·50
295 $2 Islanders singing farewell hymn and present church (1954) . . . . 3·75 4·25

1987. Ships (2nd series). As T **105**. Multicoloured.
296 50c. "Samoan Reefer" (freighter) . . . . 1·00 2·25
297 50c. "Brussel" (container ship) . . . . 1·00 2·25
298 50c. "Australian Exporter" (container ship) (48 × 35 mm) . . . . . . 1·00 2·25
299 50c. "Taupo" (cargo liner) (48 × 35 mm) . . . . . . 1·00 2·25

1987. Pitcairn Island Homes.
300 **109** 70c. black, dp violet & vio 50 60
301 – 70c. black, yellow & brn 50 60
302 – 70c. black, blue & dp blue 50 60
303 – 70c. black, green and deep green 50 60
DESIGNS: Nos. 301/3, different houses.

1987. Trees of Pitcairn Islands (2nd series). As T **99**. Multicoloured.
304 40c. Leaves and flowers from "Erythrina variegata" . . . 1·10 1·50
305 40c. "Erythrina variegata" tree . . . . 1·10 1·50
306 $1.80 Leaves from "Aleurites moluccana" and nut torch 1·90 2·75
307 $1.80 "Aleurites moluccana" tree . . . . 1·90 2·75

1987. 19th-century Paintings (2nd series). Paintings by Lt. Conway Shipley in 1848. As T **103**. Multicoloured.
308 20c. "House and Tomb of John Adams" 55 60
309 40c. "Bounty Bay" 80 85
310 90c. "School House and Chapel" . . . . 1·40 2·00
311 $1.80 "Pitcairn Island" (48 × 31 mm) . . . . . . 2·25 3·75

1988. Bicentenary of Australian Settlement. Sheet 112 × 76 mm.
MS314 **110** $3 multicoloured . . 4·25 2·75

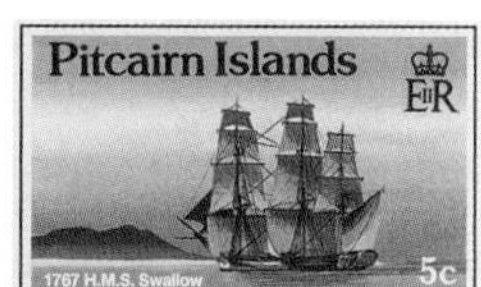

111 H.M.S. "Swallow" (survey ship), 1767

1988. Ships. Multicoloured.
315 5c. Type **111** 50 70
316 10c. H.M.S. "Pandora" (frigate), 1791 . . . . . . 50 70
317 15c. H.M.S. "Briton" and H.M.S. "Tagus" (frigates), 1814 . . . . 55 80
318 20c. H.M.S. "Blossom" (survey ship), 1825 . . . . 60 85
319 30c. "Lucy Anne" (barque), 1831 . . . . 70 90
320 35c. "Charles Doggett" (whaling brig), 1831 . . . 70 90
321 40c. H.M.S. "Fly" (sloop), 1838 . . . . 75 95
322 60c. "Camden" (missionary brig.), 1840 . . . . 1·00 1·40
323 90c. H.M.S. "Virago" (paddle-sloop), 1853 . . . 1·25 1·50
324 $1.20 "Rakaia" (screw-steamer), 1867 . . . . . . 1·50 1·75
325 $1.80 H.M.S. "Sappho" (screw-sloop), 1882 . . . . 1·75 2·25
326 $5 H.M.S. "Champion" (corvette), 1893 . . . . . 4·50 5·00

112 Raising the Union Jack, 1838

113 Angel

1988. 150th Anniv of Pitcairn Island Constitution. Each showing different extract from original Constitution. Multicoloured.
327 20c. Type **112** 15 20
328 40c. Signing Constitution on board H.M.S. "Fly", 1838 30 35
329 $1.05 Voters at modern polling station 75 80
330 $1.80 Modern classroom . . 1·25 1·40

1988. Christmas. Multicoloured.
331 90c. Type **113** 65 70
332 90c. Holy Family 65 70
333 90c. Two Polynesian Wise Men 65 70
334 90c. Polynesian Wise Man and shepherd 65 70

114 Loading Stores, Deptford

1989. Bicentenary of Pitcairn Island Settlement (1st issue). Multicoloured.
335 20c. Type **114** . . . . 1·10 1·10
336 20c. H.M.S. "Bounty" leaving Spithead . . . . . 1·10 1·10
337 20c. H.M.S. "Bounty" at Cape Horn . . . . 1·10 1·10
338 20c. Anchored in Adventure Bay, Tasmania . . . . . . 1·10 1·10
339 20c. Crew collecting breadfruit . . . . 1·10 1·10
340 20c. Breadfruit in cabin . . . 1·10 1·10
See also Nos. 341/7, 356/61 and 389/94.

1989. Bicentenary of Pitcairn Island Settlement (2nd issue). As T **114**. Multicoloured.
341 90c. H.M.S. "Bounty' leaving Tahiti . . . . 2·50 2·25
342 90c. Bligh awoken by mutineers . . . . 2·50 2·25
343 90c. Bligh before Fletcher Christian . . . . 2·50 2·25
344 90c. Provisioning "Bounty's" launch . . . . 2·50 2·25
345 90c. "Mutineers casting Bligh adrift" (Robert Dodd) . . 2·50 2·25
346 90c. Mutineers discarding breadfruit plants . . . . . 2·50 2·25
MS347 110 × 85 mm. 90c. No. 345; 90c. Isle of Man 1989 35p. Mutiny stamp; 90c. Norfolk Island 39c. Mutiny stamp . . . . 3·75 4·00

115 R.N.Z.A.F. Lockheed Orion making Mail Drop, 1985

1989. Aircraft. Multicoloured.
348 20c. Type **115** . . . . 1·10 60
349 80c. Beech 80 Queen Air on photo-mission, 1983 . . . 2·25 1·25
350 $1.05 Boeing-Vertol Chinook helicopter landing diesel fuel from U.S.S. "Breton", 1969 . . . . 2·50 1·50
351 $1.30 R.N.Z.A.F. Lockheed Hercules dropping bulldozer, 1983 . . . . . 2·50 1·75

116 Ducie Island

1989. Islands of Pitcairn Group. Mult.
352 15c. Type **116** 50 50
353 90c. Henderson Island . . . 1·60 1·25
354 $1.05 Oeno Island . . . . . 1·75 1·75
355 $1.30 Pitcairn Island . . . . 1·75 1·75

1990. Bicentenary of Pitcairn Island Settlement (3rd issue). As T **114**. Multicoloured.
356 40c. Mutineers sighting Pitcairn Island . . . . . . 1·00 85
357 40c. Ship's boat approaching landing . . . . 1·00 85
358 40c. Exploring island . . . . 1·00 85
359 40c. Ferrying goods ashore 1·00 85
360 40c. Burning of H.M.S. "Bounty" . . . . 1·00 85
361 40c. Pitcairn Island village . . 1·00 85

117 Ennerdale, Cumbria, and Peter Heywood

1990. "Stamp World London '90" International Stamp Exhibition, London. Designs showing English landmarks and "Bounty" crew members. Multicoloured.
362 80c. Type **117** 75 80
363 90c. St. Augustine's Tower, Hackney, and John Adams 85 90
364 $1.05 Citadel Gateway, Plymouth, and William Bligh . . . . 1·00 1·25
365 $1.30 Moorland Close, Cockermouth, and Fletcher Christian . . . . 1·25 1·40

117a Queen Elizabeth, 1937

119 Stephen's Lory ("Redbreast")

118 "Bounty" Chronometer and 1940 1d. Definitive

1990. 90th Birthday of Queen Elizabeth the Queen Mother.
378 **117a** 40c. multicoloured . . . 75 85
379 – $3 black and red . . . . 3·00 3·75
DESIGN—29 × 37 mm: $3 King George VI and Queen Elizabeth on way to Silver Wedding Service, 1948.

1990. 50th Anniv of Pitcairn Islands Stamps. Multicoloured.
380 20c. Type **118** 80 80
381 80c. "Bounty" Bible and 1958 4d. definitive . . . . 1·60 1·75
382 90c. "Bounty" Bell and 1969 30c. definitive . . . . . . 1·75 1·90
383 $1.05 Mutiny on the "Bounty" and 1977 $1 definitive . . . . 2·00 2·50
384 $1.30 Penny Black and 1988 15c. definitive . . . . . . 2·25 2·75

1990. "Birdpex '90" International Stamp Exhibition, Christchurch, New Zealand. Multicoloured.
385 20c. Type **119** 75 75
386 90c. Henderson Island fruit dove ("Wood Pigeon") . . 1·50 1·60
387 $1.30 Pitcairn warbler ("Sparrow") . . . . 1·75 2·75
388 $1.80 Henderson Island crake ("Chicken Bird") . . . . . 2·00 3·00

1991. Bicent of Pitcairn Island Settlement (4th issue). Celebrations. As T **114**. Multicoloured.
389 80c. Re-enacting landing of mutineers . . . . 2·00 2·50
390 80c. Commemorative plaque 2·00 2·50
391 80c. Memorial church service 2·00 2·50
392 80c. Cricket match . . . . . 2·00 2·50
393 80c. Burning model of "Bounty" . . . . 2·00 2·50
394 80c. Firework display . . . . 2·00 2·50

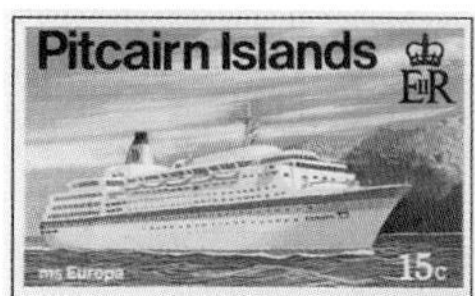

120 "Europa"

1991. Cruise Liners. Multicoloured.
395 15c. Type **120** . . . . 1·00 60
396 80c. "Royal Viking Star" . . 2·00 1·75
397 $1.30 "World Discoverer" . . 2·50 2·75
398 $1.80 "Sagafjord" . . . . . 3·00 3·50

1991. 65th Birthday of Queen Elizabeth II and 70th Birthday of Prince Philip. As T **120a** of Pitcairn Islands. Multicoloured.
399 20c. Prince Philip (vert) . . . 40 30
400 $1.30 Queen in robes of the Order of St. Michael and St. George (vert) . . . . . 1·60 1·25

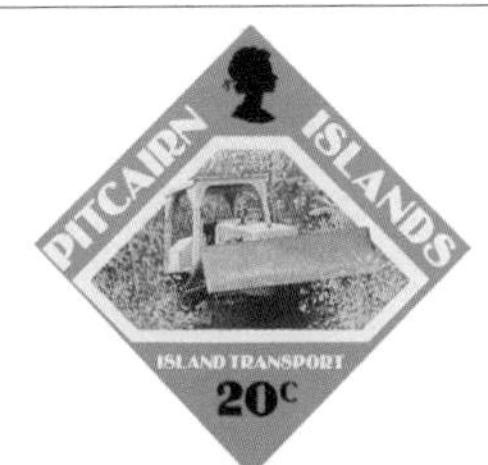

121 Bulldozer

1991. Island Transport. Multicoloured.
401 20c. Type **121** 40 30
402 80c. Two-wheeled motorcycle 1·25 1·00
403 $1.30 Tractor . . . . 1·25 1·40
404 $1.80 Three-wheeled motorcycle . . . . 2·00 2·25

122 The Annunciation

1991. Christmas. Multicoloured.
405 20c. Type **122** 30 30
406 80c. Shepherds and lamb . . 90 90
407 $1.30 Holy Family . . . . . 1·25 1·25
408 $1.80 Three Wise Men . . . 1·75 1·75

122c Bounty Bay

1992. 40th Anniv of Queen Elizabeth II's Accession. Multicoloured.
409 20c. Type **122c** 25 25
410 60c. Sunset over Pitcairn . . 70 70
411 90c. Pitcairn coastline 90 90
412 $1 Three portraits of Queen Elizabeth 95 95
413 $1.80 Queen Elizabeth II . . 1·60 1·60

123 Insular Shark

1992. Sharks. Multicoloured.
414 20c. Type **123** 80 50
415 $1 Sand tiger . . . . 2·00 1·50
416 $1.50 Black-finned reef shark 2·25 2·00
417 $1.80 Grey reef shark . . . . 2·50 2·00

124 "Montastrea sp." and "Acropora spp." (corals)

1992. The Sir Peter Scott Memorial Expedition to Henderson Island. Multicoloured.
418 20c. Type **124** 80 60
419 $1 Henderson sandalwood . . 1·75 1·50
420 $1.50 Murphy's petrel . . . 3·00 2·75
421 $1.80 Henderson hawkmoth 3·00 3·00

125 Bligh's Birthplace at St. Tudy, Cornwall

1992. 175th Death Anniv of William Bligh. Multicoloured.
422 20c. Type **125** 50 60
423 $1 Bligh on "Bounty" . . . 1·50 1·50
424 $1.50 Voyage in "Bounty's" launch . . . . 2·00 2·75
425 $1.80 "William Bligh" (R. Combe) and epitaph 2·25 3·00

126 H.M.S. "Chichester" (frigate)

1993. Modern Royal Navy Vessels. Mult.
426 15c. Type **126** 75 50
427 20c. H.M.S. "Jaguar" (frigate) 75 50
428 $1.80 H.M.S. "Andrew" (submarine) . . . . 3·25 3·25
429 $3 H.M.S. "Warrior" (aircraft carrier) and Westland Dragonfly helicopter . . . . 5·75 5·50

127 Queen Elizabeth II in Coronation Robes

1993. 40th Anniv of Coronation.
430 **127** $5 multicoloured . . . . 6·00 6·50

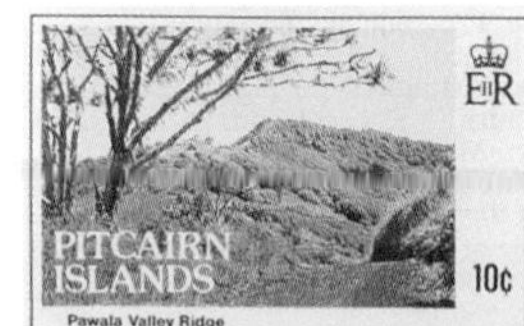

128 Pawala Valley Ridge

1993. Island Views. Multicoloured.
431 10c. Type **128** 20 20
432 90c. St. Pauls 90 90
433 $1.20 Matt's Rocks from Water Valley . . . . . . 1·25 1·50
434 $1.50 Ridge Rope to St. Paul's Pool . . . . . . 1·50 1·75
435 $1.80 Ship Landing Point . . 1·75 2·25

129 Indo-Pacific Tree Gecko

1993. Lizards. Multicoloured.
436 20c. Type **129** 80 50
437 45c. Stump-toed gecko . . . 1·00 1·25
438 45c. Mourning gecko . . . . 1·00 1·25
439 $1 Moth skink . . . . 2·00 1·50
440 $1.50 Snake-eyed skink . . . 2·50 2·75
441 $1.50 White-bellied skink . . 2·50 2·75

1994. "Hong Kong '94" International Stamp Exhibition. Nos. 437/8 and 440/1 optd **HONG KONG '94** and emblem.
442 45c. Stump-toed gecko . . . 80 90
443 45c. Mourning gecko 80 90
444 $1.50 Snake-eyed skink . . . 2·25 2·75
445 $1.50 White-bellied skink . . 2·25 2·75

130 Friday October Christian

131 Landing Stores from Wreck of "Wildwave", Oeno Island, 1858

1994. Early Pitcairners. Multicoloured.
446 5c. Type **130** 20 30
447 20c. Moses Young 50 40
448 $1.80 James Russell McCoy 2·25 2·75
449 $3 Rosalind Amelia Young 3·75 5·00

1994. Shipwrecks. Multicoloured.
450 20c. Type **131** 65 60
451 90c. Longboat trying to reach "Cornwallis", Pitcairn Island, 1875 . . . . 1·75 1·75
452 $1.80 "Acadia" aground, Ducie Island, 1881 . . . . 3·00 3·50
453 $3 Rescuing survivors from "Oregon", Oeno Island, 1883 . . . . 4·25 4·50

132 Fire Coral

133 Angel and "Ipomoea acuminata"

1994. Corals. Multicoloured.
454 20c. Type **132** 80 70
455 90c. Cauliflower coral and arc-eyed hawkfish (horiz) 2·00 2·00
456 $1 Lobe coral and high-finned rudderfish . . . . . 2·00 2·00
MS457 100 × 70 mm. $3 Coral garden and mailed butterflyfish 4·00 5·00

1994. Christmas. Flowers. Multicoloured.
458 20c. Type **133** 35 25
459 90c. Shepherds and "Hibiscus rosa-sinensis" (vert) . . . 1·25 1·40
460 $1 Star and "Plumeria rubra" 1·25 1·40
461 $3 Holy Family and "Alpinia speciosa" (vert) . . . . . 3·00 3·25

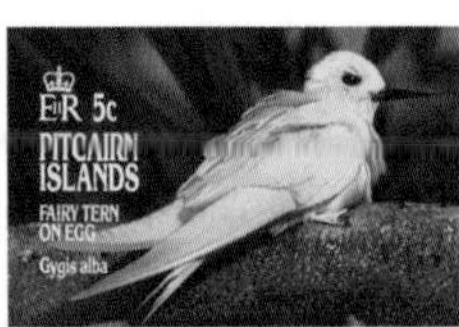

134 White ("Fairy") Tern on Egg

1995. Birds. Multicoloured.
462 5c. Type **134** 30 40
463 10c. Red-tailed tropic bird chick (vert) 30 40
464 15c. Henderson Island crake with chick 40 55
465 20c. Red-footed booby feeding chick (vert) 40 55
466 45c. Blue-grey noddy 60 70
467 50c. Pitcairn ("Henderson Reed") warbler in nest . . 65 75
468 90c. Common noddy . . . . 1·00 1·00
469 $1 Blue-faced ("Masked") booby and chick (vert) . . 1·10 1·10
470 $1.80 Henderson Island fruit dove . . . . 1·50 1·75
471 $2 Murphy's petrel . . . . . 1·75 2·00
472 $3 Christmas Island shearwater . . . . 2·25 2·50
473 $5 Red-tailed tropic bird juvenile . . . . 3·50 4·00

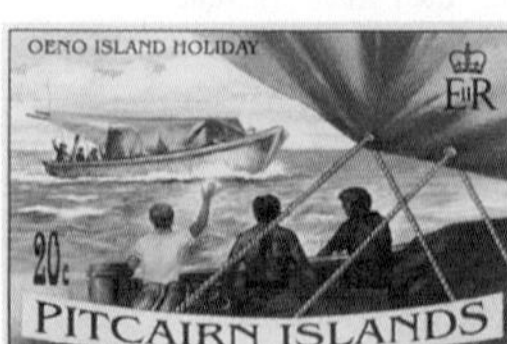

135 Islanders in Longboats

1995. Oeno Island Holiday. Multicoloured.
474 20c. Type **135** 40 60
475 90c. Playing volleyball on beach . . . . 1·25 1·25
476 $1.80 Preparing picnic . . . 2·25 3·00
477 $3 Singsong . . . . 3·50 4·75

136 Queen Elizabeth the Queen Mother

1995. 95th Birthday of Queen Elizabeth the Queen Mother. Sheet 75 × 90 mm.
MS478 **136** $5 multicoloured . . 5·50 5·00

137 Guglielmo Marconi and Early Wireless, 1901

1995. Centenary of First Radio Transmission. Multicoloured.
479 20c. Type **137** 40 60
480 $1 Pitcairn radio transmitter, c. 1938 . . . . 1·10 1·25
481 $1.50 Satellite Earth Station equipment, 1994 . . . . . 1·75 2·75
482 $3 Communications satellite in orbit, 1992 . . . . . . 3·25 4·50

137a United Nations Float, Lord Mayor's Show

1995. 50th Anniv of United Nations. Multicoloured.
483 20c. Type **137a** 30 30
484 $1 R.F.A. "Brambleleaf" (tanker) . . . . 1·40 1·25
485 $1.50 U.N. Ambulance . . . 2·00 2·25
486 $3 R.A.F. Lockheed L-1011 TriStar . . . . 3·50 3·75

138 Early Morning at the Jetty

1996. Supply Ship Day. Multicoloured.
487 20c. Type **138** 25 30
488 40c. Longboat meeting "America Star" (freighter) 45 55
489 90c. Loading supplies into longboats . . . . 1·00 1·10
490 $1 Landing supplies on jetty 1·10 1·25
491 $1.50 Sorting supplies at the Co-op . . . . 1·75 2·25
492 $1.80 Tractor towing supplies 1·90 2·25

1996. 70th Birthday of Queen Elizabeth II. As T **55** of Tokelau, each incorporating a different photograph of the Queen. Multicoloured.
493 20c. Bounty Bay 45 45
494 90c. Jetty and landing point, Bounty Bay . . . . 1·40 1·40
495 $1.80 Matt's Rocks . . . . . 2·25 2·50
496 $3 St. Pauls . . . . 4·00 4·50

139 Chinese junk

1996. "CHINA '96" 9th Asian International Stamp Exhibition, Peking. Multicoloured.
497 $1.80 Type **139** . . . . . . 2·25 2·50
498 $1.80 H.M.S. "Bounty" . . . 2·25 2·50
MS499 80 × 79 mm. 90c. China 1984 8f. Year of the Rat stamp; 90c. Polynesian rat eating banana 2·00 2·00

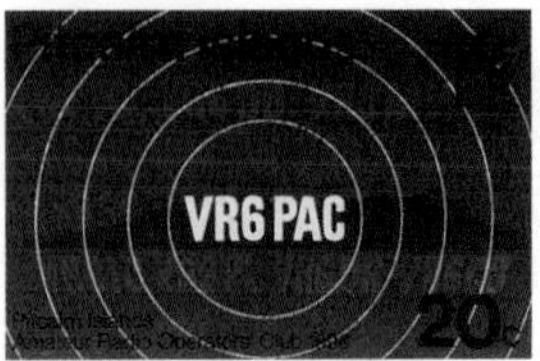

140 Island Profile and Radio Call Signs

1996. Amateur Radio Operations from Pitcairn Islands. Multicoloured.
500 20c. Type **140** 45 45
501 $1.50 Radio operator calling for medical assistance . . . 2·00 2·25
502 $1.50 Doctors giving medical advice by radio . . . . . 2·00 2·25
503 $2.50 Andrew Young (first radio operator), 1938 . . . 2·75 3·00

141 Pitcairn Warbler ("Henderson Island Reed Warbler") 142 Coat of Arms

1996. Endangered Species. Local Birds. Mult.
504 5c. Type **141** 30 30
505 10c. Stephen's lory ("Stephen's Lorikeet") . . 30 30
506 20c. Henderson Island crake ("Henderson Island Rail") 50 50
507 90c. Henderson Island fruit dove . . . . 1·25 1·25
508 $2 White tern (horiz) . . . . 2·00 2·25
509 $2 Blue-faced booby ("Masked Booby") (horiz) 2·00 2·25

1997. "HONG KONG '97" International Stamp Exhibition. Chinese New Year ("Year of the Ox"). Sheet 82 × 87 mm.
MS510 **142** $5 multicoloured . . 5·00 5·50

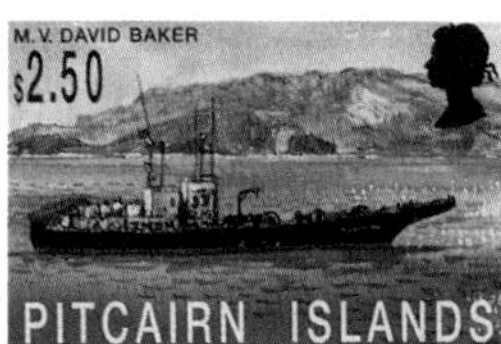

143 "David Barker" (supply ship)

1997. 50th Anniv of South Pacific Commission. Sheet 115 × 56 mm, containing T **143** and similar horiz design. Multicoloured.
MS511 $2.50 Type **143**; $2.50 "McLachlan" (fishing boat) . . 7·00 6·00

144 Health Centre

1997. Island Health Care. Multicoloured.
512 20c. Type **144** 30 25
513 $1 Nurse treating patient . . 1·00 1·00
514 $1.70 Dentist treating woman 1·75 1·90
515 $3 Evacuating patient by longboat . . . . 3·00 3·25

1997. Golden Wedding of Queen Elizabeth and Prince Philip. As T **316a** of Papua New Guinea. Multicoloured.
516 20c. Prince Philip driving carriage 30 40
517 20c. Queen Elizabeth 30 40
518 $1 Prince Philip at Royal Windsor Horse Show, 1996 1·00 1·25
519 $1 Queen Elizabeth with horse . . . . 1·00 1·25
520 $1.70 Queen Elizabeth and Prince Philip at the Derby, 1991 . . . . 1·50 1·75
521 $1.70 Prince Charles hunting, 1995 . . . . 1·50 1·75
Nos. 516/17, 518/19 and 520/21 respectively were printed together, se-tenant, with the backgrounds forming composite designs.

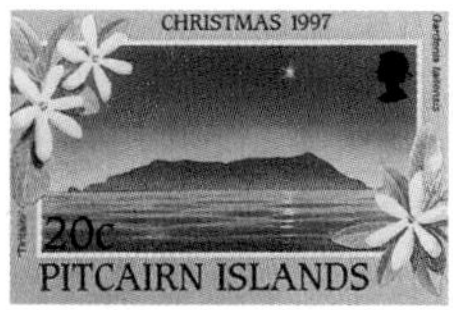

145 Island and Star

1997. Christmas. Multicoloured.
522 20c. Type **145** 35 25
523 80c. Hand ringing bell . . . 1·00 80
524 $1.20 Presents in baskets . . 1·40 1·50
525 $3 Families outside church 2·75 3·00

146 Christian's Cave

1997. Christian's Cave. Multicoloured.
526 5c. Type **146** 15 20
527 20c. View from the beach . . 35 35
528 35c. Cave entrance (vert) . . 50 50
529 $5 Pathway through forest (vert) . . . . 3·75 5·00

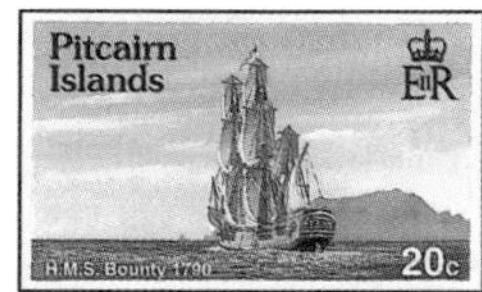

147 H.M.S. "Bounty" (Bligh), 1790

1998. Millennium Commemoration (1st issue). Sailing Ships. Multicoloured.
530 20c. Type **147** 40 40
531 90c. H.M.S. "Swallow" (Carteret), 1767 . . . . 1·00 1·00
532 $1.80 H.M.S. "Briton" and H.M.S. "Tagus" (frigates), 1814 . . . . 1·50 1·60
533 $3 H.M.S. "Fly" (sloop), 1838 . . . . 2·50 2·75
See also Nos. 549/52 and 577/80.

1998. Diana, Princess of Wales Commemoration. Sheet, 145 × 70 mm, containing vert designs as T **91** of Kiribati. Multicoloured.
MS534 90c. Wearing pearl choker and red evening dress; 90c. Wearing white hat and pearl necklace; 90c. Carrying bouquet; 90c. Wearing white dress and hat (*sold at $3.60+40c. charity premium*) . . . . 3·50 3·75

148 "Bidens mathewsii"

1998. Flowers. Multicoloured.
535 20c. Type **148** 60 40
536 90c. "Hibiscus" sp. . . . . . 1·40 1·00
537 $1.80 "Osteomeles anthyllidifolia" . . . . . . 2·25 1·75
538 $3 "Ipomoea littoralis" . . . 3·25 2·75

149 Fishing

1998. International Year of the Ocean. Multicoloured.
539 20c. Type **149** 60 50
540 90c. Diver at wreck of "Cornwallis" (vert) . . . . 1·25 1·00
541 $1.80 Reef fish . . . . 2·00 1·75
542 $3 Murphy's petrel and great frigate bird (vert) . . . . . 3·50 2·75
MS543 86 × 86 mm. Nos. 539/42 7·00 7·50

150 George Nobbs and Class, 1838

1999. Development of Local Education. Mult.
544 20c. Type **150** 60 60
545 90c. Children outside thatched school, 1893 . . . 1·40 1·40
546 $1.80 Boy in wheelbarrow outside wooden school, 1932 . . . . 2·25 2·50
547 $3 Modern classroom with computer . . . . 3·00 3·50

151 H.M.S. "Bounty" and Anchor

1999. "Australia '99" World Stamp Exhibition, Melbourne. Pitcairn Archaeology Project. Sheet, 190 × 80 mm, containing T **151** and similar diamond-shaped designs. Multicoloured.
MS548 50c. Type **151**; $1 "Bounty" approaching Pitcairn and cannon; $1.50, "Bounty" on fire and chronometer; $2 "Bounty" sinking and metal bucket . . . . . . 5·50 5·50

152 John Adams (survivor of "Bounty" crew) and Bounty Bay

1999. Millennium Commemoration (2nd issue). Multicoloured.
549 20c. Type **152** 40 60
550 90c. "Topaz" (sealer), 1808 90 1·10
551 $1.80 George Hunn Nobbs and Norfolk Island . . . . 1·75 2·50
552 $3 H.M.S "Champion" (corvette), 1893 . . . . . 2·50 3·25

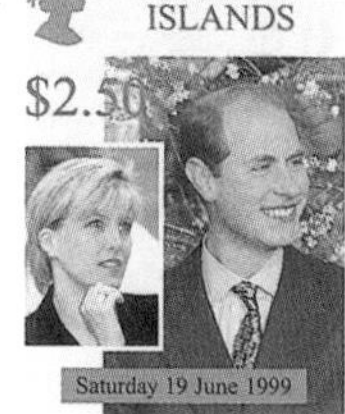

153 Prince Edward and Miss Sophie Rhys-Jones

1999. Royal Wedding. Multicoloured.
553 $2.50 Type **153** . . . . . . 1·90 2·50
554 $2.50 Engagement photograph . . . . 1·90 2·50

154 Bee-keepers at Work

1999. Bee-keeping. Multicoloured. Self-adhesive.
555 20c. Type **154** 65 65
556 $1 Bee on passion flower . . 1·40 1·40
557 $1.80 Bees in honeycomb . . 2·25 2·50
558 $3 Bee on flower and jar of "Mutineer's Dream" honey 3·00 3·25
MS559 74 × 100 mm. No. 556 . . 1·50 2·00
No. **MS**559 includes the "China '99" International Stamp Exhibition emblem on the sheet margin.

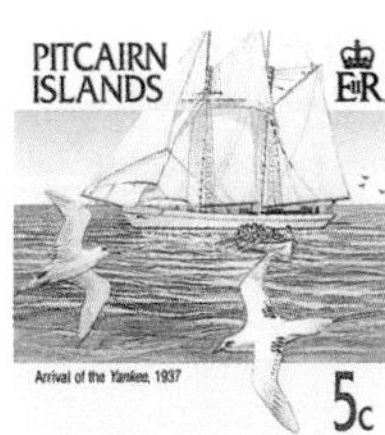

155 Arrival of "Yankee" (schooner), 1937

2000. Protection of "Mr. Turpen" (Galapagos Tortoise on Pitcairn). Multicoloured.
560 5c. Type **155** 65 90
561 20c. Off-loading Mr. Turpen at Bounty Bay . . . . . . 80 1·00
562 35c. Mr. Turpen . . . . . . 90 1·10
563 $5 Head of Mr. Turpen . . . 3·75 4·00
Nos. 560/3 were printed together, se-tenant, with the background forming a composite design.

156 *Guettarda speciosa* (flower)

2000. Flowers of Pitcairn Islands. Multicoloured.
564 10c. Type **156** 10 10
565 15c. *Hibiscus tiliaceus* 10 15
566 20c. *Selenicereus grandiflorus* 15 20
567 30c. *Metrosideros collina* . . 20 25
568 50c. *Alpinia zerumbet* 30 35
569 $1 *Syzygium jambos* 65 70
570 $1.50 *Commelina diffusa* . . . 95 1·00
571 $1.80 *Canna indica* . . . . . 1·10 1·25
572 $2 *Allamanda cathartica* . . . 1·25 1·40
573 $3 *Calophyllum inophyllum* 1·90 2·00
574 $5 *Ipomea indica* . . . . . . 3·25 3·50
575 $10 *Bauhinia monandra* (40 × 40 mm) . . . . . . 7·00 7·25

2000. "The Stamp Show 2000" International Stamp Exhibition, London. Sheet, 120 × 80 mm, containing Nos. 570 and 572.
MS576 $1.50 Commelina diffusa; $2 Allamanda cathartica . . . . 3·25 3·50

157 Longboat

2000. Millennium Commemoration (3rd issue). Communications. Multicoloured.
577 20c. Type **157** 50 50
578 90c. Landing and Longboat House . . . . 1·10 1·10
579 $1.80 Honda quad with trailer of watermelons . . . 2·00 2·25
580 $3 Woman with printer at Satellite Station . . . . . 2·50 2·75

158 Surveyor and Helicopter

2000. "EXPO 2000" World Stamp Exhibition, Anaheim, U.S.A. Anglo-American Joint Satellite Recovery Survey Mission, Henderson Island, 1966. Sheet, 120 × 180 mm, containing T **158** and similar vert design. Multicoloured.
MS581 $2.50 Type **158**; $2.50 Survey team and U.S.S. *Sunnyvale* (satellite recovery vessel) . . . 3·50 4·00
No. **MS**581 was issued folded in half horizontally with the issue title, "CLASSIFIED INFORMATION" and seal printed on the gum of the top panel. Details of the survey appear on the other side of this section.

159 Queen Elizabeth the Queen Mother

2000. Queen Elizabeth the Queen Mother's 100th Birthday. Sheet, 127 × 95 mm (oval-shaped), containing T **159** and similar vert design. Multicoloured.
MS582 $2 Type **159**; $3 Queen Mother wearing plum outfit . . 3·75 4·00

160 Wrapping Presents

2000. Christmas. Multicoloured.
583 20c. Type **160** 40 40
584 80c. Ringing island bell . . . 90 90
585 $1.50 Making decorations . . 1·50 1·60
586 $3 Opening presents . . . . 2·50 2·75

161 *Europa* (liner)

2001. Cruise Ships. Multicoloured.
587 $1.50 Type **161** . . . . . . 1·50 1·60
588 $1.50 *Rotterdam VI* . . . . 1·50 1·60
589 $1.50 *Saga Rose* . . . . . . 1·50 1·60
590 $1.50 *Bremen* . . . . 1·50 1·60

162 Coconut

2001. Tropical Fruits. Multicoloured.
591 20c. Type **162** 30 30
592 80c. Pomegranate 75 75
593 $1 Passion fruit 90 90
594 $3 Pineapple . . . . 2·25 2·50
MS595 103 × 70mm. Nos. 592 and 594 . . . . 3·00 3·50

163 Keyboard

2001. Introduction of Pitcairn Islands Internet Domain Name. Multicoloured. Self-adhesive.
596 20c. Type **163** 30 40
597 50c. Circuit board 55 60
598 $1 Microchip 90 95
599 $5 Mouse . . . . 4·25 5·00

164 Ornate Butterflyfish (*Chaetodon ornatissimus*)

165 Man carrying Driftwood

2001. Reef Fish. Multicoloured.
600 20c. Type **164** 30 35
601 80c. Mailed butterflyfish (*Chaetodon reticulatus*) . . 65 65
602 $1.50 Racoon butterflyfish (*Chaetodon lunula*) . . . . 1·10 1·25
603 $2 *Henochus chrysostomus* . . 1·40 1·60
MS604 87 × 120 mm. Nos. 600 and 603 . . . . 1·75 2·00
No. **MS**604 has the paper around the outlines of fish along the upper edge of the sheet cut away.

2001. Woodcarving. Multicoloured.
605 20c. Type **165** 45 60
606 50c. Carver at work . . . . 80 1·10
607 $1.50 Working on wood lathe 1·40 1·60
608 $3 Taking carvings to *World Discoverer* (cruise liner) for sale . . . . 2·25 2·50
Nos. 605/8 were printed together, se-tenant, with the backgrounds forming a composite design.

166 *Cypraea argus* Shell

2001. Cowrie Shells. Multicoloured.
609 20c. Type **166** 30 35
610 80c. *Cypraea isabella* 65 65
611 $1 *Cypraea mappa* 75 75
612 $3 *Cypraea mauritiana* . . . 2·00 2·50

2002. Golden Jubilee. Sheet, 162 × 95 mm, containing designs as T **153** of Nauru.
MS613 50c. black, violet and gold; $1 multicoloured; $1.20 black, violet and gold; $1.50 multicoloured; $2 multicoloured 4·50 5·00
DESIGNS—HORIZ: 50c. Queen Elizabeth with Princesses Elizabeth and Margaret; $1 Queen Elizabeth in evening dress; $1.20 Princess Elizabeth in evening dress; $1.50 Queen Elizabeth in blue hat and coat. VERT (38 × 51 mm)—$2 Queen Elizabeth after Annigoni.

167 James McCoy (President of Island Council)

2002. Pitcairn Islands Celebrities. Multicoloured.
614 $1.50 Type **167** . . . . . . 1·00 1·10
615 $1.50 Admiral Sir Fairfax Moresby . . . . 1·00 1·10
616 $1.50 Gerald DeLeo Bliss (postmaster, Cristobal, Panama Canal Zone) . . . 1·00 1·10
617 $1.50 Captain Arthur Jones of Shaw Savill Line . . . . 1·00 1·10

168 "Simba Christian" (cat)

2002. Pitcairn Cats. Multicoloured.
618 20c. Type **168** 15 10
619 $1 "Miti Christian" 65 70
620 $1.50 "Nala Brown" . . . . 95 1·00
621 $3 "Alicat Palau" . . . . . 1·90 2·00
MS622 92 × 86 mm. Nos. 618 and 621 . . . . 2·00 2·10

2002. Queen Elizabeth the Queen Mother Commemoration. As T **156** of Nauru.
623 40c. black, gold and purple 25 30
624 $1 brown, gold and purple 65 70
625 $1.50 multicoloured . . . . 95 1·00
626 $2 multicoloured . . . . . . 1·25 1·40
MS627 145 × 70 mm. Nos. 624 and 626 . . . . 1·90 2·00
DESIGNS: 40c. Lady Elizabeth Bowes-Lyon, 1910; $1 Lady Elizabeth Bowes-Lyon, 1923; $1.50, Queen Mother at Leatherhead, 1970; $2 Queen Mother at Scrabster. Designs as Nos. 624 and 626 in No. **MS**627 omit the "1900-2002" inscription and the coloured frame.

169 Woman cutting Palm Fronds and Fan

2002. Weaving. Multicoloured.
628 40c. Type **169** 25 30
629 80c. Woman preparing leaves and woven bag 50 55
630 $1.50 Millie Christian weaving basket . . . . . 95 1·00
631 $2.50 Thelma Brown at basket stall in the Square 1·60 1·75
Nos. 628/31 were printed together, se-tenant, with the backgrounds forming a composite design.

170 Dudwi Nut Tree (*Aleurites moluccana*)

2002. Trees. Multicoloured.
632 40c. Type **170** 25 30
633 $1 Toa (*Cordia subcordata*) 65 70
634 $1.50 Miro (*Thespesia populnea*) . . . . 95 1·00
635 $3 Hulianda (*Cerbera manghas*) . . . . 1·90 2·00

171 *America Star* (container ship) and Island Longboat

2003. 21 Years of Blue Star Line Service to Pitcairn Islands. Sheet 158 × 75 mm.
MS636 **171** $5 multicoloured . . 3·25 3·50

172 *Conus geographus* Shell

2003. Conus Shells. Multicoloured.
637 40c. Type **172** 25 30
638 80c. *Conus textile* 50 55
639 $1 *Conus striatus* 65 70
640 $1.20 *Conus marmoreus* . . . 75 80
641 $3 *Conus litoglyphus* . . . . 1·90 2·00

POLAND Pt. 5

A country lying between Russia and Germany, originally independent, but divided between Prussia, Austria and Russia in 1772/95. An independent republic since 1918. Occupied by Germany from 1939 to 1945.

1860. 100 kopeks = 1 rouble.
1918. 100 pfennig = 1 mark.
1918. 100 halerzy = 1 korona.
100 fenigow = 1 marka.
1924. 100 groszy = 1 zloty.

1 Russian Arms

2 Sigismund III Vasa Column, Warsaw

1860.
1b **1** 10k. blue and red . . . . . £675 80·00

1918. Surch **POCZTA POLSKA** and value in fen. as in T **2**.
2 **2** 5f. on 2g. brown 45 70
3 – 10f. on 6g. green 45 65
4 – 25f. on 10g. red . . . . . . 1·60 1·40
5 – 50f. on 20g. blue . . . . . . 3·50 4·00
DESIGNS: 6g. Arms of Warsaw; 10g. Polish eagle; 20g. Jan III Sobieski Monument, Warsaw.

1918. Stamps of German Occupation of Poland optd **Poczta Polska** or surch also.
9 **10** 3pf. brown . . . . 10·00 7·00
10 5pf. green 50 35
6 **24** 5 on 2½pf. grey 30 20
7 **10** 5 on 3pf. brown . . . . . 1·75 1·25
11 10pf. red 20 20
12 **24** 15pf. violet 25 25
13 **10** 20pf. blue 25 25
8 **24** 25 on 7½pf. orange 30 20
14 **10** 30pf. black & orange on buff 20 20
15 40pf. black and red . . . . 1·00 50
16 60pf. mauve 40 40

1918. Stamps of Austro-Hungarian Military Post (Nos. 69/71) optd **POLSKA POCZTA** and Polish eagle.
17 10h. green . . . . 4·75 6·25
18 20h. red . . . . 4·75 6·25
19 45h. blue . . . . 4·75 6·25

1918. As stamps of Austro-Hungarian Military Post of 1917 optd **POLSKA POCZTA** and Polish eagle or surch also.
20b 3h. on 3h. olive . . . . . . 19·00 13·00
21 3h. on 15h. red . . . . . . 3·50 2·25
22 10h. on 30h. green . . . . . 3·75 2·75
23 25h. on 40h. olive . . . . . 5·00 2·75
24 45h. on 60h. red . . . . . . 3·50 3·50
25 45h. on 80h. blue . . . . . 6·00 5·00
28 50h. green . . . . 28·00 21·00
26 50h. on 60h. red . . . . . . 3·50 4·00
29 90h. violet . . . . 4·75 3·50

1919. Stamps of Austria optd **POCZTA POLSKA**, No. 49 also surch **25**.
30 **49** 3h. violet £200 £190
31 5h. green £200 £190
32 6h. orange . . . . 15·00 16·00
33 10h. purple £200 £190
34 12h. blue . . . . 18·00 21·00
35 **60** 15h. red . . . . 10·00 6·75
36 20h. green . . . . 80·00 70·00
37 25h. blue £650 £600
49 **51** 25 on 80h. brown . . . . 2·25 3·00
38 **60** 30h. violet £140 £110
39 **51** 40h. green . . . . 13·50 10·00
40 50h. green . . . . 4·50 5·25
41 60h. blue . . . . 2·75 5·75
42 80h. brown . . . . 3·75 5·00
43 90h. purple £550 £600
44 1k. red on yellow . . . . 6·75 10·50
45 **52** 2k. blue . . . . 4·25 4·75
46 3k. red . . . . 45·00 60·00
47 4k. green . . . . 75·00 85·00
48a 10k. violet £3500 £3750

11

15

16

17 Agriculture

18 Ploughing in peace

19 Polish Uhlan

1919. Imperf.
50 **11** 2h. grey 35 60
51 3h. violet 35 60
52 5h. green 15 35
53 6h. orange . . . . 12·50 22·00
54 10h. red 15 35
55 15h. brown 15 15
56 20h. olive 35 55
57 25h. red 15 15
58 50h. blue 25 35
59 70h. blue 35 60
60 1k. red and grey 60 85

1919. For Southern Poland. Value in halerzy or korony. Imperf or perf.
68 **15** 3h. brown 10 10
69 5h. green 10 10
70 10h. orange 10 10
71 15h. red 10 10
72 **16** 20h. brown 10 10
85 25h. blue 10 10
86 50h. brown 10 10
75 **17** 1k. green 20 10
88 1k.50 brown 70 10
89 2k. blue 90 10
90 **18** 2k.50 purple 90 35
91 **19** 5k. blue . . . . 1·40 45

1919. For Northern Poland. Value in fenigow or marki. Imperf or perf.
104 **15** 3f. brown 10 10
105 5f. green 10 10
179 5f. blue 30 60
106 10f. purple 10 10
129 10f. brown 10 10
107 15f. red 10 10
108 **16** 20f. blue 10 10
181 20f. red 30 60
109 25f. green 10 10
110 50f. green 10 10
183 50f. orange 30 60
137 **17** 1m. violet 20 10
112 1m.50 green 50 25
138 2m. brown 20 10
114 **18** 2m.50 brown 90 55
139 3m. brown 30 10
140 **19** 5m. purple 10 10
141 6m. red 10 10
142 10m. red 25 15
143 20m. green 60 35

1919. 1st Polish Philatelic Exhibition and Polish White Cross Fund. Surch **I POLSKA WYSTAWA MAREK**, cross and new value. Imperf or perf.
116 **15** 5+5f. green 20 20
117 10+5f. purple 50 20
118 15+5f. red 20 20
119 **16** 25+5f. olive 30 20
120 50+5f. green 75 55

20

21 Prime Minster Paderewski

22 A. Trampezynski

23 Eagle and Sailing Ship

24

1919. 1st Session of Parliament in Liberated Poland. Dated "1919".
121 **20** 10f. mauve 25 15
122 **21** 15f. red 25 15
123 **22** 20f. brown (21 × 25 mm) 65 30
124 20f. brown (17 × 20 mm) 1·25 1·25
125 – 25f. green 40 15
126 **23** 50f. blue 40 25
127 – 1m. violet 65 55
DESIGN—As Type **21**: 25f. Gen. Pilsudski. As Type **23**: 1m. Griffin and fasces.

1920.
146 **24** 40f. violet 10 10
182 40f. brown 30 60
184 75f. green 30 60

1920. As T **15**, but value in marks ("Mk").
147 **15** 1m. red 10 10
148 2m. green 10 10
149 3m. blue 10 10
150 4m. red 10 10
151 5m. purple 10 10
152 8m. brown 65 20

1921. Surch **3 Mk** and bars.
153 **24** 3m. on 40f. violet 20 10

1921. Red Cross Fund. Surch with cross and **30MK**.
154 **19** 5m.+30m. purple . . . . . 3·50 7·50
155 6m.+30m. red . . . . . 3·50 7·50
156 10m.+30m. red . . . . . 7·00 15·00
157 20m.+30m. green . . . . . 28·00 70·00

28 Sun of Peace

29 Agriculture

1921. New Constitution.
158 **28** 2m. green . . . . 1·10 1·90
159 3m. blue . . . . 1·10 1·90
160 4m. red 55 55
161 **29** 6m. red 55 65
162 10m. green 90 65
163 – 25m. violet . . . . 2·40 2·00
164 – 50m. green and buff . . . 1·60 1·00
DESIGN: 25, 50m. "Peace" (Seated women).

31 Sower

32

1921. Peace Treaty with Russia.
165 **31** 10m. blue 10 10
166 15m. brown 10 10
167 20m. red 10 10

1921.
170 **32** 25m. violet and buff . . . 10 10
171 50m. red and buff 10 10
172 100m. brown and orange 10 10
173 200m. pink and black . . . 10 10
174 300m. green 10 10
175 400m. brown 10 10
176 500m. purple 10 10
177 1000m. orange 10 10
178 2000m. violet 10 10

33 Silesian Miner

1922.
185 **33** 1m. black 30 60
186 1m.25 green 30 60
187 2m. red 30 60
188 3m. green 30 60
189 4m. blue 30 60
190 5m. brown 30 60
191 6m. orange . . . . 30 1·50
192 10m. brown 30 60
193 20m. purple 30 60
194 50m. olive . . . . 30 3·75
195 80m. red . . . . 95 4·50
196 100m. violet . . . . 95 4·50
197 200m. orange . . . . . . 1·90 7·50
198 300m. blue . . . . 5·00 15·00

34 Copernicus

39

1923. 450th Birth Anniv of Copernicus (astronomer) and 150th Death Anniv of Konarski (educationist).
199 **34** 1,000m. slate 55 45
200 – 3,000m. brown 25 45
201 **34** 5,000m. red 55 55
DESIGN: 3,000m. Konarski.

1923. Surch.
202 **32** 10 TYSIECY (= 10000) on 25m. violet and buff . . 10 10
206 **15** 20,000m. on 2m. green (No. 148) 35 40
204 **31** 25,000m. on 20m. red . . . 10 10
205 50,000m. on 10m. blue . . 20 20
207 **15** 100,000m. on 5m. purple (No. 151) 10 10

1924.
208 **39** 10,000m. purple 30 30
209 20,000m. green 10 25
210 30,000m. red 70 35
211 50,000m. green 70 35
212 100,000m. brown 55 30
213 200,000m. blue 55 25
214 300,000m. mauve 55 45
215 500,000m. brown . . . . 55 1·90
216 1,000,000m. pink . . . . 55 5·25
217 2,000,000m. green . . . . 90 23·00

40

41 President Wojciechowski

1924. New Currency.
218 **40** 1g. brown 45 40
219 2g. brown 45 10
220 3g. orange 55 10
221 5g. green 70 10
222 10g. green 70 10
223 15g. red 70 10
224 20g. blue . . . . 2·75 10
225 25g. red . . . . 3·50 15
226 30g. violet . . . . 17·50 20
227 40g. blue . . . . 4·00 30
228 50g. purple . . . . 2·75 25
229 **41** 1z. red . . . . 22·00 2·40

42

43 Holy Gate, Vilna

44 Town Hall, Pozan

48 Galleon

1925. National Fund.
230 **42** 1g.+50g. brown . . . . . 15·00 22·00
231 2g.+50g. brown . . . . . 15·00 22·00
232 3g.+50g. orange . . . . . 15·00 22·00
233 5g.+50g. green . . . . . 15·00 22·00
234 10g.+50g. green . . . . . 15·00 22·00
235 15g.+50g. red . . . . . . 15·00 22·00
236 20g.+50g. blue . . . . . . 15·00 22·00
237 25g.+50g. red . . . . . . 15·00 22·00
238 30g.+50g. violet . . . . . 15·00 22·00
239 40g.+50g. blue . . . . . . 15·00 22·00
240 50g.+50g. purple . . . . . 15·00 22·00

1925.
241 **43** 1g. brown 30 10
242 – 2g. olive 45 35
243a – 3g. blue . . . . 1·40 10
244a **44** 5g. green . . . . 1·10 10
245a – 10g. violet . . . . 1·10 10
246 – 15g. red . . . . 1·10 10
247 **48** 20g. red . . . . 6·50 10
248 **43** 24g. blue . . . . 7·00 70
249 – 30g. blue . . . . 3·75 10
250 – 40g. blue . . . . 3·00 10
251 **48** 45g. mauve . . . . 13·00 1·10
DESIGNS—As Type **43**: VERT: 2, 30g. Jan III Sobieski Statuc, Lwow. As Type **44**: 3, 10g. King Sigismund Vasa Column, Warsaw. HORIZ: 15, 40g. Wawel Castle, Cracow.

49 LVG Schneider Biplane

50 Chopin

1925. Air.
252 **49** 1g. blue . . . . 45 4·75
253 2g. orange . . . . 45 4·75
254 3g. brown . . . . 45 4·75
255 5g. brown 45 55
256 10g. green . . . . 1·40 65
257 15g. mauve . . . . 1·60 75
258 20g. olive . . . . 12·50 4·75
259 30g. red . . . . 6·50 1·75
260 45g. lilac . . . . 8·50 3·50

1927.
261 **50** 40g. blue . . . . 12·00 2·40

51 Marshal Pilsudski

52 Pres. Moscicki

1927.
262 **51** 20g. red . . . . 2·00 25
262a 25g. brown . . . . 2·00 25

1927.
263 **52** 20g. red . . . . 6·00 70

53

54 Dr. Karl Kaczkowki

1927. Educational Funds.
264 **53** 10g.+5g. purple on green 7·50 10·00
265 20g.+5g. blue on yellow . . 7·50 10·00

1927. 4th Int Military Medical Congress, Warsaw.
266 **54** 10g. green . . . . 2·75 2·10
267 25g. red . . . . 5·25 4·00
268 40g. blue . . . . 7·00 3·00

55 J. Slowacki (poet)

56 Marshal Pilsudski

57 Pres. Moscicki

58 Gen. Joseph Bem

1927. Transfer of Slowacki's remains to Cracow.
269 **55** 20g. red . . . . 4·50 75

1928.
272 **56** 50g. grey . . . . 2·75 20
272a 50g. green . . . . 6·50 25
273 **57** 1z. black on cream . . . 8·50 20

1928.
271 **58** 25g. red . . . . 2·25 25

59 H. Sienkiewicz

60 Slav God, "Swiatowit"

1928. Henryk Sienkiewicz (author).
274 **59** 15g. blue . . . . 1·75 25

1929. National Exhibition, Poznan.
275 **60** 25g. brown . . . . 1·75 25

61

62 King Jan III Sobieski

63

1929.
276 **61** 5g. violet 20 20
277 10g. green 55 20
278 25g. brown 35 25

1930. Birth Tercentenary of Jan III Sobieski.
279 **62** 75g. purple . . . . 5·00 25

1930. Centenary of "November Rising" (29 November 1830).
280 **63** 5g. purple 55 20
281 15g. blue . . . . 2·40 35
282 25g. lake . . . . 1·50 20
283 30g. red . . . . 8·00 3·50

64 Kosciusko, Washington and Pulaski

65

1932. Birth Bicentenary of George Washington.
284 **64** 30g. brown on cream . . . 2·25 35

1932.
284a **65** 5g. violet 20 20
285 10g. green 20 20
285a 15g. red 20 20
286 20g. grey 45 20
287 25g. bistre 45 20
288 30g. red . . . . 1·90 20
289 60g. blue . . . . 20·00 20

67 Town Hall, Torun

68 Franciszek Zwirko (airman) and Stanislaw Wigura (aircraft designer)

1933. 700th Anniv of Torun.
290 **67** 60g. blue on cream . . . . 28·00 1·10

1933. Victory in Flight round Europe Air Race, 1932.
292 **68** 30g. green . . . . 16·00 1·75

1933. Torun Philatelic Exhibition.
293 **67** 60g. red on cream . . . . 18·00 15·00

69 Altar-piece, St. Mary's Church, Cracow

1933. 4th Death Centenary of Veit Stoss (sculptor).
294 **69** 80g. brown on cream . . . 14·00 2·00

70 "Liberation of Vienna" by J. Matejko

1933. 250th Anniv of Relief of Vienna.
295 **70** 1z.20 blue on cream . . . 35·00 12·50

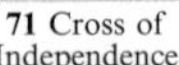

71 Cross of Independence

73 Marshal Pilsudski and Legion of Fusiliers Badge

1933. 15th Anniv of Proclamation of Republic.
296 **71** 30g. red . . . . 8·00 40

1934. Katowice Philatelic Exhibition. Optd **Wyst. Filat. 1934 Katowice**.
297 **65** 20g. grey . . . . 35·00 29·00
298 30g. red . . . . 35·00 29·00

1934. 20th Anniv of Formation of Polish Legion[illegible]
299 **73** 25g. blue 70 35
300 30g. brown . . . . 2·00 40

1934. Int Air Tournament. Optd **Challenge 1934**.
301 **49** 20g. olive . . . . 12·00 10·00
302 **68** 30g. green . . . . 7·50 2·50

1934. Surch in figures.
303 **69** 25g. on 80g. brown on cream . . . . 5·00 60
304 **65** 55g. on 60g. blue . . . . . 4·50 35
305 **70** 1z. on 1z.20 blue on cream 18·00 4·75

77 Marshal Pilsudski

1935. Mourning Issue.
306 **77** 5g. black 75 25
307 15g. black 75 30
308 25g. black . . . . 1·25 25
309 45g. black . . . . 4·00 2·00
310 1z. black . . . . 7·00 4·25

1935. Optd **Kopiec Marszalka Pilsudskiego**.
311 **65** 15g. red 80 65
312 **73** 25g. blue . . . . 2·75 2·00

79 Pieskowa Skala (Dog's Rock)

80 Pres. Moscicki

1935.
313 **79** 5g. blue 50 10
317 – 5g. violet 25 10
314 – 10g. green 50 10
318 – 10g. green 65 10
315 – 15g. blue . . . . 2·75 10
319 – 15g. lake 35 10
316 – 20g. black . . . . 1·00 10
320 – 20g. orange 55 10
321a – 25g. green 80 10
322 – 30g. red . . . . 1·75 10
323a – 45g. mauve . . . . . . 1·60 10
324a – 50g. black . . . . 2·50 10
325 – 55g. blue . . . . 6·25 40
326 – 1z. brown . . . . 3·50 70
327 **80** 3z. brown . . . . 2·50 3·50

DESIGNS: 5g. (No. 317) Monastery of Jasna Gora, Czestochowa; 10g. (314) Lake Morskie Oko; 10g. (318) "Batory" (liner) at sea passenger terminal, Gdynia; 15g. (315) "Pilsudski" (liner); 15g. (319) University, Lwow; 20g. (316) Pieniny-Czorsztyn; 20g. (320) Administrative Buildings, Katowice; 25g. Belvedere Palace, Warsaw; 30g. Castle at Mir; 45g. Castle at Podhorce; 50g. Cloth Hall, Cracow; 55g. Raczynski Library, Poznan; 1z. Vilna Cathedral.

1936. 10th Anniv of Moscicki Presidency. As T **57** but inscr "1926. 3. VI. 1936" below design.
328 **57** 1z. blue . . . . 5·00 6·00

1936. Gordon-Bennett Balloon Race. Optd **GORDON-BENNETT 30. VIII. 1936**.
329 30g. red (No. 322) . . . . . 11·00 5·75
330 55g. blue (No. 325) . . . . . 11·00 5·75

82 Marshal Smigly-Rydz

83 Pres. Moscicki

1937.
331 **82** 25g. blue 35 10
332 55g. blue 50 10

1938. President's 70th Birthday.
333 **83** 15g. grey 40 10
334 30g. purple 60 10

84 Kosciuszko, Paine and Washington

1938. 150th Anniv of U.S. Constitution.
335 **84** 1z. blue . . . . 1·10 1·40

85a

86 Marshal Pilsudski

1938. 20th Anniv of Independence.
336 – 5g. orange 10 10
337 – 10g. green 10 10
338 **85a** 15g. brown (A) 15 15
357 15g. brown (B) 35 25
339 – 20g. blue 40 10
340 – 25g. purple 10 10
341 – 30g. red 50 10
342 – 45g. black 90 65
343 – 50g. mauve . . . . 1·75 10
344 – 55g. blue 50 10
345 – 75g. green . . . . 2·25 1·90
346 – 1z. orange . . . . 2·25 1·90
347 – 2z. red . . . . 8·50 11·00
348 **86** 3z. blue . . . . 8·50 14·00

DESIGNS—VERT: 5g. Boleslaw the Brave; 10g. Casimir the Great; 20g. Casimir Jagiellon; 25g. Sigismund August; 30g. Stefan Batory; 45g. Chodkiewicz and Zolkiewski; 50g. Jan III Sobieski; 55g. Symbol of Constitution of May 3rd, 1791; 75g. Kosciuszko, Poniatowski and Dabrowski; 1z. November Uprising 1830–31; 2z. Romuald Traugutt.
(A) Type **85a**. (B) as Type **85a** but crossed swords omitted.

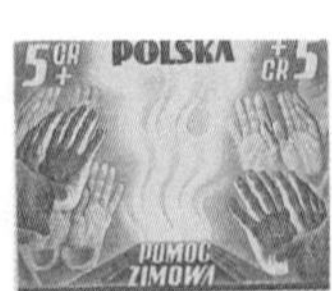

87 Teschen comes to Poland

88 "Warmth"

1938. Acquisition of Teschen.
349 **87** 25g. purple . . . . 1·50 35

1938. Winter Relief Fund.
350 **88** 5g.+5g. orange . . . . . 40 1·40
351 25g.+10g. purple . . . . 85 3·25
352 55g.+15g. blue . . . . . 1·40 3·50

89 Tatra Mountaineer

1939. International Ski Championship, Zakopane.
353 **89** 15g. brown . . . . 1·10 80
354 25g. purple . . . . 1·40 1·10
355 30g. red . . . . 1·90 1·50
356 55g. blue . . . . 7·50 5·00

90 Pilsudski and Polish Legionaries

1939. 25th Anniv of 1st Battles of Polish Legions.
358 **90** 25g. purple . . . . 1·10 45

1939–1945. GERMAN OCCUPATION.

1939. T **94** of Germany surch **Deutsche Post OSTEN** and value.
359 **94** 6g. on 3pf. brown 20 40
360 8g. on 4pf. blue 20 40
361 12g. on 6pf. green 20 40
362 16g. on 8pf. red 65 75
363 20g. on 10pf. brown . . . 20 40
364 24g. on 12pf. red 20 40
365 30g. on 15pf. purple . . . 65 65
366 40g. on 20pf. blue 65 40
367 50g. on 25pf. blue 65 65
368 60g. on 30pf. green 80 40
369 80g. on 40pf. mauve . . . 80 65
370 1z. on 50pf. black & green 1·90 1·00
371 2z. on 100pf. black & yell 3·50 2·50

1940. Surch **General-Gouvernement**, Nazi emblem and value.
372 – 2g. on 5g. orge (No. 336) 30 35
373 [illegible] (No. 336) 30 35
374 – 6g. on 10g. grn (No. 337) 30 35
375 – 8g. on 10g. grn (No. 337) 30 35
376 – 10g. on 10g. green (No. 337) 30 35
377 **107** 12g. on 15g. brown (No. 338) 30 35
378 16g. on 15g. brown (No. 338) 30 35
379 **104** 24g. on 25g. blue . . . 2·50 2·50
380 – 24g. on 25g. purple (No. 340) 30 35
381 – 30g. on 30g. red (No. 341) 45 30
382 **110** 30g. on 5g.+5g. orange 45 30
383 **105** 40g. on 30g. purple . . 65 1·00
384 **110** 40g. on 25g.+10g. pur 65 50
385 – 50g. on 50g. mauve (No. 343) 65 50
386 **104** 50g. on 55g. blue . . . 30 50
386a **D 88** 50g. on 20g. green . . 1·90 1·90
386b 50g. on 25g. green . . 12·50 11·50
386c 50g. on 30g. green . . 25·00 28·00
386d 50g. on 50g. green . . 1·90 1·60
386e 50g. on 1z. green . . . 1·90 1·60
387 – 60g. on 55g. blue (No. 344) . . . . . 9·50 6·25
388 – 80g. on 75g. green (No. 345) . . . . . 9·50 7·25
388a **110** 1z. on 55g.+15g. blue 7·50 8·25
389 – 1z. on 1z. orge (No. 346) . . . . . 9·50 6·25
390 – 2z. on 2z. red (No. 347) . . . . . 6·25 3·75
391 **108** 3z. on 3z. blue . . . . 6·25 3·75
Nos. 386a/e are postage stamps.

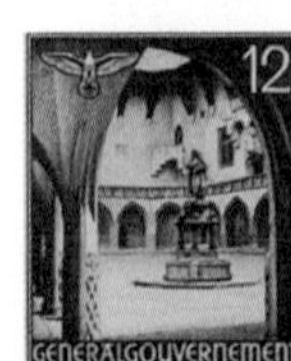

93 Copernicus Memorial, Cracow

95

1940.
392 – 6g. brown 25 55
393 – 8g. brown 25 55
394 – 8g. black 25 30
395 – 10g. green 25 20
396 **93** 12g. green . . . . 2·50 25
397 12g. violet 25 25
398 – 20g. brown 20 10
399 – 24g. red 20 10
400 – 30g. violet 20 10
401 – 30g. purple 20 30
402 – 40g. black 20 15
403 – 48g. brown . . . . 65 1·10
404 – 50g. blue 20 15
405 – 60g. green 20 20
406 – 80g. violet 45 25
407 – 1z. purple . . . . 1·90 80
408 – 1z. green 65 65

DESIGNS: 6g. Florian gate, Cracow; 8g. Castle Keep, Cracow; 10g. Cracow Gate, Lublin; 20g. Church of the Dominicans, Cracow; 24g. Wawel Castle, Cracow; 30g. Old Church in Lublin; 40g. Arcade, Cloth Hall, Cracow; 48g. Town Hall, Sandomir; 50g. Town Hall, Cracow; 60g. Court-yard of Wawel Castle, Cracow; 80g. St. Mary's Church, Cracow; 1z. Bruhl Palace, Warsaw.

1940. Red Cross Fund. As last, new colours, surch with Cross and premium in figures.
409 12g.+8g. green . . . . . . 2·40 3·25
410 24g.+16g. green . . . . . 2·40 3·25
411 50g.+50g. green . . . . . 3·50 4·50
412 80g.+80g. green . . . . . 3·50 4·50

1940. 1st Anniv of German Occupation.
413 **95** 12g.+38g. green on yellow 2·00 2·50
414 – 24g.+26g. red on yellow . . 2·00 2·50
415 – 30g.+20g. violet on yellow 3·00 3·50
DESIGNS: 24g. Woman with scarf; 30g. Fur-capped peasant as Type **96**.

96

1940. Winter Relief Fund.
416 **96** 12g.+8g. green . . . . . 1·00 75
417 24g.+16g. red . . . . . 1·40 1·25
418 30g.+30g. brown . . . . 1·40 1·90
419 50g.+50g. blue . . . . . 2·40 2·50

97 Cracow

1941.
420 **97** 10z. grey and red . . . . 1·25 1·90

98 The Barbican, Cracow

99 Adolf Hitler

1941.
421 **98** 2z. blue 25 60
422 – 4z. green 50 95
DESIGN: 4z. Tyniec Monastery.
See also Nos. 465/8.

1941.
423 **99** 2g. grey 20 25
424 6g. brown 20 25
425 8g. blue 20 25
426 10g. green 20 10
427 12g. violet 20 25
428 16g. orange 25 15
429 20g. brown 25 20
430 24g. red 20 20
431 30g. purple 20 10
432 32g. green 20 35
433 40g. blue 20 20
434 48g. brown 35 40
435 50g. blue 15 55
436 60g. green 15 55
437 80g. purple 15 55
441 1z. green 45 50
442 1z.20 brown 45 75
443 1z.60 blue 40 90

1942. Hitler's 53rd Birthday. As T **99**, but premium inserted in design.
444 30g.+1z. purple on yellow . . 25 50
445 50g.+1z. blue on yellow . . . 25 50
446 1z.20+1z. brown on yellow 25 50

100 Modern Lublin

1942. 600th Anniv of Lublin.
447 – 12g.+8g. purple 10 25
448 **100** 24g.+6g. brown 10 25
449 – 50g.+50g. blue 15 35
450 **100** 1z.+1z. green 30 65
DESIGN: 12, 50g. Lublin, after an ancient engraving.

101 Copernicus **102** Adolf Hitler

1942. 3rd Anniv of German Occupation.
451 – 12g.+18g. violet 10 30
452 – 24g.+26g. red 10 30
453 – 30g.+30g. purple 10 30
454 – 50g.+50g. blue 10 30
455 **101** 1z.+1z. green 40 70
DESIGNS: 12g. Veit Stoss (Vit Stvosz); 24g. Hans Durer; 30g. J. Schuch; 50g. J. Elsner.

1943. Hitler's 54th Birthday.
456 **102** 12g.+1z. violet 20 50
457 24g.+1z. red 20 50
458 84g.+1z. green 20 50

1943. 400th Death Anniv of Nicolas Copernicus (astronomer). As No. 455, colour changed, optd **24. MAI 1543 24. MAI 1943.**
459 **101** 1z.+1z. purple 60 75

103 Cracow Gate, Lublin **103a** Lwow

1943. 3rd Anniv of Nazi Party in German-occupied Poland.
460 **103** 12g.+38g. green 15 10
461 – 24g.+76g. red 15 10
462 – 30g.+70g. purple 15 10
463 – 50g.+1z. blue 15 10
464 – 1z.+2z. grey 60 25
DESIGNS: 24g. Cloth Hall, Cracow; 30g. Administrative Building, Radom; 50g. Bruhl Palace, Warsaw; 1z. Town Hall, Lwow.

1943.
465 – 2z. green 20 10
466 – 4z. violet 25 35
467 **103a** 6z. brown 35 40
468 – 10z. grey and brown 50 40
DESIGNS: 2z. The Barbican, Cracow; 4z. Tyniec Monastery; 10z. Cracow.

104 Adolf Hitler **105** Konrad Celtis

1944. Hitler's 55th Birthday.
469 **104** 12z.+1z. green 10 15
470 24z.+1z. brown 10 15
471 84z.+1z. violet 20 15

1944. Culture Funds.
472 **105** 12g.+18g. green 10 10
473 – 24g.+26g. red 10 10
474 – 30g.+30g. purple 10 10
475 – 50g.+50g. blue 25 25
476 – 1z.+1z. brown 25 25
PORTRAITS: 24g. Andreas Schluter; 30g. Hans Boner; 50g. Augustus the Strong; 1z. Gottlieb Pusch.

105a Cracow Castle

1944. 5th Anniv of German Occupation.
477a **105a** 10z.+10z. black and red 6·00 10·00

1941–45. ISSUES OF EXILED GOVERNMENT IN LONDON.

For correspondence on Polish sea-going vessels and, on certain days, from Polish Military camps in Great Britain.

106 Ruins of Ministry of Finance, Warsaw **107** Vickers-Armstrong Wellington and Hawker Hurricanes used by Poles in Great Britain

1941.
478 – 5g. violet 1·00 1·40
479 **106** 10g. green 1·50 1·50
480 – 25g. grey 1·75 2·00
481 – 55g. blue 2·25 2·00
482 – 75g. olive 5·75 6·50
483 – 80g. red 5·75 6·50
484 **107** 1z. blue 5·75 6·50
485 – 1z.50 brown 5·75 6·50
DESIGNS—VERT: 5g. Ruins of U.S. Embassy, Warsaw; 25g. Destruction of Mickiewicz Monument, Cracow; 1z.50, Polish submarine "Orzel". HORIZ: 55g. Ruins of Warsaw; 75g. Polish machine-gunners in Great Britain; 80g. Polish tank in Great Britain.

108 Vickers-Armstrong Wellington and U-boat **109** Merchant Navy

1943.
486 **108** 5g. red 85 1·10
487 **109** 10g. green 1·10 1·40
488 – 25g. violet 1·10 1·40
489 – 55g. blue 1·50 1·90
490 – 75g. brown 3·00 3·25
491 – 80g. red 3·00 3·25
492 – 1z. olive 3·00 3·25
493 – 1z.50 black 3·75 6·75
DESIGNS—VERT: 25g. Anti-tank gun in France; 55g. Poles at Narvik; 1z. Saboteurs damaging railway line. HORIZ: 75g. The Tobruk road; 80g. Gen. Sikorski visiting Polish troops in Middle East; 1z.50, Underground newspaper office.

1944. Capture of Monte Casino. Nos. 482/5 surch **MONTE CASSINO 18 V 1944** and value and bars.
494 – 45g. on 75g. olive 13·00 16·00
495 – 55g. on 80g. red 13·00 16·00
496 **107** 80g. on 1z. blue 13·00 16·00
497 – 1z.20 on 1z.50 brown 13·00 16·00

111 Polish Partisans **112** Romuald Traugutt

1945. Relief Fund for Survivors of Warsaw Rising.
498 **111** 1z.+2z. green 7·00 9·25

1944. INDEPENDENT REPUBLIC.

1944. National Heroes.
499 **112** 25g. red 48·00 65·00
500 – 50g. green 48·00 65·00
501 – 1z. blue 48·00 80·00
PORTRAITS: 50g. Kosciuszko; 1z. H. Dabrowski.

113 White Eagle **114** Grunwald Memorial, Cracow

1944.
502 **113** 25g. red 1·40 1·10
503 **114** 50g. green 1·40 75

1944. No. 502 surch with value **31.XII., 1943** or **1944** and **K.R.N., P.K.W.N.** or **R.T.R.P.**
504 **113** 1z. on 25g. red 2·50 3·50
505 2z. on 25g. red 2·50 3·50
506 3z. on 25g. red 2·50 3·50

1945. 82nd Anniv of 1863 Revolt against Russia. Surch with value and **22.I.1863.**
507 **112** 5z. on 25g. brown 42·00 65·00

1945. Liberation. No. 502 surch **3zl**, with town names and dates as indicated.
508 3z. on 25g. Bydgoszcz 23.1.1945 5·75 9·75
509 3z. on 25g. Czestochowa 17.1.1945 5·75 9·75
510 3z. on 25g. Gniezno 22.1.1945 5·75 9·75
511 3z. on 25g. Kalisz 24.1.1945 5·75 9·75
512 3z. on 25g. Kielce 15.1.1945 5·75 9·75
513 3z. on 25g. Krakow 19.1.1945 5·75 9·75
514 3z. on 25g. Lodz 19.1.1945 5·75 9·75
515 3z. on 25g. Radom 16.1.1945 5·75 9·75
516 3z. on 25g. Warszawa 17.1.1945 14·50 20·00
517 3z. on 25g. Zakopane 29.1.1945 8·00 13·50

120 Flag-bearer and War Victim **121** Lodz Factories

1945. Liberation of Warsaw.
518 **120** 5z. red 2·25 2·25

1945. Liberation of Lodz.
519 **121** 1z. blue 80 40

1945. 151st Anniv of Kosciuszko's Oath of Allegiance. No. 500 surch **5zl. 24.III.1794.**
520 5z. on 50g. green 11·50 17·00

123 Grunwald Memorial, Cracow **125** H.M.S. "Dragon" (cruiser)

1945. Cracow Monuments. Inscr "19.1.1945".
521 **123** 50g. purple 25 15
522 – 1z. brown 30 15
523 – 2z. blue 1·10 15
524 – 3z. violet 95 40
525 – 5z. green 6·00 6·75
DESIGNS—VERT: 1z. Kosciuszko Statue; 3z. Copernicus Memorial. HORIZ: 2z. Cloth Hall; 5z. Wawel Castle.

1945. 25th Anniv of Polish Maritime League.
526 **125** 50g.+2z. orange 7·00 10·50
527 – 1z.+3z. blue 4·00 7·50
528 – 2z.+4z. red 2·75 7·00
529 – 3z.+5z. olive 2·75 7·00
DESIGNS—VERT: 1z. "Dar Pomorza" (full-rigged cadet ship); 2z. Naval ensigns. HORIZ: 3z. Crane and tower, Gdansk.

126 Town Hall, Poznan

1945. Postal Employees Congress.
530 **126** 1z.+5z. green 19·00 32·00

127 Kosciuszko Memorial, Lodz **128** Grunwald, 1410

1945.
531 **127** 3z. purple 70 25

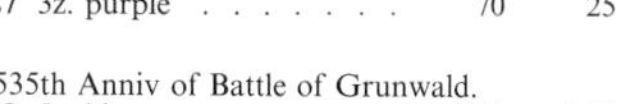

1945. 535th Anniv of Battle of Grunwald.
532 **128** 5z. blue 6·75 6·25

129 Eagle and Manifesto **133** Crane Tower, Gdansk

130 Westerplatte

1945. 1st Anniv of Liberation.
533 **129** 3z. red 10·00 16·00

1945. 6th Anniv of Defence of Westerplatte.
534 **130** 1z.+9z. slate 21·00 27·00

1945. Surch with new value and heavy bars.
535 **114** 1z. on 50g. green 55 30
536a **113** 1z.50 on 25g. red 55 30

1945. Liberation of Gdansk (Danzig). Perf or imperf.
537 **133** 1z. olive 20 20
538 – 2z. blue 30 20
539 – 3z. purple 90 20
DESIGNS—VERT: 2z. Stock Exchange, Gdansk. HORIZ: 3z. High Gate, Gdansk.

135 St. John's Cathedral

1945. "Warsaw, 1939–1945". Warsaw before and after destruction. Imperf.
540 – 1z.50 red 20 10
541 **135** 3z. blue 20 10
542 – 3z.50 green 1·25 45
543 – 6z. grey 25 20
544 – 8z. brown 2·75 55
545 – 10z. purple 55 55
DESIGNS: 1z.50, Royal Castle; 3z.50, City Hall; 6z. G.P.O.; 8z. War Ministry; 10z. Church of the Holy Cross.

136 United Workers

1945. Trades' Union Congress.
546 **136** 1z.50+8z.50 grey 6·75 8·75

137 Soldiers of 1830 and Jan III Sobieski Statue

1945. 115th Anniv of 1830 Revolt against Russia.
547 **137** 10z. grey 8·50 12·50

1946. 1st Anniv of Warsaw Liberation. Nos. 540/5 optd **WARSZAWA WOLNA 17 Styczen 1945–1946.** Imperf.
548 1z.50 red 1·90 4·25
549 3z. blue 1·90 4·25
550 3z.50 green 1·90 4·25
551 6z. grey 1·90 4·25
552 8z. brown 1·90 4·25
553 10z. purple 1·90 4·25

139 Insurgent

140 Lisunov Li-2 over Ruins of Warsaw

1946. 83rd Anniv of 1863 Revolt.
554 **139** 6z. blue . . . . 7·50 10·50

1946. Air.
555 **140** 5z. grey 35 10
556 10z. purple 45 25
557 15z. blue . . . . 2·75 25
558 20z. purple . . . . 1·10 25
559 25z. green . . . . 2·10 35
560 30z. red . . . . 3·50 50

141 Fighting in Spain

1946. Polish Legion in the Spanish Civil War.
561 **141** 3z.+5z. red . . . . 6·00 8·75

142 Bydgoszcz

143 "Death" over Majdanek Concentration Camp

1946. 600th Anniv of City of Bydgoszcz.
562 **142** 3z.+2z. grey . . . . . . 7·25 13·00

1946. Majdanek Concentration Camp.
563 **143** 3z.+5z. green . . . . . . 2·75 4·00

144 Shield and Soldiers

145 Infantry

1946. Uprisings in Upper Silesia (1919–23) and Silesian Campaign against the Germans (1939–45).
564 **144** 3z.+7z. brown . . . . . 95 1·10

1946. 1st Anniv of Peace.
565 **145** 3z. brown 45 35

146 Polish Coastline

148 Bedzin Castle

147 Pres. Bierut, Premier O. Morawski and Marshal Zymierski

1946. Maritime Festival.
566 **146** 3z.+7z. blue . . . . . . 2·50 3·75

1946. 2nd Anniv of Polish Committee of National Liberation Manifesto.
567 **147** 3z. violet . . . . 3·50 6·00

1946. Imperf (5z., 10z.) or perf (6z.).
568 **148** 5z. olive 25 15
568a 5z. brown 45 15
569 – 6z. black 35 10
570 – 10z. blue 80 25
DESIGNS—VERT: 6z. Tombstone of Henry IV. HORIZ: 10z. Castle at Lanckorona.

149 Crane, Monument and Crane Tower, Gdansk

1946. The Fallen in Gdansk.
571 **149** 3z.+12z. grey . . . . . . 2·25 3·00

150 Schoolchildren at Desk

1946. Polish Work for Education and Fund for International Bureau of Education.
571a **150** 3z.+22z. red . . . . . . 30·00 55·00
571b – 6z.+24z. blue . . . . . . [illegible] [illegible]
571c – 11z.+19z. green . . . . 30·00 55·00
DESIGNS: 6z. Court of Jagiellonian University, Cracow; 11z. Gregory Piramowicz (1735–1801), founder of the Education Commission.

152 Stojalowski, Bojko, Stapinski and Witos

1946. 50th Anniv of Peasant Movement and Relief Fund.
572 **152** 5z.+10z. green . . . . . 2·25 3·00
573 5z.+10z. blue . . . . . . 2·25 3·00
574 5z.+10z. olive . . . . . . 2·25 3·00

1947. Opening of Polish Parliament. Surch **+7 SEJM USTAWODAWCZY 19.1.1947**.
575 **147** 3z.+7z. violet . . . . . . 7·50 12·00

1947. 22nd National Ski Championships, Zakopane. Surch **5+15 zl XXII MISTRZOSTWA NARCIARSKIE POLSKI 1947**.
576 **113** 5+15z. on 25g. red . . . 3·25 5·00

1947. No. 569 surch **5 ZL** in outlined figure and capital letters between stars.
577 5z. on 6z. black 65 25

156 Home of Emil Zegadlowicz

157 Frederic Chopin (musician)

158 Boguslawski, Modrzejewska and Jaracz (actors)

159 Wounded Soldier, Nurse and Child

1947. Emil Zegadlowicz Commemoration.
578 **156** 5z.+15z. green . . . . . 2·25 3·25

1947. Polish Culture. Imperf or perf.
579 – 1z. blue 20 25
580 – 1z. grey 20 10
581 – 2z. brown 25 10
582 – 2z. orange 15 10
583 **157** 3z. green 60 25
584 3z. olive . . . . 1·90 25
585 **158** 5z. black 60 10
586 5z. brown 20 10
587 – 6z. grey . . . . 1·00 10
588 – 6z. red 35 10
589 – 10z. grey . . . . 1·25 10
590 – 10z. blue . . . . 1·50 30
591 – 15z. violet . . . . . . 1·60 30
592 – 15z. brown 35 70
593 – 20z. black . . . . . . 2·50 50
594 – 20z. purple . . . . . . 1·10 50
PORTRAITS—HORIZ: 1z. Matejko, Malczewski and Chelmonski (painters); 6z. Swietochowski, Zeromski and Prus (writers); 15z. Wyspianski, Slowacki and Kasprowicz (poets). VERT: 2z. Brother Albert of Cracow; 10z. Marie Curie (scientist); 20z. Mickiewicz (poet).

1947. Red Cross Fund.
595 **159** 5z.+5z. grey and red . . . 3·00 5·00

161 Steelworker

163 Brother Albert of Cracow

1947. Occupations.
596 **161** 5z. lake . . . . 1·40 [illegible]
597 – 10z. green 45 20
598 – 15z. blue 90 30
599 – 20z. black . . . . 1·40 30
DESIGNS: 10z. Harvester; 15z. Fisherman; 20z. Miner.

1947. Air. Surch **LOTNICZA**, bars and value.
600 **114** 40z. on 50g. green . . . . 2·10 65
602 **113** 50z. on 25g. red . . . . . 3·25 1·60

1947. Winter Relief Fund.
603 **163** 2z.+18z. violet . . . . . 1·25 4·50

164 Sagittarius

165 Chainbreaker

1948. Air.
604 **164** 15z. violet . . . . 1·60 25
605 25z. blue . . . . 1·10 20
606 30z. brown . . . . 1·10 45
607 50z. green . . . . 2·25 45
608 75z. black . . . . 2·25 55
609 100z. orange . . . . . . 2·25 55

1948. Revolution Centenaries.
610 **165** 15z. brown 45 10
611 – 30z. brown . . . . 1·50 25
612 – 35z. green . . . . 3·25 55
613 – 60z. red . . . . 1·75 65
PORTRAITS—HORIZ: 30z. Generals H. Dembinski and J. Bem; 35z. S. Worcell, P. Sciegienny and E. Dembowski; 60z. F. Engels and K. Marx.

167 Insurgents

168 Wheel and Streamers

1948. 5th Anniv of Warsaw Ghetto Revolt.
614 **167** 15z. black . . . . 2·00 3·50

1948. Warsaw–Prague Cycle Race.
615 **168** 15z. red and blue . . . . 3·25 45

169 Cycle Race

170 "Oliwa" under Construction

1948. 7th Circuit of Poland Cycle Race.
616 **169** 3z. black . . . . 1·75 4·00
617 6z. brown . . . . 1·75 4·25
618 15z. green . . . . 2·50 5·50

1948. Merchant Marine.
619 **170** 6z. violet . . . . 1·40 2·00
620 – 15z. red . . . . 1·75 3·00
621 – 35z. grey . . . . 2·00 5·00
DESIGNS—HORIZ: 15z. Freighter at wharf; 35z. "General M. Zaruski" (cadet ketch).

173 Firework Display

174 "Youth"

1948. Wroclaw Exhibition.
622 **173** 6z. blue 55 30
623 15z. red 90 25
624 18z. red . . . . 1·40 45
625 35z. brown . . . . 1·40 45

1948. International Youth Conf, Warsaw.
626 **174** 15z. blue 65 25

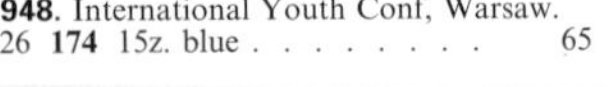

175 Roadway, St. Anne's Church and Palace

176 Torun Ramparts and Mail Coach

1948. Warsaw Reconstruction Fund.
627 **175** 15z.+5z. green 25 25

1948. Philatelic Congress, Torun.
628 **176** 15z. brown . . . . 1·00 25

177 Streamlined Steam Locomotive No. Pm36-1 (1936), Clock and Winged Wheel

178 President Bierut

1948. European Railway Conference.
629 **177** 18z. blue . . . . 6·00 18·00

1948.
629a **178** 2z. orange 15 10
629b 3z. green 15 10
630 5z. brown 15 10
631 6z. black 95 10
631a 10z. violet 25 10
632 15z. red 80 10
633 18z. green . . . . 1·10 10
634 30z. blue . . . . 1·90 25
635 35z. purple . . . . . . 3·00 50

179 Workers and Flag

1948. Workers' Class Unity Congress. (a) Dated "8 XII 1948".
636 **179** 5z. red 85 65
637 – 15z. violet 85 65
638 – 25z. brown 85 65

(b) Dated "XII 1948".
639 **179** 5z. plum . . . . 2·00 1·60
640 – 15z. blue . . . . 2·00 1·60
641 – 25z. green . . . . 2·75 2·25
DESIGNS: 15z. Flags and portraits of Engels, Marx, Lenin and Stalin; 25z. Workers marching and portrait of L. Warynski.

180 Baby

180a Pres. Franklin D. Roosevelt

1948. Anti-tuberculosis Fund. Portraits of babies as T **180**.

642 **180** 3z.+2z. green . . . . . . 4·00 4·75
643 – 5z.+5z. brown . . . . . 4·00 4·75
644 – 6z.+4z. purple . . . . . 2·25 4·75
645 – 15z.+10z. red . . . . . . 2·00 3·00

1948. Air. Honouring Presidents Roosevelt, Pulaski and Kosciuszko.

645a **180a** 80z. violet . . . . . . 21·00 21·00
645b – 100z. purple (Pulaski) 21·00 21·00
645c – 120z. blue (Kosciuszko) 21·00 21·00

181 Workers

1949. Trades' Union Congress, Warsaw.

646 **181** 3z. red . . . . 1·10 1·25
647 – 5z. blue . . . . 1·10 1·25
648 – 15z. green . . . . 1·50 1·50

DESIGNS: 5z. inscr "PRACA" (Labour), Labourer and tractor; 15z. inscr "POKOJ" (Peace), Three labourers.

182 Banks of R. Vistula

183 Pres. Bierut

1949. 5th Anniv of National Liberation Committee.

649 **182** 10z. black . . . . 2·10 2·00
650 **183** 15z. mauve . . . . 2·10 2·00
651 – 35z. blue . . . . 2·10 2·00

DESIGN—VERT: 35z. Radio station, Rasyn.

184 Mail Coach and Map

185 Worker and Tractor

1949. 75th Anniv of U.P.U.

652 **184** 6z. violet . . . . 1·25 2·00
653 – 30z. blue (liner) . . . . 2·25 2·00
654 – 80z. green (airplane) . . . 4·25 4·75

1949. Congress of Peasant Movement.

655 **185** 5z. red 95 25
656 10z. red 25 10
657 15z. green 25 10
658 35z. brown . . . . 1·25 1·25

186 Frederic Chopin

187 Mickiewicz and Pushkin

1949. National Celebrities.

659 – 10z. purple . . . . 2·40 2·10
660 **186** 15z. red . . . . 3·25 2·40
661 – 35z. blue . . . . 2·40 2·40

PORTRAITS: 10z. Adam Mickiewicz; 35z. Julius Slowacki.

1949. Polish–Russian Friendship Month.

662 **187** 15z. violet . . . . 3·50 4·25

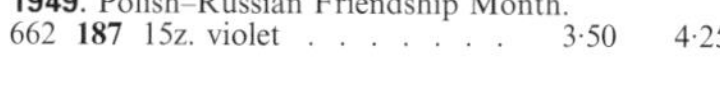

188 Postman

189 Mechanic, Hangar and Aeroplane

1950. 3rd Congress of Postal Workers.

663 **188** 15z. purple . . . . 2·10 2·75

1950. Air.

664 **189** 500z. lake . . . . 4·50 6·50

190

195a

1950. (a) With frame.

665 **190** 15z. red 60 10

(b) Without frame. Values in "zloty".

673 **195a** 5z. green 15 10
674 10z. red 15 10
675 15z. blue 95 50
676 20z. violet 45 35
677 25z. brown 45 35
678 30z. red 65 40
679 40z. brown 80 50
680 50z. olive . . . . 1·60 1·00

For values in "groszy" see Nos. 687/94.

191 J. Marchlewski

192 Workers

1950. 25th Death Anniv of Julian Marchlewski (patriot).

666 **191** 15z. black 70 35

1950. Reconstruction of Warsaw.

667 **192** 5z. brown 15 15

See also No. 695.

193 Worker and Flag

194 Statue

1950. 60th Anniv of May Day Manifesto.

668 **193** 10z. mauve . . . . 1·75 40
669 – 15z. olive . . . . 1·75 25

DESIGN—VERT: 15z. Three workers and flag.

1950. 23rd International Fair, Poznan.

670 **194** 15z. brown 35 10

195 Dove and Globe

196 Industrial and Agricultural Workers

1950. International Peace Conference.

671 **195** 10z. green 85 25
672 15z. brown 35 15

1950. Six Year Reconstruction Plan.

681 **196** 15z. blue 25 10

See also Nos. 696/e.

197 Hibner, Kniewski and Rutkowski

198 Worker and Dove

1950. 25th Anniv of Revolutionaries' Execution.

682 **197** 15z. grey . . . . 2·50 65

1950. 1st Polish Peace Congress.

683 **198** 15z. green 50 25

REVALUATION SURCHARGES. Following a revaluation of the Polish currency, a large number of definitive and commemorative stamps were locally overprinted "Groszy" or "gr". There are 37 known types of overprint and various colours of overprint. We do not list them as they had only local use, but the following is a list of the stamps which were duly authorised for overprinting: Nos. 579/94, 596/615 and 619/58. Overprints on other stamps are not authorized.

Currency Revalued: 100 old zlotys = 1 new zloty.

199 Dove (after Picasso)

1950. 2nd World Peace Congress, Warsaw.

684 **199** 40g. blue . . . . 1·75 35
685 45g. red 35 15

200 General Bem and Battle of Piski

1950. Death Centenary of General Bem.

686 **200** 45g. blue . . . . 2·50 2·00

1950. As T **195a**. Values in "groszy".

687 **195a** 5g. violet 10 10
688 10g. green 10 10
689 15g. olive 10 10
690 25g. red 10 10
691 30g. red 15 10
692 40g. orange 15 10
693 45g. blue . . . . 1·25 10
694 75g. brown 70 10

1950. As No. 667 but value in "groszy".

695 **192** 15g. green 10 10

1950. As No. 681 but values in "groszy" or "zlotys".

696 **196** 45g. blue 15 10
696b 75g. brown 30 10
696d 1z.15 green 95 10
696e 1z.20 red 70 10

201 Woman and Doves

202 Battle Scene and J. Dabrowski

1951. Women's League Congress.

697 **201** 45g. red 45 35

1951. 80th Anniv of Paris Commune.

698 **202** 45g. green 30 10

1951. Surch **45 gr**.

699 **199** 45g. on 15z. red 55 15

204 Worker with Flag

205 Smelting Works

1951. Labour Day.

700 **204** 45g. red 45 15

1951.

701 **205** 40g. blue 25 10
702 45g. black 25 10
702a 60g. brown 25 10
702c 90g. lake 85 10

206 Pioneer and Badge

207 St. Staszic

1951. Int Children's Day. Inscr "I-VI-51".

703 **206** 30g. olive . . . . 1·10 65
704 – 45g. blue (Boy, girl and map) . . . . 6·25 65

1951. 1st Polish Scientific Congress. Inscr "KONGRES NAUKI POLSKIEJ".

705 **207** 25g. red . . . . 3·75 2·75
706 – 40g. blue 60 20
707 – 45g. violet . . . . 8·00 1·60
708 – 60g. green 60 20
709 – 1z.15 purple . . . . . . 1·00 55
710 – 1z.20 grey . . . . 1·75 20

DESIGNS—As Type **207**: 40g. Marie Curie; 60g. M. Nencki; 1z.15, Copernicus; 1z.20, Dove and book. HORIZ—36 × 21 mm: 45g. Z. Wroblewski and Olszewski.

209 F. Dzerzhinsky

211 Young People and Globe

210 Pres. Bierut, Industry and Agriculture

1951. 25th Death Anniv of Dzerzhinsky (Russian politician).

711 **209** 45g. brown 30 25

1951. 7th Anniv of People's Republic.

712 **210** 45g. red . . . . 1·10 15
713 60g. green . . . . 16·00 5·25
714 90g. blue . . . . 3·50 65

1951. 3rd World Youth Festival, Berlin.

715 **211** 40g. blue . . . . 1·10 25

1951. Surch **45 gr**.

716 **195a** 45g. on 35z. orange . . 30 25

213 Sports Badge

214 Stalin

1951. Spartacist Games.

717 **213** 45g. green . . . . 1·25 1·10

1951. Polish–Soviet Friendship.

718 **214** 45g. red 15 10
719 90g. black . . . . 1·10 60

215 Chopin and Moniuszko

216 Mining Machinery

1951. Polish Musical Festival.

720 **215** 45g. black 40 20
721 90g. red . . . . 1·50 55

1951. Six Year Plan (Mining).

722 **216** 90g. brown 30 15
723 1z.20 blue 30 15
724 1z.20+15g. orange 45 20

217 Building Modern Flats

218 Installing Electric Cables

1951. Six Year Plan (Reconstruction).

725 **217** 30g. green 10 10
726 30g.+15g. red 25 10
727 1z.15 purple 25 10

1951. Six Year Plan (Electrification).

728 **218** 30g. black 10 10
729 45g. red 20 10
730 45g.+15g. brown 55 10

219 M. Nowotko

220 Women and Banner

1952. 10th Anniv of Polish Workers' Coalition.

731	**219**	45g.+15g. lake	20	10
732	–	90g. brown	45	30
733	–	1z.15 orange	45	65

PORTRAITS: 90g. P. Finder; 1z.15, M. Fornalska.

1952. International Women's Day.

734	**220**	45g.+15g. brown	45	10
735		1z.20 red	50	35

221 Gen. Swierczewski

222 Ilyushin Il-12 over Farm

1952. 5th Death Anniv of Gen. Swierczewski.

736	**221**	45g.+15g. brown	45	10
737		90g. blue	50	30

1952. Air. Aeroplanes and views.

738	–	55g. blue (Tug and freighters)	35	30
739	**222**	90g. green	35	30
740	–	1z.40 purple (Warsaw)	45	45
741	–	5z. black (Steelworks)	1·40	55

223 President Bierut

224 Cyclists and City Arms

1952. Pres. Bierut's 60th Birthday.

742	**223**	45g.+15g. red	45	35
743		90g. green	80	80
744		1z.20+15g. blue	1·00	35

1952. 5th Warsaw–Berlin–Prague Peace Cycle Race.

745	**224**	40g. blue	1·50	90

225 Workers and Banner

226 Kraszewski

1952. Labour Day.

746	**225**	45g.+15g. red	20	15
747		75g. green	55	35

1952. 140th Birth Anniv of Jozef Ignacy Kraszewski (writer).

748	**226**	25g. purple	50	25

227 Maria Konopnicka

228 H. Kollataj

1952. 110th Birth Anniv of Maria Konopnicka (poet).

749	**227**	30g.+15g. green	50	15
750		1z.15 brown	80	55

1952. 140th Death Anniv of Hugo Kollataj (educationist and politician).

751	**228**	45g.+15g. brown	35	15
752		1z. green	50	35

229 Leonardo da Vinci

231 N. V. Gogol

230 President Bierut and Children

1952. 500th Birth Anniv of Leonardo da Vinci (artist).

753	**229**	30g.+15g. blue	70	50

1952. International Children's Day.

754	**230**	45g.+15g. blue	2·50	70

1952. Death Centenary of Nikolai Gogol (Russian writer).

755	**231**	25g. green	85	60

232 Cement Works

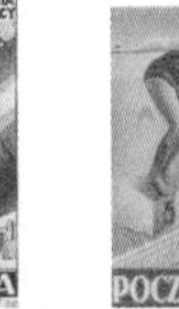
233 Swimmers

1952. Construction of Concrete Works, Wierzbica.

756	**232**	3z. black	2·10	35
757		10z. red	2·50	35

1952. Sports Day.

758	**233**	30g.+15g. blue	4·25	1·10
759	–	45g.+15g. violet	1·50	20
760	–	1z.15 green	1·40	1·50
761	–	1z.20 red	80	80

DESIGNS: 45g. Footballers; 1z.15, Runners; 1z.20, High jumper.

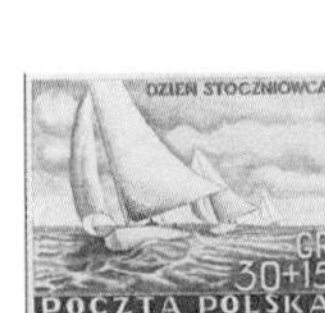
234 Yachts

235 Young Workers

1952. Shipbuilders' Day.

762	**234**	30g.+15g. green	3·25	70
763	–	45g.+15g. blue	70	25
764	–	90g. plum	70	1·25

DESIGNS—VERT: 45g. Full-rigged cadet ship "Dar Pomorza"; 90g. "Brygada Makowskiego" (freighter) under construction.

1952. Youth Festival, Warsaw.

765	**235**	30g.+15g. green	40	25
766	–	45g.+15g. red	70	15
767	–	90g. brown	40	35

DESIGNS—HORIZ: 45g. Girl and boy students; 90g. Boy bugler.

236 "New Constitution"

237 L. Warynski

1952. Adoption of New Constitution.

768	**236**	45g.+15g. green & brown	1·10	15
769		3z. violet and brown	40	35

1952. 70th Anniv of Party "Proletariat".

770	**237**	30g.+15g. red	55	15
771		45g.+15g. brown	55	15

238 Jaworzno Power Station

239 Frydman

1952. Electricity Power Station, Jaworzno.

772	**238**	45g.+15g. red	70	10
773		1z. black	65	50
774		1z.50 green	65	20

1952. Pleniny Mountain Resorts.

775	**239**	45g.+15g. purple	55	10
776	–	60g. green (Grywald)	35	45
777	–	1z. red (Niedzica)	1·00	15

240 Pilot and Glider

241 Avicenna

1952. Aviation Day.

778	**240**	3g.+15g. green	1·25	10
779	–	45g.+15g. red	2·00	70
780	–	90g. blue	35	35

DESIGNS: 45g. Pilot and Yakovlev Yak-18U; 90g. Parachutists descending.

1952. Birth Millenary of Avicenna (Arab physician).

781	**241**	75g. red	35	25

242 Victor Hugo

243 Shipbuilding

1952. 150th Birth Anniv of Victor Hugo (French author).

782	**242**	90g. brown	35	25

1952. Gdansk Shipyards.

783	**243**	5g. green	15	10
784		15g. red	15	10

244 H. Sienkiewicz (author)

245 Assault on Winter Palace, Petrograd

1952.

785	**244**	45g.+15g. brown	35	15

1952. 35th Anniv of Russian Revolution. Perf or Imperf.

786	**245**	45g.+15g. red	90	20
787		60g. brown	35	30

246 Lenin

247 Miner

1952. Polish–Soviet Friendship Month.

788	**246**	30g.+15g. purple	35	15
789		45g.+15g. brown	70	30

1952. Miners' Day.

790	**247**	45g.+15g. black	20	10
791		1z.20+15g. brown	70	35

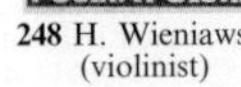
248 H. Wieniawski (violinist)

249 Car Factory, Zeran

1952. 2nd Wieniawski Int Violin Competition.

792	**248**	30g.+15g. green	1·00	60
793		45g.+15g. violet	2·75	55

1952.

800	–	30g.+15g. blue	30	10
794	**249**	45g.+15g. green	20	10
801	–	60g.+20g. purple	30	10
795	**249**	1z.15 brown	70	35

DESIGN: 30, 60g. Lorry factory, Lublin.

250 Dove of Peace

251 Soldier and Flag

1952. Peace Congress, Vienna.

796	**250**	30g. green	75	30
797		60g. blue	1·40	45

1952. 10th Anniv of Battle of Stalingrad.

798	**251**	60g. red and green	5·00	1·60
799		80g. red and grey	65	50

253 Karl Marx

254 Globe and Flag

1953. 70th Death Anniv of Marx.

802	**253**	60g. blue	20·00	11·50
803		80g. brown	1·10	45

1953. Labour Day.

804	**254**	60g. red	5·75	3·75
805		80g. red	45	15

255 Cyclists and Arms of Warsaw

256 Boxer

1953. 6th International Peace Cycle Race.

806	–	80g. green	85	40
807	**255**	80g. brown	85	40
808	–	80g. red	13·50	9·25

DESIGNS: As Type **255**, but Arms of Berlin (No. 806) or Prague (No. 808).

1953. European Boxing Championship, Warsaw. Inscr "17-24. V. 1953".

809	**256**	40g. lake	1·00	45
810		80g. orange	10·00	4·75
811	–	95g. purple	85	60

DESIGN: 95g. Boxers in ring.

257 Copernicus (after Matejko)

1953. 480th Birth Anniv of Copernicus (astronomer).

812	**257**	20g. brown	1·75	40
813	–	80g. blue	13·50	13·50

DESIGN—VERT: 80g. Copernicus and diagram.

258 "Dalmor" (trawler)

259 Warsaw Market-place

1953. Merchant Navy Day.

814	**258**	80g. green	1·60	10
815	–	1z.35 blue	1·60	3·25

DESIGN: 1z.35, "Czech" (freighter).

1953. Polish National Day.

816	**259**	20g. lake	25	20
817		2z.35 blue	4·25	3·25

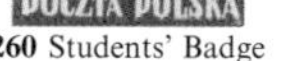

260 Students' Badge **261** Nurse Feeding Baby

1953. 3rd World Students' Congress, Warsaw. Inscr "III SWIATOWY KONGRESS STUDENTOW".
(a) Postage. Perf.
818 – 40g. brown 15 15
819 **260** 1z.35 green 70 15
820 – 1z.50 blue . . . . 2·50 2·75
(b) Air. Imperf.
821 **260** 55g. plum . . . . 1·75 60
822 75g. red . . . . 90 1·60
DESIGNS—HORIZ: 40g. Students and globe. VERT: 1z.50, Woman and dove.

1953. Social Health Service.
823 **261** 80g. red . . . . 8·75 5·25
824 – 1z.75 green 40 40
DESIGN: 1z.75, Nurse, mother and baby.

262 M. Kalinowski **263** Jan Kochanowski (poet)

1953. 10th Anniv of Polish People's Army.
825 **262** 45g. brown . . . . 3·75 3·00
826 – 80g. red 80 10
827 – 1g.75 olive 80 10
DESIGNS—HORIZ: 80g. Russian and Polish soldiers. VERT: 1z.75, R. Pazinski.

1953. "Renaissance" Commemoration. Inscr "ROK ODRODZENIA".
828 **263** 20g. brown 15 10
829 – 80g. purple 60 10
830 – 1z.35 blue . . . . 2·75 1·75
DESIGNS—HORIZ: 80g. Wawel Castle. VERT: 1z.35, Mikolaj Rej (writer).

264 Palace of Science and Culture **265** Dunajec Canyon, Pieniny Mountains

1953. Reconstruction of Warsaw. Inscr "WARSZAWA".
831 **264** 80g. red . . . . 9·75 1·50
832 – 1z.75 blue . . . . 1·90 45
833 – 2z. purple . . . . 5·00 3·50
DESIGNS: 1z.75, Constitution Square; 2z. Old City Market, Warsaw.

1953. Tourist Series.
834 – 20g. lake and blue 10 10
835 – 80g. lilac and green . . . 3·25 1·25
836 **265** 1z.75 green and brown . . 70 10
837 – 2z. black and red . . . . 1·10 10
DESIGNS—HORIZ: 20g. Krynica Spa; 2z. Clechocinek Spa. VERT: 80g. Morskie Oko Lake, Tatra Mountains.

266 Skiing **267** Infants playing

1953. Winter Sports.
838 – 80g. blue . . . . 1·50 40
839 **266** 95g. green . . . . 1·25 40
840 – 2z.85 red . . . . 4·00 2·10
DESIGNS—VERT: 80g. Ice-skating; 2z.85, Ice-hockey.

1953. Children's Education.
841 **267** 10g. violet 60 15
842 – 80g. red 90 30
843 – 1z.50 green . . . . 6·00 2·25
DESIGNS: 80g. Girls and school; 1z.50, Two Schoolgirls writing.

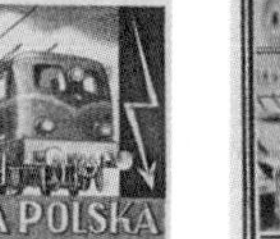

268 Class EP 02 Electric Locomotive **269** Mill Girl

1954. Electrification of Railways.
844 – 60g. blue . . . . 8·00 4·75
845 **268** 80g. brown 90 25
DESIGN: 60g. Class EW54 electric commuter train.

1954. International Women's Day.
846 **269** 20g. green . . . . 2·45 1·50
847 – 40g. blue 60 10
848 – 80g. brown 60 10
DESIGNS: 40g. Postwoman; 80g. Woman driving tractor.

270 Flags and Mayflowers **271** "Warsaw–Berlin–Prague"

1954. Labour Day.
849 **270** 40g. brown 70 40
850 60g. blue 70 25
851 80g. red 70 25

1954. 7th International Peace Cycle Race. Inscr "2-17 MAJ 1954".
852 **271** 80g. brown 80 25
853 – 80g. blue (Dove and cycle wheel) 80 25

272 Symbols of Labour **273** Glider and Flags

1954. 3rd Trades' Union Congress, Warsaw.
854 **272** 25g. blue . . . . 1·25 1·10
855 80g. lake 40 25

1954. International Gliding Competition.
856 – 45g. green 65 15
857 **273** 60g. violet . . . . 1·90 70
858 60g. brown . . . . 1·25 15
859a – 1z.35 blue . . . . 2·40 25
DESIGNS: 45g. Glider and clouds in frame; 1z.35, Glider and sky.

274 Paczkow **275** Fencing

1954. Air. Inscr "POCZTA LOTNICZA".
860 **274** 60g. green 25 10
861 – 80g. red 35 10
862 – 1z.15 black . . . . . . 1·75 1·60
863 – 1z.50 red 80 10
864 – 1z.55 blue 80 10
865 – 1z.95 brown . . . . . . 1·00 10
DESIGNS—Ilyushin Il-12 airplane over: 80g. Market-place, Kazimierz Dolny; 1z.15, Wawel Castle, Cracow; 1z.50, Town Hall, Wroclaw; 1z.55, Lazienki Palace, Warsaw; 1z.95, Cracow Tower, Lublin.

1954. 2nd Spartacist Games (1st issue). Inscr "II OGOLNOPOLSKA SPARTAKIADA".
866 **275** 25g. purple . . . . 1·25 50
867 – 60g. turquoise . . . . . 1·25 35
868 – 1z. blue . . . . 2·40 70
DESIGNS—VERT: 60g. Gymnastics. HORIZ: 1z. Running.

276 Spartacist Games Badge **277** Battlefield

1954. 2nd Spartacist Games (2nd issue).
869 **276** 60g. brown . . . . 1·10 35
870 1z.55 grey . . . . 1·10 60

1954. 10th Anniv of Liberation and Battle of Studzianki.
871 **277** 60g. green . . . . 1·60 40
872 – 1z. blue . . . . 5·50 3·00
DESIGN—HORIZ: 1z. Soldier, airman and tank.

278 Steel Works

1954. 10th Anniv of Second Republic.
873 – 10g. sepia and brown . . 65 10
874 – 20g. green and red . . . 35 10
876 **278** 25g. black and buff . . . 1·00 45
877 – 40g. brown and yellow . . 45 15
878 – 45g. purple and mauve . . 45 15
880 – 60g. purple and green . . 40 25
881 – 1z.15 black and turquoise 6·00 15
882 – 1z.40 brown and orange 12·50 2·50
883 – 1z.55 blue and indigo . . 2·50 65
884 – 2z.10 blue and cobalt . . 3·50 1·25
DESIGNS: 10g. Coal mine; 20g. Soldier and flag; 40g. Worker on holiday; 45g. House-builders; 60g. Tractor and binder; 1z.15, Lublin Castle; 1z.40, Customers in bookshop; 1z.55, "Soldek" (freighter) alongside wharf; 2z.10, Battle of Lenino.

279 Steam Train and Signal **280** Picking Apples

1954. Railway Workers' Day.
885 **279** 40g. blue . . . . 3·00 60
886 – 60g. black . . . . 2·50 75
DESIGN: 60g. Steam night express.

1954. Polish–Russian Friendship.
887 **280** 40g. violet . . . . 1·60 1·10
888 60g. black 70 25

281 Elblag **282** Chopin and Grand Piano

1954. 500th Anniv of Return of Pomerania to Poland.
889 **281** 20g. red on blue . . . . 1·40 70
890 – 45g. brown on yellow . . 15 10
891 – 60g. green on yellow . . 20 10
892 – 1z.40 blue on pink . . . 50 10
893 – 1z.55 brown on cream . . 70 10
VIEWS: 45g. Gdansk; 60g. Torun; 1z.40, Malbork; 1z.55, Olsztyn.

1954. 5th International Chopin Piano Competition, Warsaw (1st issue).
894 **282** 45g. brown 25 10
895 60g. green 60 10
896 1z. blue . . . . 1·75 80
See also Nos. 906/7.

283 Battle Scene

1954. 160th Anniv of Kosciuszko's Insurrection.
897 **283** 40g. olive 45 10
898 – 60g. brown 60 10
899 – 1z.40 black . . . . 1·50 95
DESIGNS: 60g. Kosciuszko on horseback, with insurgents; 1z.40, Street battle.

284 European Bison **285** "The Liberator"

1954. Protected Animals.
900 **284** 45g. brown and green . . 35 10
901 – 60g. brown and green . . 35 10
902 – 1z.90 brown and blue . . 70 10
903 – 3z. brown and turquoise 1·10 55
ANIMALS: 60g. Elk; 1z.90, Chamois; 3z. Eurasian beaver.

1955. 10th Anniv of Liberation of Warsaw.
904 **285** 40g. brown . . . . 1·60 70
905 – 60g. blue . . . . 1·60 45
DESIGN: 60g. "Spirit of Poland".

286 Bust of Chopin (after L. Isler) **287** Mickiewicz Monument

1955. 5th International Chopin Piano Competition (2nd issue).
906 **286** 40g. brown 55 25
907 60g. blue . . . . 1·60 80

1955. Warsaw Monuments.
908 – 5g. green on yellow . . . 20 10
909 – 10g. purple on yellow . . 20 10
910 – 15g. black on green . . . 20 10
911 – 20g. blue on pink 20 10
912 – 40g. violet on lilac . . . 60 10
913 – 45g. brown on orange . . 1·25 25
914 **287** 60g. blue on grey 20 10
915 – 1z.55 green on grey . . . 1·90 25
MONUMENTS: 5g. "Siren"; 10g. Dzerzhinski Statue; 15g. King Sigismund III Statue; 20g. "Brotherhood in Arms"; 40g. Copernicus; 45g. Marie Curie Statue; 1z.55, Kilinski Statue.

288 Flags and Tower **289**

1955. 10th Anniv of Russo-Polish Treaty of Friendship.
916 **288** 40g. red 35 10
917 40g. brown 85 55
918 – 60g. brown 35 10
919 – 60g. turquoise 35 10
DESIGN: 60g. Statue of "Friendship".

1955. 8th International Peace Cycle Race.
920 **289** 40g. brown 45 25
921 – 60g. blue 25 10
DESIGN: 60g. "VIII" and doves.

290 Town Hall, Poznan **291** Festival Emblem

1955. 24th International Fair, Poznan.
922 **290** 40g. blue 25 25
923 60g. red 10 10

1955. Cracow Festival.
924 **291** 20g. multicoloured . . . 35 10
925 – 40g. multicoloured . . . 10 10
926 **291** 60g. multicoloured . . . 70 25
No. 925 is as T **291** but horiz and inscr "FESTIWAL SZTUKI", etc.

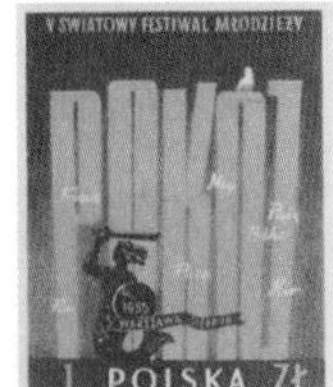

292 "Peace" **293** Motor Cyclists

1955. 5th International Youth Festival, Warsaw.
927 – 25g. brown, pink & yellow 25 10
928 – 40g. grey and blue . . . 25 10
929 – 45g. red, mauve and yellow 45 10
930 **292** 60g. ultramarine and blue 35 10
931 – 60g. black and orange . . 35 10
932 **292** 1z. purple and blue . . . 80 80
DESIGNS: 25, 45g. Pansies and dove; 40, 60g. (No. 931) Dove and tower.

1955. 13th International Tatra Mountains Motor Cycle Race.
933 **293** 40g. brown 25 25
934 60g. green 10 10

294 Stalin Palace of Culture and Science, Warsaw **295** Athletes

1955. Polish National Day.
935 **294** 60g. blue 10 10
936 60g. grey 10 10
937 75g. green 55 25
938 75g. brown 55 25

1955. 2nd International Games. Imperf or perf.
939 **295** 20g. brown 10 10
940 – 40g. purple 15 10
941 – 60g. blue 25 10
942 – 1z. red 45 10
943 – 1z.35 lilac 55 10
944 – 1z.55 green . . . . 1·10 80
DESIGNS—VERT: 40g. Throwing the hammer; 1z. Netball; 1z.35, Sculling; 1z.55, Swimming. HORIZ: 60g. Stadium.

296 Szczecin **297** Peasants and Flag

1955. 10th Anniv of Return of Western Territories.
945 **296** 25g. green 10 10
946 – 40g. red (Wroclaw) . . . 25 10
947 – 60g. blue (Zielona Gora) 55 10
948 – 95g. black (Opole) . . . . 1·50 60

1955. 50th Anniv of 1905 Revolution.
949 **297** 40g. brown 55 45
950 60g. red 25 25

298 Mickiewicz **299** Statue

1955. Death Cent of Adam Mickiewicz (poet).
951 **298** 20g. brown 20 10
952 **299** 40g. brown and orange 20 10
953 – 60g. brown and green . . 25 10
954 – 95g. black and red . . . 1·40 45
DESIGNS—As Type **299**: 60g. Sculptured head; 95g. Statue.

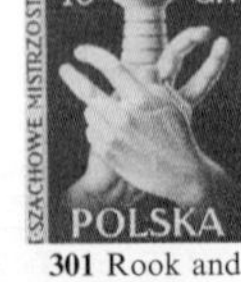

300 Teacher and Pupil **301** Rook and Hands

1955. 50th Anniv of Polish Teachers' Union.
955 **300** 40g. brown . . . . 1·60 35
956 – 60g. blue . . . . 2·75 80
DESIGN: 60g. Open book and lamp.

1956. 1st World Chess Championship for the Deaf and Dumb, Zakopane.
957 **301** 40g. red . . . . 2·25 80
958 – 60g. blue . . . . 1·40 10
DESIGN: 60g. Knight and hands.

302 Ice Skates **304** Racing Cyclist

303 Officer and "Kilinski" (freighter)

1956. 11th World Students' Winter Sports Championship.
959 **302** 20g. black and blue . . . 3·25 1·60
960 – 40g. blue and green . . . 80 10
961 – 60g. red and mauve . . . 80 10
DESIGNS: 40g. Ice-hockey sticks and puck; 60g. Skis and ski sticks.

1956. Merchant Navy.
962 **303** 5g. green 15 10
963 – 10g. red 20 10
964 – 20g. blue 25 10
965 – 45g. brown 90 55
966 – 60g. blue 20 55
DESIGNS: 10g. Tug and barges; 20g. "Pokoj" (freighter) in dock; 45g. Building "Marceii Nowatka" (freighter); 60g. "Fryderyk Chopin" (freighter) and "Radunia" (trawler).

1956. 9th International Peace Cycle Race.
967 **304** 40g. blue . . . . 1·10 70
968 60g. green 20 10

305 Lodge, Tatra Mountains **307** Ghetto Heroes' Monument

1956. Tourist Propaganda.
969 **305** 30g. green 10 10
970 – 40g. brown 10 10
971 – 60g. blue . . . . 1·60 60
972 – 1z.15 purple 55 10
DESIGNS: 40g. Compass, rucksack and map; 60g. Canoe and map; 1z.15, Skis and mountains.

1956. No. 829 surch.
973 10g. on 80g. purple 70 35
974 40g. on 80g. purple 45 10
975 60g. on 80g. purple 45 10
976 1z.35 on 80g. purple . . . . 2·25 1·00

1956. Warsaw Monuments.
977 **307** 30g. black 10 10
978 – 40g. brown on green . . . 70 35
979 – 1z.55 purple on pink . . . 55 10
STATUES: 40g. Statue of King Jan III Sobieski; 1z.55, Statue of Prince Joseph Poniatowski.

308 "Economic Co-operation" **309** Ludwika Wawrzynska (teacher)

1956. Russo-Polish Friendship Month.
980 – 40g. brown and pink . . . 45 35
981 **308** 60g. red and bistre . . . 25 10
DESIGN: 40g. Polish and Russian dancers.

1956. Ludwika Wawrzynska Commemoration.
982 **309** 40g. brown . . . . 95 1·50
983 60g. blue 35 10

310 "Lady with a Weasel" (Leonardo da Vinci) **311** Honey Bee and Hive

1956. International Campaign for Museums.
984 – 40g. green . . . . 2·25 1·40
985 – 60g. violet 95 10
986 **310** 1z.55 brown . . . . . . 1·90 25
DESIGNS: 40g. Niobe (bust); 60g. Madonna (Vit Stvosz).

1956. 50th Death Anniv of Jan Dzierzon (apiarist).
987 **311** 40g. brown on yellow . . 1·10 25
988 – 60g. brown on yellow . . 25 10
DESIGN: 60g. Dr. J. Dzierzon.

312 Fencing **313** 15th-century Postman

1956. Olympic Games. Inscr "MELBOURNE 1956".
989 **312** 10g. brown and grey . . . 20 10
990 – 20g. lilac and brown . . . 25 10
991 – 25g. black and blue . . . 70 25
992 – 40g. brown and green . . 35 10
993 – 60g. brown and red . . . 60 10
994 – 1z.55 brown and violet . . 2·75 1·10
995 – 1z.55 brown and orange 1·25 35
DESIGNS: No. 990, Boxing; 991, Rowing; 992, Steeplechase; 993, Javelin throwing; 994, Gymnastics; 995, Long jumping (Elizabeth Dunska-krzesinska's gold medal).

1956. Re-opening of Postal Museum, Wroclaw.
996 **313** 60g. black on blue . . . . 3·00 2·75

314 Snow Crystals and Skier of 1907 **315** Apple Tree and Globe

1957. 50 Years of Skiing in Poland.
997 **314** 40g. blue 20 10
998 – 60g. green 20 10
999 – 1z. purple 45 35
DESIGNS (with snow crystals)—VERT: 60g. Skier jumping. HORIZ: 1z. Skier standing.

1957. U.N.O. Commemoration.
1000 **315** 5g. red and turquoise . . 25 10
1001 – 15g. blue and grey . . . 45 10
1002 – 40g. green and grey . . 80 60
DESIGNS—VERT: 15g. U.N.O. emblem; 40g. U.N.O. Headquarters, New York.

316 Skier **317** Winged Letter

1957. 12th Death Annivs of Bronislaw Czech and Hanna Marusarzowna (skiers).
1003 **316** 60g. brown 90 35
1004 60g. blue 45 10

1957. Air. 7th Polish National Philatelic Exhibition, Warsaw.
1005 **317** 4z.+2z. blue . . . . . . 3·00 3·00

318 Foil, Sword and Sabre on Map **319** Dr. S. Petrycy (philosopher)

1957. World Youth Fencing Championships, Warsaw.
1006 **318** 40g. purple 45 10
1007 – 60g. red 20 10
1008 – 60g. blue 20 10
DESIGNS: Nos. 1007/8 are arranged in se-tenant pairs in the sheet and together show two fencers duelling.

1957. Polish Doctors.
1009 **319** 10g. brown and blue . . 10 10
1010 – 20g. lake and green . . . 10 10
1011 – 40g. black and red . . . 10 10
1012 – 60g. purple and blue . . 45 25
1013 – 1z. blue and yellow . . . 20 10
1014 – 1z.35 brown and green 15 10
1015 – 2z.50 violet and red . . 35 10
1016 – 3z. brown and violet . . 45 10
PORTRAITS: 20g. Dr. W. Oczko; 40g. Dr. J. Sniadecki; 60g. Dr. T. Chalubinski; 1z. Dr. W. Bieganski; 1z.35, Dr. J. Dietl; 2z.50, Dr. B. Dybowski; 3z. Dr. H. Jordan.

320 Cycle Wheel and Flower **321** Fair Emblem

1957. 10th International Peace Cycle Race.
1017 **320** 60g. blue 25 10
1018 – 1z.50 red (Cyclist) . . . 45 25

1957. 26th International Fair, Poznan.
1019 **321** 60g. blue 25 25
1020 2z.50 green 25 25

322 Carline Thistle **323** Fireman

1957. Wild Flowers.
1021 **322** 60g. yellow, green & grey 35 10
1022 – 60g. green and blue . . . 35 10
1023 – 60g. olive and grey . . . 35 10
1024 – 60g. purple and green . . 60 35
1025 – 60g. purple and green . . 35 10
FLOWERS—VERT: No. 1022, Sea holly; 1023, Edelweiss; 1024, Lady's slipper orchid; 1025, Turk's cap lily.

1957. International Fire Brigades Conference, Warsaw. Inscr "KONGRES C.T.I.F. WARSZAWA 1957".
1026 **323** 40g. black and red . . . 10 10
1027 – 60g. green and red . . . 10 10
1028 – 2z.50 violet and red . . 25 10
DESIGNS: 60g. Flames enveloping child; 2z.50, Ear of corn in flames.

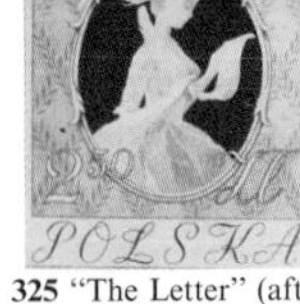

324 Town Hall, Leipzig **325** "The Letter" (after Fragonard)

1957. 4th Int Trade Union Congress, Leipzig.
1029 **324** 60g. violet 25 10

1957. Stamp Day.
1030 **325** 2z.50 green 60 10

326 Red Banner

327 Karol Libelt (founder)

1957. 40th Anniv of Russian Revolution.
1031 **326** 60g. red and blue . . . 10 10
1032 – 2z.50 brown and black 25 10
DESIGN: 2z.50, Lenin Monument, Poronin.

1957. Centenary of Poznan Scientific Society.
1033 **327** 60g. red 25 10

328 H. Wieniawski (violinist)
329 Ilyushin Il-14P over Steel Works

1957. 3rd Wieniawski Int Violin Competition.
1034 **328** 2z.50 blue 35 15

1957. Air.
1035 **329** 90g. black and pink . . 15 10
1036 – 1z.50 brown and salmon 15 10
1037 – 3z.40 sepia and buff . . 45 10
1038 – 3z.90 brown and yellow 90 60
1039 – 4z. blue and green . . . 45 10
1039a – 5z. lake and lavender 55 10
1039b – 10z. brown and turquoise 90 35
1040 – 15z. violet and blue . . 1·50 45
1040a – 20z. violet and yellow 1·60 80
1040b – 30z. olive and buff . . 2·75 1·10
1040c – 50z. blue and drab . . 8·25 1·10
DESIGNS—Ilyushin Il-14P over: 1z.50, Castle Square, Warsaw; 3z.40, Market, Cracow; 3z.90, Szczecin; 4z. Karkonosze Mountains; 5z. Old Market, Gdansk; 10z. Liw Castle; 15z. Lublin; 20z. Cable railway, Kasprowy Wierch; 30z. Porabka Dam; 50z. "Batory" (liner).
For stamp as No. 1039b, but printed in purple only, see No.1095.

330a J. A. Komensky (Comenius)

331 A. Strug

1957. 300th Anniv of Publication of Komensky's "Opera Didactica Omnia".
1041 **330a** 2z.50 red 35 10

1957. 20th Death Anniv of Andrzej Strug (writer).
1042 **331** 2z.50 brown 25 10

332 Joseph Conrad and Full-rigged Sailing Ship "Torrens"

1957. Birth Centenary of Joseph Conrad (Korzeniowski) (author).
1043 **332** 60g. brown on green . . 10 10
1044 2z.50 blue on pink . . . 50 10

333 Postman of 1558

334 Town Hall, Biecz

1958. 400th Anniv of Polish Postal Service (1st issue).
1045 **333** 2z.50 purple and blue . . 35 10
For similar stamps see Nos. 1063/7.

1958. Ancient Polish Town Halls.
1046 **334** 20g. green 10 10
1047 – 40g. brown (Wroclaw) 10 10
1048 – 60g. blue (Tarnow) (horiz) 10 10
1049 – 2z.10 lake (Gdansk) . . 15 10
1050 – 2z.50 violet (Zamosc) . . 55 35

335 Zander

336 Warsaw University

1958. Fishes.
1051 **335** 40g. yellow, black & blue 15 10
1052 – 60g. blue, indigo & green 25 10
1053 – 2z.10 multicoloured . . . 45 10
1054 – 2z.50 green, black & violet . . . . 1·50 45
1055 – 6z.40 multicoloured . . . 45 45
DESIGNS—VERT: 60g. Atlantic salmon; 2z.10, Northern pike; 2z.50, Brown trout. HORIZ 6z.40, European grayling.

1958. 140th Anniv of Warsaw University.
1056 **336** 2z.50 blue 35 10

337 Fair Emblem

338

1958. 27th International Fair, Poznan.
1057 **337** 2z.50 red and black . . . 35 10

1958. 7th International Gliding Championships.
1058 **338** 60g. black and blue . . . 10 10
1059 – 2z.50 black and grey . . 25 10
DESIGN: 2z.50, As Type **338** but design in reverse.

339 Armed Postman

340 Polar Bear on Iceberg

1958. 19th Anniv of Defence of Gdansk Post Office.
1060 **339** 60g. blue 10 10

1958. I.G.Y. Inscr as in T **340**.
1061 **340** 60g. black 15 10
1062 – 2z.50 blue 70 10
DESIGN: 2z.50, Sputnik and track of rocket.

341 Tomb of Prosper Prowano (First Polish Postmaster)

342 Envelope, Quill and Postmark

1958. 400th Anniv of Polish Postal Service (2nd issue).
1063 **341** 40g. purple and blue . . 55 10
1064 – 60g. black and lilac . . . 15 10
1065 – 95g. violet and yellow . . 15 10
1066 – 2z.10 blue and grey . . . 80 45
1067 – 3z.40 brown & turquoise 55 35
DESIGNS: 60g. Mail coach and Church of Our Lady, Cracow; 95g. Mail coach (rear view); 2z.10, 16th-century postman; 3z.40, Kogge.
Nos. 1064/7 show various forms of modern transport in clear silhouette in the background.

1958. Stamp Day.
1068 **342** 60g. green, red and black 55 55

343 Partisans' Cross

345 Galleon

344 "Mail Coach in the Kielce District" (after painting by A. Kedzierskiego)

1958. 15th Anniv of Polish People's Army. Polish decorations.
1069 **343** 40g. buff, black and green 15 10
1070 – 60g. multicoloured . . . 15 10
1071 – 2z.50 multicoloured . . . 55 25
DESIGNS: 60g. Virtuti Military Cross; 2z.50, Grunwald Cross.

1958. Polish Postal Service 400th Anniv Exhibition.
1072 **344** 2z.50 black on buff . . . 90 1·10

1958. 350th Anniv of Polish Emigration to America.
1073 **345** 60g. green 25 10
1074 – 2z.50 red (Polish emigrants) 45 55

346 UNESCO Headquarters, Paris

347 S. Wyspianski (dramatist and painter)

1958. Inauguration of UNESCO Headquarters Building, Paris.
1075 **346** 2z.50 black and green . . 70 55

1958. Famous Poles.
1076 **347** 60g. violet 10 10
1077 – 2z.50 green 25 35
PORTRAIT: 2z.50, S. Moniuszko (composer).

348 "Human Rights"

349 Party Flag

1958. 10th Anniv of Declaration of Human Rights.
1078 **348** 2z.50 lake and brown . . 60 10

1958. 40th Anniv of Polish Communist Party.
1079 **349** 60g. red and purple . . . 10 10

350 Yacht

351 The "Guiding Hand"

1959. Sports.
1080 **350** 40g. ultramarine and blue 35 10
1081 – 60g. purple and salmon 35 10
1082 – 95g. purple and green . . 70 25
1083 – 2z. blue and green . . . 35 10
DESIGNS: 60g. Archer; 95g. Footballers; 2z. Horseman.

1959. 3rd Polish United Workers' Party Congress.
1084 **351** 40g. black, brown and red 10 10
1085 – 60g. multicoloured . . . 10 10
1086 – 1z.55 multicoloured . . . 45 25
DESIGNS—HORIZ: 60g. Hammer and ears of corn. VERT: 1z.55, Nowa Huta foundry.

352 Death Cap

1959. Mushrooms.
1087 **352** 20g. yellow, brown & green . . . . 2·25 10
1088 – 30g. multicoloured . . . 25 10
1089 – 40g. multicoloured . . . 55 10
1090 – 60g. multicoloured . . . 55 10
1091 – 1z. multicoloured 80 10
1092 – 2z.50 brown, green & bl 1·10 25
1093 – 3z.40 multicoloured . . . 1·25 35
1094 – 5z.60 brown, grn & yell 3·50 1·10
MUSHROOMS: 30g. Butter mushroom; 40g. Cep; 60g. Saffron milk cap; 1z. Chanterelle; 2z.50, Field mushroom; 3z.40, Fly agaric; 5z.60, Brown beech bolete.

1959. Air. 65 Years of Philately in Poland and 6th Polish Philatelic Assn Congress, Warsaw. As No. 1039b but in one colour only.
1095 10z. purple . . . . 3·25 3·75

353 "Storks" (after Chelmonski)

354 Miner

1959. Polish Paintings.
1096 **353** 40g. green 15 10
1097 – 60g. purple 35 10
1098 – 1z. black 35 10
1099 – 1z.50 brown 70 25
1100 – 6z.40 blue . . . . 3·25 1·10
PAINTINGS—VERT: 60g. "Motherhood" (Wyspianski); 1z. "Madame de Romanet" (Rodakowski); 1z.50, "Death" (Maiczewski). HORIZ: 6z.40, "The Sandmen" (Gierymski).

1959. 3rd Int Miners' Congress, Katowice.
1101 **354** 2z.50 multicoloured . . . 60 25

355 Sheaf of Wheat ("Agriculture")

356 Dr. L. Zamenhof

1959. 15th Anniv of People's Republic.
1102 **355** 40g. green and black . . 10 10
1103 – 60g. red and black . . . 10 10
1104 – 1z.50 blue and black . . 20 10
DESIGNS: 60g. Crane ("Building"); 1z.50, Corinthian column, and book ("Culture and Science").

1959. International Esperanto Congress, Warsaw and Birth Centenary of Dr. Ludwig Zamenhof (inventor of Esperanto).
1105 **356** 60g. black & green on green 15 10
1106 – 1z.50 green, red and violet on grey 80 35
DESIGN: 1z.50, Esperanto Star and globe.

357 "Flowering Pink" (Map of Austria)

358

1959. 7th World Youth Festival, Vienna.
1107 **357** 60g. multicoloured . . . 10 10
1108 2z.50 multicoloured . . . 45 45

1959. 30th Anniv of Polish Airlines "LOT".
1109 **358** 60g. blue, violet and black 15 10

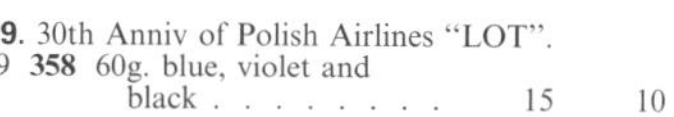

359 Parliament House, Warsaw

1959. 48th Inter-Parliamentary Union Conf, Warsaw.
1110 **359** 60g. green, red and black 10 10
1111 2z.50 purple, red & black 55 35

1959. Baltic States' International Philatelic Exhibition, Gdansk. No. 890 optd **BALPEX I - GDANSK 1959**.
1112 45g. brown on lemon . . . 70 70

361 Dove and Globe 362 Nurse with Bag

1959. 10th Anniv of World Peace Movement.
1113 **361** 60g. grey and blue . . . 20 10

1959. 40th Anniv of Polish Red Cross. Cross in red.
1114 **362** 40g. black and green . . 20 10
1115 – 60g. brown 20 10
1116 – 2z.50 black and red . . . 90 45
DESIGNS—VERT: 60g. Nurse with bottle and bandages. SQUARE—23 × 23 mm: 2z.50, J. H. Dunant.

363 Emblem of Polish–Chinese Friendship Society 364

1959. Polish–Chinese Friendship.
1117 **363** 60g. multicoloured . . . 45 10
1118 2z.50 multicoloured . . . 25 10

1959. Stamp Day.
1119 **364** 60g. red, green & turq 15 10
1120 2z.50 blue, green and red 25 10

365 Sputnik "3"

1959. Cosmic Flights.
1121 **365** 40g. black and blue . . . 15 10
1122 – 60g. black and lake . . . 25 10
1123 – 2z.50 blue and green . . 1·10 60
DESIGNS: 60g. Rocket "Mieczta" encircling Sun; 2z.50, Moon rocket "Lunik 2".

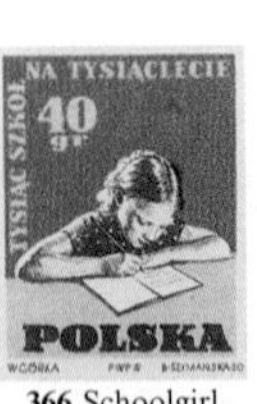

366 Schoolgirl 367 Darwin

1959. "1000 Schools for Polish Millennium". Inscr as in T **366**.
1124 **366** 40g. brown and green . . 15 10
1125 – 60g. red, black and blue 15 10
DESIGN: 60g. Children going to school.

1959. Famous Scientists.
1126 **367** 20g. blue 10 10
1127 – 40g. olive (Mendeleev) 10 10
1128 – 60g. purple (Einstein) . . 15 10
1129 – 1z.50 brown (Pasteur) . . 25 10
1130 – 1z.55 green (Newton) . . 55 10
1131 – 2z.50 violet (Copernicus) 90 70

368 Costumes of Rzeszow 369 Costumes of Rzeszow

1959. Provincial Costumes (1st series).
1132 **368** 20g. black and green . . 10 10
1133 **369** 20g. black and green . . 10 10
1134 – 60g. brown and pink . . 15 10
1135 – 60g. brown and pink . . 15 10
1136 – 1z. red and blue 15 10
1137 – 1z. red and blue 15 10
1138 – 2z.50 green and grey . . 35 10
1139 – 2z.50 green and grey . . 35 10
1140 – 5z.60 blue and yellow . . 1·40 55
1141 – 5z.60 blue and yellow . . 1·40 55
DESIGNS—Male and female costumes of: Nos. 1134/5, Kurpic; 1136/7, Silesia; 1138/9, Mountain regions; 1140/1, Szamotuly.
See also Nos. 1150/9.

370 Piano 371 Polish 10k. Stamp of 1860 and Postmark

1960. 150th Birth Anniv of Chopin and Chopin Music Competition, Warsaw.
1142 **370** 60g. black and violet . . 45 10
1143 – 1z.50 black, red and blue 70 10
1144 – 2z.50 brown . . . . . . 2·25 1·50
DESIGNS—As Type **370**: 1z.50, Portion of Chopin's music. 25 × 39½ mm: 2z.50, Portrait of Chopin.

1960. Stamp Centenary.
1145 **371** 40g. red, blue and black 15 10
1146 – 60g. blue, black and violet 25 10
1147 – 1z.35 blue, red and grey 70 45
1148 – 1z.55 red, black & green 80 35
1149 – 2z.50 green, black & ol 1·40 70
DESIGNS: 1z.35, Emblem inscr "1860 1960". Reproductions of Polish stamps: 60g. No. 356; 1z.55, No. 533; 2z.50, No. 1030. With appropriate postmarks.

1960. Provincial Costumes (2nd series). As T **368/69**.
1150 40g. red and blue 10 10
1151 40g. red and blue 10 10
1152 2z. blue and yellow 15 10
1153 2z. blue and yellow 15 10
1154 3z.10 turquoise and green 25 10
1155 3z.10 turquoise and green 25 10
1156 3z.40 brown and turquoise 35 25
1157 3z.40 brown and turquoise 35 25
1158 6z.50 violet and green . . . 1·10 45
1159 6z.50 violet and green . . . 1·10 45
DESIGNS—Male and female costumes of: Nos. 1150/1, Cracow; 1152/3, Lowicz; 1154/5, Kujawy; 1156/7, Lublin; 1158/9, Lubusz.

372 Throwing the Discus 373 King Wladislaw Jagiello's Tomb, Wawel Castle

1960. Olympic Games, Rome. Rings and inscr in black.
1160 60g. blue (T **372**) 15 10
1161 60g. mauve (Running) . . . 15 10
1162 60g. violet (Cycling) 15 10
1163 60g. turq (Show jumping) 15 10
1164 2z.50 blue (Trumpeters) . . 70 35
1165 2z.50 brown (Boxing) . . . 70 35
1166 2z.50 red (Olympic flame) 70 35
1167 2z.50 green (Long jump) . . 70 35
Stamps of the same value were issued together, se-tenant, forming composite designs illustrating a complete circuit of the stadium track.

1960. 550th Anniv of Battle of Grunwald.
1168 **373** 60g. brown 25 10
1169 – 90g. green 60 35
1170 – 2z.50 black . . . . . . 2·75 1·50
DESIGNS—As Type **373**: 90g. Proposed Grunwald Monument. HORIZ: 78 × 35½ mm: 2z.50, "Battle of Grunwald" (after Jan Matejko).

374 1860 Stamp and Postmark 375 Lukasiewicz (inventor of petrol lamp)

1960. International Philatelic Exn, Warsaw.
1171 **374** 10z.+10z. red, black and blue . . . . 6·25 8·00

1960. Lukasiewicz Commemoration and 5th Pharmaceutical Congress. Poznan.
1172 **375** 60g. black and yellow . . 15 10

376 "The Annunciation" 377 Paderewski

1960. Altar Wood Carvings of St. Mary's Church, Cracow, by Veit Stoss.
1173 **376** 20g. blue 25 10
1174 – 30g. brown 15 10
1175 – 40g. violet 25 10
1176 – 60g. green 25 10
1177 – 2z.50 red . . . . 1·10 25
1178 – 5z.60 brown . . . . . . 4·25 4·75
DESIGNS: 30g. "The Nativity"; 40g. "Homage of the Three Kings"; 60g. "The Resurrection"; 2z.50, "The Ascension"; 5z.60, "The Descent of the Holy Ghost".

1960. Birth Centenary of Paderewski.
1179 **377** 2z.50 black 35 35

1960. Stamp Day. Optd **DZIEN ZNACZKA 1960**.
1180 **371** 40g. red, blue and black 1·25 70

379 Gniezno 380 Great Bustard

1960. Old Polish Towns as T **379**.
1181 5g. brown 10 10
1182 10g. green 10 10
1183 20g. brown 10 10
1184 40g. red 10 10
1185 50g. violet 10 10
1186 60g. lilac 10 10
1187 60g. blue 10 10
1188 80g. blue 15 10
1189 90g. brown 15 10
1190 95g. green 35 10
1191 1z. red and lilac 15 10
1192 1z.15 green and orange . . 35 10
1193 1z.35 mauve and green . . . 15 10
1194 1z.50 brown and blue . . . 35 10
1195 1z.55 lilac and yellow . . . 35 10
1196 2z. blue and lilac 20 10
1197 2z.10 brown and yellow . . 20 10
1198 2z.50 violet and green . . . 25 10
1199 3z.10 red and grey 35 35
1200 5z.60 grey and green 60 35
TOWNS: 10g. Cracow; 20g. Warsaw; 40g. Poznan; 50g. Plock; 60g. mauve, Kalisz; 60g. blue, Tczew; 80g. Frombork; 90g. Torum; 95g. Puck; 1z. Slupsk; 1z.15, Gdansk; 1z.35, Wroclaw; 1z.50, Szczecin; 1z.55, Opole; 2z. Kolobrzeg; 2z.10, Legnica; 2z.50, Katowice; 3z.10, Lodz; 5z.60, Walbrzych.

1960. Birds. Multicoloured.
1201 10g. Type **380** 10 10
1202 20g. Common Raven . . . 10 10
1203 30g. Great cormorant . . . 10 10
1204 40g. Black stork 25 10
1205 50g. Eagle owl 55 10
1206 60g. White-tailed sea eagle 55 10
1207 75g. Golden eagle 55 10
1208 90g. Short-toed eagle . . . 60 35
1209 2z.50 Rock thrush . . . . 3·25 1·75
1210 4z. River kingfisher . . . . 2·75 1·25
1211 5z.60 Wallcreeper . . . . . 4·50 1·40
1212 6z.50 European roller . . . 6·50 3·25

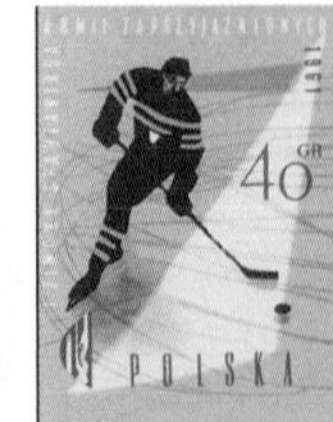

381 Front page of Newspaper "Proletaryat" (1883) 382 Ice Hockey

1961. 300th Anniv of Polish Newspaper Press.
1213 – 40g. green, blue and black 55 25
1214 **381** 60g. yellow, red and black 55 25
1215 – 2z.50 blue, violet & black . . . . 3·25 2·75
DESIGNS—Newspaper front page: 40g. "Mercuriusz" (first issue, 1661); 2z.50, "Rzeczpospolita" (1944).

1961. 1st Winter Military Spartakiad.
1216 **382** 40g. black, yellow & lilac 35 10
1217 – 60g. multicoloured . . . 95 15
1218 – 1z. multicoloured . . . . 5·25 2·75
1219 – 1z.50 black, yell & turq 90 35
DESIGNS: 60g. Ski jumping; 1z. Rifle-shooting; 1z.50, Slalom.

383 Congress Emblem 384 Yuri Gagarin

1961. 4th Polish Engineers' Conference.
1220 **383** 60g. black and red . . . 15 10

1961. World's 1st Manned Space Flight.
1221 **384** 40g. black, red and brown 60 10
1222 – 60g. red, black and blue 60 35
DESIGN: 60g. Globe and star.

385 Fair Emblem

1961. 30th International Fair, Poznan.
1223 **385** 40g. black, red and blue 10 10
1224 1z.50 black, blue and red 25 10

386 King Mieszko I

1961. Famous Poles (1st issue).
1225 **386** 60g. black and blue . . . 10 10
1226 – 60g. black and red . . . 10 10
1227 – 60g. black and green . . 10 10
1228 – 60g. black and violet . . 80 25
1229 – 60g. black and brown . . 10 10
1230 – 60g. black and olive . . 10 10
PORTRAITS: No. 1226, King Casimire the Great; 1227, King Casmir Jagiellon; 1228, Copernicus; 1229, A. F. Modrzewski; 1230, Kosciuszko.
See also Nos. 1301/6 and 1398/1401.

387 "Leskov" (trawler support ship)

1961. Shipbuilding Industry. Multicoloured.
1231 60g. Type **387** 25 10
1232 1z.55 "Severodvinsk" (depot ship) 35 10
1233 2z.50 "Rambutan" (coaster) 60 35
1234 3z.40 "Krynica" (freighter) 90 45
1235 4z. "B 54" freighter . . . . 1·25 70
1236 5z.60 "Bavsk" (tanker) . . . 4·25 1·90
SIZES: 2z.50, As Type **387**; 5z.60, 108 × 21 mm; Rest, 81 × 21 mm.

388 Posthorn and Telephone Dial 389 Opole Seal

1961. Communications Ministers' Conference, Warsaw.
1237 **388** 40g. red, green and blue 10 10
1238 – 60g. violet, yellow & purple 15 10
1239 – 2z.50 ultram, blue & bis 55 10
DESIGNS: 60g. Posthorn and radar screen; 2z.50, Posthorn and conference emblem.

1961. Polish Western Provinces.
1240 40g. brown on buff 15 10
1241 40g. brown on buff 15 10
1242 60g. violet on pink 15 10
1243 60g. violet on pink 15 10

1243a 95g. green on blue 25 25
1243b 95g. green on blue 25 25
1244 2z.50 sage on green . . . 45 25
1245 2z.50 sage on green . . . 45 25
DESIGNS—VERT: No. 1240, Type **389**; 1242, Henry IV's tomb; 1243a, Seal of Conrad II; 1244, Prince Barnim's seal. HORIZ: No. 1241, Opole cement works; 1243, Wroclaw apartment-house, 1243b, Factory interior, Zielona Gora; 1245, Szczecin harbour.
See also Nos. 1308/13.

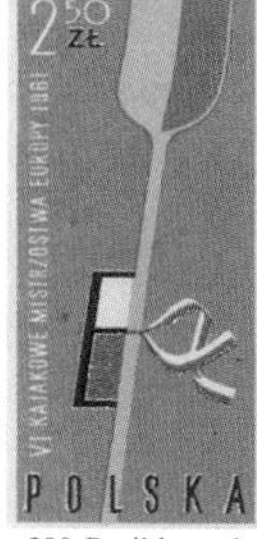

390 Beribboned Paddle

391 Titov and Orbit within Star

1961. 6th European Canoeing Championships. Multicoloured.
1246 40g. Two canoes within letter "E" (horiz) 15 10
1247 60g. Two four-seater canoes at finishing post (horiz) 15 10
1248 2z.50 Type **390** . . . . . . 1·25 60

1961. 2nd Russian Manned Space Flight.
1249 **391** 40g. black, red and pink 45 10
1250 – 60g. blue and black . . . 45 10
DESIGN: 60g. Dove and spaceman's orbit around globe.

392 Monument

393 P.K.O. Emblem and Ant

1961. 40th Anniv of 3rd Silesian Uprising.
1251 **392** 60g. grey and green . . 10 10
1252 – 1z.55 grey and blue . . 25 10
DESIGN: 1z.55, Cross of Silesian uprisers.

1961. Savings Month.
1253 – 40g. red, yellow and black 15 10
1254 **393** 60g. brown, yellow & black 15 10
1255 – 60g. blue, violet and pink 15 10
1256 – 60g. green, red and black 15 10
1257 – 2z.50 mauve, grey & black . . . . 2·25 1·25
DESIGNS: No. 1253, Savings Bank motif; 1255, Bee; 1256, Squirrel; 1257, Savings Bank book.

394 "Mail Cart" (after J. Chelmonski)

1961. Stamp Day and 40th Anniv of Postal Museum.
1258 **394** 60g. brown 25 10
1259 60g. green 25 10

395 Congress Emblem

396 Emblem of Kopasyni Mining Family, 1284

1961. 5th W.F.T.U. Congress, Moscow.
1260 **395** 60g. black 15 10

1961. Millenary of Polish Mining Industry.
1261 **396** 40g. purple and orange 15 10
1262 – 60g. grey and blue . . . 15 10
1263 – 2z.50 green and black . . 55 25
DESIGNS: 60g. 14th-century seal of Bytom; 2z.50, Emblem of Int Mine Constructors' Congress, Warsaw, 1958.

397 Child and Syringe

398 Cogwheel and Wheat

1961. 15th Anniv of UNICEF.
1264 **397** 40g. black and blue . . . 10 10
1265 – 60g. black and orange 10 10
1266 – 2z.50 black and turquoise 60 25
DESIGNS—HORIZ: 60g. Children of three races. VERT: 2z.50, Mother and child, and feeding bottle.

1961. 15th Economic Co-operative Council Meeting, Warsaw.
1267 **398** 40g. red, yellow and blue 15 10
1268 – 60g. red, blue & ultram 15 10
DESIGN: 60g. Oil pipeline map, E. Europe.

399 Caterpillar-hunter

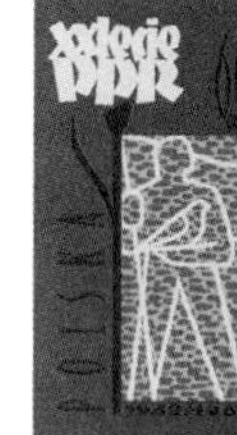

400 Worker with Flag and Dove

1961. Insects. Multicoloured.
1269 20g. Type **399** 15 10
1270 30g. Violet ground beetle . . 15 10
1271 40g. Alpine longhorn beetle 15 10
1272 50g. "Cerambyx cerdo" (longhorn beetle) 15 10
1273 60g. "Carabus auronitens" (ground beetle) 15 10
1274 80g. Stag beetle 25 10
1275 1z.15 Clouded apollo (butterfly) 55 10
1276 1z.35 Death's-head hawk moth 35 10
1277 1z.50 Scarce swallowtail (butterfly) 60 10
1278 1z.55 Apollo (butterfly) . . 60 10
1279 2z.50 Red wood ant . . . . 1·10 45
1280 5z.60 White-tailed bumble bee . . . . 5·75 3·50
Nos. 1275/80 are square, $36\frac{1}{2} \times 36\frac{1}{2}$ mm.

1962. 20th Anniv of Polish Workers' Coalition.
1281 **400** 60g. brown, black and red 10 10
1282 – 60g. bistre, black and red 10 10
1283 – 60g. blue, black and red 10 10
1284 – 60g. grey, black and red 10 10
1285 – 60g. blue, black and red 10 10
DESIGNS: No. 1282, Steersman; 1283, Worker with hammer; 1284, Soldier with weapon; 1285, Worker with trowel and rifle.

401 Two Skiers Racing

1962. F.I.S. Int Ski Championships, Zakopane.
1286 **401** 40g. blue, grey and red 10 10
1287 40g. blue, brown and red 90 25
1288 – 60g. blue, grey and red 20 10
1289 – 60g. blue, brown and red 1·10 60
1290 – 1z.50 blue, grey and red 35 10
1291 – 1z.50 violet, grey and red 1·75 60
DESIGNS—HORIZ: 60g. Skier racing. VERT: 1z.50, Ski jumper.

402 Majdanek Monument

1962. Concentration Camp Monuments.
1292 – 40g. blue 10 10
1293 **402** 60g. black 25 10
1294 – 1z.50 violet 35 15
DESIGNS—VERT: (20 × 31 mm): 40g. Broken carnations and portion of prison clothing (Auschwitz camp); 1z.50, Treblinka monument.

403 Racing Cyclist

1962. 15th International Peace Cycle Race.
1295 **403** 60g. black and blue . . . 25 10
1296 – 2z.50 black and yellow 55 10
1297 – 3z.40 black and violet . . 90 45
DESIGNS—$74\frac{1}{2} \times 22$ mm: 2z.50, Cyclists & "XV". As Type **403**: 3z.40, Arms of Berlin, Prague and Warsaw, and cycle wheel.

405 Lenin Walking

406 Gen. K. Swierczewski-Walter (monument)

1962. 50th Anniv of Lenin's Sojourn in Poland.
1298 **405** 40g. green and light green 45 10
1299 – 60g. lake and pink . . . 15 10
1300 – 2z.50 brown and yellow 45 10
DESIGNS: 60g. Lenin; 2z.50, Lenin wearing cap, and St. Mary's Church, Cracow.

1962. Famous Poles (2nd issue). As T **386**.
1301 60g. black and green 10 10
1302 60g. black and brown . . . 10 10
1303 60g. black and blue 40 10
1304 60g. black and bistre . . . 10 10
1305 60g. black and purple . . 10 10
1306 60g. black and turquoise . . 10 10
PORTRAITS: No. 1301, A. Mickiewicz (poet); 1302, J. Slowacki (poet); 1303, F. Chopin (composer); 1304, R. Traugutt (patriot); 1305, J. Dabrowski (revolutionary); 1306, Maria Konopnicka (poet).

1962. 15th Death Anniv of Gen. K. Swierczewski-Walter (patriot).
1307 **406** 60g. black 15 10

1962. Polish Northern Provinces. As T **389**.
1308 60g. blue and grey 10 10
1309 60g. blue and grey 10 10
1310 1z.55 brown and yellow . . 20 10
1311 1z.55 brown and yellow . . 20 10
1312 2z.50 slate and grey 55 35
1313 2z.50 slate and grey 55 35
DESIGNS—VERT: No. 1308, Princess Elizabeth's seal; 1310, Gdansk Governor's seal; 1312, Frombork Cathedral. HORIZ: No. 1309, Insulators factory, Szczecinek; 1311, Gdansk shipyard; 1313, Laboratory of Agricultural College, Kortowo.

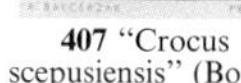

407 "Crocus scepusiensis" (Borb)

408 "The Poison Well", after J. Malczewski

1962. Polish Protected Plants. Plants in natural colours.
1314 **407** 60g. yellow 15 10
1315 A 60g. brown 70 35
1316 B 60g. pink 15 10
1317 C 90g. green 25 10
1318 D 90g. olive 25 10
1319 E 90g. green 25 10
1320 F 1z.50 blue 35 10
1321 G 1z.50 green 45 10
1322 H 1z.50 turquoise 35 10
1323 I 2z.50 green 80 55
1324 J 2z.50 turquoise 80 55
1325 K 2z.50 blue . . . . 1·10 55
PLANTS: A, "Platanthera bifolia" (Rich); B, "Aconitum callibotryon" (Rchb.); C, "Gentiana clusii" (Perr. et Song); D, "Dictamnus albus" (L.); E, "Nymphaca alba" (L.); F, "Daphne mezereum" (L.); G, "Pulsatilla vulgaris" (Mill.); H, "Anemone silvestris" (L.); I, "Trollius europaeus" (L.); J, "Galanthus nivalis" (L.); K, "Adonis vernalis" (L.).

1962. F.I.P. Day ("Federation Internationale de Philatelie").
1326 **408** 60g. black on cream . . 25 25

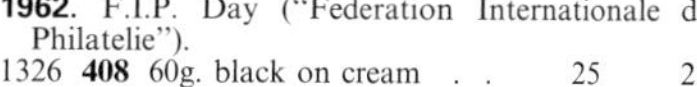

409 Pole Vault

1962. 7th European Athletic Championships, Belgrade. Multicoloured.
1327 40g. Type **409** 10 10
1328 60g. 400 m relay 10 10
1329 90g. Throwing the javelin 10 10
1330 1z. Hurdling 10 10
1331 1z.50 High-jumping 10 10
1332 1z.55 Throwing the discus 10 10
1333 2z.50 100 m final 45 15
1334 3z.40 Throwing the hammer 95 35

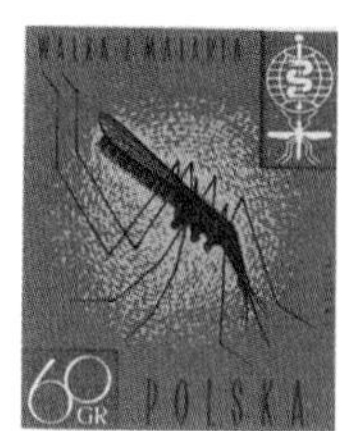

410 "Anopheles sp."

411 Cosmonauts "in flight"

1962. Malaria Eradication.
1335 **410** 60g. brown and turquoise 10 10
1336 – 1z.50 multicoloured . . . 15 10
1337 – 2z.50 multicoloured . . . 60 25
DESIGNS: 1z.50, Malaria parasites in blood; 2z.50, Cinchona plant.

1962. 1st "Team" Manned Space Flight.
1338 **411** 60g. green, black & violet 15 10
1339 – 2z.50 red, black and turquoise 45 25
DESIGN: 2z.50, Two stars (representing space-ships) in orbit.

412 "A Moment of Determination" (after painting by A. Kamienski)

413 Mazovian Princes' Mansion, Warsaw

1962. Stamp Day.
1340 **412** 60g. black 10 10
1341 2z.50 brown 45 20

1962. 25th Anniv of Polish Democratic Party.
1342 **413** 60g. black on red . . . 15 10

414 Cruiser "Aurora"

1962. 45th Anniv of Russian Revolution.
1343 **414** 60g. blue and red . . . 15 10

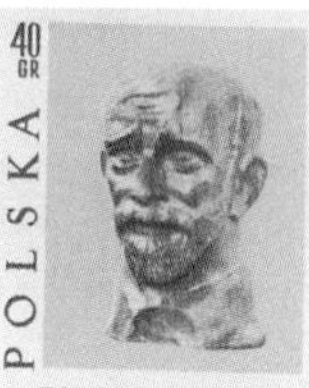

415 J. Korczak (bust after Dunikowski)

1962. 20th Death Anniv of Janusz Korczak (child educator).
1344 **415** 40g. sepia, bistre & brn 15 10
1345 – 60g. multicoloured . . . 35 10
1346 – 90g. multicoloured . . . 35 10
1347 – 1z. multicoloured 35 10
1348 – 2z.50 multicoloured . . . 70 10
1349 – 5z.60 multicoloured . . . 2·40 40
DESIGNS: 60g. to 5z.60, Illustrations from Korczak's children's books.

416 Old Town, Warsaw

1962. 5th T.U. Congress, Warsaw.
1350 **416** 3z.40 multicoloured . . . 70 25

417 Master Buncombe

419 Tractor and Wheat

418 R. Traugutt (insurgent leader)

1962. Maria Konopnicka's Fairy Tale "The Dwarfs and Orphan Mary". Multicoloured.
1351 40g. Type **417** 45 10
1352 60g. Lardie the Fox and Master Buncombe . . . . 1·40 1·00
1353 1z.50 Bluey the Frog making music 55 10
1354 1z.55 Peter's kitchen 55 25
1355 2z.50 Saraband's concert in Nightingale Valley 70 70
1356 3z.40 Orphan Mary and Subearthy . . . . 2·25 1·00

1963. Centenary of January (1863) Rising.
1357 **418** 60g. black, pink & turq 15 10

1963. Freedom from Hunger. Multicoloured.
1358 40g. Type **419** 15 10
1359 60g. Millet and hoeing . . . 80 25
1360 2z.50 Rice and mechanical harvester 70 35

420 Cocker Spaniel

1963. Dogs.
1361 **420** 20g. red, black and lilac 10 10
1362 – 30g. black and red . . . 10 10
1363 – 40g. ochre, black and lilac 25 10
1364 – 50g. ochre, black and blue 25 10
1365 – 60g. black and blue . . . 25 10
1366 – 1z. black and green . . . 70 25
1367 – 2z.50 brown, yell & blk 1·10 45
1368 – 3z.40 black and red . . . 3·00 1·40
1369 – 6z.50 black and yellow 6·00 3·75
DOGS—HORIZ: 30g. Sheep-dog; 40g. Boxer; 2z.50, Gun-dog "Ogar"; 6z.50, Great Dane. VERT: 50g. Airedale terrier; 60g. French bulldog; 1z. French poodle; 3z.40, Podhale sheep-dog.

421 Egyptian Galley (15th century B.C.)

422 Insurgent

1963. Sailing Ships (1st series).
1370 **421** 5g. brown on bistre . . . 10 10
1371 – 10g. turquoise on green 15 10
1372 – 20g. blue on grey . . . 15 10
1373 – 30g. black on olive . . . 20 10
1374 – 40g. blue on blue 20 10
1375 – 60g. purple on brown . . 35 10
1376 – 1z. black on blue 40 10
1377 – 1z.15 green on pink . . 65 10
SHIPS: 10g. Phoenician merchantman (15th cent B.C.); 20g. Greek trireme (5th cent B.C.); 30g. Roman merchantman (3rd cent A.D.); 40g. "Mora" (Norman ship, 1066); 60g. Hanse kogge (14th cent); 1z. Hulk (16th cent); 1z.15, Carrack (15th cent).
See also Nos. 1451/66.

1963. 20th Anniv of Warsaw Ghetto Uprising.
1378 **422** 2z.50 brown and blue . . 30 10

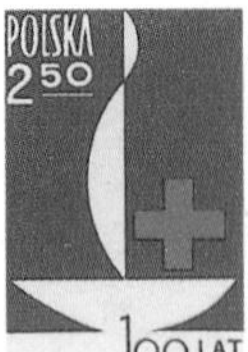

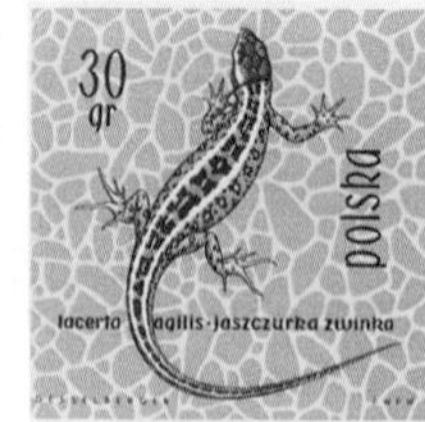

423 Centenary Emblem

424 Lizard

1963. Red Cross Centenary.
1379 **423** 2z.50 red, blue and yellow 65 20

1963. Protected Reptiles and Amphibians. Reptiles in natural colours: inscr in black: background colours given.
1380 **424** 30g. green 10 10
1381 – 40g. olive 10 10
1382 – 50g. brown 10 10
1383 – 60g. grey 10 10
1384 – 90g. green 10 10
1385 – 1z.15 grey 10 10
1386 – 1z.35 blue 10 10
1387 – 1z.50 turquoise 30 15
1388 – 1z.55 pale blue 30 10
1389 – 2z.50 lavender 30 20
1390 – 3z. green 75 20
1391 – 3z.40 purple . . . . . . 1·90 1·90
DESIGNS: 40g. Copperhead (snake); 50g. Marsh tortoise; 60g. Grass snake; 90g. Blindworm; 1z.15, Tree toad; 1z.35, Mountain newt; 1z.50, Crested newt; 1z.55, Green toad; 2z.50, "Bombina" toad; 3z. Salamander; 3z.40, "Natterjack" (toad).

425 Epee, Foil, Sabre and Knight's Helmet

1963. World Fencing Championships, Gdansk.
1392 **425** 20g. yellow and brown 10 10
1393 – 40g. light blue and blue 10 10
1394 – 60g. vermilion and red 10 10
1395 – 1z.15 light green & green 10 10
1396 – 1z.55 red and violet . . 35 10
1397 – 6z.50 yellow, pur & bis 1·25 60
DESIGNS—HORIZ: Fencers with background of: 40g. Knights jousting; 60g. Dragoons in sword-fight; 1z.15, 18th-century duellists; 1z.55, Old Gdansk. VERT: 6z.50, Inscription and Arms of Gdansk.

1963. Famous Poles (3rd issue). As T **386**.
1398 60g. black and brown . . . 10 10
1399 60g. black and brown . . . 10 10
1400 60g. black and turquoise . . 10 10
1401 60g. black and green 10 10
PORTRAITS: No. 1398, L. Warynski (patriot); 1399, L. Krzywicki (economist); 1400, M. Sklodowska-Curie (scientist); 1401, K. Swierczewski (patriot).

426 Bykovsky and "Vostok 5"

1963. 2nd "Team" Manned Space Flights.
1402 **426** 40g. black, green and blue 10 10
1403 – 60g. black, blue and green 10 10
1404 – 6z.50 multicoloured . . . 90 30
DESIGNS: 60g. Tereshkova and "Vostok 6"; 6z.50, "Vostoks 5 and 6" in orbit.

427 Basketball

1963. 13th European (Men's) Basketball Championships, Wroclaw.
1405 **427** 40g. multicoloured . . . 10 10
1406 – 50g. green, black and pink 10 10
1407 – 60g. black, green and red 10 10
1408 – 90g. multicoloured . . . 10 10
1409 – 2z.50 multicoloured . . . 20 10
1410 – 5z.60 multicoloured . . . 1·50 40
DESIGNS: 50g. to 2z.50, As Type **427** but with ball, players and hands in various positions; 5z.60, Hands placing ball in net.

428 Missile

1963. 20th Anniv of Polish People's Army. Multicoloured.
1411 20g. Type **428** 10 10
1412 40g. "Blyskawica" (destroyer) 10 10
1413 60g. PZL-106 Kruk (airplane) 10 10
1414 1z.15 Radar scanner 10 10
1415 1z.35 Tank 10 10
1416 1z.55 Missile carrier 10 10
1417 2z.50 Amphibious troop carrier 10 10
1418 3z. Ancient warrior, modern soldier and two swords 30 20

429 "A Love Letter" (after Czachorski)

1963. Stamp Day.
1419 **429** 60g. brown 20 10

1963. Visit of Soviet Cosmonauts to Poland. Nos. 1402/4 optd **23-28. X. 1963** and **w Polsce** together with Cosmonauts' names.
1420 **426** 40g. black, green and blue 20 10
1421 – 60g. black, blue and green 30 10
1422 – 6z.50 multicoloured . . . 1·40 75

431 Tsiolkovsky's Rocket and Formula

432 Mazurian Horses

1963. "The Conquest of Space". Inscr in black.
1423 **431** 30g. turquoise 10 10
1424 – 40g. olive 10 10
1425 – 50g. violet 10 10
1426 – 60g. brown 10 10
1427 – 1z. turquoise 10 10
1428 – 1z.50 red 10 10
1429 – 1z.55 blue 10 10
1430 – 2z.50 purple 10 10
1431 – 5z.60 green 65 30
1432 – 6z.50 turquoise . . . . 1·10 30
DESIGNS: 40g. "Sputnik 1"; 50g. "Explorer 1"; 60g. Banner carried by "Lunik 2"; 1z. "Lunik 3"; 1z.50, "Vostok 1"; 1z.55, "Friendship 7"; 2z.50, "Vostoks 3 and 4"; 5z.60, "Mariner 2"; 6z.50, "Mars 1".

1963. Polish Horse-breeding. Multicoloured.
1433 20g. Arab stallion "Comet" 15 10
1434 30g. Wild horses 15 10
1435 40g. Sokolski horse 20 10
1436 50g. Arab mares and foals 20 10
1437 60g. Type **432** 20 10
1438 90g. Steeplechasers 45 10
1439 1z.55 Arab stallion "Witez II" 80 10
1440 2z.50 Head of Arab horse (facing right) . . . . . 1·50 10
1441 4z. Mixed breeds . . . . . 3·75 60
1442 6z.50 Head of Arab horse (facing left) . . . . . . 5·25 2·40
SIZES—TRIANGULAR (55 × 27½ mm): 20, 30, 40g. HORIZ: (75 × 26 mm): 50, 90g., 4z. VERT: as Type **432**: 1z.55, 2z.50, 6z.50.

433 Ice Hockey

1964. Winter Olympic Games, Innsbruck. Mult.
1443 20g. Type **433** 10 10
1444 30g. Slalom 10 10
1445 40g. Downhill skiing 10 10
1446 60g. Speed skating 10 10
1447 1z. Ski-jumping 10 10
1448 2z.50 Tobogganing 10 10
1449 5z.60 Cross-country skiing 75 60
1450 6z.50 Pairs, figure skating 1·50 80

1964. Sailing Ships (2nd series). As T **421** but without coloured backgrounds. Some new designs.
1451 **421** 5g. brown 10 10
1452 – 10g. green 10 10
1453 – 20g. blue 10 10
1454 – 30g. bronze 10 10
1455 – 40g. blue 10 10
1456 – 60g. purple 10 10
1457 – 1z. brown 15 10
1458 – 1z.15 brown 15 10
1459 – 1z.35 blue 15 10
1460 – 1z.50 purple 15 10
1461 – 1z.55 black 15 10
1462 – 2z. violet 15 10
1463 – 2z.10 green 15 10
1464 – 2z.50 mauve 20 10
1465 – 3z. olive 30 10
1466 – 3z.40 brown 30 10
SHIPS—HORIZ: 10g. to 1z.15, As Nos. 1370/7; 1z.50, "Ark Royal" (English galleon, 1587); 2z.10, Ship of the line (18th cent); 2z.50, Sail frigate (19th cent); 3z. "Flying Cloud" (clipper, 19th cent). VERT: 1z.35, Columbus's "Santa Maria"; 1z.55, "Wodnik" (Polish warship, 17th cent); 2z. Dutch fleute (17th cent); 3z.40, "Dar Pomorza" (cadet ship).

434 "Flourishing Tree"

1964. 20th Anniv of People's Republic (1st issue).
1467 **434** 60g. multicoloured . . . 10 10
1468 – 60g. black, yellow and red 10 10
DESIGN: No. 1468, Emblem composed of symbols of agriculture and industry.
See also Nos. 1497/1506.

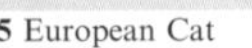

435 European Cat

436 Casimir the Great (founder)

1964. Domestic Cats. As T **435**.
1469 30g. black and yellow . . . 15 10
1470 40g. multicoloured 15 10
1471 50g. black, turquoise & yellow 15 10
1472 60g. multicoloured 35 10
1473 90g. multicoloured 30 10
1474 1z.35 multicoloured 30 10
1475 1z.55 multicoloured 50 10
1476 2z.50 yellow, black and violet 80 45
1477 3z.40 multicoloured . . . . 1·90 80
1478 6z.50 multicoloured . . . . 3·75 1·90
CATS—European: 30, 40, 60g., 1z.55, 2z.50, 6z.50. Siamese: 50g. Persian: 90g., 1z.35, 3z.40.
Nos. 1472/5 are horiz.

1964. 600th Anniv of Jagiellonian University, Cracow.
1479 **436** 40g. purple 10 10
1480 – 40g. green 10 10
1481 – 60g. violet 10 10
1482 – 60g. blue 10 10
1483 – 2z.50 sepia 65 10
PORTRAITS: No. 1480, Hugo Kollataj (educationist and politician); 1481, Jan Dlugosz (geographer and historian); 1482, Copernicus (astronomer); 1483 (36 × 37 mm), King Wladislaw Jagiello and Queen Jadwiga.

437 Northern Lapwing

1964. Birds. Multicoloured.
1484 30g. Type **437** 15 10
1485 40g. Bluethroat 15 10
1486 50g. Black-tailed godwit . . 15 10
1487 60g. Osprey (vert) 20 10
1488 90g. Grey heron (vert) . . . 30 10
1489 1z.35 Little gull (vert) . . . 45 10
1490 1z.55 Common shoveler . . 45 10
1491 5z.60 Black-throated diver 1·00 30
1492 6z.50 Great crested grebe . . 1·40 65

438 Red Flag on Brick Wall

1964. 4th Polish United Workers' Party Congress, Warsaw. Inscr "PZPR". Multicoloured.
1493 60g. Type **438** 10 10
1494 60g. Beribboned hammer . . 10 10
1495 60g. Hands reaching for Red Flag 10 10
1496 60g. Hammer and corn emblems 10 10

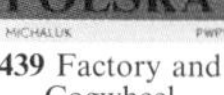

439 Factory and Cogwheel **441** Battle Scene

440 Gdansk Shipyard

1964. 20th Anniv of People's Republic (2nd issue).
1497 **439** 60g. black and blue . . . 10 10
1498 – 60g. black and green . . 10 10
1499 – 60g. red and orange . . 10 10
1500 – 60g. blue and grey . . . 10 10
1501 **440** 60g. blue and green . . . 10 10
1502 – 60g. violet and mauve 10 10
1503 – 60g. brown and violet . . 10 10
1504 – 60g. bronze and green 10 10
1505 – 60g. purple and red . . . 10 10
1506 – 60g. brown and yellow 10 10
DESIGNS—As Type **439**: No. 1498, Tractor and ear of wheat; 1499, Mask and symbols of the arts; 1500, Atomic symbol and book. As Type **440**: No. 1502, Lenin Foundry, Nowa Huta; 1503, Cement Works, Chelm; 1504, Turoszow power station; 1505, Petro-chemical plant, Plock; 1506, Tarnobrzeg sulphur mine.

1964. 20th Anniv of Warsaw Insurrection.
1507 **441** 60g. multicoloured . . . 10 10

442 Relay-racing **443** Congress Emblem

1964. Olympic Games, Tokyo. Multicoloured.
1508 20g. Triple-jumping 10 10
1509 40g. Rowing 10 10
1510 60g. Weightlifting 10 10
1511 90g. Type **442** 10 10
1512 1z. Boxing 10 10
1513 2z.50 Football 30 10
1514 5z.60 High jumping (women) 90 30
1515 6z.50 High-diving . . . . . 1·40 45
SIZES: DIAMOND—20g. to 60g. SQUARE—90g. to 2z.50. VERT: (23½ × 36 mm)—5z.60, 6z.50.

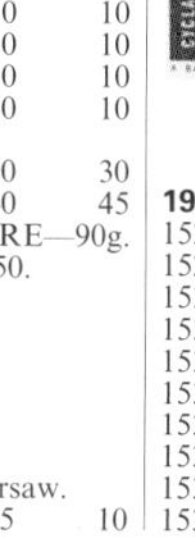

1964. 15th Int Astronautical Congress, Warsaw.
1516 **443** 2z.50 black and violet . . 35 10

444 Hand holding Hammer **445** S. Zeromski

1964. 3rd Congress of Fighters for Freedom and Democracy Association, Warsaw.
1517 **444** 60g. red, black and green 10 10

1964. Birth Cent of Stefan Zeromski (writer).
1518 **445** 60g. brown 10 10

446 Globe and Red Flag **448** Eleanor Roosevelt

447 18th-century Stage Coach (after Brodowski)

1964. Centenary of "First International".
1519 **446** 60g. black and red . . . 10 10

1964. Stamp Day.
1520 **447** 60g. green 20 10
1521 60g. brown 20 10

1964. 80th Birth Anniv of Eleanor Roosevelt.
1522 **448** 2z.50 brown 20 10

449 Battle of Studzianki (after S. Zoltowski)

1964. "Poland's Struggle" (World War II) (1st issue).
1523 – 40g. black 10 10
1524 – 40g. violet 10 10
1525 – 60g. blue 10 10
1526 – 60g. green 10 10
1527 **449** 60g. bronze 10 10
DESIGNS—VERT: No. 1523, Virtuti Militari Cross; 1524, Westerplatte Memorial, Gdansk; 1525, Bydogoszez Memorial. HORIZ: No. 1526, Soldiers crossing the Oder (after S. Zoltowski).
See also Nos. 1610/12.

450 Cyclamen **451** Spacecraft of the Future

1964. Garden Flowers. Multicoloured.
1528 20g. Type **450** 10 10
1529 30g. Freesia 10 10
1530 40g. Rose 10 10
1531 50g. Peony 10 10
1532 60g. Lily 10 10
1533 90g. Poppy 10 10
1534 1z.35 Tulip 10 10
1535 1z.50 Narcissus 65 30
1536 1z.55 Begonia 20 10
1537 2z.50 Carnation 45 10
1538 3z.40 Iris 75 30
1539 5z.60 Japanese camelia . . . 1·25 60
Nos. 1534/9 are smaller, 26½ × 37 mm.

1964. Space Research. Multicoloured.
1540 20g. Type **451** 10 10
1541 30g. Launching rocket . . . 10 10
1542 40g. Dog "Laika" and rocket 10 10
1543 60g. "Lunik 3" and Moon 10 10
1544 1z.55 Satelite 10 10
1545 2z.50 "Elektron 2" 35 10
1546 5z.60 "Mars 1" 50 10
1547 6z.50+2z. Gagarin seated in capsule . . . . 3·50 30

452 "Siren of Warsaw"

1965. 20th Anniv of Liberation of Warsaw.
1548 **452** 60g. green 10 10

453 Edaphosaurus

1965. Prehistoric Animals (1st series). Mult.
1549 20g. Type **453** 10 10
1550 30g. Cryptocleidus (vert) . . 10 10
1551 40g. Brontosaurus 10 10
1552 60g. Mesosaurus (vert) . . . 10 10
1553 90g. Stegosaurus 10 10
1554 1z.15 Brachiosaurus (vert) 10 10
1555 1z.35 Styracosaurus 20 10
1556 3z.40 Corythosaurus (vert) 50 10
1557 5z.60 Rhamphorhynchus (vert) . . . . 1·40 45
1558 6z.50 Tyrannosaurus . . . . 1·90 1·10
See also Nos. 1639/47.

454 Petro-chemical Works, Plock, and Polish and Soviet Flags

1965. 20th Anniv of Polish–Soviet Friendship Treaty. Multicoloured.
1559 60g. Seal (vert, 27 × 38½ mm) 10 10
1560 60g. Type **454** 10 10

455 Polish Eagle and Civic Arms

1965. 20th Anniv of Return of Western and Northern Territories to Poland.
1561 **455** 60g. red 10 10

456 Dove of Peace **457** I.T.U. Emblem

1965. 20th Anniv of Victory.
1562 **456** 60g. red and black . . . 10 10

1965. Centenary of I.T.U.
1563 **457** 2z.50 black, violet & blue 45 10

458 Clover-leaf Emblem and "The Friend of the People" (journal) **459** "Dragon" Dinghies

1965. 70th Anniv of Peasant Movement. Mult.
1564 40g. Type **458** 10 10
1565 60g. Ears of corn and industrial plant (horiz) . . 10 10

1965. World Finn Sailing Championships, Gdynia. Multicoloured.
1566 30g. Type **459** 10 10
1567 40g. "5.5 m." dinghies . . . 10 10
1568 50g. "Finn" dinghies (horiz) 10 10
1569 60g. "V" dinghies 10 10
1570 1z.35 "Cadet" dinghies (horiz) 20 10
1571 4z. "Star" yachts (horiz) . . 65 35
1572 5z.60 "Flying Dutchman" dinghies . . . . 1·25 60
1573 6z.50 "Amethyst" dinghies (horiz) . . . . 1·90 1·90

460 Marx and Lenin **461** 17th-cent Arms of Warsaw

1965. Postal Ministers' Congress, Peking.
1574 **460** 60g. black on red . . . 10 10

1965. 700th Anniv of Warsaw.
1575 **461** 5g. red 10 10
1576 – 10g. green 10 10
1577 – 20g. blue 10 10
1578 – 40g. brown 10 10
1579 – 60g. orange 10 10
1580 – 1z.50 black 10 10
1581 – 1z.55 blue 10 10
1582 – 2z.50 purple 10 10
DESIGNS—VERT: 10g. 13th-cent antiquities. HORIZ: 20g. Tombstone of last Masovian dukes; 40g. Old Town Hall; 60g. Barbican; 1z.50, Arsenal; 1z.55, National Theatre; 2z.50, Staszic Palace.

463 I.Q.S.Y. Emblem

1965. International Quiet Sun Year. Multicoloured. Background colours given.
1584 **463** 60g. blue 10 10
1585 60g. violet 10 10
1586 – 2z.50 red 30 10
1587 – 2z.50 brown 30 10
1588 – 3z.40 orange 45 10
1589 – 3z.40 olive 45 10
DESIGNS: 2z.50, Solar scanner; 3z.40, Solar System.

464 "Odontoglossum grande" **465** Weightlifting

1965. Orchids. Multicoloured.
1590 20g. Type **464** 10 10
1591 30g. "Cypripedium hibridum" 10 10
1592 40g. "Lycaste skinneri" . . 10 10
1593 50g. "Cattleya warzewicza" 10 10
1594 60g. "Vanda sanderiana" . . 10 10
1595 1z.35 "Cypripedium hibridum" (different) . . . 30 10

1596	4z. "Sobralia"	45	30
1597	5z.60 "Disa grandiflora"	1·25	45
1598	6z.50 "Cattleya labiata"	1·90	50

1965. Olympic Games, Tokyo. Polish Medal Winners. Multicoloured.

1599	30g. Type **465**	10	10
1600	40g. Boxing	10	10
1601	50g. Relay-racing	10	10
1602	60g. Fencing	10	10
1603	90g. Hurdling (women's 80 m)	10	10
1604	3z.40 Relay-racing (women's)	45	10
1605	6z.50 "Hop, step and jump"	90	60
1606	7z.10 Volleyball (women's)	1·25	45

466 "The Post Coach" (after P. Michalowski)

1965. Stamp Day.

1607	**466** 60g. brown	20	10
1608	– 2z.50 green	30	10

DESIGN: 2z.50, "Coach about to leave" (after P. Michalowski).

467 U.N. Emblem **468** Memorial, Holy Cross Mountains

1965. 20th Anniv of U.N.O.

1609	**467** 2z.50 blue	30	10

1965. "Poland's Struggle" (World War II) (2nd issue).

1610	**468** 60g. brown	10	10
1611	– 60g. green	10	10
1612	– 60g. brown	10	10

DESIGNS—VERT: No. 1611, Memorial Plaszow. HORIZ: No. 1612, Memorial, Chelm-on-Ner.

469 Wolf

1965. Forest Animals. Multicoloured.

1613	20g. Type **469**	10	10
1614	30g. Lynx	10	10
1615	40g. Red fox	10	10
1616	50g. Eurasian badger	10	10
1617	60g. Brown bear	10	10
1618	1z.50 Wild boar	35	10
1619	2z.50 Red deer	35	10
1620	5z.60 European bison	90	30
1621	7z.10 Elk	1·50	50

470 Gig

1965. Horse-drawn Carriages in Lancut Museum. Multicoloured.

1622	20g. Type **470**	10	10
1623	40g. Coupe	10	10
1624	50g. Ladies' "basket" (trap)	10	10
1625	60g. "Vis-a-vis"	10	10
1626	90g. Cab	10	10
1627	1z.15 Berlinka	15	10
1628	2z.50 Hunting brake	45	10
1629	6z.50 Barouche	1·25	30
1630	7z.10 English brake	1·75	50

Nos. 1627/9 are 77 × 22 mm and No. 1630 is 104 × 22 mm.

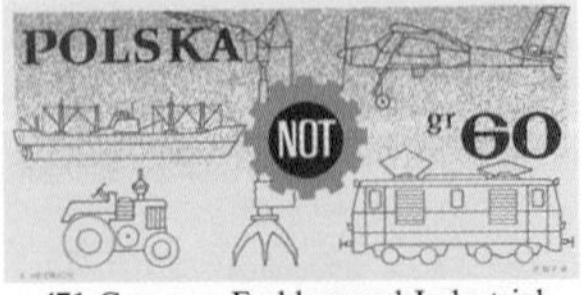

471 Congress Emblem and Industrial Products

1966. 5th Polish Technicians' Congress, Katowice.

1631	**471** 60g. multicoloured	10	10

1966. 20th Anniv of Industrial Nationalization. Designs similar to T **471**. Multicoloured.

1632	60g. Pithead gear (vert)	10	10
1633	60g. "Henryk Jedza" (freighter)	10	10
1634	60g. Petro-chemical works, Plock	10	10
1635	60g. Combine-harvester	10	10
1636	60g. Class EN 57 electric train	10	10
1637	60g. Exhibition Hall, 35th Poznan Fair	10	10
1638	60g. Crane (vert)	10	10

1966. Prehistoric Animals (2nd series). As T **453**. Multicoloured.

1639	20g. Terror fish	10	10
1640	30g. Lobefin	10	10
1641	40g. Ichthyostega	10	10
1642	50g. Mastodonsaurus	10	10
1643	60g. Cynognathus	10	10
1644	2z.50 Archaeopteryx (vert)	10	10
1645	3z.40 Brontotherium	60	10
1646	6z.50 Machairodus	90	45
1647	7z.10 Mammuthus	2·10	50

472 H. Sienkiewicz (novelist) **473** Footballers (Montevideo, 1930)

1966. 50th Death Anniv of Henryk Sienkiewicz.

1648	**472** 60g. black on buff	10	10

1966. World Cup Football Championship. Mult.

1649	20g. Type **473**	10	10
1650	40g. Rome, 1934	10	10
1651	60g. Paris, 1938	10	10
1652	90g. Rio de Janeiro, 1950	10	10
1653	1z.50 Berne, 1954	60	10
1654	3z.40 Stockholm, 1958	60	10
1655	6z.50 Santiago, 1962	1·25	10
1656	7z.10 "London", 1966 (elimination match, Glasgow, 1965)	1·75	35

Football scenes represent World Cup finals played at the cities stated.

475 Soldier with Flag, and Dove of Peace **476** Women's Relay-racing

1966. 21st Anniv of Victory Day.

1658	**475** 60g. red and black on silver	10	10

1966. 8th European Athletic Championships, Budapest. Multicoloured.

1659	20g. Runner starting race (vert)	10	10
1660	40g. Type **476**	10	10
1661	60g. Throwing the javelin	10	10
1662	90g. Women's hurdles	10	10
1663	1z.35 Throwing the discus (vert)	10	10
1664	3z.40 Finish of race	45	10
1665	6z.50 Throwing the hammer (vert)	75	35
1666	7z.10 High-jumping	1·10	60

478 White Eagle **479** Flowers and Produce

1966. Polish Millenary (1st issue). Each red and black on gold.

1668	60g. Type **478**	10	10
1669	60g. Polish flag	10	10
1670	2z.50 Type **478**	10	10
1671	2z.50 Polish flag	10	10

See also Nos. 1717/18.

1966. Harvest Festival. Multicoloured.

1672	40g. Type **479**	20	10
1673	60g. Woman and loaf	20	10
1674	3z.40 Festival bouquet	50	35

The 3z.40 is 49 × 48 mm.

480 Chrysanthemum **481** Tourist Map

1966. Flowers. Multicoloured.

1675	10g. Type **480**	10	10
1676	20g. Poinsettia	10	10
1677	30g. Centaury	10	10
1678	40g. Rose	10	10
1679	60g. Zinnia	10	10
1680	90g. Nasturtium	10	10
1681	5z.60 Dahlia	90	30
1682	6z.50 Sunflower	80	45
1683	7z.10 Magnolia	1·90	50

1966. Tourism.

1684	**481** 10g. red	10	10
1685	– 20g. olive	10	10
1686	– 40g. blue	10	10
1687	– 60g. brown	10	10
1688	– 60g. black	10	10
1689	– 1z.15 green	15	10
1690	– 1z.35 red	10	10
1691	– 1z.55 violet	10	10
1692	– 2z. green	40	10

DESIGNS: 20g. Hela Lighthouse; 40g. Yacht; 60g. (No. 1687), Poniatowski Bridge, Warsaw; 60g. (No. 1688), Mining Academy, Kielce; 1z.15, Dunajec Gorge; 1z.35, Old oaks, Rogalin; 1z.55, Silesian Planetarium; 2z. "Batory" (liner).

482 Roman Capital

1966. Polish Culture Congress.

1693	**482** 60g. red and brown	10	10

483 Stable-man with Percherons

1966. Stamp Day.

1694	**483** 60g. brown	10	10
1695	– 2z.50 green	10	10

DESIGN: 2z.50, Stablemen with horses and dogs.

484 Soldier in Action

1966. 30th Anniv of Jaroslav Dabrowski Brigade.

1696	**484** 60g. black, green and red	10	10

485 Woodland Birds

1966. Woodland Birds. Multicoloured.

1697	10g. Type **485**	15	10
1698	20g. Green woodpecker	15	10
1699	30g. Jay	20	10
1700	40g. Golden oriole	20	10
1701	60g. Hoopoe	20	10
1702	2z.50 Common redstart	45	35
1703	4z. Spruce siskin	1·50	35
1704	6z.50 Chaffinch	1·50	60
1705	7z.10 Great tit	1·50	60

486 Ram (ritual statuette) **487** "Vostok 1"

1966. Polish Archaeological Research.

1706	**486** 60g. blue	10	10
1707	– 60g. green	10	10
1708	– 60g. brown	10	10

DESIGNS—VERT: No. 1707, Plan of Biskupin settlement. HORIZ: No. 1708, Brass implements and ornaments.

1966. Space Research. Multicoloured.

1709	20g. Type **487**	10	10
1710	40g. "Gemini"	10	10
1711	60g. "Ariel 2"	10	10
1712	1z.35 "Proton 1"	10	10
1713	1z.50 "FR 1"	20	10
1714	3z.40 "Alouette"	35	10
1715	6z.50 "San Marco 1"	1·25	10
1716	7z.10 "Luna 9"	1·50	30

488 Polish Eagle and Hammer

1966. Polish Millenary (2nd issue).

1717	**488** 40g. purple, lilac and red	10	10
1718	– 60g. purple, green and red	10	10

DESIGN: 60g. Polish eagle and agricultural and industrial symbols.

489 Dressage

1967. 150th Anniv of Racehorse Breeding in Poland. Multicoloured.

1719	10g. Type **489**	15	10
1720	20g. Cross-country racing	15	10
1721	40g. Horse-jumping	15	10
1722	60g. Jumping fence in open country	30	10
1723	90g. Horse-trotting	30	10
1724	5z.90 Playing polo	90	10
1725	6z.60 Stallion "Ofir"	1·40	45
1726	7z. Stallion "Skowronek"	2·10	45

490 Black-wedged Butterflyfish

1967. Exotic Fishes. Multicoloured.

1727	5g. Type **490**	10	10
1728	10g. Emperor angelfish	10	10
1729	40g. Racoon butterflyfish	10	10
1730	60g. Clown triggerfish	10	10
1731	90g. Undulate triggerfish	10	10
1732	1z.50 Picasso triggerfish	20	10
1733	4z.50 Black-finned melon butterflyfish	75	10
1734	6z.60 Semicircle angelfish	95	45
1735	7z. Saddle butterflyfish	1·25	75

491 Auschwitz Memorial

1967. Polish Martyrdom and Resistance, 1939–45.
1736 **491** 40g. brown 10 10
1737 – 40g. black 10 10
1738 – 40g. violet 10 10
DESIGNS—VERT: No. 1737, Auschwitz-Monowitz Memorial; 1738, Memorial guide's emblem.
See also Nos. 1770/2, 1798/9 and 1865/9.

492 Cyclists

1967. 20th International Peace Cycle Race.
1739 **492** 60g. multicoloured . . . 10 10

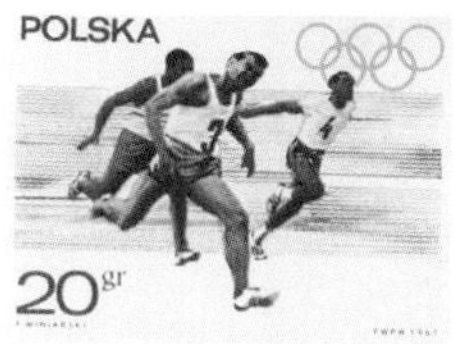

493 Running

1967. Olympic Games (1968). Multicoloured.
1740 20g. Type **493** 10 10
1741 40g. Horse-jumping 10 10
1742 60g. Relay-running 10 10
1743 90g. Weight-lifting 10 10
1744 1z.35 Hurdling 10 10
1745 3z.40 Gymnastics 45 15
1746 6z.60 High-jumping 60 35
1747 7z. Boxing . . . . 1·10 65

494 Socialist Symbols

1967. Polish Trade Unions Congress, Warsaw.
1749 **494** 60g. multicoloured . . . 10 10

495 "Arnica montana"

1967. Protected Plants. Multicoloured.
1750 40g. Type **495** 10 10
1751 60g. "Aquilegia vulgaris" . . 10 10
1752 3z.40 "Gentiana punctata" . 35 10
1753 4z.50 "Lycopodium clavatum" 35 10
1754 5z. "Iris sibirica" 60 10
1755 10z. "Azalea pontica" . . . 1·10 30

496 Katowice Memorial **497** Marie Curie

1967. Inauguration of Katowice Memorial.
1756 **496** 60g. multicoloured . . . 10 10

1967. Birth Centenary of Marie Curie.
1757 **497** 60g. lake 10 10
1758 – 60g. brown 10 10
1759 – 60g. violet 10 10
DESIGNS: No. 1758, Marie Curie's Nobel Prize diploma; 1759, Statue of Marie Curie, Warsaw.

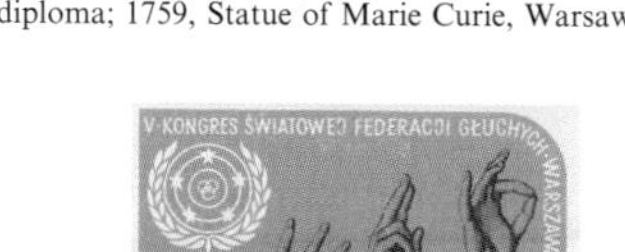

498 "Fifth Congress of the Deaf" (sign language)

1967. 5th World Federation of the Deaf Congress, Warsaw.
1760 **498** 60g. black and blue . . . 10 10

499 Bouquet

1967. "Flowers of the Meadow". Multicoloured.
1761 20g. Type **499** 10 10
1762 40g. Red poppy 10 10
1763 60g. Field bindweed 10 10
1764 90g. Wild pansy 10 10
1765 1z.15 Tansy 10 10
1766 2z.50 Corn cockle 20 10
1767 3z.40 Field scabious 45 30
1768 4z.50 Scarlet pimpernel . . 1·40 35
1769 7z.90 Chicory . . . . 1·50 30

1967. Polish Martyrdom and Resistance, 1939–45 (2nd series). As T **491**.
1770 40g. blue 10 10
1771 40g. green 10 10
1772 40g. black 10 10
DESIGNS—HORIZ: No. 1770, Stutthof Memorial. VERT: No. 1771, Walez Memorial; 1772, Lodz-Radogoszez Memorial.

500 "Wilanow Palace" (from painting by W. Kasprzycki)

1967. Stamp Day.
1773 **500** 60g. brown and blue . . 10 10

501 Cruiser "Aurora"

1967. 50th Anniv of October Revolution. Each black, grey and red.
1774 60g. Type **501** 10 10
1775 60g. Lenin 10 10
1776 60g. "Luna 10" 10 10

502 Peacock **503** Kosciuszko

1967. Butterflies. Multicoloured.
1777 10g. Type **502** 10 10
1778 20g. Swallowtail 10 10
1779 40g. Small tortoiseshell . . . 10 10
1780 60g. Camberwell beauty . . 15 10
1781 2z. Purple emperor 30 10
1782 2z.50 Red admiral 35 10
1783 3z.40 Pale clouded yellow 35 10
1784 4z.50 Marbled white . . . . 1·75 80
1785 7z.90 Large blue . . . . . 1·90 80

1967. 150th Death Anniv of Tadeusz Kosciuszko (national hero).
1786 **503** 60g. chocolate and brown 10 10
1787 2z.50 green and red . . . 20 10

504 "The Lobster" (Jean de Heem)

1967. Famous Paintings.
1788 – 20g. multicoloured . . . 20 10
1789 – 40g. multicoloured . . . 10 10
1790 – 60g. multicoloured . . . 10 10
1791 – 2z. multicoloured 30 20
1792 – 2z.50 multicolured . . . 30 20
1793 – 3z.40 multicoloured . . . 60 20
1794 **504** 4z.50 multicoloured . . . 1·10 60
1795 – 6z.60 multicoloured . . . 1·40 75
DESIGNS (Paintings from the National Museums, Warsaw and Cracow). VERT: 20g. "Lady with a Weasel" (Leonardo da Vinci); 40g. "The Polish Lady" (Watteau); 60g. "Dog fighting Heron" (A. Hondius); 2z. "Fowler tuning Guitar" (J. B. Greuze); 2z.50, "The Tax Collectors" (M. van Reymerswaele); 3z.40, "Daria Fiodorowna" (F. S. Rokotov). HORIZ: 6z.60, "Parable of the Good Samaritan" (landscape, Rembrandt).

505 W. S. Reymont

1967. Birth Centenary of W. S. Reymont (novelist).
1796 **505** 60g. brown, red and ochre 10 10

506 J. M. Ossolinski (medallion), Book and Flag

1967. 150th Anniv of Ossolineum Foundation.
1797 **506** 60g. brown, red and blue 10 10

1967. Polish Martyrdom and Resistance, 1939–45 (3rd series). As T **491**.
1798 40g. red 10 10
1799 40g. brown 10 10
DESIGNS—VERT: No. 1798, Zagan Memorial. HORIZ: No. 1799, Lambinowice Memorial.

507 Ice Hockey

1968. Winter Olympic Games, Grenoble. Mult.
1800 40g. Type **507** 10 10
1801 60g. Downhill 10 10
1802 90g. Slalom 10 10
1803 1z.35 Speed-skating 10 10
1804 1z.55 Ski-walking 10 10
1805 2z. Tobogganing 20 20
1806 7z. Rifle-shooting on skis . . 50 45
1807 7z.90 Ski-jumping (different) 95 60

508 "Puss in Boots" **510** "Peace" (poster by H. Tomaszewski)

509 "Passiflora quadrangularis"

1968. Fairy Tales. Multicoloured.
1808 20g. Type **508** 10 10
1809 40g. "The Raven and the Fox" 10 10
1810 60g. "Mr. Twardowski" . . 10 10
1811 2z. "The Fisherman and the Fish" 20 10
1812 2z.50 "Little Red Riding Hood" 30 10
1813 3z.40 "Cinderella" 45 10
1814 5z.50 "The Waif" . . . . . 1·25 45
1815 7z. "Snow White" . . . . . 1·50 60

1968. Flowers. Multicoloured.
1816 10g. "Clianthus dampieri" 10 10
1817 20g. Type **509** 10 10
1818 30g. "Strelitzia reginae" . . 10 10
1819 40g. "Coryphanta vivipara" 10 10
1820 60g. "Odontonia" 10 10
1821 90g. "Protea cyneroides" . . 10 10
1822 4z.+2z. "Abutilon" 20 10
1823 8z.+4z. "Rosa polyantha" 1·90 30

1968. 2nd Int Poster Biennale, Warsaw. Mult.
1824 60g. Type **510** 10 10
1825 2z.50 Gounod's "Faust" (poster by Jan Lenica) . . 10 10

511 Zephyr Glider

1968. 11th World Gliding Championships, Leszno. Gliders. Multicoloured.
1826 60g. Type **511** 10 10
1827 90g. Stork 10 10
1828 1z.50 Swallow 15 10
1829 3z.40 Fly 35 20
1830 4z. Seal 80 30
1831 5z.50 Pirate 95 30

512 Child with "Stamp" **513** Part of Monument

1968. "75 years of Polish Philately". Multicoloured.
1832 60g. Type **512** 10 10
1833 60g. Balloon over Poznan 10 10

1968. Silesian Insurrection Monument, Sosnowiec.
1834 **513** 60g. black and purple . . 10 10

514 Relay-racing

1968. Olympic Games, Mexico. Multicoloured.
1835 30g. Type **514** 10 10
1836 40g. Boxing 10 10
1837 60g. Basketball 10 10
1838 90g. Long-jumping 10 10
1839 2z.50 Throwing the javelin 15 10
1840 3z.40 Gymnastics 30 10
1841 4z. Cycling 35 10
1842 7z.90 Fencing 65 10
1843 10z.+5z. Torch runner and Aztec bas-relief (56 × 45 mm) . . . . . . 1·75 30

515 "Knight on a Bay Horse" (P. Michalowski)

1968. Polish Paintings. Multicoloured.
1844 40g. Type **515** 10 10
1845 60g. "Fisherman" (L. Wyczolkowski) . . . 10 10
1846 1z.15 "Jewish Woman with Lemons" (A. Gierymski) 10 10
1847 1z.35 "Eliza Parenska" (S. Wyspianski) 15 10
1848 1z.50 "Manifesto" (W. Weiss) 20 10
1849 4z.50 "Stanczyk" (Jan Matejko) (horiz) 50 10

1850 5z. "Children's Band" (T. Makowski) (horiz) . . 80 10
1851 7z. "Feast II" (Z. Waliszewski) (horiz) 90 35

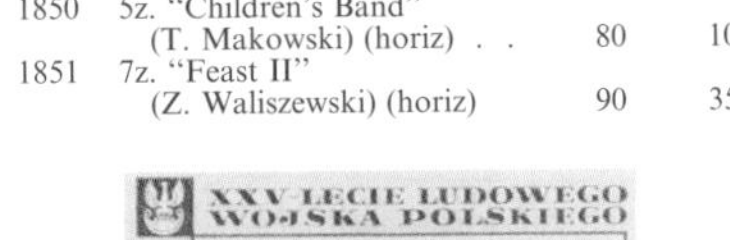

516 "September, 1939" (Bylina)

1968. 25th Anniv of Polish People's Army. Designs show paintings.
1852 40g. violet and olive on yellow 10 10
1853 40g. blue and violet on lilac 10 10
1854 40g. green and blue on grey 10 10
1855 40g. black and brown on orange 10 10
1856 40g. purple & green on green 10 10
1857 60g. brown & ultram on bl 10 10
1858 60g. purple & green on green 10 10
1859 60g. olive and red on pink 10 10
1860 60g. green and brown on red 20 10
1861 60g. blue & turquoise on blue 30 10

PAINTINGS AND PAINTERS: No. 1852, Type **516**; 1853, "Partisans" (Maciag); 1854, "Lenino" (Bylina); 1855, "Monte Cassino" (Boratynski); 1856, "Tanks before Warsaw" (Garwatowski); 1857, "Neisse River" (Bylina); 1858, "On the Oder" (Mackiewicz); 1859, "In Berlin" (Bylina); 1860, "Blyskawica" (destroyer) (Mokwa); 1861, "Pursuit" (Mikoyan Gurevich MiG-17 aircraft) (Kulisiewicz).

517 "Party Members" (F. Kowarski)

1968. 5th Polish United Workers' Party Congress, Warsaw. Multicoloured designs showing paintings.
1862 60g. Type **517** 10 10
1863 60g. "Strike" (S. Lentz) (vert) 10 10
1864 60g. "Manifesto" (W. Weiss) (vert) 10 10

1968. Polish Martyrdom and Resistance, 1939–45 (4th series). As T **491**.
1865 40g. grey 10 10
1866 40g. brown 10 10
1867 40g. brown 10 10
1868 40g. blue 10 10
1869 40g. brown 10 10

DESIGNS—HORIZ: No. 1865, Tomb of Unknown Soldier, Warsaw; 1866, Guerillas' Monument, Kartuzy. VERT: No. 1867, Insurgents' Monument, Poznan; 1868, People's Guard Insurgents' Monument, Polichno; 1869, Rotunda, Zamosc.

518 "Start of Hunt" (W. Kossak)

1968. Paintings. Hunting Scenes. Multicoloured.
1870 20g. Type **518** 10 10
1871 40g. "Hunting with Falcon" (J. Kossak) 10 10
1872 60g. "Wolves' Raid" (A. Wierusz-Kowalski) . . 10 10
1873 1z.50 "Home-coming with a Bear" (J. Falat) 30 10
1874 2z.50 "The Fox-hunt" (T. Sutherland) 20 10
1875 3z.40 "The Boar-hunt" (F. Snyders) 30 10
1876 4z.50 "Hunters' Rest" (W. G. Pierow) . . . . . 1·25 45
1877 8z.50 "Hunting a Lion in Morocco" (Delacroix) . . 1·25 90

519 Maltese Terrier

520 House Sign

1969. Pedigree Dogs. Multicoloured.
1878 20g. Type **519** 10 10
1879 40g. Wire-haired fox-terrier (vert) 20 10
1880 60g. Afghan hound 20 20
1881 1z.50 Rough-haired terrier 20 10
1882 2z.50 English setter 45 10
1883 3z.40 Pekinese 50 20
1884 4z.50 Alsatian (vert) . . . . 1·10 30
1885 8z.50 Pointer (vert) . . . . 2·25 65

1969. 9th Polish Democratic Party Congress.
1886 **520** 60g. red, black and grey 10 10

521 "Dove" and Wheat-ears

522 Running

1969. 5th Congress of United Peasant's Party.
1887 **521** 60g. multicoloured . . . 10 10

1969. 75th Anniv of International Olympic Committee and 50th Anniv of Polish Olympic Committee. Multicoloured.
1888 10g. Type **522** 10 10
1889 20g. Gymnastics 10 10
1890 40g. Weightlifting 10 10
1891 60g. Throwing the javelin 10 10
1892 2z.50+50g. Throwing the discus 10 10
1893 3z.40+1z. Running 20 10
1894 4z.+1z.50 Wrestling 60 30
1895 7z.+2z. Fencing . . . . . . 1·10 35

523 Pictorial Map of Swietokrzyski National Park

1969. Tourism (1st series). Multicoloured.
1896 40g. Type **523** 10 10
1897 60g. Niedzica Castle (vert) 10 10
1898 1z.35 Kolobrzeg Lighthouse and yacht 20 10
1899 1z.50 Szczecin Castle and Harbour 20 10
1900 2z.50 Torun and Vistula River 15 10
1901 3z.40 Klodzko, Silesia (vert) 20 20
1902 4z. Sulejow 35 30
1903 4z.50 Kazimierz Dolny market-place (vert) . . . 35 30

See also Nos. 1981/5.

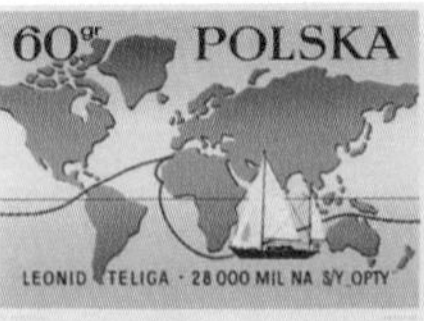

524 Route Map and "Opty"

1969. Leonid Teliga's World Voyage in Yacht "Opty".
1904 **524** 60g. multicoloured . . . 10 10

525 Copernicus (after woodcut by T. Stimer) and Inscription

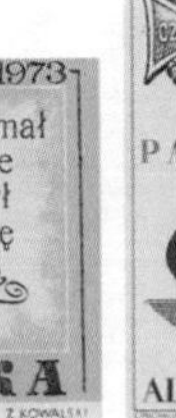

526 "Memory" Flame and Badge

1969. 500th Birth Anniv (1973) of Copernicus (1st issue).
1905 **525** 40g. brown, red & yellow 10 10
1906 – 60g. blue, red and green 10 10
1907 – 2z.50 olive, red & purple 35 30

DESIGNS: 60g. Copernicus (after J. Falck) and 15th-century globe; 2z.50, Copernicus (after painting by J. Matejko) and diagram of heliocentric system.

See also Nos. 1995/7, 2069/72, 2167/70, 2213/14 and 2217/21.

1969. 5th National Alert of Polish Boy Scout Association.
1908 **526** 60g. black, red and blue 10 10
1909 – 60g. red, black and green 10 10
1910 – 60g. black, green and red 10 10

DESIGN: No. 1909, "Defence" eagle and badge; 1910, "Labour" map and badge.

528 Coal-miner

1969. 25th Anniv of Polish People's Republic. Multicoloured.
1911 60g. Frontier guard and arms 10 10
1912 60g. Plock petro-chemical plant 10 10
1913 60g. Combine-harvester . . 10 10
1914 60g. Grand Theatre, Warsaw 10 10
1915 60g. Curie statue and University, Lublin 10 10
1916 60g. Type **528** 10 10
1917 60g. Sulphur-worker 10 10
1918 60g. Steel-worker 10 10
1919 60g. Shipbuilder 10 10

Nos. 1911/5 are vert and have white arms embossed in the top portion of the stamps.

529 Astronauts and Module on Moon

1969. 1st Man on the Moon.
1920 **529** 2z.50 multicoloured . . . 60 45

530 "Motherhood" (S. Wyspianski)

1969. Polish Paintings. Multicoloured.
1921 20g. Type **530** 10 10
1922 40g. "Hamlet" (J. Malczewski) 10 10
1923 60g. "Indian Summer" (J. Chelmonski) 10 10
1924 2z. "Two Girls" (Olga Bonznanska) (vert) . . . 20 10
1925 2z.50 "The Sun of May" (J. Mehoffer) (vert) . . . 10 10
1926 3z.40 "Woman combing her Hair" (W. Slewinski) . . 30 30
1927 5z.50 "Still Life" (J. Pankiewicz) 60 30
1928 7z. "Abduction of the King's Daughter" (W. Wojtkiewicz) . . . . 1·25 45

531 "Nike" statue

533 Krczonow (Lublin) Costumes

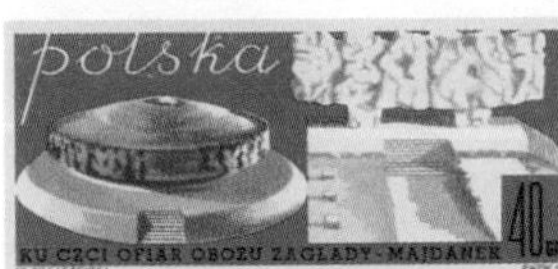

532 Majdanek Memorial

1969. 4th Congress of Fighters for Freedom and Democracy Association.
1929 **531** 60g. red, black and brown 10 10

1969. Inauguration of Majdanek Memorial.
1930 **532** 40g. black and mauve . . 10 10

1969. Provincial Costumes. Multicoloured.
1931 40g. Type **533** 10 10
1932 60g. Lowicz (Lodz) 10 10
1933 1z.15 Rozbasrk (Katowice) 10 10
1934 1z.35 Lower Silesia (Wroclaw) 10 10
1935 1z.50 Opoczno (Lodz) . . . 30 10
1936 4z.50 Sacz (Cracow) 60 15
1937 5z. Highlanders, Cracow . . 45 30
1938 7z. Kurple (Warsaw) 65 35

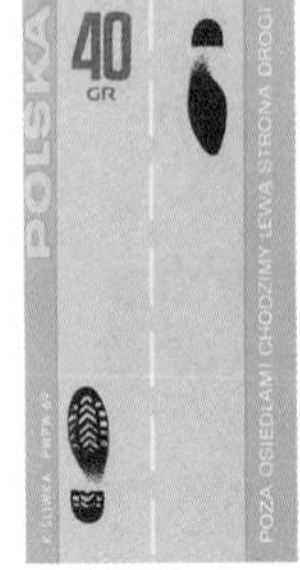

534 "Pedestrians Keep Left"

535 "Welding" and I.L.O. Emblem

1969. Road Safety. Multicoloured.
1939 40g. Type **534** 10 10
1940 60g. "Drive Carefully" (horses on road) 10 10
1941 2z.50 "Do Not Dazzle" (cars on road at night) . . 15 10

1969. 50th Anniv of I.L.O.
1942 **535** 2z.50 blue and gold . . . 20 10

536 "The Bell-founder"

537 "Angel" (19th-century)

1969. Miniatures from Behem's Code of 1505. Multicoloured.
1943 40g. Type **536** 10 10
1944 60g. "The Painter" 10 10
1945 1z.35 "The Woodcarver" . . 10 10
1946 1z.55 "The Shoemaker" . . 20 10
1947 2z.50 "The Cooper" 20 10
1948 3z.40 "The Baker" 20 20
1949 4z.50 "The Tailor" 60 30
1950 7z. "The Bowyer" . . . . . 1·00 60

1969. Polish Folk Sculpture. Multicoloured.
1951 20g. Type **537** 10 10
1952 40g. "Sorrowful Christ" (19th-century) 10 10
1953 60g. "Sorrowful Christ" (19th-cent) (different) . . 10 10
1954 2z. "Weeping Woman" (19th-century) 20 10
1955 2z.50 "Adam and Eve" (F. Czajkowski) 20 10
1956 3z.40 "Girl with Birds" (L. Kudla) 30 10
1957 5z.50+1z.50 "Choir" (A. Zegadlo) 75 35
1958 7z.+1z. "Organ-grinder" (Z. Skretowicz) 80 50

Nos. 1957/8 are larger, size 25 × 35 mm.

538 Leopold Staff

1969. Modern Polish Writers.
1959 **538** 40g. black, olive & green 10 10
1960 – 60g. black, red and pink 10 10
1961 – 1z.35 black, deep blue and blue 10 10
1962 – 1z.50 black, violet & lilac 10 10
1963 – 1z.55 black, deep green and green 10 10
1964 – 2z.50 black, deep blue and blue 20 10
1965 – 3z.40 black, brn & flesh 30 25

DESIGNS: 60g. Wladyslaw Broniewski; 1z.35, Leon Kruczkowski; 1z.50, Julian Tuwim; 1z.55, Konstanty Ildefons Galczynski; 2z.50, Maria Dabrowska; 3z.40, Zofia Nalkowska.

539 Nike Monument

1970. 25th Anniv of Liberation of Warsaw.
1966 **539** 60g. multicoloured . . . 20 10

540 Early Printing Works and Colour Dots

1970. Centenary of Printers' Trade Union.
1967 **540** 60g. multicoloured . . . 10 10

541 Mallard

1970. Game Birds. Multicoloured.

1968	40g. Type **541**	10	10
1969	60g. Common pheasant . .	30	10
1970	1z.15 Eurasian woodcock	20	10
1971	1z.35 Ruff	30	10
1972	1z.50 Wood pigeon	30	10
1973	3z.40 Black grouse	35	10
1974	7z. Grey partridge	1·90	45
1975	8z.50 Western capercaillie	2·75	50

542 Lenin at Desk

1970. Birth Centenary of Lenin.

1976 **542**	40g. grey and red . . .	10	10
1977 –	60g. brown and red . . .	10	10
1978 –	2z.50 black and red . . .	10	10

DESIGNS: 60g. Lenin addressing meeting; 2z.50, Lenin at Party conference.

543 Polish and Russian Soldiers in Berlin

1970. 25th Anniv of Liberation.
1980 **543** 60g. multicoloured . . . 10 10

1970. Tourism (2nd series). As T **523**, but with imprint "PWPW 70". Multicoloured.

1981	60g. Town Hall, Wroclaw (vert)	10	10
1982	60g. View of Opol	10	10
1983	60g. Legnica Castle	10	10
1984	60g. Bolkow Castle	10	10
1985	60g. Town Hall, Brzeg . . .	10	10

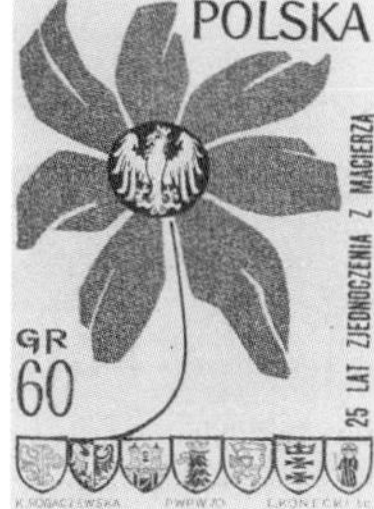

544 Polish "Flower"

1970. 25th Anniv of Return of Western Territories.
1986 **544** 60g. red, silver and green 10 10

545 Movement Flag

546 U.P.U. Emblem and New Headquarters

1970. 75th Anniv of Peasant Movement.
1987 **545** 60g. multicoloured . . . 10 10

1970. New U.P.U. Headquarters Building, Berne.
1988 **546** 2z.50 blue and turquoise 20 10

547 Footballers

548 Hand with "Lamp of Learning"

1970. Gornik Zabrze v. Manchester City, Final of European Cup-winners Cup Championship.
1989 **547** 60g. multicoloured . . . 20 10

1970. 150th Anniv of Plock Scientific Society.
1990 **548** 60g. olive, red and black 10 10

549 "Olympic Runners" (from Greek amphora)

1970. 10th Session of Int Olympic Academy.

1991 **549**	60g. red, yellow and black	10	10
1992 –	60g. violet, blue and black	10	10
1993 –	60g. multicoloured . . .	10	10

DESIGNS: No. 1992, "The Archer"; 1993, Modern runners.

550 Copernicus (after miniature by Bacciarelli) and Bologna

1970. 500th Birth Anniv (1973) of Copernicus (2nd issue).

1995 **550**	40g. green, orange & lilac	10	10
1996 –	60g. lilac, green & yellow	10	10
1997 –	2z.50 brown, blue & green	35	10

DESIGNS: 60g. Copernicus (after miniature by Lesseur) and Padua; 2z.50, Copernicus (by N. Zinck, after lost Goluchowska portrait) and Ferrara.

551 "Aleksander Orlowski" (self-portrait)

1970. Polish Miniatures. Multicoloured.

1998	20g. Type **551**	10	10
1999	40g. "Jan Matejko" (self-portrait)	10	10
2000	60g. "Stefan Batory" (unknown artist)	10	10
2001	2z. "Maria Leszczynska" (unknown artist)	10	10
2002	2z.50 "Maria Walewska" (Marie-Victorie Jacquetot)	20	10
2003	3z.40 "Tadeusz Kosciuszko" (Jan Rustem)	20	10
2004	5z.50 "Samuel Linde" (G. Landolfi)	65	40
2005	7z. "Michal Oginski" (Nanette Windisch) . . .	1·40	20

552 U.N. Emblem within "Eye"

1970. 25th Anniv of United Nations.
2006 **552** 2z.50 multicoloured . . . 20 10

553 Piano Keyboard and Chopin's Signature

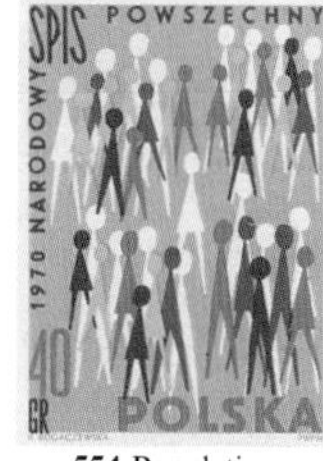

554 Population Pictograph

1970. 8th International Chopin Piano Competition.
2007 **553** 2z.50 black and violet . . 20 10

1970. National Census. Multicoloured.

2008	40g. Type **554**	10	10
2009	60g. Family in "house" . .	10	10

555 Destroyer "Piorun" (½-size illustration)

1970. Polish Warships, World War II.

2010 **555**	40g. brown	10	10
2011 –	60g. black	10	10
2012 –	2z.50 brown	35	10

DESIGNS: 60g. "Orzel" (submarine); 2z.50, H.M.S. "Garland" (destroyer loaned to Polish Navy).

556 "Expressions" (Maria Jarema)

1970. Stamp Day. Contemporary Polish Paintings. Multicoloured.

2013	20g. "The Violin-cellist" (J. Nowosielski) (vert) . .	10	10
2014	40g. "View of Lodz" (B. Liberski) (vert) . . .	10	10
2015	60g. "Studio Concert" (W. Taranczewski) (vert)	10	10
2016	1z.50 "Still Life" (Z. Pronaszko) (vert) . .	10	10
2017	2z. "Hanging-up Washing" (A. Wroblewski) (vert) . .	10	10
2018	3z.40 Type **556**	20	10

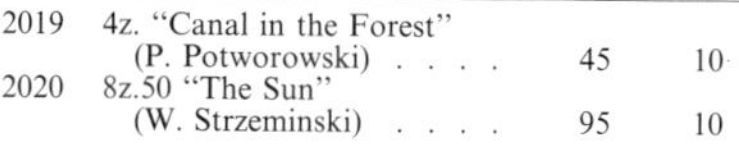

2019	4z. "Canal in the Forest" (P. Potworowski)	45	10
2020	8z.50 "The Sun" (W. Strzeminski)	95	10

557 "Luna 16" landing on Moon

558 "Stag" (detail from "Daniel" tapestry)

1970. Moon Landing of "Luna 16".
2021 **557** 2z.50 multicoloured . . . 30 10

1970. Tapestries in Wawel Castle. Multicoloured.

2022	60g. Type **558**	10	10
2023	1z.15 "White Stork" (detail)	30	10
2024	1z.35 "Panther fighting Dragon"	10	10
2025	2z. "Man's Head" (detail, "Deluge" tapestry) . . .	20	10
2026	2z.50 "Child with Bird" (detail, "Adam Tilling the Soil" tapestry)	25	10
2027	4z. "God, Adam and Eve" (detail, "Happiness in Paradise" tapestry) . . .	45	30
2028	4z.50 Royal Monogram tapestry	75	30

559 Cadet ship "Dar Pomorza"

1971. Polish Ships. Multicoloured.

2030	40g. Type **559**	10	10
2031	60g. Liner "Stefan Batory"	10	10
2032	1z.15 Ice-breaker "Perkun"	15	10
2033	1z.35 Lifeboat "R-1" . . .	20	10
2034	1z.50 Bulk carrier "Ziemia Szczecinska"	30	10
2035	2z.50 Tanker "Beskidy" . .	30	10
2036	5z. Freighter "Hel"	65	20
2037	8z.50 Ferry "Gryf"	1·40	50

560 Checiny Castle

1971. Polish Castles. Multicoloured.

2038	20g. Type **560**	10	10
2039	40g. Wisnicz	10	10
2040	60g. Bedzin	10	10
2041	2z. Ogrodzieniec	15	10
2042	2z.50 Niedzica	15	10
2043	3z.40 Kwidzyn	35	10
2044	4z. Pieskowa Skala	35	10
2045	8z.50 Lidzbark Warminski	90	30

561 Battle of Pouilly, J. Dabrowski and W. Wroblewski

1971. Centenary of Paris Commune.
2046 **561** 60g. brown, blue and red 10 10

562 Plantation

563 "Bishop Marianos"

1971. Forestry Management. Multicoloured.
2047 40g. Type **562** 10 10
2048 60g. Forest (27 × 47 mm) 10 10
2049 1z.50 Tree-felling 20 10

1971. Fresco. Discoveries made by Polish Expedition at Faras, Nubia. Multicoloured.
2050 40g. Type **563** 10 10
2051 60g. "St. Anne" 10 10
2052 1z.15 "Archangel Michael" 10 10
2053 1z.35 "The Hermit, Anamon" 10 10
2054 1z.50 "Head of Archangel Michael" 10 10
2055 4z.50 "Evangelists' Cross" 35 10
2056 5z. "Christ protecting a nobleman" 60 20
2057 7z. "Archangel Michael" (half-length) 75 45

564 Revolutionaries

1971. 50th Anniv of Silesian Insurrection.
2058 **564** 60g. brown and gold 10 10

565 "Soldiers"

1971. 25th Anniv of UNICEF Children's Drawings. Multicoloured.
2060 20g. "Peacock" (vert) 10 10
2061 40g. Type **565** 10 10
2062 60g. "Lady Spring" (vert) 10 10
2063 2z. "Cat and Ball" 10 10
2064 2z.50 "Flowers in Jug" (vert) 20 10
2065 3z.40 "Friendship" 30 10
2066 5z.50 "Clown" (vert) 70 30
2067 7z. "Strange Planet" 80 35

566 Fair Emblem

567 Copernicus's House, Torun

1971. 40th International Fair, Poznan.
2068 **566** 60g. multicoloured 10 10

1971. 500th Birth Anniv (1973) of Copernicus (3rd issue). Multicoloured.
2069 40g. Type **567** 10 10
2070 60g. Collegium Naius, Jagiellonian University, Cracow (horiz) 10 10
2071 2z.50 Olsztyn Castle (horiz) 20 10
2072 4z. Frombork Cathedral 70 20

568 Folk Art Pattern

569 "Head of Worker" (X. Dunikowski)

1971. Folk Art. "Paper Cut-outs" showing various patterns.
2073 **568** 20g. black, green and blue 10 10
2074 – 40g. blue, green & cream 10 10
2075 – 60g. brown, blue and grey 10 10
2076 – 1z.15 purple, brn & buff 10 10
2077 – 1z.35 green, red & yellow 10 10

1971. Modern Polish Sculpture. Multicoloured.
2078 40g. Type **569** 10 10
2079 40g. "Foundryman" (X. Dunikowski) 10 10
2080 60g. "Miners" (M. Wiecek) 10 10
2081 60g. "Harvester" (S. Horno-Poplawski) 10 10

570 Congress Emblem and Computer Tapes

1971. 6th Polish Technical Congress, Warsaw.
2083 **570** 60g. violet and red 10 10

571 "Angel" (J. Mehoffer)

573 PZL P-11C Fighters

572 "Mrs. Fedorowicz" (W. Pruszkowski)

1971. Stained Glass Windows. Multicoloured.
2084 20g. Type **571** 10 10
2085 40g. "Lillies" (S. Wyspianski) 10 10
2086 60g. "Iris" (S. Wyspianski) 10 10
2087 1z.35 "Apollo" (S. Wyspianski) 10 10
2088 1z.55 "Two Wise Men" (14th-century) 10 10
2089 3z.40 "The Flight into Egypt" (14th-century) 30 10
2090 5z.50 "Jacob" (14th-century) 50 10
2091 8z.50+4z. "Madonna" (15th-century) 80 10

1971. Contemporary Art from National Museum, Cracow. Multicoloured.
2092 40g. Type **572** 10 10
2093 50g. "Woman with Book" (T. Czyzeski) 10 10
2094 60g. "Girl with Chrysanthemums" (O. Boznanska) 10 10
2095 2z.50 "Girl in Red Dress" (J. Pankiewicz) (horiz) 10 10
2096 3z.40 "Reclining Nude" (L. Chwistek) (horiz) 20 10
2097 4z.50 "Strange Garden" (J. Mehoffer) 35 10
2098 5z. "Wife in White Hat" (Z. Pronaszko) 45 10
2099 7z.+1z. "Seated Nude" (W. Weiss) 65 45

1971. Polish Aircraft of World War II. Mult.
2100 90g. Type **573** 10 10
2101 1z.50 PZL 23A Karas fighters 20 10
2102 3z.40 PZL P-37 Los bomber 30 20

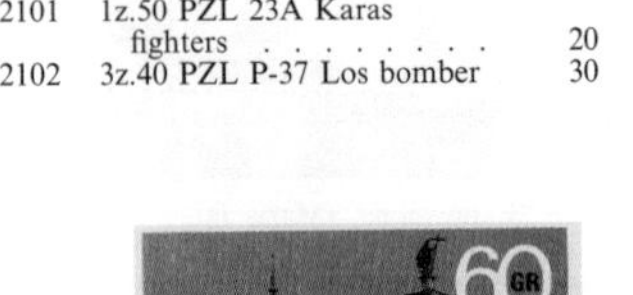

574 Royal Castle, Warsaw (pre-1939)

1971. Reconstruction of Royal Castle, Warsaw.
2103 **574** 60g. black, red and gold 10 10

575 Astronauts in Moon Rover

576 "Lunokhod 1"

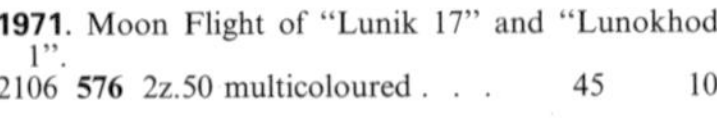

1971. Moon Flight of "Apollo 15".
2104 **575** 2z.50 multicoloured 45 10

1971. Moon Flight of "Lunik 17" and "Lunokhod 1".
2106 **576** 2z.50 multicoloured 45 10

577 Worker at Wheel

578 Ship-building

1971. 6th Polish United Workers' Party Congress.
(a) Party Posters.
2108 **577** 60g. red, blue and grey 10 10
2109 60g. red and grey (Worker's head) 10 10

(b) Industrial Development. Each in gold and red.
2110 60g. Type **578** 10 10
2111 60g. Building construction 10 10
2112 60g. Combine-harvester 10 10
2113 60g. Motor-car production 10 10
2114 60g. Pit-head 10 10
2115 60g. Petro-chemical plant 10 10

579 "Prunus cerasus"

1971. Flowers of Trees and Shrubs. Multicoloured.
2117 10g. Type **579** 10 10
2118 20g. "Malusniedzwetzskyana" 10 10
2119 40g. "Pyrus L." 10 10
2120 60g. "Prunus persica" 10 10
2121 1z.15 "Magnolia kobus" 10 10
2122 1z.35 "Crategus oxyacantha" 10 10
2123 2z.50 "Malus M." 10 10
2124 3z.40 "Aesculus carnea" 20 10
2125 5z. "Robinia pseudacacia" 75 20
2126 8z.50 "Prunus avium" 1·40 50

580 "Worker" (sculpture, J. Januszkiewicz)

1972. 30th Anniv of Polish Workers' Coalition.
2127 **580** 60g. black and red 10 10

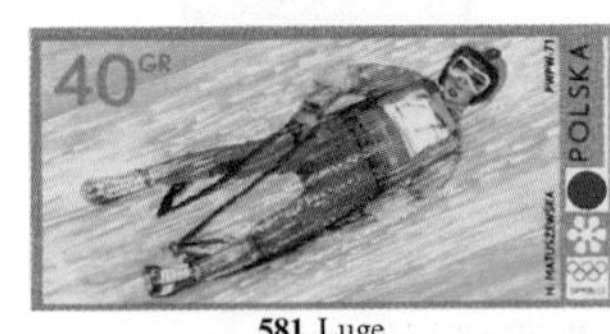

581 Luge

1972. Winter Olympic Games, Sapporo, Japan. Multicoloured.
2128 40g. Type **581** 10 10
2129 60g. Slalom (vert) 10 10
2130 1z.65 Biathlon (vert) 20 10
2131 2z.50 Ski jumping 35 25

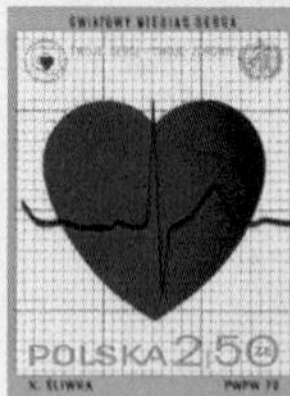

582 "Heart" and Cardiogram Trace

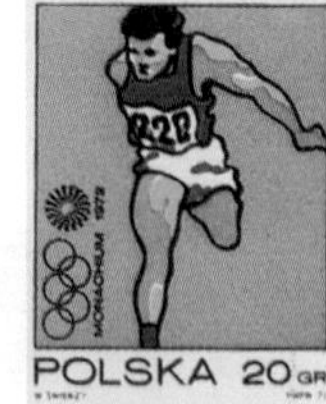

583 Running

1972. World Heart Month.
2133 **582** 2z.50 multicoloured 20 10

1972. Olympic Games, Munich. Multicoloured.
2134 20g. Type **583** 10 10
2135 30g. Archery 10 10
2136 40g. Boxing 10 10
2137 60g. Fencing 10 10
2138 2z.50 Wrestling 10 10
2139 3z.40 Weightlifting 10 10
2140 5z. Cycling 60 10
2141 8z.50 Shooting 95 20

584 Cyclists

585 Polish War Memorial, Berlin

1972. 25th International Peace Cycle Race.
2143 **584** 60g. multicoloured 10 10

1972. "Victory Day, 1945".
2144 **585** 60g. green 10 10

586 "Rodlo" Emblem

587 Polish Knight of 972 A.D.

1972. 50th Anniv of Polish Posts in Germany.
2145 **586** 60g. ochre, red and green 10 10

1972. Millenary of Battle of Cedynia.
2146 **587** 60g. multicoloured 10 10

588 Cheetah

1972. Zoo Animals. Multicoloured.
2147 20g. Type **588** 10 10
2148 40g. Giraffe (vert) 20 10
2149 60g. Toco toucan 30 10
2150 1z.35 Chimpanzee 20 10
2151 1z.65 Common gibbon 30 10
2152 3z.40 Crocodile 35 10
2153 4z. Red kangaroo 65 10
2154 4z.50 Tiger (vert) 2·75 60
2155 7z. Mountain zebra 3·00 1·25

589 L. Warynski. (founder)

590 F. Dzerzhinsky

1972. 90th Anniv of Proletarian Party.
2156 **589** 60g. multicoloured . . . 10 10

1972. 95th Birth Anniv of Feliks Dzerzhinsky (Russian politician).
2157 **590** 60g. black and red . . . 10 10

591 Global Emblem

592 Scene from "In Barracks" (ballet)

1972. 25th Int Co-operative Federation Congress.
2158 **591** 60g. multicoloured . . . 10 10

1972. Death Centenary of Stanislaus Moniuszko (composer). Scenes from Works.
2159 **592** 10g. violet and gold . . 10 10
2160 – 20g. black and gold . . 10 10
2161 – 40g. green and gold . . 10 10
2162 – 60g. blue and gold . . . 10 10
2163 – 1z.15 blue and gold . . . 10 10
2164 – 1z.35 blue and gold . . . 10 10
2165 – 1z.55 green and gold . . 20 10
2166 – 2z.50 brown and gold . . 20 10
DESIGNS: 20g. "The Countess" (opera); 40g. "The Haunted Manor" (opera); 60g. "Halka" (opera); 1z.15, "New Don Quixote" (ballet); 1z.35, "Verbum Nobile"; 1z.55, "Ideal" (operetta); 2z.50, "Pariah" (opera).

593 "Copernicus the Astronomer"

1972. 500th Birth Anniv (1973) of Nicolas Copernicus. (4th issue).
2167 **593** 40g. black and blue . . . 10 10
2168 – 60g. black and orange 10 10
2169 – 2z.50 black and red . . . 10 10
2170 – 3z.40 black and green . . 15 10
DESIGNS: 60g. Copernicus and Polish eagle; 2z.50, Copernicus and Medal; 3z.40, Copernicus and page of book.

594 "The Amazon" (P. Michalowski)

1972. Stamp Day. Polish Paintings. Multicoloured.
2172 30g. Type **594** 10 10
2173 40g. "Ostafi Laskiewicz" (J. Metejko) 10 10
2174 60g. "Summer Idyll" (W. Gerson) 10 10
2175 2z. "The Neapolitan Woman" (A. Kotsis) . . 10 10
2176 2z.50 "Girl Bathing" (P. Szyndler) 10 10
2177 3z.40 "The Princess of Thum" (A. Grottger) . . 10 10
2178 4z. "Rhapsody" (S. Wyspianski) 15 30
2179 8z.50+4z. "Young Woman" (J. Malczewski) (horiz) . . 35 35

1972. Nos. 1578/9 surch.
2180 50g. on 40g. brown 10 10
2181 90g. on 40g. brown 10 10

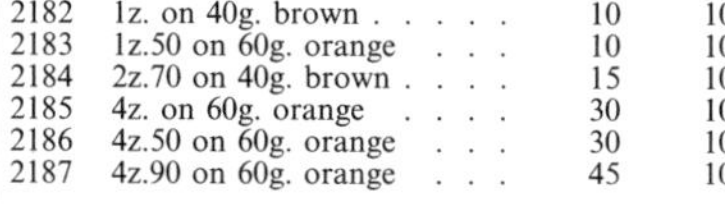
2182 1z. on 40g. brown 10 10
2183 1z.50 on 60g. orange . . . 10 10
2184 2z.70 on 40g. brown 15 10
2185 4z. on 60g. orange 30 10
2186 4z.50 on 60g. orange . . . 30 10
2187 4z.90 on 60g. orange . . . 45 10

596 "The Little Soldier" (E. Piwowarski)

1972. Children's Health Centre.
2188 **596** 60g. black and pink . . 10 10

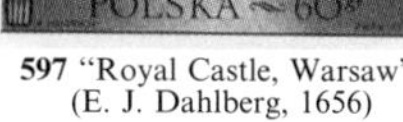

597 "Royal Castle, Warsaw". (E. J. Dahlberg, 1656)

598 Chalet, Chocholowska Valley

1972. Restoration of Royal Castle, Warsaw.
2189 **597** 60g. black, violet and blue 10 10

1972. Tourism. Mountain Chalets. Multicoloured.
2190 40g. Type **598** 10 10
2191 60g. Hala Ornak (horiz) . . 10 10
2192 1z.55 Hala Gasienicowa . . 10 10
2193 1z.65 Valley of Five Lakes (horiz) 15 10
2194 2z.50 Morskie Oko 30 10

599 Trade Union Banners

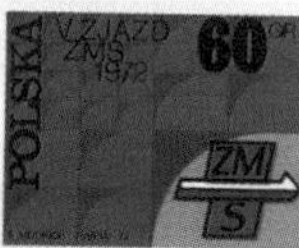

600 Congress Emblem

1972. 7th Polish Trade Union Congresses.
2195 **599** 60g. multicoloured . . . 10 10

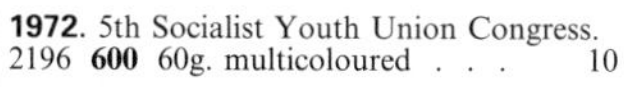

1972. 5th Socialist Youth Union Congress.
2196 **600** 60g. multicoloured . . . 10 10

601 Japanese Azalea

1972. Flowering Shrubs. Multicoloured.
2197 40g. Type **601** 10 10
2198 50g. Alpine rose 10 10
2199 60g. Pomeranian honeysuckle 10 10
2200 1z.65 Chinese quince 10 10
2201 2z.50 Korean cranberry . . 25 10
2202 3z.40 Pontic azalea 35 10
2203 4z. Delavay's white syringa 75 20
2204 8z.50 Common lilac ("Massena") . . . . 1·60 65

602 Piast Knight (10th-century)

603 Copernicus

1972. Polish Cavalry Through the Ages. Mult.
2205 20g. Type **602** 10 10
2206 40g. 13th-century knight . . 10 10
2207 60g. Knight of Wladyslaw Jagiello's Army (15th-century) (horiz) . . 10 10
2208 1z.35 17th-century hussar . . 10 10
2209 4z. Lancer of National Guard (18th-century) . . 50 10
2210 4z.50 "Congress Kingdom" cavalry officer 50 10
2211 5z. Trooper of Light Cavalry (1939) (horiz) . . 1·10 10
2212 7z. Trooper of People's Army (1945) . . . . . . 1·10 60

1972. 500th Birth Anniv (1973) of Copernicus (5th issue).
2213 **603** 1z. brown 15 10
2214 1z.50 ochre 20 10

604 Couple with Hammer and Sickle

605 "Copernicus as Young Man" (Bacciarelli)

1972. 50th Anniv of U.S.S.R. Multicoloured.
2215 40g. Type **604** 10 10
2216 60g. Red star and globe . . 10 10

1973. 500th Birth Anniv of Copernicus (6th issue). Multicoloured.
2217 1z. Type **605** 10 10
2218 1z.50 "Copernicus" (anon) 10 10
2219 2z.70 "Copernicus" (Zinck Nor) 20 10
2220 4z. "Copernicus" (from Strasbourg clock) 45 30
2221 4z.90 "Copernicus" (Jan Matejko) (horiz) 60 30

606 Coronation Sword

607 Statue of Lenin

1973. Polish Art. Multicoloured.
2222 50g. Type **606** 10 10
2223 1z. Kruzlowa Madonna (detail) 10 10
2224 1z. Armour of hussar . . . 10 10
2225 1z.50 Carved head from Wavel Castle 10 10
2226 1z.50 Silver cockerel 10 10
2227 2z.70 Armorial eagle 30 10
2228 4z.90 Skarbimierz Madonna 60 35
2229 8z.50 "Portrait of Tenczynski" (anon) . . . 95 60

1973. Unveiling of Lenin's Statue, Nowa Huta.
2230 **607** 1z. multicoloured 10 10

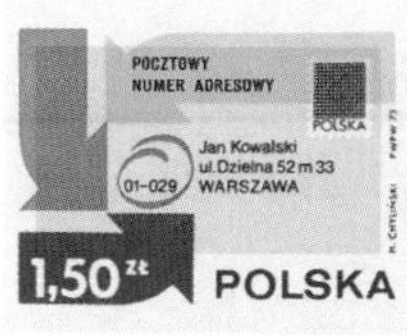

608 Coded Letter

1973. Introduction of Postal Codes.
2231 **608** 1z. multicoloured 10 10

609 Wolf

1973. International Hunting Council Congress and 50th Anniv of Polish Hunting Association. Game Animals. Multicoloured.
2232 50g. Type **609** 10 10
2233 1z. Mouflon 10 10
2234 1z.50 Elk 10 10
2235 2z.70 Western capercaillie 10 10
2236 3z. Roe deer 10 10
2237 4z.50 Lynx 55 10
2238 4z.90 Red deer . . . . . . 1·10 35
2239 5z. Wild boar . . . . 1·25 45

610 "Salyut"

611 Open Book and Flame

1973. Cosmic Research. Multicoloured.
2240 4z.90 Type **610** 35 30
2241 4z.90 "Copernicus" (U.S. satellite) 35 30

1973. 2nd Polish Science Congress, Warsaw.
2242 **611** 1z.50 multicoloured . . . 10 10

612 Ancient Seal of Poznan

613 M. Nowotko

1973. "Polska 73" Philatelic Exhibition, Poznan. Multicoloured.
2243 1z. Type **612** 10 10
2244 1z.50 Tombstone of N. Tomicki 10 10
2245 2z.70 Kalisz paten 20 10
2246 4z. Bronze gates, Gniezno Cathedral (horiz) 30 10

1973. 80th Birth Anniv of Marceli Nowotko (party leader).
2249 **613** 1z.50 black and red . . . 10 10

614 Cherry Blossom

1973. Protection of the Environment. Mult.
2250 50g. Type **614** 10 10
2251 90g. Cattle in meadow . . . 10 10
2252 1z. White stork on nest . . 30 10
2253 1z.50 Pond life 10 10
2254 2z.70 Meadow flora 15 10
2255 4z.90 Ocean fauna 35 10
2256 5z. Forest life . . . . 1·90 30
2257 6z.50 Agricultural produce 1·25 50

615 Motor-cyclist

1973. World Speedway Race Championships, Chorzow.
2258 **615** 1z.50 multicoloured . . . 10 10

616 "Copernicus" (M. Bacciarelli)

1973. Stamp Day.

2259 **616** 4z.+2z. multicoloured . . 45 30

617 Tank

1973. 30th Anniv of Polish People's Army. Mult.

2260 1z. Type **617** 10 10

2261 1z. Mikoyan Gurevich MiG-21D airplane 10 10

2262 1z.50 Guided missile 10 10

2263 1z.50 "Puck" (missile boat) 15 10

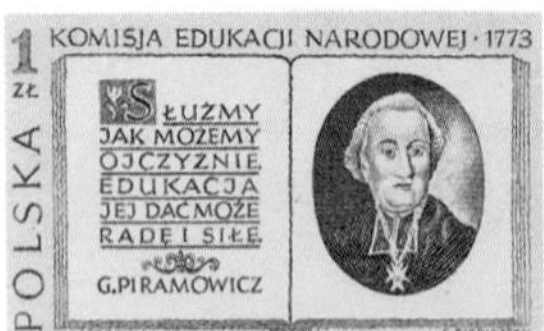

618 G. Piramowicz and Title Page

1973. Bicent of Nat Educational Commission.

2264 **618** 1z. brown and yellow . . 10 10

2265 – 1z.50 green, & light green 10 10

DESIGN: 1z.50, J. Sniadecki, H. Kollataj and J. U. Niemcewicz.

619 Pawel Strzelecki (explorer) and Red Kangaroo

620 Polish Flag

1973. Polish Scientists. Multicoloured.

2266 1z. Type **619** 10 10

2267 1z. Henryk Arctowski (Polar explorer) and Adelie penguins 20 10

2268 1z.50 Stefan Rogozinski (explorer) and "Lucy-Margaret" (schooner) . . 15 10

2269 1z.50 Benedykt Dybowski (zoologist) and sable, Lake Baikal 10 10

2270 2z. Bronislaw Malinowski (anthropologist) and New Guinea dancers 10 10

2271 2z.70 Stefan Drzewiecki (oceanographer) and submarine 20 10

2272 3z. Edward Strasburger (botanist) and classified plants 20 10

2273 8z. Ignacy Domeyko (geologist) and Chilean desert landscape 80 30

1973. 25th Anniv of Polish United Workers' Party.

2274 **620** 1z.40 red, blue and gold 10 10

621 Jelcz-Berliet Coach

1973. Polish Motor Vehicles. Multicoloured.

2275 50g. Type **621** 10 10

2276 90g. Jelcz "316" truck . . . 10 10

2277 1z. Polski-Fiat "126p" saloon 10 10

2278 1z.50 Polski-Fiat "125p" saloon and mileage records 10 10

2279 4z. Nysa "M-521" utility van 30 25

2280 4z.50 Star "660" truck . . . 60 30

622 Iris

623 Cottage, Kurpie

1974. Flowers. Drawings by S. Wyspianski.

2281 **622** 50g. purple 10 10

2282 – 1z. green 10 10

2283 – 1z.50 red 10 10

2284 – 3z. violet 30 10

2285 – 4z. blue 30 10

2286 – 4z.50 green 45 10

FLOWERS: 1z. Dandelion; 1z.50, Rose; 3z. Thistle; 4z. Cornflower; 4z.50, Clover.

1974. Wooden Architecture. Multicoloured.

2287 1z. Type **623** 10 10

2288 1z.50 Church, Sekowa . . . 10 10

2289 4z. Town Hall, Sulmierzycc 20 10

2290 4z.50 Church, Lachowice . . 30 10

2291 4z.90 Windmill, Sobienie Jeziory 45 20

2292 5z. Orthodox Church, Ulucz 50 20

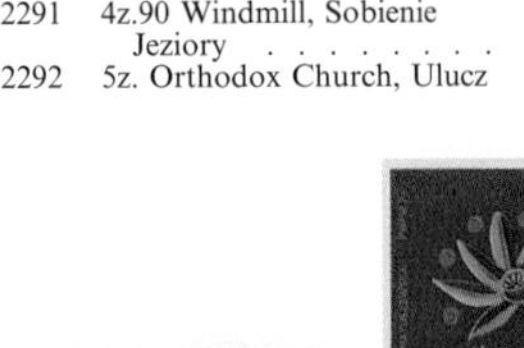

624 19th-century Mail Coach

625 Cracow Motif

1974. Centenary of Universal Postal Union.

2293 **624** 1z.50 multicoloured . . . 10 10

1974. "SOCPHILEX IV" Int Stamp Exn, Katowice. Regional Floral Embroideries. Multicoloured.

2294 50g. Type **625** 10 10

2295 1z.50 Lowicz motif 10 10

2296 4z. Silesian motif 20 10

626 Association Emblem

627 Soldier and Dove

1974. 5th Congress of Fighters for Freedom and Democracy Association, Warsaw.

2298 **626** 1z.50 red 10 10

1974. 29th Anniv of Victory over Fascism in Second World War.

2299 **627** 1z.50 multicoloured . . . 10 10

628 "Comecon" Headquarters, Moscow

1974. 25th Anniv of Council for Mutual Economic Aid.

2300 **628** 1z.50 brown, red & blue 10 10

629 World Cup Emblem

1974. World Cup Football Championship, West Germany. Multicoloured.

2301 4z.90 Type **629** 25 15

2302 4z.90 Players and Olympic Gold Medal of 1972 . . . 25 15

630 Model of 16th-century Galleon

631 Title page of "Chess" by J. Kochanowski

1974. Sailing Ships. Multicoloured.

2304 1z. Type **630** 10 10

2305 1z.50 Sloop "Dal" (1934) 10 10

2306 2z.70 Yacht "Opty" (Teliga's circumnavigation, 1969) 10 10

2307 4z. Cadet ship "Dar Pomorza", 1972 . . . . . 40 10

2308 4z.90 Yacht "Polonez" (Baranowski's circumnavigation, 1973) 55 25

1974. 10th Inter-Chess Festival, Lublin. Mult.

2309 1z. Type **631** 10 15

2310 1z.50 "Education" (18th-century engraving, D. Chodowiecki) 20 15

632 Lazienkowska Road Junction

1974. Opening of Lazienkowska Flyover.

2311 **632** 1z.50 multicoloured . . . 15 15

633 Face and Map of Poland

634 Strawberries

1974. 30th Anniv of Polish People's Republic.

2312 **633** 1z.50 black, gold and red 15 10

2313 – 1z.50 multicoloured (silver background) . . 15 10

2314 – 1z.50 multicoloured (red background) 15 10

DESIGN—31 × 43 mm: Nos. 2313/14, Polish "Eagle".

1974. 19th International Horticultural Congress, Warsaw. Fruits, Vegetables and Flowers. Mult.

2316 50g. Type **634** 10 10

2317 90g. Blackcurrants 10 10

2318 1z. Apples 10 10

2319 1z.50 Cucumbers 20 10

2320 2z.70 Tomatoes 30 10

2321 4z.50 Green peas 75 10

2322 4z.90 Pansies . . . . 1·10 20

2323 5z. Nasturtiums . . . . . . 1·50 30

635 Civic Militia and Security Service Emblem

636 "Child in Polish Costume" (L. Orlowski)

1974. 30th Anniv of Polish Civic Militia and Security Service.

2324 **635** 1z.50 multicoloured . . . 10 10

1974. Stamp Day. "The Child in Polish Costume" Painting. Multicoloured.

2325 50g. Type **636** 10 10

2326 90g. "Girl with Pigeon" (anon) 10 10

2327 1z. "Portrait of a Girl" (S. Wyspianski) 10 10

2328 1z.50 "The Orphan from Poronin" (W. Slewinski) 10 10

2329 3z. "Peasant Boy" (K. Sichulski) 20 10

2330 4z.50 "Florence Page" (A. Gierymski) 35 10

2331 4z.90 "Tadeusz and Dog" (P. Michalowski) 45 30

2332 6z.50 "Boy with Doe" (A. Kotsis) 60 35

637 "The Crib", Cracow

1974. Polish Art. Multicoloured.

2333 1z. Type **637** 10 10

2334 1z.50 "The Flight to Egypt" (15th-century polyptych) 10 10

2335 2z. "King Sigismund III Vasa" (16th-century miniature) 20 10

2336 4z. "King Jan Olbracht" (16th-century title-page) 75 30

638 Angler and Fish

639 "Pablo Neruda" (O. Guayasamin)

1974. Polish Folklore. 16th-century Woodcuts (1st series).

2337 **638** 1z. black 10 10

2338 – 1z.50 blue 10 10

DESIGN: 1z.50, Hunter and wild animals.

See also Nos. 2525/6.

1974. 70th Birth Anniv of Pablo Neruda (Chilean poet).

2339 **639** 1z.50 multicoloured . . . 10 10

640 "Nike" Memorial and National Opera House

1975. 30th Anniv of Warsaw Liberation.

2340 **640** 1z.50 multicoloured . . . 10 10

641 Male Lesser Kestrel

642 Broken Barbed Wire

1975. Birds of Prey. Multicoloured.

2341 1z. Type **641** 25 10

2342 1z. Lesser kestrel (female) 25 10

2343 1z.50 Western red-footed falcon (male) 25 10

2344 1z.50 Western red-footed falcon (female) 25 10

2345 2z. Northern hobby 30 10

2346 3z. Common kestrel 55 10

2347 4z. Merlin . . . . 1·40 75

2348 8z. Peregrine falcon . . . . 2·10 1·50

1975. 30th Anniv of Auschwitz Concentration Camp Liberation.

2349 **642** 1z.50 black and red . . . 10 10

643 Hurdling

1975. 6th European Indoor Athletic Championships, Katowice. Multicoloured.
2350 1z. Type **643** 10 10
2351 1z.50 Pole vault 10 10
2352 4z. Triple jump 30 10
2353 4z.90 Running 30 10

644 "St. Anne" (Veit Stoss)

1975. "Arphila 1975" International Stamp Exhibition, Paris.
2355 **644** 1z.50 multicoloured . . . 10 10

645 Globe and "Radio Waves"

1975. International Amateur Radio Union Conference, Warsaw.
2356 **645** 1z.50 multicoloured . . . 10 10

646 Stone, Pine and Tatra Mountains
647 Hands holding Tulips and Rifle

1975. Centenary of Mountain Guides' Association. Multicoloured.
2357 1z. Type **646** 10 10
2358 1z. Gentians and Tatra Mountains 10 10
2359 1z.50 Sudety Mountains (horiz) 10 10
2360 1z.50 Branch of yew (horiz) 10 10
2361 4z. Beskidy Mountains . . . 30 15
2362 4z. Arnica blossoms 30 10

1975. 30th Anniv of Victory over Fascism.
2363 **647** 1z.50 multicoloured . . . 15 10

648 Flags of Member Countries

1975. 20th Anniv of Warsaw Treaty Organization.
2364 **648** 1z.50 multicoloured . . . 10 10

649 Hens

1975. 26th European Zoo-technical Federation Congress, Warsaw. Multicoloured.
2365 50g. Type **649** 10 10
2366 1z. Geese 10 10
2367 1z.50 Cattle 10 10
2368 2z. Cow 10 10
2369 3z. Wielkopolska horse . . 30 20
2370 4z. Pure-bred Arab horses 30 20
2371 4z.50 Pigs . . . . 1·10 80
2372 5z. Sheep . . . . 1·75 1·10

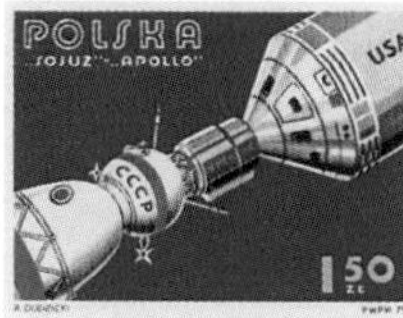

650 "Apollo" and "Soyuz" Spacecraft linked

1975. "Apollo–Soyuz" Space Project. Mult.
2373 1z.50 Type **650** 10 10
2374 4z.90 "Apollo" spacecraft 45 10
2375 4z.90 "Soyuz" spacecraft . . 45 25

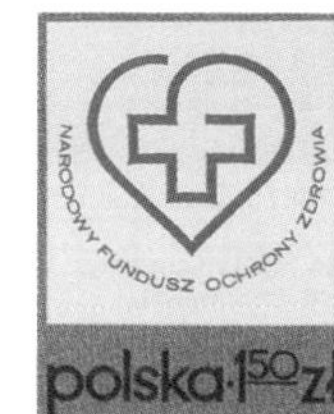

651 Organization Emblem

1975. National Health Protection Fund.
2377 **651** 1z.50 blue, black & silver 10 10

652 U.N. Emblem

1975. 30th Anniv of U.N.O.
2378 **652** 4z. multicoloured 30 10

653 Polish Flag within "E" for Europe

1975. European Security and Co-operation Conference, Helsinki.
2379 **653** 4z. red, blue and black 30 25

654 "Bolek and Lolek"

1975. Children's Television Characters. Mult.
2380 50g. Type **654** 10 15
2381 1z. "Jacek" and "Agatka" 10 15
2382 1z.50 "Reksio" (dog) . . . 10 15
2383 4z. "Telesfor" (dragon) . . 45 15

655 Institute Emblem
656 Women's Faces

1975. 40th Session of International Statistics Institute.
2384 **655** 1z.50 multicoloured . . . 10 10

1975. International Women's Year.
2385 **656** 1z.50 multicoloured . . . 10 10

657 Albatros Biplane

1975. 50th Anniv of First Polish Airmail Stamps. Multicoloured.
2386 2z.40 Type **657** 15 15
2387 4z.90 Ilyushin Il-62 airplane 40 15

658 "Mary and Margaret" and Polish Settlers
659 Frederic Chopin

1975. Bicentenary of American Revolution. Poles in American Life. Multicoloured.
2388 1z. Type **658** 15 10
2389 1z.50 Polish glass-works, Jamestown 10 10
2390 2z.70 Helena Modrzejewska (actress) 10 10
2391 4z. K. Pulaski (soldier) . . . 25 10
2392 6z.40 T. Kosciuzko (soldier) 60 30

1975. 9th International Chopin Piano Competition.
2394 **659** 1z.50 black, lilac & gold 10 20

660 "Self-portrait"
661 Market Place, Kazimierz Dolny

1975. Stamp Day. Birth Centenary of Xawery Dunikowski (sculptor). Multicoloured.
2395 50g. Type **660** 10 10
2396 1z. "Breath" 10 10
2397 1z.50 "Maternity" 15 10
2398 8z.+4z. "Silesian Insurrectionists" 90 35

1975. European Architectural Heritage Year.
2399 **661** 1z. green 10 10
2400 – 1z.50 brown 10 10
DESIGN—VERT: 1z.50, Town Hall, Zamosc.

662 "Lodz" (W. Strzeminski)
664 Symbolized Figure "7"

663 Henry IV's Eagle Gravestone Head (14th-century)

1975. "Lodz 75" National Stamp Exhibition.
2401 **662** 4z.50 multicoloured . . . 30 20

1975. Piast Dynasty of Silesia.
2403 **663** 1z. green 10 10
2404 – 1z.50 brown 10 10
2405 – 4z. violet 25 10
DESIGNS: 1z.50, Seal of Prince Boleslaw of Legnica; 4z. Coin of last Prince, Jerzy Wilhelm.

1975. 7th Congress of Polish United Workers Party.
2406 **664** 1z. multicoloured 10 10
2407 – 1z.50 red, blue and silver 10 10
DESIGN: 1z.50, Party initials "PZPR".

665 Ski Jumping

1976. Winter Olympic Games, Innsbruck. Mult.
2408 50g. Type **665** 10 10
2409 1z. Ice hockey 10 10
2410 1z.50 Skiing 10 10
2411 2z. Skating 10 10
2412 4z. Tobogganing 30 10
2413 6z.40 Biathlon 40 30

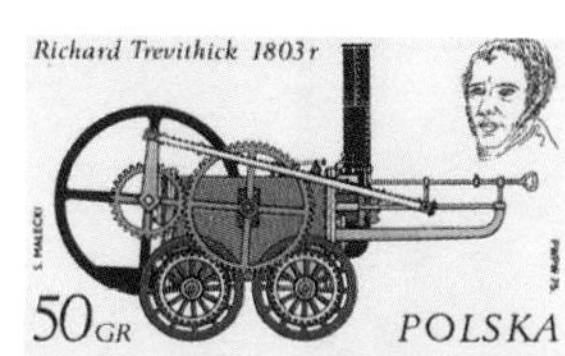

666 Richard Trevithick and his Locomotive, 1803

1976. History of the Railway Locomotive. Mult.
2414 50g. Type **666** 10 10
2415 1z. Murray and Blenkinsop's steam locomotive and carriage, 1810 . . . . 10 10
2416 1z.50 George Stephenson and his locomotive "Rocket", 1829 . . . . . 10 10
2417 1z.50 Polish "Universal" electric locomotive No. ET22-001, 1969 . . . . . 10 10
2418 2z.70 Robert Stephenson and his locomotive "North Star", 1837 . . . 10 10
2419 3z. Joseph Harrison and his locomotive, 1840 . . . . 15 10
2420 4z.50 Locomotive "Thomas Rogers", 1855, U.S.A. . . 75 45
2421 4z.90 A. Xiezopolski and Series Ok22 steam locomotive, 1922 . . . . 75 45

667 Flags of Member Countries

1976. 20th Anniv of Institute for Nuclear Research (C.M.E.A.).
2422 **667** 1z.50 multicoloured . . . 15 10

668 Early Telephone, Satellite and Radar

1976. Telephone Centenary.
2423 **668** 1z.50 multicoloured . . . 10 10

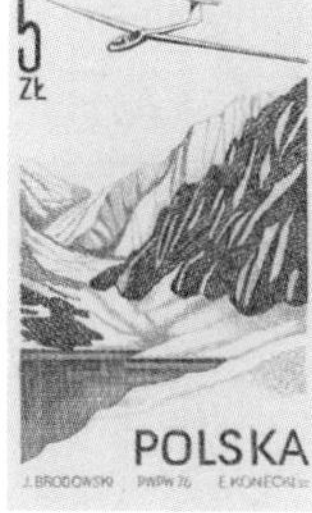

669 Jantar Glider
670 Player

1976. Air. Contemporary Aviation.
2424 **669** 5z. blue 35 10
2425 – 10z. brown 75 10
2425a – 20z. olive . . . . . . 1·50 10
2425b – 50z. lake . . . . . . 3·50 60
DESIGN: 10z. Mil Mi-6 helicopter; 20z. PZL-106A agricultural airplane; 50z. PZL-Mielec TS-11 Iskra jet trainer over Warsaw Castle.

1976. World Ice Hockey Championships, Katowice. Multicoloured.
2426 1z. Type **670** 10 10
2427 1z.50 Player (different) . . . 10 10

671 Polish U.N. Soldier

1976. Polish Troops in U.N. Sinai Force.

2428	**671**	1z.50 multicoloured . . .	10	10

672 "Glory to the Sappers" (S. Kulon) 673 "Interphil 76"

1976. War Memorials. Multicoloured.

2429	1z. Type **672**	10	10
2430	1z. 1st Polish Army Monument, Sandau, Laba (B. Koniuszy)	10	10

1976. "Interphil '76" Int Stamp Exn, Philadelphia.

2431	**673**	8z.40 multicoloured . . .	55	30

674 Wielkopolski Park and Tawny Owl

1976. National Parks. Multicoloured.

2432	90g. Type **674**	30	10
2433	1z. Wolinski Park and white-tailed sea eagle . .	30	10
2434	1z.50 Slowinski Park and seagull	35	10
2435	4z.50 Bieszezadzki Park and lynx	30	10
2436	5z. Ojcowski Park and bat	30	20
2437	6z. Kampinoski Park and elk	35	30

675 Peace Dove within Globe

1976. 25th Anniv of U.N. Postal Administration.

2438	**675**	8z.40 multicoloured . . .	60	25

676 Fencing 677 National Theatre

1976. Olympic Games, Montreal. Multicoloured.

2439	50g. Type **676**	10	10
2440	1z. Cycling	10	10
2441	1z.50 Football	10	10
2442	4z.20 Boxing	30	10
2443	6z.90 Weightlifting	55	15
2444	8z.40 Athletics	60	25

1976. Cent of National Theatre, Poznan.

2446	**677**	1z.50 green and orange	15	10

678 Aleksander Czekanowski and Baikal Landscape 679 "Sphinx"

1976. Death Centenary of Aleksander Czekanowski (geologist).

2447	**678**	1z.50 multicoloured . . .	15	15

1976. Stamp Day. Corinthian Vase Paintings (7th century B.C.). Multicoloured.

2448	1z. Type **679**	10	10
2449	1z.50 "Siren" (horiz)	10	10
2450	2z. "Lion" (horiz)	15	10
2451	4z.20 "Bull" (horiz)	30	10
2452	4z.50 "Goat" (horiz)	30	25
2453	8z.+4z. "Sphinx" (different)	1·00	45

680 Warszawa "M 20"

1976. 25th Anniv of Zeran Motor-car Factory, Warsaw. Multicoloured.

2454	1z. Type **680**	10	10
2455	1z.50 Warszawa "223" . . .	10	10
2456	2z. Syrena "104"	15	10
2457	4z.90 Polski - Fiat "125P"	40	15

681 Molten Steel Ladle

1976. Huta Katowice Steel Works.

2459	**681**	1z.50 multicoloured . . .	15	15

682 Congress Emblem 683 "Wirzbieto Epitaph" (painting on wood, 1425)

1976. 8th Polish Trade Unions Congress.

2460	**682**	1z.50 orange, bistre and brown	15	15

1976. Polish Art. Multicoloured.

2461	1z. Type **683**	10	15
2462	6z. "Madonna and Child" (painted carving, c.1410)	40	15

684 Tanker "Zawrat" at Oil Terminal, Gdansk

1976. Polish Ports. Multicoloured.

2463	1z. Type **684**	10	10
2464	1z. Ferry "Gryf" at Gdansk	10	10
2465	1z.50 Loading container ship "General Bem", Gdynia	20	10
2466	1z.50 Liner "Stefan Batory" leaving Gdynia	20	10
2467	2z. Bulk carrier "Ziemia Szczecinska" loading at Szczecin	25	10
2468	4z.20 Loading coal, Swinoujscie	30	10
2469	6z.90 Pleasure craft, Kolobrzeg	40	30
2470	8z.40 Coastal map	60	30

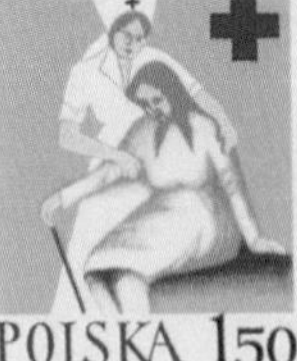

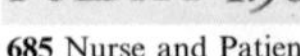

685 Nurse and Patient 686 Order of Civil Defence Service

1977. Polish Red Cross.

2471	**685**	1z.50 multicoloured . . .	10	10

1977. Polish Civil Defence.

2472	**686**	1z.50 multicoloured . . .	10	10

687 Ball in Road

1977. Child Road Safety Campaign.

2473	**687**	1z.50 multicoloured . . .	10	10

688 Dewberries 689 Computer Tape

1977. Wild Fruits. Multicoloured.

2474	50g. Type **688**	10	10
2475	90g. Cowberries	10	10
2476	1z. Wild strawberries . . .	10	10
2477	1z.50 Bilberries	15	10
2478	2z. Raspberries	15	10
2479	4z.50 Sloes	30	10
2480	6z. Rose hips	40	10
2481	6z.90 Hazelnuts	45	30

1977. 30th Anniv of Russian–Polish Technical Co-operation.

2482	**689**	1z.50 multicoloured . . .	10	10

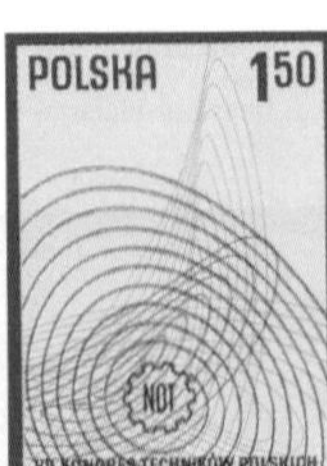

690 Pendulum Traces and Emblem

1977. 7th Polish Congress of Technology.

2483	**690**	1z.50 multicoloured . . .	10	10

691 "Toilet of Venus"

1977. 400th Birth Anniv of Peter Paul Rubens. Multicoloured.

2484	1z. Type **691**	10	10
2485	1z.50 "Bathsheba at the Fountain"	10	10
2486	5z. "Helena Fourment with Fur Coat"	30	10
2487	6z. "Self-portrait"	45	30

692 Dove 694 Wolf

693 Cyclist

1977. World Council of Peace Congress.

2489	**692**	1z.50 blue, yellow & black	10	10

1977. 30th International Peace Cycle Race.

2490	**693**	1z.50 multicoloured . . .	10	10

1977. Endangered Animals. Multicoloured.

2491	1z. Type **694**	10	10
2492	1z.50 Great bustard	30	15
2493	1z.50 Common kestrel . . .	30	15
2494	6z. European otter	40	25

695 "The Violinist" (J. Toorenvliet) 697 H. Wieniawski and Music Clef

696 Midsummer's Day Bonfire

1977. "Amphilex 77" Stamp Exhibition, Amsterdam.

2495	**695**	6z. multicoloured	40	30

1977. Folk Customs. 19th-century Wood Engravings. Multicoloured.

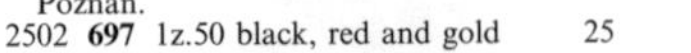

2496	90g. Type **696**	10	10
2497	1z. Easter cock (vert) . . .	10	10
2498	1z.50 "Smigus" (dousing of women on Easter Monday, Miechow district) (vert)	10	10
2499	3z. Harvest Festival, Sandomierz district (vert)	25	10
2500	6z. Children with Christmas crib (vert)	40	10
2501	8z.40 Mountain wedding dance	55	25

1977. Wieniawski International Music Competitions, Poznan.

2502	**697**	1z.50 black, red and gold	25	10

698 Apollo ("Parnassius apollo")

1977. Butterflies. Multicoloured.

2503	1z. Type **698**	30	10
2504	1z. Large tortoiseshell ("Nymphalis polychloros")	30	10
2505	1z.50 Camberwell beauty ("Nymphalis antiopa") . .	40	10
2506	1z.50 Swallowtail ("Papilio machaon")	40	10
2507	5z. High brown fritillary . .	1·10	10
2508	6z.90 Silver-washed fritillary	1·90	45

699 Keyboard and Arms of Slupsk **700** Feliks Dzerzhinsky

1977. Piano Festival, Slupsk.
2509 **699** 1z.50 mauve, blk & grn 15 10

1977. Birth Centenary of Feliks Dzerzhinsky (Russian politician).
2510 **700** 1z.50 brown and ochre 15 15

701 "Sputnik" circling Earth **702** Silver Dinar (11th century)

1977. 60th Anniv of Russian Revolution and 20th Anniv of 1st Artificial Satellite (1st issue).
2511 **701** 1z.50 red and blue . . . 15 15
See also No. 2527.

1977. Stamp Day. Polish Coins. Multicoloured.
2513 50g. Type **702** 10 10
2514 1z. Cracow grosz, 14th-century 10 10
2515 1z.50 Legnica thaler, 17th-century 10 10
2516 4z.20 Gdansk guilder, 18th-century 30 10
2517 4z.50 Silver 5z. coin, 1936 30 10
2518 6z. Millenary 100z. coin, 1966 . . . . 55 25

703 Wolin Gate, Kamien Pomorski **704** "Sputnik 1" and "Mercury" Capsule

1977. Architectural Monuments. Multicoloured.
2519 1z. Type **703** 10 10
2520 1z. Larch church, Debno . . 10 10
2521 1z.50 Monastery, Przasnysz (horiz) 10 10
2522 1z.50 Plock cathedral (horiz) 10 10
2523 6z. Kornik castle (horiz) . . 45 10
2524 6z.90 Palace and garden, Wilanow (horiz) 55 30

1977. Polish Folklore. 16th-century woodcuts (2nd series). As T **638**.
2525 4z. sepia 25 30
2526 4z.50 brown 30 10
DESIGNS: 4z. Bird snaring; 4z.50, Bee-keeper and hives.

1977. 20th Anniv of 1st Space Satellite (2nd issue).
2527 **704** 6z.90 multicoloured . . . 45 40

705 DN Category Iceboats

1978. 6th World Ice Sailing Championships.
2528 **705** 1z.50 black, grey & blue 15 10
2529 – 1z.50 black, grey & blue 25 10
DESIGN: No. 2529, Close-up of DN iceboat.

706 Electric Locomotive and Katowice Station

1978. Railway Engines. Multicoloured.
2530 50g. Type **706** 10 10
2531 1z. Steam locomotive No. Py27 and tender No. 721, Znin-Gasawa railway . . 10 10
2532 1z. Streamlined steam locomotive No. Pm36-1 (1936) and Cegielski's factory, Poznan 10 10
2533 1z.50 Electric locomotive and Otwock station . . . 10 10
2534 1z.50 Steam locomotive No. 17 KDM and Warsaw Stalowa station 10 10
2535 4z.50 Steam locomotive No. Ty51 and Gdynia station 30 10
2536 5z. Steam locomotive No. Tr21 and locomotive works, Chrzanow 40 10
2537 6z. Cockerill steam locomotive and Vienna station 55 30

707 Czeslaw Tanski and Glider

1978. Aviation History and 50th Anniv of Polish Aero Club. Multicoloured.
2538 50g. Type **707** 10 10
2539 1z. Franciszek Zwirko and Stanislaw Wigura with RWD-6 aircraft (vert) . . 10 10
2540 1z.50 Stanislaw Skarzynski and RWD-5 bis monoplane (vert) 10 10
2541 4z.20 Mil Mi-2 helicopter (vert) 25 10
2542 6z.90 PZL-104 Wilga 35 monoplane 75 25
2543 8z.40 SZD-45 Ogar powered glider 60 25

708 Tackle

1978. World Cup Football Championship, Argentina. Multicoloured.
2544 1z.50 Type **708** 10 10
2545 6z.90 Ball on field (horiz) 45 30

709 Biennale Emblem

1978. 7th International Poster Biennale, Warsaw.
2546 **709** 1z.50 mauve, yell & vio 15 15

711 Polonez Saloon Car

1978. Car Production.
2548 **711** 1z.50 multicoloured . . . 10 10

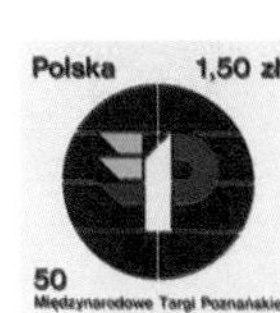

712 Fair Emblem **713** Miroslaw Hermaszewski

1978. 50th International Fair, Poznan.
2549 **712** 1z.50 multicoloured . . . 10 10

1978. 1st Pole in Space. Multicoloured. With or without date.
2550 1z.50 Type **713** 10 10
2551 6z.90 M. Hermaszewski and globe 55 25

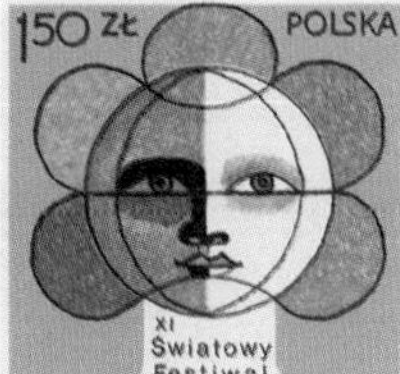

714 Globe containing Face

1978. 11th World Youth and Students Festival, Havana.
2552 **714** 1z.50 multicoloured . . . 10 10

716 Mosquito and Malaria Organisms **717** Pedunculate Oak

1978. 4th International Congress of Parasitologists, Warsaw and Cracow. Multicoloured.
2554 1z.50 Type **716** 10 10
2555 6z. Tsetse fly and sleeping sickness organism 40 40

1978. Environment Protection. Trees. Mult.
2556 50g. Norway Maple 10 10
2557 1z. Type **717** 10 10
2558 1z.50 White Poplar 10 10
2559 4z.20 Scots Pine 25 10
2560 4z.50 White Willow 25 10
2561 6z. Birch 40 15

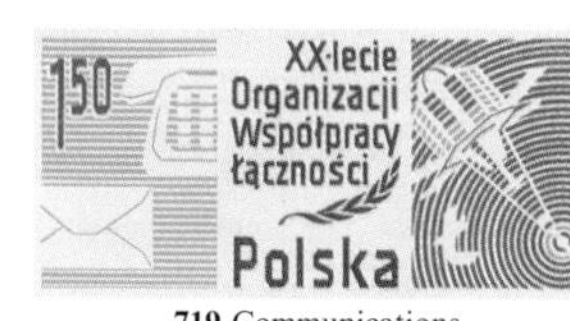

719 Communications

1978. 20th Anniv of Socialist Countries Communications Organization.
2563 **719** 1z.50 red, lt blue & blue 10 10

720 "Peace" (Andre Le Brun)

1978.
2564 **720** 1z. violet 10 10
2565 1z.50 turquoise 10 10
2565a 2z. brown 10 10
2565b 2z.50 blue 25 10

721 Polish Unit of U.N. Middle East Force

1978. 35th Anniv of Polish People's Army. Mult.
2566 1z.50 Colour party of Tadeusz Kosciuszko 1st Warsaw Infantry Division 10 10
2567 1z.50 Mechanized Unit colour party 10 10
2568 1z.50 Type **721** 10 10

722 "Portrait of a Young Man" (Raphael)

1978. Stamp Day.
2569 **722** 6z. multicoloured 40 30

723 Janusz Korczak with Children

1978. Birth Centenary of Janusz Korczak (pioneer of children's education).
2570 **723** 1z.50 multicoloured . . . 25 10

724 Wojciech Boguslawski

1978. Polish Dramatists. Multicoloured.
2571 50g. Type **724** 10 10
2572 1z. Aleksander Fredro . . . 10 10
2573 1z.50 Juliusz Slowacki . . . 10 10
2574 2z. Adam Mickiewicz . . . 10 10
2575 4z.50 Stanislaw Wyspianski 30 10
2576 6z. Gabriela Zapolska . . . 45 25

725 Polish Combatants' Monument and Eiffel Tower

1978. Monument to Polish Combatants in France, Paris.
2577 **725** 1z.50 brown, blue & red 20 10

726 Przewalski Horses

1978. 50th Anniv of Warsaw Zoo. Multicoloured.
2578 50g. Type **726** 10 10
2579 1z. Polar bears 10 10
2580 1z.50 Indian elephants . . . 25 10
2581 2z. Jaguars 30 10
2582 4z.20 Grey seals 30 10
2583 4z.50 Hartebeests 30 10
2584 6z. Mandrills 45 30

727 Party Flag

1978. 30th Anniv of Polish Workers' United Party.
2585 **727** 1z.50 red, gold and black 10 10

728 Stanislaw Dubois

1978. Leaders of Polish Workers' Movement.
2586 **728** 1z.50 blue and red . . . 10 10
2587 – 1z.50 lilac and red . . . 10 10
2588 – 1z.50 olive and red . . . 10 10
2589 – 1z.50 brown and red . . 10 10
DESIGNS: No. 2587, Aleksander Zawadzki; 2588, Julian Lenski; 2589, Aldolf Warski.

729 Ilyushin Il-62M and Fokker F.VIIb/3m

1979. 50th Anniv of LOT Polish Airlines.
2590 **729** 6z.90 multicoloured . . . 55 25

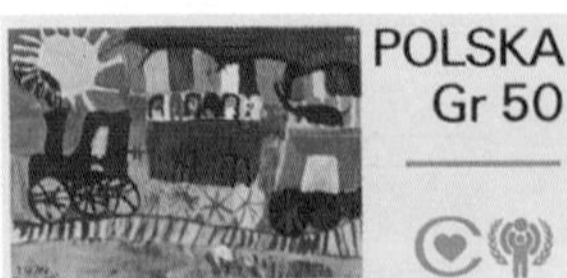

730 Steam Train

1979. International Year of the Child. Children's Paintings. Multicoloured.
2591 50g. Type **730** 10 10
2592 1z. "Mother with Children" 10 10
2593 1z.50 Children playing . . . 10 10
2594 6z. Family Group 40 25

731 "Portrait of Artist's Wife with Foxgloves" (Karol Mondrala)

1979. Contemporary Graphics.
2595 – 50g. lilac 10 10
2596 **731** 1z. green 10 10
2597 – 1z.50 blue 10 10
2598 – 4z.50 brown 30 10
DESIGNS—HORIZ: 50g. "Lightning" (Edmund Bartlomiejezyk). VERT: 1z.50, "The Musicians" (Tadeusz Kulisiewicz); 4z.50, "Head of a Young Man" (Wladyslaw Skoczylas).

732 A. Frycz Modrzewski (political writer), King Stefan Batory and Jan Zamoyski (chancellor)

1979. 400th Anniv (1978) of Royal Tribunal in Piotrkow Trybunalski.
2599 **732** 1z.50 brown and deep brown 10 10

733 Pole Vaulting

1979. 60th Anniv of Polish Olympic Committee. Multicoloured.
2600 1z. Type **733** 10 10
2601 1z.50 High jump 10 10
2602 6z. Skiing 40 10
2603 8z.40 Horse riding 60 25

734 European Flounder

1979. Centenary of Polish Angling. Multicoloured.
2605 50g. Type **734** 10 10
2606 90g. Eurasian perch . . . 10 10
2607 1z. European grayling . . . 10 10
2608 1z.50 Atlantic salmon . . . 10 10
2609 2z. Brown trout 15 10
2610 4z.50 Northern pike 30 10
2611 5z. Common carp 45 10
2612 6z. Wels 45 20

735 "30 Years of RWPG"

1979. 30th Anniv of Council of Mutual Economic Aid.
2613 **735** 1z.50 red, ultram & blue 10 10

736 Soldier, Civilian and Congress Emblem

738 Pope and Auschwitz Concentration Camp Memorial

737 St. George's Church, Sofia

1979. 6th Congress of Association of Fighters for Liberty and Democracy.
2614 **736** 1z.50 red and black . . . 10 10

1979. "Philaserdica 79" International Stamp Exhibition, Sofia, Bulgaria.
2615 **737** 1z.50 orange, brn & red 10 10

1979. Visit of Pope John Paul II. Multicoloured.
2616 1z.50 Pope and St. Mary's Church, Cracow 25 10
2617 8z.40 Type **738** 70 30

739 River Paddle-steamer "Ksiaze Ksawery" and Old Warsaw

1979. 150th Anniv of Vistula River Navigation. Multicoloured.
2619 1z. Type **739** 10 10
2620 1z.50 River paddle-steamer "General Swierczewski" and Gdansk 10 10
2621 4z.50 River tug "Zubr" and Plock 25 10
2622 6z. Passenger launch "Syrena" and modern Warsaw 45 25

740 Statue of Tadeusz Kosciuszko (Marian Konieczny)

741 Mining Machinery

1979. Monument to Tadeusz Kosciuszko in Philadelphia.
2623 **740** 8z.40 multicoloured . . . 40 25

1979. Wieliczka Salt Mine.
2624 **741** 1z. brown and black . . 10 10
2625 – 1z.50 turquoise and black 10 10
DESIGN: 1z.50, Salt crystals.

742 Heraldic Eagle

743 Rowland Hill and 1860 Stamp

1979. 35th Anniv of Polish People's Republic.
2626 – 1z.50 red, silver and black 15 10
2627 **742** 1z.50 red, silver and blue 15 10
DESIGN: No. 2626, Girl and stylized flag.

1979. Death Centenary of Sir Rowland Hill.
2629 **743** 6z. blue, black and orange 40 10

745 Wojciech Jastrzebowski

1979. 7th Congress of International Ergonomic Association, Warsaw.
2631 **745** 1z.50 multicoloured . . . 15 10

746 Monument (Wincenty Kucma)

1979. Unveiling of Monument to Defenders of Polish Post, Gdansk, and 40th Anniv of German Occupation.
2632 **746** 1z.50 multicoloured . . . 15 10

747 Radio Mast and Telecommunications Emblem

1979. 50th Anniv of International Radio Communication Advisory Committee.
2634 **747** 1z.50 multicoloured . . . 15 10

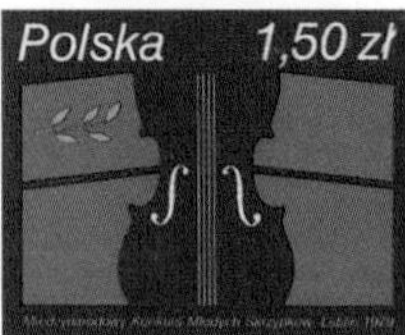

748 Violin

1979. Wieniawski Young Violinists' Competition, Lublin.
2635 **748** 1z.50 blue, orange & green 15 10

749 Statue of Kazimierz Pulaski, Buffalo (K. Danilewicz)

750 Franciszek Jozwiak (first Commander)

1979. Death Bicentenary of Kazimierz Pulaski (American Revolution Hero).
2636 **749** 8z.40 multicoloured . . . 60 30

1979. 35th Anniv of Civic Militia and Security Force.
2637 **750** 1z.50 blue and gold . . . 15 10

751 Post Office in Rural Area

1979. Stamp Day. Multicoloured.
2638 1z. Type **751** 10 10
2639 1z.50 Parcel sorting machinery 10 10
2640 4z.50 Loading containers on train 45 10
2641 6z. Mobile post office . . . 60 25

752 "The Holy Family" (Ewelina Peksowa)

753 "Soyuz 30-Salyut 6" Complex and Crystal

1979. Polish Folk Art. Glass Paintings. Mult.
2642 2z. Type **752** 10 10
2643 6z.90 "The Nativity" (Zdzislaw Walczak) . . . 45 25

1979. Space Achievements. Multicoloured.
2644 1z. Type **753** (1st anniv of 1st Pole in space) 10 10
2645 1z.50 "Kopernik" and "Copernicus" satellites . . 10 10
2646 1z. "Lunik 1" and "Ranger 7" spacecraft (20th anniv of 1st unmanned Moon landing) 10 10
2647 4z.50 Yuri Gagarin and "Vostok 1" 10 10
2648 6z.90 Neil Armstrong, lunar module and "Apollo 11" (10th anniv of first man on Moon) 25 30

754 Coach and Four

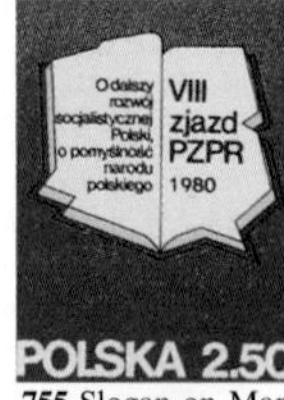

755 Slogan on Map of Poland

1980. 150th Anniv of Sierakow Stud Farm. Mult.
2650 1z. Type **754** 10 10
2651 2z. Horse and groom . . . 10 10
2652 2z.50 Sulky racing 10 10
2653 3z. Hunting 25 10
2654 4z. Horse-drawn sledge . . 30 10
2655 6z. Haywain 45 10
2656 6z.50 Grooms exercising horses 55 25
2657 6z.90 Show jumping 60 30

1980. 8th Polish United Workers' Party Congress. Multicoloured.
2658 2z.50 Type **755** 25 10
2659 2z.50 Janusz Stann (26 × 46 mm) 25 10

756 Horse Jumping

1980. Olympic Games, Moscow, and Winter Olympic Games, Lake Placid. Multicoloured.
2660 2z. Type **756** 10 10
2661 2z.50 Archery 25 10
2662 6z.50 Skiing 45 10
2663 8z.40 Volleyball 60 30

757 Town Plan and Old Town Hall

1980. 400th Anniv of Zamosc.
2665 **757** 2z.50 buff, green & brn . . . 15 10

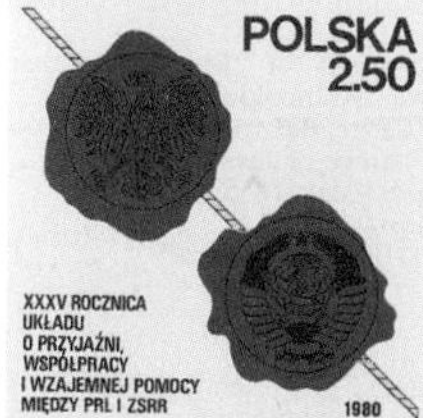

759 Seals of Poland and Russia

1980. 35th Anniv of Soviet–Polish Friendship Treaty.
2667 **759** 2z.50 multicoloured . . . 25 10

760 "Lenin in Cracow" (Zbigniew Pronaszko)

1980. 110th Birth Anniv of Lenin.
2668 **760** 2z.50 multicoloured . . . 25 10

761 Workers with Red Flag

1980. 75th Anniv of Revolution of 1905.
2669 **761** 2z.50 red, black & yellow 25 10

762 Dove

763 Shield with Crests of Member Nations

1980. 35th Anniv of Liberation.
2670 **762** 2z.50 multicoloured . . . 25 10

1980. 25th Anniv of Warsaw Pact.
2671 **763** 2z. grey and red 25 10

764 Speleological Expedition, Cuba

1980. Polish Scientific Expeditions. Multicoloured.
2672 2z. Type **764** 10 10
2673 2z. Antarctic 30 10
2674 2z.50 Archaeology, Syria . . 25 10
2675 2z.50 Ethnology, Mongolia 25 10
2676 6z.50 Mountaineering, Nepal 40 10
2677 8z.40 Paleontology, Mongolia 55 25

765 School and Arms
766 "Clathrus ruber"

1980. 800th Anniv of Malachowski School, Plock.
2678 **765** 2z. green and black . . . 15 10

1980. Fungi. Multicoloured.
2679 2z. Type **766** 20 10
2680 2z. "Xerocomus parasiticus" 20 10
2681 2z.50 Old man of the woods ("Strobilomyces floccopus") 25 10
2682 2z.50 "Phallus hadriani" . . 25 10
2683 8z. Cauliflower fungus . . . 40 20
2684 10z.50 Giant puff-ball . . . 40 45

767 T. Ziolowski and "Lwow"

1980. Polish Merchant Navy School. Cadet Ships and their Captains.
2685 **767** 2z. black, mauve and violet 20 10
2686 – 2z.50 black, light blue and blue 25 10
2687 – 6z. black, pale green and green 30 10
2688 – 6z.50 black, yellow and grey 40 10
2689 – 6z.90 black, grey and green 45 25
2690 – 8z.40 black, blue and green 55 25
DESIGNS: 2z.50, A. Garnuszewski and "Antoni Garnuszewski"; 6z. A. Ledochowski and "Zenit"; 6z.50, K. Porebski and "Jan Turleski"; 6z.90, G. Kanski and "Horyzont"; 8z.40, Maciejewicz and "Dar Pomorza".

768 Town Hall
769 "Atropa belladonna"

1980. Millenary of Sandomir.
2691 **768** 2z.50 brown and black 15 10

1980. Medicinal Plants. Multicoloured.
2692 2z. Type **769** 15 10
2693 2z.50 "Datura innoxia" . . 20 10
2694 3z.40 "Valeriana officinalis" 25 10
2695 5z. "Menta piperita" . . . 30 10
2696 6z.50 "Calendula officinalis" 40 25
2697 8z. "Salvia officinalis" . . . 55 30

770 Jan Kochanowski
771 U.N. General Assembly

1980. 450th Birth Anniv of Jan Kochanowski (poet).
2698 **770** 2z.50 multicoloured . . . 25 15

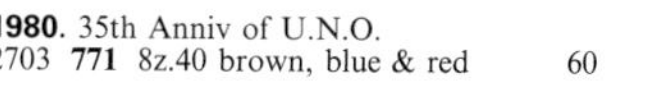

1980. 35th Anniv of U.N.O.
2703 **771** 8z.40 brown, blue & red 60 30

772 Chopin and Trees

1980. 10th International Chopin Piano Competition, Warsaw.
2704 **772** 6z.90 multicoloured . . . 45 30

773 Postman emptying Post Box

1980. Stamp Day. Multicoloured.
2705 2z. Type **773** 20 10
2706 2z.50 Mail sorting 20 10
2707 6z. Loading mail onto aircraft 45 10
2708 6z.50 Letter boxes 55 25

774 Child embracing Dove

1980. United Nations Declaration on the Preparation of Societies for Life in Peace.
2710 **774** 8z.40 multicoloured . . . 60 30

775 "Battle of Olszynka Grochowska" (Wojciech Kossak)

1980. 150th Anniv of Battle of Olszynka Grochowska.
2711 **775** 2z.50 multicoloured . . . 25 15

776 Fire Engine

1980. Warsaw Horse-drawn Vehicles. Mult.
2712 2z. Type **776** 15 10
2713 2z.50 Omnibus 20 10
2714 3z. Brewery dray 25 10
2715 5z. Sledge-cab 30 10
2716 6z. Horse tram 40 30
2717 6z.50 Droshky cab 50 45

777 "Honour to the Silesian Rebels" (statue by Jan Borowczak)
778 Picasso

1981. 60th Anniv of Silesian Rising.
2718 **777** 2z.50 green 15 10

1981. Birth Centenary of Pablo Picasso (artist).
2719 **778** 8z.40 multicoloured . . . 60 30

779 Balloon of Pilatre de Rozier and Romain, 1785
780 "Iphigenia" (Anton Maulbertsch)

1981. Balloons. Multicoloured.
2721 2z. Type **779** 20 10
2722 2z. Balloon of J. Blanchard and J. Jeffries, 1785 . . . 20 10
2723 2z.50 Eugene Godard's quiintuple "acrobatic" balloon, 1850 . . . . . 25 10
2724 3z. F. Hynek and Z. Burzynski's "Kosciuszko", 1933 . . . 25 10
2725 6z. Z. Burzynski and N. Wyescki's "Polonia II", 1935 . . . . 45 25
2726 6z.50 Ben Abruzzo, Max Anderson and Larry Newman's "Double Eagle II", 1978 . . . . 45 25

1981. "WIPA 1981" International Stamp Exhibition, Vienna.
2728 **780** 10z.50 multicoloured . . 85 30

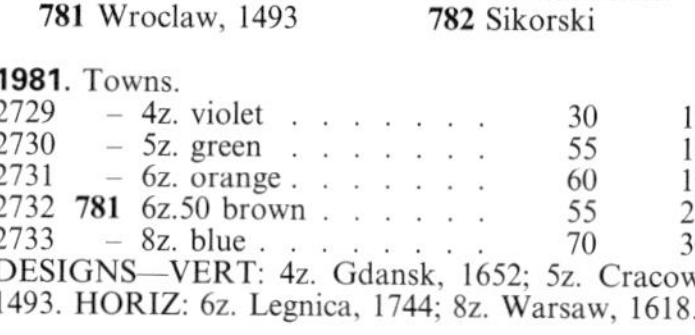

781 Wroclaw, 1493
782 Sikorski

1981. Towns.
2729 – 4z. violet 30 15
2730 – 5z. green 55 15
2731 – 6z. orange 60 15
2732 **781** 6z.50 brown 55 25
2733 – 8z. blue 70 30
DESIGNS—VERT: 4z. Gdansk, 1652; 5z. Cracow, 1493. HORIZ: 6z. Legnica, 1744; 8z. Warsaw, 1618.

1981. Birth Centenary of General Wladyslaw Sikorski (statesman).
2744 **782** 6z.50 multicoloured . . . 55 25

783 Faience Vase
784 Congress Emblem

1981. Pottery. Multicoloured.
2745 1z. Type **783** 15 10
2746 2z. Porcelain cup and saucer in "Baranowka" design 25 10
2747 2z.50 Porcelain jug, Korzec manufacture 25 10
2748 5z. Faience plate with portrait of King Jan III Sobieski by Thiele 45 25
2749 6z.50 Faience "Secession" vase 60 25
2750 8z.40 Porcelain dish, Cmielow manufacture . . 75 30

1981. 14th International Architects' Union Congress, Warsaw.
2751 **784** 2z. yellow, black and red 25 10

785 Wild Boar, Rifle and Oak Leaves
786 European Bison

1981. Game Shooting. Multicoloured.

2752	2z. Type **785**	15	10
2753	2z. Elk, rifle and fir twigs	15	10
2754	2z.50 Red fox, shotgun, cartridges and fir branches	25	10
2755	2z.50 Roe deer, feeding rack, rifle and fir branches	25	10
2756	6z.50 Mallard, shotgun, basket and reeds	70	55
2757	6z.50 Barnacle goose, shotgun and reeds (horiz)	70	55

1981. Protection of European Bison. Mult.

2758	6z.50 Type **786**	70	30
2759	6z.50 Two bison, one grazing	70	30
2760	6z.50 Bison with calf	70	30
2761	6z.50 Calf Feeding	70	30
2762	6z.50 Two bison, both looking towards right	70	30

787 Tennis Player

1981. 60th Anniv of Polish Tennis Federation.

2763	**787**	6z.50 multicoloured	55	30

788 Boy with Model Airplane

1981. Model Making. Multicoloured.

2764	1z. Type **788**	15	10
2765	2z. Model of "Atlas 2" tug	30	10
2766	2z.50 Cars	30	10
2767	4z.20 Man with gliders	30	10
2768	6z.50 Racing cars	60	20
2769	8z. Boy with yacht	70	20

789 Disabled Pictogram **791** H. Wieniawski and Violin Head

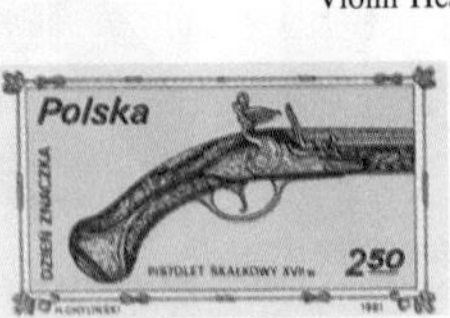

790 17th-cent Flint-lock Pistol

1981. International Year of Disabled Persons.

2770	**789**	8z.40 green, light green and black	70	30

1981. Stamp Day. Antique Weapons. Mult.

2771	2z.50 Type **790**	25	10
2772	8z.40 17th-century gala sabre	70	25

1981. Wieniawski Young Violinists' Competition.

2773	**791**	2z.50 multicoloured	25	15

792 Bronislaw Wesolowski **793** F.A.O. Emblem and Globe

1981. Activists of Polish Workers' Movement.

2774	**792**	50g. green and black	10	10
2775	–	2z. blue and black	15	10
2776	–	2z.50 brown and black	20	10
2777	–	6z.50 mauve and black	70	25

DESIGNS: 2z. Malgorzata Fornalska; 2z.50, Maria Koszutska; 6z.50, Marcin Kasprzak.

1981. World Food Day.

2778	**793**	6z.90 brown, orange & yellow	55	25

794 Helena Modrzejewska (actress)

1981. Bicentenary of Cracow Old Theatre.

2779	**794**	2z. purple, grey and violet	15	10
2780	–	2z.50 blue, stone & brn	25	10
2781	–	6z.50 violet, blue & grn	55	25
2782	–	8z. brown, green and red	85	25

DESIGNS: 2z.50, Stanislaw Kozmian (politician, writer and theatre director); 6z.50, Konrad Swinarski (stage manager and scenographer); 8z. Old Theatre building.

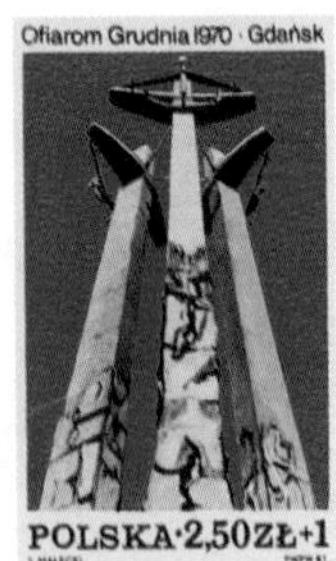

796 Gdansk Memorial

1981. Memorials to the Victims of the 1970 Uprisings.

2784	**796**	2z.50+1z. grey, black and red	30	10
2785	–	6z.50+1z. grey, black and blue	75	30

DESIGN: 6z.50, Gdynia Memorial.

797 "Epiphyllopsis gaertneri"

1981. Succulent Plants. Multicoloured.

2786	90g. Type **797**	15	10
2787	1z. "Cereus tonduzii"	15	10
2788	2z. "Cylindropuntia leptocaulis"	15	10
2789	2z.50 "Cylindropuntia fulgida"	25	10
2790	2z.50 "Coralluma lugardi"	25	10
2791	6z.50 "Nopalea cochenillifera"	1·60	30
2792	6z.50 "Lithops helmutii"	60	30
2793	10z.50 "Cylindropuntia spinosior"	1·00	40

798 Writing on Wall **799** Faience Plate

1982. 40th Anniv of Polish Workers' Coalition.

2794	**798**	2z.50 pink, red and black	25	15

1982. Polish Ceramics. Multicoloured.

2795	1z. Type **799**	15	15
2796	2z. Porcelain cup and saucer, Korzec	25	15
2797	2z.50 Porcelain tureen and sauce-boat, Barnowka	25	15
2798	6z. Porcelain inkpot, Horodnica	55	30
2799	8z. Faience "Hunter's Tumbler", Lubartow	65	30
2800	10z.50 Faience figurine of nobleman, Biala Podlaska	1·10	45

800 Ignacy Lukasiewicz and Lamp **801** Karol Szymanowski

1982. Death Centenary of Ignacy Lukasiewicz (inventor of petroleum lamp).

2801	**800**	1z. multicoloured	15	10
2802	–	2z. multicoloured	25	10
2803	–	2z.50 multicoloured	30	10
2804	–	3z.50 multicoloured	30	10
2805	–	9z. multicoloured	85	30
2806	–	10z. multicoloured	90	35

DESIGNS: 2z. to 10z. Different designs showing lamps.

1982. Birth Centenary of Karol Szymanowski (composer).

2807	**801**	2z.50 brown and gold	25	25

802 RWD 6, 1932

1982. 50th Anniv of Polish Victory in Tourist Aircraft Challenge Competition. Multicoloured.

2808	27z. Type **802**	75	25
2809	31z. RWD 9 (winner of 1934 Challenge)	1·00	30

803 Henryk Sienkiewicz (literature, 1905) **804** Football as Globe

1982. Polish Nobel Prize Winners.

2811	**803**	3z. green and black	10	10
2812	–	15z. brown and black	40	15
2813	–	25z. blue	90	25
2814	–	31z. grey and black	75	45

DESIGNS: 15z. Wladyslaw Reymont (literature, 1924); 25z. Marie Curie (physics, 1903, and chemistry, 1911); 31z. Czeslaw Milosz (literature, 1980).

1982. World Cup Football Championship, Spain. Multicoloured.

2815	25z. Type **804**	75	30
2816	27z. Bull and football (35 × 28 mm)	85	55

806 Stanislaw Sierakowski and Boleslaw Domanski (former Association presidents) **807** Text around Globe

1982. 60th Anniv of Association of Poles in Germany.

2818	**806**	4z.50 red and green	40	15

1982. 2nd U.N. Conference on the Exploration and Peaceful Uses of Outer Space, Vienna.

2819	**807**	31z. multicoloured	75	40

1982. No. 2732 surch **10** °°.

2820	10z. on 6z.50 brown	30	10

809 Father Augustyn Kordecki (prior) **810** Marchers with Banner

1982. 600th Anniv of "Black Madonna" (icon) of Jasna Gora. Multicoloured.

2821	2z.50 Type **809**	10	10
2822	25z. "Siege of Jasna Gora by Swedes, 1655" (detail) (horiz)	40	10
2823	65z. "Black Madonna"	1·10	45

1982. Centenary of Proletarian Party.

2825	**810**	6z. multicoloured	30	15

811 Norbert Barlicki **812** Dr. Robert Koch

1982. Activists of Polish Workers' Movement.

2826	**811**	5z. light blue, blue and black	10	15
2827	–	6z. deep green, green and black	10	15
2828	–	15z. pink, red and black	25	15
2829	–	20z. mauve, violet and black	40	15
2830	–	29z. light brown, brown and black	45	15

DESIGNS: 6z. Pawel Finder; 15z. Marian Buczek; 20z. Cezaryna Wojnarowska; 29z. Ignacy Daszynski.

1982. Centenary of Discovery of Tubercle Bacillus. Multicoloured.

2831	10z. Type **812**	25	15
2832	25z. Dr. Odo Bujwid	85	30

813 Carved Head of Woman **813a** Head of Ruler

1982. Carved Heads from Wawel Castle.

2835	**813a**	3z.50 brown	15	10
2836	–	5z. green	15	10
2837	–	5z. red	10	10
2838	–	10z. blue	15	10
2839	–	15z. brown	15	10
2840	–	20z. grey	45	10
2841	**813a**	20z. blue	15	10
2842	–	40z. brown	75	10
2833	**813**	60z. orange and brown	1·25	25
2843	–	60z. green	15	10
2834	–	100z. ochre and brown	2·75	40
2843a	–	200z. black	2·25	30

DESIGNS—As T **813**: 100z. Man. As T **813a**: 5z. (2836), Warrior; 5z. (2837), 15z. Woman wearing chaplet; 10z. Man in cap; 20z. (2840), Thinker; 40z. Man in beret; 60z. Young man; 200z. Man.

814 Maximilian Kolbe (after M. Koscielniak)

1982. Sanctification of Maximilian Kolbe (Franciscan concentration camp victim).

2844	**814**	27z. multicoloured	1·00	40

815 Polar Research Station

1982. 50th Anniv of Polish Polar Research.
2845 **815** 27z. multicoloured . . . 1·10 40

816 "Log Floats on Vistula River" (drawing by J. Telakowski)

817 Stanislaw Zaremba

1982. Views of the Vistula River.
2846 **816** 12z. blue 25 10
2847 – 17z. blue 30 10
2848 – 25z. blue 40 25
DESIGNS: 17z. "Kazimierz Dolny" (engraving by Andriollo); 25z. "Danzig" (18th-cent engraving).

1982. Mathematicians.
2849 **817** 5z. lilac, blue and black 25 15
2850 – 6z. orange, violet and black 25 15
2851 – 12z. blue, brown and black 40 15
2852 – 15z. yellow, brown and black 60 25
DESIGNS: 6z. Waclaw Sierpinski; 12z. Zygmunt Janiszewski; 15z. Stefan Banach.

818 Military Council Medal

1982. 1st Anniv of Military Council.
2853 **818** 2z.50 multicoloured . . . 25 15

819 Deanery Gate

1982. Renovation of Cracow Monuments (1st series).
2854 **819** 15z. black, olive & green 45 15
2855 – 25z. black, purple & mauve 55 25
DESIGN: 25z. Gateway of Collegium.
See also Nos. 2904/5, 2968/9, 3029/30, 3116 and 3153.

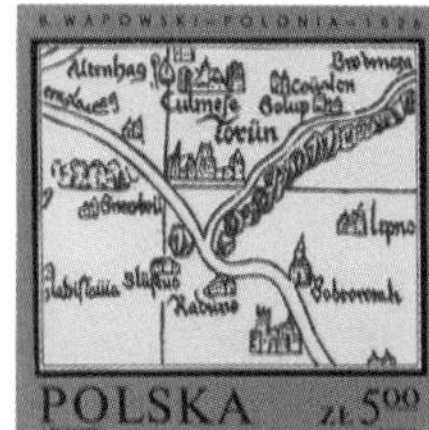

820 Bernard Wapowski Map, 1526

1982. Polish Maps.
2857 **820** 5z. multicoloured 10 10
2858 – 6z. brown, black and red 15 10
2859 – 8z. multicoloured 20 10
2860 – 25z. multicoloured . . . 55 30
DESIGNS: 6z. Map of Prague, 1839; 8z. Map of Poland from Eugen Romer's Atlas, 1908; 25z. Plan of Cracow by A. Buchowiecki, 1703, and Astrolabe.

821 "The Last of the Resistance" (Artur Grottger)

1983. 120th Anniv of January Uprising.
2861 **821** 6z. brown 15 10

822 "Grand Theatre, Warsaw, 1838" (Maciej Zaleski)

1983. 150th Anniv of Grand Theatre, Warsaw.
2862 **822** 6z. multicoloured 15 10

823 Wild Flowers

1983. Environmental Protection. Multicoloured.
2863 5z. Type **823** 15 10
2864 6z. Mute swan and river fishes 30 15
2865 17z. Hoopoe and trees . . . 90 35
2866 30z. Sea fishes 90 45
2867 31z. European bison and roe deer 90 45
2868 38z. Fruit 90 60

824 Karol Kurpinski (composer)

1983. Celebrities.
2869 **824** 5z. light brown and brown 25 10
2870 – 6z. purple and violet . . 25 10
2871 – 17z. light green and green 60 30
2872 – 25z. light brown and brown 65 30
2873 – 27z. light blue and blue 75 30
2874 – 31z. lilac and violet . . . 85 30
DESIGNS: 6z. Maria Jasnorzewska Pawlikowska (poetess); 17z. Stanislaw Szober (linguist); 25z. Tadeusz Banachiewicz (astronomer and mathematician); 27z. Jaroslaw Iwaskiewicz (writer); 31z. Wladyslaw Tatarkiewicz (philosopher and historian).

825 3000 Metres Steeplechase

1983. Sports Achievements.
2875 **825** 5z. pink and violet . . . 25 15
2876 – 6z. pink, brown and black 25 15
2877 – 15z. yellow and green . . 45 15
2878 – 27z.+5z. light blue, blue and black . . . . . . 1·00 30
DESIGNS: 6z. Show jumping; 1z. Football; 27z.+5z. Pole vault.

826 Ghetto Heroes Monument (Natan Rappaport)

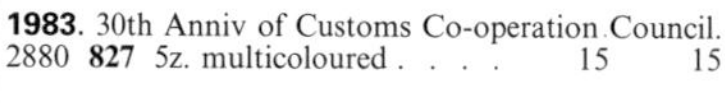

827 Customs Officer and Suitcases

1983. 40th Anniv of Warsaw Ghetto Uprising.
2879 **826** 6z. light brown & brown 25 15

1983. 30th Anniv of Customs Co-operation Council.
2880 **827** 5z. multicoloured 15 15

828 John Paul II and Jasna Gora Sanctuary

829 Dragoons

1983. Papal Visit. Multicoloured.
2881 31z. Type **828** 85 40
2882 65z. Niepokalanow Church and John Paul holding crucifix . . . . 1·90 75

1983. 300th Anniv of Polish Relief of Vienna (1st issue). Troops of King Jan III Sobieski. Mult.
2884 5z. Type **829** 15 10
2885 5z. Armoured cavalryman 15 10
2886 6z. Infantry non-commissioned officer and musketeer 25 10
2887 15z. Light cavalry lieutenant 30 30
2888 27z. "Winged" hussar and trooper with carbine . . . 90 45
See also Nos. 2893/6.

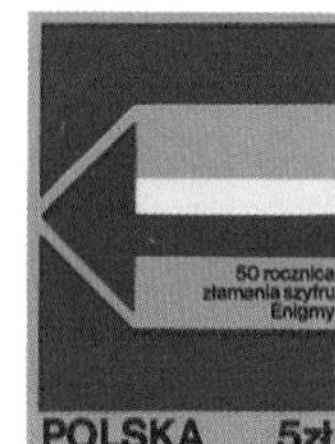

830 Arrow piercing "E"

1983. 50th Anniv of Deciphering "Enigma" Machine Codes.
2889 **830** 5z. red, grey and black 15 15

831 Torun

1983. 750th Anniv of Torun.
2890 **831** 6z. multicoloured 25 15

832 Child's Painting

1983. "Order of the Smile" (Politeness Publicity Campaign).
2892 **832** 6z. multicoloured 25 15

833 King Jan III Sobieski

1983. 300th Anniv of Relief of Vienna (2nd issue). Multicoloured.
2893 5z. Type **833** 25 15
2894 6z. King Jan III Sobieski (different) 25 15
2895 6z. "King Jan III Sobieski on Horseback" (Francesco Trevisani) . . 25 15
2896 25z. "King Jan III Sobieski" (Jerzy Eleuter) 90 30

834 Wanda Wasilewska

835 Profiles and W.C.Y. Emblem

1983. 40th Anniv of Polish People's Army. Multicoloured.
2898 **834** 5z. multicoloured 10 10
2899 – 5z. deep green, green and black 10 10
2900 – 6z. multicoloured 25 10
2901 – 6z. multicoloured 25 10
DESIGNS—VERT: No. 2899, General Zygmunt Berling; 2900, "The Frontier Post" (S. Poznanski). HORIZ: No. 2901, "Taking the Oath" (S. Poznanski).

1983. World Communications Year.
2902 **835** 15z. multicoloured . . . 45 25

836 Boxing

1983. 60th Anniv of Polish Boxing Federation.
2903 **836** 6z. multicoloured 25 15

1983. Renovation of Cracow Monuments (2nd series). As T **819**.
2904 5z. brown, purple and black 15 10
2905 6z. black, green and blue . . 15 15
DESIGNS—HORIZ: 5z. Cloth Hall. VERT: 6z. Town Hall tower.

837 Biskupiec Costume

838 Hand with Sword (poster by Zakrzewski and Krolikowski, 1945)

1983. Women's Folk Costumes. Multicoloured.
2906 5z. Type **837** 15 10
2907 5z. Rozbark 15 10
2908 6z. Warmia & Mazuria . . 25 10
2909 6z. Cieszyn 25 10
2910 25z. Kurpie 90 30
2911 38z. Lubusk . . . . 1·25 55

1983. 40th Anniv of National People's Council.
2912 **838** 6z. multicoloured 25 10

839 Badge of "General Bem" Brigade

840 Dulcimer

1983. 40th Anniv of People's Army.
2913 **839** 5z. multicoloured 25 10

1984. Musical Instruments (1st series). Mult.
2914 5z. Type **840** 15 10
2915 6z. Kettle drum and tambourine 25 15
2916 10z. Accordion 40 30
2917 15z. Double bass 45 40
2918 17z. Bagpipe 55 45
2919 29z. Country band (wood carvings by Tadeusz Zak) 90 65

841 Wincenty Witos

842 "Clematis lanuginosa"

1984. 110th Birth Anniv of Wincenty Witos (leader of Peasants' Movement).
2920 **841** 6z. brown and green . . 25 10

1984. Clematis. Multicoloured.
2921 5z. Type **842** 20 10
2922 6z. "C. tangutica" 25 10
2923 10z. "C. texensis" 30 10
2924 17z. "C. alpina" 45 15
2925 25z. "C. vitalba" 90 30
2926 27z. "C. montana" . . . . 1·00 45

843 "The Ecstasy of St. Francis" (El Greco)

1984. "Espana 84" International Stamp Exhibition, Madrid.
2927 **843** 27z. multicoloured . . . 90 40

844 Handball

1984. Olympic Games, Los Angeles, and Winter Olympics, Sarajevo. Multicoloured.
2928 5z. Type **844** 10 10
2929 6z. Fencing 15 10
2930 15z. Cycling 45 25
2931 16z. Janusz Kusocinski winning 10,000 m race, 1932 Olympics, Los Angeles 60 30
2932 17z. Stanislawa Walasiewiczowna winning 100 m race, 1932 Olympics, Los Angeles . . 60 30
2933 31z. Women's slalom (Winter Olympics) . . . . 1·00 45

845 Monte Cassino Memorial Cross and Monastery

846 "German Princess" (Lucas Cranach)

1984. 40th Anniv of Battle of Monte Cassino.
2935 **845** 15z. olive and red . . . 55 25

1984. 19th U.P.U. Congress, Hamburg.
2936 **846** 27z.+10z. multicoloured 55 1·90

847 "Warsaw from the Praga Bank" (Canaletto)

1984. Paintings of Vistula River. Multicoloured.
2937 5z. Type **847** 25 25
2938 6z. "Trumpet Festivity" (A. Gierymski) 25 25
2939 25z. "The Vistula near Bielany District" (J. Rapacki) 90 65
2940 27z. "Steamship Harbour in the Powisle District" (F. Kostrzewski) . . . . 1·00 75

848 Order of Grunwald Cross

849 Group of Insurgents

1984. 40th Anniv of Polish People's Republic. Multicoloured.
2941 5z. Type **848** 25 10
2942 6z. Order of Revival of Poland 25 10
2943 10z. Order of Banner of Labour, First Class . . . 30 10
2944 16z. Order of Builders of People's Poland 60 30

1984. 40th Anniv of Warsaw Uprising. Mult.
2946 4z. Type **849** 25 10
2947 5z. Insurgent on postal duty 25 10
2948 6z. Insurgents fighting . . . 25 10
2949 25z. Tending wounded . . . 95 30

850 Defence of Oksywie Holm and Col. Stanislaw Dabek

1984. 45th Anniv of German Invasion. Mult.
2950 5z. Type **850** 25 10
2951 6z. Battle of Bzura River and Gen. Tadeusz Kutrzeba 25 10
See also Nos. 3004/5, 3062, 3126/8, 3172/4 and 3240/3.

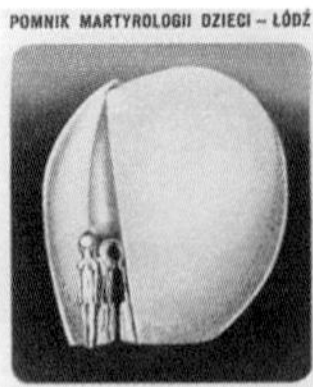

851 "Broken Heart" (monument, Lodz Concentration Camp)

1984. Child Martyrs.
2952 **851** 16z. brown, blue and deep brown 45 25

852 Militiaman and Ruins

1984. 40th Anniv of Security Force and Civil Militia. Multicoloured.
2953 5z. Type **852** 15 10
2954 6z. Militiaman in control centre 25 10

853 First Balloon Flight, 1784 (after Chostovski)

1984. Polish Aviation.
2955 **853** 5z. black, green & mauve 25 10
2956 – 5z. multicoloured 25 10
2957 – 6z. multicoloured 25 10
2958 – 10z. multicoloured . . . 30 10
2959 – 16z. multicoloured . . . 40 15
2960 – 27z. multicoloured . . . 90 30
2961 – 31z. multicoloured . . . 1·10 50
DESIGNS: No. 2956, Michal Scipio del Campo and biplane (1st flight over Warsaw, 1911); 2957, Balloon "Polonez" (winner, Gordon Bennett Cup, 1983); 2958, PWS 101 and Jantar gliders (Lilienthal Medal winners); 2959, PZL-104 Wilga airplane (world precise flight champion, 1983); 2960, Jan Nagorski and Farman M.F.7 floatplane (Arctic zone flights, 1914); 2961, PZL P-37 Los and PZL P-7 aircraft.

854 Weasel

1984. Fur-bearing Animals. Multicoloured.
2962 4z. Type **854** 15 10
2963 5z. Stoat 15 10
2964 5z. Beech marten 25 10
2965 10z. Eurasian beaver 25 10
2966 10z. Eurasian otter 25 10
2967 65z. Alpine marmot . . . . 1·90 60

1984. Renovation of Cracow Monuments (3rd series). As T **819**.
2968 5z. brown, black and green 15 10
2969 15z. blue, brown and black 30 15
DESIGNS—VERT: 5z. Wawel cathedral. HORIZ: 15z. Wawel castle (royal residence).

855 Protestant Church, Warsaw

1984. Religious Architecture. Multicoloured.
2970 5z. Type **855** 10 10
2971 10z. Saint Andrew's Roman Catholic church, Krakow 25 10
2972 15z. Greek Catholic church, Rychwald 40 10
2973 20z. St. Maria Magdalena Orthodox church, Warsaw 55 10
2974 25z. Tykocin synagogue, Kaczorow (horiz) 60 30
2975 31z. Tatar mosque, Kruszyiany (horiz) . . . 75 30

856 Steam Fire Hose (late 19th century)

1985. Fire Engines. Multicoloured.
2976 4z. Type **856** 10 10
2977 10z. "Polski Fiat", 1930s . . 25 10
2978 12z. "Jelcz 315" fire engine 30 10
2979 15z. Manual fire hose, 1899 40 10
2980 20z. "Magirus" fire ladder on "Jelcz" chassis 55 30
2981 30z. Manual fire hose (early 18th century) 84 40

857 "Battle of Raclawice" (Jan Styka and Wojciech Kossak)

1985.
2982 **857** 27z. multicoloured . . . 60 30

858 Wincenty Rzymowski

859 Badge on Denim

1985. 35th Death Anniv of Wincenty Rzymowski (founder of Polish Democratic Party).
2983 **858** 10z. violet and red . . . 30 15

1985. International Youth Year.
2984 **859** 15z. multicoloured . . . 40 15

860 Boleslaw III, the Wry-mouthed, and Map

1985. 40th Anniv of Return of Western and Northern Territories to Poland. Multicoloured.
2985 5z. Type **860** 10 10
2986 10z. Wladyslaw Gomulka (vice-president of first postwar government) and map 30 15
2987 20z. Piotr Zaremba (Governor of Szczecin) and map 60 25

861 "Victory, Berlin 1945" (Joesf Mlynarski)

1985. 40th Anniv of Victory over Fascism.
2988 **861** 5z. multicoloured 15 15

862 Warsaw Arms and Flags of Member Countries

864 Cadet Ship "Iskra"

863 Wolves in Winter

1985. 30th Anniv of Warsaw Pact.

2989	**862**	5z. multicoloured	15	15

1985. Protected Animals. The Wolf. Mult.

2990	5z. Type **863**	15	10
2991	10z. She-wolf with cubs . .	30	25
2992	10z. Close-up of wolf . . .	30	25
2993	20z. Wolves in summer . .	60	45

1985. Musical Instruments (2nd series). As T **840**. Multicoloured.

2994	5z. Rattle and tarapata . .	15	10
2995	10z. Stick rattle and berlo	30	10
2996	12z. Clay whistles	40	10
2997	20z. Stringed instruments . .	60	25
2998	25z. Cow bells	85	25
2999	31z. Wind instruments . . .	1·00	30

1985. 40th Anniv of Polish Navy.

3000	**864**	5z. blue and yellow . . .	15	10

865 Tomasz Nocznicki

1985. Leaders of Peasants' Movement.

3001	**865**	10z. green	25	10
3002	–	20z. brown	45	25

DESIGN: 20z. Maciej Rataj.

866 Hockey Players

1985. 60th Anniv (1986) of Polish Field Hockey Association.

3003	**866**	5z. multicoloured	15	10

1985. 46th Anniv of German Invasion. As T **850**. Multicoloured.

3004	5z. Defence of Wizna and Capt. Wladyslaw Raginis	15	10
3005	10z. Battle of Mlawa and Col. Wilhelm Liszka-Lawicz	30	10

867 Type 20k Goods Wagon

1985. PAFAWAG Railway Rolling Stock. Mult.

3006	5z. Type **867**	15	10
3007	10z. Electric locomotive No. ET22-001, 1969	25	10
3008	17z. Type OMMK wagon	40	25
3009	20z. Type 111A passenger carriage	55	30

869 Green-winged Teal

1985. Wild Ducks. Multicoloured.

3011	5z. Type **869**	15	10
3012	5z. Garganey	15	10
3013	10z. Tufted duck	30	10
3014	15z. Common goldeneye . .	40	10
3015	25z. Eider	65	30
3016	29z. Red-crested pochard . .	1·00	30

870 U.N. Emblem and "Flags"

1985. 40th Anniv of U.N.O.

3017	**870**	27z. multicoloured . . .	60	30

871 Ballerina

872 "Marysia and Burek in Ceylon"

1985. Bicentenary of Polish Ballet.

3018	**871**	5z. green, orange and red	15	10
3019	–	15z. brown, violet & orange	45	10

DESIGN: 15z. Male dancer.

1985. Birth Centenary of Stanislaw Ignacy Witkiewicz (artist). Multicoloured.

3020	5z. Type **872**	15	10
3021	10z. "Woman with Fox" (horiz)	30	10
3022	10z. "Self-portrait"	30	10
3023	20z. "Compositions (1917–20)"	55	30
3024	25z. "Nena Stachurska" . .	65	30

874 Human Profile

1986. Congress of Intellectuals for Defence of Peaceful Future of the World, Warsaw.

3026	**874**	10z. ultramarine, violet and blue	30	10

875 Michal Kamienski and Planetary and Comet's Orbits

1985. Appearance of Halley's Comet.

3027	**875**	25z. blue and brown . .	60	30
3028	–	25z. deep blue, blue and brown	60	30

DESIGN: No. 3028, "Vega", "Planet A", "Giotto" and "Ice" space probes and comet.

1986. Renovation of Cracow Monuments (4th series). As T **819**.

3029	5z. dp brown, brown & black	10	10
3030	10z. green, brown and black	25	10

DESIGNS: 5z. Collegium Maius (Jagiellonian University Museum); 10z. Kazimierz Town Hall.

876 Sun

877 Grey Partridge

1986. International Peace Year.

3031	**876**	25z. yellow, light blue and blue	45	25

1986. Game. Multicoloured.

3032	5z. Type **877**	30	30
3033	5z. Common rabbit	10	10
3034	10z. Common pheasants (horiz)	55	55
3035	10z. Fallow deer (horiz) . .	15	10
3036	20z. Hare	30	30
3037	40z. Argali	65	65

878 Kulczynski

880 Paderewski (composer)

879 "Warsaw Fire Brigade, 1871" (detail, Jozef Brodowski)

1986. 10th Death Anniv (1985) of Stanislaw Kulczynski (politician).

3038	**878**	10z. light brown and brown	25	10

1986. 150th Anniv of Warsaw Fire Brigade.

3039	**879**	10z. dp brown & brown	25	10

1986. "Ameripex '86" International Stamp Exhibition, Chicago.

3040	**880**	65z. blue, black and grey	1·40	45

881 Footballers

1986. World Cup Football Championship, Mexico.

3041	**881**	25z. multicoloured . . .	45	30

882 "Wilanow"

1986. Passenger Ferries. Multicoloured.

3042	10z. Type **882**	25	15
3043	10z. "Wawel"	25	15
3044	15z. "Pomerania"	30	15
3045	25z. "Rogalin"	55	25

883 A. B. Dobrowolski, Map and Research Vessel "Kopernik"

885 "The Paulinite Church on Skalka in Cracow" (detail), 1627

1986. 25th Anniv of Antarctic Agreement.

3047	**883**	5z. green, black and red	10	15
3048	–	40z. lavender, violet and orange	1·90	30

DESIGN: 40z. H. Arctowski, map and research vessel "Profesor Siedlecki".

1986. 10th Polish United Workers' Party Congress, Warsaw.

3049	**884**	10z. blue and red	25	10

1986. Treasures of Jasna Gora Monastery. Mult.

3050	5z. Type **885**	15	10
3051	5z. "Tree of Jesse", 17th-century	15	10
3052	20z. Chalice, 18th-century	40	25
3053	40z. "Virgin Mary" (detail, chasuble column), 15th-century	1·10	30

886 Precision Flying (Waclaw Nycz)

1986. 1985 Polish World Championship Successes. Multicoloured.

3054	5z. Type **886**	15	10
3055	10z. Windsurfing (Malgorzata Palasz-Piasecka)	40	10
3056	10z. Glider areobatics (Jerzy Makula)	30	10
3057	15z. Wrestling (Bogdan Daras)	30	10
3058	20z. Individual road cycling (Lech Piasecki)	45	25
3059	30z. Women's modern pentathlon (Barbara Kotowska)	75	30

887 "Bird" in National Costume carrying Stamp

888 Schweitzer

1986. "Stockholmia '86" International Stamp Exhibition.

3060	**887**	65z. multicoloured . . .	1·40	45

1986. 47th Anniv of German Invasion. As T **850**. Multicoloured.

3062	10z. Battle of Jordanow and Col. Stanislaw Maczek . .	25	10

1986. 10th Death Anniv (1985) of Albert Schweitzer (medical missionary).

3063	**888**	5z. brown, lt brown & blue	15	10

889 Airliner and Postal Messenger

890 Basilisk

1986. World Post Day.

3064	**889**	40z. brown, blue and red	75	30

1986. Folk Tales. Multicoloured.

3066	5z. Type **890**	15	15
3067	5z. Duke Popiel (vert) . . .	15	15
3068	10z. Golden Duck	25	15
3069	10z. Boruta the Devil (vert)	25	15
3070	20z. Janosik the Robber (vert)	40	15
3071	50z. Lajkonik (vert)	1·10	40

891 Kotarbinski

892 20th-century Windmill, Zygmuntow

884 Workers and Emblem

1986. Birth Centenary of Tadeusz Kotarbinski (philosopher).
3072 **891** 10z. deep brown and brown 25 30

1986. Wooden Architecture. Multicoloured.
3073 5z. Type **892** 15 10
3074 5z. 17th-century church, Baczal Dolny 15 10
3075 10z. 19th-century Oravian cottage, Zubrzyca Gorna 25 10
3076 15z. 18th-century Kashubian arcade cottage, Wdzydze 25 15
3077 25z. 19th-century barn, Grzawa 55 25
3078 30z. 19th-century watermill, Siolkowice Stare 75 30

893 Mieszko (Mieczyslaw) I

1986. Polish Rulers (1st series). Drawings by Jan Matejko.
3079 **893** 10z. brown and green . . 30 30
3080 – 25z. black and purple . . 75 45
DESIGN: 25z. Queen Dobrawa (wife of Mieszko I).
See also Nos. 3144/5, 3193/4, 3251/2, 3341/2, 3351/2, 3387/8, 3461/4, 3511/12, 3548/51, 3641/4, 3705/8, 3732/5, 3819/22 and 3887/91.

894 Star

1986. New Year.
3081 **894** 25z. multicoloured . . . 45 30

895 Trip to Bielany, 1887

1986. Centenary of Warsaw Cyclists' Society.
3082 **895** 5z. multicoloured 10 15
3083 – 5z. brown, light brown and black 10 15
3084 – 10z. multicoloured . . . 25 15
3085 – 10z. multicoloured . . . 25 15
3086 – 30z. multicoloured . . . 60 30
3087 – 50z. multicoloured . . . 1·10 45
DESIGNS: No. 3083, Jan Stanislaw Skrodaki (1895 touring record holder); 3084, Dynasy (Society's headquarters, 1892–1937); 3085, Mieczyslaw Baranski (1896 Kingdom of Poland road cycling champion); 3086, Karolina Kociecka; 3087, Henryk Weiss (Race champion).

896 Lelewel

1986. Birth Bicentenary of Joachim Lelewel (historian).
3088 **896** 10z.+5z. multicoloured 30 15

897 Krill and "Antoni Garnuszewski" (cadet freighter)

1987. 10th Anniv of Henryk Arctowski Antarctic Station, King George Island, South Shetlands. Multicoloured.
3089 5z. Type **897** 10 10
3090 5z. Antarctic toothfish, marbled rockfish and "Zulawy" (supply ship) 10 10
3091 10z. Southern fulmar and "Pogoria" (cadet brigantine) 30 10
3092 10z. Adelie penguin and "Gedania" (yacht) 30 10
3093 30z. Fur seal and "Dziunia" (research vessel) 40 10
3094 40z. Leopard seals and "Kapitan Ledochowski" (research vessel) 45 30

898 "Portrait of a Woman"

1987. 50th Death Anniv (1986) of Leon Wyczolkowski (artist). Multicoloured.
3095 5z. "Cineraria Flowers" (horiz) 10 10
3096 10z. Type **898** 15 10
3097 10z. "Wooden Church" (horiz) 15 10
3098 25z. "Beetroot Lifting" . . 40 10
3099 30z. "Wading Fishermen" (horiz) 45 15
3100 40z. "Self-portrait" (horiz) 60 40

899 "Ravage" (from "War Cycle") and Artur Grottger

1987. 150th Birth Anniv of Artur Grottger (artist).
3101 **899** 15z. brown and stone . . 25 10

900 Swierczewski **901** Strzelecki

1987. 90th Birth Anniv of General Karol Swierczewski.
3102 **900** 15z. green and olive . . 25 10

1987. 190th Birth Anniv of Pawel Edmund Strzelecki (scientist and explorer of Tasmania).
3103 **901** 65z. green 60 30

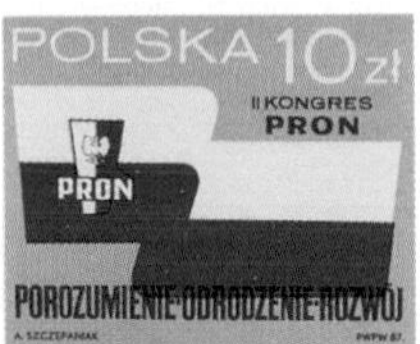

902 Emblem and Banner

1987. 2nd Patriotic Movement for National Revival Congress.
3104 **902** 10z. red, blue and brown 15 10

903 CWS "T-1" Motor Car, 1928

1987. Polish Motor Vehicles. Multicoloured.
3105 10z. Type **903** 10 10
3106 10z. Saurer-Zawrat bus, 1936 . . . . 10 10
3107 15z. Ursus-A lorry, 1928 . . 25 10
3108 15z. Lux-Sport motor car, 1936 . . . . 25 10
3109 25z. Podkowa "100" motor cycle, 1939 . . . . 30 10
3110 45z. Sokol "600 RT" motor cycle, 1935 . . . . 55 55

904 Royal Palace, Warsaw

1987.
3111 **904** 50z. multicoloured . . . 60 30

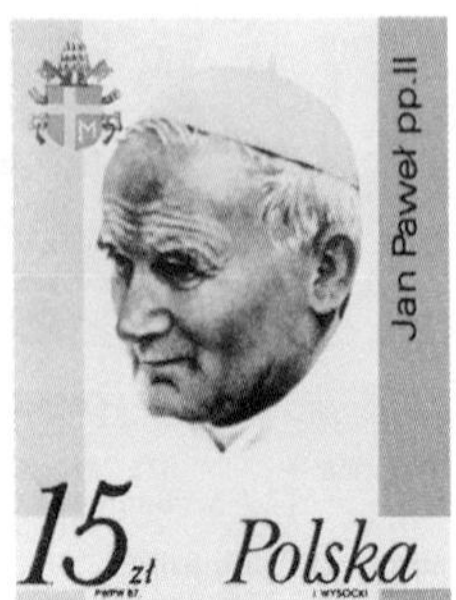

905 Pope John Paul II

1987. 3rd Papal Visit. Multicoloured.
3112 15z. Type **905** 25 15
3113 45z. Pope and signature . . 45 30

906 Polish Settler at Kasubia, Ontario

1987. "Capex '87" International Stamp Exhibition, Toronto.
3115 **906** 50z.+20z. multicoloured 75 40

1987. Renovation of Cracow Monuments (5th series). As T **819**.
3116 10z. lilac, black and green 15 10
DESIGN: 10z. Barbican.

907 Ludwig Zamenhof (inventor) and Star

1987. Cent of Esperanto (invented language).
3117 **907** 5z. brown, green & black 60 25

908 "Poznan Town Hall" (Stanislaw Wyspianski) **909** Queen Bee

1987. "Poznan 87" National Stamp Exhibition.
3118 **908** 15z. brown and orange 25 15

1987. "Apimondia 87" International Bee Keeping Congress, Warsaw. Multicoloured.
3119 10z. Type **909** 15 10
3120 10z. Worker bee 15 10
3121 15z. Drone 25 10
3122 15z. Hive in orchard 25 10
3123 40z. Worker bee on clover flower 60 25
3124 50z. Forest bee keeper collecting honey 75 30

1987. 48th Anniv of German Invasion. As T **850**. Multicoloured.
3126 10z. Battle of Mokra and Col. Julian Filipowicz . . 15 10
3127 10z. Fighting at Oleszyce and Brig.-Gen. Jozef Rudolf Kustron 15 10
3128 15z. PZL P-7 aircraft over Warsaw and Col. Stefan Pawlikowski 30 10

911 Hevelius and Sextant **912** High Jump (World Acrobatics Championships, France)

1987. 300th Death Anniv of Jan Hevelius (astronomer). Multicoloured.
3129 15z. Type **911** 25 10
3130 40z. Hevelius and map of constellations (horiz) . . . 55 25

1987. 1986 Polish World Championship Successes. Multicoloured.
3131 10z. Type **912** 15 10
3132 15z. Two-man canoe (World Canoeing Championships, Canada) 25 10
3133 20z. Marksman (Free pistol event, World Marksmanship Championships, East Germany) 30 15
3134 25z. Wrestlers (World Wrestling Championships, Hungary) 45 15

914 Warsaw Post Office and Ignacy Franciszek Przebendowski (Postmaster General)

1987. World Post Day.
3136 **914** 15z. green and red . . . 25 10

915 "The Little Mermaid" **916** Col. Stanislaw Wieckowski (founder)

1987. "Hafnia 87" International Stamp Exhibition, Copenhagen. Hans Christian Andersen's Fairy Tales. Multicoloured.
3137 10z. Type **915** 15 10
3138 10z. "The Nightingale" . . 15 10
3139 20z. "The Wild Swans" . . 25 15
3140 20z. "The Little Match Girl" 25 15
3141 30z. "The Snow Queen" . . 40 30
3142 40z. "The Tin Soldier" . . . 55 15

1987. 50th Anniv of Democratic Clubs.
3143 **916** 15z. black and blue . . . 25 10

1987. Polish Rulers (2nd series). As T **893**. Drawings by Jan Matejko.
3144 10z. green and blue 15 15
3145 15z. blue and ultramarine 40 30
DESIGNS: 10z. Boleslaw I, the Brave; 15z. Mieszko (Mieczyslaw) II.

917 Santa Claus with Christmas Trees

1987. New Year.
3146 **917** 15z. multicoloured . . . 15 15

918 Emperor Dragonfly

1988. Dragonflies. Multicoloured.
3147 10z. Type **918** 15 10
3148 15z. Four-spotted libellula ("Libellula quadrimaculata") (vert) 30 10
3149 15z. Banded agrion ("Calopteryx splendens") 30 10
3150 20z. "Condulegaster annulatus" (vert) 30 10
3151 30z. "Sympetrum pedemontanum" 40 25
3152 50z. "Aeschna viridis" (vert) 65 30

1988. Renovation of Cracow Monuments (6th series). As T **819**.
3153 15z. yellow, brown and black 15 10
DESIGN: 15z. Florianska Gate.

919 Composition

1988. International Year of Graphic Design.
3154 **919** 40z. multicoloured . . . 40 40

920 17th-century Friesian Wall Clock with Bracket Case

1988. Clocks and Watches. Multicoloured.
3155 10z. Type **920** 15 10
3156 10z. 20th-century annual clock (horiz) 15 10
3157 15z. 18th-century carriage clock 15 10
3158 15z. 18th-century French rococo bracket clock . . 15 10
3159 20z. 19th-century pocket watch (horiz) 25 10
3160 40z. 17th-cent tile-case clock from Gdansk by Benjamin Zoll (horiz) . . 40 15

921 Atlantic Salmon and Reindeer

1988. "Finlandia 88" International Stamp Exhibition, Helsinki.
3161 **921** 45z.+30z. multicoloured 60 30

922 Triple Jump

924 Wheat as Graph on VDU

1988. Olympic Games, Seoul. Multicoloured.
3162 15z. Type **922** 25 10
3163 20z. Wrestling 25 10
3164 20z. Canoeing 25 10
3165 25z. Judo 25 10
3166 40z. Shooting 40 15
3167 55z. Swimming 55 30

1988. 16th European Conference of Food and Agriculture Organization, Cracow. Multicoloured.
3169 15z. Type **924** 15 10
3170 40z. Factory in forest . . . 30 10

925 PZL P-37 Los Bomber

1988. 70th Anniv of Polish Republic (1st issue). 60th Anniv of Polish State Aircraft Works.
3171 **925** 45z. multicoloured . . . 30 10
See also Nos. 3175, 3177, 3181/88 and 3190/2.

1988. 49th Anniv of German Invasion. As T **850**. Multicoloured.
3172 15z. Battle of Modlin and Brig.-Gen. Wiktor Thommee 25 10
3173 20z. Battle of Warsaw and Brig.-Gen. Walerian Czuma 25 10
3174 20z. Battle of Tomaszow Lubelski and Brig.-Gen. Antoni Szylling 25 10

1988. 70th Anniv of Polish Republic (2nd issue). 50th Anniv of Stalowa Wola Ironworks. As T **925**. Multicoloured.
3175 15z. View of plant 15 10

926 Postal Emblem and Tomasz Arciszewski (Postal Minister, 1918–19)

1988. World Post Day.
3176 **926** 20z. multicoloured . . . 15 10

1988. 70th Anniv of Polish Republic (3rd issue). 60th Anniv of Military Institute for Aviation Medicine. As T **925**. Multicoloured.
3177 20z. Hanriot XIV hospital aircraft (38 × 28 mm) . . 15 10

927 On the Field of Glory Medal

1988. Polish People's Army Battle Medals (1st series). Multicoloured.
3178 20z. Type **927** 15 10
3179 20z. Battle of Lenino Cross 15 10
See also Nos. 3249/50.

928 "Stanislaw Malachowski" and "Kazimierz Nestor Sapieha"

1988. Bicentenary of Four Years Diet (political and social reforms). Paintings of Diet Presidents by Jozef Peszko.
3180 **928** 20z. multicoloured . . . 15 10

929 Ignacy Daszynski (politician)

1988. 70th Anniv of Polish Republic (4th issue). Personalities.
3181 **929** 15z. green, red and black 10 10
3182 – 15z. green, red and black 10 10
3183 – 20z. brown, red and black 15 10
3184 – 20z. brown, red and black 15 10
3185 – 20z. brown, red and black 15 10
3186 – 200z. purple, red & black 1·40 55
3187 – 200z. purple, red & black 1·40 55
3188 – 200z. purple, red & black 1·40 55
DESIGNS: No. 3182, Wincenty Witos (politician); 3183, Julian Marchlewski (trade unionist and economist); 3184, Stanislaw Wojciechowski (politician); 3185, Wojciech Korfanty (politician); 3186, Ignacy Paderewski (musician and politician); 3187; Marshal Jozef Pilsudski; 3188, Gabriel Narutowicz (President, 1922).

1988. 70th Anniv of Polish Republic (5th issue). As T **925**. Multicoloured.
3190 15z. Coal wharf, Gdynia Port (65th anniv) (38 × 28 mm) 10 10
3191 20z. Hipolit Cegielski (founder) and steam locomotive (142nd anniv of H. Cegielski Metal Works, Poznan) (38 × 28 mm) 15 10
3192 40z. Upper Silesia Tower (main entrance) (60th anniv of International Poznan Fair) 30 10

1988. Polish Rulers (3rd series). Drawings by Jan Matejko. As T **893**.
3193 10z. deep brown and brown 30 10
3194 15z. deep brown and brown 45 10
DESIGNS: 10z. Queen Rycheza; 15z. Kazimierz (Karol Odnowiciel) I.

930 Snowman

1988. New Year.
3195 **930** 20z. multicoloured . . . 15 10

931 Flag

932 "Blysk"

1988. 40th Anniv of Polish United Workers' Party.
3196 **931** 20z. red and black . . . 15 10

1988. Fire Boats. Multicoloured.
3197 10z. Type **932** 10 10
3198 15z. "Plomien" 10 10
3199 15z. "Zar" 10 10
3200 20z. "Strazak II" 25 10
3201 20z. "Strazak 4" 25 10
3202 45z. "Strazak 25" 40 30

933 Ardennes

1989. Horses. Multicoloured.
3203 15z. Lippizaner (horiz) . . . 10 10
3204 15z. Type **933** 10 10
3205 20z. English thoroughbred (horiz) 25 10
3206 20z. Arab 25 10
3207 30z. Great Poland race-horse (horiz) 40 10
3208 70z. Polish horse 75 30

934 Wire-haired Dachshund

1989. Hunting Dogs. Multicoloured.
3209 15z. Type **934** 10 10
3210 15z. Cocker spaniel 10 10
3211 20z. Czech fousek pointer 10 10
3212 20z. Welsh terrier 10 10
3213 25z. English setter 15 10
3214 45z. Pointer 30 30

935 Gen. Wladyslaw Anders and Plan of Battle

936 Marianne

1989. 45th Anniv of Battle of Monte Cassino.
3215 **935** 80z. multicoloured . . . 40 30
See also Nos. 3227, 3247, 3287 and 3327.

1989. Bicentenary of French Revolution.
3216 **936** 100z. black, red and blue 40 25

937 Polonia House

1989. Opening of Polonia House (cultural centre), Pultusk.
3218 **937** 100z. multicoloured . . . 45 25

938 Monument (Bohdan Chmielewski)

1989. 45th Anniv of Civic Militia and Security Force.
3219 **938** 35z. blue and brown . . 25 15

939 Xaweri Dunikowski (artist)

941 Firemen

940 Astronaut

1989. Recipients of Order of Builders of the Republic of Poland. Multicoloured.
3220 35z. Type **939** 15 10
3221 35z. Stanislaw Mazur (farmer) 15 10

3222 35z. Natalia Gasiorowska (historian) 15 10
3223 35z. Wincenti Pstrowski (initiator of worker performance contests) . . 15 10

1989. 20th Anniv of First Manned Landing on Moon.
3224 **940** 100z. multicoloured . . . 45 25

1989. World Fire Fighting Congress, Warsaw.
3226 **941** 80z. multicoloured . . . 30 10

1989. 45th Anniv of Battle of Falaise. As T **935**. Multicoloured.
3227 165z. Plan of battle and Gen. Stanislaw Maczek (horiz) 60 30

942 Daisy

943 Museum Emblem

1989. Plants. (a) Perf.
3229 **942** 40z. green 15 10
3230 – 60z. violet 15 10
3231 **942** 150z. red 30 10
3232 – 500z. mauve 30 10
3233 – 700z. green 15 10
3234 – 1000z. blue 90 30

(b) Self-adhesive. Imperf.
3297 – 2000z. green 40 25
3298 – 5000z. violet 85 40

DESIGNS: 60z. Juniper; 500z. Wild rose; 700z. Lily of the valley; 1000z. Blue cornflower; 2000z. Water lily; 5000z. Iris.

1989. 50th Anniv of German Invasion. As T **850**.
3240 25z. grey, orange and black 25 10
3241 25z. multicoloured 25 10
3242 35z. multicoloured 40 30
3243 35z. multicoloured 40 30

DESIGNS: No. 3240, Defence of Westerplatte and Captain Franciszek Dabrowski; 3241, Defence of Hel and Captain B. Przybyszewski; 3242, Battle of Kock and Brig.-Gen. Franciszek Kleeberg; 3243, Defence of Lwow and Brig.-Gen. Wladyslaw Langner.

1989. Caricature Museum.
3244 **943** 40z. multicoloured . . . 15 10

944 Rafal Czerwiakowski (founder of first university Surgery Department)

945 Emil Kalinski (Postal Minister, 1933–39)

1989. Polish Surgeons' Society Centenary Congress, Cracow.
3245 **944** 40z. blue and black . . . 25 10
3246 – 60z. green and black . . 25 10

DESIGN: 60z. Ludwik Rydygier (founder of Polish Surgeons' Society).

1989. 45th Anniv of Landing at Arnhem. As T **935**. Multicoloured.
3247 210z. Gen. Stanislaw Sosabowski and plan of battle 75 45

1989. World Post Day.
3248 **945** 60z. multicoloured . . . 25 25

1989. Polish People's Army Battle Medals (2nd series). As T **927**. Multicoloured.
3249 60z. "For Participation in the Struggle for the Rule of the People" 25 15
3250 60z. Warsaw 1939–45 Medal 25 15

1989. Polish Rulers (4th series). As T **893**. Drawings by Jan Matejko.
3251 20z. black and grey 30 10
3252 30z. sepia and brown . . . 30 30

DESIGNS: 20z. Boleslaw II, the Bold; 30z. Wladyslaw I Herman.

946 Stamps

1989. "World Stamp Expo '89" International Stamp Exhibition, Washington D.C.
3253 **946** 500z. multicoloured . . . 1·10 65

947 Cross and Twig

949 Photographer and Medal depicting Maksymilian Strasz

948 Ignacy Paderewski and Roman Dmowski (Polish signatories)

1989. 70th Anniv of Polish Red Cross.
3254 **947** 200z. red, green and black 45 25

1989. 70th Anniv of Treaty of Versailles.
3255 **948** 350z. multicoloured . . . 60 60

1989. 150th Anniv of Photography. Multicoloured.
3256 40z. Type **949** 15 10
3257 60z. Lens shutter as pupil of eye (horiz) 15 10

1989. No. 2729 surch **500**.
3258 500z. on 4z. violet 90 45

951 Painting by Jan Ciaglinski

1989. Flower Paintings by Artists Named. Mult.
3259 25z. Type **951** 10 10
3260 30z. Wojciech Weiss 10 10
3261 35z. Antoni Kolasinski . . . 15 10
3262 50z. Stefan Nacht-Samborski 15 10
3263 60z. Jozef Pankiewicz . . . 15 10
3264 85z. Henryka Beyer 25 25
3265 110z. Wladyslaw Slewinski 30 30
3266 190z. Czeslaw Wdowiszewski 40 40

952 Christ

1989. Icons (1st series). Multicoloured.
3267 50z. Type **952** 15 10
3268 60z. Two saints with books 15 10
3269 90z. Three saints with books 25 15
3270 150z. Displaying scriptures (vert) 40 40
3271 200z. Madonna and child (vert) 45 45
3272 350z. Christ with saints and angels (vert) 45 45

See also Nos. 3345/50.

1990. No. 2839 surch **350 zl**.
3273 350z. on 15z. brown 60 30

954 Krystyna Jamroz

955 High Jumping

1990. Singers. Multicoloured.
3274 100z. Type **954** 25 25
3275 150z. Wanda Werminska . . 25 25
3276 350z. Ada Sari 40 40
3277 500z. Jan Kiepura 45 45

1990. Sports. Multicoloured.
3278 100z. Yachting 15 25
3279 200z. Rugby 15 30
3280 400z. Type **955** 15 30
3281 500z. Ice skating 15 40
3282 500z. Diving 15 45
3283 1000z. Gymnastics 25 30

956 Kozlowski

1990. Birth Centenary (1989) of Roman Kozlowski (palaeontologist).
3284 **956** 500z. brown and red . . 15 25

957 John Paul II

1990. 70th Birthday of Pope John Paul II.
3285 **957** 1000z. multicoloured . . 30 30

1990. 50th Anniv of Battle of Narvik. As T **935**. Multicoloured.
3287 1500z. Gen. Zygmunt Bohusz-Szyszko and plan of battle 30 25

959 Ball and Colosseum

1990. World Cup Football Championship, Italy.
3288 **959** 1000z. multicoloured . . 15 25

1990. No. 3230 surch **700 zl**.
3289 700z. on 60z. violet 15 15

961 Memorial

963 Stagnant Pond Snail

962 People and "ZUS"

1990. 34th Anniv of 1956 Poznan Uprising.
3290 **961** 1500z. multicoloured . . 25 15

1990. 70th Anniv of Social Insurance.
3291 **962** 1500z. blue, mauve & yellow 30 25

1990. Shells. No value expressed.
3292 – B (500z.) lilac 25 10
3293 **963** A (700z.) green 45 10

DESIGN: B, River snail.

964 Cross

1990. 50th Anniv of Katyn Massacre.
3294 **964** 1500z. black and red . . 25 10

965 Weather Balloon

1990. Polish Hydrology and Meteorology Service. Multicoloured.
3295 500z. Type **965** 10 10
3296 700z. Water-height gauge . . 25 10

966 Women's Kayak Pairs

1990. 23rd World Canoeing Championships. Mult.
3305 700z. Type **966** 25 10
3306 1000z. Men's kayak singles 30 30

967 Victory Sign

968 Jacob's Ladder

1990. 10th Anniv of Solidarity Trade Union.
3307 **967** 1500z. grey, black and red 25 30

1990. Flowers. Multicoloured.
3308 200z. Type **968** 10 10
3309 700z. Floating heart water fringe ("Nymphoides peltata") 15 10
3310 700z. Dragonhead ("Dracocephalum ruyschiana") 15 10
3311 1000z. "Helleborus purpurascens" 25 10
3312 1500z. Daphne cneorum . . 45 40
3313 1700z. Campion 65 45

969 Serving Dish, 1870–87

1990. Bicentenary of Cmieow Porcelain Works. Multicoloured.
3314 700z. Type **969** 15 10
3315 800z. Plate, 1887–90 (vert) 25 10
3316 1000z. Cup and saucer, 1887 30 10
3317 1000z. Figurine of dancer, 1941–44 (vert) 30 10
3318 1500z. Chocolate box, 1930–90 . . . . 55 25
3319 2000z. Vase, 1979 (vert) . . 60 40

970 Little Owl

972 Collegiate Church, Tum (12th century)

971 Walesa

1990. Owls. Multicoloured.
3320 200z. Type **970** 15 10
3321 500z. Tawny owl (value at left) 35 10
3322 500z. Tawny owl (value at right) 35 10
3323 1000z. Short-eared owl . . . 50 25
3324 1500z. Long-eared owl . . . 80 30
3325 2000z. Barn owl . . . . . 1·10 40

1990. Lech Walesa, 1984 Nobel Peace Prize Winner and new President.
3326 **971** 1700z. multicoloured . . 40 25

1990. 50th Anniv of Battle of Britain. As T **935**. Multicoloured.
3327 1500z. Emblem of 303 Squadron, Polish Fighter Wing R.A.F. and Hawker Hurricane 45 45

1990. Historic Architecture. Multicoloured.
3328 700z. Type **972** 25 20
3329 800z. Reszel Castle (11th century) 25 25
3330 1500z. Chelmno Town Hall (16th century) 60 60
3331 1700z. Church of the Nuns of the Visitation, Warsaw (18th century) 60 60

973 "King Zygmunt II August" (anon)

974 Silver Fir

1991. Paintings. Multicoloured.
3332 500z. Type **973** 15 10
3333 700z. "Adoration of the Magi" (Pultusk Codex) 25 10
3334 1000z. "St Matthew" (Pultusk Codex) 30 10
3335 1500z. "Expelling of Merchants from Temple" (Nikolai Haberschrack) 45 30
3336 1700z. "The Annunciation" (miniature) 55 30
3337 2000z. "Three Marys" (Nikolai Haberschrack) 60 40

1991. Cones. Multicoloured.
3338 700z. Type **974** 15 10
3339 1500z. Weymouth pine . . . 25 25
See also Nos. 3483/4.

975 Radziwill Palace

977 Chmielowski

1991. Admission of Poland into European Postal and Telecommunications Conference.
3340 **975** 1500z. multicoloured . . 30 25

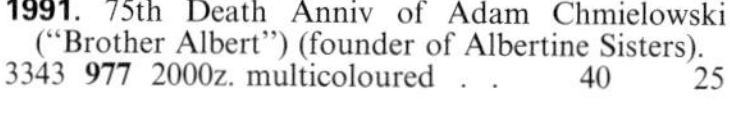

1991. Polish Rulers (5th series). Drawings by Jan Matejko. As T **893** but surch.
3341 1000z. on 40z. black & green 40 25
3342 1500z. on 50z. black and red 55 30
DESIGNS: 1000z. Boleslaw III, the Wry Mouthed; 1500z. Wladyslaw II, the Exile.
Nos. 3341/2 were not issued unsurcharged.

1991. 75th Death Anniv of Adam Chmielowski ("Brother Albert") (founder of Albertine Sisters).
3343 **977** 2000z. multicoloured . . 40 25

978 Battle (detail of miniature, Schlackenwerth Codex, 1350)

1991. 750th Anniv of Battle of Legnica.
3344 **978** 1500z. multicoloured . . 30 25

1991. Icons (2nd series). As T **952**. Mult.
3345 500z. "Madonna of Nazareth" 10 10
3346 700z. "Christ the Acheirophyte" 15 10
3347 1000z. "Madonna of Vladimir" 25 10
3348 1500z. "Madonna of Kazan" 40 15
3349 2000z. "St. John the Baptist" 55 25
3350 2200z. "Christ the Pentocrator" 85 30

1991. Polish Rulers (6th series). Drawings by Jan Matejko. As T **893**.
3351 1000z. black and red 30 25
3352 1500z. black and blue . . . 45 25
DESIGNS: 1000z. Boleslaw IV, the Curly; 1500z. Mieszko (Mieczyslaw) III, the Old.

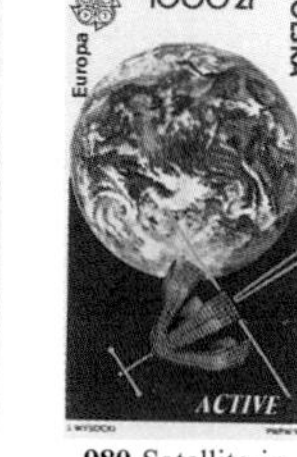

979 Title Page of Constitution

980 Satellite in Earth Orbit

1991. Bicentenary of 3rd May Constitution.
3353 **979** 2000z. brown, buff & red 40 30
3354 – 2500z. brown, stone & red 55 40
DESIGNS: 2500z. "Administration of Oath by Gustav Taubert" (detail, Johann Friedrich Bolt).

1991. Europa. Europe in Space.
3356 **980** 1000z. multicoloured . . 25 25

981 Map and Battle Scene

1991. 50th Anniv of Participation of "Piorun" (destroyer) in Operation against "Bismarck" (German battleship).
3357 **981** 2000z. multicoloured . . 45 30

982 Arms of Cracow

983 Pope John Paul II

1991. European Security and Co-operation Conference Cultural Heritage Symposium, Cracow.
3358 **982** 2000z. purple and blue 40 30

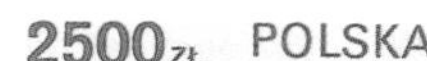

1991. Papal Visit. Multicoloured.
3359 1000z. Type **983** 25 10
3360 2000z. Pope in white robes 40 30

984 Bearded Penguin

985 Making Paper

1991. 30th Anniv of Antarctic Treaty.
3361 **984** 2000z. multicoloured . . 40 30

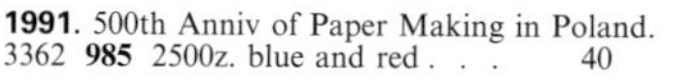

1991. 500th Anniv of Paper Making in Poland.
3362 **985** 2500z. blue and red . . . 40 30

986 Prisoner

1991. Commemoration of Victims of Stalin's Purges.
3363 **986** 2500z. red and black . . 40 30

988 Ball and Basket

1991. Centenary of Basketball.
3365 **988** 2500z. multicoloured . . 55 30

989 "Self-portrait" (Leon Wyczolkowski)

1991. "Bydgoszcz '91" National Stamp Exn.
3366 **989** 3000z. green and brown 55 40

990 Twardowski

1991. 125th Birth Anniv of Kazimierz Twardowski (philosopher).
3368 **990** 2500z. black and grey . . 60 40

991 Swallowtail

1991. Butterflies and Moths. Multicoloured.
3369 1000z. Type **991** 25 25
3370 1000z. Dark crimson underwing ("Mormonia sponsa") 25 25
3371 1500z. Painted lady ("Vanessa cardui") . . . 30 25
3372 1500z. Scarce swallowtail ("Iphiclides podalirius") 30 25
3373 2500z. Scarlet tiger moth ("Panaxia dominula") . . 55 40
3374 2500z. Peacock ("Nymphalis io") 55 40

992 "The Shepherd's Bow" (Francesco Solimena)

1991. Christmas.
3376 **992** 1000z. multicoloured . . 30 25

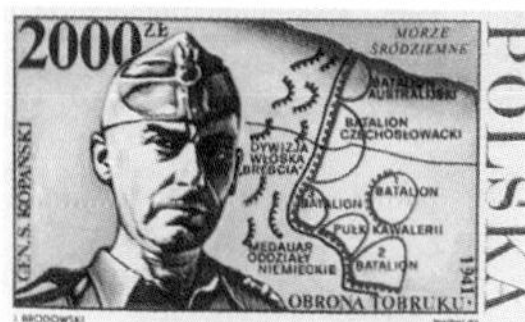

993 Gen. Stanislaw Kopanski and Battle Map

1991. 50th Anniv of Participation of Polish Troops in Battle of Tobruk.
3377 **993** 2000z. multicoloured . . 40 45

994 Brig.-Gen. Michal Tokarzewski-Karaszewicz

995 Lord Baden-Powell (founder)

1991. World War II Polish Underground Army Commanders.
3378 **994** 2000z. black and red . . 40 25
3379 – 2500z. red and violet . . 45 30
3380 – 3000z. violet and mauve 55 40
3381 – 5000z. brown and green 90 60
3382 – 6500z. dp brown & brn 1·10 75
DESIGNS: 2500z. Gen. Broni Kazimierz Sosnkowski; 3000z. Lt.-Gen. Stefan Rowecki; 5000z. Lt.-Gen. Tadeusz Komorowski; 6500z. Brig.-Gen. Leopold Okulicki.

1991. 80th Anniv of Scout Movement in Poland.
3383 **995** 1500z. yellow and green 30 10
3384 – 2000z. blue and yellow 45 30
3385 – 2500z. violet and yellow 55 30
3386 – 3500z. brown and yellow 65 45
DESIGNS: 2000z. Andrzej Malkowski (Polish founder); 2500z. "Watch on the Vistula" (Wojciech Kossak); 3500z. Polish scout in Warsaw Uprising, 1944.

1992. Polish Rulers (7th series). As T **893**.
3387 1500z. brown and green . . 40 25
3388 2000z. black and blue . . . 55 40
DESIGNS: 1500z. Kazimierz II, the Just; 2000z. Leszek I, the White.

996 Sebastien Bourdon

1992. Self-portraits. Multicoloured.
3389 700z. Type **996** 15 10
3390 1000z. Sir Joshua Reynolds 25 10
3391 1500z. Sir Godfrey Kneller 25 10
3392 2000z. Bartolome Esteban Murillo 40 25
3393 2200z. Peter Paul Rubens 45 25
3394 3000z. Diego de Silva y Velazquez 60 45

997 Skiing

1992. Winter Olympic Games, Albertville. Mult.
3395 1500z. Type **997** 25 25
3396 2500z. Ice hockey 45 30

998 Manteuffel

1992. 90th Birth Anniv of Tadeusz Manteuffel (historian).
3397 **998** 2500z. brown 45 30

999 Nicolas Copernicus (astronomer)

1992. Famous Poles. Multicoloured.
3398 1500z. Type **999** 25 10
3399 2000z. Frederic Chopin (composer) 40 25
3400 2500z. Henryk Sienkiewicz (writer) 45 25
3401 3500z. Marie Curie (physicist) 60 30

1000 Columbus and Left-hand Detail of Map

1992. Europa. 500th Anniv of Discovery of America by Columbus. Multicoloured.
3403 1500z. Type **1000** 25 25
3404 3000z. "Santa Maria" and right-hand detail of Juan de la Costa map, 1500 . . 55 45
Nos. 3403/4 were issued together, se-tenant, forming a composite design.

1001 River Czarna Wiselka

1003 Family and Heart

1002 Prince Jozef Poniatowski

1992. Environmental Protection. River Cascades. Multicoloured.
3405 2000z. Type **1001** 45 15
3406 2500z. River Swider 60 40
3407 3000z. River Tanew 60 30
3408 3500z. Mickiewicz waterfall 60 40

1992. Bicentenary of Order of Military Virtue. Multicoloured.
3409 1500z. Type **1002** 25 25
3410 3000z. Marshal Jozef Pilsudski 40 30

1992. Children's Drawings. Multicoloured.
3412 1500z. Type **1003** 25 10
3413 3000z. Butterfly, sun, bird and dog 60 30

1004 Fencing

1992. Olympic Games, Barcelona. Multicoloured.
3414 1500z. Type **1004** 25 10
3415 2000z. Boxing 40 30
3416 2500z. Running 45 30
3417 3000z. Cycling 55 40

1006 Statue of Korczak

1992. 50th Death Anniv of Janusz Korczak (educationist).
3419 **1006** 1500z. black, brown & yellow 30 30

1007 Flag and "V"

1008 Wyszinski

1992. 5th Polish Veterans World Meeting.
3420 **1007** 3000z. multicoloured . . 55 54

1992. 11th Death Anniv of Stefan Wyszinski (Primate of Poland) (3421) and 1st Anniv of World Youth Day (3422). Multicoloured.
3421 1500z. Type **1008** 30 15
3422 3000z. Pope John Paul II embracing youth 60 45

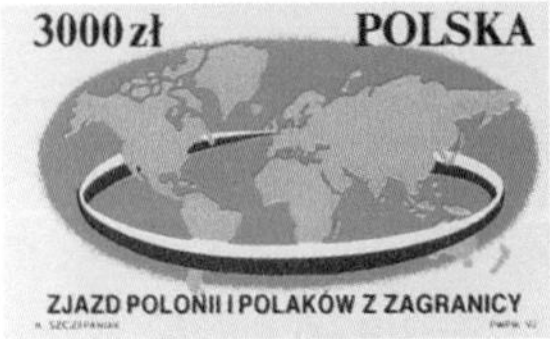

1009 National Colours encircling World Map

1992. World Meeting of Expatriate Poles, Cracow.
3423 **1009** 3000z. multicoloured . . 60 45

1010 Polish Museum, Adampol

1992. 150th Anniv of Polish Settlement at Adampol, Turkey.
3424 **1010** 3500z. multicoloured . . 60 45

1011 18th-century Post Office Sign, Slonim

1992. World Post Day.
3425 **1011** 3500z. multicoloured . . 60 45

1012 "Dedication" (self-portrait)

1992. Birth Centenary of Bruno Schulz (writer and artist).
3426 **1012** 3000z. multicoloured . . 55 45

1013 "Seated Girl" (Henryk Wicinski)

1992. Polish Sculptures. Multicoloured.
3427 2000z. Type **1013** 40 15
3428 2500z. "Portrait of Tytus Czyzewski" (Zbigniew Pronaszko) 45 30
3429 3000z. "Polish Nike" (Edward Wittig) 60 45
3430 3500z. "The Nude" (August Zamoyski) 60 45

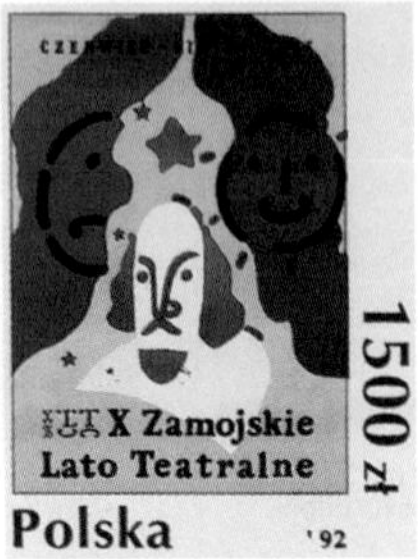

1014 "10th Theatrical Summer in Zamosc" (Jan Mlodozeniec)

1992. Poster Art (1st series). Multicoloured.
3432 1500z. Type **1014** 25 10
3433 2000z. "Red Art" (Franciszek Starowieyski) 45 30
3434 3000z. "Circus" (Waldemar Swierzy) 50 45
3435 3500z. "Mannequins" (Henryk Tomaszewski) . . 65 55
See also Nos. 3502/3, 3523/4, 3585/6 and 3712/15.

1015 Girl skipping with Snake

1992. "Polska '93" International Stamp Exn, Poznan (1st issue). Multicoloured.
3436 1500z. Type **1015** 25 10
3437 2000z. Boy on rocking horse with upside-down runners 45 25
3438 2500z. Boy firing bird from bow 45 30
3439 3500z. Girl placing ladder against clockwork giraffe 65 55
See also Nos. 3452, 3453/6 and 3466/9.

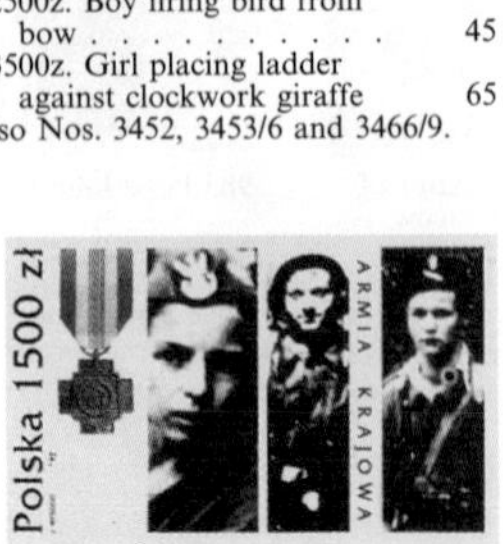

1016 Medal and Soldiers

1992. 50th Anniv of Formation of Polish Underground Army. Multicoloured.
3440 1500z. Type **1016** 25 25
3441 3500z. Soldiers 60 55

1017 Church and Star

1018 Wheat

1992. Christmas.
3443 **1017** 1000z. multicoloured . . 15 10

1992. International Nutrition Conference, Rome. Multicoloured.
3444 1500z. Type **1018** 25 10
3445 3500z. Glass, bread, vegetables and jug on table 55 45

1019 Arms of Sovereign Military Order

1020 Arms, 1295

1992. Postal Agreement with Sovereign Military Order of Malta.
3446 **1019** 3000z. multicoloured . . 55 45

1992. History of the White Eagle (Poland's arms). Each black, red and yellow.
3447 2000z. Type **1020** 40 10
3448 2500z. 15th-century arms . . 45 30
3449 3000z. 18th-century arms . . 60 30
3450 3500z. Arms, 1919 . . . . 65 40
3451 5000z. Arms, 1990 . . . . 90 55

1021 Exhibition Emblem and Stylized Stamp

1992. Centenary of Polish Philately and "Polska '93" International Stamp Exhibition, Poznan (2nd issue).
3452 **1021** 1500z. multicoloured . . 25 10

1022 Amber

1993. "Polska '93" International Stamp Exhibition, Poznan (3rd issue). Amber. Multicoloured.
3453 1500z. Type **1022** 25 10
3454 2000z. Pinkish amber . . . 40 25
3455 2500z. Amber in stone . . . 45 45
3456 3000z. Amber containing wasp 60 55

1023 Downhill Skier

1024 Flower-filled Heart

1993. Winter University Games, Zakopane.
3458 **1023** 3000z. multicoloured . . 45 45

1993. St. Valentine's Day. Multicoloured.
3459 1500z. Type **1024** 25 25
3460 3000z. Heart in envelope . . 55 45

1993. Polish Rulers (8th series). As T **983** showing drawings by Jan Matejko.
3461 1500z. brown and green . . 30 25
3462 2000z. black and mauve . . 55 30
3463 2500z. black and green . . . 65 40
3464 3000z. deep brown and brown 85 55
DESIGNS: 1500z. Wladyslaw Laskonogi; 2000z. Henryk I; 2500z. Konrad I of Masovia; 3000z. Boleslaw V, the Chaste.

1025 Arsenal

1993. 50th Anniv of Attack by Szare Szeregi (formation of Polish Scouts in the resistance forces) on Warsaw Arsenal.
3465 **1025** 1500z. multicoloured . . 30 30

1026 Jousters with Lances

1993. "Polska '93" International Stamp Exhibition, Poznan (4th issue). Jousting at Golub Dobrzyn. Designs showing a modern and a medieval jouster. Multicoloured.
3466 1500z. Type **1026** 25 10
3467 2000z. Jousters 30 30
3468 2500z. Jousters with swords 75 40
3469 3500z. Officials 65 40

1027 Szczecin **1028** Jew and Ruins

1993. 750th Anniv of Granting of Town Charter to Szczecin.
3470 **1027** 1500z. multicoloured . . 30 30

1993. 50th Anniv of Warsaw Ghetto Uprising.
3471 **1028** 4000z. black, yellow & blue 90 60

1029 Works by A. Szapocznikow and J. Lebenstein

1993. Europa. Contemporary Art. Multicoloured.
3472 1500z. Type **1029** 25 25
3473 4000z. "CXCIX" (S. Gierawski) and "Red Head" (B. Linke) 65 55

1030 "King Alexander Jagiellonczyk in the Sejm" (Jan Laski, 1505)

1993. 500th Anniv of Parliament.
3474 **1030** 2000z. multicoloured . . 30 30

1031 Nullo

1993. 130th Death Anniv of Francesco Nullo (Italian volunteer in January 1863 Rising).
3475 **1031** 2500z. multicoloured . . 45 45

1033 Cap **1034** Copernicus and Solar System

1993. 3rd World Congress of Cadets of the Second Republic.
3477 **1033** 2000z. multicoloured . . 30 30

1993. 450th Death Anniv of Nicolas Copernicus (astronomer).
3478 **1034** 2000z. multicoloured . . 40 40

1035 Fiki Miki and Lion

1993. 40th Death Anniv of Kornel Makuszynski (writer of children's books). Multicoloured.
3479 1500z. Type **1035** 30 25
3480 2000z. Billy goat 45 30
3481 3000z. Fiki Miki 60 45
3482 5000z. Billy goat riding ostrich . . . . 1·00 60

1993. Cones. As T **974**. Multicoloured.
3483 10000z. Arolla pine . . . . 1·40 85
3484 20000z. Scots pine . . . . . 3·00 1·50

1036 Eurasian Tree Sparrow

1993. Birds. Multicoloured.
3485 1500z. Type **1036** 30 15
3486 2000z. Pied wagtail 40 25
3487 3000z. Syrian woodpecker 60 45
3488 4000z. Eurasian goldfinch 85 65
3489 5000z. Common starling . . 90 85
3490 6000z. Northern bullfinch 1·25 90

1037 Soldiers Marching

1993. Bicentenary of Dabrowski's "Mazurka" (national anthem) (1st issue).
3491 **1037** 1500z. multicoloured . . 30 30
See also Nos. 3526, 3575, 3639 and 3700.

1038 "Madonna and Child" (St. Mary's Basilica, Lesna Podlaska)

1993. Sanctuaries to St. Mary. Multicoloured.
3492 1500z. Type **1038** 25 25
3493 2000z. "Madonna and Child" (St. Mary's Church, Swieta Lipka) . . 40 30

1039 Handley Page Halifax and Parachutes

1993. The Polish Rangers (Second World War air troop).
3494 **1039** 1500z. multicoloured . . 30 30

1040 Trumpet Player

1993. "Jazz Jamboree '93" International Jazz Festival, Warsaw.
3495 **1040** 2000z. multicoloured . . 40 30

1041 Postman **1042** St. Jadwiga (miniature, Schlackenwerther Codex)

1993. World Post Day.
3496 **1041** 2500z. brown, grey and blue 40 40

1993. 750th Death Anniv of St. Jadwiga of Silesia.
3497 **1042** 2500z. multicoloured . . 45 45

1044 Golden Eagle and Crown **1045** St. Nicholas

1993. 75th Anniv of Republic.
3499 **1044** 4000z. multicoloured . . 65 55

1993. Christmas.
3501 **1045** 1500z. multicoloured . . 30 30

1993. Poster Art (2nd series). As T **1014**. Mult.
3502 2000z. "Come and see Polish Mountains" (M. Urbaniec) 30 30
3503 5000z. Production of Alban Berg's "Wozzeck" (J. Lenica) 75 60

1046 Daisy shedding Petals **1047** Cross-country Skiing

1994. Greetings Stamp.
3504 **1046** 1500z. multicoloured . . 40 40

1994. Winter Olympic Games, Lillehammer, Norway. Multicoloured.
3505 2500z. Type **1047** 45 45
3506 5000z. Ski jumping 85 75

1048 Bem and Cannon

1994. Birth Bicentenary of General Jozef Bem.
3508 **1048** 5000z. multicoloured . . 75 75

1049 Jan Zamojski (founder) **1050** Cracow Battalion Flag and Scythes

1994. 400th Anniv of Zamojski Academy, Zamosc.
3509 **1049** 5000z. grey, black and brown 75 60

1994. Bicentenary of Tadeusz Kosciuszko's Insurrection.
3510 **1050** 2000z. multicoloured . . 40 40

1994. Polish Rulers (9th series). Drawings by Jan Matejko. As T **893**.
3511 2500z. black and blue . . . 45 25
3512 5000z. black, deep violet and violet 85 90
DESIGN: 2500z. Leszek II, the Black; 5000a. Przemysl II.

1051 Oil Lamp, Open Book and Spectacles **1052** "Madonna and Child"

1994. Europa. Inventions and Discoveries. Mult.
3513 2500z. Type **1051** (invention of modern oil lamp by Ignacy Lukasiewicz) . . . 45 40
3514 6000z. Illuminated filament forming "man in the moon" (astronomy) . . . 1·10 85

1994. St. Mary's Sanctuary, Kalwaria Zebrzydowska.
3515 **1052** 4000z. multicoloured . . 60 45

1053 Abbey Ruins and Poppies

1994. 50th Anniv of Battle of Monte Cassino.
3516 **1053** 6000z. multicoloured . . 75 60

1054 Mazurka

1994. Traditional Dances. Multicoloured.
3517 3000z. Type **1054** 30 30
3518 4000z. Coralski 40 40
3519 9000z. Krakowiak 85 75

1055 Cogwheels

1994. 75th Anniv of International Labour Organization.
3520 **1055** 6000z. deep blue, blue and black 60 55

1056 Optic Fibre Cable

1994. 75th Anniv of Polish Electricians Association.
3521 **1056** 4000z. multicoloured . . 55 40

1057 Map of Americas on Football

1994. World Cup Football Championship, U.S.A.
3522 **1057** 6000z. multicoloured . . 75 75

1994. Poster Art (3rd series). As T **1014**. Mult.
3523 4000z. "Monsieur Fabre" (Wiktor Gorka) 45 55
3524 6000z. "8th OISTAT Congress" (Hurbert Hilscher) (horiz) 75 75

1058 Znaniecki
1059 Polish Eagle and Ribbon

1994. 36th Death Anniv of Professor Florian Znaniecki.
3525 **1058** 9000z. green, bistre & yellow . . . . 1·25 85

1994. Bicentenary of Dabrowski's Mazurka (2nd issue). As T **1037**. Multicoloured.
3526 2500z. Troops preparing to charge 45 40

1994. 50th Anniv of Warsaw Uprising.
3527 **1059** 2500z. multicoloured . . 45 35

1060 "Stamp" protruding from Pocket
1061 Basilica of St. Brigida, Gdansk

1994. "Philakorea 1994" International Stamp Exhibition, Seoul.
3528 **1060** 4000z. multicoloured . . 60 45

1994. Sanctuaries.
3529 **1061** 4000z. multicoloured . . 60 40

1062 "Nike" (goddess of Victory)

1994. Centenary of International Olympic Committee.
3530 **1062** 4000z. multicoloured . . 60 40

1063 Komeda and Piano Keys

1994. 25th Death Anniv of Krzysztof Komeda (jazz musician).
3531 **1063** 6000z. multicoloured . . 60 50

1064 Long-finned Bristle-mouthed Catfish
1065 Arms of Polish Post, 1858

1994. Fishes. Multicoloured.
3532 4000z. Type **1064** 60 45
3533 4000z. Freshwater angelfish ("Pterophyllum scalare") 60 45
3534 4000z. Red swordtail ("Xiphophorus helleri"), neon tetra ("Paracheirodon innesi") and Berlin platy 60 45
3535 4000z. Neon tetra ("Poecilia reticulata") and guppies 60 45
Nos. 3532/5 were issued together, se-tenant, forming a composite design.

1994. World Post Day.
3536 **1065** 4000z. multicoloured . . 45 40

1066 Kolbe

1994. Maximilian Kolbe (concentration camp victim) Year.
3537 **1066** 2500z. multicoloured . . 45 40

1067 Pigeon

1994. Pigeons. Multicoloured.
3538 4000z. Type **1067** 25 30
3539 4000z. Friar pigeon 25 30
3540 6000z. Silver magpie pigeon 40 50
3541 6000z. Danzig pigeon (black) 40 50

1068 Musicians playing Carols

1994. Christmas.
3543 **1068** 2500z. multicoloured . . 35 30

1069 Landscape and E.U. Flag

1994. Application by Poland for Membership of European Union.
3544 **1069** 6000z. multicoloured . . 90 70

Currency reform. 10000 (old) zlotys = 1 (new) zloty

1070 "I Love You" on Pierced Heart

1995. Greetings Stamp.
3545 **1070** 35g. red and blue . . . 25 30

1071 Rain, Sun and Water

1995. 75th Anniv of Hydrological-Meteorological Service.
3546 **1071** 60g. multicoloured . . 50 40

1072 Flag and Sea
1073 St. John

1995. 75th Anniv of Poland's "Marriage to the Sea" (symbolic ceremony commemorating renewal of access to sea).
3547 **1072** 45g. multicoloured . . 40 30

1995. Polish Rulers (10th series). As T **893** showing drawings by Jan Matejko.
3548 35g. deep brown, brown and light brown 25 25
3549 45g. olive, deep green and green 35 30
3550 60g. brown and ochre . . . 45 40
3551 80g. black and blue 60 60
DESIGNS: 35g. Waclaw II; 45g. Wladyslaw I; 60g. Kazimierz III, the Great; 80g. Ludwik Wegierski.

1995. 500th Birth Anniv of St. John of God (founder of Order of Hospitallers).
3552 **1073** 60g. multicoloured . . 45 30

1074 Eggs

1995. Easter. Decorated Easter eggs. Mult, background colours given.
3553 **1074** 35g. red 25 25
3554 – 35g. lilac 25 25
3555 – 45g. blue 35 40
3556 – 45g. green 35 40

1995. Cones. As T **974**. Multicoloured.
3557 45g. European larch 30 35
3558 80g. Mountain pine 60 60

1075 Polish Officer's Button and Leaf

1995. Katyn Commemoration Year.
3559 **1075** 80g. multicoloured . . 60 50

1076 Rose and Barbed Wire

1995. Europa. Peace and Freedom. Multicoloured.
3560 35g. Type **1076** (liberation of concentration camps) 30 35
3561 80g. Flowers in helmet . . . 60 55

1077 Commom Cranes

1995. 50th Anniv of Return of Western Territories.
3562 **1077** 45g. multicoloured . . 60 40

1078 Pope and Wadowice Church Font

1995. 75th Birthday of Pope John Paul II.
3563 **1078** 80g. multicoloured . . 40 45

1079 Puppets under Spotlight ("Miromagia")

1995. 50th Anniv of Groteska Fairy Tale Theatre. Multicoloured.
3564 35g. Type **1079** 30 25
3565 35g. Puppets in scene from play 30 25
3566 45g. Puppet leaning on barrel ("Thomas Fingerchen") (vert) . . . 40 30
3567 45g. Clown ("Bumstara Circus") 40 30

1080 Cockerill Steam Locomotive and Train, 1845, Warsaw–Vienna

1995. 150th Anniv of Polish Railways. Mult.
3568 35g. Type **1080** 30 20
3569 60g. "Lux-Torpedo" diesel railcar, 1927 . . . . . . 50 35
3570 80g. Electric freight train . . 70 45
3571 1z. Eurocity "Sobieski" express, 1992, Warsaw–Vienna 85 55

1081 Symbols of Nations

1995. 50th Anniv of U.N.O.
3572 **1081** 80g. multicoloured . . 60 50

1082 Bank

1995. 125th Anniv of Warsaw Commercial Bank.
3573 **1082** 45g. multicoloured . . 40 40

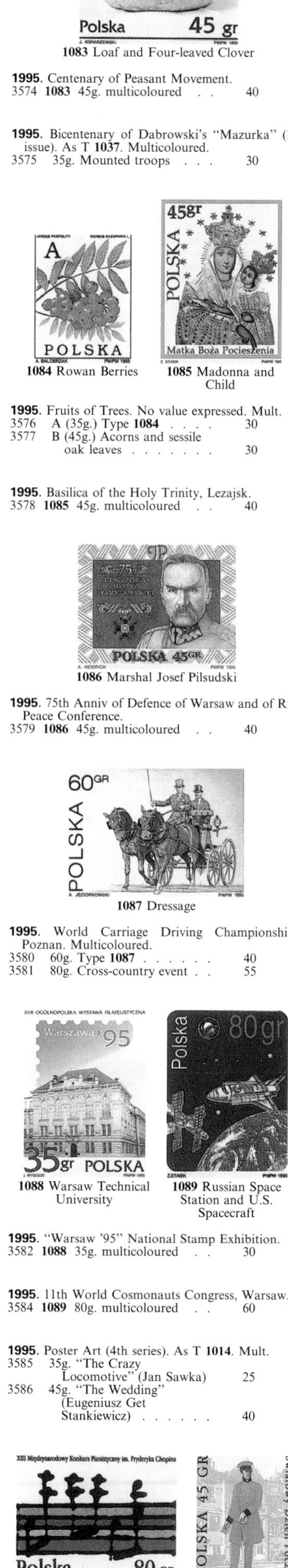

1083 Loaf and Four-leaved Clover

1995. Centenary of Peasant Movement.
3574 **1083** 45g. multicoloured . . 40 40

1995. Bicentenary of Dabrowski's "Mazurka" (3rd issue). As T **1037**. Multicoloured.
3575 35g. Mounted troops . . . 30 40

1084 Rowan Berries **1085** Madonna and Child

1995. Fruits of Trees. No value expressed. Mult.
3576 A (35g.) Type **1084** 30 25
3577 B (45g.) Acorns and sessile oak leaves 30 35

1995. Basilica of the Holy Trinity, Lezajsk.
3578 **1085** 45g. multicoloured . . 40 35

1086 Marshal Josef Pilsudski

1995. 75th Anniv of Defence of Warsaw and of Riga Peace Conference.
3579 **1086** 45g. multicoloured . . 40 40

1087 Dressage

1995. World Carriage Driving Championships, Poznan. Multicoloured.
3580 60g. Type **1087** 40 40
3581 80g. Cross-country event . . 55 55

1088 Warsaw Technical University **1089** Russian Space Station and U.S. Spacecraft

1995. "Warsaw '95" National Stamp Exhibition.
3582 **1088** 35g. multicoloured . . 30 40

1995. 11th World Cosmonauts Congress, Warsaw.
3584 **1089** 80g. multicoloured . . 60 50

1995. Poster Art (4th series). As T **1014**. Mult.
3585 35g. "The Crazy Locomotive" (Jan Sawka) 25 25
3586 45g. "The Wedding" (Eugeniusz Get Stankiewicz) 40 40

1090 Bar from Polonaise (Frederic Chopin) **1091** Postman

1995. 13th International Chopin Piano Competition.
3587 **1090** 80g. multicoloured . . 60 50

1995. Post Day. Multicoloured.
3588 45g. Type **1091** 40 25
3589 80g. Feather fixed to envelope by seal 60 55

1092 Acrobatic Pyramid **1094** Crib

1093 Groszkowski and Formula

1995. World Acrobatic Sports Championships, Wroclaw.
3590 **1092** 45g. multicoloured . . 40 40

1995. 11th Death Anniv of Professor Janusz Groszkowski (radio-electronic scientist).
3591 **1093** 45g. multicoloured . . 40 40

1995. Christmas. Multicoloured.
3592 35g. Type **1094** 40 25
3593 45g. Wise men, Christmas tree and star of Bethlehem 40 25

Nos. 3592/3 were issued together, se-tenant, forming a composite design.

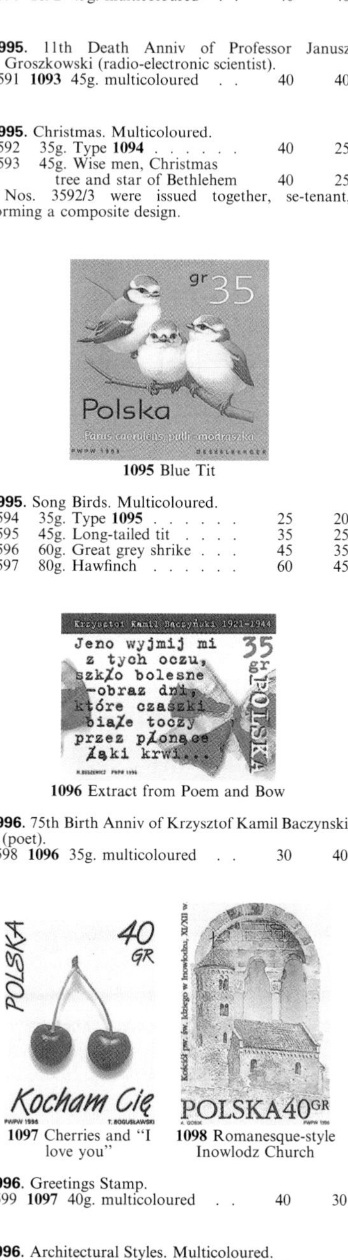

1095 Blue Tit

1995. Song Birds. Multicoloured.
3594 35g. Type **1095** 25 20
3595 45g. Long-tailed tit 35 25
3596 60g. Great grey shrike . . . 45 35
3597 80g. Hawfinch 60 45

1096 Extract from Poem and Bow

1996. 75th Birth Anniv of Krzysztof Kamil Baczynski (poet).
3598 **1096** 35g. multicoloured . . 30 40

1097 Cherries and "I love you" **1098** Romanesque-style Inowlodz Church

1996. Greetings Stamp.
3599 **1097** 40g. multicoloured . . 40 30

1996. Architectural Styles. Multicoloured.
3600 40g. Type **1098** 40 30
3601 55g. Gothic-style St. Mary the Virgin's Church, Cracow 45 35
3602 70g. Renaissance-style St. Sigismund's Chapel, Wawel Castle 60 50
3603 1z. Baroque-style Church of the Order of the Holy Sacrament, Warsaw . . . 90 75

1099 "Oceania"

1996. Sailing Ships. Multicoloured.
3604 40g. Type **1099** 30 30
3605 55g. "Zawisza Czarny" (cadet schooner) 45 40
3606 70g. "General Zaruski" (cadet ketch) 55 55
3607 75g. "Fryderyk Chopin" (cadet brig) 60 55

1100 16th-century Warsaw **1101** Bull (Taurus)

1996. 400th Anniv of Warsaw.
3608 **1100** 55g. multicoloured . . 45 35

1996. Signs of the Zodiac. Multicoloured.
3609 5g. Workman in water (Aquarius) 15 15
3610 10g. "Fish-person" holding fish (Pisces) 15 15
3611 20g. Type **1101** 10 10
3612 25g. Twins looking through keyhole (Gemini) 15 15
3613 30g. Crab smoking pipe (Cancer) 15 15
3614 40g. Maid and cogwheels (Virgo) 25 25
3615 50g. Lion in military uniform (Leo) 30 25
3616 55g. Couple with head and shoulders as scales (Libra) 30 30
3617 70g. Ram with ram-head (Aries) 45 25
3618 1z. Woman with scorpion's tail hat (Scorpio) 70 35
3619 2z. Archer on motor cycle (Sagittarius) . . . . . . 1·40 75
3620 5z. Office worker shielding face with paper mask (Capricorn) . . . . 3·25 1·60

1102 Hanka Ordonowna (singer)

1996. Europa. Famous Women. Multicoloured.
3621 40g. Type **1102** 30 25
3622 1z. Pola Negri (actress) . . 70 65

1103 Flag of Osiek and Old Photographs forming "1921"

1996. 75th Anniv of Silesian Uprising.
3623 **1103** 55g. red, green and black 40 40

1104 "On Bergamuty Islands"

1996. 50th Anniv of UNICEF. Scenes from Fairy Tales by Jan Brzechwa. Multicoloured.
3624 40g. Type **1104** 35 30
3625 40g. Waiters carrying trays of apples (nursery rhyme) 35 30
3626 55g. Vegetable characters ("At the Market Stall") 55 40
3627 55g. Chef holding duck ("Wacky Duck") 55 40

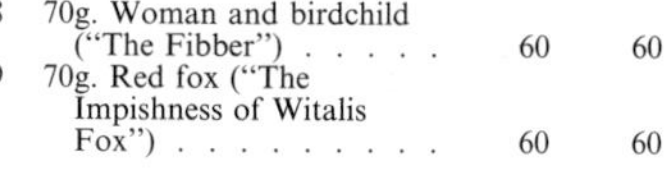

3628 70g. Woman and birdchild ("The Fibber") 60 60
3629 70g. Red fox ("The Impishness of Witalis Fox") 60 60

1105 "City Walls and Building"

1996. Paintings by Stanislaw Noakowski. Mult.
3630 40g. Type **1105** 30 25
3631 55g. "Renaissance Bedroom" 40 35
3632 70g. "Rural Gothic Church" 50 50
3633 1z. "Renaissance Library" 70 65

1106 Discus on Ribbon **1108** St. Mary of Przeczycka

1107 Tweezers holding Stamp showing Emblem

1996. Olympic Games, Atlanta, and Centenary of Modern Olympic Games. Multicoloured.
3634 40g. Type **1106** (gold medal, Halina Konopacka, 1928) 25 25
3635 55g. Tennis ball (horiz) . . 40 35
3636 70g. Polish Olympic Committee emblem (horiz) 50 45
3637 1z. Bicycle wheel 70 50

1996. "Olymphilex '96" International Sports Stamp Exhibition, Atlanta.
3638 **1107** 1z. multicoloured . . . 70 65

1996. Bicentenary of Dabrowski's Mazurka (4th issue). As T **1037**. Multicoloured.
3639 40g. Charge of Polish cavalry at Somosierra . . 45 30

1996. St. Mary's Church, Przeczycka.
3640 **1108** 40g. multicoloured . . 45 35

1996. Polish Rulers (11th series). As T **893**.
3641 40g. brown and bistre . . . 30 25
3642 55g. lilac and mauve 45 35
3643 70g. deep grey and grey . . 55 50
3644 1z. deep green, green and yellow 80 65

DESIGNS: 40g. Queen Jadwiga (wife of Wladyslaw II); 55g. Wladyslaw II Jagiello; 70g. Wladyslaw III Warnenczyk; 1z. Kazimierz IV Jagiellonczyk.

1109 Mt. Giewont and Edelweiss

1996. The Tatra Mountains. Multicoloured.
3645 40g. Type **1109** 30 20
3646 40g. Mt. Krzesanica and spring gentian 30 20
3647 55g. Mt. Koscielec and leopard's bane 45 25
3648 55g. Mt. Swinica and clusius gentian 45 25
3649 70g. Mt. Rysy and ragwort 55 30
3650 70g. Mieguszowieckie peaks and pine trees 55 30

1110 Seifert

1996. 50th Birth Anniv of Zbigniew Seifert (jazz musician).
3651 **1110** 70g. multicoloured . . 75 45

1111 "Changing of Horses at Post Station" (detail, Mieczyslaw Watorski)

1996. World Post Day. 75th Anniv of Post and Telecommunications Museum, Wroclaw. Paintings.
3652 **1111** 40g. multicoloured . . 30 25

1112 Father Christmas on Horse-drawn Sleigh
1113 Head of Male

1996. Christmas. Multicoloured.
3654 40g. Type **1112** 25 10
3655 55g. Carol singers with star lantern 35 25

1996. The European Bison. Multicoloured.
3656 55g. Type **1113** 40 40
3657 55g. Head of female 40 40
3658 55g. Pair of bison 40 40
3659 55g. Male 40 40

1114 Wislawa Szymborska

1996. Award of Nobel Prize for Literature to Wislawa Szymborska (poet).
3660 **1114** 1z. multicoloured . . . 75 65

1115 "I Love You" on King of Hearts Playing Card

1997. Greetings Stamps. Multicoloured.
3661 B (40g.) Type **1115** 30 25
3662 A (55g.) Queen of hearts playing card . . . . . . 45 1·00

Nos. 3661/2 were issued together, se-tenant, forming a composite design.

No. 3661 was sold at the rate for postcards and No. 3662 for letters up to 20 grams.

1116 Blessing the Palms

1997. Easter. Traditional Customs. Multicoloured.
3663 50g. Type **1116** 30 25
3664 60g. Woman and child painting Easter eggs . . . 40 35
3665 80g. Priest blessing the food 55 45
3666 1z.10 Man throwing water over woman's skirts on Easter Monday 65 45

1117 Long Market and Town Hall (after Mateusz Deisch)

1997. Millenary of Gdansk.
3667 **1117** 50g. brown, cinnamon and red 60 40

1118 St. Adalbert and Monks addressing Pagans

1997. Death Millenary of St. Adalbert (Bishop of Prague).
3669 **1118** 50g. brown 30 25
3670 – 60g. green 40 35
3671 – 1z.10 lilac 70 40

DESIGNS—VERT: 60g. St. Adalbert and anniversary emblem; 1z.10, St. Adalbert.

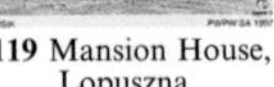

1119 Mansion House, Lopuszna
1120 The Crock of Gold

1997. Polish Manor Houses. Multicoloured.
3671a 10g Lipkowie, Warsaw . . 10 10
3672 50g. Type **1119** 20 10
3673 55g. Henryk Sienkewicz Museum, Oblegorek . . 35 20
3674 60g. Zyrzyn 50 20
3675 65g. Stanislaw Wyspianski Museum, Bronowice, near Cracow 60 20
3675a 70g. Modlnica 65 35
3675b 80g. Grabonog, Gostyn . . 75 35
3676 90g. Obory, near Warsaw 90 60
3676a 1z. Krzelawice 95 45
3677 1z.10 Ozarow . . . . . . 1·00 35
3678 1z.20 Jozef Krasnewski Museum, Biala 65 35
3678a 1z.40 Winna Gora 75 80
3678b 1z.50 Sulejowku, Warsaw 45 15
3678c 1z.55 Zelazowa Wola . . . 80 80
3678d 1z.60 Potok Zloty 80 95
3678e 1z.65 Sucha, Wegrow . . . 90 95
3679 1z.70 Tulowice . . . . . . 95 1·00
3679a 1z.85 Kasna Dolna 90 80
3679b 1z.90 Petrykozach Mszczonowa 60 20
3680 2z.20 Kuznocin . . . . . 1·10 95
3681 2z.65 Liwia, Wegrow . . . 1·50 1·10
3682 3z. Janowcu, Pulaw . . . 90 30
3683 10z. Koszuty . . . . . . 5·50 4·00

See also Nos. 3727/8.

1997. Europa. Tales and Legends. Multicoloured.
3685 50g. Type **1120** 30 35
3686 1z.10 Wars, Sawa and mermaid-siren 70 80

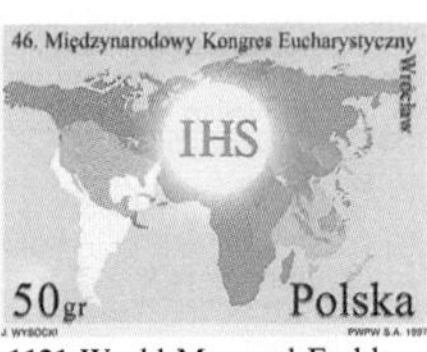

1121 World Map and Emblem

1997. 46th International Eucharistic Congress, Wroclaw.
3687 **1121** 50g. multicoloured . . 30 35

1122 San Francisco–Oakland Bay Bridge

1997. "Pacific 97" International Stamp Exhibition, San Francisco.
3688 **1122** 1z.30 multicoloured . . 75 75

1124 European Long-eared Bat

1997. Bats. Multicoloured.
3690 50g. Type **1124** 30 20
3691 60g. Common noctule . . . 40 25
3692 80g. Brown bat 50 35
3693 1z.30 Red bat 85 55

1125 "Founding of the Main School" (Jan Matejko)

1997. 600th Anniv of Faculty of Theology, Jagiellonian University, Cracow.
3694 **1125** 80g. multicoloured . . 60 55

1126 Map highlighting Settled Area

1997. Centenary of Polish Migration to Argentina.
3695 **1126** 1z.40 multicoloured . . 80 75

1127 "Return from War to the Village"

1997. Paintings by Juliusz Kossak. Multicoloured.
3696 50g. Type **1127** 30 25
3697 60g. "Cracowian Wedding" 35 35
3698 80g. "In the Stable" 50 45
3699 1z.10 "Stablehand with Pair of Horses" 65 60

1997. Bicentenary of Dabrowski's "Mazurka" (5th issue). As T **1037**.
3700 50g. Dabrowski and Wybicki's arrival in Poznan, 1806 . . . . . . 35 35

1128 Strzelecki and Route Map around Australia

1997. Birth Bicentenary of Pawel Strzelecki (explorer).
3702 **1128** 1z.50 multicoloured . . 90 90

1129 Flooded Houses
1130 "Holy Mother of Consolation" (icon)

1997. Flood Relief Fund.
3703 **1129** 60g.+30g. multicoloured 75 65

1997. Church of the Holy Mother of Consolation and St. Michael the Archangel, Gorka Duchowa.
3704 **1130** 50g. multicoloured . . 30 40

1997. Polish Rulers (12th series). As T **893**.
3705 50g. agate, brown and bistre 35 30
3706 60g. purple and blue 45 40
3707 80g. green, deep green and olive 60 50
3708 1z.10 purple and lilac . . . 80 65

DESIGNS: 50g. Jan I Olbracht; 60g. Aleksander Jagiellonczyk; 80g. Zygmunt I, the Old; 1z.10, Zygmunt II August.

1131 Kosz
1132 Globe and posthorn

1997. 24th Death Anniv of Mieczyslaw Kosz (jazz musician).
3709 **1131** 80g. multicoloured . . 60 50

1997. World Post Day.
3710 **1132** 50g. multicoloured . . 35 35

1133 St. Basil's Cathedral, Moscow

1997. "Moskva 97" International Stamp Exhibition, Moscow.
3711 **1133** 80g. multicoloured . . 60 70

1997. Poster Art (5th series). As T **1014**.
3712 50g. multicoloured 35 25
3713 50g. black 35 25
3714 60g. multicoloured 40 45
3715 60g. multicoloured 40 45

POSTERS—HORIZ: No. 3712, Advertisement for Radion washing powder (Tadeusz Gronowski). VERT: No. 3713, Production of Stanislaw Witkiewicz's play "Shoemakers" (Roman Cieslewicz); 3714, Production of Aleksander Fredro's play "A Husband and a Wife" (Andrzej Pagowski); 3715, Production of ballet "Goya" (Wiktor Sadowski).

1134 Nativity

1997. Christmas. Multicoloured.
3716 50g. Type **1134** 25 20
3717 60g. Christmas Eve feast (horiz) 35 25
3718 80g. Family going to church for Midnight Mass (horiz) 45 30
3719 1z.10 Waits (carol singers representing animals) . . 60 40

1135 Common Shelducks

1997. Praecocial Chicks. Multicoloured.
3720 50g. Type **1135** 35 35
3721 50g. Goosanders ("Mergus merganser") 35 35

3722 50g. Common snipes ("Gallinago gallinago") 35 35
3723 50g. Moorhens ("Gallinula chloropus") 35 35

1136 Ski Jumping

1137 Dog wearing Cat T-shirt inscr "I Love You"

1998. Winter Olympic Games, Nagano, Japan.
3724 **1136** 1z.40 multicoloured . . 80 75

1998. Greetings Stamps. No value expressed. Multicoloured.
3725 B (55g.) Type **1137** 35 25
3726 A (65g.) Cat wearing dog T-shirt 35 35

1998. Polish Manor Houses. No value expressed. As T **1119**. Multicoloured.
3727 B (55g.) Gluchy 35 25
3728 A (65g.) Jan Kochanwoski Museum, Czarnolas . . . 35 35

1138 Paschal Lamb

1140 Grey Seal

1139 Polish National Guard and Civilians at Lvov Barricades

1998. Easter. Multicoloured.
3729 55g. Type **1138** 35 20
3730 65g. The Resurrected Christ 35 20

1998. 150th Anniv of 1848 Revolutions.
3731 **1139** 55g. brown 45 25

1998. Polish Rulers (13th series). As T **893**.
3732 55g. brown and light brown 35 20
3733 65g. purple, deep purple and mauve 40 35
3734 80g. deep green and green 50 45
3735 90g. lilac, purple and mauve 60 45
DESIGNS: 55g. Henryk Walezy; 65g. Queen Anna Jagiellonka (wife of Stefan I); 80g. Stefan I Batory; 90g. Zygmunt III Wasa.

1998. Protection of Baltic Sea. Marine Life. Mult.
3736 65g. Type **1140** 45 35
3737 65g. "Patoschistus microps" (fish), jellyfish and shells 45 35
3738 65g. Twaite shad ("Alosa fallax") and pipefish ("Syngnathus typhle") . . 45 35
3739 65g. Common sturgeon ("Acipenser sturio") . . . 45 35
3740 65g. Atlantic salmon ("Salmo salar") 45 35
3741 65g. Common porpoise . . 45 35
Nos. 3736/41 were issued together, se-tenant, forming a composite design.

1141 Exhibition Emblem and 1948 Israeli 500 m. Stamp

1998. "Israel '98" International Stamp Exhibition, Tel Aviv.
3743 **1141** 90g. multicoloured . . 75 80

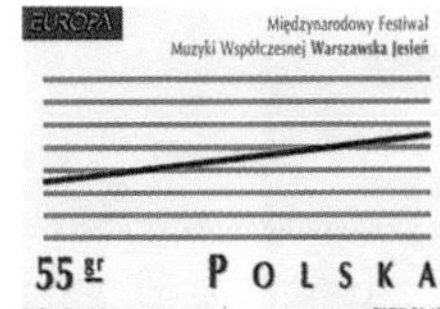

1142 Festival Emblem

1998. Europa. National Festivals.
3744 **1142** 55g. multicoloured . . 55 50
3745 – 1z.20 black, red and blue 90 95
DESIGNS: 55g. Type **1142** ("Warsaw Autumn" International Festival of Music); 1z.20, State flag and opening bars of "Welcome the May Dawn" (3rd of May Constitution Day).

1144 "Longing Holy Mother"

1145 "Triple Self-portrait"

1998. Coronation of "Longing Holy Mother" (icon in Powsin Church).
3752 **1144** 55g. multicoloured . . 45 75

1998. 30th Death Anniv of Nikifor (Epifan Drowniak) (artist). Multicoloured.
3753 55g. Type **1145** 35 40
3754 65g. "Cracow Office" . . . 40 50
3755 1z.20 "Orthodox Church" 75 80
3756 2z.35 "Ucrybow Station" . . 1·50 1·60

1146 Anniversary Inscription

1998. 80th Anniv of Main Board of Statistics.
3757 **1146** 55g. multicoloured . . 45 40

1147 "Madonna and Child"

1998. Basilica of the Visitation of St. Mary the Virgin, Sejny.
3758 **1147** 55g. multicoloured . . 45 40

1148 Jesus (stained glass window)

1998. Bicentenary of Diocese of Warsaw.
3759 **1148** 65g. multicoloured . . 45 50

1150 Pierre and Marie Curie (physicists)

1998. Centenary of Discovery of Polonium and Radium.
3761 **1150** 1z.20 multicoloured . . 70 80

1151 Mazowsze Dancers

1998. 50th Anniv of Mazowsze Song and Dance Group. Multicoloured.
3762 65g. Type **1151** 40 50
3763 65g. Dancers (different) . . 40 50
Nos. 3762/3 were issued together, se-tenant, forming a composite design.

1152 Mniszchow Palace

1998. Belgium Embassy, Warsaw.
3764 **1152** 1z.20 multicoloured . . 70 75

1153 "King Sigismund" (Studio of Rubens)

1154 Coloured Envelopes

1998. 400th Anniv of Battle of Stangebro.
3765 **1153** 1z.20 brown . . . . . 70 1·00

1998. World Post Day.
3766 **1154** 65g. multicoloured . . 45 50

1155 Pope John Paul II and People of Different Races

1157 "Nativity"

1156 State Flags and 1919 Seal

1998. 20th Anniv of Selection of Karol Wojtyla to Papacy.
3767 **1155** 65g. multicoloured . . 45 50

1998. 80th Anniv of Independence.
3768 **1156** 65g. black, red and gold 45 50

1998. Christmas. Polyptych, Grudziadz. Mult.
3769 55g. Type **1157** 40 40
3770 65g. "Adoration of the Wise Men" 40 50

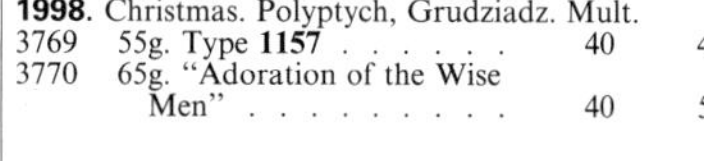

1158 Anniversary Emblem

1998. 50th Anniv of Universal Declaration of Human Rights.
3771 **1158** 1z.20 blue and ultramarine 75 80

1159 Maryla Wereszczakowna and Moonlit Night

1998. Birth Bicentenary of Adam Mickiewicz (poet). Multicoloured.
3772 55g. Type **1159** 30 35
3773 65g. Cranes flying over tomb of Maria Potocka 40 45
3774 90g. Burning candles and cross 45 60
3775 1z.20 House, field of flowers and uhlan's shako 60 75

1160 "Piorun" (destroyer), 1942–46

1999. 80th Anniv (1998) of Polish Navy. Mult.
3777 55g. Type **1160** 40 35
3778 55g. "Piorun" (missile corvette), 1994 . . . . . 40 35

1161 Dominoes

1999. Greetings stamps. Value expressed by letter. Multicoloured.
3779 B (60g.) Type **1161** 40 35
3780 A (65g.) Dominoes (different) 40 45

1162 Ernest Malinowski and Railway Bridge over Varrugas Canyon

1999. Polish Engineers. Multicoloured.
3781 1z. Type **1162** (death cent) 55 60
3782 1z.60 Rudolf Modrzejewski and Benjamin Franklin Bridge over Delaware River, Philadelphia . . . 85 95

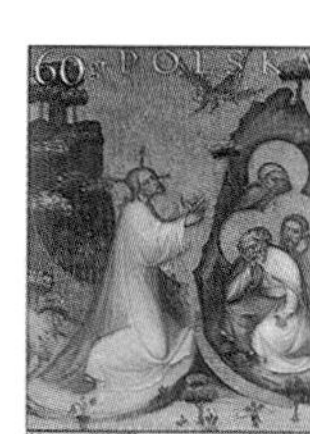

1163 "Prayer in Ogrojec"

1165 "Victorious St. Mary of Kozielsk" (sculpture)

1999. Easter. Multicoloured.
3783 60g. Type **1163** 30 35
3784 65g. "Carrying the Cross" 30 35
3785 1z. "Pieta" 50 55
3786 1z.40 "Resurrection" . . . 75 70
Nos. 3783/4 and 3786 show details of the Grudzic polyptych.

1999. Images of Virgin Mary made by Polish Prisoners of War. Multicoloured.
3788 60g. Type **1165** 30 35
3789 70g. "St. Mary of Katyn" (bas-relief, Stanislaw Balos) 40 35

1166 Jan Skrzetuski passing Zbara Fortress (“With Fire and Sword”)

1999. “Heroes of the Trilogy ” (novels) by Henryk Sienkiewicz. Multicoloured.

3790	70g. Type **1166**	35	35
3791	70g. Onufry Zagloba and 17th-century map of Poland (all three parts)	35	35
3792	70g. Longinus Podbipieta defending Zbara and three Tartars (“With Fire and Sword”)	35	35
3793	70g. Bohun with Helena Kuncewiczowna on way to Czarci Jar (“With Fire and Sword”)	35	35
3794	70g. Andrzej Kmicic and cannon at Jasna Gora Monastery (“The Deluge”)	35	35
3795	70g. Michal Jerzy Wolodyjowski and Basia Jeziorkowska fencing (“Pan Michael”)	35	35

1167 Polish Flag and N.A.T.O. Emblem

1999. 50th Anniv of North Atlantic Treaty Organization and Accession of Poland.

3796	**1167** 70g. multicoloured . .	45	35

1168 Anniversary Emblem and Headquarters, Strasbourg

1999. 50th Anniv of Council of Europe.

3797	**1168** 1z. multicoloured . . .	55	60

1169 Three-toed Woodpecker

1999. Europa. Parks and Gardens. Bialowieski National Park.

3798	**1169** 1z.40 multicoloured . .	75	90

1170 Mountain Biking

1999. Youth Sports. Multicoloured.

3799	60g. Type **1170**	40	35
3800	70g. Snowboarding	40	50
3801	1z. Skateboarding	60	60
3802	1z.40 Rollerblading	85	1·00

1171 St. Mary's Church, Cracow, Pope John Paul II and Crowd

1999. 6th Papal Visit to Poland. Multicoloured.

3803	60g. Type **1171**	35	30
3804	70g. Pope and crowd with crosses	40	40
3805	1z. Pope and cheering teenagers	60	50
3806	1z.40 Eiffel Tower (Paris), “Christ the Saviour” (statue, Rio de Janeiro), Pope and church at Fatima, Portugal	80	65

1172 Ignacy Paderewski and Roman Dmowski (signatories)

1999. 80th Anniv of Treaty of Versailles.

3807	**1172** 1z.40 multicoloured . .	85	1·00

1173 “St. Mary Carefully Listening” (icon)

1174 Great Diving Beetle (“Dytiscus marginalis”)

1999. St. Mary's Sanctuaries. Multicoloured.

3808	60g. Type **1173** (church of St. Mary Queen of Poland, Rokitno)	40	40
3809	70g. “Mary” (statue, Ms. Jazlowiecka), Convent of Order of the Immaculate Conception, Szymanow	40	50

1999. Insects. Multicoloured.

3810	60g. Type **1174**	30	35
3811	60g. “Corixa punctata” . .	30	35
3812	70g. “Limnophilus”	40	45
3813	70g. “Perla marginata” . .	40	45
3814	1z.40 Emperor dragonfly (“Anax imperator”) . . .	80	95
3815	1z.40 “Ephemera vulgata”	80	95

1176 Red Deer

1999. Eastern Carpathian Mountains International Biosphere Reserve (covering Polish, Ukrainian and Slovakian National Parks). Multicoloured.

3817	1z.40 Type **1176**	70	90
3818	1z.40 Wild cat	70	90

1999. Polish Rulers (14th series). As T **893**.

3819	60g. black and green	35	20
3820	70g. brown and light brown	40	35
3821	1z. black and blue	60	40
3822	1z.40 deep purple and purple	80	45

DESIGNS: 60g. Wladyslaw IV Waza; 70g. Jan II Kazimierz; 1z. Michal Korybut Wisniowiecki; 1z.40, Jan III Sobieski.

1177 U.P.U. Emblem

1999. 125th Anniv of Universal Postal Union.

3823	**1177** 1z.40 multicoloured . .	70	85

1178 Chopin and Academy of Fine Arts, Warsaw

1999. 150th Death Anniv of Frederic Chopin (composer).

3824	**1178** 1z.40 green	70	85

1179 Popieluszko

1182 Polish Museum, Rapperswil Castle, Switzerland

1181 Angel (“Silent Night”)

1999. 15th Death Anniv of Father Jerzy Popieluszko.

3825	**1179** 70g. multicoloured . .	40	50

1999. Christmas. Inscr in Polish with the opening lines of carols. Multicoloured.

3827	60g. Type **1181**	35	25
3828	70g. Angel (“Sleep, Jesus Baby”)	40	25
3829	1z. Angel (“Let's Go Everybody to the Stable”)	55	40
3830	1z.40 Angel (“The God is Born”)	80	60

1999. Polish Overseas Cultural Buildings. Mult.

3831	1z. Type **1182**	60	40
3832	1z.40 Marian Priests' Museum, Fawley Court, England	80	60
3833	1z.60 Polish Library, Paris, France	[illegible]	[illegible]
3834	1z.80 Polish Institute and Gen. Sikorski Museum, London, England	1·10	75

1183 “Proportions of Man” (Da Vinci)

1185 Otto III granting Crown to Boleslaw I

1184 Bronislaw Malinowski (sociologist)

2000. New Year 2000.

3835	**1183** A (70g.) multicoloured	55	50

2000. Polish Personalities. Multicoloured.

3836	1z.55 Type **1184**	75	75
3837	1z.95 Jozef Zwierzycki (geologist)	1·10	1·00

2000. 1000th Anniv of the Gniezno Summit and the Catholic Church in Poland. Multicoloured.

3838	70g. Type **1185**	45	45
3839	80g. Archbishop of Gnesna, and Bishops of Cracovina, Wratislavia and Colberga	45	45

1186 Jesus in Tomb

2000. Easter. Multicoloured.

3841	70g. Type **1186**	45	45
3842	80g. Resurrected Christ . .	45	45

1187 Saurolophus

2000. Prehistoric Animals. Multicoloured.

3843	70g. Type **1187**	40	45
3844	70g. Gallimimus	40	45
3845	80g. Saichania	45	50
3846	80g. Protoceratops	45	50
3847	1z.55 Prenocephale	85	1·00
3848	1z.55 Velociraptor	85	1·00

1188 Wajda

2000. Presentation of American Film Academy Award to Andrzej Wajda (film director).

3849	**1188** 1z.10 black	60	95

1189 Pope John Paul kneeling, St. Peter's Basilica, Rome

2000. Holy Year 2000 Opening of Holy Door, St. Peter's Basilica, Rome.

3850	**1189** 80g. multicoloured . .	45	45

1190 Artist and Model, Poster for *Wesele* (play), and Building

2000. Crakow, European City of Culture. Mult.

3851	70g. Type **1190**	40	45
3852	1z.55 Jagiellonian University, Pope John Paul II, Queen Jadwiga and Krzysztof Penderecki (composer)	95	90

1191 Dying Rose

2000. “Stop Drug Addiction” Campaign.

3854	**1191** 70g. multicoloured . .	40	45

1192 “Building Europe”

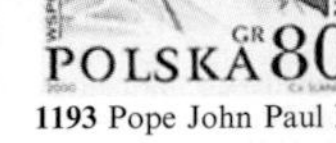

1193 Pope John Paul II

2000. Europa.
3855 **1192** 1z.55 multicoloured . . 90 75

2000. 80th Birthday of Pope John Paul II.
3856 **1193** 80g. violet 45 45
3857 – 1z.10 multicoloured . . 60 60
3858 – 1z.55 green 75 90
DESIGNS: No. 3857, Holy Mother, Czestochowa; 3858, Pastoral Staff.

1194 Woman's Face and Fan

2000. "Espana 2000" International Stamp Exhibition, Madrid.
3859 **1194** 1z.55 multicoloured . . 90 85

1195 Family

2000. Parenthood.
3860 **1195** 70g. multicoloured . . 40 45

1197 Karol Marcinkowski

2000. Personalities. Multicoloured.
3862 70g. Type **1197** (founder of Scientific Assistance Association) 35 20
3863 80g. Josemaria Escriva de Balaguer (founder of Priests' Association of St. Cross, 1943) 35 30

1198 Gerwazy and the Count

2000. *Pan Tadeusz* (poem by Adam Mickiewicz). Illustrations by Michal Elwiro Andriolli from the 1882 edition.
3864 **1198** 70g. brown 40 15
3865 – 70g. brown 40 15
3866 – 80g. green 45 20
3867 – 80g. green 45 20
3868 – 1z.10 purple 60 30
3869 – 1z.10 purple 60 30
DESIGNS: No. 3865, Telimenta reclining and the Judge; 3866, Father Robak, Judge and Gerwazy; 3867, Gathering in forest; 3868, Jankiel playing musical instrument; 3869, Zosia and Tadeusz.

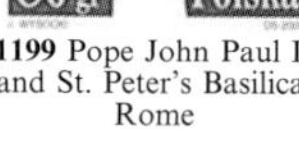

1199 Pope John Paul II and St. Peter's Basilica, Rome

1200 "Self-portrait"

2000. National Pilgrimage to Rome. Multicoloured.
3870 80g. Type **1199** 45 30
3871 1z.55 Cross and Colosseum 85 60

2000. Birth Bicentenary of Piotr Michalowski (artist). Multicoloured.
3872 70g. Type **1200** 70 25
3873 80g. "Portrait of a Boy in a Hat" 80 30
3874 1z.10 "Stable-boy Bridling Percherons" (horiz) . . . 1·10 40
3875 1z.55 "Horses with Cart" (horiz) . . . . 1·50 55

1201 Mary and Jesus (painting), Rozanystok

2000. St. Mary's Sanctuaries. Multicoloured.
3876 70g. Type **1201** 25 10
3877 1z.55 Mary with crown supported by angels, Lichen 55 20

1202 John Bosco (founder of movement)

2000. Salesian Society (religious educational institution) in Poland.
3878 **1202** 80g. multicoloured . . 45 30

1204 Running

2000. Olympic Games, Sydney. Multicoloured.
3880 70g. Type **1204** 35 25
3881 80g. Diving, wind-surfing, sailing and kayaking . . . 40 30
3882 1z.10 Weight lifting, high jumping and fencing . . . 55 40
3883 1z.55 Athletics, basketball and judo 80 55

1205 Postman (Tomasz Wistuba)

1207 Priest and Cross

2000. World Post Day. Winning Entries in Children's Painting Competition. Multicoloured.
3884 70g. Type **1205** 40 30
3885 80g. Customers and flying stork in Post Office (Katarzyna Chrzanowska) (horiz) 45 30
3886 1z.10 Post Office on "stamp" (Joanna Zbik) (horiz) 60 40
3887 1z.55 Woman at Post Office counter (Katarzyna Lonak) (horiz) 85 55

2000. Polish Rulers (15th series). As T **893**.
3889 70g. black, green and olive 40 30
3890 80g. black and purple . . . 45 30
3891 1z.10 black, blue and cobalt 60 40
3892 1z.55 black and brown . . . 85 55
DESIGNS; 70g. August II; 80g. Stanislaw Leszczynski; 1z.10, August III; 1z.55, Stanislaw August Poniatowski.

2000. 60th Anniv of Katyn Massacre. Mult.
3893 70g. Type **1207** 35 20
3894 80g. Pope John Paul II kneeling at monument, Muranow 40 30

1208 Nativity

2000. Christmas. Multicoloured.
3895 70g. Type **1208** 35 30
3896 80g. Wedding at Cana . . . 40 35
3897 1z.10 The Last Supper . . . 55 45
3898 1z.55 The Ascension 80 85

1209 Building Facade

1210 Privately Issued Stamp

2000. Centenary of Warsaw Art Gallery.
3899 **1209** 70g. multicoloured . . 45 40

2000. Underground Post during Martial Law, 1982–89.
3900 **1210** 80g. multicoloured . . 45 35

1211 Pope John Paul II, Emblem and Crowd

2001. End of Holy Year 2000. Value expressed by letter.
3901 **1211** A (1z.10) mult 40 15

1212 Mountains reflected in Ski Goggles

2001. 20th University Games, Zakopane.
3902 **1212** 1z. multicoloured . . . 35 10

1213 Computer Mouse

2001. The Internet.
3903 **1213** 1z. multicoloured . . . 35 10

1214 Adam Malysz (ski jumper)

2001. World Classic Seniors Championships. Multicoloured.
3904 1z. Type **1214** 35 10
3905 1z. As Type **1214** but additionally inscribed "Adam Malysz" 35 10
3906 1z. As No. 3905 but additionally inscribed "Mistrzem Swiata" . . . 35 10

1215 Tomb of the Resurrected Christ

2001. Easter. Multicoloured.
3907 1z. Type **1215** 35 10
3908 1z.90 Resurrected Christ and Apostles 35 10

1216 Emblem and Basketball Players

2001. 12th Salesian Youth World Championships, Warsaw.
3909 **1216** 1z. multicoloured . . . 35 10

1217 Water Droplet

2001. Europa. Water Resources.
3910 **1217** 1z.90 multicoloured . . 65 20

1218 Man and Mermaid on Beach ("Holiday Greetings")

2001. Greetings Stamps. Multicoloured.
3911 1z. Type **1218** 35 10
3912 1z. Man presenting bouquet to woman ("Best Wishes") 35 10

1219 "Christ Blessing Children of Wrzesnia" (Marian Turwid) (stained-glass window), Parish Church, Wrzesnia

2001. Centenary of Support of Wrzesnia Schoolchildren for the Language.
3913 **1219** 1z. multicoloured . . . 35 10

1220 Polish Scientific Institute and Wanda Stachiewicz Library,Montreal, Canada

2001. Polish Institutions Abroad. Multicoloured.
3914 1z. Type **1220** 35 10
3915 1z.90 Bust of Josef Pilsudski, Josef Pilsudski Institute, New York . . . 65 20

3916 2z.10 Polonia Museum, Archives and Library, Orchard Lake, Michigan . . . 75 25
3917 2z.20 Polish Museum, Chicago 75 25

1221 Snowdrop (*Galanthus nivalis*) and European Lynx (*Lynx lynx*)

2001. Convention on International Trade of Wild Animals and Plants Threatened with Extinction (C.I.T.E.S.). Multicoloured.
3918 1z. Type **1221** 35 10
3919 1z. Apollo butterfly (*Parnassius apollo*) and orchid (*Orchis sambucina*) 35 10
3920 1z. Northern eagle owl (*Bubo bubo*) and *Adonis vernalis* (plant) 35 10
3921 1z.90 Lady's slipper orchid (*Cypripedium calceolus*) and brown bear (*Ursus arctos*) 65 20
3922 1z.90 Peregrine falcon (*Falco peregrinus*) and *Orchis pallens* 65 20
3923 1z.90 Wide leaf orchid (*Orchis latifolia*) and European otter (*Lutra lutra*) 65 20

1222 Cardinal Wyszynski and Text

2001. Birth Centenary of Cardinal Stefan Wyszynski (Primate of Poland, 1948–81).
3925 **1222** 1z. multicoloured . . . 35 10

1223 Father Kolbe and Handwriting

2001. 60th Death Anniv of Maksymilian Maria Kolbe (founder of Knighthood of the Immaculate, and concentration camp victim).
3926 **1223** 1z. multicoloured . . . 35 10

1224 "St. Mary of the Beautiful Love" (icon)

1225 Model of Sanctuary

2001. St. Mary's Sanctuaries. Multicoloured.
3927 1z. Type **1224** (Cathedral of St. Martin and St. Nicolas, Bydgoszcz) 35 10
3928 1z. St. Mary of Ludzmierz, Basilica of the Assumption of St. Mary, Ludzmierz 35 10
3929 1z.90 St. Mary the Winner, Church of St. Mary in Piasek, Wroclaw 65 20

2001. Completion of Section of God's Mercy Sanctuary at Cracow-Lagiewniki.
3930 **1225** 1z. multicoloured . . . 35 10

1226 Ligia, Vinius and Petrinius

2001. *Quo Vadis* (film directed by Jerzy Kawalerowicz). Depicting scenes from the film. Multicoloured.
3931 1z. Type **1226** 35 10
3932 1z. Nero singing at feast . . 35 10
3933 1z. St. Peter in the catacombs and the baptism of Chilon Chilonides 35 10
3934 1z. Chilon Chilonides and crowd fleeing 35 10
3935 1z. Liga tied to the back of a bull and in the arms of Ursus 35 10
3936 1z. St. Peter blessing Vincius and Liga 35 10

1227 Copper Furnace

2001. "Euro Cuprum 2001" European Stamp Exhibition, Lubin. Multicoloured.
3937 1z. Type **1227** 35 10
3938 1z.90 Engraver at work and men dressing copper sheets 65 20
3939 2z. Inking plates and engraving press 70 20

1228 "Battle of Chocim" (detail, Stanislaw Batowski-Kaczor) and Breast-plate of Stanislaw Skorkowski's Armour

2001. "One Century Passes it Over to Another Century" Exhibition, Polish Military Museum, Warsaw.
3941 **1228** 1z. multicoloured . . . 35 10

1229 Steam and Electric Locomotives

2001. 75th Anniv of Polish State Railways.
3942 **1229** 1z. multicoloured . . . 35 10

1230 Street Scene (Marcin Kuron)

2001. Winners of "Poland in 21st Century" (children's painting competition). Multicoloured.
3943 1z. Type **1230** 35 10
3944 1z.90 Rockets behind girl and boy (Agata Grzyb) 65 20
3945 2z. Futuristic car and house on wheels (Joanna Sadrakula) 70 25

1231 Football and Players

1232 Children encircling Globe

2001. Qualification of Poland for World Cup Football Championship, Japan and South Korea.
3946 **1231** 1z. multicoloured . . . 35 10

2001. World Post Day. United Nations Year of Dialogue among Civilizations.
3947 **1232** 1z.90 multicoloured . . 65 20

1234 Violin Peg Box and Scroll

2001. 12th Henryk Wieniawski International Violin Competition, Poznan.
3949 **1234** 1z. multicoloured . . . 35 10

1235 Pope John Paul II

2001. Papal Day.
3950 **1235** 1z. multicoloured . . . 35 10

1236 Building Facade

2001. Centenary of National Philharmonic Orchestra.
3951 **1236** 1z. multicoloured . . . 35 10

1237 Pope John Paul II

2001. New Millennium. Multicoloured.
3952 1z. Type **1237** 35 10
3953 1z. President Lech Walesa and cover of 1791 constitution 35 10
3954 1z. Covers of *Glos Wolny Wolnosc Ubespieczaiacy*, *Kultura*, *Zniewolony umysl* and *O skutecznym rad sposobie* (magazines) . . . 35 10
3955 1z. Wojciech Boguslawski (actor and dramatist) and Jerzy Grotowski (director) 35 10
3956 1z. General Jozef Pilsudski (soldier and President 1918–22) and posters (1989) 35 10
3957 1z. N.A.T.O. emblem and General Kazimierz Pulaski (soldier) 35 10
3958 1z. Nicolaus Copernicus and Aleksander Wolszczan (astronomers) 35 10
3959 1z. Jan of Glogow (wood engraving) (mathematician and astronomer) and Tadeusz Kotarbinski (physicist) 35 10
3960 1z. "Do Broni" (poster, 1920) and "Bitwa pod Grunwaldem" (detail) (painting, Jan Matejko) 35 10
3961 1z. Leaders of November Uprising, 1830 . . . . . 35 10
3962 1z. Head of John the Apostle (detail) (wooden altarpiece, Wit Stwosz) and sculpture by Magdalena Abakanowicz 35 10
3963 1z. Frederik Chopin, Krzysztof Penderecki (composers) and score of *Mazurka No. 10* by Karol Szymanowski 35 10
3964 1z. Royal Castle, Warsaw and view of Cracow (wood engraving) 35 10
3965 1z. Jan III Sobieski (painting) and emblem of European Union 35 10
3966 1z. Wislawa Szymborska (Nobel Prizewinner for Literature) and Mikolaj Rej (poet) 35 10
3967 1z. Janusz Kusocinski and Robert Korzeniowski (athletes) 35 10

1238 Lower Silesian Crib

2001. Christmas. Multicoloured.
3968 1z. Type **1238** 35 10
3969 1z.90 Lower Silesian Crib (different) 35 10

1239 Radio Station Building and Virgin Mary (statue)

2001. 10th Anniv of "Radio Maryja" (religious broadcasting station).
3970 **1239** 1z. multicoloured . . . 35 10

1240 Pear and Apple

2002. Valentine's Day.
3972 **1240** 1z.10 multicoloured . . 25 10

1241 Downhill, Biathlon, Ice-skating, and Ski Jumping

2002. Winter Olympic Games, Salt Lake City, U.S.A.
3973 **1241** 1z.10 multicoloured . . 25 10

1242 Jan Czerski

2002. Explorers. Multicoloured.
3974 2z. Type **1242** 50 15
3975 2z. Bronislaw Pilsudski . . . 50 15

1243 Gniezno

1244 Flowers

2002. Polish Cities. Multicoloured.
3975a 1z.80 Kalisz 40 10
3976 2z. Type **1243** 50 15
3977 2z.10 Krakow 50 15
3977a 2z.60 Pfock (horiz) 60 20
3978 3z.20 Warsaw 75 25

2002. Easter. Multicoloured.
3979 1z.10 Type **1244** 25 10
3980 2z. Chicks 50 15

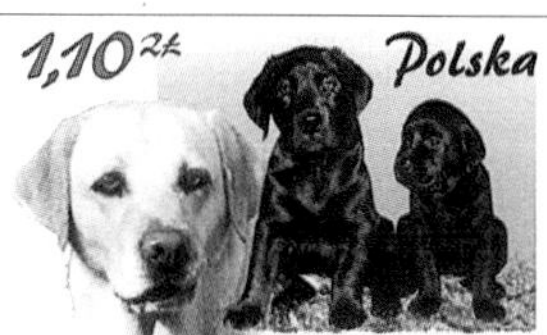

1245 Labrador Retriever and Puppies

2002. Domestic and Wild Animals. Multicoloured.
3981 1z.10 Type **1245** 25 10
3982 1z.10 Cat and kittens . . . 25 10
3983 1z.10 Wolf and cubs 25 10
3984 1z.10 Lynx and kittens . . . 25 10

1246 Soldiers marching

2002. 60th Anniv of Evacuation of General Wladislaw Ander's Army from U.S.S.R.
3985 **1246** 1z.10 multicoloured . . 25 10

1247 Trees (Amanda Zejmis)

1249 Radio Microphone

1248 Stylized Figures

2002. Paintings. Multicoloured.
3986 1z.10 Type **1257** 25 10
3987 1z.10 Vase and ornaments (Henryk Paraszczuk) . . . 25 10
3988 2z. Landscape (Lucjan Matula) (horiz) 50 15
3989 3z.20 Basket of flowers (Jozefa Laciak) (horiz) . . 75 25

2002. National Census.
3990 **1248** 1z.10 multicoloured . . 25 10

2002. 50th Anniv of "Radio Free Europe".
3991 **1249** 2z. multicoloured . . . 50 15

1250 Fireman

2002. 10th Anniv of State Fire Brigade.
3992 **1250** 1z.10 multicoloured . . 25 10

1251 Circus Artist

2002. Europa. Circus.
3993 **1251** 2z. multicoloured . . . 50 15

1252 "Madonna with the Child, St. John the Baptist and the Angel" (Sandro Botticelli)

2002. 140th Anniv of the National Gallery, Warsaw.
3994 **1252** 1z.10 multicoloured . . 25 10

1253 Maria Konopnicka

1254 Scooter

2002. 160th Birth Anniv of Maria Konopnicka (poet and writer).
3995 **1253** 1z.10 brown, ochre and green 25 10

2002. Children's Games. Multicoloured.
3996 1z.10 Type **1254** 25 10
3997 1z.10 Flying kite 25 10
3998 1z.10 Badminton 25 10

1255 Football and Globe

2002. World Cup Football Championship, Japan and South Korea. Multicoloured.
3999 1z.10 Type **1255** 25 10
4000 2z. Player chasing ball . . . 50 15

1256 Domeyko and Santiago University, Chile

2002. Birth Bicentenary of Ignacego Domeyki (scientist).
4015 **1256** 2z.60 multicoloured . . 60 20

1257 Hibiscus and Tulips

2002. "Philakorea 2002" International Philatelic Exhibition, Seoul and "Amphilex 2002" International Philatelic Exhibition, Amsterdam.
4016 **1257** 2z. multicoloured . . . 50 15

1258 Pope John Paul II and Basilica of Virgin Mary of the Angel, Kalwaria Zebrzydowska

2002. 7th Papal Visit To Poland (1st issue). Multicoloured.
4017 1z.10 Type **1258** 25 10
4018 1z.80 Pope John Paul II and Sanctuary of God's Mercy, Sisters of Virgin Mary's Convent, Lagiewniki 40 10
See also No. **MS**4022.

1259 "Holy Lady of Assistance"

2002. St. Mary's Sanctuaries. Multicoloured.
4019 1z.10 Type **1259** (Church of the Holy Lady of Assistance, Jaworzno) . . 25 10
4020 1z.10 "Holy Virgin of Opole" (Cathedral of Holy Cross, Opole) . . . 25 10
4021 2z. "Holy Virgin of Trabki" (Church of the Assumption of the Holy Lady, Trabki Wielkie) . . 50 15

1260 Pope John Paul II and Wawel Castle, Cracow

2002. 7th Papal Visit To Poland (2nd issue). Sheet 73 × 57 mm.
MS4022 1260 3z.20 black 75 75

1261 Spa Building, Ciechocinku

2002. 18th Polish Philatelic Association Convention, Ciechocinku. Sheet 74 × 105 mm.
MS4023 1261 3z.20 brown . . . 75 75

1262 Czesnik Raptusiewicz and Dyndalski

2002. "Zemsta" (Revenge) (film directed by Andrzej Wajda). Sheet 177 × 137 mm containing T **1262**, Showing scenes from the film. Multicoloured.
MS4024 1z.10 Type **1262**; 1z.10 Klara and Waclaw; 1z.10 Papkin; 1z.10 Regent Milczek and Papkin; 1z.10 Regent Milczek and Czesnik Raptusiewicz; 1z.10 Podstolina and Klara . . . . 1·60 1·60

1263 Schwarzkopf Okl-359

2002. Steam Locomotives. Showing locomotives from Wolsztyn Railway Museum. Multicoloured.
4025 1z.10 Type **1263** 25 10
4026 1z.10 Fablok 0149-7 . . . . 25 10
4027 2z. Krolewiec Tki3-87 . . . 50 15
4028 2z. Express locomotive Pm 36-2 . . . . 50 15

1264 Hands holding Pens

2002. World Post Day.
4029 **1264** 2z. multicoloured . . . 50 15

1265 Emblem

2002. Anti-Cancer Campaign.
4030 **1265** 1z.10 multicoloured . . 25 10

1266 Emblem

2002. 50th Anniv of Polish Television. Sheet 185 × 115 mm containing T **1266** Showing emblems of television programmes. Multicoloured.
MS4031 1z.10 Type **1266** (TV News); 1z.10 TV Theatre; 1z.10 "Pegaz" (cultural programme); 1z.10 "Teleranek" (children's programme) . . . . 1·00 1·00

1267 St. Stanislaw

2002. Saints. Sheet 136 × 165 mm containing T **1267** and similar vert designs. Multicoloured.
MS4032 1z.10 Type **1267**; 1z.10 St. Kazimierz; 1z.10 St. Faustyna Kowalska; 1z.10 St. Benedict; 1z.10 St. Cyril and St. Methody; 1z.10 St. Catherine of Siena . . 1·60 1·60

1268 Christmas Tree Baubles

2002. Christmas. Multicoloured.
4033 1z.10 Type **1268** 25 10
4034 2z. Small purple and large yellow baubles 50 15

MILITARY POST

I. Polish Corps in Russia, 1918.

1918. Stamps of Russia optd **POCZTA Pol. Korp.** and eagle. Perf or imperf. (70k.).
M 1 **22** 3k. red . . . . 55·00 55·00
M 2 **23** 4k. red . . . . 55·00 55·00
M 3 **22** 5k. red . . . . 17·00 13·50
M 4 **23** 10k. blue . . . . 17·00 13·50
M 5 **22** 10k. on 7k. blue (No.151) £425 £500
M 6 **10** 15k. blue and purple . . . 3·75 3·75
M 7 **14** 20k. red and blue . . . . 6·75 5·50
M 8 **10** 25k. mauve and green . . 85·00 70·00
M 9 35k. green and purple . . 3·75 3·75
M10 **14** 40k. green and purple . . 13·50 9·75
M11 **10** 70k. orge & brn (No. 166) £275 £225

1918. Stamps of Russia surch **Pol. Korp.**, eagle and value. (a) Perf on Nos. 92/4.
M12A **22** 10k. on 3k. red . . . . 3·50 3·50
M13A 35k. on 1k. orange . . . 50·00 50·00
M14A 50k. on 2k. green . . . 3·50 3·50
M15A 1r. on 3k. red . . . . . 70·00 65·00

(b) Imperf on Nos. 155/7.
M12B **22** 10k. on 3k. red . . . . 1·40 1·40
M13B 35k. on 1k. orange . . . 55 55
M14B 50k. on 2k. green . . . 1·40 1·40
M15B 1r. on 3k. red . . . . 3·25 2·40

II. Polish Army in Russia, 1942.

M 3 "We Shall Return"

1942.
M16 M **3** 50k. brown £170 £425

NEWSPAPER STAMPS

1919. Newspaper stamps of Austria optd **POCZTA POLSKA**. Imperf.
N50 N **53** 2h. brown . . . . . . 8·75 10·50
N51 4h. green . . . . 1·75 2·25
N52 6h. blue . . . . 1·75 2·25
N53 10h. orange . . . . . 35·00 42·00
N54 30h. red . . . . 3·75 5·50

OFFICIAL STAMPS

O 24 O 70

1920.
O128 O **24** 3f. red 10 25
O129 5f. red 10 10
O130 10f. red 10 10
O131 15f. red 10 10
O132 25f. red 10 10
O133 50f. red 10 10
O134 100f. red 25 25
O135 150f. red 30 30
O136 200f. red 30 35
O137 300f. red 30 35
O138 600f. red 40 50

1933. (a) Inscr "ZWYCZAJNA".
O295 O **70** (No value) mauve . . 15 15
O306 (No value) blue . . . 20 20
(b) Inscr "POLECONA".
O307 O **70** (No value) red 20 20

O 93

1940. (a) Size 31 × 23 mm.
O392 O **93** 6g. brown . . . . . . 1·25 1·60
O393 8g. grey . . . . . . 1·25 1·60
O394 10g. green . . . . . 1·25 1·60
O395 12g. green . . . . . 1·25 1·60
O396 20g. brown . . . . . 1·25 2·25
O397 24g. red . . . . . . 9·50 45
O398 30g. red . . . . . . 1·60 2·25
O399 40g. violet . . . . . 1·60 3·75
O400 48g. green . . . . . 5·00 3·75
O401 50g. blue . . . . . . 1·25 2·25
O402 60g. green . . . . . 1·25 1·75
O403 80g. purple . . . . . 1·25 1·75
(b) Size 35 × 26 mm.
O404 O **93** 1z. purple and grey . . 3·75 4·50
O405 3z. brown and grey . . 3·75 4·50
O406 5z. orange and grey . . 5·00 5·75
(c) Size 21 × 16 mm.
O407 O **93** 6g. brown . . . . . . 65 1·00
O408 8g. grey . . . . . . 1·25 1·75
O409 10g. green . . . . . 1·90 1·90
O410 12g. green . . . . . 1·90 1·60
O411 20g. brown . . . . . 95 1·00
O412 24g. red 95 85
O413 30g. red . . . . . . 1·25 2·25
O414 40g. violet . . . . . 1·90 2·00
O415 50g. blue . . . . . . 1·90 2·00

O 102 O 128 O 277

1943.
O456 O **102** 6g. brown 30 60
O457 8g. blue 30 60
O458 10g. green 30 60
O459 12g. violet 30 60
O460 16g. orange 30 60
O461 20g. green 30 60
O462 24g. red 30 60
O463 30g. purple 30 60
O464 40g. blue 30 60
O465 60g. green 30 60
O466 80g. purple 30 60
O467 100g. grey 30 95

1945. No value. (a) With control number below design. Perf or imperf.
O534 O **128** (5z.) blue 45 25
O535 (10z.) red 45 25
(b) Without control number below design. Perf.
O748 O **128** (60g.) pale blue . . . 35 25
O805 (60g.) indigo . . . 55 25
O806 (1.55z.) red 55 25
The blue and indigo stamps are inscr "ZWYKLA" (Ordinary) and the red stamps "POLECONA" (Registered).

1954. No value.
O871 O **277** (60g.) blue 20 15
O872 (1.55z.) red ("POLECONA") 40 15

POSTAGE DUE STAMPS

1919. Postage Due Stamps of Austria optd **POCZTA POLSKA**.
D50 D **55** 5h. red . . . . 5·50 5·00
D51 10h. red £1750 £2750
D52 15h. red . . . . 3·25 2·50
D53 20h. red £550 £550
D54 25h. red . . . . 19·00 17·00
D55 30h. red £950 £950
D56 40h. red £220 £220
D57 D **56** 1k. blue £2000 £2500
D58 5k. blue £2000 £2500
D59 10k. blue £9750 £9000

1919. Postage Due Provisionals of Austria optd **POCZTA POLSKA**.
D60 **50** 15 on 36h. (No. D287) . . £300 £325
D61 50 on 42h. (No. D289) . . 30·00 25·00

D 20 D 28 D 63

1919. Sold in halerzy or fenigow.
D 92 D **20** 2h. blue 10 10
D 93 4h. blue 10 10
D 94 5h. blue 10 10
D 95 10h. blue 10 10
D 96 20h. blue 10 10
D 97 30h. blue 10 10
D 98 50h. blue 10 10
D145 100h. blue 20 10
D146 200f. blue 75 10
D147 500h. blue 75 10
The 20, 100 and 500 values were sold in both currencies.

1919. Sold in fenigow.
D128 D **20** 2f. red 10 25
D129 4f. red 10 10
D130 5f. red 10 10
D131 10f. red 10 10
D132 20f. red 10 10
D133 30f. red 10 10
D134 50f. red 25 25
D135 100f. red 30 30
D136 200f. red 30 35

1921. Stamps of 1919 surch with new value and **doplata**. Imperf.
D154 **11** 6m. on 15h. brown . . . 70 90
D155 6m. on 25h. red 50 55
D156 20m. on 10h. red . . . . 1·90 2·10
D157 20m. on 50h. blue . . . 1·00 1·75
D158 35m. on 70h. blue . . . 8·75 12·50

1921. Value in marks. (a) Size 17 × 22 mm.
D159 D **28** 1m. blue 20 10
D160 2m. blue 20 10
D161 4m. blue 20 10
D162 6m. blue 20 10
D163 8m. blue 20 10
D164 20m. blue 20 10
D165 50m. blue 20 10
D166 100m. blue 20 10
(b) Size 19 × 24 mm.
D199 D **28** 50m. blue 10 10
D200 100m. blue 10 10
D201 200m. blue 10 10
D202 500m. blue 10 10
D203 1000m. blue 10 10
D204 2000m. blue 10 10
D205 10,000m. blue 10 10
D206 20,000m. blue 10 10
D207 30,000m. blue 10 10
D208 50,000m. blue 10 10
D209 100,000m. blue . . . 10 10
D210 200,000m. blue . . . 10 10
D211 300,000m. blue . . . 30 20
D212 500,000m. blue . . . 40 40
D213 1,000,000m. blue . . . 75 55
D214 2,000,000m. blue . . . 1·10 90
D215 3,000,000m. blue . . . 1·40 1·10

1923. Surch.
D216 D **28** 10,000 on 8m. blue . . 10 15
D217 20,000 on 20m. blue 10 35
D218 50,000 on 2m. blue . . 1·25 60

1924. As Type D **28** but value in "groszy" or "zloty". (a) Size 20 × 25½ mm.
D229 D **28** 1g. brown 10 10
D230 2g. brown 20 10
D231 4g. brown 20 10
D232 6g. brown 20 10
D233 10g. brown . . . . . 3·25 10
D234 15g. brown . . . . . 3·25 10
D235 20g. brown . . . . . 6·75 10
D236 25g. brown . . . . . 4·75 10
D237 30g. brown 95 10
D238 40g. brown . . . . . 1·40 10
D239 50g. brown . . . . . 1·40 10
D240 1z. brown 90 10
D241 2z. brown 90 25
D242 3z. brown . . . . . . 1·40 45
D243 5z. brown . . . . . . 1·40 30
(b) Size 19 × 24 mm.
D290 D **28** 1g. brown 20 10
D291 2g. brown 20 10
D292 10g. brown 90 10
D293 15g. brown . . . . . 1·40 10
D294 20g. brown . . . . . 3·25 10
D295 25g. brown . . . . . 30·00 10

1930.
D280 D **63** 5g. brown 35 20

1934. Nos. D79/84 surch.
D301 D **28** 10g. on 2z. brown . . 20 15
D302 15g. on 2z. brown . . 20 15
D303 20g. on 1z. brown . . 20 15
D304 20g. on 5z. brown . . 1·75 35
D305 25g. on 40g. brown . . 60 35
D306 30g. on 40g. brown . . 65 45
D307 50g. on 40g. brown . . 65 45
D308 50g. on 3z. brown . . 2·10 60

1934. No. 273 surch **DOPLATA** and value.
D309 10g. on 1z. black on cream 70 20
D310 20g. on 1z. black on cream 1·50 55
D311 25g. on 1z. black on cream 70 20

D 88

D 97

1938.
D350 D **88** 5g. green 15 10
D351 10g. green 15 10
D352 15g. green 15 10
D353 20g. green 40 10
D354 25g. green 10 10
D355 30g. green 10 10
D356 50g. green 45 50
D357 1z. green . . . . . . 2·25 1·75

1940. German Occupation.
D420 D **97** 10g. orange 25 75
D421 20g. orange . . . . . 25 1·00
D422 30g. orange . . . . . 25 1·00
D423 50g. orange . . . . . 70 2·00

D 126

D 190

1945. Size 26 × 19½ mm. Perf.
D530 D **126** 1z. brown 10 10
D531 2z. brown 20 10
D532 3z. brown 25 20
D533 5z. brown 40 25

1946. Size 29 × 21½ mm. Perf or imperf.
D646 D **126** 1z. brown 10 10
D647 2z. brown 10 10
D572 3z. brown 10 10
D573 5z. brown 10 10
D574 6z. brown 10 10
D575 10z. brown 10 10
D649 15z. brown 10 10
D577 25z. brown 50 20
D651 100z. brown 55 35
D652 150z. brown 80 45

1950.
D665 D **190** 5z. red 15 15
D666 10z. red 15 15
D667 15z. red 15 15
D668 20z. red 15 15
D669 25z. red 30 15
D670 50z. red 45 15
D671 100z. red 55 30

1951. Value in "groszy" or "zloty".
D701 D **190** 5g. red 10 10
D702 10g. red 10 10
D703 15g. red 10 10
D704 20g. red 10 10
D705 25g. red 10 10
D706 30g. red 10 10
D707 50g. red 10 10
D708 60g. red 10 10
D709 90g. red 25 10
D710 1z. red 25 10
D711 2z. red 45 25
D712 5z. purple 95 30

1953. As last but with larger figures of value and no imprint below design.
D804 D **190** 5g. brown 10 10
D805 10g. brown 10 10
D806 15g. brown 10 10
D807 20g. brown 10 10
D808 25g. brown 10 10
D809 30g. brown 10 10
D810 50g. brown 10 10
D811 60g. brown 10 10
D812 90g. brown 25 10
D813 1z. brown 25 10
D814 2z. brown 45 10

1980. As Type D **190** but redrawn without imprint.
D2699 1z. red 10 10
D2700 2z. drab 10 10
D2701 3z. violet 30 10
D2702 5z. brown 50 30

D 1143

1998.
D3746 D **1143** 5g. blue, vio & yell 10 10
D3747 10g. blue, turq & yell 10 10
D3748 20g. bl, grn & yell 10 10
D3749 50g. black & yell 15 10
D3750 80g. bl, orge & yell 25 10
D3751 1z. blue, red & yell 35 15

POLISH POST IN DANZIG Pt. 5

For Polish post in Danzig, the port through which Poland had access to the sea between the two Great Wars.

100 groszy = 1 zloty.

Stamps of Poland optd **PORT GDANSK**.

1925. Issue of 1924.
R 1 **40** 1g. brown . . . . 30 1·50
R 2 2g. brown . . . . 30 3·50
R 3 3g. orange . . . . 30 1·50
R 4 5g. green . . . . 9·50 6·50
R 5 10g. green . . . . . . 3·50 3·25
R 6 15g. red . . . . 19·00 5·00
R 7 20g. blue . . . . 1·50 1·50
R 8 25g. red . . . . 1·00 1·50
R 9 30g. violet . . . . . . 1·00 1·50
R10 40g. blue . . . . 1·00 1·50
R11 50g. purple . . . . . . 2·75 1·75

1926. Issues of 1925–28.
R14 **44** 5g. green . . . . 70 3·00
R15 – 10g. violet (No. 245a) . . 70 3·00
R16 – 15g. red (No. 246) . . . 2·10 3·50
R17 **48** 20g. red . . . . 1·75 1·75
R18 **51** 25g. brown . . . . . . 2·75 1·75
R19 **57** 1z. black and cream . . . 19·00 23·00

1929. Issues of 1928/9.
R21 **61** 5g. violet . . . . 1·00 1·50
R22 10g. green . . . . . . 1·00 1·50
R23 **59** 15g. blue . . . . 2·45 4·50
R24 **61** 25g. brown . . . . . . 2·10 1·50

1933. Stamp of 1928 with vert opt.
R25 **57** 1z. black on cream . . . . 60·00 90·00

1934. Issue of 1932.
R26 **65** 5g. violet . . . . 2·40 3·50
R27 10g. green . . . . . . 23·00 90·00
R28 15g. red . . . . 2·40 3·50

1936. Issue of 1935.
R29 **79** 5g. blue (No. 313) . . . . 2·10 3·50
R31 – 5g. violet (No. 317) . . . 70 1·75
R30 – 15g. blue (No. 315) . . . 2·10 5·00
R32 – 15g. lake (No. 319) . . . 70 1·75
R33 – 25g. green (No. 321a) . . 2·10 3·50

R 6 Port of Danzig

1938. 20th Anniv of Polish Independence.
R34 R **6** 5g. orange . . . . . . 40 1·50
R35 15g. brown . . . . . 40 1·50
R36 25g. purple . . . . . 40 1·50
R37 55g. blue . . . . . . 70 2·75

POLISH POST OFFICE IN TURKEY Pt. 5

Stamps used for a short period for franking correspondence handed in at the Polish Consulate, Constantinople.

100 fenigow = 1 marka.

1919. Stamps of Poland of 1919 optd **LEVANT**. Perf.
1 **15** 3f. brown . . . . 35·00
2 5f. green . . . . 35·00
3 10f. purple . . . . . . 35·00
4 15f. red . . . . 35·00
5 20f. blue . . . . 35·00

6		25f. olive	35·00	
7		50f. green	35·00	
8	17	1m. violet	40·00	
9		1m.50 green	40·00	
10		2m. brown	40·00	
11	18	2m.50 brown	40·00	
12	19	5m. purple	40·00	

PONTA DELGADA Pt. 9

A district of the Azores, whose stamps were used from 1868, and again after 1905.

1000 reis = 1 milreis.

1892. As T **26** of Portugal but inscr "PONTA DELGADA".

6		5r. yellow	2·25	1·50
7		10r. mauve	2·25	1·50
8		15r. brown	2·75	2·25
9		20r. lilac	2·75	2·25
3		25r. green	5·75	1·00
12		50r. blue	5·75	3·25
25		75r. pink	5·75	5·25
14		80r. green	9·00	9·00
15		100r. brown on yellow	9·00	5·25
28		150r. red on pink	45·00	29·00
16		200r. blue on blue	48·00	42·00
17		300r. blue on brown	48·00	42·00

1897. "King Carlos" key-types inscr "PONTA DELGADA".

29	S	2½r. grey	45	35
30		5r. orange	45	35
31		10r. green	45	35
32		15r. brown	5·75	5·75
45		15r. green	1·50	1·10
33		20r. lilac	1·60	1·10
34		25r. green	2·25	1·10
46		25r. red	1·25	40
35		50r. blue	2·40	1·10
48		65r. blue	1·00	45
36		75r. pink	5·00	1·10
49		75r. brown on yellow	10·00	6·00
37		80r. mauve	1·25	1·10
38		100r. blue on blue	2·75	1·10
50		115r. brown on pink	1·60	1·25
51		130r. brown on cream	1·60	1·25
39		150r. brown on yellow	1·60	1·25
52		180r. grey on pink	1·60	1·25
40		200r. purple on pink	5·25	5·00
41		300r. blue on pink	5·25	5·00
42		500r. black on blue	11·00	9·75

POONCH Pt. 1

A state in Kashmir, India. Now uses Indian stamps.

12 pies = 1 anna;
16 annas = 1 rupee.

1 4

1876. Imperf.

1	1	6p. red	£6000	£120
2		½a. red	—	£3250

1880. Imperf.

32	1	1p. red	2·25	2·75
12	4	½a. red	2·25	3·00
50		1a. red	1·75	3·00
52		2a. red (22×22 mm)	3·00	3·00
31		4a. red (28×27 mm)	3·75	4·00

These stamps were printed on various coloured papers.

OFFICIAL STAMPS

1888. Imperf.

O1	1	1p. black	2·00	2·25
O2	4	½a. black	2·50	3·25
O3		1a. black	2·25	2·50
O4		2a. black	3·50	3·50
O5		4a. black	5·50	9·00

PORT LAGOS Pt. 6

French Post Office in the Turkish Empire. Closed in 1898.

25 centimes = 1 piastre.

1893. Stamps of France optd **Port-Lagos** and the three higher values surch also in figures and words.

75	10	5c. green	19·00	17·00
76		10c. black on lilac	32·00	29·00
77		15c. blue	35·00	55·00
78		1p. on 25c. black on pink	65·00	65·00
79		2p. on 50c. red	£100	80·00
80		4p. on 1f. green	60·00	60·00

PORT SAID Pt. 6

French Post Office in Egypt. Closed 1931.

1902. 100 centimes = 1 franc.
1921. 10 milliemes = 1 piastre.

1899. Stamps of France optd **PORT SAID**.

101	10	1c. black on blue	30	1·00
102		2c. brown on buff	50	1·60
103		3c. grey	50	2·75
104		4c. brown on grey	35	2·75
105		5c. green	65	2·75
107		10c. black on lilac	4·00	4·75
109		15c. blue	3·25	7·75
110		20c. red on green	4·25	10·00
111		25c. black on pink	1·75	30
112		30c. brown	7·00	10·00
113		40c. red on yellow	8·25	7·50
115		50c. red	14·00	12·50
116		1f. green	20·00	17·00
117		2f. brown on blue	38·00	55·00
118		5f. mauve on lilac	60·00	80·00

1899. No. 107 surch. (a) **25c VINGT-CINQ**.

119	10	25c. on 10c. black on lilac	£325	£130

(b) **VINGT-CINQ** only.

121	10	25c. on 10c. black on lilac	95·00	23·00

1902. "Blanc", "Mouchon" and "Merson" key-types inscr "PORT SAID".

122	A	1c. grey	10	85
123		2c. purple	40	1·40
124		3c. red	15	1·75
125		4c. brown	25	1·40
126a		5c. green	1·40	1·50
127	B	10c. red	1·10	30
128		15c. red	1·60	2·50
128a		15c. orange	3·75	3·75
129		20c. brown	90	2·50
130		25c. blue	70	15
131		30c. mauve	3·00	2·75
132	C	40c. red and blue	2·00	3·50
133		50c. brown and lilac	1·75	2·25
134		1f. red and green	7·25	8·25
135		2f. lilac and buff	5·50	14·50
136		5f. blue and buff	20·00	35·00

1915. Red Cross. Surch **5c** and red cross.

137	B	10c.+5c. red	50	3·00

1921. Surch with value in figures and words (without bars).

151a	A	1m. on 1c. grey	2·25	2·75
152		2m. on 5c. green	1·50	2·75
153	B	4m. on 10c. red	85	3·25
166a	A	5m. on 1c. grey	7·00	11·00
167		5m. on 2c. purple	13·00	13·00
154		5m. on 3c. red	6·25	10·00
141		5m. on 4c. brown	8·50	11·00
155	B	6m. on 15c. orange	1·25	3·50
156		6m. on 15c. red	11·50	14·00
157		8m. on 20c. brown	1·50	3·50
168	A	10m. on 2c. purple	11·00	12·50
142		10m. on 4c. brown	20·00	24·00
158	B	10m. on 25c. blue	2·25	2·00
159		10m. on 30c. mauve	3·75	7·50
144		12m. on 30c. mauve	30·00	42·00
145	A	15m. on 4c. brown	8·00	9·25
169	B	15m. on 15c. red	60·00	60·00
170		15m. on 20c. brown	55·00	55·00
146	C	15m. on 40c. red and blue	55·00	65·00
160		15m. on 50c. brown and lilac	3·25	5·50
161	B	15m. on 50c. blue	4·25	3·75
162		30m. on 1f. red and green	2·75	7·75
171	C	30m. on 50c. brown & lilac	£225	£225
172		60m. on 50c. brown and lilac	£225	£225
149		60m. on 2f. lilac and buff	70·00	70·00
164		60m. on 2f. red and green	6·00	11·00
173		150m. on 50c. brown and lilac	£250	£250
165		150m. on 5f. blue and buff	6·25	10·50

1925. Surch with value in figures and words and bars over old value.

174	A	1m. on 1c. grey	25	3·00
175		2m. on 5c. green	1·60	3·00
176	B	4m. on 10c. red	1·10	3·00
177	A	5m. on 3c. red	65	2·25
178	B	6m. on 15c. orange	1·25	3·25
179		8m. on 20c. brown	1·40	3·25
180		10m. on 25c. blue	1·40	3·25
181		15m. on 50c. blue	1·75	2·25
182	C	30m. on 1f. red and green	1·75	2·75
183		60m. on 2f. red and green	1·25	3·50
184		150m. on 5f. blue and buff	3·00	4·25

1927. Altered key-types. Inscr "Mm" below value.

185	A	3m. orange	2·25	3·25
186	B	15m. blue	1·10	2·50
187		20m. mauve	2·25	3·75
188	C	50m. red and green	3·25	4·75
189		100m. blue and yellow	2·00	6·00
190		250m. green and red	7·00	10·00

1927. "French Sinking Fund" issue. As No. 186 (colour changed) surch **+5 Mm Caisse d'Amortissement**.

191	B	15m.+5m. orange	1·75	4·50
192		15m.+5m. mauve	2·25	4·50
193		15m.+5m. brown	2·25	4·50
194		15m.+5m. lilac	3·25	6·75

POSTAGE DUE STAMPS

1921. Postage Due stamps of France surch in figures and words.

D174	D 11	2m. on 5c. blue	38·00	48·00
D175		4m. on 10c. brown	42·00	48·00
D176		10m. on 30c. red	42·00	48·00
D166		12m. on 10c. brown	38·00	45·00
D167		15m. on 5c. blue	40·00	55·00
D177		15m. on 50c. purple	55·00	60·00
D168		30m. on 20c. olive	48·00	60·00
D169		30m. on 50c. purple	£1800	£2000

For 1928 issues, see Alexandria.

PORTUGAL Pt. 9

A country on the S.W. coast of Europe, a kingdom until 1910, when it became a republic.

1853. 1000 reis = 1 milreis.
1912. 100 centavos = 1 escudo.
2002. 100 cents = 1 euro.

1 Queen Maria II 5 King Pedro V 9 King Luis

1853. Various frames. Imperf.

1	1	5r. brown	£2250	£550
4		25r. blue	£700	11·50
6		50r. green	£2500	£600
8		100r. lilac	£26000	£1300

1855. Various frames. Imperf.

18a	5	5r. brown	£375	46·00
21		25r. blue	£300	8·50
22		25r. pink	£225	3·25
13		50r. green	£400	49·00
15		100r. lilac	£600	55·00

1862. Various frames. Imperf.

24	9	5r. brown	£100	16·00
28		10r. yellow	£110	29·00
30		25r. pink	80·00	3·00
32		50r. green	£550	50·00
34		100r. lilac	£650	60·00

14 King Luis 15

1866. With curved value labels. Imperf.

35	14	5r. black	70·00	6·00
36		10r. yellow	£160	£100
38		20r. bistre	£140	40·00
39		25r. pink	£160	5·75
41		50r. green	£275	43·00
43		80r. orange	£200	43·00
45		100r. purple	£225	65·00
46		120r. blue	£225	39·00

1867. With curved value labels. Perf.

52	14	5r. black	95·00	29·00
54		10r. yellow	£200	60·00
56		20r. bistre	£225	75·00
57		25r. pink	50·00	4·25
60		50r. green	£190	70·00
61		80r. orange	£275	75·00
62		100r. lilac	£200	70·00
64		120r. blue	£225	47·00
67		240r. lilac	£750	£275

1870. With straight value labels. Perf.

69	15	5r. black	42·00	3·25
70		10r. yellow	60·00	17·00
158		10r. green	90·00	21·00
74		15r. brown	80·00	18·00
76		20r. bistre	60·00	15·00
143		20r. red	£250	36·00
80		25r. red	44·00	2·00
115		50r. green	£120	26·00
117		50r. blue	£225	43·00
148		80r. orange	90·00	13·50
153		100r. mauve	55·00	6·50
93		120r. blue	£200	44·00
95		150r. blue	£275	75·00
155		150r. yellow	60·00	11·00
99		240r. lilac	£1200	£700
156		300r. mauve	85·00	22·00
128		1000r. black	£250	55·00

16 King Luis 17

1880. Various frames for T **16**.

185	16	5r. black	21·00	2·50
188		25r. grey	22·00	1·80
190		25r. brown	22·00	1·90
180	17	25r. grey	£250	22·00
184	16	50r. blue	£250	8·75

19 King Luis

26 King Carlos

1882. Various frames.

229	19	5r. black	11·00	70
231		10r. green	28·00	2·20
232		20r. red	33·00	8·25
212		25r. brown	22·00	1·30
234		25r. mauve	22·00	1·40
236		50r. blue	35·00	1·50
216		500r. black	£375	£200
217		500r. mauve	£170	38·00

1892.

271	26	5r. orange	9·25	1·50
239		10r. mauve	22·00	2·50
256		15r. brown	26·00	4·75
242		20r. lilac	26·00	5·25
275		25r. green	30·00	1·50
244		50r. blue	26·00	7·25
245		75r. red	38·00	6·25
262		80r. green	65·00	43·00
248		100r. brown on buff	50·00	4·00
265		150r. red on pink	£120	33·00
252		200r. blue on blue	£100	34·00
267		300r. blue on brown	£130	49·00

1892. Optd **PROVISORIO**.

284	19	5r. black	12·50	5·00
283		10r. green	12·50	5·75
297	15	15r. brown	16·00	7·75
290	19	20r. red	31·00	15·00
291		25r. mauve	11·00	3·25
292		50r. blue	60·00	45·00
293	15	80r. orange	80·00	60·00

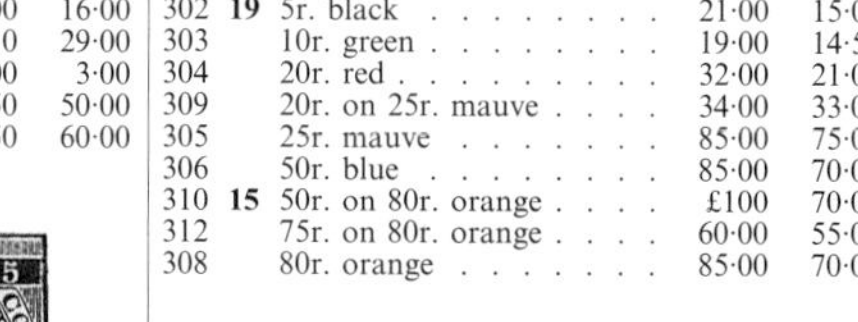

1893. Optd **1893 PROVISORIO** or surch also.

302	19	5r. black	21·00	15·00
303		10r. green	19·00	14·50
304		20r. red	32·00	21·00
309		20r. on 25r. mauve	34·00	33·00
305		25r. mauve	85·00	75·00
306		50r. blue	85·00	70·00
310	15	50r. on 80r. orange	£100	70·00
312		75r. on 80r. orange	60·00	55·00
308		80r. orange	85·00	70·00

32 Prince Henry in his Caravel and Family Motto

1894. 500th Birth Anniv of Prince Henry the Navigator.

314	32	5r. orange	2·75	70
315		10r. red	2·75	70
316		15r. brown	8·75	2·30
317		20r. lilac	8·75	2·50
318	–	25r. green	7·75	90
319	–	50r. blue	22·00	4·25
320	–	75r. red	42·00	8·75
321	–	80r. green	42·00	9·25
322	–	100r. brown on buff	15·00	8·25
323	–	150r. red	95·00	17·00
324	–	300r. blue on buff	£100	21·00
325	–	500r. purple	£225	48·00
326	–	1000r. black on buff	£400	75·00

DESIGNS: 25r. to 100r. Prince Henry directing movements of his fleet; 150r. to 1000r. Prince Henry's studies.

35 St. Anthony's Vision 37 St. Anthony ascending into Heaven

1895. 700th Birth Anniv of St. Anthony (Patron Saint). With a prayer in Latin printed on back.

327	35	2½r. black	3·25	80
328	–	5r. orange	3·25	80
329	–	10r. mauve	10·50	5·00
330	–	15r. brown	11·50	6·25
331	–	20r. lilac	11·50	6·75
332	–	25r. purple and green	10·00	80
333	37	50r. brown and blue	25·00	16·00
334		75r. brown and red	39·00	30·00
335		80r. brown and green	50·00	47·00
336		100r. black and brown	44·00	23·00
337	–	150r. red and bistre	£130	65·00
338	–	200r. blue and bistre	£120	75·00
339	–	300r. grey and bistre	£170	80·00
340	–	500r. brown and green	£300	£200
341	–	1000r. lilac and green	£500	£250

DESIGNS—HORIZ: 5r. to 25r. St. Anthony preaching to fishes. VERT: 150r. to 1000r. St. Anthony from picture in Academy of Fine Arts, Paris.

39 King Carlos

1895. Numerals of value in red (Nos. 354 and 363) or black (others).
342 **39** 2½r. grey 20 10
343 5r. orange 20 10
344 10r. green 35 10
345 15r. green . . . . 34·00 1·50
346 15r. brown . . . . 65·00 3·00
347 20r. lilac 55 20
348 25r. green . . . . 48·00 15
349 25r. red 20 10
351 50r. blue 40 15
352 65r. blue 40 15
353 75r. red . . . . 65·00 2·50
354 75r. brown on yellow . . . 1·20 35
355 80r. mauve . . . . 1·70 60
356 100r. blue on blue 70 30
357 115r. brown on pink . . . 3·75 1·00
358 130r. brown on cream . . 5·50 75
359 150r. brown on yellow . . £110 15·00
360 180r. grey on pink . . . . 12·00 4·75
361 200r. puple on pink . . . 8·00 1·80
362 300r. blue on pink . . . . 3·00 1·10
363 500r. black on blue . . . . 7·50 1·90

40 Departure of Fleet

43 Muse of History

44 Da Gama and Camoens and "Sao Gabriel" (flagship)

1898. 4th Centenary of Discovery of Route to India by Vasco da Gama.
378 **40** 2½r. green . . . . 1·00 15
379 – 5r. red . . . . 1·00 20
380 – 10r. purple . . . . 6·75 2·10
381 **43** 25r. green . . . . 4·00 20
382 **44** 50r. blue . . . . 8·25 1·90
383 – 75r. brown . . . . 35·00 7·25
384 – 100r. brown . . . . 24·00 6·75
385 – 150r. brown . . . . 55·00 19·00
DESIGNS—HORIZ: 5r. Arrival at Calicut; 10r. Embarkation at Rastello; 100r. Flagship "Sao Gabriel"; 150r. Vasco da Gama. VERT: 75r. Archangel Gabriel, Patron Saint of the Expedition.

48 King Manoel II

49

1910.
390 **48** 2½r. lilac 20 15
391 5r. black 15 15
392 10r. green 25 15
393 15r. brown . . . . 2·10 90
394 20r. red 75 50
395 25r. brown 45 15
396 50r. blue . . . . 1·20 45
397 75r. brown . . . . 7·25 4·00
398 80r. grey . . . . 1·90 1·70
399 100r. brown on green . . . 6·75 1·90
400 200r. green on orange . . . 4·00 3·00
401 300r. black on blue . . . . 4·75 3·25
402 **49** 500r. brown and green . . 10·50 7·75
403 1000r. black and blue . . . 24·00 16·00

1910. Optd **REPUBLICA**.
404 **48** 2½r. lilac 25 15
405 5r. black 20 15
406 10r. green . . . . 2·20 65
407 15r. brown 75 60
408 20r. red . . . . 3·00 1·40
409 25r. brown 65 15
410 50r. blue . . . . 4·00 1·50
411 75r. brown . . . . 6·25 3·00
412 80r. grey . . . . 2·10 1·60
413 100r. brown on green . . . 1·50 70
414 200r. green on orange . . . 1·60 1·20
415 300r. black on blue . . . . 2·75 1·80
416 **49** 500r. brown and green . . 7·50 5·50
417 1000r. black and blue . . . 16·00 16·00

1911. Optd **REPUBLICA** or surch also.
441 **40** 2½r. green 30 10
442a D **48** 5r. black 60 30
443a 10r. mauve 90 60
444 – 15r. on 5r. red (No. 379) 55 25
445a D **48** 20r. orange . . . . . 4·00 2·20
446 **43** 25r. green 30 15
447 **44** 50r. blue . . . . . . 2·30 80
448 – 75r. brown (No. 383) 30·00 18·00
449 – 80r. on 150r. (No. 385) 8·25 3·00
450 – 100r. brown (No. 384) 8·25 1·40
451 D **48** 200r. brown on buff . . 85·00 44·00
452 300r. on 50r. grey . . . 60·00 27·00
453 500r. on 100r. red on pink . . . . 32·00 16·00
454 – 1000r. on 10r. (No. 380) . . . . . 43·00 29·00

1911. Vasco da Gama stamps of Madeira optd **REPUBLICA** or surch also.
455 2½r. green . . . . 9·25 5·50
456 15r. on 5r. red . . . . . . 1·90 1·70
457 25r. green . . . . 4·75 4·00
458 50r. blue . . . . 8·75 6·50
459 75r. brown . . . . 8·75 4·50
460 80r. on 150r. brown . . . . 10·00 6·75
461 100r. brown . . . . 30·00 6·00
462 1000r. on 10r. purple . . . . 29·00 48·00

56 Ceres

60 Presidents of Portugal and Brazil and Airmen Gago Coutinho and Sacadura Cabral

1912.
484 **56** ¼c. brown 30 10
485 ½c. black 35 10
486 1c. green 95 25
515 1c. brown 10 10
488 1½c. brown . . . . 5·50 1·80
516 1½c. green 15 15
490 2c. red . . . . 5·50 1·10
517 2c. yellow 60 15
702 2c. brown 10 10
492 2½c. lilac 45 10
521 3c. red 30 20
703 3c. blue 10 10
495 3½c. green 25 10
523 4c. green 10 10
704 4c. orange 10 10
497 5c. blue . . . . 5·50 40
705 5c. brown 10 10
527 6c. purple 70 35
706 6c. brown 10 10
815 6c. red 25 15
500 7½c. brown . . . . 6·75 1·60
529 7½c. blue 25 15
530 8c. grey 35 20
531 8c. green 40 30
532 8c. orange 40 30
503 10c. brown . . . . 14·00 50
707 10c. red 10 10
504 12c. blue . . . . 1·00 45
534 12c. green 40 20
535 13½c. blue 90 65
481 14c. blue on yellow . . . . 1·40 1·00
536 14c. purple 50 35
505 15c. brown . . . . 1·70 70
708 15c. black 20 10
709 16c. blue 20 10
474 20c. brown on green . . . 13·00 1·20
475 20c. brown on buff . . . . 14·00 3·25
539 20c. brown 50 25
540 20c. green 35 25
541 20c. grey 45 20
542 24c. blue 40 20
543 25c. pink 35 15
710 25c. grey 20 10
819 25c. green 40 20
476 30c. brown on pink . . . . 80·00 8·75
477 30c. brown on yellow . . . 7·00 1·70
545 30c. brown 45 15
820 32c. green 40 20
548 36c. red . . . . 1·20 25
549 40c. blue 75 50
550 40c. brown 45 20
712 40c. green 30 10
713 48c. pink 95 75
478 50c. orange on orange . . 13·00 1·00
553 50c. yellow . . . . 1·20 45
554 50c. red . . . . 1·40 60
554 60c. blue . . . . 1·30 40
715 64c. blue . . . . 1·50 1·20
826 75c. red . . . . 1·20 60
510 80c. pink . . . . 1·30 75
558 80c. lilac 90 40
827 80c. green . . . . 1·50 60
559 90c. blue . . . . 1·30 60
717 96c. red . . . . 1·50 75
480 1e. green on blue . . . . . 15·00 1·00
561 1e. lilac . . . . 3·00 1·40
565 1e. blue . . . . 4·00 1·40
566 1e. purple . . . . 1·30 55
829 1e. red . . . . 3·00 60
562 1e.10 brown . . . . 3·00 1·30
563 1e.20 green . . . . 1·60 85
830 1e.20 brown . . . . 2·40 70
831 1e.25 blue . . . . 1·90 60
568 1e.50 lilac . . . . 13·50 2·40
720 1e.60 blue . . . . 1·80 25
721 2e. green . . . . 11·50 55
833 2e. mauve . . . . 12·00 3·75
572 2e.40 green £160 £100
573 3e. pink . . . . £160 90·00
722 3e.20 green . . . . 4·25 65
723 4e.50 yellow . . . . 4·25 80
575 5e. green . . . . 28·00 7·00
724 5e. brown . . . . 65·00 1·90
725 10e. red . . . . 6·75 1·20
577 20e. blue £275 £130

1923. Portugal–Brazil Trans-Atlantic Flight.
578 **60** 1c. brown 15 35
579 2c. orange 15 40
580 3c. blue 15 40
581 4c. green 20 40
582 5c. brown 20 40
583 10c. brown 20 40
584 15c. black 20 40
585 20c. green 20 40
586 25c. red 25 30
587 30c. brown . . . . 80 1·20
588 40c. brown 20 40
589 50c. yellow 40 55
590 75c. purple 40 65
591 1e. blue . . . . 45 1·20
592 1e.50 grey . . . . 75 1·50
593 2e. green . . . . 80 3·50

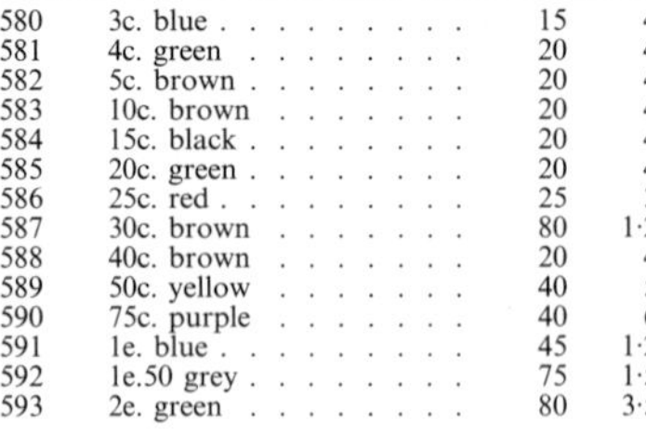

62 Camoens at Ceuta

63 Saving the "Lusiad"

1924. 400th Birth Anniv of Camoens (poet). Value in black.
600 **62** 2c. blue 10 10
601 3c. orange 10 10
602 4c. grey 10 10
603 5c. green 10 10
604 6c. red 10 10
605 **63** 8c. brown 10 10
606 10c. violet 10 10
607 15c. green 10 10
608 16c. purple 15 15
609 20c. orange 25 15
610 – 25c. violet 25 15
611 – 30c. brown 25 15
612 – 32c. green 65 70
613 – 40c. blue 20 30
614 – 48c. red . . . . 1·00 1·30
615 – 50c. red . . . . 1·10 90
616 – 64c. green . . . . 1·10 85
617 – 75c. lilac . . . . 1·10 90
618 – 80c. brown 85 90
619 – 96c. red 85 85
620 – 1e. turquoise 85 80
621 – 1e.20 brown . . . . 4·00 4·25
622 – 1e.50 red 95 90
623 – 1e.60 blue 95 95
624 – 2e. green . . . . 4·00 4·50
625 – 2e.40 green on green . . . 2·75 2·20
626 – 3e. blue on blue . . . . . 1·20 1·10
627 – 3e.20 black on turquoise . 1·20 1·00
628 – 4e.50 black on yellow . . 3·25 2·30
629 – 10e. brown on pink . . . 7·25 7·25
630 – 20e. violet on mauve . . 7·25 5·75
DESIGNS—VERT: 25c. to 48c. Luis de Camoens; 50c. to 96c. 1st Edition of "Lusiad"; 20e. Monument to Camoens. HORIZ: 1e. to 2e. Death of Camoens; 2e.40 to 10e. Tomb of Camoens.

65 Branco's House at S. Miguel de Seide

67 Camilo Castelo Branco

1925. Birth Centenary of Camilo Castelo Branco (novelist). Value in black.
631 **65** 2c. orange 15 10
632 3c. green 15 10
633 4c. blue 15 10
634 5c. red 15 10
635 6c. purple 15 10
636 8c. brown 15 10
637 A 10c. blue 15 25
638 **67** 15c. green 15 15
639 A 16c. orange 20 30
640 20c. violet 20 15
641 **67** 25c. red 20 30
642 A 30c. bistre 20 30
643 32c. green 85 70
644 **67** 40c. black and green . . . 55 40
645 A 48c. red . . . . 2·40 1·90
646 B 50c. green 55 60
647 64c. brown . . . . 2·40 1·90
648 75c. grey 45 60
649 **67** 80c. brown 45 75
650 B 96c. red . . . . 1·20 95
651 1e. lilac . . . . 1·20 1·10
652 1e.20 green . . . . 1·20 1·50
653 C 1e.50 blue on blue . . . . 20·00 9·00
654 **67** 1e.60 blue . . . . 3·75 2·50
655 C 2e. green on green . . . . 5·00 2·75
656 2e.40 red on orange . . . 42·00 21·00
657 3e. red on blue . . . . . 55·00 27·00
658 3e.20 black on green . . . 25·00 21·00
659 **67** 4e.50 black and red . . . . 9·75 3·00
660 C 10e. brown on buff . . . 10·00 3·00
661 D 20e. black on orange . . . 11·00 3·00
DESIGNS—HORIZ: A, Branco's study. VERT: B, Teresa de Albuquerque; C, Mariana and Joao da Cruz; D, Simao de Botelho. Types B/D shows characters from Branco's "Amor de Peredicao".

76 Afonso I, first King of Portugal, 1140

80 Goncalo Mendes da Maia

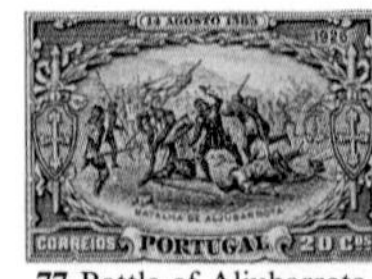

77 Battle of Aljubarrota

1926. 1st Independence issue. Dated 1926. Centres in black.
671 **76** 2c. orange 15 15
672 – 3c. blue 15 15
673 **76** 4c. green 15 15
674 – 5c. brown 15 15
675 **76** 6c. orange 15 15
676 – 15c. green 15 15
677 **76** 16c. blue 55 45
678 **77** 20c. violet 55 70
679 – 25c. red 55 75
680 **77** 32c. green 70 65
681 – 40c. brown 40 50
682 – 46c. red . . . . 2·75 2·20
683 – 50c. bistre . . . . 2·75 2·20
684 – 64c. green . . . . 3·50 3·00
685 – 75c. brown . . . . 3·50 3·00
686 – 96c. red . . . . 5·50 6·25
687 – 1e. violet . . . . 5·50 5·75
688 **77** 1e.60 blue . . . . 7·50 7·50
689 – 3e. purple . . . . 22·00 21·00
690 – 4e.50 green . . . . 27·00 27·00
691 **77** 10e. red . . . . 44·00 38·00
DESIGNS—VERT: 25, 40, 50, 75c. Philippa de Vilhena arms her sons; 64c., 1e. Don Joao IV, 1640; 96c., 3e., 4e.50, Independence Monument, Lisbon. HORIZ: 3, 5, 15, 46c. Monastery of D. Joao I.

1926. 1st Independence issue surch. Centres in black.
692 2c. on 5c. brown 90 90
693 2c. on 46c. red 90 75
694 2c. on 64c. green . . . . . . 1·10 90
695 3c. on 75c. brown . . . . . 1·10 90
696 3c. on 96c. red . . . . . . 1·60 1·30
697 3c. on 1e. violet . . . . . . 1·30 1·10
698 4c. on 1e.60 blue . . . . . 9·00 8·50
699 4c. on 3e. purple . . . . . 3·25 3·25
700 6c. on 4e.50 green . . . . . 3·25 3·25
701 6c. on 10e. red . . . . . . 3·25 3·00

1927. 2nd Independence issue. Dated 1927. Centres in black.
726 **80** 2c. brown 15 10
727 – 3c. blue 15 10
728 **80** 4c. orange 15 10
729 – 5c. brown 15 10
730 – 6c. brown 15 10
731 – 15c. brown 35 40
732 – 16c. blue 85 45
733 **80** 25c. grey 95 95
734 – 32c. green . . . . 2·00 1·60
735 – 40c. green 40 45
736 **80** 48c. red . . . . 9·00 6·75
737 – 80c. violet . . . . 6·50 5·25
738 – 96c. red . . . . 11·50 11·50
739 – 1e.60 blue . . . . 12·00 11·50
740 – 4e.50 brown . . . . 18·00 19·00
DESIGNS—HORIZ: 3, 15, 80c. Gulmaraes Castle; 6, 32c. Battle of Montijo. VERT: 5, 16c., 1e.50, Joao das Regras; 40, 96c. Brites de Aimelda; 4e.50, J. P. Ribeiro.

1928. Surch.
742 **56** 4c. on 8c. orange 30 20
743 4c. on 30c. brown 30 25
744 10c. on ¼c. brown 40 20
745 10c. on ½c. black 40 30
746 10c. on 1c. brown 40 30
747 10c. on 4c. green 30 30
748 10c. on 4c. orange 30 30
749 10c. on 5c. brown 30 30
751 15c. on 16c. blue 85 65
752 15c. on 20c. brown . . . . 22·00 22·00
753 15c. on 20c. grey 30 15
754 15c. on 24c. blue . . . . 1·50 1·30
755 15c. on 25c. pink 30 20
756 15c. on 25c. grey 30 15
757 16c. on 32c. green 60 60
758 40c. on 2c. yellow 30 20
760 40c. on 2c. brown 30 20
761 40c. on 3c. blue 30 20
762 40c. on 50c. yellow 30 20
763 40c. on 60c. blue 60 45
764 40c. on 64c. blue 80 80
765 40c. on 75c. pink 70 65
766 40c. on 80c. lilac 50 40
767 40c. on 90c. blue . . . . 3·00 2·20
768 40c. on 1e. grey 55 60
769 40c. on 1e.10 brown . . . 60 60
770 80c. on 6c. purple . . . . 1·00 60
771 80c. on 6c. brown 55 45
772 80c. on 48c. pink 80 80
773 80c. on 1e.50 lilac . . . . 1·30 85
774 96c. on 1e.20 green . . . 2·50 1·70
775 96c. on 1e.20 buff . . . . 2·50 2·00
777 1e.60 on 2e. green . . . 26·00 16·00
778 1e.60 on 3e.20 green . . . 6·25 4·75
779 1e.60 on 20e. blue . . . . 9·00 6·25

84 Storming of Santarem

1928. 3rd Independence issue. Dated 1928. Centres in black.

No.	Type	Description	Unused	Used
780	–	2c. blue	10	10
781	**84**	3c. green	10	10
782	–	4c. red	10	10
783	–	5c. green	10	10
784	–	6c. brown	10	10
785	**84**	15c. grey	50	65
786	–	16c. purple	50	70
787	–	25c. blue	50	65
788	–	32c. green	2·40	3·00
789	–	40c. brown	50	65
790	–	50c. red	6·25	4·50
791	**84**	80c. grey	6·50	5·75
792	–	96c. red	11·50	14·50
793	–	1e. mauve	19·00	21·00
794	–	1e.60 blue	8·75	9·00
795	–	4e.50 yellow	9·25	10·50

DESIGNS—VERT: 2, 25c., 1e.60, G. Paes; 6, 32, 96c. Joana de Gouveia; 4e.50, Matias de Albuquerque. HORIZ: 4, 16, 50c. Battle of Rolica; 5, 40c., 1e. Battle of Atoleiros.

1929. Optd **Revalidado**.

No.	Type	Description	Unused	Used
805	**56**	10c. red	30	25
806		15c. black	40	20
807		40c. brown	50	35
808		40c. green	35	35
810		96c. red	3·50	2·75
811		1e.60 blue	16·00	9·75

1929. Telegraph stamp surch **CORREIO 1$60** and bars.

No.	Type	Description	Unused	Used
812	–	1e.60 on 5c. brown	10·00	6·50

88 Camoens' Poem "Lusiad"

89 St. Anthony's Birthplace

1931.

No.	Type	Description	Unused	Used
835	**88**	4c. brown	20	10
836		5c. brown	20	10
837		6c. grey	20	10
838		10c. mauve	20	10
839		15c. black	20	10
840		16c. blue	1·00	45
841		25c. green	2·50	15
841a		25c. blue	2·75	15
841b		30c. green	1·40	20
842		40c. red	4·00	10
843		48c. brown	1·00	75
844		50c. brown	25	10
845		75c. red	4·00	75
846		80c. green	35	10
846a		95c. red	11·00	3·75
847		1e. purple	20·00	10
848		1e.20 green	1·70	70
849		1e.25 blue	1·60	10
849a		1e.60 blue	19·00	2·30
849b		1e.75 blue	55	15
850		2e. mauve	60	10
851		4e.50 orange	1·20	10
852		5e. green	1·20	10

1931. 700th Death Anniv of St. Anthony.

No.	Type	Description	Unused	Used
853	**89**	15c. purple	40	15
854	–	25c. myrtle and green	55	15
855	–	40c. brown and buff	40	15
856	–	75c. pink	14·00	11·00
857	–	1e.25 grey and blue	37·00	18·00
858	–	4e.50 purple and mauve	16·00	2·50

DESIGNS—VERT: 25c. Saint's baptismal font; 40c. Lisbon Cathedral; 75c. St. Anthony; 1e.25, Santa Cruz Cathedral, Coimbra. HORIZ: 4e.50, Saint's tomb, Padua.

90 Don Nuno Alvares Pereira

94 President Carmona

1931. 5th Death Centenary of Pereira.

No.	Type	Description	Unused	Used
859	**90**	15c. black	70	80
860		25c. green and black	6·75	60
861		40c. orange	1·60	40
862		75c. red	14·00	12·50
863		1e.25 light blue and blue	16·00	12·50
864		4e.50 green and brown	80·00	33·00

1933. Pereira issue of 1931 surch.

No.	Type	Description	Unused	Used
865	**90**	15c. on 40c. orange	45	40
866		40c. on 15c. black	2·50	1·80
867		40c. on 25c. green & black	65	50
868		40c. on 75c. red	5·75	2·50
869		40c. on 1e.25 light blue and blue	5·75	3·25
870		40c. on 4e.50 green and brown	5·75	3·25

1933. St. Anthony issue of 1931 surch.

No.	Type	Description	Unused	Used
871	–	15c. on 40c. brown and buff	60	45
872	**89**	40c. on 15c. purple	1·70	90
873	–	40c. on 25c. myrtle and green	1·40	45
874	–	40c. on 75c. pink	5·75	3·75
875	–	40c. on 1e.25 grey and blue	5·75	3·50
876	–	40c. on 4e.50 purple and mauve	5·75	4·25

1934.

No.	Type	Description	Unused	Used
877	**94**	40c. violet	14·00	25

95

96 Queen Maria

1934. Colonial Exhibition.

No.	Type	Description	Unused	Used
878	**95**	25c. brown	2·10	75
879		40c. red	16·00	25
880		1e.60 blue	19·00	7·00

1935. 1st Portuguese Philatelic Exhibition.

No.	Type	Description	Unused	Used
881	**96**	40c. red	1·10	10

97 Temple of Diana at Evora

98 Prince Henry the Navigator

99 "All for the Nation"

100 Coimbra Cathedral

1935.

No.	Type	Description	Unused	Used
882	**97**	4c. black	20	10
883		5c. blue	35	10
884		6c. brown	55	20
885	**98**	10c. green	50	10
886		15c. red	25	10
887	**99**	25c. blue	4·00	15
888		40c. brown	1·30	10
889		1e. red	7·50	25
890	**100**	1e.75 blue	50·00	65
890a	**99**	10e. grey	14·50	2·20
890b		20e. blue	21·00	1·70

102 Shield and Propeller

103 Symbol of Medicine

1937. Air.

No.	Type	Description	Unused	Used
891	**102**	1e.50 blue	50	30
892		1e.75 red	70	25
893		2e.50 red	75	30
893a		3e. blue	9·75	8·75
893b		4e. green	13·00	12·50
894		5e. red	1·40	60
895		10e. purple	2·50	80
895a		15e. orange	8·00	5·50
896		20e. brown	6·75	1·70
896a		50e. purple	£110	50·00

1937. Centenary of Medical and Surgical Colleges at Lisbon and Oporto.

No.	Type	Description	Unused	Used
897	**103**	25c. blue	6·75	65

104 Gil Vicente

106 Grapes

107 Cross of Avis

1937. 400th Death Anniv of Gil Vicente (poet).

No.	Type	Description	Unused	Used
898	**104**	40c. brown	12·00	10
899		1e. red	1·50	10

1938. Wine and Raisin Congress.

No.	Type	Description	Unused	Used
900	**106**	15c. violet	85	35
901		25c. brown	2·10	90
902		40c. mauve	7·50	25
903		1e.75 blue	20·00	13·00

1940. Portuguese Legion.

No.	Type	Description	Unused	Used
904	**107**	5c. buff	20	10
905		10c. violet	20	10
906		15c. blue	20	10
907		25c. brown	12·00	55
908		40c. green	20·00	15
909		80c. green	1·20	35
910		1e. red	30·00	1·90
911		1e.75 blue	4·25	1·30

109 Portuguese World Exhibition

113 Sir Rowland Hill

1940. Portuguese Centenaries.

No.	Type	Description	Unused	Used
912	**109**	10c. purple	15	10
913	–	15c. blue	15	10
914	–	25c. green	85	15
915	–	35c. green	65	25
916	–	40c. brown	1·70	10
917	**109**	80c. purple	3·25	15
918	–	1e. red	7·75	95
919	–	1e.75 blue	4·25	1·50

DESIGNS—VERT: 15, 35c. Statue of King Joao IV; 25c., 1e. Monument of Discoveries, Belem; 40c., 1e.75, King Afonso Henriques.

1940. Centenary of First Adhesive Postage Stamps.

No.	Type	Description	Unused	Used
920	**113**	15c. purple	15	10
921		25c. red	20	10
922		35c. green	20	10
923		40c. purple	25	10
924		50c. green	11·00	2·75
925		80c. blue	1·30	80
926		1e. red	12·50	2·20
927		1e.75 blue	3·75	2·10

114 Fish-woman of Nazare

115 Caravel

1941. Costumes.

No.	Type	Description	Unused	Used
932	**114**	4c. green	10	10
933	–	5c. brown	10	10
934	–	10c. purple	2·00	90
935	–	15c. green	10	10
936	–	25c. purple	1·50	50
937	–	40c. green	10	10
938	–	80c. blue	2·20	2·10
939	–	1e. red	5·75	1·20
940	–	1e.75 blue	6·50	3·00
941	–	2e. orange	25·00	19·00

DESIGNS: 5c. Woman from Coimbra; 10c. Vine-grower of Saloio; 15c. Fish-woman of Lisbon; 25c. Woman of Olhao; 40c. Woman of Aveiro; 80c. Shepherdess of Madeira; 1e. Spinner of Viana do Castelo; 1e.75, Horsebreeder of Ribatejo; 2e. Reaper of Alentejo.

1943.

No.	Type	Description	Unused	Used
942	**115**	5c. black	10	10
943		10c. brown	10·00	10·00
944		15c. grey	10	10
945		20c. violet	10	10
946		30c. purple	10	10
947		35c. green	15	10
948		50c. purple	10	10
948a		80c. green	2·75	15
949		1e. red	4·25	10
949a		1e. lilac	2·50	10
949b		1e.20 red	3·00	15
949c		1e.50 green	24·00	20
950		1e.75 blue	13·50	15
950a		1e.80 orange	29·00	2·50
951		2e. brown	1·10	10
951a		2e. blue	4·00	25
952		2e.50 red	1·70	10
953		3e.50 blue	8·75	35
953a		4e. orange	42·00	1·60

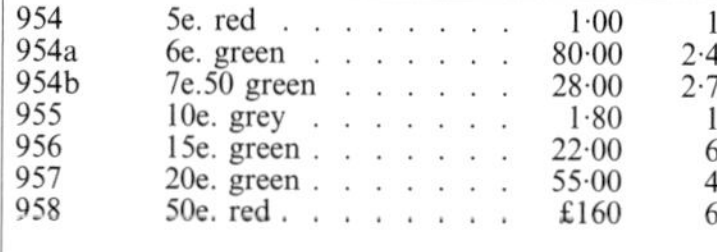

No.	Type	Description	Unused	Used
954		5e. red	1·00	10
954a		6e. green	80·00	2·40
954b		7e.50 green	28·00	2·75
955		10e. grey	1·80	10
956		15e. green	22·00	60
957		20e. green	55·00	40
958		50e. red	£160	65

116 Labourer

117 Mounted Postal Courier

1943. 1st Agricultural Science Congress.

No.	Type	Description	Unused	Used
959	**116**	10c. blue	70	15
960		50c. red	1·00	20

1944. 3rd National Philatelic Exhibition, Lisbon.

No.	Type	Description	Unused	Used
961	**117**	10c. brown	20	10
962		50c. violet	20	10
963		1e. red	3·00	40
964		1e.75 blue	3·00	1·00

118 Felix Avellar Brotero

120 Vasco da Gama

1944. Birth Bicentenary of Avellar Brotero (botanist).

No.	Type	Description	Unused	Used
965	**118**	10c. brown	15	10
966	–	50c. green	1·10	10
967	–	1e. red	6·50	80
968	**118**	1e.75 blue	6·50	1·10

DESIGN: 50c., 1e. Brotero's statue, Coimbra.

1945. Portuguese Navigators.

No.	Type	Description	Unused	Used
969	–	10c. brown	10	10
970	–	30c. orange	10	10
971	–	35c. green	30	20
972	**120**	50c. green	1·20	15
973	–	1e. red	3·00	60
974	–	1e.75 blue	3·75	1·20
975	–	2e. black	4·25	1·70
976	–	3e.50 red	9·00	2·40

PORTRAITS: 10c. Gil Eanes; 30c. Joao Goncalves Zarco; 35c. Bartolomeu Dias; 1e. Pedro Alvares Cabral; 1e.75, Fernao de Magalhaes (Magellan); 2e. Frey Goncalo Velho; 3e.50, Diogo Cao.

121 President Carmona

122

1945.

No.	Type	Description	Unused	Used
977	**121**	10c. violet	20	10
978		30c. brown	20	10
979		35c. green	20	10
980		50c. green	35	10
981		1e. red	9·25	95
982		1e.75 blue	7·50	2·10
983		2e. purple	42·00	3·50
984		3e.50 grey	27·00	4·25

1945. Naval School Centenary.

No.	Type	Description	Unused	Used
985	**122**	10c. brown	10	10
986		50c. green	25	10
987		1e. red	2·75	50
988		1e.75 blue	3·25	1·60

123 Almourol Castle

1946. Portuguese Castles.

No.	Type	Description	Unused	Used
989	–	10c. purple	10	10
990	–	30c. brown	10	10
991	–	35c. green	10	10
992	–	50c. grey	30	10
993	**123**	1e. red	19·00	75
994	–	1e.75 blue	11·00	1·40
995	–	2e. green	36·00	3·00
996	–	3e.50 brown	17·00	2·75

DESIGNS: Castles at Silves (10c.); Leiria (30c.); Feira (35c.); Guimaraes (50c.); Lisbon (1e.75); Braganza (2e.) and Ourem (3e.50).

124 "Decree Founding National Bank" 125 Madonna and Child

1946. Centenary of Bank of Portugal.

997	124	50c. blue	50	10

1946. Tercentenary of Proclamation of St. Mary of Castile as Patron Saint of Portugal.

998	125	30c. grey	20	10
999		50c. green	20	10
1000		1e. red	2·50	60
1001		1e.75 blue	4·50	1·30

126 Caramulo Shepherdess 127 Surrender of the Keys of Lisbon

1947. Regional Costumes.

1002	126	10c. mauve	10	10
1003	–	30c. red	10	10
1004	–	35c. green	15	10
1005	–	50c. brown	35	10
1006	–	1e. red	12·00	35
1007	–	1e.75 blue	13·00	2·50
1008	–	2e. blue	43·00	2·50
1009	–	3e.50 green	32·00	4·50

COSTUMES: 30c. Malpique timbrel player; 35c. Monsanto flautist; 50c. Woman of Avintes; 1e. Maia field labourer; 1e.75, Woman of Algarve; 2e. Miranda do Douro bastonet player; 3e.50, Woman of the Azores.

1947. 800th Anniv of Recapture of Lisbon from the Moors.

1010	127	5c. green	10	10
1011		20c. red	10	10
1012		50c. violet	15	10
1013		1e.75 blue	5·25	3·50
1014		2e.50 brown	7·50	4·75
1015		3e.50 black	13·00	8·50

128 St. Joao de Brito

1948. Birth Tercentenary of St. Joao de Brito.

1016	128	30c. green	10	10
1017	–	50c. brown	15	10
1018	128	1e. red	7·00	1·20
1019	–	1e.75 blue	8·50	1·80

DESIGN: 50c., 1e.75, St. Joao de Brito (different).

130 "Architecture and Engineering" 131 King Joao I

1948. Exhibition of Public Works and National Congress of Engineering and Architecture.

1020	130	50c. purple	50	10

1949. Portraits.

1021	131	10c. violet and buff	15	10
1022	–	30c. green and buff	15	10
1023	–	35c. green and olive	30	10
1024	–	50c. blue and light blue	1·40	10
1025	–	1e. lake and red	1·10	10
1026	–	1e.75 black and grey	18·00	8·75
1027	–	2e. blue and light blue	5·25	1·10
1028	–	3e.50 chocolate & brown	33·00	12·50

PORTRAITS: 30c. Queen Philippa; 35c. Prince Fernando; 50c. Prince Henry the Navigator; 1e. Nun Alvares; 1e.75, Joao da Regras; 2e. Fernao Lopes; 3e.50, Afonso Domingues.

132 Statue of Angel 133 Hands and Letter

1949. 16th Congress of the History of Art.

1029	132	1e. red	9·00	10
1030		5e. brown	2·10	10

1949. 75th Anniv of U.P.U.

1031	133	1e. lilac	30	10
1032		2e. blue	90	15
1033		2e.50 green	4·50	60
1034		4e. brown	10·00	2·50

134 Our Lady of Fatima 135 Saint and Invalid

1950. Holy Year.

1035	134	50c. green	60	15
1036		1e. brown	2·20	15
1037		2e. blue	3·25	1·30
1038		5e. lilac	70·00	21·00

1950. 400th Death Anniv of San Juan de Dios.

1039	135	20c. violet	20	10
1040		50c. red	30	15
1041		1e. green	1·30	20
1042		1e.50 orange	10·00	2·20
1043		2e. blue	8·75	1·40
1044		4e. brown	35·00	6·50

136 G. Junqueiro 137 Fisherman with Meagre

1951. Birth Centenary of Junqueiro (poet).

1045	136	50c. brown	3·75	20
1046		1e. blue	95	15

1951. Fisheries Congress.

1047	137	50c. green on buff	3·00	45
1048		1e. purple on buff	80	10

138 Dove and Olive Branch 139 15th century Colonists

1951. Termination of Holy Year.

1049	138	20c. brown and buff	30	10
1050		90c. green and yellow	10·50	1·20
1051	–	1e. purple and pink	10·50	15
1052	–	2e.30 green and blue	11·50	1·70

PORTRAIT: 1e., 2e.30, Pope Pius XII.

1951. 500th Anniv of Colonization of Terceira, Azores.

1053	139	50c. blue on flesh	1·70	40
1054		1e. brown on buff	1·00	40

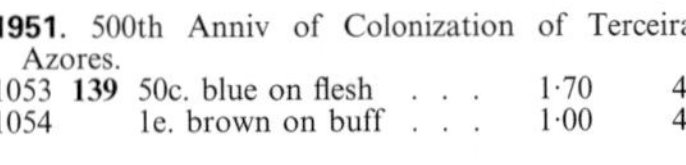

140 Revolutionaries

1951. 25th Anniv of National Revolution.

1055	140	1e. brown	7·50	10
1056		2e.30 blue	4·50	95

141 Coach of King Joao VI

1952. National Coach Museum.

1057	–	10c. purple	15	10
1058	141	20c. green	15	10
1059	–	50c. green	55	10
1060	–	90c. green	2·30	1·30
1061	–	1e. orange	90	10
1062	–	1e.40 pink	5·25	3·50
1063	141	1e.50 brown	5·25	2·00
1064	–	2e.30 blue	3·00	1·70

DESIGNS (coaches of): 10, 90c. King Felippe II; 50c., 1e.40, Papal Nuncio to Joao V; 1e., 2e.30, King Jose.

142 "N.A.T.O." 143 Hockey Players

1952. 3rd Anniv of N.A.T.O.

1065	142	1e. green and deep green	10·00	35
1066		3e.50 grey and blue	£250	15·00

1952. 8th World Roller-skating Hockey Championship.

1067	143	1e. black and blue	3·25	10
1068		3e.50 black and brown	4·50	1·80

144 Teixeira 145 Marshal Carmona Bridge

1952. Birth Centenary of Prof. Gomes Teixeira (mathematician).

1069	144	1e. mauve and pink	60	10
1070		2e.30 deep blue and blue	5·75	3·00

1952. Centenary of Ministry of Public Works.

1071	145	1e. brown on stone	45	10
1072	–	1e.40 lilac on stone	10·00	4·00
1073	–	2e. green on stone	6·00	1·80
1074	–	3e.50 blue on stone	10·50	3·25

DESIGNS: 1e.40, 28th May Stadium, Braga; 2e. Coimbra University; 3e.50, Salazar Barrage.

146 St. Francis Xavier 147 Medieval Knight

1952. 4th Death Centenary of St. Francis Xavier.

1075	146	1e. blue	45	15
1076		2e. purple	1·60	30
1077		3e.50 blue	19·00	8·50
1078		5e. lilac	35·00	3·00

1953.

1079	147	5c. green on yellow	15	10
1080		10c. grey on pink	15	10
1081		20c. orange on yellow	15	10
1081a		30c. purple on buff	20	10
1082		50c. black	15	10
1083		90c. green on yellow	13·50	45
1084		1e. brown on pink	35	10
1085		1e.40 red	14·00	85
1086		1e.50 red on yellow	55	10
1087		2e. black	60	10
1088		2e.30 blue	18·00	60
1089		2e.50 black on pink	1·20	10
1089a		2e.50 green on yellow	1·20	10
1090		5e. purple on yellow	1·30	05
1091		10e. blue on yellow	7·75	15
1092		20e. brown on yellow	15·00	10
1093		50e. lilac	4·50	20

148 St. Martin of Dume 149 G. Gomes Fernandes

1953. 14th Centenary of Landing of St. Martin of Dume on Iberian Peninsula.

1094	148	1e. black and grey	1·20	10
1095		3e.50 brown and yellow	9·75	4·25

1953. Birth Centenary of Fernandes (fire-brigade chief).

1096	149	1e. purple and cream	80	10
1097		2e.30 blue and cream	8·50	4·50

150 Club Emblems, 1903 and 1953 151 Princess St. Joan

1953. 50th Anniv of Portuguese Automobile Club.

1098	150	1e. deep green and green	60	10
1099		3e.50 brown and buff	10·50	4·50

1953. 5th Centenary of Birth of Princess St. Joan.

1100	151	1e. black and green	1·60	10
1101		3e.50 deep blue and blue	16·00	5·25

152 Queen Maria II

1953. Centenary of First Portuguese Stamps. Bottom panel in gold.

1102	152	50c. red	30	10
1103		1e. brown	30	10
1104		1e.40 purple	1·60	60
1105		2e.30 blue	4·00	1·70
1106		3e.50 blue	4·00	1·60
1107		4e.50 green	2·75	1·30
1108		5e. green	6·25	1·20
1109		20e. violet	55·00	6·00

153 154

1954. 150th Anniv of Trade Secretariat.

1110	153	1e. blue and light blue	45	05
1111		1e.50 brown and buff	2·40	55

1954. People's Education Plan.

1112	154	50c. blue and light blue	30	10
1113		1e. red and pink	30	10
1114		2e. deep green and green	27·00	95
1115		2e.50 brown and light brown	22·00	95

155 Cadet and College Banner 156 Father Manuel da Nobrega

1954. 150th Anniv of Military College.

1116	155	1e. brown and green	1·30	10
1117		3e.50 blue and green	5·00	2·10

1954. 400th Anniv of Sao Paulo.

1118	156	1e. brown	55	10
1119		2e.30 blue	47·00	18·00
1120		3e.50 green	13·00	2·10
1121		5e. green	39·00	3·50

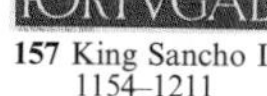

157 King Sancho I, 1154–1211 **158** Telegraph Poles

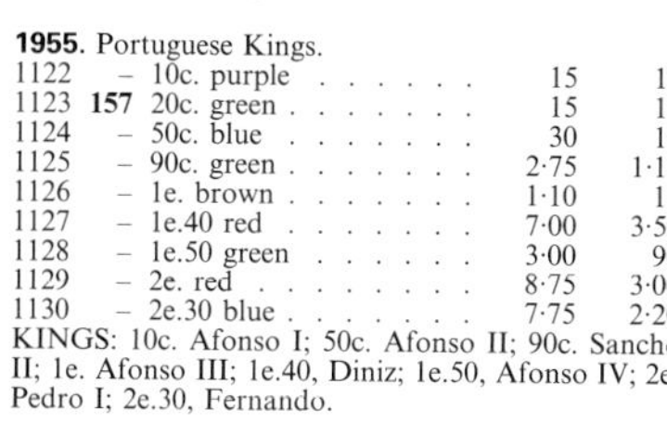

1955. Portuguese Kings.
1122 – 10c. purple 15 10
1123 **157** 20c. green 15 10
1124 – 50c. blue 30 10
1125 – 90c. green . . . . . . 2·75 1·10
1126 – 1e. brown . . . . . . 1·10 15
1127 – 1e.40 red . . . . . . 7·00 3·50
1128 – 1e.50 green . . . . . . 3·00 90
1129 – 2e. red . . . . . . 8·75 3·00
1130 – 2e.30 blue . . . . . . 7·75 2·20
KINGS: 10c. Afonso I; 50c. Afonso II; 90c. Sancho II; 1e. Afonso III; 1e.40, Diniz; 1e.50, Afonso IV; 2e. Pedro I; 2e.30, Fernando.

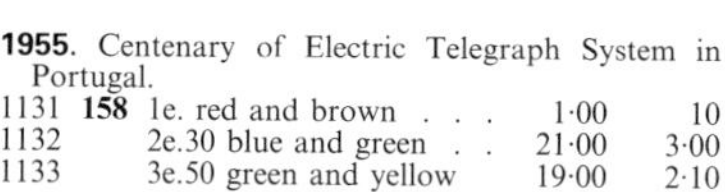

1955. Centenary of Electric Telegraph System in Portugal.
1131 **158** 1e. red and brown . . . 1·00 10
1132 2e.30 blue and green . . 21·00 3·00
1133 3e.50 green and yellow 19·00 2·10

159 A. J. Ferreira da Silva **160** Steam Locomotive, 1856

1956. Birth Centenary of Ferreira da Silva (teacher).
1134 **159** 1e. deep blue, blue and azure 30 10
1135 2e.30 deep green, emerald and green . . 12·50 4·00

1956. Centenary of Portuguese Railways.
1136 **160** 1e. olive and green . . . 50 10
1137 – 1e.50 blue and green . . 3·75 40
1138 – 2e. brown and bistre . . 27·00 95
1139 **160** 2e.50 brown and deep brown . . . . 37·00 1·60
DESIGN: 1e.50, 2e. Class 2500 electric locomotive, 1956.

161 Madonna and Child **162** Almeida Garrett (after Barata Feyo)

1956. Mothers' Day.
1140 **161** 1e. sage and green . . . 30 10
1141 1e.50 lt brown and brown 80 15

1957. Almeida Garrett (writer) Commem.
1142 **162** 1e. brown 55 10
1143 2e.30 lilac . . . . 36·00 7·00
1144 3e.50 green . . . . . . 7·75 1·00
1145 5e. red . . . . 65·00 8·00

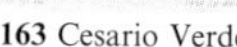

163 Cesario Verde **164** Exhibition Emblem

1957. Cesario Verde (poet) Commem.
1146 **163** 1e. brown, buff and green 30 10
1147 3e.30 black, olive and green . . . . 1·50 80

1958. Brussels International Exhibition
1148 **164** 1e. multicoloured 30 10
1149 3e.30 multicoloured . . . 1·40 1·10

165 St. Elizabeth **166** Institute of Tropical Medicine, Lisbon

1958. St. Elizabeth and St. Teotonio Commem.
1150 **165** 1e. red and cream . . . 15 10
1151 – 2e. green and cream . . 45 25
1152 **165** 2e.50 violet and cream 4·25 60
1153 – 5e. brown and cream . . 5·50 80
PORTRAIT: 2, 5e. St. Teotonio.

1958. 6th Int Congress of Tropical Medicine.
1154 **166** 1e. green and grey . . . 1·90 15
1155 2e.50 blue and grey . . . 6·00 1·00

167 Liner **168** Queen Leonora

1958. 2nd National Merchant Navy Congress.
1156 **167** 1e. brown, ochre & sepia 5·25 15
1157 4e.50 violet, lilac and blue . . . . 3·75 1·80

1958. 500th Birth Anniv of Queen Leonora. Frames and ornaments in bistre, inscriptions and value tablet in black.
1158 **168** 1e. blue and brown . . . 15 10
1159 1e.50 turquoise and blue 3·25 55
1160 2e.30 blue and green . . 3·00 95
1161 4e.10 blue and grey . . . 2·75 1·20

169 Arms of Aveiro **170**

1959. Millenary of Aveiro.
1162 **169** 1e. multicoloured . . . . 1·40 15
1163 5e. multicoloured . . . . 10·50 1·60

1960. 10th Anniv of N.A.T.O.
1164 **170** 1e. black and lilac . . . 30 10
1165 3e.50 green and grey . . 2·50 1·20

171 "Doorway to Peace" **172** Glider

1960. World Refugee Year. Symbol in black.
1166 **171** 20c. yellow, lemon & brn 10 10
1167 1e. yellow, green and blue 40 10
1168 1e.80 yellow and green 90 1·00

1960. 50th Anniv of Portuguese Aero Club. Multicoloured.
1169 1e. Type **172** 15 10
1170 1e.50 Light monoplane . . . 55 15
1171 2e. Airplane and parachutes 1·00 55
1172 2e.50 Model glider . . . . 2·10 95

173 Padre Cruz (after M. Barata) **174** University Seal

1960. Death Centenary of Padre Cruz.
1173 **173** 1e. brown 15 10
1174 4e.30 blue . . . . 7·00 5·00

1960. 400th Anniv of Evora University.
1175 **174** 50c. blue 10 10
1176 1e. brown and yellow . . 30 10
1177 1e.40 purple . . . . . . 2·20 1·20

175 Prince Henry's Arms **175a** Conference Emblem

1960. 5th Death Centenary of Prince Henry the Navigator. Multicoloured.
1178 1e. Type **175** 25 10
1179 2e.50 Caravel . . . . 2·75 30
1180 3e.50 Prince Henry the Navigator . . . . 4·00 1·00
1181 5e. Motto . . . . 6·50 60
1182 8e. Barketta . . . . 1·50 70
1183 10e. Map showing Sagres 11·00 1·60

1960. Europa.
1184 **175a** 1e. light blue and blue 15 10
1185 3e.50 red and lake . . . 2·75 1·50

176 Emblems of Prince Henry and Lisbon

1960. 5th National Philatelic Exhibition, Lisbon.
1186 **176** 1e. blue, black and green 30 10
1187 3e.30 blue, black and light blue . . . . . . 4·25 2·75

177 Portuguese Flag **178** King Pedro V

1960. 50th Anniv of Republic.
1188 **177** 1e. multicoloured 20 10

1961. Cent of Lisbon University Faculty of Letters.
1189 **178** 1e. green and brown . . 20 10
1190 6e.50 brown and blue . . 2·75 75

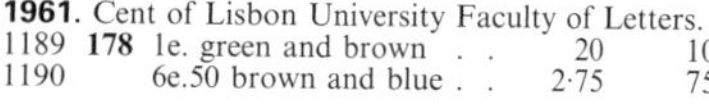

179 Arms of Setubal **180**

1961. Centenary of Setubal City.
1191 **179** 1e. multicoloured 30 10
1192 4e.30 multicoloured . . . 15·00 5·25

1961. Europa.
1193 **180** 1e. light blue, blue and deep blue 10 10
1194 1e.50 light green, green and deep green . . . 1·10 1·10
1195 3e.50 pink, red and lake 1·30 1·20

181 Tomar Gateway **182** National Guardsman

1961. 800th Anniv of Tomar.
1196 – 1e. multicoloured 10 10
1197 **181** 3e.50 multicoloured . . . 1·10 95
DESIGN: 1e. As Type **181** but without ornamental background.

1962. 50th Anniv of National Republican Guard.
1198 **182** 1e. multicoloured 10 10
1199 2e. multicoloured . . . . 1·70 60
1200 2e.50 multicoloured . . . 1·70 45

183 St. Gabriel (Patron Saint of Telecommunications) **184** Scout Badge and Tents

1962. St. Gabriel Commemoration.
1201 **183** 1e. brown, green and olive 55 10
1202 3e.50 green, brown & ol 40 35

1962. 18th International Scout Conference (1961).
1203 **184** 20c. multicoloured . . . 10 10
1204 50c. multicoloured . . . 10 10
1205 1e. multicoloured 50 10
1206 2e.50 multicoloured . . . 3·25 30
1207 3e.50 multicoloured . . . 75 40
1208 6e.50 multicoloured . . . 95 70

185 Children with Ball **186** Europa "Honeycomb"

1962. 10th International Paediatrics Congress, Lisbon. Centres in black.
1209 – 50c. yellow and green . . 10 10
1210 – 1e. yellow and grey . . . 1·00 10
1211 **185** 2e.80 yellow and brown 1·90 85
1212 – 3e.50 yellow and purple 4·00 1·50
DESIGNS: 50c. Children with book; 1e. Inoculating child; 3e.50, Weighing baby.

1962. Europa. "EUROPA" in gold.
1213 **186** 1e. ultramarine, light blue and blue 15 10
1214 1e.50 deep green, light green and green . . . 1·10 55
1215 3e.50 purple, pink and claret . . . . 1·30 1·10

187 St. Zenon (the Courier) **188** Benfica Emblem and European Cup

1962. Stamp Day. Saint in yellow and pink.
1216 **187** 1e. black and purple . . 10 10
1217 2e. black and green . . . 75 55
1218 2e.80 black and bistre . . 1·50 1·40

1963. Benfica Club's Double Victory in European Football Cup Championship (1961–62).
1219 **188** 1e. multicoloured 65 10
1220 4e.30 multicoloured . . . 1·00 1·20

189 Campaign Emblem

1963. Freedom from Hunger.
1221 **189** 1e. multicoloured 10 10
1222 3e.30 multicoloured . . . 1·10 90
1223 3e.50 multicoloured . . . 1·00 65

190 Mail Coach **191** St. Vincent de Paul

1963. Centenary of Paris Postal Conference.
1224 **190** 1e. blue, light blue and grey 10 10
1225 1e.50 multicoloured . . . 1·60 35
1226 5e. brown, lilac & lt brown 45 20

1963. 300th Death Anniv of St. Vincent de Paul. Inscr in gold.
1227 **191** 20c. ultramarine and blue 10 10
1228 1e. blue and grey 30 10

1229 2e.80 black and green . . 3·50 1·40
1230 5e. grey and mauve . . . 2·75 1·00

192 Medieval Knight

1963. 800th Anniv of Military Order of Avis.
1231 **192** 1e. multicoloured 10 10
1232 1e.50 multicoloured . . . 45 35
1233 2e.50 mulitcoloured . . . 1·10 60

193 Europa "Dove"

1963. Europa.
1234 **193** 1e. grey, blue and black 20 10
1235 2e.50 grey, green & black 2·00 90
1236 3e.50 grey, red and black 3·50 1·80

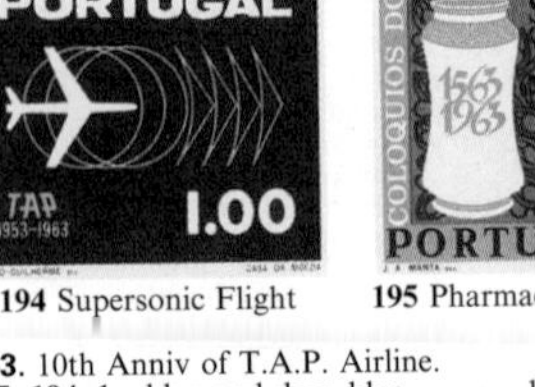

194 Supersonic Flight 195 Pharmacist's Jar

1963. 10th Anniv of T.A.P. Airline.
1237 **194** 1e. blue and deep blue 10 10
1238 2e.50 light green & green 1·00 45
1239 3e.50 orange and red . . 1·30 80

1964. 400th Anniv of Publication of "Coloquios dos Simples" (Dissertation on Indian herbs and drugs) by Dr. G. d'Orta.
1240 **195** 50c. brown, black & bis 20 10
1241 1e. purple, black and red 20 10
1242 4e.30 blue, black & grey 3·50 3·25

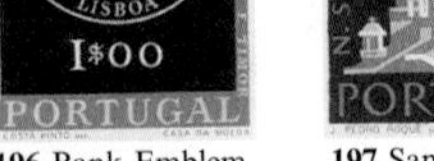

196 Bank Emblem 197 Sameiro Shrine (Braga)

1964. Centenary of National Overseas Bank.
1243 **196** 1e. yellow, green and blue 10 10
1244 2e.50 yellow, olive & grn 2·00 75
1245 3e.50 yellow, green & brn . . . . 1·60 95

1964. Centenary of Sameiro Shrine.
1246 **197** 1e. yellow, brown and red 10 10
1247 2e. yellow, light brown and brown . . . . . 2·75 55
1248 5e. yellow, green and blue . . . . 1·80 90

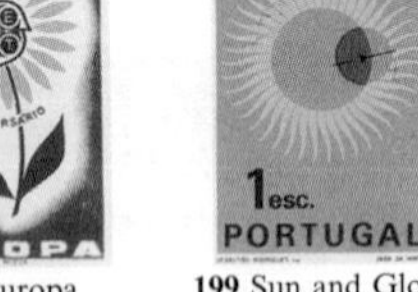

198 Europa "Flower" 199 Sun and Globe

1964. Europa.
1249 **198** 1e. deep blue, light blue and blue 30 10
1250 3e.50 brown, light brown and purple . . . . . 2·40 90
1251 4e.30 deep green, light green and green . . . 3·25 2·75

1964. International Quiet Sun Years.
1252 **199** 1e. multicoloured 15 10
1253 8e. multicoloured . . . . 1·10 85

200 Olympic "Rings"

201 E. Coelho (founder)

1964. Olympic Games, Tokyo.
1254 **200** 20c. multicoloured . . . 10 10
1255 1e. multicoloured 15 10
1256 1e.50 multicoloured . . . 1·30 75
1257 6e.50 multicoloured . . . 2·20 1·40

1964. Centenary of "Diario de Noticias" (newspaper).
1258 **201** 1e. multicoloured 15 10
1259 5e. mutlicoloured . . . . 2·75 85

202 Traffic Signals 203 Dom Fernando (second Duke of Braganza)

1965. 1st National Traffic Congress Lisbon.
1260 **202** 1e. yellow, red and green 15 1·80
1261 3e.30 green, red & yellow 4·75 3·00
1262 3e.50 red, yellow & green 3·00 95

1965. 500th Anniv of Braganza.
1263 **203** 1e. red and black 10 10
1264 10e. green and black . . 2·10 60

204 Angel and Gateway 205 I.T.U. Emblem

1965. 900th Anniv of Capture of Coimbra from the Moors.
1265 **204** 1e. multicoloured 10 10
1266 2e.50 multicoloured . . . 1·70 1·20
1267 5e. multicoloured . . . . 1·70 1·60

1965. Centenary of I.T.U.
1268 **205** 1e. green and brown . . 10 10
1269 3e.50 purple and green 1·30 10
1270 6e.50 blue and green . . 1·10 1·00

206 C. Gulbenkian 207 Red Cross Emblem

1965. 10th Death Anniv of Calouste Gulbenkian (oil industry pioneer and philanthropist).
1271 **206** 1e. multicoloured 50 10
1272 8e. multicoloured 45 45

1965. Centenary of Portuguese Red Cross.
1273 **207** 1e. red, green and black 15 10
1274 4e. red, green and black 2·00 1·10
1275 4e.30 red, light red & black . . . . 9·75 6·00

208 Europa "Sprig" 209 North American F-86 Sabre Jet Fighter

1965. Europa.
1276 **208** 1e. lt blue, black and blue 15 10
1277 3e.50 flesh, brown & red 4·50 1·10
1278 4e.30 light green, black and green . . . . . . 11·50 5·25

1965. 50th Anniv of Portuguese Air Force.
1279 **209** 1e. red, green and olive 15 10
1280 2e. red, green and brown 1·10 60
1281 5e. red, green and blue 2·10 1·30

210 211 Monogram of Christ

1965. 500th Birth Anniv of Gil Vicente (poet and dramatist). Designs depicting characters from Vicente's poems.
1282 **210** 20c. multicoloured . . . 10 10
1283 – 1e. multicoloured 55 10
1284 – 2e.50 multicoloured . . . 2·50 45
1285 – 6e.50 multicoloured . . . 90 70

1966. International Committee for the Defence of Christian Civilisation Congress, Lisbon.
1286 **211** 1e. violet, gold and bistre 20 10
1287 3e.30 black, gold & pur 5·00 3·00
1288 5e. black, gold and red 3·25 95

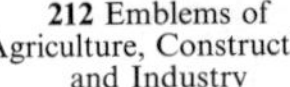

212 Emblems of Agriculture, Construction and Industry 213 Giraldo the "Fearless"

1966. 40th Anniv of National Revolution.
1289 **212** 1e. black, blue and grey 15 10
1290 3e.50 brown, light brown and bistre . . . . . . 2·20 95
1291 4e. purple, red and pink 2·20 90

1966. 800th Anniv of Reconquest of Evora.
1292 **213** 1e. multicoloured 25 10
1293 8e. multicoloured 90 55

214 Salazar Bridge 215 Europa "Ship"

1966. Inauguration of Salazar Bridge, Lisbon.
1294 **214** 1e. red and gold 15 10
1295 2e.50 blue and gold . . . 1·00 65
1296 – 2e.80 blue and silver . . 1·70 1·60
1297 – 4e.30 green and silver . . 1·80 1·80
DESIGN—VERT: 2e.80, 4e.30, Salazar Bridge (different view).

1966. Europa.
1298 **215** 1e. multicoloured 20 10
1299 3e.50 multicoloured . . . 7·00 1·30
1300 4e.50 multicoloured . . . 7·25 2·75

216 C. Pestana (bacteriologist) 217 Bocage

1966. Portuguese Scientists. Portraits in brown and bistre; background colours given.
1301 **216** 20c. green 10 10
1302 – 50c. orange 10 10
1303 – 1e. yellow 15 10
1304 – 1e.50 brown 30 10
1305 – 2e. brown . . . . 1·40 10
1306 – 2e.50 green . . . . . . 1·60 45
1307 – 2e.80 orange . . . . . . 1·80 1·60
1308 – 4e.30 blue . . . . 3·00 2·30
SCIENTISTS: 50c. E. Moniz (neurologist); 1e. E. A. P. Coutinho (botanist); 1e.50, J. C. da Serra (botanist); 2e. R. Jorge (hygienist and anthropologist); 2e.50, J. L. de Vasconcelos (ethnologist); 2e.80, M. Lemos (medical historian); 4e.30, J. A. Serrano (anatomist).

1966. Birth Bicentenary (1965) of Manuel M. B. du Bocage (poet).
1309 **217** 1e. black, green and bistre 10 10
1310 2e. black, green & brown 70 35
1311 6e. black, green and grey 1·00 70

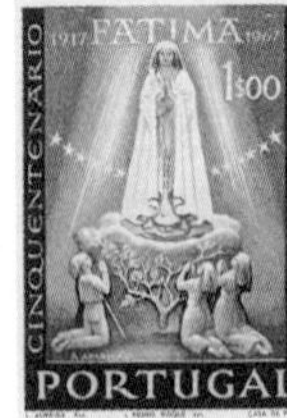

218 Cogwheels 219 Adoration of the Virgin

1967. Europa.
1312 **218** 1e. blue, black & lt blue 20 10
1313 3e.50 brown, black and orange . . . . 5·00 1·00
1314 4e.30 green, black and light green . . . . . 8·00 2·00

1967. 50th Anniv of Fatima Apparitions. Mult.
1315 1e. Type **219** 10 10
1316 2e.80 Fatima Church . . . 45 45
1317 3e.50 Virgin of Fatima . . . 55 15
1318 4e. Chapel of the Apparitions 80 30

220 Roman Senators 221 Lisnave Shipyard

1967. New Civil Law Code.
1319 **220** 1e. red and gold 10 10
1320 2e.50 blue and gold . . . 1·70 90
1321 4e.30 green and gold . . 1·20 95

1967. Inauguration of Lisnave Shipyard, Lisbon.
1322 **221** 1e. multicoloured 10 10
1323 – 2e.80 multicoloured . . . 2·10 95
1324 **221** 3e.50 multicoloured . . . 1·20 55
1325 – 4e.30 multicoloured . . . 1·90 95
DESIGN: 2e.80, 4e.30, Section of ship's hull and location map.

222 Serpent Symbol 223 Flags of EFTA Countries

1967. 6th European Rheumatological Congress, Lisbon.
1326 **222** 1e. multicoloured 10 10
1327 2e. multicoloured 95 55
1328 5e. multicoloured . . . . 1·40 1·20

1967. European Free Trade Association.
1329 **223** 1e. multicoloured 10 10
1330 3e.50 multicoloured . . . 95 85
1331 4e.30 multicoloured . . . 2·50 3·00

224 Tombstones 225 Bento de Goes

1967. Centenary of Abolition of Death Penalty in Portugal.
1332 **224** 1e. green 10 10
1333 2e. brown . . . . 1·00 70
1334 5e. green . . . . 1·80 1·40

1968. Bento de Goes Commemoration.
1335 **225** 1e. blue, brown and green 55 10
1336 8e. purple, green & brown . . . . 1·10 50

226 Europa "Key" 227 "Maternal Love"

1968. Europa.
1337 **226** 1e. multicoloured 20 10
1338 3e.50 multicoloured . . . 4·50 1·20
1339 4e.30 multicoloured . . . 8·25 3·00

1968. 30th Anniv of Organization of Mothers for National Education (O.M.E.N.).
1340 **227** 1e. black, orange and grey 10 10
1341 2e. black, orange and pink . . . . 1·30 55
1342 5e. black, orange and blue . . . . 2·50 1·30

228 "Victory over Disease"

1968. 20th Anniv of W.H.O.
1343 **228** 1e. multicoloured 10 10
1344 3e.50 multicoloured . . . 1·10 45
1345 4e.30 multicoloured . . . 5·75 4·50

229 Vineyard, Girao

1968. "Lubrapex 1968" Stamp Exhibition. Madeira—"Pearl of the Atlantic". Multicoloured.
1346 50c. Type **229** 10 10
1347 1e. Firework display 15 10
1348 1e.50 Landscape 30 10
1349 2e.80 J. Fernandes Vieira (liberator of Pernambuco) (vert) . . . . 1·80 1·60
1350 3e.50 Embroidery (vert) . . 1·20 90
1351 4e.30 J. Goncalves Zarco (navigator) (vert) . . . . 6·50 6·00
1352 20e. "Muschia aurea" (vert) 3·25 95

230 Pedro Alvares Cabral (from medallion)

1969. 500th Birth Anniv of Pedro Alvares Cabral (explorer).
1353 **230** 1e. blue 15 10
1354 – 3e.50 purple . . . . . . 3·50 1·80
1355 – 6e.50 multicoloured . . . 2·00 2·00
DESIGNS—VERT: 3e.50, Cabral's arms. HORIZ: 6e.50, Cabral's fleet (from contemporary docu-ments).

231 Colonnade

232 King Joseph I

1969. Europa.
1356 **231** 1e. multicoloured 20 10
1357 3e.50 multicoloured . . . 4·75 1·50
1358 4e.30 multicoloured . . . 9·75 4·00

1969. Centenary of National Press.
1359 **232** 1e. multicoloured 10 10
1360 2e. multicoloured 70 45
1361 8e. multicoloured 80 75

233 I.L.O. Emblem

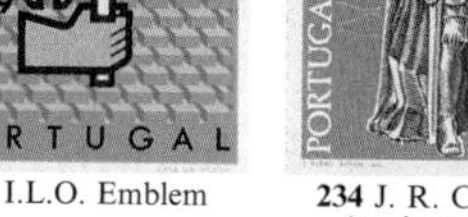

234 J. R. Cabrilho (navigator and colonizer)

1969. 50th Anniv of I.L.O.
1362 **233** 1e. multicoloured 10 10
1363 3e.50 multicoloured . . . 1·30 65
1364 4e.30 multicoloured . . . 2·10 1·40

1969. Bicentenary of San Diego, California.
1365 **234** 1e. dp green, yellow & grn 10 10
1366 2e.50 brown, light brown and blue . . . . . . 1·30 45
1367 6e.50 deep brown, green and brown . . . . . 1·50 95

235 Vianna da Motta (from painting by C. B. Pinheiro)

1969. Birth Centenary (1968) of Jose Vianna da Motta (concert pianist).
1368 **235** 1e. multicoloured 70 10
1369 9e. multicoloured 75 70

236 Coutinho and Fairey IIID Seaplane

1969. Birth Centenary of Gago Coutinho (aviator). Multicoloured.
1370 1e. Type **236** 10 10
1371 2e.80 Coutinho and sextant 1·60 1·10
1372 3e.30 Type **236** . . . . . . 1·90 1·50
1373 4e.30 As No. 1371 . . . . 1·80 1·60

237 Vasco da Gama

1969. 500th Birth Anniv of Vasco da Gama. Multicoloured.
1374 1e. Type **237** 15 10
1375 2e.50 Arms of Vasco da Gama . . . . 2·40 2·00
1376 3e.50 Route map (horiz) . . 1·80 85
1377 4e. Vasca da Gama's fleet (horiz) . . . . 1·60 70

238 "Flaming Sun"

239 Distillation Plant and Pipelines

1970. Europa.
1378 **238** 1e. cream and blue . . . 20 10
1379 3e.50 cream and brown 5·25 1·00
1380 4e.30 cream and green 9·25 4·00

1970. Inauguration of Porto Oil Refinery.
1381 **239** 1e. blue and light blue 10 10
1382 – 2e.80 black and green . . 2·00 1·60
1383 **239** 3e.30 green and olive . . 1·30 1·20
1384 – 6e. brown and light brown . . . . 1·10 90
DESIGN: 2e.80, 6e. Catalytic cracking plant and pipelines.

240 Marshal Carmona (from sculpture by L. de Almeida)

1970. Birth Centenary of Marshal Carmona.
1385 **240** 1e. green and black . . . 10 10
1386 2e.50 blue, red and black 1·50 60
1387 7e. blue and black . . . 1·30 90

241 Station Badge

1970. 25th Anniv of Plant-breeding Station.
1388 **241** 1e. multicoloured 10 10
1389 2e.50 multicoloured . . . 1·10 35
1390 5e. multicoloured . . . . 1·40 65

242 Emblem within Cultural Symbol

1970. Expo 70. Multicoloured.
1391 1e. Compass (postage) . . . 15 10
1392 5e. Christian symbol . . . . 1·20 50
1393 6e.50 Symbolic initials . . . 3·00 2·30
1394 3e.50 Type **242** (air) 55 35

243 Wheel and Star

1970. Centenaries of Covilha (Nos. 1395/6) and Santarem (Nos. 1397/8). Multicoloured.
1395 1e. Type **243** 10 10
1397 1e. Castle . . . . 2·30 80
1396 2e.80 Ram and weaving frame . . . . 10 1·10
1398 4e. Two knights . . . . . . 1·10 70

244 "Great Eastern" laying Cable

1970. Centenary of Portugal–England Submarine Telegraph Cable.
1399 **244** 1e. black, blue and green 10 10
1400 2e.50 black, green & buff 1·40 45
1401 – 2e.80 multicoloured . . . 2·75 2·50
1402 – 4e. multicoloured . . . . 1·30 70
DESIGN: 2e.80, 4e. Cable cross-section.

245 Harvesting Grapes

246 Mountain Windmill, Bussaco Hills

1970. Port Wine Industry. Multicoloured.
1403 50c. Type **245** 10 10
1404 1e. Harvester and jug . . . 15 10
1405 3e.50 Wine-glass and wine barge 75 10
1406 7e. Wine-bottle and casks 85 55

1971. Portuguese Windmills.
1407 **246** 20c. brown, black & sepia 10 10
1408 – 50c. brown, black & blue 10 10
1409 – 1e. purple, black and grey 15 10
1410 – 2e. red, black and mauve 65 15
1411 – 3e.30 chocolate, black and brown . . . . . 2·10 1·60
1412 – 5e. brown, black & green 1·90 60
WINDMILLS: 50c. Beira Litoral Province; 1e. "Saloio" type Estremadura Province; 2e. St. Miguel Azores; 3e.30, Porto Santo, Madeira; 5e. Pico, Azores.

247 Europa Chain

1971. Europa.
1413 **247** 1e. green, blue and black 20 10
1414 3e.50 yellow, brn & blk 4·00 60
1415 7e.50 brown, green & blk 7·50 1·30

248 F. Franco

249 Pres. Salazar

1971. Portuguese Sculptors.
1416 **248** 20c. black 10 10
1417 – 1e. red 20 10
1418 – 1e.50 brown 45 45
1419a – 2e.50 blue 80 30
1420 – 3e.50 mauve . . . . . 1·10 40
1421 – 4e. green . . . . 2·10 1·60
DESIGNS: 1e. A. Lopes; 1e.50, A. de Costa Mota; 2e.50, R. Gameiro; 3e.50, J. Simoes de Almeida (the Younger); 4e. F. dos Santos.

1971. Pres. Antonio Salazar Commemoration
1422 **249** 1e. brown, green & orge 15 10
1423 5e. brown, purple & orge 1·30 40
1424 10e. brown, blue & orge 2·10 95

250 Wolframite

1971. 1st Spanish–Portuguese–American Congress of Economic Geology. Multicoloured.
1425 1e. Type **250** 10 10
1426 2e.50 Arsenopyrite . . . . 1·60 45
1427 3e.50 Beryllium 55 35
1428 6e.50 Chalcopyrite 95 35

251 Town Gate

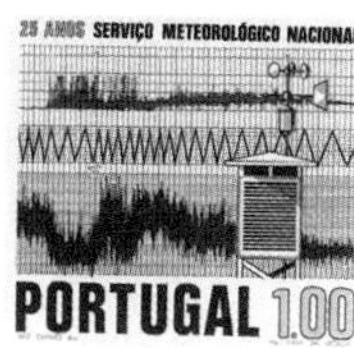

252 Weather Equipment

1971. Bicentenary of Castelo Branco. Mult.
1429 1e. Type **251** 10 10
1430 3e. Town square and monument . . . . 1·10 55
1431 12e.50 Arms of Castelo Branco (horiz) 95 55

1971. 25th Anniv of Portuguese Meteorological Service. Multicoloured.
1432 1e. Type **252** 10 10
1433 4e. Weather balloon . . . . 1·80 85
1434 6e.50 Weather satellite . . . 1·20 45

253 Drowning Missionaries

254 Man and his Habitat

1971. 400th Anniv of Martyrdom of Brazil Missionaries.
1435 **253** 1e. black, blue and grey 10 10
1436 3e.30 black, purple & brn . . . . 1·60 1·20
1437 4e.80 black, grn & olive 1·70 1·10

1971. Nature Conservation. Multicoloured.
1438 1e. Type **254** 10 10
1439 3e.30 Horses and trees ("Earth") 50 35
1440 3e.50 Birds ("The Atmosphere") 55 30
1441 4e.50 Fishes ("Water") . . . 2·10 1·60

255 Clerigos Tower, Oporto

1972. Buildings and Views.
1442 – 5c. grey, black and green 10 15
1443 – 10c. black, green & blue 10 10
1444 – 30c. sepia, brown & yell 10 10
1445 – 50c. blue, orange & blk 15 10
1446p **255** 1e. black, brown & grn 15 10
1447 – 1e.50 brown, blue & blk 15 10
1448p – 2e. black, brown & pur 15 10
1449p – 2e.50 brown, light brown and grey . . . 15 10
1450 – 3e. yellow, black & brn 15 10
1451p – 3e.50 green, orge & brn 15 10
1452 – 4e. black, yellow & blue 45 10
1453 – 4e.50 black, brn & grn 65 10
1454 – 5e. green, brown & black . . . . 4·50 10
1455 – 6e. bistre, green & black . . . . 1·70 25
1456 – 7e.50 black, orge & grn 90 10
1457 – 8e. bistre, black & green 90 10
1458 – 10e. multicoloured . . 40 10
1459 – 20e. multicoloured . . 3·00 25
1460 – 50e. multicoloured . . 1·50 30
1461 – 100e. multicoloured . . 4·50 75
DESIGNS—As T **255**: 5c. Aguas Livres aqueduct, Lisbon; 10c. Lima Bridge; 30c. Monastery interior, Alcobaca; 50c. Coimbra University; 1e.50, Belem Tower, Lisbon; 2e. Domus Municipalis, Braganza; 2e.50, Castle, Vila de Feira; 3e. Misericord House, Viana do Castelo; 3e.50, Window, Tomar Convent; 4e. Gateway, Braga; 4e.50, Dolmen of Carrazeda; 5e. Roman Temple, Evora; 6e. Monastery, Leca do Balio; 7e.50, Almourol Castle; 8e. Ducal Palace, Guimaraes. 31 × 22 mm: 10e. Cape Girao, Madeira; 20e. Episcopal Garden, Castelo Branco; 50e. Town Hall, Sintra; 100e. Seven Cities' Lake, Sao Miguel, Azores.

256 Arms of Pinhel **257** Heart and Pendulum

1972. Bicentenary of Pinhel's Status as a City. Multicoloured.
1464 1e. Type **256** 10 10
1465 2e.50 Balustrade (vert) . . . 1·40 40
1466 7e.50 Lantern on pedestal (vert) . . . . 1·10 50

1972. World Heart Month.
1467 **257** 1e. red and lilac 10 10
1468 – 4e. red and green . . . . 2·50 85
1469 – 9e. red and brown . . . 1·20 60
DESIGNS: 4e. Heart in spiral; 9e. Heart and cardiogram trace.

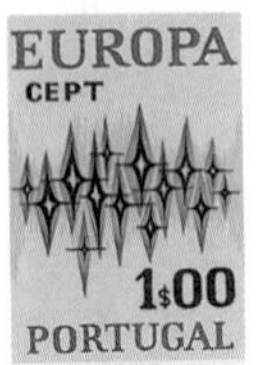

258 "Communications" **259** Container Truck

1972. Europa.
1470 **258** 1e. multicoloured 20 10
1471 3e.50 multicoloured . . . 2·50 40
1472 6e. multicoloured . . . . 7·00 1·40

1972. 13th International Road Transport Union Congress, Estoril. Multicoloured.
1473 1e. Type **259** 10 10
1474 4e.50 Roof of taxi-cab . . . 1·60 1·10
1475 8e. Motor-coach . . . . . 1·40 70

260 Football

1972. Olympic Games, Munich. Multicoloured.
1476 50c. Type **260** 10 10
1477 1e. Running 10 10
1478 1e.50 Show jumping 45 20
1479 3e.50 Swimming 85 30
1480 4e.50 Yachting . . . . . . 1·20 85
1481 5e. Gymnastics . . . . . . 2·20 90

261 Marquis de Pombal **262** Tome de Sousa

1972. Pombaline University Reforms. Multicoloured.
1482 1e. Type **261** 10 10
1483 2e.50 "The Sciences" (emblems) . . . . 1·20 75
1484 8e. Arms of Coimbra University. . . . . 1·30 95

1972. 150th Anniv of Brazilian Independence. Mult.
1485 1e. Type **262** 10 10
1486 2e.50 Jose Bonifacio 55 30
1487 3e.50 Dom Pedro IV . . . 55 30
1488 6e. Dove and globe . . . . 1·30 70

263 Sacadura, Cabral, Gago, Coutinho and Fairey III D Seaplane

1972. 50th Anniv of 1st Lisbon–Rio de Janeiro Flight. Multicoloured.
1489 1e. Type **263** 10 10
1490 2e.50 Route map 60 30
1491 2e.80 Type **263** 85 75
1492 3e.80 As 2e.50 . . . . . . 1·30 1·00

264 Camoens

1972. 400th Anniv of Camoens' "Lusiads" (epic poem).
1493 **264** 1e. yellow, brown & black 10 10
1494 – 3e. blue, green and black 1·10 50
1495 – 10e. brown, purple & blk 1·30 70
DESIGNS: 3e. "Saved from the Sea"; 10e. "Encounter with Adamastor".

265 Graph and Computer Tapes

1973. Portuguese Productivity Conference, Lisbon. Multicoloured.
1496 1e. Type **265** 10 10
1497 4e. Computer scale . . . . 1·00 55
1498 9e. Graphs . . . . 1·00 55

266 Europa "Posthorn" **268** Child Running

267 Pres. Medici and Arms

1973. Europa.
1499 **266** 1e. multicoloured 35 10
1500 4e. multicoloured . . . . 7·25 1·10
1501 6e. multicoloured . . . . 8·50 1·70

1973. Visit of Pres. Medici of Brazil. Mult.
1502 1e. Type **267** 10 10
1503 2e.80 Pres. Medici and globe 60 55
1504 3e.50 Type **267** 65 45
1505 4e.80 As No. 1503 . . . . 65 55

1973. "For the Child".
1506 **268** 1e. dp blue, blue & brown 10 10
1507 – 4e. purple, mauve & brn 1·20 50
1508 – 7e.50 orange, ochre and brown . . . . 1·20 1·00
DESIGNS: 4e. Child running (to right); 7e.50, Child jumping.

269 Transport and Weather Map

1973. 25th Anniv of Ministry of Communications. Multicoloured.
1509 1e. Type **269** 10 10
1510 3e.80 "Telecommunications" 35 30
1511 6e. "Postal Services" 90 55

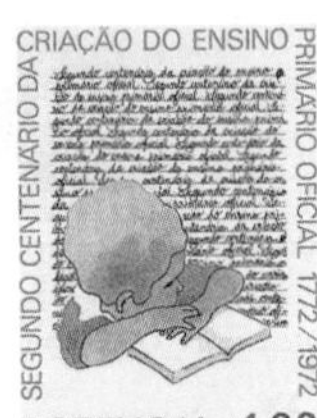

270 Child and Written Text

1973. Bicentenary of Primary State School Education. Multicoloured.
1512 1e. Type **270** 10 10
1513 4e.50 Page of children's primer . . . . 1·30 35
1514 5e.30 "Schooldays" (child's drawing) (horiz) . . . . 1·00 65
1515 8e. "Teacher and children" (horiz) . . . . 2·75 1·10

271 Electric Tramcar **272** League Badge

1973. Centenary of Oporto's Public Transport System. Multicoloured.
1516 1e. Horse tram 10 10
1517 3e.50 Modern bus . . . . . 1·70 1·10
1518 7e.50 Type **271** . . . . . . 1·90 90
Nos. 1516/17 are $31\frac{1}{2} \times 31\frac{1}{2}$ mm.

1973. 50th Anniv of Servicemen's League. Multicoloured.
1519 1e. Type **272** 10 10
1520 2e.50 Servicemen . . . . . 1·70 60
1521 11e. Awards and medals . . 1·40 55

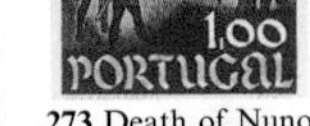

273 Death of Nuno Goncalves **274** Damiao de Gois (after Durer)

1973. 600th Anniv of Defence of Faria Castle by the Alcaide, Nuno Goncalves.
1522 **273** 1e. green and yellow . . 20 10
1523 10e. purple and yellow 1·70 85

1974. 400th Death Anniv of Damiao de Gois (scholar and diplomat). Multicoloured.
1524 1e. Type **274** 10 10
1525 4e.50 Title-page of "Chronicles of Prince Dom Joao" . . . . . . 1·90 55
1526 7e.50 Lute and "Dodecahordon" score 1·00 50

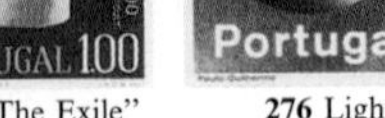

275 "The Exile" (A. Soares dos Reis) **276** Light Emission

1974. Europa
1527 **275** 1e. green, blue and olive 35 25
1528 4e. green, red and yellow 9·25 1·00
1529 6e. dp green, green & blue . . . . 11·50 1·50

1974. Inauguration of Satellite Communications Station Network.
1530 **276** 1e.50 green 10 10
1531 – 4e.50 blue . . . . 1·00 60
1532 – 5e.30 purple . . . . . . 1·60 95
DESIGNS: 4e.50, Spiral Waves; 5e.30, Satellite and Earth.

277 "Diffusion of Hertzian Radio Waves"

1974. Birth Centenary of Guglielmo Marconi (radio pioneer). Multicoloured.
1533 1e.50 Type **277** 10 10
1534 3e.30 "Radio waves across Space" . . . . 1·60 75
1535 10e. "Radio waves for Navigation" . . . . . . 1·00 45

278 Early Post-boy and Modern Mail Van

1974. Centenary of U.P.U. Multicoloured.
1536 1e.50 Type **278** 10 10
1537 2e. Hand with letters . . . 65 10
1538 3e.30 Sailing packet and modern liner 30 20
1539 4e.50 Dove and airliner . . 1·10 45
1540 5e.30 Hand with letter . . . 40 40
1541 20e. Steam and electric locomotives . . . . . . 2·00 1·20

279 Luisa Todi **280** Arms of Beja

1974. Portuguese Musicians.
1543 **279** 1e.50 purple 10 10
1544 – 2e. red 95 30
1545 – 2e.50 brown 65 20
1546 – 3e. blue 95 40
1547 – 5e.30 green 65 50
1548 – 11e. red 70 55
PORTRAITS: 2e. Joao Domingos Bomtempo; 2e.50,Carlos Seixas; 3e. Duarte Lobo; 5e.30, Joaode Sousa Carvalho; 11e. Marcos Portugal.

1974. Bimillenary of Beja. Multicoloured.
1549 1e.50 Type **280** 10 10
1550 3e.50 Beja's inhabitants through the ages . . . . 1·90 90
1551 7e. Moorish arches . . . . 1·90 95

281 "The Annunciation" **282** Rainbow and Dove

1974. Christmas. Multicoloured.

1552 1e.50 Type **281** 10 10
1553 4e.50 "The Nativity" . . . 2·50 45
1554 10e. "The Flight into Egypt" . . . . 1·90 75

1974. Portuguese Armed Forces Movement of 25 April.

1555 **282** 1e.50 multicoloured . . . 10 10
1556 3e.50 multicoloured . . . 2·75 1·30
1557 5e. multicoloured . . . . 1·50 55

283 Egas Moniz

284 Farmer and Soldier

1974. Birth Centenary of Professor Egas Moniz (brain surgeon).

1558 **283** 1e.50 brown and orange 20 10
1559 – 3e.30 orange and brown 1·10 45
1560 – 10e. grey and blue . . . 4·00 60

DESIGNS: 3e.30, Nobel Medicine and Physiology Prize medal, 1949; 10e. Cerebral angiograph, 1927.

1975. Portuguese Cultural Progress and Citizens' Guidance Campaign.

1561 **284** 1e.50 multicoloured . . . 10 10
1562 3e. multicoloured . . . . 1·50 55
1563 4e.50 multicoloured . . . 2·10 90

285 Hands and Dove of Peace

286 "The Hand of God"

1975. 1st Anniv of Portuguese Revolution. Multicoloured.

1564 1e.50 Type **285** 10 10
1565 4e.50 Hands and peace dove 2·10 60
1566 10e. Peace dove and emblem 2·50 90

1975. Holy Year. Multicoloured.

1567 1e.50 Type **286** 10 10
1568 4e.50 Hand with cross . . . 2·75 75
1569 10e. Peace dove . . . . . . 3·25 95

287 "The Horseman of the Apocalypse" (detail of 12th-cent manuscript)

1975. Europa. Multicoloured.

1570 1e.50 Type **287** 55 10
1571 10e. "Fernando Pessoa" (poet) (A. Negreiros) . . 19·00 95

288 Assembly Building

1975. Opening of Portuguese Constituent Assembly.

1572 **288** 2e. black, red and yellow 20 10
1573 20e. black, green & yellow . . . . 4·50 1·10

289 Hiking

1975. 36th International Camping and Caravanning Federation Rally. Multicoloured.

1574 2e. Type **289** 70 10
1575 4e.50 Boating and swimming 2·20 90
1576 5e.30 Caravanning . . . . 1·00 1·00

290 Planting Tree

1975. 30th Anniv of U.N.O. Multicoloured.

1577 2e. Type **290** 35 10
1578 4e.50 Releasing peace dove 1·20 45
1579 20e. Harvesting corn . . . . 2·75 1·20

291 Lilienthal Glider and Modern Space Rocket

1975. 26th International Astronautical Federation Congress, Lisbon. Multicoloured.

1580 2e. Type **291** 35 10
1581 4e.50 "Apollo"–"Soyuz" space link . . . . 1·60 65
1582 5e.30 R. H. Goddard, R. E. Pelterie, H. Oberth and K. E. Tsiolkovsky (space pioneers) 75 70
1583 10e. Astronaut and spaceships (70 × 32 mm) 3·50 1·10

292 Surveying the Land

1975. Centenary of National Geographical Society, Lisbon. Multicoloured.

1584 2e. Type **292** 15 10
1585 8e. Surveying the sea . . . 1·10 70
1586 10e. Globe and people . . . 2·40 1·20

293 Symbolic Arch

294 Nurse in Hospital Ward

1975. European Architectural Heritage Year.

1587 **293** 2e. grey, blue & deep blue 20 10
1588 – 8e. grey and red . . . . 2·50 70
1589 – 10e. multicoloured . . . 2·50 1·30

DESIGNS: 8e. Stylized building plan; 10e. Historical building being protected from development.

1975. International Women's Year. Multicoloured

1590 50c. Type **294** 10 10
1591 2e. Woman farm worker . . 80 30
1592 3e.50 Woman office worker 80 45
1593 8e. Woman factory worker 1·30 95

295 Pen-nib as Plough Blade

1976. 50th Anniv of National Writers Society.

1595 **295** 3e. blue and red 35 10
1596 20e. red and blue . . . . 3·00 1·10

296 First Telephone Set

1976. Telephone Centenary.

1597 **296** 3e. black, green & dp grn 70 10
1598 – 10e.50 black, red and pink . . . . 1·20 75

DESIGNS: 10e.50, Alexander Graham Bell.

297 "Industrial Progress"

298 Carved Olive-wood Spoons

1976. National Production Campaign.

1599 **297** 50c. red 15 10
1600 – 1e. green 35 10

DESIGN: 1e. Consumer goods

1976. Europa. Multicoloured.

1601 3e. Type **298** . . . . . . 2·00 30
1602 20e. Gold ornaments . . . 31·00 5·75

299 Stamp Designing

1976. "Interphil 76" International Stamp Exhibition, Philadelphia. Multicoloured.

1603 3e. Type **299** 15 10
1604 7e.50 Stamp being hand-cancelled 85 55
1605 10e. Stamp printing . . . . 1·20 75

300 King Fernando promulgating Law

1976. 600th Anniv of Law of "Sesmarias" (uncultivated land). Multicoloured.

1606 3e. Type **300** 10 10
1607 5e. Plough and farmers repelling hunters . . . . 1·30 40
1608 10e. Corn harvesting . . . . 1·50 65

301 Athlete with Olympic Torch

1976. Olympic Games, Montreal. Multicoloured.

1610 3e. Type **301** 15 10
1611 7e. Women's relay . . . . . 1·20 1·00
1612 10e.50 Olympic flame . . . 1·70 85

302 "Speaking in the Country"

1976. Literacy Campaign. Multicoloured.

1613A 3e. Type **302** 45 10
1614A 3e. "Speaking at Sea" . . 45 10
1615A 3e. "Speaking in Town" . . 45 10
1616B 3e. "Speaking at Work" 65 10

303 Azure-winged Magpie

304 "Lubrapex" Emblem and Exhibition Hall

1976. "Portucale 77" Thematic Stamp Exhibition, Oporto (1st issue). Flora and Fauna. Mult.

1618 3e. Type **303** 15 10
1619 5e. Lynx 95 25
1620 7e. Portuguese laurel cherry and blue tit . . . . . . 1·00 80
1621 10e.50 Little wild carnation and lizard . . . . 1·00 1·00

See also Nos 1673/8.

1976. "Lubrapex 1976" Luso-Brazilian Stamp Exhibition. Multicoloured.

1622 3e. Type **304** 20 10
1623 20e. "Lubrapex" emblem and "stamp" . . . . . . 1·90 1·20

305 Bank Emblem

1976. Centenary of National Trust Fund Bank.

1625 **305** 3e. multicoloured 10 10
1626 7e. multicoloured . . . . 1·60 70
1627 15e. multicoloured . . . 2·50 1·00

306 Sheep Grazing

307 "Liberty"

1976. Water Conservation. Protection of Humid Zones. Multicoloured.

1628 1e. Type **306** 15 10
1629 3e. Marshland 70 25
1630 5e. Sea trout . . . . 1·60 35
1631 10e. Mallards . . . . 3·00 75

1976. Consolidation of Democratic Institutions.

1632 **307** 3e. grey, green and red 55 15

308 Examining Child's Eyes

1976. World Health Day. Detection and Prevention of Blindness. Multicoloured.

1633 3e. Type **308** 15 10
1634 5e. Welder wearing protective goggles . . . . 1·60 30
1635 10e.50 Blind person reading Braille . . . . 1·30 90

309 Hydro-electric Power

1976. Uses of Natural Energy. Multicoloured.

1636 1e. Type **309** 10 10
1637 4e. Fossil fuel (oil) 45 10
1638 5e. Geo-thermic sources . . 60 25
1639 10e. Wind power . . . . . 1·20 50
1640 15e. Solar energy . . . . . 2·10 1·40

310 Map of Member Countries

1977. Admission of Portugal to the Council of Europe.

1641 **310** 8e.50 multicoloured . . . 1·00 1·00
1642 10e. multicoloured . . . 1·00 1·00

311 Bottle inside Human Body

1977. 10th Anniv of Portuguese Anti-Alcoholic Society. Multicoloured.

1643 3e. Type **311** 10 10
1644 5e. Broken body and bottle 75 35
1645 15e. Sun behind prison bars and bottle . . . . 1·80 1·10

312 Forest

1977. Natural Resources. Forests. Multicoloured.
1646 1e. Type **312** 10 10
1647 4e. Cork oaks 55 15
1648 7e. Logs and trees . . . . . 1·20 1·10
1649 15e. Trees by the sea . . . 1·20 1·00

313 Exercising

315 John XXI Enthroned

314 Southern Plains

1977. International Rheumatism Year.
1650 – 4e. orange, brown & blk 15 10
1651 **313** 6e. ultramarine, blue and black 95 85
1652 – 10e. red, mauve and black 85 55
DESIGNS: 4e. Rheumatism victim; 10e. Group exercising.

1977. Europa. Multicoloured.
1653 4e. Type **314** 20 10
1654 8e.50 Northern terraced mountains . . . . 1·20 65

1977. 7th Death Centenary of Pope John XXI. Multicoloured.
1656 4e. Type **315** 15 10
1657 15e. Pope as doctor 55 35

316 Compass

1977. Camoes Day.
1658 **316** 4e. multicoloured 15 10
1659 8e.50 multicoloured . . . 90 90

317 Child and Computer

1977. Permanent Education. Multicoloured.
1660 4e. Type **317** 30 10
1661 4e. Flautist and dancers . . 30 10
1662 4e. Farmer and tractor . . . 30 10
1663 4e. Students and atomic construction 30 10

318 Pyrite

1977. Natural Resources. The Subsoil. Mult.
1665 4e. Type **318** 15 10
1666 5e. Marble 75 30
1667 10e. Iron ore 80 45
1668 20e. Uranium . . . . 1·80 95

319 Alexandre Herculano

1977. Death Centenary of Alexandre Herculano (writer and politician).
1669 **319** 4e. multicoloured 35 10
1670 15e. multicoloured . . . 1·30 50

320 Early Steam Locomotive and Peasant Cart (ceramic panel, J. Colaco)

1977. Centenary of Railway Bridge over River Douro. Multicoloured.
1671 4e. Type **320** 20 10
1672 10e. Maria Pia bridge (Eiffel) . . . . 1·70 1·30

321 Poviero (Northern coast)

1977. "Portucale 77" Thematic Stamp Exhibition, Oporto (2nd issue). Coastal Fishing Boats. Multicoloured.
1673 2e. Type **321** 35 10
1674 3e. Sea-going rowing boat, Furadouro 20 10
1675 4e. Rowing boat from Nazare 20 10
1676 7e. Caicque from Algarve 40 15
1677 10e. Tunny fishing boat, Algarve 65 45
1678 15e. Boat from Buarcos . . 1·00 70

322 "The Adoration" (Maria do Sameiro A. Santos)

1977. Christmas. Children's Paintings. Mult.
1680 4e. Type **322** 15 10
1681 7e. "Star over Bethlehem" (Paula Maria L. David) 85 35
1682 10e. "The Holy Family" (Carla Maria M. Cruz) (vert) . . . . 1·00 45
1683 20e. "Children following the Star" (Rosa Maria M. Cardoso) (vert) . . . 1·10 90

323 Medical Equipment and Operating Theatre

1978. (a) Size 22 × 17 mm.
1684 **323** 50c. green, black and red 10 10
1685 – 1e. blue, orange and black 10 10
1686 – 2e. blue, green & brown 10 10
1687 – 3e. brown, green and black 10 10
1688 – 4e. green, blue & brown 10 10
1689 – 5e. blue, green & brown 10 10
1690 – 5e.50 brown, buff and green 15 10
1691 – 6e. brown, yellow & grn 15 10
1692 – 6e.50 blue, deep blue and green 15 10
1693 – 7e. black, grey and blue 15 10
1694 – 8e. ochre, brown and grey 15 10
1694a – 8e.50 brn, blk & lt brn 20 10
1695 – 9e. yellow, brown & blk 20 10
1696 – 10e. brown, black & grn 20 10
1697 – 12e.50 blue, red and black 25 10
1698 – 16e. brown, black and violet 25 10

(b) Size 30 × 21 mm.
1699 – 20e. multicoloured 40 10
1700a – 30e. multicoloured 45 15
1701 – 40e. multicoloured 50 30
1702 – 50e. multicoloured 80 15
1703 – 100e. multicoloured . . . 1·30 40
1703a – 250e. multicoloured . . . 3·50 65

DESIGNS: 1e. Old and modern kitchen equipment; 2e. Telegraph key and masts, microwaves and dish aerial; 3e. Dressmaking and ready-to-wear clothes; 4e. Writing desk and computer; 5e. Tunny fishing boats and modern trawler; 5e.50, Manual and mechanical weaver's looms; 6e. Plough and tractor; 6e.50, Monoplane and B.A.C. One Eleven airliner; 7e. Hand press and modern printing press; 8e. Carpenter's hand tools and mechanical tool; 8e.50, Potter's wheel and modern ceramic machinery; 9e. Old cameras and modern cine and photo cameras; 10e. Axe, saw and mechanical saw; 12e.50, Navigation and radar instruments; 16e. Manual and automatic mail sorting; 20e. Hand tools and building site; 30e. Hammer, anvil, bellows and industrial complex; 40e. Peasant cart and lorry; 50e. Alembic, retorts and modern chemical plant; 100e. Carpenter's shipyard, modern shipyard and tanker; 250e. Survey instruments.

324 Mediterranean Soil

1978. Natural Resources. The Soil. Mult.
1704 4e. Type **324** 20 10
1705 5e. Rock formation 40 15
1706 10e. Alluvial soil 80 45
1707 20e. Black soil . . . . . . 2·10 75

325 Pedestrian on Zebra Crossing

1978. Road Safety.
1708 **325** 1e. blue, black and orange 10 10
1709 – 2e. blue, black and green 20 10
1710 – 2e.50 blue, black & lt bl 55 10
1711 – 5e. blue, black and red 1·00 15
1712 – 9e. blue, black & ultram 1·90 50
1713 – 12e.50 blue and black . . 2·75 1·20
DESIGNS: 2e. Motor cyclist; 2e.50, Children in back of car; 5e. Driver in car; 9e. View of road from driver's seat; 12e.50, Road victim ("Don't drink and drive").

326 Roman Tower of Centum Cellas, Belmonte
327 Roman Bridge, Chaves

1978. Europa. Multicoloured.
1714 10e. Type **326** 85 15
1715 40e. Belem Monastery, Lisbon . . . . 2·40 1·30

1978. 19th Century of Chaves (Aquae Flaviae). Multicoloured.
1717 5e. Type **327** 35 10
1718 20e. Inscribed tablet from bridge . . . . 1·90 80

328 Running

1978. Sport for All. Multicoloured.
1719 5e. Type **328** 15 10
1720 10e. Cycling 30 20
1721 12e.50 Swimming 70 65
1722 15e. Football 70 70

329 Pedro Nunes

1978. 400th Death Anniv of Pedro Nunes (cosmographer). Multicoloured.
1723 5e. Type **329** 10 10
1724 20e. Nonio (navigation instrument) and diagram 1·10 35

330 Trawler, Crates of Fish and Lorry

1978. Natural Resources. Fishes. Multicoloured.
1725 5e. Type **330** 15 10
1726 9e. Trawler and dockside cranes 50 15
1727 12e.50 Trawler, radar and lecture 95 80
1728 15e. Trawler with echo-sounding equipment and laboratory . . . . 1·50 1·20

331 Post Rider

1978. Introduction of Post Code. Multicoloured.
1729 5e. Type **331** 25 10
1730 5e. Pigeon with letter . . . 25 10
1731 5e. Sorting letters 25 10
1732 5e. Pen nib and post codes 25 10

332 Symbolic Figure

1978. 30th Anniv of Declaration of Human Rights. Multicoloured.
1733 14e. Type **332** 55 35
1734 40e. Similar symbolic figure, but facing right . . . . . 1·40 90

333 Sebastiao Magalhaes Lima

1978. 50th Death Anniv of Magalhaes Lima (journalist and pacifist).
1736 **333** 5e. multicoloured 20 10

334 Portable Post Boxes and Letter Balance

1978. Centenary of Post Museum. Multicoloured.
1737 4e. Type **334** 20 10
1738 5e. Morse equipment . . . 20 10
1739 10e. Printing press and Portuguese stamps of 1853 (125th anniv) . . . 85 15
1740 14e. Books, bookcase and entrance to Postal Library (centenary) . . . . 2·00 1·20

335 Emigrant at Railway Station

1979. Portuguese Emigrants. Multicoloured.
1742 5e. Type **335** 15 10
1743 14e. Emigrants at airport . . 55 50
1744 17e. Man greeting child at railway station . . . . . 85 1·00

336 Traffic

1979. Fight Against Noise. Multicoloured.
1745 4e. Type **336** 15 10
1746 5e. Pneumatic drill 55 10
1747 14e. Loud hailer . . . . . 1·20 50

337 N.A.T.O. Emblem

1979. 30th Anniv of N.A.T.O.
1748 **337** 5e. blue, red and brown 20 10
1749 50e. blue, yellow and red 2·30 2·10

338 Door-to-door Delivery

1979. Europa. Multicoloured.
1751 14e. Postal messenger delivering letter in cleft stick 45 20
1752 40e. Type **338** . . . . . . 1·00 1·00

339 Children playing Ball

1979. International Year of the Child. Multicoloured.
1754 5e.50 Type **339** 15 10
1755 6e.50 Mother, baby and dove 20 10
1756 10e. Child eating 35 30
1757 14e. Children of different races 80 85

340 Saluting the Flag

1979. Camoes Day.
1759 **340** 6e.50 multicoloured . . . 30 10

341 Pregnant Woman

1979. The Mentally Handicapped. Multicoloured.
1761 6e.50 Type **341** 25 10
1762 17e. Boy sitting in cage . . 65 45
1763 20e. Face, and hands holding hammer and chisel 85 70

342 Children reading Book

1979. 50th Anniv of International Bureau of Education. Multicoloured.
1764 6e.50 Type **342** 30 10
1765 17e. Teaching a deaf child 1·40 70

343 Water Cart, Caldas de Monchique

1979. "Brasiliana 79" International Stamp Exhibition. Portuguese Country Carts. Mult.
1766 2e.50 Type **343** 10 15
1767 5e.50 Wine sledge, Madeira 15 15
1768 6e.50 Wine cart, Upper Douro 30 10
1769 16e. Covered cart, Alentejo 70 65
1770 19e. Cart, Mogadouro . . . 95 1·00
1771 20e. Sand cart, Murtosa . . 95 35

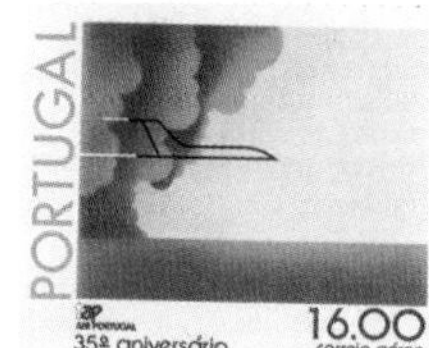

344 Aircraft flying through Storm Cloud

1979. 35th Anniv of TAP National Airline. Multicoloured.
1772 16e. Type **344** 90 45
1773 19e. Aircraft and sunset . . 95 75

345 Antonio Jose de Almeida

346 Family Group

1979. Republican Personalities (1st series).
1774 **345** 5e.50 mauve, grey and red 25 10
1775 – 6e.50 red, grey and carmine 25 10
1776 – 10e. brown, grey and red 45 15
1777 – 16e. blue, grey and red 75 45
1778 – 19e.50 green, grey and red . . . . 1·20 1·00
1779 – 20e. purple, grey and red 1·00 35
DESIGNS: 6e. Afonso Costa; 10e. Teofilo Braga; 16e. Bernardino Machado; 19e.50, Joao Chagas; 20e. Elias Garcia.
See also Nos. 1787/92.

1979. Towards a National Health Service. Mult.
1780 6e.50 Type **346** 25 05
1781 20e. Doctor examining patient . . . . 1·10 45

347 "The Holy Family"

1979. Christmas. Tile Pictures. Multicoloured.
1782 5e.50 Type **347** 30 15
1783 6e.50 "Adoration of the Shepherds" 30 15
1784 16e. "Flight into Egypt" . . 90 60

348 Rotary Emblem and Globe

1980. 75th Anniv of Rotary International. Mult.
1785 16e. Type **348** 80 45
1786 50e. Rotary emblem and torch . . . . 2·20 1·30

349 Jaime Cortesao

1980. Republican Personalities (2nd series).
1787 – 3e.50 orange and brown 15 10
1788 – 5e.50 green, olive and deep olive 20 10
1789 – 6e.50 lilac and violet . . 20 10
1790 **349** 11e. multicoloured . . . 1·20 1·00
1791 – 16e. ochre and brown . . 80 55
1792 – 20e. green, blue & lt blue 80 30
DESIGNS: 3e.50, Alvaro de Castro; 5e.50, Antonio Sergio; 6e.50, Norton de Matos; 16e. Teixeira Gomes; 20e. Jose Domingues dos Santos.

350 Serpa Pinto

352 Luis Vaz de Camoes

351 Barn Owl

1980. Europa, Multicoloured.
1793 16e. Type **350** 55 20
1794 60e. Vasco da Gama . . . . 1·70 85

1980. Protection of Species. Animals in Lisbon Zoo. Multicoloured.
1796 6e.50 Type **351** 20 10
1797 16e. Red fox 65 35
1798 19e.50 Wolf 90 50
1799 20e. Golden eagle 90 40

1980. 400th Death Anniv of Luis Vaz de Camoes (poet).
1801 **352** 6e.50 multicoloured . . . 40 10
1802 20e. multicoloured . . . 95 55

353 Pinto in Japan

1980. 400th Anniv of Fernao Mendes Pinto's "A Peregrinacao" (The Pilgrimage). Multicoloured.
1803 6e.50 Type **353** 25 10
1804 10e. Sea battle 80 45

354 Lisbon and Statue of St. Vincent (Jeronimos Monastery)

1980. World Tourism Conference, Manila, Philippines. Multicoloured.
1805 6e.50 Type **354** 25 10
1806 8e. Lantern Tower, Evora Cathedral 30 15
1807 11e. Mountain village and "Jesus with Top-hat" (Mirando do Douro Cathedral) 65 40
1808 16e. Canicada dam and "Lady of the Milk" (Braga Cathedral) . . . . 1·10 65
1809 19e.50 Aveiro River and pulpit from Santa Cruz Monastery, Coimbra . . 1·40 75
1810 20e. Rocha beach and ornamental chimney, Algarve . . . . 1·20 45

355 Caravel

1980. "Lubrapex 80" Portuguese–Brazilian Stamp Exhibition, Lisbon. Multicoloured.
1811 6e.50 Type **355** 20 10
1812 8e. Nau 55 30
1813 16e. Galleon . . . . 1·10 45
1814 19e.50 Early paddle-steamer with sails . . . . 1·50 55

356 Lightbulbs

1980. Energy Conservation. Multicoloured.
1816 6e.50 Type **356** 20 10
1817 16e. Speeding car . . . . . 1·50 50

357 Duke of Braganza and Open Book

1980. Bicentenary of Academy of Sciences, Lisbon. Multicoloured.
1818 6e.50 Type **357** 20 10
1819 19e.50 Uniformed academician, Academy and sextant . . . . 1·10 55

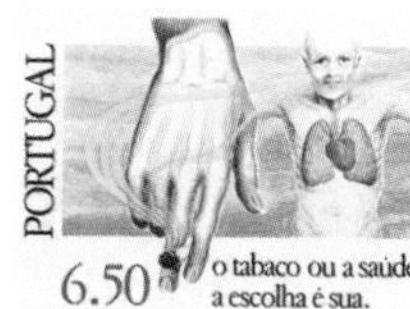

358 Cigarette contaminating Lungs

1980. Anti-Smoking Campaign. Multicoloured.
1820 6e.50 Type **358** 20 10
1821 19e.50 Healthy figure pushing away hand with cigarette . . . . 1·40 90

359 Head and Computer Punch-card

1981. National Census. Multicoloured.
1822 6e.50 Type **359** 20 10
1823 16e. Houses and punch-card 1·10 70

360 Fragata, River Tejo

1981. River Boats. Multicoloured.
1824 8e. Type **360** 20 10
1825 8e.50 Rabelo, River Douro 20 10
1826 10e. Moliceiro, Aveiro River 40 15
1827 16e. Barco, River Lima . . 1·10 35
1828 19e.50 Carocho, River Minho 70 40
1829 20e. Varino, River Tejo . . 65 30

361 "Rajola" Tile from Setubal Peninsula (15th century)

1981. Tiles (1st series).
1830 **361** 8e.50 multicoloured . . . 55 10
See also Nos. 1843, 1847, 1862, 1871, 1885, 1893, 1902, 1914, 1926, 1935, 1941, 1952, 1970, 1972, 1976, 1983, 1993, 2020 and 2031.

362 Agua Dog

1981. 50th Anniv of Kennel Club of Portugal. Multicoloured.
1832 7e. Type **362** 35 10
1833 8e.50 Serra de Aires 35 10
1834 15e. Perdigueiro 60 10
1835 22e. Podengo 90 55
1836 25e.50 Castro Laboreiro . . 1·40 80
1837 33e.50 Serra de Estrela . . . 1·80 70

363 "Agriculture"

364 Dancer and Tapestry

1981. May Day. Multicoloured.
1838 8e.50 Type **363** 20 05
1839 25e.50 "Industry" . . . . . 1·10 70

1981. Europa. Multicoloured.
1840 22e. Type **364** . . . . . . 1·10 35
1841 48e. Painted boat prow, painted plate and shipwright with model boat . . . . 2·20 1·20

1981. Tiles (2nd series). Horiz design as T **361**.
1843 8e.50 multicoloured 55 10
DESIGN: 8e.50, Tracery-pattern tile from Seville (16th century).

365 St. Anthony Writing

1981. 750th Death Anniv of St. Anthony of Lisbon. Multicoloured.
1845 8e.50 Type **365** 35 10
1846 70e. St. Anthony giving blessing . . . . 3·00 1·40

1981. Tiles (3rd series). As T **361**. Mult.
1847 8e.50 Arms of Jaime, Duke of Braganca (Seville, 1510) 55 10

366 King Joao II and Caravels

1981. 500th Anniv of King Joao II's Accession. Multicoloured.
1849 8e.50 Type **366** 35 10
1850 27e. King Joao II on horseback . . . . 1·90 70

367 "Dom Luiz", 1862

1981. 125th Anniv of Portuguese Railways. Multicoloured.
1851 8e.50 Type **367** 50 10
1852 19e. Pacific steam locomotive, 1925 . . . . 1·50 90
1853 27e. Alco 1500 diesel locomotive, 1948 . . . . 1·60 80
1854 33e.50 Alsthom BB 2600 electric locomotive, 1974 2·20 75

368 "Perrier" Pump, 1856

1981. Portuguese Fire Engines. Multicoloured.
1855 7e. Type **368** 35 10
1856 8e.50 Ford fire engine, 1927 45 10
1857 27e. Renault fire pump, 1914 . . . . 1·70 85
1858 33e.50 Ford "Snorkel" combined hoist and pump, 1978 . . . . . . 2·20 90

369 "Virgin and Child"

1981. Christmas. Crib Figures. Multicoloured.
1859 7e. Type **369** 40 30
1860 8e.50 "Nativity" 55 15
1861 27e. "Flight into Egypt" . . 1·80 1·10

1981. Tiles (4th series). As T **361**. Multicoloured.
1862 8e.50 "Pisana" tile, Lisbon (16th century) 55 10

370 St. Francis with Animals

371 Flags of E.E.C. Members

1982. 800th Birth Anniv of St. Francis of Assisi. Multicoloured.
1865 8e.50 Type **370** 30 10
1866 27e. St. Francis helping to build church . . . . . . 1·80 1·00

1982. 25th Anniv of European Economic Community.
1867 **371** 27e. multicoloured . . . 1·00 60

372 Fort St. Catherina, Lighthouse and Memorial Column

1982. Centenary of Figueira da Foz City. Mult.
1869 10e. Type **372** 40 10
1870 19e. Tagus Bridge, shipbuilding yard and trawler . . . . 1·30 75

1982. Tiles (5th series). As T **361**. Multicoloured.
1871 10e. Italo-Flemish pattern tile (17th century) 55 10

373 "Sagres I" (cadet barque)

374 Edison Gower Bell Telephone, 1883

1982. Sporting Events. Multicoloured.
1873 27e. Type **373** (Lisbon sailing races) . . . . . . 1·50 60
1874 33e.50 Roller hockey (25th World Championship) . . 1·60 75
1875 50e. "470" dinghies (World Championships) . . . . . 2·30 1·10
1876 75e. Football (World Cup Football Championship, Spain) . . . . 3·75 1·30

1982. Centenary of Public Telephone Service. Multicoloured.
1877 10e. Type **374** 35 10
1878 27e. Consolidated telephone, 1887 . . . . 1·00 1·10

375 Embassy of King Manuel to Pope Leo X

1982. Europa.
1879 **375** 33e.50 multicoloured . . 2·30 80

376 Pope John Paul II and Shrine of Fatima

377 Dunlin

1982. Papal Visit. Multicoloured.
1881 10e. Type **376** 35 10
1882 27e. Pope and Sameiro Sanctuary . . . . 1·60 90
1883 33e.50 Pope and Lisbon Cathedral . . . . 1·70 70

1982. Tiles (6th series). As T **361**. Multicoloured.
1885 10e. Altar front panel depicting oriental tapestry (17th century) 60 10

1982. "Philexfrance 82" International Stamp Exhibition, Paris. Birds. Multicoloured.
1887 10e. Type **377** 40 10
1888 19e. Red-crested pochard . . 1·20 45
1889 27e. Greater flamingo . . . 1·50 70
1890 33e.50 Black-winged stilt . . 1·70 85

378 Dr. Robert Koch

1982. Centenary of Discovery of Tubercle Bacillus. Multicoloured.
1891 27e. Type **378** . . . . . . 1·20 95
1892 33e.50 Lungs . . . . 1·30 95

1982. Tiles (7th series). As T **361**. Multicoloured.
1893 10e. Polychromatic quadrilobate pattern, 1630–40 . . . . 55 10

379 Wine Glass and Stop Sign

1982. "Don't Drink and Drive".
1895 **379** 10e. multicoloured . . . 40 10

380 Fairey IIID Seaplane "Lusitania"

1982. "Lubrapex 82" Brazilian–Portuguese Stamp Exhibition, Curitiba. Multicoloured.
1896 10e. Type **380** 25 10
1897 19e. Dornier Do-J Wal flying boat "Argus" . . . 1·00 65
1898 33e.50 Douglas DC-7C "Seven Seas" airliner . . 1·40 75
1899 50e. Boeing 747-282B jetliner . . . . 1·90 80

381 Marquis de Pombal

1982. Death Bicentenary of Marquis de Pombal (statesman and reformer).
1901 **381** 10e. multicoloured . . . 40 10

1982. Tiles (8th series). As T **361**. Multicoloured.
1902 10e. Monochrome quadrilobate pattern, 1670–90 . . . . 55 10

382 Gallic Cock and Tricolour

1983. Centenary of French Alliance (French language teaching association).
1905 **382** 27e. multicoloured . . . 1·20 60

383 Lisnave Shipyard

1983. 75th Anniv of Port of Lisbon Administration.
1906 **383** 10e. multicoloured . . . 40 10

384 Export Campaign Emblem

1983. Export Promotion
1907 **384** 10e. multicoloured . . . 40 10

385 Midshipman, 1782, and Frigate "Vasco da Gama"

386 W.C.Y. Emblem

1983. Naval Uniforms. Multicoloured.
1908 12e.50 Type **385** 40 10
1909 25e. Seaman and steam corvette "Estefania", 1845 1·10 30
1910 30e. Marine sergeant and cruiser "Adamastor", 1900 . . . . 1·30 45
1911 37e.50 Midshipman and frigate "Joao Belo", 1982 1·60 45

1983. World Cummunications Year. Mult.
1912 10e. Type **386** 40 10
1913 33e.50 W.C.Y. emblem (diff) 1·30 85

1983. Tiles (9th series). As T **361**. Multicoloured.
1914 12e.50 Hunter killing white bull (tile from Saldanha Palace, Lisbon, 17/18th century) 65 10

387 Portuguese Helmet (16th century)

1983. "Expo XVII" Council of Europe Exhibition. Multicoloured.
1916 11e. Type **387** 40 15
1917 12e.50 Astrolabe (16th century) 55 10
1918 25e. Portuguese caravels (from 16th-century Flemish tapestry) . . . . 1·20 30
1919 30e. Carved capital (12th century) . . . . 1·50 30
1920 37e.50 Hour glass (16th century) . . . . 1·70 75
1921 40e. Detail from Chinese panel painting (16th–17th century) . . . . 1·80 65

388 Egas Moniz (Nobel Prize winner and brain surgeon)

1983. Europa.
1923 **388** 37e.50 multicoloured . . 1·70 55

389 Passenger in Train

1983. European Ministers of Transport Conference.
1925 **389** 30e. blue, deep blue and silver . . . . 1·80 45

1983. Tiles (10th series). As T **361**. Multicoloured.
1926 12e.50 Tiles depicting birds (18th century) 65 10

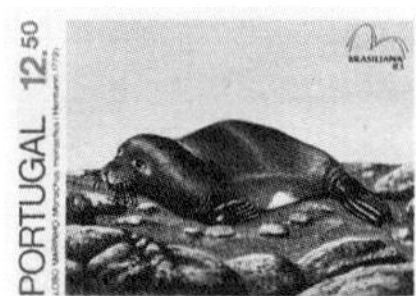

390 Mediterranean Monk Seal

1983. "Brasiliana 83" International Stamp Exhibition, Rio de Janeiro. Marine Mammals. Multicoloured.
1928 12e.50 Type **390** 65 10
1929 30e. Common dolphin . . . 1·70 40
1930 37e.50 Killer whale . . . . 2·20 75
1931 80e. Humpback whale . . . 3·50 75

391 Assassination of Spanish Administrator by Prince John

393 "Adoration of the Magi"

392 Bartolomeu de Gusmao and Model Balloon, 1709

1983. 600th Anniv of Independence. Mult.
1933 12e.50 Type **391** 60 10
1934 30e. Prince John proclaimed King of Portugal . . . . 2·00 95

1983. Tiles (11th series). As T **361**. Multicoloured.
1935 12e.50 Flower pot by Gabriel del Barco (18th century) 65 10

1983. Bicentenary of Manned Flight. Mult.
1937 16e. Type **392** 65 10
1938 51e. Montgolfier balloon, 1783 . . . . 1·50 80

1983. Christmas. Stained Glass Windows from Monastery of Our Lady of Victory, Batalha. Multicoloured.
1939 12e.50 Type **393** 45 10
1940 30e. "The Flight into Egypt" . . . . 1·70 80

1983. Tiles (12th series). As T **361**. Multicoloured.
1941 12e.50 Turkish horseman (18th century) 65 10

394 Siberian Tiger

1983. Centenary of Lisbon Zoo. Multicoloured.
1944 16e. Type **394** . . . . . . 1·20 25
1945 16e. Cheetah . . . . 1·20 25
1946 16e. Blesbok . . . . 1·20 25
1947 16e. White rhino . . . . . 1·20 25

395 Fighter Pilot and Hawker Hurricane Mk II, 1954

1983. Air Force Uniforms. Multicoloured.
1948 16e. Type **395** 40 10
1949 35e. Pilot in summer uniform and Republic F-84G Thunderjet, 1960 1·60 35
1950 40e. Paratrooper in walking-out uniform and Nord 250ID Noratlas military transport plane, 1966 . . 1·50 55
1951 51e. Pilot in normal uniform and Vought A-70 Corsair II bomber, 1966 . . . . 1·90 60

1984. Tiles (13th series). As T **361**. Multicoloured.
1952 16e. Coat of arms of King Jose I (late 18th century) 70 10

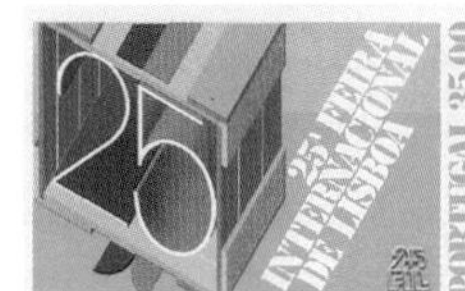

396 "25" on Crate (25th Lisbon International Fair)

1984. Events.
1954 35e. Type **396** . . . . . . 1·30 65
1955 40e. Wheat rainbow and globe (World Food Day) 1·40 55
1956 51e. Hand holding stylized flower (15th World Congress of International Rehabilitation) (vert) . . 1·80 70

397 National Flag

1984. 10th Anniv of Revolution.
1957 **397** 16e. multicoloured . . . 1·20 10

398 Bridge

1984. Europa.
1958 **398** 51e. multicoloured . . . 1·80 90

399 "Panel of St. Vincent"

1984. "Lubrapex 84" Portuguese–Brazilian Stamp Exhibition. Multicoloured.
1960 16e. Type **399** 50 10
1961 40e. "St. James" (altar panel) . . . . 1·70 45
1962 51e. "View of Lisbon" (painting) . . . . 2·50 65
1963 66e. "Head of Youth" (Domingos Sequeira) . . 2·50 90

400 Fencing

1984. Olympic Games, Los Angeles, and 75th Anniv of Portuguese Olympic Committee. Multicoloured.
1965 35e. Type **400** . . . . . . 1·20 30
1966 40e. Gymnastics . . . . . . 1·50 45
1967 51e. Running . . . . 2·10 65
1968 80e. Pole vaulting . . . . . 2·30 90

1984. Tiles (14th series). As T **361**. Multicoloured.
1970 16e. Pictorial tile from Pombal Palace, Lisbon (late 18th century) 65 10

1984. Tiles (15th series). As T **361**. Multicoloured.
1972 16e. Four art nouveau tiles (late 19th century) 65 10

401 Gil Eanes

1984. Anniversaries. Multicoloured.
1974 16e. Type **401** (550th anniv of rounding of Cape Bojador) 35 10
1975 51e. King Pedro IV of Portugal and I of Brazil (150th death anniv) . . . 1·90 85

1984. Tiles (16th series). As T **361**. Multicoloured.
1976 16e. Grasshoppers and wheat (R. Bordalo Pinheiro, 19th century) . . 65 10

402 Infantry Grenadier, 1740, and Regiment in Formation

1985. Army Uniforms. Multicoloured.
1979 20e. Type **402** 40 10
1980 46e. Officer, Fifth Cavalry, 1810, and cavalry charge 1·80 35
1981 60e. Artillery corporal, 1891, and Krupp 9 mm gun and crew . . . . 1·90 65
1982 100e. Engineer in chemical protection suit, 1985, and bridge-laying armoured car . . . . 2·30 1·10

1985. Tiles (17th series). As T **361**. Multicoloured.
1983 20e. Detail of panel by Jorge Barrados in Lisbon Faculty of Letters (20th century) 65 10

403 Calcada R. dos Santos Kiosk

1985. Lisbon Kiosks. Multicoloured.
1985 20e. Type **403** 85 10
1986 20e. Tivoli kiosk, Avenida da Liberdade 85 10
1987 20e. Porto de Lisboa kiosk 85 10
1988 20e. Rua de Artilharia Um kiosk 85 10

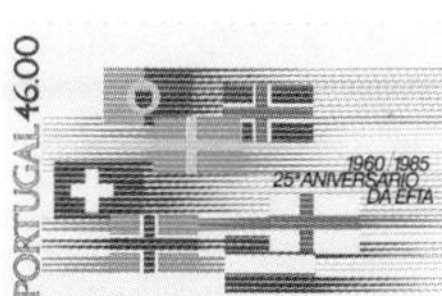

404 Flags of Member Countries

1985. 25th Anniv of European Free Trade Assn.
1989 **404** 46e. multicoloured . . . 1·10 50

405 Profiles

1985. International Youth Year.
1990 **405** 60e. multicoloured . . . 1·40 65

406 Woman holding Adufe (tambourine)

1985. Europa.
1991 **406** 60e. multicoloured . . . 2·75 1·00

1985. Tiles (18th series). As T **361**. Multicoloured.
1993 20e. Detail of panel by Maria Keil on Avenida Infante Santo (20th century) 65 10

407 Knight on Horseback

1985. Anniversaries. Multicoloured.
1995 20e. Type **407** (600th anniv of Battle of Aljubarrota) 55 50
1996 46e. Queen Leonor and hospital (500th anniv of Caldas da Rainha thermal hospital) . . . . 1·70 45
1997 60e. Pedro Reinel (500th anniversary of first Portuguese sea-chart) . . 1·80 65

408 Farmhouse, Minho

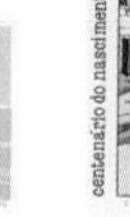

409 Aquilino Ribeiro (writer)

1985. Architecture.
1998 – 50c. black, bistre and blue 10 10
1999 – 1e. black, yellow & green 10 10
2000 – 1e.50 black, green and emerald 10 10
2001 – 2e.50 brown, orange & bl 10 10
2002 – 10e. black, purple & pink 15 10
2003 **408** 20e. brn, yell & dp yell 25 10
2004 – 22e.50 brown, blue and ochre 25 10
2005 – 25e. brown, yellow & grn 30 10
2006 – 27e. black, grn & yell . . 40 10
2007 – 29e. black, yellow & orge 40 10
2008 – 30e. black, blue & brown 40 10
2009 – 40e. black, yellow & grn 60 10
2010 – 50e. black, blue & brown 60 10
2011 – 55e. black, yellow & grn 80 10
2012 – 60e. black, orange & blue 80 15
2013 – 70e. black, yellow & orge 90 15
2014 – 80e. brown, green and red 90 30
2015 – 90e. brown, yellow & grn 1·00 30
2016 – 100e. brown, yellow & bl 1·20 30
2017 – 500e. black, grey and blue . . . . 5·00 70

DESIGNS: 50e. Saloia house, Estremadura; 1e. Beira inland house; 1e.50, Ribatejo house; 2e.50, Tras-os-montes houses; 10e. Minho and Douro coast house; 22e.50, Alentejo houses; 25e. Sitio house, Algarve; 27e. Beira inland house (different); 29e. Tras-os-montes house; 30e. Algarve house; 40e. Beira inland house (different); 50e. Beira coasthouse; 55e. Tras-os-montes house (different); 60e. Beira coast house (different); 70e. South Estramadura and Alentejo house; 80e. Estremadura house; 90e. Minho house; 100e. Monte house, Alentejo; 500e. Terraced houses, East Algarve.

1985. Tiles (19th series). As T **361**. Multicoloured.
2020 20e. Head of woman by Querubim Lapa (20th century) 65 20

1985. Anniversaries. Multicoloured.
2022 20e. Type **409** (birth centenary) 85 20
2023 46e. Fernando Pessoa (poet 50th death anniv) . . . . 1·40 45

410 Berlenga National Reserve

1985. National Parks and Reserves. Multicoloured.
2024 20e. Type **410** 35 10
2025 40e. Estrela Mountains National Park . . . . . 1·20 45
2026 46e. Boquilobo Marsh National Reserve . . . . 1·90 70
2027 80e. Formosa Lagoon National Reserve . . . . 1·90 60

411 "Nativity"

412 Post Rider

1985. Christmas. Illustrations from "Book of Hours of King Manoel I". Multicoloured.
2029 20e. Type **411** 40 10
2030 46e. "Adoration of the Three Wise Men" . . . . 1·40 45

1985. Tiles (20th series). As T **361**. Multicoloured.
2031 20e. Detail of panel by Manuel Cargaleiro (20th century) 65 10

1985. No value expressed.
2034 **412** (–) green and deep green 65 10

413 Map and Flags of Member Countries

1985. Admission of Portugal and Spain to European Economic Community. Multicoloured.
2035 20e. Flags of Portugal and Spain uniting with flags of other members 45 10
2036 57e.50 Type **413** . . . . . 1·80 75

414 Feira Castle

1986. Castles (1st series). Multicoloured.
2037 22e.50 Type **414** 65 05
2038 22e.50 Beja Castle 65 10
See also Nos. 2040/1, 2054/5, 2065/6, 2073/4, 2086/7 2093/4, 2102/3 and 2108/9.

415 Globe and Dove

1986. International Peace Year.
2039 **415** 75e. multicoloured . . . 1·90 80

1986. Castles (2nd series). As T **414**. Multicoloured.
2040 22e.50 Braganca Castle . . 65 10
2041 22e.50 Guimaraes Castle . . 65 10

416 Benz Motor Tricycle, 1886

1986. Centenary of Motor Car. Multicoloured.
2042 22e.50 Type **416** 90 10
2043 22e.50 Daimler motor car, 1886 . . . . 90 10

417 Allis Shad

1986. Europa.
2044 **417** 68e.50 multicoloured . . 1·90 80

418 Alter

1986. "Ameripex 86" International Stamp Exn, Chicago. Thoroughbred Horses. Multicoloured.
2046 22e.50 Type **418** 40 10
2047 47e.50 Lusitano . . . . . . 1·40 65
2048 52e.50 Garrano . . . . . . 1·70 85
2049 68e.50 Sorraia . . . . . . 2·00 90

420 Diogo Cao (navigator) and Monument

1986. Anniversaries. Multicoloured.
2051 22e.50 Type **420** (500th anniv of 2nd expedition to Africa) 40 10
2052 52e.50 Passos Manuel (Director) and capital (150th anniv of National Academy of Fine Arts, Lisbon) . . . . 1·30 50
2053 52e.50 Joao Baptista Ribeiro (painter and Oporto Academy Director) and drawing (150th anniv of Portuguese Academy of Fine Arts, Oporto) . . . 1·30 50

1986. Castles (3rd series). As T **414**. Multicoloured.
2054 22e.50 Belmonte Castle . . 65 10
2055 22e.50 Montemor-o-Velho Castle 65 10

421 Hand writing on Postcard

1986. Anniversaries. Multicoloured.
2057 22e.50 Type **421** (centenary of first Portuguese postcards) 65 10
2058 47e.50 Guardsman and houses (75th anniv of National Republican Guard) . . . . 1·20 55
2059 52e.50 Calipers, globe and banner (50th anniv of Order of Engineers) . . . 1·20 70

422 Seasonal Mill, Douro

1986. "Luprapex 86" Portuguese–Brazilian Stamp Exhibition, Rio de Janeiro. Multicoloured.
2060 22e.50 Type **422** 40 10
2061 47e.50 Seasonal mill, Coimbra . . . . 1·00 60
2062 52e.50 Overshot bucket mill, Gerez . . . . 1·30 90
2063 90e. Permanent stream mill, Braga . . . . 2·10 70

1987. Castles (4th series). As T **414**. Mult.
2065 25e. Silves Castle 65 05
2066 25e. Evora-Monte Castle . . 65 05

423 Houses on Stilts, Tocha

1987. 75th Anniv (1986) of Organized Tourism. Multicoloured.
2067 25e. Type **423** 40 10
2068 57e. Fishing boats, Espinho 1·70 60
2069 98e. Fountain, Arraiolos . . 2·20 65

424 Hand, Sun and Trees

1987. European Environment Year. Multicoloured.
2070 25e. Type **424** 40 10
2071 57e. Hands and flower on map of Europe . . . . . 1·10 60
2072 74e.50 Hand, sea, purple dye murex shell, moon and rainbow . . . . . . 2·00 75

1987. Castles (5th series). As T **414**. Multicoloured.
2073 25e. Leiria Castle 65 10
2074 25e. Trancoso Castle . . . 65 10

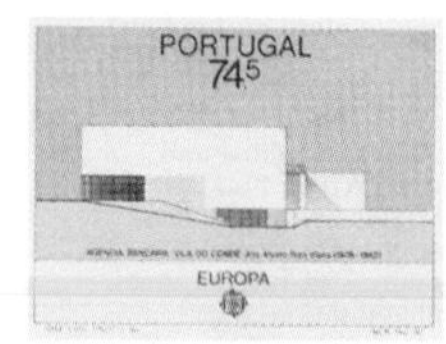

425 Bank Borges and Irmao Agency, Vila do Conde (Alvaro Siza)

1987. Europa. Architecture.
2075 **425** 74e.50 multicoloured . . 1·80 90

426 Cape Mondego

427 Souza-Cardoso (self-portrait)

1987. "Capex '87" International Stamp Exhibition Toronto. Portuguese Lighthouses. Multicoloured.
2077 25e. Type **426** 65 10
2078 25e. Berlenga 65 10
2079 25e. Aveiro 65 10
2080 25e. Cape St. Vincent . . . 65 10

1987. Birth Centenary of Amadeo de Souza-Cardoso (painter)
2081 **427** 74e.50 multicoloured . . 1·40 65

428 Clipped 400 Reis Silver Coin

1987. 300th Anniv of Portuguese Paper Currency.
2082 **428** 100e. multicoloured . . . 1·90 60

429 Dias's Fleet leaving Lisbon

1987. 500th Anniv of Bartolomeu Dias's Voyages (1st issue). Multicoloured.
2083 25e. Type **429** 70 20
2084 25e. Ships off coast of Africa 70 10
Nos. 2083/4 were printed together, se-tenant, each pair forming a composite design.
See also Nos. 2099/2100.

430 Library

1987. 150th Anniv of Portuguese Royal Library, Rio de Janeiro.
2085 **430** 125e. multicoloured . . . 2·50 95

1987. Castles (6th series). As T **414**. Multicoloured.
2086 25e. Marvao Castle 65 10
2087 25e. St. George's Castle, Lisbon 65 10

432 Angels around Baby Jesus, Tree and Kings (Jose Manuel Coutinho)

1987. Christmas. Children's Paintings. Mult.
2089 25e. Type **432** 45 10
2090 57e. Children dancing around sunburst (Rosa J. Leitao) . . . . 1·30 55
2091 74e.50 Santa Claus flying on dove (Sonya Alexandra Hilario) . . . . 1·50 85

1988. Castles (7th series). As T **414**. Multicoloured.
2093 27e. Fernandine Walls, Oporto 65 10
2094 27e. Almourol Castle . . . 65 10

433 Lynx

1988. Iberian Lynx. Multicoloured.
2095 27e. Type **433** 75 10
2096 27e. Lynx carrying rabbit 75 10
2097 27e. Pair of lynxes 75 10
2098 27e. Mother with young . . 75 10

434 King Joao II sending Pero da Covilha on Expedition

1988. 500th Anniv of Voyages of Bartolomeu Dias (2nd issue) (2099/2100) and Pero da Covilha (2101). Multicoloured.
2099 27e. Dias's ships in storm off Cape of Good Hope 65 10
2100 27e. Contemporary map . . 65 10
2101 105e. Type **434** . . . . . . 1·90 70
Nos. 2099/2100 are as T **429**.

1988. Castles (8th series). As T **414**. Multicoloured.
2102 27e. Palmela Castle 65 10
2103 27e. Vila Nova da Cerveira Castle 65 10

435 19th-century Mail Coach

1988. Europa. Transport and Communications.
2104 **435** 80e. multicoloured . . . 1·60 1·50

436 Map of Europe and Monnet

1988. Birth Centenary of Jean Monnet (statesman). "Europex 88" Stamp Exhibition.

2106	**436** 60e. multicoloured	1·10	50

1988. Castles (9th series). As T **414**. Multicoloured.

2108	27e. Chaves Castle	65	30
2109	27e. Penedono Castle	65	30

438 "Part of a Viola" (Amadeo de Souza-Cardoso)

1988. 20th-century Portuguese Paintings (1st series). Multicoloured.

2110	27e. Type **438**	40	15
2111	60e. "Acrobats" (Almada Negreiros)	1·20	55
2112	80e. "Still Life with Viola" (Eduardo Viana)	1·50	90

See also Nos. 2121/3, 2131/3, 2148/50, 2166/8 and 2206/8.

439 Archery

1988. Olympic Games, Seoul. Multicoloured.

2114	27e. Type **439**	35	10
2115	55e. Weightlifting	1·10	65
2116	60e. Judo	1·20	60
2117	80e. Tennis	1·80	70

440 "Winter" (House of the Fountains, Coimbra)

1988. Roman Mosaics of 3rd Century. Mult.

2119	27e. Type **440**	45	15
2120	80e. "Fish" (Baths, Faro)	1·40	60

1988. 20th Century Portuguese Paintings (2nd series). As T **438**. Multicoloured.

2121	27e. "Internment" (Mario Eloy)	35	10
2122	60e. "Lisbon Houses" (Carlos Botelho)	1·10	45
2123	80e. "Avejao Lirico" (Antonio Pedro)	1·40	60

441 Braga Cathedral

1989. Anniversaries. Multicoloured.

2126	30e. Type **441** (900th anniv)	60	30
2127	55e. Caravel, Fischer's lovebird and S. Jorge da Mina Castle (505th anniv)	1·00	55
2128	60e. Sailor using astrolabe (500th anniv of South Atlantic voyages)	1·40	60

Nos. 2127/8 also have the "India 89" Stamp Exhibition, New Delhi, emblem.

442 "Greetings" **443** Flags in Ballot Box

1989. Greetings Stamps. Multicoloured.

2129	29e. Type **442**	40	10
2130	60e. Airplane distributing envelopes inscribed "with Love"	85	35

1989. 20th-Century Portuguese Paintings (3rd series). As T **438**. Multicoloured.

2131	29e. "Antithesis of Calm" (Antonio Dacosta)	35	10
2132	60e. "Unskilled Mason's Lunch" (Julio Pomar)	1·10	60
2133	87e. "Simumis" (Vespeira)	1·40	90

1989. 3rd Direct Elections to European Parliament.

2135	**443** 60e. multicoloured	1·10	60

444 Boy with Spinning Top

1989. Europa. Children's Games and Toys.

2136	**444** 80e. multicoloured	1·40	80

445 Cable Railway

1989. Lisbon Transport. Multicoloured.

2138	29e. Type **445**	40	10
2139	65e. Electric tramcar	1·20	65
2140	87e. Santa Justa lift	1·40	80
2141	100e. Bus	1·70	65

446 Gyratory Mill, Ansiao

1989. Windmills. Multicoloured.

2143	29e. Type **446**	40	10
2144	60e. Stone mill, Santiago do Cacem	1·20	60
2145	87e. Post mill, Afife	1·40	65
2146	100e. Wooden mill, Caldas da Rainha	1·70	80

1989. 20th-Century Portuguese Paintings (4th series). As T **438**.

2148	29e. blue, green and black	35	25
2149	60e. multicoloured	1·10	50
2150	87e. multicoloured	1·40	80

DESIGNS: 29e. "046-72" (Fernando Lanhas); 60e. "Spirals" (Nadir Afonso); 87e. "Sim" (Carlos Calvet).

448 Luis I (death centenary) and Ajuda Palace, Lisbon

1989. National Palaces (1st series). Multicoloured.

2153	29e. Type **448**	30	10
2154	60e. Queluz Palace	1·10	65

See also Nos. 2211/14.

449 "Armeria pseudarmeria"

1989. Wild Flowers. Multicoloured.

2155	29e. Type **449**	30	10
2156	60e. "Santolina impressa"	85	55
2157	87e. "Linaria lamarckii"	1·20	80
2158	100e. "Limonium multiflorum"	1·70	1·00

450 Blue and White Plate

1990. Portuguese Faience (1st series). Mult.

2159	33e. Type **450**	40	10
2160	33e. Blue and white plate with man in centre	40	10
2161	35e. Vase decorated with flowers	55	15
2162	60e. Fish-shaped jug	95	55
2163	60e. Blue and white plate with arms in centre	95	55
2164	60e. Blue and white dish with lid	95	55

See also Nos. 2221/6 and 2262/7.

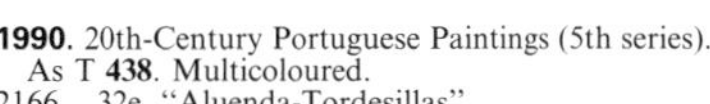

1990. 20th-Century Portuguese Paintings (5th series). As T **438**. Multicoloured.

2166	32e. "Aluenda-Tordesillas" (Joaquim Rodrigo)	35	10
2167	60e. "Painting" (Luis Noronha da Costa)	85	45
2168	95e. "Painting" (Vasco Costa)	1·40	70

451 Joao Goncalves Zarco

1990. Portuguese Navigators.

2170	**451** 2e. red, pink and black	10	10
2171	– 3e. green, blue and black	10	10
2172	– 4e. purple, red and black	10	05
2173	– 5e. brown, grey & black	10	05
2174	– 6e. deep green, green and black	10	05
2175	– 10e. dp red, red & black	10	05
2176	– 32e. green, brown & blk	35	05
2177	– 35e. red, pink and black	30	05
2178	– 38e. blue, lt blue & black	30	05
2179	– 42e. green, grey & black	35	10
2180	– 45e. green, yellow & blk	35	15
2181	– 60e. yellow, purple & blk	70	30
2182	– 65e. brown, green & blk	70	25
2183	– 70e. violet, mauve & blk	70	25
2184	– 75e. olive, green & black	65	35
2185	– 80e. orange, brn & blk	95	45
2186	– 100e. red, orange & blk	1·40	45
2187	– 200e. green, yellow & blk	1·90	60
2188	– 250e. blue, green & black	3·00	1·10
2189	– 350e. red, pink and black	3·75	1·00

DESIGNS: 3e. Pedro Lopes de Sousa; 4e. Duarto Pacheco Pereira; 5e. Tristao Vaz Teixeira; 6e. Pedro Alvares Cabral; 10e. Joao de Castro; 32e. Bartolomeu Perestrelo; 35e. Gil Eanes: 38e. Vasco da Gama; 42e. Joao de Lisboa; 45e. Joao Rodrigues Cabrilho; 60e. Nuno Tristao; 65e. Joaoda Nova; 70e. Fernao de Magalhaes (Magellan); 75e. Pedro Fernandes de Queiros; 80e. Diogo Gomes; 100e. Diogo de Silves; 200e. Estevao Gomes; 250e. Diogo Cao; 350e. Bartolomeu Dias.

452 Score and Singers

1990. Anniversaries. Multicoloured.

2191	32e. Type **452** (centenary of "A Portuguesa" (national anthem))	35	10
2192	70e. Students and teacher (700th anniv of granting of charter to Lisbon University) (vert)	1·20	65

453 Santo Tirso Post Office

1990. Europa. Post Office Buildings. Mult.

2193	**453** 80e. multicoloured	1·10	75

455 Street with Chairs under Trees

1990. Greetings Stamps. Multicoloured.

2196	60e. Type **455**	80	55
2197	60e. Hand holding bouquet out of car window	80	55
2198	60e. Man with bouquet crossing street	80	55
2199	60e. Women with bouquet behind pillar box	80	55

456 Camilo Castelo Branco (writer)

1990. Death Anniversaries. Multicoloured.

2200	65e. Type **456** (centenary)	90	55
2201	70e. Brother Bartolomeu dos Martires (Bishop of Braga, 400th anniv)	1·00	75

457 Barketta

1990. 15th-Century Explorers' Ships. Mult.

2202	32e. Type **457**	35	10
2203	60e. Carvel-built fishing boat	85	45
2204	70e. Nau	1·00	65
2205	95e. Caravel	1·40	85

1990. 20th-Century Portuguese Paintings (6th series). As T **438**. Multicoloured.

2206	32e. "Dom Sebastiao" (Costa Pinheiro)	35	10
2207	60e. "Domestic Scene with Green Dog" (Paula Rego)	80	45
2208	95e. "Homage to Magritte" (Jose de Guimaraes)	1·50	85

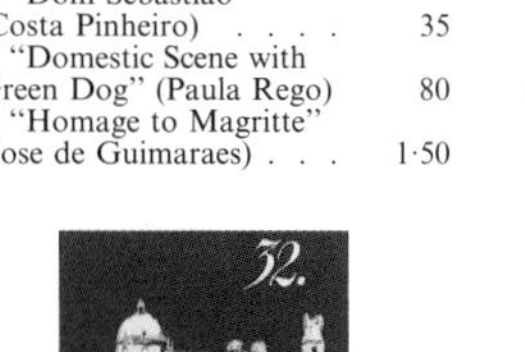

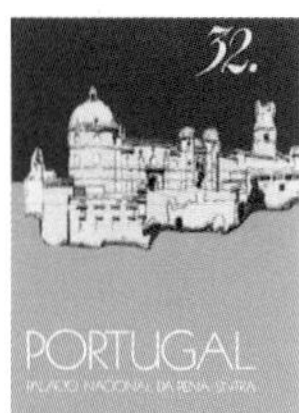

458 Pena Palace

1990. National Palaces (2nd series). Mult.

2211	32e. Type **458**	35	40
2212	60e. Vila Palace	85	50
2213	70e. Mafra Palace	1·00	65
2214	120e. Guimaraes Palace	1·40	80

459 Carneiro

1990. 10th Death Anniv of Francisco Sa Carneiro (founder of Popular Democratic Party and Prime Minister, 1980).

2215	**459** 32e. black and brown	40	15

460 Steam Locomotive No. 02, 1887

1990. Centenary of Rossio Railway Station, Lisbon, Multicoloured.

2216	32e. Type **460**	35	10
2217	60e. Steam locomotive No. 010, 1891	85	50
2218	70e. Steam locomotive No. 071, 1916	1·00	65
2219	95e. Electric train, 1956	1·40	80

1991. Portuguese Faience (2nd series). As T **450**. Multicoloured.

2221	35e. Barrel of fish and plate (Rato factory Lisbon)	40	10
2222	35e. Floral vase (Bica do Sapato factory)	40	10
2223	35e. Gargoyle (Costa Briozo factory, Coimbra)	40	10
2224	60e. Dish with leaf pattern (Juncal factory)	80	50

2225 60e. Coffee pot (Cavaquinho factory, Oporto) 80 50
2226 60e. Mug (Massarelos factory, Oporto) 80 50

461 Greater Flamingoes

1991. European Tourism Year. Multicoloured.
2228 60e. Type **461** 75 50
2229 110e. European chameleon 1·30 75

462 "Eutelsat II" Satellite

1991. Europa. Europe in Space. Multicoloured.
2231 **462** 80e. multicoloured . . . 1·10 85

463 Caravel

1991. 16th-Century Explorers' Ships. Mult.
2233 35e. Type **463** 35 10
2234 75e. Port view of nau . . . 95 55
2235 80e. Stern view of nau 1·00 60
2236 110e. Galleon . . . . 1·30 50

465 Emerald and Diamond Bow

1991. "Royal Treasures" Exhibition, Ajuda Palace (1st issue). Multicoloured.
2238 35e. Type **465** 35 10
2239 60e. Royal sceptre 80 45
2240 70e. Sash of the Grand Cross 95 60
2241 80e. Hilt of sabre . . . . . 1·10 55
2242 140e. Crown . . . . 1·60 80
See also Nos. 2270/4.

466 Antero de Quental (writer)

1991. Anniversaries. Multicoloured.
2243 35e. Type **466** (death centenary) 35 10
2244 110e. Arrival of expedition and baptism of Sonyo prince (500th anniv of first Portuguese missionary expedition to the Congo) . . . . 1·40 55

467 Faculty of Architecture, Oporto University (Siza Vieira)

1991. Architecture. Multicoloured.
2245 35e. Type **467** 35 10
2246 60e. Torre do Tombo (Arsenio Cordeiro Associates) 65 35
2247 80e. Maria Pia bridge over River Douro (Edgar Cardoso) and Donna Maria bridge . . . . . . 1·00 75
2248 110e. Setubal–Braga highway . . . . 1·30 70

468 King Manoel I creating Public Post, 1520

1991. History of Communications in Portugal. Mult.
2249 35e. Type **468** 35 10
2250 60e. Woman posting letter and telegraph operator (merging of posts and telegraph operations, 1881) 65 35
2251 80e. Postman, mail van and switchboard operator (creation of Posts and Telecommunications administration, 1911) . . 95 60

469 Show Jumping

1991. Olympic Games, Barcelona (1992) (1st issue). Multicoloured.
2253 35e. Type **469** 35 10
2254 60e. Fencing 65 35
2255 80e. Shooting . . . . 1·00 55
2256 110e. Yachting . . . . . . 1·30 50
See also Nos. 2295/8.

470 Peugeot "19", 1899

1991. Caramulo Automobile Museum. Mult.
2257 35e. Type **470** 35 10
2258 60e. Rolls Royce "Silver Ghost", 1911 . . . . . . 65 35
2259 80e. Bugatti "35B", 1930 . . 1·00 55
2260 110e. Ferrari "1965 Inter", 1950 . . . . 1·20 45
See also Nos. 2275/8.

1992. Portuguese Faience (3rd series). As T **450**. Multicoloured.
2262 40e. Jug (Viana do Castelo factory) 40 15
2263 40e. Plate with flower design ("Ratinho" faience, Coimbra) 40 15
2264 40e. Dish with lid (Estremoz factory) 40 15
2265 65e. Decorated violin by Wescislau Cifka (Constancia factory, Lisbon) 70 45
2266 65e. Figure of man seated on barrel (Calvaquinho factory, Oporto) 70 45
2267 65e. Figure of woman (Fervenca factory, Oporto) 70 30

471 Astrolabe (Presidency emblem)

1992. Portuguese Presidency of European Community.
2269 **471** 65e. multicoloured . . . 70 40

1992. "Royal Treasures" Exhibition, Ajuda Palace (2nd issue). As T **465**. Multicoloured.
2270 38e. Coral diadem 35 10
2271 65e. Faberge clock 80 90
2272 70e. Gold tobacco box studded with diamonds and emeralds by Jacqumin 65 35
2273 85e. Royal sceptre with dragon supporting crown 85 45
2274 125e. Necklace of diamond stars by Estevao de Sousa 1·10 80

1992. Oeiras Automobile Museum. As T **470**. Multicoloured.
2275 38e. Citroen "Torpedo", 1922 . . . . 35 10
2276 65e. Robert Schneider, 1914 80 40
2277 85e. Austin "Seven", 1933 95 55
2278 120e. Mercedes Benz armoured "770", 1938 . . 1·20 80

472 Portuguese Traders

1992. 450th Anniv of First Portuguese Contacts with Japan (1st issue). Details of painting attributed to Kano Domi. Multicoloured.
2280 38e. Type **472** 35 10
2281 120e. Portuguese visitors with gifts . . . . 1·20 70
See also Nos. 2342/4.

473 Portuguese Pavilion

474 Cross-staff

1992. "Expo '92" World's Fair, Seville.
2282 **473** 65e. multicoloured . . . 60 30

1992. Nautical Instruments (1st series). Mult.
2283 60e. Type **474** 55 30
2284 70e. Quadrant 70 50
2285 100e. Astrolabe 90 50
2286 120e. Compass . . . . . . 1·20 70
See also Nos. 2318/21.

475 Royal All Saints Hospital, Lisbon

1992. Anniversaries. Multicoloured.
2288 38e. Type **475** (500th anniv of foundation) 40 15
2289 70e. Lucia, Francisco and Jacinta (75th anniv of apparition of Our Lady at Fatima) 65 40
2290 120e. Crane and docks (centenary of Port of Leixoes) . . . . 1·10 70

476 Columbus with King Joao II

1992. Europa. 500th Anniv of Discovery of America by Columbus.
2291 **476** 85e. multicoloured . . . 80 65

478 Black-headed Gull flying over contaminated River

479 Running

1992. 2nd United Nations Conference on Environment and Development, Rio de Janeiro. Multicoloured.
2293 70e. Type **478** 70 55
2294 120e. River kingfisher and butterfly beside clean river 1·10 60
Nos. 2293/4 were issued together, se-tenant, forming a composite design.

1992. Olympic Games, Barcelona (2nd issue). Mult.
2295 38e. Type **479** 35 10
2296 70e. Football 70 50
2297 85e. Hurdling 85 50
2298 120e. Roller hockey . . . . 1·10 60

480 Bullfighter on Horse

1992. Centenary of Campo Pequeno Bull Ring, Lisbon. Multicoloured.
2300 38e. Type **480** 35 10
2301 65e. Bull charging at horse 65 35
2302 70e. Bullfighter attacking bull 80 45
2303 155e. Bullfighter flourishing hat . . . . 1·30 80

482 Star

1992. European Single Market.
2313 **482** 65e. multicoloured . . . 60 40

483 Industrial Safety Equipment

1992. European Year of Health, Hygiene and Safety in the Workplace.
2314 **483** 120e. multicoloured . . . 1·10 70

484 Post Office Emblem

1993. No value expressed.
2315 **484** (–) red and black 40 15
No. 2315 was sold at the current first class inland letter rate. This was 42e. at time of issue.

485 Graphic Poem

1993. Birth Centenary of Jose de Almada Negreiros (artist and poet). Multicoloured.
2316 40e. Type **485** 35 15
2317 65e. Trawlers (painting) . . 65 40

486 Sand Clock

1993. Nautical Instruments (2nd series). Mult.
2318 42e. Type **486** 35 15
2319 70e. Nocturlabio 70 35
2320 90e. Kamal 90 60
2321 130e. Back-staff . . . . . . 1·20 70

487 View from Window

1993. Europa. Contemporary Art. Untitled painting by Jose Escada.
2322 **487** 90e. multicoloured . . . 95 65

488 Rossini and "The Barber of Seville"

1993. Bicentenary of San Carlos National Theatre, Lisbon. Multicoloured.
2324 42e. Type **488** 35 15
2325 70e. Verdi and "Rigoletto" 75 40
2326 90e. Wagner and "Tristan and Isolde" 90 55
2327 130e. Mozart and "The Magic Flute" . . . . . . 1·20 60

489 Fireman's Helmet

1993. 125th Anniv of Association of Volunteer Firemen of Lisbon.
2329 **489** 70e. multicoloured . . . 65 40

490 Santos-o-Velho, Lisbon

491 "Angel of the Annunciation" (from Oporto Cathedral)

1993. Union of Portuguese-speaking Capital Cities.
2330 **490** 130e. multicoloured . . . 1·20 70

1993. Sculptures (1st series). Multicoloured.
2332 42e. Type **491** 35 10
2333 70e. "St Mark" (Cornelius de Holanda) (horiz) . . . 70 40
2334 75e. "Madonna and Child" 80 40
2335 90e. "Archangel St. Michael" 90 50
2336 130e. "Count of Ferreira" (Soares dos Reis) . . . . 1·20 65
2337 170e. "Construction" (Heldar Batista) . . . . . 1·60 90
See also Nos. 2580/5 and 2466/71.

492 Road Tanker and Electric Tanker Train

1993. Int Railways Congress, Lisbon. Mult.
2339 90e. Type **492** 75 40
2340 130e. Electric train and traffic jam . . . . 1·20 70

493 Japanese Man with Musket

1993. 450th Anniv of First Portuguese Visit to Japan (2nd issue). Multicoloured.
2342 42e. Type **493** 35 15
2343 130e. Portuguese missionaries . . . . . . 1·20 80
2344 350e. Traders carrying goods . . . . 3·00 1·90

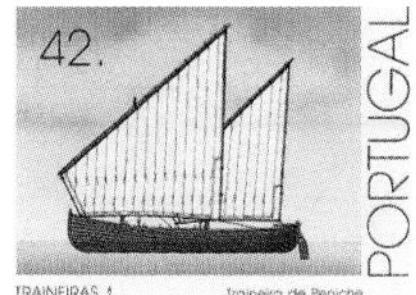

494 Peniche Trawler

1993. Trawlers (1st series). Multicoloured.
2345 42e. Type **494** 35 15
2346 70e. Peniche type trawler . . 60 35
2347 90e. "Germano 3" (steam trawler) 80 45
2348 130e. "Estrela 1" (steam trawler) . . . . 1·10 60
See also Nos. 2392/5.

495 Rural Post Bag, 1800

1993. Post Boxes. Multicoloured.
2349 42e. Type **495** 35 15
2350 70e. 19th-century wall-mounted box for railway travelling post office . . . 60 35
2351 90e. 19th-century pillar box 80 50
2352 130e. Modern multi-function post box . . . . 1·10 60

496 Imperial Eagle

1993. Endangered Birds of Prey. Multicoloured.
2354 42e. Type **496** 35 15
2355 70e. Eagle owl 80 35
2356 130e. Peregrine falcon . . . 1·20 65
2357 350e. Hen harrier . . . . . 2·75 1·90

497 Knot

1993. 40th Anniv of Brazil–Portugal Consultation and Friendship Treaty.
2358 **497** 130e. multicoloured . . . 1·10 1·00

499 Stylized Map of Member Nations

1994. 40th Anniv of Western European Union.
2360 **499** 85e. multicoloured . . . 70 45

500 Olympic Rings as Torch Flame

1994. Centenary of Int Olympic Committee. Mult.
2361 100e. Type **500** 75 70
2362 100e. "100" and rings . . . 75 70

501 Oliveira Martins (historian)

1994. Centenaries. Multicoloured.
2363 45e. Type **501** (death) . . . 35 15
2364 100e. Florbela Espanca (poet, birth) 80 50

502 Map and Prince Henry (½-size illustration)

1994. 600th Birth Anniv of Prince Henry the Navigator.
2365 **502** 140e. multicoloured . . . 1·10 75

503 Dove

1994. 20th Anniv of Revolution.
2366 **503** 75e. multicoloured . . . 60 40

504 Mounted Knight and Explorer with Model Caravel

1994. Europa. Discoveries.
2367 **504** 100e. multicoloured . . . 80 50

505 Emblem

1994. International Year of the Family.
2369 **505** 45e. red, black and lake 30 15
2370 140e. red, black and green . . . . 1·20 85

506 Footballer kicking Ball and World Map

1994. World Cup Football Championship, U.S.A. Multicoloured.
2371 100e. Type **506** 80 50
2372 140e. Ball and footballers' legs . . . . 1·10 85

507 King Joao II of Portugal and King Fernando of Spain (½-size illustration)

1994. 500th Anniv of Treaty of Tordesillas (defining Portuguese and Spanish spheres of influence).
2373 **507** 140e. multicoloured . . . 1·10 1·10

508 Music

1994. Lisbon, European Capital of Culture. Multicoloured.
2374 45e. Type **508** 30 15
2375 75e. Photography and cinema 60 35
2376 100e. Theatre and dance . . 70 50
2377 140e. Art . . . . 1·00 75

509 Emblem

1994. Portuguese Road Safety Year.
2379 **509** 45e. red, green and black 35 15

1994. Sculptures (2nd series). As T **491**. Mult.
2380 45e. Carved stonework from Citania de Briteiros (1st century) (horiz) 30 15
2381 75e. Visigothic pilaster (7th century) 40 35
2382 80e. Capital from Amorim Church (horiz) 60 40
2383 100e. Laying Christ's body in tomb (attr Joao de Ruao) (Monastery Church of Santa Cruz de Coimbra) (horiz) 70 50
2384 140e. Carved wood reliquary (Santa Maria Monastery, Alcobaca) (horiz) . . . . 1·00 75
2385 180e. Relief of Writers (Leopoldo de Almeida) (Lisbon National Library) (horiz) . . . . 1·40 80

510 Falconer, Peregrine Falcon and Dog

1994. Falconry. Designs showing a peregrine falcon in various hunting scenes. Multicoloured.
2387 45e. Type **510** 30 15
2388 75e. Falcon chasing duck . . 60 40
2389 100e. Falconer approaching falcon with dead duck . . 70 50
2390 140e. Falcons . . . . 1·00 45

511 "Maria Arminda"

1994. Trawlers (2nd series). Multicoloured.
2392 45e. Type **511** 30 15
2393 75e. "Bom Pastor" 60 30
2394 100e. Aladores trawler with triplex haulers 70 50
2395 140e. "Sueste" . . . . . . 1·00 85

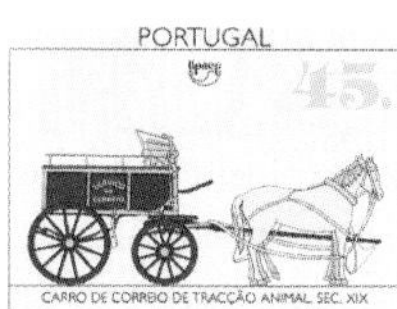

512 19th-century Horse-drawn Wagon

1994. Postal Transport. Multicoloured.
2396 45e. Type **512** 30 15
2397 75e. Travelling Post Office sorting carriage No. C7, 1910 . . . . 60 45
2398 100e. Mercedes mail van, 1910 . . . . 70 45
2399 140e. Volkswagen mail van, 1950 . . . . 1·00 75

513 Multiple Unit Set, Sintra Suburban Railway (½-size illustration)

1994. Modern Electric Locomotives (1st series). Multicoloured.
2401 45e. Type **513** 30 15
2402 75e. Locomotive No. 5611-7 (national network) 55 40
2403 140e. Lisbon Underground train . . . . 1·00 90
See also No. 2465.

514 Medal

1994. 150th Anniv of Montepio Geral Savings Bank (45e.) and World Savings Day (100e.). Mult.
2404 45e. Type **514** 35 15
2405 100e. Coins and bee 70 40

515 St. Philip's Fort, Setubal

1994. Pousadas (hotels) in Historic Buildings. Multicoloured.
2406 45e. Type **515** 30 15
2407 75e. Obidos Castle 60 40
2408 100e. Convent of Loios, Evora 70 40
2409 140e. Santa Marinha Monastery, Guimaraes . . 1·00 85

516 Businessman and Tourist

1994. American Society of Travel Agents World Congress, Lisbon.
2410 **516** 140e. multicoloured . . . 65 65

517 Statuette of Missionary, Mozambique

1994. Evangelization by Portuguese Missionaries. Multicoloured.
2411 45e. Type **517** 30 15
2412 75e. "Child Jesus the Good Shepherd" (carving), India 60 40
2413 100e. Chalice, Macao . . . 70 40
2414 140e. Carving of man in frame, Angola (horiz) . . 1·00 75

518 Africans greeting Portuguese

1994. 550th Anniv of First Portuguese Landing in Senegal.
2415 **518** 140e. multicoloured . . . 65 1·00

521 Great Bustard

1995. European Nature Conservation Year. Multicoloured.
2418 42e. Type **521** 30 15
2419 90e. Osprey 65 50
2420 130e. Schreiber's green lizard 90 60

522 St. John and Sick Man

1995. 500th Birth Anniv of St. John of God (founder of Order of Hospitallers).
2422 **522** 45e. multicoloured . . . 35 15

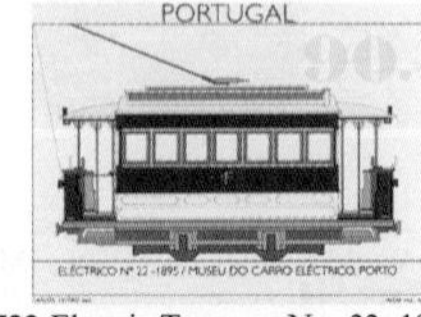

523 Electric Tramcar No. 22, 1895

1995. Centenaries of Trams and Motor Cars in Portugal. Multicoloured.
2423 90e. Type **523** 65 45
2424 130e. Panhard and Levassor motor car 90 60

524 Bread Seller

1995. 19th-century Itinerant Trades. Multicoloured.
2425 1e. Type **524** 10 10
2425a 2e. Laundryman 10 10
2426 3e. Broker 10 10
2427 5e. Broom seller 10 10
2428 10e. Fish seller 10 10
2431 20e. Spinning-wheel and spoon seller 10 10
2432 30e. Olive oil and vinegar seller 20 10
2434 40e. Seller of indulgences 20 25
2435 45e. General street trader 30 15
2436 47e. Hot chestnut seller . . 30 15
2436b 49e. Clothes mender . . . 30 25
2437 50e. Fruit seller 35 15
2437a 50e. Pottery seller 30 25
2438 51e. Knife grinder 30 25
2439 75e. Whitewasher 60 35
2440 78e. Cloth seller 50 30
2440b 80e. Carrier/messenger boy 60 40
2440c 85e. Goose seller 55 45
2440d 86e. Bread seller 50 35
2440e 95e. Coachman 60 65
2441 100e. Mussels seller 65 50
2441a 100e. Milk seller 60 40
2442 210e. Basket seller . . . . 1·40 95
2443 250e. Water seller . . . . 1·70 1·00
2447 250e. Pastry seller . . . . 1·70 1·40

526 Emblem

1995. 50th Anniv of U.N.O. Multicoloured.
2449 75e. Type **526** 50 30
2450 135e. Clouds and emblem 1·00 75

527 Evacuees from Gibraltar arriving at Madeira (½-size illustration)

1995. Europa. Peace and Freedom. Portuguese Neutrality during Second World War. Mult.
2452 95e. Type **527** 65 55
2453 95e. Refugees waiting at Lisbon for transatlantic liner and Aristides de Sousa Mendes (Portuguese Consul in Bordeaux) 65 55

528 "St. Antony holding Child Jesus"(painting)

1995. 800th Birth Anniv of St. Antony of Padua (Franciscan preacher). Multicoloured.
2454 45e. Type **528** 30 15
2455 75e. St. Antony with flowers (vert) 55 40
2456 135e. "St. Antony holding Child Jesus" (statue) . . . 95 75

529 Carpenters with Axes and Women with Water, 1395

1995. 600th Anniv of Fire Service in Portugal. Multicoloured.
2458 45e. Type **529** 30 25
2459 80e. Fire cart and men carrying barrels of water, 1834 . . . . 60 40
2460 95e. Merryweather steam-powered fire engine, 1867 70 50
2461 135e. Zoost fire engine No. 1, 1908 . . . . . . 90 75

530 Coronation

1995. 500th Anniv of Accession of King Manoel I.
2463 **530** 45e. brown, yellow and red 30 25

1995. Modern Electric Locomotives (2nd series). As T **513**.
2465 80e. multicoloured 55 40
DESIGN: 80e. Articulated trams.

1995. Sculptures (3rd series). As T **491**. Multicoloured.
2466 45e. "Warrior" (castle statue) 30 25
2467 75e. Double-headed fountain 55 40
2468 80e. "Truth" (monument to Eca de Queiros by Antonio Teixeira Lopes) 55 40
2469 95e. First World War memorial, Abrantes (Ruy Gameiro) 65 50
2470 135e. "Fernao Lopes" (Martins Correia) 90 65
2471 190e. "Fernando Pessoa" (Lagoa Henriques) . . . 1·30 95

531 "Portugal's Guardian Angel" (sculpture, Diogo Pires)

533 Archangel Gabriel

532 Queiroz

1995. Art of the Period of Discoveries (15th–16th centuries). Multicoloured.
2473 45e. Type **531** 30 25
2474 75e. Reliquary of Queen Leonor (Master Joao) . . 55 40
2475 80e. "Don Manuel" (sculpture, Nicolas Chanterenne) 55 40
2476 95e. "St. Anthony" (painting, Nuno Goncalves) 65 55
2477 135e. "Adoration of the Three Wise Men" (painting, Grao Vasco) . . 90 65
2478 190e. "Christ on the Way to Calvary" (painting, Jorge Afonso) . . . . 1·30 1·10

1995. 150th Birth Anniv of Eca de Queiroz (writer).
2480 **532** 135e. multicoloured . . . 90 60

1995. Christmas. Multicoloured. (a) With country name at foot.
2481 **533** 80e. multicoloured . . . 85 70

(b) With country name omitted.
2483 80e. Type **533** 65 75

534 Airbus Industrie A340/300

1995. 50th Anniv of TAP Air Portugal.
2485 **534** 135e. multicoloured . . . 90 40

535 King Carlos I of Portugal (½-size illustration)

1996. Centenary of Oceanographic Expeditions. Multicoloured.
2486 95e. Type **535** 65 70
2487 135e. Prince Albert I of Monaco 90 35

536 Books

1996. Anniversaries. Multicoloured.
2488 80e. Type **536** (bicentenary of National Library) . . . 55 45
2489 200e. Hand writing with quill pen (700th anniv of adoption of Portuguese as official language) . . . . 1·40 95

537 Joao de Deus (poet and author of reading primer)

1996. Writers' Anniversaries. Multicoloured.
2490 78e. Type **537** (death centenary) 55 45
2491 140e. Joao de Barros (historian, philosopher and grammarian, 500th birth) 95 85

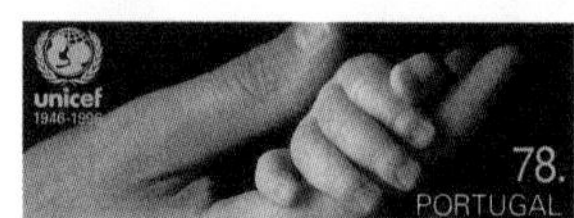

538 Holding Child's Hand (½-size illustration)

1996. 50th Anniv of UNICEF. Multicoloured.
2492 78e. Type **538** 55 60
2493 140e. Children of different races . . . . 95 1·00

539 Helena Vieira da Silva (artist, self-portrait)

1996. Europa. Famous Women.
2494 **539** 98e. multicoloured . . . 70 65

540 Match Scene

1996. European Football Championship, England. Multicoloured.
2496 78e. Type **540** 55 55
2497 140e. Match scene (different) 95 80

541 Caravel and Arms (½-size illustration)

1996. 500th Death Anniv of Joao Vaz Corte-Real (explorer).
2499 **541** 140e. multicoloured . . . 1·00 1·00

542 Wrestling

1996. Olympic Games, Atlanta. Multicoloured.
2501 47e. Type **542** 30 25
2502 78e. Show jumping 55 55
2503 98e. Boxing 70 70
2504 140e. Running 90 90

543 Hilario and Guitar

1996. Death Centenary of Augusto Hilario (fado singer).
2506 **543** 80e. multicoloured . . . 55 40

544 Antonio Silva (actor)

1996. Centenary of Motion Pictures. Multicoloured.
2507 47e. Type **544** 30 25
2508 78e. Vasco Santana (actor) 50 45
2509 80e. Laura Alves (actress) 55 50
2510 98e. Auelio Pais dos Reis (director) 65 65
2511 100e. Leitao de Barros (director) 65 70
2512 140e. Antonio Lopes Ribeiro (director) 95 85

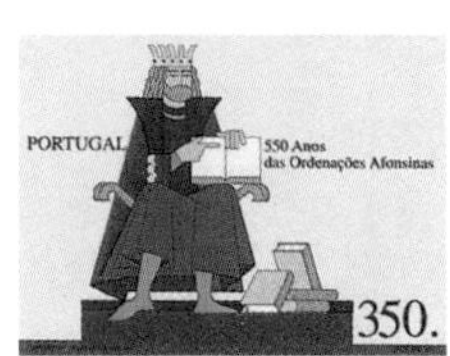

545 King Afonso V

1996. 550th Anniv of Alphonsine Collection of Statutes.
2515 **545** 350e. multicoloured . . . 2·30 1·70

546 Perdigao

1996. Birth Centenary of Jose de Azeredo Perdigao (lawyer and Council of State member).
2516 **546** 47e. multicoloured . . . 35 25

547 Aveiro

1996. District Arms (1st series). Multicoloured.
2517 47e. Type **547** 30 25
2518 78e. Beja 50 55
2519 80e. Braga 55 55
2520 98e. Braganca 65 80
2521 100e. Castelo Branco . . . 65 70
2522 140e. Coimbra . . . . . . 95 1·10
See also Nos. 2579/84 and 2648/53.

548 Henry of Burgundy (governor of Portucale) and his Wife Theresa

1996. 900th Anniv of Foundation of County of Portucale by King Afonso VI of Leon and Castille.
2524 **548** 47e. multicoloured . . . 35 25

549 Rojoes (Pork dish)

1996. Traditional Portuguese Dishes (1st series). Multicoloured.
2525 47e. Type **549** 30 25
2526 78e. Boticas trout 50 55
2527 80e. Oporto tripe 55 50
2528 98e. Baked cod with jacket potatoes 65 80
2529 100e. Aveiro eel 65 85
2530 140e. Peniche lobster . . . 95 1·10
See also Nos. 2569/74.

550 Lisbon Postman, 1821

1996. 175th Anniv of Home Delivery Postal Service. Multicoloured.
2531 47e. Type **550** 30 25
2532 78e. Postman, 1854 . . . . 50 55
2533 98e. Rural postman, 1893 65 60
2534 100e. Postman, 1939 . . . . 65 55
2535 140e. Modern postman, 1992 . . . . 95 95

551 King Manoel I in Shipyard

1996. 500th Anniv (1997) of Discovery of Sea-route to India by Vasco da Gama (1st issue). Multicoloured.
2536 47e. Type **551** 30 25
2537 78e. Departure from Lisbon 50 45
2538 98e. Fleet in Atlantic Ocean 65 55
2539 140e. Sailing around Cape of Good Hope 90 95
See also Nos. 2592/5 and 2665/79.

552 "Banknote"

1996. 150th Anniv of Bank of Portugal.
2541 **552** 78e. multicoloured . . . 45 55

553 East Timorese Couple

1996. Rights of People of East Timor. Award of 1996 Nobel Peace Prize to Don Carlos Ximenes Belo and Jose Ramos Horton.
2542 **553** 140e. multicoloured . . . 90 95

555 Portuguese Galleon

1997. Sailing Ships of the India Shipping Line. Multicoloured.
2544 49e. Type **555** 30 25
2545 80e. "Principe da Beira" (nau) 55 55
2546 100e. Bow view of "Don Fernando II e Gloria" (sail frigate) 65 75
2547 140e. Stern view of "Don Fernando II e Gloria" . . 95 95

556 Youth with Flower

1997. "No to Drugs – Yes to Life" (anti-drugs campaign).
2548 **556** 80e. multicoloured . . . 55 55

557 Arms

1997. Bicent of Managing Institute of Public Credit.
2549 **557** 49e. multicoloured . . . 35 25

558 Desman eating Worm
559 Moorish Girl guarding Hidden Treasure

1997. The Pyrenean Desman. Multicoloured.
2550 49e. Type **558** 65 25
2551 49e. Diving 65 25
2552 49e. With wet fur 65 25
2553 49e. Cleaning snout 65 25

1997. Europa. Tales and Legends.
2554 **559** 100e. multicoloured . . . 70 75

560 Surfing

1997. Adventure Sports. Multicoloured.
2556 49e. Type **560** 30 25
2557 80e. Skateboarding 55 55
2558 100e. In-line skating 65 75
2559 140e. Paragliding 95 95

561 Night Attack on Santarem Fortress
563 Indian Children and Jose de Anchieta

562 Frois with Japanese Man

1997. 850th Anniv of Capture from the Moors of Santarem and Lisbon. Multicoloured.
2561 80e. Type **561** 55 50
2562 80e. Victorious King Afonso riding past Lisbon city walls 55 50

1997. 400th Death Anniv of Father Luis Frois (author of "The History of Japan"). Multicoloured.
2564 80e. Type **562** 50 55
2565 140e. Father Frois and church (vert) 95 85
2566 140e. Father Frois and flowers (vert) 95 85

1997. Death Anniversaries of Missionaries to Brazil. Multicoloured.
2567 140e. Type **563** (400th) . . . 90 65
2568 350e. Antonio Vieira in pulpit (300th) . . . . . . 2·30 2·10

1997. Traditional Portuguese Dishes (2nd series). As T **549**. Multicoloured.
2569 10e. Scalded kid, Beira Baixa 10 10
2570 49e. Fried shad with bread-pap, Ribatejo 30 25
2571 80e. Lamb stew, Alentejo . . 50 55
2572 100e. Rich fish chowder, Algarve 65 45
2573 140e. Black scabbardfish fillets with maize, Madeira 90 85
2574 200e. Stewed octopus, Azores . . . . 1·30 1·30

565 Couple before Clerk
566 Laboratory, Lisbon

1997. 700th Anniv of Mutual Assurance in Portugal.
2576 **565** 100e. multicoloured . . . 65 60

1997. 50th Anniv of National Laboratory of Civil Engineering.
2577 **566** 80e. multicoloured . . . 50 55

567 King Dinis and Arms of Portugal and King Fernando IV and Arms of Castile and Leon

1997. 700th Anniv of Treaty of Alcanices (defining national frontiers).
2578 **567** 80e. multicoloured . . . 50 55

568 Evora

1997. District Arms (2nd series). Multicoloured.
2579 10e. Type **568** 10 10
2580 49e. Faro 30 25
2581 80e. Guarda 50 55
2582 100e. Leiria 65 75
2583 140e. Lisbon 90 85
2584 200e. Portalegre . . . . . . 1·30 1·30

569 Chart by Lopo Homem-Reineis, 1519

1997. Portuguese Charts. Multicoloured.
2586 49e. Type **569** 30 25
2587 80e. Chart by Joao Freire, 1546 . . . . 50 55
2588 100e. Planisphere by Diogo Ribeiro, 1529 . . . . . 65 60
2589 140e. Chart showing Tropic of Capricorn (anon), 1630 90 75

570 Queen Maria I and Mail Coach

1997. Bicentenary of State Postal Service.
2591 **570** 80e. multicoloured . . . 50 55

571 Erecting Landmark Monument, Quelimane

1997. 500th Anniv of Discovery of Portugal–India Sea Route (2nd issue). Multicoloured.
2592 49e. Type **571** 30 25
2593 80e. Arrival of fleet at Mozambique 50 45

2594 100e. Arrival of fleet in Mombasa 65 60
2595 140e. King of Melinde greeting Vasco da Gama 90 85

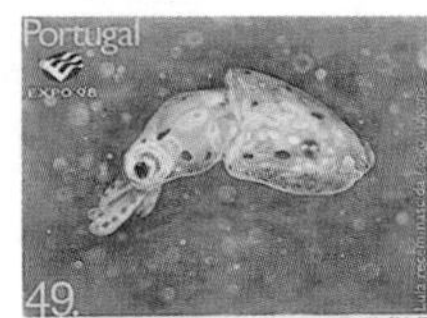

572 Squid

1997. "Expo'98" World Fair, Lisbon. Ocean Life (1st issue). Multicoloured.
2597 49e. Type **572** 30 25
2598 80e. Rock lobster larva . . 50 55
2599 100e. Adult "Pontellina plumata" (crustacean) . . 65 55
2600 140e. Senegal sole (pastlarva) 90 75

See also Nos. 2611/14, 2621/6 and 2630/41.

574 Officer and Plan of Almeida Fortress, 1848

1998. 350th Anniv of Portuguese Military Engineering. Multicoloured.
2603 50e. Type **574** 30 25
2604 80e. Officer and plan of Miranda do Oduro Fortress, 1834 . . . . . 50 55
2605 100e. Officer and plan of Moncao Fortress, 1797 65 75
2606 140e. Officer and plan of Elvas Fortress, 1806 . . . 90 85

575 Ivens and African Scene **576** Adoration of the Madonna (carving)

1998. Death Centenary of Roberto Ivens (explorer).
2607 **575** 140e. multicoloured . . . 90 85

1998. 500th Anniv of Holy Houses Misericordia (religious social relief order).
2608 80e. Type **576** 50 55
2609 100e. Attending patient (tile mural) 65 55

1998. "Expo '98" World's Fair, Lisbon (2nd issue). Ocean Life. As T **572**. Multicoloured.
2611 50e. Crab ("Pilumnus" sp.) larva 30 25
2612 85e. Monkfish ("Lophius piscatonis") larva 55 60
2613 100e. Gilthead sea bream ("Sparus aurata") larva 65 55
2614 140e. Medusa ("Cladonema radiatum") 90 75

578 Vasco da Gama Bridge

1998. Opening of Vasco da Gama Bridge (from Sacavem to Montijo).
2616 **578** 200e. multicoloured . . . 1·30 1·20

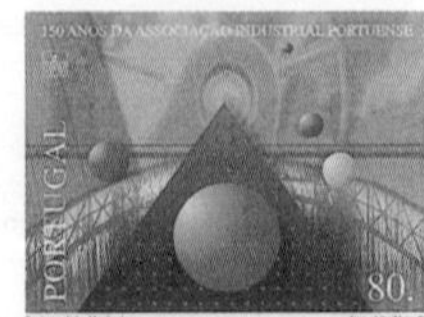

579 Coloured Balls

1998. 150th Anniv of Oporto Industrial Association.
2618 **579** 80e. multicoloured . . . 50 50

580 Seahorse

1998. International Year of the Ocean. Centenary of Vasco da Gama Aquarium. Multicoloured.
2619 50e. Type **580** 30 25
2620 80e. Angelfish and shoal . . 55 60

581 Diver and Astrolabe

1998. "Expo '98" World's Fair, Lisbon (3rd issue).
(a) The Ocean. Multicoloured.
2621 50e. Type **581** 30 25
2622 50e. Caravel 30 25
2623 85e. Fishes and coral reef (inscr "oceanario") . . . 55 60
2624 85e. Underwater exploration equipment observing fishes 55 60
2625 140e. Mermaid and sea anemones 90 65
2626 140e. Children with hands on globe 90 65

(b) As Nos. 2611/14 (but with Latin names removed) and 2621/6. Size 29 × 23 mm. Self-adhesive.
2630 50e. As No. 2612 . . . . . 30 35
2631 50e. Bioluminescent protozoan 30 35
2632 50e. As No. 2611 . . . . . 30 35
2633 50e. As No. 2613 . . . . . 30 35
2634 50e. Dinoflagellate 30 35
2635 50e. As No. 2614 . . . . . 30 35
2636 85e. Type **581** 55 60
2637 85e. As No. 2624 . . . . . 55 60
2638 85e. As No. 2626 . . . . . 55 60
2639 85e. As No. 2622 . . . . . 55 60
2640 85e. As No. 2623 but inscr "Portugal e os Oceanos" 55 60
2641 85e. As No. 2625 . . . . . 55 60

The designers' names and printer's imprints have been removed from Nos. 2630/41.

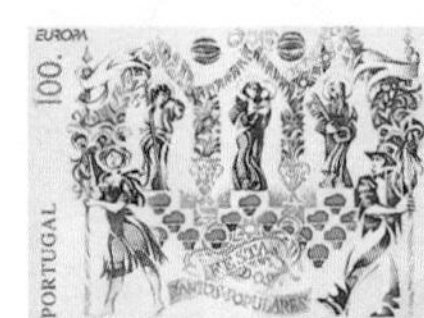

582 Revellers before Statues of St. Antony of Padua, St. John and St. Peter

1998. Europa. National Festivals.
2642 **582** 100e. multicoloured . . . 65 60

583 Marie Curie

1998. Centenary of Discovery of Radium.
2644 **583** 140e. multicoloured . . . 85 80

584 Ferreira de Castro and Illustration to "The Jungle"

1998. Birth Centenary of Jose Ferreira de Castro (writer).
2645 **584** 50e. multicoloured . . . 30 25

585 Untitled Painting

1998. Death Centenary of Bernardo Marques (artist).
2646 **585** 85e. multicoloured . . . 55 55

1998. District Arms (3rd series). As T **568**. Multicoloured.
2648 50e. Vila Real 30 25
2649 85e. Setubal 55 60
2650 85e. Viana do Castelo (150th anniv of elevation to city) 55 60
2651 100e. Santarem 60 60
2652 100e. Viseu 60 60
2653 200e. Oporto . . . . 1·20 85

587 Glass Production

1998. 250th Anniv of Glass Production in Marinha Grande. Multicoloured.
2655 50e. Type **587** 30 25
2656 80e. Heating glass and finished product 55 55
2657 100e. Bottles and factory . . 65 60
2658 140e. Blue bottles and glass-maker . . . . 1·10 80

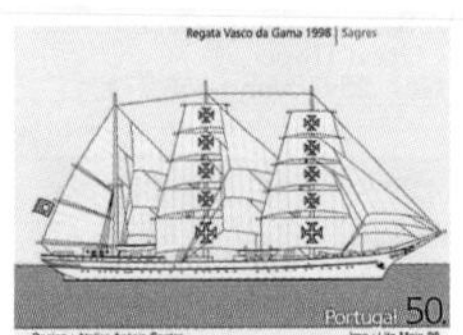

588 "Sagres II" (cadet barque), Portugal

1998. Vasco da Gama Regatta. Multicoloured.
2659 50e. Type **588** 30 25
2660 85e. "Asgard II" (Irish cadet brigantine) 55 20
2661 85e. "Rose" (American replica) 55 55
2662 100e. "Amerigo Vespucci" (Italian cadet ship) . . . 65 60
2663 100e. "Kruzenshtern" (Russian cadet barque) . . 65 60
2664 140e. "Creoula" (Portuguese cadet schooner) 85 40

589 Da Gama with Pilot Ibn Madjid

1998. 500th Anniv (1997) of Discovery of Sea-route to India by Vasco da Gama (3rd issue). Mult.
2665 50e. Type **551** 30 15
2666 50e. As No. 2537 . . . . . 30 15
2667 50e. As No. 2538 . . . . . 30 15
2668 50e. As No. 2539 . . . . . 30 35
2669 50e. Type **571** 30 35
2670 50e. As No. 2593 . . . . . 30 35
2671 50e. As No. 2594 . . . . . 30 35
2672 50e. As No. 2595 . . . . . 30 35
2673 50e. Type **589** 30 35
2674 50e. "Sao Gabriel" (flagship) in storm 30 15
2675 50e. Fleet arriving at Calicut 30 15
2676 50e. Audience with the Samorin of Calicut . . . 30 15
2677 80e. As No. 2674 . . . . . 45 55
2678 100e. As No. 2675 . . . . . 60 60
2679 140e. As No. 2676 . . . . . 90 80

590 Modern Mail Van

1998. Bicentenaries of Inauguration of Lisbon–Coimbra Mail Coach Service and of Re-organization of Maritime Mail Service to Brazil. Mult.
2681 50e. Type **590** 30 25
2682 140e. Mail coach and "Postilhao da America" (brigantine) 85 85

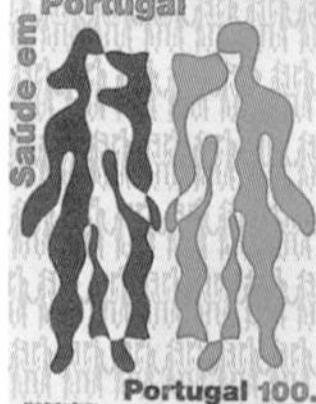

593 Male and Female Figures **595** Knife Grinder

1998. Health Awareness.
2685 **593** 100e. multicoloured . . . 70 60

DENOMINATION. From No. 2687 Portugal stamps are denominated both in escudos and in euros. As no cash for this latter is in circulation, the catalogue continues to use the escudo value.

1999. 19th-Century Itinerant Trades. Multicoloured. Self-adhesive.
2687 51e. Type **595** 30 10
2688 95e. Coachman 60 45

596 Flags of European Union Members and Euro Emblem

1999. Introduction of the Euro (European currency).
2696 **596** 95e. multicoloured . . . 60 60

597 Galleon and Aborigines

1999. "Australia 99" International Stamp Exhibition, Melbourne. The Portuguese in Australia. Multicoloured.
2697 140e. Kangaroos and galleon 85 85
2698 140e. Type **597** 85 85

Nos. 2697/8 were issued together, se-tenant, forming a composite design.

598 Norton de Matos

1999. 50th Anniv of Candidature of General Jose Norton de Matos to Presidency of the Republic.
2700 **598** 80e. multicoloured . . . 50 55

599 Almeida Garrett

1999. Birth Bicentenary of Joao Baptista Almeida Garrett (writer).
2701 **599** 95e. multicoloured . . . 60 60

600 Breguet 16 Bn2 Patria

1999. 25th Anniv of Sarmento de Beires and Brito Pais's Portugal–Macao Flight. Multicoloured.
2703 140e. Type **600** 85 85
2704 140e. De Havilland D.H.9 biplane 85 85

601 Carnation

1999. 25th Anniv of Revolution. Multicoloured.
2706 51e. Type **601** 30 35
2707 80e. National Assembly building (78 × 29 mm) . . 50 50

602 Council Emblem

1999. 50th Anniv of Council of Europe.
2709 **602** 100e. multicoloured . . . 60 55

603 Wolf and Iris (Peneda-Geres National Park)

1999. Europa. Parks and Gardens.
2710 **603** 100e. multicoloured . . . 60 75

604 Marquis de Pombal

1999. 300th Birth Anniv of Marquis de Pombal (statesman and reformer).
2712 **604** 80e. multicoloured . . . 50 50

605 Harbour

1999. "Meeting of Cultures". Return of Macao to China. Multicoloured.
2714 51e. Type **605** 30 25
2715 80e. Dancers 50 50
2716 95e. Procession of the Madonna 60 35
2717 100e. Ruins of St. Paul's Basilica 65 60
2718 140e. Garden with bust of Luis Camoes (horiz) . . . 85 85

606 De Havilland D.H.82A Tiger Moth

1999. 75th Anniv of Military Aeronautics. Multicoloured.
2719 51e. Type **606** 30 35
2720 51e. Supermarine Spitfire V6 fighter 30 35
2721 85e. Breguet Bre XIV A2 . . 55 50
2722 85e. SPAD VII-C1 . . . . 55 50
2723 95e. Caudron G-3 . . . . . 65 60
2724 95e. Junkers Ju 52/3m . . . 65 60

607 Portion by Antonio Pedro

1999. 50th Anniv of Surrealism (modern art movement) in Portugal. Designs showing details by artist named of collective painting "Cadavre Exquis". Multicoloured.
2726 51e. Type **607** 30 25
2727 80e. Vespeira 50 50
2728 95e. Moniz Pereira 60 60
2729 100e. Fernando de Azevedo 60 60
2730 140e. Antonio Domingues 85 85

608 Passenger Train on Bridge

1999. Inauguration of Railway Section of the 25th of April Bridge over River Tagus, Lisbon. Mult.
2732 51e. Type **608** 30 25
2733 95e. Passenger train on bridge (different) 60 60

609 Heinrich von Stephan (founder)

1999. 125th Anniv of Universal Postal Union. Multicoloured.
2735 95e. Type **609** 60 60
2736 140e. Globe, letter and keyboard 85 85

610 Egg Packs

1999. Convent Sweets (1st series). Multicoloured.
2738 51e. Type **610** 30 10
2739 80e. Egg pudding 45 20
2740 95e. Angel's purses 55 60
2741 100e. Abrantes straw . . . 60 25
2742 140e. Viseu chestnuts . . . 85 35
2743 210e. Honey cake . . . . . 1·20 55
See also Nos. 2785/90.

611 Portuguese Troops and Moslem Ships

1999. 750th Anniv of King Afonso III's Conquest of the Algarve.
2744 **611** 100e. multicoloured . . . 60 60

612 Camara Pestana (bacteriologist)

1999. Medical Anniversaries. Multicoloured.
2745 51e. Type **612** (death centenary) 30 25
2746 51e. Ricardo Jorge (founder of National Health Institute, 60th death anniv) 30 25
2747 80e. Francisco Gentil (oncologist, 35th death anniv) 45 50
2748 80e. Egas Moniz (neurosurgeon, 125th birth anniv) 45 50
2749 95e. Joao Cid dos Santos (surgeon, 23rd death anniv) 60 60
2750 95e. Reynaldo dos Santos (arteriography researcher, 30th death anniv (2000)) 60 60

613 Jose Diogo de Mascarenhas Neto (first General Mail Lieutenant)

1999. Bicentenary of the Provisional Mail Rules (re-organization of postal system).
2751 **613** 80e. multicoloured . . . 45 50

614 Barata, Stamps and Mural

1999. Birth Centenary of Jaime Martins Barata (artist and stamp designer).
2752 **614** 80e. multicoloured . . . 45 50

615 Wise Men following Star (Maria Goncalves)

1999. Christmas. National Association of Art and Creativity for and by Handicapped Persons. Designs with artists name in brackets. Multicoloured.
2753 51e. Type **615** 30 25
2754 95e. Father Christmas delivering presents (Marta Silva) 55 60
2755 140e. Father Christmas (Luis Farinha) 80 85
2756 210e. The Nativity (Maria Goncalves) . . . . 1·20 1·30

618 "Madonna and Child" (Alvaro Pires of Evora) Maia, Oporto)

620 Golden Eagle

619 Astronaut and Space Craft

2000. 2000th Birth Anniv of Jesus Christ.
2759 **618** 52e. multicoloured . . . 30 35

2000. The Twentieth Century. Conquest of Space.
2760 **619** 86e. multicoloured . . . 50 50

2000. Birds. (1st series). Multicoloured. (a) Ordinary gum. Size 30 × 27 mm.
2761 52e. Type **620** 30 35
2762 85e. Great crested grebe . . 50 30
2763 90e. Greater flamingo . . . 55 45
2764 100e. Northern gannet . . . 60 40
2765 215e. Green-winged teal . . 1·20 55

(b) Self-adhesive gum. Size 28 × 25 mm.
2766 52e. As No. 2761 . . . . . 25 25
2767 100e. As No. 2764 . . . . 50 65
See also Nos. 2832/9.

622 Members' Flags forming Stars

2000. Portuguese Presidency of European Union Council.
2769 **622** 100e. multicoloured . . . 60 60

623 Native Indians

2000. 500th Anniv of Discovery of Brazil. Multicoloured.
2770 52e. Type **623** 30 35
2771 85e. Native Indians watching Pedro Alvares Cabral's fleet 50 50
2772 100e. Ship's crew and sails 60 65
2773 140e. Native Indians and Portuguese sailors meeting 85 85

624 "Building Europe"

2000. Europa.
2775 **624** 100e. multicoloured . . . 60 60

625 Pope John Paul II and Children

2000. Papal Visit to Portugal. Beatification of Jacinta and Francisco Marto (Children of Fatima).
2777 **625** 52e. multicoloured . . . 30 35

626 Draisienne Bicycle, 1817

2000. "The Stamp Show 2000" International Stamp Exhibition, London. Centenary of International Cycling Union. Bicycles. Mult.
2778 52e. Type **626** 30 35
2779 85e. Michaux, 1868 . . . . 50 50
2780 100e. Ariel, 1871 . . . . . 60 60
2781 140e. Rover, 1888 . . . . . 85 85
2782 215e. BTX, 2000 . . . . . 1·30 1·30
2783 350e. GT, 2000 . . . . . . 2·10 2·10

627 Slices of Tomar

2000. Convent Sweets (2nd series). Multicoloured.
2785 52e. Type **627** 30 35
2786 85e. Rodrigo's present . . . 55 50
2787 100e. Sericaia 70 60
2788 140e. Lo bread 95 85
2789 215e. Grated bread . . . . 85 1·30
2790 350e. Royal paraiso cake . . 2·30 2·10

628 Fishing Boat and Fishes

2000. Fishermen's Day.
2791 **628** 52e. multicoloured . . . 30 35

629 Portuguese Landscapes (½-size illustration)

2000. "EXPO 2000" World's Fair, Hanover, Germany. Humanity–Nature–Technology.
2792 **629** 100e. multicoloured . . . 60 60

630 Statue and Assembly Hall

2000. 25th Anniv of Constituent Assembly.
2794 **630** 85e. multicoloured . . . 50 50

631 Fishermen and Boat

2000. Cod Fishing. Multicoloured.
2795 52e. Type **631** 30 35
2796 85e. Fishing barquentine and fisherman at ship's wheel 45 50
2797 100e. Three fishermen and boat 60 60
2798 100e. Fisherman and dories on fishing schooner . . . 60 60
2799 140e. Fisherman rowing and fishing barquentine . . . 85 85
2800 215e. Fisherman and fishing schooner . . . . 1·20 1·30

632 De Queiroz

2000. Death Centenary of Eca de Queiroz (author).
2802 **632** 85e. multicoloured . . . 50 50

633 Running

2000. Olympic Games, Sydney. Multicoloured.
2803 52e. Type **633** 30 35
2804 85e. Show jumping 50 50
2805 100e. Dinghy racing 60 60
2806 140e. Diving 80 85
Nos. 2803/6 are wrongly inscribed "Sidney".

634 Airplane and Runway

2000. Inauguration of Madeira Airport Second Runway Extension.
2808 **634** 140e. multicoloured . . . 80 35

635 Writing Letter on Computer

2000. 50th Anniv of Snoopy (cartoon character created by Charles Schulz). Postal Service. Mult.
2810 52e. Type **635** 30 35
2811 52e. Posting letter 30 35
2812 85e. Driving post van . . . 50 50
2813 100e. Sorting post 60 60
2814 140e. Delivering post . . . 85 85
2815 215e. Reading letter . . . . 1·20 1·30

636 Drawing, Telescope and Sextant

2000. 125th Anniv of Lisbon Geographic Society. Multicoloured.
2817 85e. Type **636** 50 50
2818 100e. Sextant and drawing 60 60
Nos. 2817/18 were issued together, se-tenant, forming a composite design.

637 Carolina Michaelis de Vasconcellos (teacher)

2001. The Twentieth Century. History and Culture. Multicoloured.
2819 85e. Type **637** 50 55
2820 85e. Miguel Bombarda (doctor and politician) . . 50 55
2821 85e. Bernardino Machado (politician) 50 55
2822 85e. Tomas Alcaide (lyricist) 50 55
2823 85e. Jose Regio (writer) . . 50 55
2824 85e. Jose Rodrigues Migueis (writer) 50 55
2825 85e. Vitorino Nemesio (scholar) 50 55
2826 85e. Bento de Jesus Caraca (scholar) 50 55

638 Athletics

2001. World Indoor Athletics Championship, Lisbon. Multicoloured.
2827 85e. Type **638** 50 50
2828 90e. Pole vault 55 55
2829 105e. Shot put 60 60
2830 250e. High jump . . . . . 1·40 1·50

2001. Birds (2nd series). As T **620**. Multicoloured.
(a) Ordinary gum. Size 27 × 25 mm.
2832 53e. Little bustard 30 35
2833 85e. Purple swamphen . . . 50 50
2834 105e. Collared Pratincole . . 60 25
2835 140e. Black-shouldered kite 80 35
2836 225e. Egyptian vulture . . . 1·30 1·30
(b) Self-adhesive gum. (i) Size 25 × 21 mm.
2837 53e. As No. 2832 . . . . . 35 20
2838 105e. As No. 2834 . . . . 65 35
(ii) Size 48 × 22 mm.
2839 85e. Purple swamphen . . . 50 50
No. 2839 is inscribed "CorreioAzul".

639 Decorated Dish

2001. Arab Artefacts. Multicoloured.
2840 53e. Type **639** 30 30
2841 90e. Painted tile 55 50
2842 105e. Carved stone tablet and fortress 60 60
2843 140e. Coin 80 85
2844 225e. Carved container . . . 1·30 1·30
2845 350e. Jug . . . . 2·10 2·10

640 Coastal Environment (Angela M. Lopes)

2001. "Stampin' the Future". Winning Entries in Children's International Painting Competition. Multicoloured.
2846 85e. Type **640** 50 50
2847 90e. Earth, Sun and watering can (Maria G. Silva) (vert) 55 50
2848 105e. Marine life (Joao A. Ferreira) 60 60

641 Statue, Building Facade and Stained Glass Window

2001. Centenary of National Fine Arts Society. Multicoloured.
2849 85e. Type **641** 50 55
2850 105e. Painting and woman holding palette and brush 60 55

642 Congress in Session

2001. 25th Anniv of Portuguese Republic Constitution.
2852 **642** 85e. multicoloured . . . 50 50

643 Fishes

2001. Europa. Water Resources.
2853 **643** 105e. multicoloured . . . 60 65

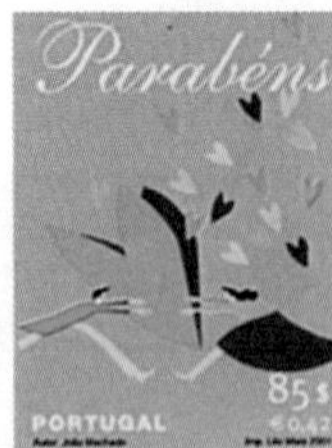

644 Couple and Heart

2001. Greetings Stamps. Multicoloured.
2855 85e. Type **644** 50 50
2856 85e. Birthday cake 50 50
2857 85e. Glasses 50 50
2858 85e. Bunch of flowers . . . 50 50

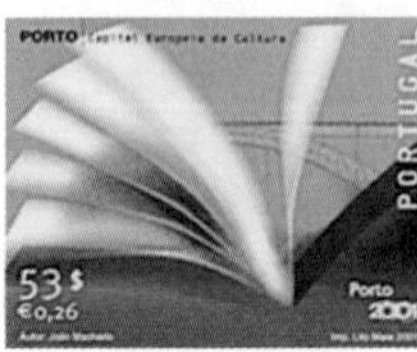

645 Open Book

2001. Porto, European City of Culture. Multicoloured.
2860 53e. Type **645** 30 35
2861 85e. Bridge and Globe . . . 50 50
2862 105e. Grand piano 60 60
2863 140e. Stage curtain 80 85
2864 225e. Picture frame . . . . 1·30 1·20
2865 350e. Firework display . . . 2·00 2·10

646 Campaign Cannon, 1773

2001. 150th Anniv of Military Museum, Lisbon. Multicoloured.
2867 85e. Type **646** 50 50
2868 105e. 16th-century armour 60 60

647 Brown Bear

2001. Lisbon Zoo. Multicoloured.
2870 53e. Type **647** 30 35
2871 85e. Emperor tamarin . . . 50 50
2872 90e. Green iguana 55 50
2873 105e. Humboldt penguin . . 60 60
2874 225e. Toco toucan . . . . . 1·30 1·30
2875 350e. Giraffe . . . . 2·00 2·10

648 Emblem

2001. 47th Lion's European Forum, Oporto.
2877 **648** 85e. multicoloured . . . 45 50

649 Azinhoso Pillory

2001. Pillories. Multicoloured.
2878 53e. Type **649** 30 40
2879 53e. Soajo 30 40
2880 53e. Braganca 30 40
2881 53e. Linhares 30 40
2882 53e. Arcos de Valdevez . . 30 40
2883 53e. Vila de Rua 30 40
2884 53e. Sernancelhe 30 40
2885 53e. Frechas 30 40

650 Faces

2001. United Nations Year of Dialogue among Civilizations.
2886 **650** 140e. multicoloured . . . 80 85

651 Disney

2001. Birth Centenary of Walt Disney (artist and film producer).
2887 **651** 53e. multicoloured . . . 30 40

652 Royal Police Guard, 1801

2001. Bicentenary of National Guard. Multicoloured.
2889 53e. Type **652** 30 35
2890 85e. Lisbon Municipal Guard bandsman, 1834 45 20

2891 90e. Infantry helmet, 1911 and modern guardsman . . . 50 50
2892 105e. Mounted division helmet of 1911 and modern guardsmen . . . 60 60
2893 140e. Guardsmen with motorcycle and car . . . 80 85
2894 350e. Customs and Excise officer and boat . . . . . 1·90 2·10

653 Chinese Junk

2001. Ships. Multicoloured.
2896 53e. Type **653** 30 40
2897 53e. Portuguese caravel . . 30 40

654 1c. Coin

2002. New Currency. Multicoloured.
2898 1c. Type **654** 10 10
2899 2c. 2c. coin 10 10
2900 5c. 5c. coin 10 10
2901 10c. 10c. coin 15 10
2902 20c. 20c. coin 30 15
2903 50c. 50c. coin 70 35
2904 €1 €1 coin . . . . 1·40 70
2905 €2 €2 coin . . . . 2·75 1·40

655 Horse-rider

2002. No value expressed.
2906 **655** A (28c.) multicoloured 40 20
No. 2906 was sold at the current first class inland letter rate.

657 European Bee-eater

2002. Birds. Multicoloured. (i) Ordinary gum. Size 30 × 26 mm.
2914 2c. Type **657** 10 10
2915 28c. Little tern 40 20
2916 43c. Eagle owl 60 30
2917 54c. Pin-tailed sandgrouse 74 40
2918 60c. Red-necked nightjar . . 85 40
2919 70c. Greater spotted cuckoo 1·00 50
(ii) Self-adhesive gum. Size 49 × 23 mm.
2920 43c. Little tern (different) . . 60 30
(iii) Self-adhesive gum. Size 29 × 24 mm.
2921 28c. As No. 2919 . . . . . 40 20
2922 54c. As No. 2916 . . . . . 75 40
(iiii) Self-adhesive gum. Size 27 × 23 mm.
2923 28c. As No. 2919 . . . . . 40 20
2924 54c. As No. 2916 . . . . . 75 40

658 De Gois

2002. 500th Birth Anniv of Damiao de Gois (writer).
2925 **658** 45c. multicoloured . . . 60 30

659 Loxodromic Curve, Ship and Globe

2002. 500th Birth Anniv of Pedro Nunes (mathematician). Multicoloured.
2926 28c. Type **659** 40 20
2927 28c. Nonius (navigational instrument) 40 20
2928 €1.15 Portrait of Nunes . . 1·60 80
MS2929 140 × 105 mm Nos. 2926/8 2·40 2·40

660 Children and Flower

2002. America. Youth, Education and Literacy. Multicoloured.
2930 70c. Type **660** . . . . . . 1·00 50
2931 70c. Children, book and letters . . . . 1·00 50
2932 70c. Children and pencil . . 1·00 50

661 Refracting Telescope and Polytechnic School Observatory, Lisbon

2002. Astronomy. Multicoloured.
2933 28c. Type **661** 40 20
2934 28c. 16th-century astrolabe and Colegio dos Nobres, Lisbon 40 20
2935 43c. Quadrant and Solar Observatory, Coimbra . . 60 30
2936 45c. Terrestrial telescope and King Pedro V 60 30
2937 45c. Cassegrain telescope and King Luis 60 30
2938 54c. Earth, refracting telescope and Observatory, Ajuda . . . 75 40
2939 €1.15 Cassegrain telescope and Saturn . . . . 1·60 80
2940 €1.75 Zeiss projector and planets . . . . 2·40 1·20
MS2941 140 × 111 mm. 70c. 18th-century armillary sphere; 70c. 19th-century theodolite . . . . 2·00 2·00

662 Square and Compass

2002. Bicentenary of Grande Oriente Lusitano (Masonic Grand Lodge).
2942 **662** 43c. multicoloured . . . 60 30

663 Clown

2002. Europa. Circus.
2943 **663** 54c. multicoloured . . . 75 40
MS2944 140 × 110 mm No. 2943 × 3 2·30 2·30

664 *Scabiosa nitens*

2002. Flowers of Azores. Multicoloured.
2945 28c. Type **664** 40 20
2946 45c. *Viburnum tinus subcordatum* 60 30
2947 54c. *Euphorbia azorica* . . . 75 40
2948 70c. *Lysimachia nemorum azorica* . . . . 1·00 50
2949 €1.15 *Bellis azorica* . . . . 1·60 80
2950 €1.75 *Spergularia azorica* 2·40 1·20
MS2951 120 × 121 mm €1.15 *Azorina vidalii*; €1.75 *Senecio malvifolius* . . . . 4·00 4·00

665 General Dynamics F-16 Fighting Falcon

2002. 50th Anniv of Portuguese Air Force. Multicoloured.
2952 28c. Type **665** 40 20
2953 43c. Sud Aviation SA 300 Puma helicopter 60 30
2954 54c. Dassault Dornier Alpha Jet A 75 40
2955 70c. Lockheed C-130 Hercules transport aircraft 1·40 70
2956 €1.25 Lockheed P-3P Orion reconnaissance aircraft . . 1·70 85
2957 €1.75 Fiat G-91 fighter aircraft . . . . 2·40 1·20
MS2958 140 × 112 mm €1.15 Four airplanes; €1.75 Aerospatiale Epsilon TB 30 . . . . 4·00 4·00

666 Gymnastics

2002. Sports and Sports Anniversaries. Multicoloured.
2959 28c. Type **666** (50th anniv of Portuguese Gymnastic Federation) 40 20
2960 28c. Walking race 40 20
2961 45c. Basketball 60 30
2962 45c. Handball 60 30
2963 54c. Roller hockey (sixth Women's World Roller Hockey Championship, Pacos de Ferriera) 75 40
2964 54c. Fencing (World Fencing Championship, Lisbon) 75 40
2965 €1.75 Footballers (World Cup Football Championship, Japan and South Korea) . . . . . . 2·40 1·20
2966 €1.75 Golf . . . . 2·40 1·20
MS2967 140 × 110 mm. €1 Footballer and part of football; €2 Torsos and legs of two players 4·25 4·25
Nos. **MS**2967 was inscribed for "PHILAKOREA 2002" International Stamp Exhibition, Seoul, in the margin.

CHARITY TAX STAMPS

Used on certain days of the year as an additional postal tax on internal letters. Other values in some of the types were for use on telegrams only. The proceeds were devoted to public charities. If one was not affixed in addition to the ordinary postage, postage due stamps were used to collect the deficiency and the fine.

1911. Optd **ASSISTENCIA**.
C455 **48** 10r. green (No. 406) . . . 7·00 1·80
C484 **56** 1c. green (No. 486) . . . 4·75 1·50

C 57 "Lisbon" **C 58** "Charity"

1913. Lisbon Festival.
C485 **C 57** 1c. green 80 65

1915. For the Poor.
C486 **C 58** 1c. red 25 20
C669 15c. red 40 35

1924. Surch **15 ctvs**.
C594 **C 58** 15c. on 1c. red 80 45

C 71 Muse of History **C 81** Hurdler

C 73 Monument to De Pombal **C 75** Marquis de Pombal

1925. Portuguese Army in Flanders, 1484 and 1918.
C662 **C 71** 10c. red 65 65
C663 10c. green . . . . . . 95 1·00
C664 10c. blue . . . . . . 95 1·00
C665 10c. brown 95 85

1925. Marquis de Pombal Commemoration.
C666 **C 73** 15c. blue and black . . 35 45
C667 – 15c. blue and black . . 85 60
C668 **C 75** 15c. blue and black . . 85 40
DESIGN: No. C677, Planning reconstruction of Lisbon.

1928. Olympic Games.
C741 **C 81** 15c. black and red . . 4·75 4·75

NEWSPAPER STAMPS

N 16 **N 17**

1876.
N180 **N 16** 2r. black . . . . . . 17·00 7·75
N178 **N 17** 2½r. green . . . . . . 11·00 85
N187 2½r. brown . . . . . 11·00 85

OFFICIAL STAMPS

1938. Optd **OFICIAL**.
O900 **99** 40c. brown 40 10

O 144

1952. No value.
O1069 **O 144** (1e.) black and stone 30 10
O1070 (1e.) black and stone 45 25
On No. O1069 "CORREIO DE PORTUGAL" is in stone on a black background, on No. O1070 it is in black on the stone background.

PARCEL POST STAMPS

P 59

1920.
P578 **P 59** 1c. brown 25 30
P579 2c. orange 25 20
P580 5c. brown 25 15
P581 10c. brown 25 30
P582 20c. blue 20 20
P583 40c. red 25 30
P584 50c. black 40 40
P585 60c. blue 40 45
P586 70c. brown . . . . . . 3·00 1·40
P587 80c. blue . . . . . . 3·00 2·20
P588 90c. violet . . . . . . 3·00 1·60
P589 1e. green . . . . . . 3·25 1·80
P591 2e. lilac . . . . . . 8·75 3·25
P592 3e. green . . . . . . 15·00 4·00
P593 4e. blue . . . . . . 34·00 5·25
P594 5e. lilac . . . . . . 43·00 4·75
P595 10e. brown . . . . . . 60·00 6·00

P 101

1936.
P891 **P 101** 50c. grey 55 50
P892 1e. brown 55 45
P893 1e.50 violet 55 45
P894 2e. purple . . . . . . 2·20 55
P895 2e.50 green . . . . . 1·90 45
P896 4e.50 purple . . . . . 4·25 55
P897 5e. violet . . . . . . 6·25 65
P898 10e. orange . . . . . 9·75 1·30

POSTAGE DUE STAMPS

D 48 Da Gama received by the Zamorin of Calicut **D 49**

1898.
D386 **D 48** 5r. black . . . . . . 1·90 1·10
D387 10r. mauve . . . . . 3·00 1·60
D388 20r. orange . . . . . 5·00 1·70
D389 50r. grey . . . . . . 40·00 7·00
D390 100r. red on pink . . 65·00 28·00
D391 200r. brown on buff 70·00 41·00

1904.

No.	Description	Mint	Used
D392 D 49	5r. brown	35	40
D393	10r. orange	2·10	65
D394	20r. mauve	6·50	3·00
D395	30r. green	4·25	2·20
D396	40r. lilac	5·50	1·90
D397	50r. red	40·00	3·75
D398	100r. blue	6·50	5·25

1911. Optd **REPUBLICA**.

No.	Description	Mint	Used
D418 D 49	5r. brown	30	30
D419	10r. orange	30	30
D420	20r. mauve	1·10	1·00
D421	30r. green	1·00	30
D422	40r. lilac	1·10	30
D423	50r. red	4·50	4·25
D424	100r. blue	5·00	3·00

1915. As Type **D 49** but value in centavos.

No.	Description	Mint	Used
D491 D 49	½c. brown	55	40
D498	1c. orange	55	40
D493	2c. purple	55	60
D499	3c. green	55	40
D500	4c. lilac	55	40
D501	5c. red	55	40
D497	10c. blue	70	60

1921.

No.	Description	Mint	Used
D578 D 49	½c. green	30	40
D579	4c. green	30	40
D580	8c. green	30	40
D581	10c. green	30	40
D582	12c. green	40	30
D583	16c. green	40	45
D584	20c. green	40	50
D585	24c. green	40	30
D586	32c. green	40	55
D587	36c. green	1·00	1·00
D588	40c. green	1·00	1·00
D589	48c. green	55	55
D590	50c. green	55	70
D591	60c. green	55	55
D592	72c. green	55	55
D593	80c. green	5·75	5·75
D594	1e.20 green	2·40	2·30

D 72 D 82

1925. Portuguese Army in Flanders, 1484 and 1918.

No.	Description	Mint	Used
D662 D 72	20c. brown	40	30

1925. De Pombal types optd **MULTA**.

No.	Description	Mint	Used
D663 C 73	30c. blue	90	75
D664 –	30c. blue	90	75
D665 C 75	30c. blue	90	75

1928. Olympic Games.

No.	Description	Mint	Used
D741 D 82	30e. black and red	1·40	1·00

D 91 D 108 D 218

1932.

No.	Description	Mint	Used
D865 D 91	5e. buff	45	40
D866	10e. blue	45	40
D867	20e. pink	1·00	75
D868	30e. blue	1·00	65
D869	40e. green	1·20	75
D870	50e. grey	1·30	75
D871	60e. pink	3·50	1·20
D872	80e. purple	6·25	3·00
D873	1e.20 green	8·50	8·50

1940.

No.	Description	Mint	Used
D912 D 108	5c. brown	40	30
D923	10c. lilac	20	10
D924	20c. red	20	10
D925	30c. violet	20	10
D926	40c. mauve	20	20
D927	50c. blue	20	10
D928	60c. green	20	10
D929	80c. red	20	10
D930	1e. brown	20	20
D931	2e. mauve	45	40
D922	5e. orange	8·75	6·25

1967.

No.	Description	Mint	Used
D1312 D 218	10c. brown, yellow and orange	10	10
D1313	20e. purple, yellow and brown	10	10
D1314	30e. brown, light yellow and yellow	10	10
D1315	40e. purple, yellow and bistre	10	10
D1316	50e. indigo, blue and light blue	10	10
D1317	60e. olive, blue and turquoise	10	10
D1318	80e. indigo, blue and light blue	10	10
D1319	1e. indigo, bl & ultram	10	10
D1320	2e. olive, light green and green	10	10
D1321	3e. deep green, light green and green	20	10
D1322	4e. deep green, green and turquoise	20	10
D1323	5e. brown, mauve and purple	20	10
D1324	9e. deep lilac, lilac and violet	20	10
D1325	10e. deep purple, grey and purple	20	15
D1326	20e. maroon, grey and purple	55	30
D1327	40e. lilac, grey and mauve	1·20	30
D1328	50e. maroon, grey and purple	1·30	65

D 481

1992. Inscr "CORREIOS DE PORTUGAL".

No.	Description	Mint	Used
D2305 D 481	1e. blue, deep blue and black	10	10
D2306	2e. light green, green and black	10	10
D2307	5e. yellow, brown and black	10	10
D2308	10e. red, orange and black	10	10
D2309	20e. green, violet and black	20	15
D2310	50e. yellow, green and black	45	35
D2311	100e. orange, red and black	55	70
D2312	200e. mauve, violet and black	50	1·50

1995. Inscr "CTT CORREIOS".

No.	Description	Mint	Used
D2445 D 481	3e. multicoloured	10	10
D2446	4e. multicoloured	10	10
D2446a	5e. multicoloured	10	10
D2447	9e. multicoloured	10	10
D2447a	10e. red, orange and black	10	10
D2447b	20e. multicoloured	15	15
D2448	40e. multicoloured	30	35
D2449	50e. multicoloured	45	35
D2450	100e. orange, red and black	70	70

D 656 "0.01"

2002. Multicoloured.

No.	Description	Mint	Used
D2907	1c. Type D 656	10	10
D2908	2c. "0.02"	10	10
D2909	5c. "0.05"	10	10
D2910	10c. "0.10"	15	10
D2911	25c. "0.25"	35	15
D2912	50c. "0.50"	70	35
D2913	€1 "1"	1·40	70

PORTUGUESE COLONIES Pt. 9

General issues for the Portuguese possessions in Africa: Angola, Cape Verde Islands, Guinea, Lourenco Marques, Mozambique, Congo, St. Thomas and Prince Islands, and Zambezia.

1898. 1000 reis = 1 milreis.
1919. 100 centavos = 1 escudo.

1898. 400th Anniv of Vasco da Gama's Discovery of Route to India. As Nos. 378/85 of Portugal but inscr "AFRICA".

No.	Description	Mint	Used
1	2½r. green	40	30
2	5r. red	40	30
3	10r. purple	30	20
4	25r. green	30	20
5	50r. blue	40	40
6	75r. brown	2·10	2·00
7	100r. brown	2·10	1·50
8	150r. brown	2·75	1·50

CHARITY TAX STAMPS

C 1

1919. Fiscal stamps optd **TAXA DE GUERRA**.

No.	Description	Mint	Used
C1 C 1	1c. black and green	30	30
C2	5c. black and green	30	30

POSTAGE DUE STAMPS

D 1

1945. Value in black.

No.	Description	Mint	Used
D1 D 1	10c. purple	10	10
D2	20c. purple	10	10
D3	30c. blue	10	10
D4	40c. brown	15	15
D5	50c. lilac	15	15
D6	1e. brown	40	40
D7	2e. green	85	85
D8	3e. red	1·50	1·50
D9	5e. yellow	2·10	2·10

PORTUGUESE CONGO Pt. 9

The area known as Portuguese Congo, now called Cabinda, was the part of Angola north of the River Congo. It issued its own stamps from 1894 until 1920

1894. 1000 reis = 1 milreis.
1913. 100 centavos = 1 escudo.

1894. "Figures" key-type inscr " CONGO".

No.	Description	Mint	Used
8 R	5r. orange	35	30
9	10r. mauve	1·00	35
10	15r. brown	1·60	1·25
12	20r. lilac	1·60	1·25
13	25r. green	40	40
22	50r. blue	1·60	1·00
5	75r. pink	2·50	2·40
6	80r. green	4·00	3·75
7	100r. brown on yellow	2·25	1·90
17	150r. red on pink	4·00	3·75
18	200r. blue on blue	4·00	3·75
19	300r. blue on brown	5·00	4·50

1898. "King Carlos" key-type inscr "CONGO".

No.	Description	Mint	Used
24 S	2½r. grey	15	10
25	5r. red	15	10
26	10r. green	25	20
27	15r. brown	75	60
66	15r. green	45	30
28	20r. lilac	55	40
29	25r. green	95	60
67	25r. red	45	25
30	50r. blue	1·00	85
68	50r. brown	1·00	65
69	65r. blue	2·75	2·50
31	75r. pink	1·60	1·50
70	75r. purple	1·10	1·00
32	80r. mauve	1·60	1·50
33	100r. blue on blue	1·25	1·00
71	115r. brown on pink	2·75	2·25
72	130r. brown on yellow	3·25	3·25
34	150r. brown on yellow	1·90	1·60
35	200r. purple on pink	2·10	2·00
36	300r. blue on pink	2·00	1·60
73	400r. blue on cream	3·00	2·75
37	500r. black on blue	5·75	4·00
38	700r. mauve on yellow	9·50	6·25

1902. Surch.

No.	Description	Mint	Used
74 S	50r. on 65r. blue	1·50	1·00
40 R	65r. on 15r. brown	1·50	1·10
41	65r. on 20r. lilac	1·50	1·10
44	65r. on 25r. green	1·25	1·00
46	65r. on 300r. blue on brn	1·60	1·60
50 V	115r. on 2½r. brown	1·25	1·00
47 R	115r. on 10r. mauve	1·25	1·00
48	115r. on 50r. blue	1·50	1·00
53	130r. on 5r. orange	1·25	1·00
54	130r. on 75r. pink	1·50	1·10
57	130r. on 100r. brn on yell	1·50	1·10
58	400r. on 80r. green	60	50
60	400r. on 150r. red on pink	60	40
61	400r. on 200r. blue on blue	60	40

1902. "King Carlos" key-type of Portuguese Congo optd **PROVISORIO**.

No.	Description	Mint	Used
62 S	15r. brown	75	15
63	25r. green	75	15
64	50r. blue	75	15
65	75r. pink	1·75	1·25

1911. "King Carlos" key-type of Angola, optd **REPUBLICA** and **CONGO** with bar (200r. also surch).

No.	Description	Mint	Used
75 S	2½r. grey	50	40
76	5r. red	75	55
77	10r. green	75	55
78	15r. green	75	55
79	25r. on 200r. purple on pink	1·10	90

1911. "King Carlos" key-type of Portuguese Congo optd **REPUBLICA**.

No.	Description	Mint	Used
80 S	2½r. grey	10	10
81	5r. orange	15	10
82	10r. green	15	10
83	15r. green	15	10
84	20r. lilac	15	15
85	25r. red	15	15
86	50r. brown	15	15
87	75r. purple	30	25
88	100r. blue on blue	30	25
89	115r. brown on pink	50	40
90	130r. brown on yellow	50	40
143	200r. purple on pink	65	55
92	400r. blue on cream	80	75
93	500r. black on blue	1·10	80
94	700r. mauve on yellow	1·10	80

1913. Surch **REPUBLICA CONGO** and value on "Vasco da Gama" stamps of (a) Portuguese Colonies.

No.	Description	Mint	Used
95	¼c. on 2½r. green	50	45
96	½c. on 5r. red	50	45
97	1c. on 10r. purple	35	35
98	2½c. on 25r. green	35	35
99	5c. on 50r. blue	50	45
100	7½c. on 75r. brown	80	65
101	10c. on 100r. brown	50	45
102	15c. on 150r. brown	50	45
	(b) Macao.		
103	¼c. on ½a. green	60	50
104	½c. on 1a. red	60	50
105	1c. on 2a. purple	50	45
106	2½c. on 4a. green	50	45
107	5c. on 8a. blue	60	50
108	7½c. on 12a. brown	90	80
109	10c. on 16a. brown	85	65
110	15c. on 24a. brown	75	50
	(c) Portuguese Timor.		
111	¼c. on ½a. green	70	60
112	½c. on 1a. red	70	60
113	1c. on 2a. purple	55	50
114	2½c. on 4a. green	55	50
115	5c. on 8a. blue	70	60
116	7½c. on 12a. brown	1·00	65
117	10c. on 16a. brown	90	60
118	15c. on 24a. brown	75	50

1914. "Ceres" key-type inscr "CONGO".

No.	Description	Mint	Used
135 U	¼c. green	20	15
120	½c. black	25	15
121	1c. green	80	55
122	1½c. brown	55	30
136	2c. red	20	15
124	2½c. violet	15	15
125	5c. blue	25	25
126	7½c. brown	40	35
127	8c. grey	50	40
128	10c. red	50	40
129	15c. purple	55	40
130	20c. green	55	50
131	30c. brown on green	1·00	75
132	40c. brown on pink	1·00	75
133	50c. orange on orange	1·10	75
134	1c. green on blue	1·60	1·00

1914. "King Carlos" key-type of Portuguese Congo optd **PROVISORIO** and **REPUBLICA**.

No.	Description	Mint	Used
146 S	15r. brown (No. 62)	20	20
147	50r. blue (No. 64)	20	20
140	75r. pink (No. 65)	65	45

1914. Provisional stamps of 1902 optd **REPUBLICA**.

No.	Description	Mint	Used
148 S	50r. on 65r. blue	20	20
150 V	115r. on 2½r. brown	30	10
151 R	115r. on 10r. mauve	20	15
154	115r. on 50r. blue	50	10
156	130r. on 5r. orange	50	10
157	130r. on 75r. pink	50	30
160	130r. on 100r. brown on yellow	30	20

NEWSPAPER STAMP

1894. "Newspaper" key-type inscr "CONGO".

No.	Description	Mint	Used
N24 V	2½r. brown	35	30

PORTUGUESE GUINEA Pt. 9

A former Portuguese territory, on the west coast of Africa, with adjacent islands. Used stamps of Cape Verde Islands from 1877 until 1881. In September 1974 the territory became independent and was renamed Guinea-Bissau.

1881. 1000 reis = 1 milreis.
1913. 100 centavos = 1 escudo.

1881. "Crown" key-type inscr "CABO VERDE" and optd **GUINE**.

No.	Description	Mint	Used
19 P	5r. black	1·40	1·25
20	10r. yellow	45·00	38·00
31	10r. green	2·50	1·60
21	20r. bistre	1·25	80
32	20r. red	2·50	1·60
13	25r. pink	80	60
28	25r. lilac	1·25	75
23	40r. blue	42·00	32·00
29	40r. yellow	75	65
24	50r. green	50·00	32·00
30	50r. blue	1·90	85
16	100r. lilac	2·25	1·90
17	200r. orange	3·75	3·00
18	300r. brown	5·00	3·75

3

24 Ceres

1886.

No.	Description	Mint	Used
35 3	5r. black	1·50	85
36	10r. green	2·00	1·40
37	20r. red	3·00	1·90
38	25r. purple	3·00	2·10
46	40r. brown	2·00	1·90
40	50r. blue	5·00	1·75
47	80r. grey	4·25	3·25
48	100r. brown	4·25	3·25

43 200r. lilac . . . . 11·00 7·00
44 300r. orange . . . . 12·50 10·00

1893. "Figures" key-type inscr "GUINE".
50 R 5r. yellow 60 50
51 10r. mauve 60 55
52 15r. brown 75 60
53 20r. lilac 75 60
54 25r. green 75 60
55 50r. blue . . . . 1·40 85
57 75r. pink . . . . 3·75 3·00
58 80r. green . . . . 3·75 3·00
59 100r. brown on buff . . . . 3·75 3·00
60 150r. red on pink . . . . 4·75 4·00
61 200r. blue on blue . . . . 4·75 4·00
62 300r. blue on brown . . . 6·00 4·50

1898. "King Carlos" key-type inscr "GUINE".
65 S 2½r. grey 15 15
66 5r. red 20 15
67 10r. green 20 15
68 15r. brown . . . . 1·10 90
114 15r. green 60 40
69 20r. lilac 50 30
70 25r. green 80 40
115 25r. red 35 25
71 50r. blue . . . . 1·10 50
116 50r. brown 60 50
117 65r. blue . . . . 2·50 2·10
72 75r. pink . . . . 5·00 2·75
118 75r. purple . . . . 1·00 75
73 80r. mauve . . . . 1·50 90
74 100r. blue on blue . . . . 1·00 50
119 115r. brown on pink . . . 2·50 1·90
120 130r. brown on yellow . . . 2·50 1·90
75 150r. brown on yellow . . . 3·00 1·50
76 200r. purple on pink . . . 3·00 1·50
77 300r. blue on pink . . . 2·50 1·50
121 400r. blue on yellow . . . 2·50 1·90
78 500r. black on blue . . . 4·25 2·50
79 700r. mauve on yellow . . . 6·50 4·25

1902. Surch.
122 S 50r. on 65r. blue . . . . . 1·40 1·10
81 3 65r. on 10r. green . . . . 2·25 1·50
84 R 65r. on 10r. mauve . . . . 1·90 1·25
85 65r. on 15r. brown . . . . 1·90 1·25
82 3 65r. on 20r. red . . . . 2·25 1·50
86 R 65r. on 20r. lilac . . . . 1·90 1·25
83 3 65r. on 25r. purple . . . . 2·25 1·50
88 R 65r. on 50r. blue . . . . 1·00 85
97 V 115r. on 2½r. brown . . . 1·90 1·25
93 R 115r. on 5r. yellow . . . . 1·60 1·10
95 115r. on 25r. green . . . . 1·90 1·10
89 3 115r. on 40r. brown . . . . 1·90 1·25
91 115r. on 50r. blue . . . . 1·90 1·25
92 115r. on 300r. orange . . . 2·50 1·90
98 130r. on 80r. grey . . . . 2·50 2·00
100 130r. on 100r. brown . . . 2·75 2·00
102 R 130r. on 150r. red on pink . . 2·00 1·10
103 130r. on 200r. blue on blue . 2·25 1·40
104 130r. on 300r. blue on brn . 2·25 1·40
105 3 400r. on 5r. black . . . . 9·00 6·75
107 R 400r. on 75r. pink . . . . 1·25 1·10
108 400r. on 80r. green 85 70
109 400r. on 100r. brn on buff . 85 70
106 3 400r. on 200r. lilac . . . . 4·25 2·75

1902. "King Carlos" key-type of Portuguese Guinea optd **PROVISORIO**.
110 S 15r. brown 85 55
111 25r. green 85 55
112 50r. blue . . . . 1·00 75
113 75r. pink . . . . 1·60 1·40

1911. "King Carlos" key-type of Portuguese Guinea optd **REPUBLICA**.
123 S 2½r. grey 25 15
124 5r. red 25 15
125 10r. green 25 15
126 15r. green 25 15
127 20r. lilac 25 15
128 25r. red 25 15
129 50r. brown 25 15
130 75r. purple 25 15
131 100r. blue on blue 45 25
132 115r. brown on pink . . . 45 25
133 130r. brown on yellow . . . 45 25
134 200r. purple on pink . . . 2·50 1·25
135 400r. blue on yellow . . . 75 45
136 500r. black on blue . . . 75 45
137 700r. mauve on yellow . . . 1·25 70

1913. Surch **REPUBLICA GUINE** and value on "Vasco da Gama" stamps. (a) Portuguese Colonies.
138 ¼c. on 2½r. green 70 70
139 ½c. on 5r. red 70 70
140 1c. on 10r. purple 60 60
141 2½c. on 25r. green 60 60
142 5c. on 50r. blue 70 70
143 7½c. on 75r. brown . . . . 1·25 1·25
144 10c. on 100r. brown 70 50
145 15c. on 150r. brown . . . . 1·50 1·40

(b) Macao.
146 ¼c. on ½a. green 80 70
147 ½c. on 1a. red 80 70
148 1c. on 2a. purple 70 60
149 2½c. on 4a. green 70 60
150 5c. on 8a. blue 80 70
151 7½c. on 12a. brown . . . . 1·25 95
152 10c. on 16a. brown . . . . 1·25 1·10
153 15c. on 24a. brown . . . . 1·25 85

(c) Portuguese Timor.
154 ¼c. on ½a. green 80 70
155 ½c. on 1a. red 80 70
156 1c. on 2a. purple 70 60
157 2½c. on 4a. green 70 60
158 5c. on 8a. blue 80 70
159 7½c. on 12a. brown . . . . 1·25 90
160 10c. on 16a. brown . . . . 1·25 1·00
161 15c. on 24a. brown . . . . 1·25 90

1913. "King Carlos" key-type of Portuguese Guinea optd **PROVISORIO** and **REPUBLICA**.
184 S 15r. brown 30 25
185 50r. blue 30 25
164 75r. pink . . . . 2·50 2·25

1914. "Ceres" key-type inscr "GUINE". Name and value in black.
204 U ¼c. green 10 10
209 ½c. black 10 10
210 1c. green 10 10
211 1½c. brown 10 10
212 2c. red 10 10
213 2c. grey 10 10
214 2½c. violet 10 10
215 3c. orange 10 10
216 4c. red 10 10
217 4½c. grey 10 10
218 5c. blue 10 10
219 6c. mauve 10 10
220 7c. blue 10 10
221 7½c. brown 10 10
222 8c. grey 10 10
223 10c. red 10 10
224 12c. green 20 15
225 15c. red 25 10
226 20c. green 10 10
227 24c. blue 75 55
228 25c. brown 75 55
180 30c. brown on green . . . 2·10 1·60
229 30c. green 30 15
181 40c. brown on pink . . . 1·00 80
230 40c. turquoise 30 15
182 50c. orange on orange . . . 1·25 80
231 50c. mauve 65 35
232 60c. blue 65 35
233 60c. red 65 35
234 80c. red 70 35
183 1e. green on blue . . . . 1·25 80
235 1e. blue 85 55
236 1e. pink 85 55
237 2e. purple . . . . 1·00 60
238 5e. bistre . . . . 5·00 3·50
239 10e. pink . . . . 8·75 6·25
240 20e. green . . . . 22·00 15·00

1915. Provisional stamps of 1902 optd **REPUBLICA**.
186 S 50r. on 65r. blue 30 25
187 V 115r. on 2½r. brown . . . 45 35
190 R 115r. on 5r. yellow . . . 35 30
191 115r. on 25r. green . . . 35 30
192 3 115r. on 40r. brown . . . 35 30
194 115r. on 50r. blue . . . 35 30
196 130r. on 80r. grey . . . 1·00 75
197 130r. on 100r. brown . . . 85 75
199 R 130r. on 150r. red on pink . 35 30
200 130r. on 200r. blue on blue . 35 30
201 130r. on 300r. blue on brn . 35 30

1920. Surch.
241 U 4c. on ¼c. green . . . . 1·50 1·00
242 6c. on ½c. black . . . . 1·50 1·00
243 S 12c. on 115r. brown on pink (No. 132) . . . . 2·10 1·75

1925. Stamps of 1902 (Nos. 107/9) surch **Republica** and new value.
244 R 40c. on 400r. on 75r. pink 45 35
245 40c. on 400r. on 80r. green 40 35
246 40c. on 400r. on 100r. brown on buff 40 35

1931. "Ceres" key-type of Portuguese Guinea surch.
247 U 50c. on 60c. red 75 50
248 70c. on 80c. red . . . . 1·25 80
249 1e.40 on 2e. purple . . . 1·90 1·40

1933.
251 24 1c. brown 10 10
252 5c. brown 10 10
253 10c. mauve 10 10
254 15c. black 10 10
255 20c. grey 10 10
256 30c. green 10 10
257 40c. red 15 10
258 45c. turquoise 30 20
259 50c. brown 30 20
260 60c. green 30 20
261 70c. brown 30 20
262 80c. green 50 25
263 85c. red 90 45
264 1e. purple 45 30
265 1e.40 blue . . . . 1·75 1·00
266 2e. mauve 80 55
267 5e. green . . . . 3·00 1·90
268 10e. brown . . . . 5·50 3·75
269 20e. orange . . . . 19·00 10·00

27 Vasco da Gama
28 Airplane over Globe

1938.
270 27 1c. green (postage) . . . 10 10
271 5c. brown 10 10
272 10c. red 10 10
273 15c. purple 10 10
274 20c. grey 15 10
275 – 30c. purple 15 10
276 – 35c. green 20 15
277 – 40c. brown 20 15
278 – 50c. mauve 20 15
279 – 60c. black 20 15
280 – 70c. violet 20 15
281 – 80c. orange 30 20
282 – 1e. red 35 15
283 – 1e.75 blue 50 35
284 – 2e. red . . . . 1·50 50
285 – 5e. green . . . . 1·90 75
286 – 10e. blue . . . . 3·50 1·00
287 – 20e. brown . . . . 10·00 2·00
288 28 10c. red (air) 20 15
289 20c. violet 20 15
290 50c. orange 20 15
291 1e. blue 40 25
292 2e. red . . . . 3·00 1·75
293 3e. green 65 40
294 5e. brown . . . . 1·75 60
295 9e. red . . . . 2·00 1·25
296 10e. mauve . . . . 5·00 1·50

DESIGNS (postage): 30c. to 50c. Mousinho de Albuquerque; 60c. to 1e. Dam; 1e.75 to 5e. Prince Henry the Navigator; 10, 20e. Afonso de Albuquerque.

31 Cacheu Castle
32 Native Huts

1946. 500th Anniv of Discovery of Portuguese Guinea.
297 31 30c. black and grey . . . . 2·00 55
298 – 50c. green and light green 90 35
299 – 50c. purple and claret . . . 90 35
300 – 1e.75 blue and light blue 6·50 90
301 – 3e.50 red and pink . . . . 10·00 1·60
302 – 5e. brown and chocolate 28·00 5·00
303 – 20e. violet and mauve . . . 48·00 9·00

DESIGNS—VERT: 50c. Nuno Tristao; 1e.75, President Grant; 3e.50, Teixeiro Pinto; 5e. Honorio Barreto. HORIZ: 20e. Church at Bissau.

1948.
304 32 5c. brown 25 15
305 – 10c. purple . . . . 5·00 1·40
306 – 20c. mauve 60 30
307 – 35c. green 80 30
308 – 50c. red 35 15
309 – 70c. blue 60 25
310 – 80c. green 80 25
311 – 1e. red 80 25
312 – 1e.75 blue . . . . 15·00 4·25
313 – 2e. blue . . . . 15·00 1·10
314 – 3e.50 brown . . . . 3·50 1·10
315 – 5e. grey . . . . 5·75 2·25
316 – 20e. violet . . . . 24·00 5·75

DESIGNS: 10c. Crowned crane; 20c., 3e.50, Youth; 35c., 5e. Woman; 50c. Musician; 70c. Man; 80c., 20e. Girl; 1, 2e. Drummer; 1e.75, Bushbuck.

33 Our Lady of Fatima
34 Letter and Globe

1948. Statue of Our Lady of Fatima.
317 33 50c. green . . . . 2·75 2·75

1949. 75th Anniv of U.P.U.
318 34 2e. orange . . . . 3·75 1·90

1950. Holy Year. As Nos. 425/6 of Macao.
319 1e. purple . . . . 1·25 90
320 3e. green . . . . 2·00 1·10

36 Our Lady of Fatima
37 Doctor examining Patient

1951. Termination of Holy Year.
321 36 1e. brown and buff 55 40

1952. 1st Tropical Medicine Congress, Lisbon.
322 37 50c. brown and purple . . 30 25

39 Exhibition Entrance
40 "Analeptes Trifasciata' (longhorn beetle)

1953. Missionary Art Exhibition.
323 39 10c. red and green 10 10
324 50c. blue and brown . . . 40 25
325 3e. black and orange . . . 1·10 65

1953. Bugs and Beetles. Multicoloured.
326 5c. Type **40** 20 15
327 10c. "Callidea panaethiopica kirk" (shieldbug) 20 15
328 30c. "Craspedophorus brevicollis" (ground beetle) 20 15
329 50c. "Anthia nimrod" (ground beetle) 20 15
330 70c. "Platypria luctuosa" (leaf beetle) 35 15
331 1e. "Acanthophorus maculatus" (longhorn beetle) 35 15
332 2e. "Cordylomera nitidipennis" (longhorn beetle) . . . . 1·00 20
333 3e. "Lycus latissimus" (powder-post beetle) . . . 2·00 25
334 5e. "Cicindeia brunet" (tiger beetle) . . . . 4·00 70
335 10e. "Colliurus dimidiata" (ground beetle) . . . . . 6·25 2·40

41 Portuguese Stamp of 1853 and Arms of Portuguese Overseas Provinces
43 Arms of Cape Verde Islands and Portuguese Guinea
42 Father M. de Nobrega and View of Sao Paulo

1953. Portuguese Stamp Centenary.
336 41 50c. multicoloured 55 55

1954. 4th Centenary of Sao Paulo.
337 42 1e. multicoloured 20 15

1955. Presidential Visit.
338 43 1e. multicoloured 25 15
339 2e.50 mulitcoloured 55 25

44 Exhibition Emblem Globe and Arms
46 Statue of Barreto at Bissau
45 "Matenus stenegalenis"

1958. Brussels International Exhibition.
340 44 2e.50 green 40 35

1958. 6th Int Congress of Tropical Medicine.
341 45 5e. multicoloured . . . . . 2·00 1·00

1959. Death Centenary of Honorio Barreto (statesman).
342 46 2e.50 multicoloured 20 15

47 Astrolabe

48 "Medical Service"

1960. 500th Death Anniv of Prince Henry the Navigator.

343	**47**	2e.50 multicoloured	15	10

1960. 10th Anniv of African Technical Co-operation Commission.

344	**48**	1e.50 multicoloured	20	15

49 Motor Racing

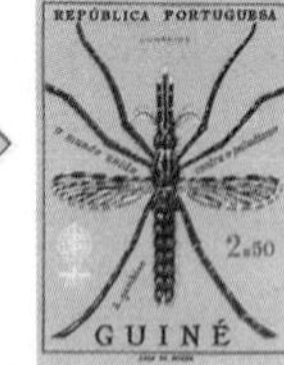

50 "Anopheles gambiae"

1962. Sports. Multicoloured.

345	50c. Type **49**	10	10
346	1e. Tennis	55	20
347	1e.50 Putting the shot	25	15
348	2e.50 Wrestling	30	20
349	3e.50 Shooting	30	20
350	15e. Volleyball	1·25	1·00

1962. Malaria Eradication.

351	**50**	2e.50 multicoloured	45	30

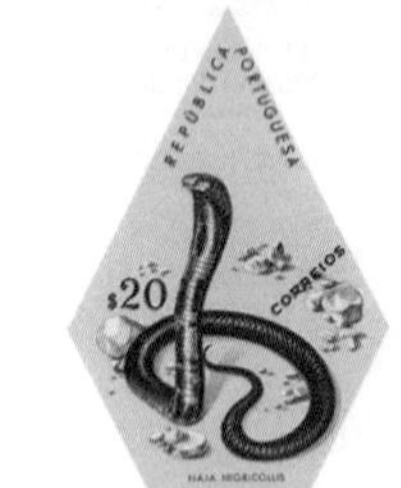

51 Common Spitting Cobra

52 Map of Africa, Boeing 707 and Lockheed L.1049G Super Constellation

1963. Snakes. Multicoloured.

352	20c. Type **51**	15	10
353	35c. African rock python . .	15	10
354	70c. Boomslang	40	25
355	80c. West African mamba . .	30	20
356	1e.50 Symthe's watersnake . .	40	10
357	2e. Common night adder . .	25	10
358	2e.50 Green swampsnake . .	1·25	25
359	3e.50 Brown house snake . .	30	20
360	4e. Spotted wolfsnake	40	25
361	5e. Common puff adder . . .	50	25
362	15e. Striped beauty snake . .	1·25	80
363	20e. African egg-eating snake	2·00	1·00

The 2e. and 20e. are horiz.

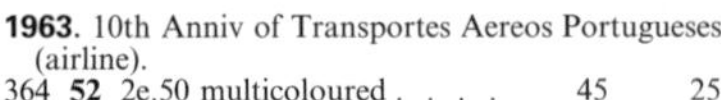

1963. 10th Anniv of Transportes Aereos Portugueses (airline).

364	**52**	2e.50 multicoloured	45	25

53 J. de A. Corvo

54 I.T.U. Emblem and St. Gabriel

1964. Centenary of National Overseas Bank.

365	**53**	2e.50 multicoloured	40	20

1965. Centenary of I.T.U.

366	**54**	2e.50 multicoloured	1·10	55

55 Soldier, 1548

1966. Portuguese Military Uniforms. Multicoloured.

367	25c. Type **55**	10	10
368	40c. Arquebusier, 1578 . . .	15	10
369	60c. Arquebusier, 1640 . . .	25	10
370	1e. Grenadier, 1721	25	10
371	2e.50 Captain of Fusiliers, 1740	50	10
372	4e.50 Infantryman, 1740 . .	1·10	25
373	7e.50 Sergeant-major, 1762	1·90	1·00
374	10e. Engineers' officer, 1806	2·50	1·25

56 B. C. Lopes School and Bissau Hospital

1966. 40th Anniv of Portuguese National Revolution.

375	**56**	2e.50 multicoloured	30	20

57 O. Muzanty and Cruiser "Republica"

1967. Centenary of Military Naval Assn. Mult.

376	50c. Type **57**	15	10
377	1e. A. de Cerqueira and destroyer "Guadiana" . .	50	30

58 Chapel of the Apparitions and Monument of the Holy Spirit

63 Pres. Tomas

1967. 50th Anniv of Fatima Apparitions.

378	**58**	50c. multicoloured	15	10

1968. Visit of President Tomas of Portugal.

396	**63**	1e. multicoloured	15	10

64 Cabral's Arms

66 Admiral Coutinho's Astrolabe

1968. 500th Birth Anniv of Pedro Cabral (explorer).

397	**64**	2e.50 multicoloured	45	20

1969. Birth Centenary of Admiral Gago Coutinho.

409	**66**	1e. multicoloured	30	15

67 Arms of Vasco da Gama

68 L. A. Rebello da Silva

1969. 500th Birth Anniv of Vasco da Gama (explorer).

410	**67**	2e.50 multicoloured	25	15

1969. Centenary of Overseas Administrative Reforms.

411	**68**	50c. multicoloured	15	15

69 Arms of King Manoel I

70 Ulysses Grant and Square, Bolama

1969. 500th Birth Anniv of Manoel I.

412	**69**	2e. multicoloured	40	15

1970. Centenary of Arbitral Judgment on Sovereignty of Bolama.

413	**70**	2e.50 multicoloured	25	15

71 Marshal Carmona

73 Camoens

1970. Birth Centenary of Marshal Carmona.

414	**71**	1e.50 multicoloured	15	10

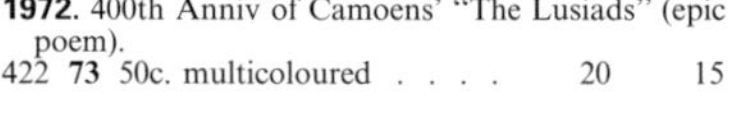

1972. 400th Anniv of Camoens' "The Lusiads" (epic poem).

422	**73**	50c. multicoloured	20	15

74 Weightlifting and Hammer-throwing

1972. Olympic Games, Munich.

423	**74**	2e.50 multicoloured	20	15

75 Fairey IIID Seaplane "Lusitania" taking-off from Lisbon

1972. 50th Anniv of 1st Lisbon–Rio de Janeiro Flight.

424	**75**	1e. multicoloured	15	15

76 W.M.O. Emblem

1973. Centenary of I.M.O./W.M.O.

425	**76**	2e. multicoloured	20	15

CHARITY TAX STAMPS

The notes under this heading in Portugal also apply here.

C 16

C 29a Arms

C 26

1919. Fiscal stamp optd **REPUBLICA TAXA DE GUERRA**.

C241	C **16**	10r. brown, buff & blk	11·00	15·00

1925. Marquis de Pombal Commem stamps of Portugal but inscr "GUINE".

C247	C **73**	15c. black and red . .	35	30
C248	–	15c. black and red . .	35	30
C249	C **75**	15c. black and red . .	35	30

1934.

C270	C **26**	50c. purple and green	3·75	2·25

1938.

C297	C **29a**	50c. yellow	3·25	2·25
C298		50c. brown and green	3·25	2·25

1942. As Type **C 29a** but smaller, 20½ × 25 mm.

C299	C **29a**	50c. black and brown	10	10
C300		50c. black and yellow	85	50
C301		50c. brown and yellow	90	75
C302		2e.50 black and blue	20	20
C303		5e. black and green	35	10
C304		10e. black and blue	75	35

Nos. C302/4 were used at several small post offices as ordinary postage stamps during a temporary shortage.

C 59

C 60

1967. National Defence. No gum.

C379	C **59**	50c. red, pink and black	40	25
C380		1e. red, green and black	55	40
C381		5e. red, grey and black	1·10	1·00
C382		10e. red, blue and black	3·25	3·25

A 50e. in the same design was for fiscal use only.

1967. National Defence. No gum.

C383	C **60**	50c. red, pink and black	15	15
C384		1e. red, green and black	15	15
C385		5e. red, grey and black	40	30
C386		10e. red, blue and black	90	65

C 61 Carved Statuette of Woman

C 65 Hands grasping Sword

1967. Guinean Artifacts from Bissau Museum. Multicoloured.

C387	50c. Type C **61**	10	10
C388	1e. "Tree of life"(carving) (horiz)	10	10
C389	2e. Cow-headed statuette	15	10
C390	2e.50 "The Magistrate" (statuette)	30	30
C391	5e. "Kneeling Servant" (statuette)	40	30
C392	10e. Stylized pelican (carving)	65	65

1968. No. C389 but inscr "TOCADOR DE BOMBOLON" surch.

C394	50c. on 2e. multicoloured	15	15
C395	1e. on 2e. multicoloured . .	15	15

1969. National Defence.

C398	C **65**	50c. multicoloured . .	15	15
C399		1e. multicoloured . . .	15	15
C400		2e. multicoloured . . .	15	15
C401		2e.50 multicoloured . .	15	15
C402		3e. multicoloured . . .	15	15
C403		4e. multicoloured . . .	20	20
C404		5e. multicoloured . . .	25	25
C405		8e. multicoloured . . .	40	40
C406		9e. multicoloured . . .	50	50
C407		10e. multicoloured . .	55	55
C408		15e. multicoloured . .	90	90

NOTE—30, 50 and 100e. stamps in the same design were for fiscal use only.

C 72 Mother and Children

1971.

C415	C **72**	50c. multicoloured . .	10	10
C416		1e. multicoloured . . .	10	10
C417		2e. multicoloured . . .	10	10
C418		3e. multicoloured . . .	15	10

C419 4e. multicoloured . . . 20 10
C420 5e. multicoloured . . . 25 15
C421 10e. multicoloured . . 50 30
Higher values were intended for fiscal use.

NEWSPAPER STAMP

1983. "Newspaper" key-type inscr "GUINE".
N50 V 2½r. brown 30 25

POSTAGE DUE STAMPS

1904. "Due" key-type inscr "GUINE". Name and value in black.
D122 W 5r. green 40 15
D123 10r. grey 40 15
D124 20r. brown 40 15
D125 30r. orange 45 35
D126 50r. brown 45 35
D127 60r. brown . . . . . . 1·25 90
D128 100r. mauve . . . . . . 1·25 90
D129 130r. blue . . . . . . 1·25 90
D130 200r. red . . . . 1·90 1·50
D131 500r. lilac . . . . 4·50 2·25

1911. "Due" key-type of Portuguese Guinea optd **REPUBLICA**.
D138 W 5r. green 10 10
D139 10r. grey 10 10
D140 20r. brown 15 10
D141 30r. orange 15 10
D142 50r. brown 15 10
D143 60r. brown 40 30
D208 100r. mauve 60 50
D145 130r. blue 75 60
D146 200r. red 75 60
D147 500r. lilac 55 45

1921. "Due" key-type of Portuguese Guinea. Currency changed.
D244 W ½c. green 15 15
D245 1c. grey 15 15
D246 2c. brown 15 15
D247 3c. orange 15 15
D248 5c. brown 15 15
D249 6c. brown 15 15
D250 10c. mauve 20 20
D251 13c. blue 20 20
D252 20c. red 20 20
D253 50c. grey 20 20

1925. Marquis de Pombal stamps, as Nos. C247/9 optd **MULTA**.
D254 C **73** 30c. black and red . . 35 30
D255 – 30c. black and red . . 35 30
D256 C **75** 30c. black and red . . 35 30

1952. As Type D **70** of Macao, but inscr "GUINE PORTUGUESA". Numerals in red, name in black (except 2e. in blue).
D323 10c. green and pink 15 15
D324 30c. violet and grey . . . 15 15
D325 50c. green and lemon . . . 15 15
D326 1e. blue and grey 15 15
D327 2e. black and olive . . . 20 20
D328 5e. brown and orange . . . 25 25

PORTUGUESE INDIA Pt. 9

Portuguese territories on the west coast of India, consisting of Goa, Damao and Diu. Became part of India in December 1961.

1871. 1000 reis = 1 milreis.
1882. 12 reis = 1 tanga; 16 tangas = 1 rupia
1959. 100 centavos = 1 escudo.

1

9

1871. Perf.
35 **1** 10r. black . . . . 3·75 2·75
33a 15r. pink . . . . 6·75 5·25
26 20r. red . . . . 6·00 4·75
21 40r. blue . . . . 13·50 32·00
22 100r. green . . . . 48·00 40·00
23 200r. yellow £130 £120
27 300r. purple . . . . . . 65·00 55·00
28 600r. purple . . . . . . 80·00 75·00
29 900r. purple . . . . . . 80·00 75·00

1877. Star above value. Imperf (241/3) or perf (others).
241 **9** 1½r. black . . . . 1·00 80
242 4½r. green . . . . 10·00 8·00
243 6r. green . . . . 10·00 7·50
48 10r. black . . . . 25·00 22·00
49 15r. pink . . . . 27·00 25·00
50 20r. red . . . . 6·75 5·75
51 40r. blue . . . . 11·50 9·25
52 100r. green . . . . 60·00 55·00
53 200r. yellow . . . . . . 65·00 60·00
54 300r. purple . . . . . . 75·00 65·00
55 600r. purple . . . . . . 75·00 65·00
56 900r. purple . . . . . . 75·00 65·00

1877. "Crown" key-type inscr "INDIA PORTUGUEZA". Perf.
65 P 5r. black . . . . 3·25 2·75
58 10r. buff . . . . 8·00 6·00
78 10r. green . . . . 7·50 6·00
67 20r. bistre . . . . 5·25 4·00
68 25r. pink . . . . 7·50 5·25
79 25r. grey . . . . 32·00 27·00
80 25r. purple . . . . 23·00 17·00
69 40r. blue . . . . 10·00 8·00
81 40r. yellow . . . . 30·00 23·00
70b 50r. green . . . . 25·00 12·00
82 50r. blue . . . . 15·00 13·50
71 100r. lilac . . . . 9·50 8·00
64 200r. orange . . . . . . 17·00 15·00
73 300r. brown . . . . 20·00 17·00
See also Nos. 204/10.

1881. Surch in figures.
213 **1** 1½ on 10r. black . . . . . — £250
215 **9** 1½ on 10r. black . . . . . — £225
90 **1** 1½ on 20r. red . . . . . . 65·00 50·00
91 **9** 1½ on 20r. red . . . . . . £120 85·00
217 **1** 4½ on 40r. blue . . . . . 17·00 17·00
223 4½ on 100r. green . . . . 30·00 26·00
96 5 on 10r. black . . . . . 4·00 4·00
98 **9** 5 on 10r. black . . . . . 27·00 22·00
101 **1** 5 on 15r. pink . . . . . . 1·90 1·90
106 5 on 20r. red . . . . . . 1·60 1·60
108 **9** 5 on 20r. red . . . . . . 3·75 3·25
224 **1** 6 on 20r. red . . . . . .
228 6 on 100r. green £150 £110
231 6 on 200r. yellow . . . . — £120
233 **9** 6 on 200r. yellow £250 £210

1881. "Crown" key-type of Portuguese India surch in figures.
199 P 1½ on 4½ on 5r. black . . . 23·00 22·00
109 1½ on 5r. black . . . . . 1·00 85
200 1½ on 6 on 10r. green . . . 38·00 35·00
110 1½ on 10r. green . . . . . 1·00 85
111 1½ on 20r. bistre . . . . . 8·75 6·75
157 1½ on 25r. grey . . . . . 23·00 22·00
158 1½ on 100r. lilac . . . . . 40·00 35·00
200a 1½ on 1t. on 20r. bistre . . — £100
201 2 on 4t. on 50r. green . . 50·00 40·00
114 4½ on 5r. black . . . . . 6·00 5·00
115 4½ on 10r. green . . . . . 90·00 85·00
116 4½ on 20r. bistre . . . . . 2·40 2·00
162 4½ on 25r. purple . . . . 7·25 6·00
118 4½ on 100r. lilac . . . . . 70·00 60·00
119a 6 on 10r. buff . . . . . . 24·00 22·00
120 6 on 10r. green . . . . . 6·00 5·00
121 6 on 20r. bistre . . . . . 10·00 8·00
167 6 on 25r. grey . . . . . . 20·00 15·00
168 6 on 25r. purple . . . . . 2·00 1·75
169 6 on 40r. blue . . . . . . 50·00 38·00
170 6 on 40r. yellow . . . . . 28·00 23·00
171 6 on 50r. green . . . . . 32·00 28·00
127 6 on 50r. blue . . . . . . 40·00 32·00
202 6 on 1t. on 10r. green . . £100
128 1t. on 10r. green . . . . 70·00 70·00
129 1t. on 20r. bistre . . . . 32·00 28·00
175 1t. on 25r. grey . . . . . 23·00 17·00
176 1t. on 25r. purple . . . . 8·00 5·75
132 1t. on 40r. blue . . . . . 13·50 10·00
178 1t. on 50r. green . . . . 35·00 32·00
134 1t. on 50r. blue . . . . . 17·00 12·00
136 1t. on 100r. lilac . . . . 17·00 10·00
137 1t. on 200r. orange . . . 28·00 23·00
139 2t. on 25r. purple . . . . 8·00 6·75
182 2t. on 25r. grey . . . . . 23·00 20·00
184 2t. on 40r. blue . . . . . 27·00 20·00
141 2t. on 40r. yellow . . . . 28·00 25·00
142a 2t. on 50r. green . . . . 11·00 8·00
143 2t. on 50r. blue . . . . . 55·00 45·00
144 2t. on 100r. lilac . . . . 8·00 6·75
188 2t. on 200r. orange . . . 23·00 20·00
189 2t. on 300r. brown . . . 23·00 20·00
190 4t. on 10r. green . . . . 10·00 8·00
191 4t. on 50r. green . . . . 8·75 7·00
148 4t. on 200r. orange . . . 28·00 20·00
193 8t. on 20r. bistre . . . . 23·00 17·00
194 8t. on 25r. pink . . . . . £100 85·00
151 8t. on 40r. blue . . . . . 28·00 23·00
196 8t. on 100r. lilac . . . . 32·00 25·00
197 8t. on 200r. orange . . . 23·00 18·00
198 8t. on 300r. brown . . . 27·00 23·00

1882. "Crown" key-type of Portuguese India.
204 P 1½r. black 40 35
205 4½r. green 40 35
206 6r. green 40 35
207 1t. pink 40 35
208 2t. blue 40 35
209 4t. purple . . . . 2·10 1·75
210 8t. orange . . . . 2·10 1·75

1886. "Embossed" key-type inscr "INDIA PORTUGUEZA".
244 Q 1½r. black . . . . 1·25 1·00
245 4½r. olive . . . . 1·60 1·10
246 6r. green . . . . 2·10 1·25
247 1t. red . . . . 2·75 2·40
248 2t. blue . . . . 5·75 3·50
249 4t. lilac . . . . 5·75 3·50
257 8t. orange . . . . 4·75 3·50

1895. "Figures" key-type inscr "INDIA".
271 R 1½r. black 70 40
259 4½r. orange 70 40
273 6r. green 70 40
274 9r. lilac . . . . 2·75 2·10
260 1t. blue 95 70
261 2t. red 95 40
262 4t. blue . . . . 1·10 70
270 8t. lilac . . . . 2·00 1·50

1898. As Vasco da Gama stamps of Portugal T **40** etc, but inscr "INDIA".
275 1½r. green 65 55
276 4½r. red 65 55
277 6r. purple 70 60
278 9r. green 80 70
279 1t. blue . . . . 1·10 1·00
280 2t. brown . . . . 1·25 1·25
281 4t. brown . . . . 1·50 1·40
282 8t. brown . . . . 2·75 2·50

DESIGNS—HORIZ: 1½r. Departure of fleet; 4½r. Arrival at Calicut; 6r. Embarkation at Rastello; 4t. Flagship "Sao Gabriel"; 8t. Vasco da Gama. VERT: 9r. Muse of History; 1t. Flagship "Sao Gabriel" and portraits of Da Gama and Camoens; 2t. Archangel Gabriel, patron saint of the expedition.

1898. "King Carlos" key-type inscr "INDIA". Value in red (No. 292) or black (others).
323 S 1r. grey 25 20
283 1½r. orange 25 20
324 1½r. grey 30 20
325 2r. orange 25 20
326 2½r. brown 30 20
327 3r. blue 30 20
284 4½r. green 55 40
285 6r. brown 55 40
328 6r. green 30 20
286 9r. lilac 55 40
287 1t. green 55 40
329 1t. red 45 20
288 2t. blue 70 40
330 2t. brown . . . . 1·25 70
331 2½t. blue . . . . 4·75 3·00
289 4t. blue on blue . . . . . 1·25 85
332 5t. brown on yellow . . . . 1·60 1·00
290 8t. purple on pink . . . . 1·25 85
291 12t. blue on pink . . . . 2·00 1·25
334 12t. green on pink . . . . 3·25 1·60
292 1rp. black on blue . . . . 4·25 2·75
335 1rp. blue on yellow . . . . 6·75 3·00
293 2rp. mauve on yellow . . . 6·75 4·00
336 2rp. black on yellow . . . . 10·00 10·50

1900. No. 288 surch **1½ Reis**.
295 S 1½r. on 2t. blue . . . . . . 1·00 70

1902. Surch.
299 R 1r. on 6r. green 30 25
298 Q 1r. on 2t. blue 40 30
300 2r. on 4½r. olive 30 25
301 R 2r. on 8t. lilac 30 25
302 Q 2½r. on 6r. green 35 25
303 R 2½r. on 9r. lilac 30 25
305 3r. on 4½r. orange . . . . 1·00 60
304 Q 3r. on 1t. red 30 25
306 R 3r. on 1t. blue 60 60
337 S 2t. on 2½t. blue and black 1·25 1·10
307 Q 2½t. on 1½r. black . . . . . 1·10 85
310 R 2½t. on 1½r. black . . . . . 1·00 70
309 Q 2½t. on 4t. lilac 95 70
315 R 5t. on 2t. red . . . . . . 1·00 70
317 5t. on 4t. blue . . . . . . 1·00 70
314 Q 5t. on 8t. orange 70 40

1902. 1898 "King Carlos" stamps optd **PROVISORIO**.
319 S 6r. brown and black . . . . 1·25 1·00
320 1t. green and black . . . . 1·25 1·00
321 2t. blue and black . . . . . 1·25 1·00

1911. 1898 "King Carlos" stamps optd **REPUBLICA**. Value in black.
338 S 1r. grey 20 20
339 1½r. grey 20 20
340 2r. orange 20 20
341 2½r. brown 25 20
342 3r. blue 25 20
343 4½r. green 25 20
344 6r. green 20 20
345 9r. lilac 25 20
346 1t. red 40 20
347 2t. brown 40 20
348 4t. blue on blue 90 85
349 5t. brown on yellow . . . . 1·00 85
350 8t. purple on pink . . . . 3·00 1·75
402 12t. green on pink . . . . 2·00 1·75
352 1rp. blue on yellow . . . . 4·25 3·25
405 2rp. black on yellow . . . 5·75 5·00
404 2rp. mauve on yellow . . . 6·50 5·00

Both unused and used prices for the following issue (Nos. 371 etc.) are for entire stamps showing both halves.

1911. Various stamps bisected by vertical perforation, and each half surch. (a) On 1898 "King Carlos" key-type.
371 S 1r. on 2r. orange and black 15 15
372 1r. on 1t. red and black . . 15 15
378 1r. on 5t. brown and black on yellow . . . . 1·00 90
374 1½r. on 2½r. brown and black 25 20
354 1½r. on 4½r. green and black . . . . 3·25 2·50
355 1½r. on 9r. lilac and black 15 15
356 1½r. on 4t. blue and black on blue 15 15
375 2r. on 2½r. brown and black 25 20
357 2r. on 4t. blue and black on blue 25 15
376 3r. on 2½r. brown and black 25 20
377 3r. on 2t. brown and black 25 20
358 6r. on 4½r. green and black 25 20
359d 6r. on 9r. lilac and black 25 20
379 6r. on 8t. purple and black on pink 50 40

(b) On 1902 Provisional issue.
360 R 1r. on 5t. on 2t. red . . . . 2·00 1·75
361 1r. on 5t. on 4t. blue . . . 1·75 1·60
363 Q 1r. on 5t. on 8t. orange . . 60 40
364 2r. on 2½r. on 6r. green . . 90 70
365 R 2r. on 2½r. on 9r. lilac . . . 5·00 4·75
366 3r. on 5t. on 2t. red . . . . 1·75 1·60
367 3r. on 5t. on 4t. blue . . . 1·75 1·60
370 Q 3r. on 5t. on 8t. orange . . 50 30

(c) On 1911 issue (optd **REPUBLICA**).
380 S 1r. on 1r. grey and black . . 15 15
381 1r. on 2r. orange and black 15 15
382 1r. on 1t. red and black . . 15 15
383 1r. on 5t. brown and black on yellow 15 15
384 1½r. on 4½r. green and black 15 15
419 3r. on 2t. brown and black 80 75
420 6r. on 4½r. green and black 30 30
386 6r. on 9r. lilac and black . . 20 20
422 6r. on 8t. purple and black on pink 50 40

1913. Nos. 275/82 optd **REPUBLICA**.
389 1½r. green 30 25
390 4½r. red 35 25
391 6r. purple 40 35
392 9r. green 40 35
393 1t. blue 70 40
394 2t. brown . . . . 1·25 95
395 4t. brown 80 60
396 8t. brown . . . . 1·40 85

1914. Stamps of 1902 optd **REPUBLICA**.
406 R 2r. on 8t. lilac . . . . . . 4·00 3·25
407 Q 2½r. on 6r. green 65 50
415 S 1t. green and black (No. 320) . . . . 5·25 3·50
458 2t. blue and black (No. 321) 80 80
459 2t. on 2½t. blue and black 1·25 80
408 R 5t. on 2t. red . . . . . . 2·00 1·60
410 5t. on 4t. blue . . . . . . 2·00 1·60
460 Q 5t. on 8t. orange . . . . . 1·40 1·10

1914. "King Carlos" key-type of Portuguese India optd **REPUBLICA** and surch.
423 S 1½r. on 4½r. green and black 30 30
424 1½r. on 9r. lilac and black 30 30
425 1½r. on 12t. green and black on pink 50 40
426 3r. on 1t. red and black . . 40 30
427 3r. on 2t. brown and black 1·25 1·10
428 3r. on 8t. purple and black on pink . . . . 1·00 90
429 3r. on 1rp. blue and black on yellow 50 40
430 3r. on 2rp. black on yellow 55 50

1914. Nos. 390 and 392/6 surch.
433 1½ on 4½r. red 30 30
434 1½r. on 9r. green 30 30
435 3r. on 1t. blue 30 30
436 3r. on 2t. brown 55 40
437 3r. on 4t. brown 30 30
438 3r. on 8t. brown . . . . . 1·00 90

1914. "Ceres" key-type inscr "INDIA". Name and value in black.
439 U 1r. green 45 35
440 1½r. green 45 35
441 2r. black 60 35
442 2½r. green 60 35
443 3r. lilac 60 35
474 4r. blue . . . . 1·00 80
444 4½r. red 60 35
445 5r. green 60 35
446 6r. brown 60 35
447 9r. blue 60 35
448 10r. red 75 45
449 1t. violet . . . . 1·10 45
481 1½t. green 90 90
450 2t. blue . . . . 1·25 45
483 2½t. turquoise 80 70
451 3t. brown . . . . 1·60 65
484 3t. 4 brown . . . . 4·00 2·50
452 4t. grey . . . . 1·25 80
453 8t. purple . . . . 3·25 3·00
454 12t. brown on green . . . . 3·00 3·00
455 1rp. brown on pink . . . . 12·50 9·25
487 1rp. brown . . . . 13·50 11·00
456 2rp. orange on orange . . . 8·50 6·75
488 2rp. yellow . . . . 13·50 11·00
457 3rp. green on blue . . . . 10·50 7·00
489 3rp. green . . . . 20·00 18·00
490 5rp. red . . . . 21·00 20·00

1922. "Ceres" key-type of Portuguese India surch with new value.
496 U 1½r. on 8t. purple and black 70 50
492 1½r. on 2r. black 40 30
497 2½t. on 3t. 4 brown and black . . . . 10·50 8·25

34 Vasco da Gama and Flagship "Sao Gabriel"

1925. 400th Death Anniv of Vasco da Gama. No gum.
493 **34** 6r. brown . . . . 3·25 1·75
494 1t. purple . . . . 3·25 2·00

36 The Signature of Francis

40 "Portugal" and Galeasse

1931. St. Francis Xavier Exhibition.
498 – 1r. green 85 65
499 **36** 2r. brown 85 65
500 – 6r. purple . . . . 1·00 65
501 – 1½t. brown . . . . 3·25 2·50
502 – 2t. blue . . . . 5·25 4·75
503 – 2½t. red . . . . 7·75 4·75

DESIGNS—VERT: 1r. Monument to St. Francis; 6r. St. Francis in surplice and cassock; 1½t. St. Francis and Cross; 2½t. St. Francis's Tomb. HORIZ: 2t. Bom Jesus Church, Goa.

1933.

504	**40**	1r. brown	20	15
505		2r. brown	20	15
506		4r. mauve	20	15
507		6r. green	20	15
508		8r. black	35	30
509		1t. grey	35	30
510		1½t. red	35	30
511		2t. brown	35	30
512		2½t. blue	1·10	50
513		3t. turquoise	1·10	50
514		5t. red	1·10	50
515		1rp. green	4·00	1·75
516		2rp. purple	7·00	3·50
517		3rp. orange	8·75	5·50
518		5rp. green	20·00	17·00

1938. As T **27** and **28** of Portuguese Guinea, but inscr "ESTADO DA INDIA".

519	**27**	1r. green (postage)	25	25
520		2r. brown	25	25
521		3r. violet	25	25
522		6r. green	25	25
523	–	10r. red	35	30
524	–	1t. mauve	35	30
525	–	1½t. red	35	30
526	–	2t. orange	35	30
527	–	2½t. blue	35	30
528	–	3t. grey	95	30
529	–	5t. purple	1·10	40
530	–	1rp. red	3·00	75
531	–	2rp. green	5·00	2·25
532	–	3rp. blue	8·00	4·25
533	–	5rp. brown	18·00	5·50

DESIGNS: 10r. to 1½t. Mousinho de Albuquerque; 2t. to 3t. Prince Henry the Navigator; 5t. to 2rp. Dam; 3, 5rp. Afonso de Albuquerque.

534	**28**	1t. red (air)	60	35
535		2½t. violet	70	35
536		3½t. orange	70	35
537		4½t. blue	1·00	40
538		7t. red	1·00	50
539		7½t. green	1·75	60
540		9t. brown	3·75	1·10
541		11t. mauve	4·00	1·10

1942. Surch.

549	**40**	1r. on 8r. black	70	70
546		1r. on 5t. red	70	70
550		2r. on 8r. black	70	70
547		3r. on 1½t. red	70	70
551		3r. on 2t. brown	70	70
552		3r. on 3rp. orange	1·60	1·50
553		6r. on 2½t. blue	1·60	1·50
554		6r. on 3t. turquoise	1·60	1·50
542		1t. on 1½t. red	3·00	1·75
548		1t. on 2t. brown	2·00	1·50
543		1t. on 1rp. green	3·00	1·75
544		1t. on 2rp. purple	3·00	1·75
545		1t. on 5rp. green	3·00	1·75

48 St. Francis Xavier **50** D. Joao de Castro

1946. Portraits and View.

555	**48**	1r. black and grey	35	25
556	–	2r. purple and pink	35	25
557	–	6r. bistre and buff	35	25
558	–	7r. violet and mauve	1·25	70
559	–	9r. brown and buff	1·25	70
560	–	1t. green and light green	1·10	65
561	–	3½t. blue and light blue	1·25	1·10
562	–	1rp. purple and bistre	4·00	1·10

DESIGNS: 2r. Luis de Camoens; 6r. Garcia de Orta; 7r. Beato Joao Brito; 9r. Vice-regal Archway; 1t. Afonso de Albuquerque; 3½t. Vasco da Gama; 1rp. D. Francisco de Almeida.

1948. Portraits.

564	**50**	3r. blue and light blue	85	55
565	–	1t. green and light green	1·40	70
566	–	1½t. purple and mauve	1·75	1·00
567	–	2½t. red and orange	2·40	1·50
568	–	7½t. purple and brown	4·00	2·00

PORTRAITS: 1t. St. Francis Xavier; 1½t. P. Jose Vaz; 2½t. D. Luis de Ataide; 7½t. Duarte Pacheco Pereira.

1948. Statue of Our Lady of Fatima. As T **33** of Portuguese Guinea.

570		1t. green	2·75	2·50

53 Our Lady of Fatima **59** Father Jose Vaz

1949. Statue of Our Lady of Fatima.

571	**53**	1r. light blue and blue	1·10	70
572		3r. yellow, orange and lemon	1·10	70
573		9r. red and mauve	2·75	1·25
574		2t. green and light green	5·50	1·50
575		9t. red and vermilion	6·25	1·60
576		2rp. brown and purple	10·00	3·00
577		5rp. black and green	19·00	5·00
578		8rp. blue and violet	40·00	10·00

1949. 75th Anniv of U.P.U. As T **34** of Portuguese Guinea.

579		2½t. red	2·75	2·00

1950. Holy Year. As Nos. 425/6 of Macao.

580	**65**	1r. bistre	1·00	40
588		1r. red	40	25
589		2r. green	40	25
590	–	3r. brown	40	25
591	**65**	6r. grey	40	25
592	–	9r. mauve	1·00	60
593	**65**	1t. blue	1·00	60
581	–	2t. green	1·25	60
594	–	2t. yellow	1·00	60
595	**65**	4t. brown	1·00	60

1950. Nos. 523 and 527 surch.

582		1real on 10r. red	40	30
583		1real on 2½t. blue	40	30
584		2reis on 10r. red	40	30
585		3reis on 2½t. blue	40	30
586		6reis on 2½t. blue	40	30
587		1tanga on 2½t. blue	40	30

1951. Termination of Holy Year. As T **36** of Portuguese Guinea.

596		1rp. blue and grey	1·00	60

1951. 300th Birth Anniv of Jose Vaz.

597	**59**	1r. grey and slate	20	15
598	–	2r. orange and brown	20	15
599	**59**	3r. grey and black	50	20
600	–	1t. blue and indigo	30	20
601	**59**	2t. purple and maroon	30	20
602	–	3t. green and black	50	20
603	**59**	9t. violet and blue	55	25
604	–	10t. violet and mauve	1·50	90
605	–	12t. brown and black	5·00	2·75

DESIGNS: 2r., 1, 3, 10t. Sancoale Church Ruins; 12t. Veneravel Altar.

60 Goa Medical School

1952. 1st Tropical Medicine Congress, Lisbon.

606	**60**	4½t. turquoise and black	3·00	1·90

1952. 4th Death Cent of St. Francis Xavier. As Nos. 452/4 of Macao but without lined background.

607		6r. multicoloured	25	15
608		2t. multicoloured	1·75	55
609		5t. green, silver and mauve	2·75	85

62 St. Francis Xavier **63** Stamp of 1871 **64** The Virgin

1952. Philatelic Exhibition, Goa.

612	**63**	3t. black	8·00	8·00
613	**62**	5t. black and lilac	8·00	8·00

1953. Missionary Art Exhibition.

614	**64**	6r. black and blue	25	20
615		1t. brown and buff	1·00	70
616		3t. lilac and yellow	2·40	1·25

1953. Portuguese Postage Stamp Centenary. As T **41** of Portuguese Guinea.

617		1t. multicoloured	90	80

66 Dr. Gama Pinto **67** Academy Buildings

1954. Birth Centenary of Dr. Gama Pinto.

618	**66**	3r. green and grey	25	20
619		2t. black and blue	40	25

1954. 4th Centenary of Sao Paulo. As T **42** of Portuguese Guinea.

620		2t. multicoloured	50	30

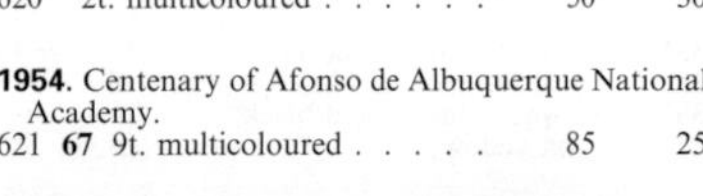

1954. Centenary of Afonso de Albuquerque National Academy.

621	**67**	9t. multicoloured	85	25

68 Mgr. Dalgado **71** M. A. de Sousa

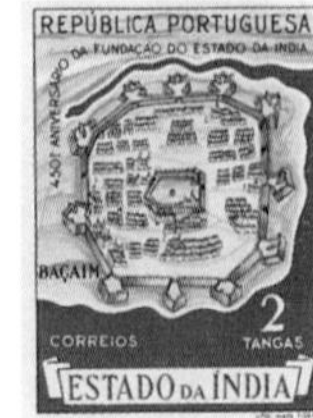

72 F. de Almeida **73** Map of Bacaim

1955. Birth Centenary of Mgr. Dalgado.

622	**68**	1r. multicoloured	15	15
623		1t. multicoloured	35	15

1956. 450th Anniv of Portuguese Settlements in India. Multicoloured. (a) Famous Men. As T **71**.

624		6r. Type **71**	30	20
625		1½t. F. N. Xavier	30	20
626		4t. A. V. Lourenco	30	20
627		8t. Father Jose Vaz	50	25
628		9t. M. G. de Heredia	50	25
629		2rp. A. C. Pacheco	1·50	1·00

(b) Viceroys. As T **72**.

630		3r. Type **72**	25	15
631		9r. A. de Albuquerque	30	20
632		1t. Vasco da Gama	30	20
633		3t. N. da Cunha	45	20
634		10t. J. de Castro	40	25
635		3rp. C. de Braganca	1·75	1·10

(c) Settlements. As T **73**.

636		2t. Type **73**	3·25	1·75
637		2½t. Mombaim	1·75	1·00
638		3½t. Damao	1·75	1·00
639		5t. Diu	1·00	55
640		12t. Cochim	1·25	70
641		1rp. Goa	2·75	1·25

74 Map of Damao, Dadra and Nagar Aveli Districts **75** Arms of Vasco da Gama

1957. Centres multicoloured.

642	**74**	3r. grey	15	10
643		6r. green	15	10
644		3t. pink	25	20
645		6t. blue	25	20
646		11t. bistre	80	55
647		2rp. lilac	1·10	80
648		3rp. yellow	1·75	1·10
649		5rp. red	2·10	1·60

1958. Heraldic Arms of Famous Men. Multicoloured.

650		2r. Type **75**	20	10
651		6r. Lopo Soares de Albergaria	20	10
652		9r. D. Francisco de Almeida	20	10
653		1t. Garcia de Noronha	20	10
654		4t. D. Afonso de Albuquerque	30	20
655		5t. D. Joao de Castro	35	20
656		11t. D. Luis de Ataide	80	55
657		1rp. Nuno da Cunha	80	55

1958. 6th International Congress of Tropical Medicine. As T **45** of Portuguese Guinea.

658		5t. multicoloured	70	50

DESIGN: 5t. "Holarrhena antidysenterica" (plant).

1958. Brussels Int Exn. As T **44** of Portuguese Guinea.

659		1rp. multicoloured	45	30

1959. Surch in new currency.

660	–	5c. on 2r. (No. 650)	25	15
661	**74**	10c. on 3r. grey	25	15
662	–	15c. on 6r. (No. 651)	25	15
663	–	20c. on 9r. (No. 652)	25	15
664	–	30c. on 1t. (No. 653)	25	15
681	–	40c. on 1½t. (No. 566)	30	20
682	–	40c. on 1½t. (No. 625)	30	20
683	–	40c. on 2t. (No. 620)	50	40
665	**73**	40c. on 2t.30	20	
666	–	40c. on 2½t. (No. 637)	40	20
667	–	40c. on 3½t. (No. 638)	30	20
668	**74**	50c. on 3t. pink	30	20
684	**64**	80c. on 3t. lilac and yellow	30	20
669	–	80c. on 3t. (No. 633)	30	20
685	–	80c. on 3½t. (No. 561)	30	20
686	–	80c. on 5t. (No. 658)	35	20
670	–	80c. on 10t. (No. 634)	60	50
687	–	80c. on 1rp. (No. 659)	85	50
671	–	80c. on 3rp. (No. 635)	70	60
672	–	1e. on 4t. (No. 654)	30	20
673	–	1e.50 on 5t. (No. 655)	30	20

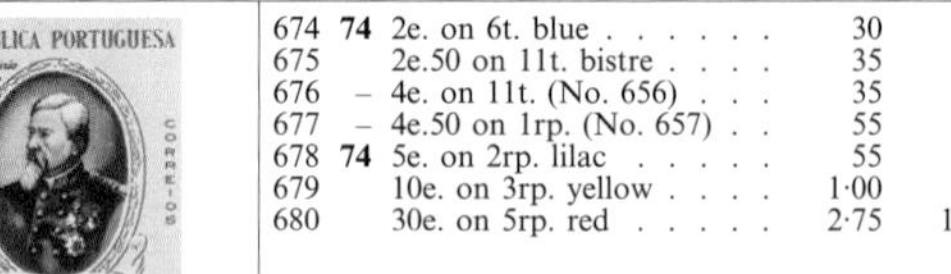

674	**74**	2e. on 6t. blue	30	20
675		2e.50 on 11t. bistre	35	20
676	–	4e. on 11t. (No. 656)	35	35
677	–	4e.50 on 1rp. (No. 657)	55	35
678	**74**	5e. on 2rp. lilac	55	30
679		10e. on 3rp. yellow	1·00	75
680		30e. on 5rp. red	2·75	1·10

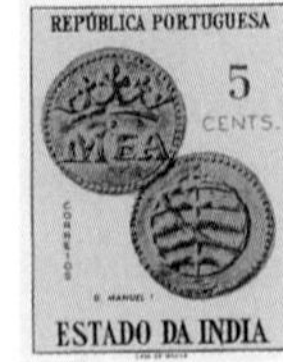

78 Coin of Manoel I **79** Prince Henry's Arms

1959. Portuguese Indian Coins. Designs showing both sides of coins of various rulers. Multicoloured.

688		5c. Type **78**	25	10
689		10c. Joao III	25	10
690		15c. Sebastiao	25	10
691		30c. Filipe I	25	10
692		40c. Filipe II	25	10
693		50c. Filipe III	25	10
694		60c. Joao IV	25	10
695		80c. Afonso VI	25	10
696		1e. Pedro II	25	10
697		1e.50 Joao V	25	10
698		2e. Jose I	50	30
699		2e.50 Maria I	50	30
700		3e. Prince Regent Joao	50	30
701		4e. Pedro IV	60	40
702		4e.40 Miguel	60	40
703		5e. Maria II	60	40
704		10e. Pedro V	1·00	70
705		20e. Luis	2·75	2·00
706		30e. Carlos	3·50	2·75
707		50e. Portuguese Republic	5·50	4·25

1960. 500th Death Anniv of Prince Henry the Navigator.

708	**79**	3e. multicoloured	70	50

The 1962 sports set and malaria eradication stamp similar to those for the other territories [illegible] issue when Portuguese India was occupied, but they were not put on sale there.

CHARITY TAX STAMPS.

The notes under this heading in Portugal also apply here.

1919. Fiscal stamp. Type C **1** of Portuguese Africa optd **TAXA DE GUERRA**.

C491	Rps. 0:00:05, 48 green	2·00	1·60
C492	Rps. 0:02:03, 43 green	4·00	2·50

1925. Marquis de Pombal Commem stamps of Portugal, but inscr "INDIA".

C495	C **73**	6r. pink	35	35
C496	–	6r. pink	35	35
C497	C **75**	6r. pink	35	35

C **52** Mother and Child C **69** Mother and Child

1948. (a) Inscr "ASSISTENCIA PUBLICA".

C571	C **52**	6r. green	2·00	1·75
C572		6r. yellow	2·25	2·00
C573		1t. red	2·00	1·75
C574		1t. orange	1·75	1·00
C575		1t. green	3·50	2·10

(b) Inscr "PROVEDORIA DE ASSISTENCIA PUBLICA".

C607	C **52**	1t. grey	2·00	1·25

1951. Surch **1 tanga**.

C606	C **52**	1t. on 6r. red	1·75	1·40

1953. Optd **"Revalidado" P. A. P.** and dotted line.

C617	C **52**	1t. red	5·00	3·75

1953. Surch as in Type C **69**.

C624	C **69**	1t. on 4t. blue	7·50	6·25

C **70** Mother and Child C **80** Arms and People

1956.
C625 C **70** 1t. black, green and red 70 45
C626 1t. blue, orange & grn 60 45

1957. Surch **6 reis**.
C650 C **70** 6r. on 1t. black, green and red 70 50

1959. Surch.
C688 C **70** 20c. on 1t. blue, orange and green 40 40
C689 40c. on 1t. blue, orange and green 40 40

1960.
C709 C **80** 20e. brown and red 40 40

POSTAGE DUE STAMPS

1904. "Due" key-type inscr "INDIA".
D337 W 2r. green 40 40
D338 3r. green 40 40
D339 4r. orange 40 40
D340 5r. grey 40 40
D341 6r. grey 40 40
D342 9r. brown 50 45
D343 1t. red 50 45
D344 2t. brown 1·00 80
D345 5t. blue 2·00 1·75
D346 10t. red 2·00 2·00
D347 1rp. lilac 6·75 5·25

1911. Nos. D337/47 optd **REPUBLICA**.
D354 W 2r. green 25 15
D355 3r. green 25 15
D356 4r. orange 25 15
D357 5r. grey 25 15
D358 6r. grey 25 20
D359 9r. brown 25 20
D360 1t. red 25 20
D361 2t. brown 55 40
D362 5t. blue 95 95
D363 10t. red 2·00 1·60
D364 1rp. lilac 2·75 2·50

1925. Marquis de Pombal stamps, as Nos. C495/7 optd **MULTA**.
D495 C **73** 1t. pink 35 35
D496 – 1t. pink 35 35
D497 C **75** 1t. pink 35 35

1943. Stamps of 1933 surch **Porteado** and new value.
D549 **40** 3r. on 2½t. blue 40 35
D550 6r. on 3t. turquoise 55 40
D551 1t. on 5t. red 1·00 90

1945. As Type D **1** of Portuguese Colonies, but optd **ESTADO DA INDIA**.
D555 2r. black and red 1·00 70
D556 3r. black and blue 1·00 70
D557 4r. black and yellow 1·00 70
D558 6r. black and green 1·00 70
D559 1t. black and brown 1·00 70
D560 2t. black and brown 1·00 70

1951. Surch **Porteado** and new value and bar.
D588 2rs. on 7r. (No. 558) 50 30
D589 3rs. on 7r. (No. 558) 50 30
D590 1t. on 1rp. (No. 562) 50 30
D591 2t. on 1rp. (No. 562) 50 30

1952. As Type D **70** of Macao, but inscr "INDIA PORTUGUESA". Numerals in red, name in black.
D606 2r. olive and brown 20 10
D607 3r. black and green 20 10
D608 6r. blue and turquoise 20 10
D609 1t. red and grey 30 20
D610 2t. orange, green and grey 60 40
D611 10t. blue, green and yellow 2·00 1·75

1959. Nos. D606/8 and D610/11 surch in new currency.
D688 5c. on 2r. multicoloured 20 20
D689 10c. on 3r. multicoloured 20 20
D690 15c. on 6r. multicoloured 20 20
D691 60c. on 2t. multicoloured 70 70
D692 60c. on 10t. multicoloured 1·40 1·25

PORTUGUESE TIMOR Pt. 9

The eastern part of Timor in the Indonesian Archipelago. Administered as part of Macao until 1896, then as a separate Portuguese Overseas Province until 1975.

Following a civil war and the intervention of Indonesian forces the territory was incorporated into Indonesia on 17 July 1976.

1885. 1000 reis = 1 milreis.
1894. 100 avos = 1 pataca.
1960. 100 centavos = 1 escudo.

1885. "Crown" key-type inscr "MACAU" optd **TIMOR**.
1 P 5r. black 70 60
12 10r. green 1·50 1·25
3 20r. red 3·25 1·75
4 25r. lilac 60 30
5 40r. yellow 1·25 1·00
6 50r. blue 70 50
7 80r. grey 1·75 1·10
8 100r. purple 70 60
19 200r. orange 1·75 1·40
20 300r. brown 1·75 1·40

1887. "Embossed" key-type inscr "CORREIO DE TIMOR".
21 Q 5r. black 1·10 70
22 10r. green 1·25 1·10
23 20r. red 2·00 1·10
24 25r. mauve 2·10 1·25
25 40r. brown 4·25 1·75
26 50r. blue 4·25 1·75
27 80r. grey 5·75 2·00
28 100r. brown 5·75 2·40
29 200r. lilac 10·00 5·00
30 300r. orange 12·00 6·00

1892. "Embossed" key-type inscr "PROVINCIA DE MACAU" surch **TIMOR 30 30**. No gum.
32 Q 30 on 300r. orange 2·75 1·60

1894. "Figures" key-type inscr "TIMOR".
33 R 5r. orange 85 50
34 10r. mauve 85 60
35 15r. brown 1·00 60
36 20r. lilac 1·00 60
37 25r. green 1·10 60
38 50r. blue 1·75 1·25
39 75r. pink 2·10 1·90
40 80r. green 2·10 1·90
41 100r. brown on buff 2·00 1·90
42 150r. red on pink 6·75 3·75
43 200r. blue on blue 6·75 3·75
44 300r. blue on brown 8·50 4·25

1894. Nos. 21/30 surch **PROVISORIO** and value in European and Chinese. No gum.
46 Q 1a. on 5r. black 85 50
47 2a. on 10r. green 1·00 85
48 3a. on 20r. red 1·25 85
49 4a. on 25r. purple 1·25 85
50 6a. on 40r. brown 1·75 85
51 8a. on 50r. blue 2·75 1·75
52 13a. on 80r. grey 4·00 4·00
53 16a. on 100r. brown 4·00 4·00
54 31a. on 200r. lilac 13·50 7·50
55 47a. on 300r. orange 15·00 11·00

1895. No. 32 further surch **5 avos PROVISORIO** and Chinese characters with bars over the original surch.
56 Q 5a. on 30 on 300r. orange 2·75 2·00

1898. 400th Anniv of Vasco da Gama's Discovery of Route to India. As Nos. 1/8 of Portuguese Colonies, but inscr "TIMOR" and value in local currency.
58 ½a. green 90 60
59 1a. red 90 60
60 2a. purple 85 60
61 4a. green 85 60
62 8a. blue 1·25 1·00
63 12a. brown 1·75 1·10
64 16a. brown 1·75 1·50
65 24a. brown 2·10 1·50

1898. "King Carlos" key-type inscr "TIMOR". Name and value in red (78a.) or black (others). With or without gum.
68 S ½a. grey 25 25
69 1a. red 25 25
71 2a. green 25 25
70 2½a. brown 25 25
72 3a. lilac 70 25
112 3a. green 85 70
73 4a. green 70 25
113 5a. red 85 70
114 6a. brown 85 70
74 8a. blue 70 25
115 9a. brown 85 70
75 10a. blue 70 25
116 10a. brown 85 70
76 12a. pink 70 25
117 12a. blue 4·25 3·75
118 13a. mauve 1·25 85
119 15a. lilac 2·00 1·75
78 16a. blue on blue 1·90 1·75
79 20a. brown on yellow 1·90 1·75
120 22a. brown on pink 2·00 1·75
80 24a. brown on buff 1·90 1·75
81 31a. purple on pink 1·90 1·75
121 31a. brown on cream 2·00 1·75
82 47a. blue on pink 3·25 2·75
122 47a. purple on pink 2·00 1·75
83 78a. black on blue 4·25 3·75
123 78a. blue on yellow 4·75 3·75

1899. Nos. 78 and 81 surch **PROVISORIO** and value in figures and bars.
84 S 10 on 16a. blue on blue 1·25 1·10
85 20 on 31a. purple on pink 1·25 1·10

1902. Surch.
88 R 5a. on 5r. orange 65 45
86 Q 5a. on 25r. mauve 1·00 60
89 R 5a. on 25r. green 65 40
90 5a. on 50r. blue 70 60
87 Q 5a. on 200r. lilac 1·60 1·00
95 V 6a. on 2½r. brown 40 30
92 Q 6a. on 10r. green 55·00 42·00
94 R 6a. on 20r. lilac 70 65
93 Q 6a. on 300r. orange 1·50 1·10
100 R 9a. on 15r. brown 70 55
98 Q 9a. on 40r. brown 1·75 1·75
101 R 9a. on 75r. pink 70 55
99 Q 9a. on 100r. brown 1·25 1·25
124 S 10a. on 12a. blue 1·25 1·10
104 R 15a. on 10r. mauve 1·00 85
102 Q 15a. on 20r. red 1·75 1·25
103 15a. on 50r. blue 50·00 42·00
105 R 15a. on 100r. brn on buff 1·00 85
106 15a. on 300r. blue on brn 1·00 85
107 Q 22a. on 80r. grey 3·25 2·75
108 R 22a. on 80r. green 1·75 1·50
109 22a. on 200r. blue on blue 1·75 1·50

1902. Nos. 72 and 76 optd **PROVISORIO**.
110 S 3a. lilac 1·00 70
111 12a. pink 2·75 2·00

1911. Nos. 68, etc, optd **REPUBLICA**.
125 S ½a. grey 15 15
126 1a. red 15 15
127 2a. green 15 15
128 3a. green 15 15
129 5a. red 30 15
130 6a. brown 30 15
131 9a. brown 30 15
132 10a. brown 70 55
133 13a. purple 70 55
134 15a. lilac 70 55
135 22a. brown on pink 70 55
136 31a. brown on cream 70 60
163 31a. purple on pink 1·25 1·10
137 47a. purple on pink 1·10 1·00
165 47a. blue on pink 1·90 1·75
167 78a. blue on yelow 1·75 1·40
168 78a. black on blue 2·25 2·00

1911. No. 112 and provisional stamps of 1902 optd **Republica**.
139 S 3a. green 1·40 1·25
140 R 5a. on 5r. orange 60 30
141 5a. on 25r. green 60 30
142 5a. on 50r. blue 1·75 1·25
144 V 6a. on 2½r. brown 1·40 80
146 R 6a. on 20r. lilac 55 60
147 9a. on 15r. brown 85 60
148 S 10a. on 12a. blue 85 60
149 R 15a. on 100r. brown on buff 90 60
150 22a. on 80r. green 1·75 1·25
151 22a. on 200r. blue on blue 1·75 1·25

1913. Provisional stamps of 1902 optd **REPUBLICA**.
192 S 3a. lilac (No. 110) 30 20
194 R 5a. on 5r. orange 30 20
195 5a. on 25r. green 30 20
196 5a. on 50r. blue 30 20
200 V 6a. on 2½r. brown 30 20
201 R 6a. on 20r. lilac 30 20
202 9a. on 15r. brown 30 20
203 9a. on 75r. pink 30 20
193 S 10a. on 10a. blue 30 20
204 R 15a. on 10r. mauve 30 20
205 15a. on 100r. brown on buff 40 20
206 15a. on 300r. blue on brn 40 20
207 22a. on 80r. green 1·00 70
208 22a. on 200r. blue on blue 1·60 1·10

1913. Vasco da Gama stamps of Timor optd **REPUBLICA** or surch also.
169 ½a. green 40 30
170 1a. red 40 30
171 2a. purple 40 30
172 4a. green 40 30
173 8a. blue 70 40
174 10a. on 12a. brown 90 85
175 16a. brown 70 60
176 24a. brown 1·00 85

1914. "Ceres" key-type inscr "TIMOR". Name and value in black.
211 U ¼a. green 30 25
212 1a. black 30 55
213 1½a. green 60 55
214 2a. green 30 25
180 3a. brown 40 30
181 4a. red 40 30
182 6a. violet 60 30
216 7a. green 90 80
217 7½a. blue 90 80
218 9a. blue 1·00 80
183 10a. blue 60 30
219 11a. grey 1·25 80
184 12a. brown 70 45
221 15a. mauve 2·50 2·10
185 16a. grey 85 60
222 18a. blue 3·00 2·10
223 19a. green 3·00 2·10
186 20a. red 6·50 2·25
224 36a. turquoise 3·00 2·10
187 40a. purple 3·75 2·00
225 54a. brown 3·00 2·10
188 58a. brown on green 3·75 2·10
226 72a. red 6·00 4·00
189 76a. brown on pink 3·75 3·25
190 1p. orange on orange 6·00 5·00
191 3p. green on blue 13·50 10·00
227 5p. red 25·00 12·50

1920. No. 196 surch ½ **Avo P. P. n.º 68 19-3-1920** and bars.
229 R ½a. on 5a. on 50r. blue 2·00 1·75

1932. Nos. 226 and 221 surch with new value and bars.
230 U 6a. on 72a. red 70 60
231 12a. on 15a. mauve 70 60

25a "Portugal" and Galeasse

1935.
232 **25a** ½a. brown 15 15
233 1a. brown 15 15
234 2a. green 15 15
235 3a. mauve 35 15
236 4a. black 35 15
237 5a. grey 35 25
238 6a. brown 35 25
239 7a. red 35 25
240 8a. turquoise 60 25
241 10a. red 60 25
242 12a. blue 60 25
243 14a. green 60 25
244 15a. purple 60 25
245 20a. orange 60 25
246 30a. green 60 25
247 40a. violet 1·75 50
248 50a. brown 1·75 50
249 1p. blue 3·25 2·50
250 2p. brown 9·00 4·25
251 3p. green 13·50 5·00
252 5p. mauve 22·00 9·25

26a Vasco da Gama
26b Airplane over globe

1938.
253 **26a** 1a. green (postage) 25 25
254 2a. brown 25 25
255 3a. violet 25 25
256 4a. green 25 25
257 – 5a. red 25 25
258 – 6a. grey 25 25
259 – 8a. purple 25 25
260 – 10a. mauve 25 25
261 – 12a. red 25 25
262 – 15a. orange 30 25
263 – 20a. blue 30 30
264 – 40a. black 40 30
265 – 50a. brown 1·00 60
266 – 1p. red 3·00 2·00
267 – 2p. olive 6·75 2·00
268 – 3p. blue 8·25 4·75
269 – 5p. brown 20·00 8·75
270 **26b** 1a. red (air) 30 30
271 2a. violet 30 30
272 3a. orange 30 30
273 5a. blue 40 30
274 10a. red 50 40
275 20a. green 1·10 70
276 50a. brown 2·10 2·00
277 70a. red 2·75 2·10
278 1p. mauve 5·75 3·75

DESIGNS—POSTAGE: 5a. to 8a. Mousinho de Albuquerque; 10a. to 15a. Prince Henry the Navigator; 20a. to 50a. Dam; 1p. to 5p. Afonso de Albuquerque.

1946. Stamps as above but inscr "MOCAMBIQUE" surch **TIMOR** and new value.
279 **26a** 1a. on 15c. purple (post) 2·40 1·60
280 – 4a. on 35c. green 2·40 1·60
281 – 8a. on 50c. mauve 2·40 1·60
282 – 10a. on 70c. violet 2·40 1·60
283 – 12a. on 1e. red 2·40 1·60
284 – 20a. on 1e.75 blue 2·40 1·60
285 **26b** 8a. on 50c. orange (air) 2·40 1·60
286 12a. on 1e. blue 2·40 1·60
287 40a. on 3e. green 2·40 1·60
288 50a. on 5e. brown 2·40 1·60
289 1p. on 10e. mauve 2·40 1·60

1947. Nos. 253/64 and 270/78 optd **LIBERTACAO**.
290 **26a** 1a. green (postage) 6·25 2·10
291 2a. brown 14·00 7·50
292 3a. violet 5·75 2·25
293 4a. green 5·75 2·25
294 – 5a. red 2·25 90
295 – 8a. purple 60 20
296 – 10a. mauve 2·25 1·00
297 – 12a. red 2·25 1·00
298 – 15a. orange 2·25 1·00
299 – 20a. blue 32·00 18·00
300 – 40a. black 7·50 4·75
301 **26b** 1a. red (air) 9·25 3·00
302 2a. violet 9·25 3·00
303 3a. orange 9·25 3·00
304 5a. blue 9·25 3·00
305 10a. red 2·25 90
306 20a. green 2·25 90
307 50a. brown 3·00 90
308 70a. red 9·25 2·50
309 1p. mauve 4·00 55

30 Girl with Gong
31 Pottery-making

1948.
310 – 1a. brown and turquoise 1·25 1·00
311 **30** 3a. brown and grey 2·25 2·00
312 – 4a. green and mauve 2·75 4·00
313 – 8a. grey and red 1·75 1·00
314 – 10a. green and brown 1·75 1·00
315 – 20a. ultramarine and blue 1·75 45
316 – 1p. blue and orange 32·00 12·00
317 – 3p. brown and violet 35·00 27·00

DESIGNS: 1a. Native woman; 4a. Girl with baskets; 8a. Chief of Aleixo de Ainaro; 10a. Timor chief; 20a. Warrior and horse; 1, 3p. Tribal chieftains.

1948. Honouring the Statue of Our Lady of Fatima. As T **33** of Portuguese Guinea.
318 8a. grey . . . . 4·00 4·00

1949. 75th Anniv of U.P.U. As T **34** of Portuguese Guinea
319 16a. brown . . . . 9·25 5·75

1950.
320 **31** 20a. blue 45 30
321 – 50a. brown (Young girl) 1·25 60

1950. Holy Year. As Nos. 425/6 of Macao.
322 40a. green 90 70
323 70a. brown . . . . 1·75 1·00

32 "Belamcanda chinensis"
34 Statue of The Virgin

1950.
324 **32** 1a. red, green and grey . . 65 30
325 – 3a. yellow, green and brown . . . . 3·75 1·50
326 – 10a. pink, green and blue 3·75 1·75
327 – 16a. multicoloured . . . . 8·00 2·50
328 – 20a. yellow, green and turquoise . . . . 3·75 1·50
329 – 30a. yellow, green and blue 3·75 1·50
330 – 70a. multicoloured . . . . 4·75 2·00
331 – 1p. red, yellow and green 8·50 4·50
332 – 2p. green, yellow and red 13·50 7·25
333 – 5p. pink, green and black 25·00 12·00
FLOWERS: 3a. "Caesalpinia pulcherrima"; 10a. "Calotropis gigantea"; 16a. "Delonix regia"; 20a. "Plumeria rubra"; 30a. "Allamanda cathartica"; 70a. "Haemanthus multiflorus"; 1p. "Bauhinia"; 2p. "Eurycles amboiniensis"; 5p. "Crinum longiflorum".

1951. Termination of Holy Year. As T **36** of Portuguese Guinea .
334 86a. blue and turquoise . . . 1·25 1·10

1952. 1st Tropical Medicine Congress, Lisbon. As T **37** of Portuguese Guinea
335 10a. brown and green 70 60
DESIGN: Nurse weighing baby.

1952. 400th Death Anniv of St. Francis Xavier. Designs as No. 452/4 of Macao.
336 1a. black and grey 15 10
337 16a. brown and buff 55 40
338 1p. red and grey . . . . . . 2·10 1·25

1953. Missionary Art Exhibition.
339 **34** 3a. brown and light brown 10 10
340 16a. brown and stone . . . 40 30
341 50a. blue and brown . . . 1·25 1·10

1954. Portuguese Stamp Centenary. As T **41** of Portuguese Guinea.
342 10a. multicoloured 70 60

1954. 400th Anniv of Sao Paulo. As T **42** of Portuguese Guinea.
343 16a. multicoloured 70 40

35 Map of Timor

38 Elephant Jar

1956.
344 **35** 1a. multicoloured 10 10
345 3a. multicoloured 10 10
346 8a. multicoloured 20 10
347 24a. multicoloured 20 10
348 32a. multicoloured 30 10
349 40a. multicoloured 60 25
350 1p. multicoloured . . . . 1·40 40
351 3p. multicoloured . . . . 4·25 2·10

1958. 6th International Congress of Tropical Medicine. As T **45** of Portuguese Guinea.
352 32a. multicoloured . . . . . 2·10 1·75
DESIGN: 32a. "Calophyllum inophyllum" (plant).

1958. Brussels International Exhibition. As T **44** of Portuguese Guinea.
353 40a. multicoloured 40 30

1960. New currency. Nos. 344/51 surch thus: **$05** and bars.
354 **35** 5c. on 1a. multicoloured 10 10
355 10c. on 3a. multicoloured 10 10
356 20c. on 8a. multicoloured 10 10
357 30c. on 24a. multicoloured 10 10
358 50c. on 32s. multicoloured 10 10
359 1e. on 40a. multicoloured 15 10
360 2e. on 40a. multicoloured 20 15
361 5e. on 1p. multicoloured 45 30
362 10e. on 3p. multicoloured 1·75 90
363 15e. on 3p. multicoloured 1·75 1·10

1960. 500th Death Anniv of Prince Henry the Navigator. As T **47** of Portuguese Guinea. Multicoloured.
364 4e.50 Prince Henry's motto (horiz) 40 25

1962. Timor Art. Multicoloured.
365 5c. Type **38** 10 10
366 10c. House on stilts 10 10
367 20c. Idol 25 10
368 30c. Rosary 25 25
369 50c. Model of outrigger canoe (horiz) 25 25
370 1e. Casket 40 30
371 2e.50 Archer 30 30
372 4e. Elephant 60 30
373 5e. Native climbing palm tree 70 30
374 10e. Statuette of woman . . 90 30
375 20e. Model of cockfight (horiz) . . . . 2·75 90
376 50e. House, bird and cat . . 6·75 2·10

1962. Sports. As T **49** of Portuguese Guinea. Multicoloured.
377 50c. Game shooting 10 10
378 1e. Horse-riding 50 15
379 1e.50 Swimming 25 10
380 2e. Athletes 25 15
381 2e.50 Football 35 25
382 15e. Big-game hunting . . . 1·25 80

1962. Malaria Eradication. Mosquito design as T **50** of Portuguese Guinea. Multicoloured.
383 2e.50 "Anopheles sundaicus" 40 30

1964. Centenary of National Overseas Bank. As T **53** of Portuguese Guinea, but portrait of M. P. Chagas.
384 2e.50 multicoloured 50 30

1965. I.T.U. Centenary. As T **54** of Portuguese Guinea.
385 1e.50 multicoloured 70 40

1966. 40th Anniv of National Revolution. As T **56** of Portuguese Guinea, but showing different buildings. Multicoloured.
386 4e.50 Dr V. Machado's College and Health Centre, Dili 60 35

1967. Centenary of Military Naval Assn. As T **57** of Portuguese Guinea. Multicoloured.
387 10c. Gago Coutinho and gunboat "Patria" 15 15
388 4e.50 Sacadura Cabral and Fairey IIID seaplane "Lusitania" . . . . 1·00 40

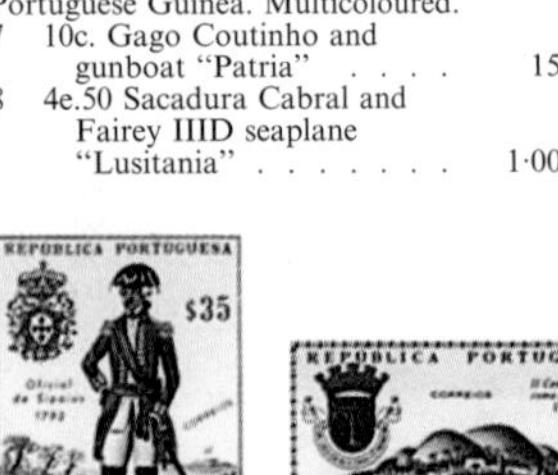

39 Sepoy Officer, 1792
40 Pictorial Map of 1834, and Arms

1967. Portuguese Military Uniforms. Mult.
389 35c. Type **39** 15 15
390 1e. Infantry officer, 1815 . . 95 25
391 1e.50 Infantryman 1879 . . . 15 15
392 2e. Infantryman, 1890 . . . 15 15
393 2e.50 Infantry officer, 1903 25 15
394 3e. Sapper, 1918 . . . . . . 35 25
395 4e.50 Commando, 1964 . . . 70 25
396 10e. Parachutist, 1964 . . . . 95 60

1967. 50th Anniv of Fatima Apparitions. As T **58** of Portuguese Guinea.
397 3e. Virgin of the Pilgrims . . 25 10

1968. 500th Birth Anniv of Pedro Cabral (explorer). As T **64** of Portuguese Guinea. Mult.
398 4e.50 Lopo Homen-Reineis' map, 1519 (horiz) 70 30

1969. Birth Centenary of Admiral Gago Coutinho. As T **66** of Portuguese Guinea. Mult.
399 4e.50 Frigate "Almirante Gago Coutinho" (horiz) . . 1·75 70

1969. Bicentenary of Dili (capital of Timor).
400 **40** 1e. multicoloured 25 15

1969. 500th Anniv of Vasco da Gama (explorer). As T **67** of Portuguese Guinea. Mult.
401 5e. Convert Medallion . . . 25 20

1969. Centenary of Overseas Administrative Reforms. As T **68** of Portuguese Guinea.
402 5e. multicoloured 25 15

1969. 500th Birth Anniv of King Manoel I. As T **69** of Portuguese Guinea. Multicoloured.
403 4e. Emblem of Manoel I in Jeronimos Monastery . . . 20 15

41 Map, Sir Ross Smith, and Arms of Britain, Timor and Australia

1969. 50th Anniv of 1st England–Australia Flight.
404 **41** 2e. multicoloured 35 25

1970. Birth Centenary of Marshal Carmona. As T **71** of Portuguese Guinea. Multicoloured.
414 1e. Portrait in civilian dress 15 15

1972. 400th Anniv of Camoens' "The Lusiads" (epic poem). As T **73** of Portuguese Guinea. Multicoloured.
415 1e. Missionaries, natives and galleon 15 15

1972. Olympic Games, Munich. As T **74** of Portuguese Guinea. Multicoloured.
416 4e.50 Football 40 25

1972. 50th Anniv of 1st Flight from Lisbon to Rio de Janeiro. As T **75** of Portuguese Guinea. Multicoloured.
417 1e. Aviators Gago Coutinho and Sacadura Cabral in Fairey IIID seaplane . . . 30 25

1973. W.M.O. Centenary. As T **76** of Portuguese Guinea.
418 20e. multicoloured . . . . . 1·10 90

CHARITY TAX STAMPS

The notes under this heading in Portugal also apply here.

1919. No. 211 surch **2 AVOS TAXA DA GUERRA**. With or without gum.
C228 U 2a. on ½a. green . . . . 2·25 1·10

1919. No. 196 surch **2 TAXA DE GUERRA** and bars.
C230 R 2 on 5a. on 50r. blue . . 28·00 16·00

1925. Marquis de Pombal Commem. As Nos. 666/8 of Portugal, but inscr "TIMOR".
C231 C **73** 2a. red 20 20
C232 – 2a. red 20 20
C233 C **75** 2a. red 20 20

1934. Educational Tax. Fiscal stamps as Type C **1** of Portuguese Colonies, with values in black, optd **Instrucao D. L. n.° 7 de 3-2-1934** or surch also. With or without gum.
C234 2a. green . . . . 1·75 1·00
C235 5a. green . . . . 2·75 1·25
C236 7a. on ½a. pink . . . . . . 2·75 1·75

1936. Fiscal stamps as Type C **1** of Portuguese Colonies, with value in black, optd **Assistencia D. L. n.° 72**. With or without gum.
C253 10a. pink . . . . 1·75 1·25
C254 10a. green . . . . 1·25 1·00

C **29**

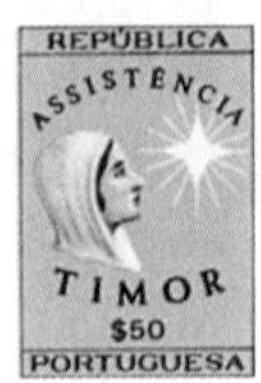

C **42** Woman and Star

1948. No gum.
C310 C **29** 10a. blue . . . . . . 1·25 1·10
C311 20a. green . . . . . . 2·00 1·25
The 20a. has a different emblem.

1960. Similar design. New currency. No gum.
C364 70c. blue . . . . 1·00 1·00
C400 1e.30 green . . . . 1·10 1·10

1969.
C405 C **42** 30c. blue and light blue 10 10
C406 50c. purple and orange 10 10
C407 1e. brown and yellow 10 10

1970. Nos. C364 and C400 surch **D. L. n.° 776** and value.
C408 30c. on 70c. blue . . . . . 2·75 2·75
C409 30c. on 1e.30 green . . . . 2·75 2·75
C410 50c. on 70c. blue . . . . . 4·00 4·00
C411 50c. on 1e.30 green . . . . 2·75 2·75
C412 1e. on 70c. blue . . . . . 4·00 4·00
C413 1e. on 1e.30 green . . . . 2·75 2·75

NEWSPAPER STAMPS

1892. "Embossed" key-type inscr "PROVINCIA DE MACAU" surch **JORNAES TIMOR 2½ 2½**. No gum.
N31 Q 2½ on 20r. red . . . . . . 1·00 60
N32 2½ on 40r. brown . . . . 1·00 60
N33 2½ on 80r. grey . . . . . 1·00 60

1893. "Newspaper" key-type inscr "TIMOR".
N36 V 2½r. brown 50 30

1894. No. N36 surch **½ avo PROVISORIO** and Chinese characters.
N58 V ½a. on 2½r. brown 30 30

POSTAGE DUE STAMPS

1904. "Due" key-type inscr "TIMOR". Name and value in black. With or without gum (1, 2a.), no gum (others).
D124 W 1a. green 30 30
D125 2a. grey 30 30
D126 5a. brown 90 75
D127 6a. orange 90 75
D128 10a. brown 90 75
D129 15a. brown . . . . . . 1·50 1·10
D130 24a. blue . . . . 3·00 2·50
D131 40a. red . . . . 3·00 2·50
D132 50a. orange . . . . . . 4·00 3·00
D133 1p. lilac . . . . 7·00 5·25

1911. "Due" key-type of Timor optd **REPUBLICA**.
D139 W 1a. green 25 25
D140 2a. grey 25 25
D141 5a. brown 25 25
D142 6a. orange 30 30
D143 10a. brown 60 40
D144 15a. brown 85 50
D145 24a. blue . . . . 1·10 90
D146 40a. red . . . . 1·40 1·10
D147 50a. orange . . . . . . 1·40 1·10
D178 1p. lilac . . . . 3·75 2·50

1925. Marquis de Pombal tax stamps. As Nos. C231/3 of Timor, optd **MULTA**.
D231 C **73** 4a. red 20 20
D232 – 4a. red 20 20
D233 C **75** 4a. red 20 20

1952. As Type D **70** of Macao, but inscr "TIMOR PORTUGUES". Numerals in red; name in black.
D336 1a. sepia and brown . . . 10 10
D337 3a. brown and orange . . . 10 10
D338 5a. green and turquoise . . 10 10
D339 10a. green and light green 15 15
D340 30a. violet and light violet 20 15
D341 1p. red and orange 55 30

For subsequent issues see **EAST TIMOR**.

PRINCE EDWARD ISLAND Pt. 1

An island off the East coast of Canada, now a province of that Dominion, whose stamps it uses.

1861. 12 pence = 1 shilling.
1872. 100 cents = 1 dollar.

1

7

1861. Queen's portrait in various frames. Values in pence.
9 **1** 1d. orange . . . . 27·00 38·00
28 2d. red . . . . 6·50 9·50
30 3d. blue . . . . 10·00 13·00
31 4d. black . . . . 4·75 27·00
18 6d. green . . . . 85·00 90·00
20 9d. mauve . . . . 70·00 70·00

1870.
32 **7** 4½d. (3d. stg.) brown . . . . 42·00 50·00

8

1872. Queen's portrait in various frames. Values in cents.
35 **8** 1c. orange . . . . 4·50 12·00
38 2c. blue . . . . 15·00 32·00
37 3c. red . . . . 15·00 21·00
40 4c. green . . . . 5·50 14·00
41 6c. black . . . . 4·25 15·00
42 12c. mauve . . . . 4·00 26·00

PRUSSIA Pt. 7

Formerly a kingdom in the N. of Germany. In 1867 it became part of the North German Confederation.

1850. 12 pfennig = 1 silbergroschen;
30 silbergroschen = 1 thaler.
1867. 60 kreuzer = 1 gulden.

1 Friedrich Wilhelm IV

3

4

1850. Imperf.

14	**1**	4pf. green	65·00	26·00
4		6pf. red	70·00	35·00
22		½sgr. (=6pf.) red	£170	£160
5		1sgr. black on pink	70·00	7·00
16		1sgr. pink	27·00	2·30
6		2sgr. black on blue	£100	14·00
18		2sgr. blue	£100	13·00
8		3sgr. black on yellow	95·00	9·50
21		3sgr. yellow	85·00	11·50

1861. Roul.

24	**3**	3pf. lilac	22·00	31·00
26		4pf. green	8·25	7·00
28		6pf. orange	8·75	10·50
31	**4**	1sgr. pink	3·50	90
35		2sgr. blue	8·25	1·80
36		3sgr. yellow	7·25	2·20

5

7

1866. Printed in reverse on back of specially treated transparent paper. Roul.

38	**5**	10sgr. pink	65·00	55·00
39	–	30sgr. blue	80·00	£130

The 30 sgr. has the value in a square.

1867. Roul.

40	**7**	1k. green	22·00	33·00
42		2k. orange	36·00	90·00
43		3k. pink	19·00	23·00
45		6k. blue	19·00	33·00
46		9k. bistre	24·00	35·00

PUERTO RICO Pt. 9; Pt. 22

A West Indian island ceded by Spain to the United States after the war of 1898. Until 1873 stamps of Cuba were in use. Now uses stamps of the U.S.A.

1873. 100 centimos = 1 peseta.
1881. 1000 milesimas = 100 centavos = 1 peso.
1898. 100 cents = 1 dollar.

A. SPANISH OCCUPATION

(2)

1873. Nos. 53/5 of Cuba optd with T **2**.

1		25c. de p. lilac	30·00	80
3		50c. de p. brown	80·00	4·00
4		1p. brown	£180	16·00

1874. No. 57 of Cuba with opt similar to T **2** (two separate characters).

5		25c. de p. blue	27·00	1·90

1875. Nos. 61/3 of Cuba with opt similar to T **2** (two separate characters).

6		25c. de p. blue	18·00	1·90
7		50c. de p. green	26·00	2·25
8		1p. brown	95·00	11·00

1876. Nos. 65a and 67 of Cuba with opt similar to T **2** (two separate characters).

9		25c. de p. lilac	3·25	1·40
10		50c. de p. blue	6·75	2·50
11		1p. black	32·00	8·75

1876. Nos. 65a and 67 of Cuba with opt as last, but characters joined.

12		25c. de p. lilac	25·00	70
13		1p. black	50·00	8·25

1877. As T **9** of Philippines, but inscr "PTO-RICO 1877".

14		5c. brown	5·25	1·75
15		10c. red	16·00	2·25
16		15c. green	24·00	9·25
17		25c. blue	9·50	1·50
18		50c. bistre	16·00	3·75

1878. As T **9** of Philippines, but inscr "PTO-RICO 1878".

19		5c. grey	12·00	12·00
20		10c. brown	£190	70·00
21		25c. green	1·50	85
22		50c. blue	5·00	2·00
23a		1p. bistre	9·50	4·00

1879. As T **9** of Philippines, but inscr "PTO-RICO 1879".

24		5c. red	10·00	4·25
25		10c. brown	10·00	4·25
26		15c. grey	10·00	4·25
27		25c. blue	3·50	1·50
28		50c. green	10·00	4·25
29		1p. lilac	48·00	19·00

1880. "Alfonso XII" key-type inscr "PUERTO-RICO 1880".

30	X	¼c. green	21·00	15·00
31		½c. red	5·50	2·00
32		1c. purple	9·50	8·00
33		2c. grey	5·50	3·75
34		3c. buff	5·50	3·75
35		4c. black	5·50	3·75
36		5c. green	2·75	1·40
37		10c. red	3·25	1·90
38		15c. brown	5·50	2·75
39		25c. lilac	2·75	1·40
40		40c. grey	11·00	1·40
41		50c. brown	21·00	12·50
42		1p. bistre	75·00	16·00

1881. "Alfonso XIII" key-type inscr "PUERTO-RICO 1881".

43	X	½m. red	20	10
45		1m. violet	40	30
46		2m. red	40	30
47		4m. green	70	20
48		6m. purple	70	40
49		8m. blue	1·60	1·00
50		1c. green	2·75	1·00
51		2c. red	3·50	2·75
52		3c. brown	7·25	4·25
53		5c. lilac	2·50	30
54		8c. brown	2·40	1·25
55		10c. grey	22·00	7·00
56		20c. bistre	28·00	12·50

1882. "Alfonso XII" key-type inscr "PUERTO-RICO".

57	X	½m. red	15	10
74		1m. red	15	10
75		1m. orange	15	10
59		2m. mauve	20	15
60		4m. purple	20	15
61		6m. brown	35	15
62		8m. green	35	15
63		1c. green	15	15
64		2c. red	1·00	15
65		3c. yellow	3·50	2·00
76		3c. brown	3·50	65
77		5c. lilac	13·00	1·00
67		8c. brown	3·25	10
68		10c. green	3·25	20
69		20c. grey	4·75	20
70		40c. blue	35·00	13·00
71		80c. bistre	50·00	18·00

1890. "Baby" key-type inscr "PUERTO-RICO".

80	Y	½m. black	15	10
95		½m. grey	15	10
111		½m. brown	15	15
124		½m. purple	15	10
81		1m. green	25	10
96		1m. purple	15	10
112		1m. blue	15	15
125		1m. brown	15	10
82		2m. red	15	10
97		2m. purple	15	10
126		2m. green	15	10
83		4m. black	9·75	5·50
98		4m. blue	15	10
114		4m. brown	15	15
127		4m. green	85	30
84		6m. brown	32·00	13·00
99		6m. red	15	10
85		8m. bistre	25·00	18·00
100		8m. green	15	10
86		1c. brown	20	10
101		1c. green	50	10
115		1c. purple	5·25	40
128		1c. red	60	10
87		2c. purple	85	80
102		2c. pink	80	10
116		2c. lilac	1·90	40
129		2c. brown	60	10
88		3c. blue	6·50	85
103		3c. orange	80	10
117		3c. grey	5·25	40
131		3c. brown	20	10
118		4c. blue	1·25	40
132		4c. brown	65	10
89		5c. purple	10·50	40
104		5c. green	80	10
133		5c. blue	20	10
120		6c. orange	40	15
134		6c. lilac	20	10
90		8c. blue	13·50	1·60
105		8c. brown	15	10
121		8c. purple	11·00	4·50
135		8c. red	2·40	1·25
106		10c. red	1·25	10
122		20c. red	1·40	40
107		20c. lilac	1·90	45
136		20c. grey	6·00	1·25
93		40c. orange	85·00	42·00
108		40c. blue	5·00	3·25
137		40c. red	6·00	1·25
94		80c. green	£400	£140
109		80c. red	13·00	10·00
138		80c. black	24·00	19·00

13 Landing of Columbus

1893. 400th Anniv of Discovery of America by Columbus.

110	**13**	3c. green	£160	40·00

1898. "Curly Head" key-type inscr "PTO RICO 1898 y 99".

139	Z	1m. brown	10	10
140		2m. brown	10	10
141		3m. brown	10	10
142		4m. brown	1·25	50
143		5m. brown	10	10
144		1c. purple	10	10
145		2c. green	10	10
146		3c. brown	10	10
147		4c. orange	1·25	85
148		5c. pink	10	10
149		6c. blue	10	10
150		8c. brown	10	10
151		10c. red	10	10
152		15c. grey	10	10
153		20c. purple	1·50	50
154		40c. lilac	1·10	1·25
155		60c. black	1·10	1·25
156		80c. brown	4·00	4·50
157		1p. green	9·00	8·75
158		2p. blue	21·00	12·00

1898. "Baby" key-type inscr "PUERTO RICO" and optd **Habilitado PARA 1898 y '99**.

159	Y	½m. purple	10·00	5·50
160		1m. brown	40	20
161		2m. green	40	20
162		4m. green	40	20
163		1c. purple	40	20
164		2c. brown	30	15
165		3c. blue	18·00	8·50
166		3c. brown	40	20
167		4c. brown	35	25
168		4c. blue	11·00	7·00
169		5c. blue	40	25
170		5c. green	5·50	4·00
172		6c. lilac	40	20
173a		8c. red	60	30
174		20c. grey	75	40
175		40c. red	3·00	50
176		80c. black	19·00	14·50

WAR TAX STAMPS

1898. 1890 and 1898 stamps optd **IMPUESTO DE GUERRA** or surch also.

W177	Y	1m. blue	2·40	1·75
W178		1m. brown	6·50	4·75
W179		2m. red	12·50	8·00
W180		2m. green	6·50	4·75
W181		4m. green	10·00	10·00
W182a		1c. brown	6·50	4·00
W183		1c. purple	11·00	10·00
W184		2c. purple	35	20
W185		2c. pink	35	20
W186		2c. lilac	85	85
W187		2c. brown	85	20
W192		2c. on 2m. red	40	25
W193c		2c. on 5c. green	2·00	1·75
W188		3c. orange	12·00	10·00
W194		3c. on 10c. red	12·00	9·50
W195		4c. on 20c. red	12·00	9·50
W189		5c. green	25	15
W196a		5c. on ½m. brown	4·75	3·25
W197		5c. on 1m. purple	35	25
W198		5c. on 1m. blue	40	40
W199	Z	5c. on 1m. brown	6·50	4·50
W200	Y	5c. on 5c. green	3·25	2·50
W191		8c. purple	19·00	16·00

B. UNITED STATES OCCUPATION

1899. 1894 stamps of United States (No. 267 etc) optd **PORTO RICO**.

202		1c. green	4·00	1·25
203		2c. red	3·75	1·00
204		5c. blue	7·00	2·10
205		8c. brown	22·00	14·50
206		10c. brown	14·00	4·50

1900. 1894 stamps of United States (No. 267 etc) optd **PUERTO RICO**.

210		1c. green	4·75	1·10
212		2c. red	4·00	90

POSTAGE DUE STAMPS

1899. Postage Due stamps of United States of 1894 optd **PORTO RICO**.

D207	**D 87**	1c. red	18·00	6·00
D208		2c. red	9·00	4·50
D209		10c. red	£130	42·00

QATAR Pt. 1, Pt. 19

An independent Arab Shaikhdom with British postal administration until 23 May 1963. The stamps of Muscat were formerly used at Doha and Urm Said. Later issues by the Qatar Post Department.

1966. 100 dirhams = 1 riyal.
1967. 100 naye paise = 1 rupee.

Stamps of Great Britain surcharged **QATAR** and value in Indian currency.

1957. Queen Elizabeth II and pictorials.

1	**157**	1n.p. on 5d. brown	10	10
2	**154**	3n.p. on ½d. orange	15	15
3		6n.p. on 1d. blue	15	15
4		9n.p. on 1½d. green	15	10
5		12n.p. on 2d. brown	20	1·75
6	**155**	15n.p. on 2½d. red	15	10
7		20n.p. on 3d. lilac	15	10
8		25n.p. on 4d. blue	40	1·25
9	**157**	40n.p. on 6d. purple	15	10
10	**158**	50n.p. on 9d. olive	40	15
11	**159**	75n.p. on 1s.3d. green	50	2·00
12		1r. on 1s.6d. blue	8·00	10
13	**166**	2r. on 2s.6d. brown	3·50	3·75
14	–	5r. on 5s. red	4·50	3·75
15	–	10r. on 10s. blue	5·50	14·00

1957. World Scout Jubilee Jamboree.

16	**170**	15n.p. on 2½d. red	35	35
17	**171**	25n.p. on 4d. blue	35	35
18	–	75n.p. on 1s.3d. green	40	40

8 Shaikh Ahmad bin All al Thani

9 Peregrine Falcon

11 Oil Derrick

1961.

27	**8**	5n.p. red	10	10
28		15n.p. black	10	10
29		20n.p. purple	10	10
30		30n.p. green	10	10
31	**9**	40n.p. red	1·00	10
32		50n.p. brown	1·40	10
33	–	75n.p. blue	60	2·25
34	**11**	1r. red	70	10
35		2r. blue	2·00	1·00
36	–	5r. green	16·00	3·50
37	–	10r. black	38·00	6·00

DESIGNS—As Type **9**: 75n.p. Dhow. As Type **11**: 5r., 10r. Mosque.

1964. Olympic Games, Tokyo. Optd **1964**, Olympic rings and Arabic inscr or surch also.

38	**9**	50n.p. brown	2·25	1·60
39	–	75n.p. blue (No. 33)	2·50	1·75
40	–	1r. on 10r. black (No. 37)	1·10	1·00
41	**11**	2r. blue	2·50	2·00
42		5r. green (No. 36)	7·00	6·00

1964. Pres. Kennedy Commem. Optd **John F Kennedy 1917–1963** in English and Arabic or surch also.

43	**9**	50n.p. brown	7·25	2·10
44	–	75n.p. blue (No. 33)	2·50	1·75
45	–	1r. on 10r. black (No. 37)	1·10	1·00
46	**11**	2r. blue	2·50	2·00
47	–	5r. green (No. 36)	7·00	5·00

15 Colonnade, Temple of Isis

16 Scouts on Parade

1965. Nubian Monuments Preservation. Mult.

48	1n.p. Type **15**	10	15
49	2n.p. Temple of Isis, Philac	10	15
50	3n.p. Trajan's Kiosk, Philac	10	15
51	1r. As 3n.p.	1·25	30
52	1r.50 As 2n.p.	2·10	50
53	2r. Type **15**	2·50	50

1965. Qatar Scouts.

54	–	1n.p. brown and green	20	15
55	–	2n.p. blue and brown	20	15
56	–	3n.p. blue and green	20	15
57	–	4n.p. brown and blue	20	15
58	–	5n.p. blue and turquoise	20	15
59	**16**	30n.p. multicoloured	50	40
60		40n.p. multicoloured	65	50
61		1r. multicoloured	1·60	1·10

DESIGNS—TRIANGULAR (60 × 30 mm): 1, 4n.p. Qatar Scout badge; 2, 3, 5n.p. Ruler, badge, palms and camp.

17 "Telstar" and Eiffel Tower

1965. I.T.U. Centenary.

62	**17**	1n.p. brown and blue	20	15
63	–	2n.p. brown and blue	20	15
64	–	3n.p. violet and green	20	15
65	–	4n.p. blue and brown	20	15
66	**17**	5n.p. brown and violet	20	15
67	–	40n.p. black and red	50	30
68	–	50n.p. brown and green	60	40
69	–	1r. red and green	1·25	80

DESIGNS: 2n.p., 1r. "Syncom 3" and pagoda; 3, 40n.p. "Relay" and radar scanner; 4, 50n.p. Post Office Tower (London), globe and satellites.

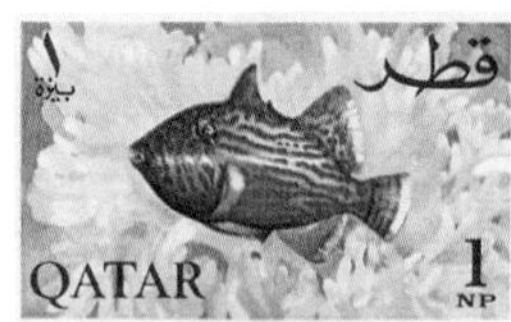

18 Jigsaw Triggerfish

1965. Fish of the Arabian Gulf. Multicoloured.

70	1n.p. Type **18**	10	10
71	2n.p. Harlequin sweetlips	10	10
72	3n.p. Saddle butterflyfish	10	10
73	4n.p. Thread-finned butterflyfish	10	10
74	5n.p. Masked unicornfish	10	10
75	15n.p. Paradise fish	35	15
76	20n.p. White-spotted surgeonfish	40	15
77	30n.p. Rio Grande cichlid	50	15
78	40n.p. Convict cichlid	65	20
79	50n.p. As 2n.p	1·00	35
80	75n.p. Type **18**	1·60	40
81	1r. As 30n.p.	2·50	40
82	2r. As 20n.p.	5·00	1·00
83	3r. As 15n.p.	7·00	2·00
84	4r. As 5n.p.	8·50	2·60
85	5r. As 4n.p.	9·25	3·50
86	10r. As 3n.p.	16·00	7·50

19 Basketball

1966. Pan-Arab Games, Cairo (1965).

87	**19**	1r. black, grey and red	90	60
88	–	1r. brown and green	90	60
89	–	1r. red and blue	90	60
90	–	1r. green and blue	90	60
91	–	1r. blue and brown	90	60

SPORTS: No. 88, Horse-jumping; No. 89, Running; No. 90, Football; No. 91, Weightlifting.

1966. Space Rendezvous. Nos. 62/9 optd with two space capsules and **SPACE RENDEZVOUS 15th. DECEMBER 1965** in English and Arabic.

92	**17**	1n.p. brown and blue	15	10
93	–	2n.p. brown and blue	15	10
94	–	3n.p. violet and green	15	10
95	–	4n.p. blue and brown	15	10
96	**17**	5n.p. brown and violet	15	10
97	–	40n.p. black and red	90	25
98	–	50n.p. brown and green	90	30
99	–	1r. red and green	1·90	55

21 Shaikh Ahmed

1966. Gold and Silver Coinage. Circular designs embossed on gold (G) or silver (S) foil, backed with "Walsall Security Paper" inscr in English and Arabic. Imperf. (a) Diameter 42 mm.

101	**21**	1n.p. bistre and purple (S)	15	15
102	–	3n.p. black and orange (S)	15	15
103	**21**	4n.p. violet and red (G)	15	15
104	–	5n.p. green and mauve (G)	15	15

(b) Diameter 55 mm.

105	**21**	10n.p. brown and violet (S)	25	15
106	–	40n.p. red and blue (S)	50	25
107	**21**	70n.p. blue & ultram (G)	85	45
108	–	80n.p. mauve and green (G)	85	45

(c) Diameter 64 mm.

109	**21**	1r. mauve and black (S)	1·50	60
110	–	2r. green and purple (S)	3·00	1·40
111	**21**	5r. purple and orange (G)	7·00	3·00
112	–	10r. blue and red (G)	14·00	6·00

The 1, 4, 10, 70n.p. and 1 and 5r. each show the obverse side of the coins as Type **21**. The remainder show the reverse side of the coins (Shaikh's seal).

22 I.C.Y. and U.N. Emblem

1966. International Co-operation Year

113	**22**	40n.p. brown, violet & bl	1·10	65
114	A	40n.p. violet, brn & turq	1·10	65
115	B	40n.p. blue, brown & vio	1·10	65
116	C	40n.p. turquoise, vio & bl	1·10	65

DESIGNS: A, Pres. Kennedy, I.C.Y. emblem and U.N. Headquarters; B, Dag Hammarskjold and U.N. General Assembly; C, Nehru and dove.

Nos. 113/16 were issued together in blocks of four, each sheet containing four blocks separated by gutter margins. Subsequently the sheets were reissued perf and imperf with the opt **U.N. 20TH ANNIVERSARY** on the stamps. The gutter margins were also printed in various designs, face values and overprints.

23 Pres. Kennedy and New York Skyline

1966. Pres. Kennedy Commemoration. Multicoloured.

118	10n.p. Type **23**	20	15
119	30n.p. Pres. Kennedy and Cape Kennedy	40	20
120	60n.p. Pres. Kennedy and Statue of Liberty	65	40
121	70n.p. Type **23**	70	55
122	80n.p. As 30n.p.	80	55
123	1r. As 60n.p.	1·50	95

24 Horse-jumping

1966. Olympic Games Preparation (Mexico). Multicoloured.

125	1n.p. Type **24**	15	15
126	4n.p. Running	15	15
127	5n.p. Throwing the javelin	15	15
128	70n.p. Type **24**	85	45
129	80n.p. Running	85	50
130	90n.p. Throwing the javelin	90	70

25 J. A. Lovell and Capsule

1966. American Astronauts. Each design showing spacecraft and astronaut. Multicoloured.

132	5n.p. Type **25**	15	15
133	10n.p. T. P. Stafford	15	15
134	15n.p. A. B. Shepard	15	15
135	20n.p. J. H. Glenn	15	15
136	30n.p. M. Scott Carpenter	30	20
137	40n.p. W. M. Schirra	30	20
138	50n.p. V. I. Grissom	45	35
139	60n.p. L. G. Cooper	65	45

Nos. 132/4 are diamond-shaped as Type **25**, the remainder are horiz designs (56 × 25 mm).

1966. Various stamps with currency names changed to dirhams and riyals by overprinting in English and Arabic. (i) Nos. 27/37 (Definitives).

141	**8**	5d. on 5n.p. red	25	10
142		15d. on 15n.p. black	35	10
143		20d. on 20n.p. purple	35	15
144		30d. on 30n.p. green	65	25
145	**9**	40d. on 40n.p. red	2·10	50
146		50d. on 50n.p. brown	2·50	65
147	–	75d. on 75n.p. blue	2·25	55
148	**11**	1r. on 1r. red	2·50	50
149		2r. on 2r. blue	5·50	2·25
150	–	5r. on 5r. green	12·50	7·00
151	–	10r. on 10r. black	21·00	10·00

(ii) Nos. 70/86 (Fish). Multicoloured.

152	1d. on 1n.p.	10	10
153	2d. on 2n.p.	10	10
154	3d. on 3n.p.	10	10
155	4d. on 4n.p.	10	10
156	5d. on 5n.p.	10	10
157	15d. on 15n.p.	35	10
158	20d. on 20n.p.	45	10
159	30d. on 30n.p.	60	15
160	40d. on 40n.p.	85	20
161	50d. on 50n.p.	1·10	30
162	75d. on 75n.p.	2·00	55
163	1r. on 1r.	2·25	70
164	2r. on 2r.	4·50	2·00
165	3r. on 3r.	7·50	3·50
166	4r. on 4r.	10·00	5·00
167	5r. on 5r.	12·50	6·00
168	10r. on 10r.	24·00	12·00

27 National Library, Doha

1966. Education Day. Multicoloured.

169	2n.p. Type **27**	10	10
170	3n.p. School and playing field	15	10
171	5n.p. School and gardens	15	10
172	1r. Type **27**	2·75	90
173	2r. As 3n.p	4·25	2·00
174	3r. As 5n.p	6·00	2·75

28 Palace, Doha

1966. Currency expressed in naye paise and rupees. Multicoloured.

175	2n.p. Type **28**	10	10
176	3n.p. Gulf Street, Shahra Al-Khalij	10	10
177	10n.p. Doha airport	30	10
178	15n.p. Garden, Rayan	20	10
179	20n.p. Head Post Office, Doha	25	10
180	30n.p. Mosque Doha (vert)	40	15
181	40n.p. Shaikh Ahmad	80	20
182	50n.p. Type **28**	90	35
183	60n.p. As 3n.p.	1·40	50
184	70n.p. As 10n.p.	2·00	75
185	80n.p. As 15n.p.	1·90	85
186	90n.p. As 20n.p.	2·25	1·40
187	1r. As 30n.p. (vert)	2·40	1·50
188	2r. As 40n.p.	5·00	3·75

29 Hands holding Jules Rimet Trophy

1966. World Cup Football Championship, England.

189	**29**	60n.p. mult (postage)	85	65
190	–	70n.p. multicoloured	1·00	80
191	–	80n.p. multicoloured	1·40	1·00
192	–	90n.p. multicoloured	1·50	1·10
193	–	1n.p. blue (air)	15	15
194	–	2n.p. blue	15	15
195	–	3n.p. blue	25	25
196	–	4n.p. blue	30	30

DESIGNS: No. 190, Jules Rimet Trophy and "football" globe; No. 191, Footballers and globe; No. 192, Wembley stadium; Nos. 193/6, Jules Rimet Trophy.

30 A.P.U. Emblem

32 Traffic Lights

31 Astronauts on Moon

1967. Admission of Qatar to Arab Postal Union.

198	**30**	70d. brown and violet	1·10	60
199		80d. brown and blue	1·40	85

1967. U.S. "Apollo" Space Missions. Mult.

200	5d. Type **31**	10	10
201	10d. "Apollo" spacecraft	10	10
202	20d. Landing module on Moon	15	10
203	30d. Blast-off from Moon	25	15
204	40d. "Saturn 5" rocket	35	20
205	70d. Type **31**	75	45
206	80d. As 10d.	85	60
207	1r. As 20d.	90	80
208	1r.20 As 30d.	1·50	1·25
209	2r. As 40d.	2·10	1·75

1967. Traffic Day.

211	**32**	20d. multicoloured	35	15
212		30d. multicoloured	70	30
213		50d. multicoloured	1·10	50
214		1r. multicoloured	3·00	1·75

33 Brownsea Island and Jamboree Camp, Idaho

1967. Diamond Jubilee of Scout Movement and World Scout Jamboree, Idaho. Multicoloured.

215	1d. Type **33**	15	10
216	2d. Lord Baden-Powell	15	10
217	3d. Pony-trekking	15	10
218	5d. Canoeing	20	10
219	15d. Swimming	60	25
220	75d. Rock-climbing	1·50	85
221	2r. World Jamboree emblem	4·75	2·40

34 Norman Ship (from Bayeux Tapestry)

1967. Famous Navigators' Ships. Multicoloured.

222	1d. Type **34**	20	10
223	2d. "Santa Maria" (Columbus)	25	10
224	3d. "Sao Gabriel" (Vasco da Gama)	30	10
225	75d. "Vitoria" (Magellan)	1·75	1·25
226	1r. "Golden Hind" (Drake)	2·75	1·25
227	2r. "Gipsy Moth IV" (Chichester)	5·75	2·10

35 Arab Scribe

1968. 10th Anniv of Qatar Postage Stamps. Multicoloured.

228	1d. Type **35**	15	10
229	2d. Pigeon post (vert)	15	10
230	3d. Mounted postman	15	10
231	60d. Rowing boat postman (vert)	1·25	85

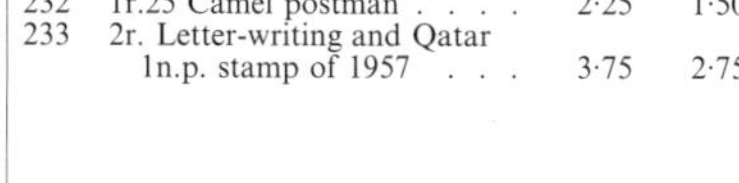

232	1r.25 Camel postman	2·25	1·50
233	2r. Letter-writing and Qatar 1n.p. stamp of 1957	3·75	2·75

36 Human Rights Emblem and Barbed Wire

1968. Human Rights Year. Multicoloured designs embodying Human Rights emblem.

234	1d. Type **36**	15	10
235	2d. Arab refugees	15	10
236	3d. Scales of justice	15	10
237	60d. Opening doors	85	50
238	1r.25 Family (vert)	1·40	1·25
239	2r. Human figures	2·40	1·75

37 Shaikh Ahmad

39 Shaikh Ahmad

38 Dhow

1968.

240	**37**	5d. green and blue	15	10
241		10d. brown and blue	15	10
242		20d. red and black	30	10
243		25d. green and purple	50	15
244	**38**	35d. green, blue and pink	1·25	20
245	–	40d. purple, blue & orange	1·00	20
246	–	60d. brown, blue and violet	2·50	45
247	–	70d. black, blue and green	1·60	55
248	–	1r. blue, yellow and green	1·90	60
249	–	1r.25 blue, pink and light blue	3·50	75
250	–	1r.50 green, blue & purple	6·50	1·40
251	**39**	2r. blue, brown and cinnamon	5·25	1·25
252		5r. purple, green and light green	11·00	4·50
253		10r. brown, ultram & blue	22·00	7·50

DESIGNS—As Type **38**: 40d. Water purification plant; 60d. Oil jetty; 70d. Qatar mosque; 1r. Palace Doha; 1r.25, Doha fort; 1r.50, Peregrine falcon.

41 Maternity Ward

1968. 20th Anniv of W.H.O. Multicoloured.

258	1d. Type **41**	15	10
259	2d. Operating theatre	15	10
260	3d. Dental surgery	15	10
261	60d. X-ray examination table	90	50
262	1r.25 Laboratory	2·50	1·50
263	2r. State Hospital Qatar	3·25	4·00

42 Throwing the Discus

1968. Olympic Games, Mexico. Multicoloured.

264	1d. Type **42**	15	10
265	2d. Olympic Flame and runner	15	10
266	3d. "68", rings and gymnast	15	10
267	60d. Weightlifting and Flame	1·25	65
268	1r.25 "Flame" in mosaic pattern (vert)	2·40	1·00
269	2r. "Cock" emblem	3·50	1·60

43 U.N. Emblem and Flags

1968. United Nations Day. Multicoloured.

270	1d. Type **43**	15	10
271	4d. Dove of Peace and world map	15	10
272	5d. U.N. Headquarters and flags	15	10
273	60d. Teacher and class	1·25	65
274	1r.50 Agricultural workers	2·40	1·00
275	2r. U. Thant and U.N. Assembly	3·50	1·60

44 Trawler "Ross Rayyan"

1969. Progress in Qatar. Multicoloured.

276	1d. Type **44**	10	10
277	4d. Primary school	10	10
278	5d. Doha International Airport	10	10
279	60d. Cement factory and road-making	1·40	50
280	1r.50 Power station and pylon	2·75	1·25
281	2r. Housing estate	3·75	1·90

45 Armoured Cars

1969. Qatar Security Forces. Multicoloured.

282	1d. Type **45**	10	10
283	2d. Traffic control	10	10
284	3d. Military helicopter	10	10
285	60d. Section of military band	1·50	70
286	1r.25 Field gun	2·75	1·50
287	2r. Mounted police	4·25	2·10

46 Tanker "Sivella" at Mooring

1969. Qatar's Oil Industry. Multicoloured.

288	1d. Type **46**	10	10
289	2d. Training school	10	10
290	3d. "Sea Shell" (oil rig) and "Shell Dolphin" (supply vessel)	10	10
291	60d. Storage tanks, Halul	1·50	85
292	1r.50 Topping plant	3·50	1·90
293	2r. Various tankers, 1890–1968	6·50	2·50

47 "Guest-house" and Dhow-building

1969. 10th Scout Jamboree, Qatar. Multicoloured.

294	1d. Type **47**	10	10
295	2d. Scouts at work	10	10
296	3d. Review and March Past	10	10
297	60d. Interior gateway	1·50	70
298	1r.25 Camp entrance	2·75	1·50
299	2r. Hoisting flag, and Shaikh Ahmad	4·00	2·10

48 Neil Armstrong

1969. 1st Man on the Moon. Multicoloured.

301	1d. Type **48**	10	10
302	2d. Edward Aldrin	10	10
303	3d. Michael Collins	10	10
304	60d. Astronaut on Moon	90	45
305	1r.25 Take-off from Moon	1·75	1·00
306	2r. Splashdown (horiz)	4·00	2·00

49 Douglas DC-8 and Mail Van

1970. Admission to U.P.U. Multicoloured.

307	1d. Type **49**	10	10
308	2d. Liner "Oriental Empress"	10	10
309	3d. Loading mail-van	10	10
310	60d. G.P.O., Doha	1·00	65
311	1r.25 U.P.U. Building, Berne	2·40	1·50
312	2r. U.P.U. Monument, Berne	3·00	1·60

50 League Emblem, Flag and Map

1970. Silver Jubilee of Arab League.

313	**50**	35d. multicoloured	45	25
314		60d. multicoloured	70	45
315		1r.25 multicoloured	1·75	85
316		1r.50 multicoloured	2·25	1·40

51 Vickers VC-10 on Runway

1970. 1st Gulf Aviation Vickers VC-10 Flight, Doha–London. Multicoloured.

317	1d. Type **51**	10	10
318	2d. Peregrine falcon and VC-10	1·10	10
319	3d. Tail view of VC-10	15	10
320	60d. Gulf Aviation emblem on map	1·00	85
321	1r.25 VC-10 over Doha	3·50	1·60
322	2r. Tail assembly of VC-10	4·50	2·25

52 "Space Achievements"

1970. International Education Year.

323	**52**	35d. multicoloured	65	25
324		60d. multicoloured	1·40	50

53 Freesias

55 Globe, "25" and U.N. Emblem

54 Toyahama Fishermen with Giant "Fish"

1970. Qatar Flowers. Multicoloured.

325 1d. Type **53** 10 10
326 2d. Azalieas 10 10
327 3d. Ixias 10 10
328 60d. Amaryllises . . . . . . 1·00 50
329 1r.25 Cinerarias . . . . . . 2·25 1·10
330 2r. Roses . . . . 3·00 1·50

1970. "EXPO 70" World Fair, Osaka. Multicoloured.

331 1d. Type **54** 10 10
332 2d. Expo emblem and map of Japan 10 10
333 3d. Fisherman on Shikoku beach 15 10
334 60d. Expo emblem and Mt. Fuji . . . . 1·40 60
335 1r.50 Gateway to Shinto Shrine . . . . 2·00 1·00
336 2r. Expo Tower and Mt. Fuji 4·25 2·75

Nos. 333, 334 and 336 are vert.

1970. 25th Anniv of U.N.O. Multicoloured.

337 1d. Type **55** 10 10
338 2d. Flowers in gun-barrel . . 10 10
339 3d. Anniversary cake 10 10
340 35d. "The U.N. Agencies" . . 1·25 45
341 1r.50 "Trumpet fanfare" . . 2·25 1·00
342 2r. "World friendship" . . . 3·50 2·00

56 Al Jahiz (philosopher) and Ancient Globe

1971. Famous Men of Islam. Multicoloured.

343 1d. Type **56** 10 10
344 2d. Saladin (soldier), palace and weapons 10 10
345 3d. Al Farabi (philosopher and musician), felucca and instruments 10 10
346 35d. Ibn Al Haithum (scientist), palace and emblems 75 40
347 1r.50 Al Motanabbi (poet), symbols and desert . . . . 3·25 2·00
348 2r. Ibn Sina (Avicenna) (physician and philosopher), medical instruments and ancient globe . . . . 4·50 2·40

57 Great Cormorant and Water Plants

1971. Qatar Fauna and Flora. Multicoloured.

349 1d. Type **57** 85 20
350 2d. Lizard and prickly pear 20 10
351 3d. Greater flamingos and palms 85 20
352 60d. Arabian oryx and yucca 1·40 80
353 1r.25 Mountain gazelle and desert dandelion . . . . . 3·50 1·75
354 2r. Dromedary, palm and bronzed chenopod . . . . 4·75 2·50

58 Satellite Earth Station, Goonhilly

1971. World Telecommunications Day. Mult.

355 1d. Type **58** 10 10
356 2d. Cable ship "Ariel" . . . 10 10
357 3d. Post Office Tower and T.V. control-room 10 10
358 4d. Modern telephones . . . 10 10
359 5d. Video-phone equipment 10 10
360 35d. As 3d. 65 35
361 75d. As 5d. . . . . 1·00 85
362 3r. Telex machine . . . . . 5·75 3·25

59 Arab Child reading Book

60 A.P.U. Emblem

1971. 10th Anniv of Education Day.

363 **59** 35d. multicoloured 40 20
364 55d. multicoloured 80 40
365 75d. multicoloured . . . . 1·25 65

1971. 25th Anniv of Arab Postal Union.

366 **60** 35d. multicoloured 50 20
367 55d. multicoloured 75 45
368 75d. multicoloured . . . . 1·10 65
369 1r.25 multicoloured . . . . 1·75 1·40

61 "Hammering Racism"

1971. Racial Equality Year. Multicoloured.

370 1d. Type **61** 10 10
371 2d. "Pushing back racism" 10 10
372 3d. War-wounded 10 10
373 4d. Working together (vert) 10 10
374 5d. Playing together (vert) . . 10 10
375 35d. Racial "tidal-wave" . . 60 30
376 75d. Type **61** . . . . 1·60 95
377 3r. As 2d. . . . . [illegible] [illegible]

62 Nurse and Child

1971. 25th Anniv of UNICEF. Multicoloured.

378 1d. Mother and child (vert) 10 10
379 2d. Child's face 10 10
380 3d. Child with book (vert) . . 10 10
381 4d. Type **62** 10 10
382 5d. Mother and baby 10 10
383 35d. Child with daffodil (vert) 60 30
384 75d. As 3d. . . . . 1·60 95
385 3r. As 1d. . . . . 4·50 3·25

63 Shaikh Ahmad, and Flags of Arab League and Qatar

1971. Independence.

386 **63** 35d. multicoloured 40 15
387 – 75d. multicoloured 95 55
388 – 1r.25 black, pink & brown 1·50 90
389 – 3r. multicoloured . . . . . 4·25 2·75

DESIGNS—HORIZ: 75d. As Type **63**, but with U.N. flag in place of Arab League flag. VERT: 1r.25, Shaikh Ahmad; 3r. Handclasp.

64 European Roller

66 Shaikh Khalifa bin Hamad al-Thani

1972. Birds. Multicoloured.

391 1d. Type **64** 25 25
392 2d. River kingfisher 25 25
393 3d. Rock thrush 25 25
394 4d. Caspian tern 40 25
395 5d. Hoopoe 40 25
396 35d. European bee eater . . 2·50 90
397 75d. Golden oriole . . . . . 7·25 3·25
398 3r. Peregrine falcon . . . . . 24·00 12·50

1972. Nos. 328/30 surch with value in English and Arabic.

399 10d. on 60d. multicoloured 1·00 15
400 1r. on 1r.25 multicoloured . . 4·25 85
401 5r. on 2r. multicoloured . . . 8·50 4·00

1972.

402 **66** 5d. blue and violet 15 10
403 10d. red and brown 15 10
404 35d. green and orange . . 55 15
405 55d. mauve and green . . 95 35
406 75d. mauve and blue . . . 1·50 50
407 – 1r. black and brown . . . 1·75 50
408 – 1r.25 black and green . . . 2·75 70
409 – 5r. black and blue . . . . 10·00 3·50
410 – 10r. black and red . . . . 17·00 6·00

The rupee values are larger, 27 × 32 mm.

For similar design but with Shaikh's head turned slightly to right, see Nos. 444a/b.

67 Book Year Emblem

1972. International Book Year.

411 **67** 35d. black and blue . . . 50 30
412 55d. black and brown . . . 75 45
413 75d. black and green . . . 1·10 75
414 1r.25 black and lilac . . . 2·00 1·25

68 Football

1972. Olympic Games, Munich. Designs depicting sportsmen's hands or feet. Multicoloured.

415 1d. Type **68** 10 10
416 2d. Running (foot on starting block) 10 10
417 3d. Cycling (hand) 10 10
418 4d. Gymnastics (hand) . . . 10 10
419 5d. Basketball (hand) 15 10
420 35d. Discus (hand) 55 30
421 75d. Type **68** . . . . 1·40 90
422 3r. As 2d. . . . . 4·50 3·25

69 Underwater Pipeline Construction

1972. "Oil from the Sea". Multicoloured.

424 1d. Drilling (vert) 10 10
425 4d. Type **69** 10 10
426 5d. Offshore rig "Sea Shell" 10 10
427 35d. Underwater "prospecting" for oil . . . 80 35
428 75d. As 1d. . . . . 1·75 85
429 3r. As 5d. . . . . 8·00 3·75

70 Administrative Building

1972. Independence Day. Multicoloured.

430 10d. Type **70** 25 10
431 35d. Handclasp and Arab League flag 65 30
432 75d. Handclasp and U.N. flag . . . . 1·10 70
433 1r.25 Shaikh Khalifa . . . . 2·00 1·25

71 Dish Aerial, Satellite and Telephone (I.T.U.)

1972. United Nations Day. Multicoloured.

435 1d. Type **71** 10 10
436 2d. Archaeological team (UNESCO) 10 10
437 3d. Tractor, produce and helicopter (F.A.O.) 10 10
438 4d. Children with books (UNICEF) 10 10
439 5d. Weather satellite (W.M.O.) 10 10
440 25d. Construction workers (I.L.O.) 70 30
441 55d. Child care (W.H.O.) . . 1·75 65
442 1r. Airliner and van (U.P.U.) 3·25 1·10

72 Emblem and Flags

72a Shaikh Khalifa

1972. 10th Session of Arab States Civil Aviation Council, Qatar.

443 **72** 25d. multicoloured 70 35
444 30d. multicoloured 95 50

1972.

444a **72a** 10d. red and brown . . 25·00 25·00
444b 25d. green and purple 25·00 25·00

73 Shaikh Khalifa

74 Clock Tower, Doha

1973.

445 **73** 5d. multicoloured 15 10
446 10d. multicoloured 15 10
447 20d. multicoloured 35 10
448 25d. multicoloured 35 10
449 35d. multicoloured 60 15
450 55d. multicoloured . . . . 1·00 35
451 **74** 75d. purple, green and blue 2·25 65
452 **73** 1r. multicoloured . . . . 2·25 55
453 5r. multicoloured . . . . 8·25 2·40
454 10r. multicoloured . . . . 16·00 5·75

Nos. 452/4 are larger, 27 × 32 mm.

75 Housing Development

1973. 1st Anniv of Shaikh Khalifa's Accession. Multicoloured.

455 2d. Road construction . . . 10 10
456 3d. Type **75** 10 10
457 4d. Hospital operating theatre 10 10
458 5d. Telephone exchange . . 10 10
459 15d. School classroom . . . 25 10
460 20d. Television studio 30 10
461 35d. Shaikh Khalifa 50 15
462 55d. Gulf Hotel, Doha . . . 95 45
463 1r. Industrial plant . . . . . 1·75 80
464 1r.35 Flour mills . . . . . . 2·25 1·40

76 Aerial Crop-spraying

1973. 25th Anniv of W.H.O. Multicoloured.

465	2d. Type **76**	10	10
466	3d. Drugs and syringe	10	10
467	4d. Woman in wheelchair (Prevention of polio)	10	10
468	5d. Mosquito (Malaria control)	10	10
469	55d. Mental patient (Mental Health Research)	1·60	80
470	1r. Dead trees (Anti-pollution)	3·00	1·60

77 Weather Ship

1973. Centenary of World Meteorological Organization. Multicoloured.

471	2d. Type **77**	10	10
472	3d. Launching radio-sonde balloon	10	10
473	4d. Hawker Siddeley H.S.125 weather plane	10	10
474	5d. Meteorological station	10	10
475	10d. Met airplane taking-off	20	10
476	1r. "Nimbus 1"	2·00	95
477	1r.55 Rocket on launch-pad	3·50	1·75

78 Handclasp

1973. Independence Day. Multicoloured.

478	15d. Type **78**	10	10
479	35d. Agriculture	20	10
480	55d. Government building	60	30
481	1r.35 View of Doha	1·50	70
482	1r.55 Illuminated fountain	1·75	1·10

79 Child planting Sapling (UNESCO)

1973. United Nations Day. Multicoloured.

483	2d. Type **79**	10	10
484	4d. U.N. Headquarters, New York, and flags	10	10
485	5d. Building construction (I.L.O.)	10	10
486	35d. Nurses in dispensary (W.H.O.)	35	10
487	1r.35 Radar control (I.T.U.)	1·75	95
488	3r. Inspection of wheat and cattle (F.A.O.)	4·00	2·50

80 "Open Gates"

1973. 25th Anniv of Declaration of Human Rights. Multicoloured.

489	2d. Type **80**	10	10
490	4d. Freedom marchers	10	10
491	5d. "Equality of Man"	10	10
492	35d. Primary education	35	15
493	1r.35 General Assembly, U.N.	1·75	70
494	3r. Flame emblem (vert)	4·00	2·25

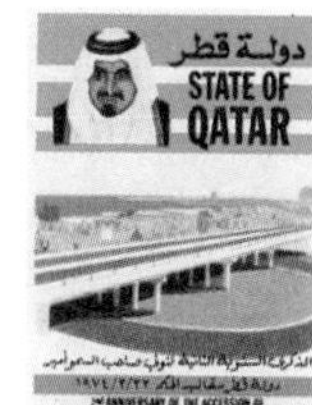

81 New Flyover, Doha

1974. 2nd Anniv of Shaikh Khalifa's Accession. Mult.

495	2d. Type **81**	10	10
496	3d. Education symbol	10	10
497	5d. Gas plant	10	10
498	35d. Gulf Hotel, Doha	40	20
499	1r.55 Space communications station	2·00	95
500	2r.25 Shaikh Khalifa	3·00	1·75

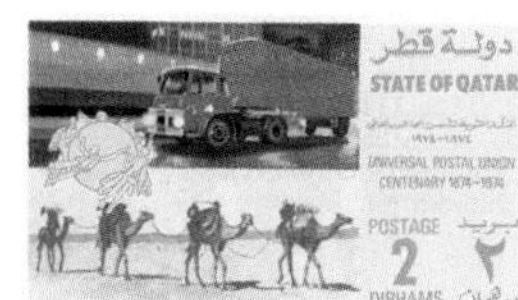

82 Camel Caravan and Articulated Mail Van

1974. Centenary of U.P.U. Multicoloured.

501	2d. Type **82**	10	10
502	3d. Early mail wagon and Japanese "Hikari" express train	20	20
503	10d. "Hindoostan" (paddle-steamer) and "Iberia" (liner)	60	20
504	35d. Early (Handley Page H.P.42) and modern (Vickers VC-10) mail planes	55	35
505	75d. Manual and mechanized mail-sorting	1·10	70
506	1r.25 Early and modern P.O. sales counters	1·75	1·25

83 Doha Hospital

1974. World Population Year. Multicoloured.

507	5d. Type **83**	10	10
508	10d. W.P.Y. emblem	15	10
509	15d. Emblem within wreath	15	10
510	35d. World population map	40	20
511	1r.75 New-born infants and clock ("a birth every minute")	2·00	90
512	2r.25 "Ideal Family" group	2·50	1·50

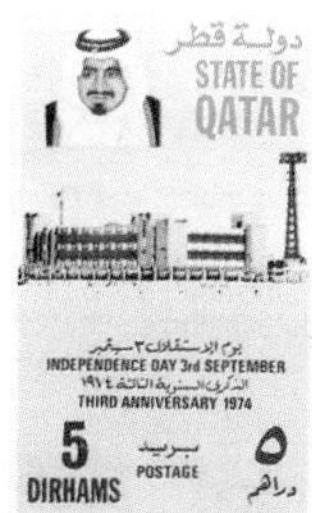

84 Television Station

1974. Independence Day. Multicoloured.

513	5d. Type **84**	10	10
514	10d. Doha palace	15	10
515	15d. Teachers' College	20	10
516	75d. Clock tower and mosque	85	40
517	1r.55 Roundabout and surroundings	1·75	1·00
518	2r.25 Shaikh Khalifa	2·50	1·50

85 Operating Theatre (W.H.O.)

1974. United Nations Day.

519	**85**	5d. orange, purple & black	10	10
520	–	10d. orange, red and black	15	10
521	–	20d. blue, green and black	25	10
522	–	25d. blue, brown and black	35	15
523	–	1r.75 blue, mauve & black	1·90	1·25
524	–	2r. blue, orange and black	2·75	1·60

DESIGNS: 10d. Satellite earth station (I.T.U.); 20d. Tractor (F.A.O.); 25d. Classroom (UNESCO); 1r.75, African open-air court (Human Rights); 2r. U.P.U. and U.N. emblems (U.P.U.).

86 Vickers VC-10 Airliner

1974. Arab Civil Aviation Day.

525	**86**	20d. multicoloured	60	20
526	–	25d. blue, green and yellow	70	30
527	–	30d. multicoloured	1·10	40
528	–	50d. red, green and purple	2·50	90

DESIGNS: 25d. Doha airport; 30, 50d. Flags of Qatar and the Arab League.

87 Clock Tower, Doha

1974. Tourism. Multicoloured.

529	5d. Type **87**	20	10
530	10d. White-cheeked terns, hoopoes and Shara'o Island (horiz)	2·25	30
531	15d. Fort Zubara (horiz)	30	10
532	35d. Dinghies and Gulf Hotel (horiz)	50	20
533	55d. Qatar by night (horiz)	85	35
534	75d. Arabian oryx (horiz)	1·60	50
535	1r.25 Khor-al-Udeid (horiz)	1·90	95
536	1r.75 Ruins Wakrah (horiz)	2·10	1·50

88 Traffic Roundabout, Doha

1975. 3rd Anniv of Shaikh Khalifa's Accession. Multicoloured.

537	10d. Type **88**	20	10
538	35d. Oil pipelines	60	20
539	55d. Laying offshore pipelines	90	35
540	1r. Oil refinery	1·60	65
541	1r.35 Shaikh Khalifa (vert)	2·40	1·10
542	1r.55 As 1r.35	3·00	1·60

89 Flintlock Pistol

1975. Opening of National Museum. Multicoloured.

543	2d. Type **89**	10	10
544	3d. Arabesque-pattern mosaic	10	10
545	35d. Museum buildings	65	35
546	75d. Museum archway (vert)	1·50	80
547	1r.25 Flint tools	2·25	1·40
548	3r. Gold necklace and pendant (vert)	4·50	3·50

90 Policeman and Road Signs

1975. Traffic Week. Multicoloured.

549	5d. Type **90**	35	15
550	15d. Traffic arrows and signal lights	90	30
551	35d. Type **90**	2·00	50
552	55d. As 15d.	3·50	1·40

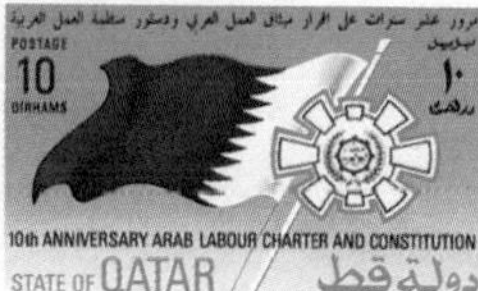

91 Flag and Emblem

1975. 10th Anniv of Arab Labour Charter.

553	**91**	10d. multicoloured	25	15
554		35d. multicoloured	1·00	40
555		1r. multicoloured	2·75	2·00

92 Government Building, Doha

1975. 4th Anniv of Independence. Multicoloured.

556	5d. Type **92**	10	10
557	15d. Museum and clock tower, Doha	30	10
558	35d. Constitution – Arabic text (vert)	55	15
559	55d. Ruler and flag (vert)	80	40
560	75d. Constitution – English text (vert)	1·10	70
561	1r.25 As 55d.	2·25	1·25

93 Telecommunications Satellite (I.T.U.)

1975. 30th Anniv of U.N.O. Multicoloured.

562	5d. Type **93**	10	10
563	15d. U.N. Headquarters, New York	15	10
564	35d. U.P.U. emblem and map	40	15
565	1r. Doctors tending child (U.N.I.C.E.F.)	1·00	55
566	1r.25 Bulldozer (I.L.O.)	1·60	90
567	2r. Students in class (U.N.E.S.C.O.)	2·75	1·50

94 Fertilizer Plant

1975. Qatar Industry. Multicoloured.

568	5d. Type **94**	15	10
569	10d. Flour mills (vert)	25	10
570	35d. Natural gas plant	50	15
571	75d. Oil refinery	1·40	70
572	1r.25 Cement works	2·00	1·25
573	1r.55 Steel mills	2·50	1·50

95 Modern Building, Doha

1976. 4th Anniv of Shaikh Khalifa's Accession.

574	**95**	5d. multicoloured	10	10
575	–	10d. multicoloured	10	10
576	–	35d. multicoloured	40	10
577	–	55d. multicoloured	70	30
578	–	75d. multicoloured	90	50
579	–	1r.55 multicoloured	2·75	1·90

DESIGNS: Nos. 575/6 and 579 show public buildings; Nos. 577/8 show Shaikh Khalifa with flag.

96 Tracking Aerial

97 Early and Modern Telephones

1976. Opening of Satellite Earth Station. Mult.
580 35d. Type **96** 65 15
581 55d. "Intelsat" satellite . . . 90 35
582 75d. Type **96** . . . . 1·50 70
583 1r. As 55d. . . . . 1·90 90

1976. Telephone Centenary.
584 **97** 1r. multicoloured . . . . . 1·40 80
585 1r.35 multicoloured . . . . 1·90 1·00

98 Tournament Emblem

100 Football

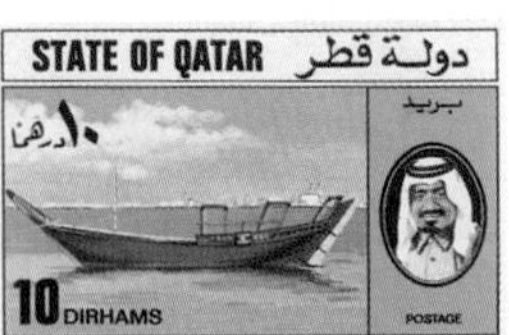
99 Qatar Dhow

1976. 4th Arabian Gulf Football Cup Tournament. Multicoloured.
586 5d. Type **98** 10 10
587 10d. Qatar Stadium 15 10
588 35d. Type **98** 75 15
589 55d. Two players with ball 1·25 35
590 75d. Player with ball . . . . 1·75 60
591 1r.25 As 10d. . . . . 3·25 1·40

1976. Dhows.
592 **99** 10d. multicoloured 25 10
593 – 35d. multicoloured 70 15
594 – 80d. multicoloured . . . . 1·60 40
595 – 1r.25 multicoloured . . . . 2·50 1·40
596 – 1r.50 multicoloured . . . . 3·25 1·75
597 – 2r. multicoloured . . . . . 4·75 2·25
DESIGNS: 35d. to 2r. Various craft.

1976. Olympic Games, Montreal, Multicoloured.
598 5d. Type **100** 10 10
599 10d. Yachting 25 10
600 35d. Show jumping 55 15
601 80d. Boxing . . . . 1·40 50
602 1r.25 Weightlifting . . . . . 2·25 1·25
603 1r.50 Basketball . . . . . . 2·50 2·10

101 Urban Housing Development

1976. United Nations Conference on Human Settlements. Multicoloured.
604 10d. Type **101** 10 10
605 35d. U.N. and conference emblems 40 15
606 80d. Communal housing development . . . . 1·10 50
607 1r.25 Shaikh Khalifa . . . . 2·25 1·25

102 Kentish Plover

1976. Birds. Multicoloured.
608 5d. Type **102** 70 25
609 10d. Great cormorant 70 25
610 35d. Osprey . . . . 3·50 65
611 80d. Greater flamingo (vert) 6·50 1·50
612 1r.25 Rock thrush (vert) . . 9·75 3·25
613 2r. Saker falcon (vert) . . . 14·00 4·50

103 Shaikh Khalifa and Flag

105 Shaikh Khalifa

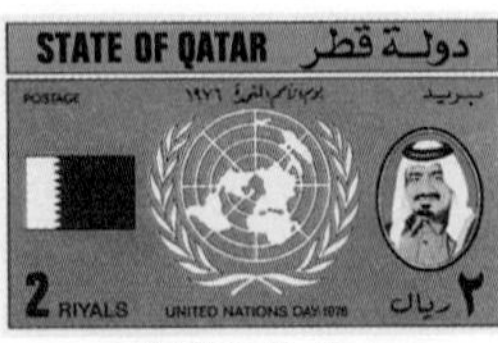
104 U.N. Emblem

1976. 5th Anniv of Independence. Multicoloured.
614 5d. Type **103** 10 10
615 10d. Type **103** 20 10
616 40d. Doha buildings (horiz) 35 15
617 80d. As 40d. 70 30
618 1r.25 "Dana" (oil rig) (horiz) 2·00 1·10
619 1r.50 United Nations and Qatar emblems (horiz) . . 2·10 1·50

1976. United Nations Day.
620 **104** 2r. multicoloured . . . . 3·00 1·75
621 3r. multicoloured . . . . 3·75 2·25

1977. 5th Anniv of Amir's Accession.
622 **105** 20d. multicoloured . . . 25 10
623 1r.80 multicoloured . . . 2·75 2·10

106 Shaikh Khalifa

107 Envelope and A.P.U. Emblem

1977.
624 **106** 5d. multicoloured 15 10
625 10d. multicoloured 20 10
626 35d. multicoloured . . . 60 15
627 80d. multicoloured . . . 1·10 35
628 1r. multicoloured . . . . 1·40 50
629 5r. multicoloured . . . . 6·75 3·25
630 10r. multicoloured . . . . 12·00 5·50
Nos. 628/30 are larger, size 25 × 31 mm.

1977. 25th Anniv of Arab Postal Union.
631 **107** 35d. multicoloured . . . 35 15
632 1r.35 multicoloured . . . 1·75 1·25

108 Shaikh Khalifa and Sound Waves

1977. International Telecommunications Day.
633 **108** 35d. multicoloured . . . 35 15
634 1r.80 multicoloured . . . 2·25 1·90

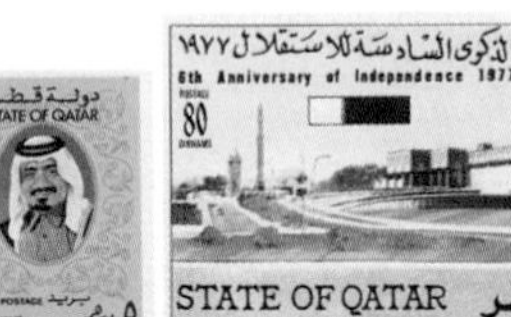
108a Shaikh Khalifa

109 Parliament Building, Doha

1977.
634a **108a** 5d. multicoloured . . . 15 15
634c 10d. multicoloured . . 25 25
634d 35d. multicoloured . . 60 60
634e 80d. multicoloured . . 1·90 1·90

1977. 6th Anniv of Independence. Multicoloured.
635 80d. Type **109** . . . . 1·10 75
636 80d. Main business district, Doha . . . . 1·10 75
637 80d. Motorway, Doha . . . 1·10 75

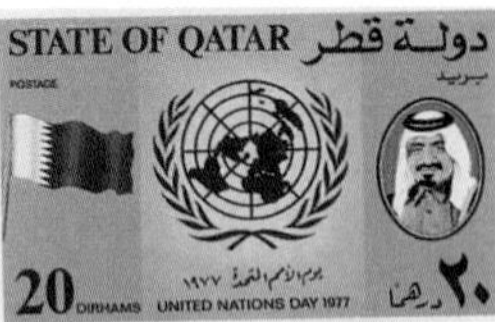
110 U.N. Emblem

1977. United Nations Day.
638 **110** 20d. multicoloured . . . 25 10
639 1r. multicoloured . . . . 1·75 1·25

111 Steel Mill

1978. 6th Anniv of Amir's Accession. Mult.
640 20d. Type **111** 20 10
641 80d. Operating theatre . . . 80 30
642 1r. Children's classroom . . . 1·00 50
643 5r. Shaikh Khalifa . . . . . 3·75 2·75

112 Oil Refinery

1978. 7th Anniv of Independence. Multicoloured.
644 35d. Type **112** 30 15
645 80d. Apartment buildings 70 30
646 1r.35 Town centre, Doha . . 1·50 1·00
647 1r.80 Shaikh Khalifa . . . . 2·00 1·40

113 Man reading Alphabet

1978. International Literacy Day.
648 **113** 35d. multicoloured . . . 30 15
649 80d. multicoloured . . . 85 60

114 U.N. Emblem and Qatar Flag

1978. United Nations Day.
650 **114** 35d. multicoloured . . . 30 15
651 80d. multicoloured . . . 85 60

115 "Human Rights Flame"

116 I.Y.C. Emblem

1978. 30th Anniv of Declaration of Human Rights. Multicoloured.
652 35d. Type **115** 30 15
653 80d. Type **115** 50 40
654 1r.25 Flame and scales of justice 85 70
655 1r.80 As 1r.25 . . . . 1·25 90

1979. International Year of the Child.
656 **116** 35d. mauve, blue and black 30 15
657 1r.80 green, blue & black 1·25 90

117 Shaikh Khalifa

118 Shaikh Khalifa and Laurel Wreath

1979.
658 **117** 5d. multicoloured 10 10
659 10d. multicoloured . . . 10 10
660 20d. multicoloured . . . 25 10
661 25d. multicoloured . . . 25 10
662 35d. multicoloured . . . 45 15
663 60d. multicoloured . . . 80 15
664 80d. multicoloured . . . 1·00 20
665 1r. multicoloured . . . . 1·10 20
666 1r.25 multicoloured . . . 1·40 30
667 1r.35 multicoloured . . . 1·60 40
668 1r.80 multicoloured . . . 2·00 55
669 5r. multicoloured . . . . 5·00 1·90
670 10r. multicoloured . . . . 8·50 2·75
Nos. 665/70 are larger, size 27 × 32½ mm.

1979. 7th Anniv of Amir's Accession.
671 **118** 35d. multicoloured . . . 25 10
672 80d. multicoloured . . . 50 25
673 1r. multicoloured 65 35
674 1r.25 multicoloured . . . 90 75

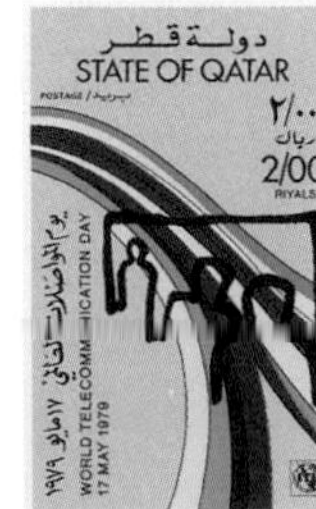
119 Wave Pattern and Television Screen

1979. World Telecommunications Day.
675 **119** 2r. multicoloured . . . . 1·25 90
676 2r.80 multicoloured . . . 1·50 1·25

120 Two Children supporting Globe

1979. 50th Anniv of Int Bureau of Education.
677 **120** 35d. multicoloured . . . 35 15
678 80d. multicoloured . . . 75 35

121 Rolling Mill

122 U.N. Emblem and Flag of Qatar

1979. 8th Anniv of Independence. Multicoloured.
679 5d. Type **121** 10 10
680 10d. Aerial view of Doha . . 10 10
681 1r.25 Qatar flag 85 60
682 2r. Shaikh Khalifa . . . . . 1·40 1·10

1979. United Nations Day.
683 **122** 1r.25 multicoloured . . . 1·25 65
684 2r. multicoloured . . . . 2·25 1·60

123 Mosque Minaret and Crescent Moon

1979. 3rd World Conference on the Prophet's Seera and Sunna.

685	123	35d. multicoloured	40	15
686		1r.80 multicoloured	2·10	1·60

124 Shaikh Khalifa

1980. 8th Anniv of Amir's Accession.

687	124	20d. multicoloured	20	10
688		60d. multicoloured	60	25
689		1r.25 multicoloured	1·40	95
690		2r. multicoloured	2·25	1·75

125 Emblem

1980. 6th Congress of Arab Towns Organization, Doha.

691	125	2r.35 multicoloured	2·50	1·75
692		2r.80 multicoloured	3·00	2·25

126 Oil Refinery

1980. 9th Anniv of Independence. Multicoloured.

693	10d. Type 126	15	10
694	35d. Doha	40	15
695	2r. Oil Rig	2·25	1·60
696	2r.35 Hospital	2·50	1·75

127 Figures supporting O.P.E.C. Emblem

1980. 20th Anniv of Organization of Petroleum Exporting Countries.

697	127	1r.35 multicoloured	90	60
698		2r. multicoloured	1·60	90

128 U.N.Emblem

129 Mosque and Kaaba, Mecca

1980. United Nations Day.

699	128	1r.35 blue, light blue and purple	90	60
700		1r.80 turquoise, green and black	1·90	1·40

1980. 1400th Anniv of Hegira.

701	129	10d. multicoloured	10	10
702		35d. multicoloured	40	20
703		1r.25 multicoloured	90	65
704		2r.80 multicoloured	2·40	1·75

130 I.Y.D.P. Emblem

1981. International Year of Disabled Persons.

705	130	2r. multicoloured	1·90	1·25
706		3r. multicoloured	3·00	1·75

131 Student

132 Shaikh Khalifa

1981. 20th Anniv of Education Day.

707	131	2r. multicoloured	1·90	1·10
708		3r. multicoloured	2·75	1·60

1981. 9th Anniv of Amir's Accession.

709	132	10d. multicoloured	10	10
710		35d. multicoloured	45	25
711		80d. multicoloured	75	45
712		5r. multicoloured	3·75	2·40

133 I.T.U. and W.H.O. Emblems and Ribbons forming Caduceus

134 Torch

1981. World Telecommunications Day.

713	133	2r. multicoloured	2·00	95
714		2r.80 multicoloured	2·75	1·25

1981. 30th International Military Football Championship.

715	134	1r.25 multicoloured	1·75	85
716		2r.80 multicoloured	3·50	2·25

135 Qatar Flag

1981. 10th Anniv of Independence.

717	135	5d. multicoloured	10	10
718		60d. multicoloured	70	30
719		80d. multicoloured	1·00	50
720		5r. multicoloured	5·25	3·50

136 Tractor gathering Crops

1981. World Food Day.

721	136	2r. multicoloured	2·10	1·40
722		2r.80 multicoloured	3·25	1·90

137 Red Crescent

1982. Qatar Red Crescent.

723	137	20d. multicoloured	40	10
724		2r.80 multicoloured	4·25	2·75

138 Shaikh Khalifa

1982. 10th Anniv of Amir's Accession.

725	138	10d. multicoloured	10	10
726		20d. multicoloured	25	10
727		1r.25 multicoloured	1·40	80
728		2r.80 multicoloured	3·25	2·00

139 Hamad General Hospital

1982. Hamad General Hospital.

729	139	10d. multicoloured	10	10
730		2r.35 multicoloured	2·50	1·90

140 Shaikh Khalifa

1982.

731	140	5d. multicoloured	10	10
732		10d. multicoloured	10	10
733		15d. multicoloured	40	10
734		20d. multicoloured	15	10
735		25d. multicoloured	20	15
736		35d. multicoloured	30	15
737		60d. multicoloured	50	15
738		80d. multicoloured	60	15
739	–	1r. multicoloured	1·00	20
740	–	1r.25 multicoloured	1·00	25
741	–	2r. multicoloured	1·40	65
742	–	5r. multicoloured	4·00	1·60
743	–	10r. multicoloured	8·00	3·50
744	–	15r. multicoloured	9·75	4·75

DESIGNS—25 × 32 mm: 1r. to 2r. Oil refinery; 5r. to 15r. Doha clock tower.

142 "Bar'zan" Container Ship

1982. 6th Anniv of United Arab Shipping Company.

745	142	20d. multicoloured	45	15
746		2r.35 multicoloured	3·50	2·25

143 A.P.U. Emblem

144 National Flag

1982. 30th Anniv of Arab Postal Union.

747	143	35d. multicoloured	50	15
748		2r.80 multicoloured	3·25	2·25

1982. 11th Anniv of Independence.

749	144	10d. multicoloured	10	10
750		80d. multicoloured	80	30
751		1r.25 multicoloured	1·25	75
752		2r.80 multicoloured	3·00	1·90

145 W.C.Y. Emblem

147 Arabic Script

146 Conference Emblem

1983. World Communications Year.

753	145	35d. multicoloured	50	15
754		2r.80 multicoloured	3·00	2·10

1983. 2nd Gulf Postal Organization Conference.

755	146	1r. multicoloured	1·25	50
756		1r.35 multicoloured	1·90	75

1983. 12th Anniv of Independence.

757	147	10d. multicoloured	10	10
758		35d. multicoloured	35	20
759		80d. multicoloured	75	40
760		2r.80 multicoloured	2·75	2·10

148 Council Emblem

1983. 4th Session of Gulf Co-operation Council Supreme Council.

761	148	35d. multicoloured	40	15
762		2r.80 multicoloured	2·25	1·90

149 Globe and Human Rights Emblem

1983. 35th Anniv of Declaration of Human Rights. Multicoloured.

763	1r.25 Type 149	1·75	70
764	2r.80 Globe and emblem in balance	3·75	1·90

150 Harbour

151 Shaikh Khalifa

1984.

765	150	15d. multicoloured	10	10
765a	151	25d. mult (22 × 27 mm)	20	15
766	150	40d. multicoloured	30	20
767		50d. multicoloured	40	25
767a	151	75d. mult (22 × 27 mm)	45	35
768		1r. multicoloured	75	35
769		1r.50 multicoloured	1·25	55
769a		2r. multicoloured	1·25	90
770		2r.50 multicoloured	1·90	85
771		3r. multicoloured	2·50	1·25
772		5r. multicoloured	4·00	2·00
773		10r. multicoloured	7·75	5·25

152 Flag and Shaikh Khalifa

1984. 13th Anniv of Independence.

774	152	15d. multicoloured	15	10
775		1r. multicoloured	85	35
776		2r.50 multicoloured	2·10	1·10
777		3r.50 multicoloured	3·00	1·60

153 Teacher and Blackboard

154 I.C.A.O. Emblem

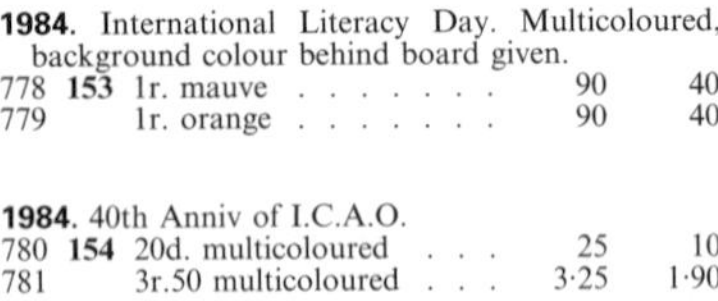

1984. International Literacy Day. Multicoloured, background colour behind board given.
778 **153** 1r. mauve 90 40
779 1r. orange 90 40

1984. 40th Anniv of I.C.A.O.
780 **154** 20d. multicoloured . . . 25 10
781 3r.50 multicoloured . . . 3·25 1·90

155 I.Y.Y. Emblem

156 Crossing the Road

1985. International Youth Year.
782 **155** 50d. multicoloured . . . 65 30
783 1r. multicoloured . . . . 1·40 45

1985. Traffic Week. Multicoloured, frame colour given.
784 **156** 1r. red . . . . 1·25 40
785 1r. blue . . . . 1·25 40

157 Emblem

1985. 40th Anniv of League of Arab States.
786 **157** 50d. multicoloured . . . 50 20
787 4r. multicoloured . . . . 3·50 2·25

158 Doha

1985. 14th Anniv of Independence. Multicoloured.
788 40d. Type **158** 30 25
789 50d. Dish aerials and microwave tower 45 30
790 1r.50 Oil refinery . . . . . . 1·25 1·00
791 4r. Cement works . . . . . 3·25 2·75

159 O.P.E.C. Emblem in "25"

1985. 25th Anniv of Organization of Petroleum Exporting Countries. Multicoloured, background colours given.
792 **159** 1r. red . . . . 1·25 70
793 1r. green . . . . 1·25 70

160 U.N. Emblem

1985. 40th Anniv of U.N.O.
794 **160** 1r. multicoloured 80 70
795 3r. multicoloured . . . . 2·00 1·90

161 Emblem

1986. Population and Housing Census.
796 **161** 1r. multicoloured 70 60
797 3r. multicoloured . . . . 2·00 1·75

162 "Qatari ibn al-Fuja'a" (container ship)

1986. 10th Anniv of United Arab Shipping Company. Multicoloured.
798 1r.50 Type **162** 90 80
799 4r. "Al Wajda" (container ship) . . . . 2·40 2·25

163 Flag and Shaikh Khalifa

1986. 15th Anniv of Independence.
800 **163** 40d. multicoloured . . . 25 20
801 50d. multicoloured . . . 35 25
802 1r. multicoloured 65 55
803 4r. multicoloured . . . . [illegible] [illegible]

164 Shaikh Khalifa

165 Palace

1987.
804 **164** 15r. multicoloured . . . . 7·25 6·50
805 20r. multicoloured . . . . 9·75 8·50
806 30r. multicoloured . . . . 14·00 12·50

1987. 15th Anniv of Amir's Accession.
807 **165** 50d. multicoloured . . . 35 25
808 1r. multicoloured 60 30
809 1r.50 multicoloured . . . 80 70
810 4r. multicoloured . . . . 2·25 1·90

166 Emblem

167 Emblem

1987. 35th Anniv of Arab Postal Union.
811 **166** 1r. yellow, green and black 50 45
812 1r.50 multicoloured . . . 1·00 70

1987. Gulf Environment Day.
813 **167** 1r. multicoloured 60 50
814 4r. multicoloured . . . . 2·40 1·90

168 Modern Complex

1987. 16th Anniv of Independence.
815 25d. Type **168** 20 10
816 75d. Aerial view of city . . . 50 35
817 2r. Modern building . . . . 1·25 90
818 4r. Oil refinery . . . . 2·40 2·00

169 Pens in Fist

170 Anniversary Emblem

1987. International Literacy Day.
819 **169** 1r.50 multicoloured . . . 90 80
820 4r. multicoloured . . . . 2·40 1·90

1988. 40th Anniv of W.H.O.
821 **170** 1r.50 yellow, black and blue 90 80
822 2r. yellow, black and pink 1·40 95

171 State Arms, Shaikh Khalifa and Flag

1988. 17th Anniv of Independence.
823 **171** 50d. multicoloured . . . 30 25
824 75d. multicoloured . . . 45 35
825 1r.50 multicoloured . . . 85 70
826 2r. multicoloured . . . . 1·10 90

172 Post Office

1988. Opening of New Doha General Post Office.
827 **172** 1r.50 multicoloured . . . 75 65
828 4r. multicoloured . . . . 1·90 1·75

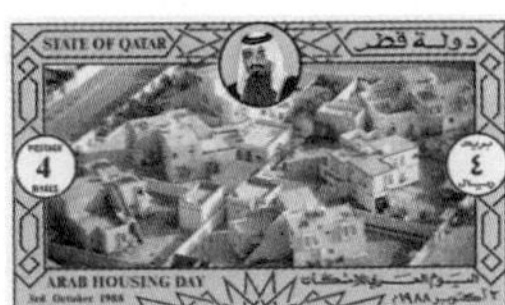

173 Housing Development

1988. Arab Housing Day.
829 **173** 1r.50 multicoloured . . . 75 70
830 4r. multicoloured . . . . 2·00 1·75

174 Hands shielding Flame

175 Dish Aerials and Arrows

1988. 40th Anniv of Declaration of Human Rights.
831 **174** 1r.50 multicoloured . . . 75 65
832 2r. multicoloured . . . . 1·00 90

1989. World Telecommunications Day.
833 **175** 2r. multicoloured 95 85
834 4r. multicoloured . . . . 1·75 1·60

176 Headquarters

1989. 10th Anniv of Qatar Red Crescent Society.
835 **176** 4r. multicoloured . . . . 1·90 1·60

177 Palace

1989. 18th Anniv of Independence.
836 **177** 75d. multicoloured . . . 35 25
837 1r. multicoloured 60 55
838 1r.50 multicoloured . . . 75 65
839 2r. multicoloured 90 85

178 Anniversary Emblem

1990. 40th Anniv of Gulf Air.
840 **178** 50d. multicoloured . . . 35 30
841 75d. multicoloured . . . 50 45
842 4r. multicoloured . . . . 2·50 2·25

179 Map and Rising Sun

1990. 19th Anniv of Independence. Multicoloured.
843 50d. Type **179** 35 30
844 75d. Map and sunburst . . . 50 45
845 1r.50 Musicians and sword dancer . . . . 1·00 90
846 2r. As No. 845 . . . . 2·00 1·75

180 Anniversary Emblem

181 Emblem and Dhow

1990. 30th Anniv of Organization of Petroleum Exporting Countries. Multicoloured.
847 50d. Type **180** 35 30
848 1r.50 Flags of member nations . . . . 1·00 90

1990. 11th Session of Supreme Council of Gulf Co-operation Council. Multicoloured.
849 50d. Type **181** 45 30
850 1r. Council heads of state and emblem 65 55
851 1r.50 State flag and Council emblem . . . . 1·00 90
852 2r. State and Council emblems . . . . 1·25 1·10

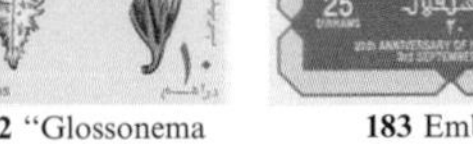

182 "Glossonema edule"

183 Emblem

1991. Plants. Multicoloured.
853 10d. Type **182** 10 10
854 25d. "Lycium shawii" 15 10
855 50d. "Acacia tortilis" 35 30
856 75d. "Acacia ehrenbergiana" 50 45
857 1r. "Capparis spinosa" . . . 65 55
858 4r. "Cymbopogon parkeri" 2·50 2·25
No. 858 is wrongly inscribed "Cymhopogon".

1991. 20th Anniv of Independence. Multicoloured.
859 25d. Type **183** 15 10
860 75d. As Type **183** but different Arabic inscription 50 45

861 1r. View of Doha (35 × 32 mm) 65 55
862 1r.50 Palace (35 × 32 mm) . . 1·00 90

184 Seabream

1991. Fishes. Multicoloured.
863 10d. Type **184** 10 10
864 15d. Pennant coralfish . . . 10 10
865 25d. Scarlet-finned squirrelfish 15 10
866 50d. Smooth houndshark . . 45 35
867 75d. Seabream 65 55
868 1r. Golden trevally 80 65
869 1r.50 Rabbitfish . . . . . . 1·25 1·10
870 2r. Yellow-banded angelfish 1·75 1·50

185 Shaikh Khalifa

1992. Multicoloured. (a) Size 22 × 28 or 28 × 22 mm.
871 10d. Type **185** 10 10
872 25d. North Field gas project 15 10
873 50d. Map of Qatar 25 20
874 75d. Petrochemical factory (horiz) 30 25
875 1r. Oil refinery (horiz) 40 35

(b) Size 25 × 32 or 32 × 25 mm.
876 1r.50 As No. 872 . . . . . . 65 60
877 2r. As No. 873 . . . . 85 75
878 3r. As No. 874 . . . . 1·40 1·25
879 4r. As No. 875 . . . . 1·75 1·50
880 5r. As No. 873 . . . . 2·10 1·75
881 10r. As No. 875 . . . . . . 4·25 3·75
882 15r. Shaikh Khalifa (different frame) . . . . 6·75 6·00
883 20r. As No. 882 . . . . . . 8·75 7·75
884 30r. As No. 882 . . . . . . 13·50 12·00

186 Shaikh Khalifa and Gateway
187 Heart in Centre of Flower

1992. 20th Anniv of Amir's Accession. Mult.
885 25d. Type **186** 15 10
886 50d. Type **186** 25 20
887 75d. Archway and "20" . . . 40 35
888 1r.50 As No 887 . . . . . . 75 65

1992. World Health Day. "Heartbeat, the Rhythm of Health". Multicoloured.
889 50d. Type **187** 25 20
890 1r.50 Heart on clockface and cardiograph (horiz) 75 65

188 Women dancing

1992. Children's Paintings. Multicoloured.
891 25d. Type **188** 15 10
892 50d. Children's playground 25 20
893 75d. Boat race 40 35
894 1r.50 Fishing fleet 90 65

189 Runner and Emblems

1992. Olympic Games, Barcelona. Multicoloured.
896 50d. Type **189** 25 20
897 1r.50 Footballer and emblems 75 65

190 Shaikh Khalifa and Script

1992. 21st Anniv of Independence. Multicoloured.
898 50d. Type **190** 25 20
899 50d. Shaikh Kalifa and "21" in English and Arabic . . 25 20
900 1r. Oil well, pen and dhow (42 × 42 mm) 50 45
901 1r. Dhow in harbour (42 × 42 mm) 50 45

191 Ball, Flag and Emblem

1992. 11th Arabian Gulf Football Championship. Multicoloured.
902 50d. Type **191** 25 20
903 1r. Ball bursting goal net (vert) 50 45

192 Emblems and Globe

1992. International Nutrition Conference, Rome. Multicoloured.
904 50d. Type **192** 25 20
905 1r. Cornucopia (horiz) . . . 50 45

193 Mosque

1993. Old Mosques. Each sepia, yellow and brown.
906 1r. Type **193** 55 45
907 1r. Mosque (minaret without balcony) 55 45
908 1r. Mosque (minaret with wide balcony) 55 45
909 1r. Mosque (minaret with narrow balcony) 55 45

194 Presenter and Dish Aerial

1993. 25th Anniv of Qatar Broadcasting. Mult.
910 25d. Type **194** 15 10
911 50d. Rocket and satellite . . 30 25
912 75d. Broadcasting House . . 40 35
913 1r. Journalists 55 45

195 Oil Refinery and Sea
196 Scroll, Quill and Paper

1993. 22nd Anniv of Independence. Multicoloured.
915 25d. Type **195** 15 10
916 50d. Flag and clock tower, Doha 30 25
917 75d. "22" in English and Arabic 40 35
918 1r.50 Flag and fort 80 70

1993. International Literacy Day. Multicoloured.
919 25d. Type **196** 15 10
920 50d. Fountain pen and flags spelling "Qatar" 30 25
921 75d. Fountain pen and Arabic characters 40 35
922 1r.50 Arabic text on scroll and fountain pen 80 70

197 Girls playing

1993. Children's Games. Multicoloured.
923 25d. Type **197** 15 10
924 50d. Boys playing with propeller (vert) 30 25
925 75d. Wheel and stick race (vert) 40 35
926 1r.50 Skipping 80 70

198 Lanner Falcon
199 Headquarters

1993. Falcons. Multicoloured.
928 25d. Type **198** 20 15
929 50d. Saker falcon 40 40
930 75d. Barbary falcon 55 50
931 1r.50 Peregrine falcon . . . . 1·25 1·00

1994. 30th Anniv of Qatar Insurance Company. Multicoloured.
933 50d. Type **199** 25 20
934 1r.50 Company emblem and international landmarks . . 70 60

200 Hands catching Drops from Tap
201 Gavel, Scales and National Flag

1994. World Water Day. Mulicoloured.
935 25d. Type **200** 10 10
936 1r. Hands catching raindrop, water tower, crops and United Nations emblem . . 50 45

1994. Qatar International Law Conference. Multicoloured.
937 75d. Type **201** 35 30
938 2r. Gavel and scales suspended from flag . . . 1·00 90

202 Society Emblem
203 Anniversary Emblem

1994. Qatar Society for Welfare and Rehabilitation of the Handicapped. Multicoloured.
939 25d. Type **202** 10 10
940 75d. Handicapped symbol and hands 35 30

1994. 75th Anniv of I.L.O. Multicoloured.
941 25d. Type **203** 10 10
942 2r. Anniversary emblem and cogwheel . . . . 1·00 90

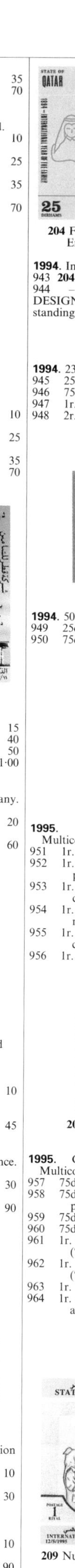

204 Family and Emblem

205 Scroll

1994. International Year of the Family.
943 **204** 25d. blue and black . . . 10 10
944 – 1r. multicoloured 50 45
DESIGN: 1r. I.Y.F. emblem and stylized family standing on U.N. emblem.

1994. 23rd Anniv of Independence. Multicoloured.
945 25d. Type **205** 10 10
946 75d. Oasis 35 30
947 1r. Industry 50 45
948 2r. Scroll (different) . . . . 1·00 90

206 Map, Airplane and Emblem

1994. 50th Anniv of I.C.A.O. Multicoloured.
949 25d. Type **206** 10 10
950 75d. Anniversary emblem . . 35 30

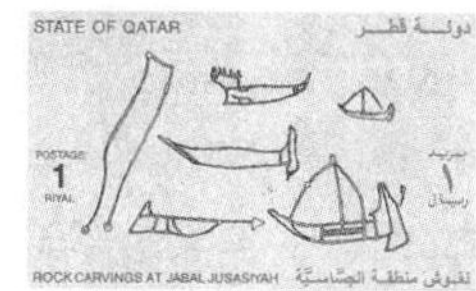

207 Ship-like Carvings

1995. Rock Carvings, Jabal Jusasiyah. Multicoloured.
951 1r. Type **207** 40 35
952 1r. Circular and geometric patterns 40 35
953 1r. Six irregular-shaped carvings 40 35
954 1r. Carvings including three multi-limbed creatures . . 40 35
955 1r. Nine multi-limbed creatures 40 35
956 1r. Fishes 70 40

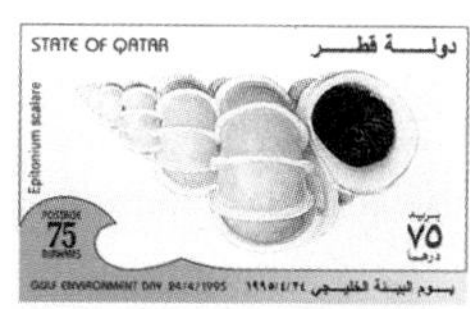

208 Precious Wentletrap ("Epitonium scalare")

1995. Gulf Environment Day. Sea Shells. Multicoloured.
957 75d. Type **208** 35 30
958 75d. Feathered cone ("Conus pennaceus") 35 30
959 75d. "Cerithidea cingulata" 35 30
960 75d. "Hexaplex kuesterianus" 35 30
961 1r. Giant spider conch ("Lambis truncata sebae") 40 35
962 1r. Woodcock murex ("Murex scolopax") . . . 40 35
963 1r. "Thais mutabilis" 40 35
964 1r. Spindle shell ("Fusinus arabicus") 40 35

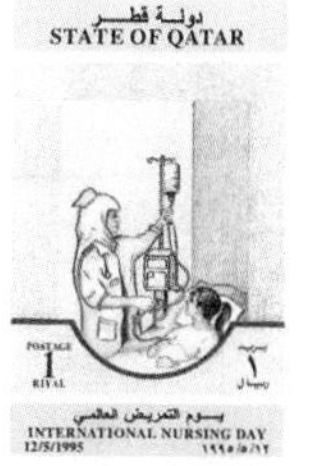

209 Nursing Patient

211 Anniversary Emblem

210 Schoolchildren

1995. International Nursing Day. Multicoloured.

No.	Description	Unused	Used
965	1r. Type **209**	40	35
966	1r.50 Vaccinating child	60	55

1995. 24th Anniv of Independence. Multicoloured.

No.	Description	Unused	Used
967	1r. Type **210**	35	30
968	1r. Palm trees	35	30
969	1r.50 Port	55	45
970	1r.50 Doha	55	45

Nos. 967/70 were issued together, se-tenant, forming a composite design.

1995. 50th Anniv of U.N.O.

No.	Description	Unused	Used
971 **211**	1r.50 multicoloured	55	45

212 Addra Gazelle

1996. Mammals. Multicoloured.

No.	Description	Unused	Used
972	25d. Type **212**	10	10
973	50d. Beira antelope	15	10
974	75d. "Gazella dorcas pelzelni"	25	20
975	1r. Dorcas gazelle	35	30
976	1r.50 Speke's gazelle	50	40
977	2r. Soemmerring's gazelle	70	55

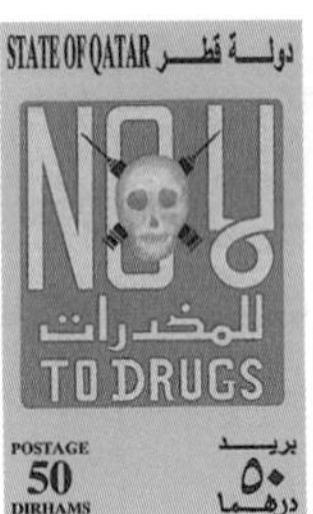

213 Syringes through Skull

214 Map of Qatar and Games Emblem

1996. International Day against Drug Abuse. Multicoloured.

No.	Description	Unused	Used
979	50d. Type **213**	15	10
980	1r. "No entry" sign over syringes in hand	35	30

1996. Olympic Games, Atlanta. Multicoloured.

No.	Description	Unused	Used
981	10d. Type **214**	10	10
982	15d. Rifle shooting	10	10
983	25d. Bowling	10	10
984	50d. Table tennis	15	10
985	1r. Running	35	30
986	1r.50 Yachting	50	40

Nos. 981/6 were issued together, se-tenant, forming a composite design.

215 Map, National Flag and Shaikh Hamad

1996. 25th Anniv of Independence.

No.	Description	Unused	Used
987 **215**	1r.50 multicoloured	50	40
988	2r. multicoloured	70	55

216 Shaikh Hamad

217 Shaikh Hamad

1996.

No.	Description	Unused	Used
990 **216**	25d. multicoloured	10	10
991	50d. multicoloured	15	10
992	75d. multicoloured	25	20
993	1r. multicoloured	35	30
994 **217**	1r.50 multicoloured	50	40
995	2r. multicoloured	70	55
997	4r. multicoloured	1·40	1·10
998	5r. multicoloured	1·75	1·40
999	10r. multicoloured	3·50	2·75
1001	20r. multicoloured	6·75	5·50
1002	30r. multicoloured	10·00	8·00

218 Doha Clock Tower, Dove and Heads of State

219 Children and UNICEF Emblem

1996. 17th Session of Gulf Co-operation Council Supreme Council, Doha. Multicoloured.

No.	Description	Unused	Used
1004	1r. Type **218**	35	30
1005	1r.50 Council emblem, dove and national flag	50	40

1996. 50th Anniv of UNICEF. Multicoloured.

No.	Description	Unused	Used
1006	75d. Type **219**	25	20
1007	75d. Children and emblem	25	20

220 Al-Wajbah

1997. Forts. Multicoloured.

No.	Description	Unused	Used
1008	25d. Type **220**	10	10
1009	75d. Al-Zubarah (horiz)	25	20
1010	1r. Al-Kout Fort, Doha (horiz)	35	30
1011	3r. Umm Salal Mohammed (horiz)	1·00	80

221 World Map and Liquid Gas Containers (½-size illustration)

1997. Inauguration of Ras Laffan Port.

No.	Description	Unused	Used
1012 **221**	3r. multicoloured	1·00	80

222 Palomino

1997. Arab Horses. Multicoloured.

No.	Description	Unused	Used
1013	25d. Type **222**	10	10
1014	75d. Black horse	25	20
1015	1r. Grey	35	30
1016	1r.50 Bay	50	40

223 Arabic Script within Wreath, Flag and Shaikh Hamad

1997. 26th Anniv of Independence. Multicoloured.

No.	Description	Unused	Used
1018	1r. Type **223**	35	30
1019	1r.50 Amir, oil refinery and Government Palace	50	40

224 Graph

1997. Middle East and Northern Africa Economic Conference, Doha.

No.	Description	Unused	Used
1020 **224**	2r. multicoloured	65	50

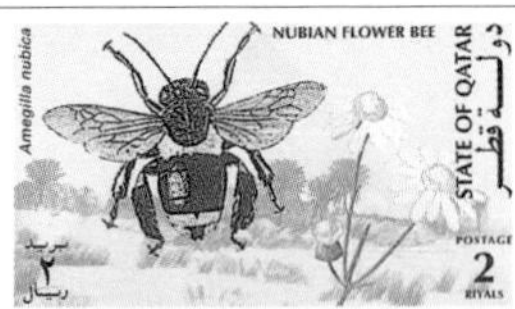

225 Nubian Flower Bee

1998. Insects. Multicoloured.

No.	Description	Unused	Used
1021	2r. Type **225**	65	50
1022	2r. Domino beetle	65	50
1023	2r. Seven-spotted ladybird	65	50
1024	2r. Desert giant ant	65	50
1025	2r. Eastern death's-head hawk moth	65	50
1026	2r. Arabian darkling beetle	65	50
1027	2r. Yellow digger	65	50
1028	2r. Mole cricket	65	50
1029	2r. Migratory locust	65	50
1030	2r. Elegant rhinoceros beetle	65	50
1031	2r. Oleander hawk moth	65	50
1032	2r. American cockroach	65	50
1033	2r. Girdled skimmer	65	50
1034	2r. Sabre-toothed beetle	65	50
1035	2r. Arabian cicada	65	50
1036	2r. Pin-striped ground weevil	65	50
1037	2r. Praying mantis	65	50
1038	2r. Rufous bombardier beetle	65	50
1039	2r. Diadem	65	50
1040	2r. Shore earwig (inscr "Earwing")	65	50

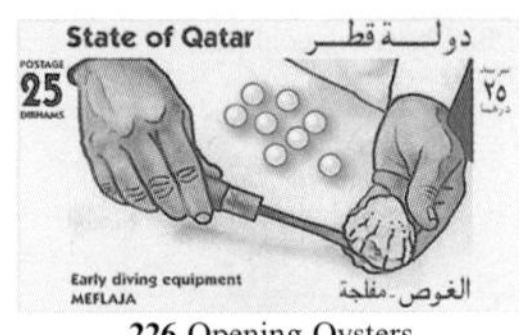

226 Opening Oysters

1998. Early Pearl-diving Equipment. Multicoloured.

No.	Description	Unused	Used
1042	25d. Type **226**	10	10
1043	75d. Opened oyster with pearl	25	20
1044	1r. Bowl for weighing pearls	35	30
1045	1r.50 Basket for keeping oysters (vert)	50	40

227 Shaikh Hamad

228 Anniversary Emblem

1998. 27th Anniv of Independence. Multicoloured.

No.	Description	Unused	Used
1047	1r. Type **227**	35	30
1048	1r.50 Shaikh Hamad (horiz)	50	40

1998. 25th Anniv of University of Qatar.

No.	Description	Unused	Used
1049 **228**	1r. multicoloured	35	30
1050	1r.50 multicoloured	50	40

229 Dromedaries

1999. Dromedaries. Multicoloured.

No.	Description	Unused	Used
1051	25d. Type **229**	10	10
1052	75d. One dromedary	25	20
1053	1r. Three dromedaries	35	30
1054	1r.50 Four young dromedaries with herd	50	40

230 Emblem

1999. General Assembly of International Equestrian Federation, Doha.

No.	Description	Unused	Used
1056 **230**	1r.50 multicoloured	50	40

231 Umayyad Dirham

1999. Coins. Multicoloured.

No.	Description	Unused	Used
1057	1r. Type **231**	35	30
1058	1r. Umayyad dirham (four small circles around edge of right-hand coin)	35	30
1059	1r. Abbasid dirham (three lines of inscr on left-hand coin)	35	30
1060	1r. Abbasid dirham (six lines of inscr on left-hand coin)	35	30
1061	1r. Umayyad dirham (five small circles around edge of right-hand coin)	35	30
1062	2r. Abbasid dirham (three lines on inscr on left-hand coin)	70	55
1063	2r. Umayyad dinar	70	55
1064	2r. Abbasid dinar (five lines of inscr on left-hand coin)	70	55
1065	2r. Murabitid dinar	70	55
1066	2r. Fatimid dinar	70	55

232 Shaikh Hamad

1999. 28th Anniv of Independence.

No.	Description	Unused	Used
1068 **232**	1r. multicoloured	35	30
1069	1r.50 multicoloured	50	45

233 Tree of Letters

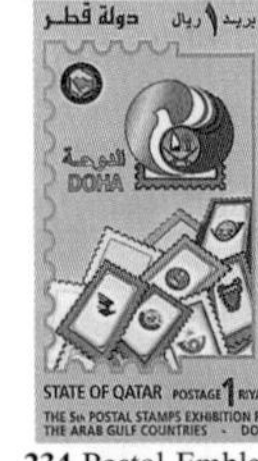

234 Postal Emblems on "Stamps"

1999. 125th Anniv of Universal Postal Union. Multicoloured.

No.	Description	Unused	Used
1070	1r. Type **233**	35	30
1071	1r.50 General Post Office, Doha (horiz)	50	45

1999. 5th Arab Gulf Countries Stamp Exhibition, Doha. Multicoloured.

No.	Description	Unused	Used
1072	1r. Type **234**	35	30
1073	1r.50 Exhibition emblem (horiz)	50	45

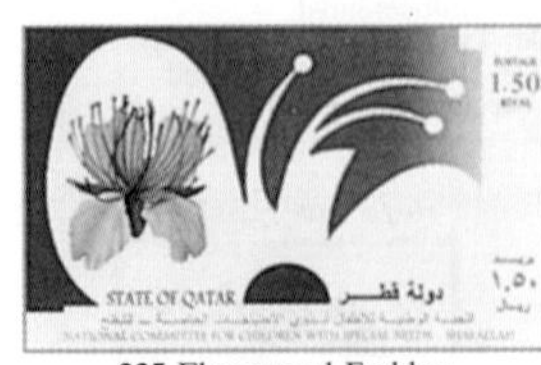

235 Flower and Emblem

1999. National Committee for Children with Special Needs.

No.	Description	Unused	Used
1074 **235**	1r.50 multicoloured	60	50

236 Clock Tower

2000. New Millennium.

No.	Description	Unused	Used
1075 **236**	1r.50 gold and red	60	50
1076	2r. gold and blue	75	60

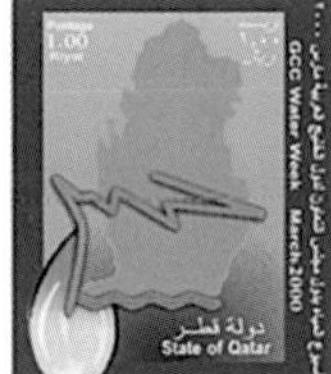

237 Emir Cup and Court — 238 Map and Water Droplet

2000. New Millennium Open Tennis Championships, Qatar. Multicoloured.

1077	1r. Type **237**	40	30
1078	1r.50 Emir Cup and racquet	60	50

2000. Gulf Co-operation Council Water Week. Mult.

1079	1r. Type **238**	40	30
1080	1r.50 Dried earth and water droplet	60	50

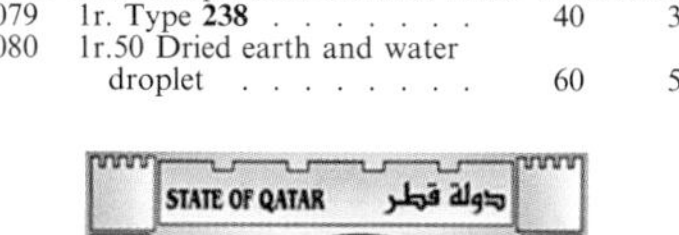

239 Bat and Ball

2000. 15th Asian Table Tennis Championship, Doha.

1081 **239**	1r.50 multicoloured	60	50

240 Shaikh Hamad, Fort and Emblem

2000. 29th Anniv of Independence. Multicoloured.

1082	1r. Type **240**	40	30
1083	1r.50 Shaikh Hamad, city and oil drilling platform	60	50

241 Emblem and Dove carrying Letter

2000. 50th Anniv of Qatar Post Office. Multicoloured.

1084	1r.50 Type **241**	60	50
1085	2r. Emblem, magnifying glass and building facade	75	60

242 Emblem

2000. 9th Islamic Summit Conference, Doha. Multicoloured.

1086	1r. Type **242**	40	30
1087	1r.50 Emblem and olive branch (47 × 30 mm)	60	50

243 Gas Terminal

2001. "Clean Environment". Multicoloured.

1088	1r. Type **243**	35	30
1089	1r.50 Oryx and gas installation	50	40
1090	2r. Flamingoes and Ras Laffan city skyline	70	55
1091	3r. Earth viewed from space	1·00	80

244 Castle, Koran and Ship

2001. 30th Anniv of Independence.

1092 **244**	1r. multicoloured	35	30
1093	1r.50 multicoloured	50	40

245 Children encircling Globe

2001. United Nations Year of Dialogue among Civilizations. Multicoloured.

1094	1r.50 Type **245**	50	40
1095	2r. Leaves	70	55

246 Building and Emblem

2001. 4th World Trade Organization Ministerial Conference, Doho, Qatar.

1096 **246**	1r. multicoloured	35	30
1097	1r.50 multicoloured	50	40

247 Door

2001. Traditional Wooden Doors. Multicoloured.

1098	25d. Type **247**	10	10
1099	75d. Small door in left-hand panel and large bolt at right	25	20
2000	1r.50 Plain doors	50	40
2001	2r. Knocker at left and smaller door in right-hand panel	70	55
MS2002	100 × 70 mm. 3r. As No. 2001	1·00	80

POSTAGE DUE STAMPS

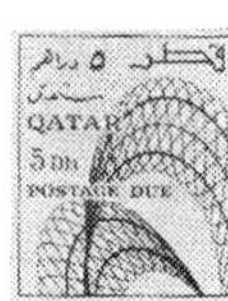

D 40

1968.

D254 **D 40**	5d. blue	13·50	13·50
D255	10d. red	16·00	16·00
D256	20d. green	20·00	20·00
D257	30d. lilac	21·00	21·00

QU'AITI STATE IN HADHRAMAUT

Pt. 1

The stamps of Aden were used in Qu'aiti State in Hadhramaut from 22 April 1937 until 1942.

1937. 16 annas = 1 rupee.
1951. 100 cents = 1 shilling.
1966. 1000 fils = 1 dinar.

(I) Issues inscribed "SHIHR and MUKALLA"

1 Sultan of Shihr and Mukalla — **2** Mukalla Harbour

1942.

1 **1**	½a. green	70	40
2	¾a. brown	1·25	30
3	1a. blue	1·00	1·00
4 **2**	1½a. red	1·25	50
5 –	2a. brown	1·50	1·75
6 –	2½a. blue	50	30
7 –	3a. brown and red	80	75
8 –	8a. red	50	40
9 –	1r. green	3·75	2·50
10 –	2r. blue and purple	12·00	8·00
11 –	5r. brown and green	15·00	11·00

DESIGNS—VERT: 2a. Gateway of Shihr; 3a. Outpost of Mukalla; 1r. Du'an. HORIZ: 2½a. Shibam; 8a. Einat; 2r. Mosque in Hureidha; 5r. Meshhed.

1946. Victory. Optd **VICTORY ISSUE 8TH JUNE 1946**.

12 **2**	1½a. red	10	75
13 –	2½a. blue	10	10

1949. Royal Silver Wedding. As T **4b/c** of Pitcairn Islands.

14	1½a. red	50	3·00
15	5r. green	15·00	9·00

1949. U.P.U. As T **4d/g** of Pitcairn Islands surch.

16	2½a. on 20c. blue	15	20
17	3a. on 30c. red	1·10	50
18	8a. on 50c. orange	25	60
19	1r. on 1s. blue	30	50

1951. Stamps of 1942 surch in cents or shillings.

20	5c. on 1a. blue	15	15
21	10c. on 2a. sepia	15	15
22	15c. on 2½a. blue	15	15
23	20c. on 3a. sepia and red	30	50
24	50c. on 8a. red	50	1·25
25	1s. on 1r. green	2·00	30
26	2s. on 2r. blue and purple	7·50	13·00
27	5s. on 5r. brown and green	12·00	18·00

1953. Coronation. As T **4h** of Pitcairn Islands.

28	15c. black and blue	1·00	55

(II) Issues inscribed "HADHRAMAUT"

11 Metal Work — **22** Metal Work

1955. Occupations. Portrait as in T **11**.

29 **11**	5c. blue	30	10
30 –	10c. black (Mat-making)	60	10
31 –	15c. green (Weaving)	50	10
32 –	25c. red (Pottery)	40	10
33 –	35c. blue (Building)	70	10
34 –	50c. orange (Date cultivation)	40	10
35 –	90c. brown (Agriculture)	50	15
36 –	1s. black and orange (Fisheries) (horiz)	50	10
37 –	1s.25 black and orange (Lime-burning) (horiz)	55	55
38 –	2s. black and blue (Dhow building) (horiz)	4·00	60
39 –	5s. black and green (Agriculture) (horiz)	5·00	1·75
40 –	10s. black and red (as No. 37) (horiz)	5·50	7·50

1963. Occupations. As Nos. 29/40 but with inset portrait of Sultan Awadh bin Saleh el Qu'aiti, as in T **22**.

41 **22**	5c. blue	10	1·25
42 –	10c. black	10	1·25
43 –	15c. green	10	1·25
44 –	25c. red	10	50
45 –	35c. blue	10	1·50
46 –	50c. orange	10	1·00
47 –	70c. brown (As No. 35)	15	60
48 –	1s. black and lilac	20	30
49 –	1s.25 black and orange	45	3·75
50 –	2s. black and blue	3·25	1·75
51 –	5s. black and green	13·00	25·00
52 –	10s. black and red	17·00	25·00

1966. Nos. 41/52 surch **SOUTH ARABIA** in English and Arabic, with value and bar.

53 **5**	5f. on 5c.	10	60
54 –	5f. on 10c.	10	60
55 –	10f. on 15c.	10	30
56 –	15f. on 25c.	10	60
57 –	20f. on 35c.	10	1·50
58 –	25f. on 50c.	10	60
59 –	35f. on 70c.	10	60
60 –	50f. on 1s.	10	30
61 –	65f. on 1s.25	1·00	30
62 –	100f. on 2s.	1·50	75
63 –	250f. on 5s.	1·50	1·50
64 –	500f. on 10s.	19·00	3·00

1966. Churchill Commemoration. Nos. 54/6 optd **1874–1965 WINSTON CHURCHILL**.

65	5f. on 10c.	5·50	10·00
66	10f. on 15c.	6·50	11·00
67	15f. on 25c.	8·50	12·00

1966. President Kennedy Commemoration. Nos. 57/9 optd **1917–63 JOHN F. KENNEDY**.

68	20f. on 35c.	1·50	6·00
69	25f. on 50c.	1·75	6·50
70	35f. on 70c.	2·25	7·50

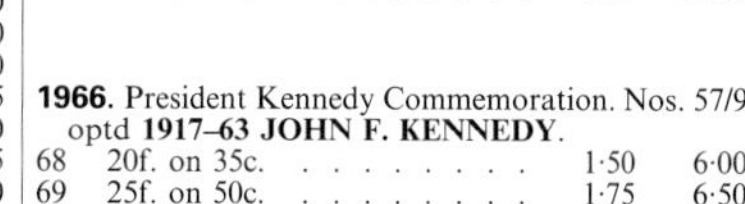

25 World Cup Emblem

1966. World Cup Football Championship.

71 **25**	5f. purple and orange	1·75	25
72 –	10f. violet and green	2·00	25
73 –	15f. purple and orange	2·25	30
74 –	20f. violet and green	2·50	30
75 **25**	25f. green and red	2·75	30
76 –	35f. blue and yellow	3·25	35
77 –	50f. green and red	3·75	40
78 **25**	65f. blue and yellow	4·50	40
MS78a	110 × 110 mm. Nos. 77/8	16·00	7·50

DESIGNS: 10, 35f. Wembley Stadium; 15, 50f. Footballers; 20f. Jules Rimet Cup and football.

29 Mexican Hat and Basket

1966. Pre-Olympic Games, Mexico (1968).

79 **29**	75f. sepia and green	1·25	75

30 Telecommunications Satellite

1966. International Co-operation Year.

80 **30**	5f. mauve, purple and green	2·25	35
81 –	10f. multicoloured	2·50	35
82 –	15f. purple, blue and red	2·75	40
83 **30**	20f. blue, purple and red	3·00	45
84 –	25f. multicoloured	3·00	50
85 **30**	35f. purple, red and blue	3·50	60
86 –	50f. purple, green and red	4·50	75
87 **30**	65f. brown, violet and red	5·00	80

DESIGNS: 10f. Olympic runner (inscr "ROME 1960"); 15f. Fishes; 25f. Olympic runner (inscr "TOKIO 1964"); 50f. Tobacco plant.

APPENDIX

The following stamps have either been issued in excess to postal needs or have not been made available to the public in reasonable quantities at face value.

1967.

Stampex, London. Postage 5, 10, 15, 20, 25f.; Air 50, 65f.

Amphilex International Stamp Exhibition, Amsterdam. Air 75f.

Olympic Games, Mexico (1968). 75f.

Paintings. Postage 5, 10, 15, 20, 25f.; Air 50, 65f.

Scout Jamboree, Idaho. Air 35f.

Space Research. Postage 10, 25, 35, 50, 75f.; Air 100, 250f.

The National Liberation Front is said to have taken control of Qu'aiti State in Hadhramaut on 17 September 1967.

QUEENSLAND Pt. 1

The north eastern state of the Commonwealth of Australia whose stamps it now uses.

12 pence = 1 shilling;
20 shillings = 1 pound.

1

7

1860. Imperf.

1	**1**	1d. red	£2750	£800
2		2d. blue	£5500	£1500
3		6d. green	£4000	£800

1860. Perf.

94	**1**	1d. red	38·00	5·00
99		2d. blue	30·00	1·00
101		3d. brown	65·00	9·00
65		3d. green	85·00	6·00
53		4d. grey	£190	23·00
55		4d. lilac	£140	18·00
103		4d. yellow	£650	24·00
27		6d. green	90·00	12·00
108		1s. purple	48·00	9·00
29		1s. grey	£160	22·00
119		2s. blue	75·00	26·00
121		2s.6d. red	£120	50·00
58		5s. red	£300	70·00
123		5s. yellow	£160	75·00
125		10s. brown	£350	£130
127		20s. red	£700	£140

1879.

134	**7**	1d. brown	40·00	6·00
135		1d. orange	23·00	4·00
136		1d. red	18·00	2·25
138		2d. blue	32·00	1·25
141		4d. yellow	£130	10·00
142		6d. green	75·00	4·50
115		1s. mauve	60·00	6·00

1880. Nos. 136 surch **Half-penny**.

151	**7**	½d. on 1d. brown	£200	£130

9

13

12

14

1882.

152	**9**	2s. blue	80·00	26·00
158		2s.6d. orange	40·00	22·00
159		5s. red	38·00	30·00
155		10s. brown	£120	40·00
161		£1 green	£180	60·00

1882. Shaded background around head.

185	**13**	½d. green	3·75	1·25
206	**12**	1d. orange	2·50	20
204		2d. blue	4·00	30
191	**14**	2½d. red	11·00	1·25
192	**12**	3d. brown	9·00	2·50
193		4d. yellow	13·00	2·25
170		6d. green	10·00	1·50
173		1s. mauve	11·00	2·25
182		2s. brown	60·00	28·00

15

16

17

1895. Head on white background.

208	**15**	½d. green	1·40	75
211	**16**	1d. red	3·75	20
212		2d. blue	8·50	35
213	**17**	2½d. red	13·00	3·75
215		5d. brown	14·00	3·75

19

21

1896.

229	**19**	1d. red	10·00	50

1897. Same designs, but figures in all four corners, as T **21**.

286	½d. green	1·75	2·00
232	1d. red	2·00	15
234	2d. blue	2·50	15
236	2½d. red	17·00	19·00
238	2½d. purple on blue	9·50	1·75
241	3d. brown	8·00	1·75
244	4d. yellow	8·00	1·75
294	4d. black	15·00	3·25
246	5d. brown	8·00	1·75
250	6d. green	6·50	1·75
298	1s. mauve	12·00	2·50
300	2s. green	32·00	16·00

26

27

1899.

262a	**26**	½d. green	2·25	1·25

1900. S. African War Charity. Inscr "PATRIOTIC FUND 1900".

264a	**27**	1d. (1s.) mauve	£120	£110
264b	–	2d. (2s.) violet (horiz)	£200	£275

28

1903.

265	**28**	9d. brown and blue	18·00	3·00

REGISTRATION STAMP

1861. Inscr "REGISTERED".

20	**1**	(No value) yellow	60·00	38·00

QUELIMANE Pt. 9

A district of Portuguese E. Africa, now part of Mozambique, whose stamps it now uses.

100 centavos = 1 escudo.

1913. Surch **REPUBLICA QUELIMANE** and new value on "Vasco da Gama" stamps of (a) Portuguese Colonies.

1	¼c. on 2½r. green	60	35
2	½c. on 5r. red	60	35
3	1c. on 10r. purple	60	35
4	2½c. on 25r. green	60	35
5	5c. on 50r. blue	60	35
6	7½c. on 75r. brown	70	60
7	10c. on 100r. brown	50	35
8	15c. on 150r. brown	50	35

(b) Macao.

9	¼c. on ½a. green	60	35
10	½c. on 1a. red	60	35
11	1c. on 2a. purple	60	35
12	2½c. on 4a. green	60	35
13	5c. on 8a. blue	60	35
14	7½c. on 12a. brown	70	60
15	10c. on 16a. brown	50	35
16	15c. on 24a. brown	50	35

(c) Portuguese Timor.

17	¼c. on ½a. green	60	35
18	½c. on 1a. red	60	35
19	1c. on 2a. purple	60	35
20	2½c. on 2a. green	60	35
21	5c. on 8a. blue	60	35
22	7½c. on 12a. brown	70	60
23	10c. on 16a. brown	50	35
24	15c. on 24a. brown	50	35

1914. "Ceres" key-type inscr "QUELIMANE".

25	U	½c. green	25	25
26		½c. black	50	35
42		1c. green	45	45
28		1½c. brown	60	40
29		2c. red	50	50
30		2¼c. violet	25	15
31		5c. blue	40	35
43		7½c. brown	45	45
33		8c. grey	50	40
44		10c. red	45	45
35		15c. purple	70	65
45		20c. green	45	45
37		30c. brown on green	1·10	85
38		40c. brown on pink	1·10	85
39		50c. orange on orange	1·10	85
40		1e. green on blue	1·10	85

RAJASTHAN Pt. 1

Formed in 1948 from states in Rajputana, India, which included Bundi, Jaipur and Kishangarh whose separate posts functioned until 1 April 1950. Now uses Indian stamps.

12 pies = 1 anna;
16 annas = 1 rupee.

BUNDI

(1)

1949. Nos. 86/92 of Bundi or optd with T **1**.

1	**21**	¼a. green	5·00	
2		½a. violet	3·50	
3		1a. green	5·00	
11	–	2a. red	5·00	65·00
12	–	4a. orange	3·00	65·00
6	–	8a. blue	5·00	
14	–	1r. brown	7·50	

Nos. 1, 2, 3 and 6 used are worth about six times the unused prices

JAIPUR

राजस्थान

RAJASTHAN
(2)

1949. Stamps of Jaipur optd with T **2**.

15	**7**	¼a. black and purple	4·75	16·00
16		½a. black and violet	3·50	17·00
17		¾a. black and orange	7·00	18·00
18		1a. black and blue	4·25	35·00
19		2a. black and orange	8·00	45·00
20		2½a. black and red	8·50	22·00
21		3a. black and green	9·00	50·00
22		4a. black and green	9·00	60·00
23		6a. black and blue	9·50	85·00
24		8a. black and brown	14·00	£120
25		1r. black and bistre	16·00	£170

KISHANGARH

1949. Stamps of Kishangarh handstamped with T **1**.
(a) On stamps of 1899.

26a	**2**	¼a. pink	—	£170
27		½a. blue	£325	
29		1a. lilac	14·00	38·00
30		4a. brown	70·00	90·00
31		1r. green	£200	£225
31a		2r. red	£227	
32		5r. mauve	£250	£250

(b) On stamps of 1904.

33	**13**	½a. brown	—	£120
33a		1a. blue	—	£160
34		4a. brown	13·00	
35	**2**	8a. grey	90·00	£140
36	**13**	8a. violet	11·00	
37		1r. green	12·00	
38		2r. yellow	19·00	
39		5r. brown	25·00	

(c) On stamps of 1912.

40	**14**	½a. green	—	£170
41		1a. red	—	£170
43		2a. purple	3·00	7·50
44		4a. blue	—	£400
45		8a. brown	5·00	
46		1r. mauve	10·00	
47		2r. green	10·00	
48		5r. brown	£300	

(d) On stamps of 1928.

56	**16**	¼a. blue	40·00	40·00
57		½a. green	28·00	30·00
58	–	1a. red	38·00	40·00
59	–	2a. purple	£130	£130
61	**16**	4a. brown	2·50	7·50
51		8a. violet	6·00	50·00
63		1r. green	6·50	
53		2r. yellow	16·00	
54		5r. red	16·00	

RAJPIPLA Pt. 1

A state of Bombay, India. Now uses Indian stamps.

12 pies = 1 anna;
12 annas = 1 rupee.

1 (1 pice)

2 (2a.)

1880.

1	**1**	1p. blue	2·75	28·00
2	**2**	2a. green	24·00	80·00
3		4a. red	13·00	48·00

RAS AL KHAIMA Pt. 19

Arab Shaikhdom in the Arabian Gulf. Ras al Khaima joined the United Arab Emirates in February 1972 and U.A.E. stamps were used in the shaikhdom from 1 January 1973.

1964. 100 naye paise = 1 rupee.
1966. 100 dirhams = 1 riyal.

1 Shaikh Saqr bin Mohamed al-Qasimi

3 Dhow

1964.

1	**1**	5n.p. brown and black	15	15
2		15n.p. blue and black	15	15
3	–	30n.p. brown and black	15	15
4	–	40n.p. blue and black	25	20
5	–	75n.p. red and black	60	50
6	**3**	1r. brown and green	1·75	90
7		2r. brown and violet	3·00	1·90
8		5r. brown and blue	6·00	5·00

DESIGNS—As Type **1**: 30n.p. to 75n.p. Seven palms.

3a Pres. Kennedy inspecting "Friendship 7"

1965. Pres. Kennedy Commemoration.

9	**3a**	2r. blue and brown	1·00	95
10	–	3r. blue and brown	1·25	1·25
11	–	4r. blue and brown	1·75	1·75

DESIGNS—HORIZ: 3r. Kennedy and wife. VERT: 4r. Kennedy and flame of remembrance.

4 Sir Winston Churchill and Houses of Parliament

1965. Churchill Commemoration.

12	**4**	2r. blue and brown	90	90
13	–	3r. blue and brown	1·25	1·25
14	–	4r. blue and brown	1·90	1·75

DESIGNS—HORIZ: 3r. Churchill and Pres. Roosevelt; 4r. Churchill, and Heads of State at his funeral.

1965. Olympic Games, Tokyo (1964). Optd **OLYMPIC TOKYO 1964** in English and Arabic and Olympic "rings".

15	3	1r. brown and green	40	40
16		2r. brown and violet	90	90
17		5r. brown and blue	2·50	2·50

1965. Death Centenary of Abraham Lincoln. Optd **ABRAHAM LINCOLN 1809-1865** in English and Arabic.

18	3	1r. brown and green	40	40
19		2r. brown and violet	90	90
20		5r. brown and blue	2·50	2·50

1965. 20th Death Anniv of Pres. Roosevelt. Optd **FRANKLIN D. ROOSEVELT 1882-1945** in English and Arabic.

21	3	1r. brown and green	40	40
22		2r. brown and violet	90	90
23		5r. brown and blue	2·50	2·50

8 Satellite and Tracking Station

1966. I.T.U. Centenary. Multicoloured.

24		15n.p. Type **8**	15	10
25		50n.p. Post Office Tower, London, "Telstar" and tracking gantry	30	15
26		85n.p. Rocket on launching-pad and "Relay"	60	20
27		1r. Type **8**	70	30
28		2r. As 50n.p.	1·25	35
29		3r. As 85n.p.	1·50	65

9 Swimming

10 Carpenter

1966. Pan-Arab Games, Cairo (1965).

31	A	1n.p. brown, pink and green	10	10
32	B	2n.p. black, grey and green	10	10
33	C	3n.p. brown, pink and green	10	10
34	D	4n.p. brown, pink and purple	10	10
35	A	5n.p. black, grey and orange	10	10
36	9	10n.p. brown, pink and blue	15	10
37	B	25n.p. brown, pink and cinnamon	15	10
38	C	50n.p. black, grey and violet	35	15
39	D	75n.p. black, grey and blue	55	15
40	9	1r. black, grey and green	70	30

DESIGNS: A, Running; B, Boxing; C, Football; D, Fencing.

1966. American Astronauts.

42	10	25n.p. black, gold and purple	15	10
43	–	50n.p. black, silver & brown	25	15
44	–	75n.p. black, silver and blue	35	20
45	–	1r. black, silver and bistre	55	35
46	–	2r. black, silver and mauve	90	70
47	–	3r. black, gold and green	1·50	1·10
48	–	4r. black, gold and red	1·75	1·25
49	–	5r. black, gold and blue	2·10	1·60

ASTRONAUTS: 50n.p. Glenn; 75n.p. Shepard; 1r. Cooper; 2r. Grissom; 3r. Schirra; 4r. Stafford; 5r. Lovell.

11 Shaikh Sabah of Kuwait and Shaikh Saqr of Ras al Khaima

1966. International Co-operation Year.

51	11	1r. black and red	50	20
52	A	1r. black and lilac	50	20
53	B	1r. black and pink	50	20
54	C	1r. black and green	50	20
55	D	1r. black and green	50	20
56	E	1r. black and yellow	50	20
57	F	1r. black and orange	50	20
58	G	1r. black and blue	50	20

SHAIKH SAQR AND WORLD LEADERS: A, Shaikh Ahmad of Qatar; B, Pres. Nasser; C, King Hussein; D, Pres. Johnson; E, Pres. De Gaulle; F, Pope Paul VI; G, Prime Minister Harold Wilson.

NEW CURRENCY SURCHARGES. During the latter half of 1966 various issues appeared surcharged in dirhams and riyals. The 1964 definitives with this surcharge are listed below as there is considerable evidence of their postal use. Nos. 24/58 also exist with these surcharges.

In August 1966 Nos. 1/14, 24/9 and 51/8 appeared surcharged in fils and rupees. As Ras Al Khaima did not adopt this currency their status is uncertain.

1966. Nos. 1/8 with currency names changed to dirhams and riyals by overprinting in English and Arabic

60	1	5d. on 5n.p. brown and black	20	15
60a	–	5d. on 75n.p. red and black	20	15
64b	3	5d. on 5r. brown and blue	20	15
61	1	15d. on 15n.p. blue & black	30	15
62	–	30d. on 30n.p. brown and black	55	20
63	–	40d. on 40n.p. blue & black	70	30
64	–	75d. on 75n.p. red and black	80	35
65	3	1r. on 1r. brown and green	90	45
66		2r. on 2r. brown and violet	2·00	1·75
67		5r. on 5r. brown and blue	4·50	3·00

15 W.H.O. Building and Flowers

1966. Inauguration of W.H.O. Headquarters, Geneva.

68	15	15d. multicoloured (postage)	20	10
69	–	35d. multicoloured	40	15
70	15	50d. multicoloured (air)	50	25
71	–	3r. multicoloured	1·75	65

DESIGN: 35d., 3r. As Type **15** but with red instead of yellow flowers at left.

16 Queen Elizabeth II presenting Jules Rimet Cup to Bobby Moore, Captain of England Team

1966. Air. England's Victory in World Cup Football Championship. Multicoloured.

73		1r. Wembley Stadium	50	15
74		2r. Goalkeeper saving ball	1·00	30
75		3r. Footballers with ball	1·50	50
76		4r. Type **16**	1·75	1·00

17 Shaikh Saqr

18 Oil Rig

1971.

78	17	5d. multicoloured		
79	18	20d. multicoloured		
80	17	30d. multicoloured		

For later issues see **UNITED ARAB EMIRATES**.

APPENDIX

The following stamps have either been issued in excess of postal needs or have not been available to the public in reasonable quantities at face value. Such stamps may later be given full listing if there is evidence of regular postal use.

1967.

"The Arabian Nights". Paintings. Air 30, 70d., 1, 2, 3r.

Cats. Postage 1, 2, 3, 4, 5d.: Air 3r.

Arab Paintings. 1, 2, 3, 4, 10, 20, 30d.

European Paintings. Air 60, 70d., 1, 2, 3, 5, 10r.

50th Birth Anniv of Pres. John F. Kennedy. Optd on 1965 Pres. Kennedy Commem. 2, 3, 4r.

World Scout Jamboree, Idaho. Postage 1, 2, 3, 4d.; Air 35, 75d., 1r.

U.S. "Apollo" Disaster. Optd on 1966 American Astronauts issue. 25d. on 25n.p., 50d. on 50n.p., 75d. on 75n.p., 1, 2, 3, 4, 5r.

Summer Olympics Preparation, Mexico 1968. Postage 10, 20, 30, 40d.; Air 1, 2r.

Winter Olympics Preparation, Grenoble 1968. Postage 1, 2, 3, 4, 5d.; Air 85d., 2, 3r.

1968.

Mothers' Day. Paintings. Postage 20, 30, 40, 50d.; Air 1, 2, 3, 4r.

International Human Rights Year. 2r. × 3.

International Museum Campaign. Paintings. 15, 15, 20, 25, 35, 40, 45, 60, 70, 80, 90d.; 1, 1r.25, 1r.50, 2r.50, 2r.75.

Winter Olympic Medal Winners, Grenoble. 50d., 1, 1r.50, 2, 2r.50, 3r.

Olympic Games, Mexico. Air 1, 2, 2, 3, 3, 4r. 5th Death Anniv of Pres. John F. Kennedy. Air. 2, 3r.

Christmas. Religious Paintings. Postage 20, 30, 40, 50, 60d., 1r.; Air 2, 3, 4r.

1969.

Famous Composers (1st series). Paintings. 25, 50, 75d., 1r.50, 2r.50.

Famous Operas. 20, 40, 60, 80d., 1, 2r.

Famous Men. Postage 20, 30, 50d.; Air 1r.50, 2, 3, 4, 5r.

International Philatelic Exhibition, Mexico 1968 (EFIMEX). Postage 10, 10, 25, 35, 40, 50, 60, 70d.; Air 1, 2, 3, 5, 5r.

Int Co-operation in Olympics. 1, 2, 3, 4r.

International Co-operation in Space. Air 1r.50, 2r.50, 3r.50, 4r.50.

Birth Bicentenary of Napoleon. Paintings. Postage 1r.75, 2r.75, 3r.75; Air 75d.

"Apollo" Moon Missions. Air 2, 2r.50, 3, 3r.50, 4, 4r.50, 5, 5r.50.

"Apollo 11" Astronauts. Air 2r.25, 3r.25, 4r.25, 5r.25.

"Apollo 12" Astronauts. Air 60d., 2r.60, 3r.60, 4r.60, 5r.60.

1970.

Christmas 1969. Religious Paintings. Postage 50d.; Air 3, 3r.50.

World Cup, Mexico. Air 1, 2, 3, 4, 5, 6r.

Easter. Religious Paintings. Postage 50d.; Air 3, 3r.50.

Paintings by Titian and Tiepolo. Postage 50, 50d.; Air 3, 3, 3r.50, 3r.50.

Winter Olympics, Sapporo 1972. Air 1, 2, 3, 4, 5, 6r.

Olympic Games, Munich 1972. Air 1, 2, 3, 4, 5, 6r.

Paul Gauguin's Paintings. Postage 50d.; Air 3, 3r.50.

Christmas. Religious Paintings. Postage 50d.; Air 3, 3r.50.

"World Cup Champions, Brazil". Optd on Mexico World Cup issue. Air 1, 2, 3, 4, 5, 6r.

"EXPO 70" World Fair, Osaka, Japan (1st issue). Postage 40, 45, 50, 55, 60, 65, 70, 75d.; Air 80, 85, 90, 95d., 1r.60, 1r.65, 1r.85, 2r.

"EXPO 70" World Fair, Osaka, Japan (2nd issue). Postage 55, 65, 75d.; Air 25, 85, 95d., 1r.50, 1r.75.

Space Programmes. Air 1r. × 6, 2r. × 6, 4r. × 6.

Famous Frenchmen. Air 1r. × 4, 2r. × 4, 2r.50 × 2, 3r. × 2, 4r. × 4, 5r.50 × 2.

Int Philatelic Exn (Philympia '70). Air 1r. × 4, 1r.50 × 4, 2r.50 × 4, 3r. × 4, 4r. × 4.

Events in the Life of Christ. Religious Paintings. 5, 10, 25, 50d., 1, 2, 5r.

"Stages of the Cross". Religious Paintings. 10, 20, 30, 40, 50, 60, 70, 80d., 1, 1r.50, 2, 2r.50, 3, 3r.50.

The Life of Mary. Religious Paintings. 10, 15, 30, 60, 75d., 3, 4r.

1971.

Easter. "Stages of the Cross" (1970) but with additional inscr "EASTER". 10, 20, 30, 40, 50, 60, 70, 80d., 1, 1r.50, 2, 2r.50, 3, 3r.50.

Charles de Gaulle Memorial. Postage 50d.; Air 1, 1r.50, 2, 3, 4r.

Safe Return of "Apollo 14". Postage 50d.; Air 1, 1r.50, 2, 3, 4r.

U.S.A.–Japan Baseball Friendship. Postage 10, 25, 30, 80d.; Air 50, 70d., 1, 1r.50.

Munich Olympics, 1972. Postage 50d.; Air 1, 1r.50, 2, 3, 4r.

Cats. 35, 60, 65, 110, 120, 160d.

13th World Jamboree, Japan. Postage 30, 50, 60, 75d.; Air 1, 1r.50, 3, 4r.

Sapporo Olympic Gold Medal Winners. Optd on 1970 Winter Olympics, Sapporo 1972, issue. Air 1, 2, 3, 4, 5, 6r.

Munich Olympic Medal Winners, Optd on 1970 Summer Olympics, Munich 1972, issue. Air 1, 2, 3, 4, 5, 6r.

Japanese Locomotives. Postage 30, 35, 75d.; Air 90d., 1, 1r.75.

"Soyuz 11" Russian Cosmonauts Memorial. Air 1, 2, 3, 4r.

"Apollo 15". Postage 50d.; Air 1, 1r.50, 2, 3, 4r.

Dogs. 5, 20, 75, 85, 185, 200d.

Durer's Paintings. Postage 50d.; Air 1, 1r.50, 2, 3, 4r.

Famous Composers (2nd series). Postage 50d.; Air 1, 1r.50, 2, 3, 4r.

"Soyuz 11" and "Salyut" Space Projects. Postage 50 d.; Air 1, 1r.50, 2, 3, 4r.

Butterflies. Postage 15, 20, 70d.; Air 1r.25, 1r.50, 1r.70.

Wild Animals. 10, 40, 80 d.; 1r.15, 1r.30, 1r.65.

Fishes. 30, 50, 60, 90d., 1r.45, 1r.55.

Ludwig van Beethoven. Portraits. Postage 50d.; Air 1, 1r.50, 2, 3, 4r.

1972.

Birds. 50, 55, 80, 100, 105, 190d.

Winter Olympics, Sapporo (1st issue). Postage 20, 30, 50d., Air 70, 90d., 2r.50

Winter Olympics, Sapporo (2nd issue). Postage 5, 60, 80, 90d.; Air 1r.10, 1r.75

Mozart. Portraits. Postage 50d.; Air 1, 1r.50, 2, 3, 4r.

Olympic Games, Munich. Postage 50d.; Air 1, 1r.50, 2, 3, 4r.

"In Memory of Charles de Gaulle". Optd on 1971 Charles de Gaulle memorial issue. Postage 50d.; Air 1, 1r.50, 2, 3, 4r.

Winter Olympics, Sapporo (3rd issue). Postage 15, 45d.; Air 65, 75d., 1r.20, 1r.25.

Horses. Postage 10, 25, 30d.; Air 1r.40, 1r.80, 1r.95.

Parrots. 40, 45, 70, 95d., 1r.35, 1r.75.

"Apollo 16". Postage 50d.; Air 1, 1r.50, 2, 3, 4r.

European Footballers. Postage 50d.; Air 1, 1r.50, 2, 3, 4r.

A number of issues on gold or silver foil also exist, but it is understood that these were mainly for presentation purposes, although valid for postage.

In common with the other states of the United Arab Emirates the Ras al Khaima stamp contract was terminated on 1st August 1972, and any further new issues released after that date were unauthorized.

REDONDA Pt. 1

A dependency of Antigua.

The following stamps were issued in anticipation of commercial and tourist development, philatelic mail being handled by a bureau in Antigua. Since at the present time the island is uninhabited, we do not list or stock these items. It is understood that the stamps are valid for the prepayment of postage in Antigua. Miniature sheets, imperforate stamps etc, are excluded from this section.

1979.

Antigua 1976 definitive issue optd **REDONDA**. 3, 5, 10, 25, 35, 50, 75c., $1, $2.50, $5, $10.

Antigua Coronation Anniversary issue optd **REDONDA**. 10, 30, 50, 90c., $2.50.

Antigua World Cup Football Championship issue optd **REDONDA**. 10, 15c., $3.

Death Centenary of Sir Rowland Hill. 50, 90c., $2.50, $3.

International Year of the Child 25, 50c., $1, $2.

Christmas. Paintings. 8, 50, 90c., $3.

1980.

Marine Life. 8, 25, 50c., $4.

75th Anniv of Rotary International. 25, 50c., $1, $2.

Birds of Redonda. 8, 10, 15, 25, 30, 50c., $1, $2, $5.

Olympic Medal Winners, Lake Placid and Moscow. 8, 25, 50c., $3.

80th Birthday of Queen Elizabeth the Queen Mother. 10c., $2.50.

Christmas Paintings. 8, 25, 50c., $4.

1981.

Royal Wedding. 25, 55c., $4.

Christmas. Walt Disney Cartoon Characters. ½, 1, 2, 3, 4, 5, 10c., $2.50, $3.

World Cup Football Championship, Spain (1982). 30c. × 2, 50c. × 2, $1 × 2, $2 × 2.

1982.

Boy Scout Annivs. 8, 25, 50c., $3, $5.

Butterflies. 8, 30, 50c., $2.

21st Birthday of Princess of Wales. $2, $4.

Birth of Prince William of Wales. Optd on Princess of Wales 21st Birthday issue. $2, $4.

Christmas. Walt Disney's "One Hundred and One Dalmatians". ½, 1, 2, 3, 4, 5, 10c., $2.50, $3.

1983.

Easter. 500th Birth Anniv of Raphael. 10, 50, 90c., $5.

Bicent of Manned Flight. 10, 50, 90c., $2.50.

Christmas. Walt Disney Cartoon Characters. "Deck the Halls". ½, 1, 2, 3, 4, 5, 10c., $2.50, $3.

1984.

Easter. Walt Disney Cartoon Characters. ½, 1, 2, 3, 4, 5, 10c., $2, $4.

Olympic Games, Los Angeles. 10, 50, 90c., $2.50.

Christmas. 50th Birthday of Donald Duck. 45, 60, 90c., $2, $4.

1985.

Birth Bicentenary of John J. Audubon (ornithologist) (1st issue). 60, 90c., $1, $3.

Life and Times of Queen Elizabeth the Queen Mother. $1, $1.50, $2.50.

Royal Visit. 45c., $1, $4.

150th Birth Anniv of Mark Twain (author). 25, 50c., $1.50, $3.

Birth Bicentenaries of Grimm Brothers (folklorists). Walt Disney cartoon characters. 30, 60, 70c., $4.

1986.

Birth Bicentenary of John J. Audubon (ornith-ologist) (2nd issue). 90c., $1, $1.50, $3.

Appearance of Halley's Comet. 5, 15, 55c., $4.

Centenary of Statue of Liberty (1st issue). 20, 25, 30c., $4.

60th Birthday of Queen Elizabeth II. 50, 60c., $4.

Royal Wedding. 60c., $1, $4.

Christmas (1st issue). Disney characters in Hans Andersen Stories. 30, 60, 70c., $4.

Christmas (2nd issue). "Wind in the Willows" (by Kenneth Grahame). 25, 50c., $1.50, $3.

1987.

"Capex '87" International Stamp Exhibition, Toronto. Disney characters illustrating Art of Animation. 25, 30, 50, 60, 70c., $1.50, $3, $4.

Birth Centenary of Marc Chagall (artist). 10, 30, 40, 60, 90c., $1, $3, $4.

Centenary of Statue of Liberty (2nd issue). 10, 15, 25, 30, 40, 60, 70, 90c., $1, $2, $3, $4.

250th Death Anniv of Sir Isaac Newton (scientist). 20c., $2.50.

750th Anniv of Berlin. $1, $4.

Bicentenary of U.S. Constitution. 30c., $3.

16th World Scout Jamboree, Australia. 10c., $4.

1988.

500th Anniv (1992) of Discovery of America by Columbus. 15, 30, 45, 60, 90c., $1, $2, $3.

"Finlandia '88" International Stamp Exhibition, Helsinki. Disney characters in Finnish scenes. 1, 2, 3, 4, 5, 6c., $5, $6.

Olympic Games, Seoul. 25, 60c., $1.25, $3.

500th Birth Anniv of Titian. 10, 25, 40, 70, 90c., $2, $3, $4.

1989.

20th Anniv of First Manned Landing on Moon. Disney characters on Moon. ½, 1, 2, 3, 4, 5c., $5, $6.

500th Anniv (1992) of Discovery of America by Columbus (2nd issue). Pre-Columbian Societies. 15, 45, 45, 50c., $2, $2, $3, $3.

Christmas. Disney Characters and Cars of 1950s. 25, 35, 45, 60c., $1, $2, $3, $4.

1990.

Christmas. Disney Characters and Hollywood cars. 25, 35, 40, 60c., $2, $3, $4, $5.

1991.

Nobel Prize Winners. 5, 15, 25, 40, 50c., $1, $2, $4.

REUNION Pt. 6

An island in the Indian Ocean, E. of Madagascar, now an overseas department of France.

100 centimes = 1 franc.

1

1852. Imperf. No gum.

No.	Type	Description	Unused	Used
1	1	15c. black on blue	£25000	£16000
2		30c. black on blue	£25000	£16000

1885. Stamps of French Colonies surch **R** and value in figures. Imperf.

No.	Type	Description	Unused	Used
5	D	5c. on 30c. brown	50·00	42·00
7	H	5c. on 30c. brown	3·00	5·50
3	A	5c. on 40c. orange	£250	£225
6	F	5c. on 40c. orange	35·00	35·00
8	H	5c. on 40c. red on yellow	70·00	85·00
9		10c. on 40c. red on yellow	3·25	4·50
10		20c. on 30c. brown	48·00	45·00
4	A	25c. on 40c. orange	50·00	38·00

1891. Stamps of French Colonies optd **REUNION**. Imperf (Types F and H) or perf (Type J).

No.	Type	Description	Unused	Used
17	J	1c. black on blue	70	2·50
18		2c. brown on buff	1·10	7·50
19		4c. brown on grey	2·75	4·25
20		5c. green on green	5·00	1·60
21		10c. black on lilac	18·00	2·25
22		15c. blue on blue	42·00	1·50
23		20c. red on green	11·50	11·50
24		25c. black on pink	35·00	1·75
13	H	30c. brown	32·00	38·00
25	J	35c. black on yellow	27·00	23·00
11	F	40c. orange	£375	£350
14	H	40c. red on yellow	30·00	14·50
26	J	40c. red on buff	70·00	60·00
15	H	75c. red	£275	£275
27	J	75c. red on pink	£500	£400
12	F	80c. pink	55·00	45·00
16	H	1f. green	50·00	42·00
28	J	1f. green	£375	£375

1891. Stamps of French Colonies surch **REUNION** and new value.

No.	Type	Description	Unused	Used
29	J	02c. on 20c. red on green	3·75	6·25
30		15c. on 20c. red on green	5·75	5·50
31		2 on 20c. red on green	2·25	2·50

1892. "Tablet" key-type inscr "REUNION".

No.	Type	Description	Unused	Used
34	D	1c. black and red on blue	50	50
35		2c. brown and blue on buff	50	45
36		4c. brown and blue on grey	1·50	60
50		5c. green and red	85	40
38		10c. black and blue on lilac	3·50	1·40
51		10c. red and blue	1·40	40
39		15c. blue and red	28·00	75
52		15c. grey and red	4·75	40
40		20c. red and blue on green	9·25	9·50
41		25c. black and red on pink	10·50	1·50
53		25c. blue and red	16·00	22·00
42		30c. brown and blue on drab	13·00	7·50
43		40c. red and blue on yellow	32·00	13·00
44		50c. red and blue on pink	70·00	21·00
54		50c. brown and red on blue	35·00	38·00
55		50c. brown and blue on blue	42·00	48·00
45		75c. brown and red on orange	49·00	35·00
46		1f. green and red	30·00	28·00

1893. Stamp of French Colonies "Commerce" type, surch **2 c.**

No.	Type	Description	Unused	Used
47	J	2c. on 20c. red on green	2·00	1·75

1901. "Tablet" key-type surch in figures.

No.	Type	Description	Unused	Used
56	D	5c. on 40c. red and blue on yellow	1·60	6·00
57		5c. on 50c. red and blue on pink	3·25	6·50
58		15c. on 75c. brown and red on orange	12·50	17·00
59		15c. on 1f. green and red	8·75	9·25

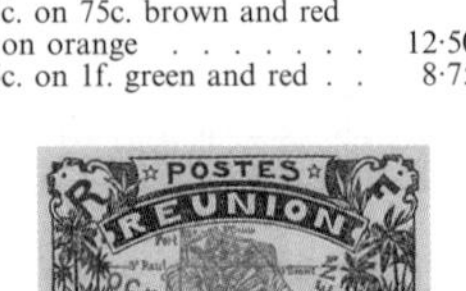

16 Map of Reunion

17 View of Saint-Denis and Arms of the Colony

18 View of St. Pierre and Crater Dolomieu

1907.

No.	Type	Description	Unused	Used
60	16	1c. red and lilac	30	25
61		2c. blue and brown	40	25
62		4c. red and green	45	50
63		5c. red and green	1·10	20
92		5c. violet and yellow	35	50
64		10c. green and red	3·25	20
93		10c. turquoise and green	50	25
94		10c. red and lake on blue	90	25
65		15c. blue and black	1·50	20
95		15c. turquoise and green	50	70
96		15c. red and blue	1·25	1·10
66	17	20c. green and olive	1·75	75
67		25c. brown and blue	3·50	45
97		25c. blue and brown	55	10
68		30c. green and brown	1·00	1·10
98		30c. pink and red	2·50	2·75
99		30c. red and grey	2·00	1·25
100		30c. light green and green	2·50	3·00
69		35c. blue and brown	1·90	1·00
101		40c. brown and green	2·25	15
70		45c. pink and violet	1·60	3·00
102		45c. red and purple	2·50	2·75
103		45c. red and mauve	2·50	4·00
71		50c. blue and brown	2·25	2·25
104		50c. ultramarine and blue	1·75	1·60
105		50c. violet and yellow	1·40	15
106		60c. brown and blue	1·60	2·75
107		65c. blue and violet	2·25	3·25
72		75c. pink and red	2·25	65
108		75c. purple and brown	3·25	4·00
109		90c. pink and red	7·50	8·25
73	18	1f. blue and brown	2·25	1·90
110		1f. blue	2·25	3·50
111		1f. lilac and brown	2·50	2·00
112		1f.10 mauve and brown	2·50	3·25
113		1f.50 lt blue & blue on bl	12·00	11·00
74		2f. green and red	4·00	1·10
114		3f. mauve on pink	11·00	9·50
75		5f. brown and pink	6·75	6·25

1912. "Tablet" key-type surch.

No.	Type	Description	Unused	Used
76	D	05 on 2c. brown and red on buff	25	25
77		05 on 15c. grey and red	25	40
78		05 on 20c. red and blue on green	2·25	3·00
79		05 on 25c. black and red on pink	70	2·50
80		05 on 30c. brown and blue on drab	35	1·75
81		10 on 40c. red and blue on yellow	30	2·50
82		10 on 50c. brown and blue on blue	1·75	3·00
83		10 on 75c. brown and red on orange	2·25	12·50

1915. Red Cross Surch **5c** and red cross.

No.	Type	Description	Unused	Used
90	16	10c.+5c. green and red	1·10	3·25

1917. Surch **0,01**.

No.	Type	Description	Unused	Used
91	16	0,01 on 4c. chestnut and brown	2·75	2·75

1922. Surch in figures only.

No.	Type	Description	Unused	Used
115	17	40 on 20c. yellow and green	55	1·60
116		50 on 45c. red and purple	2·50	1·90
117		50 on 45c. red and mauve	£200	£200
118		50 on 65c. blue and violet	2·25	3·00
119		60 on 75c. carmine and red	30	50
120	16	65 on 15c. blue and black	2·25	3·25
121		85 on 15c. blue and black	1·60	3·25
122	17	85 on 75c. pink and red	2·00	3·50
123		90 on 75c. pink and red	2·50	3·25

1924. Surch in cents and francs.

No.	Type	Description	Unused	Used
124	18	25c. on 5f. brown and pink	1·60	3·00
125		1f.25 on 1f. blue	1·40	2·75
126		1f.50 on 1f. light blue and blue on blue	1·75	40
127		3f. on 5f. blue and red	3·50	3·50
128		10f. on 5f. red and green	13·50	18·00
129		20f. on 5f. pink and brown	18·00	22·00

1931. "Colonial Exhibition" key-types inscr "REUNION".

No.	Type	Description	Unused	Used
130	E	40c. green and black	4·00	4·50
131	F	50c. mauve and black	4·50	4·50
132	G	90c. red and black	4·00	4·75
133	H	1f.50 blue and black	4·75	5·00

30 Cascade, Salazie

32 Leon Dierx Museum

31 Anchain Peak, Salazie

34 Caudron C-600 "Aiglon"

1933.

No.	Type	Description	Unused	Used
134	30	1c. purple	20	1·50
135		2c. brown	10	1·60
136		3c. mauve	25	2·00
137		4c. olive	10	2·00
138		5c. orange	10	20
139		10c. blue	10	35
140		15c. black	10	15
141		20c. blue	15	1·25
142		25c. brown	20	35
143		30c. green	75	50
144	31	35c. green	85	2·75
145		40c. blue	1·90	1·10
146		40c. brown	30	2·75
147		45c. mauve	95	3·00
148		45c. green	70	2·75
149		50c. red	65	15
150		55c. orange	2·00	3·00
151		60c. blue	25	2·75
152		65c. olive	3·00	2·25
153		70c. olive	2·25	2·75
154		75c. brown	5·25	5·75
155		80c. black	1·10	3·00
156		90c. red	3·50	3·75
157		90c. purple	1·25	2·00
158		1f. green	3·50	65
159		1f. red	95	3·00
160		1f. black	55	2·75
161	32	1f.25 brown	60	2·75
162		1f.25 red	2·00	3·00
163	30	1f.40 blue	1·60	3·00
164	32	1f.50 blue	30	15
165	30	1f.60 red	2·25	3·00
166	32	1f.75 olive	1·25	1·25
167	30	1f.75 blue	1·25	3·00
168	32	2f. red	25	2·00
169	30	2f.25 blue	3·00	3·50
170		2f.50 brown	2·00	3·00
171	32	3f. violet	1·60	1·10
172		5f. mauve	1·75	2·75
173		10f. blue	2·25	2·75
174		20f. brown	2·75	3·25

1937. Air. Pioneer Flight from Reunion to France by Laurent, Lenier and Touge. Optd **REUNION – FRANCE par avion "ROLAND GARROS"**.

No.	Type	Description	Unused	Used
174a	31	50c. red	£225	£200

1937. International Exhibition, Paris. As Nos. 168/73 of St.-Pierre et Miquelon.

No.	Type	Description	Unused	Used
175		20c. violet	1·25	3·00
176		30c. green	1·75	3·00
177		40c. red	75	2·50
178		50c. brown and agate	1·00	2·50
179		90c. red	1·40	3·00
180		1f.50 blue	1·50	3·00

1938. Air.

No.	Type	Description	Unused	Used
181	34	3f.65 blue and red	80	1·60
182		6f.65 brown and red	1·25	3·00
183		9f.65 red and blue	55	3·25
184		12f.65 brown and green	1·25	3·50

1938. International Anti-cancer Fund. As T **17a** of Oceanic Settlements.

No.	Type	Description	Unused	Used
185		1f.75+50c. blue	4·50	17·00

1939. New York World's Fair. As T **17b** of Oceanic Settlements.

No.	Type	Description	Unused	Used
186		1f.25 red	1·75	3·25
187		2f.25 blue	1·90	3·25

1939. 150th Anniv of French Revolution. As T **17c** of Oceanic Settlements.

No.	Type	Description	Unused	Used
188		45c.+25c. green and black (postage)	7·75	11·00
189		70c.+30c. brown and black	6·50	11·00
190		90c.+35c. orange and black	5·75	12·00
191		1f.25+1f. red and black	5·50	12·00
192		2f.25+2f. blue and black	6·00	12·00
193		3f.65+4f. blk & orge (air)	10·00	20·00

1943. Surch **1f.**

No.	Type	Description	Unused	Used
194	31	1f. on 65c. green	85	1·25

1943. Optd **France Libre**.

No.	Type	Description	Unused	Used
198	30	1c. purple (postage)	30	3·00
199		2c. brown	30	3·00
200		3c. purple	30	3·00
195	16	4c. red and green	1·10	4·50
201	30	4c. green	25	3·00
202		5c. red	60	3·00
203		10c. blue	25	3·00
204		15c. black	25	3·00
205		20c. blue	75	3·00
206		25c. brown	85	3·00
207		30c. green	50	3·00
208	31	35c. green	40	3·00
209		40c. blue	50	3·00
210		40c. brown	50	3·00
211		45c. mauve	40	2·75
212		45c. green	55	3·00
213		50c. red	75	3·00
214		55c. orange	35	3·00
215		60c. blue	2·25	3·25
216		65c. green	85	3·00
217		70c. green	1·75	3·75
196	17	75c. pink and red	45	3·25
218	31	75c. brown	2·00	4·50
219		80c. black	25	3·00
220		90c. purple	25	3·00
221		1f. green	95	3·00
222		1f. red	35	2·50
223		1f. black	1·75	3·75
240		1f. on 65c. green (No. 194)	65	2·50
224	32	1f.25 brown	75	3·25
225		1f.25 red	1·40	3·25
238	–	1f.25 red (No. 186)	75	4·25
226	30	1f.40 blue	95	3·25
227	32	1f.50 blue	90	3·00
228	30	1f.60 red	70	3·25
229	32	1f.75 green	60	3·00
230	30	1f.75 blue	2·25	5·00
231	32	2f. red	85	2·25
239	–	2f.25 blue (No. 187)	1·50	3·75
232	30	2f.25 blue	50	3·75
233		2f.50 brown	1·90	7·50
234	32	3f. violet	55	2·50
197	18	5f. brown and pink	42·00	42·00
235	32	5f. mauve	1·10	2·00
236		10f. blue	2·25	7·50
237		20f. brown	5·25	12·50
241	34	3f.65 blue and red (air)	3·00	5·00
242		6f.65 brown and red	2·75	5·00
243		9f.65 red and blue	2·25	5·00
244		12f.65 brown and green	3·00	5·00

37 Chief Products

1943. Free French Issue.

No.	Type	Description	Unused	Used
245	37	5c. brown	10	2·00
246a		10c. blue	90	1·10
247		25c. green	15	2·50
248		30c. red	55	2·50
249		40c. green	10	2·25
250		80c. mauve	25	2·25

251 1f. purple 30 30
252 1f.50 red 35 90
253 2f. black . . . . 30 1·75
254 2f.50 blue . . . . 55 2·00
255 4f. violet 45 40
256 5f. yellow 50 25
257 10f. brown 65 70
258 20f. green . . . . 95 1·40

1944. Air. Free French Administration. As T **19a** of Oceanic Settlements.
259 1f. orange 35 55
260 1f.50 red 50 35
261 5f. purple 60 50
262 10f. black . . . . 1·25 2·50
263 25f. blue . . . . 1·90 2·25
264 50f. green . . . . 1·50 1·25
265 100f. red . . . . 1·75 2·75

1944. Mutual Air and Red Cross Funds. As T **19b** of Oceanic Settlements.
266 5f.+20f. black . . . . 1·60 3·50

1945. Eboue. As T **20a** of Oceanic Settlements.
267 2f. black 40 80
268 25f. green . . . . 1·60 2·25

1945. Surch.
269 **37** 50c. on 5c. brown . . . . 95 2·75
270 60c. on 5c. brown . . . . 1·00 2·75
271 70c. on 5c. brown . . . . 45 2·75
272 1f.20 on 5c. brown . . . . 75 2·75
273 2f.40 on 25c. green . . . . 1·25 2·25
274 3f. on 25c. green 75 70
275 4f.50 on 25c. green . . . . 80 2·50
276 15f. on 2f.50 blue . . . . 45 1·25

1946. Air. Victory. As T **20b** of Oceanic Settlements.
277 8f. grey . . . . 25 1·10

1946. Air. From Chad to the Rhine. As T **20c** of Oceanic Settlements.
278 5f. red . . . . 1·75 3·25
279 10f. violet . . . . 1·00 3·00
280 15f. black . . . . 1·60 3·00
281 20f. red . . . . 1·60 2·75
282 25f. blue . . . . 1·50 3·25
283 50f. green . . . . 2·00 3·50

39 Cliffs

40 Banana Tree and Cliff

41 Mountain Landscape

42 Shadow of Airplane over Coast

1947.
284 **39** 10c. orange & grn (postage) . . . . 10 2·50
285 30c. orange and blue . . . 10 2·25
286 40c. orange and brown . . . 10 2·75
287 – 50c. brown and green . . . 15 2·50
288 – 60c. brown and blue . . . 15 2·75
289 – 80c. green and brown . . . 15 2·75
290 – 1f. purple and blue . . . 20 50
291 – 1f.20 grey and green . . . 45 3·00
292 – 1f.50 purple and orange . . 60 3·00
293 **40** 2f. blue and green . . . 25 30
294 3f. purple and green . . . 65 2·25
295 3f.60 pink and red . . . 85 3·25
296 4f. blue and brown . . . 1·00 2·25
297 **41** 5f. mauve and brown . . . 1·25 1·50
298 6f. blue and brown . . . 1·25 2·00
299 10f. orange and blue . . . 1·60 3·00
300 – 15f. purple and blue . . . 1·50 5·25
301 – 20f. blue and orange . . . 2·25 6·00
302 – 25f. brown and mauve . . . 1·75 5·75
303 **42** 50f. green and grey (air) . . 5·75 9·00
304 – 100f. orange and brown . . 8·25 14·00
305 – 200f. blue and orange . . . 7·25 18·00

DESIGNS—20 × 37 mm: 50c. to 80c. Cutting sugar cane; 1f. to 1f.50, Cascade. 28 × 50 mm: 100f. Douglas DC-4 airplane over Reunion. 37 × 20 mm: 15f. to 25f. "Ville de Strasbourg" (liner) approaching Reunion. 50 × 28 mm: 200f. Reunion from the air.

1949. Stamps of France surch **CFA** and value. (a) Postage. (i) Ceres.
306 **218** 50c. on 1f. red . . . . . 20 1·40
307 60c. on 2f. green . . . . 1·75 4·00

(ii) Nos. 972/3 (Arms).
308 10c. on 30c. black, red and yellow (Alsace) . . . . . 20 2·75
309 30c. on 50c. brown, yellow and red (Lorraine) . . . . 35 3·00

(iii) Nos. 981, 979 and 982/a (Views).
310 5f. on 20f. blue (Finistere) . . 2·50 45
311 7f. on 12f. red (Luxembourg Palace) . . . . 2·00 2·10
312 8f. on 25f. blue (Nancy) . . . 4·25 2·10
313 10f. on 25f. brown (Nancy) . . 1·00 55

(iv) Marianne.
314 **219** 1f. on 3f. mauve 30 25
315 2f. on 4f. green 50 40
316 2f. on 5f. green . . . . 3·50 6·00
317 2f. on 5f. violet 50 40
318 2f.50 on 5f. blue . . . . 5·50 16·00
319 3f. on 6f. red 75 30
320 3f. on 6f. green . . . . 1·25 1·40
321 4f. on 10f. violet 65 25
322 6f. on 12f. blue . . . . 1·75 80
323 6f. on 12f. orange . . . . 2·10 2·00
324 9f. on 18f. red . . . . . 2·25 7·50

(v) Conques Abbey.
325 **263** 11f. on 18f. blue . . . . 1·40 2·50

(b) Air. (i) Nos. 967/70 (Mythology).
326 – 20f. on 40f. green . . . . 1·60 90
327 **236** 25f. on 50f. pink . . . . 2·25 50
328 **237** 50f. on 100f. blue . . . . 4·50 1·90
329 – 100f. on 200f. red . . . . 20·00 11·00

(ii) Nos. 1056 and 1058/9 (Cities).
330 100f. on 200f. green (Bordeaux) . . . . 55·00 45·00
331 200f. on 500f. red (Marseilles) 40·00 30·00
332 500f. on 1000f. purple and black on blue (Paris) . . . £150 £160

1950. Stamps of France surch **CFA** and value. (a) Nos. 1050 and 1052 (Arms).
342 10c. on 50c. yellow, red and blue (Guyenne) . . . . . 15 1·60
343 1f. on 2f. red, yellow and green (Auvergne) . . . . . 2·50 5·25

(b) On Nos. 1067/8 and 1068b (Views).
344 – 5f. on 20f. red (Comminges) . . . . . 2·00 55
345 **284** 8f. on 25f. blue (Wandrille) . . . . . . 1·25 50
346 – 15f. on 30f. blue (Arbois) . . . 55 70

1951. Nos. 1123/4 of France (Arms) surch **CFA** and value.
347 50c. on 1f. red, yellow and blue (Bearn) . . . . 30 1·25
348 1f. on 2f. yellow, blue and red (Touraine) 25 30

1952. Nos. 1138 and 1144 of France surch **CFA** and value.
349 **323** 5f. on 20f. violet (Chambord) 60 30
350 **317** 8f. on 40f. violet (Bigorre) . 1·90 25

1953. Stamps of France surch **CFA** and value. (a) Nos. 1162, 1168 and 1170 (Literary Figures and National Industries).
351 3f. on 6f. lake and red (Gargantua) 95 80
352 8f. on 40f. brown and chocolate (Porcelain) . . . 90 20
353 20f. on 75f. red and carmine (Flowers) 90 60

(b) Nos. 1181/2 (Arms).
354 50c. on 1f. yellow, red and black (Poitou) . . . . . . 55 1·25
355 1f. on 2f. yellow, blue and brown (Champagne) . . . 65 3·00

1954. Stamps of France surch **CFA** and value. (a) Postage. (i) Nos. 1188 and 1190 (Sports).
356 8f. on 40f. blue and brown (Canoeing) . . . . 7·50 5·00
357 20f. on 75f. red and orange (Horse jumping) . . . . . 23·00 35·00

(ii) Nos. 1205/8 and 1210/11 (Views).
358 2f. on 6f. indigo, blue and green (Lourdes) . . . . . 55 1·25
359 3f. on 8f. green and blue (Andelys) . . . . 1·10 3·00
360 4f. on 10f. brown and blue (Royan) . . . . 60 1·40
361 6f. on 12f. lilac and violet (Quimper) . . . . 90 1·50
362 9f. on 18f. indigo, blue and green (Cheverny) . . . . 1·90 5·00
363 10f. on 20f. brown, chestnut and blue (Ajaccio) . . . . 3·00 2·75

(iii) No. 1229 (Arms).
364 1f. on 2f. yellow, red and black (Angoumois) 25 25

(b) Air. Nos. 1194/7 (Aircraft).
365 50f. on 100f. brown and blue (Mystere IV) . . . . . . 2·50 95
366 100f. on 200f. purple and blue (Noratlas) . . . . . 2·10 2·25
367 200f. on 500f. red and orange (Magister) . . . . 19·00 18·00
368 500f. on 1000f. indigo, purple and blue (Provence) . . . 11·00 20·00

1955. Stamps of France surch **CFA** and value. (a) Nos. 1262/5, 1266, 1268 and 1268b (Views).
369 2f. on 6f. red (Bordeaux) . . 75 1·25
370 3f. on 8f. blue (Marseilles) . . 1·25 1·00
371 4f. on 10f. blue (Nice) . . . 1·10 1·00
372 5f. on 12f. brown and grey (Cahors) 50 35
373 6f. on 18f. blue and green (Uzerche) 60 40
374 10f. on 25f. brown and chestnut (Brouage) 65 35
375 17f. on 70f. black and green (Cahors) . . . . 2·75 5·00

(b) No. 1273 (Arms).
376 50c. on 1f. yellow, red and blue (Comtat Venaissin) . . 20 25

1956. Nos. 1297/1300 of France (Sports) surch **CFA** and value.
377 8f. on 30f. black and grey (Basketball) . . . . 1·10 30
378 9f. on 40f. purple and brown (Pelota) . . . . 1·40 2·00
379 15f. on 50f. violet and purple (Rugby) . . . . 2·75 2·25
380 20f. on 75f. green, black and blue (Climbing) . . . . . 1·60 2·25

1957. Stamps of France surch **CFA** and value. (a) Postage. (i) Harvester.
381 **344** 2f. on 6f. brown 55 15
382 4f. on 12f. purple . . . . 1·40 1·10
383 5f. on 10f. green . . . . 1·25 65

(ii) France.
384 **362** 10f. on 20f. blue 45 15
385 12f. on 25f. red . . . . . 1·40 30

(iii) No. 1335 (Le Quesnoy).
386 7f. on 15f. black and green 95 30

(iv) Nos. 1351, 1352/3, 1354/5 and 1356a (Tourist Publicity).
387 3f. on 10f. chocolate and brown (Elysee) 70 60
388 6f. on 18f. brown and blue (Beynac) . . . . 1·00 1·75
389 9f. on 25f. brown and grey (Valencay) . . . . 80 2·25
390 17f. on 35f. mauve and red (Rouen) . . . . 1·40 2·25
391 20f. on 50f. brown and green (St. Remy) 75 30
392 25f. on 85f. purple (Evian-les-Bains) . . . . 2·00 65

(b) Air. Nos. 1319/20 (Aircraft).
393 200f. on 500f. black and blue (Caravelle) . . . . 8·50 10·00
394 500f. on 1000f. black, violet and brown (Alouette II) . . 15·00 21·00

1960. Nos. 1461, 1464 and 1467 of France (Tourist Publicity) surch **CFA** and value.
395 7f. on 15c. indigo and blue (Laon) . . . . 1·60 80
396 20f. on 50c. purple and green (Tlemcen) . . . . 11·00 3·25
397 50f. on 1f. violet, green and blue (Cilaos) . . . . 1·40 70

1961. Harvester and Sower stamps of France (in new currency) surch **CFA** and value.
398 **344** 5f. on 10c. green 95 75
400 **453** 10f. on 20c. red and turquoise 50 45

1961. "Marianne" stamp of France surch **12f. CFA.**
401 **463** 12f. on 25c. grey & purple 15 55

1961. Nos. 1457, 1457b and 1459/60 of France (Aircraft) surch **CFA** and value.
402 100f. on 2f. purple and blue (Noratlas) . . . . 4·25 1·40
403 100f. on 2f. indigo and blue (Mystere Falcon 20) . . . 1·75 1·50
404 200f. on 5f. black and blue (Caravelle) . . . . 5·00 3·75
405 500f. on 10f. black, violet and brown (Alouette II) . . . . 14·50 3·75

1962. Red Cross stamps of France (Nos. 1593/4) surch **CFA** and value.
409 10f.+5f. on 20c.+10c. . . . 1·75 2·25
410 12f.+5f. on 25c.+10c. . . . 1·75 2·25

1962. Satellite Link stamps of France surch **CFA** and value.
411 12f. on 25c. (No. 1587) . . . 45 2·00
412 25f. on 50c. (No. 1588) . . . 50 1·90

1963. Nos. 1541 and 1545 of France (Tourist Publicity) surch **CFA** and value.
413 7f. on 15c. grey, purple and blue (Saint-Paul) . . . . . 1·60 1·75
414 20f. on 45c. brown, green and blue (Sully) . . . . 1·10 40

1963. Nos. 1498b/9b and 1499e/f of France (Arms) surch **CFA** and value.
415 1f. on 2c. yellow, green and blue (Gueret) 10 50
416 2f. on 5c. mult (Oran) . . . 20 55
417 2f. on 5c. red, yellow and blue (Armiens) 30 50
418 5f. on 10c. blue, yellow and red (Troyes) 30 55
419 6f. on 18c. multicoloured (St. Denis) 15 50
420 15f. on 30c. red and blue (Paris) 40 55

1963. Red Cross stamps of France Nos. 1627/8 surch **CFA** and value.
421 10f.+5f. on 20c.+10c. . . . 2·75 4·00
422 12f.+5f. on 25c.+10c. . . . 2·75 4·00

1964. 'PHILATEC 1964' International Stamp Exhibition stamp of France surch **CFA** and value.
423 12f. on 25c. (No. 1629) . . . 1·00 75

1964. Nos. 1654/5 of France (Tourist Publicity) surch **CFA** and value.
431 20f. on 40c. chocolate, green and brown (Ronchamp) . . 1·40 2·00
432 35f. on 70c. purple, green and blue (Provins) . . . . . . 95 1·75

1964. Red Cross stamps of France Nos. 1665/6 surch **CFA** and value.
433 10f.+5f. on 20c.+10c. . . . 1·90 2·75
434 12f.+5f. on 25c.+10c. . . . 1·90 2·75

1965. No. 1621 of France (Saint Flour) surch **3F CFA.**
435 30f. on 60c. red, green & blue 1·10 1·75

1965. Nos 1684/5 and 1688 of France (Tourist Publicity) surch **CFA** and value.
436 25f. on 50c. blue, green and bistre (St. Marie) . . . . . 90 1·40
437 30f. on 60c. brown and blue (Aix les Bains) . . . . . . 75 1·75
438 50f. on 1f. grey, green and brown (Carnac) . . . . . 2·25 2·25

1965. Tercent of Colonization of Reunion. As No. 1692 of France, but additionally inscr 'CFA'.
439 15f. blue and red 85 65

1965. Red Cross stamps of France Nos. 1698/9 surch **CFA** and value.
440 12f.+5f. on 25c.+10c. . . . 2·50 2·75
441 15f.+5f. on 30c.+ 10c. . . . 2·50 2·75

1966. "Marianne" stamp of France surch **10f CFA.**
442 **476** 10f. on 20c. red and blue 2·50 2·25

1966. Launching of 1st French Satellite. Nos. 1696/7 (plus se-tenant label) of France surch **CFA** and value.
443 15f. on 30c. blue, turquoise and light blue . . . . . . 2·25 2·25
444 30f. on 60c. blue, turquoise and light blue . . . . . . 2·50 2·25

1966. Red Cross stamps of France Nos. 1733/4 surch **CFA** and value.
445 12f.+5f. on 25c.+10c. . . . 2·25 2·25
446 15f.+5f. on 30c.+10c. . . . 2·25 2·25

1967. World Fair Montreal. No. 1747 of France surch **CFA** and value.
447 30f. on 60c. . . . . 1·25 2·25

1967. No. 1700 of France (Arms of Auch) surch **2fCFA.**
448 2f. on 5c. red and blue . . . 45 1·75

1967. 50th Anniv of Lions Int. No. 1766 of France surch **CFA** and value.
449 20f. on 40c. . . . . 1·60 2·50

1967. Red Cross. Nos. 1772/3 of France surch **CFA** and value.
450 12f.+5f. on 25c.+10c. . . . 2·75 4·50
451 15f.+5f. on 30c .+ 10c. . . . 2·75 4·50

1968. French Polar Exploration. No. 1806 of France surch **CFA** and value.
452 20f. on 40c. . . . . 2·25 2·00

1968. Red Cross stamps of France Nos. 1812/13 surch **CFA** and value.
453 12f.+5f. on 25c.+10c. . . . 2·75 2·75
454 15f.+5f. on 30c.+10c. . . . 2·75 2·75

1969. Stamp Day. No. 1824 of France surch **CFA** and value.
455 15f.+5f. on 30c.+10c. . . . 2·25 2·50

1969. "Republique" stamps of France surch **CFA** and value.
456 **604** 15f. on 30c. green . . . . 1·50 2·00
457 20f. on 40c. mauve . . . 1·10 90

1969. No. 1735 of France (Arms of Saint-Lo) surch **10F CFA.**
458 10f. on 20c. multicoloured . . 1·50 1·60

1969. Birth Bicent of Napoleon Bonaparte. No. 1845 of France surch **CFA** and value.
459 35f. on 70c. green, violet & bl 2·50 2·50

1969. Red Cross stamps of France Nos. 1853/4 surch **CFA** and value.
460 20f.+7f. on 40c.+15c. . . . 2·50 2·75
461 20f.+7f. on 40c.+15c. . . . 2·50 2·75

1970. Stamp Day. No. 1866 of France surch **CFA** and value.
462 20f.+5f. on 40c +.10c. . . . 2·25 2·25

1970. Red Cross. Nos. 1902/3 of France surch **CFA** and value.

463 20f.+7f. on 40c.+15c. . . . 3·50 3·50
464 20f.+7f. on 40c.+15c. . . . 3·50 3·50

1971. "Marianne" stamp of France surch **25f CFA.**
465 **668** 25f. on 50c. mauve . . . 75 70

1971. Stamp Day. No. 1919 of France surch **CFA** and value.
466 25f.+5f. on 50c.+10c. . . . 1·75 2·00

1971. "Antoinette". No. 1920 of France surch **CFA** and value.
467 40f. on 80c. . . . . 2·50 2·50

1971. No. 1928 of France (Rural Aid) surch **CFA** and value.
468 **678** 15f. on 40c. . . . . . . 1·90 2·00

1971. Nos. 1931/2 of France (Tourist Publicity) surch **CFA** and value.
469 45f. on 90c. brown, green and ochre (Riquewihr) . . . . 1·40 2·00
470 50f. on 1f.10 brown, blue and green (Sedan) . . . . . . 1·50 1·90

1971. 40th Anniv of 1st Meeting of Crafts Guilds Association. No. 1935 of France surch **CFA** and value.
471 **680** 45c. on 90c. purple & red 2·25 2·00

63 Reunion Chameleon

64 De Gaulle in Uniform (June 1940)

1971. Nature Protection.
472 **63** 25f. green, brown & yellow 2·25 1·90

1971. De Gaulle Commemoration.
473 **64** 25f. black . . . . 2·75 2·75
474 – 25f. blue . . . . 2·75 2·75
475 – 25f. red . . . . 2·75 2·75
476 – 25f. black . . . . 2·75 2·75
DESIGNS: No. 473, De Gaulle in uniform (June, 1940); No. 474, De Gaulle at Brazzaville, 1944; No. 475, De Gaulle in Paris, 1944; No. 476, De Gaulle as President of the French Republic, 1970 (T **64**).

1971. Nos. 1942/3 of France (Red Cross Fund) surch **CFA** and value.
477 15f.+5f. on 30c.+10c. . . . 2·25 2·50
478 25f.+5f. on 50c.+10c. . . . 2·50 2·50

65 King Penguin, Map and Exploration Ships

1972. Bicentenary of Discovery of Crozet Islands and Kerguelen (French Southern and Antarctic Territories).
479 **65** 45f. black, blue and brown 4·00 4·25

1972. No. 1956 of France surch **CFA** and value.
480 **688** 25f.+5f. on 50c+10c. blue, drab and yellow . . . . 2·25 2·25

1972. No. 1966 of France (Blood Donors) surch **CFA** and value.
481 **692** 15f. on 40c. red . . . . . 1·90 2·00

1972. Air. No 1890 of France (Daurat and Vanier) surch **CFA** and value.
482 **662** 200f. on 5f. brn, grn & bl 4·75 3·25

1972. Postal Codes. Nos. 1969/70 of France surch **CFA** and value.
483 **695** 15f. on 30c. red, black and green . . . . . . 1·90 1·90
484 25f. on 50c. yell, blk & red . . . . 1·75 1·60

1972. Red Cross Fund. Nos. 1979/80 of France surch **CFA** and value.
485 **701** 15f.+5f. on 30c.+10c. . . 2·25 2·50
486 25f.+5f. on 50c.+10c. . . 2·50 2·50

1973. Stamp Day. No. 1996 of France surch **CFA** and value.
487 **707** 25f.+5f. on 50c.+10c. . . 2·75 2·50

1973. No. 2011 of France surch **CFA** and value.
488 **714** 45f. on 90c. green, violet and blue . . . . 2·75 2·75

1973. No. 2008 of France surch **CFA** and value.
489 50f. on 1f. green, brown & bl 1·60 2·25

1973. No. 1960 of France surch **CFA** and value.
490 100f. on 2f. purple and green 2·50 2·50

1973. No. 2021/2 of France surch **CFA** and value.
491 **721** 15f.+5f. on 30c.+10c. green and red . . . . . 2·25 2·75
492 25f.+5f. on 50c .+ 10c. red and black . . . . . 2·50 2·75

1973. No. 2026 of France surch **CFA** and value.
494 **725** 25f. on 50c. brown, blue and purple . . . . . . 2·00 2·00

1974. Stamp Day. No. 2031 surch **FCFA** and value.
495 **727** 25f.+5f. on 50c .+ 10c. 2·00 2·25

1974. French Art. No. 2033/6 surch **FCFA** and value.
496 100f. on 2f. multicoloured . . 2·50 3·25
497 100f. on 2f. multicoloured . . 2·25 3·25
498 100f. on 2f. brown and blue 2·75 3·25
499 100f. on 2f. multicoloured . . 2·50 3·25

1974. French Lifeboat Service. No. 2040 surch **FCFA** and value.
500 **731** 45f. on 90c. blue, red and brown . . . . 2·50 2·50

1974. Centenary of Universal Postal Union. No. 2057 surch **FCFA** and value.
501 **741** 60f. on 1f.20 green, red and blue . . . . 1·40 2·75

1974. "Marianne" stamps of France surch **FCFA** and value.
502 **668** 30f. on 60c. green . . . . 2·50 3·00
503 40f. on 80c. red . . . . . 2·50 3·00

1974. Red Cross Fund. "The Seasons". Nos. 2059/60 surch **FCFA** and value.
504 **743** 30f.+7f. on 60c.+15c. . . 2·50 2·75
505 – 40f.+7f . on 80c.+15c. . . 2·50 2·75

From 1 January 1975 the CFA franc was replaced by the French Metropolitan franc, and Reunion subsequently used unsurcharged stamps of France.

PARCEL POST STAMPS

P 5 P 20

1890.
P11 **P 5** 10c. black on yellow (black frame) £250 £150
P13 10c. black on yellow (blue frame) . . . . 24·00 18·00

1907. Receipt stamps surch as in Type **P 20.**
P76 **P 20** 10c. brown and black . . 22·00 13·00
P77 10c. brown and red . . 19·00 20·00

POSTAGE DUE STAMPS

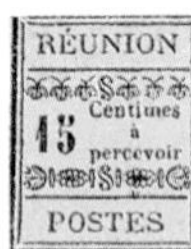

D 4 D 19

1889. Imperf.
D11 **D 4** 5c. black . . . . 17·00 4·50
D12 10c. black . . . . 9·50 4·00
D13 15c. black . . . . 38·00 18·00
D14 20c. black . . . . 50·00 5·25
D15 30c. black . . . . 45·00 5·25

1907.
D76 **D 19** 5c. red on yellow . . . 10 15
D77 10c. blue on blue . . . 15 25
D78 15c. black on grey . . . 15 1·75
D79 20c. pink 70 35
D80 30c. green on green . . 65 2·50
D81 50c. red on green . . . 25 1·75
D82 60c. pink on blue . . . 1·40 2·25
D83 1f. lilac . . . . 95 2·75

1927. Surch.
D130 **D 19** 2f. on 1f. red . . . . 3·50 3·50
D131 3f. on 1f. brown . . . 13·50 18·00

D 33 Arms of Reunion

RÉUNION 10c CHIFFRE-TAXE
D 43

1933.
D175 **D 33** 5c. purple . . . . . . 10 1·75
D176 10c. green . . . . . . 10 2·25
D177 15c. brown . . . . . . 10 1·75
D178 20c. orange . . . . . 15 2·00
D179 30c. olive . . . . . . 15 2·50
D180 50c. blue . . . . . . 20 3·00
D181 60c. brown . . . . . 25 3·00
D182 1f. violet . . . . . . 35 3·00
D183 2f. blue . . . . 35 3·00
D184 3f. red . . . . 35 3·00

1947.
D306 **D 43** 10c. mauve . . . . . 10 2·50
D307 30c. brown . . . . . 10 2·25
D308 50c. green . . . . . 10 2·50
D309 1f. brown . . . . . 1·10 3·00
D310 2f. red . . . . 2·00 2·75
D311 3f. brown . . . . . 1·60 3·00
D312 4f. blue . . . . . . 1·40 3·25
D313 5f. red . . . . 1·50 3·25
D314 10f. green . . . . . 1·60 3·00
D315 20f. blue . . . . . . 2·75 3·25

1949. As Type **D 250** of France, but inscr "TIMBRE TAXE" surch **CFA** and value.
D333 10c. on 1f. blue . . . . . 10 2·75
D334 50c. on 2f. blue . . . . . 10 2·75
D335 1f. on 3f. red . . . . . . 40 3·00
D336 2f. on 4f. violet . . . . . 85 3·50
D337 3f. on 5f. pink . . . . . . 2·00 8·50
D338 5f. on 10f. red . . . . . . 1·10 3·75
D339 10f. on 20f. brown . . . . 1·60 4·25
D340 20f. on 50f. green . . . . 3·75 6·75
D341 50f. on 100f. green . . . . 12·00 23·00

1962. Wheat Sheaves Type of France surch **CFA** and value.
D406 **D 457** 1f. on 5c. mauve . . 1·10 25
D407 10f. on 20c. brown 3·00 3·00
D408 20f. on 50c. green . . 18·00 17·00

1964. Nos. D1650/4 and D1656/7 of France surch **CFA** and value.
D424 – 1f. on 5c. . . . . . 20 1·50
D425 – 5f. on 10c. . . . . 30 1·50
D426 **D 539** 7f. on 15c. . . . . 15 1·60
D427 – 10f. on 20c. . . . 2·50 2·00
D428 – 15f. on 30c. . . . 40 1·75
D429 – 20f. on 50c. . . . 55 1·75
D430 – 50f. on 1f. . . . . 1·00 2·25

RHODESIA Pt. 1

A British territory in central Africa, formerly administered by the British South Africa Co. In 1924 divided into the territories of Northern and Southern Rhodesia which issued their own stamps (q.v). In 1964 Southern Rhodesia was renamed Rhodesia; on becoming independent in 1980 it was renamed Zimbabwe.

1890. 12 pence = 1 shilling;
20 shillings = 1 pound.
1970. 100 cents = 1 dollar.

1 Arms of the Company

1890. The pound values are larger.
18 **1** ½d. blue and red . . . . . . 2·50 3·00
1 1d. black . . . . 10·00 2·75
20 2d. green and red . . . . . 19·00 2·25
21 3d. black and green . . . . 10·00 3·50
22 4d. brown and black . . . . 21·00 2·25
3 6d. blue . . . . 26·00 3·75
23 8d. red and blue . . . . . . 10·00 10·00
4 1s. brown . . . . 35·00 7·50
5 2s. red . . . . 42·00 25·00
6 2s.6d. purple . . . . 30·00 35·00
25 3s. brown and green . . . . £140 75·00
26 4s. black and red . . . . . 32·00 50·00
8 5s. yellow . . . . 65·00 50·00
9 10s. green . . . . 80·00 £100
10 – £1 blue £180 £130
11 – £2 red £400 £150
12 – £5 green £1600 £450
13 – £10 brown £2750 £700

1891. Surch in figures.
14 **1** ½d. on 6d. blue . . . . . . 95·00 £275
15 2d. on 6d. blue £100 £400
16 4d. on 6d. blue £130 £475
17 8d. on 1s. brown £130 £500

5 **9**

1896. The ends of ribbons containing motto cross the animals' legs.
41 **5** ½d. grey and mauve . . . . 2·50 3·25
42 1d. red and green . . . . . 3·25 3·75
43 2d. brown and mauve . . . 7·50 4·50
31 3d. brown and blue . . . . 3·75 1·75
44a 4d. blue and mauve . . . . 8·00 50
46 6d. mauve and red . . . . 6·00 75
34 8d. green and mauve on buff . . . . 4·50 60
35 1s. green and blue . . . . . 15·00 2·75
47 2s. blue and green on buff 22·00 8·50
48 2s.6d. brown & pur on yell 70·00 48·00
36 3s. green and mauve on blue 65·00 32·00
37 4s. red and blue on green 48·00 2·75
49 5s. brown and green . . . . 42·00 9·00
50 10s. grey and red on rose 90·00 60·00

1896. Surch in words.
51 **1** 1d. on 3d. black and green £450 £475
52 1d. on 4s. black and red . . £250 £275
53 3d. on 5s. yellow £170 £225

1896. Cape of Good Hope stamps optd **BRITISH SOUTH AFRICA COMPANY.**
58 **6** ½d. black (No. 48) . . . . . 10·00 16·00
59 **17** 1d. red (No. 58a) . . . . . . 12·00 17·00
60 **6** 2d. brown (No. 60) . . . . 15·00 9·00
61 3d. red (No. 40) . . . . . 50·00 70·00
62 4d. blue (No. 51) . . . . . 17·00 17·00
63 **4** 6d. violet (No. 52a) . . . . 50·00 65·00
64 **6** 1s. yellow (No. 65) £140 £140

1897. The ends of motto ribbons do not cross the animals' legs.
66 **9** ½d. grey and mauve . . . . 2·25 4·50
67 1d. red and green . . . . . 3·00 4·00
68 2d. brown and mauve . . . . 6·00 1·50
69 3d. brown and blue . . . . 2·50 40
70 4d. blue and mauve . . . . 9·00 1·50
71 6d. mauve and red . . . . . 6·50 3·50
72 8d. green and mauve on buff 11·00 40
73 £1 black and brown on green £350 £225

10 **11**

1898. Nos. 90/93a are larger (24 × 28½ mm).
75a **10** ½d. green . . . . 2·25 75
77 1d. red . . . . 3·00 50
79 2d. brown . . . . 2·75 60
80 2½d. blue . . . . 4·50 80
81 3d. red . . . . 4·00 80
82 4d. olive . . . . 4·25 30
83 6d. purple . . . . 10·00 1·75

84 **11** 1s. brown . . . . 14·00 2·25
85 2s.6d. grey . . . . 45·00 75
86 3s. violet . . . . 13·00 1·50
87 5s. orange . . . . 38·00 9·50
88 7s.6d. black . . . . 65·00 16·00
89 10s. green . . . . 22·00 1·00
90 – £1 purple . . . . £225 80·00
91 £2 brown . . . . 75·00 6·50
92 – £5 blue £3000 £2250
93 – £10 lilac £3250 £2250
93a – £20 brown £14000

13 Victoria Falls

1905. Visit of British Assn. and Opening of Victoria Falls Bridge across Zambesi.
94 **13** 1d. red . . . . 3·25 4·25
95 2½d. blue . . . . 8·00 5·50
96 5d. red . . . . 22·00 48·00
97 1s. green . . . . 23·00 35·00
98 2s.6d. black £100 £150
99 5s. violet . . . . 85·00 40·00

1909. Optd **RHODESIA.** or surch also.
100 **10** ½d. green . . . . 1·75 1·25
101 1d. red . . . . 2·25 75
102 2d. brown . . . . 1·60 3·25
103 2½d. blue . . . . 1·25 70
104 3d. red . . . . 1·60 50
105 4d. olive . . . . 2·75 1·00
114 5d. on 6d. purple . . . . 6·50 12·00
106 6d. purple . . . . 5·00 3·75
116 **11** 7½d. on 2s.6d. grey . . . 3·50 3·75
117a 10d. on 2s. violet . . . . 4·00 3·75
107c 1s. brown . . . . 8·50 3·00
118 2s. on 5s. orange . . . . 12·00 7·50
108 2s.6d. grey . . . . 17·00 8·50
109 3s. violet . . . . 15·00 8·50
110 5s. orange . . . . 25·00 30·00
111 7s.6d. black . . . . . . 85·00 17·00
112 10s. green . . . . 32·00 11·00
113 – £1 purple . . . . £140 75·00
113d – £2 brown £3250 £275
113e – £5 blue £6500 £3000

17

18

1910.
119 **17** ½d. green . . . . 9·50 1·75
123 1d. red . . . . 16·00 1·75
128 2d. black and grey . . . 50·00 5·50
131a 2½d. blue . . . . 19·00 5·50
135 3d. purple and yellow . . 32·00 11·00
140 4d. black and orange . . 32·00 11·00
141 5d. purple and olive . . . 24·00 40·00
145 6d. purple and mauve . . 28·00 12·00
148 8d. black and purple . . £130 90·00
149 10d. red and purple . . . 30·00 48·00
151 1s. black and green . . . 35·00 16·00
153 2s. black and blue . . . 75·00 50·00
157 2s.6d. black and red . . . £275 £300
158 3s. green and violet . . . £150 £150
160a 5s. red and green £225 £180
160b 7s.6d. red and blue . . . £600 £425
164 10s. green and orange . . £375 £325
166 £1 red and black £1100 £350

1913.
187 **18** ½d. green . . . . 4·25 1·50
192 1d. red . . . . 3·50 1·25
198 1½d. brown . . . . 3·25 1·25
291 2d. black and grey . . . . 5·50 3·50
200 2½d. blue . . . . 4·00 23·00
259 3d. black and yellow . . . 8·00 1·75
262 4d. black and orange . . . 9·50 6·00
212 5d. black and green . . . 3·75 10·00
266 6d. black and mauve . . . 6·00 5·00
230 8d. violet and green . . . 10·00 48·00
247 10d. blue and red . . . . 6·50 26·00
272 1s. black and blue . . . . 6·50 5·50
273 2s. black and brown . . . 12·00 15·00
236 2s.6d. blue and brown . . 45·00 28·00
304 3s. brown and blue . . . . 80·00 95·00
239 5s. blue and green . . . . 48·00 55·00
252 7s.6d. mauve and grey . . £110 £160
309 10s. red and green £170 £200
242 £1 black and purple . . . £375 £500

1917. Surch **Half Penny** (without hyphen or full stop).
280 **18** ½d. on 1s. red . . . . . . 2·50 7·00

1917. Surch **Half-Penny.** (with hyphen and full stop).
281 **18** ½d. on 1d. red . . . . . . 1·75 6·50

RHODESIA

The following stamps are for the former Southern Rhodesia, renamed Rhodesia.

59 "Telecommunications"

60 Bangala Dam

1965. Centenary of I.T.U.
351 **59** 6d. violet and olive . . . . 1·25 40
352 1s.3d. violet and lilac . . . 1·25 40
353 2s.6d. violet and brown . . 2·00 4·50

1965. Water Conservation. Multicoloured.
354 3d. Type **60** 30 10
355 4d. Irrigation canal . . . . . 1·00 1·00
356 2s.6d. Cutting sugar cane . . 2·25 3·50

63 Sir Winston Churchill, Quill, Sword and Houses of Parliament

1965. Churchill Commemoration.
357 **63** 1s.3d. black and blue . . . 70 35

64 Coat of Arms **67** Emeralds

1965. "Independence".
358 **64** 2s.6d. multicoloured . . . 15 15

1966. Optd **INDEPENDENCE 11th November 1965**.
(a) On Nos. 92/105 of Southern Rhodesia.
359 **45** ½d. yellow, green and blue 10 10
360 – 1d. violet and ochre . . . 10 10
361 – 2d. yellow and violet . . . 10 10
362 – 3d. brown and blue 10 10
363 – 4d. orange and green . . . 15 10
364 **50** 6d. red, yellow and green 15 10
365 – 9d. brown, yellow and green 30 10
366 – 1s. green and ochre 40 10
367 – 1s.3d. red, violet and green 50 20
368 – 2s. blue and ochre . . . . 60 3·25
369 – 2s.6d. blue and red . . . . 60 1·00
370 **56** 5s. multicoloured . . . . . 1·50 5·50
371 – 10s. multicoloured . . . . 3·00 2·25
372 – £1 multicoloured . . . . . 1·25 2·25

(b) Surch on No. 357.
373 **63** 5s. on 1s.3d. black and blue . . . . 3·50 9·00

1966. As Nos. 92/105 of Southern Rhodesia, but inscr "RHODESIA" as in T **67**. Some designs and colours changed.
374 – 1d. violet and ochre . . . 10 10
375 – 2d. orange & grn (As No. 96) 10 10
376 – 3d. brown and blue 10 10
377 **67** 4d. green and brown . . . 1·00 10
378 **50** 6d. red, yellow and green 15 10
379 – 9d. yellow & vio (As No. 94) 15 20
380 **45** 1s. yellow, green and blue 15 10
381 – 1s.3d. bl & ochre (As No. 101) 25 15
382 – 1s.6d. brn, yell & grn (As No. 98) . . . . 2·25 25
383 – 2s. red, vio & grn (As No. 100) 40 80
384 – 2s.6d. blue, red & turquoise 1·50 20
385 **56** 5s. multicoloured 40 90
386 – 10s. multicoloured . . . . 2·75 4·00
387 – £1 multicoloured . . . . . 5·00 8·00

Nos. 379/80 are in larger format as Type **50** of Southern Rhodesia.

Stamps in these designs were later printed locally. These vary only slightly from the above in details and shade.

For Nos. 376, 380 and 382/4 in dual currency see Nos. 408/12.

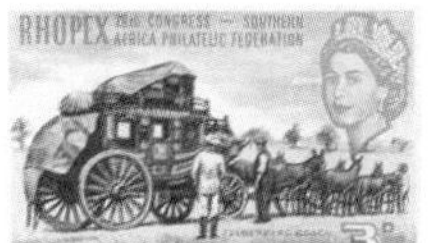

68 Zeederberg Coach, c. 1895

1966. 28th Congress of Southern Africa Philatelic Federation ("Rhopex").
388 **68** 3d. multicoloured 15 10
389 – 9d. multicoloured 15 20
390 – 1s.6d. blue and black . . . 25 30
391 – 2s.6d. pink, green and black 30 55
MS392 126 × 84 mm. Nos. 388/91 6·00 12·00

DESIGNS: 9d. Sir Rowland Hill; 1s.6d. The Penny Black; 2s.6d. Rhodesian stamp of 1892 (No. 12).

69 De Havilland Dragon Rapide (1946)

70 Kudu

1966. 20th Anniv of Central African Airways.
393 **69** 6d. multicoloured 75 35
394 – 1s.3d. multicoloured . . . 1·00 40
395 – 2s.6d. multicoloured . . . 1·75 2·00
396 – 5s. black and blue . . . . 3·00 5·00

AIRCRAFT: 1s.3d. Douglas DC-3 (1953); 2s.6d. Vickers Viscount 748 "Matopos" (1956); 5s. B.A.C. One Eleven.

1967. Dual Currency Issue. As Nos. 376, 380 and 382/4. but value in dual currency as T **70**.
408 **70** 3d./2½c. brown and blue . . 50 15
409 – 1s./10c. yellow, green and blue (No. 380) 50 25
410 – 1s.6d./15c. brown, yellow and green (No. 382) . . 3·50 70
411 – 2s./20c. red, violet and green (No. 383) . . . . 1·50 3·00
412 – 2s.6d./25c. ultramarine, red and blue (No. 384) . . . 16·00 25·00

71 Dr. Jameson (administrator)

1967. Famous Rhodesians (1st series) and 50th Death Anniv of Dr. Jameson.
413 **71** 1s.6d. multicoloured . . . 20 35

See also Nos. 426, 430, 457, 458, 469, 480, 488 and 513.

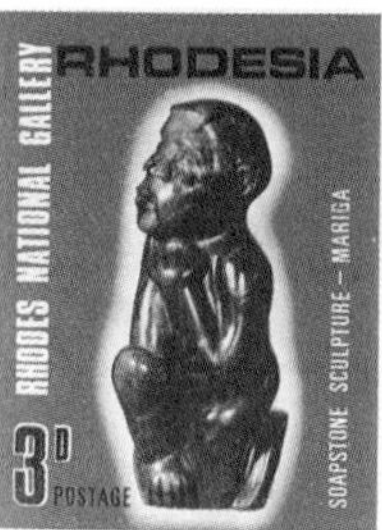

72 Soapstone Sculpture (Joram Mariga)

1967. 10th Anniv of Opening of Rhodes National Gallery.
414 **72** 3d. brown, green and black 10 10
415 – 9d. blue, brown and black 20 20
416 – 1s.3d. multicoloured . . . 20 25
417 – 2s.6d. multicoloured . . . 25 35

DESIGNS: 9d. "The Burgher of Calais" (detail, Rodin); 1s.3d. "The Knight" (stamp design wrongly inscr) (Roberto Crippa); 2s.6d. "John the Baptist" (Mossini).

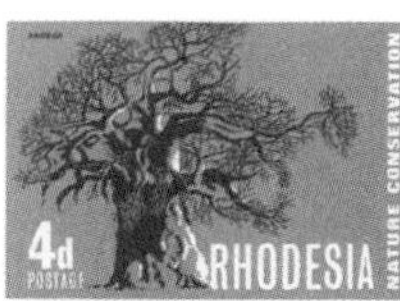

73 Baobab Tree

1967. Nature Conservation.
418 **73** 4d. brown and black . . . 10 20
419 – 4d. green and black . . . 25 20
420 – 4d. grey and black 25 20
421 – 4d. orange and black . . . 10 20

DESIGNS—HORIZ: No. 419, White rhinoceros; No. 420, African elephants. VERT: No. 421, Wild gladiolus.

74 Wooden Hand Plough

1968. 15th World Ploughing Contest, Norton, Rhodesia.
422 **74** 3d. orange, red and brown 10 10
423 – 9d. multicoloured 15 20
424 – 1s.6d. multicoloured . . . 20 55
425 – 2s.6d. multicoloured . . . 20 75

DESIGNS: 9d. Early wheel plough; 1s.6d. Steam powered tractor, and ploughs; 2s.6d. Modern tractor, and plough.

75 Alfred Beit (national benefactor)

1968. Famous Rhodesians (2nd issue).
426 **75** 1s.6d. orange, black & brn 20 30

76 Raising the Flag, Bulawayo, 1893

1968. 75th Anniv of Matabeleland.
427 **76** 3d. orange, red and black 15 10
428 – 9d. multicoloured 15 20
429 – 1s.6d. green, emerald & blk 20 60

DESIGNS: 9d. View and coat of arms of Bulawayo; 1s.6d. Allan Wilson (combatant in the Matabele War).

77 Sir William Henry Milton (administrator)

1969. Famous Rhodesians (3rd issue).
430 **77** 1s.6d. multicoloured . . . 20 55

78 2ft. Gauge Locomotive No. 15, 1897

1969. 70th Anniv of Opening of Beira–Salisbury Railway. Multicoloured.
431 3d. Type **78** 50 10
432 9d. 7th Class steam locomotive No. 43, 1903 70 40
433 1s.6d. Beyer, Peacock 15th Class steam locomotive No. 413, 1951 . . . . . 2·00 1·75
434 2s.6d. Class DE2 diesel-electric locomotive No. 1203, 1955 . . . . . 3·00 4·25

79 Low Level Bridge

1969. Bridges of Rhodesia. Multicoloured.
435 3d. Type **79** 40 10
436 9d. Mpudzi bridge 60 25
437 1s.6d. Umniati bridge . . . . 1·40 75
438 2s.6d. Birchenough bridge . . 1·75 1·50

80 Harvesting Wheat

81 Devil's Cataract, Victoria Falls

1970. Decimal Currency.
439 **80** 1c. multicoloured 10 10
440 – 2c. multicoloured 10 10
441 – 2½c. multicoloured . . . 10 10
441c – 3c. multicoloured . . . . 1·25 10
442 – 3½c. multicoloured . . . 10 10
442b – 4c. multicoloured . . . . 1·75 40
443 – 5c. multicoloured 15 10
443b – 6c. multicoloured . . . . 4·00 3·75
443c **81** 7½c. multicoloured . . . . 7·00 60
444 8c. multicoloured 75 20
445 – 10c. multicoloured . . . 60 10
446 – 12½c. multicoloured . . . 1·00 10
446a – 14c. multicoloured . . . 12·00 70
447 – 15c. multicoloured . . . 1·25 15
448 – 20c. multicoloured . . . 1·00 15
449 – 25c. multicoloured . . . 4·00 60
450 – 50c. turquoise and blue . . 1·25 55

No.	Description	Unused	Used
451	– $1 multicoloured	2·25	85
452	– $2 multicoloured	5·50	15·00

DESIGNS—As Type **80**: 2c. Pouring molten metal; 2½c. Zimbabwe Ruins; 3c. Articulated lorry; 3½c., 4c. Statue of Cecil Rhodes; 5c. Mine headgear; 6c. Hydrofoil "Seaflight". As Type **81**: 10c. Yachting on Lake McIlwaine; 12½c. Hippopotamus in river; 14c., 15c. Kariba Dam; 20c. Irrigation canal. 31 × 26 mm: 25c. Bateleurs; 50c. Radar antenna and Vickers Viscount 810; $1 "Air Rescue"; $2 Rhodesian flag.

82 Despatch Rider, c. 1890

1970. Inauguration of Posts and Telecommunications Corporation. Multicoloured.

No.	Description	Unused	Used
453	2½c. Type **82**	30	10
454	3½c. Loading mail at Salisbury airport	40	50
455	15c. Constructing telegraph line, c. 1890	45	1·25
456	25c. Telephone and modern telecommunications equipment	50	2·00

83 Mother Patrick (Dominican nurse and teacher)

1971. Famous Rhodesians (4th issue).

No.	Description	Unused	Used
457	**83** 15c. multicoloured	60	50

84 Fredrick Courteney Selous (big-game hunter, explorer and pioneer)

1971. Famous Rhodesians (5th issue).

No.	Description	Unused	Used
458	**84** 15c. multicoloured	40	70

85 Hoopoe **86** Porphyritic Granite

1971. Birds of Rhodesia (1st series). Multicoloured.

No.	Description	Unused	Used
459	2c. Type **85**	60	20
460	2½c. Half-collared kingfisher (horiz)	60	10
461	5c. Golden-breasted bunting	1·50	40
462	7½c. Carmine bee eater	1·75	45
463	8c. Red-eyed bulbul	1·75	50
464	25c. Senegal wattled plover (horiz)	3·50	2·50

See also Nos. 537/42.

1971. "Granite 71" Geological Symposium. Multicoloured.

No.	Description	Unused	Used
465	2½c. Type **86**	35	10
466	7½c. Muscovite mica seen through microscope	50	30
467	15c. Granite seen through microscope	90	1·00
468	25c. Geological map of Rhodesia	90	2·25

87 Dr. Robert Moffat (missionary)

1972. Famous Rhodesians (6th issue).

No.	Description	Unused	Used
469	**87** 13c. multicoloured	50	75

88 Bird ("Be Airwise")

1972. "Prevent Pollution". Multicoloured.

No.	Description	Unused	Used
470	2½c. Type **88**	15	10
471	3½c. Antelope ("Be Countrywise")	15	20
472	7c. Fish ("Be Waterwise")	15	30
473	13c. City ("Be Citywise")	20	55

1972. "Rhophil '72". Nos. 439, 441 and 442 with commemorative inscr in margins.

No.	Description	Unused	Used
MS474	1c. multicoloured	1·10	2·00
MS475	2½c. multicoloured	1·10	2·00
MS476	3½ c. multicoloured	1·10	2·00
MS474/6	Set of 3 sheets	3·00	5·50

89 "The Three Kings" **91** W.M.O. Emblem

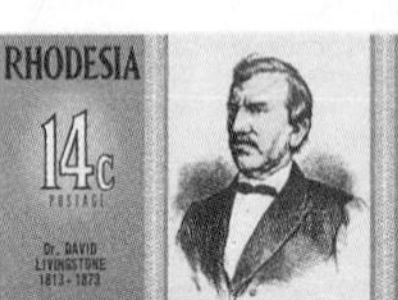

90 Dr. David Livingstone

1972. Christmas.

No.	Description	Unused	Used
477	**89** 2c. multicoloured	10	10
478	5c. multicoloured	15	20
479	13c. multicoloured	30	55

1973. Famous Rhodesians (7th issue).

No.	Description	Unused	Used
480	**90** 14c. multicoloured	50	75

1973. Centenary of I.M.O./W.M.O.

No.	Description	Unused	Used
481	**91** 3c. multicoloured	10	10
482	14c. multicoloured	30	30
483	25c. multicoloured	40	1·00

92 Arms of Rhodesia

1973. 50th Anniv of Responsible Government.

No.	Description	Unused	Used
484	**92** 2½c. multicoloured	10	10
485	4c. multicoloured	15	15
486	7½c. multicoloured	20	25
487	14c. multicoloured	35	1·25

93 George Pauling (construction engineer)

1974. Famous Rhodesians (8th issue).

No.	Description	Unused	Used
488	**93** 14c. multicoloured	50	1·25

94 Greater Kudu **95** Thunbergia

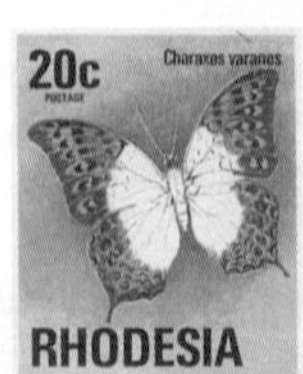

96 "Charaxes varanes"

1974. Multicoloured. (a) Antelopes.

No.	Description	Unused	Used
489	1c. Type **94**	10	10
490	2½c. Eland	75	10
491	3c. Roan antelope	10	10
492	4c. Reedbuck	30	10
493	5c. Bushbuck	30	40

(b) Wild Flowers.

No.	Description	Unused	Used
494	6c. Type **95**	30	10
495	7½c. Flame lily	75	20
496	8c. As 7½c.	30	10
497	10c. Devil thorn	30	10
498	12c. Hibiscus	50	2·00
499	12½c. Pink sabi star	1·00	35
500	14c. Wild pimpernel	1·50	35
501	15c. As 12½c.	50	75
502	16c. As 14c.	50	30

(c) Butterflies.

No.	Description	Unused	Used
503	20c. Type **96**	1·25	35
504	24c. "Precis hierta"	50	40
505	25c. As 24c.	1·75	1·75
506	50c. "Colotis regina"	50	60
507	$1 "Graphium antheus"	50	75
508	$2 "Hamanumida daedalus"	50	90

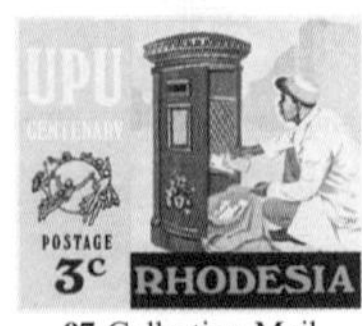

97 Collecting Mail

1974. Centenary of U.P.U. Multicoloured.

No.	Description	Unused	Used
509	3c. Type **97**	15	10
510	4c. Sorting mail	15	10
511	7½c. Mail delivery	20	20
512	14c. Weighing parcel	30	90

98 Thomas Baines (artist)

1975. Famous Rhodesians (9th issue).

No.	Description	Unused	Used
513	**98** 14c. multicoloured	50	60

99 "Euphorbia confinalis" **100** Prevention of Head Injuries

1975. Int Succulent Congress, Salisbury ("Aloe '75"). Multicoloured.

No.	Description	Unused	Used
514	2½c. Type **99**	10	10
515	3c. "Aloe excelsa"	10	10
516	4c. "Hoodia lugardii"	10	10
517	7½c. "Aloe ortholopha"	15	10
518	14c. "Aloe musapana"	30	10
519	25c. "Aloe saponaria"	50	2·00

1975. Occupational Safety. Multicoloured.

No.	Description	Unused	Used
520	2½c. Type **100**	10	10
521	4c. Bandaged hand and gloved hand	15	10
522	7½c. Broken glass and eye	15	15
523	14c. Blind man and welder with protective mask	20	55

101 Telephones, 1876 and 1976 **103** Roan Antelope

1976. Telephone Centenary.

No.	Description	Unused	Used
524	**101** 3c. grey and blue	10	10
525	– 14c. black and brown	20	55

DESIGN: 14c. Alexander Graham Bell.

1976. Nos. 495, 500 and 505 surch.

No.	Description	Unused	Used
526	8c. on 7½c. multicoloured	15	15
527	16c. on 14c. multicoloured	15	15
528	24c. on 25c. multicoloured	20	60

1976. Vulnerable Wildlife. Multicoloured.

No.	Description	Unused	Used
529	4c. Type **103**	10	10
530	6c. Brown hyena	15	60
531	8c. Hunting dog	15	10
532	16c. Cheetah	20	35

104 Msasa **105** Garden Bulbul ("Blackeyed-Bulbul")

1976. Trees of Rhodesia. Multicoloured.

No.	Description	Unused	Used
533	4c. Type **104**	10	10
534	6c. Red mahogany	10	10
535	8c. Mukwa	15	10
536	16c. Rhodesian teak	20	55

1977. Birds of Rhodesia (2nd series). Mult.

No.	Description	Unused	Used
537	3c. Type **105**	20	10
538	4c. Yellow-mantled whydah ("Yellow-mantled Wydah")	20	10
539	6c. Cape longclaw ("Orange throated longclaw")	25	60
540	8c. Magpie shrike ("Eastern Long-tailed Shrike")	30	35
541	16c. Lesser blue-eared glossy starling ("Lesser Blue-eared Starling")	35	60
542	24c. Green wood hoopoe ("Red-billed Wood hoopee")	40	1·10

106 "Lake Kyle" (Joan Evans) **107** Virgin and Child

1977. Landscape Paintings. Multicoloured.

No.	Description	Unused	Used
543	3c. Type **106**	10	10
544	4c. "Chimanimani Mountains" (Joan Evans)	10	10
545	6c. "Rocks near Bonsor Reef" (Alice Balfour)	10	30
546	8c. "A Dwala near Devil's Pass" (Alice Balfour)	10	10
547	16c. "Zimbabwe" (Alice Balfour)	15	30
548	24c. "Victoria Falls" (Thomas Baines)	25	60

1977. Christmas.

No.	Description	Unused	Used
549	**107** 3c. multicoloured	10	10
550	6c. multicoloured	10	20
551	8c. multicoloured	10	10
552	16c. multicoloured	15	30

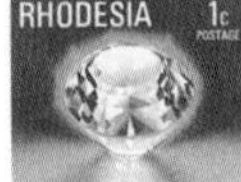

108 Fair Spire **109** Morganite

1978. Trade Fair Rhodesia, Bulawayo. Multicoloured.

No.	Description	Unused	Used
553	4c. Type **108**	10	10
554	8c. Fair Spire (different)	15	25

1978. Gemstones, Wild Animals and Waterfalls. Multicoloured.

No.	Description	Unused	Used
555	1c. Type **109**	10	10
556	3c. Amethyst	10	10
557	4c. Garnet	10	10
558	5c. Citrine	10	10
559	7c. Blue topaz	10	10
560	9c. White rhinoceros	15	10
561	11c. Lion	10	20
562	13c. Warthog	10	85
563	15c. Giraffe	15	20
564	17c. Common zebra	15	10
565	21c. Odzani Falls	15	40
566	25c. Goba Falls	15	15
567	30c. Inyangombi Falls	15	15
568	$1 Bridal Veil Falls	20	35
569	$2 Victoria Falls	30	60

Nos. 560/4 are 26 × 23 mm, and Nos. 565/9 32 × 27 mm.

112 Wright Flyer I

1978. 75th Anniv of Powered Flight. Mult.

No.	Description	Unused	Used
570	4c. Type **112**	10	10
571	5c. Bleriot XI	10	10
572	7c. Vickers Vimy "Silver Queen II"	10	10
573	9c. Armstrong Whitworth A.W.15 Atalanta	10	10
574	17c. Vickers Viking 1B "Zambezi"	10	10
575	25c. Boeing 720B	15	50

POSTAGE DUE STAMPS

D 2

D 3 Zimbabwe Bird (soapstone sculpture)

1965. Roul.
D 8 **D 2** 1d. red . . . . 50 12·00
D 9 2d. blue . . . . 40 8·00
D10 4d. green . . . . 50 8·00
D11 6d. plum . . . . 50 6·00

1966.
D12 **D 3** 1d. red . . . . 60 3·00
D13 2d. blue . . . . 75 1·50
D14 4d. green . . . . 75 3·75
D15 6d. violet . . . . 75 1·50
D16 1s. brown . . . . 75 1·50
D17 2s. black . . . . 1·00 4·50

1970. Decimal Currency. As Type D **3** but larger (26 × 22½ mm).
D18 **D 3** 1c. green . . . . 75 1·75
D19 2c. blue 75 60
D20 5c. violet . . . . 1·75 2·75
D21 6c. yellow . . . . 3·50 4·00
D22 10c. red . . . . 1·75 4·00

RHODESIA AND NYASALAND Pt. 1

Stamps for the Central African Federation of Northern and Southern Rhodesia and Nyasaland Protectorate. The stamps of the Federation were withdrawn on 19 February 1964 when all three constituent territories had resumed issuing their own stamps.

12 pence = 1 shilling;
20 shillings = 1 pound.

1 Queen Elizabeth II

2 Queen Elizabeth II

1954.
1 **1** ½d. red 15 10
2 1d. blue 15 10
3 2d. green 15 10
3a 2½d. ochre . . . . 3·50 10
4 3d. red 20 10
5 4d. brown 60 15
6 4½d. green 25 30
7 6d. purple . . . . 2·00 10
8 9d. violet . . . . 1·50 70
9 1s. grey . . . . 1·75 10
10 **2** 1s.3d. red and blue . . . . 3·00 10
11 2s. blue and brown . . . . 7·50 2·00
12 2s.6d. black and red . . . . 6·00 1·25
13 5s. violet and olive . . . . 17·00 4·50
14 – 10s. turquoise and orange 19·00 7·00
15 – £1 olive and lake . . . . . 30·00 24·00
The 10s. and £1 are as Type **2** but larger (31 × 17 mm) and have the name at top and foliage on either side of portrait.

4 De Havilland Comet 1 over Victoria Falls

5 Livingstone and Victoria Falls

1955. Cent of Discovery of Victoria Falls.
16 **4** 3d. blue and turquoise . . . 35 30
17 **5** 1s. purple and blue 55 70

6 Tea Picking

11 Lake Bangweulu

17 Rhodes Statue

1959.
18 **6** ½d. black and green . . . 60 50
19 – 1d. red and black 15 10
20 – 2d. violet and brown . . . 1·25 50
21 – 2½d. purple and blue . . . 85 50
22 – 3d. black and blue 20 10
23 **11** 4d. purple and green . . . 1·25 10
24 – 6d. blue and green 70 10
24a – 9d. brown and violet . . . 8·00 2·50
25 – 1s. green and blue 80 10
26 – 1s.3d. green and brown . . 3·00 10
27 – 2s. green and red . . . . . 3·25 60
28 – 2s.6d. blue and brown . . . 4·25 30
29 **17** 5s. brown and green . . . 9·00 2·25
30 – 10s. brown and red . . . . 25·00 15·00
31 – £1 black and violet . . . . 45·00 48·00
DESIGNS—VERT (as Type **6**): 1d. V.H.F. mast; 2d. Copper mining; 2½d. Fairbridge Memorial. (As Type **11**): 6d. Eastern Cataract, Victoria Falls. HORIZ (as Type **6**): 3d. Rhodes's grave. (As Type **11**): 9d. Rhodesian railway trains; 1s. Tobacco; 1s.3d. Lake Nyasa; 2s. Chirundu Bridge; 2s.6d. Salisbury Airport. (As Type **17**): 10s. Mlanje; £1 Federal Coat of Arms.

20 Kariba Gorge, 1955

1960. Opening of Kariba Hydro-electric Scheme.
32 **20** 3d. green and orange . . . 70 10
33 – 6d. brown and bistre . . . 70 20
34 – 1s. blue and green . . . . . 2·50 3·50
35 – 1s.3d. blue and brown . . . 2·50 2·25
36 – 2s.6d. purple and red . . . 3·50 7·50
37 – 5s. violet and turquoise . . 8·00 11·00
DESIGNS: 6d. 330 k.V. power lines; 1s. Barrage wall; 1s.3d. Barrage and lake; 2s.6d. Interior of power station; 5s. Queen Mother and barrage wall (inscr "ROYAL OPENING").

26 Miner drilling

1961. 7th Commonwealth Mining and Metallurgical Congress.
38 **26** 6d. green and brown 50 20
39 – 1s.3d. black and blue . . . 50 80
DESIGN: 1s.3d. Surface installations, Nchanga Mine.

28 De Havilland Hercules "City of Basra" on Rhodesian Airstrip

1962. 30th Anniv of 1st London–Rhodesian Airmail Service.
40 **28** 6d. green and red 35 25
41 – 1s.3d. blue, black and yellow 1·50 50
42 – 2s.6d. red and violet . . . . 4·00 4·75
DESIGNS: 1s.3d. Short S.23 flying boat "Canopus" taking off from Zambesi; 2s.6d. Hawker Siddeley Comet 4 at Salisbury Airport.

31 Tobacco Plant

1963. World Tobacco Congress, Salisbury.
43 **31** 3d. green and olive 30 10
44 – 6d. green, brown and blue 40 35
45 – 1s.3d. brown and blue . . . 60 45
46 – 2s.6d. yellow and brown . . 1·00 2·75
DESIGNS: 6d. Tobacco field; 1s.3d. Auction floor; 2s.6d. Cured tobacco.

35

1963. Centenary of Red Cross.
47 **35** 3d. red 85 10

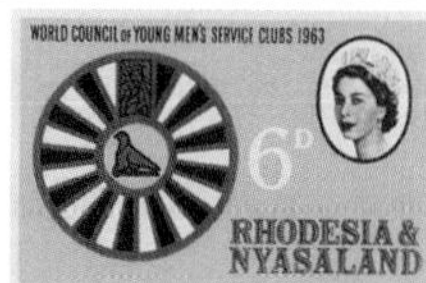
36 African "Round Table" Emblem

1963. World Council of Young Men's Service Clubs, Salisbury.
48 **36** 6d. black, gold and green 50 1·50
49 1s.3d. multicoloured . . . . 50 1·00

POSTAGE DUE STAMPS

D 1

1961.
D1 **D 1** 1d. red . . . . 3·25 5·50
D2 2d. blue . . . . 2·50 3·00
D3 4d. green . . . . 2·50 9·50
D4 6d. purple . . . . 4·50 7·50

RIAU-LINGGA ARCHIPELAGO Pt. 21

A group of islands E of Sumatra and S of Singapore. Part of Indonesia.

100 cents or sen = 1 rupiah.

1954. Optd **RIAU**. (a) On stamps of Indonesia.
1 **96** 5s. red . . . . 50·00 25·00
2 7½s. green . . . . 1·00 1·25
3 10s. blue . . . . 55·00 60·00
4 15s. violet . . . . 2·50 2·00
5 20s. red . . . . 2·50 2·00
6 25s. green . . . . £110 32·00
7 **97** 30s. red . . . . 5·00 3·75
8 35s. violet . . . . 1·00 1·25
9 40s. green . . . . 1·00 1·25
10 45s. purple . . . . 1·00 1·25
11 50s. brown . . . . £400 45·00
12 **98** 60s. brown . . . . 1·00 1·75
13 **98** 70s. grey . . . . 2·50 1·75
14 75s. blue . . . . 8·75 2·50
15 80s. purple . . . . 1·75 2·75
16 90s. green . . . . 1·75 2·50
(b) On Netherlands Indies Nos. 566/71.
17 – 1r. violet . . . . 11·50 3·75
18 – 2r. green . . . . 2·50 4·50
19 – 3r. purple . . . . 3·75 4·50
20 – 5r. brown . . . . 3·75 4·50
21 – 10r. black . . . . 5·00 7·50
22 – 25r. brown . . . . 5·00 7·50

1958. Stamps of Indonesia optd **RIAU**.
26 **115** 5s. blue 50 75
27 10s. brown (No. 714) . . . 75 75
28 15s. purple (No. 715) . . . 75 1·50
29 – 20s. green (No. 716) . . . 75 75
30 – 25s. brown (No. 717) . . . 75 75
31 – 30s. orange (No. 718) . . . 75 75
32 – 50s. brown (No. 722) . . . 75 75

1960. Stamps of Indonesia optd **RIAU**.
33 **99** 1r.25 orange . . . . 3·25 5·00
34 1r.50 brown . . . . 3·25 5·00
35 2r.50 brown . . . . 5·00 7·50
36 4r. green . . . . 90 4·75
37 6r. mauve . . . . 90 4·75
38 15r. stone . . . . 90 4·75
39 20r. purple . . . . 90 10·00
40 40r. green . . . . 90 7·00
41 50r. violet . . . . 1·75 7·50

RIO DE ORO Pt. 9

A Spanish territory on the West Coast of North Africa, renamed Spanish Sahara in 1924.

100 centimos = 1 peseta.

1905. "Curly Head" key-type inscr "COLONIA DE RIO DE ORO".
1 Z 1c. green . . . . 3·00 2·40
2 2c. red . . . . 3·00 2·40
3 3c. black . . . . 3·00 2·40
4 4c. brown . . . . 3·00 2·40
5 5c. red . . . . 3·00 2·40
6 10c. brown . . . . 3·00 2·40
7 15c. brown . . . . 3·00 2·40
8 25c. blue . . . . 60·00 26·00
9 50c. green . . . . 29·00 10·50
10 75c. violet . . . . 29·00 14·50
11 1p. brown . . . . 19·00 6·50
12 2p. orange . . . . 65·00 40·00
13 3p. lilac . . . . 42·00 14·50
14 4p. green . . . . 42·00 14·50
15 5p. blue . . . . 60·00 30·00
16 10p. red £140 £100

1906. "Curly Head" key-type surch **HABILITADO PARA 15 CENTS** in circle.
17 Z 15c. on 25c. blue . . . . . £170 55·00

3

7

11

1907.
18 **3** 1c. purple . . . . 2·40 1·90
19 2c. black . . . . 2·40 1·90
20 3c. brown . . . . 2·40 1·90
21 4c. red . . . . 2·40 1·90
22 5c. brown . . . . 2·40 1·90
23 10c. brown . . . . 2·40 1·90
24 15c. blue . . . . 2·40 1·90
25 25c. green . . . . 6·00 1·90
26 50c. purple . . . . 6·00 1·90
27 75c. brown . . . . 6·00 1·90
28 1p. buff . . . . 10·50 1·90
29 2p. lilac . . . . 3·75 1·90
30 3p. green . . . . 3·75 1·90
31 4p. blue . . . . 6·00 3·50
32 5p. red . . . . 6·00 3·50
33 10p. green . . . . 6·00 9·00

1907. Nos. 9/10 surch **1907 10 Cens**.
34 Z 10c. on 50c. green . . . . . 60·00 23·00
35 10c. on 75c. violet . . . . . 45·00 23·00

1908. Nos. 12 and 26 surch **1908** and value.
36 Z 2c. on 2p. orange . . . . . 38·00 23·00
37 **3** 10c. on 50c. purple . . . . . 17·00 3·75

1908. Surch **HABILITADO PARA 15 CENTS** in circle.
38 **3** 15c. on 25c. green . . . . . 21·00 4·00
39 15c. on 75c. brown . . . . . 28·00 7·00
40 15c. on 1p. buff . . . . . . 28·00 7·00
71 15c. on 3p. green . . . . . . £120 21·00
72 15c. on 5p. red . . . . 8·75 8·00

1908. Large Fiscal stamp inscr "TERRITORIOS ESPAÑOLES DEL AFRICA OCCIDENTAL" surch **HABILITADO PARA CORREOS RIO DE ORO 5 CENS**. Imperf.
45 5c. on 50c. green . . . . . . 55·00 23·00

1909.
47 **7** 1c. orange 55 40
48 2c. orange 55 40
49 5c. green 55 40
50 10c. red 55 40
51 15c. green 55 40
52 20c. purple . . . . 1·50 65
53 25c. blue . . . . 1·50 65
54 30c. red . . . . 1·50 65
55 40c. brown . . . . 1·50 65
56 50c. purple . . . . 2·75 65
57 1p. brown . . . . 3·75 3·25
58 4p. red . . . . 4·25 4·50
59 10p. purple . . . . 9·50 7·50

1910. Nos. 13/16 surch **1910** and value.
60 Z 10c. on 5p. blue . . . . . . 14·00 12·50
62 10c. on 10p. red . . . . . . 12·00 7·00
65 15c. on 3p. lilac . . . . . . 12·00 7·00
66 15c. on 4p. green . . . . . 12·00 7·00

1911. Surch with value in figures and words.
67 **3** 2c. on 4p. blue . . . . 8·75 7·00
68 5c. on 10p. green . . . . . 23·00 7·00
69 10c. on 2p. lilac . . . . . . 11·50 7·00
70 10c. on 3p. green . . . . . . £140 42·00

1912.
73 **11** 1c. pink 20 15
74 2c. lilac 20 15
75 5c. green 20 15
76 10c. red 20 15
77 15c. brown 20 15
78 20c. brown 20 15
79 25c. blue 20 15
80 30c. lilac 20 15
81 40c. green 20 15
82 50c. purple 20 15
83 1p. red . . . . 2·00 55
84 4p. red . . . . 4·50 2·75
85 10p. brown . . . . 6·50 4·25

12

14

15

1914.
86 **12** 1c. brown 25 15
87 2c. purple 25 15
88 5c. green 25 15
89 10c. red 25 15
90 15c. red 25 15
91 20c. red 25 15
92 25c. blue 25 15
93 30c. green 25 15
94 40c. orange 25 15
95 50c. brown 25 15
96 1p. lilac . . . . 2·25 2·40
97 4p. red . . . . 5·25 2·40
98 10p. violet . . . . 7·00 7·00

1917. Nos. 73/85 optd **1917**.
99 **11** 1c. pink . . . . 8·25 1·10
100 2c. lilac . . . . 8·25 1·10
101 5c. green . . . . 2·25 1·10
102 10c. red . . . . 2·25 1·10
103 15c. brown . . . . 2·25 1·10

104 20c. brown 2·25 1·10
105 25c. blue 2·25 1·10
106 30c. lilac 2·25 1·10
107 40c. green 2·25 1·10
108 50c. purple 2·25 1·10
109 1p. red 11·00 4·75
110 4p. red 14·50 6·75
111 10p. brown 25·00 11·00

1919.

112 **14** 1c. brown 60 40
113 2c. purple 60 40
114 5c. green 60 40
115 10c. red 60 40
116 15c. red 60 40
117 20c. orange 60 40
118 25c. blue 60 40
119 30c. green 60 40
120 40c. orange 60 40
121 50c. brown 60 40
122 1p. lilac 4·25 2·75
123 4p. red 7·00 5·25
124 10p. violet 11·00 8·00

1920.

125 **15** 1c. purple 55 35
126 2c. pink 55 35
127 5c. red 55 35
128 10c. purple 55 35
129 15c. brown 55 35
130 20c. green 55 35
131 25c. orange 55 35
132 30c. blue 3·25 3·25
133 40c. orange 1·90 1·40
134 50c. purple 1·90 1·40
135 1p. green 1·90 1·40
136 4p. red 3·75 3·25
137 10p. brown 9·00 8·00

1921. As Nos. 14/26 of La Aguera but inscr "RIO DE ORO".
138 1c. yellow 55 40
139 2c. brown 55 40
140 5c. green 55 40
141 10c. red 55 40
142 15c. green 55 40
143 20c. blue 55 40
144 25c. blue 55 40
145 30c. pink 1·10 95
146 40c. violet 1·10 95
147 50c. orange 1·10 95
148 1p. mauve [illegible] [illegible]
149 4p. purple 5·50 4·00
150 10p. brown 9·50 9·00

For later issues see **SPANISH SAHARA**.

RIO MUNI Pt. 9

A coastal settlement between Cameroun and Gabon, formerly using the stamps of Spanish Guinea. On 12 October 1968 it became independent and joined Fernando Poo to become Equatorial Guinea.

100 centimos = 1 peseta.

1 Native Boy reading Book

2 Cactus

1960.

1 **1** 25c. grey 10 10
2 50c. brown 10 10
3 75c. purple 10 10
4 1p. red 10 10
5 1p.50 green 10 10
6 2p. purple 15 10
7 3p. blue 30 10
8 5p. brown 65 10
9 10p. green 1·25 20

1960. Child Welfare Fund.
10 **2** 10c.+5c. purple 10 10
11 – 15c.+5c. brown 10 10
12 – 35c. green 10 10
13 **2** 80c. green 10 10
DESIGNS: 15c. Sprig with berries; 35c. Star-shaped flowers.

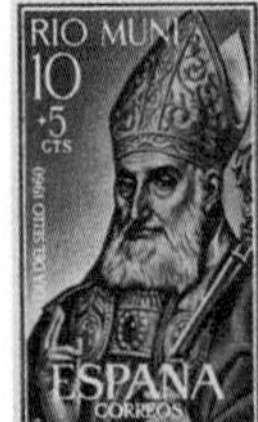

3 Bishop Juan de Ribera

4 Mandrill with Banana

1960. Stamp Day.
14 **3** 10c.+5c. red 10 10
15 – 20c.+5c. green 10 10
16 – 30c.+10c. brown 10 10
17 **3** 50c.+20c. brown 10 10
DESIGNS: 20c. Portrait of man (after Velazquez); 30c. Statue.

1961. Child Welfare. Inscr "PRO-INFANCIA 1961".
18 **4** 10c.+5c. red 10 10
19 – 25c.+10c. violet 10 10
20 **4** 80c.+20c. green 10 10
DESIGN—VERT: 25c. African elephant.

5

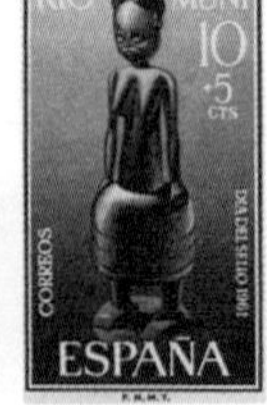

6 Statuette

1961. 25th Anniv of Gen. Franco as Head of State.
21 – 25c. grey 20 10
22 **5** 50c. brown 10 10
23 – 70c. green 10 10
24 **5** 1p. red 10 10
DESIGNS: 25c. Map; 70c. Government building.

1961. Stamp Day. Inscr "DIA DEL SELLO 1961".
25 **6** 10c.+5c. red 10 10
26 – 25c.+10c. purple 10 10
27 **6** 30c.+10c. brown 10 10
28 – 1p.+10c. orange 10 10
DESIGN: 25c., 1p. Figure holding offering.

7 Girl wearing Headdress

8 African Buffalo

1962. Child Welfare. Inscr "PRO-INFANCIA 1962".
29 **7** 25c. violet 10 10
30 – 50c. green 10 10
31 **7** 1p. brown 10 10
DESIGN: 50c. Native mask.

1962. Stamp Day. Inscr "DIA DEL SELLO 1962".
32 **8** 15c. green 10 10
33 – 35c. purple 10 10
34 **8** 1p. red 15 10
DESIGN—VERT: 35c. Gorilla.

9 Statuette

10 "Blessing"

1963. Seville Flood Relief.
35 **9** 50c. green 10 10
36 1p. brown 10 10

1963. Child Welfare. Inscr "PRO-INFANCIA 1963".
37 – 25c. violet 10 10
38 **10** 50c. green 10 10
39 – 1p. red 10 10
DESIGN: 25c., 1p. Priest.

11 Child at Prayer

12 Copal Flower

1963. "For Barcelona".
40 **11** 50c. green 10 10
41 1p. brown 10 10

1964. Stamp Day. Inscr "DIA DEL SELLO 1963".
42 **12** 25c. violet 10 10
43 – 50c. turquoise 10 10
44 **12** 1p. red 10 10
FLOWER—HORIZ: 50c. Cinchona blossom.

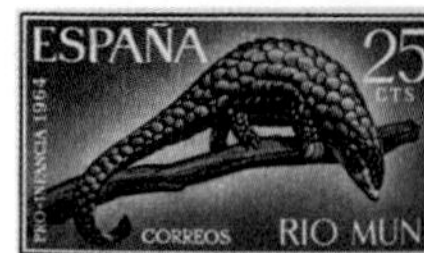

13 Giant Ground Pangolin

1964. Child Welfare. Inscr "PRO-INFANCIA 1964".
45 **13** 25c. violet 10 10
46 – 50c. green (Chameleon) 10 10
47 **13** 1p. brown 10 10

1964. Wild Life. As T **13** but without "PRO INFANCIA" inscription.
48 15c. brown 10 10
49 25c. violet 10 10
50 50c. green 10 10
51 70c. green 10 10
52 1p. brown 55 10
53 1p.50 green 55 10
54 3p. blue 1·10 10
55 5p. brown 3·00 35
56 10p. green 5·50 65
ANIMALS: 15, 70c., 3p. Crocodile; 25c., 1, 5p. Leopard; 50c., 1p.50, 10p. Black rhinoceros.

14 "Goliath" Frog

15 Woman

1964. Stamp Day.
57 **14** 50c. green 10 10
58 – 1p. red 20 10
59 **14** 1p.50 green 10 10
DESIGN—VERT: 1p. Helmeted guineafowl.

1965. 25th Anniv of End of Spanish Civil War.
60 **15** 50c. green 10 10
61 – 1p. red 10 10
62 – 1p.50 turquoise 10 10
DESIGNS: 1p. Nurse; 1p.50, Logging.

16 Goliath Beetle

1965. Child Welfare. Insects.
63 **16** 50c. green 10 10
64 – 1p. brown 10 10
65 **16** 1p.50 black 20 15
DESIGN: 1p. "Acridoxena hewaniana".

17 Leopard and Arms of Rio Muni

1965. Stamp Day.
66 – 50c. grey 35 10
67 **17** 1p. brown 30 10
68 – 2p.50 violet 2·25 50
DESIGN—VERT: 50c., 2p.50, Common pheasant.

18 African Elephant and Grey Parrot

1966. Child Welfare.
69 **18** 50c. brown 20 10
70 1p. lilac 20 10
71 – 1p.50 blue 25 10
DESIGN: 1p.50, African and lion.

19 Water Chevrotain

20 Floss Flowers

1966. Stamp Day.
72 **19** 10c. brown and ochre 10 10
73 – 40c. brown and yellow 10 10
74 **19** 1p.50 violet and red 10 10
75 – 4p. blue and green 15 10
DESIGN—VERT: 40c., 4p. Giant ground pangolin.

1967. Child Welfare.
76 **20** 10c. yellow, olive and green 10 10
77 – 40c. green, black and mauve 10 10
78 **20** 1p.50 red and blue 10 10
79 – 4p. black and green 15 10
DESIGNS: 40c., 4p. Ylang-ylang (flower).

21 Bush Pig

1967. Stamp Day.
80 **21** 1p. chestnut and brown 10 10
81 – 1p.50 brown and green 10 10
82 – 3p.50 brown and green 15 10
DESIGNS—VERT: 1p.50, Potto. HORIZ: 3p.50, African golden cat.

1968. Child Welfare. Signs of the Zodiac. As T **56a** of Spanish Sahara.
83 1p. mauve on yellow 10 10
84 1p.50 brown on pink 10 10
85 2p.50 violet on yellow 15 10
DESIGNS: 1p. Cancer (crab); 1p.50, Taurus (bull); 2p.50, Gemini (twins).

ROMAGNA Pt. 8

One of the Papal states, now part of Italy. Stamps issued prior to union with Sardinia in 1860.

100 bajocchi = 1 scudo.

1

1859. Imperf.
2 **1** ½b. black on buff 18·00 £225
3 1b. black on grey 18·00 £110
4 2b. black on buff 32·00 £120
5 3b. black on green 37·00 £250
6 4b. black on brown £500 £120
7 5b. black on lilac 46·00 £300
8 6b. black on green £250 £6000
9 8b. black on pink £180 £1400
10 20b. black on green £180 £2000

ROSS DEPENDENCY Pt. 1

A dependency of New Zealand in the Antarctic on the Ross Sea.

The post office closed on 30 September 1987, but re-opened in November 1994.

1957. 12 pence = 1 shilling;
20 shillings = 1 pound.
1967. 100 cents = 1 dollar.

3 Map of Ross Dependency and New Zealand

4 Queen Elizabeth II

1957.

1 – 3d. blue 1·00 60
2 – 4d. red 1·00 60
3 **3** 8d. red and blue 1·00 60
4 **4** 1s.6d. purple 1·00 60
DESIGNS—HORIZ (As Type **3**): 3d. H.M.S. "Erebus"; 4d. Shackleton and Scott.

5 H.M.S. "Erebus"

1967. Nos. 1/4 with values inscr in decimal currency as T **5**.
5 **5** 2c. blue 8·00 5·50
6 – 3c. red 3·50 4·75

7 **3** 7c. red and blue 3·50 6·00
8 **4** 15c. purple 3·50 9·00

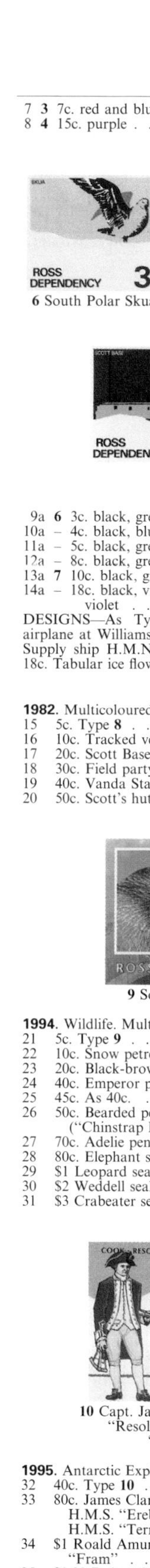

6 South Polar Skua

8 Adelie Penguins and South Polar Skua

7 Scott Base

1972.
9a **6** 3c. black, grey and blue 70 1·60
10a – 4c. black, blue and violet 15 1·60
11a – 5c. black, grey and lilac 15 1·60
12a – 8c. black, grey and brown 15 1·60
13a **7** 10c. black, green and grey 15 1·60
14a – 18c. black, violet and light violet 15 1·60

DESIGNS—As Type **6**: 4c. Lockheed Hercules airplane at Williams Field; 5c. Shackleton's Hut; 8c. Supply ship H.M.N.Z.S. "Endeavour". As Type **7**: 18c. Tabular ice flow.

1982. Multicoloured.
15 5c. Type **8** 1·25 1·40
16 10c. Tracked vehicles 20 65
17 20c. Scott Base 20 65
18 30c. Field party 20 40
19 40c. Vanda Station 20 40
20 50c. Scott's hut, Cape Evans 20 40

9 South Polar Skua

1994. Wildlife. Multicoloured.
21 5c. Type **9** 10 10
22 10c. Snow petrel chick 10 10
23 20c. Black-browed albatross 15 20
24 40c. Emperor penguins 25 30
25 45c. As 40c. 30 35
26 50c. Bearded penguins ("Chinstrap Penguins") 30 35
27 70c. Adelie penguin 45 50
28 80c. Elephant seals 50 55
29 $1 Leopard seal 65 70
30 $2 Weddell seal 1·25 1·40
31 $3 Crabeater seal pup 1·90 2·00

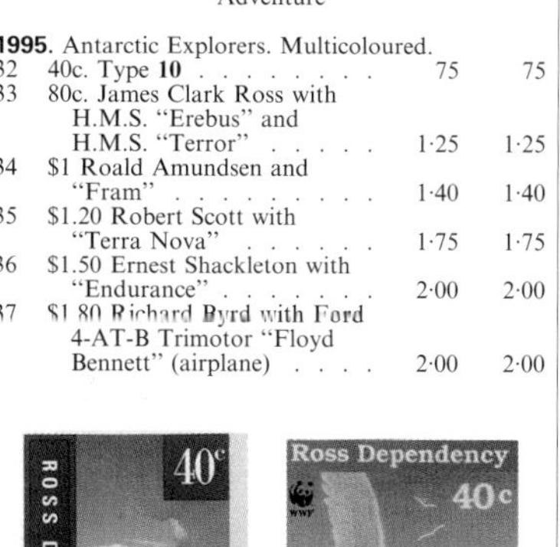

10 Capt. James Cook with H.M.S. "Resolution" and H.M.S. "Adventure"

1995. Antarctic Explorers. Multicoloured.
32 40c. Type **10** 75 75
33 80c. James Clark Ross with H.M.S. "Erebus" and H.M.S. "Terror" 1·25 1·25
34 $1 Roald Amundsen and "Fram" 1·40 1·40
35 $1.20 Robert Scott with "Terra Nova" 1·75 1·75
36 $1.50 Ernest Shackleton with "Endurance" 2·00 2·00
37 $1.80 Richard Byrd with Ford 4-AT-B Trimotor "Floyd Bennett" (airplane) 2·00 2·00

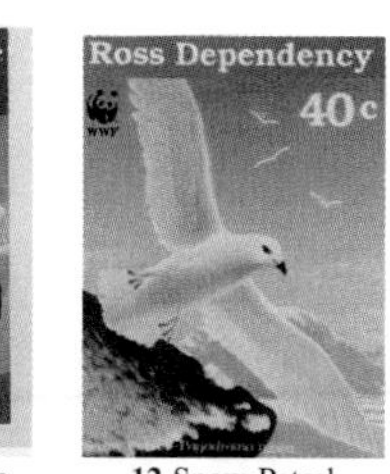

11 Inside Ice Cave

12 Snow Petrel

1996. Antarctic Landscapes. Multicoloured.
38 40c. Type **11** 40 35
39 80c. Base of glacier 70 65
40 $1 Glacier ice fall 85 80
41 $1.20 Climbers on crater rim (horiz) 1·00 95
42 $1.50 Pressure ridges (horiz) 1·25 1·25
43 $1.80 Fumarole ice tower (horiz) 1·40 1·40

1997. Antarctic Seabirds. Multicoloured. (a) With "WWF" panda emblem.
44 40c. Type **12** 70 60
45 80c. Pintado petrel ("Cape Petrel") 1·00 90
46 $1.20 Antarctic fulmar 1·40 1·25
47 $1.50 Antarctic petrel 1·40 1·25

(b) Without "WWF" panda emblem.
48 40c. Type **12** 90 80
49 80c. Pintado petrel ("Cape Petrel") 1·25 1·10
50 $1 Dove prion ("Antarctic Prion") 1·40 1·25
51 $1.20 Antarctic fulmar 1·40 1·40
52 $1.50 Antarctic petrel 1·40 1·40
53 $1.80 Antarctic tern 1·50 1·50

Nos. 48/53 were printed together, se-tenant, with the backgrounds forming a composite design.

13 Sculptured Sea Ice

1997. Ice Formation. Multicoloured.
54 40c. Type **13** 50 35
55 80c. Glacial tongue 70 60
56 $1 Stranded tabular iceberg 90 80
57 $1.20 Autumn at Cape Evans 1·00 90
58 $1.50 Sea ice in summer thaw 1·25 1·10
59 $1.80 Sunset at tubular icebergs 1·40 1·40

14 Sea Smoke, McMurdo Sound

1999. Night Skies. Multicoloured.
60 40c. Type **14** 55 45
61 80c. Alpenglow, Mount Erebus 85 75
62 $1.10 Sunset, Black Island 1·00 90
63 $1.20 Pressure ridges, Ross Sea 1·25 1·00
64 $1.50 Evening light, Ross Island 1·50 1·40
65 $1.80 Mother of pearl clouds, Ross Island 1·75 1·40

15 R.N.Z.A.F. C130 Hercules

2000. Antarctic Transport. Multicoloured.
66 40c. Type **15** 60 50
67 80c. Hagglunds BV206 All Terrain carrier 90 75
68 $1.10 Tracked 4×4 motorbike 1·25 1·00
69 $1.20 ASV track truck 1·25 1·00
70 $1.50 Squirrel helicopter 1·50 1·25
71 $1.80 Elan skidoo 1·50 1·25

2001. Penguins. As T **604** of New Zealand. Multicoloured.
72 40c. Two emperor penguins 50 50
73 80c. Two adelie penguins 70 60
74 90c. Emperor penguin leaving water 80 70
75 $1.30 Adelie penguin in water 1·25 1·00
76 $1.50 Group of emperor penguins 1·40 1·10
77 $2 Group of adelie penguins 1·60 1·50

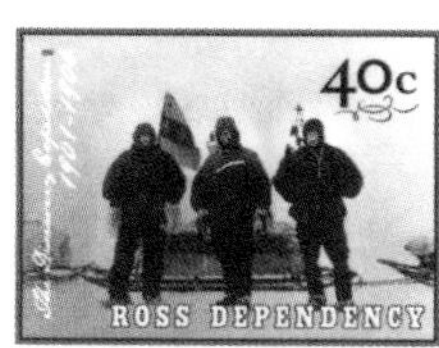

16 British Explorers by Sledge

2002. Antarctic Discovery Expedition, 1901–1904. Each black, grey and stone.
78 40c. Type **16** 25 30
79 80c. H.M.S. *Discovery*, at anchor 50 55
80 90c. H.M.S. *Discovery*, trapped in ice 60 65
81 $1.30 Sledges and tents on the ice 85 90
82 $1.50 Crew of H.M.S. *Discovery* 95 1·00
83 $2 Scott's base at Hut Point 1·25 1·40

ROUAD ISLAND (ARWAD) Pt. 6

An island in the E. Mediterranean off the coast of Syria. A French P.O. was established there during 1916.

25 centimes = 1 piastre.

1916. "Blanc" and "Mouchon" key-types inscr "LEVANT" and optd **ILE ROUAD** (vert).
1 A 5c. green £350 £180
2 B 10c. red £375 £200
3 1pi. on 25c. blue £375 £225

1916. "Blanc" "Mouchon" and "Merson" key-types inscr "LEVANT" and optd **ILE ROUAD** horiz.
4 A 1c. grey 55 3·50
5 2c. purple 40 3·25
6 3c. red 85 3·25
7 5c. green 1·90 3·25
8 B 10c. red 2·25 3·50
9 15c. red 2·00 4·00
10 20c. brown 3·00 4·50
11 1p. on 25c. blue 2·75 4·50
12 30c. lilac 3·25 4·50
13 C 40c. red and blue 4·00 7·00
14 2p. on 50c. brown & lav 6·75 10·50
15 4p. on 1f. red and yellow 11·00 15·00
16 30p. on 5f. blue and yellow 32·00 45·00

RUANDA-URUNDI Pt. 4

Part of German E. Africa, including Ruanda and Urundi, occupied by Belgian forces during the war of 1914–18 and a Trust Territory administered by Belgium until 1 July 1962. The territory then became two separate independent states, named Rwanda and Burundi.

100 centimes = 1 franc.

1916. Nos. 70/77 of Belgian Congo optd. (a) **RUANDA.**
1 **32** 5c. black and green 42·00
2 **33** 10c. black and red 42·00
3 **13** 15c. black and green 65·00
4 **34** 25c. black and blue 42·00
5 **14** 40c. black and red 42·00
6 – 50c. black and red 42·00
7 – 1f. black and brown £160
7a – 5f. black and orange £2000

(b) **URUNDI.**
8 **32** 5c. black and green 42·00
9 **33** 10c. black and red 42·00
10 **13** 15c. black and green 65·00
11 **34** 25c. black and blue 42·00
12 **14** 40c. black and red 42·00
13 – 50c. black and red 48·00
14 – 1f. black and brown £160
14a – 5f. black and orange £2000

1916. Stamps of Belgian Congo of 1915 optd **EST AFRICAIN ALLEMAND OCCUPATION BELGE. DUITSCH OOST AFRIKA BELGISCHE BEZETTING.**
15 **32** 5c. black and green 60 65
16 **33** 10c. black and red 70 70
17 **13** 15c. black and green 50 60
18 **34** 25c. black and blue 3·00 1·50
19 **14** 40c. black and lake 7·75 5·00
20 – 50c. black and lake 9·25 4·75
21 – 1f. black and olive 1·40 85
22 – 5f. black and orange 2·00 1·75

1918. Belgian Congo Red Cross stamps of 1918 optd **A. O.**
23 **32** 5c.+10c. blue and green 15 1·10
24 **33** 10c.+15c. blue and red 35 1·10
25 **13** 15c.+20c. blue and green 40 1·10
26 **34** 25c.+25c. blue 60 1·10
27 **14** 40c.+40c. blue and lake 60 1·40
28 – 50c.+50c. blue and lake 1·00 1·40
29 – 1f.+1f. blue and olive 1·75 3·00
30 – 5f.+5f. blue and orange 8·25 8·25
31 – 10f.+10f. blue and green 60·00 70·00

1922. Stamps of 1916 surch.
32 – 5c. on 50c. black and lake 1·10 3·25
33 **32** 10c. on 5c. black and green 45 85
34a **14** 25c. on 40c. black and lake 2·75 1·60
35 **33** 30c. on 10c. black and red 35 1·10
36 **34** 50c. on 25c. black and blue 80 1·00

1924. Belgian Congo stamps of 1923 optd **RUANDA URUNDI.**
37 A 5c. yellow 30 65
38 B 10c. green 20 65
39 C 15c. brown 15 40
40 D 20c. green 25 60
41 E 20c. green 15 55
42 F 25c. brown 25 20
43 **46** 30c. pink 20 55
44 30c. green 15 60
66 35c. green 35 65
45 D 40c. purple 30 70
46 G 50c. blue 20 30
47 50c. orange 25 70
48 E 75c. orange 25 30
49 75c. blue 30 25
67 **46** 75c. pink 45 80
50 H 1f. brown 35 60
51 1f. blue 60 35
68 1f. pink 85 60
69 D 1f.50 blue 1·10 1·40
71 1f.75 blue 1·25 90
52 I 3f. brown 2·50 3·50
53 J 5f. grey 4·50 5·75
54 K 10f. black 16·00 16·00

1925. Stamp of Belgian Congo optd **RUANDA-URUNDI**. Inscriptions in French or in Flemish.
61 **55** 25c.+25c. black and red 40 1·10

1925. Native cattle type of Belgian Congo optd **RUANDA-URUNDI**.
62 **56** 45c. purple 30 95
63 60c. red 35 60

1927. Belgian Congo stamps of 1923 optd **RUANDA URUNDI** in two lines, wide apart.
64 B 10c. green 25 1·00
65 C 15c. brown 1·25 2·25
66 **46** 35c. green 20 15
67 75c. red 30 25
68 H 1f. red 45 30
69 D 1f.25 blue 50 40
70 1f.50 blue 60 80
71 1f.75 blue 95 60

1927. No. 144 of Belgian Congo optd **RUANDA URUNDI**.
72 1f.75 on 1f.50 blue 40 1·00

1930. Native Fund stamps of Belgian Congo (Nos. 160/8), optd **RUANDA URUNDI**.
73 10c.+5c. red 40 1·10
74 20c.+10c. brown 90 1·50
75 35c.+15c. green 1·25 2·10
76 60c.+30c. purple 1·50 2·25
77 1f.+50c. red 2·10 3·25
78 1f.75+75c. blue 2·75 3·25
79 3f.50+1f.50 lake 5·50 7·25
80 5f.+2f.50 brown 4·00 5·75
81 10f.+5f. black 4·50 6·50

1931. Nos. 68 and 71 surch.
82 H 1f.25 on 1f. red 3·25 1·10
83 D 2f. on 1f.75 blue 4·00 2·25

10 Mountain Scenery

11 King Albert I

1931.
84 – 5c. red 20 40
85 **10** 10c. grey 10 50
86 – 15c. red 20 60
87 – 25c. purple 25 50
88 – 40c. green 60 95
89 – 50c. violet 25 45
90 – 60c. red 25 75
91 – 75c. black 45 65
92 – 1f. red 40 45
93 – 1f.25 brown 30 30
94 – 1f.50 purple 30 60
95 – 2f. blue 60 1·00
96 – 2f.50 blue 45 65
97 – 3f.25 purple 40 1·00
98 – 4f. red 65 60
99 – 5f. grey 75 75
100 – 10f. purple 1·10 1·25
101 – 20f. brown 3·00 3·25

DESIGNS—HORIZ: 15c. Warrior; 25c. Chieftain's kraal; 50c. Head of African buffalo; 1f. Wives of Urundi chiefs; 1f.50, 2f. Wooden pot hewer; 2f.50, 3f.25, Workers making tissues from ficus bark; 4f. Hutu Potter. VERT: 5, 60c., Native porter; 40c. Two cowherds; 75c. Native greeting; 1f.25, Mother and child; 5f. Ruanda dancer; 10f. Warriors; 20f. Native prince of Urundi.

1934. King Albert Mourning Stamp.
102 **11** 1f.50 black 65 60

11a Queen Astrid and Children

14a "Belgium shall rise Again"

1936. Charity. Queen Astrid Fund.
103 **11a** 1f.25+5c. brown 75 1·00
104 1f.50+10c. red 55 1·25
105 2f.50+25c. blue 80 1·60

1941. Stamps of Belgian Congo optd **RUANDA URUNDI**.
106 **78** 10c. grey 9·00 9·00
107 1f.75 orange 4·00 5·25
108 2f.75 blue 4·75 6·25

1941. Ruanda-Urundi stamps of 1931 surch.
109 – 5c. on 40c. green 3·75 5·25
110 – 60c. on 50c. violet 5·25 6·25

111 – 2f.50 on 1f.50 purple . . . 2·75 3·25
112 – 3f.25 on 2f. blue . . . . . 11·00 11·00

1941. Stamps of Belgian Congo optd **RUANDA URUNDI** and surch also.
113 – 5c. on 1f.50 black and brown (No. 222) 20 65
114 – 75c. on 90c. brown and red (No. 221) . . . . 1·50 1·90
115 **78** 2f.50 on 10f. red . . . . . 1·90 1·90

1942. War Relief.
116 **14a** 10f.+40f. red . . . . . . 2·40 3·50
117 10f.+40f. blue . . . . . 2·40 3·50
On No. 116 the French slogan is above the Flemish, on No. 117 vice versa.

1942. Nos. 107/8 of Ruanda-Urundi surch.
118 **78** 75c. on 1f.75 orange . . . 3·75 3·75
119 2f.50 on 2f.75 blue . . . . 6·00 6·25

15a Head of Warrior **17** Seated Figure

1942.
120 A 5c. red 10 45
121 10c. green 10 35
122 15c. brown 10 55
123 20c. blue 10 45
124 25c. purple 10 30
125 30c. blue 10 40
126 50c. green 20 20
127 60c. brown 10 35
128 **15a** 75c. black and lilac . . . 30 25
129 1f. black and brown . . . 35 30
130 1f.25 black and red . . . 40 50
131 B 1f.75 brown . . . . . . 1·10 1·10
132 2f. orange . . . . 1·10 75
133 2f.50 red 80 15
134 C 3f.50 green 50 20
135 5f. orange 55 35
136 6f. blue 55 35
137 7f. black 50 45
138 10f. brown 90 65
139 – 20f. black and brown . . 1·75 1·10
140 – 50f. black and red . . . 3·00 2·25
141 – 100f. black and green . . 5·25 6·00
DESIGNS—As Type **15a** (various frames): A, Oil palms; C, Askari sentry; 20f. Head of zebra. 35 × 24 mm: B, Leopard. 29 × 34 mm: 50f. Askari sentry; 100f. Head of warrior.

1944. Red Cross Fund. Nos. 126, 130, 131 and 134 surch **Au profit de la Croix Rouge Ten voordeele van het Roode Kruis** (50c., 1f.75) or with Flemish and French reversed (others) and premium.
147 50c.+50f. green . . . . . 1·40 2·50
148 1f.25+100f. black and red . . 1·90 3·50
149 1f.75+100f. brown . . . . . 1·75 2·50
150 3f.50+100f. green . . . . . 1·75 3·50

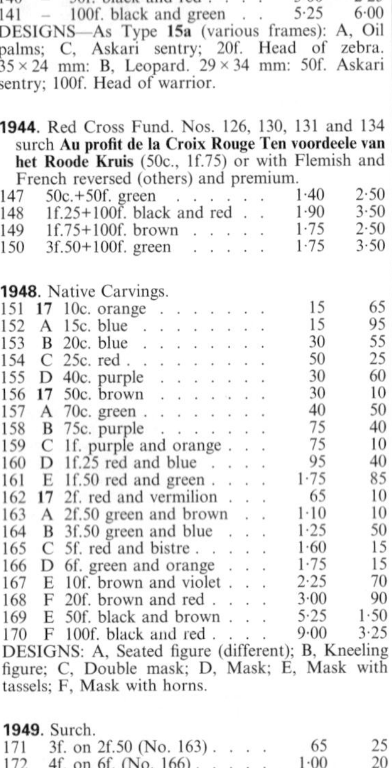

1948. Native Carvings.
151 **17** 10c. orange 15 65
152 A 15c. blue 15 95
153 B 20c. blue 30 55
154 C 25c. red 50 25
155 D 40c. purple 30 60
156 **17** 50c. brown 30 10
157 A 70c. green 40 50
158 B 75c. purple 75 40
159 C 1f. purple and orange . . . 75 10
160 D 1f.25 red and blue 95 40
161 E 1f.50 red and green . . . . 1·75 85
162 **17** 2f. red and vermilion . . . 65 10
163 A 2f.50 green and brown . . 1·10 10
164 B 3f.50 green and blue . . . 1·25 50
165 C 5f. red and bistre . . . . . 1·60 15
166 D 6f. green and orange . . . 1·75 15
167 E 10f. brown and violet . . . 2·25 70
168 F 20f. brown and red . . . . 3·00 90
169 E 50f. black and brown . . . 5·25 1·50
170 F 100f. black and red . . . . 9·00 3·25
DESIGNS: A, Seated figure (different); B, Kneeling figure; C, Double mask; D, Mask; E, Mask with tassels; F, Mask with horns.

1949. Surch.
171 3f. on 2f.50 (No. 163) 65 25
172 4f. on 6f. (No. 166) . . . . . 1·00 20
173 6f.50 on 6f. (No. 166) . . . . 1·25 30

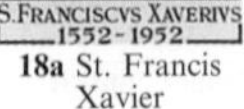

18a St. Francis Xavier **19** "Dissotis"

1953. 400th Death Anniv of St. Francis Xavier.
174 **18a** 1f.50 black and blue . . . 60 70

1953. Flowers Multicoloured.
175 10c. Type **19** 20 40
176 15c. "Protea" 20 45
177 20c. "Vellozia" 20 10
178 25c. "Littonia" 20 40
179 40c. "Ipomoea" 20 45
180 50c. "Angraecum" 35 10
181 60c. "Euphorbia" 65 60
182 75c. "Ochna" 90 40
183 1f. "Hibiscus" 90 10
184 1f.25 "Protea" . . . . 1·75 1·25
185 1f.50 "Schizoglossum" . . . 45 10
186 2f. "Ansellia" . . . . 3·50 45
187 3f. "Costus" . . . . 1·25 10
188 4f. "Nymphaea" . . . . . . 1·75 40
189 5f. "Thunbergia" . . . . . . 1·25 20
190 7f. "Gerbera" . . . . 1·75 45
191 8f. "Gloriosa" . . . . 2·25 55
192 10f. "Silene" . . . . 4·00 50
193 20f. "Aristolochia" . . . . . 7·25 85

20 King Baudouin and Mountains **20a** Mozart when a Child

1955.
194 **20** 1f.50 black and red . . . . 3·25 1·40
195 – 3f. black and green . . . . 3·25 85
196 – 4f.50 black and blue . . . 3·25 75
197 – 6f.50 black and purple . . 3·75 90
DESIGNS: 3f. Forest; 4f.50, River; 6f.50, Grassland.

1956. Birth Bicentenary of Mozart.
198 **20a** 4f.50+1f.50 violet . . . . 1·90 2·25
199 – 6f.50+2f.50 purple . . . . 4·25 3·75
DESIGN—52 × 36 mm: 6f.50, Queen Elizabeth and Mozart sonata.

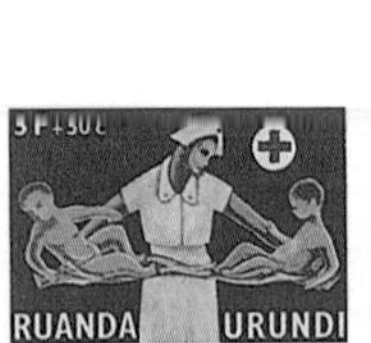

20b Nurse with Children **21** Gorilla

1957. Red Cross Fund.
200 **20b** 3f.+50c. blue . . . . . . 1·10 1·25
201 – 4f.50+50c. green . . . . . 1·25 1·40
202 – 6f.50+50c. brown . . . . 1·25 1·60
DESIGNS: 4f.50, Doctor inoculating patient; 6f.50, Nurse in tropical kit bandaging patient.

1959. Fauna.
203 10c. black, red and brown . . 10 25
204 20c. black and green 10 20
205 40c. black, olive and mauve 10 50
206 50c. brown, yellow and green 10 55
207 1f. black, blue and brown . . 10 40
208 1f.50 black and orange . . . 50 60
209 2f. black, brown and turquoise 50 45
210 3f. black, red and brown . . 60 40
211 5f. multicoloured 45 65
212 6f.50 brown, yellow and red 25 35
213 8f. black, mauve and blue . . 80 80
214 10f. multicoloured 80 75
DESIGNS—VERT: 10c., 1f. Type **21**: 40c., 2f. Eastern black and white colobus. HORIZ: 20c.1f.50, African buffaloes; 50c., 6f.50, Impala; 3, 8f. African elephants; 5, 10f. Eland and common zebras.

22 African Resources

1960. 10th Anniv of African Technical Co-operation Commission. Inscr in French or Flemish.
222 **22** 3f. salmon and blue . . . 20 60

23 High Jumping

1960. Child Welfare Fund. Olympic Games, Rome.
223 50c.+25c. blue and red . . . 20 85
224 1f.50+50c. lake and black . . 40 90
225 2f.+2f. black and red 50 95
226 3f.+1f.25 red and green . . . 1·25 1·90
227 6f.50+3f.50 green and red . . 1·40 1·90
DESIGNS: 50c. Type **23**: 1f.50, Hurdling; 2f. Football; 3f. Throwing the javelin; 6f.50, Throwing the discus.

1960. No. 210 surch.
228 3f.50 on 3f. black, red and brown 45 60

25 Leopard

1961.
229 **25** 20f. multicoloured . . . . 60 1·00
230 – 50f. multicoloured . . . . 1·25 1·70
DESIGN: 50f. Lion and lioness.

26 Usumbura Cathedral

1961. Usumbura Cathedral Fund.
231 **26** 50c.+25c. brown and buff 35 75
232 – 1f.+50c. dp green & grn . . 30 65
233 – 1f.50+75c. multicoloured 20 75
234 **26** 3f.50+1f.50 blue & lt bl . . 35 65
235 – 5f.+2f. red and orange . . 20 95
236 – 6f.50+3f. multicoloured . . 30 1·00
DESIGNS: 1, 5f. Side view of Cathedral; 1f.50, 6f.50, Stained glass windows.

POSTAGE DUE STAMPS

1924. Postage Due stamps of Belgian Congo optd **RUANDA URUNDI**.
D55 **D 54** 5c. brown 10 35
D56a 10c. red 10 50
D57 15c. violet 15 35
D58 30c. green 30 60
D59a 50c. blue 40 65
D60 1f. grey 60 95

1943. Postage Due stamps of Belgian Congo optd **RUANDA URUNDI**.
D142 **D 86** 10c. olive . . . . . 10 1·00
D143 20c. blue 15 80
D144 50c. green . . . . . 30 1·00
D145 1f. brown . . . . . 45 1·00
D146 2f. orange . . . . . 45 1·25

1959. Postage Due stamps of Belgian Congo optd **RUANDA URUNDI**.
D215 **D 99** 10c. brown 40 55
D216 20c. purple 30 70
D217 50c. green 75 80
D218 1f. blue 90 80
D219 2f. red . . . . . . 1·00 1·10
D220 4f. violet . . . . . 1·25 1·50
D221 6f. blue . . . . . . 1·25 1·75

For later issues see **BURUNDI** and **RWANDA**.

RUMANIA Pt. 3

A republic in S.E. Europe bordering on the Black Sea, originally a kingdom formed by the union of Moldavia and Wallachia.

1858. 40 parale = 1 piastre.
1867. 100 bani = 1 leu.

MOLDAVIA

1 **2**

1858. Imperf.
1 **1** 27p. black on red £19000 £6000
2 54p. blue on green £8500 £2500
3 81p. blue on blue £19000 £21000
4 108p. blue on pink £11000 £6000

1858. Imperf.
12 **2** 5p. black £140
13 40p. blue £140 £150
14 80p. red £425 £225

RUMANIA

4

1862. Imperf.
29 **4** 3p. yellow . . . . 45·00 £140
30 6p. red . . . . 32·00 £110
31 30p. blue . . . . 37·00 40·00

5 Prince Alexander Cuza **6** Prince Carol **7** Prince Carol

1865. Imperf.
49a **5** 2p. orange . . . . 25·00 £160
46 5p. blue . . . . 25·00 £150
48 20p. red . . . . 19·00 24·00

1866. Imperf.
60 **6** 2p. black on yellow . . . . 15·00 50·00
61 5p. black on blue . . . . 30·00 £300
62 20p. black on red . . . . . 12·50 11·00

1868. Imperf.
71 **7** 2b. orange . . . . 24·00 17·00
72 3b. mauve . . . . 30·00 20·00
66c 4b. blue . . . . 35·00 24·00
67 18b. red . . . . £140 16·00

8 **9** **10**

1869. Without beard. Imperf.
74 **8** 5b. orange . . . . 55·00 23·00
75 10b. blue . . . . 27·00 19·00
76 15b. red . . . . 27·00 17·00
77c 25b. blue and orange . . . 27·00 17·00
78 50b. red and blue . . . . . £120 25·00

1871. With beard. Imperf.
83 **9** 5b. red . . . . 27·00 18·00
84 10b. orange . . . . 37·00 20·00
99 10b. blue . . . . 35·00 25·00
86 15b. red . . . . £110 95·00
87 25b. brown . . . . 33·00 27·00
100 50b. red and blue £140 £160

1872. Perf.
93 **9** 5b. red . . . . 55·00 25·00
94 10b. blue . . . . 55·00 20·00
95 25b. brown . . . . 26·00 25·00

1872. Perf.
112 **10** 1½b. green . . . . 5·25 1·70
124 1½b. black . . . . 4·00 90
105 3b. green . . . . 21·00 2·20
125 3b. olive . . . . 9·50 5·00
106 5b. bistre . . . . 11·50 2·10
126 5b. green . . . . 3·25 1·00
107 10b. blue . . . . 10·00 2·40
127c 10b. red . . . . 8·50 1·00
115 15b. brown . . . . 45·00 5·00
128a 15b. red . . . . 30·00 7·00
110 25b. orange . . . . 70·00 9·00
130 25b. blue . . . . 95·00 8·75
116 30b. red . . . . £130 32·00
111 50b. red . . . . 65·00 24·00
131 50b. bistre . . . . 75·00 9·25

11 King Carol **12** King Carol **14** King Carol

1880.
146a **11** 15b. brown . . . . 9·50 95
147 25b. blue . . . . 12·50 1·20

1885. On white or coloured papers.
161 **12** 1½b. black . . . . 2·10 90
163 3b. green . . . . 3·00 90
165a 3b. violet . . . . 3·00 90
166 5b. green . . . . 3·00 90
168 10b. red . . . . 3·00 1·10
169 15b. brown . . . . 10·50 1·30
171 25b. blue . . . . 10·50 2·10
186 50b. brown . . . . 42·00 11·00

1890.
271 **14** 1½b. lake . . . . 1·10 45
272a 3b. mauve . . . . 1·20 80
273 5b. green . . . . 1·50 60
274 10b. red . . . . 7·25 65
255 15b. brown . . . . 11·50 1·90
306 25b. blue . . . . 7·50 3·50
307 50b. orange . . . . 19·00 9·25

15 **17** **19**

1891. 25th Anniv of Reign.
300 **15** 1½b. lake . . . . 2·50 3·25
293 3b. mauve . . . . 2·50 3·25
294 5b. green . . . . 4·25 4·75

295 10b. red 4·25 4·75
303 15b. brown 4·25 4·00

1893. Various frames as T **17** and **19**.
316 1 BANI brown 80 60
426 1 BAN brown 1·10 55
317 1½b. black 1·10 40
533 3b. brown 85 30
319 5b. blue 1·10 60
534 5b. green 1·50 30
320 10b. green 1·50 60
535 10b. red 1·70 45
332 15b. pink 2·50 35
400 15b. black 1·60 50
430 15b. brown 1·60 45
545 15b. violet 2·10 50
322 25b. mauve 4·00 70
701 25b. blue 50 30
421 40b. green 9·00 85
324 50b. orange 10·50 90
325 1l. pink and brown 19·00 1·20
326 2l. brown and orange 19·00 2·00
See also Nos. 532 etc.

25 Four-in-hand Postal Coach
26 New Post Office, Bucharest

1903. Opening of New Post Office in 1901.
464 **25** 1b. brown 1·30 60
465 3b. red 2·10 95
466 5b. green 3·50 1·20
467 10b. red 3·75 1·60
468 15b. black 3·75 1·30
472 **26** 15b. black 2·40 2·00
469 **25** 25b. blue 11·00 7·00
473 **26** 25b. blue 6·25 3·50
470 **25** 40b. green 16·00 7·25
474 **26** 40b. green 8·75 5·00
471 **25** 50b. orange 21·00 9·25
475 **26** 50b. orange 8·75 5·00
476 1l. brown 8·75 5·00
477 2l. red 70·00 45·00
478 5l. lilac 90·00 50·00
See also No. 1275.

1905. Various frames as T **17** and **19**.
532 1 ban black 25 25
625b 1½b. yellow 1·40 1·10
703 40b. brown 90 55
705 50b. pink 1·00 60
432 1l. black and green 21·00 1·70
706 1l. green 1·50 40
433 2l. black and brown 16·00 2·10
707 2l. orange 2·30 60

27 Queen of Rumania spinning
28 Queen of Rumania weaving

1906. Welfare Fund. Motto: "God guide our Hand".
481 **27** 3b.(+7) brown 2·50 2·50
482 5b.(+10) green 2·50 2·50
483 10b.(+10) red 9·50 7·75
484 15b.(+10) purple 9·00 4·50

1906. Welfare Fund. Motto: "Woman weaves the Future of the Country".
485 **28** 3b.(+7) brown 2·20 2·30
486 5b.(+10) green 2·20 2·30
487 10b.(+10) red 12·00 8·25
488 15b.(+10) lilac 7·75 4·25

29 Queen of Rumania nursing wounded Soldier
30

1906. Welfare Fund. Motto: "The Wounds dressed and the Tears wiped away".
489 **29** 3b.(+7) brown 2·20 2·30
490 5b.(+10) green 2·20 2·30
491 10b.(+10) red 12·00 9·00
492 15b.(+10) purple 7·75 5·75

1906. 25th Anniv of Kingdom.
493 **30** 1b. black and bistre 30 30
494 3b. black and brown 1·10 40
495 5b. black and green 70 35
496 10b. black and red 70 35
497 15b. black and violet 75 35
498 25b. black and blue 9·00 4·75
499 40b. black and brown 2·10 95
500 50b. black and brown 2·10 95
501 1l. black and red 2·10 95
502 2l. black and orange 2·10 95

31 Prince Carol at Battle of Calafat
32

1906. 40 Years' Rule of Prince and King. Dated "1906".
503 – 1b. black and bistre 15 25
504 – 3b. black and brown 30 25
505 **31** 5b. black and green 65 25
506 – 10b. black and red 30 45
507 – 15b. black and violet 30 45
508 – 25b. black and blue 3·50 2·50
508a – 25b. black and green 4·50 5·50
509 – 40b. black and brown 50 65
510 – 50b. black and brown 60 65
511 – 1l. black and red 90 90
512 – 2l. black and orange 1·20 1·30
DESIGNS—HORIZ: 1b. Prince Carol taking oath of allegiance in 1866; 3b. Prince in carriage; 10b. Meeting of Prince and Osman Pasha, 1878; 15b. Carol when Prince in 1866 and King in 1906; 25b. Rumanian Army crossing Danube, 1877; 40b. Triumphal entry into Bucharest, 1878; 50b. Prince at head of Army in 1877; 1l. King Carol at Cathedral in 1896; 2l. King at shrine of S. Nicholas, 1904.

1906. Welfare Fund. Motto: "But Glory, Honour and Peace to All that do Good".
513 **32** 3b.(+7) brown, bistre and blue 1·40 1·30
514 5b.(+10) green, red and bistre 1·40 1·30
515 10b.(+10) red, bistre and blue 2·75 2·50
516 15b.(+10) violet, bistre and blue 8·50 4·00

33 Peasant ploughing and Angel

1906. Jubilee Exhibition, Bucharest.
517 **33** 5b. black and green 2·75 85
518 10b. black and red 2·75 85
519 – 15b. black and violet 4·00 1·40
520 – 25b. black and blue 4·00 1·40
521 – 30b. brown and red 4·75 1·40
522 – 40b. brown and green 6·25 1·70
523 – 50b. black and orange 5·50 2·00
524 – 75b. sepia and brown 5·50 2·00
525 – 1l.50 brown and mauve 50·00 25·00
526 – 2l.50 brown and yellow 21·00 14·50
527 – 3l. brown and orange 16·00 14·00
DESIGNS—HORIZ: 15, 25b. Exhibition Building. VERT: 30, 40b. Farmhouse; 50, 75b. (different), Royal Family pavilion; 1l.50, 2l.50, King Carol on horseback; 3l. Queen Elizabeth (Carmen Sylva).

34 Princess Maria and her Children receiving Poor Family conducted by an Angel

1907. Welfare Fund.
528 **34** 3b.(+7) brown 4·75 2·75
529 5b.(+10) brown and green 2·75 1·40
530 10b.(+10) brown and red 2·30 1·40
531 15b.(+10) brown and blue 1·70 1·50

35
37

1908.
575 **35** 5b. green 1·40 30
562 10b. red 35 10
577 15b. violet 7·75 2·10
564 25b. blue 90 15
579 40b. green 55 15
702 40b. brown 3·50 1·60
566 50b. orange 55 15
705 50b. red 75 45
581 1l. brown 1·60 30
582 2l. red 7·75 2·40

1908.
583 **37** 1b. black 25 10
590 3b. brown 70 15
585 5b. green 25 15
592 10b. red 45 15
599 15b. violet 11·50 8·50
594 15b. olive 60 15
692 15b. brown 65 40

38
39 Troops crossing Danube

1913. Acquisition of Southern Dobruja.
626 – 1b. black 50 30
627 **38** 3b. brown and grey 1·50 60
628 **39** 5b. black and green 1·20 20
629 – 10b. black and orange 85 20
630 – 15b. violet and brown 1·10 55
631 – 25b. brown and blue 1·50 85
632 **39** 40b. red and brown 3·00 1·30
633 **38** 50b. blue and yellow 3·75 3·00
634 1l. brown and blue 9·00 7·75
635 2l. red and red 12·00 10·50
DESIGNS—VERT (As Type **38**): 1b. "Dobruja" holding flag. HORIZ (As Type **39**): 10b. Town of Constanza; 25b. Church and School in Dobruja. (24 × 16 mm): 15b. Mircea the Great and King Carol.

1918. Surch **25. BANI**.
657 **37** 25b. on 1b. black 80 80

1918. Optd **1918**.
662 **37** 5b. green 50 30
663 10b. red 50 35

TRANSYLVANIA

The Eastern portion of Hungary. Union with Rumania proclaimed in December 1918 and the final frontiers settled by the Treaty of Trianon on 4 June 1920.

The following issues for Transylvania (Nos. 747/858) were valid throughout Rumania.

BANI (**42**)
Bani (**43**)

(The "F" stands for King Ferdinand and "P.T.T." for Posts Telegraphs and Telephones).

The values "BANI", "LEU" or "LEI" appear above or below the monogram.

A. Issues for Cluj (Kolozsvar or Klausenburg).

1919. Various stamps of Hungary optd as T **42**.
(a) Flood Relief Charity stamps of 1913.
747 **7** 1l. on 1f. grey 20·00 18·00
748 1l. on 2f. yellow £100 80·00
749 1l. on 3f. orange 48·00 42·00
750 1l. on 5f. green 2·10 1·60
751 1l. on 10f. red 2·10 1·60
752 1l. on 12f. lilac on yellow 7·75 5·75
753 1l. on 16f. green 4·25 3·00
754 1l. on 25f. blue 48·00 42·00
755 1l. on 35f. purple 4·25 3·00
756 **8** 1l. on 1k. red 55·00 50·00
(b) War Charity stamps of 1916.
757 **20** 10(+2) b. red 30 20
758 – 15(+2) b. violet 30 20
759 **22** 40(+2) b. lake 40 30
(c) Harvesters and Parliament Types.
760 **18** 2b. brown 15 20
761 3b. red 30 20
762 5b. green 30 20
763 6b. blue 30 20
764 10b. red £140 £100
765 15b. violet (No. 244) 5·00 3·75
766 15b. violet 15 10
767 25b. blue 15 10
768 35b. brown 15 10
769 40b. olive 15 10
770 **19** 50b. purple 30 20
771 75b. blue 40 30
772 80b. green 40 30
773 1l. lake 40 30
774 2l. brown 55 40
775 3l. grey and violet 3·50 2·50
776 5l. brown 2·75 2·10
777 10l. lilac and brown 3·50 2·50

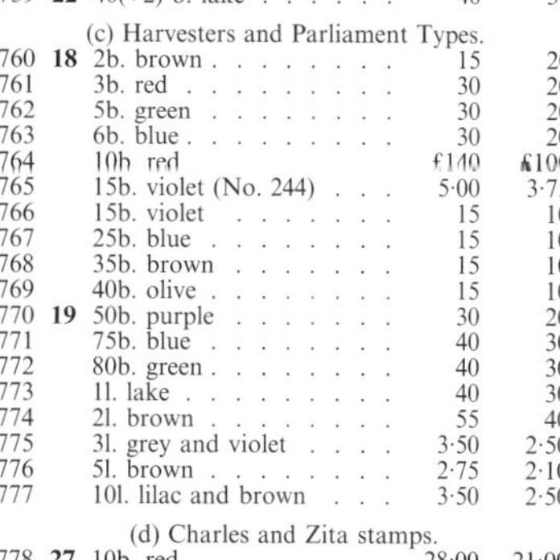

(d) Charles and Zita stamps.
778 **27** 10b. red 28·00 21·00
779 15b. violet 10·50 7·75
780 20b. brown 15 10
781 25b. blue 70 50
782 **28** 40b. green 30 20

B. Issues for Oradea (Nagyvarad or Grosswardein).

1919. Various stamps of Hungary optd as T **43**. (a) "Turul" Type.
794 **7** 2b. yellow 5·50 4·25
795 3b. orange 9·75 7·25
796 6b. drab 70 50
797 16b. green 17·00 12·50
798 50b. lake on blue 95 75
799 70b. brown and green 18·00 16·00
(b) Flood Relief Charity stamps of 1913.
800 **7** 1l. on 1f. grey 95 75
801 1l. on 2f. yellow 4·25 3·00
802 1l. on 3f. orange 1·40 1·00
803 1l. on 5l. green 30 20
804 1l. on 6f. drab 95 75
805 1l. on 10f. red 30 20
806 1l. on 12f. lilac on yellow 49·00 45·00
807 1l. on 16f. green 1·40 1·00
808 1l. on 20f. brown 6·25 4·75
809 1l. on 25f. blue 4·25 3·00
810 1l. on 35f. purple 4·25 3·00
(c) War Charity stamp of 1915.
811 **7** 5+2b. green (No. 173) 7·50 7·75
(d) War Charity stamps of 1916.
812 **20** 10(+2) b. red 30 20
813 – 15(+2) b. violet 15 10
814 **22** 40(+2) b. lake 40 30
(e) Harvesters and Parliament Types.
815 **18** 2b. brown 15 10
816 3b. red 15 10
817 5b. green 30 20
818 6b. blue 85 60
819 10b. red 1·40 1·00
820 15b. violet (No. 244) £120 £100
821 15b. violet 15 10
822 20b. brown 12·50 9·25
823 25b. blue 30 20
824 35b. brown 30 20
825 40b. olive 30 20
826 **19** 50b. purple 30 20
827 75b. blue 40 30
828 80b. green 40 30
829 1l. lake 40 30
830 2l. brown 55 40
831 3l. grey and violet 3·50 2·50
832 5l. brown 2·75 2·10
833 10l. lilac and brown 3·50 2·50
(f) Charles and Zita stamps.
834 **27** 10b. red 2·75 2·10
835 20b. brown 15 10
836 25b. blue 40 30
837 40b. green 70 50

The following (Nos. 838/58) are also optd **KOZTARSASAG**.

(g) Harvesters and Parliament Types.
838 **18** 2b. brown 1·70 1·20
839 3b. red 40 30
840 4b. grey 30 20
841 5b. green 40 30
842 6b. blue 2·10 1·60
843 10b. red 15·00 12·50
844 20b. brown 1·70 1·20
845 40b. olive 40 30
846 **19** 1l. lake 30 20
847 3l. grey and violet 1·10 85
848 5l. brown 4·75 3·75
(h) Charles and Zita stamps.
849 **27** 10b. red £120 £130
850 20b. brown 2·75 2·10
851 25b. blue 55 40
852 **28** 50b. purple 30 20
(k) Harvesters and Parliament Types inscr "MAGYAR POSTA".
853 **18** 5b. green 15 10
854 20b. red 15 10
855 20b. brown 15 10
856 25b. blue 70 50
857 40b. olive 95 75
858 **19** 5l. brown 8·25 6·25

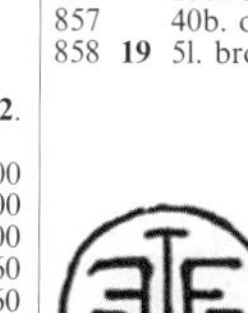

(**44**) King Ferdinand's Monogram
45 King Ferdinand
46 King Ferdinand

1919. Optd with T **44**.
873 **37** 1b. black 05 25
874 5b. green 35 50
878a 10b. red 10 15

1920.
891 **45** 1b. black 10 15
892 3b. green 10 15
893 10b. red 10 15
882 15b. brown 45 25
895 25b. blue 30 30
896 25b. brown 30 30
910 40b. brown 65 20
898 50b. pink 30 15
887 1l. green 65 20
900 1l. red 40 30
889 2l. orange 55 30
902 2l. blue 80 25
903 2l. red 2·20 1·30

1922.
923 **46** 3b. black 20 10
924 5b. black 10 10
925 10b. green 15 10
926 25b. brown 25 10
927 25b. red 30 10
928 30b. violet 30 10
929 50b. yellow 15 10
930 60b. green 1·40 50
931 1l. violet 35 10
932 2l. red 1·80 20
933a 2l. green 1·10 10
934 3l. blue 4·50 65
935a 3l. brown 4·50 60

937 3l. red . . . . 1·10 10
936a 3l. pink . . . . 7·00 1·30
938 5l. green . . . . 2·75 65
939b 5l. brown 75 10
940 6l. blue . . . . 4·50 85
941 6l. red . . . . 8·25 2·50
942 6l. olive . . . . 4·50 60
943 7l.50 blue . . . . 3·75 35
944 10l. blue . . . . 3·75 30

47 Cathedral of Alba Julia **48** King Ferdinand

49 State Arms **51** Michael the Brave and King Ferdinand

1922. Coronation.
1032 **47** 5b. black 40 25
1033 **48** 25b. brown 70 30
1034 **49** 50b. green 70 65
1035 – 1l. olive 70 45
1036 **51** 2l. red 80 50
1037 – 3l. blue . . . . 2·75 1·10
1050 – 6l. violet . . . . 9·25 5·75
DESIGNS—As Type **48**: 1l. Queen Marie as a nurse; 3l. Portrait of King but rectangular frame. Larger (21 × 33 mm): 6l. Queen Marie in coronation robes.

54 King Ferdinand **55** Map of Rumania

1926. King's 60th Birthday. Imperf or perf.
1051 **54** 10b. green 40 30
1052 25b. orange 40 30
1053 50b. brown 40 30
1054 1l. violet 40 30
1055 2l. green 40 30
1056 3l. red 40 30
1057 5l. brown 40 30
1058 6l. olive 40 30
1059 9l. grey 40 30
1060 10l. blue 40 30

1927. 50th Anniv of Rumanian Geographical Society.
1061 **55** 1+9l. violet . . . . 2·75 1·10
1062 – 2+8l. green . . . . 2·75 1·10
1063 – 3+7l. red . . . . 2·75 1·10
1064 – 5+5l. blue . . . . 2·75 1·20
1065 – 6+4l. olive . . . . 6·00 1·90
DESIGNS: 2l. Stephen the Great; 3l. Michael the Brave; 5l. Carol and Ferdinand; 6l. Adam Clisi Monument.

60 King Carol and King Ferdinand

1927. 50th Anniv of Independence.
1066 **60** 25b. red 40 10
1067 – 30b. black 30 20
1068 – 50b. green 40 20
1069 **60** 1l. blue 30 20
1070 – 2l. green 30 20
1071 – 3l. purple 30 25
1072 – 4l. brown 70 30
1073 – 4l.50 brown . . . . 2·00 1·20
1074 – 5l. brown 50 25
1075 – 6l. red . . . . 1·30 65
1076 **60** 7l.50 blue 50 25
1077 10l. blue . . . . 2·00 45
DESIGNS—HORIZ: 30b., 2, 3, 5l. King Ferdinand. VERT: 50b., 4l., 4l.50, 6l. King Ferdinand as in Type **60**.

63 King Michael **64** King Michael

1928.
1080 **63** 25b. black 35 15
1081 30b. pink 65 15
1082 50b. olive 35 15

1928. (a) Size 18½ × 24½ mm.
1083 **64** 1l. purple 45 15
1084 2l. green . . . . 1·00 15
1085 3l. red . . . . 1·00 15
1086 5l. brown . . . . 1·60 15
1087 7l.50 blue . . . . 6·75 65
1088 10l. blue . . . . 6·00 25

(b) Size 18 × 23 mm.
1129 **64** 1l. purple 85 15
1130 2l. green . . . . 1·00 20
1131 3l. red . . . . 2·10 15
1132 7l.50 blue . . . . 4·25 1·20
1133 10l. blue . . . . 16·00 6·25

65 Bessarabian Parliament House

1928. 10th Anniv of Annexation of Bessarabia.
1092 **65** 1l. green . . . . 1·40 45
1093 2l. brown . . . . 1·40 45
1094 – 3l. sepia . . . . 1·40 45
1095 – 5l. lake . . . . 1·70 55
1096 – 7l.50 blue . . . . 2·10 70
1097 – 10l. blue . . . . 3·25 1·50
1098 – 20l. violet . . . . 5·25 2·50
DESIGNS: 3, 5, 20l. Hotin Fortress; 7l.50, 10l. Fortress Cetatea Alba.

66 Bleriot SPAD 33 Biplane

1928. Air.
1099 **66** 1l. brown . . . . 6·25 4·00
1100 2l. blue . . . . 6·25 4·00
1101 5l. red . . . . 6·25 4·00

67 King Carol and King Michael

1928. 50th Anniv of Acquisition of Northern Dobruja.
1102 **67** 1l. green 55 40
1103 – 2l. brown 75 40
1104 **67** 3l. grey 85 40
1105 – 5l. mauve 85 40
1106 – 7l.50 blue . . . . 1·00 45
1107 – 10l. blue . . . . 4·25 1·10
1108 – 20l. red . . . . 5·25 1·30
DESIGNS: 2l. Constanza Harbour and Carol Lighthouse; 5l., 7l.50, Adam Clisi Monument; 10, 20l. Saligny Bridge over River Danube, Cernavoda.

68

69 The Union

1929. 10th Anniv of Union of Rumania and Transylvania.
1109 **68** 1l. purple . . . . 1·40 95
1110 **69** 2l. green . . . . 1·40 95
1111 – 3l. brown . . . . 1·50 95
1112 – 4l. red . . . . 1·40 1·00
1113 – 5l. orange . . . . 1·80 1·10
1114 – 10l. blue . . . . 3·75 2·00
DESIGNS—HORIZ: 1l. Ferdinand I, Stephen the Great, Michael the Brave, Hunyadi and Brancoveanu; 10l. Ferdinand I. VERT: 2l. Union; 3l. Avram Jancu; 4l. King Michael the Brave; 5l. Bran Castle.

1930. Stamps of King Michael optd **8 IUNIE 1930** (Accession of Carol II).
1134 **63** 25b. black (postage) . . . 35 15
1135 30b. pink 55 15
1136 50b. olive 55 15
1142 **64** 1l. purple (No. 1129) . . 45 15
1143 2l. green (No. 1130) . . 45 15
1144 3l. red (No. 1131) 55 15
1137 5l. brown 80 15
1140 7l.50 blue (No. 1087) . . 3·25 90
1145 7l.50 blue (No. 1132) . . 2·20 40
1138 10l. blue (No. 1088) . . . 4·50 1·00
1146 10l. blue (No. 1133) . . . 1·40 55
1147 **66** 1l. brown (air) . . . . . 12·00 6·00
1148 2l. blue . . . . 12·00 6·00
1149 5l. red . . . . 12·00 6·00

72 King Carol II **73** King Carol II **76** King Carol II

1930.
1172 **72** 25b. black 30 10
1173 50b. brown 70 30
1174 1l. violet 35 10
1175 2l. green 55 10
1176 **73** 3l. red . . . . 1·30 10
1177 4l. orange . . . . 1·40 10
1178 6l. red . . . . 1·60 10
1179 7l.50 blue . . . . 1·80 15
1180 – 10l. blue . . . . 3·50 10
1181 – 16l. green . . . . 8·50 15
1182 – 20l. yellow . . . . 9·25 45
DESIGN: 10l. to 20l. Portrait as Type **72**, but in plain circle, with "ROMANIA" at top.

1930. Air.
1183 **76** 1l. violet on blue . . . . 2·30 1·30
1184 2l. green on blue . . . . 2·75 1·50
1185 5l. brown on blue . . . . 5·25 2·30
1186 10l. blue on blue . . . . 9·25 4·75

77 Map of Rumania **78** Woman with Census Paper **79** King Carol II

1930. National Census.
1187 **77** 1l. violet . . . . 1·00 35
1188 **78** 2l. green . . . . 1·40 40
1189 4l. orange . . . . 2·00 20
1190 6l. red . . . . 5·00 40

1931.
1191 **79** 30l. blue and olive . . . . 1·10 55
1192 50l. blue and red . . . . 1·50 1·00
1193 100l. blue and green . . . 3·50 1·80

80 King Carol II

81 King Carol I **82** Kings Carol II, Ferdinand I and Carol I

1931. 50th Anniv of Rumanian Monarchy.
1200 **80** 1l. violet . . . . 3·00 1·40
1201 **81** 2l. green . . . . 3·50 1·60
1202 – 6l. red . . . . 7·00 2·20
1203 **82** 10l. blue . . . . 11·50 4·00
1204 – 20l. orange . . . . 14·00 5·25
DESIGNS—As Type **80**: 6l. King Carol II, facing right. As Type **81**: 20l. King Ferdinand I.

83 Naval Cadet Ship "Mircea"

1931. 50th Anniv of Rumanian Navy.
1205 **83** 6l. red . . . . 4·75 2·75
1206 – 10l. blue . . . . 6·75 3·25
1207 – 12l. green . . . . 21·00 3·50
1208 – 20l. orange . . . . 10·50 6·75
DESIGNS: 10l. Monitors "Lascar Catargiu" and "Mihail Kogalniceanu"; 16l. Monitor "Ardeal"; 20l. Destroyer "Regele Ferdinand".

84 Bayonet Attack **87** King Carol I

88 Infantry Attack **89** King Ferdinand I

1931. Centenary of Rumanian Army.
1209 **84** 25b. black . . . . 1·50 80
1210 – 50b. brown . . . . 2·20 1·10
1211 – 1l. violet . . . . 2·40 1·30
1212 **87** 2l. green . . . . 3·75 1·60
1213 **88** 3l. red . . . . 9·50 5·25
1214 **89** 7l.50 blue . . . . 10·00 11·00
1215 – 16l. green . . . . 12·00 4·50
DESIGNS: 50b. Infantryman, 1870, 20 × 33 mm: 1l. Infantry and drummer, 1830, 23 × 36 mm: 16l. King Carol II in uniform with plumed helmet, 21 × 34 mm.

91 Scouts' Encampment **92a** Farman F.121 Jaribu

1931. Rumanian Boy Scouts' Exhibition Fund.
1221 **91** 1l.+1l. red . . . . 3·00 2·50
1222 – 2l.+2l. green . . . . . . 3·50 3·50
1223 – 3l.+3l. blue . . . . . . 4·75 4·25
1224 – 4l.+4l. brown . . . . . 6·75 5·25
1225 – 6l.+6l. brown . . . . . 10·50 6·75
DESIGNS—VERT: As Type **91**: 3l. Recruiting, 22 × 37½ mm; 2l. Rescue work, 22 × 41½ mm; 4l. Prince Nicholas; 6l. King Carol II in scoutmaster's uniform.

1931. Air.
1226 **92a** 2l. green . . . . 1·30 65
1227 – 3l. red . . . . 1·60 1·00
1228 – 5l. brown . . . . 1·20 1·30
1229 – 10l. blue . . . . 4·25 2·75
1230 – 20l. violet . . . . 15·00 4·25
DESIGNS—As T **92a**: 3l. Farman F.300 and biplane; 5l. Farman F.60 Goliath; 10l. Fokker F.XII. 34 × 20 mm: 20l. Three aircraft flying in formation.

95 Kings Carol II, Ferdinand I and Carol I **96** Alexander the Good

1931.
1231 **95** 16l. green . . . . 10·50 55

1932. 500th Death Centenary of Alexander I, Prince of Moldavia.
1232 **96** 6l. red . . . . 10·50 7·50

97 King Carol II **98** Semaphore Signaller

1932.
1248 **97** 10l. blue . . . . 11·00 35

1932. Boy Scouts' Jamboree Fund.
1256 – 25b.+25b. green . . . . . 3·25 1·90
1257 **98** 50b.+50b. blue . . . . . 3·25 2·75
1258 – 1l.+1l. green . . . . . . 4·00 3·50
1259 – 2l.+2l. red . . . . 7·25 5·25
1260 – 3l.+3l. blue . . . . . . 18·00 10·50
1261 – 6l.+6l. brown . . . . . 19·00 15·00
DESIGNS—VERT: As Type **98**: 25b. Scouts in camp; 1l. On the trail; 3l. King Carol II; 6l. King Carol and King Michael when a Prince. HORIZ: 20 × 15 mm: 2l. Camp fire.

99 Cantacuzino and Gregory Chika

1932. 9th International Medical Congress.
1262 **99** 1l. red . . . . 4·75 5·25
1263 – 6l. orange . . . . 17·00 7·25
1264 – 10l. blue . . . . 30·00 12·50
DESIGNS: 6l. Congress in session; 10l. Hygeia and Aesculapius.

100 Tuberculosis Sanatorium

1932. Postal Employees' Fund.
1265 **100** 4l.+1l. green . . . . . . 3·75 2·40
1266 – 6l.+1l. brown . . . . . 5·25 2·75
1267 – 10l.+1l. blue . . . . . . 8·50 4·50
DESIGNS—VERT: 6l. War Memorial tablet. HORIZ: 10l. Convalescent home.

102 "Bull's head" **103** Dolphins **104** Arms

1932. 75th Anniv of First Moldavian Stamps. Imperf.
1268 **102** 25b. black 65 20
1269 – 1l. purple 80 40
1270 **103** 2l. green 95 50
1271 – 3l. red . . . . 1·20 65
1272 **104** 6l. red . . . . 1·30 85
1273 – 7l.50 blue . . . . 2·75 1·20
1274 – 10l. blue . . . . 5·75 2·00
DESIGNS—As Type **103**: 1l.. Lion rampant and bridge; 3l. Eagle and castles; 7l.50, Eagle; 10l. Bull's head.

1932. 30th Anniv of Opening of G.P.O., Bucharest. As T **25** but smaller.
1275 16l. green . . . . 9·25 5·00

105 Ruins of Trajan's Bridge, Arms of Turnu-Severin and Towers of Severus

1933. Centenary of Founding of Turnu-Severin.
1279 **105** 25b. green 50 35
1280 – 50b. blue 80 45
1281 – 1l. brown . . . . 1·20 65
1282 – 2l. green . . . . 1·60 1·20
DESIGNS: 50b. Trajan at the completion of bridge over the Danube; 1l. Arrival of Prince Carol at Turnu-Severin; 2l. Trajan's Bridge.

107 Carmen Sylva and Carol I

1933. 50th Anniv of Construction of Pelesch Castle, Sinaia.
1283 **107** 1l. violet . . . . 1·60 1·20
1284 – 3l. brown . . . . 1·60 1·50
1285 – 6l. red . . . . 2·00 1·70
DESIGNS: 3l. Eagle and medallion portraits of Kings Carol I, Ferdinand I and Carol II; 6l. Pelesch Castle.

108 Wayside Shrine

110 King Carol II

1934. Rumanian Women's Exhibition. Inscr "L.N.F.R. MUNCA NOASTRA ROMANEASCA".
1286 **108** 1l.+1l. brown . . . . . 1·60 1·30
1287 – 2l.+1l. blue . . . . . . 2·20 1·70
1288 – 3l.+1l. green . . . . . . 2·50 2·20
DESIGNS—HORIZ: 2l. Weaver. VERT: 3l. Spinner.

1934. Mamaia Jamboree Fund. Nos. 1256/61 optd **MAMAIA 1934** and Arms of Constanza.
1289 – 26b.+25b. green . . . . . 3·50 3·00
1290 **98** 50b.+50b. blue . . . . . 4·00 3·25
1291 – 1l.+1l. green . . . . . . 5·25 4·75
1292 – 2l.+2l. red . . . . 7·50 6·50
1293 – 3l.+3l. blue . . . . . . 15·00 11·00
1294 – 6l.+6l. brown . . . . . . 17·00 14·00

1934.
1295 – 50b. brown 80 40
1296 **110** 2l. green 85 40
1297 4l. orange . . . . 2·10 45
1298 – 6l. lake . . . . 5·75 40
DESIGNS: 50b. Profile portrait of King Carol II in civilian clothes; 6l. King Carol in plumed helmet.

112 "Grapes for Health"

113 Crisan, Horia and Closca

1934. Bucharest Fruit Exhibition.
1299 **112** 1l. green . . . . 3·00 2·10
1300 – 2l. brown . . . . 3·00 2·10
DESIGN: 2l. Woman with fruit.

1935. 150th Anniv of Death of Three Rumanian Martyrs. Portraits inscr "MARTIR AL NEAMULUI 1785".
1301 **113** 1l. violet 55 35
1302 – 2l. green (Crisan) 60 50
1303 – 6l. brown (Closca) . . . 1·60 1·00
1304 – 10l. blue (Horia) . . . . 2·40 2·10

114 Boy Scouts

1935. 5th Anniv of Accession of Carol II.
1305 – 25b. black . . . . 3·00 2·00
1306 – 1l. violet . . . . 4·50 3·50
1307 **114** 2l. green . . . . 5·75 5·25
1308 – 6l.+1l. brown . . . . . 7·00 7·25
1309 – 10l.+2l. blue . . . . . . 14·50 17·00
DESIGNS—VERT: 25b. Scout saluting; 1l. Bugler; 6l. King Carol II. HORIZ: 10l. Colour party.

1935. Portraits as T **110** but additionally inscr "POSTA".
1310 – 25b. black 15 10
1311 – 50b. brown 15 10
1312 – 1l. violet 15 10
1313 **110** 2l. green 45 10
1315 – 3l. red 75 10
1316 – 3l. blue . . . . 1·10 20
1317 **110** 4l. orange . . . . 1·20 25
1318 – 5l. red . . . . 1·10 70
1319 – 6l. lake . . . . 1·50 25
1320 – 7l.50 blue . . . . 1·80 40
1321 – 8l. purple . . . . 2·10 50
1322 **110** 9l. blue . . . . 2·50 65
1323 – 10l. blue . . . . 1·10 20
1324 – 12l. blue . . . . 1·70 85
1325 – 15l. brown . . . . . . 1·70 60
1326 – 16l. green . . . . 2·30 35
1327 – 20l. orange . . . . . . 1·40 40
1328 – 24l. red . . . . 2·50 60
PORTRAITS—IN PROFILE: 25b., 15l. In naval uniform; 50b., 3, 8, 10l. In civilian clothes. THREE-QUARTER FACE: 1, 5, 7l.50, In civilian clothes. FULL FACE: 6, 12, 16, 20, 24l. In plumed helmet.

118 King Carol II

119 Oltenia Peasant Girl

1936. Bucharest Exhibition and 70th Anniv of Hohenzollern–Sigmaringen Dynasty.
1329 **118** 6l.+1l. red . . . . 1·00 65

1936. 6th Anniv of Accession of Carol II Inscr "O.E.T.R. 8 IUNIE 1936".
1330 **119** 50b.+50b. brown . . . . 1·10 55
1331 – 1l.+1l. violet 85 60
1332 – 2l.+1l. green 85 65
1333 – 3l.+1l. red . . . . 1·20 85
1334 – 4l.+2l. red . . . . 1·40 85
1335 – 6l.+3l. grey . . . . . . 1·70 1·00
1336 – 10l.+5l. blue . . . . . . 2·75 2·50

DESIGNS (costumes of following districts)—VERT: 1l. Banat; 4l. Gori; 6l. Neamz. HORIZ: 2l. Saliste; 3l. Hateg; 10l. Suceava (Bukovina).

120 Brasov Jamboree Badge

121 Liner "Transylvania"

1936. National Scout Jamboree, Brasov.
1337 – 1l.+1l. blue . . . . . . 3·00 3·25
1338 – 3l.+3l. grey . . . . . . 4·75 4·00
1339 **120** 6l.+6l. red . . . . 6·75 4·75
DESIGNS: 1l. National Scout Badge; 3l. Tenderfoot Badge.

1936. 1st Marine Exhibition, Bucharest.
1343 – 1l.+1l. violet . . . . . . 3·00 3·75
1344 – 3l.+2l. blue . . . . . . 4·50 3·00
1345 **121** 6l.+3l. red . . . . 5·50 4·25
DESIGNS: 1l. Submarine "Delfinul"; 3l. Naval cadet ship "Mircea".

1936. 18th Anniv of Annexation of Transylvania and 16th Anniv of Foundation of "Little Entente" Nos. 1320 and 1323 optd **CEHOSLOVACIA YUGOSLAVIA 1920-1936**.
1346 7l.50 blue . . . . 2·75 3·00
1347 10l. blue . . . . 2·30 3·00

123 Creanga's Birthplace

1937. Birth Centenary of Ion Creanga (poet).
1348 **123** 2l. green 80 55
1349 – 3l. red . . . . 1·10 65
1350 **123** 4l. violet . . . . 1·60 85
1351 – 6l. brown . . . . 2·75 1·70
DESIGN: 3, 6l. Portrait of Creanga, 37 × 22 mm.

124 Footballers

1937. 7th Anniv of Accession of Carol II.
1352 **124** 25b.+25b. olive 65 25
1353 – 50b.+50b. brown 65 30
1354 – 1l.+50b. violet . . . . . 1·00 45
1355 – 2l.+1l. green . . . . . . 1·00 55
1356 – 3l.+1l. red . . . . 1·50 60
1357 – 4l.+1l. red . . . . 2·50 70
1358 – 6l.+2l. brown . . . . . 3·25 1·10
1359 – 10l.+4l. blue . . . . . . 4·00 1·60
DESIGNS—HORIZ: 50b. Swimmer; 3 1. King Carol II hunting; 10l. U.F.S.R. Inaugural Meeting. VERT: 1l. Javelin thrower; 2l. Skier; 4l. Rowing; 6l. Steeplechaser.

Premium in aid of the Federation of Rumanian Sports Clubs (U.F.S.R.).

127 Curtea de Arges Cathedral

128 Hurdling

1937. "Little Entente".
1360 **127** 7l.50 blue . . . . 1·20 75
1361 10l. blue . . . . 1·80 50

1937. 8th Balkan Games, Bucharest. Inscr as in T **115**.
1362 – 1l.+1l. violet 90 70
1363 – 2l.+1l. green . . . . . . 1·00 95
1364 **128** 4l.+1l. red . . . . 1·00 1·30
1365 – 6l.+1l. brown . . . . . 1·40 1·30
1366 – 10l.+1l. blue . . . . . . 4·25 2·40
DESIGNS: 1l. Sprinting; 2l. Throwing the javelin; 6l. Breasting the tape; 10l. High jumping.

129 Arms of Rumania, Greece, Turkey and Yugoslavia

130 King Carol II

1938. Balkan Entente.
1368 **129** 7l.50 blue . . . . 1·00 70
1369 10l. blue . . . . 1·60 50

1938. New Constitution. Profile portraits of King inscr "27 FEBRUARIE 1938". 6l. shows Arms also.
1370 **130** 3l. red 55 45
1371 – 6l. brown 95 45
1372 – 10l. blue . . . . 1·30 85

131 King Carol II and Provincial Arms

132 Dimitrie Cantemir

1938. Fund for Bucharest Exhibition celebrating 20th Anniv of Union of Provinces.
1373 **131** 6l.+1l. mauve 70 45

1938. Boy Scouts' Fund. 8th Anniv of Accession of Carol II. Inscr "STRAJA TARII 8 IUNIE 1938".
1374 **132** 25b.+25b. olive 40 40
1375 – 50b.+50b. brown 45 40
1376 – 1l.+1l. violet 60 40
1377 – 2l.+2l. green 70 40
1378 – 3l.+2l. mauve 70 40
1379 – 4l.+2l. red 75 45
1380 – 6l.+2l. brown . . . . . 1·10 50
1381 – 7l.50 blue . . . . 1·00 50
1382 – 10l. blue 95 60
1383 – 16l. green . . . . 1·60 1·60
1384 – 20l. red . . . . 2·40 1·60
PORTRAITS: 50b. Maria Doamna; 1l. Mircea the Great; 2l. Constantin Brancoveanu; 3l. Stephen the Great; 4l. Prince Cuza; 6l. Michael the Brave; 7l.50, Queen Elisabeth; 10l. King Carol II; 16l. King Ferdinand I; 20l. King Carol I.

134 "The Spring"

135 Prince Carol in Royal Carriage

1938. Birth Centenary of Nicholas Grigorescu (painter).
1385 **134** 1l.+1l. blue 75 50
1386 – 2l.+1l. green . . . . . 1·10 80
1387 – 4l.+1l. red . . . . 1·10 85
1388 – 6l.+1l. red . . . . 1·20 1·10
1389 – 10l.+1l. blue . . . . . . 2·00 1·80
DESIGNS—HORIZ: 2l. "Escorting Prisoners" (Russo-Turkish War 1877–78); 4l. "Returning from Market". VERT: 6l. "Rodica, the Water Carrier"; 10l. Self-portrait.

1939. Birth Centenary of King Carol I.
1390 **135** 25b. black 10 10
1391 – 50b. brown 10 10
1392 – 1l. violet 20 10
1393 – 1l.50 green 10 10
1394 – 2l. blue 10 10
1395 – 3l. red 10 10
1396 – 4l. red 10 10
1397 – 5l. black 10 10
1398 – 7l. black 10 10
1399 – 8l. blue 25 15
1400 – 10l. mauve 25 15
1401 – 12l. blue 30 20
1402 – 15l. blue 35 15
1403 – 16l. green 75 45
DESIGNS—HORIZ 50b. Prince Carol at Battle of Calafat; 1l.50, Sigmaringen and Pelesch Castles; 5 1. Carol I, Queen Elizabeth and Arms of Rumania. VERT: 1l. Examining plans for restoring Curtea de Arges Monastery; 2l. Carol I and Queen Elizabeth; 3l. Carol I at age of 8; 4l. In 1866; 5l. In 1877; 7l. Equestrian statue; 8l. Leading troops in 1878; 10l. In General's uniform; 12l. Bust; 16l. Restored Monastery of Curtea de Arges.

136 Rumanian Pavilion N.Y. World's Fair

137 Michael Eminescu, after painting by Joano Basarab

1939. New York World's Fair.
1407 **136** 6l. lake 45 45
1408 – 12l. blue 45 45
DESIGN: 12l. Another view of Pavilion.

1939. 50th Death Anniv of Michael Eminescu (poet).
1409 **137** 5l. black 45 40
1410 – 7l. red 45 40
DESIGN: 7l. Eminescu in later years.

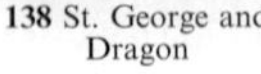
138 St. George and Dragon

139 Diesel Railcar, Class 142 Steam Locomotive (1936) and Locomotive "Calugareni" (1869)

1939. 9th Anniv of Accession of Carol II and Boy Scouts' Fund.
1411 **138** 25b.+25b. grey 45 45
1412 50b.+50b. brown 45 45
1413 1l.+1l. blue 45 45
1414 2l.+2l. green 60 45
1415 3l.+2l. purple 65 45
1416 4l.+2l. orange 1·10 65
1417 6l.+2l. red 1·10 65
1418 8l. grey 1·10 70
1419 10l. blue 1·20 75
1420 12l. blue 1·40 1·00
1421 16l. green 2·75 1·80

1939. 70th Anniv of Rumanian Railways.
1422 **139** 1l. violet 1·10 60
1423 – 4l. red 1·20 65
1424 – 5l. grey 1·20 1·00
1425 – 7l. mauve 1·60 1·00
1426 – 12l. blue 2·30 1·40
1427 – 15l. green 3·50 2·00
DESIGNS—HORIZ: 4l. Class 142 steam train crossing bridge, 1930, 13l. Railway Headquarters, Budapest. VERT: 5, 7l. Locomotive "Calugareni" (1869) leaving station; 12l. Diesel-mechanical twin set (1937) crossing bridge.

1940. Balkan Entente. As T **103** of Yugoslavia, but with Arms rearranged.
1428 12l. blue 65 55
1429 16l. blue 65 55

141 King Carol II

142 King Carol II

1940. Aviation Fund.
1430 **141** 1l.+50b. green 30 25
1431 2l.50+50b. green 35 30
1432 3l.+1l. red 55 40
1433 3l.50+50b. brown 70 45
1434 4l.+1l. orange 70 50
1435 6l.+1l. blue 1·00 30
1436 9l.+1l. blue 1·30 95
1437 14l.+1l. green 1·60 1·20

1940. 10th Anniv of Accession and Aviation Fund. Portraits of King Carol II.
1438 **142** 1l.+50b. purple 75 30
1439 4l.+1l. brown 75 45
1440 – 6l.+1l. blue 75 60
1441 – 8l. red 1·00 85
1442 – 16l. blue 1·40 1·10
1443 – 32l. brown 2·10 1·90
PORTRAITS: 6, 16l. In steel helmet; 8l. In military uniform; 32l. In flying helmet.

144 The Iron Gates of the Danube

1940. Charity. 10th Anniv of Accession of Carol II and Boy Scouts' Fund. Inscr "STRAJA TARII 8 IUNIE 1940".
1444 **144** 1l.+1l. violet 50 50
1445 – 2l.+1l. brown 55 55
1446 – 3l.+1l. green 55 60
1447 – 4l.+1l. black 65 70
1448 – 5l.+1l. orange 80 80
1449 – 8l.+1l. red 80 85
1450 – 12l.+2l. blue 90 95
1451 – 16l.+2l. grey 3·50 1·90
DESIGNS—HORIZ: 3l. Hotin Fortress; 4l. Hurez Monastery. VERT: 2l. Greco-Roman ruins; 5l. Church in Suceava; 8l. Alba Julia Cathedral; 12l. Village Church, Transylvania; 16l. Triumphal Arch, Bucharest.

145 King Michael

146 King Michael

1940.
1455 **145** 25b. green 10 10
1456 50b. olive 10 10
1457 1l. violet 10 10
1458 2l. orange 10 10
1608 3l. brown 10 10
1609 3l.50 brown 10 10
1459 4l. grey 10 10
1611 4l.50 brown 10 10
1460 5l. pink 10 10
1613 6l.50 violet 10 10
1461 7l. blue 10 10
1615 10l. mauve 10 10
1616 11l. blue 10 10
1463 12l. blue 10 10
1464 13l. purple 10 10
1618 15l. blue 10 10
1619 16l. blue 10 10
1620 20l. brown 10 10
1621 29l. blue 55 70
1467 30l. green 10 10
1468 50l. brown 10 10
1469 100l. brown 10 10

1940. Aviation Fund.
1470 **146** 1l.+50b. green 10 15
1471 2l.+50b. green 10 15
1472 2l.50+50b. green 10 15
1473 3l.+1l. violet 10 15
1474 3l.50+50b. pink 20 30
1475 4l.+50b. red 10 20
1476 4l.+1l. brown 10 20
1477 5l.+1l. red 55 45
1478 6l.+1l. blue 10 20
1479 7l.+1l. green 20 20
1480 8l.+1l. violet 20 20
1481 12l.+1l. brown 20 20
1482 14l.+1l. blue 20 20
1483 19l.+1l. mauve 95 30

147 Codreanu (founder)

148 Codreanu (founder)

1940. "Iron Guard" Fund.
1484 **147** 7l.+30l. grn (postage) 3·75 3·50
1485 **148** 20l.+5l. green (air) 1·90 1·70

149 Ion Mota

150 Library

1941. Marin and Mota (legionaries killed in Spain).
1486 – 7l.+7l. red 1·50 2·75
1487 **149** 15l.+15l. blue 5·25 5·50
PORTRAIT: 7l. Vasile Marin.

1941. Carol I Endowment Fund. Inscr "1891 1941".
1488 – 1l.50+43l.50 violet 1·30 1·40
1489 **150** 2l.+43l. red 1·30 1·40
1490 – 7l.+38l. red 1·30 1·40
1491 – 10l.+35l. green 2·20 2·00
1492 – 16l.+29l. brown 3·00 2·30
DESIGNS: 1l.50, Ex-libris; 7l. Foundation building and equestrian statue; 10l. Foundation stone; 16l. King Michael and Carol I.

1941. Occupation of Cernauti. Nos. 1488/92 optd **CERNAUTI 5 Iulie 1941**.
1493 – 1l.50+43l.50 violet 2·75 3·00
1494 **150** 2l.+43l. red 2·75 3·00
1495 – 7l.+38l. red 2·75 3·00
1496 – 10l.+35l. green 2·75 3·00
1497 – 16l.+29l. brown 3·25 3·25

1941. Occupation of Chisinau. Nos. 1488/92 optd **CHISINAU 16 Julie 1941**.
1498 – 1l.50+43l.50 violet 2·75 3·25
1499 **150** 2l.+43l. red 2·75 3·25
1500 – 7l.+38l. red 2·75 3·25
1501 – 10l.+35l. green 2·75 3·25
1502 – 16l.+29l. brown 3·25 3·25

153 "Charity"

154 Prince Voda

1941. Red Cross Fund. Cross in red.
1503 **153** 1l.50+38l.50 violet 95 90
1504 2l.+38l. red 95 90
1505 5l.+35l. olive 95 90
1506 7l.+33l. brown 95 90
1507 10l.+30l. blue 2·00 1·70

1941. Conquest of Transdniestria.
1572 **154** 3l. orange 15 45
1509 6l. brown 35 40
1510 12l. violet 35 55
1511 24l. blue 75 90

155 King Michael and Stephen the Great

1941. Anti-Bolshevik Crusade. Inscr "RAZBOIUL SFANT CONTRA BOLSEVISMULUI".
1512 **155** 10l.+30l. blue 75 1·90
1513 – 12l.+28l. red 75 1·90
1514 – 16l.+24l. brown 1·10 2·40
1515 – 20l.+20l. violet 1·10 2·40
DESIGNS: 12l. Hotin and Akkerman Fortresses; 16l. Arms and helmeted soldiers; 20l. Bayonet charge and Arms of Rumania.

1941. Fall of Odessa. Nos. 1512/15 optd **ODESA 16 Oct. 1941**.
1517 **155** 10l.+30l. blue 75 90
1518 – 12l.+28l. red 75 90
1519 – 16l.+24l. brown 1·10 2·50
1520 – 20l.+20l. violet 1·10 2·50

157 Hotin

1941. Restoration of Bessarabia and Bukovina (Suceava). Inscr "BASARABIA" or "BUCOVINA".
1522 – 25b. red 10 10
1523 **157** 50b. brown 10 10
1524 – 1l. violet 10 10
1525 – 1l.50 green 10 10
1526 – 2l. brown 10 10
1527 – 3l. olive 15 10
1528 – 5l. olive 25 10
1529 – 5l.50 brown 25 15
1530 – 6l.50 mauve 75 50
1531 **157** 9l.50 grey 75 60
1532 – 10l. purple 50 15
1533 – 13l. blue 75 20
1534 – 17l. brown 90 20
1535 – 26l. green 1·00 40
1536 – 39l. blue 1·40 55
1537 – 130l. yellow 4·00 3·00
VIEWS—VERT: 25b., 5l. Paraclis Hotin; 3l. Dragomirna; 13l. Milisauti. HORIZ: 1, 17l. Sucevita; 1l.50, Soroca; 2, 5l.50, Tighina; 6l.50, Cetatea Alba; 10, 130l. Putna; 26l. St. Nicolae, Suceava; 39l. Monastery. Rughi.

1941. Winter Relief Fund. Inscr "BASARABIA" or "BUCOVINA".
1538 – 3l.+50b. red 25 30
1539 – 5l.50+50b. orange 45 50
1540 – 5l.50+1l. black 45 50
1541 – 6l.50+1l. brown 55 65
1542 – 8l.+1l. blue 55 35
1543 – 9l.50+1l. blue 80 75
1544 – 10l.50+1l. blue 80 35
1545 – 16l.+1l. mauve 95 90
1546 **157** 25l.+1l. grey 1·20 95
VIEWS—HORIZ: 3l. Sucevita; 5l.50, (1539), Monastery, Rughi; 5l.50, (1540), Tighina; 6l.50, Soroca; 8l. St. Nicolae, Suceava; 10l.50, Putna; 16l. Cetatea Alba. VERT: 8l.50, Milisauti.

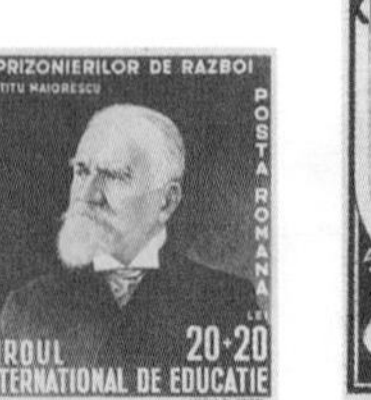
158 Titu Maiorescu

159 Coat-of-Arms of Bukovina

1942. Prisoners of War Relief Fund through International Education Office, Geneva.
1549 **158** 9l.+11l. violet 70 1·10
1550 20l.+20l. brown 90 1·90
1551 20l.+30l. blue 90 2·00

1942. 1st Anniv of Liberation of Bukovina.
1553 **159** 9l.+4l. red 1·50 2·50
1554 – 18l.+32l. blue 1·50 2·50
1555 – 20l.+30l. red 1·50 2·50
ARMORIAL DESIGNS: 18l. Castle; 20l. Mounds and crosses.

160 Map of Bessarabia, King Michael, Antonescu, Hitler and Mussolini

161 Statue of Miron Costin

1942. 1st Anniv of Liberation of Bessarabia.
1556 **160** 9l.+41l. brown 1·50 2·30
1557 – 18l.+32l. olive 1·50 2·30
1558 – 20l.+30l. blue 1·50 2·30
DESIGNS—VERT: 18l. King Michael and Marshal Antonescu below miniature of King Stephen. HORIZ: 20l. Marching soldiers and miniature of Marshal Antonescu.

1942. 1st Anniv of Incorporation of Transdniestria.
1559 **161** 6l.+44l. brown 1·00 1·70
1560 12l.+38l. violet 1·00 1·70
1561 24l.+26l. blue 1·00 1·70

162 Andrei Muresanu

163 Statue of Avram Iancu

1942. 80th Death Anniv of A. Muresanu (novelist).
1562 **162** 5l.+5l. violet 80 95

1943. Fund for Statue of Iancu (national hero).
1563 **163** 16l.+4l. brown 85 1·10

164 Nurse and wounded Soldier

165 Sword and Shield

1943. Red Cross Charity. Cross in red.
1564 **164** 12l.+88l. red 65 60
1565 16l.+84l. blue 65 60
1566 20l.+80l. olive 65 60

1943. Charity. 2nd Year of War. Inscr "22 JUNIE 1941 22 JUNIE 1943".
1568 **165** 36l.+164l. brown 1·10 2·00
1569 – 62l.+138l. blue 1·10 2·00
1570 – 76l.+124l. red 1·10 2·00
DESIGNS: 62l. Sword severing chain; 76l. Angel protecting soldier and family.

167 P. Maior

1943. Transylvanian Refugees' Fund (1st issue).
1576 **167** 16l.+134l. red 40 55
1577 – 32l.+118l. blue 40 55
1578 – 36l.+114l. purple 40 55
1579 – 62l.+138l. red 40 55
1580 – 91l.+109l. brown 40 55
PORTRAITS—VERT: 32l. G. Sincai; 36l. T. Ciparíu; 91l. G. Cosbuc. HORIZ: 62l. Horia, Closca and Crisan.
See also Nos. 1584/8.

169 King Michael and Marshal Antonescu

1943. 3rd Anniv of King Michael's Reign.
1581 **169** 16l.+24l. blue 1·30 1·60

170 Sports Shield 171 Calafat, 1877

1943. Charity. Sports Week.
1582 **170** 16l.+24l. blue 55 45
1583 16l.+24l. brown 55 45

1943. Transylvanian Refugees' Fund (2nd issue) Portraits as T **167**.
1584 16l.+134l. mauve 45 45
1585 51l.+99l. orange 45 45
1586 56l.+144l. red 45 45
1587 76l.+124l. blue 45 45
1588 77l.+123l. brown 45 45
PORTRAITS—VERT: 16l. S. Micu; 51l. G. Lazar; 56l. O. Goga; 76l. S. Barnutiu; 77l. A. Saguna.

1943. Centenary of National Artillery.
1596 **171** 1l.+1l. brown 20 30
1597 – 2l.+2l. violet 20 30
1598 – 3l.50+3l.50 blue 20 30
1599 – 4l.+4l. mauve 20 30
1600 – 5l.+5l. orange 35 45
1601 – 6l.50+6l.50 blue 35 45
1602 – 7l.+7l. purple 50 65
1603 – 20l.+20l. red 90 1·10
DESIGNS—HORIZ: (1l. to 7l. inscr battle scenes): 2l. "1916–1918"; 3l.50, Stalingrad; 4l. Crossing R. Tisza; 5l. Odessa; 6l.50, Caucasus; 7l. Sevastopol; 20l. Bibescu and King Michael.

172 Association Insignia

1943. 25th Anniv of National Engineers' Assn.
1624 **172** 21l.+29l. brown 85 65

173 Motor-cycle and Delivery Van

1944. Postal Employees' Relief Fund and Bicentenary of National Postal Service. (a) Without opt.
1625 **173** 1l.+49l. red 90 1·40
1626 – 2l.+48l. mauve 90 1·40
1627 – 4l.+46l. blue 90 1·40
1628 – 10l.+40l. purple 90 1·40

(b) Optd **1744 1944**.
1631 **173** 1l+49l. red 2·40 3·00
1632 – 2l.+48l. mauve 2·40 3·00
1633 – 4l.+46l. blue 2·40 3·00
1634 – 10l.+40l. purple 2·40 3·00
DESIGNS—HORIZ: 2l. Mail van and eight horses; 4l. Chariot. VERT: 10l. Horseman and Globe.

174 Dr. Cretzulescu 175 Rugby Player

1944. Cent of Medical Teaching in Rumania.
1637 **174** 35l.+65l. blue 80 70

1944. 30th Anniv of Foundation of National Rugby Football Association.
1638 **175** 16l.+184l. red 2·40 3·00

176 Stefan Tomsa Church, Radaseni 177 Fruit Pickers

1944. Cultural Fund. Town of Radaseni. Inscr "RADASENI".
1639 **176** 5l.+145l. blue 55 55
1640 – 12l.+138l. red 55 55
1641 **177** 15l.+135l. orange 55 55
1642 – 32l.+118l. brown 55 55
DESIGNS—HORIZ: 12l. Agricultural Institution; 32l. School.

178 Queen Helen 179 King Michael and Carol I Foundation, Bucharest

1945. Red Cross Relief Fund. Portrait in black on yellow and Cross in red.
1643 **178** 4l.50+5l.50 violet 25 20
1644 10l.+40l. brown 45 25
1645 15l.+75l. blue 70 45
1646 20l.+80l. red 85 70

1945. King Carol I Foundation Fund.
1647 **179** 20l.+180l. orange 35 35
1648 25l.+175l. slate 35 35
1649 35l.+165l. brown 35 35
1650 76l.+125l. violet 35 35

180 A. Saguna 181 A. Muresanu

1945. Liberation of Northern Transylvania. Inscr "1944".
1652 **180** 25b. red 45 40
1653 **181** 50b. orange 20 20
1654 – 4l.50 brown 25 20
1655 – 11l. blue 25 20
1656 – 15l. green 25 20
1657 – 31l. violet 25 20
1658 – 35l. grey 25 20
1659 – 41l. olive 25 75
1660 – 55l. brown 25 20
1661 – 61l. mauve 25 20
1662 – 75l.+75l. brown 30 25
DESIGNS—HORIZ: 4l.50, Samuel Micu; 31l. George Lazar; 55l. Horia, Closca and Crisan; 61l. Petru Maior; 75l. King Ferdinand and King Michael. VERT: 11l. George Sincai; 15l. Michael the Brave; 35l. Avram Iancu; 41l. Simeon Barnutiu.

182 King Michael 183 King Michael

184 King Michael 185 King Michael

1945.
1663 **182** 50b. grey 10 10
1664 **183** 1l. brown 10 10
1665 2l. violet 10 10
1666 **182** 2l. brown 10 15
1667 **183** 4l. green 10 10
1668 **184** 5l. mauve 10 10
1669 **182** 10l. blue 10 10
1670 10l. brown 10 10
1671 **183** 10l. brown 10 10
1672 **182** 15l. mauve 10 10
1673 20l. blue 10 10
1674 20l. lilac 10 10
1675 **184** 20l. purple 10 10
1676 25l. red 10 10
1677 35l. brown 10 10
1678 40l. red 10 10
1679 **183** 50l. blue 10 15
1680 55l. red 15 15
1681 **184** 75l. green 20 10
1682 **185** 80l. orange 10 10
1683 80l. blue 10 10
1684 **182** 80l. blue 10 10
1685 **185** 100l. brown 10 10
1686 **182** 137l. green 20 10
1687 **185** 160l. green 10 10
1688 160l. violet 10 10
1689 200l. green 30 15
1690 200l. red 10 10
1691 **183** 200l. red 10 10
1692 **185** 300l. blue 10 10
1693 360l. brown 20 10
1694 400l. violet 10 10
1695 **183** 400l. red 10 10
1696 **185** 480l. brown 20 10
1697 **182** 500l. mauve 20 10
1698 **185** 600l. green 10 10
1699 **184** 860l. brown 10 15
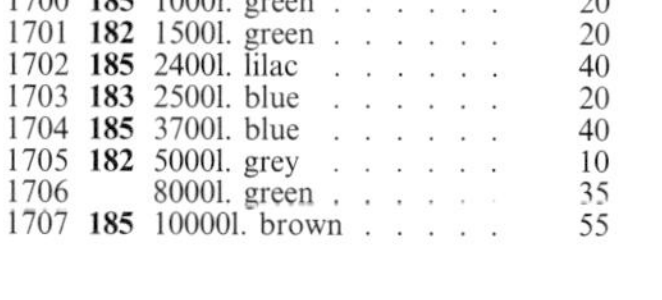
1700 **185** 1000l. green 20 10
1701 **182** 1500l. green 20 10
1702 **185** 2400l. lilac 40 10
1703 **183** 2500l. blue 20 10
1704 **185** 3700l. blue 40 10
1705 **182** 5000l. grey 10 10
1706 8000l. green 35 15
1707 **185** 10000l. brown 55 35

186 N. Jorga

1945. War Victims' Relief Fund.
1708 – 12l.+188l. blue 25 40
1709 – 16l.+184l. brown 25 40
1710 **186** 20l.+180l. brown 25 40
1711 – 32l.+168l. red 25 40
1712 – 35l.+165l. blue 25 40
1713 – 36l.+164l. violet 1·80 1·10
PORTRAITS: 12l. Ian Gheorghe Duca (Prime Minister, 1933); 16l. Virgil Madgearu (politician); 32l. Ilie Pintilie (communist); 35l. Bernath Andrei (communist); 36l. Filimon Sarbu (saboteur)..

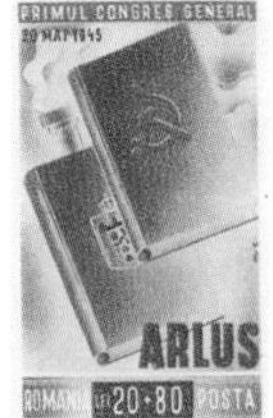

187 Books and Torch 188 Karl Marx

1945. Charity. 1st Rumanian–Soviet Congress Fund. Inscr "ARLUS".
1715 **187** 20l.+80l. olive 25 35
1716 – 35l.+165l. red 25 35
1717 – 75l.+225l. blue 25 35
1718 – 80l.+420l. brown 25 35
DESIGNS: 35l. Soviet and Rumanian flags; 75l. Drawn curtain revealing Kremlin; 80l. T. Vladimirescu and A. Nevsky.

189 Postman

1945. Trade Union Congress, Bucharest. Perf or imperf.
1720 **188** 75l.+425l. red 1·40 2·00
1723 75l.+425l. blue 3·25 5·75
1721 – 120l.+380l. blue 1·40 2·00
1724 – 120l.+380l. brown 4·00 5·75
1722 – 155l.+445l. brown 1·60 2·00
1725 – 155l.+445l. red 4·00 5·75
PORTRAITS: 120l. Engels; 155l. Lenin.

1945. Postal Employees. Inscr "MUNCA P.T.T.".
1726 **189** 100l. brown 60 45
1727 100l. olive 60 45
1728 – 150l. brown 90 70
1729 – 150l. red 90 70
1730 – 250l. olive 1·10 1·10
1731 – 250l. blue 1·10 1·10
1732 – 500l. mauve 6·25 9·25
DESIGNS: 150l. Telegraphist; 250l. Lineman; 500l. Post Office, Bucharest.

190 Throwing the Discus 192 Agricultural and Industrial Workers

1945. Charity. With shield inscr "O.S.P.". Perf or imperf.
1733 **190** 12l.+188l. olive (post) 1·60 1·80
1738 – 12l.+188l. orange 1·60 1·40
1734 – 16l.+184l. blue 1·60 1·80
1739 – 16l.+184l. purple 1·60 1·40
1735 – 20l.+180l. green 1·60 1·80
1740 – 20l.+180l. violet 1·60 1·40
1736 – 32l.+168l. mauve 1·60 1·80
1741 – 32l.+168l. green 1·60 1·40
1737 – 35l.+165l. blue 1·60 1·80
1742 – 35l.+165l. olive 1·60 1·40
1743 – 200l.+1000l. bl (air) 12·00 14·00
DESIGNS—As T **190**: 16l. Diving; 20l. Skiing; 32l. Volleyball; 35l. "Sport and work". 36 × 50 mm: 200l. Airplane and bird.

1945. 1st Anniv of Rumanian Armistice with Russia.
1744 **192** 100l.+400l. red 40 50
1745 – 200l.+800l. blue 40 50
DESIGN: 200l. King Michael, "Agriculture" and "Industry".

193 T. Vladimirescu 194 Destitute Children

1945. Charity. Patriotic Defence Fund. Inscr "APARAREA PATRIOTICA".
1746 – 20l.+580l. brown 4·75 6·75
1747 – 20l.+580l. mauve 4·75 6·75
1748 – 40l.+560l. blue 4·75 6·75
1749 – 40l.+560l. green 4·75 6·75
1750 – 55l.+545l. red 4·75 6·75
1751 – 55l.+545l. brown 4·75 6·75
1752 **193** 60l.+540l. blue 4·75 6·75
1753 60l.+540l. brown 4·75 6·75
1754 – 80l.+520l. red 4·75 6·75
1755 – 80l.+520l. mauve 4·75 6·75
1756 – 100l.+500l. green 4·75 6·75
1757 – 100l.+500l. brown 4·75 6·75
DESIGNS—HORIZ: 20l. "Political Amnesty"; 40l. "Military Amnesty"; 55l. "Agrarian Amnesty"; 100l. King Michael and "Recontruction". VERT: 80l. Nicholas Horia.

1945. Child Welfare Fund.
1758 **194** 40l. blue 30 25

195 I. Ionescu, G. Titeica, A. G. Idachimescu and V. Cristescu

1945. 50th Anniv of Founding of Journal of Mathematics.
1759 **195** 2l. brown 10 10
1760 – 80l. blue 60 65
DESIGN: 80l. Allegory of Learning.

196 Saligny Bridge

1945. 50th Anniv of Saligny Bridge over River Danube, Cernavoda.
1761 **196** 80l. black 30 30

197 Class E.18 Electric Locomotive, 1935, Germany

198

1945. Charity. 16th Congress of Rumanian Engineers. Perf or imperf. (a) Postage.
1762 **197** 10l.+490l. olive 2·10 1·90
1767 10l.+490l. blue 2·10 1·90
1763 – 20l.+480l. brown 30 45
1768 – 20l.+480l. violet 30 45
1764 – 25l.+475l. purple 30 45
1769 – 25l.+475l. green 30 45
1765 – 55l.+445l. blue 30 45
1770 – 55l.+445l. grey 30 45
1766 – 100l.+400l. brown 30 45
1771 – 100l.+400l. mauve 30 45

(b) Air. Symbolical design as T **198**. Imperf.
1772 **198** 80l.+420l. grey 1·10 1·10
1773 – 200l.+800l. blue 1·20 1·10
DESIGNS—As Type **197**: 20l. Coats of Arms; 25l. Arterial road; 55l. Oil wells; 100l. "Agriculture". As T **198**: 200l. Icarus and Lockheed 14 Super Electra airplane.

199 Globe and Clasped Hands

1945. Charity. World Trade Union Congress, Paris. Symbolical designs inscr "CONFERINTA MONDIAL LA SINDICALA DIN PARIS 25 SEPTEMVRE 1945".
1776 **199** 80l.+920l. mauve . . . . 9·00 9·75
1777 – 160l.+1840l. brown . . . 9·00 9·75
1778 – 320l.+1680l. violet . . . 9·00 9·75
1779 – 440l.+2560l. green . . . 9·00 9·75
DESIGNS: 160l. Globe and Dove of Peace; 320l. Hand and hammer; 440l. Scaffolding and flags.

1946. Nos 1444/5 surch in figures.
1780 10l.+90l. on 100l.+400l. . . 90 1·70
1781 10l.+90l. on 200l.+800l. . . 90 1·70
1782 20l.+80l. on 100l.+400l. . . 90 1·70
1783 20l.+80l. on 200l.+800l. . . 90 1·70
1784 80l.+120l. on 100l.+400l. 90 1·70
1785 80l.+120l. on 200l.+800l. 90 1·70
1786 100l.+150l. on 100l.+400l. 90 1·70
1787 100l.+150l. on 200l.+800l. 90 1·70

200 Sower

201 Distribution of Title Deeds

1946. Agrarian Reform. Inscr "REFORMA AGRARA".
1788 – 80l. blue 30 30
1789 **200** 50l.+450l. red 30 30
1790 **201** 100l.+900l. purple . . . 30 30
1791 – 200l.+800l. orange . . . 30 30
1792 – 400l.+1600l. green . . . 30 30
DESIGNS—VERT: 80l. Blacksmith and ploughman. HORIZ: 200l. Ox-drawn farm wagon; 400l. Plough and tractor.

202

1946. 25th Anniv of Bucharest Philharmonic Orchestra.
1794 **202** 10l. blue 10 10
1795 – 20l. brown 10 10
1796 – 55l. green 10 10
1797 – 80l. violet 20 20
1798 – 160l. orange 10 10
1799 **202** 200l.+800l. red 80 85
1800 – 350l.+1650l. blue . . . . 1·00 1·10
DESIGNS: 20l., 55l., 160l. "XXV" and musical score; 80l., 350l. G. Enescu.

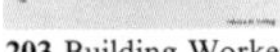

203 Building Worker **205** Sower

1946. Labour Day. Designs of workers inscr "ZIUA MUNCII".
1803 **203** 10l. red 10 50
1804 10l. green 50 45
1805 20l. blue 50 45
1806 20l. brown 10 50
1807 200l. red 20 20

1946. Youth Issue.
1809 **205** 10l.+100l. red & brn . . 10 10
1810 – 10l.+200l. pur & blue . . 1·20 1·10
1811 – 80l.+200l. brn & pur . . 10 10
1812 – 80l.+300l. mve & brn . . 10 10
1813 – 200l.+400l. red & grn . . 10 10
DESIGNS: No. 1810, Hurdling; 1811, Student; 1812, Worker and factory; 1813, Marching with flag.

206 Aviator and Aircraft **207** Football

1946. Air. Youth Issue.
1814 – 200l. blue and green . . 2·75 3·00
1815 **206** 500l. blue and orange . . 2·75 3·00
DESIGN: 200l. Airplane on ground.

1946. Sports, designs inscr "O.S.P." Perf or imperf.
1816 **207** 10l. blue (postage) . . . 30 35
1817 – 20l. red 30 35
1818 – 50l. violet 30 35
1819 – 80l. brown 30 35
1820 – 160l.+1340l. green . . . 30 35
1821 – 300l. red (air) . . . . . 1·00 1·30
1822 – 300l.+1200l. blue . . . 1·00 1·30
DESIGNS: 20l. Diving; 50l. Running; 80l. Mountaineering; 160l. Ski jumping; 300l., 300l.+1200l. Flying.

208 "Traditional Ties" **209** Banat Girl holding Distaff

1946. Rumanian–Soviet Friendship Pact.
1824 **208** 80l. brown 10 20
1825 – 100l. blue 10 20
1826 – 300l. grey 10 20
1827 – 300l.+1200l. red 80 55
DESIGNS: 100l. "Cultural ties"; 300l. "Economic ties"; 300l.+1200l. Dove.
No. 1827 also exists imperf.

1946. Charity. Women's Democratic Federation.
1829 – 80l. olive 55 10
1830 **209** 80l.+320l. red 10 10
1831 – 140l.+360l. orange . . . 10 10
1832 – 300l.+450l. green 20 20
1833 – 600l.+900l. blue 30 25
DESIGNS: 80l. Girl and handloom; 140l. Wallachian girl and wheatsheaf; 300l. Transylvanian horsewoman; 600l. Moldavian girl carrying water.

211 King Michael and Food Transport

1947. Social Relief Fund.
1845 – 300l. olive 10 20
1846 **211** 600l. mauve 30 25
1847 – 1500l.+3500l. orange . . 30 25
1848 – 3700l.+5300l. violet . . . 30 25
DESIGNS—VERT: 300l. Loaf of bread and hungry child; 1500l. Angel bringing food and clothing to destitute people; 3700l. Loaf of bread and starving family.

213 King Michael and Chariot **214** Symbols of Labour and Clasped Hands

1947. Peace.
1850 **213** 300l. purple 20 25
1851 – 600l. brown 20 25
1852 – 3000l. blue 20 25
1853 – 7200l. green 20 25
DESIGNS—VERT: 600l. Winged figure of Peace; 300l. Flags of four Allied Nations; 7200l. Dove of Peace.

1947. Trades Union Congress.
1854 **214** 200l. blue (postage) . . . 35 30
1855 300l. orange 35 30
1856 600l. red 35 30
1857 – 1100l. blue (air) 60 85
DESIGN—22 × 37 mm: 1100l. As Type **214** with Lockheed Super Electra airplane at top.

216 Worker and Torch **218** Symbolical of "Learning"

1947. Air. Trades Union Congress. Imperf.
1858 **216** 3000l.+7000l. brown . . 85 85

1947. Charity. People's Culture.
1859 – 200l.+200l. blue 15 20
1860 – 300l.+300l. brown . . . 15 20
1861 – 600l.+600l. green 15 20
1862 – 1200l.+1200l. blue . . . 15 20
1863 **218** 1500l.+1500l. red 15 20
DESIGNS—HORIZ: 200l. Boys' reading class; 300l. Girls' school; 600l. Engineering classroom; 1200l. School building.

219 King Michael

1947.
1865 **219** 1000l. blue 10 15
1869 3000l. blue 10 15
1866 5500l. green 15 15
1870 7200l. mauve 10 15
1871 15000l. blue 15 15
1867 20000l. brown 25 25
1872 21000l. mauve 15 25
1873 36000l. violet 35 30
1868 50000l. orange 40 30
Nos. 1865/8 are size 18 × 21½ mm and Nos. 1869/73 are 25 × 30 mm.

220 N. Grigorescu **221** Lisunov Li-2 Airliner

1947. Charity. Institute of Rumanian–Soviet Studies.
1874 – 1500l.+1500l. purple (postage) 25 20
1875 – 1500l.+1500l. orange . . 25 20
1876 – 1500l.+1500l. green . . . 25 20
1877 **220** 1500l.+1500l. blue . . . 25 20
1878 – 1500l.+1500l. blue . . . 25 20
1879 – 1500l.+1500l. lake . . . 25 20
1880 – 1500l.+1500l. red 25 20
1881 – 1500l.+1500l. brown . . 25 20
1882 **221** 15000l.+15000l. green (air) 75 65
PORTRAITS: No. 1874, Petru Movila; 1875, V. Babes; 1876, M. Eminescu; 1878, P. Tchaikovsky; 1879, M. Lomonosov; 1880, A. Pushkin; 1881, I. Y. Repin.
No. 1882 is imperf.

222 Miner **224** Douglas DC-4 Airliner over Black Sea

1947. Charity. Labour Day.
1883 **222** 1000l.+1000l. olive . . . 20 25
1884 – 1500l.+1500l. brown . . 15 20
1885 – 2000l.+2000l. blue . . . 15 20
1886 – 2500l.+2500l. mauve . . 15 20
1887 – 3000l.+3000l. red 20 25
DESIGNS: 1500l. Peasant; 2000l. Peasant woman; 2500l. Intellectual; 3000l. Factory worker.

1947. Air. Labour Day.
1888 – 3000l. red 25 25
1889 – 3000l. green 25 25
1890 – 3000l. brown 25 35
1891 **224** 3000l.+12,000l. blue . . 50 40
DESIGNS—24½ × 30 mm: No. 1888, Four parachutes; 1889, Air Force Monument; 1890, Douglas DC-4 over landscape.

(New currency 1 (new) leu = 100 (old) lei.)

225 King Michael and Timber Barges **227**

1947. Designs with medallion portrait of King Michael.
1892 – 50b. orange 12 10
1893 **225** 1l. brown 10 10
1894 – 2l. blue 10 10
1895 – 3l. red 10 10
1896 – 5l. blue 10 10
1897 – 10l. blue 25 15
1898 – 12l. violet 60 30
1899 – 15l. blue . . . . 1·75 30
1900 – 20l. brown . . . . . . 1·00 20
1901 – 32l. brown . . . . . . 4·75 1·90
1902 – 36l. lake . . . . 6·25 1·50
DESIGNS: 50b. Harvesting; 2l. River Danube; 3l. Reshitza Industries; 5l. Curtea de Arges Cathedral; 10l. Royal Palace, Bucharest; 12, 36l. Saligny Bridge, Cernavoda; 15, 32l. Liner "Transylvania" in Port of Constantza; 20l. Oil Wells, Prahova.

1947. Balkan Games. Surch **2+3 LEI C.B.A. 1947** and bar.
1903 **219** 2+3l. on 36,000l. violet 55 70

1947. 17th Congress of General Assn of Rumanian Engineers. With monogram as in T **227**.
1904 **227** 1l.+1l. red (postage) . . 10 10
1905 – 2l.+2l. brown 10 10
1906 – 3l.+3l. violet 25 25
1907 – 4l.+4l. olive 10 20
1908 – 5l.+5l. blue (air) 45 55
DESIGNS: 2l. Sawmill; 3l. Refinery; 4l. Steel mill; 5l. Gliders over mountains.

1947. Charity. Soviet–Rumanian Amity. As No. 1896 surch **ARLUS 1-7-XI. 1947 +5.** Imperf.
1909 5l.+5l. blue 50 45

229 Beehive **230** Food Convoy

1947. Savings Day.
1910 **229** 12l. red 15 25

1947. Patriotic Defence.
1911 **230** 1l.+1l. blue 10 20
1912 – 2l.+2l. brown 10 20
1913 – 3l.+3l. red 10 20
1914 – 4l.+4l. blue 15 20
1915 – 5l.+5l. red 25 35
SYMBOLIC DESIGNS—HORIZ: 2l. Soldiers' parcels ("Everything for the front"); 3l. Modern hospital ("Heal the wounded"); 4l. Hungry children ("Help famine-stricken regions"). VERT: 5l. Manacled wrist and flag.

231 Allegory of work

1947. Charity. Trades Union Congress, Bucharest. Inscr "C.G.M. 1947".
1916 – 2l.+10l. red (postage) . . 15 20
1917 **231** 7l.+10l. black 20 25
1918 – 11l. red and blue (air) . . 35 45
DESIGNS—As T **231**: 2l. Industrial and agricultural workers. 23 × 18 mm: 11l. Lisunov Li-2 airliner over demonstration.

233 Map of Rumania

1948. Census of 1948.
1925 **233** 12l. blue 30 20

234 Printing Works and Press

1948. 75th Anniv of Rumanian State Stamp Printing Works.

1926	**234**	6l. red	95	70
1927		7l.50 green	45	10

235 Discus Thrower **237** Industrial Worker

1948. Balkan Games, 1947. Inscr as in T **235**. Imperf or perf.

1928	**235**	1l.+1l. brown (postage)	30	35
1929	–	2l.+2l. red	45	45
1930	–	5l.+5l. blue	70	70
1931	–	7l.+7l. violet (air)	85	65
1932	–	10l.+10l. green	1·30	95

DESIGNS: 2l. Runner; 5l. Heads of two young athletes; 7, 10l. Airplane over running track.

1948. Nos. 1892/1902 optd **R.P.R.** (Republica Populara Romana).

1933		50b. orange	10	20
1934		1l. brown	10	15
1935		2l. blue	45	15
1936		3l. red	55	15
1937		5l. blue	90	15
1938		10l. blue	1·10	25
1939		12l. violet	2·10	30
1940		15l. blue	2·10	35
1941		20l. brown	1·30	35
1942		32l. brown	8·50	4·00
1943		36l. lake	6·50	2·40

1948. Young Workers' Union. Imperf or perf.

1954	**237**	2l.+2l. blue (postage)	25	30
1955	–	3l.+3l. green	25	25
1956	–	5l.+5l. brown	25	35
1957	–	8l.+8l. red	30	35
1958	–	12l.+12l. blue (air)	1·10	1·00

DESIGNS—As Type **237**: 3l. Peasant girl and wheatsheaf; 5l. Student and book. TRIANGULAR: 8l. Youths bearing Filimon Sarbu banner. 36 × 23 mm: 12l. Airplane and barn swallows.

240 "Friendship" **241** "New Constitution"

1948. Rumanian–Bulgarian Amity.

1959	**240**	32l. brown	70	45

1948. New Constitution.

1960	**241**	1l. red	15	20
1961		2l. orange	35	35
1962		12l. blue	1·60	60

242 Globe and Banner

243 Aviator and Heinkel He 116A **244** Barbed Wire Entanglement

1948. Labour Day.

1963	**242**	8l.+8l. red (postage)	1·10	2·00
1964	–	10l.+10l. green	1·90	2·50
1965	–	12l.+12l. brown	2·25	3·25
1966	**243**	20l.+20l. blue (air)	4·25	5·00

DESIGNS—HORIZ: 10l. Peasants and mountains. VERT: 12l. Worker and factory.

1948. Army Day.

1967	–	1l.50+1l.50 red (postage)	20	30
1968	**244**	2l.+2l. purple	20	30
1969	–	4l.+4l. brown	50	55
1970	–	7l.50+7l.50 black	90	1·00
1971	–	8l.+8l. violet	1·00	1·10
1972	–	3l.+3l. blue (air)	3·75	4·50
1973	–	5l.+5l. blue	6·75	6·75

DESIGNS—VERT: 1l.50, Infantry; 3l. Ilyushin Stormovik fighter planes; 5l. Petlyakov Pe-2 dive bomber Il-2M3. HORIZ: 4l. Artillery; 7l.50, Tank; 8l. Destroyer.

245 Five Portraits **246** Proclamation of Islaz

1948. Cent of 1848 Revolution. Dated "1848 1948".

1974	–	2l.+2l. purple	20	30
1975	**245**	5l.+5l. violet	25	35
1976	**246**	11l. red	40	40
1977	–	10l.+10l. green	40	30
1978	–	36l.+18l. blue	1·50	1·20

DESIGNS—22 × 38 mm. HORIZ: 10l. Balcescu, Petofi, Iancu, Barnutiu Baritiu and Murcu. VERT: 2l. Nicolas Balcescu; 36l. Balcescu, Kogalniceanu, Alecsandri and Cuza.

247 Emblem of Republic

1948.

2023	**247**	50b. red	70	30
1980		0.50l. red	15	10
1981		1l. brown	15	10
1982		2l. green	15	10
1983		3l. grey	25	10
1984		4l. brown	25	10
1985		5l. blue	25	10
2028		5l. violet	1·10	10
1986		10l. blue	65	10

No. 2023 is inscribed "BANI 0.50" (= ½ bani) and in No. 1980 this was corrected to "LEI 0.50".

248 Monimoa Gliders **249** Yachts

1948. Air Force and Navy Day. (a) Air Force (vert).

1987	**248**	2l.+2l. blue	75	95
1988	–	5l.+5l. violet	75	95
1989	–	8l.+8l. red	1·10	1·50
1990	–	10l.+10l. brown	1·90	1·90

(b) Navy (horiz).

1991	**249**	2l.+2l. green	75	95
1992	–	5l.+5l. grey	75	95
1993	–	8l.+8l. blue	1·10	1·50
1994	–	10l.+10l. red	1·90	2·00

DESIGNS—AIR FORCE: 5l. Aurel Vlaicu's No. 1 "Crazy Fly" airplane; 8l. Lisunov Li-2 airliner and tractor; 10l. Lisunov Li-2 airliner. NAVY: 5l. "Mircea" (cadet ship), 1882; 8l. "Romana Mare" (Danube river steamer); 10l. "Transylvania" (liner).

1948. Surch.

1995	**240**	31l. on 32l. brown	55	30

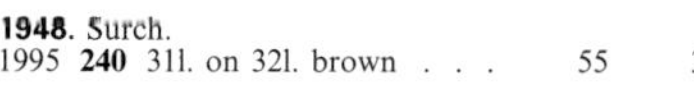

251 Newspapers and Torch **252** Soviet Soldiers' Monument

1948. Press Week. Imperf or perf.

1996	**251**	5l.+5l. red	10	10
1997		10l. brown	30	45
1998	–	10l.+10l. violet	65	60
1999	–	15l.+15l. blue	90	1·00

DESIGNS—HORIZ: 10l. (No. 1998), Flag, torch and ink-well. VERT: 15l. Alex Sahia (journalist).

1948. Rumanian–Russian Amity.

2000	**252**	10l. red (postage)	35	45
2001	–	10l.+10l. green	2·10	2·10
2002	–	15l.+15l. blue	2·40	2·75
2003	–	20l.+20l. blue (air)	7·25	7·50

DESIGNS—VERT: 10l. (No. 2001), Badge of Arlus; 15l. Kremlin. HORIZ: 20l. Lisunov Li-2 airplane.

255 Emblem of Republic

1948. Air. Designs showing aircraft.

2004	**255**	30l. red	20	10
2005	–	50l. green	30	30
2006	–	100l. blue	3·75	2·10

DESIGNS: 50l. Workers in a field; 100l. Steam train, airplane and liner.

256 Lorry

1948. Work on Communications.

2007	–	1l.+1l. black and green	30	45
2008	**256**	3l.+3l. black & brown	30	50
2009	–	11l.+11l. black & blue	1·90	1·75
2010	–	15l.+15l. black and red	4·75	3·50

DESIGNS: 1l. Dockers loading freighter; 11l. Lisunov Li-2 airliner on ground and in air; 15l. Steam train.

257 Nicolas Balcescu

1948.

2012	**257**	20l. red	40	25

258 Hands Breaking Chain

1948. 1st Anniv of People's Republic.

2013	**258**	5l. red	30	25

259 Runners **260** Lenin

1948. National Sports Organization. Imperf or perf.

2014	**259**	5l.+5l. green (postage)	2·30	2·30
2017		5l.+5l. brown	2·30	2·30
2015	–	10l.+10l. violet	4·00	4·00
2018	–	10l.+10l. red	4·00	4·00
2016	–	20l.+20l. blue (air)	16·50	15·00
2019	–	20l.+20l. green	16·50	15·00

DESIGNS—HORIZ: 10l. Parade of athletes with flags. VERT: 20l. Boy flying model airplane.

1949. 25th Death Anniv of Lenin. Perf or imperf.

2020	**260**	20l. black	20	25

261 Dancers **263** Pushkin

262 I. C. Frimu and Revolutionaries

1949. 90th Anniv of Union of Rumanian Principalities.

2021	**261**	10l. blue	30	25

1949. 30th Death Anniv of Ion Frimu (union leader and journalist). Perf or imperf.

2022	**262**	20l. red	30	25

1949. 150th Birth Anniv of A. S. Pushkin (Russian poet).

2030	**263**	11l. red	55	45
2031		30l. green	65	55

264 Globe and Posthorn

265 Forms of Transport

1949. 75th Anniv of U.P.U.

2032	**264**	20l. brown	1·20	1·00
2033	**265**	30l. blue	2·75	3·00

266 Russians entering Bucharest

1949. 5th Anniv of Russian Army's Entry into Bucharest. Perf or imperf.

2034	**266**	50l. brown on green	55	55

267 "Rumanian–Soviet Amity"

1949. Rumanian–Soviet Friendship Week. Perf or imperf.

2035	**267**	20l. red	40	40

268 Forms of Transport **269** Stalin

1949. International Congress of Transport Unions. Perf or imperf.

2036	**268**	11l. blue	65	65
2037		20l. red	1·10	90

1949. Stalin's 70th Birthday. Perf or imperf.

2038	**269**	31l. green	30	25

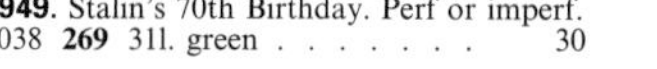

270 "The Third Letter" **271** Michael Eminescu

1950. Birth Centenary of Eminescu (poet).

2040	**270**	11l. green	75	50
2041	–	11l. brown	1·10	45
2042	–	11l. mauve	75	35

2043 – 11l. violet 75 35
2044 271 11l. blue 70 35
DESIGNS (Scenes representing poems): No. 2041, "Angel and Demon"; 2042, "Ruler and Proletariat"; 2043, "Life".

272 "Dragaica Fair"

1950. Birth Centenary of Ion Andreescu (painter). (a) Perf.
2045 272 5l. olive 70 50
2047 – 20l. brown 1·50 1·00

(b) Perf or imperf.
2046 – 11l. blue 1·10 60
DESIGNS—VERT: 11l. Andreescu. HORIZ: 20l. "The Village Well".

273 Factory and Graph 274 Worker and Flag

1950. State Plan, 1950 Inscr "PLANUL DU STAT 1950".
2048 273 11l. red 25 20
2049 – 31l. violet 85 35
DESIGN: 31l. Tractor and factories.
No. 2048 exists imperf.

1950. Labour Day. Perf or imperf.
2050 274 31l. orange 30 10

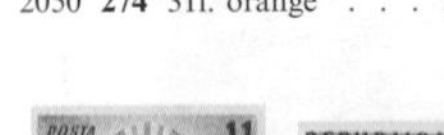

275 Emblem of Republic 276 Trumpeter and Drummer

1950.
2051 275 50b. black 25 20
2052 1l. red 20 10
2053 2l. grey 20 10
2054 3l. purple 25 10
2055 4l. mauve 20 10
2056 5l. brown 25 10
2057 6l. green 25 10
2058 7l. brown 25 10
2059 7l.50 blue 35 10
2060 10l. brown 45 10
2061 11l. red 45 10
2062 15l. blue 45 10
2063 20l. green 45 10
2064 31l. green 60 10
2065 36l. brown 1·00 45
For stamps as Type 275 but with inscriptions in white, see Nos. 2240, etc, and Nos. 2277/8.

1950. 1st Anniv of Rumanian Pioneers Organization.
2074 276 8l. blue 85 45
2075 – 11l. purple 1·30 75
2076 – 31l. red 2·40 1·50
DESIGNS: 11l. Children reading; 31l. Youth parade.

277 Engineer 278 Aurel Vlaicu and his Airplane No. 1 "Crazy Fly"

1950. Industrial Nationalization.
2077 277 11l. red 25 25
2078 11l. blue 45 25
2079 11l. brown 45 25
2080 11l. olive 15 15

1950. 40th Anniv of 1st Flight by A. Vlaicu.
2081 278 3l. green 30 20
2082 6l. blue 30 25
2083 8l. blue 40 35

279 Mother and Child

1950. Peace Congress, Bucharest.
2084 279 11l. red 20 20
2085 – 20l. brown 30 20
DESIGN: 20l. Lathe operator and graph.

280 Statue and Flags 282 Young People and Badge

1950. Rumanian–Soviet Amity.
2086 280 30l. brown 40 25

1950. Rumanian–Hungarian Amity. Optd **TRAIASCA PRIETENIA ROMANO-MAGHIARA!**.
2087 275 15l. blue 55 25

1950. GMA Complex Sports Facilities. Designs incorporating badge.
2088 – 3l. red 1·10 1·00
2089 282 5l. brown 75 70
2090 5l. blue 75 70
2091 – 11l. green 75 70
2092 – 31l. olive 1·60 1·60
DESIGNS: 3l. Agriculture and Industry; 11l. Runners, 31l. Gymnasts.

283 284 Ski-jumper

1950. 3rd Congress of "ARLUS".
2093 283 11l. orange on orange 30 25
2094 11l. blue on blue 30 25

1951. Winter Sports.
2095 284 4l. brown 45 65
2096 – 5l. red 55 55
2097 – 11l. blue 1·10 55
2098 – 20l. brown 1·10 90
2099 – 31l. green 2·75 1·60
DESIGNS: 5l. Skater; 11l. Skier; 20l. Ice hockey; 31l. Tobogganing.

286 Peasant and Tractor

1951. Agricultural and Industrial Exhibition.
2100 – 11l. brown 10 15
2101 286 31l. blue 45 25
DESIGN—VERT: 11l. Worker and machine.

287 Star of the Republic, Class I-II 288 Youth Camp

1951. Orders and Medals. Perf or imperf.
2102 – 2l. green 15 20
2103 – 4l. blue 20 25
2104 – 11l. red 30 35
2105 287 35l. brown 40 55
DESIGNS: 2l. Medal of Work; 4l. Star of the Republic, Class III–V; 11l. Order of Work.

1951. 2nd Anniv of Rumanian Pioneers Organization.
2106 288 1l. green 65 45
2107 – 11l. blue 65 45
2108 – 35l. red 85 65
DESIGNS—VERT: 11l. Children meeting Stalin. HORIZ: 35l. Decorating boy on parade.

289 Woman and Flags 290 Ion Negulici

1951. International Women's Day. Perf or imperf.
2109 289 11l. brown 40 25

1951. Death Centenary of Negulici (painter).
2110 290 35l. red 2·25 1·75

291 Cyclists

1951. Rumanian Cycle Race.
2111 291 11l. brown 1·10 70

292 F. Sarbu 294 Students

293 "Revolutionary Rumania"

1951. 10th Death Anniv of Sarbu (patriot).
2112 292 11l. brown 40 25

1951. Death Centenary of C. D. Rosenthal (painter).
2113 293 11l. green 95 55
2114 11l. orange 95 55
2115 – 11l. brown 95 55
2116 – 11l. violet 95 55
DESIGN—VERT: Nos. 2115/16, "Rumania calls to the Masses".

1951. 3rd World Youth Festival, Berlin.
2117 294 1l. red 30 35
2118 – 5l. blue 60 35
2119 – 11l. purple 1·00 75
DESIGNS: 5l. Girl, boy and flag; 11l. Young people around globe.

295 "Scanteia" Building 296 Soldier and Pithead

1951. 20th Anniv of "Scanteia" (Communist newspaper).
2120 295 11l. blue 40 25

1951. Miners' Day.
2121 296 5l. blue 30 25
2122 – 11l. mauve 45 25
DESIGN: 11l. Miner and pithead.

297 Order of Defence 298 Oil Refinery

1951. Liberation Day.
2123 297 10l. red 30 25

1951. Five-Year Plan. Dated "1951 1955".
2124 298 1l. olive (postage) 25 20
2125 – 2l. red 90 20
2126 – 3l. red 50 40
2127 – 4l. brown 35 20
2128 – 5l. green 35 15
2129 – 6l. blue 1·30 90
2130 – 7l. green 85 45
2131 – 8l. brown 55 30
2132 – 11l. blue 1·10 40
2133 – 35l. violet 75 50
2134 – 30l. green (air) 3·00 2·00
2135 – 50l. brown 6·00 4·25
DESIGNS: 2l. Miner and pithead; 3l. Soldier and pylons; 4l. Steel furnace; 5l. Combine-harvester; 6l. Canal construction; 7l. Threshing machine; 8l. Sanatorium; 11l. Dam and pylons; 30l. Potato planting; 35l. Factory; 50l. Liner, steam locomotive and Lisunov Li-2 airliner.

299 Orchestra and Dancers 300 Soldier and Arms

1951. Music Festival.
2136 299 11l. brown 30 35
2137 – 11l. blue (Mixed choir) 40 25
2138 – 11l. mauve (Lyre and dove) (vert) 30 25

1951. Army Day.
2139 300 11l. blue 30 25

301 Arms of U.S.S.R. and Rumania

1951. Rumanian–Soviet Friendship.
2140 301 4l. brown on buff 20 20
2141 35l. orange 60 50

302 P. Tcancenco 304 I. L. Caragiale

303 Open Book "1907"

1951. 25th Death Anniv of Tcancenco (revolutionary).
2142 302 10l. olive 30 45

1952. Birth Centenary of Ion Caragiale (dramatist). (a) Unissued values surch.
2143 303 20b. on 11l. red 55 40
2144 – 55b. on 11l. green 80 45
2145 304 75b. on 11l. blue 1·10 55

(b) Without surch.
2146 303 55b. red 1·00 25
2147 – 55b. green 1·00 25
2148 304 55b. blue 1·00 25
2149 – 1l. brown 2·50 1·20
DESIGNS—HORIZ: Nos. 2144, 2147, Profile of Caragiale; 1l. Caragiale addressing assembly.

1952. Currency revalued. Surch.
2174 275 3b. on 1l. red 1·30 4·50
2175 3b. on 2l. grey 1·50 90
2176 3b. on 4l. mauve 1·30 85
2177 3b. on 5l. red 1·50 90
2178 3b. on 7l.50 blue 4·25 1·30
2179 3b. on 10l. brown 1·50 90
2157a 255 3b. on 30l. red 6·25 4·75
2158 – 3b. on 50l. (No. 2005) 1·80 1·40
2159 – 3b. on 100l. (No. 2006) 6·25 3·00
2191 278 10b. on 3l. green 1·50 70
2218 301 10b. on 4l. brown on buff 80 70
2192 278 10b. on 6l. blue 1·60 70
2193 10b. on 8l. blue 1·60 70
2220 302 10b. on 10l. olive 1·75 70
2160 263 10b. on 11l. red 2·40 1·80
2164 270 10b. on 11l. green 2·40 1·80
2165 – 10b. on 11l. (No. 2041) 2·20 1·80

2166 – 10b. on 11l. (No. 2042) 2·20 1·80
2167 – 10b. on 11l. (No. 2043) 2·20 1·80
2168 **271** 10b. on 11l. blue . . . 2·20 1·80
2161 **263** 10b. on 30l. green . . . 2·50 1·80
2219 **301** 10b. on 35l. orange . . 2·00 1·20
2199 – 20b. on 2l. (No. 2102) 2·75 1·60
2200 – 20b. on 4l. (No. 2103) 2·75 1·60
2171 **273** 20b. on 11l. red . . . . 1·70 1·10
2201 – 20b. on 11l. (No. 2104) 2·75 1·60
2194 – 20b. on 20l. (No. 2085) 1·70 80
2172 – 20b. on 31l. (No. 2049) 1·70 1·10
2202 **287** 20b. on 35l. brown . . 2·75 1·60
2206 **298** 35b. on 1l. olive . . . . 2·75 95
2207 – 35b. on 2l. (No. 2125) 4·50 1·40
2208 – 35b. on 3l. (No. 2126) 3·25 1·40
2209 – 35b. on 4l. (No. 2127) 2·75 1·50
2210 – 35b. on 5l. (No. 2128) 2·75 2·30
2151 **241** 50b. on 12l. blue . . . 2·75 65
2180 **275** 55b. on 50b. black . . 4·50 1·20
2181 55b. on 3l. purple . . . 4·50 1·20
2195 – 55b. on 3l. (No. 2088) 19·00 12·00
2169 **272** 55b. on 5l. olive . . . . 7·00 3·75
2204 **295** 55b. on 5l. blue . . . . 5·75 2·75
2182 **275** 55b. on 6l. green . . . 4·50 1·20
2183 55b. on 7l. brown . . . 4·50 1·20
2188 **276** 55b. on 8l. blue . . . . 5·25 4·00
2205 **297** 55b. on 10l. red . . . . 3·00 2·40
2170 – 55b. on 11l. (No. 2046) 7·25 3·25
2189 – 55b. on 11l. (No. 2075) 4·00 3·00
2150 **233** 55b. on 12l. blue . . . 1·70 1·80
2184 **275** 55b. on 15l. blue . . . 4·00 1·20
2185 55b. on 20l. green . . . 4·25 1·80
2196 – 55b. on 20l. (No. 2098) 18·00 12·00
2186 **275** 55b. on 31l. green . . . 4·75 1·20
2173 **274** 55b. on 31l. orange . . 2·75 2·50
2190 – 55b. on 31l. (No. 2076) 4·00 4·00
2197 – 55b. on 31l. (No. 2099) 17·00 12·00
2198 **286** 55b. on 31l. blue . . . 3·00 2·75
2203 – 55b. on 35l. (No. 2108) 4·00 5·25
2187 **275** 55b. on 36l. brown . . 4·25 1·70
2211 – 1l. on 6l. (No. 2129) . . 6·00 3·75
2212 – 1l. on 7l. (No. 2130) . . 6·00 2·20
2213 – 1l. on 8l. (No. 2131) . . 4·50 2·75
2214 – 1l. on 11l. (No. 2132) 6·00 2·30
2216 – 1l. on 30l. (No. 2134) 6·75 2·10
2215 – 1l. on 35l. (No. 2133) 6·00 2·10
2217 – 1l. on 50l. (No. 2135) 13·50 4·25
2152 – 1l.75 on 2l.+2l. purple (No. 1974) . . . . . 7·00 3·00
2153 **245** 1l.75 on 5l.+5l. violet 7·00 3·00
2154 **246** 1l.75 on 11l. red . . . 7·00 3·00
2155 – 1l.75 on 10l.+10l. (No. 1977) . . . . . 7·00 3·00
2156 – 1l.75 on 36l.+18l. (No. 1978) . . . . . 7·00 3·00

1952. Air. Surch with airplane, **AERIANA** and value.
2162 **264** 3l. on 20l. brown . . . . 30·00 21·00
2163 **265** 5l. on 30l. blue . . . . 45·00 24·00

307 Railwayman  **308** Gogol and character from "Taras Bulba"

1952. Railway Day.
2229 **307** 55b. brown . . . . . . 1·75 25

1952. Death Centenary of Nikolai Gogol (Russian writer).
2230 **308** 55b. blue 85 25
2231 – 1l.75 green . . . . . . 2·75 45
DESIGN—VERT: 1l.75, Gogol and open book.

309 Maternity Medal  **310** I. P. Pavlov

1952. International Women's Day.
2232 **309** 20b. blue and purple 50 15
2233 – 55b. brown and chestnut 1·00 30
2234 – 1l.75 brown and red . . 2·50 45
MEDALS: 55b. "Glory of Maternity" medal; 1l.75, "Mother Heroine" medal.

1952. Rumanian–Soviet Medical Congress.
2235 **310** 11l. red . . . . 1·90 25

311 Hammer and Sickle Medal  **312** Boy and Girl Pioneers

1952. Labour Day.
2236 **311** 55b. brown . . . . . . 1·20 20

1952. 3rd Anniv of Rumanian Pioneers Organization.
2237 **312** 20b. brown 80 15
2238 – 55b. green . . . . . . 1·80 25
2239 – 1l.75 blue . . . . . . 3·75 35
DESIGNS—VERT: 55b. Pioneer nature-study group. HORIZ: 1l.75, Worker and pioneers.

1952. As T **275** but with figures and inscriptions in white. Bani values size 20¼ × 24¼ mm, lei values size 24½ × 29½ mm.
2240 **275** 3b. orange 25 20
2241 5b. red 35 15
2242 7b. green 40 25
2243 10b. brown 50 15
2244 20b. blue . . . . . . 1·75 15
2245 35b. brown . . . . . 1·20 15
2246 50b. green . . . . . 1·60 15
2247 55b. violet . . . . . 3·50 15
2248 1l.10 brown . . . . . 3·25 20
2249 1l.75 violet . . . . . 15·50 35
2250 2l. olive . . . . 3·25 40
2251 2l.35 brown . . . . . 3·50 35
2252 2l.55 orange . . . . . 4·50 35
2253 3l. green . . . . . . 4·75 35
2254 5l. red . . . . 6·25 60
For similar stamps with star added at top of emblem, see Nos. 2277/8.

314 "Smirdan" (after Grigorescu)  **315** Leonardo da Vinci

1952. 75th Anniv of Independence.
2255 **314** 50b. lake 55 10
2256 – 1l.10 blue 90 30
DESIGN—HORIZ: 1l.10, Rumanian and Russian soldiers.

1952. 500th Anniv of Birth of Leonardo da Vinci.
2257 **315** 55b. violet . . . . . . 2·30 35

316 Miner  **317** Students' Union Badge

1952. Miners' Day.
2258 **316** 20b. red . . . . 1·10 30
2259 55b. violet . . . . . . 1·00 25

1952. Int Students' Union Council, Bucharest.
2260 **317** 10b. blue 20 10
2261 – 20b. orange . . . . . . 1·50 25
2262 – 55b. green . . . . . . 1·50 30
2263 – 1l.75 red . . . . 2·75 75
DESIGNS—HORIZ: 20b. Student in laboratory (35½ × 22 mm); 1l.75, Six students dancing (30 × 24 mm). VERT: 55b. Students playing football (24 × 30 mm).

318 Soldier, Sailor and Airman

1952. Army Day.
2264 **318** 55b. blue 85 25

319 Statue and Flags  **320** Workers and Views of Russia and Rumania (after N. Parlius)

1952. Rumanian–Soviet Friendship.
2265 **319** 55b. red 55 10
2266 **320** 1l.75 brown . . . . . . 1·50 30

321 Rowing  **322** N. Balcescu (after C. Tattarescu)

1952. Physical Culture.
2267 **321** 20b. blue . . . . 1·90 20
2268 – 1l.75 red (Athletes) . . . 4·75 60

1952. Death Centenary of Balcescu (revolutionary).
2269 **322** 55b. grey . . . . 2·40 10
2270 1l.75 olive . . . . 6·00 75

323 Emblem and Flags  **324**

1952. New Constitution.
2271 **323** 55b. green 95 25

1952. 5th Anniv of People's Republic.
2272 **324** 55b. multicoloured . . . 1·70 40

325 Millo, Caragiale and Mme. Romanescu  **326** Foundry Worker

1953. Centenary of Caragiale National Theatre.
2273 **325** 55b. blue . . . . 1·70 25

1953. 3rd Industrial and Agricultural Congress.
2274 **326** 55b. green 60 10
2275 – 55b. orange 50 30
2276 – 55b. brown 65 10
DESIGNS—HORIZ: No. 2275, Farm workers and tractor; 2276, Workman, refinery and oil wells.

1953. As Nos. 2240, etc, but with star added at top of emblem.
2277 **275** 5b. red 35 15
2278 55b. purple . . . . . . 1·00 25

327 "The Strikers of Grivitsa" (after Nazarev)

1953. 20th Anniv of Grivitsa Strike.
2279 **327** 55b. brown . . . . . . 1·40 25

328

1953. 5th Anniv of Treaty of Friendship with Russia.
2280 **328** 55b. brown on blue . . . 1·40 25

329 Table Tennis Badge  **330** Oltenian Carpet

1953. 20th World Table Tennis Championship, Bucharest.
2281 **329** 55b. green . . . . 5·00 1·00
2282 55b. brown . . . . . . 4·25 75

1953. Rumanian Art.
2283 – 10b. green 35 10
2284 – 20b. brown 80 10
2285 – 35b. violet . . . . . . 1·40 10
2286 – 55b. blue . . . . . . 2·40 10
2287 **330** 1l. purple . . . . . . 4·25 20
DESIGNS—VERT: 10b. Pottery; 20b. Campulung peasant girl; 55b. Apuseni Mountains peasant girl. HORIZ: 35b. National dance.

331 Karl Marx  **332** Pioneers planting Tree

1953. 70th Death Anniv of Karl Marx.
2288 **331** 1l.55 brown . . . . . . 1·70 35

1953. 4th Anniv of Rumanian Pioneers Organization.
2289 **332** 35b. green 80 20
2290 – 55b. blue . . . . 1·30 20
2291 – 1l.75 brown . . . . . . 2·10 40
DESIGNS—VERT: 55b. Boy and girl flying model gliders. HORIZ: 1l.75, Pioneers and instructor.

333 Women and Flags  **334**

1953. 3rd World Congress of Women.
2292 **333** 55b. brown . . . . . . 1·20 25

1953. 4th World Youth Festival.
2293 **334** 20b. orange 55 25
2294 – 55b. blue 70 40
2295 – 65b. red 95 65
2296 – 1l.75 purple . . . . . . 3·75 1·30
DESIGNS—VERT: 55b. Students releasing dove over globe. HORIZ: 65b. Girl presenting bouquet; 1l.75, Folk dancers.

335 Cornfield and Forest  **336** V. V. Mayakovsky

1953. Forestry Month.
2297 – 20b. blue 65 55
2298 **335** 38b. green 00 80
2299 – 55b. brown . . . . . . 2·30 60
DESIGNS—VERT: 20b. Waterfall and trees; 55b. Forestry worker.

1953. 60th Birth Anniv of Vladimir Mayakovsky (Russian poet).
2300 **336** 55b. brown . . . . . . 1·20 35

337 Miner

1953. Miners' Day.
2301 **337** 1l.55 black . . . . . . 2·00 25

338 Telephonist, G.P.O. and P.O. Worker

1953. 50th Anniv of Construction of G.P.O.
2302 **338** 20b. brown 35 10
2303 – 55b. olive 60 10

2304 – 1l. blue 1·30 20
2305 – 1l.55 lake 2·00 45
DESIGNS: 55b. Postwoman and G.P.O.; 1l. G.P.O. radio transmitter and map; 1l.55, Telegraphist, G.P.O. and teletypist.

339 **340** Soldier and Flag

1953. 9th Anniv of Liberation.
2306 **339** 55b. brown 85 25

1953. Army Day.
2307 **340** 55b. olive 95 25

341 Girl and Model Glider

1953. Aerial Sports.
2308 **341** 10b. green and orange 1·90 35
2309 – 20b. olive and brown 2·75 20
2310 – 55b. purple and red 10·00 45
2311 – 1l.75 brown and purple 12·00 70
DESIGNS: 20b. Parachutists; 55b. Glider and pilot; 1l.75, Zlin Z-22 monoplane.

342 Workman, Girl and Flags

1953. Rumanian–Soviet Friendship.
2312 **342** 55b. brown 60 10
2313 – 1l.55 lake 1·50 35
DESIGN: 1l.55, Spassky Tower (Moscow Kremlin) and Volga–Don canal.

343 "Unity"

1953. 3rd World Trades' Union Congress.
2314 **343** 55b. olive 50 20
2315 – 1l.25 red 1·30 45
DESIGN—VERT: 1l.25, Workers, flags and globe.

344 C. Porumbescu **345** Agricultural Machinery

1953. Birth Centenary of Porumbescu (composer).
2316 **344** 55b. lilac 5·25 25

1953. Agricultural designs.
2317 **345** 10b. olive 15 10
2318 – 35b. green 40 10
2319 – 2l.55 brown 2·75 65
DESIGNS: 35b. Tractor drawing disc harrows; 2l.55, Cows grazing.

346 Vlaicu and his Airplane No. 1 "Crazy Fly" **347** Lenin

1953. 40th Death Anniv of Vlaicu (pioneer aviator).
2320 **346** 50b. blue 85 25

1954. 30th Death Anniv of Lenin.
2321 **347** 55b. brown 1·10 25

348 Red Deer Stag **350** O. Bancila

349 Calimanesti

1954. Forestry Month.
2322 **348** 20b. brown on yellow 4·50 35
2323 – 55b. violet on yellow 2·30 35
2324 – 1l.75 blue on yellow 4·25 75
DESIGNS: 55b. Pioneers planting tree; 1l.75, Forest.

1954. Workers' Rest Homes.
2325 **349** 5b. black on yellow 60 10
2326 – 1l.55 black on blue 2·00 20
2327 – 2l. green on pink 4·50 25
2328 – 2l.35 brown on green 3·75 90
2329 – 2l.55 brown on green 4·25 1·10
DESIGNS: 1l.55, Siniai; 2l. Predeal; 2l.35, Tusnad; 2l.55, Govora.

1954. 10th Death Anniv of Bancila (painter).
2330 **350** 55b. green and brown 2·10 1·30

351 Child and Dove of Peace **353** Stephen the Great

352 Girl Pioneer feeding Calf

1954. International Children's Day.
2331 **351** 55b. brown 85 25

1954. 5th Anniv of Rumanian Pioneer Organization.
2332 **352** 20b. black 40 15
2333 – 55b. blue 70 25
2334 – 1l.75 red 3·75 55
DESIGNS: 55b. Girl Pioneers harvesting; 1l.75, Young Pioneers examining globe.

1954. 450th Death Anniv of Stephen the Great.
2335 **353** 55b. brown 1·40 30

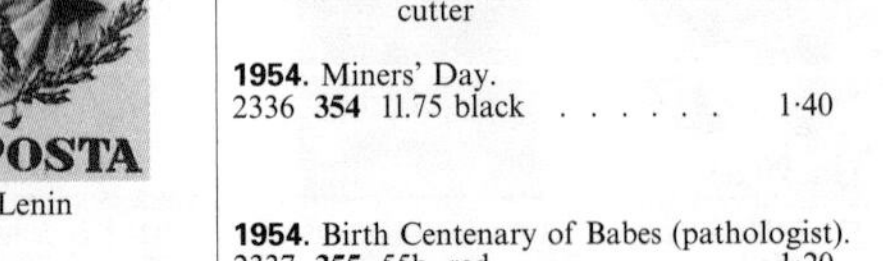

354 Miner operating Coal-cutter **355** Dr. V. Babes

1954. Miners' Day.
2336 **354** 1l.75 black 1·40 45

1954. Birth Centenary of Babes (pathologist).
2337 **355** 55b. red 1·20 25

356 Sailor, Flag and Destroyer "Regele Ferdinand" **357** Dedication Tablet

1954. Navy Day.
2338 **356** 55b. blue 95 25

1954. 5th Anniv of Mutual Aid Organization.
2339 – 20b. violet 55 10
2340 **357** 55b. brown 95 20
DESIGN: 20b. Man receiving money from counter clerk.

358 Liberation Monument **359** Recreation Centre

1954. 10th Anniv of Liberation.
2341 **358** 55b. violet and red 1·10 25

1954. Liberation Anniv Celebrations.
2342 **359** 20b. blue 25 10
2343 – 38b. violet 85 25
2344 – 55b. purple 95 20
2345 – 1l.55 brown 2·50 40
DESIGNS—38 × 22 mm: 55b. "Scanteia" offices. 24½ × 29½ mm: 38b. Opera House, Bucharest; 1l.55, Radio Station.

360 Pilot and Mikoyan Gurevich MiG-15 Jet Fighters **361** Chemical Plant and Oil Derricks

1954. Aviation Day.
2346 **360** 55b. blue 2·50 25

1954. International Chemical and Petroleum Workers Conference, Bucharest.
2347 **361** 55b. black 2·50 35

362 Dragon Pillar, Peking **363** T. Neculuta

1954. Chinese Culture Week.
2348 **362** 55b. black on yellow 2·40 35

1954. 50th Death Anniv of Dumitru Theodor Neculuta (poet).
2349 **363** 55b. violet 1·50 20

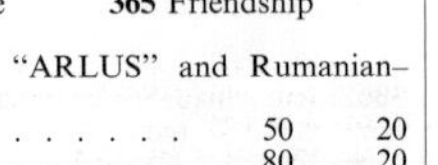

364 ARLUS Badge **365** Friendship

1954. 10th Anniv of "ARLUS" and Rumanian–Russian Friendship.
2350 **364** 55b. red 50 20
2351 **365** 65b. purple 80 20

366 G. Tattarescu **367** B. Iscovescu

1954. 60th Death Anniv of Gheorghe Tattarescu (painter).
2352 **366** 55b. red 1·60 20

1954. Death Centenary of Barbu Iscovescu (painter).
2353 **367** 1l.75 brown 2·75 40

368 Teleprinter **369** Wild Boar

1954. Cent of Telecommunications in Rumania.
2354 **368** 50b. lilac 1·00 20

1955. Forestry Month. Inscr "LUNA PADURII 1955".
2355 **369** 35b. brown 1·30 15
2356 – 65b. blue 1·40 25
2357 – 1l.20 red 4·25 50
DESIGNS: 65b. Tree planting; 1l.20, Logging.

370 Airman **371** Clasped Hands

1955. Occupations.
2358 – 3b. blue 15 10
2359 – 5b. violet 05 10
2360 **370** 10b. brown 15 10
2361 – 20b. mauve 05 10
2362 – 30b. blue 1·10 10
2363 – 35b. turquoise 30 10
2364 – 40b. blue 1·10 15
2365 – 55b. olive 75 10
2366 – 1l. violet 1·30 10
2367 – 1l.55 lake 2·10 10
2368 – 2l.35 buff 3·50 35
2369 – 2l.55 green 4·00 30
DESIGNS: 3b. Scientist; 5b. Foundryman; 20b. Miner; 30b. Tractor driver; 35b. Schoolboy; 40b. Girl student; 55b. Bricklayer; 1l. Sailor; 1l.55, Mill girl; 2l.35, Soldier; 2l.55, Telegraph linesman.

1955. International Conference of Postal Municipal Workers, Vienna.
2370 **371** 25b. red 40 25

372 Lenin **373** Dove and Globe

1955. 85th Birth Anniv of Lenin. Portraits of Lenin.
2371 **372** 20b. brown and bistre 45 20
2372 – 55b. brown (full face) 1·10 20
2373 – 1l. lake and red (half length) 1·50 30

1955. Peace Congress, Helsinki.
2374 **373** 55b. blue 85 25

374 War Memorial, Berlin **375** Children and Dove

1955. 10th Anniv of Victory over Germany.
2375 **374** 55b. blue 85 25

1955. International Children's Day.
2376 **375** 55b. brown 85 25

376 "Service" **377** People's Art Museum

1955. European Volleyball Championships.
2377 – 55b. mauve and pink . . 4·25 1·40
2378 **376** 1l.75 mauve and yellow 9·50 1·60
DESIGN: 55b. Volleyball players.

1955. Bucharest Museums.
2379 – 20b. mauve 30 15
2380 – 55b. brown 55 15
2381 **377** 1l.20 black . . . . . . 1·30 50
2382 – 1l.75 green . . . . . . 1·40 50
2383 – 2l.55 purple . . . . . . 4·25 65
MUSEUMS—30 × 24½ mm: 20b. Theodor Aman; 2l.55, Simu. 34 × 23 mm: 55b. Lenin-Stalin; 1l.75, Republican Art.

378 Mother and Child **379** "Nature Study"

1955. 1st World Mothers' Congress, Lausanne.
2384 **378** 55b. blue 95 25

1955. 5th Anniv of Pioneer Headquarters, Bucharest.
2385 – 10b. blue . . . . 1·20 10
2386 **379** 20b. green . . . . 1·10 10
2387 – 55b. purple . . . . . . 2·75 10
DESIGNS: 10b. Model railway; 55b. Headquarters building.

380 Coxed Four **381** Anton Pann (folklorist)

1955. Women's European Rowing Championships, Snagov.
2388 **380** 55b. green . . . . 5·75 65
2389 – 1l. blue (Woman sculler) 10·00 1·10

1955. Rumanian Writers.
2390 – 55b. blue 95 30
2391 – 55b. grey 95 30
2392 **381** 55b. olive 95 30
2393 – 55b. violet 95 30
2394 – 55b. purple 95 30
PORTRAITS—No. 2390, Dimitrie Cantemir (historian); 2391, Metropolitan Dosoftei (religious writer); 2393, Constantin Cantacuzino (historian); 2394, Ienachita Vacarescu (poet, grammarian and historian).

382 Marksman **383** Fire Engine

1955. European Sharpshooting Championships, Bucharest.
2395 **382** 1l. brown and light brown . . . . 3·25 45

1955. Firemen's Day.
2396 **383** 55b. red . . . . 1·40 40

384 **385** Spraying Fruit Trees

1955. 10th Anniv of W.F.T.U.
2397 **384** 55b. olive 45 10
2398 – 1l. blue 80 20
DESIGN: 1l. Workers and flag.

1955. Fruit and Vegetable Cultivation.
2399 **385** 10b. green 40 15
2400 – 20b. red 70 30
2401 – 55b. blue . . . . 1·40 30
2402 – 1l. lake . . . . 4·25 90
DESIGNS: 20b. Fruit picking; 55b. Harvesting grapes; 1l. Gathering vegetables.

386 **387** Michurin

1955. 4th ARLUS Congress.
2403 **386** 20b. blue and buff . . . 55 15

1955. Birth Cent of Ivan Michurin (Russian botanist).
2404 **387** 55b. blue 95 15

388 Cotton **389** Sheep and Shepherd blowing Bucium

1955.
2405 – 10b. purple (Sugar beet) 45 20
2406 **388** 20b. grey 70 20
2407 – 55b. blue (Linseed) . . . 2·10 45
2408 – 1l.55 brown (Sunflower) 4·25 85

1955.
2409 **389** 5b. brown and green . . 1·10 15
2410 – 10b. violet and bistre . . 1·30 25
2411 – 35b. brown and salmon 2·75 55
2412 – 55b. brown and bistre 5·00 70
DESIGNS: 10b. Pigs and farm girl; 35b. Cows and dairy maid; 55b. Horses and groom.

390 Johann von Schiller (novelist) **391** Bank and Book

1955. Literary Anniversaries.
2413 – 20b. blue 40 10
2414 – 55b. blue . . . . 1·20 20
2415 **390** 1l. grey . . . . 1·80 20
2416 – 1l.55 brown . . . . . . 4·25 90
2417 – 1l.75 violet . . . . . . 4·50 90
2418 – 2l. lake . . . . 5·25 1·40
DESIGNS: 20b. Hans Christian Andersen (children's writer, 150th birth anniv); 55b. Adam Mickiewicz (poet, death centenary); 1l. Type **390** (150th death anniv); 1l.55, Baron de Montesquieu (philosopher, death bicentenary); 1l.75, Walt Whitman (centenary of publication of "Leaves of Grass"); 2l. Miguel de Cervantes (350th anniv of publication of "Don Quixote").

1955. Savings Bank.
2419 **391** 55b. blue . . . . 2·10 20
2420 55b. violet . . . . 5·50 3·50

392 Family **393** Brown Hare

1956. National Census.
2421 – 55b. orange 30 10
2422 **392** 1l.75 brown and green 1·50 55
DESIGNS: 55b. "21 FEBRUARIE 1956" in circle.

1956. Wild Life
2423 **393** 20b. black and green . . 2·40 1·90
2424 – 20b. black and olive . . 3·00 1·90
2425 – 35b. black and blue . . 2·40 1·90
2426 – 50b. brown and blue . . 2·40 1·90
2427 – 55b. green and bistre . . 3·00 1·90
2428 – 55b. brown and turquoise . . . . . . 3·00 1·90
2429 – 1l. lake and green . . . 5·50 4·25
2430 – 1l.55 lake and blue . . 5·75 4·25
2431 – 1l.75 brown and green 8·00 6·50
2432 – 2l. brown and blue . . . 28·00 20·00
2433 – 3l.25 black and green . . 28·00 20·00
2434 – 4l.25 brown and salmon 28·00 20·00
DESIGNS—VERT: No. 2424, Great bustard; 35b. Brown trout; 1l.55, Eurasian red squirrel; 1l.75, Western capercaillie; 4l.25, Red deer. HORIZ: 50b. Wild boar; No. 2427, Common pheasant; No. 2428, Brown bear; 1l. Lynx; 2l. Chamois; 3l.25, Pintail.
See also Nos. 2474/85.

394 Insurgents **395** Boy and Globe

1956. 85th Anniv of Paris Commune.
2435 **394** 55b. red 95 40

1956. International Children's Day.
2436 **395** 55b. violet . . . . . . 1·20 35

396 Red Cross Nurse **397** Tree

1956. 2nd Rumanian Red Cross Congress.
2437 **396** 55b. olive and red . . . 1·70 35

1956. Forestry Month.
2438 **397** 20b. grey on green . . . 65 20
2439 – 55b. black on green . . 5·00 30
DESIGN: 55b. Lumber train.

398 Woman Speaking **399** Academy Buildings

1956. International Women's Congress, Bucharest.
2440 **398** 55b. green 95 35

1956. 90th Anniv of Rumanian People's Academy.
2441 **399** 55b. green and buff . . . 95 25

400 Vuia, Biplane, Vuia No. 1 and Yakovlev Yak-25 Fighters

1956. 50th Anniv of 1st Flight by Traian Vuia (pioneer airman).
2442 **400** 55b. brown and olive . . 1·10 35

401 Georgescu and Statues **402** Farm Girl

1956. Birth Centenary of Ion Georgescu (sculptor).
2443 **401** 55b. brown and green 1·40 25

1956. Collective Farming. (a) Inscr "1951–1956".
2444 **402** 55b. plum . . . . 6·00 5·50

(b) Inscr "1949–56".
2445 **402** 55b. plum 85 25

403 Black-veined White **404** Striker

1956. Insect Pests.
2446 **403** 10b. cream, black and violet . . . . 6·50 40
2447 – 55b. orange and brown 8·00 65
2448 – 1l.75 lake and olive . . . 12·00 7·50
2449 – 1l.75 brown and olive . . 15·00 1·30
PESTS: 55b. Colorado potato beetle; 1l.75 (2), May beetle.

1956. 50th Anniv of Dockers' Strike at Galatz.
2450 **404** 55b. brown on pink . . 95 25

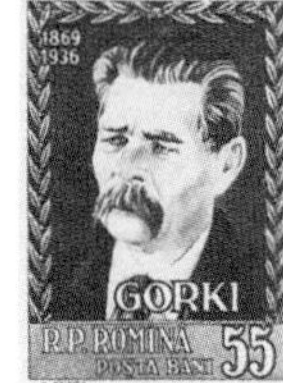

405 **406** Gorky

1956. 25th Anniv of "Scanteia" (Communist newspaper).
2451 **405** 55b. blue 85 25

1956. 20th Death Anniv of Maksim Gorky.
2452 **406** 55b. brown . . . . . . 1·40 35

407 T. Aman **408** Snowdrops and Polyanthus

1956. 125th Birth Anniv of Aman (painter).
2453 **407** 55b. grey . . . . 1·40 45

1956. Flowers. Designs multicoloured. Colours of backgrounds given.
2454 **408** 5b. blue 60 20
2455 – 55b. black . . . . 1·70 40
2456 – 1l.75 blue . . . . 4·50 55
2457 – 3l. green . . . . 8·75 95
FLOWERS: 55b. Daffodil and violets; 1l.75, Antirrhinums and campanulas; 3l. Poppies and lilies of the valley.

409 Janos Hunyadi **410** Olympic Flame

1956. 500th Death Anniv of Hunyadi.
2458 **409** 55b. violet 95 40

1956. Olympic Games.
2459 **410** 20b. red 70 20
2460 – 55b. blue . . . . 1·20 25
2461 – 1l. mauve . . . . 1·40 30
2462 – 1l.55 turquoise . . . . . 2·20 35
2463 – 1l.75 violet . . . . . . 2·75 45
DESIGNS: 55b. Water-polo; 1l. Ice-skating; 1l.55, Canoeing; 1l.75, High-jumping.

411 George Bernard Shaw (dramatist) **412** Ilyushin Il-18 Airliner over City

1956. Cultural Anniversaries.
2464 – 20b. blue 45 10
2465 – 35b. red 55 15
2466 **411** 40b. brown 55 20
2467 – 50b. brown 70 50
2468 – 55b. olive . . . . 1·20 50
2469 – 1l. turquoise . . . . . . 1·30 20
2470 – 1l.55 violet . . . . . . 2·50 20
2471 – 1l.75 blue . . . . 3·25 20
2472 – 2l.55 purple . . . . . . 4·00 35
2473 – 3l.25 blue . . . . 4·50 70

DESIGNS: 20b. Benjamin Franklin (U.S. statesman and journalist, 250th birth anniv); 35b. Toyo Oda (painter, 450th death anniv); 40b. Type **411** (birth centenary); 50b. Ivan Franco (writer, birth centenary); 55b. Pierre Curie (physicist, 50th death anniv); 1l. Henrik Ibsen (dramatist, 50th death anniv); 1l.55, Fyodor Dostoevsky (novelist, 75th death anniv); 1l.75, Heinrich Heine (poet, death centenary); 2l.55, Wolfgang Amadeus Mozart (composer, birth bicentenary); 3l.25, Rembrandt (artist, 350th birth anniv).

1956. Wild Life. As Nos. 2423/34 but colours changed. Imperf.

2474 20b. brown and green . . . 2·30 2·20
2475 20b. black and blue . . . . 3·75 3·50
2476 35b. black and blue . . . . 2·30 2·40
2477 50b. black and brown . . . 2·30 2·40
2478 55b. black and violet . . . 3·50 3·75
2479 55b. brown and green . . . 2·30 2·40
2480 1l. brown and blue . . . . 2·30 2·40
2481 1l.55 brown and bistre . . . 2·30 2·40
2482 1l.75 purple and green . . . 3·25 3·50
2483 2l. black and blue . . . . . 2·30 2·20
2484 3l.25 brown and green . . . 6·50 7·25
2485 4l.25 brown and violet . . . 3·50 3·25

1956. Air. Multicoloured.

2486 20b. Type **412** 50 40
2487 55b. Ilyushin Il-18 over mountains 75 40
2488 1l.75 Ilyushin Il-18 over cornfield . . . . 3·50 60
2489 2l.55 Ilyushin Il-18 over seashore . . . . 4·00 1·20

413 Georgi Enescu **414** "Rebels" (after Octav Bancila)

1956. 75th Birth Anniv of Enescu (musician).

2490 – 55b. blue . . . . 1·10 25
2491 **413** 1l.75 purple . . . . . . 1·70 35

DESIGN: 55b. Enescu when a child, holding violin.

1957. 50th Anniv of Peasant Revolt.

2492 **414** 55b. grey 85 25

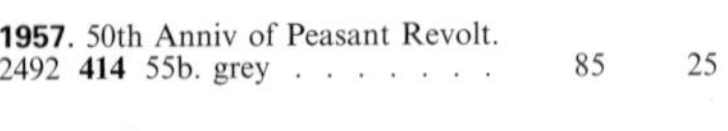

415 Stephen the Great **416** Gheorghe Marinescu (neurologist) and Institute of Medicine

1957. 500th Anniv of Accession of Stephen the Great.

2493 **415** 55b. brown 50 35
2494 55b. olive 50 50

1957. National Congress of Medical Sciences, Bucharest, and Centenary of Medical and Pharmaceutical Teaching in Bucharest (1l.75).

2495 **416** 20b. green 25 20
2496 – 35b. brown 35 20
2497 – 55b. purple . . . . . . 1·00 30
2498 – 1l.75 red and blue . . . 3·75 1·20

DESIGNS: As T **416**: 35b. Ioan Cantacuzino (bacteriologist) and Cantacuzino Institute; 55b. Victor Babes (pathologist and bacteriologist) and Babes Institute. 66 × 23 mm: 1l.75, Nicolae Kretzulescu and Carol Dairla (physicians) and Faculty of Medicine, Bucharest.

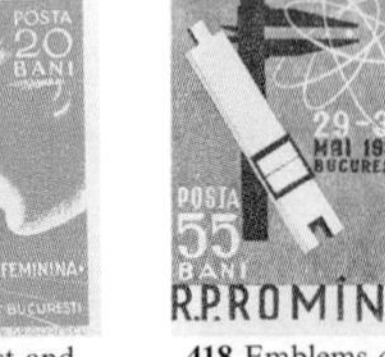

417 Gymnast and Spectator **418** Emblems of Atomic Energy

1957. 1st European Women's Gymnastic Championships, Bucharest.

2499 **417** 20b. green 35 10
2500 – 35b. red 65 20
2501 – 55b. blue . . . . 1·20 30
2502 – 1l.75 purple . . . . . . 3·50 65

DESIGNS—HORIZ: 35b. On asymmetric bars; 55b. Vaulting over horse. VERT: 1l.75, On beam.

1957. 2nd A.S.I.T. Congress.

2503 **418** 55b. brown . . . . . . 1·10 25
2504 55b. blue . . . . 1·30 25

419 Dove and Handlebars **420** Rhododendron

1957. 10th International Cycle Race.

2505 **419** 20b. blue 25 15
2506 – 55b. brown . . . . . . 1·00 25

DESIGN: 55b. Racing cyclist.

1957. Flowers of the Carpathian Mountains.

2513 **420** 5b. red and grey 25 10
2514 – 10b. green and grey . . 35 10
2515 – 20b. orange and grey . . 40 10
2516 – 35b. olive and grey . . . 65 20
2517 – 55b. blue and grey . . . 80 20
2518 – 1l. red and grey . . . . 1·90 50
2519 – 1l.55 yellow and grey . . 2·40 35
2520 – 1l.75 violet and grey . . 4·00 45

FLOWERS: 10b. Daphne; 20b. Lily; 35b. Edelweiss; 55b. Gentian; 1l. Dianthus; 1l.55, Primula; 1l.75, Anemone.

421 N. Grigorescu

1957. 50th Death Anniv of Nicolae Grigorescu (painter).

2521 – 20b. green 50 15
2522 **421** 55b. brown . . . . . . 1·00 25
2523 – 1l.75 blue . . . . 4·50 65

DESIGNS—HORIZ: 20b. "Ox-cart"; 1l.75, "Attack on Smirdan".

422 Festival Visitors **423** Festival Emblem

1957. 6th World Youth Festival, Moscow.

2524 **422** 20b. purple 25 10
2525 – 55b. green 75 10
2526 **423** 1l. orange . . . . 1·40 45
2527 – 1l.75 blue . . . . 1·80 25

DESIGNS: 55b. Girl with flags (22 × 38 mm); 1l.75, Dancers (49 × 20 mm).

424 Destroyer "Stalingrad" **425** "The Trumpeter" (after N. Grigorescu)

1957. Navy Day.

2528 **424** 1l.75 blue . . . . 1·80 25

1957. 80th Anniv of War of Independence.

2529 **425** 20b. violet 85 25

426 Soldiers Advancing **427** Child with Dove

1957. 40th Anniv of Battle of Marasesti.

2530 **426** 1l.75 brown . . . . . . 1·20 25

1957. Red Cross.

2531 **427** 55b. green and red . . . 85 25

428 Sprinter and Bird **429** Ovid

1957. Int Athletic Championships, Bucharest.

2532 **428** 20b. black and blue . . 60 10
2533 – 55b. black and yellow . . 1·50 20
2534 – 1l.75 black and red . . . 4·00 45

DESIGNS: 55b. Javelin-thrower and bull; 1l.75, Runner and stag.

1957. Birth Bimillenary of Ovid (Latin poet).

2535 **429** 1l.75 blue . . . . 1·75 45

430 Congress Emblem **431** Oil Refinery, 1957

1957. 4th W.F.T.U. Congress, Leipzig.

2536 **430** 55b. blue 55 10

1957. Centenary of Rumanian Petroleum Industry.

2537 **431** 20b. brown 50 10
2538 20b. blue 50 10
2539 – 55b. purple 75 35

DESIGN: 55b. Oil production, 1857 (horse-operated borer).

432 Lenin, Youth and Girl **433** Artificial Satellite encircling Globe

1957. 40th Anniv of Russian Revolution.

2540 **432** 10b. red 10 15
2541 – 35b. purple 40 15
2542 – 55b. brown 60 30

DESIGNS—HORIZ: 35b. Lenin and flags; 55b. Statue of Lenin.

1957. Air. Launching of Artificial Satellite by Russia.

2543 **433** 25b. blue 50 50
2545 25b. blue 50 35
2544 – 3l.75 green . . . . . . 4·50 95
2546 – 3l.75 blue . . . . 4·50 95

DESIGN: 3l.75 (2), Satellite's orbit around Globe. See also Nos. 2593/6.

434 Peasant Soldiers **435** Endre Ady

1957. 520th Anniv of Bobilna Revolution.

2547 **434** 50b. purple 25 15
2548 – 55b. grey 35 20

DESIGN—VERT: 55b. Bobilna Memorial.

1957. 80th Birth Anniv of Endre Ady (Hungarian poet).

2549 **435** 55b. olive 70 25

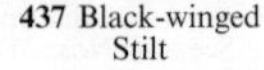

436 Laika and "Sputnik 2" **437** Black-winged Stilt

1957. Space Flight of Laika (dog).

2550 **436** 1l.20 blue and brown . . 2·25 50
2551 1l.20 blue and brown . . 2·25 50

1957. Fauna of the Danube Delta.

2552 **437** 5b. grey & brown (postage) 30 10
2553 – 10b. orange and green 40 10
2554 – 20b. orange and red . . 45 10
2555 – 50b. orange and green 15 10
2556 – 55b. blue and purple . . 40 10
2557 – 1l.30 orange and violet 2·00 20
2558 – 3l.30 grey and blue (air) 3·00 75
2559 – 5l. orange and red . . . 5·00 1·10

DESIGNS—VERT: 10b. Great egret; 20b. White spoonbill; 50b. Stellate sturgeon. HORIZ: 55b. Stoat; 1l.30, Eastern white pelican; 3l.30, Black-headed gull; 5l. White-tailed sea eagle.

438 Emblem of Republic and Flags

1957. 10th Anniv of People's Republic.

2560 **438** 25b. buff, red and blue 15 10
2561 – 55b. yellow 65 20
2562 – 1l.20 red 75 35

DESIGNS: 55b. Emblem, Industry and Agriculture; 1l.20, Emblem, the Arts and Sports.

439 Republican Flag

1958. 25th Anniv of Strike at Grivitsa.

2563 **439** 1l. red and brown on buff 50 25
2564 1l. red and blue on buff 50 25

440 "Telecommunications"

1958. Socialist Countries' Postal Ministers Conference, Moscow.

2565 **440** 55b. violet 50 25
2566 – 1l.75 purple 85 25

DESIGN: 1l.75, Telegraph pole and pylons carrying lines.

441 Nicolae Balcescu (historian) **442** Fencer

1958. Rumanian Writers.

2567 **441** 5b. blue 25 15
2568 – 10b. black 30 20
2569 – 35b. blue 45 20
2570 – 55b. brown 55 20
2571 – 1l.75 black . . . . . . 1·10 35
2572 – 2l. green . . . . 1·30 35

DESIGNS: 10b. Ion Creanga (folklorist); 35b. Alexandru Vlahuta (poet); 55b. Mihail Eminescu (poet); 1l.75, Vasile Alecsandri (poet and dramatist); 2l. Barbu Delavrancea (short-story writer and dramatist).

1958. World Youth Fencing Championships, Bucharest.

2573 **442** 1l.75 mauve 95 25

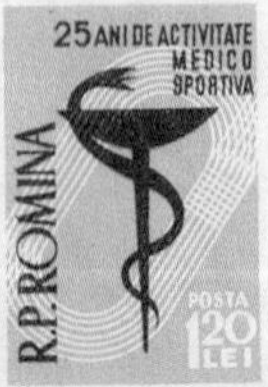

443 Symbols of Medicine and Sport **444**

1958. 25th Anniv of Sports Doctors' Service.
2574 **443** 1l.20 red and green . . . 95 25

1958. 4th Int Congress of Democratic Women.
2575 **444** 55b. blue 55 25

445 Linnaeus (botanist)

446 Parasol Mushroom

1958. Cultural Anniversaries (1957).
2576 **445** 10b. blue 20 15
2577 – 20b. brown 30 15
2578 – 40b. mauve 40 20
2579 – 55b. blue 90 15
2580 – 1l. mauve 90 20
2581 – 1l.75 blue . . . . 1·50 30
2582 – 2l. brown . . . . 2·50 35
DESIGNS: 10b. Type **445** (250th birth anniv); 20b. Auguste Comte (philosopher, death centenary); 40b. William Blake (poet and artist, birth bicentenary); 55b. Mikhail Glinka (composer, death centenary); 1l. Henry Longfellow (poet, 150th birth anniv); 1l.75, Carlo Goldoni (dramatist, 250th birth anniv); 2l. John Komensky, Comenius (educationist, 300th death anniv).

1958. Mushrooms. As T **446**.
2583 **446** 5b. brown, lt brn & blue 20 15
2584 – 10b. brown, buff and bronze 20 15
2585 – 20b. red, yellow and grey 20 15
2586 – 30b. brown, orge & green 20 20
2587 – 35b. brown, lt brn & bl 30 15
2588 – 55b. brown, red and green 50 15
2589 – 1l. brown, buff and green . . . . 1·10 20
2590 – 1l.55 pink, drab and grey 1·90 25
2591 – 1l.75 brown, buff and green . . . . 2·25 35
2592 – 2l. yellow, brown and green . . . . 4·25 35
MUSHROOMS: 10b. "Clavaria aurea"; 20b. Caesar's mushroom; 30b. Saffron milk cap; 35b. Honey fungus; 55b. Shaggy ink cap; 1l. "Morchella conica"; 1l.55, Field mushroom; 1l.75, Cep; 2l. Chanterelle.

1958. Brussels International Exhibition. Nos. 2543/4 and 2545/6 optd **EXPOZITIA UNIVERSALA BRUXELLES 1958** and star or with star only.
2593 **433** 25b. green . . . . 2·50 1·80
2595 25b. blue . . . . 18·00 13·00
2594 – 3l.75 green . . . . . . 2·50 1·40
2596 – 3l.75 blue . . . . 17·00 13·00

448 Racovita and "Belgica" (Gerlache expedition, 1897)

1958. 10th Death Anniv (1957) of Emil Racovita (naturalist and explorer).
2597 **448** 55b. indigo and blue . . 2·25 25
2598 – 1l.20 violet and olive . . 1·40 20
DESIGN: 1l.20, Racovita and grotto.

449 Sputnik encircling Globe

1958. Air. Launching of Third Artificial Satellite by Russia.
2599 **449** 3l.25 buff and blue . . . 3·25 1·00

450 Servicemen's Statue

1958. Army Day.
2600 **450** 55b. brown (postage) . . 20 15
2601 – 75b. purple 30 15
2602 – 1l.75 blue 50 20
2603 – 3l.30 violet (air) . . . . 1·30 45
DESIGNS: 75b. Soldier guarding industrial plant; 1l.75, Sailor hoisting flag, and "Royal Ferdinand" destroyer; 3l.30, Pilot and Mikoyan Gurevich MiG-17 jet fighters.

451 Costume of Oltenia

452 Costume of Oltenia

1958. Provincial Costumes.
2604 **451** 35b. red, black and yellow (female) 20 25
2605 **452** 35b. red, black and yellow (male) 20 40
2606 – 40b. red, brown and light brown (female) 20 30
2607 – 40b. red, brown and light brown (male) . . 20 30
2608 – 50b. brown, red and lilac (female) 25 25
2609 – 50b. brown, red and lilac (male) 25 25
2610 – 55b. red, brown and drab (female) 35 25
2611 – 55b. red, brown and drab (male) 35 25
2612 – 1l. carmine, brown and red (female) 90 30
2613 – 1l. carmine, brown and red (male) 90 30
2614 – 1l.75 red, brown and blue (female) . . . . 1·20 50
2615 – 1l.75 red, brown and blue (male) . . . . . 1·20 50
PROVINCES: Nos. 2606/7, Tara Oasului; 2608/9, Transylvania; 2610/11, Muntenia; 2612/3, Banat; 2614/5, Moldova.

453 Stamp Printer

454 Runner

1958. Rumanian Stamp Centenary. Inscr "1858 1958".
2617 **453** 35b. blue 20 15
2618 – 55b. brown 30 15
2619 – 1l.20 blue 60 30
2620 – 1l.30 plum 65 35
2621 – 1l.55 brown 90 20
2622 – 1l.75 red . . . . 1·25 25
2623 – 2l. violet . . . . 1·50 45
2624 – 3l.30 brown . . . . . . 2·10 55
DESIGNS: 55b. Scissors and Moldavian stamps of 1858; 1l.20, Driver with whip and mail coach; 1l.30, Postman with horn and mounted courier; 1l.55 to 3l.30, Moldavian stamps of 1858 (Nos. 1/4).

1958. 3rd Youth Spartacist Games.
2627 **454** 1l. brown 65 25

455 Revolutionary Emblem

456 Boy Bugler

1958. 40th Anniv of Workers' Revolution.
2628 **455** 55b. red 40 25

1958. 10th Anniv of Education Reform.
2629 **456** 55b. red 40 25

457 Alexandru Cuza

1959. Centenary of Union of Rumanian Provinces.
2630 **457** 1l.75 blue 85 20

458 First Cosmic Rocket

1959. Air. Launching of 1st Cosmic Rocket.
2631 **458** 3l.25 blue on salmon . . 8·00 1·20

459 Charles Darwin (naturalist)

460 Maize

1959. Cultural Anniversaries.
2633 **459** 55b. black (postage) . . 30 15
2634 – 55b. blue 30 15
2635 – 55b. red 30 15
2636 – 55b. purple 30 15
2637 – 55b. brown . . . . . . 30 5·75
2638 – 3l.25 blue (air) . . . . . 3·00 50
DESIGNS—No. 2633, Type **459** (150th birth anniv); 2634, Robert Burns (poet, birth bicentenary); 2635, Aleksandr Popov (radio pioneer, birth centenary); 2636, Sholem Aleichem (writer, birth centenary); 2637, Frederick Handel (composer, death bicentenary); 2638, Frederic Joliot-Curie (nuclear physicist, 10th anniv of World Peace Council).

1959. 10th Anniv of Collective Farming in Rumania.
2639 **460** 55b. green 30 20
2640 – 55b. orange 30 20
2641 – 55b. purple 30 20
2642 – 55b. olive 30 20
2643 – 55b. brown 30 20
2644 – 55b. bistre 30 20
2645 – 55b. blue 30 20
2646 – 55b. bistre 30 20
2647 – 5l. red . . . . 3·00 75
DESIGNS—VERT: No. 2640, Sunflower with bee; 2641, Sugar beet. HORIZ: No. 2642, Sheep; 2643, Cattle; 2644, Rooster and hens; 2645, Farm tractor; 2646, Farm wagon and horses; 2647 (38 × 26½ mm), Farmer and wife, and wheatfield within figure "10".

461 Rock Thrush

462 Young Couple

1959. Air. Birds in natural colours. Inscriptions in grey. Colours of value tablets and backgrounds given.
2648 **461** 10b. grey on buff . . . 15 10
2649 – 20b. grey on grey . . . 15 10
2650 – 35b. grey on deep grey 15 10
2651 – 40b. red on pink 20 15
2652 – 55b. grey on green . . . 30 10
2653 – 55b. grey on cream . . . 30 10
2654 – 55b. green on azure . . 30 10
2655 – 1l. red on yellow . . . 60 20
2656 – 1l.55 red on pink . . . . 1·10 20
2657 – 5l. grey on green . . . . 6·25 1·20
BIRDS—HORIZ: No. 2649, Golden oriole; 2656, Long-tailed tit; 2657, Wallcreeper. VERT: No. 2650, Northern lapwing; 2651, Barn swallow; 2652, Great spotted woodpecker; 2653, Eurasian goldfinch; 2654, Great tit; 2655, Northern bullfinch.

1959. 7th World Youth Festival, Vienna. Inscr "26 VII-4 VIII 1959".
2658 **462** 1l. blue 50 20
2659 – 1l.60 red 50 20
DESIGN: 1l.60, Folk-dancer in national costume.

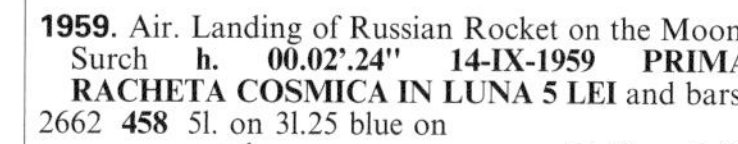

463 Workers and Banners

(466)

1959. 15th Anniv of Liberation.
2660 **463** 55b. multicoloured . . . 40 25

1959. Air. Landing of Russian Rocket on the Moon. Surch **h. 00.02'.24" 14-IX-1959 PRIMA RACHETA COSMICA IN LUNA 5 LEI** and bars.
2662 **458** 5l. on 3l.25 blue on salmon . . . . 14·00 2·50

1959. 8th Balkan Games. Optd with T **466** in silver.
2663 **454** 1l. brown . . . . 14·00 12·50

467 Prince Vlad Tepes and Charter

1959. 500th Anniv of Bucharest.
2664 **467** 20b. black and blue . . 35 25
2665 – 40b. black and brown . . 1·20 25
2666 – 55b. black and bistre . . 90 30
2667 – 55b. black and purple . . 95 30
2668 – 1l.55 black and lilac . . 3·75 85
2669 – 1l.75 black and turquoise 3·25 1·10
DESIGNS—HORIZ: 40b. Peace Buildings, Bucharest; 55b. (No. 2666), Atheneum; 55b. (No 2667), "Scanteia" Printing House; 1l.55, Opera House; 1l.75, "23 August" Stadium.

468 Football

469 "Lenin"

1959. International Sport. Multicoloured.
2671 20b. Type **468** (postage) . . 15 10
2672 35b. Motor-cycle racing (horiz) 20 10
2673 40b. Ice-hockey (horiz) . . . 30 20
2674 55b. Handball 30 10
2675 1l. Horse-jumping 45 10
2676 1l.50 Boxing 90 20
2677 1l.55 Rugby football (horiz) 1·00 10
2678 1l.60 Tennis (horiz) . . . . 1·20 25
2679 2l.80 Hydroplaning (horiz) (air) . . . . 1·75 75

1959. Launching of Atomic Ice-breaker "Lenin".
2680 **469** 1l.75 violet . . . . . . 1·50 35

STAMP DAY ISSUES. The annual issues for Stamp Day in November together with the stamp issued on 30 March 1963 for the Rumanian Philatelists' Conference are now the only stamps which carry a premium which is expressed on se-tenant labels. This was for the Association of Rumanian Philatelists. These labels were at first seperated by a vertical perforation but in the issues from 1963 to 1971 the label is an integral part of the stamp.

470 Stamp Album and Magnifier

1959. Stamp Day.
2681 **470** 1l.60(+40b.) blue 70 60

471 Foxglove

472 Cuza University

1959. Medicinal Flowers. Multicoloured.
2682 20b. Type **471** 15 10
2683 40b. Peppermint 20 20
2684 55b. False camomile 25 10
2685 55b. Cornflower 30 10
2686 1l. Meadow saffron 40 20
2687 1l.20 Monkshood 85 20
2688 1l.55 Common poppy . . . 95 20
2689 1l.60 Silver lime . . . . . . 1·10 30
2690 1l.75 Dog rose . . . . . . 2·10 30
2691 3l.20 Yellow pheasant's-eye 1·50 45

1959. Centenary of Cuza University, Jassy.
2692 **472** 55b. brown 40 25

473 Rocket, Dog and Rabbit

474 G. Cosbuc

1959. Air. Cosmic Rocket Flight.

2693	**473**	1l.55 blue	1·90	30
2694	–	1l.60 blue on cream	2·40	40
2695	–	1l.75 blue	2·40	40

DESIGNS—HORIZ: (52 × 29½ mm): 1l.60, Picture of "invisible" side of the Moon, with lists of place-names in Rumanian and Russian. VERT—(As Type **473**): 1l.75, Lunik 3's trajectory around the Moon.

1960. Rumanian Authors.

2696	**474**	20b. blue	20	20
2697	–	40b. purple	55	20
2698	–	50b. brown	65	20
2699	–	55b. purple	65	20
2700	–	1l. violet	1·30	20
2701	–	1l.55 blue	2·20	35

PORTRAITS: 40b. I. L. Caragiale; 50b. G. Alexandrescu; 55b. A. Donici; 1l. C. Negruzzi; 1l.55, D. Bolintineanu.

475 Huchen

476 Woman and Dove

1960. Rumanian Fauna.

2702	**475**	20b. blue (postage)	10	10
2703	–	55b. brown (Tortoise)	20	10
2704	–	1l.20 lilac (Common shelduck)	1·60	45
2705	–	1l.30 blue (Golden eagle) (air)	2·20	45
2706	–	1l.75 green (Black grouse)	2·20	45
2707	–	2l. red (Lammergeier)	2·30	65

1960. 50th Anniv of International Women's Day.

2708	**476**	55b. blue	60	30

477 Lenin (after painting by M. A. Gerasimov)

478 "Victory"

1960. 90th Birth Anniv of Lenin.

2709	**477**	40b. purple	35	15
2710	–	55b. blue (Statue of Lenin by Boris Carogea)	40	15

1960. 15th Anniv of Victory.

2712	**478**	40b. blue	50	10
2714		40b. purple	2·30	2·50
2713	–	55b. blue	50	10
2715	–	55b. purple	2·30	2·50

DESIGN: 55b. Statue of soldier with flag.

479 Rocket Flight

1960. Air. Launching of Soviet Rocket.

2716	**479**	55b. blue	1·80	30

480 Diving

481 Gymnastics

1960. Olympic Games, Rome (1st issue). Mult.

2717	40b. Type **480**	70	95
2718	55b. Gymnastics	90	1·00
2719	1l.20 High jumping	1·30	1·20
2720	1l.60 Boxing	2·00	1·30
2721	2l.45 Canoeing	2·10	1·40
2722	3l.70 Canoeing	4·50	3·25

Nos. 2717/9 and 2720/1 are arranged together in "brickwork" fashion, se-tenant, in sheets forming complete overall patterns of the Olympic rings.

No. 2722 is imperf.

1960. Olympic Games, Rome (2nd issue).

2723	–	20b. blue	15	10
2724	**481**	40b. purple	30	15
2725	–	55b. blue	55	10
2726	–	1l. red	70	10
2727	–	1l.60 purple	2·00	35
2728	–	2l. lilac	4·50	75

DESIGNS: 20b. Diving; 55b. High-jumping; 1l. Boxing; 1l.60, Canoeing; 2l. Football.

482 Industrial Scholars

483 Vlaicu and his Airplane No. 1 "Crazy Fly"

484 I.A.R. 817 Flying Ambulance

485 Pilot and Mikoyan Gurevich MiG-17 Jet Fighters

1960.

2731	**482**	3b. mauve (postage)	10	10
2732	–	5b. brown	30	10
2733	–	10b. purple	10	10
2734	–	20b. blue	10	10
2735	–	30b. red	15	10
2736	–	35b. red	15	10
2737	–	40b. bistre	25	10
2738	–	50b. violet	25	10
2739	–	55b. blue	30	10
2740	–	60b. green	30	10
2741	–	75b. olive	60	10
2742	–	1l. red	75	10
2743	–	1l.20 black	60	10
2744	–	1l.50 purple	1·10	10
2745	–	1l.55 turquoise	1·00	10
2746	–	1l.60 blue	90	10
2747	–	1l.75 brown	1·10	10
2748	–	2l. brown	1·30	15
2749	–	2l.40 violet	1·50	10
2750	–	3l. blue	2·00	15
2751	–	3l.20 blue (air)	4·50	10

DESIGNS—VERT: 5b. Diesel train; 10b. Dam; 20b. Miner; 30b. Doctor; 35b. Textile worker; 50b. Children at play; 55b. Timber tractor; 1l. Atomic reactor; 1l.20, Petroleum refinery; 1l.50, Iron-works; 1l.75, Mason; 2l. Road-roller; 2l.40, Chemist; 3l. Radio communications and television. HORIZ: 40b. Grand piano and books; 60b. Combine harvester; 75b. Cattle-shed; 1l.55, Dock scene; 1l.60, Runner; 3l.20, Baneasa Airport, Bucharest.

1960. 50th Anniv of 1st Flight by A. Vlaicu and Aviation Day.

2752	**483**	10b. brown and yellow	15	10
2753	–	20b. brown and orange	20	10
2754	**484**	35b. red	30	10
2755	–	40b. violet	35	10
2756	**485**	55b. blue	50	10
2757	–	1l.60 multicoloured	1·30	20
2758	–	1l.75 multicoloured	1·70	35

DESIGNS—As T **483**: 20b. Vlaicu in flying helmet and his No. 2 airplane; 40b. Antonov An-2 biplane spraying crops. 59 × 22 mm: 1l.60, Ilyushin Il-18 airliner and Baneasa airport control tower; 1l.75, Parachute descents.

486 Worker and Emblem

1960. 3rd Workers' Party Congress.

2759	**486**	55b. orange and red	55	25

487 Leo Tolstoy (writer)

488 Tomis (Constantza)

1960. Cultural Anniversaries.

2760	**487**	10b. purple	10	10
2761	–	20b. brown	10	10
2762	–	35b. blue	15	10
2763	–	40b. green	20	10
2764	–	55b. brown	35	10
2765	–	1l. green	65	25
2766	–	1l.20 purple	75	10
2767	–	1l.55 grey	1·20	15
2768	–	1l.75 brown	1·90	30

DESIGNS: 10b. Type **487** (50th death anniv); 20b. Mark Twain (writer, 50th death anniv); 35b. Katsushika Hokusai (painter, birth bicentenary); 40b. Alfred de Musset (poet, 150th birth anniv); 55b. Daniel Defoe (writer, 300th birth anniv); 1l. Janos Bolyai (mathematician, death centenary); 1l.20, Anton Chekhov (writer, birth centenary); 1l.55, Robert Koch (bacteriologist, 50th death anniv); 1l.75, Frederic Chopin (composer, 150th birth anniv).

1960. Black Sea Resorts. Multicoloured.

2769	20b. Type **488** (postage)	15	10
2770	35b. Constantza	30	10
2771	40b. Vasile Roaita	30	10
2772	55b. Mangalia	60	10
2773	1l. Eforie	1·00	25
2774	1l.60 Eforie (different)	1·10	20
2775	2l. Mamaia (air)	2·10	50

489 Globe and Flags

490 Viennese Emperor Moth

1960. International Puppet Theatre Festival, Bucharest. Designs (24 × 28½ mm, except 20b.) show puppets. Multicoloured.

2776	20b. Type **489**	20	10
2777	40b. Petrushka	25	10
2778	55b. Punch	30	10
2779	1l. Kaspar	45	10
2780	1l.20 Tindarica	55	10
2781	1l.75 Vasilache	1·00	20

1960. Air. Butterflies and Moths. Multicoloured.

2782	10b. Type **490**	25	10
2783	20b. Poplar admiral	25	10
2784	40b. Scarce copper	30	10
2785	55b. Swallowtail	55	15
2786	1l.60 Death's-head hawk moth	1·70	25
2787	1l.75 Purple emperor	2·10	35

SIZES: TRIANGULAR—36½ × 21½ mm: 20, 40b. VERT—23½ × 34 mm: 55b., 1l.60. HORIZ—34 × 23½ mm: 1l.75.

491 Children tobogganing

1960. Village Children's Games. Multicoloured.

2788	20b. Type **491**	10	10
2789	35b. "Oina" (ball-game) (horiz)	15	10
2790	55b. Ice-skating (horiz)	25	10
2791	1l. Running	50	10
2792	1l.75 Swimming (horiz)	1·40	15

492 Striker and Flag

1960. 40th Anniv of General Strike.

2793	**492**	55b. red and lake	45	20

493 Compass Points and Ilyushin Il-18 Airliner

1960. Air. Stamp Day.

2794	**493**	55b.(+45b.) blue	60	35

494 "XV", Globe and "Peace" Banner

496 Woman tending Vine (Cotnari)

495 Black Sea Herrings

1960. 15th Anniv of World Democratic Youth Federation.

2795	**494**	55b. yellow and blue	45	15

1960. Fishes.

2796	–	10b. brown, yell & grn	[illegible]	10
2797	–	20b. multicoloured	25	10
2798	–	40b. brn, lt brn & yell	40	10
2799	**495**	55b. grey, blue & orge	55	10
2800	–	1l. multicoloured	1·10	15
2801	–	1l.20 multicoloured	1·40	20
2802	–	1l.60 multicoloured	2·10	25

FISHES: 10b. Common carp; 20b. Zander; 40b. Black Sea turbot; 1l. Wels; 1l.20, Sterlet; 1l.60, Beluga.

1960. Rumanian Vineyards. Multicoloured.

2803	20b. Dragasani	10	10
2804	30b. Dealul Mare (horiz)	25	10
2805	40b. Odobesti (horiz)	35	10
2806	55b. Type **496**	55	10
2807	75b. Tirnave	75	20
2808	1l. Minis	1·30	25
2809	1l.20 Murfatlar	1·90	40

497 "Furnaceman" (after I. Irimescu)

498 Slalom Racer

1961. Rumanian Sculptures.

2811	**497**	5b. red	10	10
2812	–	10b. violet	10	10
2813	–	20b. black	20	10
2814	–	40b. bistre	25	10
2815	–	50b. brown	35	10
2816	–	55b. red	50	10
2817	–	1l. purple	85	15
2818	–	1l.55 blue	1·30	25
2819	–	1l.75 green	1·70	25

SCULPTURES—VERT: 10b. "Gh. Doja" (I. Vlad); 20b. "Reunion" (B. Caragea); 40b. "Enescu" (G. Anghel); 50b. "Eminescu" (C. Baraschi); 1l. "Peace" (I. Jalea); 1l.55, "Constructive Socialism" (C. Medrea); 1l.75, "Birth of an Idea" (A. Szobotka). HORIZ: 55b. "Peasant Uprising, 1907" (M. Constantinescu).

1961. Air. 50th Anniv of Rumanian Winter Sports.

(a) Perf.

2820	–	10b. olive and grey	20	15
2821	**498**	20b. red and grey	20	15
2822	–	25b. turquoise and grey	35	15
2823	–	40b. violet and grey	40	15
2824	–	55b. blue and grey	50	15
2825	–	1l. red and grey	70	20
2826	–	1l.55 brown and grey	1·70	30

(b) Imperf.

2827	–	10b. blue and grey	10	10
2828	**498**	20b. brown and grey	20	10
2829	–	25b. olive and grey	25	10
2830	–	40b. red and grey	50	10
2831	–	55b. turquoise and grey	65	55
2832	–	1l. violet and grey	1·00	90
2833	–	1l.55 red and grey	1·70	1·80

DESIGNS—HORIZ: Skier: racing (10b.), jumping (55b.), walking (1l.55). VERT: 25b. Skiers climbing slope; 40b. Toboggan; 1l. Rock-climber.

499 Petru Poni (chemist) **500** Yuri Gagarin in Capsule

1961. Rumanian Scientists. Inscr "1961". Portraits in sepia.
2834 **499** 10b. brown and pink . . 10 10
2835 – 20b. purple and yellow 25 10
2836 – 55b. red and blue . . . 40 15
2837 – 1l.55 violet and orange 1·20 35
PORTRAITS: 20b. Anghel Saligny (engineer) and Saligny Bridge, Cernavoda; 55b. Constantin Budeanu (electrical engineer); 1l.55, Gheorghe Titeica (mathematician).

1961. Air. World's First Manned Space Flight. Inscr "12 IV 1961". (a) Perf.
2838 – 1l.35 blue 55 20
2839 **500** 3l.20 blue . . . . 1·10 55

(b) Imperf.
2840 **500** 3l.20 red . . . . 5·50 2·10
DESIGN—VERT: 1l.35, Yuri Gagarin.

501 Freighter "Galati"

1961. Merchant Navy. Multicoloured.
2841 20b. Type **501** 35 10
2842 40b. "Oltenita" (Danube passenger vessel) 35 10
2843 55b. "Tomis" (hydrofoil) . . 55 10
2844 1l. "Arad" (freighter) . . . 80 10
2845 1l.55 "N. Cristea" (tug) . . 1·30 25
2846 1l.75 "Dobrogea" (freighter) 1·50 30

502 Red Flag with Marx, Engels and Lenin

1961. 40th Anniv of Rumanian Communist Party.
2847 **502** 35b. multicoloured . . . 50 10
2848 – 55b. multicoloured . . . 85 10
DESIGN: 55b. Two bill-posters.

503 Eclipse over Scanteia Building and Observatory **504** Roe Deer

1961. Air. Solar Eclipse.
2850 – 1l.60 blue . . . . 1·10 15
2851 **503** 1l.75 blue . . . . 1·30 15
DESIGN: 1l.60, Eclipse over Palace Square, Bucharest.

1961. Forest Animals. Inscr "1961". Multicoloured.
2852 10b. Type **504** 10 15
2853 20b. Lynx (horiz) 15 15
2854 35b. Wild boar (horiz) . . . 25 20
2855 40b. Brown bear (horiz) . . 45 20
2856 55b. Red deer 60 20
2857 75b. Red fox (horiz) 70 20
2858 1l. Chamois 95 20
2859 1l.55 Brown hare . . . . . 1·40 35
2860 1l.75 Eurasian badger . . . 1·70 30
2861 2l. Roe deer . . . . 2·40 55

505 George Enescu

1961. 2nd International George Enescu Festival.
2862 **505** 3l. lavender and brown 1·40 30

506 Yuri Gagarin and German Titov **507** Iris

1961. Air. 2nd Soviet Space Flight.
2863 – 55b. blue 35 10
2864 – 1l.35 violet 70 20
2865 **506** 1l.75 red . . . . 1·30 25
DESIGNS—VERT: 55b. "Vostok 2" in flight; 1l.35, G. S. Titov.

1961. Centenary of Bucharest Botanical Gardens. Flowers in natural colours. Background and inscription colours given. Perf or imperf.
2866 – 10b. yellow and brown 10 10
2867 – 20b. green and red . . . 10 10
2868 – 25b. blue, green and red 15 10
2869 – 35b. lilac and grey . . . 25 10
2870 **507** 40b. yellow and violet 30 10
2871 – 55b. blue and ultramarine 45 10
2872 – 1l. orange and blue . . . 75 15
2873 – 1l.20 blue and brown . . 95 15
2874 – 1l.55 brown and lake . . 1·10 15
FLOWERS—HORIZ: 10b. Primula; 35b. Opuntia; 1l. Hepatica. VERT: 20b. Dianthus; 25b. Peony; 55b. Ranunculus; 1l.20, Poppy; 1l.55, Gentian.

508 Cobza Player **509** Heraclitus (Greek philosopher)

1961. Musicians. Multicoloured.
2876 10b. Pan piper 10 10
2877 20b. Alpenhorn player (horiz) 15 10
2878 40b. Flautist 30 10
2879 55b. Type **508** 50 10
2880 60b. Bagpiper 65 15
2881 1l. Cembalo player 85 25

1961. Cultural Anniversaries.
2882 **509** 10b. purple 30 20
2883 – 20b. brown 30 20
2884 – 40b. green 35 20
2885 – 55b. mauve 50 20
2886 – 1l.35 blue 85 25
2887 – 1l.75 violet . . . . . . 1·10 30
DESIGNS: 20b. Sir Francis Bacon (philosopher and statesman, 400th birth anniv); 40b. Rabindranath Tagore (poet and philosopher, birth centenary); 55b. Domingo Sarmiento (writer, 150th birth anniv); 1l.35, Heinrich von Kleist (dramatist, 150th death anniv); 1l.75, Mikhail Lomonosov (writer, 250th birth anniv).

510 Olympic Flame **512** Tower Building, Republic Palace Square, Bucharest

511 "Stamps Round the World"

1961. Olympic Games 1960. Gold Medal Awards. Inscr "MELBOURNE 1956" or "ROMA 1960". Perf or imperf.
2888 – 10b. turquoise and ochre 15 15
2889 **510** 20b. red 20 15
2890 – 20b. grey 20 15
2891 – 35b. brown and ochre 30 15
2892 – 40b. purple and ochre 30 15
2893 – 55b. blue 40 15
2894 – 55b. blue 40 15
2895 – 55b. red and ochre . . . 40 15
2896 – 1l.35 blue and ochre 1·10 25
2897 – 1l.75 red and ochre . . . 1·80 35
DESIGNS (Medals)—DIAMOND: 10b. Boxing; 35b. Pistol-shooting; 40b. Rifle-shooting; 55b. (No. 2895), Wrestling; 1l.35, High-jumping. VERT: as Type **510**: 20b. (No. 2890), Diving; 55b. (No. 2893), Water-polo; 55b. (No. 2894), Women's high-jumping. HORIZ—45 × 33 mm: 1l.75, Canoeing.

1961. Air. Stamp Day.
2899 **511** 55b.(+45b.) blue, brown and red 95 40

1961. Air. Modern Rumanian Architecture. Mult.
2900 20b. Type **512** 25 10
2901 40b. Constantza Railway Station (horiz) 90 15
2902 55b. Congress Hall, Republic Palace, Bucharest (horiz) 40 10
2903 75b. Rolling mill, Hunedoara (horiz) 45 10
2904 1l. Apartment blocks, Bucharest (horiz) 60 15
2905 1l.20 Circus Building, Bucharest (horiz) 65 35
2906 1l.75 Workers' Club, Mangalia (horiz) 60 20

513 U.N. Emblem **514** Workers with Flags

1961. 15th Anniv of U.N.O. Perf or imperf.
2907 – 20b. multicoloured . . . 15 10
2908 – 40b. multicoloured . . . 45 10
2909 **513** 55b. multicoloured . . . 65 15
DESIGNS (bearing U.N. emblem): 20b. Peace dove over Eastern Europe; 40b. Peace dove and youths of three races.

1961. 5th W.F.T.U. Congress, Moscow.
2910 **514** 55b. red 60 20

515 Cock and Savings Book **516** Footballer

1962. Savings Day. Inscr "1962". Multicoloured.
2911 40b. Type **515** 20 10
2912 55b. Savings Bank book, bee and "honeycombs" of agriculture, housing and industry 45 10

1962. European Junior Football Competition, Bucharest.
2913 **516** 55b. brown and green . . 95 25

517 Ear of Corn, Map and Tractor **518** Handball Player

1962. Completion of Agricultural Collectivisation Project. Inscr "1962".
2914 **517** 40b. red and orange . . 15 10
2915 – 55b. lake and yellow . . 20 10
2916 – 1l.55 yellow, red and blue 45 15
DESIGNS: 55b. Commemorative medal; 1l.55, Wheatsheaf, and hammer and sickle emblem.

1962. Women's World Handball Championships, Bucharest.
2917 **518** 55b. violet and yellow 95 20

519 Canoe Race **520** Jean Jacques Rousseau

1962. Boating and Sailing. Inscr "1962". (a) Perf.
2918 **519** 10b. blue and mauve . . 15 10
2919 – 20b. blue and brown . . 20 10
2920 – 40b. blue and brown . . 25 10
2921 – 55b. blue and ultramarine 35 15
2922 – 1l. blue and red 70 15
2923 – 1l.20 blue and purple . . 90 15
2924 – 1l.55 blue and red . . . 1·10 15
2925 – 3l. blue and violet . . . 1·70 35

(b) Imperf. Colours changed.
2926 **519** 10b. blue and ultramarine 20 20
2927 – 20b. blue and mauve . . 30 20
2928 – 40b. blue and red . . . 45 30
2929 – 55b. blue and brown . . 50 40
2930 – 1l. blue and brown . . . 90 40
2931 – 1l.20 blue and violet . . 1·00 50
2932 – 1l.55 blue and red . . . 1·00 55
2933 – 3l. blue and purple . . . 2·50 95
DESIGNS: 20b. Kayak; 40b. Racing "eight"; 55b. Sculling; 1l. "Star" yachts; 1l.20, Power boats; 1l.55, "Flying Dutchman" dinghy; 3l. Canoe slalom.

1962. Cultural Anniversaries (writers).
2934 **520** 40b. green 20 10
2935 – 55b. purple 25 15
2936 – 1l.75 blue 65 10
DESIGNS—As T **520**: 40b. Type **520** (250th birth anniv); 55b. Ion Caragiale (dramatist, 50th death anniv); 1l.75, Aleksandr Herzen (150th birth anniv).

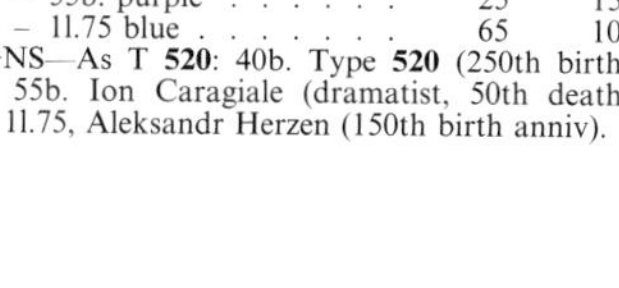

521 Flags and Globes

1962. World Youth Festival, Helsinki.
2938 **521** 55b. multicoloured . . . 65 20

522 Traian Vuia (aviator) **523** Anglers by Pond

1962. Rumanian Celebrities.
2939 **522** 15b. brown 15 10
2940 – 20b. red 20 10
2941 – 35b. purple 20 10
2942 – 40b. blue 30 15
2943 – 55b. blue 35 10
2944 – 1l. blue 55 10
2945 – 1l.20 red 70 25
2946 – 1l.35 turquoise 95 25
2947 – 1l.55 violet . . . . . . 1·10 15
PORTRAITS: 20b. Alexandru Davila (writer); 35b. Vasile Pirvan (archaeologist); 40b. Ion Negulici (painter); 55b. Grigore Cobilcescu (geologist); 1l. Dr. Gheorghe Marinescu (neurologist); 1l.20, Dr. Ion Cantacuzino (bacteriologist); 1l.35, Dr. Victor Babes (bacteriologist and pathologist); 1l.55, Dr. Constantin Levaditi (medical researcher).

1962. Fishing Sport. Multicoloured.
2948 10b. Rod-fishing in fishing punts 10 10
2949 25b. Line-fishing in mountain pool 15 10
2950 40b. Type **523** 25 10
2951 55b. Anglers on beach . . . 30 10
2952 75b. Line-fishing in mountain stream 45 10
2953 1l. Shore-fishing 50 20
2954 1l.75 Freshwater-fishing . . 85 20
2955 3l.25 Fishing in Danube delta . . . . 1·50 25

524 Dove and "Space" Stamps of 1957/58 **527** "Vostok 3" and "4" in Orbit

1962. Air. Cosmic Flights.
2956 **524** 35b. brown 15 10
2957 – 55b. green 25 10
2958 – 1l.35 blue 60 15
2959 – 1l.75 red . . . . 1·00 35
DESIGNS—Dove and: 55b. "Space" stamps of 1959; 1l.35, "Space" stamps of 1957 ("Laika"), 1959 and 1960; 1l.75, "Spacemen" stamps of 1961.

1962. Rumanian Victory in European Junior Football Competition, Bucharest. Surch **1962. Campioana Europeana 2 lei**.
2961 **516** 2l. on 55b. brown & grn 1·90 1·80

1962. Rumanian Victory in Women's World Handball Championships, Bucharest. Surch **Campioana Mondiala 5 lei**.
2962 **518** 5l. on 55b. vio& yell . . 4·00 2·40

1962. Air. 1st "Team" Manned Space Flight.
2963 – 55b. violet 35 10
2964 **527** 1l.60 blue 85 20
2965 – 1l.75 purple . . . . . . 1·20 25
DESIGNS: 55b. Andrian Nikolaev (cosmonaut); 1l.75, Pavel Popovich (cosmonaut).

528 Child and Butterfly **529** Pottery

1962. Children.
2966 **528** 20b. blue, brown and red 15 10
2967 – 30b. yellow, blue and red 20 10
2968 – 40b. blue, red & turquoise 25 10
2969 – 55b. olive, blue and red 50 10
2970 – 1l.20 red, brown & blue 1·00 20
2971 – 1l.55 ochre, blue and red 1·30 25
DESIGNS—VERT: 30b. Girl feeding dove; 40b. Boy with model yacht; 1l.20, Boy violinist and girl pianist. HORIZ: 55b. Girl teaching boy to write; 1l.55, Pioneers around camp-fire.

1962. 4th Sample Fair, Bucharest. Inscr "AL IV-LEA PAVILION DE MOSTRE BUCURESTI 1962". Multicoloured.
2972 5b. Type **529** (postage) . . . 30 15
2973 10b. Preserved foodstuffs . . 30 15
2974 20b. Chemical products . . 30 15
2975 40b. Ceramics 40 10
2976 55b. Leather goods 50 10
2977 75b. Textiles . . . . 70 2·50
2978 1l. Furniture and fabrics . . 85 10
2979 1l.20 Office equipment . . . 1·20 10
2980 1l.55 Needlework . . . . . 1·40 10
2981 1l.60 Fair pavilion (horiz) (air) . . . . 2·00 20

530 Lenin and Red Flag

1962. 45th Anniv of Russian Revolution.
2982 **530** 55b. brown, red and blue 65 20

531 "The Coachmen" (after Szatmay)

1962. Air. Stamp Day and Centenary of 1st Rumanian Stamps.
2983 **531** 55b.(+45b.) black and blue . . . . 1·00 30

532 Lamb

1962. Prime Farm Stock.
2984 **532** 20b. black and blue . . 15 10
2985 – 40b. brown, yellow & blue 15 10
2986 – 55b. green, buff and orange 25 10
2987 – 1l. brown, buff and grey 35 10
2988 – 1l.35 brown, black & green 50 15
2989 – 1l.55 brown, black & red 60 20
2990 – 1l.75 brown, cream & blue . . . . 1·00 35
DESIGNS—HORIZ: 40b. Ram; 1l.55, Heifer; 1l.75, Sows. VERT: 55b. Bull; 1l. Pig; 1l.35, Cow.

533 Arms, Industry and Agriculture

1962. 15th Anniv of People's Republic.
2991 **533** 1l.55 multicoloured . . . 95 25

534 Strikers

1963. 30th Anniv of Grivitsa Strike.
2992 **534** 1l.75 multicoloured . . . 1·30 25

535 Tractor-driver

1963. Freedom from Hunger.
2993 **535** 40b. blue 20 10
2994 – 55b. brown 30 10
2995 – 1l.55 red 65 10
2996 – 1l.75 green 75 20
DESIGNS (each with F.A.O. emblem): 55b. Girl harvester; 1l.55, Child with beaker of milk; 1l.75, Girl vintager.

1963. Air. Rumanian Philatelists' Conference, Bucharest. No. 2983 optd **A.F.R.** surrounded by **CONFERINTA PE TARA BUCURESTI 30-III-1963** in diamond shape.
2997 **531** 55b.(+45b.) blk & bl . . 2·75 2·50
The opt is applied in the middle of the se-tenant pair—stamp and 45b. label.

537 Sighisoara Glass Factory **538** Tomatoes

1963. Air. "Socialist Achievements".
2998 **537** 30b. blue and red . . . 25 10
2999 – 40b. green and violet . . 25 15
3000 – 55b. red and blue . . . 40 10
3001 – 1l. violet and brown . . 60 15
3002 – 1l.55 red and blue . . . 85 20
3003 – 1l.75 blue and purple . . 85 25
DESIGNS: 40b. Govora soda works; 55b. Tirgul-Jiu wood factory; 1l. Savinesti chemical works; 1l.55, Hunedoara metal works; 1l.75, Brazi thermic power station.

1963. Vegetable Culture. Multicoloured.
3004 35b. Type **538** 15 10
3005 40b. Hot peppers 25 10
3006 55b. Radishes 25 10
3007 75b. Aubergines 45 15
3008 1l.20 Mild peppers 65 20
3009 3l.25 Cucumbers (horiz) . . 1·30 30

539 Moon Rocket "Luna 4" **540** Chick

1963. Air. Launching of Soviet Moon Rocket "Luna 4". The 1l.75 is imperf.
3010 **539** 55b. red and blue . . . 20 15
3011 1l.75 red and violet . . . 95 15

1963. Domestic Poultry.
3012 **540** 20b. yellow and blue . . 20 10
3013 – 30b. red, blue and brown 25 10
3014 – 40b. blue, orange & brn 30 10
3015 – 55b. multicoloured . . . 35 10
3016 – 70b. blue, red and purple 40 10
3017 – 1l. red, grey and blue . . 45 15
3018 – 1l.35 red, blue and ochre 60 15
3019 – 3l.20 multicoloured . . . 1·20 35
POULTRY: 30b. Cockerel; 40b. Duck; 55b. White Leghorn; 70b. Goose; 1l. Rooster; 1l.35, Turkey (cock); 3l.20, Turkey (hen).

541 Diving **542** Congress Emblem

1963. Swimming. Bodies in drab.
3020 **541** 25b. green and brown . . 15 10
3021 – 30b. yellow and olive . . 20 10
3022 – 55b. red and turquoise 35 10
3023 – 1l. red and green 45 15
3024 – 1l.35 mauve and blue . . 50 15
3025 – 1l.55 orange and violet 90 20
3026 – 2l. yellow and mauve . . 90 50
DESIGNS—HORIZ: 30b. Crawl; 55b. Butterfly; 1l. Back stroke; 1l.35, Breast stroke. VERT: 1l.55, Swallow diving; 2l. Water polo.

1963. International Women's Congress, Moscow.
3027 **542** 55b. blue 45 20

543 Valery Bykovsky and Globe

1963. Air. 2nd "Team" Manned Space Flights.
3028 **543** 55b. blue 25 10
3029 – 1l.75 red . . . . 1·00 25
DESIGN: 1l.75, Valentina Tereshkova and globe.

544 Class 142 Steam Locomotive, 1936

1963. Air. Transport. Multicoloured.
3031 40b. Type **544** 50 15
3032 55b. Class 060-DA diesel-electric locomotive, 1959 50 15
3033 75b. Trolley bus 50 25
3034 1l.35 "Oltenita" (Danube passenger vessel) . . . . 1·30 30
3035 1l.75 Ilyushin Il-18 airplane 1·40 20

545 William Thackeray (novelist)

1963. Cultural Anniversaries. Inscr "MARILE ANNIVERSARI CULTURALE 1963".
3036 **545** 40b. black and lilac . . . 20 15
3037 – 50b. black and brown . . 30 15
3038 – 55b. black and olive . . 40 15
3039 – 1l.55 black and red . . . 80 15
3040 – 1l.75 black and blue . . 85 20
PORTRAITS: 40b. Type **545** (death centenary); 50b. Eugene Delacroix (painter, death centenary); 55b. Gheorghe Marinescu (neurologist, birth centenary); 1l.55, Giuseppe Verdi (composer, 150th birth anniv); 1l.75, Konstantin Stanislavsky (actor and stage director, birth centenary).

546 Walnuts **548** Volleyball

1963. Fruits and Nuts. Multicoloured.
3041 10b. Type **546** 25 10
3042 20b. Plums 25 10
3043 40b. Peaches 45 10
3044 55b. Strawberries 55 10
3045 1l. Grapes 60 10
3046 1l.55 Apples 80 15
3047 1l.60 Cherries . . . . 1·10 25
3048 1l.75 Pears . . . . 1·20 25

1963. Air. 50th Death Anniv of Aurel Vlaicu (aviation pioneer). No. 2752 surch **1913–1963 50 ani de la moarte 1,75 lei**.
3049 **483** 1l.75 on 10b. brn & yell 2·20 90

1963. European Volleyball Championships.
3050 **548** 5b. mauve and grey . . 20 10
3051 – 40b. blue and grey . . . 25 10
3052 – 55b. turquoise and grey 35 15
3053 – 1l.75 brown and grey . . 95 20
3054 – 3l.20 violet and grey . . 1·40 20
DESIGNS: 40b. to 1l.75, Various scenes of play at net; 3l.20, European Cup.

549 Rumanian 1l.55 "Centenary" Stamp of 1958

1963. Air. Stamp Day and 15th U.P.U. Congress. Inscr "AL XV-LEA CONGRESS", etc.
3055 **549** 20b. brown and blue . . 15 10
3056 – 40b. blue and mauve . . 15 10
3057 – 55b. mauve and blue . . 20 10
3058 – 1l.20 violet and buff . . 40 15
3059 – 1l.55 green and red . . . 1·10 20
3060 – 1l.60+50b. mult . . . . 1·00 30
DESIGNS (Rumanian stamps): 40b. (1l.20) "Laika", 1957 (blue); 55b. (3l.20) "Gagarin", 1961; 1l.20, (55b.) "Nikolaev" and (1l.75) "Popovich", 1962; 1l.55, (55b.) "Postwoman", 1953; 1l.60, U.P.U. Monument, Berne, globe, map of Rumania and aircraft (76 × 27 mm).

551 Ski Jumping

1963. Winter Olympic Games, Innsbruck, 1964.
(a) Perf.
3061 **551** 10b. blue and red . . . 25 15
3062 – 20b. brown and blue . . 35 15
3063 – 40b. brown and green . . 40 10
3064 – 55b. brown and violet 50 15
3065 – 60b. blue and brown . . 75 20
3066 – 75b. blue and mauve . . 90 20
3067 – 1l. blue and ochre . . . 1·10 25
3068 – 1l.20 blue and turquoise 1·40 30
(b) Imperf. Colours changed.
3069 **551** 10b. brown and green . . 60 55
3070 – 20b. brown and violet 60 55
3071 – 40b. blue and red . . . 60 55
3072 – 55b. brown and blue . . 60 55
3073 – 60b. blue and turquoise 60 55
3074 – 75b. blue and ochre . . 60 55
3075 – 1l. blue and mauve . . . 60 55
3076 – 1l.20 blue and brown . . 60 55
DESIGNS: 20b. Speed skating; 40b. Ice hockey; 55b. Figure skating; 60b. Slalom; 75b. Biathlon; 1l. Bobsleighing; 1l.20, Cross-country skiing.

552 Cone, Fern and Conifer **553** Silkworm Moth

1963. 18th Anniv of Reafforestation Campaign.
3078 **552** 55b. green 20 10
3079 – 1l.75 blue 40 15
DESIGN: 1l.75, Chestnut trees.

1963. Bee-keeping and Silkworm-breeding. Mult.
3080 10b. Type **553** 25 10
3081 20b. Moth emerging from chrysalis 35 10
3082 40b. Silkworm 45 10
3083 55b. Honey bee (horiz) 55 10
3084 60b. Honey bee on flower 70 20
3085 1l.20 Honey bee approaching orange flowers (horiz) 90 25
3086 1l.35 Honey bee approaching pink flowers (horiz) 1·20 35
3087 1l.60 Honey bee and sunflowers (horiz) 1·40 35

554 Carved Pillar

556 George Stephanescu (composer)

555 Yuri Gagarin

1963. Village Museum, Bucharest.
3088 **554** 20b. purple 20 10
3089 – 40b. blue (horiz) 25 10
3090 – 55b. violet (horiz) 30 10
3091 – 75b. green 40 10
3092 – 1l. red and brown 60 10
3093 – 1l.20 green 75 15
3094 – 1l.75 blue and brown 1·20 15
DESIGNS: Various Rumanian peasant houses.

1964. Air. "Space Navigation". Soviet flag, red and yellow; U.S. flag, red and blue; backgrounds, light blue; portrait and inscription colours below. (a) Perf.
3095 **555** 5b. blue 20 10
3096 – 10b. violet 25 10
3097 – 20b. bronze 30 10
3098 – 35b. grey 35 10
3099 – 40b. violet 40 15
3100 – 55b. violet 50 20
3101 – 60b. brown 50 20
3102 – 75b. blue 55 20
3103 – 1l. purple 75 25
3104 – 1l.40 purple 1·20 45

(b) Imperf. Colours changed.
3105 **555** 5b. violet 10 10
3106 – 10b. blue 10 10
3107 – 20b. grey 20 10
3108 – 35b. bronze 45 25
3109 – 40b. purple 60 30
3110 – 55b. purple 80 35
3111 – 60b. blue 80 50
3112 – 75b. brown 1·10 70
3113 – 1l. violet 1·30 85
3114 – 1l.40 violet 1·70 1·30
PORTRAITS (with flags of their countries)—As Type **555**: 10b. German Titov; 20b. John Glenn; 35b. Scott Carpenter; 60b. Walter Schirra; 75b. Gordon Cooper. 35½ × 33½ mm: 40b. Andrian Nikolaev; 55b. Pavel Popovich; 1l. Valery Bykovsky; 1l.40, Valentina Tereshkova.

1964. Rumanian Opera Singers and their stage roles. Portraits in brown.
3116 **556** 10b. olive 25 10
3117 – 20b. blue 35 10
3118 – 35b. green 35 10
3119 – 40b. light blue 40 10
3120 – 55b. mauve 50 10
3121 – 75b. violet 50 10
3122 – 1l. blue 60 15
3123 – 1l.35 violet 65 15
3124 – 1l.55 red 1·10 25
DESIGNS: 20b. Elena Teodorini in "Carmen"; 35b. Ion Bajenaru in "Petru Rares"; 40b. Dimitrie Popovici-Bayreuth as Alberich in "Ring of the Nibelung"; 55b. Haricled Dardee in "Tosca"; 75b. George Folescu in "Boris Godunov"; 1l. Jean Athanasiu in "Rigoletto"; 1l.35, Traian Grosarescu as Duke in "Rigoletto"; 1l.55, Nicolae Leonard as Hoffmann in "Tales of Hoffmann".

557 Prof. G. M. Murgoci

558 "Ascalaphus macaronius" (owl-fly)

1964. 8th International Soil Congress, Bucharest.
3125 **557** 1l.60 indigo, ochre and blue 60 20

1964. Insects. Multicoloured.
3126 5b. Type **558** 15 10
3127 10b. "Ammophila sabulosa" (digger wasp) 20 10
3128 35b. "Scolia maculata" (dagger wasp) 20 10
3129 40b. Swamp tiger moth 35 10
3130 55b. Gypsy moth 40 10
3131 1l.20 Great banded grayling 60 20
3132 1l.55 "Carabus fabricii malachiticus" (ground beetle) 70 20
3133 1l.75 "Procerus gigas" (ground beetle) 1·30 25

559 "Nicotiana alata"

560 Cross Country

1964. Rumanian Flowers. Multicoloured.
3134 10b. Type **559** 15 15
3135 20b. "Pelargonium" 20 15
3136 40b. "Fuchsia gracilis" 30 15
3137 55b. "Chrysanthemum indicum" 35 15
3138 75b. "Dahlia hybrida" 40 15
3139 1l. "Lilium croceum" 60 15
3140 1l.25 "Hosta ovata" 75 25
3141 1l.55 "Tagetes erectus" 80 25

1964. Horsemanship.
3142 – 40b. multicoloured 25 10
3143 **560** 55b. brown, red and lilac 30 10
3144 – 1l.35 brown, red & green 80 20
3145 – 1l.55 mauve, blue & bis 1·10 20
DESIGNS—HORIZ: 40b. Dressage; 1l.55, Horse race. VERT: 1l.35, Show jumping.

561 Brown Scorpionfish

562 M. Eminescu (poet)

1964. Constantza Aquarium. Fish designs. Mult.
3146 5b. Type **561** 10 10
3147 10b. Peacock blenny 10 10
3148 20b. Black Sea horse-mackerel 10 10
3149 40b. Russian sturgeon 20 10
3150 50b. Short-snouted seahorse 30 15
3151 55b. Tub gurnard 35 15
3152 1l. Beluga 50 15
3153 3l.20 Common stingray 2·10 30

1964. Cultural Anniversaries. Portraits in brown.
3154 **562** 5b. green 15 10
3155 – 20b. red 15 10
3156 – 35b. red 20 10
3157 – 55b. bistre 65 10
3158 – 1l.20 blue 1·00 15
3159 – 1l.75 violet 2·00 40
DESIGNS: Type **562** (75th death anniv); 20b. Ion Creanga (folklorist, 75th death anniv); 35b. Emil Girleanu (writer, 50th death anniv); 55b. Michelangelo (artist, 400th death anniv); 1l.20, Galileo Galilei (astronomer, 400th birth anniv); 1l.75, William Shakespeare (dramatist, 400th birth anniv).

563 Cheile Bicazului (gorge)

564 High Jumping

1964. Mountain Resorts.
3160 **563** 40b. lake 20 10
3161 – 55b. blue 35 10
3162 – 1l. purple 45 10
3163 – 1l.35 brown 50 10
3164 – 1l.75 green 85 15
DESIGNS—VERT: 55b. Cabin on Lake Bilea; 1l. Poiana Brasov ski-lift; 1l.75, Alpine Hotel. HORIZ: 1l.35, Lake Bicaz.

1964. Balkan Games. Multicoloured.
3165 30b. Type **564** 15 10
3166 40b. Throwing the javelin 15 10
3167 55b. Running 25 10
3168 1l. Throwing the discus 50 10
3169 1l.20 Hurdling 50 15
3170 1l.55 Flags of competing countries (24 × 44 mm) 55 20

565 Arms and Flag

1964. 20th Anniv of Liberation. Multicoloured.
3171 55b. Type **565** 20 10
3172 60b. Industrial plant (horiz) 20 10
3173 75b. Harvest scene (horiz) 30 10
3174 1l.20 Apartment houses (horiz) 55 20

566 High Jumping

1964. Olympic Games, Tokyo. Multicoloured. (a) Perf.
3176 20b. Type **566** 25 10
3177 30b. Wrestling 35 10
3178 35b. Volleyball 35 10
3179 40b. Canoeing 40 15
3180 55b. Fencing 50 15
3181 1l.20 Gymnastics 85 25
3182 1l.35 Football 1·00 25
3183 1l.55 Rifle-shooting 1·20 30

(b) Imperf. Colours changed and new values.
3184 20b. Type **566** 20 10
3185 30b. Wrestling 25 10
3186 35b. Volleyball 45 10
3187 40b. Canoeing 45 15
3188 55b. Fencing 90 30
3189 1l.60 Gymnastics 1·80 80
3190 2l. Football 1·90 1·00
3191 2l.40 Rifle-shooting 2·40 1·50

567 George Enescu

568 Python

1964. 3rd International George Enescu Festival.
3193 **567** 10b. green 20 10
3194 – 55b. purple 30 10
3195 – 1l.60 purple 75 30
3196 – 1l.75 blue 95 20
DESIGNS (Portraits of Enescu): 55b. At piano; 1l.60, Medallion; 1l.75, When an old man.

1964. Bucharest Zoo. Multicoloured.
3197 5b. Type **568** 10 10
3198 10b. Black swans 45 10
3199 35b. Ostriches 75 10
3200 40b. Crowned cranes 75 15
3201 55b. Tigers 35 10
3202 1l. Lions 55 10
3203 1l.55 Grevy's zebras 80 15
3204 2l. Bactrian camels 1·20 25

569 Brincoveanu, Cantacuzino, Lazar and Academy

570 Soldier

1964. Anniversaries. Multicoloured.
3205 20b. Type **569** 10 10
3206 40b. Cuza and seal 10 10
3207 55b. Emblems and the Arts (vert) 20 10
3208 75b. Laboratory workers and class 25 15
3209 1l. Savings Bank building 40 20
EVENTS, etc—HORIZ: 20b. 270th Anniv of Domneasca Academy; 40b., 75b. Bucharest University centenary; 1l. Savings Bank centenary. VERT: 55b. "Fine Arts" centenary (emblems are masks, curtain, piano keyboard, harp, palette and brushes).

1964. Centenary of Army Day.
3210 **570** 55b. blue and light blue 35 20

571 Post Office of 19th and 20th Centuries

1964. Air. Stamp Day.
3211 **571** 1l.60+40b. blue, red and yellow 95 25
No. 3211 is a two-part design, the two parts being arranged vert, imperf between.

572 Canoeing Medal (1956)

573 Strawberries

1964. Olympic Games—Rumanian Gold Medal Awards. Medals in brown and bistre (Nos. 3218/19 and 3226/7 in sepia and gold). (a) Perf.
3212 **572** 20b. red and blue 20 10
3213 – 30b. green and blue 35 15
3214 – 35b. turquoise and blue 45 15
3215 – 40b. lilac and blue 55 25
3216 – 55b. orange and blue 60 20
3217 – 1l.20 green and blue 70 25
3218 – 1l.35 brown and blue 1·10 30
3219 – 1l.55 mauve and blue 2·40 30

(b) Imperf. Colours changed and new values.
3220 **572** 20b. orange and blue 10 15
3221 – 30b. turquoise and blue 30 20
3222 – 35b. green and blue 30 20
3223 – 40b. green and blue 35 30
3224 – 55b. red and blue 40 30
3225 – 1l.60 lilac and blue 1·30 1·00
3226 – 2l. mauve and blue 2·00 1·30
3227 – 2l.40 brown and blue 2·50 1·70
MEDALS: 30b. Boxing (1956); 35b. Pistol-shooting (1956); 40b. High-jumping (1960); 55b. Wrestling (1960); 1l.20, 1l.60, Rifle-shooting (1960); 1l.35, 2l. High-jumping (1964); 1l.55, 2l.40, Throwing the javelin (1964).

1964. Forest Fruits. Multicoloured.
3229 5b. Type **573** 15 10
3230 35b. Blackberries 20 10
3231 40b. Raspberries 25 10
3232 55b. Rosehips 30 10
3233 1l.20 Blueberries 60 15
3234 1l.35 Cornelian cherries 70 15
3235 1l.55 Hazel nuts 80 10
3236 2l.55 Cherries 1·20 25

574 "Syncom 3"

575 U.N. Headquarters, New York

1965. Space Navigation. Multicoloured.
3237 30b. Type **574** 15 10
3238 40b. "Syncom 3" (different) 20 10
3239 55b. "Ranger 7" (horiz) . . 35 10
3240 1l. "Ranger 7" (different) (horiz) 40 15
3241 1l.20 "Voskhod 1" (horiz) 70 10
3242 5l. Konstantin Feoktistov, Vladimir Komarov and Boris Yegorov (cosmonauts) and "Voskhod 1" (52 × 29 mm) . . . . 1·70 60

1965. 20th Anniv of U.N.O.
3243 **575** 55b. gold, blue and red 15 10
3244 – 1l.60 multicoloured . . . 55 25
DESIGN: 1l.60, Arms and U.N. emblem on Rumanian flag.

576 Spur-thighed Tortoise

1965. Reptiles. Multicoloured.
3245 5b. Type **576** 10 10
3246 10b. Crimean lizard 15 10
3247 20b. Three-lined lizard . . . 15 10
3248 40b. Snake-eyed skink . . . 20 10
3249 55b. Slow worm 25 10
3250 60b. Sand viper 40 10
3251 1l. Arguta 45 15
3252 1l.20 Orsini's viper 55 15
3253 1l.35 European whip snake 70 15
3254 3l.25 Four-lined rat snake 2·30 35

577 Tabby Cat

1965. Domestic Cats. Multicoloured.
3255 5b. Type **577** 10 10
3256 10b. Ginger tomcat 10 10
3257 40b. White Persians (vert) 20 15
3258 55b. Kittens with shoe (vert) 30 10
3259 60b. Kitten with ball of wool (vert) 45 10
3260 75b. Cat and two kittens (vert) 60 10
3261 1l.35 Siamese (vert) . . . . 1·10 20
3262 3l.25 Heads of three cats (62 × 29 mm) . . . . . . 2·00 50

1965. Space Flight of "Ranger 9" (24.3.65). No. 3240 surch **RANGER 9 24-3-1965 5 Lei** and floral emblem over old value.
3263 5l. on 1l. multicoloured . . 17·00 17·00

579 Ion Bianu (philologist)

1965. Cultural Anniversaries. Portraits in sepia.
3264 **579** 40l. blue 15 10
3265 – 55b. ochre 15 10
3266 – 60b. purple 20 10
3267 – 1l. red 50 10
3268 – 1l.35 olive 45 15
3269 – 1l.75 red 70 25
PORTRAITS, etc: 40b. Type **579** (30th death anniv); 55b. Anton Bacalbasa (writer, birth cent); 60b. Vasile Conta (philosopher, 120th birth anniv); 1l. Jean Sibelius (composer, birth cent); 1l.35, Horace (Roman poet, birth bimillenary); 1l.75, Dante Alighieri (poet, 700th birth anniv).

580 I.T.U. Emblem and Symbols

1965. Centenary of I.T.U.
3270 **580** 1l.75 blue 70 20

581 Derdap Gorge (The Iron Gate)

1965. Inaug of Derdap Hydro-electric Project.
3271 **581** 30b. (25d.) green and grey 15 10
3272 – 55b. (50d.) red and grey 25 10
DESIGN: 55b. Derdap Dam.
Nos. 3271/72 were issued simultaneously in Yugoslavia.

582 Rifleman

583 "Fat-Frumos and the Beast"

1965. European Shooting Championships, Bucharest. Multicoloured. (a) Perf.
3274 20b. Type **582** 10 10
3275 40b. Prone rifleman 20 15
3276 55b. Pistol shooting 25 10
3277 1l. "Free" pistol shooting 45 15
3278 1l.60 Standing rifleman . . 65 15
3279 2l. Various marksmen . . . 85 30

(b) Imperf. Colours changed and new values.
3280 40b. Prone rifleman 15 10
3281 55b. Pistol shooting 20 10
3282 1l. "Free" pistol shooting 35 15
3283 1l.60 Standing rifleman . . 50 15
3284 3l.25 Type **582** . . . . . . 1·00 35
3285 5l. Various marksmen . . . 1·50 60
Apart from Type **582** the designs are horiz, the 2l. and 5l. being larger, 51½ × 28½ mm.

1965. Rumanian Fairy Tales. Multicoloured.
3286 20b. Type **583** 20 10
3287 40b. "Fat-Frumos and Ileana Cosinzeana" . . . 20 10
3288 55b. "Harap Alb" (horseman and bear) . . . 25 10
3289 1l. "The Moralist Wolf" . . 45 10
3290 1l.35 "The Ox and the Calf" 70 20
3291 2l. "The Bear and the Wolf" (drawing a sledge) 95 25

584 Honey Bee on Flowers

585 Pavel Belyaev, Aleksei Leonov, "Voskhod 2" and Leonov in Space

1965. 20th International Bee-keeping Association Federation ("Apimondia") Congress, Bucharest.
3292 **584** 55b. black, red and yellow 30 10
3293 – 1l.60 multicoloured . . . 95 15
DESIGN—HORIZ: 1l.60, Congress Hall.

1965. Space Achievements. Multicoloured.
3294 5b. "Proton 1" 10 10
3295 10b. "Sonda 3" (horiz) . . . 15 20
3296 15b. "Molnia 1" 20 20
3297 1l.75 Type **585** 60 10
3298 2l.40 "Early Bird" satellite 1·00 20
3299 3l.20 "Gemini 3" and astronauts in capsule . . 1·90 30

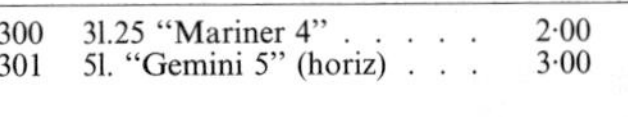
3300 3l.25 "Mariner 4" . . . . . 2·00 30
3301 5l. "Gemini 5" (horiz) . . . 3·00 75

586 Marx and Lenin

588 V. Alecsandri

587 Common Quail

1965. Socialist Countries' Postal Ministers' Congress, Peking.
3302 **586** 55b. multicoloured . . . 35 20

1965. Migratory Birds. Multicoloured.
3303 5b. Type **587** 15 10
3304 10b. Eurasian woodcock . . 25 10
3305 20b. Common snipe 30 10
3306 40b. Turtle dove 30 10
3307 55b. Mallard 40 10
3308 60b. White fronted goose . . 50 10
3309 1l. Common crane 60 15
3310 1l.20 Glossy ibis 75 15
3311 1l.35 Mute swan . . . . . 1·30 20
3312 3l.25 Eastern white pelican (32 × 73 mm) . . . . . . 3·75 55

1965. 75th Death Anniv of Vasile Alecsandri (poet).
3313 **588** 55b. multicoloured . . . 35 20

589 Zanzibar Water-lily

1965. Cluj Botanical Gardens. Multicoloured.
3314 5b. Bird-of-paradise flower (vert) 10 10
3315 10b. "Stanhopea tigrina" (orchid) (vert) 15 10
3316 20b. "Paphiopedilum insigne" (orchid) (vert) . . 15 10
3317 30b. Type **589** 25 10
3318 40b. "Ferocactus glaucescens" (cactus) . . 30 10
3319 55b. Tree-cotton 30 10
3320 1l. "Hibiscus rosa sinensis" 40 15
3321 1l.35 "Gloxinia hibrida" (vert) 60 15
3322 1l.75 Amazon water-lily . . 1·20 20
3323 2l.30 Hibiscus, water-lily, bird-of-paradise flower and botanical building (52 × 30 mm) . . . . . . 1·40 30

590 Running

592 Pigeon on TV Aerial

591 Pigeon and Horseman

1965. Spartacist Games. Multicoloured.
3324 55b. Type **590** 20 15
3325 1l.55 Football 55 20
3326 1l.75 Diving 60 20
3327 2l. Mountaineering (inscr "TURISM") 70 30
3328 5l. Canoeing (inscr "CAMPIONATELLE EUROPENE 1965") (horiz) . . . . 1·60 40

1965. Stamp Day.
3329 **591** 55b.+45b. blue & mve 35 10
3330 **592** 1l. brown and green . . 35 20
3331 – 1l.75 brown and green 80 20
DESIGN: As Type **592**: 1l.75, Pigeon in flight.

593 Chamois

1965. "Hunting Trophies".
3332 **593** 55b. brown, yell & mve 35 10
3333 – 1l. brown, green and red 60 10
3334 – 1l.60 brown, blue & orange . . . . 1·20 25
3335 – 1l.75 brown, red & green 1·60 25
3336 – 3l.20 multicoloured . . . 2·00 50
DESIGNS—37 × 23 mm: 1l. Brown bear; 1l.60, Red deer stag; 1l.75, Wild boar. 49 × 37½ mm: 3l.20, Trophy and antlers of red deer.

594 Dachshund

1965. Hunting Dogs. Multicoloured.
3337 5b. Type **594** 10 20
3338 10b. Spaniel 10 20
3339 40b. Retriever with eurasian woodcock 55 20
3340 55b. Fox terrier 25 20
3341 60b. Red setter 35 20
3342 75b. White setter 60 20
3343 1l.55 Pointers . . . . 1·30 45
3344 3l.25 Duck-shooting with retriever . . . . 2·30 1·20
SIZES: DIAMOND—47½ × 47½ mm: 10b. to 75b. HORIZ—43½ × 29 mm: 1l.55, 3l.25.

595 Pawn and Globe

596 Tractor, Corn and Sun

1966. World Chess Championships, Cuba. Mult.
3345 20b. Type **595** 25 10
3346 40b. Jester and bishop . . . 30 10
3347 55b. Knight and rook . . . 50 10
3348 1l. As No. 3347 . . . . . . 65 10
3349 1l.60 Type **595** . . . . . . 1·40 20
3350 3l.25 As No. 3346 . . . . . 2·75 1·00

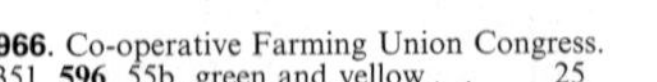
1966. Co-operative Farming Union Congress.
3351 **596** 55b. green and yellow . . 25 20

597 G. Gheorghiu-Dej

598 Congress Emblem

1966. 1st Death Anniv of Gheorghe Gheorghiu-Dej (President 1961–65).
3352 **597** 55b. black and gold . . 25 20

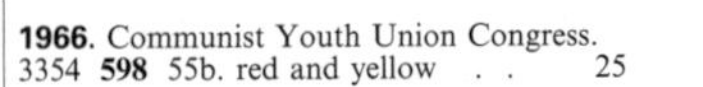
1966. Communist Youth Union Congress.
3354 **598** 55b. red and yellow . . 25 20

599 Dance of Moldova

1966. Rumanian Folk-dancing.
3355 **599** 30b. black and purple . . 20 10
3356 – 40b. black and red . . . 35 25
3357 – 55b. black and turquoise 45 10
3358 – 1l. black and lake . . . 55 10
3359 – 1l.60 black and blue . . 90 15
3360 – 2l. black and green . . . 1·80 70
DANCES OF: 40b. Oltenia; 55b. Maramures; 1l. Muntenia; 1l.60, Banat; 2l. Transylvania.

600 Footballers **601** "Agriculture and Industry"

1966. World Cup Football Championship, England.
3361 **600** 5b. multicoloured . . . 10 15
3362 – 10b. multicoloured . . . 20 15
3363 – 15b. multicoloured . . . 25 15
3364 – 55b. multicoloured . . . 50 15
3365 – 1l.75 multicoloured . . . 1·30 40
3366 – 4l. multicoloured . . . . 2·75 2·75
DESIGNS: 10b. to 1l.75, Various footballing scenes; 4l. Jules Rimet Cup.

1966. Trade Union Congress, Bucharest.
3368 **601** 55b. multicoloured . . . 25 20

602 Red-breasted Flycatcher **603** "Venus 3"

1966. Song Birds. Multicoloured.
3369 5b. Type **602** 20 15
3370 10b. Red crossbill 35 15
3371 15b. Great reed warbler . . 55 15
3372 20b. Common redstart . . . 60 15
3373 55b. European robin 90 15
3374 1l.20 Bluethroat . . . . . 1·20 15
3375 1l.55 Yellow wagtail . . . . 1·70 30
3376 3l.20 Penduline tit . . . . . 2·75 1·60

1966. Space Achievements. Multicoloured.
3377 10b. Type **603** 20 15
3378 20b. "FR 1" satellite 25 15
3379 1l.60 "Luna 9" . . . . . . 1·10 30
3380 5l. "Gemini 6" and "7" . . 2·50 1·00

604 Urechia Nestor (historian) **606** "Hottonia palustris"

605 "House" (after Petrascu)

1966. Cultural Anniversaries.
3381 – 5b. blue, black and green 10 10
3382 – 10b. green, black and red 10 10
3383 **604** 20b. purple, black & green 10 10
3384 – 40b. brown, black & blue 10 10
3385 – 55b. green, black & brn 15 10
3386 – 1l. violet, black and bistre 50 10
3387 – 1l.35 olive, black & blue 75 15
3388 – 1l.60 purple, blk & green 1·20 30
3389 – 1l.75 purple, blk & orge 80 15
3390 – 3l.25 lake, black and blue . . . . 1·50 30

PORTRAITS: 5b. George Cosbuc (poet, birth cent); 10b. Gheorghe Sincai (historian, 150th death anniv); 20b. Type **604** (birth cent); 40b. Aron Pumnul (linguist, death cent); 55b. Stefan Luchian (painter, 50th death anniv); 1l. Sun Yat-sen (Chinese statesman, birth cent); 1l.35, Gottfried Leibnitz (philosopher, 250th death anniv); 1l.60, Romain Rolland (writer, birth cent); 1l.75, Ion Ghica (revolutionary and diplomat, 150th birth anniv); 3l.25, Constantin Cantacuzino (historian, 250th death anniv).

1966. Paintings in National Gallery, Bucharest. Multicoloured.
3391 5b. Type **605** 15 15
3392 10b. "Peasant Girl" (Grigorescu) (vert) 20 15
3393 20b. "Midday Rest" (Rescu) 30 15
3394 55b. "Portrait of a Man" (Van Eyck) (vert) 75 20
3395 1l.55 "The 2nd Class Compartment" (Daumier) 3·75 55
3396 3l.25 "The Blessing" (El Greco) (vert) . . . . . . 4·25 3·75

1966. Aquatic Flora. Multicoloured.
3397 5b. Type **606** 10 10
3398 10b. "Ceratophyllum submersum" 10 10
3399 20b. "Aldrovanda vesiculosa" 10 10
3400 40b. "Callitriche verna" . . 30 10
3401 55b. "Vallisneria spiralis" 20 10
3402 1l. "Elodea canadensis" . . 30 10
3403 1l.55 "Hippuris vulgaris" . . 50 20
3404 3l.25 "Myriophyllum spicatum" (28 × 49½ mm) 2·75 1·10

607 Diagram showing one metre in relation to quadrant of Earth **608** Putna Monastery

1966. Centenary of Metric System in Rumania.
3405 **607** 55b. blue and brown 15 10
3406 – 1l. violet and green . . . 30 20
DESIGN: 1l. Metric abbreviations and globe.

1966. 500th Anniv of Putna Monastery.
3407 **608** 2l. multicoloured 75 30

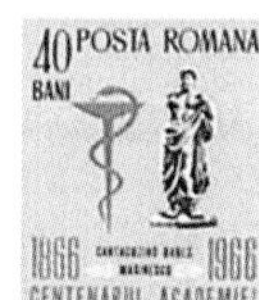

609 "Medicine"

1966. Centenary of Rumanian Academy.
3408 **609** 40b. multicoloured . . . 15 10
3409 – 55b. multicoloured . . . 20 10
3410 – 1l. brown, gold and blue 30 10
3411 – 3l. brown, gold & yellow 1·10 70
DESIGNS—As Type **609**: 55b. "Science" (formula). 22½ × 33½ mm: 1l. Gold medal. 67 × 27 mm: 3l. Ion Radulescu (writer), Mihail Kogalniceanu (historian) and Traian Savulescu (biologist).

610 Crayfish

1966. Crustaceans and Molluscs. Mult.
3412 5b. Type **610** 10 10
3413 10b. Netted nassa (vert) . . 15 10
3414 20b. Marbled rock crab . . 15 10
3415 40b. "Campylaea trizona" (snail) 25 10
3416 55b. Lucorum helix 40 10
3417 1l.35 Mediterranean blue mussel 95 20
3418 1l.75 Stagnant pond snail 1·20 20
3419 3l.25 Swan mussel . . . . . 2·75 1·10

611 Bucharest and Mail Coach

1966. Stamp Day.
3420 **611** 55b.+45b. mult 65 30
No. 3420 is a two-part design arranged horiz, imperf between.

612 "Ursus spelaeus"

1966. Prehistoric Animals.
3421 **612** 5b. blue, brown and green 10 10
3422 – 10b. violet, bistre & green 10 10
3423 – 15b. brown, purple & green 10 10
3424 – 55b. violet, bistre & green 25 10
3425 – 1l.55 blue, brown & grn 1·40 20
3426 – 4l. mauve, bistre & green 2·75 50
ANIMALS: 10b. "Mamuthus trogontherii"; 15b. "Bison priscus"; 55b. "Archidiscodon"; 1l.55, "Megaceros eurycerus". (43 × 27 mm): 4l. "Deinotherium gigantissimum".

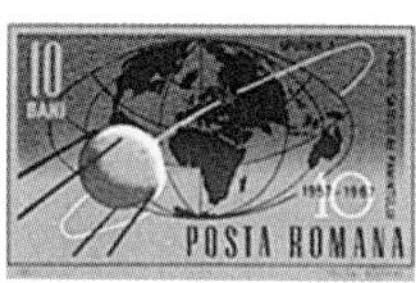

613 "Sputnik 1" orbiting Globe

1967. 10 Years of Space Achievements. Mult.
3427 10b. Type **613** (postage) . . 15 10
3428 20b. Yuri Gagarin and "Vostok 1" 15 10
3429 25b. Valentina Tereshkova ("Vostok 6") 20 10
3430 40b. Andrian Nikolaev and Pavel Popovich ("Vostok 3" and "4") 25 10
3431 55b. Aleksei Leonov in space ("Voskhod 2") . . 35 10
3432 1l.20 "Early Bird" (air) . . 75 20
3433 1l.55 Photo transmission ("Mariner 4") . . . . . 1·00 20
3434 3l.25 Space rendezvous ("Gemini 6" and "7") . . 1·40 40
3435 5l. Space link up ("Gemini 8") . . . . 1·90 1·40

614 Barn Owl

1967. Birds of Prey. Multicoloured.
3442 10b. Type **614** 35 10
3443 20b. Eagle owl 55 10
3444 40b. Saker falcon 55 10
3445 55b. Egyptian vulture . . . 65 10
3446 75b. Osprey 75 10
3447 1l. Griffon vulture . . . . . 1·20 10
3448 1l.20 Lammergeier . . . . 2·20 20
3449 1l.75 Cinereous . . . . . . 2·50 95

615 "Washerwoman" (after I. Steriadi)

1967. Paintings.
3450 – 10b. blue, gold and red 15 10
3451 **615** 20b. green, gold & ochre 20 10
3452 – 40b. red, gold and blue 30 20
3453 – 1l.55 purple, gold & blue 50 25
3454 – 3l.20 brown, gold & brn 1·80 40
3455 – 5l. brown, gold & orange 2·20 1·50
PAINTINGS—VERT: 10b. "Model in Fancy Dress" (I. Andreescu); 40b. "Peasants Weaving" (S. Dimitrescu); 1l.55, "Venus and Cupid" (L. Cranach); 5l. "Haman beseeching Esther" (Rembrandt). HORIZ: 3l.20, "Hercules and the Lion" (Rubens).

616 Woman's Head **618** "Infantryman" (Nicolae Grigorescu)

617 Copper and Silver Coins of 1867

1967. 10th Anniv of C. Brancusi (sculptor). Sculptures.
3456 **616** 5b. brown, yellow and red 10 10
3457 – 10b. black, green & violet 15 10
3458 – 20b. black, green and red 15 10
3459 – 40b. black, red & green 15 20
3460 – 55b. black, olive and blue 30 20
3461 – 1l.20 brown, violet and orange 65 25
3462 – 3l.25 black, green and mauve . . . . 3·25 95
DESIGNS—HORIZ: 10b. Sleeping muse; 40b. "The Kiss"; 3l.25, Gate of Kisses, Targujiu. VERT: 20b. "The Endless Column"; 55b. Seated woman; 1l.20, "Miss Pogany".

1967. Centenary of Rumanian Monetary System.
3463 **617** 55b. multicoloured . . . 20 20
3464 – 1l.20 multicoloured . . . 40 50
DESIGN: 1l.20, Obverse and reverse of modern silver coin (1966).

1967. 90th Anniv of Independence.
3465 **618** 55b. multicoloured . . . 70 75

619 Peasants attacking (after Octav Bancila) **620** "Centaurca pinnatifida"

1967. 60th Anniv of Peasant Rising.
3466 **619** 40b. multicoloured . . . 30 50
3467 – 1l.55 multicoloured . . . 85 1·10
DESIGN—HORIZ: 1l.55, Peasants marching (after S. Luchian).

1967. Carpathian Flora. Multicoloured.
3468 20b. Type **620** 10 15
3469 40b. "Erysimum transsilvanicum" 15 15
3470 55b. "Aquilegia transsilvanica" 20 15
3471 1l.20 Alpine violet 55 20
3472 1l.75 Bellflower 95 25
3473 4l. Mountain avens (horiz) 2·20 1·30

621 Towers, Sibiu

1967. Historic Monuments and International Tourist Year. Multicoloured.
3474 20b. Type **621** 20 15
3475 40b. Castle at Cris 20 15
3476 55b. Wooden church, Plopis 40 15
3477 1l.60 Ruins, Neamtului . . 65 25
3478 1l.75 Mogosoaia Palace, Bucharest 90 25
3479 2l.25 Church, Voronet . . . 1·30 1·30
No. 3479 is horiz, 48½ × 36 mm.

623 "Battle of Marasesti" (E. Stoica)

1967. 50th Anniv of Battles of Marasesti, Marasti and Oituz.
3481 **623** 55b. brown, blue and grey 40 25

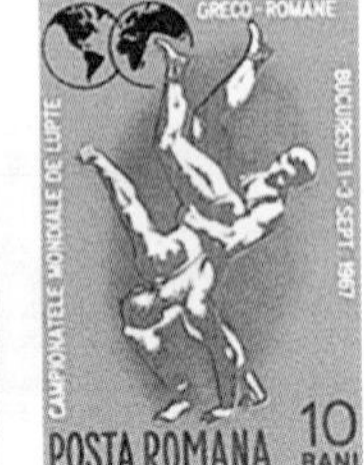

624 Dinu Lipatti (composer and pianist)

625 Wrestling

1967. Cultural Anniversaries.
3482 **624** 10b. violet, blue and black 10 10
3483 – 20b. blue, brown & black 10 10
3484 – 40b. brown, turq & blk 10 10
3485 – 55b. brown, red and black 15 10
3486 – 1l.20 brown, olive & black 25 15
3487 – 1l.75 green, blue & black 75 55
DESIGNS: 10b. Type **624** (50th birth anniv); 20b. Alexandru Orascu (architect, 150th birth anniv); 40b. Grigore Antipa (biologist, birth cent); 55b. Mihail Kogalniceanu (politician and historian, 150th birth anniv); 1l.20, Jonathan Swift (satirist, 300th birth anniv); 1l.75, Marie Curie (physicist, birth cent).

1967. World Wrestling Championships, Bucharest. Designs showing wrestlers and globes.
3488 **625** 10b. multicoloured . . . 10 10
3489 – 20b. mult (horiz) 15 10
3490 – 55b. multicoloured . . . 20 10
3491 – 1l.20 multicoloured . . . 50 15
3492 – 2l. multicoloured (horiz) 90 60

626 Inscription on Globe

1967. International Linguists' Congress, Bucharest.
3493 **626** 1l.60 ultramarine, red and blue 60 20

627 Academy

1967. Centenary of Book Academy, Bucharest.
3494 **627** 55b. grey, brown and blue 40 20

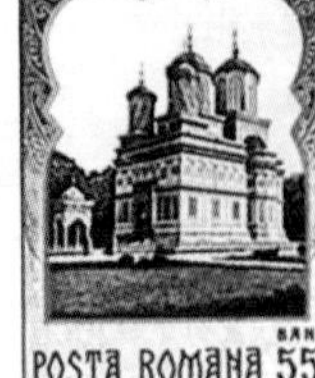

628 Dancing on Ice

629 Curtea de Arges Monastery

1967. Winter Olympic Games, Grenoble. Mult.
3495 20b. Type **628** 10 10
3496 40b. Skiing 20 10
3497 55b. Bobsleighing 30 10
3498 1l. Downhill skiing 50 20
3499 1l.55 Ice hockey 80 20
3500 2l. Games emblem . . . . . 1·10 40
3501 2l.30 Ski jumping . . . . . 1·50 1·10

1967. 450th Anniv of Curtea de Arges Monastery.
3503 **629** 55b. multicoloured . . . 35 25

630 Karl Marx and Title Page

631 Lenin

1967. Centenary of Karl Marx's "Das Kapital".
3504 **630** 40b. black, yellow and red 25 20

1967. 50th Anniv of October Revolution.
3505 **631** 1l.20 black, gold and red 40 15

632 Arms of Rumania

633 Telephone Dial and Map

1967. (a) T**632**.
3506 **632** 40b. blue 20 10
3507 55b. yellow 50 20
3508 1l.60 red 50 10

(b) T **633** and similar designs.
3509 – 5b. green 10 15
3510 – 10b. red 10 15
3511 – 20b. grey 35 15
3512 – 35b. blue 20 15
3513 – 40b. blue 10 15
3514 – 50b. orange 15 15
3515 – 55b. red 20 15
3516 – 60b. brown 35 15
3517 – 1l. green 35 15
3518 – 1l.20 violet 20 15
3519 – 1l.35 blue 70 15
3520 – 1l.50 red 35 15
3521 – 1l.55 brown 35 15
3522 – 1l.75 green 35 15
3523 – 2l. yellow 40 15
3524 – 2l.40 blue 40 15
3525 **633** 3l. turquoise 50 15
3526 – 3l.20 ochre . . . . . . 1·40 15
3527 – 3l.25 blue . . . . 1·60 15
3528 – 4l. mauve . . . . 2·00 15
3529 – 5l. violet . . . . 1·60 15
DESIGNS—23 × 17 mm: 5b. "Carpati" lorry; 20b. Railway Travelling Post Office coach; 35b. Zlin Z-226A Akrobat plane; 60b. Electric parcels truck. As Type **633**: 1l.20, Motorcoach; 1l.35, Mil Mi-4 helicopter; 1l.75, Lakeside highway; 2l. Postal van; 3l.20, Ilyushin Il-18 airliner; 4l. Electric train; 5l. Telex instrument and world map. 17 × 23 mm: 10b. Posthorn and telephone emblem; 40b. Power pylons; 50b. Telephone handset; 55b. Dam. As T **633** but vert: 1l. Diesel-electric train; 1l.50, Trolley-bus; 1l.55, Radio station; 2l.40, T.V. relay station; 3l.25, Liner "Transylvania".
No. 3525 also commemorates the 40th anniv of the automatic telephone service.
For Nos. 3517/29 in smaller format see Nos. 3842/57.

634 "Crossing the River Buzau" (lithograph by Raffet) (½-size illustration)

1967. Stamp Day.
3530 **634** 55b.+45b. blue and ochre 55 30

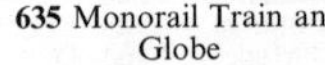

635 Monorail Train and Globe

636 Arms and Industrial Scene

1967. World Fair, Montreal. Multicoloured.
3531 55b. Type **635** 20 10
3532 1l. Expo emblem within atomic symbol 25 10
3533 1l.60 Gold cup and world map 35 10
3534 2l. Expo emblem 55 45

1967. 20th Anniv of Republic. Multicoloured.
3535 40b. Type **636** 15 10
3536 55b. Arms of Rumania . . 15 10
3537 1l.60 Rumanian flag (34 × 48 mm) 40 20
3538 1l.75 Arms and cultural emblems 65 60

637 I.A.R. 817 Flying Ambulance

1968. Air. Rumanian Aviation.
3539 – 40b. multicoloured . . . 10 10
3540 **637** 55b. multicoloured . . . 25 10
3541 – 1l. multicoloured 30 10
3542 – 2l.40 multicoloured . . . 80 40
DESIGNS—VERT: 40b. Antonov An-2 biplane spraying crops; 1l. "Aviasan" emblem and airliner; 2l.40, Mircea Zorileanu (pioneer aviator) and biplane.

638 "Angelica and Medor" (S. Ricci)

1968. Paintings in Rumanian Galleries. Mult.
3543 40b. "Young Woman" (Misu Pop) (vert) 30 20
3544 55b. "Little Girl in Red Scarf" (N. Grigorescu) (vert) 40 20
3545 1l. "Old Nicholas, the Cobza-player" (S. Luchian) (vert) 65 25
3546 1l.60 "Man with Skull" (Dierick Bouts) (vert) . . 90 25
3547 2l.40 Type **638** . . . . . . 1·10 45
3548 3l.20 "Ecce Homo" (Titian) (vert) . . . . 2·50 2·75
See also Nos. 3583/8, 3631/6, 3658/63, 3756/61 and 3779/84.

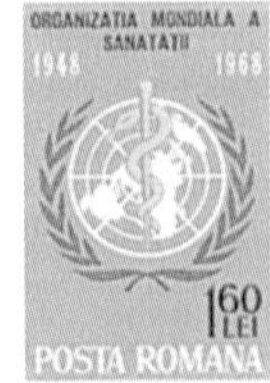

640 Human Rights Emblem

641 W.H.O. Emblem

1968. Human Rights Year.
3551 **640** 1l. multicoloured 55 20

1968. 20th Anniv of W.H.O.
3552 **641** 1l.60 multicoloured . . . 70 20

642 "The Hunter" (after N. Grigorescu)

1968. Hunting Congress, Mamaia.
3553 **642** 1l.60 multicoloured . . . 60 20

643 Pioneers and Liberation Monument

1968. Young Pioneers. Multicoloured.
3554 5b. Type **643** 10 10
3555 40b. Receiving scarves . . . 15 10
3556 55b. With models 20 10
3557 1l. Operating radio sets . . 30 10
3558 1l.60 Folk-dancing 55 20
3559 2l.40 In camp 60 45

644 Prince Mircea

645 Ion Ionescu de la Brad (scholar)

1968. 550th Death Anniv of Prince Mircea (the Old).
3560 **644** 1l.60 multicoloured . . . 70 20

1968. Cultural Anniversaries.
3561 **645** 40b. multicoloured . . . 15 10
3562 – 55b. multicoloured . . . 30 10
PORTRAITS AND ANNIVS: 40b. Type **645** (150th birth anniv); 55b. Emil Racovita (scientist, birth cent).

646 "Pelargonium zonale"

648 Throwing the Javelin

647 "Nicolae Balcescu" (Gheorghe Tattarescu)

1968. Garden Geraniums. Multicoloured.
3563 10b. Type **646** 10 10
3564 20b. "Pelargonium zonale" (orange) 10 10
3565 40b. "Pelargonium zonale" (red) 15 10
3566 55b. "Pelargonium zonale" (pink) 15 10
3567 60b. "Pelargonium grandiflorum" (red) 30 10
3568 1l.20 "Pelargonium peltatum" (red) 30 15
3569 1l.35 "Pelargonium peltatum" (pink) 40 15
3570 1l.60 "Pelargonium grandiflorum" (pink) . . 55 40

1968. 120th Anniv of 1848 Revolution. Paintings. Multicoloured.
3571 55b. Type **647** 20 10
3572 1l.20 "Avram Iancu" (B. Iscovescu) 40 10
3573 1l.60 "Vasile Alecsandri" (N. Livaditti) 80 50

1968. Olympic Games, Mexico. Multicoloured.
3574 10b. Type **648** 10 10
3575 20b. Diving 10 10
3576 40b. Volleyball 15 10
3577 55b. Boxing 20 10
3578 60b. Wrestling 20 10
3579 1l.20 Fencing 35 10
3580 1l.35 Punting 45 20
3581 1l.60 Football 85 35

1968. Paintings in the Fine Arts Museum, Bucarest. Multicoloured.
3583 10b. "The Awakening of Rumania" (G. Tattarescu) (28 × 49 mm) 10 10
3584 20b. "Composition" (Teodorescu Sionion) . . 10 10
3585 35b. "The Judgement of Paris" (H. van Balen) . . 20 10
3586 60b. "The Mystical Betrothal of St. Catherine" (L. Sustris) 35 10
3587 1l.75 "Mary with the Child Jesus" (J. van Bylert) . . 95 20
3588 3l. "The Summer" (J. Jordaens) . . . . . . 1·40 1·10

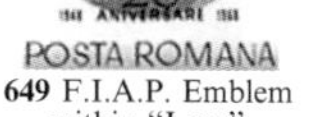

649 F.I.A.P. Emblem within "Lens" **650** Academy and Harp

1968. 20th Anniv of International Federation of Photographic Art (F.I.A.P.).
3589 **649** 1l.60 multicoloured . . . 60 20

1968. Centenary of Georgi Enescu Philharmonic Academy.
3590 **650** 55b. multicoloured . . . 40 15

651 Triumph of Trajan (Roman metope)

1968. Historic Monuments.
3591 **651** 10b. green, blue and red 10 10
3592 – 40b. blue, brown and red 15 10
3593 – 55b. violet, brown & green 20 10
3594 – 1l.20 purple, grey and ochre 35 20
3595 – 1l.55 blue, green & pur 50 20
3596 – 1l.75 brown, bistre and orange 60 40
DESIGNS—HORIZ: 40b. Monastery Church, Moldovita; 55b. Monastery. Church, Cozia; 1l.20, Tower and Church, Tirgoviste; 1l.55, Palace of Culture, Jassy; 1l.75, Corvinus Castle, Hunedoara.

652 Old Bucharest (18th-cent painting) (Illustration reduced. Actual size 76 × 28 mm)

1968. Stamp Day.
3597 **652** 55b.+45b. multicoloured 70 55

653 Mute Swan **655** Neamtz Costume (female)

654 "Entry of Michael the Brave into Alba Julia" (E. Stoica)

1968. Fauna of Nature Reservations. Multicoloured.
3598 10b. Type **653** 30 10
3599 20b. Black-winged stilt . . . 35 10
3600 40b. Common shelduck . . 45 10
3601 55b. Great egret 50 10
3602 60b. Golden eagle 65 10
3603 1l.20 Great bustard . . . . 1·30 20
3604 1l.35 Chamois 55 20
3605 1l.60 European bison . . . 70 30

1968. 50th Anniv of Union of Transylvania with Rumania. Multicoloured.
3606 55b. Type **654** 15 15
3607 1l. "Union Dance" (T. Aman) 25 15
3608 1l.75 "Alba Julia Assembly" 55 35

1968. Provincial Costumes (1st series). Mult.
3610 5b. Type **655** 10 10
3611 40b. Neamtz (male) 10 10
3612 55b. Hunedoara (female) . . 20 10
3613 1l. Hunedoara (male) . . . 35 10
3614 1l.60 Brasov (female) . . . 55 20
3615 2l.40 Brasov (male) 80 65
See also Nos. 3617/22.

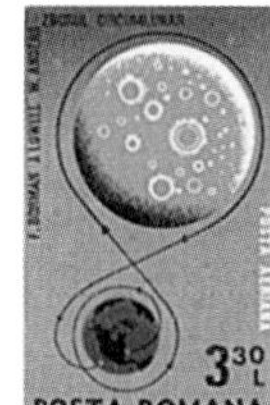

656 Earth, Moon and Orbital Track of "Apollo 8"

1969. Air. Flight of "Apollo 8" around the Moon.
3616 **656** 3l.30 black, silver & blue 1·20 1·10

1969. Provincial Costumes (2nd series). As T **655**. Multicoloured.
3617 5b. Doli (female) 10 10
3618 40b. Doli (male) 10 10
3619 55b. Arges (female) 20 10
3620 1l. Arges (male) 35 10
3621 1l.60 Timisoara (female) . . 60 20
3622 2l.40 Timisoara (male) . . . 90 65

657 Fencing

1969. Sports.
3623 **657** 10b. grey, black & brown 10 10
3624 – 20b. grey, black and violet 10 10
3625 – 40b. grey, black and blue 10 10
3626 – 55b. grey, black and red 20 10
3627 – 1l. grey, black and green 20 10
3628 – 1l.20 grey, black and blue 25 15
3629 – 1l.60 grey, black and red 35 20
3630 – 2l.40 grey, black & green 70 50
DESIGNS: 20b. Throwing the javelin; 40b. Canoeing; 55b. Boxing; 1l. Volleyball; 1l.20, Swimming; 1l.60, Wrestling; 2l.40, Football.

1969. Nude Paintings in the National Gallery. As T **638**. Multicoloured.
3631 10b. "Nude" (C. Tattarescu) 10 10
3632 20b. "Nude" (T. Pallady) 10 10
3633 35b. "Nude" (N. Tonitza) 10 10
3634 60b. "Venus and Cupid" (Flemish School) 30 15
3635 1l.75 "Diana and Endymion" (M. Liberi) 75 45
3636 3l. "The Three Graces" (J. H. von Achen) . . . . 1·70 1·10
SIZES—36 × 49 mm: 10b., 35b., 60b., 1l.75. 27 × 49 mm: 3l. 49 × 36 mm: 20b.

1969. Air. Space Link-up of "Soyuz 4" and "Soyuz 5".
3638 **658** 3l.30 multicoloured . . . 1·70 1·50

658 "Soyuz 4" and "Soyuz 5" **659** I.L.O. Emblem

1969. 50th Anniv of International Labour Office.
3639 **659** 55b. multicoloured . . . 35 15

1969. Inter-European Cultural Economic Co-operation.
3640 **660** 55b. multicoloured . . . 30 40
3641 1l.50 multicoloured . . . 75 80

1969. Postal Ministers' Conference, Bucharest.
3642 **661** 55b. deep blue and blue 25 15

660 Stylized Head **662** Referee introducing Boxers

661 Posthorn

1969. European Boxing Championships, Bucharest. Multicoloured.
3643 35b. Type **662** 10 10
3644 40b. Sparring 15 10
3645 55b. Leading with punch . . 20 10
3646 1l.75 Declaring the winner 70 40

663 "Apollo 9" and Module over Earth

1969. Air. "Apollo" Moon Flights. Multicoloured.
3647 60b. Type **663** 15 10
3648 2l.40 "Apollo 10" and module approaching Moon (vert) 70 20

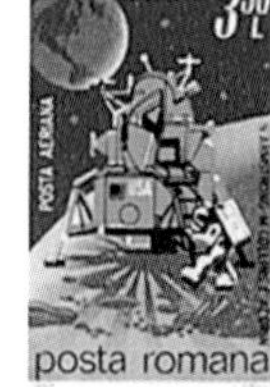

664 Lesser Purple Emperor **665** Astronaut and Module on Moon

1969. Butterflies and Moths. Multicoloured.
3649 5b. Type **664** 10 10
3650 10b. Willow-herb hawk moth 10 10
3651 20b. Eastern pale clouded yellow 10 10
3652 40b. Large tiger moth . . . 15 10
3653 55b. Pallas's fritillary . . . 20 10
3654 1l. Jersey tiger moth 40 10
3655 1l.20 Orange-tip 55 20
3656 2l.40 Meleager's blue . . . 1·10 75

1969. Air. First Man on the Moon.
3657 **665** 3l.30 multicoloured . . . 1·20 1·20

1969. Paintings in the National Gallery, Bucharest. Multicoloured. As T **638**.
3658 10b. "Venetian Senator" (School of Tintoretto) . . 10 10
3659 20b. "Sofia Kretzulescu" (G. Tattarescu) 10 10
3660 35b. "Philip IV" (Velasquez) 15 10
3661 35b. "Man Reading" (Memling) 30 10
3662 1l.75 "Lady D'Aguesseau" (Vigee-Lebrun) 55 20
3663 3l. "Portrait of a Woman" (Rembrandt) . . . . . . 1·40 80

666 Communist Flag **667** Symbols of Learning

1969. 10th Rumanian Communist Party Congress.
3665 **666** 55b. multicoloured . . . 30 15

1969. National "Economic Achievements" Exhibition, Bucharest. Multicoloured.
3666 35b. Type **667** 10 10
3667 40b. Symbols of Agriculture and Science 10 10
3668 1l.75 Symbols of Industry 60 15

668 Liberation Emblem **669** Juggling on Trick-cycle

1969. 25th Anniv of Liberation. Multicoloured.
3669 10b. Type **668** 10 10
3670 55b. Crane and trowel . . . 10 10
3671 60b. Flags on scaffolding . . 15 10

1969. Rumanian State Circus. Multicoloured.
3672 10b. Type **669** 10 10
3673 20b. Clown 10 10
3674 35b. Trapeze artists 15 10
3675 60b. Equestrian act 20 10
3676 1l.75 High-wire act 45 15
3677 3l. Performing tiger . . . . 1·10 50

670 Forces' Memorial

1969. Army Day and 25th Anniv of People's Army.
3678 **670** 55b. black, gold and red 25 15

671 Electric Train (1965) and Steam Locomotive "Calugareni" (1869)

1969. Centenary of Rumanian Railways.
3679 **671** 55b. multicoloured . . . 40 20

672 "Courtyard" (M. Bouquet) (¾-size illustration)

1969. Stamp Day.
3680 **672** 55b.+45b. multicoloured 55 60

673 Branesti Mask **674** "Apollo 12" above Moon

1969. Folklore Masks. Multicoloured.
3681 40b. Type **673** 15 10
3682 55b. Tudora mask 15 10
3683 1l.55 Birsesti mask 40 20
3684 1l.75 Rudaria mask 55 30

1969. Moon Landing of "Apollo 12".
3685 **674** 1l.50 multicoloured . . . 40 60

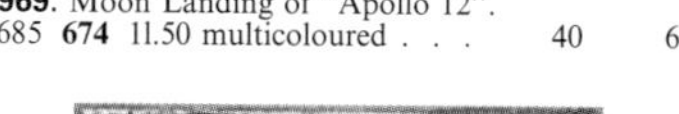

675 "Three Kings" (Voronet Monastery)

1969. Frescoes from Northern Moldavian Monasteries (1st series). Multicoloured.
3686 10b. Type **675** 10 10
3687 20b. "Three Kings" (Sucevita) 10 10
3688 35b. "Holy Child in Manger" (Voronet) . . . 15 10
3689 60b. "Ship" (Sucevita) (vert) 25 10
3690 1l.75 "Walled City" (Moldovita) 55 25
3691 3l. "Pastoral Scene" (Voronet) (vert) . . . . . 1·20 70
See also Nos. 3736/42 and 3872/8.

676 "Old Mother Goose", Capra

678 Small Pasque Flower

677 Players and Emblem

1969. New Year. Children's Celebrations. Mult.
3692 40b. Type **676** 15 10
3693 55b. Decorated tree, Sorcova 55 10
3694 1l.50 Drummers, Buhaiul . . 40 10
3695 2l.40 Singer and bellringer, Plugusorul 65 40

1970. World Ice Hockey Championships (Groups B and C), Bucharest. Multicoloured.
3696 20b. Type **677** 10 10
3697 55b. Goalkeeper 15 10
3698 1l.20 Two players 25 10
3699 2l.40 Goalmouth melee . . 60 35

1970. Flowers. Multicoloured.
3700 5b. Type **678** 10 10
3701 10b. Yellow pheasant's-eye 10 10
3702 20b. Musk thistle 10 10
3703 40b. Dwarf almond 10 10
3704 55b. Dwarf bearded iris . . 10 10
3705 1l. Flax 20 10
3706 1l.20 Sage 30 15
3707 2l.40 Peony . . . . 1·40 65

679 Japanese Woodcut

681 Lenin

680 B.A.C. One Eleven Series 475 Jetliner and Silhouettes of Aircraft

1970. World Fair, Osaka, Japan. Expo 70. Mult.
3714 20b. Type **679** 15 15
3715 1l. Japanese pagoda (29 × 92 mm) 45 35

1970. 50th Anniv of Rumanian Civil Aviation. Multicoloured.
3717 60b. Type **680** 25 10
3718 2l. Tail of B.A.C. One Eleven Series 475 and control tower at Otopeni Airport, Bucharest . . . 55 25

1970. Birth Centenary of Lenin.
3719 **681** 40b. multicoloured . . . 20 15

682 "Camille" (Monet) and Maximum Card

683 "Prince Alexander Cuza" (Szathmary)

1970. Maximafila Franco–Rumanian Philatelic Exn, Bucharest.
3720 **682** 1l.50 multicoloured . . . 65 25

1970. 150th Birth Anniv of Prince Alexandru Cuza.
3721 **683** 55b. multicoloured . . . 35 20

684 "Co-operation" Map

685 Victory Monument, Bucharest

1970. Inter-European Cultural and Economic Co-operation.
3722 **684** 40b. green, brown & black 35 40
3723 1l.50 blue, brown & blk 75 80

1970. 25th Anniv of Liberation.
3724 **685** 55b. multicoloured . . . 30 20

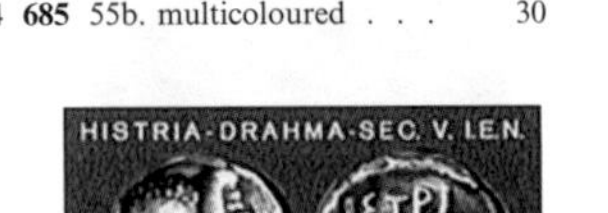

686 Greek Silver Drachma, 5th cent B.C.

1970. Ancient Coins.
3725 **686** 10b. black and blue . . . 10 10
3726 – 20b. black and red . . . 10 10
3727 – 35b. bronze and green 10 10
3728 – 60b. black and brown . . 15 10
3729 – 1l.75 black and blue . . 60 10
3730 – 3l. black and red . . . . 1·00 40
DESIGNS—HORIZ: 20b. Getic-Dacian silver didrachm, 2nd—1st-cent B.C.; 35b. Copper sestertius of Trajan, 106 A.D.; 60b. Mircea ducat, 1400; 1l.75, Silver groschen of Stephen the Great, 1460. VERT: 3l. Brasov klippe-thaler, 1601.

687 Footballers and Ball

1970. World Cup Football Championship, Mexico.
3731 **687** 40b. multicoloured . . . 10 10
3732 – 55b. multicoloured . . . 15 10
3733 – 1l.75 multicoloured . . . 40 20
3734 – 3l.30 multicoloured . . . 80 50
DESIGNS: Nos. 3732/4, various football scenes as Type **687**.

1970. Frescoes from Northern Moldavian Monasteries (2nd series). As T **675**. Mult.
3736 10b. "Prince Petru Rares and Family" (Moldovita) 10 10
3737 20b. "Metropolitan Grigore Rosca" (Voronet) (28 × 48 mm) 10 10
3738 40b. "Alexander the Good and Family" (Sucevita) 15 10
3739 55b. "The Last Judgement" (Voronet) (vert) 25 10
3740 1l.75 "The Last Judgement" (Voronet) (different) . . . 65 25
3741 3l. "St. Anthony" (Voronet) 1·40 70

688 "Apollo 13" Spashdown

689 Engels

1970. Air. Space Flight of "Apollo 13".
3743 **688** 1l.50 multicoloured . . . 1·50 95

1970. 150th Birth Anniv of Friedrich Engels.
3744 **689** 1l.50 multicoloured . . . 50 15

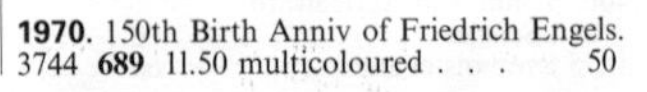

690 Exhibition Hall

1970. National Events. Multicoloured.
3745 35b. "Iron Gates" Dam . . 10 10
3746 55b. Freighter and flag . . . 30 10
3747 1l.50 Type **690** 30 10
EVENTS: 35b. Danube navigation projects; 55b. 75th anniv of Rumanian Merchant Marine; 1l.50, 1st International Fair, Bucharest.

691 New Headquarters Building

1970. New U.P.U. Headquarters Building, Berne.
3748 **691** 1l.50 blue and ultramarine 55 15

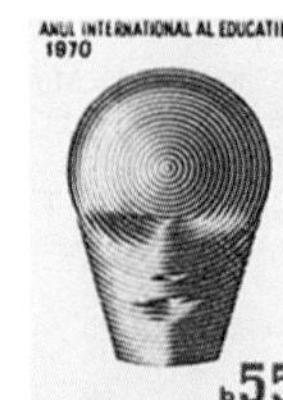

692 Education Year Emblem

693 "Iceberg"

1970. International Education Year.
3749 **692** 55b. plum, black and red 30 20

1970. Roses. Multicoloured.
3750 20b. Type **693** 10 10
3751 35b. "Wiener Charme" . . 10 10
3752 55b. "Pink Lustre" 15 10
3753 1l. "Piccadilly" 45 10
3754 1l.50 "Orange Delbard" . . 55 10
3755 2l.40 "Sibelius" 90 75

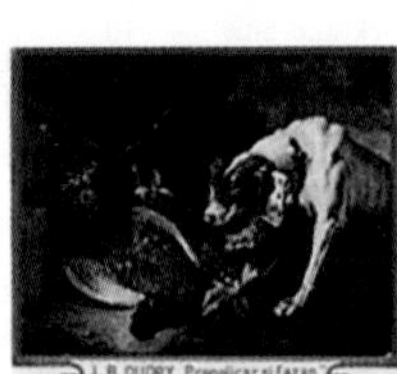

694 "Spaniel and Pheasant" (J. B. Oudry)

695 Refugee Woman and Child

1970. Paintings in Rumanian Galleries. Mult.
3756 10b. "The Hunt" (D. Brandi) (38 × 50 mm) 10 10
3757 20b. Type **694** 10 10
3758 35b. "The Hunt" (Jan Fyt) (38 × 50 mm) 10 10
3759 60b. "After the Chase" (Jordaens) (As T **694**) . . 25 10
3760 1l.75 "The Game Dealer" (F. Snyders) (50 × 38 mm) 60 20
3761 3l. "The Hunt" (A. de Gryeff) (As T **694**) . . . 1·20 70

1970. Danube Flood Victims (1st issue).
3763 **695** 55b. black, blue and green (postage) . . . 15 10
3764 – 1l.50 multicoloured . . . 35 20
3765 – 1l.75 multicoloured . . . 75 70
3766 – 60b. black, drab and blue (air) 35 10
DESIGNS: 60b. Helicopter rescue; 1l.50, Red Cross post; 1l.75, Building reconstruction.
See also No. 3777.

696 U.N. Emblem

698 Beethoven

697 Arab Horse

1970. 25th Anniv of United Nations.
3767 **696** 1l.50 multicoloured . . . 35 20

1970. Horses. Multicoloured.
3768 20b. Type **697** 10 10
3769 35b. American trotter . . . 10 10
3770 55b. Ghidran 10 10
3771 1l. Hutul 30 10
3772 1l.50 Thoroughbred 45 20
3773 2l.40 Lippizaner . . . . . . 1·60 80

1970. Birth Bicentenary of Ludwig van Beethoven (composer).
3774 **698** 55b. multicoloured . . . 60 20

699 "Mail-cart in the Snow" (E. Volkers) (½-size illustration)

1970. Stamp Day.
3775 **699** 55b.+45b. mult 55 60

700 Henri Coanda's Model Airplane

1970. Air. 60th Anniv of First Experimental Turbine-powered Airplane.
3776 **700** 60b. multicoloured . . . 55 20

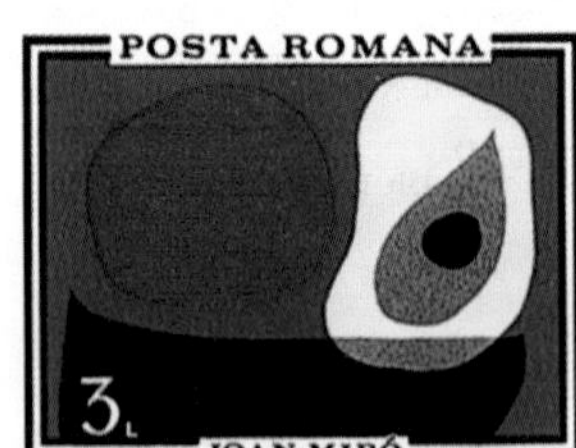

701 "The Flood" (abstract, Joan Miro)

1970. Danube Flood Victims (2nd issue).
3777 **701** 3l. multicoloured . . . . 1·60 1·60

702 "Sight" (G. Coques)

1970. Paintings from the Bruckenthal Museum, Sibiu. Multicoloured.
3779 10b. Type **702** 10 10
3780 20b. "Hearing" 10 10
3781 35b. "Smell" 10 10
3782 60b. "Taste" 20 10
3783 1l.75 "Touch" 40 15
3784 3l. Bruckenthal Museum . . 1·00 65
Nos. 3779/84 show a series of pictures by Coques entitled "The Five Senses".

703 Vladimirescu (after Theodor Aman)

705 Alsatian

704 "Three Races"

1971. 150th Death Anniv of Tudor Vladimirescu (Wallachian revolutionary).
3786 **703** 1l.50 multicoloured . . . 50 20

1971. Racial Equality Year.
3787 **704** 1l.50 multicoloured . . . 55 20

1971. Dogs. Multicoloured.
3788 20b. Type **705** 10 10
3789 35b. Bulldog 10 10
3790 55b. Fox terrier 15 10
3791 1l. Setter 40 10
3792 1l.50 Cocker spaniel 60 20
3793 2l.40 Poodle . . . . 1·90 1·20

706 "Luna 16" leaving Moon

707 Proclamation of the Commune

1971. Air. Moon Missions of "Luna 16" and "Luna 17". Multicoloured.
3794 3l.30 Type **706** . . . . . . 1·70 95
3795 3l.30 "Lunokhod 1" on Moon . . . . 1·70 95

1971. Centenary of Paris Commune.
3796 **707** 40b. multicoloured . . . 30 15

708 Astronaut and Moon Trolley

1971. Air. Moon Mission of "Apollo 14".
3797 **708** 3l.30 multicoloured . . . 1·10 1·00

709 "Three Fists" Emblem and Flags

710 "Toadstool" Rocks, Babele

1971. Trade Union Congress, Bucharest.
3798 **709** 55b. multicoloured . . . 30 15

1971. Tourism. Multicoloured.
3799 10b. Gorge, Cheile Bicazului (vert) 10 10
3800 40b. Type **710** 10 10
3801 55b. Winter resort, Poiana Brasov 15 10
3802 1l. Fishing punt and tourist launch, Danube delta . . 40 10
3803 1l.50 Hotel, Baile Sovata . . 55 10
3804 2l.40 Venus, Jupiter and Neptune Hotels, Black Sea (77 × 29 mm) 85 55

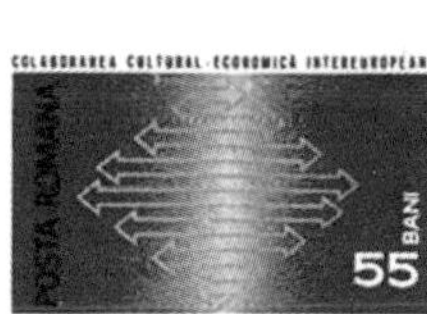

711 "Arrows"

712 Museum Building

1971. Inter-European Cultural Economic Co-operation. Multicoloured.
3805 55b. Type **711** 85 90
3806 1l.75 Stylized map of Europe . . . . 1·30 1·30

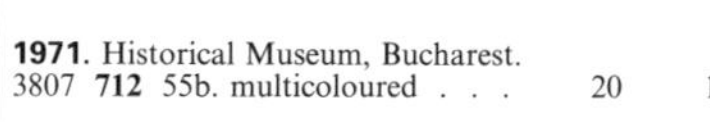

1971. Historical Museum, Bucharest.
3807 **712** 55b. multicoloured . . . 20 15

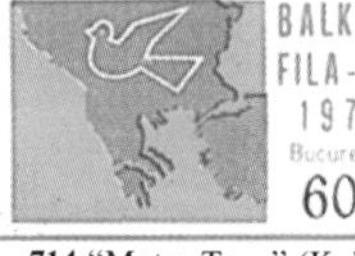

713 "The Secret Printing-press" (S. Szonyi)

714 "Motra Tone" (Kole Idromeno)

1971. 50th Anniv of Rumanian Communist Party. Multicoloured.
3808 35b. Type **713** 10 10
3809 40b. Emblem and red flags (horiz) 10 10
3810 55b. "The Builders" (A. Anastasiu) 15 10

1971. "Balkanfila III". International Stamp Exhibition, Bucharest. Multicoloured.
3811 1l.20+60b. Type **714** . . . 60 65
3812 1l.20+60b. "Maid" (Vladimir Dimitrov-Maistora) 60 65
3813 1l.20+60b. "Rosa Botzaris" (Joseph Stieler) 60 65
3814 1l.20+60b. "Portrait of a Lady" (Katarina Ivanovic) 60 65
3815 1l.20+60b. "Agreseanca" (C. Popp de Szathmary) 60 65
3816 1l.20+60b. "Woman in Modern Dress" (Calli Ibrahim) 60 65

Each stamp has a premium-carrying "tab" as shown in Type **714**.

715 Pomegranate

1971. Flowers. Multicoloured.
3818 20b. Type **715** 10 10
3819 35b. "Calceolus speciosum" 10 10
3820 55b. "Life jagra" 10 10
3821 1l. Blood-drop emlets . . . 30 10
3822 1l.50 Dwarf morning glory 45 20
3823 2l.40 "Phyllocactus phyllanthoides" (horiz) . . 1·00 30

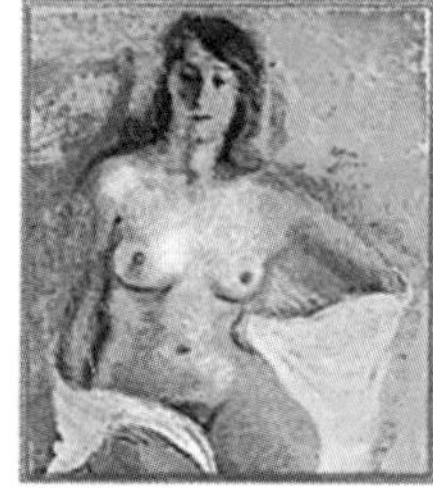

716 "Nude" (J. Iser)

1971. Paintings of Nudes. Multicoloured.
3824 10b. Type **716** 10 10
3825 20b. "Nude" (C. Ressu) (29 × 50 mm) 10 10
3826 35b. "Nude" (N. Grigorescu) 10 10
3827 60b. "Odalisque" (Delacroix) (horiz) 10 10
3828 1l.75 "Nude in a Landscape" (Renoir) . . 60 25
3829 3l. "Venus and Cupid" (Il Vecchio) (horiz) . . . . . 1·20 65

718 Astronauts and Lunar Rover on Moon

1971. Air. Moon Flight of "Apollo 15".
3833 **718** 1l.50 multicoloured (blue background) . . . . . 1·20 1·30

No. 3833 also exists imperforate, with background colour changed to green, from a restricted printing.

719 "Fishing Boats" (M. W. Arnold)

1971. Marine Paintings. Multicoloured.
3835 10b. "Coastal Storm" (B. Peters) 10 10
3836 20b. "Seascape" (I. Backhuysen) 10 10
3837 35b. "Boat in Stormy Seas" (A. van de Eertvelt) . . . 10 10
3838 60b. Type **719** 20 10
3839 1l.75 "Seascape" (I. K. Aivazovsky) 50 20
3840 3l. "Fishing boats, Braila" (J. A. Steriadi) . . . . . 1·20 50

1971. As Nos. 3517/29 and three new designs but in smaller format, 17 × 23 or 23 × 17 mm.
3842 1l. green 45 15
3843 1l.20 violet 25 15
3844 1l.35 blue 75 15
3845 1l.50 red 35 15
3846 1l.55 brown 35 15
3847 1l.75 green 35 15
3848 2l. yellow 40 15
3849 2l.40 blue 50 15
3850 3l. blue 60 15
3851 3l.20 brown 50 15
3852 3l.25 blue 75 15
3853 3l.60 blue 80 15
3854 4l. mauve . . . . 1·80 15
3855 4l.80 blue . . . . 1·00 15
3856 5l. violet . . . . 1·30 15
3857 6l. mauve . . . . 1·50 15

NEW DESIGNS—VERT: 3l.60, Clearing letter box; 4l.80, Postman on round; 6l. Postal Ministry, Bucharest.

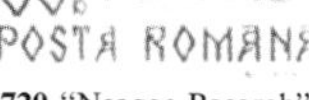

720 "Neagoe Basarab" (fresco, Curtea de Arges)

721 "T. Pallady" (self-portrait)

1971. 450th Death Anniv of Prince Neagoe Basarab, Regent of Wallachia.
3858 **720** 60b. multicoloured . . . 25 15

1971. Artists' Anniversaries.
3859 **721** 40b. multicoloured . . . 10 10
3860 – 55b. black, stone and gold 10 10
3861 – 1l.50 black, stone & gold 25 10
3862 – 2l.40 multicoloured . . . 55 30

DESIGNS (self-portraits: 40b. Type **721** (birth centenary); 55b. Benevenuto Cellini (400th death anniv); 1l.50, Jean Watteau (250th death anniv); 2l.40, Albrecht Durer (500th birth anniv).

722 Persian Text and Seal

723 Figure Skating

1971. 2500th Anniv of Persian Empire.
3863 **722** 55b. multicoloured . . . 35 15

1971. Winter Olympic Games, Sapporo, Japan (1972). Multicoloured.
3864 10b. Type **723** 10 15
3865 20b. Ice-hockey 10 15
3866 40b. Biathlon 10 15
3867 55b. Bobsleighing 10 15
3868 1l.75 Downhill skiing . . . 50 25
3869 3l. Games emblem . . . . . 1·00 60

724 "Lady with Letter" (Sava Hentia)

1971. Stamp Day.
3871 **724** 1l.10+90b. mult 70 70

1971. Frescoes from Northern Moldavian Monasteries (3rd series). As T **675**. Multicoloured.
3872 10b. "St. George and The Dragon" (Moldovita) (vert) 10 10
3873 20b. "Three Kings and Angel" (Moldovita) (vert) 10 10
3874 40b. "The Crucifixion" (Moldovita) (vert) 10 10
3875 55b. "Trial" (Voronet) (vert) 10 10
3876 1l.75 "Death of a Martyr" (Voronet) (vert) 60 20
3877 3l. "King and Court" (Arborea) . . . . 1·20 85

725 Matei Millo (dramatist, 75th death anniv)

726 Magellan and Ships (450th death anniv)

1971. Famous Rumanians. Multicoloured.
3879 55b. Type **725** 15 10
3880 1l. Nicolae Iorga (historian, birth cent) 20 10

1971. Scientific Anniversaries.
3881 **726** 40b. mauve, blue & green 35 10
3882 – 55b. blue, green and lilac 10 10
3883 – 1l. multicoloured 25 10
3884 – 1l.50 green, blue & brn 30 15

DESIGNS AND ANNIVERSARIES: 55b. Kepler and observatory (400th birth anniv); 1l. Gagarin, rocket and Globe (10th anniv of first manned space flight); 1l.50, Lord Rutherford and atomic symbol (birth cent).

727 Lynx Cubs

1972. Young Wild Animals. Multicoloured.
3885 20b. Type **727** 10 30
3886 35b. Red fox cubs 10 30
3887 55b. Roe deer fawns 20 30
3888 1l. Wild piglets 45 15
3889 1l.50 Wolf cubs 80 15
3890 2l.40 Brown bear cubs . . . 2·50 95

728 U.T.C. Emblem

730 Stylized Map of Europe

729 Wrestling

1972. 50th Anniv of Communist Youth Union (U.T.C.).
3891 **728** 55b. multicoloured . . . 25 15

1972. Olympic Games, Munich (1st issue). Mult.
3892 10b. Type **729** 10 10
3893 20b. Canoeing 10 10
3894 55b. Football 10 10
3895 1l.55 High-jumping 35 10
3896 2l.90 Boxing 60 10
3897 6l.70 Volleyball . . . . . . 1·60 85
See also Nos. 3914/19 and 3926.

1972. Inter-European Cultural and Economic Co-operation.
3899 **730** 1l.75 gold, black & mve 1·10 85
3900 – 2l.90 gold, black & green 1·30 1·10
DESIGN: 2l.90, "Crossed arrows" symbol.

731 Astronauts in Lunar Rover

732 Modern Trains and Symbols

1972. Air. Moon Flight of "Apollo 16".
3901 **731** 3l. blue, green and pink 1·40 1·20

1972. 50th Anniv of International Railway Union.
3902 **732** 55b. multicoloured . . . 45 20

734 "Paeonia romanica"

1972. Scarce Rumanian Flowers.
3904 **734** 20b. multicoloured . . . 10 10
3905 – 40b. purple, green & brown 10 10
3906 – 55b. brown and blue . . 20 10
3907 – 60b. red, green and light green 20 10
3908 – 1l.35 multicoloured . . . 45 10
3909 – 2l.90 multicoloured . . . 95 35

DESIGNS: 40b. "Dianthus callizonus"; 55b. Edelweiss; 60b. Vanilla orchid; 1l.35, "Narcissus stellaris"; 2l.90, Lady's slipper.

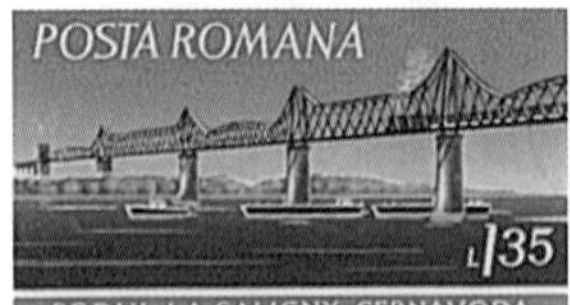

735 Saligny Bridge, Cernavoda

1972. Danube Bridges. Multicoloured.
3910 1l.35 Type **735** 50 10
3911 1l.75 Giurgeni Bridge, Vadul Oii 30 15
3912 2l.75 Friendship Bridge, Giurgiu–Ruse (Bulgaria) 2·50 25

736 North Railway Station, Bucharest, 1872

1972. Cent of North Railway Station, Bucharest.
3913 **736** 55b. multicoloured . . . 45 20

737 Water-polo

1972. Olympic Games, Munich (2nd issue). Mult.
3914 10b. Type **737** 10 10
3915 20b. Pistol-shooting 15 10
3916 55b. Throwing the discus . . 15 10
3917 1l.55 Gymnastics 35 10
3918 2l.75 Canoeing 85 20
3919 6l.40 Fencing . . . . 1·60 90

738 Rotary Stamp-printing Press

740 Runner with Torch

739 "E. Stoenescu" (Stefan Popescu)

1972. Centenary of State Stamp-printing Works.
3921 **738** 55b. multicoloured . . . 30 15

1972. Rumanian Art. Portraits. Multicoloured.
3922 55b. Type **739** 10 10
3923 1l.75 Self-portrait (Octav Bancila) 20 10
3924 2l.90 Self-portrait (Gheorghe Petrascu) 40 10
3925 6l.50 Self-portrait (Ion Andreescu) 85 35

1972. Olympic Games, Munich (3rd issue). Olympic Flame.
3926 **740** 55b. purple & blue on silver 45 20

741 Aurel Vlaicu, his Airplane No. 1 "Crazy Fly" and Silhouette of Boeing 707 Jetliner

1972. Air. Rumanian Aviation Pioneers. Mult.
3927 60b. Type **741** 15 10
3928 3l. Traian Vuia, Vuia No. 1 and silhouette of Boeing 707 jetliner 80 40

742 Cluj Cathedral

743 Satu Mare

1972.
3929 **742** 1l.85 violet (postage) . . 25 10
3930 – 2l.75 grey 35 15
3931 – 3l.35 red 45 10
3932 – 3l.45 green 50 10
3933 – 5l.15 blue 70 10
3934 – 5l.60 blue 75 10
3935 – 6l.20 mauve 80 10
3936 – 6l.40 brown . . . . . . 1·00 10
3937 – 6l.80 red . . . . 1·00 10
3938 – 7l.05 black . . . . . . 1·10 10
3939 – 8l.45 red . . . . 1·10 10
3940 – 9l.05 green . . . . . . 1·30 10
3941 – 9l.10 blue . . . . 1·30 10
3942 – 9l.05 green . . . . . . 1·20 10
3943 – 10l. brown . . . . . . 1·30 10
3944 – 11l.90 blue . . . . . . 1·50 15
3945 – 12l.75 violet . . . . . . 1·80 15
3946 – 13l.30 red . . . . 2·00 15
3947 – 16l.20 green . . . . . . 2·50 15
3948 – 14l.60 blue (air) . . . . 3·00 30
DESIGNS—HORIZ: (As Type **742**): 2l.75, Sphinx Rock, Mt. Bucegi; 3l.45, Sinaia Castle; 5l.15, Hydro-electric power station, Arges; 6l.40, Hunidoara Castle; 6l.80, Bucharest Polytechnic complex; 9l.05, Coliseum, Sarmisegtetuza; 9l.10, Hydro-electric power station, Iron Gates. (29 × 21 mm): 11l.90, Palace of the Republic, Bucharest; 13l.30, City Gate, Alba Julia; 14l.60, Otopeni Airport, Bucharest. VERT: (As Type **742**): 3l.35, Heroes' Monument, Bucharest; 5l.60, Iasi-Biserica; 6l.20, Bran Castle; 7l.05, Black Church, Brasova; 8l.45, Atheneum, Bucharest; 9l.85, Decebal's statue, Cetatea Deva. (20 × 30 mm): 10l. City Hall Tower, Sibiu; 12l.75, T.V. Building, Bucharest; 16l.20, Clock Tower, Sighisoara.

1972. Millenium of Satu Mare.
3949 **743** 55b. multicoloured . . . 30 15

744 Davis Cup on Racquet

1972. Final of Davis Cup Men's Team Tennis Championship, Bucharest.
3950 **744** 2l.75 multicoloured . . . 85 35

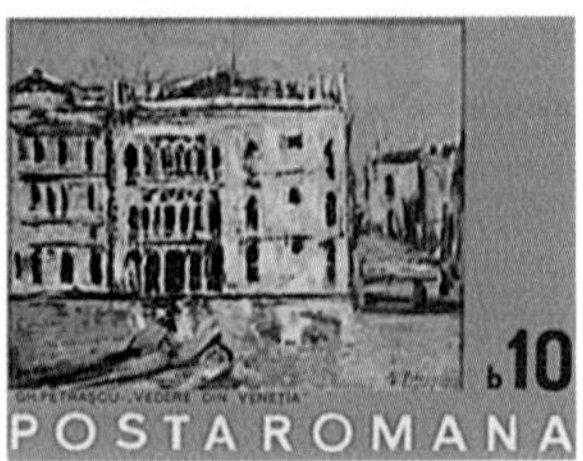

745 "Venice" (Gheorghe Petrascu)

1972. U.N.E.S.C.O. "Save Venice" Campaign. Paintings of Venice. Multicoloured.
3951 10b. Type **745** 10 15
3952 20b. Gondolas (N. Darascu) 10 15
3953 55b. Palace (Petrascu) . . . 15 15
3954 1l.55 Bridge (Marius Bunescu) 40 15
3955 2l.75 Palace (Darascu) (vert) 95 70
3956 6l.40 Canal (Bunesca) . . . 2·40 1·00

746 Fencing and Bronze Medal

748 Flags and "25"

747 "Travelling Romanies" (E. Volkers) (⅔-size illustration)

1972. Munich Olympic Games Medals. Mult.
3958 10b. Type **746** 10 15
3959 20b. Handball and Bronze Medal 10 10
3960 35b. Boxing and Silver Medal 15 10
3961 1l.45 Hurdling and Silver Medal 35 10
3962 2l.75 Shooting, Silver and Bronze Medals 70 25
3963 6l.20 Wrestling and two Gold Medals . . . . . . 1·80 80

1972. Stamp Day.
3965 **747** 1l.10+90b. mult 80 60

1972. 25th Anniv of Proclamation of Republic. Multicoloured.
3966 55b. Type **748** 15 10
3967 1l.20 Arms and "25" 40 15
3968 1l.75 Industrial scene and "25" 35 15

749 "Apollo 1", "2" and "3"

750 European Bee Eater

1972. "Apollo" Moon Flights. Multicoloured.
3969 10b. Type **749** 20 10
3970 35b. Grissom, Chaffee and White 20 10
3971 40b. "Apollo 4, 5, 6" . . . 30 10
3972 55b. "Apollo 7, 8" 40 10
3973 1l. "Apollo 9, 10" 55 10
3974 1l.20 "Apollo 11, 12" . . . 75 10
3975 1l.85 "Apollo 13, 14" . . . 95 15
3976 2l.75 "Apollo 15, 16" . . . 1·70 15
3977 3l.60 "Apollo 17" . . . . . 2·40 55

1973. Protection of Nature. Multicoloured. (a) Birds.
3979 1l.40 Type **750** 70 15
3980 1l.85 Red-breasted goose . . 85 20
3981 2l.75 Peduline tit . . . . . 1·20 40

(b) Flowers.
3982 1l.40 Globe flower 25 10
3983 1l.85 Martagon lily 30 30
3984 2l.75 Gentian 40 30

751 Copernicus

752 Suceava Costume (female)

1973. 500th Birth Anniv of Copernicus (astronomer).
3985 **751** 2l.75 multicoloured . . . 80 35

1973. Regional Costumes. Multicoloured.
3986 10b. Type **752** 10 15
3987 40b. Suceava (male) 10 15
3988 55b. Harghila (female) . . . 10 15
3989 1l.75 Harghila (male) . . . 30 15
3990 2l.75 Gorj (female) 50 20
3991 6l.40 Gorj (male) . . . . . 1·00 70

753 Dimitrie Paciurea (sculptor) **754** Map of Europe

1973. Anniversaries. Multicoloured.
3992 10b. Type **753** (birth centenary) 10 10
3993 40b. Ioan Slavici (writer, 125th birth anniv) 10 10
3994 55b. Gheorghe Lazar (educationist, death cent) 10 10
3995 6l.40 Alexandru Flechtenmacher (composer, birth cent) 1·50 60

1973. Inter-European Cultural and Economic Co-operation.
3996 **754** 3l.35 gold, blue & purple 90 85
3997 – 3l.60 gold and purple 1·10 1·20
DESIGN: 3l.60, Emblem.

756 Hand with Hammer and Sickle **757** W.M.O. Emblem and Weather Satellite

1973. Anniversaries. Multicoloured.
3999 40b. Type **756** 15 20
4000 55b. Flags and bayonets 25 20
4001 1l.75 Prince Cuza 55 20
EVENTS: 40b. 25th anniv of Rumanian Workers and Peasant Party; 55b. 40th anniv of National Anti-Fascist Committee; 1l.75, Death cent of Prince Alexandru Cuza.

1973. Centenary of W.M.O.
4002 **757** 2l. multicoloured 60 20

758 "Dimitri Ralet" (anon) **759** Prince Dimitri Cantemir

1973. "Socfilex III" Stamp Exhibition, Bucharest. Portrait Paintings. Multicoloured.
4003 40b. Type **758** 10 10
4004 60b. "Enacheta Vacarescu" (A. Chladek) 10 10
4005 1l.55 "Dimitri Aman" (C. Lecca) 20 10
4006 4l.+2l. "Barbat at his Desk" (B. Iscovescu) 1·20 60

1973. 300th Birth Anniv of Dimitri Cantemir, Prince of Moldavia (writer). Multicoloured.
4008 **759** 1l.75 multicoloured 50 25

760 Fibular Brooches

1973. Treasures of Pietroasa. Multicoloured.
4010 10b. Type **760** 10 15
4011 20b. Golden figurine and bowl (horiz) 10 15
4012 55b. Gold oil flask 10 15
4013 1l.55 Brooch and bracelets (horiz) 45 15
4014 2l.75 Gold platter 65 20
4015 6l.80 Filgree cup holder (horiz) 1·40 70

762 Oboga Jar **763** "Postilion" (A. Verona)

1973. Rumanian Ceramics. Multicoloured.
4018 10b. Type **762** 10 10
4019 20b. Vama dish and jug 10 10
4020 55b. Maginea bowl 10 10
4021 1l.55 Sibiu Saschiz jug and dish 35 10
4022 2l.75 Pisc pot and dish 55 20
4023 6l.80 Oboga "bird" vessel 1·60 45

1973. Stamp Day.
4024 **763** 1l.10+90b. mult 60 65

764 "Textile Workers" (G. Saru) **765** Town Hall, Craiova

1973. Paintings showing Workers. Multicoloured.
4025 10b. Type **764** 10 10
4026 20b. "Construction Site" (M. Bunescu) (horiz) 10 10
4027 55b. "Shipyard Workers" (H. Catargi) (horiz) 10 10
4028 1l.55 "Working Man" (H. Catargi) 20 10
4029 2l.75 "Miners" (A. Phoebus) 40 15
4030 6l.80 "The Spinner" (N. Grigorescu) 1·00 55

1974. (a) Buildings.
4032 **765** 5b. red 10 10
4033 – 10b. blue 10 10
4034 – 20b. orange 10 10
4035 – 35b. green 10 10
4036 – 40b. violet 10 10
4037 – 50b. blue 10 10
4038 – 55b. brown 10 10
4039 – 60b. red 10 10
4040 – 1l. blue 10 10
4041 – 1l.20 green 10 10

(b) Ships.
4042 – 1l.35 black 25 10
4043 – 1l.45 blue 25 10
4044 – 1l.50 red 25 10
4045 – 1l.55 blue 35 10
4046 – 1l.75 green 40 10
4047 – 2l.20 blue 45 10
4048 – 3l.65 lilac 75 10
4049 – 4l.70 purple 1·20 15
DESIGNS—VERT: 10b. "Column of Infinity", Tirgu Jiu; 40b. Romanesque church, Densus; 50b. Reformed Church, Dej; 1l. Curtea de Arges Monastery. HORIZ: 20b. Heroes' Monument, Marasesti; 35b. Citadel, Risnov; 55b. Castle, Maldarasti; 60b. National Theatre, Jassy; 1l.20, Fortress and church, Tirgu Mures; 1l.35, Danube Tug "Impingator"; 1l.45, Freighter "Dimbovita"; 1l.50, Danube passenger vessel "Muntenia"; 1l.55, Cadet barque "Mircea"; 1l.75, Liner "Transylvania"; 2l.20, Bulk carrier "Oltul"; 3l.65, Trawler "Mures"; 4l.70, Tanker "Arges".

767 "Boats at Honfleur" (Monet)

1974. Impressionist Paintings. Multicoloured.
4056 20b. Type **767** 10 10
4057 40b. "Moret Church" (Sisley) (vert) 10 10
4058 55b. "Orchard in Blossom" (Pissarro) 10 10
4059 1l.75 "Jeanne" (Pissarro) (vert) 25 10
4060 2l.75 "Landscape" (Renoir) 45 20
4061 3l.60 "Portrait of a Girl" (Cezanne) (vert) 1·10 35

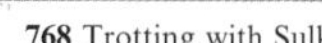

768 Trotting with Sulky **769** Nicolas Titulescu (Rumanian League of Nations Delegate)

1974. Cent of Horse-racing in Rumania. Mult.
4063 40b. Type **768** 10 10
4064 55b. Three horses racing 10 10
4065 60b. Horse galloping 10 10
4066 1l.55 Two trotters racing 30 10
4067 2l.75 Three trotters racing 55 20
4068 3l.45 Two horses racing 85 30

1974. Interparliamentary Congress Session, Bucharest.
4069 **769** 1l.75 multicoloured 35 20

771 "Anniversary Parade" (Pepene Cornelia)

1974. 25th Anniv of Rumanian Pioneers Organization.
4071 **771** 55b. multicoloured 40 15

772 "Europe"

1974. Inter-European Cultural and Economic Co-operation. Multicoloured.
4072 2l.20 Type **772** 1·10 85
4073 3l.45 Satellite over Europe 1·30 1·10

1974. Rumania's Victory in World Handball Championships. No. 3959 surch **ROMANIA CAMPIOANA MONDIALA 1974 175L.**
4074 1l.75 on 20b. multicoloured 2·00 1·80

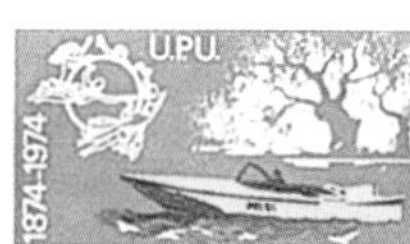

774 Postal Motor Boat

1974. U.P.U. Centenary. Multicoloured.
4075 20b. Type **774** 10 15
4076 40b. Loading mail train 40 15
4077 55b. Loading Ilyushin Il-62M mail plane 10 15
4078 1l.75 Rural postman delivering letter 30 15
4079 2l.75 Town postman delivering letter 35 25
4080 3l.60 Young stamp collectors 60 25

775 Footballers

1974. World Cup Football Championship, West Germany.
4082 **775** 20b. multicoloured 10 10
4083 – 40b. multicoloured 10 10
4084 – 55b. multicoloured 10 10
4085 – 1l.75 multicoloured 20 10
4086 – 2l.75 multicoloured 50 15
4087 – 3l.60 multicoloured 65 25
DESIGNS: Nos. 4083/7, Football scenes similar to Type **775**.

776 Anniversary Emblem **777** U.N. and World Population Emblems

1974. 25th Anniv of Council for Mutual Economic Aid.
4089 **776** 55b. multicoloured 25 20

1974. World Population Year Conference, Bucharest.
4090 **777** 2l. multicoloured 35 20

778 Emblem on Map of Europe

1974. "Euromax 1974" International Stamp Exhibition, Bucharest.
4091 **778** 4l.+3l. yellow, bl & red 1·10 35

779 Hand drawing Peace Dove **780** Prince John of Wallachia (400th birth anniv)

1974. 25th Anniv of World Peace Movement.
4092 **779** 2l. multicoloured 35 20

1974. Anniversaries.
4093 **780** 20b. blue 10 10
4094 – 55b. red 10 10
4095 – 1l. blue 10 10
4096 – 1l.10 brown 20 10
4097 – 1l.30 purple 30 10
4098 – 1l.40 violet 35 20
DESIGNS AND ANNIVERSARIES—VERT: 1l. Iron and Steel Works, Hunedoara (220th anniv); 1l.10, Avram Iancu (revolutionary, 150th anniv); 1l.30, Dr. C. I. Parhon (birth cent); 1l.40, Dosoftel (metropolitan) (350th birth anniv). HORIZ: 55b. Soldier guarding industrial installations (Rumanian People's Army, 30th anniv).

781 Rumanian and Soviet Flags as "XXX" **783** "Centaurea nervosa"

1974. 30th Anniv of Liberation. Multicoloured.
4099 40b. Type **781** 10 10
4100 55b. Citizens and flags (horiz) 10 20

1974. Nature Conservation. Wild Flowers. Mult.
4102 20b. Type **783** 10 10
4103 40b. "Fritillaria montana" 10 10
4104 55b. Yew 60 10
4105 1l.75 "Rhododendron kotschyi" 30 15
4106 2l.75 Alpine forget-me-not 40 20
4107 3l.60 Pink 65 30

784 Bust of Isis

1974. Rumanian Archaeological Finds. Sculpture. Multicoloured.

4108	20b. Type **784**	10	10
4109	40b. Glykon serpent	10	10
4110	55b. Head of Emperor Decius	10	10
4111	1l.75 Rumanian Woman	25	10
4112	2l.75 Mithras	40	25
4113	3l.60 Roman senator	65	30

785 Sibiu Market Place

1974. Stamp Day.
4114 **785** 2l.10+1l.90 mult 90 40

1974. "Nationala 74" Stamp Exhibition. No. 4114 optd **EXPOZITIA FILATELICA "NATIONALA '74" 15–24 noiembrie Bucuresti**.
4115 **786** 2l.10+1l.90 mult . . . . 1·50 1·50

787 Party Emblem

1974. 11th Rumanian Communist Party Congress, Bucharest.

4116	**787**	55b. multicoloured	15	10
4117	–	1l. multicoloured	20	20

DESIGN: 1l. Similar to Type **787**, showing party emblem and curtain.

788 "The Discus-thrower" (Myron)

1974. 60th Anniv of Rumanian Olympic Committee.
4118 **788** 2l. multicoloured 50 30

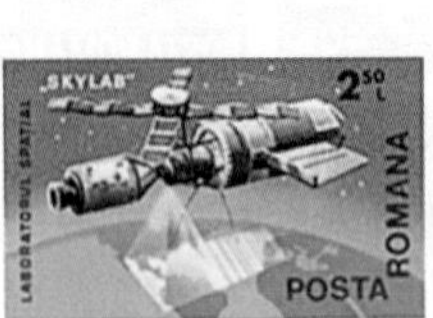

789 "Skylab"

790 Dr. Albert Schweitzer

1974. "Skylab" Space Laboratory Project.
4119 **789** 2l.50 multicoloured . . . 2·20 80

1974. Birth Centenary of Dr. Albert Schweitzer (Nobel Peace Prize-winner).
4120 **790** 40b. brown 15 20

791 Handball

793 Torch and Inscription

792 "Rocks and Birches"

1975. World Universities Handball Championships, Rumania.

4121	**791**	55b. multicoloured	10	10
4122	–	1l.75 multicoloured (vert)	20	10
4123	–	2l.20 multicoloured	40	30

DESIGNS: 1l.75, 2l.20, similar designs to Type **791**.

1975. Paintings by Ion Andreescu. Multicoloured.

4124	20b. Type **792**	10	10
4125	40b. "Peasant Woman with Green Kerchief"	10	10
4126	55b. "Winter in the Forest"	10	10
4127	1l.75 "Winter in Barbizon"	[illegible]	[illegible]
4128	2l.75 Self-portrait	45	25
4129	3l.50 "Main Road" (horiz)	90	40

1975. 10th Anniv of Rumanian Socialist Republic.
4130 **793** 40b. multicoloured . . . 20 15

794 "Battle of the High Bridge" (O. Obedeanu)

1975. 500th Anniv of Victory over the Ottomans at High Bridge.
4131 **794** 55b. multicoloured . . . 20 15

795 "Peasant Woman Spinning" (Nicolae Grigorescu)

796 "Self-portrait"

1975. International Women's Year.
4132 **795** 55b. multicoloured . . . 20 15

1975. 500th Birth Anniv of Michelangelo.
4133 **796** 5l. multicoloured 85 50

798 Mitsui Children's Science Pavilion, Okinawa

1975. International Exposition, Okinawa.
4135 **798** 4l. multicoloured 70 30

799 "Peonies" (Nicolae Tonitza)

1975. Inter-European Cultural and Economic Co-operation. Multicoloured.

4136	2l.20 Type **799**	80	80
4137	3l.45 "Chrysanthemums" (Stefan Luchian)	95	1·00

800 Dove with Coded Letter

1975. Introduction of Postal Coding.
4138 **800** 55b. multicoloured . . . 15 15

801 Convention Emblem on "Globe"

1975. Centenary of International Metre Convention.
4139 **801** 1l.85 multicoloured . . . 40 20

802 Mihail Eminescu and Museum

1975. 125th Birth Anniv of Mihail Eminescu (poet).
4140 **802** 55b. multicoloured . . . 15 15

803 Roman Coins and Stone Inscription

805 Ana Ipatescu

1975. Bimillenary of Alba Julia.
4141 **803** 55b. multicoloured . . . 15 20

1975. Death Cent of Ana Ipatescu (revolutionary).
4143 **805** 55b. mauve 20 20

806 Turnu-Severin

1975. European Architectural Heritage Year. Roman Antiquities.

4144	–	55b. black and brown	10	10
4145	–	1l.20 black, lt bl & bl	15	15
4146	–	1l.55 black and green	40	15
4147	–	1l.75 black and red	45	20
4148	**806**	2l. black and ochre	55	20
4149	–	2l.25 black and blue	70	50

DESIGNS—VERT: 55b. Emperor Trajan; 1l.20, Trajan's Column, Rome; 1l.55, Decebalus (sculpture); 10l. Roman remains, Gradiste. HORIZ: 1l.75, Imperial monument, Adam Clissi; 2l.25, Trajan's Bridge.

807 "Apollo" and "Soyuz" Spacecraft

1975. Air. "Apollo"–"Soyuz" Space Link. Mult.

4151	1l.75 Type **807**	1·10	65
4152	3l.25 "Apollo" and "Soyuz" linked together	1·50	85

808 "Michael the Brave" (Aegidius Sadeler)

1975. 375th Anniv of First Political Union of Rumanian States. Multicoloured.

4153	55b. Type **808**	10	10
4154	1l.20 "Ottoman Envoys bringing gifts to Michael the Brave" (T. Aman) (horiz)	15	10
4155	2l.75 "Michael the Brave at Calugareni" (T. Aman)	45	15

810 Larkspur

812 Policeman using Walkie-talkie

1975. Flowers. Multicoloured.

4157	20b. Type **810**	10	10
4158	40b. Long-headed poppy	10	10
4159	55b. Common immortelle	10	10
4160	1l.75 Common rock-rose	25	15
4161	2l.75 Meadow clary	45	20
[illegible]	[illegible]	[illegible]	[illegible]

1975. International Philatelic Fair, Riccione (Italy). Optd **Tîrg international de mârci postale Riccione – Italia 23-25 august 1975**.
4163 **796** 5l. multicoloured . . . . 2·40 2·20

1975. Road Safety.
4164 **812** 55b. blue 25 20

813 Text on Map of Pelendava

1975. 1750th Anniv of First Documentary Attestations of Daco-Getian Settlements of Pelendava and 500th Anniv of Craiova. Multicoloured.

4165	20b. Type **813**	15	15
4166	55b. Map of Pelendava showing location of Craiova (82 × 33 mm)	15	15
4167	1l. Text on map of Pelendava	20	15

Nos. 4165/7 were issued together, se-tenant, forming a composite design.

814 Muntenia Carpet

1975. Rumanian Traditional Carpets. Mult.

4168	20b. Type **814**	10	10
4169	40b. Banat	10	10
4170	55b. Oltenia	10	10
4171	1l.75 Moldova	30	10
4172	2l.75 Oltenia (different)	45	25
4173	3l.60 Maramures	55	30

815 T.V. "12M" Minibus

1975. Rumanian Motor Vehicles. Multicoloured.

4174 20b. Type **815** 10 10
4175 40b. L.K.W. "19 A.L.P." Oil tanker 10 10
4176 55b. A.R.O. "240" Field car 10 10
4177 1l.75 L.K.W. "R 8135 F" Truck 35 10
4178 2l.75 P.K.W. "Dacia 1300" Saloon car 50 25
4179 3l.60 L.K.W. "R 19215 D.F.K." Tipper truck . . 65 30

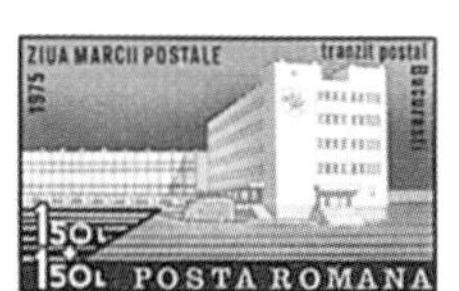

816 Postal Transit Centre, Bucharest

1975. Stamp Day. Multicoloured.

4180 1l.50+1l.50 Type **816** . . . 70 40
4181 2l.10+1l.90 Aerial view of P.T.C. . . . . 1·30 65

818 Tobogganing

1976. Winter Olympics Games, Innsbruck. Mult.

4183 20b. Type **818** 10 15
4184 40b. Rifle-shooting (biathlon) (vert) 10 15
4185 55b. Downhill skiing (slalom) 20 15
4186 1l.75 Ski jumping 35 20
4187 2l.75 Figure skating (women's) 50 30
4188 3l.60 Ice hockey 70 45

819 "Washington at Valley Forge" (W. Trego)

1976. Bicent of American Revolution. Mult.

4190 20b. Type **819** 10 10
4191 40b. "Washington at Trenton" (Trumbull) (vert) 10 10
4192 55b. "Washington crossing the Delaware" (Leutze) 15 10
4193 1l.75 "Capture of the Hessians" (Trumbull) . . 25 20
4194 2l.75 "Jefferson" (Sully) (vert) 45 25
4195 3l.60 "Surrender of Cornwallis at Yorktown" (Trumbull) 60 40

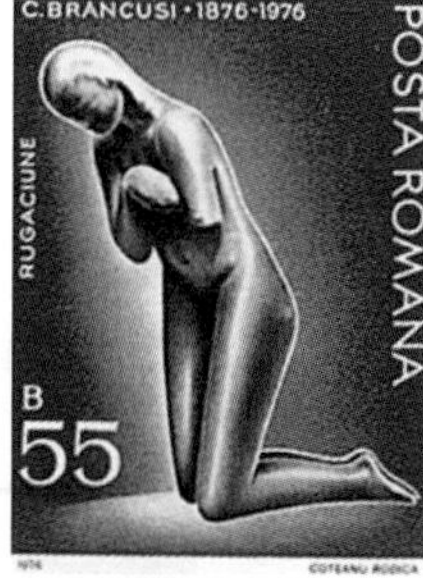

820 "Prayer"

1976. Birth Centenary of Constantin Brancusi (sculptor). Multicoloured.

4197 55b. Type **820** 10 15
4198 1l.75 Architectural Assembly, Tg. Jiu 25 20
4199 3l.60 C. Brancusi 65 20

821 Anton Davidoglu (mathematician) (birth cent)

823 Dr. Carol Davila

822 Inscribed Tablets, Tibiscum (Banat)

1976. Anniversaries. Multicoloured.

4200 40b. Type **821** 10 10
4201 55b. Prince Vlad Tepes (500th death anniv) . . . 10 10
4202 1l.20 Costache Negri (patriot—death centenary) 20 10
4203 1l.75 Gallery, Archives Museum (50th anniv) . . 25 10

1976. Daco-Roman Archaeological Finds. Mult.

4204 **822** 20b. multicoloured . . . 10 10
4205 – 40b. black, grey and red 10 10
4206 – 55b. multicoloured . . . 10 10
4207 – 1l.75 multicoloured . . . 40 10
4208 – 2l.75 black, grey and red 50 20
4209 – 3l.60 black, grey & green 70 35

DESIGNS: 40b. Sculptures (Banat); 55b. Inscribed tablet, coins and cup (Crisana); 1l.75, Pottery (Crisana); 2l.75, Altar and spears, Maramures (Banat); 3l.60, Vase and spears, Maramures.

1976. Centenary of Rumanian Red Cross. Mult.

4211 55b. Type **823** (postage) . . 10 10
4212 1l.75 Nurse and patient . . 10 10
4213 2l.20 First aid 15 10
4214 3l.35 Blood donors (air) . . 55 20

824 King Decebalus Vase

825 Rumanian Arms

1976. Inter-European Cultural and Economic Co-operation. Vases from Cluj-Napoca porcelain factory. Multicoloured.

4215 2l.20 Type **824** 50 40
4216 3l.45 Vase with portrait of King Michael the Brave 1·10 1·00

1976.

4217 **825** 1l.75 multicoloured . . . 45 20

826 De Havilland D.H.9C

1976. Air. 50th Anniv of Romanian Airline. Mult.

4218 20b. Type **826** 10 10
4219 40b. I.C.A.R. Comercial . . 15 10
4220 60b. Douglas DC-3 . . . . 25 10
4221 1l.75 Antonov An-24 . . . 40 10
4222 2l.75 Ilyushin Il-62 jetliner 60 20
4223 3l.60 Boeing 707 jetliner . . 90 20

827 Gymnastics

828 Spiru Haret

1976. Olympic Games, Montreal. Multicoloured.

4224 20b. Type **827** 10 10
4225 40b. Boxing 10 10
4226 55b. Handball 20 10
4227 1l.75 Rowing (horiz) 35 15
4228 2l.75 Gymnastics (different) (horiz) 50 20
4229 3l.60 Canoeing (horiz) . . . 65 20

1976. 125th Birth Anniv of Spiru Haret (mathematician).

4231 **828** 20b. multicoloured . . . 20 20

829 Daco-Getian Sculpture on Map of Buzau

1976. 1600th Anniv of Buzau State.

4232 **829** 55b. multicoloured . . . 20 20

1976. Philatelic Exhibition, Bucharest. No. 4199 surch **EXPOZITIA FILATELICA BUCURESTI 12–19 IX 1976 1,80+**.

4233 3l.60+1l.80 multicoloured 4·00 3·50

831 Red Deer

1976. Endangered Animals. Multicoloured.

4234 20b. Type **831** 10 10
4235 40b. Brown bear 10 10
4236 55b. Chamois 15 10
4237 1l.75 Wild boar 25 10
4238 2l.75 Red fox 50 25
4239 3l.60 Lynx 65 35

832 Cathedral, Milan

1976. "Italia '76" International Philatelic Exhibition, Milan.

4240 **832** 4l.75 multicoloured . . . 80 20

833 D. Grecu (gymnast) and Bronze Medal

1976. Olympic Games, Montreal. Rumanian Medal Winners. Multicoloured.

4241 20b. Type **833** 10 10
4242 40b. Fencing (Bronze Medal) 10 10
4243 55b. Javelin (Bronze Medal) 15 10
4244 1l.75 Handball (Silver Medal) 25 10
4245 2l.75 Boxing (Silver and Bronze Medals) (horiz) . . 40 15
4246 3l.60 Wrestling (Silver and Bronze Medals) (horiz) . . 60 35
4247 5l.70 Nadia Comaneci (gymnastics – 3 Gold, 1 Silver and 1 Bronze Medals) (27 × 42 mm) . . 1·90 95

834 "Carnations and Oranges"

1976. Floral Paintings by Stefan Luchian. Mult.

4249 20b. Type **834** 10 10
4250 40b. "Flower Arrangement" 10 10
4251 55b. "Immortelles" 10 10
4252 1l.75 "Roses in Vase" . . . 20 10
4253 2l.75 "Cornflowers" 25 20
4254 3l.60 "Carnations in Vase" 60 25

835 "Elena Cuza" (T. Aman)

836 Arms of Alba

1976. Stamp Day.

4255 **835** 2l.10+1l.90 mult 85 80

1976. Rumanian Districts' Coats of Arms (1st series). Multicoloured.

4256 55b. Type **836** 20 15
4257 55b. Arad 20 15
4258 55b. Arges 20 15
4259 55b. Bacau 20 15
4260 55b. Bihor 20 15
4261 55b. Bistrita Nasaud 20 15
4262 55b. Botosani 20 15
4263 55b. Brasov 20 15
4264 55b. Braila 20 15
4265 55b. Buzau 20 15
4266 55b. Caras-Severin 20 15
4267 55b. Cluj 20 15
4268 55b. Constanta 20 15
4269 55b. Covasna 20 15
4270 55b. Dimbovita 20 15

See also Nos. 4307/31, 4496/520 and 4542/63.

837 "Ox Cart"

1977. Paintings by Nicolae Grigorescu. Mult.

4271 55b. Type **837** 15 10
4272 1l. "Self-portrait" (vert) . . 15 10
4273 1l.50 "Shepherdess" 20 10
4274 2l.15 "Girl with Distaff" . . 30 10
4275 3l.40 "Shepherd" (vert) . . 35 20
4276 4l.80 "Halt at the Well" . . 55 25

838 Telecommunications Station, Cheia

1977.

4277 **838** 55b. multicoloured . . . 15 15

839 I.C.A.R.1

1977. Air. Rumanian Gliders. Multicoloured.

4278 20b. Type **839** 10 10
4279 40b. IS-3d 10 10
4280 55b. RG-5 . . . . 10 10
4281 1l.50 IS-11 . . . . 25 10

4282 3l. IS-29D 50 20
4283 3l.40 IS-28B 90 35

840 Red Deer

1977. Protected Animals. Multicoloured.
4284 55b. Type **840** 10 10
4285 1l. Mute swan 30 10
4286 1l.50 Egyptian vulture . . . 45 10
4287 2l.15 European bison . . . 35 10
4288 3l.40 White-headed duck . . 85 20
4289 4l.80 River kingfisher . . . 1·00 45

841 "The Infantryman" (Oscar Obedeanu)

1977. Cent of Independence. Paintings. Mult.
4290 55b. Type **841** 10 10
4291 1l. "Artillery Battery at Calafat" (S. Hentia) (horiz) 10 10
4292 1l.50 "Soldiers Attacking" (Stefan Luchian) 15 10
4293 2l.15 "Battle of Plevna" (horiz) 30 10
4294 3l.40 "The Artillerymen" (Nicolae Grigorescu) (horiz) 40 20
4295 4l.80+2l. "Battle of Rahova" (horiz) 90 45

842 Sinaia, Carpathians

843 Petru Rares, Prince of Moldavia

1977. Inter-European Cultural and Economic Co-operation. Views. Multicoloured.
4297 2l. Type **842** 55 30
4298 2l.40 Auroa, Black Sea . . . 75 40

1977. Anniversaries. Multicoloured.
4299 40b. Type **843** (450th anniv of accession) 15 20
4300 55b. Ion Caragiale (dramatist, 125th birth anniv) 15 20

844 Nurse with Children and Emblems

1977. 23rd Int Red Cross Conference, Bucharest.
4301 **844** 1l.50 multicoloured . . . 30 20

845 Triumphal Arch, Bucharest

1977. 60th Anniv of Battles of Marasti, Marasesti and Oituz.
4302 **845** 2l.15 multicoloured . . . 50 20

847 Postwoman and Letters

1977. Air.
4304 20l. Type **847** . . . . . . 3·00 1·00
4305 30l. Douglas DC-10 jetliner and mail . . . . 4·50 1·70

848 Mount Titano Castle, San Marino

1977. Centenary of San Marino Postage Stamps.
4306 **848** 4l. multicoloured 85 15

1977. Rumanian District Coats of Arms (2nd series). As T **836**. Multicoloured.
4307 55b. Dolj 15 10
4308 55b. Galati 15 10
4309 55b. Gorj 15 10
4310 55b. Harghita 15 10
4311 55b. Hunedoara 15 10
4312 55b. Ialomita 15 10
4313 55b. Iasi 15 10
4314 55b. Ilfov 15 10
4315 55b. Maramures 15 10
4316 55b. Mehedinti 15 10
4317 55b. Mures 15 10
4318 55b. Neamt 15 10
4319 55b. Olt 15 10
4320 55b. Prahova 15 10
4321 55b. Salaj 15 10
4322 55b. Satu Mare 15 10
4323 55b. Sibiu 15 10
4324 55b. Suceava 15 10
4325 55b. Teleorman 15 10
4326 55b. Timis 15 10
4327 55b. Tulcea 15 10
4328 55b. Vaslui 15 10
4329 55b. Vilcea 15 10
4330 55b. Vrancea 15 10
4331 55b. Rumanian postal emblem 15 10

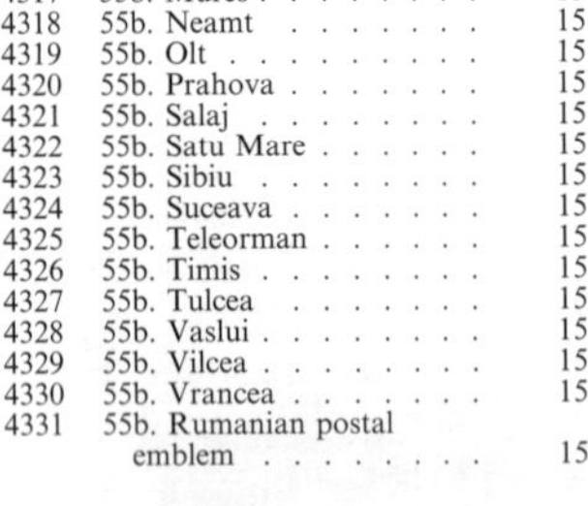

849 Gymnast on Vaulting Horse

850 Dispatch Rider and Army Officer

1977. Gymnastics. Multicoloured.
4332 20b. Type **849** 10 10
4333 40b. Floor exercise 10 10
4334 55b. Gymnast on parallel bars 10 10
4335 1l. Somersault on bar . . . 15 15
4336 2l.15 Gymnast on rings . . 30 25
4337 4l.80 Gymnastic exercise . . 1·10 65

1977. Stamp Day.
4338 **850** 2l.10+1l.90 mult 90 85

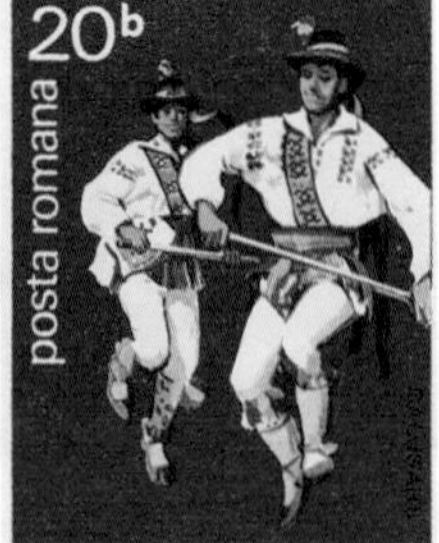

851 Two Dancers with Sticks

1977. Calusarii Folk Dance. Multicoloured.
4339 20b. Type **851** 10 10
4340 40b. Leaping dancer with stick 10 10
4341 55b. Two dancers 10 10
4342 1l. Dancer with stick . . . 15 10
4343 2l.15 Leaping dancers . . . 25 20
4344 4l.80 Leaping dancer . . . 95 50

852 "Carpati" at Cazane

1977. European Navigation on the Danube. Mult.
4346 55b. Type **852** 20 10
4347 1l. "Mircesti" near Orsova 25 10
4348 1l.50 "Oltenita" near Calafat 35 10
4349 2l.15 Hydrofoil at Giurgiu port 40 20
4350 3l. "Herculiani" at Tulcea 30 25
4351 3l.40 "Muntenia" at Sulina 60 30
4352 4l.80 Map of Danube delta 1·40 80

853 Arms and Flag of Rumania

1977. 30th Anniv of Rumanian Republic. Mult.
4354 55b. Type **853** 10 15
4355 1l.20 Rumanian-built computers 20 20
4356 1l.75 National Theatre, Craiova 35 20

854 Firiza Dam

1978. Rumanian Dams and Hydro-electric Installations. Multicoloured.
4357 20b. Type **854** 10 10
4358 40b. Negovanu dam 10 10
4359 55b. Piatra Neamt power station 15 10
4360 1l. Izvorul Montelui Bicaz dam 20 10
4361 2l.15 Vidraru dam 30 20
4362 4l.80 Danube barrage and navigation system, Iron Gates 65 40

855 LZ-1 over Lake Constance

1978. Air. Airships. Multicoloured.
4363 60b. Type **855** 10 10
4364 1l. Santos Dumont's "Ballon No. 6" over Paris 20 10
4365 1l.50 Beardmore R-34 over Manhattan Island 25 10
4366 2l.15 N.4 "Italia" at North Pole 35 10
4367 3l.40 "Graf Zeppelin" over Brasov 50 20
4368 4l.80 "Graf Zeppelin" over Sibiu 95 30

856 Footballers and Emblem

1978. World Cup Football Championship, Argentina.
4370 **856** 55b. blue 10 10
4371 – 1l. orange 10 10
4372 – 1l.50 yellow 20 10
4373 – 2l.15 red 30 10
4374 – 3l.40 green 50 20
4375 – 4l.80 mauve 75 30
DESIGNS: Nos. 4371/5, Footballers and emblem, similar to Type **856**.

857 King Decebalus of Dacia

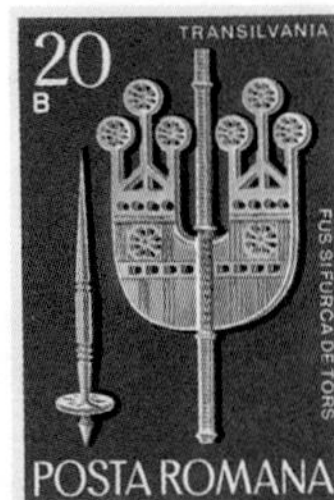

858 Worker and Factory

1978. Inter-European Cultural and Economic Co-operation. Multicoloured.
4377 1l.30 Type **857** 55 50
4378 3l.40 Prince Mircea the Elder . . . . 1·50 1·50

1978. 30th Anniv of Nationalization of Industry.
4379 **858** 55b. multicoloured . . . 15 15

859 Spindle and Fork Handle, Transylvania

1978. Wood-carving. Multicoloured.
4380 20b. Type **859** 10 10
4381 40b. Cheese mould, Muntenia 10 10
4382 55b. Spoons, Oltenia . . . 10 10
4383 1l. Barrel, Moldavia 15 10
4384 2l.15 Ladle and mug, Transylvania 25 20
4385 4l.80 Water bucket, Oltenia 60 35

860 Danube Delta

1978. Tourism. Multicoloured.
4386 55b. Type **860** 65 30
4387 1l. Bran Castle (vert) . . . 10 10
4388 1l.50 Moldavian village . . 15 10
4389 2l.15 Muierii caves 20 10
4390 3l.40 Cable car at Boiana Brasov 40 10
4391 4l.80 Mangalia (Black Sea resort) 60 25

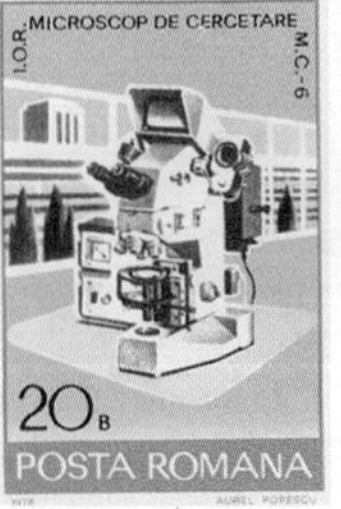

861 MC-6 Electron Microscope

862 Polovraci Cave

1978. Rumanian Industry. Multicoloured.
4393 20b. Type **861** 10 10
4394 40b. Hydraulic excavator 10 10
4395 55b. Power station control room 10 10
4396 1l.50 Oil drillheads 15 10
4397 3l. C-12 combine harvester (horiz) 35 15
4398 3l.40 Petro-chemical combine, Pitesti 40 15

1978. Caves and Caverns. Multicoloured.
4399 55b. Type **862** 10 10
4400 1l. Topolnita 15 10
4401 1l.50 Ponoare 15 10
4402 2l.15 Ratei 25 10
4403 3l.40 Closani 45 15
4404 4l.80 Epuran 65 25

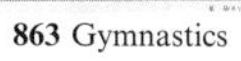

863 Gymnastics **865** Symbols of Equality

864 Zoomorphic Gold Plate

1978. "Daciada" Rumanian Games. Multicoloured.
4405 55b. Type **863** 10 10
4406 1l. Running 15 10
4407 1l.50 Skiing 20 10
4408 2l.15 Horse jumping 25 10
4409 3l.40 Football 40 15
4410 4l.80 Handball 65 25

1978. Daco-Roman Archaeology. Multicoloured.
4411 20b. Type **864** 10 10
4412 40b. Gold torque 10 10
4413 55b. Gold cameo ring 10 10
4414 1l. Silver bowl 20 10
4415 2l.15 Bronze eagle (vert) 35 10
4416 4l.80 Silver armband 40 25

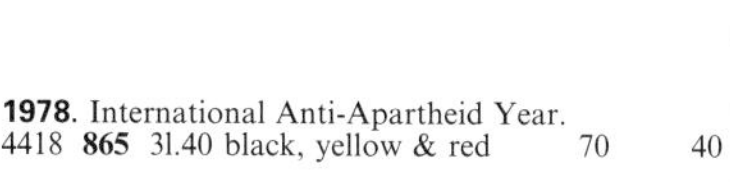

1978. International Anti-Apartheid Year.
4418 **865** 3l.40 black, yellow & red 70 40

867 Ptolemaic Map of Dacia (2000th anniv of first record of Ziridava)

1978. Anniversaries in the History of Arad. Mult.
4420 40b. Type **867** 10 10
4421 55b. Meeting place of National Council (60th anniv of unified Rumania) 10 10
4422 1l.75 Ceramic pots (950th anniv of first documentary evidence of Arad) 20 15

868 Dacian Warrior

1978. Stamp Day.
4423 **868** 6l.+3l. multicoloured 95 80
No. 4423 was issued se-tenant with a premium-carrying tab as shown in Type **868**.

869 Assembly at Alba Julia **871** Dacian Warrior

870 Wright Brothers and Wright Type A

1979. 60th Anniv of National Unity. Mult.
4424 55b. Type **869** 10 10
4425 1l. Open book, flag and sculpture 15 10

1979. Air. Pioneers of Aviation. Multicoloured.
4426 55b. Type **870** 10 10
4427 1l. Louis Bleriot and Bleriot XI monoplane 15 10
4428 1l.50 Anthony Fokker and Fokker F.VIIa/3m "Josephine Ford" 20 10
4429 2l.15 Andrei Tupolev and Tupolev ANT-25 30 10
4430 3l. Otto Lilienthal and Lilienthal monoplane glider 35 15
4431 3l.40 Traian Vuia and Vuia No. 1 40 20
4432 4l.80 Aurel Vlaicu and No. 1 "Crazy Fly" 50 30

1979. 2050th Anniv of Independent Centralized Dacic State. Details from Trajan's Column. Multicoloured.
4434 5b. Type **871** 10 10
4435 1l.50 Dacian warrior on horseback 25 10

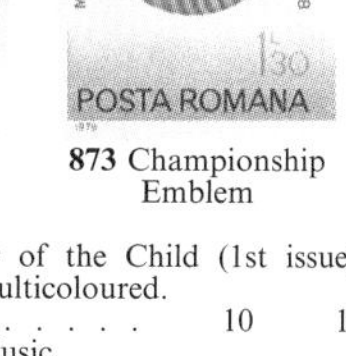

872 "The Heroes from Vaslui" **873** Championship Emblem

1979. International Year of the Child (1st issue). Children's Paintings. Multicoloured.
4436 55b. Type **872** 10 10
4437 1l. "Tica's Folk Music Band" 10 10
4438 1l.50 "Buildingsite" 10 10
4439 2l.15 "Industrial Landscape" (horiz) 20 10
4440 3l.40 "Winter Holiday" (horiz) 35 15
4441 4l.80 "Pioneers' Celebration" (horiz) 55 20
See also Nos. 4453/6.

1979. European Junior Ice Hockey Championship, Miercurea-Ciuc, and World Championship, Galati. Multicoloured.
4442 1l.30 Type **873** 20 20
4443 3l.40 Championship emblem (different) 35 20

874 Dog's tooth Violet **876** Oil Derrick

875 Street with Mail Coach and Post-rider

1979. Protected Flowers. Multicoloured.
4444 55b. Type **874** 10 10
4445 1l. Alpine violet 10 10
4446 1l.50 "Linum borzaeanum" 15 10
4447 2l.15 "Convolvulus persicus" 20 10
4448 3l.40 Auricula 35 15
4449 4l.80 "Aquilegia transsylvanica" 45 25

1979. Inter-European Cultural and Economic Co-operation.
4450 1l.30 Type **875** (postage) 55 30
4451 3l.40 Boeing 707 and motorcycle postman (air) 65 35

1979. International Petroleum Congress, Bucharest.
4452 **876** 3l.40 multicoloured 35 15

877 Children with Flowers **878** Young Pioneer

1979. International Year of the Child (2nd issue). Multicoloured.
4453 40b. Type **877** 10 20
4454 1l. Children at creative play 15 20
4455 2l. Children with hare 30 20
4456 4l.60 Young pioneers 65 50

1979. 30th Anniv of Rumanian Young Pioneers.
4457 **878** 55b. multicoloured 20 15

879 "Woman in Garden" **881** Stefan Gheorghiu

880 Brasov University

1979. Paintings by Gh. Tattarescu. Multicoloured.
4458 20b. Type **879** 10 10
4459 40b. "Muntenian Woman" 10 10
4460 55b. "Muntenian Man" 10 10
4461 1l. "General G. Magheru" 20 10
4462 2l.15 "The Artist's Daughter" 40 20
4463 4l.80 "Self-portrait" 75 25

1979. Contemporary Architecture. Multicoloured.
4464 20b. State Theatre, Tirgu Mures 10 10
4465 40b. Type **880** 10 10
4466 55b. Administration Centre, Baia Mare 10 10
4467 1l. Stefan Gheorghiu Academy, Bucharest 15 10
4468 2l.15 Adminstration Centre, Botosani 30 20
4469 4l.80 House of Culture, Tirgoviste 65 25

1979. Anniversaries. Multicoloured.
4470 40b. Type **881** (birth cent) 10 10
4471 55b. Statue of Gheorghe Lazar (poet) (birth bicent) 10 10
4472 2l.15 Fallen Workers monument (Strike at Lupeni, 50th anniv) 20 15

882 Moldavian and Wallachian Women and Monuments to Union **883** Party and National Flags

1979. 120th Anniv of Union of Moldavia and Wallachia.
4473 **882** 4l.60 multicoloured 60 20

1979. 25th Anniv of Liberation. Multicoloured.
4474 55b. Type **883** 15 10
4475 1l. "Workers' Militia" (L. Suhar) (horiz) 20 10

884 Freighter "Galati" **885** "Snapdragons"

1979. Ships. Multicoloured.
4476 55b. Type **884** 15 10
4477 1l. Freighter "Bucharesti" 20 10
4478 1l.50 Bulk carrier "Resita" 25 10
4479 2l.15 Bulk carrier "Tomis" 35 30
4480 3l.40 Tanker "Dacia" 50 15
4481 4l.80 Tanker "Independenta" 65 20

1979. "Socfilex 79" Stamp Exhibition, Bucharest. Flower Paintings by Stefan Luchian. Mult.
4482 40b. Type **885** 10 10
4483 60b. "Carnations" 15 10
4484 1l.55 "Flowers on a Stairway" 25 10
4485 4l.+2l. "Flowers of the Field" 75 70

888 Olympic Stadium, Melbourne (1956 Games)

1979. Olympic Games, Moscow (1980). Olympic Stadia. Multicoloured.
4489 55b. Type **888** 10 10
4490 1l. Rome (1960) 15 10
4491 1l.50 Tokyo (1964) 25 10
4492 2l.15 Mexico City (1968) 30 10
4493 3l.40 Munich (1972) 45 20
4494 4l.80 Montreal (1978) 70 20

1979. Municipal Coats of Arms. As T **836**. Mult.
4496 1l.20 Alba Julia 15 10
4497 1l.20 Arad 15 10
4498 1l.20 Bacau 15 10
4499 1l.20 Baia Mare 15 10
4500 1l.20 Birlad 15 10
4501 1l.20 Botosani 15 10
4502 1l.20 Brasov 15 10
4503 1l.20 Braila 15 10
4504 1l.20 Buzau 15 10
4505 1l.20 Calarasi 15 10
4506 1l.20 Cluj 15 10
4507 1l.20 Constanta 15 10
4508 1l.20 Craiova 15 10
4509 1l.20 Dej 15 10
4510 1l.20 Deva 15 10
4511 1l.20 Drobeta Turnu Severin 15 10
4512 1l.20 Focsani 15 10
4513 1l.20 Galati 15 10
4514 1l.20 Gheorghe Gheorghiu Dej 15 10
4515 1l.20 Giurgiu 15 10
4516 1l.20 Hunedoara 15 10
4517 1l.20 Iasi 15 10
4518 1l.20 Lugoj 15 10
4519 1l.20 Medias 15 10
4520 1l.20 Odorheiu Secuiesc 15 10

889 Costumes of Maramures (female)

891 Figure Skating

890 Post Coding Desks

1979. Costumes. Multicoloured.
4521 20b. Type **889** 10 10
4522 40b. Maramures (male) . . 10 10
4523 55b. Vrancea (female) . . . 10 10
4524 1l.50 Vrancea (male) 20 10
4525 3l. Padureni (female) 40 20
4526 3l.40 Padureni (male) . . . 45 30

1979. Stamp Day.
4527 **890** 2l.10+1l.90 mult 45 20

1979. Winter Olympic Games, Lake Placid (1980). Multicoloured.
4528 55b. Type **891** 10 10
4529 1l. Downhill skiing 10 10
4530 1l.50 Biathlon 20 10
4531 2l.15 Bobsleighing 25 10
4532 3l.40 Speed skating 45 20
4533 4l.80 Ice hockey 65 25

892 Locomotive "Calugareni", 1869

893 Dacian Warrior

1979. International Transport Exhibition, Hamburg. Multicoloured.
4535 55b. Type **892** 10 10
4536 1l. Steam locomotive "Orleans" 20 10
4537 1l.50 Steam locomotive No. 1059 . . . . 20 10
4538 2l.15 Steam locomotive No. 150211 . . . . . . 30 10
4539 3l.40 Steam locomotive No. 231085 . . . . 45 20
4550 4l.80 Class 060-EA electric locomotive 20 10

1980. Arms (4th series). As T **836**. Multicoloured.
4542 1l.20 Oradea 20 10
4543 1l.20 Petrosani 20 10
4544 1l.20 Piatra Neamt 20 10
4545 1l.20 Pitesti 20 10
4546 1l.20 Ploiesti 20 10
4547 1l.20 Resita 20 10
4548 1l.20 Rimnicu Vilcea 20 10
4549 1l.20 Roman 20 10
4550 1l.20 Satu Mare 15 10
4551 1l.20 Sibiu 20 10
4552 1l.20 Sighetu Marmatiei . . 20 10
4553 1l.20 Sighisoara 20 10
4554 1l.20 Suceava 20 10
4555 1l.20 Tecuci 20 10
4556 1l.20 Timisoara 20 10
4557 1l.20 Tirgoviste 20 10
4558 1l.20 Tirgu Jiu 20 05
4559 1l.20 Tirgu-Mures 20 10
4560 1l.20 Tulcea 20 10
4561 1l.20 Turda 20 10
4562 1l.20 Turnu Magurele . . . 20 10
4563 1l.20 Bucharest 20 10

1980. 2050th Anniv of Independent Centralized Dacian State under Burebista.
4564 55b. Type **893** 10 10
4565 1l.50 Dacian fighters with flag 20 10

894 River Kingfisher

1980. European Nature Protection Year. Mult.
4566 55b. Type **894** 25 10
4567 1l. Great egret (vert) 40 10
4568 1l.50 Red-breasted goose . . 45 10
4569 2l.15 Red deer (vert) 35 10
4570 3l.40 Roe deer fawn 35 20
4571 4l.80 European bison (vert) 55 30

895 Scarborough Lily

896 Tudor Vladimirescu

1980. Exotic Flowers from Bucharest Botanical Gardens. Multicoloured.
4573 55b. Type **895** 10 10
4574 1l. Floating water hyacinth 15 10
4575 1l.50 Jacobean lily 20 10
4576 2l.15 Rose of Sharon . . . 30 10
4577 3l.40 Camellia 35 20
4578 4l.80 Lotus 60 25

1980. Anniversaries. Multicoloured.
4579 40b. Type **896** (revolutionary leader) (birth bicent) 10 10
4580 55b. Mihail Sadoveanu (writer) (birth cent) . . . 10 10
4581 1l.50 Battle of Posada (650th anniv) 20 10
4582 2l.15 Tudor Arghezi (poet) (birth cent) 25 15
4583 3l. Horea (leader, Transylvanian uprising) (250th birth anniv) . . . 40 20

898 Dacian Fruit Dish

899 Throwing the Javelin

1980. Bimillenary of Dacian Fortress, Petrodava (now Piatra Neamt).
4585 **898** 1l. multicoloured 15 15

1980. Olympic Games, Moscow. Multicoloured.
4586 55b. Type **899** 10 10
4587 1l. Fencing 15 10
4588 1l.50 Pistol shooting 20 10
4589 2l.15 Single kayak 30 10
4590 3l.40 Wrestling 40 20
4591 4l.80 Single skiff 60 30

901 Congress Emblem

902 Fireman carrying Child

1980. 15th International Congress of Historical Sciences.
4594 **901** 55b. deep blue and blue 15 15

1980. Firemen's Day.
4595 **902** 55b. multicoloured . . . 15 15

903 Chinese and Rumanian Stamp Collectors

906 Dacian Warrior

905 Rooks and Chessboard

1980. Rumanian–Chinese Stamp Exhibition, Bucharest.
4596 **903** 1l. multicoloured 15 15

1980. 24th Chess Olympiad, Malta. Multicoloured.
4598 55b. Knights and chessboard 15 10
4599 1l. Type **905** 20 10
4600 2l.15 Male head and chessboard 40 10
4601 4l.80 Female head and chessboard 75 25

1980. Military Uniforms. Multicoloured.
4602 20b. Type **906** 10 10
4603 40b. Moldavian soldier (15th century) 10 10
4604 55b. Wallachian horseman (17th century) 10 10
4605 1l. Standard bearer (19th century) 10 10
4606 1l.50 Infantryman (19th century) 15 10
4607 2l.15 Lancer (19th century) 25 15
4608 4l.80 Hussar (19th century) 65 30

907 Burebista (sculpture, P. Mercea)

908 George Oprescu

1980. Stamp Day and 2050th Anniv of Independent Centralized Dacic State.
4609 **907** 2l. multicoloured 25 15

1981. Celebrities' Birth Anniversaries. Mult.
4610 1l.50 Type **908** (historian and art critic, centenary) 20 10
4611 2l.15 Marius Bunescu (painter, centenary) . . . 25 10
4612 3l.40 Ion Georgescu (sculptor, 125th anniv) . . 35 20

909 St. Bernard

1981. Dogs. Multicoloured.
4613 40b. Mountain sheepdog (horiz) 10 15
4614 55b. Type **909** 10 15
4615 1l. Fox terrier (horiz) . . . 15 15
4616 1l.50 Alsatian (horiz) . . . 25 15
4617 2l.15 Boxer (horiz) 35 15
4618 3l.40 Dalmatian (horiz) . . 55 20
4619 4l.80 Poodle 70 30

910 Paddle-steamer "Stefan cel Mare"

1981. 125th Anniv of European Danube Commission. Multicoloured.
4620 55b. Type **910** 15 10
4621 1l. "Prince Ferdinand de Roumanie" steam launch 20 20
4622 1l.50 Paddle-steamer "Tudor Vladimirescu" 30 20
4623 2l.15 Dredger "Sulina" . . . 35 25
4624 3l.40 Paddle-steamer "Republica Populara Romana" 45 30
4625 4l.80 Freighter in Sulina Channel 80 65

911 Bare-neck Pigeon

912 Party Flag and Oak Leaves

1981. Pigeons. Multicoloured.
4627 40b. Type **911** 10 10
4628 55b. Orbetan pigeon 10 10
4629 1l. Craiova chestnut pigeon 15 10
4630 1l.50 Timisoara pigeon . . . 35 10
4631 2l.15 Homing pigeon . . . 55 20
4632 3l.40 Salonta giant pigeon 80 20

1981. 60th Anniv of Rumanian Communist Party.
4633 **912** 1l. multicoloured 20 15

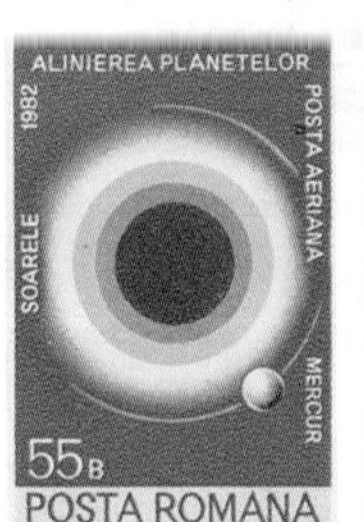

914 "Soyuz 40"

1981. Air. Soviet–Rumanian Space Flight. Mult.
4635 55b. Type **914** 15 10
4636 3l.40 "Soyuz"–"Salyut" link-up 40 10

915 Sun and Mercury

916 Industrial Symbols

1981. Air. The Planets. Multicoloured.
4638 55b. Type **915** 10 10
4639 1l. Venus, Earth and Mars 20 20
4640 1l.50 Jupiter 25 25
4641 2l.15 Saturn 35 30
4642 3l.40 Uranus 50 40
4643 4l.80 Neptune and Pluto . . 80 45

1981. "Singing Rumania" National Festival. Mult.
4645 55b. Type **916** 10 10
4646 1l.50 Technological symbols 25 10
4647 2l.15 Agricultural symbols 35 15
4648 3l.40 Cultural symbols . . . 70 30

917 Book and Flag

918 "Woman in an Interior"

1981. "Universiada" Games, Bucharest. Mult.
4649 1l. Type **917** 10 10
4650 2l.15 Games emblem 25 20
4651 4l.80 Stadium (horiz) . . . 55 65

1981. 150th Birth Anniv of Theodor Aman (painter). Multicoloured.
4652 40b. "Self-portrait" 10 10
4653 55b. "Battle of Giurgiu" (horiz) 10 10
4654 1l. "Family Picnic" (horiz) 15 10
4655 1l.50 "The Painter's Studio" (horiz) 20 10
4656 2l.15 Type **918** 30 10
4657 3l.10 Aman Museum, Bucharest (horiz) 50 10

919 "The Thinker of Cernavoda" (polished stone sculpture)

920 Blood Donation

1981. 16th International Congress of Historical Sciences.
4658 **919** 3l.40 multicoloured . . . 45 35

1981. Blood Donor Campaign.
4659 **920** 55b. multicoloured . . . 15 15

921 Central Military Hospital

1981. 150th Anniv of Central Military Hospital, Bucharest.
4660 **921** 55b. multicoloured . . . 15 15

922 Paul Constantinescu

923 Children at Stamp Exhibition

1981. Rumanian Musicians and Composers. Mult.
4661 40b. George Enescu 10 10
4662 55b. Type **922** 10 10
4663 1l. Dinu Lipatti 15 10
4664 1l.50 Ionel Perlea 20 10
4665 2l.15 Ciprian Porumbescu 30 15
4666 3l.40 Mihail Jora 45 20

1981. Stamp Day.
4667 **923** 2l. multicoloured 25 20

924 Hopscotch

925 Football Players

1981. Children's Games and Activities. Mult.
4668 40b. Type **924** (postage) . . 10 10
4669 55b. Football 10 10
4670 1l. Children with balloons and hobby horse 15 15
4671 1l.50 Fishing 20 15
4672 2l.15 Dog looking through school window at child 30 25
4673 3l. Child on stilts 40 35
4674 4l. Child tending sick dog 55 45
4675 4l.80 Children with model gliders (air) 70 75

Nos. 4671/15 are from illustrations by Norman Rockwell.

1981. World Cup Football Championship, Spain (1982). Multicoloured.
4676 55b. Type **925** 10 10
4677 1l. Goalkeeper saving ball 15 10
4678 1l.50 Player heading ball . . 20 15
4679 2l.15 Player kicking ball over head 30 30
4680 3l.40 Goalkeeper catching ball 50 40
4681 4l.80 Player kicking ball . . 70 45

926 Alexander the Good, Prince of Moldavia

927 Entrance to Union Square Station

1982. Anniversaries. Multicoloured.
4683 1l. Type **926** (550th death anniv) 10 15
4684 1l.50 Bodgan P. Hasdeu (historian, 75th death anniv) 15 10
4685 2l.15 Nicolae Titulescu (diplomat and politician, birth centenary) 35 10

1982. Inauguration of Bucharest Underground Railway. Multicoloured.
4686 60b. Type **927** 10 10
4687 2l.40 Platforms and train at Heroes' Square station . . 35 15

928 Dog rescuing Child from Sea

1982. Dog, Friend of Mankind. Multicoloured.
4688 55b. Type **928** 10 20
4689 1l. Shepherd and sheepdog (vert) 10 15
4690 3l. Gundog (vert) 30 15
4691 3l.40 Huskies 40 15
4692 4l. Dog carrying woman's basket (vert) 45 30
4693 4l.80 Dog guiding blind person (vert) 55 30
4694 5l. Dalmatian and child with doll 60 40
4695 6l. St. Bernard 75 35

929 Dove, Banner and Crowd

1982. 60th Anniv of Communist Youth Union. Mult.
4696 1l. Type **929** 15 15
4697 1l.20 Construction worker 15 15
4698 1l.50 Farm workers 20 15
4699 2l. Laboratory worker and students 25 20
4700 2l.50 Labourers 40 20
4701 3l. Choir, musicians and dancers 45 15

932 Harvesting Wheat

1982. 20th Anniv of Agricultural Co-operatives. Multicoloured.
4704 50b. Type **932** (postage) . . 10 10
4705 1l. Cows and milking equipment 15 10
4706 1l.50 Watering apple trees 20 10
4707 2l.50 Cultivator in vineyard 35 20
4708 3l. Watering vegetables . . . 40 25
4709 4l. Helicopter spraying cereal crop (air) 65 35

933 Vladimir Nicolae's Standard 1 Hang-glider

1982. Air. Hang-gliders. Multicoloured.
4711 50b. Type **933** 10 10
4712 1l. Excelsior D 20 10
4713 1l.50 Dedal-1 . . . . 25 10
4714 2l.50 Entuziast 40 15
4715 4l. AK-22 . . . . 60 30
4716 5l. Grifrom 85 35

934 Baile Felix

936 Vlaicu Monument, Banesti-Prahova

935 "Legend"

1982. Spas and Health Resorts. Multicoloured.
4717 50b. Type **934** 10 10
4718 1l. Predeal (horiz) 10 10
4719 1l.50 Baile Herculane . . . 20 10
4720 2l.50 Eforie Nord (horiz) . . 40 10
4721 3l. Olimp (horiz) 50 10
4722 5l. Neptun (horiz) 70 20

1982. Paintings by Sabin Balasa. Multicoloured.
4723 1l. Type **935** 10 15
4724 1l.50 "Contrasts" 20 15
4725 2l.50 "Peace Relay" 50 25
4726 4l. "Genesis of the Rumanian People" (vert) 55 35

1982. Air. Birth Centenary of Aurel Vlaicu (aviation pioneer). Multicoloured.
4727 50b. Vlaicu's glider, 1909 (horiz) 10 10
4728 1l. Type **936** 20 10
4729 2l.50 Air Heroes' Monument 45 20
4730 3l. Vlaicu's No. 1 airplane "Crazy Fly", 1910 (horiz) 50 15

938 Central Exhibition Pavilion

1982. "Tib '82" International Fair, Bucharest.
4732 **938** 2l. multicoloured 25 10

939 Young Pioneer with Savings Book and Books

940 Postwoman delivering Letters

1982. Savings Week. Multicoloured.
4733 1l. Type **939** 15 10
4734 2l. Savings Bank advertisement (Calin Popovici) 20 10

1982. Stamp Day. Multicoloured.
4735 1l. Type **940** 15 10
4736 2l. Postman 20 10

941 "Brave Young Man and the Golden Apples" (Petre Ispirescu)

942 Symbols of Industry, Party Emblem and Programme

1982. Fairy Tales. Multicoloured.
4737 50b. Type **941** 10 10
4738 1l. "Bear tricked by the Fox" (Ion Creanga) . . . 20 10
4739 1l.50 Warrior fighting bird ("Prince of Tears" (Mihai Eminescu)) 25 10
4740 2l.50 Hen with bag ("Bag with Two Coins" (Ion Creanga)) 35 10
4741 3l. Rider fighting three-headed dragon ("Ileana Simziana" (Petre Ispirescu)) 45 20
4742 5l. Man riding devil ("Danila Prepeleac" (Ion Creanga)) 75 30

1982. Rumanian Communist Party National Conference, Bucharest. Multicoloured.
4743 1l. Type **942** 15 15
4744 2l. Wheat symbols of industry and Party emblem and open programme 25 15

943 Wooden Canteen from Suceava

944 Wheat, Cogwheel, Flask and Electricity Emblem

1982. Household Utensils.
4745 **943** 50b. red 10 10
4746 – 1l. blue 15 15
4747 – 1l.50 orange 20 10
4748 – 2l. blue 40 15
4749 – 3l. green 50 15
4750 – 3l.50 green 55 10
4751 – 4l. brown 70 15
4752 – 5l. blue 80 10
4753 – 6l. blue . . . . 1·00 15
4754 – 7l. purple . . . . . . 1·10 15
4755 – 7l.50 mauve . . . . . 1·20 15
4756 – 8l. green . . . . . . 1·20 15
4757 – 10l. red . . . . 1·20 15
4758 – 20l. violet . . . . . . 2·50 15
4759 – 30l. blue . . . . 3·50 15
4760 – 50l. brown . . . . . . 7·25 25

DESIGNS: As T **943**—VERT: 1l. Ceramic plates from Radauti; 2l. Jug and plate from Vama-Maramures; 3l. Wooden churn and pail from North Moldavia; 4l. Wooden spoons and ceramic plate from Cluj; 5l. Ceramic bowl and pot from Marginea-Suceava. HORIZ: 1l.50, Wooden dipper from Valea Mare; 3l.50, Ceramic plates from Leheceni-Crisana. 29 × 23 mm: 10l. Wooden tubs from Hunedoara and Suceava; 30l. Wooden spoons from Alba. 23 × 29 mm: 6l. Ceramic pot and jug from Bihor; 7l. Distaff and spindle from Transylvania; 7l.50, Double wooden pail from Suceava; 8l. Pitcher and ceramic plate from Oboga and Horezu; 20l. Wooden canteen and six glasses from Horezu; 50l. Ceramic plates from Horezu.

1982. 35th Anniv of People's Republic. Mult.
4767 1l. Type **944** 15 10
4768 2l. National flag and oak leaves 20 10

945 H. Coanda and Diagram of Jet Engine

1983. Air. 25 Years of Space Exploration. Mult.
4769 50b. Type **945** 10 10
4770 1l. H. Oberth and diagram of rocket 10 10
4771 1l.50 "Sputnik 1", 1957 (first artificial satellite) . . 20 10
4772 2l.50 "Vostok 1", (first manned flight) 45 15

4773 4l. "Apollo 11, 1969 (first Moon landing) 65 20
4774 5l. Space shuttle "Columbia" 85 25

946 Rombac One Eleven 500 Jetliner

947 Matei Millo in "The Discontented" by Vasile Alecsandri

1983. Air. First Rumanian-built Jetliner.
4776 **946** 11l. blue . . . . 2·00 50

1983. Rumanian Actors.
4777 **947** 50b. red and black . . . 10 15
4778 – 1l. green and black . . . 10 10
4779 – 1l.50 violet and black . . 20 15
4780 – 2l. brown and black . . 30 15
4781 – 2l.50 green and black . . 40 10
4782 – 3l. blue and black . . . 45 15
4783 – 4l. green and black . . . 55 25
4784 – 5l. lilac and black . . . 75 40
DESIGNS: 1l. Mihail Pascaly in "Director Millo" by Vasile Alecsandri; 1l.50, Aristizza Romanescu in "The Dogs" by H. Lecca; 2l. C. I. Nottara in "Blizzard" by B. S. Delavrancea; 2l.50, Grigore Manolescu in "Hamlet" by William Shakespeare; 3l. Agatha Birsescu in "Medea" by Lebouvet; 4l. Ion Brezeanu in "The Lost Letter" by I. L. Caragiale; 5l. Aristide Demetriad in "The Despotic Prince" by Vasile Alecsandri.

948 Hugo Grotius

949 Aro "10"

1983. 400th Birth Anniv of Hugo Grotius (Dutch jurist).
4785 **948** 2l. brown 30 10

1983. Rumanian-built Vehicles. Multicoloured.
4786 50b. Type **949** 10 10
4787 1l. Dacia "1300" Break . . 20 10
4788 1l.50 Aro "242" 25 10
4789 2l.50 Aro "244" 45 10
4790 4l. Dacia "1310" 70 15
4791 5l. Oltcit "Club" 95 25

951 National and Communist Party Flags

953 Bluethroat

952 Loading Mail into Boeing 707

1983. 50th Anniv of 1933 Workers' Revolution.
4793 **951** 2l. multicoloured 30 10

1983. Air. World Communications Year.
4794 **952** 2l. multicoloured 50 10

1983. Birds of the Danube Delta. Multicoloured.
4795 50b. Type **953** 15 10
4796 1l. Rose-coloured starling 45 10
4797 1l.50 European roller . . . 55 10
4798 2l.50 European bee eater . . 90 25
4799 4l. Reed bunting . . . . . 1·60 30
4800 5l. Lesser grey shrike . . . 2·00 40

954 Kayak

1983. Water Sports. Multicoloured.
4801 50b. Type **954** 10 15
4802 1l. Water polo 15 15
4803 1l.50 Canoeing 20 15
4804 2l.50 Diving 45 20
4805 4l. Rowing 70 25
4806 5l. Swimming (start of race) 95 40

955 Postman on Bicycle

1983. Stamp Day. Multicoloured.
4807 1l. Type **955** 15 10
4808 3l.50(+3l.) National flag as stamp 95 50

No. 4808 was issued se-tenant with a premium-carrying tab showing the Philatelic Association emblem.

956 "Geum reptans"

1983. European Flora and Fauna. Multicoloured.
4810 1l. Type **956** 20 30
4811 1l. Long-headed poppy . . 20 15
4812 1l. Stemless carline thistle 20 30
4813 1l. "Paeonia peregrina" . . 20 30
4814 1l. "Gentiana excisa" . . . 20 15
4815 1l. Eurasian red squirrel . . 20 30
4816 1l. "Grammia quenselii" (butterfly) 50 20
4817 1l. Middle-spotted woodpecker 50 45
4818 1l. Lynx 50 30
4819 1l. Wallcreeper 70 45

957 "Girl with Feather"

958 Flag and Oak Leaves

1983. Paintings by Corneliu Baba. Multicoloured.
4820 1l. Type **957** 20 15
4821 2l. "Congregation" 35 15
4822 3l. "Farm Workers" 65 20
4823 4l. "Rest in the Fields" (horiz) 85 30

1983. 65th Anniv of Union of Transylvania and Rumania. Multicoloured.
4824 1l. Type **958** 15 15
4825 2l. National and Communist Party Flags and Parliament building, Bucharest 30 15

959 Postman and Post Office

961 Cross-country Skiing

1983. "Balkanfila IX '83" Stamp Exhibition, Bucharest. Multicoloured.
4826 1l. Type **959** 15 15
4827 2l. Postwoman and Athenaeum Concert Hall 30 15

1984. Winter Olympic Games, Sarajevo. Mult.
4830 50b. Type **961** 10 10
4831 1l. Biathlon 10 20
4832 1l.50 Ice skating 15 20
4833 2l. Speed skating 20 30
4834 3l. Ice hockey 30 35
4835 3l.50 Bobsleighing 40 15
4836 4l. Luge 45 55
4837 5l. Downhill skiing 55 65

963 Palace of Udriste Nasturel (Chancery official)

967 Flowering Rush

966 Sunflower

1984. Anniversaries.
4839 50b. green, pink and silver 10 10
4840 1l. violet, green and silver 20 10
4841 1l.50 multicoloured 30 15
4842 2l. brown, blue and silver 45 10
4843 3l.50 multicoloured 80 20
4844 4l. multicoloured . . . . . 1·00 20
DESIGNS: 50b. Type **963** (325th death anniv); 1l. Miron Costin (poet, 350th birth anniv); 1l.50, Crisan (Giurgiu Marcu) (leader of peasant revolt, 250th birth anniv); 2l. Simion Barnutiu (scientist, 175th birth anniv); 3l.50, Diuliu Zamfirescu (writer, 125th birth anniv); 4l. Nicolae Milescu at Great Wall of China (explorer, 275th death anniv).

1984. Protection of Environment. Multicoloured.
4847 1l. Type **966** 15 10
4848 2l. Red deer 25 15
4849 3l. Carp 35 20
4850 4l. Jay . . . . 1·70 40

1984. Flowers of the Danube. Multicoloured.
4851 50b. Arrowhead 10 10
4852 1l. Yellow iris 10 10
4853 1l.50 Type **967** 20 10
4854 3l. White water lily 45 20
4855 4l. Fringed water lily (horiz) 65 20
4856 5l. Yellow water lily (horiz) 80 30

968 Crowd with Banners

970 Congress Emblem

969 High Jumping

1984. 45th Anniv of Anti-Fascist Demonstration.
4857 **968** 2l. multicoloured 35 30

1984. Olympic Games, Los Angeles (1st issue). Multicoloured.
4858 50b. Type **969** 10 10
4859 1l. Swimming 15 10
4860 1l.50 Running 20 15
4861 3l. Handball 50 35
4862 4l. Rowing 75 55
4863 5l. Canoeing 95 70
See also Nos. 4866/73.

1984. 25th Ear, Nose and Throat Association Congress, Bucharest.
4864 **970** 2l. multicoloured 30 15

1984. Olympic Games, Los Angeles (2nd issue). As T **969**. Multicoloured.
4866 50b. Boxing 10 10
4867 1l. Rowing 10 10
4868 1l. Handball 15 10
4869 2l. Judo 20 10
4870 3l. Wrestling 35 15
4871 3l.50 Fencing 45 20
4872 4l. Kayak 55 25
4873 5l. Swimming 65 35

972 Mihai Ciuca (bacteriologist, cent)

974 Flags, Flame and Power Station

973 Lockhead 14 Super Electra

1984. Birth Anniversaries. Dated "1983".
4874 **972** 1l. purple, blue and silver 15 15
4875 – 2l. brown and silver . . 30 15
4876 – 3l. green, brown and silver 45 25
4877 – 4l. violet, green and silver 65 40
DESIGNS: 2l. Petre S. Aurelian (agronomist, 150th anniv); 3l. Alexandru Vlahuta (writer, 125th anniv); 4l. Dimitrie Leonida (engineer, centenary).

1984. Air. 40th Anniv of International Civil Aviation Organization. Multicoloured.
4878 50b. Type **973** 15 10
4879 1l.50 Britten Norman Islander 30 10
4880 3l. Rombac One Eleven 500 jetliner 60 20
4881 6l. Boeing 707 jetliner . . . 1·10 30

1984. 40th Anniv of Liberation.
4882 **974** 2l. multicoloured 50 30

975 Lippizaner

1984. Horses. Multicoloured.
4883 50b. Type **975** 10 10
4884 1l. Hutul 15 10
4885 1l.50 Bukovina 20 10
4886 2l.50 Nonius 40 10
4887 4l. Arab 65 20
4888 5l. Rumanian halfbreed . . 80 25

977 Memorial, Alba Julia

978 "Portrait of a Child" (Th. Aman)

1984. Bicentenary of Horea, Closa and Crisan Uprisings.
4890 **977** 2l. multicoloured 30 15

1984. Paintings of Children. Multicoloured.
4891 50b. Type **978** 10 15
4892 1l. "The Little Shepherd" (N. Grigorescu) 10 10
4893 2l. "Lica with an Orange" (St. Luchian) 30 10
4894 3l. "Portrait of a Child" (N. Tonitza) 45 20
4895 4l. "Portrait of a Boy" (S. Popp) 65 25
4896 5l. "Portrait of Young Girl" (I. Tuculescu) 90 30

979 Stage Coach and Rumanian Philatelic Association Emblem

1984. Stamp Day.
4897 **979** 2l.(+1l.) multicoloured . . . 45 50
No. 4897 was issued with premium-carrying label as shown in T **979**.

981 Dalmatian Pelicans

982 Dr. Petru Groza (former President)

1984. Protected Animals. Dalmatian Pelicans. Mult.
4899 50b. Type **981** 20 15
4900 1l. Pelican on nest 50 35
4901 1l. Pelicans on lake 50 35
4902 2l. Pelicans roosting . . . . 1·00 80

1984. Anniversaries. Multicoloured.
4903 50b. Type **982** (birth centenary) 25 15
4904 1l. Alexandru Odobescu (writer) (150th birth anniv) 55 10
4905 2l. Dr. Carol Davila (physician) (death centenary) 35 10
4906 3l. Dr. Nicolae Gh. Lupu (physician) (birth centenary) 55 15
4907 4l. Dr. Daniel Danielopolu (physician) (birth centenary) 65 25
4908 5l. Panait Istrati (writer) (birth centenary) 85 35

983 Generator

985 August Treboniu Laurian (linguist and historian)

1984. Centenary of Power Station and Electric Street Lighting in Timisoara. Multicoloured.
4909 1l. Type **983** 15 15
4910 2l. Street lamp 35 10

1985. Anniversaries. Multicoloured.
4912 50b. Type **985** (175th birth anniv) 10 15
4913 1l. Grigore Alexandrescu (writer) (death centenary) 20 15
4914 1l.50 Gheorghe Pop de Basesti (politician) (150th birth anniv) 30 15
4915 2l. Mateiu Caragiale (writer) (birth centenary) 35 10
4916 3l. Gheorghe Ionescu-Sisesti (scientist) (birth centenary) 55 20
4917 4l. Liviu Rebreanu (writer) (birth centenary) 85 25

986 Students in Science Laboratory

987 Racoon Dog

1985. International Youth Year. Multicoloured.
4918 1l. Type **986** 10 10
4919 2l. Students on construction site 35 10

1985. Protected Animals. Multicoloured.
4921 50b. Type **987** 10 10
4922 1l. Grey partridge 40 10
4923 1l.50 Snowy owl . . . . . 1·00 15
4924 2l. Pine marten 20 10
4925 3l. Eurasian badger 30 10
4926 3l.50 Eurasian otter 30 20
4927 4l. Western Capercaillie . . 1·60 25
4928 5l. Great bustard . . . . . 2·20 35

988 Flags and Victory Monument, Bucharest

989 Union Emblem

1985. 40th Anniv of Victory in Europe Day.
4929 **988** 2l. multicoloured 50 25

1985. Communist Youth Union Congress.
4930 **989** 2l. multicoloured 40 15

990 Route Map and Canal

1985. Danube–Black Sea Canal. Multicoloured.
4931 1l. Type **990** 25 10
4932 2l. Canal and bridge, Cernavoda . . . . 1·10 25
4933 3l. Road over Canal, Medgidia 95 15
4934 4l. Canal control tower, Agigea . . . . 1·10 25

991 Brown Pelican

992 "Fire"

1985. Birth Bicentenary of John J. Audubon (ornithologist). Multicoloured.
4936 50b. American robin (horiz) 15 10
4937 1l. Type **991** 30 10
4938 1l.50 Yellow-crowned night heron 45 15
4939 2l. Northern oriole 65 15
4940 3l. Red-necked grebe . . . 95 30
4941 4l. Mallard (horiz) . . . . 1·10 40

1985. Paintings by Ion Tuculescu. Multicoloured.
4942 1l. Type **992** 10 15
4943 2l. "Circulation" 35 15
4944 3l. "Interior of Peasant's Home" (horiz) 50 20
4945 4l. "Sunset" (horiz) 70 25

993 Peacock

1985. Butterflies and Moths. Multicoloured.
4946 50b. Type **993** 10 10
4947 1l. Swallowtail 25 10
4948 2l. Red admiral 40 15
4949 3l. Emperor moth 55 20
4950 4l. Hebe tiger moth 80 30
4951 5l. Eyed hawk moth 95 45

994 Transfagarasan Mountain Road

1985. 20th Anniv of Election of General Secretary Nicolae Ceausescu and 9th Communist Party Congress. Multicoloured.
4952 1l. Type **994** 20 15
4953 2l. Danube–Black Sea Canal 60 25
4954 3l. Bucharest underground railway 90 40
4955 4l. Irrigating fields 90 45

995 Rumanian Crest, Symbols of Agriculture and "XX"

997 "Senecio glaberrimus"

1985. 20th Anniv of Rumanian Socialist Republic. Multicoloured.
4956 1l. Type **995** 25 25
4957 2l. Crest, symbols of industry and "XX" . . . 55 35

1985. 50th Anniv of Retezat National Park. Mult.
4959 50b. Type **997** 10 10
4960 1l. Chamois 20 10
4961 2l. "Centaurea retezatensis" 40 20
4962 3l. Violet 55 20
4963 4l. Alpine marmot 80 30
4964 5l. Golden eagle . . . . . 3·25 90

998 Universal "530 DTC"

1985. Rumanian Tractors. Multicoloured.
4966 50b. Type **998** 10 10
4967 1l. Universal "550 M HC" 25 10
4968 1l.50 Universal "650 Super" 35 10
4969 2l. Universal "850" 45 20
4970 3l. Universal "S 1801 IF" tracked front loader . . . 65 20
4971 4l. Universal "A 3602 IF" front loader 95 30

999 Costume of Muscel (female)

1985. Costumes (1st series). Multicoloured.
4972 50b. Type **999** 10 10
4973 50b. Muscel (male) 10 10
4974 1l.50 Bistrita-Nasaud (female) 25 20
4975 1l.50 Bistrita-Nasaud (male) 25 20
4976 2l. Vrancea (female) 35 10
4977 2l. Vrancea (male) 35 10
4978 3l. Vilcea (female) 55 25
4979 3l. Vilcea (male) 55 25
See also Nos. 5143/5150.

1000 Footballer attacking Goal

1985. World Cup Football Championship, Mexico (1986) (1st issue). Multicoloured.
4980 50b. Type **1000** 10 15
4981 1l. Player capturing ball . . 20 15
4982 1l.50 Player heading ball . . 25 25
4983 2l. Player about to tackle . . 40 25
4984 3l. Player heading ball and goalkeeper 65 35
4985 4l. Player kicking ball overhead . . . . 1·00 45
See also Nos. 5038/43.

1001 U.N. Emblem and "40"

1002 Copper

1985. 40th Anniv of U.N.O. (4986) and 30th Anniv of Rumanian Membership (4987).
4986 2l. Type **1001** 30 20
4987 2l. U.N. building, New York, U.N. emblem and Rumanian crest 30 20

1985. Minerals. Multicoloured.
4988 50b. Quartz and calcite . . 10 15
4989 1l. Type **1002** 10 15
4990 2l. Gypsum 25 15
4991 3l. Quartz 40 20
4992 4l. Stibium 60 30
4993 5l. Tetrahedrite 90 40

1003 Posthorn

1985. Stamp Day.
4994 **1003** 2l.(+1l.) multicoloured 50 40

1004 Goofy as Hank waking to find himself at Camelot

1985. 150th Birth of Mark Twain (writer). Scenes from "A Connecticut Yankee in King Arthur's Court" (film). Multicoloured.
4995 50b. Type **1004** . . . . . 2·40 1·60
4996 50b. Hank at the stake and Merlin (Mickey Mouse) 2·40 1·60
4997 50b. Hank being hoisted onto horseback in full armour . . . . 2·40 1·60
4998 50b. Pete as Sir Sagramoor on horseback . . . . . 2·40 1·60

1985. Birth Bicentenaries of Grimm Brothers (folklorists). Scenes from "The Three Brothers". As T **1004**. Multicoloured.
5000 1l. Father (Donald Duck) bidding farewell to the brothers (Huey, Louie and Dewey) . . . . 3·00 2·75
5001 1l. Louie as fencing master brother . . . . 3·00 2·75
5002 1l. Louie keeping rain off his father with sword . . 3·00 2·75
5003 1l. Huey as blacksmith brother shoeing galloping horse . . . . 3·00 2·75
5004 1l. Dewey as barber brother shaving Brer Rabbit on the run . . . . 3·00 2·75

1005 Wright Brothers (aviation pioneers) and Wright Flyer 1

1985. Explorers and Pioneers. Multicoloured.

5006	1l. Type **1005**	15	10
5007	1l.50 Jacques Yves Cousteau (undersea explorer) and "Calypso"	45	10
5008	2l. Amelia Earhart (first woman trans-Atlantic flyer) and Fokker F.VIIb/3m seaplane "Friendship"	35	10
5009	3l. Charles Lindbergh (first solo trans-Atlantic flyer) and Ryan NYP Special "Spirit of St. Louis"	45	20
5010	3l.50 Sir Edmund Hillary (first man to reach summit of Everest)	45	25
5011	4l. Robert Peary and Emil Racovita (polar explorers)	50	25
5012	5l. Richard Byrd (polar explorer and aviator) and polar supply ship	1·20	40
5013	6l. Neil Armstrong (first man on Moon) and Moon	65	45

1006 Edmond Halley and Comet

1986. Air. Appearance of Halley's Comet.

5014	2l. Type **1006**	30	20
5015	4l. Comet, orbit and space probes	60	30

No. 5014 is wrongly inscr "Edmund".

1007 "Nina in Green" **1010** Hotel Diana, Baile Herculane

1009 Goofy playing Clarinet

1986. Paintings by Nicolae Tonitza. Multicoloured.

5016	1l. Type **1007**	10	15
5017	2l. "Irina"	30	20
5018	3l. "Forester's Daughter"	45	30
5019	4l. "Woman on Veranda"	70	30

1986. 50th Anniv of Colour Animation. Scenes from "Band Concert" (cartoon film). Mult.

5021	50b. Type **1009**	2·40	1·70
5022	50b. Clarabelle playing flute	2·40	1·70
5023	50b. Mickey Mouse conducting	2·40	1·70
5024	50b. Paddy and Peter Pig playing euphonium and trumpet	2·40	1·70
5025	1l. Conductor Mickey and flautist Donald Duck	2·75	2·75
5026	1l. Donald caught in trombone slide	2·75	2·75
5027	1l. Horace playing drums	2·75	2·75
5028	1l. Donald selling ice cream	2·75	2·75
5029	1l. Mickey and euphonium caught in tornado	2·75	2·75

1986. Spa Hotels. Multicoloured.

5031	50b. Type **1010**	10	10
5032	1l. Hotel Termal, Baile Felix	15	10
5033	2l. Hotels Delfin, Meduza and Steaua de Mare, North Eforie	35	10
5034	3l. Hotel Caciulata, Calimanesti-Caciulata	50	20
5035	4l. Villa Palas, Slanic Moldova	75	30
5036	5l. Hotel Bradet, Sovata	85	35

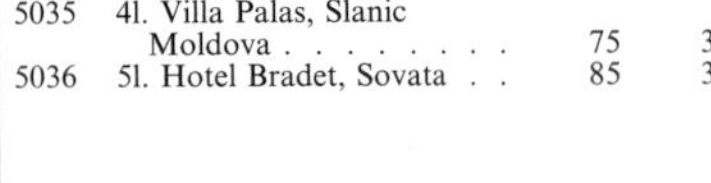

1011 Ceausescu and Red Flag

1986. 65th Anniv of Rumanian Communist Party

5037	**1011** 2l. multicoloured	80	35

1012 Italy v. Bulgaria

1986. World Cup Football Championship, Mexico (2nd issue). Multicoloured.

5038	50b. Type **1012**	10	15
5039	1l. Mexico v. Belgium	10	15
5040	2l. Canada v. France	30	20
5041	3l. Brazil v. Spain	40	20
5042	4l. Uruguay v. W. Germany	60	35
5043	5l. Morocco v. Poland	70	40

1014 "Tulipa gesneriana"

1986. Garden Flowers. Multicoloured.

5045	50b. Type **1014**	10	15
5046	1l. "Iris hispanica"	10	15
5047	2l. "Rosa hybrida"	35	15
5048	3l. "Anemone coronaria"	50	20
5049	4l. "Freesia refracta"	70	30
5050	5l. "Chrysanthemum indicum"	80	40

1015 Mircea the Great and Horsemen

1986. 600th Anniv of Mircea the Great's Accession.

5051	**1015** 2l. multicoloured	30	25

1016 Thatched House with Veranda, Alba

1986. 50th Anniv of Museum of Historic Dwellings, Bucharest. Multicoloured.

5052	50b. Type **1016**	10	35
5053	1l. Stone-built house, Arges	10	35
5054	2l. House with veranda, Constanta	35	40
5055	3l. House with tiled roof and steps, Timis	50	40
5056	4l. House with ramp to veranda, Neamt	70	20
5057	5l. Two storey house with first floor veranda, Gorj	80	30

1017 Julius Popper (Tierra del Fuego, 1886–93)

1986. Polar Research. Multicoloured.

5058	50b. Type **1017**	15	10
5059	1l. Bazil Gh. Assan (Spitzbergen, 1896)	35	10
5060	2l. Emil Racovita and "Belgica" (barque) (Antarctic, 1897–99)	80	10
5061	3l. Constantin Dumbrava (Greenland, 1927–28)	60	20
5062	4l. Rumanian participation in 17th Soviet Antarctic Expedition, 1971–72	1·60	25
5063	5l. 1977 "Sinoe" and 1979–80 "Tirnava" krill fishing expeditions	1·20	30

1019 The Blusher **1020** Group of Cyclists

1986. Fungi. Multicoloured.

5065	50b. Type **1019**	15	10
5066	1l. Oak mushroom	20	10
5067	2l. Peppery milk cap	45	15
5068	3l. Shield fungus	70	35
5069	4l. The charcoal burner	1·00	40
5070	5l. "Tremiscus helvelloides"	1·10	55

1986. Cycle Tour of Rumania. Multicoloured.

5071	1l. Type **1020**	10	15
5072	2l. Motor cycle following cyclist	30	15
5073	3l. Jeep following cyclists	40	25
5074	4l. Winner	65	25

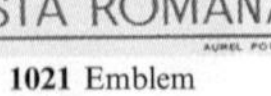

1021 Emblem **1022** Petru Maior (historian) (225th birth anniv)

1986. 40th Anniv of U.N.E.S.C.O. and 30th Anniv of Rumanian Membership.

5076	**1021** 4l. multicoloured	60	45

1986. Birth Anniversaries.

5077	**1022** 50b. purple, gold and green	10	10
5078	– 1b. green, gold and mauve	10	10
5079	– 2l. red, gold and blue	30	10
5080	– 3l. blue, gold and brown	55	20

DESIGNS: 1l. George Topirceanu (writer, centenary); 2l. Henri Coanda (engineer, centenary); 3l. Constantin Budeanu (engineer, centenary).

1023 Coach and Horses ($\frac{1}{2}$-size illustration)

1986. Stamp Day.

5081	**1023** 2l.(+1l.) multicoloured	50	40

No. 5081 includes the se-tenant premium-carrying tab shown in Type **1023**.

1024 F 300 Oil Drilling Rigs **1026** Tin Can and Motor Car ("Recycle metals")

1025 "Goat"

1986. Industry. Multicoloured.

5082	50b. Type **1024**	10	10
5083	1l. "Promex" excavator (horiz)	10	10
5084	2l. Petrochemical refinery, Pitesti	35	10
5085	3l. Tipper "110 t" (horiz)	50	20
5086	4l. "Coral" computer	70	25
5087	5l. 350 m.w. turbine (horiz)	80	35

1986. New Year Folk Customs. Multicoloured.

5088	50b. Type **1025**	10	10
5089	1l. Sorcova	10	10
5090	2l. Plugusorul	35	10
5091	3l. Buhaiul	50	15
5092	4l. Caiutii	70	25
5093	5l. Uratorii	80	35

1986. "Save Waste Materials".

5094	**1026** 1l. red and orange	15	10
5095	– 2l. light green and green	40	20

DESIGN: 2l. Trees and hand with newspaper ("Recycle waste paper").

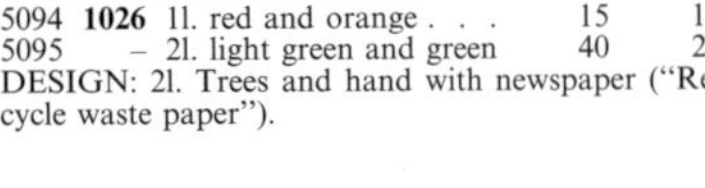

1027 Flags and Young People **1028** Anniversary Emblem

1987. 65th Anniv of Communist Youth Union. Multicoloured.

5096	1l. Type **1027**	15	40
5097	2l. Anniversary emblem	45	55
5098	3l. Flags and young people (different)	65	70

1987. 25th Anniv of Agricultural Co-operatives.

5099	**1028** 2l. multicoloured	30	30

1030 "Birch Trees by Lake" (Ion Andreescu)

1987. Paintings. Multicoloured.

5101	50b. Type **1030**	10	15
5102	1l. "Young Peasant Girls spinning" (N. Grigorescu)	15	15
5103	2l. "Washerwoman" (St. Luchian)	30	15
5104	3l. "Interior" (St. Dimitrescu)	55	20
5105	4l. "Winter Landscape" (Al. Ciucurencu)	65	25
5106	5l. "Winter in Bucharest" (N. Tonitza) (vert)	85	35

1031 "1907" and Peasants

1987. 80th Anniv of Peasant Uprising.
5107 **1031** 2l. multicoloured . . . 30 30

1032 Players **1033** 1 Leu Coin

1987. 10th Students World Men's Handball Championship.
5108 **1032** 50b. multicoloured . . 10 15
5109 – 1l. multicoloured (horiz) 45 15
5110 – 2l. multicoloured . . . 30 15
5111 – 3l. multicoloured (horiz) 55 25
5112 – 4l. multicoloured . . . 70 30
5113 – 5l. multicoloured (horiz) 85 40
DESIGNS: 1l. to 5l. Various match scenes.

1987. Currency.
5114 **1033** 1l. multicoloured . . . 20 15

1034 Eastern White Pelicans in the Danube Delta

1987. Tourism. Multicoloured.
5116 50b. Type **1034** 25 10
5117 1l. Cable car above Transfagarasan mountain road 25 10
5118 2l. Cheile Bicazului 45 10
5119 3l. Ceahlau mountains . . . 75 20
5120 4l. Lake Capra, Fagaras mountains 90 25
5121 5l. Borsa orchards . . . . . 1·10 35

1035 Henri August's Glider, 1909

1987. Air. Aircraft. Multicoloured.
5122 50b. Type **1035** 10 10
5123 1l. Sky diver jumping from IS-28 B2 glider 15 10
5124 2l. IS-29 D2 glider 25 15
5125 3l. IS-32 glider 50 15
5126 4l. I.A.R.35 light airplane 65 25
5127 5l. IS-28 M2 aircraft 90 30

1036 Youth on Winged Horse

1987. Fairy Tales by Petre Ispirescu. Multicoloured.
5128 50b. Type **1036** 10 15
5129 1l. King and princesses ("Salt in the Food") . . . 15 15
5130 2l. Girl on horse fighting lion ("Ileana Simziana") 25 15
5131 3l. Youth with bow and arrow aiming at bird ("The Youth and the Golden Apples") 50 20
5132 4l. George and dead dragon ("George the Brave") . . 65 15
5133 5l. Girl looking at sleeping youth ("The Enchanted Pig") 90 20

1037 Class L 45H Diesel Shunter

1987. Railway Locomotives. Multicoloured.
5135 50b. Type **1037** 10 10
5136 1l. Class LDE 125 diesel goods locomotive 20 10
5137 2l. Class LDH 70 diesel goods locomotive 30 10
5138 3l. Class LDE 2100 diesel locomotive 50 20
5139 4l. Class LDE 3000 diesel locomotive 60 15
5140 5l. Class LE 5100 electric locomotive 80 20

1987. Costumes (2nd series). As T **999**. Mult.
5143 1l. Tirnave (female) 20 15
5144 1l. Tirnave (male) 20 15
5145 2l. Buzau (female) 35 15
5146 2l. Buzau (male) 35 15
5147 3l. Dobrogea (female) . . . 50 25
5148 3l. Dobrogea (male) 50 25
5149 4l. Ilfov (female) 65 25
5150 4l. Ilfov (male) 65 25

1040 Postal Services (½-size illustration)

1987. Stamp Day.
5151 **1040** 2l.(+1l.) multicoloured 50 30
No. 5151 includes the se-tenant premium-carrying tab shown in Type **1040**, the stamp and tab forming a composite design.

1041 Honey Bee on Flower

1987. Bee-keeping. Multicoloured.
5152 1l. Type **1041** 15 15
5153 2l. Honey bee, sunflowers and hives 45 15
5154 3l. Hives in Danube delta 50 25
5155 4l. Apiculture Complex, Bucharest 65 30

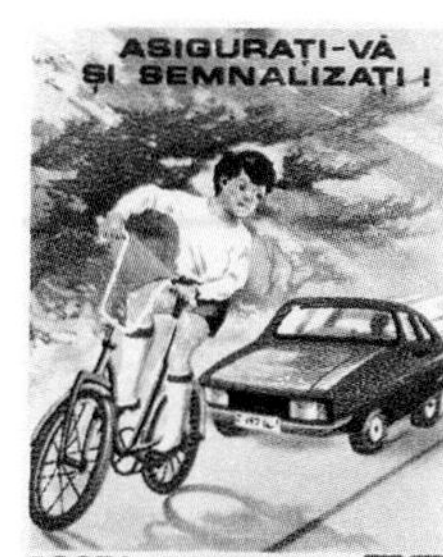

1042 Car behind Boy on Bicycle

1987. Road Safety. Multicoloured.
5156 50b. Type **1042** 10 15
5157 1l. Children using school crossing 10 15
5158 2l. Driver carelessly opening car door 15 15
5159 3l. Hand holding crossing sign and children using zebra crossing 55 25
5160 4l. Speedometer and crashed car 80 30
5161 5l. Child's face and speeding car . . . . 1·10 50

1043 Red Flag and Lenin

1987. 70th Anniv of Russian Revolution.
5162 **1043** 2l. multicoloured . . . 50 25

1044 Biathlon **1045** Crest and National Colours

1987. Winter Olympic Games, Calgary (1988). Multicoloured.
5163 50b. Type **1044** 10 15
5164 1l. Slalom 70 15
5165 1l.50 Ice hockey 15 15
5166 2l. Luge 15 15
5167 3l. Speed skating 30 15
5168 3l.50 Figure skating 55 25
5169 4l. Downhill skiing 60 30
5170 5l. Two-man bobsleigh . . . 75 40

1987. 40th Anniv of People's Republic.
5171 **1045** 2l. multicoloured . . . 40 35

1046 Pres. Ceausescu and Flags

1988. 70th Birthday and 55 Years of Revolutionary Activity of Pres. Ceausescu.
5172 **1046** 2l. multicoloured . . . 75 60

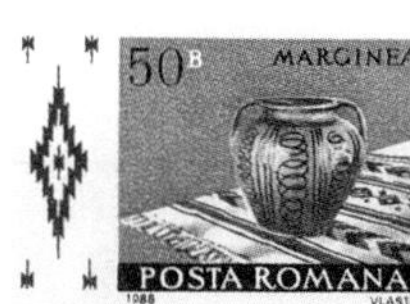

1047 Wide-necked Pot, Marginea

1988. Pottery. Multicoloured.
5173 50b. Type **1047** 10 10
5174 1l. Flask, Oboga 10 10
5175 2l. Jug and saucer, Horezu 20 10
5176 3l. Narrow-necked pot, Curtea de Arges 50 25
5177 4l. Jug, Birsa 70 25
5178 5l. Jug and plate, Vama . . 80 35

1049 Ceramic Clock **1051** Constantin Brincoveanu

1988. Clocks in Ploiesti Museum. Multicoloured.
5180 50b. Type **1049** 10 15
5181 1l.50 Gilt clock with sun at base 10 15
5182 2l. Clock with pastoral figure 20 15
5183 3l. Gilt clock surmounted by figure 50 15
5184 4l. Vase-shaped clock . . . 70 25
5185 5l. Clock surmounted by porcelain figures 80 40

1988. 300th Anniv of Election of Constantin Brincoveanu as Ruler of Wallachia.
5187 **1051** 2l. multicoloured . . . 35 25

1052 Gymnastics

1988. Olympic Games, Seoul (1st issue). Mult.
5188 50b. Type **1052** 10 15
5189 1l.50 Boxing 15 15
5190 2l. Lawn tennis 20 20
5191 3l. Judo 50 25
5192 4l. Running 70 35
5193 5l. Rowing 80 45
See also Nos. 5197/5204.

1053 Postal Emblems and Roses

1988. Rumanian–Chinese Stamp Exhibition, Bucharest.
5194 **1053** 2l. multicoloured . . . 30 25

1056 Running

1988. Olympic Games, Seoul (2nd issue). Mult.
5197 50b. Type **1056** 10 15
5198 1l. Canoeing 10 15
5199 1l.50 Gymnastics 10 15
5200 2l. Double kayak 15 15
5201 3l. Weightlifting 40 25
5202 3l.50 Swimming 45 25
5203 4l. Fencing 55 35
5204 5l. Double sculls 65 40

1058 Past and Present Postal Services (½-size illustration)

1988. Stamp Day.
5206 **1058** 2l.(+1l.) multicoloured 50 40
No. 5206 includes the se-tenant premium-carrying tab shown in T **1058**.

1060 State Arms

1988. 70th Anniv of Union of Transylvania and Rumania.
5208 **1060** 2l. multicoloured . . . 50 45

1061 Athenaeum Concert Hall, Bucharest (centenary)

1988. Rumanian History. Multicoloured.
5209 50b. Type **1061** 10 15
5210 1l.50 Roman coin showing Drobeta Bridge 15 15
5211 2l. Ruins (600th anniv of Suceava as capital of Moldavian feudal state) 20 15
5212 3l. Scroll, arms and town (600th anniv of first documentary reference to Pitesti) 50 25
5213 4l. Dacian warriors from Trajan's Column 70 25
5214 5l. Thracian gold helmet from Cotofenesti-Prahova 80 35

1062 Zapodeni, 17th century

1989. Traditional House Architecture. Mult.
5215 50b. Type **1062** 10 15
5216 1l.50 Berbesti, 18th century 15 15
5217 2l. Voitinel, 18th century 20 15
5218 3l. Chiojdu Mic, 18th century 50 25
5219 4l. Cimpanii de Sus, 19th century 70 25
5220 5l. Naruja, 19th century 80 35

1063 Red Cross Worker

1989. Life-saving Services. Multicoloured.
5221 50b. Type **1063** 10 15
5222 1l. Red Cross orderlies giving first aid to girl (horiz) 10 15
5223 1l.50 Fireman carrying child 15 15
5224 2l. Rescuing child from earthquake damaged building 20 15
5225 3l. Mountain rescue team transporting casualty on sledge (horiz) 45 25
5226 3l.50 Rescuing climber from cliff face 55 25
5227 4l. Rescuing child from river 65 25
5228 5l. Lifeguard in rowing boat and children playing in sea (horiz) 75 35

1064 Tasca Bicaz Cement Factory

1989. Industrial Achievements. Multicoloured.
5229 50b. Type **1064** 15 10
5230 1l.50 New railway bridge, Cernavoda 35 10
5231 2l. Synchronous motor, Resita 35 15
5232 3l. Bucharest underground 40 20
5233 4l. Mangalia–Constanta train ferry 1·10 25
5234 5l. "Gloria" (oil drilling platform) 1·10 30

1065 Flags and Symbols of Industry and Agriculture

1989. 50th Anniv of Anti-Fascist Demonstration.
5235 **1065** 2l. multicoloured 60 40

1068 Ion Creanga (writer, death centenary)

1989. Anniversaries. Multicoloured.
5239 1l. Type **1068** 15 10
5240 2l. Mihai Eminescu (poet, death centenary) 25 10
5241 3l. Nicolae Teclu (scientist, 150th birth anniv) 60 10

1069 State and Communist Party Flags and Symbols of Industry and Agriculture

1989. 45th Anniv of Liberation.
5242 **1069** 2l. multicoloured 50 30

1070 "Pin-Pin"

1989. Rumanian Cartoon Films. Multicoloured.
5243 50b. Type **1070** 10 15
5244 1l. "Maria" 10 15
5245 1l.50 "Gore and Grigore" 15 15
5246 2l. "Pisoiul, Balanel, Manole, Monk" 20 10
5247 3l. "Gruia lui Novac" 50 15
5248 3l.50 "Mihaela" 60 20
5249 4l. "Harap Alb" 65 25
5250 5l. "Homo Sapiens" 85 25

1071 Globe, Letter and Houses(½-size illustration)

1989. Stamp Day.
5251 **1071** 2l.(+1l.) multicoloured 45 20
No. 5251 includes the se-tenant premium-carrying tab as illustrated in T **1071**.

1072 Storming of the Bastille

1989. Bicentenary of French Revolution. Mult.
5252 50b. Type **1072** 10 10
5253 1l.50 Street boy and Marianne 15 10
5254 2l. Maximilien de Robespierre 20 10
5255 3l. Rouget de Lisle singing the "Marseillaise" 50 15
5256 4l. Denis Diderot (encyclopaedist) 70 20
5257 5l. Crowd with banner 85 25

1073 Conrad Haas and Diagram

1989. Air. Space Pioneers. Multicoloured.
5259 50b. Type **1073** 10 10
5260 1l.50 Konstantin Tsiolkovski and diagram 20 10
5261 2l. Hermann Oberth and equation 30 10
5262 3l. Robert Goddard and diagram 45 10
5263 4l. Sergei Pavlovich Korolev, Earth and satellite 70 20
5264 5l. Wernher von Braun and landing module 85 25

1075 State and Party Flags and Emblem

1989. 14th Communist Party Congress, Bucharest.
5266 **1075** 2l. multicoloured 60 40

1076 Date, Flag, Victory Sign and Candles

1990. Popular Uprising (1st issue).
5268 **1076** 2l. multicoloured 35 10
See also Nos. 5294/5301.

1077 Flags and Footballers

1990. World Cup Football Championship, Italy (1st issue).
5269 **1077** 50b. multicoloured 10 15
5270 – 1l.50 multicoloured 20 15
5271 – 2l. multicoloured 35 15
5272 – 3l. multicoloured 50 25
5273 – 4l. multicoloured 80 30
5274 – 5l. multicoloured 1·00 40
DESIGNS: 1l.50 to 5l. Showing flags and footballers.
See also Nos. 5276/83.

1079 Footballers

1990. World Cup Football Championship, Italy (2nd issue).
5276 **1079** 50b. multicoloured 10 15
5277 – 1l. multicoloured 15 15
5278 – 1l.50 multicoloured 20 15
5279 – 2l. multicoloured 30 15
5280 – 3l. multicoloured 45 25
5281 – 3l.50 multicoloured 20 10
5282 – 4l. multicoloured 30 10
5283 – 5l. multicoloured 20 10
DESIGNS: 1l. to 5l. Different football scenes.

1080 German Shepherds

1990. International Dog Show, Brno. Mult.
5284 50b. Type **1080** 10 15
5285 1l. English setter 20 15
5286 1l.50 Boxers 25 15
5287 2l. Beagles 30 15
5288 3l. Dobermann pinschers 50 20
5289 3l.50 Great Danes 55 30
5290 4l. Afghan hounds 60 30
5291 5l. Yorkshire terriers 75 30

1081 Fountain, Brunnen

1990. "Riccione 90" International Stamp Fair.
5292 **1081** 2l. multicoloured 30 15

1082 Athenaeum Concert Hall, Bucharest, and Chinese Temple

1990. Rumanian–Chinese Stamp Exhibition, Bucharest.
5293 **1082** 2l. multicoloured 30 15

1083 Soldiers and Crowd at Television Headquarters, Bucharest

1990. Popular Uprising (2nd issue). Multicoloured.
5294 50b.+50b. Republic Palace ablaze, Bucharest (horiz) 10 15
5295 1l.+1l. Crowd in Opera Square, Timisoara 15 15
5296 1l.50+1l. Soldiers joining crowd in Town Hall Square, Tirgu Mures (horiz) 20 15
5297 2l.+1l. Type **1083** 25 15
5298 3l.+1l. Mourners at funeral, Timisoara (horiz) 30 20
5299 3l.50+1l. Crowd celebrating, Brasov 40 20

5300 4l.+1l. Crowd with banners, Sibiu (horiz) 40 30
5301 5l.+2l. Cemetery, Bucharest (horiz) 60 35

1084 "Nicolae Cobzarul" (Stefan Luchian)

1990. Paintings damaged during the Uprising. Mult.
5303 50b. Type **1084** 25 10
5304 1l.50 "Woman in White" (Ion Andreescu) 20 10
5305 2l. "Florist" (Luchian) . . . 25 10
5306 3l. "Vase of Flowers" (Jan Brueghel, the elder) . . . 40 20
5307 4l. "Spring" (Pieter Brueghel, the elder) (horiz) 55 25
5308 5l. "Madonna and Child" (G. B. Paggi) 65 30

1085 size illustration Flag Stamps encircling Globe (⅔-size illustration)

1990. Stamp Day.
5309 **1085** 2l.(+1l.) multicoloured 40 20
No. 5309 includes the se-tenant premium-carrying tab as shown in Type **1085**.

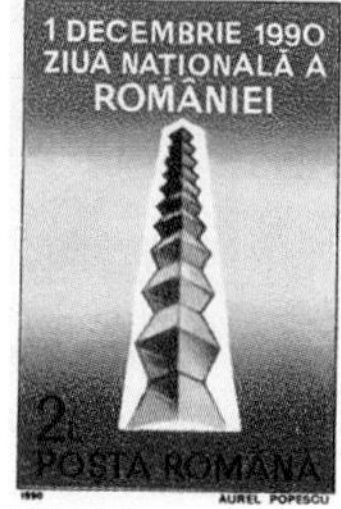

1086 Constantin Cantacuzino (historian, 350th birth anniv) **1087** Column of Infinity

1990. Anniversaries.
5310 **1086** 50b. brown and blue . . 10 10
5311 – 1l.50 green and mauve 20 10
5312 – 2l. red and blue 25 10
5313 – 3l. blue and brown . . 40 15
5314 – 4l. brown and blue . . 55 20
5315 – 5l. violet and green . . 70 25
DESIGNS: 1l.50, Ienachita Vacarescu (writer, 250th birth anniv); 2l. Titu Maiorescu (politician, 150th birth anniv); 3l. Nicolae Iorga (historian, 50th death anniv); 4l. Martha Bibescu (writer, birth centenary); 5l. Stefan Procupiu (scientist, birth centenary).

1990. National Day.
5316 **1087** 2l. multicoloured . . . 30 10

1990. 1st Anniv of Popular Uprising. No. 5268 surch **L4 UN AN DE LA VICTORIA REVOLUTIEI**.
5317 **1076** 4l. on 2l. multicoloured 60 20

1089 "Irises"

1991. Death Centenary of Vincent van Gogh (painter). Multicoloured.
5318 50b. Type **1089** 10 10
5319 2l. "The Artist's Room" . . 10 10
5320 3l. "Illuminated Coffee Terrace" (vert) 20 10
5321 3l.50 "Orchard in Blossom" 30 10
5322 5l. "Sunflowers" (vert) . . . 40 10

1090 Greater Black-backed Gull **1091** Crucifixion

1991. Water Birds.
5323 **1090** 50b. blue 10 10
5324 – 1l. green 10 10
5325 – 1l.50 bistre 10 10
5326 – 2l. blue 15 10
5327 – 3l. green 25 10
5328 – 3l.50 green 30 10
5329 – 4l. violet 35 10
5330 – 5l. brown 35 10
5331 – 6l. brown 50 10
5332 – 7l. blue 60 15
DESIGNS. 1l. Common tern; 1l.50, Pied avocet; 2l. Pomarine skua; 3l. Northern lapwings; 3l.50, Red-breasted merganser; 4l. Little egret; 5l. Dunlin; 6l. Black- tailed godwit; 7l. Whiskered tern.

1991. Easter.
5333 **1091** 4l. multicoloured . . . 20 10

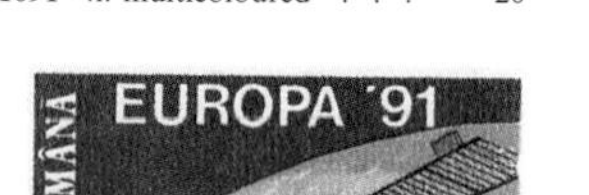

1092 "Eutelsat 1" Communications Satellite

1991. Europa. Europe in Space.
5334 **1092** 4l.50 multicoloured . . 35 20

1093 Posthorn **1094** Rings Exercise

1991.
5335 **1093** 4l.50 blue 25 10

1991. Gymnastics. Multicoloured.
5336 1l. Type **1094** 10 15
5337 1l. Parallel bars 10 15
5338 4l.50 Vaulting 30 15
5339 4l.50 Asymmetric bars . . . 30 15
5340 8l. Floor exercises 45 25
5341 9l. Beam 55 30
For similar design to No. 5341, surcharged 90l. on 5l., see No. 5431.

1095 Curtea de Arges Monastery **1096** Hotel Continental, Timisoara

1991. Monasteries. Multicoloured.
5342 1l. Type **1095** 10 10
5343 1l. Putna 10 10
5344 4l.50 Varatec 30 10
5345 4l.50 Agapia (horiz) 30 10
5346 8l. Golia (horiz) 45 10
5347 9l. Sucevita (horiz) 55 10

1991. Hotels.
5349 **1096** 1l. blue 05 10
5350 – 2l. green 10 10
5351 – 4l. red 15 10
5352 – 5l. violet 30 10
5353 – 6l. brown 20 10
5354 – 8l. brown 15 10
5355 – 9l. red 50 10
5356 – 10l. green 55 10
5357 – 18l. red 65 10
5358 – 20l. orange 65 10
5359 – 25l. blue 90 10
5360 – 30l. purple . . . . . 1·50 10
5361 – 45l. blue . . . . . . 1·00 10
5362 – 60l. brown . . . . . 1·20 10
5363 – 80l. violet . . . . . . 1·50 10
5364b – 120l. blue and grey . . 1·80 50
5365 – 160l. red and pink . . 2·30 40
5366 – 250l. blue and grey . . 2·75 50
5367 – 400l. brown and ochre 5·00 95
5368 – 500l. deep green & green . . . . . . 6·50 1·10
5369 – 800l. mauve and pink 9·00 1·80
DESIGNS—As T **1096**: HORIZ: 2l. Valea Caprei Chalet, Mt. Fagaras; 5l. Hotel Lebada, Crisan; 6l. Muntele Rosu Chalet, Mt. Ciucas; 8l. Trans-silvania Hotel, Cluj-Napoca; 9l. Hotel Orizont, Predeal; 20l. Alpin Hotel, Poiana Brasov; 25l. Constanta Casino; 30l. Miorita Chalet, Mt. Bucegi; 45l. Sura Dacilor Chalet, Poiana Brasov; 60l. Valea Draganului Tourist Complex; 80l. Hotel Florica, Venus. VERT: 4l. Intercontinental Hotel, Bucharest; 10l. Hotel Roman, Baile Herculcane; 18l. Rarau Chalet, Mt. Rarau. 26 × 40 mm: 120l. International Complex, Baile Felix; 160l. Hotel Egreta, Tulcea. 40 × 26 mm: 250l. Valea de Pesti Motel, Jiului Valley; 400l. Baisoara Tourist Complex; 500l. Bradul Hotel, Covasna; 800l. Gorj Hotel, Jiu.
Nos. 5362/9 have no frame.

1097 Gull and Sea Shore

1991. "Riccione 91" Stamp Exhibition, Riccione, Italy.
5381 **1097** 4l. multicoloured . . . 20 10

1098 Vase decorated with Scarlet and Military Macaws **1099** Academy Emblem

1991. Rumanian–Chinese Stamp Exhibition. Mult.
5382 5l. Type **1098** 40 10
5383 5l. Vase with peony decoration 40 10

1991. 125th Anniv of Rumanian Academy.
5384 **1099** 1l. blue 15 10

1100 "Flowers" (Nicu Enea) **1102** Map with House and People

1991. "Balcanfila '91" Stamp Exhibition, Bacau. Multicoloured.
5385 4l. Type **1100** 20 10
5386 5l.(+2l.) "Peasant Girl of Vlasca" (Georghe Tattarescu) 35 10

1991. Population and Housing Census.
5389 **1102** 5l. multicoloured . . . 25 10

1103 Bridge

1991. "Phila Nippon '91" International Stamp Exhibition, Tokyo.
5390 **1103** 10l. ochre, brown & red 45 15
5391 – 10l. multicoloured . . . 45 15
DESIGN: No. 5391, Junk.

1105 Running

1991. World Athletics Championships, Tokyo. Multicoloured.
5393 1l. Type **1105** 10 10
5394 4l. Long jumping 20 10
5395 5l. High jumping 25 10
5396 5l. Athlete in starting blocks 25 10
5397 9l. Hurdling 45 20
5398 10l. Throwing the javelin . . 55 20

1106 Mihail Kogalniceanu (policitian and historian, death cent)

1991. Anniversaries.
5399 **1106** 1l. brown, blue & dp blue 10 10
5400 – 4l. green, lilac and violet 20 10
5401 – 5l. brown, blue & ultramarine 25 10
5402 – 5l. blue, brown and red 35 10
5403 – 9l. red, blue & deep blue 60 20
5404 – 10l. black, lt brn & brn 70 20
DESIGNS: No. 5400, Nicolae Titulescu (politician and diplomat, 50th death anniv); 5401, Andrei Mureseanu (poet, 175th birth anniv); 5402, Aron Pumnul (writer, 125th death anniv); 5403, George Bacovia (writer, 110th birth anniv); 5404, Perpessicius (literature critic, birth centenary).

1107 Library Building

1991. Centenary of Central University Library.
5405 **1107** 8l. brown 50 20

1108 Coach and Horses (⅔-size illustration)

1991. Stamp Day.
5406 **1108** 8l.(+2l.) multicoloured 45 30
No. 5406 includes the se-tenant premium-carrying label shown in Type **1108**.

1109 "Nativity" (17th-century icon) **1110** Biathlon

1991. Christmas.
5407 **1109** 8l. multicoloured . . . 45 20

1992. Winter Olympic Games, Albertville. Mult.
5408 4l. Type **1110** 10 10
5409 5l. Downhill skiing 10 10
5410 8l. Cross-country skiing . . 15 10
5411 10l. Two-man luge 20 10
5412 20l. Speed skating 45 10
5413 25l. Ski-jumping 60 20
5414 30l. Ice hockey 75 20
5415 45l. Men's figure skating . . 1·10 30

1112 Jug, Plate, Tray and Bowl

1992. Rumanian Porcelain from Cluj Napoca. Multicoloured.
5419 4l. Type **1112** 10 15
5420 5l. Tea set 10 15
5421 8l. Jug and goblet (vert) . . 10 15
5422 30l. Tea set (different) . . . 50 20
5423 45l. Vase (vert) 70 35

1113 Atlantic Mackerels

1992. Fishes. Multicoloured.
5424 4l. Type **1113** 10 15
5425 5l. Tench 10 15
5426 8l. Brook charr 10 15
5427 10l. Rumanian bullhead perch 10 15
5428 30l. Nase 45 25
5429 45l. Black Sea red mullet . . 90 40

1114 Vase decorated with Scarlet and Military Macaws

1115 Gymnast on Beam

1992. Apollo Art Gallery. Unissued stamp surch.
5430 **1114** 90l. on 5l. multicoloured . . . . 1·60 40

1992. Individual Gymnastic Championships, Paris. Unissued stamp surch.
5431 **1115** 90l. on 5l. multicoloured . . . . 1·20 40
For similar 9l. value, see No. 5341.

1116 Dressage

1118 "Descent into Hell" (icon)

1992. Horses. Multicoloured.
5432 6l. Type **1116** 10 10
5433 7l. Racing (horiz) 10 10
5434 10l. Rearing 15 10
5435 25l. Jumping gate 35 10
5436 30l. Stamping foot (horiz) 40 20
5437 50l. Winged horse 75 25

1992. Easter.
5439 **1118** 10l. multicoloured . . . 15 10

1120 Tower and Hand Pump

1992. Centenary of Bucharest Fire Tower.
5441 **1120** 10l. multicoloured . . . 20 10

1121 Filipino Vinta and Rook

1992. 30th Chess Olympiad, Manila, Philippines. Multicoloured.
5442 10l. Type **1121** 15 10
5443 10l. Exterior of venue and chessmen 15 10

1122 Post Rider approaching Town

1992. Stamp Day.
5445 **1122** 10l.+4l. pink, violet and blue 15 10

1123 Pistol shooting

1124 Ion Bratianu

1992. Olympic Games, Barcelona. Multicoloured.
5446 6l. Type **1123** 10 10
5447 7l. Weightlifting 10 10
5448 9l. Two-man kayak (horiz) 10 10
5449 10l. Handball 10 10
5450 25l. Wrestling (horiz) . . . 20 15
5451 30l. Fencing (horiz) 25 20
5452 50l. Running 45 30
5453 55l. Boxing (horiz) 50 30

1992. 130th Anniv of Foreign Ministry. Designs showing former Ministers.
5455 **1124** 10l. violet, green and deep green 10 05
5456 – 25l. purple, blue & dp blue 20 10
5457 – 30l. blue, purple & brn 25 10
DESIGNS: 25l. Ion Duca; 30l. Grigore Gafencu.

1125 "The Thinker of Cernavoda" (sculpture)

1992. "Expo 92" World's Fair, Seville. "Era of Discovery". Multicoloured.
5458 6l. Type **1125** 10 10
5459 7l. Trajan's bridge, Turnu-Severin 10 10
5460 10l. House on stilts 10 10
5461 25l. Saligny Bridge, Cernavoda 35 10
5462 30l. Traian Vuia's No. 1 airplane 35 10
5463 55l. Hermann Oberth's rocket 25 15

1126 Doves posting Letters in Globe

1992. World Post Day.
5465 **1126** 10l. multicoloured . . . 15 10

1127 "Santa Maria" and Bust of Columbus

1992. 500th Anniv of Discovery of America by Columbus. Multicoloured.
5466 6l. Type **1127** 15 10
5467 10l. "Nina" 15 10
5468 25l. "Pinta" 25 10
5469 55l. Columbus claiming New World 35 20

1128 Post Office Emblem

1992. 1st Anniv of Establishment of R.A. Posta Romana (postal organization).
5471 **1128** 10l. multicoloured . . . 15 10

1129 Jacob Negruzzi (writer, 150th birth anniv)

1130 American Bald Eagle

1992. Anniversaries.
5472 **1129** 6l. green and violet . . 10 10
5473 – 7l. mauve, purple and green 10 10
5474 – 9l. blue and mauve . . 10 10
5475 – 10l. light brown, brown and blue 10 10
5476 – 25l. blue and brown . . 20 15
5477 – 30l. green and blue . . 20 15
DESIGNS: 7l. Grigore Antipa (biologist, 125th birth anniv); 9l. Alexe Mateevici (poet, 75th death anniv); 10l. Cezar Petrescu (writer, birth centenary); 25l. Octav Onicescu (mathematician, birth centenary); 30l. Ecaterina Teodoroiu (First World War fighter, 75th death anniv).

1992. Animals. Multicoloured.
5478 6l. Type **1130** 10 15
5479 7l. Spotted owl 10 15
5480 9l. Brown bear 15 15
5481 10l. American black oystercatcher (horiz) . . . 15 15
5482 25l. Wolf (horiz) 25 15
5483 30l. White-tailed deer (horiz) 25 15
5484 55l. Elk (horiz) 50 30

1131 Arms

1133 Nativity

1132 Buildings and Street, Mogosoaiei

1992. New State Arms.
5486 **1131** 15l. multicoloured . . . 15 10

1992. Anniversaries. Multicoloured.
5487 7l. Type **1132** (300th anniv) 10 10
5488 9l. College building and statue, Roman (600th anniv) 10 10
5489 10l. Prince Basaral, monastery and Princess Despina (475th anniv of Curtea de Arges Monastery) 10 10
5490 25l. Bucharest School of Architecture (80th anniv) 20 10

1992. Christmas.
5491 **1133** 15l. multicoloured . . . 15 10

1134 Globe and Key-pad on Telephone

1992. New Telephone Number System.
5492 **1134** 15l. black, red and blue 15 10

1136 Mihai Voda Monastery

1993. Destroyed Bucharest Buildings. Mult.
5494 10l. Type **1136** 10 10
5495 13l. Vacaresti Monastery . . 10 10
5496 25l. Unirii Hall 20 10
5497 30l. Mina Minovici Medico-legal Institute 30 10

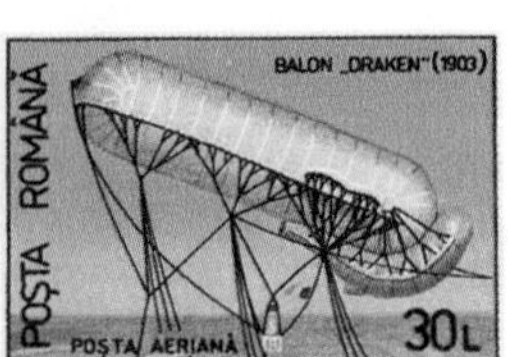

1137 Parseval Sigsfeld Kite-type Observation Balloon "Draken"

1993. Air. Balloons. Multicoloured.
5498 30l. Type **1137** 15 15
5499 90l. Caquot observation balloon, 1917 . . . . . . 50 15

1138 Crucifixion

1139 Hawthorn

1993. Easter.
5500 **1138** 15l. multicoloured . . . 15 10

1993. Medicinal Plants. Multicoloured.
5501 10l. Type **1139** 10 10
5502 15l. Gentian 10 10
5503 25l. Sea buckthorn 10 10
5504 30l. Billberry 15 10
5505 50l. Arnica 25 20
5506 90l. Dog rose 45 30

1140 Stanescu

1141 Mounted Courier

1993. 60th Birth Anniv of Nichita Stanescu (poet).
5507 **1140** 15l. multicoloured . . . 15 10

1993. Stamp Day.
5508 **1141** 15l.+10l. multicoloured 15 10

1143 Black-billed Magpie

1993. Birds.
5510 **1143** 5l. black and green . . 15 10
5511 – 10l. black and red . . . 15 10
5512 – 15l. black and red . . . 15 10
5513 – 20l. black and brown 20 10
5514 – 25l. black and red . . . 20 10
5515 – 50l. black and yellow 40 10
5516 – 65l. black and red . . . 55 10
5517 – 90l. black and red . . . 75 10
5518 – 160l. black and blue . . 1·30 15
5519 – 250l. black and mauve 2·10 25
DESIGNS—HORIZ: 10l. Golden eagle. VERT: 15l. Northern bullfinch; 20l. Hoopoe; 25l. Great spotted woodpecker; 50l. Golden oriole; 65l. White winged crossbill; 90l. Barn swallows; 160l. Azure tit; 250l. Rose-coloured starling.

1144 Long-hair **1147** Pine Marten

1146 Adder

1993. Cats. Multicoloured.
5520 10l. Type **1144** 10 20
5521 15l. Tabby-point long-hair 10 20
5522 30l. Red long-hair 15 20
5523 90l. Blue Persian 35 30
5524 135l. Tabby 55 25
5525 160l. Long-haired white Persian 65 30

1993. Protected Animals. Multicoloured.
5527 10l. Type **1146** 10 15
5528 15l. Lynx (vert) 10 15
5529 25l. Common shelduck . . . 15 15
5530 75l. Huchen 25 15
5531 105l. Poplar admiral 35 20
5532 280l. Alpine longhorn beetle 95 70

1993. Mammals.
5533 **1147** 10l. black and yellow 20 10
5534 – 15l. black and brown 20 10
5535 – 20l. red and black . . . 20 10
5536 – 25l. black and brown 25 10
5537 – 30l. black and red . . . 25 10
5538 – 40l. black and red . . . 25 10
5539 – 75l. black and yellow 55 10
5540 – 105l. black and brown 75 10
5541 – 150l. black and orange 1·10 10
5542 – 280l. black and yellow 1·80 25
DESIGNS—HORIZ: 15l. Common rabbit; 30l. Red fox; 150l. Stoat; 280l. Egyptian mongoose. VERT: 20l. Eurasian red squirrel; 25l. Chamois; 40l. Argali; 75l. Small spotted genet; 105l. Garden dormouse.

1148 Brontosaurus

1993. Prehistoric Animals. Multicoloured.
5543 29l. Type **1148** 10 15
5544 46l. Plesiosaurus 15 15
5545 85l. Triceratops 30 15
5546 171l. Stegosaurus 60 25
5547 216l. Tyannosaurus 80 30
5548 319l. Archaeopteryx . . . . 1·10 55

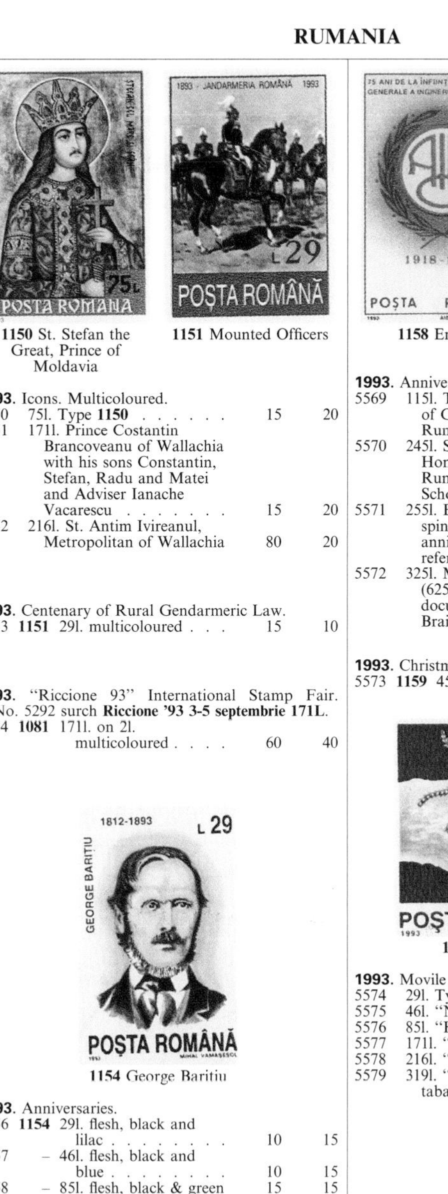

1150 St. Stefan the Great, Prince of Moldavia **1151** Mounted Officers

1993. Icons. Multicoloured.
5550 75l. Type **1150** 15 20
5551 171l. Prince Costantin Brancoveanu of Wallachia with his sons Constantin, Stefan, Radu and Matei and Adviser Ianache Vacarescu 15 20
5552 216l. St. Antim Ivireanul, Metropolitan of Wallachia 80 20

1993. Centenary of Rural Gendarmeric Law.
5553 **1151** 29l. multicoloured . . . 15 10

1993. "Riccione 93" International Stamp Fair. No. 5292 surch **Riccione '93 3-5 septembrie 171L**.
5554 **1081** 171l. on 2l. multicoloured 60 40

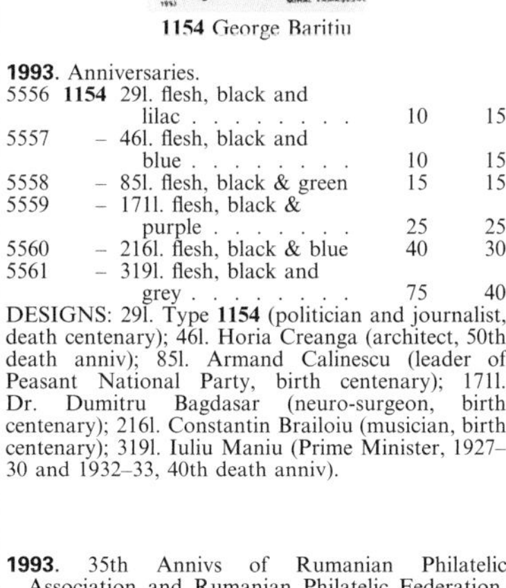

1154 George Baritiu

1993. Anniversaries.
5556 **1154** 29l. flesh, black and lilac 10 15
5557 – 46l. flesh, black and blue 10 15
5558 – 85l. flesh, black & green 15 15
5559 – 171l. flesh, black & purple 25 25
5560 – 216l. flesh, black & blue 40 30
5561 – 319l. flesh, black and grey 75 40
DESIGNS: 29l. Type **1154** (politician and journalist, death centenary); 46l. Horia Creanga (architect, 50th death anniv); 85l. Armand Calinescu (leader of Peasant National Party, birth centenary); 171l. Dr. Dumitru Bagdasar (neuro-surgeon, birth centenary); 216l. Constantin Brailoiu (musician, birth centenary); 319l. Iuliu Maniu (Prime Minister, 1927–30 and 1932–33, 40th death anniv).

1993. 35th Annivs of Rumanian Philatelic Association and Rumanian Philatelic Federation. No. 5445 surch **35 ANI DE ACTIVITATE AFR-FFR 1958–1993 70L+45L**.
5562 **1122** 70l.+45l. on 10l.+4l. pink, violet and blue 50 40

1157 Iancu Flondor (Bukovinan politician)

1993. 75th Anniv of Union of Bessarabia, Bukovina and Transylvania with Rumania.
5564 **1157** 115l. brown, blue and black 15 10
5565 – 245l. violet, yellow and green 25 20
5566 – 255l. multicoloured . . 45 20
5567 – 325l. brown, pink and deep brown 80 25
DESIGNS: 245l. Ionel Bratianu (Prime Minister, 1918–19, 1922–26 and 1927); 255l. Iuliu Maniu (Prime Minister, 1927–30 and 1932–33); 325l. Panteleimon Halippa (Bessarabian politician).

1158 Emblem **1159** "Nativity" (17th-century icon)

1993. Anniversaries. Multicoloured.
5569 115l. Type **1158** (75th anniv of General Association of Rumanian Engineers) . . 15 20
5570 245l. Statue of Johannes Honterus (450th anniv of Rumanian Humanist School) 25 25
5571 255l. Bridge, arms on book spine and seal (625th anniv of first documentary reference to Slatina) . . . 40 25
5572 325l. Map and town arms (625th anniv of first documentary reference to Braila) 75 35

1993. Christmas.
5573 **1159** 45l. multicoloured . . . 15 10

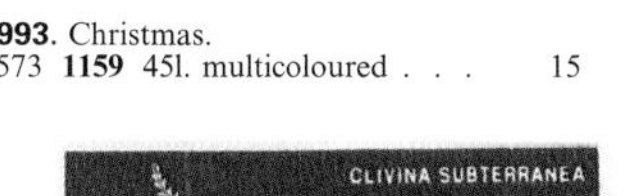

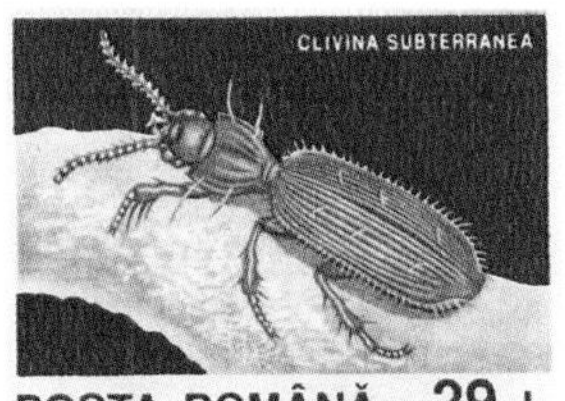

1160 "Clivina subterranea"

1993. Movile Cave Animals. Multicoloured.
5574 29l. Type **1160** 10 10
5575 46l. "Nepa anophthalma" 15 10
5576 85l. "Haemopis caeca" . . 20 15
5577 171l. "Lascona cristiani" . . 30 20
5578 216l. "Semisalsa dobrogica" 45 25
5579 319l. "Armadilidium tabacarui" 75 35

1161 Prince Alexandru Ioan Cuza and Seal

1994. 130th Anniv of Court of Accounts.
5581 **1161** 45l. multicoloured . . . 15 10

1162 Opera House

1994. Destroyed Buildings of Bucharest. Mult.
5582 115l. Type **1162** 10 15
5583 245l. Church of Vacaresti Monastery (vert) 30 25
5584 255l. St. Vineri's Church . . 35 25
5585 325l. Cloisters of Vacaresti Monastery 50 30

1164 Speed Skating **1165** Sarichioi Windmill, Tulcea

1994. Winter Olympic Games, Lillehammer, Norway. Multicoloured.
5588 70l. Type **1164** 10 10
5589 115l. Skiing 15 10
5590 125l. Bobsleighing 15 10
5591 245l. Cross-country skiing 40 15
5592 255l. Ski jumping 45 15
5593 325l. Figure skating 60 20

1994. Mills. Multicoloured.
5595 70l. Type **1165** 10 15
5596 115l. Nucarilor Valley windmill, Tulcea 10 15
5597 125l. Caraorman windmill, Tulcea 20 15
5598 245l. Romanii de Jos watermill, Valcea 40 25
5599 255l. Enisala windmill, Tulcea (horiz) 50 30
5600 325l. Nistoresti watermill, Vrancea 60 40

1166 Calin the Backward **1167** "Resurrection of Christ" (17th-century icon)

1994. Fairy Tales. Multicoloured.
5601 70l. Type **1166** 10 15
5602 115l. Ileana Cosanzeana flying 15 15
5603 125l. Ileana Cosanzeana seated 20 15
5604 245l. Ileana Cosanzeana and castle 40 25
5605 255l. Agheran the Brave . . 50 30
5606 325l. The Enchanted Wolf carrying Ileana Cosanzeana 60 35

1994. Easter.
5607 **1167** 60l. multicoloured . . . 15 10

1168 "Struthiosaurus transylvanicus"

1994. Prehistoric Animals. Multicoloured.
5608 90l. Type **1168** 10 15
5609 130l. Megalosaurus 15 15
5610 150l. Parasaurolophus . . . 30 15
5611 280l. Stenonychosaurus . . 30 20
5612 500l. Camarasaurus 55 40
5613 635l. Gallimimus 70 45

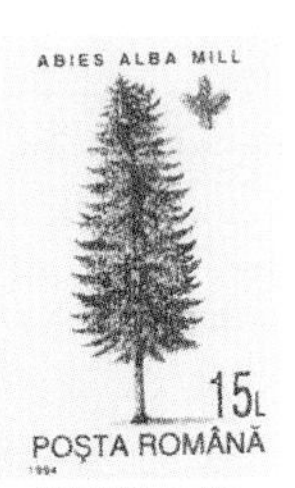

1170 Silver Fir **1171** Players and Flags of U.S.A., Switzerland, Colombia and Rumania

1994. Trees. Each green and black.
5615 15l. Type **1170** 10 10
5616 35l. Scots pine 10 10
5617 45l. White poplar 10 10
5618 60l. Pedunculate oak . . . 15 10
5619 70l. European larch 15 10
5620 125l. Beech 20 10
5621 350l. Sycamore 35 10
5622 940l. Ash . . . . 1·10 45
5623 1440l. Norway spruce . . . 1·50 70
5624 3095l. Large-leaved lime . . 2·75 1·50

1994. World Cup Football Championship, U.S.A. Designs showing various footballing scenes and flags of participating countries. Multicoloured.
5625 90l. Type **1171** 10 10
5626 130l. Brazil, Russia, Cameroun and Sweden (Group B) 10 10
5627 150l. Germany, Bolivia, Spain and South Korea (Group C) 15 10
5628 280l. Argentina, Greece, Nigeria and Bulgaria (Group D) 25 10

5629 500l. Italy, Ireland, Norway and Mexico (Group E) . . 55 30
5630 635l. Belgium, Morocco, Netherlands and Saudi Arabia (Group F) 70 35

1172 Torch-bearer and Centenary Emblem

1994. Centenary of International Olympic Committee. Ancient Greek Athletes. Mult.
5632 150l. Type **1172** 15 10
5633 280l. Discus-thrower and International Sports Year emblem 30 10
5634 500l. Wrestlers and Olympic Peace emblem 60 15
5635 635l. Arbitrator and "Paris 1994" centenary congress emblem 75 20

1173 National History Museum (former Postal Headquarters, Bucharest)

1176 Turning Fork

1175 Traian Vuia's Airplane No. 1, 1906

1994. Stamp Day.
5637 **1173** 90l.+60l. multicoloured 25 15

1994. Air. 50th Anniv of I.C.A.O.
5639 **1175** 110l. brown, black & blue 15 30
5640 – 350l. multicoloured . . 45 30
5641 – 500l. multicoloured . . 70 30
5642 – 635l. black, ultramarine and blue 85 30
DESIGNS: 350l. Rombac One Eleven; 500l. Boeing 737-300; 635l. Airbus Industrie A310.

1994. "Philakorea 1994" International Stamp Exhibition, Seoul.
5643 **1176** 60l. black, orange and mauve 15 10

1177 Beluga

1994. Environmental Protection of Danube Delta. Multicoloured.
5645 150l. Type **1177** 20 10
5646 280l. Orsini's viper 35 15
5647 500l. White-tailed sea eagle 60 35
5648 635l. European mink . . . 80 45

1994. Victory of Rumanian Team in European Gymnastics Championships, Stockholm. Nos. 5338/9 surch **Echipa Romaniei Compioana Europeana Stockholm 1994** and value.
5650 150l. on 4l.50 multicoloured 20 25
5651 525l. on 4l.50 multicoloured 75 40

1179 Elephant

1994. The Circus. Multicoloured.
5652 90l. Type **1179** 10 15
5653 130l. Balancing bear (vert) 10 15
5654 150l. Cycling monkeys . . . 15 15
5655 280l. Tiger jumping through hoop 30 25
5656 500l. Clown on tightrope balancing dogs 60 35
5657 635l. Clown on horseback 80 45

1994. World Post Day. No. 5465 surch **150LEI 1994 Posta - cea mai buna alegere**.
5658 **1126** 150l. on 10l. mult . . . 25 20

1181 Emblem

1183 Snake

1182 Sterlet

1994. 20th International Fair, Bucharest.
5659 **1181** 525l. multicoloured . . 55 20

1994. Sturgeons.
5660 150l. Type **1182** 20 25
5661 280l. Russian sturgeon . . . 40 25
5662 500l. Stellate sturgeon . . . 65 45
5663 635l. Common sturgeon . . 85 55

1994. Rumanian–Chinese Stamp Exhibition, Timisoara and Cluj-Napoca. Multicoloured.
5664 150l. Type **1183** 20 10
5665 1135l. Dragon . . . . . . 1·40 45

1184 Early Steam Train, Bucharest–Giurgii Line

1994. 125th Anniv of Rumanian Railway Administration.
5666 **1184** 90l. multicoloured . . . 15 10

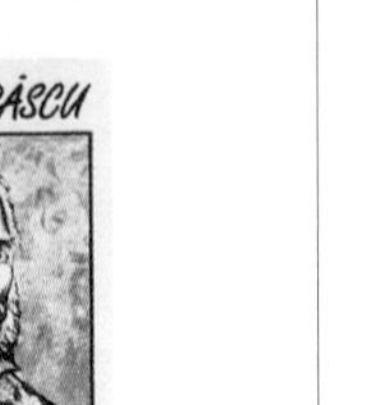

1185 Alexandru Orascu (architect and mathematician)

1994. Anniversaries. Multicoloured.
5667 30l. Type **1185** (death centenary) 10 15
5668 60l. Gheorghe Polizu (physician, 175th birth anniv) 10 15
5669 150l. Iulia Hasdeu (writer, 125th birth anniv) 20 15
5670 280l. S. Mehedinti (scientist, 125th birth anniv) 25 15
5671 350l. Camil Petrescu (writer, birth centenary) 35 25
5672 500l. N. Paulescu (physician, 125th birth anniv) 45 35
5673 940l. L. Grigorescu (painter, birth centenary) 95 50
See also No. 5684.

1186 Nativity

1994. Christmas.
5674 **1186** 60l. multicoloured . . . 15 10

1187 St. Mary's Church, Cleveland, U.S.A.

1994.
5675 **1187** 610l. multicoloured . . 65 15

1188 Anniversary Emblem

1994. 20th Anniv of World Tourism Organization.
5676 **1188** 525l. blue, orange & black 55 20

1190 Kittens

1191 Emblem

1994. Young Domestic Animals. Multicoloured.
5678 90l. Type **1190** 10 20
5679 130l. Puppies 15 20
5680 150l. Kid 25 20
5681 280l. Foal 50 20
5682 500l. Rabbit kittens 85 30
5683 635l. Lambs . . . . 1·10 50

1994. Death Centenary of Gheorghe Tattarescu (painter). As T **1185**. Multicoloured.
5684 90l. Tattarescu 15 10

1995. Save the Children Fund.
5685 **1191** 60l. blue 15 10

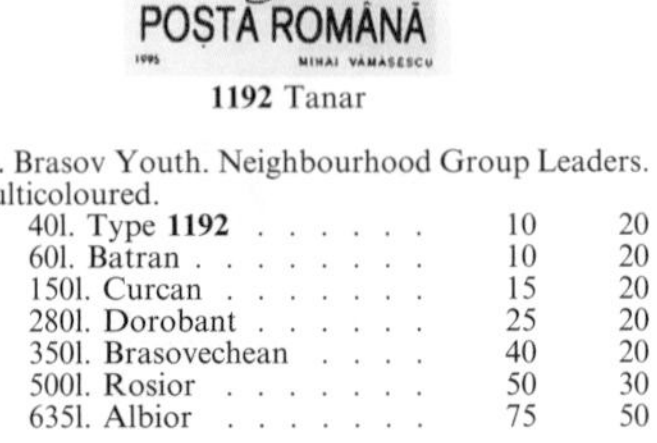

1192 Tanar

1995. Brasov Youth. Neighbourhood Group Leaders. Multicoloured.
5686 40l. Type **1192** 10 20
5687 60l. Batran 10 20
5688 150l. Curcan 15 20
5689 280l. Dorobant 25 20
5690 350l. Brasovechean 40 20
5691 500l. Rosior 50 30
5692 635l. Albior 75 50

1193 Hand and Barbed Wire

1995. 50th Anniv of Liberation of Concentration Camps.
5693 **1193** 960l. black and red . . 60 30

1194 Emblems of French and Rumanian State Airlines

1995. Air. 75th Anniv of Founding of Franco-Rumanian Air Company.
5694 **1194** 60l. blue and red . . . 55 10
5695 – 960l. blue and black . . 60 20
DESIGN: 960l. Potez IX biplane and Paris–Bucharest route map.

1195 Ear of Wheat

1995. 50th Anniversaries. Multicoloured.
5696 675l. Type **1195** (F.A.O.) . . 40 30
5697 960l. Anniversary emblem (U.N.O.) 60 35
5698 1615l. Hand holding pen showing members' flags (signing of U.N. Charter) 1·10 55

1196 "Resurrection" (icon)

1995. Easter.
5699 **1196** 60l. multicoloured . . . 15 10

1197 "Youth without Age and Life without Death"

1995. Fairy Tales. Multicoloured.
5700 90l. Type **1197** 10 20
5701 130l. "The Old Man's Servant and the Old Woman's Servant" (vert) 10 20
5702 150l. "The Prince with the Golden Hair" 10 20
5703 280l. "Son of the Red King" 15 20
5704 500l. "Praslea the Brave and the Golden Apples" (vert) 35 20
5705 635l. "King Dafin" (drawn by golden horses) 40 25

1198 Enescu

1995. 40th Death Anniv of George Enescu (composer).
5706 **1198** 960l. orange and black 60 15

1199 Dove with Section of Rainbow

1200 Blaga

1995. Europa. Peace and Freedom. Multicoloured.

5707	150l. Type **1199**	10	15
5708	4370l. Dove wings forming "EUROPA" around rainbow	3·25	2·30

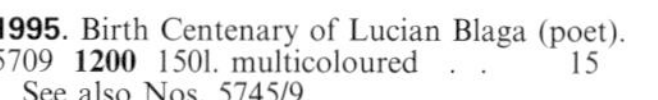

1995. Birth Centenary of Lucian Blaga (poet).

5709	**1200** 150l. multicoloured	15	10

See also Nos. 5745/9.

1201 Bucharest Underground Railway, 1979

1995. Transport.

5712	**1201** 470l. yellow and black (postage)	45	10
5713	– 630l. red and blue	35	10
5714	– 675l. red and black	40	10
5715	– 755l. blue and black	50	10
5716	– 1615l. green and black	1·00	15
5717	– 2300l. green and black	1·10	20
5718	– 2550l. black and red	1·60	25
5719	– 285l. green and black (air)	15	10
5720	– 715l. red and blue	45	10
5721	– 965l. black and blue	55	10
5722	– 1575l. green and black	95	15
5723	– 3410l. blue and black	1·90	1·60

DESIGNS—HORIZ: 285l. I.A.R. 80 aircraft (70th anniv of Rumanian aeronautical industry); 630l. "Masagerul" (post boat); 715l. I.A.R. 316 Red Cross helicopter; 755l. "Razboieni" (container ship); 965l. Sud Aviation SA 330 Puma helicopter; 1575l. I.A.R. 818H seaplane; 2300l. Trolleybus, 1904; 2550l. Steam train, 1869; 3410l. Boeing 737-300 (75th anniv of Rumanian air transport). VERT: 675l. Cable-car, Brasov; 1615l. Electric tram, 1894.

1202 "Dacia" (liner)

1203 Fallow Deer

1995. Centenary of Rumanian Maritime Service. Multicoloured.

5735	90l. Type **1202**	10	20
5736	130l. "Imparatul Traian" (Danube river steamer) (horiz)	10	20
5737	150l. "Romania" (Danube river steamer) (horiz)	10	20
5738	280l. "Costinesti" (tanker) (horiz)	20	20
5739	960l. "Caransebes" (container ship) (horiz)	60	30
5740	3410l. "Tutova" (car ferry) (horiz)	2·30	1·20

1995. European Nature Conservation Year. Mult.

5741	150l. Type **1203**	10	15
5742	280l. Great bustard	25	15
5743	960l. Lady's slipper	65	20
5744	1615l. Stalagmites	1·00	45

1995. Anniversaries. As T **1200**. Multicoloured.

5745	90l. D. Rosca (birth centenary)	10	25
5746	130l. Vasile Conta (150th birth anniv)	10	25
5747	280l. Ion Barbu (birth centenary)	20	25
5748	960l. Iuliu Hatieganu (110th birth anniv)	60	35
5749	1650l. Dimitrie Brandza (botanist) (death centenary)	95	60

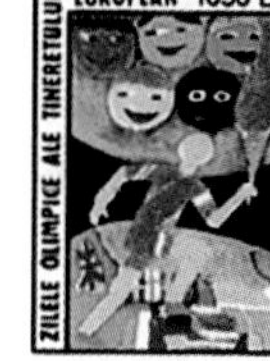

1204 Youths and Torch-bearer

1995. European Youth Olympic Days.

5750	**1204** 1650l. multicoloured	15	15

1205 Post Wagon (½-size illustration)

1995. Stamp Day. Centenary of Upper Rhine Local Post.

5751	**1205** 960l.(+715l.) mult	75	60

No. 5751 includes the se-tenant premium-carrying tab shown in Type **1205**.

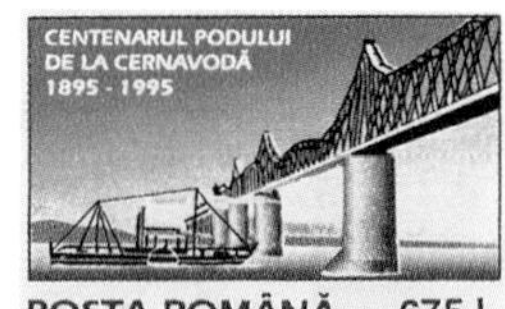

1206 Saligny Bridge

1995. Centenary of Saligny Bridge, Cernavoda.

5752	**1206** 675l. multicoloured	50	20

1207 Mallard

1208 General Dr. Victor Anastasiu

1995. Domestic Birds. Multicoloured.

5753	90l. Type **1207**	10	15
5754	130l. Red junglefowl (hen)	10	15
5755	150l. Helmeted guineafowl	10	15
5756	280l. Common turkey	20	15
5757	960l. Greylag goose	60	25
5758	1650l. Red junglefowl (cock)	1·10	40

1995. 75th Anniv of Institute of Aeronautics Medicine.

5759	**1208** 960l. ultramarine, blue and red	50	10

1209 Battle Scene

1995. 400th Anniv of Battle of Calugareni.

5760	**1209** 100l. multicoloured	25	10

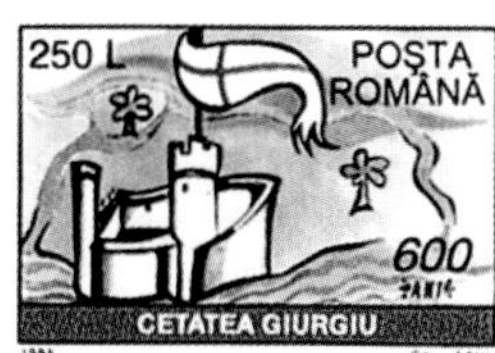

1210 Giurgiu Castle

1995. Anniversaries. Multicoloured.

5761	250l. Type **1210** (600th anniv)	15	15
5762	500l. Neamtului Castle (600th anniv) (vert)	30	15
5763	960l. Sebes-Alba Mill (700th anniv)	50	25
5764	1615l. Dorohoi Church (500th anniv) (vert)	85	40
5765	1650l. Military observatory, Bucharest (centenary) (vert)	85	40

1211 Moldovita Monastery

1212 Racket

1995. U.N.E.S.C.O. World Heritage Sites. Mult.

5766	675l. Type **1211**	35	20
5767	960l. Hurez Monastery	50	25
5768	1615l. Biertan Castle (horiz)	80	45

1995. 5th Open Tennis Championships, Bucharest.

5769	**1212** 1020l. multicoloured	50	15

1213 Ion Ionescu (editor)

1995. Centenary of Mathematics Gazette.

5770	**1213** 100l. pink and brown	15	10

1214 "Albizzia julibrissin"

1995. Plants from Bucharest Botanical Garden. Multicoloured.

5771	50l. Type **1214**	10	10
5772	100l. Yew	10	10
5773	150l. "Paulownia tomentosa"	10	10
5774	500l. Bird of Paradise flower	30	10
5775	960l. Amazon water-lily	55	15
5776	2300l. Azalea	1·50	45

1215 St. John's Church

1216 George Apostu (sculptor, 10th death (1996))

1995. 600th Anniv of First Documentary Reference to Piatra-Neamt.

5777	**1215** 250l. multicoloured	30	15

1995. Anniversaries.

5778	**1216** 150l. green and black	10	20
5779	– 250l. blue and black	15	20
5780	– 500l. light brown, brown and black	35	20
5781	– 960l. rose, purple and black	65	25
5782	– 1650l. brown and black	1·10	50

DESIGNS: 250l. Emil Cioran (philosopher, death in 1995); 500l. Eugen Ionescu (writer, 1st death anniv); 960l. Elena Vacarescu (poetess, 130th birth (1996)); 1650l. Mircea Eliade (philosopher, 10th death (1996)).

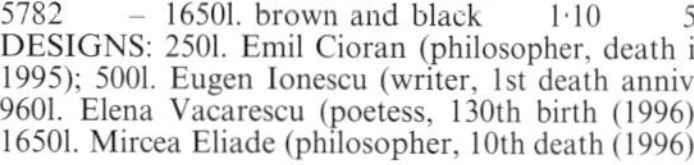

1217 Running

1995. Olympic Games, Atlanta (1996) (1st issue). Multicoloured.

5783	50l. Type **1217**	10	15
5784	100l. Gymnastics	10	15
5785	150l. Canoeing	10	15
5786	500l. Fencing	30	15

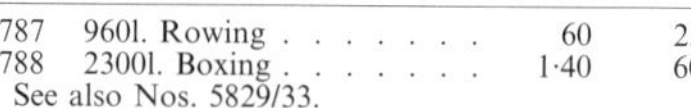

5787	960l. Rowing	60	25
5788	2300l. Boxing	1·40	60

See also Nos. 5829/33.

1218 Nativity

1995. Christmas.

5790	**1218** 100l. multicoloured	15	10

1219 Masked Person

1996. Folk Masks of Maramures (250l.) and Moldavia (others).

5791	**1219** 250l. multicoloured	10	20
5792	– 500l. multicoloured	15	20
5793	– 960l. mult (vert)	25	20
5794	– 1650l. mult (vert)	45	35

DESIGNS: 500l. to 1650l. Different masks.

1220 Tristan Tzara

1221 "Resurrection" (icon)

1996. Writers' Birth Anniversaries. Multicoloured.

5795	150l. Type **1220** (centenary)	10	20
5796	1500l. Anton Pann (bicentenary)	90	30

1996. Easter.

5797	**1221** 150l. multicoloured	15	10

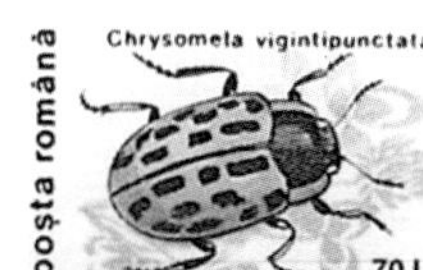

1223 "Chrysomela vigintipunctata" (leaf beetle)

1996. Beetles.

5799	**1223** 70l. yellow and black	10	10
5800	– 220l. red and black	10	10
5801	– 370l. brown and black	25	10
5802	– 650l. black, red & grey	35	10
5803	– 700l. red, black and green	40	10
5804	– 740l. black and yellow	30	10
5805	– 960l. black and red	40	10
5806	– 1000l. yellow and black	45	10
5807	– 1500l. black and brown	70	20
5808	– 2500l. red, black & green	1·00	25

DESIGNS: 220l. "Cerambyx cerdo" (longhorn beetle); 370l. "Entomoscelis adonidis"; 650l. Ladybird; 700l. Caterpillar-hunter; 740l. "Hedobia imperialis"; 960l. European rhinoceros beetle; 1000l. Bee chafer; 1500l. "Purpuricenus kaehleri" (longhorn beetle); 2500l. "Anthaxia salicis".

1225 Arbore Church

1996. U.N.E.S.C.O. World Heritage Sites. Mult.

5810	150l. Type **1225**	10	25
5811	1500l. Voronet Monastery	70	35
5812	2550l. Humor Monastery	1·00	60

1226 Ana Aslan (doctor)

1996. Europa. Famous Women. Multicoloured.
5813 370l. Type **1226** 25 25
5814 4140l. Lucia Bulandra (actress) . . . . 2·30 1·70

1227 "Mother and Children" (Oana Negoita)

1996. 50th Anniv of U.N.I.C.E.F. Prize-winning Children's Paintings. Multicoloured.
5815 370l. Type **1227** 15 25
5816 740l. "Winter Scene" (Badea Cosmin) 35 25
5817 1500l. "Children and Sun over House" (Nicoleta Georgescu) 75 40
5818 2550l. "House on Stilts" (Biborka Bartha) (vert) 1·20 70

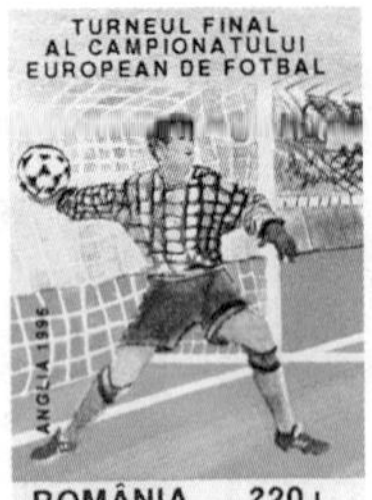

1228 Goalkeeper with Ball

1996. European Football Championship, England. Multicoloured.
5819 220l. Type **1228** 10 10
5820 370l. Player with ball . . . 15 10
5821 740l. Two players with ball 35 10
5822 1500l. Three players with ball 70 15
5823 2550l. Player dribbling ball 1·10 25
Nos. 5819/23 were issued together, se-tenant, forming a composite design of the pitch and stadium.

1229 Metropolitan Toronto Convention Centre (venue) **1232** Boxing

1230 Factory

1996. "Capex'96" International Stamp Exhibition, Toronto, Canada.
5825 **1229** 150l. multicoloured . . 15 10

1996. 225th Anniv of Resita Works.
5827 **1230** 150l. brown 15 10

1996. 5th Anniv of Establishment of R.A. Posta Romana (postal organization). No. 5471 surch **1996 - 5 ANI DE LA INFIINTARE L150**.
5828 **1128** 150l. on 10l. multicoloured 50 60

1996. Centenary of Modern Olympic Games and Olympic Games, Atlanta (2nd issue). Mult.
5829 220l. Type **1232** 10 10
5830 370l. Running 15 10
5831 740l. Rowing 30 10
5832 1500l. Judo 75 15
5833 2550l. Gymnastics (asymmetrical bars) . . . 1·10 25

1233 Postman, Keyboard and Stamp under Magnifying Glass (⅔-size illustration)

1996. Stamp Day.
5835 **1233** 1500l.(+650l.) mult . . 95 50
No. 5835 includes the se-tenant premium-carrying tab shown in Type **1233**.

1234 White Spruce

1996. Coniferous Trees. Multicoloured.
5836 70l. Type **1234** 15 10
5837 150l. Serbian spruce 15 10
5838 220l. Blue Colorado spruce 15 10
5839 740l. Sitka spruce 40 10
5840 1500l. Scots pine 95 20
5841 3500l. Maritime pine . . . 2·10 45

1235 Grass Snake **1236** Madonna and Child

1996. Animals. Multicoloured.
5842 70l. Type **1235** 15 10
5843 150l. Hermann's tortoise . . 15 10
5844 220l. Eurasian sky lark (horiz) 15 10
5845 740l. Red fox (horiz) 40 10
5846 1500l. Common porpoise . . 95 20
5847 3500l. Golden eagle (horiz) 2·10 45

1996. Christmas.
5848 **1236** 150l. multicoloured . . 15 10

1237 Stan Golestan (composer, 40th) **1241** Bow

1240 Stoat

1996. Death Anniversaries.
5849 **1237** 100l. pink and black . . 30 30
5850 – 150l. purple and black 30 30
5851 – 370l. orange and black 65 30
5852 – 1500l. red and black . . 2·50 60
DESIGNS: 150l. Corneliu Coposu (politician, 1st); 370l. Horia Vintila (writer, 4th); 1500l. Alexandru Papana (test pilot, 50th).

1997. Fur-bearing Mammals. Multicoloured.
5855 70l. Type **1240** 20 40
5856 150l. Arctic fox 20 40
5857 220l. Racoon-dog 20 40
5858 740l. European otter 30 40
5859 1500l. Muskrat 65 40
5860 3500l. Pine marten . . . . 1·50 80

1997. 26th Anniv of Greenpeace (environmental organization). The "Rainbow Warrior" (campaign ship). Multicoloured.
5861 150l. Type **1241** 20 25
5862 370l. Ship and ice 20 25
5863 1940l. Ship cruising past beach 90 25
5864 2500l. Rainbow and ship . . 1·10 25

1242 Thomas Edison (inventor)

1997. Birth Anniversaries. Multicoloured.
5866 200l. Type **1242** (150th anniv) 15 30
5867 400l. Franz Schubert (composer, bicentenary) 15 30
5868 3600l. Miguel de Cervantes Saavedra (writer, 450th anniv) . . . . 1·40 60

1243 Emblem **1244** Surdesti

1997. Inauguration of Mobile Telephone Network in Rumania.
5869 **1243** 400l. multicoloured . . 20 10

1997. Churches. Each brown, agate and green.
5870 200l. Type **1244** 15 15
5871 400l. Plopis 15 15
5872 450l. Bogdan Voda 15 15
5873 850l. Rogoz 30 15
5874 3600l. Calinesti . . . . . . 1·30 30
5875 6000l. Birsana . . . . . . 2·30 50

1245 Al. Demetrescu Dan in "Hamlet", 1916 **1246** Vlad Tepes Dracula (Voivode of Wallachia)

1997. 2nd Shakespeare Festival, Craiova. Mult.
5876 200l. Type **1245** 15 45
5877 400l. Constantin Serghie in "Othello", 1855 . . . . . 15 45
5878 2400l. Gheorghe Cozorici in "Hamlet", 1957 . . . . . 90 45
5879 3600l. Ion Manolescu in "Hamlet", 1924 . . . . . 1·30 90

1997. Europa. Tales and Legends. Dracula. Mult.
5880 400l. Type **1246** 25 45
5881 4250l. Dracula the myth . . 2·75 90

1247 "Dolichothele uberiformis"

1997. Cacti. Multicoloured.
5882 100l. Type **1247** 15 30
5883 250l. "Rebutia" 15 30
5884 450l. "Echinofossulocactus lamellosus" 15 30
5885 500l. "Ferocactus glaucescens" 15 30
5886 650l. "Thelocactus" 25 30
5887 6150l. "Echinofossulocactus albatus" . . . . 2·40 90

1248 National Theatre, Cathedral and Statue of Mihai Viteazul

1997. "Balcanmax'97" Maximum Cards Exhibition, Cluj-Napoca.
5888 **1248** 450l. multicoloured . . 15 10

1249 19th-century Postal Transport (½-size illustration)

1997. Stamp Day.
5889 **1249** 3600l.(+1500l.) multicoloured . . . . 1·90 1·20
No. 5889 includes the se-tenant premium-carrying tab shown in Type **1249**.

1997. Nos. 5349/55 and 5357 surch.
5890 250l. on 1l. blue 20 20
5891 250l. on 2l. green 20 20
5892 250l. on 4l. red 20 20
5893 450l. on 5l. violet 20 20
5894 450l. on 6l. brown 20 20
5895 450l. on 18l. red 20 20
5896 950l. on 9l. red 40 20
5897 3600l. on 8l. brown . . . . 1·60 40

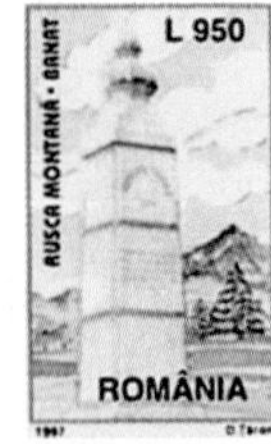

1251 Archway of Vlad Tepes Dracula's House **1252** Tourism Monument

1997. Sighisoara. Multicoloured.
5898 250l. Type **1251** 20 30
5899 650l. Town Hall clocktower 30 30
5900 3700l. Steps leading to fortress and clocktower 1·60 60

1997. Rusca Montana, Banat.
5901 **1252** 950l. multicoloured . . 35 20

1253 Printing Works **1254** Emil Racovita (biologist) and "Belgica" (polar barque)

1997. 125th Anniv of Stamp Printing Works.
5902 **1253** 450l. red, brown and blue 20 10

1997. Centenary of Belgian Antarctic Expedition.
5903 **1254** 450l. blue, grey and black 15 30
5904 – 650l. red, yellow and black 25 30
5905 – 1600l. green, pink and black 60 30
5906 – 3700l. brown, yellow and black . . . . 1·40 55
DESIGNS: 650l. Frederick Cook (anthropologist and photographer) and "Belgica" at sea; 1600l. Roald Amundsen and "Belgica" in port; 3700l. Adrien de Gerlache (expedition commander) and "Belgica" ice-bound.

1997. "Aeromfila '97" Stamp Exhibition, Brasov. No. 5334 surch **1050 L AEROMFILA'97 Brasov** and airplane.
5907 **1292** 1050l. on 41.50 mult . . 45 30

1256 Campsite

1258 Ion Mihalache (politician)

1997. Rumanian Scout Association. Multicoloured.
5908 300l. Type **1256** 20 30
5909 700l. Rumanian Scout Association emblem . . . 25 30
5910 1050l. Joined hands 40 30
5911 1750l. Carvings 65 30
5912 3700l. Scouts around campfire . . . . 1·50 60
Nos. 5908/12 were issued together, se-tenant, forming a composite design.

1997. 9th Rumanian–Chinese Stamp Exhibition, Bucharest. No. 5293 surch **A IX-a editie a expozitiei filatelice romano-chineza 1997 500 L**.
5913 **1082** 500l. on 2l. mult . . . 30 20

1997. Anniversaries. Multicoloured.
5914 500l. Type **1258** (34th death anniv) 20 25
5915 1050l. King Carol I (131st anniv of accession) (black inscriptions and face value) 75 25
5916 1050l. As No. 5915 but mauve inscriptions and face value . . . . 1·00 25
5917 1050l. As No. 5915 but blue inscriptions and face value 1·00 25
5918 1050l. As No. 5915 but brown inscriptions and face value . . . . 1·00 25

1259 Rugby

1997. Sports. Multicoloured.
5919 500l. Type **1259** 20 35
5920 700l. American football (vert) 30 35
5921 1750l. Oina (Rumanian bat and ball game) 65 35
5922 3700l. Mountaineering (vert) 1·60 75

1260 New Building

1998. 130th Anniv of Bucharest Chamber of Commerce and Industry.
5923 **1260** 700l. multicoloured . . 30 10

1261 Biathlon

1263 Four-leaved Clover (Good luck and Success)

1998. Winter Olympic Games, Nagano, Japan. Mult.
5924 900l. Type **1261** 30 20
5925 3900l. Figure skating . . . 1·40 40

1998. Europa. National Festivals.
5927 **1263** 900l. green and red . . 2·40 2·30
5928 – 3900l. red, orange and green . . . . 10·00 4·50
DESIGN: 3900l. Butterfly (youth and suaveness).

1264 Alfred Nobel

1265 Shrine, Cluj

1998. The 20th-century (1st series). Multicoloured.
5929 700l. Type **1264** (establishment of Nobel Foundation, 1901) 25 30
5930 900l. Guglielmo Marconi (first radio-telegraphic trans-Atlantic link, 1901) 35 30
5931 1500l. Albert Einstein (elaboration of Theory of Relativity, 1905) 55 30
5932 3900l. Traian Vuia (his first flight, 1906) . . . . . . 1·50 60
See also Nos. 5991/5, 6056/9, 6060/3, 6128/31, 6133/6, 6205/8 and 6230/3.

1998. Roadside Shrines. Multicoloured.
5933 700l. Type **1265** 30 10
5934 900l. Crucifixion, Prahovac 35 10
5935 1500l. Shrine, Arges 55 10

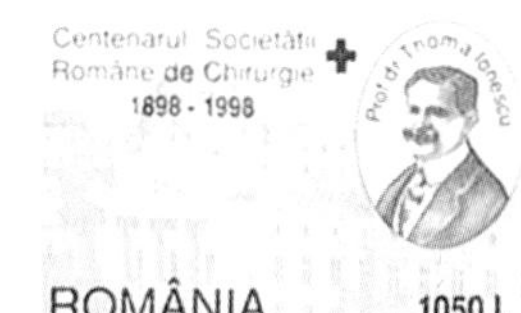

1267 Dr. Thoma Ionescu (founder) and Coltea Hospital, Bucharest

1998. Centenary of Rumanian Surgery Society.
5937 **1267** 1050l. grey, brown and red 45 15

1998. Nos. 5350/1, 5353/4 and 5357 surch, the old value cancelled by a clover leaf.
5938 50l. on 2l. green 25 10
5939 100l. on 8l. brown 25 10
5940 200l. on 4l. red 25 10
5941 400l. on 6l. brown 25 10
5942 500l. on 18l. red 25 10

1998. Nos. 5615/17 and 5620 surch, the old value cancelled by a hare.
5944 – 700l. on 125l. green and black 40 45
5945 – 800l. on 35l. green and black 40 45
5946 – 1050l. on 45l. green and black 40 45
5947 **1170** 4150l. on 15l. green and black . . . . 1·60 70

1998. Nos. 5352 and 5355 surch, the old value cancelled by a heart.
5948 1000l. on 9l. red 45 60
5949 1500l. on 5l. violet 70 60

1272 Brown Kiwi

1998. Nocturnal Birds. Multicoloured.
5950 700l. Type **1272** 25 25
5951 1500l. Barn owl 50 25
5952 1850l. Water rail 65 25
5953 2450l. European nightjar . . 80 25

1998. No. 5361 surch, the old value cancelled by a sign of the zodiac.
5954 250l. on 45l. blue (Aries) . . 20 25
5955 350l. on 45l. blue (Taurus) 20 25
5956 400l. on 45l. blue (Gemini) 20 25
5957 450l. on 45l. blue (Cancer) 20 25
5958 850l. on 45l. blue (Leo) . . 30 25
5959 900l. on 45l. blue (Aquarius) 40 25
5960 1000l. on 45l. blue (Libra) 40 25
5961 1600l. on 45l. blue (Scorpio) 60 25
5962 2500l. on 45l. blue (Sagittarius) 95 25

1274 81p. Stamp and Waslui Cancellation

1998. 140th Anniv of Bull's Head Issue of Moldavia. Multicoloured.
5963 700l. Type **1274** 30 25
5964 1050l. 27p. stamp and Jassy cancellation 40 25

1275 Soldiers and Revolutionaries fighting

1998. 150th Anniv of the 1848 Revolutions.
5966 **1275** 1050l. black, yellow and red 40 30

1276 Nikolaus Lenau (poet)

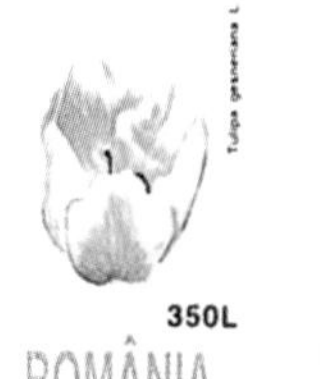

1277 Diver and Marine Life

1998. German Personalities of Banat.
5967 **1276** 800l. orange, black and pink 50 30
5968 – 1850l. orange, black and green . . . . . 1·20 30
5969 – 4150l. orange, black and blue . . . . . . 2·75 45
DESIGNS: 1850l. Stefan Jager (artist); 4150l. Adam Muller-Guttenbrunn (writer).

1998. International Year of the Ocean.
5970 **1277** 1100l. multicoloured . . 40 30

1998. Nos. 5336/7 surch, the old value cancelled by a sporting emblem.
5971 **1094** 50l. on 1l. multicoloured (Figure skater) 40 45
5972 – 50l. on 1l. multicoloured (Trophy) 40 45

1279 "Tulipa gesneriana"

1281 "Proportions of Man" (Leonardo da Vinci)

1998. Flowers. Multicoloured.
5973 350l. Type **1279** 25 25
5974 850l. "Dahlia variabilis" "Rubin" 35 25
5975 1100l. Martagon lily 45 25
5976 4450l. "Rosa centifolia" . . 1·90 50
No. 5975 commemorates the 50th anniv of the Horticulture Institute, Bucharest.

1998. Various stamps surch. (a) Nos. 5399/5404, the old value cancelled by a transport emblem.
5977 **1106** 50l. on 1l. brown, blue and deep blue (Car) 15 15
5978 – 50l. on 4l. green, lilac and violet (Steam locomotive) 15 15
5979 – 50l. on 5l. brown, blue and ultramarine (Lorry) 15 15
5980 50l. on 5l. blue, brown and red (Helicopter) 15 15
5981 – 50l. on 9l. red, blue and deep blue (Airplane) 15 15
5982 – 50l. on 10l. black, light brown and brown (Ship) 15 15

(b) Nos. 5472/5 and 5477, the old value cancelled by a bird.
5983 **1129** 50l. on 6l. green and violet (Cockerel) . . 15 15
5984 – 50l. on 7l. mauve, purple and green (Duck) 15 15
5985 – 50l. on 9l. blue and mauve (Swan) . . . 15 15
5986 – 50l. on 10l. light brown, brown and blue (Dove) 15 15
5987 – 50l. on 30l. green and blue (Swallow) . . . 15 15

1998. 50th Anniv of Universal Declaration of Human Rights.
5988 **1281** 50l. multicoloured . . . 25 15

1282 Paciurea

1998. 125th Birth Anniv of Dimitrie Paciurea (sculptor).
5989 **1282** 850l. multicoloured . . 30 15

1283 Eclipse

1998. Total Eclipse of the Sun (1999) (1st issue).
5990 **1283** 1100l. multicoloured . . 70 20
See also No. 6050.

1284 Sinking of "Titanic" (liner), 1912

1998. The 20th century (2nd series).
5991 **1284** 350l. black, bl & red . . 30 30
5992 – 1100l. multicoloured . . 50 30
5993 – 1600l. multicoloured . . 65 30
5994 – 2000l. multicoloured . . 65 30
5995 – 2600l. blk, grey & red 95 30
DESIGNS: 1100l. Henri Coanda and his turbine-powered model airplane, 1910; 1600l. Louis Bleriot and his "Bleriot XI" airplane (first powered flight across English Channel, 1909); 2000l. Freighter in locks and map of American sea routes (opening of Panama Canal, 1914); 2600l. Prisoners in courtyard (Russian October revolution, 1917).

1998. Christmas. Nos. 5491 and 5674 surch with the old value cancelled by a Christmas emblem.
5996 **1133** 2000l. on 15l. multicoloured (Christmas tree) . . . 55 40
5997 **1186** 2600l. on 60l. multicoloured (Father Christmas) 85 40

1286 Gonovez Lighthouse

1998. Lighthouses. Multicoloured.
5998 900l. Type **1286** 20 30
5999 1000l. Constanta 20 30
6000 1100l. Sfantu Gheorghe . . 30 30
6001 2600l. Sulina 65 30

1287 Arnota Monastery

1999. Monasteries. Multicoloured.
6002 500l. Type **1287** 25 25
6003 700l. Bistrita 25 25
6004 1100l. Dintr'un Lemn . . . 35 25
6005 2100l. Govora 60 25
6006 4850l. Tismana . . . . . . 1·10 25

1999. No. 5492 surch with the old value cancelled by various fungi.
6007 **1134** 50l. on 15l. black, red and blue 20 25
6009 400l. on 15l. black, red and blue 20 25
6010 2300l. on 15l. black, red and blue 55 25
6011 3200l. on 15l. black, red and blue 75 25

1999. No. 5384 surch with the old value cancelled by a musical instrument.
6012 **1099** 100l. on 1l. blue (guitar) 20 25
6013 250l. on 1l. blue (saxophone) 20 25

1290 "Magnolia soulangiana"

1999. Shrubs. Multicoloured.
6014 350l. Type **1290** 30 25
6015 1000l. "Stewartia malacodendron" 30 25
6016 1100l. "Hibiscus rosa-sinensis" 45 25
6017 5350l. "Clematis patens" . . 1·80 25

1292 Easter Eggs

1999. Easter.
6023 **1292** 1100l. multicoloured . . 30 15

1999. No. 5799 surch with the old value cancelled by a dinosaur emblem.
6024 **1223** 100l. on 70l. yellow and black (Brontosaurus) 20 20
6025 200l. on 70l. yellow and black (Iguanodon) . . 20 20
6026 200l. on 70l. yellow and black (Allosaurus) . . 20 20
6027 1500l. on 70l. yellow and black (Diplodocus) 25 20
6028 1600l. on 70l. yellow and black (Tyrannosaurus) . . 35 20
6029 3200l. on 70l. yellow and black (Stegosaurus) 65 20
6030 6000l. on 70l. yellow and black (Plateosaurus) . . . [illegible] [illegible]

1294 Girdle of Keys (Padureni)

1295 Scarlet Macaw

1999. Jewellery. Multicoloured.
6031 1200l. Type **1294** 20 30
6032 2100l. Pendant of keys (Ilia, Hunedoara) 35 30
6033 2600l. Jewelled bib (Maramures) 40 30
6034 3200l. Necklace (Banat) (horiz) 50 30

1999. Birds. Multicoloured.
6035 1100l. Type **1295** 20 35
6036 2700l. White peafowl . . . 50 35
6037 3700l. Common peafowl . . 70 35
6038 5700l. Sulphur-crested cockatoo . . . . 1·10 55

1296 Council Flag and Headquarters, Strasbourg

1999. 50th Anniv of Council of Europe.
6039 **1296** 2300l. multicoloured . . 50 15

1297 St. Peter's Cathedral, Rome

1298 Northern Shoveler

1999. Papal Visit.
6040 **1297** 1300l. mauve and black 40 30
6041 – 1600l. mauve and black 50 30
6042 – 2300l. multicoloured . . 65 30
6043 – 6300l. multicoloured . . 1·70 50

DESIGNS: 1600l. Patriarchal Cathedral, Bucharest; 2300l. Father Teoctist (patriarch of Rumanian Orthodox church); 6300l. Pope John Paul II (after Dina Bellotti).

1999. Europa. Parks and Gardens: the Danube Delta Nature Reserve. Multicoloured.
6044 1100l. Type **1298** 35 40
6045 5700l. Black stork . . . . . 1·40 60

1299 Gheorghe Cartan (historian, 150th birth anniv)

1999. Anniversaries.
6046 **1299** 600l. green, black & red 20 20
6047 – 1100l. purple, blk & red 25 20
6048 – 2600l. blue, black & red 50 20
6049 – 7300l. brown, blk & red 80 40

DESIGNS: 1100l. George Calinescu (critic and novelist, birth centenary); 2600l. Johann Wolfgang von Goethe (dramatist, 250th birth anniv); 7300l. Honore de Balzac (novelist, birth bicentenary).

1300 Moon eclipsing Sun

1999. Total Eclipse of the Sun (2nd issue).
6050 **1300** 1100l. multicoloured . . 35 20

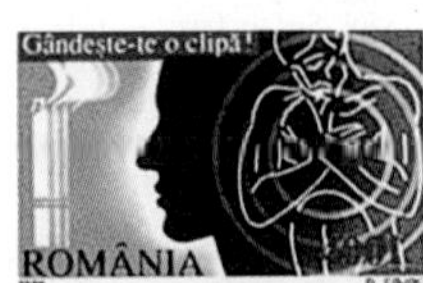

1301 Cigarette and Man with Arms Crossed

1999. Public Health Awareness Campaign. Mult.
6051 400l. Type **1301** (anti-smoking) 15 15
6052 800l. Bottles and man cradling glass and bottle (alcohol abuse) 15 15
6053 1300l. Cannabis leaf, pills and man injecting arm (drugs) 25 15
6054 2500l. Profiles and man on intravenous drip (HIV) . . 45 15

1302 Eclipse and Pavarotti (opera singer)

1999. Luciano Pavarotti's Concert on Day of Eclipse, Bucharest.
6055 **1302** 8100l. multicoloured . . 1·70 1·00

1303 Alexander Fleming (bacteriologist)

1999. The 20th century (3rd series). Multicoloured.
6056 800l. Type **1303** (discovery of penicillin, 1928) 20 30
6057 3000l. "Swords into Ploughshares" (sculpture) and map of Europe, Africa and Asia (foundation of League of Nations, 1920) 65 30
6058 7300l. Harold Clayton Urey (chemist) (discovery of heavy water, 1932) . . . 1·50 55
6059 17000l. Deep sea drilling (first oil platform, Beaumont, Texas, 1934) 2·75 1·10

1304 Karl Landsteiner (pathologist)

1999. The 20th-century (4th series).
6060 **1304** 1500l. orange, black and yellow 15 25
6061 – 3000l. ochre, black and brown 45 25
6062 – 7300l. multicoloured . . 55 55
6063 – 17000l. multicoloured 2·75 1·20

DESIGNS: 1500l. Type **1304** (discovery of blood groups, 1900–02); 3000l. Nicolae Paulescu (biochemist) (discovery of insulin, 1921); 7300l. Otto Hahn (radiochemist) (discovery of nuclear fission, 1938); 17000l. Ernst Ruska (electrical engineer) (designer of first electron microscope, 1931).

1305 Posthorn in Envelope and Berne

1306 Grigore Vasiliu Birlic

1999. 125th Anniv of Universal Postal Union.
6064 **1305** 3100l. multicoloured . . 60 30

1999. Comic Actors. Each purple, black and red.
6065 900l. Type **1306** 15 25
6066 1500l. Toma Caragiu . . . 25 25
6067 3100l. Constantin Tanase . . 50 25
6068 7950l. Charlie Chaplin . . . 1·30 45
6069 8850l. Stan Laurel and Oliver Hardy (horiz) . . . 1·40 75

1307 Monastery

1999. 275th Anniv of Stavropoleos Church.
6070 **1307** 2100l. brown, stone and black 35 20

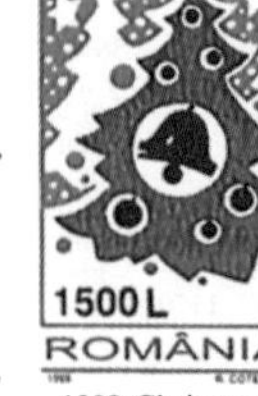

1308 Snowboarding

1309 Christmas Tree and Bell

1999. New Olympic Sports. Multicoloured.
6071 1600l. Type **1308** 35 35
6072 1700l. Softball 35 35
6073 7950l. Taekwondo . . . . . 1·40 70

1999. Christmas. Multicoloured.
6074 1500l. Type **1309** 25 25
6075 3100l. Father Christmas with presents 55 25

1310 Child as Flower (Antonela Vieriu)

1999. 10th Anniv of U.N. Convention on the Rights of the Child. Multicoloured.
6076 900l. Type **1310** 70 95
6077 3400l. Girl writing numbers (Ana-Maria Bulete) (vert) 55 35
6078 8850l. Group of people (Maria-Luiza Rogojeanu) 1·50 70

1311 Diana, Princess of Wales

1999. Diana, Princess of Wales Commemoration.
6079 **1311** 6000l. multicoloured . . 1·20 45

1312 Ferrari 365 GTB/4, 1968

1999. Birth Centenary (1998) of Enzo Ferrari (car designer). Multicoloured.
6080 1500l. Type **1312** 25 25
6081 1600l. Dino 246 GT, 1970 25 25
6082 1700l. 365 GT/4BB, 1973 . . 30 25
6083 7950l. Mondial 3.2, 1985 . . 1·40 50
6084 8850l. F 355, 1994 . . . . 1·50 75
6085 14500l. 456 MGT, 1998 . . 2·75 95

1313 Child with Rumanian Flag

1999. 10th Anniv of Popular Uprising.
6086 **1313** 2100l. multicoloured . . 35 20

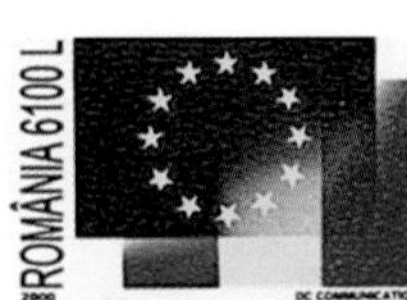

1314 European Union Flag

1316 Cupid

2000. European Union Membership Negotiations.
6087 **1314** 6100l. multicoloured . . 95 70

2000. St. Valentine's Day. Multicoloured.
6089 1500l. Type **1316** 25 50
6090 7950l. Couple . . . . 1·50 50

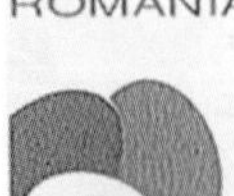

1317 Easter Eggs

2000. Easter.
6091 **1317** 1700l. blue, green and orange 35 20

2000. Nos. 5855 and 5842 surch, the old value cancelled by a different emblem.
6092 1700l. on 70l. multicoloured (crown) 30 20
6093 1700l. on 70l. multicoloured (snake) 30 20

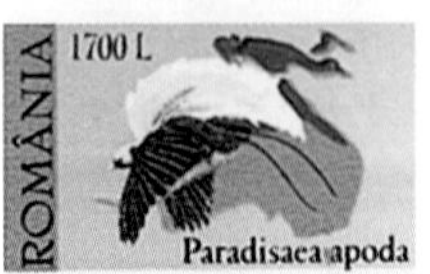

1319 Greater Bird of Paradise

2000. Birds of Paradise. Multicoloured.
6094 1700l. Type **1319** 25 45
6095 2400l. Magnificent bird of paradise 35 45
6096 9050l. Superb bird of paradise . . . . 1·30 75
6097 10050l. King bird of paradise . . . . 1·50 1·00

2000. Nos. 5342/3 surch.
6098 1900l. on 1l. multicoloured 35 20
6099 2000l. on 1l. multicoloured 35 20

2000. Nos. 5310/14 surch, the old value cancelled by various book and quill emblems.
6100 1700l. on 50b. brown and black 30 20
6101 1700l. on 1l.50 green and mauve 30 20
6102 1700l. on 2l. red and blue 30 20
6103 1700l. on 3l. blue and brown 30 20
6104 1700l. on 4l. brown and blue 30 20

1322 Cineraria

1324 "Building Europe"

2000. Flowers. Multicoloured.
6105 1700l. Type **1322** 30 40
6106 3100l. Indoor lily 55 40
6107 5800l. Plumeria 95 40
6108 10050l. Fuchsia . . . . . . 1·60 85

2000. Nos. 5303/7 surch, the old value cancelled by an easel with palette emblem.
6109 1700l. on 50b. multicoloured 30 20
6110 1700l. on 1l.50 multicoloured 30 20
6111 1700l. on 2l. multicoloured 30 20
6112 1700l. on 3l. multicoloured 30 20
6113 1700l. on 4l. multicoloured 30 20

2000. Europa.
6114 **1324** 10150l. multicoloured 1·70 1·00

2000. Death Centenary of Vincent van Gogh (artist). Nos. 5318 and 5321 surch, the old value cancelled by paint palette emblem.
6115 1700l. on 50b. multicoloured 30 20
6116 1700l. on 3l.50 multicoloured 30 20

2000. No. 5642 surch, the old value cancelled by an airship.
6117 1700l. on 635l. black, ultramarine and blue . . 25 40
6118 2000l. on 635l. black, ultramarine and blue . . 25 40
6119 3900l. on 635l. black, ultramarine and blue . . 60 40
6120 9050l. on 635l. black, ultramarine and blue . . 1·30 60

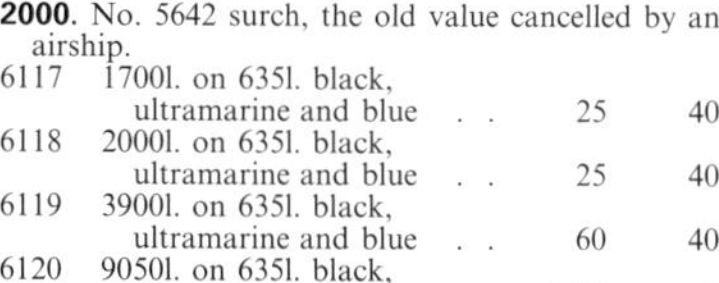

1327 Mihai the Brave and Soldiers

2000. Anniversaries. Multicoloured.
6121 3800l. Type **1327** (400th anniv of first union of the Rumanian provinces (Wallachia, Transylvania and Moldavia)) 55 45
6122 9050l. Printing press (550th anniv of the 42 line Bible (first Bible printed in Latin)) (36 × 23 mm) . . . 1·20 70

2000. No. 5801 surch, the old value cancelled by a flower.
6123 10000l. on 370l. brown and black . . . . 1·40 45
6124 19000l. on 370l. brown and black . . . . 2·50 95
6125 34000l. on 370l. brown and black . . . . 4·50 1·50

1330 Ferdinand von Zeppelin and Airship

2000. Centenary of First Zeppelin Flight.
6127 **1330** 2100l. multicoloured . . 35 20

1331 Enrico Fermi (physicist) and Mathematical Equation

2000. The 20th Century (5th series).
6128 **1331** 2100l. black, grey and red 30 25
6129 – 2200l. black and grey 30 25
6130 – 2400l. red and black . . 35 25
6131 – 6000l. multicoloured . . 90 25

DESIGNS: 2100l. Type **1331** (construction of first nuclear reactor, 1942); 2200l. United Nations Charter (signing of charter, 1945); 2400l. Edith Piaf (singer) (release of *La Vie en Rose* (song), 1947); 6000l. Sir Edmund Percival Hillary (mountaineer) (conquest of Mt. Everest, 1953).

2000. No. 5365 surch, the old value cancelled by a bird.
6132 1700l. on 160l. red and pink 25 15

1333 Globe and "Sputnik 1" Satellite

2000. The Twentieth Century (6th series).
6133 **1333** 1700l. multicoloured . . 25 30
6134 – 3900l. multicoloured . . 50 30
6135 – 6400l. black and red . . 90 30
6136 – 11300l. multicoloured 1·50 50
DESIGNS: 1700l. Type**1333** (launch of first man-made satellite, 1957); 3900l. Yuri Gagarin (first manned space flight, 1961); 6400l. Surgeons operating (first heart transplant operation, 1967); 11300l. Edwin E. Aldrin and Moon (first manned landing on Moon, 1969).

1334 Boxing

2000. Olympic Games, Sydney. Multicoloured.
6137 1700l. Type **1334** 35 45
6138 2200l. High jump 35 45
6139 3900l. Weight lifting 65 45
6140 6200l. Gymnastics . . . . . 1·20 45

1336 Palace of Agriculture Ministry

1340 Ilie Ilascu (political prisoner)

2000. Bucharest Palaces.
6143 **1336** 1700l. black and grey 25 20
6144 – 2200l. black and stone (horiz) 25 20
6145 – 2400l. black and green (horiz) 25 20
6146 – 3900l. black and brown (horiz) 55 20
DESIGNS: 2200l. Cantacuzino Palace (now George Enescu Museum); 2400l. Grigore Ghica Palace; 3900l. Stirbei Palace (now Museum of Ceramics and Glass).

2000. No. 5836 surch, the old value cancelled by a house.
6147 300l. on 70l. multicoloured 15 10

2000. No. 5349 surch.
6148 300l. on 1l. blue 15 10

2000. Air. No. 5695 surch.
6149 2000l. on 960l. blue & black 25 50
6150 4200l. on 960l. blue & black 60 50
6151 4600l. on 960l. blue & black 65 50
6152 6500l. on 960l. blue & black 95 50

2000. 50th Anniv of United Nations Convention on Human Rights.
6153 **1340** 11300l. multicoloured 1·60 85

2000. No. 5700 surch, the old value cancelled by an inkwell and quill emblem.
6154 2000l. on 90l. multicoloured 25 15

2000. No. 5556 surch.
6155 2000l. on 29l. flesh, blk & lil 25 15

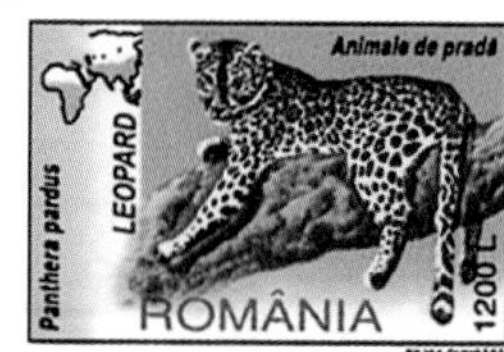

1343 Leopard

2000. Big Cats
6156 **1343** 1200l. multicoloured . . 15 20
6157 – 2000l. blue and black 25 20
6158 – 2200l. multicoloured . . 25 20
6159 – 2300l. multicoloured . . 25 20
6160 – 4200l. brown, bl & blk 55 20
6161 – 6500l. multicoloured . . 90 20

DESIGNS: 2000l. Snow leopard; 2200l. Lion; 2300l. Bobcat; 4200l. Mountain lion; 6500l. Tiger.

1344 Camil Ressu

1345 Christmas Tree

2000. Self-portraits. Multicoloured.
6163 2000l. Type **1344** 25 30
6164 2400l. Jean Al Steriadi . . . 35 30
6165 4400l. Nicolae Tonitza . . . 55 30
6166 15000l. Nicolae Grigorescu 2·00 85

2000. Christmas.
6167 **1345** 4400l. multicoloured . . 65 35

1346 Jesus Christ and Angel

1349 Globe and Fireworks

2000. Birth Bimillenary of Jesus Christ. Mult.
6168 2000l. Type **1346** 25 25
6169 7000l. Jesus Christ and dove (22 × 38 mm) 95 40

2000. No. 5624 surch, the previous value cancelled by different animals.
6170 7000l. on 3095l. Large-leaved lime (Pig) 85 45
6171 10000l. on 3095l. Large-leaved lime (Bear) . . . . 1·20 60
6172 11500l. on 3095l. Large-leaved lime (Cow) . . . . 1·70 90

2001. New Millennium.
6176 **1349** 11500l. multicoloured 1·40 85

1350 Sculpture

1352 Ribbons forming Heart

2001. 125th Birth Anniv of Constantin Brancusi (sculptor). Multicoloured.
6177 4600l. Type **1350** 45 40
6178 7200l. Display of sculptures 65 40
Nos. 6177/8 were issued together, se-tenant, forming a composite design.

2001. No. 5542 surch, the previous value cancelled by different snakes.
6179 7400l. on 280l. black & yell 70 55
6180 13000l. on 280l. black & yell 1·30 90

2001. St. Valentine's Day. Each red and grey.
6181 2200l. Type **1352** 40 80
6182 11500l. Pierced heart . . . 1·80 80

2001. Nos. 5595/6 and 5598 surch, the previous value cancelled by an ear of corn.
6183 1300l. on 245l. mult 30 40
6184 2200l. on 115l. mult 30 40
6185 5000l. on 115l. mult 55 40
6186 16500l. on 70l. mult . . . . 2·00 60

1354 Hortensia Papadat-Bengescu

2001. Birth Anniversaries. Multicoloured.
6187 1300l. Type **1354** 30 05
6188 2200l. Eugen Lovinescu (writer, 120th anniv) . . . 30 05
6189 2400l. Ion Minulescu (poet, 120th anniv) 30 05
6190 4600l. Andre Malraux (writer, centenary) 45 05
6191 7200l. George H. Gallup (opinion pollster and journalist, centenary) . . 75 05
6192 35000l. Walt Disney (artist and film producer, centenary) . . . . 4·00 20

1355 Chick inside Egg

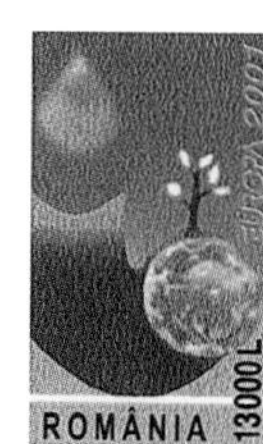

1356 Sloe (*Prunus spinosa*)

2001. Easter.
6193 **1355** 2200l. multicoloured . . 25 15

2001. Berries. Multicoloured.
6194 2200l. Type **1356** 10 10
6195 4600l. Red currant (*Ribes rubrum L.*) 20 10
6196 7400l. Gooseberry (*Ribes uva-crispa*) 30 10
6197 11500l. Mountain cranberry (*Vaccinium vitis-idaea L.*) 45 10

1357 Hagi

1358 Water Droplet and Globe surmounted by Tree

2001. Retirement of George Hagi (footballer).
6198 **1357** 2200l. multicoloured . . 10 10

2001. Europa. Water Resources.
6199 **1358** 13000l. multicoloured 50 15

1359 Collie

2001. Dogs. Multicoloured.
6200 1300l. Type **1359** 10 10
6201 5000l. Basset hound 20 10
6202 8000l. Siberian husky . . . 30 10
6203 13500l. Ciobanesc mioritic 50 15

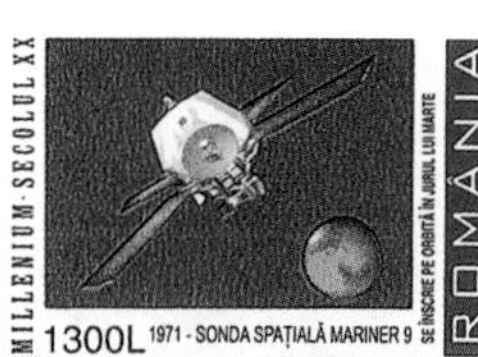

1360 Goddess Europa

1362 George Palade (Nobel Prize winner for medicine, 1974)

1361 Mariner 9 (spacecraft) and Mars

2001. Rumanian Presidency of Organization for Security and Co-operation in Europe.
6204 **1360** 11500l. multicoloured 40 10

2001. The 20th Century (7th series). Multicoloured.
6205 1300l. Type **1361** (first orbit of Mars, 1979) 10 10
6206 2400l. Bull (discovery of Paleolithic cave paintings, Ardeche, 1994) 10 10

6207 5000l. Nadia Comaneci (gymnast) (first "10" for gymnastics, Olympic Games, Montreal, 1976) 20 10
6208 8000l. Wall (fall of the Berlin wall, 1989) 30 10

2001. 50th Anniv of United Nations High Commissioner for Refugees.
6209 **1362** 13500l. multicoloured 50 15

2001. Various stamps surch the previous values cancelled by various emblems as stated.
6210 **1100** 300l. on 4l. multicoloured (candlestick) 10 10
6211 **1110** 300l. on 4l. multicoloured (bobsled) 10 10
6212 **1132** 300l. on 7l. multicoloured (harp) 10 10
6213 – 300l. on 9l. multicoloured (No. 5488) (lyre) . . 10 10
6214 **1168** 300l. on 90l. multicoloured (lizard) 10 10
6215 **1190** 300l. on 90l. multicoloured (computer mouse) . . 10 10
6216 **1202** 300l. on 90l. multicoloured (fish) 10 10
6217 – 300l. on 90l. multicoloured (No. 5745) (chess knight) 10 10
6218 **1207** 300l. on 90l. multicoloured (fungi) 10 10
6219 **1157** 300l. on 115l. brown, blue and black (scroll) 10 10
6220 **1158** 300l. on 115l. multicoloured (train) 10 10
6221 **1162** 300l. on 115l. multicoloured (rectangle) 10 10
6222 – 300l. on 115l. multicoloured (No. 5602) (kite) . . 10 10

2001. Nos. 5715/16 and 5720 surch, the previous values cancelled by a sign of the zodiac.
6223 2500l. on 755l. blue and black (Pisces) (postage) 10 10
6224 2500l. on 1615l. green and black (Capricorn) 10 10
6225 2500l. on 715l. red and blue (Aquarius) (air) 10 10

1365 Trap Racing

2001. Equestrian Competitive Events. Mult.
6226 1500l. Type **1365** 10 10
6227 2500l. Dressage 10 10
6228 5300l. Show jumping . . . 20 10
6229 8300l. Flat racing 30 10

1366 Augustin Maior and Drawing

2001. The 20th Century (8th series). Multicoloured.
6230 1500l. Type **1366** (invention of multiple telephony, 1906) 10 10
6231 5300l. Pioneer 10 (satellite) (launched, 1972) 20 10
6232 13500l. Microchip (introduction of first microprocessor, 1971) . . 50 15
6233 15500l. Hubble space telescope (launched, 1990) 60 15

1367 Finger Coral (*Porites porites*)

2001. Corals and Sea Anemones. Multicoloured.
6234 2500l. Type **1367** 10 10
6235 8300l. Giant sea anemone (*Condylactis gigantia*) . . 30 10
6236 13500l. Northern red anemone (*Anemonia telia*) 50 15
6237 37500l. Common sea fan (*Gorgonia ventalina*) . . . 1·40 35

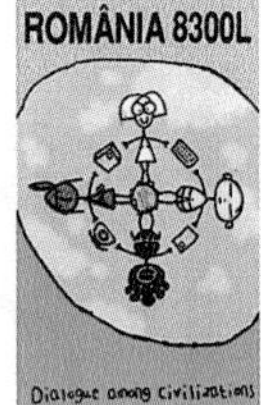
1368 Children encircling Globe

2001. United Nations Year of Dialogue among Civilizations.
6238 **1368** 8300l. multicoloured . . 30 10

1369 King, Bear and Cat

2001. Comics. Multicoloured.
6239 13500l. Type **1369** 50 15
6240 13500l. Fox beating drum and kicking cat 50 15
6241 13500l. King sleeping and fox beating drum 50 15
6242 13500l. Cat giving fox drum 50 15
6243 13500l. Drum exploding . . 50 15

1370 Top of Wreath with Baubles

2001. Christmas. Multicoloured.
6244 2500l. Type **1370** 10 10
6245 2500l. Bottom of wreath with stars 25 10
Nos. 6244/5 were issued together, se-tenant, forming a composite design of a wreath.

1371 Scorpio

2001. Signs of the Zodiac. Multicoloured.
6246 1500l. Type **1371** 10 10
6247 2500l. Libra 10 10
6248 5500l. Capricorn 20 10
6249 9000l. Pisces 35 10
6250 13500l. Aquarius 50 15
6251 16500l. Sagittarius 65 15

1372 Building

2001. Centenary of Central Post Headquarters, Bucharest. Multicoloured.
6252 5500l. Type **1372** 20 10
6253 5500l. Obverse of medal showing building, 1901 (vert) 20 10

EXPRESS LETTER STAMPS

1919. Transylvania. Cluj Issue. No. E245 of Hungary optd as T **42**.
E784 **E 18** 2b. olive and red . . . 30 45

1919. Transylvania. Oradea Issue. No. E245 of Hungary optd as T **42**.
E860 **E 18** 2b. olive and red . . . 40 70

FRANK STAMPS

F 38

1913. Silistra Commemoration Committee.
F626 **F 38** (–) brown . . . . . . 4·25 5·25

F **108** Mail Coach and Biplane

1933. For free postage on book "75th Anniv of Introduction of Rumanian Postage Stamp".
F1286 **F 108** (–) green . . . . . . 1·50 2·10

1946. For Internees' Mail via Red Cross. Nos. T1589/95 optd **SCUTIT DE TAXA POSTALA SERVICIUL PRIZONIERILOR DE RAZBOI** and cross.
F1809 **T 171** (–) on 50t. orange . . 25
F1810 (–) on 1l. lilac . . . 25
F1811 (–) on 2l. brown . . 25
F1812 (–) on 4l. blue . . . 25
F1813 (–) on 5l. violet . . . 25
F1814 (–) on 8l. green . . . 25
F1815 (–) on 10l. brown . . 25

F **209** Queen Helen

1946. For Internees' Mail via Red Cross. Perf or imperf.
F1829 **F 209** (–) green and red . . 50
F1830 (–) purple and red 50
F1831 (–) red and carmine 50

F **227** King Michael

F **228** Torch and Book

1947. King Michael's Fund. Perf or imperf.
(a) Postage.
F1904 **F 227** (–) purple . . . . . 1·50 1·90
F1905 **F 228** (–) blue . . . . . . 1·50 1·90
F1906 – (–) brown . . . . . 1·50 1·90

(b) Air. No. F1904 overprinted "**PRIN AVION**".
F1907 **F 227** (–) purple . . . . . 1·80 3·25
DESIGN: As Type **227** but horiz—No. F1906, Man writing and couple reading.

NEWSPAPER STAMPS

1919. Transylvania. Cluj Issue. No. N136 of Hungary optd as T **42**.
N783 **N 9** 2b. orange 35 50

1919. Transylvania. Oradea Issue. No. 136 of Hungary optd as T **43**.
N859 **N 9** 2b. orange 50 70

OFFICIAL STAMPS

O **71** Rumanian Eagle and National Flag

O **80**

1929.
O1115 **O 71** 25b. orange 20 15
O1116 50b. brown 20 15
O1117 1l. violet 15 10
O1118 2l. green 15 10
O1119 3l. red 30 10
O1120 4l. olive 25 15
O1221 6l. blue . . . . . . 1·20 20
O1222 10l. blue 35 25
O1223 25l. red . . . . . . 1·00 60
O1224 50l. violet . . . . . 3·00 1·70

1930. Optd **8 IUNIE 1930**.
O1150 **O 71** 25b. orange 15 15
O1151 50b. brown 15 15
O1152 1l. violet 15 15
O1153 2l. green 15 15
O1159 3l. red 25 10
O1154 4l. olive 35 15
O1155 6l. blue 40 30
O1161 10l. blue 50 10
O1166 25l. red 25 10
O1157 50l. violet . . . . . 3·00 1·90

1931.
O1243 **O 80** 25b. black 10 10
O1195 1l. purple 20 10
O1196 2l. green 35 20
O1197 3l. red 30 25
O1247 6l. red 85 40

PARCEL POST STAMPS

1895. As Type D **12** but inscr at top "TAXA DE FACTAGIU".
P353 25b. brown . . . . 4·50 50
P479 25b. red . . . . 4·50 80

1928. Surch **FACTAJ 5 LEI**.
P1078 **46** 5l. on 10b. green 85 25

POSTAGE DUE STAMPS
A. Ordinary Postage Due Stamps

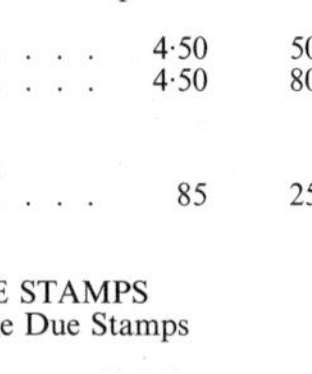

D 12

D 38

1881.
D152 **D 12** 2b. brown . . . . . . 2·75 1·30
D153 5b. brown . . . . . . 15·00 2·20
D200 10b. brown . . . . . 7·00 50
D201 30b. brown . . . . . 7·00 50
D156 50b. brown . . . . . 12·00 3·00
D157 60b. brown . . . . . 14·00 4·25

1887.
D448 **D 12** 2b. green 45 15
D449 5b. green 30 15
D450 10b. green 30 15
D451 30b. green 30 15
D371 50b. green . . . . . . 1·30 1·00
D458 60b. green . . . . . . 3·00 80

1911.
D617 **D 38** 2b. blue on yellow . . 15 15
D618 5b. blue on yellow . . 15 15
D619 10b. blue on yellow . . 15 15
D604 15b. blue on yellow . . 15 15
D621 20b. blue on yellow . . 15 15
D622 30b. blue on yellow . . 40 15
D623 50b. blue on yellow . . 55 15
D624 60b. blue on yellow . . 60 15
D609 2l. blue on yellow . . 80 40

1918. Optd **TAXA DE PLATA**.
D675 **37** 5b. green 80 35
D676 10b. red 80 35

1918. Re-issue of Type D **38**. On greenish or white paper.
D1001 **D 38** 5b. black 10 10
D 722 10b. black 10 10
D 995 20b. black 10 10
D 735 30b. black 15 15
D 736 50b. black 20 30
D 998 60b. black 15 10
D1007 1l. black 25 15
D1010 2l. black 35 10
D 991 3l. black 10 10
D 992 6l. black 25 10
D1547 50l. black 35 10
D1548 100l. black 35 15

1919. Transylvania. Cluj Issue. No. D190 etc of Hungary optd as T **42**.
D786 **D 9** 1b. red and green . . . £225 £225
D787 2b. red and green . . . 45 45
D788 5b. red and green . . . 42 50·00
D789 10b. red and green . . 20 20
D790 15b. red and green . . 8·00 8·00
D791 20b. red and green . . 20 20
D792 30b. red and green . . 13·50 13·50
D793 50b. red and green . . 5·50 6·25

1919. Transylvania. Oradea Issue. No. D190, etc of Hungary optd as T **43**.
D861 **D 9** 1b. red and green . . . 23·00 23·00
D862 2b. red and green . . . 20 20
D863 5b. red and green . . . 3·50 3·50
D864 6b. red and green . . . 2·30 2·30
D865 10b. red and green . . 25 25
D866 12b. red and green . . 35 35
D867 15b. red and green . . 35 35
D868 20b. red and green . . 20 20
D869 30b. red and green . . 50 60

1930. Optd **8 IUNIE 1930**.
D1168 **D 38** 1l. black 40 15
D1169 2l. black 40 15
D1170 3l. black 50 25
D1171 6l. black 90 35

D 98

D 233

1932.
D1249 **D 98** 1l. black 10 10
D1250 2l. black 10 10
D1251 3l. black 20 10
D1252 6l. black 20 10
D1835 20l. black 20 10
D1839 50l. black 25 25
D1840 80l. black 60 45
D1841 100l. black 55 30

D1842 200l. black 90 55
D1843 500l. black 1·40 90
D1844 5000l. black 1·70 1·10

1947. Type D 233 (without opts) perforated down centre.
D1919 2l. red 35
D1920 4l. blue 55
D1921 5l. black 90
D1922 10l. brown 1·80

The left half of Nos. D1919/22, showing Crown, served as a receipt and was stuck in the postman's book and so does not come postally used.

Prices for Nos. D1919/22 are for unused horizontal pairs.

1948. Nos. D1919/22, optd as in Type D **233**.
D1944 2l. red 35 20
D1945 4l. blue 55 25
D1946 5l. black 90 55
D1947 10l. brown 1·40 60

Prices for Nos. D1944 to D4055 are for unused and used horizontal pairs.

D **276** Badge and Postwoman

1950.
D2066 D **276** 2l. red 90 90
D2067 4l. blue 90 90
D2068 5l. green 1·40 1·40
D2069 10l. brown 1·80 1·80

1952. Currency revalued. Nos. D2066/9 surch **4 Bani** on each half.
D2221 D **276** 4b. on 2l. red 65 65
D2222 10b. on 4l. blue 65 65
D2223 20b. on 5l. green 1·40 1·40
D2224 50b. on 10l. brown 1·40 1·40

D **420** G.P.O., Bucharest and Posthorn

1957.
D2507 D **420** 3b. black 20 10
D2508 5b. orange 20 10
D2509 10b. purple 20 10
D2510 20b. red 20 10
D2511 40b. green 65 25
D2512 1l. blue 1·80 45

D **614**

1967.
D3436 D **614** 3b. green 10 10
D3437 5b. blue 10 10
D3438 10b. mauve 10 10
D3439 20b. red 10 10
D3440 40b. brown 20 10
D3441 1l. violet 55 20

D **766** Postal Emblems and Postman

1974.
D4050 D **766** 5b. blue 10 10
D4051 10b. green 10 10
D4052 – 20b. red 10 10
D4053 – 40b. violet 20 10
D4054 – 50b. brown 35 10
D4055 – 1l. orange 55 10

DESIGNS: 20b., 40b. Dove with letter and Hermes with posthorn; 50b., 1l. G.P.O., Bucharest and emblem with mail van.

Prices for Nos. D4050/55 are for unused horizontal pairs.

1982. As Type D **766**.
D4761 – 25b. violet 10 10
D4762 D **766** 50b. yellow 10 10
D4763 – 1l. red 25 10
D4764 – 2l. green 55 10
D4765 D **766** 3l. brown 80 10
D4766 – 4l. blue 1·20 20

DESIGNS: 25b., 1l. Dove with letter and Hermes with posthorn; 2, 4l. G.P.O., Bucharest and emblem with mail van.

D **1111**

1992.
D5417 D **1111** 4l. red 20 10
D5418 8l. blue 45 20

D **1163**

1994.
D5586 D **1163** 10l. brown 10 10
D5587 45l. orange 10 10

1999. Nos. D4762/4 and D4766 surch.
D6018 50l. on 50b. yellow 10 10
D6019 50l. on 1l. red 10 10
D6020 100l. on 2l. green 10 10
D6021 700l. on 1l. red 10 10
D6022 1100l. on 4l. blue 20 20

2001. Nos. D5417 and D5587 surch on both stamps in the pair.
D6173 500l. on 4l. red 10 10
D6174 1000l. on 4l. red 10 10
D6175 2000l. on 45l. orange 10 10

B. Postal Tax Due Stamps

1915. Optd **TIMBRU DE AJUTOR**.
TD643 D **38** 5b. blue on yellow 45 20
TD644 10b. blue on yellow 65 25

TD **42** TD **106**

1917. Green or white paper.
TD655 TD **42** 5b. brown 25 25
TD738 5b. red 45 25
TD654 10b. red 25 25
TD741 10b. brown 45 25

1918. Optd **TAXA DE PLATA**.
TD680 T **40** 5b. black 70 45
TD681 10b. brown 70 35

1922. As Type TD **42** but inscr "ASSISTENTA SOCIALA". On green or white paper.
TD1028 10b. brown 10 10
TD1029 20b. brown 10 10
TD1030 25b. brown 15 15
TD1031 50b. brown 10 10

1931. Aviation Fund. Optd **TIMBRUL AVIATIEI**.
TD1219 D **38** 1l. black 20 10
TD1220 2l. black 10 10

1932.
TD1278 TD **106** 3l. black 1·00 90

POSTAL TAX STAMPS

The following stamps were for compulsory use at certain times on inland mail to raise money for various funds. In some instances where the stamps were not applied the appropriate Postal Tax Postage Due stamps were applied.

Other denominations exist but these were purely for revenue purposes and were not applied to postal matter.

Soldiers' Families Fund

1915. Optd **TIMBRU DE AJUTOR**.
T638 **37** 5b. green 25 10
T639 10b. red 55 20

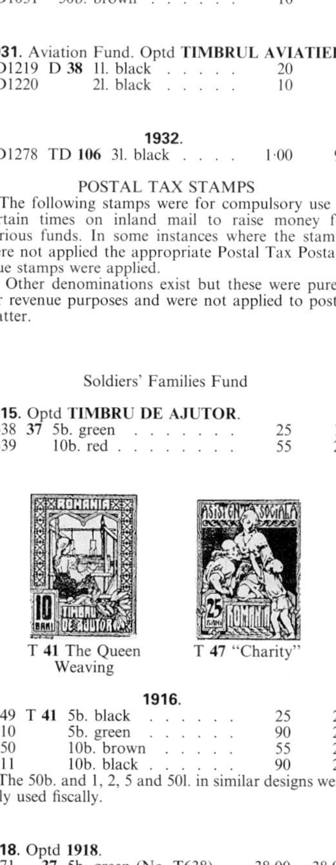

T **41** The Queen Weaving T **47** "Charity"

1916.
T649 T **41** 5b. black 25 20
T710 5b. green 90 20
T650 10b. brown 55 25
T711 10b. black 90 20

The 50b. and 1, 2, 5 and 50l. in similar designs were only used fiscally.

1918. Optd **1918**.
T671 **37** 5b. green (No. T638) 38·00 38·00
T667 T **41** 5b. black 90 65
T672 **37** 10b. red (No. T639) 38·00 38·00
T668 T **41** 10b. brown 1·40 55

1921. Social Welfare.
T978 T **47** 10b. green 20 10
T979 25b. black 20 10

Aviation Fund

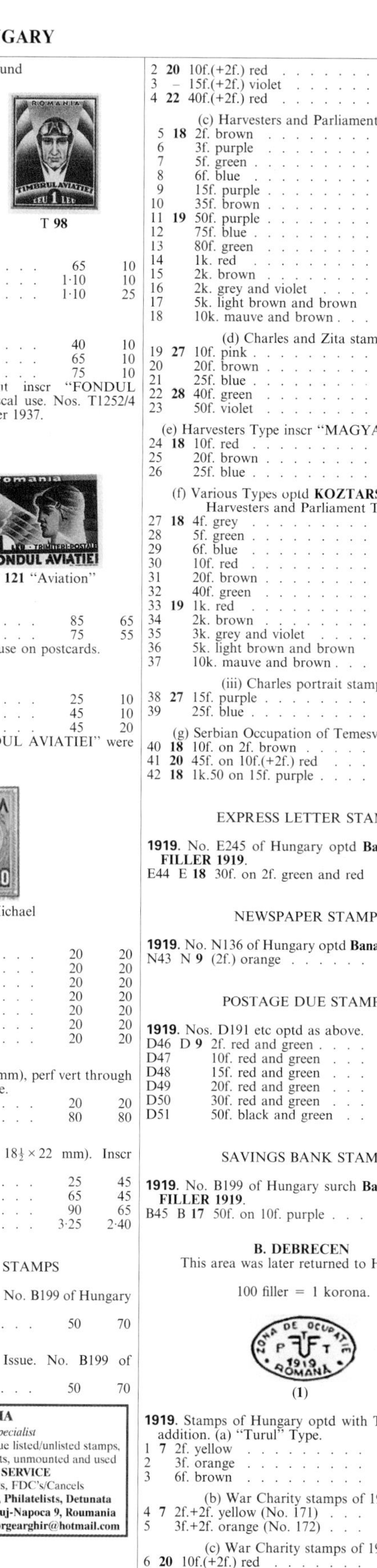

T **91** T **98**

1931.
T1216 T **91** 50b. green 65 10
T1217 1l. brown 1·10 10
T1218 2l. blue 1·10 25

1932.
T1253 T **98** 50b. green 40 10
T1254 1l. brown 65 10
T1255 2l. blue 75 10

Stamps as Type **98** but inscr "FONDUL AVIATIEI" were only for fiscal use. Nos. T1252/4 could only be used fiscally after 1937.

T **105** T **121** "Aviation"

1932. Cultural Fund.
T1276 T **105** 2l. blue 85 65
T1277 2l. brown 75 55

These were for compulsory use on postcards.

1936.
T1340 T **121** 50b. green 25 10
T1341 1l. brown 45 10
T1342 2l. blue 45 20

Other stamps inscr "FONDUL AVIATIEI" were only for fiscal use.

T **171** King Michael

1943.
T1589 T **171** 50b. orange 20 20
T1590 1l. lilac 20 20
T1591 2l. brown 20 20
T1592 4l. blue 20 20
T1593 5l. violet 20 20
T1594 8l. green 20 20
T1595 10l. brown 20 20

1947. Fiscal stamps (22 × 18½ mm), perf vert through centre surch **IOVR** and value.
T1923 1l. on 2l. red 20 20
T1924 5l. on 1l. green 80 80

1948. Vert designs (approx 18½ × 22 mm). Inscr "I.O.V.R.".
T1948 1l. red 25 45
T1949 1l. violet 65 45
T1950 2l. blue 90 65
T1951 5l. yellow 3·25 2·40

SAVINGS BANK STAMPS

1919. Transylvania. Cluj Issue. No. B199 of Hungary optd as T **42**.
B785 B **17** 10b. purple 50 70

1919. Transylvania. Oradea Issue. No. B199 of Hungary optd as T **43**.
B861 B **17** 10b. purple 50 70

RUMANIAN OCCUPATION OF HUNGARY Pt. 2

A. BANAT BACSKA

The following stamps were issued by the Temesvar postal authorities between the period of the Serbian evacuation and the Rumanian occupation. This area was later divided, the Western part going to Yugoslavia and the Eastern part going to Rumania.

100 filler = 1 korona.

1919. Stamps of Hungary optd **Banat Bacska 1919**. (a) "Turul" Type.
1 **7** 50f. red on blue 11·50 11·50

(b) War Charity stamps of 1916.
2 **20** 10f.(+2f.) red 40 40
3 – 15f.(+2f.) violet 40 40
4 **22** 40f.(+2f.) red 40 40

(c) Harvesters and Parliament Types.
5 **18** 2f. brown 55 55
6 3f. purple 55 55
7 5f. green 55 55
8 6f. blue 55 55
9 15f. purple 55 55
10 35f. brown 11·50 11·50
11 **19** 50f. purple 11·50 11·50
12 75f. blue 55 55
13 80f. green 55 55
14 1k. red 55 55
15 2k. brown 55 55
16 2k. grey and violet 19·00 19·00
17 5k. light brown and brown 1·10 1·10
18 10k. mauve and brown 2·30 2·30

(d) Charles and Zita stamps.
19 **27** 10f. pink 40 40
20 20f. brown 40 40
21 25f. blue 40 40
22 **28** 40f. green 40 40
23 50f. violet 40 40

(e) Harvesters Type inscr "MAGYAR POSTA".
24 **18** 10f. red 11·50 11·50
25 20f. brown 11·50 11·50
26 25f. blue 13·00 13·00

(f) Various Types optd **KOZTARSASAG**. (i) Harvesters and Parliament Types.
27 **18** 4f. grey 55 55
28 5f. green 55 55
29 6f. blue 55 55
30 10f. red 13·00 13·00
31 20f. brown 11·50 11·50
32 40f. green 25 25
33 **19** 1k. red 55 55
34 2k. brown 11·50 11·50
35 3k. grey and violet 11·50 11·50
36 5k. light brown and brown 11·50 11·50
37 10k. mauve and brown 11·50 11·50

(iii) Charles portrait stamps.
38 **27** 15f. purple 11·50 11·50
39 25f. blue 2·30 2·30

(g) Serbian Occupation of Temesvar stamps.
40 **18** 10f. on 2f. brown 55 55
41 **20** 45f. on 10f.(+2f.) red 75 75
42 **18** 1k.50 on 15f. purple 2·30 2·30

EXPRESS LETTER STAMP

1919. No. E245 of Hungary optd **Banat Bacska 30 FILLER 1919**.
E44 E **18** 30f. on 2f. green and red 1·50 1·50

NEWSPAPER STAMP

1919. No. N136 of Hungary optd **Banat Bacska 1919**.
N43 N **9** (2f.) orange 55 55

POSTAGE DUE STAMPS

1919. Nos. D191 etc optd as above.
D46 D **9** 2f. red and green 55 55
D47 10f. red and green 55 55
D48 15f. red and green 11·50 11·50
D49 20f. red and green 55 55
D50 30f. red and green 9·25 9·25
D51 50f. black and green 13·00 13·00

SAVINGS BANK STAMP

1919. No. B199 of Hungary surch **Banat Bacska 50 FILLER 1919**.
B45 B **17** 50f. on 10f. purple 1·50 1·50

B. DEBRECEN

This area was later returned to Hungary.

100 filler = 1 korona.

(1)

1919. Stamps of Hungary optd with **T1** or surch in addition. (a) "Turul" Type.
1 **7** 2f. yellow 22·00 14·00
2 3f. orange 28·00 28·00
3 6f. brown 4·50 4·50

(b) War Charity stamps of 1915.
4 **7** 2f.+2f. yellow (No. 171) 27·00 27·00
5 3f.+2f. orange (No. 172) 27·00 27·00

(c) War Charity stamps of 1916.
6 **20** 10f.(+2f.) red 40 40
7 – 15f.(+2f.) lilac 1·90 1·90
8 **22** 40f.(+2f.) red 90 90

(d) Harvesters and Parliament Types.
9 **18** 2f. brown 15 15
10 3f. purple 10 10
11 5f. green 40 40
12 6f. blue 15 15
13 10f. red (No. 243) 18·00 18·00
14 15f. violet (No. 244) 25·00 25·00
15 15f. purple 10 10
16 20f. brown 14·00 14·00
17 25f. blue 75 75
18 35f. brown 5·00 5·00
19 35f. on 3f. purple 25 25
20 40f. green 60 60
21 45f. on 2f. brown 25 25
22 **19** 50f. purple 60 60
23 75f. blue 15 15
24 80f. green 40 40
25 1k. red 40 40
26 2k. brown 15 15
27 3k. grey and violet 3·75 3·75
28 3k. on 75f. blue 2·10 2·10

29 5k. light brown and brown 3·75 3·75
30 5k. on 75f. blue 75 75
31 10k. mauve and brown . . . 45·00 15·00
32 10k. on 80f. green . . . . . 1·40 1·40

(e) Charles and Zita stamps.

33 **27** 10f. pink . . . . 4·50 4·25
34 15f. purple . . . . 16·00 16·00
35 20f. brown 75 75
36 25f. blue 50 50
37 **28** 40f. green 35 35
38 50f. purple . . . . 3·75 3·75

(f) Harvesters and Parliament Types inscr "MAGAR POSTA".

39 **18** 5f. green 10 10
40 6f. blue . . . . 2·50 2·50
41 10f. red 10 10
42 20f. brown 10 10
43 25f. blue 10 10
44 45f. orange . . . . 2·50 2·50
45 **19** 5k. brown 00

(g) Various Types optd **KOZTARSASAG**. (i) Harvesters and Parliament Types.

46 **18** 2f. brown 25 25
47 3f. purple . . . . 4·75 4·75
48 4f. grey 15 15
49 5f. green 10 10
50 10f. red . . . . 4·00 4·00
51 20f. brown 40 40
52 40f. green 25 25
53 **19** 1k. red 25 25
54 2k. brown . . . . 6·75 6·75
55 3k. grey and violet . . . . 1·40 1·40
56 5k. light brown and brown 60·00 60·00

(ii) War Charity stamps of 1916.

57 **20** 10f.(+2f.) red . . . . 4·75 4·75
58 – 15f.(+2f.) lilac . . . . . . 19·00 19·00
59 **22** 40f.(+2f.) red . . . . 1·40 1·40

(iii) Charles and Zita stamps.

60 **27** 10f. pink . . . . 4·25 4·25
61 15f. purple . . . . 7·50 7·50
62 20f. brown . . . . 1·10 1·10
63 25f. blue 50 50
64 **28** 50f. purple 70 70

2

4

1920. Types **2** and **4** and similar design, optd with inscr as T **1** but in circle.

65 **2** 2f. brown 15 15
66 3f. brown 15 15
67 4f. violet 15 15
68 5f. green 10 10
69 6f. grey 15 15
70 10f. red 10 10
71 15f. violet 25 25
72 20f. brown 10 10
73 – 25f. blue 80 80
74 – 30f. brown 80 80
75 – 35f. purple 80 80
76 – 40f. green 80 80
77 – 45f. red 80 80
78 – 50f. mauve 80 80
79 – 60f. green 80 80
80 – 75f. blue 80 80
81 **4** 80f. green 15 15
82 1k. red 25 25
83 1k.20 orange . . . . 4·25 4·25
84 2k. brown 75 75
85 3k. brown 75 75
86 5k. brown 75 75
87 10k. purple 75 75

DESIGN: Nos. 73/80, Horseman using lasso.

5

1920. War Charity. Type **5** with circular opt, and "Segely belyeg" at top.

88 **5** 20f. green 75 75
89 20f. green on blue 25 25
90 50f. brown . . . . 1·00 1·00
91 50f. brown on mauve 15 15
92 1k. green 80 80
93 1k. green on green 80 80
94 2k. green . . . . 1·10 1·10

EXPRESS LETTER STAMP

1919. No. E245 of Hungary optd with T **1**.

E66 E **18** 2f. green and red . . . 25 25

NEWSPAPER STAMP

1919. No. N136 of Hungary optd with T **1**.

N65 N **9** 2f. orange 20 20

POSTAGE DUE STAMPS

1919. (a) Nos. D190 etc of Hungary optd with T **1**.

D68 D **9** 1f. red and green . . . . 5·75 5·75
D69 2f. red and green 15 15
D70 5f. red and green . . . . 65·00 65·00
D71 6f. red and green . . . . 26·00 26·00
D72 10f. red and green . . . 15 15
D73 12f. red and green . . . 26·00 26·00
D74 15f. red and green . . . 1·30 1·30
D75 20f. red and green . . . 1·30 1·30
D76 30f. red and green . . . 1·30 1·30

(b) With **KOZTARSASAG** opt.

D77 D **9** 2f. red and green . . . . 3·25 3·25
D78 3f. red and green . . . . 3·25 3·25
D79 10f. red and green . . . 3·25 3·25
D80 20f. red and green . . . 3·25 3·25
D81 40f. red and green . . . 3·25 3·25
D82 50f. red and green . . . 3·25 3·25

D 6

1920.

D95 D **6** 5f. green 35 30
D96 10f. green 35 30
D97 20f. green 35 30
D98 30f. green 35 30
D99 40f. green 35 30

SAVINGS BANK STAMP

1919. No. B199 of Hungary optd with T **1**.

B67 B **17** 10f. purple . . . . . . 5·25 5·25

C. TEMESVAR

After being occupied by Serbia this area was then occupied by Rumania. It later became part of Rumania and was renamed Timisoara.

100 filler = 1 korona.

1919. Stamps of Hungary surch. (a) Harvesters Type.

6 **18** 30 on 2f. brown 15 15
7 1k. on 4f. grey (optd **KOZTARSASAG**) 15 15
8 150 on 3f. purple 10 10
9 150 on 5f. green 15 15

(b) Express Letter Stamp.

10 E **18** 3 KORONA on 2f. green and red 25 25

POSTAGE DUE STAMPS

1919 Charity stamp of Hungary surch **PORTO 40**.

D11 40 on 15+(2f.) lilac (No. 265) 30 30

(D **8**)

1919. Postage Due stamps of Hungary surch with Type D **8**.

D12 D **9** 60 on 2f. red and green 2·25 2·25
D13 60 on 10f. red and green 60 60

RUMANIAN POST OFFICES IN THE TURKISH EMPIRE Pt. 16

Rumanian P.O.s in the Turkish Empire including Constantinople. Now closed.

I. GENERAL ISSUES

40 paras = 1 piastre.

1896. Stamps of Rumania of 1893 surch in "PARAS".

9 10pa. on 5b. blue (No. 319) 11·00 11·00
10 20pa. on 10b. green (No. 320) 11·00 11·00
11 1pi. on 25b. mauve (No. 322) 11·00 11·00

II. CONSTANTINOPLE

100 bani = 1 leu.

(1)

1919. Stamps of Rumania of 1893–1908 optd with T **1**.

18 **37** 5b. green 50 50
19 10b. red 60 60
20 15b. brown 75 75
30 – 25b. blue (No. 701) 80 80
31 – 40b. brown (No. 703) . . . 2·50 2·50

1919. 1916 Postal Tax stamp of Rumania optd with T **1**.

33 T **41** 5b. green . . . . 1·60 1·80

RUSSIA Pt. 10

A country in the E. of Europe and N. Asia. An empire until 1917 when the Russian Socialist Federal Soviet Republic was formed. In 1923 this became the Union of Soviet Socialist Republics (U.S.S.R.), eventually comprising 15 constituent republics.

In 1991 the U.S.S.R. was dissolved and subsequent issues were used in the Russian Federation only.

100 kopeks = 1 rouble.

1

5

8

9

10

11

1858. Imperf.

No.	Type	Description	Unused	Used
1	1	10k. blue and brown	£4000	£400

1858. Perf.

No.	Type	Description	Unused	Used
21	1	10k. blue and brown	32·00	25
22		20k. orange and blue	55·00	7·50
23		30k. green and red	75·00	25·00

1863.

No.	Type	Description	Unused	Used
8	5	5k. black and blue	20·00	£140

No. 8 was first issued as a local but was later authorised for general use.

1864.

No.	Type	Description	Unused	Used
18	9	1k. black and yellow	3·00	35
30		2k. black and red	6·50	60
19b		3k. black and green	4·00	45
20		5k. black and lilac	7·50	25

1875.

No.	Type	Description	Unused	Used
31	8	7k. red and grey	6·00	25
32		8k. red and grey	9·00	40
33		10k. blue and brown	25·00	3·00
34		20k. orange and blue	30·00	2·50

12 No thunderbolts

1883. Posthorns in design without thunderbolts, as T 12.

No.	Type	Description	Unused	Used
38	9	1k. orange	3·00	45
39		2k. green	4·00	45
41		3k. red	4·25	30
42b		5k. purple	3·50	15
43b		7k. blue	3·75	15
44	10	14k. red and blue	9·00	35
45		35k. green and purple	20·00	4·00
46		70k. orange and brown	40·00	4·00
47	11	3r.50 grey and black	£425	£275
48		7r. yellow and black	£450	£375

14

15

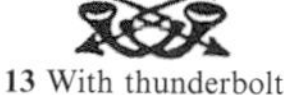
13 With thunderbolts

1889. Posthorns in design with thunderbolts as T 13. Perf.

No.	Type	Description	Unused	Used
50	9	1k. orange	25	10
51		2k. green	25	10
52		3k. red	30	10
53	14	4k. red	40	10
54	9	5k. purple	70	10
55		7k. blue	35	10
56	14	10k. blue	70	10
114A	10	14k. red and blue	10	10
100		15k. blue and purple	10	10
116A	14	20k. red and blue	10	10
102	10	25k. violet and green	10	10
103		35k. green and purple	10	10
119A	14	50k. green and purple	10	10
120A	10	70k. orange and brown	10	10
121A	15	1r. orange and brown	10	10
79	11	3r.50 grey and black	9·00	3·00
122A		3r.50 green and red	20	30
80		7r. yellow and black	8·50	5·00
124bA		7r. pink and green	20	50

For imperf stamps, see Nos. 107B/125aB.

16 Monument to Admiral Kornilov at Sevastopol

1905. War Orphans Fund (Russo-Japanese War).

No.	Type	Description	Unused	Used
88	16	3 (6) k. brown, red and green	2·75	2·00
82	–	5 (8) k. purple and yellow	2·75	2·50
83	–	7 (10) k. blue, lt blue & pink	3·50	3·00
87	–	10 (13) k. blue, lt bl & yell	5·00	3·75

DESIGNS: 5(8) k. Monument to Minin and Pozharsky, Moscow; 7(10) k. Statue of Peter the Great, St. Petersburg; 10(13) k. Moscow Kremlin.

22

23

20

1906.

No.	Type	Description	Unused	Used
107A	22	1k. orange	10	10
93		2k. green	10	10
94		3k. red	10	10
95	23	4k. red	10	10
96	22	5k. red	10	10
97		7k. blue	10	10
98a	23	10k. blue	10	10
123Aa	20	5r. blue and green	30	30
125Aa		10r. grey, red and yellow	60	65

For imperf stamps, see Nos. 107B/125aB.

25 Nicholas II

26 Elizabeth

27 The Kremlin

1913. Tercentenary of Romanov Dynasty. Views as T 27 and portraits as T 25/26.

No.	Type	Description	Unused	Used
126		1k. orange (Peter I)	30	15
127		2k. green (Alexander II)	40	15
128		3k. red (Alexander III)	40	15
129		4k. red (Peter I)	40	15
130		7k. brown (Type 25)	40	15
131		10k. blue (Nicholas II)	50	15
132		14k. green (Katherine II)	50	20
133		15k. brown (Nicholas I)	75	30
134		20k. olive (Alexander I)	1·10	30
135		25k. red (Alexis)	1·75	50
136		35k. green and violet (Paul I)	1·75	60
137		50k. grey and brown (T 26)	3·50	60
138		70k. brown and green (Michael I, the first Russian tsar)	3·50	1·25
139		1r. green (Type 27)	8·50	2·25
140		2r. brown	10·00	3·75
141		3r. violet	24·00	8·00
142		5r. brown	32·00	18·00

DESIGNS—As T 27: 2r. The Winter Palace; 3r. Romanov House, Moscow (birthplace of first Romanov tsar). 23 × 29 mm: 5r. Nicholas II.

31 Russian hero, Ilya Murometz

1914. War Charity.

No.	Type	Description	Unused	Used
151	31	1 (2) k. green & red on yell	60	1·50
144	–	3 (4) k. green and red on red	50	1·25
145	–	7 (8) k. green and brown on buff	50	2·75
161	–	10 (11) k. brown and blue on blue	1·00	2·00

DESIGNS: 3k. Cossack shaking girl's hand; 7k. Symbolical of Russia surrounded by her children; 10k. St. George and Dragon.

1915. As last. Colours changed.

No.	Type	Description	Unused	Used
155	31	1 (2) k. grey and brown	1·00	2·00
156	–	3 (4) k. black and red	1·00	2·50
158	–	10 (11) k. brown and blue	1·00	2·00

35

39

41

45 Cutting the Fetters

1915. Nos. 131, 133 and 134 printed on card with inscriptions on back as T 35. No gum.

No.	Type	Description	Unused	Used
165		10k. blue	1·50	5·00
166		15k. brown	1·50	5·00
167		20k. olive	1·50	5·00

1916. Various types surch.

No.	Type	Description	Unused	Used
168	–	10k. on 7k. brown (No. 130)	40	25
170	22	10k. on 7k. blue	40	15
169	–	20k. on 14k. green (No. 132)	40	20
171	10	20k. on 14k. red and blue	40	15

1917. Various earlier types, but imperf.

No.	Type	Description	Unused	Used
107B	22	1k. orange	10	10
108B		2k. green	10	10
109B		3k. red	10	10
110B	23	4k. red	15	25
111B	22	5k. lilac	10	10
113B	23	10k. blue	10·00	27·00
115B	10	15k. blue & pur (No. 100)	10	10
116B	14	20k. red and blue	15	30
117Bd	10	25k. vio & grn (No. 102)	50	1·00
118B		35k. grn & pur (No. 103)	15	25
119B	14	50k. green and purple	15	25
120B	10	70k. orange and brown (No. 120)	10	30
121B	15	1r. orange and brown	10	10
122B	11	3r.50 green and red	20	30
123Ba	20	5r. blue and green	30	60
124B	11	7r. pink and green	50	1·40
125B	20	10r. grey, red and yellow	22·00	30·00

1916. Types of 1913 printed on card with surch on back as T 39 or 41, or optd with figure "1" or "2" in addition on front. No gum.

No.	Type	Description	Unused	Used
172	39	1k. orange (No. 126)	20·00	35·00
175		1 on 1k. orange (No. 126)	1·00	5·00
177	41	1 on 1k. orange (No. 126)	75	4·50
173	39	2k. green (No. 127)	40·00	45·00
176		2 on 2k. green (No. 127)	1·00	5·00
178	41	2 on 2k. green (No. 127)	75	4·75
174	39	3k. red (No. 128)	1·00	4·00
179	41	3k. red (No. 128)	75	4·50

1918.

No.	Type	Description	Unused	Used
187	45	35k. blue	1·50	4·00
188		70k. brown	1·50	5·00

46 Agriculture and Industry

47 Triumph of Revolution

48 Agriculture

49 Industry

55 Science and Arts

56

64 Industry

1921. Imperf.

No.	Type	Description	Unused	Used
195	48	1r. orange	1·25	7·50
196		2r. brown	1·25	7·50
197	49	5r. blue	1·50	7·50
198	46	20r. blue	2·50	4·00
199	47	40r. blue	2·50	4·00
214	48	100r. yellow	10	10
215		200r. brown	10	25
216	55	250r. purple	10	10
217	48	300r. green	20	40
218	49	500r. blue	25	45
219		1000r. red	10	10
256	64	5000r. violet	50	85
257	46	7500r. blue	30	30
259		7500r. blue on buff	50	35
258	64	10000r. blue	5·00	10·00
260		22500r. purple on buff	50	50

1921. 4th Anniv of October Revolution. Imperf.

No.	Type	Description	Unused	Used
227	56	100r. orange	50	2·00
228		250r. violet	50	2·00
229		1000r. purple	50	2·00

57 Famine Relief Work

58

Р. С. Ф. С. Р.
ГОЛОДАЮЩИМ
250 р.+250 р.
(62)

1921. Charity. Volga Famine. Imperf.

No.	Type	Description	Unused	Used
230	57	2250r. green	5·00	7·50
231		2250r. red	3·75	8·00
232		2250r. brown	7·50	11·00
233	58	2250r. blue	10·00	15·00

1922. Surch. Imperf.

No.	Type	Description	Unused	Used
239	48	5000r. on 1r. orange	1·00	2·00
240		5000r. on 2r. brown	1·00	2·00
236	49	5000r. on 5r. blue	1·00	2·50
242	46	5000r. on 20r. blue	2·00	2·75
243	47	10000r. on 40r. blue	1·50	3·00

1922. Famine Relief. Surch as T 62. Perf.

No.	Type	Description	Unused	Used
245	45	100r.+100r. on 70k. brown	80	1·50
247		250r.+250r. on 25k. blue	80	1·75

(63)

1922. Surch as T 63. Imperf.

No.	Type	Description	Unused	Used
250	55	7500r. on 250r. purple	20	15
251		100000r. on 250r. purple	15	30

65

1922. Obligatory Tax. Rostov-on-Don issue. Famine Relief. Various sizes. Without gum. Imperf.

261	**65**	2T. (2000r.) green	32·00	£200
262	–	2T. (2000r.) red	25·00	£200
263	–	4T. (4000r.) red	50·00	£200
264	–	6T. (6000r.) green	40·00	£200

DESIGNS: 2T. red, Worker and family (35 × 42 mm); 4T. Clasped hands (triangular, 57 mm each side); 6T. Sower (29 × 59 mm).

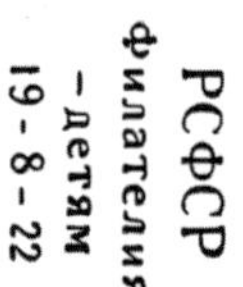

(**70** "Philately for the children")

1922. Optd with T **70**. Perf or imperf.

273	**22**	1k. orange	£200	£300
274		2k. green	18·00	20·00
275		3k. red	10·00	12·00
276		5k. red	8·00	12·00
277	**23**	10k. blue	8·00	15·00

71

73

1922. 5th Anniv of October Revolution. Imperf.

279	**71**	5r. black and yellow	60	45
280		10r. black and brown	60	45
281		25r. black and purple	2·50	1·25
282		27r. black and red	6·00	5·50
283		45r. black and blue	4·00	5·00

1922. Air. Optd with airplane. Imperf.

284	**71**	45r. black and green	22·00	45·00

1922. Famine Relief. Imperf.

285	**73**	20r.+5r. lilac	60	2·00
286	–	20r.+5r. violet	60	2·00
287	–	20r.+5r. blue	1·00	2·50
288	–	20r.+5r. blue	3·50	15·00

DESIGNS—HORIZ: No. 286, Freighter; No. 287, Steam train. VERT: No. 288, Airplane.

(77)

78 Worker

79 Soldier

1922. Surch as T **77**. Imperf or perf.

289	**14**	5r. on 20k. red and blue	3·50	20·00
290	**10**	20r. on 15k. blue & purple	3·75	20·00
291		20r. on 70k. orange and brown	15	30
292a	**14**	30r. on 50k. green & pur	35	35
293	**10**	40r. on 15k. blue & pur	15	15
294		100r. on 15k. blue & pur	15	20
295		200r. on 15k. blue & pur	15	20

1922. Imperf or perf.

303	**78**	10r. blue	10	15
304	**79**	50r. brown	10	15
305		70r. purple	10	15
310		100r. red	15	15

1 мая
1923 г. Филателия —
Трудящимся,
1 р.+1 р.
(80)

1923. Charity. Surch as T **80**. Imperf.

315	**71**	1r.+1r. on 10r. black and brown	30·00	40·00
317	**55**	2r.+2r. on 250r. purple	30·00	40·00
318	**64**	4r.+4r. on 5000r. violet	45·00	55·00

83 Worker

84 Peasant

85 Soldier

1923. Perf.

320	**85**	3r. red	10	10
321	**83**	4r. brown	10	10
322	**84**	5r. blue	10	10
323	**85**	10r. grey	15	15
324		20r. purple	25	25

86 Reaper

88 Tractor

1923. Agricultural Exn, Moscow. Imperf or perf.

325	**86**	1r. brown and orange	2·00	6·00
326	–	2r. green and light green	2·00	6·00
327	**88**	5r. blue and light blue	2·00	6·00
328	–	7r. rose and pink	2·00	6·00

DESIGNS: As Type **86**: 2r. Sower; 7r. Exhibition buildings.

90 Worker

91 Peasant

92 Soldier

93

94

95

1923. Perf (some values also imperf).

335	**90**	1k. yellow	40	25
359	**91**	2k. green	30	15
360	**92**	3k. brown	35	15
361	**90**	4k. red	35	15
434		5k. purple	55	15
363	**91**	6k. blue	60	15
364	**92**	7k. brown	60	15
437	**90**	8k. olive	90	15
366	**91**	9k. red	90	40
341	**92**	10k. blue	55	15
385	**90**	14k. grey	1·00	20
386	**91**	15k. yellow	1·25	90
442	**92**	18k. violet	1·75	55
443	**90**	20k. green	2·00	30
444	**91**	30k. violet	2·75	40
445	**92**	40k. grey	4·00	60
343	**91**	50k. brown	4·50	60
447	**92**	1r. red and brown	4·75	80
375	**93**	2r. green and red	6·50	3·00
449	**94**	3r. green and brown	14·00	4·00
450	**95**	5r. brown and blue	17·00	5·00

96 Lenin

97 Fokker F.III Airplane

1924. Lenin Mourning. Imperf or perf.

413	**96**	3k. black and red	2·00	1·75
414		6k. black and red	2·00	1·75
411		12k. black and red	5·00	75
412		20k. black and red	2·75	85

1924. Air. Surch. Imperf.

417	**97**	5k. on 3r. blue	3·50	1·75
418		10k. on 5r. green	3·50	1·50
419		15k. on 1r. brown	2·00	1·50
420		20k. on 10r. red	2·50	1·25

С. С. С. Р.
пострадавшему
от наводнения
Ленинграду.
3 к. + 10 к.
(**99** Trans "For the victims of the flood in Leningrad")

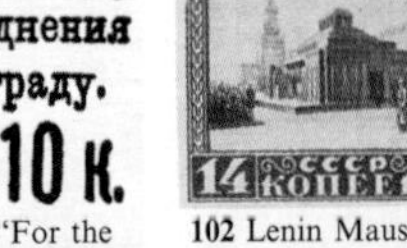
102 Lenin Mausoleum, Moscow

1924. Leningrad Flood Relief. Surch as T **99**. Imperf.

421	**48**	3+10k. on 100r. yellow	1·50	1·75
422		7+20k. on 200r. brown	1·50	1·75
423		14+30k. on 300r. green	2·75	2·50
424	**49**	12+40k. on 500r. blue	2·75	3·00
425		20+50k. on 1000r. red	2·75	2·75

1925. 1st Death Anniv of Lenin. Imperf or perf.

426	**102**	7k. blue	3·50	2·75
427		14k. olive	4·50	4·00
428		20k. red	5·00	4·00
429		40k. brown	7·50	4·00

104 Lenin

106 Prof. Lomonosov and Academy of Sciences, Leningrad

1925.

451	**104**	1r. brown	8·00	3·00
452		2r. brown	7·50	2·50
850		3r. green	2·25	75
851		5r. brown	3·50	1·50
852		10r. blue	7·50	5·00

1925. Bicentenary of Academy of Sciences.

456b	**106**	3k. brown	4·00	2·00
457		15k. olive	6·00	4·00

107 A. S. Popov

110 Moscow Barricade

1925. 30th Anniv of Popov's Radio Discoveries.

458	**107**	7k. blue	2·50	1·40
459		14k. green	4·00	2·25

1925. 20th Anniv of 1905 Rebellion. Imperf or perf.

463b	–	3k. green	3·00	1·75
464c	–	7k. brown	4·00	2·50
465a	**110**	14k. red	3·50	2·25

DESIGNS—VERT: 3k. Postal rioters; 7k. Orator and crowd.

111 "Decembrists in Exiles" (detail, A. Moravov)

112 Senate Square, St. Petersburg, 1825

1925. Centenary of Decembrist Rebellion. Imperf or perf.

466b	**111**	3k. green	2·50	2·25
467	**112**	7k. brown	4·00	3·25
468	–	14k. red	5·00	3·50

DESIGN—VERT: 14k. Medallion with heads of Pestel, Ryleev, Bestuzhev-Ryumin, Muravev-Apostol and Kakhovsky.

114

1926. 6th International Proletarian Esperanto Congress.

471	**114**	7k. red and green	5·00	3·00
472		14k. violet and green	5·00	1·75

115 Waifs

116 Lenin when a Child

1926. Child Welfare.

473	**115**	10k. brown	90	45
474	**116**	20k. blue	2·50	95

1927. Same type with new inscriptions.

475	**115**	8k.+2k. green	80	35
476	**116**	18k.+2k. red	1·75	65

ПОЧТОВАЯ
МАРКА
КОП. 8 КОП.
(117)

1927. Postage Due stamps surch with T **117**.

491	D **104**	8k. on 1k. red	1·50	2·75
492		8k. on 2k. violet	1·50	2·75
493		8k. on 3k. blue	1·50	2·75
494		8k. on 7k. yellow	1·50	2·75
494c		8k. on 8k. green	1·00	2·25
494d		8k. on 10k. blue	1·50	2·75
494f		8k. on 14k. brown	1·50	2·75

1927. Various types of 7k. surch (some values imperf or perf).

495	**92**	8k. on 7k. brown	6·00	6·00
523	**107**	8k. on 7k. blue	3·00	3·25
524	–	8k. on 7k. brn (No. 464c)	6·00	5·00
527	**112**	8k. on 7k. brown	6·00	6·50
526	**114**	8k. on 7k. red and green	12·00	14·00

119 Dr. Zamenhof

1927. 40th Anniv of Publication of Zamenhof's "Langue Internationale" (Esperanto).

498	**119**	14k. green and brown	3·00	2·00

120 Tupolev ANT-3 Biplane and Map

1927. 1st Int Air Post Congress, The Hague.

499	**120**	10k. blue and brown	14·00	5·00
500		15k. red and olive	16·00	10·00

121 Worker, Soldier and Peasant

124 Sailor and Worker

122 Allegory of Revolution

1927. 10th Anniv of October Revolution.

501	**121**	3k. red	2·50	75
502	**122**	5k. brown	6·00	2·00
503	–	7k. green	8·00	2·50
504	**124**	8k. black and brown	4·25	85
505	–	14k. red and blue	6·00	1·25
506	–	18k. blue	4·00	1·00
507	–	28k. brown	13·00	8·00

DESIGNS—HORIZ: (As Type **122**): 7k. Smolny Institute; 14k. Map of Russia inscr "C.C.C.P."; 18k. Various Russian races; 28k. Worker, soldier and peasant.

128 Worker

129 Peasant

130 Lenin

1927.

508	**128**	1k. orange	90	50
509	**129**	2k. green	90	20
510	**128**	4k. blue	90	20
511	**129**	5k. brown	90	20
512		7k. red	4·50	1·00
513	**128**	8k. green	2·50	20
514		10k. brown	2·00	20
515	**130**	14k. green	2·25	45
516		18k. olive	3·00	40
517		18k. blue	5·00	70
518	**129**	20k. olive	2·75	35
519	**128**	40k. red	6·00	60
520	**129**	50k. blue	8·00	1·00
521	**128**	70k. olive	13·00	1·40
522	**129**	80k. orange	24·00	5·00

131 Infantryman, Lenin Mausoleum and Kremlin

1928. 10th Anniv of Red Army.

No.	Type	Description	Unused	Used
529	**131**	8k. brown	1·60	45
530	–	14k. blue	3·00	50
531	–	18k. red	3·00	1·75
532	–	28k. green	4·00	4·00

DESIGNS: 14k. Sailor and cruiser "Aurora"; 18k. Cavalryman; 28k. Airman.

135 Young Factory Workers

137 Trumpeter sounding the Assembly

1929. Child Welfare.

No.	Type	Description	Unused	Used
536	**135**	10k.+2k. brown & sepia	1·75	1·10
537	–	20k.+2k. blue & brown	2·75	2·75

DESIGN: 20k. Children in harvest field.

See also Nos. 567/8.

1929. 1st All-Union Gathering of Pioneers.

No.	Type	Description	Unused	Used
538	**137**	10k. brown	12·00	8·00
539		14k. blue	6·00	4·00

138 Worker (after I. Shadr) **139** Factory Girl **140** Peasant

141 Farm Girl **142** Guardsman **143** Worker, Soldier and Peasant (after I. Smirnov)

144 Lenin **242a** Miner **242b** Steel foundryman

242c Infantryman **242d** Airman **242e** Arms of U.S.S.R.

149 Central Telegraph Office, Moscow

150 Lenin Hydro-electric Power Station

743a Farm Girl **743b** Architect **744** Furnaceman

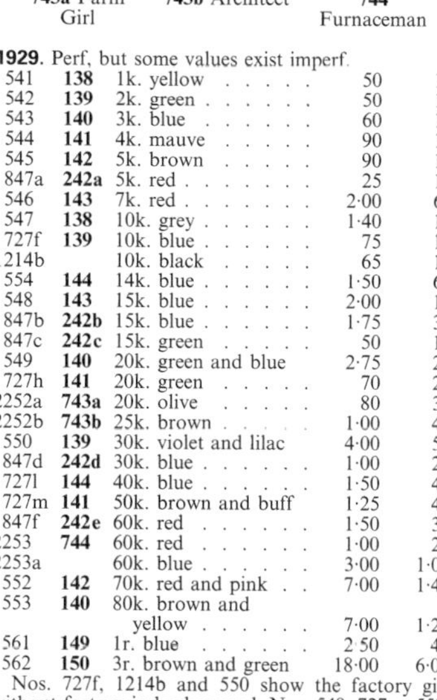

1929. Perf, but some values exist imperf.

No.	Type	Description	Unused	Used
541	**138**	1k. yellow	50	15
542	**139**	2k. green	50	10
543	**140**	3k. blue	60	10
544	**141**	4k. mauve	90	15
545	**142**	5k. brown	90	10
847a	**242a**	5k. red	25	10
546	**143**	7k. red	2·00	60
547	**138**	10k. grey	1·40	10
727f	**139**	10k. blue	75	15
1214b		10k. black	65	15
554	**144**	14k. blue	1·50	60
548	**143**	15k. blue	2·00	10
847b	**242b**	15k. blue	1·75	30
847c	**242c**	15k. green	50	15
549	**140**	20k. green and blue	2·75	20
727h	**141**	20k. green	70	25
2252a	**743a**	20k. olive	80	30
2252b	**743b**	25k. brown	1·00	45
550	**139**	30k. violet and lilac	4·00	50
847d	**242d**	30k. blue	1·00	20
727l	**144**	40k. blue	1·50	40
727m	**141**	50k. brown and buff	1·25	40
847f	**242e**	60k. red	1·50	30
2253	**744**	60k. red	1·00	20
2253a		60k. blue	3·00	1·00
552	**142**	70k. red and pink	7·00	1·40
553	**140**	80k. brown and yellow	7·00	1·25
561	**149**	1r. blue	2·50	40
562	**150**	3r. brown and green	18·00	6·00

Nos. 727f, 1214b and 550 show the factory girl without factory in background. Nos. 549, 727m, 552, 553 have designs like those shown but with unshaded background.

151 Industry

153 "More metal more machines"

1929. Industrial Loan Propaganda.

No.	Type	Description	Unused	Used
563	**151**	5k. brown	2·00	1·25
564	–	10k. olive	2·50	2·00
565	**153**	20k. green	9·00	3·25
566	–	28k. violet	5·00	3·25

DESIGNS—HORIZ: 10k. Tractors. VERT: 28k. Blast furnace and graph of pig-iron output.

1930. Child Welfare.

No.	Type	Description	Unused	Used
567	**135**	10k.+2k. olive	1·50	1·75
568	–	20k.+2k. grn (as No. 537)	2·50	3·50

155 Cavalrymen (after M. Grekov)

1930. 10th Anniv of 1st Red Cavalry.

No.	Type	Description	Unused	Used
569	**155**	2k. green	2·50	1·40
570	–	5k. brown	2·50	1·40
571	–	10k. olive	5·00	3·00
572	–	14k. blue and red	2·50	2·50

DESIGNS: 5k. Cavalry attack (after Yu. Merkulov); 10k. Cavalry facing left (after M. Grekov); 14k. Cavalry charge (after Yu. Merkulov).

159 Group of Soviet Pupils

1930. Educational Exhibition, Leningrad.

No.	Type	Description	Unused	Used
573	**159**	10k. green	2·00	1·00

160

1930. Air. "Graf-Zeppelin" (airship) Flight to Moscow.

No.	Type	Description	Unused	Used
574	**160**	40k. blue	30·00	18·00
575		80k. red	35·00	13·00

162 Battleship "Potemkin"

1930. 25th Anniv of 1905 Rebellion. Imperf or perf.

No.	Type	Description	Unused	Used
576	**162**	3k. red	1·75	50
577	–	5k. blue	1·50	60
578	–	10k. red and green	2·75	1·10

DESIGNS—HORIZ: 5k. Barricade and rebels. VERT: 10k. Red flag at Presnya barricade.

165 From the Tundra (reindeer) to the Steppes (camel)

166 Above Dnieprostroi Dam

1931. Airship Construction Fund. Imperf or perf.

No.	Type	Description	Unused	Used
579c	**165**	10k. violet	4·00	2·50
580b	**166**	15k. blue	22·00	12·00
581c	–	20k. red	3·50	3·00
582b	–	50k. brown	3·50	3·00
583c	–	1r. green	5·50	5·00

DESIGNS—As Type **165**. VERT: 20k. Above Lenin's Mausoleum. HORIZ: 1r. Airship construction. As Type **166**: 50k. Above the North Pole.

See also No. E592.

170 "Graf Zeppelin" over Ice breaker "Malygin"

1931. Air. "Graf Zeppelin" (airship) North Pole Flight. Imperf or perf.

No.	Type	Description	Unused	Used
584	**170**	30k. purple	25·00	15·00
585b		35k. green	25·00	15·00
586		1r. black	25·00	15·00
587		2r. blue	25·00	15·00

172 Maksim Gorky

173 Storming the Winter Palace

1932. 40th Anniv of Publication of "Makar Chadra".

No.	Type	Description	Unused	Used
590	**172**	15k. brown	5·00	3·50
591		35k. blue	18·00	10·00

1932. Airship Construction Fund. Imperf or perf.

No.	Type	Description	Unused	Used
592	**166**	15k. black	3·50	1·50

1932. 15th Anniv of October Revolution.

No.	Type	Description	Unused	Used
593	–	3k. violet	1·25	50
594	**173**	5k. brown	1·25	50
595	–	10k. blue	3·25	1·25
596	–	15k. green	1·75	1·25
597	–	20k. red	7·25	1·75
598	–	30k. grey	9·00	1·90
599	–	35k. brown	60·00	45·00

DESIGNS—HORIZ: 10k. Dnieper Dam; 15k. Harvesting with combines; 20k. Industrial works, Magnitogorsk; 30k. Siberians listening to Moscow broadcast. VERT: 3k. Lenin's arrival in Petrograd; 35k. People of the World hailing Lenin.

175 "Liberation"

1932. 10th Anniv of International Revolutionaries' Relief Organization.

No.	Type	Description	Unused	Used
600	**175**	50k. red	14·00	6·00

176 Museum of Fine Arts

1932. 1st All-Union Philatelic Exn, Moscow.

No.	Type	Description	Unused	Used
601	**176**	15k. brown	24·00	13·00
602		35k. blue	40·00	20·00

177 Trier, Marx's Birthplace

1933. 50th Death Anniv of Marx.

No.	Type	Description	Unused	Used
603	**177**	3k. green	4·00	90
604	–	10k. brown	7·00	1·40
605	–	35k. purple	10·00	12·50

DESIGNS—VERT: 10k. Marx's grave, Highgate Cemetery; 35k. Marx.

1933. Leningrad Philatelic Exhibition. Surch **LENINGRAD 1933** in Russian characters and premium.

No.	Type	Description	Unused	Used
606	**176**	15k.+30k. black & brn	80·00	40·00
607		35k.+70k. blue	95·00	50·00

182

183

1933. Ethnographical Issue. Racial types.

No.	Type	Description	Unused	Used
608	–	1k. brown (Kazakhs)	1·75	40
609	**183**	2k. blue (Lesgins)	1·75	40
610	–	3k. green (Crimean Tatars)	1·75	40
611	–	4k. brown (Jews of Birobidzhan)	1·25	60
612	–	5k. red (Tungusians)	1·25	40
613	–	6k. blue (Buryats)	1·25	40
614	–	7k. brown (Chechens)	1·25	40
615	–	8k. red (Abkhazians)	1·75	55
616	–	9k. blue (Georgians)	3·00	60
617	–	10k. brown (Samoyedes)	4·00	1·50
618	–	14k. green (Yakuts)	3·50	40
619	–	15k. purple (Ukrainians)	4·00	1·25
620	–	15k. black (Uzbeks)	4·00	80
621	–	15k. blue (Tadzhiks)	4·00	75
622	–	15k. brown (Transcaucasians)	4·00	75
623	–	15k. green (Byelorussians)	3·50	60
624	–	15k. orange (Great Russians)	3·50	80
625	–	15k. red (Turkmens)	4·50	1·00
626	–	20k. blue (Koryaks)	9·00	1·60
627	–	30k. red (Bashkirs)	10·00	1·75
628	**182**	35k. brown (Chuvashes)	16·00	2·25

SIZES: Nos. 608, 610/11, 614/17, 626/7, As T **182**: Nos. 612/13, 618. As T **183**: Nos. 619/24, 48 × 22 mm. No. 625, 22 × 48 mm.

186 V. V. Vorovsky

1933. Communist Party Activists. Dated "1933", "1934" or "1935".

No.	Type	Description	Unused	Used
629	**186**	1k. green	65	50
718b	–	2k. violet	4·50	25
630	–	3k. blue	1·40	60
719	–	4k. purple	5·00	4·00
631	–	5k. brown	3·00	1·90
632	–	10k. blue	16·00	6·00
633	–	15k. red	40·00	20·00
720	–	40k. brown	9·00	5·00

DESIGNS: 2k. M. Frunze; 3k. V. M. Volodarsky; 4k. N. E. Bauman; 5k. M. S. Uritsky; 10k. Iacov M. Sverdlov; 15k. Viktor P. Nogin; 40k. S. M. Kirov.

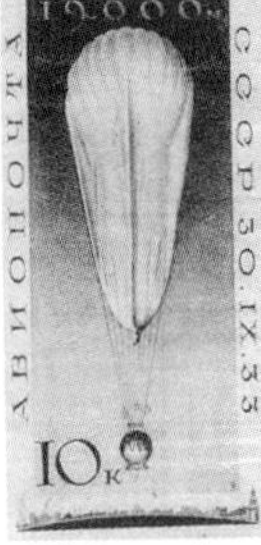

187 Stratosphere Balloon "U.S.S.R.-1" over Moscow

188 Massed Standard Bearers

1933. Air. Stratosphere record (19000 m).

No.	Type	Description	Mint	Used
634	187	5k. blue	80·00	19·00
635		10k. red	55·00	9·00
636		20k. violet	28·00	6·75

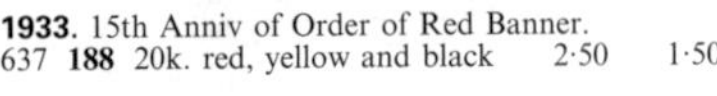

1933. 15th Anniv of Order of Red Banner.

No.	Type	Description	Mint	Used
637	188	20k. red, yellow and black	2·50	1·50

189 Commissar Shaumyan

190 Tupolev ANT-9 PS9 over Oilfield

1934. 15th Death Anniv of 26 Baku Commissars.

No.	Type	Description	Mint	Used
638	189	4k. brown	5·00	1·50
639	–	5k. black	5·00	1·50
640	–	20k. violet	3·00	85
641	–	35k. blue	18·00	4·00
642	–	40k. red	14·00	4·00

DESIGNS: 5k. Commissar Dzhaparidze. HORIZ: 20k. The 26 condemned commissars; 35k. Monument in Baku; 40k. Workman, peasant and soldier dipping flags in salute.

1934. Air. 10th Anniv of Soviet Civil Aviation and U.S.S.R. Airmail Service.

No.	Type	Description	Mint	Used
643	–	5k. blue	10·00	4·00
644	190	10k. green	10·00	4·00
645	–	20k. red	20·00	5·50
646	–	50k. blue	30·00	9·00
647	–	80k. violet	16·00	7·00

DESIGNS: Tupolev ANT-9 PS9 airplane over: 5k. Furnaces at Kuznetsk; 20k. Harvesters; 50k. Volga–Moscow Canal; 80k. Ice breaker "OB" in the Arctic.

191 New Lenin Mausoleum

1934. 10th Death Anniv of Lenin.

No.	Type	Description	Mint	Used
648	191	5k. brown	2·00	75
649		10k. blue	6·50	2·50
650		15k. red	6·00	2·00
651		20k. green	1·75	80
652		35k. brown	6·00	2·75

192 Fyodorov Monument, Moscow, and Hand and Rotary Presses

1934. 350th Death Anniv of Ivan Fyodorov (first Russian printer).

No.	Type	Description	Mint	Used
653	192	20k. red	8·00	3·75
654		40k. blue	8·00	3·00

194 Dmitri Mendeleev

1934. Birth Centenary of Dmitri Mendeleev (chemist).

No.	Type	Description	Mint	Used
655	–	5k. green	5·00	1·50
656	194	10k. brown	15·00	5·00
657		15k. red	13·00	4·50
658	–	20k. blue	7·50	2·50

DESIGN—VERT: 5k., 20k. Mendeleev seated.

195 A. V. Vasenko and "Osoaviakhim"

1934. Air. Stratosphere Balloon "Osoaviakhim" Disaster Victims.

No.	Type	Description	Mint	Used
659	–	5k. purple	22·00	5·00
660	195	10k. brown	55·00	6·00
661	–	20k. violet	60·00	8·00
1042	–	1r. green	8·50	3·00
1043	195	1r. green	8·50	3·00
1044	–	1r. blue	8·50	3·00

DESIGNS: 5k., 1r. (No. 1042). I. D. Usyskin; 20k., 1r. (No. 1044), P. F. Fedoseenko.

The 1r. values, issued in 1944, commemorated the 10th anniv of the disaster.

196 Airship "Pravda"

1934. Air. Airship Travel Propaganda.

No.	Type	Description	Mint	Used
662	196	5k. red	12·00	3·00
663	–	10k. lake	12·00	3·00
664	–	15k. brown	30·00	12·00
665	–	20k. black	16·00	7·50
666	–	30k. blue	55·00	26·00

DESIGNS—HORIZ: 10k. Airship landing; 15k. Airship "Voroshilov"; 30k. Airship "Lenin" and route map. VERT: 20k. Airship's gondolas and mooring mast.

199 Stalin and Marchers inspired by Lenin

1934. "Ten Years without Lenin". Portraits inscr "1924–1934".

No.	Type	Description	Mint	Used
667	–	1k. black and blue	1·50	75
668	–	3k. black and blue	1·50	80
669	–	5k. black and blue	3·50	1·40
670	–	10k. black and blue	4·25	2·50
671	–	20k. blue and orange	6·00	3·25
672	199	30k. red and orange	24·00	6·00

DESIGN—VERT: 1k. Lenin aged 3; 3k. Lenin as student; 5k. Lenin as man; 10k. Lenin as orator. HORIZ: 20k. Red demonstration, Lenin's Mausoleum.

200 "War Clouds"

1935. Anti-War. Inscr "1914–1934".

No.	Type	Description	Mint	Used
673	200	5k. black	4·50	90
674	–	10k. blue	7·50	3·75
675	–	15k. green	13·00	5·00
676	–	20k. brown	10·00	2·75
677	–	35k. red	22·00	13·00

DESIGNS: 10k. "Flight from a burning village"; 15k. "Before war and afterwards"; 20k. "Ploughing with the sword"; 35k. "Fraternization".

202 Capt. Voronin and Ice-breaker "Chelyuskin"

1935. Air. Rescue of "Chelyuskin" Expedition.

No.	Type	Description	Mint	Used
678	202	1k. orange	4·00	1·00
679	–	3k. red	4·75	1·40
680	–	5k. green	5·00	1·40
681	–	10k. brown	7·25	1·75
682	–	15k. black	9·25	2·50
683	–	20k. purple	14·50	2·50
684	–	25k. blue	42·00	11·00
685	–	30k. green	45·00	13·00
686	–	40k. violet	32·00	3·75
687	202	50k. blue	35·00	9·00

DESIGNS—HORIZ: 3k. Prof. Schmidt and Schmidt Camp; 50k. Schmidt Camp deserted. VERT: 5k. A. V. Lyapidevsky; 10k. S. A. Levanevsky; 15k. M. G. Slepnev; 20k. I. V. Doronin; 25k. M. V. Vodopyanov; 30k. V. S. Molokov; 40k. N. P. Kamanin.

205 Underground Station

1935. Opening of Moscow Underground.

No.	Type	Description	Mint	Used
688	–	5k. orange	8·50	3·25
689	–	10k. blue	10·00	3·25
690	205	15k. red	80·00	24·00
691	–	20k. green	17·00	9·00

DESIGNS—As Type 205: 5k. Excavating tunnel; 10k. Section of tunnel, escalator and station. $48\frac{1}{2} \times 23$ mm: 20k. Train in station.

207 Rowing

1935. Spartacist Games.

No.	Type	Description	Mint	Used
692	–	1k. blue and orange	2·75	80
693	–	2k. blue and black	2·75	80
694	207	3k. brown and green	3·50	1·50
695	–	4k. blue and red	3·00	90
696	–	5k. brown and violet	3·00	1·00
697	–	10k. purple and red	14·00	3·00
698	–	15k. brown and black	30·00	8·00
699	–	20k. blue and brown	22·00	3·25
700	–	35k. brown and blue	30·00	13·00
701	–	40k. red and brown	24·00	6·00

DESIGNS: 1k. Running; 2k. Diving; 4k. Football; 5k. Skiing; 10k. Cycling; 15k. Lawn tennis; 20k. Skating; 35k. Hurdling; 40k. Parade of athletes.

208 Friedrich Engels

Перелет Москва— Сан-Франциско через Сев. полюс 1935 1 Р.

(209)

1935. 40th Death Anniv of F. Engels.

No.	Type	Description	Mint	Used
702	208	5k. red	6·00	60
703		10k. green	3·00	2·00
704		15k. blue	7·50	2·75
705		20k. black	5·00	3·00

1935. Air. Moscow–San Francisco via North Pole Flight. Surch with T 209.

No.	Type	Description	Mint	Used
706		1r. on 10k. brown (No. 681)	£300	£400

210 A "Lion Hunt" from a Sassanian Silver Plate

211 M. I. Kalinin

1935. 3rd International Congress of Persian Art and Archaeology, Leningrad.

No.	Type	Description	Mint	Used
707	210	5k. orange	7·00	1·00
708		10k. green	7·00	1·75
709		15k. purple	8·00	3·00
710		35k. brown	14·00	5·50

1935. Pres. Kalinin's 60th Birthday. Autographed portraits inscr "1875–1935".

No.	Type	Description	Mint	Used
711	–	3k. purple	75	20
712	–	5k. green	1·25	25
713	–	10k. blue	1·25	60
714	211	20k. brown	1·60	70

DESIGNS: 3k. Kalinin as machine worker; 5k. Harvester; 10k. Orator.

See also No. 1189.

212 Tolstoi

213 Pioneers securing Letter-box

1935. 25th Death Anniv of Tolstoi (writer).

No.	Type	Description	Mint	Used
715b	–	3k. violet and black	75	25
716b	212	10k. brown and blue	1·50	45
717b	–	20k. brown and green	3·50	1·75

DESIGNS: 3k. Tolstoi in 1860; 20k. Monument in Moscow.

1936. Pioneer Movement.

No.	Type	Description	Mint	Used
721b	213	1k. green	1·10	30
722		2k. red	1·00	70
723b	–	3k. blue	1·25	1·60
724b	–	5k. red	1·25	55
725b	–	10k. blue	2·00	2·50
726	–	15k. brown	6·50	3·00

DESIGNS: 3, 5k. Pioneer preventing another from throwing stones; 10k. Pioneers disentangling kite line from telegraph wires; 15k. Girl pioneer saluting.

214 N. A. Dobrolyubov

215 Pushkin (after T. Paita)

1936. Birth Centenary of N. Dobrolyubov (author and critic).

No.	Type	Description	Mint	Used
727b	214	10k. purple	5·00	1·00

1937. Death Centenary of A. S. Pushkin (poet).

No.	Type	Description	Mint	Used
728	215	10k. brown	55	30
729		20k. green	60	30
730		40k. red	1·25	50
731	–	50k. blue	2·75	75
732a	–	80k. red	2·25	1·00
733a	–	1r. green	4·50	1·00

DESIGN: 50k. to 1r. Pushkin's Monument, Moscow (A. Opekushin).

217 Meyerhold Theatre

218 F. E. Dzerzhinsky

1937. 1st Soviet Architectural Congress.

No.	Type	Description	Mint	Used
734	217	3k. red	1·25	20
735	–	5k. lake	1·25	20
736	217	10k. brown	1·75	25
737	–	15k. black	2·00	25
738	–	20k. olive	1·10	40
739	–	30k. black	1·75	70
740	–	40k. violet	2·25	1·25
741	–	50k. brown	3·75	1·50

DESIGNS—As T 217: 5, 15k. G.P.O.; 20, 50k. Red Army Theatre. 45×27 mm: 30k. Hotel Moscow; 40k. Palace of Soviets.

1937. 10th Death Anniv of Feliks Dzerzhinsky.

No.	Type	Description	Mint	Used
742	218	10k. brown	40	20
743		20k. green	60	35
744		40k. red	1·75	55
745		80k. red	2·50	70

219 Yakovlev Ya-7 Air 7

1937. Air. Air Force Exhibition.

No.	Type	Description	Mint	Used
746	219	10k. black and brown	1·75	30
747	–	20k. black and green	1·75	30
748	–	30k. black and brown	2·75	40
749	–	40k. black and purple	5·00	90
750	–	50k. black and violet	6·50	1·50
751	–	80k. brown and blue	7·50	2·00
752	–	1r. black, orange & brown	11·00	4·00

DESIGNS—As T 219: 20k. Tupolev ANT-9; 30k. Tupolev ANT-6 bomber; 40k. O.S.G.A. 101 flying boat; 50k. Tupolev ANT-4 TB-1 bomber. 60×26 mm: 80k. Tupolev ANT-20 "Maksim Gorki"; 1r. Tupolev ANT-14 "Pravda".

220 Arms of Ukraine — **221** Arms of U.S.S.R.

1937. New U.S.S.R. Constitution. Arms of Constituent Republics.

753 – 20k. blue (Armenia) . . . 1·50 50
754 – 20k. purple (Azerbaijan) 1·50 50
755 – 20k. brown (Byelorussia) 1·50 50
756 – 20k. red (Georgia) . . . . 1·50 50
757 – 20k. green (Kazakhstan) 1·50 50
758 – 20k. red (Kirghizia) . . . 1·50 50
759 – 20k. red (Tadzhikistan) 1·50 50
760 – 20k. red (Turkmenistan) 1·50 50
761 **220** 20k. red (Ukraine) . . . 1·50 50
762 – 20k. orange (Uzbekistan) 1·50 50
763 – 20k. blue (R.S.F.S.R.) . . 1·50 50
764 **221** 40k. red (U.S.S.R.) . . . 5·00 1·50

222 "Worker and Collective Farmer" (sculpture, Vera Mukhina) — **223** Russian Pavilion, Paris Exhibition

1938. Paris International Exhibition.

765 **222** 5k. red . . . . 1·00 40
766 **223** 20k. red . . . . 1·40 40
767 **222** 50k. blue . . . . 3·50 1·00

224 Shota Rustaveli

1938. 750th Anniv of Poem "Knight in Tiger Skin".

768 **224** 20k. green . . . . 1·50 40

225 Route of North Pole Flight — **227** Infantryman

1938. North Pole Flight.

769 **225** 10k. black and brown . . 2·40 30
770 20k. black and grey . . 3·75 40
771 – 40k. red and green . . . 8·50 1·40
772 – 80k. red and deep red . . 2·75 1·10

DESIGN: 40k., 80k. Soviet Flag at North Pole.

1938. 20th Anniv of Red Army.

773 **227** 10k. black and red . . . 50 20
774 – 20k. black and red . . . 85 25
775 – 30k. black, red and blue 1·25 25
776 – 40k. black, red and blue 1·75 75
777 – 50k. black and red . . . 2·25 75
778a – 80k. black and red . . . 4·75 75
779 – 1r. black and red . . . 2·75 75

DESIGNS—VERT: 20k. Tank driver; 30k. Sailor; 40k. Airman; 50k. Artilleryman. HORIZ: 80k. Stalin reviewing cavalry; 1r. Machine gunners.

229 G. Baidukov, V. Chkalov and A. Belyakov — **230** M. Gromov, A. Yumashov and S. Danilin

1938. 1st Flight over North Pole.

780 **229** 10k. red and black . . . 2·00 50
781 20k. red and black . . . 2·25 70
782 40k. red and brown . . . 4·00 1·40
783 50k. red and purple . . . 7·25 1·75

1938. 2nd Flight over North Pole.

784 **230** 10k. purple . . . . 4·00 45
785 20k. black . . . . 4·00 90
786 50k. purple . . . . 7·75 1·25

231 Ice-breaker "Murman" approaching Survivors

1938. Rescue of Papanin's North Pole Meteorological Party.

787 **231** 10k. purple . . . . 4·00 60
788 20k. blue . . . . 4·00 70
789 – 30k. brown . . . . 7·00 1·25
790 – 50k. blue . . . . 8·00 2·50

DESIGNS—VERT: 30, 50k. Papanin survivors.

233 Nurse weighing Baby — **234** Children visiting Statue of Lenin

1938. Soviet Union Children.

791 **233** 10k. blue . . . . 1·25 30
792 **234** 15k. blue . . . . 1·25 35
793 – 20k. purple . . . . 1·50 35
794 – 30k. red . . . . 1·90 45
795 – 40k. brown . . . . 2·40 55
796 – 50k. blue . . . . 6·00 1·50
797 – 80k. green . . . . 7·00 2·00

DESIGNS—HORIZ: 20, 40k. Biology class; 30k. Health camp; 50, 80k. Young inventors at play.

235 Crimean landscape

1938. Views of Crimea and Caucasus.

798 **235** 5k. black . . . . 1·10 40
799 A 5k. brown . . . . 1·10 40
800 B 10k. green . . . . 2·25 45
801 C 10k. brown . . . . 2·25 50
802 D 15k. black . . . . 3·75 60
803 A 15k. black . . . . 3·75 60
804 E 20k. brown . . . . 4·00 70
805 C 30k. black . . . . 4·00 75
806 F 40k. brown . . . . 4·75 90
807 G 50k. green . . . . 4·75 1·75
808 H 80k. brown . . . . 6·50 2·25
809 I 1r. green . . . . 9·00 6·00

DESIGNS—HORIZ: A, Yalta (two views); B, Georgian military road; E, Crimean resthouse; F, Alupka; H, Crimea; I, Swallows' Nest Castle. VERT: C, Crimea (two views); D, Swallows' Nest Castle; G, Gurzuf Park.

236 Schoolchildren and Model Tupolev ANT-6 Bomber

1938. Aviation.

810 **236** 5k. purple . . . . 1·75 75
811 – 10k. brown . . . . 1·75 75
812 – 15k. red . . . . 2·25 75
813 – 20k. blue . . . . 2·25 75
814 – 30k. red . . . . 4·00 1·25
815 – 40k. blue . . . . 7·00 1·25
816 – 50k. green . . . . 12·00 1·75
817 – 80k. brown . . . . 8·00 3·25
818 – 1r. green . . . . 14·00 3·25

DESIGNS—HORIZ: 10k. Glider in flight; 40k. Yakovlev VT-2 seaplane; 1r. Tupolev ANT-6 bomber. VERT: 15k. Captive observation balloon; 20k. Airship "Osoaviakhim" over Kremlin; 30k. Parachutists; 30k. Balloon in flight; 80k. Stratosphere balloon.

237 Underground Railway

1938. Moscow Underground Railway Extension.

819 – 10k. violet . . . . 2·40 85
820 – 15k. brown . . . . 3·00 85
821 – 20k. black . . . . 3·75 85
822 – 30k. violet . . . . 4·00 1·25
823 **237** 40k. black . . . . 6·00 1·40
824 – 50k. brown . . . . 5·50 2·25

DESIGNS—VERT: 10k. Mayakovskaya station; 15k. Sokol station; 20k. Kievsskaya station. HORIZ: 30k. Dynamo station; 50k. Revolutskaya station.

238 Miner and Pneumatic Drill — **239** Diving

1938. 20th Anniv of Federation of Young Lenin Communists.

825 – 20k. blue 90 30
826 **238** 30k. purple . . . . 1·75 30
827 – 40k. purple . . . . 1·50 30
828 – 50k. red . . . . 1·90 90
829 – 80k. blue . . . . 6·00 1·25

DESIGNS—VERT: 20k. Girl parachutist; 50k. Students and university. HORIZ: 40k. Harvesting; 80k. Airman, sailor and battleship "Marat".

1938. Soviet Sports.

830 **239** 5k. red . . . . 2·00 30
831 – 10k. black . . . . 2·75 50
832 – 15k. brown . . . . 4·50 85
833 – 20k. green . . . . 4·50 80
834 – 30k. purple . . . . 9·00 1·25
835 – 40k. green . . . . 10·00 80
836 – 50k. blue . . . . 9·00 2·25
837 – 80k. blue . . . . 9·00 3·50

DESIGNS: 10k. Discus throwing; 15k. Tennis; 20k. Motor cycling; 30k. Skiing; 40k. Sprinting; 50k. Football; 80k. Athletic parade.

241 Council of People's Commissars Headquarters and Hotel Moscow

1939. New Moscow. Architectural designs as T **241**.

838 – 10k. brown . . . . 1·10 70
839 **241** 20k. green . . . . 1·40 70
840 – 30k. purple . . . . 1·90 1·00
841 – 40k. blue . . . . 2·75 1·00
842 – 50k. red . . . . 5·00 2·00
843 – 80k. olive . . . . 5·00 2·00
844 – 1r. blue . . . . 9·50 2·75

DESIGNS—HORIZ: 10k. Gorky Avenue; 30k. Lenin Library; 40k. Crimea suspension and 50k. Arched bridges over River Moskva; 80k. Khimki river station. VERT: 1r. Dynamo underground station.

242 Paulina Osipenko — **243** Russian Pavilion, N.Y. World's Fair

1939. Women's Moscow–Far East Flight.

845 **242** 15k. green . . . . 2·25 80
846 – 30k. purple . . . . 2·25 1·00
847 – 60k. red . . . . 4·50 1·50

PORTRAITS: 30k. Marina Raskova; 60k. Valentina Grisodubova.

1939. New York World's Fair.

848 – 30k. red and black . . . 2·00 50
849 **243** 50k. brown and blue . . . 4·00 85

DESIGN—VERT: (26×41½ mm): 30k. Statue over Russian pavilion.

244 T. G. Shevchenko in early Manhood — **245** Milkmaid

1939. 125th Birth Anniv of Shevchenko (Ukrainian poet and painter).

853 **244** 15k. black and brown . . 1·75 50
854 – 30k. black and red . . . 2·75 70
855 – 60k. brown and green . . 5·00 2·00

DESIGNS: 30k. Last portrait of Shevchenko; 60k. Monument to Shevchenko, Kharkov.

1939. All Union Agricultural Fair.

856 **245** 10k. red 75 25
857 – 15k. red 75 15
858a – 20k. grey . . . . 1·00 15
859 – 30k. orange 90 25
860 – 30k. violet 90 25
861 – 45k. green . . . . 1·75 35
862 – 50k. brown . . . . 2·50 40
863a – 60k. violet . . . . 3·00 60
864 – 80k. violet . . . . 3·00 60
865 – 1r. blue . . . . 5·00 1·25

DESIGNS—HORIZ: 15k. Harvesting; 20k. Sheep farming; 30k. (No. 860) Agricultural Fair Pavilion. VERT: 30k. (No. 859) Agricultural Fair Emblem; 45k. Gathering cotton; 50k. Thoroughbred horses; 60k. "Agricultural Wealth"; 80k. Girl with sugar beet; 1r. Trapper.

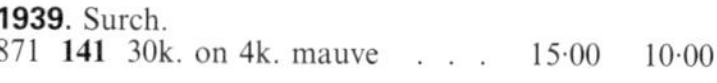

(**247**)

1939. Aviation Day. As Nos. 811, 814/16 and 818 (colours changed) optd with T **247**.

866 10k. red . . . . 2·25 55
867 30k. blue . . . . 2·25 55
868 40k. green . . . . 3·50 55
869 50k. violet . . . . 4·50 1·25
870 1r. brown . . . . 8·00 4·00

1939. Surch.

871 **141** 30k. on 4k. mauve . . . 15·00 10·00

249 Saltykov-Shchedrin — **250** Kislovodsk Sanatorium

1939. 50th Death Anniv of M. E. Saltykov-Shchedrin (writer and satirist).

872 **249** 15k. red 60 15
873 – 30k. green 80 20
874 **249** 45k. brown . . . . 1·00 35
875 – 60k. blue . . . . 1·50 70

DESIGN: 30, 60k. Saltykov-Shchedrin in later years.

1939. Caucasian Health Resorts.

876 **250** 5k. brown 30 15
877 – 10k. red 50 20
878 – 15k. green 55 30
879 – 20k. green . . . . 1·00 30
880 – 30k. blue . . . . 1·10 30
881 – 50k. black . . . . 2·00 35
882 – 60k. purple . . . . 2·50 90
883 – 80k. red . . . . 3·25 1·10

DESIGNS: 10, 15, 30, 50, 80k. Sochi Convalescent Homes; 20k. Abkhazia Sanatorium, Novyi Afon; 60k. Sukumi Rest Home.

251 M. I. Lermontov — **252** N. G. Chernyshevsky

1939. 125th Birth Anniv of Lermontov (poet and novelist).

884 **251** 15k. brown and blue . . . 1·10 30
885 – 30k. black and green . . 2·75 55
886 – 45k. blue and red . . . . 3·00 95

1939. 50th Death Anniv of N. G. Chernyshevsky (writer and politician).

887b **252** 15k. green 50 30
888 30k. violet 90 40
889b 60k. green . . . . . . 2·00 70

253 A. P. Chekhov — **254** Welcoming Soviet Troops

1940. 80th Birth Anniv of Chekhov (writer).

890 **253** 10k. green 40 15
891 15k. blue 40 15

892 – 20k. violet 80 30
893 – 30k. brown 2·00 55
DESIGN: 20, 30k. Chekhov with hat on.

1940. Occupation of Eastern Poland.
893a **254** 10k. red 1·00 35
894 – 30k. green 1·00 35
895 – 50k. black 1·50 55
896 – 60k. blue 2·00 1·00
897 – 1r. red 4·50 1·75
DESIGNS: 30k. Villagers welcoming tank crew; 50, 60k. Soldier distributing newspapers to crowd; 1r. People waving to column of tanks.

255 Ice-breaker "Georgy Sedov" and Badigin and Trofimov

1940. Polar Research.
898 – 15k. green 2·25 40
899 **255** 30k. violet 3·00 70
900 – 50k. brown 5·00 1·75
901 – 1r. blue 9·00 2·25
DESIGNS: 15k. Ice-breaker "Iosif Stalin" and portraits of Papanin and Belousov; 50k. Badgin and Papanin meeting. LARGER. (46 × 26 mm): 1r. Route of drift of "Georgy Sedov".

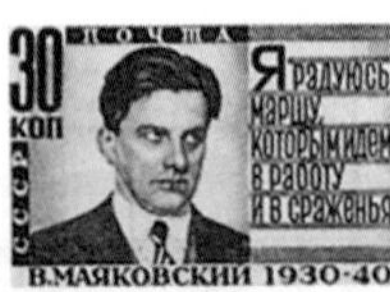
256 V. Mayakovsky

1940. 10th Death Anniv of Mayakovsky (poet).
902 **256** 15k. red 30 15
903 30k. brown 55 20
904 – 60k. violet 1·00 45
905 – 80k. blue 80 45
DESIGN—VERT: 60, 80k. Mayakovsky in profile wearing a cap.

257 Timiryazev

1940. 20th Death Anniv of K. A. Timiryazev (scientist).
906 – 10k. blue 50 20
907 – 15k. violet 50 25
908 **257** 30k. brown 80 30
909 – 60k. green 2·50 1·10
DESIGNS—HORIZ: 10k. Miniature of Timiryazev and Academy of Agricultural Sciences, Moscow; 15k. Timiryazev in laboratory. VERT: 60k. Timiryazev's statue (by S. Merkurov), Moscow.

258 Relay Runner

259 Tchaikovsky and Passage from his "Fourth Symphony"

1940. 2nd All Union Physical Culture Festival.
910 **258** 15k. red 1·10 35
911a – 30k. purple 2·00 30
912a – 50k. blue 3·00 55
913 – 60k. blue 4·50 60
914 – 1r. green 6·00 1·40
DESIGNS—HORIZ: 30k. Girls parade; 60k. Skiing; 1r. Grenade throwing. VERT: 50k. Children and sports badges.

1940. Birth Cent of Tchaikovsky (composer).
915 – 15k. green 1·50 20
916 **259** 20k. brown 1·50 20
917 30k. blue 1·75 35
918 – 50k. red 2·50 60
919 – 60k. red 2·75 85
DESIGNS: 15, 50k. Tchaikovsky's house at Klin; 60k. Tchaikovsky and excerpt from "Eugene Onegin".

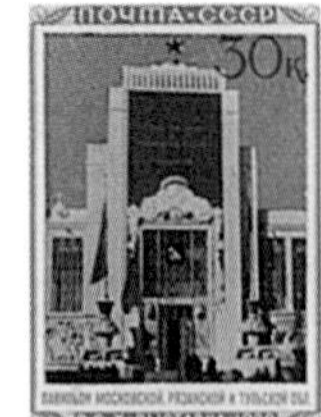
260 Central Regions Pavilion

ПАВИЛЬОН «ПОВОЛЖЬЕ»
No. 920

ПАВИЛЬОН «ДАЛЬНИЙ ВОСТОК»
No. 921

ВОРТА ПАВИЛЬОНА „ЛЕНИНГРАД И СЕВЕРО-ВОСТОК РСФСР"
No. 922

ПАВИЛЬОН МОСКОВСКОЙ, РЯЗАНСКОЙ И ТУЛЬСКОЙ ОБЛ.
No. 923

ПАВИЛЬОН УКРАИНСКОЙ ССР
No. 924

ПАВИЛЬОН БЕЛОРУССКОЙ ССР
No. 925

ПАВИЛЬОН АЗЕРБАЙДЖАНСКОЙ ССР
No. 926

ПАВИЛЬОН ГРУЗИНСКОЙ ССР
No. 927

ПАВИЛЬОН АРМЯНСКОЙ ССР
No. 928

ВХОДА В ПАВИЛЬОН УЗБЕКСКОЙ ССР
No. 929

ПАВИЛЬОН ТУРКМЕНСКОЙ ССР
No. 930

ПАВИЛЬОН ТАДЖИКСКОЙ ССР
No. 931

ПАВИЛЬОН КИРГИЗСКОЙ ССР
No. 932

ПАВИЛЬОН КАРЕЛО-ФИНСКОЙ ССР
No. 933

ПАВИЛЬОН КАЗАХСКОЙ ССР
No. 934

ГЛАВНЫЙ ПАВИЛЬОН
No. 935

ПАВИЛЬОН МЕХАНИЗАЦИИ
No. 936

1940. All Union Agricultural Fair, Coloured reproductions of Soviet Pavilions in green frames as T **260**. Inscriptions at foot as illustrated.
920 10k. Volga provinces (RSFSR) (horiz) 2·50 90
921 15k. Far East 1·75 90
922 30k. Leningrad and North East RSFSR 1·90 90
923 30k. Three Central Regions (RSFSR) 1·90 90
924 30k. Ukrainian SSR 1·90 90
925 30k. Byelorussian SSR 1·90 90
926 30k. Azerbaijan SSR 1·90 90
927 30k. Georgian SSR (horiz) 1·90 90
928 30k. Armenian SSR 1·90 90
929 30k. Uzbek SSR 1·90 90
930 30k. Turkmen SSR (horiz) 1·90 90
931 30k. Tadzhik SSR 1·90 90
932 30k. Kirgiz SSR 1·90 90
933 30k. Karelo-Finnish SSR 3·25 90
934 30k. Kazakh SSR 1·90 90
935 50k. Main Pavilion 3·00 2·00
936 60k. Mechanization Pavilion and the statue of Stalin 4·00 2·25

261 Grenade Thrower

262 Railway Bridge and Moscow–Volga Canal, Khimka

1940. 20th Anniv of Wrangel's Defeat at Perekop (Crimea). Perf or imperf.
937b – 10k. green 1·40 30
938 **261** 15k. red 50 15
939 – 30k. brown and red 75 20
940b – 50k. purple 70 50
941 – 60k. blue 1·75 55
942 – 1r. black 4·00 1·40
DESIGNS—VERT: 10k. Red Army Heroes Monument; 30k. Map of Perekop and portrait of M. V. Frunze; 1r. Victorious soldier. HORIZ: 50k. Soldiers crossing R. Sivash; 60k. Army H.Q. at Stroganovka.

1941. Industrial and Agricultural Records.
943 – 10k. blue 30 15
944 – 15k. mauve 30 15
945 **262** 20k. blue 2·25 1·00
946 – 30k. brown 2·75 1·00
947 – 50k. brown 60 15
948 – 60k. brown 1·25 55
949 – 1r. green 1·60 80
DESIGNS—VERT: 10k. Coal-miners and pithead; 15k. Blast furnace; 1r. Derricks and petroleum refinery. HORIZ: 30k. Steam locomotives; 50k. Harvesting; 60k. Ball-bearing vehicles.

263 Red Army Ski Corps

264 N. E. Zhukovsky and Air Force Academy

1941. 23rd Anniv of Red Army. Designs with Hammer, Sickle and Star Symbol.
950a **263** 5k. violet 1·60 15
951 – 10k. blue 1·25 15
952 – 15k. green 45 15
953a – 20k. red 45 15
954a – 30k. brown 45 15
955a – 45k. green 1·90 70
956 – 50k. blue 70 75
957 – 1r. green 1·00 80
957b – 3r. green 6·50 3·00
DESIGNS—VERT: 10k. Sailor; 20k. Cavalry; 30k. Automatic Rifle Squad; 50k. Airman; 1, 3r. Marshal's star. HORIZ: 15k. Artillery; 45k. Clearing a hurdle.

1941. 20th Death Anniv of Zhukovsky (scientist).
958 – 15k. blue 65 20
959 **264** 30k. red 1·50 30
960 – 50k. red 2·00 55
DESIGNS—VERT: 15k. Zhukovsky; 50k. Zhukovsky lecturing.

265 Thoroughbred Horses

266 Arms of Karelo-Finnish S.S.R.

1941. 15th Anniv of Kirghiz S.S.R.
961 **265** 15k. brown 3·00 85
962a – 30k. violet 4·00 1·25
DESIGN: 30k. Coal miner and colliery.

1941. 1st Anniv of Karelo-Finnish Republic.
963 **266** 30k. red 1·00 45
964 45k. green 1·00 75

267 Marshal Suvorov

268 Spassky Tower, Kremlin

1941. 150th Anniv of Battle of Izmail.
965 – 10k. green 80 35
966 – 15k. red 80 45
967 **267** 30k. blue 1·90 40
968 1r. brown 2·75 1·25
DESIGN: 10, 15k. Storming of Izmail.

1941.
970 **268** 1r. red 2·00 55
971 – 2r. brown 4·50 1·10
DESIGN—HORIZ: 2r. Kremlin Palace.

269 "Razin on the Volga"

1941. 25th Death Anniv of Surikov (artist).
972 – 20k. black 1·50 1·00
973 **269** 30k. red 3·50 1·00
974 – 50k. purple 6·00 2·75
975 **269** 1r. green 9·00 4·00
976 – 2r. brown 16·00 5·00
DESIGNS—VERT: 20, 50k. "Suvorov's march through Alps, 1799"; 2r. Surikov.

270 Lenin Museum (interior)

271 M. Yu. Lermontov

1941. 5th Anniv of Lenin Museum.
977 **270** 15k. red 2·75 1·50
978 – 30k. violet on mauve 22·00 16·00
979 **270** 45k. green 3·50 2·50
980 – 1r. red on rose 16·00 12·00
DESIGN: 30k., 1r. Exterior of Lenin Museum.

1941. Death Centenary of M. Yu. Lermontov (poet and novelist).
981 **271** 15k. grey 4·50 3·75
982 30k. violet 8·00 6·00

272 Poster by L. Lisitsky

273 Mass Enlistment

1941. Mobilization.
983a **272** 30k. red 18·00 20·00

1941. National Defence.
984 **273** 30k. blue 55·00 50·00

274 Alishir Navoi

275 Lt. Talalikhin ramming Enemy Bomber

289a Five Heroes

1942. 5th Centenary of Uzbek poet Mir Ali Shir (Alishir Navoi).
985 **274** 30k. brown 14·00 8·50
986 1r. purple 16·00 18·00

1942. Russian Heroes (1st issue).
987 **275** 20k. blue 50 25
988 A 30k. grey 60 35
989 B 30k. black 60 30
990 C 30k. black 60 35
991 D 30k. black 60 40
1048c **275** 30k. green 1·00 30
1048d A 30k. blue 1·00 30
1048e C 30k. green 1·00 30
1048f D 30k. purple 1·00 30
1048g **289a** 30k. blue 1·00 30
992 C 1r. green 5·00 3·25
993 D 2r. green 9·00 5·00
DESIGNS: A, Capt. Gastello and burning fighter plane diving into enemy petrol tanks; B, Maj-Gen. Dovator and Cossack cavalry in action; C, Shura Chekalin guerrilla fighting; D, Zoya Kosmodemyanskaya being led to death.
See also Nos. 1072/6.

276 Anti-tank Gun

1942. War Episodes (1st series).
994 **276** 20k. brown 1·75 75
995 – 30k. blue 1·75 75
996 – 30k. green 1·75 75
997 – 30k. red 1·75 75
998 – 60k. grey 2·50 1·75
999 – 1r. brown 5·00 4·50
DESIGNS—HORIZ: 30k. (No. 996), Guerrillas attacking train; 30k. (No. 997), Munition worker; 1r. Machine gunners. VERT: 30k. (No. 995), Signallers; 60k. Defenders of Leningrad.

277 Distributing Gifts to Soldiers

1942. War Episodes (2nd series).
1000 **277** 20k. blue . . . . 1·75 75
1001 – 20k. purple . . . . . . 1·75 75
1002 – 30k. purple . . . . . . 2·25 1·40
1003 – 45k. red . . . . 4·00 2·75
1004 – 45k. blue . . . . 5·00 3·75
DESIGNS—VERT: No. 1001, Bomber destroying tank; No. 1002, Food packers; No. 1003, Woman sewing; No. 1004, Anti-aircraft gun.
See also Nos. 1013/17.

278 Munition Worker

1943. 25th Anniv of Russian Revolution.
1005 **278** 5k. brown 55 25
1006 – 10k. brown 80 15
1007 – 15k. blue 65 20
1008 – 20k. blue 65 20
1009 – 30k. brown 85 20
1010 – 60k. brown . . . . . . 1·50 45
1011 – 1r. red . . . . 2·25 1·25
1012 – 2r. brown . . . . 4·00 1·50
DESIGNS: 10k. Lorry convoy; 15k. Troops supporting Lenin's banner; 20k. Leningrad seen through an archway; 30k. Spassky Tower, Lenin and Stalin; 60k. Tank parade; 1r. Lenin speaking; 2r. Star of Order of Lenin.

279 Nurses and Wounded Soldier

1943. War Episodes (3rd series).
1013 **279** 30k. green . . . . 1·50 1·00
1014 – 30k. green (Scouts) . . . 1·50 1·00
1015 – 30k. brown (Mine-thrower) . . . . . . 1·50 1·00
1016 – 60k. green (Anti-tank troops) . . . . . . 2·50 1·00
1017 – 60k. blue (Sniper) . . . 2·50 1·00

280 Routes of Bering's Voyages

1943. Death Bicent of Vitus Bering (explorer).
1018 – 30k. blue . . . . 1·60 30
1019 **280** 60k. grey . . . . 3·00 60
1020 – 1r. green . . . . 4·25 90
1021 **280** 2r. brown . . . . 7·75 1·75
DESIGN: 30k., 1r. Mt. St. Ilya.

281 Gorky

1943. 75th Birth Anniv of Maksim Gorky (novelist).
1022 **281** 30k. green . . . . 1·00 25
1023 60k. blue . . . . 1·50 25

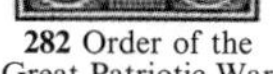

282 Order of the Great Patriotic War

(**a**) Order of Suvorov

1943. War Orders and Medals (1st series), Medals with ribbon attached.
1024 **282** 1r. black . . . . 2·75 2·00
1025 a 10r. olive . . . . 9·00 7·50
See also Nos. 1051/8, 1089/94, 1097/99a, 1172/86, 1197/1204 and 1776/80a.

283 Karl Marx

284 Naval Landing Party

1943. 125th Birth Anniv of Marx.
1026 **283** 30k. blue . . . . 1·50 40
1027 60k. green . . . . 2·50 60

1943. 25th Anniv of Red Army and Navy.
1028 **284** 20k. brown 30 20
1029 – 30k. green 40 15
1030 – 60k. green . . . . 1·25 40
1031 **284** 3r. blue . . . . 3·00 90
DESIGNS: 30k. Sailors and anti-aircraft gun; 60k. Tanks and infantry.

285 Ivan Turgenev

286 Loading a Gun

1943. 125th Birth Anniv of Ivan Turgenev (novelist).
1032 **285** 30k. green . . . . . . 12·00 10·00
1032a 60k. violet . . . . . . 18·00 16·00

1943. 25th Anniv of Young Communist League.
1033 **286** 15k. blue 60 15
1034 – 20k. orange 60 15
1035 – 30k. brown and red . . 75 15
1036a – 1r. green . . . . 1·25 35
1037 – 2r. green . . . . 2·50 75
DESIGNS—As T **286**: 20k. Tank and banner; 1r. Infantrymen; 2r. Grenade thrower. 22½ × 28½ mm: 30k. Bayonet fighter and flag.

287 V. V. Mayakovsky

288 Memorial Tablet and Allied Flags

1943. 50th Birth Anniv of Mayakovsky (poet).
1038 **287** 30k. orange 65 20
1039 60k. blue . . . . 1·00 40

1943. Teheran Three Power Conference and 26th Anniv of Revolution.
1040 **288** 30k. black . . . . 1·10 50
1041 3r. blue . . . . 4·00 1·25

289 Defence of Odessa

1944. Liberation of Russian Towns.
1045 – 30k. brown and red . . 65 25
1046 – 30k. blue 65 25
1047 – 30k. green 65 25
1048 **289** 30k. green 65 25
DESIGNS: No. 1045, Stalingrad; No. 1046, Sevastopol; No. 1047, Leningrad.

АВИАПОЧТА
1944 г.
1 РУБЛЬ

(**290**)

291 Order of Kutusov

(**b**) Order of Patriotic War

(**c**) Order of Aleksandr Nevsky

(**d**) Order of Suvorov

(**e**) Order of Kutusov

1944. Air. Surch with T **290**.
1049 **275** 1r. on 30k. grey . . . . 2·00 50
1050 A 1r. on 30k. blue (No. 1048d) . . . . . 2·00 50

1944. War Orders and Medals (2nd series). Various Stars without ribbons showing as Types **b** to **e**. Perf or imperf. (a) Frames as T **291**.
1051 b 15k. red 50 15
1052 c 20k. blue 50 15
1053 d 30k. green . . . . 1·00 25
1054 e 60k. red . . . . 1·50 40

(b) Frames as T **282**.
1055 b 1r. black 80 30
1056 c 3r. blue . . . . 3·25 60
1057 e 5r. green . . . . 4·00 1·00
1058 d 10r. red . . . . 4·00 1·50

293 Lenin Mausoleum and Red Square, Moscow

1944. "Twenty Years without Lenin". As Nos. 667/72, but inscr "1924–1944", and T **293**.
1059 – 30k. black and blue . . 50 20
1060 **199** 30k. red and orange . . 50 20
1061 – 45k. black and blue . . 65 25
1062 – 50k. black and blue . . 80 25
1063 – 60k. black and blue . . 1·75 50
1064 **293** 1r. brown and blue . . . 2·00 60
1065 **199** 3r. black and orange . . 4·00 1·75
DESIGNS—VERT: Lenin at 3 years of age (No. 1059): at school (45k.); as man (50k.); as orator (60k.).

294 Allied Flags

295 Rimsky-Korsakov and Bolshoi Theatre

1944. 14 June (Allied Nations' Day).
1066 **294** 60k. black, red and blue 1·50 45
1067 3r. blue and red . . . . 6·00 1·75

1944. Birth Centenary of Rimsky-Korsakov (composer). Imperf or perf.
1068 **295** 30k. grey 40 10
1069 60k. green 60 10
1070 1r. green . . . . 1·25 25
1071 3r. violet . . . . 2·50 50

296 Nuradilov and Machine-gun

297 Polivanova and Kovshova

298 S. A. Chaplygin

1944. War Heroes (3rd issue).
1072 **296** 30k. green 45 15
1073 – 60k. violet 85 15
1074 – 60k. blue 85 15
1075 **297** 60k. green . . . . 1·50 45
1076 – 60k. black . . . . 1·75 45
DESIGNS—HORIZ: No. 1073, Matrosov defending a snow-trench; 1074, Luzak hurling a hand grenade. VERT: No. 1076, B. Safonev, medals and aerial battle over the sea.

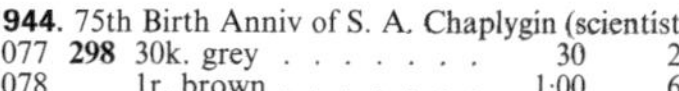

1944. 75th Birth Anniv of S. A. Chaplygin (scientist).
1077 **298** 30k. grey 30 20
1078 1r. brown . . . . 1·00 60

299 V. I. Chapaev

300 Repin (self-portrait)

301 "Reply of the Cossacks to Sultan Mahmoud IV"

302 I. A. Krylov

1944. Heroes of 1918 Civil War.
1079 **299** 30k. green . . . . 1·00 25
1080 – 30k. black (N. Shchors) 1·00 25
1081 – 30k. green (S. Lazo) . . 1·00 25
For 40k. stamp as Type **299**, see No. 1531.
See also Nos. 1349/51.

1944. Birth Centenary of Ilya Refimovich Repin (artist). Imperf or perf.
1082 **300** 30k. green 85 25
1083 **301** 50k. green 85 25
1084 60k. blue 85 25
1085 **300** 1r. brown . . . . 1·25 50
1086 **301** 2r. violet . . . . 2·75 1·00

1944. Death Centenary of Krylov (fabulist).
1087 **302** 30k. brown 60 15
1088 1r. blue . . . . 1·25 40

(**f**) Partisans' Medal

(**g**) Medal for Bravery

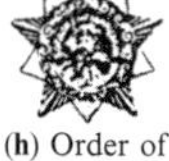

(**h**) Order of Bogdan Chmielnitsky

(**j**) Order of Victory

(**k**) Order of Ushakov

(**l**) Order of Nakhimov

1945. War Orders and Medals (3rd series). Frame as T **291** with various centres as Types **f** to **l**. Perf or imperf.
1089 f 15k. black 45 15
1090 g 30k. blue 65 20
1091 h 45k. blue . . . . 1·50 40
1092 j 60k. red . . . . 2·40 45
1093 k 1r. blue . . . . 3·25 1·00
1094 l 1r. green . . . . 3·25 1·00

303 Griboedov (after P. Karatygin)

305 Soldier

1945. 150th Birth Anniv of Aleksander S. Griboedov (author).
1095 **303** 30k. green . . . . 1·50 20
1096 60k. brown . . . . . . 2·00 35

1945. War Orders and Medals (4th series). Frames as T **282**. Various centres.
1097 g 1r. black . . . . 1·60 65
1098 h 2r. black . . . . 7·50 1·75
1098a 2r. purple . . . . 42·00 14·00
1098b 2r. olive . . . . 6·00 2·00
1099 j 3r. red . . . . 4·25 1·25
1099a 3r. purple . . . . 6·25 3·00

1945. Relief of Stalingrad.
1100 **305** 60k. black and red . . . 1·40 85
1101 3r. black and red . . . . 3·50 1·60

306 Standard Bearer

308 Attack

1945. Red Army Victories.
1102 **306** 20k. green, red and black . . . 40 15
1103 – 30k. black and red . . . 40 15
1104 – 1r. green and red . . . . 2·25 1·40
DESIGN—HORIZ: 30k. Infantry v. Tank; 1r. Infantry charge.

1945. Liberation of Russian Soil.
1105 **308** 30k. blue 40 15
1106 – 60k. red . . . . 1·00 55
1107 – 1r. green . . . . 2·40 1·25
DESIGNS: 60k. Welcoming troops; 1r. Grenade thrower.

309 Badge and Guns

310 Barricade

1945. Red Guards Commemoration.
1108 **309** 60k. red . . . . 2·75 1·00

1945. Battle of Moscow.
1109 – 30k. blue 40 20
1110 **310** 60k. black 80 45
1111 – 1r. black . . . . 1·50 60
DESIGNS: 30k. Tanks in Red Square, Moscow. 1r. Aerial battle and searchlights.

311 Prof. Lomonosov and Academy of Sciences, Leningrad

312 Popov

1945. 220th Anniv of Academy of Sciences.
1112 – 30k. blue . . . . 1·00 35
1113 **311** 2r. black . . . . 3·25 80
DESIGN—VERT: 30k. Moscow Academy, inscr "1725–1945".

1945. 50th Anniv of Popov's Radio Discoveries.
1114 **312** 30k. blue 70 30
1115 60k. red . . . . 1·25 40
1116 – 1r. brown (Popov) . . . 1·90 65

314 Motherhood Medal

315 Motherhood Medal

1945. Orders and Medals of Motherhood. Imperf or perf.
1117b **314** 20k. brown on blue . . 35 20
1118b – 30k. brown on green . . 60 20
1119b – 60k. red . . . . 1·40 20
1120 **315** 1r. black on green . . . 1·75 20
1121 – 2r. blue . . . . 2·75 50
1122 – 3r. red on blue . . . . 4·00 90
DESIGNS: 30k., 2r. Order of Motherhood Glory; 60k., 3r. Order of Heroine-Mother.

316 Petlyakov Pe-2 Dive Bombers

317 Ilyushin Il-2M3 Stormovik Fighters

318 Petlyakov Pe-8 TB-7 Bomber

1945. Air. Aviation Day.
1123 **316** 1r. brown . . . . 3·50 1·00
1124 **317** 1r. brown . . . . 3·50 1·00
1125 – 1r. red . . . . 3·50 1·00
1126 – 1r. black . . . . 3·50 1·00
1127 – 1r. blue . . . . 3·50 1·00
1128 – 1r. green . . . . 3·50 1·00
1129 **318** 1r. grey . . . . 3·50 1·00
1130 – 1r. brown . . . . 3·50 1·00
1131 – 1r. red . . . . 3·50 1·00
DESIGNS—As Type **317**: No. 1125, Lavochkin La-7 fighter shooting tail off enemy plane; 1126, Ilyushin Il-4 DB-3 bombers dropping bombs; 1127, Tupolev ANT-60 Tu-2 bombers in flight; 1128, Polikarpov Po-2 biplane. As Type **318**: No. 1130, Yakovlev Yak-3 fighter destroying Messerschmitt BF 109 fighter; 1131, Yakovlev Yak-9 fighter destroying Henschel Hs 129B fighter.
See also Nos. 1163/71.

ПРАЗДНИК
ПОБЕДЫ

9 мая
1945 года
(**319**)

1945. VE Day. No. 1099 optd with T **319**.
1132 j 3r. red . . . . 4·00 1·50

320 Lenin

321 Lenin

1945. 75th Birth Anniv of Lenin.
1133 **320** 30k. blue 40 20
1134 – 50k. brown . . . . . . 1·00 20
1135 – 60k. red . . . . 1·00 30
1136 **321** 1r. black . . . . 1·90 35
1137 – 3r. brown . . . . 3·75 1·75
DESIGNS—VERT: (inscr "1870–1945"). 50k. Lenin at desk; 60k. Lenin making a speech; 3r. Portrait of Lenin.

322 Kutuzov (after R. Volkov)

323 A. I. Herzen

1945. Birth Bicentenary of Mikhail Kutuzov (military leader).
1138 **322** 30k. blue . . . . 1·00 25
1139 60k. brown . . . . . . 1·60 50

1945. 75th Death Anniv of Herzen (author and critic).
1140 **323** 30k. brown 85 20
1141 2r. black . . . . 1·90 55

324 I. I. Mechnikov

325 Friedrich Engels

1945. Birth Centenary of Mechnikov (biologist).
1142 **324** 30k. brown 70 15
1143 1r. black . . . . 1·40 35

1945. 125th Birth Anniv of Engels.
1144 **325** 30k. brown 80 20
1145 60k. green . . . . . . 1·25 45

326 Observer and Guns

327 Heavy Guns

1945 Artillery Day.
1146 **326** 30k. brown . . . . . . 1·75 1·40
1147 **327** 60k. black . . . . 4·00 2·75

328 Tank Production

1945. Home Front.
1148 **328** 20k. blue and brown . . 2·25 50
1149 – 30k. black and brown . . 2·00 75
1150 – 60k. brown and green . . 3·25 1·40
1151 – 1r. blue and brown . . . 4·75 1·50
DESIGNS: 30k. Harvesting; 60k. Designing aircraft; 1r. Firework display.

329 Victory Medal

330 Soldier with Victory Flag

1946. Victory Issue.
1152 **329** 30k. violet 30 15
1153 30k. brown 30 15
1154 60k. black 55 20
1155 60k. brown 55 20
1156 **330** 60k. black and red . . . 1·75 85

331 Arms of U.S.S.R.

332 Kremlin, Moscow

1946. Supreme Soviet Elections.
1157 **331** 30k. red 30 10
1158 **332** 45k. red 50 30
1159 **331** 60k. green . . . . 2·00 80

333 Tank Parade

334 Infantry Parade

1946. 28th Anniv of Red Army and Navy.
1160 **333** 60k. brown . . . . . . 1·00 15
1161 2r. violet . . . . 2·00 50
1162 **334** 3r. black and red . . . . 5·00 1·40

1946. Air. As Nos. 1123/31.
1163 – 5k. violet (as No. 1130) 65 60
1164 **316** 10k. red 65 60
1165 **317** 15k. red 70 65
1166 **318** 15k. green 70 65
1167 – 20k. black (as No. 1127) 70 65
1168 – 30k. violet (as No. 1127) 1·40 95
1169 – 30k. brown (as No. 1128) . . . . . 1·40 95
1170 – 50k. blue (as No. 1125) 2·00 1·50
1171 – 60k. blue (as No. 1131) 4·00 1·75

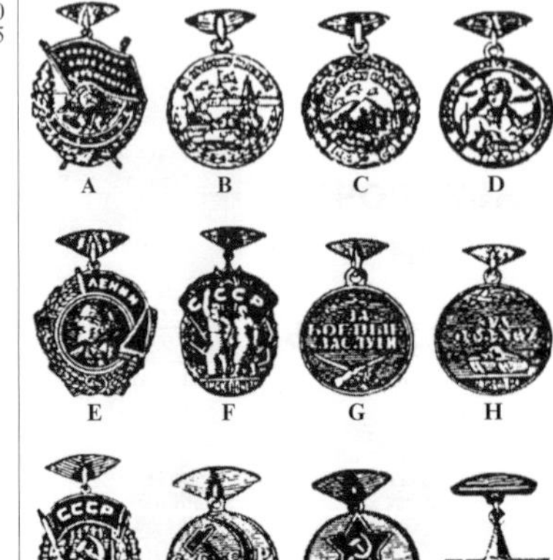
A B C D E F G H J K L M

N

O

P

1946. War Orders with Medals (5th series). Frames as T **291** with various centres as Types A to P.
1172 A 60k. red . . . . 1·60 1·25
1173 B 60k. red . . . . 1·60 1·25
1174 C 60k. green . . . . 1·60 1·25
1175 D 60k. green . . . . 1·60 1·25
1176 E 60k. green . . . . 1·60 1·25
1177 F 60k. blue . . . . 1·60 1·25
1178 G 60k. blue . . . . 1·60 1·25
1179 H 60k. violet . . . . 1·60 1·25
1180 J 60k. purple . . . . 1·60 1·25
1181 K 60k. brown . . . . 1·60 1·25
1182 L 60k. brown . . . . 1·60 1·25
1183 M 60k. purple . . . . 1·60 1·25
1184 N 60k. red . . . . 1·60 1·25
1185 O 60k. blue . . . . 1·60 1·25
1186 P 60k. purple . . . . 1·60 1·25

336 P. L. Chebyshev

337 Gorky

1946. 125th Birth Anniv of Chebyshev (mathematician).
1187 **336** 30k. brown 50 20
1188 60k. black 90 45

1946. Death of President Kalinin. As T **211**, but inscr "3-VI-1946".
1189 20k. black . . . . 1·90 75

1946. 10th Death Anniv of Maksim Gorky (novelist).
1190 **337** 30k. brown 55 15
1191 – 60k. green 80 20
DESIGN: 60k. Gorky and laurel leaves.

338 Gagry

340 Partisan Medal

339 Stalin and Parade of Athletes

1946. Health Resorts.
1192 – 15k. brown 40 15
1193 **338** 30k. green 60 25
1194 – 30k. green 70 25
1195 – 45k. brown . . . . . . 1·00 40
DESIGNS—HORIZ: 15k. Sukumi; 45k. Novy Afon. VERT: 30k. (No. 1194) Sochi.

1946. Sports Festival.
1196 **339** 30k. green . . . . 7·25 4·00

1946. War Medals (6th series). Frames as T **282** with various centres.
1197 **340** 1r. red . . . . 1·90 95
1198 B 1r. green . . . . 1·90 95
1199 C 1r. brown . . . . 1·90 95
1200 D 1r. blue . . . . 1·90 95
1201 G 1r. grey . . . . 1·90 95
1202 H 1r. red . . . . 1·90 95
1203 K 1r. purple . . . . 1·90 95
1204 L 1r. red . . . . 1·90 95

341 Moscow Opera House

342 Tanks in Red Square

1946. Moscow Buildings.

1205	–	5k. brown	40	15
1206	341	10k. grey	50	15
1207	–	15k. brown	40	15
1208	–	20k. brown	70	20
1209	–	45k. green	85	50
1210	–	50k. brown	95	75
1211	–	60k. violet	1·50	1·10
1212	–	1r. brown	2·25	1·75

DESIGNS—VERT: 5k. Church of Ivan the Great and Kremlin; 1r. Spassky Tower (larger). HORIZ: 15k. Hotel Moscow; 20k. Theatre and Sverdlov Square; 45k. As 5k. but horiz; 50k. Lenin Museum; 60k. St. Basil's Cathedral and Spassky Tower (larger).

1946. Heroes of Tank Engagements.

1213	342	30k. green	2·25	1·75
1214		60k. brown	3·50	2·25

343 "Iron" **345** Lenin and Stalin

344 Soviet Postage Stamps

1946. 4th Stalin "Five-Year Reconstruction Plan". Agriculture and Industry.

1215	–	5k. olive	30	10
1216	–	10k. green	40	10
1217	–	15k. brown	50	15
1218	–	20k. violet	80	20
1219	343	30k. brown	1·10	30

DESIGNS—HORIZ: 5k. "Agriculture"; 15k. "Coal". VERT: 10k. "Oil"; 20k. "Steel".

1946. 25th Anniv of Soviet Postal Services.

1220	–	15k. black and red	1·75	40
1221	–	30k. brown and green	2·50	1·00
1222	344	60k. black and green	4·25	1·60

DESIGNS: 15k. ($48\frac{1}{2}\times23$ mm). Stamps on map of U.S.S.R.; 30k. ($33\times22\frac{1}{2}$ mm). Reproduction of Type **47**.

1946. 29th Anniv of Russian Revolution. Imperf or Perf.

1223b	345	30k. orange	3·00	2·75
1224b		30k. green	3·00	2·75

346 N. A. Nekrasov **347** Stalin Prize Medal

1946. 125th Birth Anniv of Nekrasov (poet).

1225	346	30k. black	1·10	25
1226		60k. brown	1·60	55

1946. Stalin Prize.

1227	347	30k. green	2·75	1·00

348 Dnieperprostroi Dam

1946. Restoration of Dnieperprostroi Hydro-electric Power Station.

1228	348	30k. black	1·75	65
1229		60k. blue	3·00	1·00

349 A. Karpinsky **350** N. E. Zhukovsky

1947. Birth Centenary of Karpinsky (geologist).

1230	349	30k. green	1·25	65
1231		50k. black	2·75	90

1947. Birth Centenary of Zhukovsky (scientist).

1232	350	30k. black	1·75	55
1233		60k. blue	2·50	85

351 Lenin Mausoleum **352** Lenin

1947. 23rd Death Anniv of Lenin.

1234	351	30k. green	90	50
1235		30k. blue	90	50
1236	352	50k. brown	3·25	1·00

For similar designs inscr "1924/1948" see Nos. 1334/6.

353 Nikolai M. Przhevalsky **354** Arms of R.S.F.S.R.

356 Arms of U.S.S.R.

1947. Centenary of Soviet Geographical Society.

1237	–	20k. brown	2·00	50
1238	–	20k. blue	2·00	50
1239	353	60k. olive	3·50	1·40
1240	–	60k. brown	3·50	1·40

DESIGN: 20k. Miniature portrait of F. P. Litke and full-rigged ship "Senyavin".

1947. Supreme Soviet Elections. Arms of Constituent Republics. As T **354**.

1241	354	30k. red (Russian Federation)	70	50
1242	–	30k. brown (Armenia)	70	50
1243	–	30k. bistre (Azerbaijan)	70	50
1244	–	30k. green (Byelorussia)	70	50
1245	–	30k. grey (Estonia)	70	50
1246	–	30k. brown (Georgia)	70	50
1247	–	30k. purple (Karelo-Finnish S.S.R.)	70	50
1248	–	30k. orange (Kazakhstan)	70	50
1249	–	30k. purple (Kirgizia)	70	50
1250	–	30k. brown (Latvia)	70	50
1251	–	30k. green (Lithuania)	70	50
1252	–	30k. purple (Moldavia)	70	50
1253	–	30k. green (Tadzhikistan)	70	50
1254	–	30k. black (Turkmenistan)	70	50
1255	–	30k. blue (Ukraine)	70	50
1256	–	30k. brown (Uzbekistan)	70	50
1257	356	1r. multicoloured	2·75	85

A hammer and sickle in the centre of No. 1247 and at the base of No. 1249 should assist identification.

357 Russian Soldier **359** A. S. Pushkin

1947. 29th Anniv of Soviet Army. Perf or imperf.

1258b	357	20k. black	60	20
1259b	–	30k. blue	55	15
1260b	–	30k. brown	65	20

DESIGNS—VERT: No. 1259, Military cadet. HORIZ: No. 1260, Soldier, sailor and airman.

1947. 110th Death Anniv of Pushkin (poet).

1261	359	30k. black	90	45
1262		50k. green	1·50	1·00

360 Schoolroom

1947. International Women's Day.

1263	360	15k. blue	3·50	2·25
1264	–	30k. red	6·00	2·75

DESIGN—$26\frac{1}{2}\times39\frac{1}{2}$ mm: 30k. Women students and banner.

362 Moscow Council Building **364** Yakovlev Yak-9 Fighter and Flag

363 May Day Procession

1947. 30th Anniv of Moscow Soviet. Perf or imperf.

1265b	362	30k. red, blue and black	2·25	1·50

1947. May Day.

1266	363	30k. red	1·50	1·25
1267		1r. green	3·75	2·50

1947. Air Force Day.

1268	364	30k. violet	80	20
1269		1r. blue	2·25	55

365 Yakhromsky Lock

1947. 10th Anniv of Volga–Moscow Canal.

1270	–	30k. black	70	10
1271	365	30k. lake	70	10
1272	–	45k. red	90	25
1273	–	50k. blue	1·25	30
1274	–	60k. red	1·25	30
1275	–	1r. violet	2·50	60

DESIGNS—HORIZ: 30k. (No. 1270), Karamyshevsky Dam; 45k. Yakhromsky Pumping Station; 50k. Khimki Pier; 1r. Lock No. 8. VERT: 60k. Map of Volga–Moscow Canal.

800 лет Москвы
1147—1947 гг.
(366)

367 Izmailovskaya Station

1947. 800th Anniv of Moscow (1st issue). Optd as T **366**.

1276		20k. brown (No. 1208)	55	15
1277		50k. brown (No. 1210)	90	35
1278		60k. violet (No. 1211)	1·50	60
1279		1r. brown (No. 1212)	3·75	1·90

See also Nos. 1286/1300.

1947. Opening of New Moscow Underground Stations. Inscr "M".

1280	367	30k. blue	70	20
1281	–	30k. brown	70	20
1282	–	45k. brown	1·25	40
1283	–	45k. violet	1·25	40
1284	–	60k. green	2·50	65
1285	–	60k. red	2·50	65

DESIGNS—HORIZ: No. 1281, Power plant; No. 1282, Sokol underground station; No. 1283, Stalinskaya underground station; No. 1284, Kievskaya underground station. VERT: No. 1285, Maya Kovskaya underground station.

368 Crimea Bridge, Moscow

1947. 800th Anniv of Moscow (2nd issue).

1286	368	5k. brown and blue	50	10
1287	–	10k. black and brown	30	10
1288	–	30k. grey	1·50	25
1289	–	30k. blue	1·50	25
1290	–	30k. brown	55	25
1291	–	30k. green	55	25
1292	–	30k. green	55	25
1293	–	50k. green	1·40	70
1294	–	60k. blue	2·00	55
1295	–	60k. black and brown	2·00	55
1296	–	1r. purple	3·25	80
		Centre in yellow, red and blue.		
1297	–	1r. blue	5·50	1·75
1298	–	2r. red	8·50	2·50
1299	–	3r. blue	13·50	3·50
1300	–	5r. blue	25·00	7·50

DESIGNS—VERT: 10k. Gorky Street, Moscow; 30k. (No. 1292), Pushkin Place; 60k. (No. 1294), 2r. Kremlin; 1r. (No. 1296), "Old Moscow" after A. M. Vasnetsov; 1r. (No. 1279), St. Basil Cathedral. HORIZ: 30k. (No. 1288), Kiev railway station; 30k. (No. 1289), Kazan railway station; 30k. (No. 1290), Central Telegraph Offices; 30k. (No. 1291), Kaluga Street; 50k. Kremlin; 3r. Kremlin; 5r. Government Buildings. ($54\frac{1}{2}\times24\frac{1}{2}$ mm): 60k. (No. 1295), Bridge and Kremlin.

369 "Ritz", Gagry **370** "Zapadugol", Sochi

1947. U.S.S.R. Health Resorts. (a) Vertical.

1301	369	30k. green	75	20
1302	–	30k. green (Sukhumi)	75	20
		(b) Horizontal.		
1303	370	30k. black	75	20
1304	–	30k. brown ("New Riviera", Sochi)	75	20
1305	–	30k. purple ("Voroshilov", Sochi)	75	20
1306	–	30k. violet ("Gulripsh", Sukhumi)	75	20
1307	–	30k. blue ("Kemeri", Riga)	75	20
1308	–	30k. brown ("Abkhazia", Novyi Afon)	75	20
1309	–	30k. bistre ("Krestyansky", Livadia)	75	20
1310	–	30k. blue ("Kirov", Kislovodsk)	75	20

371 1917 Revolution

1947. 30th Anniv of Revolution. Perf or imperf.

1311b	371	30k. black and red	30	15
1312b	–	50k. blue and red	1·60	20
1313b	371	60k. black and red	1·00	30
1314b	–	60k. brown and red	1·00	30
1315b	–	1r. black and red	2·75	50
1316b	–	2r. green and red	3·00	1·00

DESIGNS: 50k., 1r. "Industry"; 60k. (No. 1314), 2r. "Agriculture".

372 Metallurgical Works **373** Spassky Tower, Kremlin

1947. Post-War Five Year Plan. Horiz industrial designs. All dated "1947" except No. 1324. Perf or imperf.

1317	372	15k. brown	40	20
1318	–	20k. brown (Foundry)	50	30
1319	372	30k. purple	1·00	30
1320	–	30k. green (Harvesting machines)	75	50
1321	–	30k. brown (Tractor)	1·00	30
1322	–	30k. brown (Tractors)	75	30
1323	–	60k. bistre (Harvesting machines)	1·10	60
1324	–	60k. purple (Builders)	1·10	60
1325	–	1r. orange (Foundry)	2·25	1·25

1326 – 1r. red (Tractor) . . . . 3·75 1·75
1327 – 1r. violet (Tractors) . . . 2·50 1·25

1947.
1328 **373** 60k. red . . . . 10·00 5·50
1329a 1r. red . . . . 1·75 35

374 Peter I Monument

376 Government Building, Kiev

1948. 4th Anniv of Relief of Leningrad.
1330 – 30k. violet 50 15
1331 **374** 50k. green 80 30
1332 – 60k. black . . . . 1·60 55
1333 – 1r. violet . . . . 2·10 1·10
DESIGNS—HORIZ: 30k. Winter Palace; 60k. Peter and Paul Fortress; 1r. Smolny Institute.

1948. 24th Death Anniv of Lenin. As issue of 1947, but dated "1924 1928".
1334 **351** 30k. red 85 50
1355 60k. blue . . . . 1·40 70
1336 **352** 60k. green . . . . 2·75 1·10

1948. 30th Anniv of Ukrainian S.S.R. Various designs inscr "XXX" and "1917–1947".
1337 **376** 30k. blue 55 15
1338 – 50k. violet . . . . . . 1·00 50
1339 – 60k. brown . . . . . . 1·25 75
1340 – 1r. brown . . . . 3·00 1·90
DESIGNS: 50k. Dnieper hydro-electric power station; 60k. Wheatfield and granary; 1r. Metallurgical works and colliery.

377 Vasily I. Surikov

378 Skiing

1948. Birth Centenary of Surikov (artist).
1341 **377** 30k. brown . . . . . . 1·60 65
1342 60k. green . . . . 2·40 1·40

1948. R.S.F.S.R. Games.
1343 **378** 15k. blue . . . . 2·25 25
1344 – 20k. blue . . . . 3·25 50
DESIGN—VERT: 20k. Motor cyclist crossing stream.

379 Artillery

381 Karl Marx and Friedrich Engels

380 Bulganin and Military School

1948. 30th Anniv of Founding of Soviet Defence Forces and of Civil War. (a) Various designs with arms and inscr "1918 XXX 1948".
1345 **379** 30k. brown . . . . . . 1·00 35
1346 – 30k. grey . . . . 1·25 35
1347 – 30k. blue . . . . 1·60 35
1348 **380** 60k. brown . . . . . . 2·50 70
DESIGNS—VERT: No. 1346, Navy. HORIZ: No. 1347, Air Force.

(b) Portraits of Civil War Heroes as Nos. 1079/81.
1349 **299** 60k. brown (Chapaev) 1·50 1·10
1350 – 60k. green (Shchors) . . 1·50 1·10
1351 – 60k. blue (Lazo) . . . . 1·50 1·10

1948. Centenary of Publication of "Communist Manifesto".
1352 **381** 30k. black 45 15
1353 50k. brown 65 25

382 Miner

384b Arms of U.S.S.R.

384d Spassky Tower, Kremlin

1948.
1354 **382** 5k. black . . . . . 1·75 90
1355 – 10k. violet (Sailor) 1·75 90
1356 – 15k. blue (Airman) 5·50 2·50
1361i **382** 15k. black 20 10
1357 – 20k. brown (Farm girl) . . . . 5·50 2·50
1361j – 20k. green (Farm girl) 30 10
1361ka – 25k. blue (Airman) 50 10
1358 **384b** 30k. brown . . . . . 7·00 3·75
1361l – 30k. brown (Scientist) 60 10
1361n **384b** 40k. red . . . . . . 2·50 10
1359 – 45k. violet (Scientist) 11·00 5·50
1361f **384d** 50k. blue . . . . . 14·50 5·00
1361 – 60k. green (Soldier) 26·00 13·00

385 Parade of Workers

1948. May Day.
1362 **385** 30k. red . . . . 1·10 55
1363 60k. blue . . . . 1·90 1·10

386 Belinsky (after K. Gorbunov)

1948. Death Centenary of Vissarion Grigorievich Belinsky (literary critic and journalist).
1364 **386** 30k. brown . . . . . . 1·10 35
1365 50k. green . . . . 2·75 1·00
1366 60k. violet . . . . . . 2·25 1·10

387 Ostrovsky

388 Ostrovsky (after V. Perov)

1948. 125th Birth Anniv of Aleksandr Ostrovsky (dramatist).
1367 **387** 30k. green . . . . 1·25 50
1368 **388** 60k. brown . . . . . . 1·60 1·00
1369 1r. violet . . . . 3·25 1·75

389 I. I. Shishkin (after I. Kramskoi)

391 Factories

390 "Rye Field"

1948. 50th Death Anniv of Shishkin (landscape painter).
1370 **389** 30k. brown and green . . 1·40 30
1371 **390** 50k. yellow, red and blue 3·00 55
1372 – 60k. multicoloured . . . 4·50 75
1373 **389** 1r. blue and brown . . . 5·00 1·75
DESIGN—HORIZ: 60k. "Morning in the Forest".

1948. Leningrad Workers' Four-Year Plan.
1374 **391** 15k. brown and red . . 2·50 1·00
1375 – 30k. black and red . . . 2·25 1·50
1376 **391** 60k. brown and red . . 6·50 3·00
DESIGN—HORIZ (40 × 22 mm): 30k. Proclamation to Leningrad workers.

392 Arms and People of the U.S.S.R.

393 Caterpillar drawing Seed Drills

1948. 25th Anniv of U.S.S.R.
1377 **392** 30k. black and red . . . 1·60 65
1378 60k. olive and red . . . 2·75 1·40

1948. Five Year Agricultural Plan.
1379 **393** 30k. red 65 25
1380 30k. green 75 25
1381 – 45k. brown . . . . . . 1·40 60
1382 **393** 50k. black . . . . 2·10 1·00
1383 – 60k. green . . . . 1·60 40
1384 – 60k. green . . . . 1·60 40
1385 – 1r. violet . . . . 5·25 2·25
DESIGNS: 30k. (No. 1380), 1r. Harvesting sugar beet; 45, 60k. (No. 1383), Gathering cotton; 60k. (No. 1384), Harvesting machine.

ИЮЛЬ
1948
года
(394)

395 Miners

396 A. Zhdanov

1948. Air Force Day. Optd with T **394**.
1386 **364** 30k. violet . . . . . . 4·50 2·50
1387 1r. blue . . . . 4·50 2·50

1948. Miners' Day.
1388 **395** 30k. blue 80 40
1389 – 60k. violet . . . . . . 1·50 65
1390 – 1r. green . . . . 3·50 1·00
DESIGNS: 60k. Inside a coal mine; 1r. Miner's emblem.

1948. Death of A. A. Zhdanov (statesman).
1391 **396** 40k. blue . . . . 2·75 1·10

397 Sailor

398 Football

1948. Navy Day.
1392 **397** 30k. green . . . . 2·25 1·10
1393 60k. blue . . . . 3·25 1·60

1948. Sports.
1394 – 15k. violet . . . . . . 1·25 15
1395a **398** 30k. brown . . . . . . 2·50 15
1396 – 45k. brown . . . . . . 2·75 35
1397a – 50k. blue . . . . 3·75 35
DESIGNS—VERT: 15k. Running; 50k. Diving. HORIZ: 45k. Power boat racing.

399 Tank and Drivers

1948. Tank Drivers' Day.
1398 **399** 30k. black . . . . 2·00 1·40
1399 – 1r. red . . . . 4·75 2·00
DESIGN: 1r. Parade of tanks.

400 Horses and Groom

1948. Five Year Livestock Development Plan.
1400 **400** 30k. black . . . . 2·00 1·40
1401 – 60k. green . . . . 3·25 1·90
1402 **400** 1r. brown . . . . 6·00 2·75
DESIGN: 60k. Dairy farming.

401 Steam and Electric Locomotives

1948. Five Year Transport Plan.
1403 **401** 30k. brown . . . . . . 4·00 1·25
1404 50k. green . . . . 6·75 4·00
1405 – 60k. blue . . . . 5·75 4·00
1406 – 1r. violet . . . . 9·00 5·00
DESIGNS: 60k. Road traffic; 1r. Liner "Vyacheslav Molotov".

402 Iron Pipe Manufacture

1948. Five Year Rolled Iron, Steel and Machine-building Plan.
1407 – 30k. violet . . . . . . 1·75 90
1408 – 30k. purple . . . . . . 1·75 90
1409 – 50k. brown . . . . . . 2·75 1·40
1410 – 50k. black . . . . . . 2·75 1·40
1411 – 60k. brown . . . . . . 3·75 2·50
1412 **402** 60k. red . . . . 3·75 2·50
1413 1r. blue . . . . 5·75 3·25
DESIGNS—HORIZ: Nos. 1407, 1410, Foundry; No. 1408/9, Pouring molten metal; No. 1411, Group of machines.

403 Abovyan

404 Miner

1948. Death Centenary of Khachatur Abovyan (writer).
1414 **403** 40k. purple . . . . . . 2·25 1·60
1415 50k. green . . . . 3·25 2·25

1948. Five Year Coal Mining and Oil Extraction Plan.
1416 **404** 30k. black . . . . 1·50 70
1417 60k. brown . . . . . . 3·00 1·60
1418 – 60k. brown . . . . . . 4·25 1·75
1419 – 1r. green . . . . 6·25 4·00
DESIGN: Nos. 1418/19, Oil wells and tanker train.

405 Farkhadsk Power Station

406 Flying Model Aircraft

1948. Five Year Electrification Plan.
1420 **405** 30k. green . . . . 1·40 1·10
1421 – 60k. red . . . . 3·00 2·25
1422 **405** 1r. red . . . . 5·00 2·50
DESIGN: 60k. Zuevsk Power Station.

1948. Government Care of School Children's Summer Vacation.
1423 **406** 30k. green . . . . 3·25 95
1424 – 45k. red . . . . 6·50 5·00
1425 – 45k. violet . . . . . . 3·25 2·00
1426 – 60k. blue . . . . 9·00 5·00
1427 – 1r. blue . . . . 17·00 6·00
DESIGNS—VERT: No. 1424, Boy and girl saluting; 60k. Boy trumpeter. HORIZ: No. 1425, Children marching; 1r. Children round camp fire.

407 Children in School

408 Flag of U.S.S.R.

1948. 30th Anniv of Lenin's Young Communist League.
1428 – 20k. purple . . . . . . 3·00 1·10
1429 – 25k. red . . . . 2·00 1·10
1430 – 40k. brown and red . . 4·75 2·00
1431 **407** 50k. green . . . . . . 4·75 2·50
1432 **408** 1r. multicoloured . . . . 15·00 10·00
1433 – 2r. violet . . . . 15·00 10·00
DESIGNS—HORIZ: 20k. Youth parade. VERT: 25k. Peasant girl; 40k. Young people and flag; 2r. Industrial worker.

409 Interior of Theatre

410 Searchlights over Moscow

1948. 50th Anniv of Moscow Arts Theatre.
1434 **409** 50k. blue . . . . 2·75 2·25
1435 – 1r. purple . . . . 5·00 4·00
DESIGN: 1r. Stanislavsky and Dantchenko.

1948. 31st Anniv of October Revolution.
1436 **410** 40k. red . . . . 2·25 1·60
1437 1r. green . . . . 5·00 3·25

411 Artillery Barrage

1948. Artillery Day.
1438 **411** 30k. blue . . . . 2·75 2·25
1439 1r. red . . . . 4·50 3·25

412 Trade Union Building (venue)

1948. 16th World Chess Championship, Moscow.
1440 **412** 30k. blue . . . . 4·00 65
1441 – 40k. violet . . . . . . 9·00 1·00
1442 **412** 50k. brown . . . . . . 9·00 1·75
DESIGN—VERT: 40k. Players' badge showing chessboard and rook.

413 Stasov and Building

1948. Death Centenary of Stasov (architect).
1443 – 40k. brown . . . . . . 1·40 1·25
1444 **413** 1r. black . . . . 3·25 3·00
DESIGN—VERT: 40k. Portrait of Stasov.

414 Yakovlev Yak-9 Fighters and Flag

415 Statue of Ya. M. Sverdlov

1948. Air Force Day.
1445a **414** 1r. blue . . . . 7·25 1·90

1948. 225th Anniv of Sverdlovsk City. Imperf or perf.
1446b **415** 30k. blue 65 15
1447b – 40k. purple . . . . . . 1·60 50
1448b **415** 1r. green . . . . 1·90 60
DESIGN: 40k. View of Sverdlovsk.

416 Sukhumi

417 State Emblem

1948. Views of Crimea and Caucasus.
1449 **416** 40k. green . . . . 1·00 30
1450 – 40k. violet . . . . . . 1·00 30
1451 – 40k. mauve . . . . . . 1·00 30
1452 – 40k. brown . . . . . . 1·00 30
1453 – 40k. purple . . . . . . 1·00 30
1454 – 40k. green . . . . 1·00 30
1455 – 40k. blue . . . . 1·00 30
1456 – 40k. green . . . . 1·00 30
DESIGNS—VERT: No. 1450, Gardens, Sochi; 1451, Eagle-topped monument, Pyatigorsk; 1452, Cliffs, Crimea. HORIZ: No. 1453, Terraced gardens, Sochi; 1454, Roadside garden, Sochi; 1455, Colonnade, Kislovodsk; 1456, Seascape, Gagry.

1949. 30th Anniv of Byelorussian Soviet Republic.
1457 **417** 40k. red . . . . 1·90 1·60
1458 1r. green . . . . 3·50 2·25

418 M. V. Lomonosov

419 Lenin Mausoleum

1949. Establishment of Lomonosov Museum of Academy of Sciences.
1459 **418** 40k. brown . . . . . . 1·60 1·10
1460 50k. green . . . . 1·90 1·10
1461 – 1r. blue . . . . 4·25 2·75
DESIGN—HORIZ: 1r. Museum.

1949. 25th Death Anniv of Lenin.
1462 **419** 40k. brown and green . . 5·50 5·00
1463 1r. brown & deep brown 10·50 9·50

420 Dezhnev's Ship

1949. 300th Anniv of Dezhnev's Exploration of Bering Strait.
1464 – 40k. green . . . . 10·00 8·50
1465 **420** 1r. grey . . . . 20·00 12·50
DESIGN: 40k. Cape Dezhnev.

421 "Women in Industry"

422 Admiral S. O. Makarov

1949. International Women's Day.
1466 **421** 20k. violet 35 10
1467 – 25k. blue 40 10
1468 – 40k. red 55 15
1469 – 50k. grey . . . . 1·10 30
1470 – 50k. brown . . . . . . 1·10 30
1471 – 1r. green . . . . 3·50 50
1472 – 2r. red . . . . 5·25 80
DESIGNS—HORIZ: 25k. Kindergarten; 50k. grey, Woman teacher; 50k. brown, Women in field; 1r. Women sports champions. VERT: 40k., 2r. Woman broadcasting.

1949. Birth Centenary of Admiral S. O. Makarov (naval scientist).
1473 **422** 40k. blue . . . . 1·60 1·00
1474 1r. red . . . . 3·50 3·00

423 Soldier

1949. 31st Anniv of Soviet Army.
1475 **423** 40k. red . . . . 12·50 10·00

424 Kirov Military Medical Academy

1949. 150th Anniv of Kirov Military Medical Academy.
1476 **424** 40k. red . . . . 1·25 1·10
1477 – 50k. blue . . . . 1·75 1·60
1478 **424** 1r. green . . . . 4·25 3·00
DESIGN: 50k. Professors Botkin, Pirogov and Sechenov and Kirov Academy.

425 V. R. Williams

425a Three Russians with Flag

1949. Agricultural Reform.
1479 **425** 25k. green . . . . 3·25 2·25
1480 50k. brown . . . . . . 5·50 4·50

1949. Labour Day.
1481 **425a** 40k. red . . . . 1·75 1·25
1482 1r. green . . . . 3·25 2·00

426 Newspapers and Books

427 A. S. Popov and Radio Equipment

1949. Press Day. Inscr "5 MAR 1949".
1483 **426** 40k. red . . . . 3·00 4·75
1484 – 1r. violet . . . . 6·25 8·25
DESIGN: 1r. Man and boy reading newspaper.

1949. Radio Day.
1485 **427** 40k. violet . . . . . . 1·75 1·40
1486 – 50k. brown . . . . . . 3·25 2·50
1487 **427** 1r. green . . . . 5·50 4·25
DESIGN—HORIZ: 50k. Popov demonstrating receiver to Admiral Makarov.

428 A. S. Pushkin

429 "Pushkin reading Poems to Southern Society" (Dmitry Kardovsky)

1949. 150th Birth Anniv of Pushkin (poet).
1488 **428** 25k. black and grey . . 1·10 50
1489 – 40k. black and brown . . 1·75 1·50
1490 **429** 40k. purple and red . . 4·00 1·50
1491 – 1r. grey and brown . . . 5·25 5·00
1492 **429** 2r. blue and brown . . . 8·00 7·00
DESIGNS—VERT: No. 1489, Pushkin portrait after Kiprensky. HORIZ: 1r. Pushkin museum, Boldino.

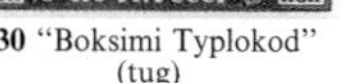
430 "Boksimi Typlokod" (tug)

431 I. V. Michurin

1949. Centenary of Krasnoe Sormovo Machine-building and Ship-building Plant, Gorky.
1493 **430** 40k. blue . . . . 6·75 5·25
1494 – 1r. brown . . . . 10·00 8·25
DESIGN: 1r. Freighter "Bolshaya Volga".

1949. Agricultural Reform.
1495 **431** 40k. blue . . . . 1·75 1·10
1496 1r. green . . . . 2·75 1·90

432 Yachting

1949. National Sports.
1497 **432** 20k. blue . . . . 1·25 10
1498 – 25k. green . . . . 1·25 15
1499 – 30k. violet . . . . . . 1·75 20
1500 – 40k. brown . . . . . . 2·25 40
1501 – 40k. green . . . . 2·25 40
1502 – 50k. grey . . . . 2·25 50
1503 – 1r. red . . . . 5·00 1·00
1504 – 2r. black . . . . 8·50 2·25
DESIGNS: 25k. Canoeing; 30k. Swimming; 40k. (No. 1500), Cycling; 40k. (No. 1501), Football; 50k. Mountaineering; 1r. Parachuting; 2r. High jumping.

433 V. V. Dokuchaev

1949. Soil Research.
1505 **433** 40k. brown . . . . . . 1·25 30
1506 1r. green . . . . 2·50 50

434 V. I. Bazhenov

435 A. N. Radischev

1949. 150th Death Anniv of V. I. Bazhenov (architect).
1507 **434** 40k. violet . . . . . . 1·40 45
1508 1r. brown . . . . 3·25 90

1949. Birth Bicent of A. N. Radischev (writer).
1509 **435** 40k. green . . . . 1·60 1·40
1510 1r. grey . . . . 2·75 2·25

436 Green Cape Sanatorium, Makhindzhauri

1949. State Sanatoria. Designs showing various buildings.
1511 **436** 40k. green 75 20
1512 – 40k. green 75 20
1513 – 40k. blue 75 20
1514 – 40k. violet 75 20
1515 – 40k. red 75 20
1516 – 40k. orange 75 20
1517 – 40k. brown 75 20
1518 – 40k. brown 75 20
1519 – 40k. black 75 20
1520 – 40k. black 75 20
DESIGNS—HORIZ: No. 1512, VTsSPS No. 41, Zheleznovodsk; No. 1513, Energetics, Hosta; No. 1514, VTsSPS No. 3, Kislovodsk; No. 1515, VTsSPS No. 3, Hosta; No. 1516, State Theatre, Sochi; No. 1517, Clinical, Tskhaltubo; No. 1518, Frunze, Sochi; No. 1519, VTsSPS No. 1, Kislovodsk; No. 1520, Communication, Hosta.

437 I. P. Pavlov

1949. Birth Centenary of I. P. Pavlov (scientist).
1521 **437** 40k. brown . . . . . . 1·00 20
1522 1r. black . . . . 2·25 60

438 Globe and Letters

1949. 75th Anniv of U.P.U. Perf or imperf.
1523b **438** 40k. blue and brown . . 2·25 25
1524b 50k. violet and blue . . 2·25 25

439 Tree Planting Machines

440 Map of S. W. Russia

1949. Forestry and Field Conservancy.
1525 **439** 25k. green 75 30
1526 – 40k. violet 90 30
1527 **440** 40k. green and black . . 90 60
1528 – 50k. blue . . . . 1·40 1·00
1529 **439** 1r. black . . . . 4·50 2·40
1530 – 2r. brown . . . . 7·25 4·75
DESIGNS—33 × 22½ mm: 40k. violet, Harvesters; 50k. River scene. 33 × 19½ mm: 2r. Old man and children.

1949. 30th Death Anniv of V. I. Chapaev (military strategist).
1531 **299** 40k. orange . . . . . . 10·50 10·00

442 I. S. Nikitin (after P. Borel)

443 Malyi Theatre, Moscow

1949. 125th Birth Anniv of Nikitin (poet).
1532 **442** 40k. brown . . . . . . 1·10 35
1533 1r. blue . . . . 2·25 60

1949. 125th Anniv of Malyi Theatre, Moscow.
1534 **443** 40k. green . . . . 1·25 25
1535 50k. orange . . . . . . 1·75 30
1536 – 1r. brown . . . . 4·00 80
DESIGN: 1r. Five portraits and theatre.

444 Crowd with Banner

1949. 32nd Anniv of October Revolution.
1537 **444** 40k. red . . . . 2·50 2·25
1538 1r. green . . . . 4·50 4·00

445 Sheep and Cows

1949. Cattle-breeding Collective Farm.
1539 **445** 40k. brown . . . . . . 1·25 40
1540 1r. violet . . . . 2·50 80

446 Lenin Hydro-electric Station, Caucasus

448 Ski Jumping

447 Ilyushin Il-12 Airliners and Map

1949. Air. Aerial views and map.
1541 **446** 50k. brown on yellow . . 1·90 1·00
1542 – 60k. brown on buff . . . 2·00 1·50
1543 – 1r. orange on yellow . . 6·00 1·90
1544 – 1r. brown on buff . . . 5·50 1·90
1545 – 1r. blue on blue . . . . 5·50 1·90
1546 **447** 1r. blue, red and grey . . 10·00 5·50
1547 – 2r. red on blue . . . . . 12·00 5·50
1548 – 3r. green on blue . . . . 23·00 13·50
DESIGNS—Ilyushin Il-12 airplane over: HORIZ: No. 1542, Farm; 1543, Sochi. VERT: 1544, Leningrad; 1545, Aleppo; 1547, Moscow; 1548, Arctic.

1949. National Sports.
1549 **448** 20k. green . . . . 1·00 15
1550 – 40k. orange . . . . . . 3·00 75
1551 – 50k. blue . . . . 2·75 60
1552 – 1r. red . . . . 5·25 60
1553 – 2r. violet . . . . 9·00 1·50
DESIGNS: 40k. Girl gymnast; 50k. Ice hockey; 1r. Weightlifting; 2r. Shooting wolves.

449 Diesel-electric Train

450 Arms of U.S.S.R.

1949. Modern Railway Development.
1554 – 25k. red . . . . 2·00 35
1555 **449** 40k. violet . . . . . . 2·50 45
1556 – 50k. brown . . . . . . 3·50 60
1557 **449** 1r. green . . . . 9·00 1·40
DESIGNS: 25k. Electric tram; 50k. Steam train.

1949. Constitution Day.
1558 **450** 40k. red . . . . 7·00 5·00

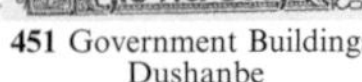
451 Government Buildings, Dushanbe

452 People with Flag

1949. 20th Anniv of Republic of Tadzhikstan.
1559 – 20k. blue 70 10
1560 – 25k. green 80 10
1561 **451** 40k. red 90 30
1562 – 50k. violet . . . . . . 1·40 30
1563 **451** 1r. black . . . . 2·25 85
DESIGNS: 20k. Textile mills; 25k. Irrigation canal; 50k. Medical University.

1949. 10th Anniv of Incorporation of West Ukraine and West Byelorussia in U.S.S.R.
1564 **452** 40k. red . . . . 9·00 9·00
1565 – 40k. orange . . . . . . 9·00 9·00
DESIGN—VERT: No. 1565, Ukrainians and flag.

453 Worker and Globe

454 Government Buildings, Tashkent

1949. Peace Propaganda.
1566 **453** 40k. red 85 25
1567 50k. blue . . . . 1·10 35

1950. 25th Anniv of Uzbek S.S.R.
1568 – 20k. blue 45 20
1569 – 25k. black 45 20
1570 **454** 40k. red . . . . 1·00 20
1571 – 40k. violet . . . . . . 1·40 40
1572 – 1r. green . . . . 2·75 75
1573 – 2r. brown . . . . 5·00 1·60
DESIGNS: 20k. Teachers' College; 25k. Opera and Ballet House, Tashkent; 40k. (violet) Navots Street, Tashkent; 1r. Map of Fergana Canal; 2r. Lock, Fergana Canal.

455 Dam

456 "Lenin at Rozliv" (sculpture, V. Pinchuk)

1950. 25th Anniv of Turkmen S.S.R.
1574 – 25k. black . . . . 3·25 3·25
1575 **455** 40k. brown . . . . . . 1·75 1·50
1576 – 50k. green . . . . 4·00 3·75
1577 **455** 1r. violet . . . . 8·75 6·00
DESIGNS: 25k. Textile factory, Ashkhabad; 50k. Carpet-making.

1950. 26th Death Anniv of Lenin.
1578 **456** 40k. brown and grey . . 85 25
1579 – 50k. red, brown and green . . . . 1·40 60
1580 – 1r. buff, green and brown . . . . 3·25 85
DESIGNS—HORIZ: 50k. Lenin's Office, Kremlin; 1r. Lenin Museum, Gorky.

457 Film Show

458 Voter

1950. 30th Anniv of Soviet Film Industry.
1581 **457** 25k. brown . . . . . . 16·00 13·50

1950. Supreme Soviet Elections. Inscr "12 MAPTA 1950".
1582 **458** 40k. green on yellow . . 3·75 2·75
1583 – 1r. red . . . . 5·50 4·50
DESIGN: 1r. Kremlin and flags.

459 Monument (I. Rabinovich)

460 Lenin Central Museum

1950. Unveiling of Monument in Moscow to Pavlik Morozov (model Soviet youth).
1584 **459** 40k. black and red . . . 4·00 3·25
1585 1r. green and red . . . . 6·50 5·00

1950. Moscow Museums. Buildings inscr "MOCKBA 1949".
1586 **460** 40k. olive . . . . 1·25 25
1587 – 40k. red . . . . 1·25 25
1588 – 40k. turquoise . . . . . 1·25 25
1589 – 40k. brown . . . . . . 1·25 25
1590 – 40k. mauve . . . . . . 1·25 25
1591 – 40k. blue (no tree) . . . 1·25 25
1592 – 40k. brown . . . . . . 1·25 25
1593 – 40k. blue (with tree) . . 1·25 25
1594 – 40k. red . . . . 1·25 25
DESIGNS—HORIZ: (33½ × 23½ mm): No. 1587, Revolution Museum; 1588, Tretyakov Gallery; 1589, Timiryazev Biological Museum; No. 1591, Polytechnic Museum; 1593, Oriental Museum. (39½ × 26½ mm): No. 1590, Pushkin Pictorial Arts Museum. VERT: (22½ × 33½ mm): No. 1592, Historical Museum; 1594, Zoological Museum.

461 Hemispheres and Wireless Mast

1950. International Congress of P.T.T. and Radio Trade Unions, London.
1595 **461** 40k. green on blue . . . 3·25 2·75
1596 50k. blue on blue . . . 4·75 4·25

462 Three Workers

463 A. S. Shcherbakov

1950. Labour Day.
1597 **462** 40k. red and black . . . 3·25 2·75
1598 – 1r. red and black . . . . 6·00 5·25
DESIGN—HORIZ: 1r. Four Russians and banner.

1950. 5th Death Anniv of Shcherbakov (statesman).
1599 **463** 40k. black . . . . 1·40 1·10
1600 1r. green on pink . . . . 3·00 2·75

464 Suvorov (after N. Utkin)

465 Statue

1950. 150th Death Anniv of Suvorov.
1601 **464** 40k. blue on pink . . . 3·50 1·90
1602 – 50k. brown on pink . . 4·75 3·25
1603 – 60k. black on blue . . . 4·75 3·25
1604 **464** 1r. brown on yellow . . 6·00 4·50
1605 – 2r. green . . . . 11·00 7·00
DESIGNS—32½ × 47 mm: 50k. "Suvorov crossing the Alps" (V. I. Surikov). 24½ × 39½ mm—60k. Order of Suvorov and military parade (after portrait by N. Smdyak). 19½ × 33½ mm—2r. "Suvorov in the Alps" (N. Abbakumov).

1950. 5th Anniv of Victory over Germany.
1606 **465** 40k. red and brown . . 4·00 2·75
1607 – 1r. red . . . . 6·50 4·00
DESIGN—22½ × 33 mm: 1r. Medal for the Victory over Germany (profile of Stalin and Order of Victory).

466 Sowing on Collective Farm

1950. Agricultural Workers.
1608 – 40k. green on blue . . . 3·00 1·75
1609 **466** 40k. brown on pink . . . 3·00 1·75
1610 1r. blue on yellow . . . 4·75 3·75
DESIGNS: No. 1608, Collective farmers studying.

467 G. M. Dimitrov

468 State Opera and Ballet House, Baku

1950. 1st Death Anniv of Bulgarian Premier, Dimitrov.
1611 **467** 40k. black on yellow . . 1·75 1·40
1612 1r. black on orange . . . 4·25 2·75

1950. 30th Anniv of Azerbaijan S.S.R.
1613 **468** 25k. green on yellow . . 1·60 1·40
1614 – 40k. brown on red . . . 3·25 2·50
1615 – 1r. black on orange . . . 5·50 4·50
DESIGNS: 40k. Science Academy; 1r. Stalin Avenue, Baku.

469 Lenin Street, Stalingrad

1950. Stalingrad Reconstruction.
1616 – 20k. blue . . . . 1·00 90
1617 **469** 40k. green . . . . 2·00 1·25
1618 – 50k. orange . . . . . . 4·25 3·25
1619 – 1r. black . . . . 5·00 4·00
DESIGNS—VERT: 20k. Pobeda Cinema. HORIZ: 50k. Gorky Theatre; 1r. Pavlov House and Tank Memorial.

470 Kaluzhskaya Station **472** Trade Union Building

471 National Flags and Civilians

1950. Underground Railway Stations.
1620 **470** 40k. green on buff . . . 1·00 35
1621 A 40k. red . . . . 1·00 35
1622 B 40k. blue on buff . . . . 1·00 35
1623 C 1r. brown on yellow . . 3·00 1·10
1624 D 1r. violet on blue . . . . 3·00 1·10
1625 A 1r. green on yellow . . . 3·00 1·10
1626 E 1r. black on orange . . . 3·00 1·10
DESIGNS—HORIZ: (34 × 22½ mm): A, Culture Park; B, Taganskaya; C, Kurskaya; D, Paveletskaya. (34 × 18½ mm): E, Taganskaya.

1950. Unconquerable Democracy. Flags in red, blue and yellow.
1627 **471** 40k. black . . . . 1·10 20
1628 50k. brown . . . . 2·25 30
1629 1r. green . . . . 2·50 45

1950. 10th Anniv of Latvian S.S.R.
1630 **472** 25k. brown 90 60
1631 – 40k. red . . . . 1·40 90
1632 – 50k. green . . . . 2·10 1·40
1633 – 60k. blue . . . . 2·50 1·90
1634 – 1r. violet . . . . 4·50 3·00
1635 – 2r. brown . . . . 7·50 5·00
DESIGNS—VERT: 40k. Cabinet Council Offices; 50k. Monument to Jan Rainis (poet); 2r. Academy of Sciences. HORIZ: 60k. Theatre, Riga; 1r. State University, Riga.

473 Marite Melnikaite **474** Stalingrad Square, Tallinn

1950. 10th Anniv of Lithuanian S.S.R.
1636 – 25k. blue . . . . 1·25 70
1637 **473** 40k. brown . . . . . . 2·40 1·40
1638 – 1r. red . . . . 6·50 3·50
DESIGNS—HORIZ: 25k. Academy of Sciences; 1r. Cabinet Council Offices.

1950. 10th Anniv of Estonian S.S.R.
1639 **474** 25k. green . . . . 1·00 60
1640 – 40k. red . . . . 1·40 90
1641 – 50k. blue on yellow . . . 2·25 1·60
1642 – 1r. brown on blue . . . 7·00 5·50
DESIGNS—HORIZ: 40k. Government building; 50k. Opera and Ballet Theatre, Tallin. VERT: 1r. Viktor Kingisepp (revolutionary).

475 Signing Peace Appeal

1950. Peace Conference.
1643 **475** 40k. red on pink . . . . 1·60 1·10
1644 – 40k. black . . . . . . 1·60 1·10
1645 – 50k. red . . . . 3·50 3·00
1646 **475** 1r. brown on pink . . . 5·50 4·75
DESIGNS—VERT: 40k. black, Children and teacher; 50k. Young people with banner.

476 Bellingshausan Lazarev and Globe **477** Frunze (after I. Brodsky)

1950. 130th Anniv of 1st Antarctic Expedition.
1647 **476** 40k. red on blue . . . . 18·00 11·00
1648 – 1r. violet on blue . . . . 32·00 15·00
DESIGN—VERT: 1r. "Mirnyi" and "Vostok" (ships) and map of Antarctica.

1950. 25th Death Anniv of M.V. Frunze (military strategist).
1649 **477** 40k. blue on pink . . . 3·50 2·75
1650 1r. brown on blue . . . 8·25 6·00

478 M. I. Kalinin **479** Picking Grapes

1950. 75th Birth Anniv of Kalinin (statesman).
1651 **478** 40k. green . . . . 1·25 85
1652 1r. brown . . . . 2·75 1·60
1653 5r. violet . . . . 7·25 6·50

1950. 30th Anniv of Armenian S.S.R.
1654 **479** 20k. blue on pink . . . 1·50 1·10
1655 – 40k. orange on blue . . 2·75 1·60
1656 – 1r. black on yellow . . . 5·75 3·75
DESIGNS—HORIZ: (33 × 16 mm): 40k. Government Offices. VERT: (21½ × 33 mm): 1r. G. M. Sundukian (dramatist).

480 Kotelnicheskaya Quay **481** Spassky Tower, Kremlin

1950. Moscow Building Projects.
1657 **480** 1r. brown on pink . . . 35·00 25·00
1658 – 1r. black on pink . . . 35·00 25·00
1659 – 1r. brown on blue . . . 35·00 25·00
1660 – 1r. green on yellow . . . 35·00 25·00
1661 – 1r. blue on pink . . . . 35·00 25·00
1662 – 1r. black . . . . 35·00 25·00
1663 – 1r. orange . . . . 35·00 25·00
1664 – 1r. green on blue . . . . 35·00 25·00
DESIGNS—HORIZ: No. 1659, Vosstaniya Square; 1660, Smolenskaya Square; 1662, Krasnye Vorota; 1664, Moscow University. VERT: No. 1658, Hotel Ukraine, Dorogomilovskaya Quay; 1661, Hotel Leningrad; 1663, Zaryade.

1950. 33rd Anniv of October Revolution.
1665 **481** 1r. red, yellow and green 16·00 9·00

482 "Golden Autumn"

1950. 50th Death Anniv of Levitan (painter).
1666 **482** 40k. multicoloured . . . 4·00 85
1667 – 50k. brown . . . . . . 5·00 85
DESIGN: 50k. Portrait of Levitan by V. Serov.

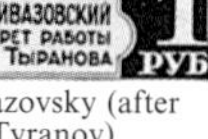

483 Aivazovsky (after A. Tyranov) **484** Newspapers "Iskra" and "Pravda"

1950. 50th Death Anniv of Aivazovsky (painter). Multicoloured centres.
1668 – 40k. brown . . . . . . 3·00 40
1669 – 50k. brown . . . . . . 4·00 65
1670 **483** 1r. blue . . . . 7·75 1·40
PAINTINGS—HORIZ: 40k. "Black Sea"; 50k. "Ninth Wave".

1950. 50th Anniv of Newspaper "Iskra".
1671 – 40k. red and black . . . 12·00 10·50
1672 **484** 1r. red and black . . . . 16·00 13·00
DESIGN: 40k. Newspapers and banners.

485 Government Offices

1950. 30th Anniv of Kazakh S.S.R.
1673 **485** 40k. black on blue . . . 4·75 2·50
1674 – 1r. brown on yellow . . 6·25 3·50
DESIGN: 1r. Opera House, Alma-Ata.

486 Decembrists and "Decembrist Rising in Senate Square, St. Petersburg, 14 December 1825" (K. Kolman)

1950. 125th Anniv of Decembrist Rising.
1675 **486** 1r. brown on yellow . . 7·25 5·50

487 Govt Offices, Tirana

1951. Friendship with Albania.
1676 **487** 40k. green on blue . . . 20·00 15·00

488 Greeting Soviet Troops

1951. Friendship with Bulgaria.
1677 **488** 25k. black on blue . . . 2·25 1·90
1678 – 40k. orange on pink . . 6·00 3·25
1679 – 60k. brown on orange 6·75 4·25
DESIGNS: 40k. Lenin Square, Sofia; 60k. Monument to Soviet fighters, Kolarovgrad.

489 Lenin at Razliv

1951. 27th Death Anniv of Lenin. Multicoloured centres.
1680 **489** 40k. green . . . . 2·75 65
1681 – 1r. blue . . . . 5·50 1·00
DESIGN: 1r. Lenin talking to young Communists.

490 Horses

1951. 25th Anniv of Kirghiz S.S.R.
1682 **490** 25k. brown on blue . . . 5·00 4·50
1683 – 40k. green on blue . . . 7·25 6·75
DESIGN—33 × 22½ mm: 40k. Government Offices, Frunze.

490a Gathering Lemons

1951. 30th Anniv of Georgia S.S.R.
1683a – 20k. green on yellow 1·75 1·25
1683b **490a** 25k. orange and violet 2·75 2·00
1683c – 40k. brown on blue 4·50 3·00
1683d – 1r. green and brown 11·00 6·00
DESIGNS—VERT: 20k. State Opera and Ballet Theatre, Tbilisi. HORIZ: 40k. Rustaveli Avenue, Tbilisi; 1r. Plucking tea.

491 University, Ulan Bator

1951. Friendship with Mongolia.
1684 **491** 25k. violet on orange . . 1·75 75
1685 – 40k. orange on yellow 2·50 1·10
1686 – 1r. multicoloured . . . . 7·25 4·00
DESIGNS—HORIZ: (37 × 25 mm): 40k. State Theatre, Ulan Bator. VERT: (22 × 33 mm): 1r. State Emblem and Mongolian Flag.

492 D. A. Furmanov **493** Soviet Soldiers Memorial, Berlin (E. Buchetich)

1951. 25th Death Anniv of D. A. Furmanov (writer).
1687 **492** 40k. brown on blue . . . 1·90 1·40
1688 – 1r. black on orange . . . 4·25 3·25
DESIGN—HORIZ: 1r. Furmanov writing.

1951. Stockholm Peace Appeal.
1689 **493** 40k. green and red . . . 4·25 3·25
1690 1r. black and red . . . . 9·00 7·50

494 Factories

1951. 150th Anniv of Kirov Machine-building Factory, Leningrad.
1691 **494** 40k. brown on yellow . . 6·75 5·00

495 Bolshoi State Theatre

1951. 175th Anniv of State Theatre.
1692 **495** 40k. multicoloured . . . 5·00 55
1693 – 1r. multicoloured . . . . 7·25 1·40
DESIGN: 1r. Theatre and medallions of Glinka, Tchaikovsky, Moussorgsky, Rimsky-Korsakov, Borodin and theatre.

496 National Museum, Budapest

1951. Hungarian Peoples' Republic. Buildings in Budapest.
1694 – 25k. green . . . . 1·40 1·10
1695 – 40k. blue . . . . 1·50 90
1696 **496** 60k. black . . . . . . 2·50 1·25
1697 – 1r. black on pink . . . . 5·75 3·50
DESIGNS—HORIZ: 25k. Liberty Bridge; 40k. Parliament buildings. VERT: 1r. Liberation Monument.

497 Harvesting

1951. Agricultural Scenes.
1698 **497** 25k. green 90 50
1699 – 40k. green on blue . . . 1·75 60
1700 – 1r. brown on yellow . . 3·00 2·75
1701 – 2r. green on pink . . . . 5·25 4·75
DESIGNS: 40k. Apiary; 1r. Gathering citrus fruit; 2r. Harvesting cotton.

498 M. I. Kalinin

499 F. E. Dzerzhinsky

1951. 5th Death Anniv of Pres. Kalinin.
1702 – 20k. black, sepia & brown 75 35
1703 **498** 40k. brown, dp grn & grn . . . . 1·60 50
1704 – 1r. black, bl & ultram 3·25 90
DESIGNS—HORIZ: 20k. Kalinin Museum. VERT: 1r. Statue of Kalinin (G. Alekseev).

1951. 25th Death Anniv of Dzerzhinsky (founder of Cheka).
1705 **499** 40k. red . . . . 2·40 60
1706 – 1r. black (Portrait in uniform) . . . . . . 4·50 1·60

500 P. K. Kozlov

501 Kalinnikov

1951. Russian Scientists.
1707 **500** 40k. orange . . . . . . 1·50 25
1708 – 40k. orange on pink . . 1·50 25
1709 – 40k. orange on blue . . 4·50 1·10
1710 – 40k. brown . . . . . . 1·50 25
1711 – 40k. brown on pink (facing left) . . . . . 1·50 25
1712 – 40k. brown on pink (facing right) . . . . 1·50 25
1713 – 40k. grey . . . . 1·50 25
1714 – 40k. grey on pink . . . 1·50 25
1715 – 40k. grey on blue . . . 4·50 1·10
1716 – 40k. green . . . . . . 1·50 25
1717 – 40k. green on pink . . . 1·50 25
1718 – 40k. blue . . . . 1·50 25
1719 – 40k. blue on pink . . . 1·50 25
1720 – 40k. blue on blue . . . 1·50 25
1721 – 40k. violet . . . . . . 1·50 25
1722 – 40k. violet on pink . . . 1·50 25
PORTRAITS: No. 1708, N. N. Miklukho-Makai; 1709, A. M. Butlerov; 1710, N. I. Lobachevsky; 1711, K. A. Timiryazev; 1712, N. S. Kurnakov; 1713, P. N. Yablochkov; 1714, A. N. Severtsov; No. 1715, K. E. Tsiolkovsky; 1716, A. N. Lodygin; 1717, A. G. Stoletov; 1718, P. N. Lebedev; 1719, A. O. Kovalesky; 1720, D. I. Mendeleev; 1721, S. P. Krasheninnikov; 1722, S. V. Kovalevskaya.

1951. Russian Composers.
1723 **501** 40k. grey on pink . . . 10·00 8·25
1724 – 40k. brown on pink . . 10·00 8·25
PORTRAIT: No. 1724, A. Alyabev (after N. Andreev).

502 Aviation Society Badge

503 Vasnetsov (after I. Kramskoi)

1951. Aviation Developement.
1725 **502** 40k. multicoloured . . . 1·25 15
1726 – 60k. multicoloured . . . 2·00 20
1727 – 1r. multicoloured . . . . 3·25 85
1728 – 2r. multicoloured . . . . 6·25 1·50
DESIGNS—VERT: 60k. Boys and model gliders; 1r. Parachutists descending. HORIZ: (45 × 25 mm): 2r. Flight of Yakovlev Yak-18U trainers.

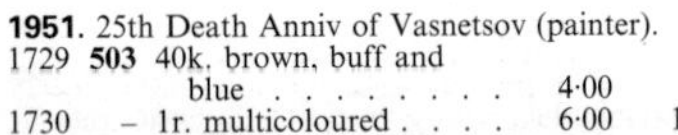
1951. 25th Death Anniv of Vasnetsov (painter).
1729 **503** 40k. brown, buff and blue . . . . 4·00 60
1730 – 1r. multicoloured . . . 6·00 1·10
DESIGN (47 × 33 mm): 1r. "Three Heroes".

504 Lenin, Stalin and Dnieperprostroi Dam

1951. 34th Anniv of October Revolution.
1731 **504** 40k. blue and red . . . 6·00 3·25
1732 – 1r. brown and red . . . 8·00 5·50
DESIGN: 1r. Lenin, Stalin and Spassky Tower.

505 Volga–Don Canal

1951. Construction of Hydro-electric Power Stations.
1733 – 20k. multicoloured . . . 4·00 2·00
1734 **505** 30k. multicoloured . . . 4·50 3·50
1735 – 40k. multicoloured . . . 5·50 4·00
1736 – 60k. multicoloured . . . 8·50 4·50
1737 – 1r. multicoloured . . . . 13·00 8·00
DESIGNS—VERT: (32 × 47 mm): 20k. Khakhovsky power station. HORIZ: (47 × 32 mm); 40k. Stalingrad dam; 60k. Excavator and map of Turkmen canal; 1r. Kuibyshev power station.

506 Signing Peace Petition

507 M. V. Ostrogradsky

1951. 3rd U.S.S.R. Peace Conference.
1738 **506** 40k. red and brown . . 9·25 7·25

1951. 150th Birth Anniv of Ostrogradsky (mathematician).
1739 **507** 40k. brown on pink . . 7·25 4·50

508 Zhizka Monument, Prague (B. Kafka)

509 Volkhovsky Hydro-electric Station and Lenin Monument

1951. Friendship with Czechoslovakia.
1740 **508** 20k. blue on pink . . . 2·00 1·25
1741 – 25k. red on yellow . . . 4·50 1·75
1742 – 40k. orange on orange 2·25 1·50
1743 – 60k. grey on pink . . . 5·25 2·75
1744 – 1r. grey on cream . . . 8·00 5·00
DESIGNS—VERT: 25k. Soviet Army Monument, Ostrava; 40k. J. Fucik by M. Shvabinsky; 60k. Smetana Museum, Prague. HORIZ: 1r. Soviet Soldiers Monument, Prague.

1951. 25th Anniv of Lenin Volkhovsky Hydro-electric Station.
1745a **509** 40k. yellow, indigo and blue . . . . 1·10 35
1746 1r. yellow, indigo and violet . . . . 2·25 50

510 Lenin when a Student (after V. Prager)

511 P. P. Semenov-Tian-Shansky

1952. 28th Death Anniv of Lenin. Multicoloured centres.
1747 **510** 40k. green . . . . 2·25 75
1748 – 60k. blue . . . . 2·75 90
1749 – 1r. brown . . . . 3·25 1·40
DESIGNS—HORIZ: 60k. Lenin and children (after A. Varlamov); 1r. Lenin talking to peasants (after V. Serov).

1952. 125th Birth Anniv of Semenov-Tian-Shansky (scientist).
1750 **511** 1r. brown on blue . . . 3·75 2·50

512 Skaters

513 V. O. Kovalevsky

1952. Winter Sports.
1751 **512** 40k. multicoloured . . . 3·25 45
1752 – 60k. multicoloured (Skiers) . . . . 4·00 75

1952. Birth Centenary of Kovalevsky (scientist).
1753 **513** 40k. brown on yellow . . 6·25 5·00

514 Gogol (after F. Moller) and Character from "Taras Bulba"

1952. Death Centenary of Nikolai Gogol (writer).
1754 **514** 40k. black on blue . . . 1·00 20
1755 – 60k. orange and black 1·40 30
1756 – 1r. multicoloured . . . . 2·75 1·40
DESIGNS: 60k. Gogol and Belinsky (after B. Lebedev); 1r. Gogol and Ukrainian peasants.

515 G. K. Ordzhonikidze

516 Workers and Flag

1952. 15th Death Anniv of Ordzhonikidze (statesman).
1757 **515** 40k. green on pink . . . 5·50 3·25
1758 1r. black on blue . . . . 7·25 5·00

1952. 15th Anniv of Stalin Constitution.
1759 **516** 40k. red and black on cream . . . . 5·50 3·75
1760 – 40k. red and green on green . . . . 5·50 3·75
1761 – 40k. red and brown on blue . . . . 5·50 3·75
1762 – 40k. red and black . . . 5·50 3·75
DESIGNS—HORIZ: No. 1760, Chess players at recreation centre; 1761, Old people and banners. VERT: No. 1762, Schoolgirl and Spassky Tower, Kremlin.

517 Novikov-Priboy and Battleship "Orel"

1952. 75th Birth Anniv of Novikov-Priboy (writer).
1763 **517** 40k. grey, yellow & green . . . . 3·25 1·10

518 Victor Hugo

519 Yulaev (after T. Nechaevoi)

1952. 150th Birth Anniv of Victor Hugo (French writer).
1764 **518** 40k. black, blue & brown . . . . 1·75 50

1952. Birth Bicent of Yulaev (Bashkirian hero).
1765 **519** 40k. red on pink . . . . 1·75 55

520 G. Ya. Sedov

521 Arms and Flag of Rumania

1952. 75th Birth Anniv of Sedov (Arctic explorer).
1766 **520** 40k. brown, blue & green . . . . 10·50 8·00

1952. Friendship with Rumania.
1767 **521** 40k. multicoloured . . . 1·40 65
1768 – 60k. green on pink . . . 2·50 1·50
1769 – 1r. blue . . . . 3·00 2·25
DESIGNS—VERT: 60k. Soviet Soldiers' Monument, Bucharest. HORIZ: 1r. University Square, Bucharest.

522 Zhukovsky (after K. Bryullov)

523 Bryullov (after V. Tropilin)

1952. Death Centenary of V. Zhukovsky (poet).
1770 **522** 40k. black on blue . . . 1·10 55

1952. Death Centenary of K. Bryullov (artist).
1771 **523** 40k. green on blue . . . 1·10 55

524 Ogarev (after M. Lemmel)

525 Uspensky (after N. Yaroshenko)

1952. 75th Death Anniv of Ogarev (revolutionary writer).
1772 **524** 40k. green 65 35

1952. 50th Death Anniv of Uspensky (writer).
1773 **525** 40k. brown and blue . . 1·75 75

526 Nakhimov (after V. Timm)

527 Tartu University

1952. 150th Birth Anniv of Admiral Nakhimov.
1774 **526** 40k. multicoloured . . . 3·75 1·60

1952. 150th Anniv of Extension of Tartu University.
1775 **527** 40k. black on salmon . . 2·75 1·60

1952. War Orders and Medals (7th series). Frame as T **282** with various centres.
1776 F 1r. brown . . . . 12·00 9·00
1777 P 2r. red . . . . 1·90 1·00
1778 J 3r. violet 90 70
1779a A 5r. lake . . . . 1·25 85
1780 E 10r. red . . . . 1·75 1·00

528 Kayum Nasyri

529 A. N. Radishchev

1952. 50th Death Anniv of Nasyri (educationist).
1781 **528** 40k. brown on yellow . . 2·75 1·60

1952. 150th Death Anniv of Radishchev (writer).
1782 **529** 40k. black and red . . . 2·25 75

530 Entrance to Volga–Don Canal

531 P. A. Fedotov

1952. 35th Anniv of Russian Revolution.
1783 **530** 40k. multicoloured . . . 5·00 3·25
1784 – 1r. yellow, red and brown . . . . 7·25 5·00
DESIGN: 1r. Lenin, Stalin, Spassky Tower and flags.

1952. Death Centenary of Fedotov (painter).
1785 **531** 40k. brown and lake . . 2·25 65

532 Polenov (after I. Repin)

534 Odoevsky (after N. Bestuzhev)

533 "Moscow Courtyard" (painting)

1952. 25th Death Anniv of Polenov (painter).
1786 **532** 40k. lake and buff . . . 1·60 55
1787 **533** 1r. blue and grey . . . . 3·75 1·25

1952. 150th Birth Anniv of A. I. Odoevsky (poet).
1788 **534** 40k. black and red . . . 1·75 50

535 Mamin-Sibiryak

536 V. M. Bekhterev

1952. Birth Centenary of D. N. Mamin-Sibiryak (writer).
1789 **535** 40k. green on yellow . . 1·10 25

1952. 25th Death Anniv of Bekhterev (psychiatrist).
1790 **536** 40k. black, grey and blue 1·40 55

537 Komsomolskaya Koltsevaya Station

1952. Underground Stations. Multicoloured centres.
1791 – 40k. violet . . . . . . 2·00 40
1792 – 40k. blue . . . . 2·00 40
1793 – 40k. grey . . . . 2·00 40
1794 **537** 40k. green . . . . 2·00 40
STATIONS: No. 1791, Belorussia Koltsevaya; 1792, Botanical Gardens; 1793, Novoslo-bodskaya.

538 U.S.S.R. Arms and Flags

1952. 30th Anniv of U.S.S.R.
1795 **538** 1r. brown, red and green 4·50 3·25

539 Lenin and Flags (after A. Gerasimov)

1953. 29th Death Anniv of Lenin.
1796 **539** 40k. multicoloured . . . 5·00 4·25

540 Peace Prize Medal

541 V. V. Kuibyshev

1953. Stalin Peace Prize.
1797 **540** 40k. yellow, blue & brown . . . . 5·50 5·00

1953. 65th Birth Anniv of Kuibyshev (statesman).
1798 **541** 40k. black and lake . . . 1·90 1·25

542 V. V. Mayakovsky

543 N. G. Chernyshevsky

1953. 60th Birth Anniv of Mayakovsky (poet).
1799 **542** 40k. black and red . . . 2·75 2·25

1953. 125th Birth Anniv of Chernyshevsky (writer).
1800 **543** 40k. brown and buff . . 2·75 2·25

544 R. Volga Lighthouse

1953. Volga–Don Canal. Multicoloured.
1801 40k. Type **544** . . . . . . 1·60 60
1802 40k. Lock No. 9 . . . . . 1·60 60
1803 40k. Lock No. 13 . . . . . 1·60 60
1804 40k. Lock No. 15 . . . . . 1·90 60
1805 40k. Tsimlyanskaya hydro-electric station . . . . . 1·60 60
1806 1r. "Iosif Stalin" (river vessel) . . . . 3·00 1·40

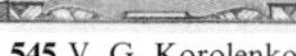

545 V. G. Korolenko

546 Tolstoi (after N. Ge)

1953. Birth Centenary of Korolenko (writer).
1807 **545** 40k. brown . . . . . . 1·10 25

1953. 125th Birth Anniv of Leo Tolstoi (writer).
1808 **546** 1r. brown . . . . 6·50 3·25

547 Lomonosov University and Students

548 Peoples of the U.S.S.R.

1953. 35th Anniv of "Komsomol" (Russian Youth Organization). Multicoloured.
1809 40k. Type **547** . . . . . . 2·25 1·40
1810 1r. Four medals and "Komsomol" badge . . . 4·50 2·75

1953. 36th Anniv of Russian Revolution. Mult.
1811 40k. Type **548** . . . . . . 7·25 5·50
1812 60k. Lenin and Stalin in Smolny Institute, 1917 . . 12·50 9·50

549 Lenin Medallion

550 Lenin Statue

551 Peter I Monument

1953. 50th Anniv of Communist Party.
1813 **549** 40k. multicoloured . . . 3·50 2·75

1953. Views of Leningrad as T **550/1**.
1814 **550** 40k. black on yellow . . 2·00 1·00
1815 40k. brown on pink . . 2·00 1·00
1816 – 40k. brown on yellow . . 1·25 45
1817 – 40k. black on buff . . . 1·75 85
1818 **551** 1r. brown on blue . . . 3·00 1·10
1819 1r. violet on yellow . . 3·00 1·40
1820 – 1r. green on pink . . . 3·00 2·25
1821 – 1r. brown on blue . . . 3·50 2·40
DESIGNS: As Type **550**: Nos. 1816/17, Admiralty. As Type **551**: 1820/1, Smolny Institute.

552 Lenin and Book "What is to be Done?"

553 Pioneers and Moscow University Model

1953. 50th Anniv of 2nd Social Democratic Workers' Party Congress.
1822 **552** 1r. brown and red . . . 7·75 6·50

1953. Peace Propaganda.
1823 **553** 40k. black, olive and grey . . . . 3·75 2·75

554 Griboedov (after I. Kramskoi)

555 Kremlin

1954. 125th Death Anniv of A. S. Griboedov (author).
1824 **554** 40k. purple on buff . . 1·60 50
1825a 1r. black on green . . . 2·25 1·00

1954. General Election.
1826 **555** 40k. grey and red . . . 2·75 2·00

556 V. P. Chkalov

557 "Lenin in Smolny Institute" (after I. Brodsky)

1954. 50th Birthday of Chkalov (aviator).
1827 **556** 1r. multicoloured . . . . 4·00 1·60

1954. 30th Death Anniv of Lenin. Multicoloured.
1828 40k. Lenin (after M. Rundaltsov) (26 × 38 mm) . . . . . 2·50 1·40
1829 40k. Type **557** . . . . . . 2·50 1·40
1830 40k. Cottage Museum, Ulyanovsk (after I. Sokolov) . . . . . . 2·50 1·40
1831 40k. "Lenin proclaims Soviet Regime" (V. Serov) (48 × 35 mm) . . . . . . 2·50 1·40
1832 40k. "Lenin at Kazan University" (A. Pushnin) (48 × 35 mm) . . . . . . 2·50 1·40

558 Stalin

559 Supreme Soviet Buildings in Kiev and Moscow

1954. 1st Death Anniv of Stalin.
1833 **558** 40k. brown . . . . . . 3·50 2·25

1954. Tercentenary of Reunion of Ukraine with Russia. Multicoloured. (a) Designs as T **559** inscr "1654–1954".
1834 40k. Type **559** . . . . . . 1·10 40
1835 40k. Shevchenko Memorial, Kharkhov (vert) . . . . 1·10 25
1836 40k. State Opera House, Kiev . . . . 1·10 25
1837 40k. Shevchenko University, Kiev . . . . 1·10 25
1838 40k. Academy of Sciences, Kiev . . . . 1·50 25
1839 60k. Bogdan Chmielnitsky Memorial, Kiev (vert) . . 1·60 25
1840 1r. Flags of R.S.F.S.R. and Ukrainian S.S.R. (vert) 3·50 55
1841 1r. Shevchenko Monument, Kanev (vert) . . . . . . 2·50 35
1842 1r. Pereyaslavskaya Rada 3·50 45

(b) No. 1098b optd with five lines of Cyrillic characters as inscr at top of T **559**.
1843 h 2r. green . . . . 7·50 1·75

561 Running

1954. Sports. Frames in brown.
1844 **561** 40k. black and stone . . 1·00 20
1845 – 40k. black and blue . . 1·25 20
1846 – 40k. brown and buff . . 1·00 20
1847 – 40k. black and blue . . 1·00 20
1848 – 40k. black . . . . . . 1·00 20
1849 – 1r. grey and blue . . . . 5·00 1·50
1850 – 1r. black and blue . . . 5·00 1·50
1851 – 1r. brown and drab . . 5·00 1·50
DESIGNS—HORIZ: No. 1845, "Soling" yachts; 1846, Cycling; 1847, Swimming; 1848, Hurdling; 1849, Mountaineering; 1850, Skiing. VERT: No. 1851, Basketball.

562 Cattle

563 A. P. Chekhov

1954. Agriculture.
1852 **562** 40k. blue, brown & cream . . . . 2·40 50
1853 – 40k. green, brown & buff 2·40 50
1854 – 40k. black, blue and green . . . . 2·40 50
DESIGNS: No. 1853, Potato cultivation; 1854, Collective farm hydro-electric station.

1954. 50th Death Anniv of Chekhov (writer).
1855 **563** 40k. brown and green . . 1·10 40

564 Bredikhin, Struve, Belopolsky and Observatory

565 M. I. Glinka

1954. Rebuilding of Pulkov Observatory.
1856 **564** 40k. black, blue and violet . . . . 8·00 1·60

1954. 150th Birth Anniv of Glinka (composer).
1857 **565** 40k. brown, pink and red . . . . 2·25 35
1858 – 60k. multicoloured . . . 3·25 65
DESIGN—HORIZ: (38 × 23½ mm). 60k. "Glinka playing piano for Pushkin and Zhukovsky" (V. Artamonov).

566 Exhibition Emblem

567 N. A. Ostrovsky

1954. Agricultural Exhibition. Multicoloured.
1859 40k. Type **566** 85 35
1860 40k. Agricultural Pavilion 85 35
1861 40k. Cattle breeding Pavilion 85 35
1862 40k. Mechanization Pavilion 85 35
1863 1r. Exhibition Entrance . . 3·00 1·40
1864 1r. Main Pavilion . . . . . 3·00 1·40
Nos. 1860/3 are horiz, 1860/1 being 41 × 30½ mm, 1862, 40 × 30 mm and 1863 41 × 33 mm. No. 1864 is vert, 29 × 41 mm.

1954. 50th Birth Anniv of Ostrovsky (writer).
1865 **567** 40k. multicoloured . . . 1·75 45

568 Monument

569 Marx, Engels, Lenin and Stalin

1954. Centenary of Defence of Sevastopol.
1866 **568** 40k. black, brown & grn 1·40 40
1867 – 60k. black, brown & buff 1·60 60
1868 – 1r. multicoloured . . . . 3·50 1·00
DESIGNS—HORIZ: 60k. Heroes of Sevastopol (after V. Timm). VERT: 1r. Admiral Nakhimov (after V. Timm).

1954. 37th Anniv of October Revolution.
1869 **569** 1r. brown, red and orange . . . . 5·50 3·50

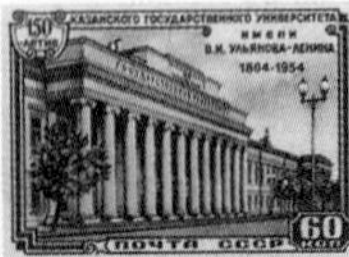
570 Kazan University

1954. 150th Anniv of Kazan University.
1870 **570** 40k. blue on blue . . . 1·00 45
1871 60k. red . . . . 1·75 55

571 Salomea Neris

1954. 50th Birth Anniv of Salomea Neris (poetess).
1872 **571** 40k. multicoloured . . . 1·25 35

572 Cultivating Vegetables

573 Stalin

1954. Agriculture. Multicoloured.
1873 40k. Type **572** . . . . . . 1·50 30
1874 40k. Tractor and plough . . 1·50 30
1875 40k. Harvesting flax (49 × 25½ mm) . . . . . 1·50 30
1876 60k. Harvesting sunflowers (49 × 25½ mm) . . . . . 3·00 65

1954. 75th Birth Anniv of Stalin.
1877 **573** 40k. purple . . . . . . 1·50 50
1878 1r. blue . . . . 3·50 1·40

574 Rubinstein (after I. Repin)

1954. 125th Birth Anniv of Rubinstein (composer).
1879 **574** 40k. black and purple . . 2·00 40

575 V. M. Garshin

576 Ilyushin Il-12 over Landscape

1955. Birth Centenary of Garshin (writer).
1880 **575** 40k. black, brown & grn 1·10 35

1955. Air.
1881 – 1r. multicoloured . . . . 1·75 40
1882 **576** 2r. black and green . . . 3·75 60
DESIGN: 1r. Ilyushin Il-12 over coastline.

577 Savitsky (after N. Frandkovsky) and "Construction of Railway"

1955. 50th Death Anniv of Savitsky (painter).
1883 **577** 40k. brown . . . . . . 1·75 30

578 Clasped Hands

579 Pushkin and Mickiewicz

1955. International Conference of Postal and Municipal Workers, Vienna.
1884 **578** 50k. multicoloured . . . 1·10 30

1955. 10th Anniv of Russo–Polish Friendship Agreement.
1885 **579** 40k. multicoloured . . . 2·25 30
1886 – 40k. black . . . . 2·25 30
1887 – 1r. multicoloured . . . . 4·00 85
1888 – 1r. multicoloured . . . . 6·00 1·25
DESIGNS: No. 1886, "Brotherhood in Arms" Monument, Warsaw (26½ × 39 mm); No. 1887, Palace of Science, Warsaw (37½ × 25½ mm); No. 1888, Copernicus and Matejko (39 × 26½ mm).

580 Lenin at Shushenskoe (after V. Basov)

1955. 85th Birth Anniv of Lenin. Multicoloured centres.
1889 **580** 60k. red . . . . 2·00 30
1890 – 1r. red . . . . 4·00 60
1891 – 1r. red . . . . 4·00 60
DESIGNS: No. 1890, Lenin in secret printing house (after F. Golubkov) (26½ × 39 mm). As Type **580**: No. 1891, Lenin and Krupskaya at Gorky (after N. Sysoev).

581 Schiller

582 Ilyushin Il-12 over Globe

1955. 150th Death Anniv of Schiller (poet).
1892 **581** 40k. brown . . . . . . 1·50 65

1955. Air.
1893 **582** 2r. brown . . . . 6·75 1·25
1894 2r. blue . . . . 3·50 55

583 V. Mayakovsky

1955. 25th Death Anniv of Mayakovsky (poet).
1895 **583** 40k. multicoloured . . . 1·10 30

584 Tadzhik S.S.R. Pavilion

1955. Agricultural Exhibition. Soviet Pavilion. Multicoloured designs with green frames.
1896 40k. R.S.F.S.R. 80 25
1897 40k. Byelorussian S.S.R. . . 80 25
1898 40k. Type **584** 80 25
1899 40k. Azerbaijan S.S.R. . . . 80 25
1900 40k. Latvian S.S.R. 80 25
1901 40k. Lithuanian S.S.R. . . . 80 25
1902 40k. Karelo-Finnish S.S.R. 80 25
1903 40k. Estonian S.S.R. 80 25
1904 40k. Armenian S.S.R. . . . 80 25
1905 40k. Ukrainian S.S.R. . . . 80 25
1906 40k. Georgian S.S.R. . . . 80 25
1907 40k. Kazakh S.S.R. 80 25
1908 40k. Turkmen S.S.R. . . . 80 25
1909 40k. Kirgiz S.S.R. 80 25
1910 40k. Uzbek S.S.R. 80 25
1911 40k. Moldavian S.S.R. . . . 80 25

585 M. V. Lomonosov and University

1955. Bicentenary of Lomonosov University. Multicoloured.
1912 40k. Type **585** . . . . . . 1·10 30
1913 1r. Lomonosov University 1·90 55

586 A. G. Venetsianov (self-portrait) and "The Labours of Spring"

1955. 175th Birth Anniv of Venetsianov (painter). Multicoloured centre.
1914 **586** 1r. black . . . . 2·75 55

587 A. Lyadov

1955. Birth Centenary of Lyadov (composer).
1915 **587** 40k. multicoloured . . . 1·60 55

588 A. S. Popov

589 Lenin

590 "Capture of Winter Palace" (detail, P. Sokolov-Skalya)

1955. 60th Anniv of Popov's Radio Discoveries. Multicoloured centres.
1916 **588** 40k. blue . . . . 1·50 20
1917 1r. brown . . . . 2·75 50

1955. 38th Anniv of Russian Revolution.
1918 **589** 40k. multicoloured . . . 2·25 1·10
1919 **590** 40k. multicoloured . . . 2·25 1·10
1920 – 1r. multicoloured . . . . 5·00 2·25
DESIGN: As T **590**: 1r. Lenin speaking to revolutionaries (after D. Nalbandyan).

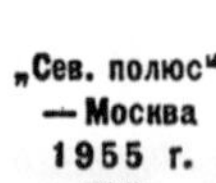

(591)

592 Magnitogorsk

1955. Air. Opening of North Pole Scientific Stations. Nos. 1881/2 optd with T **591**.
1921 – 1r. multicoloured . . . . 9·00 6·00
1922 **576** 2r. black and green . . . 13·50 6·50

1955. 25th Anniv of Magnitogorsk.
1923 **592** 40k. multicoloured . . . 1·60 35

593 Mil Mi-4 Helicopter over Station

594 Shubin (self-portrait)

1955. North Pole Scientific Stations.
1924 **593** 40k. multicoloured . . . 3·25 30
1925 60k. multicoloured . . . 3·50 65
1926 – 1r. multicoloured . . . . 5·50 1·00
DESIGN: 1r. Meteorologist taking observations.

1955. 150th Death Anniv of Shubin (sculptor).
1927 **594** 40k. multicoloured . . . 90 20
1928 1r. multicoloured . . . . 1·50 40

595 A. N. Krylov

596 Racing

1956. 10th Death Anniv of Krylov (scientist).
1929 **595** 40k. multicoloured . . . 1·10 20

1956. International Horse Racing.
1930 **596** 40k. sepia and brown . . 1·25 25
1931 60k. blue and green . . 1·50 30
1932 – 1r. purple and blue . . . 2·75 55
DESIGN—HORIZ: 1r. Trotting.

597 Badge and Stadium

1956. 5th Spartacist Games.
1933 **597** 1r. purple and green . . 1·75 45

598 Atomic Power Station

1956. Foundation of Atomic Power Station of Russian Academy of Sciences.
1934 **598** 25k. multicoloured . . . 85 20
1935 – 60k. yellow, turq & brn 2·00 35
1936 **598** 1r. yellow, red and blue 2·75 70
DESIGN: 60k. Top of atomic reactor.

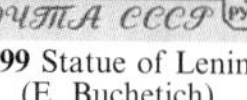

599 Statue of Lenin (E. Buchetich)

600 Kh. Abovyan

1956. 20th Communist Party Congress.
1937 **599** 40k. multicoloured . . . 90 35
1938 1r. multicoloured . . . . 1·75 55

1956. 150th Birth Anniv of Khatchatur Abovyan (Armenian writer).
1939 **600** 40k. black on blue . . . 1·10 20

601 Revolutionaries (after N. Tereshchenko)

602

1956. 50th Anniv of 1905 Revolution.
1940 **601** 40k. multicoloured . . . 4·25 1·60

ПАВИЛЬОН «УРАЛ»
No. 1941

ПАВИЛЬОН СЕВЕРО-ВОСТОЧНЫХ ОБЛАСТЕЙ
No. 1942

ПАВИЛЬОН ЦЕНТРАЛЬНЫХ ЧЕРНОЗЕМНЫХ ОБЛАСТЕЙ
No. 1943

ПАВИЛЬОН «ЛЕНИНГРАД-СЕВЕРО-ЗАПАД»
No. 1944

ПАВИЛЬОН МОСКОВСКОЙ, ТУЛЬСКОЙ, КАЛУЖСКОЙ, РЯЗАНСКОЙ И БРЯНСКОЙ ОБЛАСТЕЙ
No. 1945

ПАВИЛЬОН БАШКИРСКОЙ АССР
No. 1946

ПАВИЛЬОН ДАЛЬНЕГО ВОСТОКА
No. 1947

ПАВИЛЬОН ТАТАРСКОЙ АССР
No. 1948

ПАВИЛЬОН ЦЕНТРАЛЬНЫХ ОБЛАСТЕЙ
No. 1949

ПАВИЛЬОН ЮНЫХ НАТУРАЛИСТОВ
No. 1950

ПАВИЛЬОН СЕВЕРНОГО КАВКАЗА
No. 1951

ПАВИЛЬОН «СИБИРЬ»
No. 1952

ПАВИЛЬОН «ПОВОЛЖЬЕ»
No. 1953

Inscr at foot as shown above.

1956. Agricultural Exhibition. Multicoloured. Views of Pavilions of U.S.S.R. regions as T **602**. Inscr "BCXB".
1941 1r. Ural . . . . 1·50 40
1942 1r. North East . . . . . . 1·50 40
1943 1r. Central Black Soil Region . . . . 1·50 40
1944 1r. Leningrad . . . . 1·50 40
1945 1r. Moscow-Tula-Kaluga-Ryazan-Bryansk . . . . 1·50 40
1946 1r. Bashkir . . . . 1·50 40
1947 1r. Far East . . . . 1·50 40
1948 1r. Tatar . . . . 1·50 40
1949 1r. Central Regions . . . . 1·50 40
1950 1r. Young Naturalists . . . 1·50 40
1951 1r. North Caucasus . . . . 1·50 40
1952 1r. Siberia . . . . 1·50 40
1953 1r. Volga . . . . 1·50 40

603 N. A. Kasatkin (painter)

1956. Kasatkin Commemoration.
1954 **603** 40k. red 85 25

604 A. E. Arkhipov and Painting "On the Oka River"

1956. Arkhipov Commemoration.
1955 **604** 40k. multicoloured . . . 1·50 20
1956 1r. multicoloured . . . . 2·75 45

605 I. P. Kulibin

1956. 220th Birth Anniv of Kulibin (inventor).
1957 **605** 40k. multicoloured . . . 1·25 35

606 "Fowler" (after Perov)

1956. Perov Commemoration. Inscr "1956". Multicoloured centres.
1958 – 40k. green . . . . 1·75 25
1959 **606** 1r. brown . . . . 3·50 70
1960 – 1r. brown . . . . 3·50 70
DESIGNS—VERT: No. 1958, Self-portrait. HORIZ: No. 1960, "Hunters Resting".

607 Lenin (after P. Vasilev)

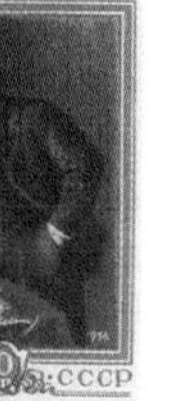

608 N. I. Lobachevsky (after L. Kryukov)

1956. 86th Birth Anniv of Lenin.
1961 **607** 40k. multicoloured . . . 9·25 5·25

1956. Death Cent of Lobachevsky (mathematician).
1962 **608** 40k. brown 80 15

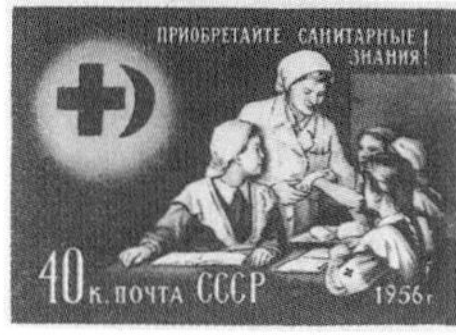

609 Student Nurses

1956. Red Cross.
1963 **609** 40k. red, blue and brown 1·00 30
1964 – 40k. red, olive & turquoise . . . . . . 1·00 30
DESIGN—37½ × 25½ mm: No. 1964, Nurse and textile factory.

610 Scientific Station

1956. Air. Opening of North Pole Scientific Station No. 6.
1965 **610** 1r. multicoloured . . . . 4·25 1·40

611 Sechenov (after I. Repin)

1956. 50th Death Anniv (1995) of I. Sechenov (naturalist).
1966 **611** 40k. multicoloured . . . 1·60 35

612 Arsenev

1956. V. K. Arsenev (writer).
1967 **612** 40k. black, violet & pink 2·00 70

613 I. V. Michurin

1956. Birth Centenary of Michurin (naturalist). Multicoloured centres.
1968 **613** 25k. brown 45 15
1969 – 60k. green . . . . 1·10 25
1970 **613** 1r. blue . . . . 2·00 45
DESIGN—47½ × 26½ mm: 60k. Michurin and children.

614 Savrasov (after V. Perov)

615 N. K. Krupskaya (Lenin's wife)

1956. 125th Birth Anniv (1955) of A. K. Savrasov (painter).
1971 **614** 1r. brown and yellow . . 1·50 60

1956. Krupskaya Commemoration.
1972 **615** 40k. brown, black & blue . . . . 1·50 30

616 S. M. Kirov

617 A. A. Blok

1956. 70th Birth Anniv of Kirov (statesman).
1973 **616** 40k. multicoloured . . . 65 15

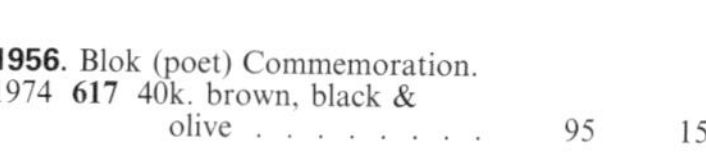

1956. Blok (poet) Commemoration.
1974 **617** 40k. brown, black & olive 95 15

618 N. S. Leskov

1956. 125th Birth Anniv of Leskov (writer).
1975 **618** 40k. multicoloured . . . 65 15
1976 1r. multicoloured . . . . 1·75 40

619 Factory Building

1956. 25th Anniv of Rostov Agricultural Machinery Works.
1977 **619** 40k. multicoloured . . . 90 25

620 G. N. Fedotova (actress)

1956. Fedotova Commemoration.
1978 **620** 40k. multicoloured . . . 80 25
For similar stamp see No. 2159.

621 P. M. Tretyakov (after I. Repin) and Art Gallery

1956. Centenary of Tretyakov Art Gallery, Moscow.
1979 **621** 40k. multicoloured . . . 2·25 60
1980 – 40k. multicoloured . . . 1·50 50
DESIGN—VERT: No. 1980, "Rooks have arrived" (painting by Savrasov).

622 Relay-race

1956. Spartacist Games.
1981 **622** 10k. red 30 10
1982 – 25k. brown 40 15
1983 – 25k. multicoloured . . . 40 15
1984 – 25k. blue 40 15
1985 – 40k. blue 65 15
1986 – 40k. green 65 15
1987 – 40k. brown and green . . 65 15
1988 – 40k. deep brown, brown and green 65 15
1989 – 40k. red, green and light green 65 15
1990 – 40k. brown 65 15
1991 – 40k. multicoloured . . . 65 15
1992 – 60k. violet . . . . . . 1·75 25
1993 – 60k. violet . . . . . . 1·75 25
1994 – 1r. brown . . . . 3·25 55
DESIGNS—VERT: No. 1982, Volleyball; 1983, Swimming; 1984, Rowing; 1985, Diving; 1989, Flag and stadium; 1990, Tennis; 1991, Medal; 1993, Boxing. HORIZ: No. 1986, Cycle racing; 1987, Fencing; 1988, Football; 1992, Gymnastics; 1994, Netball.

623 Parachutist Landing **624** Construction Work

1956. 3rd World Parachute-jumping Competition.
1995 **623** 40k. multicoloured . . . 1·00 25

1956. Builders' Day.
1996a **624** 40k. orange 65 25
1997 – 60k. brown 80 30
1998 – 1r. blue . . . . 2·50 50
DESIGNS: 60k. Plant construction; 1r. Dam construction.

625 Self-portrait and "Volga River Boatmen"

626 "Reply of the Cossacks to Sultan Mahmoud IV"

1956. 26th Death Anniv of I. E. Repin (artist).
1999 **625** 40k. multicoloured . . . 3·75 60
2000 **626** 1r. multicoloured . . . . 7·25 1·00

627 Robert Burns **628** Ivan Franko

1956. 160th Death Anniv of Burns (Scots poet).
2001 **627** 40k. brown . . . . . . 7·50 5·25
2002 40k. brown and blue . . 5·25 3·25

1956. Birth Cent of Franko (writer) (1st issue).
2003 **628** 40k. purple 85 40
2004 1r. blue . . . . 1·40 50
See also No. 2037.

1956. Lesya Ukrainka Commemoration. As T **615** but portrait of Ukrainka (author).
2005 40k. black, brown and green 85 50

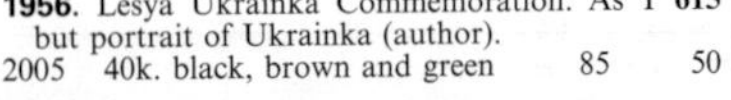

629 M. Aivazov (farmer) **630** Statue of Nestor (M. Antokol)

1956. 148th Birthday of Aivazov. (a) Wrongly inscr "Muhamed" (7 characters).
2006 **629** 40k. green . . . . 23·00 21·00

(b) Corrected to "Makmud" (6 characters).
2006a **629** 40k. green . . . . . . 11·50 8·25

1956. 900th Birth Anniv of Nestor (historian).
2007 **630** 40k. multicoloured . . . 1·10 30
2008 1r. multicoloured . . . . 2·10 50

631 Ivanov (after S. Postnikov)

1956. 150th Birth Anniv of A. A. Ivanov (painter).
2009 **631** 40k. brown and grey . . 85 25

632 Feeding Poultry

1956. Agriculture. Multicoloured.
2010 10k. Type **632** 35 10
2011 10k. Harvesting 35 10
2012 25k. Gathering maize . . . 65 20
2013 40k. Maize field . . . . . . 1·25 20
2014 40k. Tractor station . . . . 1·25 20
2015 40k. Cattle grazing . . . . 1·25 20
2016 40k. "Agriculture and Industry" . . . . 1·25 20
SIZES: Nos. 2010, 2014/15, 37 × 25½ mm. Nos. 2011/13, 37 × 28 mm. No. 2016, 37 × 21 mm.

633 Mozart **634** Mirnyi Base and Supply Ship "Lena"

1956. Cultural Anniversaries.
2017 40k. blue (Type **633**) . . . . 3·50 60
2018 40k. green (Curie) . . . . . 3·50 60
2019 40k. lilac (Heine) . . . . . 1·50 40
2020 40k. brown (Ibsen) . . . . 1·50 40
2021 40k. green (Dostoevsky) . . 1·50 40
2022 40k. brown (Franklin) . . . 1·50 40
2023 40k. black (Shaw) . . . . . 3·00 60
2024 40k. orange (Sessku-Toyo Oda) . . . . 1·50 40
2025 40k. black (Rembrandt) . . 1·50 40
Nos. 2022/5 are larger, 25 × 38 mm.

1956. Soviet Scientific Antarctic Expedition.
2026 **634** 40k. turquoise, red & grey . . . . 5·50 80

1956. Julia Zhemaite Commemoration. As T **615** but portrait of Zhemaite (author).
2027 40k. green, brown and sepia 1·00 35

635 F. A. Bredikhin **636** G. I. Kotovsky

1956. 125th Birth Anniv of Bredikhin (astronomer).
2028 **635** 40k. multicoloured . . . 5·00 1·25

1956. 75th Birth Anniv of Kotovsky (military leader).
2029a **636** 40k. mauve . . . . . . 1·60 65

637 Shatura Electric Power Station **638** Marshal Suvorov (after Utkin)

1956. 30th Anniv of Shatura Electric Power Station.
2030 **637** 40k. multicoloured . . . 90 35

1956. 225th Birth Anniv of Marshal Suvorov.
2031 **638** 40k. lake and orange . . 85 35
2032 1r. brown and olive . . 1·60 50
2033 3r. black and brown . . 4·25 1·10

639 Kryakutni's Ascent (after G. Savitsky)

1956. 225th Anniv of First Balloon Flight by Kryakutni.
2034 **639** 40k. multicoloured . . . 2·00 55

640 Vasnetsov (after S. Malyutin) and "Dawn at the Voskresenski Gate"

1956. 30th Death Anniv of A. M. Vasnetsov (artist).
2035 **640** 40k. multicoloured . . . 1·60 55

641 Y. M. Shokalsky (oceanographer) **642** Franko (after I. Trush)

1956. Birth Cent of Shokalsky.
2036 **641** 40k. brown and blue . . 2·25 50

1956. Birth Centenary of Franko (writer) (2nd issue).
2037 **642** 40k. green 75 25

643 Indian Temple and Books **644** F. G. Vokov (actor) (after A. Losenko) and State Theatre

1956. Kalidasa (Indian poet) Commemoration.
2038 **643** 40k. red 75 25

1956. Bicentenary of Leningrad State Theatre.
2039 **644** 40k. black, red and yellow 60 20

645 Lomonosov (after L. Miropolsky) at St. Petersburg University

1956. Russian Writers.
2040 **645** 40k. multicoloured . . . 1·00 25
2041 – 40k. multicoloured . . . 1·00 25
2042 – 40k. brown and blue . . 1·00 25
2043 – 40k. olive, brown & black . . . . 1·00 25
2044 – 40k. brown and turquoise . . . . 1·00 25
2045 – 40k. purple and brown . . 1·00 25
2046 – 40k. olive and blue . . . 1·00 25
DESIGNS: No. 2041, Gorky (after V. Efanov) and scene from "Mother" (novel); 2042, Pushkin and statue of Peter the Great, Leningrad (illustrating poem "Bronze Horseman"); 2043, Rustavely and episode from "The Knight in the Tiger Skin" (poem); 2044, Tolstoy and scene from "War and Peace" (novel); 2045, V. G. Belinsky and titles of literary works; 2046, M. Y. Lermontov and Daryal Pass.
See also Nos. 2076, 2089/90, 2256, 2316/22 and 2458.

646 Vitus Bering and Routes of his Voyages **647** Mendeleev

1956. 275th Birth Anniv of Bering (explorer).
2047 **646** 40k. multicoloured . . . 3·00 50

1957. 50th Death Anniv of Dmitri Mendeleev (chemist).
2048 **647** 40k. brown, grey & black . . . . 2·25 65

648 M. I. Glinka **649** Youth Festival Emblem

1957. Death Centenary of Glinka (composer). Mult.
2049a 40k. Type **648** . . . . . . 1·40 25
2050a 1r. Scene from "Ivan Susanin" . . . . 2·50 55

1957. All Union Festival of Soviet Youth.
2051 **649** 40k. multicoloured . . . 50 20

650 Ice Hockey Player **651** Youth Festival Emblem and Pigeon

1957. 23rd World and 35th European Ice Hockey Championships, Moscow.
2052a – 25k. violet 75 15
2053a **650** 40k. blue 90 15
2054a – 60k. green . . . . . . 1·00 30
DESIGNS: 25k. Championship emblem; 60k. Goalkeeper.

1957. 6th World Youth Festival, Moscow (1st issue). Perf or imperf.
2055 **651** 40k. multicoloured . . . 85 15
2056 60k. multicoloured . . . 1·40 30
See also Nos. 2084/7 and 2108/11.

652 Factory Plant **653** Sika Deer

1957. Cent of "Red Proletariat" Plant. Moscow.
2057 **652** 40k. multicoloured . . . 1·00 30

1957. Russian Wildlife. Multicoloured.
2057a 10k. Grey partridge . . . 80 25
2058 15k. Black grouse . . . . 1·00 10
2058a 15k. Polar bear 70 15
2059 20k. Type **653** 75 15
2059a 20k. Brown hare 60 25
2059b 25k. Tiger 75 25
2059c 25k. Wild horse 75 25
2060 30k. Mallard . . . . . . 1·25 25
2061 30k. European bison . . . 75 20
2062 40k. Elk . . . . 1·90 35
2063 40k. Sable . . . . 1·90 35
2063a 40k. Eurasian red squirrel 80 30
2063b 40k. Yellow-throated marten 80 30
2063c 60k. Hazel grouse . . . . 2·00 90
2063d 1r. Mute swan . . . . . 2·50 1·75
Nos. 2058/a, 2059a/62, 2063a/b and 2063d are horiz.
See also Nos. 2534/6.

654 Vologda Lace-making **655** G. V. Plekhanov

1957. Regional Handicrafts. Multicoloured.
2064 40k. Moscow wood-carving 1·75 40
2065 40k. Woman engraving vase . . . . 1·75 40
2066 40k. Type **654** . . . . . 1·75 40
2067 40k. Northern bone-carving . . . . 1·75 40
2067a 40k. Wood-block engraving 1·25 45
2067b 40k. Turkmen carpet-weaving . . . . 1·25 45

1957. Birth Centenary of Plekhanov (politician).
2068 **655** 40k. plum . . . . 1·00 35

656 A. N. Bakh **657** L. Euler

1957. Birth Centenary of Bakh (biochemist).
2069a **656** 40k. multicoloured . . 1·10 25

1957. 250th Birth Anniv of Euler (mathematician).
2070a **657** 40k. black and purple 1·50 35

658 Lenin in Meditation **659** Dr. William Harvey

1957. 87th Birth Anniv of Lenin. Multicoloured.
2071 40k. Type **658** . . . . . . 1·00 20
2072 40k. Lenin carrying pole . . 1·00 20
2073 40k. Talking with soldier and sailor . . . . 1·00 20

1957. 300th Death Anniv of Dr. William Harvey (discoverer of circulation of blood).
2074 **659** 40k. brown 75 15

660 M. A. Balakirev **661** 12th-century Narrator

1957. 120th Birth Anniv of Balakirev (composer).
2075 **660** 40k. black . . . . 1·25 20

1957. "The Tale of the Host of Igor".
2076 **661** 40k. multicoloured . . . 80 20

662 Agricultural Medal **663** A. I. Herzen (after N. Ge) and N. P. Ogarev (after M. Lemmel) (founders)

1957. Cultivation of Virgin Soil.
2077 **662** 40k. multicoloured . . . 1·10 30

1957. Centenary of Publication of Magazine "Kolokol".
2078 **663** 40k. brown, black & blue . . . . 1·00 30

664 Monument

250 лет
Ленинграда
(**665**)

1957. 250th Anniv of Leningrad. Vert designs as T **664** and stamps as Nos. 1818 and 1820 optd as T **665**.
2079 **664** 40k. green 50 15
2080 – 40k. violet 50 15
2081 – 40k. brown 65 15
2082 **551** 1r. brown on green . . . 1·40 25
2083 – 1r. green on salmon . . 1·40 25
DESIGNS: No. 2080, Nevsky Prospect, Leningrad; No. 2081, Lenin Statue.

666 Youths with Banner

1957. 6th World Youth Festival, Moscow (2nd issue). Multicoloured. Perf or imperf.
2084 10k. Type **666** 30 10
2084c 20k. Sculptor with statue 50 15
2085 25k. Type **666** 80 25
2086 40k. Dancers 85 25
2087 1r. Festival emblem and fireworks over Moscow State University . . . . 1·10 50

667 A. M. Lyapunov **668** T. G. Shevchenko (after I. Repin) and Scene from "Katharina"

1957. Birth Centenary of Lyapunov (mathematician).
2088 **667** 40k. brown . . . . . . 5·50 2·75

1957. 19th-Century Writers. Multicoloured.
2089 40k. Type **668** 85 20
2090 40k. N. G. Chernyshevsky and scene from "What is to be Done?" 85 20

669 Henry Fielding **670** Racing Cyclists

1957. 250th Birth Anniv of Fielding (novelist).
2091 **669** 40k. multicoloured . . . 50 20

1957. 10th International Cycle Race.
2092 **670** 40k. multicoloured . . . 1·25 25

671 Interior of Observatory

1957. International Geophysical Year (1st issue).
2093 **671** 40k. brown, yellow and blue . . . . 1·75 45
2094 – 40k. indigo, yellow and blue . . . . 2·50 45
2095 – 40k. violet and lavender 2·25 45
2095a – 40k. blue . . . . . . 2·25 30
2095b – 40k. green . . . . . . 2·50 40
2095c – 40k. yellow and blue 2·25 30
DESIGNS—As T **671**: No. 2094, Meteor in sky; 2095a, Malakhit radar scanner and balloon (meteorology); 2095b, "Zarya" (non-magnetic research schooner) (geo-magnetism); 2095c, Northern Lights and C-180 camera. 15 × 21 mm: No. 2095, Rocket.
See also Nos. 2371/3a.

672 Gymnast

1957. 3rd International Youth Games.
2096 **672** 20k. brown and blue . . 30 15
2097 – 25k. red and green . . 35 15
2098 – 40k. violet and red . . . 70 30
2099 – 40k. olive, red and green 70 30
2100 – 60k. brown and blue . . 1·60 50
DESIGNS—As Type **672**: No. 2097, Wrestlers; 2098, Young athletes; 2099, Moscow Stadium; 2100, Throwing the javelin.

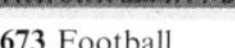

673 Football **674** Yanka Kupala

1957. Russian Successes at Olympic Games, Melbourne.
2101 – 20k. brown, blue & black 35 15
2102 – 20k. red and green . . . 35 15
2103 – 25k. blue and orange . . 40 20
2104 **673** 40k. multicoloured . . . 75 20
2105 – 40k. brown and purple 75 20
2106 – 60k. brown and violet 1·00 50
DESIGNS—VERT: No. 2101, Throwing the javelin; 2102, Running; 2103, Gymnastics; 2105, Boxing; 2106, Weightlifting.

1957. 75th Birth Anniv of Kupala (poet).
2107 **674** 40k. brown . . . . . . 4·00 1·75

675 Moscow State University

1957. 6th World Youth Festival (3rd issue). Moscow Views.
2108 – 40k. black and brown . . 55 15
2109 – 40k. black and purple . . 55 15
2110 – 1r. black and blue . . . 1·25 30
2111 **675** 1r. black and red . . . . 1·25 30
DESIGNS—HORIZ: No. 2108, Kremlin; 2109, Stadium; 2110, Bolshoi State Theatre.

676 Lenin Library

1957. Int Philatelic Exn, Moscow. Perf or imperf.
2112 **676** 40k. turquoise 75 20

677 Dove of Peace encircling Globe **678** P. Beranger

1957. "Defence of Peace".
2113 **677** 40k. multicoloured . . . 1·10 40
2114 1r. multicoloured . . . . 2·25 95

1957. Birth Centenary of Clara Zetkin (German revolutionary). As T **615** but portrait of Zetkin.
2115 40k. multicoloured . . . . 1·10 35

1957. Death Centenary of Beranger (French poet).
2116 **678** 40k. green . . . . 1·10 30

679 Krengholm Factory, Narva **680** Factory Plant and Statue of Lenin (M. Kharlamov)

1957. Centenary of Krengholm Textile Factory, Narva, Estonia.
2117 **679** 40k. brown . . . . 1·10 30

1957. Centenary of Krasny Vyborzhetz Plant, Leningrad.
2118 **680** 40k. blue 50 25

681 Stasov (after I. Repin) **682** Pigeon with Letter

1957. 50th Death Anniv of Stasov (art critic).
2119 **681** 40k. brown 55 15
2120 1r. blue . . . . 1·40 20

1957. International Correspondence Week.
2121 **682** 40k. blue 35 20
2122 60k. purple 55 25

683 K. E. Tsiolkovsky

1957. Birth Centenary of Tsiolkovsky (scientist).
2123 **683** 40k. multicoloured . . . 4·00 70

684 Congress Emblem

1957. 4th World T.U.C., Leipzig.
2124 **684** 40k. blue on blue . . . 45 20

685 Students

686 Workers and Emblem (Ukraine)

1957. 40th Anniv of Russian Revolution. (a) 1st issue. As T **685**. Multicoloured. Perf or imperf.

2125		10k. Type **685**	20	10
2126		40k. Railway worker (horiz)	70	20
2127		40k. Portrait of Lenin on banner	45	10
2128		40k. Lenin and workers with banners	45	10
2129		60k. Harvester (horiz)	1·25	60

1957. 40th Anniv of Russian Revolution (2nd issue). Multicoloured.

2130		40k. Type **686**	65	30
2131		40k. Estonia	65	30
2132		40k. Uzbekistan	65	30
2133		40k. R.S.F.S.R. (horiz)	1·10	30
2134		40k. Belorussia (horiz)	65	30
2135		40k. Lithuania (horiz)	65	30
2136		40k. Armenia (horiz)	65	30
2137		40k. Azerbaijan (horiz)	65	30
2138		40k. Georgia (horiz)	65	30
2139		40k. Kirghizia (horiz)	65	30
2140		40k. Turkmenistan (horiz)	65	30
2141		40k. Tadzhikistan (horiz)	65	30
2142		40k. Kazakhstan (horiz)	65	30
2143		40k. Latvia (horiz)	65	30
2144		40k. Moldavia (horiz)	65	30

687 Lenin (after G. Goldstein)

688 Satellite encircling Globe

1957. 40th Anniv of Russian Revolution (3rd issue). As T **687**.

2145	**687**	40k. blue	1·50	65
2146	–	60k. red	2·25	95

DESIGN—HORIZ: 60k. Lenin at desk.

1957. Launching of 1st Artifical Satellite.

2147	**688**	40k. indigo on blue	3·25	85
2148		40k. blue	3·25	85

689 Meteor Falling

690 Kuibyshev Power Station Turbine

1957. Sikhote-Alin Meteor.

2149	**689**	40k. multicoloured	2·75	1·10

1957. All Union Industrial Exhibition (1st issue).

2150	**690**	40k. brown	75	20

See also Nos. 2168.

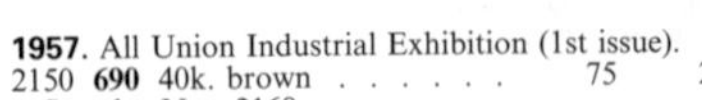
4/X-57 г. Первый в мире искусств. спутник Земли
(691)

692 Soviet War Memorial, Berlin (after Ye. Bunchetich)

1957. 1st Artificial Satellite of the World. Optd with T **691**.

2151	**683**	40k. multicoloured	35·00	22·00

1957. Bicentenary of Academy of Arts, Moscow.

2152	–	40k. black on salmon	40	10
2153	**692**	60k. black	80	15
2154	–	1r. black on pink	1·60	35

DESIGNS—$25\frac{1}{2}\times37\frac{1}{2}$ mm: 40k. Academy and portraits of K. Bryullov, I. Repin and V. Surikov (after I. Repin). $21\frac{1}{2}\times32$ mm: 1r. "Worker and Collective Farmer", Moscow (sculpture, Vera Mukhina).

693 Arms of Ukraine

694 Garibaldi

1957. 40th Anniv of Ukraine S.S.R.

2155	**693**	40k. multicoloured	85	15

1957. 150th Birth Anniv of Garibaldi.

2156	**694**	40k. purple, maroon and green	75	20

695 Edvard Grieg

696 Borovikovsky (after I. Bugaevsky-Blagodarny)

1957. 50th Death Anniv of Grieg (composer).

2157	**695**	40k. black on salmon	1·25	20

1957. Birth Bicent of Borovikovsky (painter).

2158	**696**	40k. brown	80	20

1967. M. N. Ermolova (actress) Commemoration. As T **620** but portrait of Ermolova.

2159		40k. brown and violet	1·00	40

698 Kolas

699 Mitskyavichyus-Kapsukas

700 G. Z. Bashindzhagian

1957. 75th Birth Anniv of Yakyb Kolas (poet).

2160	**698**	40k. black	2·40	1·50

1957. 22nd Death Anniv of V. S. Mitskyavichyus-Kapsukas (Communist Party leader).

2161	**699**	40k. brown	2·25	1·10

1957. Bashindzhagian (artist) Commemoration.

2162	**700**	40k. brown	2·25	1·10

701 Kuibyshev Hydro-electric Station

702 "To the Stars" (Ye. Buchetich)

1957. 40th Anniv of Kuibyshev Hydro-electric Station.

2163	**701**	40k. blue on flesh	1·10	25

1957. Launching of 2nd Artificial Satellite.

2164	**702**	20k. red and black	1·00	10
2165		40k. green and black	1·50	15
2166		60k. brown and black	2·00	25
2167		1r. blue and black	3·00	60

703 Allegory of Industry

704 Tsi Bai-shi

1958. All Union Industrial Exn (2nd issue).

2168	**703**	60k. red, black & lavender	1·00	30

1958. Rosa Luxemburg Commemoration. As T **615** but portrait of Luxemburg (German revolutionary).

2169		40k. brown and blue	1·00	35

1958. Tsi Bai-shi (Chinese artist) Commem.

2170	**704**	40k. violet	55	20

705 Linnaeus (Carl von Linne)

706 Tolstoi

1958. 250th Birth Anniv of Linnaeus.

2171	**705**	40k. brown	3·25	1·10

1958. 75th Birth Anniv of A. N. Tolstoi (writer).

2172	**706**	40k. bistre	65	20

707 Soldier, Sailor and Airman

708 E. Charents

1958. 40th Anniv of Red Army. Multicoloured.

2173		25k. Battle of Narva, 1918	40	15
2174		40k. Type **707**	60	20
2175		40k. Soldier and blast-furnaceman (vert)	60	20
2176		40k. Soldier and sailor (vert)	60	20
2177		60k. Storming the Reichstag, 1945	1·75	60

1958. Charents (Armenian poet) Commemoration.

2178	**708**	40k. brown	2·40	1·40

709 Henry W. Longfellow

710 Blake

1958. 150th Birth Anniv of Longfellow.

2179	**709**	40k. black	2·40	1·40

1958. Birth Bicentenary of William Blake (poet).

2180	**710**	40k. black	2·50	1·40

711 Tchaikovsky

712 Admiral Rudnev and Cruiser "Varyag"

1958. Tchaikovsky International Music Competition, Moscow.

2181	**711**	40k. multicoloured	1·25	30
2182	–	40k. multicoloured	1·25	30
2183a	–	1r. purple and green	3·50	75

DESIGNS—HORIZ: No. 2182, Scene from "Swan Lake" ballet. VERT: No. 2183, Pianist, violinist and inset portrait of Tchaikovsky.

1958. 45th Death Anniv of Admiral Rudnev.

2184	**712**	40k. multicoloured	1·90	45

713 Gorky (after I. Brodsky)

714 Congress Emblem and Spassky Tower, Kremlin

1958. 90th Death Anniv of Maksim Gorky (writer).

2185	**713**	40k. multicoloured	1·00	20

1958. 13th Young Communists' League Congress, Moscow.

2186	**714**	40k. violet on pink	65	15
2187		60k. red on flesh	1·00	25

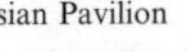
715 Russian Pavilion

716 J. A. Komensky ("Comenius")

1958. Brussels Int Exhibition. Perf or imperf.

2188	**715**	10k. multicoloured	20	10
2189		40k. multicoloured	65	15

1958. Komensky Commem.

2190	**716**	40k. green	3·25	1·10

717 Lenin

200 лет Академии художеств СССР. 1957
(718)

1958. Lenin Commemoration.

2191	**717**	40k. blue	60	10
2192		60k. red	85	15
2193		1r. brown	1·60	40

1958. Bicentenary of Russian Academy of Artists. Optd with T **718**.

2194	**557**	40k. multicoloured	6·00	1·75

719 C. Goldoni

720 Lenin Prize Medal

1958. 250th Birth Anniv of C. Goldoni (Italian dramatist).

2195	**719**	40k. brown and blue	1·00	15

1958. Lenin Prize Medal.

2196	**720**	40k. red, yellow & brown	80	15

721 Karl Marx

1958. Karl Marx Commemoration.

2197	**721**	40k. brown	85	15
2198		60k. blue	1·00	25
2199		1r. red	2·10	35

722 Federation Emblem

723 Radio Beacon, Airliner and Freighter

1958. 4th International Women's Federation Congress.

2200	**722**	40k. blue and black	65	15
2201		60k. blue and black	1·00	20

1958. Radio Day.

2202	**723**	40k. green and red	2·25	30

724 Chavchavadze (after G. Gabashvili)

725 Flags of Communist Countries

1958. Chavchavadze (Georgian poet) Commem.

2203	**724**	40k. black and blue	75	25

1958. Socialist Countries' Postal Ministers Conference, Moscow.

2204	**725**	40k. multicoloured (A)	17·00	6·25
2205		40k. multicoloured (B)	11·00	5·50

Central flag to left of inscription is in red, white and mauve. (A) has red at top and white at foot, (B) is vice versa.

726 Camp Bugler

727 Negro, European and Chinese Children

1958. "Pioneers" Day. Inscr "1958".
2206 **726** 10k. multicoloured . . . 35 10
2207 – 25k. multicoloured . . . 50 20
DESIGN: 25k. Pioneer with model airplane.

1958. International Children's Day. Inscr "1958".
2208 **727** 40k. multicoloured . . . 65 20
2209 – 40k. multicoloured . . . 65 20
DESIGN: No. 2209, Child with toys, and atomic bomb.

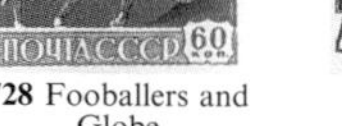
728 Fooballers and Globe

729 Rimsky-Korsakov

1958. World Cup Football Championship, Sweden. Perf or imperf.
2210 **728** 40k. multicoloured . . . 85 20
2211 60k. multicoloured . . . 1·40 40

1958. Rimsky-Korsakov (composer) Commem.
2212 **729** 40k. brown and blue . . 1·50 20

730 Athlete

1958. 14th World Gymnastic Championships, Moscow. Inscr "XIV". Multicoloured.
2213 40k. Type **730** 60 15
2214 40k. Gymnast 60 15

731 Young Construction Workers

1958. Russian Youth Day.
2215 **731** 40k. orange and blue . . 50 15
2216 60k. orange and green 60 20

732 Atomic Bomb, Globe, Sputniks, Atomic Symbol and "Lenin" (atomic ice-breaker)

733 Kiev Arsenal Uprising, 1918

1958. International Disarmament Conf, Stockholm.
2217 **732** 60k. black, orange & blue . . . . 3·50 65

1958. 40th Anniv of Ukrainian Communist Party.
2218 **733** 40k. violet and red . . . 1·10 20

734 Silhouette of Moscow State University

1958. 5th Int Architects Union Congress, Moscow.
2219 **734** 40k. blue and red . . . 90 15
2220 – 60k. multicoloured . . . 1·40 25

DESIGN—VERT: 60k. "U.I.A. Moscow 1958" in square panel of bricks and "V" in background.

735 Sadruddin Aini

1958. 80th Birth Anniv of Sadruddin Aini (Tadzhik writer).
2221 **735** 40k. red, black and buff 55 15

736 Third Artificial Satellite

737 Conference Emblem

1958. Launching of 3rd Artificial Satellite.
2222a **736** 40k. red, blue and green 1·60 50

1958. 1st World T.U. Young Workers' Conf, Prague.
2223 **737** 40k. blue and purple . . 40 20

738 Tupolev Tu-110 Jetliner

1958. Civil Aviation. Perf or imperf.
2224 – 20k. black, red and blue 50 10
2225 – 40k. black, red and green 75 15
2226 – 40k. black, red and blue 75 15
2227 – 60k. red, buff and blue 80 20
2228 **738** 60k. black and red . . . 80 20
2229 – 1r. black, red and orange 2·00 30
2230 – 2r. black, red and purple 2·75 45
DESIGNS—Russian aircraft flying across globe: No. 2224, Ilyushin Il-14M; 2225, Tupolev Tu-104; 2226, Tupolev Tu-114 Rossiya; 2229, Antonov An-10 Ukraina; 2230, Ilyushin Il-18B; No. 2227, Global air routes.

739 L. A. Kulik (scientist)

1958. 50th Anniv of Tunguz Meteor.
2231 **739** 40k. multicoloured . . . 2·25 40

740 Crimea Observatory

741 15th-century Scribe

1958. 10th International Astronomical Union Congress, Moscow.
2232 **740** 40k. turquoise and brown . . . . 1·25 20
2233 – 60k. yellow, violet & blue . . . . 1·60 30
2234 – 1r. brown and blue . . . 2·25 50
DESIGNS—HORIZ: 60k. Moscow University. VERT: 1r. Telescope of Moscow Observatory.

1958. Centenary of 1st Russian Postage Stamp.
2235 **741** 10k. multicoloured . . . 15 10
2236 – 10k. multicoloured . . . 15 10
2237 – 25k. blue, black and green 30 10
2238 – 25k. black and blue . . 30 10
2239 – 40k. brown, purple & sep 50 15
2240 – 40k. lake and brown . . 50 15
2241 – 40k. black, orange and red 50 15
2242 – 60k. turquoise, blk & vio 1·75 40
2243 – 60k. black, turquoise and purple . . . . . . 1·25 35
2244 – 1r. multicoloured . . . . 1·75 50
2245 – 1r. purple, black and orange . . . . . . 2·25 65

DESIGNS—HORIZ: No. 2236, 16th-century courier; 2237, Ordin-Nashchokin (17th-century postal administrator) (after Kh. Gusikov) and postal sleigh coach; 2238, 18th-century mail coach; 2239, Reproduction of Lenin portrait stamp of 1947; 2240, 19th-century postal troika (three-horse sleigh); 2241, Tupolev Tu-104 jetliner; 2242, Parcel post train; 2243, V. N. Podbelsky (postal administrator, 1918–20) and postal scenes; 2244, Parcel post Tupolev Tu-104; 2245, Globe and modern forms of mail transport.

741a Facade of Exhibition Building

742 Vladimir Gateway

1958. Stamp Cent Philatelic Exhibition, Leningrad.
2246 **741a** 40k. brown & lt brown 55 20

1958. 850th Anniv of Town of Vladimir. Mult.
2247 40k. Type **742** 50 15
2248 60k. Street scene in Vladimir 90 20

743 Chigorin

745 Red Cross Nurse and Patient

1958. 50th Death Anniv of Mikhail Ivanovich Chigorin (chess player).
2249 **743** 40k. green and black . . 1·75 20

1958. 40th Anniv of Red Cross and Crescent Societies.
2254 **745** 40k. multicoloured . . . 85 20
2255 – 40k. red, yellow and brown 85 20
DESIGN: No. 2255, Convalescent home.

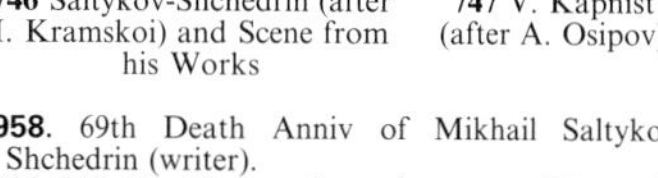
746 Saltykov-Shchedrin (after I. Kramskoi) and Scene from his Works

747 V. Kapnist (after A. Osipov)

1958. 69th Death Anniv of Mikhail Saltykov-Shchedrin (writer).
2256 **746** 40k. black and purple . . 70 20
For similar stamps see Nos. 2316/22 and 2458.

1958. Birth Bicentenary of V. Kapnist (poet).
2257 **747** 40k. black and blue . . 1·10 20

748 Yerevan, Armenia

1958. Republican Capitals.
2258 40k. brown (T **748**) 70 20
2259 40k. violet (Baku, Azerbaijan) 70 20
2260 40k. brown (Minsk, Byelorussia) 70 20
2261 40k. blue (Tbilisi, Georgia) 70 20
2262 40k. green (Tallin, Estonia) 70 20
2263 40k. green (Alma-Ata, Kazakhstan) 70 20
2264 40k. blue (Frunze, Kirgizia) 70 20
2265 40k. brown (Riga, Latvia) 70 20
2266 40k. red (Vilnius, Lithuania) 70 20
2267 40k. bistre (Kishinev, Moldavia) 70 20
2268 40k. violet (Moscow, R.S.F.S.R.) 70 20
2269 40k. blue (Stalinabad, Tadzhikistan) 70 20
2270 40k. green (Ashkhabad, Turkmenistan) . . . 70 20
2271 40k. mauve (Kiev, Ukraine) 70 20
2272 40k. black (Tashkent, Uzbekistan) 70 20
See also No. 2940.

749 Open Book, Torch, Lyre and Flowers

750 Rudaki

1958. Asian-African Writers' Conference, Tashkent.
2273 **749** 40k. orange, black and olive . . . . 1·00 15

1958. 1100th Birth Anniv of Rudaki (Tadzhik poet and musician).
2274 **750** 40k. multicoloured . . . 60 15

751 Statue of Founder Vakhtang I Gorgasal (E. Amashukeli)

1958. 1500th Anniv of Founding of Tbilisi (Georgian capital).
2275 **751** 40k. multicoloured . . . 1·25 30

752 Chelyabinsk Tractor Plant

1958. 25th Anniv of Industrial Plants.
2276 **752** 40k. green and yellow . . 80 20
2277 – 40k. blue and light blue 55 20
2278 – 40k. lake and light orange 80 20
DESIGNS: No. 2277, Ural machine construction plant; No. 2278, Zaporozhe foundry plant.

753 Young Revolutionary

754 Marx and Lenin (bas-relief)

1958. 40th Anniv of Young Communists League. Multicoloured.
2279 10k. Type **753** 20 10
2280 20k. Riveters 30 10
2281 25k. Soldier 40 15
2282 40k. Harvester 60 15
2283 60k. Builder . . . . 1·00 20
2284 1r. Students . . . . 2·40 75

1958. 41st Anniv of October Revolution.
2285 **754** 40k. black, yellow and red 85 25
2286 – 1r. multicoloured . . . . 1·10 40
DESIGN—HORIZ: 1r. Lenin (after N. Andreev) with student, peasant and miner.

755 "Human Rights"

756 Yesenin

1958. 10th Anniv of Declaration of Human Rights.
2287 **755** 60k. blue, black and buff 70 20

1958. 30th Death Anniv of Sergei Yesenin (poet).
2288 **756** 40k. multicoloured . . . 55 20

757 Kuan Han-ching

758 Ordzhonikidze

1958. Kuan Han-ching (Chinese playwright) Commemoration.
2289 **757** 40k. black and blue . . 55 20

1958. 21st Death Anniv of G. K. Ordzhonikidze (statesman).
2290 **758** 40k. multicoloured . . . 70 15

759 John Milton

760 Lenin's Statue, Minsk (M. Manizes)

1958. 350th Birth Anniv of John Milton (poet).
2291 **759** 40k. brown . . . . . . 1·10 15

1958. 40th Anniv of Byelorussian Republic.
2292 **760** 40k. brown, grey and red 70 15

761 Fuzuli

762 Census Emblem

1958. Fuzuli (Azerbaijan poet). Commemoration.
2293 **761** 40k. bistre and turquoise 1·00 15

1958. All Union Census, 1959. Multicoloured.
2294 40k. Type **762** 35 15
2295 40k. Census official with worker's family 35 15

763 Eleonora Duse

764 Rule

1958. Birth Centenary of Eleonora Duse (Italian actress).
2296 **763** 40k. black, grey and green . . . . 1·00 20

1958. Death Centenary of K. F. Rule (naturalist).
2297 **764** 40k. black and blue . . 1·00 30

765 Atomic Ice-breaker "Lenin"

766 Moon Rocket and Sputniks

1958. All-Union Industrial Exhibition. Mult.
2298 40k. Type **765** . . . . . . 2·50 65
2299 60k. Class TE 3 diesel-electric frieght locomotive 4·75 75

1959. 21st Communist Party Congress, Moscow.
2300 – 40k. multicoloured . . . 55 25
2301 – 60k. multicoloured . . . 65 40
2302 **766** 1r. multicoloured . . . . 2·75 80
DESIGNS: 40k. Lenin (after N. Andreev), Red Banner and Kremlin view; 60k. Workers beside Lenin hydro-electric plant, Volga River.

767 E. Torricelli

768 Ice Skater

1959. 350th Birth Anniv of Torricelli (physicist).
2303 **767** 40k. black and green . . 1·00 20

1959. Women's World Ice Skating Championships, Sverdlovsk.
2304 **768** 25k. multicoloured . . . 50 10
2305 40k. black, blue and grey 85 20

769 Charles Darwin

770 N. Gamaleya

1959. 150th Birth Anniv of Charles Darwin (naturalist).
2306 **769** 40k. brown and blue . . 1·10 15

1959. Birth Centenary of Gamaleya (microbiologist).
2307 **770** 40k. black and red . . . 1·10 25

771 Sholem Aleichem

Победа баскетбольной команды СССР. Чили 1959 г.
(**772**)

1959. Birth Centenary of Aleichem (Jewish writer).
2308 **771** 40k. brown 90 20

1959. Russian (Unofficial) Victory in World Basketball Championships, Chile. No. 1831 optd with T **772**.
2309 1r. brown and drab . . . . 9·50 8·00

1959. Birth Bicent of Robert Burns. Optd **1759 1959**.
2310 **627** 40k. brown and blue . . 17·00 15·00

774 Selma Lagerlof

775 P. Cvirka

1959. Birth Centenary of Selma Lagerlof (Swedish writer).
2311 **774** 40k. black, brown and cream 95 20

1959. 50th Birth Anniv of Cvirka (Lithuanian poet).
2312 **775** 40k. black and red on yellow 55 15

776 F. Joliot-Curie (scientist)

777 Popov and Polar Rescue by Ice-breaker "Ermak"

1959. Joliot-Curie Commemoration.
2313 **776** 40k. black and turquoise 1·25 30

1959. Birth Centenary of A. S. Popov (radio pioneer).
2314 **777** 40k. brown, black & blue . . . . 1·00 40
2315 – 60k. multicoloured . . . 1·50 55
DESIGN: 60k. Popov and radio tower.

1959. Writers as T **746**. Inscr "1959".
2316 40k. grey, black and red . . 1·10 20
2317 40k. brown, sepia and yellow . . . . 1·10 20
2318 40k. brown and violet . . . 1·10 20
2319 40k. multicoloured . . . . 1·10 20
2320 40k. black, olive and yellow 1·10 20
2321 40k. multicoloured 90 20
2322 40k. slate and violet . . . 1·10 20
PORTRAITS (with scene from works): No. 2316, Anton Chekhov; 2317, Ivan Krylov (after K. Bryullov); 2318, Aleksandr Ostrovsky; 2319, Aleksandr Griboedov (after I. Kramskoi); 2320, Nikolai Gogol (after F. Moller); 2321, Sergei Aksakov (after I. Kramskoi); 2322, Aleksei Koltsov (after K. Gorbunov).

778 Saadi (Persian poet)

1959. Saadi Commemoration.
2323 **778** 40k. black and blue . . 55 15

779 Orbeliani (Georgian writer)

780 "Hero riding Dolphin"

1959. Orbeliani Commemoration.
2324 **779** 40k. black and red . . . 55 15

1959. Birth Tercentenary of Ogata Korin (Japanese artist).
2325 **780** 40k. multicoloured . . . 2·50 2·00

781 "Rossiya" on Odessa-Batum Service

1959. Russian Liners. Multicoloured.
2326 10k. "Sovetsky Soyuz" on Vladivostok–Kamchatka service 30 15
2327 20k. "Feliks Dzerzhinsky" on Odessa–Latakia service 50 15
2328 40k. Type **781** 80 15
2329 40k. "Kooperatsiya" on Murmansk–Tyksi service 80 15
2330 60k. "Mikhail Kalinin" leaving Leningrad . . . . 1·10 20
2331 1r. "Baltika" on Leningrad–London service . . . . 1·50 40

782 Trajectory of Moon Rocket

783 Lenin

1959. Launching of Moon Rocket. Inscr "2-1-1959".
2332 **782** 40k. brown and pink . . 1·00 30
2333 – 40k. blue and light blue 1·00 30
DESIGN: No. 2333, Preliminary route of moon rocket after launching.

1959. 89th Birth Anniv of Lenin.
2334 **783** 40k. brown . . . . . . 1·00 35

784 M. Cachin

785 Youths with Banner

1959. 90th Birth Anniv of Marcel Cachin (French communist leader).
2335 **784** 60k. brown 90 30

1959. 10th Anniv of World Peace Movement.
2336 **785** 40k. multicoloured . . . 65 30

786 A. von Humboldt

1959. Death Centenary of Alexander von Humboldt (German naturalist).
2337 **786** 40k. brown and violet 1·00 20

787 Haydn

788 Mountain Climbing

1959. 150th Death Anniv of Haydn (Austrian composer).
2338 **787** 40k. brown and blue . . 1·25 20

1959. Tourist Publicity. Multicoloured.
2339 40k. Type **788** 75 25
2340 40k. Map reading 75 25
2341 40k. Cross country skiing 75 25
2342 40k. Canoeing (horiz) . . . 75 25

789 Exhibition Emblem and New York Coliseum

790 Statue of I. Repin (painter), Moscow (M. Manizer)

1959. Russian Scientific, Technological and Cultural Exhibition, New York.
2343 **789** 20k. multicoloured . . . 35 15
2344 40k. multicoloured . . . 70 20

1959. Cultural Celebrities. Inscr "1959". Statues in black.
2345 **790** 10k. ochre 15 10
2346 – 10k. red 15 10
2347 – 20k. lilac 40 10
2348 – 25k. turquoise 65 15
2349 – 60k. green 90 20
2350 – 1r. blue . . . . 1·40 50
STATUES: 10k. (No. 2346), Lenin, Ulanovsk (M. Manizer); 80k. V. Mayakosky (poet), Moscow (A. Kibalnikov); 25k Aleksandr Pushkin (writer), Leningrad, (M. Anikushin; 60k. Maksim Gorky (writer), Moscow (Vera Mukhina); Ir. Tchaikovsky (composer), Moscow (Vera Mukhina).

791 Russian Sturgeon

792 Louis Braille

1959. Fisheries Protection.
2350a – 20k. black and blue . . 40 10
2350b – 25k. brown and lilac . . 50 10
2351 **791** 40k. black and turquoise 70 20
2351a – 40k. purple and mauve 90 20
2352 – 60k. black and blue . . 1·40 40
DESIGNS: 20k. Zander; 25k. Northern fur seals; 40k. (No. 2351a), Common whitefish; 60k. Chum salmon and map.

1959. 150th Birth Anniv of Braille (inventor of Braille).
2353 **792** 60k. brown, yell & turq 70 25

793 Musa Djalil (Tatar poet)

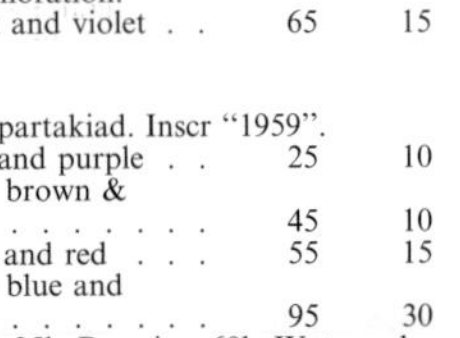

794 Vaulting

1959. Djalil Commemoration.
2354 **793** 40k. black and violet . . 65 15

1959. 2nd Russian Spartakiad. Inscr "1959".
2355 **794** 15k. grey and purple . . 25 10
2356 – 25k. grey, brown & green 45 10
2357 – 30k. olive and red . . . 55 15
2358 – 60k. grey, blue and yellow 95 30
DESIGNS—HORIZ: 25k. Running; 60k. Water polo. VERT: 30k. Athletes supporting Spartakiad emblem.

795

796 Steel Worker

1959. 2nd International T.U. Conference, Leipzig.
2359 **795** 40k. red, blue and yellow . . . 65 15

1959. Seven Year Plan.
2360 – 10k. red, blue and violet 10 10
2361 – 10k. lt red, dp red & yell 10 10
2362 – 15k. red, yellow & brn 15 10
2363 – 15k. brown, green & bis 15 10
2364 – 20k. red, yellow & green 25 10
2365 – 20k. multicoloured . . 25 10
2366 – 30k. red, flesh & purple 40 10
2366a – 30k. multicoloured . . 40 10
2367 **796** 40k. orange, yellow & bl 50 15
2368 – 40k. red, pink and blue 50 15
2369 – 60k. red, blue and yellow 95 35
2370 – 60k. red, buff and blue 95 35
DESIGNS: 2360, Chemist; 2361, Spassky Tower, hammer and sickle; 2362, Builder's labourer; 2363, Farm girl; 2364, Machine minder; No. 2365, Tractor driver; 2366, Oil technician; 2366a, Cloth production; . 2368, Coal miner; 2369, Iron moulder; 2370, Power station.

797 Glaciologist

798 Novgorod

1959. International Geophysical Year (2nd issue).
2371 **797** 10k. turquoise 60 15
2372 – 25k. red and blue . . . 1·25 15
2373 – 40k. red and blue . . . 2·75 20
2373a – 1r. blue and yellow . . 2·50 75
DESIGNS: 25k. Oceanographic survey ship "Vityaz"; 40k. Antarctic map, camp and emperor penguin; 1r. Observatory and rocket.

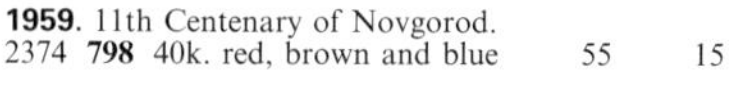

1959. 11th Centenary of Novgorod.
2374 **798** 40k. red, brown and blue 55 15

799 Schoolboys in Workshop

800 Exhibition Emblem

1959. Industrial Training Scheme for School-leavers. Inscr "1959".
2375 **799** 40k. violet 40 15
2376 – 1r. blue . . . . 1·00 30
DESIGN: 1r. Children at night-school.

1959. All Union Exhibition.
2377 **800** 40k. multicoloured . . . 55 20

801 Russian and Chinese Students

1959. 10th Anniv of Chinese Peoples' Republic.
2378 **801** 20k. multicoloured . . . 20 15
2379 – 40k. multicoloured . . . 65 20
DESIGN: 40k. Russian miner and Chinese foundryman.

802 Postwoman

803 Mahtumkuli (after A. Khadzhiev)

1959. International Correspondence Week.
2380 **802** 40k. multicoloured . . . 50 15
2381 60k. multicoloured . . . 75 20

1959. 225th Birth Anniv of Mahtumkuli (Turkestan writer).
2382 **803** 40k. brown 65 15

804 Arms and Workers of the German Democratic Republic

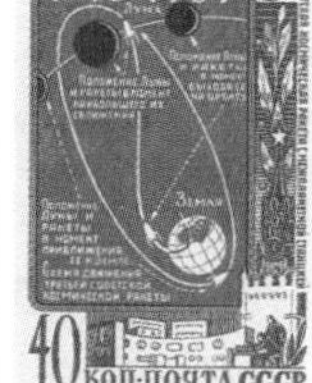
805 Lunik 3's Trajectory around the Moon

1959. 10th Anniv of German Democratic Republic.
2383 **804** 40k. multicoloured . . . 45 15
2384 – 60k. purple and cream 65 20
DESIGN—VERT: 60k. Town Hall, East Berlin.

1959. Launching of "Lunik 3" Rocket.
2385 **805** 40k. violet . . . . . . 1·90 30

806 Republican Arms and Emblem

807 Red Square, Moscow

1959. 30th Anniv of Tadzhikistan Republic.
2386 **806** 40k. multicoloured . . . 1·25 25

1959. 42nd Anniv of October Revolution.
2387 **807** 40k. red 65 15

808 Capitol, Washington and Kremlin, Moscow

1959. Visit of Russian Prime Minister to U.S.A.
2388 **808** 60k. blue and yellow . . 1·00 30

809 Mil Mi-1 Helicopter

1959. Military Sports.
2389 **809** 10k. red and violet . . . 30 10
2390 – 25k. brown and blue . . 55 10
2391 – 40k. blue and brown . . 60 15
2392 – 60k. bistre and blue . . 90 25
DESIGNS: 25k. Skin diver; 40k. Racing motor cyclist; 60k. Parachutist.

810 Track of Moon Rocket

811 Liberty Monument (Zs. Kisfaludy-Strobl), Budapest

1959. Landing of Russian Rocket on Moon. Inscr "14.IX.1959". Multicoloured.
2393 40k. Type **810** . . . . . . 1·00 25
2394 40k. Diagram of flight trajectory . . . . 1·00 25

1959. 15th Anniv of Hungarian Republic. Mult.
2395 20k. Sandor Petofi (Hungarian poet) (horiz) 35 15
2396 40k. Type **811** 70 20

812 Manolis Glezos (Greek Communist)

1959. Glezos Commemoration.
2397 **812** 40k. brown and blue . . 15·00 11·50

813 A. Voskresensky (chemist)

814 River Chusovaya

1959. Voskresensky Commemoration.
2398 **813** 40k. brown and blue . . 75 20

1959. Tourist Publicity. Inscr "1959".
2399 **814** 10k. violet 15 10
2400 – 10k. mauve 15 10
2401 – 25k. blue 30 10
2402 – 25k. red 30 10
2403 – 25k. olive 30 10
2404 – 40k. red 50 10
2405 – 60k. turquoise 65 15
2406 – 1r. green . . . . 2·00 70
2407 – 1r. orange . . . . . . 1·25 60
DESIGNS: No. 2400, Riza Lake, Caucasus; 2401, River Lena; 2402, Iskanderkuly Lake; 2403, Coastal region; 2404, Lake Baikal; . 2405, Beluha Mountains, Altay; 2406, Khibinsky Mountains; 2407, Gursuff region, Crimea.

815 "The Trumpeters of the First Horse Army" (M. Grekov)

1959. 40th Anniv of Russian Cavalry.
2408 **815** 40k. multicoloured . . . 85 20

816 A. P. Chekhov and Moscow Residence

817 M. V. Frunze

1960. Birth Centenary of Chekhov (writer).
2409 **816** 20k. red, brown & vio 35 15
2410 – 40k. brown, blue & sepia 75 25
DESIGN: 40k. Chekhov and Yalta residence.

1960. 75th Birth Anniv of M. V. Frunze (military leader).
2411 **817** 40k. brown 65 15

818 G. N. Gabrichevsky

819 Vera Komissarzhevskaya

1960. Birth Centenary of G. N. Gabrichevsky (microbiologist).
2412 **818** 40k. brown and violet 1·00 25

1960. 50th Death Anniv of V. F. Komissarzhevskaya (actress).
2413 **819** 40k. brown 65 15

820 Free-skating

1960. Winter Olympic Games.
2414 – 10k. blue and orange . . 50 10
2415 – 25k. multicoloured . . . 75 10
2416 – 40k. orange, blue & pur 90 15
2417 **820** 60k. violet, brown & grn 1·40 20
2418 – 1r. blue, red and green 2·25 50
DESIGNS: 10k. Ice hockey; 25k. Ice skating; 40k. Skiing; 1r. Ski jumping.

821 Timur Frunze (fighter pilot) and Air Battle

822 Mil Mi-4 Helicopter over Kremlin

1960. War Heroes. Multicoloured.
2419 40k. Type **821** . . . . . 1·75 55
2420 1r. Gen. Chernyakhovksy and battle scene . . . . . 1·40 40

1960. Air.
2421 **822** 60k. blue . . . . 1·25 25

823 Women of Various Races

824 "Swords into Ploughshares" (Ye. Buchetich)

1960. 50th Anniv of International Women's Day.
2422 **823** 40k. multicoloured . . . 85 25

1960. Presentation of Statue by Russia to U.N.
2423 **824** 40k. yellow, bistre and blue 65 15

15 лет освобождения Венгрии
(825)

826 Lenin when a Child

1960. 15th Anniv of Liberation of Hungary. Optd with T **825**.
2424 **811** 40k. multicoloured . . . 5·00 3·25

1960. 90th Birth Anniv of Lenin. Portraits of Lenin. Multicoloured.
2425 **826** 10k. multicoloured . . . 10 10
2426 – 20k. multicoloured . . . 20 10
2427 – 30k. multicoloured . . . 40 15
2428 – 40k. multicoloured . . . 55 20
2429 – 60k. multicoloured . . . 1·40 35
2430 – 1r. brown, blue and red 1·60 50
DESIGNS: Lenin: 20k. holding child (after N. Zhukov); 30k. and revolutionary scenes; 40k. with party banners; 60k. and industrial scenes; 1r. with globe and rejoicing people (after A. Seral).

827 "Lunik 3" photographing Moon
828 Government House, Baku

1960. Flight of "Lunik 3". Inscr "7.X.1959".
2431 **827** 40k. yellow and blue . . 1·10 35
2432 – 60k. yellow, blue & indigo . . . . 1·10 35
DESIGN: 60k. Lunar map.

1960. 40th Anniv of Azerbaijan Republic.
2433 **828** 40k. brown, bistre & yell 65 15

829 "Fraternization" (K. Pokorny)
830 Furnaceman

1960. 15th Anniv of Czechoslovak Republic.
2434 **829** 40k. black and blue . . 50 10
2435 – 60k. brown and yellow 85 15
DESIGN: 60k. Charles Bridge, Prague.

1960. Completion of First Year of Seven Year Plan.
2436 **830** 40k. brown and red . . 50 15

831 Popov Museum, Leningrad

1960. Radio Day.
2437 **831** 40k. multicoloured . . . 1·00 30

832 Robert Schumann
833 Sverdlov

1960. 150th Birth Anniv of Schumann (composer).
2438 **832** 40k. black and blue . . 1·00 20

1960. 75th Birth Anniv of Ya. M. Sverdlov (statesman).
2439 **833** 40k. sepia and brown . . 85 15

834 Magnifier and Stamp

1960. Philatelists' Day.
2440 **834** 60k. multicoloured . . . 1·10 30

835 Petrozavodsk (Karelian Republic)

1960. Capitals of Autonomous Republic (1st issue).
2441 **835** 40k. turquoise 80 20
2442 – 40k. blue 80 20
2443 – 40k. green 80 20
2444 – 40k. purple 80 20
2445 – 40k. red 80 20
2446 – 40k. blue 80 20
2447 – 40k. brown 80 20
2448 – 40k. brown 80 20
2449 – 40k. red 80 20
2450 – 40k. brown 80 20

CAPITALS: Nos. 2442, Batumi (Adzharian); 2443, Izhevsk (Udmurt); 2444, Grozny (Chechen-Ingush); 2445, Cheboksary (Chuvash); 2446, Yakutsk (Yakut); 2447, Ordzhonikidze (North Ossetian); 2448, Nukus (Kara-Kalpak); 2449, Makhachkala (Daghestan); 2450, Yoshkar-Ola (Mari).
See also Nos. 2586/92 and 2703/5.

836 Children of Different Races
838 Rocket

1960. International Children's Day. Multicoloured.
2451 10k. Type **836** 15 10
2452 20k. Children on farm (vert) 25 15
2453 25k. Children with snowman 40 15
2454 40k. Children in zoo gardens 65 20

1960. 40th Anniv of Karelian Autonomous Republic. Optd **40 лет КАССР 8.VI.1960**.
2455 **835** 40k. turquoise . . . . . 2·25 90

1960. Launching of Cosmic Rocket "Spacecraft 1" (first "Vostok" type spacecraft).
2456 **838** 40k. red and blue . . . 1·75 50

839 I.F.A.C. Emblem

1960. 1st International Automation Control Federation Congress, Moscow.
2457 **839** 60k. brown and yellow 1·90 40

1960. Birth Centenary (1959) of Kosta Khetagurov (poet). As T **746**. Inscr "1960".
2458 40k. brown and blue 80 15
DESIGN: 40k. Portrait of Khetagurov and scene from his works.

840 Cement Works, Belgorod

1960. 1st Plant Construction of Seven Year Plan.
2459 **840** 25k. black and blue . . 25 10
2460 – 40k. black and red . . . 50 10
DESIGN. 40k. Metal works, Novokrivorog.

841 Capstans and Cogwheel

1960. Industrial Mass-Production Plant.
2461 **841** 40k. turquoise 70 10
2462 – 40k. purple (Factory plant) 70 10

842 Vilnius (Lithuania)

1960. 20th Anniv of Soviet Baltic Republics. Multicoloured.
2463 40k. Type **842** 65 10
2464 40k. Riga (Latvia) 65 10
2465 40k. Tallin (Estonia) 65 10

843 Running

Международная ярмарка в Риччоне
(**844**)

1960. Olympic Games. Inscr "1960". Multicoloured.
2466 5k. Type **843** 15 10
2467 10k. Wrestling 20 10
2468 15k. Basketball 35 10
2469 20k. Weightlifting 35 10
2470 25k. Boxing 35 10
2471 40k. High diving 50 15
2472 40k. Fencing 50 15
2473 40k. Gymnastics 50 20
2474 60k. Canoeing 80 25
2475 1r. Horse jumping . . . . . 2·25 55

1960. 20th Anniv of Moldavian Republic. As T **842**.
2476 40k. multicoloured 65 10
DESIGN: 40k. Kishinev (capital).

1960. International Exhibition, Riccione. No. 2471 optd with T **844**.
2477 40k. multicoloured . . . . 16·00 11·00

845 "Agriculture and Industry"
846 G. H. Minkh

1960 15th Anniv of Vietnam Democratic Republic.
2478 40k. Type **845** 55 15
2479 60k. Book Museum, Hanoi (vert) 85 20

1960. 125th Birth Anniv of G. H. Minkh (epidemiologist).
2480 **846** 60k. brown and bistre 70 15

847 "March" (after I. Levitan)

1960. Birth Centenary of I. Levitan (painter).
2481 **847** 40k. black and olive . . 95 15

848 "Forest" (after Shishkin)

1960. 5th World Forestry Congress, Seattle.
2482 **848** 1r. brown . . . . 2·40 70

849 Addressing Letter

1960. International Correspondence Week.
2483 **849** 40k. multicoloured . . . 40 10
2484 60k. multicoloured . . . 70 20

850 Kremlin, Dogs "Belka" and "Strelka" and Rocket Trajectory

1960. 2nd Cosmic Rocket Flight.
2485 **850** 40k. purple and yellow 1·10 20
2486 1r. blue and orange . . . 1·75 30

851 Globes
852 People of Kazakhstan

1960. 15th Anniv of W.F.T.U.
2487 **851** 60k. blue, drab and lilac 80 15

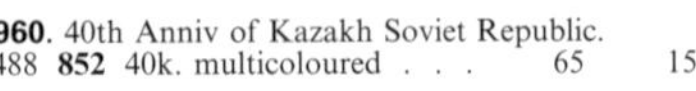

1960. 40th Anniv of Kazakh Soviet Republic.
2488 **852** 40k. multicoloured . . . 65 15

853 "Karl Marx"

1960. River Boats. Multicoloured.
2489 25k. Type **853** 40 10
2490 40k. "Lenin" 70 15
2491 60k. "Raketa" (hydrofoil) 1·40 25

854 A. N. Voronikhin and Leningrad Cathedral

1960. Birth Bicentenary of A. N. Voronikhin (architect).
2492 **854** 40k. black and grey . . 65 15

855 Motor Coach

1960. Russian Motor Industry.
2493 – 25k. black and blue . . 40 10
2494 – 40k. blue and olive . . . 55 15
2495 – 60k. red and turquoise 1·10 20
2496 **855** 1r. multicoloured . . . . 1·75 35
DESIGNS: 25k. Lorry; 40k. "Volga" car; 60k. "Moskvich" car.

856 J. S. Gogebashvily

1960. 120th Birth Anniv of J. S. Gogebashvily (Georgian teacher).
2497 **856** 40k. black and lake . . . 65 15

857 Industrial Plant and Power Plant
858 Federation Emblem

1960. 43rd Anniv of October Revolution.
2498 **857** 40k. multicoloured . . . 65 20

1960. 15th Anniv of International Federation of Democratic Women.
2499 **858** 60k. red and grey . . . 80 20

859 Youth of Three Races

40 лет Удмуртской АССР 4/XI 1960.
(**860**)

1960. 15th Anniv of World Democratic Youth Federation.
2500 **859** 60k. multicoloured . . . 80 20

1960. 40th Anniv of Udmurt Autonomous Republic. No. 2443 optd with T **860**.
2501 40k. green . . . . 2·75 1·10

861 Tolstoi and his Moscow Residence

1960. 50th Death Anniv of Leo Tolstoi (writer).
2502 **861** 20k. multicoloured . . . 30 15
2503 – 40k. brown, sepia & blue 55 15
2504 – 60k. multicoloured . . . 1·10 25
DESIGNS—HORIZ: 40k. Tolstoi and his country estate. VERT: 60k. Full face portrait.

862 Government House, Yerevan

1960. 40th Anniv of Armenian Republic.
2205 **862** 40k. multicoloured . . . 65 15

863 Students and University

864 Tulip

1960. Opening of Friendship University, Moscow.
2506 **863** 40k. purple 65 15

1960. Russian Flowers. Multicoloured.
2507 20k. Type **864** 30 10
2508 20k. Autumn crocus 30 10
2509 25k. Marsh marigold . . . 35 10
2510 40k. Tulip 45 10
2511 40k. Panax 45 10
2512 60k. Hypericum 90 25
2513 60k. Iris 90 25
2514 1r. Wild rose . . . . 1·60 45

865 Engels

867 N. Pirogov

866 Mark Twain

1960. 140th Birth Anniv of Engels.
2515 **865** 60k. grey . . . . 1·40 30

1960. 125th Birth Anniv of Mark Twain.
2516 **866** 40k. bistre and orange 2·75 1·75

1960. 150th Birth Anniv of N. Pirogov (surgeon).
2517 **867** 40k. brown and green . . 65 15

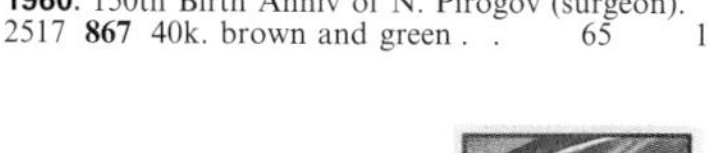

868 Chopin (after Eugene Delacroix)

869 North Korean Flag and Emblem

1960. 150th Birth Anniv of Chopin.
2518 **868** 40k. bistre and buff . . 1·50 20

1960. 15th Anniv of Korean Liberation.
2519 **869** 40k. multicoloured . . . 95 20

870 Lithuanian Costumes

871 A. Tseretely

1960. Provincial Costumes (1st issue). Inscr "1960". Multicoloured.
2520 10k. Type **870** 35 15
2521 60k. Uzbek costumes . . . 1·40 25
See also Nos. 2537/45, 2796 and 2835/8.

1960. 120th Birth Anniv of A. Tseretely (Georgian poet).
2522 **871** 40k. purple and lilac . . 1·00 20

Currency Revalued.
10 (old) Kopeks = 1 (new) Kopek.

872 Worker

873 "Ruslan and Lyudmila" (Pushkin)

1961. Inscr "1961".
2523 **872** 1k. bistre 70 10
2524 – 2k. green 25 10
2525 – 3k. violet . . . . . . 2·00 10
2526 – 4k. red 60 10
2526a – 4k. brown . . . . . . 3·00 1·40
2527 – 6k. red . . . . 4·50 45
2528 – 6k. claret . . . . . . 1·40 10
2529 – 10k. orange . . . . . 2·40 10
2533a – 12k. purple . . . . . . 2·00 25
2530 – 16k. blue . . . . 3·50 70
DESIGNS: 2k. Combine harvester; 3k. Cosmic rocket; 4k. Soviet Arms and Flag; 6k. Spassky Tower and Kremlin; 10k. "Worker and Collective Farmer" (sculpture, Vera Mukhina); 12k. Monument to F. Minin and D. Pozharsky and Spassky Tower; 16k. Airliner over power station.

1961. Russian Wild Life. As T **653** but inscr "1961". Centres in natural colours. Frame colours given.
2534 1k. sepia (Brown bear) . . . 25 15
2535 6k. black (Eurasian beaver) 1·00 20
2536 10k. black (Roe deer) . . . 1·25 55
The 1k. is vert and the rest horiz.

1961. Provincial Costumes (2nd issue). As T **870** but inscr "1961".
2537 2k. red, brown and stone . . 25 10
2538 2k. multicoloured 25 10
2539 3k. multicoloured 50 10
2540 3k. multicoloured 50 10
2541 3k. multicoloured 50 10
2542 4k. multicoloured 60 15
2543 6k. multicoloured 70 20
2544 10k. multicoloured . . . . 1·40 30
2545 12k. multicoloured . . . . 2·25 35
COSTUMES: No. 2337, Moldavia; 2538, Georgia; 2539, Ukraine; 2540, Byelorussia; 2541, Kazakhs; 2542, Koryaks; 2543, Russia; 2544, Armenia; 2545, Estonia.

1961. Scenes from Russian Fairy Tales. Mult.
2546 1k. "Geese Swans" 25 10
2547 3k. "The Fox, the Hare and the Cock" 55 15
2548 4k. "The Little Humpbacked Horse" . . 75 15
2549 6k. "The Muzhik and the Bear" . . . . 1·10 20
2550 10k. Type **873** . . . . . . 1·60 40

874 Lenin, Map and Power Station

1961. 40th Anniv of State Electricity Plan.
2551 **874** 4k. brown, yellow & blue 60 15
2552 10k. black, purple and salmon . . . . 1·25 25

875 Tractor

876 Dobrolyubov (after P. Borel)

1961. Soviet Agricultural Achievements. Inscr "1961".
2553 – 3k. mauve and blue . . 40 15
2554 **875** 4k. black and green . . 45 10
2555 – 6k. brown and blue . . . 55 25
2556 – 10k. purple and olive . . 1·10 15
DESIGNS: 3k. Dairy herd; 6k. Agricultural machinery; 10k. Fruit picking.

1961. 125th Birth Anniv of N. A. Dobrolyubov (writer).
2557 **876** 4k. buff, black and blue 55 20

877 N. D. Zelinsky

1961. Birth Centenary of N. D. Zelinsky (chemist).
2558 **877** 4k. purple and mauve . . 55 20

878 Georgian Republic Flag

1961. 40th Anniv of Georgian Republic.
2559 **878** 4k. multicoloured . . . 30 10

879 Sgt. Miroshnichenko and Battle

1961. War Hero.
2560 **879** 4k. blue and purple . . . 65 20
See also Nos. 2664/5.

880 Self-portrait and Birthplace

881 A. Rublev

1961. Death Centenary of T. G. Shevchenko (Ukrainian poet and painter).
2561 **880** 3k. brown and violet . . 35 10
2562 – 6k. purple and green . . 65 15
DESIGN: 6k. Shevchenko in old age (after I. Kramskoi), pen, book and candle.
See also Nos. 2956/62.

1961. 600th Birth Anniv of Rublev (painter).
2563 **881** 4k. multicoloured . . . 60 20

882 Statue of Shevchenko (poet), Kharkov (M. Manizer)

883 N. V. Sklifosovsky

1961. Cultural Celebrities.
2564 – 2k. brown and blue . . . 25 10
2565 **882** 4k. brown and black . . 30 15
2566 – 4k. brown and purple . . 35 15
DESIGNS: 2k. Shchors Monument, Kiev (M. Lysenko); 4k. (No. 2566), Kotovsky Monument, Kishinev (L. Dubinovsky).

1961. 125th Birth Anniv of N. Y. Sklifosovsky (surgeon).
2567 **883** 4k. black and blue . . . 40 10

884 Robert Koch

885 Zither-player and Folk Dancers

1961. 50th Death Anniv of Robert Koch (German microbiologist).
2568 **884** 6k. brown 60 20

1961. 50th Anniv of Russian National Choir.
2569 **885** 4k. multicoloured . . . 35 10

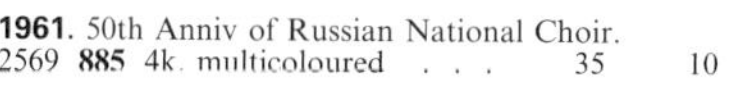

886 "Popular Science"

1961. Cent of "Vokrug Sveta" (science magazine).
2570 **886** 6k. brown, blue and deep blue . . . . . . 1·10 75

887 Venus Rocket

1961. Launching of Venus Rocket.
2571 **887** 6k. orange and blue . . 1·40 20
2572 – 10k. blue and yellow . . 1·90 40
DESIGN: 10k. Capsule and flight route.

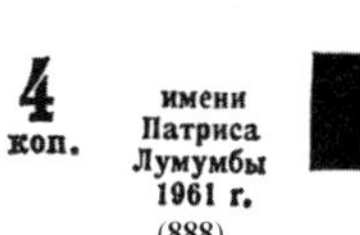

(**888**)

1961. Patrice Lumumba (Congolese politician) Commemoration (1st issue). Surch with T **888**.
2573 **863** 4k. on 40k. purple . . . 1·25 85
See also No. 2593.

889 African breaking Chains

1961. Africa Freedom Day. Inscr "1961".
2574 **889** 4k. multicoloured . . . 20 10
2575 – 6k. purple, orange and blue 45 20
DESIGN: 6k. Hands clasping Torch of Freedom, and map.

891 Yuri Gagarin

892 Lenin

1961. World's First Manned Space Flight. Inscr "12-IV-1961". Perf or imperf.
2576 **891** 3k. blue 45 10
2577 – 6k. blue, violet and red 65 20
2578 – 10k. red, green & brown 1·25 30
DESIGNS—37 × 26 mm: 6k. Rocket and Spassky Tower; 10k. Rocket, Gagarin and Kremlin.

1961. 91st Birth Anniv of Lenin.
2579 **892** 4k. blk, salmon and red 30 10

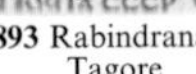

893 Rabindranath Tagore

894 Garibaldi

1961. Birth Centenary of Tagore (Indian writer).
2580 **893** 6k. black, bistre and red 50 15

1961. International Labour Exhibition, Turin.
2581 – 4k. salmon and red . . . 40 10
2582 **894** 6k. salmon and lilac . . 45 10
DESIGN: 4k. "To the Stars" (statue, G. Postnikov).

895 Lenin

896 Patrice Lumumba

1961.
2583 **895** 20k. green and brown . . 1·40 85
2584 – 30k. blue and brown . . 2·50 1·10
2585 – 50k. red and brown . . 4·00 1·90
PORTRAITS (Lenin): 30k. In cap; 50k. Profile.

1961. Capitals of Autonomous Republics (2nd issue). As T 835
2586 4k. deep violet 40 15
2587 4k. blue 40 15
2588 4k. orange 40 15
2589 4k. black 40 15
2590 4k. lake 40 15
2591 4k. green 40 15
2592 4k. deep purple 40 15
CAPITALS: No. 2586, Nalchik (Kabardino-Balkar); 2587, Ulan-Ude (Buryat); 2588, Sukhumi (Abkhazia); 2589, Syktyvkar (Komi); 2590, Nakhichevan (Nakhichevan); 2591, Rodina Cinema, Elista (Kalmyk); 2592, Ufa (Bashkir).

1961. Lumumba Commemoration (2nd issue).
2593 **896** 2k. multicoloured . . . 30 10

897 Kindergarten

898 Chernushka and Rocket

1961. International Children's Day.
2594 **897** 2k. blue and orange . . 20 10
2595 – 3k. violet and ochre . . 30 10
2596 – 4k. drab and red 45 15
DESIGNS—HORIZ: 3k. Children in Pioneer camp. VERT: 4k. Children with toys and pets.

1961. 4th and 5th "Spacecraft" Flights.
2597 – 2k. black, blue and violet 35 15
2598 **898** 4k. turquoise and blue 65 15
DESIGN—HORIZ: 2k. Dog "Zvezdochka", rocket and controller (inscr "25.III.1961").

899 Belinsky (after I. Astafev)

900

1961. 150th Birth Anniv of Vissarion Grigorievich Belinsky (literary critic and journalist).
2599 **899** 4k. black and red . . . 30 15

1961. 40th Anniv of Soviet Hydro-meteorological Service.
2600 **900** 6k. multicoloured . . . 90 25

901 D. M. Karbyshev

902 Glider

1961. Lieut-Gen. Karbyshev (war hero).
2601 **901** 4k. black, red and yellow 30 10

1961. Soviet Spartakiad.
2602 **902** 4k. red and grey 30 10
2603 – 6k. red and grey 55 15
2604 – 10k. red and grey . . . 90 35
DESIGNS: 6k. Inflatable motor boat; 10k. Motor cyclists.

903 Sukhe Bator Monument and Govt. Buildings, Ulan Bator

904 S. I. Vavilov

1961. 40th Anniv of Revolution in Mongolia.
2605 **903** 4k. multicoloured . . . 65 20

1961. 70th Birthday of Vavilov (scientist).
2606 **904** 4k. brown, bistre & green 30 15

905 V. Pshavela

906 "Youth Activities"

1961. Birth Cent of Pshavela (Georgian poet).
2607 **905** 4k. brown and cream . . 30 10

1961. World Youth Forum.
2608 – 2k. brown and orange 30 10
2609 – 4k. green and lilac . . . 35 10
2610 **906** 6k. blue and ochre . . . 65 20
DESIGNS—HORIZ: 2k. Youths pushing tank into river. VERT: 4k. "Youths and progress".

907

908

1961. 5th Int Biochemical Congress, Moscow.
2611 **907** 6k. multicoloured . . . 65 15

1961. Centenary of "Kalevipoeg" (Estonian Saga).
2612 **908** 4k. yellow, turq & blk 30 15

909 Javelin Thrower

1961. 7th Soviet Trade Union Sports.
2613 **909** 6k. red 55 20

910 A.D. Zakharov (after S. Shchukin)

1961. Birth Bicentenary of Zakharov (architect).
2614 **910** buff, brown and blue . . 80 25

911 Counter-attack (after P. Krivonogov)

1961. War of 1941–45 (1st issue). Inscr "1961".
2615 **911** 4k. multicoloured . . . 55 15
2616 – 4k. multicoloured . . . 55 15
2617 – 4k. indigo and brown . . 65 15
DESIGNS: No. 2616, Sailor with bayonet; No. 2617, Soldier with tommy gun.
See also Nos. 2717 and 2851/5.

912 Union Emblem

1961. 15th Anniv of International Union of Students.
2617a **912** 6k. violet and red . . . 45 10

913 Stamps commemorating Industry

1961. 40th Anniv of First Soviet Stamp. Centres multicoloured.
2618 **913** 2k. ochre and brown . . 30 15
2619 – 4k. blue and indigo 45 15
2620 – 6k. green and olive . . . 90 25
2621 – 10k. buff and brown . . 1·40 45
DESIGNS (stamps commemorating): 4k. Electrification; 8k. Peace; 10k. Atomic energy.

914 Titov and "Vostok 2"

1961. 2nd Manned Space Flight. Perf or imperf.
2622 – 4k. blue and purple . . . 70 20
2623 **914** 6k. orange, green & brn 1·00 30
DESIGN: 4k. Space pilot and globe.

915 Angara River Bridge

1961. Tercentenary of Irkutsk, Siberia.
2624 **915** 4k. black, lilac and bistre 55 15

916 Letters and Mail Transport

1961. International Correspondence Week.
2625 **916** 4k. black and mauve . . 55 10

917 Workers and Banners

1961. 22nd Communist Party Congress (1st issue).
2626 **917** 2k. brown, yellow and red 15 10
2627 – 3k. blue and orange . . 90 15
2628 – 4k. red, buff and purple 25 10
2629 – 4k. orange, black & mve 40 10
2630 – 4k. sepia, brown and red 25 10
DESIGNS: No. 2627, Moscow University and obelisk; 2628, Combine harvester; 2629, Workmen and machinery; 2630, Worker and slogan.
See also No. 2636.

918 Soviet Monument, Berlin

1961. 10th Anniv of International Federation of Resistance Fighters.
2631 **918** 4k. grey and red 35 10

919 Adult Education

1961. Communist Labour Teams.
2632 – 2k. purple & red on buff 20 10
2633 **919** 3k. brown & red on buff 20 10
2634 – 4k. blue and red on cream 35 15
DESIGNS: 2k. Worker at machine; 4k. Workers around piano.

920 Rocket and Globes

1961. Cosmic Flights. Aluminium-surfaced paper.
2635 **920** 1r. red and black on silver . . . . 22·00 22·00

XXII съезд
КПСС
(921)

1961. 22nd Communist Party Congress (2nd issue). Optd with T **921**.
2636 **920** 1r. red and black on silver . . . . 19·00 20·00

922 Imanov (after A. Kasteev)

923 Liszt, Piano and Music

1961. 42nd Death Anniv of Amangeldy Imanov (Kazakh Leader).
2637 **922** 4k. sepia, brown & green 35 10

1961. 150th Birth Anniv of Liszt.
2638 **923** 4k. brown, purple & yell 75 15

924 Flags, Rocket and Skyline

1961. 44th Anniv of October Revolution.
2639 **924** 4k. red, purple and yellow 70 15

925 Congress Emblem

926 Statue of Lomonosov (N. Tomsky) and Lomonosov University

1961. 5th W.F.T.U. Congress, Moscow. Inscr "МОСКВА 1961".
2640 **925** 2k. red and bistre . . . 25 10
2641 – 2k. violet and grey . . . 25 10
2642 – 4k. brown, purple & blue 50 15
2643 – 4k. red, blue and violet 50 15
2644 **925** 6k. red, bistre and green 75 20
2645 – 6k. blue, purple and bistre 75 20
DESIGNS—HORIZ: Nos. 2641, 2645, Negro breaking chains. VERT: No. 2642, Hand holding hammer; 2643, Hands holding globe.

1961. 250th Birth Anniv of Mikhail Lomonosov (scientist).
2646 **926** 4k. brown, green and blue 45 15
2647 – 6k. blue, buff and green 65 20
2648 – 10k. brown, blue & pur 1·40 40
DESIGNS—VERT: 6k. Lomonosov at desk (after M. Shreier). HORIZ: 10k. Lomonosov (after L. Miropolsky), his birthplace, and Leningrad Academy of Science.

927 Power Workers **928** Scene from "Romeo and Juliet" (Prokotiev)

1961. Young Builders of Seven Year Plan. Inscr "1961".
2649 **927** 3k. grey, brown and red 50 15
2650 – 4k. brown, blue and red 45 15
2651 – 6k. grey, brown and red 75 20
DESIGNS: 4k. Welders; 6k. Engineer with theodolite.

1961. Russian Ballet (1st issue). Multicoloured.
2652 6k. Type **928** . . . . 1·10 20
2653 10k. Scene from "Swan Lake" (Tchaikovsky) . . 1·50 45
See also Nos. 2666/7.

929 Hammer and Sickle **930** A. Pumpur

1961. 25th Anniv of Soviet Constitution.
2654 **929** 4k. lake, yellow and red 40 15

1961. 120th Birth Anniv of Pumpur (Lettish poet).
2655 **930** 4k. purple and grey . . . 25 10

1961. Air. Surch **1961 r. 6 kon.** and wavy lines.
2656 **822** 6k. on 60k. blue 90 20

932 "Bulgarian Achievements"

1961. 15th Anniv of Bulgarian Republic.
2657 **932** 4k. multicoloured . . . 35 10

933 Nansen and "Fram"

1961. Birth Centenary of Nansen (explorer).
2658 **933** 6k. brown, blue and black . . . . 1·75 15

934 M. Dolivo-Dobrovolsky **935** A. S. Pushkin (after O. Kiprensky)

1962. Birth Centenary of Dolivo-Dobrovolsky (electrical engineer).
2659 **934** 4k. blue and bistre . . . 35 10

1962. 125th Death Anniv of Pushkin (poet).
2660 **935** 4k. black, red and buff 30 10

936 Soviet Woman

1962. Soviet Women.
2661 **936** 4k. black, bistre & orange 35 10

937 People's Dancers

1962. 25th Anniv of Soviet People's Dance Ensemble.
2662 **937** 4k. brown and red . . . 35 10

938 Skaters

1962. Ice Skating Championships, Moscow.
2663 **938** 4k. blue and orange . . 40 10

1962. War Heroes. As T **879** but inscr "1962".
2664 4k. brown and blue 90 15
2665 6k. turquoise and brown . . 1·25 20
DESIGNS: 4k. Lieut. Shalandin, tanks and Yakovlev Yak-9T fighters; 6k. Capt. Gadzhiev, "K-3" submarine and sinking ship.

1962. Russian Ballet (2nd issue). As T **928** but inscr "1962".
2666 2k. multicoloured 60 15
2667 3k. multicoloured 65 15
DESIGNS: Scenes from—2k. "Red Flower" (Glier); 3k. "Paris Flame" (Asafev).

СОВЕТСКИЕ КОНЬКОБЕЖЦЫ— ЧЕМПИОНЫ МИРА
(**939**)

1962. Soviet Victory in Ice Skating Championships. Optd with T **939**.
2668 **938** 4k. blue and orange . . 2·75 1·50

940 Skiing

1962. 1st People's Winter Games, Sverdlovsk.
2669 **940** 4k. violet and red . . . 45 15
2670 – 6k. turquoise and purple 60 20
2671 – 10k. red, black and blue 1·25 30
DESIGN: 6k. Ice Hockey; 10k. Figure skating.

941 A. I. Herzen (after N. Ge) **942** Lenin on Banner

1962. 150th Birth Anniv of A. I. Herzen (writer).
2672 **941** 4k. flesh, black and blue 35 10

1962. 14th Leninist Young Communist League Congress. Inscr "1962".
2673 **942** 4k. red, yellow and purple 20 10
2674 – 6k. purple, orange & blue 35 10
DESIGN—HORIZ: 6k. Lenin (after A. Mylnikov) on flag.

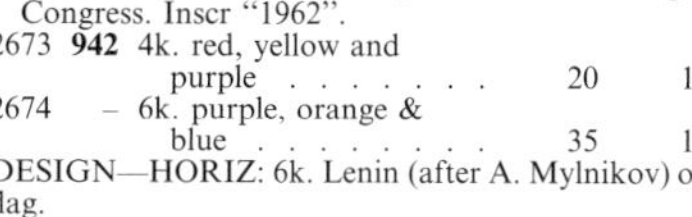

943 Rocket and Globe **944** Tchaikovsky (after sculpture by Z. M. Vilensky)

1962. 1st Anniv of World's First Manned Space Flight. Perf or imperf.
2675 **943** 10k. multicoloured . . . 1·10 35

1962. 2nd Int Tchaikovsky Music Competition.
2676 **944** 4k. drab, black and blue 50 10

945 Youth of Three Races

1962. International Day of "Solidarity of Youth against Colonialism".
2677 **945** 6k. multicoloured . . . 45 10

946 The Ulyanov (Lenin's) Family

1962. 92nd Birth Anniv of Lenin.
2678 **946** 4k. brown, grey and red 40 15
2679 – 10k. purple, red and black . . . . 1·00 30
DESIGN: 10k. Bust of Lenin (N. Sokolov).

947 "Cosmos 3"

1962. Cosmic Research.
2680 **947** 6k. black, violet and blue 65 15

948 Charles Dickens

1962. 150th Birth Anniv of Charles Dickens.
2681 **948** 6k. purple, turq & brn 85 20

949 J. J. Rousseau **950** Karl Marx Monument, Moscow (L. Kerbel)

1962. 250th Birth Anniv of Rousseau.
2682 **949** 6k. bistre, purple and grey 70 20

1962. Karl Marx Commemoration.
2683 **950** 4k. grey and blue . . . 35 10

951 Lenin reading "Pravda" **952** Mosquito and Campaign Emblem

1962. 50th Anniv of "Pravda" Newspaper.
2684 **951** 4k. purple, red and buff 30 15
2685 – 4k. multicoloured . . . 30 15
2686 – 4k. multicoloured . . . 30 15
DESIGNS—25 × 38 mm: No. 2685, Statuary and front page of first issue of "Pravda"; No. 2686, Lenin (after A. Mylnikov) and modern front page of "Pravda".

1962. Malaria Eradication. Perf (6k. also imperf).
2687 **952** 4k. black, turquoise & red 40 10
2688 6k. black, green and red 70 10

953 Model Rocket Construction

1962. 40th Anniv of All Union Lenin Pioneer Organization. Designs embody Pioneer badge. Multicoloured.
2689 2k. Lenin and Pioneers giving Oath 25 10
2690 3k. Lenya Golikov and Valya Kotik (pioneer heroes) 25 10
2691 4k. Type **953** 35 10
2692 4k. Hygiene education . . . 40 15
2693 6k. Pioneers marching . . . 90 25

954 M. Mashtotz **955** Ski Jumping

1962. 1600th Birth Anniv of Mesrop Mashtotz (author of Armenian Alphabet).
2694 **954** 4k. brown and yellow . . 35 10

1962. F.I.S. International Ski Championships, Zakopane (Poland).
2695 **955** 2k. red, brown and blue 20 10
2696 – 10k. blue, black and red 90 35
DESIGN—VERT: 10k. Skier.

956 I. Goncharov (after I. Kramskoi) **957** Cycle Racing

1962. 150th Birth Anniv of I. Goncharov (writer).
2697 **956** 4k. brown and grey . . 35 10

1962. Summer Sports Championships.
2698 **957** 2k. black, red and brown 40 10
2699 – 4k. black, yellow & brn 75 20
2700 – 10k. black, lemon & blue 80 30
2701 – 12k. brown, yellow & bl 95 40
2702 – 16k. multicoloured . . . 1·50 50
DESIGN—VERT: 4k. Volleyball; 10k. Rowing; 16k. Horse jumping. HORIZ: 12k. Football (goal keeper).

1962. Capitals of Autonomous Republics. 3rd issue. As T **835**.
2703 4k. black 50 15
2704 4k. purple 50 15
2705 4k. green 50 15
CAPITALS: No. 2703, Kazan (Tatar); No. 2704, Kyzyl (Tuva); No.2705, Saransk (Mordovian).

958 Lenin Library, 1862

1962. Centenary of Lenin Library.
2706 **958** 4k. black and grey . . . 35 15
2707 – 4k. black and grey . . . 35 15
DESIGN: No. 2707, Modern library building.

959 Fur Bourse, Leningrad and Ermine

1962. Fur Bourse Commemoration.
2708 **959** 6k. multicoloured . . . 65 30

960 Pasteur — 961 Youth and Girl with Book

1982. Centenary of Pasteur's Sterilization Process.
2709 **960** 6k. brown and black . . 60 15

1962. Communist Party Programme. Mult.
2710 2k. Type **961** 20 10
2711 4k. Workers of three races and dove 35 10

962 Hands breaking Bomb

1962. World Peace Congress, Moscow.
2712 **962** 6k. bistre, black and blue 30 15

963 Ya. Kupala and Ya. Kolas

1962. Byelorussian Poets Commemoration.
2713 **963** 4k. brown and yellow . . 30 10

964 Sabir — 965 Congress Emblem

1962. Birth Centenary of Sabir (Azerbaijan poet).
2714 **964** 4k. brown, buff and blue 30 10

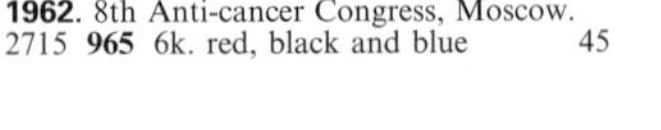

1962. 8th Anti-cancer Congress, Moscow.
2715 **965** 6k. red, black and blue 45 15

966 N. N. Zinin

1962. 150th Birth Anniv of N. N. Zinin (chemist).
2716 **966** 4k. brown and violet . . 30 10

1962. War of 1941–45 (2nd issue). As T **911** inscr "1962".
2717 4k. multicoloured 55 15
DESIGN: Sailor throwing petrol bomb (Defence of Sevastopol, after A. Deinekin).

967 M. V. Nesterov (painter) (after P. Korin)

1962. Russian Artists Commemoration.
2718 **967** 4k. multicoloured . . . 45 15
2719 – 4k. brown, purple & grey 45 15
2720 – 4k. black and brown . . 45 15
PORTRAITS—VERT: No. 2719, I. N. Kramskoi (painter) (after N. Yovoshenko). HORIZ: No. 2220, I. D. Shadr (sculptor).

968 "Vostok-2" — 969 Nikolaev and "Vostok 3"

1962. 1st Anniv of Titov's Space Flight. Perf or imperf.
2721 **968** 10k. purple, black & blue . . . . 1·10 35
2722 10k. orange, black & blue . . . . 1·10 35

1962. 1st "Team" Manned Space Flight. Perf or imperf.
2723 **969** 4k. brown, red and blue 90 20
2724 – 4k. brown, red and blue 90 20
2725 – 6k. multicoloured . . . 1·50 25
DESIGNS: No. 2724, As Type **969** but with Popovich and "Vostok-4"; No. 2725 (47 × 28½ mm), Cosmonauts in flight.

970 House of Friendship

1962. People's House of Friendship, Moscow.
2726 **970** 6k. grey and blue . . . 30 10

971 Lomonosov University and Atomic Symbols

1962. "Atoms for Peace".
2727 **971** 4k. multicoloured . . . 35 10
2728 – 6k. multicoloured . . . 75 20
DESIGN: 6k. Map of Russia, Atomic symbol and "Peace" in ten languages.

972 Common Carp and Bream — 973 F. E. Dzerzhinsky

1962. Fish Preservation Campaign.
2729 **972** 4k. yellow, violet and blue 50 10
2730 – 6k. blue, black and orange 75 20
DESIGN: 6k. Atlantic salmon.

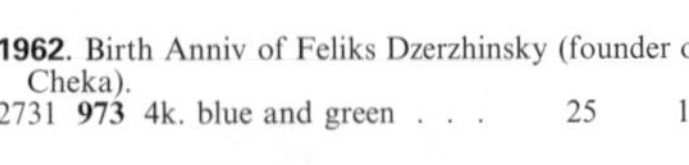

1962. Birth Anniv of Feliks Dzerzhinsky (founder of Cheka).
2731 **973** 4k. blue and green . . . 25 10

974 O. Henry

1962. Birth Cent of O. Henry (American writer).
2732 **974** 6k. black, brown & yell 45 10

975 Field Marshals Barclay de Tolly, Kutuzov and Bagration

1962. 150th Anniv of Patriotic War of 1812.
2733 **975** 3k. brown 40 10
2734 – 4k. blue 55 15
2735 – 6k. slate 65 20
2736 – 10k. violet 90 25
DESIGNS: 4k. D. V. Davydov and partisans; 6k. Battle of Borodino; 10k. Partisan Vasilisa Kozhina escorting French prisoners of war.

976 Lenin Street, Vinnitsa

1962. 600th Anniv of Vinnitsa.
2737 **976** 4k. black and bistre . . 30 10

977 Transport, "Stamp" and "Postmark" — 978 Cedar

1962. International Correspondence Week.
2738 **977** 4k. black, purple & turq 30 10

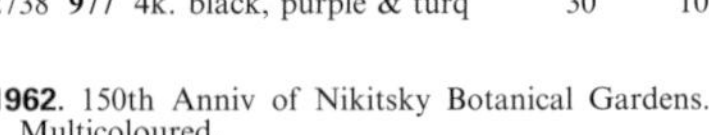

1962. 150th Anniv of Nikitsky Botanical Gardens. Multicoloured.
2739 3k. Type **978** 35 10
2740 4k. "Vostok-2" canna (plant) 55 10
2741 6k. Strawberry tree (arbutus) 70 15
2742 10k. "Road to the Stars" (chrysanthemum) 95 25

979 Builder — 981 Akhundov (after N. Ismailov)

980 "Sputnik 1"

1962. "The Russian People". Multicoloured.
2743 4k. Type **979** 30 15
2744 4k. Textile worker 30 15
2745 4k. Surgeon 30 15
2746 4k. Farm girl 30 15
2747 4k. P. T. instructor 30 15
2748 4k. Housewife 30 15
2749 4k. Rambler 30 15

1962. 5th Anniv of Launching of "Sputnik 1".
2750 **980** 10k. multicoloured . . . 1·10 30

1962. 150th Birth Anniv of Mirza Akhundov (poet).
2751 **981** 4k. brown and green . . 35 10

982 Harvester — 983 N. N. Burdenko

1962. "Settlers on Virgin Lands". Multicoloured.
2752 4k. Type **982** 55 20
2753 4k. Surveyors, tractors and map 55 20
2754 4k. Pioneers with flag . . . 55 20

1962. Soviet Scientists. Inscr "1962". Multicoloured.
2755 4k. Type **983** 30 10
2756 4k. V. P. Filatov (wearing beret) 35 10

984 Lenin Mausoleum

1962. 92nd Birth Anniv of Lenin.
2757 **984** 4k. multicoloured . . . 30 10

985 Worker with Banner — 986 "Into Space" (sculpture, G. Postnikov)

1962. 45th Anniv of October Revolution.
2758 **985** 4k. multicoloured . . . 30 10

1962. Space Flights Commem. Perf or imperf.
2759 **986** 6k. black, brown and blue 60 15
2760 10k. ultram, bis & vio 1·00 20

(987) — 988 T. Moldo (Kirghiz poet)

1962. Launching of Rocket to Mars (1st issue). Optd with T **987**.
2761 **986** 10k. blue, bistre and violet . . . . 3·25 1·75
See also No. 2765.

1962. Poets' Anniversaries.
2762 **988** 4k. black and red . . . 40 10
2763 – 4k. black and blue . . . 40 10
DESIGN: No. 2763, Sayat-Nova (Armenian poet) with musical instrument (after G. Ruthkyan).

989 Hammer and Sickle

1962. 40th Anniv of U.S.S.R.
2764 **989** 4k. yellow, red and crimson 30 10

990 Mars Rocket in Space (⅔-size illustration)

1962. Launching of Rocket to Mars (2nd issue).
2765 **990** 10k. violet and red . . . 1·10 30

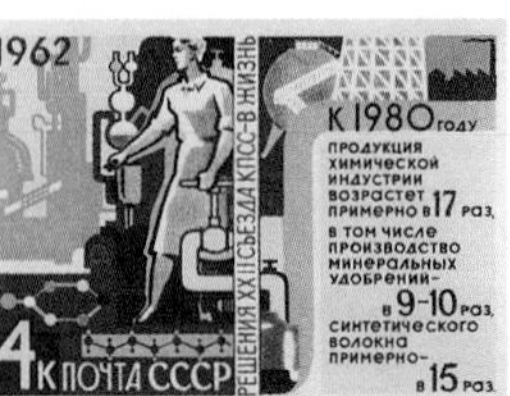

991 Chemical Industry and Statistics

1962. 22nd Communist Party Congress. "Achievements of the People". Multicoloured.
2766 4k. Type **991** 55 20
2767 4k. Engineering (machinery and atomic symbol) . . . 55 20

2768 4k. Hydro-electric power . . 55 20
2769 4k. Agriculture (harvester) 55 20
2770 4k. Engineering (surveyor and welder) 55 20
2771 4k. Communications (telephone installation) . . 55 20
2772 4k. Heavy industry (furnace) 55 20
2773 4k. Transport (signalman, etc) 65 20
2774 4k. Dairy farming (milkmaid, etc) 55 20

All the designs show production targets relating to 1980.

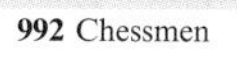

992 Chessmen   **994** V. K. Blucher (military commander)

993 Four Soviet Cosmonauts (½-size illustration)

1962. 30th Soviet Chess Championships, Yerevan.
2775 **992** 4k. black and ochre . . 75 20

1962. Soviet Cosmonauts Commem. Perf or imperf.
2776 **993** 1r. black and blue . . . 8·00 8·00

1962. V. K. Blucher Commemoration.
2777 **994** 4k. multicoloured . . . 40 10

995 V. N. Podbelsky   **996** A. Gaidar

1962. 75th Birth Anniv of V. N. Podbelsky (postal administrator, 1918–20).
2778 **995** 4k. violet and brown . . 25 10

1962. Soviet Writers.
2779 **996** 4k. buff, black and blue 30 10
2780 – 4k. multicoloured . . . 30 10
DESIGN: No. 2780, A. S. Makharenko.

997 Dove and Christmas Tree

1962. New Year. Perf or imperf.
2781 **997** 4k. multicoloured . . . 35 10

998 D. N. Pryanishnikov (agricultural chemist)   **999** Rose-coloured Starlings

1962. D. N. Pryanishnikov Commemoration.
2782 **998** 4k. multicoloured . . . 30 10

1962. Birds.
2783 **999** 3k. black, red and green 40 15
2784 – 4k. black, brown & orge 55 15
2785 – 6k. blue, black and red 65 20
2786 – 10k. blue, black and red 1·00 40
2787 – 16k. red, blue and black 1·50 65
BIRDS: 4k. Red-breasted geese; 6k. Snow geese; 10k. Great white cranes; 16k. Greater flamingos.

1000 F.I.R. Emblem and Handclasp   **1001** Badge and Yakovlev Yak-9 Fighters

1962. 4th International Federation of Resistance Heroes Congress.
2788 **1000** 4k. violet and red . . . 30 10
2789 6k. turquoise and red 45 15

1962. 20th Anniv of French Air Force "Normandy-Niemen" Unit.
2790 **1001** 6k. red, green and buff 65 15

1002 Map and Savings Book

1962. 40th Anniv of Soviet Banks.
2791 **1002** 4k. multicoloured . . . 25 10
2792 – 6k. multicoloured . . . 45 15
DESIGN: 6k. Savings book and map containing savers.

1003 Fertilizer Plant, Rustavi, Georgia

1962. Heavy Industries.
2793 **1003** 4k. black, lt blue & blue 40 15
2794 – 4k. black, turquoise & grn 40 15
2795 – 4k. black, blue and grey 40 15
DESIGNS: No. 2794, Construction of Bratsk hydro-electric station; 2795, Volzhskaya hydro-electric station, Volgograd.

1962. Provincial Costumes (3rd issue). As T **870**. Inscr "1962".
2796 3k. red, brown and drab . . 40 15
COSTUME: 3k. Latvia.

1004 K. S. Stanislavsky   **1005** A. S. Serafimovich

1963. Russian Stage Celebrities.
2797 **1004** 4k. green on pale green 35 10
2798 – 4k. brown 35 10
2799 – 4k. brown 35 10
PORTRAITS AND ANNIVERSARIES: No. 2797, Type **1004** (actor, birth cent); 2798, M. S. Shchepkin (actor, death cent); 2799, V. D. Durov (animal trainer and circus artiste, birth cent).

1963. Russian Writers and Poets.
2800 **1005** 4k. brown, sepia & mve 35 10
2801 – 4k. brown and purple 35 10
2802 – 4k. brown, red and buff 35 10
2803 – 4k. brown and green . . 35 10
2804 – 4k. brown, sepia & mve 35 10
2805 – 4k. multicoloured . . 35 10
PORTRAITS AND ANNIVERSARIES: 2800, (birth cent); 2801, Demyan Bednyi (80th birth anniv); 2802, G. I. Uspensky (120th birth anniv); 2803, N. P. Ogarev (150th birth anniv); 2804, V. Ya. Bryusov (90th birth anniv); 2805, F. V. Gladkov (80th birth anniv).

1006 Children in Nursery   **1007** Dolls and Toys

1963. Child Welfare.
2806 **1006** 4k. black and orange 30 10
2807 – 4k. purple, blue & orge 30 10
2808 – 4k. bistre, red and green 30 10
2809 – 4k. purple, red & orange 30 10
DESIGNS: No. 2807, Children with nurse; 2808, Young pioneers; 2809, Students at desk and trainee at lathe.

1963. Decorative Arts. Multicoloured.
2810 4k. Type **1007** 35 10
2811 6k. Pottery 45 15
2812 10k. Books 75 20
2813 12k. Porcelain . . . . . . 1·10 30

1008 Ilyushin Il-62 Jetliner

1962. 40th Anniv of "Aeroflot" Airline.
2814 **1008** 10k. black, brown & red 80 15
2815 – 12k. multicoloured . . 1·00 30
2816 – 16k. red, black and blue 1·40 60
DESIGNS: 12k. "Aeroflot" emblem; 16k. Tupolev Tu-124 airliner.

1009 M. N. Tukhachevsky   **1010** M. A. Pavlov (scientist)

1963. 45th Anniv of Red Army and War Heroes.
2817 **1009** 4k. green and turquoise 30 10
2818 – 4k. black and brown . . 30 10
2819 – 4k. brown and blue . . 30 10
2820 – 4k. black and red . . . 30 10
2821 – 4k. violet and mauve 30 10
DESIGNS (Army heroes and battle scenes): 2817, Type **1009** (70th birth anniv); 2818, U. M. Avetisyan; 2819, A. M. Matrosov; 2820, I. V. Panfilov; 2821, Ya. F. Fabricius.

1963. Academy of Sciences Members.
2822 **1010** 4k. blue, grey and brown 30 10
2823 – 4k. brown and green . . 30 10
2824 – 4k. multicoloured . . . 30 10
2825 – 4k. brown, red and blue 30 10
2826 – 4k. multicoloured . . . 30 10
PORTRAITS: No. 2823, I. V. Kurchatov; No. 2824, V. I. Vernadsky. LARGER (23½ × 30 mm): No. 2825, A. Krylov; No. 2826, V. Obruchev. All commemorate birth centenaries except No. 2823 (60th anniv of birth).

1011 Games Emblem

Советские хоккеисты-чемпионы мира и Европы. Стокгольм. 1963 г.

(**1012**)

1963. 5th Soviet T.U. Winter Sports.
2827 **1011** 4k. orange, black & blue 30 10

1963. Soviet Victory in Swedish Ice Hockey Championships. No. 2670 optd with T **1012**.
2828 6k. turquoise and purple . . 1·60 60

1013 V. Kingisepp   **1014** R. M. Blauman

1963. 75th Birth Anniv of Victor Kingisepp (Estonian Communist Party Leader).
2829 **1013** 4k. brown and blue . . 25 10

1963. Birth Centenary of Rudolf Blauman (Latvian writer).
2830 **1014** 4k. purple and blue . . 25 10

1015 Globe and Flowers   **1016** Lenin (after I. Brodsky)

1963. "World without Arms and Wars". Perf or imperf.
2831 **1015** 4k. green, blue and red 35 10
2832 – 6k. lilac, green and red 55 10
2833 – 10k. violet, blue and red . . . . 1·10 25
DESIGNS: 6k. Atomic emblem and pylon; 10k. Sun and rocket.

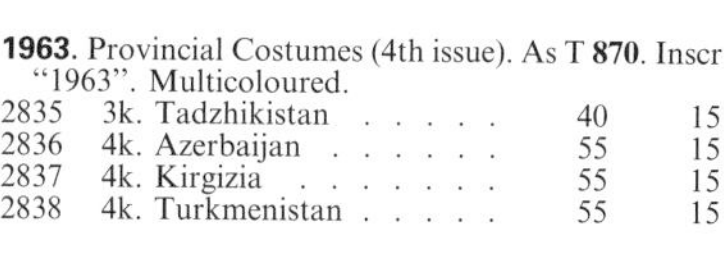

1963. 93rd Birth Anniv of Lenin.
2834 **1016** 4k. brown and red . . 3·75 1·40

1963. Provincial Costumes (4th issue). As T **870**. Inscr "1963". Multicoloured.
2835 3k. Tadzhikistan 40 15
2836 4k. Azerbaijan 55 15
2837 4k. Kirgizia 55 15
2838 4k. Turkmenistan 55 15

1017 "Luna 4" Rocket

1963. Launching of "Luna 4" Space Rocket. Perf or imperf.
2839 **1017** 6k. red, black and blue 70 20
See also No. 3250.

1018 Woman and Lido

1963. 5th Anniv of World Health Day. Mult.
2840 2k. Type **1018** 20 10
2841 4k. Man and stadium . . . 35 10
2842 10k. Child and school . . . 85 20

1019 Sputniks and Globe

1963. Cosmonautics Day.
2843 **1019** 10k. blue, black and purple (white figures of value) 75 20
2843b 10k. blue, black and purple (blue figures) 75 20
2844 – 10k. purple, black and blue (white figures) 75 20
2844a 10k. purple, black and blue (purple figures) 75 20
2845 – 10k. red, black and yellow (white figures) 75 20
2845a 10k. red, black and yellow (yellow figures) 75 20
DESIGNS: Nos. 2844/a, "Vostok 1" and Moon; Nos. 2845/a, Space rocket and Sun.

1021 Cuban Horsemen with Flag

1963. Cuban-Soviet Friendship.
2846 **1021** 4k. black, red and blue 40 10
2847 – 6k. black, blue and red 50 10
2848 – 10k. blue, red and black 65 20
DESIGNS: 6k. Hands, weapon, book and flag; 10k. Crane, hoisting tractor and flags.

1022 J. Hasek **1023** Karl Marx

1963. 40th Death Anniv of Jaroslav Hasek (writer).
2849 **1022** 4k. black 65 15

1963. 80th Death Anniv of Karl Marx.
2850 **1023** 4k. black and brown . . 30 10

1963. War of 1941–45 (3rd issue). As T **911** inscr "1963".
2851 4k. multicoloured 45 15
2852 4k. multicoloured 45 15
2853 4k. multicoloured 45 15
2854 4k. sepia and red 45 15
2855 6k. olive, black and red . . 70 20
DESIGNS: No. 2851, Woman making shells (Defence of Leningrad, 1942); 2852, Soldier in winter kit with tommy gun (20th anniv of Battle of the Volga); 2853, Soldiers attacking (Liberation of Kiev, 1943); 2854, Tanks and map indicating Battle of Kursk, 1943; 2855, Tank commander and tanks.

1024 International P.O. Building

1963. Opening of Int Post Office, Moscow.
2856 **1024** 6k. brown and blue . . 65 10

1025 Medal and Chessmen

1963. World Chess Championship, Moscow. Perf or imperf.
2857 **1025** 4k. multicoloured . . . 60 15
2858 – 6k. blue, mauve and ultramarine 70 20
2859 – 16k. black, mauve & pur . . . . 1·50 50
DESIGNS: 6k. Chessboard and pieces; 16k. Venue and pieces.

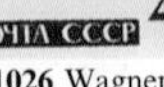

1026 Wagner **1027** Boxers on "Glove"

1963. 150th Birth Anniv of Wagner and Verdi (composers).
2860 **1026** 4k. black and red . . . 50 15
2861 – 4k. purple and red . . 50 15
DESIGN: No. 2861, Verdi.

1963. 15th European Boxing Championships, Moscow. Multicoloured.
2862 4k. Type **1027** 30 10
2863 6k. Referee and winning boxer on "glove" 55 15

1028 Bykovsky and "Vostok 5"

1963. Second "Team" Manned Space Flights (1st issue). Perf or imperf.
2864 **1028** 6k. brown and purple 55 20
2865 – 6k. red and green . . . 55 20
2866 – 10k. red and blue . . . 1·00 30
DESIGNS: No. 2865, Tereshkova and "Vostok 6"; No. 2866, Allegory—"Man and Woman in Space".
See also Nos. 2875/7.

Всемирный
конгресс
женщин.

(**1029**)

1030 Cycling

1963. International Women's Congress, Moscow. Optd with T **1029**.
2867 **1015** 4k. green, blue and red 55 30

1963. 3rd People's Spartakiad. Multicoloured. Perf or imperf.
2868b 3k. Type **1030** 25 10
2869b 4k. Athletics 30 15
2870b 6k. Swimming (horiz) . . . 45 15
2871b 12k. Basketball 85 35
2872b 16k. Football . . . . . . 1·25 50

1031 Globe, Film and Camera **1032** V. V. Mayakovsky

1963. International Film Festival, Moscow.
2873 **1031** 4k. blue, black & brown 30 10

1963. 70th Birth Anniv of Mayakovsky (poet).
2874 **1032** 4k. brown 40 15

1033 Tereshkova **1034** Ice Hockey Player

1963. 2nd "Team" Manned Space Flights (2nd issue). Multicoloured.
2875 4k. Bykovsky (horiz) . . . 40 20
2876 4k. Tereshkova (horiz) . . . 40 20
2877 10k. Type **1033** . . . . . . 1·60 35

1963. Russian Ice Hockey Championships.
2878 **1034** 6k. blue and red . . . 75 20

1035 Lenin **1037** Guibozo (polo)

1036 Freighter and Crate

1963. 60th Anniv of 2nd Socialist Party Congress.
2879 **1035** 4k. black and red . . . 30 10

1963. Red Cross Centenary.
2880 **1036** 6k. red and green . . . 60 15
2881 – 12k. red and blue . . . 1·25 30
DESIGN: 12k. Centenary emblem.

1963. Regional Sports.
2882 – 3k. multicoloured . . . 30 10
2883 **1037** 4k. black, red and ochre 40 10
2884 – 6k. red, brown & yellow 65 15
2885 – 10k. black, brn & olive 90 25
DESIGNS—HORIZ: 3k. Lapp reindeer racing; 6k. Buryat archery. VERT: 10k. Armenian wrestling.

1038 Aleksandr Mozhaisky and his Monoplane

1963. Aviation Celebrities.
2886 **1038** 6k. black and blue . . 60 10
2887 – 10k. black and blue . . 80 15
2888 – 16k. black and blue . . 1·25 35
DESIGNS: 10k. Pyotr Nesterov and "looping the loop"; 16k. N. E. Zhukovsky and "aerodynamics".

1039 S. S. Gulak-Artemovsky (composer, 150th birth anniv) **1040** Olga Kobilyanska (writer) (birth centenary)

1963. Celebrities.
2889 **1039** 4k. black and red . . . 40 15
2890 – 4k. brown and purple 40 15
2891 – 4k. brown and violet 40 15
2892 **1040** 4k. mauve and brown 40 15
2893 – 4k. mauve and green 40 15
DESIGNS AND ANNIVERSARIES: As Type **1039**: No. 2893, M. I. Petraskas (Lithuanian composer) and scene from one of his works (90th birth anniv). As Type **1040**: No. 2890, G. D. Eristavi (writer, death cent, 1964); No. 2891, A. S. Dargomizhsky (composer, 150th birth anniv).

1041 Antarctic Map and Supply Ship "Ob" **1043** E. O. Paton

1042 Letters and Transport

1963. Arctic and Antarctic Research. Mult.
2894 3k. Type **1041** . . . . . . 1·75 25
2895 4k. Convoy of snow tractors and map . . . . 1·00 30
2896 6k. Globe and aircraft at polar base . . . . 1·75 30
2897 12k. "Sovetskaya Ukraina" (whale factory ship), whale catcher and whale 4·00 50

1963. International Correspondence Week.
2898 **1042** 4k. violet, orange & blk 35 10

1963. 10th Death Anniv of Paton (engineer).
2899 **1043** 4k. black, red and blue 30 10

1045 D. Diderot **1046** "Peace"

1963. 250th Birth Anniv of Denis Diderot (French philosopher).
2900 **1045** 4k. brown, blue & bistre 30 10

1963. "Peace—Brotherhood—Liberty—Labour". All black, red and lake.
2901 4k. Type **1046** 35 15
2902 4k. Worker at desk and couple consulting plan ("Labour") 35 15
2903 4k. Artist and couple ("Liberty") 35 15
2904 4k. Voters ("Equality") . . 35 15
2905 4k. Man shaking hands with couple with banner ("Brotherhood") 35 15
2906 4k. Family group ("Happiness") 35 15

1047 Academy of Sciences, Frunze

1963. Centenary of Union of Kirgizia and Russia.
2907 **1047** 4k. blue, yellow and red 30 10

1049 Lenin and Congress Building **1050** Ilya Mechnikov

1963. 13th Soviet Trade Unions' Congress, Moscow.
2908 **1049** 4k. red and black . . . 25 10
2909 – 4k. red and black . . . 25 10
DESIGN: No. 2909, Lenin with man and woman workers.

1963. 75th Anniv of Pasteur Institute, Paris.
2910 **1050** 4k. green and bistre . . 35 10
2911 – 6k. violet and bistre . . 55 15
2912 – 12k. blue and bistre . . 1·25 30
PORTRAITS: 6k. Pasteur; 12k. Calmette.

1051 Cruiser "Aurora" and Rockets **1052** Gur Emi Mausoleum

1963. 46th Anniv of October Revolution.
2913 **1051** 4k. black, orange & lake 45 10
2914 4k. black, red and lake 65 30

1963. Ancient Samarkand Buildings. Mult.
2915 4k. Type **1052** 50 10
2916 4k. Shachi-Zinda Mosque 50 10
2917 6k. Registan Square (55 × 28½ mm) 65 20

1053 Inscription, Globe and Kremlin **1054** Pushkin Monument, Kiev (A. Kovalev)

1963. Signing of Nuclear Test-ban Treaty, Moscow.
2918 **1053** 6k. violet and pale blue 60 15

1963.
2919 **1054** 4k. brown 30 10

1056 Shukhov and Radio Tower, Moscow **1057** Ya. Steklov and "Izvestia"

1963. 110th Birth Anniv of V. G. Shukhov (engineer).
2920 **1056** 4k. black and green . . 30 10

1963. 90th Birth Anniv of Ya. M. Steklov (first editor of "Izvestia").
2921 **1057** 4k. black and mauve 30 10

1058 Buildings and Emblems of Moscow (and U.S.S.R.) and Prague (and Czechoslovakia)

1963. 20th Anniv of Soviet-Czech Friendship Treaty.
2922 **1058** 6k. red, bistre and blue 45 10

1059 F. A. Poletaev (soldier) and Medals

1963. Poletaev Commemoration.
2923 **1059** 4k. multicoloured . . . 30 10

1062 J. Grimau (Spanish Communist)
1063 Rockets

1963. Grimau Commemoration.
2924 **1062** 6k. violet, red and cream 40 10

1963. New Year (1st issue).
2925 **1063** 6k. multicoloured . . . 50 10

1064 "Happy New Year"
1067 Topaz

1963. New Year (2nd issue).
2926 **1064** 4k. red, blue and green 40 10
2927 6k. red, blue and green 55 10

1963. "Precious Stones of the Urals". Multicoloured.
2928 2k. Type **1067** 25 10
2929 4k. Jasper 50 10
2030 6k. Amethyst 70 15
2931 10k. Emerald 75 25
2932 12k. Ruby . . . . 1·00 45
2933 16k. Malachite . . . . . . 1·25 55

1068 Sputnik 7
1071 Flame and Rainbow

1069 Dushanbe Putovsky Square

1963. "First in Space". Gold, vermilion and grey.
2934 10k. Type **1068** 90 30
2935 10k. Moon landing 90 30
2936 10k. Back of Moon 90 30
2937 10k. Vostok 7 . . . . . . 90 30
2938 10k. Twin flight 90 30
2939 10k. Seagull (first woman in space) 90 30

1963. Dushanbe, Capital of Tadzhikistan.
2940 **1069** 4k. blue 40 10

1963. 15th Anniv of Declaration of Human Rights.
2941 **1071** 6k. multicoloured . . . 45 10

1072 F. A, Sergeev ("Artem")

1963. 80th Birth Anniv of Sergeev (revolutionary).
2942 **1072** 4k. brown and red . . 30 10

1073 Sun and Globe
1074 K. Donelaitis

1964. International Quiet Sun Year.
2943 – 4k. black, orange & mve 30 10
2944 **1073** 6k. blue, yellow and red 45 10
2945 – 10k. violet, red and blue 60 20
DESIGNS—HORIZ: 4k. Giant telescope and sun; 10k. Globe and Sun.

1964. 250th Birth Anniv of K. Donelaitis (Lithuanian poet).
2946 **1074** 4k. black and myrtle . . 30 10

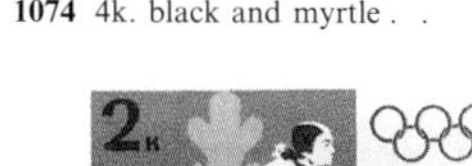

1075 Speed Skating

1964. Winter Olympic Games, Innsbruck.
2947b **1075** 2k. black, mauve & bl 25 10
2948b – 4k. black, blue & mve 40 15
2949b – 6k. red, black and blue 60 20
2950b – 10k. black, mve & grn 85 25
2951b – 12k. black, grn & mve 1·00 35
DESIGNS: 4k. Skiing; 6k. Games emblem; 10k. Rifle shooting (biathlon); 12k. Figure skating (pairs).
See also Nos. 2969/73.

1076 Golubkina (after N. Ulyanov) and Statue, Tolstoi
1077 "Agriculture"

1964. Birth Cent of A. S. Golubkina (sculptress).
2952 **1076** 4k. sepia and grey . . . 30 10

1964. Heavy Chemical Industries. Multicoloured.
2953 4k. Type **1077** 40 10
2954 4k. "Textiles" 40 10
2955 4k. "Tyre Production" . . . 40 10

(1078)
1079 Shevchenko's Statue, Kiev (M. Manizer)

1964. 150th Birth Anniv of T. G. Shevchenko (Ukrainian poet and painter). No. 2561 optd with T **1078** and designs as T **1079**.
2956 **880** 3k. brown and violet 1·50 75
2959 **1079** 4k. green 25 10
2960 4k. red 25 10
2961 – 6k. blue 40 10
2962 – 6k. brown 40 10
2957 – 10k. violet and brown 80 20
2958 – 10k. brown and bistre 80 20
DESIGNS: Nos. 2957/8, Portrait of Shevchenko by I. Repin; Nos. 2961/2, Self-portrait.

1080 K. S. Zaslonov

1964. War Heroes.
2963 **1080** 4k. sepia and brown . . 55 15
2964 – 4k. purple and blue . . 35 15
2965 – 4k. blue and red . . . 35 15
2966 – 4k. brown and blue . . 35 15
PORTRAITS: No. 2964, N. A. Vilkov; 2965, Yu. V. Smirnov; 2966, V. Z. Khoruzhaya.

1081 Fyodorov printing the first Russian book, "Apostle"

1964. 400th Anniv of First Russian Printed Book. Multicoloured.
2967 4k. Type **1081** 30 10
2968 6k. Statue of Ivan Fyodorov, Moscow (S. Volnukin), books and newspapers 45 20

(1082)
1083 Ice Hockey Player

1964. Winter Olympic Games, Soviet Medal Winners.
(a) Nos. 2947/51 optd with T **1082** or similarly.
2969 2k. black, mauve and blue 25 10
2970 4k. black, blue and mauve 40 10
2971 6k. red, black and blue . . 40 15
2972 10k. black, mauve and green 80 25
2973 12k. black, green and mauve 1·00 30

(b) New designs.
2974 **1083** 3k. red, black & turquoise 45 10
2975 – 16k. orange and brown 1·40 40
DESIGN: 16k. Gold medal and inscr "Triumph of Soviet Sport–11 Gold, 8 Silver, 6 Bronze medals".

1084 Militiaman and Factory Guard

1964. "Public Security".
2976 **1084** 4k. blue, red and black 30 10

1085 Lighthouse, Odessa and Sailor

1964. 20th Anniv of Liberation of Odessa and Leningrad. Multicoloured.
2977 4k. Type **1085** 35 10
2978 4k. Lenin Statue, Leningrad 35 10

1086 Sputniks
1087 N. I. Kibalchich

1964. "The Way to the Stars". Imperf or perf.
(a) Cosmonautics. As T **1086**.
2979 4k. green, black and red . . 50 10
2980 6k. black, blue and red . . 70 20
2981 12k. turquoise, brown & black . . . . 1·40 30
DESIGNS: 6k. "Mars I" space station; 12k. Gagarin and space capsule.

(b) Rocket Construction Pioneers. As T **1087**.
2982b 10k. black, green and violet . . . . 1·10 30
2983b 10k. black, turquoise and red . . . . 1·10 30
2984b 10k. black, turquoise and red . . . . 1·10 30
2985b 10k. black and blue . . . 1·00 30
DESIGNS: No. 2982, Type **1087**; 2983, F. A. Zander; 2984, K. E. Tsiolkovsky; 2985, Pioneers' medallion and Saransk memorial.

1088 Lenin

1964. 94th Birth Anniv of Lenin.
2986a **1088** 4k. black, blue & mve 3·25 2·50

1089 Shakespeare (400th Birth Anniv)

1964. Cultural Anniversaries.
2987 – 6k. yellow, brn & sepia 90 15
2988 **1089** 10k. brown and olive 1·40 25
2989 – 12k. green and brown 1·60 35
DESIGNS AND ANNIVERSARIES: 6k. Michelangelo (400th death anniv); 12k. Galileo (400th birth anniv).

1090 Crop-watering Machine and Produce

1964. "Irrigation".
2990 **1090** 4k. multicoloured . . . 30 10

1091 Gamarnik

1964. 70th Birth Anniv of Ya. B. Gamarnik (Soviet Army commander).
2991 **1091** 4k. brown, blue & black 30 10

1092 D. I. Gulia (Abhazian poet)
1094 Indian Elephant

1093 A. Gaidar

1964. Cultural Anniversaries.
2992 **1092** 4k. black, green and light green 30 15
2993 – 4k. black, verm & red 30 15
2994 – 4k. black, brown & bis 30 15
2995 – 4k. black, yellow & brn 30 15
2996 – 4k. multicoloured . . . 30 15
2997 – 4k. black, yellow & brn 30 15
DESIGNS: No. 2993, Nijazi (Uzbek writer, composer and painter); 2994, S. Seifullin (Kazakh poet); 2995, M. M. Kotsyubinsky (writer); 2996, S. Nazaryan (Armenian writer); 2997, T. Satylganov (Kirghiz poet).

1964. 60th Birth Annivs of Writers A. P. Gaidar and N. A. Ostrovsky.
2998 **1093** 4k. red and blue . . . 30 10
2999 – 4k. green and red . . . 35 10
DESIGN: No. 2999, N. Ostrovsky and battle scene.

1964. Centenary of Moscow Zoo. Multicoloured. Imperf or perf.
3000 1k. Type **1094** 10 10
3001 2k. Giant panda 20 10
3002 4k. Polar bear 45 10
3003 6k. Elk 55 10
3004 10k. Eastern white pelican 1·25 25
3005 12k. Tiger . . . . 2·00 30
3006 16k. Lammergeier . . . . . 1·50 40
The 2k. and 12k. are horiz; the 4k. and 10k. are "square", approx 26½ × 28 mm.

150 лет вхождения
в состав России
1964

4
коп.

(1095)

1964. 150th Anniv of Union of Azerbaijan and Russia. Surch with T **1095**.
3007 **328** 4k. on 40k. brown, bistre and yellow . . . . . 3·25 1·90

1096 Rumanian Woman and Emblems on Map
1097 Maize

1964. 20th. Anniv of Rumanian–Soviet Friendship Treaty.
3008 **1096** 6k. multicoloured . . . 50 15

1964. Agricultural Crops. Multicoloured. Imperf or perf.
3009b 2k. Type **1097** 15 10
3010b 3k. Wheat 20 10
3011b 4k. Potatoes 25 10
3012b 6k. Peas 35 20
3013b 10k. Sugar beet 70 25
3014b 12k. Cotton . . . . 1·00 30
3015b 16k. Flax . . . . 1·50 40

1098 Flag and Obelisk
1099 Leningrad G.P.O.

1964. 20th Anniv of Liberation of Byelorussia.
3016 **1098** 4k. multicoloured . . . 30 10

1964. 250th Anniv of Leningrad's Postal Service.
3017 **1099** 4k. black, bistre and red 30 10

1100 Map of Poland and Emblems

1964. 20th Anniv of Polish People's Republic.
3018 **1100** 6k. multicoloured . . . 45 10

1101 Horse-jumping

1102 M. Thorez (French Communist leader)

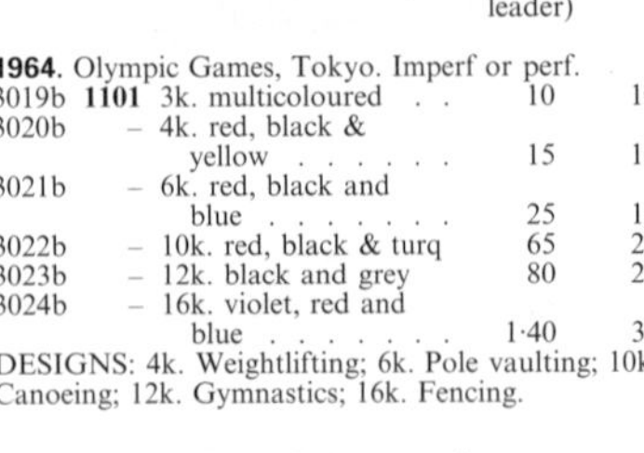

1964. Olympic Games, Tokyo. Imperf or perf.
3019b **1101** 3k. multicoloured . . 10 10
3020b – 4k. red, black & yellow 15 10
3021b – 6k. red, black and blue 25 15
3022b – 10k. red, black & turq 65 20
3023b – 12k. black and grey 80 25
3024b – 16k. violet, red and blue . . . . 1·40 30
DESIGNS: 4k. Weightlifting; 6k. Pole vaulting; 10k. Canoeing; 12k. Gymnastics; 16k. Fencing.

1964. Maurice Thorez Commemoration.
3025 **1102** 4k. black and red . . . 1·00 35

1103 Three Races

1104 Jawaharlal Nehru

1964. International Anthropologists and Ethnographers Congress, Moscow.
3026 **1103** 6k. black and yellow . . 40 15

1964. Nehru Commemoration.
3027 **1104** 4k. brown and grey . . 45 15

1105 Globe and Banner

1106 A. V. Vishnevsky (surgeon)

1964. Centenary of "First International".
3028 **1105** 4k. red, bistre and blue 30 10
3029 – 4k. red, olive and black 30 10
3030 – 4k. drab, red and lake 30 10
3031 – 4k. red, black and blue 30 10
3032 – 4k. multicoloured . . . 30 10
DESIGNS: No. 3029, Communist Party manifesto; 3030, Marx and Engels; 3031, Chain breaker; 3032, Lenin.

1964. "Outstanding Soviet Physicians".
3033 **1106** 4k. brown and purple 35 10
3034 – 4k. brown, red & yellow 35 10
3035 – 4k. brown, blue & bistre 35 10
DESIGNS: No. 3034, N. A. Semashko (public health pioneer). Both are 90th birth anniversaries. No. 3035, D. I. Ivanovsky and siphon (25 × 32 mm).

1107 Bulgarian Flag, Rose and Emblems

1108 P. Togliatti (Italian Communist leader)

1964. 20th Anniv of Bulgarian People's Republic.
3036 **1107** 6k. red, green and drab 45 15

1964. Togliatti Commemoration.
3037 **1108** 4k. black and red . . . 30 10

1110 Globe and Letters

1964. International Correspondence Week.
3038 **1110** 4k. mauve, blue & brn 30 10

1111 Soviet and Yugoslav Soldiers

1112 East German Arms, Industrial Plants, Freighter "Havel" and Electric Goods Train

1964. 20th Anniv of Liberation of Belgrade.
3039 **1111** 6k. multicoloured . . . 45 15

1964. 15th Anniv of German Democratic Republic.
3040 **1112** 6k. multicoloured . . . 45 15

1113 Woman holding Bowl of Produce (Moldavian Republic)

40 лет Советскому Таджикистану
1964 год

(1115)

1964. 40th Anniv of Soviet Republic. (a) As T **1113**.
3041 **1113** 4k. brown, green and red 30 10
3042 – 4k. multicoloured . . . 35 10
3043 – 4k. red, purple & yellow 35 10

(b) Optd with T **1115**.
3044 **1069** 4k. blue . . . . 1·10 60
DESIGNS—VERT: No. 3042, Woman holding Arms (Turkmenistan); 3043, Man and woman holding produce (Uzbekistan); 3044, commemorates the Tadzhikistan Republic.

1116 Yegorov

1964. Three-manned Space Flight. (a) Portraits in black, orange and turquoise.
3045 4k. Type **1116** 40 10
3046 4k. Feoktistov 40 10
3047 4k. Komarov 40 10
These can be identified by the close proximation of the Russian names on the stamps to the English versions.

(b) Designs 73½ × 22½ mm.
3048 6k. purple and violet . . . 75 15
3049 10k. violet and blue . . . . 1·10 30
DESIGNS: 6k. The three cosmonauts; 10k. Space ship "Voskhod 1".

1117 Soldier and Flags

1964. 20th Anniv of Liberation of Ukraine.
3050 **1117** 4k. multicoloured . . . 25 10

1119 Lermontov's Birthplace

1121 N. K. Krupskaya (Lenin's wife)

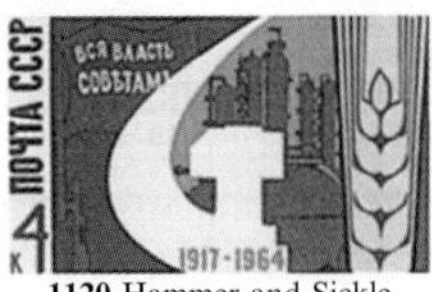
1120 Hammer and Sickle

1964. 150th Birth Anniv of M. Lermontov (poet).
3051 **1119** 4k. violet 30 10
3052 – 6k. black 45 10
3053 – 10k. brown and flesh 85 25
DESIGNS: 6k. Lermontov (after K. Gorbunov); 10k. Lermontov talking with V. Belinsky.

1964. 47th Anniv of October Revolution.
3054 **1120** 4k. multicoloured . . . 25 10

1964. Birth Anniversaries.
3055 **1121** 4k. multicoloured . . . 30 10
3056 – 4k. multicoloured . . . 30 10
DESIGNS: 3055 (95th anniv); 3056, A. I. Yelizarova-Ulyanova (Lenin's sister) (cent).

1122 Mongolian Woman and Lamb

1124 Butter Mushroom

1964. 40th Anniv of Mongolian People's Republic.
3057 **1122** 4k. multicoloured . . . 45 15

1964. Mushrooms. Multicoloured.
3058 2k. Type **1124** 30 10
3059 4k. Chanterelle 50 10
3060 6k. Ceps 65 15
3061 10k. Red-capped sacker stalk . . . . 1·10 40
3062 12k. Saffron milk cap . . . 1·40 50

1125 A. P. Dovzhenko

1126 Christmas Tree, Star and Globe

1964. 70th Birth Anniv of Dovzhenko (film producer).
3063 **1125** 4k. blue and grey . . . 30 10

1964. New Year.
3064 **1126** 4k. multicoloured . . . 75 25

1127 Struve

1128 Ivanov (after O. Braz) and "March of the Moscovites. 16th Century"

1964. Death Centenary of V. Ya. Struve (scientist).
3065 **1127** 4k. brown and blue . . 60 15

1964. Birth Centenary of S. V. Ivanov (painter).
3066 **1128** 4k. brown and black . . 65 15

1129 Scene from Film

1964. 30th Anniv of Film "Chapaev".
3067 **1129** 6k. black and green . . 50 15

1130 Test-tubes, Jar and Agricultural Scenes

1964. Chemistry for the National Economy.
3068 **1130** 4k. purple and olive . . 25 15
3069 – 6k. black and blue . . 45 10
DESIGN: 6k. Chemical plant.

1131 Cranberries

1132 Library

1964. Woodland Fruits. Multicoloured.
3070 1k. Type **1131** 15 10
3071 3k. Bilberries 20 10
3072 4k. Rowanberries 30 10
3073 10k. Blackberries 70 20
3074 16k. Red bilberries . . . . 1·10 40

1964. 250th Anniv of Academy of Sciences Library, Leningrad.
3075 **1132** 4k. black, green and red 40 10

1133 Congress Palace and Spassky Tower

1134 Mt Khan-Tengri

1964.
3076 **1133** 1r. blue . . . . 7·00 1·60

1964. Mountaineering. Multicoloured.
3077 4k. Type **1134** 30 10
3078 6k. Mt Kazbek (horiz) . . . 45 15
3079 12k. Mt Ushba 90 30

1136 Bowl

1964. Kremlin Treasures. Multicoloured.
3080 4k. Helmet 45 15
3081 6k. Quiver 65 20
3082 10k. Coronation headgear 1·00 35
3083 12k. Ladle . . . . 1·40 45
3084 16k. Type **1136** . . . . . . 1·75 80

1137 I. M. Sivko

1138 Dante

1965. War Heroes.
3085 **1137** 4k. black and violet . . 40 15
3086 – 4k. brown and blue . . 40 15
DESIGN: No. 3086, General I. S. Polbin.

1965. 700th Birth Anniv of Dante.
3087 **1138** 4k. black, bistre and purple 60 15

1139 Blood Donor

1140 N. P. Kravkov

1965. Blood Donors. Multicoloured.
3088 4k. Type **1139** 35 15
3089 4k. Hand holding red carnation 35 15

1965. Birth Cent of N. Kravkov (pharmacologist).
3090 **1140** 4k. multicoloured . . . 35 10

1141 Figure Skaters

1142 Alsatian

1965. European Figure Skating Championships, Moscow.
3091 **1141** 6k. red, black and green 55 15
See also No. 3108.

1965. World Ice Hockey Championships, Moscow. Designs similar to T **1141** but depicting ice hockey players.
3092 4k. red, blue and bistre . . 40 15

1965. Hunting and Service Dogs.
3093 – 1k. black, yellow and red 15 10
3097 – 2k. brown, blue & black 20 10
3098 **1142** 3k. black, red and yellow 20 10
3099 – 4k. black, brown & grn 30 10
3100 – 4k. black, orange & grn 30 10
3101 – 6k. black, brown & blue 40 20
3102 – 6k. black, red and blue 40 20
3104 – 10k. multicoloured . . 75 25
3095 – 12k. black, brown & vio 90 35
3096 – 16k. multicoloured . . 1·40 45
DESIGNS—HORIZ: 1k. Hound; 2k. Setter; 4k. (3099) (value in green) Fox terrier; 4k. (3100) (value in orange) Pointer; 6k. (3101) Borzoi; 12k. Husky. VERT: 6k. (3102) Sheepdog; 10k. Collie; 16k. Caucasian sheepdog.

1143 R. Sorge

1965. Richard Sorge (Soviet secret agent) Commem.
3103 **1143** 4k. black and red . . . 55 15

1144 I.T.U. Emblem and Telecommunications Symbol

1965. Centenary of I.T.U.
3104 **1144** 6k. violet and blue . . 65 15

1145 Leonov in Space (½-size illustration)

1965. Space Flight of "Voskhod 2" (1st issue). Imperf or perf.
3105 **1145** 10k. orange, black & bl 1·25 30
See also Nos. 3138/9.

1965. Ice Hockey Championships. Optd **ТАМПЕРЕ 1965 г.**
3107 **1034** 6k. blue and red . . . 1·75 50

(1147)

1148 Soldier and Woman

1965. Soviet Victory in European Figure Skating Championships. Optd with T **1147**.
3108 **1141** 6k. red, black and green 1·75 50

1965. 20th Anniversaries.
3109 **1148** 6k. multicoloured . . . 40 15
3110 – 6k. multicoloured . . . 45 15
3111 – 6k. ochre and red . . . 40 15
3112 – 6k. multicoloured . . . 40 15
3113 – 6k. multicoloured . . . 40 15
DESIGNS: No. 3109, Type **1148** (Czech Liberation); 3110, Statue and emblems of development (Friendship with Hungary); 3111, Polish and Soviet arms (Polish–Soviet Friendship Treaty); 3112, Viennese buildings and Russian soldier (Freeing of Vienna); 3113, Liberation medal, Polish flag and building reconstruction (Freeing of Warsaw)
See also Nos. 3182 and 3232.

1149 Statue Rockets and Globe

1150 Rockets and Radio-telescope

1965. National Cosmonautics Day. Nos. 3117/18 on aluminium-surfaced paper.
3114 **1149** 4k. green, black and red 25 10
3115 – 12k. purple, red and blue 80 15
3116 – 16k. multicoloured . . 1·10 30
3117 **1150** 20k. red, black and green on silver . . . 7·00 5·00
3118 – 20k. red, black and blue on silver . . . . . . 7·00 5·00
DESIGNS: 12k. Statue and Globe; 16k. Rockets and Globe; No. 3118, Globe, satellite and cosomonauts.

1151 Lenin (after bas-relief by V. Sayapin)

1965. Lenin's 95th Birth Anniv.
3119 **1151** 10k. blue, black & brn 75 30

1152 Poppies

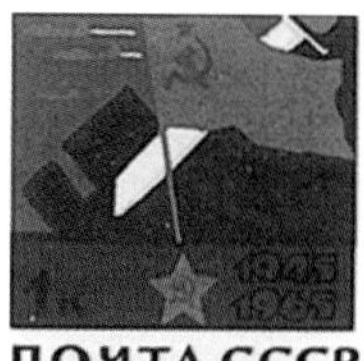

1153 Red Flag, Reichstag Building and Broken Swastika

1965. Flowers.
3120 **1152** 1k. red, lake and green 10 10
3121 – 3k. yellow, brown & grn 30 10
3122 – 4k. lilac, black and green 40 15
3123 – 6k. red, deep green and green 60 15
3124 – 10k. yellow, pur & grn 1·10 25
FLOWERS: 3k. Marguerite; 4k. Peony; 6k. Carnation; 10k. Tulips.

1965. 20th Anniv of Victory.
3125 **1153** 1k. black, gold and red 20 10
3126 – 2k. red, black and gold 25 15
3127 – 3k. blue and gold . . . 40 15
3128 – 4k. violet and gold . . 55 15
3129 – 4k. green and gold . . 60 15
3130 – 6k. purple, green & gold . . . . 1·25 20
3131 – 10k. purple, brn & gold 1·75 25
3132 – 12k. black, red and gold . . . . 2·25 30
3133 – 16k. red and gold . . . 2·50 40
3134 – 20k. black, red and gold . . . . 3·00 75
DESIGNS: 2k. Soviet mother holding manifesto (poster by I. Toidze); 3k. "The Battle for Moscow" (V. Bogatkin); 4k. (No. 3128), "Partisan Mother" (from S. Gerasimov's film); 4k. (No. 3129), "Red Army Soldiers and Partisans" (from Yu. Neprintsev's film); 6k. Soldiers and flag (poster by V. Ivanov); 10k. "Mourning the Fallen Hero" (from F. Bogorodsky's film); 12k. Soldier and worker holding bomb (poster by V. Korestsky); 16k. Victory celebrations, Red Square, Moscow (from K. Yuon's film); 20k. Soldier and machines of war.

1154 Marx and Lenin

1965. Marxism and Leninism.
3136 **1154** 6k. black and red . . . 40 10
No. 3136 is similar in design to those issued by China and Hungary for the Postal Ministers' Congress, Peking, but this event is not mentioned on the stamp or in the Soviet philatelic bulletins.

1155 Bolshoi Theatre

1965. International Theatre Day.
3137 **1155** 6k. ochre, black & turq 55 15

1156 Leonov

1157 Yakov Sverdlov (revolutionary)

1965. "Voskhod 2" Space Flight (2nd issue).
3138 **1156** 6k. violet and silver . . 45 15
3139 – 6k. purple and silver . . 45 15
DESIGN: No. 3139, Belyaev.

1965. 80th Birth Anniversaries.
3140 **1157** 4k. black and brown . . 35 10
3141 – 4k. black and violet . . 35 10
PORTRAIT: No. 3141, J. Akhunbabaev (statesman).

1158 Otto Grotewohl (1st death anniv)

1159 Telecommunications Satellite

1965. Annivs of Grotewohl and Thorez (Communist leaders).
3142 **1158** 4k. black and purple . . 35 10
3143 – 6k. brown and red . . 55 15
DESIGN: 6k. Maurice Thorez (65th birth anniv).

1965. International Co-operation Year. Mult.
3144 3k. Type **1159** 20 10
3145 6k. Star and sputnik 50 15
3146 6k. Foundry ladle, iron works and map of India 50 15
No. 3145 signifies peaceful uses of atomic energy and No. 3146 co-operation with India.

1160 Congress Emblem, Chemical Plant and Symbols

1965. 20th International Congress of Pure and Applied Chemistry, Moscow.
3147 **1160** 4k. red, black and blue 25 10

1161 V. A. Serov (after I. Repin)

1965. Birth Centenary of V. A. Serov (painter).
3148 **1161** 4k. black, brn & stone 95 20
3149 – 6k. black and drab . . 1·50 25
DESIGN: 6k. Full length portrait of Chaliapin (singer) by Serov.

1162 Vsevolod Ivanov and Armoured Train

1965. Famous Writers.
3150 **1162** 4k. black and purple . . 45 15
3151 – 4k. black and violet . . 40 15
3152 – 4k. black and blue . . 40 15
3153 – 4k. black and grey . . 40 15
3154 – 4k. black, red and green 40 15
3155 – 4k. black and brown . . 40 15
WRITERS AND ANNIVERSARIES: No. 3150, (70th birth anniv); 3151, A. Kunanbaev and military parade; 3152, J. Rainis (Lettish poet: 90th birth anniv); 3153, E. J. Vilde (Estonian author): 90th birth anniv); 3154, M. Ch. Abegjan (Armenian writer and critic: 90th birth anniv); 3155, M. L. Kropivnitsky and scene from play (Ukrainian playwright).

1163 Festival Emblem

1965. Film Festival, Moscow.
3156 **1163** 6k. black, gold and blue 50 15

1164 Concert Arena, Tallin

1165 Hand holding "Peace Flower"

1965. 25th Anniv of Incorporation of Estonia, Lithuania and Latvia in the U.S.S.R.
3157 **1164** 4k. multicoloured . . . 40 10
3158 – 4k. brown and red . . 40 10
3159 – 4k. brown, red and blue 40 10
DESIGNS—VERT: No. 3158, Lithuanian girl and Arms. HORIZ: No. 3159, Latvian Flag and Arms.

1965. Peace Issue.
3160 **1165** 6k. yellow, black & blue 45 10

1167 "Potemkin" Sailors Monument (V. Bogdanov), Odessa

1965. 60th Anniv of 1905 Rebellion.
3161 **1167** 4k. blue and red . . . 30 15
3162 – 4k. green, black and red 30 15
3163 – 4k. green, black and red 30 15
3164 – 4k. brown, black and red 30 15
DESIGNS: No. 3162, Demonstrator up lamp post; 3163, Defeated rebels; 3164, Troops at street barricade.

1168 G. Gheorgi-Dej (Rumanian Communist)

1169 Power Station

1965. G. Gheorgi-Dej Commemoration.
3165 **1168** 4k. black and red . . . 25 10

1965. Industrial Progress.
3166 **1169** 1k. multicoloured . . . 10 10
3167 – 2k. black, orange & yell 20 10
3168 – 3k. violet, yell & ochre 20 10
3169 – 4k. deep blue, blue and red 35 10
3170 – 6k. blue and bistre . . 45 10
3171 – 10k. brown, yellow and orange 70 20
3172 – 12k. turquoise and red 1·10 20
3173 – 16k. purple, blue & blk 1·40 40
DESIGNS: 2k. Steel works; 3k. Chemical works and formula; 4k. Machine tools production; 6k. Building construction; 10k. Agriculture; 12k. Communications and transport; 16k. Scientific research.

1170 Relay Racing
1171 Gymnastics

1965. Trade Unions Spartakiad. Multicoloured.
3174 4k. Type **1170** 35 15
3175 4k. Gymnastics 35 15
3176 4k. Cycling 35 15

1965. Schoolchildren's Spartakiad.
3177 **1171** 4k. red and blue . . . 30 10
3178 – 6k. red, brown & turq 50 15
DESIGN: 6k. Cycle racing.

1172 Throwing the Javelin and Running

1173 Star, Palms and Lotus

1965. American–Soviet Athletic Meeting, Kiev.
3179 **1172** 4k. red, brown and lilac 20 10
3180 – 6k. red, brown and green 45 10
3181 – 10k. red, brown and grey 60 15
DESIGNS: 6k. High jumping and putting the shot; 10k. Throwing the hammer and hurdling.

1965. 20th Anniv of North Vietnamese People's Republic.
3182 **1173** 6k. multicoloured . . . 40 15

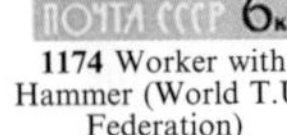

1174 Worker with Hammer (World T.U. Federation)

1176 P. K. Sternberg (astonomer: birth cent)

1965. 20th Anniv of International Organizations.
3183 **1174** 6k. drab and plum . . 35 15
3184 – 6k. brown, red and blue 35 15
3185 – 6k. lt brown & turquoise 35 15
DESIGNS: No. 3184, Torch and heads of three races (World Democratic Youth Federation); No. 3185, Woman holding dove (International Democratic Women's Federation).

1965. Scientists' Anniversaries.
3186 **1176** 4k. brown and blue . . 50 15
3187 – 4k. black and purple . . 50 15
3188 – 4k. black, purple & yell 50 15
PORTRAITS: No. 3187, Ch. Valikhanov (scientific writer: death cent); 3188, V. A. Kistyakovsky (scientist: birth cent).

1177 "Battleship 'Potemkin'" (dir. Sergei Eisenshtein)

1965. Soviet Cinema Art. Designs showing scenes from films. Multicoloured.
3189 4k. Type **1177** 35 10
3190 6k. "Young Guard" (dir. S. Coesinov) 50 15
3191 12k. "A Soldier's Ballad" (dir. G. Chuthrai) . . . . 1·00 25

1178 Mounted Postman and Map

1965. History of the Russian Post Office.
3192 **1178** 1k. green, brown & vio 25 10
3193 – 1k. brown, ochre & grey 25 10
3194 – 2k. brown, blue and lilac 40 10
3195 – 4k. black, ochre & pur 45 10
3196 – 6k. black, green & brn 65 15
3197 – 12k. sepia, brown & blue . . . . 1·10 25
3198 – 16k. plum, red and grey 1·40 45
DESIGNS: No. 3193, Mail coach and map; 2k. Early steam train and medieval kogge; 4k. Mail lorry and map; 6k. Diesel-electric train and various transport; 12k. Moscow Post Office electronic facing sorting and cancelling machines; 16k. Airports and Lenin.

1179 "Vostok" and "Mirnyi" (Antarctic exploration vessels)

1965. Polar Research Annivs.
3199 – 4k. black, orange & blue 90 15
3200 – 4k. black, orange & blue 90 15
3201 – 6k. sepia and violet . . 75 25
3202 **1179** 10k. black, drab and red . . . . 1·75 35
3203 – 16k. black, violet & brn 1·25 65
DESIGNS—HORIZ: 37½ × 25½ mm: No. 3199, Ice breakers "Taimyr" and "Vaigach" in Arctic (50th anniv); 3200, Atomic ice breaker "Lenin"; 3201, Dikson settlement (50th anniv); 3203, Vostok Antarctic station. SQUARE. No. 3202, (145th anniv of Lazarev–Bellingshausen Expedition).
Nos. 3199/200 were issued together, se-tenant, forming a composite design.

1181 Agricultural Academy

1965. Centenary of Academy of Agricultural Sciences, Moscow.
3205 **1181** 4k. violet, red and drab 30 15

1183 N. Poussin (self-portrait)

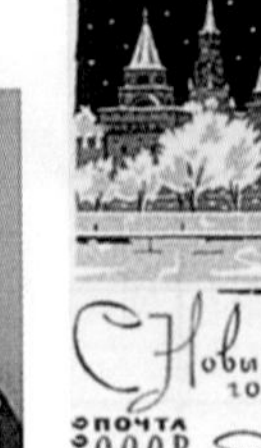

1184 Kremlin

1965. 300th Death Anniv of Nicolas Poussin (French painter).
3207 **1183** 4k. multicoloured . . . 50 10

1965. New Year.
3208 **1184** 4k. red, silver and black 40 10

1185 M. I. Kalinin

1966. 90th Birth Anniv of Kalinin (statesman).
3209 **1185** 4k. lake and red . . . 30 10

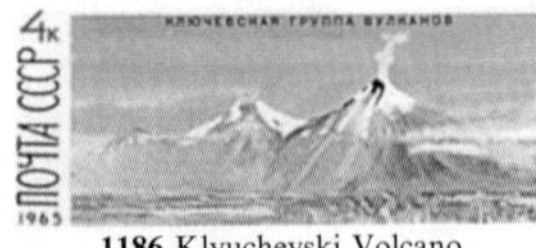

1186 Klyuchevski Volcano

1965. Soviet Volcanoes. Multicoloured.
3210 4k. Type **1186** 40 15
3211 12k. Karumski Volcano (vert) . . . . 1·00 30
3212 16k. Koryaski Volcano . . 1·10 45

1187 Oktyabrskaya Station, Moscow

1965. Soviet Metro Stations.
3213 **1187** 6k. blue 40 10
3214 – 6k. brown 40 10
3215 – 6k. brown 40 10
3216 – 6k. green 40 10
STATIONS: No. 3214, Leninksy Prospekt, Moscow; 3215, Moscow Gate, Leningrad; 3216, Bolshevik Factory, Kiev.

1188 Common Buzzard

1189 "Red Star" (medal) and Scenes of Odessa

1965. Birds of Prey. Birds in black.
3217 **1188** 1k. grey 30 10
3218 – 2k. brown 40 15
3219 – 3k. olive 45 15
3220 – 4k. drab 55 15
3221 – 10k. brown . . . . . . 1·10 30
3222 – 12k. blue . . . . 1·40 50
3223 – 14k. blue . . . . 1·50 65
3224 – 16k. purple . . . . . . 2·00 75
BIRDS—VERT: 2k. Common kestrel; 3k. Tawny eagle; 4k. Red kite; 10k. Peregrine falcon; 16k. Gyr falcon. HORIZ: 12k. Golden eagle; 14k. Lammergeier.

1965. Heroic Soviet Towns. Multicoloured.
3225 10k. Type **1189** 55 25
3226 10k. Leningrad 55 25
3227 10k. Kiev 55 25
3228 10k. Moscow 55 25
3229 10k. Brest-Litovsk 55 25
3230 10k. Volgograd 55 25
3231 10k. Sevastopol 55 25

1190 Flag, Map and Parliament Building, Belgrade

1965. 20th Anniv of Yugoslavia Republic.
3232 **1190** 6k. multicoloured . . . 45 15

1191 Tupolev Tu-134 Jetliner

1965. Soviet Civil Aviation. Multicoloured.
3233 6k. Type **1191** 55 10
3234 10k. Antonov An-24 . . . . 80 15
3235 12k. Mil Mi-10 helicopter 95 25
3236 16k. Beriev Be-10 flying boat . . . . 1·40 40
3237 20k. Antonov An-22 Anteus 1·90 45

1192 "The Proposal of Marriage" (P. Fedotov, 150th birth anniv)

1965. Soviet Painters' Annivs.
3238 – 12k. black and red . . 1·50 25
3239 **1192** 16k. blue and red . . . 2·40 40
DESIGN—VERT: 12k. "A Collective Farm Watchman" (S. Gerasimov, 80th birth anniv).

1193 Crystallography Congress Emblem

1966. International Congresses, Moscow.
3240 **1193** 6k. black, blue and bistre 35 15
3241 6k. black, red and blue 35 15
3242 – 6k. purple, grey & black 35 15
3243 – 6k. black and blue . . 35 15
3244 – 6k. black, red and yellow 35 15
CONGRESS EMBLEMS: No. 3241, Microbiology; 3242, Poultry-raising; 3243, Oceanography; 3244, Mathematics.

1194 Postman and Milkmaid (19th-century statuettes, des A. Venetsianov)

1966. Bicentenary of Dmitrov Ceramic Works. Multicoloured.
3245 6k. Type **1194** 30 15
3246 10k. Modern tea set 65 25

1195 Rolland (after A. Yar-Kravchenko)

1966. Birth Centenary of Romain Rolland (French writer) and 150th Birth Anniv of Eugene Potier (French poet).
3247 **1195** 4k. brown and blue . . 30 15
3248 – 4k. brown, red and black 30 15
DESIGN: No. 3248, Potier and revolutionary scene.

1196 Mongol Horseman

1966. 20th Anniv of Soviet–Mongolian Treaty.
3249 **1196** 4k. multicoloured . . . 30 10

„ЛУНА-9" — НА ЛУНЕ!
3.2.1966
(**1197**)

1966. Landing of "Luna 9" Rocket on Moon. Optd with T **1197**.
3250 **1017** 6k. red, black and blue 4·50 4·50

1198 Supply Ship "Ob"

1966. 10th Anniv of Soviet Antarctic Expedition.
3251 **1198** 10k. lake and silver . . 2·00 1·60
3252 – 10k. lake, silver and blue . . . . 2·25 50
3253 – 10k. lake, silver and blue . . . . 2·25 50
DESIGNS—TRIANGULAR: No. 3252, Snow vehicle. DIAMOND: No. 3253, Antarctic map. This stamp is partly perf across the centre.

1199 Mussa Dyalil and Scene from Poem

1966. Writers.
3254 **1199** 4k. black and brown . . 30 10
3255 – 4k. black and green . . 30 10
3256 – 4k. black and green . . 30 10
WRITERS: No. 3254 (Azerbaijan writer: 60th birth anniv); 3255, Akob Akopyan (Armenian poet: birth cent); 3256, Djalil Mamedkulizade (Azerbaijan writer: birth cent).

1200 Lenin (after bust by Kibalnikov)

1966. Lenin's 96th Birth Anniv
3257 **1200** 10k. gold and green . . 1·10 65
3258 10k. silver and red . . 1·10 25

1201 N. Ilin

1202 Scene from "Alive and Dead" (dir. A. Stolper)

1966. War Heroes.
3259 **1201** 4k. violet and red . . . 30 15
3260 – 4k. lilac and blue . . . 30 15
3261 – 4k. brown and green . . 30 15
PORTRAITS: No. 3260, G. P. Kravchenko; 3261, A. Uglovsky.

1966. Soviet Cinema Art.
3262 **1202** 4k. black, green and red 25 10
3263 – 10k. black and blue . . 60 20
DESIGN: 10k. Scene from "Hamlet" (dir. G. Kozintsev).

1203 Kremlin and Inscription

Учредительная конференция
Всесоюзного общества
филателистов. 1966
(**1204**)

1966. 23rd Soviet Comunist Party Congress, Moscow (1st issue).
3264 **1203** 4k. gold, red and blue 30 10
See also Nos. 3337/41.

1966. Philatelists All-Union Society Conference. No. 3198 optd with T **1204**.
3265 16k. plum, red and grey . . 2·75 1·75

1205 Ice Skating

1966. 2nd People's Winter Spartakiad.
3266 **1205** 4k. blue, red and olive 30 15
3267 – 6k. red, lake and lilac 50 20
3268 – 10k. lake, red and blue 75 30
DESIGNS: Inscription emblem and 6k. Ice hockey; 10k. Skiing.
Nos. 3266/8 are each perf across the centre.

1206 Liner "Aleksandr Pushkin"

1207 Government Building, Frunze

1966. Soviet Transport.
3269 – 4k. multicoloured . . . 55 10
3270 – 6k. multicoloured . . . 45 10
3271 – 10k. multicoloured . . 65 20
3272 **1206** 12k. multicoloured . . 1·00 20
3273 – 16k. multicoloured . . 1·00 25
DESIGNS—HORIZ: 4k. Electric train; 6k. Map of Lenin Volga–Baltic canal system; 16k. Silhouette of liner "Aleksandr Pushkin" on globe. VERT: 10k. Canal lock (Volga–Baltic canal).
Nos. 3271/3 commemorate the inauguration of Leningrad–Montreal Sea Service.

1966. 40th Anniv of Kirgizia.
3274 **1207** 4k. red 30 10

1208 S. M. Kirov (80th Birth Anniv)

1210 A. Fersman (mineralogist)

1966. Soviet Personalities.
3275 **1208** 4k. brown 30 10
3276 – 4k. green 30 10
3277 – 4k. violet 30 10
PORTRAITS: No. 3276, G. I. Ordzhonikidze (80th birth anniv); 3277, Ion Yakir (military commander, 70th birth anniv).

1966. Soviet Scientists. Multicoloured. Colours of name panels below.
3279 **1210** 4k. blue 60 15
3280 – 4k. brown 60 15
3281 – 4k. violet 60 15
3282 – 4k. brown and blue . . 60 15
PORTRAITS: No. 3280, D. K. Zabolotnyi (microbiologist); 3281, M. A. Shatelen (electrical engineer); 3282, O. Yu. Shmidt (arctic explorer).

„Луна-10"—XXIII съезду КПСС
(**1211**)

1966. Launching of "Luna 10". As No. 3284, but imperf, optd with T **1211**.
3283 **1212** 10k. multicoloured . . 3·75 3·00

1212 Arrowheads, "Luna 9" and Orbit

1966. Cosmonautics Day. Multicoloured.
3284 10k. Type **1212** 60 25
3285 12k. Rocket launching and different orbit 65 30

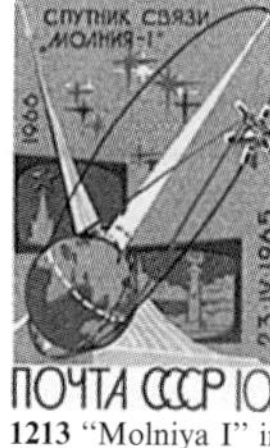

1213 "Molniya I" in Orbit

1214 Ernst Thalmann (80th birth anniv)

1966. Launching of "Molniya I" Telecommunications Satellite.
3286 **1213** 10k. multicoloured . . 55 20

1966. Prominent Leaders.
3287 **1214** 6k. red 45 10
3288 – 6k. violet 45 10
3289 – 6k. brown 45 10
PORTRAITS: No. 3288, Wilhelm Pieck (90th birth anniv); 3289, Sun Yat-sen (birth cent).

1216 Spaceman and Soldier

1966. 15th Young Communist League Congress.
3290 **1216** 4k. black and red . . . 30 10

1217 Ice Hockey Player

1966. Soviet Victory in World Ice Hockey Championships.
3291 **1217** 10k. multicoloured . . 60 25

1218 N. I. Kuznetsov

1219 Tchaikovsky

1966. War Heroes. Guerrilla Fighters.
3292 **1218** 4k. black and green . . 20 10
3293 – 4k. black and yellow . . 20 10
3294 – 4k. black and blue . . 20 10
3295 – 4k. black and purple . . 20 10
3296 – 4k. black and violet . . 20 10
PORTRAITS: No. 3293, I. Y. Sudmalis; 3294, A. A. Morozova; No. 3295, F. E. Strelets; 3296, T. P. Bumazhkov.

1966. 3rd International Tchaikovsky Music Competition, Moscow.
3297 – 4k. black, red and yellow 35 10
3298 **1219** 6k. black, red and yellow 55 10
3299 – 16k. black, red and blue 1·40 35
DESIGNS: 4k. Moscow State Conservatoire of Music; 16k. Tchaikovsky's house and museum, Klin.

1220 Running

1966. Sports Events.
3300 **1220** 4k. brown, olive & green 20 15
3301 – 6k. black, bistre & orge 45 15
3302 – 12k. black, bistre & blue 65 25
DESIGNS: 6k. Weightlifting; 12k. Wrestling.

1222 Gold Medal and Chess Pieces

1966. World Chess Championship, Moscow.
3303 **1222** 6k. multicoloured . . . 1·40 20

1223 Jules Rimet Cup and Football

1966. World Cup Football Championship (England) and World Fencing Championships (Moscow).
3304 **1223** 4k. black, gold and red . . 20 10
3305 – 6k. multicoloured . . . 35 10
3306 – 12k. multicoloured . . 70 20
3307 – 16k. multicoloured . . 1·10 40
DESIGNS: 6k. Footballers; 12k. Fencers; 16k. Fencer and fencing emblems.

1224 Sable, Lake Baikal and Animals (½-size illustration)

1966. Barguzin Nature Reserve.
3308 **1224** 4k. black and blue . . 60 15
3309 – 6k. black and purple . . 90 25
DESIGN: 6k. Map of reserve, and brown bear.

1225 Lotus Plants

1226 "Venus 3" Medal, Globe and Flight Trajectory

1966. 125th Anniv of Sukhumi Botanical Gardens.
3310 **1225** 3k. red, yellow and green 25 10
3311 – 6k. bistre, brown & blue 45 10
3312 – 12k. red, green & turq 70 30
DESIGNS: 6k. Palms and cypresses; 12k. Water lilies.

1966. Space Achievements.
3313 **1226** 6k. black, silver and red 50 20
3314 – 6k. deep blue, blue and brown 50 20
3315 – 6k. ochre and blue . . 50 20
3316 – 6k. multicoloured . . . 60 20
3317 – 6k. pink, mauve & black 60 20
DESIGNS: No. 3314, Spacedogs, Ugolek and Veterok; 3315, "Luna 10"; 3316, "Molniya I"; 3317, "Luna 2's" pennant, Earth and Moon.

1227 Itkol

1966. Tourist Resorts. Multicoloured.
3318 1k. Type **1227** 10 10
3319 4k. Cruise ship on the Volga 30 10
3320 6k. Archway, Leningrad (27½ × 28mm) 35 10
3321 10k. Castle, Kislovodsk . . 55 15
3322 12k. Ismail Samani Mausoleum, Bokhara . . 80 20
3323 16k. Kavkaz Hotel, Sochi (Black Sea) . . . . 1·25 30

1230 Congress Emblem

1231 Peace Dove and Japanese Crane

1966. 7th Consumers' Co-operative Societies Congress, Moscow.
3325 **1230** 4k. yellow and brown 40 10

1966. Soviet–Japanese Meeting, Khabarovsk.
3326 **1231** 6k. black and red . . . 50 20

1232 "Avtandil at a Mountain Spring", after engraving by S. Kabulazde

1966. 800th Birth Anniv of Shota Rustaveli (Georgian poet).
3327 – 3k. black on green . . 35 10
3328 – 4k. brown on yellow . . 45 10
3329 **1232** 6k. black on blue . . . 55 15
DESIGNS: 3k. Scene from poem "The Knight in the Tiger's Skin" (after I. Toidze); 4k. Rustaveli, (after bas-relief by Ya. Nikoladze).

1234 Arms, Moscow Skyline and Fireworks

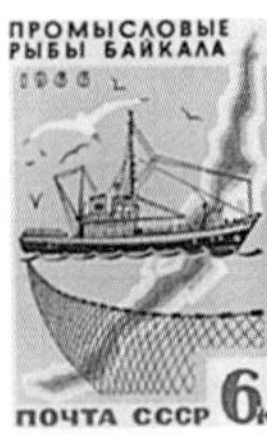

1235 Trawler, Net and Map of Lake Baikal

1966. 49th Anniv of October Revolution.
3331 **1234** 4k. multicoloured . . . 30 10

1966. Fish Resources of Lake Baikal. Mult.
3332 2k. Baikal grayling (horiz) 25 10
3333 4k. Baikal sturgeon (horiz) 30 10
3334 6k. Type **1235** 35 10
3335 10k. Omul (horiz) 70 20
3336 12k. Baikal whitefish (horiz) 85 25

1236 "Agriculture and Industry"

1966. 23rd Soviet Communist Party Congress, Moscow (3rd issue).
3337 **1236** 4k. silver and brown . . 20 10
3338 – 4k. silver and blue . . . 20 10
3339 – 4k. silver and red . . . 20 10
3340 – 4k. silver and red . . . 20 10
3341 – 4k. silver and green . . 20 10
DESIGN (Map as Type **1236** with symbols of): No. 3338, "Communications and Transport"; 3339, "Education and Technology"; 3340, "Increased Productivity"; 3341, "Power Resources".

1237 Government Buildings, Kishinev

1966. 500th Anniv of Kishinev (Moldavian Republic).
3342 **1237** 4k. multicoloured . . . 30 10

1238 Clouds, Rain and Decade Emblem

1239 Nikitin Monument (S. Orlov and A. Zavalor), Kalinin

1966. International Hydrological Decade.
3343 **1238** 6k. multicoloured . . . 40 15

1966. 50th Anniv of Afanasy Nikitin's Voyage to India.
3344 **1239** 4k. black, green & yell 30 10

1240 Scene from "Nargiz" (Muslim Magomaev)

1966. Azerbaijan Operas.
3345 **1240** 4k. ochre and black . . 35 15
3346 – 4k. green and black . . 35 15
DESIGN: No. 3346, Scene from "Kehzoglu" (Uzeir Gadzhibekov).

1241 "Luna 9" and Moon

1242 Agricultural and Chemical Symbols

1966.
3347 – 1k. brown 10 10
3348 **1241** 2k. violet 10 10
3349 – 3k. purple 20 10
3350 – 4k. red 20 10
3351 – 6k. blue 60 10
3563 – 10k. olive 90 35
3353 – 12k. brown 70 10
3354 – 16k. blue 90 15
3355 – 20k. red, blue and drab 1·10 20
3566 – 20k. red . . . . . . 1·75 40
3356 **1242** 30k. green . . . . . . 1·75 40
3357 – 50k. ultram, blue & grey . . . . 3·00 50
3568 – 50k. blue . . . . . . 5·00 1·00
3358 – 1r. black and red . . . 5·25 1·50
3569 – 1r. brown and black . . 8·25 1·50
DESIGNS—As Type **1241**: 1k. Palace of Congresses, Kremlin; 3k. Youth, girl and Lenin emblem; 4k. Arms and hammer and sickle emblem; 6k. "Communications" (Antonov An-10A Ukrainia airplane and sputnik); 10k. Soldier and star emblem; 12k. Furnaceman; 16k. Girl with dove. As Type **1242**: 20k. Workers' demonstration and flower; 50k. "Postal communications"; 1r. Lenin and industrial emblems.

1243 "Presenting Arms"

1245 Campaign Meeting

1966. 25th Anniv of People's Voluntary Corps.
3359 **1243** 4k. brown and red . . 30 10

1966. "Hands off Vietnam".
3360 **1245** 6k. multicoloured . . . 30 10

1246 Servicemen

1966. 30th Anniv of Spanish Civil War.
3361 **1246** 6k. black, red and ochre 35 10

1247 Ostankino TV Tower, "Molniya I" (satellite) and "1967"

1249 Statue, Tank and Medal

1248 Flight Diagram

1966. New Year and "50th Year of October Revolution".
3362 **1247** 4k. multicoloured . . . 40 10

1966. Space Flight and Moon Landing of "Luna 9".
3363 **1248** 10k. black and silver . . 70 25
3364 – 10k. red and silver . . 70 25
3365 – 10k. black and silver . . 70 25
DESIGNS—SQUARE (25 × 25 mm): No. 3364, Arms of Russia and lunar pennant. HORIZ: No. 3365, "Lunar 9" on Moon's surface.

1966. 25th Anniv of Battle of Moscow.
3366 – 4k. brown 30 10
3367 **1249** 6k. ochre and sepia 30 15
3368 – 10k. yellow and brown 60 20
DESIGNS—HORIZ: (60 × 28 mm): 4k. Soviet troops advancing; 10k. "Moscow at peace"– Kremlin, Sun and "Defence of Moscow" medal.

1250 Cervantes and Don Quixote

1966. 350th Death Anniv of Cervantes.
3369 **1250** 6k. brown, green and deep green 40 15

1252 Bering's Ship "Sv. Pyotr" and Map of Komandor Islands

1966. Soviet Far Eastern Territories. Mult.
3370 1k. Type **1252** 40 10
3371 2k. Medny Island and map 45 10
3372 4k. Petropavlovsk Harbour, Kamchatka 65 10
3373 6k. Geyser, Kamchatka (vert) 80 10
3374 10k. Avatchinskaya Bay, Kamchatka . . . . . . 1·00 15
3375 12k. Northern fur seals, Bering Is . . . . 1·00 35
3376 16k. Common guillemot colony, Kurile Islands . . 1·50 75

1254 "The Lute Player" (Caravaggio)

1966. Art Treasures of the Hermitage Museum, Leningrad.
3377 – 4k. black on yellow . . 20 10
3378 – 6k. black on grey . . . 40 10
3379 – 10k. black on lilac . . . 65 15
3380 – 12k. black on green . . 85 20
3381 **1254** 16k. black on buff . . . 1·10 35
DESIGNS—HORIZ: 4k. "Golden Stag" (from Scythian battle shield (6th cent B.C.). VERT: 6k. Persian silver jug (5th cent A.D.; 10k. Statue of Voltaire (Houdon, 1781); 12k. Malachite vase (Urals, 1840).

1255 Sea-water Distilling Apparatus

1967. World Fair, Montreal.
3382 **1255** 4k. black, silver & green 20 10
3383 – 6k. multicoloured . . . 35 15
3384 – 10k. multicoloured . . 60 20
DESIGNS—VERT: 6k. "Atomic Energy" (explosion and symbol). HORIZ: 10k. Space station "Proton 1".

1256 Lieut. B. I. Sizov

1967. War Heroes.
3386 **1256** 4k. brown on yellow . . 30 10
3387 – 4k. brown on drab . . 30 10
DESIGN: No. 3387, Private V. V. Khodyrev.

1257 Woman's Face and Pavlov Shawl

1967. International Women's Day.
3388 **1257** 4k. red, violet and green 30 10

1258 Cine-camera and Film "Flower"

1967. 5th International Film Festival, Moscow.
3389 **1258** 6k. multicoloured . . . 40 10

1259 Factory Ship "Cheryashevsky"

1967. Soviet Fishing Industry. Multicoloured.
3390 6k. Type **1259** 45 15
3391 6k. Refrigerated trawler . . 45 15
3392 6k. Crab canning ship . . . 45 15
3393 6k. Trawler 45 15
3394 6k. Seine-fishing boat, Black Sea 45 15

1260 Newspaper Cuttings, Hammer and Sickle

1261 I.S.O. Congress Emblem

1967. 50th Anniv of Newspaper "Izvestiya".
3395 **1260** 4k. multicoloured . . . 30 10

1967. Moscow Congresses.
3396 6k. turquoise, black and blue 30 10
3397 6k. red, black and blue . . 30 10
DESIGNS: No. 3396, Type **1261** (7th Congress of Int Standards Assn "I.S.O."; 3397, "V" emblem of 5th Int Mining Congress.

1262 I.T.Y. Emblem

1967. International Tourist Year.
3398 **1262** 4k. black, silver and blue 30 10

Вена - 1967
(**1263**)

1265 "Lenin as Schoolboy" (V. Tsigal)

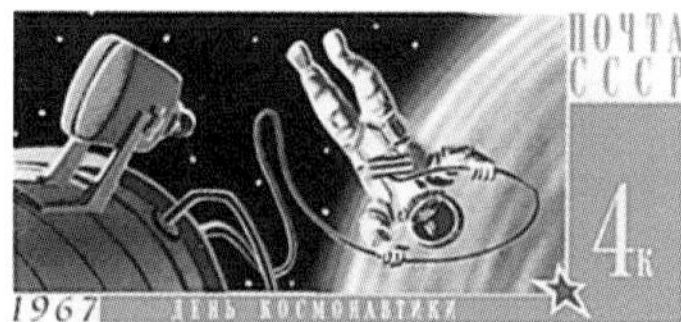

1264 A. A. Leonov in Space

1967. Victory in World Ice Hockey Championship. No. 3291 optd with T **1263**.
3399 **1217** 10k. multicoloured . . 2·75 1·40

1967. Cosmonautics Day. Multicoloured.
3400 4k. Type **1264** 35 10
3401 10k. Rocket and Earth . . . 80 15
3402 16k. "Luna 10" over Moon 1·00 35

1967. Lenin's 97th Birth Anniv.
3403 **1265** 2k. brown, yellow & grn 25 10
3404 – 3k. brown and lake . . 45 10
3405 – 4k. green, yellow and olive 60 15
3406 – 6k. silver, black and blue 90 20
3407 – 10k. blue, black & silver . . . . 2·10 45
3408 – 10k. black and gold . . 70 30
SCULPTURES—VERT: 3k. Lenin's monument, Ulyanovsk; 6k. Bust of Lenin (G. and Yu. Neroda); 10k. (both) "Lenin as Leader" (N. Andreev). HORIZ: 4k. "Lenin at Razliv" (V. Pinchuk).

1266 M. F. Shmyrev

1967. War Heroes.
3409 **1266** 4k. sepia and brown . . 20 10
3410 – 4k. brown and blue . . 20 10
3411 – 4k. brown and violet 20 10
DESIGNS: No. 3410, Major-General S. V. Rudnev; 3411, First Lieut. M. S. Kharchenko.

1267 Transport crossing Ice on Lake Ladoga

1967. Siege of Leningrad, 1941–42.
3412 **1267** 4k. grey, red and cream 20 10

1268 Marshal Biryuzov

1270 Red Cross and Tulip

1269 Minsk Old and New

1967. Biryuzov Commemoration.
3413 **1268** 4k. green and yellow . . 20 10

1967. 900th Anniv of Minsk.
3414 **1269** 4k. green and black . . 30 10

1967. Centenary of Russian Red Cross.
3415 **1270** 4k. red and ochre . . . 30 10

1271 Russian Stamps of 1918 and 1967

1967. 50th Anniv of U.S.S.R. Philatelic Exn, Moscow.
3416 **1271** 20k. green and blue . . 1·50 65

1272 Komsomolsk-on-Amur and Map

1967. 35th Anniv of Komsomolsk-on-Amur.
3418 **1272** 4k. brown and red . . 50 10

1273 Motor Cyclist (International Motor Rally, Moscow)

1967. Sports and Pastimes. International Events.
3419 – 1k. brown, bistre & grn 20 10
3420 – 2k. brown 20 10
3421 – 3k. blue 20 10
3422 – 4k. turquoise 20 10
3423 – 6k. purple and bistre 30 10
3424 **1273** 10k. purple and lilac . . 75 30
DESIGNS AND EVENTS: 1k. Draughts board and players (World Draughts Championships); 2k. Throwing the javelin; 3k. Running; 4k. Long jumping (all preliminary events for Europa Cup Games); 6k. Gymnast (World Gymnastics Championships).

1275 G. D. Gai (soldier)

1276 Games Emblem and Cup

1967. Commander G. D. Gai Commemoration.
3426 **1275** 4k. black and red . . . 30 10

1967. All Union Schoolchildren's Spartakiad.
3427 **1276** 4k. red, black and silver 20 10

1277 Spartakiad Emblem and Cup

1967. 4th People's Spartakiad.
3428 4k. black, red and silver . . 25 10
3429 4k. black, red and silver . . 25 10
3430 4k. black, red and silver . . 25 10
3431 4k. black, red and silver . . 25 10
DESIGNS: Each with Cup. No. 3428, Type **1277**; No. 3429, Gymnastics; 3430, Diving; 3431, Cycling.

1278 V. G. Klochkov (Soviet hero)

1967. Klochkov Commemoration.
3432 **1278** 4k. black and red . . . 25 10

1279 Crest, Flag and Capital of Moldavia

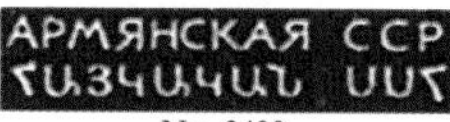

No. 3433

АЗЕРБАЙДЖАНСКАЯ ССР
АЗӘРБАЈҸАН ССР
No. 3434

БЕЛОРУССКАЯ ССР
БЕЛАРУСКАЯ ССР
No. 3435

ЭСТОНСКАЯ ССР
EESTI NSV
No. 3436

ГРУЗИНСКАЯ ССР
No. 3437

No. 3438

КИРГИЗСКАЯ ССР
КЫРГЫЗ ССР
No. 3439

ЛАТВИЙСКАЯ ССР
LATVIJAS PSR
No. 3440

ЛИТОВСКАЯ ССР
LIETUVOS TSR
No. 3441

МОЛДАВСКАЯ ССР
РСС МОЛДОВЕНЯСКЭ
No. 3442

РОССИЙСКАЯ СОВЕТСКАЯ ФЕДЕРАТИВНАЯ СОЦИАЛИСТИЧЕСКАЯ РЕСПУБЛИКА
No. 3443

ТАДЖИКСКАЯ ССР
РСС ТОҶИКИСТОН
No. 3444

ТУРКМЕНСКАЯ ССР
ТУРКМЕНИСТАН ССР
No. 3445

УКРАИНСКАЯ ССР
УКРАЇНСЬКА РСР
No. 3446

УЗБЕКСКАЯ ССР
ЎЗБЕКИСТОН ССР
No. 3447

Inscr at foot as shown above

1967. 50th Anniv of October Revolution (1st issue). Designs showing crests, flags and capitals of the Soviet Republics. Multicoloured.
3433 4k. Armenia 20 10
3434 4k. Azerbaijan 20 10

3435 4k. Belorussia 20 10
3436 4k. Estonia 20 10
3437 4k. Georgia 20 10
3438 4k. Kazakhstan 20 10
3439 4k. Kirgizia 20 10
3440 4k. Latvia 20 10
3441 4k. Lithuania 20 10
3442 4k. Type **1279** 20 10
3443 4k. Russia 20 10
3444 4k. Tadjikistan 20 10
3445 4k. Turkmenistan 20 10
3446 4k. Ukraine 20 10
3447 4k. Uzbekistan 20 10
3448 4k. Soviet Arms 20 10
No. 3448 is size 47 × 32 mm.
See also Nos. 3473/82.

1280 Telecommunications Symbols

1967. "Progress of Communism".
3449 **1280** 4k. red, purple and silver . . . . 3·25 1·40

1281 Manchurian Crane and Dove

1967. Soviet–Japanese Friendship.
3450 **1281** 16k. brown, black & red 90 35

1282 Karl Marx and Title Page

1967. Centenary of Karl Marx's "Das Kapital".
3451 **1282** 4k. brown and red . . 40 10

1283 Arctic Fox **1285** Krasnodon Memorial

1284 Ice Skating

1967. Fur-bearing Animals.
3452 **1283** 2k. blue, black & brown 20 10
3453 – 4k. blue, black and drab 30 10
3454 – 6k. ochre, black & green 45 10
3455 – 10k. brown, black & grn 60 15
3456 – 12k. black, ochre & vio 70 25
3457 – 16k. brown, black & yell 85 35
3458 – 20k. brown, black & turq . . . . 1·10 50
DESIGNS—VERT: 4k. Red fox; 12k. Stoat; 16k. Sable. HORIZ: 6k. Red fox; 10k. Muskrat; 20k. European mink.

1967. Winter Olympic Games, Grenoble (1968). Multicoloured.
3459 2k. Type **1284** 15 10
3460 3k. Ski jumping 25 10
3461 4k. Games emblem (vert) . . 30 10
3462 10k. Ice hockey 70 15
3463 12k. Skiing 90 30

1967. 25th Anniv of Krasnodon Defence.
3464 **1285** 4k. black, yellow & pur 20 10

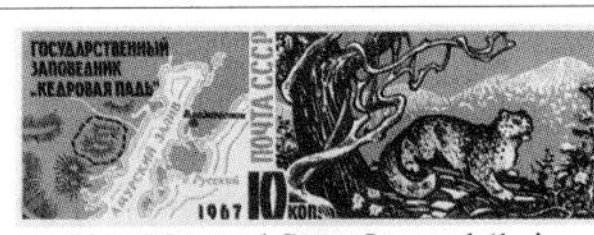
1285a Map and Snow Leopard (½-size illustration)

1967. Cedar Valley Nature Reserve.
3465 **1285a** 10k. black and bistre 75 30

1286 Badge and Yakovlev Yak-9 Fighters **1288** Cosmonauts in Space

1287 Militiaman and Soviet Crest

1967. 25th Anniv of French "Normandie-Niemen" Fighter Squadron.
3466 **1286** 6k. red, blue and gold 40 15

1967. 50th Anniv of Soviet Militia.
3467 **1287** 4k. red and blue . . . 30 10

1967. Space Fantasies. Multicoloured.
3468 4k. Type **1288** 25 10
3469 6k. Men on the Moon (horiz) 40 10
3470 10k. Cosmic vehicle 65 15
3471 12k. Planetary landscape (horiz) 80 20
3472 16k. Imaginary spacecraft 90 30

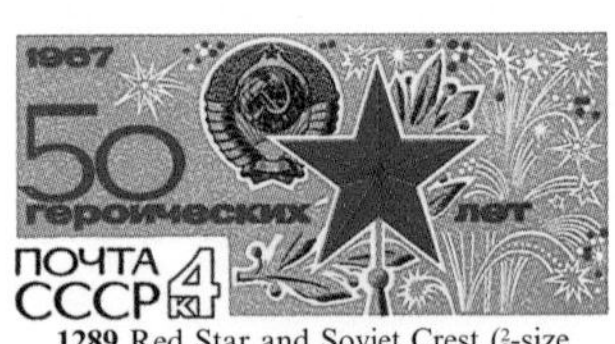

1289 Red Star and Soviet Crest (⅔-size illustration)

1967. 50th Anniv of October Revolution (2nd issue). "50 Heroic Years". Designs showing paintings and Soviet Arms. Multicoloured.
3473 4k. Type **1289** 25 15
3474 4k. "Lenin addressing Congress" (Serov—1955) 25 15
3475 4k. "Lenin explaining the GOELRO map" (Schmatko—1957) 25 15
3476 4k. "The First Cavalry" (Grekov—1924) 25 15
3477 4k. "Students" (Yoganson—1928) 25 15
3478 4k. "People's Friendship" (Karpov—1924) 25 15
3479 4k. "Dawn of the Five Year Plan" (construction work, Romas—1934) 60 15
3480 4k. "Farmers' Holiday" (Gerasimov—1937) . . . 25 15
3481 4k. "Victory in World War II" (Korolev—1965) . . . 25 15
3482 4k. "Builders of Communism" (Merpert and Skripkov—1965) . . 25 15

1290 S. Katayama **1293** Narva-Joesuu (Estonia)

1292 T.V. Tower, Moscow

1967. Katayama (founder of Japanese Communist Party) Commemoration.
3484 **1290** 6k. green 25 10

1967. Opening of Ostankino T.V. Tower, Moscow.
3486 **1292** 16k. black, silver & orge . . . . 1·00 20

1967. Baltic Health Resorts. Multicoloured.
3487 4k. Yurmala (Latvia) . . . 20 10
3488 6k. Type **1293** 30 10
3489 10k. Druskininkai (Lithuania) 55 15
3490 12k. Zelenogradsk (Kaliningrad) (vert) . . . 70 20
3491 16k. Svetlogorsk (Kaliningrad) (vert) . . . 1·00 25

1294 K.G.B. Emblem **1295** Moscow View

1967. 50th Anniv of State Security Commission (K.G.B.).
3492 **1294** 4k. red, silver and blue 25 10

1967. New Year.
3493 **1295** 4k. brown, pink and silver 30 10

1296 Revolutionaries at Kharkov, and Monument

1967. 50th Anniv of Ukraine Republic.
3494 **1296** 4k. multicoloured . . . 20 10
3495 – 6k. multicoloured . . . 60 10
3496 – 10k. multicoloured . . 70 15
DESIGNS: 6k. Hammer and sickle and industrial and agricultural scenes; 10k. Unknown Soldier's monument, Kiev, and young Ukrainians with welcoming bread and salt.

1297 Armoury, Commandant and Trinity Towers **1299** Unknown Soldier's Tomb, Kremlin

1298 Moscow Badge, Lenin's Tomb and Rockets

1967. Kremlin Buildings.
3497 **1297** 4k. brown, purple & grn 20 10
3498 – 6k. brown, green & yell 30 10
3499 – 10k. brown and grey 55 15
3500 – 12k. green, violet and cream 80 30
3501 – 16k. brown, red and light brown 90 30
DESIGNS—HORIZ: 6k. Cathedral of the Annunciation. VERT: 10k. Konstantino-Yelenin, Alarm and Spassky Towers; 12k. Ivan the Great's bell tower; 16k. Kutafya and Trinity Towers.

1967. "50 Years of Communist Development".
3502 **1298** 4k. lake 25 10
3503 – 4k. brown 30 10
3504 – 4k. green 25 10
3505 – 4k. blue 25 10
3506 – 4k. blue 30 10
DESIGNS—HORIZ: No. 3503, Computer-tape cogwheel and industrial scene; 3504, Ear of wheat and grain silo; 3505, Microscope, radar antennae and Moscow University. VERT: No. 3506, T.V. Tower, "Aleksandr Pushkin" (liner), railway bridge and jet airliner.

1967. "Unknown Soldier" Commemoration.
3507 **1299** 4k. red 30 10

1300 "The Interrogation of Communists" (B. Ioganson)

1967. Paintings in the Tretyakov Gallery, Moscow. Multicoloured.
3508 3k. Type **1300** 20 10
3509 4k. "The Sea-shore" (I. Aivazovsky) 30 10
3510 4k. "The Lace Maker" (V. Tropinin) (vert) . . . 30 10
3511 6k. "The Bakery" (T. Yablonskaya) (60 × 34 mm) 40 10
3512 6k. "Aleksandr Nevsky" (part of triptych by P. Korin) (34 × 60 mm) 40 10
3513 6k. "Boyarynya Morozova" (V. Surikov) (60 × 34 mm) 40 10
3514 10k. "The Swan Maiden" (M. Vrubel) (vert) 80 20
3515 10k. "The Arrest of a Propagandist" (I. Repin) 80 20
3516 16k. "Moscow Suburb in February" (G. Nissky) . . 2·25 45

1301 Congress Emblem

1968. 14th Soviet Trade Unions Congress, Moscow.
3517 **1301** 6k. red and green . . . 30 10

1302 Lieut. S. G. Baikov

1968. War Heroes.
3518 **1302** 4k. black and blue . . 30 10
3519 – 4k. blue and green . . 20 10
3520 – 4k. black and red . . . 20 10
PORTRAITS: No. 3519, Lieut. P. L. Guchenko; No. 3520, A. A. Pokaltchuk.

1303 Racehorses **1304** M. Ulyanova

1968. Soviet Horse Breeding.
3521 **1303** 4k. black, purple & blue 25 10
3522 – 6k. black, blue and red 35 10
3523 – 10k. black, brn & turq 60 15
3524 – 12k. black, green & brn 65 20
3525 – 16k. black, red and green 90 30
DESIGNS (each with horse's head and horses "in the field"). VERT: 6k. Show horses; 12k. Show jumpers. HORIZ: 10k. Trotters; 16k. Hunters.

1968. 90th Birth Anniv of M. I. Ulyanova (Lenin's sister).
3526 **1304** 4k. blue and green . . 25 10

1305 Red Star and Forces' Flags

1968. 50th Anniv of Soviet Armed Forces. Multicoloured.
3527 4k. Type **1305** 25 10
3528 4k. Lenin addressing recruits (horiz) 25 10
3529 4k. Recruiting poster (D. Moor) and volunteers (horiz) 25 10
3530 4k. Red Army entering Vladivostok, 1922, and monument (L. Shervud) (horiz) 25 10
3531 4k. Dnieper Dam and statue "On Guard" (horiz) . . . 25 10
3532 4k. "Liberators" poster (V. Ivanov) and tanks in the Ukraine (horiz) . . . 25 10
3533 4k. "To the East" poster and retreating Germans fording river (horiz) . . . 25 10
3534 4k. Stalingrad battle monument and German prisoners-of-war 25 10
3535 4k. Victory parade, Red Square, Moscow, and monument, Treptow (Berlin) (horiz) 25 10
3536 4k. Rockets, tank, warships and Red Flag 25 10

1306 Gorky (after Serov)

1307 Fireman and Appliances

1968. Birth Centenary of Maksim Gorky (writer).
3538 **1306** 4k. brown and drab . . 25 10

1968. 50th Anniv of Soviet Fire Services.
3539 **1307** 4k. black and red . . . 20 10

1308 Linked Satellites

1309 N. N. Popudrenko

1968. Space Link of "Cosmos" Satellites.
3540 **1308** 6k. black, gold & purple 30 10

1968. War Heroes.
3541 **1309** 4k. black and green . . 20 10
3542 – 4k. black and lilac . . 20 10
DESIGN: No. 3542, P. P. Vershigora.

1310 Protective Hand

1968. "Solidarity with Vietnam".
3543 **1310** 6k. multicoloured . . . 25 10

1311 Leonov filming in Space

1968. Cosmonautics Day. Multicoloured.
3544 4k. Type **1311** 35 15
3545 6k. "Kosmos 186" and "Kosmos 188" linking in space 55 15
3546 10k. "Venera 4" space probe 1·00 15

1312 Lenin

1968. Lenin's 98th Birth Anniv.
3547 **1312** 4k. multicoloured . . . 85 15
3548 – 4k. black, red and gold 85 15
3549 – 4k. brown, red and gold 85 15
DESIGNS: No. 3548, Lenin speaking in Red Square; No. 3549, Lenin in peaked cap speaking from lorry during parade.

1313 Navoi (after V. Kaidalov)

1314 Karl Marx

1968. 525th Birth Anniv of Alisher Navoi (Uzbek poet).
3550 **1313** 4k. brown 25 10

1968. 150th Birth Anniv of Karl Marx.
3551 **1314** 4k. black and red . . . 30 10

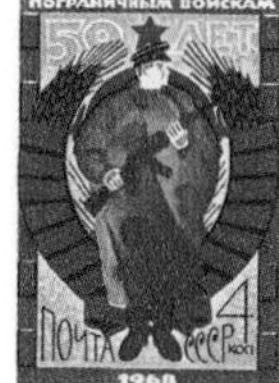
1315 Frontier Guard

1316 Gem and Congress Emblem

1968. 50th Anniv of Soviet Frontier Guards. Multicoloured.
3552 4k. Type **1315** 25 10
3553 6k. Jubilee badge 40 10

1968. "International Congresses and Assemblies".
3554 **1316** 6k. deep blue, blue and green 25 15
3555 – 6k. gold, orange & brn 25 15
3556 – 6k. gold, black and red 25 15
3557 – 6k. orange, black & mve 25 15
DESIGNS: No. 3554, Type **1316** (8th Enriched Minerals Congress); 3555, Power stations, pylon and emblem (7th World Power Conference); 3556, "Carabus schaenherri" (ground beetle) and emblem (13th Entomological Congress); 3557, Roses and emblem (4th Congress on Volatile Oils).

1317 S. Aini

1319 "Kiev Uprising" (after V. Boroday)

1318 Congress Emblem and Postrider

1968. 90th Birth Anniv of Sadriddin Aini (Tadzhik writer).
3570 **1317** 4k. purple and bistre 30 10

1968. Meeting of U.P.U. Consultative Commission, Moscow.
3571 **1318** 6k. red and grey . . . 30 10
3572 – 6k. red and yellow . . 30 10
DESIGN: No. 3572, Emblem and transport.

1968. 50th Anniv of Ukraine Communist Party.
3573 **1319** 4k. red, purple and gold 20 10

1320 Athletes and "50"

1321 Handball

1968. Young Communist League's 50th Anniv Games.
3574 **1320** 4k. red, drab and yellow 25 10

1968. Various Sports Events.
3575 **1321** 2k. multicoloured . . . 20 10
3576 – 4k. multicoloured . . . 30 10
3577 – 6k. multicoloured . . . 40 10
3578 – 10k. red, black & bistre 45 20
3579 – 12k. multicoloured . . 80 25
DESIGNS AND EVENTS—VERT: Type **1321** (World Handball Games, Moscow); 6k. Yachting (20th Baltic Regatta); 10k. Football (70th anniv of Russian soccer). HORIZ: 4k. Table tennis (All European Juvenile Competitions); 12k. Underwater swimming (European Underwater Sports Championships, Alushta, Ukraine).

1322 Girl Gymnasts

1323 Gediminas Tower, Vilnius (Vilna)

1968. Olympic Games, Mexico. Backgrounds in gold.
3580 **1322** 4k. turquoise and blue 20 10
3581 – 6k. violet and red . . . 30 10
3582 – 10k. green and turquoise 55 10
3583 – 12k. brown and orange 70 15
3584 – 16k. blue and pink . . 1·00 30
DESIGNS: 6k. Weightlifting; 10k. Rowing; 12k. Women's hurdles; 16k. Fencing match.

1968. 50th Anniv of Soviet Lithuania.
3586 **1323** 4k. red, drab and purple 30 10

1324 Tbilisi University

1325 "Death of Laocoon and his Sons" (from sculpture by Agesandre, Polidor and Asinodor)

1968. 50th Anniv of Tbilisi University.
3587 **1324** 4k. beige and green . . 25 10

1968. "Promote Solidarity with the Greek Democrats".
3588 **1325** 6k. drab, purple & brn 4·50 3·50

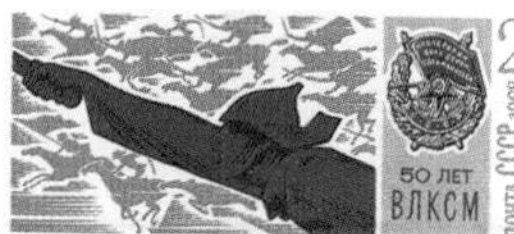

1326 Cavalryman

1968. 50th Anniv of Leninist Young Communist League (Komsomol) (1st issue). Multicoloured.
3589 2k. Type **1326** 10 10
3590 3k. Young workers 15 10
3591 4k. Army officer 20 10
3592 6k. Construction workers . . 25 10
3593 10k. Agricultural workers 40 20
See also No. 3654.

1327 Institute and Molecular Structure

1968. 50th Anniv of N. S. Kurnakov Institute of Chemistry.
3595 **1327** 4k. purple, black and blue 20 10

1328 Letter

1968. Int Correspondence Week and Stamp Day.
3596 **1328** 4k. brown, red and lake 20 10
3597 – 4k. blue, ochre and deep blue 20 10
DESIGN: No. 3597, Russian stamps.

1329 "The 26 Baku Commissars" (statue, S. Merkurov)

1330 T. Antikainen

1968. 50th Anniv of Execution of 26 Baku Commissars.
3598 **1329** 4k. multicoloured . . . 20 10

1968. 70th Birthday of Toivo Antikainen (Finnish Communist leader).
3599 **1330** 6k. brown and grey . . 25 10

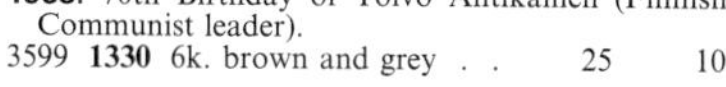

1331 Liner "Ivan Franko"

1333 P. P. Postyshev (1887–1940)

1332 Order of the October Revolution

1968. Soviet Merchant Marine.
3600 **1331** 6k. red, dp blue & blue 35 10

1968. 51st Anniv of October Revolution.
3601 **1332** 4k. multicoloured . . . 20 10

1968. Soviet Personalities.
3602 **1333** 4k. black 15 10
3603 – 4k. black 15 10
3604 – 4k. black 15 10
DESIGNS: No. 3603, S. G. Shaumian (1878–1918); 3604, A. Ikramov (1898–1938).

1334 Statuette of Warrior and Ararat Mountains

1335 I. S. Turgenev

1968. 2,750th Anniv of Yerevan (Armenian capital).
3605 **1334** 4k. blk & brn on grey 25 10
3606 – 12k. brn & sepia on yell 60 25
DESIGN: 12k. David Sasunsky Monument (Ye. Kochar).

1968. 150th Birth Anniv of Ivan Turgenev (writer).
3607 **1335** 4k. green 25 10

1336 American Bison and Common Zebra

1968. Fauna. Soviet Wildlife Reservations. Mult.
3608 4k. Type **1336** 30 10
3609 4k. Purple swamphen and lotus 30 15
3610 6k. Great egrets (vert) . . . 35 15
3611 6k. Ostrich and golden pheasant (vert) 35 15
3612 10k. Eland and guanaco . . 55 25
3613 10k. Glossy ibis and white spoonbill 60 25

1337 Building and Equipment

1968. 50th Anniv of Lenin Radio-laboratory, Gorky.
3614 **1337** 4k. blue and ochre . . 20 10

1338 Prospecting for Minerals

1339 Djety-Oguz Kirgizia

1968. Geology Day. Multicoloured.
3615 4k. Type **1338** 30 10
3616 6k. "Tracking down" metals 30 20
3617 10k. Oil derrick 85 20

1968. Central Asian Spas. Multicoloured.
3618 4k. Type **1339** 20 10
3619 4k. Borovoe, Kazakhstan (horiz) 20 10
3620 6k. Issyk-kul, Kirgizia (horiz) 30 15
3621 6k. Borovoe, Kazakhstan . . 30 15

1340 Silver Medal, "Philatec", Paris 1964

1968. Awards to Soviet Post Office at Foreign Stamp Exhibitions.
3622 4k. black, silver and purple 20 10
3623 6k. black, gold and blue . . 25 10
3624 10k. black, gold and blue 55 15
3625 12k. black, silver & turquoise 45 15
3626 16k. black, gold and red . . 75 30
3627 20k. black, gold and blue 90 40
3628 30k. black, gold and brown 1·40 85
DESIGNS: 4k. Type **1340**; 6k. Plaque, "Debria", Berlin, 1959; 10k. Cup and medals, Riccione, 1952, 1968; 12k. Diploma and medal, "Thematic Biennale", Buenos Aires, 1965; 16k. Trophies and medals, Rome, 1952, 1954; 20k. Medals and plaques, "Wipa", Vienna, 1966; 30k. Glass trophies, Prague, 1950, 1955, 1962.

1341 V. K. Lebedinsky

1342 Soldier with Flag

1968. Birth Centenary of Lebedinsky (physicist).
3629 **1341** 4k. multicoloured . . . 30 10

1968. 50th Anniv of Estonian Workers' Commune.
3630 **1342** 4k. black and red . . . 20 10

1344 Moscow Buildings and Fir Branch

1968. New Year.
3632 **1344** 4k. multicoloured . . . 35 10

1345 G. Beregovoi (cosmonaut)

1346 Electric Train, Map and Emblem

1968. Flight of "Soyuz 3".
3633 **1345** 10k. black, red and blue 55 20

1968. Soviet Railways.
3634 **1346** 4k. orange and mauve 25 15
3635 – 10k. brown and green 65 25
DESIGN: 10k. Track-laying train.

1347 Red Flag, Newspapers and Monument at Minsk

1348 "The Reapers" (A. Venetsianov)

1968. 50th Anniv of Byelorussian Communist Party.
3636 **1347** 4k. black, brown and red 20 10

1968. Paintings in State Museum, Leningrad. Mult.
3637 1k. Type **1348** 15 10
3638 2k. "The Last Days of Pompeii" (K. Bryullov) (61 × 28 mm) 35 10
3639 3k. "A Knight at the Crossroads" (V. Vasentsov) (61 × 28 mm) 40 10
3640 4k. "Conquering a Town in Winter" (V. Surikov) (61 × 28 mm) 50 10
3641 6k. "The Lake" (I. Levitan) (61 × 28 mm) 70 10
3642 10k. "The Year 1919: Alarm" (K. Petrov-Vodkin) 85 15
3643 16k. "The Defence of Sevastopol" (A. Deineka) (61 × 28 mm) . . . . . . 1·00 20
3644 20k. "Homer's Bust (G. Korzhev) . . . . . . 1·25 25
3645 30k. "The Celebration in Uritsky Square" (B. Kustodiev) (61 × 28 mm) . . . . . . 1·40 30
3646 50k. "The Duel between Peresvet and Chelumbei" (M. Avilov) (61 × 28 mm) 2·00 80

1349 House, Onega Region

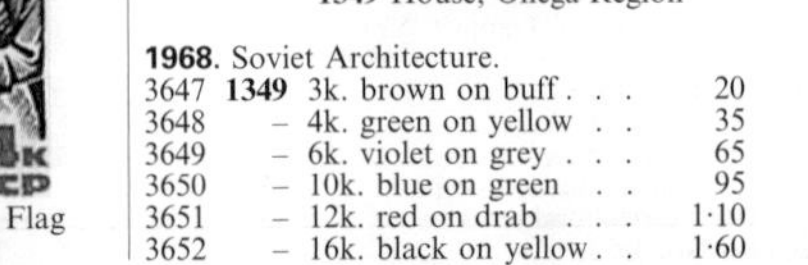

1968. Soviet Architecture.
3647 **1349** 3k. brown on buff . . . 20 10
3648 – 4k. green on yellow . . 35 10
3649 – 6k. violet on grey . . . 65 15
3650 – 10k. blue on green . . 95 35
3651 – 12k. red on drab . . . 1·10 60
3652 – 16k. black on yellow . . 1·60 80
DESIGNS: 4k. Farmhouse door, Gorky region; 6k. Wooden church, Kishi; 10k. Citadel, Rostov-Yaroslavl; 12k. Entrance gate, Tsaritzino; 16k. Master builder Rossi's Street, Leningrad.

1968. 50th Death Anniv of N. G. Markin (1893–1918) (revolutionary). As T **1333**.
3653 4k. black 20 10

1350 Flags and Order of October Revolution

1968. 50th Anniv of Leninist Young Communist League (Komsomol) (2nd issue).
3654 **1350** 12k. multicoloured . . 55 15

1351 "Declaration of Republic"

1969. 50th Anniv of Belorussian Republic. Mult.
3655 2k. Type **1351** 10 10
3656 4k. Partisans at war, 1941–45 . . . . 20 10
3657 6k. Reconstruction workers 30 10

1352 Red Guard in Riga (statue)

1354 University Buildings

1969. 50th Anniv of Soviet Revolution in Latvia.
3658 **1352** 4k. red and orange . . 20 10

1969. 150th Anniv of Leningrad University.
3660 **1354** 10k. black and lake . . 45 20

1355 Krylov (after K. Bryullov)

1356 N. D. Filchenkov

1969. Birth Bicent of Ivan Krylov (fabulist).
3661 **1355** 4k. multicoloured . . . 20 10

1969. War Heroes.
3662 **1356** 4k. brown and red . . 20 10
3663 – 4k. brown and green . . 20 10
DESIGN: No. 3663, A. A. Kosmodemiansky.

1357 "The Wheel Turns Round Again" (sculpture, Zs. Kisfaludi-Strobl)

1969. 50th Anniv of 1st Hungarian Soviet Republic.
3664 **1357** 6k. black, red and green 30 10

1358 Crest and Symbols of Petro-chemical Industry

1969. 50th Anniv of Bashkir Autonomous Soviet Socialist Republic.
3665 **1358** 4k. multicoloured . . . 20 10

1359 "Vostok 1" on Launching-pad

1969. Cosmonautics Day. Multicoloured.
3666 10k. Type **1359** 60 20
3667 10k. "Zond 5" in Lunar orbit (horiz) 60 20
3668 10k. Sergei Pavlovich Korolev (space scientist) (horiz) 60 20

1360 Lenin University, Kazan

1969. Buildings connected with Lenin. Mult.
3670 4k. Type **1360** 20 10
3671 4k. Lenin Museum, Kuibyshev 20 10
3672 4k. Lenin Museum, Pskov 20 10
3673 4k. Lenin Museum, Shushenskaya 20 10
3674 4k. "Hay Hut", Razliv . . . 20 10
3675 4k. Lenin Museum, Gorky Park, Leningrad 20 10
3676 4k. Smolny Institute, Leningrad 20 10
3677 4k. Lenin's Office, Kremlin 20 10
3678 4k. Library, Ulyanovsk (wrongly inscr "Lenin Museum") 20 10
3679 4k. Lenin Museum, Ulyanovsk 20 10

1361 Telephone and Radio Set

1969. 50th Anniv of VEF Electrical Works, Riga.
3680 **1361** 10k. brown and red . . 50 15

1362 I.L.O. Emblem

1969. 50th Anniv of Int Labour Organization.
3681 **1362** 6k. gold and red . . . 30 10

1363 Otakar Jaros

1364 P. E. Dybenko

1969. Otakar Jaros (Czech war hero) Commem.
3682 **1363** 4k. black and blue . . 25 10

1969. Soviet Personalities. 80th Birth Annivs.
3683 **1364** 4k. red 20 10
3684 – 4k. blue 20 10
DESIGN: No. 3684, S. V. Kosior (1889–1939).

1365 Suleiman Stalsky

1969. Birth Centenary of Suleiman Stalsky (Dagestan poet).
3685 **1365** 4k. green and brown . . 30 10

1366 Rose "Clear Glade"

1969. Academy of Sciences Botanical Gardens, Moscow. Multicoloured.
3686 2k. Type **1366** 15 10
3687 4k. Lily "Slender" 20 10
3688 10k. "Cattleya hybr" (orchid) 50 15
3689 12k. Dahlia "Leaves Fall" 60 25
3690 14k. Gladiolus "Ural Girl" 90 40

1367 Scientific Centre

1969. 50th Anniv of Ukraine Academy of Sciences, Kiev.
3691 **1367** 4k. purple and yellow 30 10

1368 Gold Medal within Film "Flower"
1369 Congress Emblem

1969. Cine and Ballet Events, Moscow. Mult.
3692 6k. Type **1368** (6th Int Cinema Festival) 30 15
3693 6k. Ballet dancers (1st Int Ballet Competitions) . . . 30 15

1969. 3rd Int Protozoologists Congress, Leningrad.
3694 **1369** 6k. multicoloured . . . 90 20

1370 Estonian Singer

1969. Centenary of Estonian Choir Festival.
3695 **1370** 4k. red and ochre . . . 35 10

1371 Mendeleev (after N. Yarashenko) and Formula

1969. Centenary of Mendeleev's Periodic Law of Elements.
3696 **1371** 6k. brown and red . . 50 20

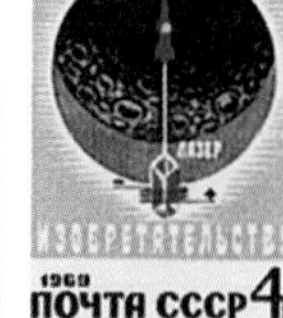

1372 Peace Banner and World Landmarks
1373 Rocket on Laser Beam, and Moon

1969. 20th Anniv of World Peace Movement.
3698 **1372** 10k. multicoloured . . 40 15

1969. "50 Years of Soviet Inventions".
3699 **1373** 4k. red, black and silver 20 10

1374 Kotlyarevsky (1375)

1969. Birth Bicentenary of Ivan Kotlyarevsky (Ukrainian writer).
3700 **1374** 4k. black, brown & grn 20 10

1969. Soviet Ice Hockey Victory in World Championships, Stockholm. No. 2828 further optd with **1375**.
3701 6k. turquoise and purple . . 3·25 2·00

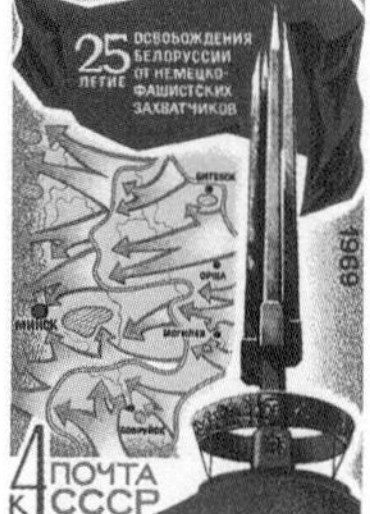

1376 War Memorial in Minsk (A. Bembel) and Campaign Map
1377 Hands holding Torch, and Bulgarian Arms

1969. 25th Anniv of Belorussian Liberation.
3702 **1376** 4k. red, purple and olive 20 10

1969. 25th Anniv of Bulgarian and Polish Peoples' Republics.
3703 **1377** 6k. multicoloured . . . 30 10
3704 – 6k. red and ochre . . . 30 10
DESIGN: No. 3704, Polish map, flag and arms.

1378 Registan Square, Samarkand

1969. 2,500th Anniv of Samarkand. Mult.
3705 4k. Type **1378** 25 10
3706 6k. Intourist Hotel, Samarkand 40 15

1379 Liberation Monument, Nikolaev
1380 Volleyball (European Junior Championships)

1969. 25th Anniv of Liberation of Nikolaev.
3707 **1379** 4k. red, violet and black 25 10

1969. International Sporting Events.
3708 **1380** 4k. red, brown & orange 20 10
3709 – 6k. multicoloured . . . 40 10
DESIGN: 6k. Canoeing (European Championships).

1381 M. Munkacsy and detail of painting, "Peasant Woman churning Butter"
1382 Miners' Statue, Donetsk

1969. 125th Birth Anniv of Mihaly Munkacsy (Hungarian painter).
3710 **1381** 6k. black, orange & brn 30 10

1969. Centenary of Donetsk.
3711 **1382** 4k. mauve and grey . . 20 10

1383 "Horse-drawn Machine-guns" (M. Grekov)

1969. 50th Anniv of 1st Cavalry Army.
3712 **1383** 4k. brown and red . . 40 15

1384 Ilya Repin (self-portrait)
1385 Running

1969. 125th Birth Anniv of Ilya Repin (painter). Multicoloured.
3713 4k. "Barge-haulers on the Volga" 25 10
3714 6k. "Unexpected" 35 15
3715 10k. Type **1384** 40 15
3716 12k. "The Refusal of Confession" 55 20
3717 16k. "Dnieper Cossacks" . . 75 30

1969. 9th Trade Unions' Games, Moscow.
3718 **1385** 4k. black, green and red 15 10
3719 – 10k. black, blue & green 35 10
DESIGN: 10k. Gymnastics.

1386 V. L. Komarov
1387 O. Tumanyan and Landscape

1969. Birth Cent of V. L. Komarov (botanist).
3721 **1386** 4k. brown and olive . . 25 10

1969. Birth Cent of O. Tumanyan (Armenian poet).
3722 **1387** 10k. black and blue . . 50 15

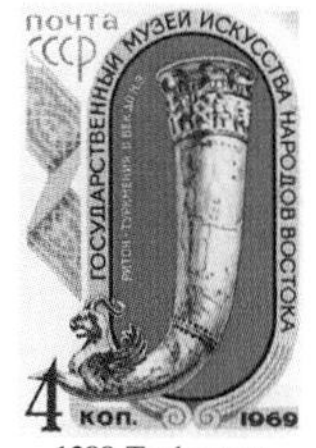

1388 Turkoman Drinking- horn (2nd-cent B.C.)
1389 Mahatma Gandhi

1969. Oriental Art Treasures, State Museum of Oriental Art, Moscow. Multicoloured.
3723 4k. Type **1388** 25 10
3724 6k. Simurg vessel, Persia (13th-century) 35 10
3725 12k. Statuette, Korea (8th-century) 50 15
3726 16k. Bodhisatva statuette, Tibet (7th-century) . . . 70 20
3727 20k. Ebisu statuette, Japan (17th-century) . . . . . 1·00 50

1969. Birth Centenary of Mahatma Gandhi.
3728 **1389** 6k. brown 55 15

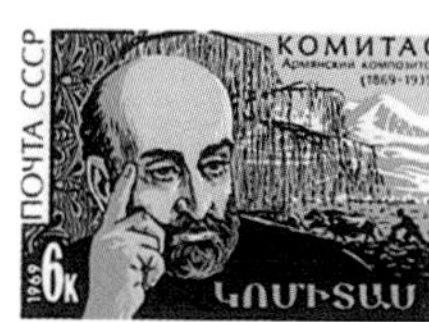

1390 Black Stork at Nest

1969. Belovezhaskaya Pushcha Nature Reserve. Multicoloured.
3729 4k. Type **1390** 30 15
3730 6k. Red deer and fawn . . . 45 15
3731 10k. European bison fighting 65 20
3732 12k. Lynx and cubs 75 20
3733 16k. Wild boar and young 90 35
No. 3731 is larger, 76 × 24 mm.

1391 "Komitas" and Rural Scene

1969. Birth Cent of "Komitas" (S. Sogomonyan, Armenian composer).
3734 **1391** 6k. black, flesh and grey 35 15

1392 Sergei Gritsevets (fighter-pilot)
1393 I. Pavlov (after portrait by A. Yar-Kravchenko)

1969. Soviet War Heroes.
3735 **1392** 4k. black and green . . 30 10
3736 – 4k. brown, red & yellow 20 10
3737 – 4k. brown and green . . 20 10
DESIGNS: As Type **1392**. No. 3737, Lisa Chaikina (partisan). (35½ × 24 mm); No. 3736, A. Cheponis, Y. Alexonis and G. Boris (Kaunas resistance fighters).

1969. 120th Birth Anniv of Ivan P. Pavlov (physiologist).
3738 **1393** 4k. multicoloured . . . 25 10

1394 D.D.R. Arms and Berlin Landmarks
1395 A. V. Koltsov (from portrait by A. Yar-Kravchenko)

1969. 20th Anniv of German Democratic Republic.
3739 **1394** 6k. multicoloured . . . 25 10

1969. 160th Birth Anniv of A. V. Koltsov (poet).
3740 **1395** 4k. brown and blue . . 25 10

1396 Arms of Ukraine and Memorial
1397 Kremlin, and Hammer and Sickle

1969. 25th Anniv of Ukraine Liberation.
3741 **1396** 4k. red and gold . . . 30 15

1969. 52nd Anniv of October Revolution.
3742 **1397** 4k. multicoloured . . . 25 10

1398 G. Shonin and V. Kubasov ("Soyuz 6")

1969. Triple Space Flights.
3744 **1398** 10k. green and gold . . 55 15
3745 – 10k. green and gold . . 55 15
3746 – 10k. green and gold . . 55 15
DESIGNS: No. 3745, A. Filipchenko, V. Volkov and V. Gorbatko ("Soyuz 7"); No. 3746, V. Shatalov and A. Yeliseev ("Soyuz 8").

1399 Lenin when a Youth (after V. Tsigal) and Emblems
1400 Corps Emblem on Red Star

1969. U.S.S.R. Youth Philatelic Exhibition to commemorate Lenin's Birth Centenary, Kiev.
3747 **1399** 4k. lake and pink . . . 25 15

1969. 50th Anniv of Red Army Communications Corps.
3748 **1400** 4k. red, brown & bistre 25 15

1401 "Worker and Collective Farmer" (sculpture, Vera Mukhina) and Title-page

1969. 3rd Soviet Collective Farmers' Congress, Moscow.
3749 **1401** 4k. brown and gold . . 20 10

1402 "Vasilisa, the Beauty" (folk tale)

1969. Russian Fairy Tales. Multicoloured.
3750 4k. Type **1402** 35 30
3751 10k. "Maria Morevna" (folk tale) 85 60
3752 16k. "The Golden Cockerel" (Pushkin) (horiz) . . . . 1·25 75
3753 20k. "Finist, the Fine Fellow" (folk tale) . . . . 1·50 1·00
3754 50k. "Tale of the Tsar Saltan" (Pushkin) . . . . 2·75 2·00

1403 Venus Plaque and Radio-telescope

1969. Space Exploration.
3755 **1403** 4k. red, brown and black 35 10
3756 – 6k. purple, grey & black 45 15
3757 – 10k. multicoloured . . 70 20
DESIGNS: 6k. Space station and capsule in orbit; 10k. Photograph of the Earth taken by "Zond 7".

1404 Soviet and Afghan Flags
1405 Red Star and Arms

1969. 50th Anniv of U.S.S.R.–Afghanistan Diplomatic Relations.
3759 **1404** 6k. red, black and green 35 10

1969. Coil Stamp.
3760 **1405** 4k. red . . . . 1·75 80

1406 Mikoyan Gurevich MiG-3 and MiG-23 Fighters

1969. "30 Years of MiG Aircraft".
3761 **1406** 6k. black, grey and red 70 15

1407 Lenin

1969. New Year.
3762 **1407** 4k. multicoloured . . . 25 10

1408 Tupolev ANT-2

1969. Development of Soviet Civil Aviation.
3763 **1408** 2k. multicoloured . . . 20 10
3764 – 3k. multicoloured . . . 25 10
3765 – 4k. multicoloured . . . 25 10
3766 – 6k. black, red and purple 25 10
3767 – 10k. multicoloured . . 55 15
3768 – 12k. multicoloured . . 60 20
3769 – 16k. multicoloured . . 80 25
3770 – 20k. multicoloured . . 95 35
AIRCRAFT: 3k. Polikarpov Po-2; 4k. Tupolev ANT-9; 6k. TsAGI 1-EA helicopter; 10k. Tupolev ANT-20 "Maksim Gorky"; 12k. Tupolev Tu-104; 16k. Mil Mi-10 helicopter; 20k. Ilyushin Il-62.

1409 Model Gliders

1969. Technical Sports.
3772 **1409** 3k. purple 15 10
3773 – 4k. green 20 10
3774 – 6k. brown 30 10
DESIGNS: 4k. Speed boat racing; 6k. Parachuting.

1410 Rumanian Arms and Soviet Memorial, Bucharest
1411 TV Tower, Ostankino

1969. 25th Anniv of Rumanian Liberation.
3775 **1410** 6k. red and brown . . 30 15

1969. Television Tower, Ostankino, Moscow.
3776 **1411** 10k. multicoloured . . 45 20

1412 "Lenin" (after N. Andreev)

1970. Birth Centenary of V. I. Lenin (1st issue). Multicoloured.
3777 4k. Type **1412** 25 10
3778 4k. "Marxist Meeting, Petrograd" (A. Moravov) 25 10
3779 4k. "Second RSDRP Congress" (Yu. Vinogradov) 25 10
3780 4k. "First Day of Soviet Power" (N. Babasyak) . . 25 10
3781 4k. "Visiting Lenin" (F. Modorov) 25 10
3782 4k. "Conversation with Ilich" (A. Shirokov) . . . 25 10
3783 4k. "May Day 1920" (I. Brodsky) 25 10
3784 4k. "With Lenin" (V. Serov) 25 10
3785 4k. "Conquerors of the Cosmos" (A. Deyineka) 25 10
3786 4k. "Communism Builders" (A. Korentsov, Ye. Merkulov, V. Burakov) 25 10
See also Nos. 3812/21.

1413 F. V. Sychkov and Painting "Tobogganing"

1970. Birth Centenary of F. V. Sychkov (artist).
3787 **1413** 4k. blue and brown . . 40 15

1414 "Vostok", "Mirnyi" and Antarctic Map
1415 V. I. Peshekhonov

1970. 150th Anniv of Antarctic Expedition by Bellinghausen and Lazarev.
3788 **1414** 4k. turquoise, mauve & bl . . . . 1·25 25
3789 – 16k. red, green & purple . . . . 2·50 55
DESIGN: 16k. Modern polar-station and map.

1970. Soviet War Heroes.
3790 **1415** 4k. purple and black . . 20 10
3791 – 4k. brown and olive . . 20 10
DESIGN: No. 3791, V. B. Borsoev (1906–1945).

1416 Geographical Society Emblem
1417 "The Torch of Peace" (A. Dumpe)

1970. 125th Anniv of Russian Geographical Society.
3792 **1416** 6k. multicoloured . . . 35 10

1970. 60th Anniv of Int Women's Solidarity Day.
3793 **1417** 6k. drab and turquoise 35 10

1418 Ivan Bazhov (folk hero) and Crafts
1419 Lenin

1970. World Fair "Expo 70", Osaka, Japan.
3794 **1418** 4k. black, red and green 15 10
3795 – 6k. silver, red and black 30 10
3796 – 10k. multicoloured . . 45 15
DESIGNS: 6k. U.S.S.R. Pavilion; 10k. Boy and model toys.

1970. Lenin Birth Centenary. All-Union Philatelic Exhibition, Moscow.
3798 **1419** 4k. black, gold and red 25 10

1420 Friendship Tree

1970. Friendship Tree, Sochi.
3800 **1420** 10k. multicoloured . . 45 20

1421 Ice Hockey Players

1970. World Ice Hockey Championships, Stockholm, Sweden.
3801 **1421** 6k. green and blue . . 60 15

1422 Hammer, Sickle and Azerbaijan Emblems

1970. 50th Anniv of Soviet Republics.
3802 **1422** 4k. red and gold . . . 20 10
3803 – 4k. brown and silver . . 20 10
3804 – 4k. purple and gold . . 20 10
DESIGNS: No. 3803, Woman and motifs of Armenia; 3804, Woman and emblem of Kazakh Republic.

1423 Worker and Book
1424 D. N. Medvedev

1970. U.N.E.S.C.O. "Lenin Centenary" Symposium.
3805 **1423** 6k. ochre and lake . . 20 10

1970. Partisan War Heroes.
3806 **1424** 4k. brown 20 10
3807 – 4k. brown 20 10
PORTRAIT: No. 3807, K. P. Orlovsky.

(1425)

1426 Hungarian Arms and Budapest View

1970. Russian Victory in World Ice Hockey Championships, Stockholm. No. 3801 optd with T **1425**.
3808 **1421** 6k. green and blue . . 70 20

1970. 25th Anniv of Hungarian and Czech Liberation. Multicoloured.
3809 6k. Type **1426** 20 10
3810 6k. Czech Arms and Prague view 20 10

1427 Cosmonauts' Emblem

1428 Lenin, 1891

1970. Cosmonautics Day.
3811 **1427** 6k. multicoloured . . . 20 10

1970. Birth Centenary of Lenin (2nd issue).
3812 **1428** 2k. green 10 10
3813 – 2k. olive 10 10
3814 – 4k. blue 15 10
3815 – 4k. lake 15 10
3816 – 6k. brown 35 10
3817 – 6k. lake 35 10
3818 – 10k. purple 50 15
3819 – 10k. brown 50 15
3820 – 12k. black and silver . . 55 20
3821 – 12k. red and gold . . . 55 20
PORTRAITS OF LENIN: No. 3813, In 1900; 3814, In 1914; 3815, In 1916; 3816, 3817, 3818, In 1918; 3819, In 1920; 3820, Sculptured head by Yu. Kolesnikov; 3821, Sculptured head by N. Andreev.

1429 Order of Victory

1431 Lenin (sculpture, Yu. Kolesnikov)

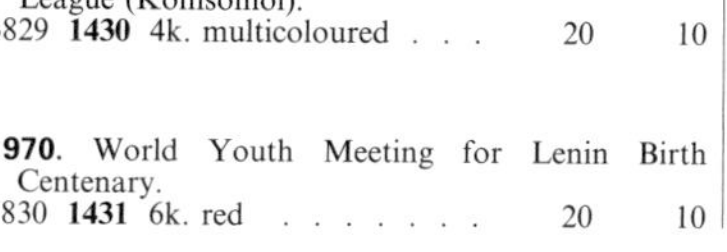

1430 Komsomol Badge

1970. 25th Anniv of Victory in Second World War.
3823 **1429** 1k. gold, grey and purple 10 10
3824 – 2k. purple, brn & gold 10 10
3825 – 3k. red, black and gold 15 10
3826 – 4k. red, brown and gold 20 10
3827 – 10k. gold, red & purple 55 30
DESIGNS: 2k. Eternal Flame; 3k. Treptow Monument, Berlin; 4k. Home Defence Order; 10k. Hero of the Soviet Union and Hero of Socialist Labour medals.

1970. 16th Congress of Leninist Young Communist League (Komsomol).
3829 **1430** 4k. multicoloured . . . 20 10

1970. World Youth Meeting for Lenin Birth Centenary.
3830 **1431** 6k. red 20 10

1432 "Young Workers" and Federation Emblem

1970. 25th Anniv of World Democratic Youth Federation.
3831 **1432** 6k. black and blue . . 35 10

1433 Arms and Government Building, Kazan

1970. 50th Anniv of Russian Federation Autonomous Soviet Socialist Republics.
3832 **1433** 4k. blue 30 10
3833 – 4k. green 30 10
3834 – 4k. red 30 10
3835 – 4k. brown 30 10
3836 – 4k. green 30 10
3837 – 4k. brown 30 10
DESIGNS: Arms and Government Buildings. No. 3832, (Tatar Republic); 3833, Petrozavodzk (Karelian Republic); 3834, Cheboksary (Chuvash Republic); 3835, Elista (Kalmyk Republic); 3836, Izhevsk (Udmurt Republic); 3837, Ioshkar-Ola (Mari Republic).
See also Nos. 3903/7, 4052/3, 4175, 4253, 4298, 4367 and 4955.

1434 Gymnast on Bar (World Championships, Yugoslavia)

1435 "Swords into Ploughshares" (sculpture by E. Vuchetich)

1970. International Sporting Events.
3838 **1434** 10k. red and drab . . . 50 15
3839 – 16k. brown and green 80 30
DESIGN: 16k. Three footballers (World Cup Championship, Mexico).

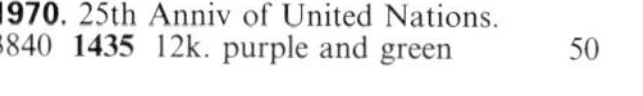

1970. 25th Anniv of United Nations.
3840 **1435** 12k. purple and green 50 10

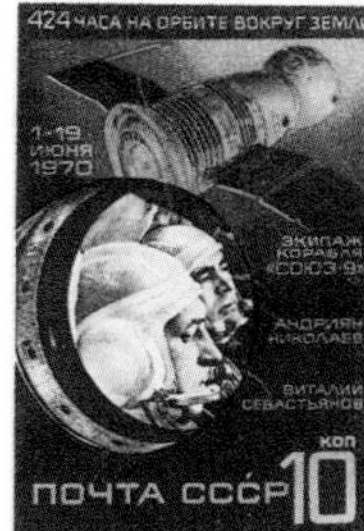

1436 Cosmonauts and "Soyuz 9"

1970. Space Flight by "Soyuz 9".
3841 **1436** 10k. black, red & purple 50 10

1437 Engels

1970. 150th Birth Anniv of Friedrich Engels.
3842 **1437** 4k. brown and red . . 20 10

1438 Cruiser "Aurora"

1970. Soviet Warships.
3843 **1438** 3k. pink, lilac and black 30 10
3844 – 4k. black and yellow . . 35 10
3845 – 10k. blue and mauve 85 20
3846 – 12k. brown and buff . . 1·10 25
3847 – 20k. purple, blue & turq . . . . 1·60 40
DESIGNS: 4k. Missile cruiser "Groznyi"; 10k. Cruiser "Oktyabrskaya Revolyutsiya"; 12k. Missile cruiser "Varyag"; 20k. Nuclear submarine "Leninsky Komsomol".

1439 Soviet and Polish Workers

1440 Allegory of the Sciences

1970. 25th Anniv of Soviet-Polish Friendship Treaty.
3848 **1439** 6k. red and blue . . . 20 10

1970. 13th Int Historical Sciences Congress, Moscow.
3849 **1440** 4k. multicoloured . . . 20 10

1441 Mandarins

1442 Magnifying Glass, "Stamp" and Covers

1970. Fauna of Sikhote-Alin Nature Reserve. Multicoloured.
3850 4k. Type **1441** 30 15
3851 6k. Yellow-throated marten 45 15
3852 10k. Asiatic black bear (vert) 60 15
3853 16k. Red deer 70 25
3854 20k. Tiger . . . . 1·00 35

1970. 2nd U.S.S.R. Philatelic Society Congress, Moscow.
3855 **1442** 4k. silver and red . . . 25 10

1443 V. I. Kikvidze

1444 University Building

1970. 75th Birth Anniv of V. J. Kikvidze (Civil War hero).
3856 **1443** 4k. brown 20 10

1970. 50th Anniv of Yerevan University.
3857 **1444** 4k. red and blue . . . 20 10

1445 Pioneer Badge

1446 Library Book-plate (A. Kuchas)

1970. Pioneer Organization.
3858 **1445** 1k. gold, red and grey 10 10
3859 – 2k. grey and brown . . 10 10
3860 – 4k. multicoloured . . . 20 10

DESIGNS: 2k. "Lenin with Children" (sculpture, N. Scherbakov), 4k. Red Star and scarf.

1970. 400th Anniv of Vilnius (Vilna) University Library (Lithuania).
3861 **1446** 4k. black, grey and silver 20 10

1447 Woman with Bouquet

1970. 25th Anniv of International Democratic Women's Federation.
3862 **1447** 6k. brown and blue . . 20 10

1448 Milkmaid and Cows ("Livestock")

1970. Soviet Agriculture. Multicoloured.
3863 4k. Type **1448** 20 10
3864 4k. Driver, tractor and harvester ("Mechanization") . . . 20 10
3865 4k. Lock-operator and canal ("Irrigation and Chemical Research") 20 10

1449 Lenin addressing Meeting

1970. 53rd Anniv of October Revolution.
3866 **1449** 4k. gold and red . . . 20 10

50 лет
ленинному плану
ГОЭЛРО • 1970

(1450)

1970. 50th Anniv of GOELRO Electrification Plan. No. 3475 optd with T **1450**.
3868 4k. multicoloured 85 40

1451 Spassky Tower, Kremlin

1452 A. A. Baikov

1970. New Year.
3869 **1451** 6k. multicoloured . . . 20 10

1970. Birth Centenary of A. A. Baikov (metallurgic scientist).
3870 **1452** 4k. black and brown . . 20 10

1453 Tsyurupa (after A. Yar-Kravchenkol)

1454 St. Basil's Cathedral, Red Square, Moscow

1970. Birth Centenary of A. D. Tsyurupa (Vice-Chairman of Soviet People's Commissars).
3871 **1453** 4k. brown and yellow 20 10

1970. Tourism.
3872 **1454** 4k. multicoloured . . . 20 10
3873 – 6k. blue, indigo & brown 35 10
3874 – 10k. brown and green 45 15
3875 – 12k. multicoloured . . 55 15
3876 – 14k. blue, red and brown 70 20
3877 – 16k. multicoloured . . 80 30
DESIGNS: 6k. Scene from ballet "Swan Lake" (Tchaikovsky); 10k. Sika deer; 12k. Souvenir handicrafts; 14k. "Swords into Ploughshares" (sculpture by Ye. Vuchetich); 16k. Tourist and camera.

1455 Camomile

1970. Flowers. Multicoloured.
3878 4k. Type **1455** 15 10
3879 6k. Dahlia 30 10
3880 10k. Phlox 45 10
3881 12k. Aster . . . . 1·00 20
3882 16k. Clematis 70 30

1456 African Woman and Child **1457** Beethoven

1970. 10th Anniv of U.N. Declaration on Colonial Independence.
3883 **1456** 10k. brown and blue . . 40 10

1970. Birth Bicentenary of Beethoven (composer).
3884 **1457** 10k. purple and pink 1·25 35

1458 "Luna 16" in Flight **1459** Speed Skating

1970. Flight of "Luna 16".
3885 **1458** 10k. green 50 15
3886 – 10k. purple 50 15
3887 – 10k. green 50 15
DESIGNS: No. 3886, "Luna 16" on Moon's surface; 3887, Parachute descent.

1970. Trade Unions' Winter Games (1971).
3889 **1459** 4k. blue, red and grey 20 10
3890 – 10k. green, brn & grey 60 15
DESIGN: 10k. Cross-country skiing.

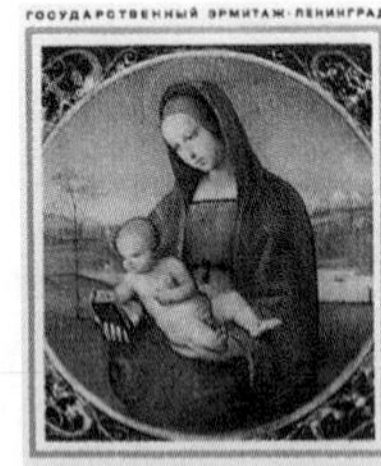

1460 "The Conestabile Madonna" (Raphael)

1970. Foreign Paintings in Soviet Galleries. Mult.
3891 3k. Type **1460** 20 10
3892 4k. "Saints Peter and Paul" (El Greco) 30 10
3893 10k. "Perseus and Andromeda" (Rubens) (horiz) 60 15
3894 12k. "The Return of the Prodigal Son" (Rembrandt) 70 15
3895 16k. "Family Portrait" (Van Dyck) 95 25
3896 20k. "The Actress Jeanne Samary" (Renoir) . . . . 1·10 35
3897 30k. "Woman with Fruit" (Gauguin) . . . . 1·50 85

1461 Harry Pollitt and Freighter "Jolly George"

1970. 80th Birth Anniv of H. Pollitt (British Communist).
3899 **1461** 10k. brown and purple 40 15

1462 "75" Emblem **1464** "50", State Emblem and Flag

1463 Sculptured Head of Lenin (A. Belostotsky and E. Fridman)

1970. 75th Anniv of Int Co-operative Alliance.
3900 **1462** 12k. red and green . . 55 15

1971. 24th Soviet Union Communist Party Congress.
3901 **1463** 4k. red and gold . . . 20 10

1971. 50th Anniv of Georgian Soviet Republic.
3902 **1464** 4k. multicoloured . . . 20 10

1971. 50th Anniv of Autonomous Soviet Socialist Republics. Similar designs to T **1433**, but dated "1971".
3903 4k. turquoise 25 10
3904 4k. red 25 10
3905 4k. red 25 10
3906 4k. blue 25 10
3907 4k. green 25 10
DESIGNS: No. 3903, Russian Federation Arms and Supreme Soviet building (Dagestan Republic); 3904, National emblem and symbols of agriculture and industry (Abkhazian Republic); 3905, Arms, produce and industry (Adjarian Republic); 3906, Arms and State building (Kabardino-Balkar Republic); 3907, Arms, industrial products and Government building (Komi Republic).

1465 Genua Fortress and Cranes

1971. 2500th Anniv of Feodosia (Crimean city).
3908 **1465** 10k. multicoloured . . 50 15

1466 Palace of Culture, Kiev **1467** "Features of National Economy"

1971. 24th Ukraine Communist Party Congress, Kiev.
3909 **1466** 4k. multicoloured . . . 20 10

1971. 50th Anniv of Soviet State Planning Organization.
3910 **1467** 6k. red and brown . . 35 10

1468 N. Gubin, I. Chernykh and S. Kosinov (dive-bomber crew)

1971. Soviet Air Force Heroes.
3911 **1468** 4k. brown and green . . 20 10

1469 Gipsy Dance

1971. State Folk Dance Ensemble. Multicoloured.
3912 10k. Type **1469** 55 20
3913 10k. Russian "Summer" dance (women in circle) 55 20
3914 10k. Ukraine "Gopak" dance (dancer leaping) . . 55 20
3915 10k. Adjar "Khorumi" dance (with drummer) . . 55 20
3916 10k. "On the Ice" (ballet) 55 20

1470 L. Ukrainka **1472** Fighting at the Barricades

1471 "Luna 17" Module on Moon

1971. Birth Centenary of Lesya Ukrainka (Ukrainian writer).
3917 **1470** 4k. red and brown . . 20 10

1971. Soviet Moon Exploration.
3918 **1471** 10k. brown and violet 40 15
3919 – 12k. brown and blue . . 70 20
3920 – 12k. brown and blue . . 70 20
3921 – 16k. brown and violet 95 30
DESIGNS: No. 3919, Control room and radio telescope; 3920, Moon trench; 3921, "Lunokhod 1" Moon-vehicle.

1971. Centenary of Paris Commune.
3923 **1472** 6k. black, brown and red 20 10

1473 Hammer, Sickle and Development Emblems **1475** E. Birznieks-Upitis

1474 Gagarin Medal, Spaceships and Planets

1971. 24th Soviet Communist Party Congress, Moscow.
3924 **1473** 6k. red, bistre & brown 20 10

1971. 10th Anniv of First Manned Space Flight (1st issue) and Cosmonautics Day.
3925 **1474** 10k. olive, yellow & brn 45 15
3926 – 12k. purple, blue & grey 60 20
DESIGN: 12k. Spaceship over Globe and economic symbols.
See also No. 3974.

1971. Birth Centenary of E. Birznieks-Upitis (Lithuanian writer).
3927 **1475** 4k. red and green . . . 20 10

1476 Honey Bee on Flower

1971. 23rd Int Bee-keeping Congress, Moscow.
3928 **1476** 6k. multicoloured . . . 40 15

1478 Memorial Building

1971. Lenin Memorial Building, Ulyanovsk.
3930 **1478** 4k. olive and red . . . 20 10

1479 Lieut-Col. N. I. Vlasov **1480** Khafiz Shirazi

1971. 26th Anniv of Victory in 2nd World War.
3931 **1479** 4k. brown and green . . 20 10

1971. 650th Birth Anniv of Khafiz Shirazi (Tadzhik writer).
3932 **1480** 4k. multicoloured . . . 20 10

1481 "GAZ-66" Truck

1971. Soviet Motor Vehicles.
3933 **1481** 2k. multicoloured . . . 15 10
3934 – 3k. multicoloured . . . 15 10
3935 – 4k. blue, black and lilac 20 10
3936 – 4k. green, purple & drab 20 10
3937 – 10k. red, black and lilac 55 15
DESIGNS: 3k. "BelAZ-540" tipper truck; 4k. (3935) "Moskvitch-412" 4-door saloon; 4k. (3936) "Zaporozhets ZAZ-968" 2-door saloon; 10k. "Volga GAZ-24" saloon.

1482 Bogomolets (after A. Yar-Kravchenko) **1483** Commemorative Scroll

1971. 90th Birth Anniv of A. A. Bogomolets (medical scientist).
3938 **1482** 4k. black, pink & orange 20 10

1971. International Moscow Congresses.
3939 **1483** 6k. brown and green . . 35 10
3940 – 6k. multicoloured . . . 35 10
3941 – 6k. multicoloured . . . 25 10
DESIGNS AND EVENTS—HORIZ: No. 3939, (13th Science History Congress); 3940, Oil derrick and symbols (8th World Oil Congress). VERT: No. 3941, Satellite over globe (15th General Assembly of Geodesics and Geophysics Union).

1484 Sukhe Bator Statue, Ulan Bator

1971. 50th Anniv of Revolution in Mongolia.
3942 **1484** 6k. grey, gold and red 20 10

1485 Defence Monument (E. Guirbulis)

1486 Treaty Emblem

1971. 30th Anniv of Defence of Liepaja, Latvia.
3943 **1485** 4k. brown, black & grey 20 10

1971. 10th Anniv of Antarctic Treaty and 50th Anniv of Soviet Hydrometeorological Service.
3944 **1486** 6k. deep blue, black and blue 75 30
3945 – 10k. violet, black & red 1·00 35
DESIGN: 10k. Hydrometeorological map.

1487 "Motherland" (sculpture, Yu. Vuchetich)

1488 Throwing the Discus

1971. 20th Anniv of "Federation Internationale des Resistants".
3946 **1487** 6k. green and red . . . 20 10

1971. 5th Summer Spartakiad.
3947 **1488** 3k. blue on pink . . . 10 10
3948 – 4k. green on flesh . . . 15 10
3949 – 6k. brown on green . . 30 10
3950 – 10k. purple on blue . . 55 20
3951 – 12k. brown on yellow 60 20
DESIGNS: 4k. Archery; 6k. Horse-riding (dressage); 10k. Basketball; 12k. Wrestling.

1489 "Benois Madonna" (Leonardo da Vinci)

1971. Foreign Paintings in Russian Museums. Multicoloured.
3952 2k. Type **1489** 10 10
3953 4k. "Mary Magdalene confesses her Sins" (Titian) 20 10
3954 10k. "The Washerwoman" (Chardin) (horiz) 40 15
3955 12k. "Young Man with Glove" (Hals) 50 20
3956 14k. "Tancred and Erminia" (Poussin) (horiz) 65 20
3957 16k. "Girl Fruit-seller" (Murillo) 80 35
3958 20k. "Child on Ball" (Picasso) . . . . 1·25 50

1490 Lenin Badge and Kazakh Flag

1971. 50th Anniv of Kazakh Communist Youth Assn.
3959 **1490** 4k. brown, red and blue 20 10

1491 Posthorn within Star

1971. International Correspondence Week.
3960 **1491** 4k. black, blue and green 20 10

1492 A. Spendiarov (Armenian composer) (after M. Saryan)

1971. Birth Anniversaries. Multicoloured.
3961 4k. Type **1492** (cent) 20 10
3962 4k. Nikolai Nekrasov (after I. Kramskoi) (poet, 150th anniv) 20 10
3963 10k. Fyodor Dostoevsky (after V. Perov) (writer, 150th anniv) 60 25

1493 Z. Paliashvili

1494 Emblem, Gorky Kremlin and Hydrofoil

1971. Birth Centenary of Z. Paliashvili (Georgian composer).
3964 **1493** 4k. brown 20 10

1971. 750th Anniv of Gorky (formerly Nizhni-Novgorod) (1st issue).
3965 **1494** 16k. multicoloured . . 65 20
See also No. 3974.

1495 Students and Globe

1971. 25th Anniv of Int Students Federation.
3966 **1495** 6k. blue, red and brown 20 10

1496 Atlantic White-sided Dolphins

1497 Star and Miners' Order

1971. Marine Fauna. Multicoloured.
3967 4k. Type **1496** 30 10
3968 6k. Sea otter 40 10
3969 10k. Narwhals 50 15
3970 12k. Walrus 75 20
3971 14k. Ribbon seals . . . . . 1·10 45

1971. 250th Anniv of Coal Discovery in Donetz Basin.
3972 **1497** 4k. red, brown and black 20 10

1498 Lord Rutherford and Atomic Formula

1499 Statue of Maksim Gorky (Vera Mukhina) and View

1971. Birth Cent of Lord Rutherford (physicist).
3973 **1498** 6k. brown and purple 35 15

1971. 750th Anniv of Gorky (formerly Nizhni-Novgorod) (2nd issue).
3974 **1499** 4k. multicoloured . . . 20 10

1500 Santa Claus in Troika

1971. New Year.
3975 **1500** 10k. red, gold and black 35 15

1501 Workers and Marx Books ("International Socialist Solidarity") (½-size illustration)

1971. 24th Soviet Union Communist Party Congress Resolutions.
3976 **1501** 4k. blue, ultram & red 25 10
3977 – 4k. red, yellow & brown 25 10
3978 – 4k. lilac, black and red 25 10
3979 – 4k. bistre, brown and red 25 10
3980 – 4k. red, green and yellow 25 10
DESIGNS: No. 3977, Farmworkers and wheatfield ("Agricultural Production"); 3978, Factory production line ("Increased Productivity"); 3979, Heavy industry ("Industrial Expansion"); 3980, Family in department store ("National Welfare").

1502 "Meeting" (V. Makovsky)

1503 V. V. Vorovsky

1971. Russian Paintings. Multicoloured.
3982 2k. Type **1502** 20 10
3983 4k. "Girl Student" (N. Yaroshenko) 25 10
3984 6k. "Woman Miner" (N. Kasatkin) 85 10
3985 10k. "Harvesters" (G. Myasoedov) (horiz) 55 15
3986 16k. "Country Road" (A. Savrasov) 80 30
3987 20k. "Pine Forest" (I. Shishkin) (horiz) . . . 1·25 40
See also Nos. 4064/70.

1971. Birth Centenary of V. V. Vorovsky (diplomat).
3989 **1503** 4k. brown 20 10

1504 Dobrovolsky, Volkov and Patsaev

1971. "Soyuz 11" Cosmonauts Commemoration.
3990 **1504** 4k. black, purple & orge 25 10

1505 Order of the Revolution and Building Construction

1971. 54th Anniv of October Revolution.
3991 **1505** 4k. multicoloured . . . 20 10

1506 E. Vakhtangov (founder) and characters from "Princess Turandot"

1507 "Dzhambul Dzhabaiev" (A. Yar-Kravchenko)

1971. 50th Anniv of Vakhtangov Theatre, Moscow.
3992 **1506** 10k. red and lake . . . 50 15
3993 – 10k. yellow and brown 50 15
3994 – 10k. orange and brown 50 15
DESIGNS—HORIZ: No. 3993, B. Shchukin (actor) and scene from "The Man with the Rifle"; 3994, R. Simonov (director) and scene from "Cyrano de Bergerac".

1971. 125th Anniv of Dzhambul Dzhabaiev (Kazakh poet).
3995 **1507** 4k. brown, yell & orge 20 10

1508 Pskov Kremlin

1971. Historical Buildings. Multicoloured.
3996 3k. Type **1508** 15 10
3997 4k. Novgorod kremlin . . . 20 10
3998 6k. Smolensk fortress and Liberation Monument . . 25 10
3999 10k. Kolomna kremlin . . . 40 15

1509 William Foster

1971. 90th Birth Anniv of Foster (American communist).
4001 **1509** 10k. black and brown 15·00 15·00
4002 10k. black and brown 50 15
No. 4001 shows the incorrect date of death "1964"; 4002 shows the correct date, "1961".

1510 Fadeev and Scene from "The Rout" (novel)

1971. 70th Birth Anniv of Aleksandr Fadeev (writer).
4003 **1510** 4k. orange and blue . . 20 10

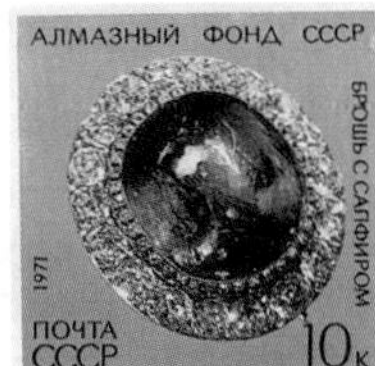

1511 Sapphire Brooch

1971. Diamonds and Jewels. Multicoloured.
4004 10k. Type **1511** 60 15
4005 10k. "Shah" diamond . . . 60 15
4006 10k. "Narcissi" diamond brooch 60 15
4007 20k. Amethyst pendant . . 90 40
4008 20k. "Rose" platinum and diamond brooch 90 40
4009 30k. Pearl and diamond pendant . . . . 1·40 60

1512 Vanda Orchid **1514** Ice Hockey Players

1513 Peter the Great's Imperial Barge, 1723

1971. Tropical Flowers. Multicoloured.
4010 1k. Type **1512** 15 10
4011 2k. "Anthurium scherzerianum" 15 10
4012 4k. "Cactus epiphyllum" . . 30 10
4013 12k. Amaryllis 60 30
4014 14k. "Medinilla magnifica" 75 35

1971. History of the Russian Navy (1st series). Multicoloured.
4016 1k. Type **1513** 15 10
4017 4k. Galleon "Orel", 1668 (vert) 35 10
4018 10k. Ship of the line "Poltava", 1712 (vert) . . 75 15
4019 12k. Ship of the line "Ingermanland", 1715 (vert) . . . . 1·10 30
4020 16k. Steam frigate "Vladimir", 1848 . . . . 1·40 50
See also Nos. 4117/21, 4209/13 and 4303/6.

1971. 25th Anniv of Soviet Ice Hockey.
4021 **1514** 6k. multicoloured . . . 50 10

1515 Baku Oil Installations **1516** G. M. Krzhizhanovsky

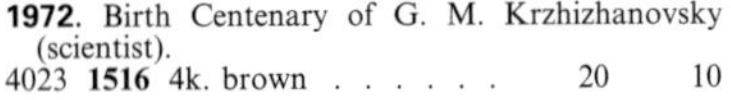

1971. Baku Oil Industry.
4022 **1515** 4k. black, red and blue 30 10

1972. Birth Centenary of G. M. Krzhizhanovsky (scientist).
4023 **1516** 4k. brown 20 10

1517 Scriabin **1518** Red-faced Cormorant

1972. Birth Centenary of Aleksandr Scriabin (composer).
4024 **1517** 4k. blue and green . . 30 10

1972. Sea Birds. Multicoloured.
4025 4k. Type **1518** 40 15
4026 6k. Ross's gull (horiz) . . . 60 25
4027 10k. Pair of barnacle geese 75 35
4028 12k. Pair of spectacled eiders (horiz) . . . . . . 1·10 60
4029 16k. Mediterranean gull . . 1·25 75

1519 Speed Skating **1520** Heart Emblem

1972. Winter Olympic Games, Sapporo, Japan. Multicoloured.
4030 4k. Type **1519** 15 10
4031 6k. Figure skating 20 10
4032 10k. Ice hockey 50 15
4033 12k. Ski jumping 65 20
4034 16k. Cross-country skiing 75 30

1972. World Heart Month.
4036 **1520** 4k. red and green . . . 20 10

1521 Fair Emblem **1522** Labour Emblems

1973. 50th Anniv of Soviet Participation in Leipzig Fair.
4037 **1521** 16k. gold and red . . . 85 30

1972. 15th Soviet Trade Unions Congress, Moscow.
4038 **1522** 4k. brown, red and pink 20 10

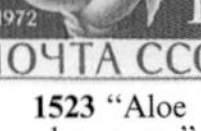

1523 "Aloe arborescens" **1524** Alexandra Kollontai (diplomat) (birth cent)

1972. Medicinal Plants. Multicoloured.
4039 1k. Type **1523** 10 10
4040 2k. Yellow horned poppy 10 10
4041 4k. Groundsel 20 10
4042 6k. Nephrite tea 30 10
4043 10k. Kangaroo apple . . . 55 15

1972. Birth Anniversaries.
4044 **1524** 4k. brown 20 10
4045 – 4k. lake 20 10
4046 – 4k. bistre 20 10
CELEBRITIES: No. 4045, G. Chicherin (Foreign Affairs Commissar) (birth cent); 4046, "Kamo" (S. A. Ter-Petrosyan—revolutionary) (90th birth anniv).

1526 "Salyut" Space-station and "Soyuz" Spacecraft

1972. Cosmonautics Day. Multicoloured.
4048 6k. Type **1526** 30 20
4049 6k. "Mars 2" approaching Mars 30 20
4050 16k. Capsule, "Mars 3" . . 75 30

1527 Factory and Products

1972. 250th Anniv of Izhora Factory.
4051 **1527** 4k. purple and silver . . 20 10

1972. 50th Anniv of Russian Federation Autonomous Soviet Socalist Republics. Designs similar to T **1433**, but dated "1972".
4052 4k. blue 35 10
4053 4k. mauve 25 10
DESIGNS: No. 4052, Arms, natural resources and industry (Yakut Republic); 4053, Arms, agriculture and industry (Checheno-Ingush Republic).

1528 L. Sobinov and scene from "Eugene Onegin"

1972. Birth Centenary of L. Sobinov (singer).
4054 **1528** 10k. brown 50 15

1529 Symbol of Knowledge and Children reading Books

1972. International Book Year.
4055 **1529** 6k. multicoloured . . . 30 10

1530 Pavlik Morosov Monument (I. Rabinovich) and Pioneers Saluting

1972. 50th Anniv of Pioneer Organization.
4056 **1530** 1k. multicoloured . . . 10 10
4057 – 2k. purple, red and green 10 10
4058 – 3k. blue, red and brown 20 10
4059 – 4k. red, blue and green 20 10
DESIGNS: 2k. Girl laboratory worker and Pioneers with book; 3k. Pioneer Place, Chukotka, and Pioneers at work; 4k. Pioneer parade.

1531 Pioneer Trumpeter

1972. "50th Anniv of Pioneer Organization" Youth Stamp Exhibition, Minsk.
4061 **1531** 4k. purple, red & yellow 20 10

1532 "World Security"

1972. European Security Conference, Brussels.
4062 **1532** 6k. blue, turquoise & gold 75 55

1533 M. S. Ordubady **1534** G. Dimitrov

1972. Birth Centenary of M. S. Ordubady (Azerbaijan writer).
4063 **1533** 4k. purple and orange 20 10

1972. Russian Paintings. As T **1502**, but dated "1972". Multicoloured.
4064 2k. "Cossack Hetman" (I. Nikitin) 10 10
4065 4k. "F. Volkov" (A. Lossenko) 20 10
4066 6k. "V. Majkov" (F. Rokotov) 25 10
4067 10k. "N. Novikov" (D. Levitsky) 40 10
4068 12k. "G. Derzhavin" (V. Borovikovsky) 55 15
4069 16k. "Peasants' Dinner" (M. Shibanov) (horiz) . . 75 25
4070 20k. "Moscow View" (F. Alexeiev) (horiz) . . . 1·10 45

1972. 90th Birth Anniv of Georgi Dimitrov (Bulgarian statesman).
4071 **1534** 6k. brown and bistre 20 10

1535 Congress Building and Emblem

1972. 9th Int Gerontology Congress, Kiev.
4072 **1535** 6k. brown and blue . . 20 10

1536 Fencing

1972. Olympic Games, Munich.
4073 **1536** 4k. purple and gold . . 25 10
4074 – 6k. green and gold . . 35 10
4075 – 10k. blue and gold . . 50 10
4076 – 14k. blue and gold . . 70 20
4077 – 16k. red and gold . . . 85 65
DESIGNS: 6k. Gymnastics; 10k. Canoeing; 14k. Boxing; 16k. Running.

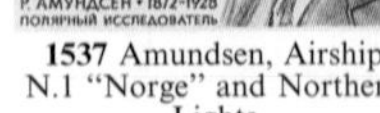

1537 Amundsen, Airship N.1 "Norge" and Northern Lights **1538** Market-place, Lvov (Lemberg)

1972. Birth Centenary of Roald Amundsen (Polar explorer).
4079 **1537** 6k. blue and brown . . 1·50 30

1972. Ukraine's Architectural Monuments. Mult.
4080 4k. Type **1538** 15 10
4081 6k. 17th-century house, Tchernigov (horiz) 30 15
4082 10k. Kovnirovsky building, Kiev (horiz) 45 20
4083 16k. Kamenetz-Podolsk Castle 75 30

1539 Indian Flag and Asokan Capital **1540** Liberation Monument, Vladivostok, and Cavalry

1972. 25th Anniv of India's Independence.
4084 **1539** 6k. red, blue and green 30 10

1972. 50th Anniv of Liberation of Far Eastern Territories.
4085 **1540** 3k. grey, orange and red 15 10
4086 – 4k. grey, yellow & ochre 20 10
4087 – 6k. grey, pink and red 30 15
DESIGNS: 4k. Labour Heroes Monument, Khabarovsk, and industrial scene; 6k. Naval statue, Vladivostok, "Vladivostok" (cruiser) and jet fighters.

1541 Miners' Day Emblem

1972. 25th Anniv of Miners' Day.
4088 **1541** 4k. red, black and violet 20 10

1542 "Boy with Dog" (Murillo)

1972. Paintings by Foreign Artists in Hermitage Gallery, Leningrad. Multicoloured.
4089 4k. "Breakfast" (Velazquez) (horiz) 20 10
4090 6k. "The Milk Seller's Family" (Le Nain) (horiz) 30 10
4091 10k. Type **1542** 55 20
4092 10k. "The Capricious Girl" (Watteau) 90 35
4093 20k. "Moroccan with Horse" (Delacroix) . . . 1·10 45

1543 "Sputnik I"

1972. 15th Anniv of "Cosmic Era". Multicoloured.
4095 6k. Type **1543** 35 15
4096 6k. Launch of "Vostok I" 35 15
4097 6k. "Lunokhod" vehicle on Moon 35 15
4098 6k. Man in space 35 15
4099 6k. "Mars 3" module on Mars 35 15
4100 6k. Touch down of "Venera 7" on Venus 35 15

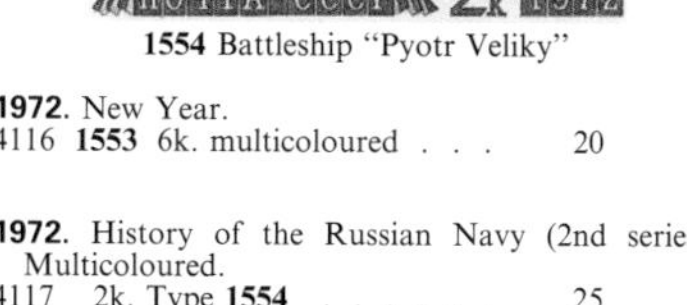

1544 Konstantin Mardzhanishvili

1545 Museum Emblem

1972. Birth Centenary of K. Mardzhanishvili (Georgian actor).
4101 **1544** 4k. green 20 10

1972. Centenary of Popov Central Communications Museum.
4102 **1545** 4k. blue, purple & green 20 10

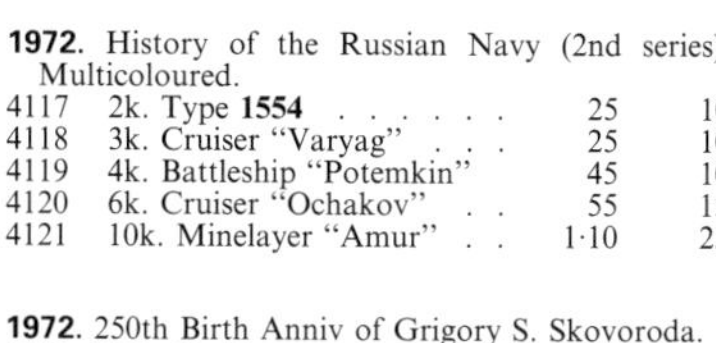

1546 Exhibition Labels

1972. "50th Anniv of U.S.S.R." Philatelic Exhibition.
4103 **1546** 4k. red & black on yell 20 10

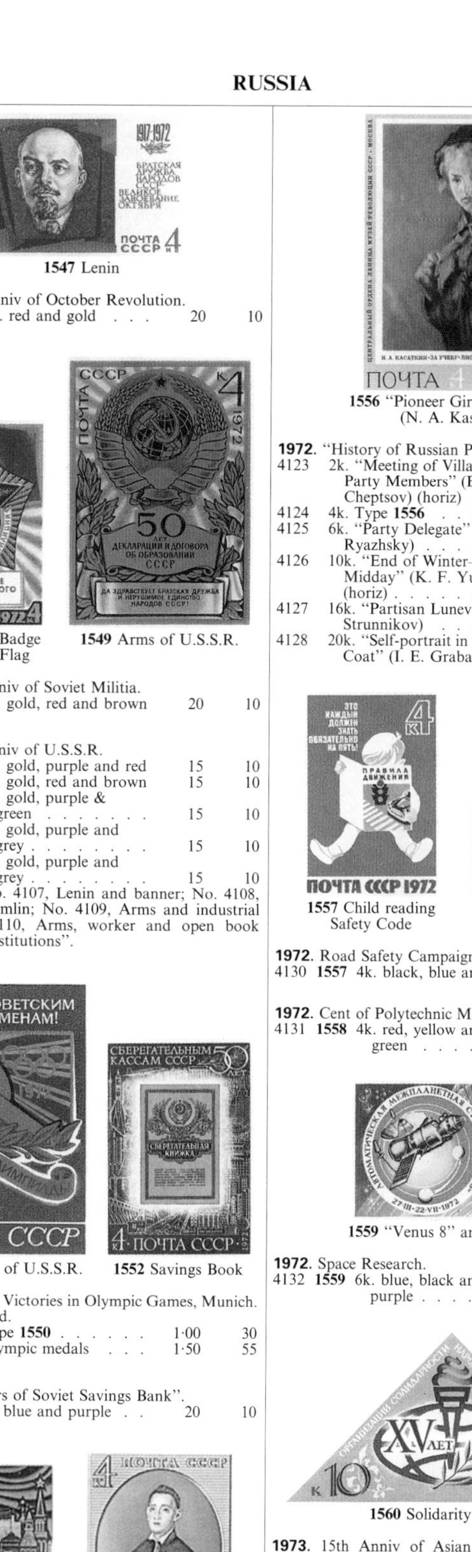

1547 Lenin

1972. 55th Anniv of October Revolution.
4104 **1547** 4k. red and gold . . . 20 10

1548 Militia Badge and Soviet Flag

1549 Arms of U.S.S.R.

1972. 55th Anniv of Soviet Militia.
4105 **1548** 4k. gold, red and brown 20 10

1972. 50th Anniv of U.S.S.R.
4106 **1549** 4k. gold, purple and red 15 10
4107 – 4k. gold, red and brown 15 10
4108 – 4k. gold, purple & green 15 10
4109 – 4k. gold, purple and grey 15 10
4110 – 4k. gold, purple and grey 15 10
DESIGNS: No. 4107, Lenin and banner; No. 4108, Arms and Kremlin; No. 4109, Arms and industrial scenes; No. 4110, Arms, worker and open book "U.S.S.R. Constitutions".

1550 Emblem of U.S.S.R.

1552 Savings Book

1972. U.S.S.R. Victories in Olympic Games, Munich. Multicoloured.
4112 20k. Type **1550** . . . . . . 1·00 30
4113 30k. Olympic medals . . . 1·50 55

1972. "50 Years of Soviet Savings Bank".
4115 **1552** 4k. blue and purple . . 20 10

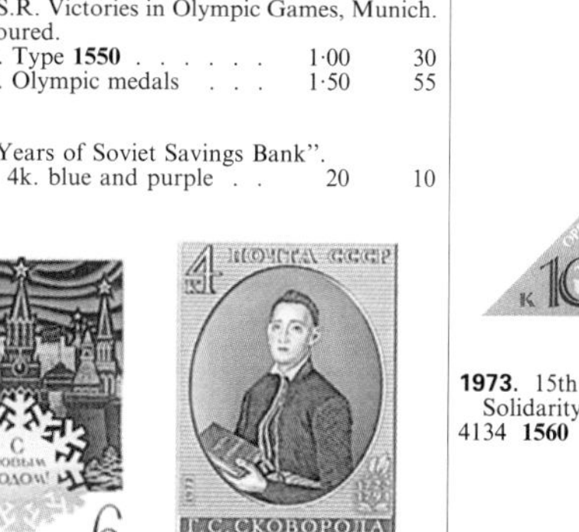

1553 Kremlin and Snowflakes

1555 Skovoroda (after P. Meshcheryakov)

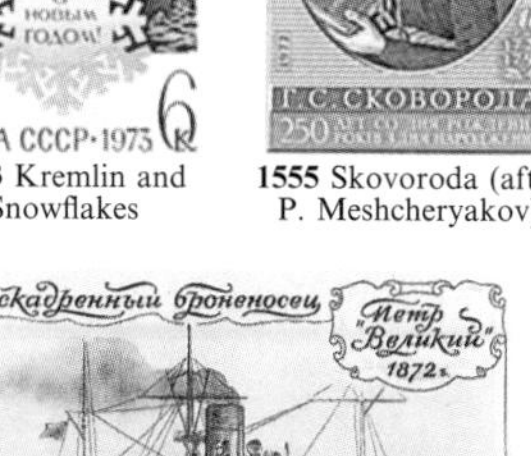

1554 Battleship "Pyotr Veliky"

1972. New Year.
4116 **1553** 6k. multicoloured . . . 20 10

1972. History of the Russian Navy (2nd series). Multicoloured.
4117 2k. Type **1554** 25 10
4118 3k. Cruiser "Varyag" . . . 25 10
4119 4k. Battleship "Potemkin" 45 10
4120 6k. Cruiser "Ochakov" . . 55 15
4121 10k. Minelayer "Amur" . . 1·10 25

1972. 250th Birth Anniv of Grigory S. Skovoroda.
4122 **1555** 4k. blue 20 10

1556 "Pioneer Girl with Books" (N. A. Kasatkin)

1972. "History of Russian Painting". Mult.
4123 2k. "Meeting of Village Party Members" (E. M. Cheptsov) (horiz) 15 10
4124 4k. Type **1556** 20 15
4125 6k. "Party Delegate" (G. G. Ryazhsky) 25 15
4126 10k. "End of Winter— Midday" (K. F. Yuon) (horiz) 35 20
4127 16k. "Partisan Lunev" (N. I. Strunnikov) 70 35
4128 20k. "Self-portrait in Fur Coat" (I. E. Grabar) . . 1·10 50

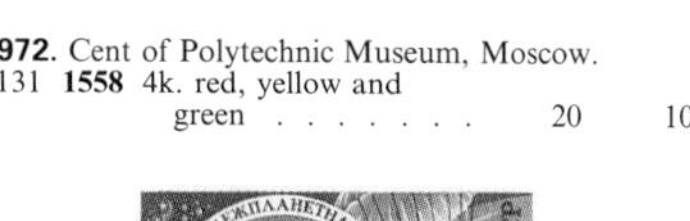

1557 Child reading Safety Code

1558 Emblem of Technology

1972. Road Safety Campaign.
4130 **1557** 4k. black, blue and red 20 10

1972. Cent of Polytechnic Museum, Moscow.
4131 **1558** 4k. red, yellow and green 20 10

1559 "Venus 8" and Parachute

1972. Space Research.
4132 **1559** 6k. blue, black and purple 25 10

1560 Solidarity Emblem

1973. 15th Anniv of Asian and African People's Solidarity Organization.
4134 **1560** 10k. blue, red and brown 35 15

1561 Town and Gediminas Tower

1562 I. V. Babushkin

1973. 650th Anniv of Vilnius (Vilna).
4135 **1561** 10k. red, black and green 35 15

1973. Birth Cent of I. V. Babushkin (revolutionary).
4136 **1562** 4k. black 20 10

1563 Tupolev Tu-154 Jetliner

1973. 50th Anniv of Soviet Civil Aviation.
4137 **1563** 6k. multicoloured . . . 45 15

1564 "30" and Admiralty Spire, Leningrad

1565 Portrait and Masks (Mayakovsky Theatre)

1973. 30th Anniv of Relief of Leningrad.
4138 **1564** 4k. black, orange & brn 20 10

1973. 50th Anniv of Moscow Theatres.
4139 **1565** 10k. multicoloured . . 30 10
4140 – 10k. red and blue . . . 30 10
DESIGN: No. 4140, Commemorative panel (Mossoviet Theatre).

1566 Prishvin (after A. Kirillov)

1973. Birth Centenary of Mikhail Prishvin (writer).
4141 **1566** 4k. multicoloured . . . 30 10

1567 Heroes' Square, Volgograd

1973. 30th Anniv of Stalingrad Victory. Detail from Heroes' Memorial.
4142 – 3k. black, yellow & orge 20 10
4143 **1567** 4k. yellow and black . . 20 10
4144 – 10k. multicoloured . . 40 15
4145 – 12k. black, light red and red 60 20
DESIGNS—VERT: 3k. Soldier and Allegory; 12k. Hand with torch. HORIZ: 10k. Mother mourning for child.

1568 Copernicus and Planetary Chart

1973. 500th Birth Anniv of Copernicus (astronomer).
4147 **1568** 10k. brown and blue . . 55 15

1569 Chaliapin (after K. Korovin)

1973. Birth Centenary of Fyodor Chaliapin (opera singer).
4148 **1569** 10k. multicoloured . . 45 15

1570 Ice Hockey Players

1571 Athletes

1973. World Ice Hockey Championships, Moscow.
4149 **1570** 10k. brown, blue & gold 60 15

1973. 50th Anniv of Central Red Army Sports Club.
4151 **1571** 4k. multicoloured . . . 20 10

1572 Red Star, Tank, and Map

1573 N. E. Bauman

1973. 30th Anniv of Battle of Kursk.
4152 **1572** 4k. black, red and grey 20 10

1973. Birth Centenary of Nikolai Bauman (revolutionary).
4153 **1573** 4k. brown 25 10

1574 Red Cross and Red Crescent

1973. International Co-operation.
4154 **1574** 4k. red, black and green 15 10
4155 – 6k. light blue, red and blue 20 10
4156 – 16k. green, red and mauve 80 25

DESIGNS AND EVENTS: 4k. (50th anniv of Soviet Red Cross and Red Crescent Societies Union); 6k. Mask, emblem and theatre curtain (15th Int Theatre Institution Congress); 16k. Floral emblem (10th World Festival of Youth, Berlin).

1575 Ostrovsky (after V. Perov)

1576 Satellites

1973. 150th Birth Anniv of Aleksandr Ostrovsky (writer).
4157 **1575** 4k. multicoloured . . . 20 10

1973. Cosmonautics Day. Multicoloured.
4158 6k. Type **1576** 20 10
4159 6k. "Lunokhod 2" 20 10

1577 "Guitarist" (V. Tropinin)

1578 Athlete and Emblems

1973. "History of Russian Painting". Mult.
4162 2k. Type **1577** 15 10
4163 4k. "The Young Widow" (P. Fedotov) 20 10
4164 6k. "Self-portrait" (O. Kiprensky) 30 10
4165 10k. "An Afternoon in Italy" (K. Bryullov) . . . 45 20
4166 12k. "That's My Father's Dinner!" (boy with dog) (A. Venetsianov) 55 30
4167 16k. "Lower Gallery of Albano" (A. Ivanov) (horiz) 75 35
4168 20k. "Yermak conquering Siberia" (V. Surikov) (horiz) . . . . 1·00 50

1973. 50th Anniv of Dynamo Sports Club.
4169 **1578** 4k. multicoloured . . . 20 10

1580 Liner "Mikhail Lermontov"

1582 Sports

1581 E. T. Krenkel and Polar Scenes

1973. Inauguration of Leningrad–New York Trans-Atlantic Service.
4171 **1580** 16k. multicoloured . . 70 30

1973. 70th Birth Anniv of E. T. Krenkel (Polar explorer).
4172 **1581** 4k. brown and blue . . 75 20

1973. "Sport for Everyone".
4173 **1582** 4k. multicoloured . . . 20 10

1583 Girls' Choir

1973. Centenary of Latvian Singing Festival.
4174 **1583** 10k. multicoloured . . 35 10

1973. 50th Anniv of Russian Federation Autonomous Soviet Socialist Republics. Design similar to T **1433**, but dated "1973".
4175 4k. blue 20 10
DESIGN: No. 4175, Arms and industries of Buryat Republic.

1584 Throwing the Hammer

1973. Universiade Games, Moscow. Mult.
4176 2k. Type **1584** 10 10
4177 3k. Gymnastics 10 10
4178 4k. Swimming 15 10
4179 16k. Fencing 85 25

1586 European Bison

1973. Caucasus and Voronezh Nature Reserves. Multicoloured.
4182 1k. Type **1586** 10 10
4183 3k. Ibex 15 10
4184 4k. Caucasian snowcocks . . 1·25 20
4185 6k. Eurasian beaver with young 35 10
4186 10k. Red deer with fawns 55 20

1587 Lenin, Banner and Membership Card

1973. 70th Anniv of 2nd Soviet Social Democratic Workers Party Congress.
4187 **1587** 4k. multicoloured . . . 20 10

1588 A. R. al-Biruni (after M. Nabiev)

1590 "Portrait of the Sculptor S. T. Konenkov" (P. Korin)

1589 Schaumberg Palace, Bonn, and Spassky Tower, Moscow

1973. Millennium of Abu Reihan al-Biruni (astronomer and mathematician).
4188 **1588** 6k. brown 30 15

1973. General Secretary Leonid Brezhnev's Visits to West Germany, France and U.S.A. Multicoloured.
4189 **1589** 10k. mauve, brn & buff 40 15
4190 – 10k. brown, ochre and yellow 40 15
4191 – 10k. red, grey and brown 40 15
DESIGNS: No. 4190, Eiffel Tower, Paris, and Spassky Tower; 4191, White House, Washington, and Spassky Tower.
See also Nos. 4245 and 4257.

1973. "History of Russian Paintings". Mult.
4193 2k. Type **1590** 10 10
4194 4k. "Farm-workers' Supper" (A. Plastov) 15 10
4195 6k. "Letter from the Battle-front" (A. Laktionov) . . 25 15
4196 10k. "Mountain Landscape" (M. Saryan) 45 25
4197 16k. "Wedding on Tomorrow's Street" (Yu. Pimenov) 75 35
4198 20k. "Ice Hockey" (mosaic, A. Deineka) . . . . . . 1·10 45

1591 Lenin Museum

1592 Steklov

1973. Inaug of Lenin Museum, Tashkent.
4200 **1591** 4k. multicoloured . . . 20 10

1973. Birth Centenary of Y. Steklov (statesman).
4201 **1592** 4k. brown, red and pink 20 10

1593 "The Eternal Pen"

1594 "Oplopanax elatum"

1973. Afro-Asian Writers' Conference, Alma-Ata.
4202 **1593** 6k. multicoloured . . . 20 10

1973. Medicinal Plants. Multicoloured.
4203 1k. Type **1594** 10 10
4204 2k. Ginseng 15 10
4205 4k. Spotted orchid 20 10
4206 10k. Arnica 40 20
4207 12k. Lily of the valley . . . 55 25

1595 I. Nasimi (after M. Abdullaev)

1973. 600th Birth Anniv of Imadeddin Nasimi (Azerbaijan poet).
4208 **1595** 4k. brown 20 10

1596 Cruiser "Kirov"

1973. History of Russian Navy (3rd series). Multicoloured.
4209 3k. Type **1596** 20 10
4210 4k. Battleship "Oktyabrskaya Revolyutsiya" 25 10
4211 6k. Submarine "Krasnogvardeets" . . . 30 15
4212 10k. Destroyer "Soobrazitelnyi" 60 25
4213 16k. Cruiser "Krasnyi Kavkaz" . . . . 1·10 35

1597 Pugachev and Battle Scene

1973. Bicentenary of Peasant War.
4214 **1597** 4k. multicoloured . . . 20 10

1598 Red Flag encircling Globe

1973. 15th Anniv of Magazine "Problems of Peace and Socialism".
4215 **1598** 6k. red, gold and green 25 10

1599 Leningrad Mining Institute

1973. Bicentenary of Leningrad Mining Institute.
4216 **1599** 4k. multicoloured . . . 20 10

1600 Laurel and Hemispheres

1601 Elena Stasova

1973. World Congress of "Peaceful Forces", Moscow.
4217 **1600** 6k. multicoloured . . . 25 10

1973. Birth Centenary of Yelena Stasova (party official).
4218 **1601** 4k. mauve 20 10

1602 Order of People's Friendship

1603 Marshal Malinovsky

1973. Foundation of Order of People's Friendship.
4219 **1602** 4k. multicoloured . . . 20 10

1973. 75th Birth Anniv of Marshal R. Malinovsky.
4220 **1603** 4k. grey 20 10

1604 Workers and Red Guard

1605 D. Cantemir

1973. 250th Anniv of Sverdlovsk.
4221 **1604** 4k. black, gold and red 20 10

1973. 300th Birth Anniv of Dmitri Cantemir (Moldavian scientist and encyclopaedist).
4222 **1605** 4k. red 20 10

1606 Pres. Allende of Chile

1973. Allende Commemoration.
4223 **1606** 6k. black and brown . . 30 10

1607 Kremlin

1608 N. Narimanov

1973. New Year.
4224 **1607** 6k. multicoloured . . . 20 10

1973. Birth Centenary (1970) of Nariman Narimanov (Azerbaijan politician).
4225 **1608** 4k. green 20 10

1609 "Russobalt" Touring Car (1909)

1973. History of Soviet Motor Industry (1st series). Multicoloured.
4226 2k. Type **1609** 15 10
4227 3k. "AMO-F15" lorry (1924) 15 10
4228 4k. Spartak "NAMI-1" tourer (1927) 20 10
4229 12k. Yaroslavsky "Ya-6" bus (1929) 55 20
4230 16k. Gorkovsky "GAZ-A" tourer (1932) 75 40
See also Nos. 4293/7, 4397/401 and 4512/16.

1610 "Game and Lobster" (Sneiders)

1973. Foreign Paintings in Soviet Galleries. Mult.
4231 4k. Type **1610** 20 10
4232 6k. "Young Woman with Ear-rings" (Rembrandt) (vert) 20 10
4233 10k. "Sick Woman and Physician" (Steen) (vert) 35 15
4234 12k. "Attributes of Art" (Chardin) 45 20
4235 14k. "Lady in a Garden" (Monet) 50 25
4236 16k. "Village Lovers" (Bastien-Lepage) (vert) . . 60 30
4237 20k. "Girl with Fan" (Renoir) (vert) 75 40

1611 Great Sea Gate, Tallin

1612 Picasso

1973. Historical Buildings of Estonia, Latvia and Lithuania.
4239 **1611** 4k. black, red and green 20 10
4240 – 4k. brown, red and green 20 10
4241 – 4k. multicoloured . . . 20 10
4242 – 10k. multicoloured . . 50 20
DESIGNS: No. 4240, Organ pipes and Dome Cathedral, Riga; 4241, Traku Castle, Lithuania; 4242, Town Hall and weather-vane, Tallin.

1973. Pablo Picasso Commemoration.
4243 **1612** 6k. green, red and gold 30 10

1613 Petrovsky

1973. I. G. Petrovsky (mathematician and Rector of Moscow University) Commemoration.
4244 **1613** 4k. multicoloured . . . 20 10

1973. Brezhnev's Visit to India. As T **1589**, but showing Kremlin, Red Fort, Delhi and flags.
4245 4k. multicoloured 20 10

1614 Soviet Soldier and Title Page

1616 Oil Workers

1615 Siege Monument and Peter the Great Statue, Leningrad

1974. 50th Anniv of "Red Star" Newspaper.
4246 **1614** 4k. black, red and gold 20 10

1974. 30th Anniv of Soviet Victory in Battle for Leningrad.
4247 **1615** 4k. multicoloured . . . 30 10

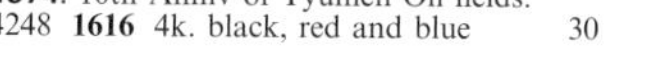

1974. 10th Anniv of Tyumen Oil fields.
4248 **1616** 4k. black, red and blue 30 10

1617 "Comecon" Headquarters, Moscow

1618 Skaters and Stadium

1974. 25th Anniv of Council for Mutual Economic Aid.
4249 **1617** 16k. green, red & brown 45 20

1974. European Women's Ice Skating Championships, Medeo, Alma-Ata.
4250 **1618** 6k. red, blue and slate 20 10

1619 Kunstkammer Museum, Leningrad, Text and Academy

1620 L. A. Artsimovich

1974. 250th Anniv of Russian Academy of Sciences.
4251 **1619** 10k. multicoloured . . 25 10

1974. 1st Death Anniv of Academician L. A. Artsimovich (physicist).
4252 **1620** 4k. brown and green . . 20 10

1974. 50th Anniv of Autonomous Soviet Socialist Republics. Design similar to T **1433**, but dated "1974".
4253 4k. brown 20 10
DESIGN: No. 4253, Arms and industries of Nakhichevan ASSR (Azerbaijan).

1621 K. D. Ushinsky

1622 M. D. Millionshchikov

1974. 150th Birth Anniv of K. D. Ushinsky (educationalist).
4254 **1621** 4k. brown and green . . 20 10

1974. 1st Death Anniv of M. D. Millionshchikov (scientist).
4255 **1622** 4k. brown, pink & green 20 10

1623 Spartakiad Emblem

1624 Young Workers and Emblem

1974. 3rd Winter Spartakiad Games.
4256 **1623** 10k. multicoloured . . 25 15

1974. General Secretary Leonid Brezhnev's Visit to Cuba. As T **1589** but showing Kremlin, Revolution Square, Havana and Flags.
4257 4k. multicoloured 20 10

1974. Scientific and Technical Youth Work Review.
4258 **1624** 4k. multicoloured . . . 20 10

1625 Theatre Facade

1626 Globe and Meteorological Activities

1974. Cent of Azerbaijan Drama Theatre, Baku.
4259 **1625** 6k. brown, red & orange 20 10

1974. Cosmonautics Day.
4260 **1626** 6k. blue, red and violet 20 10
4261 – 10k. brown, red and blue 40 15
4262 – 10k. black, red & yellow 40 15
DESIGNS: No. 4261, V. G. Lazarev and O. G. Makarov, and launch of "Soyuz 12"; 4262, P. I. Klimuk and V. V. Lebedev, and "Soyuz 13".

1627 "Odessa by Moonlight" (Aivazovsky)

1974. Marine Paintings by Ivan Aivazovsky. Mult.
4263 2k. Type **1627** 10 10
4264 4k. "Battle of Chesme" (vert) 15 10
4265 6k. "St. George's Monastery" 20 10
4266 10k. "Storm at Sea" 35 15
4267 12k. "Rainbow" 65 20
4268 16k. "Shipwreck" 80 30

1628 Young Communists

1974. 17th Leninist Young Communist League (Komsomol) Congress (4270) and 50th Anniv of Naming League after Lenin (4271). Multicoloured.
4270 4k. Type **1628** 20 10
4271 4k. "Lenin" (from sculpture by V. Tsigal) 20 10

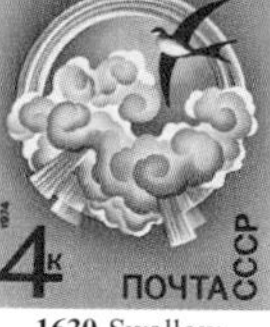

1630 Swallow ("Atmosphere")

1631 "Cobble-stone, Proletarian Weapon" (sculpture, I. Shadr)

1974. "EXPO 74" World Fair, Spokane, U.S.A. "Preserve the Environment".
4273 **1630** 4k. black, red and lilac 15 10
4274 – 6k. yellow, black & blue 20 10
4275 – 10k. black, violet and red 45 15
4276 – 16k. blue, green & black 65 20
4277 – 20k. black, brn & orge 90 40
DESIGNS: 6k. Fish and globe ("The Sea"); 10k. Crystals ("The Earth"); 16k. Rose bush ("Flora"); 20k. Young red deer ("Fauna").

1974. 50th Anniv of Central Museum of the Revolution.
4279 **1631** 4k. green, red and gold 20 10

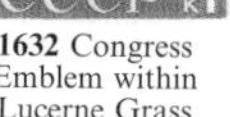

1632 Congress Emblem within Lucerne Grass

1634 Tchaikovsky and Competition Emblem

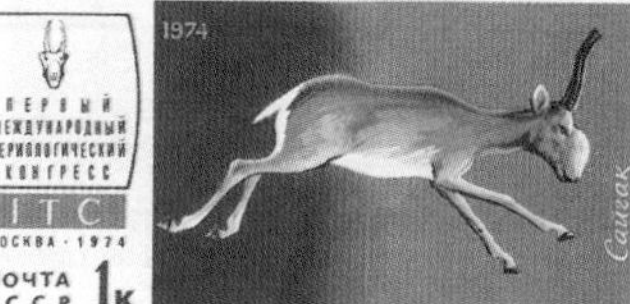

1633 Saiga

1974. 12th International Congress of Meadow Cultivation, Moscow.
4280 **1632** 4k. red, green & dp green 20 10

1974. 1st International Theriological Congress, Moscow. Fauna. Multicoloured.
4281 1k. Type **1633** 10 10
4282 3k. Asiatic wild ass 15 10
4283 4k. Russian desman 25 10
4284 6k. Northern fur seal . . . 35 15
4285 10k. Bowhead whale 75 25

1974. 5th Int Tchaikovsky Music Competition.
4286 **1634** 6k. black, violet & green 35 10

1636 Marshal F. I. Tolbukhin

1638 Runner and Emblem

1637 K. Stanislavsky, V. Nemirovich-Danchenko and Theatre Curtain

1974. 80th Birth Anniv of Marshal F. I. Tolbukhin.
4288 **1636** 4k. green 20 10

[illegible]
4289 **1637** 10k. multicoloured . . 35 15

1974. 13th Soviet Schools Spartakiad, Alma Ata.
4290 **1638** 4k. multicoloured . . . 25 10

1639 Modern Passenger Coach

1640 Shield and Monument on Battle Map

1974. Centenary of Yegorov Railway Wagon Works, Leningrad.
4291 **1639** 4k. multicoloured . . . 30 10

1974. 30th Anniv of Liberation of Belorussia.
4292 **1640** 4k. multicoloured . . . 20 10
See also No. 4301.

1974. History of Soviet Motor Industry (2nd series). As T **1609**. Multicoloured.
4293 2k. Gorkovsky "GAZ-AA" lorry (1932) 15 10
4294 3k. Gorkovsky "GAZ-03-30" bus (1933) 15 10
4295 4k. Moscow Auto Works "ZIS-5" lorry (1933) . . . 20 10
4296 14k. Moscow Auto Works "ZIS-8" bus (1934) . . . 65 20
4297 16k. Moscow Auto Works "ZIS-101" saloon car (1936) 80 25

1974. 50th Anniv of Soviet Republics. As T **1433**, dated "1974".
4298 4k. red 20 10
DESIGN: 4k. Arms and industries of North Ossetian Republic.
No. 4298 also commemorates the 200th anniv of Ossetia's merger with Russia.

1641 Liberation Monument (E. Kuntsevich) and Skyline

1644 Admiral Isakov

1642 Flag and "Nike" Memorial, Warsaw

1974. 800th Anniv of Poltava.
4299 **1641** 4k. red and brown . . 20 10

1974. 30th Anniv of Polish People's Republic.
4300 **1642** 6k. brown and red . . 25 10

1974. 30th Anniv of Liberation of Ukraine. As T **1640**, but background details and colours changed.
4301 4k. multicoloured 20 10

1974. 80th Birth Anniv of Admiral I. S. Isakov.
4302 **1644** 4k. blue 20 10

1645 Minesweeper

1974. History of the Russian Navy (4th series). Modern Warships. Multicoloured.
4303 3k. Type **1645** 25 10
4304 4k. Aligator II tank landing ship 30 10
4305 6k. "Moskova" helicopter carrier 45 15
4306 16k. Destroyer "Otvazhny" 1·25 30

1646 Pentathlon Sports

1647 D. Ulyanov

1974. World Modern Pentathlon Championships, Moscow.
4307 **1646** 16k. brown, gold & blue 60 20

1974. Birth Centenary of D. Ulyanov (Lenin's brother).
4308 **1647** 4k. green 20 10

1648 V. Menzhinsky

1650 S. M. Budennyi

1649 "Lilac" (P. P. Konchalovsky)

1974. Birth Cent of V. Menzhinsky (statesman).
4309 **1648** 4k. maroon 20 10

1974. Soviet Paintings. Multicoloured.
4310 4k. Type **1649** 15 10
4311 6k. "Towards the Wind" (sailing) (E. Kalnins) . . . 25 15
4312 10k. "Spring" (young woman) (O. Zardaryan) 45 20
4313 16k. "Northern Harbour" (G. Nissky) 75 30
4314 20k. "Daughter of Soviet Kirgiz" (S. Chuikov) (vert) 90 35

1974. Marshal S. M. Budennyi Commemoration.
4315 **1650** 4k. green 20 10

1651 Page of First Russian Dictionary

1652 Flags and Soviet War Memorial, (K. Baraski), Bucharest

1974. 400th Anniv of First Russian Primer.
4316 **1651** 4k. red, black and gold 20 10

1974. 30th Anniv of Rumanian Liberation.
4317 **1652** 6k. blue, yellow and red 20 10

1653 Vitebsk

1974. Millenary of Vitebsk.
4318 **1653** 4k. red and green . . . 15 10

1654 Kirgizia

1655 Bulgarian Crest and Flags

1974. 50th Anniv of Soviet Republics. Flags, Agricultural and Industrial Emblems. Mult. Background colours given.
4319 **1654** 4k. blue 15 10
4320 – 4k. purple 15 10
4321 – 4k. blue 15 10
4322 – 4k. yellow 15 10
4323 – 4k. green 15 10
DESIGNS: No. 4320, Moldavia; 4321, Tadzhikistan; 4322, Turkmenistan; 4323, Uzbekistan.

1974. 30th Anniv of Bulgarian Revolution.
4324 **1655** 6k. multicoloured . . . 20 10

1656 G.D.R. Crest and Soviet War Memorial, Treptow, Berlin

1658 Theatre and Laurel Wreath

1974. 25th Anniv of German Democratic Republic.
4325 **1656** 6k. multicoloured . . . 20 10

1974. 150th Anniv of Maly State Theatre, Moscow.
4327 **1658** 4k. gold, red and black 20 10

1659 "Guests from Overseas"

1974. Birth Centenary of Nikolai K. Rorich (painter).
4328 **1659** 6k. multicoloured . . . 25 10

1660 Soviet Crest and U.P.U. Monument, Berne

1974. Centenary of U.P.U. Multicoloured.
4329 10k. Type **1660** 45 15
4330 10k. Ukraine crest, U.P.U. Emblem and U.P.U. H.Q., Berne 45 15
4331 10k. Byelorussia crest, U.P.U. emblem and mail transport 45 15

1661 Order of Labour Glory

1974. 57th Anniv of October Revolution. Mult.
4333 4k. Type **1661** 25 10
4334 4k. Kamaz truck (vert) . . . 15 10
4335 4k. Hydro-electric power station, Nurek (vert) . . . 15 10

1662 Soviet "Space Stations" over Mars

1974. Soviet Space Exploration. Multicoloured.
4336 6k. Type **1662** 25 10
4337 10k. P. R. Popovich and Yu. P. Artyukhin ("Soyuz 14" cosomonauts) 45 15
4338 10k. I. V. Sarafanov and L. S. Demin ("Soyuz 15" cosmonauts) 45 15
SIZES—VERT: No. 4337, 28 × 40 mm. HORIZ: No. 4338, 40 × 28 mm.

1663 Mongolian Crest Flag

1664 Commemorative Inscription

1974. 50th Anniv of Mongolian People's Republic.
4339 **1663** 6k. multicoloured . . . 20 10

1974. 30th Anniv of Estonian Liberation.
4340 **1664** 4k. multicoloured . . . 20 10

1665 Liner "Aleksandr Pushkin", Freighter and Tanker

1974. 50th Anniv of Soviet Merchant Navy.
4341 **1665** 4k. multicoloured . . . 30 10

1666 Spassky Clock-tower, Kremlin, Moscow

1974. New Year.
4342 **1666** 4k. multicoloured . . . 20 10

1667 "The Market Place" (Beuckelaar)

1974. Foreign Paintings in Soviet Galleries. Mult.
4343 4k. Type **1667** 15 10
4344 6k. "Woman selling Fish" (Pieters) (vert) 25 10
4345 10k. "A Goblet of Lemonade" (Terborsh) (vert) 35 15
4346 14k. "Girl at Work" (Metsu) (vert) 50 25
4347 16k. "Saying Grace" (Chardin) (vert) 55 30
4348 20k. "The Spoilt Child" (Greuze) (vert) 80 35

1668 "Ostrowskia magnifica" **1669** Nikitin (after P. Borel)

1974. Flowers. Multicoloured.
4350 1k. Type **1668** 10 10
4351 2k. "Paeonia intermedia" . . 10 10
4352 4k. "Roemeria refracta" . . 20 10
4353 10k. "Tulipia dasystemon" . . 45 20
4354 12k. "Dianthus versicolor" . . 55 25

1974. 150th Birth Anniv of I. S. Nikitin (poet).
4355 **1669** 4k. black, green & olive 20 10

1670 Leningrad Mint Building

1974. 250th Anniv of Leningrad Mint.
4356 **1670** 6k. multicoloured . . . 35 10

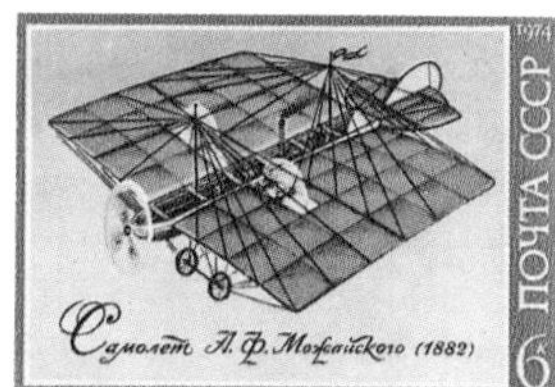

1671 Mozhaisky's Monoplane, 1884

1974. Early Russian Aircraft (1st series). Mult.
4357 6k. Type **1671** 30 15
4358 6k. Grizidubov No. 2 biplane, 1910 . . . . . . 30 15
4359 6k. Sikorsky "Russia A", 1910 . . . . 30 15
4360 6k. Sikorsky Russky Vityaz, 1913 . . . . 30 15
4361 6k. Grigorovich M-5 flying boat, 1914 . . . . 30 15
See also Nos. 4580/4, 4661/6 and 4791/6.

1673 Komsomol Emblem and Rotary Press ("Komsomolskaya Pravda")

1975. 50th Anniv of Children's Newspapers.
4363 **1673** 4k. red, black and blue 20 10
4364 – 4k. red, black and silver 20 10
DESIGN—VERT: No. 4364, Pioneer emblem and newspaper sheet ("Pioneerskaya Pravda").

1674 Emblem and Skiers (8th Trade Unions' Games)

1975. Winter Spartakiads.
4365 **1674** 4k. orange, black & blue 15 10
4366 – 16k. bistre, black & blue 55 20
DESIGN—HORIZ: 16k. Emblem, ice hockey player and skier (5th Friendly Forces Military Games).

1975. "50th Anniv of Automomous Soviet Socialist Republics. Designs similar to T **1433**, but dated "1975".
4367 4k. green 20 10
DESIGN: No. 4367, Arms, industries and produce of Karakalpak ASSR (Uzbekistan).

1675 "David"

1975. 500th Birth Anniv of Michelangelo.
4368 **1675** 4k. deep green and green 20 15
4369 – 6k. brown and ochre 25 15
4370 – 10k. deep green & green 35 15
4371 – 14k. brown and ochre 60 30
4372 – 20k. deep green & green 1·00 30
4373 – 30k. brown and ochre 1·50 30
DESIGNS: 6k. "Crouching Boy"; 10k. "Rebellious Slave"; 14k. "Creation of Adam" (detail, Sistine Chapel ceiling); 20k. Staircase of Laurentiana Library, Florence; 30k. Christ and the Virgins (detail of "The Last Judgement", Sistine Chapel).

1676 Mozhaisky, his Monoplane (1884) and Tupolev Tu-144 Jetliner

1975. 150th Birth Anniv of Aleksandr Mozhaisky (aircraft designer).
4375 **1676** 6k. brown and blue . . 40 10

1677 Convention Emblem

1975. Cent of International Metre Convention.
4376 **1677** 6k. multicoloured . . . 20 10

1678 Games Emblem

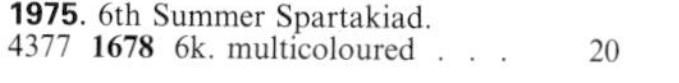

1975. 6th Summer Spartakiad.
4377 **1678** 6k. multicoloured . . . 20 10

1679 Towers of Charles Bridge, Prague (Czechoslovakia)

1975. 30th Anniv of Liberation. Multicoloured.
4378 6k. Type **1679** 15 10
4379 6k. Liberation Monument and Parliament Buildings, Budapest (Hungary) . . . 15 10

1680 French and Soviet Flags **1681** Yuri Gagarin (bust by L. Kerbel)

1975. 50th Anniv of Franco-Soviet Diplomatic Relations.
4380 **1680** 6k. multicoloured . . . 20 10

1975. Cosmonautics Day.
4381 **1681** 6k. red, silver and blue 20 10
4382 – 10k. red, black and blue 35 15
4383 – 16k. multicoloured . . 55 20
DESIGNS—HORIZ: 10k. A. A. Gubarev, G. M. Grechko ("Soyuz 17") and "Salyut 4"; 16k. A. V. Filipchenko, N. N. Rukavishnikov and "Soyuz 16".

1682 Treaty Emblem **1684** Lenin

1683 Emblem and Exhibition Hall, Sokolniki, Moscow

1975. 20th Anniv of Warsaw Treaty.
4384 **1682** 6k. multicoloured . . . 20 10

1975. "Communication 75" International Exhibition, Moscow.
4385 **1683** 6k. red, silver and blue 20 10

1975. 30th Anniv of Victory in Second World War. Multicoloured.
4386 4k. Type **1684** 15 10
4387 4k. Eternal flame and Guard of Honour 15 10
4388 4k. Woman in ammunition factory 15 10
4389 4k. Partisans 15 10
4390 4k. "Destruction of the enemy" 15 10
4391 4k. Soviet forces 15 10

1685 "Lenin" (V. G. Tsyplakov) **1686** Victory Emblems

1975. 105th Birth Anniv of Lenin.
4393 **1685** 4k. multicoloured . . . 20 10

1975. "Sozfilex 75" International Stamp Exhibition.
4394 **1686** 6k. multicoloured . . . 20 10

1687 "Apollo"–"Soyuz" Space Link

1975. "Apollo"–"Soyuz" Space Project.
4396 **1687** 20k. multicoloured . . 75 25

1975. History of Soviet Motor Industry (3rd series). As T **1609**.
4397 2k. black, orange and blue 15 10
4398 3k. black, brown and green 15 10
4399 4k. black, blue and green . . 15 10
4400 12k. black, buff and purple 45 20
4401 16k. black, green and olive 60 30
DESIGNS: 2k. Gorkovsky "GAZ-M1" saloon, 1936; 3k. Yaroslavsky "YAG-6" truck, 1936; 4k. Moscow Auto Works "ZIS-16" bus, 1938; 12k. Moscow KIM Works "KIM-10" saloon, 1940; 16k. Gorkovsky "GAZ-67B" field car, 1943.

1688 Irrigation Canal and Emblem **1689** Flags and Crests of Poland and Soviet Union

1975. 9th Int Irrigation Congress, Moscow.
4402 **1688** 6k. multicoloured . . . 20 10

1975. 30th Anniv of Soviet–Polish Friendship.
4403 **1689** 6k. multicoloured . . . 20 10

1690 A. A. Leonov in Space **1691** Ya. M. Sverdlov

1975. 10th Anniv of First Space Walk by A. A. Leonov.
4404 **1690** 6k. multicoloured . . . 25 10

1975. 90th Birth Anniv of Ya. M. Sverdlov (statesman).
4405 **1691** 4k. brown, buff & silver 15 10

1692 Congress Emblem

1975. 8th Int Plant Conservation Congress, Moscow.
4406 **1692** 6k. multicoloured . . . 20 10

1693 Emblem and Plants

1975. 12th Int Botanical Congress, Leningrad.
4407 **1693** 6k. multicoloured . . . 60 15

1695 Festival Emblem

1975. 9th International Film Festival, Moscow.
4409 **1695** 6k. multicoloured . . . 20 10

1696 Crews of "Apollo" and "Soyuz"

1975. "Apollo"–"Soyuz" Space Link. Mult.
4410 10k. Type **1696** 35 10
4411 12k. "Apollo" and "Soyuz 19" in docking procedure 35 20
4412 12k. "Apollo" and "Soyuz 19" linked together . . . 55 20
4413 16k. Launch of "Soyuz 19" (vert) 75 20

1697 Russian Sturgeon

1975. Int Exposition, Okinawa. Marine Life.
4415 **1697** 3k. bistre, black and blue 25 10
4416 – 4k. lilac, black and blue 30 10
4417 – 6k. purple, black & green 35 10
4418 – 10k. brown, black & bl 1·00 10
4419 – 16k. green, black & purple 70 25
4420 – 20k. blue, pur & stone 85 30
DESIGNS: 4k. Thomas rapa whelk; 6k. European eel; 10k. Long-tailed duck; 16k. Crab; 20k. Grey damselfish.

1698 "Parade in Red Square, Moscow" (K. F. Yuon)

1975. Birth Centenaries of Soviet Painters. Mult.
4422 1k. Type **1698** 10 10
4423 2k. "Winter Morning in Industrial Moscow" (K. P. Yuon) 15 10
4424 6k. "Soldiers with Captured Guns" (E. E. Lansere) . . 25 10
4425 10k. "Excavating the Metro Tunnel" (E. E. Lansere) 75 20
4426 16k. "A. A. Pushkin and N. N. Pushkina at Palace Ball" (N. P. Ulyanov) (vert) 60 30
4427 20k. "Lauriston at Kutuzov's Headquarters" (N. P. Ulyanov) 80 40

1699 Conference Emblem

1700 Isaakjan (after M. Sargan)

1975. European Security and Co-operation Conf, Helsinki.
4428 **1699** 6k. black, gold and blue 30 10

1975. Birth Centenary of Avetic Isaakjan (Armenian poet).
4429 **1700** 4k. multicoloured . . . 20 10

1701 M. K. Ciurlionis

1702 J. Duclos

1975. Birth Centenary of M. K. Ciurlionis (Lithuanian composer).
4430 **1701** 4k. gold, green & yellow 20 10

1975. Jacques Duclos (French communist leader) Commemoration.
4431 **1702** 6k. purple and silver . . 20 10

1703 Al Farabi (after L. Leontev)

1704 Ruffs

1975. 1100th Birth Anniv of Al Farabi (Persian philosopher).
4432 **1703** 6k. multicoloured . . . 20 10

1975. 50th Anniv of Berezinsky and Stolby Nature Reserves. Multicoloured.
4433 1k. Type **1704** 20 10
4434 4k. Siberian musk deer . . . 30 10
4435 6k. Sable 30 10
4436 10k. Western capercaillie . . 60 30
4437 16k. Eurasian badger . . . 70 30

1705 Korean Crest with Soviet and Korean Flags

1707 Yesenin

1706 Cosmonauts, "Soyuz 18" and "Salyut 4" Linked

1975. 30th Anniversaries. Multicoloured.
4438 6k. Type **1705** (Korean liberation) 20 10
4439 6k. Vietnamese crest, Soviet and Vietnamese flags (Vietnam Democratic Republic) 20 10

1975. Space Flight of "Soyuz 18–Salyut 4" by Cosmonauts P. Klimuk and V. Sevastyanov.
4440 **1706** 10k. black, red and blue 30 10

1975. 80th Birth Anniv of Yesenin (poet).
4441 **1707** 6k. brown, yell & grey 20 10

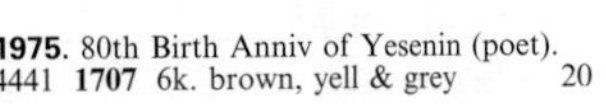

1708 Standardization Emblems

1975. 50th Anniv of Soviet Communications Standardization Committee.
4442 **1708** 4k. multicoloured . . . 15 10

1709 Astrakhan Lamb

1710 M. P. Konchalovsky

1975. 3rd International Astrakhan Lamb Breeding Symposium, Samarkand.
4443 **1709** 6k. black, green & stone 20 10

1975. Birth Centenary of M. P. Konchalovsky (therapeutist).
4444 **1710** 4k. brown and red . . 15 10

1711 Exhibition Emblem

1712 I.W.Y. Emblem and Rose

1975. 3rd All-Union Philatelic Exhibition, Yerevan.
4445 **1711** 4k. red, brown and blue 15 10

1975. International Women's Year.
4446 **1712** 6k. red, blue & turquoise 20 10

1713 Parliament Buildings, Belgrade

1714 Title-page of 1938 Edition

1975. 30th Anniv of Yugoslav Republic.
4447 **1713** 6k. blue, red and gold 20 10

1975. 175th Anniv of Publication of "Tale of the Host of Igor".
4448 **1714** 4k. red, grey and bistre 15 10

1715 M. I. Kalinin (statesman)

1975. Celebrities' Birth Centenaries.
4449 **1715** 4k. brown 15 10
4450 – 4k. brown 15 10
DESIGN: No. 4450, A. V. Lunacharsky (politician).

1716 Torch and Inscription

1975. 70th Anniv of Russian 1905 Revolution.
4451 **1716** 4k. red and brown . . 15 10

1717 Track-laying Machine and Baikal-Amur Railway

1719 Star of Spassky Tower

1718 "Decembrists in Senate Square" (D. N. Kardovsky) (⅔-size illustration)

1975. 58th Anniv of October Revolution. Mult.
4452 4k. Type **1717** 35 10
4453 4k. Rolling mill, Novolipetsk steel plant (vert) 20 10
4454 4k. Formula and ammonia plant, Nevynomyssk chemical works (vert) . . 20 10

1975. 150th Anniv of Decembrist Rising.
4455 **1718** 4k. multicoloured . . . 20 10

1975. New Year.
4456 **1719** 4k. multicoloured . . . 15 10

1720 "Village Street"

1975. 125th Birth Anniv of F. A. Vasilev (painter). Multicoloured.
4457 2k. Type **1720** 10 10
4458 5k. "Forest Path" 15 10
4459 6k. "After the Thunderstorm" 25 10
4460 10k. "Forest Marsh" (horiz) 45 15
4461 12k. "In the Crimean Mountains" 65 20
4462 16k. "Wet Meadow" (horiz) 1·00 30

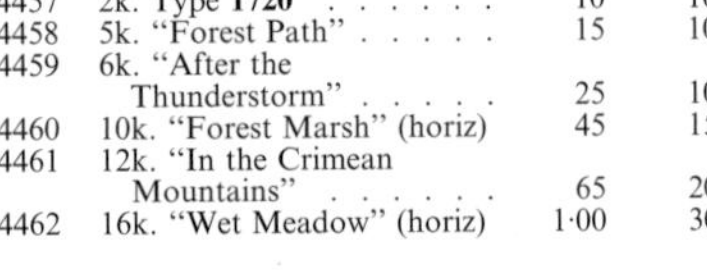
1721 "Venus" Spacecraft

1975. Space Flights of "Venus 9" and "Venus 10".
4464 **1721** 10k. multicoloured . . 35 15

1722 G. Sundukyan

1975. 150th Birth Anniv of G. Sundukyan (Armenian playwright).
4465 **1722** 4k. multicoloured . . . 15 10

1723 Iceland Poppy

1724 A. L. Mints

1975. Flowers (1st series). Multicoloured.
4466 4k. Type **1723** 30 10
4467 6k. Globe flower 25 10

4468 10k. Yellow anemone . . . 35 15
4469 12k. Snowdrop windflower 40 20
4470 16k. "Eminium lehemannii" 50 30
See also Nos. 4585/9.

1975. A. L. Mints (scientist) Commemoration.
4471 **1724** 4k. brown and gold . . 15 10

1725 "Demon" (A. Kochupalov)

1726 Pieck

1975. Miniatures from Palekh Art Museum (1st series). Multicoloured.
4472 4k. Type **1725** 20 10
4473 6k. "Vasilisa the Beautiful" (I. Vakurov) 30 10
4474 10k. "The Snow Maiden" (T. Zubkova) 45 15
4475 16k. "Summer" (K. Kukulieva) 65 25
4476 20k. "Fisherman and Goldfish" (I. Vakurov) (horiz) 90 30
See also Nos. 4561/5.

1975. Birth Centenary of Wilhelm Pieck (President of German Democratic Republic).
4477 **1726** 6k. black 20 10

1727 Saltykov-Shchedrin (after I. Kramskoi)

1728 Congress Emblem

1976. 150th Birth Anniv of M. Saltykov-Shchedrin (writer).
4478 **1727** 4k. multicoloured . . . 15 10

1976. 25th Communist Party Congress, Moscow (1st issue).
4479 **1728** 4k. gold, brown and red 15 10
See also Nos. 4489 and 4556/60.

1729 Lenin (statue, S. Merkurov), Kiev

1976. 25th Ukraine Communist Party Congress, Kiev.
4481 **1729** 4k. black, red and blue 15 10

1730 Ice Hockey

1976. Winter Olympic Games, Innsbruck (1st series). Multicoloured.
4482 2k. Type **1730** 15 10
4483 4k. Skiing 20 10
4484 6k. Figure skating 25 10
4485 10k. Speed skating 35 15
4486 20k. Tobogganing 75 35

1731 Marshal C. E. Voroshilov

1732 Congress Hall and Red Banner

1976. 95th Birth Anniv of Marshal C. E. Voroshilov.
4488 **1731** 4k. green 15 10

1976. 25th Communist Party Congress, Moscow (2nd issue).
4489 **1732** 20k. orange, red & green . . . . 3·50 2·25

1733 "Lenin on Red Square" (P. Vasilev)

1976. 106th Birth Anniv of Lenin.
4490 **1733** 4k. multicoloured . . . 20 10

1734 Atomic Symbol and Institute Emblem

1976. 20th Anniv of Joint Institute of Nuclear Research, Dubna.
4491 **1734** 6k. multicoloured . . . 20 10

1736 Bolshoi Theatre

1976. Bicentenary of Bolshoi Theatre.
4493 **1736** 10k. blue, brn & ochre 30 15

1737 "Back from the Fair"

1976. Birth Centenary of P. P. Konchalovsky (painter). Multicoloured.
4494 1k. Type **1737** 10 10
4495 2k. "The Green Glass" . . 10 10
4496 6k. "Peaches" 25 10
4497 16k. "Meat, Game and Vegetables by the Window" 70 30
4498 20k. Self-portrait (vert) . . . 95 40

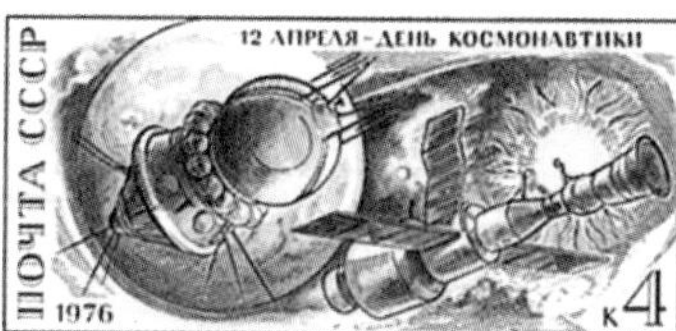

1738 "Vostok", "Salyut" and "Soyuz" Spacecraft

1976. 15th Anniv of First Manned Space Flight by Yuri Gagarin.
4499 4k. Type **1738** 15 10
4500 6k. "Meteor" and "Molniya" satellites . . . 25 10
4501 10k. Cosmonauts on board "Salyut" space-station . . 45 15
4502 12k. "Interkosmos" satellite and "Apollo"–"Soyuz" space link 55 20

1739 I. A. Dzhavakhishvili

1740 S. Vurgun

1976. Birth Centenary of I. A. Dzhavakhishvili (scientist).
4504 **1739** 4k. black, stone and green 15 10

1976. 70th Birth Anniv of Samed Vurgun (Azerbaijan poet).
4505 **1740** 4k. black, brown & green 15 10

1741 Festival Emblem

1742 F. I. P. Emblem

1976. 1st All-Union Amateur Art Festival.
4506 **1741** 4k. multicoloured . . . 15 10

1976. 50th Anniv of International Philatelic Federation.
4507 **1742** 6k. red and blue . . . 20 10

1744 Dnepropetrovsk Crest

1745 N. N. Burdenko

1976. Bicentenary of Dnepropetrovsk.
4509 **1744** 4k. multicoloured . . . 15 10

1976. Birth Centenary of N. N. Burdenko (neurologist).
4510 **1745** 4k. brown and red . . 15 10

1746 K. A. Trenev

1748 Electric Railway Train

1747 Canoeing

1976. Birth Centenary of K. A. Trenev (playwright).
4511 **1746** 4k. multicoloured . . . 15 10

1976. History of Soviet Motor Industry (4th series). As T **1609**.
4512 2k. black, red and green . . 10 10
4513 3k. black, orange and bistre 15 10
4514 4k black, buff and blue . . 15 10
4515 12k. black, green and brown 45 20
4516 16k. black, red and yellow 65 30
DESIGNS: 2k. Moscow Auto Works "ZIS-110" saloon, 1945; 3k. Gorkovsky "GAZ-51" truck, 1946; 4k. Gorkovsky "GAZ-M20 (Pobeda)" saloon, 1946; 12k. Moscow Auto Works "ZIS-150" truck, 1947; 16k. Moscow Auto Works "ZIS-154" bus, 1947.

1976. Olympic Games, Montreal. Multicoloured.
4517 4k. Type **1747** 10 10
4518 6k. Basketball (vert) 20 10
4519 10k. Graeco-Roman wrestling 30 15
4520 14k. Discus throwing (vert) 45 15
4521 16k. Rifle-shooting 55 20

1976. 50th Anniv of Soviet Railway Electrification.
4523 **1748** 4k. black, red and green 30 10

1749 L. M. Pavlichenko

1750 L. E. Rekabarren

1976. 60th Birth Anniv of L. M. Pavlichenko (war heroine).
4524 **1749** 4k. brown, yellow and silver 15 10

1976. Birth Centenary of Luis Rekabarren (founder of Chilean Communist Party).
4525 **1750** 6k. black, red and gold 15 10

1751 "Fresh Partner"

1976. Russian Art. Paintings by P. A. Fedotov. Multicoloured.
4526 2k. Type **1751** 10 10
4527 4k. "Fastidious Fiancee" (horiz) 15 10
4528 6k. "Aristocrat's Breakfast" 20 10
4529 10k. "The Gamblers" (horiz) 50 20
4530 16k. "The Outing" 70 30

1752 S. S. Nemetkin

1753 Soviet Armed Forces Order

1754 Marx and Lenin (sculpture, Ye. Belostotsky and E. Fridman)

1976. Birth Centenary of Sergei S. Nemetkin (chemist).
4532 **1752** 4k. black, yellow & blue 15 10

1976. (a) As T **1753**.
4669 1k. olive 10 10
4670 2k. mauve 10 10
4671 3k. red 10 10
4672 4k. red 15 10
4673 6k. blue 20 10
4674 10k. green 35 10
4675 12k. blue 40 10
4676 15k. blue 70 10
4677 16k. green 50 15

(b) As T **1754**.
4678 20k. red 55 10
4679 30k. red 85 20
4680 32k. blue . . . . 1·60 45
4681 50k. brown . . . . 1·40 40
4682 1r. blue . . . . 3·00 1·00
DESIGNS: 2k. Gold Star (military) and Hammer and Sickle (labour) decorations; 3k. "Worker and Collective Farmer" (sculpture, Vera Mukhina); 4k. Soviet crest; 6k. Globe and Tupolev Tu-154 jetliner (Soviet postal communications); 10k. Soviet Reputation for Work Order; 23k. Yuri Gagarin and rocket (space exploration); 15k. Ostankino T.V. tower and globe; 16k. International Lenin Prize medal (international peace and security); 30k. Council for Mutual Economic Aid building; 32k. Ilyushin Il-76 airplane and compass rose; 50k. Lenin (after P. Zhukov); 1r. Satellites orbiting globe.

The 6 and 32k. are airmail stamps.

1755 Cattle Egret

1976. Water Birds. Multicoloured.

4545	1k. Type **1755**	15	15
4546	3k. Black-throated diver	20	20
4547	4k. Black coot	45	40
4548	6k. Atlantic puffin	85	40
4549	10k. Slender-billed gull	1·40	45

1756 Peace Dove with Laurel

1976. 2nd Stockholm World Peace Appeal.
4550 **1756** 4k. blue, yellow and gold 15 10

1757 Federation Emblem

1976. 25th Anniv of International Resistance Movement Federation.
4551 **1757** 6k. black, gold and blue 15 10

1759 Soviet and Indian Flags

1761 UNESCO Emblem

1760 B. V. Volynov and V. M. Zholobov

1976. Soviet–Indian Friendship.
4553 **1759** 4k. multicoloured . . . 15 10

1976. Space Flight of "Soyuz 21".
4554 **1760** 10k. black, blue & brn 30 15

1976. 30th Anniv of UNESCO.
4555 **1761** 16k. brown, bistre & blue 45 20

1762 "Industry"

1976. 25th Communist Party Congress (3rd issue).

4556	**1762**	4k. brown, red & yellow	15	10
4557	–	4k. green, red & orange	15	10
4558	–	4k. violet, red and pink	15	10
4559	–	4k. deep red, red and grey	20	10
4560	–	4k. violet, red and blue	15	10

DESIGNS: No. 4557, "Agriculture"; 4558, "Science and Technology"; 4559, "Transport and Communications"; 4560, "International Co-operation".

1763 "The Ploughman" (I. Golikov)

1976. Minatures from Palekh Art Museum (2nd series). Multicoloured.

4561	2k. Type **1763**	10	10
4562	4k. "The Search" (I. Markichev) (vert)	15	10
4563	12k. "The Firebird" (A. Kotukhin)	40	20
4564	14k. "Folk Festival" (A. Vatagin) (vert)	55	25
4565	20k. "Victory" (I. Vakurov) (vert)	90	35

1764 Shostakovich and Part of 7th Symphony

1765 G. K. Zhukov

1976. 70th Birth Anniv of Dmitri Shostakovich (composer).
4566 **1764** 6k. blue 30 10

1976. 80th Birth Anniversaries of Soviet Marshals.
4567 **1765** 4k. green 15 10
4568 – 4k. brown 15 10
DESIGN: No. 4568, K. K. Rokossovsky.

1766 "Interkosmos 14" Satellite

1767 V. I. Dal

1976. International Co-operation in Space Research.

4569	**1766**	6k. blue, gold and black	20	10
4570	–	10k. violet, gold & black	25	10
4571	–	12k. purple, gold & black	40	15
4572	–	16k. green, gold & black	50	20
4573	–	20k. mauve, gold & black	90	25

DESIGNS: 10k. "Aryabhata" (Indian satellite); 12k. "Apollo"–"Soyuz" space link; 16k. "Aureole" (French satellite); 20k. Globe and spacecraft.

1976. 175th Birth Anniv of V. I. Dal (scholar).
4574 **1767** 4k. green 15 10

1768 Electric Power Station

1976. 59th Anniv of October Revolution. Mult.

4575	4k. Type **1768**	15	10
4576	4k. Balashovo fabrics factory	15	10
4577	4k. Irrigation ditch construction	15	10

1769 Medicine Emblem

1770 M. A. Novinsky (oncologist)

1976. 50th Anniv of Petrov Institute of Cancer Research.
4578 **1769** 4k. lilac, gold and blue 20 10

1976. Centenary of Cancer Research.
4579 **1770** 4k. brown, blue and buff 20 10

1771 Hakkel VII Biplane, 1911

1976. Early Russian Aircraft (2nd series). Mult.

4580	3k. Type **1771**	10	10
4581	6k. Hakkel IX monoplane, 1912	20	10
4582	12k. Steglau No. 2, 1912	35	15
4583	14k. Dybovsky Dolphin, 1913	50	15
4584	16k. Sikorsky Ilya Mourometz, 1914	55	25

See also Nos. 4661/6 and 4791/6.

1976. Flowers (2nd series). As T **1723**. Mult.

4585	1k. Safflower	10	10
4586	2k. Anemone	10	10
4587	3k. Gentian	10	10
4588	4k. Columbine	15	10
4589	6k. Fitillaria	25	15

1772 New Year Greeting

1976. New Year.
4590 **1772** 4k. multicoloured . . . 15 10

1773 "Parable of the Vineyard"

1976. 370th Birth Anniv of Rembrandt. Mult.

4591	4k. Type **1773**	15	10
4592	6k. "Danae"	25	10
4593	10k. "David and Jonathan" (vert)	35	15
4594	14k. "The Holy Family" (vert)	55	20
4595	20k. "Andrian" (vert)	85	30

1774 "Luna 24" and Emblem

1976. "Luna 24" Unmanned Space Flight to Moon.
4597 **1774** 10k. brown, yellow & blue 30 15

1775 "Pailot'

1976. Russian Ice-breakers (1st series). Mult.

4598	4k. Type **1775**	40	10
4599	6k. "Ermak" (vert)	50	10
4600	10k. "Fyodor Litke"	70	15
4601	16k. "Vladmir Ilich" (vert)	95	25
4602	20k. "Krassin"	1·25	50

See also Nos. 4654/60, 4843/8 and 5147.

1776 "Raduga" Experiment and Cosmonauts

1976. "Soyuz 22" Space Flight by V. F. Bykovsky and V. V. Aksenov.
4603 **1776** 10k. green, blue and red 30 15

1777 Olympic Torch

1976. Olympic Games, Moscow (1980).

4604	**1777**	4k.+2k. black, red and blue	30	10
4605	–	10k.+5k. black, blue and red	65	25
4606	–	16k.+6k. black, mauve and yellow	1·25	40

DESIGNS: 10, 16k. Games emblem.

1778 Society Emblem and "Red Star"

1779 S. P. Korolev Memorial Medallion

1977. 50th Anniv of Red Banner Forces Voluntary Society.
4608 **1778** 4k. multicoloured . . . 15 10

1977. 70th Birth Anniv of S. P. Korolev (scientist and rocket pioneer).
4609 **1779** 4k. gold, black and blue 15 10

1780 Congress Emblem

1977. World Peace Congress, Moscow.
4610 **1780** 4k. gold, ultramarine and blue 15 10

1781 Sedov and "Sv. Foka"

1977. Birth Cent of G. Y. Sedov (polar explorer).
4611 **1781** 4k. multicoloured . . . 1·10 20

1782 Working Class Monument, Red Flag and Newspaper Cover

1783 Ship on Globe

1977. 60th Anniv of Newspaper "Izvestiya".
4612 **1782** 4k. black, red and silver 15 10

1977. 24th International Navigation Congress, Leningrad.
4613 **1783** 6k. blue, black and gold 20 10

1784 Kremlin Palace of Congresses, Moscow

1785 L. A. Govorov

1977. 16th Soviet Trade Unions Congress.
4614 **1784** 4k. gold, black and red . . . 15 10

1977. 80th Birth Anniv of Marshal L. A. Govorov.
4615 **1785** 4k. brown 15 10

1786 Academy Emblem, Text and Building

1977. 150th Anniv of Grechko Naval Academy, Leningrad.
4616 **1786** 6k. multicoloured . . . 15 10

1787 J. Labourbe

1788 Chess Pieces

1977. Birth Centenary of Jeanne Labourbe (French communist).
4617 **1787** 4k. black, blue and red . . . 15 10

1977. 6th European Chess Team Championship, Moscow.
4618 **1788** 6k. multicoloured . . . 50 10

1789 "Soyuz 23" and Cosmonauts

1977. "Soyuz 23" Space Flight by V. D. Zudov and V. I. Rozhdestvensky.
4619 **1789** 10k. red, black & brown 35 15

1790 Novikov-Priboi

1791 "Welcome" (N. M. Soloninkin)

1977. Birth Centenary of Aleksei Novikov-Priboi (writer).
4620 **1790** 4k. black, orange & blue 15 10

1977. Folk Paintings from Fedoskino Village. Multicoloured.
4621 4k. Type **1791** 15 10
4622 6k. "Along the Street" (V. D. Antonov) (horiz) 20 10
4623 10k. "Northern Song" (J. V. Karapaev) 40 15
4624 12k. "Fairy Tale about Tzar Sultan" (A. I. Kozlov) . . 40 15
4625 14k. "Summer Troika" (V. A. Nalimov) (horiz) 50 20
4626 16k. "Red Flower" (V. D. Lipitsky) 60 25

1792 Congress Emblem

1977. World Electronics Congress, Moscow.
4627 **1792** 6k. red, grey and blue . . . 15 10

1793 "In Red Square" (K. V. Filatov)

1977. 107th Birth Anniv of Lenin.
4628 **1793** 4k. multicoloured . . . 15 10

1794 Yuri Gagarin and Spacecraft

1977. Cosmonautics Day.
4629 **1794** 6k. blue, lilac and purple 25 15

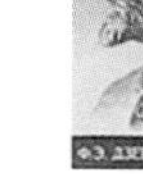

1795 N. I. Vavilov

1796 F. E. Dzerzhinsky

1977. 90th Birth Anniv of N. I. Vavilov (biologist).
4630 **1795** 4k. black and brown . . 15 10

1977. Birth Centenary of Feliks Dzerzhinsky (founder of Cheka).
4631 **1796** 4k. black 15 10

1797 Mountain Saxifrage

1798 V. V. Gorbatko and Yu. N. Glazkov (cosmonauts)

1977. Flowers. Multicoloured.
4632 2k. Type **1797** 10 10
4633 3k. Pinks 10 10
4634 4k. "Novosieversia glacialis" 15 10
4635 6k. "Cerastium maximum" 20 25
4636 16k. "Rhododendron aureum" 65 30

1977. "Soyuz 24–Salyut 5" Space Project.
4637 **1798** 10k. black, red and blue . . . 40 15

1799 I. S. Konev

1800 Festival Emblem

1977. 80th Birth Anniv of Soviet Marshals.
4638 **1799** 4k. green 15 10
4639 – 4k. black 15 10
4640 – 4k. brown 15 10

DESIGNS: No. 4639, V. D. Sokolovsky; 4640, K. A. Meretskov.

1977. 10th International Film Festival, Moscow.
4641 **1800** 6k. gold, red and lake . . . 15 10

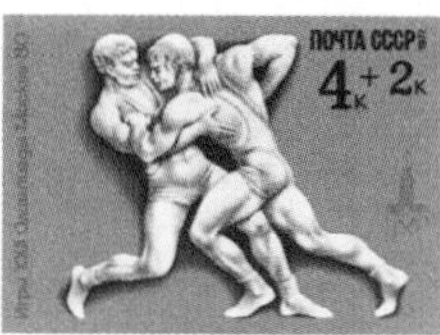

1801 Greco-Roman Wrestling

1977. Olympic Sports (1st series).
4642 **1801** 4k.+2k. black, ochre and gold 20 10
4643 – 6k.+3k. black, green and gold 30 10
4644 – 10k.+5k. black, mauve and gold 45 20
4645 – 16k.+6k. black, blue and gold 70 30
4646 – 20k.+10k. black, brown and gold . . . . . . 1·75 65

DESIGNS: 6k. Free-style wrestling; 10k. Judo; 16k. Boxing; 29k. Weightlifting.
See also Nos. 4684/9, 4749/53, 4820/4, 4870/4, 4896/4900, 4962/6 and 4973/7.

1802 "Portrait of a Chambermaid"

1804 Stamps and Emblem

1977. 400th Birth Anniv of Rubens. Multicoloured.
4647 4k. Type **1802** 20 10
4648 6k. "The Lion Hunt" (horiz) 25 10
4649 10k. "Stone Carriers" (horiz) 35 10
4650 12k. "Water and Earth Alliance" 60 15
4651 20k. "Landscape with Rainbow" (horiz) 95 35

1977. Soviet Ice-breakers (2nd series). As T **1775**. Multicoloured.
4654 4k. "Aleksandr Sibiryakov" 25 10
4655 6k. "Georgy Sedov" 30 10
4656 10k. "Sadko" 55 15
4657 12k. "Dezhnev" 65 15
4658 14k. "Sibur" 75 20
4659 16k. "Lena" 90 30
4660 20k. "Amguema" . . . . . 1·10 40

1977. Air. Early Soviet Aircraft (3rd series). As T **1771** but dated 1977.
4661 4k. black, brown and blue 15 10
4662 6k. black, orange and green 25 10
4663 10k. black, mauve and blue 30 10
4664 12k. black, blue and red . . 35 15
4665 16k. multicoloured 50 15
4666 20k. black, green and blue 70 20

DESIGNS: 4k. Porokhovshchikov P-IV bis biplane trainer, 1917; 6k. Kalinin AK-1, 1924; 10k. Tupolev ANT-3 R-3, 1925; 12k. Tupolev ANT-4 TB-1 bomber, 1929; 16k. Polikarpov R-5 biplane, 1929; 20k. Shavrov Sh-2 flying boat, 1930.

1977. "60th Anniv of October Revolution" Philatelic Exhibition, Moscow.
4667 **1804** 4k. red, blue and brown . . . 15 10

1805 Buildings and Arms, Stavropol

1807 Yuri Gagarin and "Vostok" Spacecraft

1977. Bicentenary of Stavropol.
4668 **1805** 6k. gold, red and green . . . 20 10

1977. Olympic Sports (2nd series). As T **1801**.
4684 4k.+2k. black, gold and red 20 10
4685 6k.+3k. black, gold & blue 45 15
4686 10k.+5k. black, gold & grn 75 20
4687 16k.+6k. black, gold & olive 1·00 30
4688 20k.+10k. black, gold & pur 1·75 65

DESIGNS—HORIZ: 4k. Cycling; 10k. Rifle shooting; 16k. Horse-jumping; 20k. Fencing. VERT: 6k. Archery.

1977. 20th Anniv of Space Exploration.
4690 **1807** 10k. red, blue and brown 40 15
4691 – 10k. brown, blue & violet 40 15
4692 – 10k. red, purple & green 40 15
4693 – 20k. green, brown & red 70 25
4694 – 20k. purple, red and blue 70 25
4695 – 20k. red, blue and green 70 25

DESIGNS: No. 4691, Space walking; 4692, "Soyuz" spacecraft and "Salyut" space station linked; 4693, "Proton 4" satellite; 4694, "Luna Venus" and "Mars" space stations; 4695, "Intercosmos 10" satellite and "Apollo" and "Soyuz" spacecraft linked

1808 Carving from St. Dmitri's Cathedral, Vladimir (12th-cent)

1977. Russian Art. Multicoloured.
4697 4k. Type **1808** 15 10
4698 6k. Bracelet, Ryazan (12th cent) 20 15
4699 10k. Detail of Golden Gate from Nativity Cathedral, Suzdal (13th-cent) 30 15
4700 12k. Detail from "Archangel Michael" (icon) (A. Rublev) (15th-cent) 40 15
4701 16k. Gold and marble chalice made by I. Fomin (15th-cent) 55 20
4702 20k. St. Basil's Cathedral, Moscow (16th-cent) . . . 70 20

1809 "Snowflake and Fir Twig"

1810 Cruiser "Aurora"

1977. New Year.
4703 **1809** 4k. multicoloured . . . 15 10

1977. 60th Anniv of October Revolution.
4704 **1810** 4k. multicoloured . . . 15 10
4705 – 4k. black, red and gold 15 10
4706 – 4k. black, red and gold 15 10
4707 – 4k. multicoloured . . . 15 10

DESIGNS: No. 4705, Statue of Lenin; 4706, Page of "Izvestiya", book by Brezhnev and crowd; 4707, Kremlin spire, star and fireworks.

1811 First Clause of U.S.S.R. Constitution

1977. New Constitution.
4709 **1811** 4k. yellow, red & brown 15 10
4710 – 4k. multicoloured . . . 15 10

DESIGN: No. 4710, People of the U.S.S.R. welcoming new constitution.

1813 Postwoman and Post Code

1977. Postal Communications. Multicoloured.
4713 4k. Type **1813** 15 10
4714 4k. Letter collection 15 10
4715 4k. "Map-O" automatic sorting machine 15 10

4716 4k. Mail transport 15 10
4717 4k. Delivering the mail . . . 15 10

1814 Red Fort, Delhi and Asokan Capital

1815 Monument, Kharkov

1977. 30th Anniv of Indian Independence.
4718 **1814** 6k. gold, purple and red 20 10

1977. 60th Anniv of Establishment of Soviet Power in the Ukraine.
4719 **1815** 6k. multicoloured . . . 15 10

1816 Adder

1977. Snakes and Protected Animals. Mult.
4720 1k. Type **1816** 10 10
4721 4k. Levantine viper 15 10
4722 6k. Saw-scaled viper 20 10
4723 10k. Central Asian viper . . 30 15
4724 12k. Central Asian cobra . . 30 15
4725 16k. Polar bear and cub . . 40 25
4726 20k. Walrus and young . . 50 25
4727 30k. Tiger and cub 85 30

1817 Olympic Emblem and Arms of Vladimir

1977. 1980 Olympics. "Tourism around the Golden Ring" (1st issue). Multicoloured.
4728 1r.+50k. Type **1817** . . . . 4·50 2·25
4729 1r.+50k. Vladimir Hotel . . 4·50 2·25
4730 1r.+50k. Arms of Suzdal . . 4·50 2·25
4731 1r.+50k. Pozharsky monument . . . . 4·50 2·25
4732 1r.+50k. Arms of Ivanovo and Frunze monument . . 4·50 2·25
4733 1r.+50k. Monument to Revolutionary Fighters . . 4·50 2·25
See also Nos. 4828/31, 4850/3, 4914/17, 4928/9, 4968/9, 4981/2 and 4990/5.

1818 Combine Harvester

1819 Kremlin Palace of Congresses

1978. 50th Anniv of "Gigant" Collective Farm, Rostov.
4734 **1818** 4k. brown, red & yellow 15 10

1978. 18th Leninist Young Communist League (Komsomol) Congress.
4735 **1819** 4k. multicoloured . . . 15 10

1820 Globe, Obelisk and Emblem

1978. 8th International Federation of Resistance Fighters Congress, Minsk.
4736 **1820** 6k. red, blue and black 15 10

1821 Red Army Detachment and Modern Sailor, Airman and Soldier

1978. 60th Anniv of Soviet Military Forces. Mult.
4737 4k. Type **1821** 15 10
4738 4k. Defenders of Moscow monument (detail), Lenin banner and Order of Patriotic War 15 10
4739 4k. Soviet soldier 15 10

1822 "Celebration in a Village" (½-size illustration)

1978. Birth Centenary of Boris M. Kustodiev (artist). Multicoloured.
4740 4k. Type **1822** 15 10
4741 6k. "Shrovetide" 20 10
4742 10k. "Morning" (50 × 36 mm) 30 15
4743 12k. "Merchant's Wife drinking Tea" (50 × 36 mm) 40 15
4744 20k. "Bolshevik" (50 × 36 mm) 55 25

1823 Gubarev and Remek at Launch Pad

1824 "Soyuz" Capsules linked to "Salyut" Space Station

1978. Soviet–Czech Space Flight. Multicoloured.
4746 6k. Type **1823** 15 10
4747 15k. "Soyuz-28" docking with "Salyut-6" space station 45 15
4748 32k. Splashdown . . . . . 1·00 35

1978. Olympic Sports (3rd series). As T **1801**. Multicoloured.
4749 4k.+2k. Swimmer at start 20 10
4750 6k.+3k. Diving (vert) . . . 35 10
4751 10k.+5k. Water polo . . . 70 15
4752 10k.+6k. Canoeist . . . . . 1·00 20
4753 20k.+10k. Single sculls . . . 1·60 70

1978. Cosmonautics Day.
4755 **1824** 6k. gold, blue and deep blue 15 10

1825 Shield and Laurel Wreath

1826 E. A. and M. E. Cherepanov and their Locomotive, 1833

1978. 9th World Congress of Trade Unions.
4756 **1825** 6k. multicoloured . . . 15 10

1978. Russian Locomotives (1st series). Mult.
4757 1k. Type **1826** 20 10
4758 2k. Series D locomotive, 1845 . . . . 20 10
4759 3k. Series V locomotive (first passenger train, 1845) . . 20 10
4760 16k. Series Gv locomotive, 1863–67 . . . . 95 25
4761 20k. Series Bv locomotive, 1863–67 . . . . 1·25 30
Nos. 4758/61 are horizontal designs.
See also Nos. 4861/5.

1828 "XI" and Laurel Branch

1830 I.M.C.O. Emblem

1829 Tulip "Bolshoi Theatre"

1978. 11th World Youth and Students Festival, Havana.
4763 **1828** 4k. multicoloured . . . 15 10

1978. Moscow Flowers. Multicoloured.
4764 1k. Type **1829** 10 10
4765 2k. Rose "Moscow Morning" 10 10
4766 4k. Dahlia "Red Star" . . . 10 10
4767 10k. Gladiolus "Moscovite" 40 15
4768 12k. Iris "To Il'ich's Anniversary" 45 20

1978. 20th Anniv of Intergovernment Maritime Consultative Organization and World Maritime Day.
4769 **1830** 6k. multicoloured . . . 15 10

1831 "Salyut-6" Space Station performing Survey Work

1978. "Salyut-6" Space Station. Multicoloured.
4770 15k. Type **1831** 50 30
4771 15k. Yu. V. Romanenko and G. M. Grechko . . . 50 30
Nos. 4770/1 were issued in se-tenant pairs forming a composite design.

1832 "Space Meteorology"

1978. Space Research. Multicoloured.
4772 10k. Type **1832** 30 15
4773 10k. "Soyuz" orbiting globe ("Natural resources") . . 30 15
4774 10k. Radio waves, ground station and "Molniya" satellite ("Communication") . . . 30 15
4775 10k. Human figure, "Vostok" orbiting Earth ("Medicine and biology") 30 15

1833 Transporting Rocket to Launch Site

1978. Soviet–Polish Space Flight. Multicoloured.
4777 6k. Type **1833** 15 10
4778 15k. Crystal (Sirena experiment) 50 15
4779 32k. Space station, map and scientific research ship "Kosmonavt Vladimir Komarov" . . . . 1·10 35

1834 Komsomol Awards

1835 M. V. Zakharov

1978. 60th Anniv of Leninist Young Communist League (Komsomol). Multicoloured.
4780 4k. Type **1834** 10 10
4781 4k. Products of agriculture and industry 30 10

1978. 80th Birth Anniv of Marshal M. V. Zakharov.
4782 **1835** 4k. brown 10 10

1836 N. G. Chernyshevsky

1978. 150th Birth Anniv of Nikolai G. Chernyshevsky (revolutionary).
4783 **1836** 4k. brown and yellow 10 10

1837 Snow Petrel

1978. Antarctic Fauna. Multicoloured.
4784 1k. Snares Island penguin (horiz) 60 15
4785 3k. Type **1837** 75 15
4786 4k. Emperor penguin . . . 95 15
4787 6k. Antarctic icefish . . . . 1·25 15
4788 10k. Southern elephant-seal (horiz) . . . . 1·25 15

1838 Torch and Flags

1839 William Harvey

1978. Construction of Orenburg–U.S.S.R. Western Frontier Gas Pipe-line.
4789 **1838** 4k. multicoloured . . . 15 10

1978. 400th Birth Anniv of William Harvey (discoverer of blood circulation).
4790 **1839** 6k. green, black and blue 15 10

1978. Air. Early Russian Aircraft (3rd series). As T **1771**.
4791 4k. green, brown and black 15 10
4792 6k. multicoloured 25 10
4793 10k. yellow, blue and black 45 15
4794 12k. orange, blue and black 55 15
4795 16k. blue, deep blue and black 70 15
4796 20k. multicoloured 90 20

DESIGNS: 4k. Polikarpov Po-2 biplane, 1928; 6k. Kalinin K-5, 1929; 10k. Tupolev ANT-6 TB-3 bomber, 1930; 12k. Putilov Stal-2, 1931; 16k. Beriev Be-2 MBR-2 reconnaissance seaplane, 1932; 20k. Polikarpov I-16 fighter, 1934.

1840 "Bathing of Red Horse"

1978. Birth Centenary of K. S. Petrov-Vodkin (painter). Multicoloured.

4797	4k. Type **1840**	10	10
4798	6k. "Petrograd, 1918" . . .	15	10
4799	10k. "Commissar's Death"	30	15
4800	12k. "Rose Still Life" . . .	40	15
4801	16k. "Morning Still Life"	60	15

1841 Assembling "Soyuz 31"

1978. Soviet–East German Space Flight. Mult.

4803	6k. Type **1841**	15	10
4804	15k. Space photograph of Pamir mountains	55	15
4805	32k. Undocking from space station	1·10	35

1842 "Molniya 1" Satellite, "Orbita" Ground Station and Tupolev Tu-134 Jetliner

1978. "PRAGA 78" International Stamp Exhibition.
4806 **1842** 6k. multicoloured . . . 15 10

1843 Tolstoi

1978. 150th Birth Anniv of Leo Tolstoi (novelist).
4807 **1843** 4k. green . . . . 1·25 75

1844 Union Emblem — **1845** Bronze Figure, Erebuni Fortress

1978. 14th General Assembly of International Union for the Protection of Nature and Natural Resources, Ashkhabad.
4808 **1844** 4k. multicoloured . . . 15 10

1978. Armenian Architecture. Multicoloured.

4809	4k. Type **1845**	10	10
4810	6k. Echmiadzin Cathedral	15	10
4811	10k. Khachkary (carved stones)	25	10
4812	12k. Matenadaran building (repository of manuscripts) (horiz) . . .	35	15
4813	16k. Lenin Square, Yerevan (horiz)	45	20

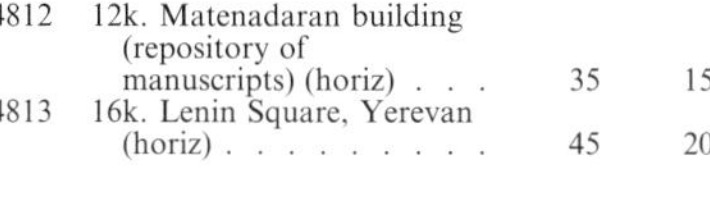

1846 Monument (P. Kufferge) — **1847** Emblem, Ostankino TV Tower and Hammer and Sickle

1978. 70th Anniv of Russian Aid to Messina Earthquake Victims.
4814 **1846** 6k. multicoloured . . . 20 10

1978. 20th Anniv of Organization for Communications Co-operation.
4815 **1847** 4k. multicoloured . . . 10 10

(**1848**)

1978. "60th Anniv of Komsomol" Philatelic Exhibition. Optd with T **1848**.
4816 **1834** 4k. multicoloured . . . 1·00 50

1851 Shaumyan — **1852** "Star" Yacht

1978. Birth Centenary of Stephan Georgievich Shaumyan (Commissar).
4819 **1851** 4k. green 10 10

1978. Olympic Sports (4th series). Sailing Regatta, Tallin. Multicoloured.

4820	4k.+2k. Type **1852**	20	10
4821	6k.+3k. "Soling" yacht . .	30	10
4822	10k.+5k. "470" dinghy . . .	50	15
4823	16k.+6k. "Finn" dinghy . .	80	25
4824	20k.+10k. "Flying Dutchman" dinghy . . .	1·25	55

1853 Industrial Structures and Flags — **1854** Black Sea Ferry

1978. 61st Anniv of October Revolution.
4826 **1853** 4k. multicoloured . . . 10 10

1978. Inauguration of Ilichevsk–Varna, Bulgaria, Ferry Service.
4827 **1854** 6k. multicoloured . . . 15 10

1855 Zagorsk

1978. 1980 Olympics. "Tourism around the Golden Ring" (2nd issue). Multicoloured.

4828	1r.+50k. Type **1855**	4·75	2·75
4829	1r.+50k. Palace of Culture, Zagorsk	4·75	2·75
4830	1r.+50k. Kremlin, Rostov-Veliki	4·75	2·75
4831	1r.+50k. View of Rostov-Veliki	4·75	2·75

1856 Church of the Intercession on River Nerl

1978. "Masterpieces of Old Russian Culture". Mult.

4832	6k. Golden crater (horiz) . .	15	10
4833	10k. Type **1856**	25	15
4834	12k. "St. George and the Dragon" (15th-century icon)	35	15
4835	16k. Tsar Cannon (horiz)	45	20

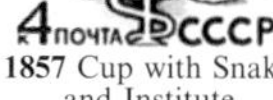

1857 Cup with Snake and Institute — **1859** Spassky Tower, Kremlin

1858 Nestor Pechersky and "Chronicle of Past Days"

1978. 75th Anniv of Herzen Oncology Research Institute, Moscow.
4836 **1857** 4k. gold, purple & black 15 10

1978. History of the Russian Posts. Multicoloured.

4837	4k. Type **1858**	10	10
4838	6k. Birch-bark letter	15	10
4839	10k. Messenger with trumpet	30	15
4840	12k. Mail sledges	35	15
4841	16k. Interior of Prikaz Post Office	45	20

1978. New Year.
4842 **1859** 4k. multicoloured . . . 15 10

1978. Soviet Ice breakers (3rd series). As T **1775**. Multicoloured.

4843	4k. "Vasily Pronchishchev"	20	10
4844	6k. "Kapitan Belousov" (vert)	25	10
4845	10k. "Moskva"	30	15
4846	12k. "Admiral Makarov"	45	15
4847	16k. "Lenin" atomic ice-breaker (vert)	65	20
4848	20k. "Arktika" atomic ice-breaker	80	35

1860 V. Kovalenok and A. Ivanchenkov

1978. "140 Days in Space".
4849 **1860** 10k. multicoloured . . 30 15

1978. 1980 Olympics "Tourism around the Golden Ring" (3rd issue). As T **1855**. Multicoloured.

4850	1r.+50k. Alexander Nevsky Monument, Pereslavl-Zalessky	4·00	2·50
4851	1r.+50k. Peter I Monument, Pereslavl-Zalessky	4·00	2·50
4852	1r.+50k. Monastery of the Transfiguration, Yaroslavl	4·00	2·50
4853	1r.+50k. Ferry terminal and Eternal Glory Monument, Yaroslavl	4·00	2·50

1862 Cuban Flags — **1863** Government Building, Minsk

1979. 20th Anniv of Cuban Revolution.
4855 **1862** 6k. multicoloured . . . 15 10

1979. 60th Anniv of Byelorussian Soviet Socialist Republic and Communist Party.
4856 **1863** 4k. multicoloured . . . 15 10

1864 Flags and Reunion Monument — **1865** Old and New University Buildings

1979. 325th Anniv of Reunion of Ukraine with Russia.
4857 **1864** 4k. multicoloured . . . 15 10

1979. 400th Anniv of Vilnius University.
4858 **1865** 4k. black and pink . . 15 10

1866 Exhibition Hall and First Bulgarian Stamp

1979. "Philaserdica 79" International Stamp Exhibition, Sofia.
4859 **1866** 15k. multicoloured . . 50 15

1867 Satellites "Radio 1" and "Radio 2"

1979. Launching of "Radio" Satellites.
4860 **1867** 4k. multicoloured . . . 35 10

1868 Series A Locomotive, 1878

1979. Railway Locomotives (2nd series). Mult.

4861 2k. Type **1868** 15 10
4862 3k. Class Shch steam locomotive, 1912 . . . . 15 10
4863 4k. Class Lp steam locomotive, 1915 . . . . 25 10
4864 6k. Class Su steam locomotive, 1925 . . . . 45 15
4865 15k. Class L steam locomotive, 1947 . . . . 1·10 40

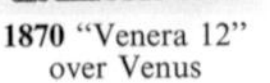

1870 "Venera 12" over Venus **1871** Albert Einstein

1979. "Venera" Flights to Venus.

4867 **1870** 10k. red, lilac and purple 35 10

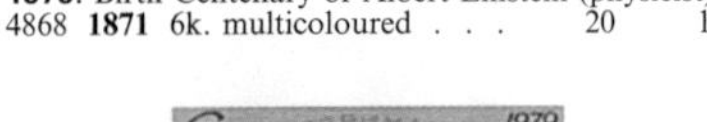

1979. Birth Centenary of Albert Einstein (physicist).

4868 **1871** 6k. multicoloured . . . 20 10

1872 Congress Emblem

1979. 21st World Veterinary Congress, Moscow.

4869 **1872** 6k. multicoloured . . . 15 10

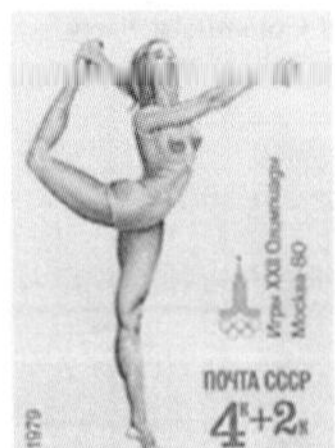

1873 Free Exercise

1979. Olympic Sports (5th series). Gymnastics.

4870 **1873** 4k.+2k. brown, stone and orange 15 10
4871 – 6k.+3k. blue, grey and violet 20 10
4872 – 10k.+5k. red, stone and brown 30 15
4873 – 16k.+6k. mauve, grey and purple 75 40
4874 – 20k.+10k. red, stone and brown . . . . . 1·60 65

DESIGNS: 6k. Parallel bars; 10k. Horizontal bar; 16k. Beam; 20k. Asymmetric bars.

1874 "To Arms" (poster by R. Beren)

1979. 60th Anniv of First Hungarian Socialist Republic.

4876 **1874** 4k. multicoloured . . . 10 10

1875 Cosmonauts at Yuri Gagarin Training Centre

1979. Soviet–Bulgarian Space Flight. Mult.

4877 6k. Type **1875** 20 10
4878 32k. Landing of cosmonauts 90 35

1876 "Intercosmos"

1979. Cosmonautics Day.

4879 **1876** 15k. multicoloured . . 50 15

1878 Exhibition Emblem

1979. U.S.S.R. Exhibition, London.

4881 **1878** 15k. multicoloured . . 40 15

1880 Antonov An-28

1979. Air. Soviet Aircraft. Multicoloured.

4883 2k. Type **1880** 10 10
4884 3k. Yakovlev Yak-42 . . . 15 10
4885 10k. Tupolev Tu-134 . . . 40 15
4886 15k. Ilyushin Il-76 . . . . . 60 20
4887 32k. Ilyushin Il-86 . . . . . 1·00 40

1882 "Tent" Monument, Mining Institute, Pushkin Theatre and Blast Furnace **1883** Child and Apple Blossom

1979. 50th Anniv of Magnitogorsk City.

4889 **1882** 4k. multicoloured . . . 15 10

1979. International Year of the Child (1st issue).

4890 **1883** 4k. multicoloured . . . 15 10

See also Nos. 4918/21.

1884 Bogorodsk Wood-carvings

1979. Folk Crafts. Multicoloured.

4891 2k. Type **1884** 10 10
4892 3k. Khokhloma painted dish and jars 10 10
4893 4k. Zhostovo painted tray 15 10
4894 6k. Kholmogory bone-carvings 25 15
4895 15k. Vologda lace 50 35

1885 Football

1979. Olympic Sports (6th series). Multicoloured.

4896 **1885** 4k.+2k. blue, grey and orange 30 10
4897 – 6k.+3k. yellow, orange and blue 40 10
4898 – 10k.+5k. green, red and mauve 50 15
4899 – 16k.+6k. purple, blue and green 60 25
4900 – 20k.+10k. yellow, red and green . . . . . 1·25 60

DESIGNS—VERT: 6k. Basketball; 10k. Volleyball. HORIZ: 16k. Handball; 20k. Hockey.

1886 Lenin Square Underground Station

1979. Tashkent Underground Railway.

4901 **1886** 4k. multicoloured . . . 25 10

1887 V. A. Dzhanibekov and O. G. Makarov **1888** Council Building and Flags of Member Countries

1979. "Soyuz 27"–"Salyut 6"–"Soyuz 26" Orbital Complex.

4902 **1887** 4k. multicoloured . . . 20 10

1979. 30th Anniv of Council of Mutual Economic Aid.

4903 **1888** 16k. multicoloured . . 30 15

1889 Scene from "Battleship Potemkin" **1892** Exhibition Hall and Film Still

1979. 60th Anniv of Soviet Films (1st issue) and 11th International Film Festival, Moscow.

4904 **1889** 15k. multicoloured . . 50 15

See also No. 4907.

1979. 60th Anniv of Soviet Films (2nd issue).

4907 **1892** 4k. multicoloured . . . 15 10

1893 "Lilac" (K. A. Korovin) **1894** John McClean

1979. Flower Paintings. Multicoloured.

4908 1k. "Flowers and Fruits" (I. F. Khrutsky) (horiz) 10 10
4909 2k. "Phloxes" (I. N. Kramskoi) 15 10
4910 3k. Type **1893** 20 10
4911 15k. "Bluebells" (S. V. Gerasimov) 50 20
4912 32k. "Roses" (P. P. Konchalovsky) (horiz) . . 95 40

1979. Birth Centenary of John McClean (first Soviet consul for Scotland).

4913 **1894** 4k. black and red . . . 15 10

1979. 1980 Olympics. "Tourism around the Golden Ring" (4th issue). As T **1855**. Multicoloured.

4914 1r.+50k. Narikaly Fortress, Tbilisi . . . . 4·00 2·50
4915 1r.+50k. Georgian Philharmonic Society Concert Hall and "Muse" (sculpture), Tbilisi . . . . 4·00 2·50
4916 1r.+50k. Chir-Dor Mosque, Samarkand . . . . 4·00 2·50
4917 1r.+50k. People's Friendship Museum and "Courage" monument, Tashkent . . 4·00 2·50

1895 "Friendship" (Lena Liberda)

1979. International Year of the Child (2nd issue). Children's Paintings. Multicoloured.

4918 2k. Type **1895** 10 10
4919 3k. "After Rain" (Daniya Akhmetshina) 10 10
4920 4k. "Dance of Friendship" (Liliya Elistratova) . . . 20 10
4921 15k. "On the Excursion" (Vika Smalyuk) 45 20

1896 Golden Oriole

1979. Birds. Multicoloured.

4922 2k. Type **1896** 15 10
4923 3k. Lesser spotted woodpecker 20 10
4924 4k. Crested tit 20 10
4925 10k. Barn owl 60 15
4926 15k. European nightjar . . 80 35

1897 Soviet Circus Emblem **1898** Marx, Engels, Lenin and View of Berlin

1979. 60th Anniv of Soviet Circus.

4927 **1897** 4k. multicoloured . . . 15 10

1979. 1980 Olympics. "Tourism around the Golden Ring" (5th issue). As T **1855**. Multicoloured.

4928 1r.+50k. Relics of Yerevan's origin . . . . 4·00 2·00
4929 1r.+50k. Armenian State Opera and Ballet Theatre, Yerevan . . . . 4·00 2·00

1979. 30th Anniv of German Democratic Republic.

4930 **1898** 6k. multicoloured . . . 15 10

1899 V. A. Lyakhov, V. V. Ryumin and "Salyut 6"

1979. Lyakhov and Ryumin's 175 Days in Space. Multicoloured.

4931 15k. Type **1899** 40 20
4932 15k. Radio telescope mounted on "Salyut 6" 40 20

Nos. 4931/2 were issued together, se-tenant, forming a composite design.

1900 Hammer and Sickle **1901** Communications Equipment and Signal Corps Emblem

1979. 62nd Anniv of October Revolution.
4933 **1900** 4k. multicoloured . . . 15 10

1979. 60th Anniv of Signal Corps.
4934 **1901** 4k. multicoloured . . . 15 10

1902 "Katherine" (T. G. Shevchenko)

1903 Shabolovka Radio Mast, Moscow

1979. Ukrainian Paintings. Multicoloured.
4935 2k. Type **1902** 10 10
4936 3k. "Into Service" (K. K. Kostandi) 25 10
4937 4k. "To Petrograd" (A. M. Lopukhov) 55 10
4938 10k. "Return" (V. N. Kostetsky) 30 15
4939 15k. "Working Morning" (M. G. Belsky) 40 25

1979. 50th Anniv of Radio Moscow.
4940 **1903** 32k. multicoloured . . 1·00 35

1904 Misha (Olympic mascot)

1905 "Peace" and Hammer and Sickle

1979. New Year.
4941 **1904** 4k. multicoloured . . . 25 10

1979. "Peace Programme in Action". Mult.
4942 4k. Type **1905** 15 10
4943 4k. Hand holding demand for peace 15 10
4944 4k. Hands supporting emblem of peace 15 10

1906 Traffic Policeman

1909 Industrial Landscape

1907 "Vulkanolog"

1979. Road Safety. Multicoloured.
4945 3k. Type **1906** 10 10
4946 4k. Child playing in road . . 15 10
4947 6k. Speeding car out of control 25 10

1979. Soviet Scientific Research Ships. Mult.
4948 1k. Type **1907** 10 10
4949 2k. "Professor Bogorov" . . 10 10
4950 4k. "Ernst Krenkel" 15 10
4951 6k. "Kosmonavt Vladislav Volkov" 30 15
4952 10k. "Kosmonavt Yuri Gagarin" 60 25
4953 15k. "Akademik Kurchatov" 85 35

1980. 50th Anniv of Mordovian ASSR of Russian Federation.
4955 **1909** 4k. red 15 10

1910 Speed Skating

1912 N. I. Podvoisky

1911 Running

1980. Winter Olympic Games, Lake Placid.
4956 **1910** 4k. blue, lt blue & orange 15 10
4957 – 6k. violet, blue & orange 15 10
4958 – 10k. red, blue and gold 40 15
4959 – 15k. brown, blue & turquoise 50 15
4960 – 20k. turquoise, blue and red 60 25
DESIGNS—HORIZ: 6k. Figure skating (pairs); 10k. Ice hockey; 15k. Downhill skiing. VERT: 20k. Luge.

1980. Olympic Sports (7th series). Athletics. Mult.
4962 4k.+2k. Type **1911** 20 10
4963 6k.+3k. Hurdling 25 10
4964 10k.+5k. Walking (vert) . . 50 20
4965 16k.+6k. High jumping . . 75 20
4966 20k.+10k. Long jumping . . 1·10 60

1980. Birth Centenary of Nikolai Ilich Podvoisky (revolutionary).
4967 **1912** 4k. brown 10 10

1980. 1980 Olympics. "Tourism around the Golden Ring" (6th issue). Moscow. As T **1855**. Mult.
4968 1r.+50k. Kremlin . . . . . 4·50 2·75
4969 1r.+50k. Kalinin Prospect 4·50 2·75

1913 "Rainbow" (A. K. Savrasov) (⅔-size illustration)

1980. Birth Annivs of Soviet Artists. Mult.
4970 6k. "Harvest Summer" (A. G. Venetsianov (bicent)) (vert) 20 10
4971 6k. Type **1913** (150th anniv) 20 10
4972 6k. "Old Yerevan" (M. S. Saryan) (centenary) . . . 20 10

1980. Olympic Sports (8th series). Athletics. As T **1911**. Multicoloured.
4973 4k.+2k. Pole vaulting . . . 20 10
4974 6k.+3k. Discus throwing . . 25 10
4975 10k.+5k. Javelin throwing 50 20
4976 16k.+6k. Hammer throwing 75 20
4977 20k.+10k. Putting the shot 1·10 60

1915 Georg Ots

1916 Order of Lenin

1980. 60th Birth Anniv of Georg K. Ots (artist).
4980 **1915** 4k. blue 10 10

1980. 1980 Olympics. "Tourism around the Golden Ring" (7th issue). As T **1855**. Multicoloured.
4981 1r.+50k. St. Isaac's Cathedral, Leningrad . . 4·50 2·75
4982 1r.+50k. Monument to the Defenders of Leningrad 4·50 2·75

1980. 50th Anniv of Order of Lenin.
4983 **1916** 4k. multicoloured . . . 10 10

1919 "Motherland" (detail of Heroes Monument, Volgograd)

1920 Government House, Arms and Flag of Azerbaijan

1980. 35th Anniv of World War II Victory. Mult.
4986 4k. Type **1919** 15 10
4987 4k. Victory Monument, Treptow Park, Berlin . . 15 10
4988 4k. Victory Parade, Red Square, Moscow 15 10

1980. 60th Anniv of Azerbaijan Soviet Republic.
4989 **1920** 4k. multicoloured . . . 10 10

1980. 1980 Olympics. "Tourism around the Golden Ring" (8th issue). As T **1855**. Multicoloured.
4990 1r.+50k. Bogdan Khmelnitsky Monument and St. Sophia Monastery, Kiev . . . . 4·50 2·75
4991 1r.+50k. Underground bridge over River Dnieper, Kiev . . . . . 5·00 3·00
4992 1r.+50k. Sports Palace and War Memorial, Minsk . . 4·50 2·75
4993 1r.+50k. House of Cinematograhy, Minsk . . 4·50 2·75
4994 1r.+50k. Old City, Tallin . . 4·50 2·75
4995 1r.+50k. Hotel Viru, Tallin 4·50 2·75

1921 Monument, Ivanovo

1922 Shield and Industrial Complexes

1980. 75th Anniv of First Soviet of Workers Deputies, Ivanovo.
4996 **1921** 4k. multicoloured . . . 10 10

1980. 25th Anniv of Warsaw Treaty.
4997 **1922** 32k. multicoloured . . 1·25 65

1923 Yakovlev Yak-24 Helicopter, 1953

1980. Helicopters. Multicoloured.
4998 1k. Type **1923** 10 10
4999 2k. Mil Mi-8, 1962 . . . . 10 10
5000 3k. Kamov Ka-26, 1965 . . 20 10
5001 6k. Mil Mi-6, 1957 . . . . 30 15
5002 15k. Mil Mi-10K, 1965 . . 80 25
5003 32k. Mil Mi-V12, 1969 . . . 1·90 55

1924 Title Page of Book

1925 Medical Check-up of Cosmonauts

1980. 1500th Birth Anniv of David Anacht (Armenian philosopher).
5004 **1924** 4k. multicoloured . . . 10 10

1980. Soviet–Hungarian Space Flight. Mult.
5005 6k. Type **1925** 15 10
5006 15k. Crew meeting on "Salyut-6" space station 45 15
5007 32k. Press conference . . . 1·00 50

1926 Red Fox

1927 Kazan

1980. Fur-bearing Animals. Multicoloured.
5008 2k. Type **1926** 10 10
5009 4k. Artic fox (horiz) 15 10
5010 6k. European mink 25 10
5011 10k. Coypu 45 20
5012 15k. Sable (horiz) 60 30

1980. 60th Anniv of Tatar Republic.
5013 **1927** 4k. multicoloured . . . 10 10

1928 College and Emblem

1929 Ho Chi Minh

1980. 150th Anniv of Bauman Technical College, Moscow.
5014 **1928** 4k. multicoloured . . . 10 10

1980. 90th Birth Anniv of Ho Chi Minh (Vietnamese leader).
5015 **1929** 6k. multicoloured . . . 20 10

1930 Arms, Monument and Modern Buildings

1980. 40th Anniv of Soviet Socialist Republics of Lithuania, Latvia and Estonia. Multicoloured.
5016 **1930** 4k. Lithuania 10 10
5017 – 4k. Latvia 10 10
5018 – 4k. Estonia 10 10

1933 Crew of "Soyuz 27" at Launching Site

1934 Avicenna (after E. Sokdov and M. Gerasimov)

1980. Soviet–Vietnamese Space Flight. Mult.
5019 6k. Type **1933** 15 10
5020 15k. Cosmonauts at work in space 45 20
5021 32k. Cosmonauts returning to Earth . . . . 1·75 70

1980. Birth Millenary of Avicenna (Arab philosopher and physician).
5022 **1934** 4k. multicoloured . . . 10 10

1935 "Khadi-7" Gas turbine Car

1980. Racing cars designed by Kharkov Automobile and Road-building Institute. Mult.
5023 2k. Type **1935** 10 10
5024 6k. "Khadi-10" piston engined car 25 10
5025 15k. "Khadi-11 E" electric car 65 25
5026 32k. "Khadi-13 E" electric car . . . . 1·25 60

1936 Arms, Flags, Government House and Industrial Complex

1980. 60th Anniv of Kazakh Soviet Socialist Republic.
5027 **1936** 4k. multicoloured . . . 10 10

1937 "Self-portrait" and "The Spring"

1980. Birth Bicent of Jean Ingres (French painter).
5028 **1937** 32k. multicoloured . . 1·00 45

1938 "Morning on Kulikovo Field" (A. Bubnov)

1980. 600th Anniv of Battle of Kulikovo.
5029 **1938** 4k. multicoloured . . . 10 10

1939 Town Hall

1940 Yuri V. Malyshev and Valdimir V. Aksenov

1980. 950th Anniv of Tartu, Estonia.
5030 **1939** 4k. multicoloured . . . 10 10

1980. "Soyuz T-2" Space Flight.
5031 **1940** 10k. multicoloured . . 35 15

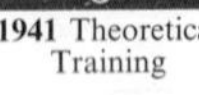

1941 Theoretical Training

1942 Crew Training

1980. 20th Anniv of Gagarin Cosmonaut Training Centre. Multicoloured.
5032 6k. Type **1941** 20 10
5033 15k. Practical training . . . 40 15
5034 32k. Physical endurance tests 95 50

1980. Soviet–Cuban Space Flight. Multicoloured.
5035 6k. Type **1942** 20 10
5036 15k. Physical exercise on board space complex . . 40 15
5037 32k. Returned cosmonauts and space capsule 95 50

1943 "Bargaining" (Nevrev) (⅔-size illustration)

1980. 150th Birth Anniv of N. V. Nevrev and K. D. Flavitsky (painters). Multicoloured.
5038 6k. Type **1943** 20 10
5039 6k. "Princess Tarakanova" (Flavitsky) 20 10

1944 Vasilevsky

1945 Banner

1980. 85th Birth Anniv of Marshal A. M. Vasilevsky.
5040 **1944** 4k. green 10 10

1980. 63rd Anniv of October Revolution.
5041 **1945** 4k. red, gold and purple 10 10

1946 Guramishvili

1947 Ioffe

1980. 275th Birth Anniv of David Guramishvili (Georgian poet).
5042 **1946** 4k. green, silver and black 10 10

1980. Birth Centenary of A. F. Ioffe (physicist).
5043 **1947** 4k. brown and buff . . 15 10

1948 Siberian Cedar

1980. Trees. Multicoloured.
5044 2k. Type **1948** 10 10
5045 4k. Pedunculate oak 10 10
5046 6k. Lime (vert) 20 10
5047 10k. Sea buckthorn 35 20
5048 15k. Ash 50 30

1950 Suvorov (after N. Utkin)

1980. 250th Birth Anniv of Field Marshal A. V. Suvorov.
5050 **1950** 4k. blue 15 10

1951 State Emblem and Republican Government House

1952 Blok (after K. Somov)

1980. 60th Anniv of Armenian Soviet Socialist Republic.
5051 **1951** 4k. multicoloured . . . 10 10

1980. Birth Cent of Aleksandr Aleksandrovich Blok (poet).
5052 **1952** 4k. multicoloured . . . 10 10

1980. Soviet Scientific Research Ships (2nd series). As T **1907**. Multicoloured.
5053 2k. "Ayu-Dag" 10 10
5054 3k. "Valerian Uryvaev" . . 10 10
5055 4k. "Mikhail Somov" . . . 20 10
5056 6k. "Akademik Sergei Korolev" 25 10
5057 10k. "Otto Schmidt" . . . 40 20
5058 15k. "Akademik Mstislav Keldysh" 65 30

1953 Spassky Tower and Kremlin Palace of Congresses

1955 Sable in Cedar

1980. New Year.
5059 **1953** 4k. multicoloured . . . 15 10

1980. Perf or imperf (2r.), perf (others).
5060 – 3k. orange 10 10
5061 – 5k. blue 15 10
5063 **1955** 35k. olive . . . . . . 1·00 35
5064 – 45k. brown . . . . . . 1·40 40
5066 – 50k. green . . . . . . 1·60 10
5067a – 2r. black 25 10
5068 – 3r. black . . . . 8·00 4·00
5069 – 3r. green . . . . 2·00 1·00
5071 – 5r. blue . . . . 3·25 1·60
DESIGNS—14 × 22 mm: 3k. State flag; 5k. Forms of transport. 22 × 33 mm: 45k. Spassky Tower; 50k. Vodovzodny Tower and Grand Palace, Moscow Kremlin; 2r. "Arklika" atomic ice-breaker; 3r. Globe, child and olive branch; 5r. Globe and feather ("Peace").

1957 Institute Building

1980. 50th Anniv of Institute for Advanced Training of Doctors.
5075 **1957** 4k. multicoloured . . . 15 10

1958 Lenin Monument, Leningrad, and Dneproges Hydro-electric Station

1959 Nesmeyanov

1980. 60th Anniv of GOELRO (electrification plan).
5076 **1958** 4k. multicoloured . . . 10 10

1980. Academician A. N. Nesmeyanov (organic chemist) Commemoration.
5077 **1959** 4k. multicoloured . . . 10 10

1960 Nagatinsky Bridge

1980. Moscow Bridges. Multicoloured.
5078 4k. Type **1960** 15 10
5079 6k. Luzhniki underground railway bridge 35 10
5080 15k. Kalininsky bridge . . . 45 20

1961 Timoshenko

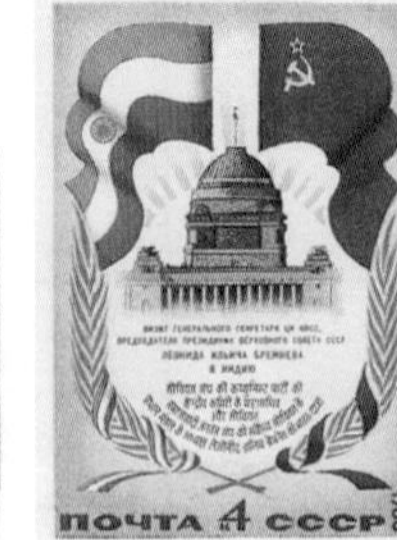

1962 Indian and Russian Flags with Government House, New Delhi

1980. 10th Death Anniv of Marshal S. K. Timoshenko.
5081 **1961** 4k. purple 10 10

1980. President Brezhnev's Visit to India.
5082 **1962** 4k. multicoloured . . . 25 10

1963 Antarctic Research Station

1964 Arms and Symbols of Agriculture and Industry

1981. Antarctic Exploration. Multicoloured.
5083 4k. Type **1963** 15 10
5084 6k. Antennae, rocket, weather balloon and tracked vehicle (Meteorological research) 50 10
5085 15k. Map of Soviet bases and supply ship "Ob" . . 2·25 40

1981. 60th Anniv of Dagestan Autonomous Soviet Socialist Republic.
5086 **1964** 4k. multicoloured . . . 10 10

1965 Hockey Players and Emblem

1981. 12th World Hockey Championships, Khabarovsk.
5087 **1965** 6k. multicoloured . . . 20 10

1966 Banner and Star

1981. 26th Soviet Communist Party Congress. Multicoloured.
5088 4k. Type **1966** 10 10
5089 20k. Kremlin Palace of Congresses and Lenin (51 × 36 mm) . . . . . . 1·25 80

1967 Lenin and Congress Building

1968 Keldysh

1981. 26th Ukraine Communist Party Congress.
5090 **1967** 4k. multicoloured . . . 10 10

1981. 70th Birth Anniv of Academician Mtislav Vsevolodovich Keldysh (mathematician).
5091 **1968** 4k. multicoloured . . . 10 10

1970 Baikal–Amur Railway

1981. Construction Projects of the 10th Five Year Plan. Multicoloured.

5093	4k. Type **1970**	25	10
5094	4k. Urengoi gas field	15	10
5095	4k. Sayano-Shushenakaya hydro-electric dam	15	10
5096	4k. Atommash Volga–Don atomic reactor	15	10
5097	4k. Syktyvkar paper mill	15	10
5098	4k. Giant excavator, Ekibastuz	25	10

1971 Freighter and Russian and Indian Flags

1981. 25th Anniv of Soviet–Indian Shipping Line.
5099 **1971** 15k. multicoloured . . 55 20

1972 Arms, Monument and Building

1981. 60th Anniv of Georgian Soviet Socialist Republic.
5100 **1972** 4k. multicoloured . . . 10 10

1973 Arms and Abkhazian Scenes

1974 Institute Building

1981. 60th Anniv of Abkhazian Autonomous Soviet Socialist Republic.
5101 **1973** 4k. multicoloured . . . 10 10

1981. 60th Anniv of Moscow Electrotechnical Institute of Communications.
5102 **1974** 4k. multicoloured . . . 10 10

1975 Communications Equipment and Satellite

1976 L. I. Popov and V. V. Ryumin

1981. 30th All-Union Amateur Radio Exhibition.
5103 **1975** 4k. multicoloured . . . 20 10

1981. 185 Days in Space of Cosmonauts Popov and Ryumin. Multicoloured.

5104	15k. Type **1976**	45	20
5105	15k. "Salyut 6"–"Soyuz" complex	45	20

1977 O. G. Makarov, L. D. Kizim and G. M. Strekalov

1961. "Soyuz T-3" Space Flight.
5106 **1977** 10k. multicoloured . . 35 15

1978 Rocket Launch

1981. Soviet–Mongolian Space Flight. Mult.

5107	6k. Type **1978**	20	10
5108	15k. Mongolians watching space flight on television	40	15
5109	32k. Re-entry stages	1·00	40

1979 Bering

1980 Yuri Gagarin and Globe

1981. 300th Birth Anniv of Vitus Bering (navigator).
5110 **1979** 4k. blue 25 10

1981. 20th Anniv of First Manned Space Flight. Multicoloured.

5111	6k. Type **1980**	20	10
5112	15k. S. P. Korolev (spaceship designer)	45	15
5113	32k. Statue of Gagarin and "Interkosmos" emblem	1·00	50

1981 "Salyut" Orbital Space Station

1983 Prokofiev

1981. 10th Anniv of First Manned Space Station.
5115 **1981** 32k. multicoloured . . 1·25 50

1981. 90th Birth Anniv of S. S. Prokofiev (composer).
5117 **1983** 4k. lilac 30 10

1984 New Hofburg Palace, Vienna

1985 Arms, Industrial Complex and Docks

1981. "WIPA 1981" International Stamp Exhibition, Vienna.
5118 **1984** 15k. multicoloured . . 50 20

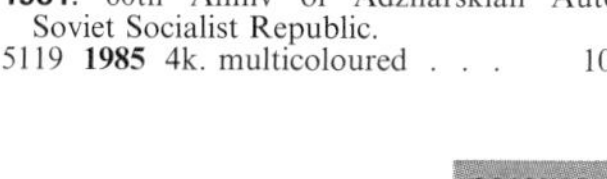

1981. 60th Anniv of Adzharskian Autonomous Soviet Socialist Republic.
5119 **1985** 4k. multicoloured . . . 10 10

1986 N. N. Benardos

1987 Congress Emblem

1981. Centenary of Invention of Welding.
5120 **1986** 6k. multicoloured . . . 15 10

1981. 14th Congress of International Union of Architects, Warsaw.
5121 **1987** 15k. multicoloured . . 50 20

1988 "Albanian Girl in Doorway" (A. A. Ivanov)

1981. Paintings. Multicoloured.

5122	10k. Type **1988**	40	15
5123	10k. "Sunset over Sea at Livorno" (N. N. Ge) (horiz)	40	15
5124	10k. "Demon" (M. A. Vrubel) (horiz)	40	15
5125	10k. "Horseman" (F. A. Rubo)	40	15

1989 Flight Simulator

1981. Soviet–Rumanian Space Flight. Mult.

5126	6k. Type **1989**	20	10
5127	15k. "Salyut"–"Soyuz" space complex	45	15
5128	32k. Cosmonauts greeting journalists after return	1·00	50

1990 "Primula minima"

1981. Flowers of the Carpathians. Multicoloured.

5129	4k. Type **1990**	15	10
5130	6k. "Carlina acaulis"	20	10
5131	10k. "Parageum montanum"	35	15
5132	15k. "Atragene alpina"	55	20
5133	32k. "Rhododendron kotschyi"	1·25	50

1991 Gyandzhevi

1992 Longo

1981. 840th Birth Anniv of Nizami Gyandzhevi (poet and philosopher).
5134 **1991** 4k. brown, yellow & green 10 10

1981. Luigi Longo (Italian politician). Commem.
5135 **1992** 6k. multicoloured . . . 15 10

1993 Running

1994 Flag and Arms of Mongolia

1981. Sports. Multicoloured.

5136	4k. Type **1993**	15	10
5137	6k. Football	15	10
5138	10k. Throwing the discus	35	20
5139	15k. Boxing	60	25
5140	32k. Swimmer on block	1·25	60

1981. 60th Anniv of Revolution in Mongolia.
5141 **1994** 6k. multicoloured . . . 15 10

1995 Spassky Tower and Film encircling Globe

1996 "Lenin"

1981. 12th International Film Festival, Moscow.
5142 **1995** 15k. multicoloured . . 50 20

1981. River Ships. Multicoloured.

5143	4k. Type **1996**	20	10
5144	6k. "Kosmonavt Gagarin" (tourist ship)	25	10
5145	15k. "Valerian Kuibyshev" (tourist ship)	60	25
5146	32k. "Baltysky" (freighter)	1·40	55

1981. Russian Ice-breakers (4th issue). As T **1775**. Multicoloured.
5147 15k. "Malygin" 65 15

1997 Industry

1981. Resolutions of the 26th Party Congress. Multicoloured.

5148	4k. Type **1997**	20	10
5149	4k. Agriculture	15	10
5150	4k. Energy	15	10
5151	4k. Transport and communications	20	10
5152	4k. Arts and science	15	10
5153	4k. International co-operation	15	10

1998 Ulyanov

2000 Brushes, Palette and Gerasimov

1999 Facade of Theatre

1981. 150th Birth Anniv of I. N. Ulyanov (Lenin's father).
5154 **1998** 4k. brown, black & green 10 10

1981. 225th Anniv of Pushkin Drama Theatre, Leningrad.
5155 **1999** 6k. multicoloured . . . 15 10

1981. Birth Centenary of A. M. Gerasimov (artist).
5156 **2000** 4k. multicoloured . . . 10 10

2001 Institute Building

1981. 50th Anniv of Institute of Physical Chemistry, Academy of Sciences, Moscow.
5157 **2001** 4k. multicoloured . . . 10 10

2002 Severtzov's Tit Warbler

1981. Song Birds. Multicoloured.

5158	6k. Type **2002**	20	10
5159	10k. Asiatic paradise flycatcher (vert)	30	15
5160	15k. Jankowski's bunting	50	35
5161	20k. Vinous-throated parrotbill (vert)	65	45
5162	32k. Hodgson's bushchat (vert)	1·10	70

2003 Arms and Industrial Scenes

1981. 60th Anniv of Komi A.S.S.R.
5163 **2003** 4k. multicoloured . . . 30 10

2004 Orbiting Satellite and Exhibition Emblem

1981. "Svyaz 81" Communications Exhibition.
5164 **2004** 4k. multicoloured . . . 15 10

2005 Buildings, Arms and Monument

2006 Soviet Soldier (monument, Treptow Park, Berlin)

1981. 60th Anniv of Kabardino-Balkar A.S.S.R.
5165 **2005** 4k. multicoloured . . . 10 10

1981. 25th Anniv of Soviet War Veterans Committee.
5166 **2006** 4k. multicoloured . . . 10 10

2007 Four-masted Barque "Tovarishch"

1981. Cadet Sailing Ships. Multicoloured.

5167	4k. Type **2007**	15	10
5168	6k. Barquentine "Vega"	25	10
5169	10k. Schooner "Kodor" (vert)	35	15
5170	15k. Three-masted barque "Tovarishch"	55	20
5171	20k. Four-masted barque "Kruzenshtern"	85	40
5172	32k. Four-masted barque "Sedov" (vert)	1·25	75

2008 Russian and Kazakh Citizens with Flags

2009 Lavrentev

1981. 250th Anniv of Unification of Russia and Kazakhstan.
5173 **2008** 4k. multicoloured . . . 10 10

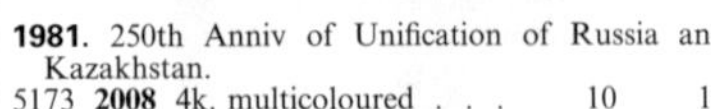

1981. Academician Mikhail Alekseevich Lavrentev (mathematician) Commemoration.
5174 **2009** 4k. multicoloured . . . 10 10

2010 Kremlin Palace of Congresses, Moscow, and Arch of the General Staff, Leningrad

1981. 64th Anniv of October Revolution.
5175 **2010** 4k. multicoloured . . . 10 10

2011 Transmitter, Dish Aerial and "Ekran" Satellite

1981. "Ekran" Television Satellite.
5176 **2011** 4k. multicoloured . . . 10 10

2012 V. V. Kovalyonok and V. P. Savinykh

2014 Merkurov

1981. "Soyuz T-4"–"Salyut 6" Space Complex. Multicoloured.

5177	10k. Type **2012**	30	15
5178	10k. Microscope slide, crystal and text	30	15

1981. Birth Centenary of Sergei Dmitrievich Merkurov (sculpture).
5180 **2014** 4k. brown, green & bis 10 10

2015 "Autumn" (Nino A. Piromanashvili)

2016 Arms and Saviour Tower, Moscow

1981. Paintings by Georgian Artists. Multicoloured.

5181	4k. Type **2015**	15	10
5182	6k. "Gurian Woman" (Sh. G. Kikodze)	15	10
5183	10k. "Travelling Companions" (U. M. Dzhaparidze) (horiz)	35	15
5184	15k. "Shota Rustaveli" (S. S. Kobuladze)	60	35
5185	32k. "Tea Pickers" (V. D. Gudiashvili" (horiz))	1·25	55

1981. New Year.
5186 **2016** 4k. multicoloured . . . 10 10

2017 Horse-drawn Sleigh (19th century)

1981. Moscow Municipal Transport.

5187	**2017**	4k. brown and silver	15	10
5188	–	6k. green and silver	35	10
5189	–	10k. lilac and silver	30	15
5190	–	15k. black and silver	45	25
5191	–	20k. brown and silver	60	30
5192	–	32k. red and silver	1·25	50

DESIGNS: 6k. Horse tram (19th century); 10k. Horse-drawn cab (19th century); 15k. Taxi, 1926; 20k. British Leyland bus, 1926; 32k. Electric tram, 1912.

2019 Modern Kiev

1982. 1500th Anniv of Kiev.
5194 **2019** 10k. multicoloured . . 35 15

2020 S. P. Korolev

2021 Arms and Industrial Complex

1982. 75th Birth Anniv of Academician S. P. Korolev (spaceship designer).
5195 **2020** 4k. multicoloured . . . 15 10

1982. 60th Anniv of Checheno-Ingush A.S.S.R.
5196 **2021** 4k. multicoloured . . . 15 10

2022 Arms and Construction Sites

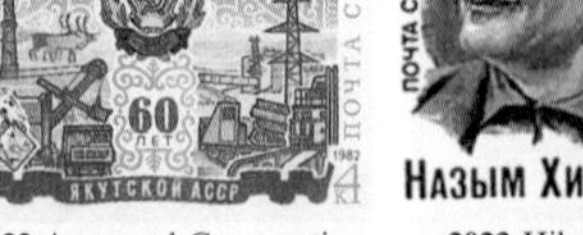
2023 Hikmet

1982. 60th Anniv of Yakut A.S.S.R.
5197 **2022** 4k. multicoloured . . . 15 10

1982. 80th Birth Anniv of Nazim Hikmet (Turkish poet).
5198 **2023** 6k. multicoloured . . . 15 10

2024 "The Oaks"

1982. 150th Birth Anniv of I. I. Shishkin (artist).
5199 **2024** 6k. multicoloured . . . 20 10

2025 Trade Unionists and World Map

1982. 10th World Trade Unions Congress, Havana.
5200 **2025** 15k. multicoloured . . 45 20

2026 Kremlin Palace of Congresses and Flag

2027 "Self-portrait"

1982. 17th Soviet Trade Unions Congress.
5201 **2026** 4k. multicoloured . . . 10 10

1982. 150th Birth Anniv of Edouard Manet (artist).
5202 **2027** 32k. multicoloured . . 1·10 40

2028 Show Jumping

1982. Soviet Horse breeding. Multicoloured.

5203	4k. Type **2028**	30	10
5204	6k. Dressage	30	10
5205	15k. Racing	60	25

2029 Tito

2030 University, Book and Monument

1982. President Tito of Yugoslavia Commemoration.
5206 **2029** 6k. brown and black . . 15 10

1982. 350th Anniv of University of Tartu.
5207 **2030** 4k. multicoloured . . . 10 10

2031 Heart on Globe

1982. 9th Int Cardiologists Conference, Moscow.
5208 **2031** 15k. multicoloured . . 45 20

2033 Blackberry

1982. Wild Berries. Multicoloured.

5210	4k. Type **2033**	15	10
5211	6k. Blueberries	20	10
5212	10k. Cranberry	30	15
5213	15k. Cherry	60	25
5214	32k. Strawberry	1·25	55

2034 "Venera 13" and "14"

2035 "M. I. Lopukhina" (V. L. Borovikovsky)

1982. "Venera" Space Flights to Venus.
5215 **2034** 10k. multicoloured . . 30 15

1982. Paintings. Multicoloured.
5216 6k. Type **2035** 20 10
5217 6k. "E. V. Davydov" (O. A. Kiprensky) 20 10
5218 6k. "The Unequal Marriage" (V. V. Pukirev) 20 10

2036 Chukovsky

2039 Solovev-Sedoi

2037 Rocket, "Soyuz" Spaceship, Globe and Space Station

1982. Birth Cent of K. I. Chukovsky (author).
5219 **2036** 4k. black and grey . . 15 10

1982. Cosmonautics Day.
5220 **2037** 6k. multicoloured . . . 20 10

1982. 75th Birth Anniv of V. P. Solovev-Sedoi (composer).
5222 **2039** 4k. brown 15 10

2040 Dimitrov

2041 Masthead

1982. Birth Centenary of Georgi Dimitrov (Bulgarian statesman).
5223 **2040** 6k. green 15 10

1982. 70th Anniv of "Pravda" (Communist Party Newspaper).
5224 **2041** 4k. multicoloured . . . 15 10

2042 Congress Emblem and Ribbons

2043 Globe and Hands holding Seedling

1982. 19th Congress of Leninist Young Communist League (Komsomol).
5225 **2042** 4k. multicoloured . . . 15 10

1982. 10th Anniv of U.N. Environment Programme.
5226 **2043** 6k. multicoloured . . . 15 10

2044 Pioneers

2045 I.T.U. Emblem, Satellite and Receiving Station

1982. 60th Anniv of Pioneer Organization.
5227 **2044** 4k. multicoloured . . . 10 10

1982. I.T.U. Delegates' Conference, Nairobi.
5228 **2045** 15k. multicoloured . . 50 25

2046 Class VL-80t Electric Locomotive

1982. Locomotives. Multicoloured.
5229 4k. Type **2046** 25 10
5230 6k. Class TEP-75 diesel . . 30 10
5231 10k. Class TEM-7 diesel . . 60 20
5232 15k. Class VL-82m electric 90 30
5233 32k. Class EP-200 electric 1·90 60

2047 Players with Trophy and Football

1982. World Cup Football Championship, Spain.
5234 **2047** 20k. lilac, yellow and brown 65 30

2048 Hooded Crane

1982. 18th International Ornithological Congress, Moscow. Multicoloured.
5235 2k. Type **2048** 10 10
5236 4k. Steller's sea eagle . . . 20 15
5237 6k. Spoon-billed sandpiper 25 15
5238 10k. Bar-headed goose . . . 45 25
5239 15k. Sociable plover 65 30
5240 32k. White stork . . . . . 1·50 65

2049 Buildings and Workers with Picks

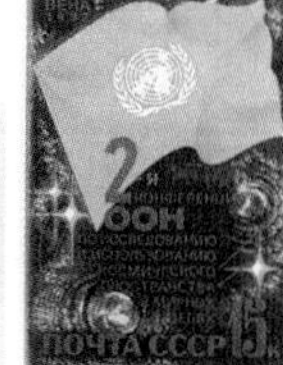
2051 U.N. Flag

2050 "The Cart"

1982. 50th Anniv of Komsomolsk-on-Amur.
5241 **2049** 4k. multicoloured . . . 15 10

1982. Birth Centenary of M. B. Grekov (artist).
5242 **2050** 6k. multicoloured . . . 40 10

1982. Second U.N. Conference on the Exploration and Peaceful Uses of Outer Space, Vienna.
5243 **2051** 15k. multicoloured . . 50 20

2052 Scientific Research in Space

1982. Soviet–French Space Flight. Multicoloured.
5244 6k. Type **2052** 15 10
5245 20k. Rocket and trajectory 60 30
5246 45k. Satellites and globe . . 1·40 75

2053 "Legend of the Golden Cockerel" (P. I. Sosin)

1982. Lacquerware Paintings. Multicoloured.
5248 6k. Type **2053** 20 10
5249 10k. "Minin's Appeal to Count Pozharsky" (I. A. Fomichev) 30 20
5250 15k. "Two Peasants" (A. F. Kotyagin) 45 25
5251 20k. "The Fisherman" (N. P. Klykov) 60 35
5252 32k. "Arrest of the Propagandists" (N. I. Shishakov) 95 55

2054 Early Telephone, Moscow, Leningrad, Odessa and Riga

2055 P. Schilling (inventor)

1982. Telephone Centenary.
5253 **2054** 4k. multicoloured . . . 15 10

1982. 150th Anniv of Electro-magnetic Telegraph in Russia.
5254 **2055** 6k. multicoloured . . . 15 10

2056 Gymnast and Television Screen

2058 Garibaldi

2057 Mastyazhart Glider, 1923

1982. Intervision Cup Gymnastics Contest.
5255 **2056** 15k. multicoloured . . 40 20

1982. Gliders (1st series). Multicoloured.
5256 4k. Type **2057** 20 10
5257 6k. Red Star, 1930 . . . . 20 10
5258 10k. TsAGI-2, 1934 . . . . 40 15
5259 20k. Stakhanovets, 1939 (60 × 27 mm) 90 35
5260 32k. GR-29, 1941 (60 × 27 mm) . . . . . . 1·40 55
See also Nos. 5301/5.

1982. 175th Birth Anniv of Giuseppe Garibaldi.
5261 **2058** 6k. multicoloured . . . 15 10

2059 Emblem

2060 F.I.D.E. Emblem, Chess Symbol for Queen and Equestrian Statue

1982. 25th Anniv of International Atomic Energy Agency.
5262 **2059** 20k. multicoloured . . 55 30

1982. World Chess Championship Interzone Tournaments for Women (Tbilisi) and Men (Moscow). Multicoloured.
5263 6k. Type **2060** 35 15
5264 6k. F.I.D.E. emblem, chess symbol for King and Kremlin tower 35 15

2061 Shaposhnikov

2062 Clenched Fist

1982. Birth Cent of Marshal B. M. Shaposhnikov.
5265 **2061** 4k. brown 15 10

1982. 70th Anniv of African National Congress.
5266 **2062** 6k. multicoloured . . . 15 10

2063 Botkin

А. КАРПОВ —
обладатель восьми
„Шахматных Оскаров"
(2065)

1982. 150th Birth Anniv of S. P. Botkin (therapeutist).
5267 **2063** 4k. green 15 10

1982. Anatoly Karpov's Victory in World Chess Championship. No. 5264 optd with T **2065**.
5269 6k. multicoloured 50 35

2066 Submarine "S-56"

1982. Soviet Naval Ships. Multicoloured.
5270 4k. Type **2066** 20 10
5271 6k. Minelayer "Gremyashchy" 20 10
5272 15k. Minesweeper "Gafel" 65 25
5273 20k. Cruiser "Krasnyi Krim" 90 40
5274 45k. Battleship "Sevastopol" 1·90 85

2067 Flag and Arms

1982. 65th Anniv of October Revolution.
5275 **2067** 4k. multicoloured . . . 10 10

2068 House of the Soviets, Moscow

1982. 60th Anniv of U.S.S.R. Multicoloured.
5276 10k. Type **2068** 30 20
5277 10k. Dneiper Dam and statue 30 20
5278 10k. Soviet war memorial and resistance poster . . 30 20
5279 10k. Newspaper, worker holding peace text, and sun illuminating city . . . 30 20
5280 10k. Workers' Monument, Moscow, rocket, Ilyushin Il-86 jetliner and factories 30 20
5281 10k. Soviet arms and Kremlin tower 30 20

Всесоюзная филателистическая выставка
(2069)

1982. All-Union Stamp Exhibition, Moscow. No. 5280 optd with T **2069**.
5282 10k. multicoloured 60 30

2070 "Portrait of an Actor" (Domenico Fetti)

2072 Hammer and Sickle, Clock and Date

1982. Italian Paintings in the Hermitage Museum, Leningrad. Multicoloured.
5283 4k. Type **2070** 15 10
5284 10k. "St. Sebastian" (Pietro Perugino) 35 15
5285 20k. "Danae" (Titian) (horiz) 65 30
5286 45k. "Portrait of a Woman" (Correggio) . . . . 1·40 75
5287 50k. "Portrait of a Young Man" (Capriolo) . . . . 1·60 85

1982. New Year.
5289 **2072** 4k. multicoloured . . . 10 10

2075 Kherson Lighthouse, Black Sea

2076 F. P. Tolstoi

1982. Lighthouses (1st series). Multicoloured.
5292 6k. Type **2075** 40 15
5293 6k. Vorontsov lighthouse, Odessa, Black Sea 40 15
5294 6k. Temryuk lighthouse, Sea of Azov 40 15
5295 6k. Novorossiisk lighthouse, Black Sea 40 15
5296 6k. Dneiper harbour light 40 15
See also Nos. 5362/6 and 5449/53.

1983. Birth Bicentenary of Fyodor Petrovich Tolstoi (artist).
5297 **2076** 4k. multicoloured . . . 15 10

2077 Masthead of "Iskra"

2078 Army Star and Flag

1983. 80th Anniv of 2nd Social Democratic Workers' Congress.
5298 **2077** 4k. multicoloured . . . 10 10

1983. 65th Anniv of U.S.S.R. Armed Forces.
5299 **2078** 4k. multicoloured . . . 15 10

1983. Gliders (2nd series). As T **2057**. Mult.
5301 2k. Antonov A-9, 1948 . . . 10 10
5302 4k. Sumonov KAU-12, 1957 15 10
5303 6k. Antonov A-15, 1960 . . 25 10
5304 20k. SA-7, 1970 . . . . . . 80 35
5305 45k. LAK-12, 1979 . . . . 1·75 80

2080 "The Holy Family"

2081 B. N. Petrov

1983. 500th Birth Anniv of Raphael (artist).
5306 **2080** 50k. multicoloured . . 1·50 75

1983. 70th Birth Anniv of Academician B. N. Petrov (chairman of Interkosmos).
5307 **2081** 4k. multicoloured . . . 10 10

2082 Tashkent Buildings

1983. 2000th Anniv of Tashkent.
5308 **2082** 4k. multicoloured . . . 25 10

2083 Popov, Serebrov and Savitskaya

1983. "Soyuz T-7"–"Salyut 7"–"Soyuz T-5" Space Flight.
5309 **2083** 10k. multicoloured . . 45 15

2085 Aleksandrov and Bars of Music

1983. Birth Centenary of A. V. Aleksandrov (composer).
5311 **2085** 4k. multicoloured . . . 25 10

2086 "Portrait of an Old Woman"

1983. Rembrandt Paintings in Hermitage Museum, Leningrad. Multicoloured.
5312 4k. Type **2086** 20 10
5313 10k. "Portrait of a Learned Man" 40 15
5314 20k. "Old Warrior" 80 30
5315 45k. "Portrait of Mrs B. Martens Doomer" . . 1·50 75
5316 50k. "Sacrifice of Abraham" 1·75 1·00

2089 A. N. Berezovoi and V. V. Lebedev

1983. 211 Days in Space of Berezovoi and Lebedev. Multicoloured.
5320 10k. Type **2089** 40 20
5321 10k. "Salyut 7"–"Soyuz T" space complex 40 20

2090 Marx

1983. Death Centenary of Karl Marx.
5322 **2090** 4k. multicoloured . . . 15 10

2091 Memorial, Building and Hydrofoil

1983. Rostov-on-Don.
5323 **2091** 4k. multicoloured . . . 15 10

2092 Kirov Theatre

1983. Bicentenary of Kirov Opera and Ballet Theatre, Leningrad.
5324 **2092** 4k. black, blue and gold 20 10

2093 Arms, Communications and Industrial Complex

1983. 60th Anniv of Buryat A.S.S.R.
5325 **2093** 4k. multicoloured . . . 20 10

2094 Sports Vignettes

1983. 8th Summer Spartakiad.
5326 **2094** 6k. multicoloured . . . 15 10

2095 Khachaturyan

1983. 80th Birth Anniv of Aram I. Khachaturyan (composer).
5327 **2095** 4k. brown 30 10

2096 Tractor and Factory

1983. 50th Anniv of Lenin Tractor Factory, Chelyabinsk.
5328 **2096** 4k. multicoloured . . . 15 10

2097 Simon Bolivar

1983. Birth Bicentenary of Simon Bolivar.
5329 **2097** 6k. deep brown, brown and black 15 10

2098 18th-century Warship and modern Missile Cruiser "Groznyi"

1983. Bicentenary of Sevastopol.
5330 **2098** 5k. multicoloured . . . 40 15

2099 Snowdrops

2101 P. N. Pospelov

2100 "Vostok 6" and Tereshkova

1983. Spring Flowers. Multicoloured.
5331 4k. Type **2099** 15 10
5332 6k. Siberian squills 20 10
5333 10k. "Anemone hepatica" 45 15
5334 15k. Cyclamen 60 25
5335 20k. Yellow star of Bethlehem . . . . 1·10 45

1983. 20th Anniv of First Woman Cosmonaut Valentina V. Tereshkova's Space Flight.
5336 **2100** 10k. multicoloured . . 35 15

1983. 85th Birth Anniv of Pyotr Nicolaievich Pospelov (scientist).
5337 **2101** 4k. multicoloured . . . 10 10

2102 Congress Emblem

2103 Film around Globe and Festival Emblem

1983. 10th European Rheumatologists' Congress, Moscow.
5338 **2102** 4k. multicoloured . . . 20 10

1983. 13th International Film Festival, Moscow.
5339 **2103** 20k. multicoloured . . 55 25

2104 Vakhtangov

1983. Birth Centenary of Ye. B. Vakhtangov (producer and actor).
5340 **2104** 5k. multicoloured . . . 20 10

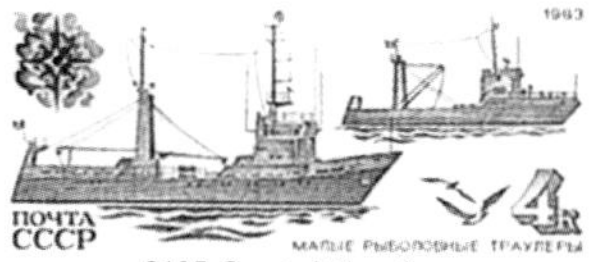

2105 Coastal Trawlers

1983. Fishing Vessels. Multicoloured.

5341	4k. Type **2105**	20	10
5342	6k. Refrigerated trawler	25	10
5343	10k. "Pulkovsky Meridian" (deep-sea trawler)	45	15
5344	15k. Refrigerated freighter	60	30
5345	20k. "50 Let SSR" (factory ship)	1·00	50

2106 "U.S.S.R.-1"  **2107** Sockeye Salmon

1983. 50th Anniv of Stratosphere Balloon's Record Altitude Flight.
5346 **2106** 20k. multicoloured . . 85 30

1983. Fishes. Multicoloured.

5347	4k. Type **2107**	15	10
5348	6k. Zerro	25	10
5349	15k. Spotted wolffish	60	20
5350	20k. Round goby	85	40
5351	45k. Starry flounder	1·75	90

2108 Exhibition Emblem  **2110** S.W.A.P.O. Flag and Emblem

1983. "Sozphilex 83" Stamp Exhibition, Moscow.
5352 **2108** 6k. multicoloured . . . 15 10

1983. Namibia Day.
5355 **2110** 5k. multicoloured . . . 15 10

2111 Palestinian with Flag  **2112** Emblem and Ostankino TV Tower, Moscow

1983. Palestinian Solidarity.
5356 **2111** 5k. multicoloured . . . 30 10

1983. 1st European Radio-telegraphy Championship, Moscow.
5357 **2112** 6k. multicoloured . . . 20 10

2113 Council Session Emblem  **2114** Mohammed al-Khorezmi

1983. 4th UNESCO International Communications Development Programme Council Session, Tashkent.
5358 **2113** 10k. blue, mauve & black 30 15

1983. 1200th Birth Anniv of Mohammed al-Khorezmi (astronomer and mathematician).
5359 **2114** 4k. multicoloured . . . 10 10

2115 Yegorov  **2116** Treaty

1983. Birth Centenary of Marshal A. I. Yegorov.
5360 **2115** 4k. purple 10 10

1983. Bicentenary of First Russian–Georgian Friendship Treaty.
5361 **2116** 6k. multicoloured . . . 10 10

1983. Lighthouses (2nd series). As Type **2075**. Multicoloured.

5362	1k. Kipu lighthouse, Baltic Sea	10	10
5363	5k. Keri lighthouse, Gulf of Finland	25	10
5364	10k. Stirsudden lighthouse, Gulf of Finland	40	25
5365	12k. Takhkun lighthouse, Baltic Sea	55	30
5366	20k. Tallin lighthouse, Gulf of Finland	75	45

2117 "Wife's Portrait with Flowers" (I. F. Khrutsky)

1983. Byelorussian Paintings. Multicoloured.

5367	4k. Type **2117**	15	10
5368	6k. "Early spring" (V. K. Byalynitsky-Birulya)	20	10
5369	15k. "Young Partisan" (E. A. Zaitsev) (vert)	50	20
5370	20k. "Partisan Madonna" (M. A. Savitsky) (vert)	70	30
5371	45k. "Corn Harvest" (V. K. Tsvirko)	1·50	70

2118 Steel Mill

1983. Centenary of Hammer and Sickle Steel Mill.
5372 **2118** 4k. multicoloured . . . 10 10

2119 Grain Production  **2120** Banner and Symbols of Economic Growth

1983. Food Programme. Multicoloured.

5373	5k. Type **2119**	15	10
5374	5k. Cattle breeding	15	10
5375	5k. Fruit and vegetable production	15	10

1983. 66th Anniv of October Revolution.
5376 **2120** 4k. multicoloured . . . 10 10

2121 Ivan Fyodorov

1983. 400th Death Anniv of Ivan Fyodorov (printer) and 420th Anniv of Publication of "The Apostle" (first Russian printed book).
5377 **2121** 4k. black 15 10

2122 Pipeline Construction

1983. Inaug of Urengoi–Uzhgorod Gas Pipeline.
5378 **2122** 5k. multicoloured . . . 15 10

2123 Sidorenko  **2124** Marchers pushing Nuclear Weapons off Globe

1983. Academician A. V. Sidorenko (geologist) Commemoration.
5379 **2123** 4k. multicoloured . . . 15 10

1983. Nuclear Disarmament.
5380 **2124** 5k. multicoloured . . . 15 10

2125 Makhtumkuli  **2126** "Madonna and Child under Apple Tree" (Cranach the Elder)

1983. 250th Birth Anniv of Makhtumkuli (Turkmen poet).
5381 **2125** 5k. multicoloured . . . 15 10

1983. German Paintings in the Hermitage Museum. Multicoloured.

5382	4k. Type **2126**	15	10
5383	10k. "Self-portrait" (Anton Raphael Mengs)	35	15
5384	20k. "Self-portrait" (Jurgens Ovens)	70	30
5385	45k. "On Board a Sailing Vessel" (Caspar David Friedrich)	1·40	60
5386	50k. "Rape of the Sabine Women" (Johann Schonfeld) (horiz)	1·60	80

2127 Sukhe Bator  **2128** Globe and Hand holding Baby

1983. 90th Birth Anniv of Sukhe Bator (Mongolian statesman).
5388 **2127** 5k. multicoloured . . . 15 10

1983. International Association of Physicians against Nuclear War.
5389 **2128** 5k. multicoloured . . . 15 10

2129 Moscow Kremlin Tower Star

1983. New Year.
5390 **2129** 5k. multicoloured . . . 15 10

2130 Children's Music Theatre

1983. New Buildings in Moscow.

5391	**2130** 3k. green	10	10
5392	– 4k. blue	15	10
5393	– 6k. brown	15	10
5394	– 20k. green	60	30
5395	– 45k. green	1·40	70

DESIGNS—VERT: 4k. Hotel and Tourist Centre. HORIZ: 6k. Russian Federation Soviet (parliament building); 20k. Hotel Izmailovo; 45k. Novosti News and Press Agency.

2132 Cuban Flag  **2133** Broadcasting Station

1984. 25th Anniv of Cuban Revolution.
5397 **2132** 5k. multicoloured . . . 15 10

1984. 50th Anniv of Moscow Broadcasting Network.
5398 **2133** 4k. multicoloured . . . 15 10

2134 Speed Skating

1984. Women's European Skating Championship, Alma-Ata.
5399 **2134** 5k. multicoloured . . . 20 10

2135 "T-34" Medium Tank

1984. World War II Armoured Vehicles. Mult.

5400	10k. Type **2135**	40	20
5401	10k. "KV" heavy tank	40	20
5402	10k. "IS-2" heavy tank	40	20
5403	10k. "SU-100" self-propelled gun	40	20
5404	10k. "ISU-152" heavy self-propelled gun	40	20

2136 Biathlon

1984. Winter Olympic Games, Sarajevo. Mult.
5405 5k. Type **2136** 15 10
5406 10k. Speed skating 35 15
5407 20k. Ice hockey 65 30
5408 45k. Figure skating . . . . 1·25 60

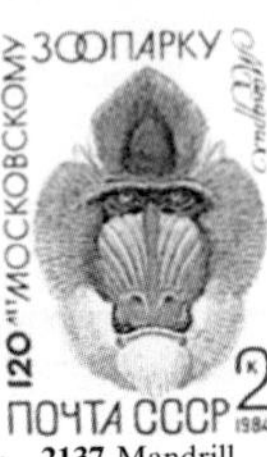
2137 Mandrill

1984. 120th Anniv of Moscow Zoo. Multicoloured.
5409 2k. Type **2137** 10 10
5410 3k. Blesbok 10 10
5411 4k. Snow leopard 15 10
5412 5k. South African crowned crane 20 15
5413 20k. Blue and yellow macaw 60 60

2138 Gagarin

1984. 50th Birth Anniv of Yuri Alekseevich Gagarin (first man in Space).
5414 **2138** 15k. blue 45 20

2140 "E. K. Vorontsova" (George Hayter)

2141 Ilyushin

1984. English Paintings in Hermitage Museum, Leningrad. Multicoloured.
5416 4k. Type **2140** 15 10
5417 10k. "Portrait of Mrs. Harriet Greer" (George Romney) 35 15
5418 20k. "Approaching Storm" (George Morland) (horiz) 70 25
5419 45k. "Portrait of an Unknown Man" (Marcus Gheeraerts, the younger) 1·50 85
5420 50k. "Cupid untying the Robe of Venus" (Joshua Reynolds) . . . . 1·75 1·00

1984. 90th Birth Anniv of Academician S. V. Ilyushin (aircraft designer).
5422 **2141** 5k. light brown, brown and black 15 10

2142 Bubnov

2143 Launching Site of "M-100" Meteorological Station

1984. Birth Centenary of Andrei Sergeevich Bubnov (Communist Party Leader).
5423 **2142** 5k. light brown, brown and black 15 10

1984. Soviet–Indian Space Co-operation. Mult.
5424 5k. Type **2143** 15 10
5425 20k. Satellite and observatory (space geodesy) 60 30
5426 45k. Rocket, satellites and dish aerials (Soviet–Indian space flight) . . . . . . 1·40 65

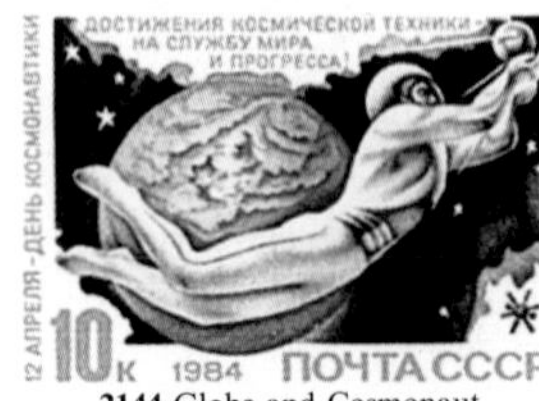
2144 Globe and Cosmonaut

1984. Cosmonautics Day.
5428 **2144** 10k. multicoloured . . 30 15

2145 "Chelyuskin" (ice-breaker) and Route Map

1984. 50th Anniv of Murmansk–Vladivostok Voyage of "Chelyuskin". Multicoloured.
5429 6k. Type **2145** 25 10
5430 15k. Evacuation of sinking ship 60 25
5431 45k. Air rescue of crew . . 1·75 75

2148 Lotus

2149 Globe and Peace March (left)

1984. Aquatic Flowers. Multicoloured.
5434 1k. Type **2148** 10 10
5435 2k. Euriala 10 10
5436 3k. Yellow water lilies (horiz) 15 10
5437 10k. White water lilies (horiz) 40 20
5438 20k. Marshflowers (horiz) 80 45

1984. Peace.
5439 **2149** 5k. multicoloured . . . 15 10
5440 – 5k. red, gold and black 15 10
5441 – 5k. multicoloured . . . 15 10
DESIGNS: No. 5440, Hammer and sickle and text; 5441, Globe and peace march (right).

2150 Welder

2151 Communications Emblem

1984. 50th Anniv of E. O. Paton Institute of Electric Welding, Kiev.
5442 **2150** 10k. multicoloured . . 25 15

1984. 25th Conference of Community for Mutual Economic Aid Electrical and Postal Communications Standing Committee, Cracow.
5443 **2151** 10k. multicoloured . . 25 15

2152 Emblem and Symbols of Match Venues

2153 Maurice Bishop

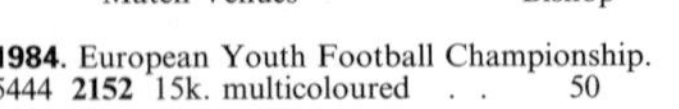

1984. European Youth Football Championship.
5444 **2152** 15k. multicoloured . . 50 20

1984. 40th Birth Anniv of Maurice Bishop (former Prime Minister of Grenada).
5445 **2153** 5k. brown 20 10

2154 Lenin and Museum

2155 Freighter, Monument and Aurora Borealis

1984. 60th Anniv of Lenin Central Museum, Moscow.
5446 **2154** 5k. multicoloured . . . 15 10

1984. 400th Anniv of Archangel.
5447 **2155** 5k. multicoloured . . . 15 10

2156 Headquarters and Spassky Tower, Moscow

2158 Liner

2157 Vladimir A. Lyakhov and Aleksandr Aleksandrov

1984. Council of Mutual Economic Aid Conference, Moscow.
5448 **2156** 5k. blue, red and black 15 10

1984. Lighthouses (3rd series). As T **2075**. Mult.
5449 1k. Petropavlovsk lighthouse, Kamchatka . . 10 10
5450 2k. Tokarev lighthouse, Sea of Japan 10 10
5451 4k. Basargin lighthouse, Sea of Japan 20 10
5452 5k. Kronotsky lighthouse, Kamchatka 20 10
5443 10k. Marekan lighthouse, Sea of Okhotsk 35 15

1984. 150 Days in Space of "Salyut 7"–"Soyuz T-9" Cosmonauts.
5454 **2157** 15k. multicoloured . . 45 20

1984. 60th Anniv of Morflot (Soviet merchant fleet).
5455 **2158** 10k. multicoloured . . 35 15

2159 Komsomol Badge and Banner

1984. 60th Anniv of Naming of Young Communist League (Komsomol) after Lenin.
5456 **2159** 5k. multicoloured . . . 15 10

2160 Memorial, Minsk

1984. 40th Anniv of Byelorussian Liberation.
5457 **2160** 5k. multicoloured . . . 15 10

2161 Congress Emblem

2162 Polish Arms and Flag

1984. 27th International Geological Congress, Moscow.
5458 **2161** 5k. blue, gold and deep blue 20 10

1984. 40th Anniv of Republic of Poland.
5459 **2162** 5k. multicoloured . . . 15 10

2163 Asafev

1984. Birth Centenary of Boris Vladimirovich Asafev (composer).
5460 **2163** 5k. green 20 10

2164 Russian and Mexican Flags and Scroll

1984. 60th Anniv of U.S.S.R.–Mexico Diplomatic Relations.
5461 **2164** 5k. multicoloured . . . 15 10

2165 Title Page of "The Princess-Frog"

1984. Folk Tales. Illustration by I. Bilibin. Mult.
5462 5k. Type **2165** 20 15
5463 5k. Hunter and frog in marshland 20 15
5464 5k. Old man and hunter in forest 20 15
5465 5k. Crowd and mute swans 20 20
5466 5k. Title page of "Ivan the Tsarevich, the Fire-bird and the Grey Wolf" . . . 20 15
5467 5k. Ivan and the Fire-bird 20 15
5468 5k. Grave and Ivan on horse 40 15
5469 5k. Ivan and princess . . . 20 15
5470 5k. Title page of "Vasilisa the Beautiful" 20 15
5471 5k. Knight on horse 20 15
5472 5k. Tree-man in forest . . . 40 15
5473 5k. Vasilisa and skulls . . . 40 15

2166 Basketball

1984. "Friendship 84" Sports Meetings. Mult.
5474 1k. Type **2166** 10 10
5475 5k. Gymnastics (vert) . . . 15 10
5476 10k. Weightlifting 30 10
5477 15k. Wrestling 50 20
5478 20k. High jumping 75 30

2167 Flag and Soviet Soldiers' Monument, Bucharest

2168 Emblem, Chess Symbol for Queen and Motherland Statue

1984. 40th Anniv of Rumania's Liberation.
5479 **2167** 5k. multicoloured . . . 15 10

1984. World Chess Championship Finals for Women (Volgograd) and Men (Moscow).
5480 **2168** 15k. gold, red and black 70 25
5481 – 15k. multicoloured . . 70 25
DESIGN: No. 5481, Emblem, chess symbol for king and Spassky tower, Moscow Kremlin

2169 Party House and Soviet Army Monument, Sofia, and State Emblem

1984. 40th Anniv of Bulgarian Revolution.
5482 **2169** 5k. multicoloured . . . 15 10

2170 Arms and Flag

1984. 10th Anniv of Ethiopian Revolution.
5483 **2170** 5k. multicoloured . . . 15 10

2171 Excavator

1984. 50th Anniv of Lenin Machine-building Plant, Novokramatorsk.
5484 **2171** 5k. multicoloured . . . 15 10

2172 Arms and Symbols of Industry and Agriculture

1984. 60th Anniv of Nakhichevan A.S.S.R.
5485 **2172** 5k. multicoloured . . . 15 10

2174 "Luna 3" photographing Moon

1984. 25th Anniv of Photography in Space. Mult.
5487 5k. Type **2174** 15 10
5488 20k. "Venera-9" and control centre 60 25
5489 45k. "Meteor" meteorological satellite and Earth . . . . 1·40 60

2175 Arms and Flag

1984. 35th Anniv of German Democratic Republic.
5491 **2175** 5k. multicoloured . . . 15 10

2176 Arms and Motherland Statue, Kiev

1984. 40th Anniv of Liberation of the Ukraine.
5492 **2176** 5k. multicoloured . . . 15 10

2177 Town, Arms and Countryside

1984. 60th Anniv of Moldavian Soviet Socialist Republic.
5493 **2177** 5k. multicoloured . . . 15 10

2178 Arms, Power Station and Mountains

1984. 60th Anniv of Kirgizia Soviet Socialist Republic.
5494 **2178** 5k. multicoloured . . . 15 10

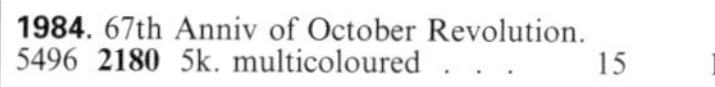
2179 Arms and Symbols of Industry and Agriculture

2180 Flags and Spassky Tower

1984. 60th Anniv of Tadzhikistan Soviet Socialist Republic.
5495 **2179** 5k. multicoloured . . . 15 10

1984. 67th Anniv of October Revolution.
5496 **2180** 5k. multicoloured . . . 15 10

2181 Arms, State Building and Dam

1984. 60th Anniv of Uzbekistan Soviet Socialist Republic.
5497 **2181** 5k. multicoloured . . . 15 10

2182 Arms, Flag and State Building

1984. 60th Anniv of Turkmenistan Soviet Socialist Republic.
5498 **2182** 5k. multicoloured . . . 15 10

2183 Medal, Workers, Diesel Train and Route Map

2184 Ilyushin Il-86 Jetliner, Rocket, "Soyuz"–"Salyut" Complex and Museum

1984. Completion of Baikal–Amur Railway.
5499 **2183** 5k. multicoloured . . . 30 10

1984. 60th Anniv of M. V. Frunze Central House of Aviation and Cosmonautics, Moscow.
5500 **2184** 5k. multicoloured . . . 15 10

2185 "Girl in Hat" (Jean-Louis Voile)

2186 Mongolian Arms and Flag

1984. French Paintings in Hermitage Museum, Leningrad. Multicoloured.
5501 4k. Type **2185** 15 10
5502 10k. "The Stolen Kiss" (Jean-Honore Fragonard) (horiz) 35 15
5503 20k. "Woman at her Toilette" (Edgar Degas) 70 30
5504 45k. "Pygmalion and Galatea" (Francois Boucher) (horiz) . . . . 1·50 60
5505 50k. "Landscape with Polyphemus" (Nicolas Poussin) (horiz) . . . . . 1·75 85

1984. 60th Anniv of Mongolian People's Republic.
5507 **2186** 5k. multicoloured . . . 15 10

2187 Spassky Tower and Snowflakes

1984. New Year.
5508 **2187** 5k. multicoloured . . . 15 10

2189 Horse-drawn Crew Wagon (19th-century)

1984. Fire Engines (1st series). Multicoloured.
5510 3k. Type **2189** 15 10
5511 5k. 19th-century horse-drawn steam pump . . . 25 10
5512 10k. "Freze" fire engine, 1904 . . . . 45 15
5513 15k. "Lessner" fire engine, 1904 . . . . 75 25
5514 20k. "Russo-Balt" fire engine, 1913 . . . . . . 1·00 35
See also Nos. 5608/12.

2190 Space Observatory and Flight Trajectory

1984. International Venus–Halley's Comet Space Project (1st issue).
5515 **2190** 15k. multicoloured . . 45 20
See also Nos. 5562 and 5630.

2191 Indira Gandhi

2192 Heroes of December Revolution Monument, Moscow

1984. Indira Gandhi (Indian Prime Minister) Commemoration.
5516 **2191** 5k. light brown & brown 30 10

1985. 80th Anniv of 1905 Revolution.
5517 **2192** 5k. multicoloured . . . 15 10

2193 Jubilee Emblem

2194 Frunze

1985. 25th Anniv of Patrice Lumumba University, Moscow.
5518 **2193** 5k. multicoloured . . . 15 10

1985. Birth Centenary of Mikhail Vasilievich Frunze (military strategist).
5519 **2194** 5k. stone, black and blue 15 10

2195 Arms and Industrial Landscape

2196 Ice Hockey Player

1985. 60th Anniv of Karakalpak A.S.S.R.
5520 **2195** 5k. multicoloured . . . 15 10

1985. 10th Friendly Armies Winter Spartakiad.
5521 **2196** 5k. multicoloured . . . 15 10

2197 Dulcimer Player and Title Page

2198 Pioneer Badge

1985. 150th Anniv of "Kalevala" (Karelian poems collected by Elino Lonnrot).
5522 **2197** 5k. brown, blue & black 20 10

1985. 60th Anniv of "Pionerskaya Pravda" (children's newspaper).
5523 **2198** 5k. multicoloured . . . 20 10

2199 Maria Aleksandrovna Ulyanova

2200 "Young Madonna Praying" (Francisco de Zurbaran)

1985. 150th Birth Anniv of Maria Aleksandrovna Ulyanova (Lenin's mother).
5524 **2199** 5k. black 20 10

1985. Spanish Paintings in Hermitage Museum, Leningrad. Multicoloured.
5525 4k. Type **2200** 15 10
5526 10k. "Still Life" (Antonio Pereda) (horiz) 30 15
5527 20k. "The Immaculate Conception" (Bartolome Esteban Murillo) 65 30
5528 45k. "The Grinder" (Antonio Puga) (horiz) . . 1·50 70
5529 50k. "Count Olivares" (Diego Velazquez) . . . . 1·75 85

2201 Cosmonauts and Globe

2203 Hungarian Arms and Budapest

1985. "Expo 85" World's Fair, Tsukuba, Japan. Multicoloured.
5531 5k. Type **2201** 15 10
5532 10k. "Molniya-I" communications satellite 30 15
5533 20k. Energy sources of the future 65 30
5534 45k. Futuristic city . . . . 1·40 60

1985. 40th Anniv of Hungary's Liberation.
5537 **2203** 5k. multicoloured . . . 20 10

2204 Emblem and Text

2206 Young People of Different Races

2205 Cosmonauts, "Soyuz T" Training Model and Gagarin

1985. 60th Anniv of Union of Soviet Societies of Friendship and Cultural Relations with Foreign Countries.
5538 **2204** 15k. multicoloured . . 45 20

1985. Cosmonautics Day. 25th Anniv of Yuri A. Gagarin Cosmonauts Training Centre.
5539 **2205** 15k. multicoloured . . 45 20

1985. 12th World Youth and Students' Festival, Moscow. Multicoloured.
5540 1k. Type **2206** 10 10
5541 3k. Girl with festival emblem in hair 10 10
5542 5k. Rainbow and girl . . . 15 10
5543 20k. Youth holding camera 65 30
5544 45k. Festival emblem . . . 1·50 65

2207 Soviet Memorial, Berlin-Treptow

Всесоюзная филателистическая выставка
„40 лет Великой Победы"
(**2209**)

2208 Lenin and Paris Flat

1985. 40th Anniv of Victory in Second World War (1st issue). Multicoloured.
5545 5k. Type **2207** 20 15
5546 5k. Partisans 20 15
5547 5k. Lenin, soldier and Moscow Kremlin 20 15
5548 5k. Soldiers and military equipment 20 15
5549 5k. Woman worker, tank, tractor and assembly of Ilyushin Il-2M3 Stormovik fighter 20 15
See also No. 5555.

1985. 115th Birth Anniv of Lenin. Multicoloured.
5551 5k. Type **2208** 20 15
5552 5k. Lenin and Lenin Museum, Tampere, Finland 20 15

1985. "Second World War Victory" Philatelic Exhibition. No. 5545 optd with T **2209**.
5554 **2207** 5k. multicoloured . . . 25 20

2210 Victory Order (½-size illustration)

1985. 40th Anniv of Victory in Second World War (2nd issue).
5555 **2210** 20k. multicoloured . . 65 35

2211 Czechoslovakian Arms and Prague Buildings

2212 Members' Flags on Shield

1985. 40th Anniv of Czechoslovakia's Liberation.
5556 **2211** 5k. multicoloured . . . 20 10

1985. 30th Anniv of Warsaw Pact Organization.
5557 **2212** 5k. multicoloured . . . 20 10

2213 Sholokhov and Books

2214 Sverdlov

1985. 80th Birth Anniv of Mikhail Aleksandrovich Sholokhov (writer).
5558 **2213** 5k. multicoloured . . . 20 10
5559 – 5k. multicoloured . . . 20 10
5560 – 5k. black, gold and brown 20 10
DESIGNS—As T **2213**. No. 5559, Sholokhov and books (different). 36 × 51 mm: No. 5560, Sholokhov.

1985. Birth Centenary of Ya. M. Sverdlov (Communist Party Leader).
5561 **2214** 5k. brown and red . . 15 10

1985. International Venus–Halley's Comet Space Project (2nd issue). As T **2190**. Multicoloured.
5562 15k. "Vega" space probe and Venus 55 30

2215 Battleship "Potemkin"

1985. 80th Anniv of Mutiny on Battleship "Potemkin".
5563 **2215** 5k. black, red and gold 20 10

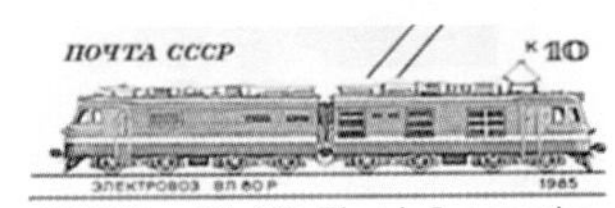

2216 Class VL-80R Electric Locomotive

1985. Locomotives and Rolling Stock.
5564 **2216** 10k. green 55 20
5565 – 10k. brown 55 20
5566 – 10k. blue 55 20
5567 – 10k. brown 55 20
5568 – 10k. blue 55 20
5569 – 10k. blue 55 20
5570 – 10k. brown 55 20
5571 – 10k. green 55 20
DESIGNS: No. 5565, Coal wagon; 5566, Oil tanker wagon; 5567, Goods wagon; 5568, Refrigerated wagon; 5569, Class TEM-2 diesel locomotive; 5570, Type SV passenger carriage; 5571, Mail van.

2217 Camp and Pioneer Badge

1985. 60th Anniv of Artek Pioneer Camp.
5572 **2217** 4k. multicoloured . . . 25 10

2218 Leonid Kizim, Vladimir Solovyov and Oleg Atkov

1985. "237 Days in Space".
5573 **2218** 15k. multicoloured . . 55 20

2219 Youths of different Races

2220 "Beating Swords into Ploughshares" (sculpture) and U.N. Emblem

1985. International Youth Year.
5574 **2219** 10k. multicoloured . . 30 15

1985. 40th Anniv of U.N.O. (1st issue).
5575 **2220** 45k. blue and gold . . 1·40 70
See also No. 5601.

2222 Larkspur

2224 Cecilienhof Palace and Flags

2223 V. A. Dzhanibekov, S. E. Savitskaya and I. P. Volk

1985. Plants of Siberia. Multicoloured.
5577 2k. Type **2222** 10 10
5578 3k. "Thermopsis lanceolata" 10 10
5579 5k. Rose 20 10
5580 20k. Cornflower 70 30
5581 45k. Bergenia . . . . 1·40 75

1985. 1st Anniv of First Space-walk by Woman Cosmonaut.
5582 **2223** 10k. multicoloured . . 35 15

1985. 40th Anniv of Potsdam Conference.
5583 **2224** 15k. multicoloured . . 40 20

2225 Finland Palace

2226 Russian and N. Korean Flags and Monument

1985. 10th Anniv of European Security and Co-operation Conference, Helsinki.
5584 **2225** 20k. multicoloured . . 75 25

1985. 40th Anniv of Liberation of Korea.
5585 **2226** 5k. multicoloured . . . 15 10

2227 Pamir Shrew

2228 A. G. Stakhanov and Industrial Scenes

1985. Protected Animals. Multicoloured.
5586 2k. Type **2227** 10 10
5587 3k. Satunin's jerboa (horiz) 10 10
5588 5k. Desert dormouse . . . 15 10
5589 20k. Caracal (47 × 32 mm) 65 30
5590 45k. Goitred gazelle (47 × 32 mm) . . . . . . 1·50 75

1985. 50th Anniv of Stakhanov Movement (for high labour productivity).
5592 **2228** 5k. yellow, red and black 15 10

2229 Cup, Football, F.I.F.A. Emblem and Kremlin Tower

2230 Chess Pieces

1985. World Junior Football Championship, Moscow.
5593 **2229** 5k. multicoloured . . . 20 10

1985. World Chess Championship Final between Anatoly Karpov and Gary Kasparov.
5594 **2230** 10k. multicoloured . . 55 20

2231 Vietnam State Emblem

2232 Immortality Monument and Buildings

1985. 40th Anniv of Vietnamese Independence.
5595 **2231** 5k. multicoloured . . . 15 10

1985. Millenary of Bryansk.
5596 **2232** 5k. multicoloured . . . 15 10

2233 Title Page

1985. 800th Anniv of "Song of Igor's Campaigns".
5597 **2233** 10k. multicoloured . . 35 15

2234 Lutsk Castle

2235 Gerasimov

1985. 900th Anniv of Lutsk.
5598 **2234** 5k. multicoloured . . . 15 10

1985. Birth Centenary of Sergei Vasilievich Gerasimov (artist).
5599 **2235** 5k. multicoloured . . . 15 10

2236 Globe, Cruiser "Aurora" and 1917

2237 Headquarters, New York, and Flag

1985. 68th Anniv of October Revolution.
5600 **2236** 5k. multicoloured . . . 20 10

1985. 40th Anniv of U.N.O. (2nd issue).
5601 **2237** 15k. green, blue and black 45 20

2238 Krisjanis Barons

1985. 150th Birth Anniv of Krisjanis Barons (writer).
5602 **2238** 5k. black and brown . . 15 10

2239 Lenin and Worker breaking Chains

1985. 90th Anniv of Petersburg Union of Struggle for Liberating the Working Class.
5603 **2239** 5k. multicoloured . . . 15 10

2240 Telescope

1985. 10th Anniv of World's Largest Telescope.
5604 **2240** 10k. blue 30 15

2241 Angolan Arms and Flag

2242 Yugoslav Arms, Flag and Parliament Building

1985. 10th Anniv of Independence of Angola.
5605 **2241** 5k. multicoloured . . . 15 10

1985. 40th Anniv of Federal People's Republic of Yugoslavia.
5606 **2242** 5k. multicoloured . . . 15 10

2243 Troitsky Tower and Palace of Congresses

2244 Samantha Smith

1985. New Year.
5607 **2243** 5k. multicoloured . . . 15 10

1985. Fire Engines (2nd series). As T **2189**. Mult.
5608 3k. "AMO-F15", 1926 . . . 15 10
5609 5k. "PMZ-1", 1933 . . . . 25 10
5610 10k. "ATs-40", 1977 . . . . 45 15
5611 20k. "AL-30" with automatic ladder, 1970 . . 80 30
5612 45k. "AA-60", 1978 . . . . 1·60 60

1985. Samantha Smith (American schoolgirl peace campaigner) Commemoration.
5613 **2244** 5k. brown, blue and red 35 10

2245 N. M. Emanuel

2246 Family and Places of Entertainment

1985. Academician N. M. Emanuel (chemist) Commemoration.
5614 **2245** 5k. multicoloured . . . 15 10

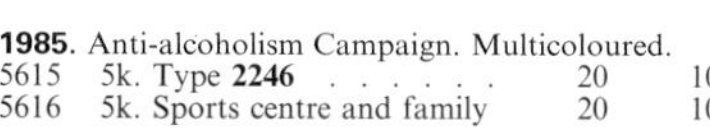

1985. Anti-alcoholism Campaign. Multicoloured.
5615 5k. Type **2246** 20 10
5616 5k. Sports centre and family 20 10

2247 Emblem

2248 Banners and Kremlin Palace of Congresses

1986. International Peace Year.
5617 **2247** 20k. blue, green & silver 55 25

1986. 27th Soviet Communist Party Congress.
5618 **2248** 5k. multicoloured . . . 15 10
5619 – 20k. multicoloured . . 55 25

DESIGNS—36 × 51 mm: 20k. Palace of Congresses, Spassky Tower and Lenin.

2249 1896 Olympics Medal

2250 Tulips

1986. 90th Anniv of First Modern Olympic Games.
5621 **2249** 15k. multicoloured . . 45 20

1986. Plants of Russian Steppes. Multicoloured.
5622 4k. Type **2250** 15 10
5623 5k. Grass (horiz) 20 10
5624 10k. Iris 35 15
5625 15k. Violets 55 25
5626 20k. Cornflower 70 30

2251 Voronezh and Arms

2252 Bela Kun

1986. 400th Anniv of Voronezh.
5627 **2251** 5k. multicoloured . . . 15 10

1986. Birth Centenary of Bela Kun (Hungarian Communist Party leader).
5628 **2252** 10k. blue 25 15

2253 Pozela

2255 Crimson-spotted Moth

1986. 90th Birth Anniv of Karolis Pozela (founder of Lithuanian Communist Party).
5629 **2253** 5k. grey 15 10

1986. International Venus–Halley's Comet Space Project (3rd issue). As T **2190**. Multicoloured.
5630 15k. "Vega 1" and Halley's Comet 50 20

1986. Butterflies and Moths listed in U.S.S.R. Red Book (1st series). Multicoloured.
5632 4k. Type **2255** 15 10
5633 5k. Eastern festoon 20 10
5634 10k. Sooty orange-tip . . . 45 15
5635 15k. Dark crimson underwing 75 25
5636 20k. "Satyrus bischoffi" . . 95 40
See also Nos. 5726/30.

2256 Globe and Model of Space Complex

2257 Kirov

1986. "Expo '86" World's Fair, Vancouver.
5637 **2256** 20k. multicoloured . . 60 30

1986. Birth Centenary of S. M. Kirov (Communist Party Secretary).
5638 **2257** 5k. black 15 10

2258 Tsiolkovsky

1986. Cosmonautics Day. Multicoloured.
5639 5k. Type **2258** 15 10
5640 10k. Sergei Pavlovich Korolev (rocket designer) and "Vostok" rocket (vert) 30 15
5641 15k. Yuri Gagarin, "Vega", sputnik and globe (25th anniv of first man in space) 55 25

2259 Ice Hockey Player

2260 Thalmann

1986. World Ice Hockey Championship, Moscow.
5642 **2259** 15k. multicoloured . . 50 20

1986. Birth Centenary of Ernst Thalmann (German politician).
5643 **2260** 10k. brown 30 15

2261 Lenin Museum, Leipzig

1986. 116th Birth Anniv of Lenin.
5645 **2261** 5k. multicoloured . . . 15 10
5646 – 5k. olive, brown & black 15 10
5647 – 5k. multicoloured . . . 15 10

DESIGNS: No. 5646, Lenin (after P. Belousov) and Lenin Museum, Prague; 5647, Lenin Museum, Poronine, Poland.

2262 Tambov and Arms

1986. 350th Anniv of Tambov.
5648 **2262** 5k. multicoloured . . . 15 10

2263 Dove with Olive Branch and Globe

2264 Emblem and Cyclists

1986. 25th Anniv of Soviet Peace Fund.
5649 **2263** 10k. multicoloured . . 35 20

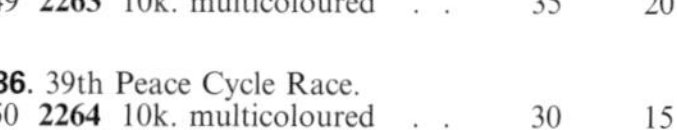

1986. 39th Peace Cycle Race.
5650 **2264** 10k. multicoloured . . 30 15

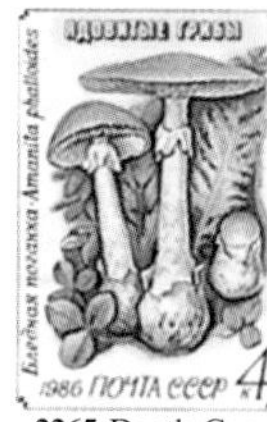
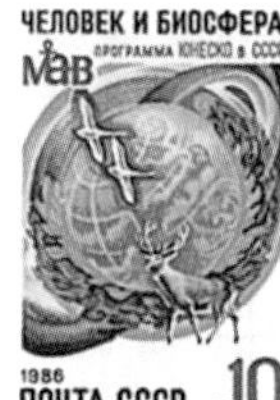

2265 Death Cap

2266 Globe and Wildlife

1986. Fungi. Multicoloured.
5651 4k. Type **2265** 15 10
5652 5k. Fly agaric 25 10

5653 10k. Panther cap 45 15
5654 15k. Bitter bolete 75 25
5655 20k. Clustered woodlover 95 45

1986. UNESCO Man and Biosphere Programme.
5656 **2266** 10k. multicoloured . . 35 15

2267 Torch and Runner

2268 Kuibyshev

1986. 9th People's Spartakiad.
5657 **2267** 10k. multicoloured . . 35 15

1986. 400th Anniv of Kuibyshev (formerly Samara).
5658 **2268** 5k. multicoloured . . . 15 10
No. 5658 depicts the Lenin Museum, Eternal Glory and V. I. Chapaev monuments and Gorky State Theatre.

2269 Ostankino T.V. Tower

2270 Footballers

1986. "Communication 86" International Exhibition, Moscow.
5659 **2269** 5k. multicoloured . . . 15 10

1986. World Cup Football Championship, Mexico. Multicoloured.
5660 5k. Type **2270** 20 10
5661 10k. Footballers (different) 40 15
5662 15k. Championship medal 50 20

2271 "Lane in Albano" (M. I. Lebedev)

2272 Arms and City

1986. Russian Paintings in Tretyakov Gallery, Moscow. Multicoloured.
5663 4k. Type **2271** 15 10
5664 5k. "View of the Kremlin in foul Weather" (A. K. Savrasov) (horiz) 20 10
5665 10k. "Sunlit Pine Trees" (I. I. Shishkin) 30 15
5666 15k. "Journey Back" (A. E. Arkhipov) (69 × 33 mm) 50 25
5667 45k. "Wedding Procession in Moscow" (A. P. Ryabushkin) (69 × 33 mm) 1·50 70

1986. 300th Anniv of Irkutsk City Status.
5668 **2272** 5k. multicoloured . . . 15 10

2273 World Map, Stadium and Runners

2274 Globe, Punched Tape and Keyboard

1986. International Goodwill Games, Moscow.
5669 **2273** 10k. blue, brown & black 35 15

1986. UNESCO Programmes in U.S.S.R. Mult.
5671 5k. Type **2274** 20 10
5672 10k. Landscape and geological section (geological correlation) . . 35 15
5673 15k. Oceanographic research vessel, albatross and ocean (Inter-governmental Oceanographic Commission) 55 30
5674 35k. Fluvial drainage (International Hydrological Programme) 1·00 55

2275 Arms and Town Buildings

1986. 400th Anniv of Tyumen, Siberia.
5675 **2275** 5k. multicoloured . . . 15 10

2276 Olof Palme

2277 Hands, Ball and Basket

1986. Olof Palme (Swedish Prime Minister) Commemoration.
5676 **2276** 10k. blue, black & brn 35 15

1986. 10th Women's Basketball Championship.
5677 **2277** 15k. brown, black & red 45 20

2278 "Ural-375D"

1986. Lorries. Multicoloured.
5678 4k. Type **2278** 15 10
5679 5k. "GAZ-53A" 20 10
5680 10k. "KrAZ-256B" 35 15
5681 15k. "MAZ-515B" 55 25
5682 20k. "ZIL-133GYa" 70 35

2279 Lenin Peak

1986. U.S.S.R. Sports Committee's International Mountaineers' Camps (1st series). Multicoloured.
5683 4k. Type **2279** 15 10
5684 5k. E. Korzhenevskaya Peak 20 10
5685 10k. Belukha Peak 30 15
5686 15k. Communism Peak . . 55 25
5687 30k. Elbrus Peak 95 55
See also Nos. 5732/5.

2281 Lenin Monument and Drama Theatre

2282 "Mukran", Maps and Flags

1986. 250th Anniv of Chelyabinsk City.
5689 **2281** 5k. multicoloured . . . 15 10

1986. Opening of Mukran (East Germany)–Klaipeda (U.S.S.R.) Railway Ferry.
5690 **2282** 15k. multicoloured . . 75 25

2283 Victory Monument and Buildings

2284 Lenin Monument and Moscow Kremlin

1986. 750th Anniv of Siauliai, Lithuania.
5691 **2283** 5k. buff, brown and red 15 10

1986. 69th Anniv of October Revolution.
5692 **2284** 5k. multicoloured . . . 30 15

2285 Ice-breaker "Vladivostok", Mil Mi-4 Helicopter, Satellite and Map

15.III—26.VII.1985
Дрейф во льдах Антарктики
(2286)

1986. Antarctic Drift of "Mikhail Somov" (research vessel). (a) As Type **2285**.
5693 5k. blue, black and red . . 25 10
5694 10k. multicoloured 50 20

(b) No. 5055 optd with T **2286**.
5696 4k. multicoloured 20 10
DESIGN—As T **2285**: 10k. Map and "Mikhail Somov".
Nos. 5693/4 were printed together, se-tenant, forming a composite design.

2287 Class Eu No. 684–37, Slavyansk

1986. Steam Locomotive as Monuments. Mult.
5697 4k. Type **2287** 20 10
5698 5k. Class FD No. 3000, Novosibirsk 20 10
5699 10k. Class Ov No. 5109, Volgograd 40 15
5700 20k. Class SO No. 17-1613, Dnepropetrovsk 75 30
5701 30k. Class FDp No. 20-578, Kiev . . . . 1·25 50

2288 G. K. Ordzhonikidze

2289 Novikov and Score

1986. Birth Centenary of Grigory Konstantinovich Ordzhonikidze (revolutionary).
5702 **2288** 5k. grey 15 10

1986. 90th Birth Anniv of Anatoli Novikov (composer).
5703 **2289** 5k. brown 20 10

2290 U.N. and UNESCO Emblem

2291 Sun Yat-sen

1986. 40th Anniv of UNESCO.
5704 **2290** 10k. silver and blue . . 35 15

1986. 120th Birth Anniv of Sun Yat-sen (first President of Chinese Republic).
5705 **2291** 5k. black and grey . . 15 10

2292 Lomonosov

1986. 275th Birth Anniv of Mikhail Vasilievich Lomonosov (scientist).
5706 **2292** 5k. brown 20 10

2293 Ya-1, 1927

1986. Sports Aircraft designed by Aleksandr Yakovlev. Multicoloured.
5707 4k. Type **2293** 15 10
5708 5k. VT-2 trainer, 1935 . . . 15 10
5709 10k. Yak-18, 1946 . . . . . 35 15
5710 20k. Yak-50, 1972 . . . . . 75 30
5711 30k. Yak-55, 1981 . . . . . 1·10 50

2294 Spassky, Senate and Nikolsky Towers, Kremlin

2295 Computer and Terminal

1986. New Year.
5712 **2294** 5k. multicoloured . . . 15 10

1986. Resolutions of 27th Communist Party Congress. Multicoloured.
5713 5k. Type **2295** (scientific and technical progress) 20 10
5714 5k. Construction engineer and building project . . . 20 10
5715 5k. City (welfare of people) 20 10
5716 5k. Peace demonstration at Council for Mutual Economic Aid building (peace) 20 10
5717 5k. Spassky Tower and Kremlin Palace, Moscow Kremlin (unity of party and people) 20 10

2296 Parkhomenko

2297 Machel

1986. Birth Centenary of Aleksandr Parkhomenko (revolutionary).
5718 **2296** 5k. black 15 10

1986. Samora Moizes Machel (President of Mozambique) Commemoration.
5719 **2297** 5k. brown and black . . 20 10

2298 Russian State Museum (Mikhailovsky Palace)

1986. Palace Museums of Leningrad.
5720 **2298** 5k. brown and green . . 20 15
5721 – 10k. green and blue . . 30 15
5722 – 15k. blue and green . . 50 20
5723 – 20k. green and brown 60 30
5724 – 50k. brown and blue . . 1·50 70

DESIGNS: 10k. Hermitage Museum (Winter Palace); 15k. Grand Palace Museum (Petrodvorets); 20k. Catherine Palace Museum (Pushkin); 50k. Palace Museum (Pavlovsk).

2299 Couple and Industrial Landscape

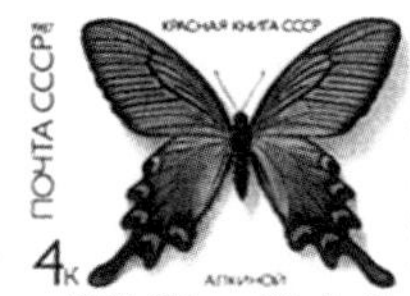
2300 Chinese Windmill

1987. 18th Soviet Trades Union Congress, Moscow.
5725 **2299** 5k. multicoloured . . . 15 10

1987. Butterflies listed in U.S.S.R. Red Book (2nd series). Multicoloured.
5726 4k. Type **2300** 20 10
5727 5k. Swallowtail 20 10
5728 10k. Southern swallowtail . . . 35 15
5729 15k. "Papilio maackii" . . . 60 25
5730 30k. Scare swallowtail . . . 95 55

2301 Karlis Miesnieks

2302 Stasys Simkus

1987. Birth Centenary of Karlis Miesnieks (Latvian artist).
5731 **2301** 5k. multicoloured . . . 15 10

1987. U.S.S.R. Sports Committee's International Mountaineers' Camps (2nd series). As T **2279**. Multicoloured.
5732 4k. Chimbulak Gorge . . . 15 10
5733 10k. Shavla Gorge 30 15
5734 20k. Donguz-Orun and Nakra-Tau, Caucasus . . 70 30
5735 35k. Kazbek, Caucasus . . 1·25 60

1987. Birth Centenary of Stasys Simkus (Lithuanian composer).
5736 **2302** 5k. purple and yellow 20 10

2303 V. I. Chapaev

2304 Lenin

1987. Birth Cent of Vasily Ivanovich Chapaev (revolutionary).
5737 **2303** 5k. brown 15 10

1987. 20th Leninist Young Communist League (Komsomol) Congress, Moscow.
5738 **2304** 5k. multicoloured . . . 15 10

2305 Heino Eller

2306 Orbeli

1987. Birth Centenary of Heino Eller (Estonian composer).
5740 **2305** 5k. light brown & brown 20 10

1987. Birth Centenary of Academician Iosif Abgarovich Orbeli (first President of Armenian Academy of Sciences).
5741 **2306** 5k. brown and pink . . 15 10

2307 Bears in and out of Water

1987. Polar Bears. Multicoloured.
5742 5k. Type **2307** 20 10
5743 10k. Mother and cubs . . . 40 15
5744 20k. Mother and cubs (different) 75 30
5745 35k. Bears . . . . 1·25 55

2308 "Sputnik 1" and Globe

2309 Emblem and Headquarters, Bangkok

1987. Cosmonautics Day. Multicoloured.
5746 10k. Type **2308** (30th anniv of launching of first artificial satellite) 35 15
5747 10k. "Vostok-3", "Vostok-4" and globe (25th anniv of first group space flight) 35 15
5748 10k. "Mars-1" and globe (25th anniv of launching of automatic interplanetary station) . . 35 15

1987. 40th Anniv of U.N. Economic and Social Commission for Asia and the Pacific Ocean.
5749 **2309** 10k. multicoloured . . 35 15

2310 "Birthday" (N. A. Sysoev)

1987. 117th Birth Anniv of Lenin. Multicoloured.
5750 5k. Type **2310** 15 10
5751 5k. "V. I. Lenin with Delegates to the Third Congress of the Young Communist League" (P. P. Belousov) 15 10

2311 Gymnast on Rings

2312 Cyclists and "40"

1987. European Gymnastics Championships, Moscow.
5753 **2311** 10k. multicoloured . . 30 15

1987. 40th Peace Cycle Race.
5754 **2312** 10k. multicoloured . . 40 15

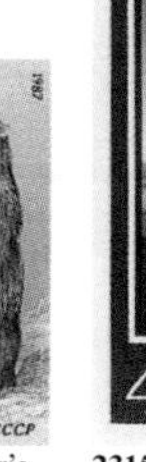
2313 Menzbir's Marmot

2315 "Portrait of a Woman" (Lucas Cranach the Elder)

2314 "Maksim Gorky"

1987. Mammals listed in U.S.S.R. Red Book. Multicoloured.
5755 5k. Type **2313** 20 10
5756 10k. Ratel (horiz) 35 15
5757 15k. Snow leopard (32 × 47 mm) 70 25

1987. River Tourist Ships. Multicoloured.
5758 5k. Type **2314** 25 10
5759 10k. "Aleksandr Pushkin" 40 15
5760 30k. "Sovetsky Soyuz" . . . 1·00 45

1987. West European Art in Hermitage Museum, Leningrad. Multicoloured.
5761 4k. Type **2315** 15 10
5762 5k. "St. Sebastian" (Titian) 15 10
5763 10k. "Justice" (drawing, Albrecht Durer) 30 15
5764 30k. "Adoration of the Magi" (Peter Breughel the younger) (horiz) . . . . . 1·00 45
5765 50k. "Statue of Ceres" (Peter Paul Rubens) . . . 1·75 80

2316 Car Production Line and Lenin Hydro-electric Power Station

2317 Pushkin (after T. Rait)

1987. 250th Anniv of Togliatti (formerly Stavropol).
5766 **2316** 5k. multicoloured . . . 15 10

1987. 150th Death Anniv of Aleksandr S. Pushkin (poet).
5767 **2317** 5k. deep brown, yellow and brown 15 10

2318 Kovpak

2319 Congress Emblem

1987. Birth Centenary of Major-General Sidor Artemevich Kovpak.
5768 **2318** 5k. black 15 10

1987. World Women's Congress, Moscow.
5769 **2319** 10k. multicoloured . . 35 15

2320 Arms, Kremlin, Docks, Drama Theatre and Yermak Monument

2321 Party Flag and Mozambican

1987. 400th Anniv of Tobolsk, Siberia.
5770 **2320** 5k. multicoloured . . . 15 10

1987. 25th Anniv of Mozambique Liberation Front (FRELIMO) (5771) and 10th Anniv of U.S.S.R.–Mozambique Friendship and Co-operation Treaty (5772). Multicoloured.
5771 5k. Type **2321** 15 10
5772 5k. Mozambique and U.S.S.R. flags 15 10

2322 "Scolopendrium vulgare"

2323 Moscow Kremlin and Indian Coin

1987. Ferns. Multicoloured.
5773 4k. Type **2322** 15 10
5774 5k. "Ceterach officinarum" 20 10
5775 10k. "Salvinia natans" (horiz) 35 15
5776 15k. "Matteuccia struthiopteris" 55 25
5777 50k. "Adiantum pedatum" 1·50 70

1987. Indian Festival in U.S.S.R. (5778) and U.S.S.R. Festival in India (5779). Multicoloured.
5778 5k. Type **2323** 15 10
5779 5k. Hammer, sickle, open book, satellite and Red Fort, Delhi 15 10

2324 Rossiya Hotel (venue), Globe and Film

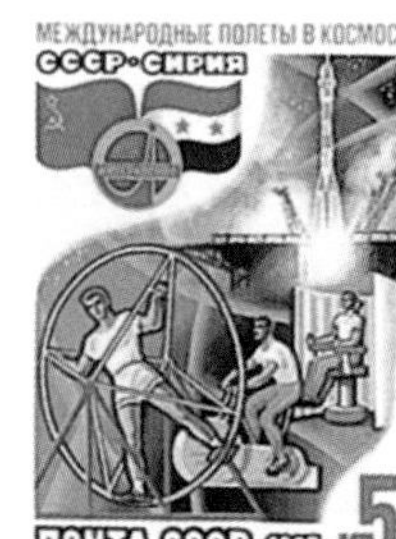
2325 Cosmonauts training

1987. 15th International Film Festival, Moscow.
5780 **2324** 10k. multicoloured . . 35 15

1987. Soviet–Syrian Space Flight. Multicoloured.
5781 5k. Type **2325** 20 10
5782 10k. Moscow–Damascus satellite link and cosmonauts watching television screen 35 15
5783 15k. Cosmonauts at Gagarin monument, Zvezdny . . . 55 25

2326 Emblem and Vienna Headquarters

1987. 30th Anniv of Int Atomic Energy Agency.
5785 **2326** 20k. multicoloured . . 70 30

2327 14th–16th Century Messenger

1987. Russian Postal History.
5786 **2327** 4k. black and brown . . 15 10
5787 – 5k. black and brown . . 20 10
5788 – 10k. black and brown 35 15
5789 – 30k. black and brown 1·40 45
5790 – 35k. black and brown 3·00 50

DESIGNS: 5k. 17th–19th century horse-drawn sledge and 17th-century postman; 10k. 16th-century and 18th-century sailing packets; 30k. 19th-century railway mail vans; 35k. 1905 post car and 1926 "AMO-F-15" van.

2328 "V. I. Lenin" (P. V. Vasilev)

1987. 70th Anniv of October Revolution. Mult.
5792 5k. Type **2328** 20 10
5793 5k. "V. I. Lenin proclaims Soviet Power" (V. A. Serov) 20 10

5794 5k. "Long Live the Socialist Revolution!" (V. V. Kuznetsov) 20 10
5795 5k. "Storming the Winter Palace" (V. A. Serov) (69 × 32 mm) 20 10
5796 5k. "On the Eve of the Storm" (portraying Lenin, Sverdlov and Podvoisky) (V. V. Pimenov) (69 × 32 mm) 20 10

2330 Postyshev

2331 Yuri Dolgoruky (founder) Monument

1987. Birth Centenary of Pavel Petrovich Postyshev (revolutionary).
5799 **2330** 5k. blue 15 10

1987. 840th Anniv of Moscow.
5800 **2331** 5k. brown, yell & orge 15 10

2332 Ulugh Beg (astronomer and mathematician)

1987. Scientists.
5801 **2332** 5k. multicoloured . . . 20 15
5802 – 5k. black, green and blue 20 15
5803 – 5k. deep brown, brown and blue 20 15
DESIGNS: No. 5801, Type **2332** (550th anniv of "New Astronomical Tables"); 5802, Isaac Newton (300th anniv of "Principia Mathematica"); 5803, Marie Curie (120th birth anniv).

Всесоюзная
филателистическая выставка
„70 лет Великого Октября"
(**2334**)

1987. "70th Anniv of October Revolution" All-Union Stamp Exhibition. No. 5795 optd with T **2334**.
5805 5k. multicoloured 25 20

2335 "There will be Cities in the Taiga" (A. A. Yakovlev)

2336 Reed

1987. Soviet Paintings of the 1980s. Multicoloured.
5806 4k. Type **2335** 15 10
5807 5k. "Mother" (V. V. Shcherbakov) 15 10
5808 10k. "My Quiet Homeland" (V. M. Sidorov) (horiz) 30 15
5809 30k. "In Yakutsk, Land of Pyotr Alekseev" (A. N. Osipov) (horiz) 90 40
5810 35k. "Ivan's Return" (V. I. Yerofeev) (horiz) . . . . 1·00 50

1987. Birth Centenary of John Reed (American journalist and founder of U.S. Communist Party).
5812 **2336** 10k. brown, yell & blk 30 15

2337 Marshak

1987. Birth Centenary of Samuil Yakovlevich Marshak (poet).
5813 **2337** 5k. brown 15 10

2338 Chavchavadze

1987. 150th Anniv of Ilya Grigoryevich Chavchavadze (writer).
5814 **2338** 5k. blue 15 10

2339 Indira Gandhi

2340 Vadim N. Podbelsky (revolutionary)

1987. 70th Birth Anniv of Indira Gandhi (Indian Prime Minister, 1966–77 and 1980–84).
5815 **2339** 5k. brown and black . . 20 10

1987. Birth Centenaries.
5816 **2340** 5k. black 15 10
5817 – 5k. blue 15 10
DESIGN: No. 5817, Academician Nikolai Ivanovich Vavilov (geneticist).

2341 Tokamak Thermonuclear System

2342 Bagramyan

1987. Science.
5818 **2341** 5k. brown and grey . . 20 10
5819 – 10k. green, blue and black 35 15
5820 – 20k. black, stone and drab 60 30
DESIGNS: 10k. Kola borehole; 20k. "Ratan-600" radio telescope.

1987. 90th Birth Anniv of Marshal Ivan Khristoforovich Bagramyan.
5821 **2342** 5k. brown 15 10

2343 Moscow Kremlin

2344 Flags, Spassky Tower, Moscow, and Capitol, Washington

1987. New Year.
5822 **2343** 5k. multicoloured . . . 15 10

1987. Soviet–American Intermediate and Short-range Nuclear Weapons Treaty.
5823 **2344** 10k. multicoloured . . 30 15

2345 Grigori Andreevich Spiridov and "Tri Svyatitelya"

1987. Russian Naval Commanders (1st series).
5824 **2345** 4k. blue and deep blue 15 10
5825 – 5k. purple and blue . . 20 10
5826 – 10k. purple and blue . . 35 15
5827 – 25k. blue and deep blue 85 35
5828 – 30k. blue and deep blue 95 45
DESIGNS: 5k. Fyodor Fyodorovich Ushakov and "Sv. Pavel"; 10k. Dmitri Nikolaevich Senyavin, Battle of Afon and "Tverdyi" (battleship); 25k. Mikhail Petrovich Lazarev and "Azov"; 30k. Pavel Stepanovich Nakhimov and "Imperatritsa Maria".
See also Nos. 6091/6.

2346 Torch

2347 Biathlon

1987. 30th Anniv of Asia–Africa Solidarity Organization.
5829 **2346** 10k. multicoloured . . 25 15

1988. Winter Olympic Games, Calgary. Mult.
5830 5k. Type **2347** 20 10
5831 10k. Cross-country skiing 35 15
5832 15k. Slalom 45 25
5833 20k. Figure skating (pairs) 65 30
5834 30k. Ski jumping . . . . . 1·10 45

2348 1918 Stamps

2349 Emblem

1988. 70th Anniv of First Soviet Postage Stamps.
5836 **2348** 10k. blue, brown and gold 35 15
5837 10k. brown, blue and gold 35 15
On No. 5836 the lower stamp depicted is the 35k. in blue, on No. 5837 the lower stamp is the 70k. in brown.

1988. 40th Anniv of W.H.O.
5838 **2349** 35k. gold, blue and black . . . . 1·00 40

2350 Byron

1988. Birth Bicentenary of Lord Byron (English poet).
5839 **2350** 15k. black, green and blue 45 25

2351 Exchange Activities and National Flags

2352 Lomov-Oppokov

1988. 30th Anniv of Agreement on Cultural, Technical and Educational Exchanges with U.S.A.
5840 **2351** 20k. multicoloured . . 60 30

1988. Birth Centenary of Georgy Ippolitovich Lomov-Oppokov (Communist party official).
5841 **2352** 5k. black and brown . . 15 10

2353 "Little Humpbacked Horse" (dir. I. Ivanov-Vano, animated L. Milchin)

1988. Soviet Cartoon Films. Multicoloured.
5842 1k. Type **2353** 10 10
5843 3k. "Winnie the Pooh" (dir. F. Khitruk, animated V. Zuikov and E. Nazarov) 10 10
5844 4k. "Gena the Crocodile" (dir. R. Kachanov, animated L. Shartsmann) 15 10
5845 5k. "Just You Wait!" (dir. V. Kotyonochkin, animated S. Rusakov) . . 25 15
5846 10k. "Hedgehog in a Mist" (dir. Yu. Norshtein, animated F. Yarbusova) 45 25

2354 Bonch-Bruevich

2355 Nurse and Emblems

1988. Birth Centenary of Mikhail Alexandrovich Bonch-Bruevich (radio engineer).
5848 **2354** 10k. black and brown 30 15

1988. 125th Anniv of International Red Cross and Red Crescent.
5849 **2355** 15k. black, blue and red 45 25

2356 Skater

1988. World Speed Skating Championships, Alma-Ata.
5850 **2356** 15k. blue, violet and [illegible] black 45 25

2357 Makarenko

1988. Birth Centenary of Anton Semenovich Makarenko (educationist and writer).
5851 **2357** 10k. green 30 15

2358 Skorina

2359 Banners and Globe

1988. 500th Birth Anniv of Frantsisk Skorina (printer).
5852 **2358** 5k. black 15 10

1988. Labour Day.
5853 **2359** 5k. multicoloured . . . 15 10

2360 Kingisepp

2361 Track and Athlete

1988. Birth Centenary of Victor Eduardovich Kingisepp (revolutionary).
5854 **2360** 5k. green 15 10

1988. Centenary of Russian Athletics.
5855 **2361** 15k. multicoloured . . 45 25

2362 M. S. Shaginyan

1988. Birth Centenary of Marietta Sergeevna Shaginyan (writer).
5856 **2362** 10k. brown 30 10

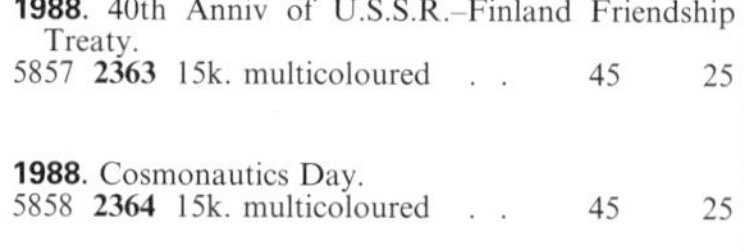

2363 Palace of Congresses, Moscow, Finlandia Hall, Helsinki, and National Flags

2364 "Mir"–"Soyuz TM" Space Complex and "Progress" Spacecraft

1988. 40th Anniv of U.S.S.R.–Finland Friendship Treaty.
5857 **2363** 15k. multicoloured . . 45 25

1988. Cosmonautics Day.
5858 **2364** 15k. multicoloured . . 45 25

2365 Sochi

1988. 150th Anniv of Sochi.
5859 **2365** 5k. multicoloured . . . 25 10

2366 "Victory" (P. A. Krivonogov)

1988. V. E. Day.
5860 **2366** 5k. multicoloured . . . 15 10

2367 Lenin Museum, Moscow

1988. 118th Birth Anniv of Lenin. Designs showing branches of Lenin Central Museum.
5861 **2367** 5k. brown, deep brown and gold 15 10
5862 – 5k. red, purple and gold 15 10
5863 – 5k. ochre, brown & gold 15 10
5864 – 5k. yellow, green & gold 15 10
DESIGNS: No. 5862, Kiev; 5863, Leningrad; 5864, Krasnoyarsk.
See also Nos. 5990/2 and 6131/3.

2368 Akulov

2369 Soviet Display Emblem

1988. Birth Centenary of Ivan Alekseevich Akulov (Communist Party official).
5865 **2368** 5k. blue 15 10

1988. "Expo 88" World's Fair, Brisbane.
5866 **2369** 20k. multicoloured . . 60 30

2370 Marx

2373 Shvernik

2371 Soldiers and Workers

1988. 170th Birth Anniv of Karl Marx.
5867 **2370** 5k. brown 15 10

1988. Perestroika (Reformation).
5868 **2371** 5k. multicoloured . . . 15 10
5869 – 5k. brown, red & orange 15 10
DESIGN: No. 5869, Banner, industrial scenes and worker.

1988. Birth Centenary of Nikolai Mikhailovich Shvernik (politician).
5871 **2373** 5k. black 15 10

2374 Russian Borzoi

1988. Hunting Dogs. Multicoloured.
5872 5k. Type **2374** 20 10
5873 10k. Kirgiz borzoi 30 25
5874 15k. Russian hound 45 25
5875 20k. Russian spaniel 60 30
5876 35k. East Siberian husky . . 1·25 50

2375 Flags, Spassky Tower and Handshake

2376 Kuibyshev

1988. Soviet–American Summit, Moscow.
5877 **2375** 5k. multicoloured . . . 15 10

1988. Birth Centenary of Valerian Vladimirovich Kuibyshev (politician).
5878 **2376** 5k. brown 15 10

2377 Flags, "Mir" Space Station and "Soyuz TM" Spacecraft

2378 Crowd and Peace Banners

1988. Soviet–Bulgarian Space Flight.
5879 **2377** 15k. multicoloured . . 50 25

1988. "For a Nuclear-free World".
5880 **2378** 5k. multicoloured . . . 15 10

2379 Red Flag, Hammer and Sickle and Laurel Branch

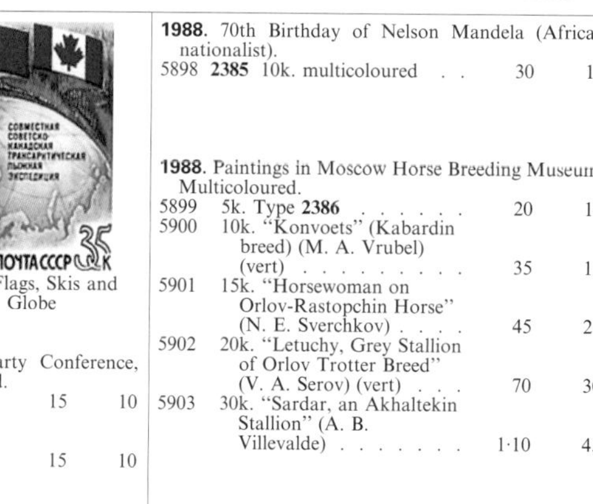

2380 Flags, Skis and Globe

1988. 19th Soviet Communist Party Conference, Moscow (1st issue). Multicoloured.
5881 5k. Type **2379** 15 10
5882 5k. Lenin on red flag and interior of Palace of Congresses (35 × 23 mm) 15 10
See also Nos. 5960/2.

1988. Soviet–Canadian Transarctic Ski Expedition.
5884 **2380** 35k. multicoloured . . 1·25 50

2381 Hurdling

2382 Giant Bellflower

1988. Olympic Games, Seoul. Multicoloured.
5885 5k. Type **2381** 20 10
5886 10k. Long jumping 30 15
5887 15k. Basketball 45 25
5888 20k. Gymnastics 60 30
5889 30k. Swimming 95 45

1988. Deciduous Forest Flowers. Multicoloured.
5891 5k. Type **2382** 20 10
5892 10k. Spring pea (horiz) . . . 30 15
5893 15k. Lungwort 45 25
5894 20k. Turk's cap lily 60 30
5895 35k. "Ficaria verna" . . . . 1·40 50

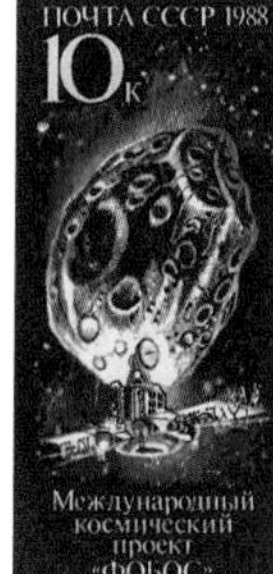

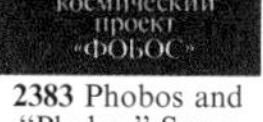

2383 Phobos and "Phobos" Space Probe

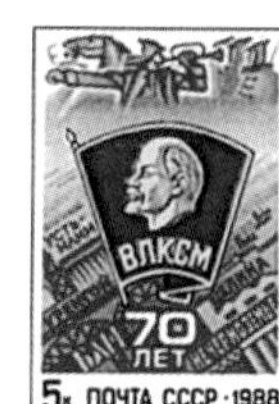

2384 Komsomol Badge

1988. Phobos (Mars Moon) International Space Project.
5896 **2383** 10k. multicoloured . . 30 15

1988. 70th Anniv of Leninist Young Communist League (Komsomol).
5897 **2384** 5k. multicoloured . . . 15 10

2385 Mandela

Филвыставка. Москва
(2387)

2386 "Obeyan Serebryanyi, Light Grey Arab Stallion" (N. E. Sverchkov)

1988. 70th Birthday of Nelson Mandela (African nationalist).
5898 **2385** 10k. multicoloured . . 30 15

1988. Paintings in Moscow Horse Breeding Museum. Multicoloured.
5899 5k. Type **2386** 20 10
5900 10k. "Konvoets" (Kabardin breed) (M. A. Vrubel) (vert) 35 15
5901 15k. "Horsewoman on Orlov-Rastopchin Horse" (N. E. Sverchkov) 45 25
5902 20k. "Letuchy, Grey Stallion of Orlov Trotter Breed" (V. A. Serov) (vert) . . . 70 30
5903 30k. "Sardar, an Akhaltekin Stallion" (A. B. Villevalde) . . . . 1·10 45

1988. Stamp Exhibition, Moscow. No. 5897 optd with T **2387**.
5904 **2384** 5k. multicoloured . . . 20 10

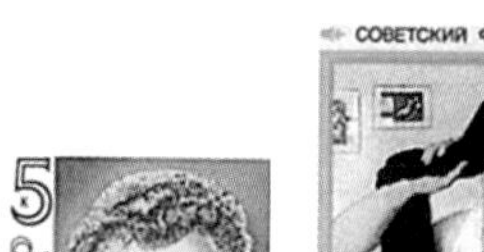

2388 Voikov

2389 "Portrait of O. K. Lansere" (Z. E. Serebryakova)

1988. Birth Centenary of Pyotr Lazarevich Voikov (diplomat).
5905 **2388** 5k. black 15 10

1988. Soviet Culture Fund. Multicoloured.
5906 10k.+5k. Type **2389** 45 25
5907 15k.+7k. "Boyarynya (noblewoman) looking at Embroidery Design" (K. V. Lebedev) (horiz) 65 35
5908 30k.+15k. "Talent" (N. P. Bogdanov-Belsky) . . . . 1·40 70

2390 Envelopes and U.P.U. Emblem

2391 "Mir" Space Station and "Soyuz-TM" Spacecraft

1988. International Correspondence Week.
5910 **2390** 5k. turquoise, blue & black 15 10

1988. Soviet–Afghan Space Flight.
5911 **2391** 15k. green, red and black 55 25

2392 Emblem and Open Book

2393 Kviring

1988. 30th Anniv of "Problems of Peace and Socialism" (magazine).
5912 **2392** 10k. multicoloured . . 30 15

1988. Birth Centenary of Emmanuil Ionovich Kviring (politician).
5913 **2393** 5k. black 15 10

2394 "Ilya Muromets" (Russia) (R. Smirnov)

2395 "Appeal of the Leader" (detail, I. M. Toidze)

1988. Epic Poems of Soviet Union (1st series). Illustrations by artists named. Multicoloured.

5914 10k. Type **2394** 30 15
5915 10k. "Cossack Golota" (Ukraine) (M. Deregus) (horiz) 30 15
5916 10k. "Musician-Magician" (Byelorussia) (N. Poplavskaya) 30 15
5917 10k. "Koblandy Batyr" (Kazakhstan) (I. Isabaev) (horiz) 30 15
5918 10k. "Alpamysh" (Uzbekistan) (R. Khalilov) 30 15

See also Nos. 6017/21 and 6139/43.

1988. 71st Anniv of October Revolution.

5919 **2395** 5k. multicoloured . . . 15 10

2396 Bolotov

2397 Tupolev

1988. 250th Birth Anniv of Andrei Timofeevich Bolotov (agriculturalist).

5920 **2396** 10k. brown 30 15

1988. Birth Centenary of Academician Andrei Nikolaevich Tupolev (aircraft designer).

5921 **2397** 10k. blue 30 15

2398 Bear

2399 "Sibir" (atomic ice-breaker)

1988. Zoo Relief Fund. Multicoloured.

5922 10k.+5k. Type **2398** 45 25
5923 10k.+5k. Wolf 45 25
5924 10k.+10k. Fox 95 45
5925 20k.+10k. Wild boar . . . 95 45
5926 20k.+10k. Lynx 95 45

1988. Soviet Arctic Expedition.

5927 **2399** 20k. multicoloured . . 90 60

2400 Ustinov

2401 National Initials

1988. 80th Birth Anniv of Marshal Dmitri Fyodorovich Ustinov.

5928 **2400** 5k. brown 15 10

1988. 10th Anniv of U.S.S.R.–Vietnam Friendship Treaty.

5929 **2401** 10k. multicoloured . . 30 15

2402 Building Facade

1988. 50th Anniv of State House of Broadcasting and Sound Recording.

5930 **2402** 10k. multicoloured . . 30 15

2403 Emblem

1988. 40th Anniv of Declaration of Human Rights.

5931 **2403** 10k. multicoloured . . 30 15

2404 Life Guard of Preobrazhensky Regt. with Peter I's New Year Decree

1988. New Year.

5932 **2404** 5k. multicoloured . . . 15 10

2405 Flags and Cosmonauts

1988. Soviet–French Space Flight.

5933 **2405** 15k. multicoloured . . 55 25

2406 "Skating Rink" (Olya Krutova)

2407 Lacis

1988. Lenin Soviet Children's Fund. Children's Paintings. Multicoloured.

5934 5k.+2k. Type **2406** 25 15
5935 5k.+2k. "Cock" (Nasta Shcheglova) 25 15
5936 5k.+2k. "May is flying over the Meadows, May is flying over the Fields" (Larisa Gaidash) 25 15

1988. Birth Cent of Martins Lacis (revolutionary).

5937 **2407** 5k. green 15 10

(**2408**)

2410 Post Messenger

1988. "Space Post". No. 4682 optd with T **2408**.

5938 1r. blue . . . . 5·50 3·50

1988.

6072 **2410** 1k. brown 10 10
6073 – 2k. brown 10 10
6074 – 3k. green 10 10
6075 – 4k. blue 10 10
6076 – 5k. red 15 10
6077a – 7k. blue 20 10
6078 – 10k. brown 35 15
6079 – 12k. purple 40 20
6080 – 13k. violet 50 20
6081 – 15k. blue 50 25
6082 – 20k. brown 70 25
6083 – 25k. green 85 35
6084 – 30k. blue 80 60
6085 – 35k. brown . . . . . 1·00 50
6086 – 50k. blue . . . . . . 1·25 95
6087 – 1r. blue . . . . . . 3·50 1·40

DESIGNS: 2k. Old mail transport (sailing packet, steam train and mail coach); 3k. "Aurora" (cruiser); 4k. Spassky Tower and Lenin's Tomb, Red Square, Moscow; 5k. State emblem and flag; 7k. Modern mail transport (Ilyushin Il-86 jetliner, Mil Mi-2 helicopter, "Aleksandr Pushkin" (liner), train and mail van); 10k. "The Worker and the Collective Farmer" (statue, Vera Mukhina); 12k. Rocket on launch pad; 13k. Satellite; 15k. "Orbit" dish aerial; 20k. Symbols of art and literature; 25k. "The Discus-thrower" (5th-century Greek statue by Miron); 30k. Map of Antarctica and emperor penguins; 35k. "Mercury" (statue, Giovanni da Bologna); 50k. Great white cranes; 1r. Universal Postal Union emblem.

2411 Great Cascade and Samson Fountain

2412 1st-cent B.C. Gold Coin of Tigran the Great

1988. Petrodvorets Fountains. Each green and grey.

5952 5k. Type **2411** 20 10
5953 10k. Adam fountain (D. Bonazza) 30 15
5954 15k. Golden Mountain cascade (Niccolo Michetti and Mikhail Zemtsov) . . 50 25
5955 30k. Roman fountains (Bartolomeo Rastrelli) . . 1·00 45
5965 50k. Oaklet trick fountain (Rastrelli) . . . . 1·60 1·00

1988. Armenian Earthquake Relief. Armenian History. Multicoloured.

5957 20k.+10k. Type **2412** . . . 95 45
5958 30k.+15k. Rispsime Church 1·25 65
5959 50k.+25k. "Madonna and Child" (18th-century fresco, Ovnat Ovnatanyan) . . . . . . 2·25 1·25

2413 Hammer and Sickle

1988. 19th Soviet Communist Party Conference, Moscow (2nd issue). Multicoloured.

5960 5k. Type **2413** 15 10
5961 5k. Hammer and sickle and building girders 15 10
5962 5k. Hammer and sickle and wheat 15 10

2415 "Vostok" Rocket, "Lunar 1", Earth and Moon

2416 Virtanen

1989. 30th Anniv of First Russian Moon Flight.

5964 **2415** 15k. multicoloured . . 35 25

1989. Birth Centenary of Jalmari Virtanen (poet).

5965 **2416** 5k. brown and bistre 15 10

2417 Headquarters Building, Moscow

1989. 40th Anniv of Council for Mutual Economic Aid.

5966 **2417** 10k. multicoloured . . 30 15

2418 Forest Protection

2419 18th-century Samovar

1989. Nature Conservation. Multicoloured.

5967 5k. Type **2418** 50 20
5968 10k. Arctic preservation . . 35 15
5969 15k. Anti-desertification campaign 50 20

1989. Russian Samovars in State Museum, Leningrad. Multicoloured.

5970 5k. Type **2419** 20 10
5971 10k. 19th-century barrel samovar by Ivan Lisitsin of Tula 30 15
5972 20k. 1830s Kabachok travelling samovar by Sokolov Brothers factory, Tula 55 30
5973 30k. 1840s samovar by Nikolai Malikov factory, Tula 85 45

2420 Mussorgsky (after Repin) and Scene from "Boris Godunov"

2421 Dybenko

1989. 150th Birth Anniv of Modest Petrovich Mussorgsky (composer).

5974 **2420** 10k. purple and brown 30 15

1989. Birth Centenary of Pavel Dybenko (military leader).

5975 **2421** 5k. black 15 10

2422 Shevchenko

2423 "Lilium speciosum"

1989. 175th Birth Anniv of Taras Shevchenko (Ukrainian poet and painter).

5976 **2422** 5k. brown, green & black 15 10

1989. Lilies. Multicoloured.

5977 5k. Type **2423** 20 10
5978 10k. "African Queen" . . . 35 15
5979 15k. "Eclat du Soir" 45 20
5980 30k. "White Tiger" . . . . 1·10 45

2424 Marten

1989. Zoo Relief Fund. Multicoloured.

5981 10k.+5k. Type **2424** 45 20
5982 10k.+5k. Squirrel 45 20
5983 20k.+10k. Hare . . . . . . 1·00 45
5984 20k.+10k. Hedgehog . . . . 1·00 45
5985 20k.+10k. Badger . . . . . 1·00 45

2426 "Victory Banner" (P. Loginov and V. Pamfilov)

1989. Victory Day.

5987 **2426** 5k. multicoloured . . . 15 10

2427 "Mir" Space Station

1989. Cosmonautics Day.

5988 **2427** 15k. multicoloured . . 45 20

2428 Emblem and Flags **2430** Statue

1989. U.S.–Soviet Bering Bridge Expedition.
5989 **2428** 10k. multicoloured . . 35 15

1989. 119th Birth Anniv of Lenin. As T **2367**. Branches of Lenin Central Museum.
5990 5k. brown, ochre and gold 15 10
5991 5k. deep brown, brn & gold 15 10
5992 5k. multicoloured 15 10
DESIGNS: No. 5990, Frunze; 5991, Kazan; 5992, Kuibyshev.

1989. 70th Anniv of First Hungarian Soviet Republic.
5994 **2430** 5k. multicoloured . . . 15 10

2431 "Motherland Statue" **2432** Drone

1989. 400th Anniv of Volgograd (formerly Tsaritsyn).
5995 **2431** 5k. multicoloured . . . 15 10

1989. Honey Bees. Multicoloured.
5996 5k. Type **2432** 20 10
5997 10k. Bees, flowers and hive 30 15
5998 20k. Bee on flower 60 30
5999 35k. Feeding queen bee . . 1·25 45

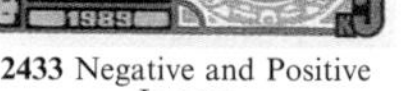

2433 Negative and Positive Images **2434** Map above Dove as Galley

1989. 150th Anniv of Photography.
6000 **2433** 5k. multicoloured . . . 15 10

1989. "Europe—Our Common Home". Mult.
6001 5k. Type **2434** 20 10
6002 10k. Laying foundations of Peace 30 15
6003 15k. White storks' nest . . . 65 55

2435 Mukhina modelling "God of Northern Wind" (after M. Nesterov) **2436** Racine

1989. Birth Centenary of Vera Mukhina (sculptress).
6004 **2435** 5k. blue 15 10

1989. 150th Birth Anniv of Jean Racine (dramatist).
6005 **2436** 15k. multicoloured . . 45 20

2437 Rabbit

1989. Lenin Soviet Children's Fund. Children's Paintings. Multicoloured.
6006 5k.+2k. Type **2437** 20 10
6007 5k.+2k. Cat 20 10
6008 5k.+2k. Nurse 20 10
See also Nos. 6162/4.

2438 Kuratov

1989. 150th Birth Anniv of Ivan Kuratov (writer).
6009 **2438** 5k. deep brown & brown 15 10

2439 Emblem **2440** Common Shelduck

1989. 13th World Youth and Students' Festival, Pyongyang.
6010 **2439** 10k. multicoloured . . 30 15

1989. Ducks (1st series). Multicoloured.
6011 5k. Type **2440** 15 10
6012 15k. Green-winged teal . . . 40 30
6013 20k. Ruddy shelduck . . . 55 35
See also Nos. 6159/61 and 6264/6.

2441 "Storming of Bastille" (Gelman after Monnet)

1989. Bicentenary of French Revolution.
6014 **2441** 5k. multicoloured . . . 20 10
6015 – 15k. blue, black and red 45 20
6016 – 20k. blue, black and red 60 25
DESIGNS: 15k. Jean-Paul Marat, Georges Danton and Maximilien Robespierre; 20k. "Marseillaise" (relief by F. Rude from Arc de Triomphe).

1989. Epic Poems of Soviet Union (2nd series). Illustrations by named artists. As T **2394**. Mult.
6017 10k. "Amirani" (Georgia) (V. Oniani) 35 15
6018 10k. "Koroglu" (Azerbaijan) (A. Gadzhiev) 35 15
6019 10k. "Fir, Queen of Grass Snakes" (Lithuania) (A. Makunaite) 35 15
6020 10k. "Mioritsa" (Moldavia) (I. Bogdesko) 35 15
6021 10k. "Lachplesis" (Lettish) (G. Wilks) 35 15

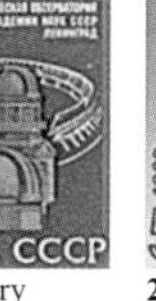

2442 Observatory **2443** Hemispheres, Roses in Envelope and Posthorn

1989. 150th Anniv of Pulkovo Observatory.
6022 **2442** 10k. multicoloured . . 30 15

1989. International Letter Week.
6023 **2443** 5k. multicoloured . . . 15 10

2444 Lynx **2446** Buildings, Container Ship and Bicentenary Emblem

1989. 50th Anniv of Tallin Zoo.
6024 **2444** 10k. multicoloured . . 30 15

1989. Bicentenary of Nikolaev.
6026 **2446** 5k. multicoloured . . . 20 10

2447 Nkrumah **2448** 1921 40r. Stamp

1989. 80th Birth Anniv of Kwame Nkrumah (first Prime Minister and President of Ghana).
6027 **2447** 10k. multicoloured . . 30 15

1989. 6th All-Union Philatelic Society Congress, Moscow.
6028 **2448** 10k. multicoloured . . 35 15

2449 Cooper

1989. Birth Bicentenary of James Fenimore Cooper (writer) (1st issue).
6029 **2449** 15k. multicoloured . . 45 20
See also Nos. 6055/9.

2450 V. L. Durov (trainer) and Sealions

1989. 70th Anniv of Soviet Circus. Multicoloured.
6030 1k. Type **2450** 10 10
6031 3k. M. N. Rumyantsev (clown "Karandash") with donkey 10 10
6032 4k. V. I. Filatov (founder of Bear Circus) and bears on motor cycles 15 10
6033 5k. E. T. Kio (illusionist) and act 25 10
6034 10k. V. E. Lazarenko (clown and acrobat) and act . . 45 20

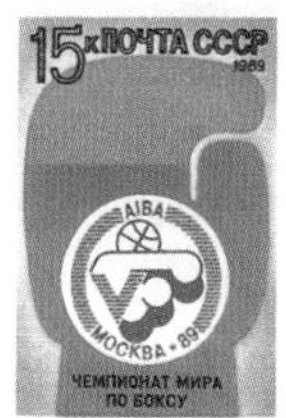

2451 Emblem on Glove **2452** Li Dazhao

1989. International Amateur Boxing Association Championship, Moscow.
6036 **2451** 15k. multicoloured . . 45 20

1989. Birth Centenary of Li Dazhao (co-founder of Chinese Communist Party).
6037 **2452** 5k. brown, stone & black 20 10

2453 Khetagurov

1989. 130th Birth Anniv of Kosta Khetagurov (Ossetian writer).
6038 **2453** 5k. brown 15 10

2454 "October Guardsmen" (M. M. Chepik)

1989. 72nd Anniv of October Revolution.
6039 **2454** 5k. multicoloured . . . 15 10

2455 Russian Spoons, Psaltery, Balalaika, Zhaleika and Accordion

1989. Traditional Musical Instruments (1st series). Multicoloured.
6040 10k. Type **2455** 35 15
6041 10k. Ukrainian bandura, trembita, drymba, svyril (pipes) and dulcimer . . . 35 15
6042 10k. Byelorussian tambourine, bastlya (fiddle), lera and dudka (pipe) 35 15
6043 10k. Uzbek nagors (drums), rubab, zang, karnai and gidzhak 35 15
See also Nos. 6183/6 and 6303/5.

2456 "Demonstration of First Radio Receiver, 1895" (N. A. Sysoev) **2457** National Flag and Provincial Arms

1989. 130th Birth Anniv of Aleksandr Stepanovich Popov (radio pioneer).
6044 **2456** 10k. multicoloured . . 30 15

1989. 40th Anniv of German Democratic Republic.
6045 **2457** 5k. multicoloured . . . 15 10

2458 Polish National Colours forming "45" **2459** Kosior

1989. 45th Anniv of Liberation of Poland.
6046 **2458** 5k. multicoloured . . . 15 10

1989. Birth Centenary of Stanislav Vikentievich Kosior (vice-chairman of Council of People's Commissars).
6047 **2459** 5k. black 15 10

2460 Nehru **2461** "Village Market" (A. V. Makovsky)

1989. Birth Centenary of Jawaharlal Nehru (Indian statesman).
6048 **2460** 15k. brown 45 20

1989. Soviet Culture Fund. Multicoloured.
6049 4k.+2k. Type **2461** 20 10
6050 5k.+2k. "Lady in Hat" (E. L. Zelenin) 25 15
6051 10k.+5k. "Portrait of the Actress Bazhenova" (A. F. Sofronova) 50 20
6052 20k.+10k. "Two Women" (Hugo Shaiber) 85 65
6053 30k.+15k. 19th-century teapot and plates from Popov porcelain works . . 1·50 85

2462 Berzin — **2463** "The Hunter"

1989. Birth Centenary of Yan Karlovich Berzin (head of Red Army Intelligence).
6054 **2462** 5k. black 15 10

1989. Birth Bicentenary of James Fenimore Cooper (writer) (2nd issue). Illustrations of his novels. Multicoloured.
6055 20k. Type **2463** 60 30
6056 20k. "Last of the Mohicans" 60 30
6057 20k. "The Pathfinder" . . . 60 30
6058 20k. "The Pioneers" . . . 60 30
6059 20k. "The Prairie" 60 30
Nos. 6055/9 were printed together, se-tenant, forming a composite design.

2464 St. Basil's Cathedral and Minin and Pozharsky Statue, Moscow — **2465** Dymkovo Toy

1989. Historical Monuments (1st series). Mult.
6060 15k. Type **2464** 45 25
6061 15k. Sts. Peter and Paul Cathedral and statue of Peter I. Leningrad 45 25
6062 15k. St. Sophia's Cathedral and statue of Bogdan Chmielnitsky, Kiev . . . 45 25
6063 15k. Khodzha Ahmed Yasavi mausoleum, Turkestan 45 25
6064 15k. Khazret Khyzr Mosque, Samarkand . . . 45 25
See also Nos. 6165/72 and 6231/3.

1989. New Year.
6065 **2465** 5k. multicoloured . . . 15 10

2466 Soviet Lunar Vehicle — **2468** Acid Rain destroying Rose

1989. "Expo 89" International Stamp Exhibition, Washington D.C. Multicoloured.
6066 25k. Type **2466** 90 45
6067 25k. Astronaut and landing module on Moon 90 45
6068 25k. Cosmonauts on Mars 90 45
6069 25k. Flag and shield on Mars 90 45

1989. Russian Naval Commanders (2nd series). As T **2345**.
6091 5k. blue and brown 10 15
6092 10k. blue and brown 25 15
6093 15k. blue and deep blue . . 40 20
6094 20k. blue and deep blue . . 55 25
6095 30k. blue and brown 90 60
6096 35k. blue and brown . . . 1·40 65
DESIGNS: 5k. V. A. Kornilov and "Vladimer" (steam frigate) and "Pervaz-Bakhric" (Turkish) steam frigate); 10k. V. I. Istomin and "Parizh"; 15k. G. I. Nevelskoi and "Baikal"; 20k. G. I. Butakov and iron-clad squadron; 30k. A. A. Popov, "Pyotr Veliky" and "Vitze Admirial Popov"; 35k. S. O. Makarov, "Intibah" (Turkish warship) and "Veliky Khyaz Konstantin".

1990. Nature Conservation. Multicoloured.
6097 10k. Type **2468** 30 15
6098 15k. Oil-smeared great black-headed gull perching on globe 40 30
6099 20k. Blade sawing down tree 65 25

2469 Ladya Monument and Golden Gates, Kiev (Ukraine) — **2470** Flag and Hanoi Monument

1990. Republic Capitals. Multicoloured.
6100 5k. Lenin Palace of Culture, Government House and Academy of Sciences, Alma-Ata (Kazakhstan) 15 10
6101 5k. Library, Mollanepes Theatre and War Heroes Monument, Ashkhabad (Turkmenistan) 15 10
6102 5k. Maiden's Tower and Divan-Khane Palace, Baku (Azerbaijan) 15 10
6103 5k. Sadriddin Aini Theatre and Avicenna Monument, Dushanbe (Tadzhikistan) 15 10
6104 5k. Spendyarov Theatre and David Sasunsky Monument, Yerevan (Armenia) 15 10
6105 5k. Satylganov Philharmonic Society building and Manas Memorial, Frunze (Kirgizia) 15 10
6106 5k. Type **2469** 15 10
6107 5k. Cathedral and Victory Arch, Kishinev (Moldavia) 15 10
6108 5k. Government House and Liberation Monument, Minsk (Byelorussia) . . . 15 10
6109 5k. Konstantino-Yeleninsky Tower and Ivan the Great Bell Tower, Moscow (Russian Federation) . . 15 10
6110 5k. Cathedral, "Three Brothers" building and Freedom Monument, Riga (Latvia) 15 10
6111 5k. Herman the Long, Oliviste Church, Cathedral and Town hall towers and wall turret, Tallin (Estonia) 15 10
6112 5k. Kukeldash Medrese and University, Tashkent (Uzbekistan) 15 10
6113 5k. Metekh Temple and Vakhtang Gorgasal Monument, Tbilisi (Georgia) 15 10
6114 5k. Gediminas Tower and St. Anne's Church, Vilnius (Lithuania) . . . 15 10

1990. 60th Anniv of Vietnamese Communist Party.
6115 **2470** 5k. multicoloured . . . 15 10

2471 Ho Chi Minh — **2472** Snowy Owl

1990. Birth Cent of Ho Chi Minh (Vietnamese leader).
6116 **2471** 10k. brown and black 30 15

1990. Owls. Multicoloured.
6117 10k. Type **2472** 20 15
6118 20k. Eagle owl (vert) . . . 35 25
6119 55k. Long-eared owl . . . . 1·00 60

2473 Paddle-steamer, Posthorn and Penny Black

1990. 150th Anniv of the Penny Black.
6120 **2473** 10k. multicoloured . . 30 15
6121 – 20k. black and gold . . 55 25
6122 – 20k. black and gold . . 55 25
6123 – 35k. multicoloured . . 1·25 65
6124 – 35k. multicoloured . . 1·25 65
DESIGNS: No. 6121, Anniversary emblem and Penny Black (lettered "T P"); 6122, As No. 6121 but stamp lettered "T F"; 6123, "Stamp World London 90" International Stamp Exhibition emblem and Penny Black (lettered "V K"); 6124, As No. 6123 but stamp lettered "A H".

2474 Electric Cables

1990. 125th Anniv of I.T.U.
6126 **2474** 20k. multicoloured . . 55 30

2475 Flowers

1990. Labour Day.
6127 **2475** 5k. multicoloured . . . 15 10

2476 "Victory, 1945" (A. Lysenko)

1990. 45th Anniv of Victory in Second World War.
6128 **2476** 5k. multicoloured . . . 15 10

2477 "Mir" Space Complex and Cosmonaut — **2478** Lenin

1990. Cosmonautics Day.
6129 **2477** 20k. multicoloured . . 45 25

1990. "Leniniana '90" All-Union Stamp Exhibition.
6130 **2478** 5k. brown 15 10

1990. 120th Birth Anniv of Lenin. Branches of Lenin Central Museum. As T **2367**.
6131 5k. red, lake and gold . . . 15 10
6132 5k. pink, purple and gold 15 10
6133 5k. multicoloured 15 10
DESIGNS: No. 6131, Ulyanovsk; 6132, Baku; 6133, Tashkent.

2479 Scene from "Iolanta" (opera) and Tchaikovsky

1990. 150th Birth Anniv of Pyotr Ilich Tchaikovsky (composer).
6134 **2479** 15k. black 60 30

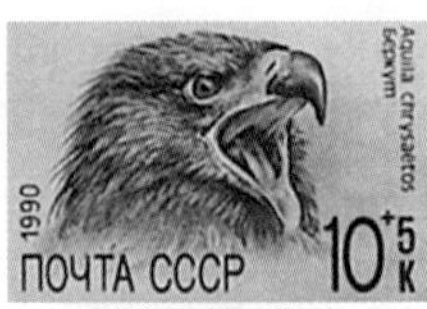

2480 Golden Eagle

1990. Zoo Relief Fund. Multicoloured.
6135 10k.+5k. Type **2480** 35 25
6136 20k.+10k. Saker falcon ("Falco cherrug") 70 65
6137 20k.+10k. Common raven ("Corvus corax") 70 65

2481 Etching by G. A. Echeistov — **2482** Goalkeeper and Players

1990. 550th Anniv of "Dzhangar" (Kalmuk folk epic).
6138 **2481** 10k. ochre, brown & black 30 15

1990. Epic Poems of Soviet Union (3rd series). Illustrations by named artists. As T **2394**. Mult.
6139 10k. "Manas" (Kirgizia) (T. Gertsen) (horiz) . . . 30 15
6140 10k. "Gurugli" (Tadzhikistan) (I. Martynov) (horiz) . . 30 15
6141 10k. "David Sasunsky" (Armenia) (M. Abegyan) 30 15
6142 10k. "Gerogly" (Turkmenistan) (I. Klychev) 30 15
6143 10k. "Kalevipoeg" (Estonia) (O. Kallis) 30 15

1990. World Cup Football Championship, Italy. Multicoloured.
6144 5k. Type **2482** 15 10
6145 10k. Players 35 15
6146 15k. Attempted tackle . . . 50 20
6147 25k. Referee and players . . 50 30
6148 35k. Goalkeeper saving ball 1·25 65

2483 Globe and Finlandia Hall, Helsinki — **2484** Competitors and Target

1990. 15th Anniv of European Security and Co-operation Conference, Helsinki.
6149 **2483** 15k. multicoloured . .

1990. 45th World Shooting Championships, Moscow.
6150 **2484** 15k. multicoloured . . 45 20

2485 Glaciology Research

1990. Soviet–Australian Scientific Co-operation in Antarctica. Multicoloured.
6151 5k. Type **2485** 15 10
6152 50k. Krill (marine biology research) . . . . 1·50 90

2486 Emblem and Sports Pictograms

1990. Goodwill Games, Seattle.
6154 **2486** 10k. multicoloured . . 35 15

2488 Greylag Geese

1990. Poultry. Multicoloured.
6156 5k. Type **2488** 10 10
6157 10k. Adlers (chickens) . . . 35 15
6158 15k. Common turkeys . . . 40 40

2489 Mallards

1990. Ducks (2nd series). Multicoloured.
6159 5k. Type **2489** 10 10
6160 15k. Common goldeneyes 40 40
6161 20k. Red-crested pochards 50 50

1990. Lenin Soviet Children's Fund. Children's Paintings. As T **2437**. Multicoloured.
6162 5k.+2k. Clown 20 10
6163 5k.+2k. Ladies in crinolines 20 10
6164 5k.+2k. Children with banner 20 10

1990. Historical Monuments (2nd series). As T **2464**. Multicoloured.
6165 15k. St. Nshan's Church, Akhpat (Armenia) 45 20
6166 15k. Shirvanshah Palace, Baku (Azerbaijan) 45 20
6167 15k. Soroki Fortress and statue of Stefan III, Kishinev (Moldavia) . . . 45 20
6168 15k. Spaso-Efrosinevsky Cathedral, Polotsk (Byelorussia) 45 20
6169 15k. St. Peter's Church and 16th-century Riga (Latvia) 45 20
6170 15k. St. Nicholas's Church and carving of city arms, Tallin (Estonia) 45 20
6171 15k. Mtatsminda Pantheon and statue of Nikoloz Baratashvili, Tbilisi (Georgia) 45 20
6172 15k. Cathedral and bell tower, Vilnius (Lithuania) 45 20

2490 Sordes

1990. Prehistoric Animals. Multicoloured.
6173 1k. Type **2490** 10 10
6174 3k. Chalicotherium (vert) . . 10 10
6175 5k. Indricotherium (vert) . . 15 10
6176 10k. Saurolophus (vert) . . 25 15
6177 20k. Cephalaspid ostracoderm 65 30

2491 "St. Basil's Cathedral and Kremlin, Moscow" (Sanjay Adhikari)

2492 Pigeon Post

1990. Indo-Soviet Friendship. Children's Paintings. Multicoloured.
6178 10k. Type **2491** 30 10
6179 10k. "Life in India" (Tanya Vorontsova) 30 10

1990. Letter Writing Week.
6180 **2492** 5k. blue 15 10

2493 Traffic on Urban Roads

2495 Killer Whales

1990. Traffic Safety Week.
6181 **2493** 5k. multicoloured . . . 25 10

1990. Traditional Musical Instruments (2nd series). As T **2455**. Multicoloured.
6183 10k. Azerbaijani balalian, shar and caz (stringed instruments), zurna and drum 40 15
6184 10k. Georgian bagpipes, tambourine, flute, pipes and chonguri (stringed instrument) 40 15
6185 10k. Kazakh flute, rattle, daubra and kobyz (stringed instruments) . . 40 15
6186 10k. Lithuanian bagpipes, horns and kankles 40 15

1990. Marine Mammals.
6187 25k. Type **2495** 75 40
6188 25k. Northern sealions . . . 75 40
6189 25k. Sea otter 75 40
6190 25k. Common dolphin . . . 75 40

2496 "Lenin among Delegates to Second Congress of Soviets" (S. V. Gerasimov)

2497 Ivan Bunin (1933)

1990. 73rd Anniv of October Revolution.
6191 **2496** 5k. multicoloured . . . 15 10

1990. Nobel Prize Winners for Literature.
6192 **2497** 15k. brown 45 20
6193 – 15k. brown 45 20
6194 – 15k. black 45 20
DESIGNS: No. 6193, Mikhail Sholokhov (1965); 6194, Boris Pasternak.

2498 "Sever 2"

1990. Research Submarines. Multicoloured.
6195 5k. Type **2498** 15 10
6196 10k. "Tinro 2" 30 15
6197 15k. "Argus" 50 20
6198 25k. "Paisis" 75 30
6199 35k. "Mir" . . . . 1·10 65

2499 "Motherland" Statue (E. Kocher), Screen and Emblem

Филателистическая выставка „Армения-90“ (**2500**)

Восстановление, милосердие, помощь (**2501**)

1990. "Armenia '90" Stamp Exhibition, Yerevan. (a) Type **2499**.
6200 **2499** 10k. multicoloured . . 30 15
(b) Nos. 5957/9 optd with T **2500** (20k.) or as T **2501**.
6201 **2412** 20k.+10k. mult 75 40
6202 – 30k.+15k. mult . . . . 1·10 70
6203 – 50k.+25k. mult . . . . 2·00 1·10

2502 S. A. Vaupshasov

2503 Soviet and Japanese Flags above Earth

1990. Intelligence Agents.
6204 **2502** 5k. dp grn, grn and blk 20 10
6205 – 5k. dp brn, brn and blk 20 10
6206 – 5k. deep blue, blue and black 20 10
6207 – 5k. brown, buff & black 20 10
6208 – 5k. brown, bistre and black 20 10
DESIGNS: No. 6205, R. I. Abel; 6206, Kim Philby; 6207, I. D. Kudrya; 6208, Konon Molodyi (alias Gordon Lonsdale).

1990. Soviet–Japanese Space Flight.
6209 **2503** 20k. multicoloured . . . 55 25

2504 Grandfather Frost and Toys

1990. New Year.
6210 **2504** 5k. multicoloured . . . 10 10

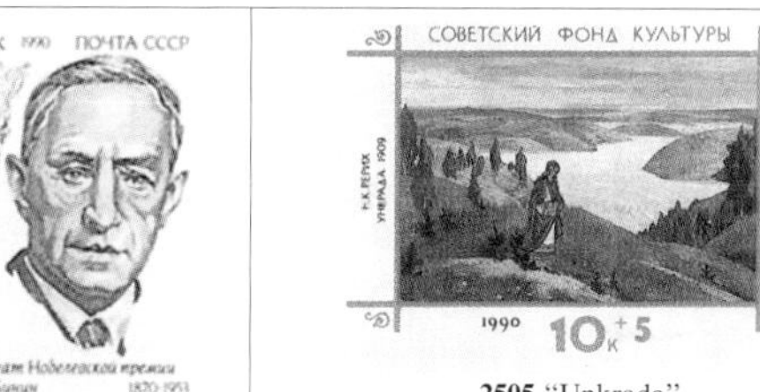

2505 "Unkrada"

1990. Soviet Culture Fund. Paintings by N. K. Rerikh. Multicoloured.
6211 10k.+5k. Type **2505** 15 10
6212 20k.+10k. "Pskovo-Pechorsky Monastery" . . 30 20

2507 Globe, Eiffel Tower and Flags

1990. "Charter for New Europe". Signing of European Conventional Arms Treaty, Paris.
6214 **2507** 30k. multicoloured . . 35 15

2508 Jellyfish

1991. Marine Animals. Multicoloured.
6215 4k. Type **2508** 10 10
6216 5k. Anemone 10 10
6217 10k. Spurdog 30 15
6218 15k. European anchovy . . 40 20
6219 20k. Bottle-nosed dolphin 45 25

2509 Keres

1991. 75th Birth Anniv of Paul Keres (chess player).
6220 **2509** 15k. brown 35 20

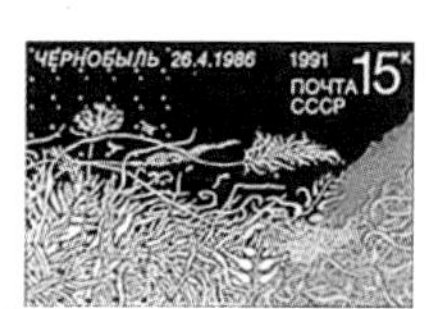

2510 Radioactive Particles killing Vegetation

1991. 5th Anniv of Chernobyl Nuclear Power Station Disaster.
6221 **2510** 15k. multicoloured . . 15 10

2511 "Sorrento Coast with View of Capri" (Shchedrin)

1991. Birth Bicentenary of Silvestr Shchedrin and 150th Birth Anniv of Arkhip Kuindzhi (painters). Multicoloured.
6222 10k. Type **2511** 15 10
6223 10k. "New Rome. View of St. Angelo's Castle" (Shchedrin) 15 10
6224 10k. "Evening in the Ukraine" (Kuindzhi) . . 15 10
6225 10k. "Birch Grove" (Kuindzhi) 15 10

2512 White Stork

1991. Zoo Relief Fund.
6226 **2512** 10k.+5k. mult 50 50

2513 Sturgeon and Bell Tower, Volga

1991. Environmental Protection. Multicoloured.
6227 10k. Type **2513** 20 10
6228 15k. Sable and Lake Baikal 15 10
6229 20k. Saiga and dried bed of Aral Sea 20 15

1991. Historical Monuments (3rd series). As T **2464**. Multicoloured.
6231 15k. Minaret, Uzgen, Kirgizia 15 10
6232 15k. Mohammed Bashar Mausoleum, Tadzhikistan 15 10
6233 15k. Talkhatan-baba Mosque, Turkmenistan 15 10

2515 G. Shelikhov and Kodiak, 1784

1991. 500th Anniv of Discovery of America by Columbus. Russian Settlements.
6234 **2515** 20k. blue and black . . 20 10
6235 – 30k. bistre, brown & blk 35 15
6236 – 50k. orange, brown & blk 55 20
DESIGNS: 30k. Aleksandr Baranov and Sitka, 1804; 50k. I. Kuskov and Fort Ross, California, 1812.

2516 Satellite and Liner

2517 Yuri Gagarin in Uniform

1991. 10th Anniv of United Nations Transport and Communications in Asia and the Pacific Programme.
6237 **2516** 10k. multicoloured . . 20 10

1991. Cosmonautics Day. 30th Anniv of First Man in Space. Each brown.
6238 25k. Type **2517** 15 10
6239 25k. Gagarin wearing space suit 15 10
6240 25k. Gagarin in uniform with cap 15 10
6241 25k. Gagarin in civilian dress 15 10

2519 "May 1945" (A. and S. Tkachev)

1991. Victory Day.
6244 **2519** 5k. multicoloured . . . 10 10

2520 "Lenin working on Book 'Materialism and Empirical Criticism' in Geneva Library" (P. Belousov)

1991. 121st Birth Anniv of Lenin.
6245 **2520** 5k. multicoloured . . . 10 10

2521 Prokofiev

1991. Birth Centenary of Sergei Prokofiev (composer).
6246 **2521** 15k. brown 10 10

2522 Lady's Slipper

2523 Ilya I. Mechnikov (medicine, 1908)

1991. Orchids. Multicoloured.
6247 3k. Type **2522** 10 10
6248 5k. Lady orchid 10 10
6249 10k. Bee orchid 10 10
6250 20k. Calypso 15 10
6251 25k. Marsh helleborine . . . 20 15

1991. Nobel Prize Winners. Each black.
6252 15k. Type **2523** 10 10
6253 15k. Ivan P. Pavlov (medicine, 1904) 10 10
6254 15k. A. D. Sakharov (peace, 1975) 10 10

2524 Soviet and British Flags in Space

1991. Soviet–British Space Flight.
6255 **2524** 20k. multicoloured . . 15 10

2525 Saroyan

1991. 10th Death Anniv of William Saroyan (writer).
6256 **2525** 1r. multicoloured . . . 60 30

2526 "The Universe"

1991. Lenin Soviet Children's Fund. Paintings by V. Lukyanets. Multicoloured.
6257 10k.+5k. Type **2526** 10 10
6258 10k.+5k. "Another Planet" 10 10

2527 Miniature from "Ostromirov Gospel" (first book written in Cyrillic), 1056–57

1991. Culture of Medieval Russia. Multicoloured.
6259 10k. Type **2527** 10 10
6260 15k. Page from "Russian Truth" (code of laws), 11th–13th century 15 10
6261 20k. Portrait of Sergy Radonezhsky (embroidered book cover), 1424 . . . . 20 10
6262 25k. "The Trinity" (icon, Andrei Rublev), 1411 . . 20 10
6263 30k. Illustration from "Book of the Apostles", 1564 . . 20 15

2528 Pintails

2529 Emblem

1991. Ducks (3rd series). Multicoloured.
6264 5k. Type **2528** 10 10
6265 15k. Greater scaups 20 10
6266 20k. White-headed ducks . . 25 15

1991. European Conference on Security and Co-operation Session, Moscow.
6267 **2529** 10k. multicoloured . . 10 10

2530 Patroness

2531 Woman in Traditional Costume

1991. Soviet Charity and Health Fund.
6268 **2530** 20k.+10k. mult 25 15

1991. 1st Anniv of Declaration of Ukrainian Sovereignty.
6269 **2531** 30k. multicoloured . . 25 15

2532 "Albatros"

2534 Girl with Letter

2533 "Sv. Pyotr" and Route Map

1991. Airships. Multicoloured.
6270 1k. Type **2532** 10 10
6271 3k. GA-42 . . . . 15 10
6272 4k. "Norge" (horiz) 15 10
6273 5k. "Pobeda" (horiz) . . . 15 10
6274 20k. LZ-127 "Graf Zeppelin" (horiz) 55 30

1991. 250th Anniv of Vitus Bering's and A. Chirkov's Expedition. Multicoloured.
6275 30k. Type **2533** 25 15
6276 30k. Sighting land 25 15

1991. Letter Writing Week.
6277 **2534** 7k. brown 10 10

2535 Bell and Bell Towers

2536 Kayak Race and "Santa Maria"

1991. Soviet Culture Fund.
6278 **2535** 20k.+10k. mult 20 10

The belfries depicted are from Kuliga-Drakonovo, Church of the Assumption in Pskov, Ivan the Great in Moscow and Cathedral of the Assumption in Rostov.

1991. Olympic Games, Barcelona (1992) (1st issue). Multicoloured.
6279 10k. Type **2536** 20 10
6280 20k. Running and Church of the Holy Family . . . 15 10
6281 30k. Football and stadium 25 15

See also Nos. 6362/4.

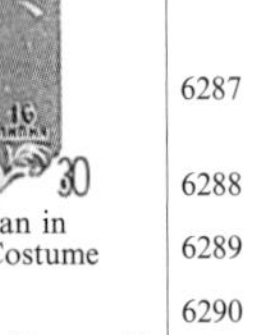
2537 Rainbow, Globe and Flags

2538 Ascension Day (Armenia)

1991. Soviet–Austrian Space Flight.
6282 **2537** 20k. multicoloured . . 15 10

1991. Folk Festivals. Multicoloured.
6283 15k. Type **2538** 15 10
6284 15k. Women carrying dishes of wheat (Novruz holiday, Azerbaijan) 15 10
6285 15k. Throwing garlands in water (Ivan Kupala summer holiday, Belorussia) 15 10
6286 15k. Stick wrestling and dancing round decorated tree (New Year, Estonia) (horiz) 15 10
6287 15k. Masked dancers (Berikaoba spring holiday, Georgia) 15 10
6288 15k. Riders with goat skin (Kazakhstan) (horiz) . . . 15 10
6289 15k. Couple on horses (Kirgizia) (horiz) 15 10
6290 15k. Couple leaping over flames (Ligo (Ivan Kupala) holiday, Latvia) (horiz) 15 10
6291 15k. Family on way to church (Palm Sunday, Lithuania) (horiz) 15 10
6292 15k. Man in beribboned hat and musicians (Plugusorul (New Year) holiday, Moldova) 15 10
6293 15k. Sledge ride (Shrovetide, Russian Federation) . . . 15 10
6294 15k. Musicians on carpet and stilt-walkers (Novruz holiday, Tajikistan) . . . 15 10
6295 15k. Wrestlers (Harvest holiday, Turkmenistan) (horiz) 15 10
6296 15k. Dancers and couple with lute and tambourine (Christmas, Ukraine) (horiz) 15 10
6297 15k. Girls with tulips (Tulip holiday, Uzbekistan) . . . 15 10

2539 Dimitry Komar

2540 Federation Government House and Flag

1991. Defeat of Attempted Coup. Multicoloured.
6298 7k. Type **2539** 10 10
6299 7k. Ilya Krichevsky 10 10
6300 7k. Vladimir Usov 10 10

Nos. 6298/6300 depict victims killed in opposing the attempted coup.

1991. Election of Boris Yeltsin as President of the Russian Federation.
6302 **2540** 7k. blue, gold and red 10 10

1991. Traditional Musical Instruments (3rd series). As T **2455**. Multicoloured.
6303 10k. Kirgiz flutes, komuzes and kyyak (string instruments) 10 10
6304 10k. Latvian ganurags and stabule (wind), tambourine, duga and kokle (string instruments) 10 10
6305 10k. Moldavian flute, bagpipes, nai (pipes), kobza and tsambal (string instruments) 10 10

2541 Decorations and Gifts

2542 Nikolai Mikhailovich Karamzin

1991. New Year.
6306 **2541** 7k. multicoloured . . . 10 10

1991. Historians' Birth Anniversaries. Mult.
6307 10k. Type **2542** (225th anniv) 10 10
6308 10k. V. O. Klyuchevsky (150th anniv) 10 10
6309 10k. Sergei M. Solovyov (171st anniv) 10 10
6310 10k. V. N. Tatishchev (after A. Osipov) (305th anniv) 10 10

RUSSIAN FEDERATION

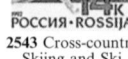

2543 Cross-country Skiing and Ski Jumping

2546 Golden Gate, Vladimir

1992. Winter Olympic Games, Albertville, France. Multicoloured.
6311 14k. Type **2543** 10 10
6312 1r. Aerobatic skiing 20 10
6313 2r. Two and four-man bobsleighing 35 20

1992.
6316 **2546** 10k. orange 10 10
6317 – 15k. brown 10 10
6318 – 20k. red 10 10
6344 – 25k. red 10 10
6319 – 30k. black 10 10
6320 – 50k. blue 10 10
6321 – 55k. turquoise 10 10
6322 – 60k. green 10 10
6323 – 80k. purple 10 10
6324 – 1r. brown 10 10
6325 – 1r.50 green 10 10
6326 – 2r. blue 10 10
6327 – 3r. red 10 10
6328 – 4r. brown 10 10
6329 – 5r. brown 10 10
6330 – 6r. blue 10 10
6331 – 10r. blue 10 10
6332 – 15r. brown 10 10
6333 – 25r. purple 10 10
6334 – 45r. black 10 10
6335 – 50r. violet 10 10
6336 – 75r. brown 10 10
6337 – 100r. green 10 10
6338 **2546** 150r. blue 10 10
6339 – 250r. green 15 10
6340 – 300r. red 25 10
6341 – 500r. purple 30 10
6341a – 750r. green 25 10
6341b – 1000r. grey 35 15
6342 – 1500r. green 55 25
6342a – 2500r. bistre 85 40
6342b – 5000r. blue . . . . . 1·75 80

DESIGNS: 15k. Pskov kremlin; 20, 50k. St. George killing dragon; 25, 55k. Victory Arch, Moscow; 30, 80k. "Millennium of Russia" monument (M. Mikeshin), Novgorod; 60k., 300r. Statue of K. Minin and D. Pozharsky, Moscow; 1, 4r. Church, Kizhky; 1r.50, 6r. Statue of Peter I, St. Petersburg; 2r. St. Basil's Cathedral, Moscow; 3r. Tretyakov Gallery, Moscow; 5r. Europe House, Moscow; 10r. St. Isaac's Cathedral, St. Petersburg; 15, 45r. "The Horse-tamer" (statue), St. Petersburg; 25, 75r. Statue of Yuri Dolgoruky, Moscow; 50r. Rostov Kremlin; 100r. Moscow Kremlin; 250r. Church, Bogulyubovo; 500r. Moscow University; 750r. State Library, Moscow; 1000r. Peter and Paul Fortress, St. Petersburg; 1500r. Pushkin Museum, Moscow; 2500r. Admiralty, St. Petersburg; 5000r. Bolshoi Theatre, Moscow.

2547 "Victory" (N. Baskakov)

2548 Western Capercaillie, Oak and Pine

1992. Victory Day.
6350 **2547** 5k. multicoloured . . . 10 10

1992. Prioksko–Terrasnyi Nature Reserve.
6351 **2548** 50k. multicoloured . . 15 15

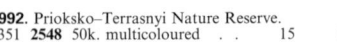

2549 "Mir" Space Station, Flags and Cosmonauts

2551 Pinocchio

1992. Russian–German Joint Space Flight.
6352 **2549** 5r. multicoloured . . . 40 30

1992. Characters from Children's Books (1st series). Multicoloured.
6354 25k. Type **2551** 10 10
6355 30k. Cipollino 10 10
6356 35k. Dunno 10 10
6357 50k. Karlson 15 10
See also Nos. 6391/5.

2552 Russian Cosmonaut and Space Shuttle

2553 Handball

1992. International Space Year. Multicoloured.
6358 25r. Type **2552** 15 10
6359 25r. American astronaut and "Mir" space station . . . 15 10
6360 25r. "Apollo" and "Vostok" spacecraft and sputnik . . 15 10
6361 25r. "Soyuz", "Mercury" and "Gemini" spacecraft 15 10
Nos. 6358/61 were issued together, se-tenant, forming a composite design.

1992. Olympic Games, Barcelona (2nd issue).
6362 **2553** 1r. multicoloured . . . 10 10
6363 – 2r. red, blue and black . . 10 10
6364 – 3r. red, green and black . 15 10
DESIGNS—HORIZ: 2r. Fencing; 3r. Judo.

2554 L. A. Zagoskin and Yukon River, Alaska, 1842–44

1992. Expeditions. Multicoloured.
6365 55k. Type **2554** 10 10
6366 70k. N. N. Miklukho-Maklai in New Guinea, 1871–74 . . . . 10 10
6367 1r. G. I. Langsdorf and route map of expedition to Brazil, 1822–28 . . . . 10 10

2555 Garganeys

1992. Ducks. Multicoloured.
6368 1r. Type **2555** 15 10
6369 2r. Common pochards . . . 30 10
6370 3r. Falcated teals 40 20

2556 "Taj Mahal Mausoleum in Agra"

1992. 150th Birth Anniv of Vasily Vasilevich Vereshchagin (painter).
6371 1r.50 Type **2556** 15 10
6372 1r.50 "Don't Touch, Let Me Approach!" 15 10

2557 "The Saviour" (icon, Andrei Rublyov)

2558 Cathedral of the Assumption

1992.
6373 **2557** 1r. multicoloured . . . 10 10

1992. Moscow Kremlin Cathedrals. Multicoloured.
6374 1r. Type **2558** 10 10
6375 1r. Cathedral of the Annunciation (15th century) 10 10
6376 1r. Archangel Cathedral (16th century) 10 10
See also Nos. 6415/17 and 6440/2.

2559 Russian "Nutcracker" Puppets

2560 "Meeting of Joachim and Anna"

1992. Centenary of First Production of Tchaikovsky's Ballet "Nutcracker". Mult.
6377 10r. Type **2559** 10 10
6378 10r. German "Nutcracker" puppets 10 10
6379 25r. Pas de deux from ballet 30 20
6380 25r. Dance of the toys . . . 30 20

1992. Icons. Multicoloured.
6381 10r. Type **2560** 10 10
6382 10r. "Madonna and Child" 10 10
6383 10r. "Archangel Gabriel" (head) 10 10
6384 10r. "Saint Nicholas" (½-length portrait) 10 10

2561 Clockface and Festive Symbols

2562 "Discovery of America" Monument (Z. Tsereteli)

1992. New Year.
6385 **2561** 50k. multicoloured . . 10 10

1992. 500th Anniv of Discovery of America by Columbus.
6386 **2562** 15r. multicoloured . . . 20 10

2563 Petipa and Scene from "Paquita"

2564 Scrub 'n' Rub

1993. 175th Birth Anniv of Marius Petipa (choreographer). Multicoloured.
6387 25r. Type **2563** 10 10
6388 25r. "Sleeping Beauty", 1890 10 10
6389 25r. "Swan Lake", 1895 . . 10 10
6390 25r. "Raimunda", 1898 . . 10 10

1993. Characters from Children's Books (2nd series). Illustrations by Kornei Chukovsky. Mult.
6391 2r. Type **2564** 10 10
6392 3r. Big Cockroach 15 10
6393 10r. The Buzzer Fly 15 10
6394 15r. Doctor Doolittle . . . 15 10
6395 25r. Barmalei 20 10
Nos. 6391/5 were issued together, se-tenant, forming a composite design.

2565 Castle

2566 Part of Diorama in Belgorod Museum

1993. 700th Anniv of Vyborg.
6396 **2565** 10r. multicoloured . . . 10 10

1993. Victory Day. 50th Anniv of Battle of Kursk.
6397 **2566** 10r. multicoloured . . . 10 10

2567 African Violet

2568 "Molniya 3"

1993. Pot Plants. Multicoloured.
6398 10r. Type **2567** 10 10
6399 15r. "Hibiscus rosa-sinensis" 10 10
6400 25r. "Cyclamen persicum" 10 10
6401 50r. "Fuchsia hybrida" . . 15 10
6402 100r. "Begonia semperflorens" 35 25

1993. Communications Satellites. Multicoloured.
6403 25r. Type **2568** 10 10
6404 45r. "Ekran M" 10 10
6405 50r. "Gorizont" 10 10
6406 75r. "Luch" 15 10
6407 100r. "Ekspress" 20 15

2569 Snuff Box (Dmitry Kolesnikov) and Tankard

2570 Map

1993. Silverware. Multicoloured.
6409 15r. Type **2569** 10 10
6410 25r. Teapot 10 10
6411 45r. Vase 10 10
6412 75r. Tray and candlestick 20 10
6413 100r. Cream jug, coffee pot and sugar basin (Aleksandr Kordes) . . . 25 15

1993. Novgorod Kremlin. As T **2558**. Mult.
6415 25r. Kukui and Knyazhaya Towers (14th–17th century) 10 10
6416 25r. St. Sophia's Cathedral (11th century) 10 10
6417 25r. St. Sophia belfry (15th–18th century) 10 10

1993. Inauguration of Denmark–Russia Submarine Cable and 500th Anniv of Friendship Treaty.
6419 **2570** 90r. green & deep green 25 15

2571 Steller's Eider

1993. Ducks. Multicoloured.
6420 90r. Type **2571** 40 15
6421 100r. Eider 45 20
6422 250r. King eider . . . . . 1·10 55

2572 Ringed Seal

1993. Marine Animals. Multicoloured.
6423 50r. Type **2572** 20 10
6424 60r. "Paralithodes brevipes" (crab) 20 10
6425 90r. Japanese common squid 50 25
6426 100r. Cherry salmon 70 30
6427 250r. Fulmar . . . . 1·00 55

2573 Ceramic Candlestick, Skopino

2574 Banknotes and Coins

1993. Traditional Art. Multicoloured.
6428 50r. Type **2573** 10 10
6429 50r. Painted tray with picture "Summer Troika", Zhostovo (horiz) 10 10
6430 100r. Painted box, lid and distaff, Gorodets 15 10
6431 100r. Enamel icon of St. Dmitry of Solun, Rostov 15 10
6432 250r. "The Resurrection" (lacquer miniature), Fedoskino 35 20

1993. 175th Anniv of Goznak (State printing works and mint).
6433 **2574** 100r. multicoloured . . 15 10

2575 Peter I and "Goto Predestinatsiya"

1993. 300th Anniv of Russian Navy (1st issue). Multicoloured.
6434 100r. Type **2575** 15 10
6435 100r. K. A. Shilder and first all-metal submarine . . . 15 10
6436 100r. I. A. Amosov and "Arkhimed" (frigate) . . 15 10
6437 100r. I. G. Bubnov and "Bars" (submarine) . . . 15 10
6438 100r. B. M. Malinin and "Dekabrist" (submarine) 15 10
6439 100r. A. I. Maslov and "Kirov" (cruiser) 15 10
See also Nos. 6502/5, 6559/62 and 6612/18.

1993. Moscow Kremlin. As T **2558**. Mult.
6440 100r. Faceted Hall (15th century) 15 10
6441 100r. Church of the Deposition of the Virgin's Robe (15th century) . . . 15 10
6442 100r. Grand Palace (17th century) 15 10

2576 Tiger

1993. The Tiger. Multicoloured.
6443 50r. Type **2576** 10 10
6444 100r. Tiger in undergrowth 15 10
6445 250r. Two tiger cubs 30 15
6446 500r. Tiger in snow 60 30

2577 Splash of Blood on Figure

2579 Indian Elephant

2578 Seasonal Decorations

1993. Anti-AIDS Campaign.
6447 **2577** 90r. red, black and lilac 10 10

1993. New Year.
6448 **2578** 25r. multicoloured . . . 10 10

1993. Animals. Multicoloured.
6449 250r. Type **2579** 30 15
6450 250r. Japanese white-naped crane 40 20
6451 250r. Giant panda 30 15
6452 250r. American bald eagle 40 20
6453 250r. Dall's porpoise . . . 30 15
6454 250r. Koala 30 15
6455 250r. Hawaiian monk seal 30 15
6456 250r. Grey whale 30 15

2580 Rimsky-Korsakov and Scene from "Sadko"

1994. 150th Birth Anniv of Nikolai Rimsky-Korsakov (composer). Scenes from his operas. Multicoloured.
6457 250r. Type **2580** 25 15
6458 250r. "The Golden Cockerel" 25 15
6459 250r. "The Tsar's Bride" . . 25 15
6460 250r. "The Snow Maiden" 25 15

2581 "Epiphyllum peacockii"

2582 York Minster, Great Britain

1994. Cacti. Multicoloured.
6461 50r. Type **2581** 10 10
6462 100r. "Mammillaria swinglei" 10 10
6463 100r. "Lophophora williamsii" 10 10
6464 250r. "Opuntia basilaris" . . 30 15
6465 250r. "Selenicereus grandiflorus" 30 15

1994. Churches. Multicoloured.
6466 150r. Type **2582** 15 10
6467 150r. Small Metropolis church, Athens 15 10
6468 150r. Roskilde Cathedral, Denmark 15 10
6469 150r. Notre Dame Cathedral, Paris 15 10
6470 150r. St. Peter's, Vatican City 15 10
6471 150r. Cologne Cathedral, Germany 15 10
6472 150r. Seville Cathedral, Spain 15 10
6473 150r. St. Basil's Cathedral, Moscow 15 10
6474 150r. St. Patrick's Cathedral, New York 15 10

2583 "Soyuz" entering Earth's Atmosphere and "TsF-18" Centrifuge

1994. Yuri Gagarin Cosmonaut Training Centre. Multicoloured.
6475 100r. Type **2583** 10 10
6476 250r. "Soyuz"–"Mir" space complex and "Mir" simulator 15 10
6477 500r. Cosmonaut on space walk and hydrolaboratory 30 15

2584 Map and Rocket Launchers (Liberation of Russia)

1994. 50th Anniv of Liberation. Multicoloured.
6478 100r. Type **2584** 10 10
6479 100r. Map and airplanes (Ukraine) 10 10
6480 100r. Map, tank and soldiers (Belorussia) . . . 10 10

2585 Beautiful Gate, Moscow

1994. Architects' Birth Anniversaries.
6481 **2585** 50r. sepia, black and brown 10 10
6482 – 100r. brown, black and flesh 10 10
6483 – 150r. green, black and olive 15 10
6484 – 300r. violet, black and grey 35 15

DESIGNS: 50r. Type **2585** (D. V. Ukhtomsky, 250th anniv); 100r. Academy of Sciences, St. Petersburg (Giacomo Quarenghi, 250th anniv); 150r. Trinity Cathedral, St. Petersburg (V. P. Stasov, 225th anniv); 300r. Church of Christ the Saviour, Moscow (K. A. Ton, bicentenary).

2586 "Christ and the Sinner"

1994. 150th Birth Anniv of Vasily Dmitrievich Polenev (painter). Multicoloured.
6485 150r. Type **2586** 15 10
6486 150r. "Golden Autumn" . . 15 10

2587 European Wigeon

2588 Games Emblem and Runners

1994. Ducks. Multicoloured.
6487 150r. Type **2587** 15 10
6488 250r. Tufted duck 25 15
6489 300r. Baikal teal 50 30

1994. 3rd Goodwill Games, St. Petersburg.
6490 **2588** 100r. multicoloured . . 10 10

2589 Pyotr Leonidovich Kapitsa

2591 Design Motifs of First Russian Stamp

2590 Olympic Flag

1994. Physics Nobel Prize Winners. Each sepia.
6491 150r. Type **2589** (1978) . . . 15 10
6492 150r. Pavel Alekseevich Cherenkov (1958) 15 10

1994. Cent of International Olympic Committee.
6493 **2590** 250r. multicoloured . . 20 10

1994. Russian Stamp Day.
6494 **2591** 125r. multicoloured . . 10 10

2592 Snuff Box (D. Vinogradov)

2593 Centre of Asia Obelisk

1994. 250th Anniv of Imperial (now M. Lomonosov) Porcelain Factory, St. Petersburg. Multicoloured.
6495 50r. Type **2592** 10 10
6496 100r. Candlestick 10 10
6497 150r. "Water-Carrier" (statuette, after S. Pimenov) 10 10
6498 250r. Sphinx vase 25 15
6499 300r. "Lady with Mask" (statuette, after K. Somov) 30 15

1994. 50th Anniv of Incorporation of Tuva into Russian Socialist Federal Soviet Republic (R.S.F.S.R.).
6501 **2593** 125r. mulitcoloured . . 10 10

2594 Vice-Admiral V. M. Golovnin (Kurile Islands, 1811)

1994. 300th Anniv of Russian Navy (2nd issue). Explorations. Multicoloured.
6502 250r. Type **2594** 20 10
6503 250r. Admiral I. F. Kruzenshtern (first Russain round-the-world expedition, 1803–06) . . . 20 10
6504 250r. Admiral Ferdinand Petrovich Vrangel (Alaska, 1829–35) 20 10
6505 250r. Admiral F. P. Litke (Novaya Zemlya, 1821–24) 20 10

2595 Horses and Grandfather Frost

1994. New Year.
6506 **2595** 125r. blue, red and black 10 10

2596 Griboedov (after N. I. Utkin)

1995. Birth Bicentenary of Aleksandr Sergeevich Griboedov (dramatist and diplomat).
6507 **2596** 250r. brown, light brown and black . . 15 10

2597 "Sheherazade"

1995. 115th Birth Anniv of Mikhail Fokine (choreographer). Scenes from Ballets. Mult.
6508 500r. Type **2597** 25 15
6509 500r. "The Fire Bird" . . . 25 15
6510 500r. "Petrushka" 25 15

2598 Kutuzov (after J. Doe) and Sculptures from Monument, Moscow

1995. 250th Birth Anniv of Field-Marshal Mikhail Ilarionovich Kutuzov, Prince of Smolensk.
6511 **2598** 300r. multicoloured . . 15 10

2599 English Yard, Varvarka Street

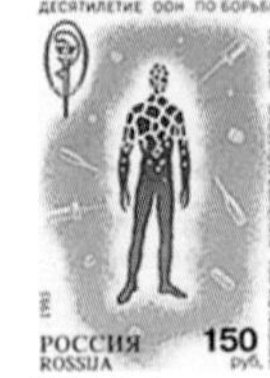

2600 Syringes and Drugs around Addict

1995. 850th Anniv (1997) of Moscow (1st issue). Multicoloured.
6512 125r. Type **2599** 10 10
6513 250r. House of Averky Kirillov (scribe), Bersenevskaya Embankment 10 10
6514 300r. Volkov house, Bolshoi Kharitonevsky Lane . . . 15 10
See also Nos. 6600/2 and 6666/75.

1995. U.N. Anti-drugs Decade.
6515 **2600** 150r. multicoloured . . 10 10

2601 Shoreline

1995. Endangered Animals. Multicoloured.
6516 250r. Type **2601** 15 10
6517 250r. Ringed seal 15 10
6518 250r. Lynx 15 10
6519 250r. Landscape 15 10

Nos. 6516/19 were issued together, se-tenant, Nos. 6516/17 and 6518/19 respectively forming composite designs.

2602 Tomb of the Unknown Soldier, Moscow

1995. 50th Anniv of End of Second World War. Multicoloured.
6520 250r. Sir Winston Churchill, U.S. Pres. Franklin Roosevelt and Iosif Stalin (Yalta Conference) (horiz) 15 10
6521 250r. Storming of the Reichstag, Berlin (horiz) 15 10
6522 250r. Flags, map of Germany and German banners (Potsdam Conference) 15 10
6523 250r. Bombers (operation against Japanese in Manchuria (horiz)) . . . 15 10
6524 250r. Urn with victims' ashes, Auschwitz, and memorial, Sachsenhausen (liberation of concentration camps) (horiz) 15 10
6525 250r. Type **2602** 15 10
6526 500r. Victory Parade, Moscow (36 × 47 mm) . . 40 20

2603 Aleksandr Popov (radio pioneer) and Radio-telegraph Equipment

2604 Spreading Bellflower

1995. Centenary of Radio.
6528 **2603** 250r. multicoloured . . 10 10

1995. Meadow Flowers. Multicoloured.
6529 250r. Type **2604** 15 10
6530 250r. Ox-eye daisy ("Leucanthemum vulgare") 15 10
6531 300r. Red clover ("Trifolium pratense") 15 10
6532 300r. Brown knapweed ("Centaurea jacea") . . . 15 10
6533 500r. Meadow cranesbill . . 25 15

2605 Eurasian Sky Lark ("Alauda arvensis")   **2606** U.S. Space Shuttle "Atlantis"

1995. Songbirds. Multicoloured.
6534 250r. Type **2605** 15 10
6535 250r. Song thrush ("Turdus philomelos") 15 10
6536 500r. Eurasian goldfinch ("Carduelis carduelis") . . 30 15
6537 500r. Bluethroat ("Cyanosylvia svecica") 30 15
6538 750r. Thrush nightingale ("Luscinia luscinia") . . . 45 25

1995. Russian–American Space Co-operation. Mult.
6539 1500r. Type **2606** 55 25
6540 1500r. "Mir" space station 55 25
6541 1500r. "Apollo" spacecraft 55 25
6542 1500r. "Soyuz" spacecraft 55 25
Nos. 6539/42 were issued together, se-tenant, forming a composite design of the spacecraft over Earth.

2607 Cathedral of the Trinity, Jerusalem   **2608** Kremlin Cathedrals

1995. Russian Orthodox Churches Abroad. Mult.
6543 300r. Type **2607** 15 10
6544 300r. Apostles Saints Peter and Paul Cathedral, Karlovy Vary, Czechoslovakia 15 10
6545 500r. St. Nicholas's Cathedral, Vienna 30 15
6546 500r. St. Nicholas's Cathedral, New York . . 30 15
6547 750r. St. Aleksei's Cathedral, Leipzig 45 20

1995. 900th Anniv of Ryazan.
6548 **2608** 250r. multicoloured . . 10 10

2609 Easter Egg with Model of "Shtandart" (yacht)

1995. Faberge Exhibits in Moscow Kremlin Museum. Multicoloured.
6549 150r. Type **2609** 10 10
6550 250r. Goblet 15 10
6551 300r. Cross pendant 20 10
6552 500r. Ladle 30 15
6553 750r. Easter egg with model of Alexander III monument 45 25

2610 Harlequin Duck

1995. Ducks. Multicoloured.
6555 500r. Type **2610** 25 15
6556 750r. Baer's pochard 40 20
6557 1000r. Goosander 60 30

2612 "The Battle of Grengam, July 27, 1720" (F. Perrault)

1995. 300th Anniv of Russian Navy (3rd issue). Paintings. Multicoloured.
6559 250r. Type **2612** 15 10
6560 300r. "Preparations for Attacking the Turkish Fleet in the Bay of Cesme, Night of June 26, 1770" (P. Hackert) . . . 20 10
6561 500r. "The Battle at the Revel Roadstead, May 2, 1790" (A. Bogolyubov) 35 20
6562 750r. "The Kronstadt Roadstead" (I. Aivazovsky) 45 25

2613 State Flag and Arms   **2614** Emblem and San Francisco Conference, 1945

1995. Constitution of the Russian Federation.
6563 **2613** 500r. multicoloured . . 25 10

1995. 50th Anniv of U.N.O.
6564 **2614** 500r. brown, blue and yellow 25 10

2615 White Storks in Nest

1995. Europa. Peace and Freedom. Multicoloured.
6565 1500r. Type **2615** 80 40
6566 1500r. Stork flying over landscape 80 40
Nos. 6565/6 were issued together, se-tenant, forming a composite design.

2616 "Birth of Christ" (icon, Assumption Cathedral, St. Cyril's Monastery, White Sea)   **2618** Semyonov

2617 Yuri Dolgoruky (1090–1157), Kiev and Building of Moscow

1995. Christmas.
6567 **2616** 500r. multicoloured . . 20 10

1995. History of Russian State (1st series). Mult.
6568 1000r. Type **2617** 45 20
6569 1000r. Aleksandr Nevsky (1220–63), Battle of Lake Peipus and as Grand Duke of Vladimir 45 20
6570 1000r. Mikhail Yaroslavich (1271–1318), Tver and torture by the Golden Horde 45 20
6571 1000r. Dmitry Donskoi (1350–89), Moscow Kremlin and Battle of Kulikovo 45 20
6572 1000r. Ivan III (1440–1505), marriage to Sophia Paleologa and Battle of Ugra River 45 20
See also Nos. 6640/3.

1996. Birth Centenary of Nikolai Semyonov (Nobel Prize winner for chemistry, 1956).
6573 **2618** 750r. grey 30 15

2619 Pansies   **2620** Tabbies

1996. Flowers. Multicoloured.
6574 500r. Type **2619** 20 10
6575 750r. Sweet-williams ("Dianthus barbatus") . . 35 15
6576 750r. Sweet peas ("Lathyrus odoratus") 35 15
6577 1000r. Crown imperial ("Fritillaria imperialis") 45 25
6578 1000r. Snapdragons ("Antirrhinum majus") . . 45 25

1996. Cats. Multicoloured.
6579 1000r. Type **2620** 40 20
6580 1000r. Russian blue 40 20
6581 1000r. White Persian . . . 40 20
6582 1000r. Sealpoint Siamese . . 40 20
6583 1000r. Siberian 40 20

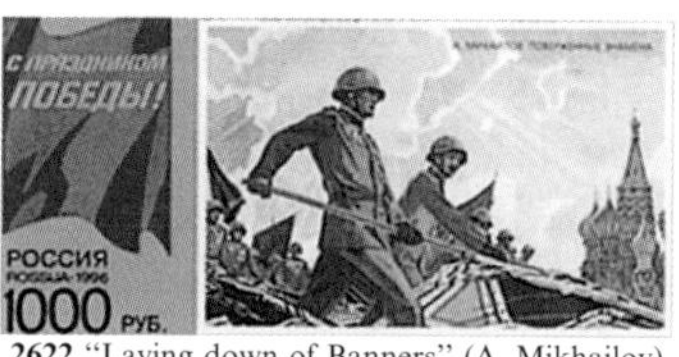

2622 "Laying down of Banners" (A. Mikhailov)

1996. Victory Day.
6585 **2622** 1000r. multicoloured . . 40 20

2623 Tula Kremlin and Monument to Peter I

1996. 850th Anniv of Tula.
6586 **2623** 1500r. multicoloured . . 60 30

2624 Putilovsky Works Tramcar, 1896

1996. Centenary of First Russian Tramway, Nizhny Novgorod. Multicoloured.
6587 500r. Type **2624** 20 10
6588 750r. Sormovo tramcar, 1912 . . . . 35 15
6589 750r. 1928 Series X tramcar, 1928 . . . . 35 15
6590 1000r. 1931 Series KM tramcar, 1931 . . . . . . 40 20
6591 1000r. Type LM-57 tramcar, 1957 . . . . 40 20
6592 2500r. Model 71-608K tramcar, 1973 . . . . . . 75 45

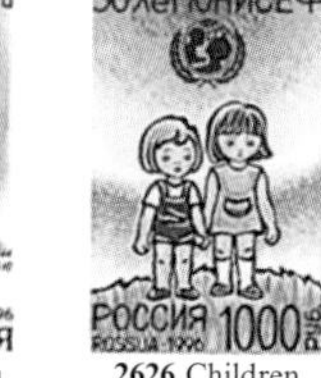

2625 Ye. Dashkova (President of Academy of Sciences)   **2626** Children walking Hand in Hand

1996. Europa. Famous Women.
6594 **2625** 1500r. green and black 60 30
6595 – 1500r. purple and black 60 30
DESIGN: No. 6594, S. Kovalevskaya (mathematician).

1996. 50th Anniv of UNICEF.
6596 **2626** 1000r. multicoloured . . 40 20

2627 "Post Troika in Snowstorm" (P. Sokolov)

1996. Post Troikas in Paintings. Mulicoloured.
6597 1500r. Type **2627** 60 30
6598 1500r. "Post Troika in Summer" (P. Sokolov) . . 60 30
6599 1500r. "Post Troika" (P. Gruzinsky) 60 30

2628 "View of Bridge over Yauza and of Shapkin House in Moscow" (J. Delabarte)

1996. 850th Anniv (1997) of Moscow (2nd issue). Paintings. Multicoloured.
6600 500r. Type **2628** 20 10
6601 500r. "View of Moscow from Balcony of Kremlin Palace" (detail, J. Delabarte) 20 10
6602 750r. "View of Voskresenskie and Nikolskie Gates and Kamenny Bridge" (F. Ya. Alekseev) 35 20
6603 750r. "Moscow Yard near Volkhonka" (anon) . . . 35 20
6604 1000r. "Varvarka Street" (anon) 40 20
6605 1000r. "Sledge Races in Petrovsky Park" 40 20

2630 Basketball   **2632** Gorsky and Scenes from "Gudula's Daughter" and "Salambo"

2631 "Yevstafy" (ship of the line), 1762

1996. Olympic Games, Atlanta, U.S.A. Mult.
6607 500r. Type **2630** 20 10
6608 1000r. Boxing 40 20
6609 1000r. Swimming 40 20
6610 1500r. Gymnastics 60 30
6611 1500r. Hurdling 60 30

1996. 300th Anniv of Russian Navy (4th issue).
(a) As T **2631**.
6612 **2631** 750r. brown and yellow 35 20
6613 – 1000r. deep blue, cobalt and blue 40 20
6614 – 1000r. purple, pink and rose 40 20
6615 – 1500r. multicoloured . . 60 30
6616 – 1500r. black, grey and stone 60 30
DESIGNS: No. 6613, "Petropavlovsk" (battleship); 6614, "Novik" (destroyer); 6615, "Tashkent" (destroyer); 6616, "S-13" (submarine).

(b) Size 35 x 24 mm. Each blue and black.
6617 1000r. "Principium" (galley) 40 20
6618 1000r. "Admiral Kuznetsov" (aircraft carrier) 40 20

1996. 125th Birth Anniv of Aleksandr Gorsky (ballet choreographer). Multicoloured.
6620 750r. Type **2632** 35 20
6621 750r. Scene from "La Bayadere" 35 20
6622 1500r. Scene from "Don Quixote" 60 30
6623 1500r. Scene from "Giselle" 60 30

2633 National Flags

1996. Formation of Community of Sovereign Republics (union of Russian Federation and Belarus).
6624 **2633** 1500r. multicoloured . . 60 30

2634 Chalice

1996. Objets d'Art. Multicoloured.

6625	1000r. Type **2634**	40	20
6626	1000r. Perfume bottles	40	20
6627	1000r. Double inkwell	40	20
6628	1500r. Coffee pot	60	30
6629	1500r. Pendent scent containers (one ladybird-shaped)	60	30

2635 Symbols of Science and Culture on Open Book

1996. 50th Anniv of UNESCO.

6631 **2635**	1000r. black, gold and blue	40	20

2636 "Madonna and Child" (icon), Moscow

2637 Clockface of Spassky Tower, Moscow Kremlin

1996. Orthodox Religion. Multicoloured.

6632	1500r. Type **2636**	60	30
6633	1500r. Stavrovouni Monastery, Cyprus	60	30
6634	1500r. "St. Nicholas" (icon), Cyprus	60	30
6635	1500r. Voskresenkie ("Resurrection") Gate, Moscow	60	30

1996. New Year.

6636 **2637**	1000r. multicoloured	35	15

2638 First Match between U.S.S.R. and Canada, 1972

1996. 50th Anniv of Ice Hockey in Russia. Mult.

6637	1500r. Type **2638**	60	30
6638	1500r. Goalkeeper and players (first match between Moscow and Prague, 1948)	60	30
6639	1500r. Players and referee (Russia versus Sweden)	60	30

1996. History of Russian State (2nd series). As T **2617**. Multicoloured.

6640	1500r. Basil III (1479–1533), removal of bell from Pskov and Siege of Smolensk, 1514	60	30
6641	1500r. Ivan IV the Terrible (1530–84), coronation in Cathedral of the Assumption (Moscow Kremlin) and executions by the Oprichnina	60	30
6642	1500r. Fyodor I Ivanovich (1557–98), with Cossacks and Siberian Kings, and election of Iove (first Russian Patriarch)	60	30
6643	1500r. Boris Godunov (1551–1605), as Tsar in 1598 and food distribution during famine, 1601–03	60	30

2639 Maule's Quince ("Chaenomeles japonica")

1997. Shrubs. Multicoloured.

6644	500r. Type **2639**	20	10
6645	500r. Ornamental almond ("Amygdalus triloba")	20	10
6646	1000r. Broom ("Cytisus scoparius")	40	20
6647	1000r. Burnet rose ("Rosa pimpinellifolia")	40	20
6648	1000r. Mock orange ("Philadelphus coronarius")	40	20

2641 Dmitri Shostakovich (composer) (from 90th birth anniv (1996) medal)

2643 Post Emblem

1997. "Shostakovich and World Musical Culture" International Music Festival.

6650 **2641**	1000r. multicoloured	35	15

1997.

6652 **2643**	100r. brown and black	10	10
6653 –	150r. mauve and black	10	10
6654 –	250r. green and black	10	10
6655 –	300r. green and black	10	10
6656 –	500r. blue and black	15	10
6657 –	750r. brown and black	20	10
6658 –	1000r. red and blue	30	15
6659 –	1500r. blue and black	43	20
6660 –	2000r. green and black	60	30
6661 –	2500r. red and black	75	35
6662 –	3000r. violet and black	90	45
6663 –	5000r. brown and black	1·50	75

DESIGNS: 100r. Combine harvesters in field; 150r. Oil rigs; 250r. White storks; 300r. Radio mast; 750r. St. George killing dragon; 1000r. State flag and arms; 1500r. Electric pylon inside generating machinery; 2000r. Class VL65 electric railway locomotive; 2500r. Moscow Kremlin; 3000r. Space satellite; 5000r. Pianist and theatre.

For these designs in revised currency, see Nos. 6718/35.

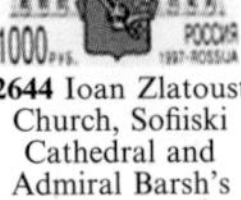
2644 Ioan Zlatoust Church, Sofiiski Cathedral and Admiral Barsh's House

2645 "Volga Svyatoslavovich" (I. Bilibin)

1997. 850th Anniv of Vologda.

6664 **2644**	1000r. multicoloured	35	15

1997. Europa. Tales and Legends.

6665 **2645**	1500r. multicoloured	55	30

2646 Jesus Christ the Saviour Cathedral

1997. 850th Anniv of Moscow (3rd issue). Mult.

6666	1000r. Type **2646**	40	20
6667	1000r. Towers and walls of Kremlin	40	20
6668	1000r. Grand Palace and cathedrals, Kremlin	40	20
6669	1000r. St. Basil's Cathedral, Spassky Tower and Trinity Church	40	20
6670	1000r. "St. George killing Dragon" (16th-century icon)	40	20
6671	1000r. First reference to Moscow in Ipatevsky Chronicle, 1147	40	20
6672	1000r. Prince Daniil Alexandrovich and Danilov Monastery	40	20
6673	1000r. "Building Moscow Kremlin, 1366" (16th-century miniature)	40	20
6674	1000r. Kazan cap and "Coronation of Ivan IV" (miniature)	40	20
6675	1000r. 16th-century plan of Moscow	40	20

Nos. 6666/75 were issued together, se-tenant, Nos. 6666/70 forming a composite design of Moscow in late 19th century.

2647 Mil Mi-14 (float)

1997. Helicopters. Multicoloured.

6676	500r. Type **2647**	20	10
6677	1000r. Mil Mi-24 (gunship)	35	15
6678	1500r. Mil Mi-26 (transport)	55	30
6679	2000r. Mil Mi-28 (gunship)	70	35
6680	2500r. Mil Mi-34 (patrol)	90	45

2648 "The Priest and Balda"

1997. Birth Bicentenary (1999) of Aleksandr Sergeevich Pushkin (poet) (1st issue). Mult.

6681	500r. Type **2648**	15	10
6682	1000r. "Tsar Saltan"	30	15
6683	1500r. "The Fisherman and the Golden Fish"	50	25
6684	2000r. "The Dead Princess and the Seven Knights"	60	30
6685	3000r. "The Golden Cockerel"	90	45

See also Nos. 6762/6 and 6827/29.

2649 Petrodvorets (St. Petersburg) National Flags and Marble Temple, Bangkok

1997. Centenary of Russia–Thailand Diplomatic Relations and of Visit of King Rama V to St. Petersburg.

6686 **2649**	1500r. multicoloured	45	20

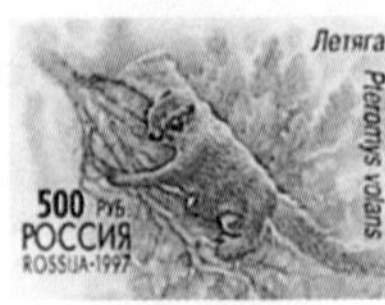
2650 Siberian Flying Squirrel

1997. Wildlife. Multicoloured.

6687	500r. Type **2650**	20	10
6688	750r. Lynx	25	10
6689	1000r. Western capercaillie	35	15
6690	2000r. European otter	70	35
6691	3000r. Western curlew	1·25	65

2651 Arkhangel Province

1997. Regions of the Russian Federation (1st series). Multicoloured.

6692	1500r. Type **2651**	50	25
6693	1500r. Kaliningrad Province (vert)	50	25
6694	1500r. Kamchatka Province	50	25
6695	1500r. Krasnodar Territory	50	25
6696	1500r. Sakha Republic (Yakutiya) (vert)	50	25

See also Nos. 6784/8, 6831/5, 6920/25 and 6980/4.

2652 Klyopa flying with Balloons

1997. Klyopa (cartoon character). Multicoloured.

6697	500r. Type **2652**	15	10
6698	1000r. Klyopa hang-gliding over Red Square	30	15
6699	1500r. Klyopa in troika (45 × 33 mm)	45	20

2653 Emblem, Mascot and Russian Federation 1992 and 20k. Stamp

2654 Indian Flag and Asokan Capital

1997. "Moscow 97" International Stamp Exhbition. Multicoloured.

6700	1500r. Russian Empire 1858 10k. and R.S.F.S.R. 1918 35k. stamps, and Spassky Tower, Moscow Kremlin	50	25
6701	1500r. Type **2653**	50	25

1997. 50th Anniv of Independence of India.

6702 **2654**	500r. multicoloured	15	10

2655 Presentation of Standard

1997. 325th Birth Anniv of Tsar Peter I. Mult.

6703	2000r. Type **2655** (creation of regular army and navy)	60	30
6704	2000r. Sea battle (access to Baltic Sea)	60	30
6705	2000r. Peter I reviewing plans (construction of St. Petersburg)	60	30
6706	2000r. Council (administrative reforms)	60	30
6707	2000r. Boy before tutor (cultural and educational reforms)	60	30

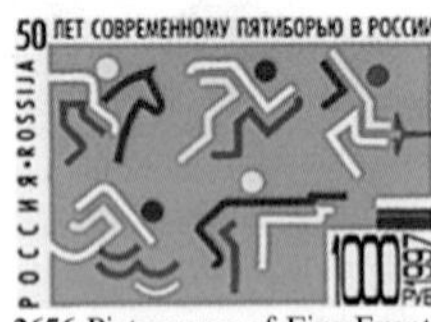
2656 Pictograms of Five Events

1997. 50th Anniv of Modern Pentathlon in Russia.

6709 **2656**	1000r. multicoloured	30	15

2657 Match Scenes

1997. Centenary of Football in Russia.

6710 **2657**	2000r. multicoloured	60	30

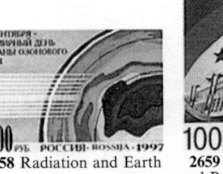

2658 Radiation and Earth

2659 National Flag and Palace of Europe, Strasbourg

1997. World Ozone Layer Day. 10th Anniv of Montreal Protocol (on reduction of use of chlorofluorocarbons).
6711 **2658** 1000r. multicoloured . . 30 15

1997. Admission of Russian Federation to European Council.
6712 **2659** 1000r. multicoloured . . 30 15

2660 "Boris and Gleb" (14th-century icon)

2663 Cross-country Skiing

2662 "Menshikov in Beresovo" (detail, Surikov)

1997. Centenary of Russian State Museum, St. Petersburg (1st issue). Multicoloured.
6713 500r. Type **2660** 15 10
6714 1000r. "Volga Boatmen" (I. Repin) (horiz) 30 15
6715 1500r. "Promenade" (Marc Chagall) 45 25
6716 2000r. "Merchant's Wife taking Tea" (B. Kustodiev) 60 30
See also Nos. 6753/6756.

1998. As Nos. 6652/63 but in reformed currency.
6718 10k. brown and black (as No. 6652) 10 10
6719 15k. mauve and black (as No. 6653) 10 10
6720 25k. green and black (as No. 6654) 10 10
6721 30k. green and black (as No. 6655) 10 10
6723 50k. blue and black (Type **2643**) 10 10
6726 1r. red and blue (as No. 6658) 15 10
6727 1r.50 blue and black (as No. 6659) 20 10
6728 2r. green and black (as No. 6660) 25 10
6729 2r.50 red and black (as No. 6661) 30 15
6730 3r. violet and black (as No. 6662) 35 20
6735 5r. brown and black (as No. 6663) 60 30

1998. 150th Birth Anniversaries of Vasily Ivanovich Surikov and V. M. Vasnetsov (artists). Multicoloured.
6741 1r.50 Type **2662** 20 10
6742 1r.50 "Morozov Boyar's Wife" (Surikov) 20 10
6743 1r.50 "Battle between Slavs and Nomads" (detail, Vasnetsov) (vert) 20 10
6744 1r.50 "Tsarevich Ivan on a Grey Wolf" (Vasnetsov) 20 10

1998. Winter Olympic Games, Nagano, Japan. Mult.
6745 50k. Type **2663** 10 10
6746 1r. Figure skating (pairs) . . 15 10
6747 1r.50 Biathlon 20 10

2664 Red-tailed Black Labeo "Epalzeorhynchus bicolor"

1998. Fishes. Multicoloured.
6748 50k. Type **2664** 10 10
6749 50k. Jewel tetra ("Hyphessobrycon callistus") 10 10
6750 1r. Galina's catfish ("Synodontis galinae") . . 15 10
6751 1r.50 "Botia kristinae" . . . 20 10
6752 1r.50 "Cichlasoma labiatum" 20 10

2665 "The Last Day of Pompeii" (K. P. Bryullov)

1998. Centenary of State Russian Museum, St. Petersburg (2nd issue). Multicoloured.
6753 1r.50 Type **2665** 20 10
6754 1r.50 "The Ninth Wave" (I. K. Aivazovsky) . . . 20 10
6755 1r.50 "Pines for Masts" (I. I. Shishkin) 20 10
6756 1r.50 "Our Lady of Tenderness for Sick Hearts" (K. S. Petrov-Vodkin) 20 10

2667 Theatre and Characters

1998. Centenary of Moscow Art Theatre.
6759 **2667** 1r.50 multicoloured . . 20 10

2668 "End of Winter" (Shrove-tide)

1998. Europa. National Festivals.
6760 **2668** 1r.50 multicoloured . . 20 10

2669 War Memorial, Venets Hotel, History Museum and Goncharovsky Pavilion

2670 "The Lyceum"

1998. 350th Anniv of Ulyanovsk (formerly Simbirsk).
6761 **2669** 1r. multicoloured . . . 15 10

1998. Birth Bicentenary (1999) of Aleksandr Sergeevich Pushkin (poet) (2nd issue). Drawings by Pushkin.
6762 **2670** 1r.50 black and blue . . 20 10
6763 – 1r.50 brown, stone & blk 20 10
6764 – 1r.50 brown, stone & blk 20 10
6765 – 1r.50 brown, stone & blk 20 10
6766 – 1r.50 black and blue . . 20 10
DESIGNS: No. 6763, "A.N. Wolf"; 6764, Self-portrait; 6765, "Tatyana" (from "Evgeny Onegin"); 6766, Knight in armour (manuscript cover from 1830).

2671 Local History Museum and Peter I Monument

1998. 300th Anniv of Taganrog.
6767 **2671** 1r. multicoloured . . . 15 10

2673 Tsar Nicholas II

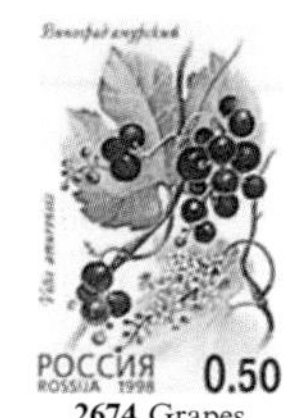

2674 Grapes

1998. 80th Death Anniv of Tsar Nicholas II.
6769 **2673** 3r. multicoloured . . . 35 20

1998. Berries. Multicoloured.
6770 50k. Type **2674** 10 10
6771 75k. Raspberry 10 10
6772 1r. Magnolia vine 15 10
6773 1r.50 Cowberrry 20 10
6774 2r. Arctic bramble 25 15

2675 Landmarks

2676 Leontina Cohen

1998. 275th Anniv of Yekaterinburg.
6775 **2675** 1r. multicoloured . . . 15 10

1998. Intelligence Agents.
6776 **2676** 1r. blue, indigo & blk 15 10
6777 – 1r. brown, yellow & blk 15 10
6778 – 1r. green, dp green & blk 15 10
6779 – 1r. purple, brown & blk 15 10
DESIGNS: No. 6777, Morris Cohen; 6778, L. R. Kvasnikov; 6779, A. A. Yatskov.

2677 Order of St. Andrew

1998. Russian Orders (1st series). Multicoloured.
6780 1r. Type **2677** 15 10
6781 1r.50 Order of St. Catherine 20 10
6782 2r. Order of St. Aleksandr Nevsky 25 15
6783 2r.50 Order of St. George 30 15
See also Nos. 6807/11.

1998. Regions of the Russian Federation (2nd series). As T **2651**. Multicoloured.
6784 1r.50 Republic of Buryatiya (vert) 20 10
6785 1r.50 Republic of Kareliya (vert) 20 10
6786 1r.50 Khabarovsk Province 20 10
6787 1r.50 Murmansk Province 20 10
6788 1r.50 Primorsky Province . . 20 10

2678 Universal Postal Union Emblem

1998. World Post Day.
6789 **2678** 1r. multicoloured . . . 15 10

2679 Anniversary Emblem

1998. 50th Anniv of Universal Declaration of Human Rights.
6790 **2679** 1r.50 multicoloured . . 20 10

2680 Headquarters, Moscow

1998. 10th Anniv of Menatep Bank.
6791 **2680** 2r. multicoloured . . . 25 15

2681 Aviation

1998. Achievements of the Twentieth Century. Multicoloured.
6792 1r. Type **2681** 15 10
6793 1r. Computers 15 10
6794 1r. Genetics 15 10
6795 1r. Nuclear energy 15 10
6796 1r. Space exploration . . . 15 10
6797 1r. Television 15 10

2682 Koshkin

1998. Birth Centenary of Mikhail Ilich Koshkin (tank designer).
6798 **2682** 1r. multicoloured . . . 15 10

2683 Grandfather Frost

1998. New Year.
6799 **2683** 1r. multicoloured . . . 15 10

2684 Telephone and Switchboard Operators

1999. Centenary of First Long-distance Telephone Link in Russia (between Moscow and St. Petersburg).
6800 **2684** 1r. multicoloured . . . 15 10

2685 Western Capercaillie

1999. Hunting. Multicoloured.
6801 1r. Type **2685** 15 10
6802 1r.50 Shooting mallard ducks from rowing boat 20 10
6803 2r. Falconry (Gyr falcon) 25 15
6804 2r.50 Wolves 30 15
6805 3r. Bears 35 20

1999. Russian Orders (2nd series). As T **2677**. Multicoloured.
6807 1r. Order of St. Vladimir . . 15 10
6808 1r.50 Order of St. Anne . . 20 10
6809 2r. Order of St. John of Jerusalem 25 15
6810 2r.50 Order of the White Eagle 30 15
6811 3r. Order of St. Stanislas . . 35 20

2688 "Family at Tea" (Sofya Kondrashina)

1999. Russia in the 21st Century. Children's paintings. Multicoloured.
6813 1r.20 Type **2688** 15 10
6814 1r.20 "My Town" (Yuri Lapushkov) 15 10
6815 1r.20 "Fantasy City" (Aleksander Khudyshin) (vert) 15 10

2690 Albrecht Durer's House

1999. "iBRA '99" International Stamp Exhibition, Nuremberg, Germany.

6817 **2690** 3r. multicoloured . . . 30 15

2691 Setting Weighted Lines

1999. Fishing. Multicoloured.

6818 1r. Type **2691** 10 10
6819 2r. Fishing by rod and line from bank and boat . . . 20 10
6820 2r. Fishing by rod and line from kayak 20 10
6821 3r. Fishing through holes in ice 30 15
6822 3r. Underwater fishing . . . 30 15

2692 Council Flag and Headquarters, Strasbourg, and Spassky Tower, Moscow

1999. 50th Anniv of Council of Europe.

6823 **2692** 3r. multicoloured . . . 30 15

2693 Oksky State Natural Biosphere Preserve

1999. Europa. Parks and Gardens.

6824 **2693** 5r. multicoloured . . . 55 30

2694 Stag

1999. Red Deer. Multicoloured.

6825 2r.50 Type **2694** 25 15
6826 2r.50 Doe and fawns . . . 25 15

2695 Pushkin, 1815 (after S. G. Chirikov)

2696 Rose "Carina" ("Happy Birthday")

1999. Birth Bicentenary of Aleksandr Sergeevich Pushkin (poet) (3rd issue). Multicoloured.

6827 1r. Type **2695** 10 10
6828 3r. Pushkin, 1826 (after I.-E. Viven) 30 15
6829 5r. Pushkin, 1836 (after Karl Bryullov) 55 25

1999. Regions of the Russian Federation (3rd series). As T **2651**. Multicoloured.

6831 2r. Republic of North Osetia-Alaniya 20 10
6832 2r. Republic of Bashkortostan (vert) . . . 20 10
6833 2r. Kirov Province 20 10
6834 2r. Evenk Autonomous Region (vert) 20 10
6835 2r. Stavropol Region . . . 20 10

1999. Greetings stamps. Roses. Multicoloured.

6836 1r.20 Type **2696** 15 10
6837 1r.20 "Gloria Dei" ("From the bottom of my heart") 15 10
6838 2r. "Candia" ("Congratulations") . . . 20 10
6839 3r. "Confidence" ("Be happy") 30 15
6840 4r. "Ave Maria" ("With love") 40 20

1999. No. 6342b surch **1.20**.

6841 1r.20 on 5000r. blue 15 10

2698 River Station, City Arms and Nativity of the Virgin Cathedral

1999. 250th Anniv of Rostov-on-Don.

6842 **2698** 1r.20 multicoloured . . 15 10

2699 Automatic Post Sorting

1999. 125th Anniv of Universal Postal Union.

6843 **2699** 3r. multicoloured . . . 30 15

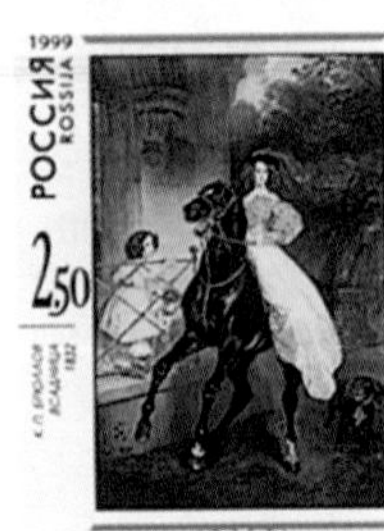

2700 "Horsewoman"

1999. Birth Bicentenary of Karl Bryullov (painter). Multicoloured.

6844 2r.50 Type **2700** 25 15
6845 2r.50 "Portrait of Yu. P. Samoilova and Amacilia Paccini" 25 15

2701 IZh-1 Motorcycle, 1929

1999. Russian Motor Cycles. Multicoloured.

6846 1r. Type **2701** 10 10
6847 1r.50 L-300, 1930 . . . . . 15 15
6848 2r. M-72, 1941 . . . . . . 20 10
6849 2r.50 M-1-A, 1945 . . . . 25 15
6850 5r. IZ–"Planeta-5", 1987 . . 55 25

2702 Suvorov's Vanguard passing Lake Klontal (after engraving by L. Hess)

1999. Bicentenary of General Aleksandr Suvorov's Crossing of the Alps. Multicoloured.

6851 2r.50 Type **2702** . . . . .
6852 2r.50 Schollenen Gorge Monument, Suvorov and soldiers . . . .

2703 Horse Racing

1999. Traditional Sports. Multicoloured.

6853 2r. Type **2703** 20 10
6854 2r. Wrestling 20 10
6855 2r. Gorodki (game with stick and blocks of wood) 20 10
6856 2r. Sleigh and deer team race 20 10
6857 2r. Weightlifting (vert) . . . 20 10

2704 Leonid Utesov

1999. Singers. Multicoloured.

6858 2r. Type **2704** 20 10
6859 2r. Lidiya Ruslanova (in costume) 20 10
6860 2r. Klavdiya Shulzhenko (with hands clasped) . . . 20 10
6861 2r. Mark Bernes (playing accordion) 20 10
6862 2r. Bulat Okudzhava (playing guitar in street scene) 20 10
6863 2r. Vladimir Vysotsky (with guitar and arms out wide) 20 10
6864 2r. Igor Talkov (with arm raised) 20 10
6865 2r. Victor Tsoi (playing guitar) 20 10

2705 Players chasing Ball and Club Badge

1999. Spartak-Alaniya, National Football Champions.

6877 **2705** 2r. multicoloured . . . 20 10

2706 Father Christmas and "2000"

1999. Christmas and New Year. Multicoloured.

6878 1r.20 Type **2706** 15 10
6879 1r.20 "2000", globe as pearl and shell 15 10

2707 "The Raising of the Daughter of Jairus" (V. D. Polenov)

2000. Bimillenary of Christianity. Religious Paintings. Multicoloured.

6880 3r. Type **2707** 30 15
6881 3r. "Christ in the Wilderness" (I. N. Kramskoy) 30 15
6882 3r. "Christ in the House of Mary and Martha" (G. I. Semiradsky) 30 15
6883 3r. "What is Truth?" (N. N. Ge) (vert) 30 15

2709 Psurtsev and Central Telegraph Office, Moscow

2000. Birth Centenary of Nikolai D. Psurtsev (statesman).

6886 **2709** 2r.50 multicoloured . . 25 15

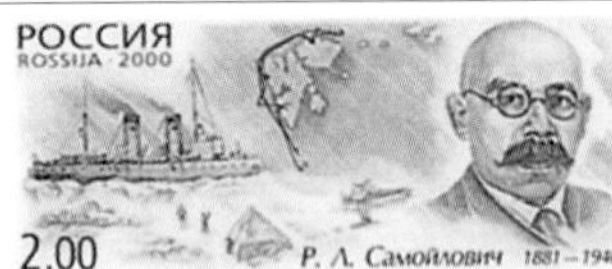

2711 R. L. Samoilovich

2000. Polar Explorers. Multicoloured.

6888 2r. Type **2711** 20 10
6889 2r. V. Yu Vize and polar station 20 10
6890 2r. M. M. Somov and ship 20 10
6891 2r. P. A. Gordienko and airplane 20 10
6892 2r. A. F. Treshnikov and tracked vehicles 20 10

2712 N. A. Panin-Kolomenkin (first Russian Olympic Ice-skating Champion, 1908)

2000. The Twentieth Century (1st issue). Sport. Multicoloured.

6893 25k. Type **2712** 10 10
6894 30k. Wrestlers (Olympic Games, Stockholm, 1912) 10 10
6895 50k. Athlete crossing finishing line (All-Russian Olympiad, 1913 and 1914) 10 10
6896 1r. Cyclists (All-Union Spartacist Games, 1928) 10 10
6897 1r.35 Emblem and parade of athletes (Sports Association for Labour and Defence, 1931) . . . 15 10
6898 1r.50 Emblem and athletes ("Honoured Master of Sports", 1934) 20 10
6899 2r. Gymnasts and shot-putter (Olympic Games, Helsinki, 1952) 20 10
6900 2r.50 V. P. Kutz and athletes (Olympic Games, Melbourne, 1956) 25 15
6901 3r. Gold Medal, goalkeeper and player (Olympic Football Champion, Melbourne Olympic Games) 30 15
6902 4r. Mikhail Botvinnik (World Chess Champion, 1948–57, 1958–60 and 1961–63) 45 25
6903 5r. Soviet Union–Canada ice hockey match, 1972 . . . 55 30
6904 6r. Stadium and emblem (Olympic Games, Moscow, 1980) 65 35

See also Nos. 6926/37, 6950/61 and 6964/76.

2714 Soldier (L. F. Golovanov)

2000. 55th Anniv of End of Second World War. Posters by named artists. Multicoloured.

6906 1r.50 Type **2714** 20 10
6907 1r.50 Mother and son (N. N. Vatolina) 20 10
6908 1r.50 Soldiers celebrating (V. V. Suryaninov) . . . 20 10
6909 1r.50 Soldier and woman (V. I. Ladyagin) 20 10
6910 5r. Soldier and emblem (V. S. Klimashin) 55 30

2715 "Apollo"–"Soyuz" Space Link, 1975

2000. International Space Co-operation. Mult.

6912 2r. Type **2715** 20 10
6913 3r. Projected international space station and flags (horiz) 30 15
6914 5r. Rocket taking off from launch pad at sea 55 30

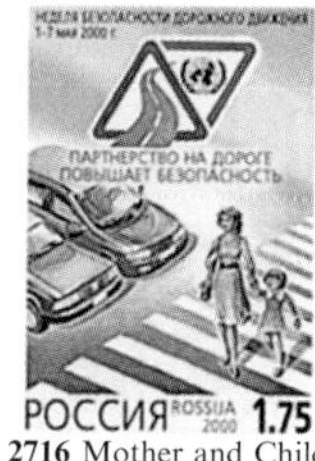

2716 Mother and Child crossing Road and Emblem

2717 Star of David, Doves and "Holocaust"

2000. World Road Safety Week.
6915 **2716** 1r.75 multicoloured . . 20 10

2000. Holocaust Victims' Commemoration.
6916 **2717** 2r. multicoloured . . . 20 10

2718 Spassky Tower and President's Flag

2719 "Building Europe"

2000. Election of President Vladimir Putin.
6917 **2718** 1r.75 multicoloured . . 20 10

2000. Europa.
6918 **2719** 7r. multicoloured . . . 75 40

2000. Regions of the Russian Federation (4th issue). As T **2651**. Multicoloured.
6920 3r. Republic of Kalmyk (vert) 30 15
6921 3r. Mari El Republic (vert) 30 15
6922 3r. Tatarstan Republic (vert) 30 15
6923 3r. Udmurt Republic (vert) 30 15
6924 3r. Chuvash Republic . . . 30 15
6925 3r. Autonomous Republic of Yamalo Nentsky 30 15

2721 V. K. Arkadjev (Observation of Ferromagnetic Resonance, 1913)

2000. The Twentieth Century (2nd issue). Science. Multicoloured.
6926 1r.30 Type **2721** (botanist and plant geneticist) . . . 15 10
6927 1r.30 Nikolai Ivanovich Vavilov (botanist and plant geneticist) and ears of corn (theory on plant divergence) 15 10
6928 1r.30 N. N. Luzin (founder of Moscow Mathematical School, 1920–30) 15 10
6929 1r.75 I. E. Tamm and chemical model (Phenoms Theory, 1929) 20 10
6930 1r.75 P. L. Kapitsa and diagram of experiment (discovery of liquid helium superfluidity, 1938) 20 10
6931 1r.75 Nikolai Nikolayevich Semenov (physical chemist) (chemical chain reactions theory, 1934) . . 20 10
6932 2r. V. I. Veksler and charged particles in accelerators, 1944–45 . . 20 10
6933 2r. Mayan text (decipherment of Mayan language by Yu V. Knorozov, 1950s) . . . 20 10
6934 2r. A. V. Ivanov (discovery of pogonophora, 1955–57) 20 10
6935 3r. Globe, Moon and Luna 3 (first photograph of Moon's dark side, 1959) 30 15
6936 3r. Scientific equipment (development of quantum electronics, 1960s) 30 15
6937 3r. N. J. Tolstoi (ethnolinguistic dictionary, 1995) 30 15

2722 Chihuahua

2723 Fencing

2000. Dogs. Multicoloured.
6938 1r. Type **2722** 10 10
6939 1r.50 Terrier 20 10
6940 2r. Poodle 20 10
6941 2r.50 French bulldog . . . 25 15
6942 3r. Japanese chin 30 15

2000. Olympic Games, Sydney. Multicoloured.
6943 2r. Type **2723** 20 10
6944 3r. Synchronized swimming 30 15
6945 5r. Volleyball 55 30

2724 Charoit

2000. Minerals. Multicoloured.
6946 1r. Type **2724** 10 10
6947 2r. Haematite 20 10
6948 3r. Rock crystal 30 15
6949 4r. Gold 45 25

2725 Ballerina and Actors

2000. The Twentieth Century (3rd series). Culture. Multicoloured.
6950 30k. Type **2725** (touring ballet and opera companies, 1908–14) . . . 10 10
6951 50k. "Black Square" (K. S. Malevich) 10 10
6952 1r. Sergi Mikhailovich Eisenstein (director) and scene from *Battleship Potemkin* (film, 1925) . . 10 10
6953 1r.30 Book and Aleksei Maksimovich Gorky (writer) 15 10
6954 1r.50 Sculptures and red star 20 10
6955 1r.75 Vladimir Vladimirovich Mayakovsky (poet and playwright) and propaganda posters, 1920s 20 10
6956 2r. V. E. Meierkhold and K. S. Stanislavsky (theatre producers) 20 10
6957 2r.50 Dmitri Dmitriyevich Shostakovich (composer) and musicians 25 15
6958 3r. Galina Sergeyevna Ulanova (ballerina) and dancers 30 15
6959 4r. A. T. Tvardovsky (poet) 45 25
6960 5r. Fountain and Great Palace, Petrodvorets (restoration of historical monuments) 55 30
6961 6r. D. S. Likhachev (literary critic) 65 35

2726 Zander (*Stizostedion lucioperca*) and Common Whitefish (*Coregonus lavaretus manaenoides*)

2000. Fish of Chudsko-Pskovskoye Lake. Mult.
6962 2r.50 Type **2726** 25 15
6963 2r.50 European smelt (*Osmerus eperlanus spirinchus*) and European cisco (*Coregonus albula*) 25 15

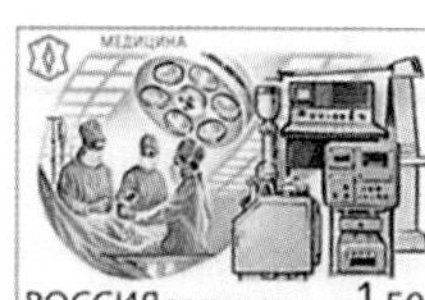

2727 Doctors Operating and Medical Equipment

2000. The Twentieth Century (4th series). Technology. Multicoloured.
6964 1r.50 Type **2727** 10 10
6965 1r.50 City skyline (construction) 10 10
6966 1r.50 Bus, car and truck (transport) 10 10
6967 2r. Dam, electricity pylons and generator (engineering) 15 10
6968 2r. Telephones, televisions and rocket and satellite (communication) 15 10
6970 2r. Space stations and rocket (space technology) 15 10
6971 3r. Civil and military airplanes (aviation) . . . 30 15
6972 3r. Steam, diesel and electric trains (rail transport) . . 30 15
6973 3r. Container ship, sailing ship and cruise liner (sea transport) 30 15
6974 4r. Furnace (metallurgy) . . 35 15
6975 4r. Oil refinery and truck (oil-refining industry) . . 35 15
6976 4r. Truck, conveyor and drill (mineral extraction) 35 15

2728 Moscow Kremlin, Pokrovsky Cathedral and Christmas Tree

2000. New Millennium.
6977 **2728** 2r. multicoloured . . . 15 10

2729 Emblem

2731 White Tulip ("Happy Birthday")

2000. 80th Anniv of Foreign Intelligence Service.
6978 **2729** 2r.50 multicoloured . . 25 15

2001. Regions of the Russian Federation (5th issue). As T **2651**. Multicoloured.
6980 3r. Republic of Dagestan . . 30 15
6981 3r. Republic of Kabardino-Balkaskaya 30 15
6982 3r. Republic of Komi (vert) 30 15
6983 3r. Samara region 30 15
6984 3r. Chita region 30 15

2001. As Nos. 6718/35 but new designs and currency expressed as "P".
6985 10p. mauve and black . . . 90 45
6986 25p. brown and black . . . 2·25 1·10
6987 50p. blue and black . . . . 4·50 2·25
6988 100p. mauve and black . . . 9·00 4·50
DESIGNS: 10p. Ballet dancer; 25p. Gymnast; 50p. Globe and computer; 100p. Universal Postal Union emblem.

2001. Greetings Stamps. Tulips. Multicoloured.
7000 2r. Type **2731** 15 10
7001 2r. Deep pink tulips ("With Love") 15 10
7002 2r. Orange tulip ("Good Luck") 15 10
7003 2r. Yellow tulip ("Congratulations") . . . 15 10
7004 2r. Magenta and white tulip ("Be Happy") 15 10

2732 I. A. Galitsin

2001. 300th Birth Anniv of Andrei Matveeich Matveev (artist) (Nos. 7005/6) and 225th Birth Anniv of Vasily Andreevich Tropinin (artist) (Nos. 7007/8). Multicoloured.
7005 3r. Type **2732** 30 15
7006 3r. A. P. Galitsina 30 15
7007 3r. P. A. Bulakhov 30 15
7008 3r. E. I. Karzinkina 30 15

2733 "Senate Square and St. Peter the Great Monument" (B. Patersen)

2001. 300th Anniv of St. Petersburg. Paintings. Multicoloured.
7009 1r. Type **2733** 10 10
7010 2r. "English embankment near Senate" (B. Patersen) 15 10
7011 3r. "Mikhailovsky Castle from Fontanka Embankment" (B. Patersen) 30 15
7012 4r. "River Moika near Stable Department" (A. E. Martynov) 35 15
7013 5r. "Neva from Peter and Paul Fortress" (K. P. Beggrov) 45 20

2734 *Pyrrhosoma numphula* (damselfly)

2001. Damselflies and Dragonflies. Multicoloured.
7014 1r. Type **2734** 10 10
7015 1r.50 *Epitheca bimaculata* (dragonfly) 10 10
7016 2r. Brown aeshna (*Aeschna grandis*) 15 10
7017 3r. *Libellula depressa* (dragonfly) 30 15
7018 5r. *Coenagrion hastulatum* (damselfly) 45 20

2735 Yuri Gagarin, S. P. Korolev (spaceship designer) and Baikonur Launch Site

2001. 40th Anniv of First Manned Space Flight. Multicoloured.
7019 3r. Type **2735** 30 15
7020 3r. Gagarin in uniform . . . 30 15
Nos. 7019/20 were issued together, se-tenant, forming a composite design.

2736 Baikal Lake

2001. Europa. Water Resources.
7021 **2736** 8r. multicoloured . . . 70 35

2737 Emblem

2001. 75th Anniv of International Philatelic Federation.
7022 **2737** 2r.50 multicoloured . . 25 10

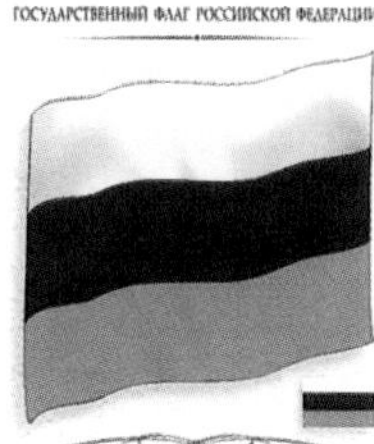

2738 Russian Flag

2001. State Emblems. Multicoloured.
7023 2r.50 Type **2738** 20 10
7024 2r.50 Russian Federation national anthem 20 10
7025 5r. State Arms 40 20
MS7026 Sheet 150 × 00 mm 2r.50 Type **2738**; 2r.50 As No. 7024; 100r. State Arms . . . . . .
The 100r. stamp in No. **MS**7026 has the arms embossed in gold foil.

2739 Map of Russian Federation and State Arms

2001. 11th Anniv of Declaration of State Sovereignty.

7027	**2739**	5r. multicoloured	40	20

2740 Cathedral of the Assumption, Vladimir (1189)

2001. Religious Architecture. Multicoloured.

7028	2r.50 Type **2740**	20	10
7029	2r.50 Cathedral of the Nativity of the Virgin, Zvenigorod (1405)	20	10
7030	2r.50 Cathedral of the Intercession of the Virgin of the Old Belief Community of Rogozhsk, Moscow (1792)	20	10
7031	2r.50 Roman Catholic Church of the Immaculate Conception of the Blessed Virgin Mary, Moscow (1911)	20	10
7032	2r.50 Lutheran Church of St. Peter, St. Petersburg (1838)	20	10
7033	2r.50 Prayer House of the Evangelical Christians (Pentecostal), Lesosibirsk (1999)	20	10
7034	2r.50 Revival Church of Evangelical Christians (Baptist), Bezhitsk, Bryansk (1996)	20	10
7035	2r.50 Church of Seventh Day Adventists, Ryazan (1996)	20	10
7036	2r.50 Armenian Cathedral Surb Khach, Rostov-on-Don (1792) and Monastery of St. Daniel, Moscow (13th-century)	20	10
7037	2r.50 First Mosque, Ufa (1830)	20	10
7038	2r.50 Hay Market Mosque, Kazan (1849)	20	10
7039	2r.50 Choral Synagogue, Moscow (1891)	20	10
7040	2r.50 Large Choral Synagogue, St. Petersburg (1893)	20	10
7041	2r.50 Buddhist Soskshin-Dugan, Ivolginsk Datsan (1976)	20	10

2741 "Sokol" (high speed passenger train)

2001. 150th Anniv of St. Petersburg–Moscow Railway. Sheet 90 × 80 mm.

MS7042	**2741**	12r. multicoloured	1·00	50

2742 G. S. Titov (cosmonaut)

2001. 40th Anniv of First Manned Space Flight.

7043	**2742**	3r. multicoloured	25	10

2743 Faina G. Ranevskaya in Cinderella

2001. Cinema Actors. Showing scenes from their films. Multicoloured.

7044	2r.50 Type **2743**	20	10
7045	2r.50 Mikhail I. Zharov in *Peter I*	20	10
7046	2r.50 Lubov P. Orlova in *Circus*	20	10
7047	2r.50 Nikolai A. Kryuchkov in *Tractor Drivers*	20	10
7048	2r.50 Yury V. Nikulin in *Diamond Arm*	20	10
7049	2r.50 Anatoly D. Papanov in *Alive and Dead*	20	10
7050	2r.50 Evgeny P. Leonov in *Stripy Voyage*	20	10
7051	2r.50 Nikolai N. Rybnikov in *Height*	20	10
7052	2r.50 Andrei A. Mironov in *Twelve Chairs*	20	10

2744 Lazarian and Institute

2001. Death Bicentenary of Horhannes Lazarian (founder of Oriental Languages Institute, Moscow).

7053	**2744**	2r.50 multicoloured	20	10

A stamp in a similar design was issued by Armenia.

EXPRESS STAMPS

E **171** Motor Cyclist

1932. Inscr "EXPRES".

E588	E **171**	5k. sepia	5·00	2·25
E589	–	10k. purple	8·50	3·50
E590	–	80k. green	35·00	14·00

DESIGNS—HORIZ: 10k. Express motor van; 80k. Class Ta steam locomotive.

E **173** Polar Region and Kalinin K-4 Airplane over Ice-breaker "Taimyr"

1932. Air Express. 2nd Int Polar Year and Franz Joseph's Land to Archangel Flight.

E591	E **173**	50k. red	42·00	18·00
E592		1r. green	60·00	20·00

POSTAGE DUE STAMPS

Доплата
1 коп.
золотом.
(D 96)

ДОПЛАТА
1 коп.
(D 99)

1924. Surch as Type D **96**.

D401b	**45**	1k. on 35k. blue	20	30
D402b		3k. on 35k. blue	20	30
D403b		5k. on 35k. blue	20	30
D404		8k. on 35k. blue	50	50
D405b		10k. on 35k. blue	30	60
D406b		12k. on 70k. brown	20	40
D407c		14k. on 35k. blue	20	40
D408b		32k. on 35k. blue	90	90
D409c		40k. on 35k. blue	1·00	90

1924. Optd with Type D **99**.

D421	**48**	1k. on 100r. yellow	4·50	10·00

D **104**

1925.

D464	D **104**	1k. red	25	30
D465		2k. mauve	25	30
D466		3k. blue	25	30
D467		7k. yellow	35	30
D468		8k. green	35	30
D469		10k. blue	40	50
D470		14k. brown	60	70

RUSSIAN POST OFFICES IN CHINA Pt. 17

Russian Post Offices were opened in various towns in Manchuria and China from 1870 onwards.

1899. 100 kopeks = 1 rouble.
1917. 100 cents = 1 dollar (Chinese).

КИТАЙ
(1)

1899. Arms types (with thunderbolts) of Russia optd with T **1**.

1	**9**	1k. orange	40	40
2		2k. green	50	40
3		3k. red	50	35
9	**14**	4k. red	3·00	1·50
4	**9**	5k. purple	65	50
5		7k. blue	70	50
6	**14**	10k. blue	75	50
30	**10**	14k. red and blue	75	1·75
31		15k. blue and brown	45	1·00
32	**14**	20k. red and blue	40	1·25
33	**10**	25k. violet and green	65	2·25
34		35k. green and purple	70	1·25
35	**14**	50k. green and purple	85	1·25
36	**10**	70k. orange and brown	60	1·50
37	**15**	1r. orange and brown	1·50	1·50
20	**11**	3r.50 grey and black	9·00	10·00
21	**20**	5r. blue and green on green	6·75	6·50
22	**11**	7r. yellow and black	12·00	11·00
23	**20**	10r. grey and red on yellow	55·00	55·00

1910. Arms types of Russia optd with T **1**.

24	**22**	1k. orange	35	60
25		2k. green	40	60
26		3k. red	30	35
27	**23**	4k. red	25	50
28	**22**	7k. blue	35	65
29	**23**	10k. blue	35	50

1917. Arms types of Russia surch in "cents" and "dollars" diagonally in one line.

42	**22**	1c. on 1k. orange	50	3·50
43		2c. on 2k. green	50	3·50
44		3c. on 3k. red	60	3·50
45	**23**	4c. on 4k. red	50	3·25
46	**22**	5c. on 5k. lilac	90	3·00
47	**23**	10c. on 10k. blue	60	3·00
48	**10**	14c. on 14k. red and blue	2·00	5·00
49		15c. on 15k. blue and purple	1·50	3·75
50	**14**	20c. on 20k. red and blue	1·75	3·50
51	**10**	25c. on 25k. violet and green	1·75	5·00
52		35c. on 35k. green & purple	1·75	6·50
53	**14**	50c. on 50k. green & purple	1·50	5·50
54	**10**	70c. on 70k. orange & brn	1·50	6·50
55	**15**	1d. on 1r. orge & brn on brn	1·50	7·00
39	**10**	3d.50 on 3r.50 grey & blk	10·00	14·00
40	**20**	5d. on 5r. bl & dp bl on grn	7·50	16·00
41	**11**	7d. on 7r. yellow and black	5·00	13·00
57	**20**	10d. on 10r. grey & red on yell	38·00	55·00

1920. Arms types of Russia surch in "cents" in two lines. Perf or imperf.

65	**22**	1c. on 1k. orange	16·00	25·00
59		2c. on 2k. green	6·00	15·00
60		3c. on 3k. red	6·00	15·00
61	**23**	4c. on 4k. red	16·00	22·00
62	**22**	5c. on 5k. lilac	18·00	28·00
63	**23**	10c. on 10k. blue	60·00	60·00
64	**22**	10c. on 10k. on 7k. blue	60·00	65·00

RUSSIAN POST OFFICES IN CRETE Pt. 3

(RETHYMNON PROVINCE)

The Russian Postal Service operated from 1 May to 29 July 1899.

4 metallik = 1 grosion (Turkish piastre).

These issues were optd with circular control marks as shown on Types R **3/4**. Prices are for stamps with these marks, but unused examples without them are known.

R **1**

R **2**

1899. Imperf.

R1	R **1**	1m. blue	45·00	12·00
R2	R **2**	1m. green	5·00	3·50
R3		2m. red	£150	£120
R4		2m. green	5·00	3·50

R **3**

R **4**

1899. Without stars in oval.

R 5	R **3**	1m. pink	55·00	35·00
R 6		2m. pink	55·00	35·00
R 7		1g. pink	55·00	35·00
R 8		1m. blue	55·00	35·00
R 9		2m. blue	55·00	35·00
R10		1g. blue	55·00	35·00
R11		1m. green	55·00	35·00
R12		2m. green	55·00	35·00
R13		1g. green	55·00	35·00
R14		1m. red	55·00	35·00
R15		2m. red	55·00	35·00
R16		1g. red	55·00	35·00
R17		1m. orange	55·00	35·00
R18		2m. orange	55·00	35·00
R19		1g. orange	55·00	35·00
R20		1m. yellow	55·00	35·00
R21		2m. yellow	55·00	35·00
R22		1g. yellow	55·00	35·00
R23		1m. black	£550	£550
R24		2m. black	£550	£550
R25		1g. black	£475	£475

1899. Starred at each side.

R26	R **4**	1m. pink	35·00	25·00
R27		2m. pink	11·00	3·25
R28		1g. pink	4·00	4·25
R29		1m. blue	18·00	10·00
R30		2m. blue	5·00	3·25
R31		1g. blue	4·00	4·25
R32		1m. green	14·00	10·00
R33		2m. green	5·00	3·25
R34		1g. green	4·00	4·25
R35		1m. red	14·00	10·00
R36		2m. red	5·00	3·25
R37		1g. red	4·00	2·25

RUSSIAN POST OFFICES IN TURKISH EMPIRE Pt. 16

General issues for Russian P.O.s in the Turkish Empire and stamps specially overprinted for use at particular offices.

1863. 100 kopeks = 1 rouble.
1900. 40 paras = 1 piastre.

1 Inscription = "Dispatch under Wrapper to the East"

1863. Imperf.

2a	**1**	6k. blue	£190	£1100

2

3

1865. Imperf.
4 **2** (10pa.) brown and blue . . . £500 £400
5 **3** (2pi.) blue and red £700 £450

4

5

1865. Imperf.
6 **4** (10pa.) red and blue . . . . . 24·00 38·00
7 **5** (2pi.) blue and red . . . . . 35·00 45·00
The values of 4/7 were 10pa. (or 2k.) and 2pi. (or 20k.).

6 Inscription = "Eastern Correspondence"

12

1868. Perf.
14 **6** 1k. brown . . . . 8·00 4·50
11 3k. green . . . . 22·00 13·00
16 5k. blue . . . . 5·50 3·25
17a 10k. red and green . . . . 4·00 3·25
See also Nos. 26/35.

1876. Surch with large figures of value.
24 **6** 7k. on 10k. red and green . . 65·00 50·00
22 8k. on 10k. red and green . . 65·00 60·00

1879.
26 **6** 1k. black and yellow . . . . 2·25 1·25
32 1k. orange 50 35
27 2k. black and red . . . . . 3·00 1·75
33 2k. green 50 35
34 5k. purple . . . . 1·25 1·00
28 7k. red and grey . . . . . . 4·50 1·10
35 7k. blue 85 35

1900. Arms types of Russia surch in "PARA" or "PIASTRES".
37 **9** 4pa. on 1k. orange 15 10
50 **22** 5pa. on 1k. orange 10 15
38 **9** 10pa. on 2k. green 40 25
51 **22** 10pa. on 2k. green 10 15
201 15pa. on 3k. red . . . . . 20 5·00
41 **14** 20pa. on 4k. red 40 40
52 **23** 20pa. on 4k. red 10 15
42 **9** 20pa. on 5k. purple 40 40
181 **22** 20pa. on 5k. purple 10 15
43 **14** 1pi. on 10k. blue 20 20
53 **23** 1pi. on 10k. blue 10 15
182 **10** 1½pi. on 15k. blue & purple 15 20
183 **14** 2pi. on 20k. red and blue 15 20
184 **10** 2½pi. on 25k. violet & green 15 20
185 3½pi. on 35k. green & pur 20 30
54 **14** 5pi. on 50k. green and lilac 50 75
55 **10** 7pi. on 70k. orange & brn 70 90
56 **15** 10pi. on 1r. orange and brown on brown . . . . 80 1·10
48 **11** 35pi. on 3r.50 grey & blk 6·00 6·00
202 **20** 50pi. on 5r. blue on green 3·25 80·00
49 **11** 70pi. on 7r. yellow & black 9·00 9·00
203 **20** 100pi. on 10r. grey and red on yellow . . . . 14·00 £275

1909. As T **14**, **15**, and **11** of Russia, but ship and date in centre as T **12**, and surch in "paras" or "piastres".
57 **14** 5pa. on 1k. orange 20 30
58 10pa. on 2k. green 30 40
59 20pa. on 4k. red 60 75
60 1pi. on 10k. blue . . . . . 70 1·10
61 5pi. on 50k. green & purple 1·25 2·50
62 7pi. on 70k. orange & brn 2·50 3·75
63 **15** 10pi. on 1r. orange & brown 3·75 6·50
64 **11** 35pi. on 3r.50 green & pur 9·00 35·00
65 70pi. on 7r. pink and green 26·00 55·00
The above stamps exist overprinted for Constantinople, Jaffa, Jerusalem, Kerassunde, Mount Athos, Salonika, Smyrna, Trebizonde, Beyrouth, Dardanelles, Mytilene and Rizeh. For full list see Part 10 (Russia) of the Stanley Gibbons Catalogue.

1913. Nos. 126/42 (Romanov types) of Russia surch.
186 5pa. on 1k. orange 40 40
187 10pa. on 3k. green 40 40
188 15pa. on 3k. red 40 40
189 20pa. on 4k. red 40 40
190 1pi. on 10k. blue 40 40
191 1½pi. on 15k. brown 60 60
192 2pi. on 20k. green 70 70
193 2½pi. on 25k. purple . . . . 1·00 1·00
194 3½pi. on 35k. green and violet 2·00 2·00
195 5pi. on 50k. grey and brown 2·25 2·25
196 7pi. on 70k. brown and green 7·00 17·00
197 10pi. on 1r. green . . . . . 8·00 17·00
198 20pi. on 2r. brown . . . . . 3·25 5·50
199 30pi. on 3r. violet . . . . . 4·50 £170
200 50pi. on 5r. brown . . . . . 90·00 £475

RWANDA Pt. 14

An independent republic established in July 1962, formerly part of Ruanda-Urundi.

100 centimes = 1 franc

1 Pres. Kayibanda and Map

1962. Independence.
1 **1** 10c. sepia and green 10 10
2 – 40c. sepia and purple 10 10
3 **1** 1f. sepia and blue 70 35
4 – 1f.50 sepia and brown 10 10
5 **1** 3f.50 sepia and orange 10 10
6 – 6f.50 sepia and blue 15 10
7 **1** 10f. sepia and olive 30 15
8 – 20f. sepia and red 60 30
DESIGN: Nos. 2, 4, 6, 8 are as Type **1** but with halo around Rwanda on map in place of "R".

1963. Admission to U.N. No. 204 of Ruanda-Urundi with coloured frame obliterating old inscr (colours below), and surch **Admission a l'O.N.U. 18-9-1962 REPUBLIQUE RWANDAISE** and new value.
9 3f.50 on 3f. grey 10 10
10 6f.50 on 3f. pink . . . . . . 1·10 90
11 10f. on 3f. blue 25 25
12 20f. on 3f. silver 40 40

1963. Flowers issue of Ruanda-Urundi (Nos. 178 etc) optd **REPUBLIQUE RWANDAISE** or surch also in various coloured panels over old inscription and values. Flowers in natural colours.
13 25c. orange and green 20 20
14 40c. salmon and green 20 20
15 60c. purple and green 20 20
16 1f.25 blue and green 90 90
17 1f.50 green and violet 90 90
18 2f. on 1f.50 green and violet 1·40 1·10
19 4f. on 1f.50 green and violet 1·40 1·10
20 5f. green and purple . . . . . 1·40 1·10
21 7f. brown and green . . . . . 1·40 1·10
22 10f. olive and purple . . . . . 1·75 1·50
The coloured panels are in various shades of silver except No. 19 which is in blue.

4 Ears of Wheat and Native Implements

1963. Freedom from Hunger.
23 **4** 2f. brown and green 10 10
24 4f. mauve and blue 10 10
25 7f. red and grey 20 10
26 10f. green and yellow 75 55

5 Coffee

6 Postal Services Emblem

5a "Post and Telecommunications"

1963. 1st Anniv of Independence.
27 **5** 10c. brown and blue 10 10
28 – 20c. yellow and blue 10 10
29 – 30c. green and orange . . . 10 10
30 **5** 40c. brown and turquoise . . 10 10
31 – 1f. yellow and purple 10 10
32 – 2f. green and blue 80 45
33 **5** 4f. brown and red 10 10
34 – 7f. yellow and green 20 15
35 – 10f. green and violet 35 30
DESIGNS: 20c., 1, 7f. Bananas; 30c., 2, 10f. Tea.

1963. 2nd Anniv of African and Malagasy Posts and Telecommunications Union.
36 **5a** 14f. multicoloured . . . . . 1·10 90

1963. Admission of Rwanda to U.P.U.
37 **6** 50c. blue and pink 10 10
38 1f.50 brown and blue 65 45
39 3f. purple and grey 10 10
40 20f. green and yellow 45 20

7 Emblem

8 Child Care

1963. 15th Anniv of Declaration of Human Rights.
41 **7** 5f. red 15 10
42 6f. violet 50 35
43 10f. blue 35 15

1963. Red Cross Centenary.
44 **8** 10c. multicoloured 10 10
45 – 20c. multicoloured 10 10
46 – 30c. multicoloured 10 10
47 – 40c. brown, red and violet . . 10 10
48 **8** 2f. multicoloured 80 60
49 – 7f. multicoloured 15 10
50 – 10f. brown, red and brown . . 20 15
51 – 20f. brown, red and orange . . 60 35
DESIGNS—HORIZ: 20c., 7f. Patient having blood test; 40, 20c. Stretcher party. VERT: 30c., 10f. Doctor examining child.

9 Map and Hydraulic Pump

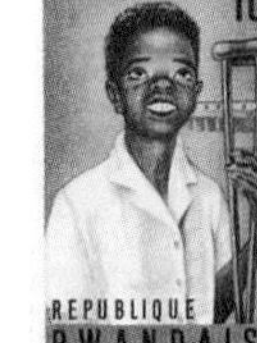

10 Boy with Crutch

1964. World Meteorological Day.
52 **9** 3f. sepia, blue and green . . 10 10
53 7f. sepia, blue and red . . . 35 20
54 10f. sepia, blue and orange 50 35

1964. Stamps of Ruanda-Urundi optd **REPUBLIQUE RWANDAISE** or surch also in black over coloured metallic panels obliterating old inscription or value.
55 10c. on 20c. (No. 204) 10 10
56 20c. (No. 204) 10 10
57 30c. on 1f.50 (No. 208) . . . 10 10
58 40c. (No. 205) 10 10
59 50c. (No. 206) 10 10
60 1f. (No. 207) 10 10
61 2f. (No. 209) 10 10
62 3f. (No. 210) 10 10
63 4f. on 3f.50 on 3f. (No. 228) 20 10
64 5f. (No. 211) 20 10
65 7f.50 on 6f.50 (No. 212) . . . 45 15
66 8f. (No. 213) . . . . 4·50 2·25
67 10f. (No. 214) 65 20
68 20f. (No. 229) . . . . 1·10 45
69 50f. (No. 230) . . . . 2·10 85

1964. Gatagara Re-education Centre.
70 **10** 10c. sepia and violet 10 10
71 – 40c. sepia and blue 10 10
72 – 4f. sepia and brown 10 10
73 **10** 7f.50 sepia and green . . . 35 15
74 – 8f. sepia and bistre . . . . 1·40 95
75 – 10f. sepia and purple . . . 45 20
DESIGNS—HORIZ: 40c., 8f. Children operating sewing machines. VERT: 4, 10f. Crippled child on crutches.

11 Running

1964. Olympic Games, Tokyo. Sportsmen in slate.
76 **11** 10c. blue 10 10
77 – 20c. red 10 10
78 – 30c. turquoise 10 10
79 – 40c. brown 10 10
80 **11** 4f. blue 10 10
81 – 5f. green . . . . 1·40 1·25
82 – 20f. purple 35 35
83 – 50f. grey . . . . 1·10 90
DESIGNS—VERT: 20c., 5f. Basketball; 40c., 50f. Football. HORIZ: 20f. High-jumping.

12 Faculties of "Letters" and "Sciences"

13 Abraham Lincoln

1965. National University. Multicoloured.
84 10c. Type **12** 10 10
85 20c. Student with microscope and building ("Medicine") (horiz) 10 10
86 30c. Scales of Justice, Hand of Law ("Social Sciences" and "Normal High School") 10 10
87 40c. University buildings (horiz) . . 10 10
88 5f. Type **12** 10 10
89 7f. As 20c. 15 10
90 10f. As 30c. . . . . 1·00 85
91 12f. As 40c. 30 15

1965. Death Centenary of Abraham Lincoln.
92 **13** 10c. green and red 10 10
93 20c. brown and blue 10 10
94 30c. violet and red 10 10
95 40c. blue and brown 10 10
96 9f. brown and purple . . . 20 15
97 40f. purple and green . . . 1·90 70

14 Marabou Storks

15 "Telstar" Satellite

1965. Kagera National Park. Multicoloured.
98 10c. Type **14** 30 15
99 20c. Common zebras 10 10
100 30c. Impalas 10 10
101 40c. Crowned cranes, hippopotami and cattle egrets 30 15
102 1f. African buffaloes 10 10
103 3f. Hunting dogs 10 10
104 5f. Yellow baboons . . . . . 4·25 1·10
105 10f. African elephant and map 20 15
106 40f. Reed cormorants and African darters . . . . . 1·75 50
107 100f. Lions . . . . 2·25 50
SIZES—As Type **14**: VERT: 30c., 2, 5f. HORIZ: 20, 40c., 3, 10f. LARGER (45 × 25½ mm): 40, 100f.

1965. Centenary of I.T.U. Multicoloured.
108 10c. Type **15** 10 10
109 40c. "Syncom" satellite . . . 10 10
110 4f.50 Type **15** . . . . 1·40 50
111 50f. "Syncom" satellite . . . 90 35

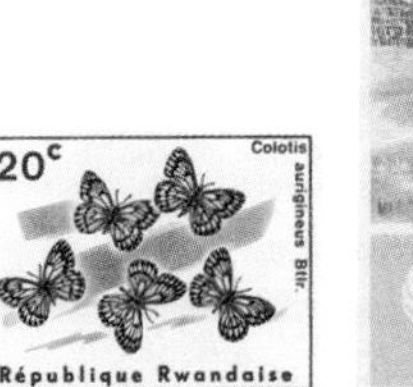

16 "Colotis aurigineus"

17 Cattle and I.C.Y. Emblem

1965. Rwanda Butterflies. Multicoloured.
112 10c. "Papilio bromius" . . . 15 20
113 15c. "Papilio hesperus" . . . 15 20
114 20c. Type **16** 15 20
115 30c. "Amphicallia pactolicus" 15 20
116 35c. "Lobobunaea phaedusa" 15 20
117 40c. "Papilio jacksoni ruandana" 15 20
118 1f.50 "Papilio dardanus" . . 15 20
119 3f. "Amaurina elliotti" . . . 4·25 1·25
120 4f. "Colias electo pseudohecate" . . . . . . 2·75 1·00
121 10f. "Bunaea alcinoe" . . . 55 30
122 50f. "Athletes gigas" . . . . 1·75 85
123 100f. "Charaxes ansorgei R" 3·50 1·25
The 10, 30, 35c., 3, 4 and 100f. are vert.

1965. International Co-operation Year.
124 **17** 10c. green and yellow . . . 10 10
125 – 40c. brown, blue and green 10 10

126 – 4f.50 green, brown & yell 1·10 50
127 – 45f. purple and brown . . 90 40
DESIGNS: 40c. Crater lake and giant plants; 4f.50, Gazelle and candelabra tree; 45f. Mt. Ruwenzori. Each with I.C.Y. emblem.

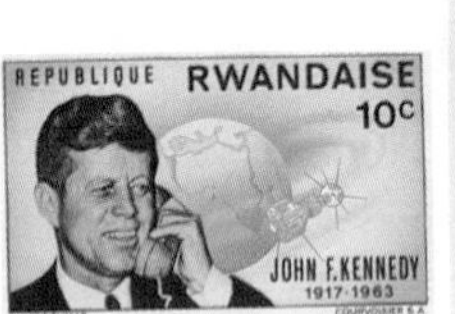

18 Pres. Kennedy, Globe and Satellites 19 Madonna and Child

1965. 2nd Anniv of Pres. Kennedy's Death.
128 **18** 10c. brown and green . . . 10 10
129 40c. brown and red 10 10
130 50c. brown and blue 10 10
131 1f. brown and olive 10 10
132 8f. brown and violet . . . 1·75 1·10
133 50f. brown and grey . . . 1·10 90

1965. Christmas.
134 **19** 10c. green and gold 10 10
135 40c. brown and gold . . . 10 10
136 50c. blue and gold 10 10
137 4f. black and gold 70 65
138 6f. violet and gold 15 10
139 30f. brown and gold . . . 65 45

20 Father Damien

1966. World Leprosy Day.
140 **20** 10c. blue and brown . . . 10 10
141 – 40c. red and blue 10 10
142 **20** 4f.50 slate and green . . . 20 15
143 – 45f. brown and red . . . . 1·75 1·25
DESIGNS: 40c., 45f. Dr. Schweitzer.

21 Pope Paul, Rome and New York

1966. Pope Paul's Visit to U.N. Organization.
144 **21** 10c. blue and brown . . . 10 10
145 – 40c. indigo and blue . . . 10 10
146 **21** 4f.50 blue and purple . . . 1·60 1·00
147 – 50f. blue and green . . . . 1·00 55
DESIGN: 40c., 50f. Pope Paul, Arms and U.N. emblem.

22 "Echinops amplexicaulis" and "E. bequaertii"

1966. Flowers. Multicoloured.
148 10c. Type **22** 10 10
149 20c. "Haemanthus multiflorus" (vert) 10 10
150 30c. "Helichrysum ericirosenii" 10 10
151 40c. "Carissa edulis" (vert) 10 10
152 1f. "Spathodea campanulata" (vert) 10 10
153 3f. "Habenaria praestans" (vert) 10 10
154 5f. "Aloe lateritia" (vert) . . 4·50 2·25
155 10f. "Ammocharis tinneana" (vert) 30 20
156 40f. "Erythrina abyssinica" 1·10 75
157 100f. "Capparis tomentosa" 2·75 1·40

23 W.H.O. Building

1966. Inaug of W.H.O. Headquarters, Geneva.
159 **23** 2f. olive 10 10
160 3f. red 20 20
161 5f. blue 10 10

24 Football 25 Mother and Child within Flames

1966. "Youth and Sports".
162 **24** 10c. black, blue and green 10 10
163 – 20c. black, green and red 10 10
164 – 30c. black, purple and blue 10 10
165 **24** 40c. black, green and bistre 10 10
166 – 9f. black, purple and grey 20 10
167 – 50f. black, blue and purple 1·10 1·00
DESIGNS: 20c., 9f. Basketball; 30c., 50f. Volleyball.

1966. Nuclear Disarmament.
168 **25** 20c. brown, red and mauve 10 10
169 30c. brown, red and green 10 10
170 50c. brown, red and blue 10 10
171 6f. brown, red and yellow 10 10
172 15f. brown, red & turquoise 65 30
173 18f. brown, red and lavender 65 40

26 Football 27 Yellow-crested Helmet Shrike and Mikeno Volcano

1966. World Cup Football Championship.
174 **26** 20c. blue and turquoise . . 10 10
175 30c. blue and violet 10 10
176 50c. blue and green 10 10
177 6f. blue and mauve 20 10
178 12f. blue and brown . . . 1·10 35
179 25f. indigo and blue . . . 2·25 60

1966. Rwanda Scenery.
180 **27** 10c. green 30 10
181 – 40c. lake 10 10
182 – 4f.50 blue 50 40
183 – 55f. purple 60 45
DESIGNS—VERT: 40c. Nyamiranga Falls (inscr "Nyamilanga"); 55f. Rusumo Falls (inscr "Rusumu"). HORIZ: 4f.50, Gahinga and Mahubura Volcanoes, and giant plants.

28 U.N.E.S.C.O. and Cultural Emblems

1966. 20th Anniv of U.N.E.S.C.O.
184 **28** 20c. mauve and blue . . . 10 10
185 – 30c. turquoise and black 10 10
186 – 50c. brown and black . . . 10 10
187 – 1f. violet and black . . . 10 10
188 **28** 5f. green and brown . . . 10 10
189 – 10f. brown and black . . . 15 10
190 – 15f. purple and blue . . . 55 35
191 – 50f. blue and black 65 50
DESIGNS: 30c., 10f. "Animal" primer; 50c., 15f. Atomic symbol and drill operator; 1, 50f. Nubian monument partly submerged in the Nile.

29 "Bitis gabonica"

1967. Snakes. Multicoloured.
192 20c. Head of mamba 20 15
193 30c. Python (vert) 20 15
194 50c. Type **29** 20 15
195 1f. "Naja melanoleuca" (vert) 20 15
196 3f. Head of python 20 15
197 5f. "Psammophis sibilans" (vert) 45 15
198 20f. "Dendroaspis jamesoni kaimosae" . . . . 1·25 50
199 70f. "Dasypeltis scabra" (vert) . . . . 1·50 70

30 Girders and Tea Flower

1967. Ntaruka Hydro-electric Project.
200 **30** 20c. blue and purple . . . 10 10
201 – 30c. brown and black . . . 10 10
202 – 50c. violet and brown . . . 10 10
203 **30** 4f. purple and green . . . 10 10
204 – 25f. green and violet . . . 50 50
205 – 50f. brown and blue . . . 1·00 1·00
DESIGNS: 30c., 25f. Power conductors and pyrethrum flower; 50c., 50f. Barrage and coffee beans.

33 "St. Martin" (Van Dyck)

1967. Paintings.
208 **33** 20c. black, gold and violet 10 10
209 – 40c. black, gold and green 10 10
210 – 60c. black, gold and red . . 10 10
211 – 80c. black, gold and blue 10 10
212 **33** 9f. black, gold and brown 90 50
213 – 15f. black, gold and red . . 35 20
214 – 18f. black, gold and bronze 35 20
215 – 26f. black, gold and lake 45 45
PAINTINGS—HORIZ: 40c., 15f. "Rebecca and Eliezer" (Murillo); 80c., 26f. "Job and his Friends" (attributed to Il Calabrese). VERT: 60c., 18f. "St. Christopher" (D. Bouts).

34 Rwanda "Round Table" Emblem and Common Zebra's Head

1967. Rwanda "Round Table" Fund for Charitable Works. Each with "Round Table" Emblem. Mult.
216 20c. Type **34** 10 10
217 40c. African elephant's head 10 10
218 60c. African buffalo's head 10 10
219 80c. Impala's head 10 10
220 18f. Ear of wheat 35 15
221 100f. Palm . . . . 1·60 90

35 "Africa Place" and Dancers

1967. World Fair, Montreal.
222 **35** 20c. blue and sepia 10 10
223 – 30c. purple and sepia . . . 10 10
224 – 50c. orange and sepia . . . 10 10
225 – 1f. green and sepia 10 10
226 – 3f. violet and sepia 10 10
227 **35** 15f. green and sepia . . . 15 15
228 – 34f. red and sepia 50 40
229 – 40f. turquoise and sepia . . 70 55
DESIGNS: "Africa Place" (two different views used alternately in order of value) and 30c., 3f. Drum and handicrafts; 50c., 40f. Dancers leaping; 1f., 34f. Spears, shields and weapons.

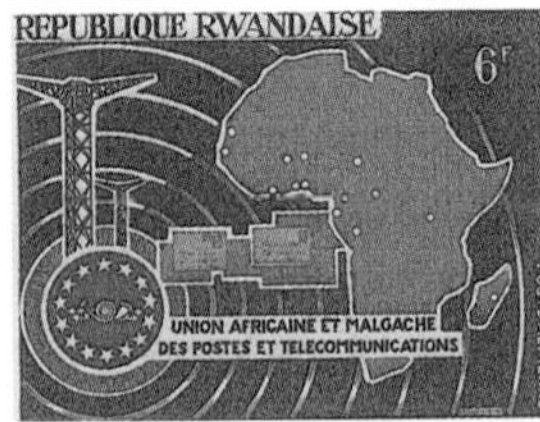

35a Map of Africa, Letters and Pylons

1967. Air. 5th Anniv of U.A.M.P.T.
230 **35a** 6f. slate, brown and lake 20 10
231 18f. purple and brown . . 65 35
232 30f. red, green and blue 1·10 65

36 Common Zebra's Head and Lion's Emblem 37 Red Bishop

1967. 50th Anniv of Lions International.
233 **36** 20c. black, blue and violet 10 10
234 80c. black, blue and green 10 10
235 1f. black, blue and red . . 10 10
236 8f. black, blue and brown 20 10
237 10f. black, blue and ultramarine 30 20
238 50f. black, blue and green 1·40 95

1967. Birds of Rwanda. Multicoloured.
239 20c. Type **37** 10 30
240 40c. Woodland kingfisher (horiz) 10 30
241 60c. Red-billed quelea . . . 10 30
242 80c. Double-toothed barbet (horiz) 10 30
243 2f. Pin-tailed whydah 25 30
244 3f. Red-chested cuckoo (horiz) 35 30
245 18f. Green wood hoopoe . . 1·40 55
246 25f. Cinnamon-chested bee eater (horiz) . . . . 2·00 90
247 80f. Regal sunbird . . . . . 4·50 2·50
248 100f. Fan-tailed whydah (horiz) . . . . 6·50 3·00

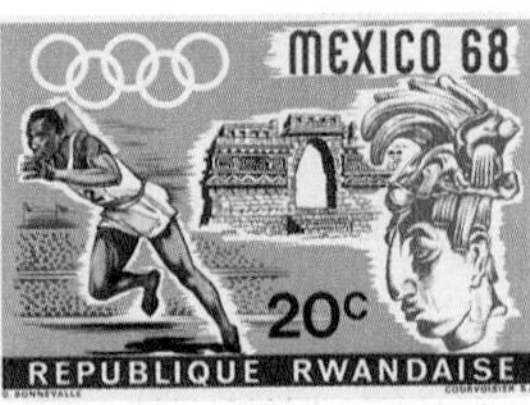

39 Running, and Mexican Antiquites

1968. Olympic Games, Mexico (1st issue). Mult.
250 20c. Type **39** 35 10
251 40c. Hammer-throwing . . . 35 10
252 60c. Hurdling 35 10
253 80c. Javelin-throwing 35 10
254 8f. Football (vert) 45 10
255 10f. Mexican horseman and cacti (vert) 45 10
256 12f. Hockey (vert) 55 10
257 18f. Cathedral (vert) 70 15
258 20f. Boxing (vert) 90 55
259 30f. Mexico City (vert) . . . 1·10 65
The 20c. to 80c. include Mexican antiquities in their designs.

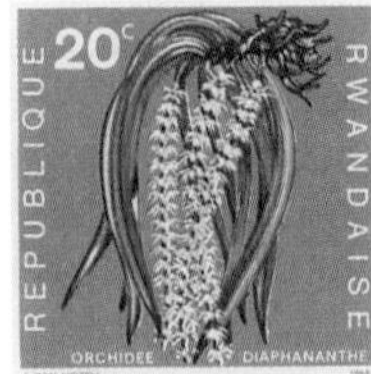

41 "Diaphananthe fragrantissima"

1968. Flowers. Multicoloured.
261 20c. Type **41** 10 10
262 40c. "Phaeomeria speciosa" 10 10
263 60c. "Ravenala madagascariensis" 10 10
264 80c. "Costus afer" 10 10
265 2f. Banana flowers 10 10
266 3f. Flowers and young fruit of pawpaw 10 10
267 18f. "Clerodendron sp." . . . 35 15
268 25f. Sweet potato flowers . . 45 30
269 80f. Baobab flower . . . . . 1·90 80
270 100f. Passion flower . . . . 2·25 1·25

42 Horse-jumping **43** Tuareg (Algeria)

1966. Olympic Games, Mexico (2nd issue).
271 **42** 20c. brown and orange . . 10 10
272 – 40c. brown and turquoise 10 10
273 – 60c. brown and purple . . 10 10
274 – 80c. brown and blue . . . 10 10
275 – 38f. brown and red 50 40
276 – 60f. brown and green . . . 1·10 65
SPORTS: 40c. Judo; 60c. Fencing; 80c. High-jumping; 38f. High-diving; 60f. Weightlifting. Each design also represents the location of previous Olympics as at left in Type **42**.

1968. African National Costumes (1st series). Mult.
277 30c. Type **43** 10 10
278 40c. Upper Volta 10 10
279 60c. Senegal 10 10
280 70c. Rwanda 10 10
281 8f. Morocco 10 10
282 20f. Nigeria 35 20
283 40f. Zambia 80 35
284 50f. Kenya . . . . 1·10 55
See also Nos. 345/52.

44a "Alexandre Lenoir" (J. L. David)

1968. Air. "Philexafrique" Stamp Exhibition, Abidjan (Ivory Coast, 1969) (1st issue).
286 **44a** 100f. multicoloured . . . 2·50 1·60

45 Rwanda Scene and Stamp of Ruanda-Urundi (1953)

1969. Air. "Philexafrique" Stamp Exn (2nd issue).
287 **45** 50f. multicoloured . . . . 1·90 1·25

46 "The Musical Angels" (Van Eyck) **47** Tuareg Tribesmen

1969. "Paintings and Music". Multicoloured.
288 20c. Type **46** (postage) . . . 10 10
289 40c. "The Angels' Concert" (M. Grunewald) 10 10
290 60c. "The Singing Boy" (Frans Hals) 10 10
291 80c. "The Lute player" (G. Terborch) 10 10
292 2f. "The Fifer" (Manet) . . . 10 10
293 6f. "Young Girls at the Piano" (Renoir) 15 10
294 50f. "The Music Lesson" (Fragonard) (air) . . . . . 1·40 85
295 100f. "Angels playing their Musical Instruments" (Memling) (horiz) . . . . 2·75 1·60

1969. African Headdresses (1st series). Mult.
297 20c. Type **47** 10 10
298 40c. Young Ovambo woman 10 10
299 60c. Ancient Guinean and Middle Congo festival headdresses 10 10
300 80c. Guinean "Dagger" dancer 10 10
301 8f. Nigerian Muslims 10 10
302 20f. Luba dancer, Kabondo (Congo) 40 20
303 40f. Senegalese and Gambian women 85 45
304 80f. Rwanda dancer . . . . 1·25 1·00
See also Nos. 408/15.

48 "The Moneylender and his Wife" (Quentin Metsys)

1969. 5th Anniv of African Development Bank.
305 **48** 30f. multicoloured on silver 55 50
306 – 70f. multicoloured on gold 1·60 1·40
DESIGN: 70f. "The Moneylender and his Wife" (Van Reymerswaele).

50 Pyrethrum **51** Revolutionary

1969. Medicinal Plants. Multicoloured.
308 20c. Type **50** 10 10
309 40c. Aloes 10 10
310 60c. Cola 10 10
311 80c. Coca 10 10
312 3f. Hagenia 10 10
313 75f. Cassia . . . . 1·40 80
314 80f. Cinchona . . . . 2·25 90
315 100f. Tephrosia . . . . . . 2·50 1·10

1969. 10th Anniv of Revolution.
316 **51** 6f. multicoloured 15 10
317 18f. multicoloured 50 45
318 40f. multicoloured . . . . 1·00 95

53 "Napoleon on Horseback" (David)

1969. Birth Bicent of Napoleon Bonaparte. Mult. Portraits of Napoleon. Artist's name given.
320 20c. Type **53** 10 10
321 40c. Debret 10 10
322 60c. Gautherot 10 10
323 80c. Ingres 10 10
324 8f. Pajou 20 15
325 20f. Gros 55 40
326 40f. Gros . . . . 1·00 55
327 80f. David . . . . 2·25 1·25

54 "The Quarryman" (O. Bonnevalle)

1969. 50th Anniv of I.L.O. Multicoloured.
328 20c. Type **54** 10 10
329 40c. "Ploughing" (detail Brueghel's "Descent of Icarus") 10 10
330 60c. "The Fisherman" (C. Meunier) 10 10
331 80c. "Ostend Slipway" (J. van Noten) 10 10
332 8f. "The Cook" (P. Aertsen) 20 10
333 10f. "Vulcan's Blacksmiths" (Velazquez) 35 15
334 50f. "Hiercheuse" (C. Meunier) . . . . . . 1·25 60
335 70f. "The Miner" (P. Paulus) 1·60 80
Nos. 330, 332 and 334/5 are vert.

55 "The Derby at Epsom" (Gericault)

1970. Paintings of Horses. Multicoloured.
336 20c. Type **55** 10 10
337 40c. "Horses leaving the Sea" (Delacroix) 10 10
338 60c. "Charles V at Muhlberg" (Titian) (vert) 10 10
339 80c. "To the Races, Amateur Jockeys" (Degas) 10 10
340 8f. "Horsemen at Rest" (Wouwermans) 20 10
341 20f. "Officer of the Imperial Guard" (Gericault) (vert) 60 30
342 40f. "Horse and Dromedary" (Bonnevalle) . . . . 1·50 45
343 80f. "The Prodigal Child" (Rubens) . . . . 2·00 80

1970. African National Costumes (2nd series). As T **43**. Multicoloured.
345 20c. Tharaka Meru woman 10 10
346 30c. Niger flautist 10 10
347 50c. Tunisian water-carrier 10 10
348 1f. Kano ceremonial (Nigeria) 10 10
349 3f. Mali troubador 10 10
350 5f. Quipongo, Angola women 10 10
351 50f. Mauritanian at prayer 95 55
352 90f. Sinehatiali dancers, Ivory Coast . . . . 2·00 1·00

58 Footballer attacking Goal

1970. World Cup Football Championship, Mexico.
353 **58** 20c. multicoloured 10 10
354 – 30c. multicoloured 10 10
355 – 50c. multicoloured 10 10
356 – 1f. multicoloured 10 10
357 – 6f. multicoloured 10 10
358 – 18f. multicoloured 45 30
359 – 30f. multicoloured 85 45
360 – 90f. multicoloured . . . . 2·00 95
Nos. 354/60 show footballers in various positions, similar to Type **58**.

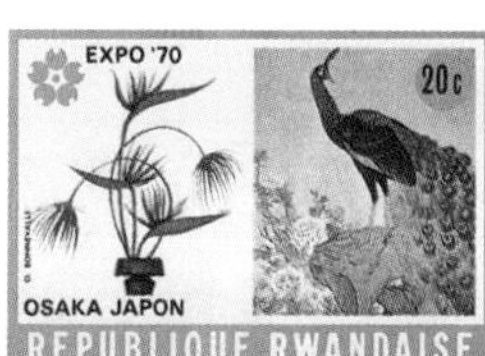

59 Flowers and Green Peafowl

1970. "EXPO 70", World Fair, Osaka, Japan. Mult.
361 20c. Type **59** 60 10
362 30c. Torii gate and "Hibiscus" (Yashuda) . . 10 10
363 50c. Dancer and "Musician" (Katayama) 10 10
364 1f. Sun Tower and "Warrior" 10 10
365 3f. House and "Seated Buddha" 10 10
366 5f. Pagoda and "Head of Girl" (Yamakawa) 10 10
367 20f. Greeting and "Imperial Palace" 55 35
368 70f. Expo emblem and "Horseman" . . . . 1·60 90

60 Two Young Gorillas

1970. Gorillas of the Mountains.
369 **60** 20c. black and green . . . 35 35
370 – 40c. black, brown & purple 35 35
371 – 60c. black, blue and brown 35 35
372 – 80c. black, orange & brown 35 35
373 – 1f. black and mauve . . . 35 35
374 – 2f. multicoloured 35 35
375 – 15f. black and sepia . . . 70 45
376 – 100f. black, brown and blue . . . . 3·75 2·25
GORILLA—VERT: 40c. Squatting; 80c. Beating chest; 2f. Eating banana; 100f. With young. HORIZ: 60c. Walking; 1f. With family; 15f. Heads.

61 Cinchona Bark

1970. 150th Anniv of Discovery of Quinine. Mult.
377 20c. Type **61** 10 10
378 80c. Pharmaceutical equipment 10 10
379 1f. Anopheles mosquito . . . 10 10
380 3f. Malaria patient and nurse 10 10
381 25f. "Attack" on mosquito 55 35
382 70f. Pelletier and Caventou (discoverers of quinine) . . 1·50 80

62 Rocket in Flight **65** Pope Paul VI

63 F. D. Roosevelt and "Brasscattleya olympia alba"

1970. Moon Missions. Multicoloured.
383 20c. Type **62** 10 10
384 30c. Separation during orbit 10 10
385 50c. Spaceship above the moon 10 10
386 1f. Module and astonauts on moon 10 10
387 3f. Take-off from the moon 10 10
388 5f. Return journey to earth 15 10
389 10f. Final separation before landing 30 15
390 80f. Splashdown . . . . . . 2·25 1·40

1970. 25th Death Anniv of F. D. Roosevelt. Portraits and Orchids.
391 **63** 20c. brown, blue and black 10 10
392 – 30c. brown, red and black 10 10
393 – 50c. brown, orange & black 10 10
394 – 1f. brown, green and black 10 10
395 – 2f. green, brown and black 10 10
396 – 6f. green, purple and black 20 15
397 – 30f. green, blue and black 1·25 40
398 – 60f. green, red and black 2·00 70
ORCHIDS: 30c. "Laeliocattleya callistoglossa"; 50c. "Chondrorrhyncha chestertoni"; 1f. "Paphiopedilum"; 2f. "Cymbidium hybride"; 6f. "Cattleya labiata"; 30f. "Dendrobium nobile"; 60f. "Laelia gouldiana".

1970. Centenary of 1st Vatican Council.
400 **65** 10c. brown and gold . . . 10 10
401 – 20c. green and gold . . . 10 10
402 – 30c. lake and gold 10 10
403 – 40c. blue and gold 10 10
404 – 1f. violet and gold 10 10
405 – 18f. purple and gold . . . 50 20
406 – 20f. orange and gold . . . 60 20
407 – 60f. brown and gold . . . 1·60 70
POPES: 20c. John XXIII; 30c. Pius XII; 40c. Pius XI; 1f. Benedict XV; 18f. Pius X; 20f. Leo XIII; 60f. Pius IX.

1971. African Headdresses (2nd series). Mult. As T **47**.
408 20c. Rendille woman 10 10
409 30c. Chad woman 10 10
410 50c. Bororo man (Niger) . . 10 10
411 1f. Masai man (Kenya) . . . 10 10
412 5f. Air girl (Niger) 10 10
413 18f. Rwanda woman 35 20
414 25f. Mauritania man 65 35
415 50f. Rwanda girls . . . . . 1·50 65

68 "Beethoven" (C. Horneman)

1971. Birth Cent (1970) of Beethoven. Portraits and funeral scene by various artists. Mult.

418 20c. Type **68** 10 10
419 30c. K. Stieler 10 10
420 50c. F. Schimon 10 10
421 3f. H. Best 10 10
422 6f. W. Fassbender 30 10
423 90f. "Beethoven's Burial" (Stober) . . . . 2·10 2·00

69 Horse-jumping

1971. Olympic Games, Munich (1972) (1st issue).

424 **69** 20c. gold and black 10 10
425 – 30c. gold and purple . . . 10 10
426 – 50c. gold and violet . . . 10 10
427 – 1f. gold and green 10 10
428 – 8f. gold and red 20 10
429 – 10f. gold and violet 30 15
430 – 20f. gold and brown 50 30
431 – 60f. gold and green . . . . 1·40 65

DESIGNS: 30c. Running (start); 50c. Basketball; 1f. High-jumping; 8f. Boxing; 10f. Pole-vaulting; 20f. Wrestling; 60f. Gymnastics.

See also Nos. 490/7.

70 U.A.M.P.T. H.Q. and Rwandaise Woman and Child

1971. Air. 10th Anniv of U.A.M.P.T.

432 **70** 100f. multicoloured . . . . 2·10 2·00

72 "Durer" (self-portrait)

1971. 500th Birth Anniv of Durer. Paintings. Multicoloured.

434 20c. "Adam" 10 10
435 30c. "Eve" 10 10
436 50c. "Portrait of H. Holzschuher" 10 10
437 1f. "Mourning the Dead Christ" 10 10
438 3f. "Madonna and Child" . . 10 10
439 5f. "St. Eustace" 10 10
440 20f. "St. Paul and St. Mark" 45 30
441 70f. Type **72** . . . . 1·60 1·00

73 Astronauts in Moon Rover

1972. Moon Mission of "Apollo 15".

442 **73** 600f. gold . . . . 95·00

74 Participation in Sport

1972. National Guard. Multicoloured.

443 4f. Type **74** 10 10
444 6f. Transport of emergency supplies 15 10
445 15f. Helicopter transport for the sick 40 20
446 25f. Participation in health service 65 35
447 50f. Guard, map and emblem (vert) . . . . 1·25 1·10

75 Ice Hockey

1972. Winter Olympic Games, Sapporo, Japan. Multicoloured.

448 20c. Type **75** 10 10
449 30c. Speed-skating 10 10
450 50c. Ski-jumping 10 10
451 1f. Figure skating 10 10
452 6f. Cross-country skiing . . . 10 10
453 12f. Slalom 15 15
454 20f. Tobogganing 45 20
455 60f. Downhill skiing . . . . 1·40 1·10

76 Savanna Monkey and Impala

1972. Akagera National Park. Multicoloured.

456 20c. Type **76** 15 10
457 30c. African buffalo 15 10
458 50c. Common zebra 15 10
459 1f. White rhinoceros 40 40
460 2f. Warthogs 15 10
461 6f. Hippopotamus 20 10
462 18f. Spotted hyenas 40 20
463 32f. Helmeted guineafowl . . 2·25 95
464 60f. Waterbucks . . . . . . 2·00 1·10
465 80f. Lion and lioness . . . . 2·75 1·75

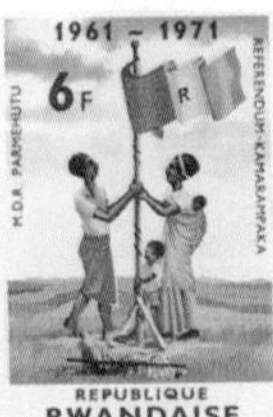

77 Family supporting Flag

78 Variable Sunbirds

1972. 10th Anniv of Referendum.

466 **77** 6f. multicoloured 10 10
467 18f. multicoloured 45 35
468 60f. multicoloured . . . . 1·25 1·10

1972. Rwanda Birds. Multicoloured.

469 20c. Common waxbills . . . 10 10
470 30c. Collared sunbird 15 10
471 50c. Type **78** 20 10
472 1f. Greater double-collared sunbird 30 10
473 4f. Ruwenzori puff-back flycatcher 35 15
474 6f. Red-billed fire finch . . . 40 20
475 10f. Scarlet-chested sunbird 70 20
476 18f. Red-headed quelea . . . 1·50 40
477 60f. Black-headed gonolek . . 4·75 1·50
478 100f. African golden oriole 8·00 2·40

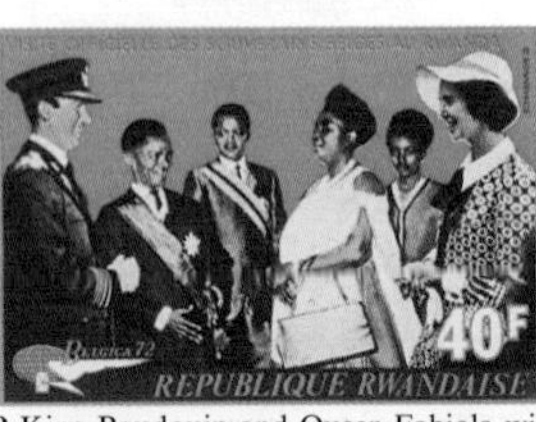

79 King Baudouin and Queen Fabiola with President and Mrs. Kayibanda in Rwanda

1972. "Belgica 72" Stamp Exhibition, Brussels.

479 – 18f. multicoloured 70 70
480 – 22f. multicoloured 90 90
481 **79** 40f. blue, black and gold 1·75 1·75

DESIGNS: 18f. Rwanda village; 22f. View of Bruges. Nos. 479/80 are smaller, size 39 × 36 mm.

80 Announcement of Independence

1972. 10th Anniv of Independence.

482 **80** 20c. green and gold 10 10
483 – 30c. purple and gold . . . 10 10
484 – 50c. sepia and gold 10 10
485 – 6f. blue and gold 10 10
486 – 10f. purple and gold . . . 15 10
487 – 15f. blue and gold 35 20
488 – 18f. brown and gold . . . 45 30
489 – 50f. green and gold . . . . 1·10 70

DESIGNS—HORIZ: 30c. Promotion ceremony, officers of the National Guard; 50c. Pres. Kayibanda, wife and family; 6f. Pres. Kayibanda casting vote in legislative elections; 10f. Pres. and Mrs. Kayibanda at "Festival of Justice"; 15f. President and members of National Assembly; 18f. Investiture of Pres. Kayibanda. VERT: 50f. President Kayibanda.

81 Horse-jumping

1972. Olympic Games, Munich (2nd issue).

490 **81** 20c. green and gold 10 10
491 – 30c. violet and gold . . . 10 10
492 – 50c. green and gold 10 10
493 – 1f. purple and gold 10 10
494 – 6f. black and gold 10 10
495 – 18f. brown and gold . . . 35 30
496 – 30f. violet and gold 80 55
497 – 44f. blue and gold . . . . 1·10 65

DESIGNS: 30c. Hockey; 50c. Football; 1f. Long-jumping; 6f. Cycling; 18f. Yachting; 30f. Hurdling; 44f. Gymnastics.

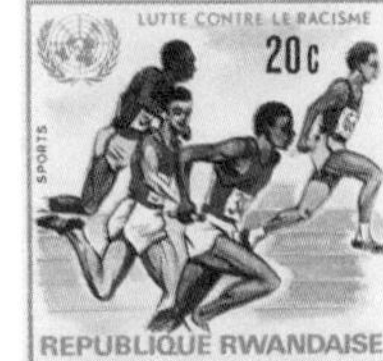

82 Runners

1972. Racial Equality Year. "Working Together". Multicoloured.

498 20c. Type **82** 10 10
499 30c. Musicians 10 10
500 50c. Ballet dancers 10 10
501 1f. Medical team in operating theatre 10 10
502 6f. Weaver and painter . . . 10 10
503 18f. Children in class 35 20
504 24f. Laboratory technicians 55 35
505 50f. U.N. emblem and hands of four races . . . . . . 1·00 65

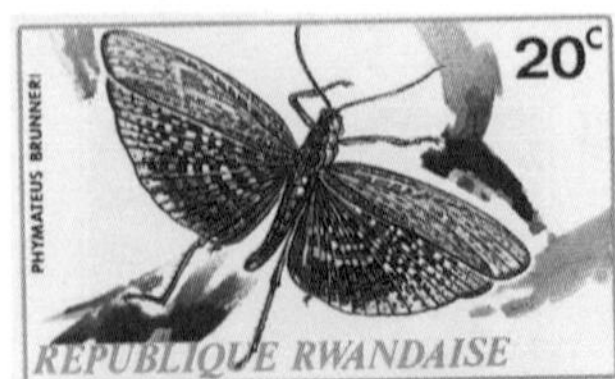

84 "Phymateus brunneri"

1973. Rwanda Insects. Multicoloured.

507 20c. Type **84** 10 10
508 30c. "Diopsis fumipennis" (vert) 10 10
509 50c. "Kitoko alberti" 10 10
510 1f. "Archibracon fasciatus" (vert) 10 10
511 2f. "Ornithacris cyanea imperialis" 10 10
512 6f. "Clitodaca fenestralis" (vert) 15 10
513 18f. "Senaspis oesacus" . . . 40 20
514 22f. "Phonoctonus grandis" (vert) 55 35
515 70f. "Loba leopardina" . . . 2·25 2·40
516 100f. "Ceratocoris distortus" (vert) . . . . 4·00 3·10

85 "Emile Zola" (Manet)

86 Longombe

1973. International Book Year. "Readers and Writers". Paintings and portraits. Multicoloured.

518 20c. Type **85** 10 10
519 30c. "Rembrandt's Mother" (Rembrandt) 10 10
520 50c. "St. Jerome removing Thorn from Lion's paw" (Colantonio) 10 10
521 1f. "St. Peter and St. Paul" (El Greco) 10 10
522 2f. "Virgin and Child" (Van der Weyden) 10 10
523 6f. "St. Jerome in his Cell" (Antonella de Messina) . . 15 10
524 40f. "St. Barbara" (Master of Flemalle) . . . . 1·00 60
525 100f. "Don Quixote" (O. Bonnevalle) . . . . . 2·40 1·90

1973. Musical Instruments. Multicoloured.

527 20c. Type **86** 10 10
528 30c. Horn 10 10
529 50c. "Xylophone" 10 10
530 1f. "Harp" 10 10
531 4f. Alur horns 10 10
532 6f. Horn, bells and drum . . 10 10
533 18f. Drums 40 40
534 90f. Gourds . . . . 2·00 1·40

87 "Rubens and Isabelle Brandt" (Rubens)

88 Map of Africa and Doves

1973. "IBRA" Stamp Exhibition, Munich. Famous Paintings. Multicoloured.

535 20c. Type **87** 10 10
536 30c. "Portrait of a Lady" (Cranach the Younger) . . 10 10
537 50c. "Woman peeling Turnips" (Chardin) 10 10
538 1f. "Abduction of the Daughters of Leucippe" (Rubens) 10 10
539 2f. "Virgin and Child" (Lippi) 10 10
540 6f. "Boys eating Fruit" (Murillo) 20 10
541 40f. "The Sickness of Love" (Steen) 90 45
542 100f. "Jesus divested of His Garments" (El Greco) . . 2·25 1·40

1973. 10th Anniv of O.A.U. Multicoloured.

544 6f. Type **88** 20 10
545 94f. Map of Africa and hands 2·25 1·90

1973. Pan-African Drought Relief. Nos. 308/13 and 315 optd **SECHERESSE SOLIDARITE AFRICAINE** and No. 315 additionally surch.

546 **50** 20c. multicoloured 10 10
547 – 40c. multicoloured 10 10
548 – 60c. multicoloured 10 10
549 – 80c. multicoloured 10 10
550 – 3f. multicoloured 10 10
551 – 75f. multicoloured . . . . 1·60 1·40
552 – 100f.+50f. multicoloured 5·00 4·00

90 Six-banded Distichodus

1973. Fishes. Multicoloured.

553 20c. Type **90** 10 10
554 30c. Lesser tigerfish 10 10
555 50c. Angel squeaker 10 10
556 1f. Nile mouthbrooder . . . 10 10
557 2f. African lungfish 15 10
558 6f. Mandeville's catfish . . . 35 10
559 40f. Congo tetra . . . . . . 1·90 95
560 150f. Golden julie . . . . . 6·25 3·50

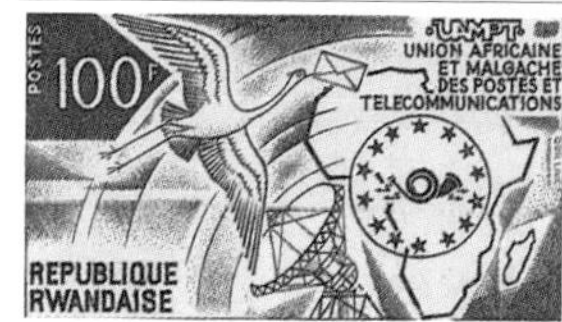

91 Crane with Letter and Telecommunications Emblem

1973. 12th Anniv of U.A.M.P.T.
562 **91** 100f. blue, brown and mauve . . . . 2·50 1·90

1973. African Fortnight, Brussels. Nos. 408/15 optd **QUINZAINE AFRICAINE BRUXELLES 15/30 SEPT. 1973** and globe.
563 20c. multicoloured 10 10
564 30c. multicoloured 10 10
565 50c. multicoloured 10 10
566 1f. multicoloured 10 10
567 5f. multicoloured 10 10
568 18f. multicoloured 40 20
569 25f. multicoloured 50 45
570 50f. multicoloured . . . . . 1·40 85

1973. Air. Congress of French-speaking Nations, Liege. No. 432 optd **LIEGE ACCUEILLE LES PAYS DE LANGUE FRANCAISE 1973** (No. 562) or congress emblem (No. 563).
571 100f. multicoloured . . . . . 4·00 2·75
572 100f. multicoloured . . . . . 4·00 2·75

1973. 25th Anniv of Declaration of Human Rights. Nos. 443/7 optd with Human Rights emblem.
574 **74** 4f. multicoloured 10 10
575 – 6f. multicoloured 10 10
576 – 15f. multicoloured 30 15
577 – 25f. multicoloured 60 40
578 – 50f. multicoloured . . . . 1·40 95

96 Copernicus and Astrolabe

97 Pres. Habyarimana

1973. 500th Birth Anniv of Copernicus. Mult.
580 20c. Type **96** 10 10
581 30c. Copernicus 10 10
582 50c. Copernicus and heliocentric system 10 10
583 1f. Type **96** 10 10
584 18f. As 30c. 65 60
585 80f. As 50c. . . . . 2·40 2·00

1974. "New Regime".
587 **97** 1f. brown, black and buff 10 10
588 2f. brown, black and blue 10 10
589 5f. brown, black and red 10 10
590 6f. brown, black and blue 10 10
591 26f. brown, black and lilac 55 45
592 60f. brown, black and green . . . . 1·25 1·00

99 Yugoslavia v Zaire

101 "Diane de Poiters" (Fontainebleau School)

100 Marconi's Steam Yacht "Elettra"

1974. World Cup Football Championship, West Germany. Players represent specified teams. Mult.
594 20c. Type **99** 10 10
595 40c. Netherlands v Sweden 10 10
596 60c. West Germany v Australia 10 10
597 80c. Haiti v Argentina . . . 10 10
598 2f. Brazil v Scotland 10 10
599 6f. Bulgaria v Uruguay . . . 10 10
600 40f. Italy v Poland 80 65
601 50f. Chile v East Germany 1·40 1·00

1974. Birth Centenary of Guglielmo Marconi (radio pioneer). Multicoloured.
602 20c. Type **100** 20 10
603 30c. Cruiser "Carlo Alberto" 20 10
604 50c. Marconi's telegraph equipment 10 10
605 4f. "Global Telecommunications" . . . 10 10
606 35f. Early radio receiver . . . 85 45
607 60f. Marconi and Poldhu radio station . . . . 1·50 1·10

1974. International Stamp Exhibitions "Stockholmia" and "Internaba". Paintings from Stockholm and Basle. Multicoloured.
609 20c. Type **101** 10 10
610 30c. "The Flute-player" (J. Leyster) 10 10
611 50c. "Virgin Mary and Child" (G. David) 10 10
612 1f. "The Triumph of Venus" (F. Boucher) 10 10
613 10f. "Harlequin Seated" (P. Picasso) 15 10
614 18f. "Virgin and Child" (15th-century) 35 15
615 20f. "The Beheading of St. John" (H. Fries) . . . 45 35
616 50f. "The Daughter of Andersdotter" (J. Hockert) 1·40 1·00

102 Monastic Messenger

105 Head of Uganda Kob

1974. Centenary of U.P.U. Multicoloured.
619 20c. Type **102** 10 10
620 30c. Inca messenger 10 10
621 50c. Moroccan postman . . . 10 10
622 1f. Indian postman 10 10
623 18f. Polynesian postman . . 55 40
624 80f. Early Rwanda messenger with horn and drum . . . 2·00 1·40

1974. 15th Anniv of Revolution. Nos. 316/18 optd **1974 15e ANNIVERSAIRE**.
625 **51** 6f. multicoloured . . . .
626 18f. multicoloured . . . .
627 40f. multicoloured . . . .
Set of 3 . . . . 11·00 9·50

1974. 10th Anniv of African Development Bank. Nos. 305/6 optd **1974 10e ANNIVERSAIRE**.
629 **48** 30f. multicoloured 85 65
630 – 70f. multicoloured . . . . 1·90 1·40

1975. Antelopes. Multicoloured.
631 20c. Type **105** 15 10
632 30c. Bongo with calf (horiz) 15 10
633 50c. Roan antelope and sable antelope heads 15 10
634 1f. Young sitatungas (horiz) 15 10
635 4f. Great kudu 15 10
636 10f. Impala family (horiz) . . 80 10
637 34f. Waterbuck head . . . . 2·00 70
638 100f. Giant eland (horiz) . . 5·75 2·50

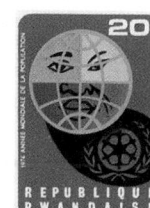

108 Pyrethrum Daisies

111 Globe and Emblem

110 Eastern White Pelicans

1975. Agricultural Labour Year. Multicoloured.
642 20c. Type **108** 10 10
643 30c. Tea plant 10 10
644 50c. Coffee berries 10 10
645 4f. Bananas 10 10
646 10f. Maize 20 10
647 12f. Sorghum 35 15
648 26f. Rice 80 45
649 47f. Coffee cultivation . . . 1·60 90

1975. Holy Year. Nos. 400/7 optd **1975 ANNEE SAINTE**.
652 **65** 10c. brown and gold . . . 10 10
653 – 20c. green and gold 10 10
654 – 30c. lake and gold 10 10
655 – 40c. blue and gold 10 10
656 – 1f. violet and gold 10 10
657 – 18f. purple and gold . . . 40 20
658 – 20f. orange and gold . . . 45 20
659 – 60f. brown and gold . . . 1·90 1·25

1975. Aquatic Birds. Multicoloured.
660 20c. Type **110** 10 10
661 30c. Malachite kingfisher . . 10 10
662 50c. Goliath herons 10 10
663 1f. Saddle-bill stork 10 10
664 4f. African jacana 40 15
665 10f. African darter 85 35
666 34f. Sacred ibis . . . . . . 2·40 1·00
667 80f. Hartlaub's duck . . . . 6·50 2·75

1975. World Population Year (1974). Mult.
669 20f. Type **111** 45 30
670 26f. Population graph 65 35
671 34f. Symbolic doorway . . . 95 50

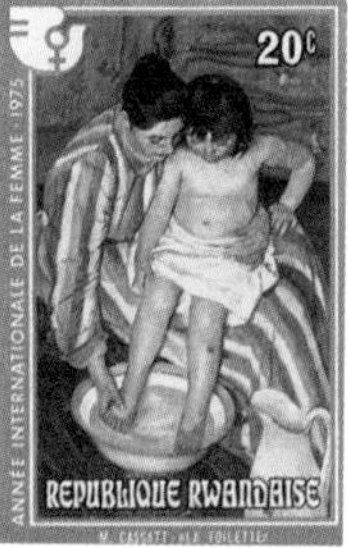

112 "La Toilette" (M. Cassatt)

113 "Arts"

1975. International Women's Year. Multicoloured.
672 20c. Type **112** 10 10
673 30c. "Mother and Child" (G. Melchers) 10 10
674 50c. "The Milk Jug" (Vermeer) 10 10
675 1f. "The Water-carrier" (Goya) 10 10
676 8f. Coffee picking 20 10
677 12f. Laboratory technician . . 35 20
678 18f. Rwandaise mother and child 55 20
679 60f. Woman carrying water jug . . . . 1·50 1·25

1975. 10th Anniv of National University. The Faculties. Multicoloured.
681 20c. Type **113** 10 10
682 30c. "Medicine" 10 10
683 1f.50 "Jurisprudence" 10 10
684 18f. "Science" 40 20
685 26f. "Commerce" 45 30
686 34f. University Building, Kigali 85 55

114 Cattle at Pool, and "Impatiens stuhlmannii"

1975. Protection of Nature. Multicoloured.
688 20c. Type **114** 10 10
689 30c. Euphorbis "candelabra" and savannah bush 10 10
690 50c. Bush fire and "Tapinanthus prunifolius" 10 10
691 5f. Lake Bulera and "Nymphaea lotus" 10 10
692 8f. Soil erosion and "Protea madiensis" 15 10
693 10f. Protected marshland and "Melanthera brownei" . . 20 15
694 26f. Giant lobelias and groundsel 55 40
695 100f. Sabyinyo volcano and "Polystachya kermesina" 2·50 2·25

1975. Pan-African Drought Relief. Nos. 345/52 optd or surch **SECHERESSE SOLIDARITE 1975** (both words share same initial letter).
696 20c. multicoloured 10 10
697 30c. multicoloured 10 10
698 50c. multicoloured 10 10
699 1f. multicoloured 10 10
700 3f. multicoloured 10 10
701 5f. multicoloured 15 10
702 50f.+25f. multicoloured . . . 1·60 1·25
703 90f.+25f. multicoloured . . . 2·40 2·00

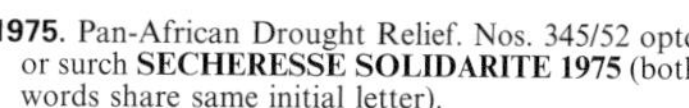

116 Loading Douglas DC-8F Jet Trader

1975. Year of Increased Production. Multicoloured.
704 20c. Type **116** 10 10
705 30c. Coffee-picking plant . . 10 10
706 50c. Lathe operator 10 10
707 10f. Farmer with hoe (vert) 15 10
708 35f. Coffee-picking (vert) . . 60 55
709 54f. Mechanical plough . . . 1·10 95

117 African Woman with Basket on Head

1975. "Themabelga" Stamp Exhibition, Brussels. African Costumes.
710 **117** 20c. multicoloured 10 10
711 – 30c. multicoloured 10 10
712 – 50c. multicoloured 10 10
713 – 1f. multicoloured 10 10
714 – 5f. multicoloured 10 10
715 – 7f. multicoloured 15 10
716 – 35f. multicoloured 70 60
717 – 51f. multicoloured . . . . 1·40 95
DESIGNS: 30c. to 51f. Various Rwanda costumes.

118 Dr. Schweitzer, Organ Pipes and Music Score

1976. World Leprosy Day.
719 – 20c. lilac, brown and black 10 10
720 – 30c. lilac, green and black 10 10
721 **118** 50c. lilac, brown and black 10 10
722 – 1f. lilac, purple and black 10 10
723 – 3f. lilac, blue and black 10 10
724 – 5f. lilac, brown and black 10 10
725 **118** 10f. lilac, blue and black 30 10
726 – 80f. lilac, red and black 1·90 1·40
DESIGNS: Dr. Schweitzer and: 20c. Piano keyboard and music; 30c. Lambarene Hospital; 1f. Lambarene residence; 3f. as 20c.; 5f. as 30 c; 80f. as 1f.

119 "Surrender at Yorktown"

1976. Bicentenary of American Revolution. Mult.
727 20c. Type **119** 10 10
728 30c. "The Sergeant-Instructor at Valley Forge" 10 10
729 50c. "Presentation of Captured Yorktown Flags to Congress" 10 10
730 1f. "Washington at Fort Lee" 10 10
731 18f. "Washington boarding a British warship" 45 30
732 26f. "Washington studying Battle plans" 55 40
733 34f. "Washington firing a Cannon" 90 55
734 40f. "Crossing the Delaware" 1·00 85

120 Sister Yohana

121 Yachting

1976. 75th Anniv of Catholic Church in Rwanda. Multicoloured.
736 20c. Type **120** 10 10
737 30c. Abdon Sabakati 10 10
738 50c. Father Alphonse Brard 10 10
739 4f. Abbe Balthazar Gafuku 10 10
740 10f. Monseigneur Bigirumwami 20 10
741 25f. Save Catholic Church (horiz) 60 45
742 60f. Kabgayi Catholic Cathedral (horiz) . . . . . 1·25 80

1976. Olympic Games, Montreal (1st issue).
743 **121** 20c. brown and green . . 10 10
744 – 30c. blue and green . . . 10 10
745 – 50c. black and green . . . 10 10
746 – 1f. violet and green . . . 10 10
747 – 10f. blue and green . . . 20 10
748 – 18f. brown and green . . 35 30
749 – 29f. purple and green . . 80 60
750 – 51f. deep green and green 1·00 80
DESIGNS: 30c. Horse-jumping; 50c. Long jumping; 1f. Hockey; 10f. Swimming; 18f. Football; 29f. Boxing; 51f. Gymnastics.
See also Nos. 767/74.

122 Bell's Experimental Telephone and Manual Switchboard

1976. Telephone Centenary.
751 **122** 20c. brown and blue . . . 10 10
752 – 30c. blue and violet . . . 10 10
753 – 50c. brown and blue . . . 10 10
754 – 1f. orange and blue . . . 10 10
755 – 4f. mauve and blue . . . 10 10
756 – 8f. green and blue . . . . 2·50 35
757 – 26f. red and blue 70 55
758 – 60f. lilac and blue . . . . 1·40 1·00
DESIGNS: 30c. Early telephone and man making call; 50c. Early telephone and woman making call; 1f. Early telephone and exchange building; 4f. Alexander Graham Bell and "candlestick" telephone; 8f. Rwanda subscriber and dial telephone; 26f. Dish aerial, satellite and modern handset; 60f. Rwanda PTT building, operator and push-button telephone.

1976. Bicentenary of Declaration of American Independence. Nos. 727/34 optd **INDEPENDENCE DAY** and Bicentennial Emblem.
759 **119** 20c. multicoloured 10 10
760 – 30c. multicoloured 10 10
761 – 50c. multicoloured 10 10
762 – 1f. multicoloured 10 10
763 – 18f. multicoloured 35 20
764 – 26f. multicoloured 65 45
765 – 34f. multicoloured 80 55
766 – 40f. multicoloured . . . . 1·10 80

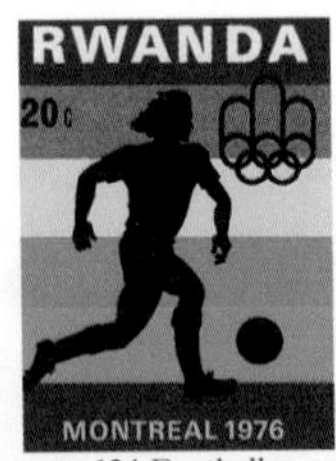

124 Football

1976. Olympic Games, Montreal (2nd issue). Mult.
767 20c. Type **124** 10 10
768 30c. Rifle-shooting 10 10
769 50c. Canoeing 10 10
770 1f. Gymnastics 10 10
771 10f. Weightlifting 15 10
772 12f. Diving 30 20
773 26f. Horse-riding 55 40
774 50f. Throwing the hammer 1·40 90

125 "Apollo" and "Soyuz" Launches and ASTP Badge

1976. "Apollo"–"Soyuz" Test Project. Mult.
776 20c. Type **125** 10 10
777 30c. "Soyuz" rocket 10 10
778 50c. "Apollo" rocket 10 10
779 1f. "Apollo" after separation 10 10
780 2f. Approach to link-up . . . 10 10
781 12f. Spacecraft docked . . . 35 15
782 30f. Sectional view of interiors . . . . 1·10 55
783 54f. "Apollo" splashdown . . 2·25 1·25

126 "Eulophia cucullata"

128 Hands embracing "Cultural Collaboration"

1976. Rwandaise Orchids. Multicoloured.
784 20c. Type **126** 10 10
785 30c. "Eulophia streptopetala" 10 10
786 50c. "Disa stairsii" 10 10
787 1f. "Aerangis kotschyana" . . 10 10
788 10f. "Eulophia abyssinica" 20 10
789 12f. "Bonatea steudneri" . . 30 15
790 26f. "Ansellia gigantea" . . . 1·10 45
791 50f. "Eulophia angolensis" 2·00 1·25

1977. World Leprosy Day. Nos. 719/26 optd with **JOURNEE MONDIALE 1977**.
793 – 20c. lilac, brown and black 10 10
794 – 30c. lilac, green and black 10 10
795 **118** 50c. lilac, brown and black 10 10
796 – 1f. lilac, purple and black 10 10
797 – 3f. lilac, blue and black 10 10
798 – 5f. lilac, brown and black 20 10
799 **118** 10f. lilac, brown and black 35 20
800 – 80f. lilac, red and black 1·60 1·60

1977. 10th OCAM Summit Meeting, Kigali. Mult.
801 10f. Type **128** 30 10
802 26f. Hands embracing "Technical Collaboration" 70 40
803 64f. Hands embracing "Economic Collaboration" 1·25 90

1977. World Water Conference. Nos. 688/95 optd **CONFERENCE MONDIALE DE L'EAU**.
805 **114** 20c. multicoloured 10 10
806 – 30c. multicoloured 10 10
807 – 50c. multicoloured 10 10
808 – 5f. multicoloured 15 10
809 – 8f. multicoloured 20 10
810 – 10f. multicoloured 40 15
811 – 26f. multicoloured . . . . 1·40 75
812 – 100f. multicoloured . . . 3·50 3·25

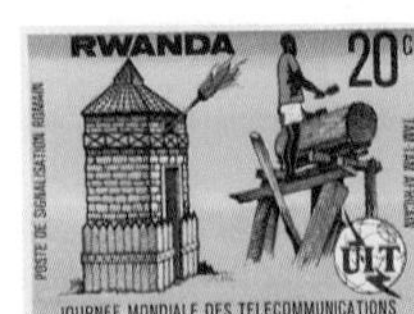

131 Roman Signal Post and African Tam-Tam

1977. World Telecommunications Day. Mult.
813 20c. Type **131** 10 10
814 30c. Chappe's semaphore and post-rider 10 10
815 50c. Morse code 10 10
816 1f. "Goliath" laying Channel cable 10 10
817 4f. Telephone, radio and television 10 10
818 18f. "Kingsport" and maritime communications satellite 75 40
819 26f. Telecommunications satellite and aerial 50 40
820 50f. "Mariner 2" satellite . . 1·40 90

132 "The Ascent to Calvary" (detail)

135 Long-crested Eagle

133 Chateau Sassenage, Grenoble

1977. 400th Birth Anniv of Peter Paul Rubens. Multicoloured.
823 20c. Type **132** 10 10
824 30c. "The Judgement of Paris" (horiz) 10 10
825 50c. "Marie de Medici, Queen of France" 10 10
826 1f. "Heads of Negroes" (horiz) 10 10
827 4f. "St. Idelfonse Triptych" (detail) 10 10
828 8f. "Helene Fourment with her Children" (horiz) . . . 15 10
829 26f. "St. Idelfonse Triptych" (different detail) 80 65
830 60f. "Helene Fourment" . . 2·50 1·75

1977. Air. 10th Anniv of International French Language Council.
831 **133** 50f. multicoloured . . . . 1·60 1·10

1977. Birds of Prey. Multicoloured.
833 20c. Type **135** 10 10
834 30c. African harrier hawk . . 10 10
835 50c. African fish eagle . . . 15 10
836 1f. Hooded vulture 15 15
837 3f. Augur buzzard 20 15
838 5f. Black kite 30 15
839 20f. Black-shouldered kite . . 1·50 70
840 100f. Bateleur . . . . 5·75 3·25

1912. Dr. Wernher von Braun Commemoration. Nos. 776/83 optd with **in memoriam WERNHER VON BRAUN 1912 - 1977**.
841 20c. Type **125** 10 10
842 30c. "Soyuz" rocket 10 10
843 50c. "Apollo" rocket 10 10
844 1f. "Apollo" after separation 10 10
845 2f. Approach to link up . . . 10 10
846 12f. Spacecraft docked . . . 40 20
847 30f. Sectional view of interiors . . . . 1·40 50
848 54f. "Apollo" after splashdown . . . . 2·50 1·50

138 Scout playing Whistle

139 Chimpanzees

1978. 10th Anniv of Rwanda Scout Association. Multicoloured.
851 20c. Type **138** 10 10
852 30c. Camp fire 10 10
853 50c. Scouts constructing a platform 10 10
854 1f. Two scouts 10 10
855 10f. Scouts on look-out . . . 20 10
856 18f. Scouts in canoe 45 35
857 26f. Cooking at camp fire . . 80 60
858 44f. Lord Baden-Powell . . . 1·50 1·25

1978. Apes. Multicoloured.
859 20c. Type **139** 10 10
860 30c. Gorilla 10 10
861 50c. Eastern black-and-white colobus 10 10
862 3f. Eastern needle-clawed bushbaby 10 10
863 10f. Mona monkey 30 10
864 26f. Potto 65 65
865 60f. Savanna monkey . . . . 1·90 1·90
866 150f. Olive baboon . . . . . 3·75 3·75

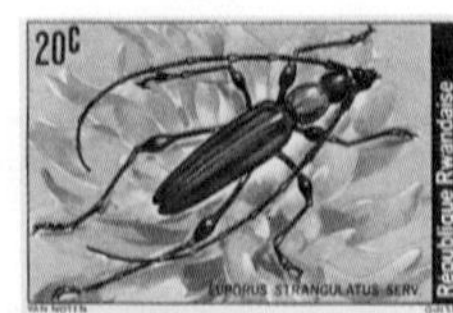

140 "Euporus strangulatus"

1978. Beetles. Multicoloured.
867 20c. Type **140** 10 10
868 30c. "Rhina afzelii" (vert) . . 10 10
869 50c. "Pentalobus palini" . . 10 10
870 3f. "Corynodes dejeani" (vert) 10 10
871 10f. "Mecynorhina torquata" 20 10
872 15f. "Mecocerus rhombeus" (vert) 55 10
873 20f. "Macrotoma serripes" 75 20
874 25f. "Neptunides stanleyi" (vert) 90 40
875 26f. "Petrognatha gigas" . . 90 40
876 100f. "Eudicella gralli" (vert) 3·25 2·50

141 Poling Boat across River of Poverty

1978. National Revolutionary Development Movement. Multicoloured.
877 4f. Type **141** 10 10
878 10f. Poling boat to right . . 15 10
879 26f. Type **141** 60 40
880 60f. As 10f. . . . . 1·10 85

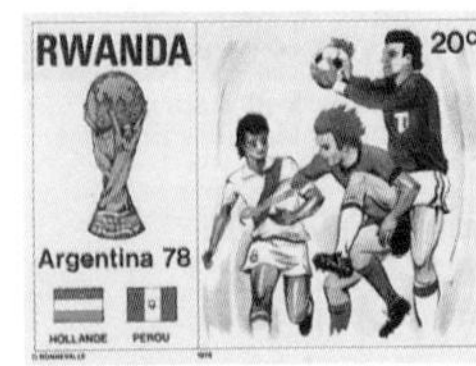

142 Footballers, Cup and Flags of Netherlands and Peru

1978. World Cup Football Championship, Argentina. Multicoloured.
881 20c. Type **142** 10 10
882 30c. Flags of FIFA, Sweden and Spain 10 10
883 50c. Mascot and flags of Scotland and Iran 10 10
884 2f. Emblem and flags of West Germany and Tunisia . . . 10 10
885 3f. Cup and flags of Italy and Hungary 10 10
886 10f. Flags of FIFA, Brazil and Austria 20 10
887 34f. Mascot and flags of Poland and Mexico 85 70
888 100f. Emblem and flags of Argentina and France . . 2·50 2·00
No. 883 shows the Union Jack.

143 Wright Brothers and Wright Flyer I, 1903

1978. Aviation History. Multicoloured.
889 20c. Type **143** 10 10
890 30c. Alberto Santos-Dumont and biplane "14 bis", 1906 10 10
891 50c. Henri Farman and Farman Voisin No. 1 bis, 1908 . . . . 10 10
892 1f. Jan Olieslagers and Bleriot XI 10 10
893 3f. General Italo Balbo and Savoia S-17 flying boat, 1919 . . . . 10 10
894 10f. Charles Lindbergh and "Spirit of St. Louis", 1927 15 10
895 55f. Hugo Junkers and Junkers Ju 52/3m, 1932 . . 1·10 55
896 60f. Igor Sikorsky and Vought-Sikorsky VS-300 helicopter prototype . . . 1·60 85

143a Great Spotted Woodpecker and Oldenburg 1852 ⅓sgr. Stamp

1978. Air. "Philexafrique" Stamp Exhibition, Libreville, Gabon and Int Stamp Fair, Essen, West Germany. Multicoloured.
898 30f. Type **143a** . . . . 1·40 90
899 30f. Greater kudu and Rwanda 1967 20c. stamp 1·40 90

1978. 15th Anniv of Organization of African Unity. Nos. 544/5 optd **1963 1978**.
901 **88** 6f. multicoloured 30 10
902 – 94f. multicoloured . . . . 1·90 1·10

146 Spur-winged Goose and Mallard

147 "Papilio demodocus"

1978. Stock Rearing Year. Multicoloured.
903 20c. Type **146** 20 10
904 30c. Goats (horiz) 10 10
905 50c. Chickens 10 10
906 4f. Rabbits (horiz) 20 10
907 5f. Pigs 20 10
908 15f. Common turkey (horiz) 90 30
909 50f. Sheep and cattle . . . . 1·50 50
910 75f. Bull (horiz) . . . . . . 1·90 70

1979. Butterflies. Multicoloured.
911 20c. Type **147** 10 10
912 30c. "Precis octavia" 10 10
913 50c. "Charaxes smaragdalis caerulea" 10 10
914 4f. "Charaxes guderiana" 15 10
915 15f. "Colotis evippe" 20 10
916 30f. "Danaus limniace petiverana" 55 30
917 50f. "Byblia acheloia" 1·50 55
918 150f. "Utetheisa pulchella" 3·75 1·40

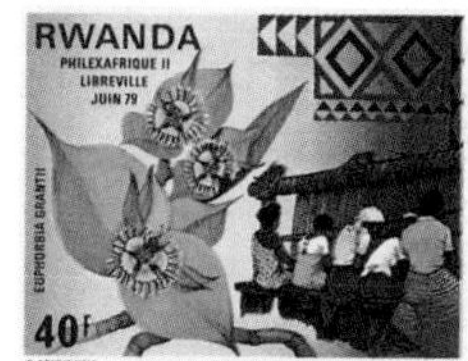

148 "Euphorbia grantii" and Women weaving

1979. "Philexafrique" Exhibition, Libreville. Mult.
919 40f. Type **148** 1·40 85
920 60f. Drummers and "Intelsat" satellite 2·25 1·10

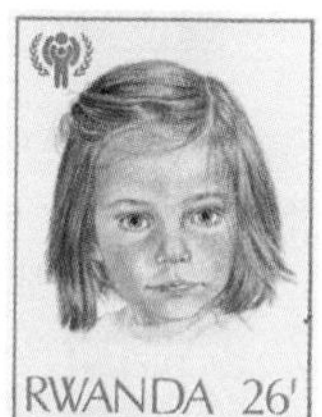

149 "Polyscias fulva" **150** European Girl

1979. Trees. Multicoloured.
921 20c. Type **149** 10 10
922 30c. "Entandrophragma excelsum" (horiz) 10 10
923 50c. "Ilex mitis" 10 10
924 4f. "Kigelia africana" (horiz) 15 10
925 15f. "Ficus thonningi" 35 10
926 20f. "Acacia senegal" (horiz) 50 20
927 50f. "Symphonia globulifera" 1·25 45
928 110f. "Acacia sieberana" (horiz) 2·50 1·25

1979. International Year of the Child. Each brown, gold and stone.
929 26f. Type **150** 65 60
930 26f. Asian 65 60
931 26f. Eskimo 65 60
932 26f. Asian boy 65 60
933 26f. African 65 60
934 26f. South American Indian 65 60
935 26f. Polynesian 65 60
936 26f. European girl (different) 65 60
937 42f. European and African (horiz) 2·00 65

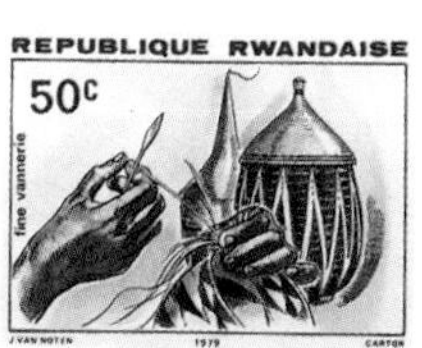

151 Basket Weaving

1979. Handicrafts. Multicoloured.
939 50c. Type **151** 10 10
940 1f.50 Wood-carving (vert) 10 10
941 2f. Metal working 10 10
942 10f. Basket work (vert) 35 10
943 20f. Basket weaving (different) 50 20
944 26f. Mural painting (vert) 65 55
945 40f. Pottery 95 65
946 100f. Smelting (vert) 2·50 1·75

153 Rowland Hill and 40c. Ruanda Stamp of 1916

1979. Death Centenary of Sir Rowland Hill. Multicoloured.
948 20c. Type **153** 10 10
949 30c. 1916 Occupation stamp 10 10
950 50c. 1918 "A.O." overprint 10 10
951 3f. 1925 overprinted 60c. stamp 10 10
952 10f. 1931 50c. African buffalo stamp 30 10
953 26f. 1942 20f. Common zebra stamp 65 15
954 60f. 1953 25f. Protea stamp 1·40 60
955 100f. 1960 Olympic stamp 2·75 1·10

154 Strange Weaver **156** Butare Rotary Club Banner, Globe and Chicago Club Emblem of 1905

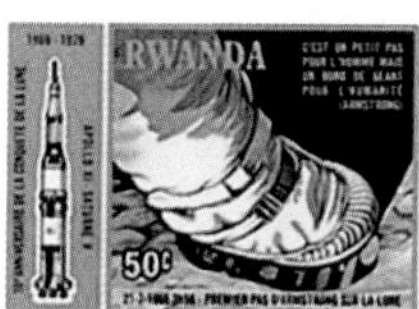

155 Armstrong's first Step on Moon

1980. Birds. Multicoloured.
956 20c. Type **154** 15 10
957 30c. Regal sunbird (vert) 15 15
958 50c. White-spotted crake 15 15
959 3f. Black-casqued hornbill 30 15
960 10f. Ituri owl (vert) 70 25
961 26f. African emerald cuckoo 1·60 65
962 60f. Black-crowned waxbill (vert) 3·00 1·50
963 100f. Crowned eagle (vert) 5·50 2·50

1980. 10th Anniv of "Apollo 11" Moon Landing. Multicoloured.
964 50c. Type **155** 10 10
965 1f.50 Aldrin descending to Moon's surface 10 10
966 8f. Planting the American flag 55 10
967 30f. Placing seisometer 95 60
968 50f. Taking samples 1·75 70
969 60f. Setting-up experiment 2·50 90

1980. 75th Anniv of Rotary International. Mult.
971 20c. Type **156** 10 10
972 30c. Kigali Rotary Club banner 10 10
973 50c. Type **156** 10 10
974 4f. As No. 972 15 10
975 15f. Type **156** 35 10
976 20f. As No. 972 45 20
977 50f. Type **156** 95 45
978 60f. As No. 972 1·10 65

157 Gymnastics

1980. Olympic Games, Moscow.
979 **157** 20c. yellow and black 10 10
980 – 30c. green and black 10 10
981 – 50c. red and black 10 10
982 – 3f. blue and black 15 10
983 – 20f. orange and black 45 20
984 – 26f. purple and black 50 25
985 – 50f. turquoise and black 1·10 45
986 – 100f. brown and black 2·50 1·10
DESIGNS: 30c. Basketball; 50c. Cycling; 3f. Boxing; 20f. Archery; 26f. Weightlifting; 50f. Javelin; 100f. Fencing.

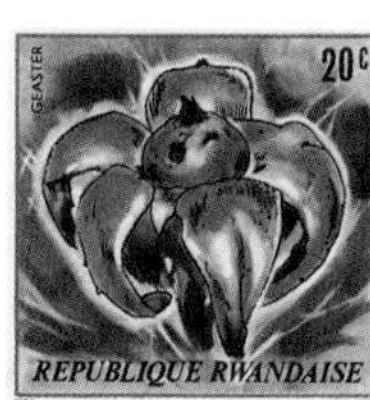

159 "Geaster"

1980. Mushrooms. Multicoloured.
988 20c. Type **159** 10 10
989 30c. "Lentinus atrobrunneus" 10 10
990 50c. "Gomphus stereoides" 10 10
991 4f. "Cantharellus cibarius" 30 10
992 10f. "Stilbothamnium dybowskii" 65 20
993 15f. "Xeromphalina tenuipes" 90 20
994 70f. "Podoscypha elegans" 3·75 80
995 100f. "Mycena" 7·50 1·60

160 "At the Theatre" (Toulouse-Lautrec)

1980. Impressionist Paintings. Multicoloured.
996 20c. "Still Life" (horiz) (Renoir) 10 10
997 30c. Type **160** 10 10
998 50c. "Seaside Garden" (Monet) (horiz) 10 10
999 4f. "Mother and Child" (Mary Cassatt) 10 10
1000 5f. "Starry Night" (Van Gogh) (horiz) 20 10
1001 10f. "Three Dancers at their Toilette" (Degas) 35 10
1002 50f. "The Card Players" (Cezanne) (horiz) 1·10 45
1003 70f. "Tahitian Girls" (Gauguin) 1·75 65
1004 100f. "La Grande Jatte" (Seurat) (horiz) 2·75 90

162 Revolutionary Scene

1980. 150th Anniv of Belgian Independence. Scenes of the Independence War from contemporary engravings.
1007 **162** 20c. green and brown 10 10
1008 – 30c. buff and brown 10 10
1009 – 50c. blue and brown 10 10
1010 – 9f. orange and brown 20 10
1011 – 10f. mauve and brown 30 10
1012 – 20f. green and brown 45 20
1013 – 70f. pink and brown 1·50 65
1014 – 90f. yellow and brown 1·90 1·00

163 Draining the Marshes

1980. Soil Protection and Conservation Year. Mult.
1015 20c. Type **163** 25 10
1016 30c. Bullock in pen (mixed farming and land fertilization) 10 10
1017 1f.50 Land irrigation and rice 10 10
1018 8f. Soil erosion and planting trees 20 10
1019 10f. Terrace 30 15
1020 40f. Crop fields 1·00 40
1021 90f. Bean crop 2·10 85
1022 100f. Picking tea 2·25 1·10

164 "Pavetta rwandensis"

1981. Flowers. Multicoloured.
1023 20c. Type **164** 10 10
1024 30c. "Cyrtorchis praetermissa" 10 10
1025 50c. "Pavonia urens" 10 10
1026 4f. "Cynorkis kassnerana" 10 10
1027 5f. "Gardenia ternifolia" 15 10
1028 10f. "Leptactina platyphylla" 20 10
1029 20f. "Lobelia petiolata" 50 15
1030 40f. "Tapinanthus brunneus" 1·25 50
1031 70f. "Impatiens niamniamensis" 1·60 95
1032 150f. "Dissotis rwandensis" 4·00 1·60

165 Mother and Child **166** Carol Singers

1981. SOS Children's Village. Multicoloured.
1033 20c. Type **165** 10 10
1034 30c. Child with pots 10 10
1035 50c. Children drawing 10 10
1036 1f. Girl sewing 10 10
1037 8f. Children playing 20 10
1038 10f. Girl knitting 20 10
1039 70f. Children making models 1·50 70
1040 150f. Mother and children 3·25 1·60

1981. Paintings by Norman Rockwell. Mult.
1041 20c. Type **166** 10 10
1042 30c. People of different races 10 10
1043 50c. Father Christmas 10 10
1044 1f. Coachman 10 10
1045 8f. Man at piano 15 10
1046 20f. "Springtime" 50 20
1047 50f. Man making donation to girl "nurse" 1·25 70
1048 70f. Clown 1·75 1·10

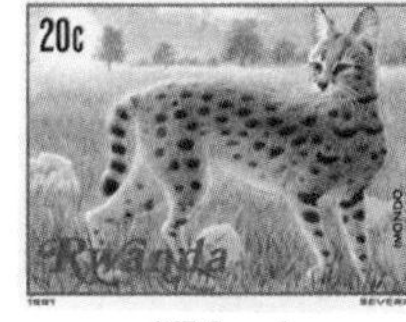

167 Serval

1981. Carnivorous Animals. Multicoloured.
1049 20c. Type **167** 10 10
1050 30c. Black-backed jackal 10 10
1051 2f. Servaline genet 10 10
1052 2f.50 Banded mongoose 10 10
1053 10f. Zorilla 20 10
1054 15f. Zaire clawless otter 55 10
1055 70f. African golden cat 1·75 1·25
1056 200f. Hunting dog (vert) 5·75 4·25

168 Drummer

1981. Telecommunications and Health. Mult.
1057 20c. Type **168** 10 10
1058 30c. Telephone receiver and world map 10 10
1059 2f. Airliner and radar screen 10 10
1060 2f.50 Satellite and computer tape 10 10
1061 10f. Satellite orbit and dish aerial 20 10
1062 15f. Tanker and radar equipment 35 25
1063 70f. Red Cross helicopter 1·90 70
1064 200f. Satellite 4·25 2·25

169 "St. Benedict leaving His Parents"

1981. 1500th Birth Anniv of St. Benedict. Mult.
1065 20c. Type **169** 10 10
1066 30c. Portrait (10th century) (vert) 10 10
1067 50c. Portrait (detail from "The Virgin of the Misericord" polyptich) (vert) 10 10
1068 4f. "St. Benedict presenting the Rules of His Order" 10 10
1069 5f. "St. Benedict and His Monks at their Meal" 15 10
1070 20f. Portrait (13th century) (vert) 45 40
1071 70f. St. Benedict at prayer (detail from "Our Lady in Glory with Sts. Gregory and Benedict") (vert) 1·75 1·40
1072 100f. "Priest bringing the Easter Meal to St. Benedict" (Jan van Coninxlo) 2·75 1·75

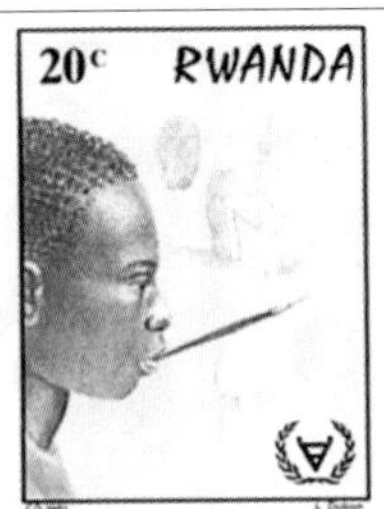

170 Disabled Child painting with Mouth

1981. International Year of Disabled Persons. Mult.
1073 20c. Type **170** 10 10
1074 30c. Boys on crutches playing football 10 10
1075 4f.50 Disabled girl knitting 10 10
1076 5f. Disabled child painting pot 15 10
1077 10f. Boy in wheelchair using saw 20 10
1078 60f. Child using sign language 1·25 60
1079 70f. Child in wheelchair playing with puzzle 1·60 70
1080 100f. Disabled child 2·00 1·10

172 Kob drinking at Pool

1981. Rural Water Supplies. Multicoloured.
1082 20c. Type **172** 10 10
1083 30c. Women collecting water (vert) 10 10
1084 50c. Constructing a pipeline 10 10
1085 10f. Woman collecting water from pipe (vert) 20 10
1086 10f. Man drinking 45 20
1087 70f. Woman collecting water (vert) 1·50 70
1088 100f. Floating pump (vert) 2·50 1·10

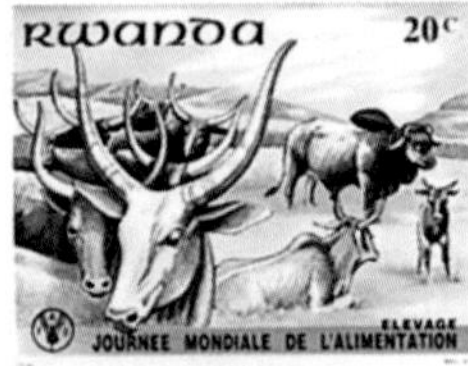

173 Cattle

1982. World Food Day. Multicoloured.
1089 20c. Type **173** 10 10
1090 30c. Bee keeping 10 10
1091 50c. Fishes 10 10
1092 1f. Avocado 10 10
1093 8f. Boy eating banana 10 10
1094 20f. Sorghum 45 15
1095 70f. Vegetables 1·50 65
1096 100f. Three generations and balanced diet 3·00 1·10

174 "Hibiscus berberidfolius"

1982. Flowers. Multicoloured.
1097 20c. Type **174** 10 10
1098 30c. "Hypericum lanceolatum" (vert) 10 10
1099 50c. "Canarina eminii" 10 10
1100 4f. "Polygala ruwenzoriensis" 10 10
1101 10f. "Kniphofia grantii" (vert) 15 10
1102 35f. "Euphorbia candelabrum" (vert) 90 60
1103 70f. "Disa erubescens" (vert) 1·75 80
1104 80f. "Gloriosa simplex" 2·40 1·10

175 Pres. Habyarimana and Flags

1982. 20th Anniv of Independence. Multicoloured.
1105 10f. Type **175** 20 10
1106 20f. Hands releasing doves (Peace) 35 20
1107 30f. Clasped hands and flag (Unity) 65 35
1108 50f. Building (Development) 1·00 50

176 Football

1982. World Cup Football Championship, Spain.
1109 **176** 20c. multicoloured 10 10
1110 – 30c. multicoloured 10 10
1111 – 1f.50 multicoloured 10 10
1112 – 8f. multicoloured 15 10
1113 – 10f. multicoloured 20 10
1114 – 20f. multicoloured 40 15
1115 – 70f. multicoloured 1·60 65
1116 – 90f. multicoloured 2·25 85
DESIGNS: 30c. to 90f. Designs show different players.

177 Microscope and Slide

1982. Centenary of Discovery of Tubercle Bacillus. Multicoloured.
1117 10f. Type **177** 15 10
1118 20f. Hand with test tube and slide 40 15
1119 70f. Lungs and slide 1·60 65
1120 100f. Dr. Robert Koch 2·25 95

180 African Elephants

1982. 10th Anniv of United Nations Environment Programme. Multicoloured.
1123 20c. Type **180** 10 10
1124 30c. Lion hunting impala 10 10
1125 50c. Flower 10 10
1126 4f. African buffalo 10 10
1127 5f. Impala 10 10
1128 10f. Flower (different) 20 10
1129 20f. Common zebra 45 15
1130 40f. Crowned cranes 1·50 35
1131 50f. African fish eagle 1·75 55
1132 70f. Woman with basket of fruit 1·60 80

181 Scout tending Injured Kob

1982. 75th Anniv of Scout Movement. Mult.
1133 20c. Type **181** 10 10
1134 30c. Tents and northern doubled-collared sunbird 35 10
1135 1f.50 Campfire 10 10
1136 8f. Scout 15 10
1137 10f. Knot 20 10
1138 20f. Tent and campfire 40 15
1139 70f. Scout cutting stake 1·90 80
1140 90f. Scout salute 2·40 1·00

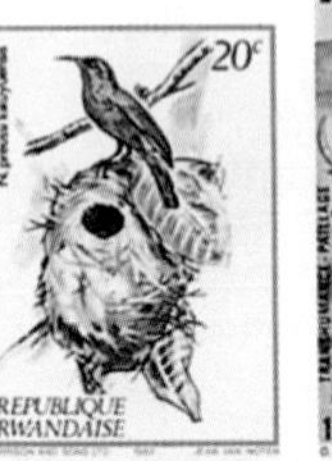

182 Northern Double-collared Sunbird

183 Driving Cattle

1983. Nectar-sucking Birds. Multicoloured.
1141 20c. Type **182** 10 10
1142 30c. Regal sunbird (horiz) 10 10
1143 50c. Red-tufted malachite sunbird 10 10
1144 4f. Bronze sunbird (horiz) 25 10
1145 5f. Collared sunbird 35 10
1146 10f. Blue-headed sunbird (horiz) 70 20
1147 20f. Purple-breasted sunbird 1·40 50
1148 40f. Coppery sunbird (horiz) 3·00 95
1149 50f. Olive-bellied sunbird 3·25 1·25
1150 70f. Red-chested sunbird (horiz) 4·50 2·00

1983. Campaign Against Soil Erosion. Mult.
1151 20c. Type **183** 10 10
1152 30c. Pineapple plantation 10 10
1153 50c. Interrupted ditches 10 10
1154 9f. Hedged terraces 20 10
1155 10f. Re-afforestation 20 10
1156 20f. Anti-erosion barriers 40 15
1157 30f. Contour planting 65 30
1158 50f. Terraces 1·00 40
1159 60f. River bank protection 1·40 60
1160 70f. Alternate fallow and planted strips 1·60 80

184 Feeding Ducks

1983. Birth Cent of Cardinal Cardijan (founder of Young Catholic Workers Movement). Mult.
1161 20c. Type **184** 10 10
1162 30c. Harvesting bananas 10 10
1163 50c. Carrying melons 10 10
1164 10f. Wood-carving 20 10
1165 19f. Making shoes 35 15
1166 20f. Children in field of millet 45 15
1167 70f. Embroidering 1·40 60
1168 80f. Cardinal Cardijan 1·60 65

185 Young Gorillas

1983. Mountain Gorillas. Multicoloured.
1169 20c. Type **185** 10 10
1170 30c. Gorilla family 10 10
1171 9f.50 Young and adult 45 30
1172 10f. Mother with young 45 30
1173 20f. Heads 65 45
1174 30f. Adult and head 90 50
1175 60f. Adult (vert) 2·00 1·40
1176 70f. Close-up of adult (vert) 2·40 1·50

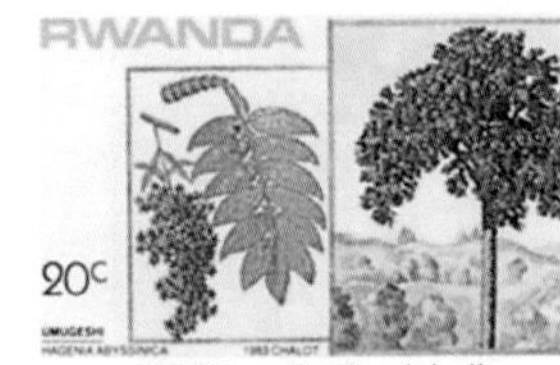

187 "Hagenia abyssinica"

1984. Trees. Multicoloured.
1178 20c. Type **187** 10 10
1179 30c. "Dracaena steudneri" 10 10
1180 50c. "Phoenix reclinata" 10 10
1181 10f. "Podocarpus milanjianus" 15 10
1182 19f. "Entada abyssinica" 40 15
1183 70f. "Parinari excelsa" 1·60 65
1184 100f. "Newtonia buchananii" 2·00 95
1185 200f. "Acacia gerrardi" (vert) 4·50 1·60

188 "Hikari" Express Train, Japan

189 "Le Martial", 1783

1984. World Communications Year. Multicoloured.
1186 20c. Type **188** 20 10
1187 30c. Liner and radar 15 10
1188 4f.50 Radio and transmitter 15 10
1189 10f. Telephone dial and cable 20 10
1190 15f. Letters and newspaper 35 10
1191 50f. Airliner and control tower 1·10 45
1192 70f. Television and antenna 1·60 65
1193 100f. Satellite and computer tape 2·50 90

1984. Bicentenary of Manned Flight. Mult.
1194 20c. Type **189** 10 10
1195 30c. De Rozier and Marquis d'Arlandes flight, 1783 10 10
1196 50c. Charles and Robert (1783) and Blanchard (1784) flights 10 10
1197 9f. M. and Mme. Blanchard 20 10
1198 10f. Blanchard and Jeffries, 1785 20 10
1199 50f. Demuyter (1937) and Piccard and Kipfer (1931) flights 1·10 40
1200 80f. Modern hot-air balloons 2·75 1·90
1201 200f. Trans-Atlantic flight, 1978 3·50 2·50

190 Equestrian

1984. Olympic Games, Los Angeles. Multicoloured.
1202 20c. Type **190** 10 10
1203 30c. Windsurfing 15 10
1204 50c. Football 10 10
1205 9f. Swimming 20 10
1206 10f. Hockey 20 10
1207 40f. Fencing 1·25 70
1208 80f. Running 2·00 1·75
1209 200f. Boxing 5·00 4·00

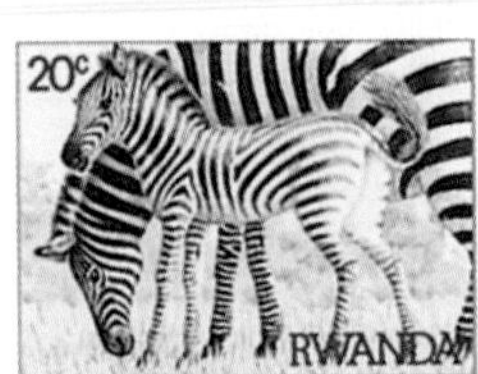

191 Mare and Foal

1984. Common Zebras and African Buffaloes. Mult.
1210 20c. Type **191** 10 10
1211 30c. Buffalo and calf (vert) 10 10
1212 50c. Pair of zebras (vert) 10 10
1213 9f. Zebras fighting 20 10
1214 10f. Close-up of buffalo (vert) 30 10
1215 80f. Herd of zebras 1·90 1·40
1216 100f. Close-up of zebras (vert) 2·50 1·75
1217 200f. Buffalo charging 4·75 3·50

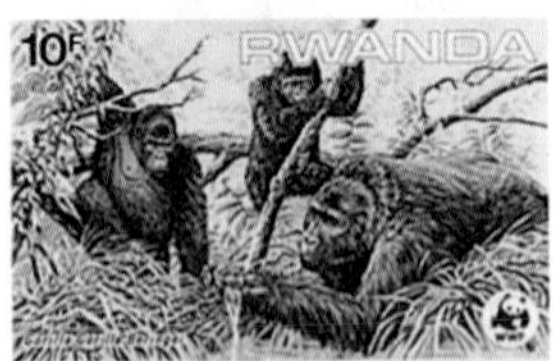

193 Gorillas at Water-hole

1985. Gorillas. Multicoloured.
1219 10f. Type **193** 1·90 80
1220 15f. Two gorillas in tree 2·75 85
1221 25f. Gorilla family 3·75 2·10
1222 30f. Three adults 4·75 3·00

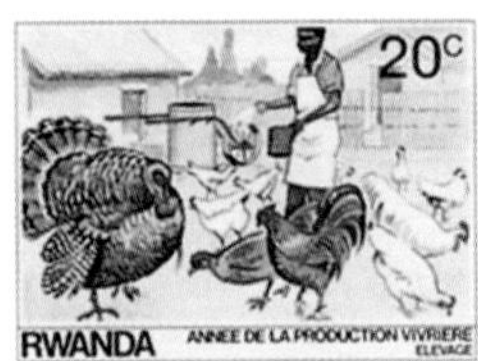

194 Man feeding Fowl

1985. Food Production Year. Multicoloured.
1224 20c. Type **194** 20 10
1225 30c. Men carrying pineapples 15 10
1226 50c. Farm animals 10 10
1227 9f. Men filling sacks with produce 20 10
1228 10f. Agricultural instruction 30 10
1229 50f. Sowing seeds 1·00 45
1230 80f. Storing produce 1·60 65
1231 100f. Working in banana plantation 2·10 80

195 Emblem

1985. 10th Anniv of National Revolutionary Redevelopment Movement.

No.		Description		
1232	**195**	10f. multicoloured	20	10
1233		30f. multicoloured	65	30
1234		70f. multicoloured	1·60	70

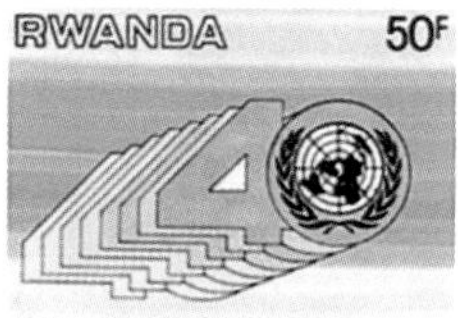

196 U.N. Emblem within "40"

1985. 40th Anniv of U.N.O.

No.		Description		
1235	**196**	50f. multicoloured	1·10	90
1236		100f. multicoloured	2·50	2·10

197 Barn Owls

1985. Birth Bicentenary of John J. Audubon (ornithologist). Multicoloured.

No.	Description		
1237	10f. Type **197**	75	30
1238	20f. White-faced scops owls	1·60	60
1239	40f. Ruby-throated humming birds	3·00	1·10
1240	80f. Eastern meadowlarks	6·75	2·40

198 "Participation, Development and Peace"

1985. International Youth Year. Multicoloured.

No.	Description		
1241	7f. Type **198**	15	10
1242	9f. Cycling	30	10
1243	44f. Youths carrying articles on head (teamwork)	1·10	45
1244	80f. Education	1·75	80

1985. 75th Anniv of Girl Guide Movement. Nos. 1133/40 optd **1910/1985** and guide emblem.

No.	Description		
1245	20c. Type **181**	10	10
1246	30c. Tents	30	10
1247	1f.50 Campfire	10	10
1248	8f. Scout	20	10
1249	10f. Knot	20	10
1250	20f. Tent and campfire	45	10
1251	70f. Scout cutting stake	1·60	65
1252	90f. Scout salute	2·50	90

201 Container Lorry (Transport)

1986. Transport and Communications. Mult.

No.	Description		
1254	10f. Type **201**	35	10
1255	30f. Handstamping cover (posts)	80	35
1256	40f. Kigali Earth Station (telecommunication)	1·10	45
1257	80f. Kigali airport (aviation) (48 × 31 mm)	1·75	1·25

1986. Intensified Agriculture Year. Nos. 1152/60 optd **ANNEE 1986 INTENSIFICATION AGRICOLE** or surch also.

No.	Description		
1258	9f. Hedged terraces	20	10
1259	10f. Re-afforestation	20	10
1260	10f. on 30c. Pineapple plantation	20	10
1261	10f. on 50c. Interrupted ditches	20	10
1262	20f. Anti-erosion barriers	45	20
1263	30f. Contour planning	65	35
1264	50f. Terraces	1·10	50
1265	60f. River bank protection	1·40	55
1266	70f. Alternate fallow and planted strips	1·60	70

203 Morocco v England

1986. World Cup Football Championship, Mexico. Multicoloured.

No.	Description		
1267	2f. Type **203**	10	10
1268	4f. Paraguay v Iraq	10	10
1269	5f. Brazil v Spain	10	10
1270	10f. Italy v Argentina	55	35
1271	40f. Mexico v Belgium	1·60	85
1272	45f. France v Russia	1·75	1·00

204 Roan Antelopes

1986. Akagera National Park. Multicoloured.

No.	Description		
1273	4f. Type **204**	15	10
1274	7f. Whale-headed storks	45	20
1275	9f. Cape eland	20	10
1276	10f. Giraffe	40	10
1277	80f. African elephant	2·50	85
1278	90f. Crocodile	3·00	1·00
1279	100f. Heuglin's masked weavers	5·00	2·75
1280	100f. Zebras and eastern white pelican	5·00	2·75

205 People of Different Races on Globe

1986. Christmas. International Peace Year. Mult.

No.	Description		
1281	10f. Type **205**	35	15
1282	15f. Dove and globe	45	15
1283	30f. Type **205**	80	35
1284	70f. As No. 1282	1·75	1·00

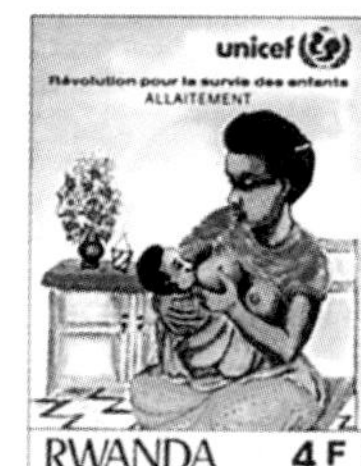

206 Mother breast-feeding Baby

1987. U.N.I.C.E.F. Child Survival Campaign. Multicoloured.

No.	Description		
1285	4f. Type **206**	15	15
1286	6f. Mother giving oral rehydration therapy to baby	20	15
1287	10f. Nurse immunizing baby	35	25
1288	70f. Nurse weighing baby and graph	1·75	1·60

207 Couple packing Baskets with Food

1987. Food Self-sufficiency Year. Multicoloured.

No.	Description		
1289	5f. Type **207**	10	10
1290	7f. Woman and baskets of food	15	10
1291	40f. Man with baskets of fish and fruits	1·75	45
1292	60f. Fruits and vegetables	2·25	80

208 Pres. Habyarimana and Soldiers

1987. 25th Anniv of Independence. Multicoloured.

No.	Description		
1293	10f. Type **208**	20	10
1294	40f. President at meeting	90	45
1295	70f. President with Pope John Paul II	2·50	85
1296	100f. Pres. Habyarimana (vert)	2·50	1·10

209 Bananas

1987. Fruits. Multicoloured.

No.	Description		
1297	10f. Type **209**	20	10
1298	40f. Pineapples (horiz)	90	45
1299	80f. Papaya (horiz)	2·25	90
1300	90f. Avocados (horiz)	2·50	1·00
1301	100f. Strawberries	2·50	1·10

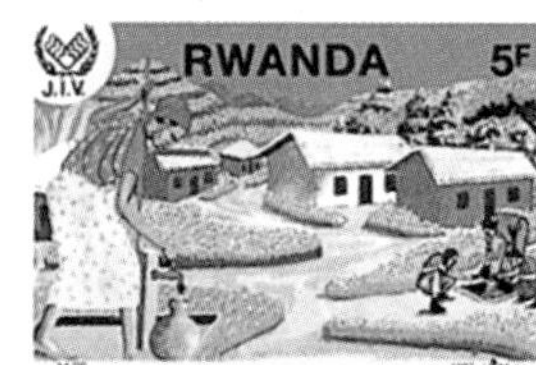

210 Mother carrying cub

1987. The Leopard. Multicoloured.

No.	Description		
1302	50f. Type **210**	2·00	1·10
1303	50f. Leopards fighting	2·00	1·10
1304	50f. Leopards with prey	2·00	1·10
1305	50f. Leopard with prey in tree	2·00	1·10
1306	50f. Leopard leaping from tree	2·00	1·10

211 Village Activities

1987. International Volunteers Day. Mult.

No.	Description		
1307	5f. Type **211**	10	10
1308	12f. Pupils in schoolroom	35	10
1309	20f. View of village	55	30
1310	60f. Woman tending oxen	1·75	85

213 Carpenter's Shop

1988. Rural Incomes Protection Year. Mult.

No.	Description		
1312	10f. Type **213**	20	10
1313	40f. Dairy farm	95	95
1314	60f. Workers in field	1·50	55
1315	80f. Selling baskets of eggs	2·10	1·50

214 Chimpanzees

1988. Primates of Nyungwe Forest. Multicoloured.

No.	Description		
1316	2f. Type **214**	25	15
1317	3f. Black and white colobus	25	15
1318	10f. Lesser bushbabies	85	50
1319	90f. Monkeys	6·00	3·00

215 Boxing

1988. Olympic Games, Seoul. Multicoloured.

No.	Description		
1320	5f. Type **215**	10	10
1321	7f. Relay race	15	10
1322	8f. Table tennis	20	10
1323	10f. Running	35	15
1324	90f. Hurdling	2·25	1·00

216 "25" on Map of Africa

1988. 25th Anniv of Organization of African Unity. Multicoloured.

No.	Description		
1325	5f. Type **216**	15	10
1326	7f. Hands clasped across map	20	10
1327	8f. Building on map	20	10
1328	90f. Words forming map	2·75	2·25

218 Newspaper Fragment and Refugees in Boat

1988. 125th Anniv of Red Cross Movement. Mult.

No.	Description		
1330	10f. Type **218**	20	10
1331	30f. Red Cross workers and patient	80	35
1332	40f. Red Cross worker and elderly lady (vert)	95	40
1333	100f. Red Cross worker and family (vert)	2·75	1·25

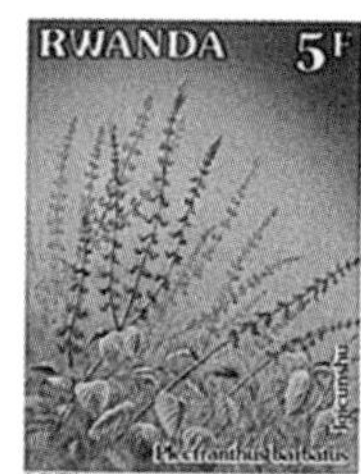

219 "Plectranthus barbatus"

1989. Plants. Multicoloured.

No.	Description		
1334	5f. Type **219**	15	20
1335	10f. "Tetradenia riparia"	50	20
1336	20f. "Hygrophila auriculata"	1·00	45
1337	40f. "Datura stramonium"	2·10	1·00
1338	50f. "Pavetta ternifolia"	2·75	1·40

220 Emblem, Dates and Sunburst

1989. Centenary of Interparliamentary Union. Mult.

No.	Description		
1339	10f. Type **220**	30	10
1340	30f. Lake	85	65
1341	70f. River	1·60	1·40
1342	90f. Sun's rays	2·25	1·75

222 Throwing Clay and Finished Pots

1989. Rural Self-help Year. Multicoloured.
1344 10f. Type **222** 30 10
1345 70f. Carrying baskets of produce (vert) . . . . . 1·60 1·40
1346 90f. Firing clay pots . . . . 2·50 2·00
1347 200f. Clearing roadway . . 5·00 3·50

223 "Triumph of Marat" (Boilly)

1990. Bicentenary of French Revolution. Mult.
1348 10f. Type **223** 30 10
1349 60f. "Rouget de Lisle singing La Marseillaise" (Pils) . . . . 1·60 1·50
1350 70f. "Oath of the Tennis Court" (Jacques Louis David) . . . . 2·00 1·75
1351 100f. "Trial of Louis XVI" (Joseph Court) . . . . . 3·00 2·75

224 Old and New Lifestyles

1990. 30th Anniv of Revolution. Multicoloured.
1352 10f. Type **224** 30 10
1353 60f. Couple holding farming implements (vert) . . . . 1·60 1·40
1354 70f. Modernization . . . . 1·75 1·40
1355 100f. Flag, map and warrior 2·50 2·50

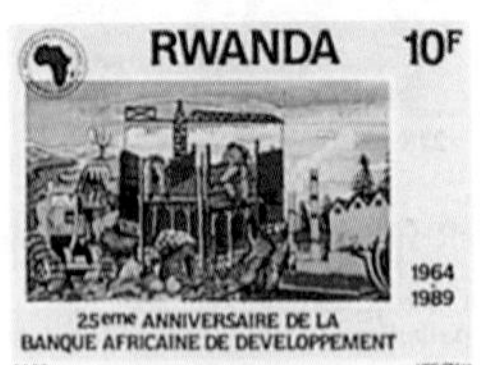

225 Construction

1990. 25th Anniv (1989) of African Development Bank. Multicoloured.
1356 10f. Type **225** 30 10
1357 20f. Tea picking 55 35
1358 40f. Road building . . . . 1·10 95
1359 90f. Tea pickers and modern housing . . . . 2·50 2·10

1990. World Cup Football Championship, Italy. Nos. 1267/72 optd **ITALIA 90**.
1361 **203** 2f. multicoloured 35 35
1362 – 4f. multicoloured 35 35
1363 – 5f. multicoloured 40 40
1364 – 10f. multicoloured . . . 65 65
1365 – 40f. multicoloured . . . 2·50 2·50
1366 – 45f. multicoloured . . . 2·75 2·75

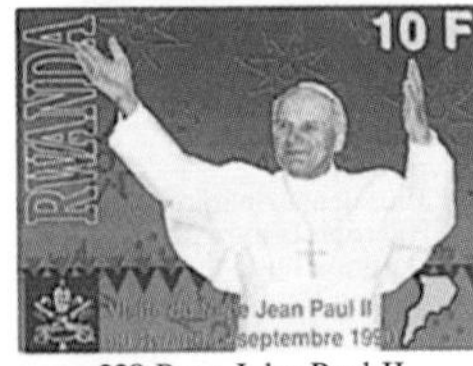

228 Pope John Paul II

1990. Papal Visits. Multicoloured.
1367 10f. Type **228** 75 75
1368 70f. Pope giving blessing . . 8·25 8·25

229 Adults learning Alphabet at School

1991. International Literacy Year (1990). Mult.
1370 10f. Type **229** 15 10
1371 20f. Children reading at school 35 20
1372 50f. Lowland villagers learning alphabet in field 90 80
1373 90f. Highland villagers learning alphabet outdoors . . . . 1·40 1·10

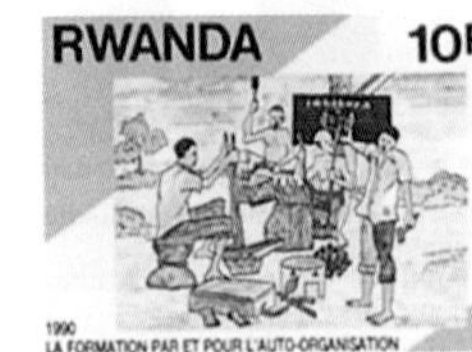

230 Tool-making

1991. Self-help Organizations. Multicoloured.
1374 10f. Type **230** 15 10
1375 20f. Rearing livestock . . . 35 20
1376 50f. Textile manufacture . . 1·40 1·10
1377 90f. Construction . . . . . 2·00 1·50

231 Statue of Madonna

1992. Death Centenary of Cardinal Lavigerie (founder of Orders of White Fathers and Sisters).
1378 **231** 5f. multicoloured . . . . 95 1·00
1379 – 15f. multicoloured . . . 2·50 2·50
1380 – 70f. black and mauve . . 12·00 12·00
1381 – 110f. black and blue . . 18·00 20·00
DESIGNS—VERT: 15f. White Sister; 110f. Cardinal [illegible] White Fathers in Uganda, 1908.

232 Fisherman

1992. Int Nutrition Conference, Rome. Mult.
1382 15f. Type **232** 80 45
1383 50f. Market fruit stall . . . 1·60 1·40
1384 100f. Man milking cow . . 3·25 2·75
1385 500f. Woman breastfeeding 17·00 14·50

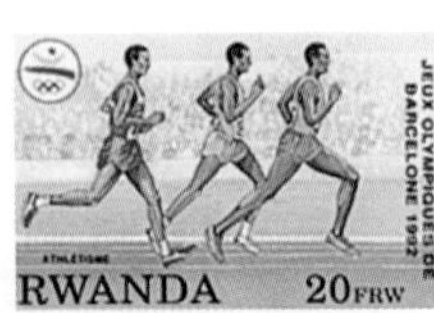

233 Running

1993. Olympic Games, Barcelona (1992). Mult.
1386 20f. Type **233** . . . . 2·50 2·50
1387 30f. Swimming . . . . . . 4·00 4·50
1388 90f. Football . . . . 12·00 10·00

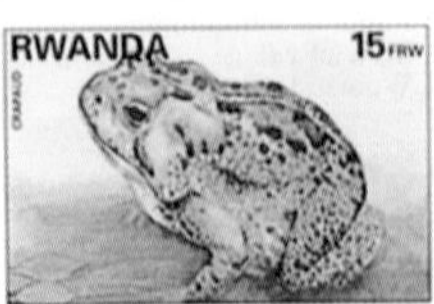

234 Toad

1998. Animals. Multicoloured.
1390 15f. Type **234** 20 30
1391 100f. Snail 80 85
1392 150f. Porcupine . . . . . . 1·25 1·25
1393 300f. Chameleon . . . . . 2·50 2·75

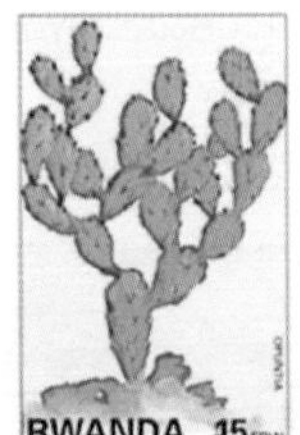

235 "Opuntia"

1998. Plants. Multicoloured.
1395 15f. Type **235** 20 30
1396 100f. "Gloriosa superba" . . 80 85
1397 150f. "Markhamia lutea" . . 1·25 1·25
1398 300f. "Hagenia abyssinica" (horiz) . . . . 2·50 2·75

RYUKYU ISLANDS Pt. 18

Group of islands between Japan and Taiwan, formerly Japanese until occupied by U.S. forces in 1945. After a period of military rule they became semi-autonomous under U.S. administration. The Amami Oshima group reverted to Japan in December 1953. The remaining islands were returned to Japan on 15 May 1972. Japanese stamps are now in use.

1948. 100 sen = 1 yen.
1958. 100 cents = 1 dollar (U.S.).

1 Cycad Palm

3 Tribute Junk

1948.
1 **1** 5s. purple . . . . 3·00 1·75
2 – 10s. green . . . . 3·50 2·25
3 **1** 20s. green . . . . 3·50 2·25
4 **3** 30s. red . . . . 3·50 2·25
5 – 40s. purple . . . . 3·00 1·75
6 **3** 50s. blue . . . . 3·50 2·50
7 – 1y. blue . . . . 3·50 2·50
DESIGNS: 10s., 40s. Easter lily; 1y. Farmer with hoe.

6 Shi-Shi Roof Tiles

12 Dove over Map of Ryukyus

1950.
8 **6** 50s. red 25 25
10 – 1y. blue . . . . 2·75 1·25
11 – 2y. purple . . . . 12·00 3·00
12 – 3y. pink . . . . 20·00 8·00
13 – 4y. grey . . . . 8·00 3·00
14 – 5y. green . . . . 10·00 4·50
DESIGNS: 1y. Shuri woman; 2y. Former Okinawa Palace, Shuri; 3y. Dragon's head; 4y. Okinawa women; 5y. Common spider and strawberry conches and radula scallop.

1950. Air.
15 **12** 8y. blue . . . . 65·00 20·00
16 12y. green . . . . 42·00 16·00
17 16y. red . . . . 18·00 12·00

14 University and Shuri Castle

15 Pine Tree

1951. Inauguration of Ryukyu University.
19 **14** 3y. brown . . . . 45·00 18·00

1951. Afforestation Week.
20 **15** 3y. green . . . . 45·00 18·00

16 Flying Goddess

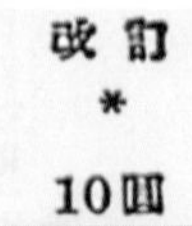

(17)

1951. Air.
21 **16** 13y. blue . . . . 2·00 40
22 18y. green . . . . 2·50 3·00
23 30y. mauve . . . . 4·00 1·25
24 40y. purple . . . . 6·00 2·25
25 50y. orange . . . . 7·50 3·25

1952. Surch as T **17**.
27 **6** 10y. on 50s. red . . . . . . 10·00 5·50
29 – 100y. on 2y. purple (No. 11) £2000 £850

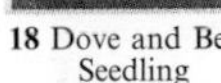

18 Dove and Bean Seedling

19 Madanbashi Bridge

1952. Establishment of Ryukyuan Government.
30 **18** 3y. red . . . . £100 20·00

1952.
31 **19** 1y. red 25 25
32 – 2y. green 30 25
33 – 3y. turquoise 60 25
34 – 6y. blue . . . . 4·00 3·25
35 – 10y. red . . . . 1·75 50
36 – 30y. green . . . . 4·75 2·50
37 – 50y. purple . . . . 6·00 2·00
38 – 100y. purple . . . . 12·00 1·50
DESIGNS: 2y. Presence Chamber, Shuri Palace; 3y. Shuri Gate; 6y. Sogenji Temple Wall; 10y. Bensaitendo Temple; 30y. Sonohyamutake Gate; 50y. Tamaudum Mausoleum, Shuri; 100y. Hosho-chai Bridge.

27 Reception at Shuri Castle

28 Perry and American Fleet at Naha Harbour

29 Chofu Ota and Matrix

1953. Centenary of Commodore Perry's Visit to Okinawa.
39 **27** 3y. purple . . . . 12·00 4·00
40 **28** 6y. blue . . . . 2·25 2·40

1953. 3rd Press Week.
41 **29** 4y. brown . . . . 12·00 5·00

30 Wine Flask to fit around Waist

33 Shigo Toma and Pen-nib

1954.
42 **30** 4y. brown 50 35
43 – 15y. red . . . . 2·25 1·75
44 – 20y. orange . . . . 3·25 2·25
DESIGNS: 15y. Tung Dar Bon (lacquer bowl); 20y. Kasuri (textile pattern).

1954. 4th Press Week.
45 **33** 4y. blue . . . . 10·00 3·50

34 Noguni Shrine and Sweet Potatoes

35 Stylized Trees

1955. 350th Anniv of Introduction of Sweet Potato Plant.
46 **34** 4y. blue . . . . 10·00 4·00

1956. Afforestation Week.
47 **35** 4y. green . . . . 8·00 3·00

38 Nidotekito Dance

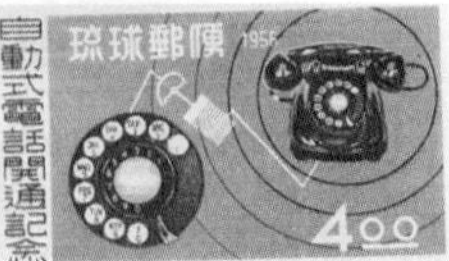

39 Telephone and Dial

1956. National Dances.
48 – 5y. purple . . . . 1·10 60
49 – 8y. violet . . . . 1·40 1·25
50 **38** 14y. brown . . . . 2·25 2·25
DESIGNS: 5y. Willow dance; 8y. Straw-hat dance.

1956. Inauguration of Telephone Dialling System.
51 **39** 4y. violet . . . . 12·00 8·00

40 Floral Garland **41** Flying Goddess

1956. New Year.
52 **40** 2y. multicoloured . . . . . 2·00 1·40

1957. Air.
53 **41** 15y. green . . . . 2·00 40
54 20y. red . . . . 4·50 3·00
55 35y. green . . . . 10·00 4·00
56 45y. brown . . . . 16·00 6·00
57 60y. grey . . . . 22·00 8·50

42 "Rocket" Pencils **43** Phoenix

1957. 7th Press Week.
58 **42** 4y. blue 55 55

1957. New Year.
59 **43** 2y. multicoloured 40 20

44 Various Ryukyuan Postage Stamps

1958. 10th Anniv of First Postage Stamps of Ryukyu Islands.
60 **44** 4y. multicoloured . . . . . 1·00 60

45 Stylized Dollar Sign over Yen Symbol

1958. With or without gum (Nos. 68/69), no gum (others).
61 **45** ½c. yellow 25 20
62 1c. green 25 20
63 2c. blue 25 25
64 3c. red 20 15
65 4c. green 60 45
66 5c. brown . . . . 2·00 50
67 10c. blue . . . . 3·25 50
68 25c. blue . . . . 3·50 80
69 50c. grey . . . . 7·00 1·00
70 $1 purple . . . . 10·00 1·25

46 Gateway of Courtesy

1958. Restoration of Shuri Gateway.
71 **46** 3c. multicoloured . . . . . 1·25 50

47 Lion Dance **48** Trees

1958. New Year.
72 **47** 1½c. multicoloured 30 25

1959. Afforestation Week.
73 **48** 3c. multicoloured . . . . . 1·50 1·25

49 Atlas Moth **50** Hibiscus

1959. Japanese Biological Teachers' Conference, Okinawa.
74 **49** 3c. multicoloured . . . . . 2·00 1·25

1959. Multicoloured. (a) Inscr as in T **50**.
75 ½c. Type **50** 30 20
76 3c. Moorish idol . . . . . . 1·10 25
77 8c. Zebra moon, banded bonnet and textile cone (shells) . . . . 8·00 2·00
78 13c. Leaf butterfly (value at left) . . . . 2·00 1·50
79 17c. Jellyfish . . . . 22·00 5·50

(b) Inscr smaller and 13c. with value at right.
87 ½c. Type **50** 30 15
88 3c. As No. 76 . . . . 2·00 20
89 8c. As No. 77 . . . . 2·50 1·00
90 13c. As No. 78 . . . . 1·75 1·00
91 17c. As No. 79 . . . . 8·00 3·25

55 Yakazi (Ryukyuan toy)

改訂 9¢
(**56**)

1959. New Year.
80 **55** 1½c. multicoloured 80 40

1959. Air. Surch as T **56**.
81 **41** 9c. on 15y. green . . . . . 2·00 40
82 14c. on 20y. red . . . . . . 3·50 3·00
83 19c. on 35y. green . . . . . 5·00 4·00
84 27c. on 45y. brown . . . . 10·00 6·00
85 35c. on 60y. grey . . . . . 14·00 8·00

57 University Badge **60** "Munjuru"

1960. 10th Anniv of University of the Ryukyus.
86 **57** 3c. multicoloured . . . . . 1·25 60

1960. Air. Surch.
92 **30** 9c. on 4y. brown . . . . . 5·00 60
93 – 14c. on 5y. purple (No. 48) 3·00 2·00
94 – 19c. on 15y. red (No. 43) . . 5·00 2·75
95 **38** 27c. on 14y. brown . . . . 6·00 4·25
96 – 35c. on 20y. orange (No. 44) 7·00 5·25

1960. Ryukyuan Dances. Mult. (a) Inscr as in T **60**.
97 1c. Type **60** . . . . 2·00 1·00
98 2½c. "Inohabushi" . . . . . 1·75 1·00
99 5c. "Hatomabushi" . . . . . 1·00 1·00
100 10c. "Hanafu" . . . . 1·50 1·00

(b) As T **60** but additionally inscr "RYUKYUS".
107 1c. Type **60** 15 15
108 2½c. As No. 98 . . . . . . 15 15
109 4c. As No. 98 . . . . 20 15
110 5c. As No. 99 . . . . 30 25
111 10c. As No. 100 . . . . . . 50 15
112 20c. "Shudun" . . . . 1·25 35
113 25c. "Haodori" . . . . 1·25 60
114 50c. "Nobori Kuduchi" . . . 1·75 60
115 $1 "Koteibushi" . . . . . . 2·25 70

65 Start of Race

1960. 8th Kyushu Athletic Meeting.
101 – 3c. red, green and blue . . 5·00 1·50
102 **65** 8c. green and orange . . . 1·75 1·00
DESIGN: 3c. Torch and coastal scene.

66 Little Egret and Rising Sun

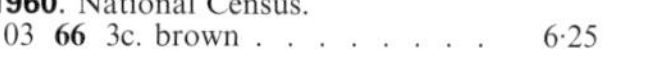
1960. National Census.
103 **66** 3c. brown . . . . 6·25 2·50

67 Bull Fight

1960. New Year.
104 **67** 1½c. brown, buff and blue 1·00 60

68 Native Pine Tree

1961. Afforestation Week.
105 **68** 3c. deep green, red & green 1·75 90

69 Naha, Junk, Liner and City Seal

1961. 40th Anniv of Naha City.
106 **69** 3c. turquoise . . . . . . 2·50 1·25

74 Flying Goddess **79** White Silver Temple

1961. Air.
116 **74** 9c. multicoloured 50 15
117 – 14c. multicoloured 70 60
118 – 19c. multicoloured . . . . 1·25 75
119 – 27c. multicoloured . . . . 1·50 75
120 – 35c. multicoloured . . . . 2·00 75
DESIGNS: 14c. Flying goddess playing flute; 19c. Wind god; 27c. Wind god (different); 35c. Flying goddess over trees.

1961. Unification of Itoman District and Takamine, Kanegushiku and Miwa Villages.
121 **79** 3c. brown . . . . 1·25 75

80 Books and Bird **81** Sunrise and Eagles

1961. 10th Anniv of Ryukyu Book Week.
122 **80** 3c. multicoloured . . . . . 1·25 75

1961. New Year.
123 **81** 1½c. red, black and gold . . 3·25 1·00

82 Govt Building, Steps and Trees **85** Shuri Gate and Campaign Emblem

1962. 10th Anniv of Ryukyu Government. Mult.
124 1½c. Type **82** 60 60
125 3c. Government building . . 90 75

1962. Malaria Eradication. Multicoloured.
126 3c. "Anopheles hyrcanus sinensis" (mosquito) . . . 70 60
127 8c. Type **85** . . . . 1·25 1·75

86 Windmill, Dolls and Horse **87** "Hibiscus lilaceus"

1962. Children's Day.
128 **86** 3c. multicoloured . . . . . 2·00 1·25

1962. Ryukyu Flowers. Multicoloured.
129 ½c. Type **87** 20 15
142 1½c. "Etithyllum strictum" . . 30 20
130 2c. "Ixora chinensis" 20 25
131 3c. "Erythrina indica" . . . 50 20
132 3c. "Caesalpinia pulcherrima" 20 20
133 8c. "Schima mertensiana" . . 75 25
134 13c. "Impatiens balsamina" . 1·00 50
135 15c. "Hamaomoto" (herb) . . 1·25 55
136 17c. "Alpinia speciosa" . . . 1·00 30
No. 142 is smaller, 18¾ × 22½ mm.

95 Akaeware Bowl **97** "Hare and Water" (textile design)

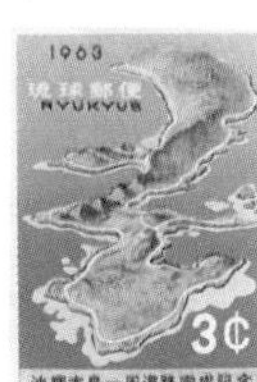

96 Kendo (Japanese Fencing)

1962. Philatelic Week.
137 **95** 3c. multicoloured . . . . . 5·00 2·25

1962. All-Japan Kendo Meeting.
138 **96** 3c. multicoloured . . . . . 5·00 2·50

1962. New Year.
139 **97** 1½c. multicoloured . . . . 2·50 1·00

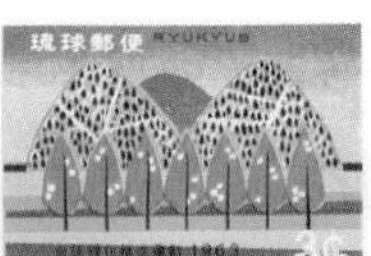

98 Reaching Maturity (clay relief) **101** Okinawa Highway

99 Trees and Wooded Hills

1963. Adults' Day.
140 **98** 3c. gold, black and blue . . 80 50

1963. Afforestation Week.
141 **99** 3c. multicoloured 80 50

1963. Opening of Okinawa Highway.
143 **101** 3c. multicoloured . . . . 1·00 60

102 Black Kites over Islands

1963. Bird Week.
144 **102** 3c. multicoloured . . . . 1·25 1·00

103 Shioya Bridge

1963. Opening of Shioya Bridge, Okinawa.
145 **103** 3c. multicoloured . . . . 1·00 60

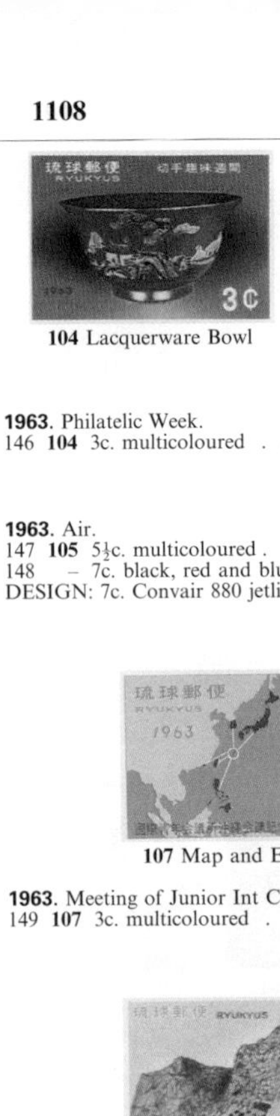

104 Lacquerware Bowl

105 Convair 880 Jetliner and Shuri Gate

1963. Philatelic Week.
146 **104** 3c. multicoloured . . . . 3·25 1·50

1963. Air.
147 **105** 5½c. multicoloured 25 20
148 – 7c. black, red and blue . . 35 30
DESIGN: 7c. Convair 880 jetliner over sea.

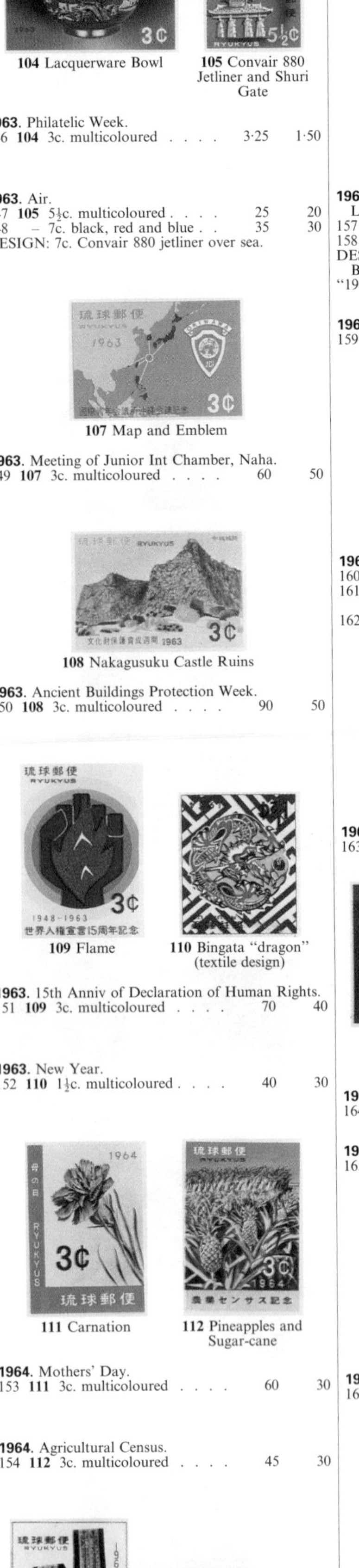

107 Map and Emblem

1963. Meeting of Junior Int Chamber, Naha.
149 **107** 3c. multicoloured 60 50

108 Nakagusuku Castle Ruins

1963. Ancient Buildings Protection Week.
150 **108** 3c. multicoloured 90 50

109 Flame

110 Bingata "dragon" (textile design)

1963. 15th Anniv of Declaration of Human Rights.
151 **109** 3c. multicoloured 70 40

1963. New Year.
152 **110** 1½c. multicoloured 40 30

111 Carnation

112 Pineapples and Sugar-cane

1964. Mothers' Day.
153 **111** 3c. multicoloured 60 30

1964. Agricultural Census.
154 **112** 3c. multicoloured 45 30

113 Hand-woven Sash

114 Girl Scout and Emblem

1964. Philatelic Week.
155 **113** 3c. brown, blue and pink 60 30

1964. 10th Anniv of Ryukyu Girl Scouts.
156 **114** 3c. multicoloured 40 25

115 Transmitting Tower

117 Shuri Gate and Olympic Torch

1964. Inauguration of Ryukyu–Jap'an Microwave Link.
157 **115** 3c. green and black . . . 1·00 85
158 – 8c. blue and black . . . . 1·40 1·00
DESIGN: 8c. "Bowl" receiving aerial.
Both stamps have "1963" cancelled by bars and "1964" inserted in black.

1964. Passage of Olympic Torch through Okinawa.
159 **117** 3c. multicoloured 40 30

118 "Naihanchi" (Karate stance)

1964. Karate ("self-defence"). Multicoloured.
160 3c. Type **118** 65 40
161 3c. "Makiwara" (karate training) 60 50
162 3c. "Kumite" exercise 55 50

121 "Miyara Dunchi" (old Ryukyuan Residence)

1964. Ancient Buildings Protection Week.
163 **121** 3c. multicoloured 40 30

122 Bingata "snake" (textile design)

123 Boy Scouts, Badge and Shuri Gate

1964. New Year.
164 **122** 1½c. multicoloured 45 35

1965. 10th Anniv of Ryukyuan Boy Scouts.
165 **123** 3c. multicoloured 50 40

124 "Samisen" (musical instrument)

1965. Philatelic Week.
166 **124** 3c. multicoloured 50 40

125 Stadium

1965. Completion of Onoyama Sports Ground.
167 **125** 3c. multicoloured 30 25

126 Kin Power Station

127 I.C.Y. Emblem and "Globe"

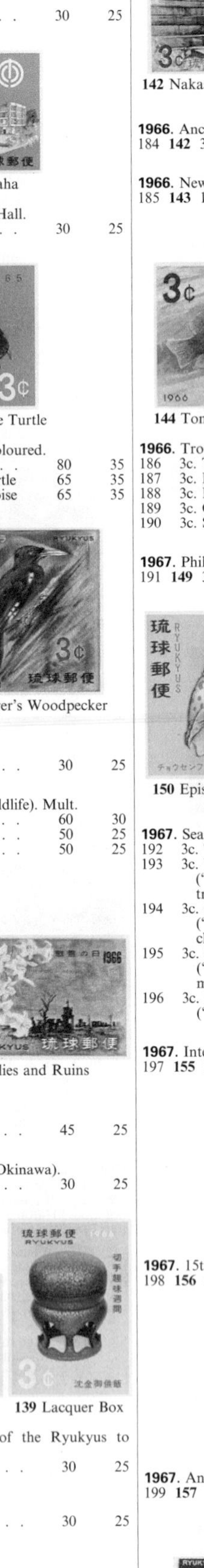

1965. Completion of Kin Power Plant.
168 **126** 3c. multicoloured 30 25

1965. International Co-operation Year and 20th Anniv of United Nations.
169 **127** 3c. multicoloured 30 25

128 City Hall, Naha

1965. Completion of Naha City Hall.
170 **128** 3c. multicoloured 30 25

129 Semaruhakogame Turtle

1965. Ryukyuan Turtles. Multicoloured.
171 3c. Type **129** 80 35
172 3c. Taimai or hawksbill turtle 65 35
173 3c. Yamagame or hill tortoise 65 35

132 Bingata "horse" (textile design)

133 Pryer's Woodpecker

1965. New Year.
174 **132** 1½c. multicoloured 30 25

1966. "Natural Monument" (Wildlife). Mult.
175 3c. Type **133** 60 30
176 3c. Sika deer 50 25
177 3c. Dugong 50 25

136 Pacific Swallow

137 Lilies and Ruins

1966. Bird Week.
178 **136** 3c. multicoloured 45 25

1966. Memorial Day (Battle of Okinawa).
179 **137** 3c. multicoloured 30 25

138 University of the Ryukyus

139 Lacquer Box

1966. Transfer of University of the Ryukyus to Government Administration.
180 **138** 3c. multicoloured 30 25

1966. Philatelic Week.
181 **139** 3c. multicoloured 30 25

140 Ryukyuan Tiled House

141 "GRI" Museum, Shuri

1966. 20th Anniv of U.N.E.S.C.O.
182 **140** 3c. multicoloured 30 25

1966. Completion of Government Museum, Shuri.
183 **141** 3c. multicoloured 30 25

142 Nakasone-Tuimya Tomb

143 Bingata "ram" (textile design)

1966. Ancient Buildings Protection Week.
184 **142** 3c. multicoloured 30 25

1966. New Year.
185 **143** 1½c. multicoloured 30 25

144 Tomato Anemonefish

149 Tsuboya Urn

1966. Tropical Fish. Multicoloured.
186 3c. Type **144** 50 30
187 3c. Blue-spotted boxfish . . . 50 30
188 3c. Long-nosed butterflyfish 50 30
189 3c. Clown triggerfish 50 30
190 3c. Saddle butterflyfish . . . 50 30

1967. Philatelic Week.
191 **149** 3c. multicoloured 40 25

150 Episcopal Mitre

155 Roof Tiles and Emblem

1967. Sea Shells. Multicoloured.
192 3c. Type **150** 40 25
193 3c. Venus comb murex ("Murex (Aranea) triremus") 40 25
194 3c. Chiragra spider conch ("Lambis (Harpago) chiragra") 60 40
195 3c. Great green turban ("Turbo (Olearia) marmoratus") 60 40
196 3c. Bubble conch ("Euprotomus bulla") . . 80 40

1967. International Tourist Year.
197 **155** 3c. multicoloured 30 25

156 Mobile Clinic

1967. 15th Anniv of Anti-T.B. Association.
198 **156** 3c. multicoloured 35 20

157 Hojo Bridge, Enkaku

1967. Ancient Buildings Protection Week.
199 **157** 3c. multicoloured 30 25

158 Bingata "monkey" (textile design)

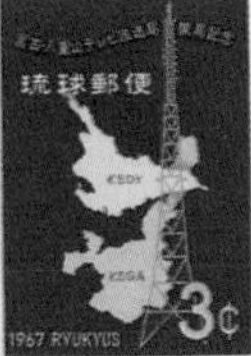

159 T.V. Tower and Map

1967. New Year.
200 **158** 1½c. multicoloured 30 25

1967. Opening of T.V. Broadcasting Stations in Miyako and Yaeyama.
201 **159** 3c. multicoloured 30 25

160 Dr. Nakachi and Assistant

161 Medicine Case (after Sokei Dana)

1968. 120th Anniv of 1st Ryukyu Vaccination (by Dr. Kijin Nakachi).
202 **160** 3c. multicoloured 30 25

1968. Philatelic Week.
203 **161** 3c. multicoloured 50 30

162 Young Man, Book, Map and Library

1968. Library Week.
204 **162** 3c. multicoloured 45 30

163 Postmen with Ryukyu Stamp of 1948

1968. 20th Anniv of 1st Ryukyu Islands Stamps.
205 **163** 3c. multicoloured 40 30

164 Temple Gate

165 Old Man Dancing

1968. Restoration of Enkaku Temple Gate.
206 **164** 3c. multicoloured 40 30

1968. Old People's Day.
207 **165** 3c. multicoloured 40 30

166 "Mictyris longicarpus"

1968. Crabs. Multicoloured.
208 3c. Type **166** 80 60
209 3c. "Uca dubia" 80 60
210 3c. "Baptozius vinosus" . . . 80 60
211 3c. "Cardisoma carnifex" . . 80 60
212 3c. "Ocypode ceratophthalma" 80 60

171 Saraswati Pavilion

172 Player

1968. Ancient Buildings Protection Week.
213 **171** 3c. multicoloured 35 25

1968. 35th All-Japan East v West Men's Softball Tennis Tournament, Onoyama.
214 **172** 3c. multicoloured 40 25

173 Bingata "cock" (textile design)

174 Boxer

1968. New Year.
215 **173** 1½c. multicoloured 30 20

1969. 20th All-Japan Boxing Championships.
216 **174** 3c. multicoloured 30 25

175 Inkwell Screen

176 UHF Antennae and Map

1969. Philatelic Week.
217 **175** 3c. multicoloured 35 25

1969. Inauguration of Okinawa–Sakishima U.H.F. Radio Service.
218 **176** 3c. multicoloured 30 25

177 Gate of Courtesy

178 "Tug of War" Festival

1969. 22nd All-Japan Formative Education Study Conference, Naha.
219 **177** 3c. multicoloured 30 25

1969. Traditional Religious Ceremonies. Mult.
220 3c. Type **178** 60 40
221 3c. "Hari" canoe race 60 40
222 3c. "Izaiho" religious ceremony 60 40
223 3c. "Ushideiku" dance . . . 60 40
224 3c. "Sea God" dance 60 40

1969. No. 131 surch.
225 ½c. on 3c. multicoloured . . . 15 25

184 Nakamura-Ke

1969. Ancient Buildings Protection Week.
226 **184** 3c. multicoloured 25 20

185 Kyuzo Toyama and Map

186 Bingata "dog and flowers" (textile design)

1969. 70th Anniv of Toyama's Ryukyu–Hawaii Emigration Project.
227 **185** 3c. multicoloured 40 35
No. 227 has "1970" cancelled by bars and "1969" inserted in black.

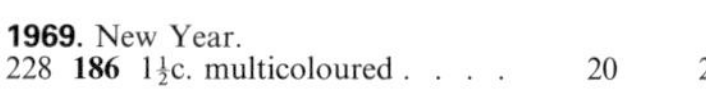

1969. New Year.
228 **186** 1½c. multicoloured 20 20

187 Sake Flask

1970. Philatelic Week.
229 **187** 3c. multicoloured 35 20

188 "Shushin-Kaneiri"

189 "Chu-nusudu"

190 "Mekarushi"

191 "Nidotichiuchi"

192 "Kokonomaki"

1970. "Kumi-Odori" Ryukyu Theatre. Mult.
230 **188** 3c. multicoloured 70 55
231 **189** 3c. multicoloured 70 55
232 **190** 3c. multicoloured 70 55
233 **191** 3c. multicoloured 70 55
234 **192** 3c. multicoloured 70 55

193 Observatory

194 Noboru Jahana (politician)

1970. Completion of Underwater Observatory, Busena-Misaki, Nago.
240 **193** 3c. multicoloured 30 25

1970. Famous Ryukyuans.
241 **194** 3c. purple 60 60
242 – 3c. green 70 60
243 – 3c. black 60 60
PORTRAITS: No. 242, Saion Gushichan Bunjaku (statesman); 243, Choho Giwan (Regent).

197 "Population

198 "Great Cycad of Une"

1970. Population Census.
244 **197** 3c. multicoloured 25 25

1970. Ancient Buildings Protection Week.
245 **198** 3c. multicoloured 40 25

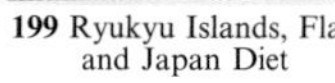
199 Ryukyu Islands, Flag and Japan Diet

200 "Wild Boar" (Bingata textile design)

1970. Election of Ryukyu Representatives to the Japanese Diet.
246 **199** 3c. multicoloured 85 60

1970. New Year.
247 **200** 1½c. multicoloured 30 25

201 "Jibata" (hand-loom)

202 "Filature" (spinning-wheel)

203 Farm-worker wearing "Shurunnu" Coat and "Kubagasa" Hat

204 Woman using "Shiri-Ushi" (rice huller)

205 Fisherman's "Umi-Fujo" (box) and "Yutui" (bailer)

1971. Ryukyu Handicrafts.
248 **201** 3c. multicoloured 40 30
249 **202** 3c. multicoloured 40 30
250 **203** 3c. multicoloured 40 30
251 **204** 3c. multicoloured 40 30
252 **205** 3c. multicoloured 40 30

206 "Taku" (container)

208 Restored Battlefield, Okinawa

207 Civic Emblem with Old and New City Views

1971. Philatelic Week.
253 **206** 3c. multicoloured 35 25

1971. 50th Anniv of Naha's City Status.
254 **207** 3c. multicoloured 30 25

1971. Government Parks. Multicoloured.
255 3c. Type **208** 30 30
256 3c. Haneji Inland Sea 30 30
257 4c. Yabuchi Island 30 30

211 Deva King, Torinji Temple

212 "Rat" (Bingata textile pattern)

1971. Anicent Buildings Protection Week.
258 **211** 4c. multicoloured 25 25

1971. New Year.
259 **212** 2c. multicoloured 30 20

213 Student-nurse and Candle

214 Islands and Sunset

1971. 25th Anniv of Nurses' Training Scheme.

260	**213**	4c. multicoloured	25	25

1972. Maritime Scenery. Multicoloured.

261	5c. Type **214**	30	70
262	5c. Coral reef (horiz)	30	70
263	5c. Island and short-tailed albatrosses	95	45

217 Dove and Flags of Japan and U.S.A

218 "Yushibin" (ceremonial sake container)

1972. Ratification of Treaty for Return of Ryukyu Islands to Japan.

264	**217**	5c. multicoloured	40	1·00

1972. Philatelic Week.

265	**218**	5c. multicoloured	50	1·00

SPECIAL DELIVERY STAMP

E **13** Sea-horse

1951.

E18	E **13**	5y. blue	30·00	15·00

INDEX

Stanley Gibbons SIMPLIFIED CATALOGUE

Stamps of the World

This popular catalogue is a straightforward listing of the stamps that have been issued everywhere in the world since the very first–Great Britain's famous Penny Black in 1840.

This edition, in which both the text and the illustrations have been captured electronically, is arranged completely alphabetically in a four-volume format. Volume 1 (Countries A–D), Volume 2 (Countries E–J), Volume 3 (Countries K–R) and Volume 4 (Countries S–Z).

Readers are reminded that the Catalogue Supplements, published in each issue of **Gibbons Stamp Monthly**, can be used to update the listings in **Stamps of the World** as well as our 22-part standard catalogue. To make the supplement even more useful the Type numbers given to the illustrations are the same in the Stamps of the World as in the standard catalogues. The first Catalogue Supplement to this Volume appeared in the September 2003 issue of **Gibbons Stamp Monthly**.

Gibbons Stamp Monthly can be obtained through newsagents or on postal subscription from Stanley Gibbons Publications, Parkside, Christchurch Road, Ringwood, Hants BH24 3SH.

The catalogue has many important features:

- The vast majority of illustrations are now in full colour to aid stamp identification.
- All Commonwealth miniature sheets are now included.
- As an indication of current values virtually every stamp is priced. Thousands of alterations have been made since the last edition.
- By being set out on a simplified basis that excludes changes of paper, perforation, shade, watermark, gum or printer's and date imprints it is particularly easy to use. (For its exact scope see "Information for users" pages following.)
- The thousands of colour illustrations and helpful descriptions of stamp designs make it of maximum appeal to collectors with thematic interests.
- Its catalogue numbers are the world-recognised Stanley Gibbons numbers throughout.
- Helpful introductory notes for the collector are included, backed by much historical, geographical and currency information.
- A very detailed index gives instant location of countries in this volume, and a cross-reference to those included in the other volumes.

Over 4,220 stamps and miniature sheets and 606 new illustrations have been added to the listings in this volume. This year's four-volumes now contain over 406,730 stamps and 97,315 illustrations.

The listings in this edition are based on the standard catalogues: Part 1, Commonwealth & British Empire Stamps 1840–1952, Part 2 (Austria & Hungary) (6th edition), Part 3 (Balkans) (4th edition), Part 4 (Benelux) (5th edition), Part 5 (Czechoslovakia & Poland) (6th edition), Part 6 (France) (5th edition), Part 7 (Germany) (6th edition), Part 8 (Italy & Switzerland) (6th edition), Part 9 (Portugal & Spain) (4th edition), Part 10 (Russia) (5th edition), Part 11 (Scandinavia) (5th edition), Part 12 (Africa since Independence A-E) (2nd edition), Part 13 (Africa since Independence F-M) (1st edition), Part 14 (Africa since Independence N-Z) (1st edition), Part 15 (Central America) (2nd edition), Part 16 (Central Asia) (3rd edition), Part 17 (China) (6th edition), Part 18 (Japan & Korea) (4th edition), Part 19 (Middle East) (5th edition), Part 20 (South America) (3rd edition), Part 21 (South-East Asia) (3rd edition) and Part 22 (United States) (5th edition).

This edition includes major repricing for all Western Europe countries in addition to the changes for Benelux Part 4, Italy and Switzerland Part 8 and Czechoslovakia & Poland Part 5. Also all thematic Bird issues have been revised for this volume.

Acknowledgements

A wide-ranging revision of prices for Western European countries has been undertaken for this edition with the intention that the catalogue should be more accurate to reflect the market for foreign issues.

Many dealers in both Great Britain and overseas have participated in this scheme by supplying copies of their retail price lists on which the research has been based.

We would like to acknowledge the assistance of the following for this edition:

ALMAZ CO
of Brooklyn, U.S.A.

AMATEUR COLLECTOR LTD, THE
of London, England

E. ANGELOPOULOS
of Thessaloniki, Greece

AVION THEMATICS
of Nottingham, England

J BAREFOOT LTD
of York, England

BELGIAN PHILATELIC SPECIALISTS INC
of Larchmont, U.S.A.

Sir CHARLES BLOMEFIELD
of Chipping Camden, England

T. BRAY
of Shipley, West Yorks, England

CENTRAL PHILATELIQUE
of Brussels, Belgium

JEAN-PIERRE DELMONTE
of Paris, France

EUROPEAN & FOREIGN STAMPS
of Pontypridd, Wales

FILATELIA LLACH SL
of Barcelona, Spain

FILATELIA RIVA RENO
of Bologna, Italy

FILATELIA TORI
of Barcelona, Spain

FORMOSA STAMP COMPANY, THE
of Koahsiung, Taiwan

FORSTAMPS
of Battle, England

ANTHONY GRAINGER
of Leeds, England

HOLMGREN STAMPS
of Bollnas, Sweden

INDIGO
of Orewa, New Zealand

ALEC JACQUES
of Selby, England

M. JANKOWSKI
of Warsaw, Poland

D.J.M. KERR
of Earlston, England

H. M. NIELSEN
of Vejle, Denmark

LEO BARESCH LTD
of Hassocks, England

LORIEN STAMPS
of Chesterfield, England

MANDARIN TRADING CO
of Alhambra, U.S.A.

MICHAEL ROGERS INC
of Winter Park, U.S.A.

PHILATELIC SUPPLIES
of Letchworth, England

PHIL-INDEX
of Eastbourne, England

PHILTRADE A/S
of Copenhagen, Denmark

PITTERI SA
of Chiasso, Switzerland

KEVIN RIGLER
of Shifnal, England

ROLF GUMMESSON AB
of Stockholm, Sweden

R. D. TOLSON
of Undercliffe, England

JAY SMITH
of Snow Camp, U.S.A.

R. SCHNEIDER
of Belleville, U.S.A.

ROBSTINE STAMPS
of Hampshire, England

SOUTHERN MAIL
of Eastbourne, England

STAMP CENTER
of Reykjavik, Iceland

REX WHITE
of Winchester, England

Western European countries will now be repriced each year in Stamps of the World and where there is no up-to-date specialised foreign volume in a country these will be the new Stanley Gibbons prices.

It is hoped that this improved pricing scheme will be extended to other foreign countries and thematic issues as information is consolidated.

Stanley Gibbons

SIMPLIFIED CATALOGUE

Stamps of the World

2004 Edition

IN COLOUR

An illustrated and priced four-volume guide to the postage stamps of the whole world, excluding changes of paper, perforation, shade and watermark

VOLUME 1

COUNTRIES A–D

STANLEY GIBBONS LTD
L

By Appointment to
Her Majesty the Queen
Stanley Gibbons Limited
London
Philatelists

69th Edition

Published in Great Britain by
Stanley Gibbons Ltd
Publications Editorial, Sales Offices and Distribution Centre
Parkside, Christchurch Road,
Ringwood, Hampshire BH24 3SH
Telephone 01425 472363

ISBN: 085259-549-2

Published as Stanley Gibbons Simplified Stamp Catalogue from 1934 to 1970, renamed Stamps of the World in 1971, and produced in two (1982-88), three (1989-2001) or four (from 2002) volumes as Stanley Gibbons Simplified Catalogue of Stamps of the World.
This volume published November 2003

S.G. Item No. 2881 (04)

Printed in Great Britain by Unwin Brothers Ltd, Old Woking, Surrey

Information for users

Aim

The aim of this catalogue is to provide a straightforward illustrated and priced guide to the postage stamps of the whole world to help you to enjoy the greatest hobby of the present day.

Arrangement

The catalogue lists countries in alphabetical order and there is a complete index at the end of each volume. For ease of reference country names are also printed at the head of each page.

Within each country, postage stamps are listed first. They are followed by separate sections for such other categories as postage due stamps, parcel post stamps, express stamps, official stamps, etc.

All catalogue lists are set out according to dates of issue of the stamps, starting from the earliest and working through to the most recent.

Scope of the Catalogue

The *Simplified Catalogue of Stamps of the World* contains listings of postage stamps only. Apart from the ordinary definitive, commemorative and air-mail stamps of each country – which appear first in each list – there are sections for the following where appropriate:

- postage due stamps
- parcel post stamps
- official stamps
- express and special delivery stamps
- charity and compulsory tax stamps
- newspaper and journal stamps
- printed matter stamps
- registration stamps
- acknowledgement of receipt stamps
- late fee and too late stamps
- military post stamps
- recorded message stamps
- personal delivery stamps

We receive numerous enquiries from collectors about other items which do not fall within the categories set out above and which consequently do not appear in the catalogue lists. It may be helpful, therefore, to summarise the other kinds of stamp that exist but which we deliberately exclude from this postage stamp catalogue.

We do *not* list the following:

Fiscal or revenue stamps: stamps used solely in collecting taxes or fees for non-postal purposes. Examples would be stamps which pay a tax on a receipt, represent the stamp duty on a contract or frank a customs document. Common inscriptions found include: Documentary, Proprietary, Inter. Revenue, Contract Note.

Local stamps: postage stamps whose validity and use are limited in area, say to a single town or city, though in some cases they provided, with official sanction, services in parts of countries not covered by the respective government.

Local carriage labels and Private local issues: many labels exist ostensibly to cover the cost of ferrying mail from one of Great Britain's offshore islands to the nearest mainland post office. They are not recognised as valid for national or international mail. Examples: Calf of Man, Davaar, Herm, Lundy, Pabay, Stroma. Items from some other places have only the status of tourist souvenir labels.

Telegraph stamps: stamps intended solely for the prepayment of telegraphic communication.

Bogus or "phantom" stamps: labels from mythical places or non-existent administrations. Examples in the classical period were Sedang, Counani, Clipperton Island and in modern times Thomond and Monte Bello Islands. Numerous labels have also appeared since the War from dissident groups as propaganda for their claims and without authority from the home governments. Common examples are labels for "Free Albania", "Free Rumania" and "Free Croatia" and numerous issues for Nagaland, Indonesia and the South Moluccas ("Republik Maluku Selatan").

Railway letter fee stamps: special stamps issued by railway companies for the conveyance of letters by rail. Example: Talyllyn Railway. Similar services are now offered by some bus companies and the labels they issue likewise do not qualify for inclusion in the catalogue.

Perfins ("perforated initials"): numerous postage stamps may be found with initial letters or designs punctured through them by tiny holes. These are applied by private and public concerns as a precaution against theft and do not qualify for separate mention.

Information for users

Labels: innumerable items exist resembling stamps but – as they do not prepay postage – they are classified as labels. The commonest categories are:

- propaganda and publicity labels: designed to further a cause or campaign;
- exhibition labels: particularly souvenirs from philatelic events;
- testing labels: stamp-size labels used in testing stamp-vending machines;
- Post Office training school stamps: British stamps overprinted with two thick vertical bars or SCHOOL SPECIMEN are produced by the Post Office for training purposes;
- seals and stickers: numerous charities produce stamp-like labels, particularly at Christmas and Easter, as a means of raising funds and these have no postal validity.

Cut-outs: items of postal stationary, such as envelopes, cards and wrappers, often have stamps impressed or imprinted on them. They may usually be cut out and affixed to envelopes, etc., for postal use if desired, but such items are not listed in this catalogue.

Collectors wanting further information about exact definitions are referred to *Philatelic Terms Illustrated*, published by Stanley Gibbons and containing many illustrations in colour.

There is also a priced listing of the postal fiscals of Great Britain in our *Commonwealth & British Empire Stamps 1840–1952* Catalogue and in Volume 1 of the *Great Britain Specialised* Catalogue (5th and later editions).

Catalogue Numbers

Stanley Gibbons catalogue numbers are recognised universally and any individual stamp can be identified by quoting the catalogue number (the one at the left of the column) prefixed by the name of the country and the letters "S.G.". Do not confuse the catalogue number with the type numbers which refer to illustrations.

Prices

Prices in the left-hand column are for unused stamps and those in the right-hand column for used. Prices are given in pence and pounds:

100 pence (p) 1 pound (£1).

Prices are shown as follows:

10 means 10p (10 pence);
1.50 means £1.50 (1 pound and 50 pence);
For £100 and above, prices are in whole pounds.

Our prices are for stamps in fine condition, and in issues where condition varies we may ask more for the superb and less for the sub-standard.

The minimum catalogue price quoted is 10p. For individual stamps prices between 10p and 45p are provided as a guide for catalogue users. The lowest price charged for individual stamps purchased from Stanley Gibbons is 50p.

The prices quoted are generally for the cheapest variety of stamps but it is worth noting that differences of watermark, perforation, or other details, outside the scope of this catalogue, may often increase the value of the stamp.

Prices quoted for mint issues are for single examples. Those in se-tenant pairs, strips, blocks or sheets may be worth more.

Where prices are not given in either column it is either because the stamps are not known to exist in that particular condition, or, more usually, because there is no reliable information as to value.

All prices are subject to change without prior notice and we give no guarantee to supply all stamps priced. Prices quoted for albums, publications, etc. advertised in this catalogue are also subject to change without prior notice.

Due to different production methods it is sometimes possible for new editions of Parts 2 to 22 to appear showing revised prices which are not included in that year's *Stamps of the World.*

Unused Stamps

In the case of stamps from *Great Britain* and the *Commonwealth*, prices for unused stamps of Queen Victoria to King George V are for lightly hinged examples; unused prices of King Edward VIII to Queen Elizabeth II issues are for unmounted mint. The prices of unused Foreign stamps are for lightly hinged examples for those issued before 1946, thereafter for examples unmounted mint.

Used Stamps

Prices for used stamps generally refer to fine postally used examples, though for certain issues they are for cancelled-to-order.

Information for users

Guarantee

All stamps supplied by us are guaranteed originals in the following terms:

If not as described, and returned by the purchaser, we undertake to refund the price paid to us in the original transaction. If any stamp is certified as genuine by the Expert Committee of the Royal Philatelic Society, London, or by B.P.A. Expertising Ltd., the purchaser shall not be entitled to make any claim against us for any error, omission or mistake in such certificate.

Consumers' statutory rights are not affected by the above guarantee.

Currency

At the beginning of each country brief details give the currencies in which the values of the stamps are expressed. The dates, where given, are those of the earliest stamp issues in the particular currency. Where the currency is obvious, e.g. where the colony has the same currency as the mother country, no details are given.

Illustrations

Illustrations of any surcharges and overprints which are shown and not described are actual size; stamp illustrations are reduced to $\frac{3}{4}$ linear, *unless otherwise stated.*

"Key-Types"

A number of standard designs occur so frequently in the stamps of the French, German, Portuguese and Spanish colonies that it would be a waste of space to repeat them. Instead these are all illustrated on page xiv together with the descriptive names and letters by which they are referred to in the lists.

Type Numbers

These are the bold figures found below each illustration. References to "Type **6**", for example, in the lists of a country should therefore be understood to refer to the illustration below which the number **"6"** appears. These type numbers are also given in the second column of figures alongside each list of stamps, thus indicating clearly the design of each stamp. In the case of Key-Types – see above – letters take the place of the type numbers.

Where an issue comprises stamps of similar design, represented in this catalogue by one illustration, the corresponding type numbers should be taken as indicating this general design.

Where there are blanks in the type number column it means that the type of the corresponding stamps is that shown by the last number above in the type column of the same issue.

A dash (–) in the type column means that no illustration of the stamp is shown.

Where type numbers refer to stamps of another country, e.g. where stamps of one country are overprinted for use in another, this is always made clear in the text.

Stamp Designs

Brief descriptions of the subjects of the stamp designs are given either below or beside the illustrations, at the foot of the list of the issue concerned, or in the actual lists. Where a particular subject, e.g. the portrait of a well-known monarch, recurs frequently the description is not repeated, nor are obvious designs described.

Generally, the unillustrated designs are in the same shape and size as the one illustrated, except where otherwise indicated.

Surcharges and Overprints

Surcharges and overprints are usually described in the headings to the issues concerned. Where the actual wording of a surcharge or overprint is given it is shown in bold type.

Some stamps are described as being "Surcharged in words", e.g. **TWO CENTS**, and others "Surcharged in figures and words", e.g. **20 CENTS**, although of course many surcharges are in foreign languages and combinations of words and figures are numerous. There are often bars, etc., obliterating old values or inscriptions but in general these are only mentioned where it is necessary to avoid confusion.

No attention is paid in this catalogue to colours of overprints and surcharges so that stamps with the same overprints in different colours are not listed separately.

Numbers in brackets after the descriptions of overprinted or surcharged stamps are the catalogue numbers of the unoverprinted stamps.

Note – the words "inscribed" or "inscription" always refer to wording incorporated in the design of a stamp and not surcharges or overprints.

Coloured Papers

Where stamps are printed on coloured paper the description is given as e.g. "4 c. black on blue" – a stamp printed in black on blue paper. No attention is paid in this catalogue to difference in the texture of paper, e.g. laid, wove.

Information for users

Watermarks

Stamps having different watermarks, but otherwise the same, are not listed separately. No reference is therefore made to watermarks in this volume.

Stamp Colours

Colour names are only required for the identification of stamps, therefore they have been made as simple as possible. Thus "scarlet", "vermilion", "carmine" are all usually called red. Qualifying colour names have been introduced only where necessary for the sake of clearness.

Where stamps are printed in two or more colours the central portion of the design is in the first colour given, unless otherwise stated.

Perforations

All stamps are perforated unless otherwise stated. No distinction is made between the various gauges of perforation but early stamp issues which exist both imperforate and perforated are usually listed separately.

Where a heading states "Imperf. or perf". or "Perf. or rouletted" this does not necessarily mean that all values of the issue are found in both conditions.

Dates of Issue

The date given at the head of each issue is that of the appearance of the earliest stamp in the series. As stamps of the same design or issue are usually grouped together a list of King George VI stamps, for example, headed "1938" may include stamps issued from 1938 to the end of the reign.

Se-tenant Pairs

Many modern issues are printed in sheets containing different designs or face values. Such pairs, blocks, strips or sheets are described as being "se-tenant" and they are outside the scope of this catalogue, although reference to them may occur in instances where they form a composite design.

Miniature Sheets

As an increasing number of stamps are now only found in miniature sheets, Stamps of the World will, in future, list these items. This edition lists all Commonwealth countries' miniature sheets, plus those of all non-Commonwealth countries which have appeared in the catalogue supplement during the past year. Earlier miniature sheets of non-Commonwealth countries will be listed in future editions.

"Appendix" Countries

We regret that, since 1968, it has been necessary to establish an Appendix (at the end of each country as appropriate) to which numerous stamps have had to be consigned. Several countries imagine that by issuing huge quantities of unnecessary stamps they will have a ready source of income from stamp collectors – and particularly from the less-experienced ones. Stanley Gibbons refuse to encourage this exploitation of the hobby and we do not stock the stamps concerned.

Two kinds of stamp are therefore given the briefest of mentions in the Appendix, purely for the sake of record. Administrations issuing stamps greatly in excess of true postal needs have the offending issues placed there. Likewise it contains stamps which have not fulfilled all the normal conditions for full catalogue listing.

These conditions are that the stamps must be issued by a legitimate postal authority, recognised by the government concerned, and are adhesives, valid for proper postal use in the class of service for which they are inscribed. Stamps, with the exception of such categories as postage dues and officials, must be available to the general public at face value with no artificial restrictions being imposed on their distribution.

The publishers of this catalogue have observed, with concern, the proliferation of 'artificial' stamp-issuing territories. On several occasions this has resulted in separately inscribed issues for various component parts of otherwise united states or territories.

Stanley Gibbons Publications have decided that where such circumstances occur, they will not, in the future, list these items in the SG catalogue without first satisfying themselves that the stamps represent a genuine political, historical or postal division within the country concerned. Any such issues which do not fulfil this stipulation will be recorded in the Catalogue Appendix only.

Stamps in the Appendix are kept under review in the light of any newly acquired information about them. If we are satisfied that a stamp qualifies for proper listing in the body of the catalogue it is moved there.

Information for users

"Undesirable Issues"

The rules governing many competitive exhibitions are set by the Federation Internationale de Philatelie and stipulate a downgrading of marks for stamps classed as "undesirable issues".

This catalogue can be taken as a guide to status. All stamps in the main listings and Addenda are acceptable. Stamps in the Appendix should not be entered for competition as these are the "undesirable issues".

Particular care is advised with Aden Protectorate States, Ajman, Bhutan, Chad, Fujeira, Khor Fakkan, Manama, Ras al Khaima, Sharjah, Umm al Qiwain and Yemen. Totally bogus stamps exist (as explained in Appendix notes) and these are to be avoided also for competition. As distinct from "undesirable stamps" certain categories are not covered in this catalogue purely by reason of its scope (see page viii). Consult the particular competition rules to see if such are admissable even though not listed by us.

Where to Look for More Detailed Listings

The present work deliberately omits details of paper, perforation, shade and watermark. But as you become more absorbed in stamp collecting and wish to get greater enjoyment from the hobby you may well want to study these matters.

All the information you require about any particular postage stamp will be found in the main Stanley Gibbons Catalogues.

Commonwealth countries before 1952 are covered by the Commonwealth & British Empire Stamps 1840–1952 published annually.

For foreign countries you can easily find which catalogue to consult by looking at the country headings in the present book.

To the right of each country name are code letters specifying which volume of our main catalogues contains that country's listing.

The code letters are as follows:

Pt. 2 Part 2

Pt. 3 Part 3 etc.

(See page xiii for complete list of Parts.)

So, for example, if you want to know more about Chinese stamps than is contained in the *Simplified Catalogue of Stamps of the World* the reference to

CHINA Pt. 17

guides you to the Gibbons Part 17 *(China)* Catalogue listing for the details you require.

New editions of Parts 2 to 22 appear at irregular intervals.

Correspondence

Whilst we welcome information and suggestions we must ask correspondents to include the cost of postage for the return of any stamps submitted plus registration where appropriate. Letters should be addressed to The Catalogue Editor at Ringwood.

Where information is solicited purely for the benefit of the enquirer we regret we cannot undertake to reply.

Identification of Stamps

We regret we do not give opinions as to the genuineness of stamps, nor do we identify stamps or number them by our Catalogue.

Users of this catalogue are referred to our companion booklet entitled *Stamp Collecting – How to Identify Stamps.* It explains how to look up stamps in this catalogue, contains a full checklist of stamp inscriptions and gives help in dealing with unfamiliar scripts.

Stanley Gibbons would like to complement your collection

At Stanley Gibbons we offer a range of services which are designed to complement your collection.

Our modern stamp shop, the largest in Europe, together with our rare stamp department has one of the most comprehensive stocks of Great Britain in the world, so whether you are a beginner or an experienced philatelist you are certain to find something to suit your special requirements.

Alternatively, through our Mail Order services you can control the growth of your collection from the comfort of your own home. Our Postal Sales Department regularly sends out mailings of Special Offers. We can also help with your wants list—so why not ask us for those elusive items?

Why not take advantage of the many services we have to offer? Visit our premises in the Strand or, for more information, write to the appropriate address on page x.

The Stanley Gibbons Group Addresses

Stanley Gibbons Limited, Stanley Gibbons Auctions

339 Strand, London WC2R 0LX
Telephone 020 7836 8444, Fax 020 7836 7342,
E-mail: enquiries@stanleygibbons.co.uk
Internet: www.stanleygibbons.com for all departments.

Auction Room and Specialist Stamp Departments.

Open Monday–Friday 9.30 a.m. to 5 p.m.

Shop. Open Monday–Friday 9 a.m. to 5.30 p.m. and Saturday 9.30 a.m. to 5.30 p.m.

Stanley Gibbons Publications

Parkside, Christchurch Road, Ringwood, Hants BH24 3SH.
Telephone 01425 472363 (24 hour answer phone service), Fax 01425 470247,
E-mail: info@stanleygibbons.co.uk

Publications Mail Order. FREEPHONE 0800 611622
Monday–Friday 8.30 a.m. to 5 p.m.

Fraser's

(a division of Stanley Gibbons Ltd)

399 Strand, London WC2R 0LX
Autographs, photographs, letters and documents

Telephone 020 7836 8444, Fax 020 7836 7342,
E-mail: info@frasersautographs.co.uk
Internet: www.frasersautographs.com

Monday–Friday 9 a.m. to 5.30 p.m. and Saturday 10 a.m. to 4 p.m.

Stanley Gibbons Publications Overseas Representation

Stanley Gibbons Publications are represented overseas by the following sole distributors (*), distributors (**) or licensees (***).

Australia
Lighthouse Philatelic (Aust.) Pty. Ltd.*
Locked Bag 5900 Botany DC, New South Wales, 2019 Australia.

Stanley Gibbons (Australia) Pty. Ltd.***
Level 6, 36 Clarence Street, Sydney, New South Wales 2000, Australia.

Belgium and Luxembourg**
Davo c/o Philac, Rue du Midi 48, Bruxelles, 1000 Belgium.

Canada*
Lighthouse Publications (Canada) Ltd., 255 Duke Street, Montreal Quebec, Canada H3C 2M2.

Denmark**
Samlerforum/Davo, Ostergade 3, DK 7470 Karup, Denmark.

Finland**
Davo c/o Kapylan Merkkiky Pohjolankatu 1 00610 Helsinki, Finland.

France*
Davo France (Casteilla), 10, Rue Leon Foucault, 78184 St. Quentin Yvelines Cesex, France.

Hong Kong**
Po-on Stamp Service, GPO Box 2498, Hong Kong.

Israel**
Capital Stamps, P.O. Box 3769, Jerusalem 91036, Israel.

Italy*
Ernesto Marini Srl, Via Struppa 300, I-16165, Genova GE, Italy.

Japan**
Japan Philatelic Co. Ltd., P.O. Box 2, Suginami-Minami, Tokyo, Japan.

Netherlands*
Davo Publications, P.O. Box 411, 7400 AK Deventer, Netherlands.

New Zealand***
Mowbray Collectables.
P.O. Box 80, Wellington, New Zealand.

Norway**
Davo Norge A/S, P.O. Box 738 Sentrum, N-0105, Oslo, Norway.

Singapore**
Stamp Inc Collectibles Pte Ltd., 10 Ubi Cresent, #01-43 Ubi Tech Park, Singapore 408564.

Sweden*
Chr Winther Soerensen AB, Box 43, S-310 Knaered, Sweden.

Switzerland**
Phila Service, Burgstrasse 160, CH 4125, Riehen, Switzerland.

Abbreviations

Anniv.	denotes	Anniversary
Assn.	,,	Association
Bis.	,,	Bistre
Bl.	,,	Blue
Bldg.	,,	Building
Blk.	,,	Black
Br.	,,	British or Bridge
Brn.	,,	Brown
B.W.I.	,,	British West Indies
C.A.R.I.F.T.A.	,,	Caribbean Free Trade Area
Cent.	,,	Centenary
Chest.	,,	Chestnut
Choc.	,,	Chocolate
Clar.	,,	Claret
Coll.	,,	College
Commem.	,,	Commemoration
Conf.	,,	Conference
Diag.	,,	Diagonally
E.C.A.F.E.	,,	Economic Commission for Asia and Far East
Emer.	,,	Emerald
E.P.T. Conference	,,	European Postal and Telecommunications Conference
Exn.		Exhibition
F.A.O.	,,	Food and Agriculture Organization
Fig.	,,	Figure
G.A.T.T.	,,	General Agreement on Tariffs and Trade
G.B.	,,	Great Britain
Gen.	,,	General
Govt.	,,	Government
Grn.	,,	Green
Horiz.	,,	Horizontal
H.Q.	,,	Headquarters
Imperf.	,,	Imperforate
Inaug.	,,	Inauguration
Ind.	,,	Indigo
Inscr.	,,	Inscribed or inscription
Int.	,,	International
I.A.T.A.	,,	International Air Transport Association
I.C.A.O.	,,	International Civil Aviation Organization
I.C.Y.	,,	International Co-operation Year
I.G.Y.	,,	International Geophysical Year
I.L.O.	,,	International Labour Office (or later, Organization)
I.M.C.O.	,,	Inter-Governmental Maritime Consultative Organization
I.T.U.	,,	International Telecommunication Union
Is.	,,	Islands
Lav.	,,	Lavender
Mar.	,,	Maroon
mm.	,,	Millimetres
Mult.	,,	Multicoloured

Mve.	denotes	Mauve
Nat.	,,	National
N.A.T.O.	,,	North Atlantic Treaty Organization
O.D.E.C.A.	,,	Organization of Central American States
Ol.	,,	Olive
Optd.	,,	Overprinted
Orge. or oran.	,,	Orange
P.A.T.A.	,,	Pacific Area Travel Association
Perf.	,,	Perforated
Post.	,,	Postage
Pres.	,,	President
P.U.	,,	Postal Union
Pur.	,,	Purple
R.	,,	River
R.S.A.	,,	Republic of South Africa
Roul.	,,	Rouletted
Sep.	,,	Sepia
S.E.A.T.O.	,,	South East Asia Treaty Organization
Surch.	,,	Surcharged
T.	,,	Type
T.U.C.	,,	Trades Union Congress
Turq.	,,	Turquoise
Ultram.	,,	Ultramarine
U.N.E.S.C.O.	,,	United Nations Educational, Scientific Cultural Organization
U.N.I.C.E.F.	,,	United Nations Children's Fund
U.N.O.	,,	United Nations Organization
U.N.R.W.A.	,,	United Nations Relief and Works Agency for Palestine Refugees in the Near East
U.N.T.E.A.	,,	United Nations Temporary Executive Authority
U.N.R.R.A.	,,	United Nations Relief and Rehabilitation Administration
U.P.U.	,,	Universal Postal Union
Verm.	,,	Vermilion
Vert.	,,	Vertical
Vio.	,,	Violet
W.F.T.U.	,,	World Federation of Trade Unions
W.H.O.	,,	World Health Organization
Yell.	,,	Yellow

Arabic Numerals

As in the case of European figures, the details of the Arabic numerals vary in different stamp designs, but they should be readily recognised with the aid of this illustration:

٠	١	٢	٣	٤
0	1	2	3	4
٥	٦	٧	٨	٩
5	6	7	8	9

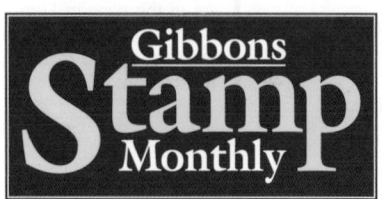

Stanley Gibbons Stamp Catalogue
Complete List of Parts

1 Commonwealth & British Empire Stamps 1840–1952 (Annual)

Foreign Countries

2 Austria & Hungary (6th edition, 2002)
Austria · U.N. (Vienna) · Hungary

3 Balkans (4th edition, 1998)
Albania · Bosnia & Herzegovina · Bulgaria · Croatia · Greece & Islands · Macedonia · Rumania · Slovenia · Yugoslavia

4 Benelux (5th edition, 2003)
Belgium & Colonies · Luxembourg · Netherlands & Colonies

5 Czechoslovakia & Poland (6th edition, 2002)
Czechoslovakia · Czech Republic · Slovakia · Poland

6 France (5th edition, 2001)
France · Colonies · Post Offices · Andorra · Monaco

7 Germany (6th edition, 2002)
Germany · States · Colonies · Post Offices

8 Italy & Switzerland (6th edition, 2003)
Italy & Colonies · Liechtenstein · San Marino · Switzerland · U.N. (Geneva) · Vatican City

9 Portugal & Spain (4th edition, 1996)
Andorra · Portugal & Colonies · Spain & Colonies

10 Russia (5th edition, 1999)
Russia · Armenia · Azerbaijan · Belarus · Estonia · Georgia · Kazakhstan · Kyrgyzstan · Latvia · Lithuania · Moldova · Tajikistan · Turkmenistan · Ukraine · Uzbekistan · Mongolia

11 Scandinavia (5th edition, 2001)
Aland Islands · Denmark · Faroe Islands · Finland · Greenland · Iceland · Norway · Sweden

12 Africa since Independence A-E (2nd edition, 1983)
Algeria · Angola · Benin · Burundi · Cameroun · Cape Verdi · Central African Republic · Chad · Comoro Islands · Congo · Djibouti · Equatorial Guinea · Ethiopia

13 Africa since Independence F-M (1st edition, 1981)
Gabon · Guinea · Guinea-Bissau · Ivory Coast · Liberia · Libya · Malagasy Republic · Mali · Mauritania · Morocco · Mozambique

14 Africa since Independence N-Z (1st edition, 1981)
Niger Republic · Rwanda · St. Thomas & Prince · Senegal · Somalia · Sudan · Togo · Tunisia · Upper Volta · Zaire

15 Central America (2nd edition, 1984)
Costa Rica · Cuba · Dominican Republic · El Salvador · Guatemala · Haiti · Honduras · Mexico · Nicaragua · Panama

16 Central Asia (3rd edition, 1992)
Afghanistan · Iran · Turkey

17 China (6th edition,1998)
China · Taiwan · Tibet · Foreign P.O.s · Hong Kong · Macao

18 Japan & Korea (4th edition, 1997)
Japan · Korean Empire · South Korea · North Korea

19 Middle East (5th edition, 1996)
Bahrain · Egypt · Iraq · Israel · Jordan · Kuwait · Lebanon · Oman · Qatar · Saudi Arabia · Syria · U.A.E. · Yemen

20 South America (3rd edition, 1989)
Argentina · Bolivia · Brazil · Chile · Colombia · Ecuador · Paraguay · Peru · Surinam · Uruguay · Venezuela

21 South-East Asia (3rd edition, 1995)
Bhutan · Burma · Indonesia · Kampuchea · Laos · Nepal · Philippines · Thailand · Vietnam

22 United States (5th edition, 2000)
U.S. & Possessions · Marshall Islands · Micronesia · Palau · U.N. (New York, Geneva, Vienna)

Thematic Catalogues

Stanley Gibbons Catalogues for use with **Stamps of the World.**
Collect Aircraft on Stamps (out of print)
Collect Birds on Stamps (5th edition, 2003)
Collect Chess on Stamps (2nd edition, 1999)
Collect Fish on Stamps (1st edition, 1999)
Collect Fungi on Stamps (2nd edition, 1997)
Collect Motor Vehicles on Stamps (in preparation)
Collect Railways on Stamps (3rd edition, 1999)
Collect Shells on Stamps (1st edition, 1995)
Collect Ships on Stamps (3rd edition, 2001)

Key-Types

(see note on page vii)

French Group

A. "Blanc."

B. "Mouchon."

C "Merson."

D. "Tablet."

E.

F.

G.

H.

"International Colonial Exhibition."

I. "Faidherbe."

J. "Palms."

K. "Balay."

L. "Natives."

M. "Figure."

German Group

N. "Yacht."

O. "Yacht."

Spanish Group

X. "Alfonso XII."

Y. "Baby."

Z. "Curly Head"

Portuguese Group

P. "Crown."

Q. "Embossed."

R. "Figures."

S. "Carlos."

T. "Manoel."

U. "Ceres."

V. "Newspaper."

W. "Due."

STANLEY GIBBONS SIMPLIFIED CATALOGUE OF STAMPS OF THE WORLD—VOLUME 1 COUNTRIES A–D

ABU DHABI — Pt. 1, Pt. 19

The largest of the Trucial States in the Persian Gulf. Treaty relations with Great Britain expired on 31 December 1966, when Abu Dhabi took over the postal services. On 18 July 1971, seven of the Gulf sheikhdoms, including Abu Dhabi, agreed to form the State of the United Arab Emirates. The federation came into being on 1 August 1972.

1964. 100 naye paise = 1 rupee.
1966. 1,000 fils = 1 dinar.

1 Shaikh Shakhbut bin Sultan

3 Ruler's Palace

1964.

No.	Type	Description	Unused	Used
1	1	5n.p. green	1·50	2·25
2		15n.p. brown	2·00	1·50
3		20n.p. blue	2·25	1·50
4		30n.p. orange	3·25	1·50
5	–	40n.p. violet	3·25	70
6	–	50n.p. bistre	4·00	2·50
7	–	75n.p. black	4·00	3·75
8	3	1r. green	4·00	1·25
9		2r. black	7·50	3·25
10	–	5r. red	17·00	10·00
11	–	10r. blue	23·00	14·00

DESIGNS: As Type **1**: 40 to 75n.p. Mountain gazelle; As Type **3**: 5, 10r. Oil rig and camels.

5 Saker Falcon

1965. Falconry.

No.	Type	Description	Unused	Used
12	5	20n.p. brown and blue	10·00	1·75
13	–	40n.p. brown and blue	13·00	2·75
14	–	2r. sepia and turquoise	22·00	13·00

DESIGNS: 40n.p., 2r. Other types of Saker falcon on gloved hand.

1966. Nos. 1/11 surch in new currency ("Fils" only on Nos. 5/7) and ruler's portrait obliterated with bars.

No.	Type	Description	Unused	Used
15	1	5f. on 5n.p. green	8·00	5·50
16		15f. on 15n.p. brown	8·00	6·00
17		20f. on 20n.p. blue	10·00	8·00
18		30f. on 30n.p. orange	9·00	14·00
19	–	40f. on 40n.p. violet	13·00	1·00
20	–	50f. on 50n.p. bistre	22·00	23·00
21	–	75f. on 75n.p. black	22·00	23·00
22	3	100f. on 1r. green	16·00	3·50
23		200f. on 2r. black	18·00	13·00
24	–	500f. on 5r. red	30·00	38·00
25	–	1d. on 10r. blue	40·00	65·00

9 Shaikh Zaid bin Sultan al Nahayyan

10

1967.

No.	Type	Description	Unused	Used
26	–	5f. red and green	20	15
27	–	15f. red and brown	30	10
28	–	20f. red and blue	50	15
29	–	35f. red and violet	60	20
30	9	40f. green	80	20
38	10	40f. green	1·10	85
31	9	50f. brown	1·00	25
39	10	50f. brown	1·40	60
32	9	60f. blue	1·10	30
40	10	60f. blue	2·40	85
33	9	100f. red	1·75	40
41	10	100f. red	6·50	1·60
34	–	125f. brown and green	3·50	1·40
35	–	200f. brown and blue	15·00	3·00
36	–	500f. violet and orange	11·00	5·50
37	–	1d. blue and green	20·00	10·00

DESIGNS—As Types **9/10**—VERT: 5f. to 35f. National flag. HORIZ: (47 × 27 mm); 125f. Mountain gazelle; 200f. Lanner falcon; 500f., 1d. Palace. Each with portrait of Ruler.

11 Human Rights Emblem and Shaikh Zaid

1968. Human Rights Year.

No.	Type	Description	Unused	Used
42	11	35f. multicoloured	1·25	50
43		60f. multicoloured	2·00	60
44		150f. multicoloured	3·75	1·40

12 Arms and Shaikh Zaid

1968. Anniv of Shaikh Zaid's Accession.

No.	Type	Description	Unused	Used
45	12	5f. multicoloured	1·25	20
46		10f. multicoloured	1·25	20
47		100f. multicoloured	3·50	1·25
48		125f. multicoloured	5·00	1·90

13 New Construction

1968. 2nd Anniv of Shaikh's Accession. "Progress in Abu Dhabi". Multicoloured.

No.	Type	Description	Unused	Used
49		5f. Type **13**	55	20
50		10f. Airport buildings (46½ × 34 mm)	1·25	50
51		35f. Shaikh Zaid, bridge and Northern goshawk (59 × 34 mm)	9·50	2·75

14 Petroleum Installations

1969. 3rd Anniv of Shaikh's Accession. Petroleum Industry. Multicoloured.

No.	Type	Description	Unused	Used
52		35f. Type **14**	75	30
53		60f. Marine drilling platform	3·25	95
54		125f. Separator platform, Zakum field	4·50	1·50
55		200f. Tank farm	5·00	2·25

15 Shaikh Zaid

1970.

No.	Type	Description	Unused	Used
56	–	5f. multicoloured	30	15
57	15	10f. multicoloured	40	15
58	–	25f. multicoloured	75	15
59	15	35f. multicoloured	1·00	15
60		50f. multicoloured	1·50	25
61	–	60f. multicoloured	1·60	30
62	15	70f. multicoloured	2·50	45
63	–	90f. multicoloured	3·25	75
64	–	125f. multicoloured	4·50	1·25
65	–	150f. multicoloured	5·50	1·50
66	–	500f. multicoloured	20·00	8·00
67	–	1d. multicoloured	35·00	13·00

DESIGNS: Nos. 56, 58, 61 and 63 as Type **15**, but frames changed, and smaller country name; 125f. Arab stallion; 150f. Mountain gazelle; 500f. Fort Jahili; 1d. Great Mosque.

No. 67 has face value in Arabic only.

17 Shaikh Zaid and "Mt. Fuji" (T. Hayashi)

1970. "Expo 70" World Fair, Osaka, Japan.

No.	Type	Description	Unused	Used
68	17	25f. multicoloured	1·00	30
69		35f. multicoloured	1·25	30
70		60f. multicoloured	2·00	1·25

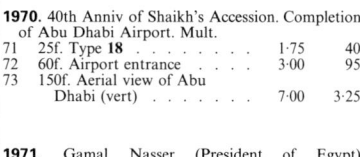

18 Abu Dhabi Airport

19 Pres. G. A. Nasser

1970. 40th Anniv of Shaikh's Accession. Completion of Abu Dhabi Airport. Mult.

No.	Type	Description	Unused	Used
71		25f. Type **18**	1·75	40
72		60f. Airport entrance	3·00	95
73		150f. Aerial view of Abu Dhabi (vert)	7·00	3·25

1971. Gamal Nasser (President of Egypt) Commemoration.

No.	Type	Description	Unused	Used
74	19	25f. black on pink	1·60	60
75		35f. black on lilac	2·25	80

20 Motorized Patrol

1971. 5th Anniv of Shaikh's Accession. Defence Force. Multicoloured.

No.	Type	Description	Unused	Used
76		35f. Type **20**	2·50	80
77		60f. Patrol-boat "Baniyas"	3·75	1·25
78		125f. Armoured car	7·00	1·75
79		150f. Hawker Hunter FGA.76 jet fighters	9·00	2·75

1971. No. 60 surch.

No.	Type	Description	Unused	Used
80	15	5f. on 50f. multicoloured	48·00	40·00

22 Dome of the Rock

1972. Dome of the Rock, Jerusalem. Multicoloured.

No.	Type	Description	Unused	Used
81		35f. Type **22**	6·25	2·25
82		60f. Mosque entrance	9·50	3·00
83		125f. Mosque dome	17·00	6·75

1972. Provisional Issue. Nos. 56/67 optd **UAE** and arabic inscr.

No.	Type	Description	Unused	Used
84	–	5f. multicoloured	1·00	1·00
85	15	10f. multicoloured	1·00	60
86	–	25f. multicoloured	1·50	1·50
87	15	35f. multicoloured	2·25	1·75
88		50f. multicoloured	3·50	3·50
89	–	60f. multicoloured	4·00	4·00
90	15	70f. multicoloured	5·00	5·00
91	–	90f. multicoloured	7·00	7·00
92	–	125f. multicoloured	22·00	22·00
93	–	150f. multicoloured	30·00	30·00
94	–	500f. multicoloured	70·00	70·00
95	–	1d. multicoloured	£130	£130

For later issues see **UNITED ARAB EMIRATES**.

ADEN — Pt. 1

Peninsula on southern coast of Arabia. Formerly part of the Indian Empire. A Crown Colony from 1 April 1937 to 18 January 1963, when Aden joined the South Arabian Federation, whose stamps it then used.

1937. 16 annas = 1 rupee.
1951. 100 cents = 1 shilling.

1 Dhow

1937.

No.	Type	Description	Unused	Used
1	1	½a. green	3·75	1·75
2		9p. green	3·75	2·00
3		1a. brown	3·75	70
4		2a. red	3·75	2·00
5		2½a. blue	4·00	80
6		3a. red	10·00	6·50
7		3½a. blue	7·50	2·75
8		8a. purple	24·00	6·00
9		1r. brown	35·00	6·50
10		2r. yellow	50·00	17·00
11		5r. purple	95·00	65·00
12		10r. olive	£300	£325

2 King George VI and Queen Elizabeth

1937. Coronation.

No.	Type	Description	Unused	Used
13	2	1a. brown	65	1·00
14		2½a. blue	75	1·40
15		3½a. blue	1·00	2·50

3 Aidrus Mosque, Crater

1939.

No.	Type	Description	Unused	Used
16	3	½a. green	50	60
17	–	¾a. brown	1·25	1·25
18	–	1a. blue	20	40
19	–	1½a. red	55	60
20	3	2a. brown	20	25
21	–	2½a. blue	40	30
22	–	3a. brown and red	60	25
23	–	8a. orange	55	40
23a	–	14a. brown and blue	2·50	1·00
24	–	1r. green	2·25	2·00
25	–	2r. blue and mauve	4·75	2·25
26	–	5r. brown and olive	11·00	8·00
27	–	10r. brown and violet	30·00	11·00

DESIGNS: ¾a., 5r. Adenese Camel Corps; 1a., 2r. Harbour; 1½a., 1r. Adenese dhow; 2½, 8a. Mukalla; 3, 14a., 10r. "Capture of Aden, 1839" (Capt. Rundle).

9 Houses of Parliament, London

1946. Victory.

No.	Type	Description	Unused	Used
28	9	1½a. red	15	1·00
29		2½a. blue	15	30

10

11 King George VI and Queen Elizabeth

1949. Royal Silver Wedding.

30	**10**	1½a. red	40	1·00
31	**11**	10r. purple	27·00	32·00

1949. 75th Anniv of U.P.U. As T **20/23** of Antigua surch with new values.

32	2½a. on 20c. blue	50	1·50
33	3a. on 30c. red	1·75	1·50
34	8a. on 50c. orange	1·10	1·50
35	1r. on 1s. blue	1·60	2·75

1951. Stamps of 1939 surch in cents or shillings.

36	5c. on 1a. blue	15	40
37	10c. on 2a. brown	15	45
38	15c. on 2½a. blue	20	1·25
39	20c. on 3a. brown and red	30	40
40	30c. on 8a. orange	30	65
41	50c. on 8a. orange	30	35
42	70c. on 14a. brown and blue	2·00	1·50
43	1s. on 1r. green	35	30
44	2s. on 2r. blue and mauve	8·00	2·75
45	5s. on 5r. brown and olive	16·00	9·50
46	10s. on 10r. brown and violet	24·00	11·00

13 Queen Elizabeth II

14 Minaret

15 Camel Transport

1953. Coronation.

47	**13**	15c. black and green	70	1·25

1953.

48	**14**	5c. green	20	10
49a		5c. turquoise	10	70
50	**15**	10c. orange	40	10
51		10c. red	10	30
52	–	15c. turquoise	1·25	60
79	–	15c. grey	30	3·50
80	–	25c. red	30	40
56	–	35c. blue	2·50	2·00
58	–	50c. blue	20	10
60	–	70c. grey	20	10
61a	–	70c. black	90	20
62	–	1s. brown and violet	30	10
63	–	1s. black and violet	1·50	10
64	–	1s.25 blue and black	2·25	60
65	–	2s. brown and red	1·25	50
66	–	2s. black and red	8·50	50
67	–	5s. brown and blue	1·50	1·00
68	–	5s. black and blue	5·00	1·25
69	–	10s. brown and green	1·75	8·00
70	–	10s. black and bronze	13·00	1·75
71	–	20s. brown and lilac	6·50	10·00
72	–	20s. black and lilac	40·00	14·00

DESIGNS—HORIZ: 15c. Crater; 25c. Mosque; 1s. Dhow building; 20s. (38 × 27 mm); Aden in 1572. VERT: 35c. Dhow; 50c. Map; 70c. Salt works; 1s.25, Colony's badge; 2s. Aden Protectorate Levy; 5s. Crater Pass; 10s. Tribesmen.

1954. Royal Visit. As No. 62 but inscr "ROYAL VISIT 1954".

73	1s. sepia and violet	30	55

1959. Revised Constitution. Optd **REVISED CONSTITUTION 1959** (in Arabic on No. 74).

74	15c. green (No. 53)	30	2·00
75	1s.25 blue and black (No. 64)	1·00	1·00

28 Protein Foods

1963. Freedom from Hunger.

76	**28**	1s.25 green	1·25	1·75

For later issues see **SOUTH ARABIAN FEDERATION**.

AFGHANISTAN Pt. 16

An independent country in Asia, to N.W. of Pakistan. Now a republic, the country was formerly ruled by monarchs from 1747 to 1973.

1871. 60 paisa = 12 shahi = 6 sanar = 3 abasi = 2 kran = 1 rupee.
1920. 60 paisa = 2 kran = 1 rupee.
1926. 100 poul (pul) = 1 afghani (rupee).

The issues from 1860 to 1892 (Types **1** to **16**) are difficult to classify because the values of each set are expressed in native script and are generally all printed in the same colour. As it is not possible to list these in an intelligible simplified form we would refer users to the detailed list in the Stanley Gibbons Part 16 (Central Asia) Catalogue.

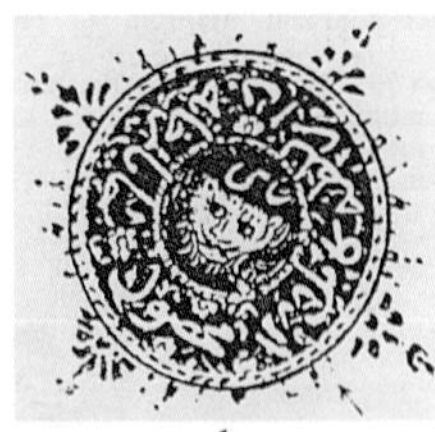
1

4

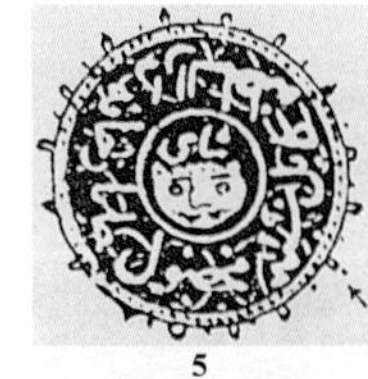
5

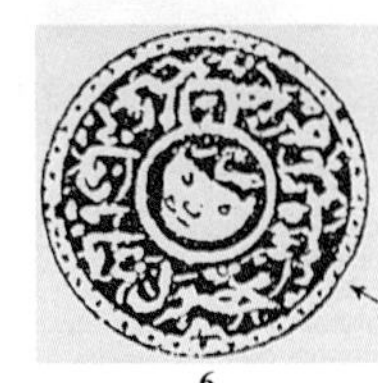
6

8

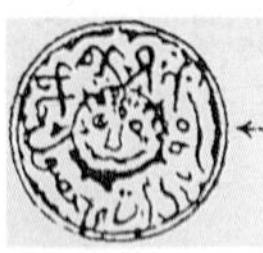
10

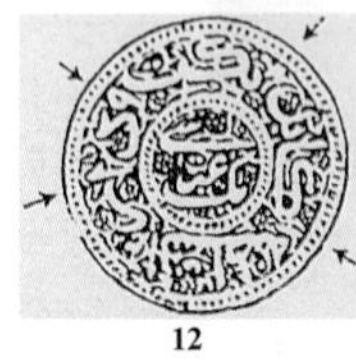
12

16

17 National Coat of Arms

1893. Dated "1310".

147	**17**	1a. black on green	2·75	2·75
148		1a. black on red	3·00	2·75
149a		1a. black on purple	3·25	3·00
150		1a. black on yellow	3·00	2·75
151		1a. black on orange	3·75	2·50
152		1a. black on blue	5·00	4·25

18 (1 Rupee)

1894. Undated.

153	**18**	2a. black on green	10·00	6·00
154		1r. black on green	12·00	7·50

20 1 Abasi

23

24 National Coat of Arms

1907. Imperf, roul or perf.

156a	**20**	1a. green	10·00	8·50
157	–	2a. blue	5·50	5·50
158	–	1r. green	7·50	9·00

The 2a. and 1r. are in similar designs.

1909. Perf.

165	**23**	2 paisa brown	2·50	3·50
166	**24**	1a. blue	4·50	1·50
168		1a. red	90	80
169	–	2a. green	2·25	2·00
170a	–	2a. bistre	1·50	2·25
171	–	1r. brown	4·00	4·25
172	–	1r. olive	5·50	5·50

The frames of the 2a. and 1r. differ from Type **24**.

27 Royal Star of Order of Independence

29 Crest of King Amanullah

(28)

1920. 1st Anniv of End of War of Independence. Size 39 × 47 mm.

173	**27**	10p. red	22·00	22·00
174		20p. purple	40·00	42·00
175		30p. green	80·00	85·00

1921. Size 23 × 29 mm.

177	**27**	10p. red	75	75
178		20p. purple	1·50	1·50
180b		30p. green	2·50	2·25

1923. 5th Independence Day. Optd with T **28**.

181	**27**	10p. red	35·00	35·00
181a		20p. brown	40·00	40·00
182		30p. green	45·00	45·00

1924. 6th Independence Day.

183	**29**	10p. brown (24 × 32 mm)	30·00	30·00

29a

30 Crest of King Amanullah

1924.

183b	**29a**	5k. blue	30·00	35·00
183c		5r. mauve	14·00	20·00

1925. 7th Independence Day.

184	**29**	10p. brown (29 × 37 mm)	30·00	28·00

1926. 7th Anniv of Independence.

185	**29**	10p. blue (26 × 33 mm)	5·50	7·50

1927. 8th Anniv of Independence.

186	**30**	10p. mauve	10·00	9·00

31

32

33

Types **31/3**, **36/37** and **41**, National Seal.

1927. Perf or imperf.

188	**31**	15p. red	85	75
189	**32**	30p. green	1·40	85
190	**33**	60p. blue	2·25	2·00

See also Nos. 207/13.

34 Crest of King Amanullah

1928. 9th Anniv of Independence.

191	**34**	15p. red	3·50	3·25

36

37

1928.

193	**36**	10p. green	85	65
194	**37**	25p. red	1·00	75
195	–	40p. blue	1·25	95
196	–	50p. red	1·75	95

The frames of the 40 and 50p. differ from Type **37**.
See also Nos. 207/13.

41

42 Independence Memorial

1929.

207	**36**	10p. brown	1·75	1·25
208	**31**	15p. blue	1·75	1·10
209	**37**	25p. blue	1·75	1·10
210	**41**	30p. green	2·25	1·25
211	–	40p. red	2·50	1·50
212	–	50p. blue	2·50	2·00
213	**33**	60p. black	2·75	2·00

1931. 13th Independence Day.

214	**42**	20p. red	3·25	2·25

46 National Assembly Building

50 Mosque at Balkh

1932. Inauguration of National Council.

215	–	40p. brown (31 × 24 mm)	65	65
216	–	60p. violet (29 × 26 mm)	95	85
217	**46**	80p. red	1·25	1·00
218	–	1a. black (24 × 27 mm)	10·00	9·00
219	–	2a. blue (36 × 25 mm)	4·50	4·25
220	–	3a. green (36 × 24 mm)	5·00	4·00

DESIGNS: Nos. 215/16, 218/19, Council Chamber; 3a. National Assembly Building (different).

1932.

221	**50**	10p. brown	50	30
222	–	15p. brown	40	35
223	–	20p. red	60	25
224	–	25p. green	75	25
225	–	30p. red	75	25
226	–	40p. orange	90	45
227	–	50p. blue	1·40	1·40
228	–	60p. blue	1·25	1·00
229	–	80p. violet	2·25	2·00
230	–	1a. blue	4·25	80

231 – 2a. purple . . . . 4·50 2·50
232 – 3a. red . . . . 5·50 3·25
DESIGNS—32 × 23 mm: 15p. Kabul Fortress; 20, 25p. Parliament House, Darul Funun, Kabul; 40p. Memorial Pillar of Knowledge and Ignorance, Kabul; 1a. Ruins at Balkh; 2a. Minarets at Herat. 32 × 16 mm: 30p. Arch of Paghman. 23 × 32 mm: 60p. Minaret at Herat. 23 × 25 mm: 30p. Arch at Qalai Bust, near Kandahar; 50p. Independence Memorial, Kabul. 16 × 32 mm: 3a. Great Buddha at Bamian.
See also Nos. 237/51.

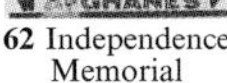

62 Independence Memorial **63** National Liberation Monument, Kabul

1932. 14th Independence Day.
233 **62** 1a. red . . . . 5·50 3·75

1932. Commemorative Issue.
234 **63** 80p. red . . . . 2·75 2·00

64 Arch of Paghman

1933. 15th Independence Day.
235 **64** 50p. blue . . . . 2·75 2·00

65 Independence Memorial

1934. 16th Independence Day.
236 **65** 50p. green . . . . 3·25 2·75

1934. As Nos. 219/20 and 221/30, but colours changed and new values.
237 **50** 10p. violet 25 15
238 – 15p. green 40 15
239 – 20p. mauve 45 15
240 – 25p. red 50 25
241 – 30p. orange 60 30
242 – 40p. black 65 35
243 – 45p. blue . . . . 2·00 1·50
244 – 45p. red 45 25
245 – 50p. red 75 25
246 – 60p. violet 80 45
247 – 75p. red . . . . 3·00 2·25
248 – 75p. blue . . . . 1·00 80
248b – 80p. brown . . . . 1·50 85
249 – 1a. mauve . . . . 2·25 2·00
250 – 2a. grey . . . . 4·25 3·00
251 – 3a. blue . . . . 4·50 3·50
DESIGNS (new values)—34 × 23 mm: 45p. Royal Palace, Kabul. 20 × 34 mm: 75p. Hunters Canyon Pass, Hindu Kush.

68 Independence Memorial **69** Firework Display

1935. 17th Independence Day.
252 **68** 50p. blue . . . . 3·25 2·75

1936. 18th Independence Day.
253 **69** 50p. mauve . . . . 3·50 2·75

70 Independence Memorial and Mohamed Nadir Shah **71** Mohamed Nadir Shah

1937. 19th Independence Day. Perf or imperf.
254 **70** 50p. brown and violet . . 2·50 2·25

1938. 20th Independence Day. Perf or imperf.
255 **71** 50p. brown and blue . . . 2·25 2·25

72 Aliabad Hospital **74** Mohamed Nadir Shah

1938. Obligatory Tax. Int Anti-cancer Fund.
256 **72** 10p. green . . . . 3·25 5·00
257 – 15p. blue . . . . 3·25 5·00
DESIGN—44 × 28 mm: 15p. Pierre and Marie Curie.

1939. 21st Independence Day.
258 **74** 50p. red . . . . 2·25 1·50

76 Darul Funun Parliament House, Kabul **79** Independence Memorial

82 Mohamed Zahir Shah

83 Sugar Mill, Baghlan

1939.
259 **76** 10p. purple (36½ × 24 mm) 25 20
260 15p. green (34 × 21 mm) 35 20
261 20p. purple (34 × 22½ mm) 40 25
262 – 25p. red 45 30
263 – 25p. green 30 25
264 – 30p. orange 40 25
265 – 35p. orange . . . . . . 1·00 65
266 – 40p. grey 80 45
267 **79** 45p. red 80 40
268 50p. orange 60 25
269 60p. violet 75 25
270 – 70p. violet . . . . . . 1·50 65
271 – 70p. purple . . . . . . 1·50 65
272 – 75p. blue . . . . 2·25 75
273 – 75p. purple . . . . . . 1·75 1·90
274 – 75p. red . . . . 2·50 2·50
275 – 80p. brown . . . . . . 1·50 80
276 **82** 1a. purple . . . . 1·50 75
277 – 1a. purple . . . . 1·50 80
278d **83** 1a.25 blue . . . . . . 1·60 70
279a – 2a. red . . . . 2·25 1·00
280 – 3a. blue . . . . 3·50 1·60
DESIGNS—31 × 19 mm: 25, 30p. Royal Palace, Kabul. 30 × 18 mm: 40p. Royal Palace, Kabul. 30 × 21 mm: 70p. Ruins at Qalai Bust, near Kandahar. 35½ × 21½ mm: 75p. Independence Memorial and Mohamed Nadir Shah. 34½ × 21 mm: 80p. As 75p. 35 × 20 mm: 1a. (No. 277), 2a. Mohamed Zahir Shah; 3a. As Type **82** but head turned more to left. 19 × 31 mm: 35p. Minarets at Herat.

85 Potez 25A2 over Kabul

1939. Air.
280a **85** 5a. orange . . . . 3·50 4·50
280b 10a. blue . . . . 3·75 4·50
280c 20a. green . . . . 6·50 7·50
See also Nos. 300/2.

86 Mohamed Nadir Shah **87** Arch of Paghman

1940. 22nd Independence Day.
281 **86** 50p. green . . . . 2·25 1·50

1941. 23rd Independence Day.
282 – 15p. green . . . . 6·00 3·75
283 **87** 50p. brown . . . . 1·75 1·50
DESIGN: (19 × 29½ mm): 15p. Independence Memorial.

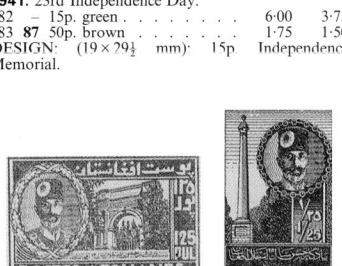

87b Mohamed Nadir Shah and Arch of Paghman **88** Independence Memorial and Mohamed Nadir Shah

1942. 24th Independence Day.
284 – 35p. green . . . . 4·25 3·75
285 **87b** 125p. blue . . . . 2·75 2·25
DESIGN—VERT: 35p. Independence Memorial in medallion.

1943. 25th Independence Day.
286 – 35p. red . . . . 12·00 9·50
287 **88** 1a.25 blue . . . . 2·50 2·25
DESIGN—HORIZ: 35p. Independence Memorial seen through archway and Mohamed Nadir Shah in oval frame.

89 Arch of Paghman **90** Independence Memorial and Mohamed Nadir Shah

1944. 26th Independence Day.
288 **89** 35p. red . . . . 1·25 75
289 **90** 1a.25 blue . . . . 2·25 2·00

91 Mohamed Nadir Shah and Independence Memorial **92** Arch of Paghman and Mohamed Nadir Shah

1945. 27th Independence Day.
290 **91** 35p. red . . . . 2·25 75
291 **92** 1a.25 blue . . . . 3·75 2·00

93 Independence Memorial **94** Mohamed Nadir Shah and Independence Memorial

1946. 28th Independence Day. Dated "1946".
292 – 15p. green . . . . 1·25 75
293 **93** 20p. mauve . . . . 2·00 85
294 – 125p. blue . . . . 3·25 2·00
DESIGNS—HORIZ: 15p. Mohamed Zahir Shah. VERT: 125p. Mohamed Nadir Shah.

1947. 29th Independence Day. Dated "1947".
295 – 15p. green . . . . 1·00 60
296 – 35p. mauve . . . . 1·25 75
297 **94** 125p. blue . . . . 3·25 2·00
DESIGNS—HORIZ: 15p. Mohamed Zahir Shah and ruins of Kandahar Fort; 35p. Mohamed Zahir Shah and Arch of Paghman.

95 Hungry Boy **96** Independence Memorial

1948. Child Welfare Fund.
298 **95** 35p. green . . . . 5·00 4·25
299 – 125p. blue . . . . 5·00 4·25
DESIGN—26 × 33½ mm: 125p. Hungry boy in vert frame.
See also No. 307.

1948. Air. As T **85** but colours changed.
300 **85** 5a. green . . . . 25·00 25·00
301 10a. orange . . . . 25·00 25·00
302 20a. blue . . . . 25·00 25·00

1948. 30th Independence Day. Dated "1948".
303 – 15p. green 75 35
304 **96** 20p. mauve . . . . 1·00 40
305 – 125p. blue . . . . 2·00 1·00
DESIGNS—VERT: 15p. Arch of Paghman. HORIZ: 125p. Mohamed Nadir Shah.

97 U.N. Symbol

1948. 3rd Anniv of U.N.O.
306 **97** 1a.25 blue . . . . 11·00 9·00

98 Hungry Boy **99** Victory Monument

1949. Obligatory Tax. Child Welfare Fund.
307 – 35p. orange . . . . 3·25 1·75
308 **98** 125p. blue . . . . 3·25 1·75
DESIGN—HORIZ: 35p. As Type **98** but 29 × 22½ mm.

1949. 31st Independence Day. Dated "1949" (Nos. 310/11).
309 **99** 25p. green 80 40
310 – 35p. mauve . . . . 1·00 45
311 – 1a.25 blue . . . . 2·25 1·25
DESIGNS—HORIZ: 35p. Mohamed Zahir Shah and ruins of Kandahar Fort; 1a.25, Independence Memorial and Mohamed Nadir Shah.

100 Arch of Paghman

1949. Obligatory Tax. 4th Anniv of U.N.O.
312 **100** 125p. green . . . . 16·00 10·00

101 King Mohamed Zahir Shah and Map of Afghanistan

1950. Obligatory Tax. Return of King Mohamed Zahir Shah from Visit to Europe.
313 **101** 125p. green . . . . 3·75 1·50

102 Hungry Boy **103** Mohamed Nadir Shah

1950. Obligatory Tax. Child Welfare Fund.
314 **102** 125p. green . . . . 4·50 2·50

1950. 32nd Independence Day.
315 **103** 35p. brown 70 45
316 125p. blue . . . . 2·25 75

104

1950. Obligatory Tax. 5th Anniv of U.N.O.

317	**104**	1a.25 blue	7·50	4·50

106

1950. 19th Anniv of Faculty of Medicine, Kabul.

318	**106**	35p. green (postage)	1·25	75
319	–	1a.25 blue	4·25	2·25
320	**106**	35p. red (obligatory tax)	1·25	60
321	–	1a.25 black	8·50	2·75

DESIGN: Nos. 319 and 321, Sanatorium. Nos. 318 and 320 measure 38½ × 25½ mm and Nos. 319 and 321, 45 × 30 mm.

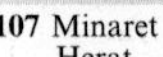

107 Minaret at Herat **109** Mohamed Zahir Shah

110 Mosque at Balkh **118**

1951.

322	**107**	10p. brown and yellow	25	20
323		15p. brown and blue	40	20
324	–	20p. black	8·00	4·25
325	**109**	25p. green	40	15
326	**110**	30p. red	45	20
327	**109**	35p. violet	50	20
328	–	40p. brown	55	20
329	–	45p. blue	55	20
330	–	50p. black	1·50	25
331	–	60p. black	1·25	25
332	–	70p. black, red and green	60	25
333	–	75p. red	1·00	40
334	–	80p. black and red	1·75	75
335	–	1a. violet and green	1·25	60
336	**118**	125p. black and purple	1·40	75
337		2a. blue	2·25	70
338		3a. blue and black	4·25	1·00

DESIGNS—19 × 29 mm: 20p. Buddha of Bamian; 45p. Maiwand Victory Monument; 60p. Victory Towers, Ghazni. 22 × 28 mm: 75, 80p., 1a. Mohamed Zahir Shah. 28 × 19 mm: 40p. Ruins at Qalai Bust; 70p. Flag. 30 × 19 mm: 50p. View of Kandahar.
See also Nos. 425/425k.

119 Douglas DC-3 over Kabul

1951. Air.

339	**119**	5a. red	3·50	75
339a		5a. green	1·60	55
340		10a. grey	8·00	1·60
341		20a. blue	12·00	2·75

See also Nos. 415a/b.

120 Shepherdess **121** Arch of Paghman

(122) (123)

1951. Obligatory Tax. Child Welfare Fund.

342	**120**	35p. green	1·50	95
343	–	125p. blue	1·50	95

DESIGN—34½ × 44 mm: 125p. Young shepherd.

1951. 33rd Independence Day. Optd with T **122**.

344	**121**	35p. black and green	1·10	60
345	–	125p. blue	2·75	1·25

DESIGN (34 × 18½ mm): 125p. Mohamed Nadir Shah and Independence Memorial.
See also Nos. 360/1b and 418/19.

IMPERF STAMPS. From 1951 many issues were made available imperf from limited printings.

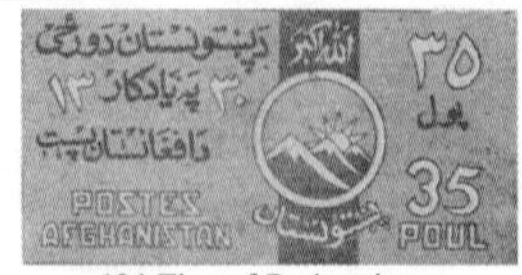

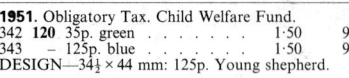

124 Flag of Pashtunistan

1951. Obligatory Tax. Pashtunistan Day.

346	**124**	35p. brown	1·75	1·00
347	–	125p. blue	3·25	2·25

DESIGN—42½ × 21½ mm: 125p. Afridi tribesman.

125 Dove and Globe **126** Avicenna (physician)

1951. Obligatory Tax. United Nations Day.

348	**125**	35p. mauve	1·00	50
349	–	125p. blue	2·50	2·00

DESIGN—VERT: 125p. Dove and globe.

1951. Obligatory Tax. 20th Anniv of Faculty of Medicine.

350	**126**	35p. mauve	3·00	1·25
351		125p. blue	1·00	3·25

127 Amir Sher Ali and First Stamp **128** Children and Postman

1951. Obligatory Tax. 76th Anniv of U.P.U.

352	**127**	35p. brown	75	50
353	–	35p. mauve	75	50
354	**127**	125p. blue	1·25	75
355	–	125p. blue	1·25	75

DESIGN: Nos. 353 and 355, Mohamed Zahir Shah and first stamp.

1952. Obligatory Tax. Child Welfare Fund.

356	**128**	35p. brown	75	60
357	–	125p. violet	1·50	85

DESIGN—HORIZ: 125p. Girl dancing (33 × 23 mm).

40 POULS

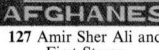

(129) **131** Soldier and Flag of Pashtunistan

1952. Obligatory Tax. Birth Millenary of Avicenna (physician and philosopher). (a) Surch with T **129**.

358	**110**	40p. on 30p. red	3·50	2·50

(b) Surch **MILLIEME ANNIVERSAIRE DE BOALI SINAI BALKI 125 POULS** in frame.

359	**110**	125p. on 30p. red	4·50	2·75

1952. 34th Independence Day. As Nos. 344/5. (a) Optd with T **123**.

360	35p. black and green	3·25	2·25
361	125p. blue	3·25	2·25

(b) Without opt.

361a	35p. black and green	1·50	65
361b	125p. blue	3·25	1·25

1952. Obligatory Tax. Pashtunistan Day.

362	**131**	35p. red	65	55
363		125p. blue	1·10	1·10

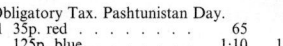

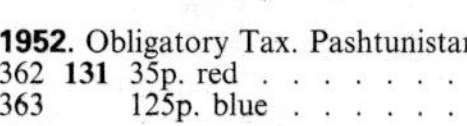

132 Orderly and Wounded Soldier **134** Staff of Aesculapius

133

1952. Obligatory Tax. Red Crescent Day.

364	**132**	10p. green	50	40

1952. Obligatory Tax. United Nations Day.

365	**133**	35p. red	75	50
366		125p. turquoise	1·75	1·25

1952. Obligatory Tax. 21st Anniv of Faculty of Medicine.

367	**134**	35p. brown	80	50
368		125p. blue	2·25	1·50

135 Stretcher Bearers and Wounded

1953. Obligatory Tax. Red Crescent Day.

369	**135**	10p. green and brown	70	70
370	–	10p. brown and orange	70	70

DESIGN: No. 370, Wounded soldier, orderly and eagle.

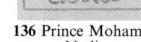

136 Prince Mohamed Nadir **138** Flags of Afghanistan and Pashtunistan

137 Mohamed Nadir Shah and Flag-bearer

1953. Obligatory Tax. Children's Day.

371	**136**	35p. orange	40	25
372		125p. blue	85	60

1953. 35th Year of Independence. Inscr "1953".

373	**137**	35p. green	40	35
374	–	125p. violet	1·10	65

DESIGN—VERT: 125p. Independence Memorial and Mohamed Nadir Shah.

1953. Obligatory Tax. Pashtunistan Day. Inscr "1953".

375	**138**	35p. red	40	20
376	–	125p. blue	85	55

DESIGN—HORIZ: 125p. Badge of Pashtunistan (26 × 20 mm).

139 U.N. Emblem **140** Mohamed Nadir Shah

1953. Obligatory Tax. United Nations Day.

377	**139**	35p. mauve	85	75
378		125p. blue	2·00	1·25

1953. Obligatory Tax. 22nd Anniv of Faculty of Medicine.

379	**140**	35p. orange	1·25	1·25
380	–	125p. blue	2·50	2·75

DESIGN: 125p. As Type **140** but inscribed "1953" and with French inscription.

No. 379 was wrongly inscribed "23rd" in Arabic (the extreme right-hand figure in the second row of the inscription) and No. 380 was wrongly inscr "XXIII" and had the words "ANNIVERSAIRE" and "MEDECINE" wrongly spelt "ANNIVERAIRE" and "MADECINE". These mistakes were subsequently corrected but the corrected stamps are much rarer than the original issue.

141 Children's Band and Map of Afghanistan

1954. Obligatory Tax. Child Welfare Fund.

381	**141**	35p. violet	50	25
382		125p. blue	1·50	1·00

142 Mohamed Nadir Shah and Cannon

1954. 36th Independence Day.

383	**142**	35p. red	75	50
384		125p. blue	2·25	1·00

143 Hoisting the Flag **144**

1954. Obligatory Tax. Pashtunistan Day.

385	**143**	35p. orange	75	50
386		125p. blue	2·00	1·10

1954. Red Crescent Day.

387	**144**	20p. red and blue	75	30

145 U.N. Flag and Map **146** Globe and Clasped Hands

1954. United Nations Day and 9th Anniv of U.N.O.

388	**145**	35p. red	1·25	1·25
389		125p. blue	3·25	3·25

1955. 10th Anniv of Signing of U.N. Charter.

390	**146**	35p. green	75	50
391	–	125p. blue	1·75	1·00

DESIGN—28½ × 36 mm. 125p. U.N. emblem and flags.
See also Nos. 403/4.

147 Amir Sher Ali and Mohamed Zahir Shah

1955. 85th Anniv of Postal Service.

392	**147**	35p.+15p. red	1·25	55
393		125p.+25p. grey	2·00	1·00

148 Children on Swing **149** Mohamed Nadir Shah (centre) and brothers

1955. Child Welfare Fund.
394 **148** 35p.+15p. green . . . . . 1·00 60
395 125p.+25p. violet . . . . 2·00 1·10

1955. 37th Year of Independence.
396 **149** 35p. blue 70 45
397 35p. mauve 70 45
398 – 125p. violet . . . . . . 1·50 1·00
399 – 125p. purple . . . . . . 1·50 1·00
DESIGN: 125p. Mohamed Zahir Shah and battle scene.

150

151 Red Crescent

1955. Obligatory Tax. Pashtunistan Day.
400 **150** 35p. brown 60 30
401 125p. green . . . . 1·75 50

1955. Obligatory Tax. Red Crescent Day.
402 **151** 20p. red and grey 40 40

152 U.N. Flag

153 Child on Slide

1955. Obligatory Tax. 10th Anniv of United Nations.
403 **152** 35p. brown 90 60
404 125p. blue . . . . 1·75 1·10

1956. Children's Day.
405 **153** 35p.+15p. blue 60 40
406 140p.+15p. brown . . . . 1·90 85

154 Independence Memorial and Mohamed Nadir Shah

155 Exhibition Building

1956. 38th Year of Independence.
407 **154** 35p. green 60 35
408 140p. blue . . . . 2·40 95

1956. International Exhibition, Kabul.
409 **155** 50p. brown 75 35
410 50p. blue 75 35

156 Pashtun Square, Kabul

157 Mohamed Zahir Shah and Crescent

1956. Pashtunistan Day.
411 **156** 35p.+15p. violet 40 25
412 140p.+15p. brown . . . . 1·00 70

1956. Obligatory Tax. Red Crescent Day.
413 **157** 20p. green and red . . . 55 25

158 Globe and Sun

159 Children on See-saw

1956. U.N. Day and 10th Anniv of Admission of Afghanistan into U.N.O.
414 **158** 35p.+15p. blue . . . . . 1·00 95
415 140p.+15p. brown . . . . 2·00 1·75

1957. Air. As Nos. 339/40, but colours changed.
415a **119** 5a. blue . . . . 2·50 60
415b 10a. violet . . . . . . 3·50 1·25

1957. Child Welfare Fund.
416 **159** 35p.+15p. red 75 55
417 140p.+15p. blue . . . . . 1·40 1·25

1957. 39th Independence Day. As Nos. 344/5 but 35p. has longer Arabic opt (19 mm) and 125p. optd **39 em Anv.**
418 **121** 35p. black and green . . 85 45
419 125p. blue . . . . 1·10 85

162 Pashtu Flag

163 Red Crescent Headquarters, Kabul

1957. Pashtunistan Day.
420 **162** 50p. red . . . . 1·00 60
421 155p. violet . . . . . . 1·50 1·10
No. 421 is inscr "JOURNEE DU PASHTUNISTAN" beneath flag instead of Pushtu characters.

1957. Obligatory Tax. Red Crescent Day.
422 **163** 20p. blue and red 50 25

164 U.N. Headquarters, New York

166 Children Bathing

165 Buzkashi Game

1957. U.N. Day.
423 **164** 35p.+15p. brown 50 40
424 140p.+15p. blue . . . . . 1·00 1·00

1957. As stamps of 1951, but colours changed and new value.
425 **110** 30p. brown 40 20
425a – 40p. red 55 20
425b – 50p. yellow 75 15
425c – 60p. blue 85 15
425d – 75p. violet 95 15
425e – 80p. brown and violet . 1·10 15
425f – 1a. blue and red . . . 75 20
425g **165** 140p. purple and green 2·25 60
425k **118** 2a. blue . . . . 5·75 50
425h 3a. black and orange . . 2·75 1·10

1958. Child Welfare Fund.
426 **166** 35p.+15p. red 65 40
427 140p.+15p. brown 75 65

167 Mohamed Nadir Shah and Old Soldier

1958. 40th Independence Day.
428 **167** 35p. green 45 25
429 140p. brown . . . . . . 1·10 85

168 Exhibition Buildings

1958. International Exhibition, Kabul.
430 **168** 35p. green 40 25
431 140p. red . . . . 1·10 65

169

170 President Bayar

1958. Pashtunistan Day.
432 **169** 35p.+15p. turquoise . . . 40 25
433 140p.+15p. brown . . . . 1·10 65

1958. Visit of Turkish President.
434 **170** 50p. blue 45 25
435 100p. brown 75 35

171 Red Crescent and Map of Afghanistan

1958. Obligatory Tax. Red Crescent Day.
436 **171** 25p. red and green . . . 35 15

172

1958. "Atoms for Peace".
437 **172** 50p. blue 50 40
438 100p. purple 85 65

173 Flags of U.N. and Afghanistan

174 U.N.E.S.C.O. Headquarters, Paris

1958. U.N. Day.
439 **173** 50p. multicoloured . . . 75 75
440 100p. multicoloured . . . 1·50 1·25

1958. Inauguration of U.N.E.S.C.O. Headquarters Building, Paris.
441 **174** 50p. green 75 65
442 100p. brown 75 75

175 Globe and Torch

1958. 10th Anniv of Declaration of Human Rights.
443 **175** 50p. mauve 40 40
444 100p. purple 60 70

176 Tug-of-War

1959. Child Welfare Fund.
445 **176** 35p.+15p. purple 45 40
446 165p.+15p. mauve . . . . 1·25 60

177 Mohamed Nadir Shah and Flags

1959. 41st Independence Day.
447 **177** 35p. red 50 40
448 165p. violet . . . . . . 1·25 60

178 Tribal Dance

1959. Pashtunistan Day.
449 **178** 35p.+15p. green 40 25
450 165p.+15p. orange . . . 1·00 65

179 Badge-sellers

180 Horseman

1959. Obligatory Tax. Red Crescent Day.
451 **179** 25p. red and violet . . . 35 15

1959. United Nations Day.
452 **180** 35p.+15p. orange 30 25
453 165p.+15p. green 65 45

181 "Uprooted Tree"

182 Buzkashi Game

183 Buzkashi Game

1960. World Refugee Year.
454 **181** 50p. orange 15 10
455 165p. blue 35 25

1960.
456 **182** 25p. pink 50 20
457 25p. violet 50 20
458 25p. olive 60 15
459 50p. turquoise . . . . . 1·25 50
460 50p. blue . . . . 1·25 15
460a 50p. orange 40 15
461 **183** 100p. olive 65 25
462 150p. orange 55 25
463 175p. brown . . . . . . 2·50 50
464 2a. green . . . . 1·25 85

184 Children receiving Ball

1960. Child Welfare Fund.
465 **184** 75p.+25p. blue 50 30
466 175p.+25p. green 80 40

185 Douglas DC-6 over Mountains

1960. Air.
467 **185** 75p. violet 65 25
468 125p. blue 75 35
469 5a. olive . . . . 1·75 60

186 Independence Monument, Kabul

188 Insecticide Sprayer

187

1960. 42nd Independence Day.
470 **186** 50p. blue 40 25
471 175p. mauve . . . . . . 1·10 35

1960. Pashtunistan Day.
472 **187** 50p.+50p. red 50 25
473 175p.+50p. blue . . . . . 1·25 95

1960. Anti-Malaria Campaign Day.
474 **188** 50p.+50p. orange . . . . 1·25 1·25
475 175p.+50p. brown . . . . 2·75 1·60

189 Mohamed Zahir Shah

1960. King's 46th Birthday.
476 **189** 50p. brown 60 50
477 150p. red . . . . 1·60 45

190 Ambulance

1960. Red Crescent Day.
478 **190** 50p.+50p. violet & red . . 75 55
479 175p.+50p. blue & red . . 1·90 1·10

191 Teacher with Globe and Children

1960. Literacy Campaign.
480 **191** 50p. mauve 45 35
481 100p. green . . . . 1·10 45

192 Globe and Flags

195 Mir Wais Nika (patriot)

1960. U.N. Day.
482 **192** 50p. purple 30 30
483 175p. blue . . . . 1·00 65

1960. Olympic Games, Rome. Optd **1960** in figures and in Arabic and Olympic Rings.
484 **183** 175p. brown . . . . . . 1·50 1·75

1960. World Refugee Year. Nos. 454/5 surch **+25 Ps**.
485 **181** 50p.+25p. orange . . . . 1·25 1·75
486 165p.+25p. blue . . . . . 1·25 1·75

1960. Mir Wais Nika Commemoration.
487 **195** 50p. mauve 65 40
488 175p. blue . . . . 1·10 55

The very numerous issues of Afghanistan which we do not list appeared between 21 April 1961 and 15 March 1964 (both dates inclusive), and were made available to the philatelic trade by an agency acting under the authority of a contract granted by the Afghanistan Government.

It later became evident that token supplies were only placed on sale in Kabul for a few hours and some of these sets contained stamps of very low denominations for which there was no possible postal use.

When the contract for the production of these stamps expired in 1963 it was not renewed and the Afghanistan Government set up a Philatelic Advisory Board to formulate stamp policy. The issues from No. 489 onwards were made in usable denominations and placed on sale without restriction in Afghanistan and distributed to the trade by the Philatelic Department of the G.P.O. in Kabul.

Issues not listed here will be found recorded in the Appendix at the end of this country. It is believed that some of the higher values from the agency sets were utilised for postage in late 1979.

196 Band Amir Lake

1961.
489 **196** 3a. blue 45 25
490 10a. purple . . . . 1·25 1·00

197 Independence Memorial

1963. 45th Independence Day.
491 **197** 25p. green 25 20
492 50p. orange 25 20
493 150p. mauve 45 25

198 Tribesmen

1963. Pashtunistan Day.
494 **198** 25p. violet 20 20
495 50p. blue 25 20
496 150p. brown 55 35

199 Assembly Building

1963. National Assembly.
497 **199** 25p. brown 15 15
498 50p. red 20 20
499 75p. brown 25 20
500 100p. olive 25 15
501 125p. lilac 30 20

200 Balkh Gate

201 Kemal Ataturk

1963.
502 **200** 3a. brown 95 25

1963. 25th Death Anniv of Kemal Ataturk.
503 **201** 1a. blue 15 20
504 3a. violet 60 40

202 Mohamed Zahir Shah

203 Afghan Stamp of 1878

1963. King's 49th Birthday.
505 **202** 25p. green 20 20
506 50p. grey 25 20
507 75p. red 25 25
508 100p. brown 35 20

1964. "Philately". Stamp Day.
509 **203** 1a.25 black, green & gold 25 20
510 5a. black, red and gold 45 35

204 Kabul International Airport

1964. Air. Inauguration of Kabul Int Airport.
511 **204** 10a. green and purple . . 75 25
512 20a. purple and green . . 1·10 40
513 50a. turquoise and blue 2·50 1·00

205 Kandahar International Airport

1964. Air. Inauguration of Kandahar Int Airport.
514 **205** 7a.75 brown 65 40
515 9a.25 blue 85 75
516 10a.50 green . . . . . . 1·10 90
517 13a.75 red . . . . 1·25 90

206 Unisphere and Flags

207 "Flame of Freedom"

1964. New York World's Fair.
518 **206** 6a. black, red and green 25 20

1964. 1st U.N. Human Rights Seminar, Kabul.
519 **207** 3a.75 multicoloured . . . 25 15

208 Snow Leopard

1964. Afghan Wildlife.
520 **208** 25p. blue and yellow . . . 55 15
521 – 50p. green and red . . . 60 15
522 – 75p. purple and blue . . . 60 15
523 – 5a. brown and green . . . 75 20
ANIMALS—VERT: 50p. Ibex. HORIZ: 75p. Argali; 5a. Yak.

209 Herat

210 Hurdling

1964. Tourist Publicity. Inscr "1964".
524 **209** 25p. brown and blue . . . 20 15
525 – 75p. blue and ochre . . . 25 15
526 – 3a. black, red and green 40 25
DESIGNS—VERT: 75p. Tomb of Gowhar Shad, Herat. HORIZ: 3a. Map and flag.

1964. Olympic Games, Tokyo.
527 **210** 25p. sepia, red and bistre 15 10
528 – 1a. sepia, red and blue . . 15 10
529 – 3a.75 sepia, red and green 40 25
530 – 5a. sepia, red and brown 50 25
DESIGNS—VERT: 1a. Diving. HORIZ: 3a.75, Wrestling; 5a. Football.

211 Afghan Flag

212 Pashtu Flag

1964. 46th Independence Day.
531 **211** 25p. multicoloured . . . 20 15
532 75p. multicoloured . . . 25 15
On the above the Pushtu inscription "33rd Anniversary" is blocked out in gold.

1964. Pashtunistan Day.
533 **212** 100p. multicoloured . . . 20 15

213 Mohamed Zahir Shah

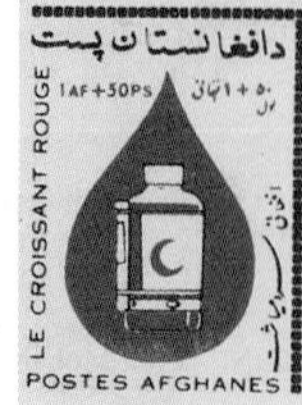

214 "Blood Transfusion"

1964. King's 50th Birthday.
534 **213** 1a.25 green and gold . . 25 20
535 3a.75 red and gold . . . 40 35
536 50a. black and gold . . . 2·75 2·00

1964. Red Crescent Day.
537 **214** 1a.+50p. red and black 20 15

215 Badges of Afghanistan and U.N.

1964. U.N. Day.
538 **215** 5a. blue, black and gold 20 15

216 Doves with Necklace

217 M. Jami

1964. Women's Day.
539 **216** 25p. blue, green and pink 15 15
540 75p. blue, green & lt blue 15 15
541 1a. blue, green and silver 25 10

1964. 550th Birth Anniv of Mowlana Jami (poet).
542 **217** 1a.50 cream, green & blk 1·00 85

218 Scaly-bellied Green Woodpecker

220 "The Red City"

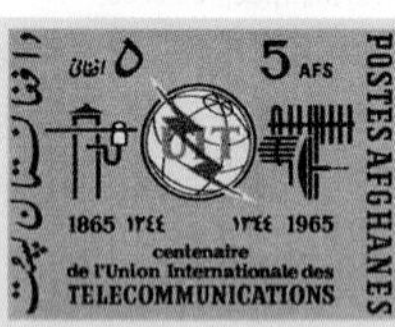

219 I.T.U. Emblem and Symbols

1965. Birds. Multicoloured.
543 1a.25 Type **218** . . . . . . 2·25 50
544 3a.75 Lanceolated jay (vert) 4·50 1·25
545 5a. Himalayan monal pheasant (vert) . . . . . . 5·25 2·40

1965. Centenary of I.T.U.
546 **219** 5a. black, red and blue . . 50 25

1965. Tourist Publicity. Inscr "1965". Mult.
547 1a. Type **220** 25 10
548 3a.75 Bami Yan (valley and mountains) 35 20
549 5a. Band-E-Amir (lake and mountains) 55 25

221 I.C.Y. Emblem

1965. International Co-operation Year.
550 **221** 5a. multicoloured 40 35

222 Douglas DC-3 and Emblem

1965. 10th Anniv of Afghan Airlines (ARIANA).
551 **222** 1a.25 multicoloured . . . 30 10
552 – 5a. black, blue & purple 85 20
553 – 10a. multicoloured . . . 1·50 50
DESIGNS: 5a. Convair CV 240; 10a. Douglas DC-6A.

223 Mohamed Nadir Shah **224** Pashtu Flag

1965. 47th Independence Day.
554 **223** 1a. brown, black & green 40 10

1965. Pashtunistan Day.
555 **224** 1a. multicoloured 35 10

225 Promulgation of New Constitution

1965. New Constitution.
556 **225** 1a.50 black and green . . 30 15

226 Mohamed Zahir Shah **227** First Aid Post

1965. King's 51st Birthday.
557 **226** 1a.25 brown, blue & pink 25 10
558 6a. indigo, purple & blue 35 30
See also Nos. 579/80, 606/7 and 637/8.

1965. Red Crescent Day.
559 **227** 1a.50+50 brn, grn & red 20 15

228 U.N. and Afghan Flags

1965. U.N. Day.
560 **228** 5a. multicoloured 20 20

229 Fat-tailed Gecko

1966. Reptiles. Multicoloured.
561 3a. Type **229** 40 20
562 4a. "Agama caucasica" (lizard) 55 20
563 8a. "Testudo horsfieldi" (tortoise) 70 35

230 Cotton **231** Footballer

1966. Agriculture Day. Multicoloured.
564 1a. Type **230** 20 10
565 5a. Silkworm moth (caterpillar) 40 20
566 7a. Oxen 45 30

1966. World Cup Football Championship, England.
567 **231** 2a. black and red 25 15
568 6a. black and blue 50 25
569 12a. black and brown . . 1·00 50

232 Independence Memorial

1966. Independence Day.
570 **232** 1a. multicoloured 15 10
571 3a. multicoloured 30 15

233 Pashtu Flag

1966. Pashtunistan Day.
572 **233** 1a. blue 25 10

234 Founding Members

1966. Red Crescent Day.
573 **234** 2a.+1a. green and red . . 25 10
574 5a.+1a. brown & mve . . 45 15

235 Map of Afghanistan

1966. Tourist Publicity. Multicoloured.
575 2a. Type **235** 20 10
576 4a. Bagh-i-Bala, former Palace of Abdur Rahman 40 20
577 8a. Tomb of Abdur Rahman, Kabul 55 40

1966. King's 52nd Birthday. Portrait similar to T **226** but with position of inscr changed. Dated "1966".
579 1a. green 25 10
580 5a. brown 35 15

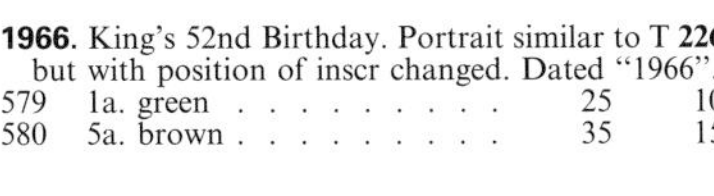

236 Mohamed Zahir Shah and U.N. Emblem

1966. U.N. Day. Inscr "20TH ANNIVERSAIRE DES REFUGIES".
581 **236** 5a. green, brown & emer 35 15
582 10a. red, green & yellow 70 25

237 Children Dancing

1966. Child Welfare Day.
583 **237** 1a.+1a. red and green . . 20 10
584 3a.+2a. brown & yell . . 40 20
585 7a.+3a. green & purple 65 40

238 Construction of Power Station **239** U.N.E.S.C.O. Emblem

1967. Afghan Industrial Development. Mult.
586 2a. Type **238** 20 10
587 5a. Handwoven carpet (vert) 25 15
588 8a. Cement works 35 25

1967. 20th Anniv (1966) of U.N.E.S.C.O.
589 **239** 2a. multicoloured 25 15
590 6a. multicoloured 40 15
591 12a. multicoloured . . . 85 20

240 I.T.Y. Emblem **241** Inoculation

1967. International Tourist Year.
592 **240** 2a. black, blue and yellow 10 10
593 – 6a. black, blue and brown 35 20
DESIGN: 6a. I.T.Y. emblem on map of Afghanistan.

1967. Anti-tuberculosis Campaign.
595 **241** 2a.+1a. black & yellow 15 10
596 5a.+2a. brown & pink . . 35 25

242 Hydroelectric Power Station, Dorunta **243** Rhesus Macaque

1967. Development of Electricity for Agriculture.
597 **242** 1a. lilac and green 10 10
598 – 6a. turquoise and brown 30 20
599 – 8a. blue and purple . . . 35 25
DESIGNS—VERT: 6a. Dam. HORIZ: 8a. Reservoir, Jalalabad.

1967. Wildlife.
600 **243** 2a. blue and buff 30 10
601 – 6a. sepia and green . . . 55 25
602 – 12a. brown and blue . . . 85 50
ANIMALS—HORIZ: 6a. Striped hyena; 12a. Goitred gazelles.

244 "Saving the Guns at Maiwand" (after R. Caton Woodville)

1967. Independence Day.
603 **244** 1a. brown and red . . . 20 10
604 2a. brown and mauve . . 30 15

245 Pashtu Dancers

1967. Pashtunistan Day.
605 **245** 2a. violet and purple . . . 25 10

1967. King's 53rd Birthday. Portrait similar to T **226** but with position of inscr changed. Dated "1967".
606 2a. brown 15 10
607 8a. blue 50 25

246 Red Crescent **247** U.N. Emblem and Fireworks

1967. Red Crescent Day.
608 **246** 3a.+1a. red, blk & ol . . 15 10
609 5a.+1a. red, blk & blue 25 15

1967. U.N. Day.
610 **247** 10a. multicoloured . . . 45 25

248 Wrestling **249** Said Jamal-ud-Din Afghan

1967. Olympic Games, Mexico City.
611 **248** 4a. purple and green . . . 25 10
612 – 6a. brown and red . . . 40 15
DESIGN: 6a. Wrestling throw.

1967. 70th Death Anniv of Said Afghan.
614 **249** 1a. purple 10 10
615 5a. brown 35 15

250 Bronze Vase **251** W.H.O. Emblem

1967. Archaeological Treasures (11th–12th century Ghasnavide era).
616 **250** 3a. brown and green . . . 25 10
617 – 7a. green and yellow . . . 45 20
DESIGN: 7a. Bronze jar.

1968. 20th Anniv of W.H.O.
619 **251** 2a. blue and bistre . . . 15 10
620 7a. blue and red 25 15

252 Karakul Sheep

1968. Agricultural Day.
621 **252** 1a. black and yellow . . . 10 10
622 6a. brown, black and blue 40 15
623 12a. brown, sepia & blue 55 25

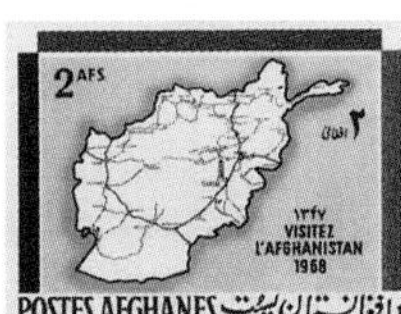
253 Road Map of Afghanistan

1968. Tourist Publicity. Multicoloured.
624 2a. Type **253** 20 10
625 3a. Victory Tower, Ghazni (21 × 31 mm) 25 10
626 16a. Mausoleum, Ghazni (21 × 31 mm) 65 35

254 Queen Humaira **255** Cinereous Vulture

1968. Mothers' Day.
627 **254** 2a.+2a. brown 15 15
628 7a.+2a. green 50 35

1968. Wild Birds. Multicoloured.
629 1a. Type **255** . . . . 1·00 40
630 6a. Eagle owl . . . . 2·25 1·25
631 7a. Greater flamingos . . . . 3·25 1·40

256 "Pig-sticking"

1968. Olympic Games, Mexico. Multicoloured.
632 2a. Olympic flame and rings (21 × 31 mm) 15 10
633 8a. Type **256** 35 20
634 12a. Buzkashi game 50 30

257 Flowers on Army Truck

1968. Independence Day.
635 **257** 6a. multicoloured 25 15

258 Pashtu Flag **259** Red Crescent

1968. Pashtunistan Day.
636 **258** 3a. multicoloured 20 10

1968. King's 54th Birthday. Portrait similar to T **226** but differently arranged and in smaller size (21 × 31 mm).
637 2a. blue 20 10
638 8a. brown 30 25

1968. Red Crescent Day.
639 **259** 4a.+1a. multicoloured . . 30 20

260 Human Rights Emblem **261** Maolala Djalalodine Balkhi

1968. U.N. Day and Human Rights Year.
640 **260** 1a. brown, bistre & green 10 10
641 2a. black, bistre & violet 15 10
642 6a. violet, bistre & purple 35 15

1968. 695th Death Anniv of Maolala Djalalodine Balkhi (historian).
644 **261** 4a. mauve and green . . . 20 10

262 Temple Painting **263** I.L.O. Emblem

1969. Archaeological Treasures (Bagram era).
645 **262** 1a. red, yellow and green 25 10
646 – 3a. purple and violet . . . 45 20
DESIGN: 3a. Carved vessel.

1969. 50th Anniv of I.L.O.
648 **263** 5a. black and yellow . . . 25 15
649 8a. black and blue 45 20

264 Red Cross Emblems **266** Mother and Child

1969. 50th Anniv of League of Red Cross Societies.
650 **264** 3a.+1a. multicoloured . . 45 20
651 5a.+1a. multicoloured . . 65 20
On Nos. 650/1 the commemorative inscr in English and Pushtu for the 50th anniv of the League of Red Cross Societies has been obliterated by gold bars.

1969. Mothers' Day.
654 **266** 1a.+1a. brown & yell . . 20 20
655 4a.+1a. violet & mve . . 40 40

267 Road Map of Afghanistan **268** Bust (Hadda era)

1969. Tourist Publicity. Badakshan and Pamir Region. Multicoloured.
657 2a. Type **267** 25 10
658 4a. Pamir landscape 25 15
659 7a. Mountain mule transport 45 25

1969. Archaeological Discoveries. Multicoloured.
661 1a. Type **268** 10 10
662 5a. Vase and jug (Bagram period) 40 15
663 10a. Statuette (Bagram period) 65 20

269 Mohamed Zahir Shah and Queen Humaira **270** Map and Rising Sun

1969. Independence Day.
664 **269** 5a. red, blue and gold . . 40 15
665 10a. green, purple & gold 55 25

1969. Pashtunistan Day.
666 **270** 2a. red and blue 25 10

271 Mohamed Zahir Shah **272** Red Crescent

1969. King's 55th Birthday.
667 **271** 2a. multicoloured 20 10
668 6a. multicoloured 45 15

1969. Red Crescent Day.
669 **272** 6a.+1a. multicoloured . . 60 20

273 U.N. Emblem, Afghan Arms and Flag

1969. United Nations Day.
670 **273** 5a. multicoloured 25 15

274 I.T.U. Emblem **275** Indian Crested Porcupine

1969. World Telecommunications Day.
671 **274** 6a. multicoloured 20 15
672 12a. multicoloured . . . 40 25

1969. Wild Animals. Multicoloured.
673 1a. Type **275** 20 10
674 3a. Wild boar 45 10
675 8a. Bactrian red deer 65 15

276 Footprint on the Moon **277** "Cancer the Crab"

1969. 1st Man on the Moon.
676 **276** 1a. multicoloured 10 10
677 3a. multicoloured 15 10
678 6a. multicoloured 20 15
679 10a. multicoloured . . . 35 30

1970. W.H.O. "Fight Cancer" Day.
680 **277** 2a. red, dp green & green 15 10
681 6a. red, deep blue & blue 25 20

278 Mirza Bedel **279** I.E.Y. Emblem

1970. 250th Death Anniv of Mirza Abdul Quader Bedel (poet).
682 **278** 5a. multicoloured 30 10

1970. International Education Year.
683 **279** 1a. black 10 10
684 6a. red 25 10
685 12a. green 30 25

280 Mother and Child **281** U.N. Emblem, Scales and Satellite

1970. Mothers' Day.
686 **280** 6a. multicoloured 25 20

1970. 25th Anniv of United Nations.
687 **281** 4a. blue, dp blue & yellow 15 15
688 6a. blue, deep blue & red 25 15

282 Road Map of Afghanistan with Location of Sites **283** Common Quail

1970. Tourist Publicity. Inscr "1970". Mult.
689 **282** 2a. black, green and blue 20 10
690 – 3a. multicoloured 25 10
691 – 7a. multicoloured 55 15
DESIGNS (36 × 26 mm): 3a. Lakeside mosque, Kabul; 7a. Arch of Paghman.

1970. Wild Birds. Multicoloured.
692 2a. Type **283** . . . . 1·40 50
693 4a. Golden eagle . . . . . . 2·75 80
694 6a. Common pheasant . . . 3·25 1·25

284 Shah Reviewing Troops

1970. Independence Day.
695 **284** 8a. multicoloured 35 35

285 Group of Pashtus

1970. Pashtunistan Day.
696 **285** 2a. blue and red 35 10

286 Mohamed Zahir Shah **287** Red Crescent Emblems

1970. King's 56th Birthday.
697 **286** 3a. violet and green . . . 15 10
698 7a. purple and blue . . . 55 15

1970. Red Crescent Day.
699 **287** 2a. black, red and gold 15 10

288 U.N. Emblem and Plaque

1970. United Nations Day.
700 **288** 1a. multicoloured 10 10
701 5a. multicoloured 15 25

289 Afghan Stamps of 1871

1970. Centenary of First Afghan Stamps.
702 **289** 1a. black, blue & orange 20 10
703 4a. black, yellow & blue 25 15
704 12a. black, blue and lilac 45 25

290 Global Emblem

1971. World Telecommunications Day.
705 **290** 12a. multicoloured . . . 50 25

291 "Callimorpha principalis" **292** Lower half of old Kushan Statue

1971. Butterflies and Moths. Multicoloured.
706 1a. Type **291** 30 10
707 3a. "Epizygaenella afghana" 45 10
708 5a. "Parnassius autocrator" 75 15

1971. U.N.E.S.C.O. Kushan Seminar.
709 **292** 6a. violet and yellow . . . 35 15
710 10a. purple and blue . . . 55 20

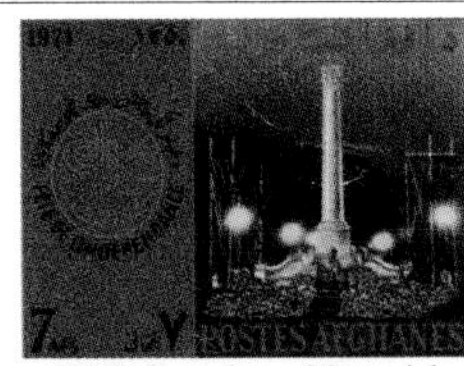
293 Independence Memorial

1971. Independence Day.
711 **293** 7a. multicoloured 40 15
712 9a. multicoloured 55 20

294 Pashtunistan Square, Kabul

1971. Pashtunistan Day.
713 **294** 5a. purple 35 15

295 Mohamed Zahir Shah and Kabul Airport

1971. Air. Multicoloured.
714 50a. Type **295** . . . . 3·25 3·00
715 100a. King, airline emblem and Boeing 727 airplane 3·50 2·50

296 Mohamed Zahir Shah

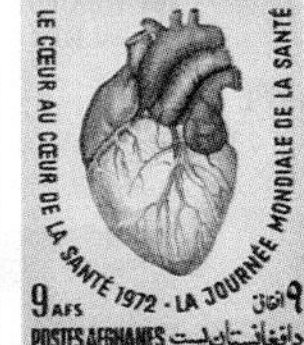
297 Map, Nurse and Patients

1971. King's 57th Birthday.
716 **296** 9a. multicoloured 40 25
717 17a. multicoloured . . . 75 35

1971. Red Crescent Day.
718 **297** 8a. multicoloured 40 15

298 Emblem of Racial Equality Year

299 Human Heart

1971. United Nations Day.
719 **298** 24a. blue . . . . 1·25 50

1972. World Health Day and World Heart Month.
720 **299** 9a. multicoloured 35 20
721 12a. multicoloured . . . 45 25

300 "Tulipa lanata"

301 Buddha of Hadda

1972. Afghan Flora and Fauna. Multicoloured.
722 7a. Type **300** 60 60
723 10a. Chukar partridge (horiz) 3·75 1·40
724 12a. Lynx (horiz) . . . . . 1·25 1·00
725 18a. "Allium stipitatum" . . 1·25 1·10

1972. Tourist Publicity.
726 **301** 3a. blue and brown . . . 25 15
727 – 7a. green and red 40 20
728 – 9a. purple and green . . . 50 25
DESIGNS: 7a. Greco-Bactrian seal, 250 B.C.; 9a. Greek temple, Ai-Khanum, 3rd–2nd century B.C.

302 King with Queen Humaira at Independence Parade

1972. Independence Day.
729 **302** 25a. multicoloured . . . 1·50 1·25

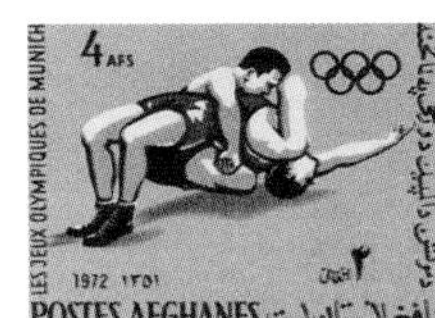
303 Wrestling

1972. Olympic Games, Munich. Various Wrestling Holds as T **303**.
730 4a. multicoloured 25 10
731 8a. multicoloured 40 20
732 10a. multicoloured 55 25
733 19a. multicoloured 75 30
734 21a. multicoloured 95 30

304 Pathan and Mountain View

305 Mohamed Zahir Shah

1972. Pashtunistan Day.
736 **304** 5a. multicoloured 40 10

1972. King's 58th Birthday.
737 **305** 7a. blue, black and gold 50 15
738 14a. brown, black & gold 90 35

306 Ruined Town and Refugees

1972. Red Crescent Day.
739 **306** 7a. black, red and blue . . 50 15

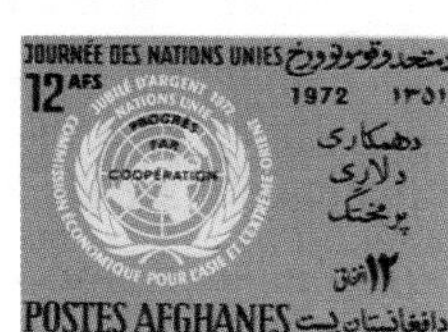
307 E.C.A.F.E. Emblem

1972. U.N. Day. 25th Anniv of U.N. Economic Commission for Asia and the Far East.
740 **307** 12a. black and blue . . . 45 25

308 Ceramics

1973. Afghan Handicrafts. Multicoloured.
741 7a. Type **308** 40 25
742 9a. Embroidered coat (vert) 55 25
743 12a. Coffee set (vert) 65 35
744 16a. Decorated boxes 90 35

309 W.M.O. and Afghan Emblems

1973. Cent of World Meteorological Organization.
746 **309** 7a. green and mauve . . . 50 15
747 14a. red and blue . . . . 1·00 30

310 Emblems and Harvester

1973. 10th Anniv of World Food Programme.
748 **310** 14a.+7a. purple & blue 1·00 1·00

311 Al-Biruni

312 Association Emblem

1973. Birth Millenary of Abu-al Rayhan al-Biruni (mathematician and philosopher).
749 **311** 10a. multicoloured . . . 60 30

1973. Family Planning Week.
750 **312** 9a. purple and orange . . 60 20

313 Himalayan Monal Pheasant

1973. Birds. Multicoloured.
751 8a. Type **313** . . . . 2·25 2·00
752 9a. Great crested grebe . . . 2·75 2·25
753 12a. Himalayan snowcock . . 3·25 3·00

314 Buzkashi Game

1973. Tourism.
754 **314** 8a. black 40 15

315 Firework Display

1973. Independence Day.
755 **315** 12a. multicoloured . . . 55 25

316 Landscape and Flag

1973. Pashtunistan Day.
756 **316** 9a. multicoloured 60 20

317 Red Crescent

1973. Red Crescent.
757 **317** 10a. multicoloured . . . 85 25

318 Kemal Ataturk

1973. 50th Anniv of Turkish Republic.
758 **318** 1a. blue 25 10
759 7a. brown 80 15

319 Human Rights Flame

1973. 25th Anniv of Declaration of Human Rights.
760 **319** 12a. blue, black and silver 40 25

320 Asiatic Black Bears

1974. Wild Animals. Multicoloured.
761 5a. Type **320** 35 10
762 7a. Afghan hound 55 20
763 10a. Goitred gazelle 70 25
764 12a. Leopard 90 30

321 "Workers"

1974. Labour Day.
766 **321** 9a. multicoloured 35 15

322 Arch of Paghman and Independence Memorial

1974. Independence Day.
767 **322** 4a. multicoloured 40 10
768 11a. multicoloured . . . 50 20

323 Arms of Afghanistan and Hands clasping Seedling

1974. 1st Anniv of Republic. Multicoloured.
769 4a. Type **323** 40 10
770 5a. Republican flag (36 × 26 mm) 50 15
771 7a. Gen. Mohammed Daoud (26 × 36 mm) 65 15
772 15a. Soldiers and arms . . . 1·00 25

324 Lesser Spotted Eagle

1974. Afghan Birds. Multicoloured.
774 1a. Type **324** . . . . 1·25 40
775 6a. White-fronted goose, ruddy shelduck and greylag goose . . . . 2·75 70
776 11a. Black crane and common coots . . . . . . 4·25 1·10

325 Flags of Pashtunistan and Afghanistan

1974. Pashtunistan Day.
777 **325** 5a. multicoloured 20 15

326 Republic's Coat of Arms

1974.
778 **326** 100p. green 65 25

327 Pres. Daoud **328** Arms and Centenary Years

1974.
779 **327** 10a. multicoloured . . . 35 20
780 16a. multicoloured . . . 1·00 40
781 19a. multicoloured . . . 65 40
782 21a. multicoloured . . . 75 35
783 22a. multicoloured . . . 1·25 50
784 30a. multicoloured . . . 1·50 50

1974. Centenary of U.P.U.
785 **328** 7a. green, black and gold 20 10

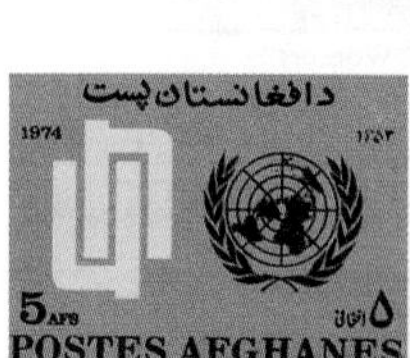

329 "UN" and U.N. Emblem **330** Pres. Daoud

1974. United Nations Day.
786 **329** 5a. blue and ultramarine 35 10

1975.
787 **330** 50a. multicoloured . . . 1·50 85
788 100a. multicoloured . . . 3·00 1·60

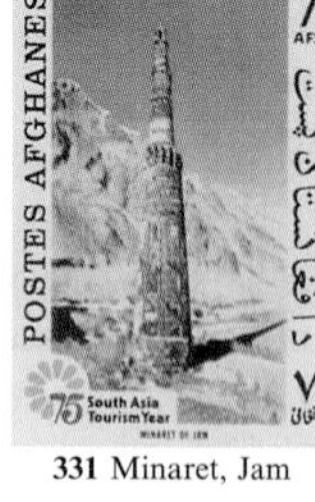

331 Minaret, Jam

1975. South Asia Tourist Year. Multicoloured.
789 7a. Type **331** 30 15
790 14a. "Griffon and Lady" (2nd century) 55 30
791 15a. Head of Buddha (4th–5th century) 65 30

332 Afghan Flag

1975. Independence Day.
793 **332** 16a. multicoloured . . . 70 25

333 Rejoicing Crowd

1975. 2nd Anniv of Revolution.
794 **333** 9a. multicoloured 45 15
795 12a. multicoloured . . . 65 20

334 I.W.Y. Emblem **335** Rising Sun and Flag

1975. International Women's Year.
796 **334** 9a. black, blue and purple 50 15

1975. Pashtunistan Day.
797 **335** 10a. multicoloured . . . 40 15

336 Wazir M. Akbar Khan

1976. 130th Death Anniv of Akbar Khan (resistance leader).
798 **336** 15a. multicoloured . . . 50 25

337 Independence Monument and Arms

1976. Independence Day.
799 **337** 22a. multicoloured . . . 60 30

338 Pres. Daoud raising Flag **339** Mountain

1976. 3rd Anniv of Republic.
800 **338** 30a. multicoloured . . . 85 50

1976. Pashtunistan Day.
801 **339** 16a. multicoloured . . . 50 30

340 Arms

1976.
802 – 25p. salmon 40 25
803 **340** 50p. green 50 15
804 1a. blue 50 10
DESIGN: 25p. As Type **340** but with Arms on left and inscription differently arranged.

341 Flag and Monuments on Open Book

1977. Independence Day.
805 **341** 20a. multicoloured . . . 45 30

342 Presidential Address

1977. Election of First President and New Constitution. Multicoloured.
806 7a. President Daoud and Election (45 × 27 mm) . . . 40 10
807 8a. Type **342** 45 10
808 10a. Inaugural ceremony . . 65 15
809 18a. Promulgation of new constitution (45 × 27 mm) 85 30

343 Medal **344** Crowd with Afghan Flag

1977. 80th Death Anniv of Sayed Jamaluddin (Afghan reformer).
811 **343** 12a. black, blue & gold 40 20

1977. Republic Day.
812 **344** 22a. multicoloured . . . 65 35

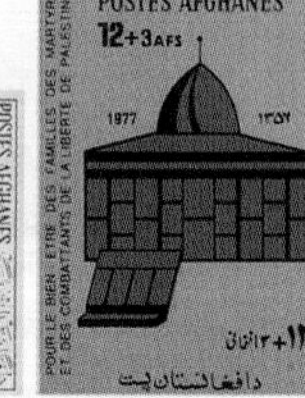

345 Dancers around Fountain **346** Dome of the Rock

1977. Pashtunistan Day.
813 **345** 30a. multicoloured . . . 90 50

1977. Palestinian Welfare.
814 **346** 12a.+3a. black, gold and pink . . . . 2·00 60

347 Arms and Carrier Pigeon

1977.
815 **347** 1a. blue and black 50 15

348 President Daoud acknowledging Crowd

1978. 1st Anniv of Presidential Election.
816 **348** 20a. multicoloured . . . 75 40

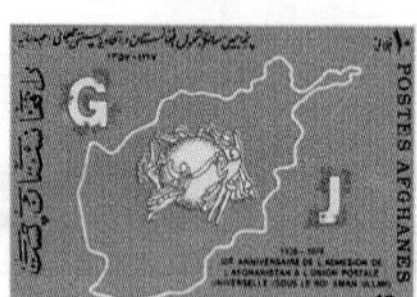

349 U.P.U. Emblem on Map of Afghanistan

1978. 50th Anniv of Admission to U.P.U.
817 **349** 10a. gold, green & black 40 15

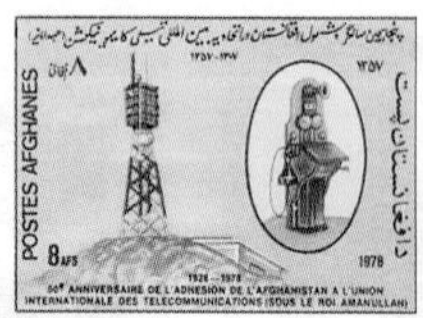

350 Transmitting Aerial and Early Telephone

1978. 50th Anniv of Admission to I.T.U.
818 **350** 8a. multicoloured 35 10

351 Red Crescent, Red Cross and Red Lion Emblems

1978. Red Crescent.
819 **351** 3a. black 40 15

352 Arms

1978.
820 **352** 1a. red and gold 45 15
821 4a. red and gold 75 10

353 Ruin, Qalai Bust

1978. Independence Day. Multicoloured.
822 16a. Buddha, Bamian 75 25
823 22a. Type **353** 85 40
824 30a. Women in national costume . . . . 1·50 75

354 Afghans with Flag

355 Crest and Symbols of the Five Senses

1978. Pashtunistan Day.
825 **354** 7a. red and blue 50 15

1978. International Literacy Day.
826 **355** 20a. red 85 35

356 Flag

1978. "The Mail is in the Service of the People".
827 **356** 8a. red, gold and brown 60 15
828 9a. red, gold and brown 90 15

357 Martyr

358 President Mohammed Taraki

1978. "The People's Democratic Party Honours its Martyrs".
829 **357** 18a. green 95 30

1978. 14th Anniv of People's Democratic Party.
830 **358** 12a. multicoloured . . . 85 10

359 Emancipated Woman

1979. Women's Day.
831 **359** 14a. blue and red 85 40

360 Farmers planting Tree

1979. Farmers' Day.
832 **360** 1a. multicoloured 45 15

361 Map and Census Taking

1979. 1st Complete Population Census.
833 **361** 3a. black, blue and red . . 50 15

362 Pres. Taraki reading "Khalq"

1979. 1st Publication of "Khalq" (party newspaper).
834 **362** 2a. multicoloured 55 15

363 Pres. Taraki and Tank

364 Pres. Taraki

1979. 1st Anniv of Sawr Revolution (1st issue).
835 **363** 50p. multicoloured . . . 60 15

1979. 1st Anniv of Sawr Revolution (2nd issue). Multicoloured.
836 4a. Type **364** 40 10
837 5a. Revolutionary H.Q. and Tank Monument, Kabul (47 × 32 mm) 55 10
838 6a. Command room, Revolutionary H.Q. (vert) 65 15
839 12a. House where first Khalq Party Congress was held (vert) 90 25

365 Carpenter and Blacksmith

1979. Workers' Solidarity.
840 **365** 10a. multicoloured . . . 85 15

366 Children on Map of Afghanistan

1979. International Year of the Child.
841 **366** 16a. multicoloured . . . 1·50 65

367 Revolutionaries and Kabul Monuments

368 Afghans and Flag

1979. Independence Day.
842 **367** 30a. multicoloured . . . 1·25 65

1979. Pashtunistan Day.
843 **368** 9a. multicoloured 75 15

369 U.P.U. Emblem and Arms on Map

1979. Stamp Day.
844 **369** 15a. multicoloured . . . 60 20

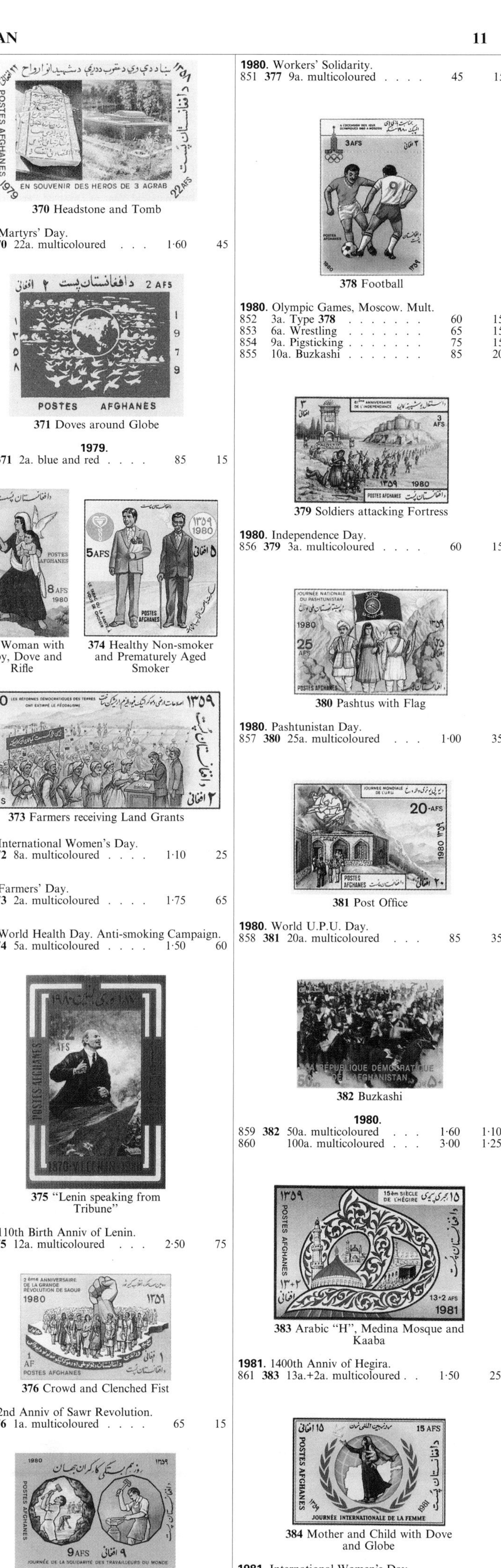

370 Headstone and Tomb

1979. Martyrs' Day.
845 **370** 22a. multicoloured . . . 1·60 45

371 Doves around Globe

1979.
845a **371** 2a. blue and red 85 15

372 Woman with Baby, Dove and Rifle

374 Healthy Non-smoker and Prematurely Aged Smoker

373 Farmers receiving Land Grants

1980. International Women's Day.
846 **372** 8a. multicoloured . . . . 1·10 25

1980. Farmers' Day.
847 **373** 2a. multicoloured . . . . 1·75 65

1980. World Health Day. Anti-smoking Campaign.
848 **374** 5a. multicoloured . . . . 1·50 60

375 "Lenin speaking from Tribune"

1980. 110th Birth Anniv of Lenin.
849 **375** 12a. multicoloured . . . 2·50 75

376 Crowd and Clenched Fist

1980. 2nd Anniv of Sawr Revolution.
850 **376** 1a. multicoloured 65 15

377 Quarry Worker and Blacksmith

1980. Workers' Solidarity.
851 **377** 9a. multicoloured 45 15

378 Football

1980. Olympic Games, Moscow. Mult.
852 3a. Type **378** 60 15
853 6a. Wrestling 65 15
854 9a. Pigsticking 75 15
855 10a. Buzkashi 85 20

379 Soldiers attacking Fortress

1980. Independence Day.
856 **379** 3a. multicoloured 60 15

380 Pashtus with Flag

1980. Pashtunistan Day.
857 **380** 25a. multicoloured . . . 1·00 35

381 Post Office

1980. World U.P.U. Day.
858 **381** 20a. multicoloured . . . 85 35

382 Buzkashi

1980.
859 **382** 50a. multicoloured . . . 1·60 1·10
860 100a. multicoloured . . . 3·00 1·25

383 Arabic "H", Medina Mosque and Kaaba

1981. 1400th Anniv of Hegira.
861 **383** 13a.+2a. multicoloured . . 1·50 25

384 Mother and Child with Dove and Globe

1981. International Women's Day.
862 **384** 15a. multicoloured . . . 95 25

385 Ox Plough, Tractor and Planting Trees

1981. Farmers' Day.
863 **385** 1a. multicoloured 80 20

386 Urial **387** Crowd and Afghan Arms

1981. Protected Wildlife.
864 **386** 12a. multicoloured . . . 75 50

1981. 3rd Anniv of Sawr Revolution.
865 **387** 50p. brown 55 10

388 Road Workers in Ravine **389** Red Crescent enclosing Scenes of Disaster and Medical Aid

1981. Workers' Day.
866 **388** 10a. multicoloured . . . 65 20

1981. Red Crescent Day.
867 **389** 1a.+4a. multicoloured . . 50 60

390 Satellite Receiving Station **391** Map enclosing playing Children

1981. World Telecommunications Day.
868 **390** 9a. multicoloured 50 15

1981. International Children's Day.
869 **391** 15a. multicoloured . . . 65 30

392 Afghans and Monument

1981. Independence Day.
870 **392** 4a. multicoloured 65 15

393 Pashtus around Flag **394** Terracotta Horseman

1981. Pashtunistan Day.
871 **393** 2a. multicoloured 55 15

1981. World Tourism Day.
872 **394** 5a. multicoloured 50 10

395 Siamese Twins and I.Y.D.P. Emblem

1981. International Year of Disabled Persons.
873 **395** 6a.+1a. multicoloured . . 65 40

396 Harvesting

1981. World Food Day.
874 **396** 7a. multicoloured 60 15

397 Peace, Solidarity and Friendship Organization Emblem **398** Heads and Clenched Fist on Globe and Emblem

1981. Afro-Asian Peoples' Solidarity Meeting.
875 **397** 8a. blue 65 15

1981. International Anti-apartheid Year.
876 **398** 4a. multicoloured 40 10

399 Lion (bas-relief at Stara Zagora)

1981. 1300th Anniv of Bulgarian State.
877 **399** 20a. stone, purple and red 1·10 40

400 Mother rocking Cradle

1982. Women's Day.
878 **400** 6a. multicoloured 45 10

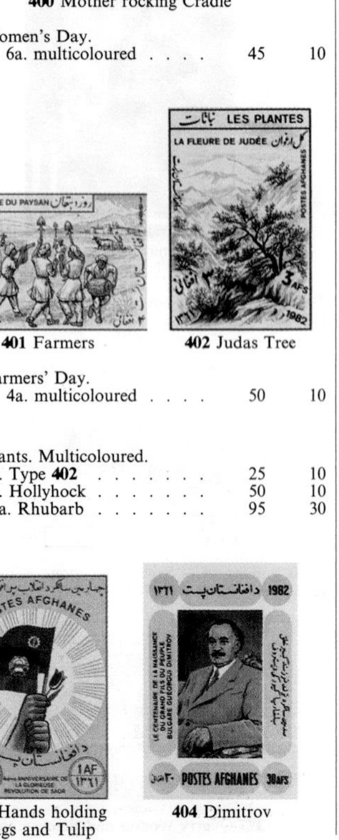

401 Farmers **402** Judas Tree

1982. Farmers' Day.
879 **401** 4a. multicoloured 50 10

1982. Plants. Multicoloured.
880 3a. Type **402** 25 10
881 4a. Hollyhock 50 10
882 16a. Rhubarb 95 30

403 Hands holding Flags and Tulip **404** Dimitrov

1982. 4th Anniv of Sawr Revolution.
883 **403** 1a. multicoloured 85 15

1982. Birth Centenary of Georgi Dimitrov (Bulgarian statesman).
884 **404** 30a. multicoloured . . . 1·50 60

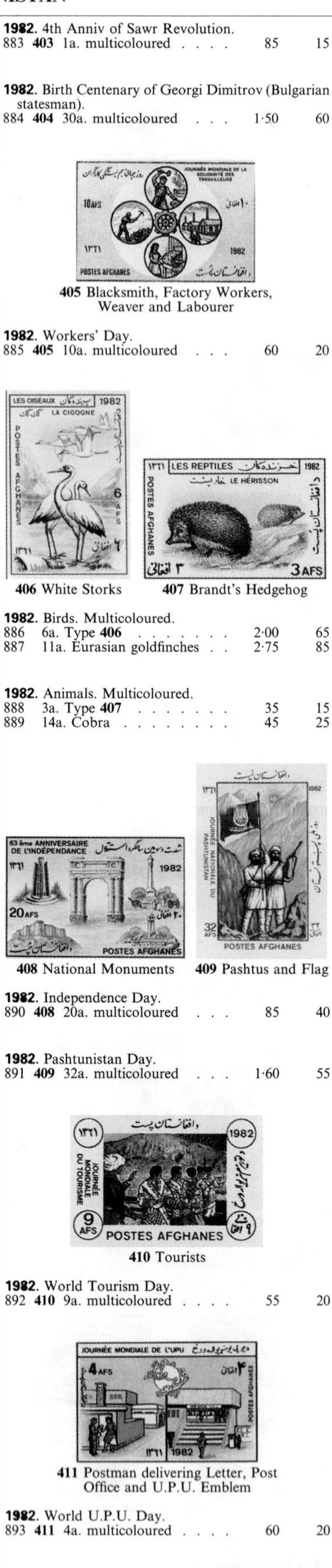

405 Blacksmith, Factory Workers, Weaver and Labourer

1982. Workers' Day.
885 **405** 10a. multicoloured . . . 60 20

406 White Storks **407** Brandt's Hedgehog

1982. Birds. Multicoloured.
886 6a. Type **406** . . . . 2·00 65
887 11a. Eurasian goldfinches . . 2·75 85

1982. Animals. Multicoloured.
888 3a. Type **407** 35 15
889 14a. Cobra 45 25

408 National Monuments **409** Pashtus and Flag

1982. Independence Day.
890 **408** 20a. multicoloured . . . 85 40

1982. Pashtunistan Day.
891 **409** 32a. multicoloured . . . 1·60 55

410 Tourists

1982. World Tourism Day.
892 **410** 9a. multicoloured 55 20

411 Postman delivering Letter, Post Office and U.P.U. Emblem

1982. World U.P.U. Day.
893 **411** 4a. multicoloured 60 20

412 Family eating Meal **413** U.N. Emblem illuminating Globe

1982. World Food Day.
894 **412** 9a. multicoloured 85 20

1982. 37th Anniv of United Nations.
895 **413** 15a. multicoloured . . . 80 30

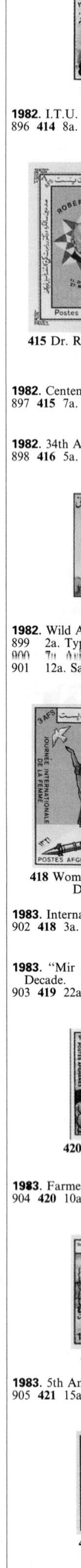

414 Earth Satellite Station

1982. I.T.U. Delegates' Conference, Nairobi.
896 **414** 8a. multicoloured 55 15

415 Dr. Robert Koch **416** Hand holding Torch, Globe and Scales

1982. Centenary of Discovery of Tubercle Bacillus.
897 **415** 7a. black, brown & pink 40 25

1982. 34th Anniv of Declaration of Human Rights.
898 **416** 5a. multicoloured 30 15

417 Lions

1982. Wild Animals. Multicoloured.
899 2a. Type **417** 20 10
900 7a. Asiatic wild ass 40 [illegible]
901 12a. Sable (vert) 85 35

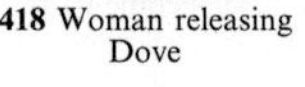

418 Woman releasing Dove **419** Mir Alicher-e-Nawai (poet)

1983. International Women's Day.
902 **418** 3a. multicoloured 20 10

1983. "Mir Alicher-e-Nawai and his Times" Study Decade.
903 **419** 22a. multicoloured . . . 65 25

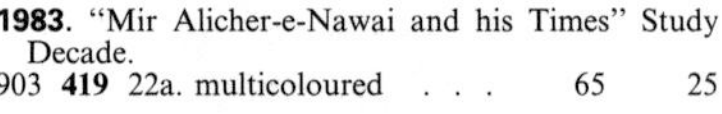

420 Distributing Land Ownership Documents

1983. Farmers' Day.
904 **420** 10a. multicoloured . . . 50 20

421 Revolution Monument

1983. 5th Anniv of Sawr Revolution.
905 **421** 15a. multicoloured . . . 45 20

422 World Map and Hands holding Cogwheel

1983. Labour Day.
906 **422** 20a. multicoloured . . . 55 20

423 Broadcasting Studio, Dish Aerial, Satellites and Television

1983. World Communications Year. Multicoloured.
907 4a. Type **423** 25 10
908 11a. Telecommunications headquarters 45 15

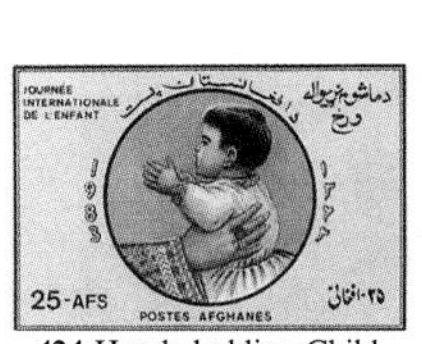

424 Hands holding Child **425** Arms and Map of Afghanistan

1983. International Children's Day.
909 **424** 25a. multicoloured 60 25

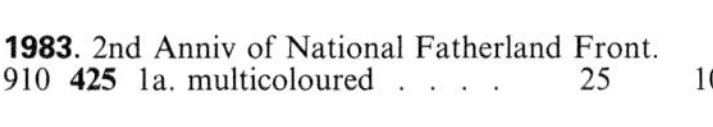

1983. 2nd Anniv of National Fatherland Front.
910 **425** 1a. multicoloured 25 10

426 Apollo **427** Racial Segregation

1983. Butterflies. Multicoloured.
911 9a. Type **426** 35 25
912 13a. Swallowtail 85 45
913 21a. Small tortoiseshell (horiz) 1·00 55

1983. Anti-apartheid Campaign.
914 **427** 10a. multicoloured 35 15

428 National Monuments **429** Pashtus with Flag

1983. Independence Day.
915 **428** 6a. multicoloured 30 10

1983. Pashtunistan Day.
916 **429** 3a. multicoloured 30 10

430 Afghan riding Camel

1983. World Tourism Day.
917 **430** 5a. multicoloured 25 10
918 – 7a. brown and black 35 15
919 – 12a. multicoloured 45 15
920 – 16a. multicoloured 65 15
DESIGNS—VERT: 7a. Stone carving. 16a. Carved stele. HORIZ: 12a. Three statuettes.

431 Winter Landscape

1983. Multicoloured.
921 50a. Type **431** 1·40 25
922 100a. Woman with camel 2·75 30

432 "Communications"

1983. World Communications Year. Mult.
923 14a. Type **432** 55 15
924 15a. Ministry of Communications, Kabul 55 15

433 Fish Breeding

1983. World Food Day.
925 **433** 14a. multicoloured 80 15

434 Football

1983. Sports. Multicoloured.
926 1a. Type **434** 10 10
927 18a. Boxing 50 15
928 21a. Wrestling 65 15

435 Jewellery

1983. Handicrafts. Multicoloured.
929 2a. Type **435** 15 10
930 8a. Polished stoneware 25 10
931 19a. Furniture 45 10
932 30a. Leather goods 95 15

436 Map, Sun, Scales and Torch

1983. 35th Anniv of Declaration of Human Rights.
933 **436** 20a. multicoloured 65 15

437 Polytechnic Buildings and Emblem

1983. 20th Anniv of Kabul Polytechnic.
934 **437** 30a. multicoloured 95 20

438 Ice Skating **439** Dove, Woman and Globe

1984. Winter Olympic Games, Sarajevo. Mult.
935 5a. Type **438** 20 10
936 9a. Skiing 25 10
937 11a. Speed skating 35 10
938 15a. Ice hockey 45 10
939 18a. Biathlon 50 10
940 20a. Ski jumping 55 10
941 22a. Bobsleigh 65 15

1984. International Women's Day.
942 **439** 4a. multicoloured 10 10

440 Ploughing with Tractor

1984. Farmers' Day. Multicoloured.
943 2a. Type **440** 10 10
944 4a. Digging irrigation channel 15 10
945 7a. Saddling donkey by water-mill 15 10
946 9a. Harvesting wheat 20 10
947 15a. Building haystack 30 10
948 18a. Showing cattle 40 10
949 20a. Ploughing with oxen and sowing seed 45 10

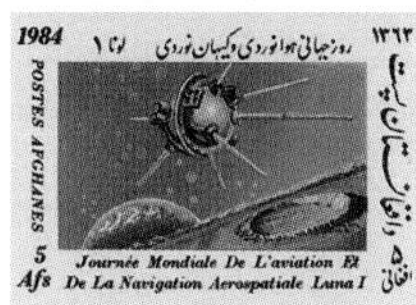

441 "Luna I"

1984. World Aviation and Space Navigation Day. Multicoloured.
950 5a. Type **441** 15 10
951 8a. "Luna II" 25 10
952 11a. "Luna III" 35 10
953 17a. "Apollo XI" 40 10
954 22a. "Soyuz VI" 55 15
955 28a. "Soyuz VII" 55 15
956 34a. "Soyuz VI", "VII" and "VIII" 75 15

442 Flags, Soldier and Workers **443** Hunting Dog

1984. 6th Anniv of Sawr Revolution.
958 **442** 3a. multicoloured 30 10

1984. Animals. Multicoloured.
959 1a. Type **443** 10 10
960 2a. Argali 20 10
961 6a. Przewalski's horse (horiz) 45 10
962 8a. Wild boar 60 10
963 17a. Snow leopard (horiz) 1·25 15
964 19a. Tiger (horiz) 1·75 20
965 22a. Indian elephant 2·25 25

444 Postal Messenger

1984. 19th U.P.U. Congress, Hamburg. Mult.
966 25a. Type **444** 75 15
967 35a. Post rider 1·10 20
968 40a. Bird with letter 1·40 20

445 Antonov AN-2

1984. 40th Anniv of Ariana Airline. Mult.
970 1a. Type **445** 10 10
971 4a. Ilyushin Il-12 15 10
972 9a. Tupolev Tu-104A 45 10
973 10a. Ilyushin Il-18 70 10
974 13a. Yakovlev Yak-42 85 10
975 17a. Tupolev Tu-154 1·10 15
976 21a. Ilyushin Il-86 1·25 15

446 Ettore Bugatti (motor manufacturer) and Bugatti Type 43 Sports car, 1927

1984. Motor Cars. Multicolored.
977 2a. Type **446** 10 10
978 5a. Henry Ford and Ford Model A two-seater, 1903 15 10

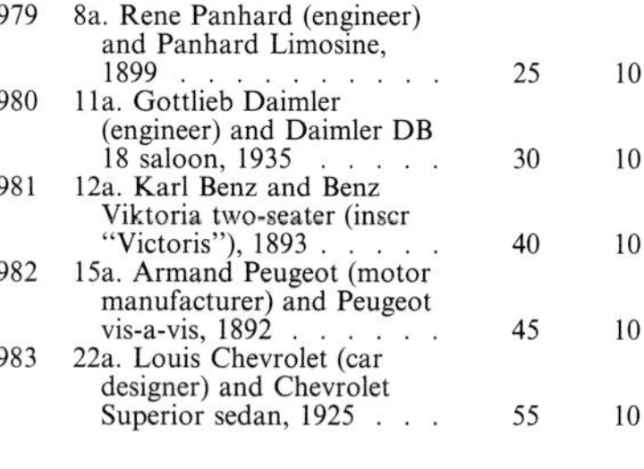

979 8a. Rene Panhard (engineer) and Panhard Limosine, 1899 25 10
980 11a. Gottlieb Daimler (engineer) and Daimler DB 18 saloon, 1935 30 10
981 12a. Karl Benz and Benz Viktoria two-seater (inscr "Victoris"), 1893 40 10
982 15a. Armand Peugeot (motor manufacturer) and Peugeot vis-a-vis, 1892 45 10
983 22a. Louis Chevrolet (car designer) and Chevrolet Superior sedan, 1925 55 10

447 Open Book showing Monuments and Fortress

1984. Independence Day.
984 **447** 6a. multicoloured 30 10

448 Truck on Mountain Road and Pashtunistan Badge

1984. Pashtunistan Day.
985 **448** 3a. multicoloured 25 10

449 Arch at Qalai Bust **450** Pine Cone

1984. World Tourism Day. Multicoloured.
986 1a. Type **449** 10 10
987 2a. Ornamented belt 15 10
988 5a. Kabul monuments 15 10
989 9a. Statuette (vert) 25 10
990 15a. Buffalo riders in snow 45 10
991 19a. Camel in ornate caparison 60 10
992 21a. Buzkashi players 65 10

1984. World Food Day. Multicoloured.
993 2a. Type **450** 10 10
994 4a. Walnuts 20 10
995 6a. Pomegranate 25 10
996 9a. Apples 35 10
997 13a. Cherries 45 10
998 15a. Grapes 55 10
999 26a. Pears 85 10

451 Globe and Emblem

1985. 20th Anniv (1984) of Peoples' Democratic Party.
1000 **451** 25a. multicoloured 85 10

452 Cattle **453** Map and Geologist

1985. Farmers' Day. Multicoloured.
1001 1a. Type **452** 10 10
1002 3a. Mare and foal 15 10
1003 7a. Galloping horse 25 10
1004 8a. Grey horse (vert) 30 10
1005 15a. Karakul sheep and sheepskins 45 10

1006 16a. Herder watching over cattle and sheep 65 10
1007 25a. Family with pack camels 85 10

1985. Geologists' Day.
1008 **453** 4a. multicoloured 25 10

454 Satellite

1985. 20th Anniv of "Intelsat" Communications Satellite. Multicoloured.
1009 6a. Type **454** 45 10
1010 9a. "Intelsat III" 55 10
1011 10a. Rocket launch (vert) 75 10

455 "Visitors for Lenin" (V. Serov)
456 Revolutionaries with Flags

1985. 115th Birth Anniv of Lenin. Multicoloured.
1012 10a. Type **455** 50 10
1013 15a. "With Lenin" (detail, V. Serov) 65 10
1014 25a. Lenin and Red Army fighters 85 10

1985. 7th Anniv of Sawr Revolution.
1016 **456** 21a. multicoloured 85 10

457 Olympic Stadium and Moscow Skyline

1985. 12th World Youth and Students' Festival, Moscow. Multicoloured.
1017 7a. Type **457** 20 10
1018 12a. Festival emblem 40 10
1019 13a. Moscow Kremlin 45 10
1020 18a. Doll 60 10

458 Soviet Memorial, Berlin-Treptow, and Tank before Reichstag

1985. 40th Anniv of End of World War II. Multicoloured.
1021 6a. Type **458** 45 10
1022 9a. "Mother Homeland" war memorial, Volgograd, and fireworks over Moscow Kremlin 60 10
1023 10a. Cecilienhof Castle, Potsdam, and flags of United Kingdom, U.S.S.R. and U.S.A. 75 10

459 Weighing Baby
460 Purple Blewit

1985. U.N.I.C.E.F. Child Survival Campaign. Mult.
1024 1a. Type **459** 10 10
1025 2a. Vaccinating child 15 10
1026 4a. Breast-feeding baby 25 10
1027 5a. Mother and child 25 10

1985. Fungi. Multicoloured.
1028 3a. Type **460** 15 10
1029 4a. Flaky-stemmed witches' mushroom 25 15
1030 7a. The blusher 35 20
1031 11a. Brown birch bolete 50 35
1032 12a. Common ink cap 60 35
1033 18a. "Hypholoma sp." 85 40
1034 20a. "Boletus aurantiacus" 90 40

461 Emblems

1985. United Nations Decade for Women.
1035 **461** 10a. multicoloured 50 10

462 Evening Primrose

1985. "Argentina "85" International Stamp Exhibition, Buenos Aires. Flowers. Multicoloured.
1036 2a. Type **462** 10 10
1037 4a. Cockspur coral tree 15 10
1038 8a. "Tillandsia aeranthos" 25 10
1039 13a. Periwinkle 40 10
1040 10a. Marvel of Peru 60 10
1041 25a. "Cypella herbertii" 85 10
1042 30a. "Clytostoma callistegioides" 1·00 10

463 Building

1985. Independence Day.
1044 **463** 33a. multicoloured 1·40 15

464 Dancers in Pashtunistan Square, Kabul

1985. Pashtunistan Day.
1045 **464** 25a. multicoloured 1·10 10

465 Guldara Stupa

1985. 10th Anniv of World Tourism Organization. Multicoloured.
1046 1a. Type **465** 10 10
1047 2a. Mirwais tomb (vert) 10 10
1048 10a. Buddha of Bamian (vert) 35 10
1049 13a. No Gumbad mosque (vert) 50 10
1050 14a. Pule Kheshti mosque 55 10
1051 15a. Arch at Qalai Bust 60 10
1052 20a. Ghazni minaret (vert) 85 10

466 Boxing

1985. Sport. Multicoloured.
1053 1a. Type **466** 10 10
1054 2a. Volleyball 15 10
1055 3a. Football (vert) 40 10
1056 12a. Buzkashi 45 10
1057 14a. Weightlifting 55 10
1058 18a. Wrestling 55 10
1059 25a. Pigsticking 75 10

467 Fruit Stall

1985. World Food Day.
1060 **467** 25a. multicoloured 75 10

468 Flags and U.N. Building, New York
469 Black-billed Magpie

1985. 40th Anniv of United Nations Organization.
1061 **468** 22a. multicoloured 75 10

1985. Birds. Multicoloured.
1062 2a. Type **469** 15 10
1063 4a. Green woodpecker 75 35
1064 8a. Common pheasants 80 35
1065 13a. Bluethroat, Eurasian goldfinch and hoopoe 1·25 65
1066 18a. Peregrine falcons 1·50 75
1067 25a. Red-legged partridge 2·10 1·10
1068 30a. Eastern white pelicans (horiz) 2·75 1·25

470 Leopard and Cubs

1985. World Wildlife Fund. The Leopard. Mult.
1070 2a. Type **470** 10 10
1071 9a. Head of leopard 35 10
1072 11a. Leopard 55 10
1073 15a. Leopard cub 85 10

471 Triumph 650 and Big Ben Tower

1985. Motorcycles. Multicoloured.
1074 2a. Type **471** 10 10
1075 4a. Motobecane and Eiffel Tower, Paris 15 10
1076 8a. Bultaco motorcycles and Don Quixote monument, Madrid 25 10
1077 13a. Honda and Mt. Fuji, Japan 40 10
1078 18a. Jawa and Old Town Hall clock, Prague 50 10
1079 25a. MZ motorcycle and T.V. Tower, Berlin 70 10
1080 30a. Motorcycle and Colosseum, Rome 85 10

472 Crowd with Flags

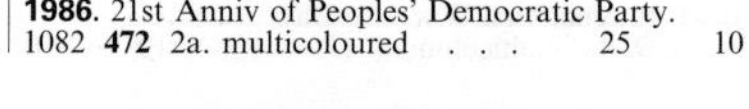

1986. 21st Anniv of Peoples' Democratic Party.
1082 **472** 2a. multicoloured 25 10

473 Lenin writing

1986. 27th Soviet Communist Party Congress, Moscow.
1083 **473** 25a. multicoloured 70 10

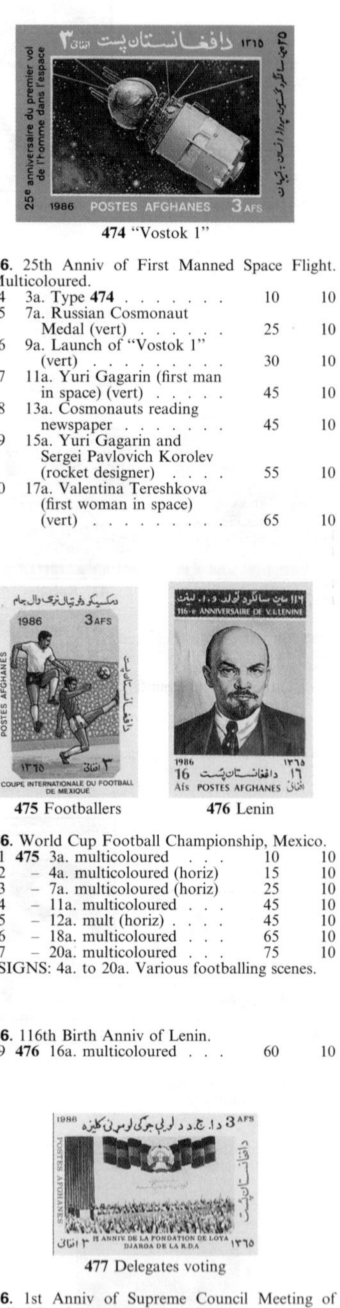

474 "Vostok 1"

1986. 25th Anniv of First Manned Space Flight. Multicoloured.
1084 3a. Type **474** 10 10
1085 7a. Russian Cosmonaut Medal (vert) 25 10
1086 9a. Launch of "Vostok 1" (vert) 30 10
1087 11a. Yuri Gagarin (first man in space) (vert) 45 10
1088 13a. Cosmonauts reading newspaper 45 10
1089 15a. Yuri Gagarin and Sergei Pavlovich Korolev (rocket designer) 55 10
1090 17a. Valentina Tereshkova (first woman in space) (vert) 65 10

475 Footballers
476 Lenin

1986. World Cup Football Championship, Mexico.
1091 **475** 3a. multicoloured 10 10
1092 – 4a. multicoloured (horiz) 15 10
1093 – 7a. multicoloured (horiz) 25 10
1094 – 11a. multicoloured 45 10
1095 – 12a. mult (horiz) 45 10
1096 – 18a. multicoloured 65 10
1097 – 20a. multicoloured 75 10
DESIGNS: 4a. to 20a. Various footballing scenes.

1986. 116th Birth Anniv of Lenin.
1099 **476** 16a. multicoloured 60 10

477 Delegates voting

1986. 1st Anniv of Supreme Council Meeting of Tribal Leaders.
1100 **477** 3a. brown, red and blue 25 10

478 Flags and Crowd
479 Worker with Cogwheel and Globe

1986. 8th Anniv of Sawr Revolution.
1101 **478** 8a. multicoloured 30 10

1986. Labour Day.
1102 **479** 5a. multicoloured 25 10

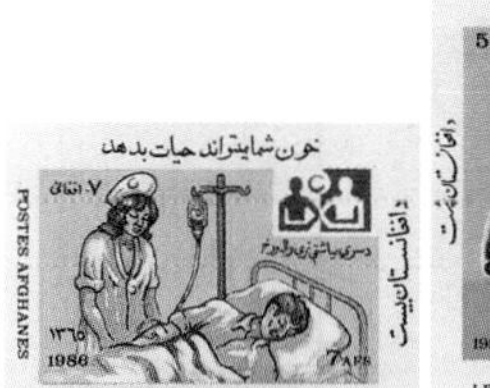

480 Patient receiving Blood Transfusion

481 St. Bernard

1986. International Red Cross/Crescent Day.
1103 **480** 7a. multicoloured . . . 45 10

1986. Pedigree Dogs. Multicoloured.
1104 5a. Type **481** 20 10
1105 7a. Rough collie 25 10
1106 8a. Spaniel 35 10
1107 9a. Long-haired dachshund 35 10
1108 11a. German shepherd 45 10
1109 15a. Bulldog 60 10
1110 20a. Afghan hound 85 10

482 Tiger Barb

483 Mother and Children

1986. Fishes. Multicoloured.
1111 5a. Type **482** 25 15
1112 7a. Mbuna 45 15
1113 8a. Clown loach 55 15
1114 9a. Lisa 65 15
1115 11a. Figure-eight pufferfish 80 15
1116 15a. Six-barred distichodus 1·10 15
1117 20a. Sail-finned molly 1·40 15

1986. World Children's Day. Multicoloured.
1118 1a. Type **483** 10 10
1119 3a. Woman holding boy and emblem 15 10
1120 9a. Circle of children on map (horiz) 30 10

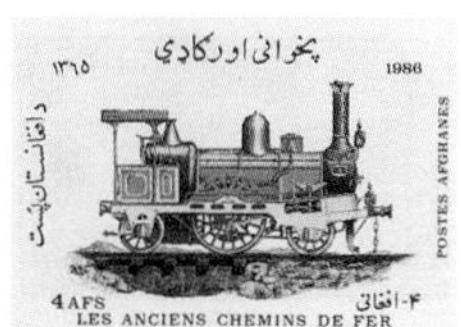

484 Italian Birkenhead Locomotive

1986. 19th-century Railway Locomotives. Mult.
1121 4a. Type **484** 40 10
1122 5a. Norris locomotive 60 10
1123 6a. Stephenson "Patentee" type locomotive 70 10
1124 7a. Bridges Adams locomotive 90 10
1125 8a. Ansoldo locomotive 1·10 10
1126 9a. Locomotive "St. David" 1·50 10
1127 11a. Jones & Potts locomotive 2·00 15

485 Cobra

1986. Animals. Multicoloured.
1128 3a. Type **485** 10 10
1129 4a. Lizards (vert) 10 10
1130 5a. Praying mantis 15 10
1131 8a. Beetle (vert) 20 15
1132 9a. Spider 25 20
1133 10a. Snake 25 20
1134 11a. Scorpions 25 20

Nos. 1130/2 and 1134 are wrongly inscr "Les Reptiles".

486 Profiles on Globe

1986. World Youth Day.
1135 **486** 15a. multicoloured . . . 90 65

487 National Monuments

1986. Independence Day.
1136 **487** 10a. multicoloured . . . 40 10

488 11th-century Ship

1986. "Stockholmia 86" International Stamp Exhibition. Sailing Ships. Multicoloured.
1137 4a. Type **488** 40 25
1138 5a. Roman galley 55 25
1139 6a. English royal kogge 85 25
1140 7a. Early dhow 90 25
1141 8a. Nao 1·00 25
1142 9a. Ancient Egyptian ship 1·10 25
1143 11a. Medieval galeasse 1·10 25

489 Tribesmen

490 State Arms

1986. Pashtunistan Day.
1145 **489** 4a. multicoloured . . . 25 10

1986. Supreme Council Meeting of Tribal Leaders.
1146 **490** 3a. gold, blue and black 25 10

491 Labourer reading

492 Dove and U.N. Emblem

1986. World Literacy Day.
1147 **491** 2a. multicoloured . . . 20 10

1986. International Peace Year.
1148 **492** 12a. black and blue . . . 40 10

493 Tulips, Flame and Man with Rifle

494 Crowd and Flags

1986. Afghanistan Youth Day.
1149 **493** 3a. red and black . . . 25 10

1987. 9th Anniv of Sawr Revolution.
1150 **494** 3a. multicoloured . . . 25 10

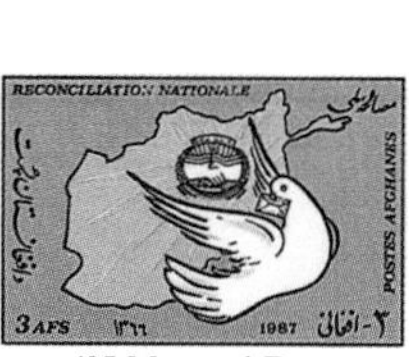

495 Map and Dove

496 Oral Rehydration

1987. National Reconciliation.
1151 **495** 3a. multicoloured . . . 25 10

1987. International Children's Day. Multicoloured.
1152 1a. Type **496** 10 10
1153 5a. Weighing babies 15 10
1154 9a. Vaccinating babies 25 10

497 Conference Delegates

498 "Pieris sp."

1987. 1st Anniv of Tribal Conference.
1155 **497** 5a. multicoloured . . . 25 10

1987. Butterflies and Moths. Multicoloured.
1156 7a. Type **498** 30 20
1157 9a. Brimstone and unidentified butterfly 35 20
1158 10a. Garden tiger moth (horiz) 40 25
1159 12a. "Parnassius sp." 45 25
1160 15a. Butterfly (unidentified) (horiz) 60 40
1161 22a. Butterfly (unidentified) (horiz) 65 40
1162 25a. Butterfly (unidentified) 75 45

499 People on Hand

1987. 1st Local Government Elections.
1163 **499** 1a. multicoloured . . . 20 10

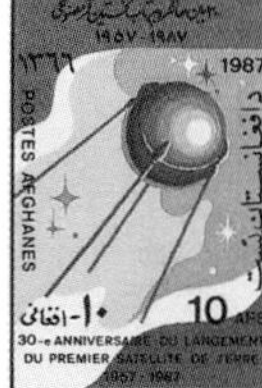

501 "Sputnik 1"

502 Old and Modern Post Offices

1987. 30th Anniv of Launch of "Sputnik 1" (first artificial satellite). Multicoloured.
1165 10a. Type **501** 35 10
1166 15a. Rocket launch 45 10
1167 25a. "Soyuz"–"Salyut" space complex 65 10

1987. World U.P.U. Day.
1168 **502** 22a. multicoloured . . . 75 10

503 Monument and Arch of Paghman

1987. Independence Day.
1169 **503** 3a. multicoloured . . . 20 10

504 "Communications"

1987. United Nations Day.
1170 **504** 42a. multicoloured . . . 3·75 75

505 Lenin

506 Castor Oil Plant

1987. 70th Anniv of Russian Revolution.
1171 **505** 25a. multicoloured . . . 95 10

1987. Plants. Multicoloured.
1172 3a. Type **506** 15 10
1173 6a. Liquorice 30 10
1174 9a. Camomile 40 10
1175 14a. Thorn apple 60 10
1176 18a. Chicory 80 10

507 Field Mice

508 Four-stringed Instrument

1987. Mice. Multicoloured.
1177 2a. Type **507** 15 10
1178 4a. Brown and white mice (horiz) 20 10
1179 8a. Ginger mice (horiz) 25 10
1180 16a. Black mice (horiz) 45 10
1181 20a. Spotted and ginger mice (horiz) 55 10

1988. Musical Instruments. Multicoloured.
1182 1a. Type **508** 10 10
1183 3a. Drums 15 10
1184 5a. Two-stringed instruments with two pegs 20 10
1185 15a. Two-stringed instrument with ten pegs 45 10
1186 18a. Two-stringed instruments with fourteen or ten pegs 60 10
1187 25a. Four-stringed bowed instruments 85 10
1188 33a. Two-stringed bowed instruments 1·25 10

509 Mixed Arrangement

510 Emblems and Means of Communication

1988. Flowers. Multicoloured.
1189 3a. Type **509** 15 10
1190 5a. Tulips (horiz) 20 10
1191 7a. Mallows 25 10
1192 9a. Small mauve flowers 35 10
1193 12a. Marguerites 50 10
1194 15a. White flowers 65 10
1195 24a. Red and blue flowers (horiz) 1·00 10

1988. 60th Anniv of Membership of U.P.U. and I.T.U.
1196 **510** 20a. multicoloured . . . 65 10

511 Tank Monument, Kabul, and Flags

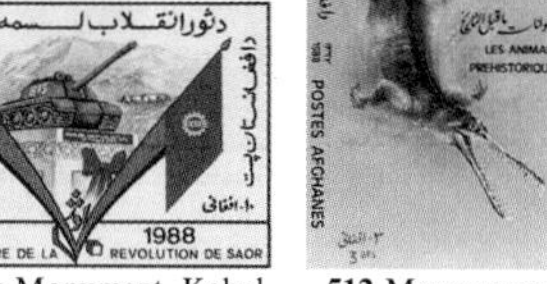

512 Mesosaurus

1988. 10th Anniv of Sawr Revolution.
1197 **511** 10a. multicoloured . . . 40 10

1988. Prehistoric Animals. Multicoloured.
1198 3a. Type **512** 15 10
1199 5a. Styracosaurus (horiz) 25 10
1200 10a. Uintatherium (horiz) 45 10
1201 15a. Protoceratops (horiz) 65 10
1202 20a. Stegosaurus (horiz) 85 10

1203 25a. Ceratosaurus . . . . . 1·10 10
1204 30a. Moa ("Dinornis maximus") . . . . 2·00 1·25

513 Baskets and Bowl of Fruit

1988. Fruit. Multicoloured.
1205 2a. Type **513** 10 10
1206 4a. Baskets of fruit 15 10
1207 7a. Large basket of fruit . . 25 10
1208 8a. Bunch of grapes on branch (vert) 25 10
1209 16a. Buying fruit from market stall 45 10
1210 22a. Arranging fruit on market stall 65 10
1211 25a. Stallholder weighing fruit (vert) 80 10

514 Memorial Pillar of Knowledge and Ignorance, Kabul

515 Heads encircled with Rope

1988. Independence Day.
1212 **514** 24a. multicoloured . . . 90 10

1988. Pashtunistan Day.
1213 **515** 23a. multicoloured . . . 80 10

516 Flags and Globe

517 Anniversary Emblem

1988. Afghan–Soviet Space Flight.
1214 **516** 32a. multicoloured . . . 90 10

1988. 125th Anniv of International Red Cross.
1215 **517** 10a. multicoloured . . . 50 10

518 Rocket and V. Tereshkova

1988. 25th Anniv of First Woman Cosmonaut Valentina Tereshkova's Space Flight. Mult.
1216 10a. Type **518** 80 20
1217 15a. Bird, globe and rocket (vert) 65 10
1218 25a. "Vostok 6" and globe 90 10

519 Decorated Metal Vessels

520 Indian Flag and Nehru

1988. Traditional Crafts. Multicoloured.
1219 2a. Type **519** 10 10
1220 4a. Pottery 15 10
1221 5a. Clothing (vert) 20 10
1222 9a. Carpets 25 10
1223 15a. Bags 45 10
1224 23a. Jewellery 65 10
1225 50a. Furniture . . . . . . 1·25 10

1988. Birth Centenary of Jawaharlal Nehru (Indian statesman).
1226 **520** 40a. multicoloured . . . 1·50 25

521 Emeralds

522 Ice Skating

1988. Gemstones. Multicoloured.
1227 13a. Type **521** 60 15
1228 37a. Lapis lazuli . . . . . 1·40 25
1229 40a. Rubies . . . . 1·75 25

1988. Winter Olympic Games, Calgary. Mult.
1230 2a. Type **522** 10 10
1231 5a. Slalom 20 10
1232 9a. Two-man bobsleigh . . 35 10
1233 22a. Biathlon 65 10
1234 37a. Speed skating . . . . 1·40 20

523 Old City

1988. International Campaign for Preservation of Old Sana'a, Yemen.
1236 **523** 32a. multicoloured . . . 90 10

524 Emblem

1989. 2nd Anniv of Move for Nat Reconciliation.
1237 **524** 4a. multicoloured . . . 20 10

525 Bishop and Game from "The Three Ages of Man" (attr. Estienne Porchier)

1989. Chess. Multicoloured.
1238 2a. Type **525** 10 10
1239 3a. Faience queen and 14th century drawing of Margrave Otto IV of Brandenburg and his wife playing chess 20 10
1240 4a. French king and game 25 10
1241 7a. King and game 35 10
1242 16a. Knight and game . . . 55 10
1243 24a. Arabian knight and "Great Chess" 85 10
1244 45a. Bishop and teaching of game . . . . 1·40 15

Nos. 1240/4 show illustrations from King Alfonso X's "Book of Chess, Dice and Tablings".

526 "The Old Jew"

527 Euphrates Jerboa

1989. Picasso Paintings. Multicoloured.
1245 4a. Type **526** 25 10
1246 6a. "The Two Harlequins" 25 10
1247 8a. "Portrait of Ambrouse Vollar" 25 10
1248 22a. "Majorcan Woman" 65 10
1249 35a. "Acrobat on Ball" . . 1·25 15

1989. Animals. Multicoloured.
1251 3a. Type **527** 20 10
1252 4a. Asiatic wild ass 25 10
1253 14a. Lynx 60 10
1254 35a. Lammergeier . . . . . 2·40 1·40
1255 44a. Markhor . . . . 1·50 20

528 Bomb breaking, Dove and Woman holding Wheat

529 Cattle

1989. International Women's Day (1988).
1257 **528** 8a. multicoloured . . . 25 10

1989. Farmers' Day. Multicoloured.
1258 1a. Type **529** 10 10
1259 2a. Ploughing with oxen and tractors 10 10
1260 3a. Picking cotton 10 10

530 Dish Aerial

1989. World Meteorology Day. Multicoloured.
1261 27a. Type **530** . . . . . . 1·00 15
1262 32a. World Meteorological Organization emblem and state arms . . . . 1·25 15
1263 40a. Data-collecting equipment (vert) . . . . 1·50 15

531 Rejoicing Crowd

1989. 11th Anniv of Sawr Revolution.
1264 **531** 20a. multicoloured . . . 75 10

532 Outdoor Class

533 Eiffel Tower and Arc de Triomphe

1989. Teachers' Day.
1265 **532** 42a. multicoloured . . . 1·50 15

1989. Bicentenary of French Revolution.
1266 **533** 25a. multicoloured . . . 90 15

534 Transmission Mast

1989. 10th Anniv of Asia-Pacific Telecommunity.
1267 3a. Type **534** 10 10
1268 27a. Dish aerial . . . . . . 1·00 15

535 National Monuments

536 Pashtu

1989. Independence Day.
1269 **535** 25a. multicoloured . . . 90 15

1989. Pashtunistan Day.
1270 **536** 3a. multicoloured . . . 10 10

537 White Spoonbill

539 Mosque

538 Duchs Tourer, 1910

1989. Birds, Multicoloured.
1271 3a. Type **537** 15 15
1272 5a. Purple swamphen . . . 35 15
1273 10a. Eurasian bittern (horiz) 60 25
1274 15a. Eastern white pelican 80 35
1275 20a. Red-crested pochard . . 1·10 40
1276 25a. Mute swan . . . . . . 1·40 50
1277 30a. Great cormorant (horiz) . . . . 1·60 60

1989. Vintage Cars. Multicoloured.
1278 5a. Type **538** 20 10
1279 10a. Ford Model T touring car, 1911 . . . . 35 10
1280 20a. Renault Type AX two-seater, 1911 . . . . . . 75 10
1281 25a. Russo-Balte tourer, 1911 . . . . 90 15
1282 30a. Fiat 509 tourer, 1926 1·00 15

1989. Multicoloured.
1283 1a. Type **539** . . . .
1284 2a. Minaret, Jam . . . . .
1285 3a. Buzkashi (horiz) . . . .
1286 4a. Airplane over Hindu Kush (horiz) . . . . . .

NEWSPAPER STAMPS

N 35

1928.
N192 N **35** 2p. blue . . . . 3·50 4·50

1929.
N205 N **35** 2p. red 25 45

N 43

1932.
N215 N **43** 2p. red 40 60
N216 2p. black 25 65
N217 2p. green 25 75
N219 2p. red 45 75

N **75** Coat-of-Arms

1939.
N259 N **75** 2p. green 15 55
N260 2p. mauve (no gum) 15 75

1969. As Type N **75**, but larger and with different Pushtu inscr.
N652 100p. green 15 20
N653 150p. brown 15 20

OFFICIAL STAMPS

O 27

O 86

1909.

O173	O 27	(–) red	1·10	1·10

1939. Design 22½ × 28 mm.

O281	O 86	15p. green	85	75
O282		30p. brown	1·25	1·25
O283		45p. red	1·00	1·00
O284		1a. mauve	1·60	1·50

1954. Design 24½ × 31 mm.

O285b	O 86	50p. red	1·00	60

1965. Design 24 × 30½ mm.

O287	O 86	50p. pink	1·25	60

PARCEL POST STAMPS

P 27

1909.

P173	P 27	3s. brown	1·00	1·50
P174		3s. green	1·50	2·50
P175		1k. green	1·50	2·50
P176		1k. red	1·50	2·25
P177		1r. orange	2·75	2·75
P178		1r. grey	20·00	
P179		1r. brown	1·50	1·50
P180		2r. red	2·75	2·75
P181		2r. blue	5·00	5·50

P 28 Old Habibia College, Kabul

1921.

P182	P 28	10p. brown	3·50	4·50
P183		15p. brown	4·50	5·50
P184		30p. purple	8·50	5·50
P185		1r. blue	10·00	10·00

1923. 5th Independence Day. Optd with T 28.

P186	P 28	10p. brown	60·00	
P187		15p. brown	65·00	
P188		30p. purple	£110	

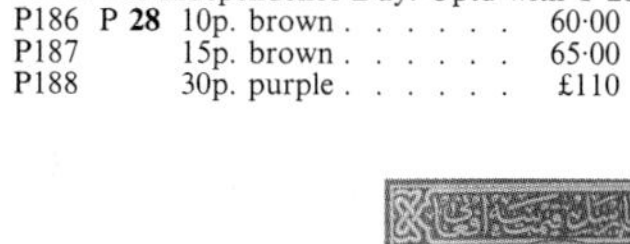

P 35

P 36

1928.

P192	P 35	2a. orange	5·50	4·25
P193	P 36	3a. green	10·00	10·00

1930.

P214	P 35	2a. green	6·50	6·50
P215	P 36	3a. brown	8·50	10·00

REGISTRATION STAMP

R 19

1894. Undated.

R155	R 19	2a. black on green	8·00	7·00

APPENDIX

The following stamps have either been issued in excess of postal needs or have not been available to the public in reasonable quantities at face value. Such stamps may later be given full listing if there is evidence of regular postal use.

1961.

Agriculture Day. Fauna and Flora. 2, 2, 5, 10, 15, 25, 50, 100, 150, 175p.

Child Welfare. Sports and Games. 2, 2, 5, 10, 15, 25, 50, 100, 150, 175p.

U.N.I.C.E.F. Surch on 1961 Child Welfare issue. 2+25, 2+25, 5+25, 10+25, 15p.+25p.

Women's Day. 50, 175p.

Independence Day. Mohamed Nadir Shah. 50, 175p.

International Exhibition, Kabul. 50, 175p.

Pashtunistan Day. 50, 175p.

National Assembly. 50, 175p.

Anti-malaria Campaign. 50, 175p.

King's 47th Birthday. 50, 175p.

Red Crescent Day. Fruits. 2, 2, 5, 10, 15, 25, 50, 100, 150, 175p.

Afghan Red Crescent Fund. 1961 Red Crescent Day issue surch 2+25, 2+25, 5+25, 10+25, 15p.+25p.

United Nations Day. 1, 2, 3, 4, 50, 75, 175p.

Teachers' Day. Flowers and Educational Scenes. 2, 2, 5, 10, 15, 25, 50, 100, 150, 175p.

U.N.E.S.C.O. 1961 Teachers' Day issue surch 2+25, 2+25, 5+25, 10+25, 15p.+25p.

1962.

15th Anniv (1961) of U.N.E.S.C.O. 2, 2, 5, 10, 15, 25, 50, 75, 100p.

Ahmed Shah Baba. 50, 75, 100p.

Agriculture Day. Animals and Products. 2, 2, 5, 10, 15, 25, 50, 75, 100, 125p.

Independence Day. Marching Athletes. 25, 50, 150p.

Women's Day. Postage 25, 50p.; Air 100, 175p.

Pashtunistan Day. 25, 50, 150p.

Malaria Eradication. 2, 2, 5, 10, 15, 25, 50, 75, 100, 150, 175p.

National Assembly. 25, 50, 75, 100, 125p.

4th Asian Games, Djakarta, Indonesia. Postage 1, 2, 3, 4, 5p.; Air 25, 50, 75, 100, 150, 175p.

Children's Day. Sports and Produce. Postage 1, 2, 3, 4, 5p.; Air 75, 150, 200p.

King's 48th Birthday. 25, 50, 75, 100p.

Red Crescent Day. Fruits and Flowers. Postage 1, 2, 3, 4, 5p.; Air 25, 50, 100p.

Boy Scouts' Day. Postage 1, 2, 3, 4p.; Air 25, 50, 75, 100p.

1st Anniv of Hammarskjold's Death. Surch on 1961 U.N.E.S.C.O. issue. 2+20, 2+20, 5+20, 10+20, 15+20, 25+20, 50+20, 75+20, 100p.+20p.

United Nations Day. Postage 1, 2, 3, 4, 5p.; Air 75, 100, 125p.

Teachers' Day. Sport and Flowers. Postage 1, 2, 3, 4, 5p.; Air 100, 150p.

World Meteorological Day. 50, 100p.

1963.

Famous Afghans Pantheon, Kabul. 50, 75, 100p.

Agriculture Day. Sheep and Silkworms. Postage 1, 2, 3, 4, 5p.; Air 100, 150, 200p.

Freedom from Hunger. Postage 2, 3, 300p.; Air 500p.

Malaria Eradication Fund. 1962 Malaria Eradication issue surch 2+15, 2+15, 5+15, 10+15, 15+15, 25+15, 50+15, 75+15, 100+15, 150+15, 175p.+15p.

World Meteorological Day. Postage 1, 2, 3, 4, 5p.; Air 200, 300, 400, 500p.

"GANEFO" Athletic Games, Djakarta, Indonesia. Postage 2, 3, 4, 5, 10p., 9a.; Air 300, 500p.

Red Cross Centenary Postage 2, 3, 4, 5, 10p.; Air 100, 200p., 4, 6a.

Nubian Monuments Preservation. Postage 100, 200, 500p.; Air 5a., 7a.50.

1964.

Women's Day (1963). 2, 3, 4, 5, 10p.

Afghan Boy Scouts and Girl Guides. Postage 2, 3, 4, 5, 10p.; Air 2, 2, 2a.50, 3, 4, 5, 12a.

Child Welfare Day (1963). Sports and Games. Postage 2, 3, 4, 5, 10p.; Air 200, 300p.

Afghan Red Crescent Society. Postage 100, 200p.; Air 5a., 7a.50.

Teachers' Day (1963). Flowers. Postage 2, 3, 4, 5, 10p.; Air 3a., 3a.50.

United Nations Day (1963). Postage 2, 3, 4, 5, 10p.; Air 100p., 2, 3a.

15th Anniv of Human Rights Declaration. Surch on 1964 United Nations Day issue. Postage 2+50, 3+50, 4+50, 5+50, 10p.+50p.; Air 100p.+50p., 2a.+50p., 3a.+50p.

U.N.I.C.E.F. (dated 1963). Postage 100, 200p.; Air 5a. 7a.50.

Malaria Eradication (dated 1963). Postage 2, 3, 4, 5p., 10p. on 4p.; Air 2, 10a.

AITUTAKI Pt. 1

Island in the South Pacific.

1903. 12 pence = 1 shilling;
20 shillings = 1 pound.
1967. 100 cents = 1 dollar.

A. NEW ZEALAND DEPENDENCY.

The British Government, who had exercised a protectorate over the Cook Islands group since the 1880s, handed the islands, including Aitutaki, to New Zealand administration in 1901. Cook Islands stamps were used from 1932 to 1972.

1903. Pictorial stamps of New Zealand surch **AITUTAKI.** and value in native language.

1	23	½d. green	4·50	6·50
2	42	1d. red	4·75	5·50
4	26	2½d. blue	11·00	12·00
5	28	3d. brown	18·00	15·00
6	31	6d. red	30·00	25·00
7	34	1s. red	55·00	85·00

1911. King Edward VII stamps of New Zealand surch **AITUTAKI.** and value in native language.

9	51	½d. green	1·00	3·25
10	53	1d. red	3·00	10·00
11	51	6d. red	45·00	£100
12		1s. red	55·00	£140

1916. King George V stamps of New Zealand surch **AITUTAKI.** and value in native language.

13a	62	6d. red	7·50	27·00
14		1s. red	20·00	90·00

1917. King George V stamps of New Zealand optd **AITUTAKI.**

19	62	½d. green	1·00	6·00
20	53	1d. red	4·00	27·00
21	62	1½d. grey	3·75	30·00
22		1½d. brown	80	7·00
15a		2½d. blue	1·75	15·00
16a		3d. brown	1·50	24·00
17a		6d. red	4·75	21·00
18a		1s. red	12·00	32·00

1920. As 1920 pictorial stamps of Cook Islands but inscr "AITUTAKI".

30	½d. black and green	2·00	12·00
31	1d. black and red	6·00	7·00
26	1½d. black and brown	6·00	12·00
32	2½d. black and blue	7·50	50·00
27	3d. black and blue	2·50	14·00
28	6d. brown and grey	5·50	14·00
29	1s. black and purple	9·50	16·00

B. PART OF COOK ISLANDS

On 9 August 1972. Aitutaki became a Port of Entry into the Cook Islands. Whilst remaining part of the Cook Islands, Aitutaki has a separate postal service.

1972. Nos. 227/8, 230, 233/4, 238, 240/1, 243 and 244 of Cook Islands optd **Aitutaki.**

33	79	½c. multicoloured	30	80
34	–	1c. multicoloured	70	1·40
35	–	2½c. multicoloured	2·25	7·00
36	–	4c. multicoloured	70	85
37	–	5c. multicoloured	2·50	7·50
38	–	10c. multicoloured	2·50	5·50
39	–	20c. multicoloured	3·75	1·00
40	–	25c. multicoloured	70	1·00
41	–	50c. multicoloured	2·75	2·75
42	–	$1 multicoloured	4·00	5·50

1972. Christmas. Nos. 406/8 of Cook Islands optd **Aitutaki.**

43	130	1c. multicoloured	10	10
44	–	5c. multicoloured	15	15
45	–	10c. multicoloured	15	25

1972. Royal Silver Wedding. As Nos. 413 and 415 of Cook Islands, but inscr "COOK ISLANDS Aitutaki".

46	131	5c. black and silver	3·50	2·75
47	–	15c. black and silver	1·50	1·50

1972. No. 245 of Cook Islands optd **AITUTAKI.**

48	$2 multicoloured	50	75

1972. Nos. 227/8, 230, 233, 234, 238, 240, 241, 243 and 244 of Cook Islands optd **AITUTAKI** within ornamental oval.

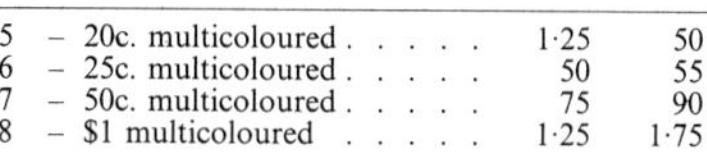

49	79	½c. multicoloured	15	10
50	–	1c. multicoloured	15	10
51	–	2½c. multicoloured	20	10
52	–	4c. multicoloured	25	15
53	–	5c. multicoloured	25	15
54	–	10c. multicoloured	35	25
55	–	20c. multicoloured	1·25	50
56	–	25c. multicoloured	50	55
57	–	50c. multicoloured	75	90
58	–	$1 multicoloured	1·25	1·75

13 "Christ Mocked" (Grunewald)

16 Red Hibiscus and Princess Anne

1973. Easter. Multicoloured.

59	1c. Type **13**	15	10
60	1c. "St. Veronica" (Van der Weyden)	15	10
61	1c. "The Crucified Christ with Virgin Mary, Saints and Angels" (Raphael)	15	10
62	1c. "Resurrection" (Piero della Francesca)	15	10
63	5c. "The Last Supper" (Master of Amiens)	20	15
64	5c. "Condemnation" (Holbein)	20	15
65	5c. "Christ on the Cross" (Rubens)	20	15
66	5c. "Resurrection" (El Greco)	20	15
67	10c. "Disrobing of Christ" (El Greco)	25	15
68	10c. "St. Veronica" (Van Oostsanen)	25	15
69	10c. "Christ on the Cross" (Rubens)	25	15
70	10c. "Resurrection" (Bouts)	25	15

1973. Silver Wedding Coinage. Nos. 417/23 of Cook Islands optd **AITUTAKI.**

71	132	1c. black, red and gold	10	10
72	–	2c. black, blue and gold	10	10
73	–	5c. black, green and silver	15	10
74	–	10c. black, blue and silver	20	10
75	–	20c. black, green and silver	30	15
76	–	50c. black, red and silver	50	30
77	–	$1 black, blue and silver	70	45

1973. 10th Anniv of Treaty Banning Nuclear Testing. Nos. 236, 238, 240 and 243 of Cook Islands optd **AITUTAKI** within ornamental oval and **TENTH ANNIVERSARY CESSATION OF NUCLEAR TESTING TREATY.**

78	8c. multicoloured	15	15
79	10c. multicoloured	15	15
80	20c. multicoloured	30	20
81	50c. multicoloured	70	50

1973. Royal Wedding. Multicoloured.

82	25c. Type **16**	25	10
83	30c. Capt. Mark Phillips and blue hibiscus	25	10
MS84	114 × 65 mm. Nos. 82/3	50	40

17 "Virgin and Child" (Montagna)

1973. Christmas. "Virgin and Child" paintings by artists listed below. Multicoloured.

85	1c. Type **17**	10	10
86	1c. Crivelli	10	10
87	1c. Van Dyck	10	10
88	1c. Perugino	10	10
89	5c. Veronese (child at shoulder)	25	10
90	5c. Veronese (child on lap)	25	10
91	5c. Cima	25	10
92	5c. Memling	25	10
93	10c. Memling	25	10
94	10c. Del Colle	25	10
95	10c. Raphael	25	10
96	10c. Lotto	25	10

18 Rose-branch Murex

1974. Sea Shells. Multicoloured.

97	½c. Type **18**	90	80
98	1c. New Caledonia nautilus	90	80
99	2c. Common or major harp	90	80
100	3c. Striped bonnet	90	80
101	4c. Mole cowrie	90	80

102 5c. Pontifical mitre 90 80
103 8c. Trumpet triton 90 80
104 10c. Venus comb murex . . . 90 80
105 20c. Red-mouth olive . . . 1·25 80
106 25c. Ruddy frog shell . . . . 1·25 80
107 60c. Widest pacific conch . . 4·00 1·25
108 $1 Maple-leaf triton or winged frog shell . . . . . 2·50 1·40
109 $2 Queen Elizabeth II and Marlin-spike auger . . . . 6·00 9·00
110 $5 Queen Elizabeth II and Tiger cowrie . . . . 29·00 10·00

The $2 and $5 are larger, 53 × 25 mm.

19 Bligh and H.M.S. "Bounty"

1974. William Bligh's Discovery of Aitutaki. Multicoloured
114 1c. Type **19** 40 40
115 1c. H.M.S. "Bounty" 40 40
116 5c. Bligh, and H.M.S. "Bounty" at Aitutaki . . . 80 80
117 5c. Aitutaki chart of 1856 . . 80 80
118 8c. Captain Cook and H.M.S. "Resolution" . . . 1·10 70
119 8c. Map of Aitutaki and inset location map . . . . . . 1·10 70

See also Nos. 123/8.

20 Aitutaki Stamps of 1903, Sand Map

1974. Centenary of U.P.U. Multicoloured.
120 25c. Type **20** 65 50
121 50c. Stamps of 1903 and 1920, and map 85 75
MS122 66 × 75 mm. Nos. 120/1 1·00 2·50

1974. Air. As Nos. 114/119 in larger size (46 × 26 mm), additionally inscr "AIR MAIL".
123 10c. Type **19** 60 55
124 10c. H.M.S. "Bounty" . . . 60 55
125 25c. Bligh, and H.M.S. "Bounty" at Aitutaki . . . 70 65
126 25c. Aitutaki chart of 1856 70 65
127 30c. Captain Cook and H.M.S. "Resolution" . . . 80 70
128 30c. Map of Aitutaki and inset location map 80 70

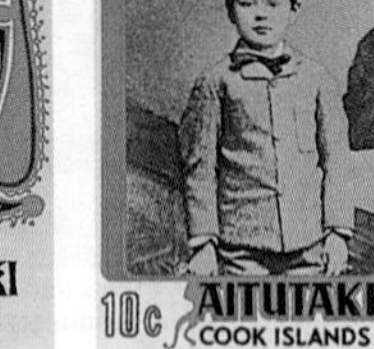

21 "Virgin and Child" (Hugo van der Goes)

22 Churchill as Schoolboy

1974. Christmas. "Virgin and Child" paintings by artists named. Multicoloured.
129 1c. Type **21** 10 10
130 5c. Bellini 10 15
131 8c. Gerard David 10 15
132 10c. Antonello da Messina 10 15
133 25c. Joos van Cleve 20 25
134 30c. Master of the Life of St. Catherine 20 25
MS135 127 × 134 mm. Nos. 129/34 1·40 1·60

1974. Birth Centenary of Sir Winston Churchill. Multicoloured.
136 10c. Type **22** 20 25
137 25c. Churchill as young man 25 40
138 30c. Churchill with troops . . 25 45
139 50c. Churchill painting . . . 30 60
140 $1 Giving "V" sign 40 75
MS141 115 × 108 mm. Nos. 136/40 1·25 1·50

1974. Children's Christmas Fund. Nos. 129/34 surch.
142 **21** 1c.+1c. multicoloured . . . 10 10
143 – 5c.+1c. multicoloured . . . 10 10
144 – 8c.+1c. multicoloured . . . 10 10
145 – 10c.+1c. multicoloured . . 10 10
146 – 25c.+1c. multicoloured . . 20 20
147 – 30c.+1c. multicoloured . . 20 20

24 Soviet and U.S. Flags

1975. "Apollo–Soyuz" Space Project. Mult.
148 25c. Type **24** 30 20
149 50c. Daedalus with space capsule 40 30
MS150 123 × 61 mm. Nos. 148/9 1·25 1·10

25 St. Francis

26 "The Descent" (detail, 15th-century Flemish School)

1975. Christmas. Multicoloured.
151 6c. Type **25** 10 10
152 6c. Madonna and Child . . . 10 10
153 6c. St. John 10 10
154 7c. King and donkey 10 10
155 7c. Madonna, Child and King 10 10
156 7c. Kings with gifts 10 10
157 15c. Madonna and Child . . 15 15
158 15c. St. Onufrius 15 15
159 15c. John the Baptist 15 15
160 20c. Shepherd and cattle . . 20 15
161 20c. Madonna and Child . . 20 15
162 20c. Shepherds 20 15
MS163 104 × 201 mm. Nos. 151/62 2·25 2·50

Stamps of the same value were printed together, se-tenant, each strip forming a composite design of a complete painting as follows: Nos. 151/3, "Madonna and Child with Saints Francis and John" (Lorenzetti); 154/6, "Adoration of the Kings" (Van der Weyden); 157/9, "Madonna and Child Enthroneth with Saints Onufrius and John the Baptist" (Montagna); 160/2, "Adoration of the Shepherds" (Reni).

1975. Children's Christmas Fund. Nos. 151/62 surch.
164 **25** 6c.+1c. multicoloured . . . 10 10
165 – 6c.+1c. multicoloured . . . 10 10
166 – 6c.+1c. multicoloured . . . 10 10
167 – 7c.+1c. multicoloured . . . 10 10
168 – 7c.+1c. multicoloured . . . 10 10
169 – 7c.+1c. multicoloured . . . 10 10
170 – 15c.+1c. multicoloured . . 15 15
171 – 15c.+1c. multicoloured . . 15 15
172 – 15c.+1c. multicoloured . . 15 15
173 – 20c.+1c. multicoloured . . 20 20
174 – 20c.+1c. multicoloured . . 20 20
175 – 20c.+1c. multicoloured . . 20 20

1976. Easter. Multicoloured.
176 15c. Type **26** 15 10
177 30c. "The Descent" (detail) 20 15
178 35c. "The Descent" (detail) 25 20
MS179 87 × 67 mm. Nos. 176/8 forming a complete picture of "The Descent" . . . . 1·00 1·25

27 Left Detail

30 "The Visitation"

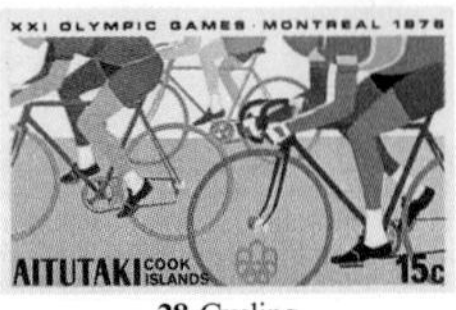

28 Cycling

1976. Bicentenary of American Revolution. Paintings by John Turnbull.
180 **27** 30c. multicoloured 25 10
181 – 30c. multicoloured 25 10
182 – 30c. multicoloured 25 10
183 – 35c. multicoloured 25 15
184 – 35c. multicoloured 25 15
185 – 35c. multicoloured 25 15
186 – 50c. multicoloured 25 15
187 – 50c. multicoloured 25 15
188 – 50c. multicoloured 25 15
MS189 132 × 120 mm. Nos. 180/8 1·75 1·10

PAINTINGS: Nos. 180/2, "The Declaration of Independence"; 183/5, "The Surrender of Lord Cornwallis at Yorktown"; 186/8, "The Resignation of General Washington".

Stamps of the same value were printed together, se-tenant, each strip forming a composite design of the whole painting.

1976. Olympic Games, Montreal. Multicoloured.
190 15c. Type **28** 60 15
191 35c. Sailing 45 20
192 60c. Hockey 90 25
193 70c. Sprinting 70 30
MS194 107 × 97 mm. Nos. 190/3 1·90 1·25

1976. Royal Visit to the U.S.A. Nos. 190/3 optd **ROYAL VISIT JULY 1976**.
195 **28** 15c. multicoloured 50 15
196 – 35c. multicoloured 45 25
197 – 60c. multicoloured 80 40
198 – 70c. multicoloured 70 45
MS199 107 × 97 mm. Nos. 195/8 2·00 1·25

1976. Christmas.
200 **30** 6c. gold and green 10 10
201 – 6c. gold and green 10 10
202 – 7c. gold and purple 10 10
203 – 7c. gold and purple 10 10
204 – 15c. gold and blue 10 10
205 – 15c. gold and blue 10 10
206 – 20c. gold and violet . . . 15 15
207 – 20c. gold and violet . . . 15 15
MS208 128 × 96 mm. As Nos. 200/7 but with borders on three sides 1·00 1·40

DESIGNS: No. 201, Angel; 202, Angel; 203, Shepherds; 204, Joseph; 205, Mary and the Child; 206, Wise Man; 207, Two Wise Men.

Stamps of the same value were printed together, se-tenant, each pair forming a composite design.

1976. Children's Christmas Fund. Nos. 200/7 surch.
209 **30** 6c.+1c. gold and green . . 10 10
210 – 6c.+1c. gold and green . . 10 10
211 – 7c.+1c. gold and purple . . 10 10
212 – 7c.+1c. gold and purple . . 10 10
213 – 15c.+1c. gold and blue . . 15 15
214 – 15c.+1c. gold and blue . . 15 15
215 – 20c.+1c. gold and violet . . 15 15
216 – 20c.+1c. gold and violet . . 15 15
MS217 128 × 96 mm. As Nos. 209/16 but with a premium of "+2c." and borders on three sides 80 1·40

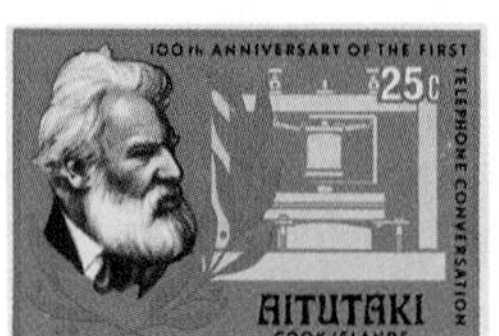

32 Alexander Graham Bell and First Telephone

1977. Centenary (1976) of Telephone.
218 **32** 25c. black, gold and red . . 20 15
219 – 70c. black, gold and lilac 40 40
MS220 116 × 59 mm. As Nos. 218/19 but with different colours 70 1·00

DESIGN: 70c. Satellite and Earth station.

33 "Christ on the Cross" (detail)

1977. Easter. 400th Birth Anniv of Rubens. Mult.
221 15c. Type **33** 45 15
222 20c. "Lamentation for Christ" 60 20
223 35c. "Christ with Straw" . . 75 25

34 Captain Bligh, George III and H.M.S. "Bounty"

1977. Silver Jubilee. Multicoloured.
225 25c. Type **34** 35 35
226 35c. Rev. Williams, George IV and Aitutaki Church . . 40 40
227 50c. Union Jack, Queen Victoria and island map . . 45 45
228 $1 Balcony scene, 1953 . . . 50 50
MS229 130 × 87 mm. As Nos. 225/8 but with gold borders 1·25 1·25

35 The Shepherds

37 Hawaiian Goddess

1977. Christmas. Multicoloured
230 6c. Type **35** 10 10
231 6c. Angel 10 10
232 7c. Mary, Jesus and ox . . . 10 10
233 7c. Joseph and donkey . . . 10 10
234 15c. Three Kings 10 10
235 15c. Virgin and Child 10 10
236 20c. Joseph 10 10
237 20c. Mary and Jesus on donkey 10 10
MS238 130 × 95 mm. Nos. 230/7 70 1·25

Stamps of the same value were printed together, se-tenant, forming composite designs.

1977. Children's Christmas Fund. Nos. 230/7 surch **+1c**.
239 6c.+1c. Type **35** 10 10
240 6c.+1c. Angel 10 10
241 7c.+1c. Mary, Jesus and ox 10 10
242 7c.+1c. Joseph and donkey 10 10
243 15c.+1c. Three Kings 15 10
244 15c.+1c. Virgin and Child . . 15 10
245 20c.+1c. Joseph 15 10
246 20c.+1c. Mary and Jesus on donkey 15 10
MS247 130 × 95 mm. As Nos. 239/46 but each with premium of "+2c." 70 85

1978. Bicentenary of Discovery of Hawaii. Mult.
248 35c. Type **37** 35 25
249 50c. Figurehead of H.M.S. "Resolution" (horiz) . . . 60 40
250 $1 Hawaiian temple figure . . 70 70
MS251 168 × 75 mm. Nos. 248/50 1·50 1·75

38 "Christ on the Way to Calvary" (Martini)

39 The Yale of Beaufort

1978. Easter. Paintings from the Louvre, Paris. Mult.
252 15c. Type **38** 15 10
253 20c. "Pieta of Avignon" (E. Quarton) 20 10
254 35c. "The Pilgrims at Emmaus" (Rembrandt) . . 25 10
MS255 108 × 83 mm. Nos. 252/4 75 75

1978. Easter. Children's Charity. Designs as Nos. 252/4, but smaller (34 × 26 mm) and without margins, in separate miniature sheets 75 × 58 mm, each with a face value of 50c. + 5c.
MS256 As Nos. 252/4 Set of 3 sheets 1·00 1·00

1978. 25th Anniv of Coronation. Multicoloured.
257 $1 Type **39** 30 50
258 $1 Queen Elizabeth II . . . 30 50
259 $1 Aitutaki ancestral statue 30 50
MS260 98 × 127 mm. Nos 257/9 × 2 75 75

Stamps from No. **MS**260 have coloured borders, the upper row in lavender and the lower in green.

40 "Adoration of the Infant Jesus"

41 "Captain Cook" (Nathaniel Dance)

1978. Christmas. 450th Death Anniv of Durer. Multicoloured.
261 15c. Type **40** 35 15
262 17c. "The Madonna with Child" 40 15

263 30c. "The Madonna with the Iris" 55 20
264 35c. "The Madonna of the Siskin" 60 25
MS265 101 × 109 mm. As Nos. 261/4 but each with premium of "+2c." 1·10 1·00

1979. Death Bicent of Captain Cook. Mult.
266 50c. Type **41** 1·00 80
267 75c. "H.M.S. 'Resolution' and 'Adventure' at Matavai Bay," Tahiti (W. Hodges) 1·75 95
MS268 94 × 58 mm. Nos. 266/7 2·00 2·25

42 Girl with Flowers
43 "Man writing a Letter" (painting by Gabriel Metsu)

1979. International Year of the Child. Multicoloured.
269 30c. Type **42** 15 15
270 35c. Boy playing guitar 20 20
271 65c. Children in canoe 30 30
MS272 104 × 80 mm. As Nos. 269/71, but each with a premium of "+3c." 70 1·00

1979. Death Centenary of Sir Rowland Hill. Multicoloured.
273 50c. Type **43** 45 45
274 50c. Sir Rowland Hill with Penny Black, 1903 ½d. and 1911 1d. stamps 45 45
275 50c. "Girl in Blue reading a Letter" (Jan Vermeer) 45 45
276 65c. "Woman writing a Letter" (Gerard Terborch) 50 50
277 65c. Sir Rowland Hill, with Penny Black, 1903 3d. and 1920 ½d. stamps 50 50
278 65c. "Lady reading a Letter" (Jan Vermeer) 50 50
MS279 151 × 85 mm. 30c. × 6. As Nos. 273/8 1·75 1·75

44 "The Burial of Christ" (left detail) (Quentin Metsys)
45 Einstein as a Young Man

1980. Easter. Multicoloured.
280 20c. Type **44** 40 25
281 30c. "The Burial of Christ" (centre detail) 50 35
282 35c. "The Burial of Christ" (right detail) 65 45
MS283 93 × 71 mm. As Nos. 280/2, but each with premium of "+2c." 75 75

1980. 25th Death Anniv of Albert Einstein (physicist). Multicoloured.
284 12c. Type **45** 50 50
285 12c. Atom and "E=mc²" equation 50 50
286 15c. Einstein in middle-age 55 55
287 15c. Cross over nuclear explosion (Test Ban Treaty, 1963) 55 55
288 20c. Einstein as an old man 65 65
289 20c. Hand preventing atomic explosion 65 65
MS290 113 × 118 mm. Nos 284/9 3·00 3·00

46 Ancestor Figure, Aitutaki
47 "Virgin and Child" (13th century)

1980. 3rd South Pacific Festival of Arts. Mult.
291 6c. Type **46** 10 10
292 6c. Staff god image, Rarotonga 10 10
293 6c. Trade adze, Mangaia 10 10
294 6c. Carved image of Tangaroa, Rarotonga 10 10
295 12c. Wooden image Aitutaki 10 10
296 12c. Hand club, Rarotonga 10 10
297 12c. Carved mace "god", Mangaia 10 10
298 12c. Fisherman's god, Rarotonga 10 10
299 15c. Ti'i image, Aitutaki 15 15
300 15c. Fisherman's god, Rarotonga (different) 15 15
301 15c. Carved mace "god", Cook Islands 15 15
302 15c. Carved image of Tangaroa, Rarotonga (different) 15 15
303 20c. Chief's headdress, Aitutaki 15 15
304 20c. Carved mace "god", Cook Islands (different) 15 15
305 20c. Staff god image, Rarotonga (different) 15 15
306 20c. Carved image of Tangaroa, Rarotonga (different) 15 15
MS307 134 × 194 mm. Nos. 291/306 1·60 1·75

1980. Christmas. Sculptures of "The Virgin and Child". Multicoloured.
308 15c. Type **47** 20 15
309 20c. 14th century 20 15
310 25c. 15th century 20 15
311 35c. 15th century (different) 30 20
MS312 82 × 120 mm. As Nos. 306/11 but each with premium of 2c. 70 80

48 "Mourning Virgin"
49 Gouldian Finch

1981. Easter. Details of Sculpture "Burial of Christ" by Pedro Roldan.
313 **48** 30c. gold and green 25 25
314 – 40c. gold and lilac 30 30
315 – 50c. gold and blue 30 30
MS316 107 × 60 mm. As Nos. 313/15 but each with premium of 2c. 75 85
DESIGNS: 40c. "Christ"; 50c. "Saint John".

1981. Birds (1st series). Multicoloured.
317 1c. Type **49** 45 30
318 1c. Common starling 45 30
319 2c. Golden whistler 50 30
320 2c. Scarlet robin 50 30
321 3c. Rufous fantail 60 30
322 3c. Peregrine falcon 60 30
323 4c. Java sparrow 70 30
324 4c. Barn owl 70 30
325 5c. Tahitian lory 70 30
326 5c. White-breasted wood swallow 70 30
327 6c. Purple swamphen 70 30
328 6c. Feral rock pigeon 70 30
329 10c. Chestnut-breasted mannikin 90 30
330 10c. Zebra dove 90 30
331 12c. Reef heron 1·00 40
332 12c. Common mynah 1·00 40
333 15c. Whimbrel (horiz) 1·25 40
334 15c. Black-browed albatross (horiz) 1·25 40
335 20c. Pacific golden plover (horiz) 1·50 55
336 20c. White tern (horiz) 1·50 55
337 25c. Pacific black duck (horiz) 1·75 70
338 25c. Brown booby (horiz) 1·75 70
339 30c. Great frigate bird (horiz) 2·00 85
340 30c. Pintail (horiz) 2·00 85
341 35c. Long-billed reed warbler 2·25 1·00
342 35c. Pomarine skua 2·25 1·00
343 40c. Buff-banded rail 2·75 1·25
344 40c. Spotted triller 2·75 1·25
345 50c. Royal albatross 3·00 1·50
346 50c. Stephen's lory 3·00 1·50
347 70c. Red-headed parrot-finch 5·50 3·00
348 70c. Orange dove 5·50 3·00
349 $1 Blue-headed flycatcher 5·50 3·75
350 $2 Red-bellied flycatcher 6·50 8·00
351 $4 Red munia 11·00 14·00
352 $5 Flat-billed kingfisher 12·00 16·00
See also Nos. 475/94.

50 Prince Charles
52 Footballers

1981. Royal Wedding. Multicoloured.
391 60c. Type **50** 30 40
392 80c. Lady Diana Spencer 40 55
393 $1.40 Prince Charles and Lady Diana (87 × 70 mm) 60 80

1981. International Year for Disabled Persons. Nos. 391/3 surch **+5c.**
394 60c.+5c. Type **50** 60 90
395 80c.+5c. Lady Diana Spencer 70 1·10
396 $1.40+5c. Prince Charles and Lady Diana 90 1·60

1981. World Cup Football Championship, Spain (1982). Football Scenes. Multicoloured.
397 12c. Ball to left of stamp 50 35
398 12c. Ball to right 50 35
399 15c. Ball to right 55 40
400 15c. Ball to left 55 40
401 20c. Ball to left 55 50
402 20c. Ball to right 55 50
403 25c. Type **52** 60 55
404 25c. "ESPANA 82" inscription 60 55
MS405 100 × 137 mm. 12c.+2c., 15c.+2c., 20c.+2c., 25c.+2c., each × 2. As Nos. 397/404 3·50 3·00

53 "The Holy Family"
54 Princess of Wales

1981. Christmas. Etchings by Rembrandt. Each brown and gold.
406 15c. Type **53** 45 45
407 30c. "Virgin with Child" 70 70
408 40c. "Adoration of the Shepherds" (horiz) 95 95
409 50c. "The Holy Family" (horiz) 1·25 1·25
MS410 Designs as Nos. 406/9 in separate miniature sheets, 65 × 82 mm or 82 × 65 mm, each with a face value of 80c.+5c. Set of 4 sheets 4·00 3·00

1982. 21st Birthday of Princess of Wales. Mult.
411 70c. Type **54** 2·00 60
412 $1 Prince and Princess of Wales 2·00 75
413 $2 Princess Diana (different) 3·25 1·50
MS414 82 × 91 mm. Nos. 411/13 5·50 2·75

1982. Birth of Prince William of Wales (1st issue). Nos. 391/3 optd.
415 60c. Type **50** 90 70
416 60c. Type **50** 90 70
417 80c. Lady Diana Spencer 1·10 80
418 80c. Lady Diana Spencer 1·10 80
419 $1.40 Prince Charles and Lady Diana 1·25 1·00
420 $1.40 Prince Charles and Lady Diana 1·25 1·00
OPTS: Nos. 415, 417 and 419, **21 JUNE 1982. PRINCE WILLIAM OF WALES.** Nos. 416, 418 and 420, **COMMEMORATING THE ROYAL BIRTH.**

1982. Birth of Prince William of Wales (2nd issue). As Nos. 411/13 but inscr "ROYAL BIRTH 21 JUNE 1982 PRINCE WILLIAM OF WALES".
421 70c. Type **54** 70 60
422 $1 Prince and Princess of Wales 80 75
423 $2 Princess Diana (different) 1·60 1·50
MS424 81 × 91 mm. Nos. 421/3 5·50 3·00

56 "Virgin and Child" (12th-century sculpture)
57 Aitutaki Bananas

1982. Christmas. Religious Sculptures. Multicoloured.
425 18c. Type **56** 60 60
426 36c. "Virgin and Child" (12th-century) 75 75
427 48c. "Virgin and Child" (13th-century) 90 90
428 60c. "Virgin and Child" (15th-century) 1·25 1·25
MS429 99 × 115 mm. As Nos. 425/8 but each with 2c. charity premium 2·50 2·75

1983. Commonwealth Day. Multicoloured.
430 48c. Type **57** 1·00 50
431 48c. Ancient Ti'i image 1·00 50
432 48c. Tourist canoeing 1·00 50
433 48c. Captain William Bligh and chart 1·00 50

58 Scouts around Campfire

1983. 75th Anniv of Boy Scout Movement. Mult.
434 36c. Type **58** 65 65
435 48c. Scout saluting 75 75
436 60c. Scouts hiking 80 80
MS437 78 × 107 mm. As Nos. 434/6 but each with premium of 3c. 1·50 1·75

1983. 15th World Scout Jamboree, Alberta, Canada. Nos. 434/6 optd **15TH WORLD SCOUT JAMBOREE.**
438 36c. Type **58** 80 45
439 48c. Scout saluting 1·00 55
440 60c. Scouts hiking 1·25 75
MS441 78 × 107 mm. As Nos. 438/40 but each with a premium of 3c. 1·50 2·00

60 Modern Sport Balloon
63 International Mail

1983. Bicentenary of Manned Flight.
442 **60** 18c. multicoloured 55 30
443 – 36c. multicoloured 75 50
444 – 48c. multicoloured 90 60
445 – 60c. multicoloured 1·00 80
MS – 446 64 × 80 mm. $2.50, mult (48½ × 28½ mm) 1·50 2·00
DESIGNS: 36c. to $2.50, showing different modern sports balloons.

1983. Various stamps surch (a) Nos. 335/48 and 352.
447 18c. on 20c. Pacific golden plover 2·75 1·00
448 18c. on 20c. White tern 2·75 1·00
449 36c. on 25c. Pacific black duck 3·75 1·25
450 36c. on 25c. Brown booby 3·75 1·25
451 36c. on 30c. Great frigate bird 3·75 1·25
452 36c. on 30c. Pintail 3·75 1·25
453 36c. on 35c. Long-billed reed warbler 3·75 1·25
454 36c. on 35c. Pomarine skua 3·75 1·25
455 48c. on 40c. Buff-banded rail 4·25 1·25
456 48c. on 40c. Spotted triller 4·25 1·25
457 48c. on 50c. Royal albatross 4·25 1·25
458 48c. on 50c. Stephen's lory 4·25 1·25
459 72c. on 70c. Red-headed parrot finch 7·50 2·50
460 72c. on 70c. Orange dove 7·50 2·50
461 $5.60 on $5 Flat-billed kingfisher (vert) 21·00 10·00

(b) Nos. 392/3 and 412/3.
462 96c. on 80c. Lady Diana Spencer 3·00 2·50
463 96c. on $1 Prince and Princess of Wales 2·75 2·00
464 $1.20 on $1.40 Prince Charles and Lady Diana 3·00 2·50
465 $1.20 on $2 Princess Diana 2·75 2·00

1983. World Communications Year. Multicoloured.
466 48c. Type **63** 65 50
467 60c. Telecommunications 95 70
468 96c. Space satellite 1·40 1·00
MS469 126 × 53 mm. Nos. 466/8 2·50 2·50

64 "Madonna of the Chair"

1983. Christmas. 500th Birth Anniv of Raphael. Multicoloured.
470 36c. Type **64** 75 40
471 48c. "The Alba Madonna" 90 50
472 60c. "Conestabile Madonna" 1·25 70
MS473 95 × 116 mm. Nos. 470/2, but each with a premium of 3c. 2·75 1·40

1983. Christmas. 500th Brith Anniv of Raphael. Children's Charity. Designs as Nos. 470/2 in separate miniature sheets 46 × 47 mm, but with different frames and a face value of 85c.+5c. Imperf.
MS474 As Nos. 470/2 Set of 3 sheets 3·75 2·75

65 Gouldian Finch **66** Javelin throwing

1984. Birds (2nd series). Multicoloured.
475 2c. Type **65** . . . . 1·75 1·00
476 3c. Common starling . . . . 1·75 1·00
477 5c. Scarlet robin . . . . . . 1·75 1·10
478 10c. Golden whistler . . . . 2·25 1·10
479 12c. Rufous fantail . . . . . 2·25 1·10
480 18c. Peregrine falcon . . . . 2·25 1·50
481 24c. Barn owl . . . . 2·25 1·50
482 30c. Java sparrow . . . . . 2·25 1·50
483 36c. White-breasted wood swallow . . . . 2·25 1·50
484 48c. Tahitian lory . . . . . 2·25 1·50
485 50c. Feral rock pigeon . . . 2·50 2·25
486 60c. Purple swamphen . . . 2·50 2·25
487 72c. Zebra dove . . . . . . 3·00 2·25
488 96c. Chestnut-breasted mannikin . . . . 3·00 2·25
489 $1.20 Common mynah . . . 3·00 3·25
490 $2.10 Reef heron . . . . . . 4·00 3·75
491 $3 Blue-headed flycatcher . . 6·50 6·00
492 $4.20 Red-bellied flycatcher 3·75 8·00
493 $5.60 Red munia . . . . . . 4·50 8·50
494 $9.60 Flat-billed kingfisher 7·50 11·00

1984. Olympic Games. Los Angeles. Multicoloured.
495 36c. Type **66** 35 35
496 48c. Shot-putting 40 45
497 60c. Hurdling 45 55
498 $2 Basketball . . . . 1·75 1·50
MS499 88 × 117 mm. As Nos. 495/8, but each with a charity premium of 5c. 3·50 3·50
DESIGNS: 48c. to $2, show Memorial Coliseum and various events.

1984. Olympic Gold Medal Winners. Nos. 495/8 optd.
500 36c. Type **66** (optd **Javelin Throw Tessa Sanderson Great Britain**) 35 35
501 48c. Shot-putting (optd **Shot Put Claudia Losch Germany**) 40 45
502 60c. Hurdling (optd **Heptathlon Glynis Nunn Australia**) 45 55
503 $2 Basketball (optd **Team Basketball United States**) 1·10 1·50

67 Captain William Bligh and Chart

1984. "Ausipex" International Stamp Exhibition, Melbourne. Multicoloured.
504 60c. Type **67** . . . . 3·75 3·50
505 96c. H.M.S. "Bounty" and map . . . . 3·75 3·75
506 $1.40 Aitutaki stamps of 1974, 1979 and 1981 with map . . . . 3·75 4·00
MS507 85 × 113 mm. As Nos. 504/6, but each with a premium of 5c. 7·50 4·00

1984. Birth of Prince Henry (1st issue). No. 391 optd **15-9-84 Birth Prince Henry** and surch also.
508 $3 on 60c. Type **50** . . . . 2·25 3·25

69 The Annunciation **70** Princess Diana with Prince Henry

1984. Christmas. Details from Altarpiece, St Paul's Church, Palencia, Spain. Multicoloured.
509 36c. Type **69** 30 35
510 48c. The Nativity 40 45
511 60c. The Epiphany 45 50
512 96c. The Flight into Egypt 75 80
MS513 Designs as Nos. 509/12 in separate miniature sheets, each 45 × 53 mm and with a face value of 90c.+7c. Imperf. Set of 4 sheets 2·50 3·25

1984. Birth of Prince Henry (2nd issue). Mult.
514 48c. Type **70** . . . . 2·50 2·00
515 60c. Prince William with Prince Henry . . . . . . 2·50 2·00
516 $2.10 Prince and Princess of Wales with children . . . 3·25 3·75
MS517 113 × 65 mm. As Nos. 514/16, but each with a face value of 96c.+7c. 7·00 3·25

71 Grey Kingbird ("Gray Kingbird")

1985. Birth Bicentenary of John J. Audubon (ornithologist). Designs showing original paintings. Multicoloured.
518 55c. Type **71** . . . . 1·10 1·10
519 65c. Bohemian waxwing . . . 1·25 1·25
520 75c. Summer tanager . . . . 1·40 1·40
521 95c. Common cardinal ("Cardinal") . . . . 1·50 1·50
522 $1.15 White-winged crossbill 1·90 1·90

72 The Queen Mother, aged Seven

1985. Life and Times of Queen Elizabeth the Queen Mother. Multicoloured.
523 55c. Type **72** 45 50
524 65c. Engagement photograph, 1922 . . . . 50 55
525 75c. With young Princess Elizabeth 60 65
526 $1.30 With baby Prince Charles . . . . 1·00 1·10
MS527 75 × 49 mm. $3 Queen Mother on her 63rd birthday 2·25 2·40

73 "The Calmady Children" (T. Lawrence)

1985. International Youth Year. Multicoloured.
528 75c. Type **73** . . . . 2·75 2·50
529 90c. "Madame Charpentier's Children" (Renoir) . . . . 2·75 2·75
530 $1.40 "Young Girls at Piano" (Renoir) . . . . 3·50 3·75
MS531 103 × 104 mm. As Nos. 528/30, but each with a premium of 10c. 4·75 3·75

74 "Adoration of the Magi" (Giotto) and "Giotto" Spacecraft

1985. Christmas. Appearance of Halley's Comet (1st issue). Multicoloured.
532 95c. Type **74** . . . . 1·50 1·50
533 95c. As Type **74** but showing "Planet A" spacecraft . . . 1·50 1·50
534 $1.15 Type **74** . . . . 1·50 1·50
535 $1.15 As No. 533 . . . . . 1·50 1·50
MS536 52 × 55 mm. $6.40. As Type **74** but without spacecraft (30 × 31 mm). Imperf 13·00 8·50

75 Halley's Comet A.D. 684 (from "Nuremberg Chronicle")

1986. Appearance of Halley's Comet (2nd issue). Multicoloured.
537 90c. Type **75** 90 90
538 $1.25 Halley's Comet, 1066 (from Bayeux Tapestry) . . 1·10 1·10
539 $1.75 Halley's Comet, 1456 (from "Lucerne Chronicles") . . . . 1·50 1·50
MS540 107 × 82 mm. As Nos. 537/9, but each with a face value of 95c. 4·00 2·50
MS541 65 × 80 mm. $4.20, "Melencolia I" (Albrecht Dürer woodcut) (61 × 76 mm). Imperf 5·50 3·50

76 Queen Elizabeth II on Coronation Day (from photo by Cecil Beaton) **78** Prince Andrew and Miss Sarah Ferguson

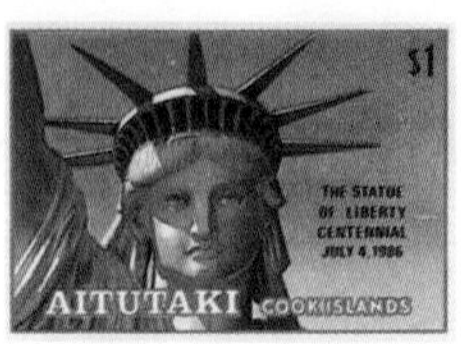

77 Head of Statue of Liberty

1986. 60th Birthday of Queen Elizabeth II.
542 **76** 95c. multicoloured . . . . 1·75 2·00
MS543 58 × 68 mm. $4.20, As T **76**, but showing more of the portrait without oval frame 5·50 5·50

1986. Centenary of Statue of Liberty. Mult.
544 $1 Type **77** . . . . 1·25 1·25
545 $2.75 Statue of Liberty at sunset . . . . 2·75 2·75
MS546 91 × 79 mm. As Nos. 544/5, but each with a face value of $1.25 3·25 2·50

1986. Royal Wedding.
547 **78** $2 multicoloured . . . . . 2·00 2·00
MS548 85 × 70 mm. Type **78** multicoloured 6·50 8·00

1986. "Stampex '86" Stamp Exhibition, Adelaide. No. **MS**507 with "Ausipex" emblems obliterated in gold.
MS549 As Nos. 504/6, but each with a premium of 5c. 10·00 11·00
The "Stampex '86" exhibition emblem is overprinted on the sheet margin.

1986. 86th Brithday of Queen Elizabeth the Queen Mother. Nos. 523/6 in miniature sheet, 132 × 82 mm.
MS550 Nos. 523/6 10·00 9·00

79 "St. Anne with Virgin and Child" **83** Angels

1986. Christmas. Paintings by Durer. Multicoloured.
551 75c. Type **79** . . . . 1·25 1·25
552 $1.35 "Virgin and Child" . . 1·75 1·75
553 $1.95 "The Adoration of the Magi" . . . . 2·25 2·25
554 $2.75 "Madonna of the Rosary" . . . . 3·00 3·00
MS555 88 × 125 mm. As Nos. 551/4, but each with a face value of $1.65 13·00 14·00

1986. Visit of Pope John Paul II to South Pacific. Nos. 551/4 optd **NOVEMBER 21-24 1986 FIRST VISIT TO SOUTH PACIFIC** and surch also.
556 75c.+10c. Type **79** . . . . . 2·75 2·50
557 $1.35+10c. "Virgin and Child" . . . . 3·25 3·00
558 $1.95+10c. "The Adoration of the Magi" . . . . . . 4·00 3·50
559 $2.75+10c. "Madonna of the Rosary" . . . . 5·00 5·00
MS560 88 × 125 mm. As Nos. 556/9, but each with a face value of $1.65+10c. 15·00 14·00

1987. Hurricane Relief Fund. Nos. 544/5, 547, 551/4 and 556/9 surch **HURRICANE RELIEF +50c**.
561 75c.+50c. Type **79** . . . . 3·00 2·75
562 75c.+10c.+50c. Type **79** . . 3·75 3·50
563 $1+50c. Type **77** . . . . . 3·25 3·00
564 $1.35+50c. "Virgin and Child" (Durer) . . . . . 3·50 3·25
565 $1.35+10c.+50c. "Virgin and Child" (Durer) . . . . . . 4·25 4·00
566 $1.95+50c. "The Adoration of the Magi" (Durer) . . . 4·25 4·00
567 $1.95+10c.+50c. "The Adoration of the Magi" (Durer) . . . . 4·75 4·50
568 $2+50c. Type **78** . . . . . 4·25 4·00
569 $2.75+50c. Statue of Liberty at sunset . . . . 4·75 4·50
570 $2.75+50c. "Madonna of the Rosary" (Durer) . . . . . 4·75 4·50
571 $2.75+10c.+50c. "Madonna of the Rosary" (Durer) . . 6·00 5·50

1987. Royal Ruby Wedding. Nos. 391/3 surch **2.50 Royal Wedding 40th Anniv**.
572 $2.50 on 60c. Type **50** . . . 2·00 2·50
573 $2.50 on 80c. Lady Diana Spencer . . . . 2·00 2·50
574 $2.50 on $1.40 Prince Charles and Lady Diana (87 × 70 mm) . . . . . . 2·00 2·50

1987. Christmas. Details of angels from "Virgin with Garland" by Rubens.
575 **83** 70c. multicoloured . . . . 2·00 2·00
576 – 85c. multicoloured . . . . 2·00 2·00
577 – $1.50 multicoloured . . . 2·25 2·25
578 – $1.85 multicoloured . . . 3·25 3·25
MS579 92 × 120 mm. As Nos. 575/8, but each with a face value of 95c. 10·00 11·00
MS580 96 × 85 mm. $6 "Virgin with Garland" (diamond, 56 × 56 mm) 10·00 11·00

84 Chariot Racing and Athletics

1988. Olympic Games, Seoul. Ancient and modern Olympic sports. Multicoloured.
581 70c. Type **84** . . . . 2·25 2·00
582 85c. Greek runners and football . . . . 2·50 2·25
583 95c. Greek wrestling and handball . . . . 2·50 2·25
584 $1.40 Greek hoplites and tennis . . . . 3·25 3·00
MS585 103 × 101 mm. As Nos. 581 and 584, but each with face value of $2 7·00 8·00

1988. Olympic Medal Winners, Los Angeles. Nos. 581/4 optd.
586 70c. Type **84** (optd **FLORENCE GRIFFITH JOYNER UNITED STATES 100 M AND 200 M**) . . . . 2·00 2·00
587 85c. Greek runners and football (optd **GELINDO BORDIN ITALY MARATHON**) . . . . . 2·00 2·00
588 95c. Greek wrestling and handball (optd **HITOSHI SAITO JAPAN JUDO**) . . 2·00 2·00
589 $1.40 Greek hoplites and tennis (optd **STEFFI GRAF WEST GERMANY WOMEN'S TENNIS**) . . 4·00 4·00

85 "Adoration of the Shepherds" (detail)

1988. Christmas. Paintings by Rembrandt. Mult.
590 55c. Type **85** . . . . 2·00 1·75
591 70c. "The Holy Family" . . 2·25 2·00
592 85c. "Presentation in the Temple" . . . . 2·50 2·25
593 95c. "The Holy Family" (different) . . . . 2·50 2·25
594 $1.15 "Presentation in the Temple" (different) . . . 2·75 2·50
MS595 85 × 101 mm. $4.50, As Type **85** but 52 × 34 mm. 5·50 6·50

86 H.M.S. "Bounty" leaving Spithead and King George III

1989. Bicentenary of Discovery of Aitutaki by Captain Bligh. Multicoloured.

596 55c. Type **86** 1·75 1·75
597 65c. Breadfruit plants 2·00 2·00
598 75c. Old chart showing Aitutaki and Captain Bligh 2·25 2·25
599 95c. Native outrigger and H.M.S. "Bounty" off Aitutaki 2·50 2·50
600 $1.65 Fletcher Christian confronting Bligh 3·00 3·00
MS601 94 × 72 mm. $4.20, "Mutineers casting Bligh adrift" (Robert Dodd) (60 × 45 mm) 8·00 9·00

87 "Apollo 11" Astronaut on Moon

1989. 20th Anniv of First Manned Landing on Moon. Multicoloured.

602 75c. Type **87** 2·50 2·00
603 $1.15 Conducting experiment on Moon 3·00 2·50
604 $1.80 Astronaut on Moon carrying equipment 3·75 3·50
MS605 105 × 86 mm. $6.40, Astronaut on Moon with U.S. flag (40 × 27 mm) 8·00 9·00

88 Virgin Mary

91 "Madonna of the Basket" (Correggio)

89 Human Comet striking Earth

1989. Christmas. Details from "Virgin in the Glory" by Titian. Multicoloured.

606 70c. Type **88** 2·25 2·00
607 85c. Christ Child 2·75 2·50
608 95c. Angel 3·00 2·75
609 $1.25 Cherubs 3·50 3·25
MS610 80 × 100 mm. $6 "Virgin in the Glory" (45 × 60 mm) 8·00 9·00

1990. Protection of the Environment. Mult.

611 $1.75 Type **89** 2·25 2·25
612 $1.75 Comet's tail 2·25 2·25
MS613 108 × 43 mm. Nos. 611/12 3·50 4·50

Nos. 611/12 were printed together, se-tenant, forming a composite design.

1990. 90th Birthday of Queen Elizabeth the Queen Mother. No. **MS**550 optd **Ninetieth Birthday**.

MS614 132 × 82 mm. Nos. 523/6 12·00 11·00

1990. Christmas. Religious Paintings. Mult.

615 70c. Type **91** 1·50 1·50
616 85c. "Virgin and Child" (Morando) 1·60 1·60
617 95c. "Adoration of the Child" (Tiepolo) 1·75 1·75
618 $1.75 "Mystic Marriage of St. Catherine" (Memling) 2·50 2·75
MS619 165 × 93 mm. $6 "Donne Triptych" (Memling) (horiz) 11·00 12·00

1990. "Birdpex '90" Stamp Exhibition, Christchurch, New Zealand. Nos. 349/50 optd **Birdpex '90** and bird's head.

620 $1 Blue-headed flycatcher 4·00 4·00
621 $2 Red-bellied flycatcher 5·50 5·50

1991. 65th Birthday of Queen Elizabeth II. No. 352 optd **COMMEMORATING 65th BIRTHDAY OF H.M. QUEEN ELIZABETH II**.

622 $5 Flat-billed kingfisher 11·00 11·00

93 "The Holy Family" (A. Mengs)

1991. Christmas. Religious Paintings. Mult.

623 80c. Type **93** 1·50 1·50
624 90c. "Virgin and the Child" (Lippi) 1·60 1·60
625 $1.05 "Virgin and Child" (A. Durer) 1·75 1·75
626 $1.75 "Adoration of the Shepherds" (G. de la Tour) 2·50 2·75
MS627 79 × 103 mm. "The Holy Family" (Michelangelo) 11·00 12·00

94 Hurdling

1992. Olympic Games, Barcelona. Mult.

628 95c. Type **94** 1·75 1·50
629 $1.25 Weightlifting 2·00 1·75
630 $1.50 Judo 2·50 2·25
631 $1.95 Football 2·75 2·75

95 Vaka Motu Canoe

1992. 6th Festival of Pacific Arts, Rarotonga. Sailing Canoes. Multicoloured.

632 30c. Type **95** 65 65
633 50c. Hamatafua 80 80
634 95c. Alia Kalia Ndrua 1·50 1·50
635 $1.75 Hokule'a Hawaiian 2·25 2·50
636 $1.95 Tuamotu Pahi 2·50 2·75

1992. Royal Visit by Prince Edward. Nos. 632/6 optd **ROYAL VISIT**.

637 30c. Type **95** 85 85
638 50c. Hamatafua 1·25 1·25
639 95c. Alia Kalia Ndrua 2·00 2·00
640 $1.75 Hokule'a Hawaiian 2·75 3·00
641 $1.95 Tuamotu Pahi 2·75 3·00

96 "Virgin's Nativity" (detail) (Reni)

1992. Christmas. Different details from "Virgin's Nativity" by Guido Reni.

642 **96** 80c. multicoloured 1·40 1·40
643 – 90c. multicoloured 1·60 1·60
644 – $1.05 multicoloured 1·75 1·75
645 – $1.75 multicoloured 2·50 2·75
MS646 101 × 86 mm. $6 multicoloured (as $1.05, but larger (36 × 46 mm)) 6·50 8·00

97 The Departure from Palos

1992. 500th Anniv of Discovery of America by Columbus. Multicoloured.

647 $1.25 Type **97** 2·25 2·50
648 $1.75 Map of voyages 2·75 3·00
649 $1.95 Columbus and crew in New World 3·25 3·50

98 Queen Victoria and King Edward VII

1993. 40th Anniv of Coronation. Mult.

650 $1.75 Type **98** 3·25 2·75
651 $1.75 King George V and King George VI 3·25 2·75
652 $1.75 Queen Elizabeth II in 1953 and 1986 3·25 2·75

99 "Madonna and Child" (Nino Pisano)

1993. Christmas. Religious Sculptures. Mult.

653 80c. Type **99** 90 90
654 90c. "Virgin on Rosebush" (Luca della Robbia) 1·00 1·00
655 $1.15 "Virgin with Child and St. John" (Juan Francisco Rustici) 1·40 1·40
656 $1.95 "Virgin with Child" (Miguel Angel) 2·25 2·25
657 $3 "Madonna and Child" (Jacopo della Quercia) (32 × 47 mm) 3·25 3·75

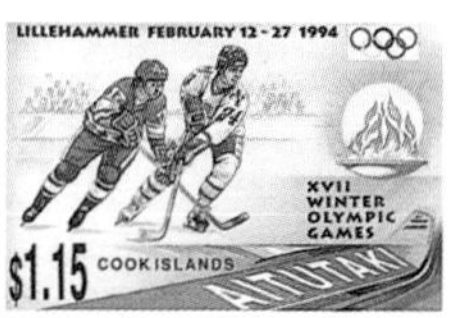

100 Ice Hockey

1994. Winter Olympic Games, Lillehammer. Multicoloured.

658 $1.15 Type **100** 3·25 2·75
659 $1.15 Ski-jumping 3·25 2·75
660 $1.15 Cross-country skiing 3·25 2·75

101 "Ipomoea pes-caprae"

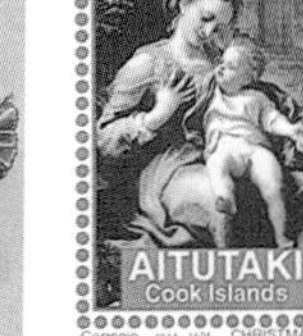

103 "The Madonna of the Basket" (Correggio)

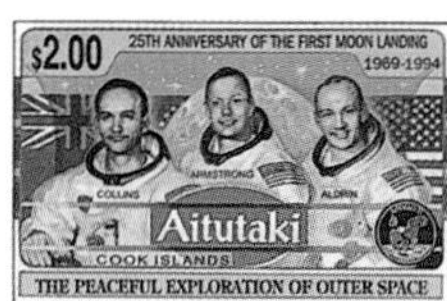

102 Cook Islands and U.S.A. Flags with Astronauts Collins, Armstrong and Aldrin

1994. Flowers. Multicoloured.

661 5c. Type **101** 10 10
662 10c. "Plumeria alba" 10 10
663 15c. "Hibiscus rosa-sinensis" 10 15
664 20c. "Allamanda cathartica" 15 20
665 25c. "Delonix regia" 15 20
666 30c. "Gardenia taitensis" 20 25
667 50c. "Plumeria rubra" 30 35
668 80c. "Ipomoea littoralis" 50 55
669 85c. "Hibiscus tiliaceus" 55 60
670 90c. "Erythrina variegata" 60 65
671 $1 "Solandra nitida" 65 70
672 $2 "Cordia subcordata" 1·25 1·40
673 $3 "Hibiscus rosa-sinensis" (different) (34 × 47mm) 1·90 2·00
674 $5 As $3 (34 × 47mm) 3·25 3·50
675 $8 As $3 (34 × 47mm) 5·00 5·25

Nos. 671/5 include a portrait of Queen Elizabeth II at top right.

1994. 25th Anniv of First Manned Moon Landing. Multicoloured.

676 $2 Type **102** 7·00 7·00
677 $2 "Apollo 11" re-entering atmosphere and landing in sea 7·00 7·00

1994. Christmas. Religious Paintings. Mult.

678 85c. Type **103** 1·00 1·10
679 85c. "The Virgin and Child with Saints" (Memling) 1·00 1·10
680 85c. "The Virgin and Child with Flowers" (Dolci) 1·00 1·10
681 85c. "The Virgin and Child with Angels" (Bergognone) 1·00 1·10
682 90c. "Adoration of the Kings" (Dosso) 1·00 1·10
683 90c. "The Virgin and Child" (Bellini) 1·00 1·10
684 90c. "The Virgin and Child" (Schiavone) 1·00 1·10
685 90c. "Adoration of the Kings" (Dolci) 1·00 1·10

No. 678 is inscribed "Corregio" in error.

104 Battle of Britain

1995. 50th Anniv of End of Second World War. Multicoloured.

686 $4 Type **104** 7·50 7·50
687 $4 Battle of Midway 7·50 7·50

105 Queen Elizabeth the Queen Mother

1995. 95th Birthday of Queen Elizabeth the Queen Mother.

688 **105** $4 multicoloured 7·00 7·50

106 Globe, Doves, United Nations Emblem and Headquarters

1995. 50th Anniv of United Nations.

689 **106** $4.25 multicoloured 5·50 6·50

107 Green Turtle

1995. Year of the Sea Turtle. Multicoloured.

690 95c. Type **107** 1·75 1·75
691 $1.15 Leatherback turtle 2·00 2·00
692 $1.50 Olive Ridley turtle 2·25 2·25
693 $1.75 Loggerhead turtle 2·50 2·50

108 Queen Elizabeth II

1996. 70th Birthday of Queen Elizabeth II.

694 **108** $4.50 multicoloured 8·00 8·00

109 Baron Pierre de Coubertin, Torch and Opening of 1896 Olympic Games

1996. Centenary of Modern Olympic Games. Multicoloured.
695 $2 Type **109** . . . . 4·50 4·50
696 $2 Athletes and American flag, 1996 . . . . 4·50 4·50

110 Princess Elizabeth and Lieut. Philip Mountbatten with King George VI and Queen Elizabeth, 1947

1997. Golden Wedding of Queen Elizabeth and Prince Philip.
697 **110** $2.50 multicoloured . . . 3·75 3·25
MS698 78 × 102 mm. **110** $6 multicoloured 6·50 7·50

111 Diana, Princess of Wales

1998. Diana, Princess of Wales Commemoration.
699 **111** $1 multicoloured . . . . 1·00 1·00
MS700 70 × 100 mm. $4 Diana, Princess of Wales 3·25 3·50

1998. Children's Charities. No. **MS**1427 surch +$1 CHILDREN'S CHARITIES.
MS701 70 × 100 mm. $4 + $1 Diana, Princess of Wales 3·75 4·25

1999. New Millennium. Nos. 632/6 optd **KIA ORANA THIRD MILLENNIUM**.
702 30c. Type **95** 50 50
703 50c. Hamatafua 60 60
704 95c. Alia Kalia Ndrua . . . 85 85
705 $1.75 Hokule'a Hawaiian . . 1·40 1·40
706 $1.95 Tuamotu Pahi . . . . 1·60 1·60

2000. Queen Elizabeth the Queen Mother's 100th Birthday. As T **277** of Cook Islands.
707 $3 blue and brown . . . . . 2·75 2·75
708 $3 multicoloured . . . . . . 2·75 2·75
709 $3 multicoloured . . . . . . 2·75 2·75
710 $3 green and brown . . . . 2·75 2·75
MS711 73 × 100 mm. $7.50, multicoloured 5·50 6·50
DESIGNS: No. 707, Queen Mother in evening dress and tiara; 708, Queen Mother in evening dress standing by table; 709, Queen Mother in Garter robes; 710, King George VI and Queen Elizabeth; **MS**711 Queen Mother holding lilies.

2000. Olympic Games, Sydney. As T **278** of Cook Islands. Multicoloured.
712 $2 Ancient Greek wrestlers 2·00 2·25
713 $2 Modern wrestlers . . . . 2·00 2·25
714 $2 Ancient Greek boxer . . . 2·00 2·25
715 $2 Modern boxers . . . . . 2·00 2·25
MS716 99 × 90 mm. $2.75, Olympic torch and Cook Island canoes 2·25 2·50

113 Blue Lorikeets and Flowers

2002. Endangered Species. Blue Lorikeet. Multicoloured.
717 80c. Type **113** 50 55
718 90c. Lorikeets and bananas 60 65
719 $1.15 Lorikeets on palm leaf 75 80
720 $1.95 Lorikeets in tree trunk 1·25 1·40

OFFICIAL STAMPS

1978. Nos. 98/105, 107/10 and 227/8 optd **O.H.M.S.** or surch also.
O 1 1c. multicoloured 90 10
O 2 2c. multicoloured . . . . . 1·00 10
O 3 3c. multicoloured . . . . . 1·00 10
O 4 4c. multicoloured . . . . . 1·00 10
O 5 5c. multicoloured . . . . . 1·00 10
O 6 8c. multicoloured . . . . . 1·25 10
O 7 10c. multicoloured . . . . . 1·50 15
O 8 15c. on 60c. multicoloured 2·75 20
O 9 18c. on 60c. multicoloured 2·75 20
O10 20c. multicoloured . . . . . 2·75 20
O11 50c. multicoloured . . . . . 1·00 55
O12 60c. multicoloured . . . . . 10·00 70
O13 $1 multicoloured (No. 108) 10·00 80
O14 $2 multicoloured . . . . . 9·00 75
O15 $4 on $1 mult (No. 228) . . 1·75 75
O16 $5 multicoloured . . . . . 11·00 1·25

1985. Nos. 351/2, 430/3, 475 and 477/94 optd **O.H.M.S.** or surch also.
O17 2c. Type **65** 90 90
O18 5c. Scarlet robin . . . . . 1·00 1·00
O19 10c. Golden whistler . . . . 1·25 1·25
O20 12c. Rufous fantail . . . . 1·40 1·40
O21 18c. Peregrine falcon . . . . 2·50 1·75
O22 20c. on 24 c Barn owl . . . 2·50 1·75
O23 30c. Java sparrow . . . . . 1·75 1·25
O24 40c. on 36c. White-breasted wood swallow . . . . . . 1·75 1·25
O25 50c. Feral rock pigeon . . . 1·75 1·25
O26 55c. on 48c. Tahitian lory . 1·75 1·25
O27 60c. Purple swamphen . . . 2·00 1·50
O28 65c. on 72c. Zebra dove . . 2·00 1·50
O38 75c. on 48c. Type **57** . . . 1·00 1·00
O39 75c. on 48c. Ancient Ti'i image . . . . 1·00 1·00
O40 75c. on 48c. Tourist canoeing . . . . 1·00 1·00
O41 75c. on 48c. Captain William Bligh and chart . . . . . 1·00 1·00
O29 80c. on 96c. Chestnut-breasted mannikin . . . . 2·00 1·50
O30 $1.20 Common mynah . . . 2·75 2·25
O31 $2.10 Reef heron . . . . . 3·75 3·50
O32 $3 Blue-headed flycatcher . . 6·00 6·00
O33 $4.20 Red-bellied flycatcher 7·00 7·00
O34 $5.60 Red munia . . . . . 8·00 8·00
O35 $9.60 Flat-billed kingfisher 12·00 12·00
O36 $14 on $4 Red munia (35 × 48 mm) . . . . . 15·00 15·00
O37 $18 on $5 Flat-billed kingfisher (35 × 48 mm) . . 17·00 17·00

AJMAN Pt. 19

One of the Trucial States in the Persian Gulf. On 18 July 1971, seven Gulf sheikhdoms, including Ajman, formed the State of the United Arab Emirates. The federation became effective on 1 August 1972.

1964. 100 naye paise = 1 rupee.
1967. 100 dirhams = 1 riyal.

1 Shaikh Rashid bin Humaid al Naimi and Arab Stallion **2** Kennedy in Football Kit

1964. Multicoloured. (a) Size 34½ × 23 mm.
1 1n.p. Type **1** 15 15
2 2n.p. Regal angelfish 15 15
3 3n.p. Dromedary 15 15
4 4n.p. Yellow-banded angelfish 15 15
5 5n.p. Tortoise 15 15
6 10n.p. Jewel cichlid 25 15
7 15n.p. White stork 40 15
8 20n.p. Black-headed gulls . . . 40 15
9 30n.p. Lanner falcon 40 15

(b) Size 42½ × 27 mm.
10 40n.p. Type **1** 20 20
11 50n.p. Regal angelfish 25 20
12 70n.p. Dromedary 25 25
13 1r. Yellow-banded angelfish 50 30
14 1r.50 Tortoise 50 50
15 2r. Jewel cichlid . . . . . . 1·25 75

(c) Size 53 × 34 mm.
16 3r. White stork . . . . 1·25 25
17 5r. Black-headed gulls . . . . 1·60 1·50
18 10r. Lanner falcon . . . . . 3·50 1·75

1964. Pres. Kennedy Commem. Perf or imperf.
19 **2** 10n.p. purple and green . . . 15 15
20 – 15n.p. violet and turquoise 15 15
21 – 50n.p. blue and brown . . . 20 20
22 – 1r. turquoise and sepia . . . 35 35
23 – 2r. olive and purple 75 65
24 – 3r. brown and green . . . . 1·25 95
25 – 5r. brown and violet . . . 2·25 2·10
26 – 10r. brown and blue . . . 5·00 3·75
DESIGNS—Various pictures of Kennedy: 15n.p. Diving; 50n.p. As naval officer; 1r. Sailing with Mrs. Kennedy; 2r. With Mrs. Eleanor Roosevelt; 3r. With wife and child; 5r. With colleagues; 10r. Full-face portrait.

3 Start of Race

1965. Olympic Games, Tokyo. Perf or imperf.
27 **3** 5n.p. slate, brown & mauve 15 15
28 – 10n.p. red, bronze and blue 15 15
29 **3** 15n.p. brown, violet & green 15 15
30 – 25n.p. black, blue and red . . 15 15
31 – 50n.p. slate, purple and blue 20 20
32 – 1r. blue, green and purple . . 70 35
33 – 1r.50 purple, violet and green 75 50
34 – 2r. blue, purple and ochre . . 1·25 90
35 – 3r. violet, brown and blue . . 2·25 1·40
36 – 5r. purple, green and yellow 2·50 2·10
DESIGNS: 10n.p., 1r.50, Boxing; 25n.p., 2r. Judo; 50n.p., 5r. Gymnastics; 1, 3r. Sailing.

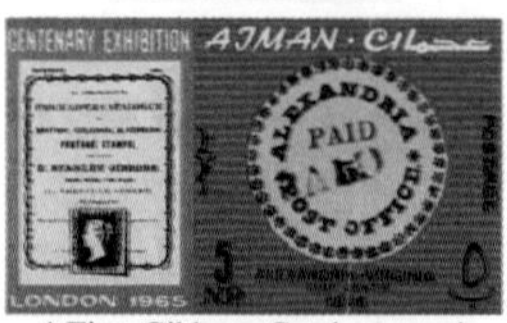

4 First Gibbons Catalogue and Alexandria (U.S.) 5c. Postmaster's Stamp

1965. Stanley Gibbons Catalogue Centenary Exhibition, London. Multicoloured.
37 5n.p. Type **4** 15 15
38 10n.p. Austria (6k.) scarlet "Mercury" newspaper stamp 15 15
39 15n.p. British Guiana "One Cent", 1856 . . . . 15 15
40 25n.p. Canada "Twelvepence Black", 1851 . . . . 15 15
41 50n.p. Hawaii "Missionary" 2c., 1851 . . . . 25 25
42 1r. Mauritius "Post Office" 2d. blue, 1847 . . . . 40 40
43 3r. Switzerland "Double Geneva" 5c.+5c., 1843 . . . 1·40 1·25
44 5r. Tuscany 3 lire, 1860 . . . 2·75 2·10
The 5, 15 and 50n.p. and 3r. also include the First Gibbons Catalogue and the others, the Gibbons "Elizabethan" Catalogue.

1965. Pan Arab Games, Cairo. Perf or imperf. Nos. 29, 31 and 33/5 optd. (a) Optd **PAN ARAB GAMES CAIRO 1965**.
45 **3** 15n.p. brown, violet & green 15 15
46 – 50n.p. slate, purple and blue 25 25
47 – 1r.50 purple, violet & green 90 90
48 – 2r. blue, red and ochre . . . 1·25 1·25
49 – 3r. violet, brown and blue . 2·00 2·00

(b) Optd as Nos. 45/9 but equivalent in Arabic.
50 **3** 15n.p. brown, violet & green 15 15
51 – 50n.p. slate, purple and blue 25 25
52 – 1r.50 purple, violet and green 90 90
53 – 2r. blue, red and ochre . . . 1·25 1·25
54 – 3r. violet, brown and blue . . 2·00 2·00

1965. Air. Designs similar to Nos. 1/9, but inscr "AIR MAIL". Mult. (a) Size 42½ × 25½ mm.
55 15n.p. Type **1** 15 15
56 25n.p. Regal angelfish 15 15
57 35n.p. Dromedary 20 15
58 50n.p. Yellow-banded angelfish 25 15
59 75n.p. Tortoise 40 20
60 1r. Jewel cichlid 75 25

(b) Size 53 × 34 mm.
61 2r. White stork . . . . 1·10 30
62 3r. Black-headed gull . . . . 1·60 30
63 5r. Lanner falcon . . . . . . 3·25 50

1966. Stamp Cent Exn, Cairo. Nos. 38/9 and 41/3 optd **STAMP CENTENARY EXHIBITION CAIRO, JANUARY 1966** and pyramid motif.
73 10n.p. multicoloured 15 15
74 15n.p. multicoloured 15 15
75 50n.p. multicoloured 25 25
76 1r. multicoloured 65 65
77 3r. multicoloured . . . . . . 1·75 1·75

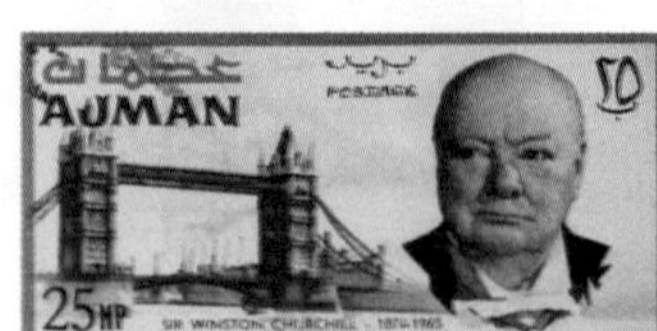

8 Sir Winston Churchill and Tower Bridge

1966. Churchill Commemoration. Each design includes portrait of Churchill. Multicoloured.
79 25n.p. Type **8** 15 15
80 50n.p. Buckingham Palace . . 25 15
81 75n.p. Blenheim Palace . . . 40 20
82 1r. British Museum 50 25
83 2r. St. Paul's Cathedral in wartime . . . . 1·00 40
84 3r. National Gallery and St. Martin in the Fields Church . . . . 1·50 60
85 5r. Westminster Abbey . . . . 2·50 90
86 7r.50 Houses of Parliament at night . . . . 3·75 1·60

9 Rocket

1966. Space Achievements. Multicoloured. (a) Postage. Size as T **9**.
88 1n.p. Type **9** 15 15
89 3n.p. Capsule 15 15
90 5n.p. Astronaut entering capsule in space 15 15
91 10n.p. Astronaut outside capsule in space 15 15
92 15n.p. Astronauts and globe 15 15
93 25n.p. Astronaut in space . . 25 15

(b) Air. Size 38 × 38 mm.
95 50n.p. As Type **9** 25 15
96 1r. Astronauts and globe . . . 40 20
97 3r. Astronaut outside capsule in space . . . . 1·25 40
98 5r. Capsule . . . . 3·25 90

1967. Various issues with currency names changed by overprinting in **Dh.** or **Riyals.** (a) Postage. Nos. 1/18 (1964 Definitives).
99 1d. on 1n.p. 15 15
100 2d. on 2n.p. 15 15
101 3d. on 3n.p. 15 15
102 4d. on 4n.p. 15 15
103 5d. on 5n.p. 15 15
104 10d. on 10n.p. 15 15
105 15d. on 15n.p. . . . . . . 1·25 15
106 20d. on 20n.p. . . . . . . 1·25 15
107 30d. on 30n.p. . . . . . . 1·25 15
108 40d. on 40n.p. 20 15
109 50d. on 50n.p. 30 15
110 70d. on 70n.p. 40 25
111 1r. on 1r. 65 25
112 1r.50 on 1r.50 . . . . . . 65 30
113 2r. on 2r. . . . . 1·50 65
114 3r. on 3r. . . . . 1·50 70
115 5r. on 5r. . . . . 2·50 1·25
116 10r. on 10r. . . . . 7·50 2·75

(b) Air. Nos. 55/63 (Airmails).
117 15d. on 15n.p. 15 15
118 25d. on 25n.p. 20 15
119 35d. on 35n.p. 25 15
120 50d. on 50n.p. 30 15
121 75d. on 75n.p. 45 25
122 1r. on 1r. 65 50
123 2r. on 2r. . . . . 1·25 70
124 3r. on 3r. . . . . 2·50 1·25
125 5r. on 5r. . . . . 3·50 2·40

NEW CURRENCY SURCHARGES. Nos. 19/44 and 79/98 are known surch in new currency (dirhams and riyals), in limited quantities, but there is some doubt as to whether they were in use locally.

11 Fiat 1500 Saloon, 1962

1967. Transport.
135 **11** 1d. brown & blk (postage) 15 15
136 – 2d. blue and brown 15 15
137 – 3d. mauve and black . . . 15 15
138 – 4d. blue and brown 15 15
139 – 5d. green and black 30 15
140 – 15d. blue and brown . . . 50 15
141 – 30d. brown and black . . . 25 15
142 – 50d. black and brown . . . 50 15
143 – 70d. violet and black . . . 65 15
144 **11** 1r. green and brown (air) 40 15
145 – 2r. mauve and black . . . 1·00 25
146 – 3r. black and brown . . . 1·60 40
147 – 5r. brown and black . . . 2·25 1·00
148 – 10r. blue and brown . . . 6·75 1·50
DESIGNS: 2d., 2r. Motor coach; 3d., 3r. Motor cyclist; 4d., 5r. Boeing 707 airliner; 5d., 10r. "Brasil" (liner); 15d. "Yankee" (sail training and cruise ship); 30d. Cameleer; 50d. Arab horse; 70d. Sikorsky S-58 helicopter.

OFFICIAL STAMPS

1965. Designs similar to Nos. 1/9, additionally inscr "ON STATE'S SERVICE". Multicoloured. (i) Postage. Size 43 × 26 mm.
O64 25n.p. Type **1** 15 15
O65 40n.p. Regal angelfish . . . 20 15
O66 50n.p. Dromedary 20 15
O67 75n.p. Yellow-banded angelfish 55 25
O68 1r. Tortoise 85 40

(ii) Air. (a) Size 43 × 26 mm.
O69 75n.p. Jewel cichlid 50 15

(b) Size 53 × 34 mm.
O70 2r. White stork . . . . . . 1·25 35
O71 3r. Black-headed gulls . . . 1·75 50
O72 5r. Lanner falcon . . . . . 5·50 1·25

1967. Nos. O64/72 with currency names changed by overprinting in **Dh.** or **Riyals**.
O126 25d. on 25n.p. 15 15
O127 40d. on 40n.p. 20 15
O128 50d. on 50n.p. 20 15
O129 75d. on 75n.p. (No. O67) 55 45
O130 75d. on 75n.p. (No. O69) 55 45
O131 1r. on 1r. 60 60
O132 2r. on 2r. . . . . 6·00 3·00
O133 3r. on 3r. . . . . 11·00 4·50
O134 5r. on 5r. . . . . 17·00 8·50
For later issues see **UNITED ARAB EMIRATES**.

APPENDIX

From June 1967 very many stamp issues were made by a succession of agencies which had been awarded contracts by the Ruler, sometimes two agencies operating at the same time. Several contradictory statements were made as to the validity of some of these issues which appeared 1967–72 and for this reason they are only listed in abbreviated form.

1967.

50th Birth Anniv of President J. F. Kennedy. Air 10, 20, 40, 70d., 1r.50, 2, 3, 5r.

Paintings. Postage. Arab Paintings 1, 2, 3, 4, 5, 30, 70d.; Air. Asian Paintings 1, 2, 3, 5r.; Indian Painting 10r.

Tales from "The Arabian Nights". Postage 1, 2, 3, 10, 30, 50, 70d.; Air 90d., 1, 2, 3r.

World Scout Jamboree, Idaho. Postage 30, 70d., 1r.; Air 2, 3, 4r.

Olympic Games, Mexico (1968). Postage 35, 65, 75d., 1r.; Air 1r.25, 2, 3, 4r.

Winter Olympic Games, Grenoble (1968). Postage 5, 35, 60, 75d.; Air 1, 1r.25, 2, 3r.

Pres. J. F. Kennedy Memorial. Die-stamped on gold foil. Air 10r.

Paintings by Renoir and Terbrugghen. Air 35, 65d., 1, 2r. × 3.

1968.

Paintings by Velasquez. Air 1r. × 2, 2r. × 2.

Winter Olympic Games, Grenoble. Die-stamped on gold foil. Air 7r.

Paintings from Famous Galleries. Air 1r. × 4, 2r. × 6.

Costumes. Air 30d. × 2, 70d. × 2, 1r. × 2, 2r. × 2.

Olympic Games, Mexico. Postage 1r. × 4; Air 2r. × 4.

Satellites and Spacecraft. Air 30d. × 2, 70d. × 2, 1r. × 2, 2r. × 2, 3r. × 2.

Paintings. Hunting Dogs. Air 2r. × 6.

Paintings. Adam and Eve. Air 2r. × 4.

Human Rights Year. Kennedy Brothers and Martin Luther King. Air 1r. × 3, 2r. × 3.

Kennedy Brothers Memorial. Postage 2r.; Air 5r.

Sports Champions. Inter-Milano Football Club. Postage 5, 10, 15, 20, 25d.; Air 10r.

Sports Champions. Famous Footballers. Postage 15, 20, 50, 75d., 1r.; Air 10r.

Cats. Postage 1, 2, 3d.; Air 2, 3r.

Olympic Games, Mexico. Die-stamped on gold foil. 5r.

5th Death Anniv of Pres. J. F. Kennedy. On gold foil. Air 10r.

Paintings of the Madonna. Air 30, 70d., 1, 2, 3r.

Space Exploration. Postage 5, 10, 15, 20, 25d.; Air 15r.

Olympic Games, Mexico. Gold Medals. Postage 2r. × 4; Air 5r. × 4.

Christmas. Air 5r.

1969.

Sports Champions. Cyclists. Postage 1, 2, 5, 10, 15, 20d.; Air 12r.

Sports Champions. German Footballers. Postage 5, 10, 15, 20, 25d.; Air 10r.

Sports Champions. Motor-racing Drivers. Postage 1, 5, 10, 15, 25d.; Air 10r.

Motor-racing Cars. Postage 1, 5, 10, 15, 25d.; Air 10r.

Sports Champions. Boxers. Postage 5, 10, 15, 20d.; Air 10r.

Sports Champions. Baseball Players. Postage 1, 2, 5, 10, 15d.; Air 10r.

Birds. Air 1r. × 11.

Roses. 1r. × 6.

Wild Animals. Air 1r. × 6.

Paintings. Italian Old Masters. 5, 10, 15, 20d., 10r.

Paintings. Famous Composers. Air 5, 10, 25d., 10r.

Paintings. French Artists. 1r. × 4.

Paintings. Nudes. Air 2r. × 4.

Three Kings Mosaic. Air 1r. × 2, 3r. × 2.

Kennedy Brothers. Air 2, 3, 10r.

Olympic Games, Mexico. Gold Medal Winners. Postage 1, 2d., 10r.; Air 10d., 5, 10r.

Paintings of the Madonna. Postage 10d.; Air 10r.

Space Flight of "Apollo 9". Optd on 1968 Space Exploration issue. Air 15r.

Space Flight of "Apollo 10". Optd on 1968 Space Exploration issue. Air 15r.

1st Death Anniv of Gagarin. Optd on 1968 Space Exploration issue. 5d.

2nd Death Anniv of Edward White. Optd on 1968 Space Exploration issue. 10d.

1st Death Anniv of Robert Kennedy. Optd on 1969 Kennedy Brothers issue. Air 2r.

European Football Championship. Optd on 1968 Famous Footballers issue. Air 10r.

Olympic Games, Munich (1972). Optd on 1969 Mexico Gold Medal Winners issue. Air 10d., 5, 10r.

Moon Landing of "Apollo 11". Air 1, 2, 5r.

Moon Landing of "Apollo 11". Circular designs on gold or silver foil. Air 3r. × 3, 5r. × 3, 10r. × 14.

Paintings. Christmas. Postage 1, 2, 3, 4, 5, 15d.; Air 2, 3r.

1970.

"Apollo" Space Flights. Postage 1, 2, 4, 5, 10d.; Air 3, 5r.

Birth Bicentenary of Napoleon Bonaparte. Die-stamped on gold foil. Air 20r.

Paintings. Easter. Postage 5, 10, 12, 30, 50, 70d.; Air 1, 2r.

Moon Landing. Die-stamped on gold foil. Air 20r.

Paintings by Michelangelo. Postage 1, 2, 4, 5, 8, 10d.; Air 3, 5r.

World Cup Football Championship, Mexico. Air 25, 50, 75d., 1, 2, 3r.

"Expo 70" World Fair, Osaka, Japan. Japanese Paintings. Postage 1, 2, 3, 4, 5, 10, 15d.; Air 1, 5r.

Birth Bicent Napoleon Bonaparte. Postage 1, 2, 4, 5, 10d.; Air 3, 5r.

Paintings. Old Masters. Postage 1, 2, 5, 6, 10d.; Air 1, 2, 3r.

Space Flight of "Apollo 13". Air 50, 75, 80d., 1, 2, 3r.

World Cup Football Championship, Mexico. Die-stamped on gold foil. Air 20r.

Olympic Games, 1960-1972. Postage 15, 30, 50, 70d.; Air 2, 5r.

"Expo 70" World Fair, Osaka, Japan. Pavilions. Postage 1, 2, 3, 4, 10, 15d.; Air 1, 3r.

Brazil's Victory in World Cup Football Championship. Optd on 1970 World Football Cup issue. Air 25, 50, 75d., 1, 2, 3r.

"Gemini" and "Apollo" Space Flights. Postage 1, 2, 3, 4, 5, 6, 8, 10, 12, 15, 20, 25, 30, 35, 40, 50d.; Air 1, 1r.50, 2, 3r.

Vintage and Veteran Cars. Postage 1, 2, 4, 5, 8, 10d.; Air 2, 3r.

Pres. D. Eisenhower Commem. Postage 30, 50, 70d.; Air 1, 2, 3r.

Paintings by Ingres. Air 25, 30, 35, 50, 70, 85d., 1, 2r.

500th Birth Anniv (1971) of Albrecht Durer. Air 25, 30, 35, 50, 70, 85d., 1, 2r.

Christmas Paintings. Air 25, 30, 35, 50, 70, 85d., 1, 2r.

Winter Olympic Games, Sapporo, Japan (1972). Die-stamped on gold foil. Air 20r.

Meeting of Eisenhower and De Gaulle, 1942. Die-stamped on gold foil. Air 20r.

General De Gaulle Commem. Air 25, 50, 75d., 1, 2, 3r.

Winter Olympic Games, Sapporo, Japan (1972). Sports. Postage 1, 2, 5, 10d.; Air 3, 5r.

J. Rindt, World Formula 1 Motor-racing Champion. Die-stamped on gold foil. Air 20r.

1971.

"Philatokyo" Stamp Exhibition, Tokyo. Japanese Paintings. Air 25, 30, 35, 50, 70, 85d., 1, 2r.

Mars Space Project. Air 50, 75, 80d., 1, 2, 3r.

Napoleonic Military Uniforms. Postage 5, 10, 15, 20, 25, 30d.; Air 2, 3r.

Olympic Games, Munich (1972). Sports. Postage 10, 15, 25, 30, 40d.; Air 1, 2, 3r.

Paintings by Modern Artists. Air 25, 30, 35, 50, 70, 85d.; 1, 2r.

Paintings by Famous Artists. Air 25, 30, 35, 50, 70, 85d., 1, 2r.

25th Anniv of United Nations. Optd on 1971 Modern Artists issue. Air 25, 30, 35, 50, 70, 85d., 1, 2r.

Olympic Games, Munich (1972). Sports. Postage 1, 2, 3, 4, 5, 6, 8, 10, 12, 15, 20, 25, 30, 35, 40, 50d.; Air 1, 1r.50, 2, 3r.

Butterflies. Air 25, 30, 35, 50, 70, 85d., 1, 2r.

Space Flight of "Apollo 14". Postage 15, 25, 50, 60, 70d.; Air 5r.

Winter Olympic Games, 1924-1968. Postage 30, 40, 50, 75d., 1r.; Air 2r.

Signs of the Zodiac. 1, 2, 5, 10, 12, 15, 25, 30, 35, 45, 50, 60d.

Famous Men. Air 65, 70, 75, 80, 85, 90d., 1, 1r.25, 1r.50, 2, 2r.50, 3r.

Death Bicent of Beethoven. 20, 30, 40, 60d., 1r.50, 2r.

Dr. Albert Schweitzer Commem. 20, 30, 40, 60d., 1r.50, 2r.

Tropical Birds. Postage 1, 2, 3, 4, 5, 10d.; Air 2, 3r.

Paintings by French Artists. Postage 1, 2, 3, 4, 5, 10d.; Air 2, 3r.

Paintings by Modern Artists. Postage 1, 2, 3, 4, 5, 10d.; Air 2, 3r.

Paintings by Degas. Postage 1, 2, 3, 4, 5, 10d.; Air 2, 3r.

Paintings by Titian. Postage 1, 2, 3, 4, 5, 10d.; Air 2, 3r.

Paintings by Renoir. Postage 1, 2, 3, 4, 5, 10d.; Air 2, 3r.

Space Flight of "Apollo 15". Postage 25, 40, 50, 60d., 1r.; Air 6r.

"Philatokyo" Stamp Exhibition, Tokyo. Stamps. Postage 10, 15, 20, 30, 35, 50, 60, 80d.; Air 1, 2r.

Tropical Birds. Postage 1, 2, 3, 5, 7, 10, 12, 15, 20, 25, 30, 40d.; Air 50, 80d., 1, 3r.

Paintings depicting Venus. Postage 1, 2, 3, 4, 5, 10d.; Air 2, 3r.

13th World Scout Jamboree, Asagiri, Japan. Scouts. Postage 1, 2, 3, 5, 7, 10, 12, 15, 20, 25, 30, 35, 40, 50, 65, 80d.; Air 1, 1r.25, 1r.50, 2r.

Lions International Clubs. Optd on 1971 Famous Paintings issue. Air 25, 30, 35, 50, 70, 85d., 1, 2r.

13th World Scout Jamboree, Asagiri, Japan. Japanese Paintings. Postage 20, 30, 40, 60, 75d.; Air 3r.

25th Anniv of U.N.I.C.E.F. Optd on 1971 Scout Jamboree (paintings) issue. Postage 20, 30, 40, 60, 75d.; Air 3r.

Christmas 1971. (1st series. Plain frames). Portraits of Popes. Postage 1, 2, 3, 4, 5, 10d.; Air 2, 3r.

Modern Cars. Postage 10, 15, 25, 40, 50d.; Air 3r.

Olympic Games, Munich (1972). Show-jumping. Embossed on gold foil. Air 20r.

Exploration of Outer Space. Postage 15, 25, 50, 60, 70d.; Air 5r.

Royal Visit of Queen Elizabeth II to Japan. Postage 1, 2, 3, 4, 5, 10d.; Air 2, 3r.

Meeting of Pres. Nixon and Emperor Hirohito of Japan in Alaska. Design as 3r. value of 1970 Eisenhower issue but value changed and optd with commemorative inscr. Air 5r. (silver opt), 5r. (gold opt).

"Apollo" Astronants. Postage 5, 20, 35, 40, 50d.; Air 1, 2, 3r.

Discoverers of the Universe. Astronomers and Space Scientists. Postage 5, 10, 15, 20, 25, 30d.; Air 2, 5r.

"ANPHILEX 71" Stamp Exn, New York. Air 2r.50.

Christmas 1971. Portraits of Popes (2nd series. Ornamental frames). Postage 1, 2, 3, 4, 5, 10d.; Air 2, 3r.

Royal Silver Wedding of Queen Elizabeth II and Prince Philip (1972). Air 1, 2, 3r.

Space Flight of "Apollo 16". Postage 20, 30, 40, 50, 60d.; Air 3, 4r.

Fairy Tales. "Baron Munchhausen" Stories. Postage 1, 2, 4, 5, 10d.; Air 3r.

World Fair, Philadelphia (1976). Paintings. Postage 25, 50, 75d.; Air 5r.

Fairy Tales. Stories of the Brothers Grimm. Postage 1, 2, 4, 5, 10d.; Air 3r.

European Tour of Emperor Hirohito of Japan. Postage 1, 2, 4, 5, 10d.; Air 6r.

13th World Scout Jamboree, Asagiri, Japan. Postage 5, 10, 15, 20, 25d.; Air 5r.

Winter Olympic Games, Sapporo, Japan (1972). Postage 5, 10, 15, 20, 25d.; Air 5r.

Olympic Games, Munich (1972). Postage 5, 10, 15, 20, 25d.; Air 5r.

"Japanese Life". Postage 10d. × 4, 20d. × 4, 30d. × 4, 40d. × 4, 50d. × 4; Air 3r. × 4.

Space Flight of "Apollo 15". Postage 5, 10, 15, 20, 25, 50d.; Air 1, 2, 3, 5r.

"Soyuz 11" Disaster. Air 50d., 1r., 1r.50.

"The Future in Space". Postage 5, 10, 15, 20, 25, 50d.

2500th Anniv of Persian Empire. Postage 10, 20, 30, 40, 50d., Air 3r.

Cats. Postage 10, 15, 20, 25d.; Air 50d., 1r.

50th Anniv of Tutankhamun Tomb Discovery. Postage 1, 2, 3, 4, 5, 6, 7, 8, 9, 10, 11, 12, 13, 14, 15, 16d.; Air 1r. × 4.

400th Birth Anniv of Johannes Kepler (astronomer). Postage 50d.; Air 5r.

Famous Men. Air. 1r. × 5.

1972.

150th Death Anniv of Napoleon Bonaparte (1971). Postage 10, 20, 30, 40d.; Air 1, 2, 3, 4r.

1st Death Anniv of General de Gaulle. Postage 10, 20, 30, 40d.; Air 1, 2, 3, 4r.

Wild Animals (1st series). Postage 5, 10, 15, 20, 25, 30, 35, 40d.

Tropical Fishes. Postage 5, 10, 15, 20, 25d.; Air 50, 75d., 1r.

Famous Musicians. Postage 5d. × 3, 10d. × 3, 15d. × 3, 20d. × 3, 25d. × 3, 30d. × 3, 35d. × 3, 40d. × 3.

Easter. Postage 5, 10, 15, 20, 25d.; Air 5r.

Wild Animals (2nd series). Postage 5, 10, 15, 20, 25d.; Air 5r.

"Tour de France" Cycle Race. Postage 5, 10, 15, 20, 25, 30, 35, 40, 45, 50, 55d.; Air 60, 65, 70, 75, 80, 85, 90, 95d., 1r.

Many other issues were released between 1 September 1971 and 1 August 1972, but their authenticity has been denied by the Ajman Postmaster-General. Certain issues of 1967–69 exist overprinted to commemorate other events but the Postmaster General states that these are unofficial.

Ajman joined the United Arab Emirates on 1 August 1972 and the Ministry of Communications assumed responsibility for the postal services. Further stamps inscribed "Ajman" issued after that date were released without authority and had no validity.

ALAND ISLANDS Pt. 11

Aland is an autonomous province of Finland. From 1984 separate stamps were issued for the area although stamps of Finland could also still be used there. On 1 January 1993 Aland assumed control of its own postal service and Finnish stamps ceased to be valid there.

1984. 100 pennia = 1 markka.
2002. 100 cents = 1 euro.

1 Fishing Boat

2 "Pommern" (barque) and Car Ferries, Mariehamn West Harbour

1984.

1	**1**	10p. mauve	10	10
2		20p. green	15	10
3		50p. green	20	25
4	–	1m. green	25	30
5	**1**	1m.10 blue	60	50
6		1m.20 black	30	40
7		1m.30 green	60	50
8	–	1m.40 multicoloured	1·25	80
9a	–	1m.50 multicoloured	90	55
10	–	1m.90 multicoloured	1·10	80
12	–	3m. blue, green and black	1·50	1·25
14	–	10m. black, chestnut & brn	4·00	3·00
15	–	13m. multicoloured	4·50	4·25

DESIGNS—20 × 29 mm: 1m.50, Midsummer pole, Storby village. 21 × 31 mm: 13m. Rug, 1793. 26 × 32 mm: 3m. Map of Aland Islands. 30 × 20 mm: 1m. Farjsund Bridge. 31 × 21 mm: 1m.40, Aland flag; 1m.90, Mariehamn Town Hall. 32 × 26 mm: 10m. Seal of Aland showing St. Olaf (patron saint).

1984. 50th Anniv of Society of Shipowners.

16	**2**	2m. multicoloured	1·50	1·75

3 Grove of Ashes and Hazels

4 Map, Compass and Measuring Instrument

1985. Aland Scenes. Multicoloured.

17	2m. Type **3**	1·10	50
18	5m. Kokar Church and shore (horiz)	1·75	1·00
19	8m. Windmill and farm (horiz)	2·75	1·50

1986. Nordic Orienteering Championships, Aland.

20	**4**	1m.60 multicoloured	1·40	1·25

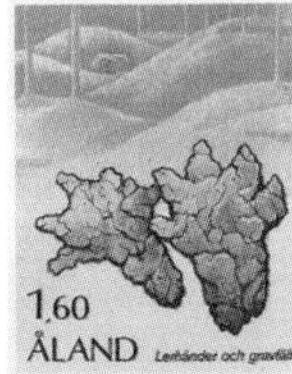

5 Clay Hands and Burial Mounds, Skamkulla

6 "Onnigeby" (drawing, Victor Westerholm)

1986. Archaeology. Multicoloured.

21	1m.60 Type **5**	1·25	70
22	2m.20 Bronze staff from Finby and Apostles	90	75
23	20m. Monument at ancient court site, Saltvik, and court in session (horiz)	6·50	6·00

1986. Centenary of Onnigeby Artists' Colony.

24	**6**	3m.70 multicoloured	1·75	1·60

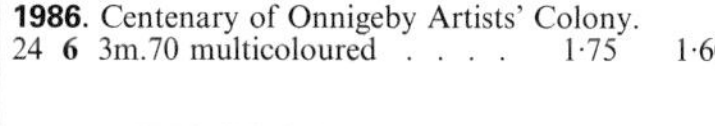

7 Eiders

8 Firemen in Horse-drawn Cart

1987. Birds. Multicoloured.

25	1m.70 Type **7**	5·50	5·25
26	2m.30 Tufted ducks	2·25	1·75
27	12m. Velvet scoters	3·75	4·50

1987. Centenary of Mariehamn Fire Brigade.

28	**8**	7m. multicoloured	3·25	4·00

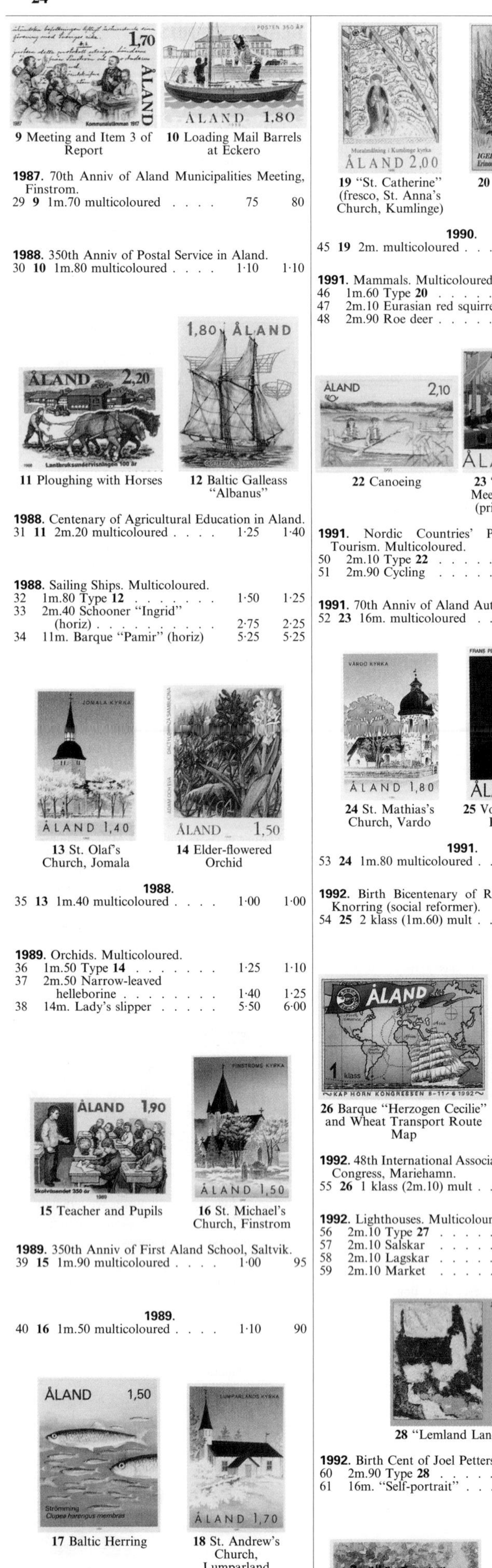

9 Meeting and Item 3 of Report — **10** Loading Mail Barrels at Eckero

1987. 70th Anniv of Aland Municipalities Meeting, Finstrom.
29 **9** 1m.70 multicoloured 75 80

1988. 350th Anniv of Postal Service in Aland.
30 **10** 1m.80 multicoloured . . . . 1·10 1·10

11 Ploughing with Horses — **12** Baltic Galleass "Albanus"

1988. Centenary of Agricultural Education in Aland.
31 **11** 2m.20 multicoloured . . . . 1·25 1·40

1988. Sailing Ships. Multicoloured.
32 1m.80 Type **12** . . . . 1·50 1·25
33 2m.40 Schooner "Ingrid" (horiz) . . . . 2·75 2·25
34 11m. Barque "Pamir" (horiz) 5·25 5·25

13 St. Olaf's Church, Jomala — **14** Elder-flowered Orchid

1988.
35 **13** 1m.40 multicoloured . . . . 1·00 1·00

1989. Orchids. Multicoloured.
36 1m.50 Type **14** . . . . 1·25 1·10
37 2m.50 Narrow-leaved helleborine . . . . 1·40 1·25
38 14m. Lady's slipper . . . . . 5·50 6·00

15 Teacher and Pupils — **16** St. Michael's Church, Finstrom

1989. 350th Anniv of First Aland School, Saltvik.
39 **15** 1m.90 multicoloured . . . . 1·00 95

1989.
40 **16** 1m.50 multicoloured . . . . 1·10 90

17 Baltic Herring — **18** St. Andrew's Church, Lumparland

1990. Fishes. Multicoloured.
41 1m.50 Type **17** 70 70
42 2m. Northern pike 90 70
43 2m.70 European flounder . . 1·25 85

1990.
44 **18** 1m.70 multicoloured 85 75

19 "St. Catherine" (fresco, St. Anna's Church, Kumlinge) — **20** West European Hedgehog

1990.
45 **19** 2m. multicoloured 75 60

1991. Mammals. Multicoloured.
46 1m.60 Type **20** 70 70
47 2m.10 Eurasian red squirrel . . 90 75
48 2m.90 Roe deer . . . . 1·10 1·25

22 Canoeing — **23** "League of Nations Meeting, Geneva, 1921" (print by F. Rackwitz)

1991. Nordic Countries' Postal Co-operation. Tourism. Multicoloured.
50 2m.10 Type **22** 85 70
51 2m.90 Cycling . . . . 1·10 70

1991. 70th Anniv of Aland Autonomy.
52 **23** 16m. multicoloured . . . . 6·00 4·75

24 St. Mathias's Church, Vardo — **25** Von Knorring (after Karl Jansson)

1991.
53 **24** 1m.80 multicoloured 85 80

1992. Birth Bicentenary of Rev. Frans Peter von Knorring (social reformer).
54 **25** 2 klass (1m.60) mult 85 80

26 Barque "Herzogen Cecilie" and Wheat Transport Route Map — **27** Ranno Lighthouse

1992. 48th International Association of Cape Horners Congress, Mariehamn.
55 **26** 1 klass (2m.10) mult . . . . 1·40 1·25

1992. Lighthouses. Multicoloured.
56 2m.10 Type **27** . . . . 2·75 1·60
57 2m.10 Salskar . . . . 2·75 1·60
58 2m.10 Lagskar . . . . 2·75 1·60
59 2m.10 Market . . . . 2·75 1·60

28 "Lemland Landscape"

1992. Birth Cent of Joel Pettersson (painter). Mult.
60 2m.90 Type **28** . . . . 1·10 70
61 16m. "Self-portrait" . . . . . 5·00 4·00

29 Delegates processing to Church Service — **30** St. Catherine's Church, Hammarland

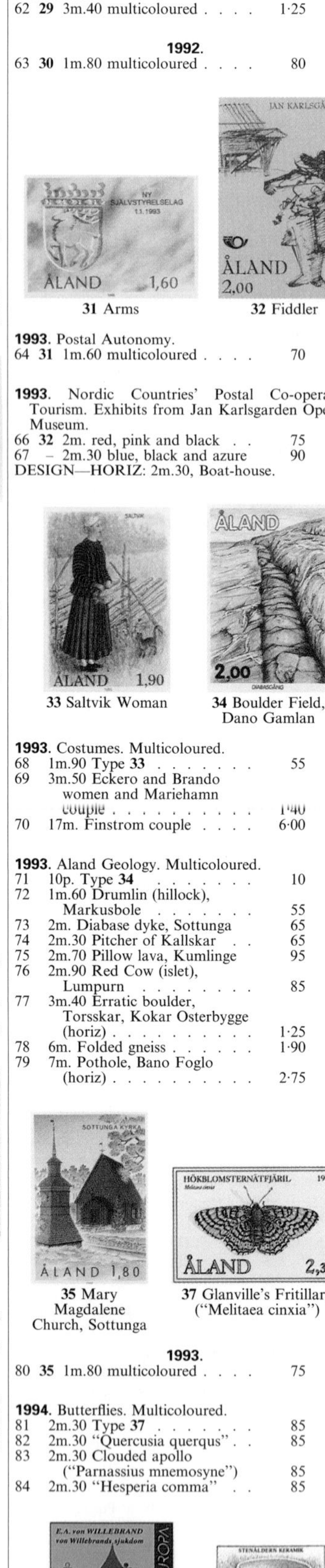

1992. 70th Anniv of First Aland Provincial Parliament.
62 **29** 3m.40 multicoloured . . . . 1·25 1·25

1992.
63 **30** 1m.80 multicoloured 80 75

31 Arms — **32** Fiddler

1993. Postal Autonomy.
64 **31** 1m.60 multicoloured 70 70

1993. Nordic Countries' Postal Co-operation. Tourism. Exhibits from Jan Karlsgarden Open-air Museum.
66 **32** 2m. red, pink and black . . 75 65
67 – 2m.30 blue, black and azure 90 70
DESIGN—HORIZ: 2m.30, Boat-house.

33 Saltvik Woman — **34** Boulder Field, Dano Gamlan

1993. Costumes. Multicoloured.
68 1m.90 Type **33** 55 70
69 3m.50 Eckero and Brando women and Mariehamn couple . . . . 1·40 1·40
70 17m. Finstrom couple . . . . 6·00 5·25

1993. Aland Geology. Multicoloured.
71 10p. Type **34** 10 10
72 1m.60 Drumlin (hillock), Markusbole 55 60
73 2m. Diabase dyke, Sottunga 65 50
74 2m.30 Pitcher of Kallskar . . 65 70
75 2m.70 Pillow lava, Kumlinge 95 70
76 2m.90 Red Cow (islet), Lumpurn 85 85
77 3m.40 Erratic boulder, Torsskar, Kokar Osterbygge (horiz) . . . . 1·25 1·10
78 6m. Folded gneiss . . . . . . 1·90 1·50
79 7m. Pothole, Bano Foglo (horiz) . . . . 2·75 2·50

35 Mary Magdalene Church, Sottunga — **37** Glanville's Fritillary ("Melitaea cinxia")

1993.
80 **35** 1m.80 multicoloured 75 75

1994. Butterflies. Multicoloured.
81 2m.30 Type **37** 85 90
82 2m.30 "Quercusia querqus" . . 85 90
83 2m.30 Clouded apollo ("Parnassius mnemosyne") 85 90
84 2m.30 "Hesperia comma" . . 85 90

38 Genetic Diagram — **39** Comb Ceramic and Pitted Ware Pottery

1994. Europa. Medical Discoveries. Multicoloured.
85 2m.30 Type **38** (discovery of Von Willebrand's disease (hereditary blood disorder)) 1·50 1·40
86 2m.90 Molecular diagram (purification of heparin by Erik Jorpes) . . . . 1·25 1·40

1994. The Stone Age.
87 **39** 2m.40 brown 55 50
88 – 2m.80 blue 85 70
89 – 18m. green . . . . 6·00 4·25

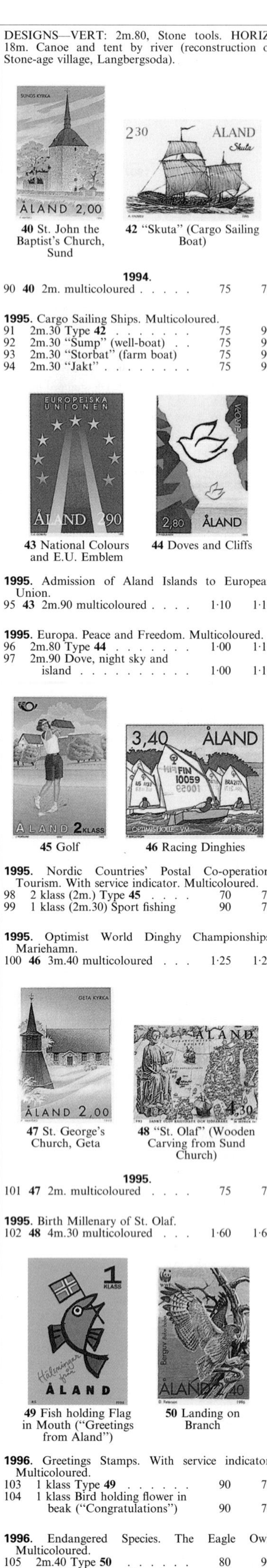

DESIGNS—VERT: 2m.80, Stone tools. HORIZ: 18m. Canoe and tent by river (reconstruction of Stone-age village, Langbergsoda).

40 St. John the Baptist's Church, Sund — **42** "Skuta" (Cargo Sailing Boat)

1994.
90 **40** 2m. multicoloured 75 70

1995. Cargo Sailing Ships. Multicoloured.
91 2m.30 Type **42** 75 90
92 2m.30 "Šump" (well-boat) . . 75 90
93 2m.30 "Storbat" (farm boat) 75 90
94 2m.30 "Jakt" 75 90

43 National Colours and E.U. Emblem — **44** Doves and Cliffs

1995. Admission of Aland Islands to European Union.
95 **43** 2m.90 multicoloured . . . . 1·10 1·10

1995. Europa. Peace and Freedom. Multicoloured.
96 2m.80 Type **44** . . . . 1·00 1·10
97 2m.90 Dove, night sky and island . . . . 1·00 1·10

45 Golf — **46** Racing Dinghies

1995. Nordic Countries' Postal Co-operation. Tourism. With service indicator. Multicoloured.
98 2 klass (2m.) Type **45** 70 70
99 1 klass (2m.30) Sport fishing 90 75

1995. Optimist World Dinghy Championships, Mariehamn.
100 **46** 3m.40 multicoloured . . . 1·25 1·25

47 St. George's Church, Geta — **48** "St. Olaf" (Wooden Carving from Sund Church)

1995.
101 **47** 2m. multicoloured 75 75

1995. Birth Millenary of St. Olaf.
102 **48** 4m.30 multicoloured . . . 1·60 1·60

49 Fish holding Flag in Mouth ("Greetings from Aland") — **50** Landing on Branch

1996. Greetings Stamps. With service indicator. Multicoloured.
103 1 klass Type **49** 90 70
104 1 klass Bird holding flower in beak ("Congratulations") 90 70

1996. Endangered Species. The Eagle Owl. Multicoloured.
105 2m.40 Type **50** 80 90
106 2m.40 Perched on branch . . 80 90

107 2m.40 Adult owl 80 90
108 2m.40 Juvenile owl 80 90
Nos. 105/6 form a composite design.

51 Sally Salminen (novelist)

1996. Europa. Famous Women. Multicoloured.
109 2m.80 Type **51** . . . . . . 1·00 65
110 2m.90 Fanny Sundstrom (politician) . . . . 1·00 70

52 Choir

53 "Haircut"

1996. "Aland 96" Song and Music Festival, Mariehamn.
111 **52** 2m.40 multicoloured . . . 95 85

1996. 150th Birth Anniv of Karl Jansson (painter).
112 **53** 18m. multicoloured . . . . 6·00 6·00

54 "Trilobita asaphus"

55 Brando Church

1996. Fossils. Multicoloured.
113 40p. Type **54** 10 10
114 9m. "Gastropoda euomophalus" . . . . . . 2·75 2·75

1996.
115 **55** 2m. multicoloured 65 70

56 Giant Isopod ("Saduria entomon") and Opossum Shrimp ("Mysis relicta")

57 Coltsfoot ("Tussilago farfara")

1997. Marine Survivors from the Ice Age. Multicoloured.
116 30p. Type **56** 10 10
117 2m.40 Four-horned sculpin ("Myotocephalus quadricornis") 70 50
118 4m.30 Ringed seal ("Phoca hispida botrica") . . . . . 1·50 1·00

1997. Spring Flowers. Multicoloured.
119 2m.40 Type **57** 80 80
120 2m.40 Blue anemone ("Hepatica nobilis") . . . 80 80
121 2m.40 Wood anemone ("Anemone nemorosa") . . 80 80
122 2m.40 Yellow anemone ("Anemone ranunculoides") 80 80

58 Floorball

59 The Devil's Dance

1997. 1st Women's Floorball World Championship, Mariehamn and Godby.
123 **58** 3m.40 multicoloured . . . 80 1·00

1997. Europa. Tales and Legends.
124 **59** 2m.90 multicoloured . . . 1·00 95

60 Kastelholm Castle and Arms

1997. 600th Anniv of Kalmar Union between Sweden, Denmark and Norway.
125 **60** 2m.40 multicoloured . . . 90 80

62 "Thornbury" (freighter)

63 St George's Church, Mariehamn

1997. Steam Freighters. Multicoloured.
127 2m.80 Type **62** 75 50
128 3m.50 "Osmo" (freighter) . . 1·40 1·40

1997. 70th Anniv of Mariehamn Church.
129 **63** 1m.90 multicoloured . . . 70 75

64 Man harvesting Apples

1998. Horticulture. Multicoloured.
130 2m. Type **64** 70 65
131 2m.40 Woman harvesting cucumbers 70 75

65 Boy on Moped

66 Midsummer Celebrations

1998. Youth Activities. Multicoloured.
132 2m.40 Type **65** 85 80
133 2m.40 Laptop computer . . . 85 80
134 2m.40 CD disk and headphones 85 80
135 2m.40 Step aerobics 85 80

1998. Europa. National Festivals.
136 **66** 4m.20 multicoloured . . . 1·50 1·40

67 "Isabella" (car ferry)

1998. Nordic Countries' Postal Co-operation. Shipping.
137 **67** 2m.40 multicoloured . . . 90 80

68 Waves breaking

1998. International Year of the Ocean.
138 **68** 6m.30 multicoloured . . . 2·10 2·00

69 Players

1998. Association of Tennis Professionals Senior Tour, Mariehamn. Self-adhesive.
139 **69** 2m.40 multicoloured . . . 85 85

70 Schooner, Compass Rose and Knots

1998. Ninth International Sea Scout Camp, Bomarsund Fortress, Aland.
140 **70** 2m.80 multicoloured . . . 95 95

71 Seffers Homestead, Onningeby

72 Eckero Church

1998. Traditional Porches. Multicoloured.
141 1m.60 Type **71** 65 55
142 2m. Labbas homestead, Storby 70 55
143 2m.90 Abras homestead, Bjorko 90 85

1998.
144 **72** 1m.90 multicoloured . . . 70 70

73 Sword and Dagger

1999. Bronze Age Relics. Multicoloured.
145 2m. Type **73** 70 70
146 2m.20 "Ship" tumulus (vert) 70 75

74 Wardrobe

1999. Folk Art. Decorated Furniture. Mult.
147 2m.40 Type **74** 85 90
148 2m.40 Distaff 85 90
149 2m.40 Chest 85 90
150 2m.40 Spinning wheel 85 90

75 "'Pamir' and 'Passat' (barques) off Port Victoria" (R. Castor)

76 Cowslip

1999. 50th Anniv of Rounding of Cape Horn by "Pamir" on Last Wheat-carrying Voyage.
151 **75** 3m.40 multicoloured . . . 1·10 1·10

1999. Provincial Plant of Aland. Self-adhesive.
152 **76** 2m.40 multicoloured . . . 75 75

77 Ido Island, Kokar

1999. Europa. Parks and Gardens.
153 **77** 2m.90 multicoloured . . . 1·00 1·00
No. 153 is denominated both in markkas and in euros.

78 Racing Yachts

79 Puffed Shield Lichen ("Hypogymnia physodes")

1999. Sailing
154 **78** 2m.70 multicoloured . . . 90 95

1999. Lichens. With service indicator. Mult.
155 2 klass (2m.) Type **79** . . . 70 75
156 1 klass (2m.40) Common orange lichen ("Xanthoria parietina") 90 90

80 Loading Mail Plane

81 St. Bridget's Church, Lemland

1999. 125th Anniv of Universal Postal Union
157 **80** 2m.90 multicoloured . . . 90 1·00

1999.
158 **81** 1m.90 multicoloured . . . 65 70

82 Runners

83 Arctic Tern (*Sterna paradisaea*)

1999. Finnish Cross-country Championships, Mariehamn.
159 **82** 3m.50 multicoloured . . . 1·10 1·10

DENOMINATION. From No. 162 Aland Islands stamps are denominated both in markkas and in euros. As no cash for the latter is in circulation, the catalogue continues to use the markka value.

2000. Sea Birds. Multicoloured.
162 1m.80 Type **83** 50 50
164 2m.20 Mew gull (*Larus canus*) (vert) 90 75
166 2m.60 Great black-backed gull (*Larus marinus*) . . . 85 85

85 Elk

86 "Building Europe"

2000. The Elk (*Alces alces*). Multicoloured.
172 2m.60 Type **85** 80 75
173 2m.60 With young 80 75
174 2m.60 Beside lake 80 75
175 2m.60 In snow 80 75

2000. Europa.
176 **86** 3m. multicoloured . . . . 90 1·00

87 Gymnast

88 Crew and *Linden* (schooner)

2000. Finno-Swedish Gymnastics Association Exhibition, Mariehamn. Self-adhesive.
177 **87** 2m.60 multicoloured . . . 80 75

2000. Visit by *Cutty Sark* Tall Ships' Race Competitors to Mariehamn.
178 **88** 3m.40 multicoloured . . . 1·10 1·00

89 Lange on prow of Longship

2000. Death Millenary of Hlodver Lange the Viking.
179 **89** 4m.50 multicoloured . . . 1·75 1·75

90 Wooden Ornamented Swiss-style House, Mariehamn

2000. 48th Death Anniv of Hilda Hongell (architect). Multicoloured.
180 3m.80 Type **90** . . . . . . 1·00 1·00
181 10m. House with central front entrance, Mariehamn 2·75 2·75

91 The Nativity

2000. 2000 Years of Christianity.
182 **91** 3m. multicoloured 95 95

92 Kokar Church **93** Steller's Eider in Flight

2000.
183 **92** 2m. multicoloured 65 70

2001. Endangered Species. The Steller's Eider (*Polysticta stelleri*). Multicoloured.
184 2m.70 Type **93** 70 80
185 2m.70 Duck and drake . . . 70 80
186 2m.70 Duck and drake swimming 70 80
187 2m.70 Drake swimming . . . 70 80

94 Swamp Horsetail (*Equisetum fluviatile*)

2001. Plants. Multicoloured.
188 1m.90 Type **94** 65 65
189 2m.80 Stiff clubmoss (*Lycopodium annotinum*) . . 90 90
190 3m.50 Polypody (*Polybodium vulgare*) . . . . 85 1·00

95 Heart and Graffiti on Brick Wall

2001. St. Valentine's Day.
200 **95** 3m.20 multicoloured . . . 85 90

96 Fisherman and Fish

2001. Europa. Water Resources.
201 **96** 3m.20 multicoloured . . . 75 90

97 Archipelago Windmill **98** Golden Retriever

2001. Windmills. Multicoloured.
202 3m. Type **97** 85 90
203 7m. Timbered windmill (horiz) . . . . 1·75 1·90
204 20m. Nest windmill (horiz) 5·00 5·50

2001. Puppies. Multicoloured.
205 2 klass (2m.30) Type **98** . . 75 75
206 1 klass (2m.70) Wire-haired dachshund 85 85

99 Foglo Church **100** Smooth Snake (*Coronella Austriaca*)

2001.
207 **99** 2m. multicoloured 55 65

New Currency: 100 cents = 1 euro

2002. Endangered Animals. Multicoloured.
208 5c. Type **100** 10 10
209 70c. Great crested newt (*Triturus cristatus*) 90 90

101 Woman pushing Shopping Trolley

2002. Euro Currency.
210 **101** 60c. multicoloured 75 75

102 Tidying up Christmasa

2002. St. Canute's Day.
211 **102** €2 multicoloured . . . . 2·50 2·50

103 Spiced Salmon and New Potatoes

2002. Traditional Dishes. Multicoloured.
212 1 klass (55c.) Type **103** . . . 70 70
213 1 klass (55c.) Fried herring, mashed potatoes and beetroot 70 70
212 1 klass (55c.) Black bread and butter 70 70
212 1 klass (55c.) Aland pancake with stewed prune sauce and whipped cream 70 70

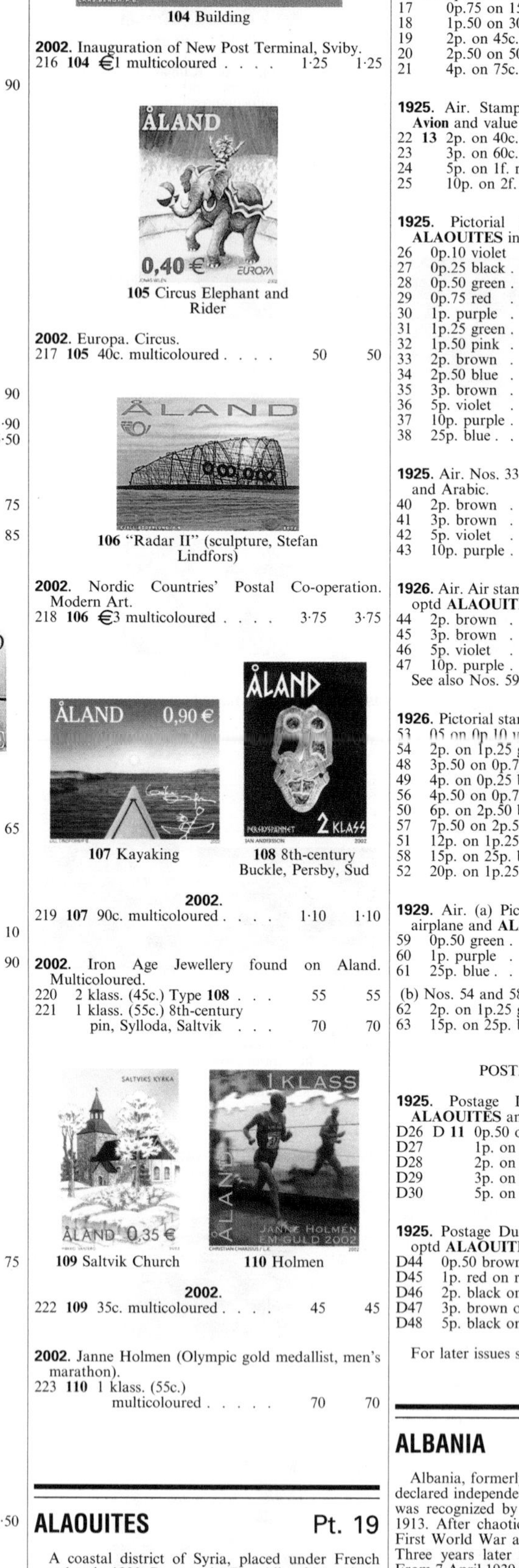

104 Building

2002. Inauguration of New Post Terminal, Sviby.
216 **104** €1 multicoloured . . . . 1·25 1·25

105 Circus Elephant and Rider

2002. Europa. Circus.
217 **105** 40c. multicoloured 50 50

106 "Radar II" (sculpture, Stefan Lindfors)

2002. Nordic Countries' Postal Co-operation. Modern Art.
218 **106** €3 multicoloured . . . . 3·75 3·75

107 Kayaking **108** 8th-century Buckle, Persby, Sud

2002.
219 **107** 90c. multicoloured . . . . 1·10 1·10

2002. Iron Age Jewellery found on Aland. Multicoloured.
220 2 klass. (45c.) Type **108** . . . 55 55
221 1 klass. (55c.) 8th-century pin, Sylloda, Saltvik . . . 70 70

109 Saltvik Church **110** Holmen

2002.
222 **109** 35c. multicoloured 45 45

2002. Janne Holmen (Olympic gold medallist, men's marathon).
223 **110** 1 klass. (55c.) multicoloured 70 70

ALAOUITES Pt. 19

A coastal district of Syria, placed under French mandate in 1920. Became the Republic of Latakia in 1930. Incorporated with Syria in 1937.

100 centimes = 1 piastre.

1925. Stamps of France surch **ALAOUITES** and value in French and Arabic.
1 **11** 0p.10 on 2c. purple . . . . 1·75 4·25
2 **18** 0p.25 on 5c. orange . . . . 2·25 3·50
3 **15** 0p.75 on 15c. green . . . . 3·00 4·50
4 **18** 1p. on 20c. brown . . . . . 2·25 3·50
5 1p.25 on 25c. blue . . . . . 2·25 2·50
6 1p.50 on 30c. red . . . . . 9·00 11·00
7 2p. on 35c. violet . . . . . 80 4·00
8 **13** 2p. on 40c. red and blue . . 3·50 5·25
9 2p. on 45c. green and blue 8·00 12·00
10 3p. on 60c. violet and blue 2·50 6·75
11 **15** 3p. on 60c. violet . . . . 10·50 11·00
12 4p. on 85c. red . . . . . . 1·60 3·25
13 **13** 5p. on 1f. red and yellow . . 4·00 8·75
14 10p. on 2f. orange & grn . . 4·50 10·00
15 25p. on 5f. blue and buff . . 8·50 8·00

1925. "Pasteur" issue of France surch **ALAOUITES** and value in French and Arabic.
16 **30** 0p.50 on 10c. green . . . . 1·75 3·50
17 0p.75 on 15c. green . . . . 1·50 3·50
18 1p.50 on 30c. red . . . . . 1·25 4·00
19 2p. on 45c. red . . . . . . 2·25 4·25
20 2p.50 on 50c. blue . . . . . 3·00 4·50
21 4p. on 75c. blue . . . . . . 2·25 5·50

1925. Air. Stamps of France optd **ALAOUITES Avion** and value in French and Arabic.
22 **13** 2p. on 40c. red and blue . . 6·25 11·00
23 3p. on 60c. violet and blue 7·25 18·00
24 5p. on 1f. red and yellow . . 6·25 10·50
25 10p. on 2f. orange & green 6·00 10·00

1925. Pictorial stamps of Syria (1925) optd **ALAOUITES** in French and Arabic.
26 0p.10 violet . . . . 45 3·00
27 0p.25 black . . . . 70 3·00
28 0p.50 green . . . . 75 1·75
29 0p.75 red . . . . 95 3·00
30 1p. purple . . . . 95 2·25
31 1p.25 green . . . . 1·75 2·25
32 1p.50 pink . . . . 95 2·25
33 2p. brown . . . . 1·75 3·75
34 2p.50 blue . . . . 1·75 3·75
35 3p. brown . . . . 95 2·50
36 5p. violet . . . . 1·75 2·75
37 10p. purple . . . . 1·90 3·00
38 25p. blue . . . . 2·50 6·75

1925. Air. Nos. 33 and 35/37 optd **AVION** in French and Arabic.
40 2p. brown . . . . 1·10 4·00
41 3p. brown . . . . 1·00 3·75
42 5p. violet . . . . 1·10 4·00
43 10p. purple . . . . 1·10 4·00

1926. Air. Air stamps of Syria with airplane overprint optd **ALAOUITES** in French and Arabic.
44 2p. brown . . . . 2·00 5·25
45 3p. brown . . . . 2·00 5·25
46 5p. violet . . . . 2·00 5·25
47 10p. purple . . . . 2·00 5·25
See also Nos. 59/60 and 63.

1926. Pictorial stamps of 1925 surcharged.
53 05 on 0p.10 violet 25 3·00
54 2p. on 1p.25 green . . . . . 8·00 7·00
48 3p.50 on 0p.75 red . . . . . 1·00 2·25
49 4p. on 0p.25 black . . . . . 85 2·25
56 4p.50 on 0p.75 red . . . . . 2·50 3·75
50 6p. on 2p.50 blue . . . . . . 1·25 2·25
57 7p.50 on 2p.50 blue . . . . . 2·50 1·90
51 12p. on 1p.25 green . . . . . 2·75 3·25
58 15p. on 25p. blue . . . . . . 7·25 6·25
52 20p. on 1p.25 green . . . . . 2·75 4·25

1929. Air. (a) Pictorial stamps of Syria optd with airplane and **ALAOUITES** in French and Arabic.
59 0p.50 green . . . . 2·00 4·25
60 1p. purple . . . . 4·50 9·00
61 25p. blue . . . . 22·00 30·00

(b) Nos. 54 and 58 of Alaouites optd with airplane.
62 2p. on 1p.25 green . . . . . 2·75 5·00
63 15p. on 25p. blue . . . . . . 19·00 25·00

POSTAGE DUE STAMPS

1925. Postage Due stamps of France surch **ALAOUITES** and value in French and Arabic.
D26 **D 11** 0p.50 on 10c. brown . . 2·10 4·75
D27 1p. on 20c. green . . . 2·10 5·00
D28 2p. on 30c. red . . . . 2·10 5·00
D29 3p. on 50c. purple . . 2·10 5·25
D30 5p. on 1f. pur on yell 2·10 5·00

1925. Postage Due stamps of Syria (Nos. D192/6) optd **ALAOUITES** in French and Arabic.
D44 0p.50 brown on yellow . . . 75 3·25
D45 1p. red on red . . . . . . 75 3·50
D46 2p. black on blue . . . . . 1·25 4·00
D47 3p. brown on red . . . . . 1·25 4·75
D48 5p. black on green . . . . . 2·40 5·00

For later issues see **LATAKIA**.

ALBANIA Pt. 3

Albania, formerly part of the Turkish Empire, was declared independent on 28 November 1912, and this was recognized by Turkey in the treaty of 30 May 1913. After chaotic conditions during and after the First World War a republic was established in 1925. Three years later the country became a kingdom. From 7 April 1939 until December 1944, Albania was occupied, firstly by the Italians and then by the Germans. Following liberation a republic was set up in 1946.

1913. 40 paras = 1 piastre or grosch.
1913. 100 qint = 1 franc.
1947. 100 qint = 1 lek.

1913. Various types of Turkey optd with double-headed eagle and **SHQIPENIA**.
3 **28** 2pa. green (No. 271) . . . £225 £200
4 5pa. brown (No. 261) . . . £225 £200
2 **25** 10pa. green (No. 252) . . . £350 £300
5 **28** 10pa. green (No. 262) . . . £190 £130
12 10pa. green (No. 289) . . . £375 £375
11 10pa. on 20pa. red £600 £600
6 20pa. red (No. 263) . . . £180 £110
13 20pa. red (No. 290) . . . £400 £350
7 1pi. blue (No. 264) £130 £120
14a 1pi. blue (No. 291) £900 £900

15 1pi. blk on red (No. D288) £1500 £1500
8 2pi. black (No. 265) . . . £250 £200
14b 2pi. black (No. 292) . . .
1 25 2½pi. brown (No. 239) . . £450 £350
9 28 5pi. purple (No. 267) . . . £700 £600
10 10pi. red (No. 268) £2500 £2500

2

1913.
16 2 10pa. violet . . . . 8·00 6·00
17 20pa. red and grey . . . . . 10·00 8·00
18 1g. grey . . . . 10·00 10·00
19 2g. blue and violet . . . . 12·00 9·50
20 5g. violet and blue . . . . 15·00 12·00
21 10g. blue and violet . . . . 15·00 12·00

3

4 Skanderbeg (after Heinz Kautsch)

1913. Independence Anniv.
22 3 10pa. black and green . . . 2·75 1·75
23 20pa. black and red . . . . 3·00 2·75
24 30pa. black and violet . . . 3·50 2·75
25 1g. black and blue . . . . . 5·00 3·50
26 2g. black . . . . 8·00 6·00

1913.
27 4 2q. brown and yellow . . . . 1·00 1·00
28 5q. green and yellow . . . . 1·00 1·00
29 10q. red . . . . 1·10 1·10
30 25q. blue . . . . 1·25 1·25
31 50q. mauve and red . . . . 5·00 4·00
32 1f. brown . . . . 8·00 8·00

1914. Arrival of Prince William of Wied. Optd **7 Mars 1461 RROFTE MBRETI 1914**.
33 4 2q. brown and yellow . . . . 22·00 18·00
34 5q. green and yellow . . . . 22·00 18·00
35 10q. red and rose . . . . . 22·00 18·00
36 25q. blue . . . . 22·00 18·00
37 50q. mauve and rose . . . . 22·00 18·00
38 1f. brown . . . . 22·00 18·00

1914. Surch.
40 4 5pa. on 2q. brown & yellow 1·75 1·75
41 10pa. on 5q. green & yellow 1·75 1·75
42 20pa. on 10q. red . . . . . 2·25 1·75
43 1g. on 25q. blue . . . . . . 2·75 2·50
44 2g. on 50q. mauve and red 3·50 3·50
45 5g. on 1f. brown . . . . . . 15·00 10·00

1914. Valona Provisional Issue. Optd **POSTE D'ALBANIE** and Turkish inscr in circle with star in centre.
45a 4 2q. brown and yellow . . . £150 £150
45b 5q. green and yellow . . .
45c 10q. red and rose . . . . . 8·50 8·50
45d 25q. blue . . . . 8·50 8·50
45e 50q. mauve and red . . . . 8·50 8·50
45f 1f. brown £475
45g 5pa. on 2q. brown & yellow 25·00 25·00
45h 10pa. on 5q. green & yellow 50·00 50·00
45i 20pa. on 10q. red and rose 13·00 13·00
45j 1gr. on 25q. blue . . . . . 7·50 7·50
45k 2gr. on 50q. mauve and red 13·00 13·00
45l 5gr. on 1f. brown . . . . . 18·00 18·00

11 12

1917. Inscribed "SHQIPERIE KORCE VETQEVERITARE" or "REPUBLIKA KORCE SHQIPETARE" or "QARKU-POSTES-I-KORCES".
75 11 1c. brown and green . . . . 2·00 4·00
76 2c. brown and green . . . . 2·00 4·00
77 3c. grey and green . . . . . 2·00 4·00
78 5c. green and black . . . . 2·75 2·50
79 10c. red and black . . . . . 2·75 2·50
72 25c. blue and black . . . . 9·00 6·25

80 50c. purple and black . . . 5·00 4·50
81 1f. brown and black . . . . 16·00 15·00

1918. No. 78 surch **QARKUI KORCES 25 CTS.**
81a 25c. on 5c. green and black 60·00 48·00

1919. Fiscal stamps used by the Austrians in Albania Handstamped with control.
83 12 (2)q. on 2h. brown . . . . 5·50 5·50
84 05q. on 16h. green . . . . 5·50 5·50
85 10q. on 8h. red . . . . . 5·50 5·50
86 25q. on 64h. blue . . . . 5·50 5·50
87a 50q. on 32h. violet . . . . 5·50 5·50
88 1f. on 1.28k. brown on blue . . . . 8·00 8·00

Three sets may be made of this issue according to whether the handstamped control is a date, a curved comet or a comet with straight tail.

1919. No. 43 optd **SHKODER 1919**.
103 4 1g. on 25q. blue . . . . . 8·00 8·00

1919. Fiscal stamps surch **POSTAT SHQIPTARE** and new value.
104 12 10q. on 2h. brown . . . 4·50 4·50
111 10q. on 8h. red . . . . . 4·50 4·50
112 15q. on 8h. red . . . . . 4·50 4·50
113 20q. on 16h. green . . . 4·50 4·50
113b 25q. on 32h. violet . . . 4·50 4·50
107 25q. on 64h. blue . . . . 4·50 4·50
108 50q. on 32h. violet . . . 4·50 4·50
113c 50q. on 64h. blue . . . . 10·00 10·00
113d 1f. on 96h. orange . . . . 6·00 6·00
113e 2f. on 160h. violet . . . . 8·50 8·50

17 Prince William I

19 Skanderberg

1920. Optd with double-headed eagle and **SHKORDA** or surch also.
114 17 1q. grey . . . . 21·00 40·00
115 2q. on 10q. red . . . . . 3·50 6·25
116 5q. on 10q. red . . . . . 3·50 6·25
117 10q. red . . . . 3·25 6·25
118 20q. brown . . . . 12·00 22·00
119 25q. blue £140 £275
120 25q. on 10q. red . . . . . 3·50 7·00
121 50q. violet . . . . 17·00 32·00
122 50q. on 10q. red . . . . . 3·50 7·00

1920. Optd with posthorn.
123 19 2q. orange . . . . 5·00 6·25
124 5q. green . . . . 6·75 11·00
125 10q. red . . . . 13·50 22·00
126 25q. blue . . . . 26·00 22·00
127 50q. green . . . . 5·00 7·50
128 1f. mauve . . . . 5·00 7·50

Stamps as Type **19** also exist optd **BESA** meaning "Loyalty".

1922. No. 123 surch with value in frame.
143 19 1q. on 2q. orange . . . . 3·50 2·00

24

1922. Views.
144 24 2q. orange (Gjinokaster) 80 1·75
145 5q. green (Kanina) 50 75
146 10q. red (Berat) 50 75
147 25q. blue (Veziri Bridge) 50 75
148 50q. green (Rozafat Fortress, Shkoder) . . . 60 75
149 1f. lilac (Korce) . . . . . 1·10 1·25
150 2f. green (Durres) . . . . 2·75 4·00

1924. Opening of National Assembly. Optd **TIRANE KALLNUER 1924** in frame with **Mbledhje Kushtetuese** above.
151 24 2q. orange . . . . 4·75 8·00
152 5q. green . . . . 4·75 8·00
153 10q. red . . . . 4·75 8·00
154 25q. blue . . . . 4·75 8·00
155 50q. green . . . . 4·75 8·00

1924. No. 144 surch with value and bars.
156 24 1 on 2q. orange . . . . . 2·50 3·75

1924. Red Cross. (a) Surch with small red cross and premium.
157 24 5q.+5q. green . . . . . . 7·50 7·50
158 10q.+5q. red . . . . . . 7·50 7·50
159 25q.+5q. blue . . . . . . 7·50 7·50
160 50q.+5q. green . . . . . . 7·50 7·50

(b) Nos. 157/60 with further surch of large red cross and premium.
161 24 5q.+5q.+5q. green . . . . 7·50 7·50
162 10q.+5q.+5q. red . . . . . 7·50 7·50
163 25q.+5q.+5q. blue . . . . 7·50 7·50
164 50q.+5q.+5q. green . . . . 7·50 7·50

1925. Return of Government to Capital in 1924. Optd **Triumf' i legalitetit 24 Dhetuer 1924**.
164a 24 1 on 2q. orange (No. 156) 2·50 3·25
165 2q. orange . . . . 2·50 3·25
166 5q. green . . . . 2·50 3·25
167 10q. red . . . . 2·50 3·25
168 25q. blue . . . . 2·50 3·25
169 50q. green . . . . 2·50 3·25
170 1f. lilac . . . . 2·50 3·25

1925. Proclamation of Republic. Optd **Republika Shqiptare 21 Kallnduer 1925**.
171 24 1 on 2q. orange (No. 156) 2·50 3·25
172 2q. orange . . . . 2·50 3·25
173 5q. green . . . . 2·50 3·25
174 10q. red . . . . 2·50 3·25
175 25q. blue . . . . 2·50 3·25
176 50q. green . . . . 2·50 3·25
177 1f. lilac . . . . 2·50 3·25

1925. Optd **Republika Shqiptare**.
178 24 1 on 2q. orange (No. 156) 65 85
179 2q. orange 65 85
180 5q. green 65 85
181 10q. red 65 85
182 25q. blue 65 85
183 50q. green 65 85
184 1f. lilac . . . . 2·75 3·75
185 2f. green . . . . 2·75 3·75

32

1925. Air.
186 32 5q. green . . . . 3·25 3·25
187 10q. red . . . . 3·50 3·50
188 25q. blue . . . . 3·50 3·50
189 50q. green . . . . 5·00 5·00
190 1f. black and violet . . . . 8·25 8·25
191 2f. violet and olive . . . . 11·00 11·00
192 3f. green and brown . . . 19·00 19·00

33 Pres. Ahmed Zogu, later King Zog I

34

1925.
193 33 1q. yellow 15 10
194 2q. brown 15 10
195 5q. green 15 10
196 10q. red 15 10
197 15q. brown 75 75
198 25q. blue 15 10
199 50q. green 75 75
200 34 1f. blue and red . . . . . 1·25 1·25
201 2f. orange and green . . . 1·75 1·25
202 3f. violet . . . . 3·50 3·00
203 5f. black and violet . . . . 4·25 4·75

1927. Air. Optd **Rep. Shqiptare**.
204 32 5q. green . . . . 10·00 10·00
205 10q. red . . . . 10·00 10·00
206 25q. blue . . . . 8·50 8·50
207 50q. green . . . . 8·00 8·00
208 1f. black and violet . . . . 8·00 8·00
209 2f. violet and olive . . . . 9·75 9·75
210 3f. green and brown . . . 17·00 17·00

1927. Optd **A.Z.** and wreath.
211 33 1q. yellow 50 65
212 2q. brown 20 25
213 5q. green . . . . 1·10 35
214 10q. red 20 20
215 15q. brown . . . . 6·00 7·00
216 25q. blue 50 25
217 50q. green 50 25
218 34 1f. blue and red 50 25
219 2f. orange and green . . . 75 50
220 3f. violet and brown . . . 1·10 1·00
221 5f. black and violet . . . . 1·75 2·00

1928. Inauguration of Vlore (Valona)-Brindisi Air Service. Optd **REP. SHQYPTARE Fluturim' i I-ar Vlone-Brindisi 21.IV.1928**.
222 32 5q. green . . . . 9·25 11·50
223 10q. red . . . . 9·25 11·50
224 25q. blue . . . . 9·25 9·50
225 50q. green . . . . 10·50 14·50
226 1f. black and violet . . . . 95·00 £110
227 2f. violet and olive £100 £110
228 3f. green and brown . . . £100 £120

1928. Surch in figures and bars.
229 33 1 on 10q. red (No. 214) . . 50 40
230 5 on 25q. blue (No. 216) 50 40

39 Pres. Ahmed Zogu, later King Zog I

40

1928. National Assembly. Optd **Kujtim i Mbledhjes Kushtetuese 25.8.28**.
231 39 1q. brown . . . . 3·50 4·25
232 2q. grey . . . . 3·50 4·25
233 5q. green . . . . 3·50 4·25
234 10q. red . . . . 3·50 4·25
235 15q. brown . . . . 9·00 14·00
236 25q. blue . . . . 4·25 3·75
237 50q. lilac . . . . 6·75 5·00
238 40 1f. black and blue . . . . 4·25 3·75

1928. Accession of King Zog I. Optd **Mbretnia-Shqiptare Zog I 1.IX.1928**.
239 39 1q. brown . . . . 8·50 13·00
240 2q. grey . . . . 8·50 13·00
241 5q. green . . . . 6·50 11·00
242 10q. red . . . . 6·00 6·25
243 15q. brown . . . . 6·00 7·50
244 25q. blue . . . . 6·00 7·50
245 50q. lilac . . . . 6·75 8·75
246 40 1f. black and blue . . . . 8·25 11·00
247 2f. black and green . . . . 8·25 11·00

1928. Optd **Mbretnia-Shqiptare** only.
248 39 1q. brown 50 50
249 2q. grey 45 35
250 5q. green . . . . 2·50 50
251 10q. red 50 35
252 15q. brown . . . . 10·00 12·00
253 25q. blue 50 35
254 50q. lilac 75 35
255 40 1f. black and blue . . . . 1·50 1·90
256 2f. black and green . . . . 1·50 2·10
257 3f. olive and red . . . . . 4·00 2·75
258 5f. black and violet . . . . 5·25 7·50

1929. Surch **Mbr. Shqiptare** and new value.
259 33 1 on 50q. green 25 40
260 5 on 25q. blue 30 40
261 15 on 10q. red 50 70

1929. King Zog's 35th Birthday. Optd **RROFT-MBRETI 8.X.1929**.
262 33 1q. yellow . . . . 4·50 6·75
263 2q. brown . . . . 4·50 6·75
264 5q. green . . . . 4·50 6·75
265 10q. red . . . . 4·50 6·75
266 25q. blue . . . . 4·50 6·75
267 50q. green . . . . 5·00 8·00
268 34 1f. blue and red . . . . . 8·00 12·00
269 2f. orange and green . . . 8·50 12·50

1929. Air. Optd **Mbr. Shqiptare**.
270 32 5q. green . . . . 8·00 12·00
271 10q. red . . . . 8·00 12·00
272 25q. blue . . . . 15·00 12·50
273 50q. green . . . . 45·00 60·00
274 1f. black and violet £250 £325
275 2f. violet and olive £275 £350
276 3f. green and brown . . . £500 £550

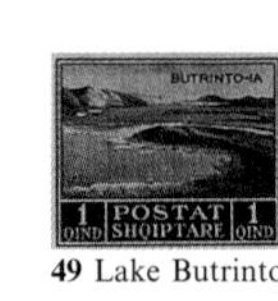
49 Lake Butrinto

50 King Zog I

1930. 2nd Anniv of Accession of King Zog I.
277 49 1q. grey 15 20
278 2q. red 15 20
279 50 5q. green 15 15
280 10q. red 25 30
281 15q. brown 25 30
282 25q. blue 20 30
283 49 50q. green 40 45
284 – 1f. violet 85 60
285 – 2f. blue . . . . 1·00 60
286 – 3f. green . . . . 2·50 95
287 – 5f. brown . . . . 3·25 2·50

DESIGNS—VERT: 1, 2f. Ahmed Zog Bridge, River Mati. HORIZ: 3, 5f. Ruins of Zogu Castle.

53 Junkers F-13 (over Tirana)

1930. Air. T **53** and similar view.
288 53 5q. green . . . . 2·10 2·10
289 15q. red . . . . 2·10 2·10
290 20q. blue . . . . 2·10 2·10
291 50q. olive . . . . 3·75 3·75
292 – 1f. blue . . . . 6·25 6·25
293 – 2f. brown . . . . 21·00 21·00
294 – 3f. violet . . . . 24·00 24·00

1931. Air. Optd **TIRANE-ROME 6 KORRIK 1931**.
295 53 5q. green . . . . 9·00 9·00
296 15q. red . . . . 9·00 9·00
297 20q. blue . . . . 9·00 9·00
298 50q. olive . . . . 9·00 9·00
299 – 1f. blue . . . . 50·00 50·00
300 – 2f. brown . . . . 50·00 50·00
301 – 3f. violet . . . . 50·00 50·00

1934. 10th Anniv of Revolution. Optd **1924-24 Dhetuer-1934**.
302 49 1q. grey . . . . 2·00 3·50
303 2q. orange . . . . 2·00 3·50
304 50 5q. green . . . . 2·00 3·50
305 10q. red . . . . 2·00 3·50
306 15q. brown . . . . 2·00 3·50
307 25q. blue . . . . 3·00 3·75
308 49 50q. turquoise . . . . . . 3·00 3·75
309 – 1f. violet (No. 284) . . . . 4·00 7·50
310 – 2f. blue (No. 285) . . . . 8·00 13·00
311 – 3f. green (No. 286) . . . . 14·00 18·00

56 Horse and Flag of Skanderbeg

57 Albania in Chains

1937. 25th Anniv of Independence.

No.	Type	Description	Mint	Used
312	56	1q. violet	15	15
313	57	2q. brown	25	20
314	–	5q. green	40	20
315	56	10q. olive	45	50
316	57	15q. red	60	45
317	–	25q. blue	1·25	1·50
318	56	50q. green	1·75	2·00
319	57	1f. violet	5·00	5·25
320	–	2f. brown	8·00	8·50

DESIGN: 5, 25q., 2f. As Type **57**, but eagle with opened wings (Liberated Albania).

58 Countess Geraldine Apponyi and King Zog

1938. Royal Wedding.

No.	Type	Description	Mint	Used
321	58	1q. purple	20	20
322		2q. brown	20	20
323		5q. green	20	25
324		10q. olive	50	50
325		15q. red	50	50
326		25q. blue	65	85
327		50q. green	3·50	2·75
328		1f. violet	4·75	3·75

59 National Emblems

60 King Zog

1938. 10th Anniv of Accession.

No.	Type	Description	Mint	Used
329	–	1q. purple	15	35
330	59	2q. red	25	35
331	–	5q. green	35	40
332	60	10q. brown	65	1·00
333	–	15q. red	65	1·00
334	60	25q. blue	85	1·10
335	59	50q. black	5·00	3·75
336	60	1f. green	7·50	5·50

DESIGN: 1, 5, 15q. As Type **60**, but Queen Geraldine's portrait.

ITALIAN OCCUPATION

1939. Optd **Mbledhja Kushtetuese 12-IV-1939 XVII.**

(a) Postage.

No.	Type	Description	Mint	Used
337	49	1q. grey	35	35
338		2q. red	35	35
339	50	5q. green	30	30
340		10q. red	30	30
341		15q. brown	70	75
342		25q. blue	80	95
343	49	50q. turquoise	1·00	1·25
344	–	1f. violet (No. 284)	2·00	2·75
345	–	2f. blue (No. 285)	2·25	3·00
346	–	3f. green	5·00	7·50
347	–	5f. brown	6·75	8·50

(b) Air. Optd as Nos. 337/47 or surch also.

No.	Type	Description	Mint	Used
348	53	5q. green	4·25	3·75
349		15q. red	3·00	3·75
350		20q. on 50q. olive	7·25	7·25

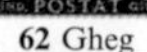
62 Gheg

64 Broken Columns, Botrint

63 King Victor Emmanuel

65 King and Fiat G18V on Tirana–Rome Service

1939.

No.	Type	Description	Mint	Used
351	62	1q. blue (postage)	40	25
352	–	2q. brown	30	10
353	–	3q. brown	30	10
354	–	5q. green	40	10
355	63	10q. brown	40	15
356		15q. red	50	15
357		25q. blue	50	25
358		30q. violet	80	60
359	–	50q. violet	1·10	60
360	–	65q. red	2·25	2·50
361	–	1f. green	2·50	1·50
362	–	2f. red	6·50	8·00
363	64	3f. black	10·00	14·50
364	–	5f. purple	12·00	18·00
365	65	20q. brown (air)	45·00	10·50

DESIGNS—SMALL: 2q. Tosk man; 3q. Gheg woman; 5, 65q. Profile of King Victor Emmanuel; 50q. Tosk woman. LARGE: 1f. Kruje Fortress; 2f. Bridge over River Kiri at Mes; 5f. Amphitheatre ruins, Berat.

66 Sheep Farming

67 King Victor Emmanuel

1940. Air.

No.	Type	Description	Mint	Used
366	66	5q. green	1·25	1·25
367	–	15q. red	1·75	1·60
368	–	20q. blue	4·00	2·40
369	–	50q. brown	4·50	4·75
370	–	1f. green	6·00	6·00
371	–	2f. black	13·50	14·00
372	–	3f. purple	55·00	24·00

DESIGNS: Savoia Marchetti S.M.75 airplane and—HORIZ: 20q. King of Italy and Durres harbour; 1f. Bridge over River Kiri at Mes. VERT: 15q. Aerial map; 50q. Girl and valley; 2f. Archway and wall, Durres; 3f. Women in North Eprius.

1942. 3rd Anniv of Italian Occupation.

No.	Type	Description	Mint	Used
373	67	5q. green	60	75
374		10q. brown	60	75
375		15q. red	75	1·25
376		25q. blue	75	1·25
377		65q. brown	1·75	2·00
378		1f. green	1·75	2·00
379		2f. purple	1·75	2·50

1942. No. 352 surch **1 QIND.**

No.	Type	Description	Mint	Used
380		1q. on 2q. brown	85	1·50

69

1943. Anti-tuberculosis Fund.

No.	Type	Description	Mint	Used
381	69	5q.+5q. green	50	85
382		10q.+10q. brown	50	85
383		15q.+10q. red	50	85
384		25q.+15q. blue	1·00	1·60
385		30q.+20q. violet	1·00	1·60
386		50q.+25q. orange	1·00	1·60
387		65q.+30q. grey	1·25	2·10
388		1f.+40q. brown	1·75	3·00

GERMAN OCCUPATION

1943. Postage stamps of 1939 optd **14 Shtator 1943** or surch also.

No.	Type	Description	Mint	Used
389	–	1q. on 3q. brn (No. 353)	1·00	3·00
390	–	2q. brown (No. 352)	1·00	3·00
391	–	3q. brown (No. 353)	1·00	3·00
392	–	5q. green (No. 354)	1·00	3·00
393	63	10q. brown	1·00	3·00
394	–	15q. red (No. 356)	1·00	3·00
395	–	25q. blue (No. 357)	1·00	3·00
396	–	30q. violet (No. 358)	1·00	3·00
397	–	50q. on 65q. brn (No. 360)	1·25	6·00
398	–	65q. red (No. 360)	1·25	6·00
399	–	1f. green (No. 361)	6·00	18·00
400	–	2f. red (No. 362)	10·00	70·00
401	64	3f. black	50·00	£225

71 War Refugees

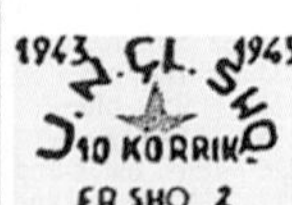
(73)

1944. War Refugees' Relief Fund.

No.	Type	Description	Mint	Used
402	71	5q.+5q. green	2·50	12·00
403		10q.+5q. brown	2·50	12·00
404		15q.+5q. red	2·50	12·00
405		25q.+10q. blue	2·50	12·00
406		1f.+50q. green	2·50	12·00
407		2f.+1f. violet	2·50	12·00
408		3f.+1f.50 orange	2·50	12·00

INDEPENDENT STATE

1945. Nos. 353/8 and 360/2 surch **QEVERIJA DEMOKRAT. E SHQIPERISE 22-X-1944** and value.

No.	Type	Description	Mint	Used
409		30q. on 3q. brown	4·25	5·00
410		40q. on 5q. green	4·25	5·00
411		50q. on 10q. brown	4·25	5·00
412		60q. on 15q. red	4·25	5·00
413		80q. on 25q. blue	4·25	5·00
414		1f. on 30q. violet	4·25	5·00
415		2f. on 65q. brown	4·25	5·00
416		3f. on 1f. green	4·25	5·00
417		5f. on 2f. red	4·25	5·00

1945. 2nd Anniv of Formation of People's Army. Surch as T **73**.

No.	Type	Description	Mint	Used
418	49	30q. on 1q. grey	2·50	3·75
419		60q. on 1q. grey	2·50	3·75
420		80q. on 1q. grey	2·75	3·75
421		1f. on 1q. grey	6·00	7·50
422		2f. on 2q. red	7·50	8·75
423		3f. on 50q. green	13·50	16·00
424	–	5f. on 2f. blue (No. 285)	20·00	25·00

1945. Red Cross Fund. Surch with Red Cross, **JAVA E K.K. SHQIPTAR 4-11 MAJ 1945** and value.

No.	Type	Description	Mint	Used
425	69	30q.+15q. on 5q.+5q. green	5·00	6·50
426		50q.+25q. on 10q.+10q. brown	5·00	6·50
427		1f.+50q. on 15q.+10q. red	14·00	16·00
428		2f.+1f. on 25q.+15q. blue	20·00	22·00

75 Labinot

77 Globe, Dove and Olive Branch

1945.

No.	Type	Description	Mint	Used
429	75	20q. green	50	85
430		30q. orange	75	1·25
431	–	40q. brown	75	1·25
432	–	60q. red	1·00	1·75
433	–	1f. red	2·00	3·75
434	–	3f. blue	12·00	15·00

DESIGNS: 40, 60q. Bridge at Berat; 1f., 3f. Permet landscape.

1946. Constitutional Assembly. Optd **ASAMBLEJA KUSHTETUESE 10 KALLNUER 1946.**

No.	Type	Description	Mint	Used
435	75	20q. green	1·25	1·25
436		30q. orange	1·75	1·75
437	–	40q. brown (No. 431)	2·00	2·00
438	–	60q. red (No. 432)	3·50	3·50
439	–	1f. red (No. 433)	12·00	12·00
440	–	3f. blue (No. 434)	20·00	20·00

PEOPLE'S REPUBLIC

1946. Int Women's Congress. Perf or imperf.

No.	Type	Description	Mint	Used
441	77	20q. mauve and red	85	85
442		40q. lilac and red	1·25	1·25
443		50q. violet and red	1·75	1·75
444		1f. blue and red	4·25	4·25
445		2f. blue and red	6·25	6·25

1946. Proclamation of Albanian People's Republic. Optd **REPUBLIKA POPULLORE E SHQIPERISE.**

No.	Type	Description	Mint	Used
446	75	20q. green	1·40	1·40
447		30q. orange	1·60	1·60
448	–	40q. brown (No. 431)	2·75	2·75
449	–	60q. red (No. 432)	5·50	5·50
450	–	1f. red (No. 433)	12·00	12·00
451	–	3f. blue (No. 434)	22·00	22·00

1946. Albanian Red Cross Congress. Surch **KONGRESI K.K.SH. 24-25-11-46** and premium.

No.	Type	Description	Mint	Used
452	75	20q.+10q. green	20·00	20·00
453		30q.+15q. orange	20·00	20·00
454	–	40q.+20q. brown	20·00	20·00
455	–	60q.+30q. red	20·00	20·00
456	–	1f.+50q. red	20·00	20·00
457	–	3f.+1f.50 blue	20·00	20·00

79 Athletes

80 Qemal Stafa

1946. Balkan Games.

No.	Type	Description	Mint	Used
458	79	1q. black	14·00	11·50
459		2q. green	14·00	11·50
460		5q. brown	14·00	11·50
461		10q. red	14·00	11·50
462		20q. blue	14·00	11·50
463		40q. lilac	16·00	11·50
464		1f. orange	32·00	30·00

1947. 5th Death Anniv of Qemal Stafa (Communist activist).

No.	Type	Description	Mint	Used
465	80	20q. dp brown & brown	9·00	9·00
466		28q. deep blue and blue	9·00	9·00
467		40q. dp brown & brown	9·00	9·00

81 Railway Construction

1947. Construction of Durres–Elbasan Railway.

No.	Type	Description	Mint	Used
468	81	1q. black and drab	5·00	1·25
469		4q. deep green and green	5·00	1·25
470		10q. dp brown & brown	5·25	1·60
471		15q. red and rose	5·25	1·60
472		20q. black and blue	12·00	1·75
473		28q. deep blue and blue	17·00	2·25
474		40q. red and purple	32·00	2·50
475		68q. dp brown & brown	40·00	22·00

82 Partisans

83 Enver Hoxha and Vasil Shanto

1947. 4th Anniv of Formation of People's Army. Inscr "1943–1947".

No.	Type	Description	Mint	Used
476	82	16q. brown	4·50	4·50
477	83	20q. brown	4·50	4·50
478	–	28q. blue	4·50	4·50
479	–	40q. brown and mauve	4·50	4·50

DESIGNS—HORIZ: 28q. Infantry column. VERT: 40q. Portrait of Vojo Kushi.

84 Ruined Conference Building

1947. 5th Anniv of Peza Conference.

No.	Type	Description	Mint	Used
480	84	2l. purple and mauve	6·00	4·00
481		2l.50 deep blue and blue	6·00	4·00

85 War Invalids

86 Peasants

1947. 1st Congress of War Invalids.

No.	Type	Description	Mint	Used
482	85	1l. red	10·00	10·00

1947. Agrarian Reform. Inscr "REFORMA AGRARE".

No.	Type	Description	Mint	Used
483	86	1l.50 purple	7·50	6·50
484	–	2l. brown	7·50	6·50
485	–	2l.50 blue	7·50	6·50
486	–	3l. red	7·50	6·50

DESIGNS—HORIZ: 2l. Banquet; 2l.50, Peasants rejoicing. VERT: 3l. Soldier being chaired.

87 Burning Village

1947. 3rd Anniv of Liberation. Inscr "29-XI-1944–1947".

No.	Type	Description	Mint	Used
487	87	1l.50 red	3·75	3·75
488	–	2l.50 purple	3·75	3·75
489	–	5l. blue	5·00	6·00
490	–	8l. mauve	12·00	8·00
491	–	12l. brown	20·00	14·00

DESIGNS: 2l.50, Riflemen; 5l. Machine-gunners; 8l. Mounted soldier; 12l. Infantry column.

1948. Nos. 429/34 surch **Lek** and value.

No.	Type	Description	Mint	Used
492	75	0l.50 on 30q. orange	35	35
493		1l. on 20q. green	90	90
494	–	2l.50 on 60q. red	2·50	2·25
495	–	3l. on 1f. red	3·00	3·00
496	–	5l. on 3f. blue	6·00	5·50
497	–	12l. on 40q. brown	15·00	12·50

88 Railway Construction

1948. Construction of Durres–Tirana Railway.
498 **88** 0l.50 red 2·50 1·00
499 1l. green 2·75 1·10
500 1l.50 red 4·25 1·10
501 2l.50 brown 5·25 2·00
502 5l. blue 10·00 2·75
503 8l. orange 16·00 4·75
504 12l. purple 20·00 8·00
505 20l. black 40·00 18·00

89 Parade of Infantrymen

90 Labourer, Globe and Flag

1948. 5th Anniv of People's Army.
506 **89** 2l.50 brown 3·00 2·50
507 5l. blue 5·00 4·50
508 – 8l. slate (Troops in action) 8·00 6·00

1949. Labour Day.
509 **90** 2l.50 brown 1·00 1·00
510 5l. blue 2·25 2·25
511 8l. purple 4·00 4·00

91 Soldier and Map

92 Albanian and Kremlin Tower

1949. 6th Anniv of People's Army.
512 **91** 2l.50 brown 1·10 1·10
513 5l. blue 2·25 2·25
514 8l. orange 4·00 4·00

1949. Albanian–Soviet Amity.
515 **92** 2l.50 brown 1·25 1·50
516 5l. blue 3·00 3·25

93 Gen. Enver Hoxha

94 Soldier and Flag

1949.
517 **93** 0l.50 purple 25 10
518 1l. green 30 10
519 1l.50 red 40 10
520 2l.50 brown 65 10
521 5l. blue 1·60 25
522 8l. purple 3·00 1·75
523 12l. purple 10·50 3·00
524 20l. slate 12·50 4·00

1949. 5th Anniv of Liberation.
525 **94** 2l.50 brown 70 70
526 – 3l. red 1·75 1·90
527 **94** 5l. violet 2·50 2·75
528 – 8l. black 5·25 5·50
DESIGN—HORIZ: 3, 8l. Street fighting.

96 Joseph Stalin

1949. Stalin's 70th Birthday.
529 **96** 2l.50 brown 1·00 1·25
530 5l. blue 1·90 2·50
531 8l. lake 4·25 5·50

97

98 Sami Frasheri

1950. 75th Anniv of U.P.U.
532 **97** 5l. blue 2·75 4·00
533 8l. purple 5·00 5·75
534 12l. black 9·00 10·00

1950. Literary Jubilee. Inscr "1950-JUBILEU I SHKRIMTAREVE TE RILINDJES".
535 **98** 2l. green 1·10 85
536 – 2l.50 brown 1·50 1·40
537 – 3l. red 1·75 2·00
538 – 5l. blue 3·00 3·00
PORTRAITS: 2l.50, A. Zako (Cajupi); 3l. Naim Frasheri; 5l. K. Kristoforidhi.

99 Vuno-Himare

100 Stafa and Shanto

1950. Air.
539 **99** 0l.50 black 90 90
540 – 1l. purple 90 90
541 – 2l. blue 1·60 1·60
542 **99** 5l. green 5·50 5·50
543 – 10l. blue 12·00 12·00
544 – 20l. violet 20·00 20·00
DESIGNS: Douglas DC-3 airplane over—1, 10l. Rozafat Shkodor; 2, 20l. Keshtjelle-Butrinto.

1950. Albanian Patriots.
545 – 2l. green 1·25 1·25
546 – 2l.50 violet 1·50 1·50
547 – 3l. red 2·50 2·25
548 – 5l. blue 3·00 2·50
549 **100** 8l. brown 8·00 7·25
PORTRAITS: 2l. Ahmet Haxhia, Hydajet Lezha, Naim Gjylbegu, Ndoc Mazi and Ndoc Deda; 2l.50, Asim Zeneli, Ali Demi, Kajo Karafili, Dervish Hakali and Asim Vokshi; 3l. Ataz Shehu, Baba Faja, Zoja Cure, Mustafa Matohiti and Gjok Doci; 5l. Perlat Rexhepi, Bako, Vojo Kushi, Reshit Collaku and Misto Mame.

101 Arms and Flags

102 Skanderbeg

1951. 5th Anniv of Republic.
550 **101** 2l.50 red 1·50 1·60
551 5l. blue 3·75 3·75
552 8l. black 5·50 5·75

1951. 483rd Death Anniv of Skanderbeg (patriot).
553 **102** 2l.50 brown 1·50 1·40
554 5l. violet 3·00 3·25
555 8l. bistre 4·75 4·75

103 Gen. Enver Hoxha and Assembly

104 Child and Globe

1951. 7th Anniv of Permet Congress.
556 **103** 2l.50 brown 90 90
557 3l. red 1·10 1·10
558 5l. blue 2·00 2·00
559 8l. mauve 3·75 3·75

1951. International Children's Day.
560 **104** 2l. green 1·50 1·10
561 – 2l.50 brown 1·75 1·50
562 – 3l. red 2·50 1·75
563 **104** 5l. blue 3·50 2·40
DESIGN—HORIZ: 2l.50, 3l. Nurse weighing baby.

105 Enver Hoxha and Meeting-house

1951. 10th Anniv of Albanian Communists.
564 **105** 2l.50 brown 55 55
565 3l. red 65 65
566 5l. blue 1·00 1·00
567 8l. black 2·25 2·25

106 Young Partisans

1951. 10th Anniv of Albanian Young Communists' Union. Inscr "1941–1951".
568 **106** 2l.50 brown 75 90
569 – 5l. blue 4·75 2·75
570 – 8l. red 3·50 3·50
DESIGNS: Schoolgirl, railway, tractor and factories; 8l. Miniature portraits of Stafa, Spiru, Mame and Kondi.

1952. Air. Surch in figures.
571 – 0.50l. on 2l. blue (No. 541) £160 £130
572 **99** 0.50l. on 5l. green 35·00 25·00
573 2l.50 on 5l. green £250 £140
574 – 2l.50 on 10l. blue (No. 543) 35·00 25·00

108 Factory

1953.
575 **108** 0l.50 brown 75 10
576 – 1l. green 75 10
577 – 2l.50 sepia 1·60 20
578 – 3l. red 2·00 35
579 – 5l. blue 3·75 90
580 – 8l. olive 4·00 1·10
581 – 12l. purple 5·50 1·40
582 – 20l. blue 12·50 3·25
DESIGNS—HORIZ: 1l. Canal; 2l.50, Girl and cotton mill; 3l. Girl and sugar factory; 5l. Film studio; 8l. Girl and textile machinery; 20l. Dam. VERT: 12l. Pylon and hydroelectric station.

109 Soldiers and Flags

1954. 10th Anniv of Liberation.
583 **109** 0l.50 lilac 15 15
584 1l. green 65 15
585 2l.50 brown 1·10 70
586 3l. red 2·00 85
587 5l. blue 2·75 1·25
588 8l. purple 5·25 3·50

110 First Albanian School

111

1956. 70th Anniv of Albanian Schools.
589 **110** 2l. purple 30 20
590 – 2l.50 green 85 30
591 – 5l. blue 1·60 1·25
592 **110** 10l. turquoise 4·25 3·50
DESIGN: 2l.50, 5l. Portraits of P. Sotiri, P. N. Luarasi and N. Naci.

1957. 15th Anniv of Albanian Workers' Party.
593 **111** 2l.50 brown 75 20
594 – 5l. blue 1·50 65
595 – 8l. purple 3·25 2·25
DESIGNS: 5l. Party headquarters, Tirana; 8l. Marx and Lenin.

112 Congress Emblem

1957. 4th World Trade Unions Congress, Leipzig.
596 **112** 2l.50 purple 50 20
597 3l. red 75 50
598 5l. blue 1·25 85
599 8l. green 3·50 2·25

113 Lenin and Cruiser "Aurora"

114 Raising the Flag

1957. 40th Anniv of Russian Revolution.
600 **113** 2l.50 brown 1·25 55
601 5l. blue 2·10 1·60
602 8l. black 3·60 2·25

1957. 45th Anniv of Proclamation of Independence.
603 **114** 1l.50 purple 75 30
604 2l.50 brown 1·10 75
605 5l. blue 3·00 1·40
606 8l. green 4·25 2·75

115 N. Veqilharxhi

116 L. Gurakuqi

1958. 160th Birth Anniv of Veqilharxhi (patriot).
607 **115** 2l.50 brown 80 30
608 5l. blue 1·50 60
609 8l. purple 3·25 1·50

1958. Removal of Ashes of Gurakuqi (patriot).
610 **116** 1l.50 green 20 20
611 2l.50 brown 75 60
612 5l. blue 1·10 75
613 8l. sepia 3·00 1·10

117 Freedom Fighters

118 Soldiers in Action

1958. 50th Anniv of Battle of Mashkullore.
614 **117** 2l.50 ochre 60 20
615 – 3l. green 80 20
616 **117** 5l. blue 1·25 75
617 – 8l. brown 2·50 1·50
DESIGN: 3, 8l. Tree and buildings.

1958. 15th Anniv of Albanian People's Army.
618 **118** 1l.50 green 20 15
619 – 2l.50 brown 60 25
620 **118** 8l. red 1·60 1·40
621 – 11l. blue 2·40 2·25
DESIGN: 2l.50, 11l. Tank-driver, sailor, infantryman and tanks.

119 Bust of Apollo and Butrinto Amphitheatre

120 F. Joliot-Curie and Council Emblem

1959. Cultural Monuments Week.
622 **119** 2l.50 brown 75 25
623 6l.50 green 3·00 1·40
624 11l. blue 4·25 2·50

1959. 10th Anniv of World Peace Council.
625 **120** 1l.50 red 2·25 80
626 2l.50 violet 5·00 2·00
627 11l. blue 10·50 6·00

121 Basketball

122 Soldier

1959. 1st National Spartacist Games.
628 **121** 1l.50 violet 75 35
629 – 2l.50 green 1·10 35
630 – 5l. red 1·75 1·40
631 – 11l. blue 6·25 3·75
DESIGNS: 2l.50, Football; 5l. Running; 11l. Runners with torches.

1959. 15th Anniv of Liberation.
632 **122** 1l.50 red 50 25
633 – 2l.50 brown . . . . . . 1·40 40
634 – 3l. green . . . . 1·60 50
635 – 6l.50 red . . . . 3·25 4·50
DESIGNS: 2l.50, Security guard. 3l. Harvester; 6l.50, Laboratory workers.

123 Mother and Child 124

1959. 10th Anniv of Declaration of Human Rights.
636 **123** 5l. blue . . . . 7·25 2·00

1960. 50th Anniv of International Women's Day.
637 **124** 2l.50 brown . . . . . . 1·00 55
638 11l. red . . . . 4·00 1·40

125 Congress Building 126 A. Moisiu 127 Lenin

1960. 40th Anniv of Lushnje Congress.
639 **125** 2l.50 brown 55 25
640 7l.50 blue . . . . 1·50 80

1960. 80th Birth Anniv of Alexandre Moisiu (actor).
641 **126** 3l. brown 65 45
642 11l. green . . . . 2·25 80

1960. 90th Birth Anniv of Lenin.
643 **127** 4l. turquoise . . . . . . 1·75 35
644 11l. red . . . . 5·50 1·25

128 Vaso Pasha 129 Frontier Guard 130 Family with Policeman

1960. 80th Anniv of Albanian Alphabet Study Association.
645 **128** 1l. olive 30 20
646 – 1l.50 brown 85 25
647 – 6l.50 blue . . . . 1·75 85
648 – 11l. red . . . . 4·25 1·60
DESIGNS: 1l.50, Jani Vreto; 6l.50, Sami Frasheri; 11l. Association statutes.

1960. 15th Anniv of Frontier Force.
649 **129** 1l.50 red 50 30
650 11l. blue . . . . 3·00 1·40

1960. 15th Anniv of People's Police.
651 **130** 1l.50 green 55 25
652 8l.50 brown . . . . 3·00 1·25

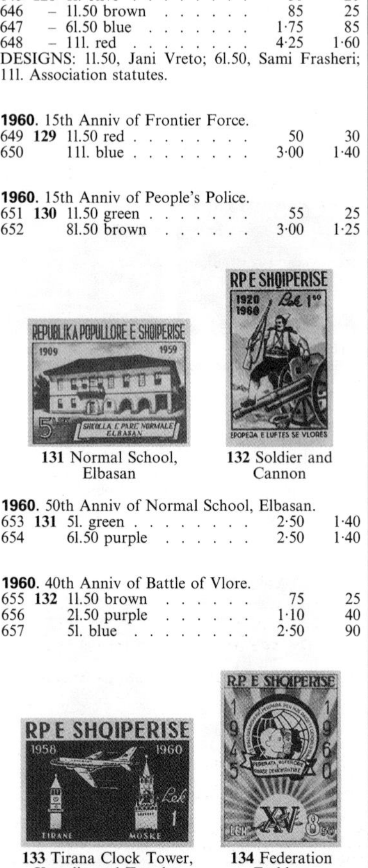

131 Normal School, Elbasan 132 Soldier and Cannon

1960. 50th Anniv of Normal School, Elbasan.
653 **131** 5l. green . . . . 2·50 1·40
654 6l.50 purple . . . . . . 2·50 1·40

1960. 40th Anniv of Battle of Vlore.
655 **132** 1l.50 brown 75 25
656 2l.50 purple . . . . . . 1·10 40
657 5l. blue . . . . 2·50 90

133 Tirana Clock Tower, Kremlin and Tupolev Tu-104A Jetliner 134 Federation Emblem

1960. 2nd Anniv of Tirana–Moscow Jet Air Service.
658 **133** 1l. brown . . . . 1·00 75
659 7l.50 blue . . . . 3·75 1·50
660 11l.50 grey . . . . 6·00 3·00

1960. 15th Anniv of World Democratic Youth Federation.
661 **134** 1l.50 blue 25 15
662 8l.50 red . . . . 1·40 55

135 Ali Kelmendi 136 Flags of Albania and Russia, and Clasped Hands 137 Marx and Lenin

1960. 60th Birth Anniv of Kelmendi (Communist).
663 **135** 1l.50 olive 55 20
664 11l. purple . . . . 1·40 85

1961. 15th Anniv of Albanian-Soviet Friendship Society.
665 **136** 2l. violet 55 20
666 8l. purple . . . . 1·75 75

1961. 4th Albanian Workers' Party Congress.
667 **137** 2l. red 55 20
668 8l. blue . . . . 1·60 80

138 Malsi e Madhe (Shkoder) Costume 139 European Otter

1961. Provincial Costumes.
669 **138** 1l. black 75 20
670 – 1l.50 purple . . . . . . 1·10 25
671 – 6l.50 blue . . . . 3·75 1·10
672 – 11l. red . . . . 7·25 2·40
COSTUMES: 1l.50, Malsi e Madhe (Shkoder) (female); 6l.50, Lume; 11l. Mirdite.

1961. Albanian Fauna.
673 **139** 2l.50 blue . . . . 4·00 1·00
674 – 6l.50 green (Eurasian badger) . . . . 8·00 2·50
675 – 11l. brown (Brown bear) 13·50 5·00

140 Dalmatian Pelicans 141 Cyclamen

1961. Albanian Birds.
676 **140** 1l.50 red on pink . . . . 3·50 60
677 – 7l.50 violet on blue . . . 5·75 1·60
678 – 11l. brown on pink . . . 8·75 2·00
BIRDS: 7l.50, Grey heron; 11l. Little egret.

1961. Albanian Flowers.
679 **141** 1l.50 purple and blue . . 2·50 50
680 – 8l. orange and purple . . 5·00 2·00
681 – 11l. red and green . . . . 8·00 2·50
FLOWERS: 8l. Forsythia; 11l. Lily.

142 M. G. Nikolla 143 Lenin and Marx on Flag

1961. 50th Birth Anniv of Nikolla (poet).
682 **142** 0l.50 brown 40 30
683 8l.50 green . . . . . . 2·00 1·40

1961. 20th Anniv of Albanian Workers' Party.
684 **143** 2l.50 red 90 25
685 7l.50 purple . . . . . . 2·00 90

144 145 Yuri Gagarin and "Vostok 1"

1961. 20th Anniv of Albanian Young Communists' Union.
686 **144** 2l.50 blue 90 25
687 7l.50 mauve . . . . . . 1·60 1·00

1962. World's First Manned Space Flight. (a) Postage.
688 **145** 0l.50 blue 90 15
689 4l. purple . . . . 3·75 90
690 11l. green . . . . 9·00 3·00

(b) Air. Optd **POSTA AJRORE**.
691 **145** 0l.50 blue on cream . . . 35·00 35·00
692 4l. purple on cream . . . 35·00 35·00
693 11l. green on cream . . . 35·00 35·00

147 P. N. Luarasi 148 Campaign Emblem

1962. 50th Death Anniv of Petro N. Luarasi (patriot).
694 **147** 0l.50 blue 75 15
695 8l.50 brown . . . . . . 3·00 75

IMPERF STAMPS. Many Albanian stamps from No. 696 onwards exist imperf and/or in different colours from limited printings.

1962. Malaria Eradication.
696 **148** 1l.50 green 15 10
697 2l.50 red 20 10
698 10l. purple . . . . 1·10 65
699 11l. blue . . . . 1·60 90

149 Camomile 150 Throwing the Javelin

1962. Medicinal Plants.
700 **149** 0l.50 yellow, green & blue 35 20
701 – 8l. green, yellow and grey 1·60 1·00
702 – 11l.50 violet, grn & ochre 2·75 1·25
PLANTS: 8l. Silver linden; 11l.50, Sage.

1962. Olympic Games, Tokyo, 1964 (1st issue). Inscr as in T **102**.
703 – 0l.50 black and blue . . . 20 15
704 – 2l.50 sepia and brown . . 70 15
705 – 3l. black and blue 90 20
706 **150** 9l. purple and red . . . . 2·50 75
707 – 10l. black and olive . . . 2·75 1·00
DESIGNS—VERT: 0l.50, Diving; 2l.50, Pole-vaulting; 10l. Putting the shot. HORIZ: 3l. Olympic flame.
See also Nos. 754/8, 818/21 and 842/51.

151 "Sputnik 1" in Orbit 152 Footballer and Ball in Net

1962. Cosmic Flights.
708 **151** 0l.50 yellow and violet . . 60 20
709 – 1l. sepia and green . . . 85 25
710 – 1l.50 yellow and red . . . 1·40 35
711 – 20l. blue and purple . . . 9·00 3·00
DESIGNS: 1l. Dog "Laika" and "Sputnik 2"; 1l.50, Artificial satellite and Sun; 20l. "Lunik 3" photographing Moon.

1962. World Cup Football Championship, Chile.
712 **152** 1l. violet and orange . . . 20 15
713 – 2l.50 blue and green . . . 1·00 20
714 **152** 6l.50 purple and brown 2·00 25
715 – 15l. purple and green . . 2·75 70
DESIGN: 2l.50, 15l. As Type **152** but globe in place of ball in net.

153 "Europa" and Albanian Maps 154 Dardhe Woman

1962. Tourist Publicity.
716 **153** 0l.50 red, yellow & green 30 30
717 – 1l. red, purple and blue 1·40 1·40
718 – 2l.50 red, purple and blue 8·00 8·00
719 **153** 11l. red, yellow and grey 16·00 16·00
DESIGN: 1, 2l.50, Statue and map.

1962. Costumes of Albania's Southern Region.
720 **154** 0l.50 red, purple and blue 25 10
721 – 1l. brown and buff . . . 30 15
722 – 2l.50 black, violet & grn 1·40 40
723 – 14l. red, brown and green 4·25 1·60
COSTUMES: 1l. Devoll man; 2l.50, Lunxheri woman; 14l. Gjirokaster man.

155 Chamois 156 Golden Eagle

1962. Albanian Animals.
724 **155** 0l.50 purple and green . . 50 15
725 – 1l. black and yellow . . . 1·40 30
726 – 1l.50 black and brown . . 2·00 35
727 – 15l. brown and green . . 20·00 3·75
ANIMALS—HORIZ. 1l. Lynx; 1l.50, Wild boar. VERT: 15l. Roe deer.

1962. 50th Anniv of Independence.
728 **156** 1l. brown and red 40 35
729 – 3l. black and brown . . 1·75 75
730 – 16l. black and mauve . . 4·75 1·90
DESIGNS: 3l. I. Qemali; 16l. "RPSH" and golden eagle.

157 Revolutionaries 158 Henri Dunant and Globe

1963. 45th Anniv of October Revolution.
731 **157** 5l. violet and yellow . . . 1·10 55
732 – 10l. black and red . . . . 2·25 1·25
DESIGN: 10l. Statue of Lenin.

1963. Red Cross Centenary. Cross in red.
733 **158** 1l.50 black and red . . . 65 20
734 2l.50 black, red and blue 85 40
735 6l. black, red and green 1·60 90
736 10l. black, red and yellow 3·50 1·75

159 Stalin and Battle 160 Nikolaev and "Vostok 3"

1963. 20th Anniv of Battle of Stalingrad.
737 **159** 8l. black & grn (postage) 9·00 2·50
738 – 7l. red and green (air) . . 9·00 2·00
DESIGN: 7l. "Lenin" flag, map, tanks, etc.

1963. 1st "Team" Manned Space Flights.
739 **160** 2l.50 brown and blue . . 75 30
740 – 7l.50 black and blue . . 1·75 1·00
741 – 20l. brown and violet . . 6·00 2·75
DESIGNS—HORIZ: 7l.50, Globe, "Vostok 3" and "Vostok 4". VERT: 20l. P. Popovic and "Vostok 4".

161 Crawling Cockchafer 162 Policeman and Allegorical Figure

1963. Insects.
742 **161** 0l.50 brown and green . . 75 30
743 – 1l. brown and blue . . . 1·50 75
744 – 8l. purple and red . . . . 6·50 1·75
745 – 10l. black and yellow . . 8·00 3·25
INSECTS: 1l.50, Stagbeetle; 8l. "Procerus gigas" (ground beetle); 10l. "Cicindela albanica" (tiger beetle).

1963. 20th Anniv of Albanian Security Police.
746 **162** 2l.50 black, purple & red 90 50
747 7l.50 black, lake and red 3·25 80

163 Great Crested Grebe
164 Official Insignia and Postmark of 1913

1963. Birds. Multicoloured.
748 0l.50 Type **163** 80 25
749 3l. Golden eagle . . . . . . 2·00 30
750 6l.50 Grey partridge . . . . 3·25 1·10
751 11l. Western capercaillie . . . 6·75 1·75

1963. 50th Anniv of First Albanian Stamps.
752 **164** 5l. multicoloured . . . . 1·90 90
753 – 10l. green, black and red 3·50 1·60
DESIGN: 10l. Albanian stamps of 1913, 1937 and 1962.

165 Boxing
166 Gen. Enver Hoxha and Labinoti Council Building

1963. Olympic Games, Tokyo (1964) (2nd issue).
754 **165** 2l. green, red and yellow 65 65
755 – 3l. brown, blue & orange 85 25
756 – 5l. purple, brown and blue . . . . 1·25 35
757 – 6l. black, grey and green 1·75 90
758 – 9l. blue and brown . . . 3·50 1·40
SPORTS: 3l. Basketball; 5l. Volleyball; 6l. Cycling; 9l. Gymnastics.

1963. 20th Anniv of Albanian People's Army.
759 **166** 1l.50 yellow, black & red 40 20
760 – 2l.50 bistre, brown & blue 1·00 30
761 – 5l. black, drab & turq . . 1·90 90
762 – 6l. blue, buff and brown 2·75 1·40
DESIGNS: 2l.50, Soldier with weapons; 5l. Soldier attacking; 6l. Peacetime soldier.

167 Gagarin

1963. Soviet Cosmonauts. Portraits in yellow and brown.
763 **167** 3l. violet . . . . 1·00 20
764 – 5l. blue . . . . 1·40 40
765 – 7l. violet and grey . . . . 2·25 65
766 – 11l. blue and purple . . . 3·75 1·00
767 – 14l. blue and turquoise . . 4·75 1·40
768 – 20l. blue . . . . 7·25 3·50
COSMONAUTS: 5l. Titov; 7l. Nikolaev; 11l. Popovich; 14l. Bykovsky; 20l. Valentina Tereshkova.

168 Volleyball (Rumania)

1963. European Sports Events, 1963.
769 **168** 2l. red, black and olive . . 85 20
770 – 3l. bistre, black and red 85 30
771 – 5l. orange, black & green 1·25 65
772 – 7l. green, black and pink 1·90 85
773 – 8l. red, black and blue . . 3·50 1·10
SPORTS: 3l. Weightlifting (Sweden); 5l. Football (European Cup); 7l. Boxing (Russia); 8l. Ladies' Rowing (Russia).

169 Celadon Swallowtail

1963. Butterflies and Moths.
774 **169** 1l. black, yellow and red 75 25
775 – 2l. black, red and blue . . 90 30
776 – 4l. black, yellow & purple 2·00 85
777 – 5l. multicoloured . . . . 2·75 75
778 – 8l. black, red and brown 4·75 1·60
779 – 10l. orange, brown & blue 6·25 2·25
DESIGNS: 2l. Jersey tiger moth; 4l. Brimstone; 5l. Death's-head hawk moth; 8l. Orange tip; 10l. Peacock.

170 Lunik 1

1963. Air. Cosmic Flights.
780 **170** 2l. olive, yellow & orange 40 25
781 – 3l. multicoloured . . . . 1·00 25
782 – 5l. olive, yellow & purple 1·60 65
783 – 8l. red, yellow and violet 2·50 1·10
784 – 12l. red, orange and blue 4·50 3·50
DESIGNS: 3l. Lunik 2; 5l. Lunik 3; 8l. Venus 1; 12l. Mars 1.

171 Food Processing Works
172 Shield and Banner

1963. Industrial Buildings.
785 **171** 2l.50 red on pink 90 20
786 – 20l. green on green . . . 4·75 1·25
787 – 30l. purple on blue . . . 7·50 1·90
788 – 50l. bistre on cream . . . 9·50 3·50
DESIGNS—VERT: 20l. Naphtha refinery; 30l. Fruit-bottling plant. HORIZ: 50l. Copper-processing works.

1963. 1st Army and Defence Aid Assn Congress.
789 **172** 2l. multicoloured 70 25
790 8l. multicoloured . . . . 2·00 1·40

173 Young Men of Three Races

1963. 15th Anniv of Declaration of Human Rights.
791 **173** 3l. black and ochre . . . 65 55
792 5l. blue and ochre . . . . 1·40 85
793 7l. violet and ochre . . . 2·25 1·40

174 Bobsleighing
175 Lenin

1963. Winter Olympic Games, Innsbruck. Inscr "1964".
794 **174** 0l.50 black and blue . . . 20 20
795 – 2l.50 black, red and grey 90 25
796 – 6l.50 black, yellow & grey 1·75 35
797 – 12l.50 red, black & green 3·50 1·60
DESIGNS—VERT: 2l.50, Skiing; 12l.50, Figure-skating. HORIZ: 6l.50, Ice-hockey.

1964. 40th Death Anniv of Lenin.
798 **175** 5l. olive and bistre . . . 1·10 35
799 10l. olive and bistre . . . 1·50 85

176 Hurdling
177 Common Sturgeon

1964. "GANEFO" Games, Djakarta (1963).
800 **176** 2l.50 blue and lilac . . . 85 25
801 – 3l. brown and green . . . 1·25 30
802 – 6l.50 red and blue . . . . 1·60 40
803 – 8l. ochre and blue . . . . 2·50 90
SPORTS—HORIZ. 3l. Running; 6l.50, Rifle-shooting. VERT: 8l. Basketball.

1964. Fishes. Multicoloured.
804 0l.50 Type **177** 30 10
805 1l. Gilthead seabream 75 20
806 1l.50 Flat-headed grey mullet 1·00 30
807 2l.50 Common carp . . . . 1·50 50
808 6l.50 Atlantic mackerel . . . 3·00 1·25
809 10l. Lake Ochrid salmon . . 5·00 2·00

178 Eurasian Red Squirrel

1964. Forest Animals. Multicoloured.
810 1l. Type **178** 30 20
811 1l.50 Beech marten 50 25
812 2l. Red fox 70 30
813 2l.50 East European hedgehog 80 30
814 3l. Brown hare . . . . . . 1·00 70
815 5l. Golden jackal . . . . . . 1·75 70
816 7l. Wild cat . . . . 3·00 90
817 8l. Wolf . . . . 4·50 1·10

179 Lighting Olympic Torch

1964. Olympic Games, Tokyo (3rd issue). Inscr "DREJT TOKIOS".
818 **179** 3l. yellow, buff and green 30 15
819 – 5l. blue, violet and red . . 65 25
820 – 7l. lt blue, blue & yellow 90 30
821 – 10l. multicoloured . . . . 1·25 85
DESIGNS: 5l. Torch and globes; 7l. Olympic flag and Mt. Fuji; 10l. Olympic Stadium, Tokyo.

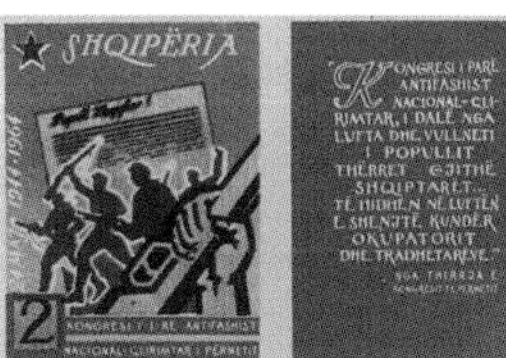

180 Soldiers, Hand clutching Rifle, and Inscription

1964. 20th Anniv of Permet Congress.
822 **180** 2l. sepia, red and orange 75 50
823 – 5l. multicoloured . . . . 2·00 1·50
824 – 8l. sepia, red and brown 3·50 3·00
DESIGNS (each with different inscription at right): 5l. Albanian Arms; 8l. Gen. Enver Hoxha.

181 Revolutionaries with Flag
183 Full Moon

1964. 40th Anniv of Revolution.
825 **181** 2l.50 black and red . . . 25 20
826 7l.50 black and mauve . . 1·00 45

1964. "Verso Tokyo" Stamp Exhibition, Rimini (Italy). Optd **Rimini 25-VI-64**.
827 10l. blue, violet, orange and black (No. 821) . . . . . 7·25 7·25

1964. Moon's Phases.
828 **183** 1l. yellow and violet . . . 30 15
829 – 5l. yellow and blue . . . 1·10 65
830 – 8l. yellow and blue . . . 1·75 85
831 – 11l. yellow and green . . 4·25 1·25
PHASES: 5l. Waxing Moon; 8l. Half-Moon; 11l. Waning Moon.

184 Winter Wren
186 Running and Gymnastics

1964. Albanian Birds. Multicoloured.
832 0l.50 Type **184** 35 25
833 1l. Penduline tit 60 30
834 2l.50 Green woodpecker . . . 85 40
835 3l. Common treecreeper . . . 1·25 40
836 4l. Eurasian nuthatch . . . . 1·40 60
837 5l. Great tit . . . . 1·75 60
838 6l. Eurasian goldfinch . . . . 2·00 60
839 18l. Golden oriole . . . . . 4·75 2·10

1964. Air. Riccione "Space" Exhibition. Optd **Riccione 23-8-1964**.
840 **170** 2l. olive, yellow & orange 10·50 10·50
841 – 8l. red, yellow and violet (No.783) . . . . 25·00 25·00

1964. Olympic Games, Tokyo.
842 **186** 1l. red, blue and green . . 20 15
843 – 2l. brown, blue and violet 25 20
844 – 3l. brown, violet and olive 35 20
845 – 4l. olive, turquoise & blue 50 25
846 – 5l. turquoise, purple & red 85 65
847 – 6l. ultram, lt blue & orge 1·00 75
848 – 7l. green, orange and blue 1·40 90
849 – 8l. grey, green and yellow 1·40 1·10
850 – 9l. lt blue, yellow & purple . . . . 1·40 1·25
851 – 10l. brown, green & turq 1·90 1·60
SPORTS: 2l. Weightlifting and judo; 3l. Horse-jumping and cycling; 4l. Football and water-polo; 5l. Wrestling and boxing; 6l. Various sports and hockey; 7l. Swimming and yachting; 8l. Basketball and volleyball; 9l. Rowing and canoeing; 10l. Fencing and pistol-shooting.

187 Chinese Republican Emblem
188 Karl Marx

1964. 15th Anniv of Chinese People's Republic. Inscr "I TETOR 1949 1964.".
852 **187** 7l. red, black and yellow 1·60 85
853 – 8l. black, red and yellow 2·75 1·25
DESIGN—HORIZ: 8l. Mao Tse-tung.

1964. Centenary of "First International".
854 **188** 2l. black, red and lavender 90 20
855 – 5l. slate . . . . 2·40 75
856 – 8l. black, red and buff . . 4·00 1·25
DESIGNS: 5l. St. Martin's Hall, London; 8l. F. Engels.

189 J. de Rada
190 Arms and Flag

1964. 150th Birth Anniv of Jeronim de Rada (poet).
857 **189** 7l. green . . . . 1·60 65
858 8l. violet . . . . 2·50 1·10

1964. 20th Anniv of Liberation.
859 **190** 1l. multicoloured 20 20
860 – 2l. blue, red and yellow 65 20
861 – 3l. brown, red and yellow 1·00 65
862 – 4l. green, red and yellow 1·40 85
863 – 10l. black, red and blue 3·50 1·60
DESIGNS—HORIZ: 2l. Industrial scene; 3l. Agricultural scene. 4l. Laboratory worker. VERT: 10l. Hands holding Constitution, hammer and sickle.

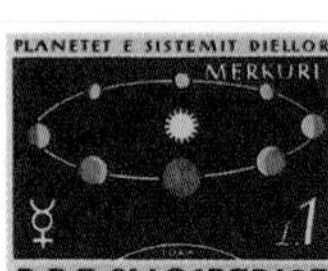

191 Mercury

192 Chestnut

1964. Solar System Planets. Multicoloured.
864 1l. Type **191** 25 20
865 2l. Venus 45 25
866 3l. Earth 70 30
867 4l. Mars 85 35
868 5l. Jupiter . . . . 1·10 40
869 6l. Saturn . . . . 1·60 50
870 7l. Uranus . . . . 1·90 65
871 8l. Neptune . . . . 2·00 1·25
872 9l. Pluto . . . . 2·10 1·60

1965. Winter Fruits. Multicoloured.
873 1l. Type **192** 25 15
874 2l. Medlars 35 20
875 3l. Persimmon 75 25
876 4l. Pomegranate 95 35
877 5l. Quince . . . . 1·60 40
878 10l. Orange . . . . 2·75 1·10

193 "Industry"

194 Buffalo Grazing

1965. 20th Anniv of Albanian Trade Unions. Inscr "B.P.S.H. 1945–1965".
879 **193** 2l. red, pink and black . . 3·50 3·00
880 – 5l. black, grey and ochre 7·00 6·00
881 – 8l. blue, lt blue & black 8·50 6·50
DESIGNS: 5l. Set square, book and dividers ("Technocracy"); 8l. Hotel, trees and sunshade ("Tourism").

1965. Water Buffaloes.
882 **194** 1l. multicoloured 50 15
883 – 2l. multicoloured . . . . 1·10 20
884 – 3l. multicoloured . . . . 1·90 30
885 – 7l. multicoloured . . . . 4·50 1·10
886 – 12l. multicoloured . . . . 8·00 2·50
DESIGNS: 2l. to 12l. As Type **194**, showing different views of buffalo.

195 Coastal View

1965. Albanian Scenery. Multicoloured.
887 1l.50 Type **195** . . . . 1·60 80
888 2l.50 Mountain forest . . . . 2·75 1·10
889 3l. Lugina Peak (vert) . . . . 3·50 1·40
890 4l. White River, Thethi (vert) 4·25 1·90
891 5l. Dry Mountain . . . . . 5·25 2·50
892 9l. Lake of Flowers, Lure . . 12·00 4·50

196 Frontier Guard

197 Rifleman

1965. 20th Anniv of Frontier Force.
893 **196** 2l.50 multicoloured . . . 1·40 85
894 12l.50 multicoloured . . . 8·00 3·50

1965. European Shooting Championships, Bucharest.
895 **197** 1l. purple, red and violet 20 15
896 – 2l. purple, ultram & blue 65 20
897 – 3l. red and pink 85 30
898 – 4l. multicoloured . . . . 1·25 30
899 – 15l. multicoloured . . . . 5·00 95
DESIGNS: 2, 15l. Rifle-shooting (different); 3l. "Target" map; 4l. Pistol-shooting.

198 I.T.U. Emblem and Symbols

199 Belyaev

1965. Centenary of I.T.U.
900 **198** 2l.50 mauve, black & grn 1·60 20
901 12l.50 blue, black & violet 6·00 1·40

1965. Space Flight of "Voskhod 2".
902 **199** 1l.50 brown and blue . . 20 10
903 – 2l. blue, ultram & lilac . . 30 15
904 – 6l.50 brown and mauve 1·25 35
905 – 20l. yellow, black & blue 4·50 1·25
DESIGNS: 2l. "Voskhod 2"; 6l.50, Leonov; 20l. Leonov in space.

200 Marx and Lenin

201 Mother and Child

1965. Postal Ministers' Congress, Peking.
907 **200** 2l.50 sepia, red & yellow 75 30
908 7l.50 green, red & yellow 3·25 1·25

1965. International Children's Day. Multicoloured.
909 1l. Type **201** 25 15
910 2l. Children planting tree . . 45 20
911 3l. Children and construction toy (horiz) 75 20
912 4l. Child on beach 90 30
913 15l. Child reading book . . . 1·25 1·75

202 Wine Vessel

203 Fuchsia

1965. Albanian Antiquities. Multicoloured.
914 1l. Type **202** 20 10
915 2l. Helmet and shield 40 15
916 3l. Mosaic of animal (horiz) 85 25
917 4l. Statuette of man . . . . 1·60 30
918 15l. Statuette of headless and limbless man . . . . . . 4·25 1·60

1965. Albanian Flowers. Multicoloured.
919 1l. Type **203** 25 15
920 2l. Cyclamen 75 20
921 3l. Lilies . . . . 1·10 25
922 3l.50 Iris . . . . 1·40 25
923 4l. Dahlia . . . . 1·60 35
924 4l.50 Hydrangea . . . . . . 1·75 35
925 5l. Rose . . . . 2·00 70
926 7l. Tulips . . . . 2·75 90

(currency revaluation 10 (old) leks = 1 (new) lek.)

1965. Surch.
927 5q. on 30l. (No. 787) 20 20
928 15q. on 30l. (No. 787) . . . 45 20
929 25q. on 50l. (No. 788) . . . 65 25
930 80q. on 50l. (No. 788) . . . 2·10 90
931 1l.10 on 20l. (No. 786) . . . 3·25 1·10
932 2l. on 20l. (No. 786) . . . . 6·25 2·10

205 White Stork

206 "War Veterans" (after painting by B. Sejdini)

1965. Migratory Birds. Multicoloured.
933 10q. Type **205** 35 35
934 20q. European cuckoo . . . 65 35
935 30q. Hoopoe . . . . 1·10 50
936 40q. European bee-eater . . . 1·75 60
937 50q. European nightjar . . . 2·00 70
938 1l.50 Common quail . . . . 6·00 2·00

1965. War Veterans Conference.
939 **206** 25q. brown and black . . 3·25 85
940 65q. blue and black . . . 7·25 1·75
941 1l.10 black . . . . 10·00 2·50

207 Hunter stalking Western Capercaillie

208 "Nerium oleander"

1965. Hunting.
942 **207** 10q. multicoloured . . . 85 25
943 – 20q. brown, sepia & grn 85 25
944 – 30q. multicoloured . . . 1·90 80
945 – 40q. purple and green . . 2·25 90
946 – 50q. brown, blue & black 2·00 55
947 – 1l. brown, bistre & green 4·25 1·00
DESIGNS: 20q. Shooting roe deer; 30q. Common pheasant; 40q. Shooting mallard; 50q. Dogs chasing wild boar; 1l. Hunter and brown hare.

1965. Mountain Flowers. Multicoloured.
948 10q. Type **208** 30 20
949 20q. "Myosotis alpestris" . . 40 20
950 30q. "Dianthus glacialis" . . 65 30
951 40q. "Nymphaea alba" . . . 1·25 40
952 50q. "Lotus corniculatus" . . 1·60 50
953 1l. "Papaver rhoeas" . . . . 3·75 1·60

209 Tourist Hotel, Fier

210 Freighter "Teuta"

1965. Public Buildings.
954 **209** 5q. black and blue . . . 10 10
955 – 10q. black and buff . . . 15 10
956 – 15q. black and green . . 20 10
957 – 25q. black and violet . . 75 15
958 – 65q. black and brown . . 1·25 35
959 – 80q. black and green . . 1·50 45
960 – 1l.10 black and purple . . 2·25 50
961 – 1l.60 black and blue . . . 3·00 1·25
962 – 2l. black and pink . . . . 4·25 1·40
963 – 3l. black and grey . . . . 8·00 2·40
BUILDINGS: 10q. Peshkopi Hotel; 15q. Sanatorium, Tirana; 25q. "House of Rest", Pogradec; 65q. Partisans Sports Palace, Tirana; 80q. "House of Rest", Dajti Mountain; 1l.10. Palace of Culture, Tirana; 1l.60, Adriatic Hotel, Durres; 2l. Migjeni Theatre, Shkoder; 3l. "A. Moisiu" Cultural Palace, Durres.

1965. Evolution of Albanian Ships.
964 **210** 10q. green and light green 40 20
965 – 20q. bistre and green . . 55 20
966 – 30q. ultramarine and blue 75 35
967 – 40q. violet and light violet 1·00 45
968 – 50q. red and rose . . . . 2·10 55
969 – 1l. brown and ochre . . . 4·25 1·00
DESIGNS: 20q. Punt; 30q. 19th-century sailing ship; 40q. 18th-century brig; 50q. Freighter "Vlora"; 1l. Illyrian galliots.

211 Head of Brown Bear

212 Championships Emblem

1965. Brown Bears. Different Bear designs as T **211**.
970 – 10q. brown and buff . . . 30 15
971 – 20q. brown and buff . . . 75 20
972 – 30q. brown, red and buff 1·00 35
973 – 35q. brown and buff . . . 1·25 40
974 – 40q. brown and buff . . . 1·60 45
975 **211** 50q. brown and buff . . . 2·50 50
976 – 55q. brown and buff . . . 3·50 85
977 – 60q. brown, red and buff 5·00 2·75
The 10q. to 40q. are vert.

1965. 7th Balkan Basketball Championships, Tirana. Multicoloured.
978 10q. Type **212** 20 10
979 20q. Competing players . . . 40 15
980 30q. Clearing ball 85 20
981 50q. Attempted goal . . . . 2·10 25
982 1l.40 Medal and ribbon . . . 4·25 1·00

213 Arms on Book

214 Cow

1966. 20th Anniv of Albanian People's Republic.
983 **213** 10q. gold, red and brown 15 10
984 – 20q. gold, blue & ultram 20 15
985 – 30q. gold, yellow and brown 75 20
986 – 60q. gold, lt grn & green 1·40 65
987 – 80q. gold, red and brown 2·25 75
DESIGNS (Arms and): 20q. Chimney stacks; 30q. Ear of corn; 60q. Hammer, sickle and open book; 80q. Industrial plant.

1966. Domestic Animals. Animals in natural colours; inscr in black: frame colours given.
988 **214** 10q. turquoise 30 20
989 – 20q. green 85 25
990 – 30q. blue . . . . 1·25 30
991 – 35q. lavender . . . . . . 1·40 35
992 – 40q. pink . . . . 1·75 35
993 – 50q. yellow . . . . 2·00 40
994 – 55q. blue . . . . 2·25 70
995 – 60q. yellow . . . . 4·50 95
ANIMALS—HORIZ. 20q. Pig; 30q. Sheep; 35q. Goat; 40q. Dog. VERT: 50q. Cat; 55q. Horse; 60q. Ass.

215 Football

216 A. Z. Cajupi

1966. World Cup Football Championships (1st series).
996 **215** 5q. orange grey & buff 15 10
997 – 10q. multicoloured . . . 20 10
998 – 15q. blue, yellow & buff 25 15
999 – 20q. multicoloured . . . 35 20
1000 – 25q. sepia, red and buff 45 20
1001 – 30q. brown, green & buff 50 30
1002 – 35q. green, blue and buff 85 30
1003 – 40q. brown red and buff 90 35
1004 – 50q. multicoloured . . . 1·00 65
1005 – 70q. multicoloured . . . 1·40 90
DESIGNS—Footballer and map showing: 10q. Montevideo (1930); 15q. Rome (1934); 20q. Paris (1938); 25q. Rio de Janeiro (1950); 30q. Berne (1954); 35q. Stockholm (1958); 40q. Santiago (1962); 50q. London (1966); 70q. World Cup and football.
See also Nos. 1035/42.

1966. Birth Centenary of Andon Cajupi (poet).
1006 **216** 40q. indigo and blue . . 1·10 55
1007 1l.10 bronze and green 2·50 1·10

217 Painted Lady

218 W.H.O. Building

1966. Butterflies and Dragonflies. Multicoloured.
1008 10q. Type **217** 35 20
1009 20q. "Calopteryx virgo" . . 50 20
1010 30q. Pale clouded yellow . . 70 20
1011 35q. Banded agrion 85 25
1012 40q. Banded agrion (different) . . . . 1·10 30
1013 50q. Swallowtail . . . . . 1·50 40
1014 55q. Danube clouded yellow 2·00 50
1015 60q. Hungarian glider . . . 5·00 1·25
The 20, 35 and 40q. are dragonflies, remainder are butterflies.

1966. Inaug of W.H.O. Headquarters, Geneva.
1016 **218** 25q. black and blue . . 45 15
1017 – 35q. blue and orange . . 1·25 20
1018 – 60q. red, blue and green 1·60 35
1019 – 80q. blue, yellow & brn 2·75 65
DESIGNS—VERT: 35q. Ambulance and patient; 60q. Nurse and mother weighing baby. HORIZ: 80q. Medical equipment.

219 Leaf Star **220** "Luna 10"

1966. "Starfish". Multicoloured.

1020 15q. Type **219** 30 15
1021 25q. Spiny Star 50 20
1022 35q. Brittle Star . . . . . . 1·10 25
1023 45q. Sea Star . . . . 1·60 30
1024 50q. Blood Star . . . . . . 1·75 40
1025 60q. Sea Cucumber . . . . 2·25 40
1026 70q. Sea Urchin . . . . . . 4·00 1·75

1966. "Luna 10". Launching.

1027 **220** 20q. multicoloured . . . 70 20
1028 – 30q. multicoloured . . . 90 25
1029 **220** 70q. multicoloured . . . 1·75 35
1030 – 80q. multicoloured . . . 3·50 1·00
DESIGN: 30, 80q. Earth, Moon and trajectory of "Luna 10".

221 Water-level Map of Albania **222** Footballers (Uruguay, 1930)

1966. International Hydrological Decade.

1031 **221** 20q. black, orge & red 50 20
1032 – 30q. multicoloured . . . 1·00 25
1033 – 70q. black and violet . . 2·10 40
1034 – 80q. multicoloured . . . 2·75 1·25
DESIGNS: 30q. Water scale and fields; 70q. Turbine and electricity pylon; 80q. Hydrological decade emblem.

1966. World Cup Football Championship (2nd series). Inscriptions and values in black.

1035 **222** 10q. purple and ochre 20 10
1036 – 20q. olive and blue . . . 30 15
1037 – 30q. slate and red . . . 75 15
1038 – 35q. red and blue . . . 85 20
1039 – 40q. brown and green . . 1·00 20
1040 – 50q. green and brown . . 1·25 50
1041 – 55q. green and mauve 1·25 95
1042 – 60q. ochre and red . . . 2·50 1·40
DESIGNS—Various footballers representing World Cup winners: 20q. Italy, 1934; 30q. Italy, 1938; 35q. Uruguay, 1950; 40q. West Germany, 1954; 50q. Brazil, 1958; 55q. Brazil, 1962; 60q. Football and names of 16 finalists in 1966 Championship.

223 Tortoise

1966. Reptiles. Multicoloured.

1043 10q. Type **223** 20 15
1044 15q. Grass snake 30 20
1045 25q. Swamp tortoise 45 25
1046 30q. Lizard 55 30
1047 35q. Salamander 70 35
1048 45q. Green lizard . . . . . 1·25 40
1049 50q. Slow-worm . . . . . 1·25 75
1050 90q. Sand viper . . . . . . 3·25 1·40

224 Siamese Cat **225** P. Budi (writer)

1966. Cats. Multicoloured.

1051 10q. Type **224** 25 15
1052 15q. Tabby 30 20
1053 25q. Kitten 90 30
1054 45q. Persian . . . . 1·75 40
1055 60q. Persian . . . . 2·25 90
1056 65q. Persian . . . . 2·50 1·00
1057 80q. Persian . . . . 3·25 1·25
Nos. 1053/7 are horiz.

1966. 400th Birth Anniv of P. Budi.

1058 **225** 25q. bronze and flesh . . 40 25
1059 1l.75 purple and green 3·25 1·90

226 U.N.E.S.C.O. Emblem

1966. 20th Anniv of U.N.E.S.C.O. Multicoloured.

1060 5q. Type **226** 20 15
1061 15q. Tulip and open book 35 20
1062 25q. Albanian dancers . . . 95 25
1063 1l.55 Jug and base of column . . . . 4·75 1·60

227 Borzoi

1966. Dogs. Multicoloured.

1064 10q. Type **227** 40 15
1065 15q. Kuvasz 50 20
1066 25q. Setter . . . . 1·25 25
1067 45q. Cocker spaniel . . . . 1·90 85
1068 60q. Bulldog . . . . 2·00 1·00
1069 65q. St. Bernard . . . . . 2·75 1·10
1070 80q. Dachshund . . . . . 3·50 1·60

228 Hand holding Book **229** Ndre Mjeda (poet)

1966. 5th Workers Party Congress, Tirana. Multicoloured.

1071 15q. Type **228** 40 15
1072 25q. Emblems of agriculture and industry 85 15
1073 65q. Hammer and sickle, wheat and industrial skyline . . . . 1·90 35
1074 95q. Hands holding banner on bayonet and implements . . . . 3·25 65

1966. Birth Centenary of Ndre Mjeda.

1075 **229** 25q. brown and blue . . 65 20
1076 1l.75 brown and green 3·75 1·40

230 Hammer and Sickle **231** Young Communists and Banner

1966. 25th Anniv of Albanian Young Communists' Union. Multicoloured.

1077 15q. Type **230** 35 10
1078 25q. Soldier leading attack 75 10
1079 65q. Industrial worker . . . 1·60 30
1080 95q. Agricultural and industrial vista . . . . . 2·75 55

1966. 25th Anniv of Young Communists' Union. Multicoloured.

1081 5q. Manifesto (vert) 10 10
1082 10q. Type **231** 20 10
1083 1l.85 Partisans and banner (vert) . . . . 3·25 1·10

232 Golden Eagle **233** European Hake

1966. Birds of Prey. Multicoloured,

1084 10q. Type **232** 75 25
1085 15q. White-tailed sea eagle 1·10 40
1086 25q. Griffon vulture . . . . 1·90 90
1087 40q. Northern sparrow hawk . . . . 2·75 1·10
1088 50q. Osprey . . . . 3·50 1·40
1089 70q. Egyptian vulture . . . 4·75 2·00
1090 90q. Common kestrel . . . 5·25 2·75

1967. Fishes. Multicoloured.

1091 10q. Type **233** 30 15
1092 15q. Striped red mullet . . . 45 15
1093 25q. Opali . . . . 1·00 20
1094 40q. Atlantic wolffish . . . 1·25 30
1095 65q. Lumpsucker . . . . . 1·60 70
1096 80q. Swordfish . . . . . . 2·50 80
1097 1l.15 Short-spined sea-scorpion . . . . 2·75 1·40

234 Dalmatian Pelicans

1967. Dalmatian Pelicans. Multicoloured.

1098 10q. Type **234** 35 25
1099 15q. Three pelicans 75 35
1100 25q. Pelican and chicks at nest . . . . 2·00 55
1101 50q. Pelicans "taking off" and airborne . . . . . . 4·25 70
1102 2l. Pelican "yawning" . . . 11·00 3·50

235 "Camellia williamsi" **236** Congress Emblem

1967. Flowers. Multicoloured.

1103 5q. Type **235** 20 10
1104 10q. "Chrysanthemum indicum" 25 15
1105 15q. "Althaea rosea" . . . 30 15
1106 25q. "Abutilon striatum" . . 90 20
1107 35q. "Paeonia chinensis" . . 1·25 20
1108 65q. "Gladiolus gandavensis" . . . . . . 2·00 40
1109 80q. "Freesia hybrida" . . . 2·50 65
1110 1l.15 "Dianthus caryophyllus" . . . . . . 2·75 1·75

1967. 6th Trade Unions Congress, Tirana.

1111 **236** 25q. red, sepia and lilac 90 15
1112 1l.75 red, green and grey 4·00 1·60

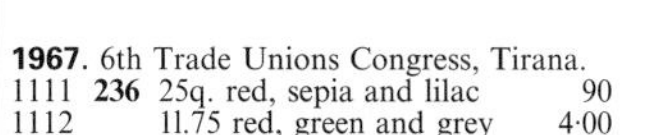

237 Rose

1967. Roses.

1113 **237** 5q. multicoloured . . . 25 10
1114 – 10q. multicoloured . . . 55 10
1115 – 15q. multicoloured . . . 70 15
1116 – 25q. multicoloured . . . 85 15
1117 – 35q. multicoloured . . . 1·00 25
1118 – 65q. multicoloured . . . 1·50 40
1119 – 80q. multicoloured . . . 1·90 50
1120 – 1l.65 multicoloured . . . 4·50 1·25
DESIGNS: 10q. to 1l.65 Various roses as Type **237**.

238 Borsh Coast

1967. Albanian Riviera. Multicoloured.

1121 15q. Butrinti (vert) 40 20
1122 20q. Type **238** 50 20
1123 25q. Piqeras village 90 30
1124 45q. Coastal view . . . . . 1·40 30
1125 50q. Himara coast . . . . . 1·60 40
1126 65q. Fishing boat, Saranda 2·25 55
1127 80q. Dhermi . . . . 2·50 1·00
1128 1l. Sunset at sea (vert) . . . 4·25 1·60

239 Fawn

1967. Roe Deer. Multicoloured.

1129 15q. Type **239** 50 15
1130 20q. Head of buck (vert) . . 50 20
1131 25q. Head of doe (vert) . . 95 20
1132 30q. Doe and fawn 95 25
1133 35q. Doe and new-born fawn . . . . 1·40 30
1134 40q. Young buck (vert) . . 1·40 35
1135 65q. Buck and doe (vert) . . 2·75 1·00
1136 70q. Running deer . . . . 3·50 1·40

240 Costumes of Malesia e Madhe Region **241** Battle Scene and Newspaper

1967. National Costumes. Multicoloured.

1137 15q. Type **240** 35 15
1138 20q. Zadrima 45 20
1139 25q. Kukesi 55 20
1140 45q. Dardhe 70 35
1141 50q. Myzeqe 75 70
1142 65q. Tirana . . . . 1·40 85
1143 80q. Dropulli . . . . 1·75 1·00
1144 1l. Laberise . . . . 2·25 1·25

1967. 25 Years of the Albanian Popular Press. Mult.

1145 25q. Type **241** 70 20
1146 75q. Newspapers and printery . . . . 1·90 50
1147 2l. Workers with newspaper 4·25 1·60

242 University, Torch and Open Book **243** Soldiers and Flag

1967. 10th Anniv of Tirana University.

1148 **242** 25q. multicoloured . . . 45 30
1149 1l.75 multicoloured . . . 2·75 1·10

1967. 25th Anniv of Albanian Democratic Front. Multicoloured.

1150 15q. Type **243** 25 15
1151 65q. Pick, rifle and flag . . 1·00 25
1152 1l.20 Torch and open book 1·90 75

244 Grey Rabbits

1967. Rabbit-breeding. Multicoloured.

1153 15q. Type **244** 20 10
1154 20q. Black and white rabbit (vert) 30 15
1155 25q. Brown hare 75 15
1156 35q. Brown rabbits . . . . 1·10 20
1157 40q. Common rabbits . . . 1·40 20
1158 50q. Grey rabbit (vert) . . . 1·75 65

1159 65q. Head of white rabbit (vert) . . . . 2·50 85
1160 1l. White rabbit . . . . . . 3·50 1·25

245 "Shkoder Wedding" (detail, Kole Idromeno)

1967. Albanian Paintings.
1161 **245** 15q. multicoloured . . . 55 10
1162 – 20q. multicoloured . . . 80 10
1163 – 25q. multicoloured . . . 1·10 10
1164 – 45q. multicoloured . . . 2·25 10
1165 – 50q. multicoloured . . . 2·40 15
1166 – 65q. multicoloured . . . 3·25 55
1167 – 80q. multicoloured . . . 4·25 80
1168 – 1l. multicoloured . . . . 7·25 1·10
DESIGNS—VERT: 20q. "Head of the Prophet David" (detail, 16th-century fresco); 45q. Ancient mosaic head (from Durres); 50q. Detail, 16th-century icon (30 × 51 mm); 1l. "Our Sister" (K. Idromeno). HORIZ (51 × 30 mm): 25q. "Commandos of the Hakmarrja Battalion" (S. Shijaku); 65q. "Co-operative" (farm women, Z. Shoshi); 80q. "Street in Korce" (V. Mio).

246 Lenin and Stalin

1967. 50th Anniv of October Revolution. Mult.
1169 15q. Type **246** 20 15
1170 25q. Lenin with soldiers (vert) 65 15
1171 50q. Lenin addressing meeting (vert) . . . . . . 1·10 25
1172 1l.10 Revolutionaries . . . 2·75 70

247 Common Turkey **248** First Aid

1967. Domestic Fowl. Multicoloured.
1173 15q. Type **247** 20 10
1174 20q. Goose 50 10
1175 25q. Hen 75 15
1176 45q. Cockerel . . . . 1·25 20
1177 50q. Helmeted guineafowl 1·40 50
1178 65q. Greylag goose (horiz) 1·90 65
1179 80q. Mallard (horiz) . . . . 2·50 85
1180 1l. Chicks (horiz) . . . . . 3·50 1·25

1967. 6th Red Cross Congress, Tirana. Mult.
1181 15q.+5q. Type **248** . . . . 1·00 65
1182 25q.+5q. Stretcher case . . 1·90 1·00
1183 65q.+25q. Heart patient . . 5·00 3·50
1184 80q.+40q. Nurse holding child . . . . 8·75 5·25

249 Arms of Skanderbeg

1967. 500th Death Anniv of Castriota Skanderbeg (patriot) (1st issue). Multicoloured.
1185 10q. Type **249** 20 10
1186 15q. Skanderbeg 20 15
1187 25q. Helmet and sword . . 50 15
1188 30q. Kruja Castle 65 20
1189 35q. Petrela Castle 75 25
1190 65q. Berati Castle . . . . . 1·40 30
1191 80q. Meeting of chiefs . . . 1·75 65
1192 90q. Battle of Albulena . . 1·90 2·25
See also Nos. 1200/7.

250 Winter Olympic Emblem

1967. Winter Olympic Games, Grenoble. Mult.
1193 15q. Type **250** 15 10
1194 25q. Ice hockey 20 15
1195 30q. Figure skating 25 15
1196 50q. Skiing (slalom) 40 20
1197 80q. Skiing (downhill) . . . 70 30
1198 1l. Ski jumping . . . . . . 1·60 40

251 Skanderbeg Memorial, Tirana

1968. 500th Death Anniv of Castriota Skanderbeg (2nd issue). Multicoloured.
1200 10q. Type **251** 25 10
1201 15q. Skanderbeg portrait . . 30 15
1202 25q. Skanderbeg portrait (different) 90 15
1203 30q. Equestrian statue, Kruja (vert) . . . . . . 1·10 20
1204 35q. Skanderbeg and mountains . . . . 1·40 20
1205 65q. Bust of Skanderbeg . . 2·50 20
1206 80q. Title page of biography 2·75 85
1207 90q. "Skanderbeg battling with the Turks" (painting) (vert) . . . . 3·50 1·25

252 Alpine Dianthus

1968. Flowers. Multicoloured.
1208 15q. Type **252** 20 10
1209 20q. Chinese dianthus . . . 25 15
1210 25q. Pink carnation 30 15
1211 50q. Red carnation and bud 85 20
1212 80q. Two red carnations . . 1·40 50
1213 1l.10 Yellow carnations . . 1·90 85

253 Ear of Wheat and Electricity Pylon

1968. 5th Agricultural Co-operative Congress. Mult.
1214 25q. Type **253** 40 15
1215 65q. Tractor (horiz) . . . . 1·25 45
1216 1l.10 Cow . . . . 1·90 40

254 Long-horned Goat

1968. Goats. Multicoloured.
1217 15q. Zane female 20 10
1218 20q. Kid 20 10
1219 25q. Long-haired capore . . 30 15
1220 30q. Black goat at rest . . . 35 15
1221 40q. Kids dancing 75 20
1222 50q. Red and piebald goats 90 20

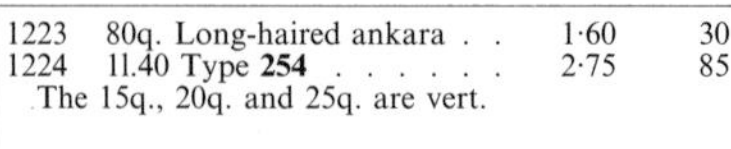
1223 80q. Long-haired ankara . . 1·60 30
1224 1l.40 Type **254** . . . . . . 2·75 85
The 15q., 20q. and 25q. are vert.

255 Zef Jubani **256** Doctor using Stethoscope

1968. 150th Birth Anniv of Zef Jubani (patriot).
1225 **255** 25q. brown and yellow 20 15
1226 1l.75 blue, black & vio 2·75 65

1968. 20th Anniv of W.H.O.
1227 **256** 25q. red and green . . . 35 10
1228 – 65q. black, blue & yellow 75 20
1229 – 1l.10 brown and black 1·25 35
DESIGNS—HORIZ: 65q. Hospital and microscope. VERT: 1l.10, Mother feeding child.

257 Servicewoman

1968. 25th Anniv of Albanian Women's Union.
1230 **257** 15q. red and orange . . 25 15
1231 – 25q. turquoise and green 35 20
1232 – 60q. brown and ochre 1·00 30
1233 – 1l. violet and light violet 1·75 55
DESIGNS: 25q. Teacher; 60q. Farm girl; 1l. Factory worker.

258 Karl Marx

1968. 150th Birth Anniv of Karl Marx. Mult.
1234 15q. Type **258** 40 20
1235 25q. Marx addressing students 85 20
1236 65q. "Das Kapital", "Communist Manifesto" and marchers . . . . . . 1·60 65
1237 95q. Karl Marx . . . . . . 3·50 85

259 Heliopsis

1968. Flowers. Multicoloured.
1238 15q. Type **259** 10 10
1239 20q. Red flax 15 10
1240 25q. Orchid 20 10
1241 30q. Gloxinia 30 15
1242 40q. Orange lily 50 15
1243 80q. Hippeastrum . . . . . 1·40 25
1244 1l.40 Purple magnolia . . . 2·75 90

260 A. Frasheri and Torch

1968. 90th Anniv of Prizren Defence League.
1245 **260** 25q. black and green . . 40 15
1246 – 40q. multicoloured . . . 95 20
1247 – 85q. multicoloured . . . 1·60 40
DESIGNS: 40q. League headquarters; 85q. Frasheri's manifesto and partisans.

261 "Shepherd" (A. Kushi)

1968. Paintings in Tirana Gallery. Multicoloured.
1248 15q. Type **261** 15 10
1249 20q. "Tirana" (V. Mio) (horiz) 20 10
1250 25q. "Highlander" (G. Madhi) 25 15
1251 40q. "Refugees" (A. Buza) 75 15
1252 80q. "Partisans at Shahin Matrakut" (S. Xega) . . . 1·40 50
1253 1l.50 "Old Man" (S. Papadhimitri) . . . . 2·75 1·00
1254 1l.70 "Shkoder Gate" (S. Rrota) . . . . 3·50 1·25

262 Soldiers and Armoured Vehicles

1968. 25th Anniv of People's Army. Multicoloured.
1256 15q. Type **262** 35 15
1257 25q. Sailor and naval craft 1·25 30
1258 65q. Pilot and Ilyushin Il-28 and Mikoyan Gurevich MiG-17 aircraft (vert) . . 2·50 85
1259 95q. Soldier and patriots . . 3·75 1·25

263 Common Squid

1968. Marine Fauna. Multicoloured.
1260 15q. Type **263** 25 10
1261 20q. Common lobster . . . 20 10
1262 25q. Common northern whelk 65 15
1263 50q. Edible crab . . . . . 1·00 40
1264 70q. Spiny lobster . . . . . 1·40 65
1265 80q. Common green crab 1·75 85
1266 90q. Norwegian lobster . . 1·90 1·40

264 Relay-racing

1968. Olympic Games, Mexico. Multicoloured.
1267 15q. Type **264** 15 10
1268 20q. Running 20 10
1269 25q. Throwing the discus . . 25 10
1270 30q. Horse-jumping 30 15
1271 40q. High-jumping 35 15
1272 50q. Hurdling 40 20
1273 80q. Football 80 30
1274 1l.40 High diving . . . . . 1·75 85

265 Enver Hoxha (Party Secretary) **266** Alphabet Book

1968. Enver Hoxha's 60th Birthday.
1276 **265** 25q. blue 35 25
1277 35q. purple 85 30
1278 80q. violet . . . . . . 1·75 90
1279 1l.10 brown . . . . . . 1·90 1·40

1968. 60th Anniv of Monastir Language Congress.
1281 **266** 15q. lake and green . . . 65 15
1282 85q. brown and green . . 3·25 55

267 Bohemian Waxwing

1968. Birds. Multicoloured.
1283 15q. Type **267** 55 20
1284 20q. Rose-coloured starling 75 20
1285 25q. River kingfishers . . . 1·10 30
1286 50q. Long-tailed tit . . . . 1·60 75
1287 80q. Wallcreeper . . . . . 3·25 90
1288 1l.10 Bearded reedling . . . 4·00 1·40

268 Mao Tse-tung

1968. Mao Tse-tung's 75th Birthday.
1289 **268** 25q. black, red and gold 85 30
1290 1l.75 black, red and gold 4·25 1·75

269 Adem Reka (dock foreman)

1969. Contemporary Heroes. Multicoloured.
1291 5q. Type **269** 10 10
1292 10q. Pjeter Lleshi (telegraph linesman) 15 10
1293 15q. M. Shehu and M. Kepi (fire victims) 20 15
1294 25q. Shkurte Vata (railway worker) . . . . 2·25 35
1295 65q. Agron Elezi (earthquake victim) . . . 95 25
1296 80q. Ismet Bruca (schoolteacher) . . . . . 1·25 40
1297 1l.30 Fuat Cela (blind Co-op leader) . . . . 1·90 50

270 Meteorological Equipment

1969. 20th Anniv of Albanian Hydro-meteorology. Multicoloured.
1298 15q. Type **270** 65 20
1299 25q. "Arrow" indicator . . 1·00 25
1300 1l.60 Meteorological balloon and isobar map . . . . . 4·75 1·50

271 "Student Revolutionaries" (P. Mele)

1969. Albanian Paintings since 1944. Mult.
1301 5q. Type **271** 15 10
1302 25q. "Partisans 1914" (F. Haxhiu) (horiz) . . . 20 10
1303 65q. "Steel Mill" (C. Ceka) (horiz) 75 15
1304 80q. "Reconstruction" (V. Kilica) (horiz) 85 30
1305 1l.10 "Harvest" (N. Jonuzi) (horiz) . . . . 1·40 35
1306 1l.15 "Seaside Terraces" (S. Kaceli) (horiz) . . . . 1·75 1·00
SIZES: The 25q., 80q., 1l.10 and 1l.15 are 50 × 30 mm.

272 "Self-portrait" **273** Congress Building

1969. 450th Death Anniv of Leonardo da Vinci.
1308 **272** 25q. agate, brown & gold 30 15
1309 – 35q. agate, brown & gold 65 20
1310 – 40q. agate, brown & gold 85 20
1311 – 1l. multicoloured . . . . 1·90 85
1312 – 2l. agate, brown & gold 3·75 1·75
DESIGNS—VERT: 35q. "Lilies"; 1l. "Portrait of Beatrice"; 2l. "Portrait of a Lady". HORIZ: 40q. Design for "Helicopter".

1969. 25th Anniv of Permet Congress. Mult.
1314 25q. Type **273** 35 25
1315 2l.25 Two partisans . . . . 4·25 2·75

274 "Viola albanica" **275** Plum

1969. Flowers. Viola Family. Multicoloured.
1317 5q. Type **274** 10 10
1318 10q. "Viola hortensis" . . . 15 10
1319 15q. "Viola heterophylla" 20 15
1320 20q. "Viola hortensis" (different) 25 20
1321 25q. "Viola odorata" . . . 35 20
1322 80q. "Viola hortensis" (different) . . . . 1·25 85
1323 1l.95 "Viola hortensis" (different) . . . . 2·25 1·75

1969. Fruit Trees. Blossom and Fruit. Mult.
1324 10q. Type **275** 15 20
1325 15q. Lemon 15 15
1326 25q. Pomegranate 50 15
1327 50q. Cherry . . . . 1·00 20
1328 80q. Apricot . . . . 1·75 85
1329 1l.20 Apple . . . . 2·75 1·40

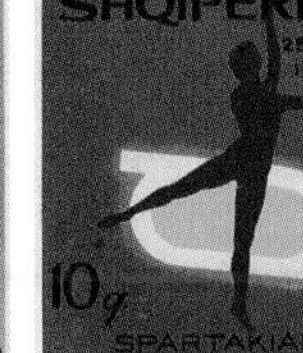

276 Throwing the Ball **277** Gymnastics

1969. 16th European Basketball Championships, Naples. Multicoloured.
1330 10q. Type **276** 20 10
1331 15q. Trying for goal 20 10
1332 25q. Ball and net (horiz) . . 35 15
1333 80q. Scoring a goal . . . . 1·10 25
1334 2l.20 Intercepting a pass . . 2·75 1·00

1969. National Spartakiad. Multicoloured.
1335 5q. Pickaxe, rifle, flag and stadium 15 10
1336 10q. Type **277** 15 10
1337 15q. Running 20 10
1338 20q. Pistol-shooting 25 15
1339 25q. Swimmer on starting block 30 15
1340 80q. Cycling . . . . 1·00 25
1341 95q. Football . . . . 1·25 45

278 Mao Tse-tung **279** Enver Hoxha

1969. 20th Anniv of Chinese People's Republic. Multicoloured
1342 25q. Type **278** . . . . . . 1·25 50
1343 85q. Steel ladle and control room (horiz) . . . . . . 4·00 1·25
1344 1l.40 Rejoicing crowd . . . 6·00 2·25

1969. 25th Anniv of 2nd National Liberation Council Meeting, Berat. Multicoloured.
1345 25q. Type **279** 25 15
1346 80q. Star and Constitution 85 20
1347 1l.45 Freedom-fighters . . . 1·60 40

280 Entry of Provisional Government, Tirana

1969. 25th Anniv of Liberation. Multicoloured.
1348 25q. Type **280** 20 10
1349 30q. Oil refinery 35 10
1350 35q. Combine harvester . . 75 15
1351 45q. Hydrolectric power station . . . . 1·10 15
1352 55q. Soldier and partisans 1·60 65
1353 1l.10 People rejoicing . . . 2·75 1·25

281 Stalin **282** Head of Woman

1969. 90th Birth Anniv of Joseph Stalin.
1354 **281** 15q. lilac 15 10
1355 25q. blue 20 15
1356 1l. brown . . . . 1·10 30
1357 1l.10 blue . . . . 1·25 35

1969. Mosaics. (1st series). Multicoloured.
1358 15q. Type **282** 15 10
1359 25q. Floor pattern 20 10
1360 80q. Bird and tree 85 20
1361 1l.10 Diamond floor pattern 1·10 30
1362 1l.20 Corn in oval pattern 1·60 35
Nos. 1359/61 are horiz.
See also Nos. 1391/6, 1564/70 and 1657/62.

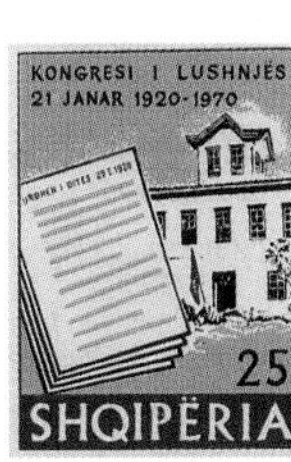

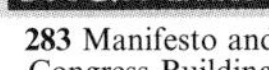

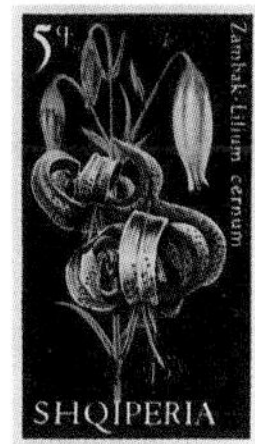

283 Manifesto and Congress Building **285** "Lilium cernum"

284 "25" and Workers

1970. 50th Anniv of Lushnje Congress.
1363 **283** 25q. black, red and grey 30 20
1364 – 1l.25 black, yell & grn 1·90 85
DESIGN: 1l.25, Lushnje postmark of 1920.

1970. 25th Anniv of Albanian Trade Unions.
1365 **284** 25q. multicoloured . . . 30 15
1366 1l.75 multicoloured . . . 1·90 90

1970. Lilies. Multicoloured.
1367 5q. Type **285** 25 10
1368 15q. "Lilium candidum" . . 40 10
1369 25q. "Lilium regale" 70 20
1370 80q. "Lilium martagon" . . 1·75 30
1371 1l.10 "Lilium tigrinum" . . 2·25 75
1372 1l.15 "Lilium albanicum" 2·50 90
Nos. 1370/2 are horiz.

286 Lenin

1970. Birth Cent of Lenin. Each blk, silver & red.
1373 5q. Type **286** 10 10
1374 15q. Lenin making speech 15 15
1375 25q. As worker 20 15
1376 95q. As revolutionary . . . 95 35
1377 1l.10 Saluting . . . . 1·40 40
Nos. 1374/6 are horiz.

287 Frontier Guard

1970. 25th Anniv of Frontier Force.
1378 **287** 25q. multicoloured . . . 50 10
1379 1l.25 multicoloured . . . 2·00 75

288 Jules Rimet Cup

1970. World Cup Football Championship, Mexico. Multicoloured.
1380 5q. Type **288** 10 10
1381 10q. Aztec Stadium 15 10
1382 15q. Three footballers . . . 20 10
1383 25q. Heading goal 25 15
1384 65q. Two footballers 40 20
1385 80q. Two footballers . . . . 1·00 25
1386 2l. Two footballers . . . . 2·50 45

289 New U.P.U. Headquarters Building

1970. New U.P.U. Headquarters Building, Berne.
1388 **289** 25q. blue, black and light blue 20 15
1389 1l.10 pink, black & orge 1·25 35
1390 1l.15 turq, blk & grn . . 1·40 45

290 Birds and Grapes

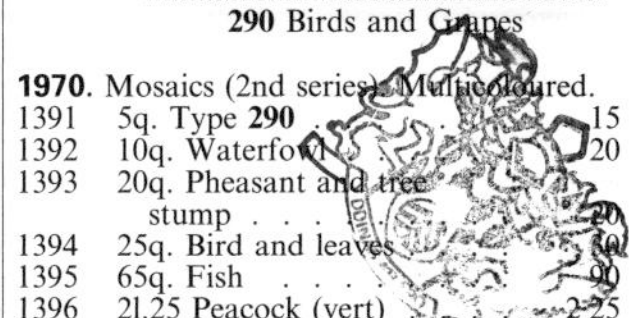

1970. Mosaics (2nd series). Multicoloured.
1391 5q. Type **290** 15
1392 10q. Waterfowl 20
1393 20q. Pheasant and tree stump 20
1394 25q. Bird and leaves 30
1395 65q. Fish 90
1396 2l.25 Peacock (vert) . . . 2·25

291 Harvesters and Dancers **292** Partisans going into Battle

1970. 25th Anniv of Agrarian Reform.
1397 **291** 15q. lilac and black . . . 20 10
1398 – 25q. blue and black . . 25 10
1399 – 80q. brown and black . . 85 20
1400 – 1l.30 brown and black 1·25 35
DESIGNS: 25q. Ploughed fields and open-air conference; 80q. Cattle and newspapers; 1l.30, Combine-harvester and official visit.

1970. 50th Anniv of Battle of Vlore.
1401 **292** 15q. brown, orge & black 20 10
1402 – 25q. brown, yell & black 30 15
1403 – 1l.60 myrtle, grn & blk 1·40 85
DESIGNS: 25q. Victory parade; 1l.60, Partisans.

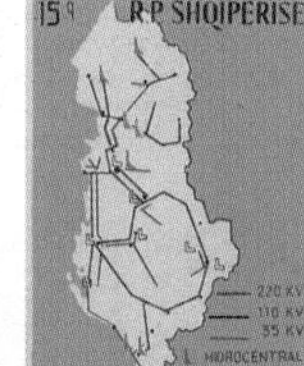

293 "The Harvesters" (I. Sulovari) **294** Electrification Map

1970. 25th Anniv of Liberation. Prize-winning Paintings. Multicoloured.
1404 5q. Type **293** 10 10
1405 15q. "Return of the Partisan" (D. Trebicka) (horiz) 15 10
1406 25q. "The Miners" (N. Zajmi) (horiz) 20 10
1407 65q. "Instructing the Partisans" (H. Nallbani) (horiz) 35 20
1408 95q. "Making Plans" (V. Kilica) (horiz) 85 50
1409 2l. "The Machinist" (Z. Shoshi) . . . . 2·50 90

1970. Rural Electrification Completion. Mult.
1411 15q. Type **294** 20 10
1412 25q. Lamp and graph . . . 25 15
1413 80q. Erecting power lines . . 85 20
1414 1l.10 Uses of electricity . . 1·40 50

295 Engels **296** Beethoven's Birthplace

295a Tractor Factory, Tirana

1970. 150th Birth Anniv of Friedrich Engels.
1415 **295** 25q. blue and bistre . . 25 15
1416 – 1l.10 purple and bistre 1·25 55
1417 – 1l.15 olive and bistre . . 1·25 70
DESIGNS: 1l.10, Engels as a young man; 1l.15, Engels making speech.

1971. Industry. Multicoloured.
1417a 10q. Type **295a** . . . . . . £130 75·00
1417b 15q. Fertiliser factory, Fier £130 75·00
1417c 20q. Superphosphate factory, Lac (vert) . . . £130 75·00
1417d 25q. Cement factory, Elbasan . . . . £130 75·00

1970. Birth Bicentenary of Beethoven.
1418 **296** 5q. violet and gold . . . 20 10
1419 – 15q. purple and silver . . 20 20
1420 – 25q. green and gold . . 50 20
1421 – 65q. purple and silver . . 1·00 50
1422 – 1l.10 blue and gold . . . 1·50 50
1423 – 1l.80 black and silver . . 3·00 1·00
DESIGNS—VERT: Beethoven: 15q. In silhouette; 25q. As young man; 65q. Full-face; 1l.10, Profile. HORIZ: 1l.80, Stage performance of "Fidelio".

297 Republican Emblem

1971. 25th Anniv of Republic.
1424 **297** 15q. multicoloured . . . 10 10
1425 – 25q. multicoloured . . . 15 10
1426 – 80q. black, gold & green 90 15
1427 – 1l.30 black, gold & brn 1·25 65
DESIGNS: 25q. Proclamation; 80q. Enver Hoxha; 1l.30, Patriots.

298 "Storming the Barricades"

1971. Centenary of Paris Commune.
1428 – 25q. blue and deep blue 40 10
1429 – 50q. green and grey . . 50 20
1430 **298** 65q. chestnut and brown 80 20
1431 – 1l.10 lilac and violet . . 1·50 80
DESIGNS—VERT: 25q. "La Marseillaise"; 50q. Women Communards. HORIZ: 1l.10, Firing squad.

299 "Conflict of Race" **300** Tulip

1971. Racial Equality Year.
1432 **299** 25q. black and brown . . 20 15
1433 – 1l.10 black and red . . . 85 25
1434 – 1l.15 black and red . . . 95 30
DESIGNS—VERT: 1l.10, Heads of three races; 1l.15, Freedom fighters.

1971. Hybrid Tulips.
1435 **300** 5q. multicoloured . . . 15 10
1436 – 10q. multicoloured . . . 15 10
1437 – 15q. multicoloured . . . 20 10
1438 – 20q. multicoloured . . . 20 10
1439 – 25q. multicoloured . . . 55 15
1440 – 80q. multicoloured . . . 1·40 20
1441 – 1l. multicoloured . . . . 1·90 65
1442 – 1l.45 multicoloured . . . 3·50 1·40
DESIGNS: 10q. to 1l.45, Different varieties of tulips.

301 "Postrider" **302** Globe and Satellite (1970)

1971. 500th Birth Anniv of Albrecht Durer (painter and engraver).
1443 **301** 10q. black and green . . 15 10
1444 – 15q. black and blue . . 30 10
1445 – 25q. black and blue . . 50 15
1446 – 45q. black and purple . . 85 15
1447 – 65q. multicoloured . . . 1·25 25
1448 – 2l.40 multicoloured . . . 3·25 1·00
DESIGNS—VERT: 15q. "Three Peasants"; 25q. "Peasant Dancers"; 45q. "The Bagpiper". HORIZ: 65q. "View of Kalchreut"; 2l.40, "View of Trient".

1971. Chinese Space Achievements. Multicoloured.
1450 60q. Type **302** 75 20
1451 1l.20 Public Building, Tirana 1·25 30
1452 2l.20 Globe and satellite (1971) . . . . 2·50 60
The date on No. 1451 refers to the passage of Chinese satellite over Tirana.

303 Mao Tse-tung

1971. 50th Anniv of Chinese Communist Party. Multicoloured.
1454 25q. Type **303** 70 20
1455 1l.05 Party Birthplace (horiz) . . . . 1·75 70
1456 1l.20 Chinese celebrations (horiz) . . . . 2·50 1·00

304 Crested Tit

1971. Birds. Multicoloured.
1457 5q. Type **304** 25 20
1458 10q. European serin 30 20
1459 15q. Linnet 40 20
1460 25q. Firecrest 60 20
1461 45q. Rock thrush 90 25
1462 60q. Blue tit . . . . 1·40 60
1463 2l.40 Chaffinch . . . . . . 5·25 4·00

305 Running

1971. Olympic Games (1972). (1st issue). Mult.
1464 5q. Type **305** 10 10
1465 10q. Hurdling 15 10
1466 15q. Canoeing 15 10
1467 25q. Gymnastics 25 15
1468 80q. Fencing 55 25
1469 1l.05 Football . . . . . . 1·10 25
1470 3l.60 Diving . . . . 4·00 1·10
See also Nos. 1522/29.

306 Workers with Banner **307** "XXX" and Red Flag

1971. 6th Workers' Party Congress. Multicoloured.
1472 25q. Type **306** 25 15
1473 1l.05 Congress hall . . . . 1·40 95
1474 1l.20 "VI", flag, star and rifle (vert) . . . . 1·75 1·25

1971. 30th Anniv of Albanian Workers' Party. Multicoloured.
1475 15q. Workers and industry (horiz) . . . . 2·50 15
1476 80q. Type **307** . . . . . . 1·00 75
1477 1l.55 Enver Hoxha and flags (horiz) . . . . 2·00 1·75

308 "Young Man" (R. Kuci)

1971. Albanian Paintings. Multicoloured.
1478 5q. Type **308** 10 10
1479 15q. "Building Construction" (M. Fushekati) 15 10
1480 25q. "Partisan" (D. Jukniu) 20 10
1481 80q. "Fighter Pilots" (S. Kristo) (horiz) . . . . 1·00 20
1482 1l.20 "Girl Messenger" (A. Sadikaj) (horiz) . . . 1·40 65
1483 1l.55 "Medieval Warriors" (S. Kamberi) (horiz) . . . 2·00 1·25

309 Emblems and Flags

1971. 30th Anniv of Albanian Young Communists' Union.
1485 **309** 15q. multicoloured . . . 15 10
1486 1l.35 multicoloured . . . 1·60 80

310 Village Girls

1971. Albanian Ballet "Halili and Hajria". Mult.
1487 5q. Type **310** 15 10
1488 10q. Parting of Halili and Hajria 20 10
1489 15q. Hajria before Sultan Suleiman 20 10
1490 50q. Hajria's marriage . . . 85 20
1491 80q. Execution of Halili . . 1·25 65
1492 1l.40 Hajria killing her husband . . . . 2·25 1·25

311 Rifle-shooting (Biathlon)

1972. Winter Olympic Games, Sapporo, Japan. Multicoloured.
1493 5q. Type **311** 10 10
1494 10q. Tobogganing 15 10
1495 15q. Ice-hockey 15 10
1496 20q. Bobsleighing 20 10
1497 50q. Speed skating 30 20
1498 1l. Slalom skiing . . . . . 1·10 30
1499 2l. Ski jumping . . . . . . 2·00 95

312 Wild Strawberries

1972. Wild Fruits. Multicoloured.
1501 5q. Type **312** 15 10
1502 10q. Blackberries 15 10
1503 15q. Hazelnuts 20 10
1504 20q. Walnuts 25 15
1505 25q. Strawberry-tree fruit . . 30 15
1506 30q. Dogwood berries . . . 45 20
1507 2l.40 Rowanberries . . . . 2·50 1·10

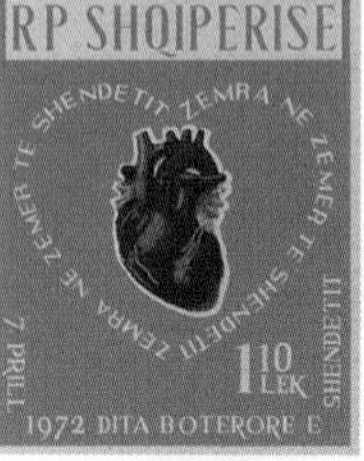

313 Human Heart **314** Congress Delegates

1972. World Health Day. Multicoloured.
1508 1l.10 Type **313** . . . . . . 1·10 30
1509 1l.20 Treatment of cardiac patient . . . . 1·25 75

1972. 7th Albanian Trade Unions Congress. Mult.
1510 25q. Type **314** 30 20
1511 2l.05 Congress Hall . . . . 1·90 1·00

315 Memorial Flame

1972. 30th Anniv of Martyrs' Day, and Death of Qemal Stafa.
1512 **315** 15q. multicoloured . . . 20 10
1513 – 25q. black, orge & grey 25 15
1514 – 1l.90 black and ochre . . 1·90 35
DESIGNS—VERT: 25q. "Spirit of Defiance" (statue). HORIZ: 1l.90, Qemal Stafa.

316 "Camellia japonica Kamelie"

1972. Camellias.
1515 **316** 5q. multicoloured . . . 15 10
1516 – 10q. multicoloured . . . 20 10
1517 – 15q. multicoloured . . . 20 10
1518 – 25q. multicoloured . . . 25 10
1519 – 45q. multicoloured . . . 40 15
1520 – 50q. multicoloured . . . 50 20
1521 – 2l.50 multicoloured . . . 3·50 2·25
DESIGNS: Nos. 1516/21, Various camellias as Type **316**.

317 High Jumping

1972. Olympic Games, Munich (2nd issue). Mult.
1522 5q. Type **317** 10 10
1523 10q. Running 10 10
1524 15q. Putting the shot . . . 15 10
1525 20q. Cycling 15 10
1526 25q. Pole-vaulting 20 10
1527 50q. Hurdling 35 15
1528 75q. Hockey 65 25
1529 2l. Swimming 90 75

318 Articulated bus

1972. Modern Transport. Multicoloured.
1531 15q. Type **318** 15 10
1532 25q. Czechoslovakian Class T699 diesel locomotive . . 2·00 15
1533 80q. Freighter "Tirana" . . 1·40 30
1534 1l.05 Motor-car 80 25
1535 1l.20 Container truck . . . 1·25 50

319 "Trial of Strength"

1972. 1st Nat Festival of Traditional Games. Mult.
1536 5q. Type **319** 10 10
1537 10q. Pick-a-back ball game 15 10
1538 15q. Leaping game 15 10
1539 25q. Rope game 20 10
1540 90q. Leap-frog 65 20
1541 2l. Women's throwing game 1·60 75

320 Newspaper "Mastheads"

1972. 30th Anniv of Press Day.
1542 **320** 15q. black and blue . . 20 10
1543 – 25q. green, red & black 25 15
1544 – 1l.90 black and mauve 1·90 95
DESIGNS: 25q. Printing-press and partisan; 1l.90, Workers with newspaper.

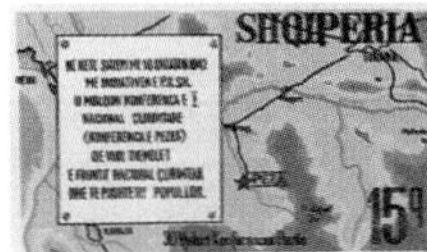

321 Location Map and Commemorative Plaque

1972. 30th Anniv of Peza Conference. Mult.
1545 15q. Type **321** 30 20
1546 25q. Partisans with flag . . 45 30
1547 1l.90 Conference Memorial 2·00 1·25

322 "Partisans Conference" (S. Capo)

1972. Albanian Paintings. Multicoloured.
1548 5q. Type **322** 10 10
1549 10q. "Head of Woman" (I. Lulani) (vert) 15 10
1550 15q. "Communists" (L. Shkreli) (vert) 15 10
1551 20q. "Nendorit, 1941" (S. Shijaku) (vert) 20 10
1552 50q. "Farm Woman" (Z. Shoshi) (vert) 65 20
1553 1l. "Landscape" (D. Trebicka) . . . . . . 1·25 50
1554 2l. "Girls with Bicycles" (V. Kilica) . . . . 2·50 1·25

323 Congress Emblem **324** Lenin

1972. 6th Congress of Young Communists' Union.
1556 **323** 25q. gold, red and silver 30 15
1557 – 2l.05 multicoloured . . . 2·00 1·00
DESIGN: 2l.05, Young worker and banner.

1972. 55th Anniv of Russian October Revolution. Multicoloured.
1558 – 1l.10 multicoloured . . . 1·25 65
1559 **324** 1l.20 red, blk & pink . . 1·25 75
DESIGN: 1l.10, Hammer and Sickle.

325 Albanian Soldiers

1972. 60th Anniv of Independence.
1560 **325** 15q. blue, red and black 15 15
1561 – 25q. black, red & yellow 25 20
1562 – 65q. multicoloured . . . 45 20
1563 – 1l.25 black and red . . . 1·00 75
DESIGNS—VERT: 25q. Ismail Qemali; 1l.25, Albanian double-eagle emblem. HORIZ: 65q. Proclamation of Independence, 1912.

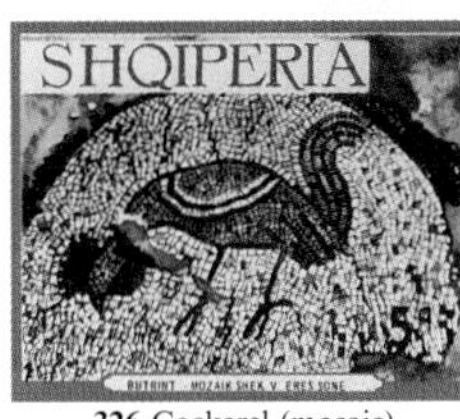

326 Cockerel (mosaic)

1972. Ancient Mosaics from Apolloni and Butrint (3rd series). Multicoloured.
1564 5q. Type **326** 10 10
1565 10q. Bird (vert) 15 10
1566 15q. Partridges (vert) . . . 20 10
1567 25q. Warrior's leg 25 15
1568 45q. Nude on dolphin (vert) 35 20
1569 50q. Fish (vert) 40 20
1570 2l.50 Warrior's head . . . . 3·25 1·75

327 Nicolas Copernicus

1973. 500th Birth Anniv of Copernicus. Mult.
1571 5q. Type **327** 10 10
1572 10q. Copernicus and signatures 15 10
1573 25q. Engraved portrait . . . 20 15
1574 80q. Copernicus at desk . . 1·00 25
1575 1l.20 Copernicus and planets 1·60 65
1576 1l.60 Planetary diagram . . 1·90 85

328 Policeman and Industrial Scene

1973. 30th Anniv of State Security Police.
1577 **328** 25q. black, blue & lt blue 30 20
1578 – 1l.80 multicoloured . . . 1·90 1·40
DESIGN: 1l.80, Prisoner under escort.

329/30 Cactus Flowers

1973. Cacti. As T **329/30**.
1579 **329** 10q. multicoloured . . . 10 10
1580 **330** 15q. multicoloured . . . 15 10
1581 – 20q. multicoloured . . . 20 10
1582 – 25q. multicoloured . . . 20 10
1583 – 30q. multicoloured . . . 4·50 1·75
1584 – 65q. multicoloured . . . 85 20
1585 – 80q. multicoloured . . . 1·00 25
1586 – 2l. multicoloured . . . . 1·90 85
Nos. 1579/86 were issued together se-tenant within the sheet and in alternate formats as Types **329/30**.

331 Common Tern

1973. Sea Birds. Multicoloured.
1587 5q. Type **331** 25 20
1588 15q. White-winged black tern 35 25
1589 25q. Black-headed gull . . . 40 25
1590 45q. Great black-headed gull 75 45
1591 80q. Slender-billed gull . . . 1·40 80
1592 2l.40 Sandwich tern . . . . 3·50 2·10

332 Postmark of 1913, and Letters

1973. 60th Anniv of First Albanian Stamps. Mult.
1593 25q. Type **332** . . . . . . 1·00 35
1594 1l.80 Postman and postmarks . . . . 4·00 1·50

333 Albanian Woman

1973. 7th Albanian Women's Congress.
1595 **333** 25q. red and pink . . . 25 15
1596 – 1l.80 black, orge & yell 1·75 1·40
DESIGN: 1l.80, Albanian female workers.

334 "Creation of the General Staff" (G. Madhi)

1973. 30th Anniv of Albanian People's Army. Mult.
1597 25q. Type **334** . . . . . . 12·00 5·00
1598 40q. "August 1949" (sculpture by Sh. Haderi) (vert) . . . . 12·00 5·00
1599 60q. "Generation after Generation" (Statue by H. Dule) (vert) . . . . . 12·00 5·00
1600 80q. "Defend Revolutionary Victories" (M. Fushekati) 12·00 5·00

335 "Electrification" (S. Hysa)

1973. Albanian Paintings. Multicoloured.
1601 5q. Type **335** 10 10
1602 10q. "Textile Worker" (E. Nallbani) (vert) . . . 15 10
1603 15q. "Gymnastics Class" (M. Fushekati) 15 10
1604 50q. "Aviator" (F. Stamo) (vert) 65 15
1605 80q. "Downfall of Fascism" (A. Lakuriqi) 90 20
1606 1l.20 "Koci Bako" (demonstrators (P. Mele)) (vert) . . . . 1·40 25
1607 1l.30 "Peasant Girl" (Z. Shoshi) (vert) . . . . 1·75 30

336 "Mary Magdalene" **338** Weightlifting

337 Goalkeeper with Ball

1973. 400th Birth Anniv of Caravaggio. Paintings. Multicoloured.
1609 5q. Type **336** 10 10
1610 10q. "The Guitar Player" (horiz) 15 10
1611 15q. Self-portrait 20 10
1612 50q. "Boy carrying Fruit" 65 20
1613 80q. "Basket of Fruit" (horiz) 90 25
1614 1l.20 "Narcissus" . . . . . 1·40 65
1615 1l.30 "Boy peeling Apple" 2·25 90

1973. World Cup Football Championship, Munich (1974) (1st issue). Multicoloured.
1617 **337** 5q. multicoloured . . . 10 10
1618 – 10q. multicoloured . . . 15 10
1619 – 15q. multicoloured . . . 15 10
1620 – 20q. multicoloured . . . 20 10
1621 – 25q. multicoloured . . . 25 15

1622 – 90q. multicoloured . . . 1·40 20
1623 – 1l.20 multicoloured . . . 1·90 30
1624 – 1l.25 multicoloured . . . 1·90 85
DESIGNS: Nos. 1618/24 are similar to Type **337**, showing goalkeepers saving goals.
See also Nos. 1663/70.

1973. World Weightlifting Championships, Havana, Cuba.
1626 **338** 5q. multicoloured . . . 10 10
1627 – 10q. multicoloured . . . 15 10
1628 – 25q. multicoloured . . . 20 10
1629 – 90q. multicoloured . . . 90 25
1630 – 1l.20 mult (horiz) . . . 1·10 35
1631 – 1l.60 mult (horiz) . . . 1·60 40
DESIGNS: Nos. 1627/31 are similar to Type **338**, showing various lifts.

339 Ballet Scene

340 Mao Tse-tung

1973. "Albanian Life and Work". Multicoloured.
1632 5q. Cement Works, Kavaje 10 10
1633 10q. Ali Kelmendi truck factory and trucks (horiz) 15 10
1634 15q. Type **339** 20 10
1635 20q. Combine-harvester (horiz) 25 15
1636 25q. "Telecommunications" 25 15
1637 35q. Skier and hotel, Dajt (horiz) 35 15
1638 60q. Llogora holiday village (horiz) 50 20
1639 80q. Lake scene 65 25
1640 1l. Textile mill (horiz) . . . 50 20
1641 1l.20 Furnacemen (horiz) . . 80 25
1642 2l.40 Welder and pipeline (horiz) . . . . 2·00 50
1643 3l. Skanderbeg Statue, Tirana . . . . 2·75 65
1644 5l. Roman arches, Durres 4·25 1·75

1973. 80th Birth Anniv of Mao Tse-tung. Mult.
1645 85q. Type **340** . . . . . . 1·00 20
1646 1l.20 Mao Tse-tung at parade . . . . 1·75 85

341 "Horse's Head" (Gericault)

1974. 150th Death Anniv of Jean-Louis Gericault (French painter).
1647 **341** 10q. multicoloured . . . 15 10
1648 – 15q. multicoloured . . . 15 10
1649 – 20q. black and gold . . 20 10
1650 – 25q. black, lilac and gold 25 15
1651 – 1l.20 multicoloured . . . 1·60 30
1652 – 2l.20 multicoloured . . . 3·50 1·25
DESIGNS—VERT: 15q. "Male Model" (Gericault); 20q. "Man and Dog"; 25q. "Head of a Negro"; 1l.20, Self-portrait. HORIZ: 2l.20, "Battle of the Giants".

342 "Lenin with Crew of the 'Aurora'" (D. Trebicka)

1974. 50th Death Anniv of Lenin. Multicoloured.
1654 25q. Type **342** 25 15
1655 60q. "Lenin" (P. Mele) (vert) . . . . 1·00 20
1656 1l.20 "Lenin" (seated) (V. Kilica) (vert) . . . . 2·00 1·25

343 Duck

1974. Ancient Mosaics from Butrint, Pogradec and Apolloni (4th series). Multicoloured.
1657 5q. Duck (different) 10 10
1658 10q. Bird and flower 15 10
1659 15q. Ornamental basket and grapes 15 10
1660 25q. Type **343** 20 10
1661 40q. Donkey and cockerel 35 20
1662 2l.50 Dragon . . . . 2·75 1·10

344 Shooting at Goal

1974. World Cup Football Championships, Munich (2nd issue).
1663 **344** 10q. multicoloured . . . 15 10
1664 – 15q. multicoloured . . . 15 10
1665 – 20q. multicoloured . . . 20 10
1666 – 25q. multicoloured . . . 25 10
1667 – 40q. multicoloured . . . 35 15
1668 – 80q. multicoloured . . . 1·00 25
1669 – 1l. multicoloured . . . . 1·25 25
1670 – 1l.20 multicoloured . . . 1·60 45
DESIGNS: Nos. 1664/70, Players in action similar to Type **344**.

345 Memorial and Arms

346 "Solanum dulcamara"

1974. 30th Anniv of Permet Congress. Mult.
1672 25q. Type **345** 20 15
1673 1l.80 Enver Hoxha and text 1·40 40

1974. Useful Plants. Multicoloured.
1674 10q. Type **346** 15 10
1675 15q. "Arbutus uva-ursi" (vert) 15 10
1676 20q. "Convallaria majalis" (vert) 15 10
1677 25q. "Colchicum autumnale" (vert) 20 10
1678 40q. "Borago officinalis" . . 75 20
1679 80q. "Saponaria officinalis" 1·40 25
1680 2l.20 "Gentiana lutea" . . . 3·50 1·40

347 Revolutionaries

1974. 50th Anniv of 1924 Revolution.
1681 **347** 25q. mauve, black & red 20 15
1682 – 1l.80 multicoloured . . . 1·25 40
DESIGN—VERT: 1l.80, Prominent revolutionaries.

348 Redwing

1974. Song Birds. Multicoloured.
1683 10q. Type **348** 20 20
1684 15q. European robin 20 20
1685 20q. Western greenfinch 20 20
1686 25q. Northern bullfinch (vert) 45 20
1687 40q. Hawfinch (vert) 55 20
1688 80q. Blackcap (vert) . . . . 1·25 60
1689 2l.20 Nightingale (vert) . . . 3·00 1·90

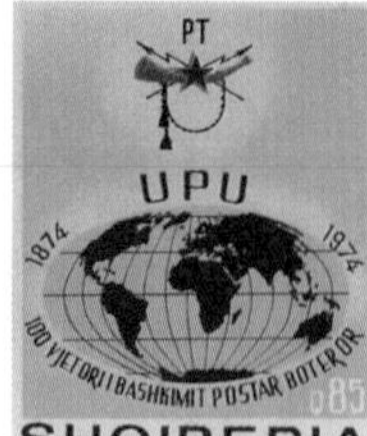

349 Globe and Post Office Emblem

1974. Centenary of Universal Postal Union. Multicoloured.
1690 **349** 85q. multicoloured . . . 1·00 50
1691 – 1l.20 green, lilac & violet 1·50 75
DESIGN: 1l.20, U.P.U. emblem.

350 "Widows" (Sali Shijaku)

1974. Albanian Paintings. Multicoloured.
1693 10q. Type **350** 10 10
1694 15q. "Road Construction" (Danish Jukniu) (vert) . . 20 10
1695 20q. "Fulfilling the Plans" (Clirim Ceka) 25 10
1696 25q. "The Call to Action" (Spiro Kristo) (vert) . . . 30 20
1697 40q. "The Winter Battle" (Sabaudin Xhaferi) . . . 40 20
1698 80q. "Three Comrades" (Clirim Ceka) (vert) . . . 80 50
1699 1l. "Step by Step, Aid the Partisans" (Guri Madhi) 1·00 60
1700 1l.20 "At the War Memorial" (Kleo Nini) 1·25 70

351 Chinese Festivities

1974. 25th Anniv of Chinese People's Republic. Multicoloured.
1702 **351** 85q. multicoloured . . . 85 25
1703 – 1l.20 black, red and gold 1·25 30
DESIGN—VERT: 1l.20, Mao Tse-tung.

352 Volleyball

353 Berat

1974. National Spartakiad. Multicoloured.
1704 10q. Type **352** 10 10
1705 15q. Hurdling 10 10
1706 20q. Hoop exercises 15 10
1707 25q. Stadium parade 15 10
1708 40q. Weightlifting 20 10
1709 80q. Wrestling 40 20
1710 1l. Rifle shooting 75 25
1711 1l.20 Football 85 25

1974. 30th Anniv of 2nd Berat Liberal Council Meeting.
1712 **353** 25q. red and black . . . 20 15
1713 – 80q. yellow, brown and black 75 20
1714 – 1l. purple and black . . 1·10 50
DESIGNS—HORIZ: 80q. "Liberation" frieze. VERT: 1l. Council members walking to meeting.

354 Security Guards patrolling Industrial Plant

1974. 30th Anniv of Liberation. Multicoloured.
1715 25q. Type **354** 15 10
1716 35q. Chemical industry . . . 20 10
1717 50q. Agricultural produce 30 15
1718 80q. Cultural activities . . . 40 20
1719 1l. Scientific technology . . 80 25
1720 1l.20 Railway construction 2·50 50

355 Head of Artemis

356 Clasped hands

1974. Archaeological Discoveries. Multicoloured.
1722 **355** 10q. black, mauve & sil 10 10
1723 – 15q. black, green and silver 15 10
1724 – 20q. black, buff & silver 15 10
1725 – 25q. black, mauve & sil 20 10
1726 – 40q. multicoloured . . . 20 10
1727 – 80q. black, blue & silver 70 20
1728 – 1l. black, green & silver 90 20
1729 – 1l.20 black, sepia & sil 1·75 75
DESIGNS: 15q. Statue of Zeus; 20q. Statue of Poseidon; 25q. Illyrian helmet; 40q. Greek amphora; 80q. Bust of Agrippa; 1l. Bust of Demosthenes; 1l.20, Bust of Bilia.

1975. 30th Anniv of Albanian Trade Unions. Mult.
1731 25q. Type **356** 20 15
1732 1l.80 Workers with arms raised (horiz) . . . . . . 1·25 50

357 "Cichorium intybus"

1975. Albanian Flowers. Multicoloured.
1733 5q. Type **357** 10 10
1734 10q. "Sempervivum montanum" 10 10
1735 15q. "Aquilegia alpina" . . 10 10
1736 20q. "Anemone hortensis" 15 10
1737 25q. "Hibiscus trionum" . . 15 10
1738 30q. "Gentiana kochiana" 20 10
1739 35q. "Lavatera arborea" . . 20 10
1740 2l.70 "Iris graminea" . . . 1·90 70

358 Head of Jesus (detail, Doni Tondo)

1975. 500th Birth Anniv of Michelangelo. Mult.
1741 **358** 5q. multicoloured . . . 10 10
1742 – 10q. brown, grey & gold 10 10
1743 – 15q. brown, grey & gold 15 10
1744 – 20q. sepia, grey and gold 20 10
1745 – 25q. multicoloured . . . 20 10
1746 – 30q. brown, grey & gold 20 10
1747 – 1l.20 brn, grey & gold 85 30
1748 – 3l.90 multicoloured . . . 2·50 1·00
DESIGNS: 10q. "The Heroic Captive"; 15q. "Head of Dawn"; 20q. "Awakening Giant" (detail); 25q. "Cumaenian Sybil" (detail, Sistine chapel); 30q. "Lorenzo di Medici"; 1l.20, Head and shoulders of "David"; 3l.90, "Delphic Sybil" (detail, Sistine chapel).

359 Horseman

1975. "Albanian Transport of the Past". Mult.
1750 5q. Type **359** 10 10
1751 10q. Horse and cart 15 10
1752 15q. Ferry 40 15

1753 20q. Barque 40 15
1754 25q. Horse-drawn cab . . . 30 15
1755 3l.35 Early car . . . . . . 2·75 85

360 Frontier Guard

1975. 30th Anniv of Frontier Force. Mult.
1756 25q. Type **360** 20 15
1757 1l.80 Guards patrolling industrial plant . . . . . 1·75 90

361 Patriot affixing Anti-fascist Placard

1975. 30th Anniv of "Victory over Fascism". Mult.
1758 25q. Type **361** 15 10
1759 60q. Partisans in battle . . . 30 10
1760 1l.20 Patriot defeating Nazi soldier . . . . 1·25 55

362 European Wigeon

1975. Albanian Wildfowl. Multicoloured.
1761 5q. Type **362** 20 20
1762 10q. Red-crested pochard 20 20
1763 15q. White-fronted goose . . 20 20
1764 20q. Pintail 20 20
1765 25q. Red-breasted merganser 20 20
1766 30q. Eider 35 20
1767 35q. Whooper swans . . . 45 20
1768 2l.70 Common shoveler . . 2·75 1·40

363 "Shyqyri Kanapari" (Musa Qarri)

1975. Albanian Paintings. People's Art Exhibition, Tirana. Multicoloured.
1769 5q. Type **363** 10 10
1770 10q. "Sea Rescue" (Agim Faja) 10 10
1771 15q. "28 November 1912" (Petri Ceno) (horiz) . . . 10 10
1772 20q. "Workers' Meeting" (Sali Shijaka) 15 10
1773 25q. "Shota Galica" (Ismail Lulani) 15 10
1774 30q. "Victorious Fighters" (Nestor Jonuzi) 20 15
1775 80q. "Partisan Comrades" (Vilson Halimi) 65 20
1776 2l.25 "Republic Day Celebration" (Fatmir Haxhiu) (horiz) . . . . . 1·60 1·25

364 Farmer with Declaration of Reform

1975. 30th Anniv of Agrarian Reform. Mult.
1778 15q. Type **364** 15 15
1779 2l. Agricultural scene . . . 1·40 75

365 Dead Man's Fingers **366** Cycling

1975. Marine Corals. Multicoloured.
1780 5q. Type **365** 10 10
1781 10q. "Paramuricea chamaeleon" 15 10
1782 20q. Red Coral 15 10
1783 25q. Tube Coral or Sea Fan 30 15
1784 3l.70 "Cladocora cespitosa" 4·25 1·75

1975. Olympic Games, Montreal (1976). Mult.
1785 5q. Type **366** 10 10
1786 10q. Canoeing 10 10
1787 15q. Handball 15 10
1788 20q. Basketball 15 10
1789 25q. Water-polo 20 10
1790 30q. Hockey 20 10
1791 1l.20 Pole vaulting 85 25
1792 2l.05 Fencing . . . . 1·40 35

367 Power Lines leading to Village

1975. 5th Anniv of Electrification of Albanian Countryside. Multicoloured.
1794 **367** 15q. multicoloured . . . 15 15
1795 – 25q. violet, red and lilac 20 15
1796 – 80q. black, turq & green 85 20
1797 – 85q. buff, brn & ochre 1·25 85
DESIGNS: 25q. High power insulators; 80q. Dam and power station; 85q. T.V. pylons and emblems of agriculture and industry.

368 Berat

1975. Air. Tourist Resorts. Multicoloured.
1798 20q. Type **368** 25 15
1799 40q. Gjirokaster 40 20
1800 60q. Sarande 70 30
1801 90q. Durres 90 40
1802 1l.20 Krujae . . . . 1·25 50
1803 2l.40 Boga . . . . 2·40 1·00
1804 4l.05 Tirana . . . . 3·50 1·75

369 Child, Rabbit and Bear planting Saplings

1975. Children's Tales. Multicoloured.
1805 5q. Type **369** 10 10
1806 10q. Mrs. Fox and cub . . 10 10
1807 15q. Ducks in school . . . 15 10
1808 20q. Bears building 15 10
1809 25q. Animals watching television 20 10
1810 30q. Animals with log and electric light bulbs 20 10
1811 35q. Ants with spade and guitar 35 15
1812 2l.70 Boy and girl with sheep and dog . . . . . 1·90 85

370 Arms and Rejoicing Crowd

1976. 30th Anniv of Albanian People's Republic. Multicoloured.
1813 25q. Type **370** 20 15
1814 1l.90 Folk-dancers . . . . . 1·40 40

371 Ice Hockey

1976. Winter Olympic Games, Innsbruck. Mult.
1815 5q. Type **371** 10 10
1816 10q. Speed skating 15 10
1817 15q. Rifle shooting (biathlon) 20 10
1818 50q. Ski jumping 30 15
1819 1l.20 Skiing (slalom) 90 25
1820 2l.30 Bobsleighing . . . . . 1·90 45

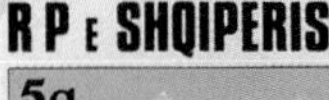

372 "Colchicum autumnale"

1976. Medicinal Plants. Multicoloured.
1822 5q. Type **372** 10 10
1823 10q. "Atropa belladonna" 15 10
1824 15q. "Gentiana lutea" . . . 15 10
1825 20q. "Aesculus hippocastanum" 15 10
1826 70q. "Polystichum filix" . . 35 20
1827 80q. "Althaea officinalis" 55 20
1828 2l.30 "Datura stamonium" 2·25 1·00

373 Wooden Bowl and Spoon

1976. Ethnographical Studies Conference, Tirana. Albanian Artifacts. Multicoloured.
1829 10q. Type **373** 10 10
1830 15q. Flask (vert) 15 10
1831 20q. Ornamental handles (vert) 20 10
1832 25q. Pistol and dagger . . . 25 10
1833 80q. Hand-woven rug (vert) 70 20
1834 1l.20 Filigree buckle and earrings . . . . 1·00 25
1835 1l.40 Jugs with handles (vert) . . . . 1·25 85

374 "Founding the Co-operatives" (Zef Shoshi)

1976. Albanian Paintings. Multicoloured.
1836 5q. Type **374** 10 10
1837 10q. "Going to Work" (Agim Zajmi) (vert) . . . 10 10
1838 25q. "Listening to Broadcast" (Vilson Kilica) 15 10
1839 40q. "Female Welder" (Sabaudin Xhaferi) (vert) 25 10
1840 50q. "Steel Workers" (Isuf Sulovari) (vert) 35 15
1841 1l.20 "1942 Revolt" (Lec Shkreli) (vert) 90 25
1842 1l.60 "Returning from Work" (Agron Dine) . . 1·25 35

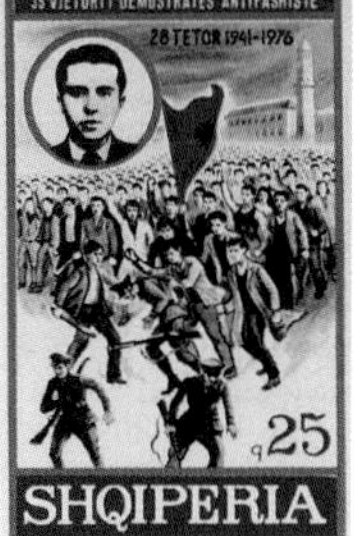

375 Demonstrators attacking Police **376** Party Flag, Industry and Agriculture

1976. 35th Anniv of Hoxha's Anti-fascist Demonstration. Multicoloured.
1844 25q. Type **375** 20 15
1845 1l.90 Crowd with flag . . . 1·40 55

1976. 7th Workers' Party Congress. Multicoloured.
1846 25q. Type **376** . . . . . . 1·75 45
1847 1l.20 Hand holding Party symbols, and flag 85 30

377 Communist Advance

1976. 35th Anniv of Workers' Party. Mult.
1848 15q. Type **377** 20 10
1849 25q. Hands holding emblems and revolutionary army . . . 20 10
1850 80q. "Reconstruction" . . . 40 20
1851 1l.20 "Heavy Industry and Agriculture" 95 30
1852 1l.70 "The Arts" (ballet) . . 1·40 40

378 Young Communist

1976. 35th Anniv of Young Communists' Union. Multicoloured.
1853 80q. Type **378** . . . . . . 1·90 45
1854 1l.25 Young Communists in action 90 40

379 Ballet Dancers

1976. Albanian Ballet "Cuca e Malexe".
1855 **379** 10q. multicoloured . . . 10 10
1856 – 15q. multicoloured . . . 15 10
1857 – 20q. multicoloured . . . 20 10
1858 – 25q. multicoloured . . . 25 10
1859 – 80q. multicoloured . . . 45 20
1860 – 1l.20 multicoloured . . . 70 25
1861 – 1l.40 multicoloured . . . 85 30
DESIGNS: 15q. to 1l.40, Various ballet scenes.

380 Bashtoves Castle

381 Skanderbeg's Shield and Spear

1976. Albanian Castles.
1863 **380** 10q. black and blue . . 10 10
1864 – 15q. black and green . . 10 10
1865 – 20q. black and grey . . 20 15
1866 – 25q. black and ochre . . 30 20
1867 – 80q. black, pink and red 90 50
1868 – 1l.20 black and blue . . 1·25 80
1869 – 1l.40 black, red & pink 1·75 90
DESIGNS: 15q. Gjirokaster; 20q. All Pash Tepelenes; 25q. Petreles; 80q. Berat; 1l.20, Durres; 1l.40, Krujes.

1977. Crest and Arms of Skanderbeg's Army. Mult.
1870 15q. Type **381** . . . . . . 1·25 70
1871 80q. Helmet, sword and scabbard . . . . 4·00 2·50
1872 1l. Halberd, spear, bow and arrows . . . . 6·00 3·00

382 Ilya Oiqi

383 Polyvinyl-chloride Plant, Vlore

1977. Albanian Heroes. Multicoloured.
1873 5q. Type **382** 10 10
1874 10q. Ilia Dashi 20 10
1875 25q. Fran Ndue Ivanaj . . . 75 30
1876 80q. Zeliha Allmetaj . . 1·25 35
1877 1l. Ylli Zaimi . . . . 1·50 50
1878 1l.90 Isuf Plloci . . . . . . 2·50 80

1977. 6th Five-year Plan. Multicoloured.
1879 15q. Type **383** 25 20
1880 25q. Naphtha plant, Ballsh 40 25
1881 65q. Hydroelectric station, Fjerzes 80 50
1882 1l. Metallurgical combinate, Elbasan . . . . 1·60 80

384 Shote Galica

385 Crowd and Martyrs' Monument, Tirana

1977. 50th Death Anniv of Shote Galica (Communist partisan).
1883 **384** 80q. red and pink . . . 80 40
1884 – 1l.25 grey and blue . . . 1·50 75
DESIGN: 1l.25, Shote Galica and father.

1977. 35th Anniv of Martyrs' Day. Multicoloured.
1885 25q. Type **385** 40 25
1886 80q. Clenched fist and Albanian flag . . . . . . 1·00 40
1887 1l.20 Bust of Qemal Stafa 1·75 70

386 Doctor calling at Village House

387 Workers outside Factory

1977. "Socialist Transformation of the Villages". Multicoloured.
1888 5q. Type **386** 10 10
1889 10q. Cowherd with cattle . . 15 10
1890 20q. Harvesting 20 20
1891 80q. Modern village . . . . 1·00 40
1892 2l.95 Tractor and greenhouse . . . . 3·50 70

1977. 8th Trade Unions Congress. Multicoloured.
1893 25q. Type **387** 25 20
1894 1l.80 Three workers with flags . . . . 1·50 80

388 Advancing Soldiers

390 Armed Worker with Book

391 "Beni Ecen Vet"

389 Two Girls with Handkerchiefs

1977. "All the People are Soldiers". Multicoloured.
1895 15q. Type **388** 20 10
1896 25q. Enver Hoxha and marching soldiers 25 10
1897 80q. Soldiers and workers 75 25
1898 1l. The Armed Forces . . . 1·00 35
1899 1l.90 Marching soldiers and workers . . . . 2·00 40

1977. National Costume Dances (1st series). Mult.
1900 5q. Type **389** 15 10
1901 10q. Two male dancers . . 15 10
1902 15q. Man and woman in kerchief dance 15 15
1903 25q. Two male dancers (different) 20 15
1904 80q. Two women dancers with kerchiefs 55 25
1905 1l.20 "Elbow dance" 85 30
1906 1l.55 Two women with kerchiefs (different) . . . 1·10 50
See also Nos. 1932/6 and 1991/5.

1977. New Constitution.
1908 **390** 25q. gold, red and black 25 15
1909 – 1l.20 gold, red and black 1·10 35
DESIGN: 1l.20, Industrial and agricultural symbols and hand with book.

1977. Albanian Films.
1910 **391** 10q. green and grey . . 20 10
1911 – 15q. multicoloured . . . 30 10
1912 – 25q. green, black & grey 40 20
1913 – 80q. multicoloured . . . 1·00 50
1914 – 1l.20 brown and grey . . 1·50 60
1915 – 1l.60 multicoloured . . . 2·50 90
DESIGNS: 15q. "Rruge te Bardha"; 25q. "Rrugicat qe Kerkonin Diell"; 80q. "Ne Fillim te Veres"; 1l.20, "Lulekuqet Mbi Mure"; 1l.60, "Zonja nga Qyteti".

392 Rejoicing Crowd and Independence Memorial, Tirana

393 "Farm Workers"

1977. 65th Anniv of Independence. Multicoloured.
1916 15q. Type **392** 15 15
1917 25q. Independence leaders marching in Tirana . . . 25 15
1918 1l.65 Albanians dancing under national flag . . . 1·25 45

1977. Paintings by V. Mio. Multicoloured.
1919 5q. Type **393** 10 10
1920 10q. "Landscape in the Snow" 10 10
1921 15q. "Sheep under a Walnut Tree, Springtime" 15 10
1922 25q. "Street in Korce" . . . 25 10
1923 80q. "Riders in the Mountains" 65 20
1924 1l. "Boats by the Seashore" 85 25
1925 1l.75 "Tractors Ploughing" 1·10 30

394 Pan Flute

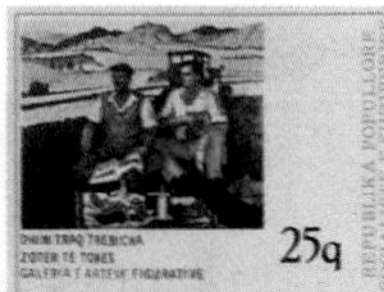

395 "Tractor Drivers" (D. Trebicka)

1978. Folk Music Instruments.
1927 **394** 15q. red, black and green 30 15
1928 – 25q. yellow, black & vio 60 25
1929 – 80q. red, black and blue 1·50 40
1930 – 1l.20 yellow, blk & blue 3·00 60
1931 – 1l.70 lilac, black & grn 5·00 1·25
DESIGNS: 25q. Single-string goat's head fiddle; 80q. Trumpet; 1l.20, Drum; 1l.70, Bagpipes.

1978. National Costume Dances (2nd series). As T **389**. Multicoloured.
1932 5q. Girl dancers with scarves 10 10
1933 25q. Male dancers 20 15
1934 80q. Kneeling dancers . . . 40 20
1935 1l. Female dancers 70 25
1936 2l.30 Male dancers with linked arms . . . . . . 1·75 50

1978. Paintings of the Working Class. Mult.
1937 25q. Type **395** 15 10
1938 80q. "Steeplejack" (S. Kristo) 30 20
1939 85q. "A Point in the Discussion" (S. Milori) . . 35 20
1940 90q. "Oil Rig Crew" (A. Cini) (vert) 45 20
1941 1l.60 "Metal Workers" (R. Karanxha) 75 30

396 Boy and Girl

1978. International Children's Day. Multicoloured.
1943 5q. Type **396** 10 10
1944 10q. Boy and girl with pickaxe and rifle 15 10
1945 25q. Children dancing . . . 25 20
1946 1l.80 Classroom scene . . . 2·00 45

397 Woman with Pickaxe and Rifle

1978. 8th Women's Union Congress.
1947 **397** 25q. red and gold . . . 30 10
1948 – 1l.95 red and gold . . . 2·50 75
DESIGN: 1l.95, Peasant, Militia Guard and industrial installation.

398 Battle of Mostar Bridge

399 Guerillas and Flag

1978. Centenary of the League of Prizren.
1949 **398** 10q. multicoloured . . . 15 10
1950 – 25q. multicoloured . . . 20 15
1951 – 80q. multicoloured . . . 45 20
1952 – 1l.20 blue, black & vio 75 30
1953 – 1l.65 multicoloured . . . 1·00 40
1954 – 2l.60 lt grn, blk & grn 1·60 60
DESIGNS: 25q. Spirit of Skanderbeg; 80q. Albanians marching under national flag; 1l.20, Riflemen; 1l.65, Abdyl Frasheri (founder); 2l.60, League Headquarters, Prizren.

1978. 35th Anniv of People's Army.
1956 5q. Type **399** 35 15
1957 25q. Men of armed forces (horiz) 75 30
1958 1l.90 Men of armed forces, civil guards and Young Pioneers . . . . 4·00 1·50

1978. International Fair, Riccione. No. 1832 surch **3.30L. RICCIONE 78 26.8.78.**
1959 3l.30 on 25q. multicoloured 10·00 3·25

401 Man with Target Rifle

402 Kerchief Dance

1978. 32nd National Shooting Championships.
1960 **401** 25q. black and yellow . . 20 15
1961 – 80q. black and orange 40 20
1962 – 95q. black and red . . . 50 25
1963 – 2l.40 black and red . . . 1·75 50
DESIGNS—VERT: 80q. Woman with machine carbine; 2l.40, Pistol shooting. HORIZ: 95q. Shooting from prone position.

1978. National Folklore Festival, Gjirokaster. Mult.
1964 10q. Type **402** 10 10
1965 15q. Musicians 15 10
1966 25q. Fiddle player 20 15
1967 80q. Singers 45 20
1968 1l.20 Sabre dance 80 25
1969 1l.90 Girl dancers . . . . . 1·40 35

403 Enver Hoxha (after V. Kilica)

404 Woman with Wheatsheaf

1978. Enver Hoxha's 70th Birthday.
1970 **403** 80q. multicoloured . . . 65 20
1971 1l.20 multicoloured . . . 90 25
1972 2l.40 multicoloured . . . 1·40 65

1978. Agriculture and Stock Raising. Multicoloured.
1974 15q. Type **404** 30 20
1975 25q. Woman with boxes of fruit 40 30
1976 80q. Shepherd and flock . . 1·25 60
1977 2l.60 Dairymaid and cattle 4·00 2·00

405 Pupils entering School

406 Dora D'Istria

1978.
1978 **405** 5q. brown, lt brn & gold 15 10
1979 – 10q. blue, lt bl & gold 20 10
1980 – 15q. violet, lilac and gold 30 15
1981 – 20q. brown, drab & gold 45 20
1982 – 25q. red, pink and gold 55 25
1983 – 60q. green, lt grn & gold 1·75 45
1984 – 80q. blue, lt blue & gold 2·50 55
1985 – 1l.20 magenta, mauve and gold . . . . . . 3·50 90
1986 – 1l.60 blue, lt blue & gold 12·00 1·40
1987 – 2l.40 grn, lt grn & gold 6·00 2·10
1988 – 3l. blue, lt blue & gold 7·50 3·75
DESIGNS: 10q. Telephone, letters, telegraph wires and switchboard operators; 15q. Pouring molten iron; 20q. Dancers, musical instruments, book and artist's materials; 25q. Newspapers, radio, television and broadcasting tower; 60q. Assistant in clothes shop; 80q. Militiamen and women, tanks, ships, aircraft and radar equipment; 1l.20, Industrial complex and symbols of industry; 1l.60, Train and truck; 2l.40, Workers hoeing fields, cattle and girl holding wheat sheaf; 3l. Microscope and nurse holding up baby.

1979. 150th Birth Anniv of Dora D'Istria (pioneer of women's rights).
1989 **406** 80q. green and black . . 85 20
1990 – 1l.10 grey and black . . 1·25 1·00
DESIGN: 1l.10, Full-face portrait.

1979. National Costume Dances (3rd series). As T **389**. Multicoloured.
1991 15q. Girl dancers with scarves 15 10
1992 25q. Male dancers 20 10
1993 80q. Girl dancers with scarves (different) 50 25
1994 1l.20 Male dancers with pistols 80 40
1995 1l.40 Female dancers with linked arms . . . . . . 1·25 45

407 Stone-built Galleried House

408 Aleksander Moissi

1979. Traditional Albanian Houses (1st series). Multicoloured.
1996 15q. Type **407** 15 10
1997 25q. Tower house (vert) . . 20 10
1998 80q. House with wooden galleries 85 25

1999 1l.20 Galleried tower house (vert) . . . . 1·25 40
2000 1l.40 Three-storied fortified house (vert) . . . . . . 1·75 65
See also Nos. 2116/19.

1979. Birth Cententary of Aleksander Moissi (actor).
2002 **408** 80q. green, black & gold 65 20
2003 – 1l.10 brown, blk & gold 1·00 25
DESIGN: 1l.10, Aleksander Moissi (different).

409 Vasil Shanto

1979. Anti-fascist Heroes (1st series). Multicoloured.
2004 15q. Type **409** 25 10
2005 25q. Qemal Stafa 30 15
2006 60q. Type **409** 80 20
2007 90q. As 25q. . . . . 1·25 60
See also Nos. 2052/5, 2090/3, 2126/9, 2167/70, 2221/4, 2274/7 and 2313/5.

410 Soldier, Crowd and Coat of Arms

1979. 35th Anniv of Permet Congress. Mult.
2008 25q. Soldier, factories and wheat 40 20
2009 1l.65 Type **410** . . . . . . 2·00 1·00

411 Albanian Flag

1979. 5th Albanian Democratic Front Congress.
2010 **411** 25q. multicoloured . . . 40 20
2011 1l.65 multicoloured . . . 2·00 1·00

412 "Ne Stervitje" (Arben Basha)

1979. Paintings. Multicoloured.
2012 15q. Type **412** 10 10
2013 25q. "Shtigje Lufte" (Ismail Lulani) 20 10
2014 80q. "Agim me Fitore" (Myrteza Fushekati) . . . 75 25
2015 1l.20 "Gjithe Populli ushtare" (Muhamet Deliu) 1·10 35
2016 1l.40 "Zjarret Ndezur Mbajme" (Jorgji Gjikopulli) . . . . 1·40 85

413 Athletes round Party Flag **414** Founder-president

1979. 35th Anniv of Liberation Spartakiad. Mult.
2018 15q. Type **413** 10 10
2019 25q. Shooting 20 10
2020 80q. Girl gymnast 65 25
2021 1l.10 Football 90 35
2022 1l.40 High jump . . . . . 1·10 35

1979. Centenary of Albanian Literary Society.
2023 – 25q. black, brown and gold 20 15
2024 **414** 80q. black, brown and gold 45 20
2025 – 1l.20 black, blue & gold 70 30
2026 – 1l.55 black, vio & gold 95 40
DESIGNS: 25q. Foundation document and seal of 1880; 1l.20, Headquarters building, 1979; 1l.55, Headquarters building, 1879.

415 Congress Building

1979. 35th Anniv of Berat Congress. Multicoloured.
2028 25q. Arms and congress document 80 50
2029 1l.65 Type **415** . . . . . . 3·00 2·00

416 Workers and Industrial Complex **417** Joseph Stalin

1979. 35th Anniv of Liberation. Multicoloured.
2030 25q. Type **416** 20 10
2031 80q. Wheat and hand grasping hammer and pickaxe 45 25
2032 1l.20 Open book, star and musical instrument . . . 60 30
2033 1l.55 Open book, compasses and gear wheel . . . . . 1·00 45

1979. Birth Centenary of Joseph Stalin.
2034 **417** 80q. blue and red . . . 40 25
2035 – 1l.10 blue and red . . . 85 40
DESIGN: 1l.10, Stalin and Enver Hoxha.

418 Fireplace and Pottery, Korce

1980. Interiors (1st series). Multicoloured.
2036 25q. Type **418** 20 20
2037 80q. Carved bed alcove and weapons, Shkoder 50 40
2038 1l.20 Cooking hearth and carved chair, Mirdite . . 1·10 85
2039 1l.35 Turkish-style chimney, dagger and embroidered jacket, Gjirokaster . . . . 1·40 90
See also Nos. 2075/8.

419 Lacework **420** Aleksander Xhuvani

1980. Handicrafts. Multicoloured.
2040 25q. Pipe and flask 20 20
2041 80q. Leather handbags . . . 55 35
2042 1l.20 Carved eagle and embroidered rug 75 60
2043 1l.35 Type **419** 95 65

1980. Birth Centenary of Dr. Aleksander Xhuvani.
2044 **420** 80q. blue, grey and black 1·00 50
2045 1l. brown, grey and black . . . . 1·50 1·00

421 Insurrectionists

1980. 70th Anniv of Kosovo Insurrection.
2046 **421** 80q. black and red . . . 1·00 50
2047 – 1l. black and red . . . 1·50 1·00
DESIGN: 1l. Battle scene.

422 "Soldiers and Workers helping Stricken Population" (D. Jukniu and L. Lulani)

1980. 1979 Earthquake Relief.
2048 **422** 80q. multicoloured . . . 1·00 50
2049 1l. multicoloured . . . . 1·50 1·00

423 Lenin

1980. 110th Birth Anniv of Lenin.
2050 **423** 80q. grey, red and pink 1·00 50
2051 1l. multicoloured . . . . 1·50 1·00

424 Misto Mame and Ali Demi

1980. Anti-fascist Heroes (2nd series). Mult.
2052 25q. Type **424** 25 10
2053 80q. Sadik Staveleci, Vojo Kushi and Xhoxhi Martini 60 30
2054 1l.20 Bule Naipi and Persefoni Kokedhima . . 90 60
2055 1l.35 Ndoc Deda, Hydajet Lezha, Naim Gjylbegu, Ndoc Mazi and Ahmet Haxhia . . . . 1·00 70

425 "Mirela"

1980. Children's Tales. Multicoloured.
2056 15q. Type **425** 10 10
2057 25q. "Shkarravina" 20 15
2058 80q. "Ariu Artist" 45 40
2059 2l.40 "Pika e Ujit" . . . . 2·25 1·40

426 "The Enver Hoxha Tractor Combine" (S. Shijaku and M. Fushekati)

1980. Paintings from Gallery of Figurative Arts, Tirana. Multicoloured.
2060 25q. Type **426** 20 15
2061 80q. "The Welder" (Harilla Dhima) 50 35
2062 1l.20 "Steel Erector (Petro Kokushta) 70 65
2063 1l.35 "Harvest Festival" (Pandeli Lena) 80 75

427 Decorated Door (Pergamen miniature)

1980. Art of the Middle Ages. Each black and gold.
2065 25q. Type **427** 15 10
2066 80q. Bird (relief) 45 25
2067 1l.20 Crowned lion (relief) 75 65
2068 1l.35 Pheasant (relief) . . . 80 75

428 Divjaka

1980. National Parks. Multicoloured.
2069 80q. Type **428** 45 30
2070 1l.20 Lura . . . . 1·00 75
2071 1l.60 Thethi . . . . 1·75 1·00

429 Flag, Arms and rejoicing Albanians

1981. 35th Anniv of Albanian People's Republic. Multicoloured.
2073 80q. Type **429** 75 30
2074 1l. Crowd and flags outside People's Party headquarters 75 45

1981. Interiors (2nd series). Multicoloured.
2075 25q. As T **418** 20 15
2076 80q. Sleeping mats and spirit keg, Labara 45 30
2077 1l.20 Fireplace and covered dish mat . . . . 1·00 50
2078 1l.35 Interior and embroidered jacket, Dibres . . . . 1·25 65

430 Wooden Cot

1981. Folk Art. Multicoloured.
2079 25q. Type **430** 20 15
2080 80q. Bucket and flask . . . 60 30
2081 1l.20 Embroidered slippers 70 40
2082 1l.35 Jugs 80 85

431 Footballers

1981. World Cup Football Championship Eliminating Rounds. Multicoloured.
2083 25q. Type **431** . . . . . . 1·25 60
2084 80q. Tackle . . . . 3·75 1·75
2085 1l.20 Player kicking ball . . 5·25 2·25
2086 1l.35 Goalkeeper saving goal 6·25 2·75

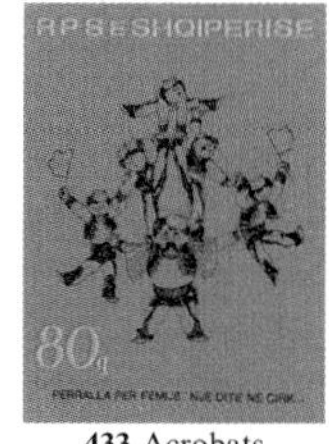

432 Rifleman **433** Acrobats

1981. Cent of Battle of Shtimje. Each purple & red.
2087 80q. Type **432** 65 35
2088 1l. Albanian with sabre . . 80 50

1981. Anti-fascist Heroes (3rd series). As T **424**. Multicoloured.
2090 25q. Perlat Rexhepi and Branko Kadia 20 15
2091 80q. Xheladin Beqiri and Hajdah Dushi 50 35
2092 1l.20 Koci Bako, Vasil Laci and Mujo Ulqinaku . . . 85 55
2093 1l.35 Mine Peza and Zoja Cure 95 70

1981. Children's Circus.
2094 – 15q. black, green & stone 15 10
2095 – 25q. black, blue and grey 20 15
2096 **433** 80q. black, mve & pink 45 35
2097 – 2l.40 black, orge & yell 1·60 1·40
DESIGNS: 15q. Monocyclists. 25q. Human pyramid; 2l.40, Acrobats spinning from marquee pole.

434 "Rallying to the Flag, December 1911" (A. Zajmi)

1981. Paintings. Multicoloured.
2098 25q. "Allies" (Sh. Hysa) (horiz) 20 15
2099 80q. "Azem Galica breaking the Ring of Turks" (A. Buza) (horiz) 50 30
2100 1l.20 Type **434** 70 45
2101 1l.35 "My Flag is my Heart" (L. Cefa) . . . . 1·10 90

435 Weightlifting

1981. Albanian Participation in Inter Sports. Mult.
2103 25q. Rifle shooting 15 10
2104 80q. Type **435** 45 30
2105 1l.20 Volleyball 65 45
2106 1l.35 Football . . . . . . 1·00 70

436 Flag and Hands holding Pickaxe and Rifle **437** Industrial and Agricultural Symbols

1981. 8th Workers' Party Congress.
2107 **436** 80q. red, brown & black 55 35
2108 – 1l. red and black 70 50
DESIGN: 1l. Party flag, hammer and sickle.

1981. 40th Anniv of Workers' Party. Mult.
2109 80q. Type **437** . . . . . . 2·00 45
2110 2l.80 Albanian flag and hand holding pickaxe and rifle . . . . 2·00 1·25

438 Pickaxe, Rifle and Young Communists Flag **439** F. S. Noli

1981. 40th Anniv of Young Communists' Union. Multicoloured.
2112 80q. Type **438** . . . . . . 1·25 40
2113 1l. Workers' Party flag and Young Communists emblem . . . . 2·00 85

1981. Birth Centenary of F. S. Noli (author).
2114 **439** 80q. green and gold . . 75 35
2115 1l.10 brown and gold . . 90 45

1982. Traditional Albanian Houses (2nd series). As T **407**, but vert. Multicoloured.
2116 25q. House in Bulqize . . . 25 15
2117 80q. House in Kosovo . . . 80 50
2118 1l.20 House in Bicaj . . . . 1·10 75
2119 1l.55 House in Mat . . . . 1·50 1·00

440 Map, Globe and Bacillus

1982. Centenary of Discovery of Tubercle Bacillus.
2120 **440** 80q. multicoloured . . . 1·75 80
2121 – 1l.10 brown & dp brown 3·00 1·50
DESIGN: 1l.10, Robert Koch (discoverer), microscope and bacillus.

441 "Prizren Castle" (G. Madhi)

1982. Paintings of Kosovo. Multicoloured.
2122 25q. Type **441** 25 20
2123 80q. "House of the Albanian League, Prizren" (K. Buza) (horiz) 75 60
2124 1l.20 "Mountain Gorge, Rogove" (K. Buza) . . . 1·25 75
2125 1l.55 "Street of the Hadhji, Zekes" (G. Madhi) . . . 1·75 1·00

1982. Anti-fascist Heroes (4th series). As T **424**. Multicoloured.
2126 25q. Hibe Palikuqi and Liri Gero 20 15
2127 80q. Mihal Duri and Kojo Karafili 60 40
2128 1l.20 Fato Dudumi, Margarita Tutulani and Shejnaze Juka 80 50
2129 1l.55 Memo Meto and Gjok Doci . . . . 1·10 75

442 Factories and Workers

1982. 9th Trade Unions Congress. Multicoloured.
2130 80q. Type **442** . . . . . . 1·50 75
2131 1l.10 Congress emblem . . . 2·00 1·00

443 Ship in Harbour

1982. Children's Paintings. Multicoloured.
2132 15q. Type **443** 25 15
2133 80q. Forest camp 75 45
2134 1l.20 House 90 70
2135 1l.65 House and garden . . 1·50 80

444 "Village Festival" (Danish Jukniu)

1982. Paintings from Gallery of Figurative Arts, Tirana. Multicoloured.
2136 25q. Type **444** 25 15
2137 80q. "The Hydroelectric Station Builders" (Ali Miruku) 60 40
2138 1l.20 "Steel Workers" (Clirim Ceka) . . . . . . 1·00 60
2139 1l.55 "Oil Drillers" (Pandeli Lena) . . . . 1·25 85

445 "Voice of the People" (party newspaper) **446** Heroes of Peza Monument

1982. 40th Anniv of Popular Press. Multicoloured.
2141 80q. Type **445** . . . . . . 65·00 65·00
2142 1l.10 Hand duplicator producing first edition of "Voice of the People" . . 65·00 65·00

1982. 40th Anniv of Democratic Front. Mult.
2143 80q. Type **446** . . . . . . 2·50 1·50
2144 1l.10 Peza Conference building and marchers with flag . . . . 3·75 2·00

447 Congress Emblem

1982. 8th Young Communists' Union Congress.
2145 **447** 80q. multicoloured . . . 3·00 1·50
2146 1l.10 multicoloured . . . 4·50 2·25

448 Tapestry

1982. Handicrafts. Multicoloured.
2147 25q. Type **448** 25 15
2148 80q. Bags (vert) 60 40
2149 1l.20 Butter churns 85 55
2150 1l.55 Jug (vert) . . . . . . 1·75 1·10

449 Freedom Fighters

1982. 70th Anniv of Independence.
2151 **449** 20q. deep red, red & blk 20 15
2152 – 1l.20 black, grn & red 85 60
2153 – 2l.40 brown, buff and red . . . . 1·90 1·50
DESIGNS: 20q. Ismail Qemali (patriot) and crowd around building; 2l.40, Six freedom fighters (58 × 55 mm).

450 Dhermi

1982. Coastal Views. Multicoloured.
2155 25q. Type **450** 20 15
2156 80q. Sarande 55 35
2157 1l.20 Ksamil 85 55
2158 1l.55 Lukove . . . . 1·10 1·00

451 Male Dancers **452** Karl Marx

1983. Folk Dance Assemblies Abroad. Mult.
2159 25q. Type **451** 15 10
2160 80q. Male dancers and drummer 50 30
2161 1l.20 Musicians 70 40
2162 1l.55 Group of female dancers . . . . 1·00 90

1983. Death Centenary of Karl Marx.
2163 **452** 80q. multicoloured . . . 1·00 50
2164 1l.10 multicoloured . . . 1·25 60

453 Electricity Generation

1983. Energy Development.
2165 **453** 80q. blue and orange . . 55 35
2166 – 1l.10 mauve and green 90 55
DESIGN: 1l.10, Gas and oil production.

1983. Anti-fascist Heroes (5th series). As T **424**. Multicoloured.
2167 25q. Asim Zeneli and Nazmi Rushiti 20 15
2168 80q. Shyqyri Ishmi, Shyqyri Alimerko and Myzafer Asqeriu 55 35
2169 1l.20 Qybra Sokoli, Qeriba Derri and Ylbere Bilibashi 90 55
2170 1l.55 Themo Vasi and Abaz Shehu . . . . 1·25 75

454 Congress Emblem **456** Soldier and Militia

455 Cycling

1983. 9th Women's Union Congress.
2171 **454** 80q. multicoloured . . . 60 50
2172 1l.10 multicoloured . . . 70 60

1983. Sport and Leisure. Multicoloured.
2173 25q. Type **455** 25 15
2174 80q. Chess . . . . 1·00 50
2175 1l.20 Gymnastics . . . . . 1·25 70
2176 1l.55 Wrestling . . . . . . 1·40 80

1983. 40th Anniv of People's Army.
2177 **456** 20q. gold and red . . . 20 15
2178 – 1l.20 gold and red . . . 85 50
2179 – 2l.40 gold and brown . . 1·75 1·40
DESIGNS: 1l.20, Soldier; 2l.40 Factory guard.

457 "Sunny Day" (Myrteza Fushekati)

1983. Paintings from Gallery of Figurative Arts, Tirana. Multicoloured.
2180 25q. Type **457** 20 15
2181 80q. "Morning Gossip" (Niko Progri) 55 40
2182 1l.20 "29th November, 1944" (Harilla Dhimo) . . 85 50
2183 1l.55 "Demolition" (Pandi Mele) . . . . 1·10 70

1983. National Folklore Festival, Gjirokaster. As T **402**. Multicoloured.
2185 25q. Sword dance 25 15
2186 80q. Kerchief dance 75 45
2187 1l.20 Musicians . . . . . . 1·10 70
2188 1l.55 Women dancers with garlands . . . . 1·25 85

458 Enver Hoxha

1983. 75th Birthday of Enver Hoxha.
2189 **458** 80q. multicoloured . . . 45 35
2190 1l.20 multicoloured . . . 75 50
2191 1l.80 multicoloured . . . 1·40 85

459 W.C.Y. Emblem and Globe

1983. World Communications Year.
2193 **459** 60q. multicoloured . . . 40 25
2194 1l.20 blue, orange & blk 65 45

460 "Combine to Triumph" (J. Keraj)

1983. Skanderbeg Epoch in Art. Multicoloured.
2195 25q. Type **460** 20 15
2196 80q. "The Heroic Resistance at Krujes" (N. Bakalli) . . 60 35
2197 1l.20 "United we are Unconquerable by our Enemies" (N. Progri) . . 90 55
2198 1l.55 "Assembly at Lezhe" (B. Ahmeti) . . . . . . 1·25 70

461 Amphitheatre, Butrint (Buthrotum)

1983. Graeco-Roman Remains in Illyria. Mult.
2200 80q. Type **461** . . . . . . 1·00 75
2201 1l.20 Colonnade, Apoloni Cesma (Apollonium) . . . 1·50 90
2202 1l.80 Vaulted gallery of amphitheatre, Dyrrah (Epidamnus) . . . . . . 1·90 1·25

462 Man's Head from Apoloni
463 Clock Tower, Gjirokaster

1984. Archaeological Discoveries (1st series). Mult.
2203 15q. Type **462** 20 15
2204 25q. Tombstone from Korce 25 15
2205 80q. Woman's head from Apoloni 55 35
2206 1l.10 Child's head from Tren 85 65
2207 1l.20 Man's head from Dyrrah 90 70
2208 2l.20 Bronze statuette of Eros from Dyrrah . . . . 1·75 1·25
See also Nos. 2258/61.

1984. Clock Towers.
2209 **463** 15q. purple 20 15
2210 – 25q. brown 25 15
2211 – 80q. violet 55 35
2212 – 1l.10 red 85 65
2213 – 1l.20 green 90 70
2214 – 2l.20 brown . . . . . . 1·75 1·25
DESIGNS: 25q. Kavaje; 80q. Elbasan; 1l.10, Tirana; 1l.20, Peqin; 2l.20, Kruje.

464 Student with Microscope

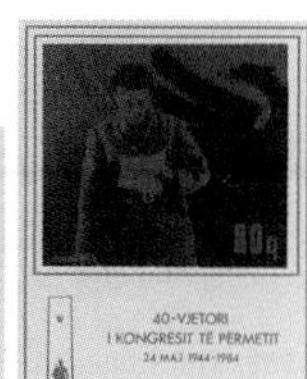

465 Enver Hoxha

1984. 40th Anniv of Liberation (1st issue). Mult.
2215 15q. Type **464** 20 15
2216 25q. Soldier with flag . . . 25 15
2217 80q. Schoolchildren 65 35
2218 1l.10 Soldier, ships, airplanes and weapons . . 95 65
2219 1l.20 Workers with flag . . 1·10 75
2220 2l.20 Armed guards on patrol . . . . 4·00 1·75
See also Nos. 2255/6.

1984. Anti-fascist Heroes (6th series). As T **424**. Multicoloured.
2221 15q. Manush Alimani, Mustafa Matohiti and Kastriot Muco 15 10
2222 25q. Zaho Koka, Reshit Collaku and Maliq Muco 20 15
2223 1l.20 Lefter Talo, Tom Kola and Fuat Babani 85 55
2224 2l.20 Myslysm Shyri, Dervish Hekali and Skender Caci . . . . . . 1·75 1·25

1984. 40th Anniv of Permet Congress.
2225 **465** 80q. brown, orge & red 1·50 80
2226 – 1l.10 black, yell & lilac 1·75 1·25
DESIGN: 1l.10, Resistance fighter (detail of monument).

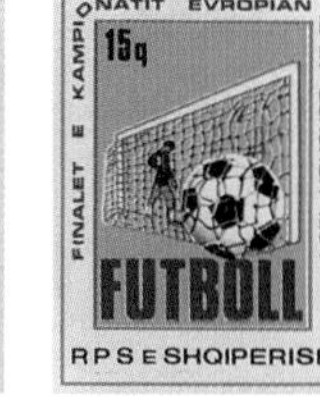

466 Children reading Comic
467 Football in Goal

1984. Children. Multicoloured.
2227 15q. Type **466** 20 15
2228 25q. Children with toys . . 25 20
2229 60q. Children gardening and rainbow 55 35
2230 2l.80 Children flying kite bearing Albanian arms . . 2·25 1·75

1984. European Football Championship Finals. Multicoloured.
2231 15q. Type **467** 40 20
2232 25q. Referee and football . . 60 30
2233 1l.20 Football and map of Europe . . . . 1·25 60
2234 2l.20 Football and pitch . . 3·50 1·75

468 "Freedom is Here" (Myrteza Fushekati)

1984. Paintings from Gallery of Figurative Arts, Tirana. Multicoloured.
2235 15q. Type **468** 20 15
2236 25q. "Morning" (Zamir Mati) (vert) 25 15
2237 80q. "My Darling" (Agim Zajmi) (vert) 70 40
2238 2l.60 "For the Partisans" (Arben Basha) . . . . . 2·00 1·75

469 Mulberry
471 Truck driving through Forest

1984. Flowers. Multicoloured.
2240 15q. Type **469** 25 15
2241 25q. Plantain 65 15
2242 1l.20 Hypericum . . . . . 3·25 1·10
2243 2l.20 Edelweiss . . . . . . 6·25 2·50

1984. Forestry. Multicoloured.
2245 15q. Type **471** 40 25
2246 25q. Transporting logs on overhead cable 75 40
2247 1l.20 Sawmill in forest . . . 2·25 75
2248 2l.20 Lumberjack sawing down trees . . . . 3·00 1·60

472 Gjirokaster
473 Football

1984. "Eurphila '84" Int Stamp Exn, Rome.
2249 **472** 1l.20 multicoloured . . . 1·10 90

1984. 5th National Spartakiad. Multicoloured.
2250 15q. Type **473** 20 15
2251 25q. Running 25 15
2252 80q. Weightlifting 65 35
2253 2l.20 Pistol shooting . . . . 1·75 1·40

474 Agriculture and Industry

1984. 40th Anniv of Liberation (2nd issue). Mult.
2255 80q. Type **474** 80 40
2256 1l.10 Soldiers and flag . . . 1·25 60

1985. Archaeological Discoveries (2nd series). As T **462**, showing Illyrian finds. Multicoloured.
2258 15q. Pot 25 15
2259 80q. Terracotta head of woman 65 35
2260 1l.20 Terracotta bust of Aphrodite . . . . 1·00 65
2261 1l.70 Bronze statuette of Nike . . . . 1·75 1·25

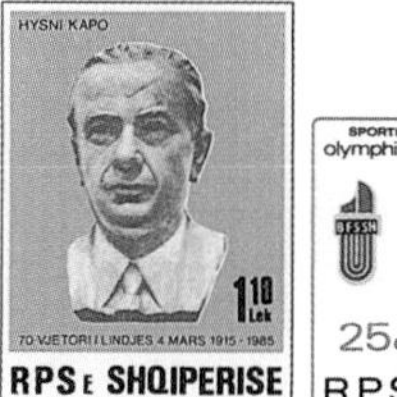

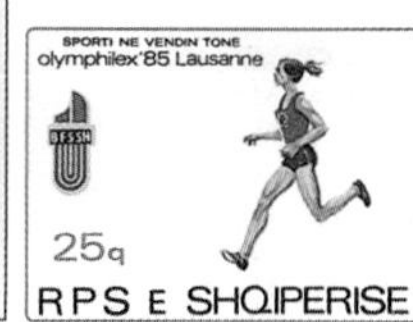

476 Kapo (bust)
477 Running

1985. 70th Birthday of Hysni Kapo (politician).
2262 **476** 90q. black and red . . . 90 60
2263 1l.10 black and blue . . 1·25 75

1985. "Olymphilex '85" Olympic Stamps Exhibition, Lausanne. Multicoloured.
2264 25q. Type **477** 25 15
2265 60q. Weightlifting 50 25
2266 1l.20 Football . . . . . . 1·10 65
2267 1l.50 Pistol shooting . . . . 1·60 1·10

478 Bach
479 Hoxha

1985. 300th Birth Anniv of Johann Sebastian Bach (composer).
2268 **478** 80q. orange, brn & blk 6·50 4·50
2269 – 1l.20 blue, dp blue & blk 7·50 5·50
DESIGN—1l.20, Bach's birthplace, Eisenach.

1985. Enver Hoxha Commemoration.
2270 **479** 80q. multicoloured . . . 1·00 80

480 Frontier Guards
481 Scarf on Rifle Barrel

1985. 40th Anniv of Frontier Force. Multicoloured.
2272 25q. Type **480** 75 50
2273 80q. Frontier guard . . . . 1·75 1·00

1985. Anti-fascist Heroes (7th series). As T **424**. Multicoloured.
2274 25q. Mitro Xhani, Nimete Progonati and Kozma Nushi 40 25
2275 40q. Ajet Xhindoli, Mustafa Kacaci and Estref Caka 60 40
2276 60q. Celo Sinani, Llambro Andoni and Meleo Gosnishti 80 50
2277 1l.20 Thodhori Mastora, Fejzi Micoli and Hysen Cino . . . . 1·50 1·00

1985. 40th Anniv of V.E. (Victory in Europe) Day. Multicoloured.
2278 25q. Type **481** 75 50
2279 80q. Crumpled swastika and hand holding rifle butt . . 1·75 1·00

482 "Primary School" (Thoma Malo)

1985. Paintings from Gallery of Figurative Arts, Tirana. Multicoloured.
2280 25q. Type **482** 25 15
2281 80q. "Heroes and Mother" (Hysen Devolli) (vert) . . 90 35
2282 90q. "Mother writing" (Angjelin Dodmasej) (vert) 1·00 70
2283 1l.20 "Women off to Work" (Ksenofen Dilo) . . . . . 1·40 70

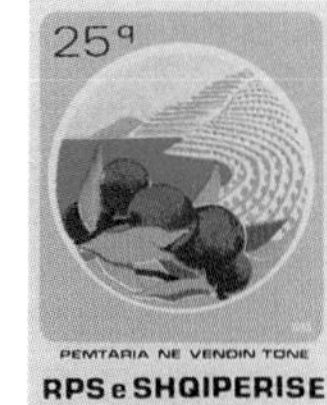

483 Scoring a Goal
484 Oranges

1985. 10th World Basketball Championship, Spain.
2285 **483** 25q. blue and black . . 25 15
2286 – 80q. green and black . . 65 35
2287 – 1l.20 violet and black . . 1·00 70
2288 – 1l.60 red and black . . . 1·60 1·10
DESIGNS: 80q. Player running with ball; 1l.20, Defending goal; 1l.60, Defender capturing ball.

1985. Fruit Trees. Multicoloured.
2289 25q. Type **484** . . . . . . 1·50 55
2290 80q. Plums . . . . 2·25 80
2291 1l.20 Apples . . . . 3·25 1·50
2292 1l.60 Cherries . . . . 6·50 2·75

485 Kruja
486 War Horse Dance

1985. Architecture.
2293 **485** 25q. black and red . . . 25 15
2294 – 80q. black, grey and brown . . . . 1·25 35
2295 – 1l.20 black, brown & bl 1·75 65
2296 – 1l.60 black, brown & red 2·50 1·10
DESIGNS: 80q. Gjirokastra; 1l.20, Berat; 1l.60, Shkoder.

1985. National Folklore Festival. Dances.
2297 **486** 25q. brown, red & black 25 15
2298 – 80q. brown, red & black 65 35
2299 – 1l.20 brown, red & blk 1·00 65
2300 – 1l.60 brown, red & blk 1·60 1·10
DESIGNS: 80q. Pillow dance; 1l.20, Ladies' kerchief dance; 1l.60, Men's one-legged pair dance.

487 State Arms **488** Dam across River Drin

1986. 40th Anniv of Albanian People's Republic.
2302 **487** 25q. gold, red and black . . . 60 40
2303 – 80q. multicoloured . . . 1·50 80
DESIGN: 80q. "Comrade Hoxha announcing the News to the People" (Vilson Kilica) and arms.

1986. Enver Hoxha Hydroelectric Power Station. Multicoloured.
2304 25q. Type **488** . . . . . . 2·50 1·00
2305 80q. Control building . . . 5·50 3·00

489 "Gymnospermium shqipetarum" **490** Maksim Gorky (writer)

1986. Flowers. Multicoloured.
2306 25q. Type **489** 60 40
2307 1l.20 "Leucojum valentinum" . . . . . . 3·00 1·50

1986. Anniversaries.
2308 **490** 25q. brown 25 15
2309 – 80q. violet . . . . . . [illegible] [illegible]
2310 – 1l.20 green . . . . . . 2·50 2·00
2311 – 2l.40 purple . . . . . . 4·25 2·75
DESIGNS: 25q. Type **490** (50th death anniv); 80q. Andre Ampere (physicist and mathematician, 150th death anniv); 1l.20, James Watt (inventor, 250th birth); 2l.40, Franz Liszt (composer, death cent).

1986. Anti-fascist Heroes (8th series). As T **424**. Multicoloured.
2313 25q. Ramiz Aranitasi, Inajete Dumi and Laze Nuro Ferraj 80 60
2314 80q. Dine Kalenja, Kozma Naska, Met Hasa and Fahri Raalbani . . . . . 2·00 1·00
2315 1l.20 Hiqmet Buzi, Bajram Tusha, Mumin Selami and Hajredin Bylyshi . . . . 3·00 2·00

491 Trophy on Globe

1986. World Cup Football Championship, Mexico. Multicoloured.
2316 25q. Type **491** 30 20
2317 1l.20 Goalkeeper's hands and ball . . . . 1·25 1·00

492 Car Tyre within Ship's Wheel, Diesel Train and Traffic Lights

1986. 40th Anniv of Transport Workers' Day.
2319 **492** 1l.20 multicoloured . . . 4·25 1·25

493 Naim Frasheri (poet)

1986. Anniversaries. Multicoloured.
2320 30q. Type **493** (140th birth anniv) 50 15
2321 60q. Ndre Mjeda (poet, 120th birth anniv) . . . . 1·00 65
2322 90q. Petro Nini Luarasi (jounalist, 75th death anniv) . . . . 1·50 1·00
2323 1l. Andon Zaka Cajupi (poet, 120th birth anniv) 1·60 1·10
2324 1l.20 Millosh Gjergj Nikolla (Migjeni) (revolutionary writer, 75th birth anniv) 2·00 1·40
2325 2l.60 Urani Rumbo (women's education pioneer, 50th death anniv) 4·25 2·75

494 Congress Emblem **495** Party Stamp and Enver Hoxha's Signature

1986. 9th Workers' Party Congress, Tirana.
2326 **494** 30q. multicoloured . . . 5·75 4·25

1986. 45th Anniv of Workers' Party.
2327 **495** 30q. red, grey and gold 1·10 55
2328 – 1l.20 red, orange & gold 4·75 2·40
DESIGNS: 1l.20, Profiles of Marx, Engels, Lenin and Stalin and Tirana house where Party was founded.

496 "Mother Albania" **497** Marble Head of Aesculapius

1986.
2329 **496** 10q. blue 10 10
2330 20q. red 10 10
2331 30q. red 10 10
2332 50q. brown 20 15
2333 60q. green 25 15
2334 80q. red 30 20
2335 90q. blue 35 25
2336 1l.20 green 45 30
2337 1l.60 purple 60 40
2338 2l.20 green 85 55
2339 3l. brown . . . . . . 1·10 75
2340 6l. yellow . . . . 2·25 1·50

1987. Archaeological Discoveries. Multicoloured.
2341 30q. Type **497** 45 30
2342 80q. Terracotta figure of Aphrodite . . . . 1·10 75
2343 1l. Bronze figure of Pan . . 1·40 95
2344 1l.20 Limestone head of Jupiter . . . . 1·75 1·10

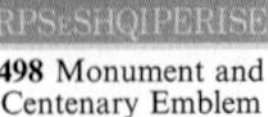

498 Monument and Centenary Emblem **499** Victor Hugo (writer, 185th birth anniv)

1987. Centenary of First Albanian School.
2345 **498** 30q. brown, lt brn & yell 30 20
2346 – 80q. multicoloured . . . 80 55
2347 – 1l.20 multicoloured . . . 1·25 85
DESIGNS: 80q. First school building; 1l.20, Woman soldier running, girl reading book and boy doing woodwork.

1987. Anniversaries.
2348 **499** 30q. vio, lavender & blk 30 20
2349 – 80q. brown, lt brn & blk 80 60
2350 – 90q. dp blue, blue & blk 90 65
2351 – 1l.30 dp grn, grn & brn 1·25 90
DESIGNS: 80q. Galileo Galilei (astronomer, 345th death); 90q. Charles Darwin (naturalist, 105th death); 1l.30. Miguel de Cervantes Saavedra (writer, 440th birth).

500 "Forsythia europaea" **501** Congress Emblem

1987. Flowers. Multicoloured.
2352 30q. Type **500** 30 20
2353 90q. "Moltkia doerfleri" . . 90 60
2354 2l.10 "Wulfenia baldacii" . . 2·10 1·40

1987. 10th Trade Unions Congress, Tirana.
2355 **501** 1l.20 dp red, red & gold 3·00 2·00

502 "The Bread of Industry" (Myrteza Fushekati)

1987. Paintings from Gallery of Figurative Arts, Tirana. Multicoloured.
2356 30q. Type **502** 25 20
2357 80q. "Partisan Gift" (Skender Kokobobo) . . 65 50
2358 1l. "Sowers" (Bujar Asllani) (horiz) 80 60
2359 1l.20 "At the Foundry" (Clirim Ceka) (horiz) . . 90 75

503 Throwing the Hammer

1987. World Light Athletics Championships, Rome. Multicoloured.
2360 30q. Type **503** 25 20
2361 90q. Running 75 55
2362 1l.10 Putting the shot . . . 95 70

504 Themistokli Germenji (revolutionary, 70th death)

1987. Anniversaries.
2364 **504** 30q. brown, red & black 35 25
2365 – 80q. red, scarlet & black 1·00 65
2366 – 90q. violet, red and black . . . . 1·10 75
2367 – 1l.30 green, red & black 1·60 1·10
DESIGNS: 80q. Bajram Curri (organizer of Albanian League, 125th birth); 90q. Aleks Stavre Drenova (poet, 40th death); 1l.30, Gjerasim Qiriazi (educational pioneer, 126th birth).

505 Emblem **506** National Flag

1987. 9th Young Communists' Union Congress, Tirana.
2368 **505** 1l.20 multicoloured . . . 4·00 2·75

1987. 75th Anniv of Independence.
2369 **506** 1l.20 multicoloured . . . 4·00 2·75

507 Post Office Emblem **508** Lord Byron (writer, bicentenary)

1987. 75th Anniv of Albanian Postal Administration. Multicoloured.
2370 90q. Type **507** . . . . . . 6·00 4·00
2371 1l.20 National emblem on bronze medallion . . . . 8·50 5·75

1988. Birth Anniversaries.
2372 **508** 30q. black and orange 2·75 2·25
2373 – 1l.20 black and mauve 10·50 8·50
DESIGN: 1l.20, Eugene Delacroix (painter, 190th anniv).

509 Oil Derrick, Tap, Houses and Wheat Ears **510** "Sideritis raeseri"

1988. 40th Anniv of W.H.O.
2374 **509** 90q. multicoloured . . . 17·00 14·00
2375 1l.20 multicoloured . . . 23·00 19·00

1988. Flowers. Multicoloured.
2376 30q. Type **510** . . . . . . 2·25 1·75
2377 90q. "Lunaria telekiana" . . 6·75 5·50
2378 2l.10 "Sanguisorba albanica" . . . . 16·00 13·00

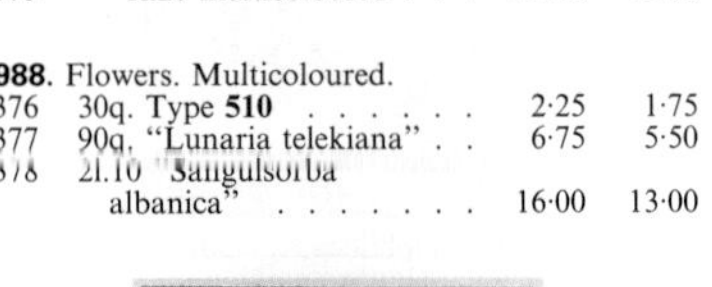

511 Flag and Woman with Book

1988. 10th Women's Union Congress, Tirana.
2379 **511** 90q. black, red & orange 7·00 6·00

512 Footballers **513** Clasped Hands

1988. 8th European Football Championship, West Germany. Multicoloured.
2380 30q. Type **512** 65 50
2381 80q. Players jumping for ball . . . . 1·75 1·25
2382 1l.20 Tackling . . . . . . 2·50 1·90

1988. 110th Anniv of League of Prizren. Mult.
2384 30q. Type **513** . . . . . . 6·50 6·50
2385 1l.20 League Headquarters, Prizren . . . . 27·00 27·00

514 Flag, Woman with Rifle and Soldier **515** Mihal Grameno (writer)

1988. 45th Anniv of People's Army. Multicoloured.
2386 60q. Type **514** . . . . . . 15·00 15·00
2387 90q. Army monument, partisans and Labinot house . . . . 23·00 23·00

1988. Multicoloured.
2388 30q. Type **515** . . . . . . 5·50 5·50
2389 90q. Bajo Topulli (revolutionary) . . . . . 16·00 16·00

2390 1l. Murat Toptani (sculptor and poet) . . . . 18·00 18·00
2391 1l.20 Jul Variboba (poet) . . 22·00 22·00

516 Migjeni

1988. 50th Death Anniv of Millosh Gjergj Nikolla (Migjeni) (writer).
2392 **516** 90q. silver and brown . . 6·75 6·00

517 "Dede Skurra"
518 Bride wearing Fezzes, Mirdita

1988. Ballads. Each black and grey.
2393 30q. Type **517** . . . . . . 5·00 5·00
2394 90q. "Young Omer" . . . . 15·00 15·00
2395 1l.20 "Gjergj Elez Alia" . . 19·00 19·00

1988. National Folklore Festival, Gjirokaster. Wedding Customs. Multicoloured.
2396 30q. Type **518** . . . . . . 9·00 9·00
2397 1l.20 Pan Dance, Gjirokaster . . . . 35·00 35·00

519 Hoxha

1988. 80th Birth Anniv of Enver Hoxha. Mult.
2398 90q. Type **519** . . . . . . 3·00 3·00
2399 1l.20 Enver Hoxha Museum (horiz) . . . . 4·00 4·00

520 Detail of Congress Document

1988. 80th Anniv of Monastir Language Congress. Multicoloured.
2400 60q. Type **520** . . . . . . 12·50 12·50
2401 90q. Alphabet book and Congress building . . . . 16·00 16·00

521 Steam Locomotive and Map showing 1947 Railway line

1989. Railway Locomotives. Multicoloured.
2402 30q. Type **521** 40 10
2403 90q. Polish steam locomotive and map of 1949 network . . . . . . 1·25 35
2404 1l.20 Diesel locomotive and 1978 network . . . . . . 1·60 45
2405 1l.80 Diesel locomotive and 1985 network . . . . . . 2·40 70
2406 2l.40 Czechoslovakian diesel-electric locomotive and 1988 network . . . . 3·25 90

522 Entrance to Two-storey Tomb

1989. Archaeological Discoveries in Illyria.
2407 **522** 30q. black, brown & grey 15 10
2408 – 90q. black and green . . 50 35
2409 – 2l.10 multicoloured . . . 1·10 75
DESIGNS: 90q. Buckle showing battle scene; 2l.10, Earring depicting head.

523 Mother mourning Son
524 "Aster albanicus"

1989. "Kostandini and Doruntina" (folk tale). Mult.
2410 30q. Type **523** 15 10
2411 80q. Mother weeping over tomb and son rising from dead 45 30
2412 1l. Son and his sister on horseback 55 35
2413 1l.20 Mother and daughter reunited 65 45

1989. Flowers. Multicoloured.
2414 30q. Type **524** 15 10
2415 90q. "Orchis paparisti" . . 50 35
2416 2l.10 "Orchis albanica" . . 1·10 75

525 Johann Strauss (composer, 90th death anniv)
526 State Arms, Workers' Party Flag and Crowd

1989. Anniversaries. Each brown and gold.
2417 30q. Type **525** 15 10
2418 80q. Marie Curie (physicist, 55th death anniv) 45 30
2419 1l. Federico Garcia Lorca (writer, 53rd death anniv) 55 35
2420 1l.20 Albert Einstein (physicist, 110th birth anniv) 65 45

1989. 6th Albanian Democratic Front Congress, Tirana.
2421 **526** 1l.20 multicoloured . . . 5·00 4·00

527 Storming of the Bastille

1989. Bicentenary of French Revolution. Mult.
2422 90q. Type **527** 40 30
2423 1l.20 Monument 55 40

528 Galley
529 Pjeter Bogdani (writer, 300th anniv)

1989. Ships.
2424 **528** 30q. green and black . . 30 15
2425 – 80q. blue and black . . 75 35
2426 – 90q. blue and black . . 95 45
2427 – 1l.30 lilac and black . . 1·25 60
DESIGNS: 80q. Kogge; 90q. Schooner; 1l.30, "Tirana" (freighter).

1989. Death Anniversaries. Multicoloured.
2428 30q. Type **529** 20 15
2429 80q. Gavril Dara (writer, centenary) 50 35
2430 90q. Thimi Mitko (writer, centenary (1990)) 60 40
2431 1l.30 Kole Idromeno (painter, 50th anniv) . . . 85 55

530 Engels, Marx and Marchers
531 Gymnastics

1989. 125th Anniv of "First International". Mult.
2432 90q. Type **530** 40 30
2433 1l.20 Factories, marchers and worker with pickaxe and rifle 55 40

1989. 6th National Spartakiad.
2434 **531** 30q. black, orange & red 15 10
2435 – 80q. black, lt grn & grn 40 25
2436 – 1l. black, blue & dp blue 50 35
2437 – 1l.20 black, pur & red 55 35
DESIGNS: 80q. Football; 1l. Cycling; 1l.20, Running.

532 Soldier
533 Chamois

1989. 45th Anniv of Liberation. Multicoloured.
2438 30q. Type **532** 15 10
2439 80q. Date 35 25
2440 1l. State arms 45 30
2441 1l.20 Young couple 50 35

1990. Endangered Animals. The Chamois. Mult.
2442 10q. Type **533** 10 10
2443 30q. Mother and young . . 25 20
2444 80q. Chamois keeping lookout 65 50
2445 90q. Head of chamois . . . 70 55

534 Eagle Mask

1990. Masks. Multicoloured.
2446 30q. Type **534** 10 10
2447 90q. Sheep 35 25
2448 1l.20 Goat 50 35
2449 1l.80 Stork 70 45

535 Caesar's Mushroom

1990. Fungi. Multicoloured.
2450 30q. Type **535** 30 15
2451 90q. Parasol mushroom . . 85 40
2452 1l.20 Cep . . . . 1·10 50
2453 1l.80 "Clathrus cancelatus" 1·60 80

536 Engraving Die

1990. 150th Anniv of the Penny Black. Mult.
2454 90q. Type **536** 50 40
2455 1l.20 Mounted postal messenger 65 55
2456 1l.80 Mail coach passengers reading letters 95 80

537 Mascot and Flags

1990. World Cup Football Championship, Italy. Multicoloured.
2457 30q. Type **537** 15 10
2458 90q. Mascot running . . . 40 25
2459 1l.20 Mascot preparing to kick ball 55 35

538 Young Van Gogh and Paintings

1990. Death Centenary of Vincent van Gogh (painter). Multicoloured.
2461 30q. Type **538** 15 10
2462 90q. Van Gogh and woman in field 40 25
2463 2l.10 Van Gogh in asylum 90 60

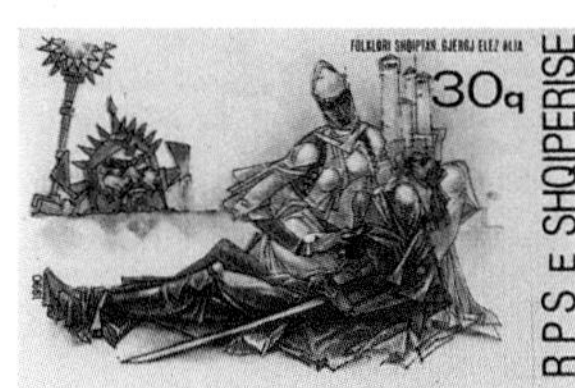

539 Gjergj Elez Alia lying wounded

1990. Gjergj Elez Alia (folk hero). Multicoloured.
2465 30q. Type **539** 15 10
2466 90q. Alia being helped onto horse 40 25
2467 1l.20 Alia fighting Bajloz . . 50 35
2468 1l.80 Alia on horseback and severed head of Bajloz . . 75 50

540 Mosque
541 Pirroja

1990. 2400th Anniv of Berat. Multicoloured.
2469 30q. Type **540** 10 10
2470 90q. Triadha's Church . . . 30 20
2471 1l.20 River 40 25
2472 1l.80 Onufri (artist) 60 40
2473 2l.40 Nikolla 80 55

1990. Illyrian Heroes. Each black.
2474 30q. Type **541** 10 10
2475 90q. Teuta 30 20
2476 1l.20 Bato 40 25
2477 1l.80 Bardhyli 65 45

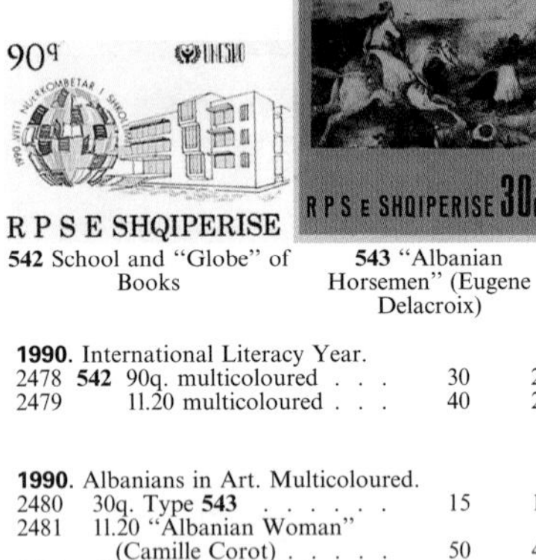

542 School and "Globe" of Books

543 "Albanian Horsemen" (Eugene Delacroix)

1990. International Literacy Year.
2478 **542** 90q. multicoloured . . . 30 20
2479 1l.20 multicoloured . . . 40 25

1990. Albanians in Art. Multicoloured.
2480 30q. Type **543** 15 10
2481 1l.20 "Albanian Woman" (Camille Corot) 50 40
2482 1l.80 "Skanderbeg" (anon) 75 55

544 Boletini

545 Armorial Eagle

1991. 75th Death Anniv of Isa Boletini (revolutionary). Multicoloured.
2483 90q. Type **544** 20 15
2484 1l.20 Boletini and flag . . . 30 25

1991. 800th Anniv (1990) of Founding of Arberi State.
2485 **545** 90q. multicoloured . . . 20 15
2486 1l.20 multicoloured . . . 30 25

546 "Woman reading"

547 "Cistus albanicus"

1991. 150th Birth Anniv of Pierre Auguste Renoir (artist). Multicoloured.
2487 30q. Type **546** 15 10
2488 90q. "The Swing" 50 40
2489 1l.20 "The Boat Club" (horiz) 85 50
2490 1l.80 Still life (detail) (horiz) 95 70

1991. Flowers. Multicoloured.
2492 30q. Type **547** 15 10
2493 90q. "Trifolium pilczii" . . 35 25
2494 1l.80 "Lilium albanicum" 75 55

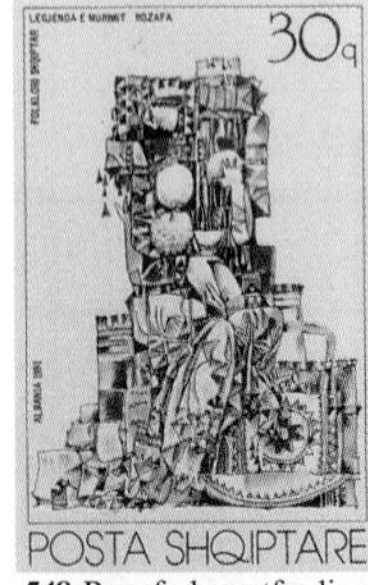

548 Rozafa breastfeeding Child

549 Mozart conducting

1991. Imprisonment of Rozafa (folk tale). Mult.
2495 30q. Type **548** 10 10
2496 90q. The three brothers talking to old man . . . 30 25
2497 1l.20 Building of walls around Rozafa 40 30
2498 1l.80 Figures symbolizing water flowing between stones 60 45

1991. Death Bicentenary of Wolfgang Amadeus Mozart (composer). Multicoloured.
2499 90q. Type **549** 30 25
2500 1l.20 Mozart and score . . 45 35
2501 1l.80 Mozart composing . . 65 50

550 Vitus Bering

1992. Explorers. Multicoloured.
2503 30q. Type **550** 10 10
2504 90q. Christopher Columbus and his flagship "Santa Maria" 50 25
2505 1l.80 Ferdinand Magellan and his flagship "Vitoria" 90 50

551 Otto Lilienthal's Biplane Glider, 1896

1992. Aircraft.
2506 **551** 30q. black, red and blue 10 10
2507 – 80q. multicoloured . . . 25 20
2508 – 90q. multicoloured . . . 30 25
2509 – 1l.20 multicoloured . . . 40 30
2510 – 1l.80 multicoloured . . . 55 40
2511 – 2l.40 black, grey & mve 75 55
DESIGNS: 80q. Clement Ader's "Avion III", 1897; 90q. Wright Brothers' Type A, 1903; 1l.20, Concorde supersonic jetliner; 1l.80, Tupolev Tu-144 jetliner (wrongly inscr "114"); 2l.40, Dornier Do-31E (wrongly inscr "Dernier").

552 Ski Jumping

1992. Winter Olympic Games, Albertville. Mult.
2512 30q. Type **552** 10 10
2513 90q. Skiing 30 25
2514 1l.20 Ice skating (pairs) . . 40 30
2515 1l.80 Luge 60 45

553 "Europe" and Doves

1992. Admission of Albania to European Security and Co-operation Conference at Foreign Ministers' Meeting, Berlin. Multicoloured.
2516 90q. Type **553** 30 25
2517 1l.20 Members' flags and map of Europe 45 35

554 Envelopes and Emblem

1992. Admission of Albania to E.P.T. Conference. Multicoloured.
2518 90q. Type **554** 30 25
2519 1l.20 Emblem and tape reels 45 35

555 Everlasting Flame

1992. National Martyrs' Day. Multicoloured.
2520 90q. Type **555** 25 20
2521 4l.10 Poppies (horiz) . . . . 1·10 85

556 Pictograms

1992. European Football Championship, Sweden.
2522 **556** 30q. light green & green 10 10
2523 – 90q. red and blue . . . 35 25
2524 – 10l.80 ochre and brown 4·00 3·00
DESIGNS: 90q., 10l.80, Different pictograms.

557 Lawn Tennis

1992. Olympic Games, Barcelona. Multicoloured.
2526 30q. Type **557** 10 10
2527 90q. Baseball 35 25
2528 1l.80 Table tennis 75 55

558 Map and Doves

1992. European Unity.
2530 **558** 1l.20 multicoloured . . . 35 25

559 Native Pony

1992. Horses. Multicoloured.
2531 30q. Type **559** 10 10
2532 90q. Hungarian nonius . . . 25 20
2533 1l.20 Arab (vert) 35 25
2534 10l.60 Haflinger (vert) . . . 3·25 2·40

560 Map of Americas, Columbus and Ships

1992. Europa. 500th Anniv of Discovery of America by Columbus. Multicoloured.
2535 60q. Type **560** 60 20
2536 3l.20 Map of Americas and Columbus meeting Amerindians . . . . . . 1·10 1·85

561 Mother Teresa and Child

562 Pope John Paul II

1992. Mother Teresa (Agnes Gonxhe Bojaxhi) (founder of Missionaries of Charity).
2538 **561** 40q. red 10 10
2539 60q. brown 10 10
2540 1l. violet 10 10
2541 1l.80 grey 10 10
2542 2l. red 15 10
2543 2l.40 green 15 10
2544 3l.20 blue 20 15
2545 5l. violet 25 20
2546 5l.60 purple 35 25
2547 7l.20 green 45 35
2548 10l. orange 55 40
2549 18l. orange 85 65
2550 20l. purple 30 25
2551 25l. green . . . . 1·00 75
2552 60l. green 85 65

1993. Papal Visit.
2555 **562** 16l. multicoloured . . . 95 70

1993. Nos. 2329/32 and 2335 surch **POSTA SHQIPTARE** and new value.
2556 **496** 3l. on 10q. blue 25 20
2557 6l.50 on 20q. red 50 35
2558 13l. on 30q. red . . . . 1·00 1·75
2559 20l. on 90q. blue . . . . 1·50 1·10
2560 30l. on 50q. brown . . . 2·25 1·75

564 Lef Nosi (first Postal Minister)

565 "Life Weighs Heavily on Man" (A. Zajmi)

1993. 80th Anniv of First Albanian Stamps.
2561 **564** 6l.50 brown and green 35 25

1993. Europa. Contemporary Art. Multicoloured.
2562 3l. Type **565** 30 25
2563 7l. "The Green Star" (E. Hila) (horiz) 70 55

566 Running

1993. Mediterranean Games, Agde and Roussillon (Languedoc), France. Multicoloured.
2565 3l. Type **566** 20 15
2566 16l. Canoeing . . . . 1·10 85
2567 21l. Cycling . . . . 1·40 1·10

567 Bardhi

568 Mascot and Flags around Stadium

1993. 350th Death Anniv of Frang Bardhi (scholar).
2569 **567** 6l.50 brown and stone 45 35

1994. World Cup Football Championship, U.S.A. Multicoloured.
2571 42l. Type **568** 50 40
2572 68l. Mascot kicking ball . . 80 60

569 Gjovalin Gjadri (construction engineer) **571** Richard Wagner

570 Emblem and Benz

1994. Europa. Discoveries and Inventions.
2573 **569** 50l. dp brn, ches & brn 70 55
2574 – 100l. dp brn, ches & brn 1·75 1·25
DESIGN: 100l. Karl Ritter von Ghega (railway engineer).

1995. 150th Birth Anniv (1994) of Karl Benz (motor manufacturer). Multicoloured.
2576 5l. Type **570** 10 10
2577 10l. Mercedes-Benz C-class saloon, 1995 Daimler motor carriage, 1886 . . . 20 15
2578 60l. First four-wheel Benz motor-car, 1886 . . . . . 1·00 75
2579 125l. Mercedes-Benz 540 K cabriolet, 1936 . . . . . 2·10 1·60

1995. Composers. Each brown and gold.
2580 3l. Type **571** 10 10
2581 6l.50 Edvard Grieg 10 10
2582 11l. Charles Gounod . . . 20 15
2583 20l. Pyotr Tchaikovsky . . 35 25

572 Intersections

1995. 50th Anniv (1994) of Liberation.
2584 **572** 50l. black and red . . . 75 55

573 Ali Pasha

1995. 250th Birth Anniv (1994) of Ali Pasha of Tepelene (Pasha of Janina, 1788–1820).
2585 **573** 60l. black, yellow & brn 95 70

574 Veskopoja, 1744 (left half) **577** Hands holding Olive Branch

576 Palace of Europe, Strasbourg

1995. 250th Anniv (1994) of Veskopoja Academy. Multicoloured.
2587 42l. Type **574** 60 45
2588 68l. Veskopoja, 1744 (right half) . . . . 1·00 75

Nos. 2587/8 were issued together, se-tenant, forming a composite design.

1995. Admission of Albania to Council of Europe. Multicoloured.
2590 25l. Type **576** 30 25
2591 85l. State arms and map of Europe . . . . 1·40 1·10

1995. Europa. Peace and Freedom. Multicoloured.
2592 50l. Type **577** 80 60
2593 100l. Dove flying over hands 1·60 1·25

578 Mice sitting around Table and Stork with Fox

1995. 300th Death Anniv of Jean de La Fontaine (writer). Multicoloured.
2595 2l. Type **578** 10 10
2596 3l. Stork with foxes around table 10 10
2597 25l. Frogs under tree . . . 45 35

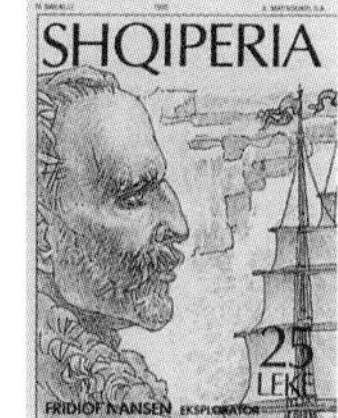

579 Bee on Flower **580** Fridtjof Nansen

1995. The Honey Bee. Multicoloured.
2599 5l. Type **579** 10 10
2600 10l. Bee and honeycomb . . 20 15
2601 25l. Bee on comb 45 35

1995. Polar Explorers. Multicoloured.
2602 25l. Type **580** 55 45
2603 25l. James Cook 55 45
2604 25l. Roald Amundsen . . . 55 45
2605 25l. Robert Scott 55 45
Nos. 2602/5 were issued together, se-tenant, forming a composite design.

581 Flags outside U.N. Building, New York

1995. 50th Anniv of U.N.O. Multicoloured.
2606 2l. Type **581** 10 10
2607 100l. Flags flying to right outside U.N. building, New York . . . . 1·60 1·25

582 Male Chorus **583** "Poet"

1995. National Folklore Festival, Berat. Mult.
2608 5l. Type **582** 10 10
2609 50l. Female participant . . . 85 65

1995. Jan Kukuzeli (11th-century poet, musician and teacher). Abstract representations of Kukuzeli. Multicoloured.
2610 18l. Type **583** 30 25
2611 20l. "Musician" 35 25

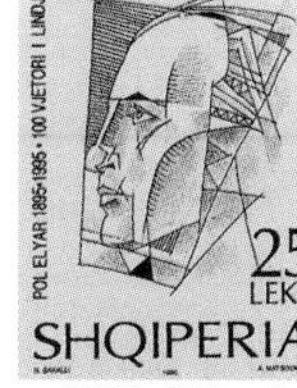

584 Church and Preacher, Berat Kruje **585** Paul Eluard

1995. 20th Anniv of World Tourism Organization. Multicoloured.
2613 18l. Type **584** 30 25
2614 20l. Street, Shkoder 35 25
2615 42l. Buildings, Gjirokaster 70 35

1995. Poets' Birth Centenaries. Multicoloured.
2616 25l. Type **585** 35 25
2617 50l. Sergei Yessenin 75 55

586 Louis, Film Reel and Projector

1995. Centenary of Motion Pictures. Lumiere Brothers (developers of cine camera). Mult.
2618 10l. Type **586** 25 20
2619 85l. Auguste, film reel and cinema audience . . . . 1·50 40

587 Presley

1995. 60th Birth Anniv of Elvis Presley (entertainer). Multicoloured.
2620 3l. Type **587** 10 10
2621 60l. Presley (different) . . . 1·00 75

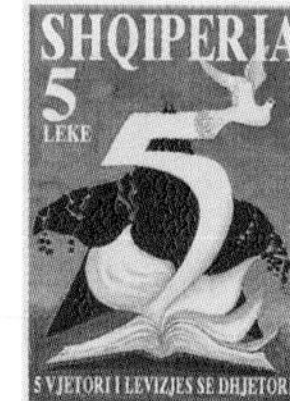

588 Banknotes of 1925 **589** "5", Crumbling Star, Open Book and Peace Dove

1995. 70th Anniv of Albanian National Bank. Mult.
2622 10l. Type **588** 20 15
2623 25l. Modern banknotes . . 45 35

1995. 5th Anniv of Democratic Movement. Mult.
2624 5l. Type **589** 10 10
2625 50l. Woman planting tree 85 65

590 Mother Teresa **591** Football, Union Flag, Map of Europe and Stadium

1996. Europa. Famous Women. Mother Teresa (founder of Missionaries of Charity).
2626 **590** 25l. multicoloured . . . 45 35
2627 100l. multicoloured . . . 1·75 1·25

1996. European Football Championship, England, Multicoloured.
2629 25l. Type **591** 65 35
2630 100l. Map of Europe, ball and player . . . . 1·75 1·25

592 Satellite and Radio Mast **593** Running

1996. Inaug of Cellular Telephone Network. Mult.
2631 10l. Type **592** 20 10
2632 60l. User, truck, container ship and mobile telephone (vert) . . . . 1·75 75

1996. Olympic Games, Atlanta, U.S.A. Mult.
2633 5l. Type **593** 10 10
2634 25l. Throwing the hammer 45 35
2635 60l. Long jumping . . . . . 1·00 75

594 Linked Hands **596** "The Naked Maja"

595 Gottfried Wilhelm Leibniz (350th)

1996. 75th Anniv of Albanian Red Cross.
2637 **594** 50l.+10l. mult . . . . . 1·00 1·00

1996. Philosopher-mathematicians' Birth Annivs. Multicoloured.
2638 10l. Type **595** 20 10
2639 85l. Rene Descartes (400th) 1·50 1·10

1996. 250th Birth Anniv of Francisco de Goya (artist). Multicoloured.
2640 10l. Type **596** 20 10
2641 60l. "Dona Isabel Cobos de Porcel" . . . . 1·00 75

597 Book Binding **598** Princess

1996. Christian Art Exhibition. Multicoloured.
2643 5l. Type **597** 10 10
2644 25l. Book clasp showing crucifixion 45 35
2645 85l. Book binding (different) 1·50 1·10

1996. 50th Anniv of U.N.I.C.E.F. Children's Paintings. Multicoloured.
2646 5l. Type **598** 10 10
2647 10l. Woman 20 15
2648 25l. Sea life 45 35
2649 50l. Harbour 85 65

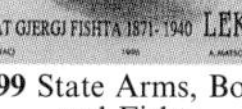

599 State Arms, Book and Fishta **600** Omar Khayyam and Writing Materials

1996. 125th Birth Anniv of Gjergj Fishta (writer and politician). Multicoloured.
2650 10l. Type **599** 20 15
2651 60l. Battle scene and Fishta 1·00 75

1997. 950th Birth Anniv of Omar Khayyam (astronomer and poet). Multicoloured.
2652 20l. Type **600** 35 25
2653 50l. Omar Khayyam and symbols of astronomy . . 85 65
Nos. 2652/3 are inscribed "850" in error.

601 Gutenberg

602 Pelicans

1997. 600th Birth Anniv of Johannes Gutenberg (printer). Multicoloured.
2654 20l. Type **601** 40 25
2655 60l. Printing press . . . . . 1·00 75
Nos. 2654/5 were issued together, se-tenant, forming a composite design.

1997. The Dalmatian Pelican. Multicoloured.
2656 10l. Type **602** 20 15
2657 80l. Pelicans on shore and in flight . . . . 1·40 45
Nos. 2656/7 were issued together, se-tenant, forming a composite design.

603 Dragon

604 Konica

1997. Europa. Tales and Legends. "The Blue Pool". Multicoloured.
2658 30l. Type 603 . . . . [illegible] 40
2659 100l. Dragon drinking from pool . . . . 1·75 1·25

1997. 55th Death Anniv of Faik Konica (writer and politician).
2660 **604** 10l. brown and black . . 20 15
2661 25l. blue and black . . . 45 35

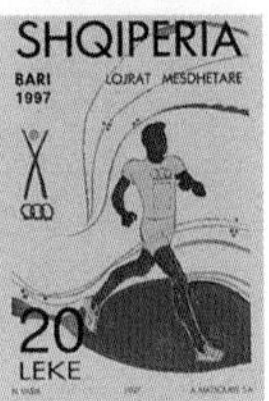

605 Male Athlete

606 Skanderbeg

1997. Mediterranean Games, Bari. Multicoloured.
2663 20l. Type **605** 35 25
2664 30l. Female athlete and rowers 50 40

1997.
2666 **606** 5l. red and brown . . . 10 10
2667 10l. green and olive . . . 10 10
2668 20l. green and deep green 20 15
2669 25l. mauve and purple 25 20
2670 30l. violet and lilac . . . 30 25
2671 50l. grey and black . . . 50 40
2672 60l. lt brown & brown 60 45
2673 80l. lt brown & brown 80 60
2674 100l. red and lake . . . 1·00 75
2675 110l. blue and deep blue 1·10 85

1997. Mother Teresa (founder of Missionaries of Charity) Commemoration. No. 2627 optd **HOMAZH 1910–1997.**
2676 **590** 100l. multicoloured . . . 1·00 75

608 Codex Aureus (11th century)

609 Twin-headed Eagle (postal emblem)

1997. Codices (1st series). Multicoloured.
2677 10l. Type **608** 10 10
2678 25l. Codex Purpureus Beratinus (7th century) showing mountain and scribe 25 20
2679 60l. Codex Purpureus Beratinus showing church and scribe 60 45
See also Nos. 2712/14.

1997. 85th Anniv of Albanian Postal Service.
2680 **609** 10l. multicoloured . . . 10 10
2681 30l. multicoloured . . . 30 25
The 30l. differs from Type **609** in minor parts of the design.

610 Nikete of Ramesiana

611 Man sitting at Table

1998. Nikete Dardani, Bishop of Ramesiana (philosopher and composer).
2682 **610** 30l. multicoloured . . . 25 20
2683 100l. multicoloured . . . 85 65
There are minor differences of design between the two values.

1998. Legend of Pogradeci Lake. Multicoloured.
2684 30l. Type **611** 25 20
2685 50l. The Three Graces . . . 40 30
2686 60l. Women drawing water 50 40
2687 80l. Man of ice 70 55

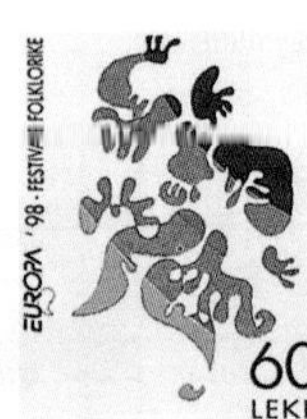

612 Stylized Dancers

1998. Europa. National Festivals. Multicoloured.
2688 60l. Type **612** 50 40
2689 100l. Female dancer 85 65

613 Abdyl Frasheri (founder)

614 Player with Ball

1998. 120th Anniv of League of Prizren. Mult.
2691 30l. Type **613** 25 15
2692 50l. Sulejman Vokshi and partisan 40 30
2693 60l. Iljaz Pashe Dibra and crossed rifles 50 35
2694 80l. Ymer Prizreni and partisans 70 50

1998. World Cup Football Championship, France. Multicoloured.
2695 60l. Type **614** 50 35
2696 100l. Player with ball (different) 85 65

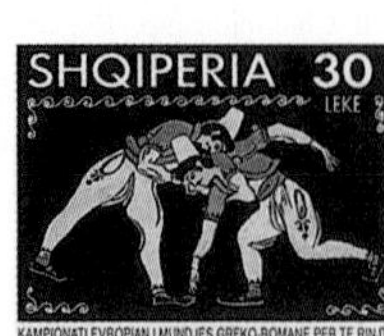

615 Wrestlers in National Costume

616 Cacej

1998. European Junior Wrestling Championship. Multicoloured.
2698 30l. Type **615** 25 15
2699 60l. Ancient Greek wrestlers 25 15

1998. 90th Birth Anniv of Eqerem Cabej (linguist).
2700 **616** 60l. black and yellow . . 25 15
2701 80l. yellow, black & red 70 50

617 Diana, Princess of Wales

1998. Diana, Princess of Wales Commemoration. Multicoloured.
2702 60l. Type **617** 55 30
2703 100l. With Mother Teresa 90 45

618 Mother Teresa holding Child

1998. Mother Teresa (founder of Missionaries of Charity) Commemoration. Multicoloured.
2704 60l. Type **618** 55 30
2705 100l. Mother Teresa (vert) 90 45

619 Detail of Painting

1998. 150th Birth Anniv of Paul Gauguin (artist). Multicoloured.
2706 60l. Type **619** 55 30
2707 80l. "Women of Tahiti" . . 70 35

620 Epitaph

1998. 625th Anniv of Epitaph of Gllavenica (embroidery of dead Christ). Multicoloured.
2709 30l. Type **620** 25 10
2710 80l. Close-up of upper body 70 35

621 Page of Codex

623 Koliqi

1998. Codices (2nd series). 11th-century Manuscripts. Multicoloured.
2712 30l. Type **621** 25 10
2713 50l. Front cover of manuscript 45 20
2714 80l. Page showing mosque 70 35

1998. 1st Death Anniv of Cardinal Mikel Koliqi (first Albanian Cardinal). Multicoloured.
2716 30l. Type **623** 25 15
2717 100l. Koliqi (different) . . . 90 45

624 George Washington (first President, 1789–97)

1999. American Anniversaries. Multicoloured.
2718 150l. Type **624** (death bicentenary) . . . . . . 1·40 70
2719 150l. Abraham Lincoln (President 1861–65, 190th birth anniv) . . . . . . 1·40 70
2720 150l. Martin Luther King Jr. (civil rights campaigner, 70th birth anniv) . . . . 1·40 70

625 Monk Seals

1999. The Monk Seal. Multicoloured.
2721 110l. Type **625** . . . . . . 1·00 50
2722 110l. Two seals (both facing left) . . . . 1·00 50
2723 150l. As No. 2722 but both facing right . . . . 1·40 70
2724 150l. As Type **625** but seal at back facing left and seal at front facing right 1·40 70
Nos. 2721/4 were issued together, se-tenant, forming a composite design.

1999. 50th Anniv of Council of Europe. No. 2590 surch **150 LEKE** and emblem.
2725 **576** 150l. on 25l. mult . . . 1·40 70

1999. "iBRA '99" International Stamp Exhibition, Nuremberg, Germany. No. 2496 surch **150 LEKE** in black (new value) and multicoloured (emblem).
2726 150l. on 90q. multicoloured 1·40 70

628 Dove, Airplane and NATO Emblem

629 Mickey Mouse

1999. 50th Anniv of North Atlantic Treaty Organization.
2727 **628** 10l. multicoloured . . . 10 10
2728 100l. multicoloured . . . 90 45

1999. Mickey Mouse (cartoon film character). Multicoloured.
2730 60l. Type **629** 55 30
2731 80l. Mickey writing letter . . 70 35
2732 110l. Mickey thinking . . . 1·00 50
2733 150l. Wearing black and red jumper . . . . 1·40 70

630 Thethi National Park, Shkoder

1999. Europa. Parks and Gardens. Multicoloured.
2734 90l. Type **630** 80 40
2735 310l. Lura National Park, Dibra . . . . 2·75 1·40

631 Coin

1999. Illyrian Coins. Multicoloured.
2737 10l. Type **631** 10 10
2738 20l. Coins from Labeateve, Bylisi and Scutari 20 10
2739 200l. Coins of King Monuni 1·75 90

1999. "Philexfrance 99" International Stamp Exhibition, Paris. No. 2512 surch with new value and Exhibition logo.
2741 **552** 150l. on 30q. mult . . . 1·40 70

633 Chaplin

634 Neil Armstrong on Moon

1999. 110th Birth Anniv of Charlie Chaplin (film actor and director). Multicoloured.
2742 30l. Type **633** 25 10
2743 50l. Raising hat 45 25
2744 250l. Dancing . . . . 2·25 1·10

1999. 30th Anniv of First Manned Moon Landing. Multicoloured.
2745 30l. Type **634** 25 10
2746 150l. Lunar module . . . . 1·40 70
2747 300l. Astronaut and American flag . . . . . 2·75 1·40
Nos. 2745/7 were issued together, se-tenant, forming a composite design.

635 Prisoner behind Bars
636 Emblem

1999. The Nazi Holocaust.
2749 **635** 30l. multicoloured . . . 25 10
2750 150l. black and yellow 1·40 70

1999. 125th Anniv of Universal Postal Union.
2751 **636** 20l. multicoloured . . . 20 10
2752 60l. multicoloured . . . 55 30

1999. "China 1999" International Stamp Exhibition, Peking. No. 2497 surch **150 LEKE**.
2753 150l. on 11.20 multicoloured 1·40 70

638 Javelin
639 Madonna and Child

1999. 70th Anniv of National Athletic Championships. Multicoloured.
2754 10l. Type **638** 10 10
2755 20l. Discus 20 10
2756 200l. Running . . . . 1·90 85

1999. Icons by Onufri Shek (artist). Multicoloured.
2757 30l. Type **639** 25 10
2758 300l. The Resurrection . . . 2·75 1·40

640 Bilal Golemi (veterinary surgeon)

1999. Birth Anniversaries. Multicoloured.
2759 10l. Type **640** (centenary) . . 10 10
2760 20l. Azem Galica (revolutionary) (centenary) 20 10
2761 50l. Viktor Eftimiu (writer) (centenary) 45 20
2762 300l. Lasgush Poradeci (poet) (centenary (2000)) 2·75 1·40

641 Carnival Mask

1999. Carnivals. Multicoloured.
2763 30l. Type **641** 25 10
2764 300l. Turkey mask . . . . 2·75 1·40

642 Bell and Flowers
643 Woman's Costume, Librazhdi

2000. New Millennium. The Peace Bell. Mult.
2765 40l. Type **642** 35 15
2766 90l. Bell and flowers (different) 80 40

2000. Regional Costumes (1st series). Mult.
2767 5l. Type **643** 10 10
2768 10l. Woman's costume, Malesia E Madhe 10 10
2769 15l. Man's costume, Malesia E Madhe 15 10
2770 20l. Man's costume, Tropoje 20 10
2771 30l. Man's costume, Dumrea 30 15
2772 35l. Man's costume, Tirana 30 15
2773 40l. Woman's costume, Tirana 35 15
2774 45l. Woman's costume, Arbereshe 40 20
2775 50l. Man's costume, Gjirokastra 45 25
2776 55l. Woman's costume, Lunxheri 50 25
2777 70l. Woman's costume, Cameria 65 30
2778 90l. Man's costume, Laberia 80 40
See also Nos. 2832/43 and 2892/2903.

644 Majer
645 Donald Duck

2000. 150th Birth Anniv of Gustav Majer (etymologist).
2779 **644** 50l. green 45 25
2780 130l. red . . . . 1·25 65

2000. Donald and Daisy Duck (cartoon film characters). Multicoloured.
2781 10l. Type **645** 10 10
2782 30l. Donald Duck 30 15
2783 90l. Daisy Duck 80 40
2784 250l. Donald Duck . . . . 2·25 1·10

646 Early Racing Car

2000. Motor Racing. Multicoloured.
2785 30l. Type **646** 30 15
2786 30l. Two-man racing car . . 30 15
2787 30l. Racing car with wire nose 30 15
2788 30l. Racing car with solid wheels 30 15
2789 30l. Car No. 1 . . . . . . 30 15
2790 30l. Car No. 2 . . . . . . 30 15
2791 30l. White Formula 1 racing car (facing left) 30 15
2792 30l. Blue Formula 1 racing car 30 15
2793 30l. Red Formula 1 racing car 30 15
2794 30l. White Formula 1 racing car (front view) 30 15

647 Ristoz of Mborja Church, Korca

2000. Birth Bimillenary of Jesus Christ. Mult.
2795 15l. Type **647** 15 10
2796 40l. St. Kolli Church, Voskopoja 35 15
2797 90l. Church of Flori and Lauri, Kosovo 80 40

648 "Building Europe"
650 Gustav Mahler (composer) (40th death anniv)

649 Wolf

2000. Europa.
2799 **648** 130l. multicoloured . . . 1·25 60

2000. Animals. Multicoloured.
2801 10l. Type **649** 10 10
2802 40l. Brown bear 35 15
2803 90l. Wild boar 80 40
2804 220l. Red fox . . . . 2·00 1·00

2000. "WIPA 2000" International Stamp Exhibition, Vienna.
2805 **650** 130l. multicoloured . . . 1·25 1·00

651 Footballer saving Ball

2000. European Football Championship, Belgium and The Netherlands. Multicoloured.
2806 10l. Type **651** 10 10
2807 120l. Footballer heading ball 1·10 55

652 Musicans

2000. Paintings by Picasso. Multicoloured.
2809 30l. Type **652** 30 15
2810 40l. Abstract face 35 15
2811 250l. Two women running along beach . . . . . . 2·25 1·10

653 Basketball
655 "Self-portrait" (Picasso)

654 *LZ-1* (first Zeppelin airship) over Lake Constance, Friedrichshafen (first flight)

2000. Olympic Games, Sydney. Multicoloured.
2813 10l. Type **653** 10 10
2814 40l. Football 40 20
2815 90l. Athletics 85 45
2816 250l. Cycling . . . . 2·40 1·25

2000. Centenary of First Zeppelin Flight. Airship Development. Multicoloured.
2817 15l. Type **654** 15 10
2818 30l. Santos-Dumont airship *Ballon No. 5* and Eiffel Tower C attempted round trip from St. Cloud via Eiffel Tower, 1901) . . . 30 15
2819 300l. Beardmore airship *R-34* over New York (first double crossing of Atlantic) . . . . 2·75 1·25

2000. "Espana 2000" World Stamp Exhibition, Madrid.
2821 **655** 130l. multicoloured . . . 1·25 65

656 Yellow Gentian (*Gentiana lutea*)
658 Mother holding Child

657 Naim Frasheri (poet) and Landscape

2000. Medicinal Plants. Multicoloured.
2822 50l. Type **656** 50 25
2823 70l. Cross-leaved gentian (*Gentiana cruciata*) . . . 65 35

2000. Personalities. Multicoloured.
2824 30l. Type **657** 20 15
2825 50l. Bajram Curri (revolutionary) and landscape 50 25
Nos. 2824/5 were issued together, se-tenant, forming a composite design.

2000. 50th Anniv of United Nations High Commission for Refugees. Multicoloured.
2826 50l. Type **658** 50 25
2827 90l. Mother breastfeeding child 85 40

659 Dede Ahmed Myftar Ahmataj
661 Southern Magnolia (*Magnolia gandiflora*)

2001. Religious Leaders. Multicoloured.
2828 90l. Type **65** 85 45
2829 90l. Dede Sali Njazi 85 45

2001. "For Kosovo". Nos. 2592/3 surch **PER KOSOVEN** and new value.
2830 80l.+10l. on 50l. multicoloured 85 45
2831 130l.+20l. on 100l. multicoloured . . . . . . 1·40 70

2001. Regional Costumes (2nd series). As T **643**. Multicoloured.
2832 20l. Man's costume, Tropoje 20 10
2833 20l. Woman's costume, Lume 20 10
2834 20l. Woman's costume, Mirdite 20 10
2835 20l. Man's costume, Lume 20 10
2836 20l. Woman's costume, Zadrime 20 10
2837 20l. Woman's costume, Shpati 20 10
2838 20l. Man's costume, Kruje 20 10
2839 20l. Woman's costume, Macukulli 20 10
2840 20l. Woman's costume, Dardhe 20 10
2841 20l. Man's costume, Lushnje 20 10
2842 20l. Woman's costume, Dropulli 20 10
2843 20l. Woman's costume, Shmili 20 10

2001. Scented Flowers. Multicoloured.
2844 10l. Type **661** 10 10
2845 20l. Virginia rose (*Rosa virginiana*) 20 10
2846 90l. *Dianthus barbatus* . . . 85 45
2847 140l. Lilac (*Syringa vulgaris*) 1·25 65

662 Goofy in Shorts

2001. Goofy (cartoon film character). Multicoloured.
2848 20l. Type **662** 20 10
2849 50l. Goofy in blue hat . . . 50 25
2850 90l. Goofy in red trousers 85 45
2851 140l. Goofy in purple waistcoat . . . . 1·25 65

663 Vincenzo Bellini

2001. Composers' Anniversaries. Multicoloured.
2852 90l. Type **663** (birth centenary) 85 45
2853 90l. Guiseppe Verdi (death centenary) 85 45

664 Cliffs and Stream

2001. Europa. Water Resources. Multicoloured.
2855 40l. Type **664** 40 20
2856 110l. Waterfall . . . . . . 1·10 55
2857 200l. Lake . . . . 1·90 95

665 Horse

2001. Domestic Animals. Multicoloured.
2859 10l. Type **665** 10 10
2860 15l. Donkey 15 10
2861 80l. Siamese cat 75 40
2862 90l. Dog 85 45

666 Swimming

2001. Mediterranean Games, Tunis. Multicoloured.
2864 10l. Type **666** 10 10
2865 90l. Athletics 85 45
2866 140l. Cycling . . . . 1·40 70

667 *Eole* (first powered take-off by Clement Ader, 1890)

2001. Aviation History. Multicoloured.
2868 40l. Type **667** 40 20
2869 40l. *Bleriot XI* (first powered crossing of English channel by Louis Bleriot, 1909) 40 20
2870 40l. *Spirit of St. Louis* (first solo non-stop crossing of North Atlantic from Paris to New York by Charles Lindbergh, 1927) 40 20
2871 40l. First flight to Tirana, 1925 . . . . 40 20
2872 40l. Antonov AH-10 (first flight, 1956) 40 20
2873 40l. Concorde (first flight, 1969) 40 20
2874 40l. Concorde (first commercial flight, 1970) 40 20
2875 40l. Space shuttle *Colombia* (first flight, 1981) 40 20

668 Tabakeve 669 Dimitri of Arber

2001. Old Bridges.
2876 **668** 10l. multicoloured . . . 10 10
2877 – 20l. multicoloured . . . 20 10
2878 – 40l. multicoloured . . . 40 20
2879 – 90l. black 85 45
DESIGNS: 20l. Kamares; 40l. Golikut; 90l. Mesit. 49 × 22 mm-21.50, Tabakeve.

2001. Arms (1st series).
2881 20l. Type **669** 20 10
2882 45l. Balsha pricipality . . . 45 25
2883 50l. Muzaka family 50 25
2884 90l. George Castriot (Skanderbeg) 85 45
See also Nos. 2921/4.

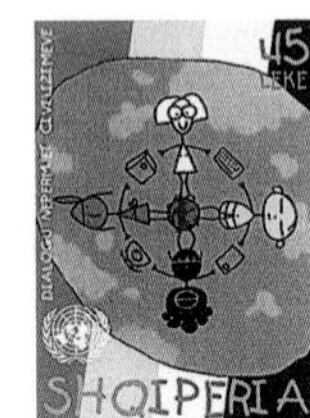

670 Children encircling Globe

2001. United Nations Year of Dialogue among Civilizations. Multicoloured, background colours given.
2885 **670** 45l. red, yellow and black 40 20
2886 50l. orange and green . . 45 20
2887 120l. black and red . . . 1·10 55
There are minor differences in Nos. 2886/7, with each colour forming a solid block above and below the central motif.

671 Award Ceremony (Medicins sans Frontieres, 1999 Peace Prize) and Medal

2001. Centenary of Nobel Prizes. Showing winners and Nobel medal. Multicoloured.
2888 10l. Type **671** 10 10
2889 20l. Wilhelm Konrad Rontgen (1901 Physics prize) 20 10
2890 90l. Ferid Murad (1998 Medicine Prize) 45 25
2891 200l. Mother Teresa (1979 Peace Prize) . . . . . . 2·00 1·00

2002. Regional Costumes (3rd series). As T **643**. Multicoloured.
2892 30l. Woman's costume, Gjakova 30 15
2893 30l. Woman's costume, Prizreni 30 15
2894 30l. Man's costume, Shkodra 30 15
2895 30l. Woman's costume, Shkodra 30 15
2896 30l. Man's costume, Berati 30 15
2897 30l. Woman's costume, Berati 30 15
2898 30l. Woman's costume, Elbasani 30 15
2899 30l. Man's costume, Elbasani 30 15
2900 30l. Woman's costume, Vlora 30 15
2901 30l. Man's costume, Vlora 30 15
2902 30l. Woman's costume, Gjirokastra 30 15
2903 30l. Woman's costume, Delvina 30 15

672 Bambi and Thumper 673 Fireplace

2002. Bambi (cartoon film character). Multicoloured.
2904 20l. Type **672** 20 40
2905 50l. Bambi alone amongst flowers 50 25
2906 90l. Bambi and Thumper looking right 90 45
2907 140l. Bambi with open mouth . . . . 1·40 70

2002. Traditional Fireplaces. T **673** and similar vert designs showing fireplaces. Multicoloured.
MS 30l. 2908 Type **673**: 40l. With columns at each side; 50l. With foliage arch; 90l. With three medallions in arch 4·25 4·25

674 Acrobatic Jugglers

2002. Europa. Circus. Multicoloured.
2909 40l. Type **674** 40 20
2910 90l. Female acrobat 90 45
2911 220l. Tightrope performers 2·25 1·10
MS2912 60 × 80 mm. 350l. Equestrienne performer (38 × 38 mm) 3·50 3·50

675 Heading the Ball

2002. Football World Championships, Japan and South Korea. Multicoloured.
2913 20l. Type **675** 20 10
2914 30l. Catching the ball . . . 30 15
2915 90l. Kicking the ball from horizontal position . . . 90 45
2916 120l. Player and ball . . . . 1·25 65
MS2917 80 × 60 mm. 360l. Emblem (50 × 30) 3·50 3·50

2002. Arms (2nd series). As T **669**. Multicoloured.
2918 20l. Gropa family 20 10
2919 45l. Skurra family 45 25
2920 50l. Bua family 50 25
2921 90l. Topia family 90 45

676 *Opuntia catingiola*

2002. Cacti. T **676** and similar triangular designs. Multicoloured.
MS 50l. 2922 Type **676**; 50l. *Neoporteria pseudoreicheana*; 50l. *Lobivia shaferi*; 50l. *Hylocereus undatus*; 50l. *Borzicactus madisoniorum* 2·50 2·50

EXPRESS LETTER STAMPS

ITALIAN OCCUPATION

E 67 King Victor Emmanuel

1940.
E373 **E 67** 25q. violet . . . . . . 2·00 2·50
E374 50q. red . . . . 4·00 6·25
No. E374 is inscr "POSTAT EXPRES".

1943. Optd **14 Shtator 1943**.
E402 **E 67** 25q. violet . . . . . . 16·00 25·00

POSTAGE DUE STAMPS

1914. Optd **TAKSE** through large letter **T**.
D33 **4** 2q. brown and yellow . . . 6·00 2·00
D34 5q. green and yellow . . . 6·00 3·75
D35 10q. red and pink . . . . 8·00 2·25
D36 25q. blue . . . . 10·00 2·50
D37 50q. mauve and red . . . . 11·00 4·50

1914. Nos. 40/4 optd **TAKSE**.
D46 **4** 10pa. on 5q. green & yell 2·75 2·50
D47 20pa. on 10q. red and pink 2·75 2·50
D48 1g. on 25q. blue . . . . . 2·75 2·50
D49 2g. on 50q. mauve and red 2·75 2·50

1919. Fiscal stamps optd **TAXE**.
D89 **12** 4q. on 4h. pink . . . . . 6·75 6·75
D90 10q. on 10k. red on grn 6·75 6·75
D91 20q. on 2k. orge on lilac 6·75 6·75
D92 50q. on 5k. brown on yell 6·75 6·75

D 20 Fortress of Shkoder D 22 D 35

1920. Optd with posthorn.
D129 **D 20** 4q. olive 75 75
D130 10q. red . . . . . . 1·50 4·75
D131 20q. brown . . . . . 1·50 2·00
D132 50q. black . . . . . . 1·50 4·75

1922.
D141 **D 22** 4q. black on red . . . 85 1·75
D142 10q. black on red . . 85 1·75
D143 20q. black on red . . 85 1·75
D144 50q. black on red . . 85 1·75

1922. Optd **Republika Shiqiptare**.
D186 **D 22** 4q. black on red . . . 1·25 1·90
D187 10q. black on red . . 1·25 1·90
D188 20q. black on red . . 1·25 1·90
D189 50q. black on red . . 1·25 1·90

1925.
D204 **D 35** 10q. blue 45 75
D205 20q. green 50 75
D206 30q. brown . . . . . 75 2·00
D207 50q. dark brown . . . 1·25 2·75

D 53 Arms of Albania D 67

1930.
D288 **D 53** 10q. blue . . . . . . 5·00 6·50
D289 20q. red . . . . . . 1·50 2·00
D290 30q. violet . . . . . . 1·50 2·00
D291 50q. green . . . . . . 1·50 2·00

1936. Optd **Takse**.
D312 **50** 10q. red . . . . 8·50 11·50

1940.
D373 **D 67** 4q. red . . . . 20·00 25·00
D374 10q. violet . . . . . 20·00 25·00
D375 20q. brown . . . . . 20·00 25·00
D376 30q. blue . . . . . . 20·00 25·00
D377 50q. red . . . . . . 20·00 25·00

ALEXANDRETTA Pt. 6

The territory of Alexandretta. Autonomous under French control from 1923 to September 1938.

1938. 100 centiemes = 1 piastre.

1938. Stamps of Syria of 1930/1 optd **Sandjak d'Alexandrette** (Nos. 1, 4, 7 and 11) or **SANDJAK D'ALEXANDRETTE** (others), Nos. 7 and 11 surch also.
1 0p.10 purple . . . . 1·60 2·50
2 0p.20 red . . . . 1·50 2·75
3 0p.50 violet . . . . 1·60 2·75
4 0p.75 red . . . . 2·00 2·75
5 1p. brown . . . . 1·50 2·50
6 2p. violet . . . . 1·60 5·25
7 2p.50 on 4p. orange . . . . 2·00 2·50
8 3p. green . . . . 2·00 3·50
9 4p. orange . . . . 2·75 2·75
10 6p. black . . . . 3·00 3·25
11 12p.50 on 15p. red (No. 267) 4·50 5·75
12 25p. purple . . . . 8·00 14·00

1938. Air. Stamps of Syria of 1937 (Nos. 322 etc) optd **SANDJAK D'ALEXANDRETTE**.
13 ½p. violet . . . . 1·50 2·50
14 1p. black . . . . 1·50 2·50
15 2p. green . . . . 2·25 3·50
16 3p. blue . . . . 3·25 4·50
17 5p. mauve . . . . 6·25 10·50
18 10p. brown . . . . 7·00 11·00
19 15p. brown . . . . 7·50 13·00
20 25p. blue . . . . 10·00 16·00

1938. Death of Kemal Ataturk. Nos. 4, 5, 7, 9 and 11 optd **10-11-1938** in frame.
27 0p.75 red . . . . 24·00 48·00
28 1p. brown . . . . 16·00 40·00
29 2p.50 on 4p. orange . . . . 12·50 10·00
30 4p. orange . . . . 8·75 9·25
31 12p.50 on 15p. red . . . . . 45·00 50·00

POSTAGE DUE STAMPS

1938. Postage Due stamps of Syria of 1925 optd **SANDJAK D'ALEXANDRETTE**.
D21 D 20 0p.50 brown on yellow 2·25 3·25
D22 1p. purple on pink 1·50 3·50
D23 2p. black on blue 2·75 3·50
D24 3p. black on red 3·25 5·75
D25 5p. black on green 4·50 5·25
D26 8p. black on blue 7·50 5·25

ALEXANDRIA Pt. 6

Issues of the French P.O. in this Egyptian port. The French Post Offices in Egypt closed on 31 March 1931.

1899. 100 centimes = 1 franc.
1921. 10 milliemes = 1 piastre.

1899. Stamps of France optd **ALEXANDRIE**.
1 10 1c. black on blue 1·25 1·10
2 2c. brown on yellow 1·75 2·50
3 3c. grey 1·40 2·25
4 4c. brown on grey 1·10 2·50
5 5c. green 2·25 2·25
7 10c. black on lilac 5·50 7·25
9 15c. blue 6·25 4·25
10 20c. red on green 7·50 7·00
11 25c. black on red 5·50 55
12 30c. brown 5·75 7·00
13 40c. red on yellow 9·75 10·00
15 50c. red 19·00 12·50
16 1f. olive 12·00 14·00
17 2f. brown on blue 70·00 75·00
18 5f. mauve on lilac 95·00 85·00

1902. "Blanc", "Mouchon" and "Merson" key-types, inscr "ALEXANDRIE".
19 A 1c. grey 1·40 1·00
20 2c. purple 45 1·50
21 3c. red 55 1·00
22 4c. brown 35 1·00
24 5c. green 1·25 70
25 B 10c. red 2·75 75
26 15c. red 3·00 1·75
27 15c. orange 85 2·00
28 20c. brown 3·25 1·25
29 25c. blue 2·00 10
30 30c. mauve 4·25 3·25
31 C 40c. red and blue 2·75 2·25
32 50c. brown and lilac 5·50 55
33 1f. red and green 9·25 1·25
34 2f. lilac and buff 13·00 4·50
35 5f. blue and buff 17·00 10·50

1915. Red Cross. Surch **5c** and Red Cross.
36 B 10c. + 5c. red 20 2·75

1921. Surch thus, **15 Mill.**, in one line (without bars).
37 A 2m. on 5c. green 3·00 6·00
38 3m. on 3c. red 6·00 7·50
39 B 4m. on 10c. red 4·00 5·00
40 A 5m. on 1c. grey 7·25 7·50
41 5m. on 4c. brown 6·75 7·75
42 B 6m. on 15c. orange 2·50 4·50
43 8m. on 20c. brown 4·00 5·25
44 10m. on 25c. blue 1·75 3·75
45 12m. on 30c. mauve 11·50 12·50
46 A 15m. on 2c. purple 6·00 3·25
47 C 15m. on 40c. red and blue 12·00 12·50
48 15m. on 50c. brown & lilac 6·00 10·00
49 30m. on 1f. red and green £120 £100
50 60m. on 2f. lilac and buff £140 £140
51 150m. on 5f. blue and buff £225 £225

1921. Surch thus, **15 MILLIEMES**, in two lines (without bars).
53 A 1m. on 1c. grey 2·50 3·50
54 2m. on 5c. green 1·75 3·25
55 B 4m. on 10c. red 3·00 4·25
65 4m. on 10c. green 2·25 3·25
56 A 5m. on 3c. orange 4·25 6·50
57 B 6m. on 15c. orange 2·25 3·50
58 8m. on 20c. brown 1·75 3·00
59 10m. on 25c. blue 1·90 2·25
60 10m. on 30c. mauve 4·25 4·25
61 C 15m. on 50c. brown & lilac 3·75 4·50
66 B 15m. on 50c. blue 2·50 2·50
62 C 30m. on 1f. red and green 3·25 3·00
63 60m. on 2f. lilac and buff £1400 £1500
67 60m. on 2f. red and green 9·75 9·75
64 150m. on 5f. blue and buff 11·00 10·00

1925. Surch in milliemes with bars over old value.
68 A 1m. on 1c. grey 15 3·00
69 2m. on 5c. orange 20 2·75
70 2m. on 5c. green 2·50 3·50
71 B 4m. on 10c. green 20 3·25
72 A 5m. on 3c. red 80 2·50
73 B 6m. on 15c. orange 55 3·25
74 8m. on 20c. brown 20 3·25
75 10m. on 25c. blue 35 1·90
76 15m. on 50c. blue 1·75 1·75
77 C 30m. on 1f. red and green 1·10 55
78 60m. on 2f. red and green 2·75 4·75
79 150m. on 5f. blue and buff 3·75 5·50

1927. Altered key-types, inscr "Mm" below value.
80 A 3m. orange 2·00 3·25
81 B 15m. blue 2·25 1·40
82 20m. mauve 4·00 5·00
83 C 50m. red and green 9·25 7·50
84 100m. blue and yellow 11·50 10·50
85 250m. green and red 17·00 17·00

1927. Sinking Fund. As No. 81, colour changed, surch **+ 5 Mm Caisse d'Amortissement**.
86 B 15m.+5m. orange 3·25 5·00
87 15m.+5m. red 4·50 5·00
88 15m.+5m. brown 7·50 10·00
89 15m.+5m. lilac 12·00 16·00

POSTAGE DUE STAMPS

1922. Postage Due Stamps of France surch in milliemes.
D65 D 11 2m. on 5c. blue 1·10 4·25
D66 4m. on 10c. brown 2·25 4·25
D67 10m. on 30c. red 2·00 4·50
D68 15m. on 50c. purple 1·50 4·75
D69 30m. on 1f. pur on yell 1·25 6·25

D 10

1928.
D90 D 10 1m. grey 1·40 3·50
D91 2m. blue 2·75 3·50
D92 4m. pink 2·75 3·75
D93 5m. olive 2·75 3·25
D94 10m. red 3·00 3·75
D95 20m. purple 3·00 3·50
D96 30m. green 5·75 6·25
D97 40m. lilac 5·00 6·25

This set was issued for use in both Alexandria and Port Said.

ALGERIA Pt. 6; Pt. 12

French territory in N. Africa. Stamps of France were used in Algeria from July 1958 until 3 July 1962, when the country achieved independence following a referendum.

1924. 100 centimes = 1 franc.
1964. 100 centimes = 1 dinar.

1924. Stamps of France optd **ALGERIE**.
1 11 ½c. on 1c. grey 35 1·75
2 1c. grey 65 2·25
3 2c. red 10 2·50
4 3c. red 40 2·25
5 4c. brown 65 2·50
6 18 5c. orange 95 75
7 11 5c. green 10 10
8 30 10c. green 1·40 1·25
9 18 10c. green 10 75
10 15 15c. green 1·50 1·40
11 30 15c. green 85 2·00
12 18 15c. brown 1·50 1·10
13 20c. brown 1·50 65
14 25c. blue 10 10
15 30 30c. red 75 70
16 18 30c. blue 10 10
17 30c. red* 30 90
18 35c. violet 1·25 1·50
19 13 40c. red and blue 1·60 1·75
20 18 40c. olive 1·25 1·90
21 13 45c. green and blue 1·25 2·25
22 30 45c. red 40 85
23 50c. blue 1·50 85
24 15 60c. violet 1·10 65
25 65c. red 25 60
26 30 75c. blue 25 45
27 15 80c. red 70 70
28 85c. red 35 50
29 13 1f. red and green 1·75 55
30 18 1f.05 red 55 1·75
31 13 2f. red and green 2·00 3·25
32 3f. violet and blue 2·00 3·00
33 5f. blue and yellow 8·00 8·50

*No. 17 was only issued pre-cancelled and the price in the unused column is for stamps with full gum.

3 Street in the Casbah

4 Mosque of Sidi Abderahman

5 Grand Mosque

6 Bay of Algiers

1926.
34 3 1c. green 40 1·25
35 2c. purple 30 1·50
36 3c. orange 10 1·40
37 5c. green 25 10
38 10c. mauve 35 10
39 4 15c. brown 10 10
40 20c. green 10 10
41 20c. red 1·40 10
43 25c. green 95 75
45 25c. blue 45 30
46 30c. blue 80 1·40
47 30c. green 1·25 40
48 35c. violet 1·25 3·25
49 40c. green 10 10
50 5 45c. purple 15 10
51 50c. blue 2·25 15
53 50c. red 1·10 10
54 60c. green 20 90
55 65c. brown 1·50 1·60
56 3 65c. blue 1·10 10
57 5 75c. red 10 20
58 75c. blue 2·50 10
59 80c. orange 35 2·10
60 90c. red 1·75 2·50
61 6 1f. purple and green 80 10
62 5 1f.05 brown 35 1·90
63 1f.10 mauve 3·50 6·00
64 6 1f.25 ultramarine and blue 1·00 3·50
65 1f.50 ultramarine and blue 70 10
66 2f. brown and green 1·40 35
67 3f. red and mauve 3·25 1·50
68 5f. mauve and red 3·75 3·00
69 10f. red and brown 48·00 32·00
70 20f. green and violet 8·00 9·00

1926. Surch ½ **centime**.
71 3 ½c. on 1c. olive 10 1·75

1927. Wounded Soldiers of Moroccan War Charity Issue. Surch with star and crescent and premium.
72 3 5c.+5c. green 95 3·25
73 10c.+10c. mauve 90 3·25
74 4 15c.+15c. brown 90 3·25
75 20c.+20c. red 90 3·25
76 25c.+25c. green 80 3·25
77 30c.+30c. blue 1·10 3·25
78 35c.+35c. violet 55 3·25
79 40c.+40c. olive 80 3·25
80 5 50c.+50c. blue 85 3·75
81 80c.+80c. orange 85 3·75
82 6 1f.+1f. purple and green 1·25 3·75
83 2f.+2f. brown and green 22·00 40·00
84 5f.+5f. mauve and red 35·00 55·00

1927. Surch in figures.
85 4 10 on 35c. violet 10 90
86 25 on 30c. blue 65 10
87 30 on 25c. green 15 10
88 5 65 on 60c. green 60 1·25
89 90 on 80c. orange 20 20
90 1f.10 on 1f.05 brown 10 15
91 6 1f.50 on 1f.25 ultramarine and blue 1·25 90

1927. Surch **5c**.
92 11 5c. on 4c. brown (No. 5) 45 1·75

11 Railway Terminus, Oran

1930. Centenary of French Occupation.
93 11 5c.+5c. orange 9·00 14·50
94 – 10c.+10c. olive 8·00 14·00
95 – 15c.+15c. brown 6·25 13·50
96 – 25c.+25c. grey 6·00 13·50
97 – 30c.+30c. red 5·75 14·00
98 – 40c.+40c. green 5·25 14·00
99 – 50c.+50c. blue 5·25 14·00
100 – 75c.+75c. purple 5·00 13·50
101 – 1f.+1f. orange 5·50 13·50
102 – 1f.50+1f.50 blue 5·75 13·50
103 – 2f.+2f. red 5·25 13·50
104 – 3f.+3f. green 5·75 13·50
105 – 5f.+5f. red and green 10·50 35·00

DESIGNS—HORIZ: 10c. Constantine; 15c. Admiralty, Algiers; 25c. Algiers; 30c. Ruins of Timgad; 40c. Ruins of Djemila. VERT: 50c. Ruins of Djemila; 75c. Tlemcen; 1f. Ghardaia; 1f.50, Tolga; 2f. Tuaregs; 3f. Native quarter, Algiers; 5f. Mosque, Algiers.

12 Bay of Algiers, after painting by Verecque

1930. N. African International Philatelic Exn.
106 12 10f.+10f. brown 24·00 30·00

15 Admiralty and Penon Lighthouse, Algiers

1936.
107 A 1c. blue 35 1·10
108 F 2c. purple 10 90
109 B 3c. green 65 1·50
110 C 5c. mauve 10 10
111 15 10c. green 70 65
112 D 15c. red 15 10
113 G 20c. green 20 10
114 E 25c. purple 2·00 20
115 C 30c. green 35 10
116 D 40c. purple 50 20
117 G 45c. blue 1·25 3·25
118 15 50c. red 2·25 10
119 A 65c. brown 6·25 8·25
120 65c. red 2·25 35
121 70c. brown 80 85
122 F 75c. slate 50 15
124 B 90c. red 85 1·50
125 E 1f. brown 30 10
126 15 1f.25 violet 1·90 60
127 1f.25 red 40 1·40
128 F 1f.50 blue 2·25 85
129 1f.50 red 3·50 3·50
130 C 1f.75 orange 95 70
131 B 2f. purple 40 10
132 A 2f.25 green 16·00 24·00
133 E 2f.25 blue 1·50 1·60
134 C 2f.50 blue 1·75 2·25
135 G 3f. mauve 55 25
136 E 3f.50 blue 2·25 2·75
137 15 5f. slate 1·25 1·50
138 F 10f. orange 75 2·00
139 D 20f. blue 1·90 3·00

DESIGNS—HORIZ: A, In the Sahara; B, Arc de Triomphe, Lambese; C, Ghardaia, Mzab; D, Marabouts, Touggourt; E, El Kebir Mosque, Algiers. VERT: F, Colomb Bechar-Oued; G, Cemetery, Tlemcen.

17 Exhibition Pavilion

18 Constantine in 1837

1937. Paris International Exhibition.
140 17 40c. green 40 30
141 50c. red 40 50
142 1f.50 blue 60 1·00
143 1f.75 black 95 1·25

1937. Centenary of Capture of Constantine.
144 18 65c. red 80 20
145 1f. brown 2·75 65
146 1f.75 blue 35 95
147 2f.15 purple 25 40

19 Ruins of Roman Villa

1938. Centenary of Philippeville.
148 19 30c. green 1·75 2·00
149 65c. blue 75 55
150 75c. purple 1·60 3·25
151 3f. red 3·75 2·50
152 5f. brown 4·25 5·00

1938. 20th Anniv of Armistice Day. No. 132 surch **1918 - 11 Nov. - 1938 0.65 + 0.35**.
153 65c.+35c. on 2f.25 green 1·00 3·75

1938. Surch **0,25**.
154 15 25c. on 50c. red 25 10

22 Caillie, Lavigerie and Duveyrier

1939. Sahara Pioneers' Monument Fund.
155 22 30c.+20c. green 2·50 3·75
156 90c.+60c. red 1·10 3·25
157 2f.25+75c. blue 8·50 2·00
158 5f.+5f. black 14·50 45·00

23 "Extavia" (freighter) in Algiers Harbour

1939. New York World's Fair.
159 23 20c. green 1·60 3·50
160 40c. purple 1·75 3·50
161 90c. brown 2·25 75
162 1f.25 red 6·00 6·50
163 2f.25 blue 2·25 2·40

1939. Surch with new values and bars or cross.
173 3 50c. on 65c. blue 30 10
173c B 90c.+60c. red (No. 124) 20 10
164 3 1f. on 90c. red 40 10

25 Algerian Soldiers

26 Algiers

1940. Soldiers' Dependants' Relief Fund. Surch **+** and premium.
166 **25** 1f.+1f. blue . . . . 2·25 3·00
167 1f.+2f. red . . . . 1·90 3·50
168 1f.+4f. green . . . . . . 2·00 3·75
169 1f.+9f. brown . . . . . . 2·25 4·25

1941.
170 **26** 30c. blue . . . . 75 1·25
171 70c. brown 15 10
172 1f. red 15 10

28 Marshal Petain

1941.
174 **28** 1f. blue . . . . 40 1·10

1941. National Relief Fund. As No. 174, but surch **+4 f** and colour changed.
175 1f.+4f. black . . . . 1·25 2·50

1942. National Relief Fund. Surch **SECOURS NATIONAL +4f.**
176 1f.+4f. blue (No. 174) . . . . 70 3·00

1942. Various altered types. (a) As T **26**, but without "RF".
177 **26** 30c. blue . . . . 20 2·75
(b) As T **5**, but without "REPUBLIQUE FRANCAISE".
178 **5** 40c. grey . . . . 25 3·00
179 50c. red . . . . 35 1·40
(c) As No. 129 but without "RF".
180 F 1f.50 red . . . . 1·10 65

32 Arms of Oran 34 Marshal Petain

1942. Coats-of-Arms.
190 A 10c. lilac . . . . 1·00 2·25
191 **32** 30c. green . . . . 1·00 3·00
181 B 40c. violet . . . . 45 2·75
192 40c. lilac . . . . 1·75 2·25
182 **32** 60c. red . . . . 1·40 1·60
194 B 70c. blue . . . . 1·25 2·25
195 A 80c. green . . . . 75 1·90
183 B 1f.20 green . . . . 1·10 2·00
184 A 1f.50 red 15 30
198 **32** 2f. blue 20 95
186 B 2f.40 red . . . . 1·25 1·00
187 A 3f. blue 20 45
188 B 4f. blue . . . . 1·00 1·10
201 **32** 4f.50 purple 80 10
189 5f. green . . . . 1·00 1·40
ARMS: A, Algiers; B, Constantine.

1943.
202 **34** 1f.50 red . . . . 15 2·50

35 "La Marseillaise" 36 Allegory of Victory

1943.
203 **35** 1f.50 red . . . . 80 2·25
204 **36** 1f.50 blue 20 60

1943. Surch **2f.**
205 **32** 2f. on 5f. orange 15 90

38 Summer Palace, Algiers 39 Mother and Children

1943.
206 **38** 15f. grey . . . . 1·10 1·90
207 20f. green . . . . 1·50 1·90
208 50f. red . . . . 90 1·50
209 100f. blue . . . . 3·00 2·75
210 200f. brown . . . . 3·50 2·75

1943. Prisoners-of-war Relief Fund.
211 **39** 50c.+4f.50 pink . . . . . 60 3·50
212 1f.50+8f.50 green . . . . 30 3·50
213 3f.+12f. blue . . . . . . 30 3·50
214 5f.+15f. brown . . . . . . 55 3·50

40 "Marianne" 41 Gallic Cock

1944.
215 **40** 10c. grey 15 75
216 30c. lilac 15 65
217 50c. red 10 15
218 80c. green . . . . 25 1·00
219 1f.20 lilac . . . . 40 1·75
220 1f.50 blue 10 10
221 2f.40 red 10 35
222 3f. violet 15 15
223 4f.50 black 25 10

1944.
224 **41** 40c. red . . . . 30 2·75
225 1f. green 15 20
226 2f. red 15 15
227 2f. brown 15 90
228 4f. blue . . . . 1·60 10
229 10f. black . . . . 1·10 2·25

1944. Surch **0f.30.**
230 **4** 0f.30 on 15c. brown 25 60
No. 230 was only issued pre-cancelled and the price in the unused column is for stamps with full gum.

1945. Types of France optd **ALGERIE.**
247 **239** 10c. black and blue . . . 10 2·75
231 **217** 40c. mauve 20 75
232 50c. blue 15 10
248 – 50c. brown, yellow and red (No. 973) 65 60
233 **218** 60c. blue 50 70
236 **136** 80c. green . . . . 1·00 1·25
237 1f. blue 80 10
234 **218** 1f. red 70 25
238 **136** 1f.20 violet . . . . . . 55 2·50
235 **218** 1f.50 lilac . . . . 70 1·50
239 **136** 2f. brown 20 10
242 **219** 2f. green 85 10
240 **136** 2f.40 red . . . . 70 1·75
241 3f. orange 55 95
243 **219** 3f. red 35 10
244 4f.50 blue . . . . 1·75 40
245 5f. green 10 25
246 10f. blue . . . . 1·75 1·25

1945. Airmen and Dependants Fund. As No. 742 of France (bombers) optd **RF ALGERIE.**
249 **169** 1f.50+3f.50 blue . . . . . 1·50 3·00

1945. Postal Employees War Victims' Fund. As No. 949 of France overprinted **ALGERIE.**
250 **223** 4f.+6f. brown . . . . . . 55 3·00

1945. Stamp Day. As No. 955 of France (Louis XI) optd **ALGERIE.**
251 **228** 2f.+3f. purple . . . . . . 1·25 2·50

1946. No. 184 surch **0f50 RF.**
252 50c. on 1f.50 red 15 30

1946. Type of France optd **ALGERIE** and surch **2F.**
253 **136** 2f. on 1f.50 brown . . . 15 10

46 Potez 56 over Algiers

1946. Air.
254 **46** 5f. red 35 50
255 10f. blue 20 10
256 15f. green 65 35
257a 20f. brown 70 10
258 25f. violet 70 20
259 40f. black . . . . 1·25 1·40

1946. Stamp Day. As No. 975 of France (De la Varane), optd **ALGERIE.**
260 **241** 3f.+2f. red . . . . 90 3·75

47 Children at Spring 49 Arms of Constantine

1946. Charity. Inscr as in T **47.**
261 **47** 3f.+17f. green . . . . . . 1·75 4·00
262 4f.+21f. red . . . . 1·25 3·75
263 8f.+27f. purple . . . . . . 3·00 9·50
264 10f.+35f. blue . . . . . . 1·75 4·00
DESIGNS—VERT: 4f. Boy gazing skywards; 8f. Laurel-crowned head. HORIZ: 10f. Soldier looking at Algerian coast.

1947. Air. Surch **-10%.**
265 **46** "-10%" on 5f. red 20 55

1947. Stamp Day. As No. 1008 of France (Louvois), optd **ALGERIE.**
266 **253** 4f.50+5f.50 blue . . . . . 35 3·25

1947. Various Arms.
267 **49** 10c. green and red . . . . 10 1·75
268 A 50c. black and orange . . 10 10
269 B 1f. blue and yellow 10 10
270 **49** 1f.30 black and blue . . . 75 3·00
271 A 1f.50 violet and yellow . . 10 10
272 B 2f. black and green 10 10
273 **49** 2f.50 black and red 90 70
274 A 3f. red and green 10 65
275 B 3f.50 green and purple . . 45 10
276 **49** 4f. brown and green . . . 10 10
277 A 4f.50 blue and red 10 10
278 5f. black and blue 10 10
279 B 6f. brown and red 20 10
280 8f. brown and blue 15 10
281 **49** 10f. pink and brown . . . 25 10
282 A 15f. black and red . . . . 1·75 10
ARMS: A, Algiers; B, Oran. See also Nos. 364/8 and 381/3.

1947. Air. 7th Anniv of Gen. de Gaulle's Call to Arms. Surch with Lorraine Cross and **18 Juin 1940 + 10 Fr.**
283 **46** 10f.+10f. blue . . . . . . 2·50 3·50

1947. Resistance Movement. Type of France surch **ALGERIE+10f.**
284 **261** 5f.+10f. grey . . . . . . 1·25 3·25

1948. Stamp Day. Type of France (Arago) optd **ALGERIE.**
285 **267** 6f.+4f. green . . . . . . 1·25 3·75

1948. Air. 8th Anniv of Gen. de Gaulle's Call to Arms. Surch with Lorraine Cross and **18 JUIN 1940 + 10 Fr.**
286 **46** 5f.+10f. red . . . . 2·50 3·50

1948. General Leclerc Memorial. Type of France surch **ALGERIE + 4f.**
287 **270** 6f.+4f. red . . . . 1·40 3·50

57 Battleship "Richelieu" 58 White Storks over Minaret

1949. Naval Welfare Fund.
288 **57** 10f.+15f. blue . . . . . . 5·25 12·50
289 – 18f.+22f. red . . . . . . 8·75 12·50
DESIGN: 18f. Aircraft-carrier "Arromanches".

1949. Air.
290 **58** 50f. green . . . . 4·00 1·10
291 – 100f. brown . . . . 2·25 40
292 **58** 200f. red . . . . 11·00 3·75
293 – 500f. blue . . . . 29·00 28·00
DESIGN—HORIZ: 100, 500f. Dewoitine D-338 trimotor airplane over valley dwellings.

1949. Stamp Day. As No. 1054 of France (Choiseul) optd **ALGERIE.**
294 **278** 15f.+5f. mauve . . . . . 45 4·50

60 French Colonials 61 Statue of Duke of Orleans

1949. 75th Anniv of U.P.U.
295 **60** 5f. green . . . . 1·60 3·75
296 15f. red . . . . 1·00 3·75
297 25f. blue . . . . 3·25 9·25

1949. Air. 25th Anniv of First Algerian Postage Stamp.
298 **61** 15f.+20f. brown . . . . . 5·75 10·00

62 Grapes 63 Foreign Legionary

1950.
299 **62** 20f. purple, green & dp pur 85 65
300 – 25f. brown, green & black 1·75 55
301 – 40f. orange, green & brown 2·75 2·50
DESIGNS: 25f. Dates; 40f. Oranges and lemons.

1950. Stamp Day. As No. 1091 of France (Postman), optd **ALGERIE.**
302 **292** 12f.+3f. brown . . . . . 1·60 4·50

1950. Foreign Legion Welfare Fund.
303 **63** 15f.+5f. green . . . . . . 85 4·50

64 R. P. de Foucauld and Gen. Laperrine

1950. 50th Anniv of French in the Sahara (25f.) and Unveiling of Monument to Abd-el-Kader (40f.).
304 **64** 25f.+5f. black and green 5·00 9·25
305 – 40f.+10f. dp brown & brn 4·75 9·25
DESIGN: 40f. Emir Abd-el-Kader and Marshal Bugeaud.

65 Col. C. d'Ornano

1951. Col. d'Ornano Monument Fund.
306 **65** 15f.+5f. purple, brn blk . . 1·25 3·75

1951. Stamp Day. As No. 1107 of France (Travelling Post Office sorting van), optd **ALGERIE.**
307 **300** 12f.+3f. brown . . . . . 3·00 4·25

66 Apollo of Cherchel 67 Algerian War Memorial

1952.
308 **66** 10f. sepia 20 25
309 – 12f. brown 35 10
310 – 15f. blue 20 10
311 – 18f. red 40 30
312 – 20f. green 45 15
313 **66** 30f. blue 50 30
STATUES: 12, 18f. Isis of Cherchel; 15, 20f. Boy and eagle.

1952. Stamp Day. As No. 1140 of France (Mail Coach), optd **ALGERIE.**
314 **319** 12f.+3f. blue . . . . . . 2·25 4·75

1952. African Army Commemoration.
315 **67** 12f. green . . . . 85 2·25

68 Medaille Militaire

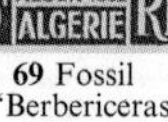

69 Fossil ("Berbericeras sekikensis")

1952. Military Medal Centenary.
316 **68** 15f.+5f. brown, yell & grn 2·50 4·75

1952. 19th Int Geological Convention, Algiers.
317 **69** 15f. red 2·50 5·00
318 – 30f. blue 1·50 3·25
DESIGN: 30f. Phonolite Dyke, Hoggar.

1952. 10th Anniv of Battle of Bir-Hakeim. As No. 1146 of France surch **ALGERIE+5 F**.
319 **325** 30f.+5f. blue 3·00 4·75

72 Bou-Nara
73 Members of Corps and Camel

1952. Red Cross Fund.
320 – 8f.+2f. red and blue 1·75 4·50
321 **72** 12f.+3f. red 2·75 6·75
DESIGN: 8f. El-Oued and map of Algeria.

1952. 50th Anniv of Sahara Corps.
322 **73** 12f. brown 2·00 3·00

1953. Stamp Day. As No. 1161 of France (Count D'Argenson), optd **ALGERIE**.
323 **334** 12f.+3f. violet 1·25 4·25

74 "Victory" of Cirta
75 E. Millon

1954. Army Welfare Fund.
324 **74** 15f.+5f. brown and sepia 70 3·25

1954. Military Health Service.
325 **75** 25f. sepia and green 95 30
326 – 40f. red and brown 90 25
327 – 50f. indigo and blue 1·25 25
DOCTORS—VERT: 40f. F. Maillot. HORIZ: 50f. A. Laveran.

1954. Stamp Day. As No. 1202 of France (Lavalette), optd **ALGERIE**.
328 **346** 12f.+3f. red 90 3·75

76 French and Algerian Soldiers
77 Foreign Legionary

1954. Old Soldiers' Welfare Fund.
329 **76** 15f.+5f. sepia 1·60 3·00

1954. Foreign Legion Welfare Fund.
330 **77** 15f.+5f. green 2·75 4·75

78
79 Darguinah Hydroelectric Station

1954. 3rd International Congress of Mediterranean Citrus Fruit Culture.
331 **78** 15f. blue and indigo 1·25 3·75

1954. 10th Anniv of Liberation. As No. 1204 of France ("D-Day") optd **ALGERIE**.
332 **348** 15f. red 75 2·25

1954. Inauguration of River Agrioun Hydroelectric Installations.
333 **79** 15f. purple 1·60 3·75

80 Courtyard of Bardo Museum

1954.
334 **80** 10f. brown & light brown 15 10
335 12f. orange and brown (I) 85 10
336 12f. orange and brown (II) 25 60
337 15f. blue and light blue 55 20
338 18f. carmine and red 30 45
339 20f. green and light green 25 1·10
340 25f. lilac and mauve 30 10
12f. "POSTES" and "ALGERIE" in orange (I) or in white (II).

1954. 150th Anniv of Presentation of First Legion of Honour. As No. 1223 of France, optd **ALGERIE**.
341 **356** 12f. green 50 3·00

81 Red Cross Nurses
82 St. Augustine

1954. Red Cross Fund. Cross in red.
342 **81** 12f.+3f. blue 3·75 6·25
343 – 15f.+5f. violet 5·50 7·75
DESIGN: 15f. J.H. Dunant and Djemila ruins.

1954. 1600th Birth Anniv of St. Augustine.
344 **82** 15f. brown 1·50 3·00

83 Earthquake Victims and Ruins
84 Statue of Aesculapius and El Kettar Hospital

1954. Orleansville Earthquake Relief Fund. Inscr as in T **83**.
345 **83** 12f.+4f. brown 1·90 4·75
346 15f.+5f. blue 2·00 4·75
347 – 18f.+6f. mauve 2·25 4·75
348 – 20f.+7f. violet 2·50 4·75
349 – 25f.+8f. lake 2·75 5·25
350 – 30f.+10f. turquoise 2·50 5·75
DESIGNS—HORIZ: 18, 20f. Red Cross workers. 25, 30f. Stretcher-bearers.

1955. Stamp Day. As No. 1245 of France (Balloon Post), optd **ALGERIE**.
351 **364** 12f.+3f. blue 1·10 4·00

1955. 30th French Medical Congress.
352 **84** 15f. red 45 1·00

85 Ruins of Tipasa
86 Widows and Children

1955. Bimillenary of Tipasa.
353 **85** 50f. brown 50 20

1955. 50th Anniv of Rotary International. As No. 1235 of France optd **ALGERIE**.
354 **361** 30f. blue 90 2·00

1955. As Nos. 1238 and 1238b of France ("France") inscr "ALGERIE".
355 **362** 15f. red 15 10
356 20f. blue 90 1·50

1955. War Victims' Welfare Fund.
357 **86** 15f.+5f. indigo and blue 1·90 2·75

87 Grand Kabylie
88

1955.
358 **87** 100f. indigo and blue 2·25 30

1956. Anti-cancer Fund.
359 **88** 15f.+5f. brown 1·90 3·25

1956. Stamp Day. As No. 1279 of France ("Francis of Taxis"), optd **ALGERIE**.
360 **383** 12f.+3f. red 1·10 3·50

89 Foreign Legion Retirement Home, Sidi Bel Abbes

1956. Foreign Legion Welfare Fund.
361 **89** 15f.+5f. green 1·90 4·25

90 Marshal Franchet d'Esperey (after J. Ebstein)

1956. Birth Cent of Marshal Franchet d'Esperey.
362 **90** 15f. indigo and blue 2·50 3·50

91 Marshal Leclerc and Memorial

1956. Marshal Leclerc Commemoration
363 **91** 15f. brown and sepia 40 3·25

1956. Various arms as T **49**.
364 1f. green and red 25 70
365 3f. blue and green 50 2·10
366 5f. blue and yellow 20 60
367 6f. green and red 50 2·50
368 12f. blue and red 90 3·25
DESIGNS: 1f. Bone; 3f. Mostaganem; 5f. Tlemcen; 6f. Algiers; 12f. Orleansville.

92 Oran

1956.
369 **92** 30f. purple 1·40 10
370 35f. red 2·00 3·50

1957. Stamp Day. As No. 1322 of France ("Felucca") optd **ALGERIE**.
371 **403** 12f.+3f. purple 2·50 3·75

93 Electric Train Crossing Viaduct

1957. Electrification of Bone-Tebessa Railway Line.
372 **93** 40f. turquoise and green 1·75 20

94 Fennec Fox

1957. Red Cross Fund. Cross in red.
373 **94** 12f.+3f. brown 4·50 12·50
374 – 15f.+5f. sepia (White storks) 6·00 12·00

1957. 17th Anniv of Gen. de Gaulle's Call to Arms. Surch **18 JUIN 1940 + 5F**.
375 **91** 15f.+5f. red and carmine 1·10 4·00

96 Beni Bahdel Barrage, Tlemcen
97 "Horseman Crossing Ford" (after Delacroix)

1957. Air.
376 **96** 200f. red 6·00 8·00

1957. Army Welfare Fund. Inscr "OEUVRES SOCIALES DE L'ARMEE".
377 **97** 15f.+5f. red 6·00 12·50
378 – 20f.+5f. green 5·25 12·50
379 – 35f.+10f. blue 5·50 12·50
DESIGNS—HORIZ: 20f. "Lakeside View" (after Fromentin). VERT: 35f. "Arab Dancer" (after Chasseriau).

1958. Stamp Day. As No. 1375 of France (Rural Postal Service), optd **ALGERIE**.
380 **421** 15f.+5f. brown 1·75 3·75

1958. Arms. As T **49** but inscr "REPUBLIQUE FRANCAISE" instead of "RF" at foot.
381 2f. red and blue 75 3·25
382 6f. green and red 32·00 42·00
383 10f. purple and green 85 3·00
ARMS: 2f. Tizi-Ouzou; 6f. Algiers; 10f. Setif.

99 "Strelitzia Reginae"
100

1958. Algerian Child Welfare Fund.
384 **99** 20f.+5f. orge, vio & grn 4·00 5·25

1958. Marshal de Lattre Foundation.
385 **100** 20f.+5f. red, grn & bl 3·75 4·25

INDEPENDENT STATE

1962. Stamps of France optd **EA** and with bars obliterating "REPUBLIQUE FRANCAISE".
386 **344** 10c. green 70 35
387 **463** 25c. grey and red 45 20
393 – 45c. violet, purple and sepia (No. 1463) 5·00 4·00
394 – 50c. pur & grn (No. 1464) 5·00 4·00
395 – 1f. brown, blue and myrtle (No. 1549) 2·25 1·10

103a Maps of Africa and Algeria

1962. War Orphans' Fund.
395a **103a** 1f.+9f. green, black and red £325

1962. As pictorial types of France but inscr "REPUBLIQUE ALGERIENNE".
396 – 5c. turquoise, grn & brn 15 10
397 **438** 10c. blue and sepia 20 10
398 – 25c. red, slate & brown 45 10
399 – 95c. blue, buff and sepia 2·75 80
400 – 1f. sepia and green 1·90 1·40
DESIGNS—VERT: 5c. Kerrata Gorges; 25c. Tlemcen Mosque; 95c. Oil derrick and pipeline at Hassi-Massaoud, Sahara. HORIZ: 1f. Medea.

104 Flag, Rifle and Olive Branch

1963. "Return of Peace". Flag in green and red. Inscription and background colours given.
401 **104** 5c. bistre 15 10
402 10c. blue 20 10
403 25c. red . . . . 1·90 10
404 95c. violet . . . . 1·40 65
405 – 1f. green . . . . 1·25 30
406 – 2f. brown . . . . 3·00 65
407 – 5f. purple . . . . 5·50 2·50
408 – 10f. black . . . . 20·00 12·00
DESIGN: 1f. to 10f. As Type **104** but with dove and broken chain added.

105 Campaign Emblem and Globe

1963. Freedom from Hunger.
409 **105** 25c. yellow, green and red 40 20

106 Clasped Hands **107** Map and Emblems

1963. National Solidarity Fund.
410 **106** 50c.+20c. red, grn & blk 1·10 55

1963. 1st Anniv of Independence.
411 **107** 25c. multicoloured 50 20

108 "Arab Physicians" (13th-century MS.) **109** Branch of Orange Tree

1963. 2nd Arab Physicians Union Congress.
412 **108** 25c. brown, green & bistre 1·60 45

1963.
413 **109** 8c. orange and bronze* 10 10
414 20c. orange and green* 15 10
415 40c. orange & turq* . . . 45 20
416 55c. orange and green* 80 45
*These stamps were only issued pre-cancelled, the unused prices being for stamps with full gum.

110 "Constitution" **111** "Freedom Fighters"

1963. Promulgation of Constitution.
417 **110** 25c. red, green and sepia 55 25

1963. 9th Anniv of Revolution.
418 **111** 25c. red, green and brown 55 20

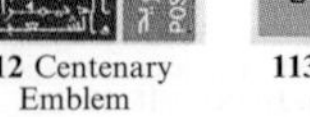

112 Centenary Emblem **113** Globe and Scales of Justice

1963. Red Cross Centenary.
419 **112** 25c. blue, red and yellow 80 55

1963. 15th Anniv of Declaration of Human Rights.
420 **113** 25c. black and blue . . . 60 20

114 Labourers **115** Map of Africa and Flags

1964. Labour Day.
421 **114** 50c. multicoloured . . . . 1·10 35

1964. 1st Anniv of Africa Day, and African Unity Charter.
422 **115** 45c. red, orange and blue 80 30

116 Tractors **117** Rameses II in War Chariot, Abu Simbel

1964.
423 **116** 5c. purple 10 10
424 – 10c. brown 10 10
425 – 12c. green 45 15
426 – 15c. blue 35 15
427 – 20c. yellow 35 10
428 **116** 25c. red 45 10
429 – 30c. violet 40 10
430 – 45c. lake 55 20
431 – 50c. blue 55 10
432 – 65c. orange 65 15
433 **116** 85c. green . . . . 1·10 20
434 – 95c. red . . . . 1·40 20
DESIGNS: 10, 30, 65c. Apprentices; 12, 15, 45c. Research scientist; 20, 50, 95c. Draughtsman and bricklayer.

1964. Nubian Monuments Preservation.
435 **117** 20c. purple, red and blue 80 35
436 – 30c. ochre, turq & red . . 90 45
DESIGN: 30c. Heads of Rameses II.

118 Hertzian-wave Radio Transmitting Pylon **119** Fair Emblems

1964. Inauguration of Algiers–Annaba Radio-Telephone Service.
437 **118** 85c. black, blue & brown 1·60 55

1964. Algiers Fair.
438 **119** 30c. blue, yellow and red 40 15

120 Gas Plant **121** Planting Trees

1964. Inaug of Natural Gas Plant at Arzew.
439 **120** 25c. blue, yellow & violet 65 45

1964. Reafforestation Campaign.
440 **121** 25c. green, red and yellow 40 20

122 Children **123** Mehariste Saddle

1964. Children's Charter.
441 **122** 15c. blue, green and red 40 20

1966. Saharan Handicrafts.
442 **123** 20c. multicoloured 45 20

124 Books Aflame **125** I.C.Y. Emblem

1965. Reconstitution of Algiers University Library.
443 **124** 20c.+5c. red, blk & grn 45 30

1965. International Co-operation Year.
444 **125** 30c. black, green and red 80 35
445 60c. black, green and blue 1·10 40

126 I.T.U. Emblem and Symbols

1965. Centenary of I.T.U.
446 **126** 60c. violet, ochre & green 80 40
447 95c. brown, ochre & lake 1·10 45

127 Musicians playing Rebbah and Lute

1965. Mohamed Racim's Miniatures (1st series). Multicoloured.
448 30c. Type **127** . . . . 1·40 55
449 60c. Musicians playing derbouka and tarr . . . . 1·90 85
450 5d. Algerian princess and sand gazelle . . . . 11·00 6·75
See also Nos. 471/3.

128 Cattle

1966. Rock-paintings of Tassili-N-Ajjer (1st series).
451 **128** 1d. brown, ochre & purple . . . . 4·00 2·25
452 – 1d. multicoloured . . . . 4·00 2·25
453 – 2d. dp brown, buff & brn 8·25 4·00
454 – 3d. multicoloured . . . . 9·00 5·00
DESIGNS—VERT: No. 452, Peuhl shepherd; 454, Peuhl girls. HORIZ: No. 453, Ostriches.
See also Nos. 474/7.

129 Pottery **130** Meteorological Instruments

1966. Grand Kahylie Handicrafts.
455 **129** 40c. brown, sepia and blue 40 20
456 – 50c. orange, green & bl 55 30
457 – 70c. black, red and blue 1·10 45
DESIGNS—HORIZ: 50c. Weaving. VERT: 70c. Jewellery.

1966. World Meteorological Day.
458 **130** 1d. purple, green and blue 1·10 40

131 Open Book, Cogwheel and Ear of Corn **132** W.H.O. Building

1966. Literacy Campaign.
459 **131** 30c. black and ochre . . . 35 20
460 – 60c. red, black and grey 55 30
DESIGN: 60c. Open primer, cogwheel and ear of corn.

1966. Inaug of W.H.O. Headquarters, Geneva.
461 **132** 30c. turq, grn & brn . . . 40 30
462 60c. slate, blue and brown 70 35

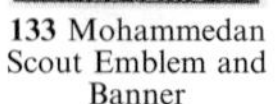

133 Mohammedan Scout Emblem and Banner **134** Soldiers and Battle Casualty

1966. 30th Anniv of Algerian Mohammedan Scouts, and 7th Arab Scout Jamboree, Jedaid (Tripoli). Multicoloured.
463 30c. Type **133** 45 30
464 1d. Jamboree emblem . . . . 1·40 55

1966. Freedom Fighters' Day.
465 **134** 30c.+10c. mult 80 55
466 95c.+10c. mult . . . . . 1·40 1·10

135 Massacre Victims **136** Emir Abd-el-Kader

1966. Deir Yassin Massacre (1948).
467 **135** 30c. black and red 45 20

1966. Return of Emir Abd-el-Kader's Remains.
468 **136** 30c. multicoloured 20 10
469 95c. multicoloured 90 35
See also Nos. 498/502.

137 U.N.E.S.C.O. Emblems **138** Bardo Museum

1966. 20th Anniv of U.N.E.S.C.O.
470 **137** 1d. multicoloured 90 35

1966. Mohamed Racim's Miniatures (2nd series). As T **127**. Multicoloured.
471 1d. Horseman . . . . 3·25 1·10
472 1d.50 Algerian bride . . . . 5·00 1·60
473 2d. Barbarossa . . . . . . 7·75 2·75

1967. Rock-paintings of Tassili-N-Ajjer (2nd series). As T **128**.
474 1d. violet, buff and purple . . 3·25 1·60
475 2d. brown, buff and purple 5·50 3·25
476 2d. brown, purple and buff 5·00 2·75
477 3d. brown, buff and black . . 8·25 4·50
DESIGNS: No. 474, Cow; No. 475, Antelope; No. 476, Archers; No. 477, Warrior.

1967. "Musulman Art". Multicoloured.
478 35c. Type **138** 35 15
479 95c. La Kalaa minaret (vert) 80 40
480 1d.30 Sedrata ruins . . . . . 1·40 55

139 Ghardaia

1967. Air.
481 **139** 1d. brown, green & purple 1·10 45
482 – 2d. brown, green and blue 2·50 1·25
483 – 5d. brown, green and blue 6·75 2·75
DESIGNS: 2d. Sud Aviation SE210 Caravelle over El Oued (Souf); 5d. Tipasa.

140 View of Moretti

1967. International Tourist Year. Multicoloured.
484 40c. Type **140** 55 35
485 70c. Tuareg, Tassili (vert) . . 1·10 45

141 Boy and Girl, and Red Crescent **142** Ostrich

1967. Algerian Red Crescent Organization.
486 **141** 30c.+10c. brn, red & grn 65 40

1967. Saharan Fauna. Multicoloured.
487 5c. Shiny-tailed Lizard (horiz) 35 30
488 20c. Type **142** . . . . 2·25 75
489 40c. Sand gazelle 90 45
490 70c. Fennec foxes (horiz) . . 1·40 80

143 Dancers with Tambourines **144** "Athletics"

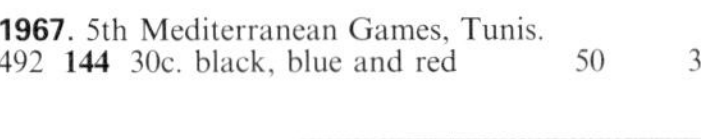

1967. National Youth Festival.
491 **143** 50c. black, yellow & blue 80 35

1967. 5th Mediterranean Games, Tunis.
492 **144** 30c. black, blue and red 50 30

145 Skiing **146** Scouts supporting Jamboree Emblem

1967. Winter Olympic Games, Grenoble (1968).
493 **145** 30c. blue, green & ultram 80 35
494 – 95c. green, violet & brown 1·40 65
DESIGN—HORIZ (36 × 26 mm): 95c. Olympic rings and competitors.

1967.
498 **136** 5c. purple 15 10
499 10c. green 10 10
500 25c. orange 20 10
501 30c. black 30 10
502 30c. violet 35 10
496 50c. red 50 15
497 70c. blue 50 20
The 10c. value exists in two versions, differing in the figures of value and inscription at bottom right.

1967. World Scout Jamboree, Idaho.
503 **146** 1d. multicoloured . . . . 1·60 65

1967. No. 428 surch.
504 **116** 30c. on 25c. red 50 15

148 Kouitra **149** Nememcha Carpet

1968. Musical Instruments. Multicoloured.
505 30c. Type **148** 45 20
506 40c. Lute 65 30
507 1d.30 Rebbah . . . . 2·25 90

1968. Algerian Carpets. Multicoloured.
509 30c. Type **149** 80 45
510 70c. Guergour . . . . 1·40 80
511 95c. Djebel-Amour . . . . . 2·25 1·00
512 1d.30 Kalaa . . . . 2·75 1·10

150 Human Rights Emblem and Globe

1968. Human Rights Year.
513 **150** 40c. red, yellow and blue 60 30

151 W.H.O. Emblem **152** Emigrant

1968. 20th Anniv of W.H.O.
514 **151** 70c. yellow, black & blue 60 30

1968. Emigration of Algerians to Europe.
515 **152** 30c. brown, slate & blue 45 15

153 Scouts holding Jamboree Emblem **154** Torch and Athletes

1968. 8th Arab Scouts Jamboree, Algiers.
516 **153** 30c. multicoloured 55 20

1968. Olympic Games, Mexico. Multicoloured.
517 30c. Type **154** 50 35
518 50c. Football 85 40
519 1d. Allegory of Games (horiz) 1·40 80

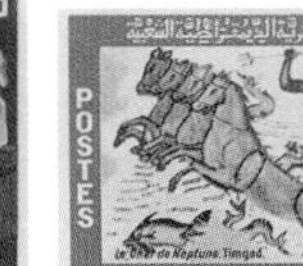

155 Barbary Sheep **156** "Neptune's Chariot", Timgad

1968. Protected Animals. Multicoloured.
520 40c. Type **155** 65 30
521 1d. Red deer . . . . 1·60 55

1968. Roman Mosaics. Multicoloured.
522 40c. "Hunting Scene" (Djemila) (vert) 50 20
523 95c. Type **156** . . . . 1·10 45

157 Miner **158** Opuntia

1968. "Industry, Energy and Mines".
524 **157** 30c. multicoloured 40 15
525 – 30c. silver and red 40 15
526 – 95c. red, black and silver 1·10 35
DESIGNS: No. 525, Coiled spring ("Industry"); No. 526, Symbol of radiation ("Energy").

1969. Algerian Flowers. Multicoloured.
527 25c. Type **158** 55 45
528 40c. Dianthus 85 55
529 70c. Rose . . . . 1·40 65
530 95c. Strelitzia . . . . 2·25 1·10
See also Nos. 621/4.

159 Djorf Torba Dam, Oued Guir

1969. Saharan Public Works. Multicoloured.
531 30c. Type **159** 45 20
532 1d.50 Route Nationale No. 51 . . . . 1·60 65

160 Desert Mail-coach of 1870 **161** The Capitol, Timgad

1969. Stamp Day.
533 **160** 1d. sepia, brown and blue 1·40 55

1969. Roman Ruins in Algeria. Multicoloured.
534 30c. Type **161** 45 15
535 1d. Septimius Temple, Djemila (horiz) . . . . . 1·10 40

162 I.L.O. Emblem **164** Carved Bookcase

1969. 50th Anniv of I.L.O.
536 **162** 95c. red, yellow and black 1·00 40

1969. No. 425 surch.
537 20c. on 12c. green 35 10

1969. Handicrafts. Multicoloured.
538 30c. Type **164** 40 20
539 60c. Copper tray 60 30
540 1d. Arab saddle . . . . . . 1·25 50

165 "Africa" Head **166** Astronauts on Moon

1969. 1st Pan-African Cultural Festival, Algiers.
541 **165** 30c. multicoloured 35 20

1969. 1st Man on the Moon.
542 **166** 50c. multicoloured 85 35

167 Bank Emblem **168** Flood Victims

1969. 5th Anniv of African Development Bank.
543 **167** 30c. black, yellow blue . . 45 20

1969. Aid for 1969 Flood Victims.
544 **168** 30c.+10c. black, flesh and blue 60 40
545 – 95c.+25c. brown, blue and purple . . . . 1·25 70
DESIGN: 95c. Helping hand for flood victims.

169 "Algerian Women" (Dinet)

1969. Dinet's Paintings. Multicoloured.
546 1d. Type **169** . . . . 1·60 65
547 1d.50 "The Look-outs" (Dinet) . . . . 2·25 1·00

170 "Mother and Child"

1969. "Protection of Mother and Child".
548 **170** 30c. multicoloured 50 30

171 "Agriculture" **172** Postal Deliveries by Donkey and Renault R4 Mail Van

1970. Four Year Plan.
549 **171** 25c. multicoloured 20 15
550 – 30c. multicoloured . . . . 1·75 15
551 – 50c. black and purple . . 45 20
DESIGNS: (LARGER, 49 × 23 mm): 30c. "Industry and Transport"; 50c. "Industry" (abstract).

1970. Stamp Day.
552 **172** 30c. multicoloured 45 20

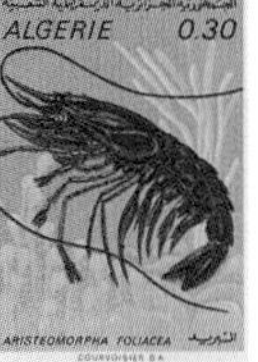

173 Royal Prawn **174** Oranges

1970. Marine Life. Multicoloured.
553 30c. Type **173** 45 20
554 40c. Noble pen (mollusc) . . 75 35
555 75c. Neptune's basket . . . . 1·10 45
556 1d. Red coral . . . . 1·60 65

1970. "Expo 70" World Fair, Osaka, Japan. Multicoloured.
557 30c. Type **174** 55 20
558 60c. Algerian Pavilion . . . 55 35
559 70c. Bunches of grapes . . . 1·10 45

175 Olives and Bottle of Olive-oil

1970. World Olive-oil Year.
560 **175** 1d. multicoloured . . . . 1·40 65

176 New U.P.U. H.Q. Building

1970. Inaug of New U.P.U. Headquarters Building.
561 **176** 75c. multicoloured 60 30

177 Crossed Muskets

1970. Algerian 18th-century Weapons. Mult.
562 40c. Type **177** 85 45
563 75c. Sabre (vert) . . . . . . 1·10 65
564 1d. Pistol . . . . 1·60 90

178 Arab League Flag, Arms and Map **179** Lenin

1970. 25th Anniv of Arab League.
565 **178** 30c. multicoloured 45 15

1970. Birth Centenary of Lenin.
566 **179** 30c. bistre and ochre . . 1·10 30

180 Exhibition Palace

1970. 7th International Algiers Fair.
567 **180** 60c. green 55 35

181 I.E.Y. and Education Emblems

1970. International Education Year. Mult.
568 30c. Type **181** 35 15
569 3d. Illuminated Koran (30 × 41 mm) . . . . . . 2·40 1·40

182 Great Mosque, Tlemcen

1970. Mosques.
570 **182** 30c. multicoloured 30 15
571 – 40c. brown and bistre . . 45 15
572 – 1d. multicoloured 85 30
DESIGNS—VERT: 40c. Ketchaoua Mosque, Algiers; 1d. Sidi-Okba Mosque.

183 "Fine Arts"

1970. Algerian Fine Arts.
573 **183** 1d. orange, grn & lt grn 90 35

184 G.P.O., Algiers **186** "Racial Equality"

185 Hurdling

1971. Stamp Day.
574 **184** 30c. multicoloured 65 30

1971. 6th Mediterranean Games, Izmir (Turkey).
575 **185** 20c. grey and blue 35 15
576 – 40c. grey and green . . . 50 30
577 – 75c. grey and brown . . . 85 40
DESIGNS—VERT: 40c. Gymnastics; 75c. Basket-ball.

1971. Racial Equality Year.
578 **186** 60c. multicoloured 60 30

187 Symbols of Learning, and Students

1971. Inaug of Technological Institutes.
579 **187** 70c. multicoloured 65 20

188 Red Crescent Banner

1971. Red Crescent Day.
580 **188** 30c.+10c. red and green 55 35

189 Casbah, Algiers

1971. Air.
581 **189** 2d. multicoloured . . . . 1·90 85
582 – 3d. violet and black . . . 2·75 1·40
583 – 4d. multicoloured . . . . 3·25 1·60
DESIGNS: 3d. Port of Oran; 4d. Rhumel Gorges.

190 Aures Costume **191** U.N.I.C.E.F. Emblem, Tree and Animals

1971. Regional Costumes (1st series). Multicoloured.
584 50c. Type **190** 90 45
585 70c. Oran . . . . 1·00 65
586 80c. Algiers . . . . 1·25 80
587 90c. Djebel-Amour . . . . . 1·60 90
See also Nos. 610/13 and 659/62.

1971. 25th Anniv of U.N.I.C.E.F.
588 **191** 60c. multicoloured 60 35

192 Lion of St. Mark's

1971. U.N.E.S.C.O. "Save Venice" Campaign. Mult.
589 80c. Type **192** 90 45
590 1 d. 15 Bridge of Sighs . . . 1·60 80

193 Cycling **194** Book and Bookmark

1972. Olympic Games, Munich. Multicoloured.
591 25c. Type **193** 35 15
592 40c. Throwing the javelin (vert) 40 20
593 60c. Wrestling (vert) 65 40
594 1d. Gymnastics (vert) . . . . 1·10 45

1972. International Book Year.
595 **194** 1d.15 red, black and brown 70 40

195 Algerian Postmen **196** Jasmine

1972. Stamp Day.
596 **195** 40c. multicoloured 45 15

1972. Flowers. Multicoloured.
597 50c. Type **196** 50 30
598 60c. Violets 55 35
599 1d.15 Tuberose . . . . . . 1·40 50

197 Olympic Stadium **198** Festival Emblem

1972. Inaug of Cheraga Olympic Stadium.
600 **197** 50c. green, brown & violet 55 30

1972. 1st Festival of Arab Youth.
601 **198** 40c. brown, yellow & grn 45 15

199 Rejoicing Algerians **201** Child posting Letter

1972. 10th Anniv of Independence.
602 **199** 1d. multicoloured 95 50

1972. Regional Costumes (2nd series). As T **190**. Multicoloured.
610 50c. Hoggar . . . . 1·10 55
611 60c. Kabylie . . . . 1·10 55
612 70c. Mzab . . . . 1·40 80
613 90c. Tlemcen . . . . 1·60 90

1973. Stamp Day.
614 **201** 40c. multicoloured 35 15

202 Ho-Chi-Minh and Map **203** Annaba Embroidery

1973. "Homage to the Vietnamese People".
615 **202** 40c. multicoloured 60 30

1973. Algerian Embroidery. Multicoloured.
616 40c. Type **203** 50 30
617 60c. Algiers embroidery . . . 70 40
618 80c. Constantine embroidery 1·00 50

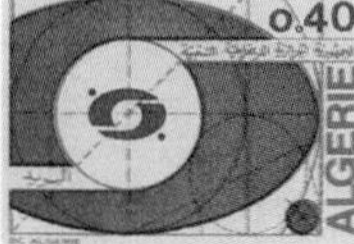

204 "Food Cultivation" **206** O.A.U. Emblem

205 Serviceman and Flag

1973. 10th Anniv of World Food Programme.
619 **204** 1d.15 multicoloured . . . 65 30

1973. National Service.
620 **205** 40c. multicoloured 45 15

1973. Algerian Flowers. As T **158**. Multicoloured.
621 30c. Type **158** 45 20
622 40c. As No. 529 . . . . . . 55 35
623 1d. As No. 528 . . . . . . 1·25 55
624 1d.15 As No. 530 . . . . . 1·60 65

1973. 10th Anniv of Organization of African Unity.
625 **206** 40c. multicoloured 45 20

207 Peasant Family

1973. Agrarian Revolution.
626 **207** 40c. multicoloured 50 20

208 Scout Badge on Map **209** P.T.T. Symbol

1973. 24th World Scouting Congress, Nairobi, Kenya.
627 **208** 80c. mauve 60 30

1973. Inauguration of New P.T.T. Symbol.
628 **209** 40c. orange and blue . . 45 15

210 Conference Emblem

211 "Skikda Harbour"

1973. 4th Summit Conference of Non-Aligned Countries, Algiers.

629 **210** 40c. multicoloured 35 15
630 80c. multicoloured 60 20

1973. Opening of Skikda Port.

631 **211** 80c. multicoloured 60 30

212 Young Workers

213 Arms of Algiers

1973. Volontariat Students' Volunteer Service.

632 **212** 40c. multicoloured 45 20

1973. Millenary of Algiers.

633 **213** 2d. multicoloured . . . . 2·25 1·10

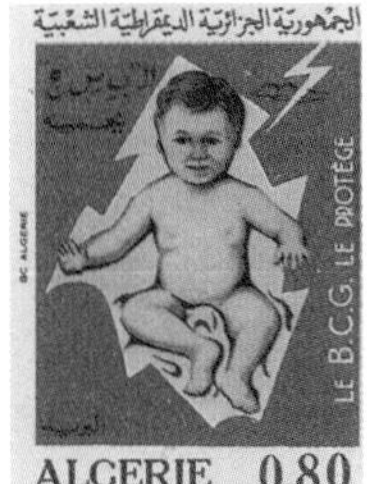

214 "Protected Infant"

1974. Anti-TB Campaign.

634 **214** 80c. multicoloured 60 30

215 Industrial Scene

1974. Four Year Plan.

635 **215** 80c. multicoloured 65 35

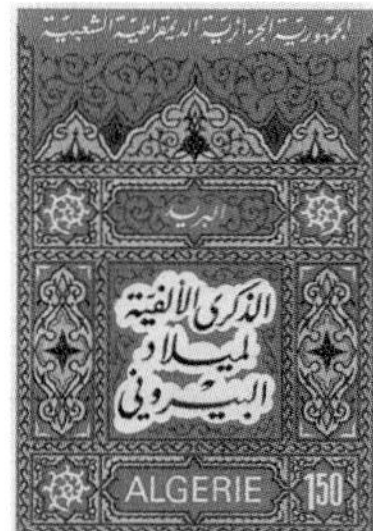

216 Arabesque Motif

1974. Birth Millenary of Abu-al Rayhan al-Biruni (mathematician and philosopher).

636 **216** 1d.50 multicoloured . . . 1·60 1·10

217 Map and Arrows

218 Upraised Weapon and Fist

1974. Meeting of Maghreb Committee for Co-ordination of Posts and Telecommunications, Tunis.

637 **217** 40c. multicoloured 45 20

1974. Solidarity with South African People's Campaign.

638 **218** 80c. black and red 55 20

219 Algerian Family

1974. Homage to Algerian Mothers.

639 **219** 85c. multicoloured 55 20

220 Urban Scene

1974. Children's Drawings. Multicoloured.

640 70c. Type **220** 60 15
641 80c. Agricultural scene . . . 70 30
642 90c. Tractor and sunrise . . 90 45
Nos. 641/2 are size 49 × 33 mm.

1974. "Floralies 1974" Flower Show, Algiers. Nos. 623/4 optd **FLORALIES 1974**.

643 1d. multicoloured . . . . . 1·25 65
644 1d.15 multicoloured . . . . 1·60 1·00

222 Automatic Stamp-vending Machine

223 U.P.U. Emblem on Globe

1974. Stamp Day.

645 **222** 80c. multicoloured 55 20

1974. Centenary of U.P.U.

646 **223** 80c. multicoloured 60 30

224 Revolutionaries

1974. 20th Anniv of Revolution. Multicoloured.

647 40c. Type **224** 35 15
648 70c. Armed soldiers (vert) . . 45 20
649 95c. Raising the flag (vert) . . 70 20
650 1d. Algerians looking to Independence 95 30

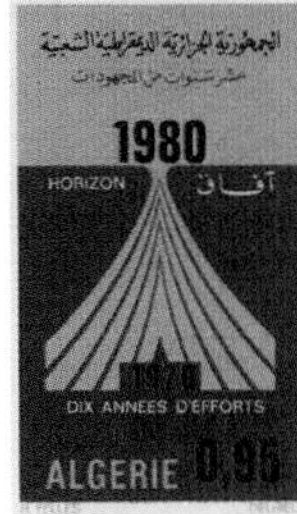

225 "Towards the Horizon"

226 Ewer

1974. "Horizon 1980".

651 **225** 95c. red, brown & black 60 30

1974. Algerian 17th-century Brassware. Mult.

652 50c. Type **226** 40 20
653 60c. Coffee pot 45 30
654 95c. Sugar basin 65 40
655 1d. Bath vessel 95 50

1975. No. 622 surch.

656 50c. on 40c. multicoloured . . 1·10 45

228 Games Emblem

1975. 7th Mediterranean Games (1st issue).

657 **228** 50c. violet, green & yellow 40 15
658 1d. orange, violet & blue 70 20
See also Nos. 671/5.

1975. Regional Costumes (3rd series). As T **190**. Multicoloured.

659 1d. Algiers . . . . 1·10 60
660 1d. The Hogger . . . . . . 1·10 60
661 1d. Oran . . . . 1·10 60
662 1d. Tlemcen . . . . 1·10 60

229 Labour Emblems

1975. 10th Anniv of Arab Labour Organization.

663 **229** 50c. brown 45 10

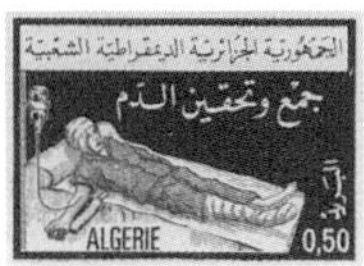

230 Transfusion

1975. Blood Collection and Transfusion Service.

664 **230** 50c. multicoloured 55 30

231 El Kantara Post Office

232 Policeman and Oil Rig on Map of Algeria

1975. Stamp Day.

665 **231** 50c. multicoloured 45 15

1975. Police Day.

666 **232** 50c. multicoloured 45 20

233 Ground Receiving Aerial

1975. Satellite Telecommunications. Mult.

667 50c. Type **233** 40 15
668 1d. Map of receiving sites . . 65 20
669 1d.20 Main and subsidiary ground stations 85 30

234 Revolutionary with Flag

235 Swimming

1975. 20th Anniv of "Skikda" Revolution.

670 **234** 1d. multicoloured 60 30

1975. 7th Mediterranean Games, Algiers (2nd issue). Multicoloured.

671 25c. Type **235** 15 10
672 50c. Wrestling 30 15
673 70c. Football (vert) 50 20
674 1d. Athletics (vert) 65 30
675 1d.20 Handball (vert) 85 45

236 "Setif-Guelma-Kherrata"

237 Map of the Maghreb and A.P.U. Emblem

1975. 30th Anniv of Setif, Guelma and Kherrata Massacres (1st issue).

677 **236** 5c. black and orange . . 10 10
678 10c. black and green . . . 10 10
679 25c. black and blue . . . 15 10
680 30c. black and brown . . 20 10
681 50c. black and green . . . 30 10
682 70c. black and red 40 15
683 1d. black and red 60 30
See also No. 698.

1975. 10th Arab Postal Union Congress, Algiers.

684 **237** 1d. multicoloured 60 30

238 Mosaic, Palace of the Bey, Constantine

1975. Historic Buildings.

685 **238** 1d. multicoloured 85 35
686 – 2d. multicoloured . . . . 1·60 80
687 – 2d.50 black and brown . . 2·25 1·10

DESIGNS—VERT: 2d. Medersa Sidi-Boumedienne Oratory, Tlemcen. HORIZ: 2d.50, Palace of the Dey, Algiers.

239 University Building

240 Red-billed Fire Finch

1975. Millenary of Al-Azhar University, Cairo.

688 **239** 2d. multicoloured . . . . 1·60 65

1976. Algerian Birds (1st series). Multicoloured.

689 50c. Type **240** . . . . 1·25 60
690 1d.40 Black-headed bush shrike (horiz) . . . . . . 2·00 1·00
691 2d. Blue-tit . . . . 2·40 1·10
692 2d.50 Black-bellied sand-grouse (horiz) . . . . . . 2·75 1·50
See also Nos. 722/5.

241 Early and Modern Telephones

242 Map and Angolan Flag

1976. Telephone Centenary.

693 **241** 1d.40 multicoloured . . . 85 40

1976. "Solidarity with Republic of Angola".

694 **242** 50c. multicoloured 45 15

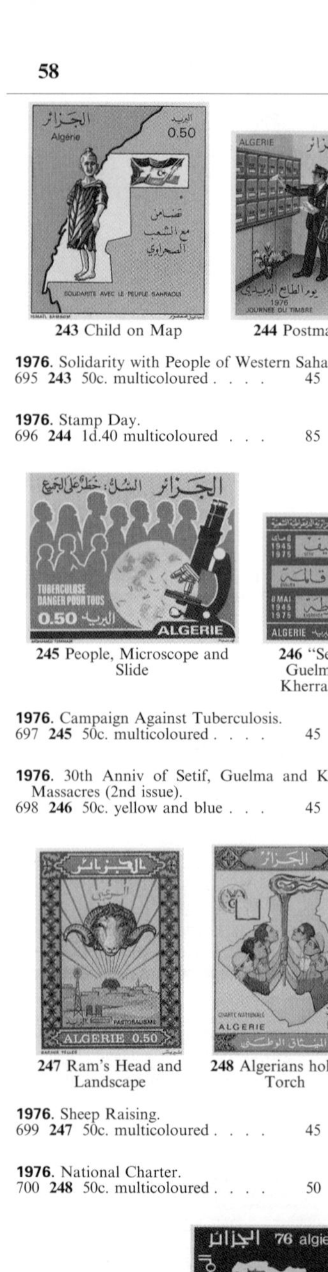

243 Child on Map 244 Postman

1976. Solidarity with People of Western Sahara.
695 **243** 50c. multicoloured 45 20

1976. Stamp Day.
696 **244** 1d.40 multicoloured . . . 85 35

245 People, Microscope and Slide 246 "Setif-Guelma-Kherrata"

1976. Campaign Against Tuberculosis.
697 **245** 50c. multicoloured 45 15

1976. 30th Anniv of Setif, Guelma and Kherrata Massacres (2nd issue).
698 **246** 50c. yellow and blue . . . 45 10

247 Ram's Head and Landscape 248 Algerians holding Torch

1976. Sheep Raising.
699 **247** 50c. multicoloured 45 20

1976. National Charter.
700 **248** 50c. multicoloured 50 15

249 Flag and Map 250 Map of Africa

1976. Solidarity with the Palestinian People.
701 **249** 50c. multicoloured 50 15

1976. 2nd Pan-African Commercial Fair, Algiers.
702 **250** 2d. multicoloured . . . . 1·40 50

251 Blind Man making Brushes 253 Soldiers planting Seedlings

252 Open Book

1976. Rehabilitation of the Blind. Multicoloured.
703 1d.20 Type **251** 80 35
704 1d.40 "The Blind Man" (E. Dinet) (horiz) . . . . . 1·10 50

1976. The Constitution.
705 **252** 2d. multicoloured . . . . 1·40 55

1976. Protection against Saharan Encroachment.
706 **253** 1d.40 multicoloured . . . 1·10 45

254 Arabic Inscription

1976. Election of President Boumedienne.
707 **254** 2d. multicoloured . . . . 1·40 55

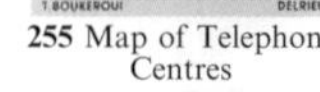

255 Map of Telephone Centres 256 "Pyramid" of Heads

1977. Inauguration of Automatic Telephone Dialling System.
708 **255** 40c. multicoloured 35 15

1977. 2nd General Population and Housing Census.
709 **256** 60c. on 50c. mult 45 15

257 Museum Building 258 El Kantara Gorges

1977. Sahara Museum, Ouargla.
710 **257** 60c. multicoloured 55 35

1977.
711 **258** 20c. green and cream . . 1·10 45
712 60c. mauve and cream . . 1·60 45
713 1d. brown and cream . . 6·00 50

259 Assembly in Session

1977. National Assembly.
714 **259** 2d. multicoloured . . . . 1·10 45

260 Soldiers with Flag 261 Soldier with Flag

1977. Solidarity with People of Zimbabwe.
715 **260** 2d. multicoloured . . . . 1·10 45

1977. Solidarity with People of Namibia.
716 **261** 3d. multicoloured . . . . 1·75 65

262 "Winter"

1977. Roman Mosaics. "The Seasons". Mult.
717 1d.20 Type **262** . . . . . . 1·25 65
718 1d.40 "Autumn" . . . . . . 1·35 65
719 2d. "Summer" . . . . . . 1·75 1·10
720 3d. "Spring" . . . . 2·40 1·40

1977. Algerian Birds (2nd series). As T **240**. Multicoloured.
722 60c. Tristram's warbler . . . 1·10 60
723 1d.40 Moussier's redstart (horiz) . . . . 1·50 75
724 2d. Temminck's horned lark (horiz) . . . . 2·25 1·10
725 3d. Hoopoe . . . . 3·50 1·60

263 Horseman 264 Ribbon and Games Emblem

1977. "The Cavaliers" (performing horsemen). Multicoloured.
726 2d. Type **263** . . . . 1·60 65
727 5d. Three horsemen (horiz) 3·75 1·60

1977. 3rd African Games, Algiers (1978) (1st issue). Multicoloured.
728 60c. Type **264** 45 20
729 1d.40 Symbolic design and emblem . . . . 1·10 45
See also Nos. 740/4.

265 Tessala el Merdja

1977. Socialist Agricultural Villages.
730 **265** 1d.40 multicoloured . . . 85 35

266 12th-century Almohad Dirham

1977. Ancient Coins. Multicolored.
731 60c. Type **266** 45 30
732 1d.40 12th-century Alomhad dinar . . . . 1·00 40
733 2d. 11th-century Almorarid dinar . . . . 1·40 70

267 Cherry ("Cerasus avium") 269 Children with Traffic Signs opposing Car

1978. Fruit Tree Blossom. Multicoloured.
734 60c. Type **267** 45 20
735 1d.20 "Persica vulgaris" (peach) 80 55
736 1d.30 "Amygdalus communis" (almond) . . . 80 55
737 1d.40 "Malus communis" (crab apple) . . . . 1·10 65

1978. Surch.
738 **236** 60c. on 50c. black & grn 55 15

1978. Road Safety for Children.
739 **269** 60c. multicoloured 50 20

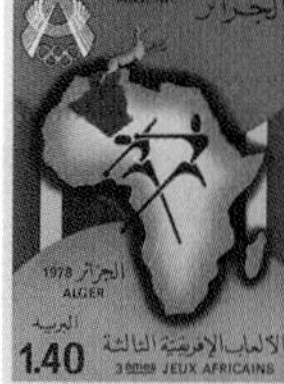

270 Boxing and Map of Africa

1978. 3rd African Games, Algiers (2nd issue). Multicoloured.
740 40c. Sports emblems and volleyball (horiz) 20 10
741 60c. Olympic rings and table tennis symbol 35 15
742 1d.20 Basketball symbol (horiz) 70 30
743 1d.30 Hammerthrowing symbol 70 40
744 1d.40 Type **270** 90 40

271 Patient returning to Family

1978. Anti-tuberculosis Campaign.
745 **271** 60c. multicoloured 50 20

272 Ka'aba, Mecca

1978. Pilgrimage to Mecca.
746 **272** 60c. multicoloured 50 10

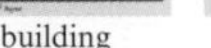

273 Road-building 274 Triangular Brooch

1978. African Unity Road.
747 **273** 60c. multicoloured 50 15

1978. Jewellery (1st series). Multicoloured.
748 1d.20 Type **274** 90 45
749 1d.35 Circular brooch . . . 1·10 55
750 1d.40 Anklet . . . . 1·40 65
See also Nos. 780/2 and 833/5.

275 President Houari Boumedienne 276 Books and Hands holding Torch

1979. President Boumedienne Commem (1st issue).
751 **275** 60c. brown, red & turq 45 20
See also No. 753.

1979. National Liberation Front Party Congress.
752 **276** 60c. multicoloured 40 15

277 President Houari Boumedienne

1979. President Boumedienne Commem (2nd issue).
753 **277** 1d.40 multicoloured . . . 95 40

278 Arabic Inscription **279** White Storks

1979. Election of President Chadli Bendjedid.
754 **278** 2d. multicoloured . . . . 1·25 35

1979. Air.
755 **279** 10d. blue, black and red 6·00 2·00

280 Ben Badis **281** Globe within Telephone Dial

1979. 90th Birth Anniv of Sheikh Abdelhamid Ben Badis (journalist and education pioneer).
756 **280** 60c. multicoloured 40 15

1979. "Telecom 79" Exhibition. Multicoloured.
757 1d.20 Type **281** 70 20
758 1d.40 Sound waves 90 35

282 Children dancing on Globe

1979. International Year of the Child. Mult.
759 60c. Picking Dates 40 10
760 1d.40 Type **282** (vert) 85 35

283 Kabylie Nuthatch **284** Fighting for the Revolution and Construction work

1979.
761 **283** 1d.40 multicoloured . . . 3·00 1·25

1979. 25th Anniv of Revolution. Multicoloured.
762 1d.40 Type **284** 80 20
763 3d. Algerians with flag . . . 1·75 65

285 Arabic Inscription

1979. 1400th Anniv of Hegira.
764 **285** 3d. gold, turquoise & blue 1·60 65

286 Return of Dionysus (right detail) **287** Books

1980. Dionysus Mosaic, Setif. Multicoloured.
765 1d.20 Type **286** 80 35
766 1d.35 Centre detail 90 45
767 1d.40 Left detail . . . . . . 1·00 65
Nos. 765/7 were issued together, se-tenant, forming a composite design.

1980. Day of Knowledge.
768 **287** 60c. brown, yellow & grn 40 10

288 Five Year Plan **289** Olympic Flame

1980. Extraordinary Congress of National Liberation Front Party.
769 **288** 60c. multicoloured 40 15

1980. Olympic Games, Moscow. Multicoloured.
770 50c. Type **289** 35 10
771 1d.40 Olympic sports (horiz) 80 30

290 Figures supporting O.P.E.C. Emblem

1980. 20th Anniv of Organization of Petroleum Exporting Countries.
772 **290** 60c. green, blue and red 40 10
773 – 1d.40 green and blue . . 95 35
DESIGN: 1d.40, O.P.E.C. emblem on world map.

291 Aures

1980. World Tourism Conference, Manila. Mult.
774 50c. Type **291** 35 15
775 1d. El Oued 65 20
776 1d.40 Tassili 90 35
777 2d. Algiers . . . . 1·40 50

292 Ibn Sina

1980. Birth Millenary of Ibn Sina (Avicenna) (philosopher).
778 **292** 3d. multicoloured . . . . 1·60 65

293 Earthquake Devastation

1980. El Asnam Earthquake Relief.
779 **293** 3d. multicoloured . . . . 1·60 45

1980. Jewellery (2nd series). As T **274**. Mult.
780 60c. Necklace 45 20
781 1d.40 Earrings and bracelet 80 45
782 2d. Diadem (horiz) . . . . . 1·25 55

294 Emblem

1981. Five Year Plan.
783 **294** 60c. multicoloured 35 10

295 Basket-worker

1981. Traditional Arts. Multicoloured.
784 40c. Type **295** 20 10
785 60c. Spinning 35 15
786 1d. Copper-smith 55 20
787 1d.40 Jeweller 80 35

296 Cedar "Cedrus atlantica"

1981. World Tree Day. Multicoloured.
788 60c. Type **296** 35 10
789 1d.40 Cypress "Cupressus dupreziana" 80 35

297 Mohamed Bachir el Ibrahimi

298 Children and Blackboard (Basic Schooling)

1981. Day of Knowledge.
790 **297** 60c. multicoloured 35 10
791 **298** 60c. multicoloured 35 10

299 Archer, Dog and Internal Organs

1981. 12th Int Hydatidological Congress, Algiers.
792 **299** 2d. multicoloured . . . . 1·40 45

300 Dish Aerial and Caduceus **301** "Disabled"

1981. World Telecommunications Day.
793 **300** 1d.40 multicoloured . . . 80 20

1981. International Year of Disabled People.
794 **301** 1d.20 blue, red & orange 65 15
795 – 1d.40 multicoloured . . . 80 15
DESIGN: 1d.40, Disabled people and hand holding flower.

302 "Papilio machaon"

1981. Butterflies. Multicoloured.
796 60c. Type **302** 45 15
797 1d.20 "Rhodocera rhamni gonepteryx rhamni" . . . 80 35
798 1d.40 "Charaxes jasius" . . . 1·00 50
799 2d. "Papilio podalirius" . . . 1·40 65

303 Mediterranean Monk Seal **304** Man holding Ear of Wheat

1981. Nature Protection. Multicoloured.
800 60c. Type **303** 55 35
801 1d.40 Barbary ape . . . . . 1·10 80

1981. World Food Day.
802 **304** 2d. multicoloured . . . . 1·00 40

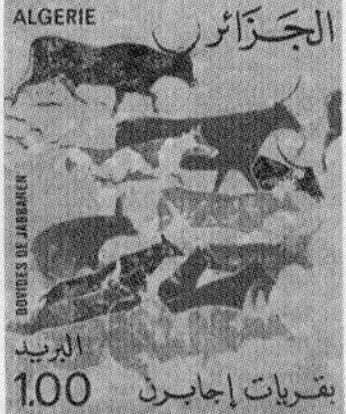

305 Cattle, Jabbaren

1981. Cave Paintings. Multicoloured.
803 60c. Mouflon, Tan Zoumaitek 35 15
804 1d. Type **305** 55 20
805 1d.60 Cattle, Iherir (horiz) . . 80 35
806 2d. One-horned bull, Jabbaren (horiz) . . . . . 1·10 40

306 Galley

1981. Algerian Ships of 17th and 18th Centuries. Multicoloured.
807 60c. Type **306** 60 25
808 1d.60 Xebec . . . . 1·50 45

307 Footballers with Cup **308** Microscope

1982. World Cup Football Championship, Spain. Multicoloured.
809 80c. Type **307** 45 15
810 2d.80 Footballers and ball (horiz) . . . . 1·40 50

1982. Centenary of Discovery of Tubercle Bacillus.
811 **308** 80c. blue, lt blue & orge 45 15

309 Mirror

1982. Popular Traditional Arts. Multicoloured.
812 80c. Type **309** 45 15
813 2d. Whatnot . . . . 1·00 40
814 2d.40 Chest (48 × 32 mm) . . 1·40 55

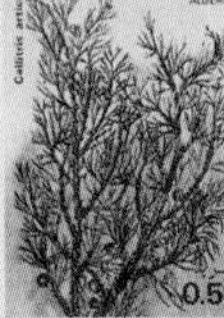

310 New Mosque, Algiers **311** "Callitris articulata"

1982. Views of Algeria before 1830 (1st series). Size 32 × 22 mm.
815 **310** 80c. brown 35 15
816 – 2d.40 violet 90 45
817 – 3d. green . . . . 1·25 55
DESIGNS: 2d.40, Sidi Boumedienne Mosque, Tlemcen; 3d. Garden of Dey, Algiers.
See also Nos. 859/62, 873/5, 880/2, 999/1001, 1054/6 and 1075/86.

1982. Medicinal Plants. Multicoloured.
818 50c. Type **311** 30 10
819 80c. "Artemisia herba-alba" 40 15
820 1d. "Ricinus communis" . . 55 20
821 2d.40 "Thymus fontanesii" 1·25 50

312 Independence Fighter **313** Congress House

1982. 20th Anniv of Independence. Mult.
822 50c. Type **312** 30 10
823 80c. Modern soldiers 40 15
824 2d. Algerians and symbols of prosperity . . . . 1·00 45

1982. Soumman Congress.
826 **313** 80c. multicoloured 45 10

314 Scout and Guide releasing Dove **315** Child

1982. 75th Anniv of Boy Scout Movement.
827 **314** 2d.80 multicoloured . . . 1·40 45

1982. Palestinian Children.
828 **315** 1d.60 multicoloured . . . 80 20

316 Waldrapp

1982. Nature Protection. Multicoloured.
829 50c. Type **316** 60 50
830 80c. Houbara bustard (vert) 75 75
831 2d. Tawny eagle . . . . . . 2·10 1·40
832 2d.40 Lammergeier (vert) . . 2·75 1·50

317 Mirror **318** "Abies numidica"

1983. Silver Work.
833 **317** 50c. silver, black and red 20 10
834 – 1d. multicoloured 45 30
835 – 2d. silver, black, & purple 90 45
DESIGNS—VERT. 1d. Perfume flasks. HORIZ: 2d. Belt buckle.

1983. World Tree Day. Multicoloured.
836 80c. Type **318** 40 15
837 2d.80 "Acacia raddiana" . . 1·50 55

319 Mineral **320** Customs Officer

1983. Mineral Resources.
838 **319** 70c. multicoloured 55 20
839 80c. multicoloured 55 30
840 1d.20 mult (horiz) 85 55
841 2d.40 mult (horiz) . . . . 1·60 90

1983. 30th Anniv of Customs Co-operation Council.
842 **320** 80c. multicoloured 55 20

321 Emir Abdelkader

1983. Death Centenary of Emir Abdelkader.
843 **321** 4d. multicoloured . . . . 1·75 70

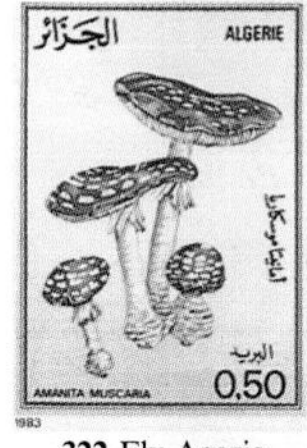

322 Fly Agaric **323** Ibn Khaldoun

1983. Mushrooms. Multicoloured.
844 50c. Type **322** 65 25
845 80c. Death cap 95 50
846 1d.40 "Pleurotus eryngii" . . 2·10 75
847 2d.80 "Terfezia leonis" . . . 3·50 1·50

1983. Ibn Khaldoun Commemoration.
848 **323** 80c. multicoloured 55 20

324 W.C.Y. Emblem and Post Office

1983. World Communications Year. Mult.
849 80c. Type **324** 45 15
850 2d.40 W.C.Y. emblem and telephone switch box . . . 1·10 40

325 Goat and Tassili Mountains

1983. Tassili World Patrimony. Multicoloured.
851 50c. Type **325** 30 10
852 80c. Touaregs 40 15
853 2d.40 Rock paintings . . . . 1·10 40
854 2d.80 Rock formation . . . 1·40 55

326 Sloughi

1983. Sloughi. Multicoloured.
855 80c. Type **326** 55 20
856 2d.40 Sloughi . . . . 1·40 65

327 Symbols of Economic Progress

1983. 5th National Liberation Front Party Congress.
857 **327** 80c. multicoloured 55 30

1984. Views of Algeria before 1830 (2nd series). As T **310**.
859 10c. blue 10 10
860 1d. purple 40 15
861 2d. blue 80 35
862 4d. red . . . . 1·60 55
DESIGNS: 10c. Oran; 1d. Sidi Abderahmane Mosque, Et Taalibi; 2d. Bejaia; 4d. Constantine.

328 Jug **329** Fountain

1984. Pottery. Multicoloured.
863 80c. Type **328** 40 20
864 1d. Dish (horiz) 50 20
865 2d. Lamp . . . . 1·00 45
866 2d.40 Jug (horiz) . . . . . . 1·25 55

1984. Fountains of Old Algiers.
867 **329** 50c. multicoloured 20 15
868 – 80c. multicoloured 40 20
869 – 2d.40 multicoloured . . . 1·00 55
DESIGNS: 80c., 2d.40, Different fountains.

330 Dove, Flames and Olympic Rings **331** Stallion

1984. Olympic Games, Los Angeles.
870 **330** 1d. multicoloured 60 30

1984. Horses. Multicoloured.
871 80c. Type **331** 45 35
872 2d.40 Mare . . . . 1·40 80

1984. Views of Algeria before 1830 (3rd series). As T **310**.
873 5c. purple 10 10
874 20c. blue 10 10
875 70c. violet 30 15
DESIGNS: 5c. Mustapha Pacha; 20c. Bab Azzoun; 70c. Mostaganem.

332 Lute

1984. Musical Instruments. Multicoloured.
876 80c. Type **332** 45 20
877 1d. Drum 55 20
878 2d.40 One-stringed instrument 1·25 55
879 2d.80 Bagpipes . . . . . . 1·40 65

1984. Views of Algeria before 1830 (4th series). As T **310**.
880 30c. red and black 15 10
881 40c. black 20 10
882 50c. brown 30 10
DESIGNS: 30c. Algiers from Admiralty; 40c. Kolea; 50c. Algiers from aqueduct.

333 Partisans in Mountains and Flag

1984. 30th Anniv of Revolution.
883 **333** 80c. multicoloured 55 20

334 Map of M'Zab Valley

1984. M'Zab Valley. Multicoloured.
885 80c. Type **334** 45 10
886 2d.40 M'Zab town . . . . . 1·25 45

335 Coffee Pot **336** Blue-finned Tuna

1985. Ornamental Tableware.
887 **335** 80c. black, silver & yellow 35 20
888 – 2d. black, silver and green 90 45
889 – 2d.40 black, silver & pink 1·25 55
DESIGNS—HORIZ: 2d. Bowl. VERT: 2d.40, Lidded jar.

1985. Fishes. Multicoloured.
890 50c. Type **336** 45 20
891 80c. Gilthead seabream . . . 70 25
892 2d.40 Dusky grouper . . . . 2·00 90
893 2d.80 Smooth hound . . . . 2·40 1·10

337 Birds in Flight and Emblem

1985. National Games.
894 **337** 80c. multicoloured 50 15

338 Stylized Trees **339** Algiers Casbah

1985. Environmental Protection. Multicoloured.
895 80c. Type **338** 40 15
896 1d.40 Stylized waves 70 20

1985.
897 **339** 20c. blue and cream . . . 10 10
898 80c. green and cream . . 45 10
899 2d.40 brown and cream 1·25 10

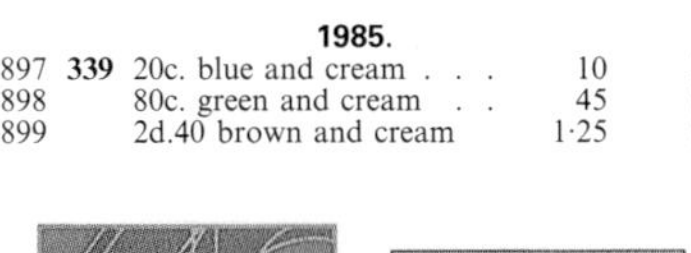

340 Dove within "40" **341** Figures linking arms and Emblem

1985. 40th Anniv of U.N.O.
900 **340** 1d. multicoloured 60 20

1985. 1st National Youth Festival.
901 **341** 80c. multicoloured 50 15

342 Figures linking arms on Globe and Dove **343** O.P.E.C. Emblem

1985. International Youth Year. Multicoloured.
902 80c. Type **342** 45 15
903 1d.40 Doves making globe with laurels 65 20

1985. 25th Anniv of Organization of Petroleum Exporting Countries.
904 **343** 80c. multicoloured 50 20

344 Mother and Children **345** Chetaibi Bay

1985. Family Planning. Multicoloured.
905 80c. Type **344** 40 15
906 1d.40 Doctor weighing baby 65 20
907 1d.70 Mother breast-feeding baby 85 30

1985. Tourist Sites.
908 **345** 80c. blue, green & brown 35 15
909 – 2d. brown, green & blue 1·00 30
910 – 2d.40 brown, green & bl 1·10 40
DESIGNS—VERT: 2d. El Meniaa. HORIZ: 2d.40, Bou Noura.

346 "Palm Grove" **347** Line Pattern

1985. Paintings by N. Dinet. Multicoloured.
911 2d. Type **346** . . . . 1·10 55
912 3d. "Palm Grove" (different) 1·60 85

1985. Weavings. Multicoloured.
913 80c. Type **347** 50 35
914 1d.40 Diamond pattern . . . 90 50
915 2d.40 Patterned horizontal stripes . . . . 1·40 85
916 2d.80 Vertical and horizontal stripes . . . . 1·90 1·40

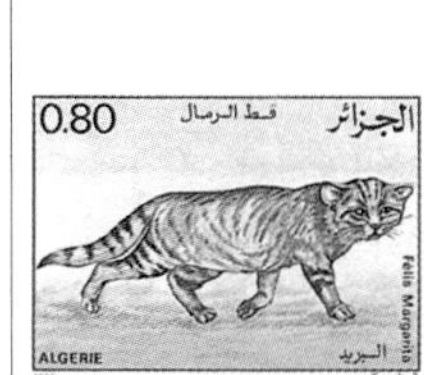

348 "Felis margarita" **349** Oral Vaccination

1986. Wild Cats. Multicoloured.
917 80c. Type **348** 45 35
918 1d. Caracal 55 45
919 2d. Wild cat . . . . 1·25 90
920 2d.40 Serval (vert) . . . . . 1·60 1·10

1986. U.N.E.S.C.O. Child Survival Campaign. Mult.
921 80c. Type **349** 45 20
922 1d.40 Sun behind mother and baby 90 35
923 1d.70 Children playing . . . 1·10 55

350 Industrial Skyline, Clasped Hands and Emblem **351** Books and Crowd

1986. 30th Anniv of Algerian General Workers' Union.
924 **350** 2d. multicoloured . . . . 1·10 45

1986. National Charter.
925 **351** 4d. multicoloured . . . . 2·25 1·00

352 Emblem on Book and Drawing Instruments **353** Children playing

1986. Disabled Persons' Day.
926 **352** 80c. multicoloured 50 20

1986. Anti-tuberculosis Campaign.
927 **353** 80c. multicoloured 55 30

354 Sombrero on Football **355** Courtyard with Fountain

1986. World Cup Football Championship, Mexico. Multicoloured.
928 2d. Type **354** . . . . 1·00 40
929 2d.40 Players and ball . . . 1·25 45

1986. Traditional Dwellings. Multicoloured.
930 80c. Type **355** 45 20
931 2d.40 Courtyard with two beds of shrubs . . . . . . 1·40 70
932 3d. Courtyard with plants in tall pot . . . . 1·75 1·00

356 Heart forming Drop over Patient **357** Transmission Mast as Palm Tree

1986. Blood Donors.
933 **356** 80c. multicoloured 90 30

1986. Opening of Hertzian Wave Communications (Southern District).
934 **357** 60c. multicoloured 35 15

358 Studded Gate

1986. Mosque Gateways. Multicoloured.
935 2d. Type **358** . . . . 1·00 45
936 2d.40 Ornate gateway . . . . 1·25 65

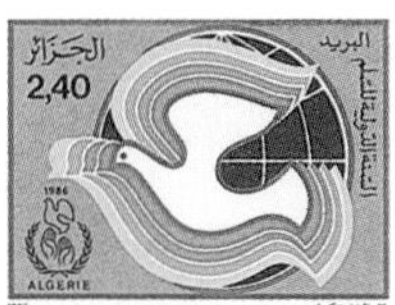

359 Dove

1986. International Peace Year.
937 **359** 2d.40 multicoloured . . . 1·25 45

360 Girl dancing **361** "Narcissus tazetta"

1986. Folk Dances. Multicoloured.
938 80c. Type **360** 45 20
939 2d.40 Woman with purple dress dancing . . . . . . 1·25 55
940 2d.80 Veiled sword dancer . . 1·25 55

1986. Flowers. Multicoloured.
941 80c. Type **361** 45 20
942 1d.40 "Iris unguicularis" . . 80 45
943 2d.40 "Capparis spinosa" . . 1·10 65
944 2d.80 "Gladiolus segetum" 1·40 90

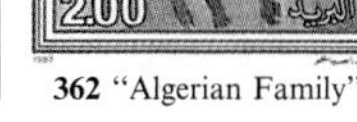

362 "Algerian Family" **363** Earrings

1987. Paintings by Mohammed Issiakhem in National Museum. Multicoloured.
945 2d. Type **362** . . . . 1·10 55
946 5d. "Man and Books" . . . 2·50 1·60

1987. Jewellery from Aures. Multicoloured.
947 1d. Type **363** 45 30
948 1d.80 Bangles 80 45
949 2d.90 Brooches . . . . . . 1·25 85
950 3d.30 Necklace (horiz) . . . . 1·40 95

364 Boy and Girl

1987. Rock Carvings. Multicoloured.
951 1d. Type **364** 55 35
952 2d.90 Goat . . . . 1·40 1·10
953 3d.30 Animals . . . . 1·60 1·10

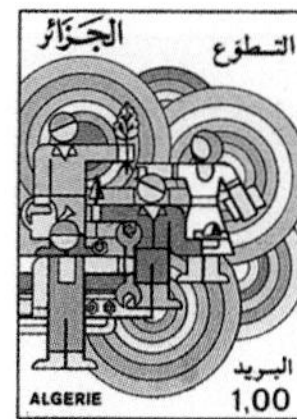

365 Baby holding Syringe "Umbrella" **366** Workers and Circles

1987. African Vaccination Year.
954 **365** 1d. multicoloured 45 20

1987. Voluntary Service.
955 **366** 1d. multicoloured 45 20

367 People and Buildings

1987. 3rd General Population Census.
956 **367** 1d. multicoloured 45 20

368 1962 War Orphans Fund Stamps and Magnifying Glass

1987. 25th Anniv of Independent Algeria Stamps.
957 **368** 1d.80 multicoloured . . . 80 50

369 Hand holding Torch **370** Actors in Spotlight

1987. 25th Anniv of Independence. Multicoloured.
958 **369** 1d. multicoloured 45 20

1987. Amateur Theatre Festival, Mostaganem. Multicoloured.
960 1d. Type **370** 40 15
961 1d.80 Theatre 70 40

371 Discus Thrower

372 Greater Flamingo

1987. Mediterranean Games, Lattaquie. Mult.
962 1d. Type **371** 40 15
963 2d.90 Tennis player (vert) . . 1·10 50
964 3d.30 Footballer . . . . . . 1·40 65

1987. Birds. Multicoloured.
965 1d. Type **372** 45 35
966 1d.80 Purple swamphen . . . 90 75
967 2d.50 Black-shouldered kite 1·75 95
968 2d.90 Red kite . . . . 1·90 1·25

373 Reservoir

374 Map, Transmitter and Radio Waves

1987. Agriculture. Multicoloured.
969 1d. Type **373** 45 15
970 1d. Forestry (36 × 28 mm) . . 45 15
971 1d. Foodstuffs (25 × 37 mm) 45 15
972 1d. Erecting hedge against desert (25 × 37 mm) 45 15

1987. African Telecommunications Day.
973 **374** 1d. multicoloured 45 20

375 Motorway

1987. Transport. Multicoloured.
974 2d.90 Type **375** . . . . . . 1·10 45
975 3d.30 Diesel locomotive and passenger train . . . . . . 2·75 1·10

376 Houari Boumedienne University, Algiers

1987. Universities. Multicoloured.
976 1d. Type **376** 40 15
977 2d.50 Oran University . . . 90 35
978 2d.90 Constantine University 1·10 45
979 3d.30 Emir Abdelkader University, Constantine (vert) . . . . 1·40 55

377 Wheat, Sun and Farmer ploughing with Oxen

378 Emblem as Sun above Factories

1988. 10th Anniv of International Agricultural Development Fund.
980 **377** 1d. multicoloured 40 20

1988. Autonomy of State-owned Utilities.
981 **378** 1d. multicoloured 40 20

379 Woman's Face and Emblem

380 Globe, Flag, Wood Pigeon and Scout Salute

1988. International Women's Day.
982 **379** 1d. multicoloured 40 20

1988. 75th Anniv of Arab Scouting.
983 **380** 2d. multicoloured 80 35

381 Bau-Hanifia

382 Running

1988. Spas. Multicoloured.
984 1d. Type **381** 40 15
985 2d.90 Chellala . . . . 1·10 45
986 3d.30 Righa-Ain Tolba . . . 1·25 50

1988. Olympic Games, Seoul.
987 **382** 2d.90 multicoloured . . . 1·00 45

383 Pencil and Globe

384 Barbary Ape

1988. International Literacy Day.
988 **383** 2d.90 multicoloured . . . 1·00 45

1988. Endangered Animals. Barbary Ape. Mult.
989 50c. Type **384** 20 10
990 90c. Ape family 35 15
991 1d. Ape's head and shoulders (vert) 40 20
992 1d.80 Ape in tree (vert) . . . 70 35

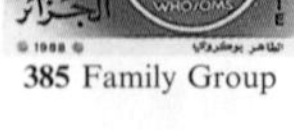

385 Family Group

386 Different Races raising Fists

1988. 40th Anniv of W.H.O.
993 **385** 2d.90 multicoloured . . . 1·00 45

1988. Anti-apartheid Campaign.
994 **386** 2d.50 multicoloured . . . 85 35

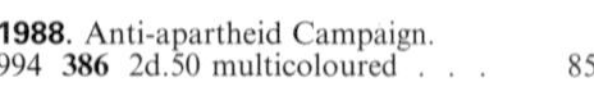

387 Emblem

388 Man irrigating Fields

1988. 6th National Liberation Front Party Congress.
995 **387** 1d. multicoloured 40 15

1988. Agriculture. Multicoloured.
996 1d. Type **388** 40 15
997 1d. Fields, cattle and man picking fruit 40 15

389 Constantine

390 Courtyard

1989.
998 **389** 1d. deep green and green 30 10

1989. Views of Algeria before 1830 (5th series). As T **310**.
999 2d.50 green 70 35
1000 2d.90 green 80 15
1001 5d. brown and black . . . . 2·00 70
DESIGNS: 2d.50, Bay; 2d.90, Harbour; 5d. View of harbour through archway.

1989. National Achievements. Multicoloured.
1002 1d. Type **390** 35 20
1003 1d. Flats (housing) 35 20
1004 1d. Gateway, Timimoun (tourism) 35 20
1005 1d. Dish aerial and telephones (communications) 35 20

391 Oran Es Senia Airport

1989. Airports. Multicoloured.
1006 2d.90 Type **391** 85 35
1007 3d.30 Tebessa airport . . . 95 45
1008 5d. Tamanrasset airport (vert) . . . . 1·60 90

392 Irrigation

393 Soldiers at Various Tasks

1989. Development of South. Multicoloured.
1009 1d. Type **392** 30 15
1010 1d.80 Ouargla secondary school 50 30
1011 2d.50 Gas complex, Hassi R'mel (vert) 70 35

1989. 20th Anniv of National Service.
1012 **393** 2d. multicoloured . . . 1·50 75

394 Locusts and Crop Spraying

1989. Anti-locusts Campaign.
1013 **394** 1d. multicoloured . . . 30 15

395 Mother and Baby

1989. International Children's Day.
1014 **395** 1d.+30c. mult 40 30

396 Moon

1989. 20th Anniv of First Manned Landing on Moon. Multicoloured.
1015 2d.90 Type **396** 85 35
1016 4d. Astronaut on moon . . 1·10 55

397 Globe and Emblem

1989. Centenary of Interparliamentary Union.
1017 **397** 2d.90 mauve, brn & gold 85 30

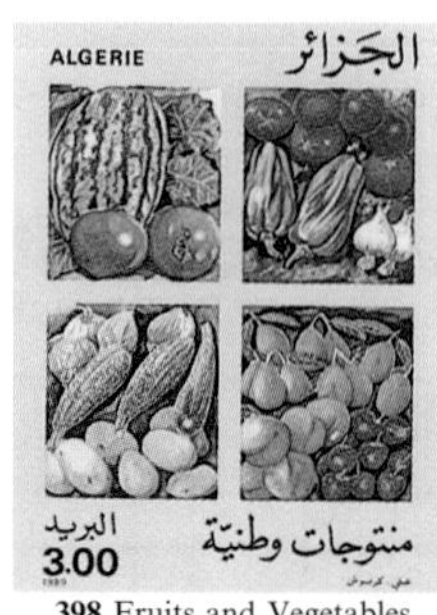

398 Fruits and Vegetables

1989. National Production.
1018 **398** 2d. multicoloured . . . 55 35
1019 – 3d. multicoloured . . . 85 50
1020 – 5d. multicoloured . . . 1·40 85
DESIGNS: 3, 5d. Various fruits and vegetables.

399 Atlantic Bonito

400 "35" and Soldier with Rifle

1989. Fishes. Multicoloured.
1021 1d. Type **399** 45 15
1022 1d.80 John dory 95 30
1023 2d.90 Red seabream . . . . 1·40 45
1024 3d.30 Swordfish . . . . . . 1·60 55

1989. 35th Anniv of Revolution.
1025 **400** 1d. multicoloured . . . 30 10

401 Bank Emblem Cogwheel, Factory and Wheat

402 Satan's Mushroom

1989. 25th Anniv of African Development Bank.
1026 **401** 1d. multicoloured . . . 30 15

1989. Fungi. Multicoloured.
1027 1d. Type **402** 60 20
1028 1d.80 Yellow stainer . . . . 1·10 40
1029 2d.90 Parasol mushroom . . 1·75 60
1030 3d.30 Saffron milk cap . . . 1·90 70

403 Emblem

404 Sun, Arm and Face

1990. 10th Anniv of Pan-African Postal Union.
1031 **403** 1d. multicoloured . . . 30 15

1990. Rational Use of Energy.
1032 **404** 1d. multicoloured . . . 30 15

405 Emblem **406** Ceramics

1990. African Nations Cup Football Championship.
1033 **405** 3d. multicoloured . . . 85 40

1990. Industries. Multicoloured.
1034 2d. Type **406** 55 30
1035 2d.90 Car maintenance . . . 85 35
1036 3d.30 Fishing . . . . 1·75 45

407 Pictogram and Olympic Rings **408** Pylons on Map

1990. World Cup Football Championship, Italy. Multicoloured.
1037 2d.90 Type **407** 85 35
1038 5d. Trophy, ball and flag . . 1·40 65

1990. Rural Electrification.
1039 **408** 2d. multicoloured . . . 55 20

409 Young Workers **410** Members Flags

1990. Youth. Multicoloured.
1040 2d. Type **409** 55 20
1041 3d. Youth in crowd (vert) 85 30

1990. Arab Maghreb Union Summit Conference.
1042 **410** 1d. multicoloured . . . 30 15

411 Anniversary Emblem

1990. 30th Anniv of O.P.E.C.
1043 **411** 2d. multicoloured . . . 50 20

412 House and Hand holding Coin **413** Flag, Rifle and Hands with Broken Manacles

1990. Savings Day.
1044 **412** 1d. multicoloured . . . 20 10

1990. Namibian Independence.
1045 **413** 3d. multicoloured . . . 60 15

414 Duck **415** Dome of the Rock and Palestinians

1990. Domestic Animals. Multicoloured.
1046 1d. Type **414** 20 10
1047 2d. Hare (horiz) 45 20
1048 2d.90 Common turkey . . . 65 35
1049 3d.30 Red junglefowl (horiz) 90 55

1990. Palestinian "Intifada" Movement.
1050 **415** 1d.+30c. mult 35 20

416 Crowd with Banners **417** Families in Countryside

1990. 30th Anniv of 11 December 1960 Demonstration.
1051 **416** 1d. multicoloured . . . 20 10

1990. Campaign against Respiratory Diseases.
1052 **417** 1d. multicoloured . . . 20 10

418 Sunburst, Torch and Open Book **419** Bejaia

1991. 2nd Anniv of Constitution.
1053 **418** 1d. multicoloured . . . 20 10

1991. Views of Algeria before 1830 (6th series). As T **310**.
1054 1d.50 red 35 10
1055 4d.20 green 90 35
DESIGNS: 1d.50, Kolea; 4d.20, Constantine.

1991. Air. Multicoloured.
1056 10d. Type **419** . . . . . . 1·90 85
1057 20d. Annaba . . . . 4·00 1·90

420 "Jasminum fruticans" **421** "Trip to the Country" (Mehdi Medrar)

1991. Flowers. Multicoloured.
1058 2d. Type **420** 45 20
1059 4d. "Dianthus crinitus" . . 90 35
1060 5d. "Cyclamen africanum" 1·10 55

1991. Children's Drawings. Multicoloured.
1061 3d. Type **421** . . . . 3·50 1·75
1062 4d. "Children playing" (Ouidad Bounab) 90 35

422 Emblem

1991. 3rd Anniv of Arab Maghreb Union Summit Conference, Zeralda.
1063 **422** 1d. multicoloured . . . 20 10

423 Figures and Emblem

1991. 40th Anniv of Geneva Convention on Status of Refugees.
1064 **423** 3d. multicoloured . . . 65 20

424 Coded Letter and Target

1991. World Post Day (1065) and "Telecom 91" International Telecommunications Exhibition, Geneva (1066). Multicoloured.
1065 1d.50 Type **424** 35 15
1066 4d.20 Exhibition and I.T.U. emblems (vert) 95 35

425 Spanish Festoon

1991. Butterflies. Multicoloured.
1067 2d. Type **425** 20 15
1068 4d. "Melitaea didyma" . . . 45 30
1069 6d. Red admiral 65 45
1070 7d. Large tortoiseshell . . . 90 65

426 Chest Ornament **427** Woman

1991. Silver Jewellery from South Algeria. Mult.
1071 3d. Necklaces 35 20
1072 4d. Type **426** 45 30
1073 5d. Enamelled ornament . . 55 45
1074 7d. Bangles (horiz) 90 70

1992. Views of Algeria before 1830. As previous issues and new values. Size 30½ × 21 mm.
1075 5c. purple 10 10
1076 10c. blue 10 10
1077 20c. blue 10 10
1078 30c. red and black 20 10
1079 50c. brown 10 10
1080 70c. lilac 10 10
1081 80c. brown 10 10
1082 1d. brown 10 10
1083 2d. blue 10 10
1084 3d. green 20 10
1085 4d. red 25 10
1086 6d.20 blue 70 20
1087 7d.50 red 85 20
DESIGNS: 5c., 6d.20, As No. 873; 10c., 7d.50, As No. 859; 20c. As No. 1000; 30c. As No. 1001; 50c. As No. 882; 70c. As No. 875; 80c. Type **310**; 1d. As No. 860; 2d. As No. 861; 3d. As No. 817; 4d. As No. 1055.

1992. International Women's Day.
1095 **427** 1d.50 multicoloured . . 20 10

428 Dorcas Gazelle **429** Algiers

1992. Gazelles. Multicoloured.
1096 1d.50 Type **428** 15 10
1097 6d.20 Edmi gazelle 70 45
1098 8d.60 Addra gazelle 95 55

1992.
1099 **429** 1d.50 brown & lt brown 15 10
1132 2d. blue 10 10
1147 3d. blue 10 10

430 Runners **431** Doves and Flags

1992. Olympic Games, Barcelona.
1100 **430** 6d.20 multicoloured . . 70 30

1992. 30th Anniv of Independence.
1101 **431** 5d. green, red and black 55 20

432 "Ajuga iva" **433** Computerized Post Office Equipment

1992. Medicinal Plants. Multicoloured.
1102 1d.50 Type **432** 15 10
1103 5d.10 Buckthorn 55 30
1104 6d.20 Milk thistle 70 35
1105 8d.60 French lavender . . . 1·00 50

1992. World Post Day. Modernization of Postal Service.
1106 **433** 1d.50 multicoloured . . 15 10

434 Boudiaf

1992. Mohammed Boudiaf (chairman of Committee of State) Commemoration.
1107 **434** 2d. multicoloured . . . 20 15
1108 8d.60 multicoloured . . 95 55

435 2nd-century B.C. Numidian Coin

1992. Coinage. Multicoloured.
1109 1d.50 Type **435** 15 10
1110 2d. 14th-century Zianide dinar 20 15
1111 5d.10 11th-century Almoravid dinar 55 20
1112 6d.20 19th-century Emir Abd-el-Kader coin . . . 70 35

436 Short-snouted Seahorse **437** Algiers Door Knocker

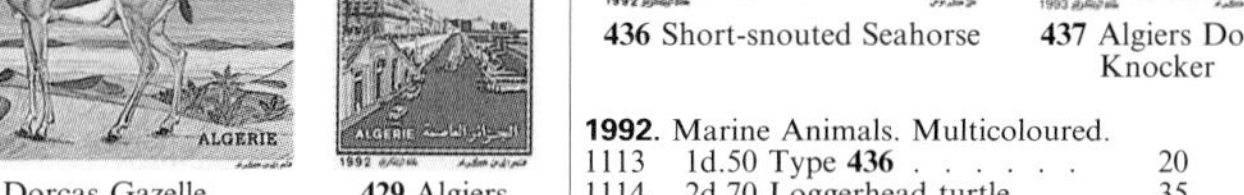

1992. Marine Animals. Multicoloured.
1113 1d.50 Type **436** 20 10
1114 2d.70 Loggerhead turtle . . 35 15

1115 6d.20 Mediterranean moray . . . 90 35
1116 7d.50 Lobster 85 50

1993. Door Knockers. Multicoloured.
1117 2d. Type **437** 10 10
1118 5d.60 Constantine 30 15
1119 8d.60 Tlemcen 50 25

438 Medlar Blossom

1993. Fruit-tree Blossom. Multicoloured.
1120 4d.50 Type **438** 25 10
1121 8d.60 Quince (vert) 50 25
1122 11d. Apricot (vert) 60 30

439 Patrol Boat, Emblem and Flag

440 Grain Storage Jar

1993. 20th Anniv of Coastguard Service.
1123 **439** 2d. multicoloured . . . 20 10

1993. Traditional Utensils. Multicoloured.
1124 2d. Type **440** 10 10
1125 5d.60 Grindstone 30 15
1126 8d.60 Oil-press 50 25

441 Mauretanian Royal Mausoleum, Tipaza

442 Jijelienne Coast

1993. Mausoleums. Multicoloured.
1127 8d.60 Type **441** 50 25
1128 12d. Royal Mausoleum, El Khroub 65 30

1993. Air.
1129 **442** 50d. green, brown & blue . . . . 2·75 1·25

443 Annaba

444 Chameleon

1993. Ports. Multicoloured.
1130 2d. Type **443** 15 10
1131 8d.60 Arzew 95 25

1993. Reptiles. Multicoloured.
1133 2d. Type **444** 10 10
1134 8d.60 Desert monitor (horiz) 50 25

445 Tipaza

446 Map, Processing Plant and Uses of Hydrocarbons

1993. Tourism. Multicoloured.
1135 2d. Type **445** 10 10
1136 8d.60 Kerzaz 25 10

1993. 30th Anniv of Sonatrach (National Society for Transformation and Commercialization of Hydrocarbons).
1137 **446** 2d. multicoloured . . . 10 10

447 Dove, Flag and "18"

448 Crown of Statue of Liberty, Football, U.S. Flag and Trophy

1994. National Chahid Day.
1138 **447** 2d. multicoloured . . . 10 10

1994. World Cup Football Championship, U.S.A.
1139 **448** 8d.60 multicoloured . . 25 10

449 Monkey Orchid

450 Hoggar Script on Stone

1994. Orchids. Multicoloured.
1140 5d.60 Type **449** 15 10
1141 8d.60 "Orphrys lutea" . . . 25 10
1142 11d. Bee orchid 35 15

1994. Ancient Communication. Multicoloured.
1143 3d. Type **450** 10 10
1144 10d. Abizar stele 30 15

451 Flags and Olympic Rings

452 Figures and City on Globe

1994. Cent of International Olympic Committee.
1145 **451** 12d. multicoloured . . . 35 15

1994. World Population Day.
1146 **452** 3d. multicoloured . . . 10 10

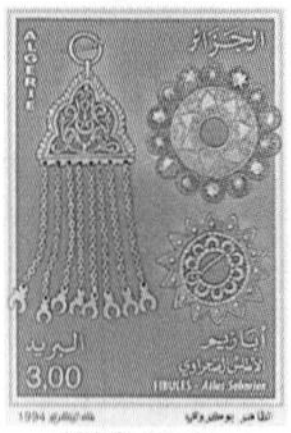

453 Sandstone

454 Brooches

1994. Minerals. Multicoloured.
1148 3d. Type **453** 10 10
1149 5d. Cipolin 15 10
1150 10d. Turitella shells in chalk 25 15

1994. Saharan Silver Jewellery. Multicoloured.
1151 3d. Type **454** 10 10
1152 5d. Belt (horiz) 15 10
1153 12d. Bracelets (horiz) . . . 30 15

455 Soldiers

456 Ladybirds on Leaves

1994. 40th Anniv of Revolution.
1154 **455** 3d. multicoloured . . . 10 10

1994. Insects. Multicoloured.
1155 3d. Type **456** 10 10
1156 12d. Beetle ("Buprestidae") on plant 30 15

457 Virus and Family

1994. World Anti-AIDS Campaign Day.
1157 **457** 3d. black, blue & mauve 10 10

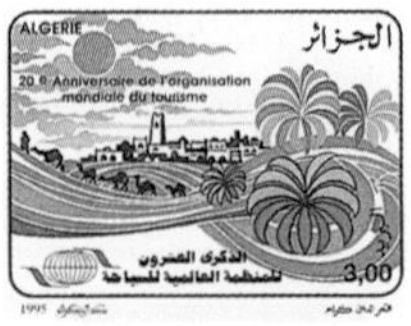

458 Algiers

459 Southern Algeria

1994. Regional Dances. Multicoloured.
1158 3d. Type **458** 10 10
1159 10d. Constantine 25 15
1160 12d. Alaoui 30 15

1995. 20th Anniv of World Tourism Organization.
1161 **459** 3d. multicoloured . . . 10 10

460 Honey Bee on Comb

461 Dahlia

1995. Bee-keeping. Multicoloured.
1162 3d. Type **460** 10 10
1163 13d. Bee on flower (horiz) 35 20

1995. Flowers. Multicoloured.
1164 3d. Type **461** 10 10
1165 10d. Zinnias 25 15
1166 13d. Lilac 35 20

462 Circular Design

463 Doves, Graves, Victims and Soldiers

1995. Stucco Work from Sedrata (4th century after Hegira).
1167 **462** 3d. brown 10 10
1168 – 4d. green 10 10
1169 – 5d. brown 15 10
DESIGNS—4d. Circular design within square; 5d. Stylized flowers.

1995. 50th Anniv of End of Second World War. Multicoloured.
1170 **463** 3d. multicoloured . . . 10 10

464 Water Pollution

465 Players and Anniversary Emblem

1995. Environmental Protection. Multicoloured.
1172 3d. Type **464** 10 10
1173 13d. Air pollution 35 20

1995. Centenary of Volleyball.
1174 **465** 3d. multicoloured . . . 10 10

466 Map and Pylon

467 Children and Schoolbag Contents

1995. Electrification.
1175 **466** 3d. multicoloured . . . 10 10

1995. National Solidarity.
1176 **467** 3d.+50c. mult 10 10

468 Doves and Anniversary Emblem

469 Pitcher from Lakhdaria

1995. 50th Anniv of U.N.O.
1177 **468** 13d. multicoloured . . . 30 15

1995. Traditional Pottery.
1178 **469** 10d. brown 20 10
1179 – 20d. brown 45 25
1180 – 21d. brown 45 25
1181 – 30d. brown 65 35
DESIGNS: 20d. Water jug (Aokas); 21d. Jar (Larbaa nath Iraten); 30d. Jar (Ouadhia).

470 Common Shelduck

1995. Water Birds. Multicoloured.
1182 3d. Type **470** 10 10
1183 5d. Common snipe 10 10

471 Doves flying over Javelin Thrower and Olympic Rings

1996. Centenary of Modern Olympic Games and Olympic Games, Atlanta.
1184 **471** 20d. multicoloured . . . 45 25

472 Fringed Bag

473 Pasteur Institute

1996. Handicrafts. Leather Bags. Multicoloured.
1185 5d. Type **472** 10 10
1186 16d. Shoulder bag with handle (vert) 35 20

1996. Centenary (1994) of Algerian Pasteur Institute.
1187 **473** 5d. multicoloured . . . 10 10

474 Arabic Script and Computer

1996. Scientific and Technical Education Day. Multicoloured.
1188 5d. Type **474** 10 10
1189 16d. Dove, fountain pen and symbols (vert) 35 20
1190 23d. Pencil, pen, dividers and satellite over Earth on pages of open book (vert) 50 25

475 Iron Ore, Djebel Quenza

1996. Minerals. Multicoloured.
1191 10d. Type **475** 20 10
1192 20d. Gold, Tirek-Amesmessa 45 25

476 "Pandoriana pandora"

1996. Butterflies. Multicoloured.
1193 5d. Type **476** 10 10
1194 10d. "Coenonympha pamphilus" 20 10
1195 20d. Painted lady 45 25
1196 23d. Marbled white 50 25

477 Globe, Drug Addict and Drugs

1996. World Anti-drugs Day.
1197 **477** 5d. multicoloured . . . 10 10

478 "Woman with Pigeons"

1996. Paintings by Ismail Samsom. Multicoloured.
1198 20d. Type **478** 40 20
1199 30d. "Interrogation" 60 30

479 Ambulance and Paramedic holding Child (Medical Aid)

480 Children, Syringe and Pens

1996. Civil Defence. Multicoloured.
1200 5d. Type **479** 10 10
1201 23d. Globe resting in cupped hands (natural disaster prevention) (vert) 45 25

1996. 50th Anniv of U.N.I.C.E.F. Multicoloured.
1202 5d. Type **480** 10 10
1203 10d. Family holding pencil, key, syringe and flower 20 10

481 Dar Hassan Pacha

482 Minbar Inscription, Nedroma Mosque

1996. Algiers Courtyards. Multicoloured.
1204 5d. Type **481** 10 10
1205 10d. Dar Kedaoudj el Amia 20 10
1206 20d. Palais des Rais 40 20
1207 30d. Villa Abdellatif 60 30

1997. Mosque Carvings. Multicoloured.
1208 5d. Type **482** 10 10
1209 23d. Doors, Ketchaoua Mosque, Algiers 45 25

483 Outline Map, Graph and Roofs over People

484 Soldiers controlling Crowd with Flags

1997. 4th General Population and Housing Census.
1210 **483** 5d. multicoloured . . . 10 10

1997. 35th Anniv of Oargla Protest.
1211 **484** 5d. multicoloured . . . 10 10

485 Doves above Crowd with Flags

1997. 35th Anniv of Victory Day.
1212 **485** 5d. multicoloured . . . 10 10

486 "Ficaria verna"

1997. Flowers. Multicoloured.
1213 5d. Type **486** 10 10
1214 16d. Honeysuckle 35 20
1215 23d. Common poppy . . . 45 25

487 "No Smoking" Sign on Map

488 Crowd and Map

1997. World No Smoking Day.
1216 **487** 5d. multicoloured . . . 10 10

1997. Legislative Elections.
1217 **488** 5d. multicoloured . . . 10 10

489 "Buthus occitanus"

1997. Scorpions. Multicoloured.
1218 5d. Type **489** 10 10
1219 10d. "Androctonus australis" 20 10

490 Crowd with Flags

1997. 35th Anniv of Independence.
1220 **490** 5d. multicoloured . . . 10 10

491 Zakaria

1997. 20th Death Anniv of Moufdi Zakaria (poet).
1222 **491** 5d. multicoloured . . . 10 10

492 Dokkali Design, Tidikelt

1997. Textiles. Multicoloured.
1223 3d. Type **492** 10 10
1224 5d. Tellis design, Aures . . 10 10
1225 10d. Bou Taleb design, M'Sila 20 10
1226 20d. Ddil design, Ait-Hichem 40 20

493 Map, Emblem and Rainbow

1997. 25th Anniv of Pan-Arab Security Forces Organization.
1227 **493** 5d. multicoloured . . . 10 10

494 Packages and Express Mail Service Emblem

1997. World Post Day.
1228 **494** 5d. multicoloured . . . 10 10

495 Rising Sun on Map

1997. Local Elections.
1229 **495** 5d. multicoloured . . . 10 10

496 Tenes Lighthouse

1997. Lighthouses. Multicoloured.
1230 5d. Type **496** 10 10
1231 10d. Cap Caxine, Algiers (vert) 20 10

497 Mail Plane and Mail Van

1997. 1st Anniv of Aeropostale.
1232 **497** 5d. multicoloured . . . 10 10

498 Variable Scallop

1997. Sea Shells. Multicoloured.
1233 5d. Type **498** 10 10
1234 10d. "Bolinus brandaris" . . 20 10
1235 20d. "Hinia reticulata" (vert) 40 20

499 National Flag and Columned Facade

500 Flag, Ballot Box, Constitution and People

1997. Inauguration of Council of the Nation (upper parliamentary chamber).
1236 **499** 5d. multicoloured . . . 10 10

1997. Completion of Government Reform. Mult.
1237 5d. Type **500** (presidential election) 10 10
1238 5d. Constitution and torch (constitution referendum) 10 10
1239 5d. Ballot box and voting papers (elections to National Assembly (lower chamber of Parliament)) 10 10
1240 5d. Flag, sun and rose (local elections) 10 10
1241 5d. Flag and Parliament (elections to National Council (upper chamber)) 10 10

Nos. 1237/41 were issued together, se-tenant, forming a composite design.

501 Exhibition Emblem

1998. "Expo '98" World's Fair, Lisbon.
1242 **501** 5d. multicoloured . . . 10 10

502 Aerial Bombardment

1998. 40th Anniv of Bombing of Sakiet Sidi Youcef.
1244 **502** 5d. multicoloured . . . 10 10

503 Archives Building

1998. National Archives.
1245 **503** 5d. multicoloured . . . 10 10

504 Lalla Fadhma N'Soumeur

1998. International Women's Day.
1246 **504** 5d. multicoloured . . . 10 10

505 Players and Eiffel Tower **506** View from Land

1998. World Cup Football Championship, France.
1247 **505** 24d. multicoloured . . . 50 25

1998. Algiers Kasbah. Multicoloured.
1248 5d. Type **506** 10 10
1249 10d. Street 20 10
1250 24d. View from sea (horiz) 50 25

507 Crescent and Flag

1998. Red Crescent.
1251 **507** 5d.+1d. red, green and black 10 10

508 Battle Scene

1998. 150th Anniv of Insurrection of the Zaatcha.
1252 **508** 5d. multicoloured . . . 10 10

509 Parent and Child and Hand holding Rose **510** "Tourism and the Environment"

1998. International Children's Day. National Solidarity. Multicoloured.
1253 5d.+1d. Type **509** 10 10
1254 5d.+1d. Children encircling emblem (horiz) 10 10

1998. Tourism. Multicoloured.
1255 5d. Type **510** 10 10
1256 10d. Young tourists and methods of transportation (horiz) 10 10
1257 24d. Taghit (horiz) 50 25

511 Map of North Africa and Arabia

1998. Arab Post Day.
1258 **511** 5d. multicoloured . . . 10 10

512 Interpol and Algerian Police Force Emblems

1998. 75th Anniv of Interpol.
1259 **512** 5d. multicoloured . . . 10 10

513 Provisional Government and State Flag

1998. 40th Anniv of Creation of Provisional Government of Algerian Republic.
1260 **513** 5d. multicoloured . . . 10 10

514 Arrows leading from Algeria around the World

1998. National Diplomacy Day.
1261 **514** 5d. multicoloured . . . 10 10

515 Dove and Olympic Rings

1998. 35th Anniv of Algerian Olympic Committee.
1262 **515** 5d. multicoloured . . . 10 10

516 Osprey

1998. Birds. Multicoloured.
1263 5d. Type **516** 10 10
1264 10d. Audouin's gull 20 10
1265 24d. Shag (vert) 45 25
1266 30d. Common cormorant (vert) 55 30

517 Anniversary Emblem and Profiles **518** Comb

1998. 50th Anniv of Universal Declaration of Human Rights. Multicoloured.
1267 5d. Type **517** 10 10
1268 24d. Anniversary emblem, dove and people 45 25

1999. Spinning and Weaving Implements. Mult.
1269 5d. Type **518** 10 10
1270 10d. Carding (horiz) 20 10
1271 20d. Spindle 35 20
1272 24d. Loom 45 25

519 Dove, Torch, Flag and Soldiers

1999. National Chahid Day.
1273 **519** 5d. multicoloured . . . 10 10

520 Pear

1999. Fruit Trees. Multicoloured.
1274 5d. Type **520** 10 10
1275 10d. Plum 20 10
1276 24d. Orange (vert) 45 25

521 Calligraphy **522** 14th-century Ceramic Mosaic, Tlemcen

1999. Presidential Election.
1277 **521** 5d. multicoloured . . . 10 10

1999. Crafts. Multicoloured.
1278 5d. Type **522** 10 10
1279 10d. 11th-century ceramic mosaic, Kalaa des Beni Hammad 20 10
1280 20d. Cradle (horiz) 35 20
1281 24d. Table with raised rim (horiz) 45 25

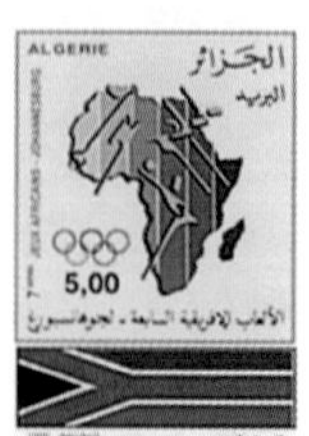
523 Pictograms on Map of Africa and South African Flag **524** Gneiss

1999. 7th African Games, Johannesburg. Mult.
1282 5d. Type **523** 10 10
1283 10d. Pictograms of athletes and South African flag (horiz) 20 10

1999. Minerals. Multicoloured.
1284 5d. Type **524** 10 10
1285 20d. Granite 35 20
1286 24d. Sericite schist 45 25

525 Emblem **526** Family and Map of Africa

1999. Organization of African Unity Summit, Algiers.
1287 **525** 5d. multicoloured . . . 10 10

1999. 40th Anniv of Organization of African Unity Convention on Refugees.
1288 **526** 5d. multicoloured . . . 10 10

527 Emblem and Police Officers

1999. Police Day.
1289 **527** 5d. multicoloured . . . 10 10

528 Linked Hands and "2000"

1999. International Year of Culture and Peace.
1290 **528** 5d. multicoloured . . . 10 10

529 Dentex Seabream

1999. Fishes. Multicoloured.
1291 5d. Type **529** 10 10
1292 10d. Striped red mullet . . . 15 10
1293 20d. Pink dentex 35 20
1294 24d. White seabream . . . 40 20

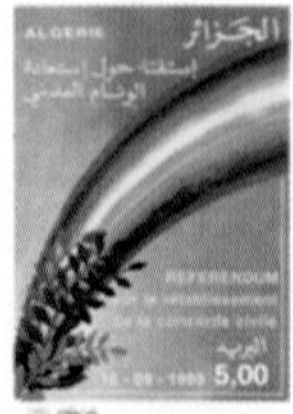
530 Rainbow

1999. Referendum.
1295 **530** 5d. multicoloured . . . 10 10

531 Emblem and Rainbow

1999. 125th Anniv of Universal Postal Union. Mult.
1296 5d. Type **531** 10 10
1297 5d. Globe, satellite and stamps 10 10

532 Woman's Face

1999. Rural Women's Day.
1298 **532** 5d. multicoloured . . . 10 10

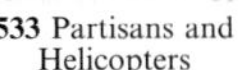

533 Partisans and Helicopters **534** Chaoui

1999. 45th Anniv of Revolution. Multicoloured.
1299 5d. Type **533** 10 10
1300 5d. Partisans and fires . . . 10 10
Nos. 1299/300 were issued together, se-tenant, forming a composite design.

1999. Folk Dances. Multicoloured.
1301 5d. Type **534** 10 10
1302 10d. Targuie 15 10
1303 24d. M'zab 40 20

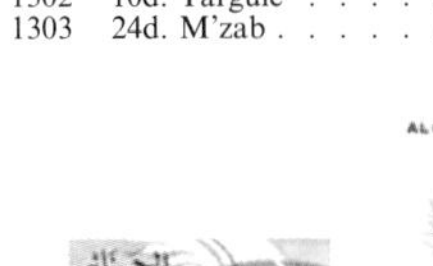

535 Doves **536** Chaffinches

2000. New Millennium. Mult. Self-adhesive.
1304 5d. Type **535** (peace) . . . 10 10
1305 5d. Plants and tree (environment) 10 10
1306 5d. Umbrella over ears of grain (food security) . . . 10 10
1307 5d. Wind farm (new energy sources) 10 10
1308 5d. Globe and ballot box (democracy) 10 10
1309 5d. Microscope (health) . . 10 10
1310 5d. Cargo ship at quayside (commerce) 10 10
1311 5d. Space satellite, dish aerial, jet plane and train (communications) 10 10
1312 5d. Astronaut and lunar buggy on Moon (space) 10 10
1313 5d. Film cave paintings, mandolin and music notes (culture) 10 10
1314 5d. Outline of dove (peace) 10 10
1315 5d. Hand above flora and fauna (environment) . . . 10 10
1316 5d. Space satellites, computer and printed circuits forming maps of Europe and Africa (communications) 10 10
1317 5d. Sun, clouds, flame and water (new energy sources) 10 10
1318 5d. Hand holding seedling (food security) 10 10
1319 5d. Staff of Aesculapius and heart (health) 10 10
1320 5d. Arrows around globe (communication) 10 10
1321 5d. Cave paintings, book, painting and violin (culture) 10 10
1322 5d. Parthenon and envelopes (democracy) 10 10
1323 5d. Space satellite, solar system, space shuttle and astronaut (space) 10 10

2000. Birds. Multicoloured.
1324 5d. Type **536** 10 10
1325 5d. Northern serin (horiz) 10 10
1326 10d. Northern bullfinch (horiz) 15 10
1327 24d. Eurasian goldfinch . . 40 20

537 Emblem

2000. "EXPO 2000" World's Fair, Hanover.
1328 **537** 5d. multicoloured . . . 10 10

538 Sydney Opera House and Sports Pictograms

2000. Olympic Games, Sydney.
1329 **538** 24d. multicoloured . . . 40 20

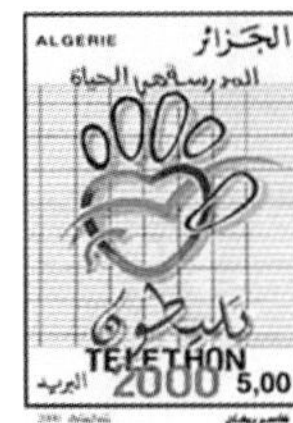

539 Emblem **540** Crowd, Linked Hands and White Doves

2000. Telethon 2000 (fundraising event).
1330 **539** 5d. multicoloured . . . 10 10

2000. "Concorde Civile". Multicoloured.
1331 5d. Type **540** 10 10
1332 10d. Hands releasing doves (horiz) 15 10
1333 20d. Flag, doves and hands forming heart (horiz) . . 35 20
1334 24d. Doves and clasped hands above flowers . . . 40 20

541 Building

2000. National Library.
1335 **541** 5d. multicoloured . . . 10 10

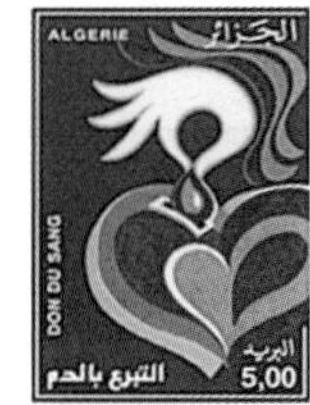

542 Hand holding Blood Droplet

2000. Blood Donation Campaign.
1336 **542** 5d. multicoloured . . . 10 10

543 Lock

2000. Touareg Cultural Heritage. Multicoloured.
1337 5d. Type **543** 10 10
1338 10d. Lock (vert) 20 10

544 Mohamed Racim (artist)

2000. Personalities. Multicoloured.
1339 10d. Type **544** 20 10
1340 10d. Mohammed Dib (writer) 20 10
1341 10d. Mustapha Kateb (theatre director) 20 10
1342 10d. Ali Maachi (musician) 20 10

545 Cock-chafer **546** Jug

2000. Insects. Multicoloured.
1343 5d. Type **545** 10 10
1344 5d. Carpet beetle 10 10
1345 10d. Drugstore beetle . . . 20 10
1346 24d. Carabus 45 25

2000. Roman Artefacts, Tipasa. Multicoloured.
1347 5d. Type **546** 10 10
1348 10d. Vase 20 10
1349 24d. Jug 45 25

547 *Limodorum abortivum*

2000. Orchids. Multicoloured.
1350 5d. Type **547** 10 10
1351 10d. *Orchis papilionacea* . . 20 10
1352 24d. *Orchis provincialis* . . . 45 25

548 Greylag Goose (*Anser anser*)

2001. Waterfowl. Multicoloured.
1353 5d. Type **548** 10 10
1354 5d. Avocet (*Recurvirostra avosetta*) (vert) 10 10
1355 10d. Eurasian bittern (*Botaurus stellaris*) (vert) 20 10
1356 24d. Western curlew (*Numenius arquata*) . . . 45 25

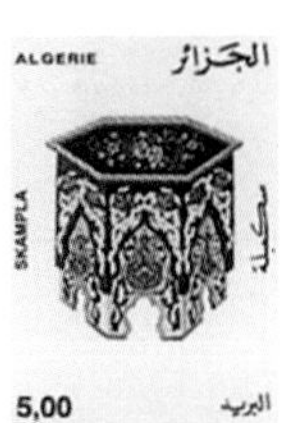
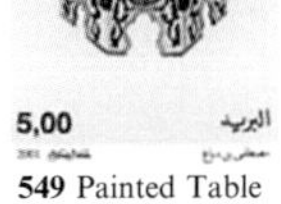

549 Painted Table **550** Forest, Belezma National Park, Batna

2001. Traditional Crafts. Multicoloured.
1357 5d. Type **549** 10 10
1358 10d. Decorated shelf (horiz) 20 10
1359 24d. Ornate mirror 45 25

2001. National Parks. Multicoloured.
1360 5d. Type **550** 10 10
1361 10d. Headland, Gouraya National Park, Bejaia (horiz) 20 10
1362 20d. Forest and mountains, Theneit el Had National Park, Tissemsilt (horiz) 35 20
1363 24d. El Tarf National Park 45 25

551 St. Augustine as Child (statue)

2001. St. Augustine of Hippo Conference, Algiers and Annaba. Multicoloured.
1364 5d. Type **551** 10 10
1365 24d. 4th-century Christian mosaic (43 × 31 mm) . . . 45 25

552 Obverse and Reverse of Ryal Boudjou, 1830

2001. Coins. Multicoloured.
1366 5d. Type **552** 10 10
1367 10d. Obverse and reverse of Double Boudjou, 1826 . . 20 10
1368 24d. Obverse and reverse of Ryal Drahem, 1771 . . . 45 25

553 Emblem and Scouts

2001. National Scouts' Day.
1369 **553** 5d. multicoloured . . . 10 10

554 Child throwing Stones **555** Asthma Sufferer

2001. Intifida.
1370 **554** 5d. multicoloured . . . 10 10

2001. National Asthma Day.
1371 **556** 5d. multicoloured . . . 10 10

556 Hopscotch

2001. Children's Games. Multicoloured.
1372 5d. Type **556** 10 10
1373 5d. Jacks 10 10
1374 5d. Spinning top 10 10
1375 5d. Marbles 10 10

557 Runners

2001. 50th Anniv of Mediterranean Games. Multicoloured.
1376 5d. Type **557** 10 10
1377 5d. Race winners and tile decoration 10 10

558 Emblem **559** Burning Lorry

2001. 15th World Festival of Youth and Students, Algiers.
1378 **558** 5d. multicoloured . . . 10 10

2001. Freedom Fighters' Day.
1379 **559** 5d. multicoloured . . . 10 10

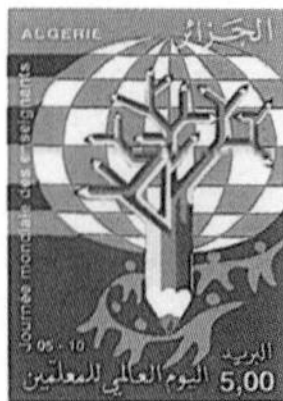

560 Tree of Pencils

561 Children encircling Globe

2001. Teacher's Day.

1380	**560**	5d. multicoloured	10	10

2001. United Nations Year of Dialogue among Civilisations.

1381	**561**	5d. multicoloured	10	10

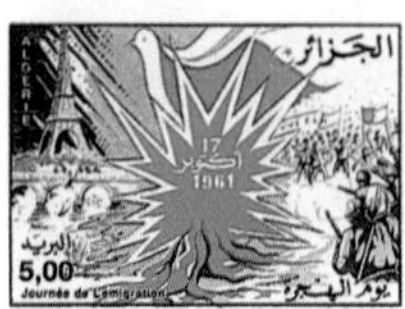

562 Dove and Explosion

2001. National Immigration Day. 40th Anniv of Demonstrations in Paris.

1382	**562**	5d. multicoloured	10	10

563 El Mokrani

564 Bab el Oued (flood damaged town)

2001. Resistance Fighters. Multicoloured.

1383		5d. Type **563**	10	10
1384		5d. Cheikh Bouamama	10	10

2001. Flood Victims Relief Fund.

1385	**564**	5d.+5d. multicoloured	15	10

POSTAGE DUE STAMPS

1926. As Postage Due stamps of France, but inscr "ALGERIE".

D 34	D **11**	5c. blue	10	2·75
D 35		10c. brown	10	95
D 36		20c. olive	85	2·75
D 37		25c. red	95	3·25
D 38		30c. red	10	20
D 39		45c. green	2·00	3·25
D 40		50c. purple	10	20
D 41		60c. green	2·00	4·50
D 42		1f. red on yellow	40	90
D249		1f.50 lilac	1·75	3·00
D 43		2f. mauve	35	1·10
D250		2f. blue	2·50	3·00
D 44		3f. blue	50	1·25
D251		5f. red	1·75	3·00
D252		5f. green	3·00	3·00

1926. As Postage Due stamps of France, but inscr "ALGERIE".

D45	D **19**	1c. olive	20	2·75
D46		10c. violet	85	1·25
D47		30c. bistre	70	30
D48		60c. red	1·10	25
D49		1f. violet	7·75	2·10
D50		2f. blue	10·50	2·50

1927. Nos. D36, D39 and D37 surch.

D92	D **11**	60 on 20c. olive	1·25	45
D93		2f. on 45c. green	1·90	4·25
D94		3f. on 25c. red	1·10	3·50

1927. Nos. D45/8 surch.

D95	D **19**	10c. on 30c. bistre	3·25	6·50
D96		1f. on 1c. olive	1·50	2·50
D97		1f. on 60c. red	18·00	15
D98		2f. on 10c. violet	7·25	23·00

1942. As 1926 issue, but without "RF".

D181	D **11**	30c. red	1·90	2·75
D182		2f. mauve	2·25	2·75

1944. No. 208 surch **TAXE P. C. V. DOUANE 20Fr.**

D230	**38**	20f. on 50f. red	2·00	3·00

1944. Surch **T 0.50**.

D231	**4**	50c. on 20c. green	1·10	2·75

1947. Postage Due Stamps of France optd **ALGERIE**.

D283		10c. brown (No. D985)	10	3·00
D284		30c. purple (No. D986)	10	2·50

D 53

1947.

D285	D **53**	20c. red	20	3·00
D286		60c. blue	45	2·75
D287		1f. brown	10	2·75
D288		1f.50 olive	1·00	3·50
D289		2f. red	20	2·25
D290		3f. violet	40	2·50
D291		5f. blue	35	1·00
D292		6f. black	40	1·75
D293		10f. purple	1·10	80
D294		15f. myrtle	2·00	3·25
D295		20f. green	1·40	95
D296		30f. red	3·00	3·25
D297		50f. black	3·75	4·00
D298		100f. blue	14·50	10·50

INDEPENDENT STATE

1962. Postage Due stamps of France optd **EA** and with bar obliterating "REPUBLIQUE FRANCAISE".

D391	D **457**	5c. mauve	11·00	11·00
D392		10c. red	11·00	11·00
D393		20c. brown	11·00	11·00
D394		50c. green	22·00	22·00
D395		1f. green	45·00	45·00

The above also exist with larger overprint applied with handstamps.

D 107 Scales of Justice

D 200 Ears of Corn

1963.

D411	D **107**	5c. red and olive	10	10
D412		10c. olive and red	10	10
D413		20c. blue and black	35	20
D414		50c. brown and green	80	55
D415		1f. violet and orange	1·40	1·25

1968. No. D415 surch.

D508	D **107**	60c. on 1f. violet and orange	55	40

1972.

D603	D **200**	10c. brown	10	10
D604		20c. brown	10	10
D605		40c. orange	20	10
D606		50c. blue	20	10
D607		80c. brown	45	20
D608		1d. green	55	35
D609		2d. blue	1·10	65
D610		3d. violet	15	10
D611		4d. purple	20	10

ALLENSTEIN Pt. 7

A district of E. Prussia retained by Germany as the result of a plebiscite in 1920. Stamps issued during the plebiscite period.

100 pfennig = 1 mark.

1920. Stamps of Germany inscr "DEUTSCHES REICH" optd **PLEBISCITE OLSZTYN ALLENSTEIN**.

1	**17**	5pf. green	15	15
2		10pf. red	15	15
3	**24**	15pf. violet	15	15
4		15pf. purple	7·00	7·75
5	**17**	20pf. blue	15	15
6		30pf. black & orge on buff	30	35
7		40pf. black and red	20	20
8		50pf. black & pur on buff	20	20
9		75pf. black and green	65	60
10	**18**	1m. red	90	1·10
11		1m.25 green	95	1·00
12		1m.50 brown	1·25	3·00
13b	**20**	2m.50 red	3·25	3·75
14	**21**	3m. black	2·00	2·40

1920. Stamps of Germany inscr "DEUTSCHES REICH" optd **TRAITE DE VERSAILLES** etc. in oval.

15	**17**	5pf. green	35	20
16		10pf. red	35	30
17	**24**	15pf. violet	20	35
18		15pf. purple	28·00	23·00
19	**17**	20pf. blue	35	35
20		30pf. black & orge on buff	40	20
21		40pf. black and red	40	20
22		50pf. black & pur on buff	25	25
23		75pf. black and green	25	25
24	**18**	1m. red	1·10	35
25		1m.25 green	1·10	50
26		1m.50 brown	1·10	50
27	**20**	2m.50 red	1·40	1·90
28	**21**	3m. black	1·40	2·50

ALSACE AND LORRAINE Pt. 7

Stamps used in parts of France occupied by the German army in the war of 1870–71, and afterwards temporarily in the annexed provinces of Alsace and Lorraine.

100 pfennig = 1 mark.

1

1870.

1	**1**	1c. green	42·00	85·00
3		2c. brown	65·00	£100
5		4c. grey	65·00	65·00
8		5c. green	40·00	6·75
10		10c. brown	45·00	10·00
14		20c. blue	55·00	8·00
16		25c. brown	90·00	65·00

For 1940 issues see separate lists for Alsace and Lorraine under German Occupations.

ALWAR Pt. 1

A state of Rajputana, N. India. Now uses Indian stamps.

12 pies = 1 anna; 16 annas = 1 rupee

1 Native Dagger

1877. Roul or perf.

1c	**1**	¼a. blue	3·25	90
5		¼a. green	3·50	2·25
2c		1a. brown	2·25	1·10

ANDORRA Pt. 6; Pt. 9

An independent state in the Pyrenees under the joint suzerainty of France and Spain.

FRENCH POST OFFICES

1931. 100 centimes = 1 franc.
2002. 100 cents = 1 euro.

1931. Stamps of France optd **ANDORRE**.

F 1	**11**	½c. on 1c. grey	45	1·25
F 2		1c. grey	45	75
F 3		2c. red	50	1·40
F 4		3c. orange	55	1·40
F 5		5c. green	1·40	2·10
F 6		10c. lilac	2·75	3·25
F 7	**18**	15c. brown	4·50	5·00
F 8		20c. mauve	7·00	7·00
F 9		25c. brown	7·75	8·00
F10		30c. green	7·00	7·25
F11		40c. blue	9·50	11·50
F12	**15**	45c. violet	15·00	15·00
F13		50c. red	10·50	9·50
F14		65c. green	21·00	23·00
F15		75c. mauve	22·00	24·00
F16	**18**	90c. red	26·00	30·00
F17	**15**	1f. blue	30·00	30·00
F18	**18**	1f.50 blue	35·00	38·00
F19	**13**	2f. red and green	23·00	27·00
F20		3f. mauve and red	75·00	85·00
F21		5f. blue and buff	£100	£130
F22		10f. green and red	£225	£275
F23		20f. mauve and green	£275	£325

F 3 Our Lady's Chapel, Meritxell

F 5 St. Michael's Church, Engolasters

1932.

F24	F **3**	1c. slate	25	95
F25		2c. violet	65	1·10
F26		3c. brown	50	90
F27		5c. green	50	1·00
F28	A	10c. lilac	1·10	1·50
F29	F **3**	15c. red	1·75	1·75
F30	A	20c. mauve	11·50	9·50
F31	F **5**	25c. brown	4·50	5·00
F32	A	25c. brown	9·50	17·00
F33		30c. green	3·25	3·00
F34		40c. blue	8·75	8·25
F35		40c. brown	1·25	1·60
F36		45c. red	10·50	10·50
F37		45c. green	4·25	6·00
F38	F **5**	50c. mauve	10·50	10·50
F39	A	50c. violet	4·25	6·50
F40		50c. green	1·75	3·00
F41		55c. violet	18·00	18·00
F42		60c. brown	1·25	1·75
F43	F **5**	65c. green	40·00	48·00
F44	A	65c. blue	14·00	13·00
F45		70c. red	1·60	2·40
F46	F **5**	75c. violet	8·00	8·50
F47	A	75c. blue	3·25	5·50
F48		80c. green	21·00	23·00
F49	B	80c. green	75	1·25
F50		90c. red	6·00	5·25
F51		90c. green	4·75	5·00
F52		1f. green	17·00	12·50
F53		1f. red	22·00	20·00
F54		1f. blue	60	95
F55		1f. 20 violet	75	1·40
F56	F **3**	1f. 25 mauve	48·00	42·00
F57		1f.25 red	5·00	4·50
F58	B	1f.30 brown	80	1·40
F59	C	1f.50 blue	18·00	17·00
F60	B	1f.50 red	70	1·40
F61		1f.75 violet	95·00	£100
F62		1f.75 blue	40·00	40·00
F63		2f. mauve	9·00	8·75
F64	F **3**	2f. red	1·25	2·40
F65		2f. green	70	1·40
F66		2f.15 violet	48·00	55·00
F67		2f.25 blue	7·50	8·50
F68		2f.40 red	80	1·40
F69		2f.50 black	8·00	9·25
F70		2f.50 blue	1·90	2·75
F71	B	3f. brown	11·50	10·50
F72	F **3**	3f. brown	90	1·40
F73		4f. blue	85	1·40
F74		4f.50 violet	1·40	2·00
F75	C	5f. brown	1·00	1·10
F76		10f. violet	1·25	1·50
F78		15f. blue	90	1·50
F79		20f. red	1·25	1·40
F81	A	50f. blue	2·10	2·40

DESIGNS—HORIZ: A, St. Anthony's Bridge; C, Andorra la Vella. VERT: B, Valley of Sant Julia.

1935. No. F38 surch **20c**.

F82	F **5**	20c. on 50c. purple	13·00	15·00

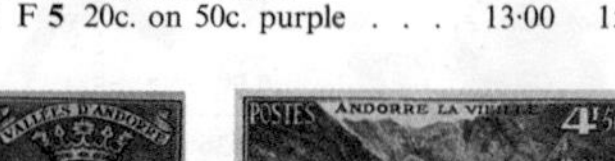

F 9

F 13 Andorra la Vella

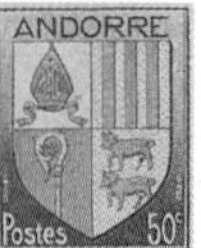

F 10

F 14 Councillor Jaume Bonell

1936.

F83	F **9**	1c. black	20	1·10
F84		2c. blue	20	1·00
F85		3c. brown	30	1·10
F86		5c. red	15	1·00
F87		10c. blue	20	1·25
F88		15c. mauve	2·25	2·40
F89		20c. green	25	1·25
F90		30c. red	45	1·50
F91		30c. black	75	1·25
F92		35c. green	50·00	60·00
F93		40c. brown	70	1·40
F94		50c. green	75	1·40
F95		60c. blue	95	1·40
F96		70c. violet	90	1·40

1944.

F 97	F **10**	10c. violet	10	90
F 98		30c. red	15	85
F 99		40c. blue	25	90
F100		50c. red	10	95
F101		60c. black	20	90
F102		70c. mauve	15	95
F103		80c. green	10	95
F104		1f. blue	60	1·25
F105	D	1f. purple	15	95
F106		1f.20 blue	10	1·10
F107		1f.50 red	10	1·10
F108		2f. green	10	80
F109	E	2f.40 red	10	95
F110		2f.50 red	4·25	2·10
F111		3f. brown	35	75
F112	D	3f. red	4·25	4·25
F113	E	4f. blue	20	1·10
F114		4f. green	80	1·60
F115	D	4f. brown	1·75	3·25
F116	E	4f.50 brown	45	1·00
F117	F **13**	4f.50 blue	5·50	5·75
F118		5f. blue	30	1·40
F119		5f. green	1·00	1·40
F120	E	5f. green	2·40	3·50
F121		5f. violet	7·00	4·50
F122	F **13**	6f. red	35	85
F123		6f. purple	35	1·25
F124	E	6f. green	4·00	3·50
F125	F **13**	8f. blue	1·10	2·10
F126	E	8f. brown	70	1·25
F127	F **13**	10f. green	25	90

F128 10f. blue . . . . 1·25 60
F129 12f. red . . . . 80 2·40
F130 12f. green . . . . . . 95 1·75
F131 F **14** 15f. purple . . . . . . 35 1·25
F132 F **13** 15f. red . . . . 55 1·25
F133 15f. brown . . . . 7·00 2·40
F134 F **14** 18f. blue . . . . 2·40 3·25
F135 F **13** 18f. red . . . . 14·00 14·00
F136 F **14** 20f. blue . . . . 80 1·25
F137 20f. violet . . . . . . 2·40 3·00
F138 25f. red . . . . 2·75 3·50
F139 25f. blue . . . . 1·40 2·10
F140 30f. blue . . . . 21·00 14·00
F141 40f. green . . . . . . 2·75 2·75
F142 50f. brown . . . . . . 1·50 1·75
DESIGNS—HORIZ: D, Church of St. John of Caselles; E, House of the Valleys.

F **15** Chamois and Pyrenees

F **16** Les Escaldes

1950. Air.
F143 F **15** 100f. blue . . . . . . 65·00 60·00

1955.
F144 F **16** 1f. blue (postage) . . . 15 90
F145 2f. green . . . . 30 1·25
F146 3f. red . . . . 35 1·10
F147 5f. brown . . . . . . 40 1·10
F148 – 6f. green . . . . . . 1·00 1·25
F149 – 8f. red . . . . 1·10 1·60
F150 – 10f. violet . . . . . . 1·25 1·40
F151 – 12f. blue . . . . . . 1·75 1·25
F152 – 15f. red . . . . 1·75 1·25
F153 – 18f. blue . . . . . . 1·60 1·75
F154 – 20f. violet . . . . . . 2·00 1·40
F155 – 25f. brown . . . . . . 2·25 2·25
F156 – 30f. blue . . . . 24·00 22·00
F157 – 35f. blue . . . . 8·75 9·00
F158 – 40f. green . . . . . . 32·00 35·00
F159 – 50f. red . . . . 3·50 2·75
F160 – 65f. violet . . . . . . 7·50 9·25
F161 – 70f. brown . . . . . . 5·25 6·25
F162 – 75f. blue . . . . 45·00 48·00

F163 – 100f. green (air) . . . 10·00 7·75
F164 – 200f. red . . . . . . 19·00 14·00
F165 – 500f. blue . . . . . . 90·00 70·00
DESIGNS—VERT: 15f. to 25f. Gothic cross, Andorra la Vella; 100f. to 500f. East Valira River. HORIZ: 6f. to 12f. Santa Coloma Church; 30f. to 75f. Les Bons village.

New currency. 100 (old) francs = 1 (new) franc.

F **21**

F **22** Gothic Cross, Meritxell

1961.
F166 F **21** 1c. grey, blue and slate (postage) . . . 10 60
F167 2c. lt orge, blk & orge 35 60
F168 5c. lt grn, blk & grn 25 60
F169 10c. pink, blk & red 25 20
F170a 12c. yell, pur & grn 1·40 1·25
F171 15c. lt bl, blk & bl . . 40 95
F172 18c. pink, blk & mve 1·10 1·40
F173 20c. lt yell, brn & yell 50 20
F174 F **22** 25c. blue, vio & grn 65 50
F175 30c. pur, red & grn 70 50
F175a 40c. green and brown 90 90
F176 45c. blue, ind & grn 17·00 15·00
F176a 45c. brown, bl & vio 90 1·40
F177 50c. multicoloured . . 1·60 1·40
F177a 60c. brown & chestnut 1·10 1·10
F178 65c. olive, bl & brn 21·00 24·00
F179 85c. multicoloured . . 21·00 22·00
F179a 90c. green, bl & brn 1·25 1·60
F180 1f. blue, brn & turq 1·50 1·50

F181 – 2f. green, red and purple (air) . . . . 1·25 1·10
F182 – 3f. purple, bl & grn 1·75 1·50
F183 – 5f. orange, pur & red 2·75 1·90
F184 – 10f. green and blue . . 5·00 3·50
DESIGNS—As Type F **22**: 60c. to 1f. Engolasters Lake; 2f. to 10f. Incles Valley.

F **23** "Telstar" Satellite and part of Globe

1962. 1st Trans-Atlantic TV Satellite Link.
F185 F **23** 50c. violet and blue . . 1·10 1·75

F **24** "La Sardane" (dance)

1963. Andorran History (1st issue).
F186 F **24** 20c. purple, mve & grn 3·75 4·50
F187 – 50c. red and green . . 6·75 8·25
F188 – 1f. green, blue & brn 12·00 13·50
DESIGNS—LARGER (48½ × 27 mm): 50c. Charlemagne crossing Andorra. (48 × 27 mm): 1f. Foundation of Andorra by Louis le Debonnaire.
See also Nos. F190/1.

F **25** Santa Coloma Church and Grand Palais, Paris

1964. "PHILATEC 1964" International Stamp Exhibition, Paris.
F189 F **25** 25c. green, pur & brn 1·40 1·90

1964. Andorran History (2nd issue). As Nos. F187/8, inscribed "1964".
F190 60c. green, chestnut and brown . . . . 10·50 15·00
F191 1f. blue, sepia and brown 14·00 17·00
DESIGNS (48½ × 27 mm): 60c. "Napoleon re-establishes the Andorran Statute, 1806"; 1f. "Confirmation of the Co-government, 1288".

F **26** Virgin of Santa Coloma

F **27** "Syncom", Morse Key and Pleumeur-Bodou centre

1964. Red Cross Fund.
F192 F **26** 25c. + 10c. red, green and blue . . . . . 17·00 23·00

1965. Centenary of I.T.U.
F193 F **27** 60c. violet, blue and red . . . . 4·50 5·00

F **28** Andorra House, Paris

F **29** Chair-lift

1965. Opening of Andorra House, Paris.
F194 F **28** 25c. brown, olive & bl 85 1·25

1966. Winter Sports.
F195 F **29** 25c. green, purple & bl 1·10 1·25
F196 – 40c. brown, blue & red 1·60 1·90
DESIGN—HORIZ: 40c. Ski-lift.

F **30** Satellite "FR 1"

1966. Launching of Satellite "FR 1".
F197 F **30** 60c. blue, emer & grn 1·40 2·00

F **31** Europa "Ship"

F **32** Cogwheels

1966. Europa.
F198 F **31** 60c. brown . . . . . . 3·25 4·00

1967. Europa.
F199 F **32** 30c. indigo and blue 2·75 2·75
F200 60c. red and purple . . 6·25 4·50

F **33** "Folk Dancers" (statue)

F **34** Telephone and Dial

1967. Centenary (1966) of New Reform.
F201 F **33** 30c. green, olive & slate 1·10 1·25

1967. Inaug of Automatic Telephone Service.
F202 F **34** 60c. black, violet & red 1·50 1·60

F **35** Andorran Family

1967. Institution of Social Security.
F203 F **35** 2f.30 brown & purple 6·25 8·50

F **36** "The Temptation"

F **37** Downhill Skiing

1967. 16th-century Frescoes in House of the Valleys (1st series).
F204 F **36** 25c. red and black . . 65 95
F205 – 30c. purple and violet 60 40
F206 – 60c. blue and indigo 95 1·50
FRESCOES: 30c. "The Kiss of Judas"; 60c. "The Descent from the Cross".
See also Nos. F210/12.

1968. Winter Olympic Games, Grenoble.
F207 F **37** 40c. purple, orge & red 90 1·40

F **38** Europa "Key"

1968. Europa.
F208 F **38** 30c. blue and slate . . 7·50 5·50
F209 60c. violet & brown . . 10·50 8·00

1968. 16th-century Frescoes in House of the Valleys (2nd series). Designs as Type F **36**.
F210 25c. deep green and green 55 1·00
F211 30c. purple and brown . . . 70 1·10
F212 60c. brown and red . . . . 1·40 1·90
FRESCOES: 25c. "The Beating of Christ"; 30c. "Christ Helped by the Cyrenians"; 60c. "The Death of Christ".

F **39** High Jumping

1968. Olympic Games, Mexico.
F213 F **39** 40c. brown and blue 1·40 1·60

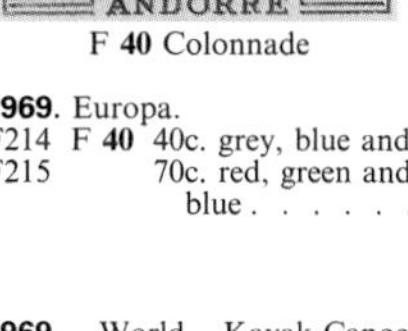

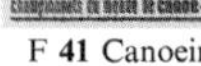

F **40** Colonnade

F **41** Canoeing

1969. Europa.
F214 F **40** 40c. grey, blue and red 8·50 5·50
F215 70c. red, green and blue . . . . 13·00 9·75

1969. World Kayak-Canoeing Championships, Bourg-St. Maurice.
F216 F **41** 70c. dp blue, bl & grn 2·10 3·00

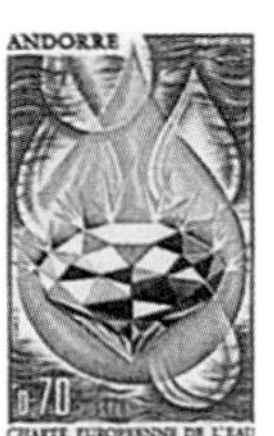

F **41a** "Diamond Crystal" in Rain Drop

F **42** "The Apocalypse"

1969. European Water Charter.
F217 F **41a** 70c. black, blue and ultramarine . . . . 4·00 5·25

1969. Altar-screen, Church of St. John of Caselles (1st series). "The Revelation of St. John".
F218 F **42** 30c. red, violet & brn 75 1·25
F219 – 40c. bistre, brn & grey 1·25 1·40
F220 – 70c. purple, lake & red 1·40 1·75
DESIGNS: 40c. Angel "clothed with cloud with face as the sun, and feet as pillars of fire" (Rev. 10); 70c. Christ with sword and stars, and seven candlesticks.
See also Nos. F225/7, F233/5 and F240/2.

F **43** Handball Player

F **44** "Flaming Sun"

1970. 7th World Handball Championships, France.
F221 F **43** 80c. blue, brn & dp bl 2·25 2·40

1970. Europa.
F222 F **44** 40c. orange . . . . . 7·00 4·25
F223 80c. violet . . . . . . 12·50 8·25

F **45** Putting the Shot

F **46** Ice Skaters

1970. 1st European Junior Athletic Championships, Paris.
F224 F **45** 80c. purple and blue 2·40 3·00

1970. Altar-screen, Church of St. John of Caselles (2nd series). Designs as Type F **42**.
F225 30c. violet, brown and red 1·00 1·40
F226 40c. green and violet . . . 90 2·10
F227 80c. red, blue and green . . 2·25 2·25
DESIGNS: 30c. Angel with keys and padlock; 40c. Angel with pillar; 80c. St. John being boiled in cauldron of oil.

1971. World Ice Skating Championships, Lyon.
F228 F **46** 80c. violet, pur & red 2·25 3·25

F 47 Western Capercaillie   F 48 Europa Chain

1971. Nature Protection.
F229 F **47** 80c. multicoloured . . 3·75 2·50
F230 – 80c. brown, green & bl 3·00 2·75
DESIGN: No. F230, Brown bear.

1971. Europa.
F231 F **48** 50c. red . . . . 8·25 5·50
F232 80c. green . . . . . . 14·00 9·00

1971. Altar-screen, Church of St. John of Caselles (3rd series). As Type F **42**.
F233 30c. green, brown and myrtle . . . . 95 1·40
F234 50c. brown, orange and lake 1·40 1·50
F235 90c. blue, purple and brown 1·90 2·50
DESIGNS: 30c. St. John in temple at Ephesus; 50c. St. John with cup of poison; 90c. St. John disputing with pagan philosophers.

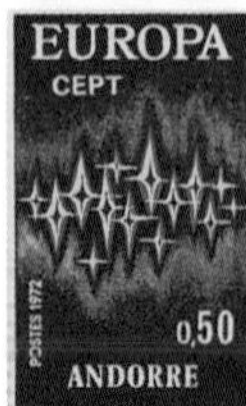

F **49** "Communications"   F **50** Golden Eagle

1972. Europa.
F236 F **49** 50c. multicoloured . . 8·00 5·75
F237 90c. multicoloured . . 14·00 9·50

1972. Nature Protection.
F238 F **50** 60c. olive, green & pur 4·00 3·50

F **51** Rifle-shooting   F **52** General De Gaulle

1972. Olympic Games, Munich.
F239 F **51** 1f. purple . . . . . . 3·00 2·50

1972. Altar-screen, Church of St. John of Caselles (4th series). As Type F **42**.
F240 30c. purple, grey and green 85 1·40
F241 50c. grey and blue . . . . 1·25 1·60
F242 90c. green and blue . . . . 1·75 2·10
DESIGNS: 30c. St. John in discussion with bishop; 50c. St. John healing a cripple; 90c. Angel with spear.

1972. 5th Anniv of Gen. De Gaulle's Visit to Andorra.
F243 F **52** 50c. blue . . . . . . 1·75 2·75
F244 – 90c. red . . . . 2·25 2·40
DESIGN: 90c. Gen. De Gaulle in Andorra la Vella, 1967.
See also Nos. F434/5.

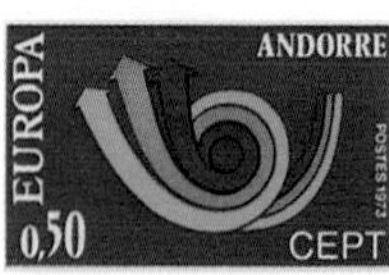

F **53** Europa "Posthorn"

1973. Europa.
F245 F **53** 50c. multicoloured . . 8·25 6·00
F246 90c. multicoloured . . 15·00 9·75

F **54** "Virgin of Canolich" (wood carving)   F **55** Lily

1973. Andorran Art.
F247 F **54** 1f. lilac, blue and drab 2·25 2·50

1973. Pyrenean Flowers (1st series). Multicoloured.
F248 30c. Type F **55** 70 90
F249 50c. Columbine . . . . . . 1·40 1·60
F250 90c. Wild pinks . . . . . . 1·10 1·40
See also Nos. F253/5 and F264/6.

F **56** Blue Tit ("Mesange Bleue")   F **57** "The Virgin of Pal"

1973. Nature Protection. Birds. Multicoloured.
F251 90c. Type F **56** . . . . . . 2·25 2·10
F252 1f. Lesser spotted woodpecker ("Pic Epeichette") . . . . . . 2·25 2·10
See also Nos. F259/60.

1974. Pyrenean Wild Flowers (2nd series). As Type F **55**. Multicoloured.
F253 45c. Iris 35 75
F254 65c. Tobacco Plant 50 85
F255 90c. Narcissus . . . . . . 95 1·25

1974. Europa. Church Sculptures. Mult.
F256 50c. Type F **57** . . . . . . 11·50 7·00
F257 90c. "The Virgin of Santa Coloma" . . . . 17·00 11·00

F **58** Arms of Andorra   F **59** Letters crossing Globe

1974. Meeting of Co-Princes, Cahors.
F258 F **58** 1f. blue, violet & orge 90 1·25

1974. Nature Protection. Birds. As Type F **56**. Multicoloured.
F259 60c. Citril finch ("Venturon Montagnard") . . . . . 3·00 2·40
F260 80c. Northern bullfinch ("Boureuil") . . . . . . 3·00 2·40

1974. Centenary of U.P.U.
F261 F **59** 1f.20 red, grey & brn 1·40 1·75

F **60** "Calvary"

1975. Europa. Paintings from La Cortinada Church. Multicoloured.
F262 80c. Type F **60** . . . . . . 7·00 6·00
F263 1f.20 "Coronation of St. Martin" (horiz) . . . 9·25 9·00

1975. Pyrenean Flowers (3rd series). As Type F **55**.
F264 60c. multicoloured 55 85
F265 80c. multicoloured . . . . 1·40 1·40
F266 1f.20 yellow, red and green 80 1·25
DESIGNS: 60c. Gentian; 80c. Anemone; 1f.20, Colchicum.

F **61** "Arphila" Motif

1975. "Arphila 75" International Stamp Exhibition, Paris.
F267 F **61** 2f. red, green and blue 1·75 2·00

F **62** Pres. Pompidou (Co-prince of Andorra)   F **63** "La Pubilla" and Emblem

1976. President Pompidou of France Commem.
F268 F **62** 80c. black and violet 85 1·25

1976. International Women's Year.
F269 F **63** 1f.20 black, pur & bl 1·40 1·50

F **64** Skier   F **65** Telephone and Satellite

1976. Winter Olympic Games, Innsbruck.
F270 F **64** 1f.20 black, green & bl 1·00 1·40

1976. Telephone Centenary.
F271 F **65** 1f. green, black and red 1·10 1·40

F **66** Catalan Forge

1976. Europa.
F272 F **66** 80c. brown, blue & grn 2·50 2·10
F273 – 1f.20 red, green & blk 4·25 3·25
DESIGN: 1f.20, Andorran folk-weaving.

F **67** Thomas Jefferson   F **68** Ball-trap (clay pigeon) Shooting

1976. Bicentenary of American Revolution.
F274 F **67** 1f.20 dp grn, brn & grn 85 1·40

1976. Olympic Games, Montreal.
F275 F **68** 2f. brown, violet & grn 1·50 1·90

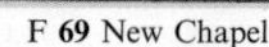

F **69** New Chapel

1976. New Chapel of Our Lady, Meritxell.
F276 F **69** 1f. green, purple & brn 80 1·25

F **70** Apollo   F **71** Stoat

1976. Nature Protection. Butterflies. Mult.
F277 80c. Type F **70** . . . . . . 3·25 2·50
F278 1f.40 Camberwell beauty . . 3·00 3·00

1977. Nature Protection.
F279 F **71** 1f. grey, black & blue 1·40 1·75

F **72** Church of St. John of Caselles   F **73** Book and Flowers

1977. Europa.
F280 F **72** 1f. purple, green & bl 3·50 2·40
F281 – 1f.40 indigo, grn & bl 5·00 3·50
DESIGN: 1f.40, St. Vicens Chateau.

1977. 1st Anniv of Institute of Andorran Studies.
F282 F **73** 80c. brown, green & bl 75 1·10

F **74** St. Roma

1977. Reredos, St. Roma's Chapel, Les Bons.
F283 F **74** 2f. multicoloured . . . 1·90 2·00

F **75** General Council Assembly Hall   F **76** Eurasian Red Squirrel

1977. Andorran Institutions.
F284 F **75** 1f.10 red, blue & brn 1·50 1·50
F285 – 2f. brown and red . . 1·50 1·60
DESIGN—VERT. 2f. Don Guillem d'Areny Plandolit.

1978. Nature Protection.
F286 F **76** 1f. brown, grn & olive 95 1·10

F **77** Escalls Bridge   F **78** Church at Pal

1978. 700th Anniv of Parity Treaties (1st issue).
F287 F **77** 80c. green, brown & bl 60 95
See also No. F292.

1978. Europa.
F288 F **78** 1f. brown, green & red 3·75 2·75
F289 1f.40 brown, bl & red 5·50 3·75
DESIGN: 1f.40, Charlemagne's House.

F **79** "Virgin of Sispony"

1978. Andorran Art.
F290 F **79** 2f. multicoloured . . . 1·50 1·50

F **80** Tribunal Meeting

1978. Tribunal of Visura.
F291 F **80** 1f.20 multicoloured . . 1·25 1·10

F **81** Treaty Text

1978. 700th Anniv of Parity Treaties (2nd issue).
F292 F **81** 1f.50 brown, grn & red 95 1·25

F **82** Chamois

F **83** Rock Ptarmigans ("Perdiu Blanca")

1978. Nature Protection.
F293 F **82** 1f. brown, lt brn & bl 60 85

1979. Nature Protection.
F294 F **83** 1f.20 multicoloured . . 1·25 1·40

F **84** Early 20th Century Postman and Church of St. John of Caselles

F **85** Wall painting, Church of St. Cerni, Nagol

1979. Europa.
F295 F **84** 1f.20 black, brn & grn 1·50 1·50
F296 – 1f.70 brown, grn & mve . . . . 2·40 2·25
DESIGN: 1f.70, Old French Post Office, Andorra.

1979. Pre-Romanesque Art.
F297 F **85** 2f. green, pink and brown . . . . 1·25 1·40
See also No. F309.

F **86** Boy with Sheep

F **87** Co-princes Monument (Luigiteruggi)

1979. International Year of the Child.
F298 F **86** 1f.70 multicoloured . . 90 1·10

1979. Co-princes Monument.
F299 F **87** 2f. dp green, grn & red 1·40 1·25

F **88** Judo

F **89** Cal Pal, La Cortinada

1979. World Judo Championships, Paris.
F300 F **88** 1f.30 black, dp bl & bl 85 1·25

1980.
F301 F **89** 1f.10 brown, bl & grn 60 1·00

F **90** Cross-country Skiing

F **91** Charlemagne

1980. Winter Olympics, Lake Placid.
F302 F **90** 1f.80 ultram, bl & red 1·25 1·60

1980. Europa.
F303 F **91** 1f.30 brn, chest & red 70 1·10
F304 – 1f.80 green and brown 1·00 1·25
DESIGN: 1f.80, Napoleon I.

F **93** Dog's-tooth Violet

F **94** Cyclists

1980. Nature Protection. Multicoloured.
F306 1f.10 Type F **93** 45 85
F305 1f.30 Pyrenean lily 55 90

1980. World Cycling Championships.
F307 F **94** 1f.20 violet, mve & brn 70 90

F **95** House of the Valleys

1980. 400th Anniv of Restoration of House of the Valleys (meeting place of Andorran General Council).
F308 F **95** 1f.40 brown, vio & grn 70 90

1980. Pre-Romanesque Art. As Type F **85**. Mult.
F309 2f. Angel (wall painting, Church of St. Cerni, Nagol) (horiz) . . . . . 1·00 1·50

F **97** Shepherds' Huts, Mereig

1981. Architecture.
F310 F **97** 1f.40 brown and blue 75 90

F **98** Bear Dance (Emcamp Carnival)

F **99** Bonelli's Warbler

1981. Europa.
F311 F **98** 1f.40 black, green & bl 75 95
F312 – 2f. black, blue and red 70 1·25
DESIGN: 2f. El Contrapas (dance).

1981. Nature Protection. Birds. Multicoloured.
F313 1f.20 Type F **99** . . . . . 70 1·00
F314 1f.40 Wallcreeper . . . . . 80 1·10

F **100** Fencing

1981. World Fencing Championships, Clermont-Ferrand.
F315 F **100** 2f. blue and black . . 70 1·10

F **101** Chasuble of St. Martin (miniature)

1981. Art.
F316 F **101** 3f. multicoloured . . 1·40 1·75

F **102** Fountain, Sant Julia de Loria

F **103** Symbolic Disabled

1981. International Decade of Drinking Water.
F317 F **102** 1f.60 blue and brown 60 95

1981. International Year of Disabled Persons.
F318 F **103** 2f.30 blue, red & grn 80 1·25

F **104** Scroll and Badge (creation of Andorran Executive Council, 1981)

F **105** Footballer running to right

1982. Europa.
F319 F **104** 1f.60 blue, brn & orge 1·10 1·00
F320 – 2f.30 blue, blk & orge 1·50 1·40
DESIGN: 2f.30, Hat and cloak (creation of Land Council, 1419).

1982. World Cup Football Championship, Spain.
F321 F **105** 1f.60 brown and red 70 1·25
F322 – 2f.60 brown and red 95 1·10
DESIGN: 2f.60, Footballer running to left.

F **107** Wall Painting, La Cortinada Church

1982. Romanesque Art.
F324 F **107** 3f. multicoloured . . 1·25 1·75

F **108** Wild Cat

F **109** Dr. Robert Koch

1982. Nature Protection.
F325 F **108** 1f.80 blk, grn & grey 1·10 1·40
F326 – 2f.60 brown & green 1·00 1·25
DESIGN: 2f.60, Scots Pine.

1982. Centenary of Discovery of Tubercle Bacillus.
F327 F **109** 2f.10 lilac . . . . . . 1·10 1·10

F **110** St. Thomas Aquinas

F **111** Montgolfier and Charles Balloons over Tuileries, Paris

1982. St. Thomas Aquinas Commemoration.
F328 F **110** 2f. deep brown, brown and grey . . . . . 90 1·10

1983. Bicentenary of Manned Flight.
F329 F **111** 2f. green, red and brown . . . . . . 75 1·10

F **112** Silver Birch

1983. Nature Protection.
F330 F **112** 1f. red, brown and green . . . . . . 1·25 1·25
F331 – 1f.50 green, bl & brn 1·00 1·25
DESIGN: 1f.50, Brown trout.

F **113** Mountain Cheesery

1983. Europa.
F332 F **113** 1f. purple and violet 1·25 1·50
F333 – 2f.60 red, mve & pur 1·50 1·75
DESIGN: 2f.60, Catalan forge.

F **114** Royal Edict of Louis XIII

1983. 30th Anniv of Customs Co-operation Council.
F334 F **114** 3f. black and slate . . 1·40 1·60

F **115** Early Coat of Arms

1983. Inscr "POSTES".

F335 F **115** 5c. green and red . . 55 60
F336 10c. dp green & green 55 60
F337 20c. violet and mauve 55 30
F338 30c. purple and violet 45 65
F339 40c. blue & ultram . . 65 65
F340 50c. black and red . . 60 60
F341 1f. lake and red . . . 65 55
F342 1f.90 green . . . . . 1·40 1·40
F343 2f. red and brown . . 1·10 60
F344 2f.10 green . . . . . 1·10 75
F345 2f.20 red 50 80
F346 2f.30 red . . . . . . 1·10 1·00
F347 3f. green and mauve 1·60 1·10
F348 4f. orange and brown 2·10 1·60
F349 5f. brown and red . . 1·50 1·40
F350 10f. red and brown 2·75 1·90
F351 15f. green & dp green 3·50 3·25
F352 20f. blue and brown 4·25 3·00

For design as Type F **115** but inscribed "LA POSTE" see Nos. F446/9.

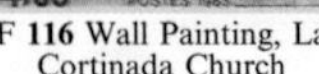

F **116** Wall Painting, La Cortinada Church F **117** Plandolit House

1983. Romanesque Art.

F354 F **116** 4f. multicoloured . . 1·60 2·00

1983.

F355 F **117** 1f.60 brown & green 55 90

F **118** Snowflakes and Olympic Torch

1984. Winter Olympic Games, Sarajevo.

F356 F **118** 2f.80 red, blue & grn 1·10 1·25

F **119** Pyrenees and Council of Europe Emblem

1984. Work Community of Pyrenees Region.

F357 F **119** 3f. blue and brown . . 1·10 1·40

F **120** Bridge

1984. Europa.

F358 F **120** 2f. green . . . . . . 1·75 1·75
F359 2f.80 red . . . . . . 2·50 2·25

F **121** Sweet Chestnut

1984. Nature Protection.

F360 F **121** 1f.70 grn, brn & pur 70 95
F361 – 2f.10 green & brown 80 1·25

DESIGN: 2f.10, Walnut.

F **122** Centre Members

1984. Pyrenean Cultures Centre, Andorra.

F362 F **122** 3f. blue, orange & red 1·00 1·40

F **123** "St. George" (detail of fresco, Church of St. Cerni, Nagol)

1984. Pre-Romanesque Art.

F363 F **123** 5f. multicoloured . . 2·25 2·10

F **124** Sant Julia Valley F **125** Title Page of "Le Val d'Andorre" (comic opera)

1985.

F364 F **124** 2f. green, olive & brn 85 1·10

1985. Europa.

F365 F **125** 2f.10 green . . . . . 2·10 1·75
F366 – 3f. brown & dp brown 3·00 2·50

DESIGN: 3f. Musical instruments within frame.

F **126** Teenagers holding up ball F **127** Mallard

1985. International Youth Year.

F367 F **126** 3f. red and brown . . 95 1·40

1985. Nature Protection. Multicoloured.

F368 1f.80 Type F **127** . . . . . 90 1·25
F369 2f.20 Eurasian goldfinch . . 1·00 1·40

F **128** St. Cerni and Angel (fresco, Church of St. Cerni, Nagol)

1985. Pre-Romanesque Art.

F370 F **128** 5f. multicoloured . . 1·75 2·75

F **130** 1979 Europa Stamp

1986. Inauguration of Postal Museum.

F381 F **130** 2f.20 brown & green 80 1·10

F **131** Ansalonga F **132** Players

1986. Europa.

F382 F **131** 2f.20 black and blue 1·50 1·40
F383 – 3f.20 black and green 2·40 2·25

DESIGN: 3f.20, Pyrenean chamois.

1986. World Cup Football Championship, Mexico.

F384 F **132** 3f. grn, blk & dp grn 1·40 1·60

F **133** Angonella Lakes

1986.

F385 F **133** 2f.20 multicoloured 80 1·10

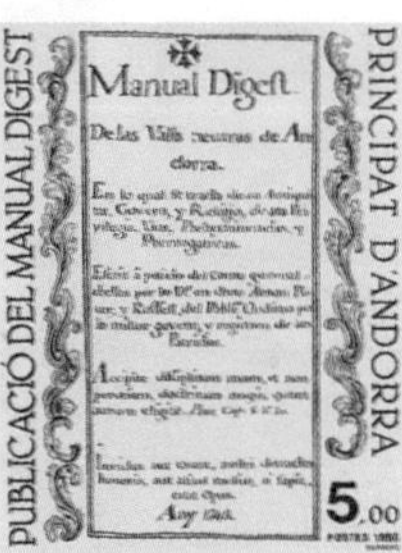

F **134** Title Page of "Manual Digest", 1748

1986. "Manual Digest".

F386 F **134** 5f. black, grn & brn 1·50 2·10

F **135** Dove with Twig F **136** St. Vincent's Chapel, Enclar

1986. International Peace Year.

F387 F **135** 1f.90 blue and indigo 90 1·25

1986.

F388 F **136** 1f.90 brn, blk & grn 80 1·25

F **137** Arms F **138** Meritxell Chapel

1987. Visit of French Co-prince (French president).

F389 F **137** 2f.20 multicoloured 1·40 2·10

1987. Europa.

F390 F **138** 2f.20 purple and red 3·00 2·25
F391 – 3f.40 violet and blue 4·50 3·25

DESIGN: 3f.40, Ordino.

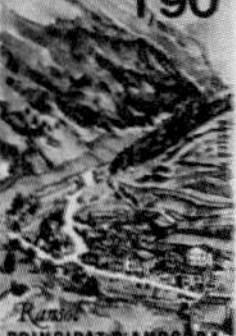

F **139** Ransol F **140** Horse

1987.

F392 F **139** 1f.90 multicoloured 90 1·40

1987. Nature Protection. Multicoloured.

F393 1f.90 Type F **140** . . . . . 1·25 1·40
F394 2f.20 Isabel (moth) . . . . 1·40 1·60

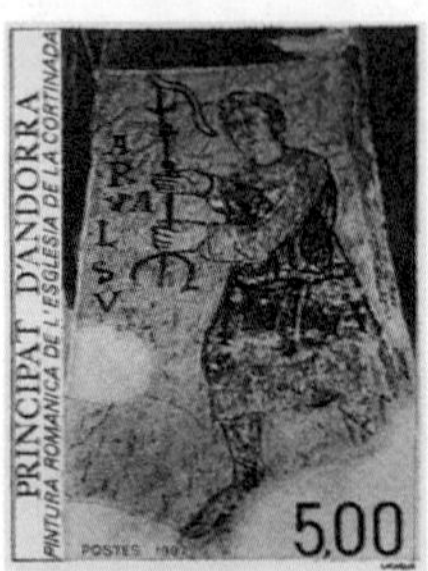

F **141** Arualsu (fresco, La Cortinada Church)

1987. Romanesque Art.

F395 F **141** 5f. multicoloured . . 1·90 2·40

F **142** Walker with Map by Signpost

1987. Walking.

F396 F **142** 2f. pur, grn & dp grn 80 1·10

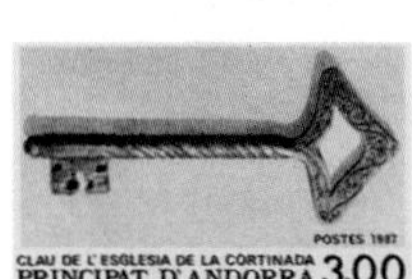

F **143** Key F **144** Arms

1987. La Cortinada Church Key.

F397 F **143** 3f. multicoloured . . 1·25 1·25

1988.

F398 F **144** 2f.20 red . . . . . . 80 1·25
F399 2f.30 red . . . . . . 1·00 1·40
F400 2f.50 red . . . . . . 1·40 1·25
F401 2f.80 red . . . . . . 1·40 1·25

Nos. F400/1 are inscribed "LA POSTE".

F **145** Bronze Boot and Mountains F **146** Players

1988. Archaeology.

F407 F **145** 3f. multicoloured . . 1·10 1·40

1988. Rugby.

F408 F **146** 2f.20 blk, yell & grn 95 1·40

F **147** Enclar Aerial F **148** Les Escaldes Hot Spring

1988. Europa. Transport and Communications. Each green, brown and blue.
F409 2f.20 Type F **147** . . . . . 1·90 1·25
F410 3f.60 Hand pointing to map on screen (tourist information) . . . . . . 2·75 3·00

1988.
F411 F **148** 2f.20 blue, brn & grn 80 1·25

F **149** Ansalonga Pass

F **150** Pyrenean Shepherd Dog

1988.
F412 F **149** 2f. blue, green & olive 75 1·10

1988. Nature Protection. Multicoloured.
F413 2f. Type F **150** . . . . . . 1·25 1·25
F414 2f.20 Hare . . . . 1·25 1·25

F **151** Fresco, Andorra La Vella Church

1988. Romanesque Art.
F415 F **151** 5f. multicoloured . . 1·90 2·10

F **152** Birds

F **153** Pal

1989. Bicentenary of French Revolution.
F416 F **152** 2f.20 violet, blk & red 1·10 1·25

1989.
F417 F **153** 2f.20 violet and blue 50 1·25

F **154** The Strong Horse

1989. Europa. Children's Games. Each brown and cream.
F418 2f.20 Type F **154** . . . . . 1·75 1·50
F419 3f.60 The Handkerchief . . 2·50 2·25

F **155** Wounded Soldiers

F **156** Archaeological Find and St. Vincent's Chapel, Enclar

1989. 125th Anniv of International Red Cross.
F420 F **155** 3f.60 brn, blk & red 1·40 1·60

1989. Archaeology.
F421 F **156** 3f. multicoloured . . 1·40 1·40

F **157** Wild Boar

1989. Nature Protection.
F422 F **157** 2f.20 blk, grn & brn 1·10 1·25
F423 – 3f.60 black, green and deep green . . . . 1·50 1·75
DESIGN: 3f.60, Palmate newt.

F **158** Retable of St. Michael de la Mosquera, Encamp

1989.
F424 F **158** 5f. multicoloured . . 1·90 2·25

F **159** La Margineda Bridge

1990.
F425 F **159** 2f.30 blue, brn & turq 85 1·10

F **160** Llorts Iron Ore Mines

1990.
F426 F **160** 3f.20 multicoloured 1·10 1·25

F **161** Exterior of Old Post Office, Andorra La Vella

1990. Europa. Post Office Buildings.
F427 F **161** 2f.30 red and black 2·25 1·75
F428 – 3f.20 violet and red 3·25 2·25
DESIGN: 3f.20, Interior of modern post office.

F **162** Censer, St. Roma's Chapel, Les Bons

F **163** Wild Roses

1990.
F429 F **162** 3f. multicoloured . . 1·10 1·40

1990. Nature Protection. Multicoloured.
F430 2f.30 Type F **163** . . . . . 1·00 1·25
F431 3f.20 Otter (horiz) . . . . 1·25 1·40

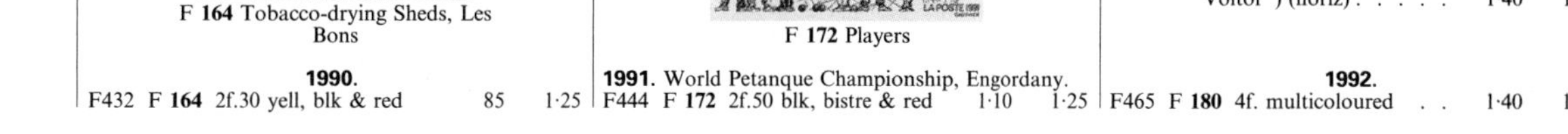

F **164** Tobacco-drying Sheds, Les Bons

1990.
F432 F **164** 2f.30 yell, blk & red 85 1·25

F **165** Part of Mural from Santa Coloma Church

1990.
F433 F **165** 5f. multicoloured . . 1·75 2·25

1990. Birth Centenary of Charles de Gaulle (French statesman). As Nos. F243/4 but values and inscriptions changed.
F434 F **52** 2f.30 blue . . . . . . 1·25 1·40
F435 3f.20 red . . . . 1·40 1·40

F **166** Coin from St. Eulalia's Church, Encamp

1990.
F436 F **166** 3f.20 multicoloured 1·00 1·40

F **167** Chapel of Sant Roma Dels Vilars

F **168** Emblem and Track

1991.
F437 F **167** 2f.50 blue, blk & grn 90 1·25

1991. 4th European Small States Games.
F438 F **168** 2f.50 multicoloured 65 1·25

F **169** Television Satellite

F **170** Bottles

1991. Europa. Europe in Space. Multicoloured.
F439 2f.50 Type F **169** . . . . . 3·00 2·10
F440 3f.50 Globe, telescope and eye (horiz) . . . . 4·00 2·75

1991. Artefacts from Tomb of St. Vincent of Enclar.
F441 F **170** 3f.20 multicoloured 1·40 1·40

F **171** Sheep

1991. Nature Protection.
F442 F **171** 2f.50 brown, bl & blk 1·25 1·10
F443 – 3f.50 brn, mve & blk 1·50 1·40
DESIGN: 3f.50, Pyrenean cow.

F **172** Players

1991. World Petanque Championship, Engordany.
F444 F **172** 2f.50 blk, bistre & red 1·10 1·25

F **173** Mozart, Quartet and Organ Pipes

1991. Death Bicentenary of Wolfgang Amadeus Mozart (composer).
F445 F **173** 3f.40 blue, blk & turq 1·60 2·10

1991. As Type F **115** but inscr "LA POSTE".
F446 F **115** 2f.20 green . . . . . 1·00 1·00
F447 2f.40 green . . . . . 1·25 1·10
F448 2f.50 red . . . . . . 1·10 1·00
F449 2f.70 green . . . . . 95 1·00
F450 2f.80 red . . . . . . 1·40 1·00
F451 3f. red 95 90

F **174** "Virgin of the Remedy of Sant Julia and Sant Germa"

F **175** Slalom

1991.
F455 F **174** 5f. multicoloured . . 1·90 1·90

1992. Winter Olympic Games, Albertville. Mult.
F456 2f.50 Type F **175** . . . . . 1·10 1·00
F457 3f.40 Figure skating . . . . 1·40 1·40

F **176** St. Andrew's Church, Arinsal

1992.
F458 F **176** 2f.50 black and buff 90 95

F **177** Navigation Instrument and Columbus's Fleet

F **178** Canoeing

1992. Europa. 500th Anniv of Discovery of America by Columbus. Multicoloured.
F459 2f.50 Type F **177** . . . . . 2·50 1·90
F460 3f.40 Fleet, Columbus and Amerindians . . . . . . 3·75 3·00

1992. Olympic Games, Barcelona. Multicoloured.
F461 2f.50 Type F **178** . . . . . 1·10 1·50
F462 3f.40 Shooting . . . . . . 1·40 1·40

F **179** Globe Flowers

F **180** "Martyrdom of St. Eulalia" (altarpiece, St. Eulalia's Church, Encamp)

1992. Nature Protection. Multicoloured.
F463 2f.50 Type F **179** . . . . . 90 1·00
F464 3f.40 Griffon vulture ("El Voltor") (horiz) . . . . . 1·40 1·40

1992.
F465 F **180** 4f. multicoloured . . 1·40 1·40

F **181** "Ordino Arcalis 91" (Mauro Staccioli)

1992. Modern Sculpture. Multicoloured.
F466 5f. Type F **181** . . . . . . 2·25 1·90
F467 5f. "Storm in a Teacup" (Dennis Oppenheim) (horiz) . . . . 2·25 1·90

F **182** Grau Roig F **183** "Estructures Autogeneradores" (Jorge du Bon)

1993. Ski Resorts. Multicoloured.
F468 2f.50 Type F **182** . . . . . 1·10 1·10
F469 2f.50 Ordino . . . . 1·10 1·10
F470 2f.50 Soldeu el Tarter . . . 1·10 1·10
F471 3f.40 Pal . . . . 1·25 1·00
F472 3f.40 Arinsal . . . . 1·25 1·00

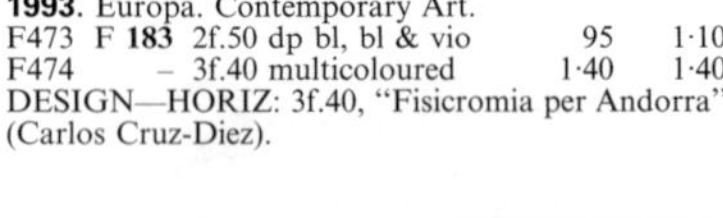
1993. Europa. Contemporary Art.
F473 F **183** 2f.50 dp bl, bl & vio 95 1·10
F474 – 3f.40 multicoloured 1·40 1·40
DESIGN—HORIZ: 3f.40, "Fisicromia per Andorra" (Carlos Cruz-Diez).

F **184** Common Blue F **185** Cyclist

1993. Nature Protection. Butterflies. Multicoloured.
F475 2f.50 Type F **184** . . . . . 1·10 1·10
F476 4f.20 "Nymphalidae" . . . 1·60 1·50

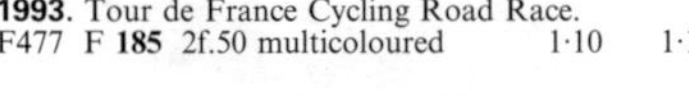
1993. Tour de France Cycling Road Race.
F477 F **185** 2f.50 multicoloured 1·10 1·10

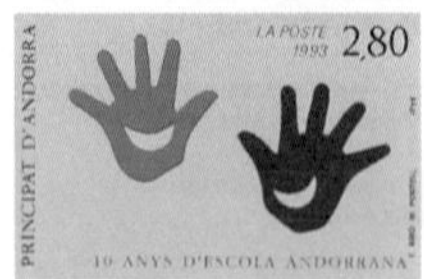
F **186** Smiling Hands

1993. 10th Anniv of Andorran School.
F478 F **186** 2f.80 multicoloured 1·10 1·10

F **187** "A Pagan Place" (Michael Warren)

1993. Modern Sculpture.
F479 F **187** 5f. black and blue . . 1·90 1·90
F480 – 5f. multicoloured . . 2·00 1·90
DESIGN: No. F480, "Pep, Lu, Canolic, Ton, Meritxell, Roma, Anna, Pau, Carles, Eugenia,...and Others" (Erik Dietman).

F **188** Cross-country Skiing F **189** Constitution Monument

1994. Winter Olympic Games, Lillehammer, Norway.
F481 F **188** 3f.70 multicoloured 1·25 1·25

1994. 1st Anniv of New Constitution.
F482 F **189** 2f.80 multicoloured 1·00 90
F483 – 3f.70 blk, yell & mve 1·40 1·25
DESIGN: 3f.70, Stone tablet.

F **190** AIDS Virus

1994. Europa. Discoveries and Inventions. Mult.
F484 2f.80 Type F **190** . . . . . 1·10 90
F485 3f.70 Radio mast . . . . . 1·50 1·25

F **191** Competitors' Flags and Football F **192** Horse Riding

1994. World Cup Football Championship, U.S.A.
F486 F **191** 3f.70 multicoloured 1·25 1·25

1994. Tourist Activities. Multicoloured.
F487 2f.80 Type F **192** . . . . . 1·00 95
F488 2f.80 Mountain biking . . . 1·00 95
F489 2f.80 Climbing . . . . . . 1·00 95
F490 2f.80 Fishing . . . . 1·00 95

F **193** Scarce Swallowtail F **194** "26 10 93"

1994. Nature Protection. Butterflies. Multicoloured.
F491 2f.80 Type F **193** . . . . . 1·10 1·00
F492 4f.40 Small tortoiseshell . . 1·90 1·60

1994. Meeting of Co-princes.
F493 F **194** 2f.80 multicoloured 95 85

F **195** Emblem F **196** Globe, Goal and Player

1995. European Nature Conservation Year.
F494 F **195** 2f.80 multicoloured 95 90

1995. 3rd World Cup Rugby Championship, South Africa.
F495 F **196** 2f.80 multicoloured 95 85

F **197** Dove and Olive Twig ("Peace")

1995. Europa. Peace and Freedom. Multicoloured.
F496 2f.80 Type F **197** . . . . . 1·40 1·10
F497 3f.70 Flock of doves ("Freedom") . . . . . . 1·60 1·40

F **198** Emblem

1995. 15th Anniv of Caritas Andorrana (welfare organization).
F498 F **198** 2f.80 multicoloured 1·00 90

F **199** Caldea Thermal Baths, Les Escaldes-Engordany

1995.
F499 F **199** 2f.80 multicoloured 1·00 90

F **200** National Auditorium, Ordino

1995.
F500 F **200** 3f.70 black and buff 1·40 1·10

F **201** "Virgin of Meritxell"

1995.
F501 F **201** 4f.40 multicoloured 1·50 1·40

F **202** Brimstone F **203** National Flag over U.N. Emblem

1995. Nature Protection. Butterflies. Multicoloured.
F502 2f.80 Type F **202** . . . . . 1·10 1·00
F503 3f.70 Marbled white (horiz) 1·60 1·40

1995. 50th Anniv of U.N.O. Multicoloured.
F504 2f.80 Type F **203** . . . . . 1·00 1·00
F505 3f.70 Anniversary emblem over flag . . . . 1·25 1·25

F **204** National Flag and Palace of Europe, Strasbourg

1995. Admission of Andorra to Council of Europe.
F506 F **204** 2f.80 multicoloured 1·00 90

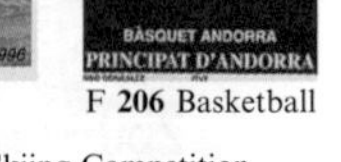
F **205** Emblem F **206** Basketball

1996. 4th Borrufa Trophy Skiing Competition.
F507 F **205** 2f.80 multicoloured 1·10 95

1996.
F508 F **206** 3f.70 red, blk & yell 1·40 1·25

F **207** Children

1996. 25th Anniv of Our Lady of Meritxell Special School.
F509 F **207** 2f.80 multicoloured 1·00 90

F **208** European Robin

1996. Nature Protection. Multicoloured.
F510 3f. Type F **208** . . . . . . 1·10 1·00
F511 3f.80 Great tit . . . . . . 1·40 1·25

F **209** Cross, St. James's Church, Engordany F **210** Ermessenda de Castellbo

1996. Religious Objects. Multicoloured.
F512 3f. Type F **209** . . . . . . 1·10 1·00
F513 3f.80 Censer, St. Eulalia's Church, Encamp (horiz) 1·40 1·25

1996. Europa. Famous Women.
F514 F **210** 3f. multicoloured . . 1·25 1·10

F **211** Chessmen F **212** Canillo

1996. Chess.
F515 F **211** 4f.50 red, black & bl 1·10 1·10

1996. No value expressed. Self-adhesive.
F516 F **212** (3f.) multicoloured . . 1·50 1·25

F **213** Cycling, Running and Throwing the Javelin

1996. Olympic Games, Atlanta.
F517 F **213** 3f. multicoloured . . 1·10 90

F **214** Singers

1996. 5th Anniv of National Youth Choir.
F518 F **214** 3f. multicoloured . . 1·10 95

F **215** Man and Boy with Animals

1996. Livestock Fair.
F519 F **215** 3f. yellow, red and black . . . . 1·10 95

F 216 St. Romá's Chapel, Les Bons
F 217 Mitterrand

1996. Churches. Multicoloured.
F520 6f.70 Type F **216** . . . . . 2·25 2·00
F521 6f.70 Santa Coloma . . . . 2·25 2·00

1997. Francois Mitterrand (President of France and Co-prince of Andorra, 1981–95) Commemoration.
F522 F **217** 3f. multicoloured . . 1·00 80

F **218** Parish Emblem
F **219** Volleyball

1997. Parish of Encamp. No value expressed. Self-adhesive.
F523 F **218** (3f.) blue 95 75

1997.
F524 F **219** 3f. multicoloured . . 1·00 90

F **220** The White Lady
F **221** House Martin approaching Nest

1997. Europa. Tales and Legends.
F525 F **220** 3f. multicoloured . . 1·10 1·10

1997. Nature Protection.
F526 F **221** 3f.80 multicoloured 1·40 1·10

F **222** Mill and Saw-mill, Cal Pal
F **223** Monstrance, St. Iscle and St. Victoria's Church

1997. Tourism. Paintings by Francesc Galobardes. Multicoloured.
F527 3f. Type F **222** . . . . . . 1·10 90
F528 4f.50 Mill and farmhouse, Sole (horiz) . . . . . . 1·60 1·40

1997. Religious Silver Work. Multicoloured.
F529 3f. Type F **223** . . . . . 1·25 95
F530 15f.50 Pax, St. Peter's Church, Aixirivall . . . . 5·00 4·00

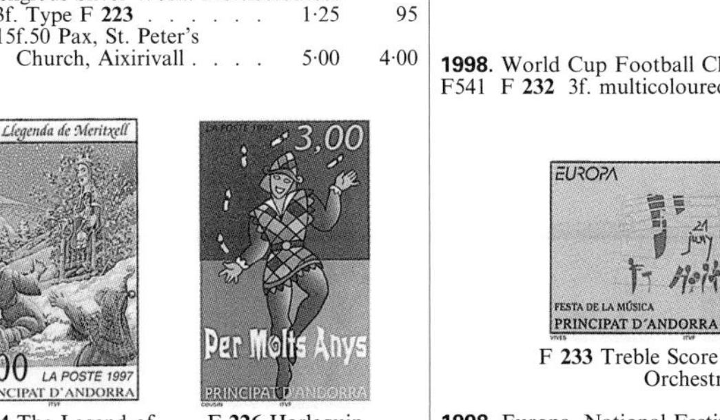

F **224** The Legend of Meritxell
F **226** Harlequin juggling Candles

F **225** St. Michael's Chapel, Engolasters

1997. Legends. Multicoloured.
F531 3f. Type F **224** . . . . . . 1·10 85
F532 3f. The Seven-armed Cross 1·10 85
F533 3f.80 Wrestlers (The Fountain of Esmelicat) 1·40 1·10

1997. International Stamp Exn, Monaco.
F534 F **225** 3f. multicoloured . . 1·00 90

1998. Birthday Greetings Stamp.
F535 F **226** 3f. multicoloured . . 1·00 80

F **227** Super Giant Slalom
F **228** Arms of Ordino

1997. Winter Olympic Games, Nagano, Japan.
F536 F **227** 4f.40 multicoloured 1·25 1·25

1998. No value expressed. Self-adhesive.
F537 F **228** (3f.) multicoloured . . 85 80

F **229** Altarpiece and Vila Church

1998.
F538 F **229** 4f.50 multicoloured 1·50 1·40

F **230** Emblem and Cogwheels

1998. 20th Anniv of Rotary Int in Andorra.
F539 F **230** 3f. multicoloured . . 1·00 90

F **231** Chaffinch and Berries
F **232** Players

1998. Nature Protection.
F540 F **231** 3f.80 multicoloured 1·25 1·00

1998. World Cup Football Championship, France.
F541 F **232** 3f. multicoloured . . 1·00 90

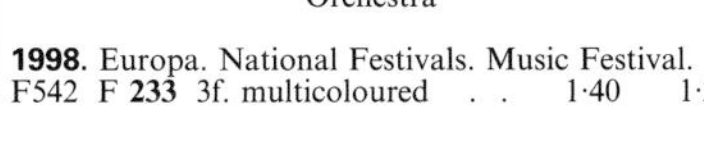
F **233** Treble Score and Stylized Orchestra

1998. Europa. National Festivals. Music Festival.
F542 F **233** 3f. multicoloured . . 1·40 1·25

F **234** River

1998. "Expo '98" World's Fair, Lisbon, Portugal.
F543 F **234** 5f. multicoloured . . 1·60 1·40

F **235** Chalice
F **237** Andorra, 1717

1998. Chalice from the House of the Valleys.
F544 F **235** 4f.50 multicoloured 1·25 1·10

1998. French Victory in World Cup Football Championship. No. F541 optd **FINAL FRANCA/ BRASIL 3-0**.
F545 F **232** 3f. multicoloured . . 1·10 1·10

1998. Relief Maps. Multicoloured.
F546 3f. Type F **237** . . . . . . 1·00 90
F547 15f.50 Andorra, 1777 (horiz) . . . . 4·50 3·50

F **238** Museum

1998. Inauguration of Postal Museum.
F548 F **238** 3f. multicoloured . . 1·00 90

F **239** Front Page of First Edition
F **240** Arms of La Massana

1998. 250th Anniv of "Manual Digest".
F549 F **239** 3f.80 multicoloured 1·25 1·10

1999. No value expressed. Self-adhesive.
F550 F **240** (3f.) multicoloured . . 80 75

F **241** House and Recycling Bins

1999. "Green World". Recycling of Waste.
F551 F **241** 5f. multicoloured . . 1·50 1·40

F **242** Vall de Sorteny (½-size illustration)

1999. Europa. Parks and Gardens.
F552 F **242** 3f. multicoloured . . 1·10 90

F **243** Council Emblem and Seat, Strasbourg

1999. 50th Anniv of Council of Europe.
F553 F **243** 3f.80 multicoloured 1·10 90

F **244** "The First Mail Coach"
F **245** Footballer and Flags

1999.
F554 F **244** 2f.70 multicoloured 95 80

1999. Andorra–France Qualifying Match for European Nations Football Championship.
F555 F **245** 4f.50 multicoloured 1·10 1·25

F **246** St. Michael's Church, Engolasters, and Emblem

1999. "Philexfrance 99" International Stamp Exhibition, Paris, France.
F556 F **246** 3f. multicoloured . . 80 95

F **247** Winter Scene

1999. Paintings of Pal by Francesc Galobardes. Multicoloured.
F557 3f. Type F **247** 80 80
F558 3f. Summer scene (horiz) . . 80 80

F **248** Emblem and "50"

1999. 50th Anniv of International Photographic Art Federation.
F559 F **248** 4f.40 multicoloured 1·10 1·10

F **249** Rull House, Sispony

1999.
F560 F **249** 15f.50 multicoloured 3·75 3·50

F **250** Chest with Six Locks

1999.
F561 F **250** 6f.70 multicoloured 1·60 1·60

F **251** Angels

1999. Christmas.
F562 F **251** 3f. multicoloured . . 80 75

F 252 Revellers F 253 Arms of La Vella

2000. New Millennium.
F563 F **252** 3f. multicoloured . . 80 75

2000. No value expressed. Self-adhesive.
F564 F **253** (3f.) multicoloured . . 80 75

F **254** Snow Boarder F **255** Emblem

2000.
F565 F **254** 4f.50 blue, brown and black . . . . 1·10 1·10

2000. Montserrat Caballe International Opera Competition, Saint Julia de Loria.
F566 F **255** 3f.80 yellow and blue 95 90

F **256** *Campanula cochlearifolia* F **257** "Building Europe"

2000.
F567 F **256** 2f.70 multicoloured 75 70

2000. Europa.
F568 F **257** 3f. multicoloured . . 80 70

F **258** Church (Canolich Festival) F **259** Sparrow

2000. Festivals. Multicoloured.
F569 3f. Type F **258** 75 75
F570 3f. People at Our Lady's Chapel, Meritxell (Meritxell Festival) . . . 95 90

2000.
F571 F **259** 4f.40 multicoloured 1·10 1·10

F **260** Hurdling F **261** Goat, Skier and Walker

2000. Olympic Games, Sydney.
F572 F **260** 5f. multicoloured . . 1·25 1·25

2000. Tourism Day.
F573 F **261** 3f. multicoloured . . 75 75

F **262** Flower, Text, Circuit Board and Emblems

2000. "EXPO 2000" World's Fair, Hanover.
F574 F **262** 3f. multicoloured . . 75 75

F **263** Stone Arch and Flag

2000. European Community.
F575 F **263** 3f.80 multicoloured 90 85

F **264** Pottery

2000. Prehistoric Pottery.
F576 F **264** 6f.70 multicoloured 1·60 1·60

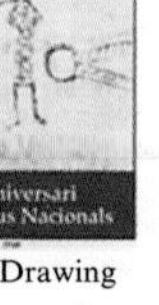

LA POSTE
COMÚ DE SANT JULIÀ DE LÒRIA
PRINCIPAT D'ANDORRA

F **265** Drawing F **266** Arms of Saint Julia de Loria

2000. 25th Anniv of National Archives.
F577 F **265** 15f.50 multicoloured 3·50 3·50

2001. No value expressed. Self-adhesive.
F578 F **266** (3f.) multicoloured . . 80 75

F **267** Ski Lift

2001. Canillo Aliga Club.
F579 F **267** 4f.50 multicoloured 1·25 1·40

F **268** Decorative Metalwork

2001. Casa Cristo Museum.
F580 F **268** 6f.70 multicoloured 1·75 1·75

F **269** Legend of Lake Engolasters F **270** Globe and Books

2001. Legends. Multicoloured.
F581 3f. Type F **269** 85 85
F582 3f. Lords before King (foundation of Andorra) 85 85

2001. World Book Day.
F583 F **270** 3f.80 multicoloured 1·00 1·00

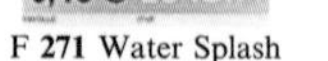

F **271** Water Splash F **272** Raspberry

2001. Europa. Water Resources.
F584 F **271** 3f. multicoloured . . 85 85

2001. Multicoloured.
F585 3f. Type F **272** 85 85
F586 4f.40 Jay (horiz) . . . . . 1·25 1·25

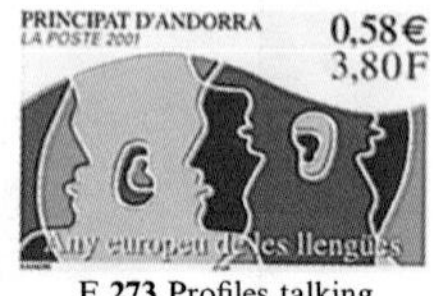

F **273** Profiles talking

2001. European Year of Languages.
F587 F **273** 3f.80 multicoloured 1·00 1·00

F **274** Trumpeter

2001. Jazz Festival, Escaldes-Engordany.
F588 F **274** 3f. multicoloured . . 60 60

F **275** Kitchen

2001.
F589 F **275** 5f. multicoloured . . 1·00 1·00

F **276** Chapel

2001. 25th Anniv of Chapel of Our Lady, Meritxell.
F590 F **276** 3f. multicoloured . . 60 60

F **277** Hotel Pla

2001.
F591 F **277** 15f. 50 black, violet and green . . . . . 3·00 3·00

PRINCIPAT D'ANDORRA
LA POSTE 0,01€

F **278** Cross F **279** State Arms

2001. Grossa Cross (boundary cross at the crossroads between Avinguda Meritxell and Carrer Bisbe Iglesias).
F592 F **278** 2f.70 multicoloured 50 50

New Currency
100 cents = 1 euro

2002. (a) With Face Value.
F593 F **279** 1c. multicoloured . . 10 10
F594 2c. multicoloured . . 10 10
F595 5c. multicoloured . . 10 10

(b) No value expressed.
F599 F **279** (46c.) multicoloured 60 60
No. F599 was sold at the rate for inland letters up to 20 grammes.

F **280** The Legend of Meritxell F **281** Pedestrians on Crossing

2002. Legends. Desings as Nos. F525, F531/3 and F581/2 but with values in new currency as Type F **280**. Multicoloured.
F600 10c. Type F **280** 10 10
F601 20c. Wrestlers (The Fountain of Esmelicat) 25 25
F602 41c. The Piper (La joyeur de cornemuse) 50 50
F603 50c. The Seven-armed Cross 65 65
F604 €1 Lords before King (foundation of Andorra) 1·25 1·25
F605 €2 Legend of Lake Engolasters . . . . . . 2·50 2·20
F606 €5 The White Lady . . . 6·25 6·25

2002. Schools' Road Safety Campaign.
F615 F **281** 69c. multicoloured . . 90 90

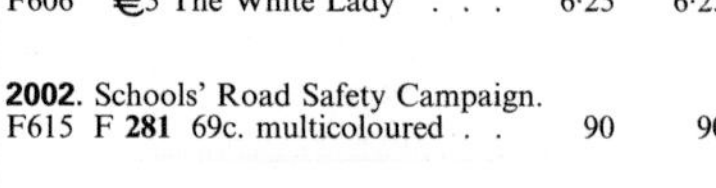

F **282** Skier

2002. Winter Olympic Games, Salt Lake City, U.S.A.
F616 F **282** 58c. multicoloured . . 75 75

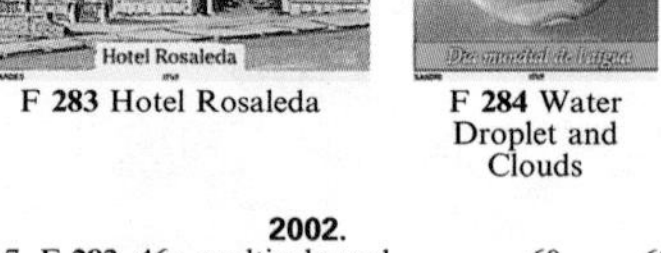

F **283** Hotel Rosaleda F **284** Water Droplet and Clouds

2002.
F617 F **283** 46c. multicoloured . . 60 60

2002. World Water Day.
F618 F **284** 67c. multicoloured . . 85 85

F **285** Clown

2002. Europa. Circus.
F619 F **285** 46c. multicoloured . . 60 60

F **286** Myrtle F **287** Seated Nude (Josep Viladomat)

2002.
F620 F **286** 46c. multicoloured . . 60 60

2002.
F621 F **287** €2.26 multicoloured 3·00 3·00

F **288** Mountains from Tunnel Entrance

2002. Completion of the Envalira Road Tunnel between Andorra and France.
F622 F **288** 46c. multicoloured . . 60 60

F **289** Mural (detail) (Santa Coloma Church, Andorra la Vella)

2002.
F623 F **289** €1.02 multicoloured 1·30 1·30

POSTAGE DUE STAMPS

1931. Postage Due stamps of France optd **ANDORRE**.
FD24 D **11** 5c. blue . . . . . . 1·25 2·50
FD25 10c. brown . . . . . 1·25 2·25
FD26 30c. red . . . . . . 60 1·25
FD27 50c. purple . . . . . 1·25 2·40
FD28 60c. green . . . . . 18·00 23·00
FD29 1f. brown on yellow 1·00 1·75
FD30 2f. mauve . . . . . . 9·25 15·00
FD31 3f. mauve . . . . . . 1·50 2·75

1931. Postage Due stamps of France optd **ANDORRE**.
FD32 D **43** 1c. green . . . . . . 1·00 2·75
FD33 10c. red . . . . . . 3·50 5·00
FD34 60c. red . . . . . . 18·00 23·00
FD35 1f. green . . . . . . 70·00 90·00
FD36 1f.20 on 2f. blue . . . 55·00 75·00
FD37 2f. brown £140 £150
FD38 5f. on 1f. purple . . . 70·00 90·00

FD **7** FD **10** FD **11** Wheat Sheaves

1935.
FD82 FD **7** 1c. green . . . . . . 2·10 3·00

1937.
FD 97 FD **10** 5c. blue . . . . . 5·00 9·50
FD 98 10c. brown . . . . 3·00 9·00
FD 99 2f. mauve . . . . 7·00 6·50
FD100 5f. orange . . . . 14·50 14·00

1943.
FD101a FD **11** 10c. brown . . . 35 1·10
FD102 30c. mauve . . . 1·00 1·50
FD103 50c. green . . . 75 1·90
FD104 1f. blue . . . . 1·10 1·40
FD105 1f.50 red . . . . 3·75 5·50
FD106 2f. blue . . . . 40 2·25
FD107 3f. red . . . . . 2·00 3·25
FD108 4f. violet . . . . 2·40 6·00
FD109 5f. mauve . . . . 2·75 5·00
FD110 10f. orange . . . 3·75 6·00
FD111 20f. brown . . . 4·75 8·25

1946. As Type **FD 11**, but inscr "TIMBRE-TAXE".
FD143 10c. brown . . . . 70 2·00
FD144 1f. blue . . . . 75 1·75
FD145 2f. blue . . . . 70 1·75
FD146 3f. brown . . . . 1·90 3·00
FD147 4f. violet . . . . 1·90 3·75
FD148 5f. red . . . . 1·60 3·00
FD149 10f. orange . . . . 2·75 3·75
FD150 20f. brown . . . . 6·25 8·50
FD151 50f. green . . . . 27·00 32·00
FD152 100f. green . . . . 80·00 95·00

1961. As Nos. FD143/52 but new values and colours.
FD185 5c. red . . . . 3·00 5·00
FD186 10c. orange . . . . . . 6·00 9·75
FD187 20c. brown . . . . . . 12·00 15·00
FD188 50c. green . . . . . . 27·00 26·00

1964. Designs as Nos. D1650/6 of France, but inscr "ANDORRE".
FD192 5c. red, green and purple 30 1·10
FD193 10c. blue, grn & pur . . . 35 1·10
FD194 15c. red, green and brown 60 1·10
FD195 20c. purple, green & turq 45 1·10
FD196 30c. blue, grn & brn . . . 55 60
FD197 40c. yellow, red and green 90 75
FD198 50c. red, green and blue 85 55

FD **129** Holly Berries

1985. Fruits.
FD371 FD **129** 10c. red and green 55 70
FD372 – 20c. brown & blue 55 70
FD373 – 30c. green and red 55 70
FD374 – 40c. brown & blk 55 75
FD375 – 50c. olive & violet 55 75
FD376 – 1f. green and blue 55 85
FD377 – 2f. red and brown 75 1·25
FD378 – 3f. purple & green 1·10 1·60
FD379 – 4f. olive and blue 1·75 2·00
FD380 – 5f. olive and red 2·00 2·25
DESIGNS: 20c. Wild plum; 30c. Raspberry; 40c. Dogberry; 50c. Blackberry; 1f. Juniper; 2f. Rose hip; 3f. Elder; 4f. Bilberry; 5f. Strawberry.

SPANISH POST OFFICES

1928. 100 centimos = 1 peseta.
2002. 100 cents = 1 euro.

1928. Stamps of Spain optd **CORREOS ANDORRA**.
1 **68** 2c. green 30 35
2 5c. red 40 50
3 10c. green 40 40
5 15c. blue . . . . 1·00 1·75
6 20c. violet . . . . 1·40 1·75
7 25c. red . . . . 1·40 6·50
8 30c. brown . . . . 7·00 8·00
9 40c. blue . . . . 8·50 5·50
10 50c. orange . . . . 9·25 7·00
11 **69** 1p. grey . . . . 11·50 11·50
12 4p. red . . . . 80·00 £140
13 10p. brown . . . . 95·00 £180

2 House of the Valleys **3** General Council of Andorra

1929.
14 **2** 2c. green . . . . 70 1·25
26 2c. brown 50 85
15 – 5c. purple . . . . 1·10 2·00
27 – 5c. brown . . . . 70 1·00
16 – 10c. green . . . . 1·10 2·00
17 – 15c. blue . . . . 1·10 3·50
30 – 15c. green . . . . 2·10 3·50
18 – 20c. violet . . . . 1·75 2·10
33 – 25c. red . . . . 1·10 2·00
20 **2** 30c. brown . . . . 50·00 70·00
34 30c. red . . . . 1·10 1·90
21 – 40c. blue . . . . 3·50 3·50
36 **2** 45c. red . . . . 70 1·25
22 – 50c. orange . . . . 3·50 3·50
38 **2** 60c. blue . . . . 1·75 2·00
23 **3** 1p. slate . . . . 9·25 14·00
39 4p. purple . . . . 40·00 26·00
40 10p. brown . . . . 40·00 30·00
DESIGNS: 5, 40c. Church of St. John of Caselles; 10, 20, 50c. Sant Julia de Loria; 15, 25c. Santa Coloma Church.

7 Councillor Manuel Areny Bons **11** Map

1948.
41 F 2c. olive 35 25
42 5c. orange 35 25
43 10c. blue 35 25
44 **7** 20c. purple . . . . 3·25 2·50
45 25c. orange . . . . 3·75 1·40
46 G 30c. green . . . . 8·50 4·50
47 H 50c. green . . . . 18·00 7·00
48 I 75c. blue . . . . 16·00 7·00
49 H 90c. purple . . . . 1·40 4·25
50 I 1p. red . . . . 16·00 6·75
51 G 1p.35 violet . . . . 6·50 7·00
52 **11** 4p. blue . . . . 11·50 12·00
53 10p. brown . . . . 20·00 14·00
DESIGNS—VERT: F. Edelweiss; G. Arms; H. Market Place, Ordino; I. Shrine near Meritxell Chapel.

12 Andorra La Vella **13** St. Anthony's Bridge

1951. Air.
54 **12** 1p. brown . . . . 18·00 12·00

1963.
55 **13** 25c. brown and black . . . 15 20
56 – 70c. black and green 20 25
57 – 1p. lilac and grey 20 50
58 – 2p. violet and lilac 35 75
59 – 2p.50 deep red and purple 25 70
60 – 3p. slate and black . . . . 60 1·00
61 – 5p. purple and brown . . . 1·60 1·90
62 – 6p. red and brown . . . . 2·00 2·00
DESIGNS—VERT: 70c. Anyos meadows (wrongly inscr "AYNOS"); 1p. Canillo; 2p. Santa Coloma Church; 2p.50, Arms; 6p. Virgin of Meritxell. HORIZ: 3p. Andorra la Vella; 5p. Ordino.

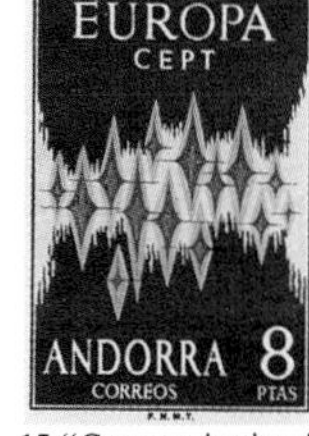
14 Daffodils **15** "Communications"

1966. Pyrenean Flowers.
63 **14** 50c. blue and slate 10 40
64 – 1p. purple and brown . . . 65 60
65 – 5p. blue and green . . . . 1·00 1·90
66 – 10p. slate and violet . . . . 65 1·50
DESIGNS: 1p. Carnation; 5p. Narcissus; 10p. Anemone (wrongly inscr "HELEBORUS CONI").

1972. Europa.
67 **15** 8p. multicoloured . . . . . 70·00 60·00

16 Encamp Valley **17** Volleyball

1972. Tourist Views. Multicoloured.
68 1p. Type **16** 35 60
69 1p.50 La Massana 50 60
70 2p. Skis and snowscape, Pas de la Casa . . . . 95 1·10
71 5p. Lake Pessons (horiz) . . . 1·25 1·10

1972. Olympic Games, Munich. Multicoloured.
72 2p. Type **17** 35 35
73 5p. Swimming (horiz) 35 55

18 St. Anthony's Auction

1972. Andorran Customs. Multicoloured.
74 1p. Type **18** 15 20
75 1p.50 "Les Caramelles" (choir) 15 20
76 2p. Nativity play (Christmas) 15 25
77 5p. Giant cigar (vert) 35 55
78 8p. Carved shrine, Meritxell (vert) 45 65
79 15p. "La Marratxa" (dance) 80 1·40

19 "Peoples of Europe" **20** "The Nativity"

1973. Europa.
80 **19** 2p. black, red and blue . . 20 35
81 – 8p. red, brown and black . . 60 70
DESIGN: 8p. Europa "Posthorn".

1973. Christmas. Frescoes from Meritxell Chapel. Multicoloured.
82 2p. Type **20** 20 30
83 5p. "Adoration of the Kings" 60 1·00

21 "Virgin of Ordino" **22** Oak Cupboard and Shelves

1974. Europa. Sculptures. Multicoloured.
84 2p. Type **21** . . . . 1·00 1·40
85 8p. Cross . . . . 1·60 2·75

1974. Arts and Crafts. Multicoloured.
86 10p. Type **22** . . . . 1·60 1·75
87 25p. Crown of the Virgin of the Roses . . . . 2·50 3·00

23 U.P.U. Monument, Berne

1974. Centenary of Universal Postal Union.
88 **23** 15p. multicoloured . . . . 1·10 1·60

24 "The Nativity"

1974. Christmas. Carvings from Meritxell Chapel. Multicoloured.
89 2p. Type **24** 60 90
90 5p. "Adoration of the Kings" 1·25 80

25 19th-century Postman and Church of St. John of Caselles **26** "Peasant with Knife"

1975. "Espana 75" Int Stamp Exhibition, Madrid.
91 **25** 3p. multicoloured 25 40

1975. Europa. 12th-century Romanesque Paintings from La Cortinada Church. Multicoloured.
92 3p. Type **26** . . . . 95 1·40
93 12p. "Christ" . . . . 1·75 3·00

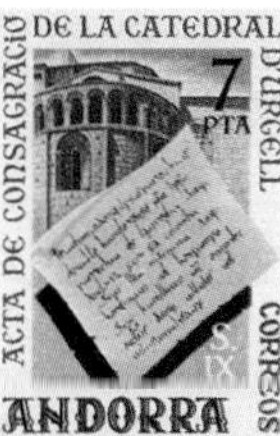
27 Cathedral and Consecration Text

1975. 1100th Anniv of Consecration of Urgel Cathedral.
94 **27** 7p. multicoloured . . . . . 1·00 1·90

28 "The Nativity"

1975. Christmas. Paintings from La Cortinada Church. Multicoloured.
95 3p. Type **28** 30 25
96 7p. "Adoration of The Kings" 35 70

29 Copper Cauldron

30 Slalom Skiing

1976. Europa. Multicoloured.
97 3p. Type **29** 20 50
98 12p. Wooden marriage chest (horiz) 60 75

1976. Olympic Games, Montreal. Multicoloured.
99 7p. Type **30** 20 40
100 15p. Canoeing (horiz) 50 80

31 "The Nativity"

1976. Christmas. Carvings from La Massana Church. Multicoloured.
101 3p. Type **31** 10 20
102 25p. "Adoration of the Kings" . . . . 50 1·10

32 Ansalonga

1977. Europa. Multicoloured.
103 3p. Type **32** 15 30
104 12p. Xuclar 45 70

33 Boundary Cross

1977. Christmas. Multicoloured.
105 5p. Type **33** 20 30
106 12p. St. Michael's Church, Engolasters 50 95

35 House of the Valleys

1978. Europa. Multicoloured.
108 5p. Type **35** 15 30
109 12p. Church of St. John of Caselles 35 70

36 Crown, Mitre and Crook

37 "Holy Family"

1978. 700th Anniv of Parity Treaties.
110 **36** 5p. multicoloured 30 50

1978. Christmas. Frescoes in St. Mary's Church, Encamp. Multicoloured.
111 5p. Type **37** 10 20
112 25p. "Adoration of the Kings" 35 50

38 Young Woman's Costume

39 Old Mail Bus

1979. Local Costumes. Multicoloured.
113 3p. Type **38** 10 10
114 5p. Young man's costume . . 10 20
115 12p. Newly-weds 25 35

1979. Europa.
116 **39** 5p. green & blue on yellow 15 25
117 – 12p. lilac and red on yellow 45 65
DESIGN: 12p. Pre-stamp letters.

40 Drawing of Boy and Girl

41 Agnus Dei, Santa Coloma Church

1979. International Year of the Child.
118 **40** 19p. blue, red and black 30 50

1979. Christmas. Multicoloured.
119 **41** 8p. Santa Coloma Church 15 20
120 25p. Type **41** 30 50

42 Pere d'Urg

43 Antoni Fiter i Rosell

1979. Bishops of Urgel, Co-princes of Andorra (1st series).
121 **42** 1p. blue and brown 10 10
122 – 5p. red and violet 10 20
123 – 13p. brown and green . . . 15 30
DESIGNS: 5p. Joseph Caixal; 13p. Joan Benlloch.
See also Nos. 137/8, 171, 182 and 189.

1980. Europa.
124 **43** 8p. brown, ochre and green 15 20
125 – 19p. black, green & dp grn 35 50
DESIGN: 19p. Francesc Cairat i Freixes.

44 Skiing

1980. Olympic Games, Moscow.
126 **44** 5p. turquoise, red and blk 10 20
127 – 8p. multicoloured 10 20
128 – 50p. multicoloured 45 70
DESIGNS: 8p. Boxing; 50p. Shooting.

45 Nativity

46 Santa Anna Dance

1980. Christmas. Multicoloured.
129 10p. Type **45** 10 20
130 22p. Epiphany 20 45

1981. Europa. Multicoloured.
131 12p. Type **46** 15 35
132 30p. Festival of the Virgin of Canolich 35 55

47 Militia Members

1981. 50th Anniv of People's Militia.
133 **47** 30p. green, grey and black 30 65

48 Handicapped Child learning to Write

1981. International Year of Disabled Persons.
134 **48** 50p. multicoloured 50 50

49 "The Nativity"

50 Arms of Andorra

1981. Christmas. Carvings from Encamp Church. Multicoloured.
135 12p. Type **49** 15 30
136 30p. "The Adoration" . . . 25 45

1981. Bishops of Urgel, Co-princes of Andorra (2nd series). As T **42**.
137 7p. purple and blue 15 20
138 20p. brown and green 25 50
DESIGNS: 7p. Salvador Casanas; 20p. Josep de Boltas.

1982. With "PTA" under figure of value.
139 **50** 1p. mauve 10 10
140 3p. brown 10 10
141 7p. red 10 10
142 12p. red 10 20
143 15p. blue 20 20
144 20p. green 20 20
145 30p. red 20 40
146 50p. green (25×31 mm) . . 65 50
147 100p. blue (25×31 mm) . . 1·40 95
See also Nos. 203/6.

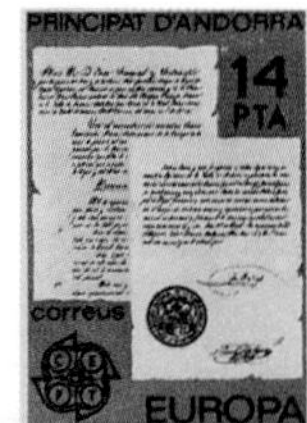

51 The New Reforms, 1866

1982. Europa. Multicoloured.
154 14p. Type **51** 30 30
155 33p. Reform of the Institutions, 1981 . . . . . 45 75

52 Footballers

1982. World Cup Football Championship, Spain. Multicoloured.
156 14p. Type **52** 45 60
157 33p. Tackle . . . . 1·40 1·40

53 Arms and 1929 1p. stamp

1982. National Stamp Exhibition.
158 **53** 14p. black and green . . . 30 50

54 Spanish and French Permanent Delegations Buildings

55 "Virgin and Child" (statue from Andorra la Vella Parish Church)

1982. Anniversaries.
159 **54** 9p. brown and blue 15 20
160 – 23p. blue and brown . . . 25 45
161 – 33p. black and green . . . 35 50
DESIGNS—VERT: 9p. Type **54** (centenary of Permanent Delegations); 23p. "St. Francis feeding the Birds" (after Ciambue) (800th birth anniv of St. Francis of Assisi); 33p. Title page of "Relacio sobre la Vall de Andorra" (birth centenary of Tomas Junoy (writer)).

1982. Christmas. Multicoloured.
162 14p. Type **55** 15 20
163 33p. Children beating log with sticks 30 55

56 Building Romanesque Church

57 "Lactarius sanguifluus"

1983. Europa.
164 **56** 16p. green, purple & black 25 25
165 – 38p. brown, blue and black 45 85
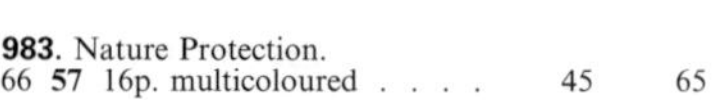
DESIGN: 38p. 16th-century water mill.

1983. Nature Protection.
166 **57** 16p. multicoloured 45 65

58 Ballot Box on Map and Government Building

1983. 50th Anniv of Universal Suffrage in Andorra.
167 **58** 10p. multicoloured 25 30

59 Mgr. Cinto Verdaguer

60 Jaume Sansa Nequi

1983. Centenary of Mgr. Cinto Verdaguer's Visit.
168 **59** 50p. multicoloured 50 80

1983. Air. Jaume Sansa Nequi (Verger-Episcopal) Commemoration.
169 **60** 20p. deep brown & brown 20 40

61 Wall Painting, Church of San Cerni, Nagol

1983. Christmas.
170 **61** 16p. multicoloured 20 35

1983. Bishops of Urgel, Co-princes of Andorra (3rd series). As T **42**.
171 26p. brown and red 30 45
DESIGN: 26p. Joan Laguarda.

62 Ski Jumping

1984. Winter Olympic Games, Sarajevo.
172 **62** 16p. multicoloured 20 40

63 Exhibition and F.I.P. Emblems

1984. "Espana 84" Int Stamp Exhibition, Madrid.
173 **63** 26p. multicoloured 30 45

64 Bridge

1984. Europa.
174 **64** 16p. brown 25 35
175 38p. blue 45 70

65 Hurdling

1984. Olympic Games, Los Angeles.
176 **65** 40p. multicoloured 45 70

66 Common Morel

1984. Nature Protection.
177 **66** 11p. multicoloured . . . . 2·00 2·00

67 Pencil, Brush and Pen

68 The Holy Family (wood carvings)

1984. Pyrenean Cultures Centre, Andorra.
178 **67** 20p. multicoloured 25 35

1984. Christmas.
179 **68** 17p. multicoloured 25 35

69 Mossen Enric Marfany and Score

1985. Europa.
180 **69** 18p. green, purple & brown 30 35
181 – 45p. brown and green . . . 60 70
DESIGN: 45p. Musician with viola (fresco detail, La Cortinada Church).

1985. Air. Bishops of Urgel, Co-princes of Andorra (4th series). As T **42**.
182 20p. brown and ochre . . . 25 35
DESIGN: 20p. Ramon Iglesias.

70 Beefsteak Morel

71 Pal

1985. Nature Protection.
183 **70** 30p. multicoloured 45 65

1985.
184 **71** 17p. deep blue and blue . . 25 35

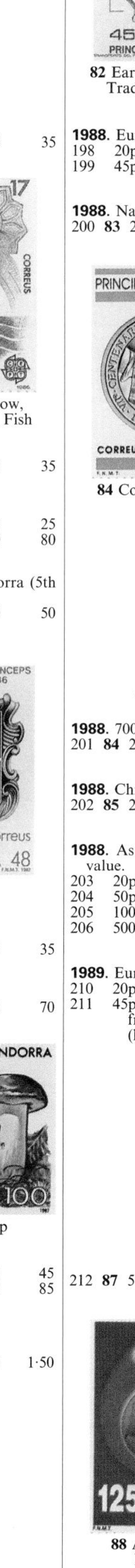

72 Angels (St. Bartholomew's Chapel)

1985. Christmas.
185 **72** 17p. multicoloured 25 35

73 Scotch Bonnet

74 Sun, Rainbow, Lighthouse and Fish

1986. Nature Protection.
186 **73** 30p. multicoloured 35 35

1986. Europa. Each blue, red and green.
187 17p. Type **74** 15 25
188 45p. Sun and trees on rocks 50 80

1986. Bishops of Urgel, Co-princes of Andorra (5th series). As T **42**.
189 35p. blue and brown 30 50
DESIGN: 35p. Justi Guitart.

75 Bell of St. Roma's Chapel, Les Bons

76 Arms

1986. Christmas.
190 **75** 19p. multicoloured 25 35

1987. Meeting of Co-princes.
191 **76** 48p. multicoloured 60 70

77 Interior of Chapel

79 Cep

1987. Europa. Meritxell Chapel.
192 **77** 19p. brown and blue . . . 30 45
193 – 48p. blue and brown . . . 70 85
DESIGN: 48p. Exterior of Chapel.

1987. Nature Protection.
195 **79** 100p. multicoloured . . . 1·25 1·50

80 Extract from "Doctrina Pueril" by Ramon Llull

1987. Christmas.
196 **80** 20p. multicoloured 25 35

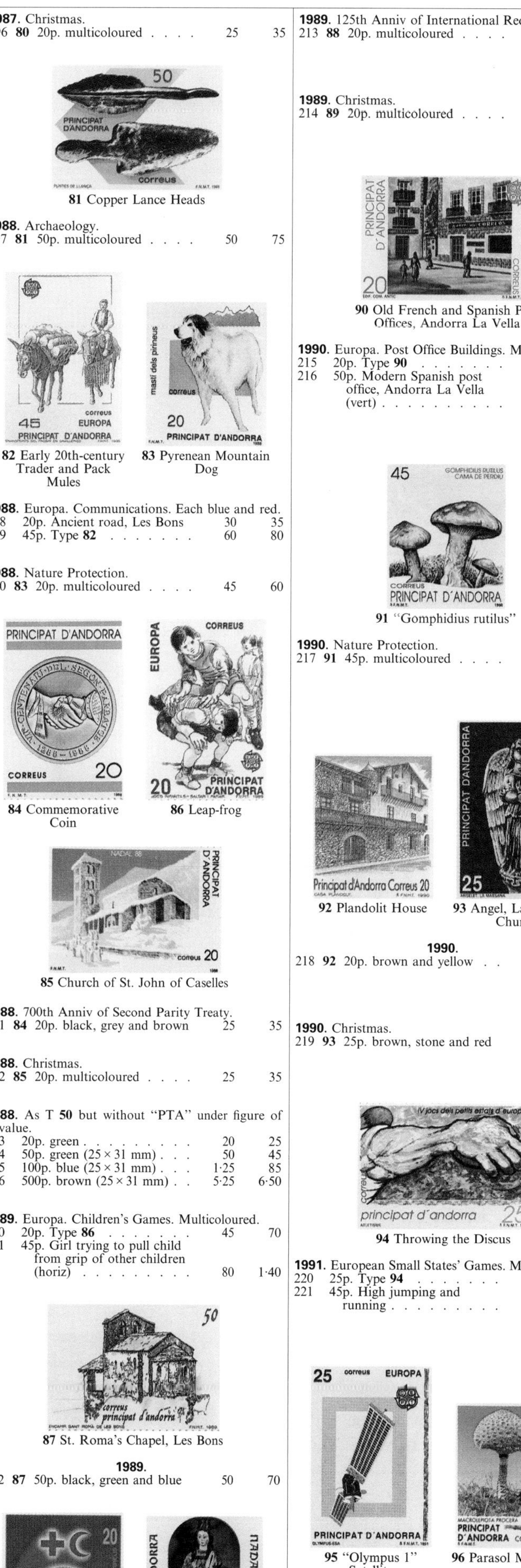

81 Copper Lance Heads

1988. Archaeology.
197 **81** 50p. multicoloured 50 75

82 Early 20th-century Trader and Pack Mules

83 Pyrenean Mountain Dog

1988. Europa. Communications. Each blue and red.
198 20p. Ancient road, Les Bons 30 35
199 45p. Type **82** 60 80

1988. Nature Protection.
200 **83** 20p. multicoloured 45 60

84 Commemorative Coin

86 Leap-frog

85 Church of St. John of Caselles

1988. 700th Anniv of Second Parity Treaty.
201 **84** 20p. black, grey and brown 25 35

1988. Christmas.
202 **85** 20p. multicoloured 25 35

1988. As T **50** but without "PTA" under figure of value.
203 20p. green 20 25
204 50p. green (25 × 31 mm) . . . 50 45
205 100p. blue (25 × 31 mm) . . . 1·25 85
206 500p. brown (25 × 31 mm) . . 5·25 6·50

1989. Europa. Children's Games. Multicoloured.
210 20p. Type **86** 45 70
211 45p. Girl trying to pull child from grip of other children (horiz) . . . . 80 1·40

87 St. Roma's Chapel, Les Bons

1989.
212 **87** 50p. black, green and blue 50 70

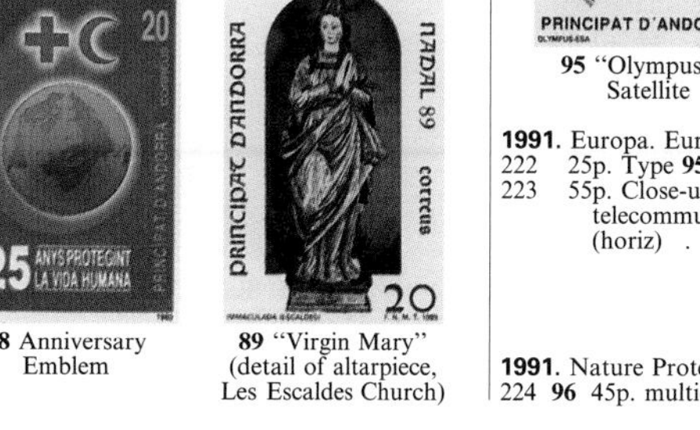

88 Anniversary Emblem

89 "Virgin Mary" (detail of altarpiece, Les Escaldes Church)

1989. 125th Anniv of International Red Cross.
213 **88** 20p. multicoloured 30 50

1989. Christmas.
214 **89** 20p. multicoloured 30 35

90 Old French and Spanish Post Offices, Andorra La Vella

1990. Europa. Post Office Buildings. Multicoloured.
215 20p. Type **90** 30 40
216 50p. Modern Spanish post office, Andorra La Vella (vert) 65 65

91 "Gomphidius rutilus"

1990. Nature Protection.
217 **91** 45p. multicoloured 60 60

92 Plandolit House

93 Angel, La Massana Church

1990.
218 **92** 20p. brown and yellow . . 25 25

1990. Christmas.
219 **93** 25p. brown, stone and red 30 45

94 Throwing the Discus

1991. European Small States' Games. Multicoloured.
220 25p. Type **94** 30 55
221 45p. High jumping and running 45 65

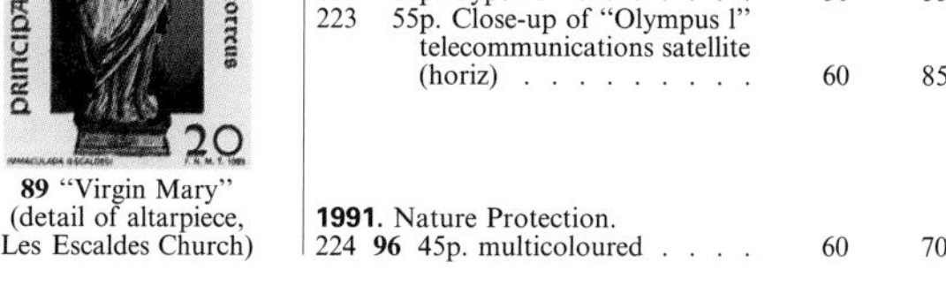

95 "Olympus 1" Satellite

96 Parasol Mushroom

1991. Europa. Europe in Space. Multicoloured.
222 25p. Type **95** 30 55
223 55p. Close-up of "Olympus 1" telecommunications satellite (horiz) 60 85

1991. Nature Protection.
224 **96** 45p. multicoloured 60 70

97 "Virgin of the Three Hands" (detail of triptych in Meritxell Chapel by Maria Assumpta Ortado i Maimo)

98 Woman fetching Water from Public Tap

1991. Christmas.
225 **97** 25p. multicoloured 30 45

1992.
226 **98** 25p. multicoloured 30 45

99 "Santa Maria"

100 White-water Canoeing

1992. Europa. 500th Anniv of Discovery of America by Columbus.
227 **99** 27p. multicoloured 35 45
228 – 45p. brown, red and orange 50 70
DESIGN—HORIZ: 45p. Engraving of King Ferdinand from map sent by Columbus to Ferdinand and Queen Isabella the Catholic.

1992. Olympic Games, Barcelona.
229 **100** 27p. multicoloured . . . 30 45

101 Benz Velo, 1894 and Sedanca de ville, 1920s

102 "Nativity" (Fra Angelico)

1992. National Motor Car Museum, Encamp.
230 **101** 27p. multicoloured . . . 30 45

1992. Christmas.
231 **102** 27p. multicoloured . . . 30 45

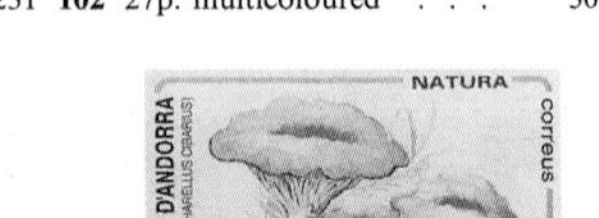

103 Chanterelle

1993. Nature Protection.
232 **103** 28p. multicoloured . . . 30 45

104 "Upstream" (J. A. Morrison)

1993. Europa. Contemporary Art. Multicoloured.
233 28p. Type **104** 35 50
234 45p. "Ritme" (Angel Calvente) (vert) 50 60

105 Society Emblem on National Colours

106 Illuminated "P" (Galceran de Vilanova Missal)

1993. 25th Anniv of Andorran Arts and Letters Circle.
235 **105** 28p. multicoloured . . . 30 45

1993. Christmas.
236 **106** 28p. multicoloured . . . 30 45

108 Sir Alexander Fleming and Penicillin

1994. Europa. Discoveries.
238 **108** 29p. multicoloured . . . 35 50
239 – 55p. blue and black . . . 60 80
DESIGN: 55p. Test tube and AIDS virus.

109 "Hygrophorus gliocyclus"

110 "Madonna and Child" (anon)

1994. Nature Protection.
240 **109** 29p. multicoloured . . . 35 45

1994. Christmas.
241 **110** 29p. multicoloured . . . 35 45

111 Madriu Valley (south)

1995. European Nature Conservation Year. Mult.
242 30p. Type **111** 35 45
243 60p. Madriu Valley (north) 60 85

112 Sun, Dove and Barbed Wire

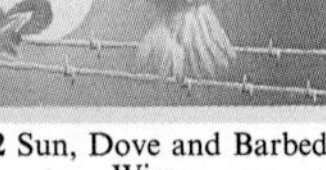

113 "Flight into Egypt" (altarpiece, St. Mark and St. Mary Church, Encamp)

1995. Europa. Peace and Freedom.
244 **112** 60p. green, orange & blk 60 60

1995. Christmas.
245 **113** 30p. multicoloured . . . 30 45

114 Palace of Europe, Strasbourg

1995. Admission of Andorra to Council of Europe.
246 **114** 30p. multicoloured . . . 30 45

115 "Ramaria aurea"

1996. Nature Protection. Multicoloured.
247 30p. Type **115** 30 45
248 60p. Black truffles 60 85

116 Isabelle Sandy (writer)

1996. Europa. Famous Women.
249 **116** 60p. multicoloured . . . 60 85

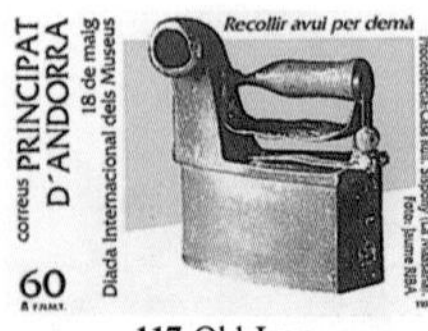

117 Old Iron

1996. International Museums Day.
250 **117** 60p. multicoloured . . . 60 85

118 "The Annunciation" (altarpiece, St. Eulalia's Church, Encamp)

1996. Christmas.
251 **118** 30p. multicoloured . . . 30 45

119 Drais Velocipede, 1818

1997. Bicycle Museum (1st series). Multicoloured.
252 32p. Type **119** 30 45
253 65p. Michaux velocipede, 1861 . . . . 65 70
See also Nos. 258/9 and 264/5.

120 The Bear and The Smugglers

121 Dove and Cultural Symbols

1997. Europa. Tales and Legends.
254 **120** 65p. multicoloured . . . 60 80

1997. National U.N.E.S.C.O. Commission.
255 **121** 32p. multicoloured . . . 30 45

122 Catalan Crib Figure

1997. Christmas.
256 **122** 32p. multicoloured . . . 30 45

123 Giant Slalom

1998. Winter Olympic Games, Nagano, Japan.
257 **123** 35p. multicoloured . . . 35 45

1998. Bicycle Museum (2nd series). As T **119**. Multicoloured
258 35p. Kangaroo bicycle, Great Britain, 1878 . . . . . . 30 45
259 70p. The Swallow, France, 1889 . . . . 65 85

124 Harlequins of Canillo

1998. Europa. National Festivals.
260 **124** 70p. multicoloured . . . 60 60

125 Front Page of First Edition and Landscape

1998. 250th Anniv of "Manual Digest".
261 **125** 35p. multicoloured . . . 30 45

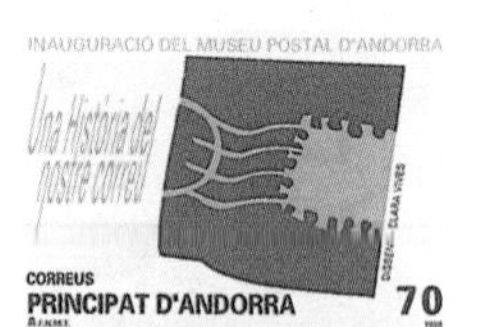

126 Emblem

1998. Inauguration of Postal Museum.
262 **126** 70p. violet and yellow . . 60 85

127 St. Lucia Fair

1998. Christmas.
263 **127** 35p. multicoloured . . . 30 45

1999. Bicycle Museum (3rd series). As T **119**. Multicoloured.
264 35p. Salvo tricycle, 1878 (vert) 30 45
265 70p. Rudge tricycle, Coventry, England 60 85

128 Mules

1999. Postal History.
266 **128** 35p. black and brown . . 30 45

129 Palace of Human Rights, Strasbourg

1999. 50th Anniv of Council of Europe.
267 **129** 35p. multicoloured . . . 30 45

130 Vall d'Incles National Park, Canillo

1999. Europa. Parks and Gardens.
268 **130** 70p. multicoloured . . . 60 85

131 Rull House, Sispony

1999.
269 **131** 35p. multicoloured . . . 30 45

132 Angel (detail of altarpiece, St. Serni's Church, Canillo)

133 Santa Coloma Church

1999. Christmas.
270 **132** 35p. brown and light brown 30 45

1999. European Heritage.
271 **133** 35p. multicoloured . . . 30 45

134 "Building Europe"

2000. Europa.
272 **134** 70p. multicoloured . . . 60 85

135 Angonella Lakes, Ordino

2000.
273 **135** 35p. multicoloured . . . 30 45

136 Casa Lacruz

2000. 131st Birth Anniv of Josep Cadafalch (architect).
274 **136** 35p. multicoloured . . . 30 45

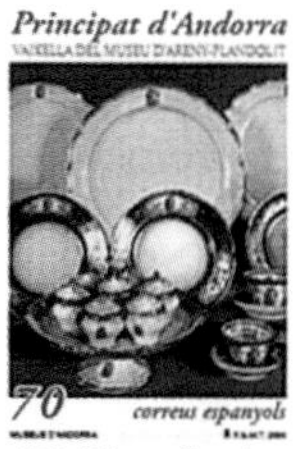

137 Dinner Service

138 Hurdling

2000. D'Areny-Plandolit Museum.
275 **137** 70p. multicoloured . . . 60 80

2000. Olympic Games, Sydney.
276 **138** 70p. multicoloured . . . 60 80

139 United Nations Headquarters, Strasbourg

2000. 50th Anniv of United Nations Declaration of Human Rights.
277 **139** 70p. multicoloured . . . 60 80

140 Gradual, St. Roma, Les Bons

141 "Quadre de les Animes" (Joan Casanovas)

2000. 25th Anniv of the National Archives.
278 **140** 35p. multicoloured . . . 30 45

2000. Christmas.
279 **141** 35p. multicoloured . . . 30 45

142 Rec del Sola

2001. Natural Heritage.
280 **142** 40p. multicoloured . . . 30 45

143 Roc del Metge (thermal spring), Escaldes-Engordany

2001. Europa. Water Resources.
281 **143** 75p. muticoloured 60 80

144 Casa Palau, Sant Julia de Loria

145 Part of Sanctuary, Meritxell

2001.
282 **144** 75p. multicoloured . . . 60 80

2001. 25th Anniv of Chapel of Our Lady, Meritxell.
283 **145** 40p. multicoloured . . . 30 45

146 Building

2001. 10th Anniv of National Auditorium, Ordino.
284 **146** 75p. multicoloured . . . 60 80

147 Angel (detail of altarpiece, Church of St. John of Caselles)

2001. Christmas.
285 **147** 40p. multicoloured . . . 30 30

New Currency
100 cents = 1 euro

148 State Arms

2002.
286 **148** 25c. orange 30 30
287 50c. red 65 65

149 Alpine Accentor (*Prunella collaris*)

2002. Native Birds. Multicoloured.
300 25c. Type **149** 30 30
301 50c. Snow finch (*Montifringilla nivalis*) . . . 65 65

150 Emblem

2002. International Year of the Mountain.
302 **150** 50c. multicoloured 65 65

151 Tightrope Walker

2002. Europa. Circus.
303 **151** 50c. multicoloured 65 65

152 Casa Fusile, Escaldes-Engordany

153 Pinette Minim

2002. Architectural Heritage. Multicoloured.
304 €1.80 Type **152** . . . . . . 2·30 2·30
305 €2.10 Farga Rossell Iron Museum, La Massana . . 2·75 2·75

2002. History of the Motor Car. Multicoloured.
306 25c. Type **153** 30 30
307 50c. Rolls Royce Silver Wraith 65 65

154 Placa Benlloch, Areny-Plandolit

2002. Christmas.
308 **154** 25c. multicoloured 30 30

156 Painted Medallion

2002. Cultural Heritage. Romanesque Murals from Santa Coloma Church, Andorra la Vella.
309 25c. Type **156** 30 30
310 50c. Part of damaged fresco showing seated figure . . . 65 65
311 75c. Frieze 95 95

EXPRESS LETTER STAMPS

1928. Express Letter stamp of Spain optd **CORREOS ANDORRA**.
E15 E **53** 20c. red . . . . 30·00 40·00

E **4** Lammergeier over Pyrenees

E **12** Eurasian Red Squirrel (after Durer) and Arms

1929.
E41 E **4** 20c. red . . . . 4·00 5·50

1949.
E54 E **12** 25c. red . . . . 3·00 4·50

ANGOLA Pt. 9; Pt. 12

Republic of Southern Africa. Independent of Portugal since 11 November 1975.

1870. 1000 reis = 1 milreis.
1913. 100 centavos = 1 escudo.
1932. 100 centavos = 1 angolar.
1954. 100 centavos = 1 escudo.
1977. 100 lweis = 1 kwanza.

1870. "Crown" key-type inscr "ANGOLA".
7 P 5r. black . . . . 1·00 95
17 10r. yellow . . . . 8·75 4·25
31 10r. green . . . . 2·75 1·25
9 20r. bistre . . . . 1·50 95
26 20r. red . . . . 4·75 3·50
10 25r. red . . . . 5·25 2·40
27 25r. purple . . . . 3·75 1·25
19b 40r. blue . . . . 80·00 48·00
33 40r. yellow . . . . 2·75 2·00
12 50r. green . . . . 20·00 7·50
30 50r. blue . . . . 12·00 1·25
21a 100r. lilac . . . . 1·40 95
22 200r. orange . . . . 1·75 1·10
23a 300r. brown . . . . 1·90 1·50

1886. "Embossed" key-type inscr "PROVINCIA DE ANGOLA".
35 Q 5r. black . . . . 4·25 2·40
36 10r. green . . . . 4·25 2·40
37 20r. red . . . . 6·50 4·50
39 25r. mauve . . . . 4·50 1·00
40 40r. brown . . . . 5·00 2·50
41 50r. blue . . . . 5·75 1·40
42 100r. brown . . . . 7·50 3·50
43 200r. violet . . . . 10·50 4·75
44 300r. orange . . . . 10·50 4·75

1894. "Figures" key-type inscr "ANGOLA".
49 R 5r. orange 85 40
62 10r. mauve . . . . 1·60 55
63 15r. brown . . . . 1·60 95
54 20r. lavender . . . . 1·90 1·10
74 25r. green . . . . 1·00 75
66 50r. blue . . . . 2·00 95
67 75r. red . . . . 4·25 2·25
68 80r. green . . . . 4·00 3·00
69 100r. brown on buff . . . . 4·25 3·00
70 150r. red on rose . . . . . 7·50 5·00
77 200r. blue on blue . . . . . 7·50 5·75
78 300r. blue on brown . . . . 7·50 5·75

1894. No. N51 with circular surch **CORREIOS DE ANGOLA 25 REIS**.
79b V 25r. on 2½r. brown . . . . 27·00 25·00

1898. "King Carlos" key-type inscr "ANGOLA".
80 S 2½r. grey 20 20
81 5r. orange 20 20
82 10r. green 20 20
83 15r. brown . . . . 1·10 55
142 15r. green 45 40
84 20r. lilac 25 20
85 25r. green 65 25
143 25r. red 30 10
86 50r. blue 95 35
144 50r. brown . . . . 2·25 1·10
145 65r. blue . . . . 3·00 2·75
87 75r. red . . . . 3·00 1·40
146 75r. purple . . . . 1·00 70
88 80r. mauve . . . . 3·00 1·40
89 100r. blue on blue 60 40
147 115r. brown on pink . . . . 3·00 2·75
148 130r. brown on yellow . . . 3·00 2·75
90 150r. brown on buff . . . . 3·00 2·25
91 200r. purple on pink . . . . 1·75 60
92 300r. blue on pink . . . . . 2·00 1·75
149 400r. blue on yellow . . . . 2·00 1·60
93 500r. black on blue . . . . 2·25 1·75
94 700r. mauve on yellow . . . 9·50 6·75

1902. "Embossed", "Figures" and "Newspaper" key-types of Angola surch.
98 R 65r. on 5r. orange . . . . 3·00 2·25
100 65r. on 10r. mauve . . . . 2·25 1·60
102 65r. on 20r. violet . . . . 4·00 2·25

104 65r. on 25r. green . . . . 2·25 1·75
95 Q 65r. on 40r. brown . . . . 3·50 2·10
96 65r. on 300r. orange . . . 3·50 2·10
106 115r. on 10r. green . . . . 4·00 2·00
109 R 115r. on 80r. green . . . . 4·50 3·50
111 115r. on 100r. brn on buff 3·75 2·10
113 115r. on 150r. red on rose 5·50 4·25
108 Q 115r. on 200r. violet . . . 4·00 1·90
120 R 130r. on 15r. brown . . . 2·25 1·50
116 Q 130r. on 50r. blue . . . . 4·25 3·00
124 R 130r. on 75r. red . . . . . 3·25 1·75
118 Q 130r. on 100r. brown . . . 2·75 1·90
126 R 130r. on 300r. blue on brn 7·50 4·75
136 V 400r. on 2½r. brown 55 50
127 Q 400r. on 5r. black . . . . 6·25 5·25
128 400r. on 20r. red . . . . . 25·00 16·00
130 400r. on 25r. mauve . . . 6·25 3·25
131 R 400r. on 50r. pale blue . . 2·75 2·00
133 400r. on 200r. blue on blue 3·50 2·40

1902. "King Carlos" key-type of Angola optd **PROVISORIO**.
138 S 15r. brown 80 45
139 25r. green 65 30
140 50r. blue . . . . 1·40 70
141 75r. red . . . . 2·00 1·50

1905. No. 145 surch **50 REIS** and bar.
150 S 50r. on 65r. blue . . . . . 1·25 75

1911. "King Carlos" key-type optd **REPUBLICA**.
151 S 2½r. grey 20 15
152 5r. orange 20 15
153 10r. green 20 15
154 15r. green 20 15
155 20r. lilac 20 15
156 25r. red 20 15
157 50r. brown 75 55
232 50r. blue (No. 140) 75 45
224 75r. purple 45 30
234 75r. red (No. 141) . . . . . 1·50 1·10
225 100r. blue on blue 95 95
160 115r. brown on pink . . . 75 45
161 130r. brown on yellow . . . 75 45
226 200r. purple on pink 85 45
163 400r. blue on yellow . . . . 1·00 50
164 500r. black on blue . . . . 1·10 50
165 700r. mauve on yellow . . . 1·40 65

1912. "King Manoel" key-type inscr "ANGOLA" optd **REPUBLICA**.
166 T 2½r. lilac 20 20
167 5r. black 20 20
168 10r. green 20 20
169 20r. red 20 20
170 25r. brown 20 20
171 50r. blue 45 35
172 75r. brown 50 45
173 100r. brown on green . . . 1·00 65
174 200r. green on pink . . . . 1·00 70
175 300r. black on blue . . . . 1·00 70

1912. "King Carlos" key-type of Angola optd **REPUBLICA** and surch.
176 S 2½ on 15r. green . . . . . 1·50 1·00
177 5 on 15r. green . . . . . . 1·25 90
178 10 on 15r. green . . . . . 1·25 80
179 25 on 75r. red (No. 141) . . 22·00 15·00
180 25 on 75r. purple . . . . . 1·60 1·25

1913. Surch **REPUBLICA ANGOLA** and value in figures on "Vasco da Gama" issues of (a) Portuguese Colonies.
181 ¼c. on 2½r. green 45 35
182 ½c. on 5r. red 45 35
183 1c. on 10r. purple 45 35
184 2½c. on 25r. green 45 35
185 5c. on 50r. blue 45 35
186 7½c. on 75r. brown . . . . . 1·90 1·60
187 10c. on 100r. brown 80 55
188 15c. on 150r. bistre 65 55

(b) Macao.
189 ¼c. on ½a. green 75 65
190 ½c. on 1a. red 75 65
191 1c. on 2a. purple 65 50
192 2½c. on 4a. green 55 45
193 5c. on 8a. blue 55 45
194 7½c. on 12a. brown . . . . . 1·90 1·10
195 10c. on 16a. brown . . . . . 1·10 65
196 15c. on 24a. bistre 85 65

(c) Timor.
197 ¼c. on ½a. green 75 65
198 ½c. on 1a. red 75 65
199 1c. on 2a. purple 65 50
200 2½c. on 4a. green 55 40
201 5c. on 8a. blue 55 50
202 7½c. on 12a. brown . . . . . 1·90 1·10
203 10c. on 16a. brown . . . . . 1·00 65
204 15c. on 24a. bistre 90 65

1914. "Ceres" key-type inscr "ANGOLA".
296 U ¼c. olive 10 10
297 ½c. black 10 10
298 1c. green 10 10
299 1½c. brown 10 10
300 2c. red 10 10
301 2c. grey 15 15
281 2½c. violet 10 10
303 3c. orange 10 10
304 4c. red 10 10
305 4½c. grey 10 10
284a 5c. blue 10 10
307 6c. mauve 10 10
308 7c. blue 10 10
309 7½c. brown 10 10
288 8c. grey 10 10
311 10c. brown 10 10
312 12c. brown 15 10
313 12c. green 15 15
291 15c. purple 15 10
314 15c. pink 15 10
315 20c. green 35 25
316 24c. blue 40 35
317 25c. brown 40 35
217 30c. brown on green . . . 1·10 75
318 30c. green 15 10
218 40c. brown on pink . . . 1·10 75
319 40c. blue 40 15
219 50c. orange on pink . . . 3·50 2·50
320 50c. purple 35 15
321 60c. blue 40 25
322 60c. red . . . . 25·00 20·00
322a 80c. pink 55 25
220 1e. green on blue . . . . 2·10 1·50
323 1e. red 50 25
325 1e. blue . . . . 1·00 55
326 2e. purple . . . . 1·10 65
327 5e. brown . . . . 4·00 3·25
328 10e. pink . . . . 11·00 8·00
329 20e. green . . . . 32·00 25·00

1914. Provisional stamps of 1902 optd **REPUBLICA**.
233 S 50r. on 65r. blue . . . . . 1·50 1·40
256 Q 115r. on 10r. green 80 60
258 R 115r. on 80r. green 65 60
261 115r. on 100r. brn on buff 55 45
263 115r. on 150r. red on rose 85 60
266 Q 115r. on 200r. violet . . . 60 40
267 R 130r. on 15r. brown 55 40
246 Q 130r. on 50r. blue . . . . 6·50 6·50
269 R 130r. on 75r. red . . . . . 1·10 55
273 Q 130r. on 100r. brown . . . 45 40
274 R 130r. on 300r. blue on brn 45 40
254 V 400r. on 2½r. brown 25 20

1919. Stamps of 1911, 1912 or 1914 surch.
332 S ½c. on 75r. purple 55 45
331 T ½c. on 75r. brown 35 30
336 1c. on 50r. blue 65 60
335 S 2½c. on 100r. blue on blue 65 30
334 2½c. on 100r. brown on grn 65 55
337 4c. on 130r. brown on yell 65 55
339 U $04 on 15c. purple 45 45
340 $04 on 15c. pink . . . . . 7·50
341 T $00.5 on 75r. brown . . . 50 45
342 U $00.5 on 7½c. brown . . . 65 55

1925. Nos. 136 and 133 surch **Republica 40 C.**
345 V 40c. on 400r. on 2½r. brn 25 25
343 R 40c. on 400r. on 200r. blue on blue 25 25

1931. "Ceres" key-type of Angola surch.
347 U 50c. on 60c. red 55 55
348 70c. on 80c. pink . . . . . 1·40 85
349 70c. on 1e. blue . . . . . 1·10 85
350 1e.40 on 2e. purple 90 55

17 Ceres

1932.
351 **17** 1c. brown 10 10
352 5c. sepia 10 10
353 10c. mauve 10 10
354 15c. black 10 10
355 20c. grey 10 10
356 30c. green 10 10
357 35c. green . . . . 3·00 1·25
358 40c. red 15 10
359 45c. blue 45 40
360 50c. brown 15 10
361 60c. olive 30 15
362 70c. brown 30 15
363 80c. green 20 10
364 85c. red . . . . 1·50 85
365 1a. red 35 10
366 1a.40 blue . . . . 3·00 1·50
367 1a.75 blue . . . . 5·75 1·60
368 2a. mauve . . . . 1·25 15
369 5a. green . . . . 2·40 50
370 10a. brown . . . . 5·75 95
371 20a. orange . . . . 14·00 1·90

1934. Surch.
380 **17** 5c. on 80c. green (A) . . . 25 10
419 5c. on 80c. green (B) . . . 30 25
413 10c. on 45c. blue 65 55
381 10c. on 80c. green 45 20
414 15c. on 45c. blue 65 55
382 15c. on 80c. green 65 25
415 20c. on 85c. red 65 55
374 30c. on 1a.40 blue . . . . 1·00 85
416 35c. on 85c. red 65 55
417 50c. on 1a.40 blue 65 55
418 60c. on 1a. red . . . . . 3·25 3·00
375 70c. on 2a. mauve . . . . 1·25 95
376 80c. on 5a. green . . . . 2·10 1·00
(A) surch **0,05 Cent.** in one line; (B) surch **5 CENTAVOS** in two lines.

1935. "Due" key-type surch **CORREIOS** and new value.
377 W 5c. on 6c. brown 85 65
378 30c. on 50c. grey 85 65
379 40c. on 50c. grey 85 65

22 Vasco da Gama

27 Airplane over Globe

1938. Name and value in black.
383 **22** 1c. olive (postage) 10 10
384 5c. brown 10 10
385 10c. red 10 10
386 15c. purple 10 10
387 20c. grey 10 10
388 – 30c. purple 15 10
389 – 35c. green 20 15
390 – 40c. brown 10 10
391 – 50c. mauve 10 10
392 – 60c. black 25 15
393 – 70c. violet 25 15
394 – 80c. orange 25 15
395 – 1a. red 25 15
396 – 1a.75 blue 70 30
397 – 2a. red . . . . 1·00 30
398 – 5a. olive . . . . 3·50 30
399 – 10a. blue . . . . 8·00 45
400 – 20a. brown . . . . 14·00 90

401 **27** 10c. red (air) 20 15
402 20c. violet 20 15
403 50c. orange 20 15
404 1a. blue 20 15
405 2a. red 30 15
406 3a. green 65 20
407 5a. brown . . . . 1·75 25
408 9a. red . . . . 2·40 70
409 10a. mauve . . . . 3·25 80
DESIGNS: 30c. to 50c. Mousinho de Albuquerque; 60c. to 1a. "Fomento" (symbolizing Progress); 1a.75, 2, 5a. Prince Henry the Navigator; 10, 20a. Afonso de Albuquerque.

28 Portuguese Colonial Column

31 Arms of Angola

1938. President's Colonial Tour.
410 **28** 80c. green . . . . 1·10 85
411 1a.75 blue . . . . 8·00 1·90
412 20a. brown . . . . 19·00 10·50

1945. Nos. 394/6 surch.
420 5c. on 80c. orange 50 30
421 50c. on 1a. red 50 30
422 50c. on 1a.75 blue 50 30

1947. Air.
423a **31** 1a. brown . . . . 4·00 1·50
423b 2a. green . . . . 4·00 1·50
423c 3a. orange . . . . . . 4·25 1·50
423d 3a.50 orange . . . . . 8·25 1·75
423e 5a. green . . . . 45·00 4·50
423f 6a. pink . . . . 45·00 7·50
423g 9a. red . . . . £130 80·00
423h 10a. green . . . . . . £120 30·00
423i 20a. blue . . . . £120 30·00
423j 50a. black . . . . . . £190 90·00
423k 100a. yellow £350 £250

32 Sao Miguel Fortress, Luanda

33 Our Lady of Fatima

1948. Tercentenary of Restoration of Angola. Inscr "Tricentenario da Restauracao de Angola 1648–1948".
424 **32** 5c. violet 10 10
425 – 10c. brown 30 15
426 – 30c. green 10 10
427 – 50c. purple 10 10
428 – 1a. red 25 10
429 – 1a.75 blue 50 10
430 – 2a. green 50 10
431 – 5a. black . . . . 1·75 30
432 – 10a. mauve . . . . 3·75 55
433 – 20a. blue . . . . 8·00 1·10
DESIGNS—HORIZ: 10c. Our Lady of Nazareth Hermitage, Luanda; 1a. Surrender of Luanda; 5a. Inscribed Rocks of Yelala; 20a. Massangano Fortress. VERT (portraits): 30c. Don John IV; 50c. Salvador Correia de Sa Benevides; 1a.75, Dioga Cao; 7a. Manuel Cerveira Pereira; 10a. Paulo Dias de Novais.

1948. Honouring Our Lady of Fatima.
434 **33** 50c. red . . . . 1·25 1·00
435 3a. blue . . . . 3·25 2·00
436 6a. orange . . . . 13·50 5·00
437 9a. red . . . . 27·00 6·50

35 River Chiumbe

36 Pedras Negras

1949.
438 **35** 20c. blue 30 15
439 **36** 40c. brown 30 10
440 – 50c. red 30 10
441 – 2a.50 blue . . . . 1·60 30
442 – 3a.50 grey . . . . 1·60 1·40
443 – 15a. green . . . . 13·50 1·40
444 – 50a. green . . . . 75·00 4·75
DESIGNS—As T **35**: 50c. Luanda; 2a.50, Bandeira; 3a.50, Mocamedes; 50a. Braganza Falls. 31 × 26 mm: 15a. River Cubal.

37 Aircraft and Globe

38 "Tentativa Feliz"

1949. Air.
445 **37** 1a. orange 30 10
446 2a. brown 65 10
447 3a. mauve 90 10
448 6a. green . . . . 2·00 50
449 9a. purple . . . . 2·75 1·10

1949. Centenary of Founding of Mocamedes.
450 **38** 1a. purple . . . . 5·25 60
451 4a. green . . . . 13·50 1·60

39 Letter and Globe

40 Reproduction of "Crown" key-type

1949. 75th Anniv of U.P.U.
452 **39** 4a. green . . . . 6·00 2·40

1950. Philatelic Exhibition and 80th Anniv of First Angolan Stamp.
453 **40** 50a. green 95 30
454 1a. red 95 45
455 4a. black . . . . 3·25 1·25

41 Bells and Dove

42 Angels holding Candelabra

1950. Holy Year.
456 **41** 1a. violet 65 10
457 **42** 4a. black . . . . 3·00 55

43 Dark Chanting Goshawk

44 Our Lady of Fatima

1951. Birds. Multicoloured.
458 5c. Type **43** 20 10
459 10c. Racquet-tailed roller . . 20 10
460 15c. Bateleur 30 10
461 20c. European bee eater . . . 35 25
462 50c. Giant kingfisher 35 10
463 1a. Anchieta's barbet 35 10
464 1a.50 African open-bill stork 50 15
465 2a. Southern ground hornbill 1·75 15
466 2a.50 African skimmer . . . 70 15
467 3a. Shikra 50 15
468 3a.50 Senham's bustard . . . 70 15
469 4a. African golden oriole . . 80 15
470 4a.50 Magpie shrike 80 15
471 5a. Red-shouldered glossy starling . . . . 3·50 35
472 6a. Sharp-tailed glossy starling . . . . 4·75 90
473 7a. Fan-tailed whydah . . . 5·25 1·25
474 10a. Half-collared kingfisher 20·00 1·40
475 12a.50 White-crowned shrike 5·75 2·00
476 15a. White-winged starling 5·25 2·00
477 20a. Southern yellow-billed hornbill . . . . 50·00 4·75
478 25a. Violet starling . . . . . 16·00 4·00
479 30a. Sulphur-breasted bush shrike . . . . 16·00 4·75

480 40a. Secretary bird 26·00 6·75
481 50a. Peach-faced lovebird 60·00 14·50
The 10, 15 and 20c., 2a.50, 3a., 4a.50, 12a.50 and 30a. are horiz, the remainder vert.

1951. Termination of Holy Year.
482 **44** 4a. orange 1·90 1·00

45 Laboratory
46 The Sacred Face

1952. 1st Tropical Medicine Congress, Lisbon.
483 **45** 1a. grey and blue 60 25

1952. Missionary Art Exhibition.
484 **46** 10c. blue and flesh 15 15
485 50c. green and stone 40 15
486 2a. purple and flesh 2·00 30

47 Leopard
48 Stamp of 1853 and Colonial Arms

1953. Angolan Fauna. Multicoloured.
487 5c. Type **47** 15 15
488 10c. Sable antelope (vert) 25 20
489 20c. African elephant (vert) 25 20
490 30c. Eland (vert) 25 20
491 40c. Crocodile 25 20
492 50c. Impala (vert) 25 20
493 1a. Mountain zebra (vert) 50 20
494 1a.50 Sitatunga (vert) 25 20
495 2a. Black rhinoceros 75 20
496 2a.30 Gemsbok (vert) 50 20
497 2a.50 Lion (vert) 75 20
498 3a. African buffalo 65 20
499 3a.50 Springbok (vert) 65 20
500 4a. Blue wildebeest (vert) 15·00 25
501 5a. Hartebeest (vert) 1·25 20
502 7a. Warthog (vert) 1·60 25
503 10a. Waterbuck (vert) 2·10 25
504 12a.50 Hippopotamus (vert) 7·00 1·60
505 15a. Greater kudu (vert) 7·00 1·60
506 20a. Giraffe (vert) 9·50 1·10

1953. Portuguese Stamp Centenary.
507 **48** 50c. multicoloured 65 45

49 Father M. da Nobrega and Sao Paulo
50 Route of President's Tour

1954. 4th Centenary of Sao Paulo.
508 **49** 1e. black and buff 40 20

1954. Presidential Visit.
509 **50** 35c. multicoloured 15 10
510 4e.50 multicoloured 1·00 45

51 Map of Angola
52 Col. A. de Paiva

1955. Map mult. Angola territory in colour given.
511 **51** 5c. white 20 15
512 20c. salmon 20 15
513 50c. blue 20 15
514 1e. orange 20 15
515 2e.30 yellow 90 30
516 4e. blue 1·75 15
517 10e. green 2·10 15
518 20e. white 3·00 1·10

1956. Birth Centenary of De Paiva.
519 **52** 1e. black, blue and orange 25 20

53 Quela Chief
54 Father J. M. Antunes

1957. Natives. Multicoloured.
520 5c. Type **53** 15 15
521 10c. Andulo flute player 15 15
522 15c. Dembos man and woman 15 15
523 20c. Quissama dancer (male) 15 15
524 30c. Quibala family 15 15
525 40c. Bocolo dancer (female) 15 15
526 50c. Quissama woman 15 15
527 80c. Cuanhama woman 20 15
528 1e.50 Luanda widow 1·60 15
529 2e.50 Bocolo dancer (male) 1·60 15
530 4e. Muquixe man 80 15
531 10e. Cabinda chief 1·40 30

1957. Birth Centenary of Father Antunes.
532 **54** 1e. multicoloured 55 30

55 Exhibition Emblem, Globe and Arms

1958. Brussels International Exhibition.
533 **55** 1e.50 multicoloured 45 40

56 "Securidaca longipedunculata"
57 Native Doctor and Patient

1958. 6th Int Tropical Medicine Congress.
534 **56** 2e.50 multicoloured 1·50 90

1958. 75th Anniv of Maria Pia Hospital, Luanda.
535 **57** 1e. brown, black and blue 30 20
536 – 1e.50 multicoloured 80 40
537 – 2e.50 multicoloured 1·50 75
DESIGNS: 1e.50, 17th-century doctor and patient; 2e.50, Present-day doctor, orderly and patients.

58 Welwitschia (plant)
59 Old Map of West Africa

1959. Centenary of Discovery of Welwitschia.
538 **58** 1e.50 multicoloured 70 30
539 – 2e.50 multicoloured 1·00 40
540 – 5e. multicoloured 1·60 40
541 – 10e. multicoloured 5·00 1·25
DESIGNS: 2e.50, 5, 10e. Various types of Welwitschia ("Welwitschia mirabilis").

1960. 500th Death Anniv of Prince Henry the Navigator.
542 **59** 2e.50 multicoloured 40 20

60 "Agriculture" (distribution of seeds)
61

1960. 10th Anniv of African Technical Co-operation Commission.
543 **60** 2e.50 multicoloured 50 20

1961. Angolan Women. As T **61**. Portraits multicoloured; background colours given.
544 10c. green 10 10
545 15c. blue 10 10
546 30c. yellow 10 10
547 40c. grey 10 10
548 60c. brown 10 10
549 1e.50 turquoise 10 10
550 2e. lilac 75 10
551 2e.50 lemon 75 10
552 3e. pink 2·75 20
553 4e. olive 1·40 20
554 5e. blue 90 20
555 7e.50 yellow 1·25 60
556 10e. buff 90 45
557 15e. brown 1·40 60
558 25e. red 1·90 90
559 50e. grey 4·25 1·90

62 Weightlifting

1962. Sports. Multicoloured.
560 50e. Flying 15 15
561 1e. Rowing 80 15
562 1e.50 Water polo 55 20
563 2e.50 Throwing the hammer 70 20
564 4e.50 High jumping 55 40
565 15e. Type **62** 1·40 1·00

63 "Anopheles funestus" (mosquito)
64 Gen. Norton de Matos (statue)

1962. Malaria Eradication.
566 **63** 2e.50 multicoloured 1·00 55

1962. 50th Anniv of Nova Lisboa.
567 **64** 2e.50 multicoloured 40 20

65 Red Locusts

1963. 15th Anniv of Int Locust Eradication Service.
568 **65** 2e.50 multicoloured 65 30

66 Arms of St. Paul of the Assumption, Luanda
67 Rear-Admiral A. Tomas

1963. Angolan Civic Arms (1st series). Mult.
569 5c. Type **66** 15 15
570 10c. Massangano 15 15
571 30c. Muxima 15 15
572 50c. Carmona 15 15
573 1e. Salazar 45 15
574 1e.50 Malanje 90 15
575 2e. Henry of Carvalho 45 15
576 2e.50 Mocamedes 2·50 40
577 3e. Novo Redondo 65 15
578 3e.50 St. Salvador (Congo) 75 15
579 5e. Luso 65 25
580 7e.50 St. Philip (Benguela) 90 75
581 10e. Lobito 1·00 65
582 12e.50 Gabela 1·25 1·00
583 15e. Sa da Bandeira 1·25 1·00
584 17e.50 Silva Porto 2·00 1·75
585 20e. Nova Lisboa 2·00 1·60
586 22e.50 Cabinda 2·00 1·75
587 30e. Serpa Pinto 2·50 2·25
See also Nos. 589/610.

1963. Presidential Visit.
588 **67** 2e.50 multicoloured 40 15

68 Arms of Sanza-Pombo
69 Map of Africa, Boeing 707 and Lockheed Super Constellation Airliners

1963. Angolan Civic Arms (2nd series). Mult.
589 15c. Type **68** 10 10
590 20c. St. Antonio do Zaire 10 10
591 25c. Ambriz 10 10
592 40c. Ambrizete 10 10
593 50c. Catete 10 10
594 70c. Quibaxe 10 10
595 1e. Maquela do Zombo 15 10
596 1e.20 Bembe 10 10
597 1e.50 Caxito 50 10
598 1e.80 Dondo 25 20
599 2e.50 Damba 1·75 10
600 4e. Cuimba 35 15
601 6e.50 Negage 35 30
602 7e. Quitexe 60 40
603 8e. Mucaba 60 50
604 9e. 31 de Janeiro 85 75
605 11e. Novo Caipemba 1·00 85
606 14e. Songo 1·10 1·00
607 17e. Quimbele 1·25 1·10
608 25e. Noqui 1·50 1·10
609 35e. Santa Cruz 2·10 1·75
610 50e. General Freire 2·75 1·50

1963. 10th Anniv of T.A.P. Airline.
611 **69** 1e. multicoloured 40 20

70 Bandeira Cathedral
71 Dr. A. T. de Sousa

1963. Angolan Churches. Multicoloured.
612 10c. Type **70** 10 10
613 20c. Landana 10 10
614 30c. Luanda (Cathedral) 10 10
615 40c. Gabela 10 10
616 50c. St. Martin, Bay of Tigers (Chapel) 10 10
617 1e. Melange (Cathedral) (horiz) 15 10
618 1e.50 St. Peter, Chibia 15 10
619 2e. Benguela (horiz) 20 10
620 2e.50 Jesus, Luanda 25 10
621 3e. Camabatela (horiz) 30 15
622 3e.50 Cabinda Mission 40 15
623 4e. Vila Folgares (horiz) 40 25
624 4e.50 Arrabida, Lobito (horiz) 50 25
625 5e. Cabinda 55 30
626 7e.50 Cacuso, Malange (horiz) 85 50
627 10e. Lubanga Mission 1·10 50
628 12e.50 Huila Mission (horiz) 1·25 70
629 15e. Island Cape, Luanda (horiz) 1·50 80

1964. Centenary of National Overseas Bank.
630 **71** 2e.50 multicoloured 55 25

72 Arms and Palace of Commerce, Luanda
73 I.T.U. Emblem and St. Gabriel

1964. Cent of Luanda Commercial Association.
631 **72** 1e. multicoloured 20 15

1965. Centenary of I.T.U.
632 **73** 2e.50 multicoloured 80 40

74 Boeing 707 over Petroleum Refinery
75 Fokker F.27 Friendship over Luanda Airport

1965. Air. Multicoloured.

633 1e.50 Type **74** 85 10
634 2e.50 Cambabe Dam 80 10
635 3e. Salazar Dam 1·10 10
636 4e. Captain Trofilo Duarte Dam 1·10 15
637 4e.50 Creveiro Lopes Dam 80 15
638 5e. Cuango Dam 80 20
639 6e. Quanza Bridge 1·25 30
640 7e. Captain Trofilo Duarte Railway Bridge 2·75 40
641 8e.50 Dr. Oliveira Salazar Bridge 2·25 70
642 12e.50 Captain Silva Carvalho Railway Bridge 3·25 1·00

Nos. 634/42 are horiz and each design includes a Boeing 707 airliner overhead.

1965. 25th Anniv of Direccao dos Transportes Aereos (Angolan airline).
643 **75** 2e.50 multicoloured 25 15

76 Arquebusier, 1539

77 St. Paul's Hospital, Luanda, and Sarmento Rodrigues Commercial and Industrial School

1966. Portuguese Military Uniforms. Multicoloured.

644 50c. Type **76** 10 10
645 1e. Arquebusier, 1640 10 10
646 1e.50 Infantry officer, 1777 15 10
647 2e. Infantry standard-bearer, 1777 20 10
648 2e.50 Infantryman, 1777 20 10
649 3e. Cavalry officer, 1783 25 10
650 4e. Trooper, 1783 30 15
651 4e.50 Infantry officer, 1807 40 20
652 5e. Infantryman, 1807 50 20
653 6e. Cavalry officer, 1807 70 20
654 8e. Trooper, 1807 1·00 30
655 9e. Infantryman, 1873 1·00 45

1966. 40th Anniv of National Revolution.
656 **77** 1e. multicoloured 20 15

78 Emblem of Brotherhood

79 Mendes Barata and Cruiser "Don Carlos I"

1966. Centenary of Brotherhood of the Holy Spirit.
657 **78** 1e. multicoloured 15 15

1967. Centenary of Military Naval Assn. Mult.

658 1e. Type **79** 70 35
659 2e.50 Augusto de Castilho and sail/steam corvette "Mindelo" 85 40

80 Basilica of Fatima

81 17th-century Map and M. C. Pereira (founder)

1967. 50th Anniv of Fatima Apparitions.
660 **80** 50c. multicoloured 15 10

1967. 350th Anniv of Benguela.
661 **81** 50c. multicoloured 15 10

82 Town Hall, Uige-Carmona

83 "The Three Orders"

1967. 50th Anniv of Uige-Carmona.
662 **82** 1e. multicoloured 15 10

1967. Portuguese Civil and Military Orders. Mult.

663 50c. Type **83** 10 10
664 1e. "Tower and Sword" 10 10
665 1e.50 "Avis" 10 10
666 2e. "Christ" 10 10
667 2e.50 "St. James of the Sword" 10 10
668 3e. "Empire" 20 10
669 4e. "Prince Henry" 25 15
670 5e. "Benemerencia" 30 25
671 10e. "Public Instruction" 60 25
672 20e. "Agricultural and Industrial Merit" 1·25 70

84 Belmonte Castle

85 Francisco Inocencio de Souza Countinho

1968. 500th Birth Anniv of Pedro Cabral (explorer). Multicoloured.

673 50c. Our Lady of Hope (vert) 15 15
674 1e. Type **84** 20 15
675 1e.50 St. Jeronimo's hermitage (vert) 25 15
676 2e.50 Cabral's fleet (vert) 70 15

1969. Bicent of Novo Redondo (Angolan city).
677 **85** 2e. multicoloured 25 15

86 Gunboat "Loge" and Admiral Coutinho

87 Compass

1969. Birth Centenary of Admiral Gago Coutinho.
678 **86** 2e.50 multicoloured 60 20

1969. 500th Birth Anniv of Vasco da Gama (explorer).
679 **87** 1e. multicoloured 15 10

88 L. A. Rebello de Silva

89 Gate of Jeronimos

1969. Cent of Overseas Administrative Reforms.
680 **88** 1e.50 multicoloured 15 10

1969. 500th Birth Anniv of King Manoel I.
681 **89** 3e. multicoloured 20 15

90 "Angolasaurus bocagei"

91 Marshal Carmona

1970. Fossils and Minerals. Multicoloured.

682 50c. Type **90** 35 15
683 1e. Ferro-meteorite 35 15
684 1e.50 Dioptase 55 35
685 2e. "Gondwanidium validium" 55 35
686 2e.50 Diamonds 55 35
687 3e. Estromatolitos 55 35
688 3e.50 Giant-toothed shark ("Procarcharodon megalodon") 1·25 55
689 4e. Dwarf lungfish ("Micro-ceratodus angolensis") 1·25 55
690 4e.50 Muscovite (mica) 90 55
691 5e. Barytes 90 55
692 6e. "Nostoceras helicinum" 1·60 75
693 10e. "Rotula orbiculus angolensis" 1·75 1·00

1970. Birth Centenary of Marshal Carmona.
694 **91** 2e.50 multicoloured 25 15

92 Cotton-picking

1970. Centenary of Malanje Municipality.
695 **92** 2e.50 multicoloured 30 20

93 Mail Steamers "Infante Dom Henrique" and "Principe Perfeito" and 1870 5r. Stamp

94 Map and Emblems

1970. Stamp Centenary. Multicoloured.

696 1e.50 Type **93** (postage) 50 25
697 4e.50 Beyer-Garratt steam locomotive and 25r. stamp of 1870 1·75 1·75
698 2e.50 Fokker F.27 Friendship and Boeing 707 mail planes and 10r. stamp of 1870 (air) 50 25

1971. 5th Regional Soil and Foundation Engineering Conference, Luanda.
700 **94** 2e.50 multicoloured 20 15

96 16th-century Galleon at Mouth of Congo

97 Sailing Yachts

1972. 400th Anniv of Camoens' "The Lusiads" (epic poem).
704 **96** 1e. multicoloured 50 15

1972. Olympic Games, Munich.
705 **97** 50c. multicoloured 30 15

98 Fairey IIID Seaplane "Santa Cruz" near Fernando de Noronha

1972. 50th Anniv of 1st Flight Lisbon–Rio de Janeiro.
706 **98** 1e. multicoloured 20 15

99 W.M.O. Emblem

1974. Centenary of W.M.O.
707 **99** 1e. multicoloured 20 15

100 Dish Aerials

1974. Inauguration of Satellite Communications Station Network.
708 **100** 2e. multicoloured 25 20

101 Doris Harp

1974. Sea Shells. Multicoloured.

709 25c. Type **101** 10 10
710 30c. West African murex 10 10
711 50c. Scaly-ridged venus 10 10
712 70c. Filose latirus 10 10
713 1e. "Cymbium cisium" 10 10
714 1e.50 West African helmet 15 10
715 2e. Rat cowrie 15 10
716 2e.50 Butterfly cone 25 10
717 3e. Bubonian conch 25 15
718 3e.50 "Tympanotonus fuscatus" 30 15
719 4e. Great ribbed cockle 30 15
720 5e. Lightning moon 40 15
721 6e. Lion's-paw scallop 45 20
722 7e. Giant tun 60 25
723 10e. Rugose donax 80 30
724 25e. Smith's distorsio 2·25 90
725 30e. "Olivancilaria acuminata" 2·25 1·00
726 35e. Giant hairy melongena 2·75 1·25
727 40e. Wavy-leaved turrid 3·50 1·40
728 50e. American sundial 4·50 1·75

1974. Youth Philately. No. 511 optd **1974 FILATELIA JUVENIL**.
729 **51** 5c. multicoloured 2·00 2·25

103 Arm with Rifle and Star

104 Diquiche-ua-Puheue Mask

1975. Independence.
730 **103** 1e.50 multicoloured 10 10

1975. Angolan Masks. Multicoloured.

731 50c. Type **104** 10 10
732 3e. Bui ou Congolo mask 15 10

105 Workers

107 Pres. Agostinho Neto

1976. Workers' Day.
733 **105** 1e. multicoloured 10 10

1976. Stamp Day. Optd **DIA DO SELO 15 Junho 1976 REP. POPULAR DE**.
734 **51** 10e. multicoloured 1·50 1·25

1976. 1st Anniv of Independence.

735 **107** 50c. black and grey 10 10
736 2e. purple and grey 10 10
737 3e. blue and grey 10 10
738 5e. brown and buff 15 10
739 10e. brown and drab 25 10

1976. St. Silvestre Games. Optd **S Silvestre Rep. Popular de**.
741 **62** 15e. multicoloured 55 35

1977. Nos. 518, 724/5 and 728 optd **REPUBLICA POPULAR DE**.

742 20e. Type **51** 3·50 3·50
743 25e. "Cymatium trigonum" 60 15
744 30e. "Olivancilaria acuminata" 75 25
745 50e. "Solarium granulatum" 1·25 40

111 Child receiving Vaccine

112 Map of Africa and Flag

1977. Polio Vaccination Campaign.
746 **111** 2k.50 blue and black 10 10

1977. MPLA Congress.
747 **112** 6k. multicoloured 20 15

113 Human Rights Flame **114** Emblem

1979. 30th Anniv of Declaration of Human Rights.
748 **113** 2k.50 yellow, red & black . . . 15 10

1979. International Anti-apartheid Year.
749 **114** 1k. multicoloured 10 10

115 Child raising Arms to Light **117** Pres. Agostinho Neto

1980. International Year of the Child (1979).
750 **115** 3k.50 multicoloured . . . 15 10

1980. Nos. 697/8 optd **REPUBLICA POPULAR DE**.
751 4e.50 multicoloured (postage) 2·75 1·75
752 2e.50 multicoloured (air) . . 15 10

1980. National Heroes Day. Multicoloured.
753 4k.50 Type **117** 15 10
754 50k. Pres. Neto with machine-gun . . . . 1·25 70

118 Arms and Workers **119** "The Liberated Angolan" (A. Vaz de Carvalho)

1980. "Popular Power".
755 **118** 40k. blue and black . . . 1·00 55

1980. 5th Anniv of Independence.
756 **119** 5k.50 multicoloured . . . 15 10

120 Running **121** Millet

1980. Olympic Games, Moscow.
757 **120** 9k. pink and red 20 10
758 – 12k. light blue and blue 30 10
DESIGN: 12k. Swimming.

1980. Angolan Produce. Multicoloured.
759 50l. Type **121** 10 10
760 5k. Coffee 15 10
761 7k.50 Sunflower 20 10
762 13k.50 Cotton 30 15
763 14k. Petroleum 30 15
764 16k. Diamonds 35 20

1981. Nos. 708, 713/16 and 718/27 with "REPUBLICA PORTUGUESA" inscr obliterated.
(a) Dish aerials.
765 **100** 2e. multicoloured 10 10

(b) Sea Shells. Multicoloured.
766 1e. "Cymbium cisium" . . . 10 10
767 1e.50 West African helmet . . 15 10
768 2e. Rat cowrie 20 10
769 2e.50 Butterfly cone 25 10
770 3e.50 "Tympanotonus fuscatus" 30 10
771 4e. Great ribbed cockle . . . 35 15
772 5e. Lightning moon 40 15
773 6e. Lion's-paw scallop . . . 45 20
774 7e. Giant tun 50 20
775 10e. Rugose donax 70 25
776 25e. Smith's distorsio . . . . 1·75 30
777 30e. "Olivancilaria acuminata" . . . . 1·90 65
778 35e. Giant hairy melongena 2·40 90
779 40e. Wavy-leaved turrid . . . 3·00 1·00

122 Prisoner and Protesting Crowd

1981. 5th Anniv of Soweto Riots in South Africa.
780 **122** 4k.50 black, red & silver 20 15

123 Basketball and Volleyball

1981. 2nd Central African Games. Multicoloured.
781 50l. Cycling and Tennis . . . 10 10
782 5k. Judo and Boxing 20 15
783 6k. Type **123** 25 15
784 10k. Handball and football 40 20

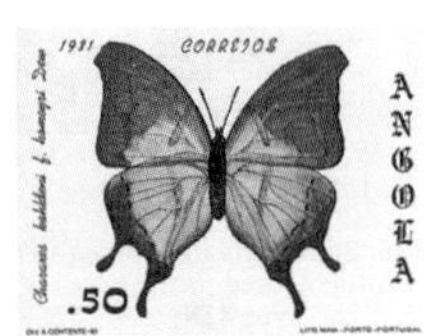

124 Statuette **125** "Charaxes kahldeni f. homeyri"

1981. "Turipex 81".
785 **124** 9k. multicoloured 40 20

1982. Butterflies. Multicoloured.
787 50l. Type **125** 10 10
788 1k. "Abantis gambesiaca" . . 10 10
789 5k. "Catacroptera cloanthe" 25 30
790 9k. "Myrina ficedula" (vert) 60 25
791 10k. "Colotis danae" 60 25
792 15k. "Acraea acrita bella" . . 80 30
793 100k. "Precis hierta cebrese" 5·25 2·40

126 "Silence of Night" **127** Worker and Building

1982. 5th Anniv of Admission to United Nations. Multicoloured.
794 5k.50 Type **126** 25 15
795 7k.50 "Cotton Fields" . . . 35 15

1982. 20th Anniv of Angola Laboratory of Engineering. Multicoloured.
797 9k. Laboratory building (horiz) 40 20
798 13k. Type **127** (Research in construction materials) . . 45 25
799 100k. Geotechnical equipment 4·00 2·25

128 "Albizzia versicolor"

1983. Flowers (1st series). Multicoloured.
800 5k. "Dichrostachys glomerata" 25 10
801 12k. "Amblygonocarpus obtusangulus" 45 20
802 50k. Type **128** . . . . . . 2·00 1·10

129 Angolan Woman and Emblem

1983. 1st Angolan Women's Organization Congress.
803 **129** 20k. multicoloured . . . 80 25

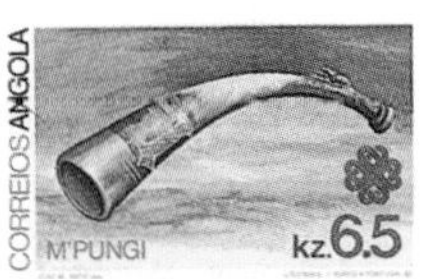

130 M'pungi (horn)

1983. World Communications Year. Multicoloured.
804 6k.50 Type **130** 25 20
805 12k. Mondu (drum) 50 45

131 Spear breaking Chain around South Africa

1983. 30th Anniv of Organization of African Unity.
806 **131** 6k.50 multicoloured . . . 30 25

132 "Antestiopsis lineaticollis intricata"

1983. "Brasiliana 83" International Stamp Exn, Rio de Janeiro. Harmful Insects. Multicoloured.
807 4k.50 Type **132** 25 15
808 6k.50 "Stephanoderes hampei" 35 25
809 10k. "Zonocerus variegatus" 60 45

133 Map of Africa and E.C.A. Emblem

1983. 25th Anniv of Economic Commission for Africa.
810 **133** 10k. multicoloured . . . 45 40

134 Collecting Mail **136** Dove

135 "Parasa karschi"

1983. 185th Anniv of Postal Service. Multicoloured.
811 50l. Type **134** 10 10
812 3k.50 Unloading mail from aircraft (horiz) 20 15
813 5k. Sorting mail (horiz) . . . 35 25
814 15k. Posting letter 85 80
815 30k. Collecting mail from private box (horiz) . . . . 1·75 1·50

1984. Moths. Multicoloured.
817 50l. Type **135** 10 10
818 1k. "Diaphone angolensis" 10 10
819 3k.50 "Choeropais jucunda" 30 15
820 6k.50 "Hespagarista rendalli" 50 35
821 15k. "Euchromia guineensis" 95 80
822 17k.50 "Mazuca roseistriga" 1·10 95
823 20k. "Utetheisa callima" . . 1·40 1·25

1984. 1st National Union of Angolan Workers Congress.
824 **136** 30k. multicoloured . . . 1·75 1·50

137 Flag and Agostinho Neto

1984. 5th National Heroes Day. Multicoloured.
825 10k.50 Type **137** 50 45
826 36k.50 Flag and Agostinho Neto (different) . . . . . 1·60 1·50

138 Southern Ground Hornbill

1984. Birds. Multicoloured.
827 10k.50 Type **138** 90 90
828 14k. Palm-nut vulture . . . . 1·25 1·25
829 16k. Goliath heron . . . . . 1·50 1·50
830 19k.50 Eastern white pelican 1·75 1·75
831 22k. African spoonbill . . . 2·00 2·00
832 26k. South African crowned crane . . . . 2·40 2·40

139 Greater Kudu

1984. Mammals. Multicoloured.
833 1k. Type **139** 10 10
834 4k. Springbok 25 15
835 5k. Chimpanzee 30 25
836 10k. African buffalo 55 50
837 15k. Sable antelope 80 65
838 20k. Aardvark . . . . 1·25 1·10
839 25k. Spotted hyena . . . . . 1·50 1·25

140 Sao Pedro da Barra Fortress

1985. Monuments. Multicoloured.
840 5k. Type **140** 25 20
841 12k.50 Nova Oerias ruins . . 60 55
842 18k. Antiga cathedral ruins, M'Banza Kongo 80 75
843 26k. Massangano fortress . . 1·25 1·10
844 39k. Escravatura museum . . 1·75 1·60

141 Flags on World Map **142** Flags and "XXV"

1985. 5th Anniv of Southern Africa Development Co-ordination Conference. Multicoloured.
845 1k. Type **141** 10 10
846 11k. Offshore drilling . . . . 1·25 50
847 57k. Conference session . . . 2·50 2·40

1985. 25th Anniv of National Union of Angolan Workers.
848 **142** 77k. multicoloured . . . 3·50 3·25

143 "Lonchocarpas sericeus"

1985. Medicinal Plants. Multicoloured.
849 1k. Type **143** 10 10
850 4k. "Gossypium sp." 20 15
851 11k. Senna 50 45
852 25k.50 "Gloriosa superba" 1·10 1·00
853 55k. "Cochlospermum angolensis" . . . . 2·50 2·40

144 Map of Angola as Dove and Conference Emblem

1984. Ministerial Conference of Non-aligned Countries, Luanda.
854 **144** 35k. multicoloured . . . 1·60 1·50

145 Dove and U.N. Emblem

1985. 40th Anniv of U.N.O.
855 **145** 12k.50 multicoloured . . 60 55

146 Cement Works

1985. 10th Anniv of Independence. Multicoloured.
856 50l. Type **146** 10 10
857 5k. Timber yard 20 15
858 7k. Quartz 30 25
859 10k. Iron works 50 45

147 Emblem, Open Book, Soldier, Farmer and Factory

1985. 2nd MPLA Congress.
861 **147** 20k. multicoloured . . . 90 85

148 Runner on Track

1985. 30th Anniv of Demostenes de Almeida Clington Races. Multicoloured.
862 50l. Type **148** 10 10
863 5k. Two runners on road . . 20 15
864 6k.50 Three runners on road 30 25
865 10k. Two runners on track 50 45

149 Map, Stadium and Players **150** Crowd

1986. World Cup Football Championship, Mexico.
866 **149** 50l. multicoloured 10 10
867 – 3k.50 multicoloured 15 15
868 – 5k. multicoloured 30 25
869 – 7k. multicoloured 35 30
870 – 10k. multicoloured . . . 50 45
871 – 18k. multicoloured . . . 85 70
DESIGNS: 3k.50 to 18k. Different footballers.

1986. 25th Anniv of Armed Independence Movement.
872 **150** 15k. multicoloured . . . 75 70

151 Soviet Space Project

1985. 25th Anniv of First Man in Space. Mult.
873 50l. Type **151** 10 10
874 1k. "Voskhod 1" 10 10
875 5k. Cosmonaut on space walk 20 15
876 10k. Moon vehicle 50 45
877 13k. "Soyuz"–"Apollo" link-up 60 55

152 National Flag and U.N. Emblem **153** People at Work

1986. 10th Anniv of Angolan Membership of U.N.O.
878 **152** 22k. multicoloured . . . 1·00 90

1986. 30th Anniv of Popular Movement for the Liberation of Angola. Multicoloured.
879 5k. Type **153** 20 15
880 5k. Emblem and people (29 × 36 mm) 20 15
881 5k. Soldiers fighting 20 15
Nos. 879/81 were printed together, se-tenant, forming a composite design.

154 Lecturer and Students (Faculty of Engineering) **155** Ouioca

1986. 10th Anniv of Agostinho Neto University. Multicoloured.
882 50l. Type **154** 10 10
883 7k. Students and Judges (Faculty of Law) 30 25
884 10k. Students using microscopes and surgeons operating (Faculty of Medicine) 50 45

1987. Traditional Hairstyles. Multicoloured.
885 1k. Type **155** 10 10
886 1k.50 Luanda 10 10
887 5k. Humbe 20 15
888 7k. Muila 35 25
889 20k. Muila (different) 80 70
890 30k. Lunda, Dilolo . . . . 1·25 1·00

156 "Lenin in the Smolny Institute" (detail, Serov) **157** Pambala Beach

1987. 70th Anniv of Russian Revolution.
891 **156** 15k. multicoloured . . . 60 25

1987. Scenic Spots. Multicoloured.
892 50l. Type **157** 10 10
893 1k.50 Quedas do Dala (waterfalls) 10 10
894 3k.50 Black Feet Rocks, Pungo Adongo (vert) . . . 15 10
895 5k. Cuango River valley . . 20 15
896 10k. Luanda shore (vert) . . 40 35
897 20k. Serra da Leba road . . 80 75

158 Emblem **159** Dancers

1988. 2nd Angolan Women's Organization Congress. Multicoloured.
898 2k. Type **158** 10 10
899 10k. Woman engaged in various pursuits 40 35

1988. 10th Anniv of Vitoria Carnival. Mult.
900 5k. Type **159** 15 10
901 10k. Revellers 40 35

160 Augusto N'Gangula (child revolutionary)

1989. Pioneers. Multicoloured.
902 12k. Type **160** (20th death anniv) 50 45
903 15k. Pioneers (25th anniv (1988) of Agostinho Neto Pioneers Organization) . . 60 55

161 Luanda 1st August Sports Club (1979–81)

1989. 10th National Football League Championship. Championship Winners. Multicoloured.
904 5k. Type **161** 15 15
905 5k. Luanda Petro Atletico (1982, 1984, 1986–88) . . . 15 15
906 5k. Benguela 1st May Sports Club (1983, 1985) 15 15

162 Watering Cabbages

1990. 10th Anniv (1987) of International Fund for Agricultural Development.
907 **162** 10k. multicoloured . . . 35 30

163 19th-century Middle-class Houses, Luanda

1990. Historical Buildings. Multicoloured.
908 1k. Type **163** 10 10
909 2k. Cidade Alta railway station, Luanda . . . . . 1·75 30
910 5k. National Anthropology Museum 20 15
911 15k. Palace of Ana Joaquina dos Santos 55 50
912 23k. Iron Palace 80 75
913 36k. Meteorological observatory (vert) . . . . 1·25 1·10
914 50k. Governor's palace . . . 1·75 1·60

164 "General Machado" and Route Map

1990. Benguela (915) and Luanda Railways. Mult.
915 5k. Type **164** 45 30
916 12k. Beyer-Garratt steam locomotive (facing left) . . 80 75
917 12k. Beyer-Garratt steam locomotive (facing right) 80 75
918 14k. Mikado steam locomotive . . . . 1·25 95

165 Hydroelectric Production

1990. 10th Anniv of Southern Africa Development Co-ordinating Conference. Multicoloured.
920 5k. Type **165** 20 15
921 9k. Oil industry 90 30

166 Map in Envelope

1990. 10th Anniv of Pan-African Postal Union. Multicoloured.
922 4k. Type **166** 15 10
923 10k. Map consisting of stamps and envelopes . . . 35 30

167 "Muxima"

1990. "Stamp World London 90" International Stamp Exn. Paintings by Raul Indipwo. Multicoloured.
924 6k. "Three Graces" (horiz) 20 15
925 9k. Type **167** 30 25

168 Antelope

1990. Protected Animals. Sable Antelope. Mult.
926 5k. Type **168** . . . . 2·40 1·90
927 5k. Male and female . . . . 2·40 1·90
928 5k. Female . . . . 2·40 1·90
929 5k. Female and young . . . 2·40 1·90

169 Porcelain Rose **170** Zebra Drinking

1990. "Belgica 90" International Stamp Exhibition, Brussels. Flowers. Multicoloured.
930 5k. Type **169** 20 15
931 8k. Indian carnation 30 25
932 10k. Allamanda 35 30

1990. International Literacy Year. Multicoloured.
934 5k. Type **170** 20 15
935 5k. Butterfly 20 15
936 5k. Horse's head 20 15

171 Flag and People

1990. 10th Anniv of People's Assembly.
938 **171** 10k. multicoloured 35 30

172 Dove, Flag and Workers **174** Marimba

173 Uniform, 1961

1990. 3rd Popular Movement for the Liberation of Angola-Labour Party Congress.
939 **172** 14k. multicoloured 50 45

1991. 30th Anniv of Armed Independence Movement. Freedom Fighters' Uniforms. Mult.
940 6k. Type **173** 20 15
941 6k. Pau N'Dulo, 1962–63 20 15
942 6k. Military uniform, 1968 20 15
943 6k. Military uniform from 1972 20 15

1991. Musical Instruments. Multicoloured.
944 6k. Type **174** 10 10
945 6k. Ngoma ya Mucupela (double-ended drum) 10 10
946 6k. Ngoma la Txina (floor-standing drum) 10 10
947 6k. Kissange 10 10

175 Iona National Park

1991. African Tourism Year. Multicoloured.
948 3k. Type **175** 10 10
949 7k. Kalandula Falls 10 10
950 35k. Lobito Bay 70 30
951 60k. "Welwitschia mirabilis" 65 55

176 Kabir of the Dembos

1991. "Espamer '91" Spain–Latin America Stamp Exhibition, Buenos Aires. Dogs. Multicoloured.
953 5k. Type **176** 10 10
954 7k. Ombua 20 10
955 11k. Kabir massongo 15 10
956 12k. Kawa tchowe 15 10

177 Judo **178** Mother and Child

1991. Olympic Games, Barcelona (1992) (1st issue). Multicoloured.
957 4k. Type **177** 10 10
958 6k. Yachting 10 10
959 10k. Marathon 15 10
960 100k. Swimming 1·10 95

1991. 13th Anniv of Angolan Red Cross. Mult.
961 20k.+5k. Type **178** 30 20
962 40k.+5k. Zebra and foal 50 40

179 Quadrant and Galleon

1991. "Iberex '91" Stamp Exhibition. Navigational Instruments. Multicoloured.
963 5k. Type **179** 15 10
964 15k. Astrolabe and caravel 30 10
965 20k. Cross-staff and caravel 50 20
966 50k. Navigation chart by Fran-cisco Rodrigues and galleon 1·50 60

180 Common Eagle Ray **181** Mukixi wa Mbwesu Mask

1992. Rays. Multicoloured.
967 40k. Type **180** 35 25
968 50k. Spotted eagle ray 40 35
969 66k. Manta ray 55 40
970 80k. Brown ray 65 50

1992. Quioca Painted Masks (1st series).
972 – 60k. orange and brown 15 10
973 – 100k. black, verm & red 25 20
974 **181** 150k. pink and orange 35 30
975 – 250k. red and brown 60 50
DESIGNS: 60k. Kalelwa mask; 100k. Mikixe wa Kino mask; 250k. Cikunza mask.
See also Nos. 1006/7 and 1021/4.

182 "Ptaeroxylon obliquum" **183** King and Missionaries

1992. "Lubrapex 92" Brazilian–Portuguese Stamp Exhibition, Lisbon. Medicinal Plants. Each brown, stone and deep brown.
976 200k. Type **182** 45 35
977 300k. "Spondias mombin" 70 55
978 500k. "Parinari curatellifolia" 1·25 1·00
979 600k. "Cochlospermum angolense" 1·40 1·10

1992. 500th Anniv (1991) of Baptism of First Angolans. Multicoloured.
980 150k. Type **183** 35 30
981 420k. Ruins of M'Banza Congo Church 1·00 80
982 470k. Muxima Church 1·10 90
983 500k. Cross superimposed on children's faces 1·25 1·00

184 Dimba House **185** Lovebirds

1992. "Expo '92" World's Fair, Seville. Traditional Houses. Multicoloured.
984 150k. Type **184** 35 30
985 330k. Cokwe house 80 65
986 360k. Mbali house 85 70
987 420k. Ambwela house 1·00 80
988 500k. House of the Upper Zambezi 1·25 1·00

1992. Nature Protection. Peach-faced Lovebirds. Multicoloured.
989 150k. Type **185** 35 30
990 200k. Birds feeding 45 35
991 250k. Bird in hand 60 50
992 300k. Bird on perch 70 55

187 Hurdling **188** Women with Nets

1992. Olympic Games, Barcelona (2nd issue). Mult.
994 120k. Type **187** 30 25
995 180k. Cycling 45 35
996 240k. Roller hockey 55 45
997 360k. Basketball 85 70

1992. Fishing. Multicoloured.
998 65k. Type **188** 20 10
999 90k. Fishermen pulling in nets 30 15
1000 100k. Fishermen checking traps 35 20
1001 120k. Fishing canoes 30 25

190 Crowd with Ballot Papers around Ballot Box **191** Mail Van

1992. 1st Free Elections. Multicoloured.
1003 120k. Type **190** 30 25
1004 150k. Doves, map, people and ballot box 35 30
1005 200k. Dove, crowd and ballot box 45 35

1992. Quioca Painted Masks (2nd series). As T **181**.
1006 72k. brown, black and yellow 15 10
1007 80k. red, black and brown 20 15
1008 120k. pink, black and red 30 25
1009 210k. black and yellow 50 40
DESIGNS: 72k. Cihongo mask; 80k. Mbwasu mask; 120k. Cinhanga mask; 210k. Kalewa mask.

1992. Introduction of Express Mail Service in Angola. Multicoloured.
1010 450k. Type **191** 55 45
1011 550k. Boeing 707 airplane 65 50

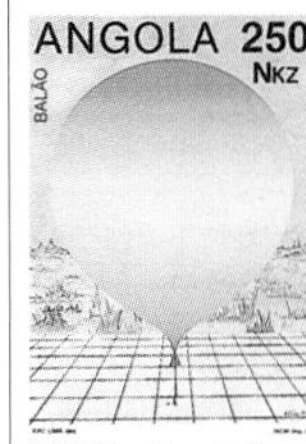

192 Weather Balloon **193** Rayed Hat

1993. World Meteorology Day. Meteorological Instruments. Multicoloured.
1012 250k. Type **192** 10 10
1013 470k. Actinometer 10 10
1014 500k. Rain-gauge 10 10

1993. Molluscs. Multicoloured.
1015 210k. Type **193** 10 10
1016 330k. Bubonian conch 15 10
1017 400k. African pelican's foot 15 10
1018 500k. White spindle 20 15

1993. Quioca Art (1st series). As T **181**.
1021 72k. grey, red and brown 10 10
1022 210k. pink and brown 10 10
1023 420k. black, brown & orge 10 10
1024 600k. black, red and brown 10 10
DESIGNS: 72k. Men with vehicles; 210k. Rider on antelope; 420k. Bird-plane; 600k. Carrying "soba".
See also Nos. 1038/41 and 1050/3.

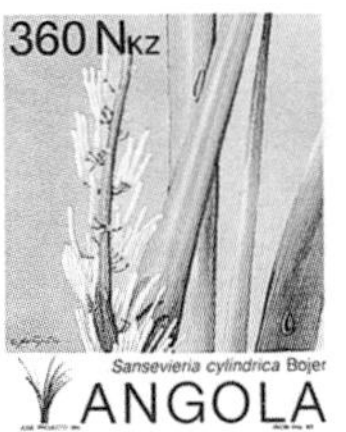

195 "Sansevieria cylindrica" **196** Atlantic Hawksbill Turtle laying Eggs and Green Turtle

1993. Cacti and Succulents. Multicoloured.
1025 360k. Type **195** 10 10
1026 400k. Milk-bush 10 10
1027 500k. Indian fig 10 10
1028 600k. "Dracaena aubryana" 10 10

1993. Sea Turtles. Multicoloured.
1029 180k. Type **196** 10 10
1030 450k. Head of Atlantic hawksbill turtle and newly hatched turtles 10 10
1031 550k. Leather-back turtle 10 10
1032 630k. Loggerhead turtles 15 10
Nos. 1029/32 were issued together, se-tenant, forming a composite design.

198 Vimbundi Pipe **199** St. George's Mushroom

1993. Tobacco Pipes. Multicoloured.
1034 72k. Type **198** 10 10
1035 200k. Vimbundi pipe (different) 10 10
1036 420k. Mutopa calabash water pipe 10 10
1037 600k. Pexi carved-head pipe 10 10

1993. Quioca Art (2nd series). As T **181**.
1038 300k. brown and orange 10 10
1039 600k. red and brown 10 10
1040 800k. black, orange and deep orange 15 10
1041 1000k. orange and brown 20 15
DESIGNS: 300k. Leopard and dog; 600k. Rabbits; 800k. Birds; 1000k. Birds and cockerel.

1993. Fungi. Multicoloured.
1042 300k. Type **199** 55 15
1043 500k. Death cap 90 30
1044 600k. "Amanita vaginata" 1·10 35
1045 1000k. Parasol mushroom 1·90 60

200 "Cinganji" (figurine of dancer, Bie province) **201** Orgy

1994. National Culture Day. "Hong Kong '94" International Stamp Exhibition. Multicoloured.
1046 500k. Type **200** 10 10
1047 1000k. Chief's staff with carved woman's head (Bie province) 20 15
1048 1200k. Statuette of traveller riding ox (Huambo province) 25 20
1049 2200k. Corn pestle (Ovimbundu) 45 35

1994. Quioca Art (3rd series). As T **181**.
1050 500k. multicoloured 10 10
1051 2000k. red and brown 40 30
1052 2500k. red and brown 50 40
1053 3000k. carmine and red 60 50
DESIGNS: 500k. Bird on plant; 2000k. Plant with roots; 2500k. Plant; 3000k. Fern.

1994. AIDS Awareness Campaign. Multicoloured.
1054 500k. Type **201** 10 10
1055 1000k. Masked figure using infected syringe passing box of condoms to young couple 10 10
1056 3000k. Victims 20 15

202 Flag, Arrows and Small Ball

1994. World Cup Football Championship, U.S.A. Multicoloured.
1057 500k. Type **202** 10 10
1058 700k. Flag, four arrows and large ball 10 10
1059 2200k. Flag, goal net and ball 10 10
1060 2500k. Flag, ball and boot 10 10

203 Brachiosaurus

1994. "Philakorea 1994" International and "Singpex '94" Stamp Exhibitions. Dinosaurs. Multicoloured.
1061 1000k. Type **203** 10 10
1062 3000k. Spinosaurus 10 10
1063 5000k. Ouranosaurus 10 10
1064 10000k. Lesothosaurus . . . 15 10

204 Brown Snake Eagle, Ostrich, Yellow-billed Stork and Pink-backed Pelican

1994. Tourism. Multicoloured.
1066 2000k. Type **204** 10 10
1067 4000k. Animals 10 10
1068 8000k. Women 10 10
1069 10000k. Men 10 10

205 Dual-service Wall-mounted Post Box

1994. Post Boxes. Multicoloured.
1070 5000k. Type **205** 10 10
1071 7500k. Wall-mounted philatelic post box 10 10
1072 10000k. Free-standing post box 10 10
1073 21000k. Multiple service wall-mounted post box . . 25 15

206 "Heliothis armigera" (moth)

1994. Insects. Multicoloured.
1074 5000k. Type **206** 10 10
1075 6000k. "Bemisia tabasi" . . 10 10
1076 10000k. "Dysdercus sp." (bug) 10 10
1077 27000k. "Spodoptera exigua" (moth) 25 15

207 "100"

1994. Cent of International Olympic Committee.
1078 **207** 27000k. red, yell & blk 25 20

208 Pot

1995. Traditional Ceramics. With service indicator. Multicoloured. (a) INLAND POSTAGE. Inscr "PORTE NACIONAL".
1079 (1°) Type **208** 10 10
1080 (2°) Pot with figure of woman on lid 10 10

(b) INTERNATIONAL POSTAGE. Inscr "PORTE INTERNACIONAL".
1081 (1°) Pot with man's head on lid 20 15
1082 (2°) Duck-shaped pot . . . 25 20

209 Making Fire

1995. The !Kung (Khoisan tribe). Multicoloured.
1083 10000k. Type **209** 10 10
1084 15000k. Tipping darts with poison 15 10
1085 20000k. Smoking 20 15
1086 25000k. Hunting 20 15
1087 28000k. Women and children 25 20
1088 30000k. Painting animals on walls 25 20

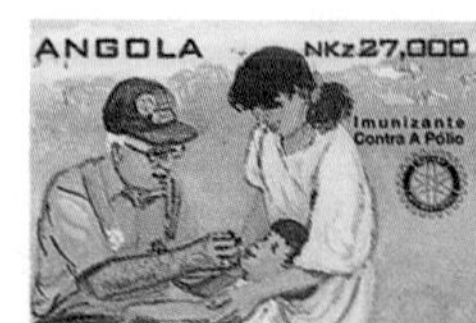

210 Vaccinating Child against Polio

1995. 90th Anniv of Rotary International. Multicoloured. (a) Inscr in Portuguese.
1089 27000k. Type **210** 15 10
1090 27000k. Examining baby . . 15 10
1091 27000k. Giving child vaccination 15 10

(b) Inscr in English.
1092 27000k. Type **210** 15 10
1093 27000k. As No. 1090 . . . 15 10
1094 27000k. As No. 1091 . . . 15 10

Nos. 1089/91 and 1092/4 respectively were issued together, se-tenant, forming composite designs.

211 "Sputnik 1" (satellite)

1995. World Telecommunications Day. Mult.
1096 27000k. Type **211** 15 10
1097 27000k. "Intelsat" satellite and space shuttle 15 10

212 Doves above Baby on Daisy-covered Map

1995. 20th Anniv of Independence.
1099 **212** 2900k. multicoloured . . 65 50

213 Child, Containers and Fork-lift Truck

1996. Goods Transportation. Multicoloured.
1100 200k. Type **213** 10 10
1101 1265k. Sailing boats and "Mount Cameroon" (ferry) 25 25
1102 2583k. Fork-lift trucks loading and unloading "Mount Cameroon" (ferry) 90 50
1103 2583k. Truck 60 50

214 Women in Agriculture

1996. 4th World Conference on Women, Peking (1995). Multicoloured.
1105 375k. Type **214** 10 10
1106 1106k. Women in education 25 20
1107 1265k. Women in business 30 25
1108 2900k. Dimba servant girl (vert) 65 50

215 Verdant Hawk Moth

1996. Flora and Fauna. Multicoloured.
1110 1500k. Type **215** 10 10
1111 1500k. Western honey buzzard 10 10
1112 1500k. Bateleur 10 10
1113 1500k. Common kestrel . . 10 10
1114 4400k. Water lily 20 15
1115 4400k. Red-crested turaco 20 15
1116 4400k. Giraffe 20 15
1117 4400k. African elephant . . 20 15
1118 5100k. Panther toad 20 15
1119 5100k. Hippopotamus . . . 20 15
1120 5100k. Cattle egret 20 15
1121 5100k. Lion 20 15
1122 6000k. African hunting ("wild") dog 25 20
1123 6000k. Helmeted turtle . . . 25 20
1124 6000k. African pygmy goose 25 20
1125 6000k. Egyptian plover . . 25 20

Nos. 1111/13, 1115/17, 1119/21 and 1123/5 respectively were issued together, se-tenant, forming composite designs.

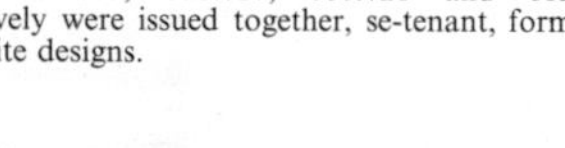

216 California Quail

1997. Birds. Multicoloured.
1127 5500k. Type **216** 20 15
1128 5500k. Prairie chicken ("Greater Prairie Chicken") 20 15
1129 5500k. Indian blue quail ("Painted Quail") 20 15
1130 5500k. Golden pheasant . . 20 15
1131 5500k. Crested wood partridge ("Roulroul Partridge") 20 15
1132 5500k. Ceylon spurfowl ("Ceylon Sourfowl") . . . 20 15
1133 5500k. Himalayan snowcock 20 15
1134 5500k. Temminck's tragopan ("Temminicks Tragopan") 20 15
1135 5500k. Lady Amherst's pheasant 20 15
1136 5500k. Great curassow . . . 20 15
1137 5500k. Red-legged partridge 20 15
1138 5500k. Himalayan monal pheasant ("Impeyan Pheasant") 20 15
1139 5500k. Anna's hummingbird 20 15
1140 5500k. Blue-throated hummingbird 20 15
1141 5500k. Broad-tailed hummingbird 20 15
1142 5500k. Costa's hummingbird 20 15
1143 5500k. White-eared hummingbird 20 15
1144 5500k. Calliope hummingbird 20 15
1145 5500k. Violet-crowned hummingbird 20 15
1146 5500k. Rufous hummingbird 20 15
1147 5500k. Crimson topaz ("Crimson Topaz Hummingbird") 20 15
1148 5500k. Broad-billed hummingbird 20 15
1149 5500k. Frilled coquette ("Frilled Coquette Hummingbird") 20 15
1150 5500k. Ruby-throated hummingbird 20 15

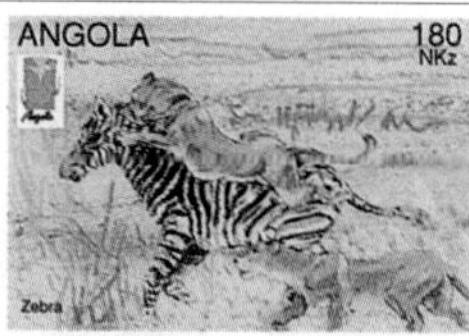

217 Lions attacking Zebra

1996. African Wildlife. Multicoloured.
1152 180k. Type **217** 10 10
1153 180k. Lions watching zebras 10 10
1154 180k. African hunting dogs attacking gnu 10 10
1155 180k. Pack of hunting dogs chasing herd of gnu . . . 10 10
1156 450k. Lions stalking isolated zebra 10 10
1157 450k. Male lion 10 10
1158 450k. Hunting dogs surrounding gnu 10 10
1159 450k. Close-up of African hunting dog 10 10
1160 550k. Cheetah 10 10
1161 550k. Cheetah chasing springbok 10 10
1162 550k. Leopard 10 10
1163 550k. Leopard stalking oryx 10 10
1164 630k. Cheetah running beside herd of springbok 10 10
1165 630k. Cheetah overpowering springbok 10 10
1166 630k. Leopard approaching oryx 10 10
1167 630k. Leopard leaping at oryx 10 10

Nos. 1152/67 were issued together, se-tenant, in sheetlets with each horizontal strip forming a composite design of lions, cheetah, hunting dogs or leopard attacking prey.

218 Couple with Elderly Woman

1996. 50th Anniv of U.N.O. Multicoloured.
1168 3500k. Type **218** 15 10
1169 3500k. Children at water pump 15 10

219 "Styrbjorn" (Swedish sail warship), 1789

1996. Ships. Multicoloured.
1171 6000k. Type **219** 35 20
1172 6000k. U.S.S. "Constellation" (United States frigate), 1797 . . . 35 20
1173 6000k. "Taureau" (French torpedo-boat), 1865 . . . 35 20
1174 6000k. French bomb ketch 35 20
1175 6000k. "Sardegna" (Italian battleship), 1881 . . . . 35 20
1176 6000k. H.M.S. "Glasgow" (frigate), 1867 . . . . . 35 20
1177 6000k. U.S.S. "Essex" (frigate), 1812 . . . . . 35 20
1178 6000k. H.M.S. "Inflexible" (battleship), 1881 . . . . 35 20
1179 6000k. H.M.S. "Minotaur" (ironclad), 1863 . . . . . 35 20
1180 6000k. "Napoleon" (French steam ship of the line), 1854 . . . . 35 20
1181 6000k. "Sophia Amalia" (Danish galleon), 1650 . . 35 20
1182 6000k. "Massena" (French battleship), 1887 . . . . 35 20

220 Mask and Drilling Platform

1996. 20th Anniv of Sonangol. Multicoloured.
1184 1000k. Type **220** 30 10
1185 1000k. Storage tanks and mask of woman's face . . 10 10
1186 2500k. Mask with beard and gas bottles 10 10
1187 5000k. Refuelling airplane and mask of monkey's face 20 15

ANGOLA KZr. 20.000.00
221 Slaves in Ship's Hold

1996. "Brapex 96" National Stamp Exhibition, Recife, Brazil. Multicoloured.
1188 20000k. Type **221** 10 10
1189 20000k. Ship capsizing 20 10
1190 30000k. Boats punting out to ship 30 15
1191 30000k. Inspection of slaves 20 15

222 Mission Church, Huila
223 Handball

1996. Churches. Multicoloured.
1193 5000k. Type **222** 10 10
1194 10000k. Church of Our Lady, PoPulo 10 10
1195 10000k. Church of Our Lady, Nazare 10 10
1196 25000k. St. Adriao's Church 10 10

1996. Olympic Games, Atlanta, U.S.A. Mult.
1197 5000k. Type **223** 10 10
1198 10000k. Swimming (horiz) 10 10
1199 25000k. Athletics 10 10
1200 35000k. Shooting (horiz) 15 10

224 Dolphins, and Angola on Map of Africa

1996. 40th Anniv of Popular Movement for the Liberation of Angola (MPLA).
1202 **224** 30000k. multicoloured 15 10
The face value of No. 1202 is wrongly inscr as "300.00.00".

225 AVE, Spain

1997. Trains. Multicoloured.
1203 100000k. Type **225** 60 50
1204 100000k. "Hikari", Japan 60 50
1205 100000k. "Warbonnet" diesel locomotives, U.S.A. 60 50
1206 100000k. "Deltic" diesel locomotive, Great Britain 60 50
1207 100000k. "Eurostar", France and Great Britain 60 50
1208 100000k. ETR 450, Italy 60 50
1209 140000k. Class E1300 diesel locomotive, Morocco 85 70
1210 140000k. ICE, Germany 85 70
1211 140000k. Class X2000, Sweden 85 70
1212 140000k. TGV, France 85 70
1213 250000k. Steam locomotive 1·10 90
1214 250000k. Garratt steam locomotive 1·10 90
1215 250000k. General Electric electric locomotive 1·10 90
Nos. 1203/8 were issued together, se-tenant, forming a composite design.

226 Thoroughbred

1997. Horses. Multicoloured.
1217 100000k. Type **226** 45 35
1218 100000k. Palomino and Appaloosa 45 35
1219 100000k. Grey and white Arabs 45 35
1220 100000k. Arab colt 45 35
1221 100000k. Thoroughbred colt 45 35
1222 100000k. Mustang (with hind quarters of another mustang) 45 35
1223 100000k. Head of mustang and hind quarters of Furioso 45 35
1224 100000k. Head and shoulders of Furioso 45 35
1225 120000k. Thoroughbred 55 45
1226 120000k. Arab and palomino 55 45
1227 120000k. Arab and Chincoteague 55 45
1228 120000k. Pintos 55 45
1229 120000k. Przewalski's Horse 55 45
1230 120000k. Thoroughbred colt 55 45
1231 120000k. Arabs 55 45
1232 120000k. New Forest pony 55 45
1233 140000k. Selle Francais 65 50
1234 140000k. Fjord 65 50
1235 140000k. Percheron 65 50
1236 140000k. Italian heavy draught horse 65 50
1237 140000k. Shagya Arab 65 50
1238 140000k. Avelignese 65 50
1239 140000k. Czechoslovakian warmblood 65 50
1240 140000k. New Forest pony 65 50
Stamps of the same value were issued together, se-tenant, Nos. 1217/24 and 1225/32 respectively forming composite designs.

227 Jules Rimet Trophy (Uruguay, 1930)

1997. World Cup Football Championship, France.
1241 **227** 100000k. black 45 35
1242 – 100000k. black 45 35
1243 – 100000k. multicoloured 45 35
1244 – 100000k. multicoloured 45 35
1245 – 100000k. black 45 35
1246 – 100000k. multicoloured 45 35
1247 – 100000k. black 45 35
1248 – 100000k. black 45 35
1249 – 100000k. multicoloured 45 35
1250 – 100000k. multicoloured 45 35
1251 – 100000k. black 45 35
DESIGNS—Victory celebrations: No. 1240, Germany (1954); 1241, Brazil (1970); 1242, Maradona holding trophy (Argentina, 1986); 1243, Brazil (1994). Official team photographs: 1244, Germany (1954); 1245, Uruguay (1958); 1246, Italy (1938); 1247, Brazil (1962); 1248, Brazil (1970); 1249, Uruguay (1930).

228 House Insurance
230 Royal Assyrian ("Terinos terpander")

229 Coral

1998. 20th Anniv of ENSA Insurance. Mult.
1254 240000k. Type **228** 1·10 90
1255 240000k. Forklift truck carrying egg (industrial risks) 1·10 90
1256 240000k. Egg on cross (personal accidents) 1·10 90
1257 240000k. Egg on waves (pleasure boating) 1·10 90

1998. "Expo '98" World's Fair, Lisbon, Portugal. Multicoloured.
1259 100000k. Type **229** 45 35
1260 100000k. Sea urchin 45 35
1261 100000k. Seahorses 45 35
1262 100000k. Sea anemone 45 35
1263 240000k. Sea slug 1·10 90
1264 240000k. Finger coral 1·10 90

1998. Butterflies. Multicoloured.
1265 120000k. Type **230** 55 45
1266 120000k. Wanderer ("Bematistes aganice") 55 45
1267 120000k. Great orange-tip ("Hebomoia glaucippe") 55 45
1268 120000k. Alfalfa butterfly ("Colias eurytheme") 55 45
1269 120000k. Red-banded perelite ("Pereute leucodrosime") 55 45
1270 120000k. Large copper ("Lycaena dispar") 55 45
1271 120000k. Malachite ("Metamorpha stelenes") 55 45
1272 120000k. Tiger swallowtail ("Papilio glaucus") 55 45
1273 120000k. Monarch ("Danaus plexippus") 55 45
1274 120000k. Grecian shoemaker ("Catonephele numili") 55 45
1275 120000k. Silver-studded blue ("Plebejus argus") 55 45
1276 120000k. Common eggfly ("Hypolimnas bolina") 55 45
1277 120000k. Brazilian dynastor ("Dynastor napolean") (horiz) 55 45
1278 120000k. Saturn butterfly ("Zeuxidia amethystus") (horiz) 55 45
1279 120000k. Pipevine swallowtail ("Battus philenor") (horiz) 55 45
1280 120000k. Orange-barred sulphur ("Phoebis philea") (horiz) 55 45
1281 120000k. African monarch ("Danaus chrysippus") (horiz) 55 45
1282 120000k. Green-underside blue ("Glaucopsyche alexis") (horiz) 55 45
Nos. 1265/70, 1271/6 and 1277/82 respectively were issued together, se-tenant, forming composite designs.

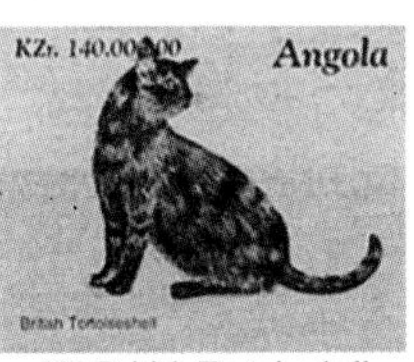

231 British Tortoiseshell

1998. Cats and Dogs. Multicoloured.
1284 140000k. Type **231** 65 55
1285 140000k. Chinchilla 65 55
1286 140000k. Russian blue 65 55
1287 140000k. Black persian (longhair) (wrongly inscribed "Longhiar") 65 55
1288 140000k. British red tabby 65 55
1289 140000k. Birman 65 55
1290 140000k. West Highland white terrier 65 55
1291 140000k. Red setter 65 55
1292 140000k. Dachshund 65 55
1293 140000k. St. John water-dog 65 55
1294 140000k. Shetland sheep-dog 65 55
1295 140000k. Dalmatian 65 55

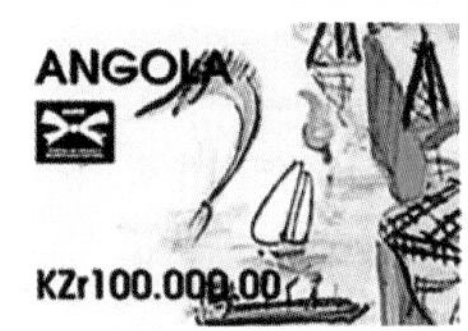

232 Dolphin, Yacht and Container Ship

1998. 1st Anniv of Government of Unity and National Reconciliation. Multicoloured.
1297 100000k. Type **232** 45 35
1298 100000k. Yacht, dolphin and container ship (different) 45 35
1299 100000k. Yacht, container ship and railway line 45 35
1300 100000k. Coastline and electricity pylons 45 35
1301 200000k. Grapes, goat and railway 95 75
1302 200000k. Village 95 75
1303 200000k. Tractor, grapes and railway 95 75
1304 200000k. Coal train 95 75
1305 200000k. Railway line with branch and pylons 95 75
1306 200000k. Elephant and tip of tree 95 75
1307 200000k. Edge of coastline with pylon 95 75
1308 200000k. Tree trunk and coastline 95 75
Nos. 1297/1308 were issued together, se-tenant, forming a composite design.

234 Lion

1998. Animals of the Grande Porte. Multicoloured.
1310 100000k. Type **234** 45 35
1311 100000k. Hippopotamus ("Hippopotamus amphibius") 45 35
1312 100000k. African elephant ("Loxodonta africana") 45 35
1313 100000k. Giraffe ("Giraffa campelopardalis") 45 35
1314 220000k. African buffalo ("Synceros caffer") 1·00 80
1315 220000k. Gorilla ("Gorilla gorilla") 1·00 80
1316 220000k. White rhinoceros ("Ceratotherium simum") 1·00 80
1317 220000k. Gemsbok ("Oryx gazella") 1·00 80
There are errors in the Latin inscriptions.

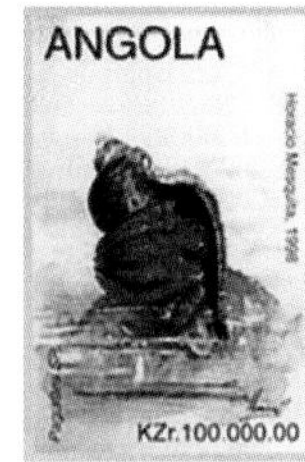

236 Diana, Princess of Wales
237 "Pagurites sp."

1998. Diana, Princess of Wales Commemoration. Multicoloured.
1319 100000k. Type **236** 45 35
1320 100000k. Wearing white balldress 45 35
1321 100000k. Holding handbag 45 35
1322 100000k. Wearing black evening dress 45 35
1323 100000k. Holding bouquet (white jacket) 45 35
1324 100000k. Wearing pearl necklace (looking down) 45 35
1325 100000k. Wearing pearl necklace (head raised) 45 35
1326 100000k. Speaking, wearing green velvet jacket 45 35
1327 100000k. Wearing sunglasses 45 35
1328 100000k. Wearing black jacket and white blouse 45 35
1329 100000k. Wearing green blouse 45 35
1330 100000k. Holding flowers (black jacket) 45 35
1331 150000k. With young girl amputee 70 55
1332 150000k. With two amputees 70 55
1333 150000k. Walking through minefield 70 55

1998. International Year of the Ocean. Mult.
1335 100000k. Type **237** 45 35
1336 100000k. "Callinectes marginatus" (crab) 45 35
1337 100000k. "Thais forbesi" 45 35
1338 100000k. "Ostrea tulipa" 45 35
1339 100000k. "Balanus amphitrite" 45 35
1340 100000k. "Uca tangeri" 45 35
1341 170000k. "Littorina angulifera" 80 65
1342 170000k. Great hairy melongena ("Semifusus morio") 80 65
1343 170000k. "Thais coronata" 80 65
1344 170000k. "Cerithium atratum" on red branch 80 65
1345 170000k. "Ostrea tulipa" (different) 80 65
1346 170000k. "Cerithium atratum" on green branch 80 65

238 Mangos

1998. "Portugal 98" International Stamp Exhibition, Lisbon. Fruit and Vegetables. Multicoloured.
1348 100000k. Type **238** 45 35
1349 100000k. Guava 45 35
1350 120000k. Chillies 55 45
1351 120000k. Sweet corn 55 45
1352 140000k. Sliced bananas 65 55
1353 140000k. Avocadoes 65 55

239 Bimba Canoe

1998. Canoes. Multicoloured.
1354 250000k. Type **239** 1·10 90
1355 250000k. Sailing canoe, Ndongo 1·10 90
1356 250000k. Building canoes in Ndongo 1·10 90

241 Ultralight Plane

1998. Aircraft. Multicoloured.
1358 150000k. Type **241** 70 55
1359 150000k. Gyroplane 70 55
1360 150000k. Business jet 70 55
1361 150000k. Convertible plane 70 55
1362 150000k. Chuterplane 70 55
1363 150000k. Twin-rotor craft 70 55
1364 150000k. Skycrane 70 55
1365 150000k. British Aerospace/ Aerospatiale Concorde Supersonic airliner 70 55
1366 150000k. Flying boat 70 55
1367 200000k. Boeing 737-100 70 55
1368 200000k. Ilyushin Il-62M 70 55
1369 250000k. Pedal-powered plane 70 55
1370 250000k. Sail plane 70 55
1371 250000k. Aerobatic plane 70 55
1372 250000k. Hang-gliding 70 55
1373 250000k. Balloon 70 55
1374 250000k. Glidercraft 70 55
1375 250000k. Model airplane 70 55
1376 250000k. Air racing 70 55
1377 250000k. Solar-celled plane 70 55

Nos. 1358/66 and 1369/77 respectively were issued together, se-tenant, forming composite designs.

242 Parasaurolophus

243 Head

1998. Prehistoric Animals. Multicoloured.
1379 120000k. Type **242** 55 45
1380 120000k. Elaphosaurus 55 45
1381 120000k. Iguanodon 55 45
1382 120000k. Maiasaura 55 45
1383 120000k. Brontosaurus 55 45
1384 120000k. Plateosaurus 55 45
1385 120000k. Brachiosaurus 55 45
1386 120000k. Anatosaurus 55 45
1387 120000k. Tyrannosaurus rex 55 45
1388 120000k. Carnotaurus 55 45
1389 120000k. Corythosaurus 55 45
1390 120000k. Stegosaurus 55 45
1391 120000k. Iguanodon (different) 55 45
1392 120000k. Hadrosaurus (horiz) 55 45
1393 120000k. Ouranosaurus (horiz) 55 45
1394 120000k. Hypsilophodon (horiz) 55 45
1395 120000k. Brachiosaurus (horiz) 55 45
1396 120000k. Shunosaurus (horiz) 55 45
1397 120000k. Amargasaurus (horiz) 55 45
1398 120000k. Tuojiangosaurus (horiz) 55 45
1399 120000k. Monoclonius 55 45
1400 120000k. Struthiosaurus (horiz) 55 45

1999. Endangered Species. The Lesser Flamingo (*Phoenicopterus minor*). Multicoloured.
1402 300000k. Type **243** 1·40 1·10
1403 300000k. Flamingo with wings outstretched 1·40 1·10
1404 300000k. Flamingo facing left 1·40 1·10
1405 300000k. Front view of flamingo 1·40 1·10

244 Hyacinth Macaw (*Anodorhynchus hyacinthinus*)

1999. Animals and Birds. Multicoloured.
1406 300000k. Type **244** 1·40 1·10
1407 300000k. Penguin (*Sphenisciformes*) (vert) 1·40 1·10
1408 300000k. Przewalski's horse (*Equus caballus przewalski*) (wrongly inscr "Equis") 1·40 1·10
1409 300000k. American bald eagle (*Haliaetus leucocephalus*) (vert) 1·40 1·10
1410 300000k. Spectacled bear (*Tremarctos ornatus*) 1·40 1·10
1411 300000k. Jay (*Aphelocoma*) 1·40 1·10
1412 300000k. Bare-legged scops owl (*Otus insularis*) 1·40 1·10
1413 300000k. Whale-headed stork (*Balaeniceps rex*) 1·40 1·10
1414 300000k. Atlantic ridley turtle (*Lepidochelys kempii*) 1·40 1·10
1415 300000k. Canadian river otter (*Lutra canadensis*) 1·40 1·10
1416 300000k. Swift fox (*Vulpes velox hebes*) 1·40 1·10
1417 300000k. Deer (*Odocoileus*) 1·40 1·10
1418 300000k. Orang-utan (*Pongo pygmaeus*) 1·40 1·10
1419 300000k. Golden lion tamarin (*Leontopithecus rosalia rosalia*) (inscr "Leontopitecus") 1·40 1·10
1420 300000k. Tiger (*Panthera tigris altaica*) 1·40 1·10
1421 300000k. Polecat (wrongly inscr "Tragelaphus eurycerus") 1·40 1·10
MS1422 Two sheets, each 110×85 mm. (a) 1000000k. Brown bear (*Ursus arctos horribilis*): (b) 1000000k. Giant panda (*Ailuropoda melanoleuca*) 9·50 9·50

245 Satellite circling Earth

1999. International Telecommunications Day.
1423 **245** 500000k. multicoloured 90 70

246 Waterfall, Andulo, Bie

1999. Waterfalls. Multicoloured.
1424 500000k. Type **246** 90 70
1425 500000k. Chiumbo, Lunda 90 70
1426 500000k. Ruacana, Cunene 90 70
1427 500000k. Coemba, Moxico 90 70

247 Emblem

1999. "Afrobasket '99" (Men's African Basketball Championship). Multicoloured.
1428 15000000k. Type **247** 70 55
1429 15000000k. Ball teetering on the edge of net, and players' hands 70 55
1430 15000000k. Hand scooping ball from edge of net 70 55
1431 15000000k. Flower holding ball 70 55
MS1432 95×83 mm. 25000000k. Enlarged detail from No. 1441 (39×29 mm) 1·25 1·25

248 African Continent

1999. South African Development Community (S.A.D.C.).
1433 **248** 1000000k. multicoloured 50 40

249 Duke and Duchess of York, 1923

250 Ekuikui II

1999. 100th Birthday of Queen Elizabeth, the Queen Mother. Multicoloured.
1434 **249** 200000k. black and gold 10 10
1435 – 200000k. mult 10 10
1436 – 200000k. mult 10 10
1437 – 200000k. mult 10 10
MS1438 154×157 mm. 500000k. Queen Mother in academic robes (37×50 mm) 25 25

DESIGNS: No. 1447, Portrait of Queen Mother wearing Star of the Garter; 1448, Queen Mother wearing fur stole; 1449, Queen Mother wearing blue hat.

1999. Rulers. Multicoloured.
1439 500000k. Type **250** 25 20
1440 500000k. Mvemba Nzinga 25 20
1441 500000k. Mwata Yamvu Nawej II 25 20
1442 500000k. Njinga Mbande 25 20
MS1443 104×76 mm. 1000000k. Mandume Ndemufayo 50 50

251 13th-century B.C. Pharaonic Barque

1999. Ships. Multicoloured.
1444 950000k. Type **251** 50 40
1445 950000k. Flemish carrack, 1480 50 40
1446 950000k. H.M.S. *Beagle* (Darwin), 1830 50 40
1447 950000k. *North Star* (paddle-steamer), 1852 50 40
1448 950000k. *Fram* (schooner, Amundsen and Nansen), 1892 50 40
1449 950000k. *Unyo Maru* (sail/ steam freighter), 1909 (inscr "Unyon") 50 40
1450 950000k. *Juan Sebastian de Elcano* (cadet schooner), 1927 50 40
1451 950000k. *Tovarishch*, (three-masted cadet barque), 1933 50 40
1452 950000k. *Bucentaur* (Venetian state galley), 1728 50 40
1453 950000k. *Clermont* (first commercial paddle-steamer), 1807 50 40
1454 950000k. *Savannah* (paddle-steamer), 1819 50 40
1455 950000k. *Dromedary* (steam tug), 1844 50 40
1456 950000k. *Iberia* (steam freighter), 1881 50 40
1457 950000k. *Gluckauf* (tanker), 1886 50 40
1458 950000k. *Cidade de Paris* (ocean steamer), 1888 50 40
1459 950000k. *Mauretania* (liner), 1906 50 40
1460 950000k. *La Gloire* (first armoured-hull ship), 1859 50 40
1461 950000k. *L'Ocean*, (French battery ship), 1868 50 40
1462 950000k. *Dandolo* (Italian cruiser), 1876 (inscr "Dandalo") and stern of H.M.S. *Dreadnought* 50 40
1463 950000k. H.M.S. *Dreadnought* (battleship), 1906 50 40
1464 950000k. *Bismarck* (battleship), 1939 and stern of U.S.S. *Cleveland* 50 40
1465 950000k. U.S.S. *Cleveland* (cruiser), 1946 50 40
1466 950000k. U.S.S. *Boston* (first guided-missile cruiser), 1942 and stern of U.S.S. *Long Beach* 50 40
1467 950000k. U.S.S. *Long Beach* (first nuclear-powered cruiser), 1959 50 40
MS1468 Four sheets, each 75×70 mm. (a) 5000000k. 18th-century junk; (b) 5000000k. *Madre de Dios* (carrack) (wrongly inscr "Deus"), 1609; (c) 5000000k. Catamaran, 1861; (d) 5000000k. *Natchez* (Mississippi paddle-steamer), 1870 9·50 9·50

Nos. 1474/5, 1476/7 and 1478/9 respectively were issued together, se-tenant, forming a composite design.

252 Fly Agaric (*Amanita muscaria*)

1999. Fungi. Multicoloured.
1469 1000000k. Type **252** (wrongly inscr "Aminita") 50 40
1470 1000000k. Bronze boletus (*Boletus*) 50 40
1471 1000000k. Lawyer's wig (*Coprinus comatus*) 50 40
1472 1000000k. The blusher (*Amanita rubescens*) (inscr "Aminita") 50 40
1473 1000000k. Slimy-branded cort (*Cortinarius collinitus*) 50 40
1474 1000000k. Devil's boletus (*Boletus satanas*) 50 40
1475 1000000k. Parasol mushroom (*Lepiota procera*) 50 40
1476 1000000k. Trumpet agaric (*Clitocybe geotropa*) 50 40
1477 1000000k. *Morchella crassipes* 50 40
1478 1000000k. *Boletus rufescens* 50 40
1479 1000000k. Death cap (*Amanita phalloides*) 50 40
1480 1000000k. *Collybia iocephala* 50 40
1481 1000000k. *Tricholoma aurantium* 50 40
1482 1000000k. *Cortinarius violaceus* 50 40
1483 1000000k. *Mycena polygramma* 50 40
1484 1000000k. *Psalliota augusta* 50 40
1485 1000000k. *Russula nigricans* 50 40
1486 1000000k. Granulated boletus (*Boletus granulatus*) 50 40
1487 1000000k. *Mycena strobilinoides* 50 40
1488 1000000k. Caesar's mushroom (*Amanita caesarea*) 50 40
1489 1000000k. Fly agaric (*Amanita muscaria*) (different) 50 40
1490 1000000k. *Boletus crocipodius* 50 40
1491 1000000k. Cracked green russula (*Russula virescens*) 50 40
1492 1000000k. Saffron milk cap (*Lactarius deliciosus*) 50 40
1493 1250000k. Caesar's mushroom (*Amanita caesarea*) (different) 60 50
1495 1250000k. Red cracked boletus (*Boletus chrysenteron*) (wrongly inscr "chyrsenteron") 60 50
1496 1250000k. Butter mushroom (*Boletus luteus*) 60 50
1497 1250000k. Lawyer's wig (*Coprinus comatus*) (different) 60 50
1498 1250000k. Witch's hat (*Hygrocybe conica*) 60 50
1499 1250000k. *Psalliota xanthoderma* 60 50
MS1500 Two sheets, each 75×105 mm. (a) 5000000k. *Mycena lilacifolia*; (b) 5000000k. *Psalliota haemorrhoidaria* 5·00 5·00

253 Mercury and Venus

1999. 30th Anniv of First Manned Moon Landing. Multicoloured.
1501 3500000k. Type **253** 70 55
1502 3500000k. Jupiter 70 55
1503 3500000k. Neptune and Pluto 70 55
1504 3500000k. Earth and Mars 70 55
1505 3500000k. Saturn 70 55
1506 3500000k. Uranus 70 55
1507 3500000k. Explorer 17 satellite, 1963 70 55
1508 3500000k. Intelsat 4A satellite, 1975 70 55
1509 3500000k. GOES-D (Geostationary Operational Environmental Satellite), 1980 70 55
1510 3500000k. Intelsat 2 satellite, 1966 70 55
1511 3500000k. Navstar 2 (Navigation System with Timing And Ranging), 1978 70 55
1512 3500000k. S.M.S. (Solar Maximum Mission) satellite, 1980 70 55
1513 3500000k. Earth and astronaut walking in space 70 55
1514 3500000k. Mariner 8 spacecraft 70 55
1515 3500000k. Viking 10 spacecraft 70 55
1516 3500000k. Ginga satellite 70 55
1517 3500000k. Soyuz 19 spacecraft (inscr "satelite") 70 55
1518 3500000k. Voyager spacecraft 70 55
1519 3500000k. Hubble space telescope (vert) 70 55
1520 3500000k. Launch of space shuttle *Atlantis* (vert) 70 55
1521 3500000k. Uhuru satellite (vert) 70 55
1522 3500000k. Mir space station (vert) 70 55
1523 3500000k. Gemini 7 spacecraft (vert) 70 55
1524 3500000k. Venera 7 spacecraft (vert) 70 55
MS1525 Five sheets (a) 95×85 mm. 6000000k. Astronaut from Apollo 17 walking on moon (vert); (b) 95×85 mm. 6000000k. Astronaut driving moon buggy (vert); (c) 85×110 mm. 12000000k. Launch of commercial satellite SBS 4 (vert); (d) 85×110 mm. Neil Armstrong (astronaut) (vert); (e) 110×85 mm. 12000000 k. Earth and *Columbia* spacecraft 10·00 10·00

No. 1523 is inscribed "GEMNI" in error.

254 "Night Attack by 47 Ronins"

1999. 150th Death Anniv of Katushika Hokusai (artist). Multicoloured.

1526	3500000k. Type **254**	70	55
1527	3500000k. "Usigafuchi no Kudan"	70	55
1528	3500000k. Sketch of seated man	70	55
1529	3500000k. Sketch of animals and birds	70	55
1530	3500000k. "Autumn Pheasant"	70	55
1531	3500000k. Rural landscape	70	55
1532	3500000k. "Survey of the region"	70	55
1533	3500000k. Kabuki theatre	70	55
1534	3500000k. Sketch of hen	70	55
1535	3500000k. Sketch of wheelwright	70	55
1536	3500000k. "Excursion to Enoshima"	70	55
1537	3500000k. Sumida River landscape	70	55
MS1538	Two sheets, each 100 × 70 mm. (a) 12000000k. Japanese calligraphy between woman and child (vert); (b) 12000000k. Woman dressing hair (vert)	5·00	5·00

APPENDIX

1995.

90th Anniv of Rotary International (on gold foil). 81000k.

CHARITY TAX STAMPS

Used on certain days of the year as an additional tax on internal letters. If one was not used in addition to normal postage, postage due stamps were used to collect the deficiency and the fine.

1925. Marquis de Pombal Commemorative stamps of Portugal but inscr "ANGOLA".

C343	C **73**	15c. violet	30	25
C344	–	15c. violet	30	25
C345	C **75**	15c. violet	30	25

C **15**

C **29**

C **52** Old Man

1929.

C347	C **15**	50c. blue	1·60	60

1939. No gum.

C413	C **29**	50c. green	1·25	10
C414		1a. red	1·60	70

1955. Heads in brown.

C646	C **52**	50c. orange	15	10
C647	–	1e. red (Boy)	15	10
C648	–	1e.50 green (Girl)	15	10
C522	–	2e.50 blue (Old woman)	50	30

1957. Surch.

C535	C **52**	10c. on 50c. orange	20	15
C534		30c. on 50c. orange	20	15

C **58** Mother and Child

C **75** "Full Employment"

C **65** Yellow, White and Black Men

1959.

C538	C **58**	10c. black and orange	15	15
C539	–	30c. black and slate	15	15

DESIGN: 30c. Boy and girl.

1962. Provincial Settlement Committee.

C568	C **65**	50c. multicoloured	20	10
C569		1e. multicoloured	40	20

1965. Provincial Settlement Committee.

C643	C **75**	50e. multicoloured	15	10
C644		1e. multicoloured	15	10
C645		2e. multicoloured	20	15

C **95** Planting Tree

1972. Provincial Settlement Committee.

C701	C **95**	50c. red and brown	15	15
C702	–	1e. black and green	15	15
C703	–	2e. black and brown	15	15

DESIGNS: 1e. Agricultural workers; 2e. Corncobs and flowers.

NEWSPAPER STAMP

1893. "Newspaper" key-type inscr "ANGOLA".

N51	V	2½r. brown	95	55

POSTAGE DUE STAMPS

1904. "Due" key-type inscr "ANGOLA".

D150	W	5r. green	15	15
D151		10r. grey	15	15
D152		20r. brown	25	20
D153		30r. orange	25	20
D154		50r. brown	30	20
D155		60r. brown	2·75	1·50
D156		100r. mauve	95	75
D157		130r. blue	95	85
D158		200r. red	3·25	1·50
D159		500r. lilac	3·00	1·50

See also Nos. D343/52.

1911. Nos. D150/9 optd **REPUBLICA**.

D166	W	5r. green	15	10
D167		10r. grey	15	10
D168		20r. brown	15	10
D169		30r. orange	20	10
D170		50r. brown	20	15
D171		60r. brown	50	30
D172		100r. mauve	50	30
D173		130r. blue	50	35
D174		200r. red	50	35
D175		500r. lilac	65	40

1921. Values in new currency.

D343	W	½c. green	10	10
D344		1c. grey	10	10
D345		2c. brown	10	10
D346		3c. orange	10	10
D347		5c. brown	10	10
D348		6c. brown	10	10
D349		10c. mauve	10	10
D350		13c. blue	20	20
D351		20c. red	20	20
D352		50c. grey	20	20

1925. Marquis de Pombal stamps of Angola, as Nos. C343/5, optd **MULTA**.

D353	C **73**	30c. violet	25	25
D354	–	30c. violet	25	25
D355	C **75**	30c. violet	25	25

1949. Surch **PORTEADO** and value.

D438	**17**	10c. on 20c. grey	25	25
D439		20c. on 30c. green	25	25
D440		30c. on 50c. brown	25	25
D441		40c. on 1a. red	50	50
D442		50c. on 2a. mauve	75	75
D443		1a. on 5a. green	85	85

D **45**

1952. Numerals in red, name in black.

D483	D **45**	10c. brown and olive	15	15
D484		30c. green and blue	15	15
D485		50c. brown & lt brn	15	15
D486		1a. blue, green & orge	15	15
D487		2a. brown and red	20	20
D488		5a. brown and blue	30	30

ANGRA Pt. 9

A district of the Azores, which used the stamps of the Azores except from 1892 to 1905.

1000 reis = 1 milreis.

1892. As T **4** of Funchal, inscr "ANGRA".

16	5r. yellow	2·25	1·40
5	10r. mauve	2·50	1·40
6	15r. brown	2·75	2·10
7	20r. violet	2·75	2·10
8	25r. green	3·50	55
9	50r. blue	5·75	3·25
10	75r. red	6·75	4·00
11	80r. green	8·00	7·75
24	100r. brown on yellow	29·00	11·00
13	150r. red on rose	40·00	32·00
14	200r. blue on blue	40·00	32·00
15	300r. blue on brown	40·00	32·00

1897. "King Carlos" key-type inscr "ANGRA".

28	S	2½r. grey	55	40
29		5r. red	55	40
30		10r. green	55	40
31		15r. brown	6·75	3·75
43		15r. green	60	45
32		20r. lilac	1·40	1·00
33		25r. green	2·10	1·00
44		25r. red	45	45
34		50r. blue	3·75	1·25
46		65r. blue	1·00	45
35		75r. red	2·50	1·25
47		75r. brown on yellow	9·75	8·50
36		80r. mauve	1·10	95
37		100r. blue on blue	2·00	1·25
48		115r. red on pink	2·00	1·60
49		130r. brown on cream	2·00	1·60
38		150r. brown on yellow	2·00	1·25
50		180r. grey on pink	2·25	2·10
39		200r. purple on pink	4·00	2·75
40		300r. blue on pink	5·75	4·50
41		500r. black on blue	13·00	10·50

ANGUILLA Pt. 1

St. Christopher, Nevis and Anguilla were granted Associated Statehood on 27 February 1967, but following a referendum Anguilla declared her independence and the St. Christopher authorities withdrew. On 7 July 1969, the Anguilla post office was officially recognised by the Government of St. Christopher, Nevis and Anguilla and normal postal communications via St. Christopher were resumed.

By the Anguilla Act of 27 July 1971, the island was restored to direct British control.

100 cents = 1 West Indian dollar.

1967. Nos. 129/44 of St. Kitts-Nevis optd **Independent Anguilla** and bar.

1	–	½c. sepia and blue	32·00	24·00
2	**33**	1c. multicoloured	35·00	7·50
3	–	2c. multicoloured	35·00	1·50
4	–	3c. multicoloured	35·00	4·50
5	–	4c. multicoloured	35·00	5·50
6	–	5c. multicoloured	£120	22·00
7	–	6c. multicoloured	60·00	10·00
8	–	10c. multicoloured	35·00	7·00
9	–	15c. multicoloured	70·00	12·00
10	–	20c. multicoloured	£110	14·00
11	–	25c. multicoloured	£100	24·00
12	–	50c. multicoloured	£2000	£450
13	–	60c. multicoloured	£2500	£850
14	–	$1 yellow and blue	£1800	£400
15	–	$2.50 multicoloured	£1600	£300
16	–	$5 multicoloured	£1600	£300

Owing to the limited stocks available for overprinting, the sale of the stamps were personally controlled by the Postmaster and no orders from the trade were accepted.

2 Mahogany Tree, The Quarter

1967.

17	**2**	1c. green, brown and orange	10	85
18	–	2c. turquoise and black	10	1·00
19	–	3c. black and green	10	10
20	–	4c. blue and black	10	10
21	–	5c. multicoloured	10	10
22	–	6c. red and black	10	10
23	–	10c. multicoloured	15	10
24	–	15c. multicoloured	1·60	20
25	–	20c. multicoloured	1·25	1·75
26	–	25c. multicoloured	60	20
27	–	40c. green, blue and black	1·00	25
28	–	60c. multicoloured	4·00	4·25
29	–	$1 multicoloured	1·75	3·25
30	–	$2.50 multicoloured	2·00	4·25
31	–	$5 multicoloured	3·00	4·25

DESIGNS: 2c. Sombrero Lighthouse; 3c. St. Mary's Church; 4c. Valley Police Station; 5c. Old Plantation House, Mt. Fortune; 6c. Valley Post Office; 10c. Methodist Church, West End; 15c. Wall Blake Airport; 20c. Beech A90 King Air aircraft over Sandy Ground; 25c. Island harbour; 40c. Map of Anguilla; 60c. Hermit crab and starfish; $1, Hibiscus; $2.50, Local scene; $5, Spiny lobster.

17 Yachts in Lagoon

1968. Anguillan Ships. Multicoloured.

32	10c. Type **17**	20	10
33	15c. Boat on beach	25	10
34	25c. Schooner "Warspite"	35	15
35	40c. Schooner "Atlantic Star"	40	20

18 Purple-throated Carib

1968. Anguillan Birds. Multicoloured.

36	10c. Type **18**	85	15
37	15c. Bananaquit	1·10	20
38	25c. Black-necked stilt (horiz)	1·40	20
39	40c. Royal tern (horiz)	1·60	30

19 Guides' Badge and Anniversary Years

1968. 35th Anniv of Anguillan Girl Guides. Mult.

40	10c. Type **19**	10	10
41	15c. Badge and silhouettes of guides (vert)	15	10
42	25c. Guides' badge and Headquarters	20	15
43	40c. Association and proficiency badges (vert)	25	15

20 The Three Kings

1968. Christmas.

44	**20**	1c. black and red	10	10
45	–	10c. black and blue	10	10
46	–	15c. black and brown	15	10
47	–	40c. black and blue	15	10
48	–	50c. black and green	20	15

DESIGNS—VERT: 10c. The Wise Men; 15c. Holy Family and manger. HORIZ: 40c. The Shepherds; 50c. Holy Family and donkey.

21 Bagging Salt

1969. Anguillan Salt Industry. Multicoloured.

49	10c. Type **21**	25	10
50	15c. Packing salt	30	10
51	40c. Salt pond	35	10
52	50c. Loading salt	35	10

1969. Expiration of Interim Agreement on Status of Anguilla. Nos. 17/22, 23, 24 and 26/7 optd **INDEPENDENCE JANUARY 1969**.

52a	1c. green, brown and orange	10	40
52b	2c. green and black	10	40
52c	3c. black and green	10	20
52d	4c. blue and black	10	20
52e	5c. multicoloured	10	20
52f	6c. red and black	10	20
52g	10c. multicoloured	10	30
52h	15c. multicoloured	90	30
52i	25c. multicoloured	80	30
52j	40c. green, blue and black	1·00	40

The remaining values of the 1967 series. Nos. 17/31 also come with this overprint but these are outside the scope of this catalogue

22 "The Crucifixion" (Studio of Massys)

1969. Easter Commemoration. Multicoloured.
53 25c. Type **22** 25 15
54 40c. "The Last Supper" (ascribed to Roberti) 35 15

23 Amaryllis

1969. Flowers of the Caribbean. Multicoloured.
55 10c. Type **23** 20 20
56 15c. Bougainvillea 25 25
57 40c. Hibiscus 50 50
58 50c. "Cattleya" orchid . . . . 1·50 1·25

24 Superb Gaza, Channelled Turban, Chestnut Turban and Carved Star Shell

1969. Sea Shells. Multicoloured.
59 10c. Type **24** 20 20
60 15c. American thorny oysters 20 20
61 40c. Scotch, royal and smooth scotch bonnets 30 30
62 50c. Atlantic trumpet triton . . 40 30

1969. Christmas. Nos. 17 and 25/8 optd with different seasonal emblems.
63 1c. green, brown and orange 10 10
64 20c. multicoloured 20 10
65 25c. multicoloured 20 10
66 40c. green, blue and black . . 25 15
67 60c. multicoloured 40 20

30 Spotted Goatfish

1969. Fishes. Multicoloured.
68 10c. Type **30** 30 15
69 15c. Blue-striped grunt 45 15
70 40c. Nassau grouper 55 20
71 50c. Banded butterflyfish . . . 65 20

31 "Morning Glory" **32** "The Crucifixion" (Masaccio)

1970. Flowers. Multicoloured.
72 10c. Type **31** 30 10
73 15c. Blue petrea 45 10
74 40c. Hibiscus 70 20
75 50c. "Flame Tree" 80 25

1970. Easter. Multicoloured.
76 10c. "The Ascent to Calvary" (Tiepolo) (horiz) 15 10
77 20c. Type **32** 20 10
78 40c. "Deposition" (Rosso Fiorentino) 25 15
79 60c. "The Ascent to Calvary" (Murillo) (horiz) 25 15

33 Scout Badge and Map

1970. 40th Anniv of Scouting in Anguilla. Multicoloured.
80 10c. Type **33** 15 15
81 15c. Scout camp, and cubs practising first aid 20 20
82 40c. Monkey bridge 25 30
83 50c. Scout H.Q. building and Lord Baden-Powell 35 30

34 Boatbuilding

1970. Multicoloured.
84 1c. Type **34** 30 40
85 2c. Road construction 30 40
86 3c. Quay, Blowing Point . . . 30 20
87 4c. Broadcaster, Radio Anguilla 30 50
88 5c. Cottage Hospital extension 40 50
89 6c. Valley Secondary School 30 50
90 10c. Hotel extension 30 30
91 15c. Sandy Ground 30 30
92 20c. Supermarket and cinema 55 30
93 25c. Bananas and mangoes . . 35 1·00
94 40c. Wall Blake Airport . . . 2·75 3·00
95 60c. Sandy Ground jetty . . . 65 3·25
96 $1 Administration buildings 1·25 1·40
97 $2.50 Livestock . . . . 1·50 3·75
98 $5 Sandy Hill Bay . . . . . . 2·75 3·75

35 "The Adoration of the Shepherds" (Reni)

1970. Christmas. Multicoloured.
99 1c. Type **35** 10 10
100 20c. "The Virgin and Child" (Gozzoli) 30 20
101 25c. "Mystic Nativity" (detail, Botticelli) 30 20
102 40c. "The Santa Margherita Madonna" (detail, Mazzola) 40 25
103 50c. "The Adoration of the Magi" (detail, Tiepolo) . . 40 25

36 "Ecce Homo" (detail, Correggio)

1971. Easter. Paintings. Multicoloured.
104 10c. Type **36** 25 10
105 15c. "Christ appearing to St Peter" (detail, Carracci) . . 25 10
106 40c. "Angels weeping over the Dead Christ" (detail, Guercino) (horiz) 30 10
107 50c. "The Supper at Emmaus" (detail, Caravaggio) (horiz) 30 15

37 "Hypolimnas misippus"

1971. Butterflies. Multicoloured.
108 10c. Type **37** . . . . 1·60 70
109 15c. "Junonia evarete" . . . 1·60 80
110 40c. "Agraulis vanillae" . . . 2·00 1·25
111 50c. "Danaus plexippus" . . 2·00 1·50

38 "Magnanime" and "Aimable" in Battle **39** "The Ansidei Madonna" (detail, Raphael)

1971. Sea-battles of the West Indies. Multicoloured.
112 10c. Type **38** . . . . 1·10 1·40
113 15c. H.M.S. "Duke", "Glorieux" and H.M.S. "Agamemnon" . . . . . . 1·25 1·60
114 25c. H.M.S. "Formidable" and H.M.S. "Namur" against "Ville de Paris" . . 1·50 1·75
115 40c. H.M.S. "Canada" . . . 1·60 1·90
116 50c. H.M.S. "St. Albans" and wreck of "Hector" . . 1·75 2·00
Nos. 112/116 were issued together, se-tenant, forming a composite design.

1971. Christmas. Multicoloured.
117 20c. Type **39** 25 30
118 25c. "Mystic Nativity" (detail, Botticelli) 25 30
119 40c. "Adoration of the Shepherds" (detail, ascr to Murillo) 30 40
120 50c. "The Madonna of the Iris" (detail, ascr to Durer) 35 45

40 Map of Anguilla and St. Martin by Thomas Jefferys, 1775 **41** "Jesus Buffeted"

1972. Caribbean Maps depicting Anguilla. Multicoloured.
121 10c. Type **40** 25 10
122 15c. Samuel Fahlberg's Map, 1814 . . . . 35 15
123 40c. Thomas Jefferys' Map, 1775 (horiz) 50 25
124 50c. Captain E. Barnett's Map, 1847 (horiz) 60 25

1972. Easter. Multicoloured.
125 10c. Type **41** 25 25
126 15c. "The Way of Sorrows" 30 30
127 25c. "The Crucifixion" . . . 30 30
128 40c. "Descent from the Cross" 35 35
129 50c. "The Burial" 40 40

42 Loblolly Tree **44** Flight into Egypt

1972. Multicoloured.
130 1c. Spear fishing 10 40
131 2c. Type **42** 10 40
132 3c. Sandy Ground 10 40
133 4c. Ferry at Blowing Point 1·75 20
134 5c. Agriculture . . . . . . 15 1·00
135 6c. St. Mary's Church . . . 25 20
136 10c. St. Gerard's Church . . 25 40
137 15c. Cottage hospital extension 25 30
138 20c. Public library 30 35
139 25c. Sunset at Blowing Point 40 2·00
140 40c. Boat building . . . . . 5·00 1·50
141 60c. Hibiscus . . . . 4·00 4·00
142 $1 Magnificent frigate bird ("Man-o'-War") . . . . . 9·00 8·00
143 $2.50 Frangipani . . . . . 6·00 10·00
144 $5 Brown pelican . . . . . 16·00 17·00
144a $10 Green-back turtle . . . 15·00 18·00

1972. Royal Silver Wedding. As T **52** of Ascension, but with Schooner and Common dolphin in background.
145 25c. green 50 75
146 40c. brown 50 75

1972. Christmas. Multicoloured.
147 1c. Type **44** 10 10
148 20c. Star of Bethlehem . . . 20 20
149 25c. Holy Family 20 20
150 40c. Arrival of the Magi . . 20 25
151 50c. Adoration of the Magi 25 25

45 "The Betrayal of Christ"

1973. Easter. Multicoloured.
152 1c. Type **45** 10 10
153 10c. "The Man of Sorrows" 10 10
154 20c. "Christ bearing the Cross" 10 15
155 25c. "The Crucifixion" . . . 15 15
156 40c. "The Descent from the Cross" 15 15
157 50c. "The Resurrection" . . 15 20

46 "Santa Maria"

1973. Columbus Discovers the West Indies. Multicoloured.
159 1c. Type **46** 10 10
160 20c. Early map . . . . . . 1·50 1·25
161 40c. Map of voyages . . . . 1·60 1·40
162 70c. Sighting land . . . . . 1·90 1·75
163 $1.20 Landing of Columbus 2·50 2·25
MS164 193 × 93 mm. Nos. 159/63 6·00 7·00

47 Princess Anne and Captain Mark Phillips **49** "The Crucifixion" (Raphael)

48 "The Adoration of the Shepherds" (Reni)

1973. Royal Wedding. Multicoloured. Background colours given.
165 **47** 60c. green 20 15
166 $1.20 mauve 30 15

1973. Christmas. Multicoloured.
167 1c. Type **48** 10 10
168 10c. "The Madonna and Child with Saints Jerome and Dominic" (Filippino Lippi) 10 10
169 20c. "The Nativity" (Master of Brunswick) 15 15
170 25c. "Madonna of the Meadow" (Bellini) 15 15
171 40c. "Virgin and Child" (Cima) 20 20
172 50c. "Adoration of the Kings" (Geertgen) 20 20
MS173 148 × 149 mm. Nos. 167/72 80 1·60

1974. Easter.
174 **49** 1c. multicoloured 10 10
175 – 15c. multicoloured 10 10
176 – 20c. multicoloured 15 15
177 – 25c. multicoloured 15 15

178 – 40c. multicoloured 15 15
179 – $1 multicoloured 20 25
MS180 123 × 141 mm. Nos. 174/9 1·00 1·25
DESIGNS: 15c. to $1, Details of Raphael's "Crucifixion".

50 Churchill Making "Victory" Sign

1974. Birth Centenary of Sir Winston Churchill. Multicoloured.
181 1c. Type **50** 10 10
182 20c. Churchill with Roosevelt 20 20
183 25c. Wartime broadcast 20 20
184 40c. Birthplace, Blenheim Palace 30 30
185 60c. Churchill's statue 30 35
186 $1.20 Country residence, Chartwell 45 55
MS187 195 × 96 mm. Nos. 181/6 1·40 2·25

51 U.P.U. Emblem

1974. Centenary of U.P.U.
188 **51** 1c. black and blue 10 10
189 20c. black and orange 15 15
190 25c. black and yellow 15 15
191 40c. black and mauve 20 25
192 60c. black and green 30 40
193 $1.20 black and blue 50 60
MS194 195 × 96 mm. Nos. 188/93 1·25 2·00

52 Anguillan pointing to Star

1974. Christmas. Multicoloured.
195 1c. Type **52** 10 10
196 20c. Child in Manger 10 20
197 25c. King's offering 10 20
198 40c. Star over map of Anguilla 15 20
199 60c. Family looking at star 15 20
200 $1.20 Angels of Peace 20 30
MS201 177 × 85 mm. Nos. 195/200 1·00 1·75

53 "Mary, John and Mary Magdalene" (Matthias Grunewald)
55 "Madonna, Child and the Infant John the Baptist" (Raphael)

54 Statue of Liberty

1975. Easter. Details from Isenheim Altarpiece, Colmar Museum. Multicoloured.
202 1c. Type **53** 10 10
203 10c. "The Crucifixion" 15 15
204 15c. "St. John the Baptist" 15 15
205 20c. "St. Sebastian and Angels" 15 20
206 $1 "The Entombment" (horiz) 20 35
207 $1.50 "St. Anthony the Hermit" 25 45
MS208 134 × 127 mm. Nos. 202/7 (imperf) 1·00 1·75

1975. Bicentenary of American Revolution. Mult.
209 1c. Type **54** 10 10
210 10c. The Capitol 20 10
211 15c. "Congress voting for Independence" (Pine and Savage) 30 15
212 20c. Washington and map 30 15
213 $1 Boston Tea Party 45 40
214 $1.50 Bicentenary logo 50 60
MS215 198 × 97 mm. Nos. 209/14 1·50 2·50

1975. Christmas. "Madonna and Child" paintings by artists named. Multicoloured.
216 1c. Type **55** 10 10
217 10c. Cima 15 15
218 15c. Dolci 20 15
219 20c. Durer 20 20
220 $1 Bellini 35 25
221 $1.50 Botticelli 45 35
MS222 130 × 145 mm. Nos. 216/21 2·00 2·25

1976. New Constitution. Nos. 130 etc optd **NEW CONSTITUTION 1976** or surch also.
223 1c. Spear fishing 30 40
224 2c. on 1c. Spear fishing 30 40
225 2c. Type **42** 7·00 1·75
226 3c. on 40c. Boat building 75 70
227 4c. Ferry at Blowing Point 1·00 1·00
228 5c. on 40c. Boat building 30 50
229 6c. St. Mary's Church 30 50
230 10c. on 20c. Public library 30 50
231 10c. St. Gerard's Church 7·00 4·75
232 15c. Cottage Hospital extension 30 90
233 20c. Public library 30 50
234 25c. Sunset at Blowing Point 30 50
235 40c. Boat building 1·00 70
236 60c. Hibiscus 70 70
237 $1 Magnificent frigate bird 6·50 2·25
238 $2.50 Frangipani 2·25 2·25
239 $5 Brown pelican 8·00 7·50
240 $10 Green-back turtle 3·00 6·00

57 Almond

1976. Flowering Trees. Multicoloured.
241 1c. Type **57** 10 10
242 10c. Autograph 20 20
243 15c. Calabash 20 20
244 20c. Cordia 20 20
245 $1 Papaya 30 45
246 $1.50 Flamboyant 35 55
MS247 194 × 99 mm. Nos. 241/6 1·50 2·00

58 The Three Marys

1976. Easter. Showing portions of the Altar Frontal Tapestry, Rheinau. Multicoloured.
248 1c. Type **58** 10 10
249 10c. The Crucifixion 10 10
250 15c. Two Soldiers 15 15
251 20c. The Annunciation 15 15
252 $1 The complete tapestry (horiz) 65 65
253 $1.50 The Risen Christ 80 80
MS254 138 × 130 mm. Nos. 248/53 (imperf) 1·75 2·10

59 French Ships approaching Anguilla

1976. Bicentenary of Battle of Anguilla. Mult.
255 1c. Type **59** 10 10
256 3c. "Margaret" (sloop) leaving Anguilla 1·25 35
257 15c. Capture of "Le Desius" 1·50 55
258 25c. "La Vaillante" forced aground 1·50 80
259 $1 H.M.S. "Lapwing" 2·00 1·25
260 $1.50 "Le Desius" burning 2·25 1·75
MS261 205 × 103 mm. Nos. 255/60 7·50 6·00

60 "Christmas Carnival" (A. Richardson)

1976. Christmas. Children's Paintings. Mult.
262 1c. Type **60** 10 10
263 3c. "Dreams of Christmas Gifts" (J. Connor) 10 10
264 15c. "Carolling" (P. Richardson) 15 15
265 25c. "Candle-light Procession" (A. Mussington) 20 20
266 $1 "Going to Church" (B. Franklin) 30 30
267 $1.50 "Coming Home for Christmas" (E. Gumbs) 40 40
MS268 232 × 147 mm. Nos. 262/7 1·50 1·75

61 Prince Charles and H.M.S. "Minerva" (frigate)

1977. Silver Jubilee. Multicoloured.
269 25c. Type **61** 15 10
270 40c. Prince Philip landing by launch at Road Bay, 1964 15 10
271 $1.20 Coronation scene 20 20
272 $2.50 Coronation regalia and map of Anguilla 25 30
MS273 145 × 96 mm. Nos. 269/72 65 90

62 Yellow-crowned Night Heron

1977. Multicoloured.
274 1c. Type **62** 30 1·00
275 2c. Great barracuda 30 1·75
276 3c. Queen or pink conch 2·00 2·75
277 4c. Spanish bayonet (flower) 40 30
278 5c. Honeycomb trunkfish 1·50 30
279 6c. Cable and Wireless building 30 30
280 10c. American kestrel ("American Sparrow Hawk") 5·00 2·50
281 15c. Ground orchid 2·75 1·75
282 20c. Stop-light parrotfish 3·25 75
283 22c. Lobster fishing boat 50 60
284 35c. Boat race 1·40 70
285 50c. Sea bean 90 50
286 $1 Sandy Island 60 50
287 $2.50 Manchineel 1·00 1·00
288 $5 Ground lizard 2·00 1·75
289 $10 Red-billed tropic bird 9·00 4·25

63 "The Crucifixion" (Massys)

1977. Easter. Paintings by Castagno ($1.50) or Ugolino (others). Multicoloured.
291 1c. Type **63** 10 10
292 3c. "The Betrayal" 10 10
293 22c. "The Way to Calvary" 20 20
294 30c. "The Deposition" 25 25
295 $1 "The Resurrection" 50 50
296 $1.50 "The Crucifixion" 65 65
MS297 192 × 126 mm. Nos. 291/6 1·60 1·75

1977. Royal Visit. Nos. 269/72 optd **ROYAL VISIT TO WEST INDIES**.
298 25c. Type **61** 10 10
299 40c. Prince Philip landing at Road Bay, 1964 10 15
300 $1.20 Coronation scene 20 25
301 $1.50 Coronation regalia and map of Anguilla 25 35
MS302 145 × 96 mm. Nos. 298/301 80 60

65 "Le Chapeau de Paille"

1977. 400th Birth Anniv of Rubens. Multicoloured.
303 25c. Type **65** 15 15
304 40c. "Helene Fourment and her Two Children" 20 25
305 $1.20 "Rubens and his Wife" 60 65
306 $2.50 "Marchesa Brigida Spinola-Doria" 75 95
MS307 90 × 145 mm. Nos. 303/6 2·00 2·10

1977. Christmas. Nos. 262/7 with old date blocked out and additionally inscr "1977", some also surch.
308 1c. Type **60** 10 10
309 5c. on 3c. "Dreams of Christmas Gifts" 10 10
310 12c. on 15c. "Carolling" 15 15
311 18c. on 25c. "Candle-light Procession" 20 20
312 $1 "Going to Church" 45 45
313 $2.50 on $1.50 "Coming Home for Christmas" 90 90
MS314 232 × 147 mm. Nos. 308/13 2·50 2·50

1978. Easter. Nos. 303/6 optd **EASTER 1978**.
315 25c. Type **65** 15 20
316 40c. "Helene Fourment with her Two Children" 15 20
317 $1.20 "Rubens and his Wife" 35 40
318 $2.50 "Marchesa Brigida Spinola-Doria" 45 60
MS319 93 × 145 mm. Nos. 315/18 1·25 1·50

68 Coronation Coach at Admiralty Arch

1978. 25th Anniv of Coronation. Multicoloured.
320 22c. Buckingham Palace 10 10
321 50c. Type **68** 10 10
322 $1.50 Balcony scene 15 15
323 $2.50 Royal coat of arms 25 25
MS324 138 × 92 mm. Nos. 320/3 60 60

1978. Anniversaries. Nos. 283/4 and 287 optd **VALLEY SECONDARY SCHOOL 1953–1978** and Nos. 285/6 and 288 optd **ROAD METHODIST CHURCH 1878–1978**, or surch also.
325 22c. Lobster fishing boat 20 15
326 35c. Boat race 30 20
327 50c. Sea bean 30 30
328 $1 Sandy Island 35 40
329 $1.20 on $5 Ground lizard 40 45
330 $1.50 on $2.50 Manchineel 45 55

71 Mother and Child

1978. Christmas. Children's Paintings. Mult.
331 5c. Type **71** 10 10
332 12c. Christmas masquerade 15 10
333 18c. Christmas dinner 15 10
334 22c. Serenading 15 10
335 $1 Child in manger 45 20
336 $2.50 Family going to church 90 40
MS337 191 × 101 mm. Nos. 331/6 1·60 1·75

1979. International Year of the Child. As Nos. 331/6, but additionally inscr "1979 INTERNATIONAL YEAR OF THE CHILD" and emblem. Borders in different colours.
338 5c. Type **71** 10 10
339 12c. Christmas masquerade 10 10
340 18c. Christmas dinner 10 10
341 22c. Serenading 10 10
342 $1 Child in manger 30 30
343 $2.50 Family going to church 50 50
MS344 205 × 112 mm. Nos. 338/43 2·25 2·50

1979. Nos. 274/7 and 279/80 surch.
345 12c. on 2c. Great barracuda 50 50
346 14c. on 4c. Spanish bayonet 40 50
347 18c. on 3c. Queen conch 80 55
348 25c. on 6c. Cable and Wireless building 55 50
349 38c. on 10c. American kestrel 2·50 70
350 40c. on 1c. Type **62** 2·50 70

73 Valley Methodist Church

1979. Easter. Church Interiors. Multicoloured.
351 5c. Type **73** 10 10
352 12c. St. Mary's Anglican Church, The Valley 10 10
353 18c. St. Gerard's Roman Catholic Church, The Valley 15 15
354 22c. Road Methodist Church 15 15
355 $1.50 St. Augustine's Anglican Church, East End 60 60
356 $2.50 West End Methodist Church 75 75
MS357 190 × 105 mm. Nos. 351/6 1·75 2·25

74 Cape of Good Hope 1d. "Woodblock" of 1881

1979. Death Centenary of Sir Rowland Hill. Multicoloured.
358 1c. Type **74** 10 10
359 1c. U.S.A. "inverted Jenny" of 1918 . . . . 10 10
360 22c. Penny Black ("V.R." Official) 15 15
361 35c. Germany 2m, "Graf Zeppelin" of 1928 . . . . 20 20
362 $1.50 U.S.A. $5 "Columbus" of 1893 . . . . 40 60
363 $2.50 Great Britain £5 orange of 1882 . . . . 60 95
MS364 187 × 123 mm. Nos. 358/63 1·25 2·10

75 Wright "Flyer I" (1st powered Flight, 1903)

1979. History of Powered Fight. Multicoloured.
365 5c. Type **75** 15 10
366 12c. Louis Bleriot at Dover after Channel crossing, 1909 . . . . 20 10
367 18c. Vickers FB-27 Vimy (1st non-stop crossing of Atlantic, 1919) 25 15
368 22c. Ryan NYP Special "Spirit of St Louis" (1st solo Atlantic flight by Charles Lindbergh, 1927) 25 20
369 $1.50 Airship LZ 127 "Graf Zeppelin", 1928 . . . . . 60 60
370 $2.50 Concorde, 1979 . . . . 2·50 90
MS371 200 × 113 mm. Nos. 365/70 3·25 2·50

76 Sombrero Island

1979. Outer Islands. Multicoloured.
372 5c. Type **76** 10 10
373 12c. Anguillita Island 10 10
374 18c. Sandy Island 15 15
375 25c. Prickly Pear Cays . . . 15 15
376 $1 Dog Island 30 40
377 $2.50 Scrub Island 50 70
MS378 180 × 91 mm. Nos. 372/7 2·25 2·25

77 Red Poinsettia

1979. Christmas. Multicoloured.
379 22c. Type **77** 15 20
380 35c. Kalanchoe 20 30
381 $1.50 Cream poinsettia . . . 40 50
382 $2.50 White poinsettia . . . 60 70
MS383 146 × 164 mm. Nos. 379/82 1·75 2·25

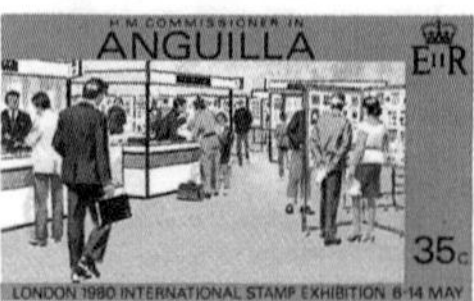

78 Exhibition Scene

1979. "London 1980" International Stamp Exhibition (1st issue). Multicoloured.
384 35c. Type **78** 15 20
385 50c. Earls Court Exhibition Centre 15 25
386 $1.50 Penny Black and Two-penny Blue stamps 25 60
387 $2.50 Exhibition Logo . . . 45 95
MS388 150 × 94 mm. Nos. 384/7 1·40 2·00
See also Nos. 407/9.

79 Games Site

1980. Winter Olympic Games, Lake Placid, U.S.A. Multicoloured.
389 5c. Type **79** 10 10
390 18c. Ice hockey 20 10
391 35c. Ice skating 20 20
392 50c. Bobsleighing 20 20
393 $1 Skiing 20 35
394 $2.50 Luge-tobogganing . . . 40 80
MS395 136 × 128 mm. Nos. 389/94 1·00 2·00

80 Salt ready for "Reaping"

1980. Salt Industry. Multicoloured.
396 5c. Type **80** 10 10
397 12c. Tallying salt 10 10
398 18c. Unloading salt flats . . 15 15
399 22c. Salt storage heap 15 15
400 $1 Salt for bagging and grinding 30 40
401 $2.50 Loading salt for export 50 70
MS402 180 × 92 mm. Nos. 396/401 1·10 1·75

1980. Anniversaries. Nos. 280, 282 and 287/8 optd **50th Anniversary Scouting 1980** (10c., $2.50) or **75th Anniversary Rotary 1980** (others).
403 10c. American kestrel . . . . 1·75 15
404 20c. Stop-light parrotfish . . 1·00 20
405 $2.50 Manchineel . . . . . 1·75 1·25
406 $5 Ground lizard . . . . . 2·50 1·90

83 Palace of Westminster and Great Britain 1970 9d. "Philympia" Commemoration

1980. "London 1980" International Stamp Exhibition (2nd issue). Multicoloured.
407 50c. Type **83** 55 65
408 $1.50 City Hall, Toronto and "Capex 1978" stamp of Canada . . . . 85 1·00
409 $2.50 Statue of Liberty and 1976 "Interphil" stamp of U.S.A. . . . . 1·10 1·40
MS410 157 × 130 mm. Nos. 407/9 2·25 2·75

84 Queen Elizabeth the Queen Mother

85 Brown Pelicans ("Pelican")

1980. 80th Birthday of The Queen Mother.
411 **84** 35c. multicoloured 70 40
412 50c. multicoloured 85 50
413 $1.50 multicoloured . . . 1·50 1·25
414 $3 multicoloured . . . . . 2·25 2·00
MS415 160 × 110 mm. Nos. 411/14 5·50 3·50

1980. Christmas. Birds. Multicoloured.
416 5c. Type **85** 30 10
417 22c. Great blue heron ("Great Grey Heron") . . 75 20
418 $1.50 Barn swallow ("Swallow") . . . . 1·75 60
419 $3 Ruby-throated hummingbird ("Hummingbird") . . . . 2·25 1·40
MS420 126 × 160 mm. Nos. 416/19 8·50 6·50

1980. Separation from St. Kitts. Nos. 274, 277, 280/9, 334 and 418/19 optd **SEPARATION 1980** or surch also.
421 1c. Type **62** 15 80
422b 2c. on 4c. Spanish bayonet 15 80
423 5c. on 15c. Ground orchid 1·00 80
424 5c. on $1.50 Barn swallow 1·00 80
425 5c. on $3 Ruby-throated hummingbird . . . . . . 1·00 80
426 10c. American kestrel . . . 1·50 80
427 12c. on $1 Sandy Island . . 20 80
428 14c. on $2.50 Manchineel 20 80
429 15c. Ground orchid . . . . 1·25 80
430 18c. on $5 Ground lizard 25 80
431 20c. Stop-light parrotfish . . 25 80
432 22c. Lobster fishing boat . . 25 80
433 25c. on 15c. Ground orchid 1·25 85
434 35c. Boat race 30 85
435 38c. on 22c. Serenading . . 30 85
436 40c. on 1c. Type **62** 30 85
437 50c. Sea bean 35 95
438 $1 Sandy Island . . . . . 50 1·25
439 $2.50 Manchineel . . . . . 1·25 3·00
440 $5 Ground lizard . . . . . 2·25 4·00
441 $10 Red-billed tropic bird 5·00 6·00
442 $10 on 6c. Cable and Wireless Building . . . . 5·00 6·00

87 First Petition for Separation, 1825

1980. Separation from St. Kitts. Multicoloured.
443 18c. Type **87** 10 10
444 22c. Referendum ballot paper, 1967 . . . . 15 10
445 35c. Airport blockade, 1967 15 15
446 50c. Anguillan flag 20 20
447 $1 Separation celebration, 1980 . . . . 30 35
MS448 178 × 92 mm. Nos. 443/7 80 1·25

88 "Nelson's Dockyard" (R. Granger Barrett)

1981. 175th Death Anniv of Lord Nelson. Mult.
449 22c. Type **88** . . . . 1·40 40
450 35c. "Ships in which Nelson Served" (Nicholas Pocock) 1·60 60
451 50c. "H.M.S. Victory" (Monamy Swaine) . . . . 1·90 85
452 $3 "Battle of Trafalgar" (Clarkson Stanfield) . . . 2·50 3·00
MS453 82 × 63 mm. $5 "Horatio Nelson" (L. F. Abbott) and coat of arms 3·00 3·25

89 Minnie Mouse being chased by Bees

1981. Easter. Walt Disney Cartoon Characters. Multicoloured.
454 1c. Type **89** 10 10
455 2c. Pluto laughing at Mickey Mouse 10 10
456 3c. Minnie Mouse tying ribbon round Pluto's neck 10 10
457 5c. Minnie Mouse confronted by love-struck bird who fancies her bonnet 10 10
458 7c. Dewey and Huey admiring themselves in mirror 10 10
459 9c. Horace Horsecollar and Clarabelle Cow out for a stroll 10 10
460 10c. Daisy Duck with hat full of Easter eggs 10 10
461 $2 Goofy unwrapping Easter hat . . . . 1·40 1·40
462 $3 Donald Duck in his Easter finery . . . . 1·60 1·60
MS463 134 × 108 mm. $5 Chip and Dale making off with hat 3·50 3·50

90 Prince Charles, Lady Diana Spencer and St. Paul's Cathedral

1981. Royal Wedding. Multicoloured.
464 50c. Type **90** 15 20
465 $2.50 Althorp 30 50
466 $3 Windsor Castle 35 60
MS467 90 × 72 mm. Buckingham Palace 1·25 1·50

91 Children playing in Tree

1981. 35th Anniv of U.N.I.C.E.F. Multicoloured.
470 5c. Type **91** 20 30
471 10c. Children playing by pool 20 30
472 15c. Children playing musical instruments 20 30
473 $3 Children playing with pets 2·50 3·00
MS474 78 × 106 mm. Children playing football (vert) 3·50 4·50

1981. Christmas. Designs as T **89** showing scenes from Walt Disney's cartoon film "The Night before Christmas".
475 1c. multicoloured 10 10
476 2c. multicoloured 10 10
477 3c. multicoloured 10 10
478 5c. multicoloured 15 10
479 7c. multicoloured 15 10
480 10c. multicoloured 15 10
481 12c. multicoloured 15 10
482 $2 multicoloured . . . . . . 3·75 1·25
483 $3 multicoloured . . . . . . 3·75 1·60
MS484 130 × 105 mm. $5 multicoloured 5·50 3·50

92 Red Grouper

1982. Multicoloured.
485 1c. Type **92** . . . . 15 1·00
486 5c. Ferry service, Blowing Point . . . . 30 1·00
487 10c. Island dinghies 20 60
488 15c. Majorettes 20 60
489 20c. Launching boat, Sandy Hill 40 60
490 25c. Corals . . . . 1·50 60
491 30c. Little Bay cliffs 30 75
492 35c. Fountain Cave interior 1·50 80
493 40c. Sunset over Sandy Island 30 75
494 45c. Landing at Sombrero . . 50 80
495 60c. Seine fishing . . . . . . 3·25 3·25
496 75c. Boat race at sunset, Sandy Ground . . . . . . 1·00 2·00
497 $1 Bagging lobster at Island Harbour . . . . 2·25 2·00
498 $5 Brown pelicans . . . . . 16·00 13·00
499 $7.50 Hibiscus . . . . 11·00 15·00
500 $10 Queen triggerfish . . . . 16·00 15·00

1982. No. 494 surch **50c.**
501 50c. on 45c. Landing at Sombrero 50 35

94 Anthurium and "Heliconius charithonia"

95 Lady Diana Spencer in 1961

1982. Easter. Flowers and Butterflies. Multicoloured.
502 10c. Type **94** 85 10
503 35c. Bird of paradise and "Junonia evarete" . . . . 1·60 40
504 75c. Allamanda and "Danaus plexippus" . . . . 1·75 70
505 $3 Orchid tree and "Biblis hyperia" . . . . 3·00 2·25
MS506 65×79 mm. $5 Amaryllis and "Dryas julia" 2·75 3·50

1982. 21st Birthday of Princess of Wales. Mult.
507 10c. Type **95** 50 20
508 30c. Lady Diana Spencer in 1968 . . . . 1·25 25
509 40c. Lady Diana in 1970 . . 50 30
510 60c. Lady Diana in 1974 . . 55 35
511 $2 Lady Diana in 1981 . . . 80 1·10
512 $3 Lady Diana in 1981 (different) . . . . 4·50 1·40
MS513 72×90 mm. $5 Princess of Wales 6·50 3·00
MS514 125×125 mm. As Nos. 507/12, but with buff borders 7·50 5·50

96 Pitching Tent

1982. 75th Anniv of Boy Scout Movement. Multicoloured.
515 10c. Type **96** 45 20
516 35c. Scout band 85 50
517 75c. Yachting . . . . 1·25 90
518 $3 On parade . . . . 3·00 2·75
MS519 90×72 mm. $5 Cooking 4·50 4·00

1982. World Cup Football Championship, Spain. Horiz designs as T **89** showing scenes from Walt Disney's cartoon film "Bedknobs and Broomsticks".
520 1c. multicoloured 10 10
521 3c. multicoloured 10 10
522 4c. multicoloured 10 10
523 5c. multicoloured 10 10
524 7c. multicoloured 10 10
525 9c. multicoloured 10 10
526 10c. multicoloured 10 10
527 $2.50 multicoloured . . . . 2·25 1·75
528 $3 multicoloured . . . . . . 2·25 2·00
MS529 126×101 mm. $5 multicoloured 6·50 6·50

1982. Commonwealth Games, Brisbane. Nos. 487, 495/6 and 498 optd **COMMONWEALTH GAMES 1982**.
530 10c. Island dinghies 15 25
531 60c. Seine fishing 45 60
532 75c. Boat race at sunset, Sandy Ground 60 80
533 $5 Brown pelicans . . . . . 3·25 3·75

1982. Birth Cent of A. A. Milne (author). As T **89**.
534 1c. multicoloured 20 15
535 2c. multicoloured 20 15
536 3c. multicoloured 20 15
537 5c. multicoloured 30 15
538 7c. multicoloured 30 25
539 10c. multicoloured 40 15
540 12c. multicoloured 50 20
541 20c. multicoloured 80 25
542 $5 multicoloured . . . . . . 7·00 8·00
MS543 120×93 mm. $5 multicoloured 7·00 7·50
DESIGNS—HORIZ: 1c. to $5 Scenes from various "Winnie the Pooh" stories.

98 Culture

1983. Commonwealth Day. Multicoloured.
544 10c. Type **98** 10 15
545 35c. Anguilla and British flags 30 30
546 75c. Economic co-operation 60 80
547 $2.50 Salt industry (salt pond) . . . . 3·75 4·25
MS548 76×61 mm. World map showing positions of Commonwealth countries 2·50 2·50

99 "I am the Lord Thy God"

101 Montgolfier Hot Air Balloon, 1783

100 Leatherback Turtle

1983. Easter. The Ten Commandments. Mult.
549 1c. Type **99** 10 10
550 2c. "Thou shalt not make any graven image" 10 10
551 3c. "Thou shalt not take My Name in vain" 10 10
552 10c. "Remember the Sabbath Day" 20 10
553 35c. "Honour thy father and mother" 55 20
554 60c. "Thou shalt not kill" . . 90 40
555 75c. "Thou shalt not commit adultery" . . . . 1·00 50
556 $2 "Thou shalt not steal" . . 2·50 1·50
557 $2.50 "Thou shalt not bear false witness" . . . . . . 2·75 1·50
558 $5 "Thou shalt not covet" . . 4·00 2·75
MS559 126×102 mm. $5 "Moses receiving the Tablets" (16th-century woodcut) 2·50 3·00

1983. Endangered Species. Turtles. Multicoloured.
560 10c. Type **100** . . . . 2·75 80
561 35c. Hawksbill turtle . . . . 5·00 1·25
562 75c. Green turtle . . . . . . 6·00 3·00
563 $1 Loggerhead turtle . . . . 7·00 7·00
MS564 93×72 mm. $5 Leatherback turtle (different) 9·00 3·00

1983. Bicentenary of Manned Flight. Multicoloured.
565 10c. Type **101** 50 50
566 60c. Blanchard and Jefferies crossing English Channel by balloon, 1785 . . . . . 1·25 85
567 $1 Henri Giffard's steam-powered dirigible airship, 1852 . . . . 1·75 1·25
568 $2.50 Otto Lillienthal and biplane glider, 1890–96 . . 2·50 2·50
MS569 72×90 mm. $5 Wilbur Wright flying round Statue of Liberty, 1909 2·75 3·50

102 Boys' Brigade Band and Flag

1983. Centenary of Boys' Brigade. Multicoloured.
570 10c. Type **102** 50 15
571 $5 Brigade members marching . . . . 3·50 2·75
MS572 96×115 mm. Nos. 570/1 3·25 4·00

1983. 150th Anniv of Abolition of Slavery (1st issue). Nos. 487, 493 and 497/8 optd **150TH ANNIVERSARY ABOLITION OF SLAVERY ACT**.
573 10c. Island dinghies 20 10
574 40c. Sunset over Sandy Island 30 25
575 $1 Bagging lobster at Island Harbour 70 50
576 $5 Brown pelicans . . . . . 6·00 2·75
See also Nos. 616/23.

104 Jiminy on Clock ("Cricket on the Hearth")

1983. Christmas. Walt Disney Cartoon Characters. Multicoloured.
577 1c. Type **104** 10 10
578 2c. Jiminy with fiddle ("Cricket on the Hearth") 10 10
579 3c. Jiminy among toys ("Cricket on the Hearth") 10 10
580 4c. Mickey as Bob Cratchit ("A Christmas Carol") . . 10 10
581 5c. Donald Duck as Scrooge ("A Christmas Carol") . . 10 10
582 6c. Mini and Goofy in "The Chimes" 10 10
583 10c. Goofy sees an imp appearing from bells ("The Chimes") 10 10
584 $2 Donald Duck as Mr. Pickwick ("The Pickwick Papers") . . . . 3·25 2·75
585 $3 Disney characters as Pickwickians ("The Pickwick Papers") . . . . 3·75 2·25
MS586 130×104 mm. Donald Duck as Mr. Pickwick with gifts ("The Pickwick Papers") 7·50 8·50

105 100 Metres Race

1984. Olympic Games, Los Angeles. Multicoloured.
(A) Inscr "1984 Los Angeles".
587A 1c. Type **105** 10 10
588A 2c. Long jumping 10 10
589A 3c. Shot-putting 10 10
590A 4c. High jumping 10 10
591A 5c. 400 metres race 10 10
592A 6c. Hurdling 10 10
593A 10c. Discus-throwing . . . 10 10
594A $1 Pole-vaulting . . . . . 3·25 1·25
595A $4 Javelin-throwing . . . . 6·00 3·50
MS596A 117×93 mm. $5 1500 metres race 7·50 4·50

(B) Inscr "1984 Olympics Los Angeles" and Olympic emblem.
587B 1c. Type **105** 10 10
588B 2c. Long jumping 10 10
589B 3c. Shot-putting 10 10
590B 4c. High jumping 10 10
591B 5c. 400 metres race 10 10
592B 6c. Hurdling 10 10
593B 10c. Discus-throwing . . . 10 10
594B $1 Pole-vaulting . . . . . 3·75 3·00
595B $4 Javelin-throwing . . . . 7·50 8·50
MS596B 117×93 mm. $5 1500 metres race 7·50 4·50

106 "Justice"

1984. Easter. Multicoloured.
597 10c. Type **106** 15 10
598 25c. "Poetry" 20 20
599 35c. "Philosophy" 30 30
600 40c. "Theology" 30 30
601 $1 "Abraham and Paul" . . 85 95
602 $2 "Moses and Matthew" . . 1·60 2·25
603 $3 "John and David" . . . . 2·25 3·00
604 $4 "Peter and Adam" . . . 2·50 3·00
MS605 83×110 mm. $5 "Astronomy" 3·50 3·00
Nos. 597/605 show details from "La Stanza della Segnatura" by Raphael.

1984. Nos. 485, 491, 498/500 surch.
606 25c. on $7.50 Hibiscus . . . 65 35
607 35c. on 30c. Little Bay cliffs 50 40
608 60c. on 1c. Type **92** 55 45
609 $2.50 on $5 Brown pelicans 3·00 1·50
610 $2.50 on $10 Queen triggerfish . . . . 1·75 1·50

108 1913 1d. Kangaroo Stamp

1984. "Ausipex 84" International Stamp Exhibition. Multicoloured.
611 10c. Type **108** 40 30
612 75c. 1914 6d. Laughing Kookaburra . . . . 1·25 1·00
613 $1 1932 2d. Sydney Harbour Bridge . . . . 1·75 1·50
614 $2.50 1938 10s. King George VI . . . . 2·25 3·00
MS615 95×86 mm. $5 £1 Bass and £2 Admiral King 4·50 6·00

109 Thomas Fowell Buxton

1984. 150th Anniv of Abolition of Slavery (2nd issue). Multicoloured.
616 10c. Type **109** 10 10
617 25c. Abraham Lincoln . . . 25 25
618 35c. Henri Christophe . . . 35 35
619 60c. Thomas Clarkson . . . 50 50
620 75c. William Wilberforce . . 60 60
621 $1 Olaudah Equiano 70 70
622 $2.50 General Charles Gordon . . . . 1·60 1·60
623 $5 Granville Sharp . . . . . 3·00 3·00
MS624 150×121 mm. Nos. 616/23 6·50 8·00

1984. Universal Postal Union Congress, Hamburg. Nos. 486/7 and 498 optd **U.P.U. CONGRESS HAMBURG 1984** or surch also (No 626).
625 5c. Ferry service, Blowing Point 30 10
626 20c. on 10c. Island dinghies 30 15
627 $5 Brown pelicans . . . . . 5·50 3·50

1984. Birth of Prince Henry. Nos. 507/12 optd **PRINCE HENRY BIRTH 15.9.84**.
628 10c. Type **95** 20 10
629 30c. Lady Diana Spencer in 1968 . . . . 40 25
630 40c. Lady Diana in 1970 . . 25 30
631 60c. Lady Diana in 1974 . . 40 45
632 $2 Lady Diana in 1981 . . . 1·00 1·25
633 $3 Lady Diana in 1981 (different) . . . . 1·50 1·75
MS634 72×90 mm. $5 Princess of Wales 2·00 3·00
MS635 125×125 mm. As Nos. 628/33, but with buff borders 2·50 4·00

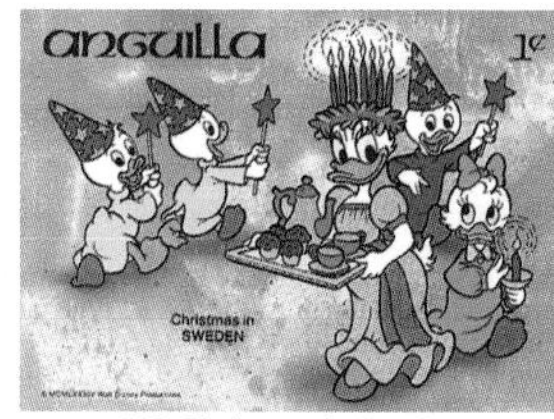

112 Christmas in Sweden

1984. Christmas. Walt Disney Cartoon Characters. National Scenes. Multicoloured.
636 1c. Type **112** 10 10
637 2c. Italy 10 10
638 3c. Holland 10 10
639 4c. Mexico 10 10
640 5c. Spain 10 10
641 10c. Disneyland, U.S.A. . . . 10 10
642 $1 Japan . . . . 3·00 2·00
643 $2 Anguilla . . . . 4·00 4·75
644 $4 Germany . . . . 6·50 8·00
MS645 126×102 mm. $5 England 7·00 5·00

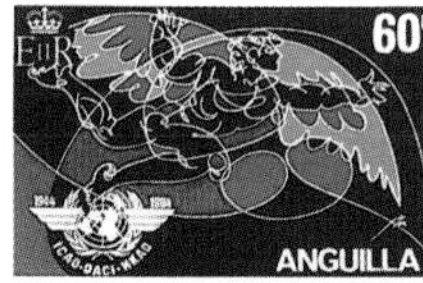

113 Icarus in Flight

1984. 40th Anniv of International Civil Aviation Authority. Multicoloured.
646 60c. Type **113** 60 75
647 75c. "Solar Princess" (abstract) 80 90
648 $2.50 I.C.A.O. emblem (vert) 2·25 3·00
MS649 65×49 mm. $5 Map of air routes serving Anguilla 3·00 4·25

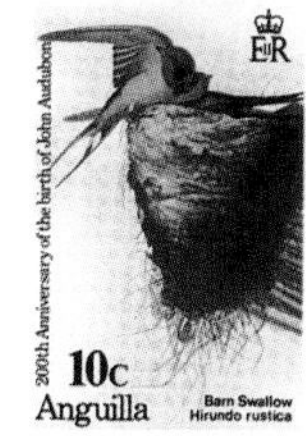

114 Barn Swallow

115 The Queen Mother visiting King's College Hospital, London

1985. Birth Bicentenary of John J. Audubon (ornithologist). Multicoloured.
650 10c. Type **114** 80 65
651 60c. American wood stork ("Woodstork") . . . . . 1·50 1·25

652 75c. Roseate tern . . . . . . 1·50 1·25
653 $5 Osprey . . . . 4·50 5·00
MS654 Two sheets, each 73 × 103 mm. $4 Western tanager (horiz); (b) $4 Solitary vireo (horiz) Set of 2 sheets 8·00 5·00

1985. Life and Times of Queen Elizabeth the Queen Mother. Multicoloured.
655 10c. Type **115** 10 10
656 $2 The Queen Mother inspecting Royal Marine Volunteer Cadets, Deal . . 80 1·25
657 $3 The Queen Mother outside Clarence House . . . . . 1·10 1·50
MS658 56 × 85 mm. $5 At Ascot, 1979 1·75 2·50

116 White-tailed Tropic Bird

1985. Birds. Multicoloured.
659 5c. Brown pelican . . . . . 1·75 1·75
660 10c. Mourning dove ("Turtle Dove") . . . . . 1·75 1·75
661 15c. Magnificent frigate bird (inscr "Man-o-War") . . 1·75 1·75
662 20c. Antillean crested hummingbird . . . . . . 1·75 1·75
663 25c. Type **116** . . . . . . 1·75 1·75
664 30c. Caribbean elaenia . . . 1·75 1·75
665 35c. Black-whiskered vireo 7·50 5·00
665a 35c. Lesser Antillean bullfinch . . . . 1·75 1·75
666 40c. Yellow-crowned night heron . . . . 1·75 1·75
667 45c. Pearly-eyed thrasher . . 1·75 1·75
668 50c. Laughing gull . . . . 1·75 1·75
669 65c. Brown booby . . . . . 1·75 1·75
670 80c. Grey kingbird . . . . 2·25 3·00
671 $1 Audubon's shearwater 2·25 3·00
672 $1.35 Roseate tern . . . . 1·75 3·00
673 $2.50 Bananaquit . . . . . 5·50 7·00
674 $5 Belted kingfisher . . . . 4·25 8·00
675 $10 Green-backed heron ("Green Heron") . . . . 7·00 10·00

1985. 75th Anniv of Girl Guide Movement. Nos. 486, 491, 496 and 498 optd **GIRL GUIDES 75TH ANNIVERSARY 1910–1985** and anniversary emblem.
676 5c. Ferry service, Blowing Point 30 30
677 30c. Little Bay cliffs 40 35
678 75c. Boat race at sunset, Sandy Ground 60 85
679 $5 Brown pelicans . . . . . 7·00 7·50

118 Goofy as Huckleberry Finn Fishing

1985. 150th Birth Anniv of Mark Twain (author). Walt Disney cartoon characters in scenes from "Huckleberry Finn". Multicoloured.
680 10c. Type **118** 65 20
681 60c. Pete as Pap surprising Huck . . . . 2·00 85
682 $1 "Multiplication tables" . . 2·50 1·25
683 $3 The Duke reciting Shakespeare . . . . 3·75 4·00
MS684 127 × 102 mm. $5 "In school but out" 7·50 7·00

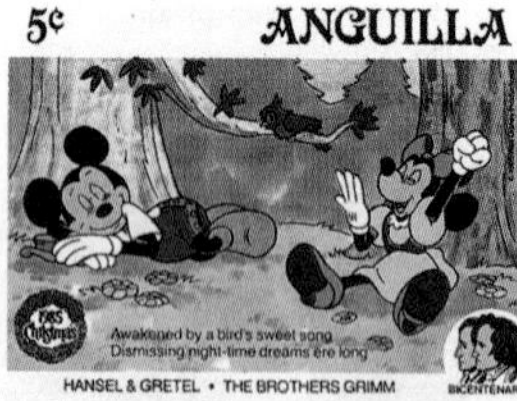

119 Hansel and Gretel (Mickey and Minnie Mouse) awakening in Forest

1985. Birth Bicentenaries of Grimm Brothers (folklorists). Designs showing Walt Disney cartoon characters in scenes from "Hansel and Gretel". Multicoloured.
685 5c. Type **119** 40 40
686 50c. Hansel and Gretel find the gingerbread house . . 1·25 45
687 90c. Hansel and Gretel meeting the Witch . . . . 1·75 1·00
688 $4 Hansel and Gretel captured by the Witch . . 3·25 4·25
MS689 128 × 101 mm. $5 Hansel and Gretel riding on swan 7·50 8·00

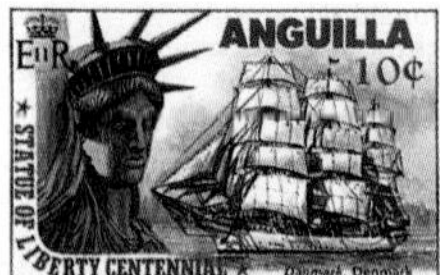

120 Statue of Liberty and "Danmark" (Denmark)

1985. Centenary of the Statue of Liberty (1986). The Statue of Liberty and Cadet ships.
690 10c. Type **120** 65 65
691 20c. "Eagle" (U.S.A.) 85 85
692 60c. "Amerigo Vespucci" (Italy) . . . . 1·25 1·50
693 75c. "Sir Winston Churchill" (Great Britain) . . . . . . 1·25 1·00
694 $2 "Nippon Maru" (Japan) 1·25 2·75
695 $2.50 "Gorch Fock" (West Germany) . . . . 1·50 2·75
MS696 96 × 69 mm. $5 Statue of Liberty (vert) 7·00 4·50

1985. 80th Anniv of Rotary (10, 35c.) and International Youth Year (others). Nos. 487, 491 and 497 optd or surch **80TH ANNIVERSARY ROTARY 1985** and emblem (10, 35c.) or **INTERNATIONAL YOUTH YEAR** and emblem ($1, $5).
697 10c. Island dinghies 25 15
698 35c. on 30c. Little Bay cliffs 55 30
699 $1 Bagging lobster at Island Harbour . . . . 1·25 80
700 $5 on 30c. Little Bay cliffs . . 4·00 4·00

123 Johannes Hevelius (astronomer) and Mayan Temple Observatory

1986. Appearance of Halley's Comet. Multicoloured.
701 5c. Type **123** 35 35
702 10c. "Viking Lander" space vehicle on Mars, 1976 . . 35 35
703 60c. Comet in 1664 (from "Theatri Cosmicum", 1668) 1·00 85
704 $4 Comet over Mississippi riverboat, 1835 (150th birth anniv of Mark Twain) . . 3·75 3·75
MS705 101 × 70 mm. $5 Halley's Comet over Anguilla 4·50 5·50

124 "The Crucifixion" **125** Princess Elizabeth inspecting Guards, 1946

1986. Easter.
706 **124** 10c. multicoloured 20 20
707 – 25c. multicoloured 35 35
708 – 45c. multicoloured 65 65
709 – $4 multicoloured . . . . 3·25 3·75
MS710 93 × 75 mm. $5 multicoloured (horiz) 5·50 7·50
DESIGNS: 25c. to $5 Different stained glass windows from Chartres Cathedral.

1986. 60th Birthday of Queen Elizabeth II.
711 **125** 20c. black and yellow . . 40 20
712 – $2 multicoloured . . . . 1·75 1·50
713 – $3 multicoloured . . . . 1·75 1·75
MS714 120 × 85 mm. $5 black and brown 2·75 3·50
DESIGNS: $2 Queen at Garter Ceremony; $3 At Trooping the Colour; $5 Duke and Duchess of York with baby Princess Elizabeth, 1926.

1986. "Ameripex" International Stamp Exhibition, Chicago. Nos. 659, 667, 671, 673 and 675 optd **AMERIPEX 1986**.
715 5c. Brown pelican 60 75
716 45c. Pearly-eyed thrasher . . 1·25 45
717 $1 Audubon's shearwater . . 2·00 1·10
718 $2.50 Bananaquit . . . . . 2·75 3·00
719 $10 Green-backed heron . . 6·50 8·50

127 Prince Andrew and Miss Sarah Ferguson **130** Christopher Columbus with Astrolabe

129 Trading Sloop

1986. Royal Wedding. Multicoloured.
720 10c. Type **127** 30 15
721 35c. Prince Andrew 60 35
722 $2 Miss Sarah Ferguson . . 1·75 1·50
723 $3 Prince Andrew and Miss Sarah Ferguson (diffferent) 2·25 2·00
MS724 119 × 90 mm. $6 Westminster Abbey 5·50 6·50

1986. International Peace Year. Nos. 616/23 optd **INTERNATIONAL YEAR OF PEACE**.
725 10c. Type **109** 50 30
726 25c. Abraham Lincoln . . . 75 45
727 35c. Henri Christophe . . . 90 55
728 60c. Thomas Clarkson . . . 1·40 80
729 75c. William Wilberforce . . 1·40 90
730 $1 Olaudah Equiano . . . . 1·40 1·00
731 $2.50 General Gordon . . . 2·50 3·50
732 $5 Granville Sharp . . . . . 3·50 4·50
MS733 150 × 121 mm. Nos. 725/32 13·00 15·00

1986. Christmas. Ships. Multicoloured.
734 10c. Type **129** . . . . 1·25 60
735 45c. "Lady Rodney" (cargo liner) . . . . 2·25 1·10
736 80c. "West Derby" (19th-century sailing ship) 3·25 2·50
737 $3 "Warspite" (local sloop) 5·50 7·00
MS738 130 × 100 mm. $4 Boat-race day (vert) 14·00 16·00

1986. 500th Anniv (1992) of Discovery of America by Columbus (1st issue). Multicoloured.
739 5c. Type **130** 60 60
740 10c. Columbus on board ship 1·00 60
741 35c. "Santa Maria" . . . . 2·00 1·10
742 80c. King Ferdinand and Queen Isabella of Spain (horiz) . . . . 1·50 1·75
743 $4 Caribbean Indians smoking tobacco (horiz) . . 3·25 5·00
MS744 Two sheets, each 96 × 66 mm. (a) $5 Caribbean manatee (horiz). (b) $5 Dragon tree Set of 2 sheets 13·00 15·00
See also Nos. 902/6.

131 "Danaus plexippus"

1987. Easter. Butterflies. Multicoloured.
745 10c. Type **131** . . . . 1·25 60
746 80c. "Anartia jatrophae" . . 3·25 2·50
747 $1 "Heliconius charithonia" 3·50 2·50
748 $2 "Junonia evarete" . . . . 5·50 7·00
MS749 90 × 69 mm. $6 "Dryas julia" 11·00 13·00

132 Old Goose Iron and Modern Electric Iron

1987. 20th Anniv of Separation from St. Kitts-Nevis. Multicoloured.
750 10c. Type **132** 50 40
751 35c. Old East End School and Albena Lake-Hodge Comprehensive College . . 55 45
752 45c. Past and present markets 65 50
753 80c. Previous sailing ferry and new motor ferry, Blowing Point . . . . . . 1·50 85
754 $1 Original mobile post office and new telephone exchange . . . . 1·25 95
755 $2 Open-air meeting, Burrowes Park and House of Assembly in session . . 1·50 2·50
MS756 159 × 127 mm. Nos. 750/5 8·00 10·00

1987. "Capex '87" International Stamp Exhibition, Toronto. Nos. 665a, 667, 670 and 675 optd **CAPEX'87**.
757 35c. Lesser Antillean bullfinch . . . . 1·50 80
758 45c. Pearly-eyed thrasher . . 1·50 80
759 80c. Grey kingbird . . . . . 2·50 1·25
760 $10 Green-backed heron . . 8·50 10·00

1987. 20th Anniv of Independence. Nos. 659, 661/4 and 665a/75 optd **20 YEARS OF PROGRESS 1967–1987**, No. 762 surch also.
761 5c. Brown pelican . . . . . 2·00 2·00
762 10c. on 15c. Magnificent frigate bird . . . . 2·00 2·00
763 15c. Magnificent frigate bird 2·25 2·25
764 20c. Antillean crested hummingbird . . . . . . 2·25 2·25
765 25c. Type **116** . . . . 2·25 2·25
766 30c. Caribbean elaenia . . . 2·25 2·25
767 35c. Lesser Antillean bullfinch . . . . 2·25 2·25
768 40c. Yellow-crowned night heron . . . . 2·25 2·25
769 45c. Pearly-eyed thrasher . . 2·25 2·25
770 50c. Laughing gull . . . . . 2·25 2·25
771 65c. Brown booby . . . . . 2·50 2·50
772 80c. Grey kingbird . . . . . 2·50 2·50
773 $1 Audubon's shearwater . . 2·50 2·50
774 $1.35 Roseate tern . . . . . 3·00 3·25
775 $2.50 Bananaquit . . . . . 3·50 4·50
776 $5 Belted kingfisher . . . . 4·75 7·00
777 $10 Green-backed heron . . 6·50 9·50

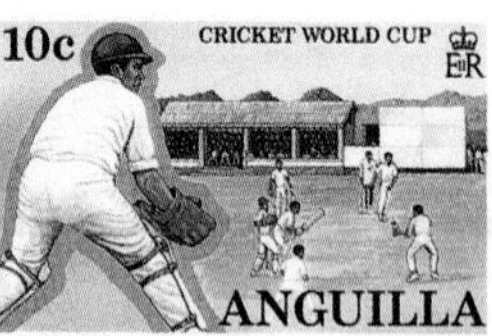

135 Wicket Keeper and Game in Progress

1987. Cricket World Cup. Multicoloured.
778 10c. Type **135** . . . . 1·25 70
779 35c. Batsman and local Anguilla team . . . . . 1·75 70
780 45c. Batsman and game in progress . . . . 1·75 75
781 $2.50 Bowler and game in progress . . . . 3·75 5·50
MS782 100 × 75 mm. $6 Batsman and game in progress (different) 12·00 13·00

136 West Indian Top Shell

1987. Christmas. Sea Shells and Crabs. Mult.
783 10c. Type **136** . . . . 1·25 55
784 35c. Ghost crab . . . . . . 1·75 60
785 50c. Spiny Caribbean vase . . 2·50 1·40
786 $2 Great land crab . . . . . 4·00 6·00
MS787 101 × 75 mm. $6 Queen or pink conch 10·00 12·00

1987. Royal Ruby Wedding. Nos. 665a, 671/2 and 675 optd **40TH WEDDING ANNIVERSARY H.M. QUEEN ELIZABETH II H.R.H. THE DUKE OF EDINBURGH**.
788 35c. Lesser Antillean bullfinch 75 40
789 $1 Audubon's shearwater . . 1·40 80
790 $1.35 Roseate tern . . . . . 1·60 90
791 $10 Green-backed heron . . 6·00 8·50

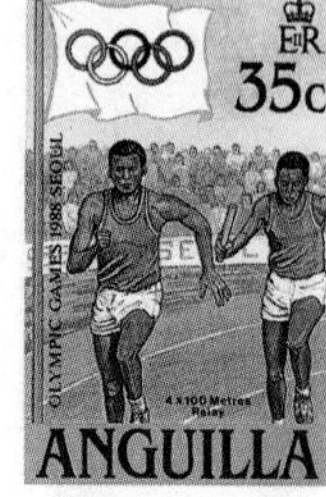

138 "Crinum erubescens" **139** Relay Racing

1988. Easter. Lilies. Multicoloured.
792 30c. Type **138** 50 25
793 45c. Spider lily 60 25

794 $1 "Crinum macowanii" . . 1·50 85
795 $2.50 Day lily . . . . 1·75 3·00
MS796 100 × 75 mm. $6 Easter lily 2·75 4·00

1988. Olympic Games, Seoul. Multicoloured.
797 35c. Type **139** 45 30
798 45c. Windsurfing 55 45
799 50c. Tennis . . . . 1·50 1·10
800 80c. Basketball . . . . 3·75 2·75
MS801 104 × 78 mm. $6 Athletics 3·00 4·00

140 Common Sea Fan

1988. Christmas. Marine Life. Multicoloured.
802 35c. Type **140** 75 30
803 80c. Coral crab . . . . . . 1·25 70
804 $1 Grooved brain coral . . . 1·60 1·00
805 $1.60 Queen triggerfish . . . 2·00 3·00
MS806 103 × 78 mm. $6 West Indian spiny lobster 3·00 4·00

1988. Visit of Princess Alexandra. Nos. 665a, 670/1 and 673 optd **H.R.H. PRINCESS ALEXANDRA'S VISIT NOVEMBER 1988**.
807 35c. Lesser Antillean bullfinch . . . . 1·75 70
808 80c. Grey kingbird . . . . . 2·25 1·40
809 $1 Audubon's shearwater . . 2·25 1·60
810 $2.50 Bananaquit . . . . . 3·75 4·75

142 Wood Slave

1989. Lizards. Multicoloured.
811 45c. Type **142** 85 50
812 80c. Slippery back . . . . . 1·40 85
813 $2.50 "Iguana delicatissima" 3·00 4·00
MS814 101 × 75 mm. $6 Tree lizard 2·75 4·00

143 "Christ Crowned with Thorns" (detail) (Bosch)

144 University Arms

1989. Easter. Religious Paintings. Multicoloured.
815 35c. Type **143** 45 20
816 80c. "Christ bearing the Cross" (detail) (Gerard David) 75 55
817 $1 "The Deposition" (detail) (Gerard David) 80 60
818 $1.60 "Pieta" (detail) (Rogier van der Weyden) . . . . . 1·25 2·00
MS819 103 × 77 mm. $6 "Crucified Christ with the Virgin Mary and Saints" (detail) (Raphael) 2·75 4·00

1989. 40th Anniv of University of the West Indies.
820 **144** $5 multicoloured . . . . 3·00 3·50

1989. 20th Anniv of First Manned Landing on Moon. Nos. 670/2 and 674 optd **20TH ANNIVERSARY MOON LANDING**.
821 80c. Grey kingbird . . . . . 1·75 90
822 $1 Audubon's shearwater . . 1·75 1·00
823 $1.35 Roseate tern . . . . . 2·00 1·75
824 $5 Belted kingfisher . . . . 5·50 7·00

146 Lone Star (house), 1930

1989. Christmas. Historic Houses. Multicoloured.
825 5c. Type **146** 35 60
826 35c. Whitehouse, 1906 . . . 75 45
827 45c. Hodges House 85 50
828 80c. Warden's Place . . . . 1·40 1·40
MS829 102 × 77 mm. $6 Wallblake House, 1787 3·25 5·00

147 Bigeye ("Blear Eye")

1990. Fishes. Multicoloured.
830B 5c. Type **147** 60 75
831B 10c. Long-spined squirrelfish ("Redman") 60 75
832A 15c. Stop-light parrotfish ("Speckletail") 60 60
833A 25c. Blue-striped grunt . . 70 80
834A 30c. Yellow jack 70 80
835B 35c. Red hind 75 75
836A 40c. Spotted goatfish . . . 90 80
837A 45c. Queen triggerfish ("Old wife") 90 60
838A 50c. Coney ("Butter fish") 90 80
839A 65c. Smooth trunkfish ("Shell fish") . . . . . . 1·00 80
840A 80c. Yellow-tailed snapper 1·25 90
841A $1 Banded butterflyfish ("Katy") . . . . 1·25 1·00
842A $1.35 Nassau grouper . . . 1·50 1·50
843A $2.50 Blue tang ("Doctor fish") . . . . 2·25 3·00
844A $5 Queen angelfish . . . . 3·00 4·50
845A $10 Great barracuda . . . 4·75 7·00

148 The Last Supper

149 G.B. 1840 Penny Black

1990. Easter. Multicoloured.
846 35c. Type **148** 75 30
847 45c. The Trial 75 30
848 $1.35 The Crucifixion . . . . 2·00 2·00
849 $2.50 The Empty Tomb . . . 2·50 3·75
MS850 114 × 84 mm. $6 The Resurrection 7·50 8·50

1990. "Stamp World London 90" International Stamp Exhibition. Multicoloured.
851 25c. Type **149** 60 25
852 50c. G.B. 1840 Twopenny Blue . . . . 1·00 50
853 $1.50 Cape of Good Hope 1861 1d. "woodblock" (horiz) . . . . 2·00 2·25
854 $2.50 G.B. 1882 £5 (horiz) . . 2·50 3·00
MS855 86 × 71 mm. $6 Penny Black and Twopence Blue (horiz) 9·00 9·50

1990. Anniversaries and Events. Nos. 841/4 optd.
856 $1 Banded butterflyfish (optd **EXPO '90**) . . . . 1·50 1·00
857 $1.35 Nassau grouper (optd **1990 INTERNATIONAL LITERACY YEAR**) . . . 1·60 1·25
858 $2.50 Blue tang (optd **WORLD CUP FOOTBALL CHAMPIONSHIPS 1990**) 4·00 4·25
859 $5 Queen angelfish (optd **90TH BIRTHDAY H.M. THE QUEEN MOTHER**) 7·00 7·50

151 Mermaid Flag

1990. Island Flags. Multicoloured.
860 50c. Type **151** . . . . 1·00 50
861 80c. New Anguilla official flag . . . . 1·50 1·00
862 $1 Three Dolphins flag . . . 1·60 1·10
863 $5 Governor's official flag . . 4·25 6·50

152 Laughing Gulls

1990. Christmas. Sea Birds. Multicoloured.
864 10c. Type **152** 60 50
865 35c. Brown booby . . . . . 1·00 50
866 $1.50 Bridled tern . . . . . 2·00 2·00
867 $3.50 Brown pelican . . . . 3·25 4·75
MS868 101 × 76 mm. $6 Least tern 7·50 9·50

1991. Easter. Nos. 846/9 optd **1991**.
869 35c. Type **148** 85 50
870 45c. The Trial 95 50
871 $1.35 The Crucifixion . . . . 2·00 1·75
872 $2.50 The Empty Tomb . . . 3·25 5·00
MS873 114 × 84 mm. $6 The Resurrection 8·00 9·00

154 Angel

155 Angels with Palm Branches outside St. Gerard's Church

1991. Christmas.
874 **154** 5c. violet, brown & black 60 70
875 – 35c. multicoloured . . . . 1·50 55
876 – 80c. multicoloured . . . . 2·50 2·00
877 – $1 multicoloured . . . . 2·50 2·00
MS878 131 × 97 mm. $5 multicoloured 7·00 8·00
DESIGNS—VERT: 35c. Father Christmas. HORIZ: 80c. Church and house; $1 Palm trees at night; $5 Anguilla village.

1992. Easter. Multicoloured.
879 30c. Type **155** 85 35
880 45c. Angels singing outside Methodist Church 95 35
881 80c. Village (horiz) . . . . . 1·75 90
882 $1 Congregation going to St. Mary's Church . . . . 1·75 1·00
883 $5 Dinghy regatta (horiz) . . 4·75 7·00

1992. No. 834 surch **$1.60**.
884 $1.60 on 30c. Yellow jack . . 2·00 1·75

157 Anguillan Flags

1992. 25th Anniv of Separation from St. Kitts-Nevis. Multicoloured.
885 80c. Type **157** . . . . 1·75 1·25
886 $1 Present official seal . . . 1·75 1·25
887 $1.60 Anguillan flags at airport . . . . 3·00 3·00
888 $2 Royal Commissioner's official seal . . . . 3·00 3·50
MS889 116 × 117 mm. $10 "Independent Anguilla" overprinted stamps of 1967 (85 × 85 mm) 9·00 10·00

158 Dinghy Race

1992. Sailing Dinghy Racing.
890 **158** 20c. multicoloured . . . . 1·00 65
891 – 35c. multicoloured . . . . 1·25 60
892 – 45c. multicoloured . . . . 1·50 60
893 – 80c. multicoloured . . . . 2·25 3·25
894 – 80c. black and blue . . . 2·25 3·25
895 – $1 multicoloured . . . . 2·25 2·50
MS896 129 × 30 mm. $6 multicoloured 6·50 7·50
DESIGNS—VERT: 35c. Stylized poster; 80c. (No. 893) "Blue Bird" in race; 80c. (No. 894) Construction drawings of "Blue Bird" by Douglas Pyle; $1 Stylized poster (different). HORIZ: 45c. Dinghies on beach. (97 × 32 mm)—$6 Composite designs as 20 and 45c. values.

159 Mucka Jumbie on Stilts

1992. Christmas. Local Traditions. Mult.
897 20c. Type **159** 55 40
898 70c. Masqueraders . . . . . 1·25 60
899 $1.05 Baking in old style oven . . . . 1·50 1·00
900 $2.40 Collecting presents from Christmas tree . . . 2·50 3·50
MS901 128 × 101 mm. $5 As No. 900 3·50 5·00

160 Columbus landing in New World

1992. 500th Anniv of Discovery of America by Columbus (2nd issue).
902 **160** 80c. multicoloured . . . . 2·00 1·25
903 – $1 black and brown . . . 2·00 1·25
904 – $2 multicoloured . . . . 3·00 3·50
905 – $3 multicoloured . . . . 3·50 4·50
MS906 78 × 54 mm. $6 multicoloured 6·50 7·50
DESIGNS—VERT: $1 Christopher Columbus; $6 Columbus and map of West Indies. HORIZ: $2 Fleet of Columbus; $3 "Pinta".

161 "Kite Flying" (Kyle Brooks)

163 Lord Great Chamberlain presenting Spurs of Charity to Queen

162 Salt Picking

1993. Easter. Children's Paintings. Mult.
907 20c. Type **161** . . . . 1·00 50
908 45c. "Clifftop Village Service" (Kara Connor) . . 1·50 50
909 80c. "Morning Devotion on Sombrero" (Junior Carty) 2·25 1·40
910 $1.50 "Hill Top Church Service" (Leana Harris) . . 3·00 4·25
MS911 90 × 110 mm. $5 "Good Friday Kites" (Marvin Hazel and Kyle Brooks) (39 × 53 mm) 4·50 5·50

1993. Traditional Industries. Mult.
912 20c. Type **162** . . . . 2·00 90
913 80c. Tobacco growing . . . 2·00 1·25
914 $1 Cotton picking . . . . . 2·00 1·25
915 $2 Harvesting sugar cane . . 3·00 4·25
MS916 111 × 85 mm. $6 Fishing 9·00 11·00

1993. 40th Anniv of Coronation. Mult.
917 80c. Type **163** . . . . 1·40 80
918 $1 The Benediction . . . . . 1·60 90
919 $2 Queen Elizabeth II in Coronation robes . . . . 2·25 2·50
920 $3 St. Edward's Crown . . . 2·75 3·50
MS921 114 × 95 mm. $6 The Queen and Prince Philip in Coronation coach 9·00 10·00

164 Carnival Pan Player

1993. Anguilla Carnival. Multicoloured.
922 20c. Type **164** 60 40
923 45c. Revellers dressed as pirates 85 40
924 80c. Revellers dressed as stars 1·40 75
925 $1 Mas dancing . . . . . . 1·40 80
926 $2 Masked couple . . . . . 2·50 3·50
927 $3 Revellers dressed as commandos . . . . 3·00 4·00
MS928 123 × 94 mm. $5 Revellers in fantasy costumes 9·00 9·50

165 Mucka Jumbies Carnival Characters

167 Princess Alexandra, 1988

166 Travelling Branch Post Van at Sandy Ground

1993. Christmas. Multicoloured.

929	20c. Type **165**	65	50
930	35c. Local carol singers	85	50
931	45c. Christmas home baking	95	50
932	$3 Decorating Christmas tree	3·50	5·00
MS933	123 × 118 mm. $4 Mucka Jumbies and carol singers (58½ × 47 mm)	3·25	4·50

1994. Delivering the Mail. Multicoloured.

934	20c. Type **166**	1·00	60
935	45c. "Betsy R" (mail schooner) at The Forest (vert)	1·75	60
936	80c. Mail van at old Post Office	2·25	1·40
937	$1 Jeep on beach, Island Harbour (vert)	2·25	1·40
938	$4 New Post Office	4·00	6·00

1994. Royal Visitors. Multicoloured.

939	45c. Type **167**	1·00	60
940	50c. Princess Alice, 1960	1·00	60
941	80c. Prince Philip, 1993	1·75	1·25
942	$1 Prince Charles, 1973	2·00	1·25
943	$2 Queen Elizabeth II, 1994	2·50	4·00
MS944	162 × 90 mm. Nos. 939/43	8·00	9·00

168 "The Crucifixion"

170 "The Nativity" (Gustave Dore)

169 Cameroun Player and Pontiac Silverdome, Detroit

1994. Easter. Stained-glass Windows. Multicoloured.

945	20c. Type **168**	40	40
946	45c. "The Empty Tomb"	55	45
947	80c. "The Resurrection"	90	90
948	$3 "Risen Christ with Disciples"	2·75	4·50

1994. World Cup Football Championship, U.S.A. Multicoloured.

949	20c. Type **169**	45	30
950	70c. Argentine player and Foxboro Stadium, Boston	85	65
951	$1.80 Italian player and RFK Memorial Stadium, Washington	1·75	2·50
952	$2.40 German player and Soldier Field, Chicago	2·00	3·25
MS953	112 × 85 mm. $6 American and Colombian players	8·00	9·00

1994. Christmas. Religious Paintings. Mult.

954	20c. Type **170**	55	50
955	30c. "The Wise Men guided by the Star" (Dore)	70	50
956	35c. "The Annunciation" (Dore)	75	50
957	45c. "Adoration of the Shepherds" (detail) (Poussin)	85	50
958	$2.40 "The Flight into Egypt" (Dore)	2·50	3·75

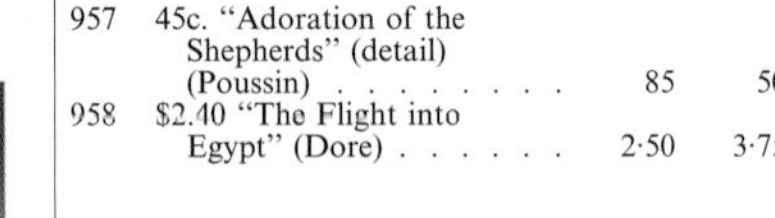

171 Pair of Zenaida Doves

1995. Easter. Zenaida Doves. Multicoloured.

959	20c. Type **171**	50	40
960	45c. Dove on branch	75	50
961	50c. Guarding nest	80	55
962	$5 With chicks	5·50	7·00

172 Trygve Lie (first Secretary-General) and General Assembly

1995. 50th Anniv of United Nations. Multicoloured.

963	20c. Type **172**	30	30
964	80c. Flag and building showing "50"	60	65
965	$1 Dag Hammarskjold and U Thant (former Secretary-Generals) and U.N. Charter	70	75
966	$5 U.N. Building (vert)	4·00	6·50

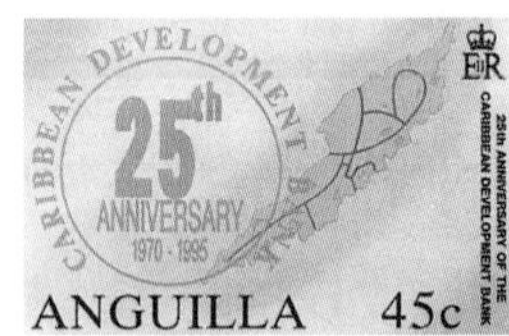

173 Anniversary Emblem and Map of Anguilla

1995. 25th Anniv of Caribbean Development Bank. Multicoloured.

967	45c. Type **173**	1·50	1·75
968	$5 Bank building and launches	3·00	4·00

174 Blue Whale

1995. Endangered Species. Whales. Multicoloured.

969	20c. Type **174**	1·75	70
970	45c. Right whale (vert)	2·00	60
971	$1 Sperm whale	2·50	1·50
972	$5 Humpback whale	7·00	8·50

175 Palm Tree

1995. Christmas. Multicoloured.

973	10c. Type **175**	60	60
974	25c. Balloons and fishes	80	50
975	45c. Shells	1·00	50
976	$5 Fishes in shape of Christmas tree	7·50	9·00

176 Deep Water Gorgonia

177 Running

1996. Corals. Multicoloured.

977	20c. Type **176**	1·25	70
978	80c. Common sea fan	2·25	1·00
979	$5 Venus sea fern	7·00	8·50

1996. Olympic Games, Atlanta. Multicoloured.

980	20c. Type **177**	65	50
981	80c. Javelin throwing and wheelchair basketball	1·75	1·00
982	$1 High jumping and hurdles	1·25	1·00
983	$3.50 Olympic rings and torch with Greek and American flags	3·50	4·25

178 Siege of Sandy Hill Fort

1996. Bicentenary of the Battle for Anguilla. Multicoloured.

984	60c. Type **178**	1·00	1·00
985	75c. French troops destroying church (horiz)	1·00	1·00
986	$1.50 Naval battle (horiz)	2·25	2·25
987	$4 French troops landing at Rendezvous Bay	3·50	4·75

179 Gooseberry

1997. Fruit. Multicoloured.

988	10c. Type **179**	10	10
989	20c. West Indian cherry	10	15
990	40c. Tamarind	20	25
991	50c. Pomme-surette	25	30
992	60c. Sea almond	30	35
993	75c. Sea grape	35	40
994	80c. Banana	40	45
995	$1 Genip	50	55
996	$1.10 Coco plum	50	55
997	$1.25 Pope	60	65
998	$1.50 Pawpaw	70	75
999	$2 Sugar apple	95	1·00
1000	$3 Soursop	1·40	1·50
1001	$4 Pomegranate	1·90	2·00
1002	$5 Cashew	2·40	2·50
1003	$10 Mango	4·75	5·00

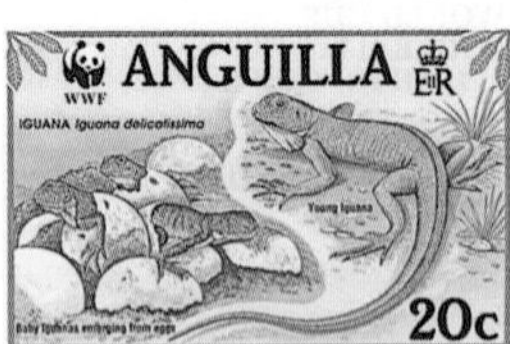

180 West Indian Iguanas hatching

1997. Endangered Species. West Indian Iguanas. Multicoloured.

1004	20c. Type **180**	1·40	1·25
1005	50c. On rock	1·60	1·40
1006	75c. On branch	1·75	1·60
1007	$3 Head of West Indian iguana	2·50	3·25

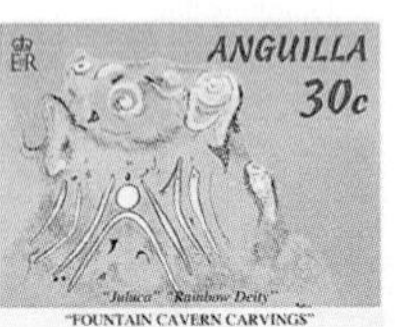

181 "Juluca, Rainbow Deity"

1997. Ancient Stone Carvings from Fountain Cavern. Multicoloured.

1008	30c. Type **181**	45	35
1009	$1.25 "Lizard with front legs extended"	90	90
1010	$2.25 "Chief"	1·60	2·25
1011	$2.75 "Jocahu, the Creator"	2·00	2·75

182 Diana, Princess of Wales

1998. Diana, Princess of Wales Commemoration. Multicoloured.

1012	15c. Type **182**	1·25	1·25
1013	$1 Wearing yellow blouse	2·00	1·60
1014	$1.90 Wearing tiara	2·25	2·50
1015	$2.25 Wearing blue short-sleeved Red Cross blouse	2·50	2·75

183 "Treasure Island" (Valarie Alix)

1998. International Arts Festival. Multicoloured.

1016	15c. Type **183**	50	50
1017	30c. "Posing in the Light" (Melsadis Fleming) (vert)	50	40
1018	$1 "Pescadores de Anguilla" (Juan Garcia) (vert)	80	80
1019	$1.50 "Fresh Catch" (Verna Hart)	1·00	1·60
1020	$1.90 "The Bell Tower of St. Mary's" (Ricky Racardo Edwards) (vert)	1·25	2·00

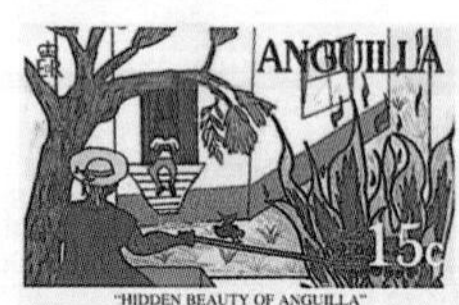

184 Roasting Corn-cobs on Fire

1998. Christmas. "Hidden Beauty of Anguilla". Children's Paintings. Multicoloured.

1021	15c. Type **184**	35	30
1022	$1 Fresh fruit and market stallholder	80	50
1023	$1.50 Underwater scene	1·00	1·25
1024	$3 Cacti and view of sea	1·60	2·50

185 University of West Indies Centre, Anguilla

1998. 50th Anniv of University of West Indies. Multicoloured.

1025	$1.50 Type **185**	80	90
1026	$1.90 Man with torch and University arms	1·10	1·50

186 Sopwith Camel and Bristol F2B Fighters

1998. 80th Anniv of Royal Air Force. Multicoloured.

1027	30c. Type **186**	65	50
1028	$1 Supermarine Spitfire Mk II and Hawker Hurricane Mk I	1·25	80
1029	$1.50 Avro Lancaster	1·60	1·60
1030	$1.90 Panavia Tornado F3 and Harrier GR7	1·75	2·25

187 Saturn 5 Rocket and "Apollo 11" Command Module

1999. 30th Anniv of First Manned Landing on Moon. Multicoloured.

1031 30c. Type **187** 55 33
1032 $1 Astronaut Edwin Aldrin, Lunar Module "Eagle" and first footprint on Moon . . . . 1·00 70
1033 $1.50 Lunar Module leaving Moon's surface . . . . . 1·00 1·00
1034 $1.90 Recovery of Command Module . . . 1·40 2·00

188 Albena Lake Hodge **189** Library and Resource Centre

1999. Anguillan Heroes and Heroines (1st series). Each black, green and cream.

1035 30c. Type **188** 40 30
1036 $1 Collins O. Hodge 80 65
1037 $1.50 Edwin Wallace Rey 1·00 1·25
1038 $1.90 Walter G. Hodge . . 1·25 2·00

1999. Modern Architecture. Multicoloured.

1039 30c. Type **189** 30 30
1040 65c. Parliamentary building and Court House 50 50
1041 $1 Caribbean Commercial Bank 70 70
1042 $1.50 Police Headquarters 1·00 1·25
1043 $1.90 Post Office . . . . . 1·10 1·75

190 Beach Barbeque and Fireworks

1999. Christmas and New Millennium. Mult.

1044 30c. Type **190** 35 30
1045 $1 Musicians around globe 80 55
1046 $1.50 Family at Christmas dinner . . . . 1·25 1·25
1047 $1.90 Celebrations around decorated shrub . . . . . 1·50 2·00

191 Shoal Bay (East)

2000. Beaches. Multicoloured.

1048 15c. Type **191** 30 40
1049 30c. Maundys Bay 35 30
1050 $1 Rendezvous Bay 75 50
1051 $1.50 Meads Bay . . . . . 1·00 1·25
1052 $1.90 Little Bay . . . . . . 1·25 1·75
1053 $2 Sandy Ground . . . . . 1·25 1·75
MS1054 144 × 144 mm. Nos. 1048/53 3·50 4·00

192 Toy Banjo (Casey Reid)

2000. Easter. Indigenous Toys. Multicoloured.

1055 25c. Type **192** 40 30
1056 30c. Spinning top (Johniela Harrigan) 40 30
1057 $1.50 Catapult (Akeem Rogers) . . . . 1·10 1·10
1058 $1.90 Roller (Melisa Mussington) . . . . . . 1·40 1·75
1059 $2.50 Killy Ban (trap) (Casey Reid) . . . . . . 1·75 2·25
MS1060 145 × 185 mm. 75c. Rag Doll (Jahia Esposito) (vert); $1 Kite (Javed Maynard) (vert); $1.25, Cricket ball (Jevon Lake) (vert); $4 Pond boat (Corvel Flemming) (vert) 4·25 4·75

193 Lanville Harrigan

2000. West Indies Cricket Tour and 100th Test Match at Lord's. Multicoloured.

1061 $2 Type **193** . . . . 1·75 1·75
1062 $4 Cardigan Connor . . . . 2·75 3·25
MS1063 119 × 102 mm. $6 Lord's Cricket Ground (horiz) 4·00 4·50

2000. "The Stamp Show 2000" International Stamp Exhibition, London. Beaches. As No. **MS**1054, but with exhibition logo on bottom margin. Mult.

MS1064 144 × 144 mm. Nos. 1048/53 3·75 4·50

194 Prince William and Royal Family after Trooping the Colour

2000. 18th Birthday of Prince William. Mult.

1065 30c. Type **194** 65 40
1066 $1 Prince and Princess of Wales with sons . . . . . 1·25 60
1067 $1.90 With Prince Charles and Prince Harry . . . . 1·75 1·75
1068 $2.25 Skiing with father and brother . . . . 2·00 2·50
MS1069 125 × 95 mm. $8 Prince William as pupil at Eton 6·00 6·50

195 Queen Elizabeth the Queen Mother and Prince William

2000. 100th Birthday of Queen Elizabeth the Queen Mother. Showing different portraits. Multicoloured.

1070 30c. Type **195** 65 40
1071 $1.50 Island scene . . . . . 1·50 1·00
1072 $1.90 Clarence House . . . 1·75 1·60
1073 $5 Castle of Mey . . . . . 3·25 4·00

196 "Anguilla Montage" (Weme Caster)

2000. International Arts Festival. Multicoloured.

1074 15c. Type **196** 30 40
1075 30c. "Serenity" (Damien Carty) 35 30
1076 65c. "Inter Island Cargo" (Paula Walden) 55 45
1077 $1.50 "Rainbow City where Spirits find Form" (Fiona Percy) . . . . 1·25 1·50
1078 $1.90 "Sailing Silver Seas" (Valerie Carpenter) . . . 1·40 2·00
MS1079 75 × 100 mm. $7 "Historic Anguilla" (Melsadis Fleming) (42 × 28 mm) 4·25 5·50

197 Dried Flower Arrangement

2000. Christmas. Flower and Garden Show.

1080 **197** 15c. multicoloured . . . 25 25
1081 – 25c. multicoloured . . . 30 25
1082 – 30c. multicoloured . . . 30 25
1083 – $1 multicoloured 75 60
1084 – $1.50 multicoloured . . 1·25 1·50
1085 – $1.90 multicoloured . . 1·50 1·75

DESIGNS: 25c. to $1.90, Different floral arrangements.

198 Winning Primary School Football Team (Bank Sponsorship)

2000. 15th Anniv of National Bank of Anguilla. Multicoloured.

1086 30c. Type **198** 30 25
1087 $1 *De-Chan* (yacht) (Bank sponsorship) (vert) . . . 70 60
1088 $1.50 Bank crest (vert) . . . 1·25 1·50
1089 $1.90 New Bank Headquarters . . . . . . 1·50 1·75

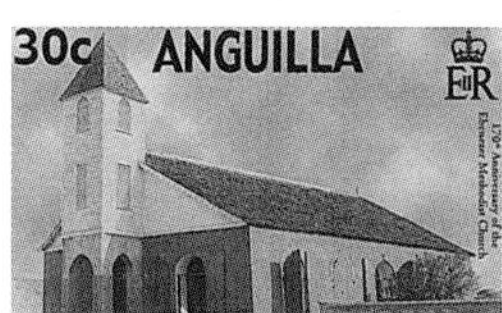

199 Ebenezer Methodist Church in 19th Century

2000. 170th Anniv of Ebenezer Methodist Church.

1090 **199** 30c. brown and black . . 30 20
1091 – $1.90 multicoloured . . 1·50 1·75

DESIGN: $1.90, Church in 2000.

200 Soroptomist Day Care Centre

2001. United Nations Women's Human Rights Campaign. Multicoloured.

1092 25c. Type **200** 30 30
1093 30c. Britannia Idalia Gumbs (Anguillan politician) (vert) 30 30
1094 $2.25 "Caribbean Woman II" (Leisel Renee Jobity) (vert) . . . . 1·60 2·25

201 John Paul Jones and U.S.S. *Ranger* (frigate)

2001. 225th Anniv of American War of Independence. Multicoloured.

1095 30c. Type **201** 40 30
1096 $1 George Washington and Battle of Yorktown . . . 70 65
1097 $1.50 Thomas Jefferson and submission of Declaration of Independence to Congress . . . . 1·00 1·10
1098 $1.90 John Adams and the signing of the Treaty of Paris . . . . 1·25 1·50

202 Bahama Pintail

2001. Anguillian Birds. Multicoloured.

1099 30c. Type **202** 50 35
1100 $1 Black-faced grassquit (vert) 70 60
1101 $1.50 Common noddy . . . 1·10 1·10
1102 $2 Black-necked stilt (vert) 1·40 1·50
1103 $3 Kentish plover ("Snowy Plover") . . . . 1·75 1·90
MS1104 124 × 88 mm. 25c. Snowy egret; 65c. Red-billed tropic bird; $1.35, Greater yellowlegs; $2.25, Sooty tern 4·00 4·00

203 "Children encircling Globe" (Urska Golob)

2001. U.N. Year of Dialogue among Civilisations.

1105 **203** $1.90 multicoloured . . 1·10 1·25

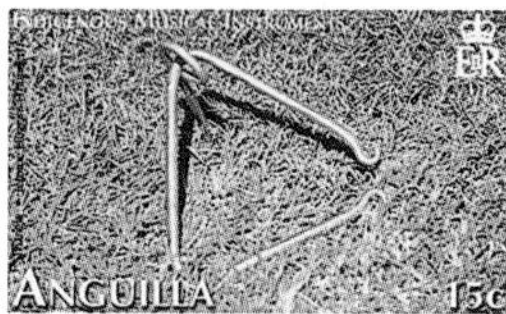

204 Triangle

2001. Christmas. Indigenous Musical Instruments. Multicoloured.

1106 15c. Type **204** 15 20
1107 25c. Maracas 25 20
1108 30c. Guiro (vert) 25 20
1109 $1.50 Marimba . . . . . . 1·00 90
1110 $1.90 Tambu (hand drum) (vert) . . . . 1·25 1·25
1111 $2.50 Bass pan . . . . . . 1·75 2·00
MS1112 110 × 176 mm. 75c. Banjo (vert); $1 Quatro (vert); $1.25, Ukelele (vert); $3 Cello (vert) 3·50 4·00

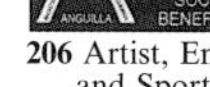

205 Sombrero Lighthouse, 1962 **206** Artist, Entertainer and Sportsmen

2002. Commissioning of New Sombrero Lighthouse. Multicoloured.

1113 30c. Type **205** 40 30
1114 $1.50 Old and new lighthouses (horiz) . . . . 1·25 1·00
1115 $1.90 New, fully-automated lighthouse, 2001 . . . . . 1·40 1·50

2002. 20th Anniv of Social Security Board. Multicoloured (except 30c.).

1116 30c. Type **206** (ultramarine and blue) 15 20
1117 75c. Anguillans of all ages 35 40
1118 $2.50 Anguillan workers (horiz) . . . . 1·25 1·40

207 H.M.S. *Antrim* (destroyer), 1967

2002. Ships of the Royal Navy. Multicoloured.

1119 30c. Type **207** 15 20
1120 50c. H.M.S. *Formidable* (aircraft carrier), 1939 . . 25 30
1121 $1.50 H.M.S. *Dreadnought* (battleship), 1906 . . . . 70 75
1122 $2 H.M.S. *Warrior* (ironclad), 1860 . . . . . 95 1·00
MS1123 102 × 77 mm. H.M.S. *Ark Royal* (aircraft carrier), 1981 (vert) 3·25 3·50

208 Princess Elizabeth with Prince Charles

2002. Golden Jubilee. Multicoloured.

1124 30c. Type **208** 15 20
1125 $1.50 Queen Elizabeth wearing white coat . . . 70 75

1126 $1.90 Queen Elizabeth in evening dress 1·40 1·50
1127 $5 Wearing yellow hat and coat 2·40 2·50
MS1128 106×75 mm. $8 Queen Elizabeth sitting at desk 3·75 4·00

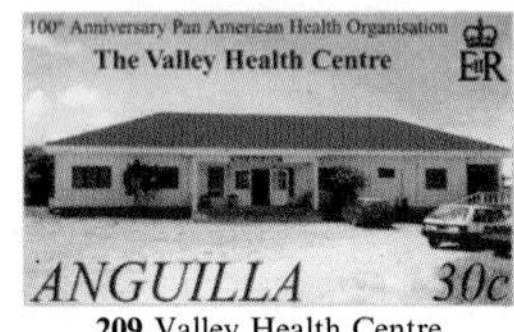

209 Valley Health Centre

2002. Centenary of Pan American Health Organization. Multicoloured.
1129 30c. Type **209** 15 20
1130 $1.50 Centenary of PAHO logo 70 75

ANJOUAN Pt. 6

One of the Comoro Is. between Madagascar and the East coast of Africa. Used stamps of Madagascar from 1914 and became part of the Comoro Islands in 1950.

100 centimes = 1 franc.

1892. "Tablet" key-type inscr "SULTANAT D'ANJOUAN".
1 D 1c. black on blue 1·00 1·75
2 2c. brown on buff 2·00 2·00
3 4c. brown on grey 2·25 2·25
4 5c. green on green 4·00 3·75
5 10c. black on lilac 4·00 4·00
14 10c. red 11·50 13·50
6 15c. blue 4·25 5·00
15 15c. grey 7·25 9·00
7 20c. red on green 5·00 6·25
8 25c. black on pink 6·00 6·25
16 25c. blue 9·00 11·00
9 30c. brown on grey 14·50 12·50
17 35c. black on yellow 5·50 5·50
10 40c. red on yellow 19·00 18·00
18 45c. black on green 75·00 65·00
11 50c. red on pink 21·00 22·00
19 50c. brown on blue 15·00 17·00
12 75c. brown on orange 29·00 24·00
13 1f. green 65·00 60·00

1912. Surch in figures.
20 D 05 on 2c. brown on buff 2·50 3·00
21 05 on 4c. brown on grey 1·25 2·50
22 05 on 15c. blue 1·25 2·50
23 05 on 20c. red on green 1·50 3·00
24 05 on 25c. black on pink 1·10 2·50
25 05 on 30c. brown on grey 2·25 2·75
26 10 on 40c. red on yellow 1·25 2·25
27 10 on 45c. black on green 95 1·75
28 10 on 50c. red on pink 2·25 4·25
29 10 on 75c. brown on orange 2·25 3·50
30 10 on 1f. green 3·25 3·75

ANNAM AND TONGKING Pt. 6

Later part of Indo-China and now included in Vietnam.

100 centimes = 1 franc.

1888. Stamps of French Colonies, "Commerce" type, surch **A & T** and value in figures.
1 J 1 on 2c. brown on yellow 38·00 32·00
2 1 on 4c. lilac on grey 32·00 25·00
3 5 on 10c. black on lilac 38·00 28·00

ANTIGUA Pt. 1

One of the Leeward Islands, Br. W. Indies. Used general issues for Leeward Islands, concurrently with Antiguan stamps until 1 July 1956. Ministerial Government introduced on 1 January 1960. Achieved Associated Statehood on 3 March 1967 and Independence within the Commonwealth on 1 November 1981.

Nos. 718/21 and 733 onwards are inscribed "Antigua and Barbuda".

1862. 12 pence = 1 shilling;
20 shillings = 1 pound.
1951. 100 cents = 1 West Indian dollar.

1

3

1862.
5 1 1d. mauve £130 50·00
25 1d. red 1·75 3·00
29 6d. green 60·00 £120

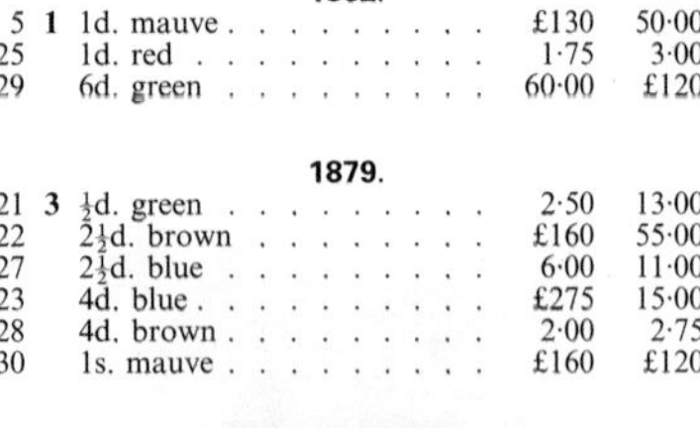

1879.
21 3 ½d. green 2·50 13·00
22 2½d. brown £160 55·00
27 2½d. blue 6·00 11·00
23 4d. blue £275 15·00
28 4d. brown 2·00 2·75
30 1s. mauve £160 £120

4

5

8

1903.
31 4 ½d. black and green 3·75 6·50
41 ½d. green 2·75 4·50
32 1d. black and red 6·50 1·25
43 1d. red 6·00 2·25
45 2d. purple and brown 4·75 29·00
34 2½d. black and blue 9·00 15·00
46 2½d. blue 12·00 15·00
47 3d. green and brown 6·50 19·00
48 6d. purple and black 7·50 48·00
49 1s. blue and purple 15·00 70·00
50 2s. green and violet 80·00 85·00
39 2s.6d. black and purple 18·00 55·00
40 5 5s. green and violet 70·00 £100

1913. Head of King George V.
51 5 5s. green and violet 70·00 £110

1916. Optd **WAR STAMP**.
52 4 ½d. green 1·50 2·50
54 1½d. orange 1·00 1·25

1921.
62 8 ½d. green 2·25 50
63 1d. red 2·25 50
64 1d. violet 4·00 1·50
67 1½d. orange 3·25 7·00
68 1½d. red 4·50 1·75
69 1½d. brown 3·00 60
70 2d. grey 2·75 75
72 2½d. yellow 2·50 17·00
73 2½d. blue 4·50 5·50
74 3d. purple on yellow 4·75 8·50
56 4d. black and red on yellow 2·25 5·50
75 6d. purple 3·50 6·50
57 1s. black on green 4·25 9·00
58 2s. purple and blue on blue 13·00 19·00
78 2s.6d. black and red on blue 24·00 28·00
79 3s. green and violet 30·00 90·00
80 4s. black and red 48·00 65·00
60 5s. green and red on yellow 8·50 50·00
61 £1 purple and black on red £180 £275

9 Old Dockyard, English Harbour

10 Government House, St. John's

1932. Tercentenary. Designs with medallion portrait of King George V.
81 9 ½d. green 2·75 7·50
82 – 1d. red 3·25 7·50
83 – 1½d. brown 3·25 4·75
84 10 2d. grey 4·25 17·00
85 2½d. blue 4·25 8·50
86 3d. orange 4·25 12·00
87 – 6d. violet 15·00 12·00
88 – 1s. olive 19·00 27·00
89 – 2s.6d. purple 40·00 60·00
90 – 5s. black and brown 90·00 £120
DESIGNS—HORIZ: 6d. to 2s.6d. Nelson's "Victory"; 5s. Sir Thomas Warner's "Conception".

13 Windsor Castle

1935. Silver Jubilee.
91 13 1d. blue and red 2·00 2·75
92 1½d. blue and grey 2·75 55
93 2½d. brown and blue 6·50 1·25
94 1s. grey and purple 8·50 12·00

1937. Coronation. As T **2** of Aden.
95 1d. red 50 1·00
96 1½d. brown 60 1·25
97 2½d. blue 1·25 1·75

15 English Harbour

16 Nelson's Dockyard

1938.
98 15 ½d. green 40 1·25
99 16 1d. red 2·75 2·00
100a 1½d. brown 2·25 1·75
101 15 2d. grey 50 50
102 16 2½d. blue 80 80
103 – 3d. orange 75 1·00
104 – 6d. violet 2·75 1·25
105 – 1s. black and brown 3·75 1·50
106a – 2s.6d. purple 22·00 10·00
107 – 5s. olive 14·00 7·50
108 16 10s. mauve 16·00 26·00
109 – £1 green 25·00 38·00
DESIGNS—HORIZ: 3d., 2s.6d., £1, Fort James. VERT: 6d., 1s., 5s. St. John's Harbour.

1946. Victory. As T **9** of Aden.
110 1½d. brown 20 10
111 3d. orange 20 30

1949. Silver Wedding. As T **10/11** of Aden.
112 2½d. blue 40 1·75
113 5s. green 8·50 7·50

20 Hermes, Globe and Forms of Transport

21 Hemispheres, Jet-powered Vickers Viking Airliner and Steamer

22 Hermes and Globe

23 U.P.U. Monument

1949. 75th Anniv of U.P.U.
114 20 2½d. blue 40 50
115 21 3d. orange 1·50 2·00
116 22 6d. purple 45 1·50
117 23 1s. brown 45 1·00

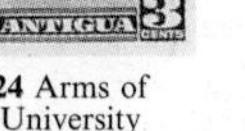

24 Arms of University

25 Princess Alice

1951. Inauguration of B.W.I. University College.
118 24 3c. black and brown 45 70
119 25 12c. black and violet 65 90

1953. Coronation. As T **13** of Aden.
120 2c. black and green 30 75

27 Martello Tower

1953. Designs as 1938 issues but with portrait of Queen Elizabeth II as in T **27**.
120a – ½c. brown 30 30
121 15 1c. grey 30 70
122 16 2c. green 30 10
123 3c. black and yellow 40 20
153 15 4c. red 30 50
154 16 5c. black and lilac 20 10
155 – 6c. yellow 60 30
156 27 8c. blue 30 20
157 – 12c. violet 40 20
129 – 24c. black and brown 2·50 15
130 27 48c. purple and blue 7·00 2·75
131 – 60c. purple 7·50 80
132 – $1.20 olive 2·25 70
133 16 $2.40 purple 11·00 12·00
134 – $4.80 slate 15·00 24·00
DESIGNS—HORIZ: ½, 6, 60c., $4.80, Fort James. VERT: 12, 24c., $1.20, St John's Harbour.

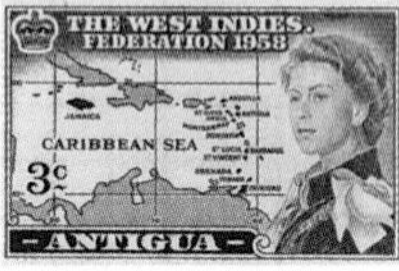

28 Federation Map

1958. Inaug of British Caribbean Federation.
135 28 3c. green 1·00 30
136 6c. blue 1·40 2·75
137 12c. red 1·60 75

1960. New Constitution. Nos. 123 and 157 optd **COMMEMORATION ANTIGUA CONSTITUTION**.
138 16 3c. black and yellow 15 15
139 – 12c. violet 15 15

30 Nelson's Dockyard and Admiral Nelson

1961. Restoration of Nelson's Dockyard.
140 30 20c. purple and brown 90 1·25
141 30c. green and blue 1·10 1·50

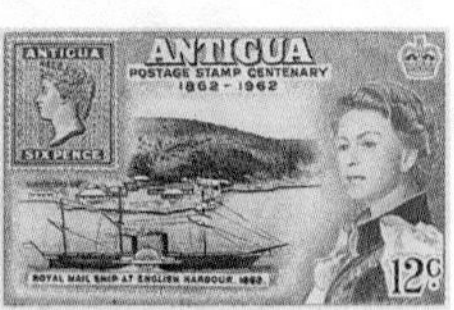

31 Stamp of 1862 and R.M.S.P. "Solent I" at English Harbour

1962. Stamp Centenary.
142 31 3c. purple and green 60 10
143 10c. blue and green 70 10
144 12c. sepia and green 80 10
145 50c. brown and green 1·50 1·75

1963. Freedom from Hunger. As T **28** of Aden.
146 12c. green 15 15

33 Red Cross Emblem

1963. Centenary of Red Cross.
147 33 3c. red and black 30 75
148 12c. red and blue 45 1·25

34 Shakespeare and Memorial Theatre, Stratford-upon-Avon

1964. 400th Birth Anniv of Shakespeare.
164 **34** 12c. brown 30 10

1965. No. 157 surch **15c.**
165 15c. on 12c. violet 10 10

36 I.T.U. Emblem

1965. Centenary of I.T.U.
166 **36** 2c. blue and red 25 15
167 50c. yellow and blue . . . 75 80

37 I.C.Y. Emblem

1965. International Co-operation Year.
168 **37** 4c. purple and turquoise 20 10
169 15c. green and lavender . . 30 20

38 Sir Winston Churchill, and St. Paul's Cathedral in Wartime

1966. Churchill Commemoration. Designs in black, red and gold with background in colours given.
170 **38** ½c. blue . . . . 10 1·75
171 4c. green 40 10
172 25c. brown . . . . 1·10 45
173 35c. violet . . . . 1·10 55

39 Queen Elizabeth II and Duke of Edinburgh

1966. Royal Visit.
174 **39** 6c. black and blue . . . . 1·25 1·10
175 15c. black and mauve . . . 1·25 1·40

40 Footballer's Legs, Ball and Jules Rimet Cup

1966. World Cup Football Championship.
176 **40** 6c. multicoloured 20 50
177 35c. multicoloured 60 25

41 W.H.O. Building

1966. Inaug of W.H.O. Headquarters, Geneva.
178 **41** 2c. black, green and blue 20 25
179 15c. black, purple & brn 80 25

42 Nelson's Dockyard

1966.
180 **42** ½c. green and blue 10 40
181 – 1c. purple and mauve . . 10 30
182 – 2c. blue and orange . . . 10 20
183a – 3c. red and black 15 15
184a – 4c. violet and brown . . . 15 15
185 – 5c. blue and green 10 10
186 – 6c. orange and purple . . 30 10
187 – 10c. green and red . . . 15 10
188a – 15c. brown and blue . . . 55 10
189 – 25c. blue and brown . . . 35 20
190a – 35c. mauve and brown . . 60 1·00
191a – 50c. green and black . . . 70 2·25
192 – 75c. blue and ultramarine 1·50 2·50
193b – $1 mauve and green . . . 1·25 5·00
194 – $2.50 black and mauve 3·50 7·00
195 – $5 green and violet . . . 6·00 6·50

DESIGNS: 1c. Old Post Office, St John's; 2c. Health Centre; 3c. Teachers' Training College; 4c. Martello Tower, Barbuda; 5c. Ruins of Officers' Quarters, Shirley Heights; 6c. Government House, Barbuda; 10c. Princess Margaret School; 15c. Air terminal building; 25c. General Post Office; 35c. Clarence House; 50c. Government House, St. John's; 75c. Administration building; $1 Court-house, St. John's; $2.50, Magistrates' Court; $5 St. John's Cathedral.

54 "Education"

55 "Science"

56 "Culture"

1966. 20th Anniv of U.N.E.S.C.O.
196 **54** 4c. violet, yellow & orange 15 10
197 **55** 25c. yellow, violet and olive 35 10
198 **56** $1 black, purple and orange . . . . 80 2·25

57 State Flag and Maps

1967. Statehood. Multicoloured.
199 4c. Type **57** 10 10
200 15c. State Flag 10 20
201 25c. Premier's Office and State Flag 10 25
202 35c. As 15c. 15 25

60 Gilbert Memorial Church

1967. Attainment of Autonomy by the Methodist Church.
203 **60** 4c. black and red 10 10
204 – 25c. black and green . . . 15 15
205 – 35c. black and blue 15 15

DESIGNS: 25c. Nathaniel Gilbert's House; 35c. Caribbean and Central American map.

63 Coat of Arms

66 Tracking Station

64 "Susan Constant" (settlers' ship)

1967. 300th Anniv of Treaty of Breda and Grant of New Arms.
206 **63** 15c. multicoloured 15 10
207 35c. multicoloured 15 10

1967. 300th Anniv of Barbuda Settlement.
208 **64** 4c. blue 30 10
209 – 6c. purple . . . . 30 1·25
210 **64** 25c. green 40 20
211 – 35c. black 40 25

DESIGN: 6, 35c. Blaeu's Map of 1665.

1968. N.A.S.A. Apollo Project. Inauguration of Dow Hill Tracking Station.
212 **66** 4c. blue, yellow and black 10 10
213 – 15c. blue, yellow and black 20 10
214 – 25c. blue, yellow and black 20 10
215 – 50c. blue, yellow and black 30 40

DESIGNS: 15c. Antenna and spacecraft taking off; 25c. Spacecraft approaching Moon; 50c. Re-entry of space capsule.

70 Limbo-dancing

1968. Tourism. Multicoloured.
216 ½c. Type **70** 10 20
217 15c. Water-skier and bathers 30 10
218 25c. Yachts and beach . . . 30 10
219 35c. Underwater swimming 30 10
220 50c. Type **70** . . . . 35 1·10

74 Old Harbour in 1768

1968. Opening of St. John's Deep Water Harbour.
221 **74** 2c. blue and red 10 40
222 – 15c. green and sepia . . . 35 10
223 – 25c. yellow and blue . . . 40 10
224 – 35c. salmon and emerald 50 10
225 **74** $1 black . . . . 90 2·00

DESIGNS: 15c. Old harbour in 1829; 25c. Freighter and chart of new harbour; 35c. New harbour.

78 Parliament Buildings

1969. Tercentenary of Parliament. Multicoloured.
226 4c. Type **78** 10 10
227 15c. Antigua Mace and bearer 20 10
228 25c. House of Representative's Room . . 20 10
229 50c. Coat of arms and Seal of Antigua . . . . 30 1·60

82 Freight Transport

1969. 1st Anniv of Caribbean Free Trade Area.
230 **82** 4c. black and purple . . . 10 10
231 15c. black and blue 20 30
232 – 25c. brown, black & ochre 25 30
233 – 35c. chocolate, blk & brn 25 30

DESIGN—VERT: 25, 35c. Crate of cargo.

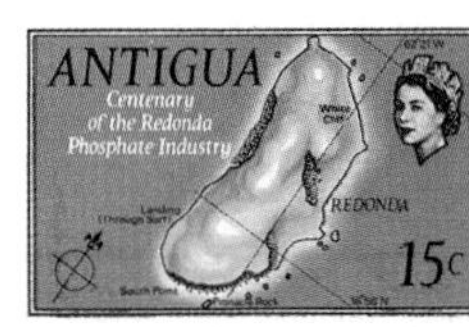

84 Island of Redonda (Chart)

1969. Centenary of Redonda Phosphate Industry. Multicoloured.
249 15c. Type **84** 20 10
250 25c. View of Redonda from the sea 20 10
251 50c. Type **84** 45 75

86 "The Adoration of the Magi" (Marcillat)

1969. Christmas. Stained Glass Windows. Mult.
252 6c. Type **86** 10 10
253 10c. "The Nativity" (unknown German artist, 15th century) 10 10
254 35c. Type **86** 25 10
255 50c. As 10c. 50 40

1970. Surch **20c** and bars.
256 20c. on 25c. (No. 189) . . . 10 10

89 Coat of Arms

90 Sikorsky S-38 Flying Boat

1970. Coil Stamps.
257A **89** 5c. blue 10 10
258A 10c. green 10 15
259A 25c. red 20 25

1970. 40th Anniv of Antiguan Air Services. Multicoloured.
260 5c. Type **90** 50 10
261 20c. Dornier Do-X flying boat . . . . 1·00 10
262 35c. Hawker Siddeley H.S.748 . . . . 1·25 10
263 50c. Douglas C-124C Globemaster II . . . . . 1·25 1·50
264 75c. Vickers Super VC-10 . . 1·50 2·00

91 Dickens and Scene from "Nicholas Nickleby"

1970. Death Centenary of Charles Dickens.
265 **91** 5c. bistre, sepia and black 10 10
266 – 20c. turq, sepia & blk . . . 20 10
267 – 35c. blue, sepia and black 30 10
268 – $1 red, sepia and black . . 75 70

DESIGNS: All stamps show Dickens and scene from: 20c. "Pickwick Papers"; 35c. "Oliver Twist"; $1 "David Copperfield".

92 Carib Indian and War Canoe

1970. Multicoloured.
323 ½c. Type **92** 20 50
270 1c. Columbus and "Nina" . . 30 1·50
271 2c. Sir Thomas Warner's emblem and "Concepcion" 40 2·25
325 3c. Viscount Hood and H.M.S. "Barfleur" . . . . 35 1·25
273 4c. Sir George Rodney and H.M.S. "Formidable" . . 40 2·25
274 5c. Nelson and H.M.S. "Boreas" 50 40
275 6c. William IV and H.M.S. "Pegasus" . . . . 1·00 2·75
276 10c. "Blackbeard" and pirate ketch 80 20
277 15c. Collingwood and H.M.S. "Pelican" . . . . 4·50 1·00
278 20c. Nelson and H.M.S. "Victory" . . . . 1·25 40
279 25c. "Solent I" (paddle-steamer) . . . . 1·25 40
280 35c. George V (when Prince George) and H.M.S. "Canada" (screw corvette) 1·75 80
281 50c. H.M.S. "Renown" (battle cruiser) . . . . . . 4·00 4·00
331 75c. "Federal Maple" (freighter) . . . . 7·50 3·00
332 $1 "Sol Quest" (yacht) and class emblem . . . . . . 3·00 1·75

333 $2.50 H.M.S. "London" (destroyer) . . . . 2·75 6·50
285 $5 "Pathfinder" (tug) . . . . 4·00 6·00

93 "The Small Passion" (detail) (Durer)

94 4th King's Own Regiment, 1759

1970. Christmas.
286 **93** 3c. black and blue 10 10
287 – 10c. purple and pink . . . 10 10
288 **93** 35c. black and red 30 10
289 – 50c. black and lilac 45 50
DESIGN: 10, 50c. "Adoration of the Magi" (detail)(Durer).

1970. Military Uniforms (1st series). Mult.
290 ½c. Type **94** 10 10
291 10c. 4th West India Regiment, 1804 . . . . . 50 10
292 20c. 60th Regiment, The Royal American, 1809 . . 75 10
293 35c. 93rd Regiment, Sutherland Highlanders, 1826–34 . . . . 1·00 10
294 75c. 3rd West India Regiment, 1851 . . . . . 1·75 2·00
MS295 128 × 164 mm. Nos. 290/4 5·50 11·00
See also Nos. 303/8, 313/18, 353/8 and 380/5.

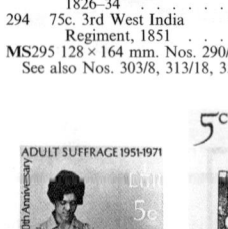

95 Market Woman casting Vote

96 "The Last Supper"

1971. 20th Anniv of Adult Suffrage.
296 **95** 5c. brown 10 10
297 – 20c. olive 10 10
298 – 35c. purple 10 10
299 – 50c. blue 15 30
DESIGNS: People voting: 20c. Executive; 35c. Housewife; 50c. Artisan.

1971. Easter. Works by Durer.
300 **96** 5c. black grey and red . . 10 10
301 – 35c. black, grey and violet 10 10
302 – 75c. black, grey and gold 20 30
DESIGNS: 35c. "The Crucifixion"; 75c. "The Resurrection".

1971. Military Uniforms (2nd series). As T **94**. Multicoloured.
303 ½c. Private, 12th Regiment, The Suffolk (1704) 10 10
304 10c. Grenadier, 38th Regiment, South Staffordshire (1751) . . . 35 10
305 20c. Light Company, 5th Regiment, Royal Northumberland Fusiliers (1778) 50 10
306 35c. Private, 48th Regiment, The Northamptonshire (1793) 60 10
307 75c. Private, 15th Regiment, East Yorks (1805) . . . . 1·00 3·00
MS308 127 × 144 mm. Nos. 303/7 4·50 6·50

97 "Madonna and Child" (detail, Veronese)

1971. Christmas. Multicoloured.
309 3c. Type **97** 10 10
310 5c. "Adoration of the Shepherds" (detail, Veronese) 10 10
311 35c. Type **97** 25 10
312 50c. As 5c. 40 30

1972. Military Uniforms (3rd series). As T **94**. Multicoloured.
313 ½c. Battalion Company Officer, 25th Foot, 1815 . . 10 10
314 10c. Sergeant, 14th Foot, 1837 . . . . 85 10
315 20c. Private, 67th Foot, 1853 1·60 15
316 35c. Officer, Royal Artillery, 1854 . . . . 1·90 20
317 75c. Private, 29th Foot, 1870 2·25 4·00
MS318 125 × 141 mm. Nos. 313/17 7·00 8·50

98 Reticulated Cowrie Helmet

1972. Shells. Multicoloured.
319 3c. Type **98** 50 10
320 5c. Measled cowrie 50 10
321 35c. West Indian fighting conch . . . . 1·40 15
322 50c. Hawk-wing conch . . . 1·60 3·00

99 St. John's Cathedral, Side View

1972. Christmas and 125th Anniv of St. John's Cathedral. Multicoloured.
335 35c. Type **99** 20 10
336 50c. Cathedral interior . . . 25 25
337 75c. St. John's Cathedral . . . 30 60
MS338 165 × 102 mm. Nos. 335/7 65 1·00

1972. Royal Silver Wedding. As T **52** of Ascension, but with floral background.
339 20c. blue 15 15
340 35c. blue 15 15

101 Batsman and Map

1972. 50th Anniv of Rising Sun Cricket Club. Multicoloured.
341 5c. Type **101** 55 15
342 35c. Batsman and wicket-keeper 65 10
343 $1 Club badge . . . . 1·00 2·25
MS344 88 × 130 mm. Nos. 341/3 3·25 7·50

102 Yacht and Map

103 "Episcopal Coat of Arms"

1972. Inauguration of Antigua and Barbuda Tourist Office in New York. Multicoloured.
345 35c. Type **102** 15 10
346 50c. Yachts 20 15
347 75c. St. John's G.P.O. . . . 25 25
348 $1 Statue of Liberty 25 25
MS349 100 × 94 mm. Nos. 346, 348 75 1·25

1973. Easter. Multicoloured.
350 **103** 5c. Type **103** 10 10
351 – 35c. "The Crucifixion" . . 15 10
352 – 75c. "Arms of 1st Bishop of Antigua" 25 30
Nos. 350/2 show different stained-glass windows from St. John's Cathedral.

1973. Military Uniforms (4th series). As T **94**. Multicoloured.
353 ½c. Private, Zachariah Tiffin's Regiment of Foot, 1701 . . 10 10
354 10c. Private, 63rd Regiment of Foot, 1759 . . . . . 40 10
355 20c. Light Company Officer, 35th Regiment of Foot, 1828 . . . . 50 15
356 35c. Private, 2nd West India Regiment, 1853 . . . . . 65 15
357 75c. Sergeant, 49th Regiment, 1858 . . . . 1·00 1·25
MS358 127 × 145 mm. Nos. 353/7 3·75 3·25

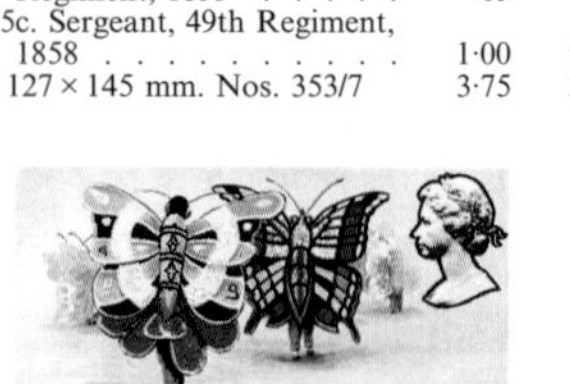

104 Butterfly Costumes

1973. Carnival. Multicoloured.
359 5c. Type **104** 10 10
360 20c. Carnival street scene . . 15 10
361 35c. Carnival troupe 20 10
362 75c. Carnival Queen 30 30
MS363 134 × 95 mm. Nos. 359/62 65 1·00

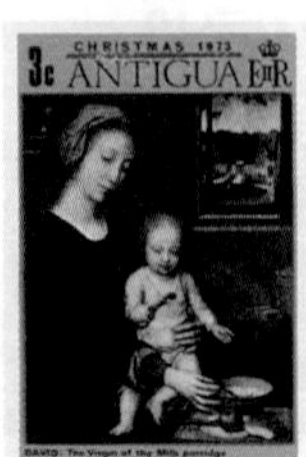

105 "Virgin of the Milk Porridge" (Gerard David)

1973. Christmas. Multicoloured.
364 3c. Type **105** 10 10
365 5c. "Adoration of the Magi" (Stomer) 10 10
366 20c. "The Granducal Madonna" (Raphael) . . . 15 10
367 35c. "Nativity with God the Father and Holy Ghost" (Battista) 20 10
368 $1 "Madonna and Child" (Murillo) 40 60
MS369 130 × 128 mm. Nos. 364/8 1·10 1·75

106 Princess Anne and Captain Mark Phillips

1973. Royal Wedding.
370 **106** 35c. multicoloured 10 10
371 – $2 multicoloured 25 25
MS372 78 × 100 mm. Nos. 370/1 50 40
The $2 is as Type **106** but has a different border.

1973. Nos. 370/1 optd **HONEYMOON VISIT DECEMBER 16TH 1973**.
373 **106** 35c. multicoloured 15 10
374 – $2 multicoloured 30 30
MS375 78 × 100 mm. Nos. 373/4 55 55

108 Coat of Arms of Antigua and University

1974. 25th Anniv of University of West Indies. Multicoloured.
376 5c. Type **108** 10 10
377 20c. Extra-mural art 15 10
378 35c. Antigua campus 20 10
379 75c. Antigua chancellor . . . 25 35

1974. Military Uniforms (5th series). As T **94**. Multicoloured.
380 ½c. Officer, 59th Foot, 1797 10 10
381 10c. Gunner, Royal Artillery, 1800 . . . . 35 10
382 20c. Private, 1st West India Regiment, 1830 . . . . . 50 10
383 35c. Officer, 92nd Foot, 1843 60 10
384 75c. Private, 23rd Foot, 1846 75 2·25
MS385 125 × 145 mm. Nos. 380/4 2·25 2·50

109 English Postman, Mailcoach and Westland Dragonfly Helicopter

1974. Centenary of U.P.U. Multicoloured.
386 ½c. Type **109** 10 10
387 1c. Bellman, mail steamer "Orinoco" and satellite . . 10 10
388 2c. Train guard, post-bus and hydrofoil 10 10
389 5c. Swiss messenger, Wells Fargo coach and Concorde 60 30
390 20c. Postilion, Japanese postmen and carrier pigeon 35 10
391 35c. Antiguan postman, Sikorsky S-88 flying boat and tracking station . . . 45 15
392 $1 Medieval courier, American express train and Boeing 747-100 . . . . . 1·75 2·00
MS393 141 × 161 mm. Nos. 386/92 3·50 2·50
On the ½c. English is spelt "Enlish" and on the 2c. Postal is spelt "Fostal".

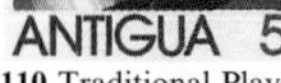

110 Traditional Player

111 Footballers

1974. Antiguan Steel Bands.
394 **110** 5c. dp red, red and black 10 10
395 – 20c. brown, lt brn & blk 10 10
396 – 35c. lt green, green & blk 10 10
397 – 75c. blue, dp blue & blk 20 85
MS398 115 × 108 mm. Nos. 394/7 35 1·00
DESIGNS—HORIZ: 20c. Traditional band; 35c. Modern band. VERT: 75c. Modern player.

1974. World Cup Football Championships.
399 **111** 5c. multicoloured 10 10
400 – 35c. multicoloured 15 10
401 – 75c. multicoloured 30 30
402 – $1 multicoloured 35 40
MS403 135 × 130 mm. Nos. 399/402 85 90
Nos. 400/2 show various footballing designs similar to Type **111**.

1974. Earthquake Relief Fund. Nos. 400/2 and 397 optd or surch **EARTHQUAKE RELIEF**.
404 35c. multicoloured 20 10
405 75c. multicoloured 30 25
406 $1 multicoloured 40 30
407 $5 on 75c. deep blue, blue and black . . . . 1·25 2·00

113 Churchill as Schoolboy and School College Building, Harrow

114 "Madonna of the Trees" (Bellini)

1974. Birth Centenary of Sir Winston Churchill. Multicoloured.
408 5c. Type **113** 15 10
409 35c. Churchill and St. Paul's Cathedral 20 10
410 75c. Coat of arms and catafalque 25 55
411 $1 Churchill, "reward" notice and South African escape route 40 90
MS412 107 × 82 mm. Nos. 408/11 90 1·50

1974. Christmas. "Madonna and Child" paintings by named artists. Multicoloured.
413 ½c. Type **114** 10 10
414 1c. Raphael 10 10
415 2c. Van der Weyden 10 10
416 3c. Giorgione 10 10
417 5c. Mantegna 10 10
418 20c. Vivarini 20 10
419 35c. Montagna 30 10
420 75c. Lorenzo Costa . . . . . 55 1·10
MS421 139 × 126 mm. Nos. 413/20 95 1·40

1975. Nos. 390/2 and 331 surch.
422 50c. on 20c. multicoloured . . 1·25 2·00
423 $2.50 on 35c. multicoloured 2·00 5·50
424 $5 on $1 multicoloured . . . 6·00 7·00
425 $10 on 75c. multicoloured . . 3·00 7·50

116 Carib War Canoe, English Harbour, 1300

1975. Nelson's Dockyard. Multicoloured.
427 5c. Type **116** 20 10
428 15c. Ship of the line, English Harbour, 1770 80 15
429 35c. H.M.S "Boreas" at anchor, and Lord Nelson, 1787 1·25 15
430 50c. Yachts during "Sailing Week", 1974 1·25 1·50
431 $1 Yacht Anchorage, Old Dockyard, 1970 1·50 2·25
MS432 130×134 mm. As Nos. 427/31, but in larger format, 43×28 mm 3·25 2·00

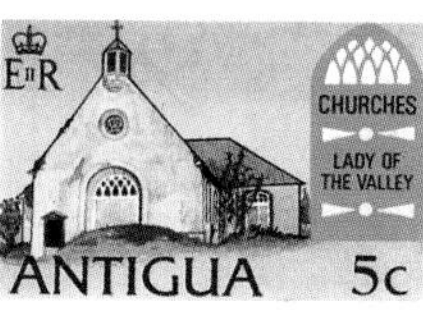

117 Lady of the Valley Church

1975. Antiguan Churches. Multicoloured.
433 5c. Type **117** 10 10
434 20c. Gilbert Memorial 10 10
435 35c. Grace Hill Moravian 15 10
436 50c. St. Phillips 20 20
437 $1 Ebenezer Methodist 35 50
MS438 91×101 mm. Nos. 435/7 65 1·25

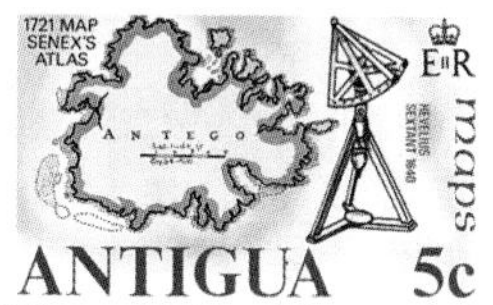

118 Map of 1721 and Sextant of 1640

1975. Maps of Antigua. Multicoloured.
439 5c. Type **118** 30 15
440 20c. Map of 1775 and galleon 55 15
441 35c. Maps of 1775 and 1955 70 15
442 $1 1973 maps of Antigua and English Harbour 1·40 2·00
MS443 130×89 mm. Nos. 439/42 3·00 3·25

119 Scout Bugler

1975. World Scout Jamboree, Norway. Mult.
444 15c. Type **119** 25 15
445 20c. Scouts in camp 30 15
446 35c. "Lord Baden-Powell" (D. Jagger) 50 20
447 $2 Scout dancers from Dahomey 1·50 2·00
MS448 145×107 mm. Nos. 444/7 3·25 3·50

120 "Eurema elathea"

1975. Butterflies. Multicoloured.
449 ½c. Type **120** 10 10
450 1c. "Danaus plexippus" 10 10
451 2c. "Phoebis philea" 10 10
452 5c. "Hypolimnas misippus" 20 10
453 20c. "Eurema proterpia" 75 60
454 35c. "Battus polydamas" 1·40 90
455 $2 "Cynthia cardui" 4·00 8·00
MS456 147×94 mm. Nos. 452/5 6·00 10·00
No. 452 is incorrectly captioned "Marpesia petreus thetys".

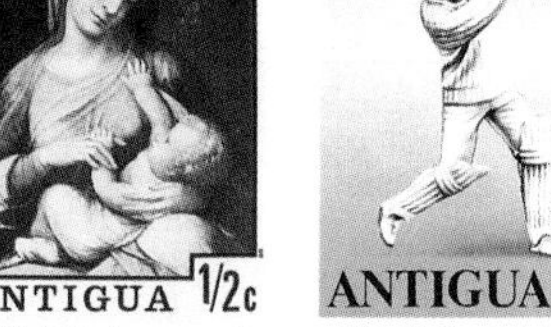

121 "Madonna and Child" (Correggio) **122** Vivian Richards

1975. Christmas. "Madonna and Child" paintings by artists named. Multicoloured.
457 ½c. Type **121** 10 10
458 1c. El Greco 10 10
459 2c. Durer 10 10
460 3c. Antonello 10 10
461 5c. Bellini 10 10
462 10c. Durer (different) 10 10
463 35c. Bellini (different) 40 10
464 $2 Durer (different again) 1·00 1·00
MS465 138×119 mm. Nos. 461/4 1·50 1·60

1975. World Cricket Cup Winners. Multicoloured.
466 5c. Type **122** 1·25 20
467 35c. Andy Roberts 2·25 60
468 $2 West Indies team (horiz) 4·25 8·00

123 Antillean Crested Hummingbird

1976. Multicoloured.
469A ½c. Type **123** 40 50
470A 1c. Imperial amazon ("Imperial Parrot") 1·00 50
471A 2c. Zenaida dove 1·00 50
472A 3c. Loggerhead kingbird 1·00 60
473A 4c. Red-necked pigeon 1·00 1·50
474A 5c. Rufous-throated solitaire 1·75 10
475A 6c. Orchid tree 30 1·50
476A 10c. Bougainvillea 30 10
477A 15c. Geiger tree 35 10
478A 20c. Flamboyant 35 35
479A 25c. Hibiscus 40 15
480A 35c. Flame of the wood 40 40
481A 50c. Cannon at Fort James 55 60
482A 75c. Premier's Office 60 1·00
483A $1 Potworks Dam 75 1·00
484A $2.50 Diamond irrigation scheme (44×28 mm) 1·00 4·25
485B $5 Government House (44×28 mm) 1·50 7·00
486A $10 Coolidge International Airport (44×28 mm) 3·50 6·50

124 Privates, Clark's Illinois Regiment

1976. Bicentenary of American Revolution. Mult.
487 ½c. Type **124** 10 10
488 1c. Rifleman, Pennsylvania Militia 10 10
489 2c. Powder horn 10 10
490 5c. Water bottle 10 15
491 35c. American flags 50 10
492 $1 "Montgomery" (American brig) 1·25 40
493 $5 "Ranger" (privateer sloop) 2·00 2·25
MS494 71×84 mm. $2.50, Congress flag 1·00 1·40

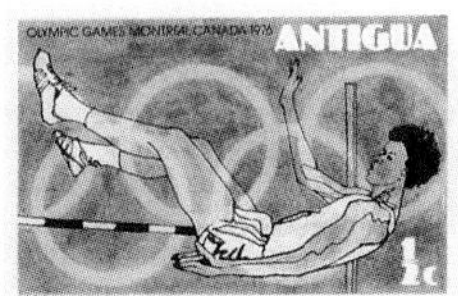

125 High Jump

1976. Olympic Games, Montreal.
495 **125** ½c. brown, yellow & black 10 10
496 – 1c. violet, blue and black 10 10
497 – 2c. green and black 10 10
498 – 15c. blue and black 15 10
499 – 30c. brown, yell & blk 20 15
500 – $1 orange, red and black 40 40
501 – $2 red and black 60 80
MS502 88×138 mm. Nos. 498/501 1·75 1·25
DESIGNS: 1c. Boxing; 2c. Pole vault; 15c. Swimming; 30c. Running; $1 Cycling; $2 Shot put.

126 Water Skiing

1976. Water Sports. Multicoloured.
503 ½c. Type **126** 10 10
504 1c. Sailing 10 10
505 2c. Snorkeling 10 10
506 20c. Deep sea fishing 50 10
507 50c. Scuba diving 75 35
508 $2 Swimming 1·25 1·25
MS509 89×114 mm. Nos. 506/8 1·75 1·75

127 French Angelfish

1976. Fishes. Multicoloured.
510 15c. Type **127** 50 15
511 30c. Yellow-finned grouper 75 30
512 50c. Yellow-tailed snapper 95 50
513 90c. Shy hamlet 1·25 80

128 The Annunciation **130** Royal Family

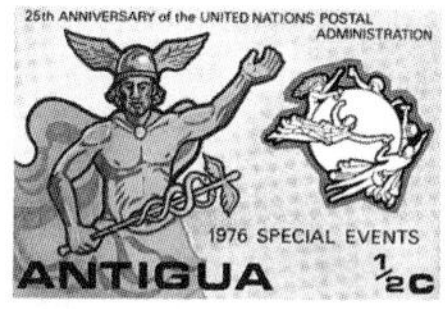

129 Mercury and U.P.U. Emblem

1976. Christmas. Multicoloured.
514 8c. Type **128** 10 10
515 10c. The Holy Family 10 10
516 15c. The Magi 10 10
517 50c. The Shepherds 20 25
518 $1 Epiphany scene 30 50

1976. Special Events, 1976. Multicoloured.
519 ½c. Type **129** 10 10
520 1c. Alfred Nobel 10 10
521 10c. Space satellite 30 10
522 50c. Viv Richards and Andy Roberts 3·50 1·75
523 $1 Bell and telephones 1·00 2·00
524 $2 Yacht "Freelance" 2·25 4·00
MS525 127×101 mm. Nos. 521/4 7·50 12·00

1977. Silver Jubilee. Multicoloured. (a) Perf.
526 10c. Type **130** 10 10
527 30c. Royal Visit, 1966 10 10
528 50c. The Queen enthroned 15 15
529 90c. The Queen after Coronation 15 25
530 $2.50 Queen and Prince Charles 30 55
MS531 116×78 mm. $5 Queen and Prince Philip 65 85

(b) Roul × imperf. Self-adhesive.
532 50c. As 90c. 35 60
533 $5 The Queen and Prince Philip 2·00 3·50
Nos. 532/3 come from booklets.

131 Making Camp

1977. Caribbean Scout Jamboree, Jamaica. Mult.
534 ½c. Type **131** 10 10
535 1c. Hiking 10 10
536 2c. Rock-climbing 10 10
537 10c. Cutting logs 15 10
538 30c. Map and sign reading 40 10
539 50c. First aid 65 25
540 $2 Rafting 1·25 2·50
MS541 127×114 mm. Nos. 538/40 3·00 3·75

132 Carnival Costume **134** "Virgin and Child Enthroned" (Tura)

1977. 21st Anniv of Carnival. Multicoloured.
542 10c. Type **132** 10 10
543 30c. Carnival Queen 20 10
544 50c. Butterfly costume 25 15
545 90c. Queen of the band 35 25
546 $1 Calypso King and Queen 35 30
MS547 140×120 mm. Nos. 542/6 1·10 1·60

1977. Royal Visit. Nos. 526/30 optd **ROYAL VISIT 28TH OCTOBER 1977**.
548 10c. Type **130** 10 10
549 30c. Royal Visit, 1966 15 10
550 50c. The Queen enthroned 20 10
551 90c. The Queen after Coronation 30 20
552 $2.50 Queen and Prince Charles 50 35
MS553 116×178 mm. $5 Queen and Prince Philip 1·00 1·00

1977. Christmas. Paintings by artists listed. Mult.
554 ½c. Type **134** 10 10
555 1c. Crivelli 10 10
556 2c. Lotto 10 10
557 8c. Pontormo 15 10
558 10c. Tura (different) 15 10
559 25c. Lotto (different) 30 10
560 $2 Crivelli (different) 85 60
MS561 144×118 mm. Nos. 557/60 1·50 2·25

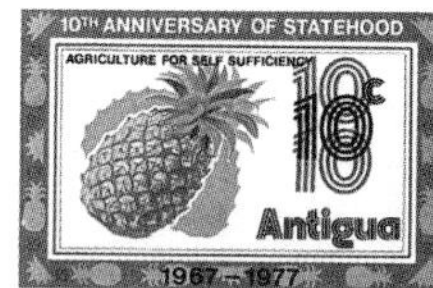

135 Pineapple

1977. 10th Anniv of Statehood. Multicoloured.
562 10c. Type **135** 10 10
563 15c. State flag 25 10
564 50c. Police band 2·25 80
565 90c. Premier V. C. Bird 55 80
566 $2 State Coat of Arms 90 1·75
MS567 129×99 mm. Nos. 563/6 3·25 2·75

136 Wright Glider III, 1902

1978. 75th Anniv of Powered Flight. Mult.
568 ½c. Type **136** 10 10
569 1c. Wright Flyer I, 1903 10 10
570 2c. Launch system and engine 10 10
571 10c. Orville Wright (vert) 30 10
572 50c. Wright Flyer III, 1905 60 15
573 90c. Wilbur Wright (vert) 80 30
574 $2 Wright Type B, 1910 1·00 80
MS575 90×75 mm. $2.50, Wright Flyer I on launch system 1·25 2·50

137 Sunfish Regatta **138** Queen Elizabeth and Prince Philip

1978. Sailing Week. Multicoloured.
576 10c. Type **137** 20 10
577 50c. Fishing and work boat race 35 20
578 90c. Curtain Bluff race 60 35
579 $2 Power boat rally 1·10 1·25
MS580 110×77 mm. $2.50, Guadeloupe–Antigua race 1·50 1·75

1978. 25th Anniv of Coronation. Mult. (a) Perf.
581 10c. Type **138** 10 10
582 30c. Crowning 10 10
583 50c. Coronation procession 15 10
584 90c. Queen seated in St. Edward's Chair 20 15
585 $2.50 Queen wearing Imperial State Crown 40 40
MS586 114×104 mm. $5 Queen and Prince Philip 80 80

(b) Roul × imperf. Self-adhesive. Horiz designs as Type **138**.
587 25c. Glass Coach 15 30
588 50c. Irish State Coach 25 50
589 $5 Coronation Coach 1·75 3·00
Nos. 587/9 come from booklets.

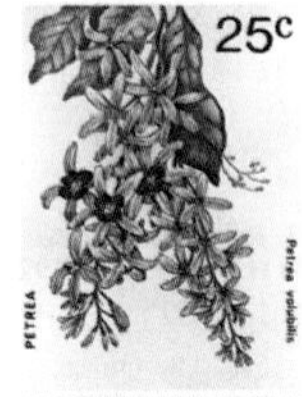

140 Player running with Ball   **141** Petrea

1978. World Cup Football Championship, Argentina. Multicoloured.

No.	Description	Unused	Used
590	10c. Type **140**	15	10
591	15c. Players in front of goal	15	10
592	$3 Referee and player	2·00	1·75
MS593	126×88 mm. 25c. Player crouching with ball; 30c. Players heading ball; 50c. Players running with ball; $2 Goalkeeper diving. All horiz	3·25	2·50

1978. Flowers. Multicoloured.

No.	Description	Unused	Used
594	25c. Type **141**	25	10
595	50c. Sunflower	35	20
596	90c. Frangipani	60	30
597	$2 Passion flower	1·25	1·10
MS598	118×85 mm. $2.50, Hibiscus	1·40	1·60

142 "St. Ildefonso receiving the Chasuble from the Virgin" (Rubens)

1978. Christmas. Multicoloured.

No.	Description	Unused	Used
599	8c. Type **142**	10	10
600	25c. "The Flight of St. Barbara" (Rubens)	20	10
601	$2 "Madonna and Child, with St. Joseph, John the Baptist and Donor"	65	55
MS602	170×113 mm. $4 "The Annunciation" (Rubens)	1·25	1·50

The painting shown on No. 601 is incorrectly attributed to Rubens on the stamp. The artist was Sebastiano del Piombo.

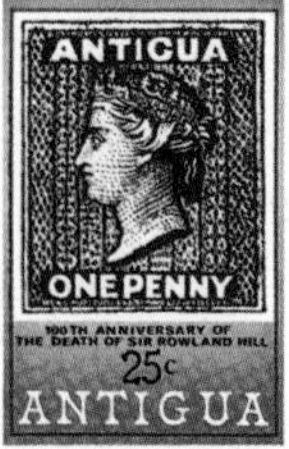

143 1d. Stamp of 1863   **144** "The Deposition from the Cross" (painting)

1979. Death Centenary of Sir Rowland Hill. Mult.

No.	Description	Unused	Used
603	25c. Type **143**	10	10
604	50c. 1840 Penny Black	20	15
605	$1 Mail coach and woman posting letter, c. 1840	30	20
606	$2 Modern transport	1·10	60
MS607	108×82 mm. $2.50, Sir Rowland Hill	80	90

1979. Easter. Works by Durer.

No.	Description	Unused	Used
608 **144**	10c. multicoloured	10	10
609 –	50c. multicoloured	35	20
610 –	$4 black, mauve and yellow	1·00	90
MS611 –	114×99 mm. $2.50, multicoloured	80	80

DESIGNS: 50c., $2.50, "Christ on the Cross–The Passion" (wood engravings) (both different); $4 "Man of Sorrows with Hands Raised" (wood engraving).

145 Toy Yacht and Child's Hand   **147** Cook's Birthplace, Marton

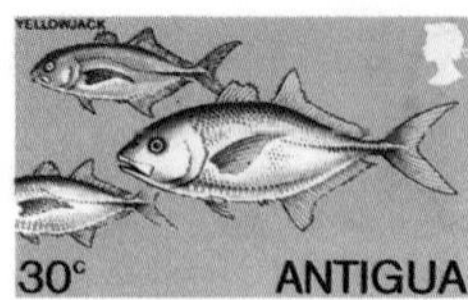

146 Yellow Jack

1979. International Year of the Child. Mult.

No.	Description	Unused	Used
612	25c. Type **145**	10	10
613	50c. Rocket	25	15
614	90c. Car	40	25
615	$2 Toy train	1·00	90
MS616	80×112 mm. $5 Aeroplane	1·10	1·10

Nos. 612/16 also show the hands of children of different races.

1979. Fishes. Multicoloured.

No.	Description	Unused	Used
617	30c. Type **146**	40	15
618	50c. Blue-finned tuna	50	25
619	90c. Sailfish	75	40
620	$3 Wahoo	2·25	1·75
MS621	122×75 mm. $2.50, Great barracuda	1·50	1·40

1979. Death Bicentenary of Captain Cook. Mult.

No.	Description	Unused	Used
622	25c. Type **147**	55	25
623	50c. H.M.S. "Endeavour"	75	60
624	90c. Marine chronometer	75	80
625	$3 Landing at Botany Bay	1·60	2·75
MS626	110×85 mm. $2.50, H.M.S. "Resolution"	2·25	1·50

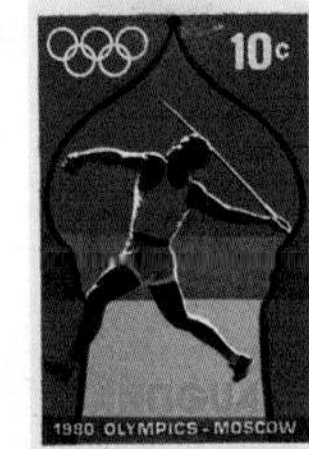

148 The Holy Family   **149** Javelin Throwing

1979. Christmas. Multicoloured.

No.	Description	Unused	Used
627	8c. Type **148**	10	10
628	25c. Virgin and Child on ass	15	10
629	50c. Shepherd and star	25	35
630	$4 Wise Men with gifts	85	2·25
MS631	113×94 mm. $3 Angel with trumpet	1·00	1·50

1980. Olympic Games, Moscow. Multicoloured.

No.	Description	Unused	Used
632	10c. Type **149**	20	10
633	25c. Running	20	10
634	$1 Pole vault	50	50
635	$2 Hurdles	70	1·75
MS636	127×96 mm. $3 Boxing (horiz)	80	90

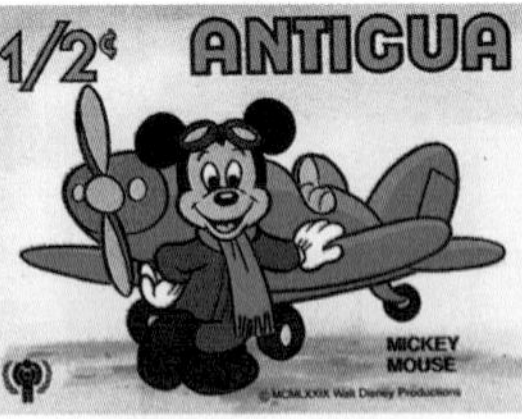

150 Mickey Mouse and Airplane

1980. International Year of the Child. Walt Disney Cartoon Characters. Multicoloured.

No.	Description	Unused	Used
637	½c. Type **150**	10	10
638	1c. Donald Duck driving car (vert)	10	10
639	2c. Goofy driving taxi	10	10
640	3c. Mickey and Minnie Mouse on motorcycle	10	10
641	4c. Huey, Dewey and Louie on a bicycle for three	10	10
642	5c. Grandma Duck and truck of roosters	10	10
643	10c. Mickey Mouse in jeep (vert)	10	10
644	$1 Chip and Dale in yacht	1·75	2·00
645	$4 Donald Duck riding toy train (vert)	3·75	6·00
MS646	101×127 mm. $2.50, Goofy flying biplane	4·50	3·25

1980. "London 1980" International Stamp Exhibition. Nos. 603/6 optd **LONDON 1980**.

No.	Description	Unused	Used
647	25c. Type **143**	25	15
648	50c. Penny Black	35	35
649	$1 Stage-coach and woman posting letter, c. 1840	60	70
650	$2 Modern mail transport	3·25	3·00

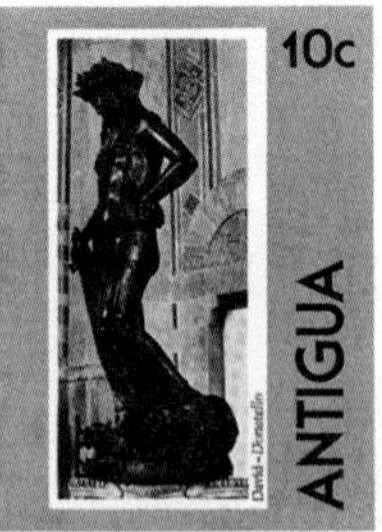

152 "David" (statue, Donatello)

1980. Famous Works of Art. Multicoloured.

No.	Description	Unused	Used
651	10c. Type **152**	10	10
652	30c. "The Birth of Venus" (painting, Botticelli) (horiz)	30	15
653	50c. "Reclining Couple" (sarcophagus), Cerveteri (horiz)	40	40
654	90c. "The Garden of Earthly Delights" (painting by Bosch) (horiz)	55	65
655	$1 "Portinari Altarpiece" (painting, van der Goes) (horiz)	65	75
656	$4 "Eleanora of Toledo and her Son, Giovanni de'Medici" (painting, Bronzino)	1·75	3·00
MS657	99×124 mm. $5 "The Holy Family" (painting, Rembrandt)	2·50	1·75

153 Anniversary Emblem and Headquarters, U.S.A.

1980. 75th Anniv of Rotary International. Mult.

No.	Description	Unused	Used
658	30c. Type **153**	30	30
659	50c. Rotary anniversary emblem and Antigua Rotary Club banner	40	50
660	90c. Map of Antigua and Rotary emblem	60	70
661	$3 Paul P. Harris (founder) and Rotary emblem	2·00	3·25
MS662	102×78 mm. $5 Antiguan flags and Rotary emblems	1·25	2·00

154 Queen Elizabeth the Queen Mother   **155** Ringed Kingfisher

1980. 80th Birthday of The Queen Mother.

No.	Description	Unused	Used
663 **154**	10c. multicoloured	40	10
664	$2.50 multicoloured	1·50	1·75
MS665	68×90 mm. As T **154**. $3 multicoloured	1·75	2·00

1980. Birds. Multicoloured.

No.	Description	Unused	Used
666	10c. Type **155**	70	30
667	30c. Plain pigeon	1·00	50
668	$1 Green-throated carib	1·50	2·00
669	$2 Black-necked stilt	2·00	3·75
MS670	73×73 mm. $2.50, Roseate tern	7·00	4·50

1980. Christmas. Walt Disney's "Sleeping Beauty". As T **150**. Multicoloured.

No.	Description	Unused	Used
671	½c. The Bad Fairy with her raven	10	10
672	1c. The good fairies	10	10
673	2c. Aurora	10	10
674	4c. Aurora pricks her finger	10	10
675	8c. The prince	10	10
676	10c. The prince fights the dragon	15	10
677	25c. The prince awakens Aurora with a kiss	20	20
678	$2 The prince and Aurora's betrothal	2·25	2·25
679	$2.50 The prince and princess	2·50	2·50
MS680	126×101 mm. $4 multicoloured (vert)	5·00	3·25

156 Diesel Locomotive No. 15

1981. Sugar Cane Railway Locomotives. Mult.

No.	Description	Unused	Used
681	25c. Type **156**	15	15
682	50c. Narrow-gauge steam locomotive	30	30
683	90c. Diesel locomotives Nos. 1 and 10	55	60
684	$3 Steam locomotive hauling sugar cane	2·00	2·25
MS685	82×111 mm. $2.50, Antiguan sugar factory, railway yard and sheds	1·75	1·75

1981. Independence. Nos. 475/6 and 478/86 optd **"INDEPENDENCE 1981"**.

No.	Description	Unused	Used
686B	6c. Orchid tree	10	10
687B	10c. Bougainvillea	10	10
688B	20c. Flamboyant	10	10
689B	25c. Hibiscus	15	15
690B	35c. Flame of the wood	20	20
691B	50c. Cannon at Fort James	35	35
692B	75c. Premier's Office	40	40
693B	$1 Potworks Dam	55	55
694B	$2.50 Irrigation scheme, Diamond Estate	75	1·25
695B	$5 Government House	1·40	2·50
696B	$10 Coolidge International Airport	3·25	5·00

158 "Pipes of Pan"

1981. Birth Centenary of Picasso. Multicoloured.

No.	Description	Unused	Used
697	10c. Type **158**	10	10
698	50c. "Seated Harlequin"	30	30
699	90c. "Paulo as Harlequin"	55	55
700	$4 "Mother and Child"	2·00	2·00
MS701	115×140 mm. $5 "Three Musicians" (detail)	2·00	2·75

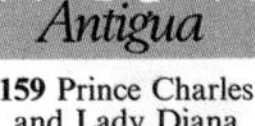

159 Prince Charles and Lady Diana Spencer   **160** Prince of Wales at Investiture, 1969

1981. Royal Wedding (1st issue). Multicoloured.

No.	Description	Unused	Used
702	25c. Type **159**	10	10
703	50c. Glamis Castle	10	10
704	$4 Prince Charles skiing	80	80
MS705	96×82 mm. $5 Glass coach	80	80

1981. Royal Wedding (2nd issue). Multicoloured. Roul×imperf. Self-adhesive.

No.	Description	Unused	Used
706	25c. Type **160**	15	25
707	25c. Prince Charles as baby, 1948	15	25
708	$1 Prince Charles at R.A.F. College, Cranwell, 1971	25	50
709	$1 Prince Charles attending Hill House School, 1956	25	50
710	$2 Prince Charles and Lady Diana Spencer	50	75
711	$2 Prince Charles at Trinity College, 1967	50	75
712	$5 Prince Charles and Lady Diana (different)	1·00	1·50

161 Irene Joshua (founder)

1981. 50th Anniv of Antigua Girl Guide Movement. Multicoloured.

No.	Description	Unused	Used
713	10c. Type **161**	15	10
714	50c. Campfire sing-song	45	35
715	90c. Sailing	75	65
716	$2.50 Animal tending	1·75	2·00
MS717	110×85 mm. $5 Raising the flag	4·50	3·00

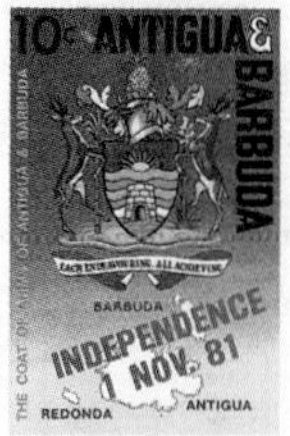

162 Antigua and Barbuda Coat of Arms

163 "Holy Night" (Jacques Stella)

1981. Independence. Multicoloured.

718 10c. Type **162** 25 10
719 50c. Pineapple, with Antigua and Barbuda flag and map 1·00 40
720 90c. Prime Minister Vere Bird 55 55
721 $2.50 St. John's Cathedral (38 × 25 mm) . . . . . . 1·50 3·25
MS722 105 × 79 mm. $5 Map of Antigua and Barbuda (42 × 42 mm) 3·75 2·75

1981. Christmas. Paintings. Multicoloured.

723 8c. Type **163** 15 10
724 30c. "Mary with Child" (Julius Schnorr von Carolfeld) 40 15
725 $1 "Virgin and Child" (Alonso Cano) 75 90
726 $3 "Virgin and Child" (Lorenzo di Credi) . . . . 1·10 3·75
MS727 77 × 111 mm. $5 "Holy Family" (Pieter von Avon) 2·50 4·50

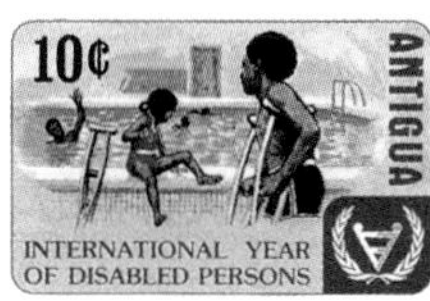

164 Swimming

1981. International Year of Disabled People. Sports for the Disabled. Multicoloured.

728 10c. Type **164** 10 10
729 50c. Discus-throwing 20 30
730 90c. Archery 40 55
731 $2 Baseball . . . . 1·00 1·40
MS732 108 × 84 mm. $4 Basketball 5·00 2·75

165 Scene from Football Match

1982. World Cup Football Championship, Spain.

733 **165** 10c. multicoloured 30 10
734 – 50c. multicoloured 60 35
735 – 90c. multicoloured . . . . 1·10 70
736 – $4 multicoloured . . . . 3·50 3·50
MS737 – 75 × 92 mm. $5 multicoloured 8·50 10·00

DESIGNS: 50c. to $5, Scenes from various matches.

166 Airbus Industrie A300

167 Cordia

1982. Coolidge International Airport. Mult.

738 10c. Type **166** 10 10
739 50c. Hawker-Siddeley H.S.748 . . . . 30 30
740 90c. De Havilland D.H.C.6 Twin Otter 60 60
741 $2.50 Britten Norman Islander . . . . 1·75 1·75
MS742 99 × 73 mm. $5 Boeing 747-100 (horiz) 2·75 4·00

1982. Death Centenary of Charles Darwin. Fauna and Flora. Multicoloured.

743 10c. Type **167** 25 10
744 50c. Small Indian mongoose (horiz) 55 40
745 90c. Corallita 85 75
746 $2 Mexican bulldog bat (horiz) . . . . 2·25 3·25
MS747 107 × 85 mm. $5 Carribbean monk seal 7·50 8·00

168 Queen's House, Greenwich

1982. 21st Birthday of Princess of Wales. Mult.

748 90c. Type **168** 45 45
749 $1 Prince and Princess of Wales 65 50
750 $4 Princess Diana . . . . . 2·75 2·00
MS751 102 × 75 mm. $5 Type **169** 3·75 2·50

170 Boy Scouts decorating Streets for Independence Parade

1982. 75th Anniv of Boy Scout Movement. Multicoloured.

752 10c. Type **170** 25 10
753 50c. Boy Scout giving helping hand during street parade 60 40
754 90c. Boy Scouts attending H.R.H. Princess Margaret at Independence Ceremony 1·00 75
755 $2.20 Cub Scout giving directions to tourists . . . 1·90 2·75
MS756 102 × 72 mm. $5 Lord Baden-Powell 5·50 5·50

1982. Birth of Prince William of Wales. Nos. 748/50 optd **ROYAL BABY 21.6.82.**

757 90c. Type **168** 45 45
758 $1 Prince and Princess of Wales 50 50
759 $4 Princess Diana . . . . . 2·00 1·50
MS760 102 × 75 mm. $5 Type **169** 2·40 2·50

172 Roosevelt in 1940

1982. Birth Centenary of Franklin D. Roosevelt. (Nos. 761, 763 and 765/6) and 250th Birth Anniv of George Washington (others). Multicoloured.

761 10c. Type **172** 20 10
762 25c. Washington as blacksmith 45 15
763 45c. Churchill, Roosevelt and Stalin at Yalta Conference 1·00 40
764 60c. Washington crossing the Delaware (vert) . . . . . 1·00 40
765 $1 "Roosevelt Special" train (vert) . . . . 1·25 90
766 $3 Portrait of Roosevelt (vert) . . . . 1·40 2·40
MS767 92 × 87 mm. $4 Roosevelt and Wife 2·00 1·75
MS768 92 × 87 mm. $4 Portrait of Washington (vert) 2·00 1·75

No. **MS**768 also exists imperf.

173 "Annunciation"

1982. Christmas. Religious Paintings by Raphael. Multicoloured.

769 10c. Type **173** 10 10
770 30c. "Adoration of the Magi" 15 15
771 $1 "Presentation at the Temple" 50 50
772 $4 "Coronation of the Virgin" . . . . 2·10 2·25
MS773 95 × 124 mm. $5 "Marriage of the Virgin" 2·75 2·50

174 Tritons and Dolphins

1983. 500th Birth Anniv of Raphael. Details from "Galatea" Fresco. Multicoloured.

774 45c. Type **174** 20 25
775 50c. Sea nymph carried off by Triton 25 30
776 60c. Winged angel steering dolphins (horiz) 30 35
777 $4 Cupids shooting arrows (horiz) . . . . 1·60 2·00
MS778 101 × 125 mm. $5 Galatea pulled along by dolphins 1·50 2·25

175 Pineapple Produce

1983. Commonwealth Day. Multicoloured.

779 25c. Type **175** 15 15
780 45c. Carnival 20 25
781 60c. Tourism 30 35
782 $3 Airport . . . . 1·00 1·50

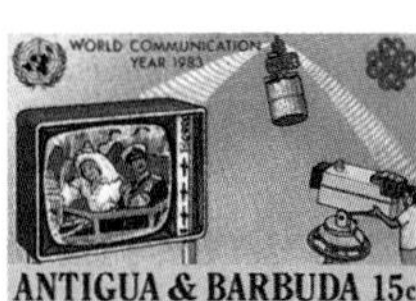

176 T.V. Satellite Coverage of Royal Wedding

1983. World Communications Year. Multicoloured.

783 15c. Type **176** 40 20
784 50c. Police communications 2·25 1·50
785 60c. House-to-train telephone call . . . . 2·25 1·50
786 $3 Satellite earth station with planets Jupiter and Saturn 4·75 5·00
MS787 100 × 90 mm. $5 "Comsat" satellite over West Indies 2·25 3·75

177 Bottle-nosed Dolphin

1983. Whales. Multicoloured.

788 15c. Type **177** 85 20
789 50c. Fin whale . . . . 1·75 1·25
790 60c. Bowhead whale . . . . 2·00 1·25
791 $3 Spectacled porpoise . . . 3·75 4·25
MS792 122 × 101 mm. $5 Narwhal 8·50 6·00

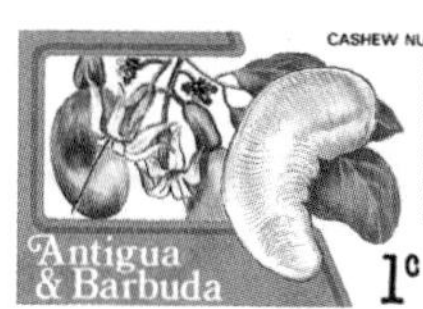

178 Cashew Nut

1983. Fruits and Flowers. Multicoloured.

793 1c. Type **178** 15 80
794 2c. Passion fruit 15 80
795 3c. Mango 15 80
796 5c. Grapefruit 20 65
797a 10c. Pawpaw 30 20
798 15c. Breadfruit 75 20
799 20c. Coconut 50 20
800a 25c. Oleander 75 20
801 30c. Banana 60 40
802a 40c. Pineapple 75 30
803a 45c. Cordia 85 40
804 50c. Cassia 90 60
805 60c. Poui . . . . 1·75 1·00
806a $1 Frangipani . . . . . . 2·25 1·50
807a $2 Flamboyant . . . . . . 3·75 4·25
808 $2.50 Lemon . . . . 4·50 6·00
809 $5 Linum vitae . . . . . . 7·00 12·00
810 $10 National flag and coat of arms . . . . 11·00 16·00

179 Dornier Do-X Flying Boat

1983. Bicentenary of Manned Flight. Mult.

811 30c. Type **179** 85 30
812 50c. Supermarine S.6B seaplane . . . . 1·00 60
813 60c. Curtiss F-9C Sparrowhawk biplane and airship U.S.S. "Akron" . . 1·25 85
814 $4 Hot-air balloon "Pro Juventute" . . . . 3·00 5·00
MS815 80 × 105 mm. $5 Airship LZ-127 "Graf Zeppelin" 2·00 2·25

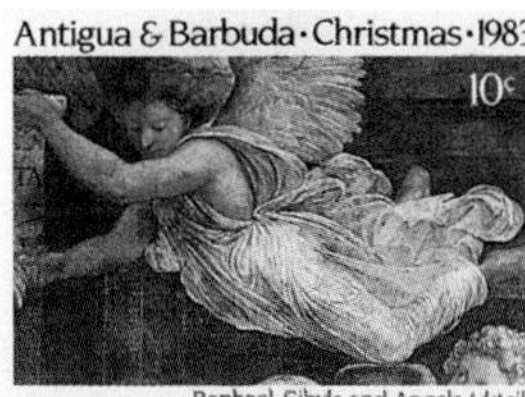

180 "Sibyls and Angels" (detail) (Raphael)

1983. Christmas. 500th Birth Anniv of Raphael.

816 **180** 10c. multicoloured 30 20
817 – 30c. multicoloured 65 35
818 – $1 multicoloured . . . . 1·50 1·25
819 – $4 multicoloured . . . . 3·00 5·00
MS820 – 101 × 103 mm. $5 multicoloured 1·50 2·25

DESIGNS—HORIZ: 10c. to $4, Different details from "Sibyls and Angels". VERT: $5 "The Vision of Ezekiel".

181 John Wesley (founder)

182 Discus

1983. Bicentenary of Methodist Church (1984). Multicoloured.

821 15c. Type **181** 25 15
822 50c. Nathaniel Gilbert (founder in Antigua) . . . 70 50
823 60c. St. John Methodist Church steeple 75 65
824 $3 Ebenezer Methodist Church, St. John's . . . . 2·00 4·00

1984. Olympic Games, Los Angeles. Multicoloured.

825 25c. Type **182** 20 15
826 50c. Gymnastics 35 30
827 90c. Hurdling 65 70
828 $3 Cycling . . . . 2·50 3·50
MS829 82 × 67 mm. $5 Volleyball 2·75 3·00

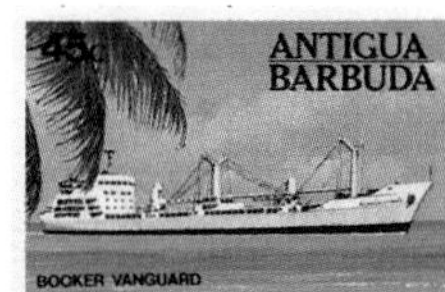

183 "Booker Vanguard" (freighter)

1984. Ships. Multicoloured.

830 45c. Type **183** . . . . 1·00 55
831 50c. S.S. "Canberra" (liner) 1·25 80
832 60c. Yachts . . . . 1·50 1·00
833 $4 "Fairwind" (cargo liner) 3·00 7·00
MS834 107 × 80 mm. $5 18th-century British man-of-war (vert) 1·75 3·50

184 Chenille

187 Abraham Lincoln

1984. Universal Postal Union Congress, Hamburg. Multicoloured.

835 15c. Type **184** 40 15
836 50c. Shell flower 80 70

837 60c. Anthurium 85 1·10
838 $3 Angels trumpet 2·75 6·50
MS839 100 × 75 mm. $5 Crown of Thorns 1·50 3·25

1984. Various stamps surch. (a) Nos. 702/4.
840 $2 on 25c. Type **159** 2·50 2·50
841 $2 on 50c. Glamis Castle 2·50 2·50
842 $2 on $4 Prince Charles skiing 2·50 2·50
MS843 96 × 82 mm. $2 on $5 Glass coach 4·00 4·00

(b) Nos. 748/50.
844 $2 on 90c. Type **168** 2·00 2·00
845 $2 on $1 Prince and Princess of Wales 2·00 2·00
846 $2 on $4 Princess Diana 2·00 2·00
MS847 102 × 75 mm. Type **169** 4·00 4·00

(c) Nos. 757/9.
848 $2 on 90c. Type **168** 2·00 2·00
849 $2 on $1 Prince and Princess of Wales 2·00 2·00
850 $2 on $4 Princess Diana 2·00 2·00
MS851 102 × 75 mm. $2 on $5 Type **169** 4·00 4·00

(d) Nos. 779/82.
852 $2 on 25c. Type **175** 2·50 1·25
853 $2 on 45c. Carnival 2·50 1·25
854 $2 on 60c. Tourism 2·50 1·25
855 $2 on $3 Airport 2·50 1·25

1984. Presidents of the United States of America. Multicoloured.
856 10c. Type **187** 15 10
857 20c. Harry S. Truman 20 15
858 30c. Dwight D. Eisenhower 30 25
859 40c. Ronald W. Reagan 50 30
860 90c. Gettysburg Address, 1863 90 75
861 $1.10 Formation of N.A.T.O.,1949 1·25 1·25
862 $1.50 Eisenhower during the war 1·60 1·75
863 $2 Reagan and Caribbean Basin Initiative 1·75 2·00

188 View of Moravian Mission

1984. 150th Anniv of Abolition of Slavery. Multicoloured.
864 40c. Type **188** 80 50
865 50c. Antigua Courthouse, 1823 90 65
866 60c. Planting sugar-cane, Monks Hill 95 75
867 $3 Boiling house, Delaps' estate 4·00 5·00
MS868 95 × 70 mm. $5 Loading sugar, Willoughby Bay 6·50 4·75

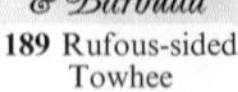

189 Rufous-sided Towhee
190 Grass-skiing

1984. Songbirds. Multicoloured.
869 40c. Type **189** 1·25 85
870 50c. Parula warbler 1·40 1·10
871 60c. House wren 1·50 1·50
872 $2 Ruby-crowned kinglet 2·00 3·75
873 $3 Common flicker ("Yellow-shafted Flicker") 2·75 5·00
MS874 76 × 76 mm. $5 Yellow-breasted chat 2·50 6·00

1984. "Ausipex" International Stamp Exhibition, Melbourne, Australian Sports. Multicoloured.
875 $1 Type **190** 1·25 1·50
876 $5 Australian football 3·75 5·50
MS877 108 × 78 mm. $5 Boomerang-throwing 2·50 4·00

191 "The Virgin and Infant with Angels and Cherubs"
192 "The Blue Dancers"

1984. 450th Death Anniv of Correggio (painter). Multicoloured.
878 25c. Type **191** 40 20
879 60c. "The Four Saints" 80 50
880 90c. "St. Catherine" 1·10 90
881 $3 "The Campori Madonna" 2·25 4·25
MS882 90 × 60 mm. $5 "St. John the Baptist" 2·00 2·75

1984. 150th Birth Anniv of Edgar Degas (painter). Multicoloured.
883 15c. Type **192** 35 15
884 50c. "The Pink Dancers" 80 60
885 70c. "Two Dancers" 1·10 85
886 $4 "Dancers at the Bar" 2·50 4·75
MS887 90 × 60 mm. "The Folk dancers" (40 × 27 mm) 2·00 2·75

ANTIGUA & BARBUDA

193 Sir Winston Churchill
194 Donald Duck fishing

1984. Famous People. Multicoloured.
888 60c. Type **193** 1·10 1·50
889 60c. Mahatma Gandhi 1·10 1·50
890 60c. John F. Kennedy 1·10 1·50
891 60c. Mao Tse-tung 1·10 1·50
892 $1 Churchill with General De Gaulle, Paris, 1944 (horiz) 1·25 1·75
893 $1 Gandhi leaving London by train, 1931 (horiz) 1·25 1·75
894 $1 Kennedy with Chancellor Adenauer and Mayor Brandt, Berlin, 1963 (horiz) 1·25 1·75
895 $1 Mao Tse-tung with Lin Piao, Peking, 1969 (horiz) 1·25 1·75
MS896 114 × 80 mm. $5 Flags of Great Britain, India, the United States and China 9·00 4·50

1984. Christmas. 50th Birthday of Donald Duck. Walt Disney Cartoon Characters. Multicoloured.
897 1c. Type **194** 10 10
898 2c. Donald Duck lying on beach 10 10
899 3c. Donald Duck and nephews with fishing rods and fishes 10 10
900 4c. Donald Duck and nephews in boat 10 10
901 5c. Wearing diving masks 10 10
902 10c. In deckchairs reading books 10 10
903 $1 With toy shark's fin 2·25 1·25
904 $2 In sailing boat 2·50 3·00
905 $5 Attempting to propel boat 5·50 6·00
MS906 Two sheets, each 125 × 100 mm. (a) $5 Nephews with crayon and paintbrushes (horiz). (b) $5 Donald Duck in deckchair Set of 2 sheets 9·00 13·00

195 Torch from Statue in Madison Square Park, 1885

1985. Centenary (1986) of Statue of Liberty (1st issue). Multicoloured.
907 25c. Type **195** 20 20
908 30c. Statue of Liberty and scaffolding ("Restoration and Renewal") (vert) 20 20
909 50c. Frederic Bartholdi (sculptor) supervising construction, 1876 30 40
910 90c. Close-up of statue 60 75
911 $1 Statue and cadet ship ("Operation Sail", 1976) (vert) 1·40 1·40
912 $3 Dedication ceremony, 1886 1·75 3·00
MS913 110 × 80 mm. $5 Port of New York 3·75 3·75
See also Nos. 1110/19.

196 Arawak Pot Sherd and Indians making Clay Utensils

1985. Native American Artefacts. Multicoloured.
914 15c. Type **196** 15 10
915 50c. Arawak body design and Arawak Indians tattooing 30 40
916 60c. Head of the god "Yocahu" and Indians harvesting manioc 40 50
917 $3 Carib war club and Carib Indians going into battle 1·25 2·50
MS918 97 × 68 mm. $5 Taino Indians worshipping stone idol 1·50 2·50

197 Triumph 2hp "Jap", 1903

1985. Centenary of the Motorcycle. Multicoloured.
919 10c. Type **197** 65 15
920 30c. "Indian Arrow", 1949 1·10 40
921 60c. BMW "R100RS", 1976 1·60 1·25
922 $4 Harley-Davidson "Model II", 1916 5·50 8·00
MS923 90 × 93 mm. $5 Laverda "Jota", 1975 5·50 7·00

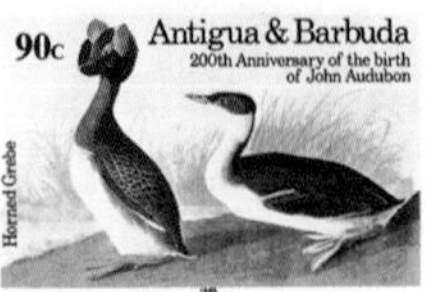

198 Slavonian Grebe ("Horned Grebe")

1985. Birth Bicentenary of John J. Audubon (ornithologist) (1st issue). Multicoloured. Designs showing original paintings.
924 90c. Type **198** 1·75 1·25
925 $1 British storm petrel ("Least Petrel") 2·00 1·25
926 $1.50 Great blue heron 2·50 3·25
927 $3 Double-crested cormorant 3·75 6·50
MS928 103 × 72 mm. $5 White-tailed tropic bird (vert) 7·00 6·00
See also Nos. 990/4.

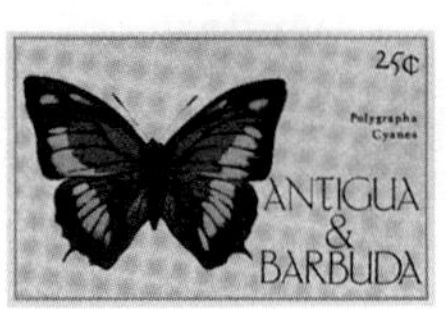

199 "Anaea cyanea"

1985. Butterflies. Multicoloured.
929 25c. Type **199** 1·00 30
930 60c. "Leodonta dysoni" 2·25 1·25
931 90c. "Junea doraete" 2·75 1·50
932 $4 "Prepona pylene" 7·50 10·50
MS933 132 × 105 mm. $5 "Caerois gerdtrudlus" 4·50 6·50

200 Cessna 172D Skyhawk

1985. 40th Anniv of International Civil Aviation Organization. Multicoloured.
934 30c. Type **200** 1·25 30
935 90c. Fokker D.VII 2·75 1·25
936 $1.50 SPAD VII 3·75 3·25
937 $3 Boeing 747-100 5·50 7·50
MS938 97 × 83 mm. $5 De Havilland D.H.C.6 twin otter 4·50 6·50

201 Maimonides
203 The Queen Mother attending Church

202 Young Farmers with Produce

1985. 850th Birth Anniv of Maimonides (physician, philosopher and scholar).
939 **201** $2 green 4·00 3·25
MS940 70 × 84 mm. Type **201** $5 brown 7·00 4·50

1985. International Youth Year. Multicoloured.
941 25c. Type **202** 20 20
942 50c. Hotel management trainees 35 50
943 60c. Girls with goat and boys with football ("Environment") 80 70
944 $3 Windsurfing ("Leisure") 2·50 4·75
MS945 102 × 72 mm. $5 Young people with Antiguan flags 2·75 3·25

1985. Life and Times of Queen Elizabeth the Queen Mother. Multicoloured.
946 $1 Type **203** 45 60
947 $1.50 Watching children playing in London garden 60 85
948 $2.50 The Queen Mother in 1979 90 1·40
MS949 56 × 85 mm. $5 With Prince Edward at Royal Wedding, 1981 4·50 3·00
Stamps as Nos. 946/8, but with face values of 90c., $1 and $3 exist from additional sheetlets with changed background colours.

204 Magnificent Frigate Bird
206 Bass Trombone

205 Girl Guides Nursing

1985. Marine Life. Multicoloured.
950 15c. Type **204** 1·00 30
951 45c. Brain coral 2·00 95
952 60c. Cushion star 2·25 1·75
953 $3 Spotted moray 7·00 9·00
MS954 110 × 80 mm. $5 Elkhorn coral 9·00 7·00

1985. 75th Anniv of Girl Guide Movement. Multicoloured.
955 15c. Type **205** 75 20
956 45c. Open-air Girl Guide meeting 1·40 60
957 60c. Lord and Lady Baden-Powell 1·75 90
958 $3 Girl Guides gathering flowers 4·25 4·50
MS959 67 × 96 mm. $5 Barn swallow (Nature study) 6·50 8·50

1985. 300th Birth Anniv of Johann Sebastian Bach (composer).
960 **206** 25c. multicoloured 1·40 55
961 – 50c. multicoloured 1·75 1·10
962 – $1 multicoloured 3·25 1·75
963 – $3 multicoloured 6·00 7·00
MS964 – 104 × 73 mm. $5 black and grey 4·50 4·75
DESIGNS:50c. English horn; $1 Violino piccolo; $3 Bass rackett; $5 Johann Sebastian Bach.

207 Flags of Great Britain and Antigua

1985. Royal Visit. Multicoloured.
965 60c. Type **207** 1·00 65
966 $1 Queen Elizabeth II (vert) 1·50 1·25
967 $4 Royal Yacht "Britannia" 3·25 6·00
MS968 110 × 83 mm. $5 Map of Antigua 3·00 3·25

1985. 150th Birth Anniv of Mark Twain (author). As T **118** of Anguilla showing Walt Disney cartoon characters in scenes from "Roughing It". Multicoloured.
969 25c. Donald Duck and Mickey Mouse meeting Indians 90 20
970 50c. Mickey Mouse, Donald Duck and Goofy canoeing 1·40 55
971 $1.10 Goofy as Pony Express rider 2·25 2·00

972 $1.50 Donald Duck and Goofy hunting buffalo . . 2·75 3·50
973 $2 Mickey Mouse and silver mine . . . . 3·25 4·25
MS974 127 × 101 mm. $5 Mickey Mouse driving stagecoach 8·00 7·50

1985. Birth Bicentenaries of Grimm Brothers (folklorists). As T **119** of Anguilla showing Walt Disney cartoon characters in scenes from "Spindle, Shuttle and Needle". Multicoloured.
975 30c. The Prince (Mickey Mouse) searches for a bride 1·00 40
976 60c. The Prince finds the Orphan Girl (Minnie Mouse) . . . . 1·50 80
977 70c. The Spindle finds the Prince . . . . 1·75 1·40
978 $1 The Needle tidies the Girl's house . . . . 2·25 1·75
979 $3 The Prince proposes . . . 4·50 6·50
MS980 125 × 101 mm. $5 The Orphan Girl and spinning wheel on Prince's horse 8·00 7·50

208 Benjamin Franklin and U.N. (New York) 1953 U.P.U. 5c. Stamp

1985. 40th Anniv of United Nations Organization. Multicoloured.
981 40c. Type **208** . . . . 1·00 70
982 $1 George Washington Carver (agricultural chemist) and 1982 Nature Conservation 28c. stamp 2·00 2·00
983 $3 Charles Lindbergh (aviator) and 1978 I.C.A.O. 25c. stamp . . . . 4·75 7·50
MS984 101 × 77 mm. $5 Marc Chagall (artist) (vert) 6·00 4·75
Nos. 981/4 each include a United Nations (New York) stamp design.

209 "Madonna and Child" (De Landi)

211 Tug

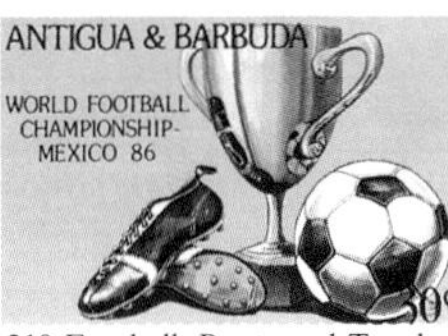
210 Football, Boots and Trophy

1985. Christmas. Religious Paintings. Mult.
985 10c. Type **209** 30 15
986 25c. "Madonna and Child" (Berlinghiero) 55 25
987 60c. "The Nativity" (Fra Angelico) 70 60
988 $4 "Presentation in the Temple" (Giovanni di Paolo) . . . . 1·75 4·25
MS989 113 × 81 mm. $5 "The Nativity" (Antoniazzo Romano) 3·00 3·75

1986. Birth Bicentenary of John J. Audubon (ornithologist) (2nd issue). As T **198** showing original paintings. Multicoloured.
990 60c. Mallard . . . . 2·25 1·50
991 90c. North American black duck ("Dusky Duck") . . 2·75 2·00
992 $1.50 Pintail ("Common Pintail") . . . . 3·50 4·50
993 $3 American wigeon ("Wigeon") . . . . 4·75 6·50
MS994 102 × 73 mm. Eider ("Common Eider") 7·00 5·50

1986. World Cup Football Championship, Mexico. Multicoloured.
995 30c. Type **210** . . . . 1·50 40
996 60c. Goalkeeper (vert) . . . 2·00 85
997 $1 Referee blowing whistle (vert) . . . . 2·50 1·75
998 $4 Ball in net . . . . 6·50 9·00
MS999 87 × 76 mm. $5 Two players competing for ball 8·50 7·50

1986. Appearance of Halley's Comet (1st issue). As T **123** of Anguilla. Multicoloured.
1000 5c. Edmond Halley and Old Greenwich Observatory 30 20
1001 10c. Messerschmitt Me 163B Komet (fighter aircraft), 1944 . . . . 30 15
1002 60c. Montezuma (Aztec emperor) and Comet in 1517 (from "Historias de las Indias de Neuva Espana") . . . . 1·50 70
1003 $4 Pocahontas saving Capt. John Smith and Comet in 1607 . . . . 4·50 5·50
MS1004 101 × 70 mm. $5 Halley's Comet over English Harbour, Antigua 3·50 3·75
See also Nos. 1047/51.

1986. 60th Birthday of Queen Elizabeth II. As T **125** of Anguilla.
1005 60c. black and yellow . . . 30 35
1006 $1 multicoloured 50 55
1007 $4 multicoloured . . . . . 1·40 1·90
MS1008 120 × 85 mm. $5 black and brown 2·00 3·00
DESIGNS: 60c. Wedding photograph, 1947; $1 Queen at Trooping the Colour; $4 In Scotland; $5 Queen Mary and Princess Elizabeth, 1927.

1986. Local Boats. Multicoloured.
1009 30c. Type **211** 25 20
1010 60c. Game fishing boat . . 45 35
1011 $1 Yacht 75 60
1012 $4 Lugger with auxiliary sail 2·50 3·25
MS1013 108 × 78 mm. $5 Boats under construction 3·00 4·00

212 "Hiawatha" express

1986. "Ameripex '86" International Stamp Exhibition, Chicago. Famous American Trains. Multicoloured.
1014 25c. Type **212** . . . . . . 1·25 50
1015 50c. "Grand Canyon" express . . . . 1·50 80
1016 $1 "Powhattan Arrow" express . . . . 1·75 1·75
1017 $3 "Empire State" express 3·00 7·00
MS1018 116 × 87 mm. $5 Southern Pacific "Daylight" express 5·50 9·50

213 Prince Andrew and Miss Sarah Ferguson

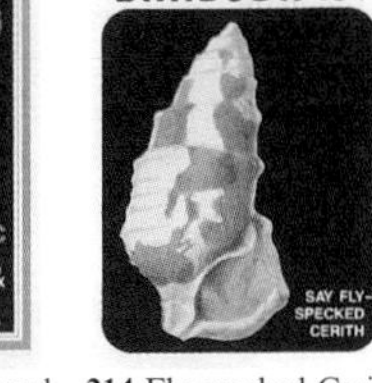
214 Fly-specked Cerith

1986. Royal Wedding. Multicoloured.
1019 45c. Type **213** 70 35
1020 60c. Prince Andrew 80 45
1021 $4 Prince Andrew with Prince Philip . . . . . . 2·75 3·50
MS1022 88 × 88 mm. $5 Prince Andrew and Miss Sarah Ferguson (different) 4·75 4·50

1986. Sea Shells. Multicoloured.
1023 15c. Type **214** 75 50
1024 45c. Smooth Scotch bonnet 1·75 1·25
1025 60c. West Indian crown conch . . . . 2·00 2·00
1026 $3 Ciboney murex . . . . . 6·50 10·00
MS1027 109 × 75 mm. $5 Colourful Atlantic moon (horiz) 7·50 8·50

215 Water Lily

1986. Flowers. Multicoloured.
1028 10c. Type **215** 20 15
1029 15c. Queen of the night . . 20 15
1030 50c. Cup of gold 55 55
1031 60c. Beach morning glory 70 70
1032 70c. Golden trumpet 80 80
1033 $1 Air plant . . . . 90 1·10
1034 $4 Purple wreath . . . . . 1·75 3·00
1035 $4 Zephyr lily . . . . . . 2·00 3·75
MS1036 Two sheets, each 102 × 72 mm. (a) $4 Dozakie. (b) $5 Four o'clock flower Set of 2 sheets 5·00 7·50

1986. World Cup Football Championship Winners, Mexico. Nos. 995/8 optd **WINNERS Argentina 3 W.Germany 2.**
1037 30c. Type **210** . . . . . . 1·00 40
1038 60c. Goalkeeper (vert) . . . 1·50 75
1039 $1 Referee blowing whistle (vert) . . . . 2·00 1·10
1040 $4 Ball in net . . . . 5·00 4·50
MS1041 87 × 76 mm. $5 Two players competing for ball 5·50 4·00

217 "Hygrocybe occidentalis var. scarletina"

(218)

1986. Mushrooms. Multicoloured.
1042 10c. Type **217** 30 25
1043 50c. "Trogia buccinalis" . . 70 55
1044 $1 "Collybia subpruinosa" 1·25 1·25
1045 $4 "Leucocoprinus brebissonii" . . . . . . 3·00 4·50
MS1046 102 × 82 mm. $5 "Pyrrhoglossum pyrrhum" 13·00 11·00

1986. Appearance of Halley's Comet (2nd issue). Nos. 1000/3 optd with T **218**.
1047 5c. Edmond Halley and Old Greenwich Observatory 15 10
1048 10c. Messerschmitt Me 163B Komet (fighter aircraft), 1944 . . . . 20 10
1049 60c. Montezuma (Aztec emperor) and Comet in 1517 (from "Historias de las Indias de Neuva Espana") . . . . 1·00 65
1050 $4 Pocahontas saving Capt. John Smith and Comet in 1607 . . . . 4·50 4·00
MS1051 101 × 70 mm. $5 Halley's Comet over English Harbour, Antigua 6·00 6·50

219 Auburn "Speedster" (1933)

1986. Centenary of First Benz Motor Car. Mult.
1052 10c. Type **219** 15 10
1053 15c. Mercury "Sable" (1986) 20 10
1054 50c. Cadillac (1959) 55 30
1055 60c. Studebaker (1950) . . . 70 45
1056 70c. Lagonda "V-12" (1939) 80 55
1057 $1 Adler "Standard" (1930) 1·10 75
1058 $3 DKW (1956) . . . . . . 2·50 2·50
1059 $4 Mercedes "500K" (1936) 3·00 3·00
MS1060 Two sheets, each 99 × 70 mm. (a) $5 Daimler (1896). (b) $5 Mercedes "Knight" (1921) Set of 2 sheets 9·00 6·50

220 Young Mickey Mouse playing Santa Claus

1986. Christmas. Designs showing Walt Disney cartoon characters as babies. Multicoloured.
1061 25c. Type **220** 60 35
1062 30c. Mickey and Minnie Mouse building snowman 70 40
1063 40c. Aunt Matilda and Goofy baking 75 45
1064 60c. Goofy and Pluto . . . 1·00 85
1065 70c. Pluto, Donald and Daisy Duck carol singing 1·10 1·00
1066 $1.50 Donald Duck, Mickey Mouse and Pluto stringing popcorn . . . . 1·75 2·50
1067 $3 Grandma Duck and Minnie Mouse . . . . . 3·00 4·50
1068 $4 Donald Duck and Pete 3·25 4·50
MS1069 Two sheets, each 127 × 102 mm. (a) $5 Goofy, Donald Duck and Minnie Mouse playing with reindeer. (b) $5 Mickey Mouse, Donald and Daisy Duck playing with toys Set of 2 sheets 11·00 13·00

221 Arms of Antigua

222 "Canada I" (1981)

1986.
1070 **221** 10c. blue 50 50
1071 – 25c. red 75 75
DESIGN: 25c. Flag of Antigua.

1987. America's Cup Yachting Championship. Multicoloured.
1072 30c. Type **222** 45 20
1073 60c. "Gretel II" (1970) . . . 60 50
1074 $1 "Sceptre" (1958) . . . . 85 1·00
1075 $3 "Vigilant" (1893) . . . . 2·25 3·00
MS1076 113 × 84 mm. $5 "Australia II" defeating "Liberty" (1983) (horiz) 4·00 5·00

223 Bridled Burrfish

1987. Marine Life. Multicoloured.
1077 15c. Type **223** . . . . . . 2·50 50
1078 30c. Common noddy ("Brown Noddy") . . . . 4·50 60
1079 40c. Nassau grouper . . . . 3·00 70
1080 50c. Laughing gull . . . . 5·50 1·50
1081 60c. French angelfish . . . 3·50 1·50
1082 $1 Porkfish . . . . 3·50 1·75
1083 $2 Royal tern . . . . 7·50 6·00
1084 $3 Sooty tern . . . . 7·50 8·00
MS1085 Two sheets, each 120 × 94 mm. (a) $5 Banded butterflyfish. (b) $5 Brown booby Set of 2 sheets 17·00 14·00
Nos. 1078, 1080 and 1083/5 are without the World Wildlife Fund logo shown on Type **223**.

224 Handball

1987. Olympic Games, Seoul (1988) (1st issue). Multicoloured.
1086 10c. Type **224** 60 10
1087 60c. Fencing 85 35
1088 $1 Gymnastics . . . . . . 1·25 75
1089 $3 Football . . . . 2·50 4·00
MS1090 100 × 72 mm. $5 Boxing gloves 3·50 4·25
See also Nos. 1222/6.

225 "The Profile"

1987. Birth Centenary of Marc Chagall (artist). Multicoloured.
1091 10c. Type **225** 30 15
1092 30c. "Portrait of the Artist's Sister" 45 30
1093 40c. "Bride with Fan" . . . 50 40
1094 60c. "David in Profile" . . 55 45
1095 90c. "Fiancee with Bouquet" 75 60
1096 $1 "Self Portrait with Brushes" 75 65
1097 $3 "The Walk" . . . . . . 1·75 2·25
1098 $4 "Three Candles" . . . . 2·00 2·50
MS1099 Two sheets, each 110 × 95 mm. (a) $5 "Fall of Icarus" (104 × 89 mm). (b) $5 "Myth of Orpheus" (104 × 89 mm). Imperf Set of 2 sheets 6·50 6·00

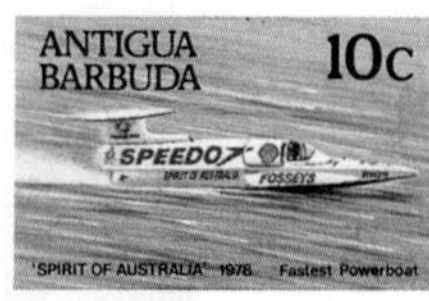

226 "Spirit of Australia" (fastest powerboat), 1978

1987. Milestones of Transportation. Multicoloured.
1100 10c. Type **226** 75 40
1101 15c. Werner von Siemens's electric locomotive, 1879 1·00 50
1102 30c. U.S.S. "Triton" (first submerged circum-navigation), 1960 . . . . 1·00 50
1103 50c. Trevithick's steam carriage (first passenger-carrying vehicle), 1801 . . 1·25 60
1104 60c. U.S.S. "New Jersey" (battleship), 1942 . . . . 1·25 70
1105 70c. Draisaine bicycle, 1818 1·25 80
1106 90c. "United States" (liner) (holder of Blue Riband), 1952 . . . . 1·25 1·00
1107 $1.50 Cierva C.4 (first autogyro), 1923 . . . . . 1·40 2·25
1108 $2 Curtiss NC-4 flying boat (first transatlantic flight), 1919 . . . . 1·50 2·50
1109 $3 "Queen Elizabeth 2" (liner), 1969 . . . . . . 2·75 4·00

227 Lee Iacocca at Unveiling of Restored Statue

228 Grace Kelly

1987. Centenary of Statue of Liberty (1986) (2nd issue). Multicoloured.
1110 15c. Type **227** 15 15
1111 30c. Statue at sunset (side view) 20 20
1112 45c. Aerial view of head . . 30 30
1113 50c. Lee Iacocca and torch 35 35
1114 60c. Workmen inside head of Statue (horiz) 35 35
1115 90c. Restoration work (horiz) 50 50
1116 $1 Head of Statue 55 55
1117 $2 Statue at sunset (front view) . . . . 1·00 1·50
1118 $3 Inspecting restoration work (horiz) . . . . . . 1·25 2·00
1119 $5 Statue at night . . . . . 2·00 3·50

1987. Entertainers. Multicoloured.
1120 15c. Type **228** 90 40
1121 30c. Marilyn Monroe . . . 2·50 80
1122 45c. Orson Welles 90 60
1123 50c. Judy Garland 90 65
1124 60c. John Lennon . . . . . 3·75 1·25
1125 $1 Rock Hudson . . . . . . 1·40 1·10
1126 $2 John Wayne . . . . . . 2·50 2·00
1127 $3 Elvis Presley . . . . . . 8·00 4·50

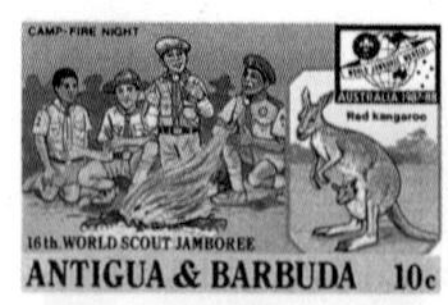

229 Scouts around Camp Fire and Red Kangaroo

1987. 16th World Scout Jamboree, Australia. Mult.
1128 10c. Type **229** 65 20
1129 60c. Scouts canoeing and blue-winged kookaburra 1·25 80
1130 $1 Scouts on assault course and ring-tailed rock wallaby . . . . 1·00 85
1131 $3 Field kitchen and koala 1·50 4·25
MS1132 103 × 78 mm. $5 Flags of Antigua, Australia and Scout Movement 3·25 3·50

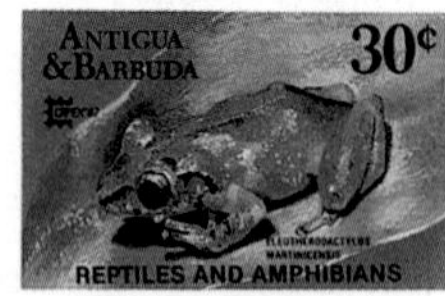

230 Whistling Frog

1987. "Capex '87" International Stamp Exhibition, Toronto. Reptiles and Amphibians. Mult.
1133 30c. Type **230** 55 20
1134 60c. Croaking lizard 75 40
1135 $1 Antiguan anole . . . . . 1·00 70
1136 $3 Red-footed tortoise . . . 2·00 3·00
MS1137 106 × 76 mm. $5 Ground lizard 2·25 2·75

1987. 10th Death Anniv of Elvis Presley (entertainer). No. 1127 optd **10th ANNIVERSARY 16th AUGUST 1987**.
1138 $3 Elvis Presley . . . . . . 6·50 4·25

232 House of Burgesses, Virginia ("Freedom of Speech")

1987. Bicentenary of U.S. Constitution. Mult.
1139 15c. Type **232** 10 10
1140 45c. State Seal, Connecticut 20 25
1141 60c. State Seal, Delaware . . 25 35
1142 $4 Governor Morris (Pennsylvania delegate) (vert) . . . . 1·75 2·25
MS1143 105 × 75 mm. $5 Roger Sherman (Connecticut delegate) (vert) 2·00 2·75

233 "Madonna and Child" (Bernardo Daddi)

234 Wedding Photograph, 1947

1987. Christmas. Religious Paintings. Mult.
1144 45c. Type **233** 50 15
1145 60c. St. Joseph (detail, "The Nativity" (Sano di Pietro)) 65 30
1146 $1 Virgin Mary (detail, "The Nativity" (Sano di Pietro)) 85 55
1147 $4 "Music-making Angel" (Melozzo da Forli) . . . 2·25 3·50
MS1148 99 × 70 mm. $5 "The Flight into Egypt" (Sano di Pietro) 2·25 2·75

1988. Royal Ruby Wedding.
1149 **234** 25c. brown, black and blue 25 15
1150 – 60c. multicoloured . . . 50 40
1151 – $2 brown, black and green . . . . 1·00 1·10
1152 – $3 multicoloured . . . . 2·75 1·60
MS1153 107 × 77 mm. $5 multicoloured 2·50 2·75
DESIGNS: 60c. Queen Elizabeth II; $2 Princess Elizabeth and Prince Philip with Prince Charles at his christening, 1948; $3 Queen Elizabeth (from photo by Tim Graham), 1980; $5 Royal family, 1952.

235 Great Blue Heron

1988. Birds of Antigua. Multicoloured.
1154 10c. Type **235** 45 50
1155 15c. Ringed kingfisher (horiz) 50 40
1156 50c. Bananaquit (horiz) . . 90 50
1157 60c. American purple gallinule ("Purple Gallinule") (horiz) 90 50
1158 70c. Blue-hooded euphonia (horiz) . . . . 1·00 55
1159 $1 Brown-throated conure ("Caribbean Parakeet") 1·25 75
1160 $3 Troupial (horiz) . . . . 2·50 3·50
1161 $4 Purple-throated carib ("Hummingbird") (horiz) 2·50 3·50
MS1162 Two sheets, each 115 × 86 mm. (a) $5 Greater flamingo. (b) $5 Brown pelican Set of 2 sheets 4·50 5·50

236 First Aid at Daycare Centre, Antigua

1988. Salvation Army's Community Service. Multicoloured.
1163 25c. Type **236** 80 65
1164 30c. Giving penicillin injection, Indonesia . . . 80 65
1165 40c. Children at daycare centre, Bolivia 90 75
1166 45c. Rehabilitation of the handicapped, India . . . 90 75
1167 50c. Training blind man, Kenya . . . . 1·00 1·25
1168 60c. Weighing baby, Ghana 1·00 1·25
1169 $1 Training typist, Zambia 1·40 1·75
1170 $2 Emergency food kitchen, Sri Lanka . . . . 2·00 3·50
MS1171 152 × 83 mm. $5 General Eva Burrows 3·75 4·50

237 Columbus's Second Fleet, 1493

1988. 500th Anniv (1992) of Discovery of America by Columbus (1st issue). Multicoloured.
1172 10c. Type **237** 60 40
1173 30c. PaiNos. Indian village and fleet 60 45
1174 45c. "Santa Mariagalante" (flagship) and PaiNos. village 70 45
1175 60c. PaiNos. Indians offering Columbus fruit and vegetables 70 50
1176 90c. PaiNos. Indian and Columbus with scarlet macaw . . . . 1·25 1·00
1177 $1 Columbus landing on island . . . . 1·25 1·00
1178 $3 Spanish soldier and fleet 2·25 3·00
1179 $4 Fleet under sail . . . . 2·50 3·00
MS1180 Two sheets, each 110 × 80 mm. (a) $5 Queen Isabella's cross. (b) $5 Gold coin of Ferdinand and Isabella Set of 2 sheets 6·50 7·00
See also Nos. 1267/71, 1360/8, 1503/11, 1654/60 and 1670/1.

Antigua & Barbuda 30c
238 "Bust of Christ"

1988. Easter. 500th Birth Anniv of Titian (artist). Multicoloured.
1181 30c. Type **238** 40 20
1182 40c. "Scourging of Christ" 45 25
1183 45c. "Madonna in Glory with Saints" 45 25
1184 50c. "The Averoldi Polyptych" (detail) . . . 45 35
1185 $1 "Christ Crowned with Thorns" 70 55
1186 $2 "Christ Mocked" . . . . 1·10 1·25
1187 $3 "Christ and Simon of Cyrene" . . . . 1·50 1·75
1188 $4 "Crucifixion with Virgin and Saints" . . . . . . 1·75 2·25
MS1189 Two sheets, each 110 × 95 mm. (a) $5 "Ecce Homo" (detail). (b) $5 "Noli me Tangere" (detail) Set of 2 sheets 7·00 8·50

239 Two Yachts rounding Buoy

1988. Sailing Week. Multicoloured.
1190 30c. Type **239** 35 20
1191 60c. Three yachts 50 40
1192 $1 British yacht under way 60 55
1193 $3 Three yachts (different) 1·10 2·50
MS1194 103 × 92 mm. $5 Two yachts 1·75 3·25

240 Mickey Mouse and Diver with Porpoise

1988. Disney EPCOT Centre, Orlando, Florida. Designs showing cartoon characters and exhibits. Multicoloured.
1195 1c. Type **240** 10 10
1196 2c. Goofy and Mickey Mouse with futuristic car (vert) 10 10
1197 3c. Mickey Mouse and Goofy as Atlas (vert) . . 10 10
1198 4c. Mickey Mouse and "Eda-phosaurus" (prehistoric reptile) . . . 10 10
1199 5c. Mickey Mouse at Journey into Imagination exhibit 10 10
1200 10c. Mickey Mouse collecting vegetables (vert) 15 10
1201 25c. Type **240** 45 25
1202 30c. As 2c. 45 25
1203 40c. As 3c. 55 30
1204 60c. As 4c. 75 50
1205 70c. As 5c. 85 60
1206 $1.50 As 10c. . . . . 1·75 1·75
1207 $3 Goofy and Mickey Mouse with robot (vert) 2·25 2·50
1208 $4 Mickey Mouse and Clarabelle at Horizons exhibit . . . . 2·25 2·50
MS1209 Two sheets, each 125 × 99 mm. (a) $5 Mickey Mouse and monorail (vert). (b) $5 Mickey Mouse flying over EPCOT Centre Set of 2 sheets 7·00 6·50

1988. Stamp Exhibitions. Nos. 1083/4 optd.
1210 $2 Royal tern (optd **Praga '88**, Prague) . . . . . . 3·50 2·50
1211 $3 Sooty tern (optd **INDEPENDENCE 40**, Israel) . . . . 3·50 3·25
MS1212 Two sheets, each 120 × 94 mm. (a) $5 Banded butterflyfish (optd **"OLYMPHILEX '88"**, Seoul). (b) $5 brown booby (optd **"FINLANDIA 88"**, Helsinki). Set of 2 sheets 9·00 7·00

242 Jacaranda

243 Gymnastics

1988. Flowering Trees. Multicoloured.
1213 10c. Type **242** 30 20
1214 30c. Cordia 40 20
1215 50c. Orchid tree 60 40
1216 90c. Flamboyant 70 50
1217 $1 African tulip tree 75 55
1218 $2 Potato tree . . . . 1·40 1·60
1219 $3 Crepe myrtle . . . . . . 1·60 2·00
1220 $4 Pitch apple . . . . 1·75 2·75
MS1221 Two sheets, each 106 × 76 mm. (a) $5 Cassia. (b) $5 Chinaberry Set of 2 sheets 5·00 6·00

1988. Olympic Games, Seoul (2nd issue). Mult.
1222 40c. Type **243** 30 25
1223 60c. Weightlifting 40 30
1224 $1 Water polo (horiz) . . . 80 50
1225 $3 Boxing (horiz) . . . . . 1·50 2·25
MS1226 114 × 80 mm. $5 Runner with Olympic torch 2·00 3·00

244 "Danaus plexippus"

1988. Caribbean Butterflies. Multicoloured.
1227 1c. Type **244** 50 70
1228 2c. "Greta diaphanus" . . 60 80
1229 3c. "Calisto archebates" . . 60 80
1230 5c. "Hamadryas feronia" 70 80
1231 10c. "Mestra dorcas" . . . 85 30
1232 15c. "Hypolimnas misippus" . . . . 1·25 30
1233 20c. "Dione juno" . . . . 1·40 30
1234 25c. "Heliconius charithonia" . . . . . . 1·40 30
1235 30c. "Eurema pyro" . . . 1·40 30
1236 40c. "Papilio androgeus" 1·40 30
1237 45c. "Anteos maerula" . . 1·40 30
1238 50c. "Aphrissa orbis" . . . 1·50 45
1239 60c. "Astraptes xagua" . . 1·75 60

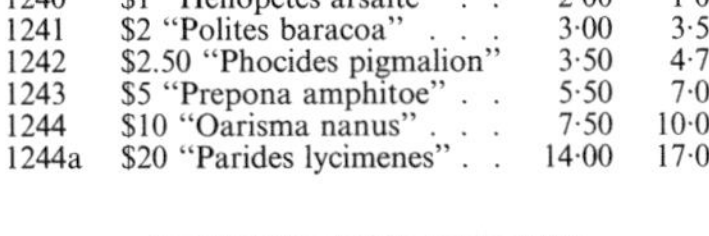

1240 $1 "Heliopetes arsalte" . . 2·00 1·00
1241 $2 "Polites baracoa" . . . 3·00 3·50
1242 $2.50 "Phocides pigmalion" 3·50 4·75
1243 $5 "Prepona amphitoe" . . 5·50 7·00
1244 $10 "Oarisma nanus" . . . 7·50 10·00
1244a $20 "Parides lycimenes" . . 14·00 17·00

245 President Kennedy and Family

1988. 25th Death Anniv of John F. Kennedy (American statesman). Multicoloured.

1245 1c. Type **245** 10 10
1246 2c. Kennedy commanding "PT109" 10 10
1247 3c. Funeral cortege 10 10
1248 4c. In motorcade, Mexico City 10 10
1249 30c. As 1c. 35 15
1250 60c. As 4c. 75 40
1251 $1 As 3c. 85 75
1252 $4 As 2c. . . . . 2·50 3·25
MS1253 105 × 75 mm. $5 Kennedy taking presidential oath of office 2·50 3·25

246 Minnie Mouse carol singing

1988. Christmas. "Mickey's Christmas Chorale". Design showing Walt Disney cartoon characters. Multicoloured.

1254 10c. Type **246** 30 30
1255 25c. Pluto 45 45
1256 30c. Mickey Mouse playing ukelele 45 45
1257 70c. Donald Duck and nephew 80 80
1258 $1 Mordie and Ferdie carol singing . . . . 80 1·00
1259 $1 Goofy carol singing . . . 80 1·00
1260 $1 Chip n'Dale sliding off roof . . . . 80 1·00
1261 $1 Two of Donald Duck's nephews at window . . . 80 1·00
1262 $1 As 10c. . . . . 80 1·00
1263 $1 As 25c. . . . . 80 1·00
1264 $1 As 30c. . . . . 80 1·00
1265 $1 As 70c. . . . . 80 1·00
MS1266 Two sheets, each 127 × 102 mm. (a) $7 Donald Duck playing trumpet and Mickey and Minnie Mouse in carriage. (b) $7 Mickey Mouse and friends singing carols on roller skates (horiz) Set of 2 sheets 8·50 8·50

Nos. 1258/65 were printed together, se-tenant, forming a composite design.

247 Arawak Warriors

1989. 500th Anniv of Discovery of America by Columbus (1992) (2nd issue). Pre-Columbian Arawak Society. Multicoloured.

1267 $1.50 Type **247** . . . . . . 1·10 1·40
1268 $1.50 Whip dancers . . . . 1·10 1·40
1269 $1.50 Whip dancers and chief with pineapple . . . 1·10 1·40
1270 $1.50 Family and camp fire 1·10 1·40
MS1271 71 × 84 mm. $6 Arawak chief 2·75 3·00

Nos. 1267/70 were printed together, se-tenant, forming a composite design.

248 De Havilland Comet 4 Airliner

1989. 50th Anniv of First Jet Flight. Mult.

1272 10c. Type **248** 80 45
1273 30c. Messerschmitt Me 262 fighter . . . . 1·40 45
1274 40c. Boeing 707 airliner . . 1·40 45
1275 60c. Canadair CL-13 Sabre (inscr "F-86") fighter . . 1·75 55
1276 $1 Lockheed F-104 Starfighters . . . . 2·00 90
1277 $2 McDonnell Douglas DC-10 airliner . . . . . 2·75 2·75
1278 $3 Boeing 747-300/400 airliner . . . . 3·00 4·25
1279 $4 McDonnell Douglas F-4 Phantom II fighter . . . 3·00 4·25
MS1280 Two sheets, each 114 × 83 mm. (a) $7 Grumman F-14A Tomcat fighter. (b) $7 Concorde airliner Set of 2 sheets 9·50 11·00

249 "Festivale"

1989. Caribbean Cruise Ships. Multicoloured.

1281 25c. Type **249** . . . . . . 1·25 40
1282 45c. "Southward" . . . . . 1·50 40
1283 50c. "Sagafjord" . . . . . 1·50 40
1284 60c. "Daphne" . . . . . . 1·50 50
1285 75c. "Cunard Countess" . . 1·75 1·00
1286 90c. "Song of America" . . 1·75 1·10
1287 $3 "Island Princess" . . . . 3·25 4·50
1288 $4 "Galileo" . . . . 3·25 4·50
MS1289 (a) 113 × 87 mm. $6 "Norway". (b) 111 × 82 mm. $6 "Oceanic" Set of 2 sheets 6·50 8·00

250 "Fish swimming by Duck half-submerged in Stream"

1989. Japanese Art. Paintings by Hiroshige. Mult.

1290 25c. Type **250** 80 30
1291 45c. "Crane and Wave" . . 1·00 40
1292 50c. "Sparrows and Morning Glories" . . . . 1·10 40
1293 60c. "Crested Blackbird and Flowering Cherry" . . . 1·25 50
1294 $1 "Great Knot sitting among Water Grass" . . 1·50 70
1295 $2 "Goose on a Bank of Water" . . . . 2·25 2·25
1296 $3 "Black Paradise Flycatcher and Blossoms" 2·75 2·75
1297 $4 "Sleepy Owl perched on a Pine Branch" . . . . . 2·75 2·75
MS1298 Two sheets, each 102 × 75 mm. (a) $5 "Bullfinch flying near a Clematis Branch". (b) $5 "Titmouse on a Cherry Branch" Set of 2 sheets 9·00 8·50

251 Mickey and Minnie Mouse in Helicopter over River Seine

1989. "Philexfrance 89" International Stamp Exhibition, Paris. Walt Disney cartoon characters in Paris. Multicoloured.

1299 1c. Type **251** 10 10
1300 2c. Goofy and Mickey Mouse passing Arc de Triomphe 10 10
1301 3c. Mickey Mouse painting picture of Notre Dame . . 10 10
1302 4c. Mickey and Minnie Mouse with Pluto leaving Metro station 10 10
1303 5c. Minnie Mouse as model in fashion show 10 10
1304 10c. Daisy Duck, Minnie Mouse and Clarabelle as Folies Bergere dancers . . 10 10
1305 $5 Mickey and Minnie Mouse shopping in street market . . . . 6·50 6·50
1306 $6 Mickey and Minnie Mouse, Jose Carioca and Donald Duck at pavement cafe . . . . 6·50 6·50
MS1307 Two sheets, each 127 × 101 mm. (a) $5 Mickey and Minnie Mouse in hot air balloon. (b) $5 Mickey Mouse at Pompidou Centre cafe (vert) Set of 2 sheets 11·00 12·00

252 Goalkeeper

1989. World Cup Football Championship, Italy (1990). Multicoloured.

1308 15c. Type **252** 85 30
1309 25c. Goalkeeper moving towards ball 90 30
1310 $1 Goalkeeper reaching for ball . . . . 2·00 1·25
1311 $4 Goalkeeper saving goal 3·50 5·00
MS1312 Two sheets, each 75 × 105 mm. (a) $5 Three players competing for ball (horiz). (b) $5 Ball and player' legs (horiz) Set of 2 sheets 8·00 9·00

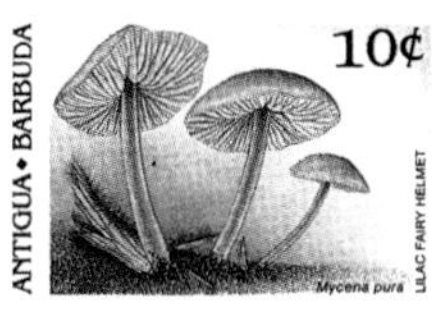

253 "Mycena pura"

1989. Fungi. Multicoloured.

1313 10c. Type **253** 75 50
1314 25c. "Psathyrella tuberculata" (vert) . . . . 1·10 40
1315 50c. "Psilocybe cubensis" . . 1·50 60
1316 60c. "Leptonia caeruleocapitata" (vert) 1·50 70
1317 75c. "Xeromphalina tenuipes" (vert) . . . . . 1·75 1·10
1318 $1 "Chlorophyllum molybdites" (vert) . . . . 1·75 1·25
1319 $3 "Marasmius haematocephalus" . . . . 2·75 3·75
1320 $4 "Cantharellus cinnabarinus" . . . . . 2·75 3·75
MS1321 Two sheets, each 88 × 62 mm. (a) $6 "Leucopaxillus gracillimus" (vert). (b) $6 "Volvariella volvacea" Set of 2 sheets 13·00 14·00

254 Desmarest's Hutia

1989. Local Fauna. Multicoloured.

1322 25c. Type **254** 80 50
1323 45c. Caribbean monk seal 2·50 1·00
1324 80c. Mustache bat (vert) . . 1·50 1·00
1325 $4 American manatee (vert) 3·50 5·50
MS1326 113 × 87 mm. $5 West Indian giant rice rat 7·00 8·50

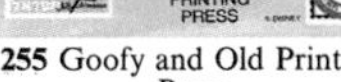

255 Goofy and Old Printing Press

258 Launch of "Apollo II"

256 Mickey Mouse and Donald Duck with Camden and Amboy Locomotive "John Bull", 1831

1989. "American Philately". Walt Disney cartoon characters with stamps and the logo of the American Philatelic Society. Multicoloured.

1327 1c. Type **255** 10 10
1328 2c. Donald Duck cancelling first day cover for Mickey Mouse 10 10
1329 3c. Donald Duck's nephews reading recruiting poster for Pony Express riders 10 10
1330 4c. Morty and Ferdie as early radio broadcasters 10 10
1331 5c. Donald Duck and water buffalo watching television 10 10
1332 10c. Donald Duck with stamp album 10 10
1333 $4 Daisy Duck with computer system . . . . 4·50 5·50
1334 $6 Donald's nephews with stereo radio, trumpet and guitar . . . . 5·50 6·50
MS1335 Two sheets, each 127 × 102 mm. (a) $5 Donald's nephews donating stamps to charity. (b) $5 Minnie Mouse flying mailplane upside down (horiz) Set of 2 sheets 11·00 12·00

1989. "World Stamp Expo '89" International Stamp Exhibition, Washington. Walt Disney cartoon characters and locomotives. Mult.

1336 25c. Type **256** 80 50
1337 45c. Mickey Mouse and friends with "Atlantic", 1832 . . . . 1·00 50
1338 50c. Mickey Mouse and Goofy with "William Crooks", 1861 . . . . . 1·00 50
1339 60c. Mickey Mouse and Goofy with "Minnetonka", 1869 . . . 1·00 65
1340 $1 Chip n'Dale with "Thatcher Perkins", 1863 1·25 75
1341 $2 Mickey and Minnie Mouse with "Pioneer", 1848 . . . . 2·00 2·25
1342 $3 Mickey Mouse and Donald Duck with cog railway locomotive "Peppersass", 1869 . . . 2·25 3·50
1343 $4 Mickey Mouse with Huey, Dewey and Louie aboard N.Y. World's Fair "Gimbels Flyer", 1939 . . 2·50 3·50
MS1344 Two sheets, each 127 × 101 mm. (a) $6 Mickey Mouse and locomotive "Thomas Jefferson", 1835 (vert). (b) $6 Mickey Mouse and friends at Central Pacific "Golden Spike" ceremony, 1869 Set of 2 sheets 7·50 8·50

1989. 20th Anniv of First Manned Landing on Moon. Multicoloured.

1346 10c. Type **258** 50 30
1347 45c. Aldrin on Moon . . . 1·25 30
1348 $1 Module "Eagle" over Moon (horiz) . . . . . . 1·75 1·10
1349 $4 Recovery of "Apollo II" crew after splashdown (horiz) . . . . 2·75 5·00
MS1350 107 × 77 mm. $5 Astronaut Neil Armstrong 4·00 4·75

259 "The Small Cowper Madonna" (Raphael)

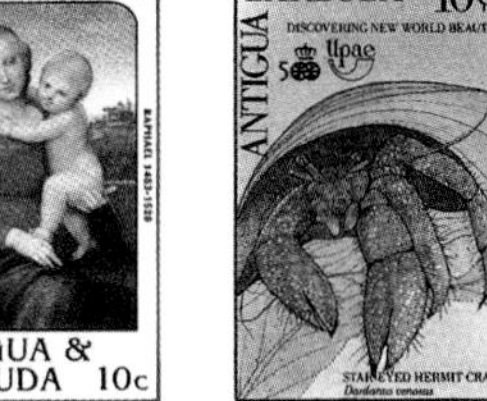

260 Star-eyed Hermit Crab

1989. Christmas. Paintings by Raphael and Giotto. Multicoloured.

1351 10c. Type **259** 30 15
1352 25c. "Madonna of the Goldfinch" (Raphael) . . 45 20
1353 30c. "The Alba Madonna" (Raphael) 45 20
1354 50c. Saint (detail, "Bologna Altarpiece") (Giotto) . . 65 30
1355 60c. Angel (detail, "Bologna Altarpiece") (Giotto) . . 70 35
1356 70c. Angel slaying serpent (detail, "Bologna Altarpiece") (Giotto) . . 80 40
1357 $4 Evangelist (detail, "Bologna Altarpiece") (Giotto) . . . . 3·00 4·25
1358 $5 "Madonna of Foligno" (detail) (Raphael) . . . . 3·00 4·25
MS1359 Two sheets, each 71 × 96 mm. (a) $5 "The Marriage of the Virgin" (detail) (Raphael). (b) $5 Madonna and Child (detail, "Bologna Altarpiece") (Giotto) Set of 2 sheets 9·00 11·00

1990. 500th Anniv (1992) of Discovery of America by Columbus (3rd issue). New World Natural History–Marine Life. Multicoloured.

1360 10c. Type **260** 45 20
1361 20c. Spiny lobster 65 25
1362 25c. Magnificent banded fanworm 65 25
1363 45c. Cannonball jellyfish . . 80 40
1364 60c. Red-spiny sea star . . . 1·00 60
1365 $2 Peppermint shrimp . . . 2·00 2·50

1366 $3 Coral crab . . . . 2·25 3·50
1367 $4 Branching fire coral . . . 2·25 3·50
MS1368 Two sheets, each 100×69 mm. (a) $5 Common sea fan. (b) $5 Portuguese man-of-war Set of 2 sheets 8·00 8·50

261 "Vanilla mexicana" **262** Queen Victoria and Queen Elizabeth II

1990. "Expo '90" International Garden and Greenery Exhibition, Osaka. Orchids. Multicoloured.
1369 15c. Type **261** 75 50
1370 45c. "Epidendrum ibaguense" . . . . 1·10 50
1371 50c. "Epidendrum secundum" . . . . 1·25 55
1372 60c. "Maxillaria conferta" 1·40 55
1373 $1 "Oncidium altissimum" 1·50 1·00
1374 $2 "Spiranthes lanceolata" 2·00 2·50
1375 $3 "Tonopsis utricularioides" . . . . . 2·25 3·50
1376 $5 "Epidendrum nocturnum" . . . . . . 3·25 4·50
MS1377 Two sheets, each 102×70 mm. (a) $6 "Octomeria graminifolia". (b) $6 "Rodriguezia lanceolata" Set of 2 sheets 6·50 8·00

1990. 150th Anniv of the Penny Black.
1378 **262** 45c. green 85 40
1379 – 60c. mauve . . . . . . 1·00 65
1380 – $5 blue . . . . 3·50 5·50
MS1381 102×80 mm. Type **262** $6 purple 4·25 5·50
DESIGNS: 60c., $5 As Type **262**, but with different backgrounds.

263 "Britannia" (mail paddle-steamer), 1840

1990. "Stamp World London '90" International Stamp Exhibition.
1382 **263** 50c. green and red . . . 85 35
1383 – 75c. brown and red . . . 1·10 90
1384 – $4 blue and red . . . . 3·75 5·50
MS1385 – 104×81 mm. $6 brown and red 3·50 5·00
DESIGNS: 75c. Travelling Post Office sorting van, 1892; $4 Short S.23 Empire "C" Class flying boat "Centaurus", 1938; $6 Post Office underground railway, London, 1927.

264 Flamefish

1990. Reef Fishes. Multicoloured.
1386 10c. Type **264** 65 55
1387 15c. Coney 80 55
1388 50c. Long-spined squirrelfish 1·25 60
1389 60c. Sergeant major . . . . 1·25 60
1390 $1 Yellow-tailed snapper . . 1·50 85
1391 $2 Rock beauty . . . . . . 2·25 2·75
1392 $3 Spanish hogfish . . . . 2·75 3·75
1393 $4 Striped parrotfish . . . . 2·75 3·75
MS1394 Two sheets, each 90×70 mm. (a) $5 Black-barred soldierfish. (b) $4 Four-eyed butterflyfish Set of 2 sheets 10·00 11·00

265 "Voyager 2" passing Saturn **266** Queen Mother in Evening Dress

1990. Achievement in Space. Multicoloured.
1395 45c. Type **265** 85 85
1396 45c. "Pioneer 11" photographing Saturn . . 85 85
1397 45c. Astronaut in transporter 85 85
1398 45c. Space shuttle "Columbia" 85 85
1399 45c. "Apollo 10" command module on parachutes . . 85 85
1400 45c. "Skylab" space station 85 85
1401 45c. Astronaut Edward White in space 85 85
1402 45c. "Apollo" spacecraft on joint mission 85 85
1403 45c. "Soyuz" spacecraft on joint mission 85 85
1404 45c. "Mariner 1" passing Venus 85 85
1405 45c. "Gemini 4" capsule . . 85 85
1406 45c. "Sputnik 1" 85 85
1407 45c. Hubble space telescope 85 85
1408 45c. North American X-15 rocket plane 85 85
1409 45c. Bell XS-1 airplane . . . 85 85
1410 45c. "Apollo 17" astronaut and lunar rock formation 85 85
1411 45c. Lunar Rover 85 85
1412 45c. "Apollo 14" lunar module 85 85
1413 45c. Astronaut Buzz Aldrin on Moon 85 85
1414 45c. Soviet "Lunokhod" lunar vehicle 85 85

1990. 90th Birthday of Queen Elizabeth the Queen Mother.
1415 **266** 15c. multicoloured . . . 55 20
1416 – 35c. multicoloured . . . 75 25
1417 – 75c. multicoloured . . . 1·00 85
1418 – $3 multicoloured . . . . 2·50 3·50
MS1419 – 67×98 mm. mult 4·00 4·50
DESIGNS: Nos. 1416/19, Recent photographs of the Queen Mother.

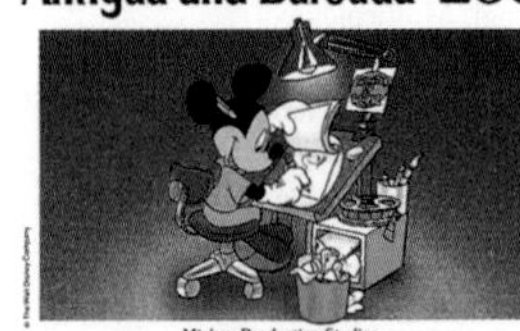

267 Mickey Mouse as Animator

1990. Mickey Mouse in Hollywood. Walt Disney cartoon characters. Multicoloured.
1420 25c. Type **267** 60 25
1421 45c. Minnie Mouse learning lines while being dressed 80 25
1422 50c. Mickey Mouse with clapper board 90 30
1423 60c. Daisy Duck making-up Mickey Mouse . . . . . 1·00 35
1424 $1 Clarabelle Cow as Cleopatra . . . . 1·25 70
1425 $2 Mickey Mouse directing Goofy and Donald Duck 1·75 2·25
1426 $3 Mickey Mouse directing Goofy as birdman . . . . 2·25 3·25
1427 $4 Donald Duck and Mickey Mouse editing film . . . . 2·25 3·25
MS1428 Two sheets, each 132×95 mm. (a) $5 Minnie Mouse, Daisy Duck and Clarabelle as musical stars. (b) $5 Mickey Mouse on set as director Set of 2 sheets. 7·00 8·00

268 Men's 20 Kilometres Walk **269** Huey and Dewey asleep ("Christmas Stories")

1990. Olympic Games, Barcelona (1992) (1st issue). Multicoloured.
1429 50c. Type **268** 75 40
1430 75c. Triple jump . . . . . 1·00 75
1431 $1 Men's 10,000 metres . . 1·25 85
1432 $5 Javelin . . . . 3·50 6·00
MS1433 100×70 mm. $6 Athlete lighting Olympic flame at Los Angeles Olympics 5·50 7·00
See also Nos. 1553/61 and 1609/17.

1990. International Literacy Year. Walt Disney cartoon characters illustrating works by Charles Dickens. Multicoloured.
1434 15c. Type **269** 65 35
1435 45c. Donald Duck as Poor Jo looking at grave ("Bleak House") . . . . 1·00 45
1436 50c. Dewey as Oliver asking for more ("Oliver Twist") 1·10 50
1437 60c. Daisy Duck as The Marchioness ("Old Curiosity Shop") . . . . 1·25 55
1438 $1 Little Nell giving nosegay to her grandfather ("Little Nell") . . . . 1·40 85
1439 $2 Scrooge McDuck as Mr. Pickwick ("Pickwick Papers") . . . . 2·00 2·25
1440 $3 Minnie Mouse as Florence and Mickey Mouse as Paul ("Dombey and Son") . . . . 2·25 3·25
1441 $5 Minnie Mouse as Jenny Wren ("Our Mutual Friend") . . . . 2·75 4·25
MS1442 Two sheets, each 126×102 mm. (a) $6 Artful Dodger picking pocket ("Oliver Twist"). (b) $6 Unexpected arrivals at Mr. Peggoty's ("David Copperfield") Set of 2 sheets 10·00 12·00

1990. World Cup Football Championship Winners, Italy. Nos. 1308/11 optd **Winners West Germany 1 Argentina 0**.
1443 15c. Type **252** 75 40
1444 25c. Goalkeeper moving towards ball 75 40
1445 $1 Goalkeeper reaching for ball . . . . 1·75 1·60
1446 $4 Goalkeeper saving goal 3·75 5·50
MS1447 Two sheets, each 75×105 mm. (a) $5 Three players competing for ball (horiz). (b) $5 Ball and players' legs (horiz) Set of 2 sheets 9·50 11·00

271 Pearly-eyed Thrasher

1990. Birds. Multicoloured.
1448 10c. Type **271** 45 30
1449 25c. Purple-throated carib 45 35
1450 50c. Common yellowthroat 50 40
1451 60c. American kestrel . . . 1·00 70
1452 $1 Yellow-bellied sapsucker 1·00 80
1453 $2 American purple gallinule ("Purple Gallinule") . . . 2·00 2·25
1454 $3 Yellow-crowned night heron . . . . 2·10 3·00
1455 $4 Blue-hooded euphonia 2·10 3·00
MS1456 Two sheets, each 76×60 mm. (a) $6 Brown pelican. (b) $6 Magnificent frigate bird Set of 2 sheets 14·00 16·00

272 "Madonna and Child with Saints" (detail, Sebastiano del Piombo)

1990. Christmas. Paintings by Renaissance Masters. Multicoloured.
1457 25c. Type **272** 60 30
1458 30c. "Virgin and Child with Angels" (detail, Grunewald) (vert) 70 30
1459 40c. "The Holy Family and a Shepherd" (detail, Titian) 80 30
1460 60c. "Virgin and Child" (detail, Lippi) (vert) . . . 1·00 40
1461 $1 "Jesus, St. John and Two Angels" (Rubens) . . . . 1·25 70
1462 $2 "Adoration of the Shepherds" (detail, Vincenzo Catena) . . . . 1·75 2·00
1463 $4 "Adoration of the Magi" (detail, Giorgione) . . . . 2·75 4·00
1464 $5 "Virgin and Child adored by Warrior" (detail, Vincenzo Catena) . . . . 2·75 4·00
MS1465 Two sheets, each 71×101 mm. (a) $6 "Allegory of the Blessings of Jacob" (detail, Rubens) (vert). (b) $6 "Adoration of the Magi" (detail, Fra Angelico) (vert) Set of 2 sheets 3·50 4·50

273 "Rape of the Daughters of Leucippus" (detail)

1991. 350th Death Anniv of Rubens. Mult.
1466 25c. Type **273** 85 40
1467 45c. "Bacchanal" (detail) . . 1·25 45
1468 50c. "Rape of the Sabine Women" (detail) . . . . 1·25 50
1469 60c. "Battle of the Amazons" (detail) . . . . 1·40 65
1470 $1 "Rape of the Sabine Women" (different detail) 1·75 1·00
1471 $2 "Bacchanal" (different detail) . . . . 2·25 2·25
1472 $3 "Rape of the Sabine Women" (different detail) 2·75 3·75
1473 $4 "Bacchanal" (different detail) . . . . 2·75 3·75
MS1474 Two sheets, each 101×71 mm. (a) $6 "Rape of Hippoda-meia" (detail). (b) $6 "Battle of the Amazons" (different detail) Set of 2 sheets 8·50 9·50

274 U.S. Troops cross into Germany, 1944

1991. 50th Anniv of Second World War. Mult.
1475 10c. Type **274** 90 55
1476 15c. Axis surrender in North Africa, 1943 . . . . . . 1·00 40
1477 25c. U.S. tanks invade Kwalajalein, 1944 . . . . 1·00 40
1478 45c. Roosevelt and Churchill meet at Casablanca, 1943 2·00 70
1479 50c. Marshal Badoglio, Prime Minister of Italian anti-fascist government, 1943 . . . . 1·25 70
1480 $1 Lord Mountbatten, Supreme Allied Commander South-east Asia, 1943 . . . . 2·50 1·25
1481 $2 Greek victory at Koritza, 1940 . . . . 2·00 2·50
1482 $4 Anglo-Soviet mutual assistance pact, 1941 . . . 2·75 3·75
1483 $5 Operation Torch landings, 1942 . . . . . 2·75 3·75
MS1484 Two sheets, each 108×80 mm. (a) $6 Japanese attack on Pearl Harbor, 1941. (b) $6 U.S.A.A.F. daylight raid on Schweinfurt, 1943 Set of 2 sheets 9·00 10·00

275 Locomotive "Prince Regent", Middleton Colliery, 1812

1991. Cog Railways. Multicoloured.
1485 25c. Type **275** . . . . . . 1·00 55
1486 30c. Snowdon Mountain Railway . . . . 1·00 55
1487 40c. First railcar at Hell Gate, Manitou Pike's Peak Railway, U.S.A . . 1·10 65
1488 60c. P.N.K.A. rack railway, Java . . . . 1·40 70
1489 $1 Green Mountain Railway, Maine, 1883 . . 1·75 1·00
1490 $2 Rack locomotive "Pike's Peak", 1891 . . . . . . 2·50 2·75
1491 $4 Vitznau–Rigi Railway, Switzerland, and Mt. Rigi hotel local post stamp . . 3·25 4·25
1492 $5 Leopoldina Railway, Brazil . . . . 3·25 4·25
MS1493 Two sheets, each 100×70 mm. (a) $6 Electric towing locomotives, Panama Canal. (b) $6 Gornergracht Railway, Switzerland (vert) Set of 2 sheets 12·00 13·00

276 "Heliconius charithonia"

1991. Butterflies. Multicoloured.
1494 10c. Type **276** 65 50
1495 35c. "Marpesia petreus" . . 1·10 50
1496 50c. "Anartia amathea" . . 1·25 60
1497 75c. "Siproeta stelenes" . . 1·50 1·00
1498 $1 "Battus polydamas" . . 1·75 1·10
1499 $2 "Historis odius" . . . . 2·25 2·75
1500 $4 "Hypolimnas misippus" 3·25 4·25
1501 $5 "Hamadryas feronia" . . 3·25 4·25
MS1502 Two sheets. (a) 73×100 mm. $6 "Vanessa cardui" caterpillar (vert) (b) 100×73 mm. $6 "Danaus plexippus" caterpillar (vert) Set of 2 sheets 14·00 16·00

277 Hanno the Phoenician, 450 B.C.

1991. 500th Anniv of Discovery of America by Columbus (1992) (4th issue). History of Exploration.

1503 **277** 10c. multicoloured . . . 60 40
1504 – 15c. multicoloured . . . 70 40
1505 – 45c. multicoloured . . . 1·00 50
1506 – 60c. multicoloured . . . 1·25 60
1507 – $1 multicoloured . . . . 1·50 85
1508 – $2 multicoloured . . . . 2·00 2·50
1509 – $4 multicoloured . . . . 2·75 3·75
1510 – $5 multicoloured . . . . 2·75 3·75
MS1511 – Two sheets, each 106 × 76 mm. (a) $6 black and red. (b) $6 black and red Set of 2 sheets 7·00 8·00

DESIGNS—HORIZ: 15c. Pytheas the Greek, 325 B.C.; 45c. Erik the Red discovering Greenland, 985 A.D.; 60c. Leif Eriksson reaching Vinland, 1000 A.D.; $1 Scylax the Greek in the Indian Ocean, 518 A.D.; $2 Marco Polo sailing to the Orient, 1259 A.D.; $4 Ship of Queen Hatshepsut of Egypt, 1493 B.C.; $5 St. Brendan's coracle, 500 A.D. VERT: $6 (No. **MS**1511a) Engraving of Columbus as Admiral; $6 (No. **MS**1511b) Engraving of Columbus bare-headed.

278 "Camille Roulin" (Van Gogh)

1991. Death Centenary (1990) of Vincent van Gogh (artist). Multicoloured.

1512 5c. Type **278** 60 75
1513 10c. "Armand Roulin" . . . 60 60
1514 15c. "Young Peasant Woman with Straw Hat sitting in the Wheat" . . 75 50
1515 25c. "Adeline Ravoux" . . . 85 50
1516 30c. "The Schoolboy" . . . 85 50
1517 40c. "Doctor Gachet" . . . 95 50
1518 50c. "Portrait of a Man" . . 1·00 50
1519 75c. "Two Children" . . . 1·60 80
1520 $2 "The Postman Joseph Roulin" . . . . 2·50 2·50
1521 $3 "The Seated Zouave" . . 3·00 3·75
1522 $4 "L'Arlesienne" . . . . . 3·25 4·00
1523 $5 "Self-Portrait, November/December 1888" . . . . 3·25 4·00
MS1524 Three sheets, each 102 × 76 mm. (a) $5 "Farmhouse in Provence" (horiz). (b) $5 "Flowering Garden" (horiz). (c) $6 "The Bridge at Trinquetaille" (horiz) Imperf Set of 3 sheets 12·00 13·00

279 Mickey Mouse as Champion Sumo Wrestler

1991. "Philanippon '91" International Stamp Exhibition, Tokyo. Walt Disney cartoon characters participating in martial arts. Multicoloured.

1525 10c. Type **279** 60 20
1526 15c. Goofy using the tonfa (horiz) 75 25
1527 45c. Donald Duck as a Ninja (horiz) . . . . . 1·25 50
1528 60c. Mickey armed for Kung fu . . . . 1·60 65
1529 $1 Goofy with Kendo sword 2·00 1·25
1530 $2 Mickey and Donald demonstrating Aikido (horiz) . . . . 2·50 2·50
1531 $4 Mickey and Donald in Judo bout (horiz) . . . . 3·25 4·50
1532 $5 Mickey performing Yabusame (mounted archery) . . . . 3·25 4·50
MS1533 Two sheets, each 127 × 102 mm. (a) $6 Mickey delivering Karate kick (horiz). (b) $6 Mickey demonstrating Tamashiwara Set of 2 sheets 9·00 10·00

280 Queen Elizabeth and Prince Philip in 1976

1991. 65th Birthday of Queen Elizabeth II. Multicoloured.

1534 15c. Type **280** 30 10
1535 20c. The Queen and Prince Philip in Portugal, 1985 30 10
1536 $2 Queen Elizabeth II . . . 1·50 1·50
1537 $4 The Queen and Prince Philip at Ascot, 1986 . . 2·75 3·25
MS1538 68 × 90 mm. $4 The Queen at National Theatre, 1986, and Prince Philip 3·00 4·00

1991. 10th Wedding Anniv of Prince and Princess of Wales. As T **280**. Multicoloured.

1539 10c. Prince and Princess of Wales at party, 1986 . . . 40 10
1540 40c. Separate portraits of Prince, Princess and sons 80 25
1541 $1 Prince Henry and Prince William . . . . 1·10 70
1542 $5 Princess Diana in Australia and Prince Charles in Hungary . . . 4·25 4·50
MS1543 68 × 90 mm. $4 Prince Charles in Hackney and Princess and sons in Majorca, 1987 5·00 5·50

281 Daisy Duck teeing-off

1991. Golf. Walt Disney cartoon characters. Mult.

1544 10c. Type **281** 70 50
1545 15c. Goofy playing ball from under trees 75 50
1546 45c. Mickey Mouse playing deflected shot . . . . . . 1·25 50
1547 60c. Mickey hacking divot out of fairway . . . . . 1·50 65
1548 $1 Donald Duck playing ball out of pond . . . . 1·75 1·10
1549 $2 Minnie Mouse hitting ball over pond . . . . . 2·50 2·75
1550 $4 Donald in a bunker . . . 3·25 4·00
1551 $5 Goofy trying snooker shot into hole . . . . . . 3·25 4·00
MS1552 Two sheets, each 127 × 102 mm. (a) $6 Grandma Duck in senior tournament. (b) $6 Mickey and Minnie Mouse on course (horiz) Set of 2 sheets 10·00 12·00

282 Moose receiving Gold Medal

1991. 50th Anniv of Archie Comics, and Olympic Games, Barcelona (1992) (2nd issue). Multicoloured.

1553 10c. Type **282** 55 40
1554 25c. Archie playing polo on a motorcycle (horiz) . . . 85 40
1555 40c. Archie and Betty at fencing class . . . . . . 1·10 45
1556 60c. Archie joining girls' volleyball team . . . . . 1·40 65
1557 $1 Archie with tennis ball in his mouth . . . . 1·75 1·10
1558 $2 Archie running marathon 2·50 3·00
1559 $4 Archie judging women's gymnastics (horiz) . . . . 3·75 4·50
1560 $5 Archie watching the cheer-leaders . . . . . . 3·75 4·50
MS1561 Two sheets, each 128 × 102 mm. (a) $6 Archie heading football. (b) $6 Archie catching baseball (horiz) Set of 2 sheets 11·00 12·00

283 Presidents De Gaulle and Kennedy, 1961

1991. Birth Centenary of Charles de Gaulle (French statesman). Multicoloured.

1562 10c. Type **283** 70 40
1563 15c. General De Gaulle with President Roosevelt, 1945 (vert) 70 40
1564 45c. President De Gaulle with Chancellor Adenauer, 1962 (vert) . . 1·10 40
1565 60c. De Gaulle at Arc de Triomphe, Liberation of Paris, 1944 (vert) . . . . 1·25 65
1566 $1 General De Gaulle crossing the Rhine, 1945 1·50 1·10
1567 $2 General De Gaulle in Algiers, 1944 . . . . . . 2·25 2·75
1568 $4 Presidents De Gaulle and Eisenhower, 1960 . . . . 3·00 4·00
1569 $5 De Gaulle returning from Germany, 1968 (vert) . . 3·00 4·00
MS1570 Two sheets. (a) 76 × 106 mm. $6 De Gaulle with crowd. (b) 106 × 76 mm. $6 De Gaulle and Churchill at Casablanca, 1943 Set of 2 sheets 12·00 13·00

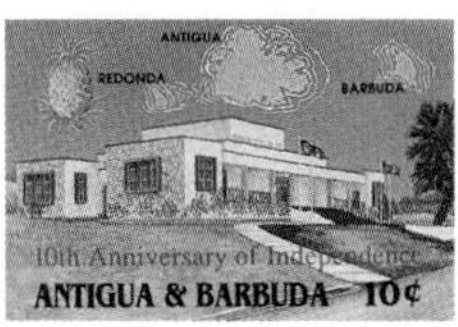

284 Parliament Building and Map

1991. 10th Anniv of Independence.

1571 **284** 10c. multicoloured . . . 75 50
MS1572 87 × 97 mm. $6 Old Post Office, St. Johns, and stamps of 1862 and 1981 (50 × 37 mm) 6·00 7·50

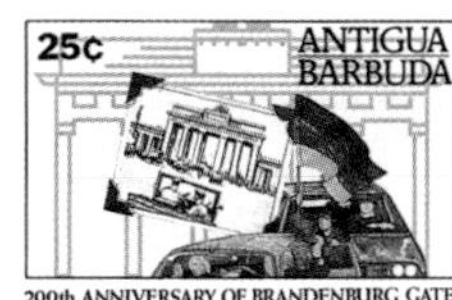

285 Germans celebrating Reunification

1991. Anniversaries and Events. Multicoloured.

1573 25c. Type **285** 30 30
1574 75c. Cubs erecting tent . . . 50 50
1575 $1.50 "Don Giovanni" and Mozart . . . . 3·50 2·25
1576 $2 Chariot driver and Gate at night . . . . 1·10 2·00
1577 $2 Lord Baden-Powell and members of 3rd Antigua Methodist cub pack (vert) 2·75 2·25
1578 $2 Lilienthal's signature and glider "Flugzeug Nr. 5" 3·00 2·25
1579 $2.50 Driver in Class P36 steam locomotive (vert) 4·00 3·25
1580 $3 Statues from podium . . 1·75 2·75
1581 $3.50 Cubs and camp fire 2·25 2·75
1582 $4 St. Peter's Cathedral, Salzburg . . . . 5·50 5·00
MS1583 Two sheets. (a) 100 × 72 mm. $4 Detail of chariot and helmet; (b) 89 × 117 mm. $5 Antiguan flag and Jamboree emblem (vert) Set of 2 sheets 8·00 10·00

ANNIVERSARIES AND EVENTS: Nos. 1573, 1576, 1580, **MS**1583a, Bicentenary of Brandenburg Gate, Germany; 1574, 1577, 1581, **MS**1583b, 17th World Scout Jamboree, Korea; 1575, 1582, Death bicentenary of Mozart (composer); 1578, Centenary of Otto Lilienthal's gliding experiments; 1579, Centenary of Trans-Siberian Railway.

286 "Nimitz" Class Carrier and "Ticonderoga" Class Cruiser

1991. 50th Anniv of Japanese Attack on Pearl Harbor. Multicoloured.

1585 $1 Type **286** . . . . . . 1·50 1·50
1586 $1 Tourist launch . . . . . 1·50 1·50
1587 $1 U.S.S. "Arizona" memorial . . . . 1·50 1·50
1588 $1 Wreaths on water and aircraft . . . . 1·50 1·50
1589 $1 White tern . . . . 1·50 1·50
1590 $1 Mitsubishi A6M Zero-Sen fighters over Pearl City . . . . 1·50 1·50
1591 $1 Mitsubishi A6M Zero-Sen fighters attacking . . 1·50 1·50
1592 $1 Battleship Row in flames 1·50 1·50

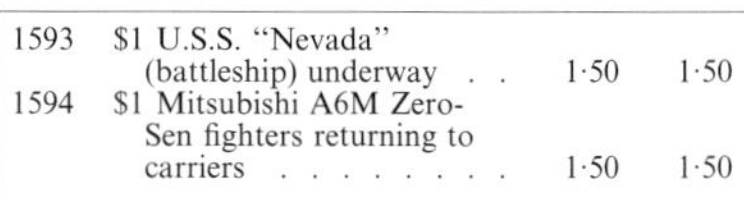
1593 $1 U.S.S. "Nevada" (battleship) underway . . 1·50 1·50
1594 $1 Mitsubishi A6M Zero-Sen fighters returning to carriers . . . . 1·50 1·50

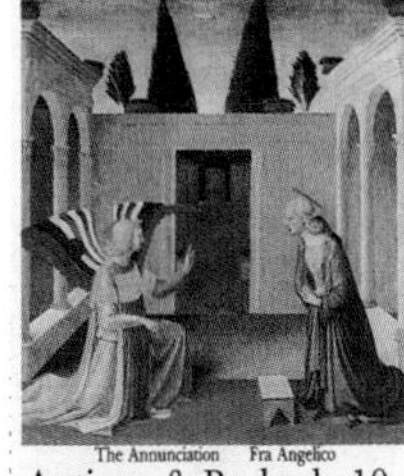

287 "The Annunciation"

1991. Christmas. Religious Paintings by Fra Angelico. Multicoloured.

1595 10c. Type **287** 40 30
1596 30c. "Nativity" 65 30
1597 40c. "Adoration of the Magi" 75 30
1598 60c. "Presentation in the Temple" . . . . 1·00 45
1599 $1 "Circumcision" . . . . 1·25 65
1600 $3 "Flight into Egypt" . . . 2·50 3·50
1601 $4 "Massacre of the Innocents" . . . . 2·50 3·75
1602 $5 "Christ teaching in the Temple" . . . . 2·50 3·75
MS1603 Two sheets, each 102 × 127 mm. (a) $6 "Adoration of the Magi" (Cook Tondo). (b) $6 "Adoration of the Magi" (different) Set of 2 sheets 11·00 13·00

288 Queen Elizabeth II and Bird Sanctuary

1992. 40th Anniv of Queen Elizabeth II's Accession. Multicoloured.

1604 10c. Type **288** 75 40
1605 30c. Nelson's Dockyard . . 90 40
1606 $1 Ruins on Shirley Heights 1·00 70
1607 $5 Beach and palm trees . . 2·75 3·75
MS1608 Two sheets, each 75 × 98 mm. (a) $6 Beach. (b) $6 Hillside foliage Set of 2 sheets 8·50 9·00

289 Mickey Mouse awarding Swimming Gold Medal to Mermaid

1992. Olympic Games, Barcelona (3rd issue). Walt Disney cartoon characters. Multicoloured.

1609 10c. Type **289** 50 30
1610 15c. Huey, Dewey and Louie with kayak 60 30
1611 30c. Donald Duck and Uncle Scrooge in yacht 75 35
1612 50c. Donald and horse playing water polo . . . 95 50
1613 $1 Big Pete weightlifting . . 1·50 85
1614 $2 Donald and Goofy fencing . . . . 2·00 2·00
1615 $4 Mickey and Donald playing volleyball . . . . 2·75 3·50
1616 $5 Goofy vaulting . . . . . 2·75 3·50
MS1617 Four sheets, each 123 × 98 mm. (a) $6 Mickey playing football. (b) $6 Mickey playing basketball (horiz). (c) $6 Minnie Mouse on uneven parallel bars (horiz). (d) $6 Mickey, Goofy and Donald judging gymnastics (horiz) Set of 4 sheets 14·00 15·00

290 Pteranodon

1992. Prehistoric Animals. Mult.

1618 10c. Type **290** 65 40
1619 15c. Brachiosaurus 65 40
1620 30c. Tyrannosaurus Rex 85 40
1621 50c. Parasaurolophus 1·00 50
1622 $1 Deinonychus (horiz) 1·50 1·00
1623 $2 Triceratops (horiz) 2·00 2·00
1624 $4 Protoceratops hatching (horiz) 2·25 2·75
1625 $5 Stegosaurus (horiz) 2·25 2·75
MS1626 Two sheets, each 100 × 70 mm. (a) $6 Apatosaurus (horiz). (b) $6 Allosaurus (horiz) Set of 2 sheets 8·50 9·50

291 "Supper at Emmaus" (Caravaggio)

1992. Easter. Religious Paintings. Multicoloured.

1627 10c. Type **291** 45 25
1628 15c. "The Vision of St. Peter" (Zurbaran) 55 25
1629 30c. "Christ driving the Money-changers from the Temple" (Tiepolo) 75 40
1630 40c. "Martyrdom of St. Bartholomew" (detail) (Ribera) 85 50
1631 $1 "Christ driving the Money-changers from the Temple" (detail) (Tiepolo) 1·50 1·00
1632 $2 "Crucifixion" (detail) (Altdorfer) 2·50 2·50
1633 $4 "The Deposition" (detail) (Fra Angelico) 3·25 4·00
1634 $5 "The Deposition" (different detail) (Fra Angelico) 3·25 4·00
MS1635 Two sheets. (a) 102 × 71 mm. $6 "The Last Supper" (detail, Masip). (b) 71 × 102 mm. $6 "Crucifixion" (detail, Altdorfer) (vert) Set of 2 sheets 9·50 11·00

292 "The Miracle at the Well" (Alonso Cano)

1992. "Granada '92" International Stamp Exhibition, Spain. Spanish Paintings. Multicoloured.

1636 10c. Type **292** 40 30
1637 15c. "The Poet Luis de Goingora y Argote" (Velazquez) 50 30
1638 30c. "The Painter Francisco Goya" (Vincente Lopez Portana) 65 40
1639 40c. "Maria de las Nieves Michaela Fourdinier" (Luis Paret y Alcazar) 75 50
1640 $1 "Carlos III eating before his Court" (Alcazar) (horiz) 1·25 1·00
1641 $2 "Rain Shower in Granada" (Antonio Munoz Degrain) (horiz) 2·00 2·50
1642 $4 "Sarah Bernhardt" (Santiago Rusinol i Prats) 3·00 3·75
1643 $5 "The Hermitage Garden" (Joaquim Mir Trinxet) 3·00 3·75
MS1644 Two sheets, each 120 × 95 mm. (a) $6 "The Ascent of Monsieur Boucle's Montgolfier Balloon in the Gardens of Aranjuez" (Antonio Carnicero) (112 × 87 mm). (b) $6 "Olympus: Battle with the Giants" (Francisco Bayeu y Subías) (112 × 87 mm). Imperf Set of 2 sheets 11·00 12·00

293 "Amanita caesarea"

1992. Fungi. Multicoloured.

1645 10c. Type **293** 70 40
1646 15c. "Collybia fusipes" 85 40
1647 30c. "Boletus aereus" 1·25 40
1648 40c. "Laccaria amethystina" 1·25 50
1649 $1 "Russula virescens" 2·00 1·25
1650 $2 "Tricholoma equestre" ("Tricholoma auratum") 2·75 2·75
1651 $4 "Calocybe gambosa" 3·50 3·75
1652 $5 "Lentinus tigrinus" ("Panus tigrinus") 3·50 3·75
MS1653 Two sheets, each 100 × 70 mm. (a) $6 "Clavariadelphus truncatus". (b) $6 "Auricularia auricula-judae" Set of 2 sheets 12·00 13·00

294 Memorial Cross and Huts, San Salvador

1992. 500th Anniv of Discovery of America by Columbus (5th issue). World Columbian Stamp "Expo '92", Chicago. Multicoloured.

1654 15c. Type **294** 30 20
1655 30c. Martin Pinzon with telescope 45 25
1656 40c. Christopher Columbus 55 35
1657 $1 "Pinta" 2·25 1·00
1658 $2 "Nina" 2·50 2·50
1659 $4 "Santa Maria" 3·25 5·00
MS1660 Two sheets, each 108 × 76 mm. (a) $6 Ship and map of West Indies. (b) $6 Sea monster Set of 2 sheets 8·50 10·00

295 Antillean Crested Hummingbird and Wild Plantain

1992. "Genova '92" International Thematic Stamp Exhibition. Hummingbirds and Plants. Multicoloured.

1661 10c. Type **295** 35 50
1662 25c. Green mango and parrot's plantain 50 40
1663 45c. Purple-throated carib and lobster claws 70 45
1664 60c. Antillean mango and coral plant 80 55
1665 $1 Vervain hummingbird and cardinal's guard 1·10 85
1666 $2 Rufous-breasted hermit and heliconia 1·75 2·00
1667 $4 Blue-headed hummingbird and red ginger 3·00 3·25
1668 $5 Green-throated carib and ornamental banana 3·00 3·25
MS1669 Two sheets, each 100 × 70 mm. (a) $6 Bee hummingbird and jungle flame. (b) $6 Western streamertail and bignonia Set of 2 sheets 10·00 11·00

296 Columbus meeting Amerindians

1992. 500th Anniv of Discovery of America by Columbus (6th issue). Organization of East Caribbean States. Multicoloured.

1670 $1 Type **296** 85 65
1671 $2 Ships approaching island 1·40 1·60

297 Ts'ai Lun and Paper

1992. Inventors and Inventions. Mult.

1672 10c. Type **297** 25 25
1673 25c. Igor Sikorsky and "Bolshoi Baltiskii" (first four-engined airplane) 1·00 40
1674 30c. Alexander Graham Bell and early telephone 55 45
1675 40c. Johannes Gutenberg and early printing press 55 45
1676 60c. James Watt and stationary steam engine 2·25 1·00
1677 $1 Anton van Leeuwenhoek and early microscope 1·25 1·10
1678 $4 Louis Braille and hands reading braille 3·75 4·50
1679 $5 Galileo and telescope 3·75 4·50
MS1680 Two sheets, each 100 × 73 mm. (a) $6 Edison and Latimer's phonograph. (b) $6 "Clermont" (first commercial paddle-steamer) Set of 2 sheets 9·50 11·00

298 Elvis looking Pensive

1992. 15th Death Anniv of Elvis Presley. Mult.

1681 $1 Type **298** 1·40 1·00
1682 $1 Wearing black and yellow striped shirt 1·40 1·00
1683 $1 Singing into microphone 1·40 1·00
1684 $1 Wearing wide-brimmed hat 1·40 1·00
1685 $1 With microphone in right hand 1·40 1·00
1686 $1 In Army uniform 1·40 1·00
1687 $1 Wearing pink shirt 1·40 1·00
1688 $1 In yellow shirt 1·40 1·00
1689 $1 In jacket and bow tie 1·40 1·00

299 Madison Square Gardens

1992. Postage Stamp Mega Event, New York. Sheet 100 × 70 mm.

MS1690 $6 multicoloured 4·25 5·50

300 "Virgin and Child with Angels" (detail) (School of Piero della Francesca)

301 Russian Cosmonauts

1992. Christmas. Details of the Holy Child from various paintings. Multicoloured.

1691 10c. Type **300** 60 30
1692 25c. "Madonna degli Alberelli" (Giovanni Bellini) 90 30
1693 30c. "Madonna and Child with St. Anthony Abbot and St. Sigismund" (Neroccio) 95 30
1694 40c. "Madonna and the Grand Duke" (Raphael) 1·00 30
1695 60c. "The Nativity" (Georges de la Tour) 1·50 60
1696 $1 "Holy Family" (Jacob Jordaens) 1·75 1·00

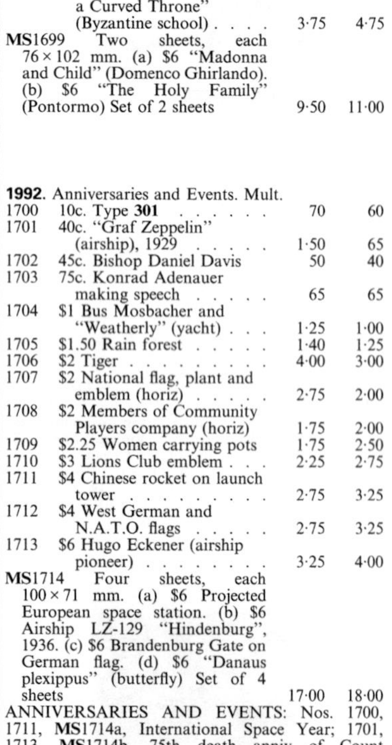

1697 $4 "Madonna and Child Enthroned" (Magaritone) 3·75 4·75
1698 $5 "Madonna and Child on a Curved Throne" (Byzantine school) 3·75 4·75
MS1699 Two sheets, each 76 × 102 mm. (a) $6 "Madonna and Child" (Domenco Ghirlando). (b) $6 "The Holy Family" (Pontormo) Set of 2 sheets 9·50 11·00

1992. Anniversaries and Events. Mult.

1700 10c. Type **301** 70 60
1701 40c. "Graf Zeppelin" (airship), 1929 1·50 65
1702 45c. Bishop Daniel Davis 50 40
1703 75c. Konrad Adenauer making speech 65 65
1704 $1 Bus Mosbacher and "Weatherly" (yacht) 1·25 1·00
1705 $1.50 Rain forest 1·40 1·25
1706 $2 Tiger 4·00 3·00
1707 $2 National flag, plant and emblem (horiz) 2·75 2·00
1708 $2 Members of Community Players company (horiz) 1·75 2·00
1709 $2.25 Women carrying pots 1·75 2·50
1710 $3 Lions Club emblem 2·25 2·75
1711 $4 Chinese rocket on launch tower 2·75 3·25
1712 $4 West German and N.A.T.O. flags 2·75 3·25
1713 $6 Hugo Eckener (airship pioneer) 3·25 4·00
MS1714 Four sheets, each 100 × 71 mm. (a) $6 Projected European space station. (b) $6 Airship LZ-129 "Hindenburg", 1936. (c) $6 Brandenburg Gate on German flag. (d) $6 "Danaus plexippus" (butterfly) Set of 4 sheets 17·00 18·00

ANNIVERSARIES AND EVENTS: Nos. 1700, 1711, **MS**1714a, International Space Year; 1701, 1713, **MS**1714b, 75th death anniv of Count Ferdinand von Zeppelin; 1702, 150th anniv of Anglican Diocese of North-eastern Caribbean and Aruba; 1703, 1712, **MS**1714c, 25th death anniv of Konrad Adenauer (German statesman); 1704, Americas Cup yachting championship; 1705/6, **MS**1714d, Earth Summit '92, Rio; 1707, 50th anniv of Inter-American Institute for Agricultural Co-operation; 1708, 40th anniv of Cultural Development; 1709, United Nations World Health Organization Projects; 1710, 75th anniv of International Association of Lions Clubs.

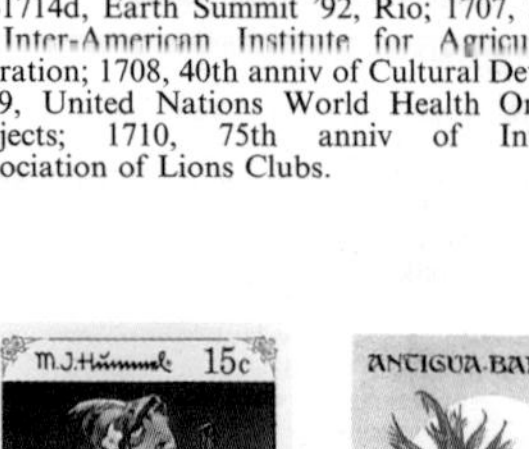

302 Boy Hiker resting

304 Cardinal's Guard

303 Goofy playing Golf

1993. Hummel Figurines. Multicoloured.

1715 15c. Type **302** 35 15
1716 30c. Girl sitting on fence 55 25
1717 40c. Boy hunter 65 35
1718 50c. Boy with umbrella 75 45
1719 $1 Hikers at signpost 1·25 75
1720 $2 Boy hiker with pack and stick 1·75 2·25
1721 $4 Girl with young child and goat 2·75 3·50
1722 $5 Boy whistling 2·75 3·50
MS1723 Two sheets, each 97 × 122 mm. (a) $1.50 × 4, As Nos. 1715/18. (b) $1.50 × 4, As Nos. 1719/22 Set of 2 sheets 13·00 14·00

1993. Opening of Euro-Disney Resort, Paris. Multicoloured.

1724 10c. Type **303** 70 30
1725 25c. Chip and Dale at Davy Crockett's campground 90 30
1726 30c. Donald Duck at the Cheyenne Hotel 90 35
1727 40c. Goofy at the Santa Fe Hotel 95 35
1728 $1 Mickey and Minnie Mouse at the New York Hotel 2·00 1·00
1729 $2 Mickey, Minnie and Goofy in car 2·50 2·50

1730 $4 Goofy at Pirates of the Caribbean . . . . 3·50 4·50
1731 $5 Donald at Adventureland 3·50 4·50
MS1732 Four sheets, each 127 × 102 mm. (a) $6 Mickey in bellboy outfit. (b) $6 Mickey on star (vert). (c) $6 Mickey on opening poster (vert) (d) $6 Mickey and balloons on opening poster (vert) Set of 2 sheets 16·00 17·00

1993. Flowers. Multicoloured.
1733 15c. Type **304** 85 30
1734 25c. Giant granadilla . . . 95 30
1735 30c. Spider flower 95 35
1736 40c. Gold vine . . . . . . 1·00 35
1737 $1 Frangipani . . . . . . 1·75 1·00
1738 $2 Bougainvillea . . . . . 2·25 2·25
1739 $4 Yellow oleander . . . . 3·25 4·00
1740 $5 Spicy jatropha . . . . . 3·25 4·00
MS1741 Two sheets, each 100 × 70 mm. (a) $6 Birdlime tree. (b) Fairy lily Set of 2 sheets 8·50 11·00

305 "The Destiny of Marie de' Medici" (upper detail)

1993. Bicentenary of the Louvre, Paris. Paintings by Peter Paul Rubens. Multicoloured.
1742 $1 Type **305** 85 85
1743 $1 "The Birth of Marie de' Medici" 85 85
1744 $1 "The Education of Marie de' Medici" 85 85
1745 $1 "The Destiny of Marie de' Medici" (lower detail) 85 85
1746 $1 "Henry VI receiving the Portrait of Marie" . . . 85 85
1747 $1 "The Meeting of the King and Marie at Lyons" 85 85
1748 $1 "The Marriage by Proxy" 85 85
1749 $1 "The Birth of Louis XIII" 85 85
1750 $1 "The Capture of Juliers" 85 85
1751 $1 "The Exchange of the Princesses" 85 85
1752 $1 "The Regency" 85 85
1753 $1 "The Majority of Louis XIII" 85 85
1754 $1 "The Flight from Blois" 85 85
1755 $1 "The Treaty of Angouleme" 85 85
1756 $1 "The Peace of Angers" 85 85
1757 $1 "The Reconciliation of Louis and Marie de' Medici" 85 85
MS1758 70 × 100 mm. $6 "Helene Faurment with a Coach" (52 × 85 mm) 5·50 7·00
Nos. 1742/57 depict details from "The Story of Marie de' Medici".

306 St. Lucia Amazon ("St. Lucia Parrot")

1993. Endangered Species. Multicoloured.
1759 $1 Type **306** 90 90
1760 $1 Cahow 90 90
1761 $1 Swallow-tailed kite . . . 90 90
1762 $1 Everglade kite ("Everglades Kite") . . . 90 90
1763 $1 Imperial amazon ("Imperial Parrot") . . . 90 90
1764 $1 Humpback whale 90 90
1765 $1 Plain pigeon ("Puerto Rican Plain Pigeon") . . 90 90
1766 $1 St. Vincent amazon ("St. Vincent Parrot") . . 90 90
1767 $1 Puerto Rican amazon ("Puerto Rican Parrot") 90 90
1768 $1 Leatherback turtle . . . 90 90
1769 $1 American crocodile . . . 90 90
1770 $1 Hawksbill turtle 90 90
MS1771 Two sheets, each 100 × 70 mm. (a) $6 As No. 1764. (b) West Indian manatee Set of 2 sheets 7·00 8·00
Nos. 1759/70 were printed together, se-tenant, with the background forming a composite design.

307 Queen Elizabeth II at Coronation (photograph by Cecil Beaton)

1993. 40th Anniv of Coronation (1st issue).
1772 **307** 30c. multicoloured . . . 50 50
1773 – 40c. multicoloured . . . 60 60
1774 – $2 blue and black . . . 1·50 1·75
1775 – $4 multicoloured . . . . 1·90 2·00
MS1776 70 × 100 mm. $6 multicoloured 4·75 5·50
DESIGNS: 40c. Queen Elizabeth the Queen Mother's Crown, 1937; $2 Procession of heralds; $4 Queen Elizabeth II and Prince Edward. (28½ × 42½ mm)—$6 "Queen Elizabeth II" (detail) (Dennis Fildes).

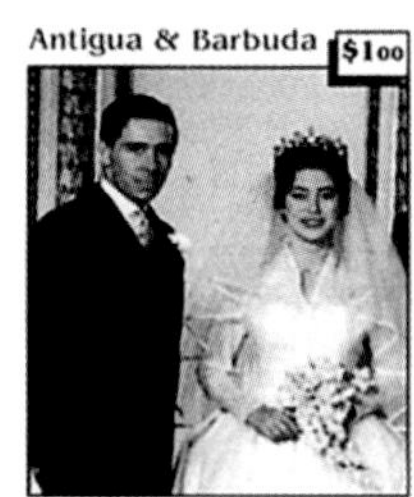

308 Princess Margaret and Antony Armstrong-Jones

1993. 40th Anniv of Coronation (2nd issue).
1777/1808 $1 × 32 either grey and black or multicoloured . . . 24·00 26·00
DESIGNS: Various views as Type **308** from each decade of the reign.

309 Edward Stanley Gibbons and Catalogue of 1865

1993. Famous Professional Philatelists (1st series).
1809 **309** $1.50 brown, black & grn . . . . 1·25 1·25
1810 – $1.50 multicoloured . . 1·25 1·25
1811 – $1.50 multicoloured . . 1·25 1·25
1812 – $1.50 multicoloured . . 1·25 1·25
1813 – $1.50 multicoloured . . 1·25 1·25
1814 – $1.50 multicoloured . . 1·25 1·25
MS1815 98 × 69 mm. $3 black; $3 black 5·50 6·00
DESIGNS: No. 1810, Theodore Champion and France 1849 1f. stamp; 1811, J. Walter Scott and U.S.A. 1918 24c. "Inverted Jenny" error; 1812, Hugo Michel and Bavaria 1849 1k. stamp; 1813, Alberto and Giulio Bolaffi with Sardinia 1851 5c. stamp; 1814, Richard Borek and Brunswick 1865 1gr. stamp; **MS**1815, Front pages of "Mekeel's Weekly Stamp News" in 1891 (misdated 1890) and 1993.
See also No. 1957.

310 Paul Gascoigne

311 Grand Inspector W. Heath

1993. World Cup Football Championship, U.S.A. (1st issue). English Players. Multicoloured.
1816 $2 Type **310** . . . . 1·50 1·40
1817 $2 David Platt . . . . . . 1·50 1·40
1818 $2 Martin Peters . . . . . 1·50 1·40
1819 $2 John Barnes . . . . . . 1·50 1·40
1820 $2 Gary Lineker . . . . . 1·50 1·40
1821 $2 Geoff Hurst . . . . . . 1·50 1·40
1822 $2 Bobby Charlton . . . . 1·50 1·40
1823 $2 Bryan Robson . . . . . 1·50 1·40
1824 $2 Bobby Moore . . . . . 1·50 1·40
1825 $2 Nobby Stiles . . . . . . 1·50 1·40
1826 $2 Gordon Banks . . . . . 1·50 1·40
1827 $2 Peter Shilton . . . . . . 1·50 1·40
MS1828 Two sheets, each 135 × 109 mm. (a) $6 Bobby Moore holding World Cup. (b) $6 Gary Lineker and Bobby Robson Set of 2 sheets 9·00 10·00
See also Nos. 2039/45.

1993. Anniversaries and Events. Multicoloured.
1829 10c. Type **311** . . . . . . 1·50 80
1830 15c. Rodnina and Oulanov (U.S.S.R.) (pairs figure skating) (horiz) 75 40
1831 30c. Present Masonic Hall, St. John's (horiz) . . . . 1·75 80
1832 30c. Willy Brandt with Helmut Schmidt and George Leber (horiz) . . 60 40
1833 30c. "Cat and Bird" (Picasso) (horiz) 60 40
1834 40c. Previous Masonic Hall, St. John's (horiz) . . . . 1·75 80
1835 40c. "Fish on a Newspaper" (Picasso) (horiz) 60 50
1836 40c. Early astronomical equipment 60 50
1837 40c. Prince Naruhito and engagement photographs (horiz) 60 50
1838 60c. Grand Inspector J. Jeffery . . . . 2·00 1·00
1839 $1 "Woman combing her Hair" (W. Slewinski) (horiz) . . . . 1·00 1·25
1840 $3 Masako Owada and engagement photographs (horiz) . . . . 2·25 2·50
1841 $3 "Artist's Wife with Cat" (Konrad Kryzanowski) (horiz) . . . . 2·25 2·50
1842 $4 Willy Brandt and protest march (horiz) . . . . . . 2·25 2·75
1843 $4 Galaxy . . . . 2·25 2·75
1844 $5 Alberto Tomba (Italy) (giant slalom) (horiz) . . 2·25 2·75
1845 $5 "Dying Bull" (Picasso) (horiz) . . . . 2·25 2·75
1846 $5 Pres. Clinton and family (horiz) . . . . 2·25 2·75
MS1847 Seven sheets. (a) 106 × 75 mm. $5 Copernicus. (b) 106 × 75 mm. $6 Womens' 1500 metre speed skating medallists (horiz). (c) 106 × 75 mm. $6 Willy Brandt at Warsaw Ghetto Memorial (horiz). (d) 106 × 75 mm. $6 "Woman with a Dog" (detail) (Picasso) (horiz). (e) 106 × 75 mm. $6 Masako Owada. (f) 70 × 100 mm. $6 "General Confusion" (S. I. Witkiewicz). (g) 106 × 75 mm. $6 Pres. Clinton taking the Oath (42½ × 57 mm) Set of 7 sheets 22·00 24·00
ANNIVERSARIES AND EVENTS: Nos. 1829, 1831, 1834, 1838, 150th anniv of St. John's Masonic Lodge No. 492; 1830, 1844, **MS**1847b, Winter Olympic Games '94, Lillehammer; 1832, 1842, **MS**1847c, 80th birth anniv of Willy Brandt (German politician); 1833, 1835, 1845, **MS**1847d, 20th death anniv of Picasso (artist); 1836, 1843, **MS**1847a, 450th death anniv of Copernicus (astronomer); 1837, 1840, **MS**1847e, Marriage of Crown Prince Naruhito of Japan; 1839, 1841, **MS**1847f, "Polska '93" International Stamp Exhibition, Poznan; 1846, **MS**1847g, Inauguration of U.S. President William Clinton.

312 Hugo Eckener and Dr. W. Beckers with Airship "Graf Zeppelin" over Lake George, New York

1993. Aviation Anniversaries. Multicoloured.
1848 30c. Type **312** . . . . . . 1·00 70
1849 40c. Chicago World's Fair from "Graf Zeppelin" . . 1·00 1·00
1850 40c. Gloster Whittle E.28/39, 1941 . . . . 1·00 1·00
1851 40c. George Washington writing balloon mail letter (vert) . . . . 1·00 1·00
1852 $4 Pres. Wilson and Curtiss JN-4 Jenny . . . . . . 3·75 4·00
1853 $5 Airship "Hindenburg" over Ebbets Field baseball stadium, 1937 . . . . . 3·75 4·00
1854 $5 Gloster Meteor in dogfight . . . . 3·75 4·00
MS1855 Three sheets. (a) 86 × 105 mm. $6 Hugo Eckener (vert). (b) 105 × 86 mm. $6 Consolidated PBY-5 Catalina flying boat (57 × 42½ mm). (c) 105 × 86 mm. $6 Alexander Hamilton, Washington and John Jay watching Blanchard's balloon, 1793 (horiz) Set of 3 sheets 16·00 17·00
ANNIVERSARIES: Nos. 1848/9, 1853, **MS**1855a, 125th birth anniv of Hugo Eckener (airship commander); 1850, 1854, **MS**1855b, 75th anniv of Royal Air Force; 1851/2, **MS**1855c, Bicentenary of first airmail flight.

313 Lincoln Continental

1993. Centenaries of Henry Ford's First Petrol Engine (Nos. 1856, 1858), and Karl Benz's First Four-wheeled Car (others). Multicoloured.
1856 30c. Type **313** . . . . . . 1·00 75
1857 40c. Mercedes racing car, 1914 . . . . 1·00 75
1858 $4 Ford "GT40", 1966 . . . 4·00 4·50
1859 $5 Mercedes Benz "gull-wing" coupe, 1954 . . . 4·00 4·50
MS1860 Two sheets. (a) 114 × 87 mm. $6 Ford's Mustang emblem. (b) 87 × 114 mm. $6 Germany 1936 12pf. Benz and U.S.A. 1968 12c. Ford stamps Set of 2 sheets 9·00 11·00

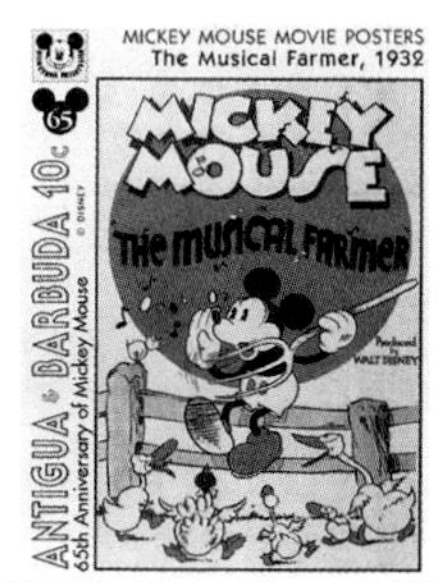

314 "The Musical Farmer", 1932

1993. Mickey Mouse Film Posters. Mult.
1861 10c. Type **314** 60 30
1862 15c. "Little Whirlwind", 1941 . . . . 70 35
1863 30c. "Pluto's Dream House", 1940 . . . . . . 80 40
1864 40c. "Gulliver Mickey", 1934 . . . . 80 40
1865 50c. "Alpine Climbers", 1936 . . . . 80 45
1866 $1 "Mr. Mouse Takes a Trip", 1940 . . . . . . 1·25 80
1867 $2 "The Nifty Nineties", 1941 . . . . 1·75 2·00
1868 $4 "Mickey Down Under", 1948 . . . . 2·50 3·50
1869 $5 "The Pointer", 1939 . . 2·50 3·50
MS1870 Two sheets, each 125 × 105 mm. (a) $6 "The Simple Things", 1953. (b) $6 "The Prince and the Pauper", 1990 Set of 2 sheets 10·00 12·00

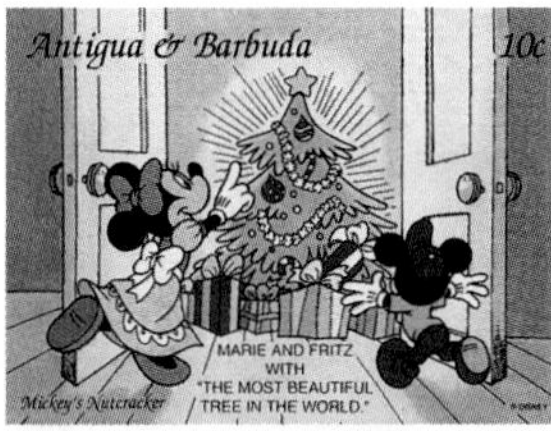

315 Marie and Fritz with Christmas Tree

1993. Christmas. Mickey's Nutcracker. Walt Disney cartoon characters in scenes from "The Nutcracker". Multicoloured.
1871 10c. Type **315** 75 40
1872 15c. Marie receives Nutcracker from Godfather Drosselmeir . . 80 40
1873 20c. Fritz breaks Nutcracker 80 40
1874 30c. Nutcracker with sword 90 40
1875 40c. Nutcracker and Marie in the snow 95 40
1876 50c. Marie and the Prince meet Sugar Plum Fairy 1·00 60
1877 60c. Marie and Prince in Crystal Hall . . . . . . 1·00 60
1878 $3 Huey, Dewey and Louie as Cossack dancers . . . 3·25 4·00
1879 $6 Mother Ginger and her puppets . . . . 4·50 6·50
MS1880 Two sheets, each 127 × 102 mm. (a) $6 Marie and Prince in sleigh. (b) $6 The Prince in sword fight (vert) Set of 2 sheets 8·50 10·00

316 "Hannah and Samuel" (Rembrandt)

1993. Famous Paintings by Rembrandt and Matisse. Multicoloured.
1881 15c. Type **316** 30 30
1882 15c. "Guitarist" (Matisse) 30 30
1883 30c. "The Jewish Bride" (Rembrandt) 40 30
1884 40c. "Jacob wrestling with the Angel" (Rembrandt) 50 30
1885 60c. "Interior with a Goldfish Bowl" (Matisse) 70 50
1886 $1 "Mlle Yvonne Landsberg" (Matisse) . . 1·00 80
1887 $4 "The Toboggan" (Matisse) . . . . 2·75 3·75
1888 $5 "Moses with the Tablets of the Law" (Rembrandt) 2·75 3·75
MS1889 Two sheets. (a) 124 × 99 mm. $6 "The Blinding of Samson by the Philistines" (detail) (Rembrandt). (b) 99 × 124 mm. $6 "The Three Sisters" (detail) (Matisse) Set of 2 sheets 8·50 10·00

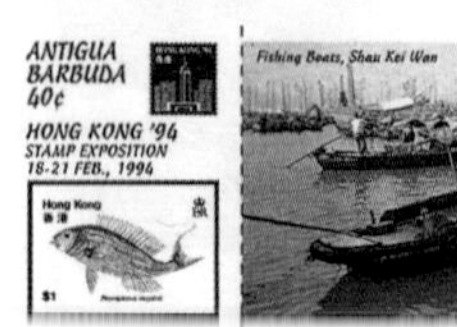

317 Hong Kong 1981 $1 Golden Threadfin Bream Stamp and Sampans, Shau Kei Wan

1994. "Hong Kong '94" International Stamp Exhibition (1st issue). Multicoloured.
1890 40c. Type **317** 80 80
1891 40c. Antigua 1990 $2 Rock beauty stamp and sampans, Shau Kei Wan 80 80
Nos. 1890/1 were printed together, se-tenant, forming a composite design.
See also Nos. 1892/7 and 1898/1905.

318 Terracotta Warriors

1994. "Hong Kong '94" International Stamp Exhibition (2nd issue). Qin Dynasty Terracotta Figures. Multicoloured.
1892 40c. Type **318** 65 65
1893 40c. Cavalryman and horse 65 65
1894 40c. Warriors in armour . . 65 65
1895 40c. Painted bronze chariot and team 65 65
1896 40c. Pekingese dog 65 65
1897 40c. Warriors with horses 65 65

319 Mickey Mouse in Junk

320 Sumatran Rhinoceros lying down

1994. "Hong Kong '94" International Stamp Exhibition (3rd issue). Walt Disney cartoon characters. Multicoloured.
1898 10c. Type **319** 70 30
1899 15c. Minnie Mouse as mandarin 75 35
1900 30c. Donald and Daisy Duck on houseboat . . . 90 45
1901 50c. Mickey holding bird in cage . . . . 1·10 60
1902 $1 Pluto and ornamental dog . . . . 1·75 1·00
1903 $2 Minnie and Daisy celebrating Bun Festival 2·50 2·50
1904 $4 Goofy making noodles 3·50 4·50
1905 $5 Goofy pulling Mickey in rickshaw . . . . 3·50 4·50
MS1906 Two sheets, each 133 × 109 mm. (a) $5 Mickey and Donald on harbour ferry (horiz). (b) $5 Mickey in traditional dragon dance (horiz) Set of 2 sheets 6·50 8·00

1994. Centenary (1992) of Sierra Club (environmental protection society). Endangered Species. Multicoloured.
1907 $1.50 Type **320** . . . . . . 1·25 1·25
1908 $1.50 Sumatran rhinoceros feeding . . . . 1·25 1·25
1909 $1.50 Ring-tailed lemur on ground . . . . 1·25 1·25
1910 $1.50 Ring-tailed lemur on branch . . . . 1·25 1·25
1911 $1.50 Red-fronted brown lemur on branch . . . . 1·25 1·25
1912 $1.50 Head of red-fronted brown lemur . . . . . . 1·25 1·25
1913 $1.50 Head of red-fronted brown lemur in front of trunk . . . . 1·25 1·25
1914 $1.50 Sierra Club Centennial emblem . . . . 1·25 1·25
1915 $1.50 Head of Bactrian camel . . . . 1·25 1·25
1916 $1.50 Bactrian camel . . . 1·25 1·25
1917 $1.50 African elephant drinking . . . . 1·25 1·25
1918 $1.50 Head of African elephant . . . . 1·25 1·25
1919 $1.50 Leopard sitting upright . . . . 1·25 1·25
1920 $1.50 Leopard in grass (emblem at right) . . . . 1·25 1·25
1921 $1.50 Leopard in grass (emblem at left) . . . . . 1·25 1·25
MS1922 Four sheets. (a) 100 × 70 mm. $1.50, Sumatran rhinoceros (horiz). (b) 70 × 100 mm. $1.50, Ring-tailed lemur (horiz). (c) 70 × 100 mm. $1.50, Bactrian camel (horiz). (d) 100 × 70 mm. $1.50, African elephant (horiz) Set of 4 sheets 5·50 7·00

321 West Highland White Terrier

1994. Dogs of the World. Chinese New Year ("Year of the Dog"). Multicoloured.
1923 50c. Type **321** 65 65
1924 50c. Beagle 65 65
1925 50c. Scottish terrier 65 65
1926 50c. Pekingese 65 65
1927 50c. Dachshund 65 65
1928 50c. Yorkshire terrier . . . 65 65
1929 50c. Pomeranian 65 65
1930 50c. Poodle 65 65
1931 50c. Shetland sheepdog . . 65 65
1932 50c. Pug 65 65
1933 50c. Shih Tzu 65 65
1934 50c. Chihuahua 65 65
1935 75c. Mastiff 65 65
1936 75c. Border collie 65 65
1937 75c. Samoyed 65 65
1938 75c. Airedale terrier 65 65
1939 75c. English setter 65 65
1940 75c. Rough collie 65 65
1941 75c. Newfoundland 65 65
1942 75c. Weimarana 65 65
1943 75c. English springer spaniel 65 65
1944 75c. Dalmatian 65 65
1945 75c. Boxer 65 65
1946 75c. Old English sheepdog 65 65
MS1947 Two sheets, each 93 × 58 mm. (a) $6 Welsh corgi. (b) $6 Labrador retriever Set of 2 sheets 9·00 10·00

322 "Spiranthes lanceolata"

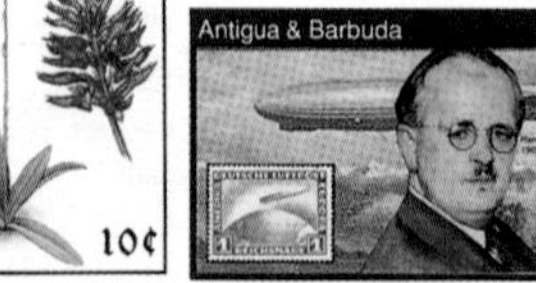

323 Hermann E. Sieger, Germany 1931 1m. Zeppelin Stamp and Airship LZ-127 "Graf Zeppelin"

1994. Orchids. Multicoloured.
1948 10c. Type **322** 55 50
1949 20c. "Ionopsis utricularioides" 75 50
1950 30c. "Tetramicra canaliculata" 85 50
1951 50c. "Oncidium picturatum" 1·00 65
1952 $1 "Epidendrum difforme" 1·50 90
1953 $2 "Epidendrum ciliare" . . 2·00 2·25
1954 $4 "Epidendrum ibaguense" 2·75 3·75
1955 $5 "Epidendrum nocturnum" . . . . . . 2·75 3·75
MS1956 Two sheets, each 100 × 73 mm. (a) $6 "Rodriguezia lanceolato". (b) $6 "Encyclia cochleata" Set of 2 sheets 9·00 10·00

1994. Famous Professional Philatelists (2nd series).
1957 **323** $1.50 multicoloured . . 1·75 1·75

324 "Danaus plexippus"

325 Bottlenose Dolphin

1994. Butterflies. Multicoloured.
1958 10c. Type **324** 75 75
1959 15c. "Appias drusilla" . . . 85 45
1960 30c. "Eurema lisa" . . . . 1·00 55
1961 40c. "Anaea troglodyta" . . 1·00 60
1962 $1 "Urbanus proteus" . . . 1·75 1·00
1963 $2 "Junonia evarete" . . . 2·25 2·25
1964 $4 "Battus polydamas" . . 3·00 4·00
1965 $5 "Heliconius charitonia" 3·00 4·00
MS1966 Two sheets, each 102 × 72 mm. (a) $6 "Phoebis sennae". (b) $6 "Hemiargus hanno" Set of 2 sheets 8·00 9·00
No. 1959 is inscribed "Appisa drusilla" and No. 1965 "Heliconius charitonius", both in error.

1994. Marine Life. Multicoloured.
1967 50c. Type **325** 65 65
1968 50c. Killer whale 65 65
1969 50c. Spinner dolphin 65 65
1970 50c. Oceanic sunfish 65 65
1971 50c. Caribbean reef shark and short fin pilot whale 65 65
1972 50c. Copper-banded butterflyfish 65 65
1973 50c. Mosaic moray 65 65
1974 50c. Clown triggerfish . . . 65 65
1975 50c. Red lobster 65 65
MS1976 Two sheets, each 106 × 76 mm. (a) $6 Seahorse. (b) $6 Swordfish ("Blue Marlin") (horiz) Set of 2 sheets 11·00 11·00

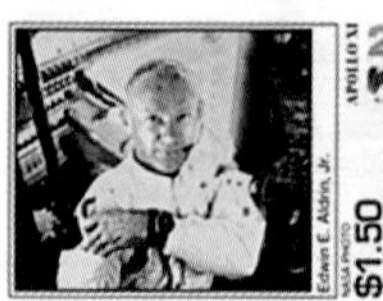

326 Edwin Aldrin (astronaut)

1994. 25th Anniv of First Manned Moon Landing. Multicoloured.
1977 $1.50 Type **326** . . . . . . 1·50 1·50
1978 $1.50 First lunar footprint 1·50 1·50
1979 $1.50 Neil Armstrong (astronaut) . . . . 1·50 1·50
1980 $1.50 Aldrin stepping onto Moon . . . . 1·50 1·50
1981 $1.50 Aldrin and equipment 1·50 1·50
1982 $1.50 Aldrin and U.S.A. flag 1·50 1·50
1983 $1.50 Aldrin at Tranquility Base . . . . 1·50 1·50
1984 $1.50 Moon plaque . . . . 1·50 1·50
1985 $1.50 "Eagle" leaving Moon 1·50 1·50
1986 $1.50 Command module in lunar orbit . . . . 1·50 1·50
1987 $1.50 First day cover of U.S.A. 1969 10c. First Man on Moon stamp . . 1·50 1·50
1988 $1.50 Pres. Nixon and astronauts . . . . 1·50 1·50
MS1989 72 × 102 mm. $6 Armstrong and Aldrin with postal official 3·50 4·50

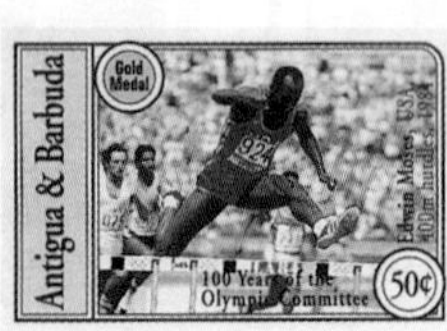

327 Edwin Moses (U.S.A.) (400 m hurdles, 1984)

1994. Centenary of International Olympic Committee. Gold Medal Winners. Multicoloured.
1990 50c. Type **327** 40 30
1991 $1.50 Steffi Graf (Germany) (tennis, 1988) . . . . . . 1·50 1·50
MS1992 79 × 110 mm. $6 Johann Olav Koss (Norway) (500, 1500 and 10,000 metre speed skating), 1994 3·25 3·75

328 Antiguan Family

1994. International Year of the Family.
1993 **328** 90c. multicoloured . . . 60 60

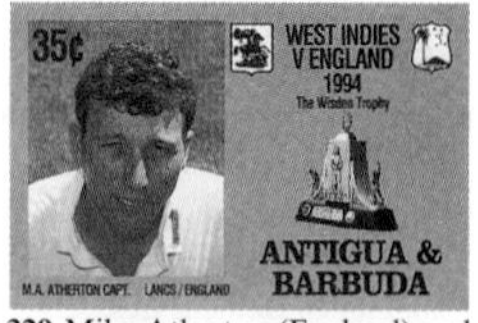

329 Mike Atherton (England) and Wisden Trophy

1994. Centenary (1995) of First English Cricket Tour to the West Indies. Multicoloured.
1994 35c. Type **329** 75 50
1995 75c. Viv Richards (West Indies) (vert) . . . . . . 1·25 80
1996 $1.20 Richie Richardson (West Indies) and Wisden Trophy . . . . 1·50 2·00
MS1997 80 × 100 mm. $3 English team, 1895 (black and brown) 2·25 2·25

330 Entrance Bridge, Songgwangsa Temple

1994. "Philakorea '94" International Stamp Exhibition, Seoul. Multicoloured.
1998 40c. Type **330** 40 40
1999 75c. Long-necked bottle . . 60 60
2000 75c. Punch'ong ware jar with floral decoration . . 60 60
2001 75c. Punch'ong ware jar with blue dragon pattern 60 60
2002 75c. Ewer in shape of bamboo shoot 60 60
2003 75c. Punch'ong ware green jar 60 60
2004 75c. Pear-shaped bottle . . . 60 60
2005 75c. Porcelain jar with brown dragon pattern . . 60 60
2006 75c. Porcelain jar with floral pattern 60 60
2007 90c. Song-op Folk Village, Cheju 60 60
2008 $3 Port Sogwipo . . . . . 1·75 2·25
MS2009 104 × 71 mm. $4 Ox herder playing flute (vert) 2·40 2·75

331 Short S.25 Sunderland (flying boat)

1994. 50th Anniv of D-Day. Multicoloured.
2010 40c. Type **331** 80 40
2011 $2 Lockheed P-38 Lightning fighters attacking train . . 2·00 2·25
2012 $3 Martin B-26 Marauder bombers . . . . 2·50 3·00
MS2013 108 × 78 mm. $6 Hawker Typhoon fighter bomber 4·50 4·75

332 Travis Tritt

1994. Stars of Country and Western Music. Multicoloured.
2014 75c. Type **332** 60 60
2015 75c. Dwight Yoakam 60 60
2016 75c. Billy Ray Cyrus 60 60
2017 75c. Alan Jackson 60 60
2018 75c. Garth Brooks 60 60
2019 75c. Vince Gill 60 60
2020 75c. Clint Black 60 60
2021 75c. Eddie Rabbit 60 60
2022 75c. Patsy Cline 60 60
2023 75c. Tanya Tucker 60 60
2024 75c. Dolly Parton 60 60
2025 75c. Anne Murray 60 60

2026 75c. Tammy Wynette . . . 60 60
2027 75c. Loretta Lynn 60 60
2028 75c. Reba McEntire 60 60
2029 75c. Skeeter Davis 60 60
2030 75c. Hank Snow 60 60
2031 75c. Gene Autry 60 60
2032 75c. Jimmie Rodgers 60 60
2033 75c. Ernest Tubb 60 60
2034 75c. Eddy Arnold 60 60
2035 75c. Willie Nelson 60 60
2036 75c. Johnny Cash 60 60
2037 75c. George Jones 60 60
MS2038 Three sheets. (a) 100×70 mm. $6 Hank Williams Jr. (b) 100×70 mm. $6 Hank Williams Sr. (c) 70×100 mm. $6 Kitty Wells (horiz) Set of 3 sheets 13·00 13·00

333 Hugo Sanchez (Mexico)

1994. World Cup Football Championship, U.S.A. (2nd issue). Multicoloured.
2039 15c. Type **333** 75 30
2040 35c. Jurgen Klinsmann (Germany) . . . . 1·25 45
2041 65c. Antiguan player . . . 1·50 55
2042 $1.20 Cobi Jones (U.S.A.) 2·00 1·75
2043 $4 Roberto Baggio (Italy) 3·25 4·00
2044 $5 Bwalya Kalusha (Zambia) . . . . 3·25 4·00
MS2045 Two sheets. (a) 72×105 mm. $6 Maldive Islands player (vert). (b) 107×78 mm. $6 World Cup trophy (vert) Set of 2 sheets 8·00 8·50
No. 2040 is inscribed "Klinsman" in error.

334 Sir Shridath Ramphal

1994. 1st Recipients of Order of the Caribbean Community. Multicoloured.
2046 65c. Type **334** 50 40
2047 90c. William Demas 65 60
2048 $1.20 Derek Walcott . . . . 1·75 1·50

335 Pair of Magnificent Frigate Birds

1994. Birds. Multicoloured.
2049 10c. Type **335** 45 45
2050 15c. Bridled quail dove . . 50 40
2051 30c. Magnificent frigate bird chick hatching 70 70
2052 40c. Purple-throated carib (vert) 70 70
2053 $1 Male magnificent frigate bird in courtship display (vert) . . . . 1·00 1·25
2054 $1 Broad-winged hawk (vert) . . . . 1·00 1·25
2055 $3 Young magnificent frigate bird . . . . 2·00 3·00
2056 $4 Yellow warbler . . . . . 2·00 3·00
MS2057 Two sheets. (a) 70×100 mm. $6 Female magnificent frigate bird (vert). (b) 100×70 mm. $6 Black-billed whistling duck ducklings Set of 2 sheets 7·00 8·00
Nos. 2049, 2051, 2053 and 2055 also show the W.W.F. Panda emblem.

336 "The Virgin and Child by the Fireside" (Robert Campin)

337 Magnificent Frigate Bird

1994. Christmas. Religious Paintings. Multicoloured.
2058 15c. Type **336** 70 30
2059 35c. "The Reading Madonna" (Giorgione) 95 30
2060 40c. "Madonna and Child" (Giovanni Bellini) . . . . 1·00 30
2061 45c. "The Litta Madonna" (Da Vinci) . . . . 1·00 30
2062 65c. "The Virgin and Child under the Apple Tree" (Lucas Cranach the Elder) 1·40 55
2063 75c. "Madonna and Child" (Master of the Female Half-lengths) . . . . . . 1·50 70
2064 $1.20 "An Allegory of the Church" (Alessandro Allori) . . . . 2·00 1·75
2065 $5 "Madonna and Child wreathed with Flowers" (Jacob Jordaens) . . . . 3·50 4·50
MS2066 Two sheets. (a) 123×88 mm. $6 "Madonna and Child with Commissioners" (detail) (Palma Vecchio) (b) 88×123 mm. $6 "The Virgin Enthroned with Child" (detail) (Bohemian master) Set of 2 sheets 7·50 8·50

1995. Birds. Multicoloured.
2067 15c. Type **337** 10 10
2068 25c. Blue-hooded euphonia 10 15
2069 35c. Eastern meadowlark ("Meadowlark") 15 20
2070 40c. Red-billed tropic bird 20 25
2071 45c. Greater flamingo . . . 20 25
2072 60c. Yellow-faced grassquit 30 35
2073 65c. Yellow-billed cuckoo 35 40
2074 70c. Purple-throated carib 35 40
2075 75c. Bananaquit 35 40
2076 90c. Painted bunting 45 50
2077 $1.20 Red-legged honeycreeper 55 60
2078 $2 Northern jacana ("Jacana") . . . . 95 1·00
2079 $5 Greater Antillean bullfinch . . . . 2·40 2·50
2080 $10 Caribbean elaenia . . . 4·75 5·00
2081 $20 Brown trembler ("Trembler") . . . . . . 9·50 9·75

338 Head of Pachycephalosaurus

1995. Prehistoric Animals. Multicoloured.
2082 15c. Type **338** 60 60
2083 20c. Head of afrovenator . . 60 60
2084 65c. Centrosaurus 80 80
2085 75c. Kronosaurus (horiz) . . 80 80
2086 75c. Ichthyosaurus (horiz) 80 80
2087 75c. Plesiosaurus (horiz) . . 80 80
2088 75c. Archelon (horiz) . . . 80 80
2089 75c. Pair of tyrannosaurus (horiz) 80 80
2090 75c. Tyrannosaurus (horiz) 80 80
2091 75c. Parasaurolophus (horiz) 80 80
2092 75c. Pair of parasaurolophus (horiz) 80 80
2093 75c. Oviraptor (horiz) . . . 80 80
2094 75c. Protoceratops with eggs (horiz) 80 80
2095 75c. Pteranodon and protoceratops (horiz) . . 80 80
2096 75c. Pair of protoceratops (horiz) 80 80
2097 90c. Pentaceratops drinking 1·00 1·00
2098 $1.20 Head of tarbosaurus 1·25 1·25
2099 $5 Head of styracosaurus 3·00 3·75
MS2100 Two sheets, each 101×70 mm. (a) $6 Head of Corythosaurus (horiz). (b) $6 Head of Carnotaurus (horiz) Set of 2 sheets 9·50 10·00

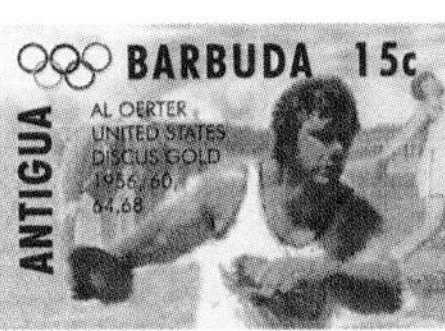

339 Al Oerter (U.S.A.) (discus – 1956, 1960, 1964, 1968)

1995. Olympic Games, Atlanta (1996). Previous Gold Medal Winners (1st issue). Multicoloured.
2101 15c. Type **339** 50 30
2102 20c. Greg Louganis (U.S.A.) (diving – 1984, 1988) . . 50 30
2103 65c. Naim Suleymanoglu (Turkey) (weightlifting – 1988) 65 50
2104 90c. Louise Ritter (U.S.A.) (high jump – 1988) . . . 90 70
2105 $1.20 Nadia Comaneci (Rumania) (gymnastics – 1976) . . . . 1·75 1·10
2106 $5 Olga Bondarenko (Russia) (10,000 metres – 1988) . . . . 3·00 4·50
MS2107 Two sheets, each 106×76 mm. (a) $6 United States crew (eight-oared shell — 1964). (b) $6 Lutz Hessilch (Germany) (cycling — 1988) (vert) Set of 2 sheets 11·00 11·00
No. 2106 is inscribed "BOLDARENKO" in error.
See also Nos. 2302/23.

340 Map of Berlin showing Russian Advance

1995. 50th Anniv of End of Second World War in Europe. Multicoloured.
2108 $1.20 Type **340** . . . . . . 1·00 1·00
2109 $1.20 Russian tank and infantry . . . . 1·00 1·00
2110 $1.20 Street fighting in Berlin . . . . 1·00 1·00
2111 $1.20 German tank exploding . . . . 1·00 1·00
2112 $1.20 Russian air raid . . . 1·00 1·00
2113 $1.20 German troops surrendering . . . . . . 1·00 1·00
2114 $1.20 Hoisting the Soviet flag on the Reichstag . . 1·00 1·00
2115 $1.20 Captured German standards . . . . 1·00 1·00
MS2116 104×74 mm. $6 Gen. Konev (vert) 4·00 4·50
See also Nos. 2132/8.

341 Signatures and Earl of Halifax

342 Woman buying Produce from Market

1995. 50th Anniv of United Nations. Multicoloured.
2117 75c. Type **341** 60 80
2118 90c. Virginia Gildersleeve 60 80
2119 $1.20 Harold Stassen . . . 60 80
MS2120 100×70 mm. $6 Pres. Franklin D. Roosevelt 3·50 4·00
Nos. 2117/19 were printed together, se-tenant, forming a composite design.

1995. 50th Anniv of F.A.O. Multicoloured.
2121 75c. Type **342** 60 80
2122 90c. Women shopping . . . 60 80
2123 $1.20 Women talking . . . 60 80
MS2124 100×70 mm. $6 Tractor 3·00 3·50
Nos. 2121/3 were printed together, se-tenant, forming a composite design.

343 Beach and Rotary Emblem

344 Queen Elizabeth the Queen Mother

1995. 90th Anniv of Rotary International.
2125 **343** $5 multicoloured . . . . 3·50 4·00
MS2126 74×104 mm. $6 National flag and emblem 3·50 4·00

1995. 95th Birthday of Queen Elizabeth the Queen Mother.
2127 – $1.50 brown, light brown and black . . . . . . 1·50 1·50
2128 **344** $1.50 multicoloured . . 1·50 1·50
2129 – $1.50 multicoloured . . 1·50 1·50
2130 – $1.50 multicoloured . . 1·50 1·50
MS2131 100×127 mm. $6 multicoloured 4·75 4·75
DESIGNS: No. 2127, Queen Elizabeth the Queen Mother (pastel drawing); 2129, At desk (oil painting); 2130, Wearing green dress; **MS**2131, Wearing blue dress.

1995. 50th Anniv of End of Second World War in the Pacific. As T **340**. Multicoloured.
2132 $1.20 Gen. Chang Kai-Shek and Chinese guerrillas . . 95 1·00
2133 $1.20 Gen. Douglas MacArthur and beach landing . . . . 95 1·00
2134 $1.20 Gen. Claire Chennault and U.S. fighter aircraft 95 1·00
2135 $1.20 Brig. Orde Wingate and supply drop . . . . 95 1·00
2136 $1.20 Gen. Joseph Stilwell and U.S. supply plane . . 95 1·00
2137 $1.20 Field-Marshal Bill Slim and loading cow into plane . . . . 95 1·00
MS2138 108×76 mm. $3 Admiral Nimitz and aircraft carrier 2·25 2·75

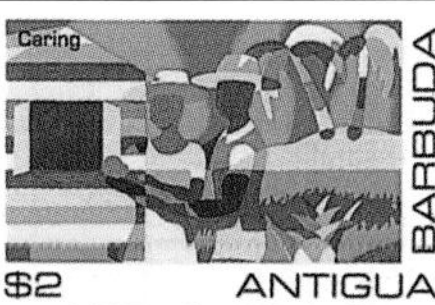

345 Family ("Caring")

1995. Tourism. Sheet 95×72 mm, containing T **345** and similar horiz designs. Multicoloured.
MS2139 $2 Type **345**; $2 Market trader ("Marketing"); $2 Workers and housewife ("Working"); $2 Leisure pursuits ("Enjoying Life") 5·50 6·50

346 Purple-throated Carib

347 Original Church, 1845

1995. Birds. Multicoloured.
2140 75c. Type **346** 85 85
2141 75c. Antillean crested hummingbird 85 85
2142 75c. Bananaquit 85 85
2143 75c. Mangrove cuckoo . . . 85 85
2144 75c. Troupial 85 85
2145 75c. Green-throated carib 85 85
2146 75c. Yellow warbler 85 85
2147 75c. Antillean euphonia ("Blue-hooded Euphonia") 85 85
2148 75c. Scaly-breasted thrasher 85 85
2149 75c. Burrowing owl 85 85
2150 75c. Carib grackle 85 85
2151 75c. Adelaide's warbler . . 85 85
2152 75c. Ring-necked duck . . . 85 85
2153 75c. Ruddy duck 85 85
2154 75c. Green-winged teal . . . 85 85
2155 75c. Wood duck 85 85
2156 75c. Hooded merganser . . 85 85
2157 75c. Lesser scaup 85 85
2158 75c. Black-billed whistling duck ("West Indian Tree Duck") 85 85
2159 75c. Fulvous whistling duck 85 85
2160 75c. Bahama pintail 85 85
2161 75c. Northern shoveler . . . 85 85
2162 75c. Masked duck 85 85
2163 75c. American wigeon . . . 85 85
MS2164 Two sheets, each 104×74 mm. (a) $6 American purple gallinule. (b) $6 Heads of Blue-winged teal Set of 2 sheets 9·50 11·00
Nos. 2140/51 and 2152/63 respectively were printed together, se-tenant, forming composite designs.

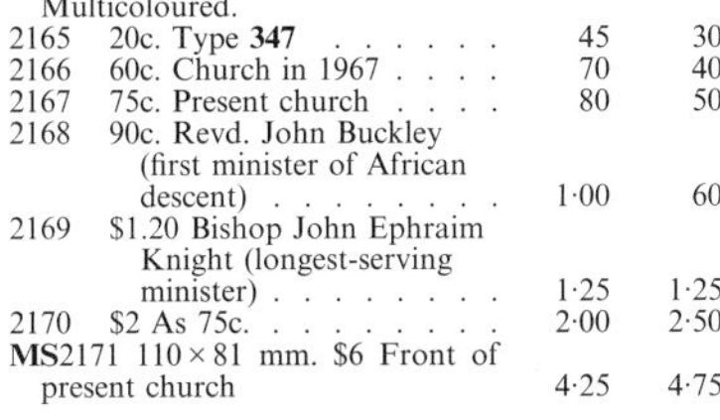

1995. 150th Anniv of Greenbay Moravian Church. Multicoloured.
2165 20c. Type **347** 45 30
2166 60c. Church in 1967 . . . . 70 40
2167 75c. Present church 80 50
2168 90c. Revd. John Buckley (first minister of African descent) . . . . 1·00 60
2169 $1.20 Bishop John Ephraim Knight (longest-serving minister) . . . . 1·25 1·25
2170 $2 As 75c. . . . . 2·00 2·50
MS2171 110×81 mm. $6 Front of present church 4·25 4·75

348 Mining Bees

1995. Bees. Multicoloured.
2172 90c. Type **348** 90 70
2173 $1.20 Solitary bee . . . . . 1·25 90
2174 $1.65 Leaf-cutter bee . . . 1·75 1·75
2175 $1.75 Honey bees . . . . . 1·75 1·75
MS2176 110×80 mm. $6 Solitary mining bee 3·50 4·00

349 Narcissus

1995. Flowers. Multicoloured.
2177 75c. Type **349** 65 65
2178 75c. Camellia 65 65

2179 75c. Iris 65 65
2180 75c. Tulip 65 65
2181 75c. Poppy 65 65
2182 75c. Peony 65 65
2183 75c. Magnolia 65 65
2184 75c. Oriental lily 65 65
2185 75c. Rose 65 65
2186 75c. Pansy 65 65
2187 75c. Hydrangea 65 65
2188 75c. Azaleas 65 65
MS2189 80 × 100 mm. $6 Calla lily 4·00 4·50

No. 2186 is inscribed "Pansie" in error.

350 Somali

1995. Cats. Multicoloured.

2190 45c. Type **350** 60 60
2191 45c. Persian and butterflies 60 60
2192 45c. Devon rex 60 60
2193 45c. Turkish angora 60 60
2194 45c. Himalayan 60 60
2195 45c. Maine coon 60 60
2196 45c. Ginger non-pedigree 60 60
2197 45c. American wirehair 60 60
2198 45c. British shorthair 60 60
2199 45c. American curl 60 60
2200 45c. Black non-pedigree and butterfly 60 60
2201 45c. Birman 60 60
MS2202 104 × 74 mm. $6 Siberian kitten (vert) 5·50 5·50

Nos. 2190/2201 were printed together, se-tenant, forming a composite design.

351 The Explorer Tent

1995. 18th World Scout Jamboree, Netherlands. Tents. Multicoloured.

2203 $1.20 Type **351** 1·40 1·40
2204 $1.20 Camper tent 1·40 1·40
2205 $1.20 Wall tent 1·40 1·40
2206 $1.20 Trail tarp 1·40 1·40
2207 $1.20 Miner's tent 1·40 1·40
2208 $1.20 Voyager tent 1·40 1·40
MS2209 Two sheets, each 76 × 106 mm. (a) $6 Scout and camp fire. (b) $6 Scout with back pack (vert) Set of 2 sheets 8·50 9·50

352 Trans-Gabon Diesel-electric Train

1995. Trains of the World. Multicoloured.

2210 35c. Type **352** 85 65
2211 65c. Canadian Pacific diesel-electric locomotive 1·25 90
2212 75c. Santa Fe Railway diesel-electric locomotive, U.S.A. 1·40 1·00
2213 90c. High Speed Train, Great Britain 1·40 1·00
2214 $1.20 TGV express train, France 1·40 1·40
2215 $1.20 Diesel-electric locomotive, Australia 1·40 1·40
2216 $1.20 Pendolino "ETR 450" electric train, Italy 1·40 1·40
2217 $1.20 Diesel-electric locomotive, Thailand 1·40 1·40
2218 $1.20 Pennsylvania Railroad Type K4 steam locomotive, U.S.A. 1·40 1·40
2219 $1.20 Beyer-Garratt steam locomotive, East African Railways 1·40 1·40
2220 $1.20 Natal Government steam locomotive 1·40 1·40
2221 $1.20 Rail gun, American Civil War 1·40 1·40
2222 $1.20 Locomotive "Lion" (red livery), Great Britain 1·40 1·40
2223 $1.20 William Hedley's "Puffing Billy" (green livery), Great Britain 1·40 1·40
2224 $6 Amtrak high speed diesel locomotive, U.S.A. 3·25 3·75
MS2225 Two sheets, each 110 × 80 mm. (a) $6 Locomotive "Iron Rooster", China (vert). (b) $6 "Indian-Pacific" diesel-electric locomotive, Australia (vert) Set of 2 sheets 10·00 10·00

353 Dag Hammarskjold (1961 Peace)

1995. Cent of Nobel Prize Trust Fund. Mult.

2226 $1 Type **353** 95 95
2227 $1 Georg Wittig (1979 Chemistry) 95 95
2228 $1 Wilhelm Ostwald (1909 Chemistry) 95 95
2229 $1 Robert Koch (1905 Medicine) 95 95
2230 $1 Karl Ziegler (1963 Chemistry) 95 95
2231 $1 Alexander Fleming (1945 Medicine) 95 95
2232 $1 Hermann Staudinger (1953 Chemistry) 95 95
2233 $1 Manfred Eigen (1967 Chemistry) 95 95
2234 $1 Arno Penzias (1978 Physics) 95 95
2235 $1 Shmuel Agnon (1966 Literature) 95 95
2236 $1 Rudyard Kipling (1907 Literature) 95 95
2237 $1 Aleksandr Solzhenitsyn (1970 Literature) 95 95
2238 $1 Jack Steinberger (1988 Physics) 95 95
2239 $1 Andrei Sakharov (1975 Peace) 95 90
2240 $1 Otto Stern (1943 Physics) 95 95
2241 $1 John Steinbeck (1962 Literature) 95 95
2242 $1 Nadine Gordimer (1991 Literature) 95 95
2243 $1 William Faulkner (1949 Literature) 95 95
MS2244 Two sheets, each 100 × 70 mm. (a) $6 Elie Wiesel (1986 Peace) (vert). (b) $6 The Dalai Lama (1989 Peace) (vert) Set of 2 sheets 7·50 8·50

354 Elvis Presley

1995. 60th Birth Anniv of Elvis Presley. Mult.

2245 $1 Type **354** 95 75
2246 $1 Holding microphone in right hand 95 75
2247 $1 In blue shirt and with neck of guitar 95 75
2248 $1 Wearing blue shirt and smiling 95 75
2249 $1 On wedding day 95 75
2250 $1 In army uniform 95 75
2251 $1 Wearing red shirt 95 75
2252 $1 Wearing white shirt 95 75
2253 $1 In white shirt with microphone 95 75
MS2254 101 × 71 mm. $6 "Ghost" image of Elvis amongst the stars 5·00 4·75

355 John Lennon and Signature

357 "Rest on the Flight into Egypt" (Paolo Veronese)

1995. 15th Death Anniv of John Lennon (entertainer). Multicoloured.

2255 45c. Type **355** 50 40
2256 50c. In beard and spectacles 50 50
2257 65c. Wearing sunglasses 55 55
2258 75c. In cap with heart badge 65 65
MS2259 103 × 73 mm. $6 As 75c. 5·50 6·50

1995. Hurricane Relief. Nos. 2203/8 optd **"Hurricane Relief"**.

2260 $1.20 Type **351** 1·25 1·25
2261 $1.20 Camper tent 1·25 1·25
2262 $1.20 Wall tent 1·25 1·25
2263 $1.20 Trail tarp 1·25 1·25
2264 $1.20 Miner's tent 1·25 1·25
2265 $1.20 Voyager tent 1·25 1·25
MS2266 Two sheets, each 76 × 106 mm. (a) $6 Scout and camp fire. (b) $6 Scout with back pack (vert) Set of 2 sheets 9·50 11·00

1995. Christmas. Religious Paintings. Multicoloured.

2267 15c. Type **357** 30 30
2268 35c. "Madonna and Child" (Van Dyck) 40 40
2269 65c. "Sacred Conversation Piece" (Veronese) 60 50
2270 75c. "Vision of St. Anthony" (Van Dyck) 70 60
2271 90c. "Virgin and Child" (Van Eyck) 80 65
2272 $6 "The Immaculate Conception" (Giovanni Tiepolo) 3·00 4·25
MS2273 Two sheets. (a) 101 × 127 mm. $5 "Christ appearing to his Mother" (detail) (Van der Weyden). (b) 127 × 101 mm. $6 "The Infant Jesus and Young St. John" (Murillo) Set of 2 sheets 7·50 9·00

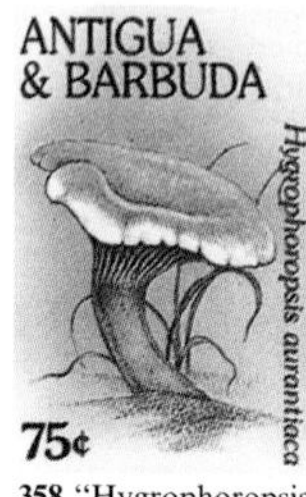

358 "Hygrophoropsis aurantiaca"

360 Florence Griffith Joyner (U.S.A.) (Gold – track, 1988)

359 H.M.S. "Resolution" (Cook)

1996. Fungi. Multicoloured.

2274 75c. Type **358** 50 60
2275 75c. "Hygrophorus bakerensis" 50 60
2276 75c. "Hygrophorus conicus" 50 60
2277 75c. "Hygrophorus miniatus" ("Hygrocybe miniata") 50 60
2278 75c. "Suillus brevipes" 50 60
2279 75c. "Suillus luteus" 50 60
2280 75c. "Suillus granulatus" 50 60
2281 75c. "Suillus caerulescens" 50 60
MS2282 Two sheets, each 105 × 75 mm. (a) $6 "Conocybe filaris". (b) $6 "Hygrocybe flavescens" Set of 2 sheets 7·00 8·00

1996. Sailing Ships. Multicoloured.

2283 15c. Type **359** 50 30
2284 25c. "Mayflower" (Pilgrim Fathers) 50 30
2285 45c. "Santa Maria" (Columbus) 70 30
2286 75c. "Aemilia" (Dutch galleon) 70 70
2287 75c. "Sovereign of the Seas" (English galleon) 70 70
2288 90c. H.M.S. "Victory" (Nelson) 80 70
2289 $1.20 As No. 2286 90 1·00
2290 $1.20 As No. 2287 90 1·00
2291 $1.20 "Royal Louis" (French galleon) 90 1·00
2292 $1.20 H.M.S. "Royal George" (ship of the line) 90 1·00
2293 $1.20 "Le Protecteur" (French frigate) 90 1·00
2294 $1.20 As No. 2288 90 1·00
2295 $1.50 As No. 2285 1·00 1·10
2296 $1.50 "Vitoria" (Magellan) 1·00 1·10
2297 $1.50 "Golden Hind" (Drake) 1·00 1·10
2298 $1.50 As No. 2284 1·00 1·10
2299 $1.50 "Griffin" (La Salle) 1·00 1·10
2300 $1.50 Type **359** 1·00 1·10
MS2301 Two sheets. (a) 102 × 72 mm. $6 U.S.S. "Constitution" (frigate). (b) 98 × 67 mm. $6 "Grande" "Hermine" (Cartier) Set of 2 sheets 7·00 8·00

1996. Olympic Games, Atlanta. Previous Medal Winners (2nd issue). Multicoloured.

2302 65c. Type **360** 60 60
2303 75c. Olympic Stadium, Seoul (1988) (horiz) 65 65
2304 90c. Allison Jolly and Lynne Jewell (U.S.A.) (Gold – yachting, 1988) (horiz) 70 70
2305 90c. Wolfgang Nordwig (Germany) (Gold – pole vaulting, 1972) 70 75
2306 90c. Shirley Strong (Great Britain) (Silver – 100 metres hurdles, 1984) 70 75
2307 90c. Sergei Bubka (Russia) (Gold – pole vault, 1988) 70 75
2308 90c. Filbert Bayi (Tanzania) (Silver – 3000 metres steeplechase, 1980) 70 75
2309 90c. Victor Saneyev (Russia) (Gold – triple jump, 1968, 1972, 1976) 70 75
2310 90c. Silke Renk (Germany) (Gold – javelin, 1992) 70 75
2311 90c. Daley Thompson (Great Britain) (Gold – decathlon, 1980, 1984) 70 75
2312 90c. Robert Richards (U.S.A.) (Gold – pole vault, 1952, 1956) 70 75
2313 90c. Parry O'Brien (U.S.A.) (Gold – shot put, 1952, 1956) 70 75
2314 90c. Ingrid Kramer (Germany) (Gold – women's platform diving, 1960) 70 75
2315 90c. Kelly McCormick (U.S.A.) (Silver – women's springboard diving, 1984) 70 75
2316 90c. Gary Tobian (U.S.A.) (Gold – men's springboard diving, 1960) 70 75
2317 90c. Greg Louganis (U.S.A.) (Gold – men's diving, 1984 and 1988) 70 75
2318 90c. Michelle Mitchell (U.S.A.) (Silver – women's platform diving, 1984 and 1988) 70 75
2319 90c. Zhou Jihong (China) (Gold – women's platform diving, 1984) 70 75
2320 90c. Wendy Wyland (U.S.A.) (Bronze – women's platform diving, 1984) 70 75
2321 90c. Xu Yanmei (China) (Gold – women's platform diving, 1988) 70 75
2322 90c. Fu Mingxia (China) (Gold – women's platform diving, 1992) 70 75
2323 $1.20 2000 metre tandem cycle race (horiz) 1·00 1·00
MS2324 Two sheets, each 106 × 76 mm. (a) $5 Bill Toomey (U.S.A.) (Gold—Decathlon, 1968) (horiz). (b) $6 Mark Lenzi (Gold – men's springboard diving, 1992) Set of 2 sheets 7·00 8·00

Nos. 2305/13 and 2314/22 respectively were printed together, se-tenant, with the background forming a composite design.

361 Black Skimmer

1996. Sea Birds. Multicoloured.

2325 75c. Type **361** 50 60
2326 75c. Black-capped petrel 50 60
2327 75c. Sooty tern 50 60
2328 75c. Royal tern 50 60
2329 75c. Pomarine skua ("Pomarine Jaegger") 50 60
2330 75c. White-tailed tropic bird 50 60
2331 75c. Northern gannet 50 60
2332 75c. Laughing gull 50 60
MS2333 Two sheets, each 105 × 75 mm. (a) $5 Magnificent frigate bird ("Great Frigate Bird"). (b) $6 Brown pelican Set of 2 sheets 7·00 8·00

362 Mickey and Goofy on Elephant ("Around the World in Eighty Days")

1996. Novels of Jules Verne. Walt Disney cartoon characters in scenes from the books. Multicoloured.

2334 1c. Type **362** 10 10
2335 2c. Mickey, Donald and Goofy entering cave ("A Journey to the Centre of the Earth") 10 10
2336 5c. Mickey and Minnie driving postcard ("Michel Strogoff") 15 15
2337 10c. Mickey, Donald and Goofy in space rocket ("From the Earth to the Moon") 20 15
2338 15c. Mickey and Goofy in balloon ("Five Weeks in a Balloon") 20 15
2339 20c. Mickey and Goofy in China ("Around the World in Eighty Days") 20 15
2340 $1 Mickey, Goofy and Pluto on island ("The Mysterious Island") 1·50 85

2341 $2 Mickey, Pluto, Goofy and Donald on Moon ("From the Earth to the Moon") . . . . 2·00 2·00
2342 $3 Mickey being lifted by bird ("Captain Grant's Children") . . . . 2·50 2·75
2343 $5 Mickey with seal and squid ("Twenty Thousand Leagues Under the Sea") 3·75 4·50
MS2344 Two sheets, each 124×99 mm. (a) $6 Mickey on "Nautilus" ("Twenty Thousand Leagues Under the Sea"). (b) $6 Mickey and Donald on raft ("A Journey to the Centre of the Earth") Set of 2 sheets 8·50 9·00

363 Bruce Lee

1996. "CHINA '96" 9th Asian International Stamp Exhibition, Peking. Bruce Lee (actor). Multicoloured.
2345 75c. Type **363** 50 55
2346 75c. Bruce Lee in white shirt and red tie 50 55
2347 75c. In plaid jacket and tie 50 55
2348 75c. In mask and uniform 50 55
2349 75c. Bare-chested 50 55
2350 75c. In mandarin jacket . . 50 55
2351 75c. In brown jumper . . . 50 55
2352 75c. In fawn shirt 50 55
2353 75c. Shouting 50 55
MS2354 76×106 mm. $5 Bruce Lee 3·00 3·25

364 Queen Elizabeth II

1996. 70th Birthday of Queen Elizabeth II. Multicoloured.
2355 $2 Type **364** . . . . 1·10 1·25
2356 $2 With bouquet . . . . . 1·10 1·25
2357 $2 In Garter robes . . . . 1·10 1·25
MS2358 96×111 mm. $6 Wearing white dress 4·25 4·50

365 Ancient Egyptian Cavalryman

1996. Cavalry through the Ages. Multicoloured.
2359 60c. Type **365** 50 55
2360 60c. 13th-century English knight 50 55
2361 60c. 16th-century Spanish lancer 50 55
2362 60c. 18th-century Chinese cavalryman 50 55
MS2363 100×70 mm. $6 19th-century French cuirassier 3·25 3·75

366 Girl in Red Sari

367 Tomb of Zachariah and "Verbascum sinuatum"

1996. 50th Anniv of U.N.I.C.E.F. Multicoloured.
2364 75c. Type **366** 60 60
2365 90c. South American mother and child 70 70
2366 $1.20 Nurse with child . . . 90 1·00
MS2367 114×74 mm. $6 Chinese child 3·25 3·75

1996. 3000th Anniv of Jerusalem. Multicoloured.
2368 75c. Type **367** 65 65
2369 90c. Pool of Siloam and "Hyacinthus orientalis" 75 75
2370 $1.20 Hurva Synagogue and "Ranunculus asiaticus" 1·10 1·10
MS2371 66×80 mm. Model of Herrod's Temple and "Cerics siliquastrum" 4·00 4·25

368 Kate Smith

1996. Cent of Radio. Entertainers. Mult.
2372 65c. Type **368** 50 50
2373 75c. Dinah Shore 60 60
2374 90c. Rudy Vallee 70 70
2375 $1.20 Bing Crosby . . . . 90 1·00
MS2376 72×104 mm. $6 Jo Stafford (28×42 mm) 3·25 3·75

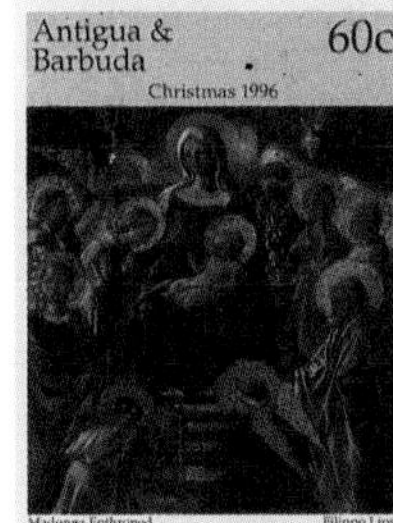

369 "Madonna Enthroned"

1996. Christmas. Religious Paintings by Filippo Lippi. Multicoloured.
2377 60c. Type **369** 50 35
2378 90c. "Adoration of the Child and Saints" 60 50
2379 $1 "The Annunciation" . . 75 55
2380 $1.20 "Birth of the Virgin" 80 80
2381 $1.60 "Adoration of the Child" . . . . 1·10 1·25
2382 $1.75 "Madonna and Child" 1·25 1·40
MS2383 Two sheets, each 76×106 mm. (a) $6 "Madonna and Child" (different). (b) $6 "The Circumcision" Set of 2 sheets 8·00 8·50

370 Robert Preston ("The Music Man")

1997. Broadway Musical Stars. Multicoloured.
2384 $1 Type **370** 60 65
2385 $1 Michael Crawford ("Phantom of the Opera") 60 65
2386 $1 Zero Mostel ("Fiddler on the Roof") 60 65
2387 $1 Patti Lupone ("Evita") 60 65
2388 $1 Raul Julia ("Threepenny Opera") 60 65
2389 $1 Mary Martin ("South Pacific") 60 65
2390 $1 Carol Channing ("Hello Dolly") 60 65
2391 $1 Yul Brynner ("The King and I") 60 65
2392 $1 Julie Andrews ("My Fair Lady") 60 65
MS2393 106×76 mm. $6 Mickey Rooney ("Sugar Babies") 3·25 3·75

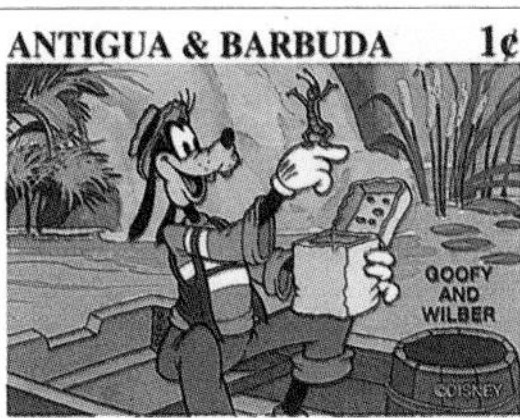

371 Goofy and Wilbur

1997. Walt Disney Cartoon Characters. Mult.
2394 1c. Type **371** 10 10
2395 2c. Donald and Goofy in boxing ring 10 10
2396 5c. Donald, Panchito and Jose Carioca 10 10
2397 10c. Mickey and Goofy playing chess 20 15
2398 15c. Chip and Dale with acorns 20 15
2399 20c. Pluto and Mickey . . . 20 15
2400 $1 Daisy and Minnie eating ice-cream 90 75
2401 $2 Daisy and Minnie at dressing table . . . . . . 1·50 1·75
2402 $3 Gus Goose and Donald 2·00 2·50
MS2403 Two sheets. (a) 102×127 mm. $6 Goofy. (b) 127×102 mm. Donald Duck playing guitar (vert) Set of 2 sheets 7·00 8·00

372 Charlie Chaplin as Young Man

1997. 20th Death Anniv of Charlie Chaplin (film star). Multicoloured.
2404 $1 Type **372** 60 65
2405 $1 Pulling face 60 65
2406 $1 Looking over shoulder 60 65
2407 $1 In cap 60 65
2408 $1 In front of star 60 65
2409 $1 In "The Great Dictator" 60 65
2410 $1 With movie camera and megaphone 60 65
2411 $1 Standing in front of camera lens 60 65
2412 $1 Putting on make-up . . . 60 65
MS2413 76×106 mm. $6 Charlie Chaplin 3·50 3·75
Nos. 2404/12 were printed together, se-tenant, with the backgrounds forming a composite design.

373 "Charaxes porthos"

1997. Butterflies. Multicoloured.
2414 90c. Type **373** 65 50
2415 $1.10 "Charaxes protoclea protoclea" 70 80
2416 $1.10 "Byblia ilithyia" . . . 70 80
2417 $1.10 Black-headed tchagra (bird) 70 80
2418 $1.10 "Charaxes nobilis" . . 70 80
2419 $1.10 "Pseudacraea boisduvali trimeni" . . . 70 80
2420 $1.10 "Charaxes smaragdalis" 70 80
2421 $1.10 "Charaxes lasti" . . . 70 80
2422 $1.10 "Pseudacrea poggei" 70 80
2423 $1.10 "Graphium colonna" 70 80
2424 $1.10 Carmine bee eater (bird) 70 80
2425 $1.10 "Pseudacraea eurytus" 70 80
2426 $1.10 "Hypolimnas monteironis" 70 80
2427 $1.10 "Charaxes anticlea" 70 80
2428 $1.10 "Graphium leonidas" 70 80
2429 $1.10 "Graphium illyris" . . 70 80
2430 $1.10 "Nephronia argia" . . 70 80
2431 $1.10 "Graphium policenes" 70 80
2432 $1.10 "Papilio dardanus" . . 70 80
2433 $1.20 "Aethiopana honorius" 75 80
2434 $1.60 "Charaxes hadrianus" 1·00 1·10
2435 $1.75 "Precis westermanni" 1·25 1·40
MS2436 Three sheets, each 106×76 mm. (a) $6 "Charaxes lactitinctus" (horiz). (b) $6 "Eupheadra neophron". (c) $6 "Euxanthe tiberius" (horiz) Set of 3 sheets 11·00 12·00

Nos. 2415/23 and 2424/32 respectively were printed together, se-tenant, with the backgrounds forming a composite design.
No. 2430 is inscribed "Nepheronia argia" in error.

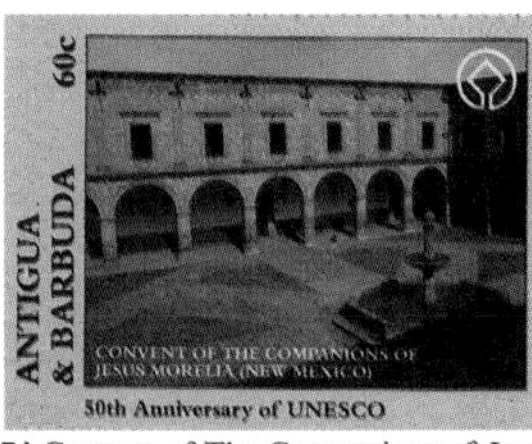

374 Convent of The Companions of Jesus, Morelia, Mexico

1997. 50th Anniv of U.N.E.S.C.O. Multicoloured.
2437 60c. Type **374** 50 35
2438 90c. Fortress at San Lorenzo, Panama (vert) 60 50
2439 $1 Canaima National Park, Venezuela (vert) 70 55
2440 $1.10 Aerial view of church with tower, Guanajuato, Mexico (vert) 70 80
2441 $1.10 Church facade, Guanajuato, Mexico (vert) 70 80
2442 $1.10 Aerial view of churches with domes, Guanajuato, Mexico (vert) 70 80
2443 $1.10 Jesuit Missions of the Chiquitos, Bolivia (vert) 70 80
2444 $1.10 Huascaran National Park, Peru (vert) 70 80
2445 $1.10 Jesuit Missions of La Santisima, Paraguay (vert) 70 80
2446 $1.10 Cartagena, Colombia (vert) 70 80
2447 $1.10 Fortification, Havana, Cuba (vert) 70 80
2448 $1.20 As No. 2444 (vert) . . 75 80
2449 $1.60 Church of San Fransisco, Guatemala (vert) . . . . 1·00 1·10
2450 $1.65 Tikal National Park, Guatemala . . . . 1·25 1·40
2451 $1.65 Rio Platano Reserve, Honduras . . . . 1·25 1·40
2452 $1.65 Ruins of Copan, Honduras . . . . 1·25 1·40
2453 $1.65 Antigua ruins, Guatemala . . . . 1·25 1·40
2454 $1.65 Teotihuacan, Mexico 1·25 1·40
2455 $1.75 Santo Domingo, Dominican Republic (vert) 1·40 1·50
MS2456 Two sheets, each 127×102 mm. (a) $6 Tikal National Park, Guatemala. (b) $6 Teotihuacan pyramid, Mexico Set of 2 sheets 7·50 8·00
No. 2446 is inscribed "Columbia" in error.

375 Red Bishop

1997. Endangered Species. Multicoloured.
2457 $1.20 Type **375** 85 90
2458 $1.20 Yellow baboon . . . 85 90
2459 $1.20 Superb starling . . . 85 90
2460 $1.20 Ratel 85 90
2461 $1.20 Hunting dog 85 90
2462 $1.20 Serval 85 90
2463 $1.65 Okapi . . . . 95 1·00
2464 $1.65 Giant forest squirrel 95 1·00
2465 $1.65 Lesser masked weaver 95 1·00
2466 $1.65 Small-spotted genet 95 1·00
2467 $1.65 Yellow-billed stork . . 95 1·00
2468 $1.65 Red-headed agama . . 95 1·00
MS2469 Three sheets, each 106×76 mm. (a) $6 South African crowned crane. (b) $6 Bat-eared fox. (c) $6 Malachite kingfisher Set of 3 sheets 10·00 11·00
Nos. 2457/62 and 2463/8 respectively were printed together, se-tenant, with the backgrounds forming composite designs.

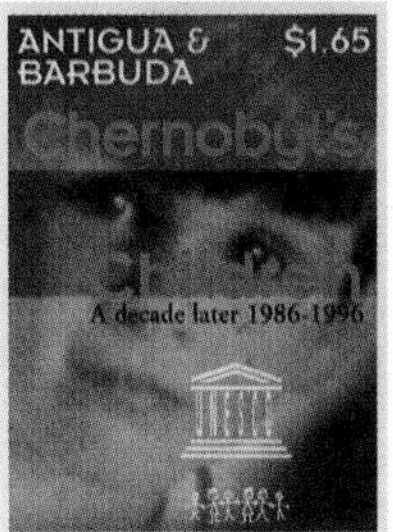

376 Child's Face and U.N.E.S.C.O. Emblem

1997. 10th Anniv of Chernobyl Nuclear Disaster. Multicoloured.
2470 $1.65 Type **376** . . . . . . 1·00 1·10
2471 $2 As Type **376**, but inscr "CHABAD'S CHILDREN OF CHERNOBYL" at foot 1·25 1·40

377 Paul Harris and James Grant

1997. 50th Death Anniv of Paul Harris (founder of Rotary International).
2472 $1.75 Type **377** . . . . . . 1·00 1·25
MS2473 78 × 107 mm. $6 Group study exchange, New Zealand 3·00 3·50

378 Queen Elizabeth II

1997. Golden Wedding of Queen Elizabeth and Prince Philip. Multicoloured.
2474 $1 Type **378** 70 75
2475 $1 Royal coat of arms . . . 70 75
2476 $1 Queen Elizabeth and Prince Philip at reception 70 75
2477 $1 Queen Elizabeth and Prince Philip in landau . . 70 75
2478 $1 Balmoral 70 75
2479 $1 Prince Philip 70 75
MS2480 100 × 71 mm. $6 Queen Elizabeth with Prince Philip in naval uniform 3·50 3·75

379 Kaiser Wilhelm I and Heinrich von Stephan

1997. "Pacific '97" International Stamp Exhibition, San Francisco. Death Centenary of Heinrich von Stephan (founder of the U.P.U.).
2481 **379** $1.75 blue . . . . 1·00 1·25
2482 – $1.75 brown . . . . . . 1·00 1·25
2483 – $1.75 mauve . . . . . . 1·00 1·25
MS2484 82 × 119 mm. $6 violet 3·50 3·75
DESIGNS: No. 2482, Von Stephan and Mercury; 2483, Carrier pigeon and loft; **MS**2484, Von Stephan and 15th-century Basle messenger.
No. 2483 is inscribed "PIDGEON" in error.

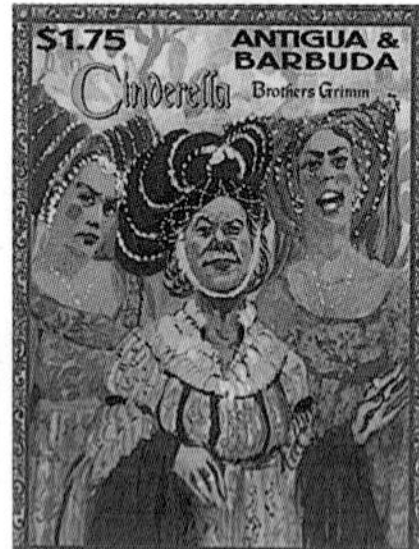

380 The Three Ugly Sisters and their Mother

1997. 175th Anniv of Brothers Grimm's Third Collection of Fairy Tales. Cinderella. Multicoloured.
2485 $1.75 Type **380** . . . . . . 1·00 1·25
2486 $1.75 Cinderella and her Fairy Godmother . . . . 1·00 1·25
2487 $1.75 Cinderella and the Prince . . . . 1·00 1·25
MS2488 124 × 96 mm. $6 Cinderella trying on slipper 3·50 3·75

381 "Marasmius rotula"

1997. Fungi. Multicoloured.
2489 45c. Type **381** 50 30
2490 65c. "Cantharellus cibarius" 60 40
2491 70c. "Lepiota cristata" . . . 60 40
2492 90c. "Auricularia mesenteric" 70 50
2493 $1 "Pholiota alnicola" . . . 75 55
2494 $1.65 "Leccinum aurantiacum" . . . . . . 1·10 1·25
2495 $1.75 "Entoloma serrulatum" . . . . . . 1·25 1·40
2496 $1.75 "Panaeolus sphinctrinus" . . . . . . 1·25 1·40
2497 $1.75 "Volvariella bombycina" . . . . . . 1·25 1·40
2498 $1.75 "Conocybe percincta" 1·25 1·40
2499 $1.75 "Pluteus cervinus" . . 1·25 1·40
2500 $1.75 "Russula foetens" . . 1·25 1·40
MS2501 Two sheets, each 106 × 76 mm. (a) $6 "Amanita cothurnata". (b) $6 "Panellus serotinus" Set of 2 sheets 7·50 8·50

382 "Odontoglossum cervantesii"

1997. Orchids of the World. Multicoloured.
2502 45c. Type **382** 50 30
2503 65c. "Phalaenopsis" Medford Star 60 40
2504 75c. "Vanda Motes" Resplendent 65 45
2505 90c. "Odontonia" Debutante 70 50
2506 $1 "Iwanagaara" Apple Blossom 75 55
2507 $1.65 "Cattleya" Sophia Martin . . . . 1·10 1·25
2508 $1.65 Dogface Butterfly . . 1·10 1·25
2509 $1.65 "Laeliocattleya" Mini Purple . . . . 1·10 1·25
2510 $1.65 "Cymbidium" Showgirl . . . . 1·10 1·25
2511 $1.65 "Brassolaeliocattleya" Dorothy Bertsch . . . . 1·10 1·25
2512 $1.65 "Disa Blackii" . . . . 1·10 1·25
2513 $1.65 "Paphiopedilum leeanum" . . . . 1·10 1·25
2514 $1.65 "Paphiopedilum macranthum" . . . . . . 1·10 1·25
2515 $1.65 "Brassocattleya" Angel Lace . . . . 1·10 1·25
2516 $1.65 "Saphrolae liocattleya" Precious Stones . . . . 1·10 1·25
2517 $1.65 Orange Theope Butterfly . . . . 1·10 1·25
2518 $1.65 "Promenaea xanthina" 1·10 1·25
2519 $1.65 "Lycasle macrobulbon" . . . . . 1·10 1·25
2520 $1.65 "Amestella philippinensis" . . . . . 1·10 1·25
2521 $1.65 "Masdevallia" Machu Picchu . . . . 1·10 1·25
2522 $1.65 "Phalaenopsis" Zuma Urchin . . . . 1·10 1·25
2523 $2 "Dendrobium victoria-reginae" . . . . 1·40 1·60
MS2524 Two sheets, each 76 × 106 mm. (a) "Mitonia" Seine. (b) "Pouphiopedilum gratrixanum" Set of 2 sheets 7·50 8·50
Nos. 2507/14 and 2515/22 respectively were printed together, se-tenant, with the backgrounds forming composite designs.

383 Maradona holding World Cup Trophy, 1986

1997. World Cup Football Championship, France (1998).
2525 **383** 60c. multicoloured . . . 50 35
2526 – 75c. brown 60 45
2527 – 90c. multicoloured . . . 70 50
2528 – $1 brown 75 75
2529 – $1 brown 75 75
2530 – $1 brown 75 75
2531 – $1 black 75 75
2532 – $1 brown 75 75
2533 – $1 brown 75 75
2534 – $1 brown 75 75
2535 – $1 brown 75 75
2536 – $1.20 multicoloured . . 75 80
2537 – $1.65 multicoloured . . 1·10 1·25
2538 – $1.75 multicoloured . . 1·10 1·40
MS2539 Two sheets, each 102 × 127 mm. (a) $6 multicoloured. (b) $6 mult Set of 2 sheets 7·50 8·50
DESIGNS—HORIZ: No. 2526, Fritzwalter, West Germany, 1954; 2527, Zoff, Italy, 1982; 2536, Moore, England, 1966; 2537, Alberto, Brazil, 1970; 2538, Matthaus, West Germany, 1990; MS2539 (b) West German players celebrating, 1990. VERT: No. 2528, Ademir, Brazil, 1950; 2529, Eusebio, Portugal, 1966; 2530, Fontaine, France, 1958; 2531, Schillaci, Italy, 1990; 2532, Leonidas, Brazil, 1938; 2533, Stabile, Argentina, 1930; 2534, Nejedly, Czechoslovakia, 1934; 2535, Muller, West Germany, 1970; MS2539 (a) Bebto, Brazil.

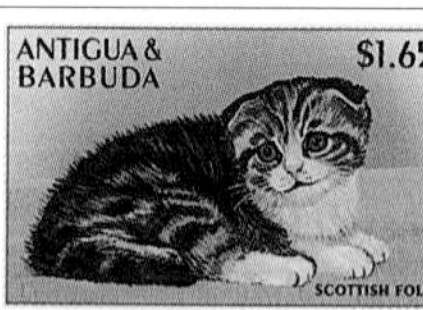

384 Scottish Fold Kitten

1997. Cats and Dogs. Multicoloured.
2540 $1.65 Type **384** . . . . . . 1·00 1·10
2541 $1.65 Japanese bobtail . . . 1·00 1·10
2542 $1.65 Tabby manx . . . . 1·00 1·10
2543 $1.65 Bicolor American shorthair . . . . 1·00 1·10
2544 $1.65 Sorrel Abyssinian . . 1·00 1·10
2545 $1.65 Himalayan blue point 1·00 1·10
2546 $1.65 Dachshund . . . . . 1·00 1·10
2547 $1.65 Staffordshire terrier 1·00 1·10
2548 $1.65 Shar-pei . . . . . . 1·00 1·10
2549 $1.65 Beagle . . . . 1·00 1·10
2550 $1.65 Norfolk terrier . . . 1·00 1·10
2551 $1.65 Golden retriever . . . 1·00 1·10
MS2552 Two sheets, each 107 × 77 mm. (a) $6 Red tabby (vert). (b) $6 Siberian husky (vert) Set of 2 sheets 7·50 8·50

385 Original Drawing by Trevithick, 1803

1997. Railway Locomotives of the World. Multicoloured.
2553 $1.65 Type **385** . . . . . . 1·00 1·10
2554 $1.65 William Hedley's "Puffing Billy", (1813–14) 1·00 1·10
2555 $1.65 Crampton locomotive of French Nord Railway, 1858 . . . . 1·00 1·10
2556 $1.65 Lawrence Machine Shop locomotive, U.S.A., 1860 . . . . 1·00 1·10
2557 $1.65 Natchez and Hamburg Railway steam locomotive "Mississippi", U.S.A., 1834 . . . . 1·00 1·10
2558 $1.65 Bury "Coppernob" locomotive, Furness Railway, 1846 . . . . . 1·00 1·10
2559 $1.65 David Joy's "Jenny Lind", 1847 . . . . . 1·00 1·10
2560 $1.65 Schenectady Atlantic locomotive, U.S.A., 1899 1·00 1·10
2561 $1.65 Kitsons Class 1800 tank locomotive, Japan, 1881 . . . . 1·00 1·10
2562 $1.65 Pennsylvania Railroad express frieght . . . . . 1·00 1·10
2563 $1.65 Karl Golsdorf's 4 cylinder locomotive, Austria . . . . 1·00 1·10
2564 $1.65 Series "E" locomotive, Russia, 1930 . . . . . 1·00 1·10
MS2565 Two sheets, each 72 × 100 mm. (a) $6 George Stephenson "Patentee" type locomotive, 1843. (b) $6 Brunel's trestle bridge over River Lynher, Cornwall Set of 2 sheets 7·50 8·50
No. 2554 is dated "1860" in error.

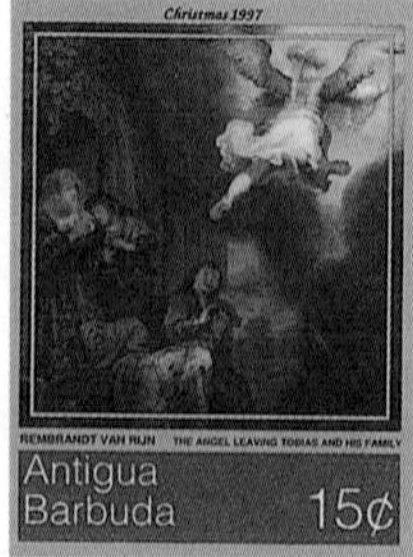

386 "The Angel leaving Tobias and his Family" (Rembrandt)

1997. Christmas. Religious Paintings. Multicoloured.
2566 15c. Type **386** 20 15
2567 25c. "The Resurrection" (Martin Knoller) 30 20
2568 60c. "Astronomy" (Raphael) 50 40
2569 75c. "Music-making Angel" (Melozzo da Forli) . . . 60 55
2570 90c. "Amor" (Parmigianino) 70 60
2571 $1.20 "Madonna and Child with Saints" (Rosso Fiorentino) 80 85
MS2572 Two sheets, each 105 × 96 mm. (a) $6 "The Wedding of Tobias" (Gianantonio and Francesco Guardi) (horiz). (b) $6 "The Portinari Altarpiece" (Hugo van der Goes) (horiz) Set of 2 sheets 7·50 8·50

387 Diana, Princess of Wales

1998. Diana, Princess of Wales Commemoration. Multicoloured (except Nos. 2574 and 2581/2).
2573 $1.65 Type **387** . . . . . . 95 1·00
2574 $1.65 Wearing hoop earrings (red and black) . . . . . 95 1·00
2575 $1.65 Carrying bouquet . . 95 1·00
2576 $1.65 Wearing floral hat . . 95 1·00
2577 $1.65 With Prince Harry . . 95 1·00
2578 $1.65 Wearing white jacket 95 1·00
2579 $1.65 In kitchen . . . . . . 95 1·00
2580 $1.65 Wearing black and white dress . . . . 95 1·00
2581 $1.65 Wearing hat (brown and black) . . . . 95 1·00
2582 $1.65 Wearing floral print dress (brown and black) 95 1·00
2583 $1.65 Dancing with John Travolta . . . . 95 1·00
2584 $1.65 Wearing white hat and jacket . . . . 95 1·00
MS2585 Two sheets, each 70 × 100 mm. (a) $6 Wearing red jumper. (b) $6 Wearing black dress for papal audience (brown and black) Set of 2 sheets 6·50 7·50

388 Yellow Damselfish

1998. Fishes. Multicoloured.
2586 75c. Type **388** 35 40
2587 90c. Barred hamlet 45 50
2588 $1 Yellow-tailed damselfish ("Jewelfish") 50 55
2589 $1.20 Blue-headed wrasse . . 55 60
2590 $1.50 Queen angelfish . . . 70 75
2591 $1.65 Jackknife-fish 80 85
2592 $1.65 Spot-finned hogfish . . 80 85
2593 $1.65 Sergeant major . . . 80 85
2594 $1.65 Neon goby 80 85
2595 $1.65 Jawfish 80 85
2596 $1.65 Flamefish 80 85
2597 $1.65 Rock beauty 80 85
2598 $1.65 Yellow-tailed snapper 80 85
2599 $1.65 Creole wrasse 80 85
2600 $1.65 Slender filefish 80 85
2601 $1.65 Long-spined squirrelfish 80 85
2602 $1.65 Royal gramma ("Fairy Basslet") 80 85
2603 $1.75 Queen triggerfish . . . 85 90
MS2604 Two sheets, each 80 × 110 mm. (a) $6 Porkfish. (b) $6 Black-capped basslet Set of 2 sheets 6·00 6·25
Nos. 2591/6 and 2597/2602 respectively were printed together, se-tenant, with the backgrounds forming composite designs.

389 First Church and Manse, 1822–40

1998. 175th Anniv of Cedar Hall Moravian Church. Multicoloured.
2605 20c. Type **389** 20 20
2606 45c. Cedar Hall School, 1840 . . . . 35 30
2607 75c. Hugh A. King, minister 1945–53 . . . . 55 45
2608 90c. Present Church building 65 50
2609 $1.20 Water tank, 1822 . . 75 75
2610 $2 Former Manse, demolished 1978 . . . . 1·25 1·50
MS2611 100 × 70 mm. $6 Present church building (different) (50 × 37 mm.) 3·25 3·75

390 Europa Point Lighthouse, Gibraltar

391 Pooh and Tigger (January)

1998. Lighthouses of the World. Multicoloured.

2612 45c. Type **390** 20 25
2613 65c. Tierra del Fuego, Argentina (horiz) 35 40
2614 75c. Point Loma, California, U.S.A. (horiz) 35 40
2615 90c. Groenpoint, Cape Town, South Africa . . . 45 50
2616 $1 Youghal, Cork, Ireland 50 55
2617 $1.20 Launceston, Tasmania, Australia . . . 55 60
2618 $1.65 Point Abino, Ontario, Canada (horiz) 80 85
2619 $1.75 Great Inagua, Bahamas 85 90
MS2620 99 × 70 mm. $6 Cap Hatteras, North Carolina, U.S.A. 3·00 3·25

No. 2613 is inscribed "Terra Del Fuego" in error.

1998. Through the Year with Winnie the Pooh. Multicoloured.

2621 $1 Type **391** 75 75
2622 $1 Pooh and Piglet indoors (February) 75 75
2623 $1 Piglet hang-gliding with scarf (March) 75 75
2624 $1 Tigger, Pooh and Piglet on pond (April) 75 75
2625 $1 Kanga and Roo with posy of flowers (May) . . 75 75
2626 $1 Pooh on balloon and Owl (June) 75 75
2627 $1 Pooh, Eeyore, Tigger and Piglet gazing at stars (July) 75 75
2628 $1 Pooh and Piglet by stream (August) 75 75
2629 $1 Christopher Robin going to school (September) . . 75 75
2630 $1 Eeyore in fallen leaves (October) 75 75
2631 $1 Pooh and Rabbit gathering pumpkins (November) 75 75
2632 $1 Pooh and Piglet skiing (December) 75 75
MS2633 Four sheets, each 126 × 101 mm. (a) $6 Pooh, Rabbit and Piglet with blanket (Spring). (b) $6 Pooh by pond (Summer). (c) $6 Pooh sweeping fallen leaves (Autumn). (d) $6 Pooh and Eeyore on ice (Winter) Set of 4 sheets 12·00 13·00

392 Miss Nellie Robinson (founder)

1998. Centenary of Thomas Oliver Robinson Memorial School.

2634 **392** 20c. green and black . . 10 15
2635 – 45c. multicoloured . . . 20 25
2636 – 65c. green and black . . 35 40
2637 – 75c. multicoloured . . . 35 40
2638 – 90c. multicoloured . . . 45 50
2639 – $1.20 brown, green and black 55 60
MS2640 106 × 76 mm. $6 brown 3·00 3·25

DESIGNS—HORIZ: 45c. School photo, 1985; 65c. Former school building, 1930–49; 75c. Children with Mrs. Natalie Hurst (present headmistress); $1.20, Present school building, 1950. VERT: 90c. Miss Ina Loving (former teacher); $6 Miss Nellie Robinson (different).

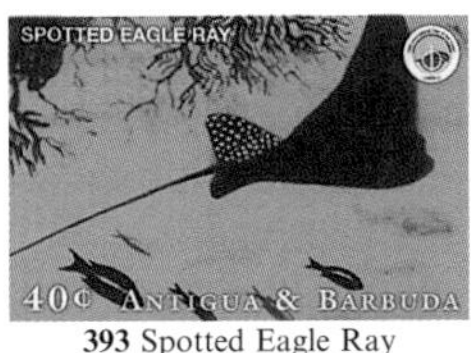

393 Spotted Eagle Ray

1998. International Year of the Ocean. Multicoloured.

2641/65 40c. × 25 Type **393**; Manta ray; Hawksbill turtle; Jellyfish; Queen angelfish; Octopus; Emperor angelfish; Regal angelfish; Porkfish; Racoon butterflyfish; Atlantic barracuda; Sea horse; Nautilus; Trumpetfish; White tip shark; Sunken Spanish galleon; Black-tip shark; Long-nosed butterflyfish; Green moray eel; Captain Nemo; Treasure chest; Hammerhead shark; Divers; Lionfish; Clownfish . . . . . .
2666/77 75c. × 12 Maroon-tailed conure; Cocoi heron; Common tern; Rainbow lory ("Rainbow Lorikeet"); Saddleback butterflyfish; Goatfish and cat shark; Blue shark and stingray; Majestic snapper; Nassau grouper; Black-cap gramma and blue tang; Stingrays; Stingrays and giant starfish . . . .
2641/77 Set of 37 . . . . 9·00 9·25
MS2678 Two sheets. (a) 68 × 98 mm. $6 Humpback whale. (b) 98 × 68 mm. $6 Fiddler ray Set of 2 sheets 6·00 6·25

Nos. 2641/65 and 2666/77 respectively were printed together, se-tenant, with the backgrounds forming composite designs.

394 "Savannah" (paddle-steamer)

1998. Ships of the World. Multicoloured.

2679 $1.75 Type **394** 85 90
2680 $1.75 Viking longship . . . 85 90
2681 $1.75 Greek galley 85 90
2682 $1.75 Sailing clipper 85 90
2683 $1.75 Dhow 85 90
2684 $1.75 Fishing catboat . . . 85 90
MS2685 Three sheets, each 100 × 70 mm. (a) $6 13th-century English warship (41 × 22 mm). (b) $6 Sailing dory (22 × 41 mm). (c) $6 Baltimore clipper (41 × 22 mm) Set of 3 sheets 9·00 9·25

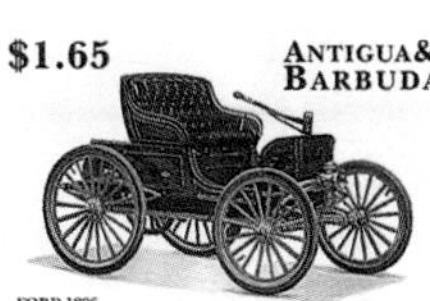

395 Flags of Antigua and CARICOM

1998. 25th Anniv of Caribbean Community.

2686 **395** $1 multicoloured 50 55

396 Ford, 1896

1998. Classic Cars. Multicoloured.

2687 $1.65 Type **396** 80 85
2688 $1.65 Ford A, 1903 . . . . 80 85
2689 $1.65 Ford T, 1928 . . . . 80 85
2690 $1.65 Ford T, 1922 . . . . 80 85
2691 $1.65 Ford Blackhawk, 1929 80 85
2692 $1.65 Ford Sedan, 1934 . . 80 85
2693 $1.65 Torpedo, 1911 . . . . 80 85
2694 $1.65 Mercedes 22, 1913 . . 80 85
2695 $1.65 Rover, 1920 . . . . . 80 85
2696 $1.65 Mercedes-Benz, 1956 80 85
2697 $1.65 Packard V-12, 1934 80 85
2698 $1.65 Opel, 1924 . . . . . 80 85
MS2699 Two sheets, each 70 × 100 mm. (a) $6 Ford, 1908 (60 × 40 mm). (b) $6 Ford, 1929 (60 × 40 mm) Set of 2 sheets 6·00 6·25

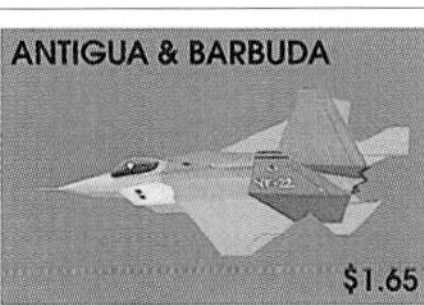

397 Lockheed-Boeing General Dynamics Yf-22

1998. Modern Aircraft. Multicoloured.

2700 $1.65 Type **397** 80 85
2701 $1.65 Dassault-Breguet Rafale BO 1 . . . . . . 80 85
2702 $1.65 MiG 29 . . . . . . 80 85
2703 $1.65 Dassault-Breguet Mirage 2000D 80 85
2704 $1.65 Rockwell B-1B "Lancer" 80 85
2705 $1.65 McDonnell-Douglas C-17A 80 85
2706 $1.65 Space Shuttle 80 85
2707 $1.65 SAAB "Grippen" . . 80 85
2708 $1.65 Eurofighter EF-2000 80 85
2709 $1.65 Sukhoi SU 27 . . . . 80 85
2710 $1.65 Northrop B-2 . . . . 80 85
2711 $1.65 Lockheed F-117 "Nighthawk" 80 85
MS2712 Two sheets, each 110 × 85 mm. (a) $6 F18 Hornet. (b) $6 Sukhoi SU 35 Set of 2 sheets 6·00 6·25

No. **MS**2712b is inscribed "Sukhi" in error.

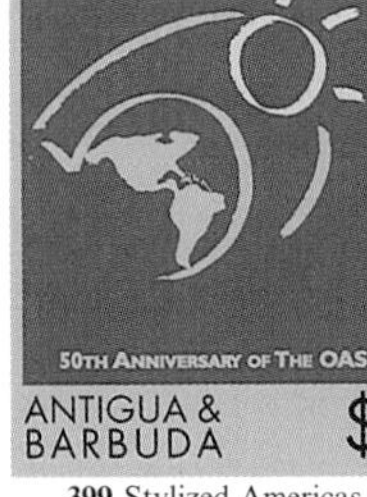

398 Karl Benz (internal-combustion engine)

399 Stylized Americas

1998. Millennium Series. Famous People of the Twentieth Century. Inventors. Multicoloured.

2713 $1 Type **398** 50 55
2714 $1 Early Benz car and Mercedes-Benz racing car (53 × 38 mm) 50 55
2715 $1 Atom bomb mushroom cloud (53 × 38 mm) . . . 50 55
2716 $1 Albert Einstein (theory of relativity) 50 55
2717 $1 Leopold Godowsky Jr. and Leopold Damrosch Mannes (Kodachrome film) 50 55
2718 $1 Camera and transparencies (53 × 38 mm) 50 55
2719 $1 Heinkel He 178 (first turbo jet plane) (53 × 38 mm) 50 55
2720 $1 Dr. Hans Pabst von Ohain (jet turbine engine) 50 55
2721 $1 Rudolf Diesel (diesel engine) 50 55
2722 $1 Early Diesel engine and forms of transport (53 × 38 mm) 50 55
2723 $1 Zeppelin airship (53 × 38 mm) 50 55
2724 $1 Count Ferdinand von Zeppelin (airship pioneer) 50 55
2725 $1 Wilhelm Conrad Rontgen (X-rays) 50 55
2726 $1 X-ray of hand (53 × 38 mm) 50 55
2727 $1 Launch of Saturn rocket (53 × 38 mm) 50 55
2728 $1 Wernher von Braun (rocket research) 50 55
MS2729 Two sheets, each 106 × 76 mm. (a) $6 Hans Geiger (Geiger counter). (b) $6 William Shockley (research into semi-conductors) Set of 2 sheets 6·00 6·25

No. 2713 is inscribed "CARL BENZ" in error.

1998. 50th Anniv of Organization of American States.

2730 **399** $1 multicoloured 50 55

400 "Figures on the Seashore"

1998. 25th Death Anniv of Pablo Picasso (painter). Multicoloured.

2731 $1.20 Type **400** 55 60
2732 $1.65 "Three Figures under a Tree" (vert) 80 85
2733 $1.75 "Two Women running on the Beach" 85 90
MS2734 126 × 102 mm. $6 "Bullfight" 3·00 3·25

401 Dino 246 GT-GTS

1998. Birth Centenary of Enzo Ferrari (car manufacturer). Multicoloured.

2735 $1.75 Type **401** . . . . . . 1·40 1·40
2736 $1.75 Front view of Dino 246 GT-GTS . . . . . . 1·40 1·40
2737 $1.75 365 GT4 BB . . . . 1·40 1·40
MS2738 104 × 72 mm. $6 Dino 246 GT-GTS (91 × 34 mm) 4·00 4·25

402 Scout Handshake

1998. 19th World Scout Jamboree, Chile. Multicoloured.

2739 90c. Type **402** 45 50
2740 $1 Scouts hiking 50 55
2741 $1.20 Scout salute 55 60
MS2742 68 × 98 mm. $6 Lord Baden-Powell 3·00 3·25

403 Mahatma Gandhi

405 Diana, Princess of Wales

404 McDonnell Douglas Phantom F-GR1

1998. 50th Death Anniv of Mahatma Gandhi. Multicoloured.

2743 90c. Type **403** 45 50
2744 $1 Gandhi seated 50 55
2745 $1.20 As young man 55 60
2746 $1.65 At primary school in Rajkot, aged 7 . . . . . 80 85
MS2747 100 × 70 mm. $6 Gandhi with staff 3·00 3·25

1998. 80th Anniv of Royal Air Force. Multicoloured.

2748 $1.75 Type **404** 85 90
2749 $1.75 Two Sepecat Jaguar GR1As 85 90
2750 $1.75 Panavia Tornado F3 85 90
2751 $1.75 McDonnell Douglas Phantom F-GR2 . . . . 85 90
MS2752 Two sheets, each 90 × 68 mm. (a) $6 Golden eagle (bird) and Bristol F2B Fighter. (b) $6 Hawker Hurricane and EF-2000 Eurofighter Set of 2 sheets 6·00 6·25

1998. 1st Death Anniv of Diana, Princess of Wales.

2753 **405** $1.20 multicoloured . . 55 60

406 Brown Pelican

1998. Sea Birds of the World. Multicoloured.

2754 15c. Type **406** 10 15
2755 25c. Dunlin 10 15
2756 45c. Atlantic puffin 20 25
2757 75c. King eider 35 40
2758 75c. Inca tern 35 40
2759 75c. Little auk ("Dovekie") 35 40
2760 75c. Ross's gull 35 40
2761 75c. Common noddy ("Brown Noddy") 35 40
2762 75c. Marbled murrelet . . . 35 40
2763 75c. Northern gannet . . . 35 40
2764 75c. Razorbill 35 40

2765 75c. Long-tailed skua ("Long-tailed Jaeger") . . 35 40
2766 75c. Black guillemot 35 40
2767 75c. Whimbrel 35 40
2768 75c. American oystercatcher ("Oystercatcher") 35 40
2769 90c. Pied cormorant 45 50
MS2770 Two sheets, each 100 × 70 mm. (a) $6 Black skimmer. (b) $6 Wandering albatross Set of 2 sheets 6·00 6·25

Nos. 2757/68 were printed together, se-tenant, with the backgrounds forming a composite design.

No. 2760 is inscribed "ROSS' BULL" in error.

407 Border Collie

1998. Christmas. Dogs. Multicoloured.
2771 15c. Type **407** 10 15
2772 25c. Dalmatian 10 15
2773 65c. Weimaraner 35 40
2774 75c. Scottish terrier 35 40
2775 90c. Long-haired dachshund 45 50
2776 $1.20 Golden retriever . . . 55 60
2777 $2 Pekingese . . . . 95 1·00
MS2778 Two sheets, each 75 × 66 mm. (a) $6 Dalmatian. (b) $6 Jack Russell terrier Set of 2 sheets 6·00 6·25

408 Mickey Mouse Sailing

1999. 70th Birthday of Mickey Mouse. Walt Disney characters participating in water sports. Multicoloured.
2779 $1 Type **408** 75 75
2780 $1 Mickey and Goofy sailing 75 75
2781 $1 Goofy windsurfing . . . 75 75
2782 $1 Mickey sailing and seagull 75 75
2783 $1 Goofy sailing 75 75
2784 $1 Mickey windsurfing . . . 75 75
2785 $1 Goofy running with surfboard 75 75
2786 $1 Mickey surfing 75 75
2787 $1 Donald Duck holding surfboard 75 75
2788 $1 Donald on surfboard (face value at right) . . . 75 75
2789 $1 Minnie Mouse surfing in green shorts 75 75
2790 $1 Goofy surfing 75 75
2791 $1 Goofy in purple shorts waterskiing 75 75
2792 $1 Mickey waterskiing . . . 75 75
2793 $1 Goofy waterskiing with Mickey 75 75
2794 $1 Donald on surfboard (face value at left) 75 75
2795 $1 Goofy in yellow shorts waterskiing 75 75
2796 $1 Minnie in pink shorts surfing 75 75
MS2797 Four sheets, each 127 × 102 mm. (a) $6 Goofy (horiz). (b) $6 Donald Duck. (c) $6 Minnie Mouse. (d) $6 Mickey Mouse Set of 4 sheets 13·00 14·00

409 Hell's Gate Steel Orchestra, 1996

1999. 50th Anniv of Hell's Gate Steel Orchestra. Multicoloured.
2798 20c. Type **409** 10 15
2799 60c. Orchestra members, New York, 1992 . . . . 30 35
2800 75c. Orchestra members with steel drums, 1950 . . 35 40
2801 90c. Eustace Henry, 1964 . . 45 50
2802 $1.20 Alston Henry playing double tenor 55 60
MS2803 Two sheets. (a) 100 × 70 mm. $4 Orchestra members, 1950 (vert). (b) 70 × 100 mm. $4 Eustace Henry, 1964 (vert) Set of 2 sheets 3·75 4·00

410 Tulips **411** Elle Macpherson

1999. Flowers. Multicoloured.
2804 60c. Type **410** 30 35
2805 75c. Fuschia 35 40
2806 90c. Morning glory (horiz) 45 50
2807 90c. Geranium (horiz) . . . 45 50
2808 90c. Blue hibiscus (horiz) . . 45 50
2809 90c. Marigolds (horiz) . . . 45 50
2810 90c. Sunflower (horiz) . . . 45 50
2811 90c. Impatiens (horiz) . . . 45 50
2812 90c. Petunia (horiz) 45 50
2813 90c. Pansy (horiz) 45 50
2814 90c. Saucer magnolia (horiz) 45 50
2815 $1 Primrose (horiz) 50 55
2816 $1 Bleeding heart (horiz) . . 50 55
2817 $1 Pink dogwood (horiz) . . 50 55
2818 $1 Peony (horiz) 50 55
2819 $1 Rose (horiz) 50 55
2820 $1 Hellebores (horiz) . . . 50 55
2821 $1 Lily (horiz) 50 55
2822 $1 Violet (horiz) 50 55
2823 $1 Cherry blossom (horiz) 50 55
2824 $1.20 Calla lily 55 60
2825 $1.65 Sweet pea 80 85
MS2826 Two sheets. (a) 76 × 100 mm. $6 Sangria lily. (b) 106 × 76 mm. $6 Zinnias Set of 2 sheets 6·00 6·25

Nos. 2806/14 and 2815/23 respectively were each printed together, se-tenant, forming composite designs

1999. "Australia '99" International Stamp Exhibition, Melbourne (1st issue). Elle Macpherson (model). Multicoloured.
2827 $1.20 Type **411** 55 60
2828 $1.20 Lying on couch . . . 55 60
2829 $1.20 In swimsuit 55 60
2830 $1.20 Looking over shoulder 55 60
2831 $1.20 Wearing cream shirt 55 60
2832 $1.20 Wearing stetson . . . 55 60
2833 $1.20 Wearing black T-shirt 55 60
2834 $1.20 Holding tree branch 55 60

See also Nos. 2875/92.

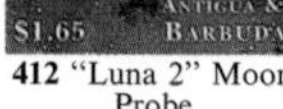

412 "Luna 2" Moon Probe **413** John Glenn entering "Mercury" Capsule, 1962

1999. Satellites and Spacecraft. Multicoloured.
2835 $1.65 Type **412** 80 85
2836 $1.65 "Mariner 2" space probe 80 85
2837 $1.65 "Giotto" space probe 80 85
2838 $1.65 Rosat satellite 80 85
2839 $1.65 International Ultraviolet Explorer . . . 80 85
2840 $1.65 "Ulysses" space probe 80 85
2841 $1.65 "Mariner 10" space probe 80 85
2842 $1.65 "Luna 9" Moon probe 80 85
2843 $1.65 Advanced X-ray Astrophysics Facility . . 80 85
2844 $1.65 "Magellan" space probe 80 85
2845 $1.65 "Pioneer – Venus 2" space probe 80 85
2846 $1.65 Infra-red Astronomy Satellite 80 85
MS2847 Two sheets, each 106 × 76 mm. (a) $6 "Salyut 1" space station (horiz). (b) $6 "MIR" space station (horiz) Set of 2 sheets 6·00 6·25

Nos. 2835/40 and 2841/46 repectively were each printed together, se-tenant, with the backgrounds forming composite designs.

1999. John Glenn's Return to Space. Multicoloured.
2848 $1.75 Type **413** 85 90
2849 $1.75 Glenn in "Mercury" mission spacesuit 85 90
2850 $1.75 Fitting helmet for "Mercury" mission . . . 85 90
2851 $1.75 Outside pressure chamber 85 90

414 Brachiosaurus

1999. Prehistoric Animals. Multicoloured.
2852 65c. Type **414** 35 40
2853 75c. Oviraptor (vert) 35 40
2854 $1 Homotherium 50 55
2855 $1.20 Macrauchenia (vert) 55 60
2856 $1.65 Struthiomimus 80 85
2857 $1.65 Corythosaurus 80 85
2858 $1.65 Dsungaripterus . . . 80 85
2859 $1.65 Compsognathus . . . 80 85
2860 $1.65 Prosaurolophus . . . 80 85
2861 $1.65 Montanoceratops . . 80 85
2862 $1.65 Stegosaurus 80 85
2863 $1.65 Deinonychus 80 85
2864 $1.65 Ouranosaurus 80 85
2865 $1.65 Leptictidium 80 85
2866 $1.65 Ictitherium 80 85
2867 $1.65 Plesictis 80 85
2868 $1.65 Hemicyon 80 85
2869 $1.65 Diacodexis 80 85
2870 $1.65 Stylinodon 80 85
2871 $1.65 Kanuites 80 85
2872 $1.65 Chriacus 80 85
2873 $1.65 Argyrolagus 80 85
MS2874 Two sheets, each 110 × 85 mm. (a) $6 Eurhinodelphis. (b) $6 Pteranodon Set of 2 sheets 6·00 6·25

Nos. 2856/64 and 2865/73 respectively were each printed together, se-tenant, with the backgrounds forming composite designs.

415 Two White Kittens

1999. "Australia '99" International Stamp Exhibition, Melbourne (2nd issue). Cats. Mult.
2875 35c. Type **415** 15 20
2876 45c. Kitten with string . . . 20 25
2877 60c. Two kittens under blanket 30 35
2878 75c. Two kittens in basket 35 40
2879 90c. Kitten with ball 45 50
2880 $1 White kitten 50 55
2881 $1.65 Two kittens playing 80 85
2882 $1.65 Black and white kitten 80 85
2883 $1.65 Black kitten and sleeping cream kitten . . 80 85
2884 $1.65 White kitten with green string 80 85
2885 $1.65 Two sleeping kittens 80 85
2886 $1.65 White kitten with black tip to tail 80 85
2887 $1.65 Kitten with red string 80 85
2888 $1.65 Two long-haired kittens 80 85
2889 $1.65 Ginger kitten 80 85
2890 $1.65 Kitten playing with mouse 80 85
2891 $1.65 Kitten asleep on blue cushion 80 85
2892 $1.65 Tabby kitten 80 85
MS2893 Two sheets, each 70 × 100 mm. (a) $6 Cat carrying kitten in mouth. (b) $6 Kitten in tree Set of 2 sheets 6·00 6·25

416 Early Leipzig–Dresden Railway Carriage and Caroline Islands 1901 Yacht Type 5m. Stamp

1999. "iBRA '99" International Stamp Exhibition, Nuremberg. Multicoloured.
2894 $1 Type **416** 50 55
2895 $1.20 Golsdorf steam locomotive and Caroline Islands 1901 Yacht type 1m. 55 60
2896 $1.65 Early Leipzig–Dresden Railway carriage and Caroline Islands 1899 20pf. optd on Germany 80 85
2897 $1.90 Golsdorf steam locomotive and Caroline Islands 1901 Yacht type 5pf. and 20pf. 90 95
MS2898 165 × 110 mm. $6 Registration label for Ponape, Caroline Islands 3·00 3·25

417 "People on Balcony of Sazaido" (Hokusai)

1999. 150th Death Anniv of Katsushika Hokusai (Japanese artist). Multicoloured.
2899 $1.65 Type **417** 80 85
2900 $1.65 "Nakahara in Sagami Province" 80 85
2901 $1.65 "Defensive Positions" (two wrestlers) 80 85
2902 $1.65 "Defensive Positions" (three wrestlers) 80 85
2903 $1.65 "Mount Fuji in Clear Weather" 80 85
2904 $1.65 "Nihonbashi in Edo" 80 85
2905 $1.65 "Asakusa Honganji" 80 85
2906 $1.65 "Dawn at Isawa in Kai Province" 80 85
2907 $1.65 "Samurai with Bow and Arrow" (with arrows on ground) 80 85
2908 $1.65 "Samurai with Bow and Arrow" (trees in background) 80 85
2909 $1.65 "Kajikazawa in Kai Province" 80 85
2910 $1.65 "A Great Wave" . . 80 85
MS2911 Two sheets, each 100 × 71 mm. (a) $6 "A Netsuke Workshop" (vert). (b) $6 "Gotenyama at Shinagawa on Tokaido Highway" (vert) Set of 2 sheets 6·00 6·25

No. 2903 is inscribed "MOUNT FUGI" in error.

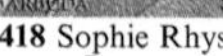

418 Sophie Rhys-Jones **419** Three Children

1999. Royal Wedding. Multicoloured.
2912 $3 Type **418** . . . . 1·40 1·50
2913 $3 Sophie and Prince Edward . . . . 1·40 1·50
2914 $3 Prince Edward . . . . . 1·40 1·50
MS2915 108 × 78 mm. $6 Prince Edward with Sophie Rhys-Jones and Windsor Castle (horiz) 3·00 3·25

1999. 10th Anniv of United Nations Rights of the Child Convention. Multicoloured.
2916 $3 Type **419** . . . . 1·40 1·50
2917 $3 Adult hand holding child's hand . . . . . . 1·40 1·50
2918 $3 Dove and U.N. Headquarters . . . . . . 1·40 1·50
MS2919 112 × 70 mm. $6 Dove 3·00 3·25

Nos. 2916/18 were printed together, se-tenant, forming a composite design.

420 Crampton Type Railway Locomotive, 1855–69

1999. "PhilexFrance '99" International Stamp Exhibition, Paris. Railway Locomotives. Two sheets, each 106 × 81 mm, containing T **420** and similar design. Multicoloured.
MS2920 (a) $6 Type **420**. (b) $6 Compound type No. 232-U1 steam locomotive, 1949 Set of 2 sheets 6·00 6·25

421 Three Archangels from "Faust"

1999. 250th Birth Anniv of Johann von Goethe (German writer).
2921 **421** $1.75 purple, mauve and black 85 90
2922 – $1.75 blue, violet and black 85 90

2923 – $1.75 green and black . . 85 90
MS2924 – 79 × 101 mm. $6 black and brown 3·00 3·25
DESIGNS: No. 2922, Von Goethe and Von Schiller; 2923, Faust reclining with spirits; **MS**2924 Wolfgang von Goethe.

422 "Missa Ferdie" (fishing launch)

423 Fiery Jewel

1999. Local Ships and Boats. Multicoloured.
2925 25c. Type **422** 10 15
2926 45c. Yachts in 32nd Annual Antigua International Sailing Week 20 25
2927 60c. "Jolly Roger" (tourist ship) 30 35
2928 90c. "Freewinds" (cruise liner) (10th anniv of first visit) 45 50
2929 $1.20 "Monarch of the Seas" (cruise liner) . . . 55 60
MS2930 98 × 62 mm. $4 "Freewinds" (11th anniv of maiden voyage) (50 × 37 mm) 1·90 2·00

1999. Butterflies. Multicoloured.
2931 65c. Type **423** 35 40
2932 75c. Hewitson's blue hairstreak 35 40
2933 $1 California dog face (horiz) 50 55
2934 $1 Small copper (horiz) . . 50 55
2935 $1 Zebra swallowtail (horiz) 50 55
2936 $1 White "M" hairstreak (horiz) 50 55
2937 $1 Old world swallowtail (horiz) 50 55
2938 $1 Buckeye (horiz) 50 55
2939 $1 Apollo (horiz) 50 55
2940 $1 Sonoran blue (horiz) . . 50 55
2941 $1 Purple emperor (horiz) 50 55
2942 $1.20 Scarce bamboo page (horiz) 55 60
2943 $1.65 Paris peacock (horiz) 80 85
MS2944 Two sheets. (a) 85 × 110 mm. $6 Monarch. (b) 110 × 85 mm. $6 Cairns birdwing (horiz) Set of 2 sheets 6·00 6·25
Nos. 2933/41 were printed together, se-tenant, forming a composite design.

424 "Madonna and Child in Wreath of Flowers" (Rubens)

1999. Christmas. Religious Paintings.
2945 **424** 15c. multicoloured . . . 10 15
2946 – 25c. black, stone & yellow 10 15
2947 – 45c. multicoloured . . . 20 25
2948 – 60c. multicoloured . . . 30 35
2949 – $2 multicoloured . . . . 95 1·00
2950 – $4 black, stone & yell . . 1·90 2·00
MS2951 – 76 × 106 mm. $6 multicoloured 3·00 3·25
DESIGNS: 25c. "Shroud of Christ held by Two Angels" (Durer); 45c. "Madonna and Child enthroned between Two Saints" (Raphael); 60c. "Holy Family with Lamb" (Raphael); $2 "The Transfiguration" (Raphael); $4 "Three Putti holding Coat of Arms (Durer); $6 "Coronation of St. Catharine" (Rubens).

425 Katharine Hepburn (actress)

2000. Senior Celebrities of the 20th Century. Mult.
2952 90c. Type **425** 45 50
2953 90c. Martha Graham (dancer) 45 50
2954 90c. Eubie Blake (jazz pianist) 45 50
2955 90c. Agatha Christie (novelist) 45 50
2956 90c. Eudora Welty (American novelist) . . . 45 50
2957 90c. Helen Hayes (actress) 45 50
2958 90c. Vladimir Horowitz (concert pianist) 45 50
2959 90c. Katharine Graham (newspaper publisher) . . 45 50
2960 90c. Pablo Casals (cellist) . . 45 50
2961 90c. Pete Seeger (folk singer) 45 50
2962 90c. Andres Segovia (guitarist) 45 50
2963 90c. Frank Lloyd Wright (architect) 45 50

426 Sir Cliff Richard

2000. 60th Birthday of Sir Cliff Richard (entertainer).
2964 **426** $1.65 multicoloured . . 80 85

427 Charlie Chaplin

2000. Charlie Chaplin (actor and director) Commemoration. Showing film scenes. Mult.
2965 $1.65 Standing in street (*Modern Times*) 80 85
2966 $1.65 Hugging man (*The Gold Rush*) 80 85
2967 $1.65 Type **427** 80 85
2968 $1.65 Wielding tools (*Modern Times*) 80 85
2969 $1.65 With hands on hips (*The Gold Rush*) 80 85
2970 $1.65 Wearing cape (*The Gold Rush*) 80 85

428 Streamertail

2000. "The Stamp Show 2000" International Stamp Exhibition, London. Birds of the Caribbean. Mult.
2971 75c. Type **428** 35 40
2972 90c. Yellow-bellied sapsucker 45 50
2973 $1.20 Rufous-tailed jacamar 55 60
2974 $1.20 Scarlet macaw 55 60
2975 $1.20 Yellow-crowned amazon ("Yellow-fronted Amazon") 55 60
2976 $1.20 Golden conure ("Queen-of-Bavaria") . . 55 60
2977 $1.20 Nanday conure . . . 55 60
2978 $1.20 Jamaican tody 55 60
2979 $1.20 Smooth-billed ani . . 55 60
2980 $1.20 Puerto Rican woodpecker 55 60
2981 $1.20 Ruby-throated hummingbird 55 60
2982 $1.20 Common ground dove 55 60
2983 $1.20 American wood ibis ("Wood Stork") 55 60
2984 $1.20 Saffron finch 55 60
2985 $1.20 Green-backed heron 55 60
2986 $1.20 Lovely cotinga 55 60
2987 $1.20 St. Vincent amazon ("St. Vincent Parrot") . . 55 60
2988 $1.20 Cuban grassquit . . . 55 60
2989 $1.20 Red-winged blackbird 55 60
2990 $2 Spectacled owl . . . . . 95 1·00
MS2991 Two sheets, each 80 × 106 mm. (a) $6 Vermillion flycatcher (50 × 37 mm). (b) $6 Red-capped manakin (37 × 50 mm) Set of 2 sheets 6·00 6·25
Nos. 2974/81 and 2982/9 were each printed together, se-tenant, with the backgrounds forming composite designs.
No. 2981 is inscribed "Arhilochus colubria" in error.

429 "Arthur Goodwin"

2000. 400th Birth Anniv of Sir Anthony Van Dyck (Flemish painter). Multicoloured.
2992 $1.20 Type **429** 55 60
2993 $1.20 "Sir Thomas Wharton" 55 60
2994 $1.20 "Mary Villiers, Daughter of Duke of Buckingham" 55 60
2995 $1.20 "Christina Bruce, Countess of Devonshire" 55 60
2996 $1.20 "James Hamilton, Duke of Hamilton" . . . 55 60
2997 $1.20 "Henry Danvers, Earl of Danby" 55 60
2998 $1.20 "Marie de Raet, Wife of Philippe le Roy" . . . 55 60
2999 $1.20 "Jacomo de Cachiopin" 55 60
3000 $1.20 "Princess Henrietta of Lorraine attended by a Page" 55 60
3001 $1.20 "Portrait of a Man" 55 60
3002 $1.20 "Portrait of a Woman" 55 60
3003 $1.20 "Philippe le Roy, Seigneur de Ravels" . . . 55 60
3004 $1.20 "Charles I in State Robes" 55 60
3005 $1.20 "Queen Henrietta Maria" (in white dress) 55 60
3006 $1.20 "Queen Henrietta Maria with Sir Jeffrey Hudson" 55 60
3007 $1.20 "Charles I in Armour" 55 60
3008 $1.20 "Queen Henrietta Maria in Profile facing right" 55 60
3009 $1.20 "Queen Henrietta Maria" (in black dress) 55 60
MS3010 Six sheets. (a) 102 × 128 mm. $5 "Charles I on Horseback". (b) 102 × 128 mm. $5 "Charles I Hunting". (c) 128 × 102 mm. $5 "Charles I with Queen Henrietta Maria". (d) 128 × 102 mm. $5 "Charles I" (from Three Aspects portrait). (e) 102 × 128 mm. $6 "William, Lord Russell". (f) 102 × 128 mm. $6 "Two Sons of Duke of Lennox" Set of 6 sheets 15·00 16·00
No. 2994 is inscribed "Mary Villers", 3002 "Portrait of a Women", 3005 "Henrieta Maria" and **MS**3010f "Duke of Lenox", all in error.

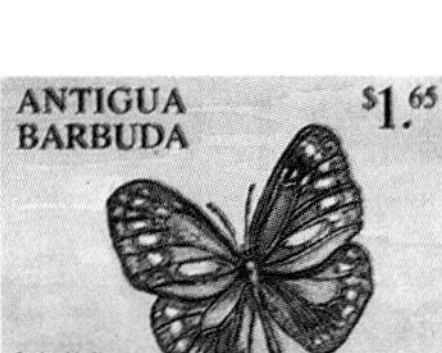

430 *Eupolea miniszeki*

2000. Butterflies. Multicoloured.
3011 $1.65 Type **430** 80 85
3012 $1.65 *Heliconius doris* . . . 80 85
3013 $1.65 *Evenus coronata* . . . 80 85
3014 $1.65 *Papilio anchisiades* . . 80 85
3015 $1.65 *Syrmatia dorilas* . . . 80 85
3016 $1.65 *Morpho patroclus* . . 80 85
3017 $1.65 *Mesosemia loruhama* 80 85
3018 $1.65 *Bia actorion* 80 85
3019 $1.65 *Anteos clorinde* . . . 80 85
3020 $1.65 *Menander menande* . . 80 85
3021 $1.65 *Catasticta manco* . . . 80 85
3022 $1.65 *Urania leilus* 80 85
3023 $1.65 *Theope eudocia* (vert) 80 85
3024 $1.65 *Uranus sloanus* (vert) 80 85
3025 $1.65 *Helicopis cupido* (vert) 80 85
3026 $1.65 *Papilio velovis* (vert) 80 85
3027 $1.65 *Graphium androcles* (vert) 80 85
3028 $1.65 *Mesene phareus* (vert) 80 85
MS3029 Three sheets. (a) 110 × 85 mm. $6 *Graphium encelades*. (b) 110 × 85 mm. $6 *Graphium milon*. (c) 85 × 110 mm. $6 *Hemlargus isola* (vert) Set of 3 sheets 9·00 9·25
Nos. 3011/16, 3017/22 and 3023/8 were each printed together, se-tenant, with the backgrounds forming composite designs.

431 Boxer

432 *Epidendrum pseudepidendrum*

2000. Cats and Dogs. Multicoloured.
3030 90c. Type **431** 45 50
3031 $1 Alaskan malamute . . . 50 55
3032 $1.65 Bearded collie 80 85
3033 $1.65 Cardigan Welsh corgi 80 85
3034 $1.65 Saluki (red) 80 85
3035 $1.65 Basset hound 80 85
3036 $1.65 White standard poodle 80 85
3037 $1.65 Boston terrier 80 85
3038 $1.65 Long-haired blue and white cat (horiz) 80 85
3039 $1.65 Snow shoe (horiz) . . 80 85
3040 $1.65 Persian (horiz) 80 85
3041 $1.65 Chocolate lynx point (horiz) 80 85
3042 $1.65 Brown and white sphynx (horiz) 80 85
3043 $1.65 White tortoiseshell (horiz) 80 85
3044 $2 Wirehaired pointer . . . 95 1·00
3045 $4 Saluki (black) . . . . . 1·90 2·00
MS3046 Two sheets. (a) 106 × 71 mm. $6 Cavalier King Charles spaniel. (b) 111 × 81 mm. $6 Lavender tortie Set of 2 sheets 6·00 6·25

2000. Flowers of the Caribbean. Multicoloured.
3047 45c. Type **432** 20 25
3048 65c. *Odontoglossum cervantesii* 35 40
3049 75c. *Cattleya dowiana* . . . 35 40
3050 90c. *Beloperone guttata* . . . 45 50
3051 $1 *Colliandra haematocephala* 50 55
3052 $1.20 *Brassavola nodosa* . . 55 60
3053 $1.65 *Pseudocalymna alliaceum* 80 85
3054 $1.65 *Datura candida* . . . 80 85
3055 $1.65 *Ipomoea tuberosa* . . 80 85
3056 $1.65 *Allamanda cathartica* 80 85
3057 $1.65 *Aspasia epidendroides* 80 85
3058 $1.65 *Maxillaria cucullata* 80 85
3059 $1.65 *Anthurium andreanum* 80 85
3060 $1.65 *Doxantha unguiscati* 80 85
3061 $1.65 *Hibiscus rosa-sinensis* 80 85
3062 $1.65 *Canna indica* 80 85
3063 $1.65 *Heliconius umilis* . . . 80 85
3064 $1.65 *Strelitzia reginae* . . . 80 85
3065 $1.65 *Masdevallia coccinea* 80 85
3066 $1.65 *Paphinia cristata* . . . 80 85
3067 $1.65 *Vanilla planifolia* . . . 80 85
3068 $1.65 *Cattleya forbesii* . . . 80 85
3069 $1.65 *Lycaste skinneri* . . . 80 85
3070 $1.65 *Cattleya percivaliana* 80 85
MS3071 Three sheets, each 74 × 103 mm. (a) $6 *Cattleya leopoldiie*. (b) $6 *Strelitzia reginae*. (c) $6 *Rossioglossum grande* Set of 3 sheets 9·00 9·25
No. 3061 is inscribed "rosa-senensis" and **MS**3071b "regenae", both in error.

433 Prince William

2000. 18th Birthday of Prince William. Multicoloured.
3072 $1.65 Prince William waving 80 85
3073 $1.65 Wearing Eton school uniform 80 85
3074 $1.65 Wearing grey suit . . 80 85
3075 $1.65 Type **433** 80 85
MS3076 100 × 80 mm. $6 Princess Diana with Princes William and Harry (37 × 50 mm) 3·00 3·25

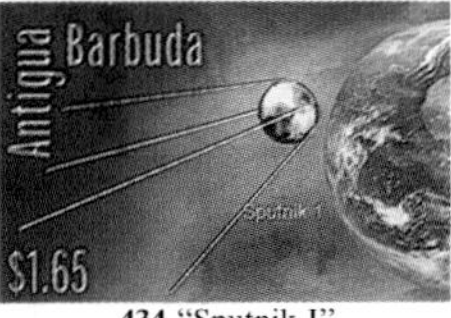

434 "Sputnik I"

2000. "EXPO 2000" World Stamp Exhibition, Anaheim, U.S.A. Space Satellites. Multicoloured.
3077 $1.65 Type **434** 80 85
3078 $1.65 "Explorer I" 80 85
3079 $1.65 "Mars Express" 80 85
3080 $1.65 "Lunik I Solnik" . . 80 85
3081 $1.65 "Ranger 7" 80 85
3082 $1.65 "Mariner 4" 80 85
3083 $1.65 "Mariner 10" 80 85

3084 $1.65 "Soho" 80 85
3085 $1.65 "Mariner 2" 80 85
3086 $1.65 "Giotto" 80 85
3087 $1.65 "Exosat" 80 85
3088 $1.65 "Pioneer Venus" . . . 80 85
MS3089 Two sheets, each 106 × 76 mm. (a) $6 "Vostok I". (b) $6 Hubble Space Telescope
Set of 2 sheets 6·00 6·25

Nos. 3077/82 and 3083/8 were each printed together, se-tenant, with the backgrounds forming composite designs.

435 Alexei Leonov (Commander of "Soyuz 19")

436 Anna Karina in *Une Femme est Une Femme*, 1961

2000. 25th Anniv of "Apollo–Soyuz" Joint Project. Multicoloured.
3090 $3 Type **435** . . . . 1·40 1·50
3091 $3 "Soyuz 19" . . . . . . 1·40 1·50
3092 $3 Valeri Kubasov ("Soyuz 19" engineer) . . . . . . 1·40 1·50
MS3093 71 × 88 mm. $6 Alexei Leonov and Thomas Stafford (Commander of "Apollo 18") 3·00 3·25

2000. 50th Anniv of Berlin Film Festival. Designs showing actors, directors and film scenes. Mult.
3094 $1.65 Type **436** 80 85
3095 $1.65 *Carmen Jones*, 1955 80 85
3096 $1.65 *Die Ratten*, 1955 . . . 80 85
3097 $1.65 *Die Vier im Jeep*, 1951 80 85
3098 $1.65 Sidney Poitier in *Lilies of the Field*, 1963 . . . . 80 85
3099 $1.65 *Invitation to the Dance*, 1956 . . . . . . 80 85
MS3100 97 × 103 mm. $6 Kate Winslet in *Sense and Sensibility*, 1996 3·00 3·25

No. 3096 is inscribed "GOLDER BERLIN BEAR" and **MS**3100 shows the award date "1966" in error.

437 George Stephenson and *Locomotion No. 1*, 1825

2000. 175th Anniv of Stockton and Darlington Line (first public railway). Multicoloured.
3101 $3 Type **437** . . . . 1·40 1·50
3102 $3 Camden and Amboy Railroad locomotive *John Bull*, 1831 . . . . 1·40 1·50

438 Statue of Johann Sebastian Bach

439 Albert Einstein

2000. 250th Death Anniv of Johann Sebastian Bach (German composer). Sheet 77 × 88 mm.
MS3103 $6 multicoloured 3·00 3·25

2000. Election of Albert Einstein (mathematical physicist) as *Time Magazine* "Man of the Century". Sheet 117 × 91 mm.
MS3104 $6 multicoloured 3·00 3·25

440 LZ-1 Airship, 1900

2000. Centenary of First Zeppelin Flight.
3105 **440** $3 brown, black and blue . . . . 1·40 1·50
3106 – $3 brown, black and blue . . . . 1·40 1·50
3107 – $3 multicoloured . . . . 1·40 1·50
MS3108 – 93 × 66 mm. $6 multicoloured 3·00 3·25

DESIGNS: No. 3106, LZ-2, 1906; 3107, LZ-3, 1906. (50 × 37 mm)—No. **MS**3108, LZ-7 *Deutschland*, 1910.

Nos. 3105/7 were printed together, se-tenant, with the backgrounds forming a composite design.

441 Marcus Latimer Hurley (cycling), St. Louis (1904)

2000. Olympic Games, Sydney. Multicoloured.
3109 $2 Type **441** . . . . 95 1·00
3110 $2 Diving . . . . 95 1·00
3111 $2 Flaminio Stadium, Rome (1960) and Italian flag . . 95 1·00
3112 $2 Ancient Greek javelin thrower . . . . 95 1·00

442 Richie Richardson

2000. West Indies Cricket Tour and 100th Test Match at Lord's. Multicoloured.
3113 90c. Type **442** 45 50
3114 $5 Viv Richards . . . . . 2·40 2·50
MS3115 121 × 104 mm. $6 Lord's Cricket Ground (horiz) 3·00 3·25

No. 3114 is inscribed "Viv Richard" in error.

443 Outreach Programme at Sunshine Home for Girls

2000. Girls Brigade. Multicoloured.
3116 20c. Type **443** 10 15
3117 60c. Ullida Rawlins Gill (International Vice President) (vert) 30 35
3118 75c. Officers and girls . . . 35 40
3119 90c. Girl with flag (vert) . . 45 50
3120 $1.20 Members of 8th Antigua Company with flag (vert) 55 60
MS3121 102 × 124 mm. $5 Girl Brigade badge (vert) 2·40 2·50

444 Lady Elizabeth Bowes-Lyon as Young Girl

445 Thumbscrew (Expansion of Inquisition, 1250)

2000. "Queen Elizabeth the Queen Mother's Century".
3122 **444** $2 multicoloured . . . . 95 1·00
3123 – $2 black and gold . . . 95 1·00
3124 – $2 black and gold . . . 95 1·00
3125 – $2 multicoloured . . . . 95 1·00
MS3126 – 153 × 157 mm. $6 multicoloured 3·00 3·25

DESIGNS: No. 3123, Queen Elizabeth in 1940; 3124, Queen Mother with Princess Anne, 1951; 3125, Queen Mother in Canada, 1989; **MS**3126, Queen Mother inspecting guard of honour.

No. **MS**3126 also shows the Royal Arms embossed in gold.

2000. New Millennium. People and Events of Thirteenth Century (1250–1300). Multicoloured (except No. 3127).
3127 60c. Type **445** (black and red) 30 35
3128 60c. Chartres Cathedral (completed, 1260) 30 35
3129 60c. Donor's sculpture, Naumberg (completed, 1260) 30 35
3130 60c. Delegates (Simon de Montfort's Parliament, 1261) 30 35
3131 60c. "Maesta" (Cimabue) (painted 1270) 30 35
3132 60c. Marco Polo (departure from Venice, 1271) . . . 30 35
3133 60c. "Divine Wind" (Kamikaze wind saves Japan from invasion, 1274) 30 35
3134 60c. St. Thomas Aquinas (died 1274) 30 35
3135 60c. Arezzo Cathedral (completed 1277) 35 35
3136 60c. Margrethe ("The Maid of Norway") (crowned Queen of Scotland, 1286) 30 35
3137 60c. Jewish refugees (Expulsion of Jews from England, 1290) 30 35
3138 60c. Muslim horseman (capture of Acre, 1291) 30 35
3139 60c. Moshe de Leon (compiles *The Zohar*, 1291) 30 35
3140 60c. Knights in combat (German Civil War, 1292–98) 30 35
3141 60c. Kublai Khan (died 1294) 30 35
3142 60c. Dante (writes *La Vita Nuova*, 1295) (59 × 39 mm) 30 35
3143 60c. "Autumn Colours on Quiao and Hua Mountains" (Zhan Mengfu) (painted 1296) 30 35

446 "Admonishing the Court Ladies" (after Ku K'ai-Chih)

2000. New Millennium. Two Thousand Years of Chinese Paintings. Multicoloured.
3144 25c. Type **446** 10 15
3145 25c. Ink on silk drawing from Zhan Jadashan . . . 10 15
3146 25c. Ink and colour on silk drawing from Mawangdui Tomb 10 15
3147 25c. "Scholars collating Texts" (attr Yang Zihua) 10 15
3148 25c. "Spring Outing" (attr Zhan Ziqian) 10 15
3149 25c. "Portrait of the Emperors" (attr Yen Liben) 10 15
3150 25c. "Sailing Boats and Riverside Mansion" (attr Li Sixun) 10 15
3151 25c. "Two Horses and Groom" (Han Kan) . . . 10 15
3152 25c. "King's Portrait" (attr Wu Daozi) 10 15
3153 25c. "Court Ladies wearing Flowered Headdresses" (attr Zhou Fang) 10 15
3154 25c. "Distant Mountain Forest" (mountain) (Juran) 10 15
3155 25c. "Mount Kuanglu" (Jiang Hao) 10 15
3156 25c. "Pheasant and Small Birds" (Huang Jucai) . . 10 15
3157 25c. "Deer among Red Maples" (anon) 10 15
3158 25c. "Distant Mountain Forest" (river and fields) (Juran) 10 15
3159 25c. "Literary Gathering" (Han Huang) (57 × 39 mm) 10 15
3160 25c. "Birds and Insects" (Huang Quan) 10 15

No. 3148 is inscribed "SPRINTING", No. 3150 "MASION" and No. 3153 "HEADRESSES", all in error.

447 King Donald III of Scotland

2000. Monarchs of the Millennium.
3161 **447** $1.65 black, stone and brown 80 85
3162 – $1.65 black, stone and brown 80 85
3163 – $1.65 black, stone and brown 80 85
3164 – $1.65 black, stone and brown 80 85
3165 – $1.65 black, stone and brown 80 85
3166 – $1.65 black, stone and brown 80 85
3167 – $1.65 multicoloured . . 80 85
3168 – $1.65 multicoloured . . 80 85
3169 – $1.65 multicoloured . . 80 85
3170 – $1.65 multicoloured . . 80 85
3171 – $1.65 multicoloured . . 80 85
3172 – $1.65 multicoloured . . 80 85
MS3173 – Two sheets, each 115 × 135 mm. (a) $6 mult. (b) $6 mult Set of 2 sheets 6·00 6·25

DESIGNS: No. 3162, King Duncan I of Scotland; 3163, King Duncan II of Scotland; 3164, King Macbeth of Scotland; 3165, King Malcolm III of Scotland; 3166, King Edgar of Scotland; 3167, King Charles I of England and Scotland; 3168, King Charles II of England and Scotland; 3169, Prince Charles Edward Stuart ("The Young Pretender"); 3170, King James II of England and VII of Scotland; 3171, King James II of Scotland; 3172, King James III of Scotland; **MS**3173a, King Robert I of Scotland; **MS**3173b, Queen Anne of Great Britain.

No. 3169 is inscribed "George III 1760–1820 Great Britain" in error.

2000. Popes of the Millennium. As T **447**. Each black, yellow and green.
3174 $1.65 Alexander VI (bare-headed) 80 85
3175 $1.65 Benedict XIII 80 85
3176 $1.65 Boniface IX 80 85
3177 $1.65 Alexander VI (wearing cap) 80 85
3178 $1.65 Clement VIII 80 85
3179 $1.65 Clement VI 80 85
3180 $1.65 John Paul II 80 85
3181 $1.65 Benedict XV 80 85
3182 $1.65 John XXIII 80 85
3183 $1.65 Pius XI 80 85
3184 $1.65 Pius XII 80 85
3185 $1.65 Paul VI 80 85
MS3186 Two sheets, each 115 × 135 mm. (a) $6 Pius II (black, yellow and black). (b) $6 Pius VII (black, yellow and black)
Set of 2 sheets 6·00 6·25

No. 3181 is inscribed "BENIDICT XV" in error.

448 Agouti

2000. Fauna of the Rain Forest. Multicoloured.
3187 75c. Type **448** 35 40
3188 90c. Capybara 45 50
3189 $1.20 Basilisk lizard 55 60
3190 $1.65 Green violetear ("Green Violet-Ear Hummingbird") 80 85
3191 $1.65 Harpy eagle 80 85
3192 $1.65 Three-toed sloth . . . 80 85
3193 $1.65 White uakari monkey 80 85
3194 $1.65 Anteater 80 85
3195 $1.65 Coati 80 85
3196 $1.75 Red-eyed tree frog . . 85 90
3197 $1.75 Black spider monkey 85 90
3198 $1.75 Emerald toucanet . . 85 90
3199 $1.75 Kinkajou 85 90
3200 $1.75 Spectacled bear . . . 85 90
3201 $1.75 Tapir 85 90
3202 $2 Heliconid butterfly . . . 95 1·00
MS3203 Two sheets. (a) 90 × 65 mm. $6 Keel-billed toucan (horiz). (b) 65 × 90 mm. $6 Scarlet macaw
Set of 2 sheets 6·00 6·25

Nos. 3190/5 and 3196/201 were printed together, se-tenant, forming composite designs.

449 "Sea Cliff" Submarine

2000. Submarines. Multicoloured.
3204 65c. Type **449** 35 40
3205 75c. "Beaver Mark IV" . . 35 40
3206 90c. "Reef Ranger" 45 50
3207 $1 "Cubmarine" 50 55
3208 $1.20 "Alvin" 55 60
3209 $2 H.M.S. *Revenge* . . . . 95 1·00
3210 $2 *Walrus*, Netherlands . . 95 1·00
3211 $2 U.S.S. *Los Angeles* . . . 95 1·00
3212 $2 *Daphne*, France . . . . 95 1·00
3213 $2 U.S.S. *Ohio* . . . . . . 95 1·00
3214 $2 U.S.S. *Skipjack* . . . . 95 1·00
3215 $3 "Argus", Russia . . . . 1·40 1·50
MS3216 Two sheets, each 107 × 84 mm. (a) $6 "Trieste". (b) $6 Type 209 U-boat, Germany
Set of 2 sheets 6·00 6·25

Nos. 3209/14 were printed together, se-tenant, with the backgrounds forming a composite design.

450 German Lookout

2000. 60th Anniv of Battle of Britain. Multicoloured (except No. 3222).

3217 $1.20 Type **450** 55 60
3218 $1.20 Children's evacuation train 55 60
3219 $1.20 Evacuating hospital patients 55 60
3220 $1.20 Hawker Hurricane (fighter) 55 60
3221 $1.20 Rescue team 55 60
3222 $1.20 Churchill cartoon (black) 55 60
3223 $1.20 King George VI and Queen Elizabeth inspecting bomb damage 55 60
3224 $1.20 Barrage balloon above Tower Bridge 55 60
3225 $1.20 Bristol Blenheim (bomber) 55 60
3226 $1.20 Prime Minister Winston Churchill 55 60
3227 $1.20 Bristol Blenheim and barrage balloons 55 60
3228 $1.20 Heinkel (fighter) . . . 55 60
3229 $1.20 Supermarine Spitfire (fighter) 55 60
3230 $1.20 German rescue launch 55 60
3231 $1.20 Messerschmitt 109 (fighter) 55 60
3232 $1.20 R.A.F. rescue launch 55 60
MS3233 Two sheets, each 90 × 60 mm. (a) $6 Junkers 87B (dive bomber). (b) $6 Supermarine Spitfires at dusk Set of 2 sheets 6·00 6·25

No. **MS**3233a is inscribed "JUNKERS 878" in error.

451 "The Defence of Cadiz" (Zurbaran)

2000. "Espana 2000" International Stamp Exhibition, Madrid. Paintings from the Prado Museum. Mult.

3234 $1.65 Type **451** 80 85
3235 $1.65 "The Defence of Cadiz" (General and galleys) 80 85
3236 $1.65 "The Defence of Cadiz" (officers) 80 85
3237 $1.65 "Vulcan's Forge" (Vulcan) (Velazquez) . . . 80 85
3238 $1.65 "Vulcan's Forge" (working metal) 80 85
3239 $1.65 "Vulcan's Forge" (workers with hammers) 80 85
3240 $1.65 "Family Portrait" (three men) (Adriaen Key) 80 85
3241 $1.65 "Family Portrait" (one man) 80 85
3242 $1.65 "Family Portrait" (three women) 80 85
3243 $1.65 "The Devotion of Rudolf I" (horseman with lantern) (Rubens and Jan Wildens) 80 85
3244 $1.65 "The Devotion of Rudolf I" (priest on horseback) 80 85
3245 $1.65 "The Devotion of Rudolf I" (huntsman) . . 80 85
3246 $1.65 "The Concert" (lute player) (Vincente Gonzalez) 80 85
3247 $1.65 "The Concert" (lady with fan) 80 85
3248 $1.65 "The Concert" (two gentlemen) 80 85
3249 $1.65 "The Adoration of the Magi" (Wise Man) (Juan Maino) 80 85
3250 $1.65 "The Adoration of the Magi" (two Wise Men) 80 85
3251 $1.65 "The Adoration of the Magi" (Holy Family) . . 80 85
MS3252 Three sheets. (a) 115 × 90 mm. $6 "The Deliverance of St. Peter" (Jose de Ribera) (horiz). (b) 110 × 90 mm. $6 "The Fan Seller" (Jose del Castillo). (c) 110 × 90 mm. $6 "Family in a Garden" (Jan van Kessel the Younger) Set of 3 sheets 9·00 9·25

Nos. 3246/8 are inscribed "Gonzlez" with No.3248 additionally inscribed "Francisco Rizi", all in error.

452 Two Angels

2000. Christmas and Holy Year. Multicoloured.

3253 25c. Type **452** 10 15
3254 45c. Heads of two angels looking down 20 25
3255 90c. Heads of two angels, one looking up 45 50
3256 $1.75 Type **452** 85 90
3257 $1.75 As 45c. 85 90
3258 $1.75 As 90c. 85 90
3259 $1.75 As $5 . . . . 85 90
3260 $5 Two angels with drapery 2·40 2·50
MS3261 110 × 120 mm. $6 Holy Child 3·00 3·25

453 "Dr. Ephraim Bueno" (Rembrandt)

2000. Bicentenary of Rijksmuseum, Amsterdam. Dutch Paintings. Multicoloured.

3262 $1 Type **453** 50 55
3263 $1 "Woman writing a Letter" (Frans van Meris de Oude) 50 55
3264 $1 "Mary Magdalen" (Jan van Scorel) 50 55
3265 $1 "Anna Coddle" (Maerten van Heemskerck) 50 55
3266 $1 "Cleopatra's Banquet" (Gerard Lairesse) 50 55
3267 $1 "Titus in Friar's Habit" (Rembrandt) 50 55
3268 $1.20 "Saskia" (Rembrandt) 55 60
3269 $1.20 "In the Month of July" (Paul Joseph Constantin Gabriel) . . . 55 60
3270 $1.20 "Maria Trip" (Rembrandt) 55 60
3271 $1.20 "Still Life with Flowers" (Jan van Huysum) 55 60
3272 $1.20 "Haesje van Cleyburgh" (Rembrandt) 55 60
3273 $1.20 "Girl in a White Kimono" (George Hendrick Breitner) . . . 55 60
3274 $1.65 "Man and Woman at a Spinning Wheel" (Pieter Pietersz) 80 85
3275 $1.65 "Self-portrait" (Rembrandt) 80 85
3276 $1.65 "Jeremiah lamenting the Destruction of Jerusalem" (Rembrandt) 80 85
3277 $1.65 "The Jewish Bride" (Rembrandt) 80 85
3278 $1.65 "Anna accused by Tobit of stealing a Kid" (Rembrandt) 80 85
3279 $1.65 "The Prophetess Anna" (Rembrandt) . . . 80 85
MS3280 Three sheets, each 118 × 88 mm. (a) $6 "Doubting Thomas" (Hendrick ter Brugghen). (b) $6 "Still Life with Cheeses" (Floris van Dijck); (c) $6 "Isaac Blessing Jacob" (Govert Flinck) Set of 3 sheets 9·00 9·25

454 "Starmie No. 121"

2001. Characters from "Pokemon" (children's cartoon series). Multicoloured.

3281 $1.75 Type **454** 85 90
3282 $1.75 "Misty" 85 90
3283 $1.75 "Brock" 85 90
3284 $1.75 "Geodude No. 74" . . 85 90
3285 $1.75 "Krabby No. 98" . . . 85 90
3286 $1.75 "Ash" 85 90
MS3287 74 × 114 mm. $6 "Charizard No. 6" 3·00 3·25

455 Blue-toothed Entoloma

456 Map and Graphs

2001. "Hong Kong 2001" Stamp Exhibition. Tropical Fungi. Multicoloured.

3288 25c. Type **455** 10 15
3289 90c. Common morel 45 50
3290 $1 Red cage fungus 50 55
3291 $1.65 Copper trumpet . . . 80 85
3292 $1.65 Field mushroom ("Meadow Mushroom") 80 85
3293 $1.65 Green gill ("Green-gilled Parasol") 80 85
3294 $1.65 The panther 80 85
3295 $1.65 Death cap 80 85
3296 $1.65 Royal boletus ("King Bolete") 80 85
3297 $1.65 Lilac fairy helmet ("Lilac Bonnet") 80 85
3298 $1.65 Silky volvar 80 85
3299 $1.65 Agrocybe mushroom ("Poplar Field Cap") . . 80 85
3300 $1.65 Saint George's mushroom 80 85
3301 $1.65 Red-stemmed tough shank 80 85
3302 $1.65 Fly agaric 80 85
3303 $1.75 Common fawn agaric ("Fawn Shield-Cap") . . 85 90
MS3304 Two sheets, each 70 × 90 mm. (a) $6 Yellow parasol. (b) $6 Mutagen milk cap Set of 2 sheets 6·00 6·25

Nos. 3291/6 and 3297/302 were each printed together, se-tenant, with the backgrounds forming composite designs.

2001. Population and Housing Census.

3305 **456** 15c. multicoloured . . . 10 15
3306 – 25c. multicoloured . . . 10 15
3307 – 65c. multicoloured . . . 35 40
3308 – 90c. multicoloured . . . 45 50
MS3309 – 55 × 50 mm. $6 multicoloured (Map and census logo) 3·00 3·25

DESIGNS: 25c. to 90c. Map and different form of graph.

457 "Yuna (Bath-house Women)" (detail)

2001. "PHILANIPPON 2001" International Stamp Exhibition, Tokyo. Traditional Japanese Paintings. Multicoloured.

3310 45c. Type **457** 20 25
3311 60c. "Yuna (Bath-house Women)" (different detail) 30 35
3312 65c. "Yuna (Bath-house Women)" (different detail) 35 40
3313 75c. "The Hikone Screen" (detail) 35 40
3314 $1 "The Hikone Screen" (different detail) 50 55
3315 $1.20 "The Hikone Screen" (different detail) 55 60
3316 $1.65 Galleon and Dutch merchants with horse . . 80 85
3317 $1.65 Galleon and merchants with tiger . . . 80 85
3318 $1.65 Merchants unpacking goods 80 85
3319 $1.65 Merchants with parasol and horse 80 85
3320 $1.65 Women packing food 80 85
3321 $1.65 Picnic under the cherry tree 80 85
3322 $1.65 Palanquins and resting bearers 80 85
3323 $1.65 Women dancing . . . 80 85

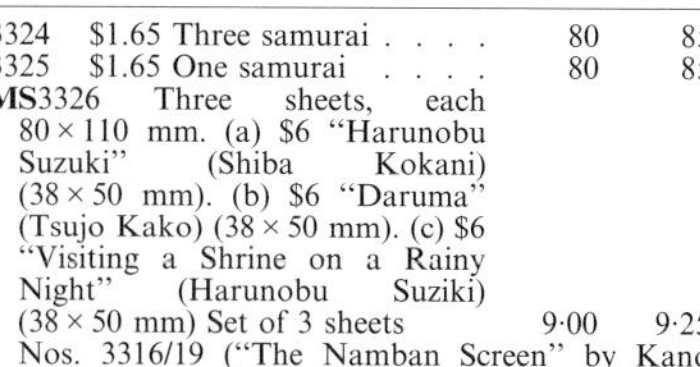

3324 $1.65 Three samurai 80 85
3325 $1.65 One samurai 80 85
MS3326 Three sheets, each 80 × 110 mm. (a) $6 "Harunobu Suzuki" (Shiba Kokani) (38 × 50 mm). (b) $6 "Daruma" (Tsujo Kako) (38 × 50 mm). (c) $6 "Visiting a Shrine on a Rainy Night" (Harunobu Suziki) (38 × 50 mm) Set of 3 sheets 9·00 9·25

Nos. 3316/19 ("The Namban Screen" by Kano Nizen) and Nos. 3320/5 ("Merry-making under the Cherry Blossoms" by Kano Naganobu) were each printed together, se-tenant, with both sheetlets forming the entire painting.

458 Lucille Ball leaning on Mantelpiece

2001. Scenes from *I Love Lucy* (American T.V. comedy series). Eight sheets each containing multicoloured design as T **458**.

MS3327 (a) 118 × 92 mm. $6 Type **458**. (b) 98 × 120 mm. $6 Desi Arnaz laughing. (c) 93 × 130 mm. $6 William Frawley at table. (d) 114 × 145 mm. $6 Lucille Ball with William Frawley. (e) 114 × 145 mm. $6 Lucille Ball in blue dress. (f) 119 × 111 mm. $6 Lucille Ball sitting at table. (g) 128 × 100 mm. $6 Lucille Ball as scarecrow. (h) 93 × 125 mm. $6 William Frawley shouting at Desi Arnaz (horiz) Set of 8 sheets 23·00 24·00

459 *Hintleya burtii*

2001. Caribbean Orchids. Multicoloured.

3328 45c. Type **459** 20 25
3329 75c. *Neomoovea irrovata* . . 35 40
3330 90c. *Comparettia speciosa* . . 45 50
3331 $1 *Cypredium crapeanum* 50 55
3332 $1.20 *Trichoceuos muralis* (vert) 55 60
3333 $1.20 *Dracula rampira* (vert) 55 60
3334 $1.20 *Psychopsis papilio* (vert) 55 60
3335 $1.20 *Lycaste clenningiana* (vert) 55 60
3336 $1.20 *Telipogon nevuosus* (vert) 55 60
3337 $1.20 *Masclecallia ayahbacana* (vert) 55 60
3338 $1.65 *Cattleya dowiana* (vert) 80 85
3339 $1.65 *Dendiobium cruentum* (vert) 80 85
3340 $1.65 *Bulbophyllum lobb* (vert) 80 85
3341 $1.65 *Chysis laevis* (vert) . . 80 85
3342 $1.65 *Ancistrochilus rothschildicanus* (vert) . . 80 85
3343 $1.65 *Angraecum sororium* (vert) 80 85
3344 $1.65 *Rhyncholaelia glanca* (vert) 80 85
3345 $1.65 *Oncidium barbatum* (vert) 80 85
3346 $1.65 *Phaius tankervillege* (vert) 80 85
3347 $1.65 *Ghies brechtiana* (vert) 80 85
3348 $1.65 *Angraecum leonis* (vert) 80 85
3349 $1.65 *Cycnoches loddigesti* (vert) 80 85
MS3350 Two sheets. (a) 68 × 104 mm. $6 *Symphalossum sanquinem* (vert). (b) 104 × 68 mm. $6 *Trichopilia fragrans* (vert) Set of 2 sheets 6·00 6·25

460 Yellowtail Damselfish

2001. Tropical Marine Life. Multicoloured.

3351 25c. Type **460** 10 15
3352 45c. Indigo hamlet 20 25
3353 65c. Great white shark . . . 35 40
3354 90c. Bottle-nose dolphin . . 45 50
3355 90c. Palette surgeonfish . . 45 50
3356 $1 Octopus 50 55
3357 $1.20 Common dolphin . . 55 60

3358 $1.20 Franklin's gull 55 60
3359 $1.20 Rock beauty 55 60
3360 $1.20 Bicoloured angelfish 55 60
3361 $1.20 Beaugregory 55 60
3362 $1.20 Banded butterflyfish 55 60
3363 $1.20 Common tern 55 60
3364 $1.20 Flying fish 55 60
3365 $1.20 Queen angelfish . . . 55 60
3366 $1.20 Blue-striped grunt . . 55 60
3367 $1.20 Porkfish 55 60
3368 $1.20 Blue tang 55 60
3369 $1.65 Red-footed booby . . 80 85
3370 $1.65 Bottle-nose dolphin 80 85
3371 $1.65 Hawksbill turtle . . . 80 85
3372 $1.65 Monk seal 80 85
3373 $1.65 Great white shark (inscr "Bull Shark") . . . 80 85
3374 $1.65 Lemon shark 80 85
3375 $1.65 Dugong 80 85
3376 $1.65 White-tailed tropicbird 80 85
3377 $1.65 Bull shark 80 85
3378 $1.65 Manta ray 80 85
3379 $1.65 Green turtle 80 85
3380 $1.65 Spanish grunt 80 85
MS3381 Four sheets. (a) 68 × 98 mm. $5 Sailfish. (b) 68 × 98 mm. $5 Brown pelican and beaugregory (vert). (c) 98 × 68 mm. $6 Queen triggerfish. (d) 96 × 68 mm. $6 Hawksbill turtle Set of 4 sheets 10·50 11·00

Nos. 3357/62, 3363/8, 3369/74 and 3375/80 were each printed together, se-tenant, the backgrounds forming composite designs.

461 *Freewinds* (liner) and Police Band, Antigua

2001. Work of *Freewinds* (Church of Scientology flagship) in Caribbean. Multicoloured.

3382 30c. Type **461** 15 20
3383 45c. At anchor off St. Barthelemy 20 25
3384 75c. At sunset 35 40
3385 90c. Off Bonaire 45 50
3386 $1.50 *Freewinds* anchored off Bequia 70 75
MS3387 Two sheets, each 85 × 60 mm. (a) $4 *Freewinds* alongside quay, Curacao. (b) $4 Decorated with lights Set of 2 sheets 3·75 4·00

462 Young Queen Victoria in Blue Dress

2001. Death Centenary of Queen Victoria. Multicoloured.

3388 $2 Type **462** . . . . 95 1·00
3389 $2 Queen Victoria wearing red head-dress . . . . . 95 1·00
3390 $2 Queen Victoria with jewelled hair ornament . . 95 1·00
3391 $2 Queen Victoria, after Chalon, in brooch . . . . 95 1·00
MS3392 70 × 82 mm. $5 Queen Victoria in old age 2·40 2·50

463 "Water Lilies"

2001. 75th Death Anniv of Claude-Oscar Monet (French painter). Multicoloured.

3393 $2 Type **463** . . . . 95 1·00
3394 $2 "Rose Portals, Giverny" 95 1·00
3395 $2 "Water Lily Pond, Harmony in Green" . . . 95 1·00
3396 $2 "Artist's Garden, Irises" 95 1·00
MS3397 136 × 111 mm. $5 "Jerusalem Artichoke Flowers" (vert) 2·40 2·50

No. 3396 is inscribed "Artists's" in error.

464 Duchess of York with Baby Princess Elizabeth (1926)

465 Verdi in Top Hat

2001. 75th Birthday of Queen Elizabeth II. Multicoloured.

3398 $1 Type **464** 50 55
3399 $1 Queen in Coronation robes (1953) 50 55
3400 $1 Young Princess Elizabeth (1938) 50 55
3401 $1 Queen Elizabeth in Garter robes (1956) . . . 50 55
3402 $1 Princess Elizabeth with pony (1939) 50 55
3403 $1 Queen Elizabeth in red dress and pearls (1985) . . 50 55
MS3404 90 × 72 mm. $6 Princess Elizabeth and Queen Elizabeth (1940) 3·00 3·25

2001. Death Centenary of Giuseppe Verdi (Italian composer). Multicoloured.

3405 $2 Type **465** . . . . 95 1·00
3406 $2 Don Carlos and part of opera score . . . . 95 1·00
3407 $2 Conductor and score for *Aida* . . . . 95 1·00
3408 $2 Musicians and score for *Rigoletto* . . . . 95 1·00
MS3409 77 × 117 mm. $5 Verdi in evening dress 2·40 2·50

Nos. 3405/8 were printed together, se-tenant, the backgrounds forming a composite design.

466 "Georges-Henri Manuel"

2001. Death Centenary of Henri de Toulouse-Lautrec (French painter). Multicoloured.

3410 $2 Type **466** . . . . 95 1·00
3411 $2 "Louis Pascal" . . . . . 95 1·00
3412 $2 "Romain Coolus" . . . 95 1·00
3413 $2 "Monsieur Fourcade" . . 95 1·00
MS3414 67 × 84 mm. $5 "Dancing at the Moulin de la Galette" 2·40 2·50

No 3412 is inscribed "ROMAN" in error.

467 Marlene Dietrich smoking

2001. Birth Centenary of Marlene Dietrich (actress and singer).

3415 **467** $2 black, purple and red 95 1·00
3416 – $2 black, purple and red 95 1·00
3417 – $2 multicoloured . . . . 95 1·00
3418 – $2 black, purple and red 95 1·00

DESIGNS: No. 3416, Marlene Dietrich, in evening gown, sitting on settee; 3417, In black dress; 3418, Sitting on piano.

468 Collared Peccary

2001. Vanishing Fauna of the Caribbean. Multicoloured.

3419 25c. Type **468** 10 15
3420 30c. Baird's tapir 15 20
3421 45c. Agouti 20 25
3422 75c. Bananaquit 35 40
3423 90c. Six-banded armadillo 45 50
3424 $1 Roseate spoonbill . . . 50 55
3425 $1.80 Mouse opossum . . . 85 90
3426 $1.80 Magnificent black frigate bird 85 90
3427 $1.80 Northern jacana . . . 85 90
3428 $1.80 Painted bunting . . . 85 90
3429 $1.80 Haitian solenodon . . 85 90
3430 $1.80 St. Lucia iguana . . . 85 90
3431 $2.50 West Indian iguana 1·25 1·40
3432 $2.50 Scarlet macaw . . . . 1·25 1·40
3433 $2.50 Cotton-topped tamarin . . . . 1·25 1·40
3434 $2.50 Kinkajou . . . . . . 1·25 1·40
MS3435 Two sheets. (a) 117 × 85 mm. $6 Ocelot (vert). (b) 162 × 116 mm. $6 King vulture (vert) Set of 2 sheets 6·00 6·25

469 Sara Crewe (*The Little Princess*) reading a Letter

2001. Shirley Temple Films. Multicoloured. Showing film scenes. (a) *The Little Princess*. Multicoloured.

3436 $1.50 Type **469** 70 75
3437 $1.50 Sara in pink dressing gown 70 75
3438 $1.50 Sara cuddling doll . . 70 75
3439 $1.50 Sara as Princess on throne 70 75
3440 $1.50 Sara talking to man in frock coat 70 75
3441 $1.50 Sara blowing out candles 70 75
3442 $1.80 Sara with Father (horiz) 85 90
3443 $1.80 Sara scrubbing floor (horiz) 85 90
3444 $1.80 Sara and friend with Headmistress (horiz) . . . 85 90
3445 $1.80 Sara with Queen Victoria (horiz) 85 90

(b) *Baby, Take a Bow*.

3447 $1.65 Shirley in dancing class (horiz) 80 85
3448 $1.65 Shirley cuddling Father (horiz) 80 85
3449 $1.65 Shirley at bedtime with parents (horiz) . . . 80 85
3450 $1.65 Shirley in yellow dress with Father (horiz) . . . 80 85
3451 $1.65 Shirley and Father at Christmas party (horiz) 80 85
3452 $1.65 Shirley and gangster looking in cradle (horiz) 80 85
3453 $1.65 Shirley in spotted dress 80 85
3454 $1.65 Shirley on steps with gangster 80 85
3455 $1.65 Shirley with gangster holding gun 80 85
3456 $1.65 Shirley with Mother 80 85
MS3457 106 × 76 mm. $6 Shirley in spotted dress 3·00 3·25

470 Rudolph Valentino in *Blood and Sand*, 1922

2001. 75th Death Anniv of Rudolph Valentino (Italian film actor).

3458 **470** $1 brown and black . . 50 55
3459 – $1 lilac and black . . . 50 55
3460 – $1 brown and black . . 50 55
3461 – $1 brown and black . . 50 55
3462 – $1 red and black 50 55
3463 – $1 lilac and black . . . 50 55
3464 – $1 multicoloured 50 55
3465 – $1 multicoloured 50 55
3466 – $1 multicoloured 50 55
3467 – $1 multicoloured 50 55
3468 – $1 multicoloured 50 55
3469 – $1 multicoloured 50 55
MS3470 Two sheets. (a) 90 × 125 mm. $6 multicoloured. (b) 68 × 95 mm. $6 multicoloured Set of 2 sheets 6·00 6·25

DESIGNS: No. 3459, In *Eyes of Youth* with Clara Kimbal Young, 1919; 3460, In *All Night Long* with Carmel Meyers, 1918; 3461, Valentino in 1926; 3462, In *Camille* with Alla Nazimova, 1921; 3463, In *Cobra* with Nita Naldi, 1925; 3464, In *The Son of the Sheik* with Vilma Banky, 1926; 3465, In *The Young Rajah*, 1922; 3466, In *The Eagle* with Vilma Banky, 1925; 3467, In *The Sheik* with Agnes Ayres, 1921; 3468, In *A Sainted Devil*, 1924; 3469, In *Monsieur Beaucaire*, 1924; **MS**3470, (a) Valentino with Natacha Rambova. (b) In *The Four Horseman of the Apocalypse*, 1921.

Nos. 3464 and 3466 are inscribed "BLANKY" and No. 3467 "AYERS", all in error.

471 Queen Elizabeth

472 Melvin Calvin, 1961

2001. Golden Jubilee (1st issue).

3471 **471** $1 multicoloured 50 55

No. 3471 was printed in sheetlets of 8, containing two vertical rows of four, separated by a large illustrated central gutter. Both the stamp and the illustration on the central gutter are made up of a collage of miniature flower photographs.

See also Nos. 3535/8.

2001. Centenary of Nobel Prizes. Chemistry Winners. Multicoloured.

3472 $1.50 Type **472** 70 75
3473 $1.50 Linus Pauling, 1954 70 75
3474 $1.50 Vincent du Vigneaud, 1955 . . . . 70 75
3475 $1.50 Richard Synge, 1952 70 75
3476 $1.50 Archer Martin, 1952 70 75
3477 $1.50 Alfred Werner, 1913 70 75
3478 $1.50 Robert Curl Jr., 1996 70 75
3479 $1.50 Alan Heeger, 2000 . . 70 75
3480 $1.50 Michael Smith, 1993 70 75
3481 $1.50 Sidney Altman, 1989 70 75
3482 $1.50 Elias Corey, 1990 . . 70 75
3483 $1.50 William Giauque, 1949 . . . . 70 75
MS3484 Three sheets, each 107 × 75 mm. (a) $6 Ernest Rutherford, 1908. (b) $6 Ernst Fischer, 1973. (c) $6 American volunteers, International Red Cross (Peace Prize, 1944) Set of 3 sheets 9·00 9·25

473 "Madonna and Child with Angels" (Filippo Lippi)

474 Final between Uruguay and Brazil, Brazil 1950

2001. Christmas. Italian Religious Paintings. Multicoloured.

3485 25c. Type **473** 10 15
3486 45c. "Madonna of Corneto Tarquinia" (Lippi) . . . 20 25
3487 50c. "Madonna and Child" (Domenico Ghirlandaio) 25 30
3488 75c. "Madonna and Child" (Lippi) 35 40
3489 $4 "Madonna Delceppo" (Lippi) . . . . 1·90 2·00
MS3490 106 × 136 mm. $6 "Madonna enthroned with Angels and Saints" (Lippi) 3·00 3·25

2001. World Cup Football Championship, Japan and Korea (2002). Multicoloured.

3491 $1.50 Type **474** 70 75
3492 $1.50 Ferenc Puskas (Hungary), Switzerland 1954 . . . . 70 75
3493 $1.50 Raymond Kopa (France), Sweden 1958 . . 70 75
3494 $1.50 Mauro (Brazil), Chile 1962 . . . . 70 75
3495 $1.50 Gordon Banks (England), England 1966 70 75
3496 $1.50 Pele (Brazil), Mexico 1970 . . . . 70 75
3497 $1.50 Daniel Passarella (Argentina), Argentina 1978 . . . . 70 75
3498 $1.50 Karl-Heinz Rummenigge (Germany), Spain 1982 . . . . 70 75
3499 $1.50 World Cup Trophy, Mexico 1986 . . . . . . 70 75
3500 $1.50 Diego Maradona (Argentina), Italy 1990 . . 70 75

3501 $1.50 Roger Milla (Cameroun), U.S.A. 1994 70 75
3502 $1.50 Zinedine Zidane (France), France 1998 . . 70 75
MS3503 Two sheets, each 88 × 75 mm. (a) $6 Detail of Jules Rimet Trophy, Uruguay, 1930. (b) $6 Detail of World Cup Trophy, Japan/Korea, 2002 Set of 2 sheets 6·00 6·25
No. 3500 is inscribed "Deigo" in error.

475 Battle of Nashville, 1864

2002. American Civil War. Multicoloured.
3504 45c. Type **475** 20 25
3505 45c. Capture of Atlanta, 1864 . . . . 20 25
3506 45c. Battle of Spotsylvania, 1864 . . . . 20 25
3507 45c. Battle of The Wilderness, 1864 . . . . 20 25
3508 45c. Battle of Chickamauga Creek, 1863 . . . . . . 20 25
3509 45c. Battle of Gettysburg, 1863 . . . . 20 25
3510 45c. Lee and Jackson at Chancellorsville, 1863 . . 20 25
3511 45c. Battle of Fredericksburg, 1862 . . 20 25
3512 45c. Battle of Antietam, 1862 . . . . 20 25
3513 45c. Second Battle of Bull Run, 1862 . . . . 20 25
3514 45c. Battle of Five Forks, 1865 . . . . 20 25
3515 45c. Seven Days' Battles, 1862 . . . . 20 25
3516 45c. First Battle of Bull Run, 1861 . . . . 20 25
3517 45c. Battle of Shiloh, 1862 20 25
3518 45c. Battle of Seven Pines, 1862 . . . . 20 25
3519 45c. Bombardment of Fort Sumter, 1861 . . . . . . 20 25
3520 45c. Battle of Chattanooga, 1863 . . . . 20 25
3521 45c. Grant and Lee at Appomattox, 1865 . . . 20 25
3522 50c. General Ulysses S. Grant (vert) 25 30
3523 50c. President Abraham Lincoln (vert) 25 30
3524 50c. President Jefferson Davis (vert) 25 30
3525 50c. General Robert E. Lee (vert) 25 30
3526 50c. General George Custer (vert) 25 30
3527 50c. Admiral Andrew Hull Foote (vert) 25 30
3528 50c. General "Stonewall" Jackson (vert) 25 30
3529 50c. General Jeb Stuart (vert) 25 30
3530 50c. General George Meade (vert) 25 30
3531 50c. General Philip Sheridan (vert) 25 30
3532 50c. General James Longstreet (vert) 25 30
3533 50c. General John Mosby (vert) 25 30
MS3534 Two sheets, each 105 × 76 mm. (a) $6 Confederate ironclad *Merrimack* attacking *Cumberland* (Federal sloop) (51 × 38 mm). (b) $6 *Monitor* (Federal ironclad) Set of 2 sheets 6·00 6·25

476 Queen Elizabeth presenting Rosettes

2002. Golden Jubilee (2nd issue). Multicoloured.
3535 $2 Type **476** . . . . 95 1·00
3536 $2 Queen Elizabeth at garden party . . . . . . 95 1·00
3537 $2 Queen Elizabeth in evening dress . . . . . . 95 1·00
3538 $2 Queen Elizabeth in cream coat . . . . 95 1·00
MS3539 76 × 108 mm. $6 Princesses Elizabeth and Margaret as brides-maids 3·00 3·25

477 U.S. Flag as Statue of Liberty and Antigua & Barbuda Flag

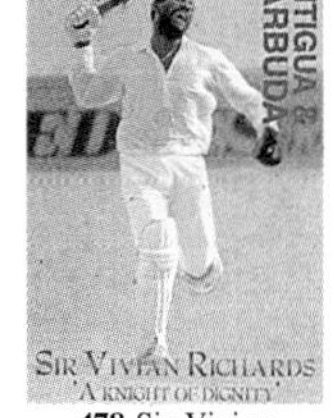

478 Sir Vivian Richards waving Bat

2002. "United We Stand". Support for Victims of 11 September 2001 Terrorist Attacks.
3540 **477** $2 multicoloured . . . . 95 1·00

2002. 50th Birthday of Sir Vivian Richards (West Indian cricketer). Multicoloured.
3541 25c. Type **478** 10 15
3542 30c. Sir Vivian Richards receiving presentation from Antigua Cricket Association 15 20
3543 50c. Sir Vivian Richards wearing sash 25 30
3544 75c. Sir Vivian Richards batting 35 40
3545 $1.50 Sir Vivian Richards and Lady Richards . . . 70 75
3546 $1.80 Sir Vivian Richards with enlarged action photograph of himself . . 85 90
MS3547 Two sheets, each 68 × 95 mm. (a) $6 Sir Vivian Richards with guard of honour. (b) $6 Sir Vivian Richards in Indian traditional dress Set of 2 sheets 6·00 6·25

479 Thick-billed Parrot

2002. Flora and Fauna. Multicoloured.
3548 50c. Type **479** 25 30
3549 75c. Lesser long-nosed bat 35 40
3550 90c. Quetzal 45 50
3551 90c. Two-toed sloth 45 50
3552 90c. Lovely cotinga 45 50
3553 90c. *Pseudolycaena marsyas* (butterfly) 45 50
3554 90c. Magenta-throated woodstar 45 50
3555 90c. *Automeris rubrescens* (moth) 45 50
3556 90c. *Bufo periglenes* (toad) 45 50
3557 90c. Collared peccary . . . 45 50
3558 90c. Tamandua anteater . . 45 50
3559 $1 St. Lucia parrot 50 55
3560 $1 Cuban kite 50 55
3561 $1 West Indian whistling-duck 50 55
3562 $1 *Eurema amelia* (butterfly) 50 55
3563 $1 Scarlet ibis 50 55
3564 $1 Black-capped petrel . . . 50 55
3565 $1 *Cnemidophorus vanzoi* (lizard) 50 55
3566 $1 Cuban solenodon 50 55
3567 $1 *Papilio thersites* (butterfly) 50 55
3568 $1.50 Montserrat oriole . . 70 75
3569 $1.80 *Leptotes perkinsae* (butterfly) 85 90
MS3570 Two sheets, each 110 × 85 mm. (a) $6 Olive Ridley turtle. (b) $6 Margay Set of 2 sheets 6·00 6·25
Nos. 3550/8 and 3559/67 were each printed together, se-tenant, with the backgrounds forming composite designs.

480 Community Players wearing Straw Hats

2002. 50th Anniv of Community Players. Multicoloured. Showing scenes from various productions.
3571 20c. Type **480** 10 10
3572 25c. Men in suits with women in long dresses . . 10 15
3573 30c. In *Pirates of Penzance* 15 20
3574 75c. Female choir 35 40
3575 90c. In Mexican dress . . . 45 50
3576 $1.50 Members at a reception 70 75
3577 $1.80 Production in the open air 85 90
MS3578 Two sheets, each 76 × 84 mm. (a) $4 Mrs. Edie Hill-Thibou (former President) (vert). (b) $4 Miss Yvonne Maginley (Acting President and Director of Music) (vert) Set of 2 sheets 3·75 4·00

481 Mount Fuji, Japan

482 Cross-country Skiing

2002. International Year of Mountains. Mult.
3579 $2 Type **481** . . . . 1·00 1·10
3580 $2 Machu Picchu, Peru . . 1·00 1·10
3581 $2 The Matterhorn, Switzerland . . . . 1·00 1·10

2002. Winter Olympic Games, Salt Lake City. Multicoloured.
3582 $2 Type **482** . . . . 1·00 1·10
3583 $2 Pairs figure skating . . . 1·00 1·10
MS3584 84 × 114 mm. Nos. 3582/3 2·00 2·25

483 Amerigo Vespucci wearing Skullcap

2002. 500th Anniv of Amerigo Vespucci's Third Voyage. Multicoloured.
3585 $2.50 Type **483** . . . . . . 1·25 1·40
3586 $2.50 Vespucci as an old man . . . . 1·25 1·40
3587 $2.50 16th-century map . . 1·25 1·40
MS3588 49 × 68 mm. $5 Vespucci holding dividers (vert) 2·40 2·50

484 *Spirit of St. Louis* and Charles Lindbergh (pilot)

2002. 75th Anniv of First Solo Transatlantic Flight. Multicoloured.
3589 $2.50 Type **484** . . . . . . 1·25 1·40
3590 $2.50 *Spirit of St. Louis* at Le Bourget, Paris, 1927 1·25 1·40
3591 $2.50 Charles Lindbergh in New York ticker-tape parade, 1927 . . . . . . 1·25 1·40
MS3592 80 × 110 mm. $6 Charles Lindbergh wearing flying helmet 2·40 2·50

485 Princess Diana

2002. 5th Death Anniv of Diana, Princess of Wales. Multicoloured.
3593 $1.80 Type **485** 85 90
3594 $1.80 Princess Diana in tiara (looking left) 85 90
3595 $1.80 Wearing hat 85 90
3596 $1.80 Princess Diana wearing pearl drop earrings and black dress 85 90
3597 $1.80 Wearing tiara (facing front) 85 90
3598 $1.80 Princess Diana wearing pearl drop earrings 85 90
MS3599 91 × 106 mm. $6 Princess Diana 3·00 3·25

486 Kennedy Brothers

2002. Presidents John F. Kennedy and Ronald Reagan Commemoration. Multicoloured.
3600 $1.50 Type **486** 70 75
3601 $1.50 John Kennedy with Danny Kaye (American entertainer) 70 75
3602 $1.50 Delivering Cuban Blockade speech, 1962 . . 70 75
3603 $1.50 With Jacqueline Kennedy 70 75
3604 $1.50 Meeting Bill Clinton (future president) 70 75
3605 $1.50 Family at John Kennedy's funeral 70 75
3606 $1.50 President and Mrs. Reagan with Pope John Paul II, 1982 . . . . . . 70 75
3607 $1.50 As George Gipp in *Knute Rockne - All American*, 1940 . . . . . 70 75
3608 $1.50 With General Matthew Ridgeway, Bitburg Military Cemetery, Germany, 1985 70 75
3609 $1.50 With George H. Bush and Secretary Mikhail Gorbachev of U.S.S.R., 1988 . . . . 70 75
3610 $1.50 Presidents Reagan, Ford, Carter and Nixon at the White House, 1981 70 75
3611 $1.50 Horse riding with Queen Elizabeth, Windsor, 1982 . . . . . 70 75
MS3612 Two sheets, each 88 × 22 mm. (a) $6 President Kennedy at press conference (vert). (b) $6 President Reagan (vert) Set of 2 sheets 3·00 3·00

487 Red-billed Tropicbird

2002. Endangered Species of Antigua. Multicoloured.
3613 $1.50 Type **487** 70 75
3614 $1.50 Brown pelican 70 75
3615 $1.50 Magnificent frigate bird 70 75
3616 $1.50 Ground lizard 70 75
3617 $1.50 West Indian whistling duck 70 75
3618 $1.50 Antiguan racer snake 70 75
3619 $1.50 Spiny lobster 70 75
3620 $1.50 Hawksbill turtle . . . 70 75
3621 $1.50 Queen conch 70 75

488 Elvis Presley

2002. 25th Death Anniv of Elvis Presley (American entertainer).
3622 **488** $1 multicoloured 50 55

489 Cheerleader Teddy

2002. Centenary of the Teddy Bear. Girl Teddies. Multicoloured.
3623 $2 Type **489** . . . . 95 1·00
3624 $2 Figure skater . . . . . 95 1·00
3625 $2 Ballet dancer . . . . . 95 1·00
3626 $2 Aerobics instructor . . . 95 1·00

490 "Croconaw No. 159"

2002. Pokemon (children's cartoon series). Mult.
3627 $1.50 Type **490** 70 75
3628 $1.50 "Mantine No. 226" 70 75
3629 $1.50 "Feraligatr No. 160" 70 75
3630 $1.50 "Qwilfish No. 211" 70 75
3631 $1.50 "Remoraid No. 223" 70 75
3632 $1.50 "Quagsire No. 195" 70 75
MS3633 80 × 106 mm. $6 "Chinchou No. 170" 3·00 3·25

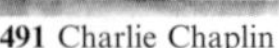

491 Charlie Chaplin **492** Bob Hope

2002. 25th Death Anniv of Charlie Chaplin (British actor). Each black, grey and light grey.
3634 $1.80 Type **491** 85 90
3635 $1.80 Wearing waistcoat and spotted bow-tie 85 90
3636 $1.80 In top hat 85 90
3637 $1.80 Wearing coat and bowler hat 85 90
3638 $1.80 Charlie Chaplin in old age 85 90
3639 $1.80 With finger on chin 85 90
MS3640 90 × 105 mm. $6 Charlie Chaplin as The Tramp 3·00 3·25

2002. Bob Hope (American entertainer) Commemoration. Designs showing him entertaining American troops. Multicoloured.
3641 $1.50 Type **492** 70 75
3642 $1.50 Wearing bush hat,Vietnam, 1972 . . . . 70 75
3643 $1.50 On board U.S.S. *John F. Kennedy* (aircraft carrier) 70 75
3644 $1.50 With hawk badge on sleeve, Berlin, 1948 . . . 70 75
3645 $1.50 Wearing desert fatigues 70 75
3646 $1.50 In white cap and stars on collar 70 75

493 Lee Strasberg **494** Marlene Dietrich

2002. 20th Death Anniv of Lee Strasberg (pioneer of "Method Acting").
3647 **493** $1 black and stone . . . 50 55

2002. 10th Death Anniv of Marlene Dietrich (actress and singer). Each black and grey.
3648 $1.50 Type **494** 70 75
3649 $1.50 Wearing top hat . . . 70 75
3650 $1.50 In chiffon dress . . . 70 75
3651 $1.50 Resting chin on left hand 70 75
3652 $1.50 In cloche hat 70 75
3653 $1.50 Wearing black evening gloves 70 75
MS3654 83 × 108 mm. $6 Marlene Dietrich wearing chiffon scarf 3·00 3·25

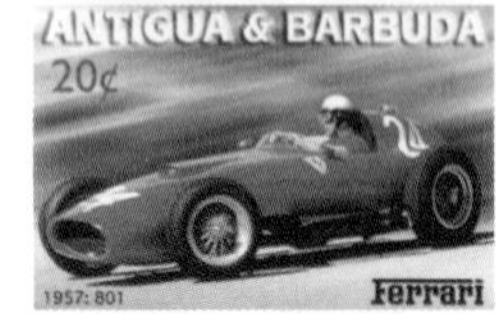

495 Ferrari 801, 1957

2002. Ferrari Racing Cars. Multicoloured.
3655 20c. Type **495** 10 10
3656 25c. Ferrari 256, 1959 . . . 10 15
3657 30c. Ferrari 246 P, 1960 . . 15 20
3658 90c. Ferrari 246, 1966 . . . 45 50
3659 $1 Ferrari 312 B2, 1971 . . 50 55
3660 $1.50 Ferrari 312, 1969 . . 70 75
3661 $2 Ferrari F310 B, 1997 . . 95 1·00
3662 $4 Ferrari F2002, 2002 . . . 1·90 2·00

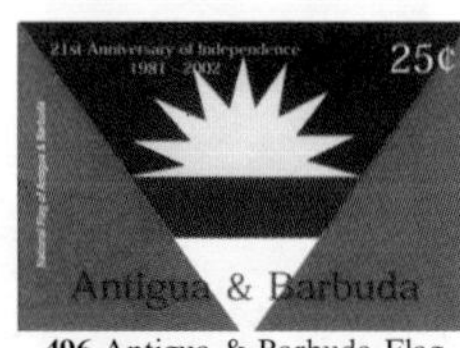

496 Antigua & Barbuda Flag

2002. 21st Anniv of Independence. Multicoloured.
3663 25c. Type **496** 10 15
3664 30c. Antigua & Barbuda coat of arms (vert) . . . 15 20
3665 $1.50 Mount St. John's Hospital under construction 70 75
3666 $1.80 Parliament Building, St. John's 85 90
MS3667 Two sheets, each 77 × 81 mm. (a) $6 Sir Vere Bird (Prime Minister, 1967–94) (38 × 51 mm) Set of 2 sheets (b) $6 Lester Bird (Prime Minister since 1994) (38 × 51 mm) 5·75 6·00

497 Juan Valeron (Spain)

2002. World Cup Football Championship, Japan and Korea. Multicoloured.
3668 $1.65 Type **497** 80 85
3669 $1.65 Iker Casillas (Spain) 80 85
3670 $1.65 Fernando Hierro (Spain) 80 85
3671 $1.65 Gary Kelly (Ireland) 80 85
3672 $1.65 Damien Duff (Ireland) 80 85
3673 $1.65 Matt Holland (Ireland) 80 85
3674 $1.65 Pyo Lee (South Korea) 80 85
3675 $1.65 Ji Sung Park (South Korea) 80 85
3676 $1.65 Jung Hwan Ahn (South Korea) 80 85
3677 $1.65 Filippo Inzaghi (Italy) 80 85
3678 $1.65 Paolo Maldini (Italy) 80 85
3679 $1.65 Dammiano Tommasi (Italy) 80 85
MS3680 Four sheets, each 82 × 82 mm. (a) $3 Jose Camacho (Spanish coach); $3 Raul Gonzales Blanco (Spain). (b) $3 Robbie Keane (Ireland); $3 Mick McCarthy (Irish coach). (c) $3 Guus Hiddink (South Korean coach); $3 Chul Sang Yoo (South Korea). (d) $3 Francesco Totti (Italy); $3 Giovanni Trapattoni (Italian coach) Set of 4 sheets 11·50 12·00
No. **MS**3680a is inscribed "Carlos Gamarra" in error.

498 "Coronation of the Virgin" (Domenico Ghirlandaio)

2002. Christmas. Religious Paintings. Multicoloured.
3681 25c. Type **498** 10 15
3682 45c. "Adoration of the Magi" (detail) (D. Ghirlandaio) 20 25
3683 75c. "Annunciation" (Simone Martini) (vert) 35 40
3684 90c. "Adoration of the Magi" (different detail) (D. Ghirlandaio) 45 50
3685 $5 "Madonna and Child" (Giovanni Bellini) . . . . 2·40 2·50
MS3686 76 × 110 mm. $6 "Madonnna and Child" (S. Martini) 3·00 3·25

499 Antiguan Racer Snake Head

2002. Endangered Species. Antiguan Racer Snake. Multicoloured.
3687 $1 Type **499** 50 55
3688 $1 Coiled Antiguan racer snake with tail at right . . 50 55
3689 $1 Antiguan racer snake with pebbles and leaves 50 55
3690 $1 Coiled Antiguan racer snake with tail at left . . 50 55

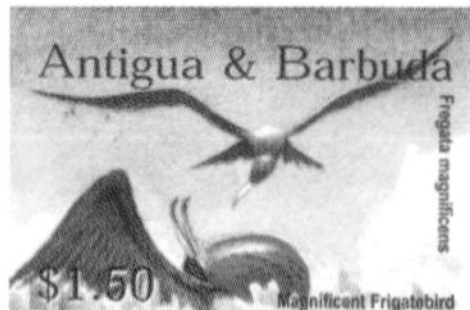

500 Magnificent Frigate Bird

2002. Fauna and Flora. Multicoloured.
3691 $1.50 Type **500** 70 75
3692 $1.50 Sooty tern 70 75
3693 $1.50 Bananaquit 70 75
3694 $1.50 Yellow-crowned night heron 70 75
3695 $1.50 Greater flamingo . . . 70 75
3696 $1.50 Belted kingfisher . . . 70 75
3697 $1.50 Killer whale 70 75
3698 $1.50 Sperm whale 70 75
3699 $1.50 Minke whale 70 75
3700 $1.50 Blainville's beaked whale 70 75
3701 $1.50 Blue whale 70 75
3702 $1.50 Cuvier's beaked whale 70 75
3703 $1.80 *Epidendrum fragans* 85 90
3704 $1.80 *Dombeya wallichii* . . 85 90
3705 $1.80 *abebuia serratifolia* . . 85 90
3706 $1.80 *Cryptostegia grandiflora* 85 90
3707 $1.80 *Hylocereus undatus* . . 85 90
3708 $1.80 *Rodriguezia lanceolata* 85 90
3709 $1.80 *Diphthera festiva* . . . 85 90
3710 $1.80 *Hypocrita dejanira* . . 85 90
3711 $1.80 *Eupseudosoma involutum* 85 90
3712 $1.80 *Composia credula* . . 85 90
3713 $1.80 *Citherania magnifica* 85 90
3714 $1.80 *Divana diva* 85 90
MS3715 Four sheets, each 75 × 45 mm. (a) $5 Snowy egret. (b) $5 *Rothschildia orizaba* (moth). (c) $6 Humpback whale. (d) $6 *Ionopsis utricularioides* (flower) Set of 4 sheets 10·50 11·00
Nos. 3691/6 (birds), 3697/702 (whales), 3703/8 (moths) and 3709/14 (flowers) were each printed together, se-tenant, with the backgrounds forming composite designs.

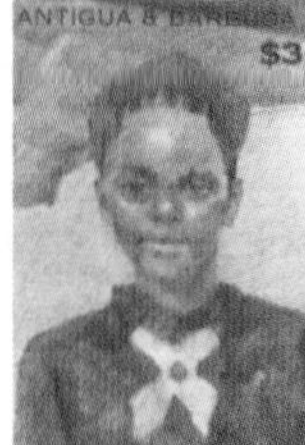

501 Dr. Margaret O'garro **502** Antiguan Brownie

2002. Centenary of Pan American Health Organization. Health Professionals. Multicoloured.
3716 $1.50 Type **501** 70 75
3717 $1.50 Ineta Wallace (nurse) 70 75
3718 $1.50 Vincent Edwards (public health official) . . 70 75

2002. 20th World Scout Jamboree, Thailand. Each lilac and brown (Nos. 3719/21) or multicoloured (others).
3719 $3 Type **502** . . . . 1·40 1·50
3720 $3 Brownie with badge on cap . . . . 1·40 1·50
3721 $3 Brownie without badge on cap . . . . 1·40 1·50
3722 $3 Robert Baden-Powell on horseback, 1896 (horiz) 1·40 1·50
3723 $3 Ernest Thompson Seton (founder, Boy Scouts of America), 1910, and American scout badge (horiz) . . . . 1·40 1·50
3724 $3 First black scout troop, Virginia, 1928 (horiz) . . 1·40 1·50
MS3725 Two sheets. (a) 80 × 113 mm. $6 Ernest Thompson Seton. (b) 110 × 83 mm. $6 Scout salute. Set of 2 sheets 3·00 3·25
Nos. 3719/21 were printed together, se-tenant, forming a composite design.

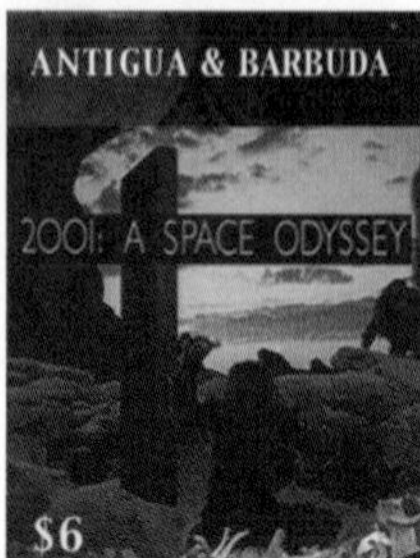

503 Scene from *2001: A Space Odyssey* (Arthur C. Clarke)

2002. Famous Science Fiction Authors. Three sheets, each 150 × 108 mm, containg vert designs as T **503**. Multicoloured
MS3726 Three sheets. (a) $6 Type **503**. (b) $6 Scene from *The Monuments of Mars* (Richard C. Hoagland). (c) $6 Nostradamus with globe. Set of 3 sheets 4·25 4·50

504 "Goat and Kids" (Liu Jiyou)

2003. Chinese New Year ("Year of the Goat").
3727 **504** $1.80 multicoloured . . 85 90

ANTIOQUIA Pt. 20

One of the states of the Granadine Confederation.
A department of Colombia from 1886, now uses Colombian stamps.

100 centavos = 1 peso.

1 5 6

1868. Various arms designs. Imperf.
1 **1** 2½c. blue £450 £225
2 – 5c. green £350 £200
3 – 10c. lilac £850 £385
4 – 1p. red £300 £185

1869. Various frames. Imperf.
5 **5** 2½c. blue . . . . 2·50 2·00
6 5c. green . . . . 3·25 3·00
8 10c. mauve . . . . 4·00 2·00
9 20c. brown . . . . 4·50 3·00
10 **6** 1p. red . . . . 7·50 7·50

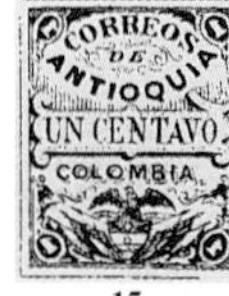

7 15

1873. Arms designs inscr "E.S." (or "Eo. So." or "Estado Soberano") "de Antioquia". Imperf.
11 **7** 1c. green . . . . 2·00 1·50
12 – 5c. green . . . . 2·50 1·60
13 – 10c. mauve . . . . 16·00 12·00
14 – 20c. brown . . . . 4·00 2·50
15 – 50c. blue . . . . 1·00 80
16 – 1p. red . . . . 2·50 2·50
17 – 2p. black on yellow . . . . 5·00 5·00
18 – 5p. black on red . . . . . . 25·00 20·00
The 5p. is larger (25½ × 31½ mm).

1875. Imperf.
20 **15** 1c. black on green 60 60
43 1c. mauve . . . . 1·00 1·00
21 1c. black 60 60
52 1c. green . . . . 1·00 1·00
22 – 2½c. blue (Arms) 80 80
23 – 5c. green ("Liberty") . . . 6·00 5·00
25 – 10c. mauve (J. Berrio) . . . 8·00 7·00

20 Condor **21** Liberty

23 Liberty **25** Liberty

1879. Imperf.
30 **20** 2½c. blue . . . . 3·00 3·00
38 2½c. green . . . . 80 1·00
45 2½c. black on buff . . . . . 3·00 3·00
39 **21** 5c. green . . . . 85 1·00
40 5c. violet . . . . 1·75 1·00
32 – 10c. violet (Arms) £250 £200
36 **23** 10c. violet . . . . 50·00 16·00

41 10c. red 1·00 1·00
42 **21** 20c. brown 1·25 1·25

1883. Various frames. Head of Liberty to left. Imperf.
53 **25** 5c. brown 4·00 2·00
47 5c. yellow 3·00 2·50
48 5c. green 55·00 40·00
49 10c. green 2·00 2·00
50 10c. mauve 3·50 3·50
55 10c. blue 4·00 3·50
51 20c. blue 2·50 2·50

28 31

1886. Imperf.
57 **28** 1c. green on pink 50 50
65 1c. red on lilac 30 30
58 2½c. black on orange 35 40
66 2½c. mauve on pink 50 40
59 5c. blue on buff 2·00 75
67 5c. red on green 2·25 2·25
68 5c. lake on buff 1·00 80
60 10c. red on buff 1·00 60
69 10c. brown on green 1·00 80
61 20c. purple on buff 1·00 60
62 50c. yellow on buff 2·00 2·00
63 1p. yellow on green 4·00 4·00
64 2p. green on lilac 4·00 4·00

1888. Various sizes and frames. Inscr "MEDELLIN". Imperf.
70 **31** 2½c. black on yellow 15·00 12·00
71 2½c. red on white 2·50 2·50
72 5c. black on yellow 2·00 2·00
73 5c. red on orange 1·75 1·75

34 35

1889. Arms in various frames.
74 **34** 1c. black on red 10 10
75 2½c. black on blue 20 15
76 5c. black on yellow 45 25
77 10c. black on green 50 40
95 10c. brown 25 25
78 20c. blue 1·00 1·00
79 50c. brown 2·00 2·00
80 50c. green 1·75 1·75
81 1p. red 1·00 1·00
82 2p. black on mauve 7·50 6·00
83 5p. black on red 10·00 7·50

1890. Perf.
84 **35** 2½c. black on buff 1·00 1·00
85 5c. black on yellow 1·00 1·00
86 10c. black on buff 4·75 4·75
87 10c. black on red 5·00 5·00
88 20c. black on yellow 5·00 5·00

36 37

1892.
89 **36** 1c. brown on buff 50 40
90 1c. blue 20 20
91 2½c. violet on lilac 30 30
92 2½c. green 30 30
93 5c. black 80 60
94 5c. red 20 20

1896.
96 **37** 2c. grey 40 40
107 2c. red 25 40
97 2½c. brown 40 40
108 2½c. blue 25 40
98 3c. red 50 50
109 3c. olive 25 40
99 5c. green 25 20
110 5c. yellow 20 30
100 10c. lilac 45 45
111 10c. brown 50 60
101 20c. brown 70 70
112 20c. blue 75 1·00
102 50c. sepia 90 90
113 50c. red 1·00 1·40
103 1p. black and blue 10·00 10·00
114 1p. black and red 10·00 10·00
104 2p. black and orange 40·00 40·00
115 2p. black and green 35·00 35·00
105 5p. black and mauve 50·00 50·00

39 Gen. Cordoba **43**

1899.
118 **39** ½c. blue 10 10
119 1c. blue 10 10
120 2c. black 10 10
121 3c. red 10 10
122 4c. brown 10 10
123 5c. green 10 10
124 10c. red 10 10
125 20c. violet 10 10
126 50c. yellow 10 10
127 1p. green 10 15
128 2p. green 10 20

1901. Various frames.
132 **43** 1c. red 10 15
133 1c. brown 25 25
134 1c. blue 25 25
Nos. 132 and 134 also exist with "CENTAVO" inside the rectangle below figure "1".

46 **47** **48** Girardot

1902.
138 **46** 1c. red 10 10
139 1c. blue 10 10
140 2c. blue 10 10
141 2c. violet 10 10
142 3c. green 10 10
143 4c. purple 10 10
144 **47** 5c. red 10 10
145 10c. mauve 10 10
147 20c. green 15 15
148 30c. red 15 10
149 **48** 40c. blue 15 10
150 50c. brown on yellow 20 20
152 – 1p. black and violet 40 45
153 – 2p. black and red 40 45
154 – 5p. black and blue 50 55
DESIGN: 1p. to 5p. Dr. J. Felix de Restrepo.
No. 145 also exists with smaller head.

54 **55** **56** Zea

1903.
159 **54** 4c. brown 10 10
160 5c. blue 10 10
161 **55** 10c. yellow 10 10
162 20c. lilac 10 10
163 30c. brown 30 30
164 40c. green 30 30
165 50c. red 10 15
166 **56** 1p. green 25 20
167 2p. mauve (Rovira) 25 20
168 3p. blue (La Pola) 30 30
169 4p. red (Restrepo) 50 30
170 5p. brown (Madrid) 50 40
171 10p. red (Corral) 2·25 2·25

ACKNOWLEDGEMENT OF RECEIPT STAMPS

AR 53

1902.
AR157 **AR 53** 5c. black on red 30 20
AR158 5c. green 10 10

REGISTRATION STAMPS

R 38

1896.
R106 **R 38** 2½c. pink 50 50
R117 2½c. blue 60 60

R 41 Gen. Cordoba **R 42**

1899.
R130 **R 41** 2½c. blue 10 10
R131 **R 42** 10c. red 10 10

R 52

1902.
R156 **R 52** 10c. violet on green 10 10

TOO LATE STAMPS

L 40 Gen. Cordoba **L 51**

1899.
L129 **L 40** 2½c. green 10 10

1901. As T **43**, but inscr "RETARDO" at sides.
L137a 2½c. purple 60 60

1902.
L155 **L 51** 2½c. lilac 10 10

ARBE Pt. 8

During the period of D'Annunzio's Italian Regency of Carnaro (Fiume), separate issues were made for Arbe (now Rab).

100 centesimi = 1 lira.

1920. No. 148, etc of Fiume optd **ARBE**.
1 5c. green 4·50 5·25
2 10c. red 10·50 11·50
3 20c. brown 24·00 18·00
4 25c. blue 14·50 18·00
5 50c. on 20c. brown 26·00 18·00
6 55c. on 5c. green 26·00 18·00

EXPRESS LETTER STAMPS

1920. Nos. E163/4 of Fiume optd **ARBE**.
E7 30c. on 20c. brown 95·00 55·00
E8 50c. on 5c. green 95·00 55·00

ARGENTINE REPUBLIC Pt. 20

A republic in the S.E. of S. America formerly part of the Spanish Empire.

1858. 100 centavos = 1 peso.
1985. 100 centavos = 1 austral.
1992. 100 centavos = 1 peso.

1 Argentine Confederation **3** Argentine Confederation

1858. Imperf.
1 **1** 5c. red 1·60 9·50
2 10c. green 2·25 55·00
3 15c. blue 16·00 £140

1862. Imperf.
10 **3** 5c. red 20·00 24·00
8 10c. green £160 75·00
9 15c. blue £325 £250

5 Rivadavia **6** Rivadavia

1864. Imperf.
24 **5** 5c. red £250 65·00
14 **6** 10c. green £1700 £1000
15 **5** 15c. blue £8000 £3500

1864. Perf.
16 **5** 5c. red 35·00 14·00
17 **6** 10c. green 80·00 35·00
18 **5** 15c. blue £160 75·00

9 Rivadavia **10** Gen. Belgrano **11** Gen. San Martin

1867. Perf.
28 **9** 5c. red 12·00 75
29 **10** 10c. green 35·00 5·00
30a **11** 15c. blue 50·00 15·00

12 Balcarce **22** Sarsfield **24** Lopez

1873. Portraits. Perf.
31 **12** 1c. violet 4·00 2·25
32 – 4c. brown (Moreno) 5·50 45
33 – 30c. orange (Alvear) £120 17·00
34 – 60c. black (Posadas) £120 5·50
35 – 90c. blue (Saavedra) 28·00 2·50

1877. Surch with large figure of value.
37 **9** 1 on 5c. red 55·00 17·00
38 2 on 5c. red £110 70·00
39 **10** 8 on 10c. green £140 35·00

1876. Roul.
36 **9** 5c. red £170 70·00
40 8c. lake 28·00 30
41 **10** 16c. green 9·00 1·25
42 **22** 20c. blue 9·50 3·50
43 **11** 24c. blue 19·00 3·50

1877. Perf.
46 **24** 2c. green 4·75 1·00
44 **9** 8c. lake 4·75 15
45 **11** 24c. blue 8·50 50
47 – 25c. lake (Alvear) 25·00 7·00

1882. Surch **1/2 (PROVISORIO)**.
51 **9** ½ on 5c. red 1·00 90

29 **33**

1882.
52 **29** ½c. brown 1·60 90
55 1c. red 4·00 1·25
54 12c. blue 65·00 10·00

1884. Surch **1884** and value in figures or words.
90 **9** ½c. on 5c. red 3·00 2·25
92 **11** ½c. on 15c. blue 2·25 1·75
94 1c. on 15c. blue 7·00 5·50
100 **9** 4c. on 5c. red 10·00 6·00

1884.
101 **33** ½c. brown 1·00 50
102 1c. red 6·00 50
103 12c. blue 28·00 1·40

34 Urquiza **45** Mitre

1888. Portrait types, inscr "CORREOS ARGENTINOS".
108 **34** ½c. blue 55 50
110 – 2c. green (Lopez) 10·00 7·00
111 – 3c. green (Celman) 1·90 70
113 – 5c. red (Rivadavia) 9·00 65
114 – 6c. red (Sarmiento) 24·00 16·00
115 – 10c. brown (Avellaneda) 16·00 1·25
116 – 15c. orange (San Martin) 16·00 1·75
117a – 20c. green (Roca) 13·00 1·40
118 – 25c. violet (Belgrano) 16·00 1·75
119 – 30c. brown (Dorrego) 24·00 2·75
120a – 40c. grey (Moreno) 24·00 3·25
121 **45** 50c. blue 85·00 9·00

60 Paz **51** Rivadavia

1888. Portrait types, inscr "CORREOS Y TELEGRAFOS" except No. 126.
137 **60** ½c. green 10 15
122 – ½c. blue (Urquiza) 30 15
123 – 1c. brown (Sarsfield) . . . 95 20
125 – 2c. violet (Derqui) 95 15
126 – 3c. green (Celman) . . . . 2·25 45
127 **51** 5c. red . . . . 3·00 20
129 – 6c. blue (Sarmiento) . . . 1·60 60
130 – 10c. brown (Avellaneda) 1·90 30
131 – 12c. blue (Alberti) . . . . 4·75 1·25
132 – 40c. grey (Moreno) . . . . 4·50 90
133 – 50c. orange (Mitre) . . . . 4·50 90
134 – 60c. black (Posadas) . . . 17·00 3·00

1890. No. 131 surch **1/4** and bars.
135 ¼ on 12c. blue 40 35

52 Rivadavia **63** La Madrid **61** Rivadavia

1890.
128a **52** 5c. red . . . . 2·25 15

1891. Portraits.
139 – 1p. blue (San Martin) . . . 45·00 6·50
140 **63** 5p. blue . . . . £225 24·00
141 – 20p. green (G. Brown) . . £325 70·00

1891.
138 **61** 8c. red . . . . 1·40 25

65 Rivadavia **66** Belgrano **67** San Martin

1892.
142 **65** ½c. blue 20 15
143 1c. brown 40 15
144 2c. green 25 15
145 3c. orange 70 15
146 5c. red 70 15
147 **66** 10c. red . . . . 5·50 15
148 12c. blue . . . . 2·75 15
149 16c. slate . . . . 6·50 60
150 24c. sepia . . . . 11·00 60
257 30c. orange . . . . 8·00 50
151 50c. green . . . . 10·00 50
188 80c. lilac . . . . 12·00 50
152a **67** 1p. red . . . . 10·00 80
190 1p.20 black . . . . 9·50 4·00
153 2p. green . . . . 17·00 8·00
154 5p. blue . . . . 42·00 3·00

70 Fleet of Columbus **71** "Liberty" and Shield

1892. 4th Centenary of Discovery of America by Columbus.
219 **70** 2c. blue . . . . 12·50 4·50
220 5c. blue . . . . 26·00 5·00

1899.
221 **71** ½c. brown 15 15
222 1c. green 10 10
223 2c. grey 10 10
224 3c. orange 95 15
225 4c. yellow . . . . 1·75 15
226 5c. red 10 10
227 6c. black . . . . 1·10 20
228 10c. green . . . . 1·75 15
229a 12c. blue . . . . 1·10 30
230 12c. green . . . . 1·10 30
231 15c. blue . . . . 3·00 15
232 16c. orange . . . . 8·50 4·25
233 20c. red . . . . 2·25 15
234 24c. purple . . . . 4·00 80
235 30c. red . . . . 4·25 20
237 50c. blue . . . . 5·50 15
238 1p. black and blue . . . 16·00 80
239 5p. black and orange . . 65·00 11·00
240 10p. black and green . . 60·00 11·00
241 20p. black and red . . . £225 32·00
The peso values are larger (19 × 32 mm).

73 Port Rosario **74** Gen. San Martin

1902. Completion of Port Rosario Docks.
290 **73** 5c. blue . . . . 80 2·00

1908.
291 **74** ½c. violet 15 10
292 1c. brown 20 10
293 2c. brown 60 10
294 3c. green 75 35
295 4c. mauve . . . . 1·50 35
296 5c. red 35 10
297 6c. green 85 25
298 10c. green . . . . 1·75 10
299 12c. brown 45 40
300 12c. blue . . . . 1·40 10
301 15c. green . . . . 1·90 90
302 20c. blue . . . . 1·40 10
303 24c. red . . . . 3·75 70
304 30c. red . . . . 6·00 70
305 50c. black . . . . 5·50 45
306 1p. red and blue . . . . 13·00 1·90
The 1p. is larger (21½ × 27 mm) with portrait at upper left.

76 Pyramid of May **80** Saavedra

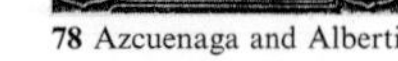

78 Azcuenaga and Alberti

1910. Cent of Deposition of the Spanish Viceroy.
366 **76** ½c. blue and grey 40 10
367 – 1c. black and green . . . 40 10
368 – 2c. black and green . . . 30 10
369 **78** 3c. green 85 10
370 – 4c. green and blue . . . 85 15
371 **80** 5c. red 70 10
372 – 10c. black and brown . . 2·00 15
373 – 12c. blue . . . . 1·60 25
374 – 20c. black and brown . . 3·75 40
375 – 24c. blue and brown . . 2·00 1·00
376 – 30c. black and lilac . . . 2·00 75
377 – 50c. black and red . . . 5·00 1·00
378 – 1p. blue . . . . 12·00 3·50
379 – 5p. purple and orange . . 80·00 35·00
380 – 10p. black and orange . . £100 75·00
381 – 20p. black and blue . . . £170 £100
DESIGNS—VERT: 50c. Crowds on 25 May 1810; 10p. Centenary Monument; 20p. San Martin. HORIZ: 1c. Pena and Vieytes; 2c. Meeting at Pena's house; 4c. Fort of the Viceroys, Buenos Aires; 10c. Distribution of cockades; 12c. Congress Building; 20c. Castelli and Matheu; 24c. First National Council; 30c. Belgrano and Larrea; 1p. Moreno and Paso; 5p. "Oath of the Junta".

90 Sarmiento **91** Ploughman

1911. Birth Centenary of Pres. Sarmiento.
382 **90** 5c. black and brown . . . 70 40

1911.
383 **91** 5c. red 40 15
384 12c. blue . . . . 4·50 20

92 Ploughman **94**

1911.
395 **92** ½c. violet 20 20
396 1c. brown 20 15
397 2c. brown 40 15
398 3c. green 50 20
399 4c. purple 40 20
400 5c. red 20 15
401 10c. green 60 15
402 12c. blue . . . . 1·60 15
403 20c. blue . . . . 5·00 1·25
404 24c. brown . . . . 3·75 20
405 30c. red . . . . 2·00 70
406 50c. black . . . . 6·00 70
408 **94** 1p. red and blue . . . . 7·00 1·10
409 5p. green and grey . . . 22·00 7·00
410 10p. blue and violet . . . 85·00 10·00
411 20p. red and blue . . . . £200 70·00

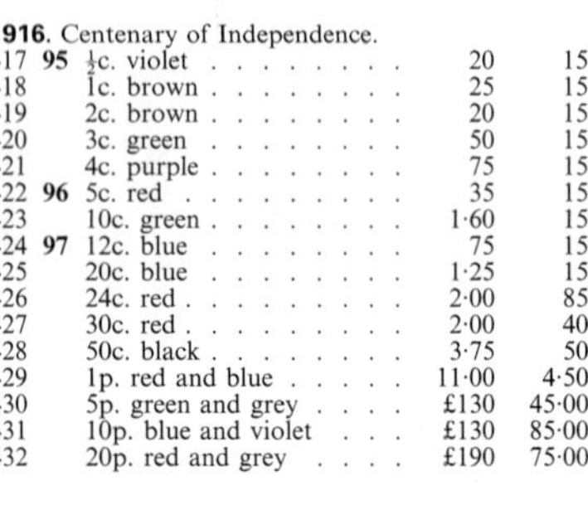

95 Dr. F. N. Laprida **97** San Martin

96 Declaration of Independence

1916. Centenary of Independence.
417 **95** ½c. violet 20 15
418 1c. brown 25 15
419 2c. brown 20 15
420 3c. green 50 15
421 4c. purple 75 15
422 **96** 5c. red 35 15
423 10c. green . . . . 1·60 15
424 **97** 12c. blue 75 15
425 20c. blue . . . . 1·25 15
426 24c. red . . . . 2·00 85
427 30c. red . . . . 2·00 40
428 50c. black . . . . 3·75 50
429 1p. red and blue . . . . 11·00 4·50
430 5p. green and grey . . . £130 45·00
431 10p. blue and violet . . . £130 85·00
432 20p. red and grey . . . . £190 75·00

98 San Martin **100** Dr. Juan Pujol

1917.
433 **98** ½c. violet 20 15
434 1c. buff 20 15
435 2c. brown 20 15
436 3c. green 70 15
454 4c. purple 30 15
455 5c. red 15 15
456 10c. green . . . . 1·75 15
457 – 12c. blue . . . . 1·40 15
458 – 20c. blue . . . . 1·75 15
459 – 24c. red . . . . 5·00 2·25
460 – 30c. red . . . . 5·00 70
461 – 50c. black . . . . 4·50 70
445 – 1p. red and blue . . . . 4·50 20
446 – 5p. green and grey . . . 19·00 3·50
447 – 10p. blue and violet . . . 45·00 11·00
448 – 20p. red and grey . . . . 81·00 17·00
The 12c. to 20p. values are larger (21 × 27 mm).

1918. Birth Centenary of Juan Pujol, 1st P.M.G. of Argentina.
449 **100** 5c. grey and bistre 80 30

102 Mausoleum of Belgrano **103** Creation of Argentine Flag

1920. Death Centenary of Gen. Manuel Belgrano.
478 **102** 2c. red 50 15
479 **103** 5c. blue and red 50 15
480 – 12c. blue and green . . . 1·00 75
DESIGN—VERT: 12c. Gen. Belgrano.

106 General Urquiza **107** General Mitre **108**

1920. Gen. Urquiza's Victory at Cepada.
488 **106** 5c. blue 30 10

1921. Birth Centenary of Gen. Mitre.
490 **107** 2c. brown 35 10
491 5c. blue 35 10

1921. 1st Pan-American Postal Congress.
492 **108** 3c. lilac . . . . 1·50 65
493 5c. blue . . . . 2·00 20
494 10c. brown . . . . 2·50 90
495 12c. red . . . . 4·50 1·90

1921. As T **108**, but smaller. Inscr "BUENOS AIRES AGOSTO DE 1921".
496 5c. red . . . . 2·25 25

1921. As No. 496, but inscr "REPUBLICA ARGENTINA" at foot.
511 5c. red . . . . 1·75 25

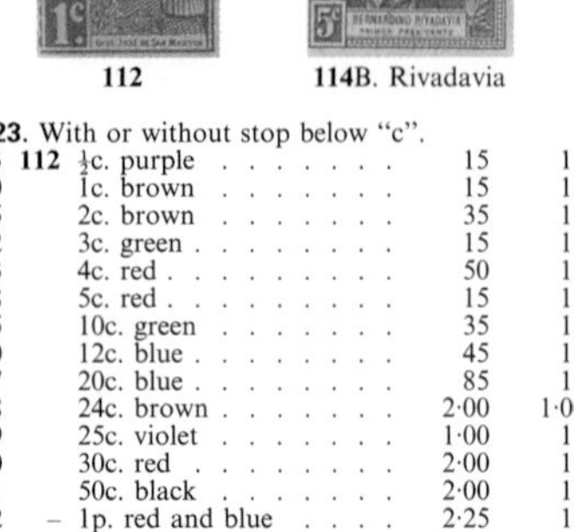

112 **114B**. Rivadavia

1923. With or without stop below "c".
513 **112** ½c. purple 15 15
530 1c. brown 15 15
515 2c. brown 35 15
532 3c. green 15 15
533 4c. red 50 15
518 5c. red 15 15
535 10c. green 35 15
520 12c. blue 45 15
537 20c. blue 85 15
538 24c. brown . . . . 2·00 1·00
539 25c. violet . . . . 1·00 15
540 30c. red . . . . 2·00 15
541 50c. black . . . . 2·00 15
542 – 1p. red and blue . . . . 2·25 15
543 – 5p. green and lilac . . . 17·00 70
544 – 10p. blue and red . . . . 38·00 3·75
545 – 20p. lake and slate . . . 55·00 8·50
The peso values are larger (21 × 27 mm).

1926. Rivadavia Centenary.
546 **114** 5c. red 50 15

115 Rivadavia **116** San Martin

117 G.P.O., 1926 **118** G.P.O., 1826

1926. Postal Centenary.
547 **115** 3c. green 15 15
548 **116** 5c. red 10 15
549 **117** 12c. blue . . . . 1·00 20
550 **118** 25c. brown . . . . 1·75 15

120 Biplane and Globe **122**

1928. Air.
558 **120** 5c. red . . . . 1·75 50
559 10c. blue . . . . 2·75 85
560 – 15c. brown . . . . 2·50 90
561 **120** 18c. violet . . . . 4·25 3·25
562 – 20c. blue . . . . 2·75 90
563 – 24c. blue . . . . 4·25 3·00
564 **122** 25c. violet . . . . 4·25 1·40
565 30c. red . . . . 5·50 1·00
566 – 35c. red . . . . 4·25 1·25
567a **120** 36c. brown . . . . 2·25 1·40
568 – 50c. black . . . . 4·50 65
569 – 54c. brown . . . . 4·25 2·10
570 – 72c. green . . . . 5·50 2·10
571 **122** 90c. purple . . . . 10·00 1·90
572 1p. red and blue . . . . 12·00 70
573 1p.08 blue and red . . . 17·00 4·75
574 – 1p.26 green and violet . . 23·00 9·00
575 – 1p.80 red and blue . . . 23·00 9·00
576 – 3p.60 blue and grey . . . 48·00 21·00
DESIGNS—VERT: 15, 20, 24, 54, 72c. Yellow-headed Caracara over sea. HORIZ: 35, 50c., 1p.26, 1p.80, 3p.60, Andean Condor on mountain top.

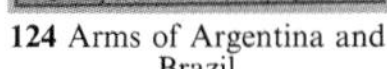

124 Arms of Argentina and Brazil

125 Torch illuminating New World

1928. Centenary of Peace with Brazil.
577 **124** 5c. red . . . . 1·00 35
578 12c. blue . . . . 1·60 70

1929. "Day of the Race" issue.
579 **125** 2c. brown 85 20
580 – 5c. red 95 15
581 – 12c. blue . . . . 2·25 75
DESIGNS: 5c. Symbolical figures, Spain and Argentina; 12c. American offering laurels to Columbus.

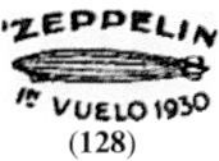

(128)

1930. Air. "Zeppelin" Europe–Pan-America Flight. Optd with T **128**.
587 – 20c. blue (No. 562) . . . 10·00 5·50
588 – 50c. black (No. 568) . . . 18·00 8·50
589 **122** 90c. purple . . . . 9·00 6·50
584 1p. red and blue . . . . 20·00 13·00
585 – 1p.80 (No. 575) . . . . . 60·00 32·00
586 – 3p.60 (No. 576) . . . . . £170 95·00

129 Soldier and Civilian Insurgents

130 The Victorious March, 6 September 30

1930. Revolution of 6 September 1930.
592 **129** ½c. violet 20 15
611 **130** ½c. mauve 15 10
593 **129** 1c. green 25 15
612 **130** 1c. black . . . . 1·00 40
594 2c. lilac 35 15
595 **129** 3c. green 50 25
613 **130** 3c. green 50 25
596 **129** 4c. violet 40 25
614 **130** 4c. lake 40 20
597 **129** 5c. red 20 15
615 **130** 5c. red 15 10
598 **129** 10c. black 85 35
616 **130** 10c. green . . . . 1·00 25
599 12c. blue 85 25
600 20c. buff 85 20
601 **130** 24c. brown . . . . 3·25 1·50
602 25c. green . . . . 4·25 1·50
603 30c. violet . . . . 6·00 2·00
604 50c. black . . . . 9·00 2·75
605 1p. red and blue . . . . 17·00 10·00
606 2p. orange and black . . 30·00 10·00
607 5p. black and green . . 90·00 40·00
608 10p. blue and lake . . . £120 50·00
609 20p. blue and green . . £325 £120
610 50p. violet and green . . £900 £650

1931. 1st Anniv of 1930 Revolution. Optd **6 Septembre 1930 - 1931**.
617 **112** 3c. green (postage) . . . 25 25
618 10c. green 70 70
619 30c. red . . . . 3·75 3·75
620 50c. black . . . . 3·75 3·75
621 1p. red and blue . . . . 4·25 3·75
623 **130** 2p. orange and black . . 15·00 8·50
622 **112** 5p. green and lilac . . . . 75·00 23·00

624 **129** 18c. violet (air) . . . . . 2·25 1·75
625 – 72c. green (No. 570) . . . 21·00 13·00
626 **122** 90c. purple . . . . 16·00 12·00
627 – 1p.80 red & bl (No. 575) 40·00 30·00
628 – 3p.60 bl & grey (No. 576) 60·00 45·00

1932. Zeppelin Air stamps. Optd **GRAF ZEPPELIN 1932**.
629 **120** 5c. red . . . . 2·50 1·60
630 18c. violet . . . . 12·00 7·50
631 **122** 90c. purple . . . . 35·00 20·00

134 Refrigerating Plant

135 Port La Plata

1932. 6th International Refrigerating Congress.
632 **134** 3c. green 50 25
633 10c. red . . . . 1·25 15
634 12c. blue . . . . 3·50 1·40

1933. 50th Anniv of La Plata City.
635 **135** 3c. brown and green . . . 1·00 25
636 – 10c. purple and orange . . 60 20
637 – 15c. blue . . . . 4·00 2·00
638 – 20c. brown and lilac . . . 2·00 1·00
639 – 30c. red and green . . . . 16·00 6·00
DESIGNS: 10c. President J. A. Roca; 15c. Municipal buildings; 20c. La Plata Cathedral; 30c. Dr. D. Rocha.

139 Christ of the Andes

141 "Liberty" with Arms of Brazil and Argentina

1934. 32nd Int Eucharistic Congress, Buenos Aires.
640 **139** 10c. red 85 25
641 – 15c. blue . . . . 1·60 55
DESIGN—HORIZ: 15c. Buenos Aires Cathedral.

1935. Visit of President Vargas of Brazil. Inscr "MAYO DE 1935".
642 **141** 10c. red 85 25
643 – 15c. blue . . . . 1·60 55
DESIGN: 15c. Clasped hands and flags.

143 D. F. Sarmiento

146 Prize Bull

151 With Boundary Lines

1935. Portraits.
644 ½c. purple (Belgrano) . . . 15 10
645 1c. brown (Type **143**) . . . 15 10
646 2c. brown (Urquiza) 15 10
647 3c. green (San Martin) . . . 15 10
648 4c. grey (G. Brown) 10 10
653b 5c. brown (Moreno) 60 10
650 6c. green (Alberdi) 15 10
653d 10c. red (Rivadavia) 25 10
651 12c. purple (Mitre) 10 10
708 15c. grey (Martin Guemes) 80 10
652 20c. blue (Juan Martin Guemes) 80 10
653 20c. blue (Martin Guemes) 80 10
See also Nos. 671 etc.

1936. Production and Industry.
676 **146** 15c. blue 60 15
677a 20c. blue (19½ × 26 mm) 15 15
755 20c. blue (22 × 33 mm) 1·50 15
656 – 25c. red and pink . . . 40 15
757 – 30c. brown and yellow 40 15
658 – 40c. purple and mauve 35 15
659 – 50c. red and salmon . . 25 15
660 **151** 1p. blue and brown . . . 19·00 75
760 – 1p. blue and brown . . . 3·00 15
661 – 2p. blue and purple . . . 85 15
662 – 5p. green and blue . . . 11·50 75
763 – 10p. black and purple . . 11·50 1·60
764 – 20p. brown and blue . . 11·00 1·60
DESIGNS—VERT: 25c. Ploughman; 50c. Oil well; 1p. (No. 760) as Type **151** but without country boundaries; 5p. Iguazu Falls; 10p. Grapes; 20p. Cotton plant. HORIZ: 30c. Patagonian ram; 40c. Sugar cane and factory; 2p. Fruit products.

157

158 Pres. Sarmiento

1936. Pan-American Peace Conference.
665 **157** 10c. red 50 15

1938. President's 50th Death Anniv.
666 **158** 3c. green 40 40
667 5c. red 40 40
668 15c. blue 75 40
669 50c. orange . . . . 2·25 80

159 "Presidente Sarmiento"

160 Allegory of the Post

1939. Last Voyage of Cadet Ship "Presidente Sarmiento".
670 **159** 5c. green 85 10

1939. Portraits as T **143**.
671 – 2½c. black 15 10
672 – 3c. grey (San Martin) . . . 40 10
672a – 3c. grey (Moreno) 15 10
673 – 4c. green 10 10
894 – 5c. brown (16½ × 22½ mm) 10 10
674 – 8c. orange 10 10
678 – 10c. purple 15 10
675 – 12c. red 10 10
895 – 20c. lilac (21 × 27 mm) . . 20 10
895b – 20c. lilac (19½ × 25½ mm) 15 10
PORTRAITS: 2½c. L. Braille; 4c. G. Brown; 5c. Jose Hernandez; 8c. N. Avellaneda; 10c. B. Rivadavia; 12c. B. Mitre; 20c. G. Brown.

1939. 11th U.P.U. Congress, Buenos Aires.
679 **160** 5c. red 15 10
680 – 15c. grey 40 25
681 – 20c. blue 40 10
682 – 25c. green 85 35
683 – 50c. brown . . . . 2·25 80
684 – 1p. purple . . . . 4·50 1·75
685 – 2p. mauve . . . . 20·00 11·50
686 – 5p. violet . . . . 46·00 23·00
DESIGNS—VERT: 20c. Seal of Argentina; 1p. Symbols of postal communications; 2p. Argentina, "Land of Promise" from a pioneer painting. HORIZ: 15c. G.P.O.; 25c. Iguazu Falls; 50c. Mt. Bonete; 5p. Lake Frias.

165 Working-class Family and New Home

167 North and South America

1939. 1st Pan-American Housing Congress.
687 **165** 5c. green 20 10

1940. 50th Anniv of Pan-American Union.
688 **167** 15c. blue 35 10

169 Airplane and Envelope

1940. Air.
689 **169** 30c. orange . . . . 7·00 10
690 – 50c. brown . . . . 9·50 15
691 **169** 1p. red . . . . 3·50 10
692 – 1p.25 green 80 10
693 **169** 2p.50 blue . . . . 2·75 40
DESIGNS—VERT: 50c. "Mercury"; 1p.25, Douglas DC-2 in clouds.

172 Gen. French, Col. Beruti and Rosette of the "Legion de Patricios"

1941. 131st Anniv of Rising against Spain.
694 **172** 5c. blue 40 10

173 Marco M. de Avellaneda

174 Statue of Gen. J. A. Roca

1941. Death Centenary of Avellaneda (patriot).
695 **173** 5c. blue 40 10

1941. Dedication of Statue of Gen. Roca.
696 **174** 5c. green 40 10

175 Pellegrini (founder) and National Bank

176 Gen. Juan Lavalle

1941. 50th Anniv of National Bank.
697 **175** 5c. lake 40 10

1941. Death Centenary of Gen. Lavalle.
698 **176** 5c. blue 40 10

177 New P.O. Savings Bank

178 Jose Manuel Estrada

1942. Inauguration of P.O. Savings Bank.
699 **177** 1c. green 40 10

1942. Birth Centenary of Estrada (patriot).
700 **178** 5c. purple 50 10

180 G.P.O., Buenos Aires

181 Proposed Columbus Lighthouse

1942. Postage and Express Stamps.
717 **180** 35c. blue . . . . 5·50 15
746 35c. blue . . . . 1·10 15
No. 717 is inscr "PALACIO CENTRAL DE CORREOS Y TELEGRAFOS" and No. 746 "PALACIO CENTRAL DE CORREOS Y TELECOMUNICACIONES".

1942. 450th Anniv of Discovery of America by Columbus.
721 **181** 15c. blue . . . . 4·00 15

182 Dr. Paz (founder of "La Prensa")

183 Flag of Argentina and Books

184 Arms of Argentina

1942. Birth Centenary of Dr. Jose C. Paz.
722 **182** 5c. blue 40 15

1943. 1st National Book Fair.
723 **183** 5c. blue 20 15

1943. Revolution of 4 June 1943.
724 **184** 5c. red 20 15
725 15c. green 60 15
726 20c. blue (larger) 80 15

185 National Independence House

186 Head of Liberty, Money-box and Laurels

1943. Restoration of Tucuman Museum.
727 **185** 5c. green 35 15

1943. 1st Savings Bank Conference.
728 **186** 5c. brown 40 10

187 Buenos Aires in 1800

1944. Export Day.
729 **187** 5c. black 40 10

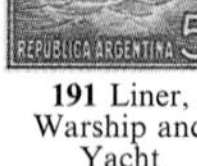

188 Postal Union of the Americas and Spain

189 Alexander Graham Bell

191 Liner, Warship and Yacht

1944. Postmen's Benefit Fund. Inscr "PRO-CARTERO".
730 – 3c.+2c. black and violet . . 1·10 1·10
731 **188** 5c.+5c. black and red . . 85 20
732 **189** 10c.+5c. black and orge 1·10 35
733 – 25c.+15c. black and brn 2·40 75
734 – 1p.+50c. black and green 10·00 7·75
DESIGNS: 3c. Samuel Morse; 25c. Rowland Hill; 1p. Columbus landing in America.

1944. Naval Week.
735 **191** 5c. blue 75 10

192 Argentina

193 Arms of Argentina

1944. San Juan Earthquake Relief Fund.
736 **192** 5c.+10c. black & olive . . 60 50
737 5c.+50c. black and red . . 3·50 1·10
738 5c.+1p. black & orange 7·00 5·50
739 5c.+20p. black & blue . . 28·00 23·00

1944. 1st Anniv of Revolution of 4 June 1943.
740 **193** 5c. blue 40 15

194 Archangel Gabriel

195 Cross of Palermo

196 Allegory of Savings

1944. 4th National Eucharistic Congress.
741 **194** 3c. green 50 15
742 **195** 5c. red 50 15

1944. 20th Anniv of Universal Savings Day.
743 **196** 5c. black 40 15

197 Reservists

1944. Reservists' Day.
744 **197** 5c. blue 40 15

198 Bernardino Rivadavia

199 Rivadavia's Mausoleum

1945. Rivadavia's Death Centenary.
770 **198** 3c. green 15 15
771 – 5c. red 15 15
772 **199** 20c. blue 15 15
DESIGN—As Type **198**: 5c. Rivadavia and Scales of Justice.

200 San Martin

201 Monument to Andes Army, Mendoza

1945.
773 **200** 5c. red 10 10

1946. "Homage to the Unknown Soldier of Independence".
776 **201** 5c. purple 15 15

202 Pres. Roosevelt

203 "Affirmation"

1946. 1st Death Anniv of Pres. Franklin Roosevelt.
777 **202** 5c. grey 10 10

1946. Installation of Pres. Juan Peron.
778 **203** 5c. blue 15 15

204 Airplane over Iguazu Falls

1946. Air.
779 **204** 15c. red 15 10
780 – 25c. green 20 10
DESIGN: 25c. Airplane over Andes.

205 "Flight"

1946. Aviation Week.
781 **205** 15c. green on green . . . 55 10
782 – 60c. purple on buff . . . 55 15
DESIGN: 60c. Hand upholding globe.

207 "Argentina and Populace"

1946. 1st Anniv of Peron's Defeat of Counter-revolution.
783 **207** 5c. mauve 20 10
784 10c. green 30 10
785 15c. blue 60 25
786 50c. brown 60 40
787 1p. red . . . . 1·25 1·10

208 Money-box and Map

209 Industry

1946. Annual Savings Day.
788 **208** 30c. red 35 10

1946. Industrial Exhibition.
789 **209** 5c. purple 10 10

210 Argentine–Brazil International Bridge

211 South Pole

1947. Opening of Bridge between Argentina and Brazil.
790 **210** 5c. green 25 25

1947. 43rd Anniv of 1st Argentine Antarctic Mail.
791 **211** 5c. violet 60 15
792 20c. red . . . . 1·25 15

212 "Justice"

213 Icarus Falling

1947. 1st Anniv of Col. Juan Peron's Presidency.
793 **212** 5c. purple and buff . . . 10 10

1947. "Week of the Wing".
794 **213** 15c. purple 15 10

214 "Presidente Sarmiento"

215 Cervantes and "Don Quixote"

1947. 50th Anniv of Launching of Cadet Ship "Presidente Sarmiento".
795 **214** 5c. blue 50 10

1947. 400th Birth Anniv of Cervantes.
796 **215** 5c. green 10 10

216 Gen. San Martin and Urn

1947. Arrival from Spain of Ashes of Gen. San Martin's Parents.
797 **216** 5c. green 10 10

217 Young Crusaders

218 Statue of Araucanian Indian

1947. Educational Crusade for Universal Peace.
798 **217** 5c. green 10 10
799 20c. brown 30 10

1948. American Indian Day.
801 **218** 25c. brown 25 10

219 Phrygian Cap and Sprig of Wheat

220 "Stop"

1948. 5th Anniv of Anti-isolationist Revolution of 4 June 1943.
802 **219** 5c. blue 10 10

1948. Safety First Campaign.
803 **220** 5c. yellow and brown . . 15 10

221 Posthorn and Oak Leaves

222 Argentine Farmers

1948. Bicent of Postal Service in Rio de la Plata.
804 **221** 5c. mauve 15 15

1948. Agriculture Day.
805 **222** 10c. brown 15 15

223 "Liberty and Plenty"

225 Statue of Atlas

226 Map, Globe and Compasses

1948. Re-election of President Peron.
806 **223** 25c. red 15 15

1948. Air. 4th Meeting of Pan-American Cartographers.
807 **225** 45c. brown 35 10
808 **226** 70c. green 65 15

227 Winged Railway Wheel

1949. 1st Anniv of Nationalization of Argentine Railways.
809 **227** 10c. blue 25 10

228 Head of Liberty

1949. Constitution Day.
810 **228** 1p. purple and red . . . 80 15

229 Trophy and Target

230 "Intercommunication"

1949. Air. International Shooting Championship.
811 **229** 75c. brown 65 15

1949. 75th Anniv of U.P.U.
812 **230** 25c. green and olive . . . 20 15

231 San Martin

233 Stamp Designer

232 San Martin at Boulogne

1950. San Martin's Death Cent. Dated "1850 1950".
813 – 10c. purple and blue . . . 15 10
814 **231** 20c. brown and red . . . 15 10
815 **232** 25c. brown 15 10
816 – 50c. blue and green . . . 40 10
817 – 75c. green and brown . . 40 10
818 – 1p. green . . . . 1·00 20
819 – 2p. purple 85 35
DESIGNS—As Type **231**: 10, 50, 75c. Portraits of San Martin; 2p. San Martin Mausoleum. As Type **232**: 1p. House where San Martin died.

1950. Int Philatelic Exhibition, Buenos Aires.
820 **233** 10c.+10c. violet (postage) 15 15
821 – 45c.+45c. blue (air) . . . 40 25
822 – 70c.+70c. brown 60 40

823 – 1p.+1p. red . . . . . . 1·75 1·60
824 – 2p.50+2p.50 olive . . . . 9·50 7·00
825 – 5p.+5p. green . . . . . . 11·00 8·50
DESIGNS: 45c. Engraver; 70c. Proofing; 1p. Printer; 2p.50, Woman reading letter; 5p. San Martin.

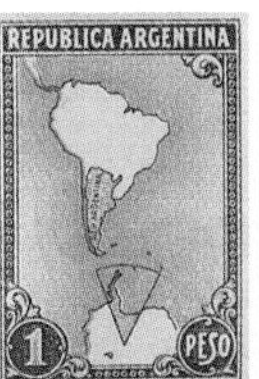

234 S. America and Antarctic **235** Douglas DC-3 and Andean Condor

1951.
826 **234** 1p. blue and brown . . . 50 15

1951. Air. 10th Anniv of State Airlines.
827 **235** 20c. olive 30 20

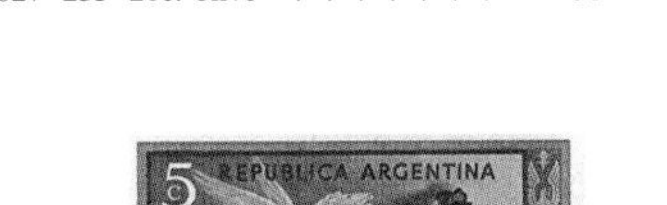

236 Pegasus and Steam Locomotive

1951. Five-year Plan.
828 **236** 5c. brown (postage) . . . 15 15
829 – 25c. green 45 10
830 – 40c. purple 40 15
831 – 20c. blue (air) 25 15
DESIGNS—HORIZ: 25c. "President Peron" (liner) and common dolphin. VERT: 20c. Douglas DC-4 and Andean condor; 40c. Head of Mercury and telephone.

237 Woman Voter and "Argentina" **238** "Piety"

1951. Women's Suffrage in Argentina.
832 **237** 10c. purple 10 10

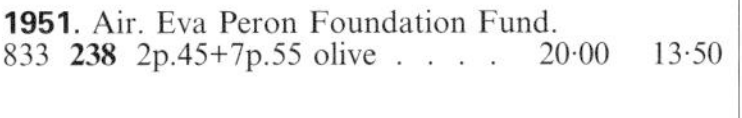

1951. Air. Eva Peron Foundation Fund.
833 **238** 2p.45+7p.55 olive . . . . 20·00 13·50

239 Eva Peron **240** Eva Peron

1952. (a) Size 20 × 26 mm.
834 **239** 1c. brown 10 10
835 5c. grey 10 10
836 10c. red 10 10
837 20c. red 10 10
838 25c. green 10 10
839 40c. purple 15 10
841 45c. blue 25 10
840 50c. bistre 25 10

(b) Size 22 × 33 mm. Without inscr "EVA PERON".
842 **240** 1p. brown 35 10
843 1p.50 green . . . . . . 1·75 10
844 2p. red 50 10
845 3p. blue 85 15

(c) Size 22 × 33 mm. Inscr "EVA PERON".
846 **240** 1p. brown 35 10
847 1p.50 green . . . . . . 1·10 10
848 2p. red . . . . 1·25 10
849 3p. blue . . . . 1·75 45

(d) Size 30½ × 40 mm. Inscr "EVA PERON".
850 **240** 5p. brown . . . . 1·75 40
851 **239** 10p. red . . . . 4·75 1·40
852 **240** 20p. green . . . . 8·00 3·25
853 **239** 50p. blue . . . . 14·00 7·75

241 Indian Funeral Urn **242** Rescue Ship "Uruguay"

1953. 4th Centenary of Santiago del Estero.
854 **241** 50c. green 15 10

1953. 50th Anniv of Rescue of the "Antarctic".
855 **242** 50c. blue . . . . 1·25 40

243 Planting Flag in S. Orkneys **244** "Telegraphs"

1954. 50th Anniv of Argentine P.O. in South Orkneys.
856 **243** 1p.45 blue 85 40

1954. International Telecommunications Conference. Symbolical designs inscr as in T **244**.
857 **244** 1p.50 purple 40 15
858 – 3p. blue . . . . 1·10 25
859 – 5p. red . . . . 1·60 35
DESIGNS—VERT: 3p. "Radio". HORIZ: 5p. "Television".

245 Pediment, Buenos Aires Stock Exchange **246** Eva Peron

1954. Centenary of Argentine Stock Exchange.
860 **245** 1p. green 30 10

1954. 2nd Death Anniv of Eva Peron.
861 **246** 3p. red . . . . 1·60 20

247 San Martin **249** Wheat

250 Mt. Fitz Roy **248** "Prosperity"

1954.
862 **247** 20c. red 10 10
863 40c. red 30 10
868 – 50c. blue (33 × 22 mm) 60 10
869 – 50c. blue (32 × 21 mm) 70 10
870 **249** 80c. brown 25 10
871 – 1p. brown 30 10
872 – 1p.50 blue 25 10
873 – 2p. red 35 10
874 – 3p. purple 35 10
875a – 5p. green . . . . 6·25 10
876 – 10p. green and grey . . 6·25 10
877 **250** 20p. violet . . . . . . 9·25 40
1018 – 22p. blue . . . . 1·40 10
878 – 50p. indigo and blue (30½ × 40½ mm) . . . 8·00 80
1023 – 50p. blue (29½ × 40 mm) 6·25 40
1287 – 50p. blue (22½ × 32½ mm) . . . 1·00 10

DESIGNS—As Type **249**: HORIZ: 50c. Port of Buenos Aires; 1p. Cattle; 2p. Eva Peron Foundation; 3p. El Nihuil Dam. As Type **250**: VERT: 1p.50, 22p. Industrial Plant; 5p. Iguazu Falls; 50p. San Martin. HORIZ: 10p. Humahuaca Ravine.
For 43p. in the design of the 1p.50 and 22p. see No. 1021.
For 65c. in same design see No. 1313.

1954. Centenary of Argentine Corn Exchange.
867 **248** 1p.50 grey 65 10

251 Clasped Hands and Congress Emblem **252** Father and Son with Model Airplane

1955. Productivity and Social Welfare Congress.
879 **251** 3p. brown 90 10

1955. 25th Anniv of Commercial Air Services.
880 **252** 1p.50 grey 80 10

253 "Liberation" **254** Forces Emblem

1955. Anti-Peronist Revolution of 16 Sept. 1955.
881 **253** 1p.50 olive 20 10

1955. Armed Forces Commemoration.
882 **254** 3p. blue 35 10

255 Gen. Urquiza (after J. M. Blanes) **256** Detail from "Antiope" (Correggio)

1956. 104th Anniv of Battle of Caseros.
883 **255** 1p.50 green 25 10

1956. Infantile Paralysis Relief Fund.
884 **256** 20c.+30c. grey 20 10

257 Coin and Die **258** Corrientes Stamp of 1856

259 Dr. J. G. Pujol **260** Cotton, Chaco

1956. 75th Anniv of National Mint.
885 **257** 2p. brown and sepia . . . 20 10

1956. Centenary of 1st Argentine Stamps.
886 **258** 40c. blue and green . . . 15 10
887 2p.40 mauve and brown 20 10
888 **259** 4p.40 blue 50 15
The 40c. shows a 1r. stamp of 1856.

1956. New Provinces.
889 – 50c. blue 10 10
890 **260** 1p. lake 20 10
891 – 1p.50 green 30 10
DESIGNS—HORIZ: 50c. Lumbering, La Pampa. VERT: 1p.50, Mate tea plant, Misiones.

261 "Liberty" **262** Detail from "Virgin of the Rocks" (Leonardo)

1956. 1st Anniv of Revolution.
892 **261** 2p.40 mauve 25 10

1956. Air. Infantile Paralysis Victims, Gratitude for Help.
893 **262** 1p. purple 30 10

264 Esteban Echeverria (writer) **265** F. Ameghino (anthropologist)

266 Roque Saenz Pena (statesman) **267** Franklin

1956.
896 **264** 2p. purple 20 10
897 **265** 2p.40 brown 30 10
898 **266** 4p.40 green 45 10

1956. 250th Birth Anniv of Benjamin Franklin.
899 **267** 40c. blue 25 10

268 "Hercules" (sail frigate) **269** Admiral G. Brown

1957. Death Cent of Admiral Guillermo Brown.
900 **268** 40c. blue (postage) . . . 50 10
901 – 2p.40 green 40 10
902 – 60c. grey (air) 75 10
903 – 1p. mauve 20 10
904 **269** 2p. brown 25 10
DESIGNS—HORIZ: 60c. "Zefiro" and "Nancy" (sail warships) at Battle of Montevideo; 1p. L. Rosales and T. Espora. VERT: 2p.40, Admiral Brown in later years.

270 Church of Santo Domingo **271** Map of the Americas and Badge of Buenos Aires

1957. 150th Anniv of Defence of Buenos Aires.
905 **270** 40c. green 10 10

1957. Air. Inter-American Economic Conference.
906 **271** 2p. purple 35 10

272 "La Portena", 1857 **273** Globe, Flag and Compass Rose

1957. Centenary of Argentine Railways.
907 **272** 40c. sepia (postage) . . . 45 10
908 – 60c. grey (air) 45 10
DESIGN: 60c. Diesel locomotive.

1957. Air. Int Tourist Congress, Buenos Aires.
909 **273** 1p. brown 15 10
910 – 2p. turquoise 20 10
DESIGN: 2p. Symbolic key of tourism.

274 Head of Liberty **275**

1957. Reform Convention.
911 **274** 40c. red 10 10

1957. Air. International Correspondence Week.
912 **275** 1p. blue 15 10

276 "Wealth in Oil" **277** La Plata Museum

1957. 50th Anniv of Argentine Oil Industry.
913 **276** 40c. blue 15 10

1958. 75th Anniv of Founding of La Plata.
914 **277** 40c. black 15 10

278 Health Emblem and Flower

1958. Air. Child Welfare.
915 **278** 1p.+50c. red 20 20

279 Stamp of 1858 and River Ferry **280** Stamp of 1858

1958. Centenary of Argentine Confederation Stamps and Philatelic Exhibition, Buenos Aires.
916 **279** 40c.+20c. purple and green (postage) 45 20
917 – 2p.40+1p.20 blue and black 40 25
918 – 4p.40+2p.20 pur & bl . . 60 40
919 **280** 1p.+50c. blue and olive (air) 40 35
920 2p.+1p. violet and red . . 55 45
921 3p.+1p.50 brown & grn 60 55
922 5p.+2p.50 red and olive 1·00 85
923 10p.+5p. sepia & olive . . 1·50 1·40
DESIGNS—HORIZ: 2p.40, Magnifier, stamp album and stamp of 1858; 4p.40, P.O. building of 1858.

281 Steam Locomotive and Arms of Argentina and Bolivia **282** Douglas DC-6 over Map of Argentine-Bolivian Frontier

1958. Argentine–Bolivian Friendship. (a) Inauguration of Yacuiba–Santa Cruz Railway.
924 **281** 40c. red and slate 35 10
(b) Exchange of Presidential Visits.
925 **282** 1p. brown 15 10

283 "Liberty and Flag" **284** Farman H.F.20 Biplane

1958. Transfer of Presidential Mandate. Head of "Liberty" in grey; inscr black; flag yellow and blue; background colours given.
926 **283** 40c. buff 10 10
927 1p. salmon 15 10
928 2p. green 25 10

1958. 50th Anniv of Argentine Aero Club.
929 **284** 2p. brown 20 10

285 National Flag Monument, Rosario **286** Map of Antarctica

1958. 1st Anniv of Inauguration of National Flag Monument.
930 **285** 40c. grey and blue 10 10

1958. International Geophysical Year.
931 **286** 40c. black and red 50 10

287 Confederation Stamp and "The Santa Fe Mail" (after J. L. Palliere)

1958. Cent of Argentine Confederation Stamps.
932 – 40c. grn & blue (postage) 15 10
933 – 80c. blue & yellow (air) 40 10
934 **287** 1p. blue and orange . . . 20 10
DESIGNS: 40c. First local Cordoba 5c. stamp of 1858 and mail coach; 80c. Buenos Aires Type **1** of 1858 and "View of Buenos Aires" (after Deroy).

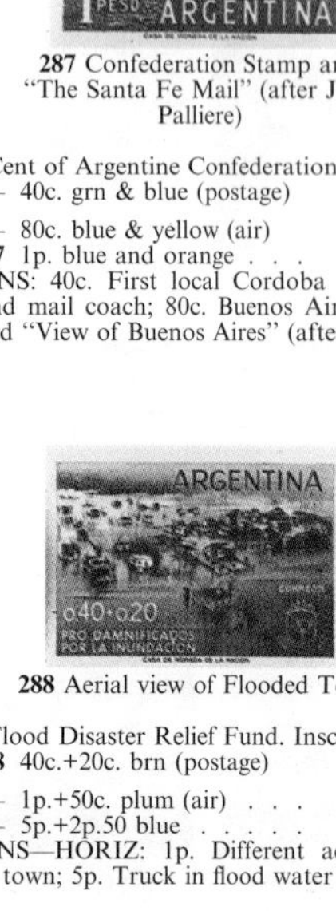

288 Aerial view of Flooded Town

1958. Flood Disaster Relief Fund. Inscr as in T **288**.
935 **288** 40c.+20c. brn (postage) 15 10
936 – 1p.+50c. plum (air) . . . 20 10
937 – 5p.+2p.50 blue 50 20
DESIGNS—HORIZ: 1p. Different aerial view of flooded town; 5p. Truck in flood water and garage.

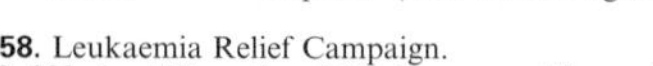

289 Child receiving Blood **290** U.N. Emblem and "Dying Captive" (after Michelangelo)

1958. Leukaemia Relief Campaign.
938 **289** 1p.+50c. red and black . . 15 10

1959. 10th Anniv of Declaration of Human Rights.
939 **290** 40c. grey and brown . . . 10 10

291 Hawker Siddeley Comet 4

1959. Air. Inauguration of Comet Jet Airliners by Argentine National Airlines.
940 **291** 5p. black and green . . . 25 10

292 Orchids and Globe **293** Pope Pius XII

1959. 1st Int Horticultural Exn, Buenos Aires.
941 **292** 1p. purple 15 10

1959. Pope Pius XII Commemoration.
942 **293** 1p. black and yellow . . . 15 10
PORTRAITS: 1p. Claude Bernard; 1p.50, Ivan P. Pavlov.

294 William Harvey

1959. 21st International Physiological Science Congress. Medical Scientists.
943 **294** 50c. green 10 10
944 – 1p. red 15 10
945 – 1p.50 brown 20 10

295 Creole Horse **296** Tierra del Fuego

1959.
946 – 10c. green 10 10
947 – 20c. purple 10 10
948 – 50c. ochre 10 10
950 **295** 1p. red 10 10
1016 – 1p. brown 10 10
1027 – 1p. brown 10 10
1035 – 2p. red 35 10
951 – 3p. blue 10 10
1036 – 4p. red 40 10
952 **296** 5p. brown 25 10
1037 – 8p. red 25 10
1286 – 10p. brown 50 10
1038 – 10p. red 70 10
1017 – 12p. purple 90 10
954 – 20p. green . . . . . . 2·40 10
1039 – 20p. red 30 10
1019 – 23p. green . . . . . 4·00 10
1020 – 25p. lilac . . . . . . 1·25 10
1021 – 43p. lake . . . . . . 5·50 10
1022 – 45p. brown . . . . . 3·25 10
1025 – 100p. blue . . . . . 6·25 20
1026 – 300p. violet . . . . . 3·25 10
1032 – 500p. green . . . . . 1·60 30
1290 – 1000p. blue . . . . . 4·50 90

DESIGNS—As Type **295**—HORIZ: 10c. Spectacled caiman; 20c. Llama; 50c. Puma. VERT: 2, 4, 8, 10p. (No 1038), 20p. (No. 1039) San Martin. As Type **296**—HORIZ: 3p. Zapata Hill, Catamarca; 300p. Mar del Plata (40 × 29½ mm). VERT: 1p. (No. 1016) Sunflowers; 1p. (No. 1027) Sunflower (22 × 32 mm); 10p. (No. 1286) Inca Bridge, Mendoza; 12, 23, 25p. Red quebracho tree; 20p. (No. 954) Lake Nahuel Huapi; 43, 45p. Industrial plant (30 × 39½ mm); 100p. Ski-jumper; 500p. Red deer (stag); 1,000p. Leaping salmon.
For these designs with face values in revalued currency, see Nos. 1300 etc.

298 Runner

299

1959. 3rd Pan-American Games, Chicago. Designs embody torch emblem. Centres and torch in black.
955 **298** 20c.+10c. green (postage) 10 10
956 – 50c.+20c. yellow 15 15
957 – 1p.+50c. purple 15 15
958 – 2p.+1p. blue (air) 30 15
959 – 3p.+1p.50 olive 45 30
DESIGNS—VERT: 50c. Basketball; 1p. Boxing. HORIZ: 2p. Rowing; 3p. High-diving.

1959. Red Cross Hygiene Campaign.
960 **299** 1p. red, blue and black 10 10

300 Child with Toys

1959. Mothers' Day.
961 **300** 1p. red and black 10 10

301 Buenos Aires 1p. stamp of 1859

1959. Stamp Day.
962 **301** 1p. blue and grey 10 10

302 B. Mitre and J. J. de Urquiza

303 Andean Condor

1959. Centenary of Pact of San Jose de Flores.
963 **302** 1p. plum 10 10

1960. Child Welfare. Birds.
964 **303** 20c.+10c. blue (postage) 70 15
965 – 50c.+20c. violet 70 15
966 – 1p.+50c. brown . . . . . 1·00 25
967 – 2p.+1p. mauve (air) . . . 70 30
968 – 3p.+1p.50 green 70 50
BIRDS: 50c. Fork-tailed flycatcher; 1p. Magellanic woodpecker; 2p. Red-winged tinamou; 3p. Greater rhea.

304 "Uprooted Tree"

305 Abraham Lincoln

1960. World Refugee Year.
969 **304** 1p. red and brown . . . 10 10
970 4p.20 purple and green . . 15 10

1960. 150th Birth Anniv of Abraham Lincoln.
972 **305** 5p. blue 25 15

306 Saavedra and Chapter Hall, Buenos Aires

307 Dr. L. Drago

1960. 150th Anniv of May Revolution.

973	**306**	1p. purple (postage)	10	10
974	–	2p. green	10	10
975	–	4p.20 green and grey	20	10
976	–	10p.70 blue and slate	40	15
977	–	1p.80 brown (air)	10	10
978	–	5p. purple and brown	30	10

DESIGNS—Chapter Hall and: 1p.80, Moreno; 2p. Paso; 4p.20, Alberti and Azcuenaga; 5p. Belgrano and Castelli; 10p.70, Larrea and Matheu.

1960. Birth Centenary of Drago.

980	**307**	4p.20 brown	15	10

308 "Five Provinces"

309 "Market Place 1810" (Buenos Aires)

1960. Air. New Argentine Provinces.

981	**308**	1p.80 blue and red	10	10

1960. Air. Inter-American Philatelic Exhibition, Buenos Aires ("EFIMAYO") and 150th Anniv of Revolution. Inscr "EFIMAYO 1960".

982	**309**	2p.+1p. lake	15	10
983	–	6p.+3p. grey	35	20
984	–	10p.70+5p.30 blue	60	35
985	–	20p.+10p. turquoise	75	60

DESIGNS: 6p. "The Water Carrier"; 10p.70, "The Landing Place"; 20p. "The Fort".

310 J. B. Alberdi

311 Seibo (Argentine National Flower)

1960. 150th Birth Anniv of J. B. Alberdi (statesman).

986	**310**	1p. green	10	10

1960. Air. Chilean Earthquake Relief Fund. Inscr "AYUDA CHILE".

987	**311**	6p.+3p. red	30	25
988	–	10p.70+5p.30 red	40	35

DESIGN: 10p.70, Copihue (Chilean national flower).

312 Map of Argentina

313 Galleon

1960. Census.

989	**312**	5p. lilac	40	10

1960. 8th Spanish-American P.U. Congress.

990	**313**	1p. green (postage)	40	10
991		5p. brown	85	20
992		1p.80 purple (air)	40	10
993		10p.70 turquoise	1·10	30

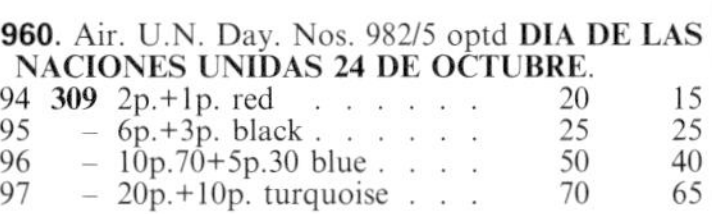

1960. Air. U.N. Day. Nos. 982/5 optd **DIA DE LAS NACIONES UNIDAS 24 DE OCTUBRE**.

994	**309**	2p.+1p. red	20	15
995	–	6p.+3p. black	25	25
996	–	10p.70+5p.30 blue	50	40
997	–	20p.+10p. turquoise	70	65

315 Blessed Virgin of Lujan

316 Jacaranda

1960. 1st Inter-American Marian Congress.

998	**315**	1p. blue	10	10

1960. International Thematic Stamp Exhibition ("TEMEX"). Inscr "TEMEX-61".

999	**316**	50c.+50c. blue	10	10
1000	–	1p.+1p. turquoise	10	10
1001	–	3p.+3p. brown	30	20
1002	–	5p.+5p. brown	50	30

FLOWERS: 1p. Passion flowers; 3p. Hibiscus; 5p. Black lapacho.

317 Argentine Scout Badge

318 "Shipment of Cereals" (after B. Q. Martin)

1961. International Scout (Patrol) Camp.

1003	**317**	1p. red and black	15	10

1961. Export Campaign.

1004	**318**	1p. brown	15	10

319 Emperor Penguin and Chick

320 "America"

1961. Child Welfare. Inscr "PRO-INFANCIA".

1005	–	4p.20+2p.10 brown (postage)	1·00	75
1006	**319**	1p.80+90c. black (air)	60	50

DESIGN: 4p.20, Blue-eyed cormorant.

1961. 150th Anniv of Battle of San Nicolas.

1007	**320**	2p. black	55	10

321 Dr. M. Moreno

322 Emperor Trajan

1961. 150th Death Anniv of Dr. M. Moreno.

1008	**321**	2p. blue	15	10

1961. Visit of President of Italy.

1009	**322**	2p. green	15	10

1961. Americas Day. Nos. 999/1002 optd **14 DE ABRIL DE LAS AMERICAS**.

1010	**316**	50c.+50c. blue	10	10
1011	–	1p.+1p. turquoise	15	10
1012	–	3p.+3p. brown	20	20
1013	–	5p.+5p. brown	40	35

324 Tagore

325 San Martin Monument, Madrid

1961. Birth Centenary of Rabindranath Tagore (Indian poet).

1014	**324**	2p. violet on green	20	10

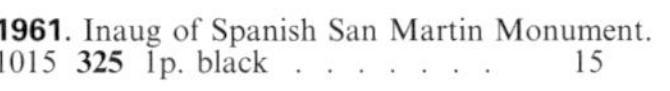

1961. Inaug of Spanish San Martin Monument.

1015	**325**	1p. black	15	10

331a Gen. Belgrano (after monument by Rocha, Buenos Aires)

1961. Gen. Manuel Belgrano Commemoration.

1034	**331a**	2p. blue	15	10

333 Antarctic Scene

1961. 10th Anniv of San Martin Antarctic Base.

1044	**333**	2p. black	50	10

334 Conquistador and Sword

335 Sarmiento Statue (Rodin)

1961. 4th Centenary of Jujuy City.

1045	**334**	2p. red and black	15	10

1961. 150th Birth Anniv of Sarmiento.

1046	**335**	2p. violet	15	10

336 Cordoba Cathedral

343 15c. Stamp of 1862

1961. "Argentina 62" International Philatelic Exn.

1047	**336**	2p.+2p. purple (postage)	20	15
1048	–	3p.+3p. green	30	15
1049	–	10p.+10p. blue	85	50
1059	**343**	6p.50+6p.50 blue and turquoise (air)	40	30

DESIGNS—HORIZ: 10p. Buenos Aires Cathedral. VERT: 3p. As Type **343** but showing 10c. value and different inscr.

337

338 "The Flight into Egypt" (after Ana Maria Moncalvo)

1961. World Town-planning Day.

1052	**337**	2p. blue and yellow	15	10

1961. Child Welfare.

1053	**338**	2p.+1p. brown & lilac	15	10
1054		10p.+5p. purple & mve	50	15

339 Belgrano Statue (C. Belleuse)

340 Mounted Grenadier

1962. 150th Anniv of National Flag.

1055	**339**	2p. blue	15	10

1962. 150th Anniv of Gen. San Martin's Mounted Grenadiers.

1056	**340**	2p. red	15	10

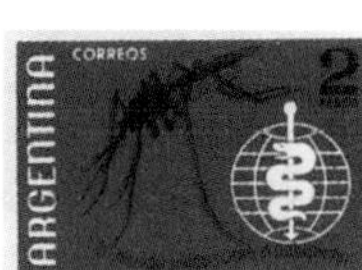

341 Mosquito and Emblem

342 Lujan Basilica

1962. Malaria Eradication.

1057	**341**	2p. black and red	10	10

1962. 75th Anniv of Coronation of the Holy Virgin of Lujan.

1058	**342**	2p. black and brown	10	10

344 Juan Jufre (founder)

345 U.N.E.S.C.O. Emblem

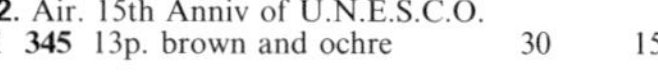

1962. 400th Anniv of San Juan.

1060	**344**	2p. blue	10	10

1962. Air. 15th Anniv of U.N.E.S.C.O.

1061	**345**	13p. brown and ochre	30	15

346 "Flight"

347 Juan Vucetich (fingerprints pioneer)

1962. 50th Anniv of Argentine Air Force.

1062	**346**	2p. blue, black & purple	15	10

1962. Vucetich Commem.

1063	**347**	2p. green	15	10

348 19th-century Mail Coach

350 U.P.A.E. Emblem

1962. Air. Postman's Day.

1064	**348**	5p.60 black and drab	15	10

1962. Air. Surch **AEREO** and value.

1065	**296**	5p.60 on 5p. brown	30	15
1066		18p. on 5p. brn on grn	1·00	20

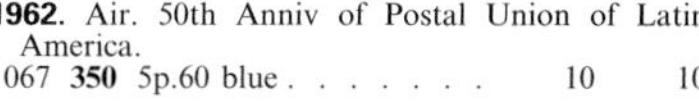

1962. Air. 50th Anniv of Postal Union of Latin America.

1067	**350**	5p.60 blue	10	10

351 Pres. Sarmiento

352 Chalk-browed Mockingbird

1962.

1073	**351**	2p. green	45	10
1069	–	4p. red	60	10
1075	–	6p. red	1·40	10
1071	–	6p. brown	10	10
1072	–	90p. bistre	2·00	15

PORTRAITS: 4, 6p. Jose Hernandez; 90p. G. Brown.

1962. Child Welfare.

1076	**352**	4p.+2p. sepia, turquoise and brown	1·25	75
1077	–	12p.+6p. brown, yellow and slate	2·00	1·25

DESIGN—VERT: 12p. Rufous-collared sparrow.

See also Nos. 1101/2, 1124/5, 1165/6, 1191/2, 1214/15, 1264/5, 1293/4, 1394/5, 1415/16 and 1441/2.

353 Skylark 3 Glider **354** "20 de Febrero" Monument, Salta

1963. Air. 9th World Gliding Championships, Junin.
1078 **353** 5p.60 black and blue . . 20 10
1079 – 11p. black, red and blue 40 10
DESIGN: 11p. Super Albatross glider.

1963. 150th Anniv of Battle of Salta.
1080 **354** 2p. green 15 10

355 Cogwheels **356** National College

1963. 75th Anniv of Argentine Industrial Union.
1081 **355** 4p. red and grey 10 10

1963. Centenary of National College, Buenos Aires.
1082 **356** 4p. black and buff . . . 10 10

357 Child drinking Milk **358** "Flight"

1963. Freedom from Hunger.
1083 **357** 4p. ochre, black and red 15 10

1963. Air. (a) As T **358**.
1084 **358** 5p.60 green, mve & pur 35 10
1085 7p. black & yellow (I) 45 10
1086 7p. black & yellow (II) 4·25 75
1087 11p. purple, green & blk 45 15
1088 18p. blue, red and mauve 1·10 25
1089 21p. grey, red and brown 1·50 35
Two types of 7p. I, "ARGENTINA" reads down, and II, "ARGENTINA" reads up as in Type **358**.

(b) As T **358** but inscr "REPUBLICA ARGENTINA" reading down.
1147 12p. lake and brown . . . . 1·50 15
1148 15p. blue and red . . . . . 1·50 15
1291 26p. ochre 25 15
1150 27p.50 green and black . . 2·25 30
1151 30p.50 brown and blue . . . 2·25 35
1292 40p. lilac . . . . 2·25 15
1153 68p. green . . . . 2·75 25
1154 78p. blue 55 35
See also Nos. 1374/80 in revalued currency.

359 Football **360** Frigate "La Argentina" (after Bouchard)

1963. 4th Pan-American Games, Sao Paulo.
1090 **359** 4p.+2p. green, black and pink (postage) 20 10
1091 – 12p.+6p. purple, black and salmon 30 25
1092 – 11p.+5p. red, black and green (air) 35 25
DESIGNS: 11p. Cycling; 12p. Show-jumping.

1963. Navy Day.
1093 **360** 4p. blue 80 10

361 Assembly House and Seal

1963. 150th Anniv of 1813 Assembly.
1094 **361** 4p. black and blue . . . 15 10

362 Battle Scene

1963. 150th Anniv of Battle of San Lorenzo.
1095 **362** 4p. black & green on grn 20 10

363 Queen Nefertari (bas-relief)

1963. U.N.E.S.C.O. Campaign for Preservation of Nubian Monuments.
1096 **363** 4p. black, green & buff 25 10

364 Government House **365** "Science"

1963. Presidential Installation.
1097 **364** 5p. brown and pink . . 15 10

1963. 10th Latin-American Neurosurgery Congress.
1098 **365** 4p. blue, black & brown 20 10

366 Blackboards **367** F. de las Carreras (President of Supreme Court)

1963. "Alliance for Progress".
1099 **366** 5p. red, black and blue 15 10

1963. Centenary of Judicial Power.
1100 **367** 5p. green 15 10

1963. Child Welfare. As T **352**. Mult.
1101 4p.+2p. Vermilion flycatcher (postage) 35 25
1102 11p.+5p. Great kiskadee (air) 75 75

368 Kemal Ataturk **369** "Payador" (after Castagnino)

1963. 25th Death Anniv of Kemal Ataturk.
1103 **368** 12p. grey 30 10

1964. 4th National Folklore Festival.
1104 **369** 4p. black, blue & ultram 15 10

370 Map of Antarctic Islands

1964. Antarctic Claims Issue.
1105 **370** 2p. bl & ochre (postage) 80 30
1106 – 4p. bistre and blue . . . 1·25 35
1107 – 18p. bl & bistre (air) . . 2·25 55
DESIGNS—VERT: (30×39½ mm): 4p. Map of Argentina and Antarctica. HORIZ: (as Type **291**): 18p. Map of "Islas Malvinas" (Falkland Islands).

371 Jorge Newbery in Airplane

1964. 50th Death Anniv of Jorge Newbery (aviator).
1108 **371** 4p. green 15 10

372 Pres. Kennedy **373** Father Brochero

1964. President Kennedy Memorial Issue.
1109 **372** 4p. blue and mauve . . 15 10

1964. 50th Death Anniv of Father J. G. Brochero.
1110 **373** 4p. brown 15 10

374 U.P.U. Monument, Berne **375** Soldier of the Patricios Regiment

1964. Air. 15th U.P.U. Congress, Vienna.
1111 **374** 18p. purple and red . . 50 20

1964. Army Day.
1112 **375** 4p. multicoloured . . . 50 15
See also Nos. 1135, 1170, 1201, 1223, 1246, 1343, 1363, 1399, 1450, 1515, 1564, 1641 and 1678.

376 Pope John XXIII **377** Olympic Stadium

1964. Pope John Commemoration
1113 **376** 4p. black and orange . . 20 10

1964. Olympic Games, Tokyo.
1114 **377** 4p.+2p. brown, yellow and red (postage) . . 15 15
1115 – 12p.+6p. black & green 30 30
1116 – 11p.+5p. blk & bl (air) 40 40
DESIGNS—VERT: 11p. Sailing; 12p. Fencing.

378 University Arms **379** Olympic Flame and Crutch

1964. 350th Anniv of Cordoba University.
1117 **378** 4p. yellow, blue & black 15 10

1964. Air. Invalids Olympic Games, Tokyo.
1118 **379** 18p.+9p. multicoloured 35 45

380 "The Discovery of America" (Florentine woodcut) **381** Pigeons and U.N. Headquarters

1964. Air. "Columbus Day" (or "Day of the Race").
1119 **380** 13p. black and drab . . 35 15

1964. United Nations Day.
1120 **381** 4p. ultramarine and blue 15 10

382 J. V. Gonzalez (medallion) **383** Gen. J. Roca

1964. Birth Centenary of J. V. Gonzalez.
1121 **382** 4p. red 15 10

1964. 50th Death Anniv of General Julio Roca.
1122 **383** 4p. blue 15 10

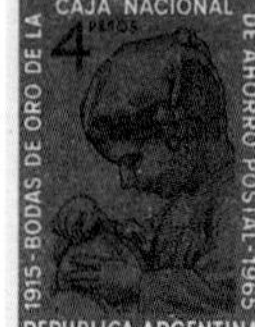

384 "Market-place, Montserrat Square" (after C. Morel) **385** Icebreaker "General San Martin" and Bearded Penguin

1964. "Argentine Painters".
1123 **384** 4p. sepia 25 10

1964. Child Welfare. As T **352**. Multicoloured.
1124 4p.+2p. Red-crested cardinal (postage) 65 35
1125 18p.+9p. Chilean swallow (air) . . . . 1·25 80

1965. "National Territory of Tierra del Fuego, Antarctic and South Atlantic Isles".
1126 – 2p. purple (postage) . . 50 10
1127 **385** 4p. blue . . . . 2·00 40
1128 – 11p. red (air) 85 15
DESIGNS: 2p. General Belgrano Base (inscr "BASE DE EJERCITO" etc); 11p. Teniente Matienzo Joint Antarctic Base (inscr "BASE CONJUNTA" etc).

1965. Air. 1st Rio Plata Philatelists' Day. Optd **PRIMERAS JORNADAS FILATELICAS RIOPLATENSES**.
1129 **358** 7p. black & yellow (II) 15 15

387 Young Saver **388** I.T.U. Emblem

1965. 50th Anniv of National Postal Savings Bank.
1130 **387** 4p. black and red . . . 10 10

1965. Air. Centenary of I.T.U.
1131 **388** 18p. multicoloured . . . 40 15

389 I.Q.S.Y. Emblem — 390 Soldier of the "Pueyrredon Hussars"

1965. Int Quiet Sun Year and Space Research.
1132 **389** 4p. black, orange and blue (postage) 15 10
1133 – 18p. red (air) 55 20
1134 – 50p. blue 80 35
DESIGNS—VERT: 18p. Rocket launching. HORIZ: 50p. Earth, trajectories and space phenomena (both inscr "INVESTIGACIONES ESPACIALES").

1965. Army Day (29 May).
1135 **390** 8p. multicoloured . . . 70 15
See also Nos. 1170, 1201, 1223, 1246, 1343, 1363, 1399, 1450, 1515, 1564 and 1641.

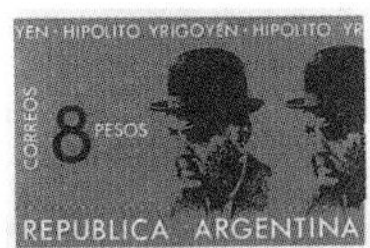

391 Ricardo Guiraldes — 392 H. Yrigoyen (statesman)

1965. Argentine Writers (1st series). Each brown.
1136 8p. Type **391** 35 10
1137 8p. E. Larreta 35 10
1138 8p. L. Lugones 35 10
1139 8p. R. J. Payro 35 10
1140 8p. R. Rojas 35 10
See also Nos 1174/8.

1965. Hipolito Yrigoyen Commemoration
1141 **392** 8p. black and red . . . 15 10

393 "Children looking through a Window"

1965. International Mental Health Seminar.
1142 **393** 8p. black and brown . . 15 10

394 Ancient Map and Funeral Urn — 395 Mgr. Dr. J. Cagliero

1965. 400th Anniv of San Miguel de Tucuman.
1143 **394** 8p. multicoloured . . . 15 10

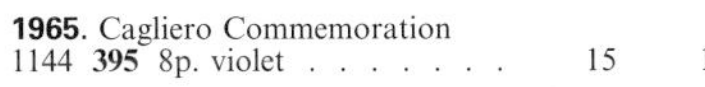

1965. Cagliero Commemoration
1144 **395** 8p. violet 15 10

396 Dante (statue in Church of the Holy Cross, Florence) — 397 Sail Merchantman "Mimosa"

1965. 700th Birth Anniv of Dante.
1145 **396** 8p. blue 15 10

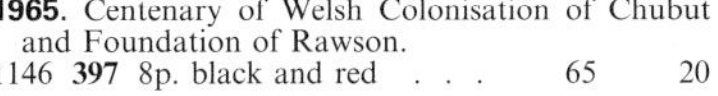

1965. Centenary of Welsh Colonisation of Chubut and Foundation of Rawson.
1146 **397** 8p. black and red . . . 65 20

398 Police Emblem on Map of Buenos Aires

1965. Federal Police Day.
1155 **398** 8p. red 15 10

399 Schoolchildren

1965. 81st Anniv of Law 1420 (Public Education).
1156 **399** 8p. black and green . . 15 10

400 St. Francis's Church, Catamarca — 401 R. Dario (Nicaraguan poet)

1965. Brother Mamerto Esquiu Commemoration.
1157 **400** 8p. brown and yellow . . 15 10

1965. 50th Death Anniv of Ruben Dario.
1158 **401** 15p. violet on grey . . . 15 10

402 "The Orange-seller" (detail)

1966. Prilidiano Pueyrredon's Paintings. Designs show details from the original works, each green.
1159 8p. Type **402** 55 45
1160 8p. "A Halt at the Village Grocer's Shop" 55 45
1161 8p. "San Fernando Landscape" 75 45
1162 8p. "Bathing Horses on the Banks of the River Plate" 55 45

403 Rocket "Centaur" and Antarctic Map — 404 Dr. Sun Yat-sen

1966. Air. Rocket Launches in Antarctica.
1163 **403** 27p.50 red, black & blue 65 25

1966. Birth Centenary of Dr. Sun Yat-sen.
1164 **404** 8p. brown 45 25

1966. Child Welfare. As T **352**, inscr "R. ARGENTINA". Multicoloured.
1165 8p.+4p. Southern lapwing (postage) . . . . 1·00 55
1166 27p.50+12p.50 Rufous hornero (air) . . . . . . 1·25 85

406 "Human Races"

1966. Inaug of W.H.O. Headquarters, Geneva.
1168 **406** 8p. black and brown . . 15 10

407 Magellan Gull

1966. Air. 50th Anniv of Naval Aviation School, Puerto Militar.
1169 **407** 12p. multicoloured . . . 40 25

1966. Army Day (29 May). As T **390**.
1170 8p. multicoloured 65 15
DESIGN: 8p. Militiaman of Guemes's "Infernals".

408 Arms of Argentina

1966. Air. "Argentina '66" Philatelic Exhibition, Buenos Aires.
1171 **408** 10p.+10p. multicoloured 1·50 1·10

410 "Charity" Emblem

1966. Argentine Charities.
1173 **410** 10p. blue, black & green 25 15

1966. Argentine Writers (2nd series). Portraits as T **391**. Each green.
1174 10p. H. Ascasubi 40 10
1175 10p. Estanislao del Campo 40 10
1176 10p. M. Cane 40 10
1177 10p. Lucio V. Lopez 40 10
1178 10p. R. Obligado 40 10

411 Anchor

1966. 25th Anniv of Argentine Mercantile Marine.
1179 **411** 4p. multicoloured . . . 25 15

412 L. Agote — 413 Map and Flags of the American States

1966. Argentine Scientists. Each violet.
1180 10p. Type **412** 40 10
1181 10p. J. B. Ambrosetti . . . 40 10
1182 10p. M. I. Lillo 40 10
1183 10p. F. P. Moreno 40 10
1184 10p. F. J. Muniz 40 10

1966. 7th American Armies Conf, Buenos Aires.
1185 **413** 10p. multicoloured . . . 15 10

414 Bank Facade — 415 La Salle Statue and College

1966. 75th Anniv of Argentine National Bank.
1186 **414** 10p. green 10 10

1966. 75th Anniv of La Salle College, Buenos Aires.
1187 **415** 10p. black and brown . . 10 10

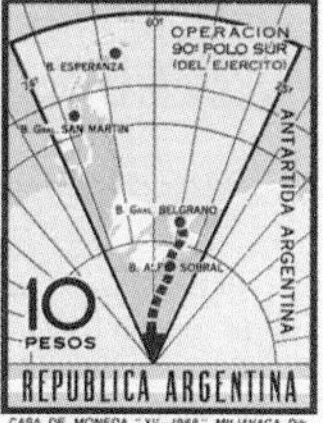

416 Antarctic Map with Expedition Route — 417 Gen. J. M. de Pueyrredon

1966. Argentine South Pole Expedition, 1965–66.
1188 **416** 10p. multicoloured . . . 80 50

1966. Gen. J. M. de Pueyrredon Commemoration
1189 **417** 10p. red 10 10

418 Gen. J. G. de Las Heras — 419 Ancient Pot

1966. Gen. Juan G. de Las Heras Commemoration.
1190 **418** 10p. black 10 10

1967. Child Welfare. As T **352**, inscr "R. ARGENTINA". Multicoloured.
1191 10p.+5p. Scarlet-headed blackbird (horiz) (postage) 80 60
1192 15p.+7p. Blue and yellow tanager (air) . . . . . . 1·25 90

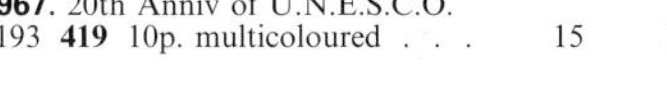

1967. 20th Anniv of U.N.E.S.C.O.
1193 **419** 10p. multicoloured . . . 15 10

420 "The Meal" (after F. Fader)

1967. Fernando Fader (painter).
1194 **420** 10p. brown 15 10

421 Juana Azurduy de Padilla — 422 Schooner "Invencible"

1967. Famous Argentine Women. Each sepia.
1195 6p. Type **421** 30 10
1196 6p. J. M. Gorriti 30 10
1197 6p. C. Grierson 30 10
1198 6p. J. P. Manson 30 10
1199 6p. A. Storni 30 10

1967. Navy Day.
1200 **422** 20p. multicoloured . . . 1·25 20

1967. Army Day (29 May). As T **390**.
1201 20p. multicoloured 75 15
DESIGN: 20p. Soldier of the Arribenos Regiment.

424 Suitcase and Dove

425 PADELAI Emblem and Sun

1967. International Tourist Year.
1203 **424** 20p. multicoloured . . . 15 10

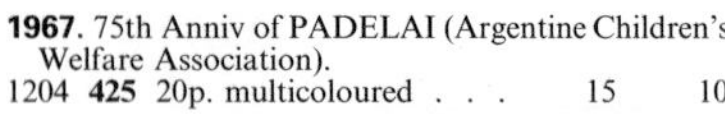

1967. 75th Anniv of PADELAI (Argentine Children's Welfare Association).
1204 **425** 20p. multicoloured . . . 15 10

426 Teodoro Fels's Bleriot XI

427 Ferreyra's Oxwagon and Skyscrapers

1967. Air. 50th Anniv of 1st Argentine–Uruguay Airmail Flight.
1205 **426** 26p. brown, olive & blue 30 10

1967. Centenary of Villa Maria.
1206 **427** 20p. multicoloured . . . 15 10

428 "General San Martin" (from statue by M. P. Nunez de Ibarra)

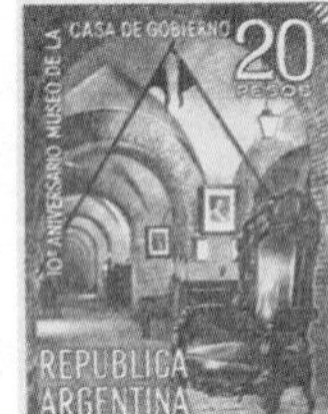

429 Interior of Museum

1967. 150th Anniv of Battle of Chacabuco.
1207 **428** 20p. brown and yellow 45 15
1208 – 40p. blue 70 15
DESIGN—(48 × 31 mm)—HORIZ: 40p. "Battle of Chacabuco" (from painting by P. Subercaseaux).

1967. 10th Anniv of Government House Museum.
1209 **429** 20p. blue 15 10

430 Pedro Zanni and "Provincia de Buenos Aires"

1967. Aeronautics Week.
1210 **430** 20p. multicoloured . . . 15 10

431 Cadet Ship "General Brown" (from painting by E. Biggeri)

432 Ovidio Lagos and Front Page of "La Capital" (newspaper)

1967. "Temex 67" Stamp Exhibition and 95th Anniv of Naval Military School.
1211 **431** 20p. multicoloured . . . 1·00 20

1967. Centenary of "La Capital".
1212 **432** 20p. brown 15 10

433 St. Barbara (from altar-painting, Segovia, Spain)

434 "Sivori's Wife"

1967. Artillery Day (4 Dec).
1213 **433** 20p. red 15 10

1967. Child Welfare. Bird designs as T **352**. Multicoloured.
1214 20p.+10p. Amazon kingfisher (postage) . . . 75 40
1215 26p.+13p. Toco toucan (air) 1·00 60

1968. 50th Death Anniv of Eduardo Sivori (painter).
1216 **434** 20p. green 15 10

435 "Almirante Brown" Scientific Station

436 Man in Wheelchair

1968. "Antarctic Territories".
1217 – 6p. multicoloured . . . 60 15
1218 **435** 20p. multicoloured . . . 85 20
1219 – 40p. multicoloured . . . 1·10 55
DESIGNS—VERT (22½ × 32 mm): 6p. Map of Antarctic radio-postal stations. HORIZ (as Type **435**): 40p. Aircraft over South Pole ("Trans-Polar Round Flight").

1968. Rehabilitation Day for the Handicapped.
1220 **436** 20p. black and green . . 20 10

437 "St. Gabriel" (detail from "The Annunciation" by Leonardo da Vinci)

438 Children and W.H.O. Emblem

1968. St. Gabriel (patron saint of army communications).
1221 **437** 20p. mauve 15 10

1968. 20th Anniv of W.H.O.
1222 **438** 20p. blue and red . . . 15 10

1968. Army Day (29 May). As T **390**.
1223 20p. multicoloured 85 15
DESIGN: 20p. Iriarte's artilleryman.

439 Full-rigged Cadet Ship "Libertad" (E. Biggeri)

1968. Navy Day.
1224 **439** 20p. multicoloured . . . 65 15

440 G. Rawson and Hospital

1968. Centenary of Guillermo Rawson Hospital.
1225 **440** 6p. bistre 15 10

441 Vito Dumas and "Legh II"

1968. Air. Vito Dumas' World Voyage in Yacht "Legh II".
1226 **441** 68p. multicoloured . . . 60 20

442 Children using Zebra crossing

1968. Road Safety.
1227 **442** 20p. multicoloured . . . 20 10

443 "O'Higgins greeting San Martin" (P. Subercaseaux)

1968. 150th Anniv of Battle of the Maipu.
1228 **443** 40p. blue 55 20

444 Dr. O. Magnasco (lawyer)

445 "The Sea" (E. Gomez)

446 "Grandmother's Birthday" (P. Lynch)

1968. Magnasco Commemoration.
1229 **444** 20p. brown 20 10

1968. Children's Stamp Design Competition.
1230 **445** 20p. multicoloured . . . 20 15
1231 **446** 20p. multicoloured . . . 20 15

447 Mar del Plata at Night

448 Mounted Gendarme

1968. 4th Plenary Assembly of Int Telegraph and Telephone Consultative Committee, Mar del Plata.
1232 **447** 20p. black, yellow and blue (postage) 25 15
1233 – 40p. black, mauve and blue (air) 35 15
1234 – 68p. multicoloured . . . 50 25
DESIGNS (as Type **447**): 40p. South America in Assembly hemisphere. (Larger, 40 × 30 mm): 68p. Assembly emblem.

1968. National Gendarmerie.
1235 **448** 20p. multicoloured . . . 30 10

449 Coastguard Cutter "Lynch"

450 A. de Anchorena and "Pampero"

1968. National Maritime Prefecture (Coastguard).
1236 **449** 20p. black, grey and blue 65 10

1968. Aeronautics Week.
1237 **450** 20p. multicoloured . . . 30 10

451 St. Martin of Tours (A. Guido)

452 Bank Emblem

1968. St. Martin of Tours (patron saint of Buenos Aires).
1238 **451** 20p. brown and lilac . . 15 10

1968. Municipal Bank of Buenos Aires.
1239 **452** 20p. black, green & yell 15 10

453 Anniversary and A.L.P.I. Emblems

1968. 25th Anniv of "Fight Against Polio Association" (A.L.P.I.).
1240 **453** 20p. green and red . . . 20 10

454 "My Grandmother's Birthday" (Patricia Lynch)

1968. 1st "Solidarity" Philatelic Exn, Buenos Aires.
1241 **454** 40p.+20p. multicoloured 75 30

455 "The Potter Woman" (Ramon Gomez Cornet)

456 Emblem of State Coalfields

1968. Cent of Whitcomb Gallery, Buenos Aires.
1242 **455** 20p. red 15 10

1968. Coal and Steel Industries. Multicoloured.
1243 20p. Type **456** 15 10
1244 20p. Ladle and emblem of Military Steel-manufacturing Agency ("FM") 15 10

457 Illustration from Schmidl's book "Journey to the River Plate and Paraguay"

1969. Ulrich Schmidl Commemoration.
1245 **457** 20p. yellow, red & black 15 10

1969. Army Day (29 May). As T **390**.
1246 20p. Sapper, Buenos Aires Army, 1856 . . . . . . 70 15

459 Sail Frigate "Hercules"

1969. Navy Day.
1247 **459** 20p. multicoloured . . . 1·00 20

460 "Freedom and Equality" (from poster by S. Zagorski)

461 I.L.O. Emblem within Honeycomb

1969. Human Rights Year.
1254 **460** 20p. black and yellow . . 15 10

1969. 50th Anniv of I.L.O.
1255 **461** 20p. multicoloured . . . 15 10

462 P. N. Arata (biologist)

463 Dish Aerial and Satellite

1969. Argentine Scientists.
1256 **462** 6p. brown on yellow . . 35 15
1257 – 6p. brown on yellow . . 35 15
1258 – 6p. brown on yellow . . 35 15
1259 – 6p. brown on yellow . . 35 15
1260 – 6p. brown on yellow . . 35 15
PORTRAITS: No. 1257, M. Fernandez (zoologist); 1258, A. P. Gallardo (biologist); 1259, C. M. Hicken (botanist); 1260, E. L. Holmberg (botanist).

1969. Satellite Communications.
1261 **463** 20p. blk & yell (postage) 25 15
1262 – 40p. blue (air) 55 20
DESIGN—HORIZ: 40p. Earth station and dish aerial.

464 Nieuport 28 and Route Map

1969. 50th Anniv of 1st Argentine Airmail Service.
1263 **464** 20p. multicoloured . . . 20 10

1969. Child Welfare. As T **352**, inscr "R. ARGENTINA". Multicoloured.
1264 20p.+10p. White-faced whistling duck (postage) 1·00 45
1265 26p.+13p. Lineated woodpecker (air) . . . . 1·00 45

465 College Entrance

466 General Pacheco (from painting by R. Guidice)

1969. Centenary of Argentine Military College.
1266 **465** 20p. multicoloured . . . 15 10

1969. Death Centenary of General Angel Pacheco.
1267 **466** 20p. green 15 10

467 Bartolome Mitre and Logotypes of "La Nacion"

468 J. Aguirre

1969. Centenary of Newspapers "La Nacion" and "La Prensa".
1268 **467** 20p. black, emer & grn 50 15
1269 – 20p. black orange & yell 50 15
DESIGN: No. 1269 "The Lantern" (masthead) and logotypes of "La Prensa".

1969. Argentine Musicians.
1270 **468** 6p. green and blue . . . 65 15
1271 – 6p. green and blue . . . 65 15
1272 – 6p. green and blue . . . 65 15
1273 – 6p. green and blue . . . 65 15
1274 – 6p. green and blue . . . 65 15
MUSICIANS: No. 1271, F. Boero; 1272, C. Gaito; 1273, C. L. Buchardo; 1274, A. Williams.

469 Hydro-electric Project on Rivers Limay and Neuquen

1969. National Development Projects. Mult.
1275 6p. Type **469** (postage) . . . 50 10
1276 20p. Parana–Santa Fe river tunnel 60 15
1277 26p. Atomic power plant, Atucha (air) . . . . . . 1·00 40

470 Lieut. B. Matienzo and Nieuport 28 Biplane

1969. Aeronautics Week.
1278 **470** 20p. multicoloured . . . 50 10

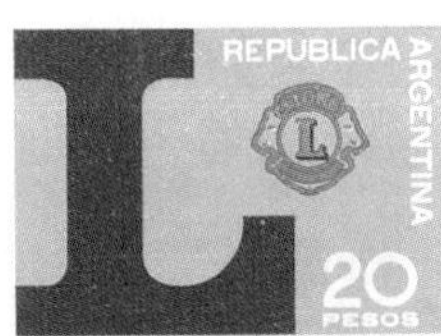

471 Capital "L" and Lions Emblem

1969. 50th Anniv of Lions International.
1279 **471** 20p. olive, orge & green 50 10

472 "Madonna and Child" (after R. Soldi)

1969. Christmas.
1280 **472** 20p. multicoloured . . . 55 15

1970. Child Welfare. As T **352**, but differently arranged and inscr "REPUBLICA ARGENTINA". Multicoloured.
1293 20c.+10c. Slender-tailed woodstar (postage) . . . 85 55
1294 40c.+20c. Chilean flamingo (air) 90 70
See also Nos. 1394/5, 1415/16 and 1441/2.

474 "General Belgrano" (lithograph by Gericault)

1970. Birth Bicent of General Manuel Belgrano.
1295 **474** 20c. brown 45 15
1296 – 50c. black, flesh & blue 80 25
DESIGN—HORIZ (56 × 15 mm): 50c. "Monument to the Flag" (bas-relief by Jose Fioravanti).

475 Early Fire Engine

1970. Air. Centenary of Buenos Aires Fire Brigade.
1297 **475** 40c. multicoloured . . . 60 10

476 Naval Schooner "Juliet", 1814

1970. Navy Day.
1298 **476** 20c. multicoloured . . . 1·25 20

477 San Jose Palace

478 General Belgrano

1970. President Justo de Urquiza Commemoration.
1299 **477** 20c. multicoloured . . . 15 10

1970. Revalued currency. Previous designs with values in centavos and pesos as T **478**. Inscr "REPUBLICA ARGENTINA" or "ARGENTINA".
1300 1c. green (No. 1016) . . 15 10
1301 – 3c. red (No. 951) . . . 15 10
1302 **296** 5c. blue 15 10
1303 **478** 6c. blue 15 10
1304 8c. green 15 10
1305 – 10c. brown (No. 1286)* 45 10
1306 – 10c. red (No. 1286) . . 1·25 10
1307 – 10c. brown (No. 1286)* 55 10
1308 **478** 10c. brown 20 10
1309 – 25c. brown 40 10
1310 **478** 30c. purple 10 10
1311 – 50c. red 80 10
1312 **478** 60c. yellow 10 10
1313 – 65c. brown (No. 878) . 85 10
1314 – 70c. blue 10 10
1315 – 90c. green (No. 878) . . 2·00 10
1316a – 1p. brown (as No. 1027, but 23 × 29 mm) 40 10
1317 – 1p.15 blue (No. 1072) 80 10
1318 – 1p.20 orange (No. 878) 80 10
1319 – 1p.20 red 35 10
1320 – 1p.80 brn (as No. 1072) 30 10
1321 **478** 1p.80 blue 20 10
1322 – 2p. brown 20 10
1323 – 2p.70 bl (as No. 878) 25 10
1323a **478** 3p. grey 15 10
1392 – 4p.50 green (as No. 1288) (G. Brown) 40 10
1325 – 5p. green (as No. 1032) 95 10
1326 – 6p. red 25 10
1327 – 6p. green 25 10
1328 – 7p.50 grn (as No. 878) 85 10
1329 – 10p. blue (as No. 1033) 1·25 10
1329a – 12p. green 25 10
1329b – 12p. red 25 10
1330 – 13p.50 red (as No. 1288) . . . . . 1·00 10
1331 – 13p.50 red (as No. 1072 but larger, 16 × 24 mm) 40 10
1332 – 15p. red 25 10
1333 – 15p. blue 25 10
1334 – 20p. red 40 10
1335 – 22p.50 blue (as No. 878) (22 × 32½ mm) . . . 1·00 10
1393 – 22p.50 blue (as No. 878) (26 × 39 mm) 40 10
1336 – 30p. red 40 10
1337 **478** 40p. green 70 15
1338 – 40p. red 40 10
1339 **478** 60p. blue 80 20
1340 – 70p. blue . . . . . . 1·00 20
1340a **478** 90p. green 55 30
1340b – 100p. red 55 25
1340c – 110p. red 35 15
1340d – 120p. red 30 20
1340e – 130p. red 40 25
DESIGNS—VERT (as Type **478**): 25, 50, 70c., 1p.20, 2, 6, 12, 15p. (No. 1332), 20, 30, 40p. (No. 1338), 100, 110, 120, 130p. General Jose de San Martin; 15p. (No. 1333), 70p. Guillermo Brown.
*No. 1307 differs from Nos. 1305/6 in being without imprint. It also has "CORREOS" at top right.

482 Wireless Set of 1920 and Radio "Waves"

1970. 50th Anniv of Argentine Radio Broadcasting.
1341 **482** 20c. multicoloured . . . 15 10

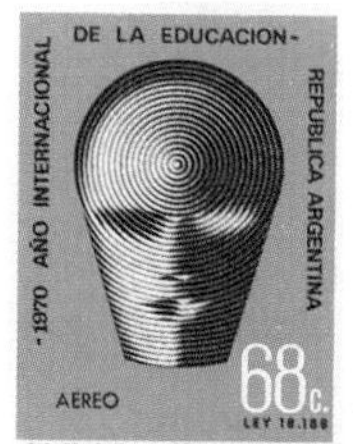

483 Emblem of Education Year

485 "United Nations"

484 "Liberation Fleet leaving Valparaiso" (A. Abel)

1970. Air. International Education Year.
1342 **483** 68c. black and blue . . . 30 15

1970. Military Uniforms. As T **390**. Multicoloured.
1343 20c. Military courier, 1879 75 25

1970. 150th Anniv of Peruvian Liberation.
1344 **484** 26c. multicoloured . . . 1·40 20

1970. 25th Anniv of U.N.
1345 **485** 20c. multicoloured . . . 15 10

486 Cordoba Cathedral

1970. 400th Anniv of Tucuman Diocese.
1346 **486** 50c. blk & grey (postage) 85 10
1347 – 40c. multicoloured (air) 85 20
DESIGN—HORIZ: 40c. Chapel, Sumampa.

487 Planetarium

1970. Air. Buenos Aires Planetarium.
1348 **487** 40c. multicoloured . . . 40 15

488 "Liberty" and Mint Building

1970. 25th Anniv of State Mint Building, Buenos Aires.
1349 **488** 20c. black, green & gold 15 10

489 "The Manger" (H. G. Gutierrez) (½-size illustration)

1970. Christmas.
1350 **489** 20c. multicoloured . . . 25 10

490 Jorge Newbery and Morane Saulnier Type L Airplane

1970. Air. Aeronautics Week.
1351 **490** 26c. multicoloured . . . 40 15

491 St. John Bosco and College Building

1970. Salesian Mission in Patagonia.
1352 **491** 20c. black and green . . 15 10

492 "Planting the Flag"

1971. 5th Anniv of Argentine Expedition to the South Pole.
1353 **492** 20c. multicoloured . . . 1·25 35

493 Dorado (½-size illustration)

1971. Child Welfare. Fishes. Multicoloured.
1354 20c.+10c. Type **493** (postage) 65 45
1355 40c.+20c. River Plate pejerry (air) 55 35

494 Einstein and Scanners **495** E. I. Alippi

1971. Electronics in Postal Development.
1356 **494** 25c. multicoloured . . . 30 10

1971. Argentine Actors and Actresses. Each black and brown.
1357 15c. Type **495** 40 10
1358 15c. J. A. Casaberta 40 10
1359 15c. R. Casaux 40 10
1360 15c. Angelina Pagano . . . 40 10
1361 15c. F. Parravicini 40 10

496 Federation Emblem

1971. Inter-American Regional Meeting of International Roads Federation.
1362 **496** 25c. black and blue . . . 15 10

1971. Army Day. As T **390**.
1363 25c. multicoloured . . . . . 1·00 15
DESIGN: 25c. Artilleryman of 1826.

1971. Navy Day. As T **476**.
1364 25c. multicoloured . . . . . 1·75 20
DESIGN: Sloop "Carmen".

498 "General Guemes" (L. Gigli)

1971. 150th Death Anniv of General M. de Guemes. Multicoloured.
1365 25c. Type **498** 55 20
1366 25c. "Death of Guemes" (A. Alice) (84 × 29 mm) 55 20

499 Order of the Peruvian Sun

1971. 150th Anniv of Peruvian Independence.
1367 **499** 31c. yellow, black & red 40 10

500 Stylized Tulip **501** Dr. A. Saenz (founder) (after Jose Gut)

1971. 3rd Int and 8th Nat Horticultural Exhibition.
1368 **500** 25c. multicoloured . . . 25 15

1971. 150th Anniv of Buenos Aires University.
1369 **501** 25c. multicoloured . . . 20 15

502 Arsenal Emblem

1971. 30th Anniv of Fabricaciones Militares (Arsenals).
1370 **502** 25c. multicoloured . . . 20 15

503 Road Transport

1971. Nationalized Industries.
1371 **503** 25c. mult (postage) . . . 35 10
1372 – 65c. multicoloured . . . 90 35
1373 – 31c. yell, blk & red (air) 45 25
DESIGNS: 31c. Refinery and formula ("Petrochemicals"); 65c. Tree and paper roll ("Paper and Cellulose").

1971. Air. Revalued currency. Face values in centavos.
1374 **358** 45c. brown . . . . . . 2·50 15
1375 68c. red 30 15
1376a 70c. blue . . . . 1·60 15
1377 90c. green . . . . . . 1·75 15
1378 1p.70 blue 55 10
1379 1p.95 green 55 15
1380 2p.65 purple 55 15

504 Constellation and Telescope

1971. Centenary of Cordoba Observatory.
1381 **504** 25c. multicoloured . . . 25 15

505 Capt. D. L. Candelaria and Morane Saulnier Type P Airplane

1971. 25th Aeronautics and Space Week.
1382 **505** 25c. multicoloured . . . 40 10

506 "Stamps" (Mariette Lydis) **507** "Christ in Majesty" (tapestry by Butler)

1971. 2nd Charity Stamp Exhibition.
1383 **506** 1p.+50c. multicoloured 35 35

1971. Christmas.
1384 **507** 25c. multicoloured . . . 20 10

1972. Child Welfare. As T **352**, but differently arranged and inscr "REPUBLICA ARGENTINA".
1394 25c.+10c. Saffron finch (vert) 90 40
1395 65c.+30c. Rufous-bellied thrush (horiz) . . . . . . 1·10 50

508 "Maternity" (J. Castagnino)

1972. 25th Anniv of U.N.I.C.E.F.
1396 **508** 25c. black and brown . . 20 15

509 Treaty Emblem, "Libertad" (liner) and Almirante Brown Base

1972. 10th Anniv of Antarctic Treaty.
1397 **509** 25c. multicoloured . . . 1·25 20

510 Postman's Mail Pouch

1972. Bicentenary of 1st Buenos Aires Postman.
1398 **510** 25c. multicoloured . . . 15 10

1972. Army Day. As T **390**. Multicoloured.
1399 25c. Sergeant of Negro and Mulatto Battalion (1806–7) 65 15

1972. Navy Day. As T **476**. Multicoloured.
1400 25c. Brigantine "Santisima Trinidad" . . . . 1·40 20

512 Sonic Balloon **513** Oil Pump

1972. National Meteorological Service.
1401 **512** 25c. multicoloured . . . 25 15

1972. 50th Anniv of State Oilfields (Y.P.F.).
1402 **513** 45c. black, blue & gold 80 10

514 Forest Centre

1972. 7th World Forestry Congress, Buenos Aires.
1403 **514** 25c. black, blue & lt bl 45 10

515 Arms and Cadet Ship "Presidente Sarmiento"

1972. Centenary of Naval School.
1404 **515** 25c. multicoloured . . . 1·25 20

516 Baron A. de Marchi, Balloon and Voisin "Boxkite" **517** Bartolome Mitre

1972. Aeronautics Week.
1405 **516** 25c. multicoloured . . . 40 10

1972. 150th Birth Anniv of General Bartolome Mitre.
1406 **517** 25c. blue 20 10

518 Heart and Flower **519** "Martin Fierro" (J. C. Castignino)

1972. World Health Day.
1407 **518** 90c. blk, violet & blue 45 15

1972. Int Book Year and Cent of "Martin Fierro" (poem by Jose Hernandez). Multicoloured.
1408 50c. Type **519** 25 15
1409 90c. "Spirit of the Gaucho" (V. Forte) 50 20

520 Iguazu Falls

1972. American Tourist Year.
1410 **520** 45c. multicoloured . . . 30 10

521 "Wise Man on Horseback" (18th-century wood-carving)
522 Cockerel Emblem

1972. Christmas.
1411 **521** 50c. multicoloured . . . 40 10

1973. 150th Anniv of Federal Police Force.
1412 **522** 50c. multicoloured . . . 20 10

523 Bank Emblem and First Coin
525 Presidential Chair

524 Douglas DC-3 Aircraft and Polar Map

1973. 150th Anniv of Provincial Bank of Buenos Aires.
1413 **523** 50c. multicoloured . . . 15 10

1973. 10th Anniv of 1st Argentine Flight to South Pole.
1414 **524** 50c. multicoloured . . . 90 20

1973. Child Welfare. As T **473**, but differently arranged and inscr "R. ARGENTINA". Mult.
1415 50c.+25c. Crested screamer (vert) 85 50
1416 90c.+45c. Saffron-cowled blackbird (horiz) . . . . 1·25 75

1973. Presidential Inauguration
1417 **525** 50c. multicoloured . . . 20 10

526 San Martin and Bolivar

1973. San Martin's Farewell to People of Peru. Multicoloured.
1418 50c. Type **526** 25 15
1419 50c. "San Martin" (after Gil de Castro) (vert) 25 15

527 "Eva Peron – Eternally with her People"

1973. Eva Peron Commemoration.
1420 **527** 70c. multicoloured . . . 20 15

528 "House of Viceroy Sobremonte" (H. de Virgilio)

1973. 4th Centenary of Cordoba.
1421 **528** 50c. multicoloured . . . 20 10

529 "Woman" (L. Spilimbergo)

1973. Philatelists' Day. Argentine Paintings. Mult.
1422 15c.+15c. "Nature Study" (A. Guttero) (horiz) . . . 50 10
1423 70c. Type **529** 80 15
1424 90c.+90c. "Nude" (M. C. Victorica) (horiz) 85 70
See also Nos. 1434/6 and 1440.

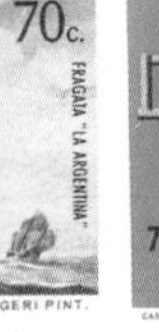

530 "La Argentina" (sail frigate)
531 Early and Modern Telephones

1973. Navy Day.
1425 **530** 70c. multicoloured . . . 1·25 20

1973. 25th Anniv of National Telecommunications Enterprise (E.N.T.E.L.).
1426 **531** 70c. multicoloured . . . 35 10

532 Quill Pen of Flags
533 Lujan Basilica

1973. 12th International Latin Notaries Congress.
1427 **532** 70c. multicoloured . . . 25 15

1973.
1428 **533** 18c. brown and yellow 15 10
1429 50c. purple and black 15 10
1429a 50c. blue and brown . . 15 10
1430 50c. purple 15 10

1973. Transfer of Presidency of General Juan Peron. No. 1318 optd **TRANSMISION DEL MANDO PRESIDENCIAL 12 OCTUBRE 1973**.
1431 1p.20 orange 80 15

535 "Virgin and Child" (stained-glass window)

1973. Christmas. Multicoloured.
1432 70c. Type **535** 30 10
1433 1p.20 "The Manger" (B. Venier) 60 15

1974. Argentine Paintings. As T **529**. Mult.
1434 50c. "Houses" (E. Daneri) (horiz) 30 10
1435 70c. "The Lama" (J. B. Planas) 35 15
1436 90c. "Homage to the Blue Grotto" (E. Pettoruti) (horiz) 50 20

536 View of Mar del Plata

1974. Centenary of Mar del Plata.
1437 **536** 70c. multicoloured . . . 30 10

537 "Fray Justo Santa Maria de Oro" (anon.)
538 Weather Contrasts

1974. Birth Bicentenary of Fray Justo Santa Maria de Oro.
1438 **537** 70c. multicoloured . . . 20 10

1974. Cent of World Meteorological Organization.
1439 **538** 1p.20 multicoloured . . 40 10

1974. "Prenfil 74" Philatelic Press Exhibition, Buenos Aires. As No. 1435.
1440 70c.+30c. multicoloured . . 20 20

1974. Child Welfare. As T **352** but differently arranged and inscr "REPUBLICA ARGENTINA". Multicoloured.
1441 70c.+30c. Double-collared seedeater 65 45
1442 1p.20+60c. Hooded siskin 1·10 65

539 B. Roldan
540 O.E.A. Member Countries

1974. Birth Centenary of Belisario Roldan (writer).
1443 **539** 70c. brown and blue . . 10 10

1974. 25th Anniv of Organization of American States' Charter.
1444 **540** 1p.38 multicoloured . . 15 10

541 Posthorn Emblem

1974. Creation of State Posts and Telecommunications Enterprise (E.N.C.O.T.E.L.).
1445 **541** 1p.20 blue, black & gold 40 10

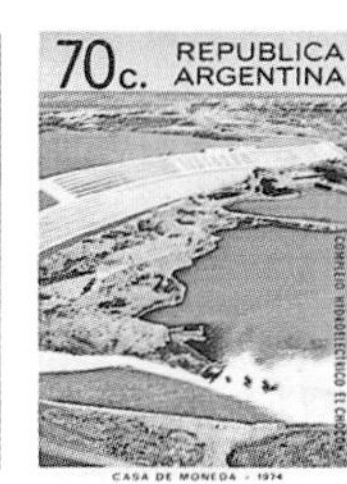

542 Flags of Member Countries
543 El Chocon Hydro-electric Complex

1974. 6th Meeting of River Plate Countries' Foreign Ministers.
1446 **542** 1p.38 multicoloured . . 15 15

1974. Nationalized Industries. Multicoloured.
1447 70c. Type **543** 35 10
1448 1p.20 Blast furnace, Somisa steel mills 55 25
1449 4p.50 General Belgrano Bridge (61 × 25 mm) . . . 2·75 60

1974. Army Day. As T **390**. Multicoloured.
1450 1p.20 Mounted Grenadier 70 15
See also Nos. 1515 and 1564.

544 A. Mascias and Bleriot XI

1974. Air Force Day.
1451 **544** 1p.20 multicoloured . . 75 15

545 Brigantine "Belgrano"

1974. 150th Anniv of San Martin's Departure into Exile.
1452 **545** 1p.20 multicoloured . . 1·25 20

546 San Francisco Convent, Santa Fe

1974. 400th Anniv of Santa Fe.
1453 **546** 1p.20 multicoloured . . 45 10

547 Symbolic Posthorn

1974. Centenary of U.P.U.
1454 **547** 2p.65 multicoloured . . 70 10

549 Congress Building, Buenos Aires

1974.
1456 **549** 30p. purple and yellow 1·50 10

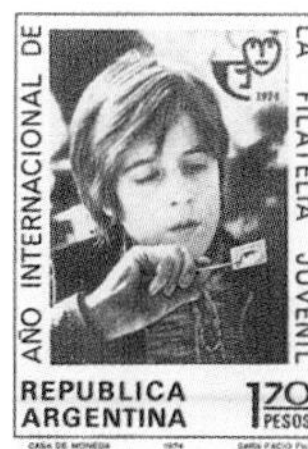

550 Boy examining Stamp

1974. International Year of Youth Philately.
1457 **550** 1p.70 black and yellow 40 10

551 "Christmas in Peace" (V. Campanella)

1974. Christmas. Multicoloured.
1458 1p.20 Type **551** 35 10
1459 2p.65 "St. Anne and the Virgin Mary" 40 15

552 "Space Monsters" (R. Forner)

1975. Contemporary Argentine Paintings. Mult.
1460 2p.70 Type **552** 80 15
1461 4p.50 "Sleep" (E. Centurion) . . . . . 1·50 25

553 Cathedral and Weaver, Catamarca (½-size illustration)

1975. Tourist Views (1st series). Multicoloured.
1462 1p.20 Type **553** 25 15
1463 1p.20 Street scene and carved pulpit, Jujuy . . . 25 15
1464 1p.20 Monastery and tree-felling, Salta 25 15
1465 1p.20 Dam and vase, Santiago del Estero . . . 25 15
1466 1p.20 Colombres Museum and farm cart, Tucuman 25 15
See also Nos. 1491/3.

554 "We're Vaccinated Now" (M. L. Alonso)
555 "Don Quixote" (Zuloaga)

1975. Children's Vaccination Campaign.
1467 **554** 2p. multicoloured . . . 50 15

1975. Air. "Espana 75" International Stamp Exhibition, Madrid.
1468 **555** 2p.75 black, yell & red 60 15

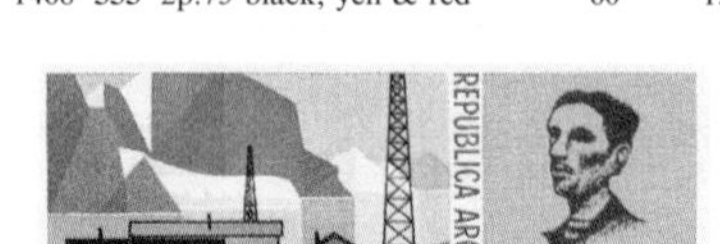

556 Hugo S. Acuna and South Orkneys Base (¾-size illustration)

1975. Antarctic Pioneers. Multicoloured.
1469 2p. Type **556** 45 10
1470 2p. Francisco P. Moreno and Quetrihue Peninsula 45 10
1471 2p. Capt. Carlos M. Moyano and Cerra Torre, Santa Cruz 45 10
1472 2p. Lt. Col. Luis Piedra Buena and naval cutter "Luisito" in the Antarctic 1·40 25
1473 2p. Ensign Jose M. Sobral and "Snow Hill" House 45 10

557 Valley of the Moon, San Juan Province
559 Eduardo Bradley and Balloon

1975.
1474 **557** 50p. multicoloured . . 1·75 10
1474a 300p. multicoloured . . 2·10 40
1474b – 500p. multicoloured . . 4·25 85
1474c – 1000p. multicoloured 3·75 1·00
DESIGNS—HORIZ: 500p. Admiral Brown Antarctic Station; 1000p. San Francisco Church, Salta.

1975. Air. Surch.
1475 **358** 9p.20 on 5p.60 green, mauve and purple . . 90 10
1476 19p.70 on 5p.60 green, mauve and purple . . 1·10 20
1477 100p. on 5p.60 green, mauve and purple . . 2·75 40

1975. Air Force Day.
1478 **559** 6p. multicoloured . . . 60 15

560 Sail Frigate "25 de Mayo"

1975. Navy Day.
1479 **560** 6p. multicoloured . . . 90 20

561 "Oath of the 33 Orientales on the Beach of La Agraciada" (J. Blanes)

1975. 150th Anniv of Uruguayan Independence.
1480 **561** 6p. multicoloured . . . 30 15

1975. Air. Surch. **REVALORIZADO** and value.
1481 **358** 9p.20 on 5p.60 green, mauve and purple . . 85 15
1482 19p.70 on 5p.60 green, mauve and purple . . 1·00 30

563 Flame Emblem

1975. 30th Anniv of Pres. Peron's Seizure of Power.
1483 **563** 6p. multicoloured . . . 35 15

1975. Surch **REVALORIZADO** and value.
1484 **533** 5p. on 18c. brown & yell 45 10

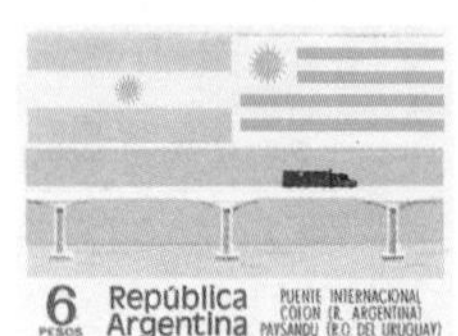

565 Bridge and Flags of Argentina and Uruguay

1975. "International Bridge" between Colon (Argentina) and Paysandu (Uruguay).
1485 **565** 6p. multicoloured . . . 50 15

566 Posthorn Emblem
568 "The Nativity" (stained-glass window)

1975. Introduction of Postal Codes.
1486 **566** 10p. on 20c. yellow, black and green . . . 35 10

1975. Nos. 951 and 1288 surch **REVALORIZADO** and value.
1487 6c. on 3p. blue 15 10
1488 30c. on 90p. bistre 15 10

1975. Christmas.
1489 **568** 6p. multicoloured . . . 30 15

569 Stylized Nurse and Child
570 "Numeral"

1975. Centenary of Children's Hospital.
1490 **569** 6p. multicoloured . . . 35 10

1975. Tourist Views (2nd series). As T **553**. Mult.
1491 6p. Mounted patrol and oil rig, Chubut 55 15
1492 6p. Glacier and sheep-shearing, Santa Cruz . . 55 15
1493 6p. Lake Lapataia, Tierra del Fuego, and Antarctic scene 55 15

1976.
1494 **570** 12c. grey and black . . . 10 10
1495 50c. slate and green . . 10 10
1496 1p. red and black . . . 10 10
1497 4p. blue and black . . . 15 10
1498 5p. yellow and black . . 15 10
1499 6p. brown and black . . 15 10
1500 10p. grey and violet . . 20 10
1501 27p. green and black . . 55 10
1502 30p. blue and black . . 75 10
1503 45p. yellow and black . . 75 10
1504 50p. green and black . . 75 10
1505 100p. green and red . . 1·10 10

571 Airliner in Flight

1976. 25th Anniv of "Aerolineas Argentinas".
1513 **571** 30p. multicoloured . . . 90 15

572 Sail Frigate "Heroina" and Map of Malvinas

1976. Argentine Claims to Falkland Islands (Malvinas).
1514 **572** 6p. multicoloured . . . 85 20

1976. Army Day. As T **390**. Multicoloured.
1515 12p. Infantryman of Conde's 7th Regiment . . 50 15

573 Louis Braille
574 Plush-crested Jay

1976. Louis Braille (inventor of characters for the Blind) Commemoration.
1516 **573** 19p.70 blue 30 15

1976. Argentine Philately. Multicoloured.
1517 7p.+3p.50 Type **574** 60 35
1518 13p.+6p.50 Yellow-collared macaw 80 35
1519 20p.+10p. "Begonia micranthera" 65 40
1520 40p.+20p. "Echinopsis shaferi" (teasel) 90 55

575 Schooner "Rio de la Plata"

1976. Navy Day.
1521 **575** 12p. multicoloured . . . 1·00 20

576 Dr. Bernardo Houssay (Medicine)

1976. Argentine Nobel Prize Winners.
1522 **576** 10p. black, orge & grey 30 10
1523 – 15p. black, yell & grey 35 15
1524 – 20p. black, brn & grey 50 25
DESIGNS: 15p. Dr. Luis Leloir (chemistry); 20p. Dr. Carlos Lamas (peace).

577 Bridge and Ship

1976. "International Bridge" between Unzue (Argentina) and Fray Bentos (Uruguay).
1525 **577** 12p. multicoloured . . . 30 10

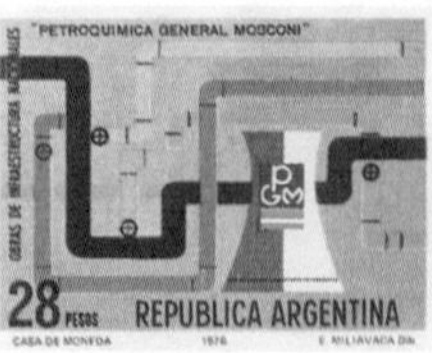

578 Cooling Tower and Pipelines

1976. General Mosconi Petrochemical Project.
1526 **578** 28p. multicoloured . . . 45 15

579 Teodoro Fels and Bleriot XI

1976. Air Force Day.
1527 **579** 15p. multicoloured . . . 40 10

580 "Nativity" (E. Chiapetto)

1976. Christmas.
1528 **580** 20p. multicoloured . . . 50 10

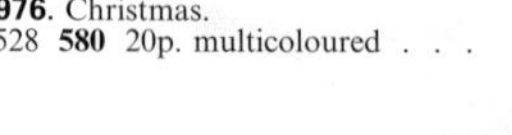

581 Dr. D. Velez Sarsfield (statesman)
582 Conference Emblem

1977. Death Cent (1975) of Dr. D. V. Sarsfield.
1529 **581** 50p. brown and red . . 60 15

1977. United Nations Water Conference.
1530 **582** 70p. multicoloured . . . 45 25

583 "The Visit" (Horacio Butler)

1977. Plastic Arts. Multicoloured.
1531 50p. Type **583** 50 15
1532 70p. "Consecration" (M. P. Caride) (vert) 70 25

584 World Cup Emblem
585 City of La Plata Museum

1977. World Cup Football Championship, Argentina. Multicoloured.
1533 30p. Type **584** 50 15
1534 70p. Stadium and flags (vert) 65 30

1977

1535 **585** 5p. black and brown 10 10
1536 – 10p. black and blue . . 10 10
1538 – 20p. black and yellow 10 10
1539 – 40p. black and blue . . 20 10
1540 – 50p. black and yellow 40 10
1541 – 50p. black and brown 25 10
1542 – 100p. black and pink 35 10
1543 – 100p. black and orange 10 10
1544 – 100p. black and green 10 10
1545 – 200p. black and blue 25 20
1546 – 280p. black and lilac 4·50 15
1547b – 300p. black and yellow 85 10
1548 – 480p. black and yellow 80 20
1549b – 500p. black and green 60 15
1550 – 520p. black and orange 90 20
1551 – 800p. black and purple 1·10 25
1552a – 1000p. black and gold 1·60 35
1553 – 1000p. black and yellow 1·25 35
1554 – 2000p. multicoloured 1·00 35

DESIGNS—HORIZ: 10p. House of Independence, Tucuman; 20p. Type **585**; 50p. (No. 1541), Cabildo, Buenos Aires; 100p. (Nos. 1542/3), Columbus Theatre, Buenos Aires; 280p., 300p. Rio Grande Museum Chapel, Tierra del Fuego; 480p., 520p., 800p. San Ignacio Mission Church ruins; 500p. Candonga Chapel; 1000p. General Post Office, Buenos Aires (No. 1552 39 × 29 mm, No. 1553 32 × 21 mm); 2000p. Civic Centre, Bariloche. VERT: 40p. Cabildo, Salta; 50p. (No. 1540), Cabildo, Buenos Aires; 200p. Monument to the Flag, Rosario.

586 Morse Key and Satellite

1977. "Argentine Philately". Multicoloured.
1560 10p.+5p. Type **586** 25 15
1561 20p.+10p. Old and modern mail vans 45 25
1562 60p.+30p. Old and modern ships . . . . 1·25 75
1563 70p.+35p. SPAD XIII and Boeing 707 aircraft . . . 85 60

1977. Army Day. As T **390**. Multicoloured.
1564 30p. Trooper of 16th Lancers 50 15

587 Schooner "Sarandi"

1977. Navy Day.
1565 **587** 30p. multicoloured . . . 1·25 20

1977. 150th Anniv of Uruguay Post Office. As No. 1325 but colour changed. Surch **100 PESOS 150 ANIV. DEL CORREO NACIONAL DEL URUGUAY**.
1566 100p. on 5p. brown 90 40

1977. "Argentina '77" Exhibition. As No. 1474c, but inscr "EXPOSICION ARGENTINA '77".
1567 160p.+80p. multicoloured 1·60 1·25

589 Admiral Guillermo Brown

1977. Birth Bicent of Admiral Guillermo Brown.
1568 **589** 30p. multicoloured . . . 40 15

590 Civic Centre, Santa Rosa (La Pampa)

1977. Provinces of the Argentine. Multicoloured.
1569 30p. Type **590** 40 20
1570 30p. Sierra de la Ventana (Buenos Aires) 40 20
1571 30p. Skiers at Chapelco, San Martin de los Andes (Neuquen) 40 20
1572 30p. Lake Fonck (Rio Negro) 40 20

591 Savoia S.16 ter Flying Boat over Rio de la Plata

1977. Air Force and 1926 Buenos Aires–New York Flight Commemoration.
1573 **591** 40p. multicoloured . . . 35 15

592 Jet Fighter Outline

1977. 50th Anniv of Military Aviation Factory.
1574 **592** 30p. blue, pale blue and black 30 10

593 "The Adoration of the Kings" (stained-glass window, Holy Sacrament Basilica, Buenos Aires)

1977. Christmas.
1575 **593** 100p. multicoloured . . 75 20

595 World Cup Emblem

1978. World Cup Football Championship, Argentina.
1577 **595** 200p. green and blue . . 55 20

596 Rosario

1978. World Cup Football Championship (3rd issue). Match Sites. Multicoloured.
1578 50p. Type **596** 20 15
1579 100p. Cordoba 40 15
1580 150p. Mendoza 50 15
1581 200p. Mar del Plata 50 25
1582 300p. Buenos Aires . . . . 2·00 75

597 Children and Institute Emblem

1978. 50th Anniv of Inter-American Children's Institute.
1583 **597** 100p. multicoloured . . 40 15

598 "The Working Day" (B. Quinquela Martin)

600 Hooded Siskin

599 Players from Argentina, Hungary, France and Italy (Group One)

1978. Argentine Art. Multicoloured.
1584 100p. Type **598** 65 15
1585 100p. "Bust of an Unknown Woman" (Orlando Pierri) 2·00 75

1978. World Cup Football Championship (4th issue).
1586 **599** 100p. multicoloured . . 35 10
1587 – 200p. multicoloured . . 40 15
1588 – 300p. multicoloured . . 65 20
1589 – 400p. multicoloured . . 1·00 30

DESIGNS: 200p. Group Two players; 300p. Group Three players; 400p. Group Four players.

1978. Inter-American Philatelic Exhibition. Mult.
1591 50p.+50p. Type **600** . . . . 1·75 1·50
1592 100p.+100p. Double-collared seedeater . . . . 2·00 2·00
1593 150p.+150p. Saffron-cowled blackbird . . . . 2·50 2·10
1594 200p.+200p. Vermilion flycatcher . . . . 2·75 2·40
1595 500p.+500p. Great kiskadee 7·00 5·75

601 Young Tree with Support

1978. Technical Co-operation among Developing Countries Conference, Buenos Aires.
1596 **601** 100p. multicoloured . . 30 15

603 Bank Emblems of 1878 and 1978

1978. Centenary of Bank of Buenos Aires.
1598 **603** 100p. multicoloured . . 30 15

604 General Manuel Savio and Steel Production

1978. 30th Death Anniv of General Manuel Savio (director of military manufacturing).
1599 **604** 100p. multicoloured . . 30 15

605 San Martin

606 Numeral

1978. Birth Bicentenary of Gen. San Martin.
1600 **605** 2000p. green . . . . . 3·25 30
1600a 10000p. blue . . . . . 3·00 35

1978.

1601 **606** 150p. blue and light blue 40 20
1602 180p. blue and light blue 40 10
1603 200p. blue and light blue 30 15

607 Chessboard, Pawn and Queen

608 Argentine Flag supporting Globe

1978. 23rd Chess Olympiad, Buenos Aires.
1604 **607** 200p. multicoloured . . 2·00 65

1978. 12th Int Cancer Congress, Buenos Aires.
1605 **608** 200p. multicoloured . . 80 20

609 "Correct Franking"

1978. Postal Publicity.
1606 **609** 20p. blue 15 10
1607 – 30p. green 15 10
1608 – 50p. red 25 10

DESIGN—VERT: 30p. "Collect postage stamps". HORIZ: 50p. "Indicate the correct post code".

610 Push-pull Tug

1978. 20th Anniv of Argentine River Fleet. Mult.
1609 100p. Type **610** 40 15
1610 200p. Tug "Legador" . . . 90 25
1611 300p. Tug "Rio Parana Mini" 95 30
1612 400p. River passenger ship "Ciudad de Parana" . . . 1·25 25

611 Bahia Blanca and Arms

1978. 150th Anniv of Bahia Blanca.
1613 **611** 200p. multicoloured . . 45 15

612 "To Spain" (Arturo Dresco)

1978. Visit of King and Queen of Spain.
1614 **612** 300p. multicoloured . . 1·75 25

613 Stained-glass Window, San Isidro Cathedral, Buenos Aires

1978. Christmas.
1615 **613** 200p. multicoloured . . 60 15

614 "Chacabuco Slope" (Pedro Subercaseaux)

1978. Birth Bicent of General Jose de San Martin.
1616 500p. Type **614** . . . . . . 1·25 35
1617 1000p. "The Embrace of Maipo" (Pedro Subercaseaux) (vert) . . . 2·25 50

615 San Martin Stamp of 1877 and U.P.U. Emblem

1979. Cent of Argentine Membership of U.P.U.
1618 **615** 200p. blue, black & brn 35 15

616 Mariano Moreno (revolutionary)

1979. Celebrities.
1619 **616** 200p. yellow, blk & red 45 15
1620 – 200p. blue, blk & dp bl 45 15
DESIGNS: No. 1620, Adolfo Alsina (statesman).

617 "Still Life" (Ernesto de la Carcova)

1979. Argentine Paintings. Multicoloured.
1621 200p. Type **617** 60 15
1622 300p. "The Washer-woman" (F. Brughetti) 80 20

618 Balcarce Antenna and Radio Waves

1979. 3rd Inter-American Telecommunications Conference.
1623 **618** 200p. multicoloured . . 35 15

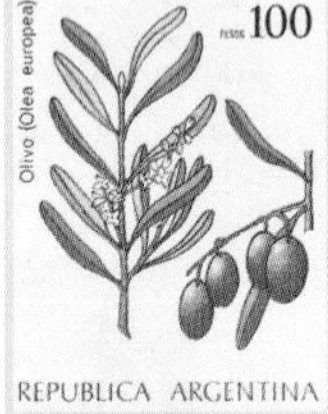

619 Rosette 620 Olives

1979.
1624 **619** 240p. blue and brown 35 10
1625 260p. blue and black 35 10
1626 290p. blue and brown 40 10
1627 310p. blue and purple 45 10
1628 350p. blue and red . . 60 15
1629 450p. blue and ultram 55 15
1630 600p. blue and green 50 20
1631 700p. blue and black 50 20
1632 800p. blue and orange 45 10
1632a 1100p. blue and grey 65 10
1632b 1500p. blue and black 40 10
1632c 1700p. blue and green 50 10

1979. Agricultural Products. Multicoloured.
1633 100p. Type **620** 25 10
1634 200p. Tea 50 25
1635 300p. Sorghum 65 40
1636 400p. Flax . . . . 1·00 55

621 "75" and Symbol

1979. 75th Anniv of Argentine Automobile Club.
1637 **621** 200p. multicoloured . . 35 15

622 Laurel Leaves and Army Emblem

1979. Naming of Village Subteniente Berdina, Tucuman.
1638 **622** 200p. multicoloured . . 30 15

623 Wheat Exchange and Emblem

1979. 125th Anniv of Wheat Exchange, Buenos Aires.
1639 **623** 200p. blue, gold & black 30 15

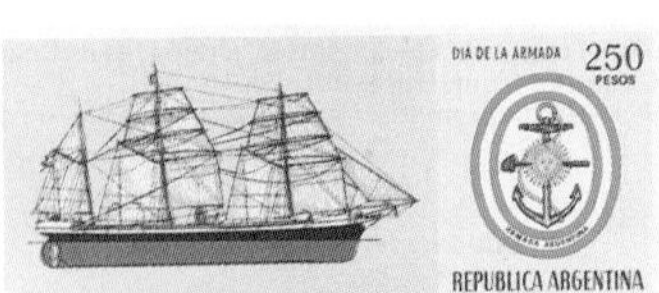

624 "Uruguay" (sail/steam gunboat)

1979. Navy Day.
1640 **624** 250p. multicoloured . . 1·00 20

1979. Army Day. As T **390**. Multicoloured.
1641 200p. Trooper of Mounted Chasseurs, 1817 . . . . . 1·00 20

625 "Comodoro Rivadavia" (hydrographic survey ship)

1979. Naval Hydrographic Service.
1642 **625** 250p. multicoloured . . 1·00 20

626 Tree and Man Symbol

1979. Ecology Day.
1643 **626** 250p. multicoloured . . 55 15

627 SPAD XIII and Vicente Almandos

1979. Air Force Day.
1644 **627** 250p. multicoloured . . 80 20

628 "Military Occupation of Rio Negro by Gen. Julio A. Roca's Expedition" (detail, J. M. Blanes)

1979. Centenary of Conquest of the Desert.
1645 **628** 250p. multicoloured . . 70 20

629 Caravel "Magdalena"

1979. "Buenos Aires '80" International Stamp Exhibition. Multicoloured.
1646 400p.+400p. Type **629** . . . 2·50 2·10
1647 500p.+500p. Three-masted sailing ship . . . . 8·50 4·50
1648 600p.+600p. Corvette "Descubierta" . . . . . 8·00 6·75
1649 1500p.+1500p. Yacht "Fortuna" . . . . 17·00 8·75

630 Rowland Hill 631 Francisco de Viedma y Narvaez Monument (A. Funes and J. Agosta)

1979. Death Centenary of Sir Rowland Hill.
1650 **630** 300p. black, grey & red 45 20

1979. Bicentenary of Founding of Viedma and Carmen de Patagones Towns.
1651 **631** 300p. multicoloured . . 45 20

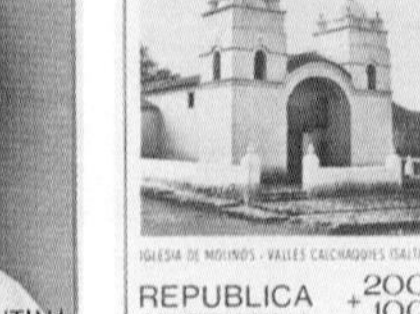

632 Pope Paul VI 633 Molinas Church

1979. Election of Pope John Paul I.
1652 **632** 500p. black 80 35
1653 – 500p. black 80 35
DESIGN: No. 1653, Pope John Paul I.

1979. Churches. Multicoloured.
1654 100p.+50p. Purmamarca Church 30 15
1655 200p.+100p. Type **633** . . . 45 20
1656 300p.+150p. Animana Church 50 35
1657 400p.+200p. San Jose de Lules Church 75 50

1979. 75th Anniv of Rosario Philatelic Society. No. 1545 optd **75 ANIV. SOCIEDAD FILATELICA DE ROSARIO.**
1658 200p. blue and black . . . 70 20

635 Children's Faces, and Sun on Map of Argentina

1979. Resettlement Policy.
1659 **635** 300p. yellow, black & bl 50 20

636 Stained-glass Window, Salta Cathedral

1979. Christmas.
1660 **636** 300p. multicoloured . . 55 20

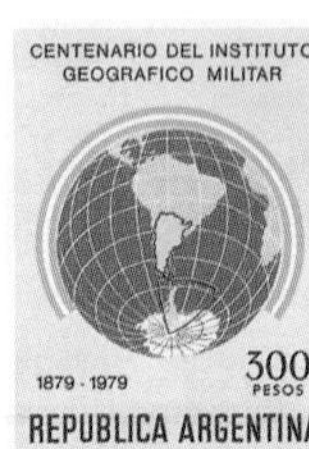

637 Institute Emblem

1979. Centenary of Military Geographical Institute.
1661 **637** 300p. multicoloured . . 70 20

638 General Mosconi and Oil Rig

1979. Birth Centenary of General Enrique Mosconi.
1662 **638** 1000p. blue and black 1·75 50

640 Rotary Emblem and Globe

1979. 75th Anniv of Rotary International.
1664 **640** 300p. multicoloured . . 1·00 25

641 Girl with Ruddy Ground Doves 642 Guillermo Brown

1979. International Year of the Child.
1665 **641** 500p. brown, blue & blk 90 40
1666 – 1000p. multicoloured . . 1·25 30
DESIGN: 1000p. "Family".

1980.
1667 **642** 5000p. black . . . . . . 2·75 20
1668 30000p. black and blue 2·00 50

643 I.T.U. Emblem and Microphone

1980. Regional Administrative Conference on Broadcasting, Buenos Aires.
1669 **643** 500p. blue, gold & ultram 80 30

644 Organization of American States Emblem

1980. Day of the Americas.
1670 **644** 500p. multicoloured . . 50 20

645 Angel

1980. Centenary of Argentinian Red Cross.
1671 **645** 500p. multicoloured . . 60 20

646 Salto Grande Hydro-electric Complex

1980. National Development Projects. Mult.
1672 300p. Type **646** 90 35
1673 300p. Zarate-Brazo Largo bridge 90 35
1674 300p. Dish aerials, Balcarce 50 20

647 Hipolito Bouchard and Sail Frigate "La Argentina"

1980. Navy Day.
1675 **647** 500p. multicoloured . . 1·25 30

648 "Villarino" and Woodcut of San Martin Theodore by Gericault

1980. Centenary of Return of General Jose de San Martin's Remains.
1676 **648** 500p. multicoloured . . 1·25 30

649 "Gazeta de Buenos-Ayres" and Signature of Dr. Mariano Moreno (first editor)

1980. Journalists' Day.
1677 **649** 500p. multicoloured . . 60 20

651 Soldier feeding Dove

1980. Army Day.
1679 **651** 500p. green, blk & gold 60 30

652 Lt. Gen. Aramburu

1980. 10th Death Anniv of Lt. Gen. Pedro Eugenio Aramburu.
1680 **652** 500p. yellow and black 50 20

653 Gen. Juan Gregorio de Las Heras

1980. National Heroes.
1681 **653** 500p. stone and black . . 60 20
1682 – 500p. yellow, blk & pur 60 20
1683 – 500p. mauve and black 60 20
DESIGNS: No. 1682, Bernardino Rivadavia; 1683, Brigadier-General Jose Matias Zapiola.

654 University of La Plata

1980. 75th Anniv of La Plata University.
1684 **654** 500p. multicoloured . . 60 20

655 Major Francisco de Arteaga and Avro 504K

1980. Air Force Day.
1685 **655** 500p. multicoloured . . 75 20

656 Flag and "Pencil" Figure

658 Congress Emblem

1980. National Census.
1686 **656** 500p. black and blue . . 1·25 20

657 King Penguin

1980. 75th Anniv of Argentine Presence in South Orkneys and 150th Anniv of Political and Military Command for the Malvinas. Multicoloured.
1687a 500p. Type **657** . . . . . 1·00 85
1687b 500p. Bearded penguin . . 1·00 85
1687c 500p. Adelie penguin . . . 1·00 85
1687d 500p. Gentoo penguin . . 1·00 85
1687e 500p. Southern elephant seals . . . . 1·00 85
1687f 500p. Kerguelen fur seals 1·00 85
1687g 500p. South Orkney Naval Station . . . . 1·00 85
1687h 500p. South Orkney Naval Station (different) . . . 1·00 85
1687i 500p. "Puerto Soledad, Falkland Islands, 1829" by Luisa Vernet . . . . 1·00 85
1687j 500p. "Puerto Soledad, Falkland Islands, 1829" by Luisa Vernet (different) . . . . . . 1·00 85
1687k 500p. Giant petrel . . . . 1·00 85
1687l 500p. Blue-eyed cormorant 1·00 85
1687m 500p. Snow petrel . . . . 1·00 85
1687n 500p. Snow sheathbill . . 1·00 85

1980. National Marian Congress, Mendoza.
1688 **658** 700p. multicoloured . . 50 15

659 Heart pierced by Cigarette

661 Radio Antenna and Call Sign

1980. Anti-smoking Campaign.
1689 **659** 700p. multicoloured . . 60 20

1980. Radio Amateurs.
1691 **661** 700p. blue, black & green 50 15

662 Academy Emblem

663 Commemorative Medallion

1980. 50th Anniv of Technical Military Academy.
1692 **662** 700p. multicoloured . . 50 15

1980. Christmas. 150th Anniv of Appearance of Holy Virgin to St. Catherine Laboure.
1693 **663** 700p. multicoloured . . 50 15

664 Plan of Lujan Cathedral and Outline of Virgin

665 Simon Bolivar

1980. Christmas. 350th Anniv of Appearance of Holy Virgin at Lujan.
1694 **664** 700p. green and brown 50 15

1980. 150th Death Anniv of Simon Bolivar.
1695 **665** 700p. multicoloured . . 50 15

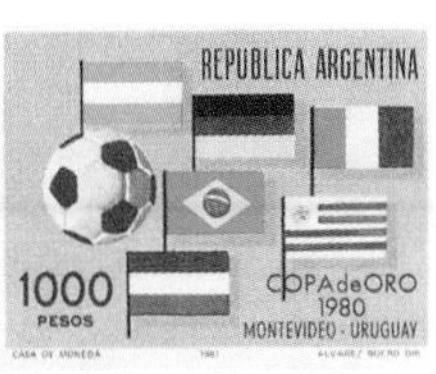

666 Football and Flags of Competing Nations

1981. Gold Cup Football Competition, Montevideo.
1696 **666** 1000p. multicoloured . . 85 20

667 "Lujan Landscape" (Marcos Tiglio)

1981. Paintings. Multicoloured.
1697 1000p. Type **667** 70 20
1698 1000p. "Effect of Light on Lines" (Miguel Angel Vidal) 70 20

668 Congress Emblem

1981. International Congress on Medicine and Sciences applied to Sport.
1699 **668** 1000p. blue, brown & blk 45 15

669 Esperanza Army Base, Antarctica

1981. 20th Anniv of Antarctic Treaty. Mult.
1700 1000p. Type **669** . . . . . 1·50 50
1701 2000p. Map of Vicecomodoro Marambio Island and De Havilland Twin Otter airplane (59½ × 25 mm) . . . . . 2·00 80
1702 2000p. Icebreaker "Almirante Irizar" . . . 3·00 95

670 Military Club

1981. Centenary of Military Club. Multicoloured.
1703 1000p. Type **670** 60 20
1704 2000p. Blunderbusses . . . 80 25

671 "Minuet" (Carlos E. Pellegrini)

1981. "Espamer '81" International Stamp Exhibition, Buenos Aires (1st issue).
1705 **671** 500p.+250p. purple, gold and brown 60 45
1706 – 700p.+350p. green, gold and brown 80 70
1707 – 800p.+400p. brown, gold and deep brown . . . 1·00 80
1708 – 1000p.+500p. mult . . . 1·25 1·10
DESIGNS: 700p. "La Media Cana" (Carlos Morel); 800p. "Cielito" (Carlos E. Pellegrini); 1000p. "El Gato" (Juan Leon Palliere).
See also Nos. 1719 and 1720/1.

672 Juan A. Alvarez de Arenales

1981. Celebrities' Anniversaries.
1709 **672** 1000p. black, yell & brn 70 20
1710 – 1000p. blk, pink & lilac 70 20
1711 – 1000p. black, pale green and green 70 20
DESIGNS: No. 1709, Type **672** (patriot, 150th death anniv); 1710, Felix G. Frias (writer and politician, death centenary); 1711, Jose E. Uriburu (statesman, 150th birth centenary).

1981. 50th Anniv of Bahia Blanca Philatelic and Numismatic Society. No. 1553 optd **50 ANIV DE LA ASOCIACION FILATELICA Y NUMISMATICA DE BAHIA BLANCA**.
1712 1000p. black and yellow . . 1·60 65

674 World Map divided into Time Zones and Sun

1981. Centenary of Naval Observatory.
1713 **674** 1000p. multicoloured . . 55 30

675 "St. Cayetano" (detail, stained-glass window, San Cayetano Basilica)

1981. 500th Death Anniv of St. Cayetano (founder of Teatino Order).
1714 **675** 1000p. multicoloured . . 45 20

676 Pablo Castaibert and Bleriot XI

1981. Air Force Day.
1715 **676** 1000p. multicoloured . . 75 20

677 First Argentine Blast Furnace, Sierra de Palpala

1981. 22nd Latin American Steel-makers Congress, Buenos Aires.
1716 **677** 1000p. multicoloured . . 45 20

678 Emblem of National Directorate for Special Education

679 Sperm Whale and Map of Argentina and Antarctica

1981. International Year of Disabled People.
1717 **678** 1000p. multicoloured . . 50 20

1981. Campaign against Indiscriminate Whaling.
1718 **679** 1000p. multicoloured . . 2·25 25

680 "Espamer 81" Emblem and 15th-century Caravel

1981. "Espamer 81" International Stamp Exhibition, Buenos Aires (2nd issue).
1719 **680** 1300p. pink, brn & blk 95 20

681 "San Martin at the Battle of Bailen" (equestrian statuette)

682 Argentine Army Emblem

1981. "Espamer 81" International Stamp Exhibition, Buenos Aires (3rd issue).
1720 **681** 1000p. multicoloured . . 20 15
1721 1500p. multicoloured . . 60 15

1981. Argentine Army. 175th Anniv of Infantry Regiment No. 1 "Patricios". Multicoloured.
1722 1500p. Type **682** 55 20
1723 1500p. "Patricios" badge . . 55 20

1981. Philatelic Services Course, Postal Union of the Americas and Spain Technical Training School, Buenos Aires. Optd **CURSO SUPERIOR DE ORGANIZACION DE SERVICIOS FILATELICOS-UPAE-BUENOS AIRES-1981**.
1724 **680** 1300p. pink, brn & blk 1·10 20

685 "Patacon" (one peso piece)

1981. Centenary of First Argentine Coins.
1726 **685** 2000p. silver, blk & pur 55 15
1727 – 3000p. gold, black & bl 70 20
DESIGN: 3000p. Argentine oro (five pesos piece)

686 Stained-glass Window, Church of Our Lady of Mercy, Tucuman

1981. Christmas.
1728 **686** 1500p. multicoloured . . 75 20

687 "Drive Carefully"

688 Francisco Luis Bernardez

1981. Road Safety. Multicoloured.
1729 1000p. "Observe traffic lights" . . . . 1·40 20
1730 2000p. Type **687** 90 25
1731 3000p. Zebra Crossing ("Cross at the white lines") (horiz) . . . . . . 1·00 35
1732 4000p. Headlights ("Don't dazzle") (horiz) . . . . . 1·25 45

1982. Authors. Multicoloured.
1733 1000p. Type **688** . . . . . 1·25 20
1734 2000p. Lucio V. Mansilla 85 25
1735 3000p. Conrado Nale Roxlo 1·10 35
1736 4000p. Victoria Ocampo . . 1·25 45

689 Emblem

690 Dr. Robert Koch

1982. 22nd American Air Force Commanders Conference, Buenos Aires.
1737 **689** 2000p. multicoloured . . 85 25

1982. 25th World Tuberculosis Conf, Buenos Aires.
1738 **690** 2000p. brown, red & blk 60 25

691 Pre-Columbian Artwork and Signature of Hernando de Lerma (founder)

1982. 400th Anniv of Salta City.
1739 **691** 2000p. green, blk & gold 80 25

1982. Argentine Invasion of the Falkland Islands. Optd **LAS MALVINAS SON ARGENTINAS**.
1741 **619** 1700p. blue and green 60 20

693 "Poseidon with Trophies of War" (sculpture) and Naval Centre Arms

1982. Centenary of Naval Centre.
1742 **693** 2000p. multicoloured . . 90 25

694 "Chorisia speciosa"

695 Juan C. Sanchez

1982. Flowers. Multicoloured.
1743 200p. "Zinnia peruviana" 10 10
1744 300p. "Ipomoea purpurea" 10 10
1745 400p. "Tillandsia aeranthos" 10 10
1746 500p. Type **694** 10 10
1747 800p. "Oncidium bifolium" 10 10
1748 1000p. "Erythrina crista-galli" 10 10
1749 2000p. "Jacaranda mimosifolia" 15 10
1750 3000p. "Bauhinia candicans" 50 10
1751 5000p. "Tecoma stans" . . 60 10
1752 10000p. "Tabebuia ipe" . . 90 15
1753 20000p. "Passiflora coerulea" . . . . 1·00 20
1754 30000p. "Aristolochia littoralis" . . . . 1·25 30
1755 50000p. "Oxalis enneaphylla" . . . . . . 2·40 40

1982. 10th Death Anniv of Lt. Gen. Juan C. Sanchez.
1761 **695** 5000p. multicoloured . . 80 25

696 Don Luis Verne (first Commander)

1982. 153rd Anniv of Political and Military Command for the Malvinas.
1762 **696** 5000p. black and brown 1·25 50
1763 – 5000p. light bl, blk & bl 90 35
DESIGN (82 × 28 mm): No. 1763, Map of the South Atlantic Islands.

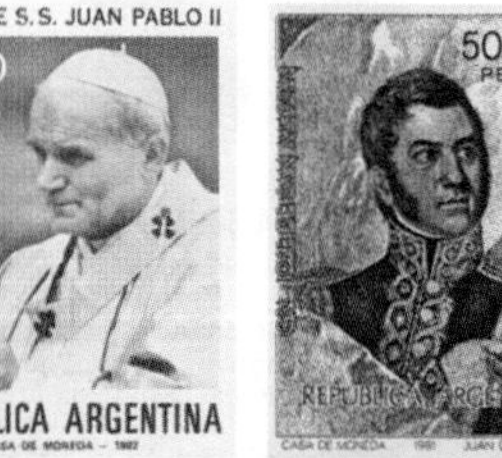

697 Pope John Paul II

698 San Martin

1982. Papal Visit.
1764 **697** 5000p. multicoloured . . 1·00 55

1982.
1765 **698** 50000p. brown and red 4·00 50

699 "The Organ Player" (detail, Aldo Severi)

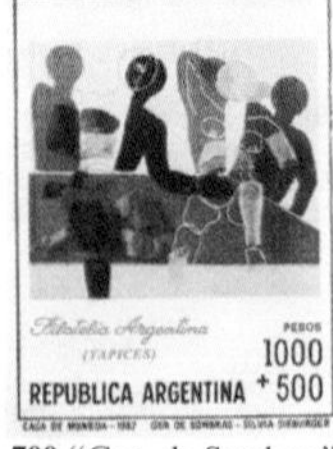

700 "Gen. de Sombras" (Sylvia Sieburger)

1982. Paintings. Multicoloured.
1766 2000p. Type **699** 65 20
1767 3000p. "Flowers" (Santiago Cogorno) 70 25

1982. "Argentine Philately". Tapestries. Mult.
1768 1000p.+500p. Type **700** . . 20 15
1769 2000p.+1000p. "Interpretation of a Rectangle" (Silke Haupt) 30 20
1770 3000p.+1500p. "Canal" (detail, Beatriz Bongliani) (horiz) . . . . 1·10 40
1771 4000p.+2000p. "Pueblito de Tilcara" (Tana Sachs) (horiz) 75 55

701 Petrol Pump and Sugar Cane

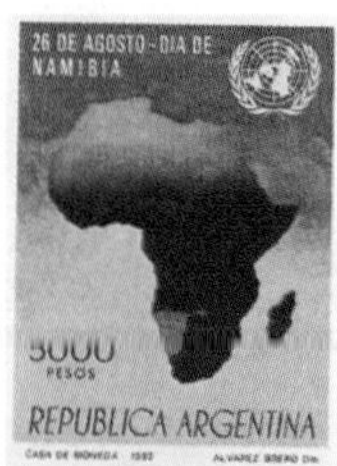

704 Map of Africa showing Namibia

703 Belt Buckle with Argentine Scout Emblem

1982. Alconafta (petrol-alcohol mixture) Campaign.
1772 **701** 2000p. multicoloured . . 40 10

1982. 50th Anniv of Tucuman Philatelic Society. No. 1751 optd **50 ANIVERSARIO SOCIEDAD FILATELICA DE TUCUMAN**.
1773 5000p. multicoloured . . . 1·60 90

1982. 75th Anniv of Boy Scout Movement.
1774 **703** 5000p. multicoloured . . 1·00 25

1982. Namibia Day.
1775 **704** 5000p. multicoloured . . 55 15

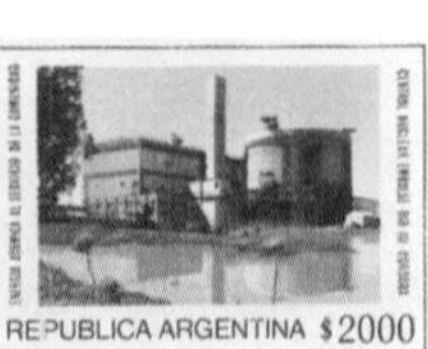

705 Rio Tercero Nuclear Power Station

1982. Atomic Energy. Multicoloured.
1776 2000p. Type **705** 40 10
1777 2000p. Control room of Rio Tercero power station . . 40 10

706 Our Lady of Itati, Corrientes

707 "Sidereal Tension" (M. A. Agatiello)

1982. Churches and Cathedrals of the North-east Provinces.
1778 **706** 2000p. green and black 50 15
1779 – 3000p. grey and purple 60 15
1780 – 5000p. blue and purple 80 20
1781 – 10000p. brown and black 1·25 40
DESIGNS—VERT: 3000p. Resistencia Cathedral, Chaco. HORIZ. 5000p. Formosa Cathedral, 10000p. Ruins of San Ignacio, Misiones.

1982. Art. Multicoloured.
1782 2000p. Type **707** 60 20
1783 3000p. "Sugerencia II" (E. MacEntyre) 70 20
1784 5000p. "Storm" (Carlos Silva) . . . . 1·00 25

708 Games Emblem and Santa Fe Bridge

1982. 2nd "Southern Cross" Games, Rosario and Santa Fe.
1785 **708** 2000p. blue and black 45 10

709 Volleyball

1982. 10th Men's Volleyball World Championship.
1786 **709** 2000p. multicoloured . . 30 10
1787 5000p. multicoloured . . 60 20

710 Road Signs

1982. 50th Anniv of National Roads Administration.
1788 **710** 5000p. multicoloured . . 60 20

711 Monument to the Army of the Andes

1982. Centenary of "Los Andes" Newspaper.
1789 **711** 5000p. multicoloured . . 50 20

712 La Plata Cathedral

714 Dr. Carlos Pellegrini (founder) (after J. Sorolla y Bastida)

713 First Oil Rig

1982. Centenary of La Plata. Multicoloured.
1790 5000p. Type **712** 50 20
1791 5000p. Municipal Palace . . 50 20

1982. 75th Anniv of Discovery of Oil in Comodoro Rivadavia.
1793 **713** 5000p. multicoloured . . 50 25

1982. Cent of Buenos Aires Jockey Club. Mult.
1794 5000p. Jockey Club emblem 55 20
1795 5000p. Type **714** 55 20

715 Cross of St. Damian, Assisi

716 "St. Vincent de Paul" (stained-glass window, Our Lady of the Miraculous Medal, Buenos Aires)

1982. 800th Birth Anniv of St. Francis of Assisi.
1796 **715** 5000p. multicoloured . . 1·00 20

1982. Christmas.
1797 **716** 3000p. multicoloured . . 1·40 40

717 Pedro B. Palacios

1982. Authors. Each red and green.
1798 1000p. Type **717** 15 10
1799 2000p. Leopoldo Marechal 20 10
1800 3000p. Delfina Bunge de Galvez 25 10
1801 4000p. Manuel Galvez . . . 50 15
1802 5000p. Evaristo Carriego . . 65 15

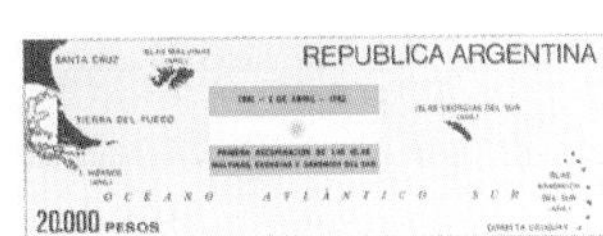

718 Argentine Flag and Map of South Atlantic Islands (½-size illustration)

1983. 1st Anniv of Argentine Invasion of Falkland Islands.
1803 **718** 20000p. multicoloured 95 35

719 Sitram (automatic message transmission service) Emblem

1983. Information Technology. Multicoloured
1804 5000p. Type **719** . . . . . 1·00 20
1805 5000p. Red Arpac (data communications system) emblem . . . . 1·00 20

720 Naval League Emblem

1983. Navy Day. 50th Anniv of Naval League.
1806 **720** 5000p. multicoloured . . 50 15

721 Allegorical Figure (Victor Rebuffo)

1983. 25th Anniv of National Arts Fund.
1807 **721** 5000p. multicoloured . . 45 15

722 Golden Saloon

1983. 75th Anniv of Columbus Theatre, Buenos Aires. Multicoloured.
1808 5000p. Type **722** 70 15
1809 10000p. Stage curtain . . . 90 20

(Currency reform. 10000 (old) pesos = 1 (new) peso.)

723 Marbles

1983. Argentine Philately. Children's Games (1st series). Multicoloured.
1810 20c.+10c. Type **723** 15 10
1811 30c.+15c. Skipping 30 15
1812 50c.+25c. Hopscotch 40 25
1813 1p.+50c. Boy with kite . . . 60 40
1814 2p.+1p. Boy with spinning top 70 55
See also Nos. 1870/4.

724 Maned Wolf

1983. Protected Animals (1st series). Mult.
1815 1p. Type **724** 35 10
1816 1p.50 Pampas deer 55 15
1817 2p. Giant anteater 60 15
1818 2p.50 Jaguar 75 25
See also Nos 1883/87.

1983. Flowers. As T **694** but inscr in new currency. Multicoloured.
1819 5c. Type **694** 40 10
1820 10c. "Erythrina crista-galli" 10 10
1821 20c. "Jacaranda mimosifolia" 10 10
1822 30c. "Bauhinia candicans" 35 10
1823 40c. "Eichhornia crassipes" 10 10
1824 50c. "Tecoma stans" . . . 10 10
1825 1p. "Tabebuia ipe" 10 10
1826 1p.80 "Mutisia retusa" . . . 15 10
1827 2p. "Passiflora coerulea" . . 20 10
1828 3p. "Aristolochia littoralis" 30 10
1829 5p. "Oxalis enneaphylla" . . 50 10
1830 10p. "Alstroemeria aurantiaca" 40 10
1831 20p. "Ipomoea purpurea" 40 10
1832 30p. "Embothrium coccineum" 40 15
1833 50p. "Tillandsia aeranthos" 45 15
1834 100p. "Oncidium bifolium" 65 15
1835 300p. "Cassia carnaval" . . 1·60 45

725 "Founding of City of Catamarca" (detail, Luis Varela Lezana)

1983. 300th Anniv of San Fernando del Valle de Catamarca.
1836 **725** 1p. multicoloured . . . 30 10

726 Brother Mamerto Esquiu

727 Bolivar (painting by Herrera Toro after engraving by C. Turner)

1983. Death Centenary of Brother Mamerto Esquiu, Bishop of Cordoba.
1837 **726** 1p. black, red and grey 30 10

1983. Birth Bicentenary of Simon Bolivar.
1838 **727** 1p. multicoloured . . . 30 10
1839 – 2p. red and black . . . 60 15
DESIGN: 2p. Bolivar (engraving by Kepper).

728 San Martin

729 Gen. Toribio de Luzuriaga

1983.
1840 **728** 10p. green and black . . 2·50 45
1841 – 20p. blue and black . . 90 40
1842 **728** 50p. brown and blue . . 2·00 45
1843 – 200p. black and blue . . 1·25 45
1844 – 500p. blue and brown . . 1·75 25
DESIGNS: 20, 500p. Guillermo Brown; 200p. Manuel Belgrano.

1983. Birth Bicentenary (1982) of Gen. Toribio de Luzuriaga.
1845 **729** 1p. multicoloured . . . 30 10

730 Grand Bourg House, Buenos Aires

1983. 50th Anniv of Sanmartinian National Institute.
1846 **730** 2p. brown and black . . 55 15

731 Dove and Rotary Emblem

1983. Rotary International South American Regional Conference, Buenos Aires.
1847 **731** 1p. multicoloured . . . 55 20

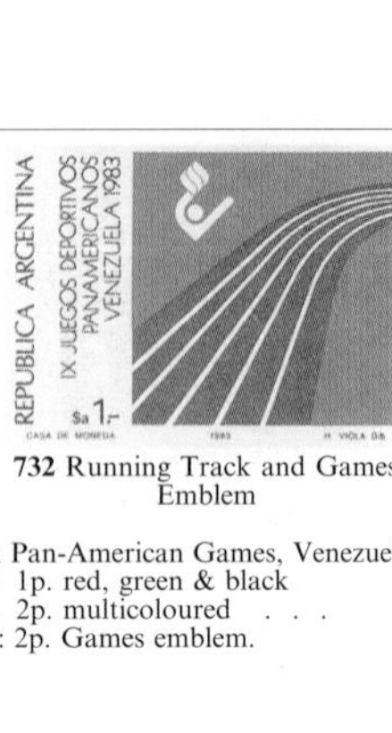

732 Running Track and Games Emblem

1983. 9th Pan-American Games, Venezuela.
1848 **732** 1p. red, green & black . . . 35 15
1849 – 2p. multicoloured . . . 60 25
DESIGN: 2p. Games emblem.

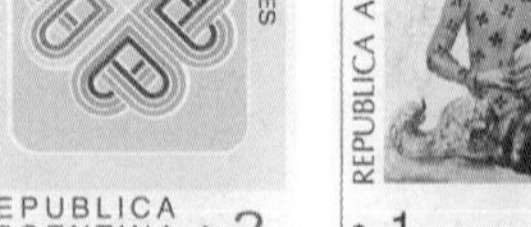

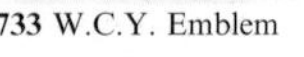
733 W.C.Y. Emblem
734 "The Squash Peddler" (Antonio Berni)

1983. World Communications Year (1st issue).
1850 **733** 2p. multicoloured . . . 55 20
See also Nos. 1853/6 and 1857.

1983. Argentine Paintings. Multicoloured.
1851 1p. Type **734** 35 10
1852 2p. "Figure in Yellow" (Luis Seoane) 55 20

735 Ox-drawn Wagon
736 "Central Post Office, Buenos Aires" (Lola Frexas)

1983. World Communications Year (2nd issue). Mail Transport. Multicoloured.
1853 1p. Type **735** 45 10
1854 2p. Horse-drawn mail cart 50 15
1855 4p. Locomotive "La Portena" . . . . 1·25 50
1856 5p. Tram . . . . 1·25 50

1983. World Communications Year (3rd issue).
1857 **736** 2p. multicoloured . . . 35 15

737 Rockhopper Penguin
738 Coin of 1813

1983. Fauna and Pioneers of Southern Argentina. Multicoloured.
1858a 2p. Type **737** 40 25
1858b 2p. Wandering albatross 40 25
1858c 2p. Black-browed albatross 40 25
1858d 2p. Macaroni penguin . . 40 25
1858e 2p. Luis Piedra Buena (after Juan R. Mezzadra) 40 15
1858f 2p. Carlos Maria Moyano (after Mezzadra) 40 15
1858g 2p. Luis Py (after Mezzadra) 40 15
1858h 2p. Augusto Lasserre (after Horacio Alvarez Boero) 40 15
1858i 2p. Light-mantled sooty albatross 40 25
1858j 2p. Leopard seal 40 15
1858k 2p. Crabeater seal 40 15
1858l 2p. Weddell seal 40 15

1983. Transfer of Presidency.
1859 **738** 2p. silver, black and blue 35 15

739 "Christmas Manger" (tapestry by Silke)

1983. Christmas. Multicoloured.
1860 2p. Type **739** 35 15
1861 3p. Stained-glass window, San Carlos de Bariloche Church 55 20

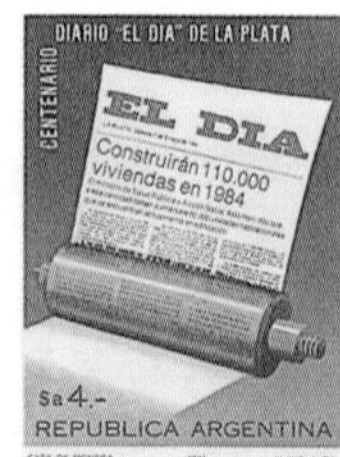

740 Printing Cylinder and Newspaper

1984. Centenary of "El Dia" Newspaper.
1862 **740** 4p. multicoloured . . . 40 15

741 Compass Rose

1984. "Espana 84" (Madrid) and "Argentina 85" (Buenos Aires) International Stamp Exhibitions (1st issue). Multicoloured.
1863 5p.+2p.50 Type **741** 50 15
1864 5p.+2p.50 Arms of Spain and Argentine Republic 50 15
1865 5p.+2p.50 Arms of Christopher Columbus . . 50 15
1866 5p.+2p.50 "Nina" . . . . . 1·25 45
1867 5p.+2p.50 "Pinta" . . . . . 1·25 45
1868 5p.+2p.50 "Santa Maria" 1·25 45
See also Nos. 1906/10, 1917/18 and 1920/4.

742 College

1984. Centenary of Alejandro Carbo Teacher Training College, Cordoba.
1869 **742** 10p. multicoloured . . . 40 15

1984. Argentine Philately. Children's Games (2nd series). As T **723**. Multicoloured.
1870 2p.+1p. Blind man's buff . . 20 15
1871 3p.+1p.50 Girls throwing hoop 30 25
1872 4p.+2p. Leap frog 40 35
1873 5p.+2p.50 Boy rolling hoop 55 45
1874 6p.+3p. Ball and stick . . . 60 55

743 Rowing and Basketball

1984. Olympic Games, Los Angeles. Mult.
1875 5p. Type **743** 25 15
1876 5p. Weightlifting and discus 25 15
1877 10p. Cycling and swimming 45 20
1878 10p. Pole vault and fencing 45 20

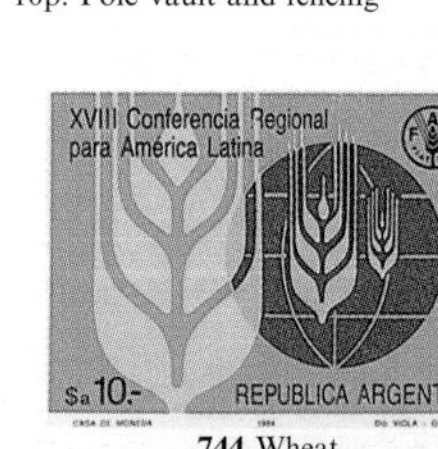

744 Wheat

1984. Food Supplies. Multicoloured.
1879 10p. Type **744** (18th F.A.O. Latin American Regional Conference, Buenos Aires) 40 20
1880 10p. Sunflowers (World Food Day) 40 20
1881 10p. Maize (3rd National Maize Congress, Pergamino) 40 20

745 Stock Exchange

1984. Centenary of Rosario Stock Exchange.
1882 **745** 10p. multicoloured . . . 40 20

1984. Protected Animals (2nd series). As T **724**. Multicoloured.
1883 20p. Brazilian merganser . . 65 20
1884 20p. Black-fronted piping guan 65 20
1885 20p. Hooded grebes 65 20
1886 20p. Vicunas 65 20
1887 20p. Chilean guemal 65 20

746 Festival Emblem

1984. 1st Latin American Theatre Festival, Cordoba.
1888 **746** 20p. multicoloured . . . 25 15

747 "Apostles' Communion" (detail, Fra Angelico)

1984. 50th Anniv of Buenos Aires International Eucharist Congress.
1889 **747** 20p. multicoloured . . . 25 15

748 Antonio Oneto and Railway Station (Puerto Deseado)

1984. City Centenaries. Multicoloured.
1890 20p. Type **748** 75 25
1891 20p. 19th-century view and sail/steam corvette "Parana" (Ushuaia) . . . 1·25 35

749 Glacier

1984. World Heritage Site. Los Glaciares National Park. Multicoloured.
1892 20p. Glacier (different) . . . 30 10
1893 30p. Type **749** 40 15

1984. 50th Anniv of Buenos Aires Philatelic Centre. No. 1830 optd **1934–50°ANIVERSARIO-1984 CENTRO FILATELICO BUENOS-AIRES**.
1894 10p. multicoloured 20 15

751 "Jesus and the Star" (Diego Aguero)

1984. Christmas. Multicoloured.
1895 20p. Type **751** 30 15
1896 30p. "The Three Kings" (Leandro Ruiz) 40 15
1897 50p. "The Holy Family" (Maria Castillo) (vert) . . 60 20

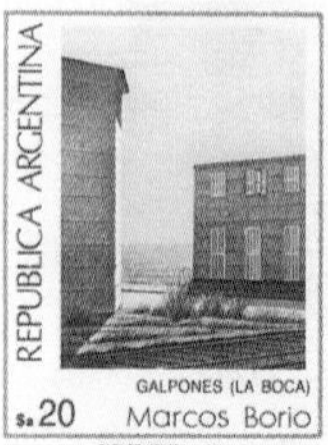

752 "Sheds (La Boca)" (Marcos Borio)
753 Angel J. Carranza (historian, 150th)

1984. Argentine Paintings. Multicoloured.
1898 20p. Type **752** 30 20
1899 20p. "View of the Zoo" (Fermin Eguia) (horiz) . . 35 20
1900 20p. "Floodlit Congress Building" (Francisco Travieso) 30 20

1985. Birth Anniversaries.
1901 **753** 10p. deep blue & blue 40 10
1902 – 20p. deep brown & brn 40 10
1903 – 30p. deep blue & blue 45 15
1904 – 40p. black and green . . 70 15
DESIGNS: 20p. Estanislao del Campo (poet, 150th); 30p. Jose Hernandez (journalist, 150th); 40p. Vicente Lopez y Planes (President of Argentine Confederation 1827–28, birth bicent).

754 Guemes and "Infernal" (soldier)

1985. Birth Bicentenary of General Martin Miguel de Guemes (Independence hero).
1905 **754** 30p. multicoloured . . . 30 15

755 Teodoro Fels's Bleriot XI Gnome

1985. "Argentina '85" International Stamp Exhibition, Buenos Aires (2nd issue). First Airmail Flights. Multicoloured.
1906 20p. Type **755** (Buenos Aires–Montevideo, 1917) 30 10
1907 40p. Junkers F-13L (Cordoba–Villa Dolores, 1925) 50 15
1908 60p. Saint-Exupery's Latecoere 25 (first Bahia Blanca-Comodoro Rivadavia, 1929) 75 25
1909 80p. "Graf Zeppelin" airship (Argentina-Germany, 1934) . . . . . 1·10 45
1910 100p. Consolidated PBY-5A Catalina amphibian (to Argentine Antarctic, 1952) 1·25 60

756 Central Bank

1985. 50th Anniv of Central Bank, Buenos Aires.
1911 **756** 80p. multicoloured . . . 40 20

757 Jose A. Ferreyra and "Munequitas Portenas"

1985. Argentine Film Directors. Multicoloured.
1912 100p. Type **757** 45 25
1913 100p. Leopoldo Torre Nilsson and "Martin Fierro" 45 25

758 "Carlos Gardel" (Hermenegildo Sabat)

1985. 50th Death Anniv of Carlos Gardel (entertainer). Multicoloured.
1914 200p. Type **758** 65 25
1915 200p. "Carlos Gardel" (Carlos Alonso) 65 25
1916 200p. "Carlos Gardel" (Aldo Severi and Martiniano Arce) 65 25

759 "The Arrival" (Pedro Figari)

1985. "Argentina '85" International Stamp Exhibition (3rd issue). Multicoloured.
1917 20c. Type **759** 65 25
1918 30c. "Mail Coach Square" (detail, Cesareo B. de Quiros) 75 25

760 Cover of 1917 Teodoro Fels Flight

1985. "Argentina '85" International Stamp Exhibition (4th issue). Multicoloured.
1920 10c. Type **760** 40 15
1921 10c. Cover of 1925 Cordoba–Villa Dolores flight 40 15
1922 10c. Cover of 1929 Saint-Exupery flight 40 15
1923 10c. Cover of 1934 "Graf Zeppelin" flight 40 15
1924 10c. Cover of 1952 Antarctic flight 40 15

1985. Flowers. As T **694** but with currency expressed as "A". Multicoloured.
1930 ½c. "Oxalis enneaphylla" 40 10
1931 1c. "Alstroemeria aurantiaca" 10 10
1932 2c. "Ipomoea purpurea" 10 10
1933 3c. "Embothrium coccineum" 10 10
1934a 5c. "Tillandsia aeranthos" 10 10
1927 8½c. "Erythrina crista-galli" 25 10
1935a 10c. "Oncidium bifolium" 40 10
1936a 20c. "Chorisia speciosa" 35 10
1937 30c. "Cassia carnaval" . . 40 10
1938 50c. "Zinnnia peruviana" 65 10
1941 1a. "Begonia micranthera var. Hieronymi" 80 10
1941a 2a. "Bauhinia candicans" 10 10
1942 5a. "Gymnocalycium bruchii" 10 10
1942a 10a. "Eichhornia crassipes" 10 10
1942b 20a. "Mutisia retusa" . . . 10 10
1942c 50a. Passion flower 10 10
1943 100a. "Alstroemeria aurantiaca" 10 10
1943a 300a. "Ipomoea purpurea" 10 10
1943b 500a. "Embothrium coccineum" 10 10
1943c 1000a. "Aristolochia littoralis" 20 10
1943d 5000a. "Erythrina crista-galli" . . . . 1·25 10
1943e 10000a. "Jacaranda mimosifolia" . . . . . 4·00 55
No. 1927 is 15 × 23 mm, the remainder 22 × 32 mm.

761 "Woman with Bird" (Juan del Prete)
762 Musical Bow

1985. Argentine Paintings. Multicoloured.
1944 20c. Type **761** 75 30
1945 30c. "Illuminated Fruits" (Fortunato Lacamera) . . 75 30

1985. Traditional Musical Instruments. Mult.
1946 20c. Type **762** 60 20
1947 20c. Long flute with drum accompaniment 60 20
1948 20c. Frame drum 60 20
1949 20c. Pan's flute 60 20
1950 20c. Jew's harp 60 20

763 Juan Bautista Alberdi (writer)

1985. Anniversaries.
1951 10c. Type **763** (death centenary (1984)) 25 15
1952 20c. Nicolas Avellaneda (President 1874–80, death centenary) 50 25
1953 30c. Brother Luis Beltran (Independence hero, birth bicentenary (1984)) . . . 75 25
1954 40c. Ricardo Levene (historian) (birth centenary) 90 25

764 Roller Skaters

1985. International Youth Year.
1955 **764** 20c. black and blue . . . 60 20
1956 – 30c. multicoloured . . . 65 30
DESIGN: 30c. "Disappointment".

765 "Rothschildia jacobaeae"

1985. Argentine Philately. Butterflies.
1958 5c.+2c. Type **765** 35 10
1959 10c.+5c. "Heliconius erato phyllis" 55 20
1960 20c.+10c. "Precis evarete hilaris" . . . . 1·10 40
1961 25c.+13c. "Cyanopepla pretiosa" . . . . 1·40 55
1962 40c.+20c. "Papilio androgeus" . . . . 1·75 90

766 Forclaz Windmill (Entre Rios)
768 "Birth of Our Lord" (Carlos Cortes)

767 Hand holding White Stick

1985. Tourism. Argentine Provinces. Mult.
1963 10c. Type **766** 40 10
1964 10c. Sierra de la Ventana (Buenos Aires) 40 10
1965 10c. Potrero de los Funes artificial lake (San Luis) 40 10
1966 10c. Church belfry (North-west Argentina) 40 10
1967 10c. Magellanic penguins, Punta Tombo (Chubut) 1·00 30
1968 10c. Sea of Mirrors (Cordoba) 40 10

1985. National Campaign for the Prevention of Blindness.
1969 **767** 10c. multicoloured . . . 40 10

1985. Christmas. Multicoloured.
1970 10c. Type **768** 30 15
1971 20c. "Christmas" (Hector Viola) 80 25

769 Rio Gallegos Cathedral

1985. Centenary of Rio Gallegos.
1972 **769** 10c. multicoloured . . . 50 10

770 Grape Harvesting

1986. 50th Anniv of Grape Harvest Nat Festival.
1973 **770** 10c. multicoloured . . . 40 10

771 House of Valentin Alsina (Italian Period)

1986. Buenos Aires Architecture, 1880–1930. Mult.
1974 20c. Type **771** 55 20
1975 20c. 1441 Calle Cerrito (French period) 55 20
1976 20c. Customs House (Academic period) (horiz) 55 20
1977 20c. House, Avenido de Mayo (Art Nouveau) . . 55 20
1978 20c. Isaac Fernandez Blanco Museum (National Restoration period) (horiz) 55 20

772 Jubany Base
773 "Foundation of Nereid" (detail, Lola Mora)

1986. Argentine Antarctic Research. Mult.
1979 10c. Type **772** 60 20
1980 10c. Kerguelen fur seal . . . 60 20
1981 10c. Southern sealion . . . 60 20
1982 10c. General Belgrano Base 60 20
1983 10c. Pintado petrel . . . . 1·00 40
1984 10c. Black-browed albatross 1·00 40
1985 10c. King penguin . . . . . 1·00 40
1986 10c. Giant petrel . . . . . 1·00 40
1987 10c. Hugo Alberto Acuna (explorer) 60 20
1988 10c. Magellanic penguin . . 1·00 40
1989 10c. Magellan snipe . . . . 1·00 40
1990 10c. Capt. Augustin Servando del Castillo (explorer) 60 20

1986. Sculpture. Multicoloured.
1991 20c. Type **773** 85 25
1992 30c. "Work Song" (detail, Rogelio Yrurtia) . . . . 1·25 40

774 Dr. Alicia Moreau de Justo (suffragist, d. 1986)
775 Dr. Francisco Narciso Laprida

1986. Anniversaries.
1993 **774** 10c. black, yellow & brn 30 10
1994 – 10c. black, turq & blue 30 10
1995 – 30c. black, red & mauve 65 30
DESIGNS: No. 1994, Dr. Emilio Ravignani (historian, birth centenary); 1995, Indira Gandhi (Prime Minister of India, 1st death anniv).

1986. Birth Bicentenaries of Independence Heroes. Each brown, yellow and black.
1996 20c. Type **775** 50 45
1997 20c. Brig. Gen. Estanislao Lopez 50 45
1998 20c. Gen. Francisco Ramirez 50 45

776 Namuncura
777 Drawing by Nazarena Pastor

1986. Birth Centenary of Ceferino Namuncura (first Indian seminary student).
1999 **776** 20c. multicoloured . . . 25 15

1986. Argentine Philately. Children's Drawings. Multicoloured.
2000 5c.+2c. Type **777** 15 15
2001 10c.+5c. Girl and boy holding flowers and balloon (Tatiana Valleistein) (horiz) 20 20
2002 20c.+10c. Boy and girl (Juan Manel Flores) 70 70
2003 25c.+13c. Town and waterfront (Marcelo E. Pezzuto) (horiz) . . . 85 85
2004 40c.+20c. Village (Esteban Diehl) (horiz) . . . . . . 1·00 1·00

1986. No. 1825 surch **A0,10**.
2005 10c. on 1p. "Tabebuia ipe" 65 30

779 Argentine Team (value top left)

1986. Argentina, World Cup Football Championship (Mexico) Winners. Multicoloured.
2006 75c. Type **779** . . . . . . 1·10 1·10
2007 75c. Argentine team (value top right) . . . . 1·10 1·10
2008 75c. Argentine team (value bottom left) . . . . . . 1·10 1·10
2009 75c. Argentine team (value bottom right) . . . . . 1·10 1·10
2010 75c. Player shooting for goal 1·10 1·10
2011 75c. Player tackling and goalkeeper on ground . . 1·10 1·10
2012 75c. Player number 11 . . . 1·10 1·10
2013 75c. Player number 7 . . . 1·10 1·10
2014 75c. Crowd and Argentina player . . . . 1·10 1·10
2015 75c. West German player . . 1·10 1·10
2016 75c. Goalkeeper on ground 1·10 1·10
2017 75c. Footballers' legs . . . 1·10 1·10
2018 75c. Hand holding World Cup trophy . . . . . . 1·10 1·10

2019 75c. Raised arm and crowded stadium . . . . 1·10 1·10
2020 75c. People with flags and cameras . . . . 1·10 1·10
2021 75c. Player's body and crowd . . . . 1·10 1·10

Nos. 2006/13 were printed together se-tenant in a sheetlet of eight stamps arranged in two blocks, each block forming a composite design. Nos. 2014/21 were similarly arranged in a second sheetlet.

780 Municipal Building

1986. Centenary of San Francisco City.
2022 **780** 20c. multicoloured . . . 50 20

781 Old Railway Station

1986. Centenary of Trelew City.
2023 **781** 20c. multicoloured . . . 1·00 45

782 Emblem and Colours

1986. Mutualism Day.
2024 **782** 20c. multicoloured . . . 25 15

783 "Primitive Retable" (Aniko Szabo)

1986. Christmas. Multicoloured.
2025 20c. Type **783** 50 10
2026 30c. "Everybody's Tree" (Franca Delacqua) . . . 60 15

784 St. Rosa of Lima **785** Municipal Building

1986. 400th Birth Anniv of St. Rosa de Lima.
2027 **784** 50c. multicoloured . . . 80 20

1986. Anniversaries. Multicoloured.
2028 20c. Type **785** (bicentenary of Rio Cuarto city) . . . 40 10
2029 20c. Palace of Justice, Cordoba (50th anniv) . . 40 10

786 Marine Biology

1987. 25th Anniv of Antarctic Treaty. Mult.
2030 20c. Type **786** 80 20
2031 30c. Study of native birds 1·75 30

787 Emblem

1987. Centenary of National Mortgage Bank.
2033 **787** 20c. yellow, brown & blk 20 15

788 Stylized Pine Trees

1987. Argentine Co-operative Movement.
2034 **788** 20c. multicoloured . . . 20 15

789 Pope

1987. 2nd Visit of Pope John Paul II.
2035 **789** 20c. blue and red 40 10
2036 – 80c. brown and green . . 1·00 55
DESIGN: 80c. Pope in robes with Crucifix.

790 Flag forming "PAZ" (peace)

1987. International Peace Year.
2038 **790** 20c. blue, dp blue & blk 45 15
2039 – 30c. multicoloured . . . 55 20
DESIGN: 30c. "Pigeon" (sculpture, Victor Kaniuka).

791 "Polo Players" (Alejandro Moy) **792** "Supplicant" (Museum of Natural Sciences, La Plata)

1987. World Polo Championships, Palermo.
2040 **791** 20c. multicoloured . . . 80 15

1987. 14th International Museums Council General Conference, Buenos Aires. Multicoloured.
2041 25c. Conference emblem . . 45 15
2042 25c. Shield of Potosi (National History Museum, Buenos Aires) 45 15
2043 25c. Statue of St. Bartholomew (Enrique Larreta Spanish Art Museum, Buenos Aires) 45 15
2044 25c. Cudgel with animal design (Patagonia Museum, San Carlos de Bariloche) 45 15
2045 25c. Type **792** 45 15
2046 25c. Grate from Argentine Confederation House (Entre Rios Historical Museum, Parana) 45 15
2047 25c. Statue of St. Joseph (Northern Historical Museum, Salta) 45 15
2048 25c. Funeral urn (Provincial Archaeological Museum, Santiago del Estero) . . . 45 15

793 Pillar Box **794** Spotted Metynis ("Metynnis maculatus")

1987. No value expressed. (a) Inscr "C" and "TARIFA INTERNA/HASTA 10 GRAMOS".
2049 **793** (18c.) red, black & yell 1·25 15

(b) Inscr "C" and "TARIFA INTERNA/DE 11 A 20 GRAMOS".
2050 **793** (33c.) black, yell & grn 1·60 15

1987. Argentine Philately. River Fishes. Mult.
2051 10c.+5c. Type **794** 35 10
2052 10c.+5c. Black-finned pearlfish ("Cynolebias nigripinnis") 35 10
2053 10c.+5c. Solar's leporinus ("Leporinus solarii") . . 35 10
2054 10c.+5c. Red-flanked bloodfin ("Aphyocharax rathbuni") 35 10
2055 10c.+5c. Bronze catfish ("Corydoras aeneus") . . 35 10
2056 10c.+5c. Giant hatchetfish ("Thoracocharax securis") 35 10
2057 10c.+5c. Black-striped pearlfish ("Cynolebias melanotaenia") 35 10
2058 10c.+5c. Chanchito cichlid ("Cichlasoma facetum") 35 10
2059 20c.+10c. Silver tetra ("Tetragonopterus argente") 65 25
2060 20c.+10c. Buenos Aires tetra ("Hemigrammus caudovittatus") 65 25
2061 20c.+10c. Two-spotted astyanax ("Astyanax bimaculatus") 65 25
2062 20c.+10c. Black widow tetra ("Gymnocorymbus ternetzi") 65 25
2063 20c.+10c. Trahira ("Hoplias malabaricus") 65 25
2064 20c.+10c. Blue-finned tetra ("Aphyocharax rubripinnis") 65 25
2065 20c.+10c. Agassiz's dwarf cichlid ("Apistogramma agassizi") 65 25
2066 20c.+10c. Fanning pyrrhulina ("Pyrrhulina rachoviana") 65 25

796 Jorge Luis Borges (writer)

1987. Anniversaries. Multicoloured.
2068 20c. Type **796** (1st death anniv) 25 10
2069 30c. Armando Discepolo, (dramatist and theatre director, birth cent) . . . 40 15
2070 50c. Dr Carlos Alberto Pueyrredon (historian, birth centenary) 65 20

797 Drawing by Leonardo da Vinci

1987. "The Post, a Medium for Communication and Prevention of Addictions".
2071 **797** 30c. multicoloured . . . 40 15

798 "The Sower" (Julio Vanzo)

1987. 75th Anniv of Argentine Farmers' Union.
2072 **798** 30c. multicoloured . . . 40 15

799 Basketball **800** Col. Maj. Ignacio Alvarez Thomas

1987. 10th Pan-American Games, Indianapolis. Multicoloured.
2073 20c. Type **799** 40 10
2074 30c. Rowing 45 15
2075 50c. Dinghies 65 15

1987. Anniversaries. Multicoloured.
2076 25c. Type **800** (birth bicent) 35 10
2077 25c. Col. Manuel Dorrego (birth bicentenary) 35 10
2078 50c. 18th-century Spanish map of Falkland Islands (death bicentenary of Jacinto de Altolaguirre, governor of Islands) (horiz) 60 20
2079 50c. "Signing the Accord" (Rafael del Villar) (50th anniv of House of Accord Museum, San Nicolas) (horiz) 60 20

801 Children as Nurse and Mother

1987. U.N.I.C.E.F. Child Vaccination Campaign.
2080 **801** 30c. multicoloured . . . 40 15

802 Balloon **803** "Nativity" (tapestry, Alisia Frega)

1987. Anniversaries. Multicoloured.
2081 50c. Type **802** (50th anniv of LRA National Radio) . . 40 20
2082 50c. Celendonio Galvan Moreno (first editor) (50th anniv of "Postas Argentinas" magazine) . . 40 20
2083 1a. Dr. Jose Marco del Pont (founder) (centenary of Argentine Philatelic Society) 60 25

1987. Christmas. Multicoloured.
2084 50c. Type **803** 35 25
2085 1a. Doves and flowers (tapestry, Silvina Trigos) 45 25

804 Crested Oropendola, Baritu National Park

1987. National Parks (1st series). Multicoloured.
2086 50c. Type **804** . . . . . . 1·00 40
2087 50c. Otter, Nahuel Huapi National Park 65 30
2088 50c. Night monkey, Rio Pilcomayo National Park 65 30
2089 50c. Kelp goose, Tierra del Fuego National Park . . 1·00 40
2090 50c. Alligator, Iguazu National Park 65 30
See also Nos. 2150/4, 2222/6 and 2295/9.

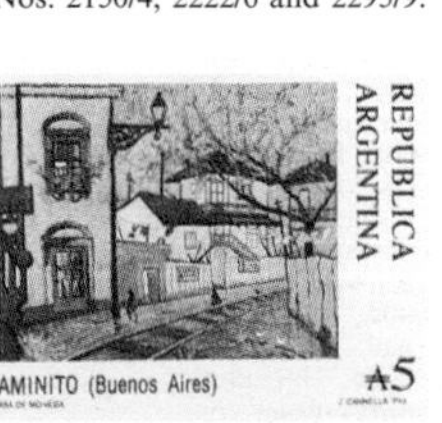

805 "Caminito" (Jose Canella)

1988. Historical and Tourist Sites. Multicoloured.
2090a 3a. "Purmamarca" (Nestor Martin) (33 × 22 mm) . . 60 20
2091 5a. Type **805** . . . . . . 1·75 30
2092 10a. "Old Almacen" (Jose Canella) (A) . . . . . . 3·25 1·50
2092a 10a. "Old Almacen" (Jose Canella) (B) . . . . . . 1·00 45
2095 20a. "Ushuaia" (Nestor Martin) (vert) . . . . . 2·75 1·10
2099 50a. Type **805** 75 10
10a. A. Inscr "Viejo Almacen". B. Inscr "El Viejo Almacen".

806 "Minstrel singing in a Grocer's Shop" (Carlos Morel)

1988. Argentine Paintings. Multicoloured.
2105 1a. Type **806** 50 15
2106 1a. "Curuzu" (detail, Candido Lopez) 50 15

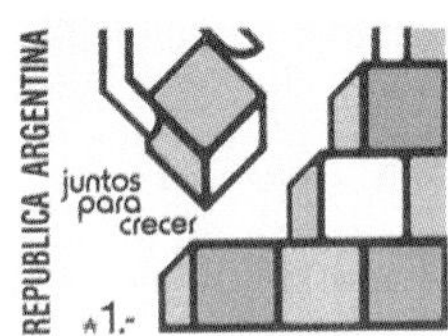

807 Hand arranging Coloured Cubes

1988. Argentine–Brazil Economic Co-operation.
2107 **807** 1a. multicoloured . . . 45 15

808 St. Anne's Chapel, Corrientes

1988. 400th Annivs of Corrientes and Alta Gracia. Multicoloured.
2108 1a. Type **808** 45 15
2109 1a. Alta Gracia church . . . 45 15

809 Men Stacking Sacks

1988. Labour Day. Details of mural "Cereals" (Nueve de Julio station, Buenos Aires underground railway). Multicoloured.
2110 50c. Type **809** 70 70
2111 50c. Sacks 70 70
2112 50c. Men unloading truck 70 70
2113 50c. Horse and cart 70 70
Nos. 2110/13 were printed together, se-tenant, forming a composite design.

810 Steam Locomotive "Yatay" and Tender, 1888 (½-size illustration)

1988. "Prenfil '88" Philatelic Literature Exhibition, Buenos Aires (1st issue). Railways. Multicoloured.
2114 1a.+50c. Type **810** 35 35
2115 1a.+50c. Electric passenger coach, 1914 . . . . . . 35 35
2116 1a.+50c. Type B-15 locomotive and tender, 1942 35 35
2117 1a.+50c. Type GT-22 diesel locomotive, 1988 . . . . 35 35
See also Nos. 2134/7.

811 Running

1988. Olympic Games, Seoul. Multicoloured.
2118 1a. Type **811** 35 10
2119 2a. Football 45 15
2120 3a. Hockey 55 20
2121 4a. Tennis 65 35

812 Bank Facade

1988. Centenary of Bank of Mendoza.
2122 **812** 2a. multicoloured . . . 20 15

813 Arms of Guemes and National Guard Emblem

814 "St. Cayetano (patron saint of workers)" (C. Quaglia)

1988. 50th Anniv of National Guard.
2123 **813** 2a. multicoloured . . . 20 15

1988. Philatelic Anniversaries and Events. Mult.
2124 2a. Type **814** (50th anniv of Liniers (Buenos Aires) Philatelic Circle) 45 15
2125 3a. "Our Lady of Carmen (patron saint of Cuyo)" (window, Carlos Quaglia) (50th anniv of West Argentina Philatelic Society) 60 20

815 Sarmiento (after Mario Chierico) and Cathedral of the North School

1988. Death Centenary of Domingo Faustino Sarmiento (President, 1868–74).
2127 **815** 3a. multicoloured . . . 35 20

816 "San Isidro" (Enrique Castro)

1988. Horse Paintings. Multicoloured.
2128 2a.+1a. Type **816** 60 60
2129 2a.+1a. "Waiting" (Gustavo Solari) 60 60
2130 2a.+1a. "Beside the Pond" (F. Romero Carranza) . . 60 60
2131 2a.+1a. "Mare and Colt" (Enrique Castro) 60 60
2132 2a.+1a. "Under the Tail" (Enrique Castro) 60 60

1988. 21st International Urological Society Congress. No. 2091 optd **XXI CONGRESO DE LA SOCIEDAD INTERNACIONAL DE UROLOGIA SIU 88**.
2133 **805** 5a. multicoloured . . . 2·00 1·50

818 Cover of "References de la Poste"

821 "Virgin of Tenderness"

820 Underground Train

1988. "Prenfil '88" Philatelic Literature Exhibition, Buenos Aires (2nd issue). Designs showing magazine covers. Multicoloured.
2134 1a.+1a. Type **818** 60 30
2135 1a.+1a. "Cronaca Filatelica" 55 20
2136 1a.+1a. "Co Fi" 75 35
2137 2a.+2a. "Postas Argentinas" 55 20

1988. 75th Anniv of Buenos Aires Underground Railway.
2139 **820** 5a. multicoloured . . . 1·25 75

1988. Christmas. Virgins in Ucrania Cathedral, Buenos Aires. Multicoloured.
2140 5a. Type **821** 60 40
2141 5a. "Virgin of Protection" 60 40

822 Ushuaia and St. John

1989. Death Centenary (1988) of St. John Bosco (founder of Salesian Brothers).
2142 **822** 5a. multicoloured . . . 35 10

823 "Rincon de los Areneros" (Justo Lynch)

1989. Paintings. Multicoloured.
2143 5a. Type **823** 35 10
2144 5a. "Blancos" (Fernando Fader) 35 10

824 "Crowning with Thorns" and Church of Our Lady of Carmen, Tandil

1989. Holy Week. Multicoloured.
2145 2a. Type **824** 15 10
2146 2a. "Jesus of Nazareth" and Buenos Aires Cathedral 15 10
2147 3a. "Our Lady of Sorrows" and Humahuaca Church, Jujuy 15 10
2148 3a. "Jesus Meets His Mother" (statue) and La Quebrada Church, San Luis 15 10

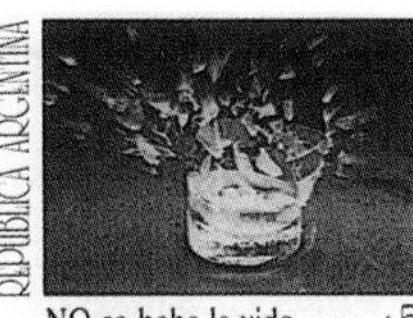

825 Shattering Drinking Glass

1989. Anti-alcoholism Campaign.
2149 **825** 5a. multicoloured . . . 25 10

1989. National Parks (2nd series). As T **804**. Mult.
2150 5a. Crested gallito ("Gallito Capeton"), Lihue Calel National Park 75 20
2151 5a. Lizard, El Palmar National Park 50 20
2152 5a. Tapirs, Calilegua National Park 60 20
2153 5a. Howler monkey, Chaco National Park 65 20
2154 5a. Magellanic woodpecker ("Carpintero Negro Patagonico"), Los Glaciares National Park 75 20

826 Emblem

1989. Cent of Argentine Membership of I.T.U.
2155 **826** 10a. multicoloured . . . 40 10

827 Class 1A Glider Entries

1989. World Model Airplane Championships, La Cruz-Embals-Cordoba. Multicoloured.
2156 5a. Type **827** 35 10
2157 5a. Class 1B rubber-powered entries 35 10
2158 10a. Class 1C petrol-engined entries 35 10

828 Otuno ("Diplomystes viedmensis")

1989. Argentine Philately. Fishes. Multicoloured.
2159 10a.+5a. Type **828** 30 25
2160 10a.+5a. Striped galaxiid ("Haplochiton taeniatus") 30 25
2161 10a.+5a. Creole perch ("Jenyns percichthys tucha") 30 25
2162 10a.+5a. River Plate galaxiid ("Galaxias platei") 30 25
2163 10a.+5a. Brown trout ("Salmo fario") 30 25

829 "All Men are Born Free and Equal"

1989. Bicentenary of French Revolution.
2164 **829** 10a. red, blue and black 35 10
2165 – 15a. black, red and blue 35 10
DESIGN: 15a. "Marianne" (Gandon) and French flag.

830 "Weser" (steamer)

1989. Immigration. Multicoloured.
2167 150a. Type **830** 90 35
2168 200a. Immigrants' hostel . . 40 35

831 "Republic" (bronze bust)

1989. Transference of Presidency. Unissued stamp surch as in T **831**.
2170 **831** 300a. on 50a. mult . . . 60 55

832 Arms of Columbus and Title Page of "Book of Privileges"

1989. "Espamer '90" Spain–Latin America Stamp Exhibition. Chronicles of Discovery. Each yellow, black and red.
2171 100a.+50a. Type **832** . . . 30 30
2172 150a.+50a. Illustration from "New Chronicle and Good Government" (Guaman Poma de Ayala) 40 40
2173 200a.+100a. Illustration from "Discovery and Conquest of Peru" (Pedro de Cieza de Leon) 60 60
2174 250a.+100a. Illustration from "A Journey to the River Plate" (Ulrico Schmidl) 70 70

833 Fr. Guillermo Furlong and Title Page of "Los Jesuitas"

1989. Birth Anniversaries.
2175 **833** 150a. black, light green and green (centenary) 30 25
2176 – 150a. black, buff and brown (centenary) . . 30 25
2177 – 200a. black, light blue and blue (bicentenary) 40 35
DESIGNS: No. 2176, Dr. Gregorio Alvarez (physician) and title page of "Canto A Chos Mala"; 2177, Brigadier Gen. Enrique Martinez and "Battle of Maipu" (detail of lithograph, Theodore Gericault).

834 Wooden Mask from Atajo

835 "Policewoman with Children" (Diego Molinari)

1989. America. Pre-Columbian Artefacts. Mult.
2178 200a. Type **834** 65 35
2179 300a. Urn from Punta de Balastro 85 55

1989. Federal Police Week. Winning entries in a schools' painting competition.
2180 100a. Type **835** 20 15
2181 100a. "Traffic policeman" (Carlos Alberto Sarago) 20 15
2182 150a. "Adults and child by traffic lights" (Roxana Andrea Osuna) 30 25
2183 150a. "Policeman and child stopping traffic at crossing" (Pablo Javier Quaglia) 30 25

836 "Dream of Christmas" (Maria Carballido)

1989. Christmas. Multicoloured.
2184 200a. Type **836** 40 35
2185 200a. "Cradle Song for Baby Jesus" (Gato Frias) 40 35
2186 300a. "Christ of the Hills" (statue, Chipo Cespedes) (vert) 85 55

837 "Battle of Vuelta de Obligado" (Ulde Todo)

1989.
2187 **837** 300a. multicoloured . . 1·25 45

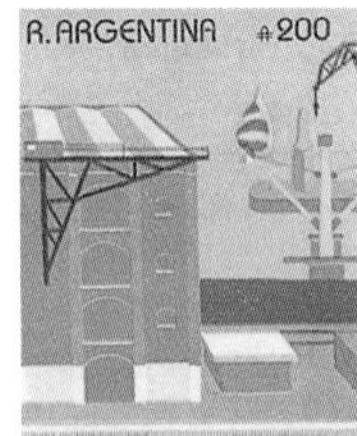

838 Port Building

1990. Cent of Buenos Aires Port. Multicoloured.
2188 200a. Type **838** . . . . . . 1·50 75
2189 200a. Crane and bows of container and sailing ships 1·50 75
2190 200a. Truck on quay and ships in dock . . . . . . 1·50 75
2191 200a. Van and building . . 1·50 75
Nos. 2188/91 were printed together, se-tenant, forming a composite design.

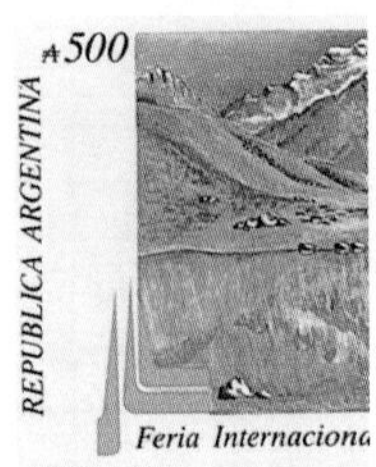

839 Aconcagua Peak and Los Horcones Lagoon

1990. Aconcagua International Fair. Mult.
2192 500a. Type **839** 60 35
2193 500a. Aconcagua Peak and Los Horcones Lagoon (right-hand detail) 60 35
Nos. 2192/3 were printed together, se-tenant, forming a composite design.

840 "75" and Girl with Savings Box

1990. 75th Anniv of National Savings and Insurance Fund.
2194 **840** 1000a. multicoloured . . 20 15

841 Footballer in Striped Shirt

1990. World Cup Football Championship, Italy. Multicoloured.
2195 2500a. Type **841** . . . . . 1·25 1·00
2196 2500a. Upper body of footballer in blue shirt . . . . 1·25 1·00
2197 2500a. Ball and footballers' legs . . . . 1·25 1·00
2198 2500a. Lower body of footballer . . . . 1·25 1·00
Nos. 2195/8 were printed together, se-tenant, forming a composite design.

842 Flowers

1990. Anti-drugs Campaign.
2199 **842** 2000a. multicoloured . . 85 30

843 School Emblem and Pellegrini

1990. Centenary of Carlos Pellegrini Commercial High School.
2200 **843** 2000a. multicoloured . . 65 30

844 "Calleida suturalis" **847** Players

845 Letters and Globe

1990. Argentine Philately. Insects. Multicoloured.
2201 1000a.+500a. Type **844** . . 60 35
2202 1000a.+500a. "Adalia bipunctata" 60 35
2203 1000a.+500a. "Hippodamia convergens" 60 35
2204 1000a.+500a. "Nabis punctipennis" 60 35
2205 1000a.+500a. "Podisus nigrispinus" 60 35

1990. International Literacy Year.
2206 **845** 2000a. multicoloured . . 85 30

1990. World Basketball Championship. Mult.
2208 **847** 2000a. multicoloured . . 85 30

848 Junkers Ju 52/3m

1990. Air. 50th Anniv of LADE (airline). Mult.
2210 2500a. Type **848** . . . . . 1·25 45
2211 2500a. Grumman SA-16 Albatross flying boat . . 1·25 45
2212 2500a. Fokker Friendship 1·25 45
2213 2500a. Fokker Fellowship 1·25 45

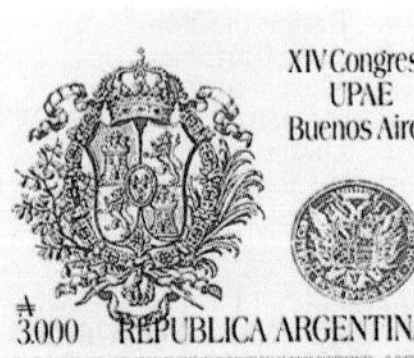

849 Arms of West Indies Maritime Post

1990. 14th Postal Union of the Americas and Spain Congress, Buenos Aires.
2214 **849** 3000a. brown & black 85 50
2215 – 3000a. multicoloured . . 1·50 75
2216 – 3000a. multicoloured . . 1·50 75
2217 – 3000a. multicoloured . . 1·25 50
DESIGNS: No. 2215, Sailing packet and despatch boat; 2216, "Rio Carcarana" (cargo liner); 2217, Boeing 707 airplane and mail van.

851 "Hamelia erecta" and Iguazu Falls

1990. America. Natural World. Multicoloured.
2219 3000a. Type **851** . . . . . 1·50 45
2220 3000a. Sea cow, Puerto Deseado . . . . 1·50 45

852 U.P.U. Emblem on "Stamp"

1990. World Post Day.
2221 **852** 3000a. multicoloured . . 95 45

1990. National Parks (3rd series). As T **804**. Mult.
2222 3000a. Anteater, El Rey National Park . . . . . 1·25 45
2223 3000a. Black-necked swans ("Cisne de Cuello Negro"), Laguna Blanca National Park . . . . . 2·00 70
2224 3000a. Black-chested buzzard eagle ("Aguila Mora"), Lanin National Park . . . . 2·00 70
2225 3000a. Armadillo, Perito Moreno National Park . . 1·25 45
2226 3000a. Pudu, Puelo National Park . . . . 1·25 45

853 Hands (after Michelangelo) and Army Emblem

1990. Cent of Salvation Army in Argentina (2227) and Nat University of the Littoral (2228). Mult.
2227 3000a. Type **853** . . . . . 1·10 50
2228 3000a. University building and emblem . . . . . . 1·10 50

854 Archangel Gabriel **856** "Landscape" (Pio Collivadino)

1990. Christmas. Stained-glass windows by Carlos Quaglia from Church of Immaculate Conception, Villaguay. Multicoloured.
2229 3000a. Dove's wing and hand 85 50
2230 3000a. Dove and Mary . . 85 50
2231 3000a. Type **854** 85 50
2232 3000a. Lower half of Mary and open book 85 50
2233 3000a. Joseph 85 50
2234 3000a. Star, shepherds and head of Mary 85 50
2235 3000a. Manger 85 50
2236 3000a. Baby Jesus in Mary's arms 85 50
2237 3000a. Joseph with two doves and Mary 85 50
2238 3000a. Simeon 85 50

2239 3000a. Lower halves of Joseph and Mary 85 50
2240 3000a. Lower half of Simeon and altar 85 50

Nos. 2229/32, 2233/6 and 2237/40 were printed together in se-tenant sheetlets of four stamps, each sheetlet forming a composite design of stained glass windows entitled "Incarnation of Son of God", "The Birth of Christ" and "Presentation of Jesus in the Temple".

1991. Paintings. Multicoloured.
2242 4000a. Type **856** 90 45
2243 4000a. "Weeping Willows" (Atilio Malinverno) (horiz) 90 45

858 Rosas

860 "Hernan, the Pirate" (Jose Salinas)

1991. Return of Remains of Brig. Gen. Juan Manuel de Rosas.
2245 **858** 4000a. multicoloured . . 80 35

1991. Comic Strips. Each black and blue.
2247 4000a. Type **860** . . . . . 1·40 70
2248 4000a. "Don Fulgencio" (Lino Palacio) . . . . . 1·40 70
2249 4000a. "Tablas Medicas de Salerno" (Oscar Conti) . . 1·40 70
2250 4000a. "Buenos Aires en Camiseta" (Alejandro del Prado) . . . . 1·40 70
2251 4000a. "Girls!" (Jose Divito) 1·40 70
2252 4000a. "Langostino" (Eduardo Ferro) . . . . 1·40 70
2253 4000a. "Mafalda" (Joaquin Lavado) . . . . 1·40 70
2254 4000a. "Mort Cinder" (Alberto Breccia) . . . . 1·40 70

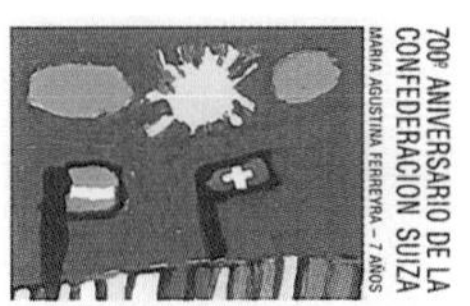

861 "Flags" (Maria Augustina Ferreyra)

1991. 700th Anniv of Swiss Confederation.
2255 **861** 4000a. multicoloured . . 80 30

862 Divine Child Mayor

1991. 400th Anniv of La Rioja City.
2256 **862** 4000a. multicoloured . . 80 30

863 Eduardo Bradley, Angel Zuloaga and Balloon "Eduardo Newbery"

1991. 75th Anniv of Crossing of Andes by Balloon.
2257 **863** 4000a. multicoloured . . 90 35

864 "Vitoria" (Magellan's galleon)

1991. America. Voyages of Discovery. Mult.
2258 4000a. Type **864** . . . . . 1·25 40
2259 4000a. Juan Diaz de Solis's fleet . . . . 1·25 40

865 "Virgin of the Valley, Catamarca" (top half)

1991. Christmas. Stained-glass Windows from Church of Our Lady of Lourdes, Santos Lugares, Buenos Aires. Multicoloured.
2260 4000a. Type **865** . . . . . 1·10 40
2261 4000a. "Virgin of the Valley" (bottom half) . . 1·10 40
2262 4000a. Church and "Virgin of the Rosary of the Miracle, Cordoba" (top half) . . . . 1·10 40
2263 4000a. "Virgin of the Rosary of the Miracle" (bottom half) . . . . . . 1·10 40

Nos. 2260/3 were issued together, se-tenant, Nos. 2260/1 and 2262/3 forming composite designs.

1889-1989

866 Enrique Pestalozzi (editor) and Masthead

1991. Centenaries. Multicoloured.
2264 4000a. Type **866** ("Argentinisches Tageblatt" (1989)) 85 40
2265 4000a. Leandro Alem (founder) and flags (Radical Civic Union) . . 85 40
2266 4000a. Marksman (Argentine Shooting Federation) 85 40
2267 4000a. Dr. Nicasio Etchepareborda (first professor) and emblem (Buenos Aires Faculty of Odontology) 85 40
2268 4000a. Dalmiro Huergo and emblem (Graduate School of Economics) 85 40

867 Gen. Juan Lavalle and Medal

1991. Anniversaries. Multicoloured.
2269 4000a. Type **867** (150th death anniv) 85 40
2270 4000a. Gen. Jose Maria Paz and Battle of Ituzaingo medal (birth bicentenary) 85 40
2271 4000a. Dr. Marco Avellaneda and opening words of "Ode to the 25th May" (politician and writer, 150th death anniv) 85 40
2272 4000a. William Henry Hudson and title page of "Far Away and Long Ago" (writer, 150th birth anniv) 85 40

868 "Castor" (rocket)

1991. "Iberoprenfil '92" Iberia–Latin America Philatelic Literature Exhibition, Buenos Aires (1st issue). Multicoloured.
2273 4000a.+4000a. Type **868** . . 2·00 1·00
2274 4000a.+4000a. "Lusat-1" satellite . . . . 2·00 1·00

See also Nos. 2313/14 and 2325/8.

869 Guiana Crested Eagle ("Morphnu guianensis")

871 Golden Tops

1991. Birds. Multicoloured.
2275 4000a. Type **869** . . . . . 1·50 1·00
2276 4000a. Green-winged macaw ("Ara chloroptera") . . . 1·50 1·00
2277 4000a. Lesser rhea ("Pterocnemia pennata") 1·50 1·00

1992. Fungi.
2279 10c. Type **871** 50 10
2280 25c. Common ink cap . . . 70 20
2281 38c. Type **871** . . . . . . 1·75 25
2282 48c. As 25c. . . . . 1·75 30
2283 50c. Granulated boletus . . 1·75 30
2284 51c. Common morel . . . . 1·75 40
2285 61c. Fly agaric . . . . . . 2·25 45
2286 68c. Lawyer's wig . . . . . 2·25 40
2289 1p. As 61c. . . . . 3·00 40
2290 1p.25 As 50c. . . . . . . 3·25 40
2293 2p. As 51c. . . . . 6·50 60

For redrawn, smaller, designs see Nos. 2365/77.

1992. National Parks (4th series). As T **804**. Multicoloured.
2295 38c. Chucao tapaculo ("Chucao"), Los Alerces National Park . . . . . 1·25 85
2296 38c. Opossum, Los Arrayanes National Park 1·00 40
2297 38c. Giant armadillo, Formosa Nature Reserve 1·00 40
2298 38c. Cavy, Petrified Forests Natural Monument . . . 1·00 40
2299 38c. James's flamingo ("Parina chica"), Laguna de los Pozuelos Natural Monument . . . . 1·25 85

872 Soldier and Truck

1992. National Heroes Commem. Multicoloured.
2300 38c. Type **872** 75 40
2301 38c. "General Belgrano" (cruiser) 90 40
2302 38c. FMA Pucara fighter . . 90 40

873 "Carnotaurus sastrei"

874 "Tileforo Areco"

1992. Dinosaurs. Multicoloured.
2303 38c.+38c. Type **873** . . . . 2·25 1·25
2304 38c.+38c. "Amargasaurus cazaui" . . . . 2·25 1·25

1992. Birth Centenary (1991) of Florencio Molina Campios (painter). Multicoloured.
2305 38c. Type **874** . . . . . . 1·10 45
2306 38c. "In the Shade" (horiz) 1·10 45

876 General Lucio N. Mansilla and "San Martin" (frigate)

1992. Birth Anniversaries. Multicoloured.
2308 38c. Type **876** (bicentenary) 1·10 50
2309 38c. Jose Manuel Estrada (historian, 150th) 85 40
2310 38c. General Jose I. Garmendia (150th) . . 85 40

877 Hearts as Flowers

1992. Anti-drugs Campaign.
2311 **877** 38c. multicoloured . . . 85 40

878 Steam Pump Fire Engine and Calaza

1992. 140th Birth Anniv of Col. Jose Calaza (founder of fire service).
2312 **878** 38c. multicoloured . . . 1·10 50

879 "The Party"

1992. "Iberoprenfil '92" Iberia–Latin America Philatelic Literature Exhibition, Buenos Aires (2nd issue). Paintings by Raul Soldi. Multicoloured.
2313 76c.+76c. Type **879** . . . . 3·50 1·75
2314 76c.+76c. "Church of St. Anne of Glew" . . . 3·50 1·75

880 Columbus, European Symbols and "Santa Maria"

1992. America. 500th Anniv of Discovery of America by Columbus. Multicoloured.
2315 38c. Type **880** . . . . . . 1·25 40
2316 38c. American symbols and Columbus . . . . 1·25 40

1992. 50th Anniv of Neuquen and Rio Negro Philatelic Centre. Unissued stamp as T **871** optd **50° ANIVERSARIO CENTRO FILATELICO DE NEUQUEN Y RIO NEGRO**. Multicoloured.
2317 1p.77 Verdigris agaric . . . 4·50 2·50

882 "God Pays You"

883 Flags of Paraguay and Argentina as Stamps

1992. Argentine Films. Advertising posters. Mult.
2318 38c. Type **882** . . . . . . 1·00 40
2319 38c. "The Turbid Waters" 1·00 40
2320 38c. "Un Guapo del 900" 1·00 40
2321 38c. "The Truce" . . . . . 1·00 40
2322 38c. "The Official Version" 1·00 40

1992. "Parafil '92" Paraguay–Argentina Stamp Exhibition, Buenos Aires.
2323 **883** 76c.+76c. mult . . . . . 3·00 1·50

884 Angel and Baby Jesus

885 Punta Mogotes Lighthouse

1992. Christmas.
2324 **884** 38c. multicoloured . . . 1·00 40

1992. "Iberoprenfil '92" Iberia–Latin America Philatelic Literature Exhibition, Buenos Aires (3rd issue). Lighthouses. Multicoloured.
2325 38c. Type **885** . . . . . . 1·00 50
2326 38c. Rio Negro . . . . . . 1·00 50
2327 38c. San Antonio . . . . . 1·00 50
2328 38c. Cabo Blanco . . . . . 1·00 50

886 Campaign Emblem

887 "Sac-B" Research Satellite

1992. Anti-AIDS Campaign.
2329 **886** 10c. black, red and blue 80 15
2330 – 26c. multicoloured . . . 1·60 25
DESIGN: 26c. AIDS cloud over house of life.

1992. International Space Year.
2331 **887** 38c. multicoloured . . . 80 40

889 Footballers and Emblem

1993. Centenary of Argentine Football Assn.
2333 **889** 38c. multicoloured . . . 1·25 60

890 Arquebusier and Arms of Francisco de Arganaras (founder)

892 Order of San Martin

1993. 400th Anniv of Jujuy.
2334 **890** 38c. multicoloured . . . 1·00 40

1993. Anniversaries. Multicoloured.
2336 38c. Type **892** (50th anniv) 85 45
2337 38c. Entrance to and emblem of National History Academy (centenary) 85 45

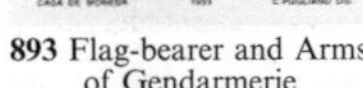

893 Flag-bearer and Arms of Gendarmerie

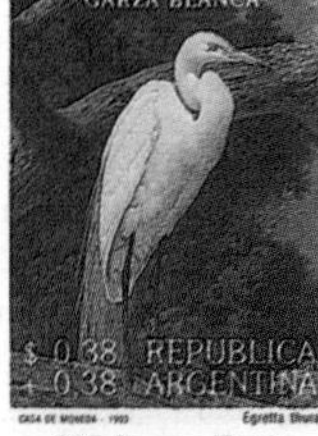

895 Snowy Egret ("Egretta thula")

894 Luis Candelaria and Morane Saulnier Type P Monoplane

1993. National Heroes Commemoration. Mult.
2338 38c. Type **893** . . . . . . 1·00 40
2339 38c. "Rio Iguazu" (coastguard corvette) . . 1·00 40

1993. 75th Anniv of First Flight over the Andes.
2340 **894** 38c. multicoloured . . . 1·25 40

1993. Paintings of Birds by Axel Amuchastegui. Multicoloured.
2341 38c.+38c. Type **895** . . . . 1·60 1·60
2342 38c.+38c. Scarlet-headed blackbird ("Amblyramphus holosericeus") . . . . . 1·60 1·60
2343 38c.+38c. Red-crested cardinal ("Paroaria coronata") . . . . 1·60 1·60
2344 38c.+38c. Amazon kingfisher ("Chloroceryle amazona") 1·60 1·60

896 "Coming Home" (Adriana Zaefferer)

1993. Paintings. Multicoloured.
2345 38c. Type **896** 90 40
2346 38c. "The Old House" (Norberto Russo) 90 40

897 Pato

1993. 40th Anniv of Declaration of Pato as National Sport.
2347 **897** 1p. multicoloured . . . 2·40 65

898 Segurola's Pacara ("Enterolobium contortisiliquum")

1993. Old Trees in Buenos Aires. Multicoloured.
2348 75c. Type **898** (Puan and Baldomero Fernandez Moreno Streets) . . . . . 1·25 40
2349 75c. Pueyrredon's carob tree ("Prosopis alba") (Pueyrredon Square) . . . 1·25 40
2350 1p.50 Alvear's coral tree ("Erythrina falcata") (Lavalle Square) . . . . 2·50 80
2351 1p.50 Avellaneda's magnolia ("Magnolia grandiflora") (Adolfo Berro Avenue) . . 2·50 80

899 Southern Right Whale

1993. America. Endangered Animals. Mult.
2352 50c. Type **899** . . . . . . 1·25 55
2353 75c. Commerson's dolphin 1·75 80

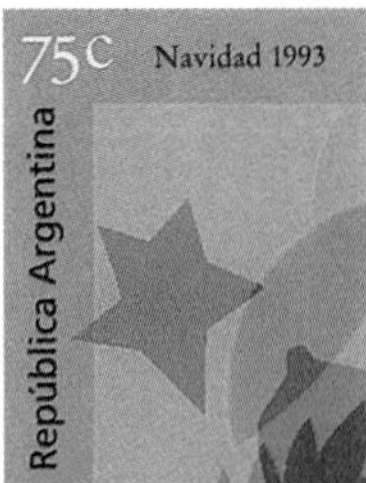

900 Star, Leaf and Bell (Christmas)

1993. Christmas and New Year. Festive Symbols. Multicoloured.
2354 75c. Type **900** . . . . . . 1·25 40
2355 75c. Leaf, sun and moon (New Year) . . . . . . 1·25 40
2356 75c. Leaf and fir tree (Christmas) . . . . 1·25 40
2357 75c. Fish and moon (New Year) . . . . 1·25 40
Nos. 2354/7 were issued together, se-tenant, forming a composite design.

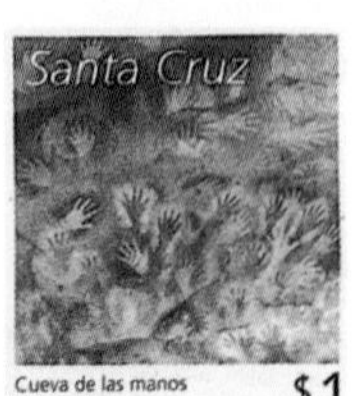

901 Cave Painting

1993. Cave of Hands, Santa Cruz.
2358 **901** 1p. multicoloured . . . 2·00 40

902 Emblem

1994. New Argentine Post Emblem.
2359 **902** 75c. multicoloured . . . 1·25 40

903 Brazil Player

904 Golden Tops

1994. World Cup Football Championship, U.S.A. (1st issue). Multicoloured.
2360 25c. German player 30 20
2361 50c. Type **903** 90 45
2362 75c. Argentine player . . . 1·40 50
2363 1p. Italian player . . . . . 1·90 75
See also Nos. 2380/3.

1994. Fungi. Multicoloured.
2365 10c. Type **904** 20 10
2366 25c. Common ink cap . . . 55 20
2369 50c. Granulated boletus . . 1·25 50
2374 1p. Fly agaric . . . . . . 2·75 1·10
2377 2p. Common morel . . . . 5·25 2·25

905 Argentine Player with Ball (Matias Taylor)

1994. World Cup Football Championship, U.S.A. (2nd issue). Winning entries in children's competition. Multicoloured.
2380 75c. Type **905** . . . . . . 1·40 50
2381 75c. Tackle (Torcuato Santiago Gonzalez Agote) 1·40 50
2382 75c. Players (Julian Lisenberg) (horiz) . . . . 1·40 50
2383 75c. Match scene (Maria Paula Palma) (horiz) . . . 1·40 50

906 Black-throated Finch

1994. Animals of the Falkland Islands (Islas Malvinas). Multicoloured.
2384 25c. Type **906** 55 40
2385 50c. Gentoo penguins . . . 1·10 75
2386 75c. Falkland Islands flightless steamer ducks 1·60 1·10
2387 1p. Southern elephant-seal 1·75 60

907 Town Arms

1994. Anniversaries. Multicoloured.
2388 75c. Type **907** (400th anniv of San Luis) . . . . . . 1·25 50
2389 75c. Arms (3rd anniv of provincial status of Tierra del Fuego, Antarctica and South Atlantic Islands) . . 1·25 50

908 Ladislao Jose Biro

1994. Inventors. Multicoloured.
2390 75c. Type **908** (ball-point pen) . . . . 1·25 50
2391 75c. Raul Pateras de Pescara (helicopter) . . . . 1·25 50
2392 75c. Quirino Cristiani (animated films) . . . . . 1·25 50
2393 75c. Enrique Finochietto (surgical instruments) . . 1·25 50

909 Star, Purple Bauble and Bell

1994. U.N.I.C.E.F. Children's Fund in Argentina. Multicoloured.
2394 50c. Type **909** 85 45
2395 75c. Bell, red bauble and star . . . . 1·25 50

910 Children holding Globe (Ivana Mirna de Caro)

1994. "Care of the Planet". Children's Painting Competition. Multicoloured.
2396 25c. Type **910** 30 20
2397 25c. Girl polishing sunbeam and boy tending tree (Elena Tsouprik) 30 20
2398 50c. Children of all races around globe (Estefania Navarro) (horiz) 60 45
2399 50c. Globe as house (Maria Belen Gidoni) (horiz) . . 60 45

911 Star and Angel (The Annunciation)

1994. Christmas. Multicoloured.
2400 50c. Type **911** 60 45
2401 75c. Madonna and Child (Nativity) . . . . 1·25 50

912 Running

1995. 12th Pan-American Games, Mar del Plata. Multicoloured.
2402 75c. Type **912** . . . . . . 1·25 45
2403 75c. Cycling . . . . 1·25 45
2404 75c. Diving . . . . 1·25 45
2405 1p.25 Football (vert) . . . . 2·00 60
2406 1p.25 Gymnastics (vert) . . 2·00 60

913 Postal Emblem

1995. Self-adhesive.
2407 **913** 25c. yellow, blue & black 3·75 50
2408 75c. yellow, blue & black 1·25 50

914 National Congress Building and "The Republic Triumphant" (statue, detail)

1995. New Constitution, August 1994.
2409 **914** 75c. multicoloured . . . 1·25 40

915 Letters and Disk

1995. 21st International Book Fair.
2410 **915** 75c. multicoloured . . . 1·25 50

916 Bay-winged Cowbird

1995. Birds. Multicoloured.
2412 5p. Hooded siskin . . . . . 10·50 7·50
2413 9p.40 Type **916** . . . . . . 21·00 15·00
2414 10p. Rufous-collared sparrow . . . . 20·00 13·50

917 Clouds seen through Atrium

1995. Centenary of Argentine Engineers' Centre, Buenos Aires.
2420 **917** 75c. multicoloured . . . 1·25 45

920 Jose Marti

1995. Revolutionaries' Anniversaries. Mult.
2423 1p. Type **920** (death cent) 1·60 45
2424 1p. Antonio de Sucre (birth bicentenary) . . . . . . 1·60 45

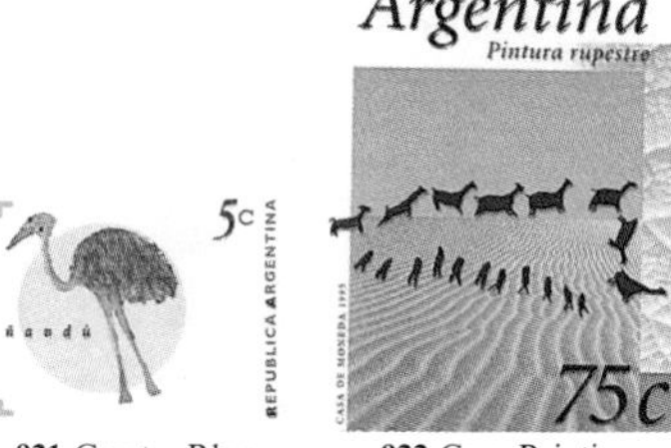

921 Greater Rhea **922** Cave Painting (Patagonia)

1995. Birds. Multicoloured.
2425 5c. Type **921** 15 10
2425a 10c. Giant wood rail ("ipecae") 15 10
2426 25c. King penguin 45 20
2427 50c. Toco toucan 85 45
2428 75c. Andean condor . . . 1·40 75
2429 1p. Barn owl . . . . . . 1·75 1·00
2430 2p. Olivaceous cormorant 3·50 2·00
2431 2p.75 Southern lapwing . . 5·00 2·75
2432 3p.25 Southern lapwing . . 4·00 3·00

1995. Animals. As T **921**. Multicoloured.
2436 25c. Alligator 30 20
2437 50c. Red fox 60 45
2438 75c. Anteater . . . . 1·25 75
2439 75c. Vicuna . . . . 1·25 75
2440 75c. Sperm whale . . . . . 1·25 75

1995. Archaeology. Multicoloured.
2441 75c. Type **922** . . . . . . 1·25 40
2442 75c. Stone mask (Tafi culture, Tucuman) . . . . 1·25 40
2443 75c. Anthropomorphic vase (Catamarca) . . . . . . 1·25 40
2444 75c. Woven cloth (North Patagonia) . . . . 1·25 40

923 Peron

1995. Birth Centenary of Juan Peron (President, 1946–55 and 1973–74).
2445 **923** 75c. blue and bistre . . . 1·25 40

924 Postal Emblem on Sunflower

1995.
2446 **924** 75c. multicoloured . . . 1·25 40

926 Christmas Tree

1995. Christmas. Multicoloured.
2448 75c. Type **926** . . . . . . 1·25 40
2449 75c. "1996" . . . . 1·25 40
2450 75c. Glasses of champagne 1·25 40
2451 75c. Present . . . . 1·25 40
2452 75c. Type **926** . . . . . . 1·25 40

927 "Les 400 Coups" (dir. Francois Truffaut)

1995. Centenary of Motion Pictures. Each black, grey and orange.
2453 75c. "Battleship Potemkin" (dir. Sergei Eisenstein) . . 1·25 40
2454 75c. "Casablanca" (dir. Michael Curtiz) . . . . . 1·25 40
2455 75c. "Bicycle Thieves" (dir. Vittorio de Sica) . . . . 1·25 40
2456 75c. Charlie Chaplin in "Limelight" . . . . . . 1·25 40
2457 75c. Type **927** . . . . . . 1·25 40
2458 75c. "Chronicle of an Only Child" (dir. Leonardo Favio) . . . . 1·25 40

928 Horse-drawn Mail Coach

1995. America (1994). Postal Transport. Mult.
2459 75c. Type **928** . . . . . . 1·25 40
2460 75c. Early postal van . . . 1·25 40

929 Dirigible Airship

1995. The Sky. Multicoloured.
2461 25c. Type **929** 55 20
2462 25c. Kite 55 20
2463 25c. Hot-air balloon 55 20
2464 50c. Balloons 85 45
2465 50c. Paper airplane 85 45
2466 75c. Airplane . . . . 1·25 45
2467 75c. Helicopter . . . . . . 1·25 45
2468 75c. Parachute . . . . . . 1·25 45

930 Ancient Greek and Modern Runners

1996. Multicoloured. (a) Centenary of Modern Olympic Games. Horiz designs.
2471 75c. Type **930** . . . . . . 1·25 35
2472 1p. "The Discus Thrower" (ancient Greek statue, Miron) and modern thrower . . . . 1·60 50

(b) Olympic Games. Vert designs.
2473 75c. Torch bearer (Buenos Aires, 2004) . . . . . . 1·25 35
2474 1p. Rowing (Atlanta, 1996) 1·60 50

931 Francisco Muniz (founder of Academy of Medicine and Public Hygiene Council)

1996. Physicians' Anniversaries. Multicoloured.
2475 50c. Type **931** (birth bicentenary (1995)) . . . 85 45
2476 50c. Ricardo Gutierrez (founder of Children's Hospital and co-founder of periodical "La Patria Argentina", death centenary) 85 45
2477 50c. Ignacio Pirovano (death centenary (1995)) 85 45
2478 50c. Esteban Maradona (birth centenary (1995) and first death anniv) . . 85 45

932 Mosaic Map of Jerusalem (left-hand detail)

1996. 3000th Anniv of Jerusalem. Multicoloured.
2479 75c. Type **932** . . . . . . 1·25 40
2480 75c. Map (right-hand detail) 1·25 40
Nos. 2479/80 were issued together, se-tenant, forming a composite design.

933 Capybaras

1996. America. Endangered Species. Mult.
2481 75c. Type **933** . . . . . . 1·50 45
2482 75c. Guanacos . . . . . . 1·50 45

934 Ramon Franco's Seaplane "Plus Ultra"

1996. "Aerofila '96" Latin American Airmail Exhibition. Aircraft. Multicoloured.
2483 25c.+25c. Type **934** . . . . 1·25 60
2484 25c.+25c. Alberto Santos-Dumont's biplane "14 bis" . . . . 1·25 60
2485 50c.+50c. Charles Lindbergh's "Spirit of St. Louis" . . . . 2·50 1·25
2486 50c.+50c. Eduardo Olivero's biplane "Buenos Aires" 2·50 1·25

1996. As Nos. 2407/8. Self-adhesive. Imperf.
2486a **913** 25c. yellow and blue . . 3·75 50
2486b 75c. yellow and blue . . 1·25 70

935 Dusky-legged Guan, Diamante National Park

1996. National Parks. Multicoloured.
2487 75c. Type **935** . . . . . . 1·25 45
2488 75c. Mountain viscacha, El Leoncito Nature Reserve 1·60 70
2489 75c. Marsh deer, Otamendi Nature Reserve . . . . . 1·25 45
2490 75c. Red-spectacled amazon, San Antonio Nature Reserve . . . . 1·60 70

936 Dragon

1996. Murals from Buenos Aires Underground Railway. Multicoloured.
2491 1p.+50c. Type **936** . . . . 3·00 1·75
2492 1p.50+1p. Bird . . . . . . 5·00 2·50

937 "San Antonio" (tank landing ship)

1996. Cent of Port Belgrano Naval Base. Mult.
2493 25c. Type **937** 65 20
2494 50c. "Rosales" (corvette) . . 1·25 45

2495 75c. "Hercules" (destroyer) 1·75 70
2496 1p. "25 de Mayo" (aircraft carrier) 2·50 1·00

938 Decorative Panel

1996. Carousel. Multicoloured.
2497 25c. Type **938** 55 20
2498 25c. Child on horse 55 20
2499 25c. Carousel 55 20
2500 50c. Fairground horses 85 20
2501 50c. Child in airplane 85 20
2502 50c. Pig 85 20
2503 75c. Child in car 1·25 45

939 Head Post Office, Buenos Aires

940 "Adoration of the Wise Men" (Gladys Rinaldi)

1996. Size 24½ × 34½ mm. Self-adhesive. Imperf.
2504 **939** 75c. multicoloured 90 70
See also Nos. 2537/8.

1996. Christmas. Tapestries. Multicoloured.
2505 75c. Type **940** 1·25 45
2506 1p. Abstract (Norma Bonet de Maekawa) (horiz) 1·60 70

941 Melchior Base

1996. Argentinian Presence in Antarctic. Mult.
2507 75c. Type **941** 1·40 45
2508 1p.25 "Irizar" (ice-breaker) 2·75 70

942 "Vahine no te Miti" (Gauguin)

1996. Cent of National Gallery of Fine Arts. Mult.
2509 75c. Type **942** 1·25 45
2510 1p. "The Nymph surprised" (Edouard Manet) 1·60 65
2511 1p. "Figure of Woman" (Amedeo Modigliani) 1·60 65
2512 1p.25 "Woman lying down" (Pablo Picasso) (horiz) 2·00 75

943 Granite Mining, Cordoba

1997. Mining Industry. Multicoloured.
2513 75c. Type **943** 1·25 45
2514 1p.25 Borax mining, Salta 2·00 65

944 "They amuse Themselves in Dancing" (Raul Soldi)

1997. America (1996). National Costume.
2515 **944** 75c. multicoloured 1·25 45

945 Arms, Sabre and Shako

1997. Centenary of Repatriation of General San Martin's Sabre.
2516 **945** 75c. multicoloured 1·25 45

946 Match Scene

1997. 29th World Rugby Youth Championship, Argentina.
2517 **946** 75c. multicoloured 1·25 45

947 "Fortuna" (yacht)

1997. 50th Anniv of Buenos Aires to Rio de Janeiro Regatta.
2518 **947** 75c. multicoloured 90 30

948 Ceres Design, France (1849–52)

1997. "Mevifil '97" First Int Exn of Philatelic Audio-visual and Computer Systems. Mult.
2519 50c.+50c. Type **948** 1·60 1·25
2520 50c.+50c. Queen Isabella II design, Spain (1851) 1·60 1·25
2521 50c.+50c. Rivadavia design, Argentine Republic (1864) 1·60 1·25
2522 50c.+50c. Paddle-steamer design, Buenos Aires (1858) 1·60 1·25
Nos. 2519/22 were issued together, se-tenant, with the centre of the block forming the composite design of an eye.

949 Museum

1997. Centenary of National History Museum, Buenos Aires.
2523 **949** 75c. multicoloured 1·25 45

950 Seal and Oak Leaf

951 Carcano (after Dolores Capdevila)

1997. Centenary of La Plata National University.
2524 **950** 75c. multicoloured 1·25 45

1997. 50th Death Anniv (1996) of Ramon Carcano (postal reformer).
2525 **951** 75c. multicoloured 1·25 45

952 Cabo Virgenes Lighthouse

1997. Lighthouses. Multicoloured.
2526 75c. Type **952** 1·25 45
2527 75c. Isla Pinguino 1·25 45
2528 75c. San Juan de Salvamento 1·25 45
2529 75c. Punta Delgada 1·25 45

953 Condor and Olympic Rings

1997. Inclusion of Buenos Aires in Final Selection Round for 2004 Olympic Games.
2530 **953** 75c. multicoloured 1·25 45

954 Lacroze Company Suburban Service, 1912

1997. Centenary of First Electric Tramway in Buenos Aires. Illustrations from "History of the Tram" by Marcelo Mayorga. Multicoloured.
2531 75c. Type **954** 1·40 70
2532 75c. Lacroze Company urban service, 1907 1·40 70
2533 75c. Anglo Argentina Company tramcar, 1930 1·40 70
2534 75c. City of Buenos Aires Transport Corporation tramcar, 1942 1·40 70
2535 75c. Fabricaciones Militares tramcar, 1956 1·40 70
2536 75c. Electricos de Sur Company tramcar, 1908 1·40 70
Nos. 2531/6 were issued together, se-tenant, showing a composite design of a tram in a city street.

1997. As No. 2504 but size 23 × 35 mm. Self-adhesive. Imperf.
2537 **939** 25c. multicoloured 70 20
2538 75c. multicoloured 1·40 20

955 Monument (by Mauricio Molina)

1997. Inauguration of Monument to Joaquin Gonzalez (politician) at La Rioja.
2539 **955** 75c. multicoloured 1·25 45

956 Alberto Ginastera (after Carlos Nine)

1997. Composers. Multicoloured.
2540 75c. Type **956** 1·25 45
2541 75c. Astor Piazzolla (after Carlos Alonso) 1·25 45
2542 75c. Anibal Troilo (after Hermenegildo Sabat) 1·25 45
2543 75c. Atahualpa Yupanqui (after Luis Scafati) 1·25 45

957 "Tren a las Nubes", Salta

1997. Trains. Multicoloured.
2544 50c.+50c. Type **957** 1·60 80
2545 50c.+50c. Preserved steam locomotive, Buenos Aires 1·60 80
2546 50c.+50c. Patagonian express "La Trochita" Rio Negro–Chubut 1·60 80
2547 50c.+50c. Austral Fueguino Railway locomotive No. 2, Tierra del Fuego 1·60 80

958 Eva Peron (after Raul Manteola)

1997. 50th Anniv of Women's Suffrage.
2548 **958** 75c. pink and grey 1·25 45

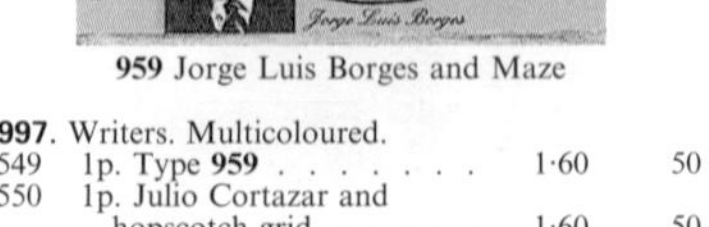

959 Jorge Luis Borges and Maze

1997. Writers. Multicoloured.
2549 1p. Type **959** 1·60 50
2550 1p. Julio Cortazar and hopscotch grid 1·60 50

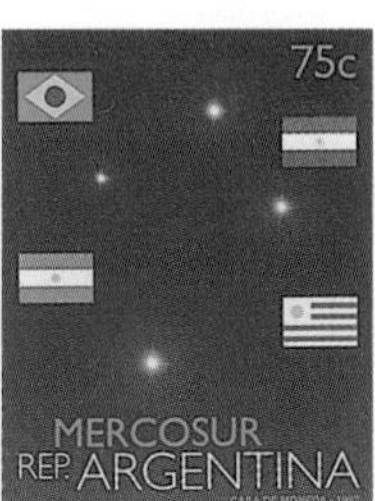

961 Members' Flags and Southern Cross

1997. Mercosur (South American Common Market).
2552 **961** 75c. multicoloured 1·25 45

962 "Presidente Sarmiento" (Hugo Leban)

1997. Centenary of Launch of "Presidente Sarmiento" (cadet ship).
2553 **962** 75c. multicoloured . . . 2·00 55

963 Guevara

1997. 30th Death Anniv of Ernesto "Che" Guevara (revolutionary).
2555 **963** 75c. brown, red & black 1·25 45

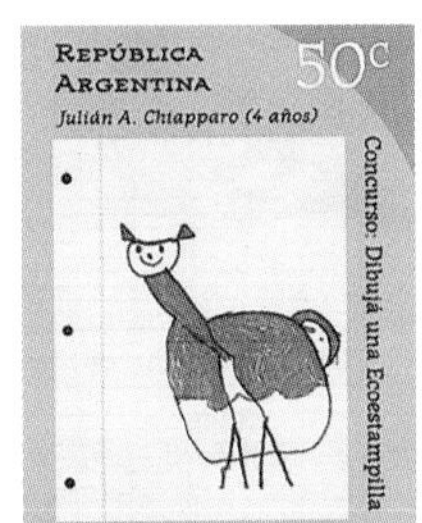

964 Vicuna (Julian Chiapparo)

1997. "Draw an Ecostamp" Children's Competition Winners. Multicoloured.
2556 50c. Type **964** 80 20
2557 50c. Vicuna (Leandro Lopez Portal) 80 20
2558 75c. Seal (Andres Lloren) (horiz) . . . . 1·25 45
2559 75c. Ashy-headed goose (Jose Saccone) (horiz) . . 1·25 45

965 "Nativity" (Mary Jose)

1997. Christmas. Tapestries of the Nativity. Designs by artists named. Mult. (a) Size 45 × 34 mm.
2560 75c. Type **965** . . . . . . 1·25 45

(b) Size 44 × 27 mm. Self-adhesive. Imperf.
2561 25c. Elena Aguilar 40 20
2562 25c. Silvia Pettachi 40 20
2563 50c. Ana Escobar 80 20
2564 50c. Alejandra Martinez . . 80 20
2565 75c. As No. 2560 but with inscriptions differently arranged . . . . 1·25 45
2566 75c. Nidia Martinez . . . . 1·25 45

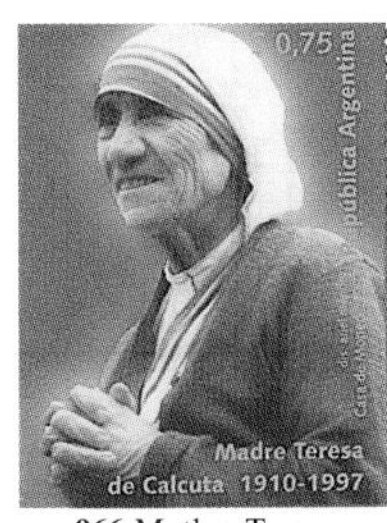

966 Mother Teresa

1997. Mother Teresa (founder of the Missionaries of Charity) Commemoration.
2567 **966** 75c. multicoloured . . . 1·25 45

967 Houssay

1998. 50th Anniv (1997) of Award to Bernardo Houssay of Nobel Prize for Medicine and Physiology.
2568 **967** 75c. multicoloured . . . 90 70

968 Mountaineers

1998. Cent of First Ascent of Mt. Aconcagua.
2569 **968** 1p.25 multicoloured . . 1·25 1·00

969 San Martin de los Andes and Lake Lacar

1998. Centenary of San Martin de los Andes.
2570 **969** 75c. multicoloured . . . 90 70

970 Grenadier Monument (Juan Carlos Ferraro)

1998. Declaration as National Historical Monument of Palermo Barracks of General San Martin Horse Grenadiers. Multicoloured.
2571 75c. Type **970** 90 70
2572 75c. Sevres urn with portrait of San Martin 90 70
2573 75c. Regiment coat of arms 90 70
2574 75c. Main facade of barracks 90 70

971 Globe and Baby

1998. Protection of Ozone Layer.
2575 **971** 75c. multicoloured . . . 90 70

972 Postman, 1920

1998. America. The Postman. Multicoloured.
2576 75c. Type **972** 90 70
2577 75c. Postman, 1998 . . . . 90 70

973 "El Reino del Reves"

1998. Stories by Maria Elena Walsh. Illustrations by Eduardo and Ricardo Fuhrmann. Multicoloured. Self-adhesive.
2578 75c. Type **973** 90 70
2579 75c. "Zoo Loco" 90 70
2580 75c. "Dailan Kifki" 90 70
2581 75c. "Manuelita" 90 70

974 St Peter's, Fiambala, Catamarca

1998. Historic Chapels. Multicoloured.
2582 75c. Type **974** 90 70
2583 75c. Huacalera, Jujuy . . . 90 70
2584 75c. St. Dominic's, La Rioja 90 70
2585 75c. Tumbaya, Jujuy . . . 90 70

975 Raised Hands

1998. White Helmets (volunteer humanitarian workers).
2586 **975** 1p. multicoloured . . . 1·25 1·00

976 Argentine Player

1998. World Cup Football Championship, France. Multicoloured.
2587 75c. Type **976** 90 70
2588 75c. Croatian player 90 70
2589 75c. Jamaican player . . . 90 70
2590 75c. Japanese player 90 70

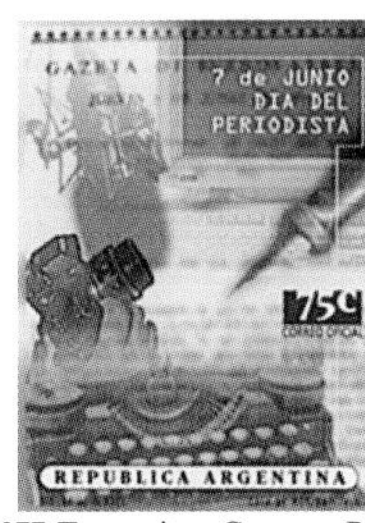

977 Typewriter, Camera, Pen, Computer and Satellite

1998. Journalism Day.
2591 **977** 75c. multicoloured . . . 90 70

978 Corrientes 1860 3c. Stamps and Postal Emblem

1998. 250th Anniv of Establishment of Regular Postal Service in Rio de la Plata (Spanish dominion in South America). Multicoloured.
2592 75c. Type **978** 90 70
2593 75c. Buenos Aires Post Office and pillar box . . . 90 70

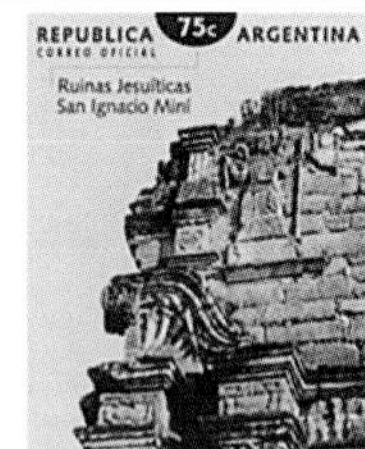

979 Jesuit Ruins, San Ignacio Mini

1998. Mercosur Missions.
2594 **979** 75c. multicoloured . . . 90 70

980 Aberdeen Angus

1998. Cattle. Multicoloured.
2595 25c. Type **980** 30 20
2596 25c. Brahman 30 20
2597 50c. Hereford 60 45
2598 50c. Criolla 60 45
2599 75c. Holando-Argentina . . 90 70
2600 75c. Shorthorn 90 70

981 Map and Base

1998. 50th Anniv of Decepcion Antarctic Base.
2601 **981** 75c. multicoloured . . . 90 70

982 Anniversary Emblem

1998. 50th Anniv of State of Israel.
2602 **982** 75c. multicoloured . . . 90 70

983 Bridge in Japanese Garden, Buenos Aires

1998. Cent of Argentina–Japan Friendship Treaty.
2603 **983** 75c. multicoloured . . . 90 70

984 Facade and clock

1998. 70th Anniv of Head Post Office, Buenos Aires. Multicoloured.
2604 75c. Type **984** 90 70
2605 75c. Capital and bench . . . 90 70

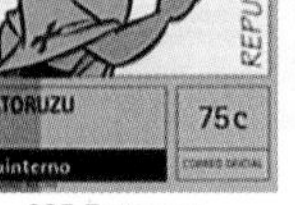

985 Patoruzu (Quinterno) **986** Heart with Arms holding Baby

1998. Comic Strip Characters. Multicoloured.
2606 75c. Type **985** 90 70
2607 75c. Matias (Sendra) 90 70
2608 75c. Clemente (Caloi) 90 70
2609 75c. El Eternauta (Oesterheld Solano Lopez) 90 70
2610 75c. Loco Chavez (Trillo Altuna) 90 70
2611 75c. Inodoro Pereyra (Fontanarrosa) 90 70
2612 75c. Tia Vicenta (Landru) 90 70
2613 75c. Gaturro (Nik) 90 70

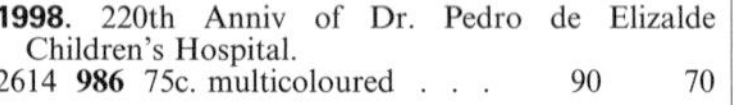

1998. 220th Anniv of Dr. Pedro de Elizalde Children's Hospital.
2614 **986** 75c. multicoloured . . . 90 70

987 Post Banner and Pennant, 1785, and Arms of Maritime Post

1998. "Espamer '98" Iberian–Latin American Stamp Exhibition, Buenos Aires. Mult. Self-adhesive.
2615 25c. Type **987** 30 20
2616 75c. Mail brigantine . . . . 1·25 70
2617 75c.+75c. Mail brigantine (different) . . . . 2·50 1·75
2618 1p.25+1p.25 Mail brig . . . 4·25 3·00

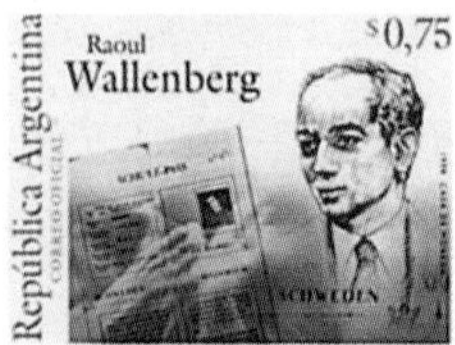

988 Passport and Wallenberg

1998. Raoul Wallenberg (Swedish diplomat in Hungary who helped Jews escape, 1944–45) Commemoration.
2619 **988** 75c. multicoloured . . . 90 70

989 Aguada Culture Bird

1998. 50th Anniv of Organization of American States.
2620 **989** 75c. multicoloured . . . 90 70

990 Eoraptor

1998. Prehistoric Animals. Multicoloured.
2621 75c. Type **990** 90 70
2622 75c. Gasparinisaura 90 70
2623 75c. Giganotosaurus 90 70
2624 75c. Patagosaurus 90 70
Nos. 2621/4 were issued together, se-tenant, forming a composite design.

991 Child as Angel, Stars and Score **993** Postman

992 Juan Figueroa (founder) and First Issue

1998. Christmas.
2625 **991** 75c. multicoloured . . . 90 70

1998. Centenary of "El Liberal" (newspaper).
2626 **992** 75c. multicoloured . . . 90 70

1998. Postmen. Size 25 × 35 mm. Multicoloured. Self-adhesive.
2627 25c. Type **993** 30 20
2628 75c. Modern postman . . . 90 70
For 75c. in reduced size see No. 2640.

1998. Birds. As T **921**. Multicoloured. Self-adhesive.
2629 60c. Red-tailed comet . . . 75 60

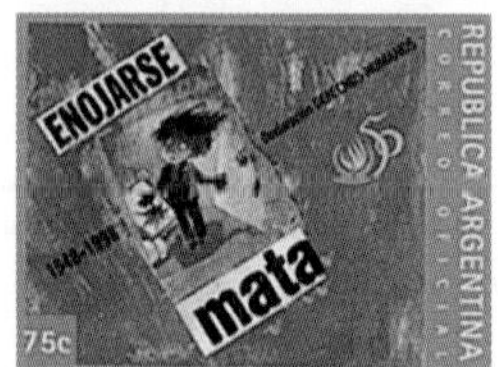

994 Child (painting, Francisco Ramirez)

1998. 50th Anniv of Universal Declaration of Human Rights.
2635 **994** 75c. multicoloured . . . 90 70

995 Enrique Julio (founder) and Newspaper Offices

1998. Cent of "La Nueva Provincia" (newspaper).
2636 **995** 75c. multicoloured . . . 90 70

996 "Haggadah" of Pessah (exhibit) and Carving on Cathedral

1998. Permanent Exhibition commemorating Holocaust Victims, Buenos Aires Cathedral.
2637 **996** 75c. multicoloured . . . 90 70

1999. Postmen. Size 21 × 27 mm. Mult. Self-adhesive.
2638 15c. Type **993** 30 20
2639 50c. Postman, 1950 . . . . 60 45
2640 75c. As No. 2628 . . . . . 90 70

997 Oil-smeared Magellanic Penguin

1999. International Year of the Ocean. Mult.
2641 50c. Type **997** 60 45
2642 75c. Dolphins (horiz) . . . 90 70

998 Buildings and Draughtsman's Instruments

1999. National Arts Fund.
2643 **998** 75c. multicoloured . . . 90 70

999 Computer and Book

1999. 25th Book Fair, Buenos Aires. Multicoloured.
2644 75c. Type **999** 90 70
2645 75c. Obelisk, compact disk case and readers 90 70
Nos. 2644/5 were issued together, se-tenant, forming a composite design.

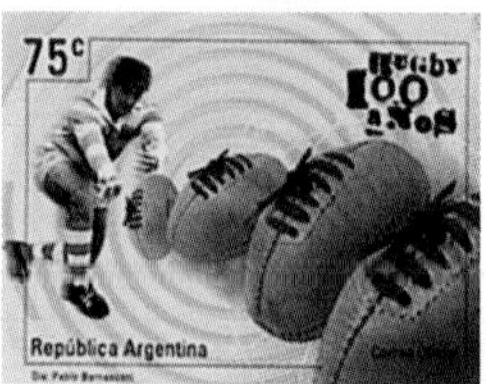

1000 Rugby Balls and Player

1999. Centenary of Argentine Rugby Union.
2646 **1000** 75c. multicoloured . . . 90 70

1001 Glass, La Giralda **1002** Pierre de Coubertin, 1924 Olympic Gold Medal and Olympic Rings

1999. Cafes. Multicoloured. Self-adhesive.
2648 25c. Type **1001** 30 20
2649 75c. Two glasses, Cafe Homero Manzi 90 70
2650 75c. Hatstand, Confitenia Ideal 90 70
2651 1p.25 Cup and saucer, Cafe Tortoni . . . . 1·50 1·00

1999. 75th Anniv of Argentine Olympic Committee.
2652 **1002** 75c. multicoloured . . . 90 70

1003 Enrico Caruso (Italian tenor)

1999. Opera. Multicoloured.
2653 75c. Type **1003** (125th birth anniv and centenary of American debut) 90 70
2654 75c. Singer and musical instruments 90 70
2655 75c. Buenos Aires Opera House 90 70
2656 75c. Scene from "El Matrero" (Felipe Boero) 90 70

1004 Rosario Vera Penaloza (educationist)

1999. America (1998). Famous Women. Mult.
2659 75c. Type **1004** 90 70
2660 75c. Julieta Lanteri (women's rights campaigner) 90 70

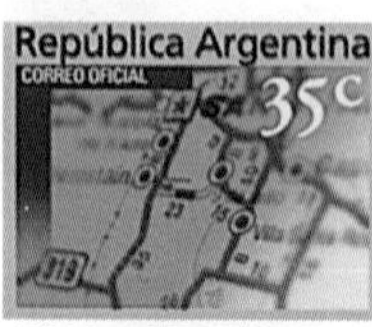

1006 Local Road Network

1999. Bulk Mailing Stamps. Mult. Self-adhesive.
2662 35c. Type **1006** 40 30
2663 40c. Town plan 50 40
2664 50c. Regional map 60 45

1007 Carrier Pigeon

1999.
2665 **1007** 75c. multicoloured . . . 90 70

1008 Boxer

1999. Dogs. Multicoloured.
2666 25c. Type **1008** 20 20
2667 25c. Old English sheepdog 30 20
2668 50c. Welsh collie 60 45
2669 50c. St. Bernard 60 45
2670 75c. German shepherd . . . 90 70
2671 75c. Siberian husky 90 70

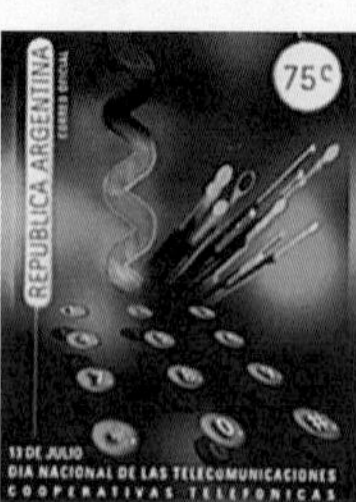

1009 Telephone Keypad

1999. National Telecommunications Day.
2672 **1009** 75c. multicoloured . . . 90 70

1010 College Gates

1999. 150th Anniv of Justo Jose de Urquiza College, Concepcion del Uruguay.
2673 **1010** 75c. multicoloured . . . 90 70

1011 Krause (engineer) and Industrial Instruments

1999. Centenary of Technical School No. 1 Otto Krause.
2674 **1011** 75c. multicoloured . . . 90 70

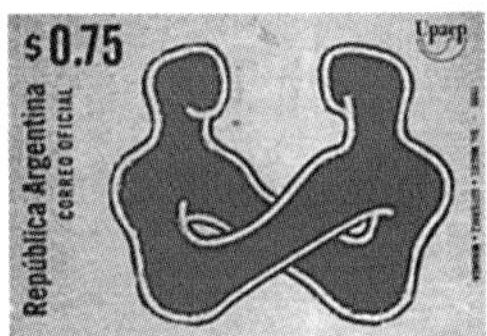

1012 Nativity

1999. Bethlehem 2000.
2675 **1012** 75c. blue, gold and red 90 70

1013 Brotherhood among Men

1999. America. A New Millennium without Arms. Multicoloured.
2676 75c. Type **1013** 90 70
2677 75c. Liberty Tree (vert) . . 90 70

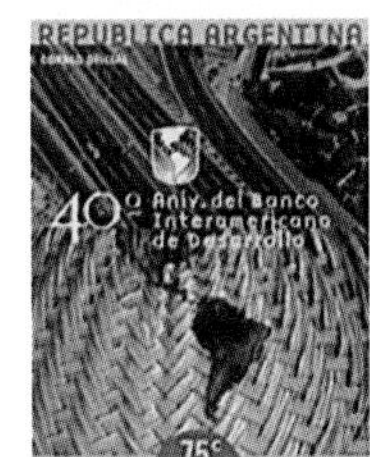

1014 Coypu ("Myocastor coypus"), Mburucuya National Park

1999. National Parks. Multicoloured.
2678 50c. Type **1014** 60 50
2679 50c. Andean condor, Quebrada de los Condoritos National Park 60 50
2680 50c. Vicuna, San Guillermo National Park 60 50
2681 75c. Puma, Sierra de las Quijadas National Park 90 70
2682 75c. Argentine grey fox ("Dusicyon griseus"), Talampaya National Park 90 70

1015 Map of the Americas, Road Network and Wickerwork

1999. 40th Anniv of Inter-American Development Bank.
2683 **1015** 75c. multicoloured . . . 90 70

1016 "Evidencias VI" (Carlos Gallardo)

1999. 125th Anniv of Universal Postal Union.
2684 **1016** 1p.50 multicoloured . . 1·75 1·40

1017 "Fournier" and Map

1999. 50th Anniv of Sinking of the "Fournier" (minesweeper) in Antarctica.
2685 **1017** 75c. multicoloured . . . 90 70

1018 "Nothofagus pumillio"

1999. Trees (1st series). Multicoloured.
2686 75c. Type **1018** 90 70
2687 75c. "Prosopis caldenia" . . 90 70
2688 75c. "Schinopsis balansae" 90 70
2689 75c. "Cordia trichotoma" 90 70
Nos. 2686/9 were issued together, se-tenant, forming a composite design.

1019 Latecoere 25 Mailplane

1999. 50th Anniv of World Record for Consecutive Parachute Jumps. Multicoloured.
2690 75c. Type **1019** 90 70
2691 75c. Parachutists 90 70

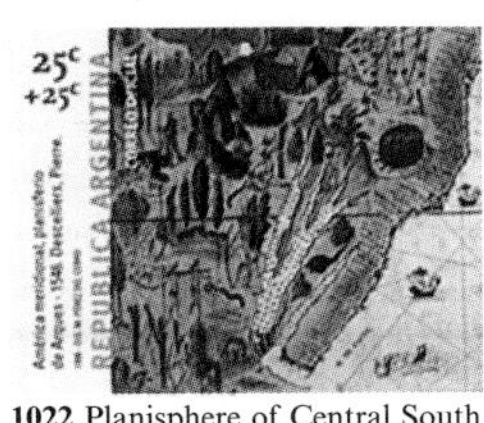

1021 Boca Juniors Club Supporters

1999. Football. Multicoloured. (a) Size 42 × 33 mm.
2693 75c. Type **1021** 90 70
2694 75c. River Plate Club supporters 90 70

(b) Size 37 × 34 mm (1p.50) or 37 × 27 mm (others)
(i) Boca Juniors
2695 25c. Two players and ball 30 25
2696 50c. Club badge 60 50
2697 50c. Players hugging 60 50
2698 75c. Supporters and balloons 90 70
2699 75c. Club banner 90 70
2700 75c. Players 90 70
2701 1p.50 Player making high kick . . . . 1·75 1·40

(ii) River Plate
2702 25c. Stadium 30 25
2703 50c. Players arriving on pitch 60 50
2704 50c. Supporters waving flags 60 50
2705 75c. Club badge 90 70
2706 75c. Trophy 90 70
2707 75c. Supporters with banner 90 70
2708 1p.50 Player preparing to kick ball . . . . 1·75 1·40
Nos. 2695/708 are self-adhesive.

1022 Planisphere of Central South America (Pierre Descelliers, 1546)

1999. Maps. Multicoloured.
2709 25c.+25c. Type **1022** 60 60
2710 50c.+50c. 17th-century map of estuary of the River Plate (Claes Voogt) . . . 1·25 1·25
2711 50c.+50c. Buenos Aires (Military Geographical Institute, 1910) . . . . . 1·25 1·25
2712 75c.+75c. Mouth of Riachuelo river and Buenos Aires harbour (satellite picture, 1999) . . 1·75 1·75

1023 Valdivielso and St. Peter's Cathedral, Rome

1999. Canonization of Hector Valdivielso Saez (Brother of the Christian Schools).
2713 **1023** 75c. multicoloured . . . 90 70

1024 "San Francisco Xavier" (brig)

1999. Bicentenary of Manuel Belgrano Naval Academy.
2714 **1024** 75c. multicoloured . . . 90 70

1026 Holy Family

1999. Christmas. Multicoloured.
2716 25c. Wise Man (29 × 29 mm) 30 25
2717 25c. Bell (29 × 29 mm) . . . 30 25
2718 50c. Two kings and camels (39 × 29 mm) 60 50
2719 50c. Holly leaf (39 × 29 mm) 60 50
2720 75c. Angel with star (39 × 30 mm) 90 70
2721 75c. Star (29 × 30 mm) . . . 90 70
2722 75c. Nativity (39 × 29 mm) 90 70
2723 75c. Tree decorations (29 × 29 mm) 90 70
2724 75c. Type **1026** 90 70

1027 Grape on Vine

2000. Wine Making. Multicoloured.
2725 25c. Type **1027** 35 30
2726 25c. Glass and bottle of wine 35 30
2727 50c. Wine bottles 70 55
2728 50c. Cork screw and cork 70 55

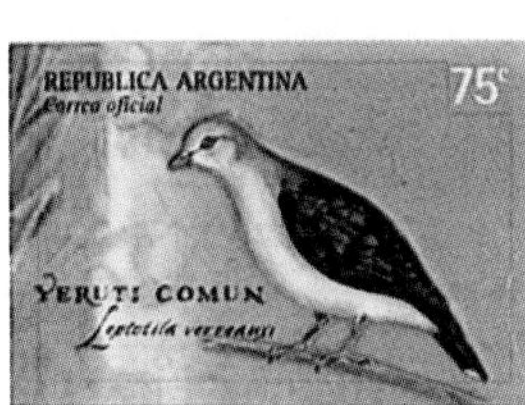

1028 Mathematical Symbol and "2000"

2000. International Mathematics Year.
2729 **1028** 75c. multicoloured . . . 1·00 80

1029 White-fronted Dove

2000. Doves and Pigeon. Mult. Self-adhesive.
2730 75c. Type **1029** . . . . . . 1·00 80
2731 75c. Picazuro pigeon (*Columba picazuro*) . . . 1·00 80
2732 75c. Picui dove (*Columbina picui*) . . . . 1·00 80
2733 75c. Eared dove (*Fenaida auriculata*) . . . . 1·00 80

1031 Open Book (CONABIP Library)

2000. Libraries. Multicoloured.
2735 25c. Type **1031** 35 35
2736 50c. Building facade (Jujuy library) 70 55
2737 75c. Hands and braille book (Argentine Library for the Blind) . . . . 1·00 80
2738 $1 Open book and building (National Library) . . . 2·10 1·60
No. 2737 has an inscription in braille across the stamp.

1032 Caravel, Compass Rose and Letter

2000. 500th Anniv of the Discovery of Brazil. Multicoloured.
2739 25c. Type **1032** 35 30
2740 75c. Pedro Alvares Cabral (discoverer) and map of South America . . . . . 1·00 80

1033 Lieutenant General Luis Maria Campos (founder)

2000. Centenary of the Higher Military Academy.
2741 **1033** 75c. multicoloured . . . 1·00 80

1035 Convention Emblem

2000. 91st Rotary International Convention, Buenos Aires.
2743 **1035** 75c. multicoloured . . . 1·00 80

1036 Futuristic Houses and Emblems (Rocio Casado)

2000. "Stampin' the Future". Winning Entries in Children's International Painting Competition. Mult.
2744 25c. Type **1036** 35 30
2745 50c. Sea and clouds (Carolina Cacerez) (vert) 70 55
2746 75c. Flower (Valeria A. Pizarro) . . . . 1·00 80
2747 $1 Flying cars (Cristina Ayala Castro) (vert) . . . 1·40 1·10

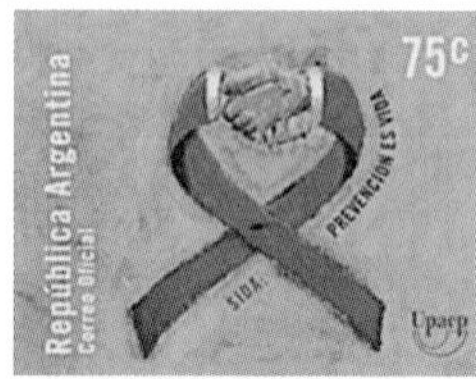

1037 Ribbon

2000. America. AIDS Awareness. Multicoloured.
2748 75c. Type **1037** . . . . . . 1·00 80
2749 75c. Arms circling faces . . 1·00 80

1038 Potez 25 Biplane

2000. Birth Centenary of Antoine de Saint-Exupery (novelist and pilot). Multicoloured.
2750 25c. Type **1038** 35 30
2751 50c. Late 28 . . . . 70 55

1039 Potez 25 Biplane

2000. "Aerofila 2000" Mercosur Air Philately Exhibition, Buenos Aires. Multicoloured.
2752 25c. As Type **1039** 35 30
2753 25c. Antoine de Saint-Exupery (novelist and pilot) (29 × 29 mm) . . . 35 30
2754 50c. Late 28 . . . . 70 55
2755 50c. Henri Guillaumet, Almonacid and Jean Mermoz (aviation pioneers) (29 × 29 mm) . . 70 55
2756 50c. Map of South America and tail of Late 25 (39 × 39 mm) 70 55
2757 $1 Late 25 and cover (39 × 29 mm) . . . . . . 1·40 1·10

1040 Illia

2000. Birth Centenary of Arturo U. Illia (President, 1963–66).
2758 **1040** 75c. multicoloured . . . 1·00 80

1041 San Martin **1042** Siku Pipes

2000. 150th Death Anniv of General Jose de San Martin.
2759 **1041** 75c. multicoloured . . . 1·00 80

2000. Argentine Culture. Multicoloured.
2760 10c. Ceremonial axe 15 10
2761 25c. Type **1042** 35 30
2762 50c. Andean loom 70 55
2763 60c. Pampeana poncho . . 80 60
2764 75c. Funeral mask . . . . . 1·00 80
2765 $1 Basket . . . . 1·40 1·10
2766 $2 Kultun ritual drum . . . 2·75 2·25
2767 $3.25 Ceremonial tiger mask 4·50 3·50
2768 $5 Funeral urn . . . . . . 7·00 5·50
2770 $9.40 Suri ceremonial costume . . . . 13·00 10·00

1043 Sarsfield, Signature and Cordoba Province Arms

2000. Birth Bicentenary of Dalmacio Velez Sarsfield (lawyer).
2775 **1043** 75c. multicoloured . . . 1·00 80

1044 Windsurfing

2000. Olympic Games, Sydney. Multicoloured.
2776 75c. Type **1044** . . . . . . 1·00 80
2777 75c. Hockey . . . . 1·00 80
2778 75c. Volleyball . . . . . . 1·00 80
2779 75c. High jump and pole vault . . . . 1·00 80

1045 Argentine Petiso

2000. "Espana 2000" International Stamp Exhibition, Madrid. Horses. Multicoloured.
2780 25c. Type **1045** 35 30
2781 25c. Carriage horse 35 30
2782 50c. Peruvian horse 70 55
2783 50c. Criolla 70 55
2784 75c. Saddle horse . . . . . 1·00 80
2785 75c. Polo horse . . . . . . 1·00 80

1046 Man on Bicycle and Las Nereidas Fountain

2000. Transportation. Multicoloured.
2787 25c.+25c. Type **1046** 70 55
2788 50c.+50c. *Graf Zeppelin* over Buenos Aires . . . . . . 1·25 1·00
2789 50c.+50c. *Ganz* (diesel locomotive) . . . . . . 1·40 1·10
2790 75c.+75c. Tram . . . . . . 2·10 1·75

1047 Nuclear Reactor

2000. 50th Anniv of National Commission for Atomic Energy.
2791 **1047** 75c. multicoloured . . . 1·00 80

1048 "Filete" (left-hand detail)

2000. Fileteado (painting genre) (Nos. 2792/3) and Tango (dance) (Nos. 2794/5). Multicoloured.
2792 75c. Type **1048** . . . . . . 1·00 80
2793 75c. "Filete" (right-hand detail) (Brunetti brothers) 1·00 80
2794 75c. Tango orchestra . . . 1·00 80
2795 75c. Couple dancing . . . . 1·00 80

1049 Human Bodies on Jigsaw

2000. 40th Anniv of Organ Donation Publicity Campaign.
2796 **1049** 75c. multicoloured . . . 1·00 60

1050 "Birth of Jesus" (stained glass window, Sanctuary of Our Lady of the Rosary, New Pompeii)

2000. Christmas.
2797 **1050** 75c. multicoloured . . . 1·00 60

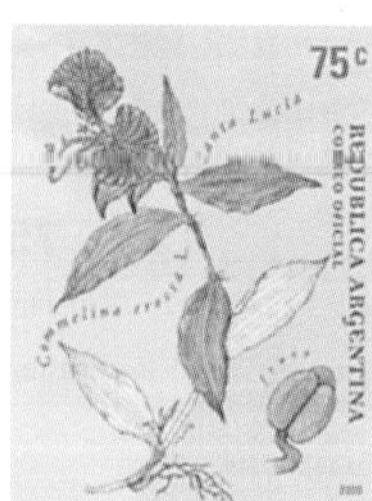

1051 *Commelina erecta*

2000. Medicinal Plants. Multicoloured.
2798 75c. Type **1051** . . . . . . 1·00 60
2799 75c. *Senna corymbosa* . . . 1·00 60
2800 75c. *Mirabilis jalapa* . . . . 1·00 60
2801 75c. *Eugenia uniflora* . . . . 1·00 60

1052 Human-shaped Vessel, Cienaga

2000. Traditional Crafts. Multicoloured.
2802 75c. Type **1052** . . . . . . 1·00 60
2803 75c. Painted human-shaped vase, Vaquerias . . . . . 1·00 60
2804 75c. Animal-shaped vessel, Condorhuasi . . . . . . 1·00 60
2805 75c. Human-shaped vase, Candelaria . . . . 1·00 60

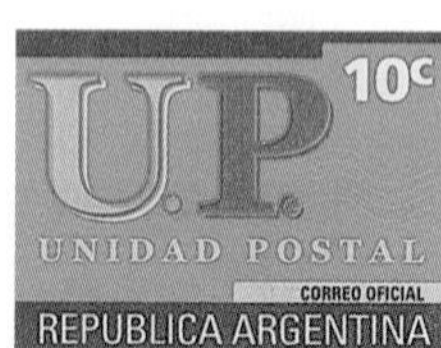

1053 "U. P." Unidad Postal

2001. Postal Agents' Stamps. Multicoloured, background colours given. Self-adhesive gum.
2806 **1053** 10c. turquoise 15 10
2807 25c. green 35 20
2808 60c. yellow 80 45
2809 75c. red . . . . 1·00 60
2810 $1 blue . . . . 1·40 80
2811 $3 red . . . . 4·00 2·40
2812 $3.25 yellow . . . . . 4·50 2·75
2813 $5.50 mauve . . . . . 7·50 4·50
Nos. 2806/13 were issued for use by Postal Agents as opposed to branches of the Argentine Post Office.

1054 *Megatherium americanum* ("Megaterio")

2001. Cainozoic Mammals. Multicoloured.
2820 75c. Type **1054** 80 45
2821 75c. *Doedicurus clavcaudatus* ("Gliptodonte") 80 45
2822 75c. *Macrauchenia patachonica* ("Macrauqueria") 80 45
2823 75c. *Toxodon platensis* ("Toxodonte") 80 45

1055 Map, South Polar Skua and San Martin Base

2001. 50th Anniv of San Martín and Brown Antarctic Bases. Multicoloured.
2824 75c. Type **1055** 80 45
2825 75c. Blue-eyed cormorant, map and Brown Base . . 80 45

1056 Bees on Clover Flower

2001. Apiculture. Multicoloured.
2826 75c. Type **1056** 80 45
2827 75c. Bees on honeycomb . . 80 45
2828 75c. Bees and bee-keeper attending hives 80 45
2829 75c. Jar of honey and swizzle 80 45
Nos. 2826/9 were issued together, se-tenant, forming a composite design.

1058 Dornier Do-j Wal Flying Boat *Plus Ultra* and Route Map

2001. 75th Anniv of Major Ramon Franco's Flight from Spain to Argentina.
2831 **1058** 75c. multicoloured . . . 80 45

1059 Horse's Bridle Fittings

2001. Silver Work. Each blue, silver and black.
2832 75c. Type **1059** 80 45
2833 75c. Stirrups 80 45
2834 75c. Spurs 80 45
2835 75c. Rastra (gaucho belt decoration) 80 45

1061 Goalkeeper catching Ball

2001. Under 20's World Youth Football Championship, Argentine Republic. Multicoloured.
2837 75c. Type **1061** 80 45
2838 75c. Player kicking ball . . 80 45

1062 People and Buildings

2001. National Census.
2839 **1062** 75c. multicoloured . . . 80 45

1063 SAC-C Satellite, Seagulls and Sunflowers

2001. Environmental Protection. Satellite Tracking Project.
2840 **1063** 75c. multicoloured . . . 80 45

1064 Puma

2001. Wild Cats. Multicoloured.
2841 25c. Type **1064** 35 20
2842 25c. Jaguar 35 20
2843 50c. Jaguarundi 70 50
2844 50c. Ocelot 70 50
2845 75c. Geoffroy's Cat 80 45
2846 75c. Kodkod 80 45

1065 "Bandoneon Recital" (painting, Aldo Severi)

2001.
2847 **1065** 75c. multicoloured . . . 80 45

1067 Discepolo

2001. Birth Centenary of Enriques Santos Discepolo (actor and lyric writer).
2849 **1067** 75c. multicoloured . . . 80 45

1068 Courtyard, Caroya Estancia, Angel and Chapel, Estancia Santa Catalina

2001. U.N.E.S.C.O. World Heritage Sites. Mult.
2850 75c. Type **1068** 80 45
2851 75c. Emblem and chapel, Estancia La Candelaria, dome of Estancia Alta Gracia and belfry, Estancia Jesus Maria . . 80 45

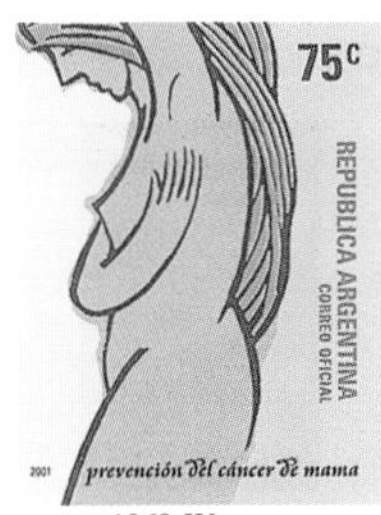

1069 Woman

2001. Breast Cancer Awareness.
2852 **1069** 75c. multicoloured . . . 80 45

1070 Burmeister's Porpoise

2001. Marine Mammals. Multicoloured.
2853 25c.+25c. Type **1070** 70 70
2854 50c.+50c. La Plata River dolphin . . . . 1·40 1·40
2855 50c.+50c. Minke whale . . . 1·40 1·40
2856 75c.+75c. Humpback whale 2·10 2·10

1071 Alfa Romeo 159 Alfetta, Spain, 1951

2001. Formula 1 Racing Cars driven by Juan Manuel Fangio. Multicoloured.
2857 75c. Type **1071** . . . . . . 1·00 60
2858 75c. Mercedes Benz W 196, France, 1954 . . . . . . 1·00 60
2859 75c. Lancia-Ferrari D50, Monaco, 1956 . . . . . 1·00 60
2860 75c. Maserati 250 F, Germany, 1957 . . . . . 1·00 60

1072 Palo Santo Tree

2001. Mercosur (South American Common Market).
2861 **1072** 75c. multicoloured . . . 1·00 60

1073 Justo Jose de Urquiza

2001. Birth Anniversaries. Multicoloured.
2862 75c. Type **1073** (politician) (bicentenary) . . . . . . 1·00 60
2863 75c. Roque Saenz Pena (President 1910—14) (150th anniv) . . . . . . 1·00 60

1075 "La Pobladora" Carriage (Enrique Udaondo Graphic Museum Complex)

2001. Museums. Multicoloured.
2865 75c. Type **1075** . . . . . . 1·00 60
2866 75c. Ebony and silver crucifix (Brigadier General Juan Martin de Pueyrredon Museum) (vert) . . . . 1·00 60
2867 75c. Funerary urn (Emilio and Duncan Wagner Museum of Anthropological and Natural Sciences) (vert) 1·00 60
2868 75c. Skeleton of Carnotaurus sastrei (Argentine Natural Science Museum) . . . . 1·00 60

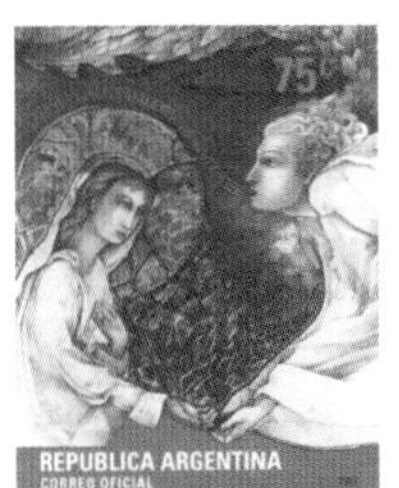

1076 "The Power of the Most High will Overshadow You" (Martin La Spina)

2001. Christmas.
2869 **1076** 75c. multicoloured . . . 1·00 60

1077 Carola Lorenzini and Focke Wulf 44-J

2001. Aviation. Multicoloured.
2870 75c. Type **1077** . . . . . . 1·00 60
2871 75c. Jean Mermoz and Arc-en-Ciel . . . . 1·00 60

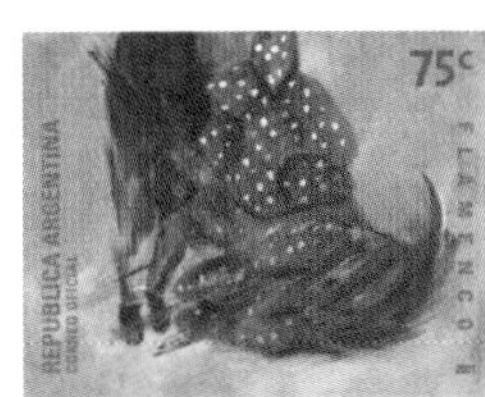

1078 Dancers (Flamenco)

2001. Dances. Multicoloured.
2872 75c. Type **1078** . . . . . . 1·00 60
2873 75c. Dancers (purple skirt) (Vals) . . . . 1·00 60
2874 75c. Dancers (orange skirt) (Zamba) . . . . 1·00 60
2875 75c. Dancers (Tango) . . . 1·00 60

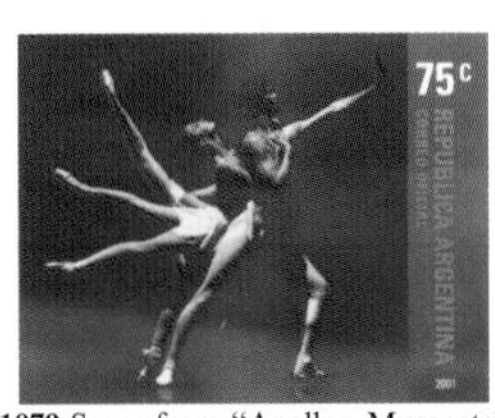

1079 Scene from "Apollon Musagete" (Igor Stravinsky)

2001. National Day of the Dancer.
2876 **1079** 75c. multicoloured . . . 1·00 60

1080 Television Set, Camera and Microphone

2001. 50th Anniv of Television in Argentina. Multicoloured.
2877 75c. Type **1080** . . . . . . 1·00 60
2878 75c. Television set and video tapes . . . . 1·00 60
2879 75c. Satellite dish and astronaut . . . . 1·00 60
2880 75c. Colour television cables and remote control . . . 1·00 60

1081 Consolidated PBY-5A Catalina (amphibian) and Cancellation

2002. 50th Anniv of Argentine Antarctic Programme. Multicoloured.
2881 75c. Type **1081** (first air and sea courier service) . . . 1·00 60
2882 75c. *Chiriguano* (minesweeper) and buildings (foundation of Esparanza Base) . . . . 1·00 60

1082 House and Flag

2002. America. Education and Literacy Campaign. Multicoloured
2883 75c. Type **1082** . . . . . . 1·00 60
2884 75c. Children playing hopscotch . . . . 1·00 60

1083 Two-banded Plover (*Charadrius falklandicus*)

2002. Birds. Multicoloured.
2885 50c. Type **1083** 70 40
2886 50c. Dolphin gull (*Larus scoresbii*) 70 40
2887 75c. Ruddy-headed goose (*Chloephaga rubidiceps*) (vert) . . . . 1·00 60
2888 75c. King penguin (*Aptenodytes patagonicus*) (vert) . . . . 1·00 60

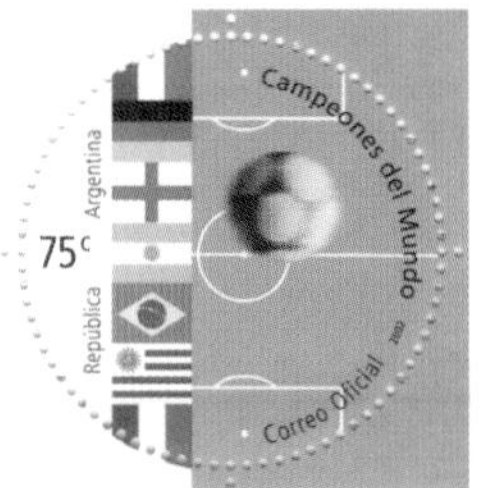

1084 Flags of Championship Winners and Football

2002. 20th-century World Cup Football Champions. Multicoloured.
2889 75c. Type **1084** . . . . . . 1·00 60
2890 75c. Argentine footballer . . 1·00 60

1085 Parana River and Emblem

2002. Anniversaries. Multicoloured.

2891	25c. Type **1085** (150th anniv of Rosario City)	35	20
2892	25c. National flag and monument	35	20
2893	50c. Mount Fitzroy (150th birth anniv of Francisco Pascasio Moreno (Perito) (explorer and founder of Argentine Scouts movement))	70	40
2894	50c. Dr. Moreno	70	40
2895	75c. Flower and view of city (centenary of foundation San Carlos de Bariloche)	1·00	60
2896	75c. Capilla San Eduardo (St. Edward's chapel) and city plan	1·00	60

BULK MAIL STAMPS

BP **999** Post Office Building, Buenos Aires

1999. Bulk Mail. Self-adhesive. Imperf.

BP2644	BP **999**	$7 black and blue	8·50	8·50
BP2645		$11 black and red	14·00	14·00
BP2646		$16 black and yellow	20·00	20·00
BP2647		$23 black and green	28·00	28·00

BP **1069**

2001. Bulk Mail. Additionally overprinted **UP.** Imperf.

BP2853	BP **1069**	$7 black and blue	8·50	8·50
BP2854		$11 black and red	14·00	14·00

EXPRESS SERVICE MAIL

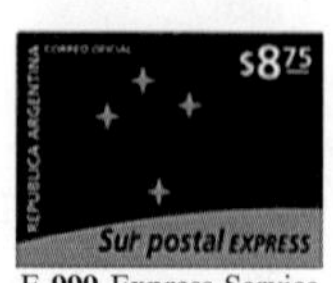
E **999** Express Service Emblem

1999. Self-adhesive.

E2644	E **999**	8p.75 blue and silver	12·00	9·50
E2645	–	17p.50 blue and gold	24·00	19·00

DESIGN: 24-hour service emblem.

No. E2644 was for express service mail and No. E2645 for use on 24-hour express service mail.

OFFICIAL STAMPS

1884. Optd **OFICIAL**.

O66	**33**	½c. brown	8·00	6·00
O69		1c. red	45	15
O70	**24**	2c. green	45	15
O71	–	4c. brown (No. 32)	45	15
O72	**9**	8c. red	45	15
O73	**10**	10c. green	42·00	22·00
O76	**33**	12c. blue	70	60
O77	**10**	16c. green	1·90	75
O78	**22**	20c. blue	8·00	6·00
O79	**11**	24c. blue (roul)	1·40	85
O80		24c. blue (perf)	1·25	70
O81	–	25c. red (No. 47)	9·50	6·50
O82	–	30c. orange (No. 33)	17·00	12·00
O83	–	60c. black (No. 34)	12·00	7·50
O84	–	90c. blue (No. 35)	8·50	6·50

O 73

1901.

O275	O **73**	1c. grey	25	10
O276		2c. brown	35	15
O277		5c. red	45	15
O278		10c. green	50	15
O279		30c. blue	3·50	85
O280		50c. orange	1·90	65

1938. (a) Optd **SERVICIO OFICIAL** in two lines.

O668	**143**	1c. brown (No. 645)	10	10
O669	–	2c. brown (No. 646)	10	10
O670	–	3c. green (No. 647)	10	10
O679	–	3c. grey (No. 672)	10	10
O771	–	3c. grey (No. 751)	3·00	1·25
O671	–	5c. brown (No. 653b)	10	10
O782	**200**	5c. red (No. 773)	10	10
O667	–	10c. red (No. 653d)	10	10
O773	–	10c. purple (No. 678)	10	10
O681	**146**	15c. blue (No. 676)	10	10
O774	–	15c. grey (No. 708)	10	10
O683	**146**	20c. blue (19½ × 26 mm)	50	10
O872	**247**	20c. red	10	10
O813	–	25c. (No. 673)	10	10
O674	–	40c. (No. 658)	10	10
O675	–	50c. (No. 659)	10	10
O676	**152**	1p. (No. 760)	10	10
O827	**234**	1p. (No. 826)	35	10
O778	–	2p. (No. 661)	10	10
O779	–	5p. (No. 662)	15	10
O780	–	10p. (No. 763)	25	10
O781	–	20p. (No. 764)	80	20

(b) Optd **SERVICIO OFICIAL** in one line.

O897	–	20c. lilac (No. 895)	15	10

1953. Eva Peron stamps optd **SERVICIO OFICIAL**.

O854	**239**	5c. grey	10	10
O855		10c. red	10	10
O856		20c. red	10	10
O857		25c. green	10	10
O858		40c. purple	10	10
O859		45c. blue	15	10
O860		50c. bistre	10	10
O862	**240**	1p. brown (No. 846)	10	10
O863		1p.50 green (No. 847)	25	10
O864		2p. red (No. 848)	20	10
O865		3p. blue (No. 849)	45	15
O866		5p. brown	70	40
O867	**239**	10p. red	4·00	3·00
O868	**240**	20p. green	32·00	20·00

1955. Stamps of 1954 optd **SERVICIO OFICIAL** in one line.

O869	**247**	20c. red	10	10
O870		40c. red	10	10
O880	–	1p. brown (No. 871)	10	10
O882	–	3p. purple (No. 874)	10	10
O883	–	5p. green (No. 875)	30	10
O884	–	10p. green and grey (No. 876)	40	10
O886	**250**	20p. violet	75	15

1955. Various stamps optd. (a) Optd **S. OFICIAL**.

O 896	–	5c. brown (No. 894)	10	10
O 955	–	10c. green (No. 946)	10	10
O 956	–	20c. purple (No. 947)	10	10
O 879	–	50c. blue (No. 868)	20	10
O 957	–	50c. ochre (No. 948)	10	10
O1034	–	1p. brn (No. 1016)	10	10
O 899	**264**	2p. purple	10	10
O1050	–	2p. red (No. 1035)	10	10
O 959	–	3p. blue (No. 951)	15	10
O1051	–	4p. red (No. 1036)	15	10
O 961	**296**	5p. brown	20	10
O1052	–	8p. red (No. 1037)	15	10
O 962	–	10p. brown (No. 1286)	15	10
O1053	–	10p. red (No. 1038)	15	10
O1036	–	12p. dull purple (No. 1028)	40	10
O 964	–	20p. green (No. 954)	50	10
O1055	–	20p. red (No. 1039)	20	10
O1037	–	22p. blue (No. 1018)	50	10
O1038	–	23p. green (No. 1019)	95	10
O1039	–	25p. lilac (No. 1020)	50	10
O1040	–	43p. lake (No. 1021)	1·40	65
O1041	–	45p. brn (No. 1022)	1·40	65
O1042	–	50p. blue (No. 1023)	2·40	95
O1043	–	50p. blue (No. 1287)	3·25	95
O1045	–	100p. blue (No. 1289)	1·60	65
O1046	–	300p. violet (No. 1026)	4·75	2·25

(b) Optd **SERVICIO OFICIAL**.

O 900	**265**	2p.40 brown	20	10
O 958	–	3p. blue (No. 951)	15	10
O 901	**266**	4p.40 green	25	10
O 960	**296**	5p. brown	20	10
O 887	–	50p. ind & bl (No. 878)	1·60	65
O1049	–	500p. grn (No. 1032)	7·75	3·75

For lists of stamps optd **M.A.**, **M.G.**, **M.H.**, **M.I.**, **M.J.I.**, **M.M.**, **M.O.P.** or **M.R.C.** for use in ministerial offices see the Stanley Gibbons Catalogue Part 20 (South America).

1963. Nos. 1068, etc., optd **S. OFICIAL**.

O1076	**351**	2p. green	20	10
O1080	–	4p. red (No. 1069)	15	10
O1081	–	6p. red (No. 1070)	25	10
O1078	–	90p. bistre (No. 1288)	4·00	2·00

RECORDED MESSAGE STAMPS

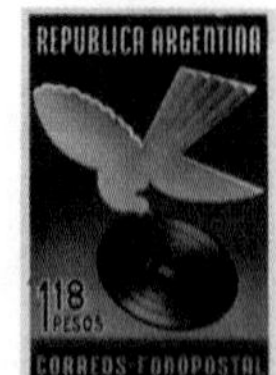
RM **166** Winged Messenger

1939. Various symbolic designs inscr "CORREOS FONOPOSTAL".

RM688	RM **166**	1p.18 blue	16·00	8·00
RM689	–	1p.32 blue	16·00	8·00
RM690	–	1p.50 brown	48·00	24·00

DESIGNS—VERT: 1p.32, Head of Liberty and National Arms. HORIZ: 1p.50, Record and winged letter.

TELEGRAPH STAMPS USED FOR POSTAGE

PT **34**

PT **35** (Sun closer to "NACIONAL")

1887.

PT104	PT **34**	10c. red	50	10
PT105	PT **35**	10c. red	50	10
PT106	PT **34**	40c. blue	60	10
PT107	PT **35**	40c. blue	60	15

ARMENIA Pt. 10

Formerly part of Transcaucasian Russia. Temporarily independent after the Russian revolution of 1917. From 12 March 1922, Armenia, Azerbaijan and Georgia formed the Transcaucasian Federation. Issues for the federation were superseded by those of the Soviet Union in 1924.

With the dissolution of the Soviet Union in 1991 Armenia once again became independent.

NOTE. Only one price is given for Nos. 3/245, which applies to unused or cancelled to order. Postally used copies are worth more.

All the overprints and surcharges were handstamped and consequently were applied upright or inverted indiscriminately, some occurring only inverted.

1919. 100 kopeks = 1 rouble.
1994. 100 luna = 1 dram.

NATIONAL REPUBLIC

28 May 1918 to 2 December 1920 and 18 February to 2 April 1921.

1919. Arms type of Russia and unissued Postal Savings Bank stamp (No. 6) surch. Imperf or perf. (a) Surch thus **k. 60 k** with or without stops.

3 22 60k. on 1k. orange 40
6 – 60k. on 1k. red on buff 10·00

(b) Surch in figures only.

7 22 60k. on 1k. orange 30·00
8 120k. on 1k. orange 30·00

(6)

(8)

1919. Stamps of Russia optd as T 6 in various sizes, with or without frame. Imperf or perf. (a) Arms types.

53B 22 1k. orange 13·00
54B 2k. green 50
55B 3k. red 50
11B 23 4k. red 25
12B 22 5k. red 25
13B 23 10k. blue 40
14B 22 10k. on 7k. blue 30
15B 10 15k. blue and purple 35
16B 14 20k. red and blue 30
17 10 25k. mauve and green 60
45B 35k. green and purple 50
19B 14 50k. green and purple 20
30B 22 60k. on 1k. orange (No. 3) 50
31B 10 70k. orange and brown 30
32B 15 1r. orange and brown 50
33B 11 3r.50 green and brown 1·00
23B 20 5r. green and blue 1·40
62 11 7r. yellow and black 25·00
24B 7r. pink and green 2·50
52B 20 10r. grey, red and yellow 3·00

(b) Romanov type.

63B 4k. red (No. 129) 2·00

(c) Unissued Postal Savings Bank stamp.

64A 1k. red on buff 3·50

1920. Stamps of Russia surch as T 8 in various types and sizes. Imperf or perf. (a) Arms types.

94B 22 1r. on 60k. on 1k. orange (No. 3) 80
65B 1r. on 1k. orange 50
66B 3r. on 3k. red 50
67B 3r. on 4k. red 6·00
97B 5r. on 2k. green 60
69B 23 5r. on 4k. red 1·00
70B 22 5r. on 5k. red 50
71B 5r. on 7k. blue 1·00
72B 23 5r. on 10k. blue 40
73B 22 5r. on 10 on 7k. blue 90
74B 10 5r. on 14k. red and blue 2·25
75B 5r. on 15k. blue and purple 75
76B 14 5r. on 20k. red and blue 1·25
76aB 10 5r. on 20 on 14k. red and blue 7·00
77B 5r. on 25k. mauve and green 7·00
111B 22 5r. on 3 r .on 5k. red 7·50
78B 10 10r. on 25k. mauve and green 1·00
79B 10r. on 35k. green and purple 65
80B 14 10r. on 50k. green and purple 1·00
80aB 9 25r. on 1k. orange 35·00
80bB 25r. on 3k. red 35·00
80cB 25r. on 5k. purple 35·00
80dB 22 25r. on 10 on 7k. blue 35·00
80eB 10 25r. on 15k. blue and purple 35·00
81B 14 25r. on 20k. red and blue 4·00
82B 10 25r. on 25k. mauve and green 4·00
83B 25r. on 35k. green and purple 3·50
84B 14 25r. on 50k. green and purple 3·50
85B 10 25r. on 70k. orange and brown 4·00
104aB 9 50r. on 1k. orange 32·00
104bB 50r. on 3k. red 32·00
85bB 10 50r. on 4k. red 38·00
104cB 14 50r. on 5k. purple 32·00
85cB 10 50r. on 15k. blue and purple 38·00
85dB 14 50r. on 20k. red and blue 38·00
85eB 10 50r. on 35k. green & purple 38·00
85fB 14 50r. on 50k. green & purple 20·00
105B 10 50r. on 70k. orange and brown 4·50
106B 15 50r. on 1r. orange and brown 1·10
107B 100r. on 1r. orange and brown 6·50
108B 11 100r. on 3r.50 green and brown 4·50
88B 20 100r. on 5r. green and blue 5·00
89B 11 100r. on 7r. yellow and black 20·00
90B 100r. on 7r. pink and green 6·75
93B 20 100r. on 10r. grey, red and yellow 6·00

(b) Romanov issue of 1913.

112 1r. on 1k. orange 7·00
113 3r. on 3k. red 5·00
114 5r. on 4k. red 3·50
115 5r. on 10 on 7k. brown 3·50
116 5r. on 14k. green 22·00
117 5r. on 20 on 14k. green 5·00
118 25r. on 4k. red 5·00
118a 100r. on 1k. orange 50·00
119 100r. on 2k. green 50·00
120 100r. on 3r. violet 55·00

(c) War Charity issues of 1914 and 1915.

121 15 25r. on 1k. green and red on yellow 38·00
122 25r. on 3k. green and red on rose 30·00
123 50r. on 7k. green and brown on buff 24·00
124 50r. on 10k. brown and blue 24·00
125 100r. on 1k. green and red on yellow 24·00
126 100r. on 1k. grey and brown 24·00
127 100r. on 3k. green and red on rose 24·00
128 100r. on 7k. green and brown on buff 24·00
129 100r. on 10k. brown and blue 24·00

1920. Arms types of Russia optd as T 6 in various sizes with or without frame, and surch as T 8 or with value only in various types and sizes. Imperf or perf.

155B 22 1r. on 60k. on 1k. orange (No. 3) 1·10
156A 3r. on 3k. red 1·50
157A 5r. on 2k. green 90
141A 23 5r. on 4k. red 3·00
158A 22 5r. on 5k. red 2·75
142A 23 5r. on 10k. blue 3·00
143A 22 5r. on 10 on 7k. blue 3·00
144A 10 5r. on 15k. blue & pur 1·25
145A 14 5r. on 20k. red and blue 1·25
132B 10 10r. on 15k. blue & pur 7·50
145aB 14 10r. on 20k. red & blue 9·00
146A 10 10r. on 25k. mauve and green 1·25
147B 10r. on 35k. green and purple 1·00
148A 14 10r. on 50k. green and purple 2·50
159A 10 10r. on 70k. orange and brown 8·75
163A 22 10r. on 5r. on 5k. red 18·00
164A 10 10r. on 5r. on 25k. mauve and green 20·00
165A 10r. on 5r. on 35k. green and purple 6·50
138A 25r. on 70k. orange and brown 5·00
161B 15 50r. on 1r. orange and brown 1·75
135B 11 100r. on 3r.50 green and brown 1·75
151A 20 100r. on 5r. green & bl 6·00
136A 11 100r. on 7r. pink and green 5·00
154aA 20 100r. on 10r. grey, red and yellow 8·00
166A 100r. on 25r. on 5r. green and blue 18·00

1920. Stamps of Russia optd as T 6 in various sizes, with or without frame and surch **10**. Perf. (a) Arms types.

168 14 10 on 20k. red and blue 18·00
169 10 10 on 25k. mauve and green 18·00
170 10 on 35k. green and purple 12·00
171 14 10 on 50k. green and purple 14·00

(b) Romanov type.

172 10 on 4k. red (No. 129) 30·00

1920. Stamps of Russia optd with monogram as in T 8 in various types and sizes and surch **10**. Imperf or perf. (a) Arms types.

173 23 10 on 4k. red 30·00
174 22 10 on 5k. red 30·00
175 10 10 on 15k. blue & purple 30·00
176 14 10 on 20k. red and blue 28·00
176a 10 10 on 20 on 14k. red and blue 14·00
177 10 on 25k. mauve & green 14·00
178 10 on 35k. green & purple 14·00
179 14 10 on 50k. green & purple 14·00

(b) Romanov type.

181 10 on 4k. red (No. 129) 38·00

11

12 Mt. Ararat

Stamps in Types **11**, **12** and a similar horizontal type showing a woman spinning were printed in Paris to the order of the Armenian National Government, but were not issued in Armenia as the Bolshevists had assumed control. (Price 10p. each).

SOVIET REPUBLIC

2 December 1920 to 18 February 1921 and 2 April 1921 to 12 March 1922.

(13)

1921. Arms types of Russia surch with T **13**. Perf.

182 15 5000r. on 1r. orange and brown 5·00
183 11 5000r. on 3r.50 grn & brn 5·00
184 20 5000r. on 5r. green & blue 5·00
185 11 5000r. on 7r. pink and green 5·00
186 20 5000r. on 10r. grey, red & yellow 5·00

14 Common Crane

16 Village Scene

1922. Unissued stamps surch in gold kopeks. Imperf.

187 14 1 on 250r. red 13·50
188 1 on 250r. slate 21·00
189 16 2 on 500r. red 4·50
190 3 on 500r. slate 1·50
191 – 4 on 1000r. red 2·75
192 – 4 on 1000r. slate 6·00
193 – 5 on 2000r. slate 24·00
194 – 10 on 2000r. red 24·00
195 – 15 on 5000r. red 12·00
196 – 20 on 5000r. slate 3·00

DESIGNS (sizes in mm): 1000r. Woman at well (17 × 26); 2000r. Erivan railway station (35 × 24½); 5000r. Horseman and Mt. Ararat (39½ × 24½).

17 Soviet Emblems

18 Wall Sculpture at Ani

19 Mt. Aragatz

1922. Unissued stamps as T **17/19** surch in gold kopeks in figures. Imperf or perf.

210 17 1 on 1r. green 3·00
198 18 2 on 2r. slate 7·50
212 – 3 on 3r. red 12·00
213 – 4 on 25r. green 2·50
201 – 5 on 50r. red 3·00
215 – 10 on 100r. orange 4·00
203 – 15 on 250r. blue 2·00
204a 19 20 on 500r. purple 2·50
205 – 35 on 20,000r. red 18·00
206a – 50 on 25,000r. green 28·00
209 – 50r. on 25,000r. blue 4·00

DESIGNS (sizes in mm): 3r. (29 × 22) and 250r. (21 × 35) Soviet emblems; 25r. (30 × 22½); 100r. (34½ × 23) and 20,000r. (43 × 27) Mythological sculptures, Ani. 50r. (25½ × 37). Armenian soldier; 25,000r. (45½ × 27½) Mt. Ararat.

The above and other values were not officially issued without the surcharges.

TRANSCAUCASIAN FEDERATION ISSUES FOR ARMENIA

1923. As T 19, etc., surch in gold kopeks in figures. Imperf or perf.

219 – 1 on 250r. blue 3·00
217 19 2 on 500r. purple 3·00
218 – 3 on 20000r. lake 8·50

26 Mt. Ararat and Soviet Emblems

28 Ploughing

1923. Unissued stamps in various designs as T **26/28** surch in Transcaucasian roubles in figures. Perf.

227 26 10,000r. on 50r. green and red 1·50
228 – 15,000r. on 300r. blue and buff 1·50
229 – 25,000r. on 400r. blue and pink 1·50
240B – 30,000r. on 500r. violet and lilac 1·50
231 – 50,000r. on 1000r. blue 1·50
232 – 75,000r. on 3000r. black and green 1·75
233 – 100,000r. on 2000r. black and grey 2·00
243 – 200,000r. on 4000r. black and brn 1·00
235 – 300,000r. on 5000r. black and red 2·75
245 28 500,000r. on 10,000r. black and red 1·25

DESIGNS (sizes in mm): 300r. (26 × 35) Star over Mt. Ararat; 400r. (26 × 34½) Soviet emblems; 500r. (26 × 34½) Crane (bird); 1000r. (19 × 25) Peasant in print; 2000r. (26 × 31) Human-headed bird from old bas-relief; 3000r. (26½ × 36) Sower; 4000r. (26 × 31½) Star and dragon; 5000r. (26 × 32) Blacksmith.

INDEPENDENT REPUBLIC

31 Mount Ararat and National Colours

1992. Independence Day.

246 31 20k. multicoloured 15 15
247 2r. multicoloured 90 90
248 5r. multicoloured 2·10 2·10

32 Dish Aerial and World Map

1992. Inauguration of International Direct-dial Telephone System.

250 32 50k. multicoloured 1·25 1·25

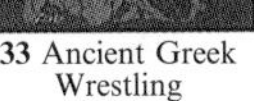
33 Ancient Greek Wrestling

34 National Flag

1992. Olympic Games, Barcelona. Multicoloured.

251 40k. Type **33** 10 10
252 3r.60 Boxing 30 30
253 5r. Weightlifting 35 35
254 12r. Gymnastics (ring exercises) 75 75

1992.

255 34 20k. multicoloured (postage) 10 10
256 – 1r. black 10 10
257 – 3r. brown 25 25
258 – 3r. brown 10 10
259 – 5r. black 40 40

260 – 20r. grey 25 25
261 – 2r. blue (air) 35 35
DESIGNS: 1r. Goddess Waroubini statuette from Orgov radio-optical telescope; 2r. Zvartnots Airport, Yerevan; 3r. (No. 257) Goddess Anahit; 3r. (No. 258) Runic inscription Karmir-Blour; 5r. U.P.U. Monument, Berne, Switzerland; 20r. Silver cup from Karashamb.
See also Nos. 275/82.

36 Engraved 10th-century Tombstone, Makenis

37 Garni Canyon

1993. Armenian Cultural History. Multicoloured.
263 40k. Type **36** 10 10
264 80k. Illuminated page from Gospel of 1295 . . . . 15 15
265 3r.60 13th-century bas-relief, Gandzasar 60 60
266 5r. "Glorious Mother of God" (18th-century painting, H. Hovnatanian) 1·00 1·00

1993. Landscapes. Multicoloured.
268 40k. Type **37** 10 10
269 80k. Shaki Falls, Zangezur 10 10
270 3r.60 River Arpa gorge, Vike 25 25
271 5r. Lake Sevan (horiz) . . . 40 40
272 12r. Mount Ararat (horiz) 90 90

38 Temple of Garni

39 Reliquary for Arm of St. Thaddeus (17th century)

1993. "YEREVAN '93" International Stamp Exn.
273 **38** 10r. red, black and brown 35 35

1994. As T **34** but new currency.
275 10l. agate and brown 10 10
277 50l. deep brown and brown 10 10
280 10d. brown and grey 25 25
282 25d. gold and red 75 75
DESIGNS: 10l. Shivini, Sun God (Karmir-Blour); 50l. Tayshaba, God of the Elements (Karmir-Blour); 10d. Khaldi, Supreme God (Karmir-Blour); 25d. National arms.

1994. Treasures of Etchmiadzin (seat of Armenian church). Multicoloured.
286 3d. Descent from the Cross (9th-century wooden panel) 10 10
287 5d. Gilded silver reliquary of Holy Cross of Khotakerats (1300) 10 10
288 12d. Cross with St. Karapet's right hand (14th century) 20 20
289 30d. Type **39** 65 65
290 50d. Gilded silver chrism vessel (1815) 90 90

(**40**)

(**41**)

1994. Stamp Exhibitions, Yerevan. (a) "Armenia '94" National Exn. No. 273 surch with T **40**.
291 **38** 40d. on 10r. red, blk & brn 1·00 1·00
(b) "Armenia–Argentina" Exhibition. No. 273 surch with T **41**.
292 **38** 40d. on 10r. red, blk & brn 1·00 1·00

42 Cancelled Stamps of 1919

43 Stadium and Arms of National Committee

1994. 75th Anniv of First Stamp Issue.
293 **42** 16d. multicoloured 30 30

1994. Olympic Committees. Multicoloured.
294 30d. Type **43** 15 15
295 40d. Olympic rings (centenary of Int Olympic Committee) 20 20

44 Haroutune Shmavonian

45 Ervand Otian

1994. Bicentenary of "Azdarar" (first Armenian periodical).
296 **44** 30d. brown and green . . . 30 30

1994. 125th Birth Anniversaries.
297 **45** 50d. drab and brown . . . 40 40
298 – 50d. brown 40 40
DESIGN—HORIZ: 50d. Levon Shant.

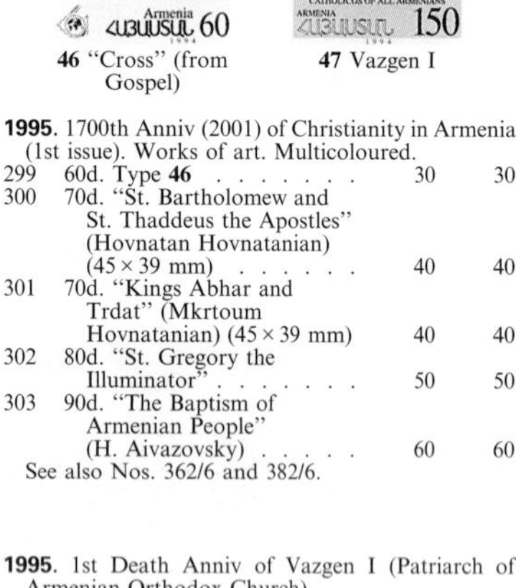

46 "Cross" (from Gospel)

47 Vazgen I

1995. 1700th Anniv (2001) of Christianity in Armenia (1st issue). Works of art. Multicoloured.
299 60d. Type **46** 30 30
300 70d. "St. Bartholomew and St. Thaddeus the Apostles" (Hovnatan Hovnatanian) (45 × 39 mm) 40 40
301 70d. "Kings Abhar and Trdat" (Mkrtoum Hovnatanian) (45 × 39 mm) 40 40
302 80d. "St. Gregory the Illuminator" 50 50
303 90d. "The Baptism of Armenian People" (H. Aivazovsky) 60 60
See also Nos. 362/6 and 382/6.

1995. 1st Death Anniv of Vazgen I (Patriarch of Armenian Orthodox Church).
305 **47** 150d. black and grey . . . 70 70

48 Black-polished Pottery

49 Red Kite and Oak

1995. Museum Artefacts (1st series). Multicoloured.
306 30d. Type **48** 10 10
307 60d. Silver horn 20 20
308 130d. Gohar carpet 50 50
See also Nos. 332/4.

1995. Birds and Trees. Multicoloured.
309 40d. Type **49** 60 60
310 60d. Golden eagle and juniper 80 80

50 Workers building "Honeycomb" Map

1995. Hyastan All-Armenian Fund.
311 **50** 90d. multicoloured 40 40

51 Rainbows around U.N. Emblem

1995. 50th Anniv of U.N.O.
312 **51** 90d. multicoloured 40 40

52 Commander P. Kitsook (408th Rifle Division)

1995. 50th Anniv of End of Second World War.
(a) Size 40 × 23 mm. Each black, orange and blue.
313 60d. Type **52** 30 30
314 60d. Commanders S. Chernikov, N. Tavartkeladze and V. Penkovsky (76th Mountain Rifle Red-banner (51st Guard) Division) . . 30 30
315 60d. Commanders S. Zakian, H. Babayan and I. Lyudnikov (390th Rifle Division) 30 30
316 60d. Commanders A. Vasilian, A. Dobrovolsky, Y. Grechany and G. Sorokin (409th Rifle Division) 30 30
317 60d. Commanders A. Sargissian and N. Safarian (89th Taman Triple Order Bearer Rifle Division) 30 30
(b) Size 23 × 35 mm. Each blue, orange and brown.
318 60d. Marshal Hovhannes Baghramian 35 35
319 60d. Admiral Hovhannes Issakov 35 35
320 60d. General Marshal Hamazasp Babajanian . . 35 35
321 60d. Marshal Sergey Khoudyakov 35 35

53 Ghevond Alishan (historian and geographer)

1995. Writers' Anniversaries.
323 **53** 90d. green and black . . . 45 45
324 – 90d. sepia, brown & yellow 45 45
325 – 90d. blue and red 45 45
DESIGNS: No. 323, Type **53** (175th birth); 324, Grigor Artsruni (journalist, 150th birth); 325, Franz Werfel (50th death).

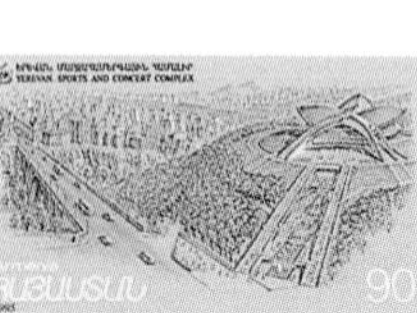

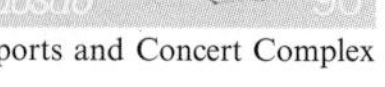

54 Sports and Concert Complex

55 Katsian and Spectators watching Flight

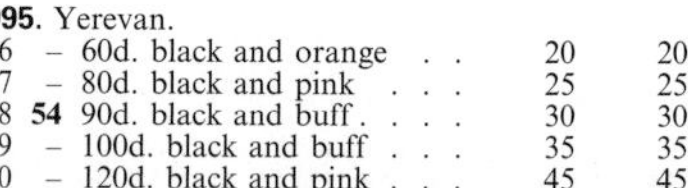

1995. Yerevan.
326 – 60d. black and orange . . 20 20
327 – 80d. black and pink . . . 25 25
328 **54** 90d. black and buff 30 30
329 – 100d. black and buff . . . 35 35
330 – 120d. black and pink . . . 45 45

DESIGNS—As T **54**: 60d. Brandy distillery and wine cellars; 80d. Abovian Street; 400d. Panoramic view of Yerevan. 60 × 23 mm: 100d. Baghramian Avenue; 120d. Republic Square.

1995. Museum Artefacts (2nd series). As T **48**. Mult.
332 40d. Four-wheeled carriages (horiz) 10 10
333 60d. Bronze model of solar system 20 20
334 90d. Tombstone from Loriberd 35 35

1995. Air. 86th Anniv of Artiom Katsian's 1909 World Record for Range and Altitude.
335 **55** 90d. ochre, brown and blue 50 50

(**56**)

57 Griboedov

1996. No. 275 surch as T **56**.
336 40d. on 10l. agate and brown 50 50
337 100d. on 10l. agate and brown . . . . 1·40 1·40
338 150d. on 10l. agate and brown . . . . 1·90 1·90
339 200d. on 10l. agate and brown . . . . 2·50 2·50

1996. Birth Bicentenary of Aleksandr Griboedov (historian).
340 **57** 90d. stone, brown and red 35 35

58 Hayrik Khrimian (patriarch of Armenian Orthodox Church, 175th birth anniv (1995))

1996. Anniversaries.
341 **58** 90d. blue & brn (postage) 35 35
342 – 90d. multicoloured 35 35
343 – 90d. grey, blue & red (air) 35 35
DESIGNS—HORIZ: No. 342, Lazar Serebryakov (Admiral of the Fleet, and 19th-century Russian warships, birth bicentenary (1995)). VERT: No. 343, Nelson Stepanian (Second World War pilot, 50th death anniv (1994)).

59 Opening Frame from First Armenian Film

1996. Centenary of Motion Pictures.
344 **59** 60d. black, grey and blue 50 75

60 Angel and Red Cross

61 Wild Goats

1996. 75th Anniv of Armenian Red Cross Society.
345 **60** 60d. multicoloured 30 30

1996. Mammals. Multicoloured.
346 40d. Type **61** 25 25
347 60d. Leopards 30 30

62 Nansen and "Fram"

1996. Centenary of Return of Fridtjof Nansen's Arctic Expedition.
348 **62** 90d. multicoloured 40 40

63 Cycling **64** Torch Bearer

1996. Olympic Games, Atlanta. Multicoloured.
349 40d. Type **63** 20 20
350 60d. Triple jumping 30 30
351 90d. Wrestling 40 40
Nos. 349/51 were issued together, se-tenant, the backgrounds forming a composite design showing ancient Greek athletes.

1996. Centenary of Modern Olympic Games.
352 **64** 60d. multicoloured 30 30

65 Genrikh Kasparian (first prize winner, "Chess in USSR" competition, 1939) **66** Tigran Petrosian (World chess champion, 1963–69) and Tigran Petrosian Chess House, Yerevan

1996. 32nd Chess Olympiad, Yerevan. Designs showing positions from previous games. Mult.
353 40d. Type **65** 40 40
354 40d. Tigran Petrosian v. Mikhail Botvinnik (World Championship, Moscow, 1963) 40 40
355 40d. Gary Kasparov v. Anatoly Karpov (World Championship, Leningrad, 1986) 40 40
356 40d. Olympiad emblem . . . 40 40

1996.
357 **66** 90d. multicoloured 50 50

67 Goats

1996. The Wild Goat. Multicoloured.
358 70d. Type **67** 30 30
359 100d. Lone female 40 40
360 130d. Lone male 50 50
361 350d. Heads of male and female . . . . 1·40 1·40

68 Church of the Holy Mother, Samarkand, Uzbekistan

1997. 1700th Anniv (2001) of Christianity in Armenia (2nd issue). Armenian Apostolic Overseas Churches. Multicoloured.
362 100d. Type **68** 35 35
363 100d. Church of the Holy Mother, Kishinev, Moldova 35 35
364 100d. St. Hripsime's Church, Yalta, Ukraine 35 35
365 100d. St. Catherine's Church, St. Petersburg, Russia . . . 35 35
366 100d. Church, Lvov, Ukraine 35 35

69 Man operating Printing Press

1997. 225th Anniv of First Printing Press in Armenia.
368 **69** 70d. multicoloured 35 35

70 Jivani and Mount Ararat

1997. 150th Birth Anniv of Jivani (folk singer).
369 **70** 90d. multicoloured 35 35

71 Babajanian and Score of "Heroic Ballad"

1997. 75th Birth Anniv (1996) of Arno Babajanian (composer and pianist).
370 **71** 90d. black, lilac & purple 35 35

72 Countryside (Gevorg Bashinjaghian)

1997. Exhibits in National Gallery of Armenia (1st series). Multicoloured.
371 150d. Type **72** 50 50
372 150d. "One of My Dreams" (Eghishe Tadevossian) . . 50 50
373 150d. "Portrait of Natalia Tehumian" (Hakob Hovnatanian) (vert) . . . 50 50
374 150d. "Salome" (Vardges Sureniants) (vert) 50 50
See also Nos. 390/2 and 512/13.

73 Mamulian **74** St. Basil's Cathedral, Moscow

1997. Birth Centenary of Rouben Mamulian (film director).
375 **73** 150d. multicoloured . . . 45 45

1997. "Moscow 97" Int Stamp Exhibition.
376 **74** 170d. multicoloured . . . 55 55

75 Hayk and Bel **76** Charents

1997. Europa. Tales and Legends. Multicoloured.
377 170d. Type **75** 55 55
378 250d. The Song of Vahagn 75 75

1997. Birth Centenary of Eghishe Charents (poet).
379 **76** 150d. brown and red . . . 45 45

77 "Iris lycotis" **78** St. Gregory the Illuminator Cathedral, Anthelias, Libya

1997. Irises. Multicoloured.
380 40d. Type **77** 15 15
381 170d. "Iris elegantissima" . . 55 55

1997. 1700th Anniv (2001) of Christianity in Armenia (3rd issue). Armenian Overseas Educational Centres. Multicoloured.
382 100d. Type **78** 30 30
383 100d. St. Khach Armenian Church, Nakhijevan, Rostov-on-Don 30 30
384 100d. St. James's Monastery, Jerusalem (horiz) 30 30
385 100d. Nercissian School, Tblisi, Georgia (60 × 21 mm) 30 30
386 100d. San Lazzaro Mekhitarian Congregation, Venice (horiz) 30 30

79 Baby Jesus, Angel and Mary **80** Eagle and Demonstrator with Flag

1997. Christmas.
388 **79** 40d. multicoloured 15 15

1998. 10th Anniv of Karabakh Movement.
389 **80** 250d. multicoloured . . . 75 75

1998. Exhibits in National Gallery of Armenia (2nd series). As T **72**. Multicoloured.
390 150d. "Family. Generations" (Yervand Kochar) (vert) 45 45
391 150d. "Tartar Women's Dance" (Alexander Bazhbeouk-Melikian) . . . 45 45
392 150d. "Spring in Our Yard" (Haroutiun Kalents) (vert) 45 45

81 Diana, Princess of Wales **82** Eiffel Tower, Ball and Pitch

1998. Diana, Princess of Wales Commemoration.
393 **81** 250d. multicoloured . . . 75 75

1998. World Cup Football Championship, France.
394 **82** 250d. multicoloured . . . 75 75

83 Couple leaping through Flames (Trndez)

1998. Europa. National Festivals. Multicoloured.
395 170d. Type **83** 55 55
396 250d. Girls in traditional costume (Ascension) . . . 75 75

84 Southern Swallowtail **85** Ayrarat Couple

1998. Insects. Multicoloured.
397 170d. Type **84** 55 55
398 250d. "Rethera komarovi" (moth) 75 75

1998. Traditional Costumes (1st series). Mult.
399 170d. Type **85** 55 55
400 250d. Vaspurakan family . . 75 75
See also Nos. 408/9.

87 Fissure in Earth's Surface

1998. 10th Anniv of Armenian Earthquake.
402 **87** 250d. black, red and lilac 75 75

88 Pyrite

1998. Minerals. Multicoloured.
403 170d. Type **88** 55 55
404 250d. Agate 75 75

89 Briusov **91** Khosrov Reserve

1998. 125th Birth Anniv of Valery Briusov (Russian translator of Armenian works).
405 **89** 90d. multicoloured 35 35

1999. Traditional Costumes (2nd series). As T **85**.
408 170d. Mother and child from Karin 40 40
409 250d. Zangezour couple . . . 60 60

1999. Europa. Parks and Gardens. Multicoloured.
410 170d. Type **91** 40 40
411 250d. Dilijan Reserve 60 60

92 Anniversary Emblem on Flag

1999. 50th Anniv of Council of Europe.
412 **92** 170d. multicoloured . . . 40 40

93 Medieval Kogge and Map

1999. Ships of the Armenian Kingdom of Cilicia (11–14th centuries). Multicoloured.
413 170d. Type **93** 40 40
414 250d. Medieval single-masted sailing ships 60 60
415 250d. As No. 414 but with emblem of "Philexfrance 99" International Stamp Exhibition, Paris, France, in lower right corner . . . 60 60

94 Armenian Gampr

1999. Domestic Pets. Multicoloured.
416 170d. Type **94** 40 40
417 250d. Turkish van cat 60 60
418 250d. As No. 417 but with emblem of "China 1999" International Stamp Exhibition, Peking, China, in lower right corner 60 60

97 House made of Envelopes

1999. 125th Anniv of Universal Postal Union.
421 **97** 270d. multicoloured 65 65

98 Karen Demirchyan (Speaker of the National Assembly)

2000. Commemoration of Victims of Attack on National Assembly. Multicoloured.
422 250d. Type **98** 60 60
423 250d. Vazgen Sargsyan (Prime Minister) 60 60

99 Sevan Trout

101 "Building Europe"

100 The Liar Hunter

2000. Fishes. Multicoloured.
425 50d. Type **99** 10 10
426 270d. Sevan barbel 70 70

2000. National Fairy Tales. Multicoloured.
427 70d. Type **100** 15 15
428 130d. The King and the Peddler 30 30

2000. Europa.
429 **101** 40d. multicoloured 10 10
430 500d. multicoloured 1·25 1·25

103 Basketball

2000. Olympic Games, Sydney. Multicoloured.
432 10d. Type **103** 10 10
433 30d. Tennis 10 10
434 500d. Weightlifting 1·25 1·25

104 Quartz

2000. Minerals. Multicoloured.
435 170d. Type **104** 40 40
436 250d. Molybdenite 60 60

105 Shnorhali

106 Adoration of the Magi

2000. 900th Birth Anniv of Nerses Shnorhali (writer and musician).
437 **105** 270d. multicoloured 70 70

2000. Christmas.
438 **106** 170d. multicoloured 40 40

107 Issahakian

2000. 125th Birth Anniv of Avetik Issahakian (poet).
439 **107** 130d. multicoloured 30 30

108 Dhol

109 Viktor Hambartsoumian (astrophysicist)

2000. Musical Instruments. Multicoloured.
440 170d. Type **108** 40 40
441 250d. Duduk (wind instrument) 60 60

2000. New Millennium. Famous Armenians. Mult.
442 110d. Type **109** 25 25
443 110d. Abraham Alikhanov (physicist) 25 25
444 110d. Andranik Iossifan (electrical engineer) 25 25
445 110d. Sargis Saltikov (metallurgist) 25 25
446 110d. Samval Kochariants (electrical engineer) 25 25
447 110d. Artem Mikoyan (aircraft designer) 25 25
448 110d. Norayr Sisisakian (biochemist) 25 25
449 110d. Ivan Knunyants (chemist) 25 25
450 110d. Nikoghayos Yenikolopian (physical chemist) 25 25
451 110d. Nikoghayos Adonts (historian) 25 25
452 110d. Manouk Abeghian (folklore scholar) 25 25
453 110d. Hovhannes Toumanian (poet) 25 25
454 110d. Hrachya Ajarian (linguist) 25 25
455 110d. Gevorg Emin (poet) 25 25
456 110d. Yervand Lalayan (anthropologist) 25 25
457 110d. Daniel Varoujan (poet) 25 25
458 110d. Paruyr Sevak (poet) 25 25
459 110d. William Saroyan (dramatist and novelist) 25 25
460 110d. Hamo Beknazarian (film director) 25 25
461 110d. Alexandre Tamanian (architect) 25 25
462 110d. Vahram Papazian (actor) 25 25
463 110d. Vasil Tahirov (viticulturist) 25 25
464 110d. Leonid Yengibarian (mime artist) 25 25
465 110d. Haykanoush Danielian (singer) 25 25
466 110d. Sergo Hambartsoumian (weight lifter) 25 25
467 110d. Hrant Shahinian (gymnast) 25 25
468 110d. Toros Toramanian (architect) 25 25
469 110d. Komitas (composer) 25 25
470 110d. Aram Khachatourian (composer) 25 25
471 110d. Martiros Sarian (artist) 25 25
472 110d. Avet Terterian (composer) 25 25
473 110d. Alexandre Spendiarian (composer) 25 25
474 110d. Arshile Gorky (artist) 25 25
475 110d. Minas Avetissian (artist) 25 25
476 110d. (Levon Orbeli physiologist) 25 25
477 110d. Hripsimeh Simonian (ceramics artist) 25 25

111 Narekatsi and Text

2001. Millenary of A Record of Lamentations by Grigor Narekatsi.
479 **111** 25d. multicoloured 10 10

112 Lake Sevan

2001. Europa. Water Resources. Multicoloured.
480 50d. Type **112** 10 10
481 500d. Spandarian Reservoir 1·25 1·25

113 Emblem

2001. Armenian Membership of Council of Europe.
482 **113** 240d. multicoloured 55 55

115 Persian Squirrel

2001. Endangered Species. Persian Squirrel (*Sciurus persicus*). Multicoloured.
484 40d. Type **115** 10 10
485 50d. Adult sitting on branch with young in tree hole 10 10
486 80d. Head of squirrel 20 20
487 120d. On ground 30 30

116 Cathedral Facade

2001. 1700th Anniv of Christianity in Armenia (7th issue). St. Gregory the Illuminator Cathedral, Yerevan. Multicoloured.
488 50d. Type **116** 10 10
489 205d. Interior elevation of Cathedral (44 × 30 mm) 50 50
490 240d. Exterior elevation of Cathedral (44 × 30 mm) 55 55

117 Lazarian and Institute

2001. Death Bicentenary of Hovhannes Lazarian (founder of Institute of Oriental Languages, Moscow).
491 **117** 300d. multicoloured 75 75
A stamp in a similar design was issued by Russia.

2001. Traditional Costumes (3rd series). As T **85**. Multicoloured.
492 50d. Javakhch couple 10 10
493 250d. Artzakh couple 60 60

118 Emblem

119 Children encircling Globe

2001. 6th World Wushu Championships, Yerevan.
494 **118** 180d. black 40 40

2001. United Nations Year of Dialogue among Civilizations.
495 **119** 275d. multicoloured 65 65

120 Emblem

2001. 10th Anniv of Commonwealth of Independent States.
496 **120** 205d. multicoloured 50 50

121 Profiles

2001. European Year of Languages.
497 **121** 350d. multicoloured 85 85

122 Flag

2001. 10th Anniv of Independence.
498 **122** 300d. multicoloured 70 70

123 Cart

2001. Transport. Multicoloured.
499 180d. Type **123** 40 40
500 205d. Phaeton 50 50

124 *Hypericum perforatum*

125 Eagle

2001. Medicinal Plants. Multicoloured.
501 85d. Type **124** 20 20
502 205d. *Thymus serpyllum* 50 50

2002.
503 **125** 10d. brown 10 10
504 25d. green 10 10
506 50d. blue 10 10

126 Calendar Belt (2000 B.C.) and Copper Works

2002. Traditional Production. Multicoloured.
510 120d. Type **126** 25 25
511 350d. Beer vessels (7th century B.C.) and modern brewing equipment 75 75

2002. Exhibits in National Gallery of Armenia (3rd series). Vert designs as T **72**.
512 200d. black, grey and green 40 40
513 200d. black, grey and red 40 40
DESIGNS: No. 512, "Lily" (Edgar Chahine); 513, "Salome" (sculpture, Hakob Gurjian).

127 Football and Maps of Japan and South Korea

2002. World Cup Football Championships, Japan and South Korea.
514 **127** 350d. multicoloured . . . 75 75

128 Pushman and "The Silent Order" (detail, painting)

2002. 125th Birth Anniv of Hovsep Pushman (artist). Sheet 75 × 65 mm.
MS515 multicoloured 1·40 1·40

129 Technical Drawings, Tevossian and Factory

2002. Birth Centenary of Hovhannes Tevossian (metallurgical engineer).
516 **129** 350d. multicoloured . . . 75 75

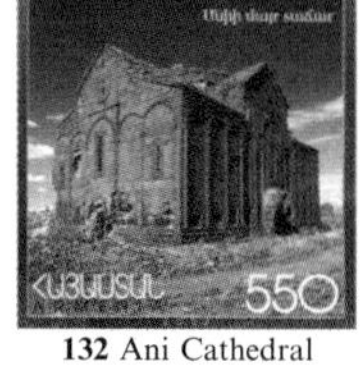

130 Birds, Playing Cards, Ribbons and Magician's Hat

132 Ani Cathedral

131 Aivazian

2002. Europa. Circus. Multicoloured.
517 70d. Type **130** 15 15
518 500d. Clown juggling . . . . 1·10 1·10

2002. Birth Centenary of Artemy Aivazian (composer).
519 **131** 600d. multicoloured . . . 1·25 1·25

2002. Sheet 90 × 60 mm.
MS520 **132** 550d. multicoloured 1·25 1·25

133 Kaputjugh Mountain

2002. International Year of Mountains.
521 **133** 350d. multicoloured . . . 75 75

134 Armenian Lizard (*Lacerta armeniaca*)

2002. Reptiles. Multicoloured.
522 170d. Type **134** 35 35
523 220d. Radde's viper (*Vipera raddei*) 50 50

ARUBA Pt. 4

An island in the Caribbean, formerly part of Netherlands Antilles. In 1986 became an autonomous country within the Kingdom of the Netherlands.

100 cents = 1 gulden.

1 Map

1986. New Constitution.
1 **1** 25c. yellow, blue and black . . 70 35
2 – 45c. multicoloured 90 70
3 – 55c. black, grey and red . . . 1·10 75
4 – 100c. multicoloured . . . . . 1·75 1·60
DESIGNS—VERT: 45c. Aruban arms; 55c. National anthem. HORIZ: 100c. Aruban flag.

2 House

1986.
5 **2** 5c. black and yellow 10 10
6 – 15c. black and blue 35 20
7 – 20c. black and grey 20 15
8 – 25c. black and violet 30 30
9 – 30c. black and red 65 45
10 – 35c. black and bistre 65 45
12 – 45c. black and blue 65 35
14 – 55c. black and grey 75 45
15 – 60c. black and blue 90 65
16 – 65c. black and blue . . . . . 1·00 85
18 – 75c. black and brown 90 70
20 – 85c. black and orange . . . 1·00 75
21 – 90c. black and green . . . . 1·10 80
22 – 100c. black and brown . . . 1·10 85
23 – 150c. black and green . . . . 2·00 1·50
24 – 250c. black and green . . . . 3·25 2·75
DESIGNS: 15c. Clock tower; 20c. Container crane; 25c. Lighthouse; 30c. Snake; 35c. Burrowing owl; 45c. Caribbean vase (shell); 55c. Frog; 60c. Water-skier; 65c. Fisherman casting net; 75c. Hurdy-gurdy; 85c. Pot; 90, 250c. Different cacti; 100c. Maize; 150c. Watapana Tree.

3 People and Two Ropes

1986. "Solidarity". Multicoloured.
25 30c.+10c. Type **3** 85 55
26 35c.+15c. People and three ropes . . . . 1·00 65
27 60c.+25c. People and one rope 1·40 1·00

4 Dove between Scenes of Peace and War

1986. International Peace Year. Multicoloured.
28 60c. Type **4** . . . . 1·00 75
29 100c. Doves flying over broken barbed wire . . . . 1·50 1·10

5 Boy and Caterpillar

6 Engagement Picture

1986. Child Welfare. Multicoloured.
30 45c.+20c. Type **5** . . . . . . 1·10 75
31 70c.+25c. Boy and shell . . . 1·60 1·10
32 100c.+40c. Girl and butterfly 2·10 1·50

1987. Golden Wedding of Princess Juliana and Prince Bernhard.
33 **6** 135c. orange, black and gold 2·10 1·40

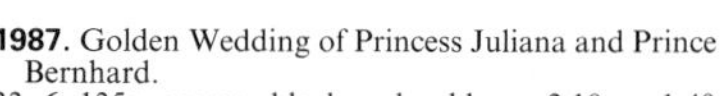

7 Queen Beatrix and Prince Claus

1987. Royal Visit. Multicoloured.
34 55c. Type **7** 90 55
35 60c. Prince Willem-Alexander 1·00 65

8 Woman looking at Beach

1987. Tourism. Multicoloured.
36 60c. Type **8** . . . . 1·10 80
37 100c. Woman looking at desert landscape . . . . 1·75 1·10

9 Child with Book on Beach

10 Plantation

1987. Child Welfare. Multicoloured.
38 25c.+10c. Type **9** 80 45
39 45c.+20c. Children drawing Christmas tree . . . . . . 1·10 70
40 70c.+30c. Child gazing at Nativity crib . . . . 1·60 1·10

1988. "Aloe vera". Multicoloured.
41 45c. Type **10** 80 55
42 60c. Stem and leaves of plant 1·00 70
43 100c. Harvesting aloes . . . . 1·60 1·00

11 25c. Coin

12 Bananaquits, Country Scene and "Love"

1988. Coins. Multicoloured.
44 25c. Type **11** 55 35
45 55c. Square 50c. coin . . . . 1·00 70
46 65c. 5c. and 10c. coins . . . . 1·25 80
47 150c. 1 gulden coin . . . . . 2·10 1·50

1988. Greetings Stamps. Multicoloured.
48 70c. Type **12** 90 65
49 135c. West Indian crown conch, West Indian chank (shells), seaside scene and "Love" . . . . 1·75 1·25

13 White Triangle on Shaded Background

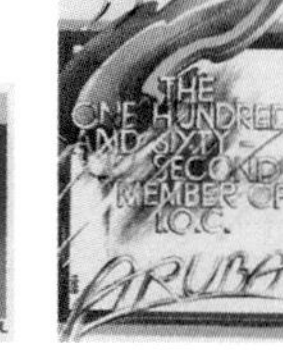

14 Torch

1988. "Solidarity". 11th Y.M.C.A. World Council. Multicoloured.
50 45c.+20c. Type **13** . . . . . 1·00 70
51 60c.+25c. Interlocking triangles 1·40 1·00
52 100c.+50c. Shaded triangle on white background . . . . . 1·90 1·40

1988. Olympic Games, Seoul. Multicoloured.
53 35c. Type **14** 70 35
54 100c. Games and Olympic emblems . . . . 1·40 1·10

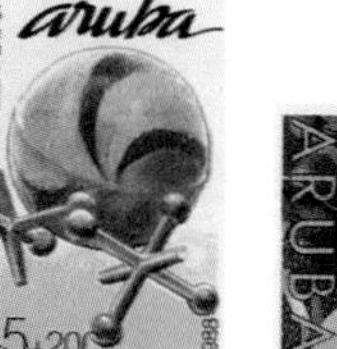

15 Jacks

16 Children

1988. Child Welfare. Toys. Multicoloured.
55 45c.+20c. Type **15** . . . . . 1·00 70
56 70c.+30c. Spinning top . . . . 70 1·00
57 100c.+50c. Kite . . . . 2·00 1·40

1989. Carnival. Multicoloured.
58 45c. Type **16** 85 55
59 60c. Girl in costume . . . . . 1·00 70
60 100c. Lights . . . . 1·90 1·10

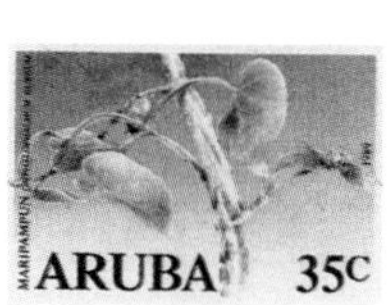

17 Maripampun

18 Emblem

1989. Maripampun. Multicoloured.
61 35c. Type **17** 70 45
62 55c. Seed pods . . . . 1·00 70
63 200c. Pod distributing seeds 2·75 2·10

1989. Universal Postal Union.
64 **18** 250c. multicoloured . . . . 3·50 2·25

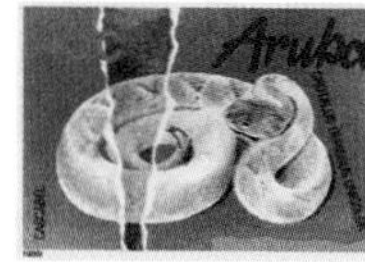

19 Snake

1989. South American Rattlesnake.
65 **19** 45c. multicoloured 70 45
66 – 55c. multicoloured 80 55
67 – 60c. multicoloured . . . . . 1·00 65
DESIGNS: 55, 60c. Snake (different).

20 Spoon in Child's Hand

21 Violin, Tambour and Cuatro Players

1989. Child Welfare. Multicoloured.
68 45c +20c. Type **20** 90 65
69 60c.+30c. Child playing football . . . . 1·10 80
70 100c.+50c. Child's hand in adult's hand (vert) . . . . . 2·00 1·40

1989. New Year. Dande Musicians. Multicoloured.
71 25c. Type **21** 55 30
72 70c. Guitar and cuatro players and singer with hat 90 65
73 150c. Cuatro, accordion and wiri players . . . . 1·75 1·40

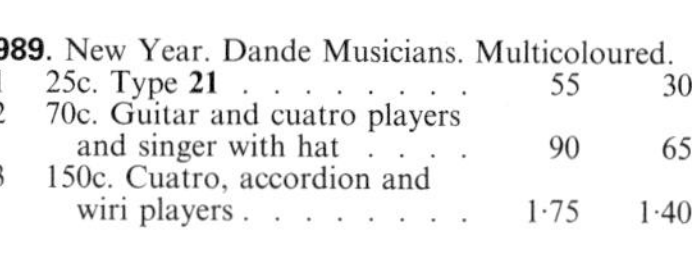

22 Tractor and Natural Vegetation

1990. Environmental Protection. Multicoloured.
74 45c. Type **22** 75 55
75 55c. Face and wildlife (vert) 90 65
76 100c. Marine life . . . . . . 1·60 1·10

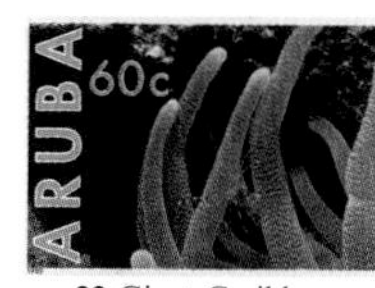

23 Giant Caribbean Anemone and Pederson's Cleaning Shrimp

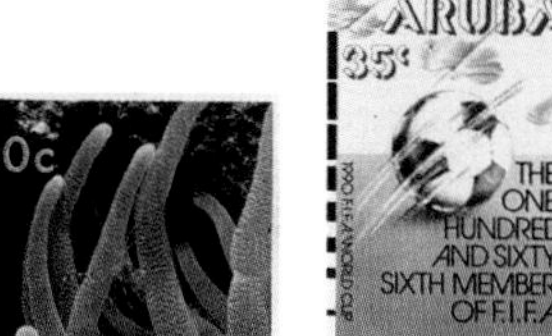

24 Ball

1990. Marine Life. Multicoloured.
77 60c. Type **23** . . . . 1·00 70
78 70c. Queen angelfish and red coral . . . . 1·10 1·00
79 100c. Banded coral shrimp, fire sponge and yellow boring sponge . . . . 1·90 1·50

1990. World Cup Football Championship, Italy. Multicoloured.
80 35c. Type **24** 65 35
81 200c. Mascot . . . . 2·75 2·10

25 Emblem of Committee of Tanki Leendert Association Youth Centre

26 Clay Painting Stamps

1990. "Solidarity". Multicoloured.
82 55c.+25c. Type **25** . . . . . 1·40 1·10
83 100c.+50c. Emblem of Foundation for Promotion of Responsible Parenthood 2·40 1·90

1990. Archaeology. Multicoloured.
84 45c. Type **26** 70 55
85 60c. Stone figure 90 70
86 100c. Dabajuroid-style jar . . 1·60 1·25

27 Sailboards and Fishes

28 Mountain and Shoreline

1990. Child Welfare. Multicoloured.
87 45c.+20c. Type **27** . . . . . 1·00 75
88 60c.+30c. Parakeets and coconut trees . . . . 1·25 1·10
89 100c.+50c. Kites and lizard . . 2·10 1·75

1991. Landscapes. Multicoloured.
90 55c. Type **28** 90 65
91 65c. Cacti and Haystack mountain . . . . 1·00 1·25
92 100c. House, mountain and ocean, Jaburibari . . . . . 1·60 1·25

29 Woman holding Herbs ("Carer")

30 "Ocimum sanctum"

1991. Women and Work. Multicoloured.
93 35c. Type **29** 65 35
94 70c. Women and kitchen ("Housewife") . . . . . . 1·00 85
95 100c. Women and telephone ("Woman in the World") 1·40 2·25

1991. Medicinal Plants. Multicoloured.
96 65c. Type **30** 85 75
97 75c. "Jatropha gossypifolia" 1·00 90
98 95c. "Croton flavens" . . . . 1·40 1·10

31 Fishing Net, Float and Needle

32 Child's Hand taking Book from Shelf

1991. Traditional Crafts.
99 **31** 35c. black, ultram & blue 65 35
100 – 250c. black, lilac & purple 3·50 2·75
DESIGNS: 250c. Hat, straw and hat-block.

1991. Child Welfare. Multicoloured.
101 45c.+25c. Type **32** . . . . . 1·00 80
102 60c.+35c. Child's finger pointing to letter "B" . . . 1·50 1·10
103 100c.+50c. Child reading . . 2·10 1·75

33 Toucan saying "Welcome"

34 Government Decree of 1892 establishing first Aruban Post Office

1991. Tourism. Multicoloured.
104 35c. Type **33** 65 45
105 70c. Aruban youth welcoming tourist . . . . 1·00 80
106 100c. Windmill and Bubali swamp . . . . 1·50 1·25

1992. Centenary of Postal Service (1st issue). Mult.
107 60c. Type **34** 90 75
108 75c. Lt.-Governor's building (mail service office, 1892–1908) (horiz) . . . . . 1·10 80
109 80c. Present Oranjestad P.O. (horiz) . . . . 1·40 1·00
See also Nos. 117/19.

35 Equality of Sexes

1992. Equality. Multicoloured.
110 100c. Type **35** . . . . 1·50 1·10
111 100c. People of different races (equality of nations) . . . 1·50 1·10

36 Aruban Flag, Guide Emblem and Girl Guides

37 Columbus, Map and Clouds

1992. "Solidarity". Multicoloured.
112 55c.+30c. Type **36** . . . . . 1·50 1·10
113 100c.+50c. Open hand with Cancer Fund emblem . . . 2·10 1·00

1992. 500th Anniv of Discovery of America by Columbus. Multicoloured.
114 30c. Type **37** 55 35
115 40c. Caravel (from navigation chart, 1525) 65 50
116 50c. Indians, queen conch shell and 1540 map . . . . 1·00 65

38 "I Love Post" (Jelissa Boekhoudt)

1992. Child Welfare. Centenary of Postal Service (2nd issue). Children's Drawings. Multicoloured.
117 50c.+30c. Type **38** . . . . . 1·25 95
118 70c.+35c. Airplane dropping letters (Marianne Fingal) 1·40 1·10
119 100c.+50c. Pigeon carrying letter in beak (Minorenti Jacobs) (vert) . . . . . . 2·10 1·75

39 Seroe Colorado Bridge

41 Rocks at Ayo

1992. Natural Bridges. Multicoloured.
120 70c. Type **39** . . . . 1·00 75
121 80c. Natural Bridge . . . . 1·25 90

1993. Rock Formations. Multicoloured.
123 50c. Type **41** 75 65
124 60c. Casibari 80 75
125 100c. Ayo (different) . . . . 1·25 1·10

42 Traditional Instruments

43 Sailfish dinghy

1993. Cock's Burial (part of St. John's Feast celebrations). Multicoloured.
126 40c. Type **42** 65 55
127 70c. "Cock's Burial" (painting, Leo Kuiperi) . . 95 80
128 80c. Verses of song, yellow flag, and calabashes . . . 1·10 1·00

1993. Sports. Multicoloured.
129 50c. Type **43** 70 65
130 65c. Land sailing 90 80
131 75c. Sailboard . . . . 1·00 90

44 Young Iguana

1993. The Iguana. Multicoloured.
132 35c. Type **44** 55 50
133 60c. Young adult 80 70
134 100c. Adult (vert) . . . . . 1·25 1·10

45 Aruban House, Landscape and Cacti

1993. Child Welfare. Multicoloured.
135 50c.+30c. Type **45** . . . . . 1·00 90
136 75c.+40c. Face, bridge and sea (vert) . . . . 1·50 1·40
137 100c.+50c. Bridge, buildings and landscape . . . . . . 1·90 1·75

46 Owls

47 Athlete

1994. The Burrowing Owl. Multicoloured.
138 5c. Type **46** 30 20
139 10c. Pair with young 50 35
140 35c. Owl with locust in claw (vert) 85 70
141 40c. Owl (vert) . . . . 1·00 90

1994. Centenary of Int Olympic Committee. Mult.
142 50c. Type **47** 70 65
143 90c. Baron Pierre de Coubertin (founder) . . . 90 1·10

48 Family in House

49 Flags of U.S.A. and Aruba, Ball and Players

1994. "Solidarity". Int Year of The Family. Mult.
144 50c.+35c. Type **48** . . . . . 1·10 1·00
145 100c.+50c. Family outside house . . . . 2·00 1·90

1994. World Cup Football Championship, U.S.A. Multicoloured.
146 65c. Type **49** 90 80
147 150c. Mascot . . . . 2·00 1·75

50 West Indian Cherry

51 Children with Umbrella sitting on Anchor (shelter and security)

1994. Wild Fruits. Multicoloured.
148 40c. Type **50** 70 55
149 70c. Geiger tree 95 80
150 85c. "Pithecellobium unguis-cati" . . . . 1·25 1·10
151 150c. Sea grape . . . . . . 2·25 1·75

1994. Child Welfare. Influence of the Family. Mult.
152 50c.+30c. Type **51** . . . . . 1·10 1·00
153 80c.+35c. Children in smiling sun (warmth of nurturing home) . . . . 1·50 1·40
154 100c.+50c. Child flying on owl (wisdom guiding the child) . . . . 1·90 1·75

52 Government Building, 1888

53 Dove, Emblem and Flags

1995. Historic Buildings. Multicoloured.
155 35c. Type **52** 50 45
156 60c. Ecury Residence, 1929 (vert) 85 70
157 100c. Protestant Church, 1846 (vert) . . . . 1·25 1·10

1995. 50th Anniv of U.N.O. Multicoloured.
158 30c. Type **53** 55 45
159 200c. Emblem, flags, globe and doves . . . . 2·50 2·40

54 Casanova II and Rosettes

55 Cowpea

1995. Interpaso Horses. Multicoloured.
160 25c. Type **54** 50 35
161 75c. Horse performing Paso Fino . . . . 1·10 90
162 80c. Horse performing Figure 8 (vert) . . . . 1·10 1·00
163 90c. Girl on horseback (vert) 1·25 1·10

1995. Vegetables. Multicoloured.
164 25c. Type **55** 40 35
165 50c. Apple cucumber 80 65
166 70c. Okra 95 80
167 85c. Pumpkin . . . . 1·25 1·00

56 Hawksbill Turtle

57 Children holding Balloons outside House (Christina Trejo)

1995. Turtles. Multicoloured.
168 15c. Type **56** 50 20
169 50c. Green turtle 80 50
170 95c. Loggerhead turtle . . . 1·50 1·10
171 100c. Leatherback turtle . . . 1·60 1·10

1995. Child Welfare. Children's Drawings. Mult.
172 50c.+25c. Type **57** . . . . . 1·10 80
173 70c.+35c. Children at seaside (Julysses Tromp) . . . . . 1·40 1·10
174 100c.+50c. Children and adults gardening (Ronald Tromp) . . . . 2·10 1·60

58 Henry Eman

59 Woman

1996. 10th Anniv of Internal Autonomy. Politicians. Multicoloured.
175 100c. Type **58** . . . . 1·25 1·10
176 100c. Juancho Irausquin . . 1·25 1·10
177 100c. Shon Eman . . . . . 1·25 1·10
178 100c. Betico Croes . . . . . 1·25 1·10

1996. America. Traditional Costumes. Mult.
179 65c. Type **59** 90 70
180 70c. Man 95 70
181 100c. Couple dancing (horiz) 1·40 1·10

60 Running

61 Mathematical Instruments, "G" and Rising Sun

1996. Olympic Games, Atlanta. Multicoloured.
182 85c. Type **60** . . . . 1·10 90
183 130c. Cycling . . . . 1·75 1·60

1996. "Solidarity". 75th Anniv of Freemasons' Lodge El Sol Naciente. Multicoloured.
184 60c.+30c. Type **61** . . . . . 1·25 1·00
185 100c.+50c. Globes on top of columns and doorway . . 1·90 1·75

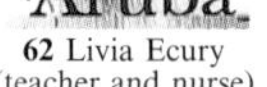

62 Livia Ecury (teacher and nurse)

63 Rabbits at Bus-stop

1996. Anniversaries. Multicoloured.
186 60c. Type **62** (5th death) . . 90 80
187 60c. Laura Wernet-Paskel (teacher and politician, 85th birth) 90 80
188 60c. Lolita Euson (poet, 2nd death) 90 80

1996. Child Welfare. Comic Strips. Multicoloured.
189 50c.+25c. Type **63** . . . . . 1·00 80
190 70c.+35c. Mother accompanying young owl to school . . . . 1·40 1·25
191 100c.+50c. Boy flying kite with friend . . . . 1·75 1·60

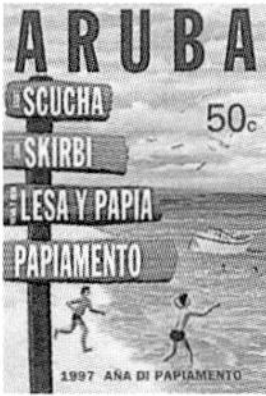
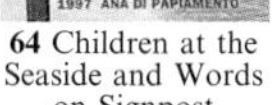

64 Children at the Seaside and Words on Signpost

65 Postman on Bicycle, 1936–57

1997. "Year of Papiamento" (Creole language). Multicoloured.
192 50c. Type **64** 75 60
193 140c. Sunrise over ocean . . 1·90 2·10

1997. America. The Postman. Multicoloured.
194 60c. Type **65** 90 80
195 70c. Postman delivering package by jeep, 1957–88 1·00 80
196 80c. Postman delivering letter from motor scooter, 1995 1·25 1·00

66 Decorated Cunucu House

1997. Aruban Architecture. Multicoloured.
197 30c. Type **66** 45 40
198 65c. Bannistered steps . . . . 1·00 80
199 100c. Arends Building (vert) 1·40 1·25

67 Merlin and Lighthouse

68 Passengers approaching Cruise Liner

1997. "Pacific 97" International Stamp Exhibition, San Francisco. Multicoloured.
200 90c. Type **67** . . . . 1·10 1·10
201 90c. Windswept trees and dolphin . . . . 1·10 1·10
202 90c. Iguana on rock and cacti 1·10 1·10
203 90c. Three types of fishes and one dolphin . . . . 1·10 1·10
204 90c. Two dolphins and fishes 1·10 1·10
205 90c. Burrowing owl on shore, turtle and lionfish . . . . 1·10 1·10
206 90c. Stingray, rock beauty, angelfishes, squirrelfish and coral reef . . . . 1·10 1·10
207 90c. Diver and stern of shipwreck . . . . 1·10 1·10
208 90c. Shipwreck, reef and fishes . . . . 1·10 1·10

Nos. 200/8 were issued together, se-tenant, forming a composite design.

1997. Cruise Tourism. Multicoloured.
209 35c. Type **68** 50 40
210 50c. Passengers disembarking 70 60
211 150c. Cruise liner at sea and launch at shore . . . . . 2·00 1·75

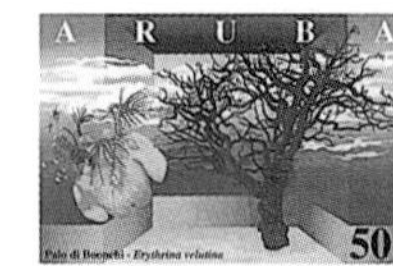

69 Coral Tree

1997. Trees. Multicoloured.
212 50c. Type **69** 70 60
213 60c. "Cordia dentata" . . . 90 80
214 70c. "Tabebuia billbergii" . . 1·00 80
215 130c. Lignum vitae . . . . . 1·75 1·60

70 Girl among Aloes

1997. Child Welfare. Child and Nature. Mult.
216 50c.+25c. Type **70** . . . . . 1·00 85
217 70c.+35c. Boy and butterfly (vert) . . . . 1·40 1·25
218 100c.+50c. Girl swimming underwater by coral reef 1·90 1·75

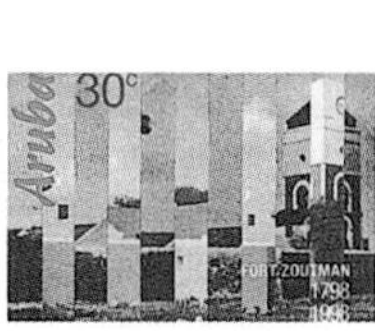

71 Fort Zoutman

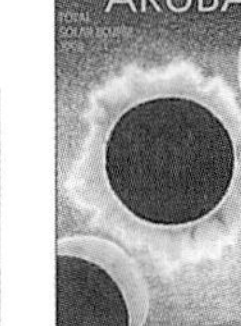

72 Stages of Eclipse

1998. Bicentenary of Fort Zoutman.
219 **71** 30c. multicoloured 50 40
220 250c. multicoloured . . . . 3·00 2·75

Each design consists of alternating strips in brown tones or black and white. When the 250c. is laid on top of the 30c., the brown strips form a composite design of the fort in its early years and the black and white strips a composite design of the fort after 1929, when various alterations were made.

1998. Total Solar Eclipse. Multicoloured.
221 85c. Type **72** . . . . 1·10 1·00
222 100c. Globe showing path of eclipse and map of Aruba plotting duration of total darkness . . . . 1·40 1·25

73 Globe, Emblem and Wheelchair balanced on Map of Aruba

1998. "Solidarity" Anniversaries. Multicoloured.
223 60c.+30c. Type **73** (50th anniv of Lions Club of Aruba) . . . . 1·25 1·00
224 100c.+50c. Boy reading, emblem and grandmother in rocking chair (60th anniv of Rotary Club of Aruba) . . . . 1·90 1·75

74 Tropical Mockingbird

1998. Birds. Multicoloured.
225 50c. Type **74** 70 65
226 60c. American kestrel (vert) 95 80
227 70c. Troupial (vert) . . . . 1·10 90
228 150c. Bananaquit . . . . . 2·10 1·90

75 Villagers processing Corn

76 Ribbon Dance

1998. World Stamp Day.
229 **75** 225c. multicoloured . . . . 3·25 2·75

1998. Child Welfare. Multicoloured.
230 50c.+25c. Type **76** . . . . . 1·00 90
231 80c.+40c. Boy playing cuarta (four-string guitar) . . . . 1·75 1·60
232 100c. + 50c. Basketball . . . 2·00 1·75

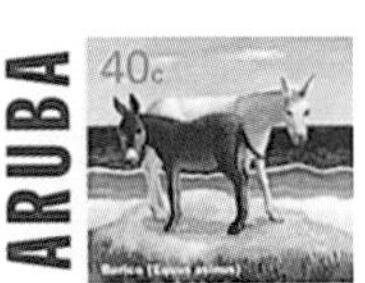

77 Two Donkeys

1999. The Donkey. Multicoloured.
233 40c. Type **77** 60 50
234 65c. Two adults and foal . . 1·00 90
235 100c. Adult and foal . . . . 1·40 1·40

78 "Opuntia wentiana"

79 Creole Dog

1999. Cacti. Multicoloured.
236 50c. Type **78** 70 65
237 60c. "Lemaireocereus griseus" 95 80
238 70c. "Cephalocereus lanuginosus" ("Cadushi di carona") . . . . 1·00 90
239 75c. "Cephalocereus lanuginosus" ("Cadushi") 1·10 1·00

1999. Creole Dogs ("Canis familiaris"). Mult.
240 40c. Type **79** 60 50
241 60c. White dog standing on rock 90 80
242 80c. Dog sitting by sea . . . 1·10 1·00
243 165c. Black and tan dog sitting on rock . . . . . . 2·10 2·00

80 Indian Cave Drawings and Antique Map

1999. 500 Years of Cultural Diversity. Mult.
244 150c. Type **80** . . . . 1·75 1·60
245 175c. Indian cave drawings and carnival headdress . . 2·10 2·00

81 Public Library and Children

1999. 50th Anniv of Public Library Service. Mult.
247 70c. Type **81** 90 80
248 100c. Library, Santa Cruz . . 1·25 1·25

82 Boy with Fisherman

83 Three Wise Men

1999. Child Welfare. Multicoloured.
249 60c.+30c. Type **82** . . . . . 1·00 1·00
250 80c.+40c. Man reading to children . . . . 1·50 1·40
251 100c.+50c. Woman with child (vert) . . . . 1·90 1·75

1999. Christmas. Multicoloured. Self-adhesive.
252 40c. Type **83** 50 45
253 70c. Shepherds 95 90
254 100c. Holy Family . . . . . 1·40 1·25

84 *Norops lineatus*

2000. Reptiles. Multicoloured.
255 40c. Type **84** 55 50
256 60c. Greeen iguana (vert) . . 90 80
257 75c. Annulated snake (vert) 1·00 90
258 150c. Racerunner . . . . . 1·75 1·75

85 Flags

2000. America. A.I.D.S. Awareness. Multicoloured.
259 75c. Type **85** 95 90
260 175c. Ribbon on globe (vert) 2·10 2·00

86 Bank Facade

2000. Anniversaries. Multicoloured.
261 150c. Type **86** (75th anniv of Aruba Bank) . . . . . . 1·90 1·75
262 165c. Chapel (250th anniv of Alto Vista Chapel) . . . . 2·25 2·00

87 West Indian Top Shell

2000. Aspects of Aruba. Multicoloured.
263 15c. Type **87** 20 20
264 25c. Guadirikiri cave 40 35
265 35c. Mud-house (vert) . . . 50 50
267 55c. Cacti 75 70
269 85c. Hooiberg . . . . 1·00 1·00
271 100c. Gold smelter, Balashi (vert) . . . . 1·25 1·25
272 250c. Rock crystal . . . . . 3·25 3·25
275 500c. Conchi . . . . 5·75 5·50

88 Children at Beach Playground

2000. "Solidarity". Multicoloured.
280 75c.+35c. Type **88** . . . . . 1·40 1·25
281 100c.+50c. Children building sandcastles . . . . 2·10 1·90

89 "Solar Energy" (Nikki Johanna Teresia Willems)

2000. Child Welfare. "Stampin' the Future". Winning Entries in Children's International Painting Competition. Multicoloured.
282 60c.+30c. Type **89** . . . . . 1·25 1·25
283 80c.+40c. "Environmental Protection" (Samantha Jeanne Tromp) . . . . . 1·50 1·40
284 100c.+50c. "Future Vehicles" (Jennifer Huntington) . . . 2·10 1·90

90 Cat

2001. Domestic Animals. Multicoloured.
285 5c. Type **90** 15 15
286 30c. Tortoise 35 35
287 50c. Rabbit 60 60
288 200c. Brown-throated conure 2·40 2·40

91 Shaman preparing for Sun Ceremony

2001. 40 Years of Mascaruba (amateur theatre group). Depicting scenes from *Macuarima*, History or Legend? (musical play). Mult.
289 60c. Type **91** 70 70
290 150c. Love scene between Guadarikiri and Blanco . . 1·75 1·75

92 Ford Model A Roadster, 1930

2001. Motor Cars. Multicoloured.
291 25c. Type **92** 30 30
292 40c. Citroen Comerciale saloon, 1933 . . . . . . 45 45
293 70c. Plymouth Pick-up, 1948 90 90
294 75c. Edsel corsair convertable, 1959 . . . . 1·00 1·00

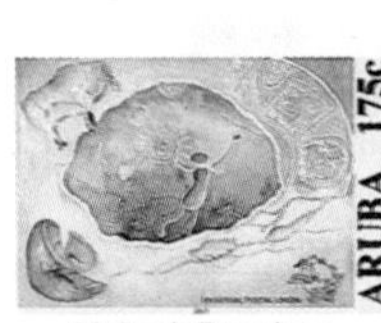

93 Rock Drawings **94** Pedestrians using Crossing

2001. Universal Postal Union. United Nations Year of Dialogue among Civilizations.
295 **93** 175c. multicoloured . . . . 2·40 2·40

2001. Child Welfare. International Year of Volunteers. Multicoloured.
296 40c. + 20c. Type **94** 80 80
297 60c. + 30c. Boys walking dogs . . . . 1·10 1·10
298 100c. + 50c. Children putting litter in bin . . . . 2·00 2·00

95 Dakota Airport, 1950

2002. Queen Beatrix Airport. Multicoloured.
299 30c. Type **95** 45 45
300 75c. Queen Beatrix Airport, 1972 . . . . 1·10 1·10
301 175c. Queen Beatrix Airport, 2000 . . . . 2·50 2·50
Dakota Airport was re-named Princess Beatrix Airport in 1955 and Queen Beatrix Airport in 1972.

96 Prince Willem-Alexander and Princess Maxima

2002. Wedding of Crown Prince Willem-Alexander to Maxima Zorreguieta. Multicoloured.
302 60c. Type **96** 85 85
303 300c. Prince Willem-Alexander and Princess Máxima facing right . . . 4·25 4·25

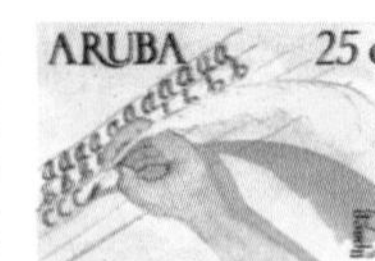

97 Tap and Water Droplet **98** Hand holding Quill Pen

2002. 70th Anniv of Water Company (W. E. B.). Multicoloured.
304 60c. Type **97** 85 85
305 85c. Water pipes (horiz) . . . 1·25 1·25
306 165c. Water meter and meter reader . . . . 2·25 2·25

2002. America. Literacy Campaign. Multicoloured.
307 25c. Type **98** 35 35
308 100c. Alphabet on wall and boy on step-ladder . . . . 1·40 1·40

99 *U-156* Submarine firing on Lago Oil Refinery **100** Boy, Iguana and Goat

2002. Second World War. Multicoloured.
309 60c. Type **99** 85 85
310 75c. *Pedernales* (oil-tanker) in flames . . . . 1·00 1·00
311 150c. "Boy" Ecury (resistance fighter) (statue) (vert) . . . 2·10 2·10

2002. Child Welfare. Animals. Multicoloured
312 40c.+20c. Type **100** 85 85
313 60c.+30c. Girl, turtle and crab (horiz) . . . . 1·00 1·00
314 100c.+50c. Pelicans, boy and parakeet . . . . 2·10 2·10

101 House at Fontein

2003. Mud Houses. Multicoloured.
315 40c. Type **101** 30 30
316 60c. House at Ari Kok . . . 45 45
317 75c. House at Fontein . . . 55 55

EXPRESS MAIL SERVICE

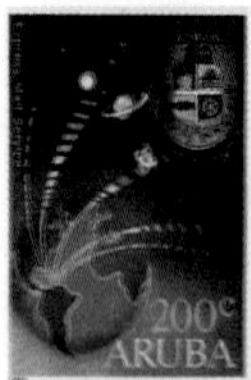

E **40** Globe, Planets and Aruban Arms

1993.
E122 E **40** 200c. multicoloured . . 2·75 2·10

ASCENSION Pt. 1

An island in South Atlantic. A dependency of St. Helena.

1922. 12 pence = 1 shilling;
20 shillings = 1 pound.
1971. 100 pence = 1 pound.

1922. Stamps of St. Helena of 1912 optd ASCENSION.
1 ½d. black and green . . . . . 4·50 16·00
2 1d. green . . . . 4·50 15·00
3 1½d. red . . . . 15·00 48·00
4 2d. black and slate . . . . . . 15·00 13·00
5 3d. blue . . . . 13·00 17·00
6 8d. black and purple . . . . . 26·00 48·00
9 1s. black on green . . . . . . 28·00 48·00
7 2s. black and blue on blue . . . 85·00 £120
8 3s. black and violet £120 £160

2 Badge of St. Helena

1924.
10 **2** ½d. black . . . . 3·50 13·00
11 1d. black and green . . . . 5·50 8·00
12 1½d. red . . . . 7·50 26·00
13 2d. black and grey . . . . 13·00 7·00
14 3d. blue . . . . 8·00 13·00
15 4d. black on yellow . . . . 48·00 80·00
15d 5d. purple and green . . . 10·00 20·00
16 6d. black and purple . . . 48·00 90·00
17 8d. black and violet . . . . 15·00 42·00
18 1s. black and brown . . . . 20·00 50·00
19 2s. black and blue on blue 55·00 85·00
20 3s. black on blue . . . . . 80·00 90·00

3 Georgetown **4** Ascension Island

1934. Medallion portrait of King George V (except 1s.).
21 **3** ½d. black and violet 90 80
22 **4** 1d. black and green . . . . 1·75 1·25
23 – 1½d. black and red . . . . . 1·75 2·25
24 **4** 2d. black and orange . . . . 1·75 2·50
25 – 3d. black and blue . . . . . 1·75 1·50
26 – 5d. black and blue . . . . . 2·25 3·25
27 **4** 8d. black and brown . . . . 4·25 4·75
28 – 1s. black and red . . . . . 18·00 6·50
29 **4** 2s.6d. black and purple . . . 45·00 32·00
30 – 5s. black and brown . . . . 45·00 55·00
DESIGNS—HORIZ: 1½d. The Pier; 3d. Long Beach; 5d. Three Sisters; 1s. Sooty tern ("Wideawake Fair"); 5s. Green mountain.

1935. Silver Jubilee. As T **13** of Antigua.
31 1½d. blue and red . . . . . . 3·50 7·00
32 2d. blue and grey . . . . . . 11·00 23·00
33 5d. green and blue . . . . . 17·00 24·00
34 1s. grey and purple . . . . . 23·00 27·00

1937. Coronation. As T **2** of Aden.
35 1d. green . . . . 50 1·10
36 2d. orange . . . . 1·00 40
37 3d. blue . . . . 1·00 50

10 The Pier

1938.
38b A ½d. black and violet . . . 70 1·75
39 B 1d. black and green . . . 40·00 8·00
39b 1d. black and orange . . . 45 60
39d C 1d. black and green . . . 60 75
40b **10** 1½d. black and red 85 80
40d 1½d. black and pink . . . 55 80
41a B 2d. black and orange . . . 80 40
41c 2d. black and red . . . . 1·00 1·25
42 D 3d. black and blue . . . . £100 27·00
42b 3d. black and grey 70 80
42d B 4d. black and blue . . . 4·50 3·00
43 C 6d. black and blue . . . . 9·00 1·75
44a A 1s. black and brown . . . 4·75 2·00
45 **10** 2s.6d. black and red . . . 42·00 9·50
46a D 5s. black and brown . . . 38·00 27·00
47a C 10s. black and purple . . . 42·00 55·00
DESIGNS: A, Georgetown; B, Green Mountain; C, Three Sisters; D, Long Beach.

1946. Victory. As T **9** of Aden.
48 2d. orange 40 60
49 4d. blue 40 30

1948. Silver Wedding. As T **10/11** of Aden.
50 3d. black 50 30
51 10s. mauve . . . . 45·00 42·00

1949. U.P.U. As T **20/23** of Antigua.
52 3d. red . . . . 1·00 1·50
53 4d. blue . . . . 3·50 1·25
54 6d. olive . . . . 2·00 3·00
55 1s. black . . . . 2·00 1·50

1953. Coronation. As T **13** of Aden.
56 3d. black and grey . . . . . 1·00 1·50

19 Water Catchment

1956.
57 **19** ½d. black and brown 10 50
58 – 1d. black and mauve . . . 2·25 70
59 – 1½d. black and orange . . . 50 70
60 – 2d. black and red . . . . . 2·25 1·00
61 – 2½d. black and brown . . . 1·00 1·50
62 – 3d. black and blue . . . . 3·50 1·25
63 – 4d. black and turquoise . . 1·25 1·75
64 – 6d. black and blue . . . . 1·25 1·50
65 – 7d. black and olive . . . . 1·25 1·00
66 – 1s. black and red . . . . . 1·00 90
67 – 2s.6d. black and purple . . 27·00 6·50
68 – 5s. black and green . . . . 35·00 17·00
69 – 10s. black and purple . . . 48·00 35·00
DESIGNS: 1d. Map of Ascension; 1½d. Georgetown; 2d. Map showing Atlantic cables; 2½d. Mountain road; 3d. White-tailed tropic bird ("Boatswain Bird"); 4d. Yellow-finned tuna; 6d. Rollers on seashore; 7d. Turtles; 1s. Land crab; 2s.6d. Sooty tern ("Wideawake"); 5s. Perfect Crater; 10s. View of Ascension from north-west.

28 Brown Booby

1963. Birds. Multicoloured.
70 1d. Type **28** 90 30
71 1½d. White-capped noddy ("Black Noddy") . . . . . 1·25 60
72 2d. White tern ("Fairy Tern") 1·25 30
73 3d. Red-billed tropic bird . . 1·25 30
74 4½d. Common noddy ("Brown Noddy") . . . . 1·25 30
75 6d. Sooty tern ("Wideawake Tern") . . . . 1·25 30
76 7d. Ascension frigate bird ("Frigate bird") . . . . . . 1·25 30
77 10d. Blue-faced booby ("White Booby") . . . . 1·25 30
78 1s. White-tailed tropic bird ("Yellow-billed Tropicbird") 1·25 30
79 1s.6d. Red-billed tropic bird 4·50 1·75
80 2s.6d. Madeiran storm petrel 8·00 9·50
81 5s. Red-footed booby (brown phase) . . . . 8·00 9·00
82 10s. Ascension frigate birds ("Frigate birds") . . . . . 13·00 10·00
83 £1 Red-footed booby (white phase) . . . . 20·00 12·00

1963. Freedom from Hunger. As T **28** of Aden.
84 1s.6d. red 75 40

1963. Centenary of Red Cross. As T **33** of Antigua.
85 3d. red and black . . . . . . 2·00 1·25
86 1s.6d. red and blue . . . . . 4·00 2·25

1965. Centenary of I.T.U. As T **36** of Antigua.
87 3d. mauve and violet 50 65
88 6d. turquoise and brown . . . 75 65

1965. I.C.Y. As T **37** of Antigua.
89 1d. purple and turquoise . . . 40 60
90 6d. green and lavender 60 90

1966. Churchill Commemoration. As T **38** of Antigua.
91 1d. blue 50 75
92 3d. green . . . . 2·75 1·25
93 6d. brown . . . . 3·50 1·50
94 1s.6d. violet . . . . 4·50 2·00

1966. World Cup Football Championship. As T **40** of Antigua.
95 3d. multicoloured . . . . . . 1·25 60
96 6d. multicoloured . . . . . . 1·50 80

1966. Inauguration of W.H.O. Headquarters, Geneva. As T **41** of Antigua.
97 3d. black, green and blue . . . 1·75 1·00
98 1s.6d. black, purple and ochre 4·25 2·00

36 Satellite Station **44** Human Rights Emblem and Chain Links

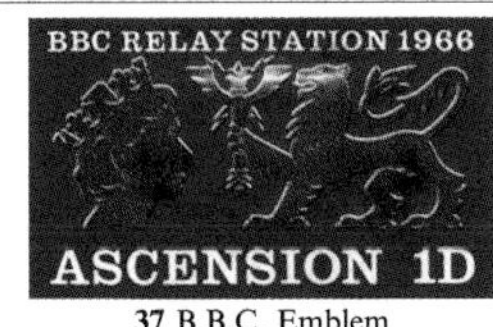

37 B.B.C. Emblem

1966. Opening of Apollo Communication Satellite Earth Station.
99 **36** 4d. black and violet . . . 10 10
100 8d. black and green . . . 15 15
101 1s.3d. black and brown . . 15 20
102 2s.6d. black and blue . . . 15 20

1966. Opening of B.B.C. Relay Station.
103 **37** 1d. gold and blue 10 10
104 3d. gold and green 15 15
105 6d. gold and violet 15 15
106 1s.6d. gold and red 15 15

1967. 20th Anniv of U.N.E.S.C.O. As T **54/56** of Antigua.
107 3d. multicoloured . . . . . 2·00 1·25
108 6d. yellow, violet and olive 2·75 1·75
109 1s.6d. black, purple and orange . . . . 4·50 2·25

1968. Human Rights Year.
110 **44** 6d. orange, red and black 15 15
111 1s.6d. blue, red and black 20 25
112 2s.6d. green, red and black 20 30

45 Black Durgon ("Ascension Black-Fish")

1968. Fishes (1st series).
113 **45** 4d. black, grey and blue . . 30 40
114 – 8d. multicoloured 35 70
115 – 1s.9d. multicoloured . . . 40 80
116 – 2s.3d. multicoloured . . . 40 85
DESIGNS: 8d. Scribbled filefish ("Leather- jacket"); 1s.9d. Yellow-finned tuna; 2s.3d. Short-finned mako.
See also Nos. 117/20 and 126/9.

1969. Fishes (2nd series). As T **45**. Multicoloured.
117 4d. Sailfish 75 90
118 6d. White seabream ("Old wife") . . . . 1·00 1·25
119 1s.6d. Yellowtail . . . . . . 1·50 2·50
120 2s.11d. Rock hind ("Jack") 2·00 3·00

46 H.M.S. "Rattlesnake"

1969. Royal Navy Crests (1st series).
121 **46** 4d. multicoloured 60 30
122 – 9d. multicoloured 75 35
123 – 1s.9d. blue and gold . . . 1·10 45
124 – 2s.3d. multicoloured . . . 1·25 55
MS125 165 × 105 mm. Nos. 121/4 6·50 12·00
DESIGNS: 9d. H.M.S. "Weston"; 1s.9d. H.M.S. "Undaunted"; 2s.3d. H.M.S. "Eagle".
See also Nos. 130/3, 149/52, 154/7 and 166/9.

1970. Fishes (3rd series). As T **45**. Multicoloured.
126 4d. Wahoo . . . . 4·50 2·75
127w 9d. Ascension jack ("Coalfish") . . . . . . 3·00 1·25
128 1s.9d. Pompouno dolphin 5·50 3·50
129w 2s.3d. Squirrelfish ("Soldier") . . . . 5·50 3·50

1970. Royal Navy Crests (2nd series). As T **46**. Multicoloured.
130 4d. H.M.S. "Penelope" . . . 1·00 1·00
131 9d. H.M.S. "Carlisle" . . . . 1·25 1·50
132 1s.6d. H.M.S. "Amphion" . . 1·75 2·00
133 2s.6d. H.M.S. "Magpie" . . 1·75 2·00
MS134 159 × 96 mm. Nos. 130/3 11·00 14·00

50 Early Chinese Rocket

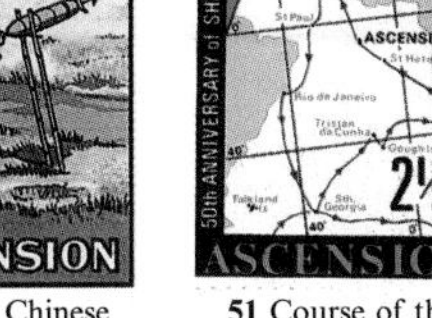

51 Course of the "Quest"

1971. Decimal Currency. Evolution of Space Travel. Multicoloured.
135 ½p. Type **50** 15 20
136 1p. Medieval Arab astronomers 20 20
137 1½p. Tycho Brahe's observatory, quadrant and supernova (horiz) 30 30
138 2p. Galileo, Moon and telescope (horiz) 40 30
139 2½p. Isaac Newton, instruments and apple (horiz) . . . . 1·00 70
140 3½p. Harrison's chronometer and H.M.S. "Deptford" (frigate), 1735 (horiz) . . . 2·00 70
141 4½p. Space rocket taking off 1·25 70
142 5p. World's largest telescope, Palomar (horiz) . . . . . 1·00 70
143 7½p. World's largest radio telescope, Jodrell Bank (horiz) . . . . 4·00 1·60
144 10p. "Mariner VII" and Mars (horiz) . . . . 3·50 1·75
145 12½p. "Sputnik II" and Space dog, Laika (horiz) . . . . 5·00 2·00
146 25p. Walking in Space . . . 6·00 2·25
147 50p. "Apollo XI" crew on Moon (horiz) . . . . . . 5·00 2·50
148 £1 Future Space Research station (horiz) . . . . . . 5·00 4·50

1971. Royal Navy Crests (3rd series). As T **46**. Mult.
149 2p. H.M.S. "Phoenix" . . . 1·00 30
150 4p. H.M.S. "Milford" . . . 1·25 55
151 9p. H.M.S. "Pelican" . . . . 1·50 80
152 15p. H.M.S. "Oberon" . . . 1·50 1·00
MS153 151 × 104 mm. Nos. 149/52 4·75 15·00

1972. Royal Navy Crests (4th series). As T **46**. Mult.
154 1½p. H.M.S. "Lowestoft" . . 50 50
155 3p. H.M.S. "Auckland" . . . 55 75
156 6p. H.M.S. "Nigeria" . . . . 60 1·25
157 17½p. H.M.S. "Bermuda" . . 90 2·50
MS158 157 × 93 mm. Nos. 154/7 2·25 7·50

1972. 50th Anniv of Shackleton's Death. Mult.
159 2½p. Type **51** 30 60
160 4p. Shackleton and "Quest" (horiz) 35 60
161 7½p. Shackleton's cabin and "Quest" (horiz) 35 65
162 11p. Shackleton statue and memorial 40 80
MS163 139 × 114 mm. Nos. 159/62 1·25 6·00

52 Land Crab and Short-finned Mako

1972. Royal Silver Wedding. Multicoloured.
164 **52** 2p. violet 15 10
165 16p. red 35 30

1973. Royal Naval Crests (5th series). As T **46**. Multicoloured.
166 2p. H.M.S. "Birmingham" 2·00 1·25
167 4p. H.M.S. "Cardiff" . . . . 2·25 1·25
168 9p. H.M.S. "Penzance" . . . 3·00 1·50
169 13p. H.M.S. "Rochester" . . . 3·25 1·50
MS170 109 × 152 mm. Nos. 166/9 28·00 10·00

53 Green Turtle

1973. Turtles. Multicoloured.
171 4p. Type **53** . . . . 2·75 1·25
172 9p. Loggerhead turtle . . . . 3·00 1·50
173 12p. Hawksbill turtle . . . . 3·25 1·75

54 Sergeant, R.M. Light Infantry, 1900

1973. 50th Anniv of Departure of Royal Marines from Ascension. Multicoloured.
174 2p. Type **54** . . . . 1·50 1·25
175 6p. R.M. Private, 1816 . . . 2·25 1·75
176 12p. R.M. Light Infantry Officer, 1880 . . . . . . 2·50 2·25
177 20p. R.M. Artillery Colour Sergeant, 1910 . . . . . 3·00 2·50

1973. Royal Wedding. As T **47** of Anguilla. Multicoloured. Background colours given.
178 2p. brown 15 10
179 18p. green 20 20

55 Letter and H.Q., Berne

1974. Centenary of Universal Postal Union. Mult.
180 2p. Type **55** 20 30
181 9p. Hermes and U.P.U. monument 30 45

56 Churchill as a Boy, and Birthplace, Blenheim Palace

1974. Birth Centenary of Sir Winston Churchill. Multicoloured.
182 5p. Type **56** 20 35
183 25p. Churchill as statesman, and U.N. Building 30 75
MS184 93 × 87 mm. Nos. 182/3 1·00 2·50

57 "Skylab 3" and Photograph of Ascension

1975. Space Satellites. Multicoloured.
185 2p. Type **57** 20 30
186 18p. "Skylab 4" Command module and photograph . . 30 40

58 U.S.A.F. Lockheed C-141A Starlifter

1975. Wideawake Airfield. Multicoloured.
187 2p. Type **58** . . . . 1·00 65
188 5p. R.A.F. Lockheed C-130 Hercules . . . . 1·00 85
189 9p. Vickers Super VC-10 . . 1·00 1·40
190 24p. U.S.A.F. Lockheed C-5A Galaxy . . . . . . 1·50 2·50
MS191 144 × 99 mm. Nos. 187/90 17·00 22·00

1975. "Apollo-Soyuz" Space Link. Nos. 141 and 145/6 optd **APOLLO-SOYUZ LINK 1975**.
192 4½p. multicoloured 15 20
193 12½p. multicoloured 15 25
194 25p. multicoloured 25 40

60 Arrival of Royal Navy, 1815

1975. 160th Anniv of Occupation. Multicoloured.
195 2p. Type **60** 25 25
196 5p. Water supply, Dampiers Drip 25 40
197 9p. First landing, 1815 . . . 25 60
198 15p. The garden on Green Mountain 35 85

61 Yellow Canaries ("Canary")

1976. Multicoloured.
199 1p. Type **61** . . . . 40 1·50
200 2p. White tern ("Fairy Tern") (vert) . . . . 50 1·50
201 3p. Common waxbill ("Waxbill") . . . . 50 1·50
202 4p. White-capped noddy ("Black Noddy") (vert) . . 50 1·50
203 5p. Common noddy ("Brown Noddy") . . . . 70 1·50
204 6p. Common mynah . . . . 70 1·50
205 7p. Madeiran storm petrel (vert) . . . . 70 1·50
206 8p. Sooty tern . . . . 70 1·50
207 9p. Blue-faced booby ("White Booby") (vert) . . . . . . 70 1·50
208 10p. Red-footed booby . . . 70 1·50
209 15p. Red-necked spurfowl ("Red-throated Francolin") (vert) . . . . 85 1·50
210 18p. Brown booby (vert) . . 85 1·50
211 25p. Red-billed tropic bird ("Red-billed Bo'sun Bird") 90 1·50
212 50p. White-tailed tropic bird ("Yellow-billed Tropic Bird") . . . . 1·25 2·25
213 £1 Ascension frigate-bird (vert) . . . . 1·25 2·75
214 £2 Boatswain Bird Island Sanctuary (50 × 38 mm) . . 2·25 5·50

63 G.B. Penny Red with Ascension Postmark

1976. Festival of Stamps, London.
215 **63** 5p. red, black and brown 15 15
216 – 9p. green, black and brown 15 20
217 – 25p. multicoloured 25 45
MS218 133 × 121 mm. No. 217 with St. Helena No. 318 and Tristan da Cunha No. 206 1·50 2·00
DESIGNS—VERT: 9p. ½d. stamp of 1922. HORIZ: 25p. "Southampton Castle" (liner).

64 U.S. Base, Ascension

1976. Bicentenary of American Revolution. Multicoloured.
219 8p. Type **64** 30 40
220 9p. NASA Station at Devils Ashpit 30 45
221 25p. "Viking" landing on Mars 40 80

65 Visit of Prince Philip, 1957

66 Tunnel carrying Water Pipe

1977. Silver Jubilee. Multicoloured.
222 8p. Type **65** 15 15
223 12p. Coronation Coach leaving Buckingham Palace (horiz) 20 20
224 25p. Coronation Coach (horiz) 35 40

1977. Water Supplies. Multicoloured.
225 3p. Type **66** 15 15
226 5p. Breakneck Valley wells 20 20
227 12p. Break tank (horiz) . . . 35 35
228 25p. Water catchment (horiz) 55 65

67 Mars Bay Location, 1877

1977. Centenary of Visit of Professor Gill (astronomer). Multicoloured.
229 3p. Type **67** 15 20
230 8p. Instrument sites, Mars Bay 20 25

231 12p. Sir David and Lady Gill . . . 30 40
232 25p. Maps of Ascension . . . 60 70

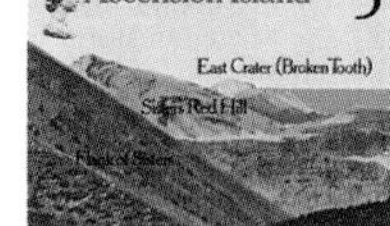

68 Lion of England **70** Flank of Sisters, Sisters' Red Hill and East Crater

1978. 25th Anniv of Coronation.
233 **68** 25p. yellow, brown and silver . . . 35 50
234 – 25p. multicoloured . . . 35 50
235 – 25p. yellow, brown and silver . . . 35 50
DESIGNS: No 234, Queen Elizabeth II; No 235, Green turtle.

1978. Ascension Island Volcanic Rock Formations. Multicoloured.
236 3p. Type **70** . . . 15 20
237 5p. Holland's Crater (Hollow Tooth) . . . 20 30
238 12p. Street Crater, Lower Valley Crater and Bear's Back . . . 25 40
239 15p. Butt Crater, Weather Post and Green Mountain . . . 30 45
240 25p. Flank of Sisters, Thistle Hill and Two Boats Village . . . 35 50
MS241 185 × 100 mm. Nos. 236/40, each × 2 . . . 2·00 5·00
Nos. 236/40 were issued as a se-tenant strip within the sheet, forming a composite design.

71 "The Resolution" (H. Roberts) **72** St. Mary's Church, Georgetown

1979. Bicentenary of Captain Cook's Voyages, 1768–79. Multicoloured.
242 3p. Type **71** . . . 30 25
243 8p. Cook's chronometer . . . 30 40
244 12p. Green turtle . . . 35 50
245 25p. Flaxman/Wedgwood medallion of Cook . . . 40 70

1979. Ascension Day. Muticoloured.
246 8p. Type **72** . . . 10 20
247 12p. Map of Ascension . . . 15 30
248 50p. "The Ascension" (painting by Rembrandt) . . . 30 90

73 Landing Cable, Comfortless Cove

1979. 80th Anniv of Eastern Telegraph Company's Arrival on Ascension.
249 **73** 3p. black and red . . . 10 10
250 – 8p. black and green . . . 15 15
251 – 12p. black and yellow . . . 20 20
252 – 15p. black and violet . . . 20 25
253 – 25p. black and brown . . . 25 35
DESIGNS—HORIZ: 8p. C.S. "Anglia"; 15p. C.S. "Seine"; 25p. Cable and Wireless earth station. VERT: 12p. Map of Atlantic cable network.

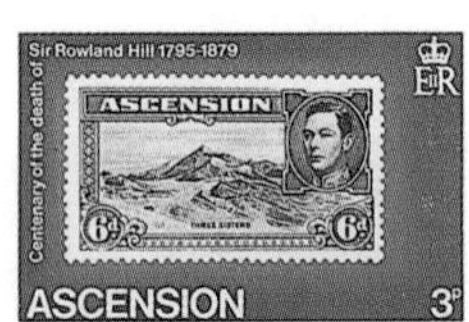

74 1938 6d. Stamp

1979. Death Centenary of Sir Rowland Hill.
254 **74** 3p. black and blue . . . 10 10
255 – 8p. black, green and pale green . . . 15 20
256 – 12p. black, blue and pale blue . . . 15 25
257 – 50p. black and red . . . 40 90
DESIGNS—HORIZ: 8p. 1956 5s. definitive. VERT: 12p. 1924 3s. stamp; 50p. Sir Rowland Hill.

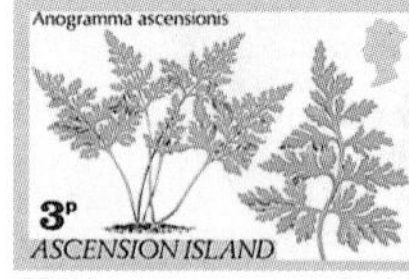

75 "Anogramma ascensionis"

1980. Ferns and Grasses. Multicoloured.
258 3p. Type **75** . . . 10 10
259 6p. "Xiphopteris ascensionense" . . . 10 15
260 8p. "Sporobolus caespitosus" . . . 10 15
261 12p. "Sporobolus durus" (vert) . . . 15 25
262 18p. "Dryopteris ascensionis" (vert) . . . 15 35
263 24p. "Marattia purpurascens" (vert) . . . 20 50

76 17th-Century Bottle Post

1980. "London 1980" International Stamp Exhibition. Multicoloured.
264 8p. Type **76** . . . 15 20
265 12p. 19th-century chance calling ship . . . 20 25
266 15p. "Garth Castle" (regular mail service from 1863) . . . 20 30
267 50p. "St. Helena" (mail services, 1980) . . . 60 90

77 H.M. Queen Elizabeth the Queen Mother

1980. 80th Birthday of The Queen Mother.
269 **77** 15p. multicoloured . . . 40 40

78 Lubbock's Yellowtail

1980. Fishes. Multicoloured.
270 3p. Type **78** . . . 30 25
271 10p. Resplendent angelfish . . . 40 25
272 25p. Bicoloured butterflyfish . . . 50 55
273 40p. Marmalade razorfish . . . 60 75

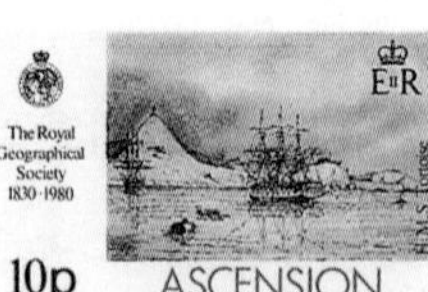

79 H.M.S. "Tortoise"

1980. 150th Anniv of Royal Geographical Society. Multicoloured.
274 10p. Type **79** . . . 20 40
275 15p. "Wideawake Fair" . . . 30 45
276 60p. Mid-Atlantic Ridge (38 × 48 mm) . . . 65 1·25

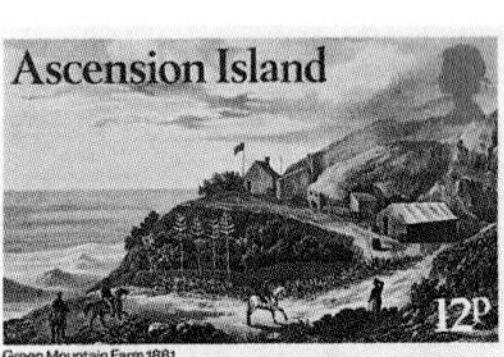

80 Green Mountain Farm, 1881

1981. Green Mountain Farm. Multicoloured.
277 12p. Type **80** . . . 15 35
278 15p. Two Boats, 1881 . . . 15 40
279 20p. Green Mountain and Two Boats, 1981 . . . 20 50
280 30p. Green Mountain Farm, 1981 . . . 30 70

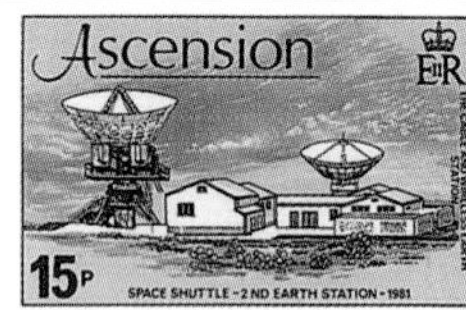

81 Cable and Wireless Earth Station

1981. "Space Shuttle" Mission and Opening of 2nd Earth Station.
281 **81** 15p. black, blue and pale blue . . . 30 35

82 Poinsettia

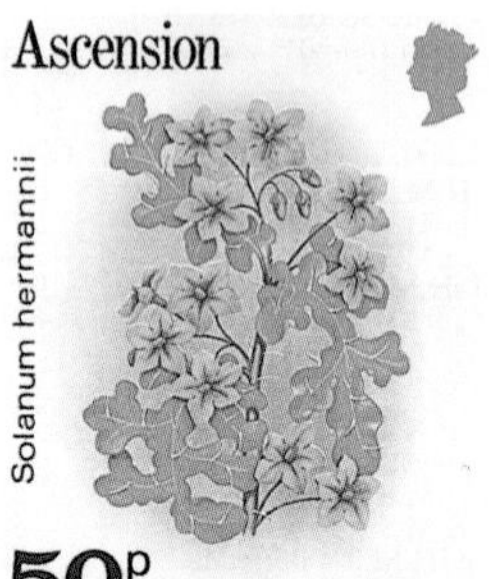

83 Solanum

1981. Flowers. Multicoloured.
282A 1p. Type **82** . . . 70 70
283B 2p. Clustered wax flower . . . 50 75
284B 3p. Kolanchoe (vert) . . . 50 75
285A 4p. Yellow pops . . . 80 75
286A 5p. Camels foot creeper . . . 80 75
287A 8p. White oleander . . . 80 80
288B 10p. Ascension lily (vert) 45 75
289A 12p. Coral plant (vert) . . . 1·50 85
290B 15p. Yellow allamanda . . . 50 75
291B 20p. Ascension euphorbia 1·00 75
292A 30p. Flame of the forest (vert) . . . 1·25 1·25
293A 40p. Bougainvillea "King Leopold" . . . 1·25 2·50
294A 50p. Type **83** . . . 1·25 2·75
295B £1 Ladies petticoat . . . 2·00 3·00
296A £2 Red hibiscus . . . 3·75 5·50
Nos. 294/6 are as Type **83**.

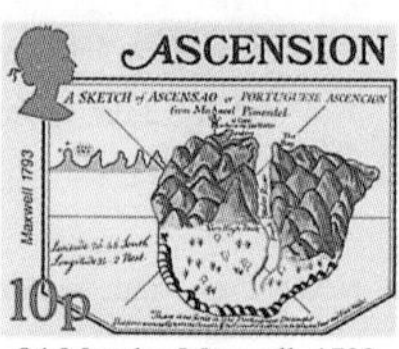

84 Map by Maxwell, 1793

1981. Early Maps of Ascension.
297 **84** 10p. black, gold and blue . . . 25 35
298 – 12p. black, gold and green . . . 25 35
299 – 15p. black, gold and stone . . . 25 35
300 – 40p. black, gold and yellow . . . 55 70
MS301 – 79 × 64 mm. 5p. × 4 multicoloured . . . 60 75
DESIGNS: 12p. Maxwell, 1793 (different); 15p. Ekeberg and Chapman, 1811; 40p. Campbell, 1819; miniature sheet, Linschoten, 1599.
Stamps from **MS**301 form a composite design.

85 Wedding Bouquet from Ascension **87** "Interest"

1981. Royal Wedding. Multicoloured.
302 10p. Type **85** . . . 15 15
303 15p. Prince Charles in Fleet Air Arm flying kit . . . 30 25
304 50p. Prince Charles and Lady Diana Spencer . . . 65 75

1981. 25th Anniv of Duke of Edinburgh Award Scheme. Multicoloured.
305 5p. Type **87** . . . 15 15
306 10p. "Physical activities" . . . 15 15
307 15p. "Service" . . . 20 20
308 40p. Duke of Edinburgh . . . 45 45

88 Scout crossing Rope Bridge

1982. 75th Anniv of Boy Scout Movement.
309 **88** 10p. black, blue and light blue . . . 15 35
310 – 15p. black, brown and yellow . . . 15 50
311 – 25p. black, mve & lt mve 20 60
312 – 40p. black, red and orange 30 85
MS313 – 121 × 121 mm. 10, 15, 25, 40p. As Nos. 309/12 (each diamond 40 × 40 mm) . . . 1·00 2·50
DESIGNS: 15p. 1st Ascension Scout Group flag; 25p. Scouts learning to use radio; 40p. Lord Baden-Powell.

89 Charles Darwin

1982. 150th Anniv of Charles Darwin's Voyage. Multicoloured.
314 10p. Type **89** . . . 25 40
315 12p. Darwin's pistols . . . 30 50
316 15p. Rock crab . . . 35 55
317 40p. H.M.S. "Beagle" . . . 75 95

90 Fairey Swordfish Torpedo Bomber

1982. 40th Anniv of Wideawake Airfield. Multicoloured.
318 5p. Type **90** . . . 1·00 35
319 10p. North American B-25C Mitchell . . . 1·25 40
320 15p. Boeing EC-135N Aria 1·50 55
321 50p. Lockheed C-130 Hercules . . . 2·25 1·10

91 Ascension Coat of Arms

1982. 21st Birthday of Princess of Wales. Mult.
322 12p. Type **91** . . . 25 25
323 15p. Lady Diana Spencer in Music Room, Buckingham Palace . . . 25 25
324 25p. Bride and Earl Spencer leaving Clarence House . . . 40 40
325 50p. Formal portrait . . . 75 75

1982. Commonwealth Games, Brisbane. Nos. 290/1 optd **1st PARTICIPATION COMMONWEALTH GAMES 1982**.
326 15p. Yellow allamanda . . . 30 40
327 20p. Ascension euphorbia . . . 40 45

94 Bush House, London

1982. Christmas. 50th Anniv of B.B.C. External Broadcasting. Multicoloured.
328 5p. Type **94** . . . 15 20
329 10p. Atlantic relay station . . . 20 30
330 25p. Lord Reith, first Director-General . . . 30 60
331 40p. King George V making his first Christmas broadcast, 1932 . . . 45 75

95 "Marasmius echinosphaerus"

1983. Fungi. Multicoloured.
332 7p. Type **95** 45 30
333 12p. "Chlorophyllum molybdites" 60 45
334 15p. "Leucocoprinus cepaestripes" 70 50
335 20p. "Lycoperdon marginatum" 80 65
336 50p. "Marasmiellus distantifolius" . . . . . . 1·25 1·25

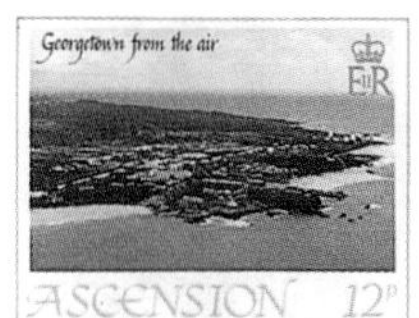

96 Aerial View of Georgetown

1983. Island Views (1st series). Multicoloured.
337 12p. Type **96** 15 25
338 15p. Green Mountain farm 15 25
339 20p. Boatswain Bird Island 20 40
340 60p. Telemetry Hill by night 40 80
See also Nos. 367/70.

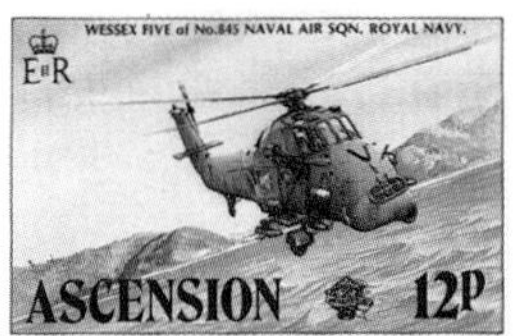

97 Westland Wessex 5 Helicopter of No. 845 Naval Air Squadron

1983. Bicentenary of Manned Flight. British Military Aircraft. Multicoloured.
341 12p. Type **97** 60 65
342 15p. Avro Vulcan B.2 of No. 44 Squadron 70 75
343 20p. Hawker Siddeley Nimrod M.R.2P of No. 20 Squadron 75 85
344 60p. Handey Page Victor K2 of No. 55 Squadron . . . 1·25 2·00

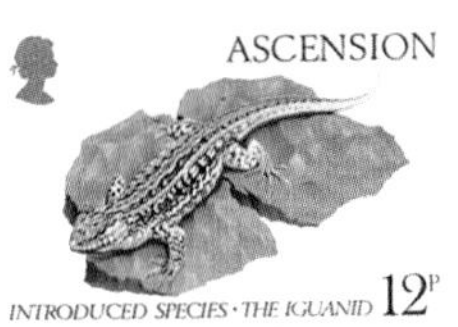

98 Iguanid

1983. Introduced Species. Multicoloured.
345 12p. Type **98** 30 30
346 15p. Common rabbit 35 35
347 20p. Cat 45 45
348 60p. Donkey . . . . 1·10 1·40

99 Speckled Tellin

1983. Sea Shells. Multicoloured.
349 7p. Type **99** 15 20
350 12p. Lion's paw scallop . . . 15 30
351 15p. Lurid cowrie 15 35
352 20p. Ascension nerite 20 45
353 50p. Miniature melo . . . . 40 1·10

100 1922 1½d. Stamp

101 Prince Andrew

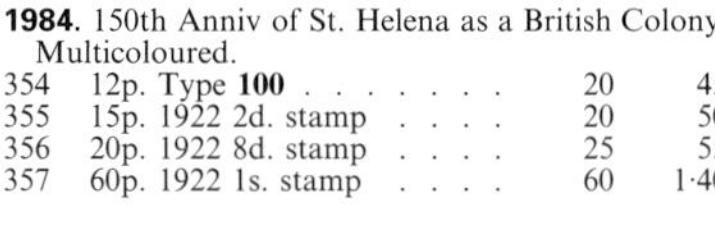
1984. 150th Anniv of St. Helena as a British Colony. Multicoloured.
354 12p. Type **100** 20 45
355 15p. 1922 2d. stamp 20 50
356 20p. 1922 8d. stamp 25 55
357 60p. 1922 1s. stamp . . . . 60 1·40

1984. Visit of Prince Andrew. Sheet 124 × 90 mm.
MS358 12p. Type **101**; 70p. Prince Andrew in naval uniform 1·40 1·60

102 Naval Semaphore

1984. 250th Anniv of "Lloyd's List" (newspaper). Multicoloured.
359 12p. Type **102** 40 30
360 15p. "Southampton Castle" (liner) 40 35
361 20p. Pier head 45 45
362 70p. "Dane" (screw steamer) 1·00 1·50

103 Penny Coin and Yellow-finned Tuna

1984. New Coinage. Multicoloured.
363 12p. Type **103** 45 35
364 15p. Twopenny coin and donkey 50 40
365 20p. Fifty pence coin and green turtle 60 50
366 70p. Pound coin and sooty tern . . . . 1·00 1·75

1984. Island Views (2nd series). As T **96**. Mult.
367 12p. The Devil's Riding-school 20 30
368 15p. St. Mary's Church . . . 25 35
369 20p. Two Boats Village . . . 25 45
370 70p. Ascension from the sea 80 1·50

104 Bermuda Cypress

105 The Queen Mother with Prince Andrew at Silver Jubilee Service

1985. Trees. Multicoloured.
371 7p. Type **104** 25 20
372 12p. Norfolk Island pine . . 30 30
373 15p. Screwpine 30 35
374 20p. Eucalyptus 30 45
375 65p. Spore tree . . . . . . 80 1·40

1985. Life and Times of Queen Elizabeth the Queen Mother. Multicoloured.
376 12p. With the Duke of York at Balmoral, 1924 . . . . 25 35
377 15p. Type **105** 25 40
378 20p. The Queen Mother at Ascot 30 55
379 70p. With Prince Henry at his christening (from photo by Lord Snowdon) . . . . . 80 1·75
MS380 91 × 73 mm. 75p. Visiting the "Queen Elizabeth 2" at Southampton, 1968 1·10 1·60

106 32 Pdr. Smooth Bore Muzzle-loader, c. 1820, and Royal Marine Artillery Hat Plate, c. 1816

1985. Guns on Ascension Island. Multicoloured.
381 12p. Type **106** 50 90
382 15p. 7 inch rifled muzzle-loader, c. 1866, and Royal Cypher on barrel . . . . 50 1·00
383 20p. 7 pdr rifled muzzle-loader, c. 1877, and Royal Artillery Badge . . . . . 50 1·25
384 70p. 5.5 inch gun, 1941, and crest from H.M.S. "Hood" 1·25 3·50

107 Guide Flag

108 "Clerodendrum fragrans"

1985. 75th Anniv of Girl Guide Movement and International Youth Year. Multicoloured.
385 12p. Type **107** 50 70
386 15p. Practising first aid . . . 50 80
387 20p. Camping 50 90
388 70p. Lady Baden-Powell . . 1·25 2·50

1985. Wild Flowers. Multicoloured.
389 12p. Type **108** 35 75
390 15p. Shell ginger 40 90
391 20p. Cape daisy 45 90
392 70p. Ginger lily . . . . . . 1·00 2·50

109 Newton's Reflector Telescope

110 Princess Elizabeth in 1926

1986. Appearance of Halley's Comet. Mult.
393 12p. Type **109** . . . . 50 1·10
394 15p. Edmond Halley and Old Greenwich Observatory . . 50 1·25
395 20p. Short's Gregorian telescope and comet, 1759 50 1·25
396 70p. Ascension satellite tracking station and ICE spacecraft . . . . 1·50 3·50

1986. 60th Birthday of Queen Elizabeth II. Mult.
397 7p. Type **110** 15 25
398 15p. Queen making Christmas broadcast, 1952 20 40
399 20p. At Garter ceremony, Windsor Castle, 1983 . . . 25 50
400 35p. In Auckland, New Zealand, 1981 . . . . . 35 80
401 £1 At Crown Agents' Head Office, London, 1983 . . . 1·00 2·25

111 1975 Space Satellites 2p. Stamp

1986. "Ameripex '86" International Stamp Exhibition, Chicago. Designs showing previous Ascension stamps. Multicoloured.
402 12p. Type **111** 30 60
403 15p. 1980 "London 1980" International Stamp Exhibition 50p. 30 70
404 20p. 1976 Bicentenary of American Revolution 8p. 35 90
405 70p. 1982 40th anniv of Wideawake Airfield 10p. 85 2·00
MS406 60 × 75 mm. 75p. Statue of Liberty 2·00 2·75

112 Prince Andrew and Miss Sarah Ferguson

1986. Royal Wedding. Multicoloured.
407 15p. Type **112** 25 35
408 35p. Prince Andrew aboard H.M.S. "Brazen" 50 75

113 H.M.S. "Ganymede" (c. 1811)

1986. Ships of the Royal Navy. Multicoloured.
409 1p. Type **113** . . . . 55 1·50
410 2p. H.M.S. "Kangaroo" (c.1811) . . . . 60 1·50
411 4p. H.M.S. "Trinculo" (c.1811) . . . . 60 1·50
412 5p. H.M.S. "Daring" (c.1811) 60 1·50
413 9p. H.M.S. "Thais" (c.1811) 70 1·50
414 10p. H.M.S. "Pheasant" (1819) . . . . 70 1·50
415 15p. H.M.S. "Myrmidon" (1819) . . . . 80 1·75
416 18p. H.M.S. "Atholl" (1825) 90 1·75
417 20p. H.M.S. "Medina" (1830) 90 1·75
418 25p. H.M.S. "Saracen" (1840) . . . . 1·00 2·00
419 30p. H.M.S. "Hydra" (c.1845) . . . . 1·00 2·00
420 50p. H.M.S. "Sealark" (1849) 1·00 2·50
421 70p. H.M.S. "Rattlesnake" (1868) . . . . 1·25 3·00
422 £1 H.M.S. "Penelope" (1889) 1·50 3·75
423 £2 H.M.S. "Monarch" (1897) 3·00 6·50

114 Cape Gooseberry

1987. Edible Bush Fruits. Multicoloured.
424 12p. Type **114** 65 90
425 15p. Prickly pear . . . . . . 65 1·00
426 20p. Guava . . . . 70 1·10
427 70p. Loquat . . . . 1·10 2·75

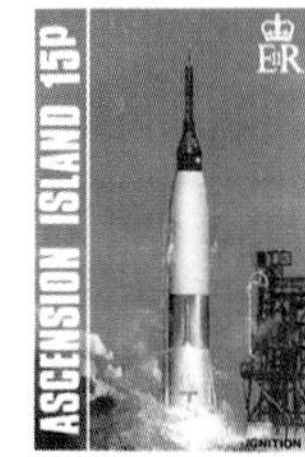

115 Ignition of Rocket Motors

116 Captains in Full Dress raising Red Ensign

1987. 25th Anniv of First American Manned Earth Orbit. Multicoloured.
428 15p. Type **115** 55 75
429 18p. Lift-off 60 80
430 25p. Re-entry 75 95
431 £1 Splashdown . . . . . . 2·50 3·25
MS432 92 × 78 mm. 70p. "Friendship 7" capsule 1·75 2·00

1987. 19th-century Uniforms (1st series). Royal Navy, 1815–20. Multicoloured.
433 25p. Type **116** 50 60
434 25p. Surgeon and seamen . . 50 60
435 25p. Seaman with water-carrying donkey 50 60
436 25p. Midshipman and gun . . 50 60
437 25p. Commander in undress uniform surveying 50 60
See also Nos. 478/82.

117 "Cynthia cardui"

1987. Insects (1st series). Multicoloured.
438 15p. Type **117** 65 65
439 18p. "Danaus chrysippus" . . 70 75
440 25p. "Hypolimnas misippus" 85 85
441 £1 "Lampides boeticus" . . . 2·25 2·50
See also Nos. 452/5 and 483/6.

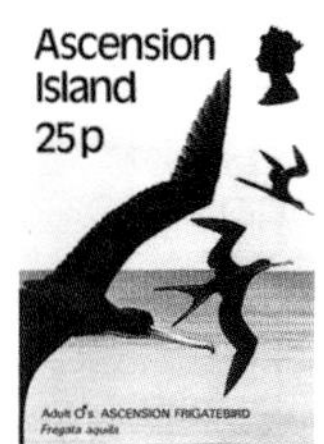

118 Male Ascension Frigate Birds

1987. Sea Birds (1st series). Multicoloured.
442 25p. Type **118** . . . . 1·60 1·90
443 25p. Juvenile Ascension frigate bird, brown booby and blue-faced boobies . . 1·60 1·90
444 25p. Male Ascension frigate bird and blue-faced boobies 1·60 1·90

445 25p. Female Ascension frigate bird . . . . 1·60 1·90
446 25p. Adult male feeding juvenile Ascension frigate bird . . . . 1·60 1·90

Nos. 442/6 were printed together, se-tenant, forming a composite design.

See also Nos. 469/73.

1987. Royal Ruby Wedding. Nos. 397/401 optd **40TH WEDDING ANNIVERSARY.**

447 7p. Type **110** 15 15
448 15p. Queen making Christmas broadcast, 1952 20 20
449 20p. At Garter ceremony, Windsor Castle, 1983 . . . 25 25
450 35p. In Auckland, New Zealand, 1981 . . . . . . 40 45
451 £1 At Crown Agents' Head Office, London, 1983 . . . 1·00 1·10

1988. Insects (2nd series). As T **117**. Multicoloured.

452 15p. "Gryllus bimaculatus" (field cricket) 50 50
453 18p. "Ruspolia differeus" (bush cricket) 55 55
454 25p. "Chilomenus lunata" (ladybird) 70 70
455 £1 "Diachrysia orichalcea" (moth) . . . . 2·25 2·25

120 Bate's Memorial, St. Mary's Church

1988. 150th Death Anniv of Captain William Bate (garrison commander, 1828–38). Multicoloured.

456 9p. Type **120** 35 35
457 15p. Commodore's Cottage 45 45
458 18p. North East Cottage . . 50 50
459 25p. Map of Ascension . . . 70 70
460 70p. Captain Bate and marines . . . . 1·75 1·75

121 H.M.S. "Resolution" (ship of the line), 1667

1988. Bicentenary of Australian Settlement. Ships of the Royal Navy. Multicoloured.

461 9p. Type **121** . . . . 1·00 45
462 18p. H.M.S. "Resolution" (Captain Cook), 1772 . . . 1·50 70
463 25p. H.M.S. "Resolution" (battleship), 1892 . . . . . 1·50 85
464 65p. H.M.S. "Resolution" (battleship), 1916 . . . . . 2·50 1·50

1988. "Sydpex '88" National Stamp Exhibition, Sydney. Nos. 461/4 optd **SYDPEX 88 30.7.88 - 7.8.88.**

465 9p. Type **121** 50 40
466 18p. H.M.S. "Resolution" (Captain Cook), 1772 . . . 75 60
467 25p. H.M.S. "Resolution" (battleship), 1892 . . . . . 85 70
468 65p. H.M.S. "Resolution" (battleship), 1916 . . . . . 1·60 1·40

1988. Sea Birds (2nd series). Sooty Tern. As T **118**. Multicoloured.

469 25p. Pair displaying . . . . 1·60 1·60
470 25p. Turning egg . . . . . . 1·60 1·60
471 25p. Incubating egg . . . . 1·60 1·60
472 25p. Feeding chick . . . . . 1·60 1·60
473 25p. Immature sooty tern . . 1·60 1·60

Nos. 469/73 were printed together, se-tenant, forming a composite design of a nesting colony.

123 Lloyd's Coffee House, London, 1688

124 Two Land Crabs

1988. 300th Anniv of Lloyd's of London. Mult.

474 8p. Type **123** 25 35
475 18p. "Alert IV" (cable ship) (horiz) 65 70

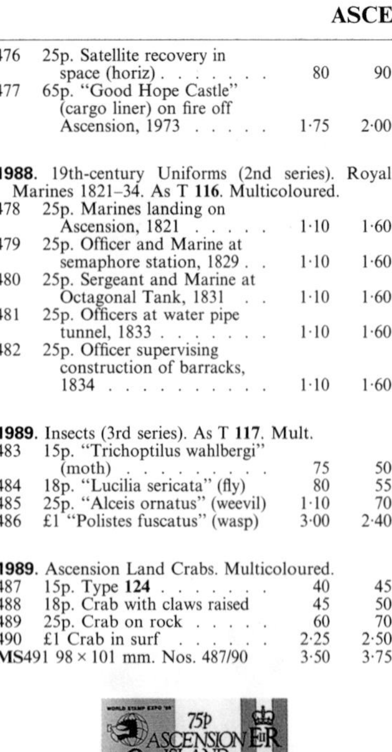

476 25p. Satellite recovery in space (horiz) 80 90
477 65p. "Good Hope Castle" (cargo liner) on fire off Ascension, 1973 . . . . . 1·75 2·00

1988. 19th-century Uniforms (2nd series). Royal Marines 1821–34. As T **116**. Multicoloured.

478 25p. Marines landing on Ascension, 1821 . . . . . 1·10 1·60
479 25p. Officer and Marine at semaphore station, 1829 . . 1·10 1·60
480 25p. Sergeant and Marine at Octagonal Tank, 1831 . . 1·10 1·60
481 25p. Officers at water pipe tunnel, 1833 . . . . 1·10 1·60
482 25p. Officer supervising construction of barracks, 1834 . . . . 1·10 1·60

1989. Insects (3rd series). As T **117**. Mult.

483 15p. "Trichoptilus wahlbergi" (moth) 75 50
484 18p. "Lucilia sericata" (fly) 80 55
485 25p. "Alceis ornatus" (weevil) 1·10 70
486 £1 "Polistes fuscatus" (wasp) 3·00 2·40

1989. Ascension Land Crabs. Multicoloured.

487 15p. Type **124** 40 45
488 18p. Crab with claws raised 45 50
489 25p. Crab on rock 60 70
490 £1 Crab in surf . . . . . . 2·25 2·50
MS491 98 × 101 mm. Nos. 487/90 3·50 3·75

125 1949 75th Anniversary of U.P.U. 1s. Stamp

1989. "Philexfrance '89" International Stamp Exhibition, Paris, and "World Stamp Expo '89", Washington (1st issue). Sheet 104 × 86 mm.

MS492 75p. multicoloured 1·50 1·75

See also Nos. 498/503.

126 "Apollo 7" Tracking Station, Ascension

127 "Queen Elizabeth 2" (liner) and U.S.S. "John F. Kennedy" (aircraft carrier) in New York Harbour

1989. 20th Anniv of First Manned Landing on Moon. Multicoloured.

493 15p. Type **126** 65 45
494 18p. Launch of "Apollo 7" (30 × 30 mm) 70 50
495 25p. "Apollo 7" emblem (30 × 30 mm) 90 70
496 70p. "Apollo 7" jettisoning expended Saturn rocket . . 1·75 1·75
MS497 101 × 83 mm. £1 Diagram of "Apollo 11" mission 2·00 2·10

1989. "Philexfrance 89" International Stamp Exhibition, Paris, and "World Stamp Expo '89", Washington (1st issue). Designs showing Statue of Liberty and Centenary celebrations. Multicoloured.

498 15p. Type **127** 35 35
499 15p. Cleaning statue 35 35
500 15p. Statue of Liberty . . . 35 35
501 15p. Crown of statue 35 35
502 15p. Warships and New York skyline 35 35
503 15p. "Jean de Vienne" (French destroyer) and skyscrapers 35 35

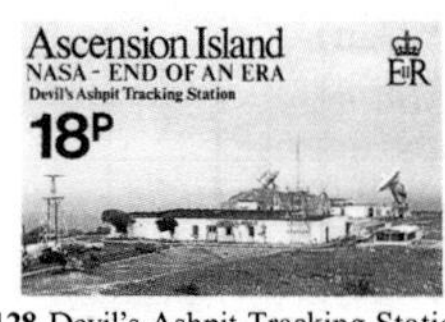

128 Devil's Ashpit Tracking Station

1989. Closure of Devil's Ashpit Tracking Station, Ascension. Multicoloured.

504 18p. Type **128** 80 50
505 25p. Launch of shuttle "Atlantis" 80 55

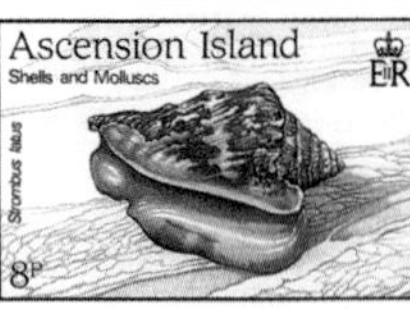

129 Bubonian Conch

1989. Sea Shells. Multicoloured.

506 8p. Type **129** 40 30
507 18p. Giant tun 70 50
508 25p. Doris loup 90 65
509 £1 Atlantic trumpet triton . . 2·75 2·50

130 Donkeys

131 Seaman's Pistol, Hat and Cutlass

1989. Ascension Wildlife. Multicoloured.

510 18p. Type **130** 60 60
511 25p. Green turtle 65 75

1990. Royal Navy Equipment, 1815–20. Mult.

512 25p. Type **131** 70 70
513 25p. Midshipman's belt plate, button, sword and hat . . 70 70
514 25p. Surgeon's hat, sword and instrument chest . . . 70 70
515 25p. Captain's hat, telescope and sword 70 70
516 25p. Admiral's epaulette, megaphone, hat and pocket 70 70

See also Nos. 541/5.

132 Pair of Ascension Frigate Birds with Young

134 "Queen Elizabeth, 1940" (Sir Gerald Kelly)

133 Penny Black and Twopence Blue

1990. Endangered Species. Ascension Frigate Bird. Multicoloured.

517 9p. Type **132** . . . . 1·50 1·00
518 10p. Fledgeling . . . . . . 1·50 1·00
519 11p. Adult male in flight . . 1·50 1·00
520 15p. Female and immature birds in flight . . . . . . 1·75 1·25

1990. "Stamp World London 90" International Stamp Exhibition. Multicoloured.

521 9p. Type **133** 50 40
522 18p. Ascension postmarks used on G.B. stamps . . . 70 60
523 25p. Unloading mail at Wideawake Airfield 95 85
524 £1 Mail van and Main Post Office . . . . 2·25 2·75

1990. 90th Birthday of Queen Elizabeth the Queen Mother.

525 **134** 25p. multicoloured . . . 75 75
526 – £1 black and lilac . . . . 2·25 2·25

DESIGN—29 × 37mm: £1 King George VI and Queen Elizabeth with Bren-gun carrier.

136 "Madonna and Child" (sculpture, Dino Felici)

137 "Garth Castle" (mail steamer), 1910

1990. Christmas. Works of Art. Multicoloured.

527 8p. Type **136** 70 70
528 18p. "Madonna and Child" (anon) . . . . 1·25 1·25
529 25p. "Madonna and Child with St. John" (Johann Gebhard) . . . . 1·75 1·75
530 65p. "Madonna and Child" (Giacomo Gritti) . . . . . 3·00 4·00

1990. Maiden Voyage of "St. Helena II". Mult.

531 9p. Type **137** 90 75
532 18p. "St. Helena I" during Falkland Islands campaign, 1982 . . . . 1·25 1·25
533 25p. Launch of "St. Helena II" . . . . 1·75 1·75
534 70p. Duke of York launching "St. Helena II" . . . . . 3·00 4·00
MS535 100 × 100 mm. £1 "St. Helena II" and outline map of Ascension 3·50 5·00

1991. 175th Anniv of Occupation. Nos. 418, 420 and 422 optd **BRITISH FOR 175 YEARS.**

536 25p. H.M.S. "Saracen" (1840) . . . . 1·75 2·25
537 50p. H.M.S. "Sealark" (1849) 2·25 3·00
538 £1 H.M.S. "Penelope" (1889) 3·25 4·50

139 Queen Elizabeth II at Trooping the Colour

1991. 65th Birthday of Queen Elizabeth II and 70th Birthday of Prince Philip. Multicoloured.

539 25p. Type **139** . . . . 1·00 1·40
540 25p. Prince Philip in naval uniform . . . . 1·00 1·40

1991. Royal Marines Equipment, 1821–1844. As T **131**. Multicoloured.

541 25p. Officer's shako, epaulettes, belt plate and button . . . . 1·10 1·50
542 25p. Officer's cap, sword, epaulettes and belt plate . . 1·10 1·50
543 25p. Drum major's shako and staff . . . . 1·10 1·50
544 25p. Sergeant's shako, chevrons, belt plate and canteen . . . . 1·10 1·50
545 25p. Drummer's shako and side-drum . . . . 1·10 1·50

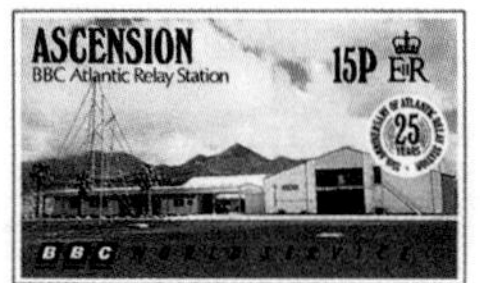

140 B.B.C. World Service Relay Station

1991. 25th Anniv of B.B.C. Atlantic Relay Station. Multicoloured.

546 15p. Type **140** . . . . 90 1·10
547 18p. Transmitters at English Bay . . . . 1·00 1·25
548 25p. Satellite receiving station (vert) . . . . 1·25 1·40
549 70p. Antenna support tower (vert) . . . . 2·50 3·50

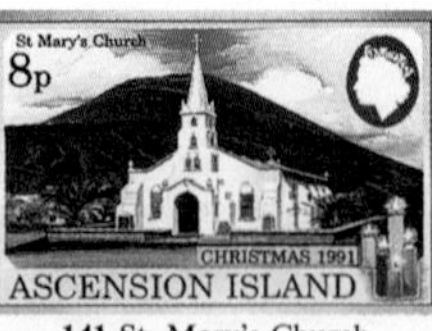

141 St. Mary's Church

1991. Christmas. Ascension Churches. Mult.

550 8p. Type **141** 55 55
551 18p. Interior of St. Mary's Church . . . . 1·00 1·00
552 25p. Our Lady of Ascension Grotto . . . . 1·25 1·25
553 65p. Interior of Our Lady of Ascension Grotto . . . . 2·75 4·50

142 Black Durgon ("Blackfish")

1991. Fishes. Multicoloured.

554 1p. Type **142** 75 60
555 2p. Sergeant major ("Five finger") 85 60
556 4p. Resplendent angelfish . . 90 70
557 5p. Derbio ("Silver fish") . . 90 70
558 9p. Spotted scorpionfish ("Gurnard") . . . . 1·25 80

559 10p. St. Helena parrotfish ("Blue dad") 1·25 80
560 15p. St. Helena butterflyfish ("Cunning fish") 1·50 1·00
561 18p. Rock hind ("Grouper") 1·50 1·00
562 20p. Spotted moray 1·50 1·25
563 25p. Squirrelfish ("Hardback soldierfish") 1·50 1·25
564 30p. Blue marlin 1·50 1·40
565 50p. Wahoo 2·00 2·00
566 70p. Yellow-finned tuna 2·25 2·75
567 £1 Blue shark 2·75 3·50
568 £2.50 Bottlenose dolphin 6·00 7·00

143 Holland's Crater

1992. 40th Anniv of Queen Elizabeth II's Accession. Multicoloured.
569 9p. Type **143** 30 30
570 15p. Green Mountain 50 50
571 18p. Boatswain Bird Island 60 60
572 25p. Three portraits of Queen Elizabeth 80 80
573 70p. Queen Elizabeth II 2·00 2·00
The portraits shown on the 25p. are repeated from the three lower values of the set.

144 Compass Rose and "Eye of the Wind" (cadet brig)

1992. 500th Anniv of Discovery of America by Columbus and Re-enactment Voyages. Mult.
574 9p. Type **144** 85 70
575 18p. Map of re-enactment voyages and "Soren Larsen" (cadet brigantine) 1·40 1·00
576 25p. "Santa Maria", "Pinta" and "Nina" 1·75 1·25
577 70p. Columbus and "Santa Maria" 3·25 2·75

145 Control Tower, Wideawake Airfield
146 Hawker Siddeley Nimrod

1992. 50th Anniv of Wideawake Airfield. Multicoloured.
578 15p. Type **145** 65 65
579 18p. Nose hangar 70 70
580 25p. Site preparation by U.S. Army engineers 90 90
581 70p. Laying fuel pipeline 2·25 2·25

1992. 10th Anniv of Liberation of Falkland Islands. Aircraft. Multicoloured.
582 15p. Type **146** 1·25 1·25
583 18p. Vickers VC-10 landing at Ascension 1·25 1·25
584 25p. Westland Wessex HU Mk 5 helicopter lifting supplies 1·75 1·50
585 65p. Avro Vulcan B.2 over Ascension 3·00 3·75
MS586 116 × 116 mm. 15p.+3p. Type **146**; 18p.+4p. As No. 583; 25p.+5p. As No. 584; 65p.+13p. As No. 585 4·75 6·00
The premiums on No. **MS**586 were for the S.S.A.F.A.

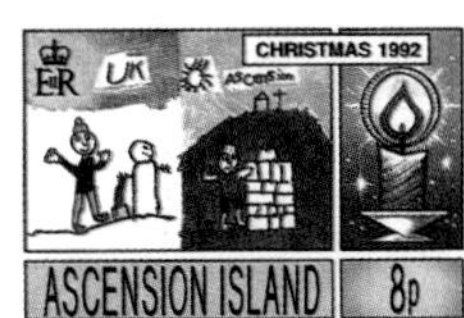

147 "Christmas in Great Britain and Ascension"

1992. Christmas. Children's Paintings. Mult.
587 8p. Type **147** 80 1·00
588 18p. "Santa Claus riding turtle" 1·25 1·50
589 25p. "Nativity" 1·50 1·75
590 65p. "Nativity with rabbit" 2·75 4·50

148 Male Canary Singing

1993. Yellow Canary. Multicoloured.
591 15p. Type **148** 75 70
592 18p. Adult male and female 85 80
593 25p. Young birds calling for food 95 95
594 70p. Adults and young birds on the wing 2·50 3·50

149 Sopwith Snipe

1993. 75th Anniv of Royal Air Force. Multicoloured.
595 20p. Type **149** 1·50 1·50
596 25p. Supermarine Southampton 1·50 1·50
597 30p. Avro Type 652 Anson 1·60 1·60
598 70p. Vickers-Armstrong Wellington 2·75 3·75
MS599 110 × 77 mm. 25p. Westland Lysander; 25p. Armstrong-Whitworth Meteor ("Gloster Meteor"); 25p. De Havilland D.H.106 Comet; 25p. Hawker Siddeley H.S.801 Nimrod 2·75 4·00

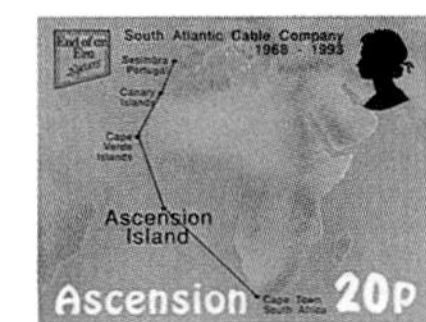

150 Map of South Atlantic Cable

1993. 25th Anniv of South Atlantic Cable Company. Multicoloured.
600 20p. Type **150** 80 80
601 25p. "Sir Eric Sharpe" laying cable 90 90
602 30p. Map of Ascension 1·00 1·00
603 70p. "Sir Eric Sharpe" (cable ship) off Ascension 2·25 2·50

151 Lanatana Camara

1993. Local Flowers. Multicoloured.
604 20p. Type **151** 1·00 70
605 25p. Moonflower 1·10 75
606 30p. Hibiscus 1·10 85
607 70p. Frangipani 2·50 2·25

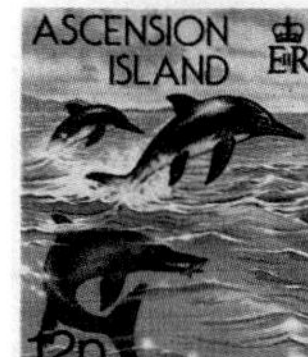

152 Posting Christmas Card to Ascension
153 Ichthyosaurus

1993. Christmas. Multicoloured.
608 12p. Type **152** 45 45
609 20p. Loading mail onto R.A.F. Lockheed TriStar at Brize Norton 75 55
610 25p. TriStar over South Atlantic 85 65
611 30p. Unloading mail at Wideawake Airfield 1·10 75
612 65p. Receiving card and Georgetown Post Office 1·60 2·00
MS613 161 × 76 mm. Nos. 608/12 7·50 7·50

1994. Prehistoric Aquatic Reptiles. Mult.
614 12p. Type **153** 70 1·00
615 20p. Metriorhynchus 85 1·10
616 25p. Mosasaurus 90 1·25
617 30p. Elasmosaurus 90 1·40
618 65p. Plesiosaurus 1·75 2·50

1994. "Hong Kong '94" International Stamp Exhibition. Nos. 614/18 optd **HONG KONG '94** and emblem.
619 12p. Type **153** 85 1·25
620 20p. Metriorhynchus 1·10 1·40
621 25p. Mosasaurus 1·10 1·60
622 30p. Elasmosaurus 1·25 1·75
623 65p. Plesiosaurus 2·25 3·25

155 Young Green Turtles heading towards Sea

1994. Green Turtles. Multicoloured.
624 20p. Type **155** 1·50 1·75
625 25p. Turtle digging nest 1·60 1·75
626 30p. Turtle leaving sea 1·75 1·75
627 65p. Turtle swimming 2·75 4·00
MS628 116 × 90 mm. 30p. Turtle leaving sea (different); 30p. Turtle digging nest (different); 30p. Young turtles heading towards sea (different); 30p. Young turtle leaving nest 7·50 8·00

156 "Yorkshireman" (tug)

1994. Civilian Ships used in Liberation of Falkland Islands, 1982. Multicoloured.
629 20p. Type **156** 1·50 1·75
630 25p. "St. Helena I" (minesweeper support ship) 1·60 1·75
631 30p. "British Esk" (tanker) 1·75 1·75
632 65p. "Uganda" (hospital ship) 2·75 4·00

157 Sooty Tern Chick

1994. Sooty Tern. Multicoloured.
633 20p. Type **157** 90 1·40
634 25p. Juvenile bird 95 1·40
635 30p. Brooding adult 1·10 1·60
636 65p. Adult male performing courting display 1·75 2·50
MS637 77 × 58 mm. £1 Flock of sooty terns 3·50 4·75

158 Donkey Mare with Foal
159 "Leonurus japonicus"

1994. Christmas. Donkeys. Multicoloured.
638 12p. Type **158** 90 90
639 20p. Juvenile 1·25 1·25
640 25p. Foal 1·25 1·25
641 30p. Adult and cattle egrets 1·40 1·40
642 65p. Adult 2·50 3·50

1995. Flowers. Multicoloured.
643 20p. Type **159** 2·00 2·00
644 25p. "Catharanthus roseus" (horiz) 2·00 2·00
645 30p. "Mirabilis jalapa" 2·25 2·25
646 65p. "Asclepias curassavica" (horiz) 3·00 4·00

160 Two Boats and Green Mountain

1995. Late 19th-century Scenes. Each in cinnamon and brown.
647 12p. Type **160** 50 70
648 20p. Island Stewards' Store 70 80
649 25p. Navy headquarters and barracks 90 1·00
650 30p. Police office 1·75 1·75
651 65p. Pierhead 2·00 3·25

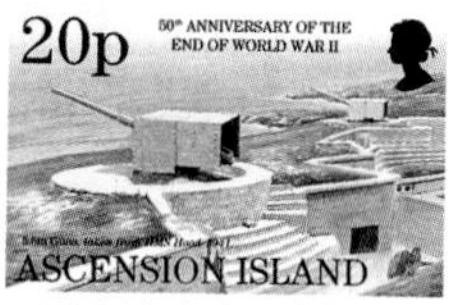

161 5.5-inch Coastal Battery

1995. 50th Anniv of End of Second World War. Multicoloured.
652 20p. Type **161** 1·00 1·50
653 25p. Fairey Swordfish aircraft 1·25 1·75
654 30p. H.M.S. "Dorsetshire" (cruiser) 1·50 2·00
655 65p. H.M.S. "Devonshire" (cruiser) 2·50 3·75
MS656 75 × 85 mm. £1 Reverse of 1939–45 War Medal (vert) 2·50 3·25

162 Male and Female "Lampides boeticus"

1995. Butterflies. Multicoloured.
657 20p. Type **162** 1·00 1·00
658 25p. "Vanessa cardui" 1·10 1·10
659 30p. Male "Hypolimnas misippus" 1·25 1·25
660 65p. "Danaus chrysippus" 2·25 2·75
MS661 114 × 85 mm. £1 "Vanessa atalanta" 3·50 3·25
No. **MS**661 includes the "Singapore '95" International Stamp Exhibition logo on the sheet margin.

163 "Santa Claus on Boat" (Phillip Stephens)

1995. Christmas. Children's Drawings. Mult.
662 12p. Type **163** 85 85
663 20p. "Santa sitting on Wall" (Kelly Lemon) 1·25 1·25
664 25p. "Santa in Chimney" (Mario Anthony) 1·40 1·40
665 30p. "Santa riding Dolphin" (Verena Benjamin) 1·40 1·40
666 65p. "Santa in Sleigh over Ascension" (Tom Butler) 2·50 3·50

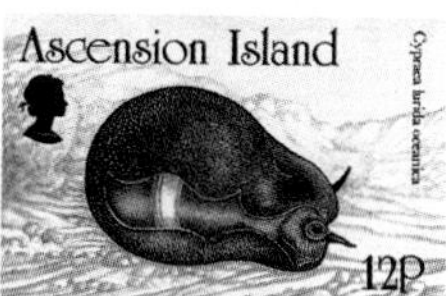

164 "Cypraea lurida oceanica"

1996. Molluscs. Multicoloured.
667 12p. Type **164** 1·75 2·00
668 25p. "Cypraea spurca sanctaehelenae" 2·00 2·25
669 30p. "Harpa doris" 2·00 2·25
670 65p. "Umbraculum umbraculum" 2·50 2·75
Nos. 667/70 were printed together, se-tenant, forming a composite design.

165 Queen Elizabeth II and St. Mary's Church

1996. 70th Birthday of Queen Elizabeth II. Mult.

671 20p. Type **165** 55 60
672 25p. The Residency 60 60
673 30p. The Roman Catholic Grotto 70 70
674 65p. The Exiles' Club . . . . 1·75 1·75

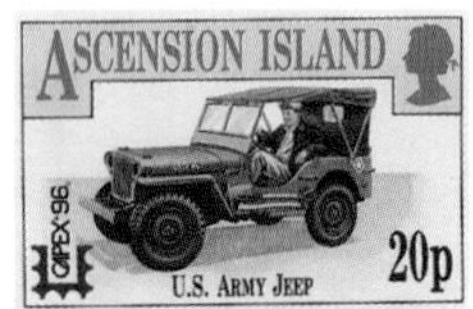

166 American Army Jeep

1996. "CAPEX '96" International Stamp Exhibition, Toronto. Island Transport. Multicoloured.

675 20p. Type **166** 75 75
676 25p. Citroen 7.5hp two-seater car, 1924 . . . . 80 80
677 30p. Austin ten tourer car, 1930 . . . . 90 90
678 65p. Series 1 Land Rover . . 1·75 1·75

167 Madeiran Storm Petrel **168** Pylons

1996. Birds and their Young. Multicoloured.

679 1p. Type **167** 50 60
680 2p. Red-billed tropic bird . . 50 60
681 4p. Common mynah 50 60
682 5p. House sparrow 50 60
683 7p. Common waxbill 65 65
684 10p. White tern 70 70
685 12p. Red-necked spurfowl . . 80 80
686 15p. Common noddy ("Brown Noddy") 90 90
687 20p. Yellow canary . . . . . 1·00 1·00
688 25p. White-capped noddy ("Black Noddy") . . . . . 1·00 1·00
689 30p. Red-footed booby . . . 1·25 1·25
690 40p. White-tailed tropic bird ("Yellow-billed Tropicbird") . . . . 1·50 1·50
691 65p. Brown booby . . . . . 2·00 2·25
692 £1 Blue-faced booby ("Masked Booby") . . . . 2·50 2·75
693 £2 Sooty tern . . . . 4·50 5·00
694 £3 Ascension frigate bird . . 6·50 7·00

See also Nos. 726/7.

1996. 30th Anniv of B.B.C. Atlantic Relay Station. Multicoloured.

695 20p. Type **168** 65 65
696 25p. Pylons (different) . . . 70 70
697 30p. Pylons and station buildings 80 80
698 65p. Dish aerial, pylon and beach . . . . 1·75 1·75

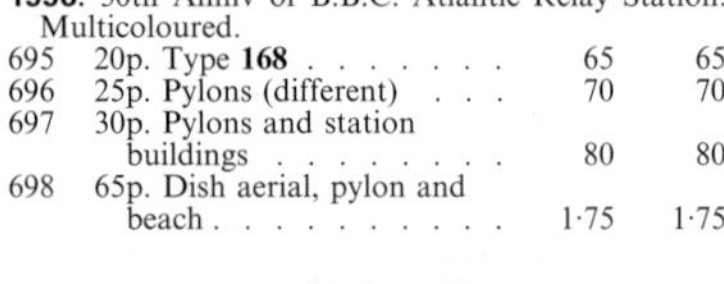

169 Santa Claus on Dish Aerial

1996. Christmas. Santa Claus. Multicoloured.

699 12p. Type **169** 35 35
700 20p. Playing golf 65 65
701 25p. In deck chair 65 65
702 30p. On top of aircraft . . . 75 75
703 65p. On funnel of "St. Helena II" (mail ship) 1·75 2·00

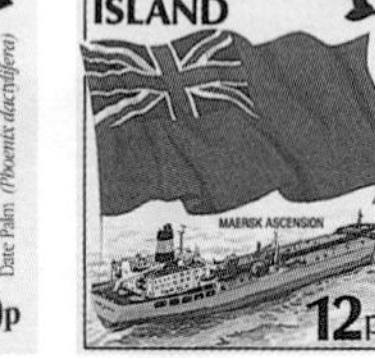

170 Date Palm **171** Red Ensign and "Maersk Ascension" (tanker)

1997. "Hong Kong '97" International Stamp Exhibition. Trees. Multicoloured.

704 20p. Type **170** 55 55
705 25p. Mauritius hemp 65 65
706 30p. Norfolk Island pine . . 75 75
707 65p. Dwarf palm . . . . . . 1·50 1·60

1997. "HONG KONG '97" International Stamp Exhibition. Sheet 130 × 90 mm containing design as No. 691. Multicoloured.

MS708 65p. Brown booby 1·50 1·50

1997. Flags. Multicoloured.

709 12p. Type **171** 60 60
710 25p. R.A.F. flag and Tristar airliner 90 90
711 30p. N.A.S.A. emblem and Space Shuttle "Atlantis" landing . . . . 1·00 1·00
712 65p. White Ensign and H.M.S. "Northumberland" (frigate) . . . . 1·75 1·75

172 "Solanum sodomaeum"

1997. Wild Herbs. Multicoloured.

713 30p. Type **172** . . . . 90 1·00
714 30p. "Ageratum conyzoides" 90 1·00
715 30p. "Leonurus sibiricus" . . 90 1·00
716 30p. "Cerastium vulgatum" 90 1·00
717 30p. "Commelina diffusa" . . 90 1·00

Nos. 713/17 were printed together, se-tenant, with the backgrounds forming a composite design.

1997. Return of Hong Kong to China. Sheet 130 × 90 mm containing design as No. 692, but with "1997" imprint date.

MS718 £1 Blue-faced booby 2·00 2·10

173 Queen Elizabeth II

1997. Golden Wedding of Queen Elizabeth and Prince Philip. Multicoloured.

719 20p. Type **173** . . . . 1·25 1·40
720 20p. Prince Philip on horseback . . . . 1·25 1·40
721 25p. Queen Elizabeth with polo pony . . . . 1·25 1·40
722 25p. Prince Philip in Montserrat . . . . 1·25 1·40
723 30p. Queen Elizabeth and Prince Philip . . . . . . 1·25 1·40
724 30p. Prince William and Prince Harry on horseback 1·25 1·40

MS725 110 × 70 mm. $1.50, Queen Elizabeth and Prince Philip in landau (horiz) 3·50 3·50

Nos. 719/20, 721/2 and 723/4 respectively were printed together, se-tenant, with the backgrounds forming composite designs.

1997. Birds and their Young. As Nos. 683 and 687, but smaller, size 20 × 24 mm. Multicoloured.

726 15p. Common waxbill . . . 75 85
727 35p. Yellow canary . . . . . 1·00 1·25

174 Black Marlin

1997. Gamefish. Multicoloured.

728 12p. Type **174** 40 50
729 20p. Atlantic sailfish 65 75
730 25p. Swordfish 75 80
731 30p. Wahoo 85 90
732 £1 Yellowfin tuna . . . . . 2·25 2·75

175 Interior of St. Mary's Church **176** "Cactoblastis cactorum" (caterpillar and moth)

1997. Christmas. Multicoloured.

733 15p. Type **175** 45 45
734 35p. Falklands memorial window showing Virgin and child 85 85
735 40p. Falklands memorial window showing Archangel 95 1·10
736 50p. Pair of stained glass windows . . . . 1·25 1·40

1998. Biological Control using Insects. Mult.

737 15p. Type **176** 90 90
738 35p. "Teleonemia scrupulosa" (lace-bug) . . . . 1·40 1·40
739 40p. "Neltumius arizonensis" (beetle) . . . . 1·40 1·40
740 50p. "Algarobius prosopis" (beetle) . . . . 1·50 1·50

177 Diana, Princess of Wales, 1985

1998. Diana, Princess of Wales Commemoration. Sheet 145 × 70 mm, containing T **177** and similar vert designs. Multicoloured.

MS741 35p. Type **177**; 35p. Wearing yellow blouse, 1992; 35p. Wearing grey jacket, 1984; 35p. Carrying bouquets (sold at £1.40 + 20p. charity premium) 3·75 3·75

178 Fairey Fawn

1998. 80th Anniv of Royal Air Force. Mult.

742 15p. Type **178** 65 65
743 35p. Vickers Vernon . . . . 1·25 1·25
744 40p. Supermarine Spitfire F.22 . . . . 1·40 1·40
745 50p. Bristol Britannia C.2 . . 1·60 1·60

MS746 110 × 77 mm. 50p. Blackburn Kangaroo; 50p. S.E.5a; 50p. Curtiss Kittyhawk III; 50p. Boeing Fortress II 4·75 4·75

179 Barn Swallow **180** Cricket

1998. Migratory Birds. Multicoloured.

747 15p. Type **179** 60 70
748 25p. House martin 80 90
749 35p. Cattle egret . . . . . . 1·00 1·25
750 40p. Eurasian swift ("Swift") 1·00 1·40
751 50p. Allen's gallinule . . . . 1·10 1·60

1998. Sporting Activities. Multicoloured.

752 15p. Type **180** . . . . 1·50 75
753 35p. Golf . . . . 2·00 1·25
754 40p. Football . . . . 1·50 1·25
755 50p. Shooting . . . . 1·50 1·25

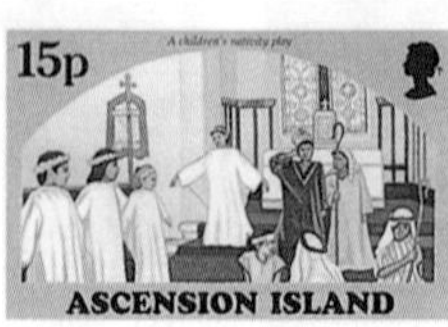

181 Children in Nativity Play

1998. Christmas. Multicoloured.

756 15p. Type **181** 75 75
757 35p. Santa Claus arriving on Ascension . . . . 1·25 1·25
758 40p. Santa Claus on carnival float . . . . 1·25 1·25
759 50p. Carol singers . . . . . 1·25 1·25

182 Curtiss C-46 Commando

1999. Aircraft. Multicoloured.

760 15p. Type **182** . . . . 75 1·00
761 35p. Douglas C-47 Dakota 1·25 1·75
762 40p. Douglas C-54 Skymaster 1·25 1·75
763 50p. Consolidated Liberator Mk. V . . . . 1·25 1·75

MS764 120 × 85 mm. $1.50, Consolidated Liberator LB-30 6·00 7·00

No. **MS**764 also commemorates the 125th birth anniv of Sir Winston Churchill.

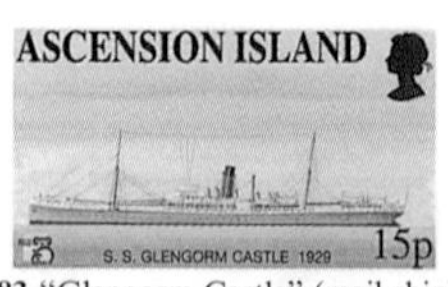

183 "Glengorm Castle" (mail ship), 1929

1999. "Australia '99" World Stamp Exhibition, Melbourne. Ships. Multicoloured.

765 15p. Type **183** . . . . 75 1·00
766 35p. "Gloucester Castle" (mail ship), 1930 . . . . 1·25 1·40
767 40p. "Durham Castle" (mail ship), 1930 . . . . 1·25 1·40
768 50p. "Garth Castle" (mail ship), 1930 . . . . 1·25 1·40

MS769 121 × 82 mm. £1 H.M.S. "Endeavour" (Cook) 2·50 2·75

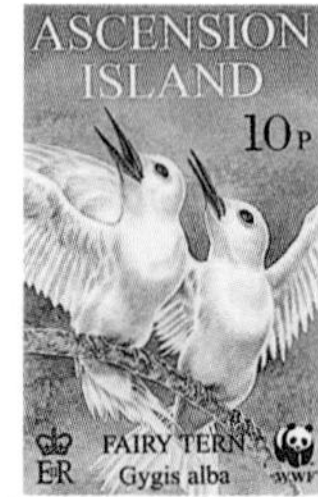

184 Pair of White Terns ("Fairy Terns")

1999. Endangered Species. White Tern ("Fairy Tern"). Multicoloured.

770 10p. Type **184** 30 40
771 10p. On branch 30 40
772 10p. Adult and fledgeling . . 30 40
773 10p. In flight 30 40

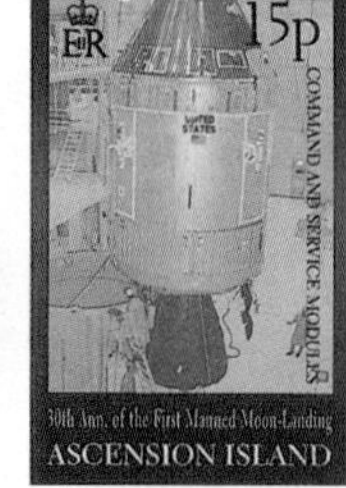

185 Prince Edward and Miss Sophie Rhys-Jones **186** Command and Service Modules

1999. Royal Wedding. Multicoloured.

774 50p. Type **185** . . . . 1·25 1·50
775 £1 Engagement photograph 2·25 2·50

1999. 30th Anniv of First Manned Landing on Moon. Multicoloured.

776 15p. Type **186** . . . . 75 1·00
777 35p. Moon from "Apollo 11" 1·25 1·40
778 40p. Devil's Ashpit Tracking Station and command module . . . . 1·25 1·40
779 50p. Lunar module leaving Moon . . . . 1·25 1·40

MS780 90 × 80 mm. $1.50, Earth as seen from Moon (circular, 40 mm diam) 3·75 4·50

187 King George VI, Queen Elizabeth and Prime Minister Winston Churchill, 1940

1999. "Queen Elizabeth the Queen Mother's Century". Multicoloured.

781 15p. Type **187** . . . . 75 1·00
782 35p. With Prince Charles at Coronation, 1953 . . . . 1·25 1·40
783 40p. On her 88th Birthday, 1988 . . . . 1·25 1·40
784 50p. With Guards' drummers, 1988 . . . . 1·25 1·40

MS785 145 × 70 mm. £1.50, Lady Elizabeth Bowes-Lyon, and "Titanic" (liner) (black) 3·50 4·50

188 Babies with Toys

1999. Christmas. Multicoloured.
786 15p. Type **188** . . . . 75 1·00
787 35p. Children dressed as clowns . . . . 1·25 1·40
788 40p. Getting ready for bed 1·25 1·40
789 50p. Children dressed as pirates . . . . 1·25 1·40

189 "Anglia" (cable ship), 1900

1999. Centenary of Cable & Wireless Communications plc on Ascension.
790 **189** 15p. black, brown and bistre . . . . 1·00 1·00
791 – 35p. black, brown and bistre . . . . 1·50 1·50
792 – 40p. multicoloured . . . 1·50 1·50
793 – 50p. black, brown and bistre . . . . 1·60 1·60
MS794 – 105 × 90 mm. £1.50, multicoloured 3·50 3·75
DESIGNS: 35p. "Cambria" (cable ship), 1910; 40p. Cable network map; 50p. "Colonia" (cable ship), 1910; £1.50, "Seine" (cable ship), 1899.

190 Baby Turtles

2000. Turtle Project on Ascension. Multicoloured.
795 15p. Type **190** . . . . 75 1·00
796 35p. Turtle on beach . . . . 1·25 1·40
797 40p. Turtle with tracking device . . . . 1·25 1·40
798 50p. Turtle heading for sea 1·40 1·40
MS799 197 × 132 mm. 25p. Head of turtle; 25p. Type **190**; 25p. Turtle on beach; 25p. Turtle entering sea (each 40 × 26 mm) 3·00 3·25

2000. "The Stamp Show 2000" International Stamp Exhibition, London. As No. **MS**799, but with "The Stamp Show 2000" added to the bottom right corner of the margin.
MS800 197 × 132 mm. 25p. Head of turtle; 25p. Type **190**; 25p. Turtle on beach; 25p. Turtle entering sea (each 40 × 26 mm) 2·75 3·00

191 Prince William as Toddler, 1983

2000. 18th Birthday of Prince William. Mult.
801 15p. Type **191** . . . . 75 1·00
802 35p. Prince William in 1994 1·25 1·40
803 40p. Skiing at Klosters, Switzerland (horiz) . . . . 1·25 1·40
804 50p. Prince William in 1997 (horiz) . . . . 1·40 1·40
MS805 175 × 95 mm. 10p. As baby with toy mouse (horiz) and Nos. 801/4 4·25 4·50

192 Royal Marine and Early Fort, 1815

2000. Forts. Multicoloured
806 15p. Type **192** . . . . 75 1·00
807 35p. Army officer and Fort Thornton, 1817 . . . . . 1·25 1·40
808 40p. Soldier and Fort Hayes, 1860 . . . . 1·25 1·40
809 50p. Naval lieutenant and Fort Bedford, 1940 . . . . 1·40 1·40

193 Ships and Dockside Crane ("I saw Three Ships")

2000. Christmas. Carols. Multicoloured.
810 15p. Type **193** 75 75
811 25p. Choir and musicians on beach ("Silent Night") . . 90 90
812 40p. Donkeys and church ("Away in a Manger") . . 1·50 1·50
813 90p. Carol singers outside church ("Hark the Herald Angels Sing") . . . . . . 2·50 3·00

194 Green Turtle

2001. "Hong Kong 2001" Stamp Exhibition. Sheet 150 × 90 mm, containing T **194**. Multicoloured.
MS814 25p. Type **194**; 40p. Loggerhead turtle 1·40 1·60

195 Captain William Dampier
196 Alfonso de Albuquerque

2001. Centenary of Wreck of the *Roebuck*. Mult.
815 15p. Type **195** 70 80
816 35p. Construction drawing (horiz) . . . . 1·10 1·25
817 40p. Cave dwelling at Dampier's Drip (horiz) . . 1·10 1·25
818 50p. Map of Ascension . . . 1·25 1·25

2001. 500th Anniv of the Discovery of Ascension Island. Multicoloured.
819 15p. Type **196** 70 80
820 35p. Portuguese caravel . . . 1·10 1·25
821 40p. Cantino map . . . . . 1·10 1·25
822 50p. Rear Admiral Sir George Cockburn . . . . 1·25 1·25

197 Great Britain 1d. Stamp used on Ascension, 1855

2001. Death Centenary of Queen Victoria. Mult.
823 15p. Type **197** 65 65
824 25p. Navy church parade, 1901 (horiz) 80 80
825 35p. H.M.S. *Phoebe* (cruiser) (horiz) . . . . 1·00 1·10
826 40p. The Red Lion, 1863 (horiz) . . . . 1·10 1·25
827 50p. "Queen Victoria" . . . 1·25 1·40
828 65p. Sir Joseph Hooker (botanist) . . . . 1·50 1·75
MS829 105 × 80 mm. £1.50, Queen Victoria's coffin on the steps of St. George's Chapel, Windsor (horiz) 3·50 4·00

198 Islander Hostel

2001. "BELGICA 2001" International Stamp Exhibition, Brussels. Tourism. Multicoloured.
830 35p. Type **198** . . . . 1·10 1·10
831 35p. The Residency . . . . . 1·10 1·10
832 40p. The Red Lion . . . . . 1·25 1·25
833 40p. Turtle Ponds . . . . . 1·25 1·25

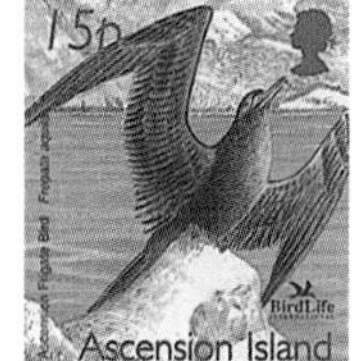

199 Female Ascension Frigate Bird

2001. Birdlife World Bird Festival. Ascension Frigate Birds. Multicoloured.
834 15p. Type **199** 75 75
835 35p. Fledgeling . . . . . . 1·10 1·25
836 40p. Male bird in flight (horiz) . . . . 1·10 1·25
837 50p. Male bird with pouch inflated (horiz) . . . . . . 1·25 1·40
MS838 175 × 80 mm. 10p. Male and female birds on rock (horiz) and Nos. 834/7 4·00 4·50

200 Princess Elizabeth and Dog

2002. Golden Jubilee.
839 **200** 15p. agate, mauve and gold 75 75
840 – 35p. multicoloured . . . 1·10 1·25
841 – 40p. multicoloured . . . 1·10 1·25
842 – 50p. multicoloured . . . 1·25 1·40
MS843 – 162 × 95 mm. Nos. 839/42 and 60p. multicoloured 5·00 5·50
DESIGNS—HORIZ: 35p. Queen Elizabeth wearing tiara, 1978; 40p. Princess Elizabeth, 1946; 50p. Queen Elizabeth visiting Henley-on-Thames, 1998. VERT: (38 × 51 mm)—50p. Queen Elizabeth after Annigoni.

201 Royal Marines landing at English Bay

2002. 20th Anniv of Liberation of the Falkland Islands. Multicoloured.
844 15p. Type **201** 45 50
845 35p. Weapons testing . . . . 90 1·00
846 40p. H.M.S. *Hermes* (aircraft carrier) . . . . 95 1·10
847 50p. R.A.F. Vulcan at Wideawake Airfield . . . . 3·25 3·50

202 Duchess of York at Harrow Hospital, 1931
204 "Ecce Ancilla Domini" (Dante Rossetti)

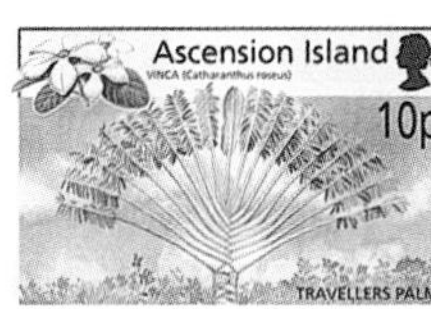

203 Travellers Palm and Vinca

2002. Queen Elizabeth the Queen Mother Commemoration.
848 **202** 35p. black, gold and purple 70 75
849 – 40p. multicoloured . . . 80 85
MS850 – 145 × 70 mm. 50p. brown and gold; £1 multicoloured 3·00 3·25
DESIGNS: 40p. Queen Mother on her birthday, 1997; 50p. Duchess of York, 1925; £1 Queen Mother, Scrabster, 1992.

2002. Island Views. Multicoloured.
851 10p. Type **203** 20 25
852 15p. Broken Tooth (volcanic crater) and Mexican poppy 30 35
853 20p. St. Mary's Church and Ascension lily 40 45
854 25p. Boatswain Bird Island and goatweed 50 55
855 30p. Cannon and Mauritius hemp 60 65
856 35p. The Guest House and frangipani 70 75
857 40p. Wideawake tern and Ascension spurge 80 85
858 50p. The Pier Head and lovechaste . . . . 1·00 1·10
859 65p. Sisters' Peak and yellowboy . . . . 1·25 1·40
860 90p. Two Boats School and Persian lilac . . . . 1·75 1·90
861 £2 Green turtle and wild currant . . . . 4·00 4·25
862 £5 Wideawake Airfield and coral tree . . . . 10·00 10·50

2002. Christmas. Religious Paintings. Multi.
863 15p. Type **204** 30 35
864 25p. "The Holy Family and Shepherd" (Titian) (horiz) 50 55
865 35p. "Christ carrying the Cross" (A. Bergognone) . . 70 75
866 75p. Sketch for "The Ascension" (Benjamin West) . . . . 1·50 1·75

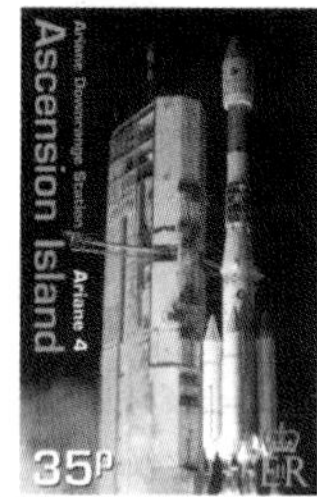

205 Ariane 4 Rocket on Gantry

2003. Ariane Downrange Station. Multicoloured.
867 35p. Type **205** 70 75
868 40p. Map of Ariane Downrange stations (horiz) 80 85
869 65p. Automated Transfer Vehicle (ATV) in Space (horiz) . . . . 1·25 1·40
870 90p. Launch of Ariane 5 . . 1·75 2·00
MS871 170 × 88 mm. Nos. 867/70 4·50 4·75

POSTAGE DUE STAMPS

D 1 Outline Map of Ascension

1986.
D1 **D 1** 1p. deep brown and brown 15 20
D2 2p. brown and orange . . 15 20
D3 5p. brown and orange . . 15 20
D4 7p. black and violet . . . 20 30
D5 10p. black and blue . . . 25 35
D6 25p. black and green . . 65 75

AUSTRALIA Pt. 1

An island continent to the S.E. of Asia. A Commonwealth consisting of the states of New S. Wales, Queensland, S. Australia, Tasmania, Victoria and W. Australia.

1913. 12 pence = 1 shilling;
20 shillings = 1 pound.
1966. 100 cents = 1 dollar.

1 Eastern Grey Kangaroo
3

1913.
1 **1** ½d. green . . . . 6·00 3·25
2 1d. red . . . . 8·50 1·00
35 2d. grey . . . . 26·00 6·50
36 2½d. blue . . . . 23·00 10·00
37 3d. green . . . . 28·00 4·50
6 4d. orange . . . . 50·00 22·00
8 5d. brown . . . . 40·00 32·00
38 6d. blue . . . . 55·00 7·50
73 6d. brown . . . . 24·00 1·75
133 9d. violet . . . . 28·00 1·25
40 1s. green . . . . 35·00 3·75
41 2s. brown . . . . £160 13·00
134 2s. purple . . . . 5·00 60
135 5s. grey and yellow . . . . £120 12·00
136 10s. grey and pink £250 £100
15 £1 brown and blue £1100 £1200
137 £1 grey £425 £160
138 £2 black and pink £1700 £350

1913.
20 **3** ½d. green . . . . 3·75 1·00
94 ½d. orange . . . . 2·25 1·40
17 1d. red . . . . 2·50 4·50
57 1d. violet . . . . 6·00 1·50

125 1d. green 1·75 20
59a 1½d. brown 6·50 60
61 1½d. green 4·00 80
77 1½d. red 2·25 40
62 2d. orange 15·00 1·00
127 2d. red 1·75 10
98 2d. brown 8·00 9·00
128 3d. blue 18·00 1·25
22 4d. orange 27·00 2·50
64 4d. violet 13·00 15·00
65 4d. blue 48·00 8·50
129 4d. green 18·00 1·25
92 4½d. violet 18·00 3·75
130 5d. brown 15·00 20
131 1s.4d. blue 50·00 3·50

4 Laughing Kookaburra

8 Parliament House, Canberra

1913.
19 **4** 6d. purple 65·00 38·00

1927. Opening of Parliament House.
105 **8** 1½d. red 50 50

1928. National Stamp Exhibition, Melbourne.
106 **4** 3d. blue 4·25 4·75
MS106a 65 × 70 mm. No. 106 × 4 £110 £200

9 De Havilland Hercules and Pastoral Scene

10 Black Swan

1929. Air.
115 **9** 3d. green 10·00 4·00

1929. Centenary of Western Australia.
116 **10** 1½d. red 1·25 1·60

11 "Capt. Chas Sturt" (J. H. Crossland)

13 The "Southern Cross" above Hemispheres

1930. Centenary of Sturt's Exploration of River Murray.
117 **11** 1½d. red 1·00 1·00
118 3d. blue 3·25 6·50

1930. Surch in words.
119 **3** 2d. on 1½d. red 1·50 75
120 5d. on 4½d. violet 6·00 9·00

1931. Kingsford Smith's Flights.
121 **13** 2d. red (postage) 1·00 1·00
122 3d. blue 4·50 5·00
123 6d. purple (air) 5·50 12·00

1931. Air. As T **13** but inscr "AIR MAIL SERVICE".
139 6d. brown 13·00 12·00

1931. Air. No. 139 optd **O S**.
139a 6d. brown 35·00 55·00

17 Superb Lyrebird

18 Sydney Harbour Bridge

1932.
140 **17** 1s. green 42·00 2·00

1932. Opening of Sydney Harbour Bridge.
144 **18** 2d. red 2·00 1·40
142 3d. blue 4·50 7·00
143 5s. green £375 £180

19 Laughing Kookaburra

20 Melbourne and River Yarra

1932.
146 **19** 6d. red 25·00 55

1934. Centenary of Victoria.
147 **20** 2d. red 2·50 1·75
148 3d. blue 4·00 5·50
149 1s. black 50·00 20·00

21 Merino Ram

22 Hermes

1934. Death Centenary of Capt. John Macarthur (founder of Australian sheep-farming).
150 **21** 2d. red 4·25 1·50
151 3d. blue 10·00 11·00
152 9d. purple 32·00 42·00

1934.
153b **22** 1s.6d. purple 2·50 1·40

23 Cenotaph, Whitehall

24 King George V on "Anzac"

1935. 20th. Anniv of Gallipoli Landing.
154 **23** 2d. red 1·00 30
155 1s. black 42·00 38·00

1935. Silver Jubilee.
156 **24** 2d. red 1·50 30
157 3d. blue 5·00 7·50
158 2s. violet 27·00 40·00

25 Amphitrite and Telephone Cable

26 Site of Adelaide, 1836; Old Gum Tree, Glenelg; King William Street, Adelaide

1936. Opening of Submarine Telephone Cable to Tasmania.
159 **25** 2d. red 75 50
160 3d. blue 2·75 2·75

1936. Centenary of South Australia.
161 **26** 2d. red 1·25 40
162 3d. blue 4·00 3·50
163 1s. green 10·00 8·50

27 Wallaroo

28 Queen Elizabeth

29 King George VI

30 King George VI

31 King George VI

33 Merino Ram

38 Queen Elizabeth

40 King George VI and Queen Elizabeth

1937.
228 **27** ½d. orange 20 10
165 **28** 1d. green 60 50
180 – 1d. green 3·00 20
181 – 1d. purple 1·50 20
182 **29** 1½d. purple 2·25 8·00
183 1½d. green 1·00 1·25
167 **30** 2d. red 60 20
184 – 2d. red 3·00 10
185 **30** 2d. purple 50 1·25
186 **31** 3d. blue 45·00 3·00
187 3d. brown 40 10
188 – 4d. green 1·00 10
189 **33** 5d. purple 50 1·50
190a – 6d. brown 1·75 10
191 – 9d. brown 1·00 20
192 – 1s. green 1·25 10
175 **31** 1s.4d. mauve 1·50 1·75
176a **38** 5s. purple 3·50 2·25
177 – 10s. purple 38·00 13·00
178 **40** £1 slate 55·00 30·00
DESIGNS—As Type **28**: 4d. Koala; 6d. Kookaburra; 1s. Lyrebird. As Type **33**: 9d. Platypus. As Type **38**: 10s. King George VI.
Nos. 180 and 184 are as Types **28** and **30** but with completely shaded background.

41 Governor Phillip at Sydney Cove (J. Alcott)

42 A.I.F. and Nurse

1937. 150th Anniv of New South Wales.
193 **41** 2d. red 2·25 20
194 3d. blue 6·00 2·25
195 9d. purple 16·00 10·00

1940. Australian Imperial Forces.
196 **42** 1d. green 1·75 2·00
197 2d. red 1·75 70
198 3d. blue 12·00 8·50
199 6d. purple 22·00 15·00

1941. Surch with figures and bars.
200 **30** 2½d. on 2d. red 60 60
201 **31** 3½d. on 3d. blue 75 1·75
202 **33** 5½d. on 5d. purple 3·50 4·75

46a Queen Elizabeth

47 King George VI

48 King George VI

49 King George VI

50 Emu

1942.
203 **46a** 1d. purple 1·00 10
204 1½d. green 1·00 10
205 **47** 2d. purple 65 1·00
206 **48** 2½d. red 30 10
207 **49** 3½d. blue 60 50
208 **50** 5½d. grey 75 10

52 Duke and Duchess of Gloucester

53 Star and Wreath

1945. Royal Visit.
209 **52** 2½d. red 10 10
210 3½d. blue 15 70
211 5½d. grey 20 70

1946. Victory. Inscr "PEACE 1945".
213 **53** 2½d. red 10 10
214 – 3½d. blue 25 75
215 – 5½d. green 30 50
DESIGNS—HORIZ: 3½d. Flag and dove. VERT: 5½d. Angel.

56 Sir Thomas Mitchell and Queensland

1946. Centenary of Mitchell's Central Queensland Exploration.
216 **56** 2½d. red 10 10
217 3½d. blue 35 1·00
218 1s. green 35 45

57 Lt. John Shortland, R.N.

58 Steel Foundry

1947. 150th Anniv of City of Newcastle.
219 **57** 2½d. lake 10 10
220 **58** 3½d. blue 40 80
221 – 5½d. green 40 45
DESIGNS—As Type **58**: HORIZ: 5½d. Coal carrier cranes.

60 Queen Elizabeth II when Princess

1947. Wedding of Princess Elizabeth.
222a **60** 1d. purple 10 10

61 Hereford Bull

61a Hermes and Globe

62 Aboriginal Art

62a Commonwealth Coat of Arms

1948.
223 **61** 1s.3d. brown 1·75 1·10
223a **61a** 1s.6d. brown 70 10
224 **62** 2s. brown 2·00 10
224a **62a** 5s. red 2·75 10
224b 10s. purple 14·00 70
224c £1 blue 30·00 3·50
224d £2 green 80·00 14·00

63 William J. Farrer

64 Ferdinand von Mueller

1948. W. J. Farrer (wheat research) Commem.
225 **63** 2½d. red 10 10

1948. Sir Ferdinand von Mueller (botanist) Commemoration.
226 **64** 2½d. red 10 10

65 Boy Scout

66 "Henry Lawson" (Sir Lionel Lindsay)

1948. Pan-Pacific Scout Jamboree, Wonga Park.
227 **65** 2½d. lake 10 10
For 3½d. value dates "1952–53", see No. 254.

1949. Henry Lawson (poet) Commemoration.
231 **66** 2½d. purple 15 10

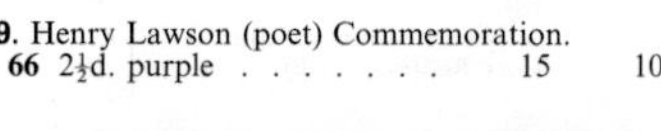

67 Mounted Postman and Convair CV 240 Aircraft

68 John, Lord Forrest of Bunbury

1949. 75th Anniv of U.P.U.

232	**67**	3½d. blue	30	50

1949. John, Lord Forrest (explorer and politician) Commemoration.

233	**68**	2½d. red	15	10

69 Queen Elizabeth

70 King George VI

81 King George VI

80 King George VI

71 Aborigine

82 King George VI

1950.

236	**69**	1½d. green	40	30
237		2d. green	15	10
234	**70**	2½d. red	10	10
237c		2½d. brown	15	30
235		3d. red	15	10
237d		3d. green	15	10
247	**81**	3½d. purple	10	10
248		4½d. red	15	1·00
249		6½d. brown	15	60
250		6½d. green	10	20
251	**80**	7½d. blue	15	60
238	**71**	8½d. brown	15	60
252	**82**	1s.0½d. blue	60	50
253	**71**	2s.6d. brown (21 × 25½ mm)	1·50	50

72 Reproduction of First Stamp of N.S.W.

73 Reproduction of First Stamp of Victoria

1950. Centenary of Australian States Stamps.

239	**72**	2½d. purple	25	10
240	**73**	2½d. purple	25	10

75 Sir Henry Parkes

77 Federal Parliament House, Canberra

1951. 50th Anniv of Commonwealth. Inscr as in T **75** and **77**.

241	**75**	3d. lake	30	10
242	–	3d. lake	30	10
243	–	5½d. blue	20	2·00
244	**77**	1s.6d. brown	35	50

DESIGNS—As Type **70**: No. 242, Sir Edmund Barton. As Type **77**: No. 243, Opening first Federal Parliament.

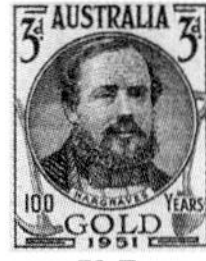

78 E. H. Hargraves

79 C. J. Latrobe

1951. Centenaries. Discovery of Gold in Australia and of Responsible Government in Victoria.

245	**78**	3d. purple	30	10
246	**79**	3d. purple	30	10

1952. Pan-Pacific Scout Jamboree, Greystanes. As T **65** but dated "1952–53".

254	**65**	3½d. lake	10	10

83 Butter

86 Queen Elizabeth II

1953. Food Production. Inscr "PRODUCE FOOD!".

255	**83**	3d. green	30	10
256	–	3d. green (Wheat)	30	10
257	–	3d. green (Beef)	30	10
258	**83**	3½d. red	30	10
259	–	3½d. red (Wheat)	30	10
260	–	3½d. red (Beef)	30	10

1953.

261	**86**	1d. purple	15	15
261a		2½d. blue	20	15
262		3d. green	20	10
263		3½d. red	20	10
263a		6½d. orange	1·75	50

87 Queen Elizabeth II

1953. Coronation.

264	**87**	3½d. red	40	10
265		7½d. violet	75	1·10
266		2s. turquoise	2·50	1·10

88 Young Farmers and Calf

1953. 25th Anniv of Australian Young Farmers' Clubs.

267	**88**	3½d. brown and green	10	10

89 Lt.-Gov. D. Collins

90 Lt.-Gov. W. Paterson

91 Sullivan Cove, Hobart, 1804

92 Stamp of 1853

1953. 150th Anniv of Settlement in Tasmania.

268	**89**	3½d. purple	30	10
269	**90**	3½d. purple	30	10
270	**91**	2s. green	1·25	2·75

1953. 1st Centenary of Tasmania Postage Stamps.

271	**92**	3d. red	10	40

93 Queen Elizabeth II and Duke of Edinburgh

94 Queen Elizabeth II

95 "Telegraphic Communications"

1954. Royal Visit.

272	**93**	3½d. red	20	10
273	**94**	7½d. purple	30	1·25
274	**93**	2s. green	60	65

1954. Centenary of Telegraph.

275	**95**	3½d. brown	10	10

96 Red Cross and Globe

97 Mute Swan

1954. 40th Anniv of Australian Red Cross Society.

276	**96**	3½d. blue and red	10	10

1954. Centenary of Western Australian Stamps.

277	**97**	3½d. black	20	10

98 Locomotives of 1854 and 1954

1954. Centenary of Australian Railways.

278	**98**	3½d. purple	30	10

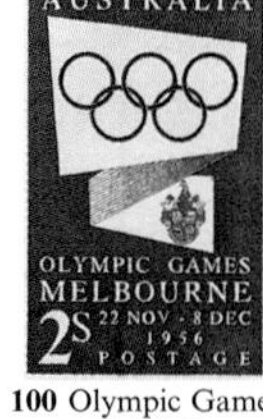

99 Territory Badge

100 Olympic Games Symbol

1954. Australian Antarctic Research.

279	**99**	3½d. black	15	10

1954. Olympic Games Propaganda.

280	**100**	2s. blue	70	80
280a		2s. green	1·75	1·75

101 Rotary Symbol, Globe and Flags

103 American Memorial, Canberra

1955. 50th Anniv of Rotary International.

281	**101**	3½d. red	10	10

1955. Australian–American Friendship.

283	**103**	3½d. blue	10	10

101a Queen Elizabeth II

102 Queen Elizabeth II

1955.

282a	**101a**	4d. lake	20	10
282b		7½d. violet	60	1·25
282c		10d. blue	60	85
282	**102**	1s.0½d. blue	1·50	75
282d		1s.7d. brown	1·50	30

104 Cobb & Co. Coach (from etching by Sir Lionel Lindsay)

1955. Mail-coach Pioneers Commemoration.

284	**104**	3½d. sepia	25	10
285		2s. brown	50	1·40

105 Y.M.C.A. Emblem and Map of the World

1955. World Centenary of Y.M.C.A.

286	**105**	3½d. green and red	10	10

106 Florence Nightingale and Young Nurse

107 Queen Victoria

1955. Nursing Profession Commemoration.

287	**106**	3½d. lilac	10	10

1955. Centenary of South Australian Postage Stamps.

288	**107**	3½d. green	10	10

108 Badges of N.S.W., Victoria and Tasmania

1956. Centenary of Responsible Government in N.S.W., Victoria and Tasmania.

289	**108**	3½d. lake	10	10

109 Arms of Melbourne

110 Olympic Torch and Symbol

111 Collins Street, Melbourne

1956. Olympic Games, Melbourne.

290	**109**	4d. red	25	10
291	**110**	7½d. blue	50	1·25
292	**111**	1s. multicoloured	60	30
293	–	2s. multicoloured	85	1·25

DESIGN—As Type **111**: 2s. Melbourne across River Yarra.

115 South Australia Coat of Arms

116 Map of Australia and Caduceus

1957. Centenary of Responsible Government in South Australia.

296	**115**	4d. brown	10	10

1957. Royal Flying Doctor Service of Australia.

297	**116**	7d. blue	15	10

117 "The Spirit of Christmas" (after Sir Joshua Reynolds)

1957. Christmas.

298	**117**	3½d. red	10	20
299		4d. purple	10	10

118 Lockheed Super Constellation Airliner

1958. Inaug of Australian "Round-the-World" Air Service.
301 **118** 2s. blue . . . . 75 1·00

119 Hall of Memory, Sailor and Airman

1958.
302 **119** 5½d. lake 40 30
303 – 5½d. lake 40 30
No. 303 shows a soldier and servicewoman instead of the sailor and airman.

120 Sir Charles Kingsford Smith and the "Southern Cross"

122 The Nativity

121 Silver Mine, Broken Hill

1958. 30th Anniv of 1st Air Crossing of the Tasman Sea.
304 **120** 8d. blue . . . . 60 1·00

1958. 75th Anniv of Founding of Broken Hill.
305 **121** 4d. brown 30 10

1958. Christmas Issue.
306 **122** 3½d. red 20 10
307 4d. violet 20 10

124 Queen Elizabeth II

126 Queen Elizabeth II

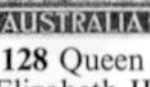
127 Queen Elizabeth II

128 Queen Elizabeth II

129 Queen Elizabeth II

1959.
308 – 1d. purple 10 10
309 **124** 2d. brown 50 20
311 **126** 3d. turquoise 15 10
312 **127** 3½d. green 15 15
313 **128** 4d. red . . . . 1·75 10
314 **129** 5d. blue 90 10
No. 308 shows a head and shoulders portrait as in Type **128** and is vert.

131 Numbat

137 Christmas Bells

142 Aboriginal Stockman

1959.
316 **131** 6d. brown . . . . 2·00 10
317 – 8d. red 75 10
318 – 9d. sepia . . . . 1·75 55
319 – 11d. blue . . . . 1·25 15
320 – 1s. green . . . . 3·00 40
321 – 1s.2d. purple . . . . . 1·25 15
322 **137** 1s.6d. red on yellow . . 2·00 90
323 – 2s. blue 70 10
324 – 2s.3d. green on yellow . 1·00 10
324a – 2s.3d. green . . . . . . 4·00 1·50
325 – 2s.5d. brown on yellow . 5·00 75
326 – 3s. red . . . . 1·00 20
327 **142** 5s. brown . . . . 22·00 1·25
DESIGNS—As Type **131**: VERT: 8d. Tiger Cat; 9d. Eastern grey kangaroo; 11d. Common rabbit bandicoot; 1s. Platypus. HORIZ: 1s.2d. Thylacine. As Type **137**: 2s. Flannel flower; 2s.3d. Wattle; 2s.5d. Banksia (plant); 3s. Waratah.

143 Postmaster Isaac Nichols boarding the Brig "Experiment"

1959. 150th Anniv of Australian P.O.
331 **143** 4d. slate 15 10

144 Parliament House, Brisbane, and Arms of Queensland

145 "The Approach of the Magi"

1959. Centenary of Queensland Self-Government.
332 **144** 4d. lilac and green 10 10

1959. Christmas.
333 **145** 5d. violet 10 10

146 Girl Guide and Lord Baden-Powell

147 "The Overlanders" (after Sir Daryl Lindsay)

1960. 50th Anniv of Girl Guide Movement.
334 **146** 5d. blue 30 15

1960. Centenary of Northern Territory Exploration.
335 **147** 5d. mauve 30 15

148 "Archer" and Melbourne Cup

149 Queen Victoria

1960. 100th Melbourne Cup Race Commemoration.
336 **148** 5d. sepia 20 10

1960. Centenary of Queensland Stamps.
337 **149** 5d. green 25 10

150 Open Bible and Candle

151 Colombo Plan Bureau Emblem

1960. Christmas Issue.
338 **150** 5d. lake 10 10

1961. Colombo Plan.
339 **151** 1s. brown 10 10

152 Melba (after bust by Sir Bertram Mackennal)

153 Open Prayer Book and Text

1961. Birth Centenary of Dame Nellie Melba (singer).
340 **152** 5d. blue 30 15

1961. Christmas Issue.
341 **153** 5d. brown 10 10

154 J. M. Stuart

155 Flynn's Grave and Nursing Sister

1962. Centenary of Stuart's South to North Crossing of Australia.
342 **154** 5d. red 15 10

1962. 50th Anniv of Australian Inland Mission.
343 **155** 5d. multicoloured 30 15

156 "Woman"

157 "Madonna and Child"

1962. "Associated Country Women of the World" Conference, Melbourne.
344 **156** 5d. green 10 10

1962. Christmas.
345 **157** 5d. violet 15 10

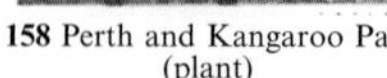

158 Perth and Kangaroo Paw (plant)

160 Queen Elizabeth II

1962. British Empire and Commonwealth Games, Perth. Multicoloured.
346 5d. Type **158** 40 10
347 2s.3d. Arms of Perth and running track . . . . . . 1·50 2·75

1963. Royal Visit.
348 **160** 5d. green 35 10
349 – 2s.3d. lake . . . . 1·50 3·00
DESIGN: 2s.3d. Queen Elizabeth II and Duke of Edinburgh.

162 Arms of Canberra and W. B. Griffin (architect)

163 Centenary Emblem

1963. 50th Anniv of Canberra.
350 **162** 5d. green 15 10

1963. Centenary of Red Cross.
351 **163** 5d. red, grey and blue . . 40 10

164 Blaxland, Lawson and Wentworth on Mount York

1963. 150th Anniv of First Crossing of Blue Mountains.
352 **164** 5d. blue 15 10

165 "Export"

1963. Export Campaign.
353 **165** 5d. red 10 10

1963. As T **160** but smaller 17½ × 21½ mm "5D" at top right replacing "ROYAL VISIT 1963" and oak leaves omitted.
354 5d. green 65 10
354c 5d. red 55 10

167 Tasman and "Heemskerk"

173 "Peace on Earth ..."

1963. Navigators.
355 **167** 4s. blue . . . . 3·00 55
356 – 5s. brown . . . . 3·25 1·50
357 – 7s.6d. olive . . . . 19·00 16·00
358 – 10s. purple . . . . 25·00 4·50
359 – £1 violet . . . . 30·00 16·00
360 – £2 sepia . . . . 55·00 75·00
DESIGNS—As Type **167**: 7s.6d. Captain Cook; 10s. Flinders and "Investigator". 20½ × 5½ mm: 5s. Dampier and "Roebuck"; £1 Bass and "Tom Thumb" (whale boat); £2 Admiral King and "Mermaid" (survey cutter).

1963. Christmas.
361 **173** 5d. blue 10 10

174 "Commonwealth Cable"

176 Black-backed Magpie

1963. Opening of COMPAC (Trans-Pacific Telephone Cable).
362 **174** 2s.3d. multicoloured . . . 1·00 2·75

1964. Birds.
363 – 6d. multicoloured 80 25
364 **176** 9d. black, grey and green 1·00 2·75
365 – 1s.6d. multicoloured . . . 75 1·40
366 – 2s. yellow, black and pink 1·40 50
367 – 2s.5d. multicoloured . . . 1·75 3·50
368 – 2s.6d. multicoloured . . . 2·50 3·75
369 – 3s. multicoloured . . . . 2·50 1·75
BIRDS—HORIZ: 6d. Yellow-tailed thornbill; 2s.6d. Scarlet robin. VERT: 1s.6d. Galah (cockatoo); 2s. Golden whistler (Thickhead); 2s.5d. Blue wren; 3s. Straw-necked ibis.

182 Bleriot XI Aircraft (type flown by M. Guillaux, 1914)

1964. 50th Anniv of 1st Australian Airmail Flight.
370 **182** 5d. green 30 10
371 2s.3d. red . . . . 1·50 2·75

183 Child looking at Nativity Scene

184 "Simpson and his Donkey"

1964. Christmas.
372 **183** 5d. red, blue, buff and black 10 10

1965. 50th Anniv of Gallipoli Landing.
373 **184** 5d. brown 50 10
374 8d. blue . . . . 75 2·50
375 2s.3d. purple . . . . 1·25 2·50

185 "Telecommunications" **186** Sir Winston Churchill

1965. Centenary of I.T.U.
376 **185** 5d. black, brown and blue . . . 40 10

1965. Churchill Commemoration.
377 **186** 5d. multicoloured 15 10

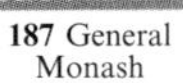

187 General Monash **188** Hargrave and "Multiplane" Seaplane (1902)

1965. Birth Centenary of General Sir John Monash (engineer and soldier).
378 **187** 5d. multicoloured 15 10

1965. 50th Death Anniv of Lawrence Hargrave (aviation pioneer).
379 **188** 5d. multicoloured 15 10

189 I.C.Y. Emblem **190** "Nativity Scene"

1965. International Co-operation Year.
380 **189** 2s.3d. green and blue . . 65 1·50

1965. Christmas.
381 **190** 5d. multicoloured 15 10

191 Queen Elizabeth II **192** Blue-faced Honeyeater

1966. Decimal currency. As earlier issues but with values in cents and dollars as in T **191/2**. Also some new designs.
382 **191** 1c. brown 25 10
383 2c. green 70 10
384 3c. green 70 10
404 3c. black, pink and green 45 90
385 4c. red 20 10
405 4c. black, brown and red 35 50
405a 5c. black, brown and blue 40 10
386 – 5c. multicoloured (as 363) 25 10
386c **191** 5c. blue 70 10
387 **192** 6c. multicoloured 80 70
387a **191** 6c. orange 65 10
388 – 7c. multicoloured 60 10
388a **191** 7c. purple . . . . 1·00 10
389 – 8c. multicoloured 60 85
390 – 9c. multicoloured 60 20
391 – 10c. multicoloured . . . 60 10
392 – 13c. multicoloured . . . 1·75 25
393 – 15c. multicoloured (as 365) . . . . 1·50 1·50
394 – 20c. yellow, black and pink (as 366) . . . . 2·50 15
395 – 24c. multicoloured . . . 65 1·25
396 – 25c. multicoloured (as 368) . . . . 3·00 30
397 – 30c. multicoloured (as 369) . . . . 7·50 1·25
398 **167** 40c. blue . . . . 3·50 10
399 – 50c. brown (as 356) . . 4·00 10
400 – 75c. olive (as 357) . . . 1·00 1·00
401 – $1 purple (as 358) . . . 1·50 20
402 – $2 violet (as 359) . . . . 7·50 1·00
403 – $4 brown (as 360) . . . 5·50 6·50
DESIGNS—VERT: 7c. White-tailed Dascyllus ("Humbug fish"); 8c. Copper-banded butterflyfish ("Coral fish"); 9c. Hermit crab; 10c. Orange clownfish ("Anemone fish"); 13c. Red-necked avocet. HORIZ: 24c. Azure kingfisher.

200 "Saving Life"

1966. 75th Anniv of Royal Life Saving Society.
406 **200** 4c. black, lt bl & bl . . . 15 10

201 "Adoration of the Shepherds" **202** "Eendracht"

1966. Christmas.
407 **201** 4c. black and olive . . . 10 10

1966. 350th Anniv of Dirk Hartog's Landing in Australia.
408 **202** 4c. multicoloured 10 10

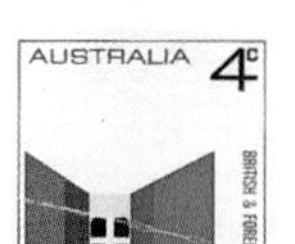

203 Open Bible **204** Ancient Keys and Modern Lock

1967. 150th Anniv of British and Foreign Bible Society in Australia.
409 **203** 4c. multicoloured 10 10

1967. 150th Anniv of Australian Banking.
410 **204** 4c. black, blue and green 10 10

205 Lions Badge and 50 Stars **206** Y.W.C.A. Emblem

1967. 50th Anniv of Lions International.
411 **205** 4c. black, gold and blue 10 10

1967. World Y.W.C.A. Council Meeting, Monash University, Melbourne.
412 **206** 4c. multicoloured 10 10

207 Anatomical Figures

1967. 5th World Gynaecology and Obstetrics Congress, Sydney.
413 **207** 4c. black, blue and violet 10 10

1967. No. 385 surch.
414 **191** 5c. on 4c. red 35 10

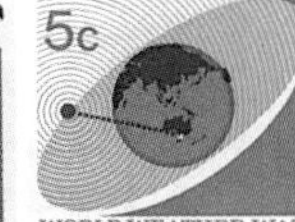

209 Christmas Bells and Gothic Arches **211** Satellite in Orbit

1967. Christmas. Multicoloured.
415 5c. Type **209** 20 10
416 25c. Religious symbols (vert) 1·00 1·75

1968. World Weather Watch. Multicoloured.
417 5c. Type **211** 30 10
418 20c. World weather map . . 1·10 2·75

213 Radar Antenna **214** Kangaroo Paw (Western Australia)

1968. World Telecommunications via Intelsat II.
419 **213** 25c. blue, black and green 1·25 2·50

1968. State Floral Emblems. Multicoloured.
420 6c. Type **214** . . . . 45 1·25
421 13c. Pink Heath (Victoria) . . 50 60
422 15c. Tasmanian Blue Gum (Tasmania) 70 20
423 20c. Sturt's Desert Pea (South Australia) . . . . 1·50 60
424 25c. Cooktown Orchid (Queensland) . . . . . . 1·10 60
425 30c. Waratah (New South Wales) 50 10

220 Soil Sample Analysis

1968. International Soil Science Congress and World Medical Association Assembly. Mult.
426 5c. Type **220** 10 10
427 5c. Rubber-gloved hands, syringe and head of Hippocrates 10 10

222 Athlete carrying Torch and Sunstone Symbol **224** Houses and Dollar Signs

1968. Olympic Games, Mexico City. Mult.
428 5c. Type **222** 30 10
429 25c. Sunstone symbol and Mexican flag . . . . . . 40 1·50

1968. Building and Savings Societies Congress.
430 **224** 5c. multicoloured 10 40

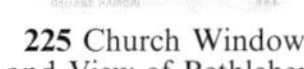

225 Church Window and View of Bethlehem **226** Edgeworth David (geologist)

1968. Christmas.
431 **225** 5c. multicoloured 10 10

1968. Famous Australians (1st series).
432 **226** 5c. green on myrtle . . . 35 20
433 – 5c. black on blue 35 20
434 – 5c. brown on buff 35 20
435 – 5c. violet on lilac 35 20
DESIGNS: No. 433, A. B. Paterson (poet); No. 434, Albert Namatjira (artist); No. 435, Caroline Chrisholm (social worker).
Nos. 432/5 were only issued in booklets and exist with one or two sides imperf.
See also Nos. 446/9, 479/82, 505/8, 537/40, 590/5, 602/7 and 637/40.

230 Macquarie Lighthouse **231** Pioneers and Modern Building, Darwin

1968. 150th Anniv of Macquarie Lighthouse.
436 **230** 5c. black and yellow . . . 30 50

1969. Centenary of Northern Territory Settlement.
437 **231** 5c. brown, olive and ochre 10 10

232 Melbourne Harbour

1969. 6th Biennial Conference of International Association of Ports and Harbours, Melbourne.
438 **232** 5c. multicoloured 15 10

233 Concentric Circles (symbolizing Management, Labour and Government)

1969. 50th Anniv of I.L.O.
439 **233** 5c. multicoloured 15 10

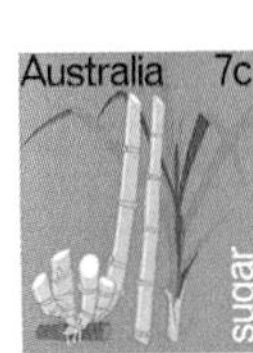

234 Sugar Cane **238** "The Nativity" (stained glass window)

1969. Primary Industries. Multicoloured.
440 7c. Type **234** . . . . 60 1·25
441 15c. Timber . . . . 1·00 2·50
442 20c. Wheat 35 60
443 25c. Wool . . . . 60 1·50

1969. Christmas. Multicoloured.
444 5c. Type **238** 20 10
445 25c. "Tree of Life", Christ in crib and Christmas Star (abstract) . . . . 1·00 2·00

240 Edmund Barton **244** Capt. Ross Smith's Vickers Vimy, 1919

1969. Famous Australians (2nd series). Prime Ministers.
446 **240** 5c. black on green 40 20
447 – 5c. black on green 40 20
448 – 5c. black on green 40 20
449 – 5c. black on green 40 20
DESIGNS: No. 447, Alfred Deakin; 448, J. C. Watson; 449, G. H. Reid.
Nos. 446/9 were only issued in booklets and only exist with one or two adjacent sides imperf.

1969. 50th Anniv of 1st England–Australia Flight.
450 **244** 5c. multicoloured 15 10
451 – 5c. red, black and green 15 10
452 – 5c. multicoloured 15 10
DESIGNS: No. 451, Lt. H. Fysh and Lt. P. McGinness on 1919 survey with Ford car; 452, Capt. Wrigley and Sgt. Murphy in Royal Aircraft Factory B.E.2E taking off to meet the Smiths.

247 Symbolic Track and Diesel Locomotive

1970. Sydney–Perth Standard Gauge Railway Link.
453 **247** 5c. multicoloured 15 10

248 Australian Pavilion, Osaka

1970. World Fair, Osaka.
454 **248** 5c. multicoloured 15 10
455 – 20c. red and black 35 65
DESIGN: 20c., "Southern Cross" and "from the Country of the south with warm feelings" (message).

251 Australian Flag

1970. Royal Visit.
456 – 5c. black and ochre . . . 35 15
457 **251** 30c. multicoloured . . . . 1·25 2·50
DESIGN: 5c. Queen Elizabeth II and Duke of Edinburgh.

252 Lucerne Plant, Bull and Sun

1970. 11th International Grasslands Congress, Queensland.
458 **252** 5c. multicoloured 10 50

253 Captain Cook and H.M.S. "Endeavour"
259 Sturt's Desert Rose

1970. Bicentenary of Captain Cook's Discovery of Australia's East Coast. Multicoloured.
459 5c. Type **253** 25 10
460 5c. Sextant and H.M.S. "Endeavour" 25 10
461 5c. Landing at Botany Bay 25 10
462 5c. Charting and exploring 25 10
463 5c. Claiming possession . . . 25 10
464 30c. Captain Cook, H.M.S. "Endeavour", sextant, aborigines and kangaroo (63 × 30 mm) . . . . . . 1·00 2·50
MS465 157 × 129 mm. Nos. 459/64. Imperf 7·50 9·00
Nos. 459/63 were issued together, se-tenant, forming a composite design.

1970. Coil Stamps. Multicoloured.
465a 2c. Type **259** 40 20
466 4c. Type **259** . . . . 85 1·50
467 5c. Golden wattle 20 10
468 6c. Type **259** . . . . 1·25 1·00
468b 7c. Sturt's desert pea . . . 40 60
468d 10c. As 7c. 60 60

264 Snowy Mountains Scheme
265 Rising Flames

1970. National Development (1st series). Mult.
469 7c. Type **264** 20 80
470 8c. Ord River scheme 10 15
471 9c. Bauxite to aluminium . . 15 15
472 10c. Oil and natural gas . . . 30 10
See also Nos. 541/4.

1970. 16th Commonwealth Parliamentary Association Conference, Canberra.
473 **265** 6c. multicoloured 10 10

266 Milk Analysis and Dairy Herd
267 "The Nativity"

1970. 18th International Dairy Congress, Sydney.
474 **266** 6c. multicoloured 10 10

1970. Christmas.
475 **267** 6c. multicoloured 10 10

268 U.N. "Plant" and Dove of Peace
269 Boeing 707 and Avro 504

1970. 25th Anniv of United Nations.
476 **268** 6c. multicoloured 15 10

1970. 50th Anniv of QANTAS Airline.
477 **269** 6c. multicoloured 30 10
478 – 30c. multicoloured . . . . 70 1·50
DESIGN: 30c. Avro 504 and Boeing 707.

1970. Famous Australians (3rd series). As T **226**.
479 6c. blue 65 20
480 6c. black on brown 65 20
481 6c. purple on pink 65 20
482 6c. red on pink 65 20
DESIGNS: No. 479, The Duigan brothers (pioneer aviators); 480, Lachlan Macquarie (Governor of New South Wales); 481, Adam Lindsay Gordon (poet); 482, E. J. Eyre (explorer).

271 "Theatre"

1971. "Australia–Asia". 28th International Congress of Orientalists, Canberra. Multicoloured.
483 7c. Type **271** 45 60
484 15c. "Music" . . . . 70 1·00
485 20c. "Sea Craft" 65 90

272 The Southern Cross
273 Market "Graph"

1971. Centenary of Australian Natives' Association.
486 **272** 6c. black, red and blue . . 10 10

1971. Centenary of Sydney Stock Exchange.
487 **273** 6c. multicoloured 10 10

274 Rotary Emblem
275 Dassault Mirage Jets and De Havilland D.H.9A Biplane

1971. 50th Anniv of Rotary International in Australia.
488 **274** 6c. multicoloured 15 10

1971. 50th Anniv of R.A.A.F.
489 **275** 6c. multicoloured 40 10

276 Draught-horse, Cat and Dog
277 Bark Painting

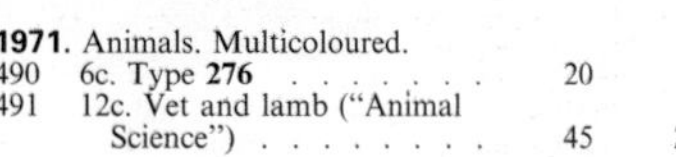

1971. Animals. Multicoloured.
490 6c. Type **276** 20 10
491 12c. Vet and lamb ("Animal Science") 45 20
492 18c. Red Kangaroo ("Fauna Conservation") 80 35
493 24c. Guide-dog ("Animals Aid to Man") . . . . . . 80 1·40
The 6c. commemorates the Centenary of the Australian R.S.P.C.A.

1971. Aboriginal Art. Multicoloured.
494 20c. Type **277** 20 20
495 25c. Body decoration 20 55
496 30c. Cave painting (vert) . . 40 20
497 35c. Grave posts (vert) . . . 30 15

278 The Three Kings and the Star
280 Cameo Brooch

1971. Christmas. Colours of star and colour of "AUSTRALIA" given.
498 **278** 7c. blue, mauve and brown 50 15
499 7c. mauve, brown and white 50 15
500 7c. mauve, white and black . . . . 2·75 80
501 7c. black, green and black 50 15
502 7c. lilac, green and mauve 50 15
503 7c. black, brown and white 50 15
504 7c. blue, mauve and green 12·00 2·25

1972. Famous Australians. (4th series). As T **240**. Prime Ministers.
505 7c. blue 30 20
506 7c. blue 30 20
507 7c. red 30 20
508 7c. red 30 20
DESIGNS: No. 505, Andrew Fisher; 506, W. M. Hughes; 507, Joseph Cook; 508, S. M. Bruce.

1972. 50th Anniv of Country Women's Association.
509 **280** 7c. multicoloured 20 10

281 Fruit
282 Worker in Wheelchair

1972. Primary Industries. Multicoloured.
510 20c. Type **281** . . . . 1·00 2·50
511 25c. Rice . . . . 1·00 4·00
512 30c. Fish . . . . 1·00 1·00
513 35c. Beef . . . . 2·25 75

1972. Rehabilitation of the Disabled.
514 **282** 12c. brown and green . . 10 10
515 – 18c. green and orange . . 85 35
516 – 24c. blue and brown . . . 15 10
DESIGNS—HORIZ: 18c. Patient and teacher. VERT: 24c. Boy playing with ball.

283 Telegraph Line
284 Athletics

1972. Centenary of Overland Telegraph Line.
517 **283** 7c. multicoloured 15 15

1972. Olympic Games, Munich. Multicoloured.
518 7c. Type **284** 20 25
519 7c. Rowing 20 25
520 7c. Swimming 20 25
521 35c. Equestrian . . . . . . 1·25 3·50

285 Numerals and Computer Circuit

1972. 10th Int Congress of Accountants, Sydney.
522 **285** 7c. multicoloured 15 15

286 Australian-built Harvester

1972. Pioneer Life. Multicoloured.
523 5c. Pioneer family (vert) . . . 10 10
524 10c. Water-pump (vert) . . . 20 10
525 15c. Type **286** 15 10
526 40c. House 15 30
527 50c. Stage-coach 35 20
528 60c. Morse key (vert) 30 80
529 80c. "Gem" (paddle-steamer) 30 80

287 Jesus with Children
288 "Length"

1972. Christmas. Multicoloured.
530 7c. Type **287** 30 10
531 35c. Dove and spectrum motif (vert) . . . . 2·75 5·00

1973. Metric Conversion. Multicoloured.
532 7c. Type **288** 40 50
533 7c. "Volume" 40 50
534 7c. "Mass" 40 50
535 7c. "Temperature" (horiz) . . 40 50

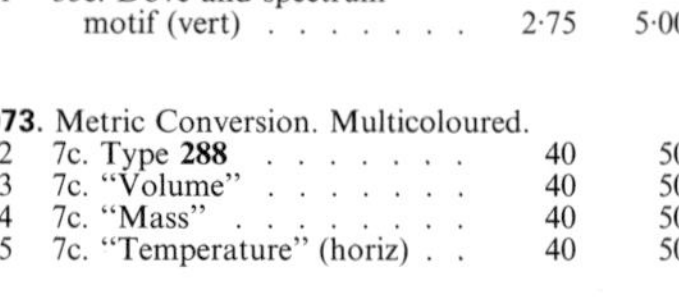

289 Caduceus and Laurel Wreath
291 Shipping

1973. 25th Anniv of World Health Organization.
536 **289** 7c. multicoloured 30 15

1973. Famous Australians (5th series). As T **226**.
537 7c. brown and black 35 45
538 7c. lilac and black 35 45
539 7c. brown and black 35 45
540 7c. lilac and black 35 45
PORTRAITS: No. 537, William Wentworth (statesman and explorer); 538, Isaac Issacs (1st Australian-born Governor-General); 539, Mary Gilmore (writer); 540, Marcus Clarke (author).

1973. National Development (2nd series). Mult.
541 20c. Type **291** . . . . . . 1·50 2·75
542 25c. Iron ore and steel . . . 1·50 2·75
543 30c. Beef roads . . . . . . 1·50 2·75
544 35c. Mapping . . . . 2·25 2·75

292 Banded Coral Shrimp
293 Children at Play

1973. Marine Life and Gemstones. Multicoloured.
545 1c. Type **292** 10 10
546 2c. Fiddler crab 10 10
547 3c. Coral crab 10 10
548 4c. Mauve stinger 15 55
549 6c. Chrysoprase (vert) . . . 15 20
550 7c. Agate (vert) 20 10
551 8c. Opal (vert) 20 10
552 9c. Rhodonite (vert) 50 15
552a 10c. Star sapphire (vert) . . 75 10

1973. 50th Anniv of Legacy (welfare organization).
553 **293** 7c. brown, red and green 30 10

294 John baptizing Jesus
295 Sydney Opera House

1973. Christmas. Multicoloured.

554	7c. Type **294**	35	10
555	30c. The Good Shepherd	1·75	2·25

1973. Architecture.

556	**295** 7c. blue and pale blue	30	15
557	– 10c. ochre and brown	60	70
558	– 40c. grey, brown and black	1·00	2·50
559	– 50c. multicoloured	1·00	2·50

DESIGNS—HORIZ: 10c. Buchanan's Hotel, Townsville; 40c. Como House, Melbourne. VERT: 50c. St. James's Church, Sydney.

296 Wireless Receiver and Speaker

297 Common Wombat

1973. 50th Anniv of Regular Radio Broadcasting.

560	**296** 7c. blue, red and black	15	10

1974. Animals. Multicoloured.

561	20c. Type **297**	25	10
562	25c. Short-nosed echidna (inscr "Spiny Anteater")	60	60
563	30c. Brush-tailed possum	40	15
564	75c. Pygmy (inscr "Feather-tailed") glider	80	85

298 "Sergeant of Light Horse" (G. Lambert)

299 Supreme Court Judge

1974. Australian Paintings. Multicoloured.

565	$1 Type **298**	1·00	10
566	$2 "Red Gums of the Far North" (H. Heysen) (horiz)	1·25	25
566a	$4 "Shearing the Rams" (Tom Roberts) (horiz)	2·00	2·25
567	$5 "McMahon's Point" (Sir Arthur Streeton)	5·00	2·25
567a	$10 "Coming South" (Tom Roberts)	5·50	3·50

1974. 150th Anniv of Australia's Third Charter of Justice.

568	**299** 7c. multicoloured	20	10

300 Rugby Football

1974. Non-Olympic Sports. Multicoloured.

569	7c. Type **300**	40	40
570	7c. Bowls	40	40
571	7c. Australian football (vert)	40	40
572	7c. Cricket (vert)	40	40
573	7c. Golf (vert)	40	40
574	7c. Surfing (vert)	40	40
575	7c. Tennis (vert)	40	40

301 "Transport of Mails"

302 Letter "A" and W. C. Wentworth (co-founder)

1974. Centenary of U.P.U. Multicoloured.

576	7c. Type **301**	40	20
577	30c. Three-part version of T **301** (vert)	85	1·90

1974. 150th Anniv of First Independent Newspaper, "The Australian".

578	**302** 7c. black and brown	40	40

1974. No. 551 surch.

579	9c. on 8c. multicoloured	15	15

304 "The Adoration of the Magi"

305 "Pre-school Education"

1974. Christmas. Woodcuts by Durer.

580	**304** 10c. black on cream	25	10
581	– 35c. black on cream	80	1·00

DESIGN: 35c. "The Flight into Egypt".

1974. Education in Australia. Multicoloured.

582	5c. Type **305**	25	40
583	11c. "Correspondence Schools"	25	60
584	15c. "Science Education"	40	40
585	60c. "Advanced Education" (vert)	50	1·75

306 "Road Safety"

307 Australian Women's Year Emblem

1975. Environment Dangers. Multicoloured.

586	10c. Type **306**	50	50
587	10c. "Pollution" (horiz)	50	50
588	10c. "Bush Fires" (horiz)	50	50

1975. International Women's Year.

589	**307** 10c. blue, green and violet	20	15

308 J. H. Scullin

309 Atomic Absorption Spectrophotometry

1975. Famous Australians (6th series). Prime Ministers. Multicoloured.

590	10c. Type **308**	25	35
591	10c. J. A. Lyons	25	35
592	10c. Earle Page	25	35
593	10c. Arthur Fadden	25	35
594	10c. John Curtin	25	35
595	10c. J. B. Chifley	25	35

1975. Scientfic Development. Multicoloured.

596	11c. Type **309**	70	60
597	24c. Radio astronomy	1·25	1·75
598	33c. Immunology	1·25	1·75
599	48c. Oceanography	1·50	2·75

310 Logo of Australian Postal Commission

1975. Inauguration of Australian Postal and Telecommunications Commissions.

600	**310** 10c. black, red and grey	25	10
601	– 10c. black, orange and grey	25	10

DESIGN: No. 601, Logo of Australian Telecommunications Commission.

311 Edith Cowan

312 "Helichrysum thomsonii"

1975. Famous Australians (7th series). Australian Women. Multicoloured.

602	10c. Type **311**	35	55
603	10c. Louisa Lawson	35	55
604	10c. "Henry Richardson" (pen name of Ethel Richardson)	35	55
605	10c. Catherine Spence	35	55
606a	10c. Constance Stone	35	55
607	10c. Truganini	35	55

1975. Wild Flowers. Multicoloured.

608	18c. Type **312**	25	10
609	45c. "Callistemon teretifolius" (horiz)	50	10

313 "Tambaran" House and Sydney Opera House

314 Epiphany Scene

1975. Independence of Papua New Guinea. Mult.

610	18c. Type **313**	20	10
611	25c. "Freedom" (bird in flight) (horiz)	50	1·25

1975. Christmas.

612	**314** 15c. multicoloured	25	10
613	– 45c. violet, blue and silver	75	2·40

DESIGN—HORIZ: 45c. "Shining Star".

315 Australian Coat of Arms

1976. 75th Anniv of Nationhood.

614	**315** 18c. multicoloured	40	20

316 Telephone-user, c. 1878

1976. Centenary of Telephone.

615	**316** 18c. multicoloured	20	15

317 John Oxley

1976. 19th Century Explorers. Multicoloured.

616	18c. Type **317**	35	50
617	18c. Hume and Hovell	35	50
618	18c. John Forrest	35	50
619	18c. Ernest Giles	35	50
620	18c. William Gosse	35	50
621	18c. Peter Warburton	35	50

318 Measuring Stick, Graph and Computer Tape

1976. 50th Anniv of Commonwealth Scientific and Industrial Research Organization.

622	**318** 18c. multicoloured	20	15

319 Football

1976. Olympic Games, Montreal. Multicoloured.

623	18c. Type **319**	20	20
624	18c. Gymnastics (vert)	20	20
625	25c. Diving (vert)	35	80
626	40c. Cycling	90	1·25

320 Richmond Bridge, Tasmania

321 Blamire Young (designer of first Australian stamp)

1976. Australian Scenes. Multicoloured.

627	5c. Type **320**	20	10
628	25c. Broken Bay, N.S.W	65	20
629	35c. Wittenoom Gorge, W.A	45	20
630	50c. Mt. Buffalo, Victoria (vert)	90	30
631	70c. Barrier Reef	1·25	1·25
632	85c. Ayers Rock, N.T	1·25	1·75

1976. National Stamp Week.

633	**321** 18c. multicoloured	15	15
MS634	101 × 112 mm. Nos. 633 × 4	75	2·00

322 "Virgin and Child" (detail, Simone Contarini)

1976. Christmas.

635	**322** 15c. mauve and blue	20	10
636	– 45c. multicoloured	50	90

DESIGN: 45c. Toy koala bear and decorations.

323 John Gould

1976. Famous Australians. (8th series). Scientists. Multicoloured.

637	18c. Type **323**	35	50
638	18c. Thomas Laby	35	50
639	18c. Sir Baldwin Spencer	35	50
640	18c. Griffith Taylor	35	50

324 "Music"

325 Queen Elizabeth II

1977. Performing Arts. Multicoloured.

641	20c. Type **324**	15	25
642	30c. Drama	20	35
643	40c. Dance	25	40
644	60c. Opera	1·25	1·75

1977. Silver Jubilee. Multicoloured.

645	18c. Type **325**	20	10
646	45c. The Queen and Duke of Edinburgh	50	80

326 Fielder and Wicket Keeper

327 Parliament House

1977. Centenary of Australia–England Test Cricket.

647	18c. Type **326**	40	65
648	18c. Umpire and batsman	40	65
649	18c. Fielders	40	65
650	18c. Batsman and umpire	40	65
651	18c. Bowler and fielder	40	65
652	45c. Batsman facing bowler	50	1·25

1977. 50th Anniv of Opening of Parliament House, Canberra.

653	**327** 18c. multicoloured	15	10

328 Trade Union Workers
329 Surfing Santa

1977. 50th Anniv of Australian Council of Trade Unions.
654 **328** 18c. multicoloured 15 10

1977. Christmas. Multicoloured.
655 15c. Type **329** 25 10
656 45c. Madonna and Child . . 75 1·25

330 National Flag

1978. Australia Day.
657 **330** 18c. multicoloured 20 15

331 Harry Hawker and Sopwith Atlantic

1978. Early Australian Aviators. Multicoloured.
658 18c. Type **331** 30 50
659 18c. Bert Hinkler and Avro Type 581 Avian 30 50
660 18c. Sir Charles Kingsford Smith and "Southern Cross" 30 50
661 18c. Charles Ulm and "Southern Cross" 30 50
MS662 100 × 112 mm. Nos. 658/61 × 2. Imperf 75 1·75

332 Piper PA-31 Navajo landing at Station Airstrip

1978. 50th Anniv of Royal Flying Doctor Service.
663 **332** 18c. multicoloured 20 15

333 Illawarra Flame Tree
334 Sturt's Desert Rose and Map

1978. Trees. Multicoloured.
664 18c. Type **333** 20 15
665 25c. Ghost gum . . . . . . 35 1·10
666 40c. Grass tree . . . . 45 1·75
667 45c. Cootamundra wattle . . 45 70

1978. Establishment of State Government for the Northern Territory.
668 **334** 18c. multicoloured 20 15

335 Hooded Plover
336 1928 3d. National Stamp Exhibition Commemorative

1978. Birds (1st series). Multicoloured.
669 1c. Spotted-sided ("Zebra") finch 10 20
670 2c. Crimson finch 10 20
671 5c. Type **335** 50 10
672 15c. Forest kingfisher (vert) 20 20
673 20c. Australian dabchick ("Little Grebe") 70 10
674 20c. Yellow robin ("Eastern Yellow Robin") 60 10
675 22c. White-tailed kingfisher (22 × 29 mm) 30 10
676 25c. Masked ("Spur-wing") plover 90 90
677 30c. Pied oystercatcher . . . 1·00 25
678 40c. Variegated ("Lovely") wren (vert) 30 45
679 50c. Flame robin (vert) . . . 85 50
680 55c. Comb-crested jacana ("Lotus-Bird") . . . . . . 1·40 60
See also Nos. 734/40.

1978. 50th Anniv of National Stamp Week, and National Stamp Exhibition.
694 **336** 20c. multicoloured 15 15
MS695 78 × 113 mm. No. 694 × 4 75 1·75

337 "The Madonna and the Child" (after van Eyck)
338 "Tulloch"

1978. Christmas. Multicoloured.
696 15c. Type **337** 30 10
697 25c. "The Virgin and Child" (Marmion) 45 55
698 55c. "The Holy Family" (del Vaga) 70 90

1978. Horse-racing. Multicoloured.
699 20c. Type **338** 30 10
700 35c. "Bernborough" (vert) . . 45 85
701 50c. "Phar Lap" (vert) . . . 60 1·25
702 55c. "Peter Pan" . . . . . . 60 1·10

339 Raising the Flag, Sydney Cove, 26 January 1788
340 "Canberra" (paddle-steamer)

1979. Australia Day.
703 **339** 20c. multicoloured 15 15

1979. Ferries and Murray River Steamers. Mult.
704 20c. Type **340** 25 10
705 35c. "Lady Denman" . . . . 45 1·00
706 50c. "Murray River Queen" (paddle-steamer) . . . . . 65 1·40
707 55c. "Curl Curl" (hydrofoil) 70 1·25

341 Port Campbell, Victoria

1979. National Parks. Multicoloured.
708 20c. Type **341** 25 25
709 20c. Uluru, Northern Territory 25 25
710 20c. Royal, New South Wales 25 25
711 20c. Flinders Ranges, South Australia 25 25
712 20c. Nambung, Western Australia 25 25
713 20c. Girraween, Queensland (vert) 25 25
714 20c. Mount Field, Tasmania (vert) 25 25

342 "Double Fairlie" Type Locomotive, Western Australia

1979. Steam Railways. Multicoloured.
715 20c. Type **342** 30 10
716 35c. Locomotive, Puffing Billy Line, Victoria 60 70
717 50c. Locomotive, Pichi Richi Line, South Australia . . . 70 1·50
718 55c. Locomotive, Zig Zag Railway, New South Wales 80 1·40

343 Symbolic Swan

1979. 150th Anniv of Western Australia.
719 **343** 20c. multicoloured 15 15

344 Children playing on Slide
345 Letters and Parcels

1979. International Year of the Child.
720 **344** 20c. multicoloured 15 10

1979. Christmas. Multicoloured.
721 15c. "Christ's Nativity" (Eastern European icon) 15 10
722 25c. Type **345** 15 65
723 55c. "Madonna and Child" (Buglioni) 25 80

346 Fly-fishing
347 Matthew Flinders

1979. Fishing.
724 **346** 20c. multicoloured 15 10
725 – 35c. blue and violet . . . 25 70
726 – 50c. multicoloured 30 90
727 – 55c. multicoloured 35 85
DESIGNS: 35c. Spinning; 50c. Deep sea game-fishing; 55c. Surf-fishing.

1980. Australia Day.
728 **347** 20c. multicoloured 20 10

348 Dingo

1980. Dogs. Multicoloured.
729 20c. Type **348** 35 10
730 25c. Border collie 35 50
731 35c. Australian terrier 40 70
732 50c. Australian cattle dog . . 70 1·75
733 55c. Australian kelpie . . . . 70 1·40

1980. Birds (2nd series). As T **335**. Multicoloured.
734 10c. Golden-shouldered parrot (vert) 50 10
734b 18c. Spotted catbird (vert) 50 1·25
735 28c. Australian bee eater ("Rainbow Bird") (vert) 50 20
736 35c. Regent bower bird (vert) 50 10
737 45c. Masked wood swallow 50 10
738 60c. Australian king parrot ("King Parrot") (vert) . . 50 15
739 80c. Rainbow pitta . . . . 1·00 75
740 $1 Black-backed magpie ("Western Magpie") (vert) 1·00 10

349 Queen Elizabeth II
350 "Once a jolly Swagman camp'd by a Billabong"

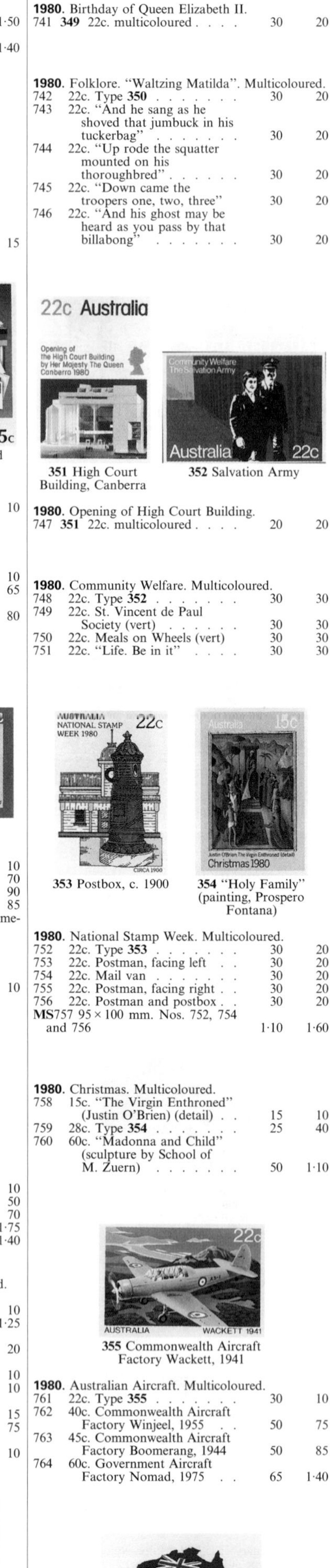

1980. Birthday of Queen Elizabeth II.
741 **349** 22c. multicoloured 30 20

1980. Folklore. "Waltzing Matilda". Multicoloured.
742 22c. Type **350** 30 20
743 22c. "And he sang as he shoved that jumbuck in his tuckerbag" 30 20
744 22c. "Up rode the squatter mounted on his thoroughbred" 30 20
745 22c. "Down came the troopers one, two, three" 30 20
746 22c. "And his ghost may be heard as you pass by that billabong" 30 20

351 High Court Building, Canberra
352 Salvation Army

1980. Opening of High Court Building.
747 **351** 22c. multicoloured 20 20

1980. Community Welfare. Multicoloured.
748 22c. Type **352** 30 30
749 22c. St. Vincent de Paul Society (vert) 30 30
750 22c. Meals on Wheels (vert) 30 30
751 22c. "Life. Be in it" 30 30

353 Postbox, c. 1900
354 "Holy Family" (painting, Prospero Fontana)

1980. National Stamp Week. Multicoloured.
752 22c. Type **353** 30 20
753 22c. Postman, facing left . . 30 20
754 22c. Mail van 30 20
755 22c. Postman, facing right . . 30 20
756 22c. Postman and postbox . . 30 20
MS757 95 × 100 mm. Nos. 752, 754 and 756 1·10 1·60

1980. Christmas. Multicoloured.
758 15c. "The Virgin Enthroned" (Justin O'Brien) (detail) . . 15 10
759 28c. Type **354** 25 40
760 60c. "Madonna and Child" (sculpture by School of M. Zuern) . . . . 50 1·10

355 Commonwealth Aircraft Factory Wackett, 1941

1980. Australian Aircraft. Multicoloured.
761 22c. Type **355** 30 10
762 40c. Commonwealth Aircraft Factory Winjeel, 1955 . . 50 75
763 45c. Commonwealth Aircraft Factory Boomerang, 1944 50 85
764 60c. Government Aircraft Factory Nomad, 1975 . . 65 1·40

356 Flag in shape of Australia

1981. Australia Day.
765 **356** 22c. multicoloured 20 20

357 Caricature of Darby Munro (jockey)

358 1931 Kingsford Smith's Flights 6d. Commemorative

1981. Sporting Personalities. Caricatures. Mult.

766 22c. Type **357** 20 10
767 35c. Victor Trumper (cricket) 40 60
768 55c. Sir Norman Brookes (tennis) . . . . 40 1·00
769 60c. Walter Lindrum (billiards) . . . . 40 1·25

1981. 50th Anniversary of Official Australia–U.K. Airmail Service.

770 **358** 22c. lilac, red and blue . . 15 10
771 – 60c. lilac, red and blue . . 40 90

DESIGN—HORIZ: 60c. As T **358**, but format changed.

359 Apex Emblem and Map of Australia

1981. 50th Anniv of Apex (young men's service club).

772 **359** 22c. multicoloured 20 20

360 Queen's Personal Standard for Australia

361 "Licence Inspected"

1981. Birthday of Queen Elizabeth II.

773 **360** 22c. multicoloured 20 20

1981. Gold Rush Era. Sketches by S. T. Gill. Mult.

774 22c. Type **361** 20 25
775 22c. "Puddling" 20 25
776 22c. "Quality of washing stuff" 20 25
777 22c. "On route to deposit gold" 20 25

362 "On the Wallaby Track" (Fred McCubbin)

1981. Paintings. Multicoloured.

778 $2 Type **362** . . . . 1·25 30
779 $5 "A Holiday at Mentone, 1888" (Charles Conder) . . 4·75 1·25

363 Thylacine

363a Blue Mountain Tree Frog

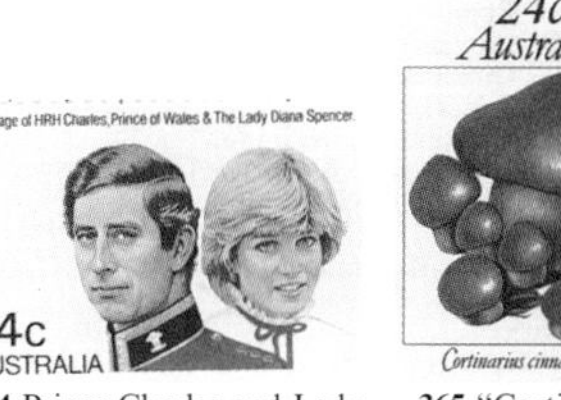

Australia 27c

ULYSSES

363b "Papilio ulysses" (butterfly)

1981. Wildlife. Multicoloured.

781 1c. Lace monitor 10 20
782 3c. Corroboree frog 10 10
783 4c. Regent skipper (butterfly) (vert) 55 80
784 5c. Queensland hairy-nosed wombat (vert) 10 10
785 10c. Cairns birdwing (butterfly) (vert) 60 10
786 15c. Eastern snake-necked tortoise . . . . 1·00 60
787 20c. MacLeay's swallowtail (butterfly) (vert) 80 35
788 24c. Type **363** 45 10
789 25c. Common rabbit-bandicoot (inscr "Greater Bilby") (vert) 40 80
790 27c. Type **363a** . . . . . . 1·25 20
791 27c. Type **363b** . . . . . . 1·00 30
792 30c. Bridle nail-tailed wallaby (vert) 90 15
792a 30c. Chlorinda hairstreak (butterfly) (vert) . . . . . 1·00 20
793 35c. Blue tiger (butterfly) (vert) . . . . 1·00 30
794 40c. Smooth knob-tailed gecko 45 30
795 45c. Big greasy (butterfly) (vert) . . . . 1·00 30
796 50c. Leadbeater's possum 50 10
797 55c. Stick-nest rat (vert) . . 50 30
798 60c. Wood white (butterfly) (vert) . . . . 1·10 30
799 65c. Yellow-faced whip snake . . . . 1·75 1·50
800 70c. Crucifix toad . . . . . 65 1·50
801 75c. Eastern water dragon 1·25 90
802 80c. Amaryllis azure (butterfly) (vert) . . . . . 1·40 2·00
803 85c. Centralian blue-tongued lizard . . . . 1·10 1·25
804 90c. Freshwater crocodile 1·60 1·25
805 95c. Thorny devil . . . . . 1·60 2·00
806 $1 Sword-grass brown (butterfly) (vert) . . . . . 1·40 30

24c Australia

Cortinarius cinnabarinus

364 Prince Charles and Lady Diana Spencer

365 "Cortinarius cinnabarinus"

1981. Royal Wedding.

821 **364** 24c. multicoloured 20 10
822 60c. multicoloured . . . . 55 1·00

1981. Australian Fungi. Multicoloured.

823 24c. Type **365** 25 10
824 35c. "Coprinus comatus" . . 45 1·10
825 55c. "Armillaria luteobubalina" . . . . . . 60 1·25
826 60c. "Cortinarius austro-venetus" . . . . 70 1·40

366 Disabled People playing Basketball

367 "Christmas Bush for His Adorning"

1981. International Year for Disabled Persons.

827 **366** 24c. multicoloured 20 20

1981. Christmas. Scenes and Verses from Carols by W. James and J. Wheeler. Multicoloured.

828 18c. Type **367** 20 10
829 30c. "The Silver Stars are in the Sky" 25 25
830 60c. "Noeltime" 40 85

Australia 24c Commonwealth Heads of Government Meeting, Melbourne 1981

24c AUSTRALIA

368 Globe depicting Australia

369 "Ragamuffin" ocean racing yacht

1981. Commonwealth Heads of Government Meeting, Melbourne.

831 **368** 24c. black, blue and gold 15 10
832 60c. black, blue and silver 45 75

1981. Yachts. Multicoloured.

833 24c. Type **369** 25 10
834 35c. "Sharpie" 40 55
835 55c. "12 Metre" . . . . 55 1·00
836 60c. "Sabot" . . . . 80 1·25

370 Aborigine, Governor Phillip (founder of N.S.W., 1788) and Post World War II Migrant

1982. Australia Day. "Three Great Waves of Migration".

837 **370** 24c. multicoloured 35 25

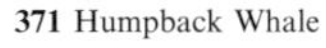

371 Humpback Whale

372 Queen Elizabeth II

1982. Whales. Multicoloured.

838 24c. Sperm whale 30 10
839 35c. Black (inscr "Southern") right whale (vert) 40 60
840 55c. Blue whale (vert) . . . . 60 1·50
841 60c. Type **371** . . . . 70 1·50

1982. Birthday of Queen Elizabeth II.

842 **372** 27c. multicoloured 35 15

373 "Marjorie Atherton"

374 Radio Announcer and 1930-style Microphone

1982. Roses. Multicoloured.

843 27c. Type **373** 30 15
844 40c. "Imp" 50 60
845 65c. "Minnie Watson" . . . 1·00 2·00
846 75c. "Satellite" . . . . 1·00 1·25

1982. 50th Anniv of ABC (Australian Broadcasting Commission). Multicoloured.

847 27c. Type **374** 30 65
848 27c. ABC logo 30 65

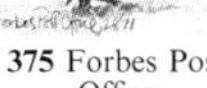

375 Forbes Post Office

376 Early Australian Christmas Card

1982. Historic Australian Post Offices. Mult.

849 27c. Type **375** 30 40
850 27c. Flemington Post Office 30 40
851 27c. Rockhampton Post Office 30 40
852 27c. Kingston S. E. Post Office (horiz) 30 40
853 27c. York Post Office (horiz) 30 40
854 27c. Launceston Post Office 30 40
855 27c. Old Post and Telegraph Station, Alice Springs (horiz) 30 40

1982. Christmas. Multicoloured.

856 21c. Bushman's Hotel with Cobb's coach arriving (horiz) 25 10
857 35c. Type **376** 40 60
858 75c. Little girl offering Christmas pudding to swagman . . . . 60 1·40

377 Boxing

1982. Commonwealth Games, Brisbane.

859 **377** 27c. stone, yellow and red 20 25
860 – 27c. yellow, stone and green 20 25
861 – 27c. stone, yellow and brown 20 25
862 – 75c. multicoloured . . . . 50 1·25
MS863 130 × 95 mm. Nos. 859/61 1·25 1·75

DESIGNS: No. 860, Archery; No. 861, Weight-lifting; No. 862, Pole-vaulting.

27c Australia

378 Sydney Harbour Bridge 5s. Stamp of 1932

379 "Yirawala" Bark Painting

1982. National Stamp Week.

864 **378** 27c. multicoloured 35 30

1982. Opening of Australian National Gallery.

865 **379** 27c. multicoloured 30 25

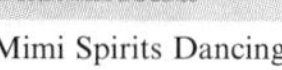

380 Mimi Spirits Dancing

381 "Eucalyptus calophylla" "Rosea"

1982. Aboriginal Culture. Music and Dance.

866 **380** 27c. multicoloured 20 10
867 – 40c. multicoloured 30 60
868 – 65c. multicoloured . . . . 45 1·00
869 – 75c. multicoloured . . . . 50 1·00

DESIGN: 40c. to 75c. Aboriginal bark paintings of Mimi Spirits.

1982. Eucalyptus Flowers. Multicoloured.

870 1c. Type **381** 10 30
871 2c. "Eucalyptus casia" . . . 10 30
872 3c. "Eucalyptus ficifolia" . . 1·25 1·75
873 10c. "Eucalyptus globulus" 1·25 1·75
874 27c. "Eucalyptus forrestiana" 30 40

382 Shand Mason Steam Fire Engine, 1891

1983. Historic Fire Engines. Multicoloured.

875 27c. Type **382** 35 10
876 40c. Hotchkiss fire engine, 1914 . . . . 45 75
877 65c. Ahrens-Fox PS2 fire engine, 1929 . . . . 70 1·50
878 75c. Merryweather manual fire appliance, 1851 . . . . 70 1·40

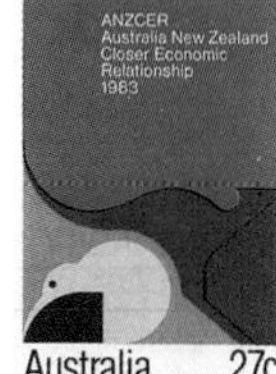

383 H.M.S. "Sirius"

384 Stylized Kangaroo and Kiwi

1983. Australia Day. Multicoloured.

879 27c. Type **383** 40 75
880 27c. H.M.S. "Supply" . . . 40 75

1983. Closer Economic Relationship Agreement with New Zealand.

881 **384** 27c. multicoloured 30 30

Australia 27c

385 Equality and Dignity

386 R.Y. "Britannia" passing Sydney Opera House

1983. Commonwealth Day. Multicoloured.

882 27c. Type **385** 20 25
883 27c. Liberty and Freedom . . 20 25
884 27c. Social Justice and Co-operation 20 25
885 75c. Peace and Harmony . . 50 1·50

1983. Birthday of Queen Elizabeth II.

886 **386** 27c. multicoloured 50 30

387 "Postal and Telecommunications Services" **388** Badge of the Order of St. John

1983. World Communications Year.
887 **387** 27c. multicoloured 30 30

1983. Centenary of St. John Ambulance in Australia.
888 **388** 27c. black and blue . . . 35 30

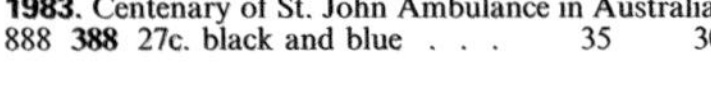

389 Jaycee Members and Badge **390** "The Bloke"

1983. 50th Anniv of Australian Jaycees.
889 **389** 27c. multicoloured 30 30

1983. Folklore. "The Sentimental Bloke" (humorous poem by C. J. Dennis). Multicoloured.
890 27c. Type **390** 40 50
891 27c. "Doreen—The Intro" . . 40 50
892 27c. "The Stror' at Coot" . . 40 50
893 27c. "Hitched" 40 50
894 27c. "The Mooch o' Life" . . 40 50

391 Nativity Scene

1983. Christmas. Children's Paintings. Mult.
895 24c. Type **391** 20 10
896 35c. Kookaburra 35 45
897 85c. Father Christmas in sleigh over beach . . . . . 90 1·40

392 Sir Paul Edmund de Strzelecki

1983. Explorers of Australia. Multicoloured.
898 30c. Type **392** 35 40
899 30c. Ludwig Leichhardt . . . 35 40
900 30c. William John Wills and Robert O'Hara Burke . . 35 40
901 30c. Alexander Forrest . . . 35 40

393 Cook Family Cottage, Melbourne

1984. Australia Day.
902 **393** 30c. black and stone . . . 30 35

394 Charles Ulm, "Faith in Australia" and Trans-Tasman Cover

1984. 50th Anniv of First Official Airmail Flights. New Zealand–Australia and Australia–Papua New Guinea. Multicoloured.
903 45c. Type **394** . . . . 1·00 1·40
904 45c. As Type **394** but showing flown cover to Papua New Guinea . . . . 1·00 1·40

395 Thomson "Steamer", 1898

1984. Veteran and Vintage Cars. Multicoloured.
905 30c. Type **395** 50 60
906 30c. Tarrant, 1906 . . . . . 50 60
907 30c. Gordon & Co "Australian Six", 1919 . . 50 60
908 30c. Summit, 1923 . . . . . 50 60
909 30c. Chic, 1924 . . . . . . 50 60

396 Queen Elizabeth II **397** "Cutty Sark"

1984. Birthday of Queen Elizabeth II.
910 **396** 30c. multicoloured 30 35

1984. Clipper Ships. Multicoloured.
911 30c. Type **397** 35 25
912 45c. "Orient" (horiz) 50 80
913 75c. "Sobraon" (horiz) . . . 70 1·75
914 85c. "Thermopylae" . . . . 70 1·50

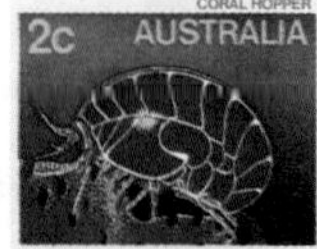

398 Freestyle **399** Coral Hopper

1984. Skiing. Multicoloured.
915 30c. Type **398** 30 45
916 30c. Downhill racer 30 45
917 30c. Slalom (horiz) 30 45
918 30c. Nordic (horiz) 30 45

1984. Marine Life. Multicoloured.
919 2c. Type **399** 10 30
920 3c. Jimble 20 30
921 5c. Tasselled frogfish ("Anglerfish") 15 10
922 10c. Rough stonefish 60 30
923 20c. Red handfish 65 40
924 25c. Orange-lipped cowrie . . 45 40
925 30c. Choat's wrasse 45 40
926 33c. Leafy seadragon 65 10
927 40c. Red velvetfish . . . . 85 1·50
928 45c. Textile or cloth of gold cone . . . . 1·25 50
929 50c. Clown surgeonfish . . . 80 50
930 55c. Bennet's nudibranch . . 80 50
931 60c. Zebra lionfish . . . . 1·25 70
932 65c. Banded stingray . . . . 1·50 1·75
933 70c. Southern blue-ringed octopus . . . . 1·50 1·75
934 80c. Pineconefish ("Pineapple fish") . . . . . . 1·25 1·75
935 85c. Royal angelfish 90 70
936 90c. Crab-eyed goby . . . . 1·60 75
937 $1 Crown of thorns starfish . . 1·50 80

400 Before the Event **401** Australian 1913 1d. Kangaroo Stamp

1984. Olympic Games, Los Angeles. Multicoloured.
941 30c. Type **400** 25 40
942 30c. During the event . . . 25 40
943 30c. After the event (vert) . . 25 40

1984. "Ausipex '84" International Stamp Exhibition, Melbourne.
944 **401** 30c. multicoloured 35 30
MS945 126×175 mm. 30c. × 7, Victoria 1850 3d. "Half Length"; New South Wales 1850 1d. "Sydney View"; Tasmania 1853 1d.; South Australia 1855 1d.; Western Australia 1854 1d. "Black Swan"; Queensland 1860 6d.; Type **401** 3·50 4·50

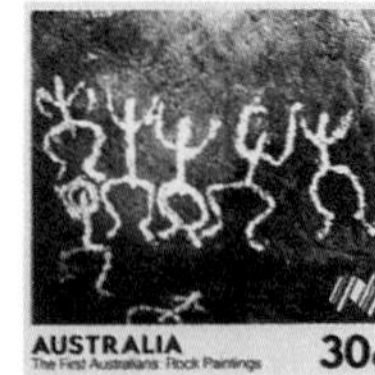

402 "Angel" (stained-glass window, St. Francis's Church, Melbourne) **403** "Stick Figures" (Cobar Region)

1984. Christmas. Stained-glass Windows. Mult.
946 24c. "Angel and Child" (Holy Trinity Church, Sydney) 20 10
947 30c. "Veiled Virgin and Child" (St. Mary's Catholic Church, Geelong) 25 10
948 40c. Type **402** 40 70
949 50c. "Three Kings" (St. Mary's Cathedral, Sydney) 50 85
950 85c. "Madonna and Child" (St. Bartholomew's Church, Norwood) . . . . 60 1·40

1984. Bicentenary (1988) of Australian Settlement (1st issue). The First Australians. Multicoloured.
951 30c. Type **403** 20 45
952 30c. "Bunjil" (large figure), Grampians 20 45
953 30c. "Quikans" (tall figures), Cape York 20 45
954 30c. "Wandjina Spirit and Baby Snakes" (Gibb River) 20 45
955 30c. "Rock Python" (Gibb River) 20 45
956 30c. "Silver Barramundi" (fish) (Kakadu National Park) 20 45
957 30c. Bicentenary emblem . . 20 45
958 85c. "Rock Possum" (Kakadu National Park) 50 1·40

See also Nos. 972/5, 993/6, 1002/7, 1019/22, 1059/63, 1064/6, 1077/81, 1090/2, 1110, 1137/41, 1145/8 and 1149.

404 Yellow-tufted Honeyeater **405** "Musgrave Ranges" (Sidney Nolan)

1984. 150th Anniv of Victoria.
959 30c. Type **404** 40 65
960 30c. Leadbeater's possum . . 40 65

1985. Australia Day. Birth Bicentenary of Dorothea Mackellar (author of poem "My Country"). Multicoloured.
961 30c. Type **405** 50 80
962 30c. "The Walls of China" (Russell Drysdale) 50 80

406 Young People of Different Races and Sun **407** Royal Victorian Volunteer Artillery

1985. International Youth Year.
963 **406** 30c. multicoloured 40 30

1985. 19th-Century Australian Military Uniforms. Multicoloured.
964 33c. Type **407** 50 65
965 33c. Western Australian Pinjarrah Cavalry 50 65
966 33c. New South Wales Lancers 50 65
967 33c. New South Wales Contingent to the Sudan 50 65
968 33c. Victorian Mounted Rifles 50 65

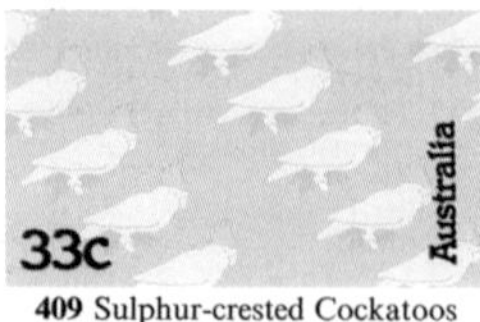

408 District Nurse of early 1900s **410** Abel Tasman and Journal Entry

409 Sulphur-crested Cockatoos

1985. Centenary of District Nursing Services.
969 **408** 33c. multicoloured 45 35

1985. Multicoloured, background colour given.
970 **409** 1c. flesh . . . . 1·50 2·25
971 33c. turquoise 45 55

1985. Bicentenary (1988) of Australian Settlement (2nd issue). Navigators. Multicoloured.
972 33c. Type **410** 45 35
973 33c. Dirk Hartog's "Eendracht" (detail, Aert Anthonisz) 45 35
974 33c. "William Dampier" (detail, T. Murray) 45 35
975 90c. Globe and hand with extract from Dampier's journal . . . . 1·00 2·50
MS976 150×115 mm. As Nos. 972/5, but with cream-coloured margins 3·25 4·50

411 Sovereign's Badge of Order of Australia **412** Tree, and Soil running through Hourglass ("Soil")

1985. Queen Elizabeth II's Birthday.
977 **411** 33c. multicoloured 40 30

1985. Conservation. Multicoloured.
978 33c. Type **412** 25 20
979 50c. Washing on line and smog ("air") 50 85
980 80c. Tap and flower ("water") . . . . 65 1·50
981 90c. Chain encircling flames ("energy") . . . . 80 2·00

413 "Elves and Fairies" (Annie Rentoul and Ida Rentoul Outhwaite) **414** Dish Aerials

1985. Classic Australian Children's Books. Mult.
982 33c. Type **413** 50 70
983 33c. "The Magic Pudding" (Norman Lindsay) 50 70
984 33c. "Ginger Meggs" (James Charles Bancks) 50 70
985 33c. "Blinky Bill" (Dorothy Wall) 50 70
986 33c. "Snugglepot and Cuddlepie" (May Gibbs) 50 70

1985. Electronic Mail Service.
987 **414** 33c. multicoloured 35 30

415 Angel in Sailing Ship

1985. Christmas. Multicoloured.
988 27c. Angel with holly wings 25 10
989 33c. Angel with bells 30 10
990 45c. Type **415** 40 35

991 55c. Angel with star 50 70
992 90c. Angel with Christmas tree bauble 75 1·75

416 Astrolabe ("Batavia", 1629)

417 Aboriginal Wandjina Spirit, Map of Australia and Egg

1985. Bicentenary (1988) of Australian Settlement (3rd issue). Relics from Early Shipwrecks. Multicoloured.
993 33c. Type **416** 35 15
994 50c. German beardman jug ("Vergulde Draeck", 1656) 60 1·00
995 90c. Wooden bobbins ("Batavia", 1629) and encrusted scissors ("Zeewijk", 1727) 1·25 3·00
996 $1 Silver and brass buckle ("Zeewijk", 1727) 1·25 2·25

1986. Australia Day.
997 **417** 33c. multicoloured 40 30

418 AUSSAT Satellite, Moon and Earth's Surface

419 H.M.S. "Buffalo"

1986. AUSSAT National Communications Satellite System. Multicoloured.
998 33c. Type **418** 40 15
999 80c. AUSSAT satellite in orbit 1·00 2·25

1986. 150th Anniv of South Australia. Mult.
1000 33c. Type **419** 70 1·00
1001 33c. "City Sign" sculpture (Otto Hajek), Adelaide 70 1·00
Nos. 1000/1 were printed together se-tenant, the background of each horiz pair showing an extract from the colony's Letters Patent of 1836.

420 "Banksia serrata"

421 Radio Telescope, Parkes, and Diagram of Comet's Orbit

1986. Bicentenary (1988) of Australian Settlement (4th issue). Cook's Voyage to New Holland. Multicoloured.
1002 33c. Type **420** 60 35
1003 33c. "Hibiscus meraukensis" 60 35
1004 50c. "Dillenia alata" 90 1·10
1005 80c. "Correa reflexa" 1·75 2·50
1006 90c. "Joseph Banks" (botanist) (Reynolds) and Banks with Dr. Solander 2·25 2·25
1007 90c. "Sydney Parkinson" (self-portrait) and Parkinson drawing 2·25 2·25

1986. Appearance of Halley's Comet.
1008 **421** 33c. multicoloured 50 35

422 Queen Elizabeth II

423 Brumbies (wild horses)

1986. 60th Birthday of Queen Elizabeth.
1009 **422** 33c. multicoloured 45 35

1986. Australian Horses. Multicoloured.
1010 33c. Type **423** 60 15
1011 80c. Mustering 1·50 2·25
1012 90c. Show-jumping 1·50 2·50
1013 $1 Child on pony 1·75 2·25

424 "The Old Shearer stands"

425 "King George III" (A. Ramsay) and Convicts

1986. Folklore. Scenes and Verses from the Folksong "Click go the Shears". Multicoloured.
1014 33c. Type **424** 55 80
1015 33c. "The ringer looks around" 55 80
1016 33c. "The boss of the board" 55 80
1017 33c. "The tar-boy is there" 55 80
1018 33c. "Shearing is all over" 55 80
Nos. 1014/18 were printed together, se-tenant, forming a composite design.

1986. Bicentenary (1988) of Australian Settlement (5th issue). Convict Settlement in New South Wales. Multicoloured.
1019 33c. Type **425** 80 50
1020 33c. "Lord Sydney" (Gilbert Stuart) and convicts 80 50
1021 33c. "Captain Arthur Phillip" (F. Wheatley) and ship 80 50
1022 $1 "Captain John Hunter" (W. B. Bennett) and aborigines 3·25 5·00

426 Red Kangaroo

427 Royal Bluebell

1986. Australian Wildlife (1st series). Mult.
1023 36c. Type **426** 60 80
1024 36c. Emu 60 80
1025 36c. Koala 60 80
1026 36c. Laughing kookaburra ("Kookaburra") 60 80
1027 36c. Platypus 60 80
See also Nos. 1072/6.

1986. Alpine Wildflowers. Multicoloured.
1028 3c. Type **427** 50 60
1029 5c. Alpine marsh marigold 1·75 2·75
1030 25c. Mount Buffalo sunray 1·75 2·75
1031 36c. Silver snow daisy 45 30

428 Pink Enamel Orchid

429 "Australia II" crossing Finishing Line

1986. Native Orchids. Multicoloured.
1032 36c. Type **428** 70 20
1033 55c. "Dendrobium nindii" 1·25 1·25
1034 90c. Duck orchid 2·00 3·50
1035 $1 Queen of Sheba orchid 2·00 2·25

1986. Australian Victory in America's Cup, 1983. Multicoloured.
1036 36c. Type **429** 75 75
1037 36c. Boxing kangaroo flag of winning syndicate 75 75
1038 36c. America's Cup trophy 75 75

430 Dove with Olive Branch and Sun

431 Mary and Joseph

1986. International Peace Year.
1039 **430** 36c. multicoloured 65 40

1986. Christmas. Scenes from children's nativity play. Multicoloured.
1040 30c. Type **431** 40 30
1041 36c. Three Wise Men leaving gifts 50 45
1042 60c. Angels (horiz) 90 1·50
MS1043 147 × 70 mm. 30 c. Three angels and shepherd (horiz); 30 c. Kneeling shepherds (horiz); 30 c. Mary, Joseph and three angels; 30 c. Innkeeper and two angels; 30 c. Three Wise Men (horiz) 3·00 3·50

432 Australian Flag on Printed Circuit Board

433 Aerial View of Yacht

1987. Australia Day. Multicoloured.
1044 36c. Type **432** 55 75
1045 36c. "Australian Made" Campaign logos 55 75

1987. America's Cup Yachting Championship. Multicoloured.
1046 36c. Type **433** 40 20
1047 55c. Two yachts tacking 90 1·25
1048 90c. Two yachts beating 1·40 2·50
1049 $1 Two yachts under full sail 1·50 1·75

434 Grapes and Melons

435 Livestock

1987. Australian Fruit. Multicoloured.
1050 36c. Type **434** 40 20
1051 65c. Tropical and sub-tropical fruits 1·00 1·50
1052 90c. Citrus fruit, apples and pears 1·40 2·50
1053 $1 Stone and berry fruits 1·40 1·60

1987. Agricultural Shows. Multicoloured.
1054 36c. Type **435** 60 20
1055 65c. Produce 1·25 1·75
1056 90c. Sideshows 1·75 2·75
1057 $1 Competitions 1·90 2·40

436 Queen Elizabeth in Australia, 1986

1987. Queen Elizabeth II's Birthday.
1058 **436** 36c. multicoloured 55 60

437 Convicts on Quay

438 "At the Station"

1987. Bicentenary (1988) of Australian Settlement (6th issue). Departure of the First Fleet. Multicoloured.
1059 36c. Type **437** 80 1·10
1060 36c. Royal Marines officer and wife 80 1·10
1061 36c. Sailors loading supplies 80 1·10
1062 36c. Officers being ferried to ships 80 1·10
1063 36c. Fleet in English Channel 80 1·10
See also Nos. 1064/6, 1077/81 and 1090/2.

1987. Bicentenary (1988) of Australian Settlement (7th issue). First Fleet at Tenerife. As T **437**. Multicoloured.
1064 36c. Ferrying supplies, Santa Cruz 70 1·00
1065 36c. Canary Islands fishermen and departing fleet 70 1·00
1066 $1 Fleet arriving at Tenerife 1·75 2·25
Nos. 1064/5 were printed together, se-tenant, forming a composite design.

1987. Folklore. Scenes and Verses from Poem "The Man from Snowy River". Multicoloured.
1067 36c. Type **438** 70 1·00
1068 36c. "Mountain bred" 70 1·00
1069 36c. "That terrible descent" 70 1·00
1070 36c. "At their heels" 70 1·00
1071 36c. "Brought them back" 70 1·00
Nos. 1067/71 were printed together, se-tenant, forming a composite background design of mountain scenery.

1987. Australian Wildlife (2nd series). As T **426**. Multicoloured.
1072 37c. Common brushtail possum 55 80
1073 37c. Sulphur-crested cockatoo ("Cockatoo") 55 80
1074 37c. Common wombat 55 80
1075 37c. Crimson rosella ("Rosella") 55 80
1076 37c. Echidna 55 80

1987. Bicentenary (1988) of Australian Settlement (8th issue). First Fleet at Rio de Janeiro. As T **437**. Multicoloured.
1077 37c. Sperm whale and fleet 80 1·00
1078 37c. Brazilian coast 80 1·00
1079 37c. British officers in market 80 1·00
1080 37c. Religious procession 80 1·00
1081 37c. Fleet leaving Rio 80 1·00
Nos. 1077/81 were printed together, se-tenant, forming a composite design.

439 Bionic Ear

440 Catching Crayfish

1987. Australian Achievements in Technology. Mult.
1082 37c. Type **439** 40 35
1083 53c. Microchips 75 60
1084 63c. Robotics 85 70
1085 68c. Ceramics 95 75

1987. "Aussie Kids". Multicoloured.
1086 37c. Type **440** 40 35
1087 55c. Playing cat's cradle 75 75
1088 90c. Young football supporters 1·25 2·00
1089 $1 Children with kangaroo 1·25 1·50

1987. Bicentenary (1988) of Australian Settlement (9th issue). First Fleet at Cape of Good Hope. As T **437**. Multicoloured.
1090 37c. Marine checking list of livestock 65 1·00
1091 37c. Loading livestock 65 1·00
1092 $1 First Fleet at Cape Town 1·50 2·25
Nos. 1090/1 were printed together, se-tenant, forming a composite design.

441 Detail of Spearthrower, Western Australia

1987. Aboriginal Crafts. Multicoloured.
1093 3c. Type **441** 1·10 1·50
1094 15c. Shield pattern, New South Wales 4·50 5·50
1095 37c. Basket weave, Queensland 1·10 1·50
1096 37c. Bowl design, Central Australia 90 1·25
1097 37c. Belt pattern, Northern Territory 1·10 1·50

442 Grandmother and Granddaughters with Candles

443 Koala with Stockman's Hat and Eagle dressed as Uncle Sam

1987. Christmas. Designs showing carol singing by candlelight. Multicoloured.

1098 30c. Type **442** 50 65
1099 30c. Father and daughters 50 65
1100 30c. Four children 50 65
1101 30c. Family 50 65
1102 30c. Six teenagers 50 65
1103 37c. Choir (horiz) 50 65
1104 63c. Father and two children (horiz) . . . . . 85 1·25

1988. Bicentenary of Australian Settlement (10th issue). Arrival of First Fleet. As T **437**. Mult.

1105 37c. Aborigines watching arrival of Fleet, Botany Bay 65 90
1106 37c. Aborigine family and anchored ships 65 90
1107 37c. Fleet arriving at Sydney Cove 65 90
1108 37c. Ship's boat 65 90
1109 37c. Raising the flag, Sydney Cove, 26 January 1788 . . 65 90

Nos. 1105/9 were printed together, se-tenant, forming a composite design.

1988. Bicentenary of Australian Settlement (11th issue). Joint issue with U.S.A.

1110 **443** 37c. multicoloured . . . 60 35

444 "Religion" (A. Horner)

445 "Government House, Sydney, 1790" (George Raper)

1988. "Living Together". Designs showing cartoons. Multicoloured (except 30c.).

1111 1c. Type **444** 50 60
1112 2c. "Industry" (P. Nicholson) 50 40
1113 3c. "Local Government" (A. Collette) 50 40
1114 4c. "Trade Unions" (Liz Honey) 10 20
1115 5c. "Parliament" (Bronwyn Halls) 50 50
1116 10c. "Transport" (Meg Williams) 30 40
1117 15c. "Sport" (G. Cook) . . 70 50
1118 20c. "Commerce" (M. Atcherson) 70 70
1119 25c. "Housing" (C. Smith) 45 40
1120 30c. "Welfare" (R. Tandberg) (black and lilac) 55 70
1121 37c. "Postal Services" (P. Viska) 60 50
1121b 39c. "Tourism" (J. Spooner) 60 50
1122 40c. "Recreation" (R. Harvey) 70 70
1123 45c. "Health" (Jenny Coopes) 70 80
1124 50c. "Mining" (G. Haddon) 70 50
1125 53c. "Primary Industry" (S. Leahy) . . . . . . 1·75 1·50
1126 55c. "Education" (Victoria Roberts) . . . . 1·50 1·00
1127 60c. "Armed Forces" (B. Green) . . . . . . 1·50 70
1128 63c. "Police" (J. Russell) 2·00 1·10
1129 65c. "Telecommunications" (B. Petty) . . . . 1·50 1·75
1130 68c. "The Media" (A. Langoulant) . . . . 2·00 2·50
1131 70c. "Science and Technology" (J. Hook) 1·75 1·00
1132 75c. "Visual Arts" (G. Dazeley) . . . . . 1·00 1·00
1133 80c. "Performing Arts" (A. Stitt) . . . . 1·25 1·00
1134 90c. "Banking" (S. Billington) . . . . . 1·50 1·00
1135 95c. "Law" (C. Aslanis) . . 1·00 1·50
1136 $1 "Rescue and Emergency" (M. Leunig) 1·10 1·00

1988. Bicentenary of Australian Settlement (12th issue). "The Early Years, 1788–1809". Mult.

1137 37c. Type **445** . . . . . . 65 1·00
1138 37c. "Government Farm, Parramatta, 1791" ("The Port Jackson Painter") . . 65 1·00
1139 37c. "Parramatta Road, 1796" (attr Thomas Watling) . . . . 65 1·00
1140 37c. "View of Sydney Cove, c. 1800" (detail) (Edward Dayes) . . . . . 65 1·00
1141 37c. "Sydney Hospital, 1803", (detail) (George William Evans) . . . . . 65 1·00

Nos. 1137/41 were printed together, se-tenant, forming a composite background design from the painting "View of Sydney from the East Side of the Cove, c. 1808" by John Eyre.

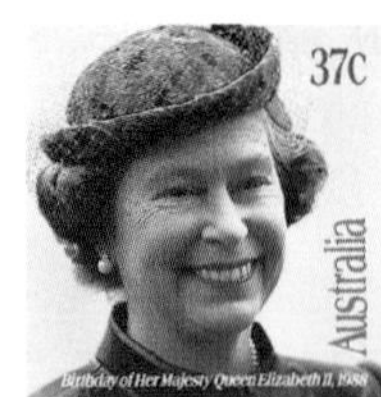

446 Queen Elizabeth II (from photo by Tim Graham)

1988. Queen Elizabeth II's Birthday.

1142 **446** 37c. multicoloured . . . 50 40

447 Expo '88 Logo

1988. "Expo '88" World Fair, Brisbane.

1143 **447** 37c. multicoloured . . . 50 40

448 New Parliament House

1988. Opening of New Parliament House, Canberra.

1144 **448** 37c. multicoloured . . . 50 40

449 Early Settler and Sailing Clipper

1988. Bicentenary of Australian Settlement (13th issue). Multicoloured.

1145 37c. Type **449** . . . . . . 75 1·00
1146 37c. Queen Elizabeth II with British and Australian Parliament Buildings . . . 75 1·00
1147 $1 W. G. Grace (cricketer) and tennis racquet . . . . 1·50 2·25
1148 $1 Shakespeare, John Lennon (entertainer) and Sydney Opera House . . 1·50 2·25

Stamps in similar designs were also issued by Great Britain.

450 Kiwi and Koala at Campfire

1988. Bicentenary of Australian Settlement (14th issue).

1149 **450** 37c. multicoloured . . . 65 40

A stamp in a similar design was also issued by New Zealand.

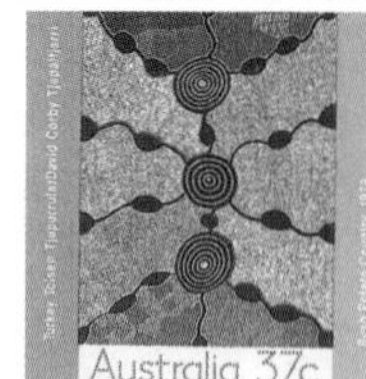

451 "Bush Potato Country" (Turkey Tolsen Tjupurrula and David Corby Tjapaltjarri)

1988. Art of the Desert. Aboriginal Paintings from Central Australia. Multicoloured.

1150 37c. Type **451** 30 30
1151 55c. "Courtship Rejected" (Limpi Puntungka Tjapangati) 55 70
1152 90c. "Medicine Story" (artist unknown) . . . . 75 2·40
1153 $1 "Ancestor Dreaming" (Tim Leura Tjapaltjarri) 80 1·50

452 Basketball

1988. Olympic Games, Seoul. Multicoloured.

1154 37c. Type **452** 50 40
1155 65c. Athlete crossing finish line . . . . 60 1·50
1156 $1 Gymnast with hoop . . . 85 1·75

453 Rod and Mace

1988. 34th Commonwealth Parliamentary Conference, Canberra.

1157 **453** 37c. multicoloured . . . 50 60

454 Necklace by Peter Tully

1988. Australian Crafts. Multicoloured.

1158 2c. Type **454** . . . . 3·50 4·50
1159 5c. Vase by Colin Levy . . 3·50 4·50
1160 39c. Teapot by Frank Bauer 50 35

455 Pinnacles Desert

1988. Panorama of Australia. Multicoloured.

1161 39c. Type **455** 50 40
1162 55c. Flooded landscape, Arnhem Land 80 90
1163 65c. Twelve Apostles, Victoria . . . . 90 1·75
1164 70c. Mountain Ash wood 1·00 1·75

456 "The Nativity" (Danielle Hush)

1988. Christmas. Multicoloured.

1165 32c. Type **456** 50 20
1166 39c. "Koala as Father Christmas" (Kylie Courtney) 55 25
1167 63c. "Christmas Cockatoo" (Benjamin Stevenson) . . 1·10 1·60

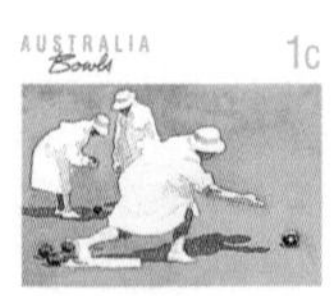

457 Sir Henry Parkes

458 Bowls

1989. Australia Day. Centenary of Federation Speech by Sir Henry Parkes (N.S.W. Prime Minister).

1168 **457** 39c. multicoloured . . . 45 40

1989. Sports. Multicoloured.

1169 1c. Type **458** 10 30
1170 2c. Tenpin-bowling 10 10
1171 3c. Australian football . . . 50 65
1172 5c. Kayaking and canoeing 15 10
1174 10c. Sailboarding 15 15
1176 20c. Tennis 20 25
1179 39c. Fishing 45 40
1180 41c. Cycling 40 35
1181 43c. Skateboarding 50 40
1184 55c. Kite-flying 40 45
1186 65c. Rock-climbing 70 60
1187 70c. Cricket . . . . 1·00 80
1188 75c. Netball 55 70
1189 80c. Squash . . . . 1·00 65
1190 85c. Diving . . . . 1·75 80
1191 90c. Soccer . . . . 1·75 80
1192 $1 Fun-run . . . . 1·00 95
1193 $1.10 Golf . . . . 1·25 90
1194 $1.20 Hang-gliding . . . . 3·25 1·10

459 Merino

1989. Sheep in Australia. Multicoloured.

1195 39c. Type **459** 70 45
1196 39c. Poll Dorset 70 45
1197 85c. Polwarth . . . . 1·40 2·25
1198 $1 Corriedale . . . . 1·40 1·50

460 Adelaide Botanic Garden

1989. Botanic Gardens. Multicoloured.

1199 $2 Noroo, New South Wales . . . . 1·50 40
1200 $5 Mawarra, Victoria . . . 4·25 60
1201 $10 Type **460** . . . . . . 7·50 1·25
1201a $20 "A View of the Artist's House and Garden in Mills Plains, Van Diemen's Land" (John Glover) . . . . 15·00 8·00

461 "Queen Elizabeth II" (sculpture, John Dowie)

462 Arrival of Immigrant Ship, 1830s

1989. Queen Elizabeth II's Birthday.

1202 **461** 39c. multicoloured . . . 55 50

1989. Colonial Development (1st issue). Pastoral Era 1810–1850. Multicoloured.

1203 39c. Type **462** 55 55
1204 39c. Pioneer cottage and wool dray 55 55
1205 39c. Squatter's homestead 55 55
1206 39c. Shepherd with flock (from Joseph Lycett's "Views of Australia") . . 55 55
1207 39c. Explorer in desert (after watercolour by Edward Frome) 55 55

See also Nos. 1254/8 and 1264/8.

463 Gladys Moncrieff and Roy Rene

464 "Impression" (Tom Roberts)

1989. Australian Stage and Screen Personalities. Multicoloured.

1208 39c. Type **463** 45 40
1209 85c. Charles Chauvel and Chips Rafferty . . . . . 1·25 1·75
1210 $1 Nellie Stewart and J. C. Williamson . . . . 1·25 1·10
1211 $1.10 Lottie Lyell and Raymond Longford . . . 1·25 1·50

1989. Australian Impressionist Paintings. Mult.

1212 41c. Type **464** 45 50
1213 41c. "Impression for Golden Summer" (Sir Arthur Streeton) 45 50
1214 41c. "All on a Summer's Day" (Charles Conder) (vert) 45 50
1215 41c. "Petit Dejeuner" (Frederick McCubbin) . . 45 50

465 Freeways

1989. The Urban Environment.

1216 **465** 41c. black, purple and green . . . . 65 1·00
1217 – 41c. black, purple and mauve . . . . 65 1·00
1218 – 41c. black, purple and blue . . . . 65 1·00

DESIGNS: No. 1217, City buildings, Melbourne; No. 1218, Commuter train at platform.

466 Hikers outside Youth Hostel

1989. 50th Anniv of Australian Youth Hostels.

1219 **466** 41c. multicoloured . . . 55 50

467 Horse Tram, Adelaide, 1878

1989. Historic Trams. Multicoloured.

1220 41c. Type **467** 60 60
1221 41c. Steam tram, Sydney, 1884 . . . . 60 60
1222 41c. Cable tram, Melbourne, 1886 . . . . 60 60
1223 41c. Double-deck electric tram, Hobart, 1893 . . . 60 60
1224 41c. Combination electric tram, Brisbane, 1901 . . . 60 60

468 "Annunciation" (15th-century Book of Hours)

469 Radio Waves and Globe

1989. Christmas. Illuminated Manuscripts. Mult.

1225 36c. Type **468** 40 15
1226 41c. "Annunciation to the Shepherds" (Wharncliffe Book of Hours, c. 1475) 50 15
1227 80c. "Adoration of the Magi" (15th-century Parisian Book of Hours) 1·25 1·90

1989. 50th Anniv of Radio Australia.

1228 **469** 41c. multicoloured . . . 55 50

470 Golden Wattle

471 Australian Wildflowers

1990. Australia Day.

1229 **470** 41c. multicoloured . . . 55 50

1990. Greetings Stamps.

1230 **471** 41c. multicoloured . . . 65 65
1231 43c. multicoloured . . . 50 50

472 Dr. Constance Stone (first Australian woman doctor), Modern Doctor and Nurses

1990. Centenary of Women in Medical Practice.

1232 **472** 41c. multicoloured . . . 50 45

473 Greater Glider

474 "Stop Smoking"

1990. Animals of the High Country. Multicoloured.

1233 41c. Type **473** 60 45
1234 65c. Tiger cat ("Spotted-tailed Quoll") . . . . . . 90 1·25
1235 70c. Mountain pygmy-possum . . . . 95 1·25
1236 80c. Brush-tailed rock-wallaby . . . . 1·10 1·25

1990. Community Health. Multicoloured.

1237 41c. Type **474** 55 55
1238 41c. "Drinking and driving don't mix" 55 55
1239 41c. "No junk food, please" 55 55
1240 41c. "Guess who's just had a check up?" 55 55

475 Soldiers from Two World Wars

476 Queen at Australian Ballet Gala Performance, London, 1988

1990. "The Anzac Tradition". Multicoloured.

1241 41c. Type **475** 50 40
1242 41c. Fighter pilots and munitions worker 50 40
1243 65c. Veterans and Anzac Day parade 85 90
1244 $1 Casualty evacuation, Vietnam, and disabled veteran . . . . 1·25 1·40
1245 $1.10 Letters from home and returning troopships 1·40 1·50

1990. Queen Elizabeth II's Birthday.

1246 **476** 41c. multicoloured . . . 65 45

477 New South Wales 1861 5s. Stamp

1990. 150th Anniv of the Penny Black. Designs showing stamps. Multicoloured.

1247 41c. Type **477** 60 75
1248 41c. South Australia 1855 unissued 1s. 60 75
1249 41c. Tasmania 1853 4d. . . 60 75
1250 41c. Victoria 1867 5s. . . . 60 75
1251 41c. Queensland 1897 unissued 6d. 60 75
1252 41c. Western Australia 1855 4d. with inverted frame 60 75
MS1253 122 × 85 mm. Nos. 1247/52 3·25 4·00

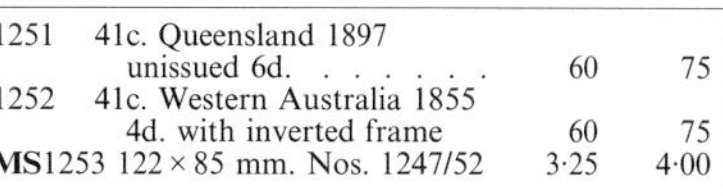

478 Gold Miners on Way to Diggings

1990. Colonial Development (2nd issue). Gold Fever. Multicoloured.

1254 41c. Type **478** 80 85
1255 41c. Mining camp 80 85
1256 41c. Panning and washing for gold 80 85
1257 41c. Gold Commissioner's tent 80 85
1258 41c. Moving gold under escort 80 85

479 Glaciology Research

1990. Australian–Soviet Scientific Co-operation in Antarctica. Multicoloured.

1261 41c. Type **479** 65 40
1262 $1.10 Krill (marine biology research) . . . . 1·60 1·50
MS1263 85 × 65 mm. Nos. 1261/2 2·25 2·25

Stamps in similar designs were also issued by Russia.

480 Auctioning Building Plots

1990. Colonial Development (3rd series). Boomtime. Multicoloured.

1264 41c. Type **480** 55 55
1265 41c. Colonial mansion . . . 55 55
1266 41c. Stock exchange 55 55
1267 41c. Fashionable society . . 55 55
1268 41c. Factories 55 55

AUSTRALIA 43c

481 "Salmon Gums" (Robert Juniper)

482 "Adelaide Town Hall" (Edmund Gouldsmith)

1990. "Heidelberg and Heritage" Art Exhibition. Multicoloured.

1269 28c. Type **481** . . . . . . 2·25 3·00
1270 43c. "The Blue Dress" (Brian Dunlop) 40 45

1990. 150th Anniv of Local Government.

1271 **482** 43c. multicoloured . . . 75 50

483 Laughing Kookaburras and Gifts

1990. Christmas. Multicoloured.

1272 38c. Type **483** 50 25
1273 43c. Baby Jesus with koalas and wallaby (vert) 50 25
1274 80c. Possum on Christmas tree . . . . 1·50 2·50

484 National Flag

485 Black-necked Stork

1991. Australia Day. 90th Anniv of Australian Flag.

1275 **484** 43c. blue, red and grey 50 40
1276 – 90c. multicoloured . . . 1·10 1·25
1277 – $1 multicoloured . . . . 1·25 1·40
1278 – $1.20 red, blue and grey 1·60 1·75

DESIGNS: 90c. Royal Australian Navy ensign; $1 Royal Australian Air Force standard; $1.20, Australian merchant marine ensign.

1991. Waterbirds. Multicoloured.

1279 43c. Type **485** 75 40
1280 43c. Black swan (horiz) . . 75 40
1281 85c. Cereopsis goose ("Cape Barren") . . . . 1·75 2·25
1282 $1 Chestnut-breasted teal ("Chestnut Teal") (horiz) 1·90 1·75

486 Recruitment Poster (Women's Services)

1991. Anzac Day. 50th Anniversaries.

1283 **486** 43c. multicoloured . . . 60 40
1284 – 43c. black, green & brn 60 40
1285 – $1.20 multicoloured . . 2·25 2·00

DESIGNS: 43c. (No. 1284) Patrol (Defence of Tobruk); $1.20, "V-P Day Canberra" (Harold Abbot) (Australian War Memorial).

487 Queen Elizabeth at Royal Albert Hall, London

489 "Bondi" (Max Dupain)

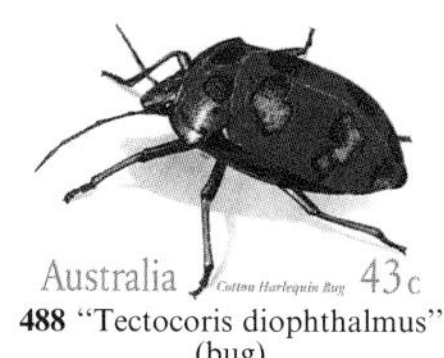

488 "Tectocoris diophthalmus" (bug)

1991. Queen Elizabeth II's Birthday.

1286 **487** multicoloured 80 50

1991. Insects. Multicoloured.

1287 43c. Type **488** 75 45
1288 43c. "Cizara ardeniae" (hawk moth) 75 45
1289 80c. "Petasida ephippigera" (grasshopper) . . . . . . 2·00 2·00
1290 $1 "Castiarina producta" (beetle) . . . . 2·00 1·50

1991. 150 Years of Photography in Australia.

1291 **489** 43c. black, brown and blue 75 65
1292 – 43c. black, green & brn 75 65
1293 – 70c. black, green & brn 1·25 1·10
1294 – $1.20 black, brn & grn 1·75 1·50

DESIGNS: No. 1292, "Gears for the Mining Industry, Vickers Ruwolt, Melbourne" (Wolfgang Sievers); 1293, "The Wheel of Youth" (Harold Cazneaux); 1294, "Teacup Ballet" (Olive Cotton).

490 Singing Group

491 Puppy

1991. Australian Radio Broadcasting. Designs showing listeners and scenes from radio programmes. Multicoloured.

1295 43c. Type **490** 60 45
1296 43c. "Blue Hills" serial . . . 60 45

1297 85c. "The Quiz Kids" . . . 1·25 1·25
1298 $1 "Argonauts' Club" children's programme . . 1·50 1·40

1991. Domestic Pets. Multicoloured.
1299 43c. Type **491** 70 45
1300 43c. Kitten 70 45
1301 70c. Pony . . . . 1·40 2·50
1302 $1 Sulphur-crested cockatoo 1·90 1·50

492 George Vancouver (1791) and Edward Eyre (1841)

493 "Seven Little Australians" (Ethel Turner)

1991. Exploration of Western Australia.
1303 **492** $1.05 multicoloured . . 1·00 1·10
MS1304 100 × 65 mm. No. 1303 1·25 1·40

1991. Australian Writers of the 1890s. Multicoloured.
1305 43c. Type **493** 50 45
1306 75c. "On Our Selection" (Steele Rudd) . . . . . . 80 1·00
1307 $1 "Clancy of the Overflow" (poem, A. B. Paterson) (vert) . . . . 1·10 1·00
1308 $1.20 "The Drover's Wife" (short story, Henry Lawson) (vert) . . . . . 1·25 1·60

494 Shepherd

1991. Christmas. Multicoloured.
1309 38c. Type **494** 40 15
1310 43c. Infant Jesus 45 15
1311 90c. Wise Man . . . . . . 1·50 1·75

495 Parma Wallaby

1992. Threatened Species. Multicoloured.
1312 45c. Type **495** 65 60
1313 45c. Ghost bat 65 60
1314 45c. Long-tailed dunnart . . 65 60
1315 45c. Little pygmy-possum 65 60
1316 45c. Dusky hopping-mouse 65 60
1317 45c. Squirrel glider 65 60

496 Basket of Wild Flowers

1992. Greetings Stamp.
1318 **496** 45c. multicoloured . . . 50 50

497 Noosa River, Queensland

1992. Wetlands and Waterways. Multicoloured.
1319 20c. Type **497** . . . . . . 1·75 2·25
1320 45c. Lake Eildon, Victoria 40 45

498 "Young Endeavour" (brigantine)

1992. Australia Day and 500th Anniv of Discovery of America by Columbus (**MS**1337). Multicoloured. Sailing Ships.
1333 45c. Type **498** 80 50
1334 45c. "Britannia" (yacht) (vert) 80 50
1335 $1.05 "Akarana" (cutter) (vert) . . . . 1·75 2·75
1336 $1.20 "John Louis" (pearling lugger) . . . . . 2·00 2·00
MS1337 147 × 64 mm. Nos. 1333/6 4·75 5·25

499 Bombing of Darwin

1992. 50th Anniv of Second World War Battles. Multicoloured.
1338 45c. Type **499** 70 45
1339 75c. Anti-aircraft gun and fighters, Milne Bay . . . 1·25 1·50
1340 75c. Infantry on Kokoda Trail . . . . 1·25 1·50
1341 $1.05 H.M.A.S. "Australia" (cruiser) and U.S.S. "Yorktown" (aircraft carrier), Coral Sea . . . . 1·50 1·75
1342 $1.20 Australians advancing, El Alamein . . . . 1·75 1·60

500 "Helix Nebula"

1992. International Space Year. Multicoloured.
1343 45c. Type **500** 60 45
1344 $1.05 "The Pleiades" . . . 1·75 1·25
1345 $1.20 "Spiral Galaxy, NGC 2997" . . . . 2·00 1·50
MS1346 133 × 70 mm. Nos. 1343/5 4·25 4·50

501 Hunter Valley, New South Wales

1992. Vineyard Regions. Multicoloured.
1347 45c. Type **501** 60 75
1348 45c. North-east Victoria . . 60 75
1349 45c. Barossa Valley, South Australia 60 75
1350 45c. Coonawarra, South Australia 60 75
1351 45c. Margaret River, Western Australia 60 75

502 3½d. Stamp of 1953

503 Salt Action

1992. Queen Elizabeth II's Birthday.
1352 **502** 45c. multicoloured . . . 80 50

1992. Land Conservation. Multicoloured.
1353 45c. Type **503** . . . . . . 65 1·00
1354 45c. Farm planning . . . . 65 1·00
1355 45c. Erosion control . . . . 65 1·00
1356 45c. Tree planting . . . . . 65 1·00
1357 45c. Dune care . . . . . . 65 1·00

504 Cycling

1992. Olympic Games and Paralympic Games (No. 1359), Barcelona. Multicoloured.
1358 45c. Type **504** 60 45
1359 $1.20 High jumping . . . . 1·50 1·60
1360 $1.20 Weightlifting . . . . 1·50 1·60

505 Echidna

506 Sydney Harbour Tunnel (value at left)

1992. Australian Wildlife (1st series). Multicoloured.
1361 30c. Saltwater crocodile . . 25 20
1362 35c. Type **505** 50 20
1363 40c. Platypus . . . . . . 1·25 25
1364 50c. Koala 60 35
1365 60c. Common bushtail possum . . . . 1·00 1·25
1366 70c. Laughing kookaburra ("Kookaburra") . . . . 1·75 1·00
1367 85c. Australian pelican ("Pelican") 65 70
1368a 90c. Eastern grey kangaroo 1·25 1·00
1369 95c. Common wombat . . 1·00 1·75
1370a $1.20 Major Mitchell's cockatoo ("Pink Cockatoo") . . . . . . 1·25 1·10
1371 $1.35 Emu . . . . 1·00 1·75
See also Nos. 1453/8.

1992. Opening of Sydney Harbour Tunnel. Mult.
1375b 45c. Type **506** . . . . . . 1·75 1·75
1376b 45c. Sydney Harbour Tunnel (value at right) 1·75 1·75
Nos. 1375/6 were printed together, se-tenant, forming a composite design.

507 Warden's Courthouse, Coolgardie

508 Bowler of 1892

1992. Centenary of Discovery of Gold at Coolgardie and Kalgoorlie. Multicoloured.
1377 45c. Type **507** 70 45
1378 45c. Post Office, Kalgoorlie 70 45
1379 $1.05 York Hotel, Kalgoorlie . . . . 1·60 1·60
1380 $1.20 Town Hall, Kalgoorlie 1·90 1·90

1992. Centenary of Sheffield Shield Cricket Tournament. Multicoloured.
1381 45c. Type **508** 85 50
1382 $1.20 Batsman and wicket-keeper . . . . 1·90 2·50

509 Children's Nativity Play

1992. Christmas. Multicoloured.
1383 40c. Type **509** 55 25
1384 45c. Child waking on Christmas Day 60 25
1385 $1 Children carol singing . . 1·90 2·00

510 "Ghost Gum, Central Australia" (Namatjira)

1993. Australia Day. Paintings by Albert Namatjira. Multicoloured.
1386 45c. Type **510** . . . . . . 90 1·40
1387 45c. "Across the Plain to Mount Giles" . . . . . . 90 1·40

511 "Wild Onion Dreaming" (Pauline Nakamarra Woods)

1993. "Dreamings". Paintings by Aboriginal Artists. Multicoloured.
1388 45c. Type **511** 60 30
1389 75c. "Yam Plants" (Jack Wunuwun) (vert) . . . . 1·10 95
1390 85c. "Goose Egg Hunt" (George Milpurrurru) (vert) . . . . 1·25 1·40
1391 $1 "Kalumpiwarra-Ngulalintji" (Rover Thomas) . . . . 1·40 1·40

512 Uluru (Ayers Rock) National Park

1993. World Heritage Sites (1st series). Multicoloured.
1392 45c. Type **512** 70 30
1393 85c. Rain forest, Fraser Island . . . . 1·75 1·60
1394 95c. Beach, Shark Bay . . . 1·75 1·60
1395 $2 Waterfall, Kakadu . . . 2·50 2·25
See also Nos. 1582/5.

513 Queen Elizabeth II on Royal Visit, 1992

514 H.M.A.S. "Sydney" (cruiser, launched 1934) in Action

1993. Queen Elizabeth II's Birthday.
1396 **513** 45c. multicoloured . . . 70 60

1993. Second World War Naval Vessels. Mult.
1397 45c. Type **514** 80 45
1398 85c. H.M.A.S. "Bathurst" (mine-sweeper) . . . . . 1·60 1·75
1399 $1.05 H.M.A.S. "Arunta" (destroyer) . . . . 1·75 2·75
1400 $1.20 "Centaur" (hospital ship) and tug . . . . . . 2·00 2·75

515 "Work in the Home"

516 "Centenary Special", Tasmania, 1971

1993. Working Life in the 1890s. Mult.
1401 45c. Type **515** 55 50
1402 45c. "Work in the Cities" 55 50
1403 $1 "Work in the Country" 1·10 1·10
1404 $1.20 Trade Union banner 1·50 2·00

1993. Australian Trains. Multicoloured.
1405 45c. Type **516** 65 75
1406 45c. "Spirit of Progress", Victoria 65 75
1407 45c. "Western Endeavour", Western Australia, 1970 65 75
1408 45c. "Silver City Comet", New South Wales 65 75
1409 45c. Cairns–Kuranda tourist train, Queensland 65 75
1410 45c. "The Ghan", Northern Territory 65 75
Nos. 1405/10 also come self-adhesive.

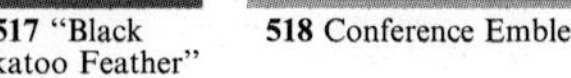

517 "Black Cockatoo Feather" (Fiona Foley)

518 Conference Emblem

1993. International Year of Indigenous Peoples. Aboriginal Art. Multicoloured
1417 45c. Type **517** 55 30
1418 75c. "Ngarrgooroon Country" (Hector Jandany) (horiz) . . . . 1·10 1·50

1419 $1 "Ngak Ngak" (Ginger Riley Munduwalawala) (horiz) . . . . 1·25 1·60
1420 $1.05 "Untitled" (Robert Cole) . . . . 1·50 2·50

1993. Inter-Parliamentary Union Conference and 50th Anniv of Women in Federal Parliament. Multicoloured.
1421 45c. Type **518** . . . . . . 1·00 1·40
1422 45c. Dame Enid Lyons and Senator Dorothy Tangney 1·00 1·40

519 Ornithocheirus

520 "Goodwill"

1993. Prehistoric Animals. Multicoloured.
1423 45c. Type **519** 60 50
1424 45c. Leaellynasaura (25 × 30 mm) 60 50
1425 45c. Timimus (26 × 33 mm) 60 50
1426 45c. Allosaurus (26 × 33 mm) 60 50
1427 75c. Muttaburrasaurus (30 × 50 mm) . . . . . . 1·00 90
1428 $1.05 Minmi (50 × 30 mm) 1·50 1·50
MS1429 166 × 73 mm. Nos. 1423/8 5·50 6·50
Nos. 1423/4 also come self-adhesive.

1993. Christmas. Multicoloured.
1432 40c. Type **520** 50 25
1433 45c. "Joy" 55 25
1434 $1 "Peace" . . . . 1·90 2·00

521 "Shoalhaven River Bank—Dawn" (Arthur Boyd)

1994. Australia Day. Landscape Paintings. Mult.
1435 45c. Type **521** 60 30
1436 85c. "Wimmera" (Sir Sidney Nolan) . . . . 1·40 1·40
1437 $1.05 "Lagoon, Wimmera" (Nolan) . . . . 1·60 1·60
1438 $2 "White Cockatoos with Flame Trees" (Boyd) (vert) . . . . 2·50 2·75

522 Teaching Lifesaving Techniques

1994. Centenary of Organized Life Saving in Australia. Multicoloured.
1439 45c. Type **522** 60 45
1440 45c. Lifeguard on watch . . 60 45
1441 95c. Lifeguard team . . . . 1·25 1·40
1442 $1.20 Lifeguards on surf boards . . . . 1·60 1·75
Nos. 1439/40 also come self-adhesive.

523 Rose

524 Bridge and National Flags

1994. Greetings Stamps. Flower photographs by Lariane Fonseca. Multicoloured.
1445 45c. Type **523** 40 45
1446 45c. Tulips 40 45
1447 45c. Poppies 40 45

1994. Opening of Friendship Bridge between Thailand and Laos.
1448 **524** 95c. multicoloured . . . 1·25 1·40

525 "Queen Elizabeth II" (Sir William Dargie)

526 "Family in Field" (Bobbie-Lea Blackmore)

1994. Queen Elizabeth II's Birthday.
1449 **525** 45c. multicoloured . . . 70 70

1994. International Year of the Family. Children's Paintings. Multicoloured.
1450 45c. Type **526** 55 30
1451 75c. "Family on Beach" (Kathryn Teoh) . . . . . 1·00 1·25
1452 $1 "Family around Fire" (Maree McCarthy) . . . 1·25 1·50

1994. Australian Wildlife (2nd series). As T **505**. Multicoloured. Ordinary or self-adhesive gum.
1453 45c. Kangaroo 80 55
1454 45c. Female kangaroo with young 80 55
1455 45c. Two kangaroos 80 55
1456 45c. Family of koalas on branch 80 55
1457 45c. Koala on ground . . . 80 55
1458 45c. Koala asleep in tree . . 80 55

527 Suffragettes

1994. Centenary of Women's Emancipation in South Australia.
1465 **527** 45c. multicoloured . . . 60 60

528 Bunyip from Aboriginal Legend

1994. The Bunyip (mythological monster). Mult.
1466 45c. Type **528** 70 70
1467 45c. Nature spirit bunyip . . 70 70
1468 90c. "The Bunyip of Berkeley's Creek" (book illustration) . . . . 1·75 1·75
1469 $1.35 Bunyip as natural history . . . . 2·25 2·25

529 "Robert Menzies" (Sir Ivor Hele)

530 Lawrence Hargrave and Box Kites

1994. Wartime Prime Ministers. Multicoloured.
1470 45c. Type **529** . . . . . . 90 1·00
1471 45c. "Arthur Fadden" (William Dargie) . . . . 90 1·00
1472 45c. "John Curtin" (Anthony Dattilo-Rubbo) 90 1·00
1473 45c. "Francis Forde" (Joshua Smith) . . . . . 90 1·00
1474 45c. "Joseph Chifley" (A. D. Colquhoun) . . . . . . 90 1·00

1994. Aviation Pioneers.
1475 **530** 45c. brown, green and cinnamon 70 50
1476 – 45c. brown, red and lilac 70 50
1477 – $1.35 brown, violet and blue . . . . 2·25 3·00
1478 – $1.80 brown, deep green and green . . . . . . 2·50 3·25
DESIGNS: No. 1476, Ross and Keith Smith with Vickers Vimy (first England–Australia flight); 1477, Ivor McIntyre, Stanley Goble and Fairey IIID seaplane (first aerial circumnavigation of Australia); 1478, Freda Thompson and De Havilland Moth Major "Christopher Robin" (first Australian woman to fly solo from England to Australia).

531 Scarlet Macaw

532 "Madonna and Child" (detail)

1994. Australian Zoos. Endangered Species. Mult.
1479 45c. Type **531** 65 55
1480 45c. Cheetah (25 × 30 mm) 65 55
1481 45c. Orang-utan (26 × 37 mm) 65 55
1482 45c. Fijian crested iguana (26 × 37 mm) 65 55
1483 $1 Asian elephants (49 × 28 mm) . . . . . 1·75 1·60
MS1484 166 × 73 mm. Nos. 1479/83 4·00 4·50
Nos. 1479/80 also come self-adhesive.

1994. Christmas. "The Adoration of the Magi" by Giovanni Toscani. Multicoloured.
1487 40c. Type **532** 60 25
1488 45c. "Wise Man and Horse" (detail) (horiz) 60 25
1489 $1 "Wise Man and St. Joseph" (detail) (horiz) 1·50 1·40
1490 $1.80 Complete painting (49 × 29 mm) . . . . . . 2·00 2·75

533 Yachts outside Sydney Harbour

534 Symbolic Kangaroo

1994. 50th Sydney to Hobart Yacht Race. Mult.
1491 45c. Type **533** 90 80
1492 45c. Yachts passing Tasmania coastline . . . 90 80
Nos. 1491/92 also come self-adhesive.

1994. Self-adhesive. Automatic Cash Machine Stamps.
1495 **534** 45c. gold, emerald and green 80 80
1496 45c. gold, green and blue 80 80
1497 45c. gold, green and lilac 80 80
1498 45c. gold, emerald and green 80 80
1499 45c. gold, emerald and green 80 80
1500 45c. gold, green and pink 80 80
1501 45c. gold, green and red 80 80
1502 45c. gold, green and brown 80 80

535 "Back Verandah" (Russell Drysdale)

1995. Australia Day. Paintings. Multicoloured.
1503 45c. Type **535** 60 45
1504 45c. "Skull Springs Country" (Guy Grey-Smith) 60 45
1505 $1.05 "Outcamp" (Robert Juniper) . . . . 1·60 1·50
1506 $1.20 "Kite Flying" (Ian Fairweather) . . . . . . 1·75 1·50

536 Red Heart and Rose

537 "Endeavour" Replica at Sea

1995. St. Valentine's Day. Multicoloured.
1507 45c. Type **536** 55 55
1508 45c. Gold and red heart with rose 55 55
1509 45c. Gold heart and roses 85 85

1995. Completion of "Endeavour" Replica. Mult.
1510 45c. Type **537** . . . . . . 1·25 1·25
1511 45c. "Captain Cook's Endeavour" (detail) (Oswald Brett) . . . . . 1·25 1·25

538 Coalport Plate and Bracket Clock, Old Government House, Parramatta

1995. 50th Anniv of Australian National Trusts.
1514 **538** 45c. blue and brown . . 45 45
1515 – 45c. green and brown . . 45 45
1516 – $1 red and blue . . . . 1·00 95
1517 – $2 green and blue . . . 1·90 1·90
DESIGNS: No. 1515, Steiner doll and Italian-style chair, Ayers House, Adelaide; 1516, "Advance Australia" teapot and parian-ware statuette, Victoria; 1517, Silver bowl and china urn, Old Observatory, Perth.

539 Light Opal (hologram)

1995. Opals. Mulitcoloured.
1518 $1.20 Type **539** . . . . . . 2·25 1·25
1519 $2.50 Black opal (hologram) 3·75 3·75

540 Queen Elizabeth II at Gala Concert, 1992

541 Sir Edward Dunlop and P.O.W. Association Badge

1995. Queen Elizabeth II's Birthday.
1520 **540** 45c. multicoloured . . . 75 75

1995. Australian Second World War Heroes (1st series). Mult. Ordinary or self-adhesive gum.
1521 45c. Type **541** 60 60
1522 45c. Mrs. Jessie Vasey and War Widows' Guild badge 60 60
1523 45c. Sgt. Tom Derrick and Victoria Cross 60 60
1524 45c. Flt. Sgt. Rawdon Middleton and Victoria Cross 60 60
See also Nos. 1545/8.

542 Children and Globe of Flags

543 "The Story of the Kelly Gang"

1995. 50th Anniv of United Nations.
1529 **542** 45c. multicoloured . . . 75 75

1995. Centenary of Cinema. Scenes from Films. Multicoloured. (a) Size 23 × 35 mm.
1530 45c. Type **543** . . . . . . 1·00 1·10
1531 45c. "On Our Selection" . . 1·00 1·10
1532 45c. "Jedda" . . . . 1·00 1·10
1533 45c. "Picnic at Hanging Rock" . . . . 1·00 1·10
1534 45c. "Strictly Ballroom" . . 1·00 1·10

(b) Self-adhesive. Size 19 × 30½ mm.
1535 45c. Type **543** . . . . . . 1·25 1·40
1536 45c. "On Our Selection" . . 1·25 1·40
1537 45c. "Jedda" . . . . 1·25 1·40
1538 45c. "Picnic at Hanging Rock" . . . . 1·25 1·40
1539 45c. "Strictly Ballroom" . . 1·25 1·40

544 Man in Wheelchair flying Kite

545 Koala with Cub

1995. People with Disabilities. Multicoloured.
1540 45c. Type **544** 90 90
1541 45c. Blind woman playing violin 90 90

1995. 50th Anniv of Peace in the Pacific. Designs as 1946 Victory Commemoration (Nos. 213/15) redrawn with new face values.
1542 **53** 45c. red 75 60
1543 – 45c. green 75 60
1544 – $1.50 blue 1·90 2·25
DESIGNS—VERT: No. 1543, Angel. HORIZ: No. 1544, Flag and dove.

1995. Australian Second World War Heroes (2nd series). As T **541**. Multicoloured.
1545 45c. Sister Ellen Savage and George Medal 85 85
1546 45c. Chief Petty Officer Percy Collins and Distinguished Service Medal and Bar 85 85
1547 45c. Lt-Comm. Leon Goldsworthy and George Cross 85 85
1548 45c. Warrant Officer Len Waters and R.A.A.F. wings 85 85

1995. Australia–China Joint Issue. Endangered Species. Multicoloured.
1549 45c. Type **545** 70 1·00
1550 45c. Giant panda with cubs 70 1·00
MS1551 Two sheets, each 106 × 70 mm. (a) No. 1549. (b) No. 1550 Set of 2 sheets 1·60 2·00

546 Father Joseph Slattery, Thomas Lyle and Walter Filmer (Radiology)

1995. Medical Scientists. Multicoloured.
1552 45c. Type **546** 90 90
1553 45c. Dame Jean Macnamara and Sir Macfarlane Burnet (viruses) 90 90
1554 45c. Fred Hollows (ophthalmology) (vert) 90 60
1555 $2.50 Sir Howard Florey (antibiotics) (vert) 4·50 5·00

547 Flatback Turtle

548 "Madonna and Child"

1995. Marine Life. Multicoloured. Ordinary or self-adhesive gum.
1556 45c. Type **547** 55 55
1557 45c. Flame angelfish and nudibranch 55 55
1558 45c. Potato grouper ("Potato cod") and hump-headed wrasse ("Maori wrasse") 55 55
1559 45c. Giant trevally 55 55
1560 45c. Black marlin 55 55
1561 45c. Mako and tiger sharks 55 55
MS1562 166 × 73 mm. Nos. 1556/61 3·50 3·00

1995. Christmas. Stained-glass Windows from Our Lady Help of Christians Church, Melbourne. Multicoloured.
1569 40c. Type **548** 60 25
1570 45c. "Angel carrying the Gloria banner" 60 25
1571 $1 "Rejoicing Angels" 2·00 2·50
No. 1569 also comes self-adhesive.

549 "West Australian Banksia" (Margaret Preston)

1996. Australia Day. Paintings. Multicoloured.
1573 45c. Type **549** 70 30
1574 85c. "The Babe is Wise" (Lina Bryans) 1·50 1·75
1575 $1 "The Bridge in Curve" (Grace Cossington Smith) (horiz) 1·75 1·75
1576 $1.20 "Beach Umbrellas" (Vida Lahey) (horiz) 2·00 2·50

550 Gold Heart and Rose

1996. St. Valentine's Day.
1577 **550** 45c. multicoloured 65 65

551 Bristol Type 156 Beaufighter and Curtiss P-40E Kittyhawk I

1996. Military Aviation. Multicoloured.
1578 45c. Type **551** 90 1·00
1579 45c. Hawker Sea Fury and Fairey Firefly 90 1·00
1580 45c. Bell Kiowa helicopters 90 1·00
1581 45c. Government Aircraft Factory Hornets 90 1·00

552 Tasmanian Wilderness

1996. World Heritage Sites (2nd series). Mult.
1582 45c. Type **552** 50 45
1583 75c. Willandra Lakes 90 1·00
1584 95c. Naracoorte Fossil Cave 1·25 1·60
1585 $1 Lord Howe Island 1·50 1·60

553 Australian Spotted Cuscus

555 North Melbourne Players

554 Head of Queen Elizabeth II

1996. Australia–Indonesia Joint Issue. Mult.
1586 45c. Type **553** 90 1·00
1587 45c. Indonesian bear cuscus 90 1·00
MS1588 106 × 70 mm. Nos. 1586/7 1·90 2·00

1996. Queen Elizabeth II's Birthday.
1589 **554** 45c. multicoloured 75 65

1996. Centenary of Australian Football League. Players from different teams. Multicoloured. Ordinary or self-adhesive gum.
1590 45c. Type **555** 70 80
1591 45c. Brisbane (red and yellow shirt) 70 80
1592 45c. Sydney (red and white shirt) 70 80
1593 45c. Carlton (black shirt with white emblem) 70 80
1594 45c. Adelaide (black, red and yellow shirt) 70 80
1595 45c. Fitzroy (yellow, red and blue shirt) 70 80
1596 45c. Richmond (black shirt with yellow diagonal stripe) 70 80
1597 45c. St. Kilda (red, white and black shirt) 70 80
1598 45c. Melbourne (black shirt with red top) 70 80
1599 45c. Collingwood (black and white vertical striped shirt) 70 80
1600 45c. Fremantle (green, red, white and blue shirt) 70 80
1601 45c. Footscray (blue, white and red shirt) 70 80
1602 45c. West Coast (deep blue shirt with yellow stripes) 70 80
1603 45c. Essendon (black shirt with red stripe) 70 80
1604 45c. Geelong (black and white horizontal striped shirt) 70 80
1605 45c. Hawthorn (black and yellow vertical striped shirt) 70 80

556 Leadbeater's Possum

1996. Fauna and Flora (1st series). Central Highlands Forest, Victoria. Multicoloured.
1622 5c. Type **556** 10 10
1623 10c. Powerful owl 10 10
1624 $2 Blackwood wattle 1·40 1·50
1625 $5 Soft tree fern and mountain ash (30 × 50 mm) 3·50 3·75
See also Nos. 1679/90, 1854/66, 2126/9, 2200/3 and 2273.

1996. "China '96" 9th Asian International Stamp Exhibition, Peking. Sheet 120 × 65 mm, containing Nos. 1453b, 1454b and 1455b. Multicoloured.
MS1626 45c. Kangaroo; 45c. Female kangaroo with young; 45c. Two kangaroos 1·75 1·90

557 Edwin Flack (800 and 1500 metres gold medal winner, 1896)

1996. Centennial Olympic Games and 10th Paralympic Games, Atlanta. Multicoloured.
1627 45c. Type **557** 70 70
1628 45c. Fanny Durack (100 metres freestyle swimming gold medal winner, 1912) 70 70
1629 $1.05 Wheelchair athletes 1·60 1·60

558 "Animalia" (Graeme Base)

1996. 50th Anniv of Children's Book Council Awards. Designs taken from book covers. Ordinary or self-adhesive gum. Multicoloured.
1630 45c. Type **558** 60 60
1631 45c. "Greetings from Sandy Beach" (Bob Graham) 60 60
1632 45c. "Who Sank the Boat?" (Pamela Allen) 60 60
1633 45c. "John Brown, Rose and the Midnight Cat" (Jenny Wagner, illustrated by Ron Brooks) 60 60

559 American Bald Eagle, Kangaroo and Olympic Flame

560 Margaret Windeyer

1996. Passing of Olympic Flag to Sydney.
1638 **559** 45c. multicoloured 55 50

1996. Centenary of the National Council of Women.
1639 **560** 45c. purple and yellow 50 50
1640 – $1 blue and yellow 1·25 2·00
DESIGN: $1 Rose Scott.

561 Pearl

1996. Pearls and Diamonds. Multicoloured.
1641 45c. Type **561** 60 50
1642 $1.20 Diamond 1·40 1·50
The pearl on the 45c. is shown as an exelgram (holographic printing on ultra thin plastic film) and the diamond on the $1.20 as a hologram, each embossed on to the stamp.

562 Silhouettes of Female Dancer and Musician on Rural Landscape

1996. 50th Anniv of Arts Councils. Multicoloured.
1643 20c. Type **562** 1·60 2·00
1644 45c. Silhouettes of musician and male dancer on landscape 35 40

563 Ginger Cats

1996. Australian Pets. Multicoloured.
1645 45c. Type **563** 60 60
1646 45c. Blue heeler dogs 60 60
1647 45c. Sulphur-crested cockatoo (30 × 25 mm) 60 60
1648 45c. Duck with ducklings (25 × 30 mm) 60 60
1649 45c. Dog and cat (25 × 30 mm) 60 60
1650 45c. Ponies (30 × 50 mm) 60 60
MS1651 166 × 73 mm. Nos. 1645/50 3·25 3·50
Nos. 1645/6 also come self-adhesive.

564 Ferdinand von Mueller

1996. Australia–Germany Joint Issue. Death Centenary of Ferdinand von Mueller (botanist).
1654 **564** $1.20 multicoloured 1·25 1·40

565 Willem de Vlamingh

566 Madonna and Child

1996. 300th Anniv of the Visit of Willem de Vlamingh to Western Australia.
1655 **565** 45c. multicoloured 75 75

1996. Christmas. Multicoloured.
1656 40c. Type **566** 55 30
1657 45c. Wise man with gift 55 30
1658 $1 Shepherd boy with lamb 1·25 1·75
No. 1656 also comes self-adhesive.

567 "Landscape '74" (Fred Williams)

1997. Australia Day. Contemporary Paintings. Multicoloured.
1660 85c. Type **567** 1·10 1·10
1661 90c. "The Balcony 2" (Brett Whiteley) 1·10 1·10
1662 $1.20 "Fire Haze at Gerringong" (Lloyd Rees) 1·40 1·40

568 Sir Donald Bradman

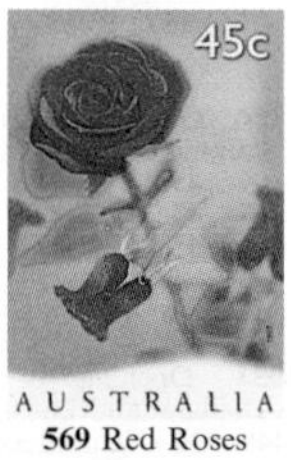

569 Red Roses

1997. Australian Legends (1st series). Sir Donald Bradman (cricketer). Multicoloured.
1663 45c. Type **568** 55 55
1664 45c. Bradman playing stroke 55 55
See also Nos. 1731/42, 1838/9, 1947/50, 2069/70, 2160/4 and 2265/8.

1997. St. Valentine's Day. Ordinary or self-adhesive gum.
1665 **569** 45c. multicoloured . . . 50 50

570 Ford Coupe Utility, 1934 **571** May Wirth and Horse

1997. Classic Cars. Multicoloured. Ordinary or self-adhesive gum.
1667 45c. Type **570** 60 60
1668 45c. GMH Holden 48-215 (FX), 1948 . . . . 60 60
1669 45c. Austin Lancer, 1958 . . 60 60
1670 45c. Chrysler Valiant "R" Series, 1962 . . . . . . 60 60

1997. 150th Anniv of the Circus in Australia. Multicoloured.
1675 45c. Type **571** 55 55
1676 45c. Con Colleano on tightrope 55 55
1677 45c. Clowns 55 55
1678 45c. Acrobats 55 55

1997. Fauna and Flora (2nd series). Kakadu Wetlands, Northern Territory. As T **556**. Mult.
1679 20c. Saltwater crocodile . . 15 20
1680 25c. Northern dwarf tree frog 20 25
1681 45c. Comb-crested jacana ("Jacana") 75 60
1682 45c. Mangrove kingfisher ("Little Kingfisher") . . . 75 60
1683 45c. Brolga 75 60
1684 45c. Black-necked stork ("Jabiru") 75 60
1685 $1 "Cressida cressida" (butterfly) 70 75
1686 $10 Kakadu Wetlands (50 × 30 mm) . . . . . . 7·00 7·25
MS1686a 106 × 70 mm. No. 1686 10·50 10·50
Nos. 1681/84 also come self-adhesive.

572 Royal Wedding 1d. Stamp of 1947 **573** Hand holding Globe and Lion's Emblem

1997. Queen Elizabeth II's Birthday.
1691 **572** 45c. purple 50 50

1997. 50th Anniv of First Australian Lions Club.
1692 **573** 45c. blue, brown and purple 50 50

574 Doll holding Teddy Bear (Kaye Wiggs) **575** Police Rescue Helicopter

1997. Dolls and Teddy Bears. Multicoloured.
1693 45c. Type **574** 45 50
1694 45c. Teddy bear standing (Jennifer Laing) 45 50
1695 45c. Doll wearing white dress with teddy bear (Susie McMahon) 45 50
1696 45c. Doll in brown dress and bonnet (Lynda Jacobson) 45 50
1697 45c. Teddy bear sitting (Helen Williams) 45 50

1997. Emergency Services. Multicoloured.
1698 45c. Type **575** 80 65
1699 45c. Emergency Service volunteers carrying victim 80 65
1700 $1.05 Fire service at fire . . 1·60 2·00
1701 $1.20 Loading casualty into ambulance . . . . 1·75 1·75

576 George Peppin Jnr (breeder) and Merino Sheep

1997. Bicentenary of Arrival of Merino Sheep in Australia. Multicoloured.
1702 45c. Type **576** 70 90
1703 45c. Pepe chair, cloth and wool logo 70 90

577 Dumbi the Owl

1997. "The Dreaming". Cartoons from Aboriginal Stories. Multicoloured.
1704 45c. Type **577** 75 30
1705 $1 The Two Willy-Willies 1·50 1·10
1706 $1.20 How Brolga became a Bird . . . . 1·75 1·75
1707 $1.80 Tuggan-Tuggan . . . 2·50 3·00

578 "Rhoetosaurus brownei" **579** Spotted-tailed Quoll

1997. Prehistoric Animals. Multicoloured.
1708 45c. Type **578** 50 50
1709 45c. "Mcnamaraspis kaprios" 50 50
1710 45c. "Ninjemys oweni" . . 50 50
1711 45c. "Paracyclotosaurus davidi" 50 50
1712 45c. "Woolungasaurus glendowerensis" 50 50

1997. Nocturnal Animals. Multicoloured.
1713 45c. Type **579** 70 70
1714 45c. Barking owl 70 70
1715 45c. Platypus (30 × 25 mm) 70 70
1716 45c. Brown antechinus (30 × 25 mm) 70 70
1717 45c. Dingo (30 × 25 mm) . . 70 70
1718 45c. Yellow-bellied glider (50 × 30 mm) 70 70
MS1719 166 × 78 mm. Nos. 1713/18 3·75 3·75
Nos. 1713/14 also come self-adhesive.

580 Woman

1997. Breast Cancer Awareness Campaign.
1722 **580** 45c. multicoloured . . . 80 50

581 Two Angels

1997. Christmas. Children's Nativity Play. Mult.
1723 40c. Type **581** 50 30
1724 45c. Mary 55 30
1725 $1 Three Kings . . . . . . 1·25 1·75
No. 1723 also comes self-adhesive.

582 "Flying Cloud" (clipper) (J. Scott)

1998. Ship Paintings. Multicoloured.
1727 45c. Type **582** 60 30
1728 85c. "Marco Polo" (full-rigged ship) (T. Robertson) . . . . . 1·00 1·00
1729 $1 "Chusan I" (steamship) (C. Gregory) . . . . . . 1·25 1·10
1730 $1.20 "Heather Belle" (clipper) . . . . 1·50 1·75

583 Betty Cuthbert (1956) **584** "Champagne" Rose

1998. Australian Legends (2nd series). Olympic Gold Medal Winners. Multicoloured. Ordinary or self-adhesive gum.
1731 45c. Type **583** 55 65
1732 45c. Betty Cuthbert running 55 65
1733 45c. Herb Elliott (1960) . . 55 65
1734 45c. Herb Elliott running . . 55 65
1735 45c. Dawn Fraser (1956, 1960 and 1964) 55 65
1736 45c. Dawn Fraser swimming 55 65
1737 45c. Marjorie Jackson (1952) 55 65
1738 45c. Marjorie Jackson running 55 65
1739 45c. Murray Rose (1956) . . 55 65
1740 45c. Murray Rose swimming 55 65
1741 45c. Shirley Strickland (1952 and 1956) 55 65
1742 45c. Shirley Strickland hurdling 55 65

1998. Greeting Stamp. Ordinary or self-adhesive gum.
1755 **584** 45c. multicoloured . . . 55 50

585 Queen Elizabeth II

1998. Queen Elizabeth II's Birthday.
1757 **585** 45c. multicoloured . . . 50 50

586 Sea Hawk (helicopter) landing on Frigate

1998. 50th Anniv of Royal Australian Navy Fleet Air Arm.
1758 **586** 45c. multicoloured . . . 50 50

587 Sheep Shearer and Sheep

1998. Farming. Multicoloured. Ordinary or self-adhesive gum.
1759 45c. Type **587** 45 50
1760 45c. Barley and silo 45 50
1761 45c. Farmers herding beef cattle 45 50
1762 45c. Sugar cane harvesting 45 50
1763 45c. Two dairy cows 45 50

588 Cardiograph Trace and Heart

1998. Heart Disease Awareness.
1769 **588** 45c. multicoloured . . . 50 50

589 Johnny OKeefe ("The Wild One", 1958)

1998. Australian Rock and Roll. Multicoloured. Ordinary or self-adhesive gum.
1770 45c. Type **589** 55 50
1771 45c. Col Joye ("Oh Yeah Uh Huh", 1959) 55 50
1772 45c. Little Pattie ("He's My Blonde Headed Stompie Wompie Real Gone Surfer Boy", 1963) . . . 55 50
1773 45c. Normie Rowe ("Shakin all Over", 1965) 55 50
1774 45c. Easybeats ("She's so Fine", 1965) 55 50
1775 45c. Russell Morris ("The Real Thing", 1969) . . . 55 50
1776 45c. Masters Apprentices ("Turn Up Your Radio", 1970) 55 50
1777 45c. Daddy Cool ("Eagle Rock", 1971) 55 50
1778 45c. Billy Thorpe and the Aztecs ("Most People I know think I'm Crazy", 1972) 55 50
1779 45c. Skyhooks ("Horror Movie", 1974) 55 50
1780 45c. AC/DC ("It's a Long Way to the Top", 1975) 55 50
1781 45c. Sherbet ("Howzat", 1976) 55 50

590 Yellow-tufted Honeyeater ("Helmeted Honeyeater")

1998. Endangered Species. Multicoloured.
1794 5c. Type **590** 35 35
1795 5c. Orange-bellied parrot . . 35 35
1796 45c. Red-tailed black cockatoo ("Red-tailed Black-Cockatoo") 75 65
1797 45c. Gouldian finch 75 65

591 French Horn and Cello Players

1998. Youth Arts, Australia. Multicoloured.
1798 45c. Type **591** 50 50
1799 45c. Dancers 50 50

592 "Phalaenopsis rosenstromii"

1998. Australia–Singapore Joint Issue. Orchids. Multicoloured.
1800 45c. Type **592** 55 40
1801 85c. "Arundina graminifolia" . . . . . . 1·00 1·00
1802 $1 "Grammatophyllum speciosum" . . . . 1·25 1·25
1803 $1.20 "Dendrobium phalaenopsis" . . . . . 1·50 1·60
MS1804 138 × 72 mm. Nos. 1800/3 3·75 3·75

593 Flying Angel with Teapot (cartoon by Michael Leunig)

1998. "The Teapot of Truth" (cartoons by Michael Leunig). Multicoloured.
1805 45c. Type **593** 50 55
1806 45c. Two birds in heart-shaped tree 50 55
1807 45c. Pouring tea 50 55
1808 $1 Mother and child (29 × 24 mm) . . . . . . 1·25 1·25
1809 $1.20 Cat with smiling face (29 × 24 mm) . . . . . . 1·50 1·60

594 Red Lacewing

595 Flinders' Telescope and Map of Tasmania

1998. Butterflies. Multicoloured. Ordinary or self-adhesive gum.
1810 45c. Type **594** 65 65
1811 45c. Dull oakblue 65 65
1812 45c. Meadow argus 65 65
1813 45c. Ulysses butterfly . . . 65 65
1814 45c. Common red-eye . . . 65 65

1998. Bicentenary of the Circumnavigation of Tasmania by George Bass and Matthew Flinders. Multicoloured.
1820 45c. Type **595** 65 50
1821 45c. Sextant and letter from Bass 65 50

596 Weedy Seadragon

597 Rose of Freedom

1998. International Year of the Ocean. Multicoloured.
1822 45c. Type **596** 65 65
1823 45c. Bottlenose dolphin . . 65 65
1824 45c. Fiery squid (24 × 29 mm) 65 65
1825 45c. Manta ray (29 × 24 mm) 65 65
1826 45c. White pointer shark (29 × 49 mm) 65 65
1827 45c. Southern right whale (49 × 29 mm) 65 65
MS1828 166 × 73 mm. Nos. 1822/7 2·75 2·75
Nos. 1822/3 also come self-adhesive.

1998. 50th Anniv of Universal Declaration of Human Rights.
1831 **597** 45c. multicoloured . . . 50 50

598 Three Kings

1998. Christmas. Multicoloured.
1832 40c. Type **598** 40 25
1833 45c. Nativity scene 40 25
1834 $1 Mary and Joseph . . . . 1·10 1·50
No. 1832 also comes self-adhesive.

599 Australian Coat of Arms

1999. 50th Anniv of Australian Citizenship. Ordinary or self-adhesive gum.
1836 **599** 45c. multicoloured . . . 50 50

600 Arthur Boyd

1999. Australian Legends (3rd series). Arthur Boyd (painter). Multicoloured. Ordinary or self-adhesive gum.
1838 45c. Type **600** 45 45
1839 45c. "Nebuchadnezzer on fire falling over Waterfall" (Arthur Boyd) 45 45

601 Red Roses

1999. Greetings Stamp. Romance. Ordinary or self-adhesive gum.
1842 **601** 45c. multicoloured . . . 50 50

602 Elderly Man and Grandmother with Boy

1999. International Year of Older Persons. Mult.
1844 45c. Type **602** 45 45
1845 45c. Elderly woman and grandfather with boy . . 45 45

603 "Polly Woodside" (barque)

604 Olympic Torch and 1956 7½d. Stamp

1999. Sailing Ships. Multicoloured.
1846 45c. Type **603** 60 35
1847 85c. "Alma Doepel" (topsail schooner) . . . . 1·00 90
1848 $1 "Enterprize" replica (topsail schooner) . . . . 1·25 1·10
1849 $1.05 "Lady Nelson" replica (topsail schooner) . . . . 1·40 1·60

1999. Australia—Ireland Joint Issue. "Polly Woodside" (barque). Sheet 137 × 72 mm. Mult.
MS1850 45c. Type **603**; 30p. Type **374** of Ireland (No. **MS**1850 was sold at $1.25 in Australia) 1·25 1·40

1999. Australia—Canada. Joint Issue. "Marco Polo" (emigrant ship). Sheet 160 × 95 mm. Mult.
MS1851 85c. As No. 1728; 46c. Type **701** of Canada (No. **MS**1851 was sold at $1.30 in Australia) 1·25 1·40

1999. "Australia '99" International Stamp Exhibition, Melbourne. Two sheets, each 142 × 76 mm, containing designs as Nos. 398/403 and all with face value of 45 c.
MS1852 (a) 45c. ultramarine (Type **167**); 45c. grey (Captain Cook); 45c. brown (Flinders). (b) 45c. red (Type **168**); 45c. brown (Bass); 45c. purple (King) Set of 2 sheets 2·50 2·75

1999. Olympic Torch Commemoration.
1853 **604** $1.20 multicoloured . . 1·10 1·10

605 "Correa reflexa" (native fuchsia)

607 "Here's Humphrey"

606 Queen Elizabeth II with The Queen Mother

1999. Fauna and Flora (3rd series). Coastal Environment. Multicoloured. Ordinary or self-adhesive gum.
1854 45c. Type **605** 50 35
1855 45c. "Hibbertia scandens" (guinea flower) 50 35
1856 45c. "Ipomoea pre-caprae" (beach morning glory) . . 50 35
1857 45c. "Wahlenbergia stricta" (Australian bluebells) . . 50 35
1858 70c. Humpback whales and zebra volute shell (29 × 24 mm) 50 55
1859 90c. Brahminy kite and checkerboard helmet shell (29 × 24 mm) 65 70
1860 90c. Fraser Island and chambered nautilus (29 × 24 mm) 65 70
1861 $1.05 Loggerhead turtle and melon shell (29 × 24 mm) 75 80
1862 $1.20 White-bellied sea eagle and Campbell's stromb shell (29 × 24 mm) 85 90
Nos. 1859/60 were printed together, se-tenant, forming a composite design.

1999. Queen Elizabeth II's Birthday.
1870 **606** 45c. multicoloured . . . 50 50

1999. Children's Television Programmes. Multicoloured. Ordinary or self-adhesive gum.
1871 45c. Type **607** 45 45
1872 45c. "Bananas in Pyjamas" 45 45
1873 45c. "Mr. Squiggle" 45 45
1874 45c. "Play School" (teddy bears) 45 45
1875 45c. "Play School" (clock, toy dog and doll) 45 45

608 Obverse and Reverse of 1899 Sovereign

1999. Centenary of the Perth Mint.
1881 **608** $2 gold, blue and green 2·00 1·75

609 Lineout against New Zealand

610 Drilling at Burn's Creek and Rock Bolting in Tumut 2 Power Station Hall

1999. Centenary of Australian Test Rugby. Mult.
1882 45c. Type **609** 40 40
1883 45c. Kicking the ball against England 40 40
1884 $1 Try against South Africa (horiz) 85 85
1885 $1.20 Passing the ball against Wales (horiz) . . 1·10 1·25
Nos. 1882/3 also come self-adhesive.

1999. 50th Anniv of Snowy Mountain Scheme (hydro-electric project). Multicoloured. Ordinary or self-adhesive gum.
1888 45c. Type **610** 55 55
1889 45c. English class for migrant workers, Cooma 55 55
1890 45c. Tumut 2 Tailwater Tunnel and Eucumbene Dam 55 55
1891 45c. German carpenters and Island Bend Dam 55 55

611 Calligraphy Pen and Letter

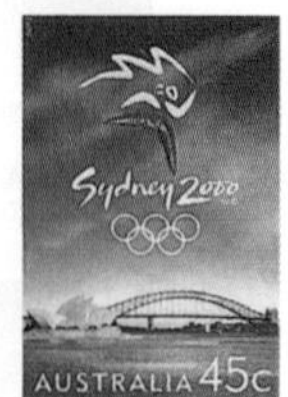

612 Sydney Olympic Emblem

1999. Greetings Stamps. Multicoloured.
1896 45c. Type **611** 55 55
1897 45c. Wedding rings 55 55
1898 45c. Birthday cake 55 55
1899 45c. Christmas decoration 55 55
1900 45c. Teddy bear 55 55
1901 $1 Koala . . . . 1·00 1·00
See also No. 1921.

1999. Olympic Games, Sydney (2000) (1st issue).
1902 **612** 45c. multicoloured . . . 60 50

613 Australia Post Symbol, 1975

1999. "Sydney Design '99" International Congress and Exhibition. Multicoloured.
1903 45c. Type **613** 45 30
1904 90c. Embryo chair, 1988 . . 80 80
1905 $1.35 Possum skin textile, c.1985 . . . . 1·25 1·25
1906 $1.50 Storey Hall, R.M.I.T. University, 1995 . . . . 1·25 1·50

614 Magnificent Tree Frog

615 Madonna and Child

1999. National Stamp Collecting Month, Small Pond Life. Multicoloured. Ordinary or self-adhesive gum.
1907 45c. Type **614** 45 40
1908 45c. Sacred kingfisher . . . 45 40
1909 45c. Roth's tree frog (29 × 24 mm) 45 40
1910 45c. Dragonfly (29 × 24 mm) 45 40
1911 50c. Javelin frog (24 × 29 mm) 50 40
1912 50c. Northern dwarf tree frog (24 × 29 mm) 50 40
MS1913 166 × 73 mm. Nos. 1907/12 2·50 2·50

1999. Christmas. Multicoloured.
1918 40c. Type **615** 45 30
1919 $1 Tree of Life (horiz) . . . 1·00 1·00
No. 1918 also comes self-adhesive.

616 Fireworks and Hologram

617 Rachel Thomson (college administrator)

1999. Millennium Greetings stamp.
1921 **616** 45c. multicoloured . . . 50 50

2000. New Millennium. "Face of Australia". Mult.
1922 45c. Nicholle and Meghan Triandis (twin babies) . . 45 50
1923 45c. David Willis (cattleman) 45 50
1924 45c. Natasha Bramley (scuba diver) 45 50
1925 45c. Cyril Watson (Aborigine boy) 45 50
1926 45c. Mollie Dowdall (wearing red hat) (vineyard worker) 45 50
1927 45c. Robin Dicks (flying instructor) 45 50
1928 45c. Mary Simons (retired nurse) 45 50
1929 45c. Peta and Samantha Nieuwerth (mother and baby) 45 50
1930 45c. John Matthews (doctor) 45 50
1931 45c. Edith Dizon-Fitzimmons (wearing drop earrings) (music teacher) 45 50
1932 45c. Philippa Weir (wearing brown hat) (teacher) . . . 45 50
1933 45c. John Thurgar (in bush hat and jacket) (farmer) 45 50
1934 45c. Miguel Alzona (with face painted) (schoolboy) 45 50
1935 45c. Type **617** 45 50
1936 45c. Necip Akarsu (wearing blue shirt) (postmaster) 45 50
1937 45c. Justin Allan (R.A.N. sailor) 45 50
1938 45c. Wadad Dennaoui (wearing checked shirt) (student) 45 50
1939 45c. Jack Laity (market gardener) 45 50
1940 45c. Kelsey Stubbin (wearing cricket cap) (schoolboy) 45 50
1941 45c. Gianna Rossi (resting chin on hand) (church worker) 45 50
1942 45c. Paris Hansch (toddler) 45 50
1943 45c. Donald George Whatham (in blue shirt and tie) (retired teacher) 45 50
1944 45c. Stacey Coull (wearing pendant) 45 50
1945 45c. Alex Payne (wearing cycle helmet) (schoolgirl) 45 50
1946 45c. John Lodge (Salvation Army member) 45 50

618 Walter Parker

2000. Australian Legends (4th series). "The Last Anzacs". Multicoloured.
1947 45c. Type **618** 55 55
1948 45c. Roy Longmore 55 55
1949 45c. Alec Campbell 55 55
1950 45c. 1914–15 Star (medal) 55 55
Nos. 1947/50 also come self-adhesive.

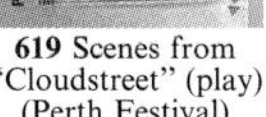

619 Scenes from "Cloudstreet" (play) (Perth Festival)
620 Coast Banksia, False Sarsaparilla and Swamp Bloodwood (plants)

2000. Arts Festivals. Multicoloured.
1955 45c. Type **619** 55 55
1956 45c. Belgian dancers from Rosas Company (Adelaide Festival) 55 55
1957 45c. "Guardian Angel" (sculpture) and dancer (Sydney Festival) 55 55
1958 45c. Musician and Balinese dancer (Melbourne Festival) 55 55
1959 45c. Members of Vusa Dance Company of South Africa (Brisbane Festival) 55 55

2000. Gardens. Multicoloured. Ordinary or self-adhesive gum.
1960 45c. Type **620** 45 50
1961 45c. Eastern spinebill on swamp bottlebrush in foreground 45 50
1962 45c. Border of cannas . . . 45 50
1963 45c. Roses, lake and ornamental bridge 45 50
1964 45c. Hibiscus with bandstand in background 45 50

621 Queen Elizabeth II in 1996

2000. Queen Elizabeth II's Birthday.
1970 **621** 45c. multicoloured . . . 50 50

622 Medals and Korean Landscape

2000. 50th Anniv of Korean War.
1971 **622** 45c. multicoloured . . . 50 50

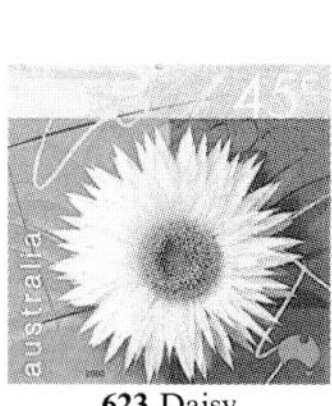

623 Daisy
624 Taking the Vote, New South Wales

2000. Nature and Nation. Greeting stamps. Mult.
1972 45c. Type **623** 45 50
1973 45c. Australia on globe . . 45 50
1974 45c. Red kangaroo and flag 45 50
1975 45c. Sand, sea and sky . . . 45 50
1976 45c. Rainforest 45 50

2000. Centenary of Commonwealth of Australia Constitution Act. Multicoloured.
1977 45c. Type **624** 45 40
1978 45c. Voters waiting for results, Geraldton, Western Australia 45 40
1979 $1.50 Queen Victoria (29 × 49 mm) . . . . . . 1·40 1·40
1980 $1.50 Women dancing ("The Fair New Nation") (29 × 49 mm) . . . . . . 1·40 1·40
MS1981 155 × 189 mm. Nos. 1977/80 2·75 3·00

625 Sydney Opera House, New South Wales

2000. International Stamps. Views of Australia (1st series). Multicoloured.
1982 50c. Type **625** 90 40
1983 $1 Nandroya Falls, Queensland . . . . 1·60 80
1984 $1.50 Sydney Harbour Bridge, New South Wales 2·00 1·25
1985 $2 Cradle Mountain, Tasmania . . . . 2·25 1·50
1986 $3 The Pinnacles, Western Australia . . . . 2·50 2·25
1987 $4.50 Flinders Ranges, South Australia (51 × 24 mm) . . . . . . 3·25 3·50
1988 $5 Twelve Apostles, Victoria (51 × 24 mm) . . . . . . 3·50 3·75
1989 $10 Devils Marbles, Northern Territory (51 × 24 mm) . . . . . . 7·25 7·50
Nos. 1982/9 were intended for international postage which, under changes in Australian tax laws from 1 July 2000, remained exempt from General Sales Tax.
See also Nos. 2121/5, 2195/7 and 2219/22.

626 Tennis Player in Wheelchair
627 Sir Neville Howse (first Australian recipient of Victoria Cross, 1900)

2000. Paralympic Games, Sydney. Multicoloured. Ordinary or self-adhesive gum.
1990 45c. Type **626** 50 50
1991 45c. Amputee sprinting . . 50 50
1992 49c. Basketball player in wheelchair 50 50
1993 49c. Blind cyclist 50 50
1994 49c. Amputee putting the shot 50 50

2000. Cent of Australia's First Victoria Cross Award.
2000 **627** 45c. multicoloured . . . 50 50
2001 – 45c. brown, gold and black 50 50
2002 – 45c. multicoloured . . . 50 50
2003 – 45c. multicoloured . . . 50 50
2004 – 45c. brown, gold and black 50 50
DESIGNS: No. 2001, Sir Roden Cutler, 1941; 2002, Victoria Cross; 2003, Private Edward Kenna, 1945; 2004, Warrant Officer Keith Payne, 1969.

628 Water Polo
629 Olympic Flag, Flame and Parthenon

2000. Olympic Games, Sydney. Multicoloured. Ordinary or self-adhesive gum. Competitors highlighted in varnish.
2005 45c. Type **628** 50 50
2006 45c. Hockey 50 50
2007 45c. Swimming 50 50
2008 45c. Basketball 50 50
2009 45c. Cycling (triathlon) . . . 50 50
2010 45c. Horse riding 50 50
2011 45c. Tennis 50 50
2012 45c. Gymnastics 50 50
2013 45c. Running 50 50
2014 45c. Rowing 50 50
Nos. 2005/14 were printed together, se-tenant, with the backgrounds forming a composite design.

2000. Transfer of Olympic Flag from Sydney to Athens. Joint issue with Greece. Multicoloured.
2025 45c. Type **629** 50 40
2026 $1.50 Olympic Flag, Flame and Sydney Opera House 1·50 1·50
Stamps in similar designs were issued by Greece.

630 Ian Thorpe (Men's 400m Freestyle Swimming)
631 Martian Terrain

2000. Australian Gold Medal Winners at Sydney Olympic Games. Multicoloured.
2027A 45c. Type **630** 45 45
2028A 45c. Australian team (Men's 4 × 100 m Freestyle Swimming Relay) . . . 45 45
2029A 45c. Michael Diamond (Men's Trap Shooting) 45 45
2030A 45c. Australian team (Three Day Equestrian Event) 45 45
2031A 45c. Susie O'Neill (Women's 200 m Freestyle Swimming) 45 45
2032A 45c. Australian team (Men's 4 × 200 m Freestyle Swimming Relay) . . . 45 45
2033A 45c. Simon Fairweather (Men's Individual Archery) 45 45
2034A 45c. Australian team (Men's Madison Cycling) 45 45
2035A 45c. Grant Hackett (Men's 1500 m Freestyle Swimming) 45 45
2036A 45c. Australian team (Women's Water Polo) 45 45
2037A 45c. Australian team (Women's Beach Volleyball) 45 45
2038A 45c. Cathy Freeman (Women's 400 m Athletics) 45 45
2039A 45c. Lauren Burns (Women's under 49 kg Taekwondo) 45 45
2040A 45c. Australian team (Women's Hockey) . . 45 45
2041A 45c. Australian crew (Women's 470 Dinghy Sailing) 45 45
2042A 45c. Australian crew (Men's 470 Dinghy Sailing) 45 45

2000. Stamp Collecting Month. Exploration of Mars. Multicoloured. (a) Ordinary gum.
2043 45c. Type **631** 45 45
2044 45c. Astronaut using thruster 45 45
2045 45c. Spacecraft (50 × 30 mm) 45 45
2046 45c. Flight crew (30 × 25 mm) 45 45
2047 45c. Launch site (30 × 50 mm) 45 45
2048 45c. Robots on kelp rod (25 × 30 mm) 45 45

(b) Self-adhesive. Designs 21 × 32 mm.
2050 45c. Type **631** 45 45
2051 45c. Astronaut using thruster 45 45

632 Cathy Freeman with Olympic Torch and Ring of Flames

2000. Opening Ceremony, Olympic Games, Sydney.
2052 **632** 45c. multicoloured . . . 50 50

633 Blind Athlete carrying Olympic Torch

2000. Paralympic Games, Sydney (2nd issue). Multicoloured.
2053 45c. Type **633** 55 50
2054 45c. Paralympic Games logo 55 50

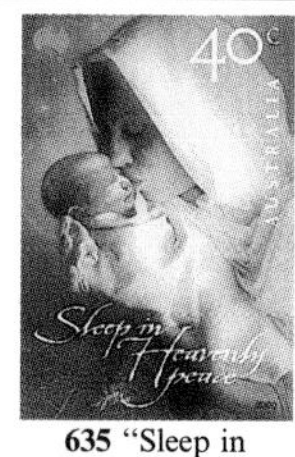

634 Siobhan Paton (swimmer)
635 "Sleep in Heavenly Peace"

2000. Siobhan Paton, Paralympian of the Year.
2055 **634** 45c. multicoloured . . . 50 50

2000. Christmas. "Silent Night" (carol). Multicoloured. (a) Ordinary gum.
2056 40c. Type **635** 45 25
2057 45c. "All is Calm, All is Bright" 50 25

(b) Self-adhesive.
2059 40c. Type **635** 45 35

(c) International Mail. As T **625** inscr "Season's Greetings".
2060 80c. Byron Bay, New South Wales 70 85

2001. International Mail. No. 1901 optd **International POST**.
2061 $1 Koala . . . . 1·25 80

637 Parade passing Federation Arch, Sydney

2001. Centenary of Federation. Multicoloured. (a) Ordinary gum.
2062 49c. Type **637** 45 40
2063 49c. Edmund Barton (first Federal Prime Minister) 45 40
2064 $2 "Australia For Ever" (song sheet) and celebration picnic (50 × 30 mm) . . . . . . 1·75 2·00
2065 $2 State Banquet, Sydney (30 × 50 mm) . . . . . . 1·75 2·00

(b) Self-adhesive.
2067 49c. Type **637** 45 40
2068 49c. Edmund Barton (first Federal Prime Minister) 45 40

638 Slim Dusty with Guitar in 1940s

2001. Australian Legends (5th series). Slim Dusty (country music singer). Multicoloured. Ordinary or self-adhesive gum.
2069 45c. Type **638** 45 45
2070 45c. Slim Dusty wearing "Sundowner" hat 45 45

639 Light Horse Parade, 1940, and Command Post, New Guinea, 1943

2001. Centenary of Australian Army. Multicoloured.
2073 45c. Type **639** 45 45
2074 45c. Soldier carrying Rwandan child and officers on the Commando Selection Course 45 45

640 Entry Canopy, Skylights and Site Plan

2001. Opening of the National Museum, Canberra. Multicoloured.
2075 49c. Type **640** 45 45
2076 49c. Skylights and "Pangk" (wallaby sculpture) . . . 45 45

2001. Sir Donald Bradman (cricketer) Commemoration. Nos. 1663/4 additionally inscribed "1908–2001" in red. Multicoloured.
2077 45c. Type **568** 45 45
2078 45c. Bradman playing stroke 45 45

641 "Khe Sanh" (Cold Chisel), 1978

2001. Australian Rock and Pop Music. Multicoloured. Ordinary or self-adhesive gum.
2079 45c. Type **641** 45 45
2080 45c. "Down Under" (Men at Work), 1981 . . . . . 45 45
2081 45c. "Power and the Passion" (Midnight Oil), 1983 . . . . 45 45
2082 45c. "Original Sin" (INXS), 1984 . . . . 45 45
2083 45c. "You're the Voice" (John Farnham), 1986 . . 45 45
2084 45c. "Don't Dream it's Over" (Crowded House), 1986 . . . . 45 45
2085 45c. "Treaty" (Yothu Yindi), 1991 . . . . . . 45 45
2086 45c. "Tomorrow" (Silverchair), 1994 . . . . 45 45
2087 45c. "Confide in Me" (Kylie Minogue), 1994 . . . . 45 45
2088 45c. "Truly, Madly, Deeply" (Savage Garden), 1997 . . 45 45

642 Queen Elizabeth II holding Bouquet

643 Party Balloons

2001. Queen Elizabeth II's Birthday.
2099 **642** 45c. multicoloured . . . 50 50

2001. "Colour My Day". Greetings Stamps. (a) Domestic Mail.
2100 45c. Type **643** 30 35
2101 45c. Smiling Flower 30 35
2102 45c. Hologram and party streamers 30 35

(b) International Mail.
2103 $1 Kangaroo and joey . . . 1·00 80
2104 $1.50 The Bayulu Banner 1·40 1·75

644 "Opening of the First Federal Parliament" (Charles Nuttall)

2001. Centenary of Federal Parliament. Paintings. Multicoloured.
2105 45c. Type **644** 45 40
2106 $2.45 "Prince George opening the First Parliament of the Commonwealth of Australia" (Tom Roberts) 2·25 2·50
MS2107 Two sheets, each 166 × 75 mm. (a) No. 2105. (b) No. 2106 Set of 2 sheets 2·50 2·75

645 Telecommunications Tower

2001. Outback Services. Multicoloured. Ordinary or self-adhesive gum.
2108 45c. Type **645** 45 45
2109 45c. Road train 45 45
2110 45c. School of the Air pupil 45 45
2111 45c. Outback family and mail box 45 45
2112 45c. Royal Flying Doctor Service aircraft and ambulance 45 45

646 Dragon Boat and Hong Kong Convention and Exhibition Centre

2001. Joint Issue with Hong Kong. Dragon Boat Racing. Multicoloured. (a) Domestic Mail.
2118 45c. Type **646** 45 45

(b) International Mail.
2119 $1 Dragon boat and Sydney Opera House . . . . . . 1·00 1·00
MS2120 115 × 70 mm. Nos. 2118/19 1·40 1·40

2001. International Stamps. Views of Australia (2nd series). As T **625**. Multicoloured.
2121 50c. The Three Sisters, Blue Mountains, New South Wales 55 40
2122 $1 The Murrumbidgee River, Australian Capital Territory . . . . 1·00 75
2123 $1.50 Four Mile Beach, Port Douglas, Queensland . . 1·50 1·25
2124 $20 Uluru Rock at dusk, Northern Territory (52 × 24 mm) . . . . . . 14·50 15·00
No. 2121 also comes self-adhesive.

647 Variegated Wren ("Variegated Fairy-Wren")

649 Christmas Tree

648 Daniel Solander (Swedish botanist) and Mango Tree

2001. Fauna and Flora (4th series). Desert Birds. Multicoloured. Ordinary or self-adhesive gum.
2126 45c. Type **647** 30 35
2127 45c. Painted finch ("Painted Firetail") 30 35
2128 45c. Crimson chat 30 35
2129 45c. Budgerigar 30 35

2001. Australia–Sweden Joint Issue. Daniel Solander's Voyage with Captain Cook. Multicoloured. (a) Domestic Mail.
2134 45c. Type **648** 50 50

(b) International Mail.
2135 $1.50 H.M.S. *Endeavour* on reef and Kapok tree . . . 1·50 1·50

2001. Christmas (1st issue). Multicoloured. (a) Domestic Mail.
2136 40c. Type **649** 30 35

(b) International Mail.
2137 80c. Star 80 90
See also Nos. 2157/8.

650 Australia on Globe

2001. Commonwealth Heads of Government Meeting (No. 2138) and Commonwealth Parliamentary Conference (No. 2139). Mult.
2138 45c. Type **650** 45 45
2139 45c. Southern Cross 45 45

651 Wedge-tailed Eagle

2001. Centenary of Birds of Australia. Birds of Prey. Multicoloured.
2140 49c. Type **651** 50 50
2141 49c. Australian kestrel ("Nankeen Kestrel") . . . 50 50
2142 98c. Red goshawk (vert) . . 95 1·10
2143 98c. Spotted harrier (vert) 95 1·10

652 Cockatoos dancing to Animal Band

653 "Adoration of the Magi"

2001. National Stamp Collecting Month. "Wild Babies" (cartoons). Multicoloured. Ordinary or self-adhesive gum.
2144 45c. Type **652** 45 45
2145 45c. Kevin Koala with birthday cake 45 45
2146 45c. Ring-tailed possums eating 45 45
2147 45c. Bilbies at foot of tree 45 45
2148 45c. James Wombat on rope ladder 45 45
2149 45c. Wallaby, echidna and platypus on rope ladder 45 45

2001. Christmas (2nd issue). Miniatures from "Wharncliffe Hours Manuscript". Multicoloured.
2157 40c. Type **653** 40 25
2158 45c. "Flight into Egypt" . . 40 35
No. 2157 also comes self-adhesive.

654 Sir Gustav Nossal (immunologist)

2002. Australian Legends. (6th series). Medical Scientists. Ordinary or self-adhesive gum. Multicoloured.
2160 45c. Type **654** 40 40
2161 45c. Nancy Millis (microbiologist) 40 40
2162 45c. Peter Doherty (immunologist) 40 40
2163 45c. Fiona Stanley (epidemiologist) 40 40
2164 45c. Donald Metcalf (haematologist) 40 40

655 Queen Elizabeth in 1953

2002. Golden Jubilee. Multicoloured.
2170 45c. Type **655** 40 35
2171 $2.45 Queen Elizabeth in Italy, 2000 . . . . 2·00 2·25

656 Steven Bradbury (Men's 1000m Short Track Speed Skating)

2002. Australian Gold Medal Winners at Salt Lake City Winter Olympic Games. Multicoloured.
2173 45c. Type **656** 40 40
2174 45c. Alisa Camplin (Women's Aerials Freestyle Skiing) 40 40

657 Austin 7 and Bugatti Type 40, Australian Grand Prix, Phillip Island, 1928

658 Macquarie Lighthouse

2002. Centenary of Motor Racing in Australia and New Zealand. Multicoloured.
2175 45c. Type **657** 40 40
2176 45c. Jaguar Mark II, Australian Touring Car Championship, Mallala, 1963 . . . . 40 40
2177 45c. Repco-Brabham, Tasman Series, Sandown, 1966 . . . . 40 40
2178 45c. Holden Torana and Ford Falcon, Hardie-Ferodo 500, Bathurst, 1972 . . . . 40 40
2179 45c. William's Ford, Australian Grand Prix, Calder, 1980 . . . . . . 40 40
2180 45c. Benetton-Renault, Australian Grand Prix, Albert Park, 2001 . . . . 40 40

2002. Lighthouses. Multicoloured.
2187 45c. Type **658** 40 35
2188 49c. Cape Naturaliste . . . 45 50
2189 49c. Troubridge Island . . . 45 50
2190 $1.50 Cape Bruny . . . . . 1·25 1·40
Nos. 2188/9 also come self-adhesive.

659 Nicolas Baudin, Kangaroo, *Geographe* (ship) and Map

2002. Australia—France Joint Issue. Bicentenary of Flinders—Baudin Meeting at Encounter Bay. Multicoloured. (a) Domestic Mail.
2193 45c. Type **659** 40 40

(b) International Mail.
2194 $1.50 Matthew Flinders, Port Lincoln Parrot, *Investigator* (ship) and Map . . . . 1·25 1·40

2002. International Stamps. Views of Australia (3rd series). As T **625**. Multicoloured.
2195 50c. Walker Flat, River Murray, South Australia 35 40
2196 $1 Mt. Roland, Tasmania 80 75
2197 $1.50 Cape Leveque, Western Australia . . . . 1·25 1·25
Nos. 2195/6 also come self-adhesive.

660 Desert Star Flower

2002. Flora and Fauna (5th series). Great Sandy Desert. Multicoloured.
2200 50c. Type **660** 35 40
2201 $1 Bilby 70 75
2202 $1.50 Thorny Devil . . . . 1·10 1·25
2203 $2 Great Sandy Desert landscape (50 × 30 mm) 1·40 1·50
No. 2200 also comes self adhesive.

661 "Ghost Gum, Mt Sonder" (Albert Namatjira)

2002. Birth Centenary of Albert Namatjira (artist). Multicoloured. Nos. 2204/7, ordinary or self-adhesive gum.
2205 45c. Type **661** 30 35
2206 45c. "Mt Hermannsburg" 30 35
2207 45c. "Glen Helen Country" 30 35
2208 45c. "Simpsons Gap" . . . 30 35
MS2209 133 × 70 mm. Nos. 2205/8 1·25 1·10

662 *Nelumbo nucifera*

2002. Australia–Thailand Joint Issue. 50th Anniv of Diplomatic Relations. Water Lilies. Multicoloured. (a) Domestic Mail.
2214 45c. Type **662** 30 35

(b) International Mail.
2215 $1 *Nymphaea immutabilis* . . 70 75
MS2216 107 × 70 mm. Nos. 2214/15 1·00 1·10

663 Star, Presents and Baubles

664 Lilly-pilly

2002. International Greetings. Multicoloured.
2217 90c. Type **663** 65 70
2218 $1.10 Koala 80 85
2219 $1.65 "Puja" (painting by Ngarralja Tommy May) 1·10 1·25

2002. International Stamps. Views of Australia (4th series). As T **625**. Multicoloured.
2220 $1.10 Coonawarra, South Australia 80 85
2221 $1.65 Gariwerd (Grampians), Victoria . . 1·10 1·25
2222 $2.20 National Library, Canberra . . . . 1·50 1·60
2223 $3.30 Cape York, Queensland . . . . 2·10 2·40

2002. "Bush Tucker". Edible Plants from the Outback. Multicoloured. Ordinary or self-adhesive gum.
2224 49c. Type **664** 35 40
2225 49c. Honey Grevillea . . . 35 40
2226 49c. Quandong 35 40
2227 49c. Acacia seeds 35 40
2228 49c. Murnong 35 40

2002. Stamp Collecting Month. *The Magic Rainforest*, (book by John Marsden). Multicoloured. Nos. 2233/8, ordinary or self-adhesive gum.
2234 45c. Type **665** 30 35
2235 45c. Fairy on branch . . . 30 35
2236 45c. Gnome with sword . . 30 35
2237 45c. Goblin with stock whip 30 35
2238 45c. Wizard 30 35
2239 45c. Sprite 30 35
MS2240 170 × 90 mm. Nos. 2234/9 1·75 1·90

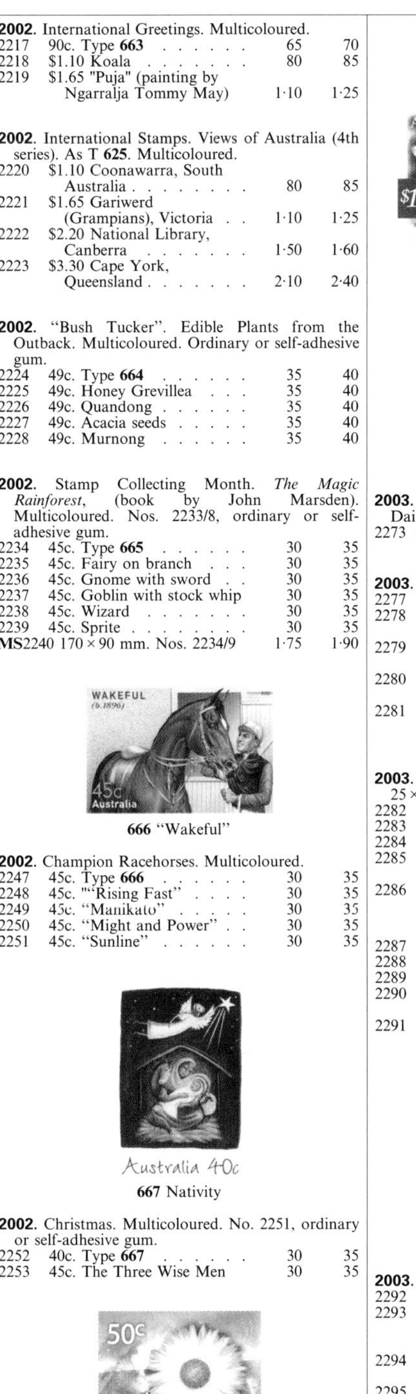

666 "Wakeful"

2002. Champion Racehorses. Multicoloured.
2247 45c. Type **666** 30 35
2248 45c. "Rising Fast" 30 35
2249 45c. "Manikato" 30 35
2250 45c. "Might and Power" . . 30 35
2251 45c. "Sunline" 30 35

667 Nativity

2002. Christmas. Multicoloured. No. 2251, ordinary or self-adhesive gum.
2252 40c. Type **667** 30 35
2253 45c. The Three Wise Men 30 35

668 Two Daisies

2003. Greetings Stamps. Some adapted from previous issues. Multicoloured.
2255 50c. Type **668** 35 40
2256 50c. Wedding rings and yellow roses 35 40
2257 50c. Hearts and pink roses 35 40
2258 50c. Birthday cake and present 35 40
2259 50c. Seated teddy bear . . . 35 40
2260 50c. Balloons 35 40
2261 50c. Red kangaroo and flag 35 40
2262 50c. Australia on globe . . 35 40
2263 50c. Sports car 35 40
2264 $1 Wedding rings and pink rose 70 75

669 Margaret Court with Wimbledon Trophy

2003. Australian Legends (7th series). Tennis Players. Ordinary or self-adhesive gum. Multicoloured.
2265 50c. Type **669** 35 40
2266 50c. Margaret Court in action 35 40
2267 50c. Rod Laver with Wimbledon Trophy . . . 35 40
2268 50c. Rod Laver in action . . 35 40

670 Blue Orchid

672 "Hari Withers" Camellia

671 Snapper and Fishing from Beach

2003. Flora and Fauna (6th series). Rainforest, Daintree National Park.
2273 **670** $1.45 multicoloured . . 1·00 1·10

2003. Angling in Australia. Multicoloured.
2277 50c. Type **671** 35 40
2278 50c. Murray cod and flooded wood 35 40
2279 50c. Brown trout and fly-fishing 35 40
2280 50c. Yellow-finned tuna and sea-fishing from launch 35 40
2281 50c. Barramundi and anglers in mangrove swamp . . . 35 40

2003. Australian Horticulture. Multicoloured. (a) Size 25 × 36 mm. Ordinary gum.
2282 50c. Type **672** 35 40
2283 50c. "Victoria Gold" rose 35 40
2284 50c. "Superb" grevillea . . 35 40
2285 50c. "Bush Tango" kangaroo paw 35 40
2286 50c. "Midnight" rhododendron 35 40

(b) Size 21 × 33 mm. Self-adhesive.
2287 50c. Type **672** 35 40
2288 50c. "Victoria Gold" rose 35 40
2289 50c. "Superb" grevillea . . 35 40
2290 50c. "Bush Tango" kangaroo paw 35 40
2291 50c. "Midnight" rhododendron 35 40

673 "Ned Kelly" (Sir Sidney Nolan)

2003. Australian Paintings (1st series). Multicoloured.
2292 $1 Type **673** 75 80
2293 $1 "Family Home, Suburban Exterior" (Howard Arkley) 75 80
2294 $1.45 "Cord Long Drawn, Expectant" (Robert Jacks) 1·00 1·10
2295 $2.45 "Girl" (Joy Hester) 1·75 2·00

OFFICIAL STAMPS

1931. Optd **O.S.** (a) Kangaroo issue.
O133 **1** 6d. brown . . . . 20·00 20·00

(b) King George V issue.
O128 **3** ½d. orange . . . . 4·75 1·50
O129 1d. green . . . . 3·25 45
O130 2d. red . . . . 8·00 55
O131 3d. blue . . . . 7·50 4·00
O126 4d. olive . . . . 16·00 3·75
O132 5d. brown . . . . 35·00 27·00

(c) Various issues.
O123 **13** 2d. red . . . . 55·00 18·00
O134 **18** 2d. red . . . . 5·00 2·00
O124 **13** 3d. blue . . . . £200 32·00
O135 **18** 3d. blue . . . . 14·00 5·00
O136 **17** 1s. green . . . . 40·00 27·00

POSTAGE DUE STAMPS

D 1

D 3

1902. White space below value at foot.
D1 **D 1** ½d. green . . . . 3·25 4·50
D2 1d. green . . . . 12·00 6·50
D3 2d. green . . . . 35·00 7·50
D4 3d. green . . . . 30·00 20·00
D5 4d. green . . . . 42·00 12·00
D6 6d. green . . . . 55·00 9·50
D7 8d. green . . . . 95·00 75·00
D8 5s. green . . . . £180 70·00

1902. White space filled in.
D22 **D 3** ½d. green . . . . 7·50 7·50
D23 1d. green . . . . 7·00 2·75
D24 2d. green . . . . 22·00 2·75
D25 3d. green . . . . 60·00 13·00
D26 4d. green . . . . 50·00 9·00
D17 5d. green . . . . 45·00 9·50
D28 6d. green . . . . 50·00 10·00
D29 8d. green . . . . £120 50·00
D18 10d. green . . . . 70·00 17·00
D19 1s. green . . . . 55·00 11·00
D20 2s. green . . . . £100 18·00
D33 5s. green . . . . £190 22·00
D43 10s. green £1600 £1300
D44 20s. green £3500 £2250

1908. As Type D 3, but stroke after figure of value, thus "5/-".
D58 **D 3** 1s. green . . . . 75·00 8·50
D60 2s. green £850 £1700
D59 5s. green . . . . £200 48·00
D61 10s. green £2000 £2750
D62 20s. green £5500 £7500

D 7

D 10

1909.
D132 **D 7** ½d. red and green . . . 2·00 2·00
D133 1d. red and green . . . 3·00 3·50
D 93 1½d. red and green . . . 1·50 9·00
D121 2d. red and green . . . 4·50 1·25
D134 3d. red and green . . . 1·75 3·00
D109 4d. red and green . . . 6·50 2·50
D124 5d. red and green . . . 12·00 3·50
D137 6d. red and green . . . 2·75 3·25
D126 7d. red and green . . . 4·25 8·50
D127 8d. red and green . . . 10·00 26·00
D139 10d. red and green . . 4·50 3·25
D128 1s. red and green . . . 18·00 1·75
D 70 2s. red and green . . . 70·00 13·00
D 71 5s. red and green . . . 90·00 15·00
D 72 10s. red and green . . . £250 £150
D 73 £1 red and green . . . £475 £275

1953.
D140 **D 10** 1s. red and green . . 6·50 3·00
D130 2s. red and green . . 18·00 12·00
D131a 5s. red and green . . 12·00 70

AUSTRALIAN ANTARCTIC TERRITORY Pt. 1

By an Order in Council of 7 February 1933, the territory S. of latitude 60°S. between 160th and 145th meridians of East longitude (excepting Adelie Land) was placed under Australian administration. Until 1957 stamps of Australia were used from the base.

1957. 12 pence = 1 shilling;
20 shillings = 1 pound.
1966. 100 cents = 1 dollar.

1 1954 Expedition at Vestfold Hills and Map

1957.
1 **1** 2s. blue 80 50

2 Members of Shackleton Expedition at S. Magnetic Pole, 1909

3 Weazel and Team

1959.
2 **2** 5d. on 4d. black and sepia . . 60 15
3 **3** 8d. on 7d. black and blue . . 1·75 2·25
4 – 1s. myrtle . . . . 2·25 2·00
5 – 2s.3d. green . . . . 7·00 4·00
DESIGNS—VERT (as Type **3**): 1s. Dog-team and iceberg; 2s.3d. Map of Antarctica and emperor penguins.

6

7 Sir Douglas Mawson (Expedition leader)

1961.
6 **6** 5d. blue 90 20

1961. 50th Anniv of 1911–14 Australian Antarctic Expedition.
7 **7** 5d. myrtle 35 20

8 Aurora and Camera Dome

11 Sastrugi (Snow Ridges)

1966. Multicoloured.
8 1c. Type **8** 70 30
9 2c. Emperor penguins . . . . 3·00 80
10 4c. Ship and iceberg 90 90
11 5c. Banding southern elephant-seals . . . . 2·75 1·75
12 7c. Measuring snow strata . . 80 80
13 10c. Wind gauges . . . . . . 1·00 1·10
14 15c. Weather balloon . . . . 5·00 2·00
15 20c. Bell Trooper helicopter (horiz) . . . . 6·00 2·50
16 25c. Radio operator (horiz) . . 2·00 2·25
17 50c. Ice-compression tests (horiz) . . . . 2·75 4·00
18 $1 Parahelion ("mock sun") (horiz) . . . . 19·00 12·00

1971. 10th Anniv of Antarctic Treaty.
19 **11** 6c. blue and black . . . . . 75 1·00
20 – 30c. multicoloured . . . . . 2·75 6·00
DESIGN: 30c. Pancake ice.

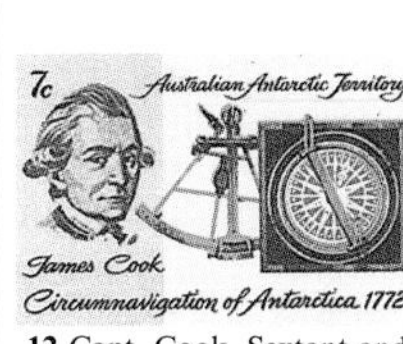

12 Capt. Cook, Sextant and Compass

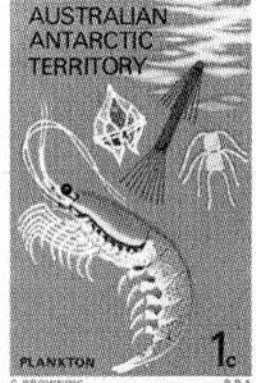

13 Plankton

1972. Bicentenary of Cook's Circumnavigation of Antarctica. Multicoloured.
21 7c. Type **12** . . . . 1·00 75
22 35c. Chart and H.M.S. "Resolution" . . . . 3·50 3·50

1973. Multicoloured.
23 1c. Type **13** 30 15
24 5c. Mawson's De Havilland Gipsy Moth, 1931 . . . . . 70 70
25 7c. Adelie penguin . . . . . 1·75 70
26 8c. De Havilland Fox Moth, 1934–37 . . . . 75 90
27 9c. Leopard seal (horiz) . . . 40 90
28 10c. Killer whale (horiz) . . . 2·75 2·00
29 20c. Wandering albatross ("Albatross") (horiz) . . . 1·00 1·00
30 25c. Wilkins's Lockheed Vega "San Francisco", 1928 (horiz) . . . . 75 1·00
31 30c. Ellsworth's Northrop Gamma "Polar Star", 1935 75 1·00
32 35c. Christensen's Avro Type 581 Avian, 1934 (horiz) . . . . 75 1·00
33 50c. Byrd's Ford Trimotor "Floyd Bennett", 1929 . . . 75 1·00
34 $1 Sperm whale . . . . 1·00 1·40

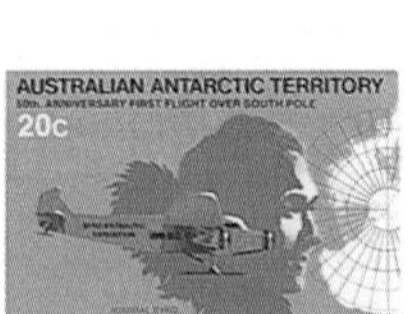

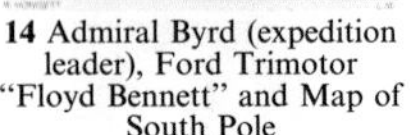

14 Admiral Byrd (expedition leader), Ford Trimotor "Floyd Bennett" and Map of South Pole

15 "Thala Dan" (supply ship)

1979. 50th Anniv of First Flight over South Pole. Multicoloured.
35 20c. Type **14** 25 60
36 55c. Admiral Byrd, aircraft and Antarctic terrain . . . 50 1·25

1979. Ships. Multicoloured.
37 1c. "Aurora" (horiz) 15 10
38 2c. "Penola" (Rymill's ship) 40 10
39 5c. Type **15** 30 40
40 10c. H.M.S. "Challenger" (survey ship) (horiz) 50 55
41 15c. "Morning" (bow view) (whaling ship) (horiz) . . . 2·00 3·00
42 15c. "Nimrod" (stern view) (Shackleton's ship) (horiz) 1·40 60
43 20c. "Discovery II" (supply ship) (horiz) . . . . 1·50 1·50
44 22c. "Terra Nova" (Scott's ship) . . . . 90 1·25
45 25c. "Endurance" (Shackleton's ship) . . . . 60 1·00
46 30c. "Fram" (Amundsen's ship) (horiz) . . . . 60 1·75
47 35c. "Nella Dan" (supply ship) (horiz) . . . . 80 1·75
48 40c. "Kista Dan" (supply ship) 1·25 1·50
49 45c. "L'Astrolabe" (D'Urville's ship) (horiz) . . . . 70 1·50
50 50c. "Norvegia" (supply ship) (horiz) 70 70
51 55c. "Discovery" (Scott's ship) 1·00 2·00
52 $1 H.M.S. "Resolution" (Cook's ship) . . . . 1·75 2·50
No. 41 is incorrectly inscr "S.Y. Nimrod".

16 Sir Douglas Mawson in Antarctic Terrain

17 Light-mantled Sooty Albatross

1982. Birth Centenary of Sir Douglas Mawson (Antarctic explorer). Multicoloured.
53 27c. Type **16** 25 25
54 75c. Sir Douglas Mawson and map of Australian Antarctic Territory . . . . 75 1·50

1983. Regional Wildlife. Multicoloured.
55 27c. Type **17** 60 90
56 27c. King cormorant ("Macquarie Island shag") 60 90
57 27c. Southern elephant seal . . 60 90
58 27c. Royal penguin 60 90
59 27c. Dove prion ("Antarctic prion") 60 90

18 Antarctic Scientist

19 Prismatic Compass and Lloyd-Creak Dip Circle

1983. 12th Antarctic Treaty Consultative Meeting. Canberra.
60 **18** 27c. multicoloured 55 55

1984. 75th Anniv of Magnetic Pole Expedition. Multicoloured.
61 30c. Type **19** 30 30
62 85c. Aneroid barometer and theodolite . . . . 70 1·25

20 Dog Team pulling Sledge

21 Prince Charles Mountains near Mawson Station

1984. Antarctic Scenes. Multicoloured.
63 2c. Summer afternoon, Mawson Station 10 50
64 5c. Type **20** 15 30
65 10c. Late summer evening, MacRobertson Land . . . 15 30
66 15c. Prince Charles Mountains 15 30
67 20c. Summer morning, Wilkesland 15 50
68 25c. Sea-ice and iceberg . . . 60 1·25
69 30c. Mount Coates 25 50
70 33c. "Iceberg Alley", Mawson 25 60
71 36c. Early winter evening, Casey Station 30 35
72 45c. Brash ice (vert) . . . . . 70 1·75
73 60c. Midwinter shadows, Casey Station 50 55
74 75c. Coastline . . . . 2·25 2·75
75 85c. Landing strip . . . . . . 2·50 3·00
76 90c. Pancake ice (vert) 75 80
77 $1 Emperor penguins . . . . 2·75 1·25

1986. 25th Anniv of Antarctic Treaty.
78 **21** 36c. multicoloured . . . . . 1·25 1·10

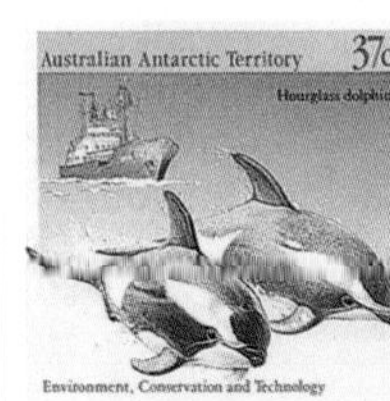

22 Hourglass Dolphins and "Nella Dan"

23 "Antarctica"

1988. Environment, Conservation and Technology. Multicoloured.
79 37c. Type **22** . . . . 1·10 1·25
80 37c. Emperor penguins and Davis Station . . . . 1·10 1·25
81 37c. Crabeater seal and Hughes 500D helicopters . . 1·10 1·25
82 37c. Adelie penguins and tracked vehicle . . . . . . 1·10 1·25
83 37c. Grey-headed albatross and photographer . . . . . 1·10 1·25

1989. Antarctic Landscape Paintings by Sir Sidney Nolan. Multicoloured.
84 39c. Type **23** . . . . 1·00 1·00
85 39c. "Iceberg Alley" . . . . . 1·00 1·00
86 60c. "Glacial Flow" . . . . . 1·75 1·50
87 80c. "Frozen Sea" . . . . . . 2·25 1·75

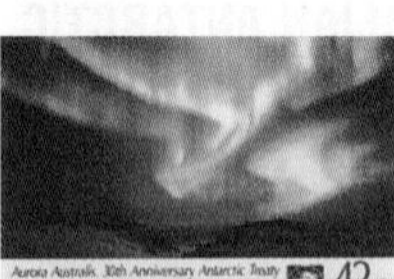

24 "Aurora Australis"

1991. 30th Anniv of Antarctic Treaty (43c.) and Maiden Voyage of "Aurora Australis" (research ship) ($1.20). Multicoloured.
88 43c. Type **24** 75 60
89 $1.20 "Aurora Australis" off Heard Island . . . . 2·75 4·00

25 Adelie Penguin and Chick

26 Head of Husky

1992. Antarctic Wildlife. Multicoloured.
90 45c. Type **25** 30 35
91 75c. Elephant seal with pup 55 60
92 85c. Hall's giant petrel ("Northern giant petrel") on nest with fledgeling 60 65
93 95c. Weddell seal and pup . . 70 75
94 $1 Royal penguin 70 75
95 $1.20 Emperor penguins with chicks (vert) 85 90
96 $1.40 Fur seal . . . . 1·00 1·10
97 $1.50 King penguin (vert) . . 1·10 1·25

1994. Departure of Huskies from Antarctica. Multicoloured.
104 45c. Type **26** . . . . 1·50 75
105 75c. Dogs pulling sledge (horiz) . . . . 1·75 2·00
106 85c. Husky in harness . . . 2·00 2·25
107 $1.05 Dogs on leads (horiz) 2·25 2·50

27 Humpback Whale with Calf

1995. Whales and Dolphins. Multicoloured.
108 45c. Type **27** . . . . 1·25 80
109 45c. Pair of hourglass dolphins (vert) . . . . . . 1·25 1·25
110 45c. Pair of minke whales (vert) . . . . 1·25 1·25
111 $1 Killer whale . . . . . . 2·00 2·00
MS112 146 × 64 mm. Nos. 108/11 4·25 4·00
Nos. 109/10 were printed together, se-tenant, forming a composite design.

28 "Rafting Sea Ice" (Christian Clare Robertson)

29 Apple Huts

1996. Paintings by Christian Clare Robertson. Multicoloured.
113 45c. Type **28** 90 70
114 45c. "Shadow on the Plateau" 90 70
115 $1 "Ice Cave" . . . . 1·90 1·40
116 $1.20 "Twelve Lake" . . . . 2·25 1·60

1997. 50th Anniv of Australian National Antarctic Research Expeditions (A.N.A.R.E.). Multicoloured.
117 45c. Type **29** 75 75
118 45c. Tuning a radio receiver 75 75
119 95c. Summer surveying . . . 1·25 1·40
120 $1.05 Scientists in cage above sea ice . . . . 1·25 1·40
121 $1.20 Scientists and tents . . 1·40 1·60

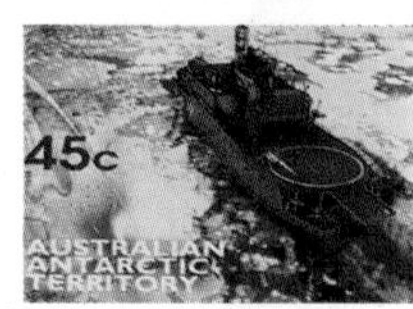

30 "Aurora Australis" (research ship)

1998. Antarctic Transport. Multicoloured.
122 45c. Type **30** . . . . 1·40 1·40
123 45c. "Skidoo" . . . . 1·40 1·40
124 $1 Helicopter lifting quad-bike (vert) . . . . 2·50 2·25
125 $2 Hagglunds tractor and trailer (vert) . . . . 2·50 2·75

31 Sir Douglas Mawson (expedition leader, 1911–14) and "Aurora" (research ship)

1999. Restoration of Mawson's Huts, Cape Denison. Each including a background drawing of a hut. Multicoloured.
126 45c. Type **31** . . . . 1·00 1·00
127 45c. Huts in blizzard . . . . 1·00 1·00
128 90c. Husky team . . . . . . 1·60 1·60
129 $1.35 Conservation in progress . . . . 1·75 1·75

32 Emperor Penguins

2000. Penguins. Multicoloured.
130 45c. Type **32** 90 90
131 45c. Adelie penguins 90 90

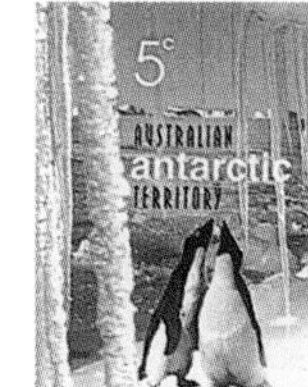

33 Adelie Penguins with Egg

2001. Centenary of Australian Antarctic Exploration. Multicoloured.
132 5c. Type **33** 25 30
133 5c. Louis Bernacchi (physicist) 25 30
134 5c. *Nimrod* (Shackleton) . . . 25 30
135 5c. Mackay, Edgeworth David and Mawson at South Magnetic Pole, 1909 25 30
136 5c. Taylor and Debenham (geologists) 25 30
137 10c. Early radio set 30 35
138 10c. Lockheed-Vega aircraft and husky team 30 35
139 10c. Sir Douglas Mawson . . 30 35
140 10c. Members of BANZARE Expedition, 1929–31 . . . 30 35
141 10c. Hoisting Union Jack . . 30 35
142 25c. Hoisting Australian flag, 1948 . . . . 35 40
143 25c. Hagglund vehicle and helicopter 35 40
144 25c. *Aurora australis* over Casey 35 40
145 25c. Scientist with weather balloon 35 40
146 25c. Modern Antarctic clothing and "apple" hut 35 40
147 45c. *Nella Dan* (supply ship) and emperor penguins . . 40 45
148 45c. Male and female scientists taking ice sample 40 45
149 45c. Scientist using satellite phone 40 45
150 45c. Weddell seal and tourists 40 45
151 45c. Satellite photograph of Antarctica 40 45
Nos. 132/51 were printed together, se-tenant, with the backgrounds forming a composite design.
Each stamp carries an inscription on the reverse, printed over the gum.

34 Female Leopard Seal and Pup

2001. Endangered Species. Leopard Seal. Mult.
152 45c. Type **34** 45 50
153 45c. Male seal on ice floe chasing adelie penguins . . 45 50
154 45c. Female seal and pup swimming underwater . . . 45 50
155 45c. Adult seal chasing adelie penguins underwater . . . 45 50

35 Light Detection and Ranging Equipment, Davis Base

2002. Antarctic Research. Multicoloured.
156 45c. Type **35** 30 35
157 45c. Magnified diatom and coastline, Casey Base . . . 30 35
158 45c. Wandering albatross, Macquarie Base 30 35
159 45c. Adelie penguin, Mawson Base 30 35

36 *Kista Dan* in Heavy Seas

2003. Antarctic Supply Ships. Multicoloured.
160 50c. Type **36** 35 40
161 50c. *Magga Dan* entering pack ice 35 40
162 $1 *Thala Dan* and iceberg (vert) 70 75
163 $1.45 *Nella Dan* unloading in Antarctic (vert) . . . . . 1·00 1·10

AUSTRIA Pt. 2

A state of Central Europe, part of the Austro-Hungarian Monarchy and Empire until 1918. At the end of the First World War the Empire was dismembered and German-speaking Austria became a Republic.

Austria was absorbed into the German Reich in 1938 and remained part of Germany until 1945. Following occupation by the four Allied Powers the Austrian Republic was re-established on 14 May 1945.

1850. 60 kreuzer = 1 gulden.
1858. 100 kreuzer = 1 gulden.
1899. 100 heller = 1 krone.
1925. 100 groschen = 1 schilling.
1938. 100 pfennig = 1 German reichsmark.
1945. 100 groschen = 1 schilling.
2002. 100 cents = 1 euro.

1 Arms of Austria — 4 — 5

1850. Imperf.

6a	1	1k. yellow	£1400	95·00
7		2k. black	£1200	60·00
8a		3k. red	£650	3·00
9		6k. brown	£900	5·50
10		9k. blue	£1200	2·50

For stamps in Type **1** with values in "CENTES", see Lombardy and Venetia.

1858.

22	5	2k. yellow	£950	42·00
23	4	3k. black	£1400	£170
24		3k. green	£1200	£120
25	5	5k. red	£375	1·00
26		10k. brown	£750	2·50
27		15k. blue	£700	1·50

For stamps in Types **4** and **5** with values in "SOLDI", see Lombardy and Venetia.

The portraits on Austrian stamps to 1906 are of the Emperor Francis Joseph I.

10 — 12 Arms of Austria

1860.

33	10	2k. yellow	£350	25·00
34		3k. green	£350	22·00
35		5k. red	£275	90·00
36		10k. brown	£350	1·60
37		15k. blue	£400	1·00

1863.

45	12	2k. yellow	£130	9·00
46		3k. green	£160	9·50
47		5k. red	48·00	30
48		10k. blue	£200	2·25
49		15k. brown	£180	1·40

A H 14 — A H 16 — 20

1867.

59	A H 14	2k. yellow	11·50	70
60		3k. green	48·00	70
62		5k. red	2·00	20
63		10k. blue	£110	50
64		15k. brown	13·00	6·25
56a		25k. grey	38·00	13·50
66	A H 16	50k. brown	25·00	75·00

1883.

70	20	2k. brown	6·00	35
71		3k. green	5·25	25
72		5k. red	26·00	20
73		10k. blue	3·50	25
74		20k. grey	50·00	3·50
75a		50k. mauve	£300	60·00

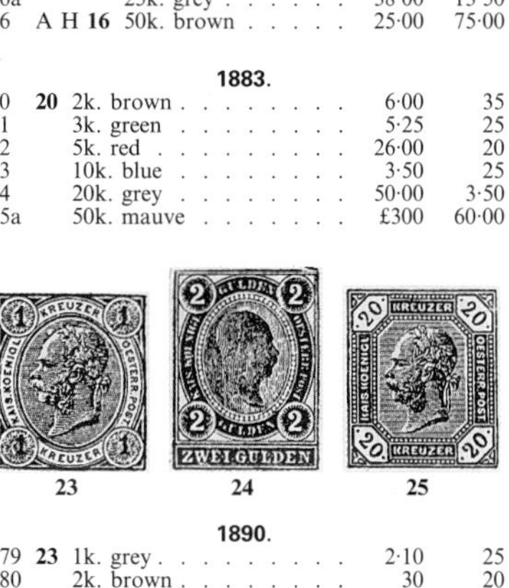
23 — 24 — 25

1890.

79	23	1k. grey	2·10	25
80		2k. brown	30	20
81		3k. green	45	20
82		5k. red	45	25
83		10k. blue	1·00	25
84		12k. purple	2·40	30
85		15k. purple	2·40	30
86		20k. green	35·00	1·90
87		24k. blue	2·50	1·10
88		30k. brown	2·50	65
89		50k. mauve	6·50	5·50
90	24	1g. blue	2·40	2·10
105		1g. lilac	42·00	4·25
91		2g. red	3·50	15·00
106		2g. green	13·50	40·00

1891. Figures in black.

92	25	20k. green	1·50	20
93		24k. blue	2·50	75
94		30k. brown	1·50	20
95		50k. mauve	1·50	35

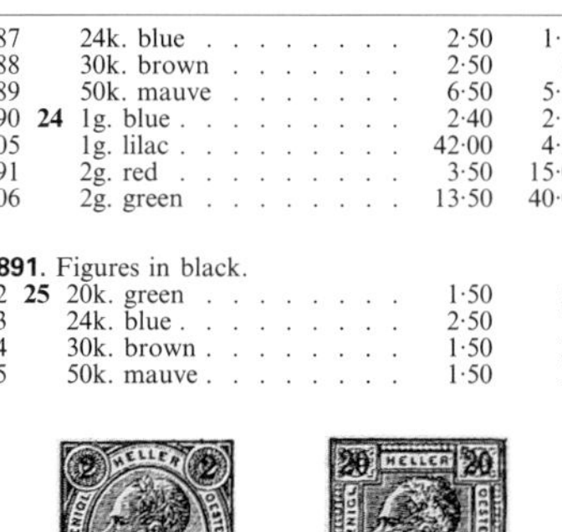
27 — 28

29 — 30

1899. Corner numerals in black on heller values.

107	27	1h. mauve	1·40	20
108		2h. grey	2·50	35
140		3h. brown	1·00	15
141		5h. green	75	15
142		6h. orange	75	15
143	28	10h. red	90	15
144		20h. brown	1·25	15
145		25h. blue	1·25	15
146		30h. mauve	3·00	90
147	29	35h. green	1·25	25
148		40h. green	3·00	4·00
149		50h. blue	7·00	7·25
150		60h. brown	3·00	80
119a	30	1k. red	5·25	20
120		2k. lilac	50·00	40
121		4k. green	8·00	10·00

33

35

1904. Types as before, but with corners containing figures altered as T **33** and **35**. Figures in black on white on 10h. to 30h. only.

169	33	1h. purple	20	35
170		2h. black	20	25
171		3h. brown	25	15
183		5h. green	30	15
173		6h. orange	40	15
160	28	10h. red	2·50	15
161		20h. brown	30·00	80
162		25h. blue	32·00	80
163		30h. mauve	42·00	1·60
178	35	35h. green	3·00	30
179		40h. purple	3·00	80
180		50h. blue	3·00	2·75
181		60h. brown	3·00	65
168		72h. red	3·00	1·60

1906. Figures on plain white ground and stamps printed in one colour.

184	28	10h. red	40	15
185		12h. violet	1·00	65
186		20h. brown	3·25	15
187		25h. blue	3·25	40
188		30h. red	7·75	25

37 Francis Joseph I

38 Francis Joseph I

41 Schonbrunn — 42 Francis Joseph I

1908. 60th Anniv of Emperor's Accession.

189	–	1h. black	30	15
190	–	2h. violet	30	15
191	–	3h. purple	50	15
192	37	5h. green	30	15
193	–	6h. brown	65	80
194	37	10h. red	25	15
195	–	12h. red	1·40	90
196	–	20h. brown	6·50	30
197	37	25h. blue	2·75	25
198	–	30h. green	10·00	30
199	–	35h. grey	2·50	25
200	38	50h. green	65	25
201	–	60h. red	30	15
202	38	72h. brown	1·90	35
203	–	1k. violet	11·00	20
204	41	2k. green and red	19·00	40
205	–	5k. purple and brown	38·00	4·25
206	42	10k. brown, blue & ochre	£150	60·00

DESIGNS—As Type **37**: 1h. Charles VI; 2h. Maria Theresa; 3h. Joseph II; 6h. Leopold II; 12h. Francis I; 20h. Ferdinand; 30h. Francis Joseph I in 1848; 35h. Same in 1878. As Type **38**: 60h. Francis Joseph I on horseback; 1k. Same in ceremonial robes. As Type **41**: 5k. Hofburg.

45

47

1910. 80th Birthday of Francis Joseph I. As issue of 1908 but with dates added as T **45**.

223		1h. black	4·50	7·75
224		2h. violet	5·50	9·50
225		3h. purple	4·75	10·50
226		5h. green	40	45
227		6h. brown	3·75	8·50
228		10h. red	20	30
229		12h. red	3·75	8·50
230		20h. brown	8·50	9·75
231		25h. blue	2·00	3·00
232		30h. green	4·25	7·25
233		35h. grey	4·25	7·00
234		50h. green	6·00	10·00
235		60h. red	6·00	10·00
236		1k. violet	7·50	11·50
237		2k. green and red	£130	£200
238		5k. purple and brown	£110	£180
239		10k. brown, blue and ochre	£180	£325

1914. War Charity Funds.

240	47	5h.+(2h.) green	20	40
241		10h.+(2h.) red	25	30

48 Cavalry

1915. War Charity Funds.

242	–	3h.+1h. brown	15	45
243	48	5h.+2h. green	15	15
244	–	10h.+2h. red	15	15
245	–	20h.+3h. green	70	2·00
246	–	35h.+3h. blue	2·00	4·75

DESIGNS: 3h. Infantry; 10h. Artillery; 20h. Battleship "Viribus Unitas" (Navy); 35h. Lohner Pfeilflieger B-1 biplane (Air Force).

49 Imperial Austrian Crown

50 Francis Joseph I

51 Arms of Austria

52

1916.

247	49	3h. violet	15	10
248		5h. green	15	10
249		6h. orange	30	75
250		10h. red	15	10
251		12h. blue	30	1·40
252	50	15h. red	45	15
253		20h. brown	2·50	20
254		25h. blue	4·25	35
255		30h. slate	3·75	65
256	51	40h. olive	25	15
257		50h. green	20	20
258		60h. blue	20	20
259		80h. brown	25	15
260		90h. purple	25	15
261		1k. red on yellow	30	20
262aa	52	2k. blue	15	25
263aa		3k. red	25	90
264a		4k. green	1·75	1·50
265aa		10k. violet	11·00	27·00

On Nos. 254/5 the portrait is full face. The 1k. has floral sprays each side of the coat-of-arms.

60 Charles I

1917.

290	60	15h. red	15	15
291a		20h. green	20	15
292		25h. blue	50	15
293		30h. violet	40	15

1918. Air. Optd **FLUGPOST** or surch also.

296	52	1k.50 on 2k. mauve	3·25	4·50
297		2k.50 on 3k. brown	10·00	24·00
298		4k. grey	5·50	14·00

1918. Optd **Deutschosterreich**.

299	49	3h. violet	15	15
300		5h. green	15	15
301		6h. orange	25	1·40
302		10h. red	15	15
303		12h. blue	30	1·75
304	60	15h. red	30	85
305		20h. green	15	15
306		25h. blue	25	20
307		30h. violet	20	20
308	51	40h. olive	20	20
309		50h. green	65	1·00
310		60h. blue	65	1·00
311		80h. brown	20	25
312		90h. red	30	40
313		1k. red on yellow	25	30
314	52	2k. blue	20	15
315		3k. red	30	80
316		4k. green	90	1·00
317		10k. violet	8·25	21·00

64 Posthorn

65 Republican Arms

66 "New Republic"

1919. Imperf or perf.

336	64	3h. grey	15	15
337	65	5h. green	15	15
338		5h. grey	15	15
339	64	6h. orange	20	45
340	65	10h. red	15	10
342	64	12h. blue	20	70
343a		15h. brown	30	30
344	66	20h. green	10	10
346	65	25h. blue	15	15
347	64	25h. violet	10	10
348	66	30h. brown	10	10
349		40h. violet	15	15
350		40h. red	10	10
351	65	45h. green	20	75
352	66	50h. blue	10	10
353	64	60h. green	10	10
354	65	1k. red on yellow	10	10
355		1k. blue	15	10

67 Parliament Building

71 Republican Arms

1919.

356	67	2k. black and red	25	55
357		2½k. bistre	35	45
358		3k. brown and blue	25	35
359		4k. black and red	25	25
360		5k. black	25	25
361		7½k. purple	30	40
362		10k. brown and green	35	50
363		20k. brown and violet	25	50
364		50k. violet on yellow	50	1·25

1920.

402	71	80h. red	15	10
403		1k. brown	15	10
404		1½k. green	30	15
405		2k. blue	30	15
406		3k. black and green	10	20
407		4k. claret and red	10	10
408		5k. red and lilac	10	10
409		7½k. brown and orange	20	25
410		10k. blue and violet	20	25

The frames of the 3 to 10k. differ.

1920. Issues for Carinthian Plebiscite. Optd **Karnten Abstimmung** (T **65/7** in new colours). (a) Perf.

411	65	5h. (+10h.) grey on yell	55	1·40
412		10h. (+20h.) red on pink	50	1·10
413	64	15h. (+30h.) brn on yell	35	1·00
414	66	20h. (+40h.) green on bl	35	90
415	64	25h. (+50h.) pur on pink	35	85
416	66	30h. (+60h.) brn on buff	1·50	3·00
417		40h. (+80h.) red on yell	40	95
418		50h. (+100h.) indigo on blue	35	55
419	64	60h. (+120h.) green on bl	1·50	3·25
420	71	80h. (+160h.) red	40	90

No.	Type	Description	Mint	Used
421		1k. (+2k.) brown	40	90
422		2k. (+4k.) blue	40	95

(b) Imperf.

No.	Type	Description	Mint	Used
423	**67**	2½k. (+5k.) brown	40	1·10
424		3k. (+6k.) green & blue	50	1·40
425		4k. (+8k.) violet & red	70	1·60
426		5k. (+10k.) blue	70	1·40
427		7½k. (+15k.) green	70	1·40
428		10k. (+20k.) red & green	70	1·40
429		20k. (+40k.) brn & lilac	75	2·00

The plebiscite was to decide whether Carinthia should be part of Austria or Yugoslavia, and the premium was for a fund to promote a vote in favour of remaining in Austria. The result was a vote for Austria.

1921. Flood Relief Fund. Optd **Hochwasser 1920** (colours changed).

No.	Type	Description	Mint	Used
430	**65**	5h. (+10h.) grey on yell	25	50
431		10h. (+20h.) brown	25	50
432	**64**	15h. (+30h.) grey	25	50
433	**66**	20h. (+40h.) green on yell	25	50
434	**64**	25h. (+50h.) blue on yell	25	50
435	**66**	30h. (+60h.) purple on bl	55	1·00
436		40h. (+80h.) brn on red	60	1·25
437		50h. (+100h.) green on bl	1·25	2·00
438	**64**	60h. (+120h.) pur on yell	20	1·00
439	**71**	80h. (+160h.) blue	45	90
440		1k. (+2k.) orange on blue	35	85
441		1½k. (+3k.) green on yell	25	50
442		2k. (+4k.) brown	25	50
443	**67**	2½k. (+5k.) blue	25	50
444		3k. (+6k.) red & green	25	50
445		4k. (+8k.) brown & lilac	75	1·75
446		5k. (+10k.) green	25	60
447		7½k. (+15k.) red	30	75
448		10k. (+20k.) green & blue	25	80
449		20k. (+40k.) pur & red	60	1·10

80 Pincers and Hammer

81 Ear of Corn

1922.

No.	Type	Description	Mint	Used
461	**81**	½k. brown	10	55
462	**80**	1k. brown	10	15
463		2k. blue	10	10
464	**81**	2½k. brown	10	10
465	**80**	4k. purple	15	90
466		5k. green	10	10
467	**81**	7½k. violet	10	10
468	**80**	10k. red	10	10
469	**81**	12½k. green	10	10
470		15k. turquoise	10	10
471		20k. blue	10	10
472		25k. red	10	10
473	**80**	30k. grey	10	10
474		45k. red	10	10
475		50k. brown	10	10
476		60k. green	10	10
477		75k. blue	15	10
478		80k. yellow	10	10
479	**81**	100k. grey	10	10
480		120k. brown	10	10
481		150k. orange	10	10
482		160k. green	15	10
483		180k. red	10	10
484		200k. pink	10	10
485		240k. violet	10	10
486		300k. blue	10	10
487		400k. green	75	10
488		500k. yellow	10	10
489		600k. slate	15	10
490		700k. brown	1·60	10
491		800k. violet	90	1·60
492	**80**	1000k. mauve	1·60	10
493		1200k. red	1·60	40
494		1500k. orange	1·60	10
495		1600k. slate	4·00	2·10
496		2000k. blue	4·25	1·10
497		3000k. blue	15·00	1·25
498		4000k. blue on blue	6·00	4·25

82

85 Mozart

1922.

No.	Type	Description	Mint	Used
499	**82**	20k. sepia	10	15
500		25k. blue	10	10
501		50k. red	10	10
502		100k. green	10	15
503		200k. purple	10	15
504		500k. orange	30	1·00
505		1000k. violet on yellow	10	10
506		2000k. green on yellow	10	15
507		3000k. red	12·00	70
508		5000k. black	3·25	1·50
509		10,000k. brown	3·75	5·00

1922. Musicians' Fund.

No.	Type	Description	Mint	Used
519	–	2½k. brown	7·25	15·00
520	**85**	5k. blue	1·00	2·00
521	–	7½k. black	1·75	3·25
522	–	10k. purple	2·00	4·00
523	–	25k. green	4·50	7·50
524	–	50k. red	2·10	4·00
525	–	100k. green	6·25	11·00

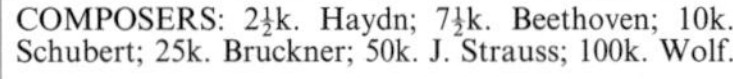
COMPOSERS: 2½k. Haydn; 7½k. Beethoven; 10k. Schubert; 25k. Bruckner; 50k. J. Strauss; 100k. Wolf.

87 Hawk

88 W. Kress

1922. Air.

No.	Type	Description	Mint	Used
546	**87**	300k. red	30	1·25
547		400k. green	4·25	16·00
548		600k. olive	20	1·10
549		900k. red	20	1·10
550	**88**	1200k. purple	20	1·10
551		2400k. slate	20	1·10
552		3000k. brown	3·25	8·00
553		4800k. blue	3·25	8·00

89 Bregenz

90 "Art the Comforter"

1923. Artists' Charity Fund.

No.	Type	Description	Mint	Used
554	**89**	100k. green	2·75	9·50
555	–	120k. blue	2·50	6·00
556	–	160k. purple	2·50	6·00
557	–	180k. purple	2·50	6·00
558	–	200k. red	2·50	6·00
559	–	240k. brown	3·00	6·00
560	–	400k. brown	2·75	6·25
561	–	600k. green	2·75	7·50
562	–	1000k. black	3·50	8·50

DESIGNS: 120k. Salzburg; 160k. Eisenstadt; 180k. Klagenfurt; 200k. Innsbruck; 240k. Linz; 400k. Graz; 600k. Melk; 1000k. Vienna.

1924. Artists' Charity Fund.

No.	Type	Description	Mint	Used
563	**90**	100k.+300k. green	3·50	7·00
564	–	300k.+900k. brown	3·50	7·25
565	–	500k.+1500k. purple	3·50	8·00
566	–	600k.+1800k. turquoise	4·50	14·00
567	–	1000k.+3000k. brown	8·00	18·00

DESIGNS: 300k. "Agriculture and Handicraft"; 500k. "Mother Love"; 600k. "Charity"; 1000k. "Fruitfulness".

91

92 Plains

93 Minorite Church, Vienna

1925.

No.	Type	Description	Mint	Used
568	**91**	1g. grey	25	10
569		2g. red	45	10
570		3g. red	45	10
571		4g. blue	1·10	10
572		5g. brown	2·00	10
573		6g. blue	2·50	10
574		7g. brown	1·90	10
575		8g. green	3·75	10
576	**92**	10g. brown	40	10
577		15g. red	40	10
578		16g. blue	40	10
579		18g. green	95	10
580	–	20g. violet	70	10
581	–	24g. red	80	40
582	–	30g. brown	60	10
583	–	40g. blue	90	10
584	–	45g. brown	1·10	20
585	–	50g. grey	1·40	25
586	–	80g. blue	5·25	4·75
587	**93**	1s. green	22·00	1·40
588	–	2s. red	7·00	11·00

DESIGN—As T **92**—20g. to 80g. Golden eagle on mountains.

96 Airman and Hansa Brandenburg C-1

97 De Havilland D.H.34 and Common Crane

1925. Air

No.	Type	Description	Mint	Used
616	**96**	2g. brown	45	70
617		5g. red	25	25
618		6g. blue	1·00	1·50
619		8g. green	1·00	1·75
620	**97**	10g. red	85	2·40
621	**96**	10g. orange	1·00	1·90
622	**97**	15g. red	65	1·25
623	**96**	15g. mauve	60	80
624		20g. brown	10·50	6·50
625		25g. violet	5·00	7·50
626	**97**	30g. purple	1·00	2·40
627	**96**	30g. bistre	8·50	8·50
628	**97**	50g. grey	1·50	2·75
629	**96**	50g. blue	18·00	12·50
630		80g. green	2·40	3·50
631	**97**	1s. blue	8·00	7·50
632		2s. green	2·00	3·75
633		3s. brown	50·00	55·00
634		5s. blue	13·00	23·00
635		10s. brown on grey (25 × 32 mm)	8·25	17·00

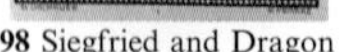
98 Siegfried and Dragon

99 Dr. Michael Hainisch

1926. Child Welfare. Scenes from the Nibelung Legend.

No.	Type	Description	Mint	Used
636	**98**	3g.+2g. brown	60	65
637	–	8g.+2g. blue	10	30
638	–	15g.+5g. red	25	35
639	–	20g.+5g. green	25	45
640	–	24g.+6g. violet	25	55
641	–	40g.+10g. brown	3·50	3·25

DESIGNS: 8g. Gunther's voyage; 15g. Kriemhild and Brunhild; 20g. Hagen and the Rhine maidens; 24g. Rudiger and the Nibelungs; 40g. Dietrich's fight with Hagen.

1928. 10th Anniv of Republic and War Orphans and Invalid Children's Fund.

No.	Type	Description	Mint	Used
642	**99**	10g. (+10g.) brown	3·25	8·50
643		15g. (+15g.) red	3·25	8·50
644		30g. (+30g.) black	3·25	8·50
645		40g. (+40g.) blue	3·25	8·50

100 Gussing

101 National Library, Vienna

1929. Views. Size 25½ × 21½ mm.

No.	Type	Description	Mint	Used
646	**100**	10g. orange	90	15
647		10g. brown	90	15
648	–	15g. purple	55	1·10
649	–	16g. black	30	10
650	–	18g. green	65	45
651	–	20g. black	70	10
653	–	24g. purple	6·00	30
654	–	30g. violet	6·00	10
655	–	40g. blue	10·00	15
656	–	50g. violet	30·00	20
657	–	60g. green	20·00	25
658	**101**	1s. brown	5·75	25
659	–	2s. green	9·50	8·25

VIEWS—As T **100**: 15g. Hochosterwitz; 16, 20g. Durnstein; 18g. Traunsee; 24g. Salzburg; 30g. Seewiesen; 40g. Innsbruck; 50g. Worthersee; 60g. Hohenems. As T **101**: 2s. St. Stephen's Cathedral, Vienna.

See also Nos. 678/91.

102 Pres. Wilhelm Miklas

104 Johann Nestroy

1930. Anti-tuberculosis Fund.

No.	Type	Description	Mint	Used
660	**102**	10g. (+10g.) brown	6·00	13·50
661		20g. (+20g.) red	6·00	13·50
662		30g. (+30g.) purple	6·00	13·50
663		40g. (+40g.) blue	6·00	13·50
664		50g. (+50g.) green	6·00	13·50
665		1s. (+1s.) brown	6·00	13·50

1930. Rotarian Congress. Optd with Rotary Int emblem and **CONVENTION WIEN 1931**.

No.	Type	Description	Mint	Used
666	**100**	10g. (+10g.) brown	32·00	40·00
667	–	20g. (+20g.) grey (No. 651)	32·00	40·00
668	–	30g. (+30g.) vio (No. 654)	32·00	40·00
669	–	40g. (+40g.) bl (No. 655)	32·00	40·00
670	–	50g. (+50g.) vio (No. 656)	32·00	40·00
671	**101**	1s. (+1s.) brown	32·00	40·00

1931. Austrian Writers and Youth Unemployment Fund.

No.	Type	Description	Mint	Used
672	–	10g. (+10g.) purple	11·00	22·00
673	–	20g. (+20g.) grey	11·00	22·00
674	**104**	30g. (+30g.) red	11·00	22·00
675	–	40g. (+40g.) blue	11·00	22·00
676	–	50g. (+50g.) green	11·00	22·00
677	–	1s. (+1s.) brown	11·00	22·00

DESIGNS: 10g. F. Raimund; 20g. E. Grillparzer; 40g. A Stifter; 50g. L. Anzengruber; 1s. P. Rosegger.

105

106 Dr. Ignaz Seipel

1932. Designs as No. 646 etc, but size reduced to 20½ × 16 mm as T **105**.

No.	Type	Description	Mint	Used
678	**105**	10g. brown	75	10
679	–	12g. green	1·75	10
680	–	18g. green	1·75	1·90
681	–	20g. black	1·00	10
682	–	24g. red	5·25	10
683	–	24g. violet	3·25	10
684	–	30g. violet	14·00	10
685	–	30g. red	5·50	10
686	–	40g. blue	20·00	75
687	–	40g. violet	7·00	25
688	–	50g. violet	22·00	30
689	–	50g. blue	7·00	25
690	–	60g. green	45·00	2·25
691	–	64g. green	11·50	30

DESIGNS (new values): 12g. Traunsee; 64g. Hohenems.

1932. Death of Dr. Seipel (Chancellor), and Ex-servicemen's Fund.

No.	Type	Description	Mint	Used
692	**106**	50g. (+50g.) blue	12·00	17·00

107 Hans Makart

108 The Climb

1932. Austrian Painters.

No.	Type	Description	Mint	Used
693	–	12g. (+12g.) green	14·00	25·00
694	–	24g. (+24g.) purple	14·00	20·00
695	–	30g. (+30g.) red	14·00	20·00
696	**107**	40g. (+40g.) grey	14·00	25·00
697	–	64g. (+64g.) brown	14·00	25·00
698	–	1s. (+1s.) red	14·00	32·00

DESIGNS: 12g. F. G. Waldmuller; 24g. Von Schwind; 30g. Alt; 64g. Klimt; 1s. A. Egger-Lienz.

1933. International Ski Championship Fund.

No.	Type	Description	Mint	Used
699	**108**	12g. (+12g.) green	6·50	13·00
700	–	24g. (+24g.) violet	75·00	£140
701	–	30g. (+30g.) red	11·00	24·00
702	–	50g. (+50g.) blue	75·00	£140

DESIGNS: 24g. Start; 30g. Race; 50g. Ski jump.

109 "The Honeymoon" (M. von Schwind)

111 John Sobieski

1933. International Philatelic Exn, Vienna (WIPA).

No.	Type	Description	Mint	Used
703	**109**	50g. (+50g.) blue	£130	£190

1933. 250th Anniv of Relief of Vienna and Pan-German Catholic Congress.

No.	Type	Description	Mint	Used
706	–	12g. (+12g.) green	21·00	32·00
707	–	24g. (+24g.) violet	19·00	25·00
708	–	30g. (+30g.) red	19·00	25·00
709	**111**	40g. (+40g.) grey	30·00	48·00
710	–	50g. (+50g.) blue	19·00	26·00
711	–	64g. (+64g.) brown	24·00	55·00

DESIGNS—VERT: 12g. Vienna in 1683; 24g. Marco d'Aviano; 30g. Count von Starhemberg; 50g. Charles of Lorraine; 64g. Burgomaster Liebenberg.

1933. Winter Relief Fund. Surch with premium and **Winterhilfe** (5g.) or **WINTERHILFE** (others).

No.	Type	Description	Mint	Used
712	**91**	5g.+2g. green	15	60
713	–	12g.+3g. blue (as 679)	25	60
714	–	24g.+6g. brn (as 682)	15	60
715	**101**	1s.+50g. red	28·00	42·00

114

115

1934.

No.	Type	Description	Mint	Used
716	**114**	1g. violet	15	10
717		3g. red	15	10
718	–	4g. green	15	10
719	–	5g. purple	15	10
720	–	6g. blue	35	10
722	–	8g. green	20	10
723	–	12g. brown	20	10
724	–	20g. brown	25	10
725	–	24g. turquoise	20	10
726	–	25g. violet	30	25
727	–	30g. red	25	10

728 – 35g. red 50 40
729 **115** 40g. grey 80 25
730 45g. brown 70 20
731 – 60g. blue 1·25 30
732 – 64g. brown 1·40 10
733 – 1s. purple 1·75 50
735 – 2s. green 3·25 6·00
736 – 3s. orange 16·00 18·00
737 – 5s. black 28·00 50·00

DESIGNS (Austrian costumes of the districts named)—As Type **114**: 1, 3g. Burgenland; 4, 5g. Carinthia; 6, 8g. Lower Austria; 12, 20g. Upper Austria; 24, 25g. Salzburg; 30, 35g. Styria (Steiermark). As Type **115**: 40, 45g. Tyrol; 60, 64g. Vorarlberg; 1s. Vienna; 2s. Army officer and soldiers. 30 × 31 mm: 3s. Harvesters; 5s. Builders.

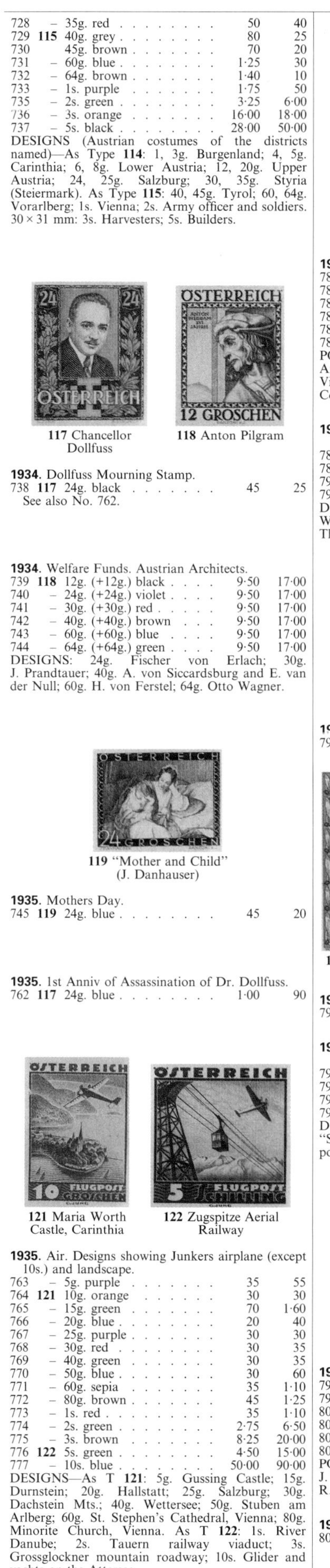

117 Chancellor Dollfuss
118 Anton Pilgram

1934. Dollfuss Mourning Stamp.
738 **117** 24g. black 45 25
See also No. 762.

1934. Welfare Funds. Austrian Architects.
739 **118** 12g. (+12g.) black 9·50 17·00
740 – 24g. (+24g.) violet 9·50 17·00
741 – 30g. (+30g.) red 9·50 17·00
742 – 40g. (+40g.) brown 9·50 17·00
743 – 60g. (+60g.) blue 9·50 17·00
744 – 64g. (+64g.) green 9·50 17·00

DESIGNS: 24g. Fischer von Erlach; 30g. J. Prandtauer; 40g. A. von Siccardsburg and E. van der Null; 60g. H. von Ferstel; 64g. Otto Wagner.

119 "Mother and Child" (J. Danhauser)

1935. Mothers Day.
745 **119** 24g. blue 45 20

1935. 1st Anniv of Assassination of Dr. Dollfuss.
762 **117** 24g. blue 1·00 90

121 Maria Worth Castle, Carinthia
122 Zugspitze Aerial Railway

1935. Air. Designs showing Junkers airplane (except 10s.) and landscape.
763 – 5g. purple 35 55
764 **121** 10g. orange 30 30
765 – 15g. green 70 1·60
766 – 20g. blue 20 40
767 – 25g. purple 30 30
768 – 30g. red 30 35
769 – 40g. green 30 35
770 – 50g. blue 30 60
771 – 60g. sepia 35 1·10
772 – 80g. brown 45 1·25
773 – 1s. red 35 1·10
774 – 2s. green 2·75 6·50
775 – 3s. brown 8·25 20·00
776 **122** 5s. green 4·50 15·00
777 – 10s. blue 50·00 90·00

DESIGNS—As T **121**: 5g. Gussing Castle; 15g. Durnstein; 20g. Hallstatt; 25g. Salzburg; 30g. Dachstein Mts.; 40g. Wettersee; 50g. Stuben am Arlberg; 60g. St. Stephen's Cathedral, Vienna; 80g. Minorite Church, Vienna. As T **122**: 1s. River Danube; 2s. Tauern railway viaduct; 3s. Grossglockner mountain roadway; 10s. Glider and yachts on the Attersee.

1935. Winter Relief Fund. As Nos. 719, 723, 725 and 733, but colours changed, surch **Winterhilfe** (778/80) or **WINTERHILFE** (781) and premium.
778 5g.+2g. green 30 60
779 12g.+3g. blue 30 1·00
780 24g.+6g. brown 30 75
781 1s.+50g. red 18·00 32·00

123 Prince Eugene of Savoy (born 1663, not 1667 as given)
124 Slalom Course Skier

1935. Welfare Funds. Austrian Heroes.
782 **123** 12g. (+12g.) brown 8·25 16·00
783 – 24g. (+24g.) green 8·25 16·00
784 – 30g. (+30g.) purple 8·25 16·00
785 – 40g. (+40g.) blue 8·25 16·00
786 – 60g. (+60g.) blue 8·25 16·00
787 – 64g. (+64g.) violet 8·25 16·00

PORTRAITS: 24g. Baron von Laudon; 30g. Archduke Charles; 40g. Field-Marshal Radetzky; 60g. Vice-Admiral von Tegetthoff; 64g. Field-Marshal Conrad von Hotzendorff.

1936. International Ski Championship Fund. Inscr "WETTKAMPFE 1936".
788 **124** 12g. (+12g.) green 2·50 3·50
789 – 24g. (+24g.) violet 4·00 4·75
790 – 35g. (+35g.) red 25·00 42·00
791 – 60g. (+60g.) blue 25·00 42·00

DESIGNS: 24g. Skier on mountain slope; 35g. Woman slalom course skier; 60g. View of Maria Theresienstrasse, Innsbruck.

125 Madonna and Child

1936. Mothers' Day.
792 **125** 24g. blue 25 30

126 Chancellor Dollfuss
127 "St. Martin sharing Cloak"

1936. 2nd Anniv of Assassination of Dr. Dollfuss.
793 **126** 10s. blue £600 £950

1936. Winter Relief Fund. Inscr "WINTERHILFE 1936/37".
794 **127** 5g.+2g. green 25 50
795 – 12g.+3g. violet 25 50
796 – 24g.+6g. blue 25 50
797 – 1s.+1s. red 5·50 10·00

DESIGNS: 12g. "Healing the sick"; 24g. "St. Elizabeth feeding the hungry"; 1s. "Warming the poor".

128 J. Ressel
129 Mother and Child

1936. Welfare Funds. Austrian Inventors.
798 **128** 12g. (+12g.) brown 3·25 6·25
799 – 24g. (+24g.) violet 3·25 6·25
800 – 30g. (+30g.) red 3·25 6·25
801 – 40g. (+40g.) black 3·25 6·25
802 – 60g. (+60g.) blue 3·25 6·25
803 – 64g. (+64g.) green 3·25 6·25

PORTRAITS: 24g. Karl Ritter von Ghega; 30g. J. Werndl; 40g. Carl Freih. Auer von Welsbach; 60g. R. von Lieben; 64g. V. Kaplan.

1937. Mothers' Day.
804 **129** 24g. red 30 25

130 "Maria Anna"
131 "Child Welfare"

1937. Centenary of Regular Danube Services of Danube Steam Navigation Co. Paddle-steamers.
805 **130** 12g. red 70 25
806 – 24g. blue 70 25
807 – 64g. green 70 85

DESIGNS: 24g. "Helios"; 64g. "Oesterreich".

1937. Winter Relief Fund. Inscr "WINTERHILFE 1937 1938"
808 **131** 5g.+2g. green 20 45
809 – 12g.+3g. brown 20 45
810 – 24g.+6g. blue 20 45
811 – 1s.+1s. red 2·75 7·25

DESIGNS: 12g. "Feeding the Children"; 24g. "Protecting the Aged"; 1s. "Nursing the Sick."

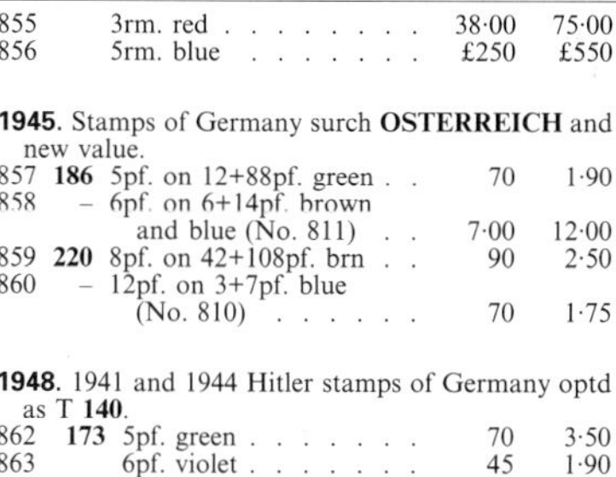

132 Steam Locomotive "Austria", 1837
133 Dr. G. Van Swieten

1937. Railway Centenary.
812 **132** 12g. brown 1·75 10
813 – 25g. violet 1·75 1·10
814 – 35g. red 1·75 2·40

DESIGNS: 25g. Steam locomotive, 1936; 35g. Electric locomotive.

1937. Welfare Funds. Austrian Doctors.
815 **133** 5g. (+5g.) brown 1·75 4·25
816 – 8g. (+8g.) red 1·75 4·25
817 – 12g. (+12g.) brown 1·75 4·25
818 – 20g. (+20g.) green 1·75 4·25
819 – 24g. (+24g.) violet 1·75 4·25
820 – 30g. (+30g.) red 1·75 4·25
821 – 40g. (+40g.) olive 1·75 4·25
822 – 60g. (+60g.) blue 1·75 4·25
823 – 64g. (+64g.) purple 1·75 4·25

DESIGNS: 8g. L. A. von Auenbrugg; 12g. K. von Rokitansky; 20g. J. Skoda; 25g. F. von Hebra; 30g. F. von Arlt; 40g. J. Hyrtl; 60g. T. Billroth; 64g. T. Meynert.

134 Nosegay and Signs of the Zodiac

1937. Christmas Greetings.
824 **134** 12g. green 10 15
825 24g. red 10 15

ALLIED OCCUPATION. Nos. 826/905 were issued in the Russian Zone of occupation and Nos. 906/22 were a joint issue for use in the British, French and American zones.

1945. Hitler portrait stamps of Germany optd.
(a) Optd **Osterreich** only.
826 **173** 5pf. green 15 90
827 8pf. red 20 60

(b) Optd **Osterreich** and bar.
828 **173** 6pf. violet 20 1·10
829 12pf. red 20 1·10

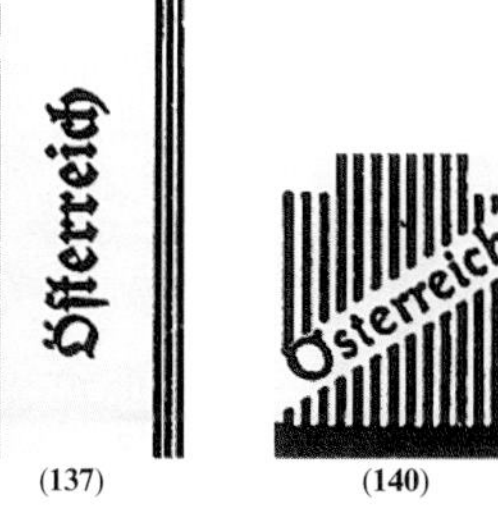

(137) (140)

1945. 1941 and 1944 Hitler stamps of Germany optd as T **137**.
830 **137** 1pf. grey 3·00 5·25
831 3pf. brown 1·90 4·50
832 4pf. grey 11·00 28·00
833 5pf. green 2·40 5·25
834 6pf. violet 30 60
835 8pf. red 1·00 1·60
836 10pf. brown 2·75 4·75
837 12pf. red 40 75
838 15pf. red 1·25 2·75
839 16pf. green 23·00 55·00
840 20pf. blue 2·75 5·50
841 24pf. brown 24·00 70·00
842 **173** 25pf. blue 2·25 4·50
843 30pf. green 2·25 4·50
844 40pf. mauve 2·50 5·00
845 **225** 42pf. green 5·00 11·25
846 **173** 50pf. green 3·50 7·00
847 60pf. brown 4·00 11·00
848 80pf. blue 3·25 9·00
853 **182** 1rm. green 21·00 38·00
850 2rm. violet 21·00 38·00
855 3rm. red 38·00 75·00
856 5rm. blue £250 £550

1945. Stamps of Germany surch **OSTERREICH** and new value.
857 **186** 5pf. on 12+88pf. green 70 1·90
858 – 6pf. on 6+14pf. brown and blue (No. 811) 7·00 12·00
859 **220** 8pf. on 42+108pf. brn 90 2·50
860 – 12pf. on 3+7pf. blue (No. 810) 70 1·75

1948. 1941 and 1944 Hitler stamps of Germany optd as T **140**.
862 **173** 5pf. green 70 3·50
863 6pf. violet 45 1·90
864 8pf. red 25 2·25
865 12pf. red 45 2·75
866 30pf. green 8·00 20·00
867a **225** 42pf. green 20·00 42·00

141 New National Arms
142 New National Arms

1945.
868 **141** 3pf. brown 10 15
869 4pf. blue 10 35
870 5pf. green 10 15
871 6pf. purple 10 15
872 8pf. orange 10 15
873 10pf. brown 10 15
874 12pf. red 10 15
875 15pf. orange 10 15
876 16pf. green 10 40
877 20pf. blue 10 25
878 24pf. orange 10 25
879 25pf. blue 10 25
880 30pf. green 15 20
881 38pf. blue 15 25
882 40pf. purple 15 20
883 42pf. grey 20 40
884 50pf. green 15 20
885 60pf. red 15 40
886 80pf. violet 15 35
887 **142** 1rm. green 20 60
888 2rm. violet 20 80
889 3rm. purple 25 90
890 5rm. brown 20 1·40

Nos. 877/86 are 24 × 28 mm.

144 Allegorical of the Home Land
145 Posthorn

1945. Austrian Welfare Charities.
905 **144** 1s.+10s. green 85 2·25

1945.
906 **145** 1g. blue 10 60
907 3g. orange 10 15
908 4g. brown 10 15
909 5g. green 10 10
910 6g. purple 10 10
911 8g. red 10 10
912 10g. grey 10 10
913 12g. brown 10 10
914 15g. red 10 15
915 20g. brown 10 15
916 25g. blue 10 15
917 30g. mauve 10 15
918 40g. blue 10 15
919 60g. olive 10 25
920 1s. violet 15 55
921 2s. yellow 35 1·40
922 5s. blue 45 1·40

146 Salzburg
148 Durnstein

1945. Views as T **146/8**.
923 – 3g. blue 10 10
924 – 4g. red 10 10
925 – 5g. red 10 10
926 **146** 6g. green 10 10
927 – 8g. brown 10 10
928 – 8g. purple 10 10
929 – 8g. green 10 10
930 – 10g. green 10 10
931 – 10g. purple 10 10
932 – 12g. brown 10 10
933 – 15g. blue 10 10
934 – 16g. brown 10 10
935 – 20g. blue 10 10
936 – 24g. green 10 10
937 – 25g. grey 10 10

938 – 30g. red 10 10
939 – 30g. blue 25 10
940 – 35g. red 10 10
941 – 38g. green 10 10
942 – 40g. grey 10 10
943 – 42g. red 10 10
944 – 45g. blue 25 10
945 – 50g. blue 15 10
946 – 50g. purple 45 40
947 – 60g. blue 15 20
948 – 60g. violet . . . . 2·25 2·75
949 – 70g. blue 25 40
950 – 80g. brown 30 55
951 – 90g. green . . . . 1·40 2·10
952 **148** 1s. brown 65 85
953 – 2s. grey . . . . 3·00 4·00
954 – 3s. green . . . . 90 1·40
955 – 5s. red . . . . 1·40 2·70

DESIGNS—As Type **146**: 3g. Lermoos; 4g. Iron-ore mine, Erzberg; 5g. Leopoldsberg, Vienna; 8g. (927), Prater Woods, Vienna; 8g. (928/9), Town Hall Park, Vienna; 10g. (930/1), Hochosterwitz; 12g. Schafberg; 15g. Forchtenstein; 16g. Gesauseeingang. 23½ × 29 mm: 20g. Gebhartsberg; 24g. Holdrichsmuhle, near Modling; 25g. Vent im Otztal; 30g. (938/9), Neusiedler Lake; 35g. Belvedere Palace, Vienna; 38g. Langbath Lake; 40g. Mariazell; 42g. Traunstein; 45g. Burg Hartenstein; 50g. (945/6), Silvretta Peaks, Vorarlberg; 60g. (947/8), Semmering; 70g. Badgastein; 80g. Kaisergebirge; 90g. Wayside shrine near Tragoss. As T **148**: 2s. St. Christof; 3s. Heiligenblut; 5s. Schonbrunn Palace, Vienna.

See also Nos. 1072/86a.

1946. 1st Anniv of U.N.O. No. 938 surch **26. JUNI 1945+20 g 26. JUNI 1946** and globe.
971 30g.+20g. red . . . . 2·10 4·25

151 Dr. Karl Renner

1946. 1st Anniv of Establishment of Renner Government.
972 **151** 1s.+1s. green . . . . . . 2·10 5·00
973 2s.+2s. violet . . . . . . 2·10 5·00
974 3s.+3s. purple . . . . . . 2·10 5·00
975 5s.+5s. brown . . . . . . 2·10 5·00

152 Dagger and Map

(153)

1946. "Anti-Fascist" Exhibition.
977 **152** 5g.+3g. sepia 45 85
978 – 6g.+4g. green 35 75
979 – 8g.+6g. orange 35 75
980 – 12g.+12g. blue 65 80
981 – 30g.+30g. violet 35 60
982 – 42g.+42g. brown 35 75
983 – 1s.+1s. red . . . . 45 1·10
984 – 2s.+2s. red . . . . 1·10 1·90

DESIGNS: 6g. Broom sweeping Nazi and Fascist emblems; 8g. St. Stephen's Cathedral in flames; 12g. Hand and barbed wire; 30g. Hand strangling snake; 42g. Hammer and broken column; 1s. Hand and Austrian flag; 2s. Eagle and smoking Nazi emblem.

1946. Congress of Society for Promotion of Cultural and Economic Relations with the Soviet Union. No. 932 optd with T **153**.
985 12g. brown 15 35

154 Mare and Foal

155 Ruprecht's Church, Vienna

1946. Austria Prize Race Fund.
986 **154** 16g.+16g. red . . . . . . 2·25 4·50
987 – 24g.+24g. violet . . . . . 1·90 4·00
988 – 60g.+60g. green . . . . . 1·90 4·00
989 – 1s.+1s. blue . . . . . . 1·90 4·00
990 – 2s.+2s. brown . . . . . 3·25 6·50

DESIGNS: 24g. Two horses' heads; 60g. Racehorse clearing hurdle; 1s. Three racehorses; 2s. Three horses' heads.

1946. 950th Anniv of First recorded use of name "Osterreich".
991 **155** 30g.+70g. red 30 85

156 Statue of Duke Rudolf

157 Franz Grillparzer (dramatic poet)

1946. St. Stephen's Cathedral Reconstruction Fund. Architectural and Sculptural designs.
992 **156** 3g.+12g. brown 20 60
993 – 5g.+20g. purple 20 60
994 – 6g.+24g. blue 20 60
995 – 8g.+32g. green 20 60
996 – 10g.+40g. blue 20 70
997 – 12g.+48g. violet . . . . 55 1·25
998 – 30g.+1s.20 red . . . . 1·00 1·75
999 – 50g.+1s.80 blue . . . . 1·25 3·50
1000 – 1s.+5s. purple . . . . . 1·60 4·50
1001 – 2s.+10s. brown . . . . 3·00 8·25

DESIGNS: 5g. Tomb of Frederick III; 6g. Pulpit; 8g. Statue of St. Stephen; 10g. Statue of Madonna and Child; 12g. Altar; 30g. Organ; 50g. Anton Pilgram; 1s. N.E. Tower; 2s. S.W. Spire.

1947. Famous Austrians.
1002 – 12g. green 20 15
1003 **157** 18g. purple 20 15
1004 – 20g. green 40 25
1005 – 40g. brown . . . . . . 8·50 4·50
1006 – 40g. green . . . . 6·50 6·50
1007 – 60g. lake 45 25

PORTRAITS: 12g. Franz Schubert (composer); 20g. Carl Michael Ziehrer (composer); 40g. (No. 1005), Adalbert Stifter (poet); 40g. (No. 1006), Anton Bruckner (composer); 60g. Friedrich Amerling (painter).

158 Harvesting

159 Airplane over Hinterstoder

1947. Vienna Fair Fund.
1009 **158** 3g.+2g. brown 40 65
1010 – 8g.+2g. green 35 65
1011 – 10g.+5g. slate 35 65
1012 – 12g.+8g. violet 35 65
1013 – 18g.+12g. olive 35 65
1014 – 30g.+10g. purple 35 65
1015 – 35g.+15g. red 40 95
1016 – 60g.+20g. blue . . . . . 40 1·00

DESIGNS: 8g. Logging; 10g. Factory; 12g. Pithead; 18g. Oil wells; 30g. Textile machinery; 35g. Foundry; 60g. Electric cables.

1947. Air.
1017 – 50g. brown 20 70
1018 – 1s. purple 25 70
1019 – 2s. green 25 90
1020 **159** 3s. brown . . . . 2·40 4·50
1021 – 4s. green . . . . 1·90 4·50
1022 – 5s. blue . . . . 1·90 4·50
1023 – 10s. blue . . . . 80 6·00

DESIGNS—Airplane over: 50g. Windmill at St. Andra; 1s. Heidentor; 2s. Gmund; 4s. Pragraten; 5s. Torsaule; 10s. St. Charles's Church, Vienna.

160 Beaker (15th century)

161 Racehorse

1947. National Art Exhibition Fund.
1024 **160** 3g.+2g. brown 25 60
1025 – 8g.+2g. green 25 60
1026 – 10g.+5g. red 25 60
1027 – 12g.+8g. violet 25 60
1028 – 18g.+12g. brown 25 70
1029 – 20g.+10g. violet 25 65
1030 – 30g.+10g. green 25 65
1031 – 35g.+15g. red 25 70
1032 – 48g.+12g. purple 25 80
1033 – 60g.+20g. blue 35 90

DESIGNS: 8g. Statue of "Providence" (Donner); 10g. Benedictine Monastery, Melk; 12g. "Wife of Dr. Brante of Vienna"; 18g. "Children in a Window" (Waldmuller); 20g. Belvedere Palace Gateway; 30g. Figure of "Egeria" on fountain at Schonbrunn; 35g. National Library, Vienna; 48g. "Copper Printer's (Ernst Rohm) Workshop" (Ferdinand Schmutzer); 60g. "Girl in Straw Hat" (Amerling).

1947. Vienna Prize Race Fund.
1034 **161** 60+20g. blue on pink . . 20 45

163 Prisoner-of-war

165 Globe and Tape Machine

1947. Prisoners-of-war Relief Fund.
1063 **163** 8g.+2g. green 15 40
1064 – 12g.+8g. brown 15 50
1065 – 18g.+12g. black 15 50
1066 – 35g.+15g. purple 15 50
1067 – 60g.+20g. blue 15 50
1068 – 1s.+40g. brown 15 70

DESIGNS: 12g. Letter from home; 18g. Gruesome camp visitor; 35g. Soldier and family reunited; 60g. Industry beckons returned soldier; 1s. Soldier sowing.

1947. Nos. 934 and 941 surch.
1069 75g. on 38g. green 25 80
1070 1s.40 on 16g. brown 15 25

1947. Telegraph Centenary.
1071 **165** 40g. violet 20 35

1947. Currency Revaluation. (a) As T **146**.
1072 3g. red (Lermoos) 20 20
1073 5g. red (Leopoldsberg) . . . 20 15
1074 10g. red (Hochosterwitz) . . 20 15
1075 15g. red (Forchtenstein) . . 1·75 1·90

(b) As T **146** but larger (23½ × 29 mm).
1076 20g. red (Gebhartsberg) . . 40 15
1077 30g. red (Neusiedler Lake) 60 25
1078 40g. red (Mariazell) 60 15
1079 50g. red (Silvretta Peaks) . . 80 15
1080 60g. red (Semmering) . . . 8·75 1·60
1081 70g. red (Badgastein) . . . 3·25 20
1082 80g. red (Kaisergebirge) . . 3·25 25
1083 90g. red (Wayside shrine, Tragoss) . . . . 3·50 80

(c) As T **148**.
1084 1s. violet (Durnstein) . . . 70 15
1085 2s. violet (St. Christof) . . 85 25
1086 3s. violet (Heiligenblut) . . 13·00 1·40
1086a 5s. violet (Schonbrunn) . . 13·00 1·75

Nos. 1072/86a in new currency replaced previous issue at rate of 3s. (old) = 1s. (new).

166 Sacred Olympic Flame

167 Laabenbach Viaduct, Neulenbach

1948. Fund for Entries to 5th Winter Olympic Games, St. Moritz.
1087 **166** 1s.+50g. blue 30 40

1948. Reconstruction Fund.
1088 **167** 10g.+5g. grey 30 30
1089 – 20g.+10g. violet 30 30
1090 – 30g.+10g. green 30 40
1091 – 40g.+20g. green 20 30
1092 – 45g.+20g. blue 20 30
1093 – 60g.+30g. red 20 30
1094 – 75g.+35g. purple 20 30
1095 – 80g.+40g. purple 20 30
1096 – 1s.+50g. blue 20 30
1097 – 1s.40+70g. lake 40 55

DESIGNS (showing reconstruction): 20g. Vermunt Lake Dam; 30g. Danube Port, Vienna; 40g. Erzberg open-cast mine; 45g. Southern Railway Station, Vienna; 60g. Flats; 75g. Vienna Gas Works; 80g. Oil refinery; 1s. Mountain roadway; 1s.40, Parliament Building.

169 Violets

170 Vorarlberg Montafon

1948. Anti-tuberculosis Fund.
1098 **169** 10g.+5g. violet, mauve and green 25 25
1099 – 20g.+10g. green, light green and yellow . . . 25 25
1100 – 30g.+10g. brown, yellow and green . . . . . . 3·00 3·00
1101 – 40g.+20g. green, yellow and orange 55 50
1102 – 45g.+20g. purple, mauve and yellow 20 25
1103 – 60g.+30g. red, mauve and green 20 25
1104 – 75g.+35g. green, pink and yellow 20 25
1105 – 80g.+40g. blue, pink and green 30 30
1106 – 1s.+50g. blue, ultramarine and green 30 30
1107 – 1s.40+70g. green, blue and yellow . . . . . 1·75 1·25

FLOWERS: 20g. Anemone; 30g. Crocus; 40g. Primrose; 45g. Pasque flower; 60g. Rhododendron; 75g. Wild rose; 80g. Cyclamen; 1s. Gentian; 1s.40, Edelweiss.

1948. Provincial Costumes.
1108 – 3g. grey 55 75
1109 – 5g. green 15 15
1110 – 10g. blue 15 15
1111 – 15g. brown 40 15
1112 **170** 20g. green 20 15
1113 – 25g. brown 20 15
1114 – 30g. red . . . . 1·40 15
1115 – 30g. violet 45 15
1116 – 40g. violet . . . . 2·10 15
1117 – 40g. green 25 15
1118 – 45g. blue . . . . 2·00 40
1119 – 50g. brown 60 15
1120 – 60g. red 30 15
1121 – 70g. green 40 15
1122 – 75g. blue . . . . 5·00 55
1123 – 80g. rose 40 15
1124 – 90g. purple . . . . . . 26·00 30
1125 – 1s. blue . . . . 6·25 15
1126 – 1s. red . . . . 55·00 15
1127 – 1s. green 40 15
1128 – 1s.20 violet 50 15
1129 – 1s.40 brown . . . . . . 2·75 25
1130 – 1s.45 red . . . . 1·00 15
1131 – 1s.50 blue . . . . 1·10 15
1132 – 1s.60 red 40 15
1133 – 1s.70 blue . . . . 2·25 60
1134 – 2s. green 80 15
1135 – 2s.20 slate . . . . . . 4·00 20
1136 – 2s.40 blue . . . . 1·10 15
1137 – 2s.50 brown . . . . . . 2·50 1·25
1138 – 2s.70 brown 65 60
1139 – 3s. lake . . . . 2·00 15
1140 – 3s.50 green . . . . . . 18·00 15
1141 – 4s.50 purple 65 70
1142 – 5s. purple . . . . 1·00 15
1143 – 7s. olive . . . . 3·75 80
1144 – 10s. grey . . . . 29·00 5·75

DESIGNS—As T **170**: 3g. "Tirol Inntal"; 5 g "Salzburg Pinzgau"; 10, 75g. "Steiermark Salzkammergut" (different designs); 15 g "Burgenland Lutzmannsburg"; 25g., 1s.60, "Wien 1850" (two different designs), 30g. (2) "Salzburg Pongau", 40g. (2) "Wien 1840"; 45 g "Karnten Lesachtal"; 50g. "Vorarlberg Bregenzerwald"; 60g. "Karnten Lavanttal"; 70g. "Niederosterreich Wachau"; 80 g "Steiermark Ennstal"; 90g. "Steiermark Mittelsteier"; 1s. (3) "Tirol Pustertal"; 1s.20, "Niederosterreich Wienerwald"; 1s.40, "Oberosterreich Innviertel"; 1s.45, "Wilter bei Innsbruck"; 1s.50, "Wien 1853"; 1s.70, "Ost Tirol Kals"; 2s. "Oberosterreich"; 2s.20, "Ischl 1820"; 2s.40, "Kitzbuhel"; 2s.50, "Obersteiermark 1850"; 2s.70, "Kleines Walsertal"; 3s. "Burgenland"; 3s.50, "Niederosterreich 1850"; 4s.50, "Gailtal"; 5s. "Zillertal"; 7s. "Steiermark Sulmtal". 25 × 35 mm: 10s. "Wien 1850".

172 Kunstlerhaus

173 Hans Makart

1948. 80th Anniv of Creative Artists' Association.
1145 **172** 20g.+10g. green . . . . 6·50 6·00
1146 **173** 30g.+15g. brown . . . . 2·50 3·00
1147 – 40g.+20g. blue . . . . . 2·50 3·00
1148 – 50g.+25g. violet . . . . 4·25 5·00
1149 – 60g.+30g. red . . . . . 5·50 4·00
1150 – 1s.+50g. blue . . . . . 5·50 5·75
1151 – 1s.40+70g. brown . . . 15·00 12·00

PORTRAITS: 40g. K. Kundmann; 50g. A. von Siccardsburg; 60g. H. Canon; 1s. W. Unger; 1s.40, Friedr. Schmidt.

174 St. Rupert

175 Pres. Renner

1948. Salzburg Cathedral Reconstruction Fund.
1152 **174** 20g.+10g. green . . . . 7·25 6·50
1153 – 30g.+15g. brown . . . . 2·50 2·50
1154 – 40g.+20g. green . . . . 2·50 2·10
1155 – 50g.+25g. brown 60 70
1156 – 60g.+30g. red 60 70
1157 – 80g.+40g. purple 50 70
1158 – 1s.+50g. blue 70 85
1159 – 1s.40+70g. green . . . 2·10 2·10

DESIGNS: 30, 40, 50, 80g. Views of Salzburg Cathedral; 60g. St. Peter's; 1s. Cathedral and Fortress; 1s.40, Madonna.

1948. 30th Anniv of Republic.
1160 **175** 1s. blue . . . . 2·00 1·75

See also Nos. 1224 and 1333.

176 F. Gruber and J. Mohr **177** Boy and Hare

1948. 130th Anniv of Composition of Carol "Silent Night, Holy Night".
1161 **176** 60g. brown . . . . . . 4·50 4·50

1949. Child Welfare Fund.
1162 **177** 40g.+10g. purple . . . . 13·00 16·00
1163 – 60g.+20g. red . . . . . 13·00 16·00
1164 – 1s.+25g. blue . . . . . 13·00 16·00
1165 – 1s.40+35g. green . . . . 16·00 17·00
DESIGNS: 60g. Two girls and apples in boot; 1s. Boy and birthday cake; 1s.40, Girl praying before candle.

178 Boy and Dove **179** Johann Strauss

1949. U.N. Int. Children's Emergency Fund.
1166 **178** 1s. blue . . . . 9·00 2·40

1949. 50th Death Anniv of Johann Strauss the Younger (composer).
1167 **179** 1s. blue . . . . 2·50 2·25
See also Nos. 1174, 1207 and 1229.

180 Esperanto Star **181** St. Gebhard

1949. Esperanto Congress, Vienna.
1168 **180** 20g. green 85 80

1949. Birth Millenary of St. Gebhard (Bishop of Vorarlberg).
1169 **181** 30g. violet . . . . 1·60 1·50

182 Seal of Duke Friedrich II, 1230 **183** Allegory of U.P.U.

1949. Prisoners-of-war Relief Fund. Arms.
1170 **182** 40g.+10g. yell & brn . . 7·00 7·50
1171 – 60g.+15g. pink & pur . . 5·75 6·00
1172 – 1s.+25g. red & blue . . 5·75 6·00
1173 – 1s.60+40g. pink and green . . . . 8·25 8·50
ARMS: 60g. Princes of Austria, 1450; 1s. Austria, 1600; 1s.60, Austria, 1945.

1949. Death Centenary of Johann Strauss the Elder (composer). Portrait as T **179**.
1174 30g. purple . . . . 1·90 1·90

1949. 75th Anniv of U.P.U.
1175 **183** 40g. green . . . . 2·50 2·75
1176 – 60g. red . . . . 3·25 2·75
1177 – 1s. blue . . . . 6·50 6·25
DESIGNS: 60g. Children holding "75"; 1s. Woman's head.

185 Magnifying Glass and Covers **186** M. M. Daffinger

1949. Stamp Day.
1206 **185** 60g.+15g. brown . . . . 2·50 2·75

1949. 50th Death Anniv of Karl Millocker (composer). Portrait as T **179**.
1207 1s. blue . . . . 11·50 8·25

1950. 160th Birth Anniv of Moritz Michael Daffinger (painter).
1208 **186** 60g. brown . . . . . . 6·00 5·50

187 A. Hofer

1950. 140th Death Anniv of Andreas Hofer (patriot).
1209 **187** 60g. violet . . . . 9·75 9·00
See also Nos. 1211, 1223, 1232, 1234, 1243, 1253, 1288 and 1386.

188 Stamp of 1850 **189** Arms of Austria and Carinthia

1950. Austrian Stamp Centenary.
1210 **188** 1s. black on yellow . . . 1·75 1·25

1950. Death Centenary of Josef Madersperger (sewing machine inventor). Portrait as T **187**.
1211 60g. violet . . . . 5·25 3·50

1950. 30th Anniv of Carinthian Plebiscite.
1212 **189** 60g.+15g. grn & brn . . 24·00 25·00
1213 – 1s.+25g. red & orange 28·00 30·00
1214 – 1s.70+40g. blue and turquoise . . . . . . 32·00 35·00
DESIGNS: 1s. Carinthian waving Austrian flag; 1s.70, Hand and ballot box.

190 Rooks **191** Philatelist

1950. Air.
1215 **190** 60g. violet . . . . 3·50 3·25
1216 – 1s. violet (Barn swallows) . . . . . . 22·00 19·00
1217 – 2s. blue (Black-headed gulls) . . . . 20·00 7·50
1218 – 3s. turquoise (Great cormorants) . . . . . £120 90·00
1219 – 5s. brown (Common buzzard) . . . . . . £120 95·00
1220 – 10s. purple (Grey heron) 55·00 45·00
1221 – 20s. sepia (Golden eagle) 8·00 2·75

1950. Stamp Day.
1222 **191** 60g.+15g. green . . . . 7·00 6·50

1950. Birth Centenary of Alexander Girardi (actor). Portrait as T **187**.
1223 30g. blue . . . . 1·50 1·10

192 Dr. Renner **193** Miner

1951. Death of Pres. Karl Renner.
1224 **192** 1s. black on lemon . . . 1·10 35

1951. Reconstruction Fund.
1225 **193** 40g.+10g. purple . . . . 11·50 12·00
1226 – 60g.+15g. green . . . . 11·50 12·00
1227 – 1s.+25g. brown . . . . 11·50 12·00
1228 – 1s.70+40g. blue . . . . 11·50 12·00
DESIGNS: 60g. Bricklayer; 1s. Bridge-builder; 1s.70, Telegraph engineer.

1951. 150th Birth Anniv of Joseph Lanner (composer). Portrait as T **179**.
1229 60g. green . . . . 3·50 2·00

194 Martin Johann Schmidt **195** Scout Badge

1951. 150th Death Anniv of Schmidt (painter).
1230 **194** 1s. red . . . . 5·00 2·75

1951. Boy Scout Jamboree.
1231 **195** 1s. red, yellow & green 4·00 3·50

1951. 10th Death Anniv of Wilhelm Kienzl (composer). Portrait as T **187**.
1232 1s.50 blue . . . . 2·75 1·40

196 Laurel Branch and Olympic Emblem **197** Schrammel

1952. 6th Winter Olympic Games, Oslo.
1233 **196** 2s.40+60g. green . . . . 15·00 16·00

1952. 150th Birth Anniv of Karl Ritter von Ghega (railway engineer). Portrait as T **187**.
1234 1s. green . . . . 7·00 1·60

1952. Birth Cent of Josef Schrammel (composer).
1235 **197** 1s.50 blue . . . . 6·00 1·60
See also No. 1239.

198 Cupid and Letter **199** Breakfast Pavilion

1952. Stamp Day.
1236 **198** 1s.50+35g. purple . . . 15·00 17·00

1952. Bicentenary of Schonbrunn Menagerie.
1237 **199** 1s.50 green . . . . . . 5·25 1·75

200 **202**

1952. Int Union of Socialist Youth Camp, Vienna.
1238 **200** 1s.50 blue . . . . 5·75 1·10

1952. 150th Birth Anniv of Nikolaus Lenau (writer). Portrait as T **197**.
1239 1s. green . . . . 6·00 1·60

1952. International Children's Correspondence.
1240 **202** 2s.40 blue . . . . 8·50 2·50

203 "Christus Pantocrator" (sculpture) **204** Hugo Wolf

1952. Austrian Catholics' Day.
1241 **203** 1s.+25g. olive . . . . . 9·00 11·00

1953. 50th Death Anniv of Wolf (composer).
1242 **204** 1s.50 blue . . . . 8·00 1·40

1953. President Korner's 80th Birthday. As T **187** but portrait of Korner.
1243 1s.50 blue . . . . 5·50 1·10
For 1s.50 black, see No. 1288.

1953. 60th Anniv of Austrian Trade Union Movement. As No. 955 (colour changed) surch **GEWERKSCHAFTS BEWEGUNG 60 JAHRE 1s+25g.**
1244 1s.+25g. on 5s. blue . . . . 2·40 2·50

206 Linz National Theatre **207** Meeting-house, Steyr

1953. 150th Anniv of Linz National Theatre.
1245 **206** 1s.50 turquoise . . . . . 13·00 2·25

1953. Vienna Evangelical School Rebuilding Fund.
1246 **207** 70g.+15g. purple 25 25
1247 – 1s.+25g. blue 30 30
1248 – 1s.50+40g. brown . . . 45 55
1249 – 2s.40+60g. green . . . . 3·00 2·50
1250 – 3s.+75g. lilac . . . . . 8·00 6·75
DESIGNS: 1s. J. Kepler (astronomer); 1s.50, Lutheran Bible, 1534; 2s.40, T. von Hansen (architect); 3s. School after reconstruction.

208 Child and Christmas Tree **209**

1953. Christmas
1251 **208** 1s. green . . . . 1·10 25
See also No. 1266.

1953. Stamp Day.
1252 **209** 1s.+25g. brown . . . . 6·25 5·50

1954. 150th Birth Anniv of M. Von Schwind (painter). As T **187** but portrait of Von Schwind.
1253 1s.50 lilac . . . . 8·00 1·90

210 Baron K. von Rokitansky **212** Surgeon with Microscope

1954. 150th Birth Anniv of Von Rokitansky (anatomist).
1254 **210** 1s.50 violet . . . . . . 14·00 2·40
See also No. 1264.

1954. Avalanche Fund. As No. 953 (colour changed) surch **LAWINENOPFER 1954 1s+20g.**
1255 1s.+20g. blue 20 20

1954. Health Service Fund.
1256 – 30g.+10g. violet . . . . 1·10 1·25
1257 **212** 70g.+15g. brown 30 25
1258 – 1s.+25g. blue 30 30
1259 – 1s.45+35g. green 45 50
1260 – 1s.50+35g. red . . . . . 5·00 5·50
1261 – 2s.40+60g. purple . . . 5·75 7·00
DESIGNS: 30g. Boy patient and sun-ray lamp; 1s. Mother and children; 1s.45, Operating theatre; 1s.50, Baby on scales; 2s.40, Red Cross nurse and ambulance.

213 Esperanto Star

214 J. M. Rottmayr von Rosenbrunn

1954. 50th Anniv of Esperanto in Austria.
1262 **213** 1s. green and brown . . 3·50 35

1954. Birth Tercentenary of Rottmayr von Rosenbrunn (painter).
1263 **214** 1s. green . . . . 9·00 3·00

1954. 25th Death Anniv of Dr. Auer von Welsbach (inventor). Portrait as T **210**.
1264 1s.50 blue . . . . 26·00 2·50

216 Great Organ, Church of St. Florian

217 18th-century River Boat

1954. 2nd International Congress of Catholic Church Music, Vienna.
1265 **216** 1s. brown . . . . 1·75 35

1954. Christmas. As No. 1251, but colour changed.
1266 **208** 1s. blue . . . . 4·00 55

1954. Stamp Day.
1267 **217** 1s.+25g. green . . . . . 5·00 5·50

218 Arms of Austria and Newspapers

1954. 150th Anniv of State Printing Works and 250th Anniv of "Wiener-Zeitung" (newspaper).
1268 **218** 1s. black and red . . . . 2·10 25

219 "Freedom"

1955. 10th Anniv of Re-establishment of Austrian Republic.
1269 – 70g. purple . . . . . . 1·25 25
1270 – 1s. blue . . . . 5·75 25
1271 **219** 1s.45 red . . . . 7·25 3·25
1272 – 1s.50 brown . . . . . . 20·00 30
1273 – 2s.40 green . . . . . . 7·25 5·00
DESIGNS: 70g. Parliament Buildings; 1s. Western Railway terminus, Vienna; 1s.50, Modern houses; 2s.40, Limberg Dam.

1955. Austrian State Treaty. As No. 888, but colour changed, optd **STAATSVERTRAG 1955**.
1274 **142** 2s. grey . . . . 2·10 40

221 "Strength through Unity"

1955. 4th World Trade Unions Congress, Vienna.
1275 **221** 1s. blue . . . . 2·10 2·00

222 "Return to Work"

1955. Returned Prisoners-of-war Relief Fund.
1276 **222** 1s.+25g. brown . . . . 2·00 1·90

223 Burgtheater, Vienna

1955. Re-opening of Burgtheater and State Opera House, Vienna.
1277 **223** 1s.50 brown . . . . . . 3·50 25
1278 – 2s.40 blue (Opera House) 4·50 2·50

224 Globe and Flags

225 Stamp Collector

1955. 10th Anniv of U.N.O.
1279 **224** 2s.40 green . . . . . . 8·00 2·75

1955. Stamp Day.
1280 **225** 1s.+25g. brown . . . . 2·75 2·75

226 Mozart

227

1956. Birth Bicentenary of Mozart (composer).
1281 **226** 2s.40 blue . . . . 3·25 1·10

1956. Admission of Austria into U.N.
1282 **227** 2s.40 brown . . . . . . 8·25 1·90

228

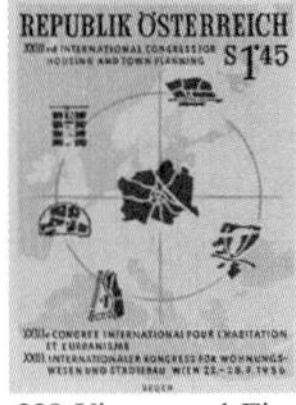

229 Vienna and Five New Towns

1956. 5th World Power Conference, Vienna.
1283 **228** 2s.40 blue . . . . 8·00 2·10

1956. 23rd International Town Planning Congress.
1284 **229** 1s.45 red, black & green 2·50 75

230 J. B. Fischer von Erlach

231 "Stamp Day"

1956. Birth Tercentenary of Fischer von Erlach (architect).
1285 **230** 1s.50 brown 85 90

1956. Stamp Day.
1286 **231** 1s.+25g. red . . . . . . 2·40 2·50

1956. Hungarian Relief Fund. As No. 1173, but colours changed, surch **1956 1.50 +50 UNGARNHILFE**.
1287 1s.50+50g. on 1s.60+40g. red and grey 55 50

1957. Death of Pres. Korner. As No. 1243, but colour changed.
1288 1s.50 black . . . . 1·60 1·40

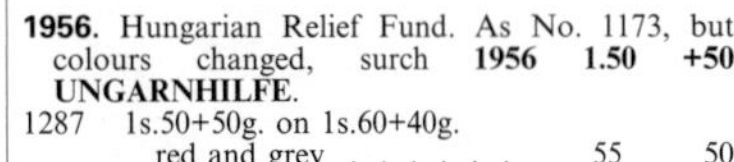

233 J. Wagner von Jauregg

234 Anton Wildgans

1957. Birth Centenary of Wagner von Jauregg (psychiatrist).
1289 **233** 2s.40 brown . . . . . . 3·50 2·00

1957. 25th Death Anniv of Anton Wildgans (poet).
1290 **234** 1s. blue 30 25

235 Daimber (1907), Graf and Stift (1957) Post Buses

1957. 50th Anniv of Postal Coach Service.
1291 **235** 1s. black on yellow . . . 40 35

237 Mt. Gasherbrum II

236 Mariazell Basilica

1957. Austrian Himalaya–Karakorum Expedition, 1956.
1293 **237** 1s.50 blue 45 30

1957. Buildings. (a) Size 20½ × 24½ mm.
1295 – 20g. purple 35 15
1296 – 30g. green 35 15
1297 – 40g. red 25 15
1298 – 50g. grey 90 15
1299 – 60g. brown 40 15
1300 – 70g. blue 35 15
1301 – 80g. brown 25 15
1302 **236** 1s. brown . . . . 1·00 15
1303 – 1s. brown 95 15
1304 – 1s.20 purple 70 25
1305 – 1s.30 green 50 15
1306 – 1s.40 blue 55 20
1307 – 1s.50 red 70 15
1308 – 1s.80 blue 80 20
1309 – 2s. blue . . . . 4·25 15
1310 – 2s. blue 85 15
1311 – 2s.20 green . . . . . . 1·00 20
1312 – 2s.50 violet . . . . . . 1·40 40
1313 – 3s. blue 90 15
1314 – 3s.40 green . . . . . . 1·10 75
1315 – 3s.50 mauve . . . . . . 1·00 15
1316 – 4s. violet . . . . 1·40 15
1317 – 4s.50 green . . . . . . 1·75 40
1318 – 5s.50 green . . . . . . 1·10 15
1319 – 6s. violet . . . . 1·50 15
1320 – 6s.40 blue . . . . 1·50 85
1321 – 8s. purple . . . . 2·10 30

(b) Larger.
1322 – 10s. green . . . . 3·50 40
1323 – 20s. purple . . . . 3·75 70

(c) Smaller, size 17½ × 21 mm.
1324 – 50g. grey 25 20
1325 **236** 1s. brown 25 20
1326 – 1s.50 purple 25 20
DESIGNS: 20g. Old Courtyard, Morbisch; 30g. Vienna Town Hall; 40g. Porcia Castle, Spittal; 50g. Heiligenstadt flats; 60g. Lederer Tower, Wells; 70g. Archbishop's Palace, Salzburg; 80g. Old farmhouse, Pinzgau; 1s. (1303) Millstatt; 1s.20, Corn Measurer's House, Bruck-on-the-Mur; 1s.30, Schattenburg Castle; 1s.40, Klagenfurt Town Hall; 1s.50, "Rabenhof" Flats, Erdberg, Vienna; 1s.80, Mint Tower, Hall-in-Tyrol; 2s. (1309) Christkindl Church; 2s. (1310) Dragon Fountain, Klagenfurt; 2s.20, Beethoven's House, Heiligenstadt, Vienna; 2s.50, Danube Bridge, Linz; 3s. "Swiss Portal", Imperial Palace, Vienna; 3s.40, Stein Gate, Krems-on-the-Danube; 3s.50, Esterhazy Palace, Eisenstadt; 4s. Vienna Gate, Hainburg; 4s.50, Schwechat Airport; 5s.50, Chur Gate, Feldkirch; 6s. Graz Town Hall; 6s.40, "Golden Roof", Innsbruck; 8s. Steyr Town Hall. 22 × 28½ mm: 10s. Heidenreichstein Castle. 28½ × 37½ mm: 20s. Melk Abbey.

238 Post Office, Linz

1957. Stamp Day.
1327 **238** 1s.+25g. green . . . . . 2·50 2·50

239 Badgastein

1958. International Alpine Ski Championships, Badgastein.
1328 **239** 1s.50 blue 25 20

240 Vickers Viscount 800

241 Mother and Child

1958. Austrian Airlines Inaugural Flight, Vienna–London.
1329 **240** 4s. red 60 30

1958. Mothers' Day.
1330 **241** 1s.50 blue 25 20

242 Walther von der Vogelweide (after 12th-century manuscript)

243 Dr. O. Redlich

1958. 3rd Austrian Choir Festival, Vienna.
1331 **242** 1s.50 multicoloured . . . 25 20

1958. Birth Cent of Dr. Oswald Redlich (historian).
1332 **243** 2s.40 blue 55 50

1958. 40th Anniv of Republic. As T **175** but inscr "40 JAHRE".
1333 **175** 1s.50 green 60 60

244 Post Office, Kitzbuhel

1958. Stamp Day.
1334 **244** 2s.40+60g. blue 80 80

245 "E" building on Map of Europe

246 Monopoly Emblem and Cigars

1959. Europa.
1335 **245** 2s.40 green 50 35

1959. 175th Anniv of Austrian Tobacco Monopoly.
1336 **246** 2s.40 brown 40 30

247 Archduke Johann

248 Western Capercailie

1959. Death Cent of Archduke Johann of Austria.
1337 **247** 1s.50 green 35 25

1959. International Hunting Congress, Vienna.
1338 **248** 1s. purple 35 15
1339 – 1s.50 blue (Roebuck) . . 50 15
1340 – 2s.40 grn (Wild boar) . . 75 85
1341 – 3s.50 brown (Red deer family) 50 45

249 Haydn

250 Tyrolean Eagle

1959. 150th Death Anniv of Haydn.
1342 **249** 1s.50 purple 45 25

1959. 150th Anniv of Tyrolese Rising.
1343 **250** 1s.50 red 25 20

251 Microwave Transmitting Aerial, Zugspitze

252 Handball Player

1959. Inaug of Austrian Microwave Network.
1344 **251** 2s.40 blue 40 25

1959. Sports.
1345 – 1s. violet 25 20
1346 **252** 1s.50 green 60 25
1347 – 1s.80 red 50 30
1348 – 2s. purple 30 30
1349 – 2s.20 blue 25 20
DESIGNS: 1s. Runner; 1s.80, Gymnast; 2s. Hurdling; 2s.20, Hammer thrower.

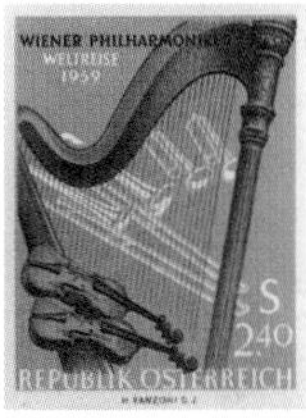

253 Orchestral Instruments

254 Roman Coach

1959. Vienna Philharmonic Orchestra's World Tour.
1350 **253** 2s.40 black and blue . . 40 30

1959. Stamp Day.
1351 **254** 2s.40+60g. blk & mve . . 60 60

255 Refugees

256 Pres. Adolf Scharf

1960. World Refugee Year.
1352 **255** 3s. turquoise 55 40

1960. President's 70th Birthday.
1353 **256** 1s.50 green 50 25

257 Youth Hostellers

258 Dr. Eiselsberg

1960. Youth Hostels Movement.
1354 **257** 1s. red 25 20

1960. Birth Cent of Dr. Anton Eiselsberg (surgeon).
1355 **258** 1s.50 sepia and cream . . 55 25

259 Gustav Mahler

260 Jakob Prandtauer

1960. Birth Centenary of Gustav Mahler (composer).
1356 **259** 1s.50 brown 55 25

1960. 300th Birth Anniv of Jakob Prandtauer (architect).
1357 **260** 1s.50 brown 55 25

261 Grossglockner Highway

262 Ionic Capital

1960. 25th Anniv of Grossglockner Alpine Highway.
1358 **261** 1s.80 blue 60 45

1960. Europa.
1359 **262** 3s. black . . . . 1·40 1·00

263 Griffen, Carinthia

1960. 40th Anniv of Carinthian Plebiscite.
1360 **263** 1s.50 green 35 25

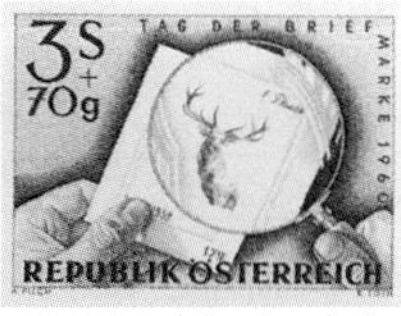

264 Examining Proof of Engraved Stamp

265 "Freedom"

1960. Stamp Day.
1361 **264** 3s.+70g. brown 80 80

1961. Austrian Freedom Martyrs' Commem.
1362 **265** 1s.50 red 25 20

266 Hansa Brandenburg C-1

267 Transport and Multi-unit Electric Train

1961. "LUPOSTA" Exhibition, Vienna, and 1st Austrian Airmail Service Commemoration.
1363 **266** 5s. blue 65 45

1961. European Transport Ministers' Meeting.
1364 **267** 3s. olive and red 45 40

268 "Mower in the Alps" (Detail, A. Egger-Lienz)

269 Observatory on Sonnblick Mountain

1961. Centenary of Kunstlerhaus, Vienna. Inscr as in T **268**.
1365 **268** 1s. purple and brown . . 15 15
1366 – 1s.50 lilac and brown . . 20 25
1367 – 3s. green and brown . . 80 75
1368 – 5s. violet and brown . . 70 60
PAINTINGS: 1s.50, "The Kiss" (after A. von Pettenkofen). 3s. "Portrait of a Girl" (after A. Romako). 5s. "The Triumph of Ariadne" (detail of Ariadne, after Hans Makart).

1961. 75th Anniv of Sonnblick Meteorological Observatory.
1369 **269** 1s.80 blue 35 30

270 Lavanttaler Colliery

271 Mercury

1961. 15th Anniv of Nationalized Industries. Inscr "JAHRE VERSTAATLICHTE UNTERNEHMUNGEN".
1370 **270** 1s. black 15 15
1371 – 1s.50 green 25 25
1372 – 1s.80 red 60 50
1373 – 3s. mauve 80 50
1374 – 5s. blue . . . . 1·25 75
DESIGNS: 1s.50, Turbine; 1s.80, Industrial plant; 3s. Steelworks, Linz; 5s. Oil refinery, Schwechat.

1961. World Bank Congress, Vienna.
1375 **271** 3s. black 50 40

272 Arms of Burgenland

273 Liszt

1961. 40th Anniv of Burgenland.
1376 **272** 1s.50 red, yellow & sepia 30 20

1961. 150th Birth Anniv of Franz Liszt (composer).
1377 **273** 3s. brown 50 40

274 Rust Post Office

1961. Stamp Day.
1378 **274** 3s.+70g. green 70 75

275 Court of Accounts

1961. Bicentenary of Court of Accounts.
1379 **275** 1s. sepia 25 20

276 Glockner-Kaprun Power Station

1962. 15th Anniv of Electric Power Nationalization. Inscr as in T **276**.
1380 **276** 1s. blue 20 15
1381 – 1s.50 purple 25 25
1382 – 1s.80 green 90 65
1383 – 3s. brown 45 40
1384 – 4s. red 50 40
1385 – 6s.40 black . . . . . . 1·40 1·90
DESIGNS: 1s.50, Ybbs-Persenbeug (Danube); 1s.80, Luner See; 3s. Grossraming (Enns River); 4s. Bisamberg Transformer Station; 6s.40, St. Andra Power Stations.

1962. Death Cent of Johann Nestroy (playwright). Portrait as T **187**.
1386 1s. violet 20 15

277 F. Gauermann

278 Scout Badge and Handclasp

1962. Death Cent of Friedrich Gauermann (painter).
1387 **277** 1s.50 blue 20 20

1962. 50th Anniv of Austrian Scout Movement.
1388 **278** 1s.50 green 45 25

279 Forest and Lake

1962. "The Austrian Forest".
1389 **279** 1s. grey 20 20
1390 – 1s.50 brown 45 35
1391 – 3s. myrtle . . . . 1·40 95
DESIGNS: 1s.50, Deciduous forest; 3s. Fir and larch forest.

280 Electric Locomotive and Steam Locomotive "Austria" (1837)

1962. 125th Anniv of Austrian Railways.
1392 **280** 3s. black and buff . . . 90 75

281 Engraving Die

282 Postal Officials of 1863

1962. Stamp Day.
1393 **281** 3s.+70g. violet . . . . . 1·25 1·10

1963. Centenary of Paris Postal Conference.
1394 **282** 3s. sepia and yellow . . 70 55

283 Hermann Bahr

284 St. Florian (statue)

1963. Birth Centenary of Hermann Bahr (writer).
1395 **283** 1s.50 sepia and blue . . 25 15

1963. Cent of Austrian Voluntary Fire Brigade.
1396 **284** 1s.50 black and pink . . 60 40

285 Flag and Emblem

1963. 5th Austrian Trade Unions Federation Congress.
1397 **285** 1s.50 red, sepia & grey 25 20

286 Crests of Tyrol and Austria

1963. 600th Anniv of Tyrol as an Austrian Province.
1398 **286** 1s.50 multicoloured . . . 25 20

287 Prince Eugene of Savoy

288 Centenary Emblem

1963. Birth Tercent of Prince Eugene of Savoy.
1399 **287** 1s.50 violet 25 20

1963. Centenary of Red Cross.
1400 **288** 3s. silver, red and black 50 40

289 Skiing (slalom)

1963. Winter Olympic Games, Innsbruck, 1964. Centres black; inscr gold; background colours given.
1401 **289** 1s. grey 15 15
1402 – 1s.20 blue 15 20
1403 – 1s.50 grey 15 20
1404 – 1s.80 purple 25 25
1405 – 2s.20 green 85 70
1406 – 3s. slate 40 30
1407 – 4s. blue . . . . 1·10 80
DESIGNS: 1s.20, Skiing (biathlon); 1s.50, Ski jumping; 1s.80, Figure skating; 2s.20, Ice hockey; 3s. Tobogganing; 4s. Bobsleighing.

290 Vienna "101" P.O. and Railway Shed

291 "The Holy Family" (Josef Stammel)

1963. Stamp Day.
1408 **290** 3s.+70g. black & drab 65 70

1963. Christmas.
1409 **291** 2s. green 40 20

292 Nasturtium

1964. Int Horticultural Exn, Vienna. Mult.
1410 1s. Type **292** 15 15
1411 1s.50 Peony 15 15
1412 1s.80 Clematis 25 20
1413 2s.20 Dahlia 60 50
1414 3s. Convolvulus 45 25
1415 4s. Mallow 70 60

293 Gothic Statue and Stained-glass Window

1964. Romanesque Art Exhibition, Vienna.
1416 **293** 1s.50 blue and black . . 25 30

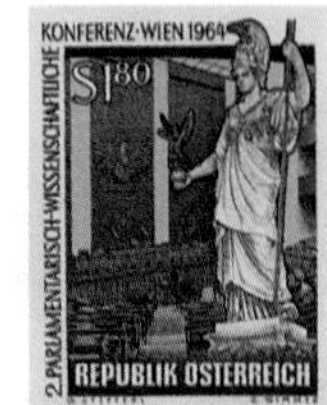

294 Pallas Athene and Interior of Assembly Hall, Parliament Building

1964. 2nd Parliamentary and Scientific Conference, Vienna.
1417 **294** 1s.80 [illegible]

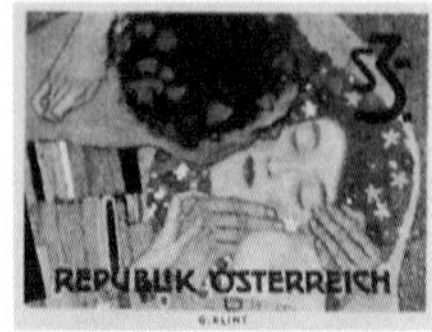

295 "The Kiss" (Gustav Klimt)

1964. Re-opening of "Viennese Secession" Exn Hall.
1418 **295** 3s. multicoloured 50 40

296 "Comforting the Sick"

1964. 350th Anniv of Order of Brothers of Mercy in Austria.
1419 **296** 1s.50 blue 25 20

297 "Bringing News of the Victory at Kunersdorf" (Bellotto)

1964. 15th U.P.U. Congress, Vienna. Paintings.
1420 **297** 1s. purple 15 15
1421 – 1s.20 brown 25 20
1422 – 1s.50 blue 25 15
1423 – 1s.80 violet 25 25
1424 – 2s.20 black 45 35
1425 – 3s. purple 35 30
1426 – 4s. green 70 60
1427 – 6s.40 purple . . . . . 1·60 1·40
PAINTINGS: 1s.20, "Changing Horses" (Hormann); 1s.50, "The Wedding Trip" (Schwind); 1s.80, "Postboys returning Home" (Raffalt); 2s.20, "The Vienna Mail Coach" (Klein); 3s. "Changing Horses" (Gauermann); 4s. "Postal Tracked-vehicle in Mountain Village" (Pilch); 6s.40, "Saalbach Post Office and Post-bus" (Pilch).

298 Vienna, from the Hochhaus (N.)

299 "Workers"

1964. "WIPA" Stamp Exhibition, Vienna (1965) (1st issue). Multicoloured.
1428 1s.50+30g. Type **298** . . . 25 25
1429 1s.50+30g. N.E. 25 25
1430 1s.50+30g. E. 25 25
1431 1s.50+30g. S.E. 25 25
1432 1s.50+30g. S. 25 25
1433 1s.50+30g. S.W. 25 25
1434 1s.50+30g. W. 25 25
1435 1s.50+30g. N.W. 25 25
The designs show a panoramic view of Vienna, looking to different points of compass (indicated on stamps). The inscription reads "Vienna welcomes you to WIPA 1965".
See also Nos. 1447/52.

1964. Centenary of Austrian Workers' Movement.
1436 **299** 1s. black 20 20

300 Europa "Flower"

301 Radio Receiver Dial

1964. Europa.
1437 **300** 3s. blue 60 40

1964. 40th Anniv of Austrian Broadcasting Service.
1438 **301** 1s. sepia and red 20 20

302 Old Printing Press

1964. 6th International Graphical Federation Congress, Vienna.
1439 **302** 1s.50 black and drab . . 25 20

303 Post-bus Station, St. Gilgen

1964. Stamp Day.
1440 **303** 3s.+70g. multicoloured 60 50

304 Dr. Adolf Scharf

305 "Reconstruction"

1965. Pres. Scharf Commemoration.
1441 **304** 1s.50 blue and black . . 25 25

1965. "20 Years of Reconstruction".
1442 **305** 1s.80 lake 25 25

306 University Seal, 1365

307 "St. George" (after engraving by Altdorfer)

1965. 600th Anniv of Vienna University.
1443 **306** 3s. red and gold 40 30

1965. Danubian Art.
1444 **307** 1s.80 blue 30 25

308 I.T.U. Emblem, Morse Key and T.V. Aerial

309 F. Raimund

1965. Centenary of I.T.U.
1445 **308** 3s. violet 40 30

1965. 175th Birth Anniv of Ferdinand Raimund (actor and playwright).
1446 **309** 3s. purple 40 20

310 Egyptian Hieroglyphs on Papyrus

311 Gymnasts with Wands

1965. "WIPA" Stamp Exhibition, Vienna (2nd issue). "Development of the Letter".
1447 **310** 1s.50+40g. black and pink 25 25
1448 – 1s.80+50g. black and yellow 25 25
1449 – 2s.20+60g. black and lilac 65 65
1450 – 3s.+80g. black & yell . . 35 40
1451 – 4s.+1s. black & blue . . 70 75
1452 – 5s.+1s.20 black & grn . . 70 80
DESIGNS: 1s.80, Cuneiform writing; 2s.20, Latin; 3c. Ancient letter and seal; 4s.19th-century letter; 5s. Typewriter.

1965. 4th Gymnaestrada, Vienna.
1453 **311** 1s.50 black and blue . . 30 25
1454 – 3s. black and brown . . 45 35
DESIGNS: 3s. Girls exercising with tambourines.

312 Dr. I. Semmelweis

313 F. G. Waldmuller (self-portrait)

1965. Death Cent of Ignaz Semmelweis (physician).
1455 **312** 1s.50 lilac 25 15

1965. Death Cent of F. G. Waldmuller (painter).
1456 **313** 3s. black 45 30

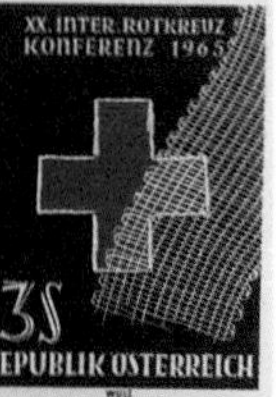

314 Red Cross and Gauze

315 Flag and Crowned Eagle

1965. Red Cross Conference, Vienna.
1457 **314** 3s. red and black 40 25

1965. 50th Anniv of Austrian Towns Union.
1458 **315** 1s.50 multicoloured . . . 20 15

316 Austrian Flag, U. N. Emblem and Headquarters

1965. 10th Anniv of Austria's Membership of U.N.O.
1459 **316** 3s. sepia, red and blue 40 30

317 University Building

318 Bertha von Suttner

1965. 150th Anniv of University of Technology, Vienna.
1460 **317** 1s.50 violet 30 15

1965. 60th Anniv of Nobel Peace Prize Award to Bertha von Suttner (writer).
1461 **318** 1s.50 black 30 20

319 Postman delivering Mail

1965. Stamp Day.
1462 **319** 3s.+70g. green 55 55

320 Postal Code Map

1966. Introduction of Postal Code System.
1463 **320** 1s.50 black, red & yell 30 15

321 P.T.T. Headquarters

322 M. Ebner-Eschenbach

1966. Centenary of Austrian Posts and Telegraphs Administration.
1464 **321** 1s.50 black on cream . . 30 20

1966. 50th Death Anniv of Maria Ebner-Eschenbach (writer).
1465 **322** 3s. purple 45 25

323 Big Wheel

324 Josef Hoffmann

1966. Bicentenary of Vienna Prater.
1466 **323** 1s.50 green 30 20

1966. 10th Death Anniv of Josef Hoffmann (architect).
1467 **324** 3s. brown 45 20

325 Bank Emblem

1966. 150th Anniv of Austrian National Bank.
1468 **325** 3s. brown, grn & drab 40 20

326 Arms of Wiener Neustadt

1966. "Wiener Neustadt 1440–93" Art Exhibition.
1469 **326** 1s.50 multicoloured . . . 30 15

327 Puppy

328 Columbine

1966. 120th Anniv of Vienna Animal Protection Society.
1470 **327** 1s.80 black and yellow 30 20

1966. Alpine Flora. Multicoloured.
1471 1s.50 Type **328** 15 15
1472 1s.80 Turk's cap 25 20
1473 2s.20 Wulfenia 45 30
1474 3s. Globe flower 45 35
1475 4s. Orange lily 60 50
1476 5s. Alpine anemone 75 55

329 Fair Building

1966. Wels International Fair.
1477 **329** 3s. blue 45 20

330 Peter Anich

1966. Death Bicent of Peter Anich (cartographer).
1478 **330** 1s.80 black 30 15

331 "Suffering"

1966. 15th International Occupational Health Congress, Vienna.
1479 **331** 3s. black and red 45 20

332 "Eunuchus" by Terence (engraving, Johann Gruninger)

1966. Austrian National Library, Vienna. Mult.
1480 1s.50 Type **332** (Theatre collection) 20 15
1481 1s.80 Detail of title page of Willem Blaeu's atlas (Cartography collection) 25 25
1482 2s.20 "Herrengasse, Vienna" (Anton Stutzinger (Pictures and portraits collection)) 35 30
1483 3s. Illustration from Rene of Anjou's "Livre du Cuer d'Amours Espris" (Manuscripts collection) 35 30

333 Young Girl

1966. Austrian "Save the Children" Fund.
1484 **333** 3s. black and blue . . . 40 20

334 Strawberries

335 16th-century Postman

1966. Fruits. Multicoloured.
1485 50g. Type 334 . . . . 25 10
1486 1s. Grapes 25 15
1487 1s.50 Apple 25 15
1488 1s.80 Blackberries 30 25
1489 2s.20 Apricots 30 25
1490 3s. Cherries 40 25

1966. Stamp Day.
1491 **335** 3s.+70g. multicoloured 50 40

336 Arms of Linz University

337 Skater of 1867

1966. Inauguration of Linz University.
1492 **336** 3s. multicoloured 45 25

1967. Centenary of Vienna Skating Assn.
1493 **337** 3s. indigo and blue . . . 45 30

338 Dancer with Violin

339 Dr. Schonherr

1967. Centenary of "Blue Danube" Waltz.
1494 **338** 3s. purple 45 25

1967. Birth Cent of Dr. Karl Schonherr (poet).
1495 **339** 3s. brown 40 25

340 Ice Hockey Goalkeeper

341 Violin and Organ

1967. World Ice Hockey Championships, Vienna.
1496 **340** 3s. blue and green . . . 45 25

1967. 125th Anniv of Vienna Philharmonic Orchestra.
1497 **341** 3s.50 blue 50 30

342 "Mother and Children" (aquarelle, Peter Fendi)

1967. Mother's Day.
1498 **342** 2s. multicoloured 30 20

343 "Madonna" (Gothic wood-carving)

1967. "Gothic Art in Austria" Exhibition, Krems.
1499 **343** 3s. green 45 20

344 Jewelled Cross

345 "The White Swan" (from Kokoschkas tapestry "Cupid and Psyche")

1967. "Salzburg Treasures" Exhibition, Salzburg Cathedral.
1500 **344** 3s.50 multicoloured . . . 40 25

1967. "Art of the Nibelungen District" Exhibition, Pochlarn.
1501 **345** 2s. multicoloured 25 20

346 Vienna

1967. 10th European Talks, Vienna.
1502 **346** 3s. black and red 45 25

347 Champion Bull

1967. Centenary of Ried Fair.
1503 **347** 2s. purple 25 20

348 Colorado Potato Beetle

1967. 6th Int Plant Protection Congress, Vienna.
1504 **348** 3s. multicoloured 40 20

349 Locomotive No. 671

350 "Christ" (fresco detail)

1967. Centenary of Brenner Railway.
1505 **349** 3s.50 green and brown . . . 50 30

1967. Lambach Frescoes.
1506 **350** 2s. multicoloured 25 20

351 Prater Hall, Vienna

352 Rector's Medallion and Chain

1967. International Trade Fairs Congress, Vienna.
1507 **351** 2s. purple and cream . . 25 20

1967. 275th Anniv of Fine Arts Academy, Vienna.
1508 **352** 2s. brown, yellow & blue 25 20

353 Bible on Rock (from commemorative coin of 1717)

355 Memorial, Vienna

354 Forest Trees

1967. 450th Anniv of the Reformation.
1509 **353** 3s.50 blue 40 35

1967. 100 Years of Austrian University Forestry Studies.
1510 **354** 3s.50 green 55 35

1967. 150th Anniv of Land Registry.
1511 **355** 2s. green 25 20

356 "St. Leopold" (stained-glass window, Heiligenkreuz Monastery)

357 "Music and Art"

1967. Margrave Leopold the Holy.
1512 **356** 1s.80 multicoloured . . . 30 25

1967. 150th Anniv of Academy of Music and Dramatic Art, Vienna.
1513 **357** 3s.50 black and violet . . 50 30

358 St. Mary's Altar, Nonnberg Convent, Salzburg

359 "The Letter-carrier" (from playing-card)

1967. Christmas.
1514 **358** 2s. green 30 20

1967. Stamp Day.
1515 **359** 3s.50+80g. mult 60 50

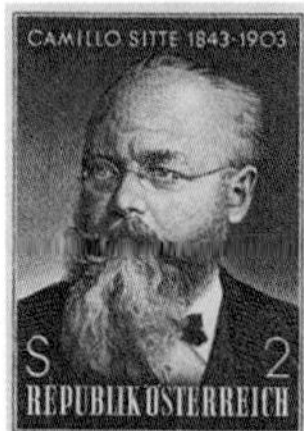

360 Ski Jump, Stadium and Mountains

1968. Winter University Games, Innsbruck.
1516 **360** 2s. blue 30 20

361 C. Sitte

362 Mother and Child

1968. 125th Birth Anniv of Camillo Sitte (architect).
1517 **361** 2s. brown 25 25

1968. Mothers' Day.
1518 **362** 2s. olive 25 25

363 "Veterinary Medicine"

364 Bride with Lace Veil

1968. Bicentenary of Vienna Veterinary College.
1519 **363** 3s.50 gold, pur & drab 40 30

1968. Centenary of Vorarlberg Lace.
1520 **364** 3s.50 blue 45 30

365 Etrich Limousine

1968. "IFA Wien 1968" Airmail Stamp Exhibition, Vienna.
1521 **365** 2s. brown 40 30
1522 – 3s.50 green 65 60
1523 – 5s. blue 85 80
DESIGNS: 3s.50, Sud Aviation Caravelle; 5s. Douglas DC-8.

366 Horse-racing

1968. Centenary of Freudenau Gallop Races.
1524 **366** 3s.50 brown 45 30

367 Landsteiner

368 P. Rosegger

1968. Birth Centenary of Dr. Karl Landsteiner (physician and pathologist).
1525 **367** 3s.50 blue 45 20

1968. 50th Death Anniv of Peter Rosegger (writer).
1526 **368** 2s. green 25 20

369 A. Kauffmann (self-portrait)

370 Statue of Young Man (Helenenberg site)

1968. Exhibition of Angelica Kauffmann's Paintings, Bregenz.
1527 **369** 2s. violet 30 25

1968. Magdalensberg Excavations, Carinthia.
1528 **370** 2s. black and green . . . 25 20

371 "The Bishop" (Romanesque carving)

372 K. Moser

1968. 750th Anniv of Graz-Seckau Diocese.
1529 **371** 2s. grey 25 20

1968. 50th Death Anniv of Koloman Moser (graphic artist).
1530 **372** 2s. brown and red . . . 25 20

373 Human Rights Emblem

374 Arms and Provincial Shields

1968. Human Rights Year.
1531 **373** 1s.50 red, green & grey 45 25

1968. 50th Anniv of Republic. Multicoloured.
1532 2s. Type **374** 35 30
1533 2s. Karl Renner (first President of Second Republic) 35 30
1534 2s. First Article of Constitution 35 30

375 Crib, Oberndorf, Salzburg

376 Mercury

1968. 150th Anniv of "Silent Night, Holy Night" (carol).
1535 **375** 2s. green 30 20

1968. Stamp Day.
1536 **376** 3s.50+80g. green 55 55

377 Fresco (Troger), Melk Monastery

378 "Madonna and Child"

1968. Baroque Frescoes. Designs showing frescoes in locations given. Multicoloured.
1537 2s. Type **377** 35 35
1538 2s. Altenburg Monastery . . 35 35
1539 2s. Rohrenbach-Greillenstein 35 35
1540 2s. Ebenfurth Castle 35 35
1541 2s. Halbthurn Castle 35 35
1542 2s. Maria Treu Church, Vienna 35 35
Nos. 1537/9 are the work of Anton Troger and Nos. 1540/2 that of Franz Maulbertsch.

1969. 500th Anniv of Vienna Diocese. Statues in St. Stephen's Cathedral, Vienna.
1543 **378** 2s. blue 35 35
1544 – 2s. grey 35 35
1545 – 2s. green 35 35
1546 – 2s. purple 35 35
1547 – 2s. black 35 35
1548 – 2s. brown 35 35
DESIGNS: No. 1544, "St. Christopher"; No. 1545, "St. George"; No. 1546, "St. Paul"; No. 1547, "St. Sebastian"; No. 1548, "St. Stephen".

379 Parliament Building, Vienna

1969. Interparliamentary Union Meeting, Vienna.
1549 **379** 2s. green 20 20

380 Colonnade

1969. Europa.
1550 **380** 2s. multicoloured 30 25

381 "Council Members"

382 Soldiers

1969. 20th Anniv of Council of Europe.
1551 **381** 3s.50 multicoloured . . . 50 40

1969. Austrian Armed Forces.
1552 **382** 2s. brown and red . . . 25 20

384 Maximilian's Armour

385 Viennese "Privilege" Seal

1969. "Maximilian I" Exhibition, Innsbruck.
1554 **384** 2s. black 25 20

1969. 19th International Union of Local Authorities Congress, Vienna.
1555 **385** 2s. red, brown & ochre 20 20

386 Young Girl
387 Hands clasping Spanner

1969. 20th Anniv of "SOS" Children's Villages Movement.
1556 **386** 2s. brown and green . . 20 20

1969. 50th Anniv of Int Labour Organization.
1557 **387** 2s. green 20 20

388 Austrian "Flag" encircling Globe
389 "El Cid killing a Bull" (Goya)

1969. "Austrians Living Abroad" Year.
1558 **388** 3s.50 red and green . . . 40 25

1969. Bicentenary of Albertina Art Collection, Vienna. Multicoloured.
1559 2s. Type **389** 35 30
1560 2s. "Young Hare" (Durer) 35 30
1561 2s. "Madonna with Pomegranate" (Raphael) 35 30
1562 2s. "The Painter and the Amateur" (Bruegel) . . . 35 30
1563 2s. "Rubens's Son, Nicholas" (Rubens) . . . 35 30
1564 2s. "Self-portrait" (Rembrandt) 35 30
1565 2s. "Madame de Pompadour" (detail, Guerin) 35 30
1566 2s. "The Artist's Wife" (Schiele) 35 30

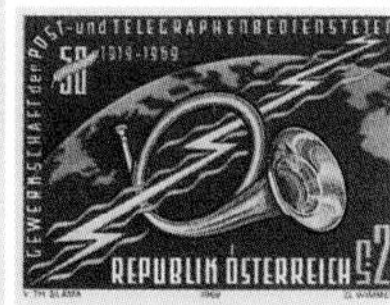

390 Pres. Jonas
391 Posthorn and Lightning over Globe

1969. Pres. Franz Jonas's 70th Birthday.
1567 **390** 2s. blue and grey 25 20

1969. 50th Anniv of Post and Telegraph Employees Union.
1568 **391** 2s. multicoloured 25 20

392 Savings Bank (c. 1450)
393 "The Madonna" (Egger-Lienz)

1969. 150th Anniv of Austrian Savings Bank.
1569 **392** 2s. green and silver . . . 25 20

1969. Christmas.
1570 **393** 2s. purple and yellow . . 25 20

394 Unken, Salzburg, Post-house Sign (after F. Zeller)
395 J. Schoffel

1969. Stamp Day.
1571 **394** 3s.50+80g. black, red and stone 55 50

1970. 60th Death Anniv of Josef Schoffel ("Saviour of the Vienna Woods").
1572 **395** 2s. purple 20 20

396 St. Clement Hofbauer
398 Krimml Waterfalls

397 Chancellor Leopold Figl

1970. 150th Death Anniv of St. Clement Hofbauer (theologian).
1573 **396** 2s. brown and green . . 20 20

1970. 25th Anniv of Austrian Republic.
1574 **397** 2s. olive 20 25
1575 – 2s. brown 20 25
DESIGN: No. 1575, Belvedere Castle.

1970. Nature Conservation Year.
1576 **398** 2s. green 55 35

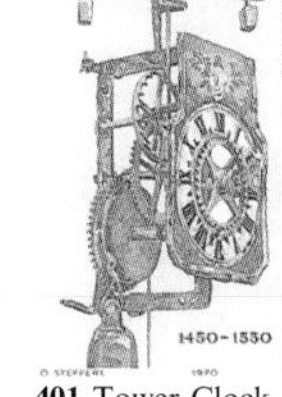

399 Oldest University Seal
401 Tower Clock, 1450–1550

400 "Musikverein" Organ

1970. 300th Anniv of Leopold Franz University, Innsbruck.
1577 **399** 2s. black and red 25 20

1970. Centenary of "Musikverein" Building.
1578 **400** 2s. purple and gold . . . 30 20

1970. Antique Clocks.
1579 **401** 1s.50 brown and cream 35 25
1580 – 1s.50 green & lt green . . 35 25
1581 – 2s. blue and pale blue . . 35 25
1582 – 2s. red and purple . . . 35 25
1583 – 3s.50 brown and buff . . 60 50
1584 – 3s.50 purple and lilac . . 60 50
DESIGNS: No. 1580, Empire "lyre" clock, 1790–1815; No. 1581, Pendant ball clock, 1600–50; No. 1582, Pocket-watch and signet, 1800–30; No. 1583, Bracket clock, 1720–60; No. 1584, "Biedermeier" pendulum clock and musical-box, 1820–50.

402 "The Beggar Student" (Millocker)
403 Scene from "The Gipsy Baron" (J. Strauss)

1970. Famous Operettas.
1585 **402** 1s.50 turquoise & green 35 25
1586 – 1s.50 blue and yellow . . 35 25
1587 – 2s. purple and pink . . 45 30
1588 – 2s. brown and green . . 45 30
1589 – 3s.50 blue and light blue 65 65
1590 – 3s.50 blue and buff . . . 65 65
OPERETTAS: No. 1586, "Die Fledermaus" (Johann Strauss the younger); 1587, "A Waltz Dream" (O. Straus); 1588, "The Birdseller" (C. Zeller); 1589, "The Merry Widow" (F. Lehar); 1590, "Two Hearts in Waltz-time" (R. Stoiz).

1970. 25th Anniv of Bregenz Festival.
1591 **403** 3s.50 blue, buff & ult . . 45 30

404 Festival Emblem
405 T. Koschat

1970. 50th Anniv of Salzburg Festival.
1592 **404** 3s.50 multicoloured . . . 45 35

1970. 125th Birth Anniv of Thomas Koschat (composer and poet).
1593 **405** 2s. brown 25 20

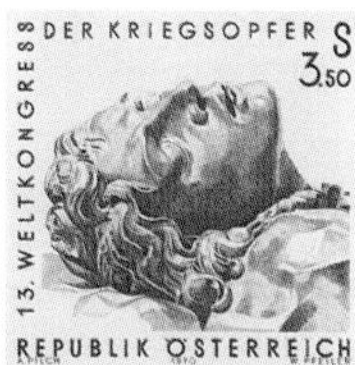

406 "Head of St. John", from sculpture "Mount of Olives", Ried Church (attributed to T. Schwanthaler)

1970. 13th World Veterans Federation General Assembly.
1594 **406** 3s.50 sepia 45 30

407 Climbers and Mountains

1970. "Walking and Mountaineering".
1595 **407** 2s. blue and mauve . . . 25 20

408 A. Cossmann

1970. Birth Cent of Alfred Cossmann (engraver).
1596 **408** 2s. brown 25 20

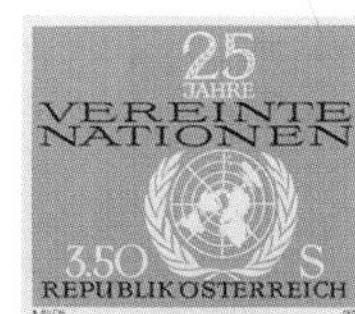

409 Arms of Carinthia
410 U.N. Emblem

1970. 50th Anniv of Carinthian Plebiscite.
1597 **409** 2s. multicoloured 25 20

1970. 25th Anniv of United Nations.
1598 **410** 3s.50 blue and black . . 45 30

411 "Adoration of the Shepherds" (carving, Garsten Monastery)

1970. Christmas.
1599 **411** 2s. blue 25 20

412 Saddle, Harness and Posthorn
413 Pres. K. Renner

1970. Stamp Day.
1600 **412** 3s.50+80g. black, yellow and grey 60 55

1970. Birth Centenary of Pres. Renner.
1601 **413** 2s. purple 20 20

414 Beethoven (after painting by Waldmuller)
415 E. Handel-Mazzetti

1970. Birth Bicentenary of Beethoven.
1602 **414** 3s.50 black and stone . . 50 40

1971. Birth Centenary of Enrica Handel-Mazzetti (novelist).
1603 **415** 2s. brown 25 20

416 "Safety for Children"

1971. Road Safety.
1604 **416** 2s. multicoloured 25 20

417 Florentine Bowl, c. 1580

1971. Austrian Art Treasures (1st series). Sculpture and Applied Art.
1605 **417** 1s.50 green and grey . . 30 25
1606 – 2s. purple and grey . . . 30 25
1607 – 3s.50 yellow, brn & grey 70 60
DESIGNS: 2s. Ivory equestrian statuette of Joseph I, 1693 (Matthias Steinle); 3s.50, Salt-cellar, c. 1570 (Cellini).
See also Nos. 1609/11, 1632/4 and 1651/3.

418 Shield of Trade Association
419 "Jacopo de Strada" (Titian)

1971. 23rd International Chamber of Commerce Congress, Vienna.
1608 **418** 3s.50 multicoloured . . . 40 25

1971. Austrian Art Treasures (2nd series).
1609 **419** 1s.50 purple 30 25
1610 – 2s. black 30 25
1611 – 3s.50 brown 60 65
PAINTINGS: 2s. "The Village Feast" (Brueghel); 3s.50, "Young Venetian Woman" (Durer).

420 Notary's Seal **421** "St. Matthew" (altar sculpture)

1971. Austrian Notarial Statute Cent Congress.
1612 **420** 3s.50 purple and brown . . . 45 35

1971. "Krems Millennium of Art" Exhibition.
1613 **421** 2s. brown and purple . . 20 20

422 Dr. A. Neilreich **423** Singer with Lyre

1971. Death Cent of Dr. August Neilreich (botanist).
1614 **422** 2s. brown 20 20

1971. International Choir Festival, Vienna.
1615 **423** 4s. blue, gold & lt blue 60 40

424 Arms of Kitzbuhel

1971. 700th Anniv of Kitzbuhel.
1616 **424** 2s.50 multicoloured . . . 30 20

425 Stock Exchange Building

1971. Bicentenary of Vienna Stock Exchange.
1617 **425** 4s. brown 50 45

426 Old and New Fair Halls **427** O.G.B. Emblem

1971. "50 Years of Vienna International Fairs".
1618 **426** 2s.50 purple 35 20

1971. 25th Anniv of Austrian Trade Unions Federation.
1619 **427** 2s. multicoloured 25 20

428 Arms and Insignia **429** "Marcus" Veteran Car

1971. 50th Anniv of Burgenland Province.
1620 **428** 4s. multicoloured 25 20

1971. 75th Anniv of Austrian Automobile, Motor Cycle and Touring Club.
1621 **429** 4s. black and green . . . 50 40

430 Europa Bridge, Brenner Highway **431** Iron-ore Workings, Erzberg

1971. Inauguration of Brenner Highway.
1622 **430** 4s. blue 50 40

1971. 25 Years of Nationalized Industries.
1623 **431** 1s.50 brown 25 25
1624 – 2s. blue 30 25
1625 – 4s. green 70 55
DESIGNS: 2s. Nitrogen Works, Linz; 4s. Iron and Steel works, Linz.

432 Electric Train on the Semmering Line **433** E. Tschermak-Seysenegg

1971. Railway Anniversaries.
1626 **432** 2s. purple 35 25

1971. Birth Centenary of Dr. E. Tshermak-Seysenegg (biologist).
1627 **433** 2s. purple and grey . . . 25 20

434 Angling **435** "The Infant Jesus as Saviour" (from miniature by Durer)

1971. Sports.
1628 **434** 2s. brown 25 20

1971. Christmas.
1629 **435** 2s. multicoloured 30 20

436 "50 Years"

1971. 50th Anniv of Austrian Philatelic Clubs Association.
1630 **436** 4s.+1s.50 pur & gold . . 75 70

437 Franz Grillparzer (from miniature by Daffinger) **438** Roman Fountain, Friesach

1972. Death Centenary of Grillparzer (dramatist).
1631 **437** 2s. black, brown & stone 30 20

1972. Austrian Art Treasures (3rd series). Fountains.
1632 **438** 1s.50 purple 25 25
1633 – 2s. brown 35 25
1634 – 2s.50 green 50 50
DESIGNS: 2s. Lead Fountain, Heiligenkreuz Abbey; 2s.50. Leopold Fountain, Innsbruck.

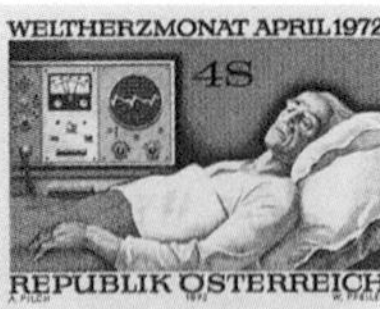

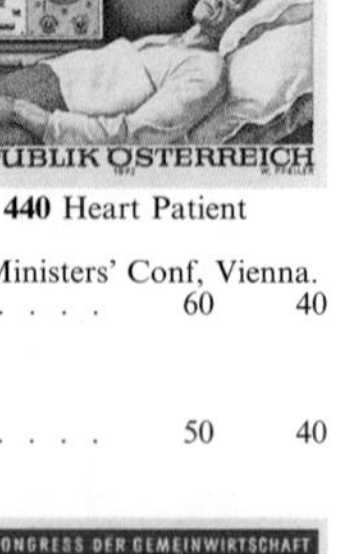

439 Hofburg Palace **440** Heart Patient

1972. 4th European Postal Ministers' Conf, Vienna.
1635 **439** 4s. violet 60 40

1972. World Heart Month.
1636 **440** 4s. brown 50 40

441 "Woman's Head" (sculpture, Gurk Cathedral) **442** Vienna Town Hall and Congress Emblem

1972. 900th Anniv of Gurk Diocese.
1637 **441** 2s. purple and gold . . . 25 20

1972. 9th International Public and Co-operative Economy Congress, Vienna.
1638 **442** 4s. black, red and yellow 50 35

443 Lienz–Pelos Pylon Line

1972. 25th Anniv of Electric Power Nationalization.
1639 **443** 70g. violet and grey . . . 15 15
1640 – 2s.50 brown and grey . . 30 30
1641 – 4s. blue and grey 60 50
DESIGNS: 2s.50, Vienna-Semmering Power Station; 4s. Zemm Dam and lake.

444 Runner with Torch **445** "Hermes" (C. Laib)

1972. Passage of the Olympic Torch through Austria.
1642 **444** 2s. brown and red . . . 25 20

1972. "Late Gothic Art" Exhibition, Salzburg.
1643 **445** 2s. purple 25 20

446 Pears **448** University Arms

1972. Amateur Gardeners' Congress, Vienna.
1644 **446** 2s.50 multicoloured . . . 30 20

1972. Cent of University of Agriculture, Vienna.
1646 **448** 2s. multicoloured 25 20

449 Old University Buildings (after F. Danreiter) **450** C. M. Ziehrer

1972. 350th Anniv of Paris Lodron University, Salzburg.
1647 **449** 4s. brown 50 30

1972. 50th Death Anniv of Carl M. Ziehrer (composer and conductor).
1648 **450** 2s. red 25 20

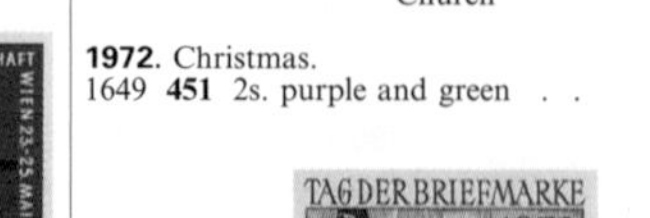

451 "Virgin and Child", Inzersdorf Church

1972. Christmas.
1649 **451** 2s. purple and green . . 25 20

452 18th-century Viennese Postman

1972. Stamp Day.
1650 **452** 4s.+1s. green 65 70

453 State Sledge of Maria Theresa

1972. Austrian Art Treasures (4th series). Carriages from the Imperial Coach House.
1651 **453** 1s.50 brown and bistre . . 25 20
1652 – 2s. green and bistre . . . 30 25
1653 – 2s.50 purple and bistre . . 50 45
DESIGNS: 2s. Coronation landau; 2s.50, Hapsburg State Coach.

454 Telephone Network **456** A. Petzold

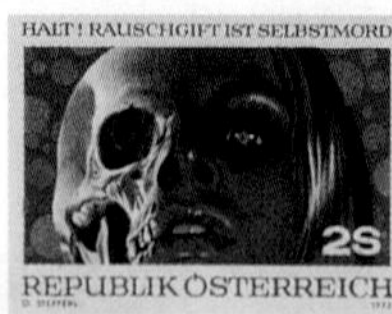

455 "Drug Addict"

1972. Completion of Austrian Telephone System Automation.
1654 **454** 2s. black and yellow . . 25 30

1973. Campaign against Drug Abuse.
1655 **455** 2s. multicoloured 35 30

1973. 50th Death Anniv of Alfons Petzold (writer).
1656 **456** 2s. purple 40 25

457 Korner **458** Douglas DC-9-80 Super Eighty

1973. Birth Centenary of Pres. Theodor Korner (President, 1951–57).
1657 **457** 2s. purple and grey . . . 25 20

1973. Austrian Aviation Anniversaries.
1658 **458** 2s. blue and red 30 20

459 Otto Loewi

460 "Succour"

1973. Birth Cent of Otto Loewi (pharmacologist).
1659 **459** 4s. violet 45 35

1973. 25th Anniv of National Federation of Austrian Social Insurance Institutes.
1660 **460** 2s. blue 25 20

461 Telephone Dial within Posthorn

463 Military Pentathlon

462 Fair Emblem

1973. Europa.
1661 **461** 2s.50 black, yell & orge 40 25

1973. 25th Dornbirn Fair.
1662 **462** 2s. multicoloured 25 25

1973. 25th Anniv of International Military Sports Council and 23rd Military Pentathlon Championships, Wiener Neustadt.
1663 **463** 4s. green 45 40

464 Leo Slezak

465 Main Entrance, Hofburg Palace

1973. Birth Centenary of Leo Slezak (operatic tenor).
1664 **464** 4s. brown 50 40

1973. 39th International Statistical Institute's Congress, Vienna.
1665 **465** 2s. brown, red and grey 25 20

466 "Admiral Tegetthof Icebound" (J. Payer)

467 I.U.L.C.S. Arms

1973. Centenary of Discovery of Franz Josef Land.
1666 **466** 2s.50 green 35 20

1973. 13th International Union of Leather Chemists' Societies Congress, Vienna.
1667 **467** 4s. multicoloured 45 40

468 "Academy of Sciences, Vienna" (B. Bellotto)

469 Max Reinhardt

1973. Cent of Int Meteorological Organization.
1668 **468** 2s.50 violet 35 25

1973. Birth Centenary of Max Reinhardt (theatrical director).
1669 **469** 2s. purple 25 20

470 F. Hanusch

1973. 50th Death Anniv of Ferdinand Hanusch (politician).
1670 **470** 2s. purple 25 20

471 Light Harness Racing

1973. Centenary of Vienna Trotting Assn.
1671 **471** 2s. green 25 20

472 Radio Operator

1973. 50th Anniv of International Criminal Police Organization (Interpol).
1672 **472** 4s. violet 50 40

473 Petzval Camera Lens

1973. "Europhot" (professional photographers) Congress, Vienna.
1673 **473** 2s.50 multicoloured . . . 35 30

474 Aqueduct, Hollen Valley

1973. Centenary of Vienna's 1st Mountain-spring Aqueduct.
1674 **474** 2s. brown, red & blue . . 25 20

475 Almsee

476 "The Nativity" (stained-glass window, St. Erhard Church, Bretenau)

1973. Views. (a) Size 23 × 29 mm.
1674a – 20g. blue and light blue 35 20
1675 – 50g. green & lt green 20 15
1676 – 1s. sepia and brown . . 30 15
1677 – 1s.50 purple and pink 30 15
1678 – 2s. indigo and blue . . 30 15
1679 – 2s.50 deep lilac & lilac 45 15
1680 – 3s. ultramarine & blue 45 15
1680a – 3s.50 brown & orange 55 30
1681 **475** 4s. violet and lilac . . . 65 15
1681a – 4s.20 black and grey . . 55 50
1682 – 4s.50 dp green & green 70 15
1683 – 5s. violet and lilac . . . 75 15
1683a – 5s.50 blue and violet . . 85 35
1683b – 5s.60 olive and green 85 90
1684 – 6s. lilac and pink . . . 85 15
1684a – 6s.50 blue & turquoise 1·00 25
1685 – 7s. deep green & green 1·00 15
1685a – 7s.50 purple & mauve 1·25 35
1686 – 8s. brown and pink . . 1·40 30

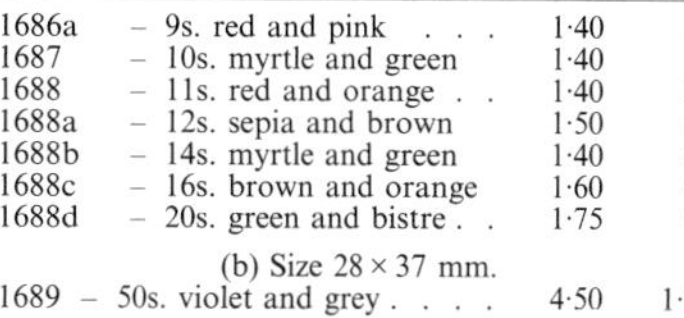
1686a – 9s. red and pink . . . 1·40 50
1687 – 10s. myrtle and green 1·40 15
1688 – 11s. red and orange . . 1·40 30
1688a – 12s. sepia and brown 1·50 45
1688b – 14s. myrtle and green 1·40 40
1688c – 16s. brown and orange 1·60 40
1688d – 20s. green and bistre . . 1·75 60

(b) Size 28 × 37 mm.
1689 – 50s. violet and grey . . . . 4·50 1·90

(c) Size 17 × 20 mm.
1690 – 3s. ultramarine and blue 45 20

DESIGNS: 20g. Friedstadt Keep, Muhlviertel; 50g. Zillertal; 1s. Kahlenbergerdorf, Vienna; 1s.50, Bludenz; 2s. Old bridge, Finstermunz; 2s.50, Murau, Styria; 3s. Bischofsmutze and Alpine farm; 3s.50, Osterkirche, Oberwart; 4s.20, Hirschegg, Kleinwalsertal; 4s.50, Windmill, Retz; 5s. Ruins of Aggstein Castle; 5s.50, Peace Chapel, Stoderzinken; 5s.60, Riezlern, Kleinwalsertal; 6s. Lindauer Hut, Ratikon Massif; 6s.50, Villach, Carinthia; 7s. Falkenstein Castle; 7s.50, Hohensalzburg Fortress; 8s. Votive column, Reiteregg, Styria; 9s. Asten valley; 10s. Neusiedlersee; 11s. Enns; 12s. Kufstein Fortress; 14s. Weiszsee, Salzburg; 16s. Bad Tatzmannsdorf open-air museum; 20s. Myra Falls, Muggendorf; 50s. Hofburg, Vienna.

1973. Christmas.
1691 **476** 2s. multicoloured 55 20

477 "Archangel Gabriel" (carving by Lorenz Luchsperger)

478 Dr. Fritz Pregl

1973. Stamp Day.
1692 **477** 4s.+1s. purple 45 50

1973. 50th Anniv of Award of Nobel Prize for Chemistry to Fritz Pregl.
1693 **478** 4s. blue 45 40

479 Telex Machine and Globe

480 Hugo Hofmannsthal

1974. 50th Anniv of Radio Austria.
1694 **479** 2s.50 blue & ultramarine 30 25

1974. Birth Cent of Hugo Hofmannsthal (writer).
1695 **480** 4s. blue 45 35

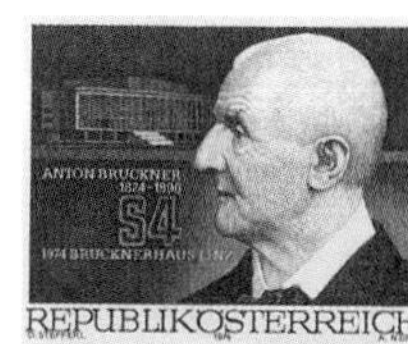
481 Anton Bruckner (composer)

1974. Inaug of Bruckner Memorial Centre, Linz.
1696 **481** 4s. brown 55 45

482 Vegetables

1974. 2nd Int Horticultural Show, Vienna. Mult.
1697 2s. Type **482** 30 25
1698 2s.50 Fruit 35 40
1699 4s. Flowers 65 60

483 Head from Ancient Seal

484 Karl Kraus

1974. 750th Anniv of Judenburg.
1700 **483** 2s. multicoloured 30 25

1974. Birth Centenary of Karl Kraus (poet).
1701 **484** 4s. red 45 40

485 "St. Michael" (wood-carving, Thomas Schwanthaler)

486 "King Arthur" (statue, Innsbruck)

1974. "Sculptures by the Schwanthaler Family" Exhibition, Reichersberg.
1702 **485** 2s.50 green 40 25

1974. Europa.
1703 **486** 2s.50 blue and brown . . 35 20

487 Early De Dion-Bouton Motor-tricycle

489 I.R.U. Emblem

488 Mask of Satyr's Head

1974. 75th Anniv of Austrian Association of Motoring, Motor Cycling and Cycling.
1704 **487** 2s. brown and grey . . . 30 25

1974. "Renaissance in Austria" Exhibition, Schallaburg Castle.
1705 **488** 2s. black, brown & gold 25 25

1974. 14th International Road Haulage Union Congress, Innsbruck.
1706 **489** 4s. black and orange . . 45 30

490 F. A. Maulbertsch

491 Gendarmes of 1849 and 1974

1974. 205th Birth Anniv of Franz Maulbertsch (painter).
1707 **490** 2s. brown 30 25

1974. 125th Anniv of Austrian Gendarmerie.
1708 **491** 2s. multicoloured 30 25

492 Fencing

1974. Sports.
1709 **492** 2s.50 black and orange 35 25

493 Transport Emblems

1974. European Transport Ministers' Conference, Vienna.
1710 **493** 4s. multicoloured 55 35

494 "St. Virgilius" (wood-carving)

495 Pres. F. Jonas

1974. 1200 Years of Christianity in Salzburg.
1711 **494** 2s. blue 30 25

1974. Pres. Franz Jonas Commemoration.
1712 **495** 2s. black 30 25

496 F. Stelzhamer

497 Diving

1974. Death Cent of Franz Stelzhamer (poet).
1713 **496** 2s. blue 30 25

1974. 13th European Swimming, Diving and Water-polo Championships.
1714 **497** 4s. brown and blue . . . 50 35

498 F. R. von Hebra (founder of German scientific dermatology)

499 A. Schonberg

1974. 30th Meeting of German-speaking Dermatologists Association, Graz.
1715 **498** 4s. brown 45 40

1974. Birth Cent of Arnold Schonberg (composer).
1716 **499** 2s.50 purple 40 25

500 Broadcasting Studios, Salzburg

501 E. Eysler

1974. 50th Anniv of Austrian Broadcasting.
1717 **500** 2s. multicoloured 30 20

1974. 25th Death Anniv of Edmund Eysler (composer).
1718 **501** 2s. green 30 25

502 19th-century Postman and Mail Transport

1974. Centenary of U.P.U.
1719 **502** 2s. brown and mauve . . 40 30
1720 – 4s. blue and grey 50 45
DESIGN: 4s. Modern postman and mail transport.

503 Sports Emblem

1974. 25th Anniv of Football Pools in Austria.
1721 **503** 70g. red, black and green 20 15

504 Steel Gauntlet grasping Rose

1974. Nature Protection.
1722 **504** 2s. multicoloured 45 30

505 C. D. von Dittersdorf

506 Mail Coach and P.O., 1905

1974. 175th Death Anniv of Carl Ditters von Dittersdorf (composer).
1723 **505** 2s. green 30 25

1974. Stamp Day.
1724 **506** 4s.+2s. blue 70 70

507 "Virgin Mary and Child" (wood-carving)

508 F. Schmidt

1974. Christmas.
1725 **507** 2s. brown and gold . . . 30 25

1974. Birth Centenary of Franz Schmidt (composer).
1726 **508** 4s. black and stone . . . 60 45

509 "St. Christopher and Child" (altarpiece)

511 Seat-belt around Skeletal Limbs

510 Slalom

1975. European Architectural Heritage Year and 125th Anniv of Austrian Commission for Preservation of Monuments.
1727 **509** 2s.50 brown and grey . . 40 30

1975. Winter Olympics, Innsbruck (1976) (1st issue). Multicoloured.
1728 1s.+50g. Type **510** 20 20
1729 1s.50+70g. Ice hockey . . . 30 30
1730 2s.+90g. Ski-jumping . . . 45 45
1731 4s.+1s.90 Bobsleighing . . . 85 80
See also Nos. 1747/50.

1975. Car Safety-belts Campaign.
1732 **511** 70g. multicoloured . . . 20 15

512 Stained-glass Window, Vienna Town Hall

513 "The Buffer State"

1975. 11th European Communities' Day.
1733 **512** 2s.50 multicoloured . . . 40 25

1975. 30th Anniv of Foundation of Austrian Second Republic.
1734 **513** 2s. black and brown . . 30 25

514 Forest Scene

1975. 50th Anniv of Foundation of Austrian Forests Administration.
1735 **514** 2s. green 35 25

515 "The High Priest" (M. Pacher)

516 Gosaukamm Cable-way

1975. Europa.
1736 **515** 2s.50 multicoloured . . . 35 25

1975. 4th International Ropeways Congress, Vienna.
1737 **516** 2s. blue and red 30 30

517 J. Misson

1975. Death Centenary of Josef Misson (poet).
1738 **517** 2s. brown and red . . . 30 30

518 "Setting Sun"

520 L. Fall

519 F. Porsche

1975. Nat Pensioners' Assn Meeting, Vienna.
1739 **518** 1s.50 multicoloured . . . 30 25

1975. Birth Centenary of Prof. Ferdinand Porsche (motor engineer).
1740 **519** 1s.50 purple & green . . 30 30

1975. 50th Death Anniv of Leo Fall (composer).
1741 **520** 2s. violet 30 30

521 Judo "Shoulder Throw"

522 Heinrich Angeli

1975. World Judo Championships, Vienna.
1742 **521** 2s.50 multicoloured . . . 30 25

1975. 50th Death Anniv of Heinrich Angeli (court painter).
1743 **522** 2s. purple 30 25

523 J. Strauss

1975. 150th Birth Anniv of Johann Strauss the Younger (composer).
1744 **523** 4s. brown and ochre . . 65 40

524 "The Cellist"

525 "One's Own House"

1975. 75th Anniv of Vienna Symphony Orchestra.
1745 **524** 2s.50 blue and silver . . 40 25

1975. 50th Anniv of Austrian Building Societies.
1746 **525** 2s. multicoloured 30 25

1975. Winter Olympic Games, Innsbruck (1976) (2nd issue). As T **510**. Multicoloured.
1747 70g.+30g. Figure-skating (pairs) 25 25
1748 2s.+1s. Cross-country skiing 30 40
1749 2s.50+1s. Tobogganing . . . 45 40
1750 4s.+2s. Rifle-shooting (biathlon) 90 90

526 Scene on Folding Fan

1975. Bicentenary of Salzburg State Theatre.
1751 **526** 1s.50 multicoloured . . . 30 25

527 Austrian Stamps of 1850, 1922 and 1945

528 "Virgin and Child" (Schottenaltar, Vienna)

1975. Stamp Day. 125th Anniv of Austrian Postage Stamps.
1752 **527** 4s.+2s. multicoloured . . 70 75

1975. Christmas.
1753 **528** 2s. lilac and gold 35 25

529 "Spiralbaum" (F. Hundertwasser)

531 Dr. R. Barany

1975. Modern Austrian Art.
1754 **529** 4s. multicoloured 90 50

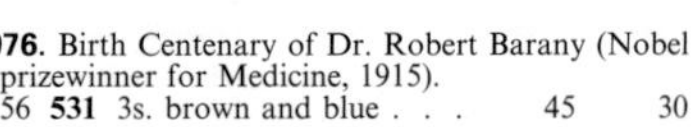

1976. Birth Centenary of Dr. Robert Barany (Nobel prizewinner for Medicine, 1915).
1756 **531** 3s. brown and blue . . . 45 30

532 Ammonite Fossil **533** 9th-century Coronation Throne

1976. Cent Exn, Vienna Natural History Museum.
1757 **532** 3s. multicoloured 50 30

1976. Millenary of Carinthia.
1758 **533** 3s. black and yellow . . 45 30

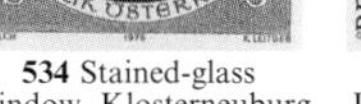

534 Stained-glass Window, Klosterneuburg **535** "The Siege of Linz" (contemporary engraving)

1976. Babenberg Exhibition, Lilienfeld.
1759 **534** 3s. multicoloured 45 30

1976. 350th Anniv of the Peasants' War in Upper Austria.
1760 **535** 4s. black and green . . . 60 40

536 Bowler delivering Ball

1976. 11th World Skittles Championships, Vienna.
1761 **536** 4s. black and orange . . 60 40

537 "St. Wolfgang" (altar painting by Michael Pacher) **538** Tassilo Cup, Kremsmunster

1976. International Art Exhibition, St. Wolfgang.
1762 **537** 6s. purple 80 50

1976. Europa.
1763 **538** 4s. multicoloured 60 50

539 Fair Emblem **540** Constantin Economo

1976. 25th Austrian Timber Fair, Klagenfurt.
1764 **539** 3s. multicoloured 50 30

1976. Birth Centenary of Constantin Economo (brain specialist).
1765 **540** 3s. brown 35 25

541 Bohemian Court Chancellery, Vienna

1976. Centenary of Administrative Court.
1766 **541** 6s. brown 70 55

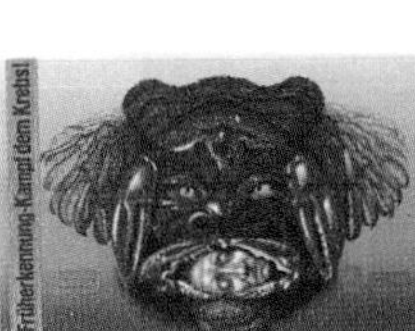

543 Cancer the Crab **544** U.N. Emblem and Bridge

1976. Fight against Cancer.
1768 **543** 2s.50 multicoloured . . . 35 25

1976. 10th Anniv of U.N. Industrial Development Organization.
1769 **544** 3s. blue and gold 45 30

545 Punched Tapes and Map of Europe

1976. 30th Anniv of Austrian Press Agency.
1770 **545** 1s.50 multicoloured . . . 20 15

546 V. Kaplan

1976. Birth Centenary of Viktor Kaplan (inventor of turbine).
1771 **546** 2s.50 multicoloured . . . 30 25

547 "The Birth of Christ" (Konrad von Friesach)

1976. Christmas.
1772 **547** 3s. multicoloured 40 25

548 Postilion's Hat and Posthorn

1976. Stamp Day.
1773 **548** 6s.+2s. black & lilac . . 1·00 1·00

549 R. M. Rilke **550** "Augustin the Piper" (Arik Brauer)

1976. 50th Death Anniv of Rainer Maria Rilke (poet).
1774 **549** 3s. violet 40 30

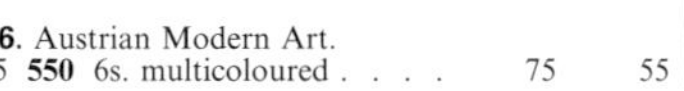

1976. Austrian Modern Art.
1775 **550** 6s. multicoloured 75 55

551 City Synagogue **552** N. J. von Jacquin

1976. 150th Anniv of Vienna City Synagogue.
1776 **551** 1s.50 multicoloured . . . 35 15

1977. 250th Birth Anniv of Nikolaus Joseph Freiherrn von Jacquin (botanist).
1777 **552** 4s. brown 40 35

553 Oswald von Wolkenstein **555** A. Kubin

554 Handball

1977. 600th Birth Anniv of Oswald von Wolkenstein (poet).
1778 **553** 3s. multicoloured 45 25

1977. World Indoor Handball Championships, Group B, Austria.
1779 **554** 1s.50 multicoloured . . . 25 20

1977. Birth Centenary of Alfred Kubin (writer and illustrator).
1780 **555** 6s. blue 75 50

556 Cathedral Spire **558** I.A.E.A. Emblem

557 F. Herzmanovsky-Orlando

1977. 25th Anniv of Re-opening of St. Stephen's Cathedral, Vienna.
1781 **556** 2s.50 brown 40 30
1782 – 3s. blue 50 45
1783 – 4s. purple 75 70
DESIGNS: 3s. West front; 4s. Interior.

1977. Birth Centenary of Fritz Herzmanovsky-Orlando (writer).
1784 **557** 6s. green and gold . . . 75 50

1977. 20th Anniv of Int Atomic Energy Agency.
1785 **558** 3s. lt blue, gold & blue 40 25

559 Arms of Schwanenstadt **561** Globe (Vincenzo Coronelli)

560 Attersee

1977. 350th Anniv of Schwanenstadt.
1786 **559** 3s. multicoloured 45 30

1977. Europa.
1787 **560** 6s. green 70 55

1977. 5th International Symposium and 25th Anniv of Coronelli World Federation of Globe Friends.
1788 **561** 3s. black and stone . . . 40 25

562 Canoeist

1977. World "White Water" Canoe Championships.
1789 **562** 4s. multicoloured 50 35

563 "The Samaritan" (Francesco Bassano)

1977. 50th Anniv of Austrian Workers' Samaritan Federation.
1790 **563** 1s.50 multicoloured . . . 25 25

564 Papermakers' Arms **565** "Freedom"

1977. 17th Conference of European Committee of Pulp and Paper Technology.
1791 **564** 3s. multicoloured 35 20

1977. Martyrs for Austrian Freedom.
1792 **565** 2s.50 blue and red . . . 35 25

566 Steam Locomotive, "Austria", 1837

1977. 140th Anniv of Austrian Railways. Mult.
1793 1s.50 Type **566** 35 30
1794 2s.50 Type 214 steam locomotive, 1928 . . . . 55 40
1795 3s. Type 1044 electric locomotive, 1974 . . . . 75 50

567 "Madonna and Child" (wood carving, Mariastein Pilgrimage Church)

1977. Christmas.
1796 **567** 3s. multicoloured 40 25

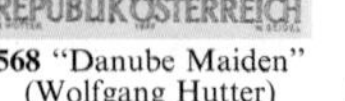

568 "Danube Maiden" (Wolfgang Hutter)
569 Emanuel Herrmann (inventor of postcard)

1977. Austrian Modern Art.
1797 **568** 6s. multicoloured 85 50

1977. Stamp Day.
1798 **569** 6s.+2s. brown and cinnamon . . . . . . 1·00 1·00

570 Egon Friedell

1978. Birth Centenary of Egon Friedell (writer).
1799 **570** 3s. black and blue . . . 45 30

571 Underground Train

1978. Opening of Vienna Underground Railway.
1800 **571** 3s. multicoloured 70 40

572 Rifleman and Skier

1978. Biathlon World Championships, Hochfilzen.
1801 **572** 4s. multicoloured 60 40

573 Aztec Feather Shield

1978. 30th Anniv of Museum of Ethnology, Vienna.
1802 **573** 3s. multicoloured 40 30

574 Leopold Kunschak
575 "Mountain Peasants"

1978. 25th Death Anniv of Leopold Kunschak (politician).
1803 **574** 3s. blue 45 30

1978. Birth Centenary of Suitbert Lobisser (wood engraver).
1804 **575** 3s. brown and stone . . 40 30

576 Black Grouse, Hunting Satchel and Fowling Piece
577 Map of Europe and Austrian Parliament Building

1978. International Hunting Exn, Marchegg.
1805 **576** 6s. blue, brown & turq 85 75

1978. 3rd Interparliamentary European Security Conference, Vienna.
1806 **577** 4s. multicoloured 55 40

578 Riegersburg Castle, Styria

1978. Europa.
1807 **578** 6s. purple 85 65

579 "Admont Pieta" (Salzburg Circle Master)
580 Ort Castle

1978. "Gothic Art in Styria" Exhibition.
1808 **579** 2s.50 black and ochre . . 30 25

1978. 700th Anniv of Gmunden Town Charter.
1809 **580** 3s. multicoloured 45 30

581 Face surrounded by Fruit and Flowers
582 Franz Lehar and Villa at Bad Ischl

1978. 25th Anniv of Austrian Association for Social Tourism.
1810 **581** 6s. multicoloured 80 55

1978. International Lehar Congress.
1811 **582** 6s. blue 90 55

583 Tools and Globe

1978. 15th Congress of International Federation of Building and Wood Workers.
1812 **583** 1s.50 black, yellow & red 25 20

584 Knights Jousting

1978. 700th Anniv of Battle of Durnkrut and Jedenspeigen.
1813 **584** 3s. multicoloured 40 30

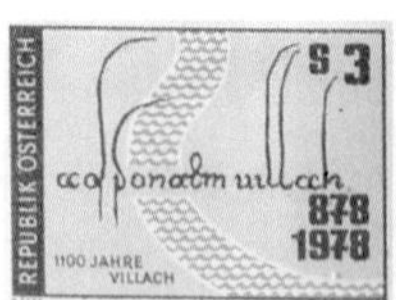

585 Bridge over River Drau
586 City Seal, 1440

1978. 1100th Anniv of Villach.
1814 **585** 3s. multicoloured 45 30

1978. 850th Anniv of Graz.
1815 **586** 4s. brown, green & grey 50 40

587 Angler
588 Distorted Pattern

1978. 25th Sport Fishing Championships, Vienna.
1816 **587** 4s. multicoloured 55 40

1978. Handicapped People.
1817 **588** 6s. black and brown . . 75 55

589 Concrete Chain
590 "Grace" (Albin Egger-Lienz)

1978. 9th International Concrete and Prefabrication Industry Congress, Vienna.
1818 **589** 2s.50 multicoloured . . . 30 25

1978. European Family Congress.
1819 **590** 6s. multicoloured 75 55

591 Lise Meitner
592 Victor Adler (bust, Anton Hamek)

1978. Birth Centenary of Lise Meitner (physicist).
1820 **591** 6s. violet 80 55

1978. 60th Death Anniv of Victor Adler (statesman).
1821 **592** 3s. black and red 40 30

593 Franz Schubert (after Josef Kriehuber)
594 "Madonna and Child" (Martino Altomonte, Wilhering Collegiate Church)

1978. 150th Death Anniv of Franz Schubert (composer).
1822 **593** 6s. brown . . . . 1·25 55

1978. Christmas.
1823 **594** 3s. multicoloured 40 25

595 Postbus, 1913

1978. Stamp Day.
1824 **595** 10s.+5s. multicoloured 1·90 1·90

596 "Archduke Johann Hut, Grossglockner" (E. T. Compton)

1978. Centenary of Austrian Alpine Club.
1825 **596** 1s.50 violet and gold . . 25 20

597 "Adam" (Rudolf Hausner)
598 Bound Hands

1978. Austrian Modern Art.
1826 **597** 6s. multicoloured 75 50

1978. 30th Anniv of Declaration of Human Rights.
1827 **598** 6s. purple 75 50

599 "CCIR"

1979. 50th Anniv of International Radio Consultative Committee.
1828 **599** 6s. multicoloured 75 50

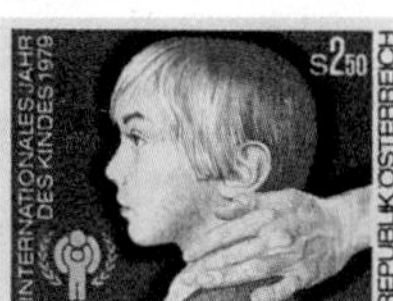

600 Adult protecting Child

1979. International Year of the Child.
1829 **600** 2s.50 multicoloured . . . 40 30

601 Air Rifle, Pistol and Target

1979. Centenary of Austrian Shooting Club, and European Air Rifle and Air Pistol Shooting Championships.
1830 **601** 6s. multicoloured 75 50

602 "Franz I" (paddle-steamer)

1979. 150th Anniv of Danube Steam Navigation Company.
1831 **602** 1s.50 blue 30 25
1832 – 2s.50 brown 50 30
1833 – 3s. red 50 40
DESIGNS: 2s.50, Pusher tug "Linz"; 3s. "Theodor Korner" (passenger vessel).

603 Skater

1979. World Ice Skating and Dancing Championships. Vienna.
1834 **603** 4s. multicoloured 50 40

604 Fashion Drawing by Theo Zache, 1900

605 Wiener Neustadt Cathedral

1979. 50th Viennese Int Ladies' Fashion Week.
1835 **604** 2s.50 multicoloured . . . 30 25

1979. 700th Anniv of Wiener Neustadt Cathedral.
1836 **605** 4s. blue and grey 55 35

606 Relief from Emperor Joseph II Monument, Vienna

607 Population Graph

1979. Bicentenary of Education for the Deaf.
1837 **606** 2s.50 green, black & gold 40 30

1979. 150th Anniv of Austrian Central Statistical Office.
1838 **607** 2s.50 multicoloured . . . 40 30

608 Laurenz Koschier (postal reformer)

609 Section through Diesel Engine

1979. Europa.
1839 **608** 6s. brown and ochre . . 75 50

1979. 13th Congress of International Combustion Engine Council.
1840 **609** 4s. multicoloured 50 35

610 Town Arms of Ried, Braunau and Scharding

1979. Bicentenary of Innviertel District.
1841 **610** 3s. multicoloured 40 30

611 Water Pollution

1979. Prevention of Water Pollution.
1842 **611** 2s.50 green and grey . . 40 30

612 Arms of Rottenmann

613 Jodok Fink

1979. 700th Anniv of Rottenmann.
1843 **612** 3s. multicoloured 40 30

1979. 50th Death Anniv of Jodok Fink (politician).
1844 **613** 3s. brown 40 30

614 Arms of Wels and Returned Soldiers League Badge

615 Flower

1979. 5th European Meeting of Returned Soldiers.
1845 **614** 4s. green and black . . . 50 35

1979. U.N. Conference on Science and Technology for Development, Vienna.
1846 **615** 4s. blue 50 35

616 Vienna International Centre

1979. Opening of U.N.O. Vienna Int Centre.
1847 **616** 6s. slate 75 55

617 Eye and Blood Vessels of Diabetic

1979. 10th World Congress of International Diabetes Federation, Vienna.
1848 **617** 2s.50 multicoloured . . . 40 30

618 Stanzer Valley seen from Arlberg Road Tunnel

1979. 16th World Road Congress, Vienna.
1849 **618** 4s. multicoloured 60 35

619 Steam-driven Printing Press

1979. 175th Anniv of State Printing Works.
1850 **619** 3s. black and stone . . . 45 30

620 Richard Zsigmondy

1979. 50th Death Anniv of Dr. Richard Zsigmondy (Nobel Prize winner for Chemistry).
1851 **620** 6s. brown 75 55

621 Bregenz Festival and Congress Hall

1979. Bregenz Festival and Congress Hall.
1852 **621** 2s.50 lilac 40 30

622 Burning Match

1979. "Save Energy".
1853 **622** 2s.50 multicoloured . . . 40 30

623 Lions Emblem

1979. 25th European Lions Forum, Vienna.
1854 **623** 4s. yellow, gold and lilac 50 35

624 Wilhelm Exner (founder)

625 "The Suffering Christ" (Hans Fronius)

1979. Centenary of Industrial Museum and Technical School, Vienna.
1855 **624** 2s.50 dp purple & purple 40 30

1979. Austrian Modern Art.
1856 **625** 4s. black and stone . . . 60 40

626 Series 52 Goods Locomotive

627 August Musger

1979. Centenary of Raab (Gyor)–Odenburg (Sopron)-Ebenfurt Railway.
1857 **626** 2s.50 multicoloured . . . 45 40

1979. 50th Death Anniv of August Musger (pioneer of slow-motion photography).
1858 **627** 2s.50 black and grey . . 40 30

628 "Nativity" (detail of icon by Moses Subotic, St. Barbara Church, Vienna)

1979. Christmas.
1859 **628** 4s. multicoloured 50 30

629 Neue Hofburg, Vienna

1979. "WIPA 1981" International Stamp Exhibition, Vienna (1st issue). Inscr "1. Phase".
1860 **629** 16s.+8s. multicoloured 3·00 3·50
See also No. 1890.

630 Arms of Baden

631 Loading Exports

1980. 500th Anniv of Baden.
1861 **630** 4s. multicoloured 60 30

1980. Austrian Exports.
1862 **631** 4s. blue, red and black 50 30

632 Rheumatic Hand holding Stick

1980. Fight against Rheumatism.
1863 **632** 2s.50 red and blue . . . 40 30

633 Emblems of 1880 and 1980

1980. Centenary of Austrian Red Cross.
1864 **633** 2s.50 multicoloured . . . 40 30

634 Kirchschlager

635 Robert Hamerling

1980. Pres. Rudolf Kirchschlager's 65th Birthday.
1865 **634** 4s. brown and red . . . 60 35

1980. 150th Birth Anniv of Robert Hamerling (writer).
1866 **635** 2s.50 green 40 30

636 Town Seal

637 "Maria Theresa as a Young Woman" (Andreas Moller)

1980. 750th Anniv of Hallein.
1867 **636** 4s. black and red 50 40

1980. Death Bicentenary of Empress Maria Theresa.
1868 **637** 2s.50 purple 45 30
1869 – 4s. blue 70 50
1870 – 6s. brown . . . . 1·00 85
DESIGNS: 4s. "Maria Theresa with St. Stephen's Crown" (Martin van Meytens); 6s. "Maria Theresa as Widow" (Joseph Ducreux).

638 Flags of Treaty Signatories

639 St. Benedict (statue, Meinrad Guggenbichler)

1980. 25th Anniv of Austrian State Treaty.
1871 **638** 4s. multicoloured 50 30

1980. Congress of Austrian Benedictine Orders, Mariazell.
1872 **639** 2s.50 green 40 30

640 "Hygieia" (Gustav Klimt)

641 Dish Aerial, Aflenz

1980. 175th Anniv of Hygiene Education.
1873 **640** 4s. multicoloured 50 35

1980. Inauguration of Aflenz Satellite Communications Earth Station.
1874 **641** 6s. multicoloured 75 55

642 Steyr (copperplate engraving, 1693)

1980. Millenary of Steyr.
1875 **642** 4s. brown, black & gold 50 35

643 Oil Driller

644 Town Seal of 1267

1980. 50th Anniv of Oil Production in Austria.
1876 **643** 2s.50 multicoloured . . . 40 30

1980. 800th Anniv of Innsbruck.
1877 **644** 2s.50 yellow, blk & red 40 30

645 Ducal Crown

1980. 800th Anniv of Elevation of Styria to Dukedom.
1878 **645** 4s. multicoloured 50 35

646 Leo Ascher

647 "Abraham" (illustration from "Viennese Genesis")

1980. Birth Cent of Leo Ascher (composer).
1879 **646** 3s. violet 45 30

1980. 10th Congress of International Organization for Study of the Old Testament.
1880 **647** 4s. multicoloured 50 35

648 Robert Stolz

649 Falkenstein Railway Bridge

1980. Europa and Birth Centenary of Robert Stolz (composer).
1881 **648** 6s. red 75 55

1980. 11th International Association of Bridge and Structural Engineering Congress, Vienna.
1882 **649** 4s. multicoloured 50 35

650 "Moon Figure" (Karl Brandstatter)

651 Customs Officer

1980. Austrian Modern Art.
1883 **650** 4s. multicoloured 50 35

1980. 150th Anniv of Customs Service.
1884 **651** 2s.50 brown and red . . 30 30

652 Masthead of 1810

1980. 350th Anniv of "Linzer Zeitung" (Linz newspaper).
1885 **652** 2s.50 black, red & gold 30 30

653 Frontispiece of Waidhofen Municipal Book

654 Heads

1980. 750th Anniv of Waidhofen.
1886 **653** 2s.50 multicoloured . . . 30 30

1980. 25th Anniv of Federal Army.
1887 **654** 2s.50 green and red . . . 30 30

655 Alfred Wegener

656 Robert Musil

1980. Birth Centenary of Alfred Wegener (explorer and geophysicist).
1888 **655** 4s. blue 50 35

1980. Birth Centenary of Robert Musil (writer).
1889 **656** 4s. brown 50 40

1980. "WIPA 1981" International Stamp Exhibition, Vienna (2nd issue). Inscr "2. Phase".
1890 **629** 16s.+8s. mult . . . . . 3·00 2·75

657 "Adoration of the Kings" (stained-glass window, Viktring Collegiate Church)

658 Ribbon in National Colours

1980. Christmas.
1891 **657** 4s. multicoloured 50 35

1981. 25th Anniv of General Social Insurance Act.
1892 **658** 2s.50 red, green & black 30 30

659 Unissued Design for 1926 Child Welfare Stamps

660 Disabled Person operating Machine Tool

1981. Birth Centenary of Wilhelm Dachauer (artist).
1894 **659** 3s. brown 40 30

1981. 3rd European Regional Conference of Rehabilitation International.
1895 **660** 6s. brown, blue and red 75 60

661 Sigmund Freud

662 Long-distance Heating System

1981. 125th Birth Anniv of Sigmund Freud (psychoanalyst).
1896 **661** 3s. purple 45 30

1981. 20th International Union of Long-distance Heat Distributors Congress, Vienna.
1897 **662** 4s. multicoloured 50 40

663 "Azzo and his Vassals" (cover of Monastery's "bearskin" Manuscript)

664 Maypole

1981. Kuenring Exhibition, Zwettl Monastery.
1898 **663** 3s. multicoloured 45 30

1981. Europa.
1899 **664** 6s. multicoloured 85 60

665 Early Telephone

1981. Centenary of Austrian Telephone System.
1900 **665** 4s. multicoloured 50 35

666 "The Frog King"

1981. Art Education in Schools.
1901 **666** 3s. multicoloured 45 30

667 Research Centre

1981. 25th Anniv of Seibersdorf Research Centre.
1902 **667** 4s. blue, dp blue & orge 50 40

668 Town Hall and Seal

669 Johann Florian Heller (chemist)

1981. 850th Anniv of St. Veit-on-Glan.
1903 **668** 4s. yellow, brown & red 50 40

1981. 11th Int Clinical Chemistry Congress, Vienna.
1904 **669** 6s. brown 75 60

670 Boltzmann

671 Otto Bauer

1981. 75th Death Anniv of Ludwig Boltzmann (physicist).
1905 **670** 3s. green 45 30

1981. Birth Centenary of Otto Bauer (writer and politician).
1906 **671** 4s. multicoloured 50 35

672 Chemical Balance

673 Impossible Construction (M. C. Escher)

1981. International Pharmaceutical Federation Congress, Vienna.
1907 **672** 6s. black, brown and red 75 50

1981. 10th International Austrian Mathematicians' Congress, Innsbruck.
1908 **673** 4s. lt blue, blue & dp blue 50 35

674 "Coronation of Virgin Mary" (detail)

675 Compass Rose

1981. 500th Anniv of Michael Pacher's Altarpiece at St. Wolfgang, Abersee.
1909 **674** 3s. blue 45 30

1981. 75th Anniv of Graz S.E. Exhibition.
1910 **675** 4s. multicoloured 50 40

676 "Holy Trinity" (illuminated MS, 12th century)

1981. 16th International Congress of Byzantine Scholars, Vienna.
1911 **676** 6s. multicoloured 75 55

677 Josef II **678** Hans Kelsen

1981. Bicentenary of Toleration Act (giving freedom of worship to Protestants).
1912 **677** 4s. black, blue & bistre 50 40

1981. Bicentenary of Hans Kelsen (law lecturer and contributor to shaping of Austrian Constitution).
1913 **678** 3s. red 45 30

679 Full and Empty Bowls and F.A.O. Emblem

1981. World Food Day.
1914 **679** 6s. multicoloured 75 55

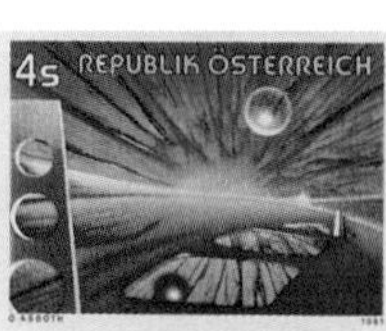

680 "Between the Times" (Oscar Asboth) **681** Workers and Emblem

1981. Austrian Modern Art.
1915 **680** 4s. multicoloured 50 35

1981. 7th International Catholic Employees' Meeting, Vienna-Lainz.
1916 **681** 3s. multicoloured 45 30

682 Hammer-Purgstall

1981. 125th Death Anniv of Josef Hammer-Purgstall (orientalist).
1917 **682** 3s. multicoloured 45 30

683 Julius Raab **684** Stefan Zweig

1981. 90th Birth Anniv of Julius Raab (politician).
1918 **683** 6s. purple 70 50

1981. Birth Centenary of Stefan Zweig (writer).
1919 **684** 4s. lilac 55 35

685 Christmas Crib, Burgenland

1981. Christmas.
1920 **685** 4s. multicoloured 50 35

686 Arms of St. Nikola

1981. 800th Anniv of St. Nikola-on-Danube.
1921 **686** 4s. multicoloured 50 40

687 Volkswagen Transporter Ambulance

1981. Cent of Vienna's Emergency Medical Service.
1922 **687** 3s. multicoloured 45 35

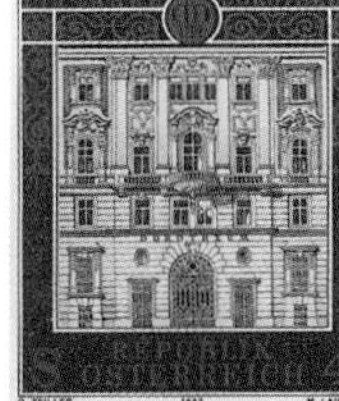

688 Skier **689** Dorotheum Building

1982. Alpine Skiing World Championship, Schladming-Haus.
1923 **688** 4s. multicoloured 50 35

1982. 275th Anniv of Dorotheum Auction, Pawn and Banking Society.
1924 **689** 4s. multicoloured 50 35

690 Lifesaving **691** St. Severin

1982. 25th Anniv of Austrian Water Lifesaving Service.
1925 **690** 5s. blue, red & light blue 65 45

1982. "St. Severin and the End of the Roman Period" Exhibition, Enns.
1926 **691** 3s. multicoloured 55 35

692 Sebastian Kneipp (pioneer of holistic medicine) **693** Printers' Coat-of-arms

1982. International Kneipp Congress, Vienna.
1927 **692** 4s. multicoloured 45 30

1982. 500th Anniv of Printing in Austria.
1928 **693** 4s. multicoloured 50 35

694 Urine Analysis from "Canon Medicinae" by Avicenna **695** St. Francis preaching to Animals (miniature)

1982. 5th European Union for Urology Congress, Vienna.
1929 **694** 6s. multicoloured 75 60

1982. "Franciscan Art and Culture in the Middle Ages" Exhibition, Krems-Stein.
1930 **695** 3s. multicoloured 40 30

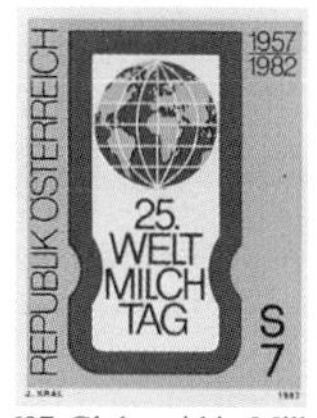

696 Haydn and Birthplace, Rohrau **697** Globe within Milk Churn

1982. "Joseph Haydn and His Time" Exhibition, Eisenstadt.
1931 **696** 3s. green 45 30

1982. World Dairying Day.
1932 **697** 7s. multicoloured 85 65

698 Town Arms (1804 flag) **699** Tennis Player

1982. 800th Anniv of Gfohl.
1933 **698** 4s. multicoloured 50 35

1982. 80th Anniv of Austrian Lawn Tennis Assn.
1934 **699** 3s. multicoloured 45 35

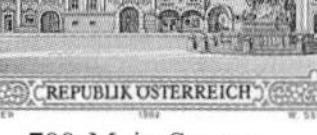

700 Main Square, Langenlois **701** Town Arms

1982. 900th Anniv of Langenlois.
1935 **700** 4s. multicoloured 50 40

1982. 800th Anniv of Weiz.
1936 **701** 4s. multicoloured 65 40

702 Linz–Freistadt–Budweis Horse-drawn Railway

1982. Europa.
1937 **702** 6s. brown 75 70

703 Ignaz Seipel **704** Postbus

1982. 50th Death Anniv of Ignaz Seipel (Federal Chancellor).
1938 **703** 3s. purple 50 30

1982. 75th Anniv of Post-bus Service.
1939 **704** 4s. multicoloured 55 45

705 Rocket Launch

1982. Second U.N. Conference on the Exploration and Peaceful Uses of Outer Space, Vienna.
1940 **705** 4s. multicoloured 55 45

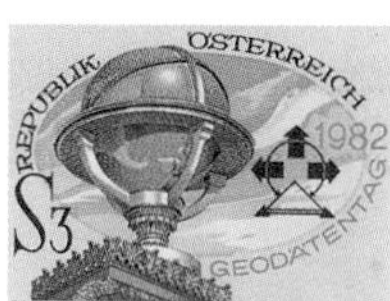

706 Globe (Federal Office for Standardization and Surveying, Vienna)

1982. Geodesists' Day.
1941 **706** 3s. multicoloured 45 30

707 Great Bustard ("Grosstrappe")

1982. Endangered Animals. Multicoloured.
1942 3s. Type **707** 50 45
1943 4s. Eurasian beaver 55 60
1944 6s. Western capercaillie ("Auerhahn") 75 90

708 Institute Building, Laxenburg

1982. 10th Anniv of International Institute for Applied Systems Analysis.
1945 **708** 3s. black and brown . . 45 30

709 St. Apollonia (patron saint of dentists)

1982. 70th International Dentists Federation Congress, Vienna.
1946 **709** 4s. multicoloured 55 45

710 Emmerich Kalman **711** Max Mell

1982. Birth Cent of Emmerich Kalman (composer).
1947 **710** 3s. blue 45 30

1982. Birth Centenary of Max Mell (writer).
1948 **711** 3s. multicoloured 45 30

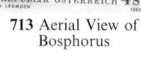

712 Christmas Crib, Damuls Church **713** Aerial View of Bosphorus

1982. Christmas.
1949 **712** 4s. multicoloured 55 45

1982. Centenary of St. George's Austrian College, Istanbul.
1950 **713** 4s. multicoloured 55 45

714 "Mainz-Weber" Mailbox, 1870

1982. Stamp Day.
1951 **714** 6s.+3s. multicoloured . . 1·40 1·60

715 "Muse of the Republic" (Ernst Fuchs)

716 Bank, Vienna

1982. Austrian Modern Art.
1952 **715** 4s. red and violet 55 40

1983. Centenary of Postal Savings Bank.
1953 **716** 4s. yellow, black and blue 55 45

717 Hildegard Burjan

1983. Birth Centenary of Hildegard Burjan (founder of Caritas Socialis (religious sisterhood)).
1954 **717** 4s. red 50 50

718 Linked Arms

1983. World Communications Year.
1955 **718** 7s. multicoloured 85 75

719 Young Girl

720 Josef Matthias Hauer

1983. 75th Anniv of Children's Friends Organization.
1956 **719** 4s. black, blue and red 55 40

1983. Birth Centenary of Josef Matthias Hauer (composer).
1957 **720** 3s. purple 45 35

721 Douglas DC-9-80 Super Eighty

1983. 25th Anniv of Austrian Airlines.
1958 **721** 6s. multicoloured 75 60

722 Hands protecting Workers

1983. Cent of Government Work Inspection Law.
1959 **722** 4s. grn, dp grn & brn . . 55 40

723 Wels (engraving, Matthaeus Merian)

1983. "Millenary of Upper Austria" Exn, Wels.
1960 **723** 3s. multicoloured 40 30

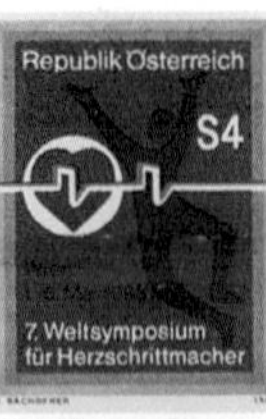

724 Human Figure, Heart and Electrocardiogram

725 Monastery Arms

1983. 7th World Symposium on Pacemakers.
1961 **724** 4s. red, mauve and blue 50 62

1983. 900th Anniv of Gottweig Monastery.
1962 **725** 3s. multicoloured 45 30

726 Weitra

1983. 800th Anniv of Weitra.
1963 **726** 4s. black, red and gold 55 40

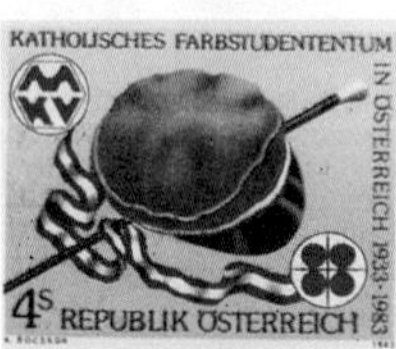

727 Cap, Stick, Ribbon and Emblems

1983. 50th Anniv of MKV and CCV Catholic Students' Organizations.
1964 **727** 4s. multicoloured 55 40

728 Glopper Castle and Town Arms

729 Hess

1983. 650th Anniv of Hohenems Town Charter.
1965 **728** 4s. multicoloured 55 40

1983. Europa. Birth Centenary of Viktor Franz Hess (physicist and Nobel Prize winner).
1966 **729** 6s. green 80 70

730 Vienna City Hall

731 Kiwanis Emblem and View of Vienna

1983. 25th Anniv of Vienna City Hall.
1967 **730** 4s. multicoloured 55 50

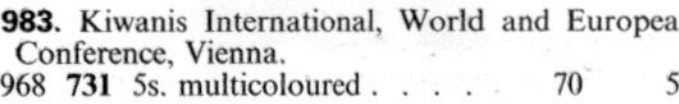

1983. Kiwanis International, World and European Conference, Vienna.
1968 **731** 5s. multicoloured 70 50

732 Congress Emblem

733 Hasenauer and Natural History Museum, Vienna

1983. 7th World Psychiatry Congress, Vienna.
1969 **732** 4s. multicoloured 55 40

1983. 150th Birth Anniv of Carl Freiherr von Hasenauer (architect).
1970 **733** 3s. brown 45 35

734 Institute for Promotion of Trade and Industry, Linz

1983. 27th International Professional Competition for Young Skilled Workers, Linz.
1971 **734** 4s. multicoloured 55 40

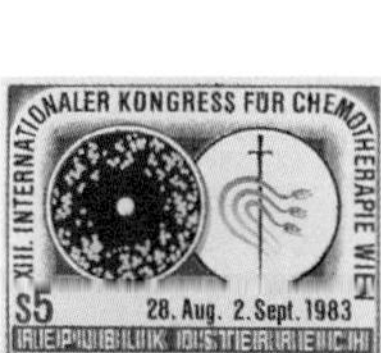

735 Symbols of Penicillin V Efficacy and Cancer

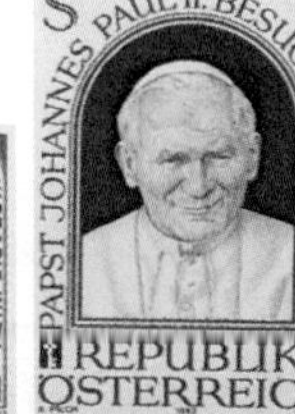

736 Pope John Paul II

1983. 13th Int Chemotherapy Congress, Vienna.
1972 **735** 5s. red and green 70 70

1983. Papal Visit.
1973 **736** 6s. black, red and gold 80 60

738 Spectrum around Cross

739 Vienna Town Hall

1983. Austrian Catholics' Day.
1975 **738** 3s. multicoloured 50 30

1983. Centenary of Vienna Town Hall.
1976 **739** 4s. multicoloured 55 40

740 Karl von Terzaghi

1983. Birth Centenary of Karl von Terzaghi (soil mechanics and foundations engineer).
1977 **740** 3s. blue 50 30

741 Initials of Federation

1983. 10th Austrian Trade Unions Federation Congress.
1978 **741** 3s. red and black 50 30

742 "Evening Sun in Burgenland" (Gottfried Kumpf)

743 Tram No. 5, 1883

1983. Austrian Modern Art.
1979 **742** 4s. multicoloured 55 60

1983. Centenary of Modling–Hinterbruhl Electric Railway.
1980 **743** 3s. multicoloured 50 45

744 Boy looking at Stamped Envelope

1983. Stamp Day.
1981 **744** 6s.+3s. multicoloured . . 1·40 1·50

745 Francisco Carolinum Museum, Linz

1983. 150th Anniv of Upper Austrian Provincial Museum.
1982 **745** 4s. multicoloured 55 40

746 Crib by Johann Giner the Elder, Kitzbuhel Church

1983. Christmas.
1983 **746** 4s. multicoloured 55 40

747 Parliament Building

748 "St. Nicholas" (Maria Freund)

1983. Centenary of Parliament Building, Vienna.
1984 **747** 4s. blue 55 40

1983. Youth Stamp.
1985 **748** 3s. multicoloured 50 35

749 Wolfgang Pauli

1983. 25th Death Anniv of Wolfgang Pauli (Nobel Prize winner for Physics).
1986 **749** 6s. brown 75 60

750 Gregor Mendel

1984. Death Cent of Gregor Mendel (geneticist).
1987 **750** 4s. ochre and brown . . 55 40

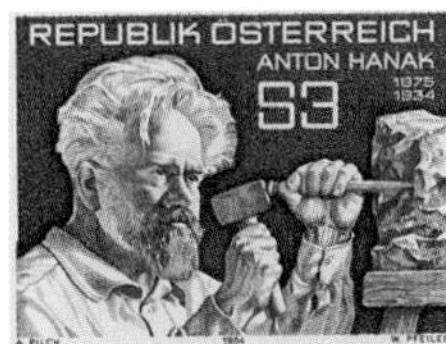

751 Hanak at Work

1984. 50th Death Anniv of Anton Hanak (sculptor).
1988 **751** 3s. brown and black . . 50 35

752 Disabled Skier

1984. 3rd World Winter Games for the Disabled, Innsbruck.
1989 **752** 4s.+2s. multicoloured . . 85 1·00

753 Memorial, Wollersdorf

1984. 50th Anniv of 1934 Insurrections.
1990 **753** 4s.50 red and black . . . 60 40

754 Founders' Stone 755 Geras Monastery

1984. 900th Anniv of Reichersberg Monastery.
1991 **754** 3s.50 stone, brown & bl 55 40

1984. Monasteries and Abbeys.

1992	–	50g. yellow, black & grey	25	20
1993	–	1s. yellow, black & mve	25	15
1994	–	1s.50 yellow, red & blue	35	20
1995	–	2s. yellow, green & black	40	20
1996	**755**	3s.50 yellow, sep & brn	40	15
1997	–	4s. yellow, purple & red	50	15
1998	–	4s.50 yellow, lilac & blue	55	15
1999	–	5s. yellow, purple & orge	75	20
2000	–	5s.50 yell, dp vio & vio	90	40
2001	–	6s. yellow, green & emer	70	15
2002	–	7s. yellow, green & blue	90	20
2003	–	7s.50 yell, dp brn & brn	90	25
2004	–	8s. yellow, blue and red	1·00	25
2005	–	10s. yellow, red & grey	1·25	25
2006	–	11s. yellow, black & brn	1·40	50
2007	–	12s. yellow, brn & orge	1·75	90
2008	–	17s. yellow, ultram & bl	2·25	75
2009	–	20s. yellow, brown & red	2·75	1·10

DESIGNS: 50g. Vorau Monastery; 1s. Wettingen Abbey, Mehrerau; 1s.50, Monastery of Teutonic Order, Vienna; 2s. Michaelbeuern Benedictine Monastery, Salzburg; 4s. Stams Monastery; 4s.50, Schlagl Monastery; 5s. St. Paul's Monastery, Lavanttal; 5s.50, St. Gerold's Priory, Vorarlberg; 6s. Rein Monastery; 7s. Loretto Monastery; 7s.50, Dominican Monastery, Vienna; 8s. Cistercian Monastery, Zwettl; 10s. Premonstratensian Monastery, Wilten; 11s. Trappist Monastery, Engelszell; 12s. Monastery of the Hospitallers, Eisenstadt; 17s. St. Peter's Abbey, Salzburg; 20s. Wernberg Convent, Carinthia.

756 Cigar Band showing Tobacco Plant 757 Kostendorf

1984. Bicentenary of Tobacco Monopoly.
2012 **756** 4s.50 multicoloured . . . 60 45

1984. 1200th Anniv of Kostendorf.
2013 **757** 4s.50 multicoloured . . . 60 45

758 Wheel Bearing

1984. 20th International Federation of Automobile Engineers' Associations World Congress, Vienna.
2014 **758** 5s. multicoloured 70 55

759 Bridge 760 Archduke Johann (after Schnorr von Carolsfeld)

1984. Europa. 25th Anniv of E.P.T. Conference.
2015 **759** 6s. blue and ultramarine 75 60

1984. 125th Death Anniv of Archduke Johann.
2016 **760** 4s.50 multicoloured . . . 60 45

761 Aragonite 762 Binding of "Das Buch vom Kaiser", by Max Herzig

1984. "Ore and Iron in the Green Mark" Exhibition, Eisenerz.
2017 **761** 3s.50 multicoloured . . . 50 35

1984. Lower Austrian "Era of Emperor Franz Joseph: From Revolution to Grunderzeit" Exhibition, Grafenegg Castle.
2018 **762** 3s.50 red and gold . . . 50 35

763 Upper City Tower and Arms 764 Dionysus (Virunum mosaic)

1984. 850th Anniv of Vocklabruch.
2019 **763** 4s.50 multicoloured . . . 60 45

1984. Centenary of Carinthia Provincial Museum, Klagenfurt.
2020 **764** 3s.50 stone, brn & grey 50 35

765 "Meeting of Austrian Army with South Tyrolean Reserves" (detail, Schnorr von Carolsfeld) 766 Ralph Benatzky

1984. "Jubilee of Tyrol Province" Exhibition.
2021 **765** 3s.50 multicoloured . . . 50 35

1984. Birth Cent of Ralph Benatzky (composer).
2022 **766** 4s. brown 60 50

767 Flood Control Barriers 768 Christian von Ehrenfels

1984. Centenary of Flood Control Systems.
2023 **767** 4s.50 green 60 50

1984. 125th Death Anniv of Christian von Ehrenfels (philosopher).
2024 **768** 3s.50 multicoloured . . . 50 35

769 Models of European Monuments

1984. 25th Anniv of Minimundus (model world), Worthersee.
2025 **769** 4s. yellow and black . . 55 40

770 Blockheide Eibenstein National Park

1984. Natural Beauty Spots.
2026 **770** 4s. pink and olive . . . 60 50

771 Electric Train on Schanatobel Bridge (Arlberg Railway Centenary)

1984. Railway Anniversaries.
2027 **771** 3s.50 brown, gold & red 60 50
2028 – 4s.50 blue, silver and red 65 55
DESIGN: 4s.50, Electric train on Falkenstein Bridge (75th anniv of Tauern Railway).

772 Johann Georg Stuwer's Ascent in Montgolfier Balloon

1984. Bicentenary of First Manned Balloon Flight in Austria.
2029 **772** 6s. multicoloured 90 65

773 Lake Neusiedl

1984. Natural Beauty Spots.
2030 **773** 4s. purple and blue . . . 60 50

774 Palace of Justice, Vienna 775 "Joseph Hyrtl" (window, Innsbruck Anatomy Institute)

1984. 20th Int Bar Assn Congress, Vienna.
2031 **774** 7s. multicoloured 85 70

1984. 7th European Anatomists' Congress, Innsbruck.
2032 **775** 6s. multicoloured 75 55

776 "Window" (Karl Korab) 777 Clock of Imms (astrolabe)

1984. Austrian Modern Art.
2033 **776** 4s. multicoloured 55 40

1984. 600th Birth Anniv of Johannes von Gmunden (astronomer and mathematician).
2034 **777** 3s.50 multicoloured . . . 55 40

778 Quill 779 Fanny Elssler

1984. 125th Anniv of Concordia Press Club.
2035 **778** 4s.50 black, gold & red 60 45

1984. Death Centenary of Fanny Elssler (dancer).
2036 **779** 4s. multicoloured 55 40

780 "Holy Family" (detail, Aggsbach Old High Altar)

1984. Christmas.
2037 **780** 4s.50 multicoloured . . . 60 45

781 Detail from Burial Chamber Wall of Seschemnofer III 782 Coat of Arms

1984. Stamp Day.
2038 **781** 6s.+3s. multicoloured . . 1·40 1·50

1985. 400th Anniv of Graz University.
2039 **782** 3s.50 multicoloured . . . 50 35

783 Dr. Lorenz Bohler

1985. Birth Centenary of Prof. Dr. Lorenz Bohler (surgeon).
2040 **783** 4s.50 purple 60 45

784 Ski Jumping, Skiing and Emblem

1985. World Nordic Skiing Championship, Seefeld.
2041 **784** 4s. multicoloured 55 40

785 Linz Cathedral **786** Alban Berg

1985. Bicentenary of Linz Diocese.
2042 **785** 4s.50 multicoloured . . . 65 50

1985. Birth Centenary of Alban Berg (composer).
2043 **786** 6s. blue 90 60

787 Institute Emblem **788** Stylized "B" and Clouds

1985. 25th Anniv of Institute for Vocational Advancement.
2044 **787** 4s.50 multicoloured . . . 60 45

1985. 2000th Anniv of Bregenz.
2045 **788** 4s. black, ultram & blue 55 45

789 1885 Registration Label **790** Josef Stefan

1985. Centenary of Registration Labels in Austria.
2046 **789** 4s.50 black, yell & grey 60 45

1985. 150th Birth Anniv of Josef Stefan (physicist).
2047 **790** 6s. brown, stone and red 75 60

791 St. Leopold (Margrave and patron saint) **792** "The Story-teller"

1985. Lower Austrian Provincial Exhibition, Klosterneuburg Monastery.
2048 **791** 3s.50 multicoloured . . . 50 35

1985. 150th Birth Anniv of Franz Defregger (artist).
2049 **792** 3s.50 multicoloured . . . 50 35

793 Barbed Wire, Broken Tree and New Shoot **794** Johann Joseph Fux (composer)

1985. 40th Anniv of Liberation.
2050 **793** 4s.50 multicoloured . . . 60 55

1985. Europa. Music Year.
2051 **794** 6s. brown and grey . . . 1·10 70

795 Flags and Caduceus **797** Bishop's Gate, St. Polten

796 Town and Arms

1985. 25th Anniv of European Free Trade Association.
2052 **795** 4s. multicoloured 60 50

1985. Millenary of Boheimkirchen.
2053 **796** 4s.50 multicoloured . . . 60 50

1985. Bicentenary of St. Polten Diocese.
2054 **797** 4s.50 multicoloured . . . 60 45

798 Johannes von Nepomuk Church, Innsbruck **799** Garsten (copperplate, George Matthaus Fischer)

1985. Gumpp Family (architects) Exn, Innsbruck.
2055 **798** 3s.50 multicoloured . . . 60 45

1985. Millenary of Garsten.
2056 **799** 4s.50 multicoloured . . . 65 55

800 U.N. Emblem and Austrian Arms

1985. 40th Anniv of U.N.O. and 30th Anniv of Austrian Membership.
2057 **800** 4s. multicoloured 55 50

801 Association Headquarters, Vienna

1985. 13th International Suicide Prevention Association Congress, Vienna.
2058 **801** 5s. brown, lt yell & yell 70 55

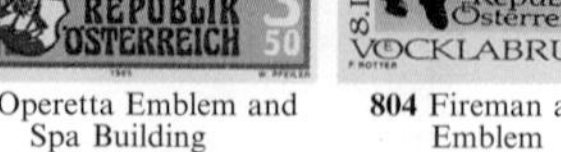
803 Operetta Emblem and Spa Building **804** Fireman and Emblem

1985. 25th Bad Ischl Operetta Week.
2060 **803** 3s.50 multicoloured . . . 65 40

1985. 8th International Fire Brigades Competition, Vocklabruck.
2061 **804** 4s.50 black, green & red 90 50

805 Grossglockner Mountain Road

1985. 50th Anniv of Grossglockner Mountain Road.
2062 **805** 4s. multicoloured 55 40

806 Chessboard as Globe **807** "Founding of Konigstetten" (August Stephan)

1985. World Chess Association Congress, Graz.
2063 **806** 4s. multicoloured 60 40

1985. Millenary of Konigstetten.
2064 **807** 4s.50 multicoloured . . . 65 45

808 Webern Church and Arms of Hofkirchen and Taufkircher

1985. 1200th Anniversaries of Hofkirchen, Weibern and Taufkirchen.
2065 **808** 4s.50 multicoloured . . . 65 50

809 Dr. Adam Politzer

1985. 150th Birth Anniv of Dr. Adam Politzer (otologist).
2066 **809** 3s.50 violet 50 35

810 Emblem and View of Vienna

1985. International Association of Forwarding Agents World Congress, Vienna.
2067 **810** 6s. multicoloured 80 60

811 "Clowns Riding High Bicycles" (Paul Flora)

1985. Austrian Modern Art.
2068 **811** 4s. multicoloured 60 50

812 St. Martin, Patron Saint of Burgenland

1985. 25th Anniv of Eisenstadt Diocese.
2069 **812** 4s.50 black, bistre & red 65 60

813 Roman Mounted Courier

1985. 50th Anniv of Stamp Day.
2070 **813** 6s.+3s. multicoloured . . 1·50 1·50

814 Hanns Horbiger **815** "Adoration of the Christ Child" (marble relief)

1985. 125th Birth Anniv of Hanns Horbiger (design engineer).
2071 **814** 3s.50 purple and gold . . 55 40

1985. Christmas.
2072 **815** 4s.50 multicoloured . . . 60 35

816 Aqueduct

1985. 75th Anniv of Second Vienna Waterline.
2073 **816** 3s.50 black, red & blue 55 40

818 Chateau de la Muette (headquarters)

1985. 25th Anniv of Organization of Economic Co-operation and Development.
2080 **818** 4s. black, gold & mauve 55 40

819 Johann Bohm

1986. Birth Centenary of Johann Bohm (founder of Austrian Trade Unions Federation).
2081 **819** 4s.50 black and red . . . 70 45

820 Dove and Globe

1986. International Peace Year.
2082 **820** 6s. multicoloured 80 60

821 Push-button Dialling

1986. Introduction of Digital Preselection Telephone System.
2083 **821** 5s. multicoloured 70 45

822 Albrechtsberger and Organ

1986. 250th Birth Anniv of Johann Georg Albrechtsberger (composer).
2084 **822** 3s.50 multicoloured . . . 70 35

823 Main Square and Arms

1986. 850th Anniv of Korneuburg.
2085 **823** 5s. multicoloured 70 40

824 Kokoschka (self-portrait) **825** Council Flag

1986. Birth Centenary of Oskar Kokoschka (artist).
2086 **824** 4s. black and pink . . . 55 40

1986. 30th Anniv of Membership of Council of Europe.
2087 **825** 6s. black, red and blue 80 60

826 Holzmeister and Salzburg Festival Hall

1986. Birth Centenary of Professor Clemens Holzmeister (architect).
2088 **826** 4s. grey, brown & lt brn 55 40

827 Road, Roll of Material, and Congress Emblem

1986. 3rd International Geotextile Congress, Vienna.
2089 **827** 5s. multicoloured 70 45

828 Schlosshof Palace (after Bernardo Bellotto) and Prince Eugene

1986. "Prince Eugene and the Baroque Era" Exhibition, Schlosshof and Niederweiden.
2090 **828** 4s. multicoloured 55 40

829 St. Florian Monastery

1986. Upper Austrian "World of Baroque" Exhibition, St. Florian Monastery.
2091 **829** 4s. multicoloured 55 40

830 Herberstein Castle and Styrian Arms

1986. "Styria – Bridge and Bulwark" Exhibition, Herberstein Castle, near Stubenberg.
2092 **830** 4s. multicoloured 55 40

831 Large Pasque Flower

1986. Europa.
2093 **831** 6s. multicoloured 90 70

832 Wagner and Scene from Opera "Lohengrin"

1986. International Richard Wagner (composer) Congress, Vienna.
2094 **832** 4s. multicoloured 85 60

833 Antimonite Crystal

1986. Burgenland "Mineral and Fossils" Exhibition, Oberpullendorf.
2095 **833** 4s. multicoloured 55 50

834 Martinswall, Zirl

1986. Natural Beauty Spots.
2096 **834** 5s. brown and blue . . . 75 50

835 Waidhofen

1986. 800th Anniv of Waidhofen on Ybbs.
2097 **835** 4s. multicoloured 55 50

836 Tschauko Falls, Ferlach

1986. Natural Beauty Spots.
2098 **836** 5s. green and brown . . 75 50

837 19th-century Steam and Modern Articulated Trams

1986. Cent of Salzburg Local Transport System.
2099 **837** 4s. multicoloured 80 50

838 Enns and Seals of Signatories

1986. 800th Anniv of Georgenberg Treaty (between Duke Leopold V of Austria and Duke Otakar IV of Styria).
2100 **838** 5s. multicoloured 70 55

839 Tandler **840** "Observatory, 1886" (A. Heilmann)

1986. 50th Death Anniv of Julius Tandler (social reformer).
2101 **839** 4s. multicoloured 55 40

1986. Centenary of Sonnblick Observatory.
2102 **840** 4s. black, blue and gold 55 40

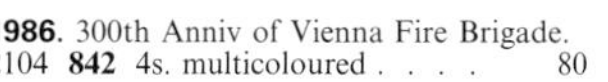

841 Man collecting Mandragora (from "Codex Tacuinum Sanitatis") **842** Fire Assistant

1986. 7th European Anaesthesia Congress, Vienna.
2103 **841** 5s. multicoloured 70 45

1986. 300th Anniv of Vienna Fire Brigade.
2104 **842** 4s. multicoloured 80 55

843 Stoessl **844** Viennese Hunting Tapestry (detail)

1986. 50th Death Anniv of Otto Stoessl (writer).
2105 **843** 4s. multicoloured 55 45

1986. 5th International Oriental Carpets and Tapestry Conference, Vienna and Budapest.
2106 **844** 5s. multicoloured 70 50

845 Minister in Pulpit **846** "Decomposition" (Walter Schmogner)

1986. 125th Anniv of Protestants Act and 25th Anniv of Protestants Law.
2107 **845** 5s. black and violet . . . 70 50

1986. Austrian Modern Art.
2108 **846** 4s. multicoloured 55 40

847 Liszt, Birthplace and Score

1986. 175th Birth Anniv of Franz Liszt (composer).
2109 **847** 5s. green and brown . . 90 55

849 Strettweg Religious Carriage

1986. 175th Anniv of Styrian Joanneum Museum.
2111 **849** 4s. multicoloured 55 40

850 "Nuremberg Letter Messenger" (16th century woodcut) **852** Headquarters

851 "Adoration of the Shepherds" (woodcut, Johann Georg Schwanthaler)

1986. Stamp Day.
2112 **850** 6s.+3s. multicoloured . . 1·40 1·50

1986. Christmas.
2113 **851** 5s. brown and gold . . . 70 50

1986. 40th Anniv of Federal Chamber of Trade and Industry.
2114 **852** 5s. multicoloured 70 50

853 Foundry Worker

1986. Austrian World of Work (1st series).
2115 **853** 4s. multicoloured 60 40
See also Nos. 2144, 2178, 2211, 2277, 2386, 2414, 2428, 2486, 2520, 2572 and 2605.

854 "The Educated Eye"

1987. Centenary of Adult Education in Vienna.
2116 **854** 5s. multicoloured 70 50

855 "Large Blue Madonna" (Anton Faistauer)

1987. Painters' Birth Centenaries. Multicoloured.
2117 4s. Type **855** 55 45
2118 6s. "Self-portrait" (Albert Paris Gutersloh) 80 70

856 Hundertwasser House, Vienna

1987. Europa and "Europalia 1987 Austria" Festival, Belgium.
2119 **856** 6s. multicoloured . . . . 1·10 1·40

857 Ice Hockey Players

1987. World Ice Hockey Championships, Vienna, and 75th Anniv of Austrian Ice Hockey Association.
2120 **857** 5s. multicoloured 70 55

858 Austria Centre

1987. Inaug of Austria Conference Centre, Vienna.
2121 **858** 5s. multicoloured 75 55

859 Salzburg

860 Machine Shop, 1920

1987. 700th Anniv of Salzburg Town Charter.
2122 **859** 5s. multicoloured 75 50

1987. Upper Austrian "Work–Men–Machines, the Route to Industrialized Society" Exhibition, Steyr.
2123 **860** 4s. black and red 55 40

861 Man and Woman

862 "Adele Bloch-Bauer I" (detail, Gustav Klimt)

1987. Equal Rights for Men and Women.
2124 **861** 5s. multicoloured 75 50

1987. Lower Austrian "Era of Emperor Franz Joseph: Splendour and Misery" Exhibition, Grafenegg Castle.
2125 **862** 4s. multicoloured 60 50

863 Archbishop and Salzburg

1987. 400th Anniv of Election of Prince Wolf Dietrich von Raitenau as Archbishop of Salzburg.
2126 **863** 4s. multicoloured 60 50

864 Schnitzler

865 Lace and Arms

1987. 125th Birth Anniv of Arthur Schnitzler (dramatist).
2127 **864** 6s. multicoloured 75 60

1987. 1100th Anniv of Lustenau.
2128 **865** 5s. multicoloured 75 50

867 Dachstein Giant Ice Cave

1987. Natural Beauty Spots.
2130 **867** 5s. green and black . . . 80 55

868 Engraver at Work

869 Dr. Karl Josef Bayer (chemist)

1987. 8th European Association of Engravers and Flexographers International Congress, Vienna.
2131 **868** 5s. brown, pink and grey 75 50

1987. 8th International Light Metal Meeting, Leoben and Vienna.
2132 **869** 5s. multicoloured 75 50

870 Passenger Ferry

871 Office Building, Vienna

1987. Centenary of 1st Achensee Steam Service.
2133 **870** 4s. multicoloured 55 50

1987. 10th Anniv of Office of Ombudsmen.
2134 **871** 5s. black, yellow and red 70 50

872 Schrodinger

873 Freistadt Town Square

1987. Birth Cent of Erwin Schrodinger (physicist).
2135 **872** 5s. brown, cream and bistre 75 50

1987. 125th Anniv of Freistadt Exhibitions.
2136 **873** 5s. multicoloured 75 50

874 Arbing Church

1987. 850th Anniv of Arbing.
2137 **874** 5s. multicoloured 75 50

875 Gauertal and Montafon Valleys, Voralberg

1987. Natural Beauty Spots.
2138 **875** 5s. brown and yellow . . 80 50

876 Cyclist

877 Emblem

1987. World Cycling Championship, Vienna and Villach.
2139 **876** 5s. multicoloured 75 50

1987. World Congress of International Institute of Savings Banks, Vienna.
2140 **877** 5s. multicoloured 75 45

878 Hofhaymer at Organ

880 Lammergeier ("Bartgeier")

879 Haydn and Salzburg

1987. 450th Death Anniv of Paul Hofhaymer (composer and organist).
2141 **878** 4s. blue, black and gold 70 40

1987. 250th Birth Anniv of Michael Haydn (composer).
2142 **879** 4s. lilac 70 40

1987. 25th Anniv of Alpine Zoo, Innsbruck.
2143 **880** 4s. multicoloured 70 40

881 Woman using Word Processor

1987. Austrian World of Work (2nd series).
2144 **881** 4s. multicoloured 55 45

882 "Tree Goddesses" (Arnulf Neuwirth)

1987. Austrian Modern Art.
2145 **882** 5s. multicoloured 80 55

883 Lottery Wheel

884 Helmer

1987. Bicentenary of Gambling Monopoly.
2146 **883** 5s. multicoloured 75 45

1987. Birth Centenary of Oskar Helmer (politician).
2147 **884** 4s. multicoloured 55 40

885 Gluck

886 Stagecoach and Passengers (lithograph, Carl Schuster)

1987. Death Bicentenary of Christoph Willibald Gluck (composer).
2148 **885** 5s. brown and ochre . . 90 55

1987. Stamp Day.
2149 **886** 6s.+3s. multicoloured . . 1·40 1·50

887 Josef Mohr and Franz Xaver Gruber (composers of "Silent Night")

1987. Christmas.
2150 **887** 5s. multicoloured 90 45

888 Bosco and Boys **889** Cross-country Sledging

1988. International Educational Congress of St. John Bosco's Salesian Brothers, Vienna.
2151 **888** 5s. purple and orange . . 75 45

1988. 4th World Winter Games for the Disabled, Innsbruck.
2152 **889** 5s.+2s.50 multicoloured 1·00 1·25

890 Mach **891** "Village with Bridge"

1988. 150th Birth Anniv of Ernst Mach (physicist and philosopher).
2153 **890** 6s. multicoloured 75 60

1988. 25th Death Anniv of Franz von Zulow (artist).
2154 **891** 4s. multicoloured 55 50

892 "The Confiscation" (Ferdinand Georg Waldmuller)

1988. "Patriotism and Protest: Viennese Biedermeier and Revolution" Exhibition, Vienna.
2155 **892** 4s. multicoloured 55 50

893 Barbed Wire, Flag and Crosses

1988. 50th Anniv of Annexation of Austria by Germany.
2156 **893** 5s. green, brown and red 75 45

894 Steam Locomotive "Aigen", Muhlkreis Railway, 1887 **895** European Bee Eater

1988. Railway Centenaries. Multicoloured.
2157 4s. Type **894** 60 60
2158 5s. Modern electric tram and Josefsplatz stop (Viennese Local Railways Stock Corporation) . . . 70 55

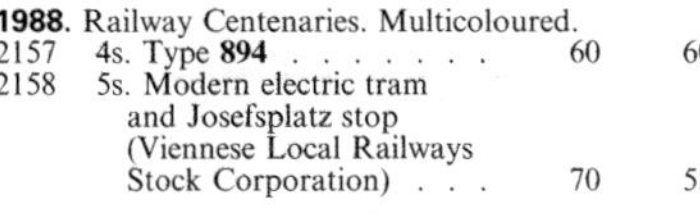

1988. 25th Anniv of World Wildlife Fund, Austria.
2159 **895** 5s. multicoloured 90 55

896 Decanter and Beaker **897** Late Gothic Silver Censer

1988. Styrian "Glass and Coal" Exn, Barnbach.
2160 **896** 4s. multicoloured 55 45

1988. Lower Austrian "Art and Monastic Life at the Birth of Austria" Exhibition, Seitenstetten Benedictine Monastery.
2161 **897** 4s. multicoloured 55 40

898 Taking Casualty to Volkswagen Transporter Ambulance and Red Cross **900** Mattsee Monastery

899 Dish Aerials, Aflenz

1988. 125th Anniv of Red Cross.
2162 **898** 12s. black, red and green 1·50 1·10

1988. Europa. Telecommunications.
2163 **899** 6s. multicoloured 85 60

1988. Salzburg "Bajuvars from Severin to Tassilo" Exhibition, Mattsee Monastery.
2164 **900** 4s. multicoloured 55 50

901 Weinberg Castle **902** Horvath

1988. Upper Austrian "Muhlviertel: Nature, Culture, Life" Exhibition, Weinberg Castle, near Kefermarkt.
2165 **901** 4s. multicoloured 55 50

1988. 50th Death Anniv of Odon von Horvath (writer).
2166 **902** 6s. black and bistre . . . 85 55

903 Stockerau Town Hall

1988. 25th Anniv of Stockerau Festival.
2167 **903** 5s. multicoloured 75 45

904 Motorway **905** Brixlegg

1988. Completion of Tauern Motorway.
2168 **904** 4s. multicoloured 55 40

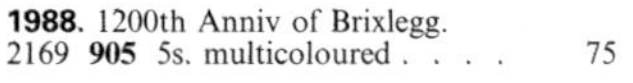

1988. 1200th Anniv of Brixlegg.
2169 **905** 5s. multicoloured 75 45

906 Klagenfurt (after Matthaus Merian)

1988. 400th Anniv of Regular Postal Services in Carinthia.
2170 **906** 5s. multicoloured 75 45

907 Parish Church and Dean's House

1988. 1200th Anniv of Brixen im Thale, Tyrol.
2171 **907** 5s. multicoloured 75 45

908 Krimml Waterfalls, Upper Tauern National Park

1988. Natural Beauty Spots.
2172 **908** 5s. black and blue . . . 75 55

909 Town Arms

1988. 1100th Anniv of Feldkirchen, Carinthia.
2173 **909** 5s. multicoloured 75 45

910 Feldbach

1988. 800th Anniv of Feldbach.
2174 **910** 5s. multicoloured 75 55

911 Ansfelden **912** Hologram of Export Emblem

1988. 1200th Anniv of Ansfelden.
2175 **911** 5s. multicoloured 75 45

1988. Federal Economic Chamber Export Congress.
2176 **912** 8s. multicoloured . . . . 1·90 2·00

913 Concert Hall

1988. 75th Anniv of Vienna Concert Hall.
2177 **913** 5s. multicoloured 75 45

914 Laboratory Assistant

1988. Austrian World of Work (3rd series).
2178 **914** 4s. multicoloured 55 50

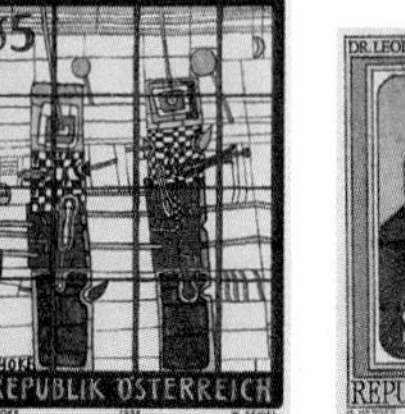

915 "Guards" (Giselbert Hoke) **916** Schonbauer

1988. Austrian Modern Art.
2179 **915** 5s. multicoloured 75 45

1988. Birth Centenary of Dr. Leopold Schonbauer (neurosurgeon and politician).
2180 **916** 4s. multicoloured 65 50

917 Carnation **918** Loading Railway Mail Van at Pardubitz Station, 1914

1988. Cent of Austrian Social Democratic Party.
2181 **917** 4s. multicoloured 55 45

1988. Stamp Day.
2182 **918** 6s.+3s. multicoloured . . 1·40 1·50

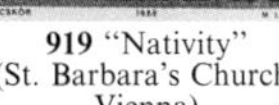

919 "Nativity" (St. Barbara's Church, Vienna) **920** "Madonna" (Lucas Cranach)

1988. Christmas.
2183 **919** 5s. multicoloured 75 45

1989. 25th Anniv of Diocese of Innsbruck.
2184 **920** 4s. multicoloured 55 50

921 Margrave Leopold II leading Abbot Sigibold and Monks to Melk (detail of fresco, Paul Troger)

1989. 900th Anniv of Melk Benedictine Monastery.
2185 **921** 5s. multicoloured 75 45

922 Marianne Hainisch **923** Glider and Paraskier

1989. 150th Birth Anniv of Marianne Hainisch (women's rights activist).
2186 **922** 6s. multicoloured 80 60

1989. World Gliding Championships, Wiener Neustadt, and World Paraskiing Championships, Damuls.
2187 **923** 6s. multicoloured 80 60

924 "The Painting" **926** Wittgenstein

925 "Bruck an der Leitha" (17th-century engraving, Georg Vischer)

1989. 50th Death Anniv of Rudolf Jettmar (painter).
2188 **924** 5s. multicoloured 75 45

1989. 750th Anniv of Bruck an der Leitha.
2189 **925** 5s. multicoloured 75 50

1989. Birth Centenary of Ludwig Wittgenstein (philosopher).
2190 **926** 5s. multicoloured 75 45

927 Holy Trinity Church, Stadl-Paura **928** Suess (after Josef Kriehuber) and Map

1989. 250th Death Anniv of Johann Michael Prunner (architect).
2191 **927** 5s. multicoloured 75 45

1989. 75th Death Anniv of Eduard Suess (geologist and politician).
2192 **928** 6s. multicoloured 80 70

929 "Judenburg" (17th-century engraving, Georg Vischer) **930** Steam Engine (Vinzenz Prick)

1989. Upper Styrian "People, Coins, Markets" Exhibition, Judenburg.
2193 **929** 4s. multicoloured 55 55

1989. Lower Austrian "Magic of Industry" Exhibition, Pottenstein.
2194 **930** 4s. blue and gold 55 55

931 Radstadt

1989. 700th Anniv of Radstadt.
2195 **931** 5s. multicoloured 75 45

932 Wooden Salt Barge from Viechtau

1989. Europa. Children's Toys.
2196 **932** 6s. multicoloured 80 75

933 "St. Adalbero and Family before Madonna and Child" (Monastery Itinerary Book) **935** Hansa Brandenburg C-1 Mail Biplane at Vienna, 1918

934 "Gisela" (paddle-steamer)

1989. Upper Austrian "Graphic Art" Exhibition and 900th Anniv of Lambach Monastery Church.
2197 **933** 4s. multicoloured 55 50

1989. 150th Anniv of Passenger Shipping on Traunsee.
2198 **934** 5s. multicoloured 75 50

1989. Stamp Day.
2199 **935** 6s.+3s. multicoloured . . 1·40 1·50

936 St. Andra (after Matthaus Merian)

1989. 650th Anniv of St. Andra.
2200 **936** 5s. multicoloured 75 45

937 Strauss **938** Locomotive

1989. 125th Birth Anniv of Richard Strauss (composer).
2201 **937** 6s. red, brown and gold 85 75

1989. Centenary of Achensee Steam Rack Railway.
2202 **938** 5s. multicoloured 80 50

939 Parliament Building, Vienna

1989. Centenary of Interparliamentary Union.
2203 **939** 6s. multicoloured 80 75

940 Anniversary Emblem

1989. Centenary of National Insurance in Austria.
2204 **940** 5s. multicoloured 75 50

941 U.N. Building, Vienna

1989. 10th Anniv of U.N. Vienna Centre.
2205 **941** 8s. multicoloured . . . . 1·00 75

942 Lusthaus Water, Prater Woods, Vienna

1989. Natural Beauty Spots.
2206 **942** 5s. black and buff . . . 75 45

943 Wildalpen and Hammerworks

1989. 850th Anniv of Wildalpen.
2207 **943** 5s. multicoloured 75 50

944 Emblem **946** "Tree of Life" (Ernst Steiner)

945 Palace of Justice, Vienna

1989. 33rd Congress of European Organization for Quality Control, Vienna.
2208 **944** 6s. multicoloured 80 75

1989. 14th Congress of Int Assn of Criminal Law.
2209 **945** 6s. multicoloured 80 60

1989. Austrian Modern Art.
2210 **946** 5s. multicoloured 75 50

947 Bricklayer **948** Ludwig Anzengruber (150th birth anniv)

1989. Austrian World of Work (4th series).
2211 **947** 5s. multicoloured 75 50

1989. Writers' Anniversaries. Multicoloured.
2212 4s. Type **948** 55 50
2213 4s. Georg Trakl (75th death anniv) 55 50

949 Fried **950** "Adoration of the Shepherds" (detail, Johann Carl von Reslfeld)

1989. 125th Birth Anniv of Alfred Fried (Peace Movement worker).
2214 **949** 6s. multicoloured 80 75

1989. Christmas.
2215 **950** 5s. multicoloured 75 40

951 "Courier" (Albrecht Durer) **952** Streif Downhill and Ganslern Slalom Runs

1990. 500th Anniv of Regular European Postal Services.
2216 **951** 5s. chocolate, cinnamon and brown 75 45

1990. 50th Hahnenkamm Ski Championships, Kitzbuhel.
2217 **952** 5s. multicoloured 75 45

953 Sulzer **954** Emich

1990. Death Centenary of Salomon Sulzer (creator of modern Synagogue songs).
2218 **953** 4s.50 multicoloured . . . 85 55

1990. 50th Death Anniv of Friedrich Emich (microchemist).
2219 **954** 6s. purple and green . . 75 70

955 Emperor Friedrich III (miniature by Ulrich Schreier)

1990. 500th Anniv of Linz as Capital of Upper Austria.
2220 **955** 5s. multicoloured 75 55

956 University Seals

1990. 625th Anniv of Vienna University and 175th Anniv of Vienna University of Technology.
2221 **956** 5s. red, gold and lilac . . 75 55

957 South Styrian Vineyards

1990. Natural Beauty Spots.
2222 **957** 5s. black and yellow . . 80 55

958 Parish Church

959 1897 May Day Emblem

1990. 1200th Anniv of Anthering.
2223 **958** 7s. multicoloured . . . . 1·40 80

1990. Centenary of Labour Day.
2224 **959** 4s.50 multicoloured . . . 70 55

960 "Our Dear Housewife of Seckau" (relief)

961 Ebene Reichenau Post Office

1990. 850th Anniv of Seckau Abbey.
2225 **960** 4s.50 blue 70 50

1990. Europa. Post Office Buildings.
2226 **961** 7s. multicoloured . . . . 1·25 80

962 Thematic Stamp Motifs

963 Makart (self-portrait)

1990. Stamp Day.
2227 **962** 7s.+3s. multicoloured . . 1·50 1·60

1990. 150th Birth Anniv of Hans Makart (painter).
2228 **963** 4s.50 multicoloured . . . 70 50

964 Schiele (self-portrait)

965 Raimund

1990. Birth Centenary of Egon Schiele (painter).
2229 **964** 5s. multicoloured 75 55

1990. Birth Bicentenary of Ferdinand Raimund (actor and playwright).
2230 **965** 4s.50 multicoloured . . . 70 50

966 "The Hundred Guilden Note" (Rembrandt)

1990. 2nd Int Christus Medicus Congress, Bad Ischl.
2231 **966** 7s. multicoloured . . . . 1·25 80

967 Hardegg

1990. 700th Anniv of Hardegg's Elevation to Status of Town.
2232 **967** 4s.50 multicoloured . . . 70 70

968 Oberdrauburg (copperplate engraving, Freiherr von Valvasor)

970 Zdarsky skiing

969 Church and Town Hall

1990. 750th Anniv of Oberdrauburg.
2233 **968** 5s. multicoloured 75 50

1990. 850th Anniv of Gumpoldskirchen.
2234 **969** 5s. multicoloured 75 50

1990. 50th Death Anniv of Mathias Zdarsky (developer of alpine skiing).
2235 **970** 5s. multicoloured 85 80

971 "Telegraph", 1880, and "Anton Chekhov", 1978

1990. 150th Anniv of Modern (metal) Shipbuilding in Austria.
2236 **971** 9s. multicoloured . . . . 1·50 1·10

972 Perkonig

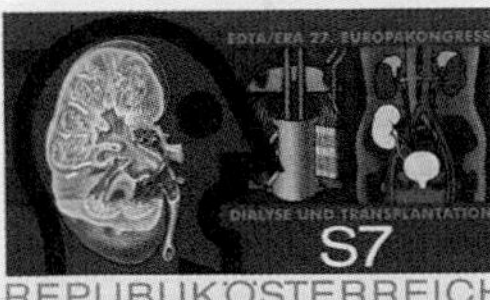

973 "Man of Rainbows" (Robert Zeppel-Sperl)

1990. Birth Centenary of Josef Friedrich Perkonig (writer).
2237 **972** 5s. sepia, brown & gold 75 50

1990. Austrian Modern Art.
2238 **973** 5s. multicoloured 75 50

974 Kidney, Dialysis Machine and Anatomical Diagram

1990. 27th European Dialysis and Transplantation Federation Congress, Vienna.
2239 **974** 7s. multicoloured . . . . 1·25 75

975 Werfel

1990. Birth Centenary of Franz Werfel (writer).
2240 **975** 5s. multicoloured 75 55

976 U.N. and Austrian Flags

1990. 30th Anniv of Austrian Participation in U.N. Peace-keeping Forces.
2241 **976** 7s. multicoloured . . . . 1·25 80

977 Arms of Provinces

1990. 45th Anniv of First Provinces Conference (established Second Republic as Federal State).
2242 **977** 5s. multicoloured 75 50

978 University Seal

979 Vogelsang

1990. 150th Anniv of Mining University, Leoben.
2243 **978** 4s.50 black, red & green 70 50

1990. Death Centenary of Karl von Vogelsang (Christian social reformer).
2244 **979** 4s.50 multicoloured . . . 70 50

980 Metal Workers

1990. Centenary of Metal, Mining and Energy Trade Union.
2245 **980** 5s. multicoloured 75 50

981 Player

982 Greenhouse

1990. 3rd World Ice Curling Championships, Vienna.
2246 **981** 7s. multicoloured . . . . 1·25 80

1990. Re-opening of Schonbrunn Greenhouse.
2247 **982** 5s. multicoloured 75 80

983 "Birth of Christ"

984 Grillparzer

1990. Christmas. Detail of Altarpiece by Master Nikolaus of Verdun, Klosterneuburg Monastery.
2248 **983** 5s. multicoloured 75 40

1991. Birth Bicent of Franz Grillparzer (dramatist).
2249 **984** 4s.50 multicoloured . . . 70 70

985 Skier

986 Kreisky

1991. World Alpine Skiing Championships, Saalbach-Hinterglemm.
2250 **985** 5s. multicoloured 75 50

1991. 80th Birth Anniv of Bruno Kreisky (Chancellor, 1970–82).
2251 **986** 5s. multicoloured 75 50

987 Schmidt and Vienna Town Hall

1991. Death Centenary of Friedrich von Schmidt (architect).
2252 **987** 7s. multicoloured . . . . 1·25 80

988 Fountain, Vienna

1991. Anniversaries. Multicoloured.
2253 4s.50 Type **988** (250th death anniv of Georg Raphael Donner (sculptor)) . . . 55 50
2254 5s. "Kitzbuhel in Winter" (birth centenary of Alfons Walde (artist and architect)) 65 55
2255 7s. Vienna Stock Exchange (death centenary of Theophil von Hansen (architect)) 80 85
See also No. 2269.

989 M. von Ebner-Eschenbach

1991. 75th Death Anniv of Marie von Ebner-Eschenbach (writer).
2256 **989** 4s.50 purple 70 50

991 Obir Stalactite Caverns, Eisenkappel

1991. Natural Beauty Spots.
2258 **991** 5s. multicoloured 75 55

992 Spittal an der Drau (after Matthaus Merian)

1991. 800th Anniv of Spittal an der Drau.
2259 **992** 4s.50 multicoloured . . . 70 50

993 "ERS-1" European Remote Sensing Satellite

1991. Europa. Europe in Space.
2260 **993** 7s. multicoloured . . . . 1·10 95

994 "Garden Party" (Anthoni Bays)

1991. Vorarlberg "Clothing and People" Exhibition, Hohenems.
2261 **994** 5s. multicoloured 75 50

995 Grein

1991. 500th Anniv of Grein Town Charter.
2262 **995** 4s.50 multicoloured . . . 70 50

996 Bedding Plants forming Arms

1991. 1200th Anniv of Tulln.
2263 **996** 5s. multicoloured 75 50

997 Military History Museum

1991. Vienna Museum Centenaries. Multicoloured.
2264 5s. Type **997** 75 60
2265 7s. Museum of Art History 95 70

998 "B" and "P"

999 Tunnel Entrance

1991. Stamp Day.
2266 **998** 7s.+3s. brown, sepia and black . . . . 1·40 1·90
This is the first of a series of ten annual stamps, each of which will illustrate two letters. The complete series will spell out the words "Briefmarke" and "Philatelie".

1991. Opening of Karawanken Road Tunnel between Carinthia and Slovenia.
2267 **999** 7s. multicoloured 85 80

1000 Town Hall

1991. 5th Anniv of St. Polten as Capital of Lower Austria.
2268 **1000** 5s. multicoloured . . . 75 55

1991. 150th Birth Anniv of Otto Wagner (architect). As T **988**. Multicoloured.
2269 4s.50 Karlsplatz Station, Vienna City Railway . . 70 50

1001 Rowing

1991. Junior World Canoeing Championships and World Rowing Championships, Vienna.
2270 **1001** 5s. multicoloured . . . 75 50

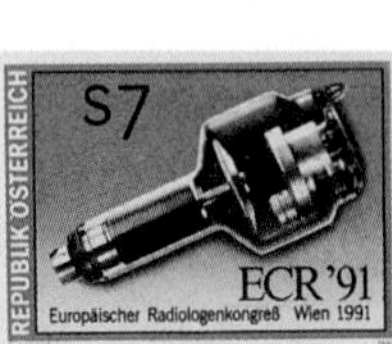

1002 X-ray Tube 1003 Paracelsus

1991. European Radiology Congress, Vienna.
2271 **1002** 7s. multicoloured . . . 90 80

1991. 450th Death Anniv of Theophrastus Bombastus von Hohenheim (Paracelsus) (physician and scientist).
2272 **1003** 4s. black, red & brown 70 50

1004 "Mir" Space Station 1005 Almabtrieb (driving cattle from mountain pastures) (Zell, Tyrol)

1991. "Austro Mir 91" Soviet–Austrian Space Flight.
2273 **1004** 9s. multicoloured . . . 1·40 1·75

1991. Folk Customs and Art (1st series). Mult.
2274 4s.50 Type **1005** 65 50
2275 5s. Vintage Crown (Neustift, Vienna) 70 60
2276 7s. Harvest monstrance (Nestelbach, Styria) . . . 90 85
See also Nos. 2305/7, 2349/51, 2363/5, 2393/5, 2418, 2432/3, 2450, 2482, 2491, 2500/1, 2508, 2524, 2546, 2550, 2552, 2568, 2581, 2587 and 2595.

1006 Weaver

1991. Austrian World of Work (5th series).
2277 **1006** 4s.50 multicoloured . . 70 50

1007 "The General" (Rudolf Pointner) 1008 Raab

1991. Austrian Modern Art.
2278 **1007** 5s. multicoloured . . . 75 55

1991. Birth Centenary of Julius Raab (Chancellor, 1953–61).
2279 **1008** 4s.50 brown & chestnut 70 50

1009 "Birth of Christ" (detail of fresco, Baumgartenberg Church)

1991. Christmas.
2280 **1009** 5s. multicoloured . . . 75 55

1010 Clerks

1992. Centenary of Trade Union of Clerks in Private Enterprise.
2281 **1010** 5s.50 multicoloured . . 75 55

1011 Emblems of Games and Olympic Rings

1992. Winter Olympic Games, Albertville, and Summer Games, Barcelona.
2282 **1011** 7s. multicoloured . . . 1·25 90

1012 Competitor

1992. 8th World Toboggan Championships on Natural Runs, Bad Goisern.
2283 **1012** 5s. multicoloured . . . 75 50

1013 Hollow Stone, Klostertal

1992. Natural Beauty Spots.
2284 **1013** 5s. multicoloured . . . 75 50

1014 Saiko 1015 "Athlete with Ball" (Christian Attersee)

1992. Birth Centenary of George Saiko (writer).
2285 **1014** 5s.50 brown 75 55

1992. Centenary of Workers' Sport Movement.
2286 **1015** 5s.50 multicoloured . . 75 60

1016 Franz Joseph Muller (chemist and mineralogist)

1992. Scientific Anniversaries. Multicoloured.
2287 5s. Type **1016** (250th birth anniv) 70 60
2288 5s.50 Paul Kitaibel (botanist, 175th death anniv) 75 70
2289 6s. Christian Doppler (physicist) (150th anniv of observation of Doppler Effect) 80 85
2290 7s. Richard Kuhn (chemist, 25th death anniv) 95 80

1018 First and Present Emblems

1992. Centenary of Railway Workers' Trade Union.
2292 **1018** 5s.50 red and black . . 75 55

1019 Hanrieder 1020 Scenes from "The Birdseller" (Zeller) and "The Beggar Student" (Millocker)

1992. 150th Birth Anniv of Norbert Hanrieder (writer).
2293 **1019** 5s.50 lilac & brown . . 75 55

1992. 150th Birth Anniversaries of Carl Zeller and Karl Millocker (composers).
2294 **1020** 6s. multicoloured . . . 90 85

1021 Foundry and Process

1992. Ironworks Day. 40th Anniv of First LD-Process Steel Works, Linz.
2295 **1021** 5s. multicoloured . . . 75 50

1022 Woodcut of the Americas by Sebastian Munster (from "Geographia Universalis" by Claudius Ptolomaus)

1992. Europa. 500th Anniv of Discovery of America by Columbus.
2296 **1022** 7s. multicoloured . . . 1·25 1·10

1023 Dredger 1024 Rieger

1992. Centenary of Treaty for International Regulation of the Rhine.
2297 **1023** 7s. multicoloured . . . 1·10 80

1992. Centenary of Adoption of Pseudonym Reimmichl by Sebastian Rieger (writer).
2298 **1024** 5s. brown 75 55

1025 Flags and Alps **1026** Dr. Anna Dengel

1992. Alpine Protection Convention.
2299 **1025** 5s.50 multicoloured . . 75 55

1992. Birth Centenary of Dr. Anna Dengel (founder of Medical Missionary Sisters).
2300 **1026** 5s.50 multicoloured . . 75 55

1027 "R" and "H"

1992. Stamp Day.
2301 **1027** 7s.+3s. multicoloured 1·10 1·60
See note below No. 2266.

1028 Town Hall

1992. 750th Anniv of First Documentation of Lienz as a Town.
2302 **1028** 5s. multicoloured . . . 75 50

1029 "Billroth in Lecture Room" (A. F. Seligmann) **1030** Waldheim

1992. Austrian Surgery Society International Congress, Eisenstadt.
2303 **1029** 6s. multicoloured . . . 80 80

1992. Presidency of Dr. Kurt Waldheim.
2304 **1030** 5s.50 black, red & grey 75 55

1992. Folk Customs and Art (2nd series). As T **1005**. Multicoloured.
2305 5s. Target with figure of Zieler, Lower Austria, 1732 . . . . 65 60
2306 5s.50 Chest, Carinthia . . . 70 70
2307 7s. Votive tablet from Venser Chapel, Vorarlberg 80 80

1031 Bridge over Canal

1992. Completion of Marchfeld Canal System.
2308 **1031** 5s. multicoloured . . . 75 50

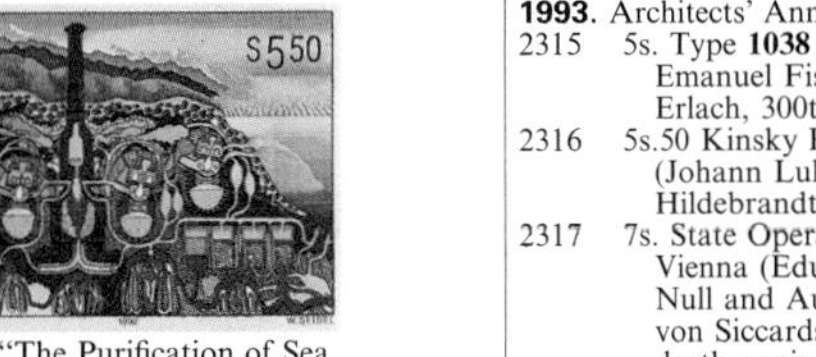

1032 "The Purification of Sea Water" (Peter Pongratz)

1992. Austrian Modern Art.
2309 **1032** 5s.50 multicoloured . . 75 65

1033 Gateway, Hofburg Palace (venue)

1992. 5th Int Ombudsmen's Conference, Vienna.
2310 **1033** 5s.50 multicoloured . . 75 55

1034 Academy Seal **1035** "The Annunciation"

1992. 300th Anniv of Academy of Fine Arts, Vienna.
2311 **1034** 5s. blue and red 75 60

1992. Death Bicentenary of Veit Koniger (sculptor).
2312 **1035** 5s. multicoloured . . . 75 50

1036 "Birth of Christ" (Johann Georg Schmidt)

1992. Christmas.
2313 **1036** 5s.50 multicoloured . . 75 50

1037 Earth and Satellite

1992. Birth Centenary of Hermann Potocnik (alias Noordung) (space travel pioneer).
2314 **1037** 10s. multicoloured . . . 1·40 1·40

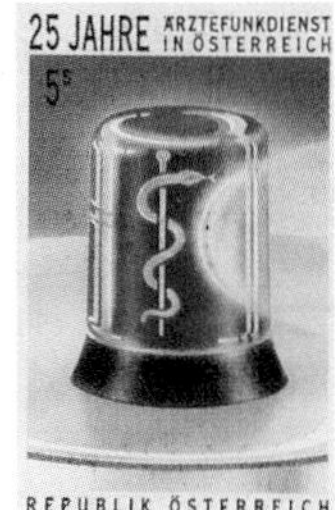

1038 Dome of Michael Wing, Hofburg Palace, Vienna **1039** Emergency Vehicle's Flashing Lantern

1993. Architects' Anniversaries. Multicoloured.
2315 5s. Type **1038** (Joseph Emanuel Fischer von Erlach, 300th birth) . . . 65 50
2316 5s.50 Kinsky Palace, Vienna (Johann Lukas von Hildebrandt, 325th birth) 70 55
2317 7s. State Opera House, Vienna (Eduard van der Null and August Siccard von Siccardsburg, 125th death annivs) 80 70

1993. 25th Anniv of Radio-controlled Emergency Medical Service.
2318 **1039** 5s. multicoloured . . . 75 55

1040 Wilder Kaiser Massif, Tyrol

1993. Natural Beauty Spots.
2319 **1040** 6s. multicoloured . . . 80 80

1041 Mitterhofer Typewriter

1993. Death Centenary of Peter Mitterhofer (typewriter pioneer).
2320 **1041** 17s. multicoloured . . . 2·00 2·10

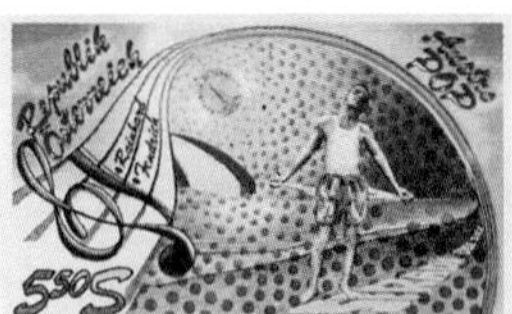

1042 "Strada del Sole" (record sleeve)

1993. "Austro Pop" (1st series). Rainhard Fendrich (singer).
2321 **1042** 5s.50 multicoloured . . 75 55
See also Nos. 2356 and 2368.

1043 Games Emblem

1993. Winter Special Olympics, Salzburg and Schladming.
2322 **1043** 6s.+3s. multicoloured 1·00 1·75

1044 Sealsfield **1045** Girl realizing her Rights

1993. Birth Bicent of Charles Sealsfield (novelist).
2323 **1044** 10s. red, blue and gold 1·40 1·10

1993. Ratification of U.N. Convention on Children's Rights.
2324 **1045** 7s. multicoloured . . . 90 85

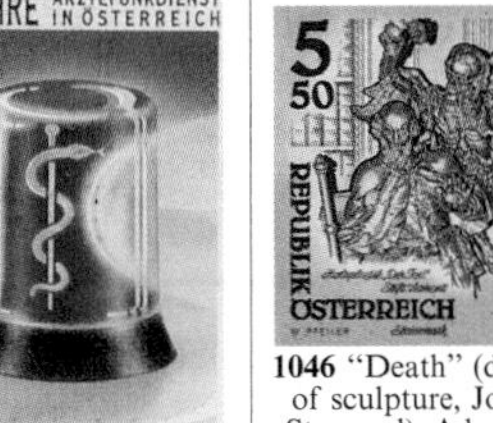

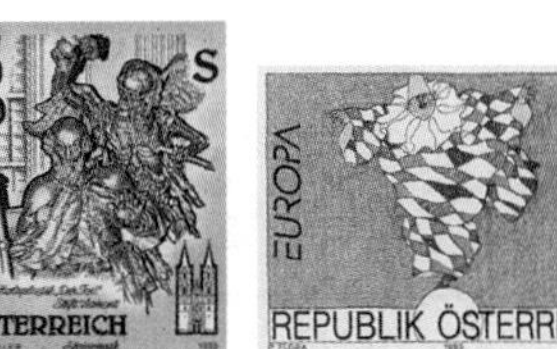

1046 "Death" (detail of sculpture, Josef Stammel), Admont Monastery, Styria **1047** "Flying Harlequin" (Paul Flora)

1993. Monasteries and Abbeys.
2325 – 1s. brown, black & grn 20 10
2328 **1046** 5s.50 black, yell & grn 75 20
2329 – 6s. black, mauve & yell 75 15
2330 – 7s. brown, black & grey 80 45
2331 – 7s.50 brown, bl & blk 90 40
2332 – 8s. orange, black & bl 1·10 55
2334 – 10s. black, blue & orge 1·40 35
2339 – 20s. black, blue & yell 1·50 65
2340 – 26s. orange, black & bis 3·25 1·90
2341 – 30s. red, yellow & black 3·50 1·25

DESIGNS: 1s. The Annunciation (detail of crosier of Abbess), St. Gabriel Benedictine Abbey, Bertholdstein; 6s. St. Benedict of Nursia (glass painting), Mariastern Abbey, Gwiggen; 7s. Marble lion, Franciscan Monastery, Salzburg; 7s.50, Virgin Mary (detail of cupola painting by Paul Troger), Altenburg Monastery; 8s. Early Gothic doorway, Wilhering Monastery; 10s. "The Healing of St. Peregrinus" (altarpiece), Maria Luggau Monastery; 20s. Hartmann Crosier, St. Georgenberg Abbey, Fiecht; 26s. "Master Dolorosa" (sculpture), Franciscan Monastery, Schwaz; 30s. Madonna and Child, Monastery of the Scottish Order, Vienna.

1993. Europa. Contemporary Art.
2345 **1047** 7s. multicoloured . . . 1·10 90

1048 Silhouette, Script and Signature **1049** "Hohentwiel" (lake steamer) and Flags

1993. 150th Birth Anniv of Peter Rosegger (writer and newspaper publisher).
2346 **1048** 5s.50 black and green 75 55

1993. Lake Constance European Region.
2347 **1049** 6s. multicoloured . . . 80 70

1050 Knights in Battle and "I"s **1051** Human Rights Emblem melting Bars

1993. Stamp Day.
2348 **1050** 7s.+3s. gold, black and blue . . . . 1·40 1·50
See note below No. 2266.

1993. Folk Customs and Art (3rd series). As T **1005**. Multicoloured.
2349 5s. Corpus Christi Day procession, Hallstatt, Upper Austria 70 50
2350 5s.50 Drawing the block (log), Burgenland 75 55
2351 7s. Aperschnalzen (whipping the snow away), Salzburg 85 85

1993. U.N. World Conf on Human Rights, Vienna.
2352 **1051** 10s. multicoloured . . . 1·40 1·10

1052 Jagerstatter **1053** Train approaching Wolfgangsee

1993. 50th Death Anniv of Franz Jagerstatter (conscientious objector).
2353 **1052** 5s.50 multicoloured . . 80 60

1993. Centenary of Schafberg Cog Railway.
2354 **1053** 6s. multicoloured . . . 1·10 75

1054 "Self-portrait with Doll"

1993. Birth Centenary of Rudolf Wacker (artist).
2355 **1054** 6s. multicoloured . . . 75 60

1993. "Austro Pop" (2nd series). Ludwig Hirsch (singer and actor). As T **1042**. Multicoloured.
2356 5s.50 "Die Omama" (record sleeve) 75 55

1055 "Concert in Dornbacher Park" (Balthasar Wigand)

1993. 150th Anniv of Vienna Male Choral Society.
2357 **1055** 5s. multicoloured . . . 70 55

1056 "Easter" (Max Weiler)

1057 "99 Heads" (detail, Friedensreich Hundertwasser)

1993. Austrian Modern Art.
2358 **1056** 5s.50 multicoloured . . 75 55

1993. Council of Europe Heads of State Conference, Vienna.
2359 **1057** 7s. multicoloured . . . 90 85

1058 Statue of Athene, Parliament Building

1060 "Birth of Christ" (Krainburg Altar, Styria)

1059 Workers

1993. 75th Anniv of Austrian Republic.
2360 **1058** 5s. multicoloured . . . 75 55

1993. Cent of 1st Austrian Trade Unions Congress.
2361 **1059** 5s.50 multicoloured . . 75 55

1993. Christmas.
2362 **1060** 5s.50 multicoloured . . 75 55

1994. Folk Customs and Art (4th series). As T **1005**. Multicoloured.
2363 5s.50 Rocking cradle, Vorarlberg 70 65
2364 6s. Carved sleigh, Styria . . 75 70
2365 7s. Godparent's bowl and lid, Upper Austria 90 90

1061 Winter Sports

1994. Winter Olympic Games, Lillehammer, Norway.
2366 **1061** 7s. multicoloured . . . 80 85

1062 Early Production of Coins

1994. 800th Anniv of Vienna Mint.
2367 **1062** 6s. multicoloured . . . 75 70

1994. "Austro Pop" (3rd series). Falco (Johann Holzel) (singer). As T **1042**. Multicoloured.
2368 6s. "Rock Me Amadeus" (record sleeve) 75 60

1063 "Reclining Lady" (detail, Herbert Boeckl)

1994. Birth Centenary of Herbert Boeckl (painter).
2369 **1063** 5s.50 multicoloured . . 75 60

1064 N.W. Tower of City Wall

1994. 800th Anniv of Wiener Neustadt.
2370 **1064** 6s. multicoloured . . . 75 55

1065 Lurgrotte (caves), Styria

1994. Natural Beauty Spots.
2371 **1065** 6s. multicoloured . . . 80 70

1066 Lake Rudolf (Teleki–Hohnel expedition to Africa, 1887)

1994. Europa. Discoveries.
2372 **1066** 7s. multicoloured . . . 1·10 85

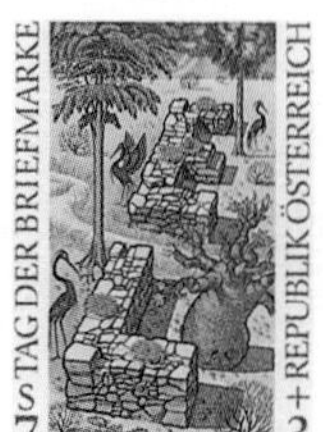
1067 "E" and "L" as Ruins in Landscape

1994. Stamp Day.
2373 **1067** 7s.+3s. multicoloured 1·40 1·60
See note below No. 2266.

1068 "Allegory of Theology, Justice, Philosophy and Medicine" (detail of fresco, National Library)

1994. 300th Birth Anniv of Daniel Gran (artist).
2374 **1068** 20s. multicoloured . . . 2·10 2·40

1069 Scene from "The Prodigal Son" (opera, Benjamin Britten)

1994. 25th Anniv of Carinthian Summer Festival, Ossiach and Villach.
2375 **1069** 5s.50 gold and red . . 75 50

1070 Steam Locomotive and Diesel Railcar (Gailtal)

1994. Railway Centenaries. Multicoloured.
2376 5s.50 Type **1070** 75 65
2377 6s. Steam locomotive and diesel railcar (Murtal) . . 90 70

1071 Gmeiner and Children

1072 Seitz (bust, G. Ambrosi)

1994. 75th Birth Anniv of Hermann Gmeiner (founder of S.O.S. children's villages).
2378 **1071** 7s. multicoloured . . . 80 80

1994. 125th Birth Anniv of Karl Seitz (acting President, 1920).
2379 **1072** 5s.50 multicoloured . . 75 65

1073 Bohm

1075 Franz Theodor Csokor (dramatist and poet)

1074 Ethnic Minorities on Map

1994. Birth Centenary of Karl Bohm (conductor).
2380 **1073** 7s. blue and gold . . . 90 1·10

1994. Legal and Cultural Protection of Ethnic Minorities.
2381 **1074** 5s.50 multicoloured . . 80 85

1994. Writers' Anniversaries. Multicoloured.
2382 6s. Type **1075** (25th death anniv) 75 70
2383 7s. Joseph Roth (novelist, birth cent) . . . . 90 1·10

1076 "Head" (Franz Ringel)

1077 Money Box

1994. Austrian Modern Art.
2384 **1076** 6s. multicoloured . . . 75 55

1994. 175th Anniv of Savings Banks in Austria.
2385 **1077** 7s. multicoloured . . . 80 85

1078 Air Hostess and Child

1994. Austrian World of Work (6th series).
2386 **1078** 6s. multicoloured . . . 75 70

1079 Coudenhove-Kalergi and Map of Europe

1994. Birth Cent of Richard Coudenhove-Kalergi (founder of Paneuropa Union).
2387 **1079** 10s. multicoloured . . . 1·40 1·10

1080 "Birth of Christ" (Anton Wollenek)

1081 Map and Austrian and E.U. Flags

1994. Christmas.
2388 **1080** 6s. multicoloured . . . 75 50

1995. Austria's Entry into E.U.
2389 **1081** 7s. multicoloured . . . 85 85

1082 Loos House, Michaelerplatz, Vienna

1995. 125th Birth Anniv of Adolf Loos (architect).
2390 **1082** 10s. multicoloured . . . 1·25 1·25

1083 Sporting Activities

1995. 50th Anniv of Austrian Gymnastics and Sports Association.
2391 **1083** 6s. multicoloured . . . 75 50

1084 Workers

1995. 75th Anniv of Workers' and Employees' Chambers (advisory body).
2392 **1084** 6s. multicoloured . . . 75 50

1995. Folk Costumes and Art (5th series). As T **1005**. Multicoloured.
2393 5s.50 Belt, Carinthia 70 55
2394 6s. Costume of Hiata (vineyard guard), Vienna 80 55
2395 7s. Gold bonnet, Wachau 90 85

1085 State Seal **1086** Heft Ironworks

1995. 50th Anniv of Second Republic.
2396 **1085** 6s. multicoloured . . . 75 50

1995. Carinthian "History of Mining and Industry" Exhibition, Heft, Huttenberg.
2397 **1086** 5s.50 multicoloured . . 75 50

1087 Hiker in Mountains

1995. Centenary of Friends of Nature.
2398 **1087** 5s.50 multicoloured . . 75 50

1088 Heidenreichstein National Park

1995. Natural Beauty Spots.
2399 **1088** 6s. multicoloured . . . 75 65

1089 Woman and Barbed Wire around Skull **1090** Map, Woman and Child and Transport

1995. Europa. Peace and Freedom.
2400 **1089** 7s. multicoloured . . . 90 80

1995. Meeting of European Ministers of Transport Conference, Vienna.
2401 **1090** 7s. multicoloured . . . 85 80

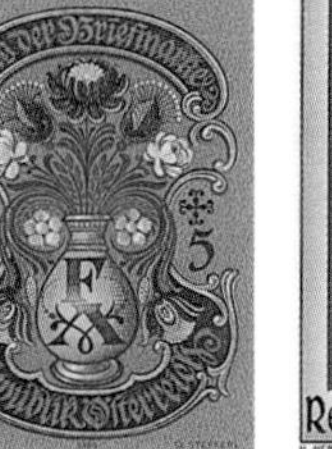

1091 "F" and "A" on Vase of Flowers **1093** St. Gebhard (stained-glass window, Martin Hausle)

1092 Set for "The Flying Dutchman"

1995. Stamp Day.
2402 **1091** 10s.+5s. mult . . . . . 1·75 2·25
See note below No. 2266.

1995. 50th Bregenz Festival.
2403 **1092** 6s. multicoloured . . . 75 70

1995. Death Millenary of St. Gebhard, Bishop of Konstanz (patron saint of Vorarlberg chuches).
2404 **1093** 7s.50 multicoloured . . 95 85

1094 Members' Flags **1095** Loschmidt

1995. 50th Anniv of U.N.O.
2405 **1094** 10s. multicoloured . . . 1·25 1·00

1995. Death Centenary of Josef Loschmidt (physical chemist).
2406 **1095** 20s. black, stone & brn 2·40 2·25

1096 K. Leichter **1097** Scene from "Jedermann" (Hugo von Hofmannsthal)

1995. Birth Cent of Kathe Leichter (sociologist).
2407 **1096** 6s. cream, black & red 75 55

1995. 75th Anniv of Salzburg Festival.
2408 **1097** 6s. multicoloured . . . 75 55

1098 "European Scene" (Adolf Frohner)

1995. Austrian Modern Art.
2409 **1098** 6s. multicoloured . . . 75 55

1099 Franz von Suppe and "The Beautiful Galatea"

1995. Composers' Anniversaries. Scenes from operettas. Multicoloured.
2410 6s. Type **1099** (death cent) 75 60
2411 7s. Nico Dostal and "The Hungarian Wedding" (birth centenary) 85 80

1100 University Building

1995. 25th Anniv of Klagenfurt University.
2412 **1100** 5s.50 multicoloured . . 75 65

1101 Hollenburg Castle

1995. 75th Anniv of Carinthian Referendum.
2413 **1101** 6s. multicoloured . . . 75 55

1102 Postman

1995. Austrian World of Work (7th series).
2414 **1102** 6s. multicoloured . . . 75 55

1103 Anton von Webern (50th death) **1104** Christ Child

1995. Composers' Anniversaries.
2415 **1103** 6s. blue and orange . . 75 55
2416 – 7s. red and orange . . 90 80
DESIGN: 7s. Ludwig van Beethoven (225th birth).

1995. Christmas. 300th Anniv of Christkindl Church.
2417 **1104** 6s. multicoloured . . . 75 55

1996. Folk Customs and Art (6th series). As T **1005**.
2418 6s. multicoloured 75 55
DESIGN: 6s. Masked figures Roller and Scheller (Imst masquerades, Tyrol).

1105 Empress Maria Theresia and Academy Building

1996. 250th Anniv of Theresian Academy, Vienna.
2419 **1105** 6s. multicoloured . . . 75 55

1106 Ski Jumping

1996. World Ski Jumping Championships, Tauplitz and Bad Mitterndorf.
2420 **1106** 7s. multicoloured . . . 90 80

1107 Terminal

1996. Completion of West Terminal, Vienna International Airport.
2421 **1107** 7s. multicoloured . . . 80 80

1108 Hohe Tauern National Park

1996. Natural Beauty Spots.
2422 **1108** 6s. multicoloured . . . 75 55

1109 "Mother and Child" (Peter Fendi) **1110** Organ and Music

1996. Artists' Birth Bicentenaries. Multicoloured.
2423 6s. Type **1109** 75 55
2424 7s. "Self-portrait" (Leopold Kupelwieser) 85 80

1996. Death Cent of Anton Bruckner (composer).
2425 **1110** 5s.50 multicoloured . . 85 70

1111 Kollmitz Castle (from copper engraving)

1996. 300th Death Anniv of Georg Vischer (cartographer and engraver).
2426 **1111** 10s. black and stone . . 1·40 1·10

1112 Old Market Square

1996. 800th Anniv of Klagenfurt.
2427 **1112** 6s. multicoloured . . . 75 60

1113 Hotel Chef and Waitress

1996. Austrian World of Work (8th series).
2428 **1113** 6s. multicoloured . . . 75 70

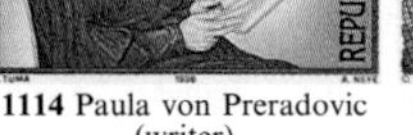
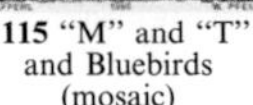

1114 Paula von Preradovic (writer)

1115 "M" and "T" and Bluebirds (mosaic)

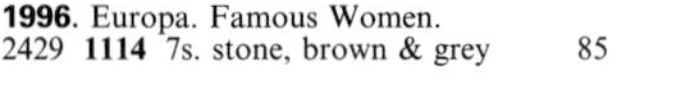

1996. Europa. Famous Women.
2429 **1114** 7s. stone, brown & grey . . . 85 80

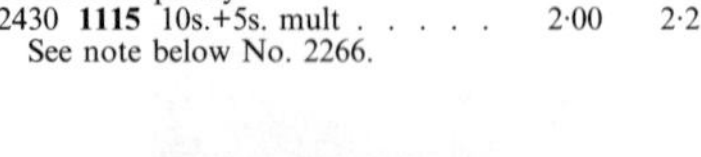

1996. Stamp Day.
2430 **1115** 10s.+5s. mult . . . . . 2·00 2·25
See note below No. 2266.

1116 Mascot with Olympic Flag

1996. Olympic Games, Atlanta.
2431 **1116** 10s. multicoloured . . . 1·40 1·10

1996. Folk Customs and Art (7th series). As T **1005**.
2432 5s.50 Flower-bedecked poles, Salzburg 80 70
2433 7s. Tyrol militia . . . . . . 90 1·00

1117 Landscape

1996. 75th Anniv of Burgenland.
2434 **1117** 6s. multicoloured . . . 80 70

1118 Mountaineers

1119 Deed of Otto III, 996

1996. Cent of Austrian Mountain Rescue Service.
2435 **1118** 6s. multicoloured . . . 80 60

1996. Millenary of Austria. Multicoloured.
2436 6s. Type **1119** 75 75
2437 6s. Archduke Joseph II (after Georg Weikert) and Archduchess Maria Theresia (after Martin van Meytens) 75 75
2438 7s. "Duke Heinrich II" (stained-glass window, Monastery of the Holy Cross) 85 90
2439 7s. Arms in flames (1848 Revolution) 85 90
2440 7s. Rudolf IV, the Founder 85 90
2441 7s. Karl Renner (first Federal Republic president) 85 90
2442 10s. Archduke Maximilian I (Holy Roman Emperor) (miniature from Statute Book of Order of the Golden Fleece) . . . . . 1·25 1·25
2443 10s. Seal and signature of Leopold Figl (State Treaty of 1955) . . . . . 1·25 1·25
2444 20s. Imperial crown of Rudolf II . . . . 2·50 2·75
2445 20s. State arms, stars of Europe and "The Horsebreaker" (bronze by Josef Lax) (Austria and Europe) . . . . 2·50 2·75

1120 "Power Station" (Reinhard Artberg)

1996. Austrian Modern Art.
2446 **1120** 7s. multicoloured . . . 90 95

1121 Children of Different Nations

1996. 50th Anniv of U.N.I.C.E.F.
2447 **1121** 10s. multicoloured . . . 1·40 1·10

1122 Nativity and Vienna Town Hall

1996. Christmas.
2448 **1122** 6s. multicoloured . . . 75 60

1123 Kramer

1997. Birth Centenary of Theodor Kramer (poet).
2449 **1123** 5s.50 blue 75 55

1997. Folk Customs and Art (8th series). As T **1005**. Multicoloured.
2450 7s. Epiphany carol singers, Eisenstadt Burgenland . . 80 80

1124 Vineyards on the Nussberg, Vienna

1997. Natural Beauty Spots.
2451 **1124** 6s. multicoloured . . . 75 55

1125 Academy and Light

1997. 150th Anniv of Austrian Academy of Sciences, Vienna.
2452 **1125** 10s. multicoloured . . . 1·40 1·10

1126 Emblem

1997. 50th Anniv of Verbund Electricity Company.
2453 **1126** 6s. multicoloured . . . 75 60

1127 The Cruel Rosalia of Forchtenstein

1128 Stage Set for "Die tote Stadt"

1997. Myths and Legends.
2459 – 6s.50 grn, pink & blk 80 60
2460 **1127** 7s. black, stone & brn 80 55
2461 – 8s. orange, blk & lilac 1·00 90
2462 – 9s. black, stone & pur 1·25 1·25
2462a – 10s. black, grey & red 1·40 1·40
2463 – 13s. black, brn & pur 1·75 1·50
2464 – 14s. black, lt blue & bl 1·75 1·75
2465 – 20s. green, blk & stone 2·25 2·25
2466 – 22s. black, bl & stone 2·50 2·50
2467 – 23s. black, ochre and green . . . . 2·50 2·50
2468 – 25s. stone, black and yellow . . . . . . 3·25 3·00
2469 – 32s. black, brn & pink 4·00 3·25
DESIGNS: 6s.50, Lindworm of Klagenfurt; 8s. The Black Lady of Hardegg; 9s. Charming Augustin; 10s. Basilisk of Vienna; 13s. The Pied Piper of Korneuburg; 14s. The Strudengau Water-nymph; 20s. St. Notburga; 22s. Witches Whirl; 23s. Loaf Agony; 25s. St. Konrad and Altems Castle; 32s. The Discovery of Erzberg (Mountain of Ore).

1997. Birth Cent of Erich Korngold (composer).
2470 **1128** 20s. black, blue & gold 2·40 1·75

1129 Stadium, Badge and Players

1997. Rapid Vienna, National Football Champions, 1995–96.
2471 **1129** 7s. multicoloured . . . 80 85

1130 Red Deer

1997. Hunting and the Environment. Deer Feeding in Winter.
2472 **1130** 7s. multicoloured . . . 80 75

1131 Canisius and Children (altar by Josef Bachlechner in Innsbruck Seminary)

1997. 400th Death Anniv of St. Petrus Canisius (patron saint of Innsbruck).
2473 **1131** 7s.50 multicoloured . . 85 90

1132 Johannes Brahms (after L. Michalek)

1997. Composers' Anniversaries.
2474 **1132** 6s. violet and gold . . . 80 75
2475 – 10s. purple and gold . . 1·40 1·25
DESIGNS: 6s. Type **1132** (death centenary); 10s. Franz Schubert (birth bicentenary).

1133 "A" and "E"

1134 The Four Friends

1997. Stamp Day.
2476 **1133** 7s. multicoloured . . . 80 85
See note below No. 2266.

1997. Europa. Tales and Legends. "The Town Band of Bremen" by the Brothers Grimm.
2477 **1134** 7s. multicoloured . . . 80 85

1135 1850 9k. Stamp and Postman

1997. "WIPA 2000" International Stamp Exhibition, Vienna (1st issue).
2478 **1135** 27s.+13s. mult . . . . 4·50 5·00
See also Nos. 2521 and 2543.

1136 Train on Hochschneeberg Line

1997. Railway Anniversaries. Multicoloured.
2479 6s. Type **1136** (centenary of Hochschneeberg rack-railway) 75 80
2480 7s.50 Steam locomotive "Licaon" and viaduct near Mattersburg (150th anniv of Odenburg–Wiener Neustadt line) . . 85 1·00

1137 Cogwheels

1138 Waggerl (self-portrait)

1997. 125th Anniv of Austrian Technical Supervisory Association.
2481 **1137** 7s. multicoloured . . . 80 85

1997. Folk Customs and Art (9th series). As T **1005**. Multicoloured.
2482 6s.50 Tyrolean brass band 80 80

1997. Birth Centenary of Karl Waggerl (writer).
2483 **1138** 7s. green, yellow & blue 80 85

1139 Adolf Lorenz (founder of German Society of Orthopaedia)

1997. Orthopaedics Congress, Vienna.
2484 **1139** 8s. multicoloured . . . 95 1·10

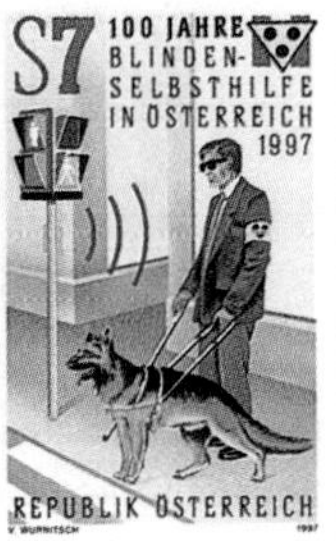

1140 Emblem

1142 Blind Man with Guide Dog

1141 Patient, Nurse and Doctor

1997. 125th Anniv of College of Agricultural Sciences, Vienna.
2485 **1140** 9s. multicoloured . . . 1·10 1·25

1997. Austrian World of Work (9th series).
2486 **1141** 6s.50 multicoloured . . 80 70

1997. Cent of Austrian Association for the Blind.
2487 **1142** 7s. multicoloured . . . 80 80

1143 "House in Wind" (Helmut Schickhofer)

1997. Austrian Modern Art.
2488 **1143** 7s. multicoloured . . . 80 75

1144 Klestil

1145 Werner

1997. 65th Birthday of Pres. Thomas Klestil.
2489 **1144** 7s. multicoloured . . . 80 85

1997. 75th Birth Anniv of Oskar Werner (actor).
2490 **1145** 7s. black, orge & grey 80 75

1997. Folk Customs and Art (10th series). As T **1005**. Multicoloured.
2491 6s.50 Tower wind-band, Upper Austria 80 75

1146 Glowing Light

1997. 25th Anniv of Light in Darkness (umbrella organization of children's charities).
2492 **1146** 7s. blue 80 85

1147 "Mariazell Madonna"

1997. Christmas.
2493 **1147** 7s. multicoloured . . . 80 75

1148 Kalkalpen National Park

1998. Natural Beauty Spots.
2494 **1148** 7s. multicoloured . . . 80 75

1149 Courting Pair

1998. Hunting and the Environment. Preservation of Breeding Habitat of the Black Grouse.
2495 **1149** 9s. multicoloured . . . 1·10 1·25

1150 Ice Skaters

1998. Winter Olympic Games, Nagano, Japan.
2496 **1150** 14s. multicoloured . . . 1·75 1·90

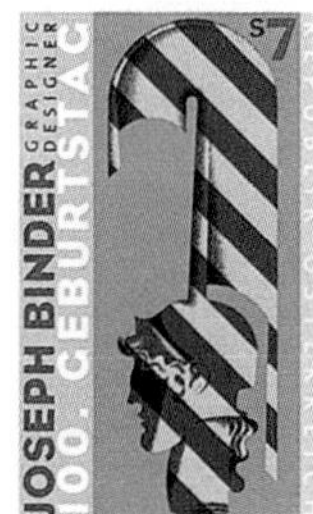

1151 Austrian Poster Exposition Advertising Poster, 1928

1152 Alois Senefelder (inventor) on Lithographic Stone

1998. Birth Cent of Joseph Binder (designer).
2497 **1151** 7s. multicoloured . . . 85 90

1998. Bicentenary of Invention of Lithography (printing process).
2498 **1152** 7s. blue, yellow & black 85 75

1153 Facade

1155 "St. Florian" (glass painting)

1154 Player and Team Emblem

1998. Centenary of Vienna Secession (exn hall).
2499 **1153** 8s. brown, gold & blue 95 1·00

1998. Folk Customs and Art (11th series). As T **1005**. Multicoloured.
2500 6s.50 Fiacre, Vienna 80 75
2501 7s. Palm Sunday procession, Thaur, Tyrol 80 85

1998. Austria Memphis Football Club.
2502 **1154** 7s. multicoloured . . . 85 85

1998. St. Florian, Patron Saint of Firemen.
2503 **1155** 7s. multicoloured . . . 85 85

1156 Rupertus Cross

1998. 1200th Anniv of Salzburg Archdiocese.
2504 **1156** 7s. multicoloured . . . 85 80

1157 Series Yv Locomotive No. 2, 1895

1998. Centenary of Completion of Ybbs Valley Railway.
2505 **1157** 6s.50 multicoloured . . 80 85

1158 "Tyrolia" (Ferdinand Cosandier)

1159 Vienna Town Hall (Viennese festive weeks)

1998. 175th Anniv of Tyrol Ferdinandeum (state museum), Innsbruck.
2506 **1158** 7s. multicoloured . . . 85 85

1998. Europa. National Festivals.
2507 **1159** 7s. multicoloured . . . 85 85

1998. Folk Customs and Art (12th series). As T **1005**. Multicoloured.
2508 6s.50 Samson and the dwarves, Salzburg 80 85

1160 Christine Lavant

1998. 25th Death Anniv of Christine Lavant (poet).
2509 **1160** 7s. multicoloured . . . 80 85

1161 Electric Railcar No. 1

1162 "R" and "L"

1998. Centenary of Postlingberg Railway.
2510 **1161** 6s.50 multicoloured . . 80 85

1998. Stamp Day.
2511 **1162** 7s. multicoloured . . . 80 1·10
See note below No. 2266.

1163 Presidency Emblem

1164 Railcar No. 5090

1998. Austrian Presidency of E.U.
2512 **1163** 7s. multicoloured . . . 80 85

1998. Centenary of Pinzgau Railway.
2513 **1164** 6s.50 multicoloured . . 80 85

1165 Volksoper, Vienna

1998. Centenary of Volksoper (theatre) and 50th Death Anniv of Franz Lehar (composer).
2514 **1165** 6s.50 multicoloured . . 80 95

1166 Empress Elisabeth (after Franz Winterhalter)

1998. Death Centenary of Empress Elisabeth.
2515 **1166** 7s. multicoloured . . . 85 85

1167 School Building

1998. Centenary of Vienna Business School.
2516 **1167** 7s. multicoloured . . . 80 95

1168 Kudlich and Farmers

1169 "My Garden" (Hans Staudacher)

1998. 175th Birth Anniv of Hans Kudlich (promoter of 1848 "Peasants' Liberation" Law).
2517 **1168** 6s.50 multicoloured . . 80 95

1998. Austrian Modern Art.
2518 **1169** 7s. multicoloured . . . 80 95

1170 Town Hall and Arms

1998. 350th Anniv of Declaration of Eisenstadt as a Free Town.
2519 **1170** 7s. multicoloured . . . 80 95

1171 Photographer and Reporter

1998. Austrian World of Work (10th series). Art, Media and Freelances.
2520 **1171** 6s.50 multicoloured . . 80 95

1172 1929 2s. Stamp and Post Van

1998. "WIPA 2000" International Stamp Exhibition, Vienna (2nd issue).
2521 **1172** 32s.+13s. mult . . . . 5·00 6·50

1173 "Nativity" (fresco, Tainach Church) **1174** Cross-country Skiing

1998. Christmas.
2522 **1173** 7s. multicoloured . . . 80 85

1999. World Nordic Skiing Championships, Ramsau.
2523 **1174** 7s. multicoloured . . . 80 95

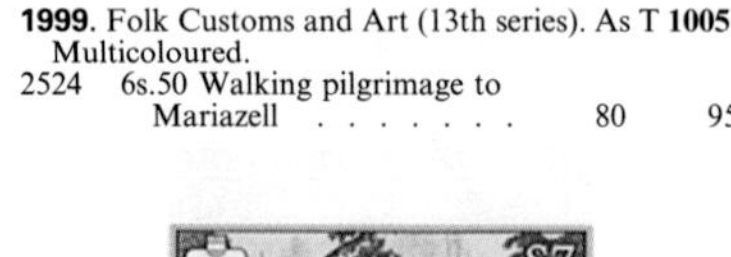

1999. Folk Customs and Art (13th series). As T **1005**. Multicoloured.
2524 6s.50 Walking pilgrimage to Mariazell 80 95

1175 Stingl Rock, Bohemian Forest

1999. Natural Beauty Spots.
2525 **1175** 7s. multicoloured . . . 80 95

1176 Books and Compact Disc

1999. Centenary of Austrian Patent Office.
2526 **1176** 7s. multicoloured . . . 80 95

1177 Player and Club Emblem

1999. SK Puntigamer Sturm Graz Football Club.
2527 **1177** 7s. multicoloured . . . 80 95

1178 Palace Facade

1999. World Heritage Site. Schonbrunn Palace, Vienna.
2528 **1178** 13s. multicoloured . . . 1·60 1·90

1179 Partridges

1999. Hunting and the Environment. Living Space for Grey Partridges.
2529 **1179** 6s.50 multicoloured . . 80 95

1180 Snowboarder

1999. 50th Anniv of Austrian General Sport Federation.
2530 **1180** 7s. multicoloured . . . 80 95

1181 Council Building, Strasbourg

1999. 50th Anniv of Council of Europe.
2531 **1181** 14s. multicoloured . . . 1·60 2·10

No. 2531 is denominated both in Austrian schillings and in euros.

1182 Steyr Type 50 Baby Saloon

1999. Birth Centenary of Karl Jenschke (engineer and car manufacturer).
2532 **1182** 7s. multicoloured . . . 80 95

1183 "St. Martin" (marble relief, Peuerbach Church)

1999. Ancient Arts and Crafts (1st series).
2533 **1183** 8s. brown, blue & orange . . . . 95 1·10

See also Nos. 2542, 2575, 2600 and 2602.

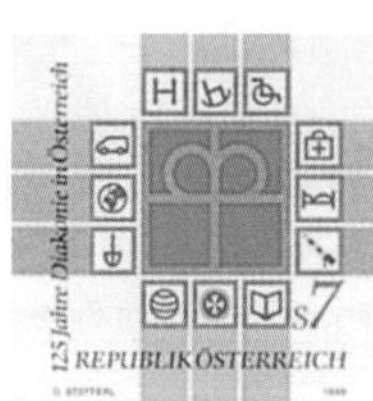
1184 Symbols of Aid and Emblem

1999. 125th Anniv of Diakonie (professional charitable services).
2534 **1184** 7s. multicoloured . . . 80 95

1185 Johann Strauss, the Younger

1999. Composers' Death Anniversaries. Mult.
2535 7s. Type **1185** (centenary) 80 95
2536 8s. Johann Strauss, the Elder (150th anniv) . . . 95 1·10

1186 Rural Gendarmes **1188** "K" and "I"

1187 Donau-auen National Park

1999. 150th Anniv of National Gendarmerie.
2537 **1186** 7s. multicoloured . . . 80 95

1999. Europa. Parks and Gardens.
2538 **1187** 7s. multicoloured . . . 80 95

1999. Stamp Day.
2539 **1188** 7s. multicoloured . . . 80 95

See note below No. 2266.

1189 Iron Stage Curtain

1999. Centenary of Graz Opera.
2540 **1189** 6s.50 multicoloured . . 80 95

1190 Couple on Bench

1999. International Year of the Elderly.
2541 **1190** 7s. multicoloured . . . 80 95

1191 "St. Anne with Mary and Child Jesus" (wood-carving, St. George's Church, Purgg)

1999. Ancient Arts and Crafts (2nd series).
2542 **1191** 9s. multicoloured . . . 1·00 1·25

1192 1949 25g. Stamp and Vienna Airport

1999. "WIPA 2000" International Stamp Exhibition, Vienna (3rd issue).
2543 **1192** 32s.+16s. mult . . . . 5·25 6·75

1193 "Security throughout Life" **1194** "Cafe Girardi" (Wolfgang Herzig)

1999. 14th Congress of Federation of Austrian Trade Unions.
2544 **1193** 6s.50 multicoloured . . 80 95

1999. Austrian Modern Art.
2545 **1194** 7s. multicoloured . . . 80 95

1999. Folk Customs and Art (14th series). As T **1005**. Multicoloured.
2546 8s. Pumpkin Festival, Lower Austria . . . . 95 1·10

1999. Folk Customs and Art (15th series). As T **1005**. Multicoloured.
2547 7s. The Pummerin (great bell of St. Stephen's Cathedral) ringing in the New Year 80 95

1195 Institute and Fossils

1999. 150th Anniv of National Institute of Geology.
2548 **1195** 7s. multicoloured . . . 80 95

1196 "Nativity" (altar painting, Pinkafeld Church)

1999. Christmas.
2549 **1196** 7s. multicoloured . . . 80 90

2000. Folk Customs and Art (16th series). As T **1005**. Multicoloured.
2550 7s. Chapel procession, Carinthia . . . . 80 1·00

2000. Folk Customs and Art (17th series). As T **1005**. Multicoloured.
2552 6s.50 Three men wearing masks (Cavalcade of Beautiful Masks, Telfs) 80 95

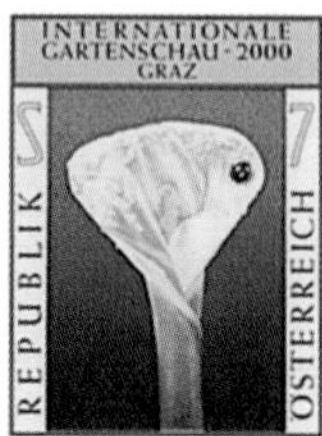

1197 *Zantadeschica aethiopica*

2000. International Garden Show, Graz.
2553 **1197** 7s. multicoloured . . . 80 1·00

1198 Ibex

2000. Hunting and the Environment. Return of Ibex to Austrian Mountains.
2554 **1198** 7s. multicoloured . . . 80 1·00

1199 Players

2000. F.C. Tirol Innsbruck, National Football Champion 2000.
2555 **1199** 7s. multicoloured . . . 80 1·00

1200 Mt. Grossglockner and Viewing Point

2000. Bicentenary of First Ascent of Mt. Grossglockner.
2556 **1200** 7s. multicoloured . . . 80 1·00

1201 Weisssee Lake

2000. Natural Beauty Spots.
2557 **1201** 7s. multicoloured . . . 80 1·00

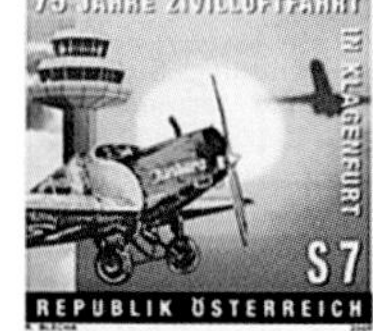
1202 "Building Europe" **1203** Junkers Airplane and Air Traffic Control Tower

2000. Europa.
2558 **1202** 7s. multicoloured . . . 80 1·00

2000. 75th Anniv of Civil Aviation at Klagenfurt Airport.
2559 **1203** 7s. multicoloured . . . 80 1·00

1204 Madonna of Altenmarkt (statue) and Glass Roof, Palm House, Burggarten, Vienna

2000. 150th Anniv of Protection of Historic Monuments.
2560 **1204** 8s. multicoloured . . . 95 1·25

1205 Illuminated Letter and Text

2000. Life of St. Malachy (treatise) by St. Bernard of Clairvaux.
2561 **1205** 9s. multicoloured . . . 1·00 1·25

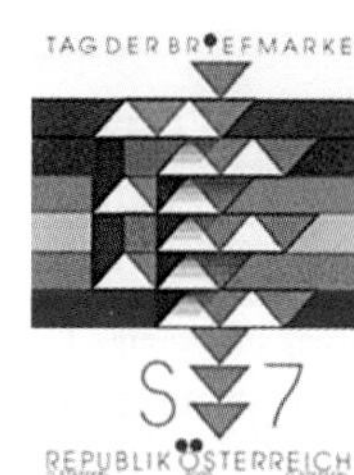
1206 "E" and "E"

2000. Stamp Day.
2562 **1206** 7s. multicoloured . . . 80 1·00
See note below No. 2266.

1207 1850 9 Kreuzer and 2000 Stamp Day Stamps

2000. 150th Anniv of Austrian Stamps.
2563 **1207** 7s. multicoloured . . . 80 1·00

1208 "Confetti"

2000. *Confetti* (children's television programme).
2565 **1208** 7s. multicoloured . . . 80 90

1210 Blood Droplets

2000. Centenary of Discovery of Blood Groups by Karl Landsteiner (pathologist).
2567 **1210** 8s. pink, silver & black 80 1·00

1211 Daimler Cannstatter Bus

2000. Centenary of First Regular Bus Route between Purkersdorf and Gablitz.
2568 **1211** 9s. black, blue and light blue . . . . 1·10 1·25

2000. Folk Customs and Art (18th series). As T **1005**. Multicoloured.
2569 7s. Men on raft (International Rafting Meeting, Carinthia) . . . 90 1·10

1212 Dachstein River and Hallstatt

2000. Natural Beauty Spots.
2570 **1212** 7s. multicoloured . . . 80 1·00

1213 String Instrument and Emblem

2000. Centenary of Vienna Symphony Orchestra.
2571 **1213** 7s. multicoloured . . . 80 1·00

1214 Dinghies

2000. Olympic Games, Sydney.
2572 **1214** 9s. multicoloured . . . 1·00 1·25

1215 Old and Modern Paper Production Methods

2000. Austrian World of Work (11th series). Printing and Paper.
2573 **1215** 6s.50 multicoloured . . 80 75

1216 "Turf Turkey" (Ida Szigethy)

2000. Austrian Modern Art.
2574 **1216** 7s. multicoloured . . . 80 1·00

1217 Codex 965 (National Library)

2000. Ancient Arts and Crafts (3rd series).
2575 **1217** 8s. multicoloured . . . 90 1·10
See also Nos. 2600 and 2602.

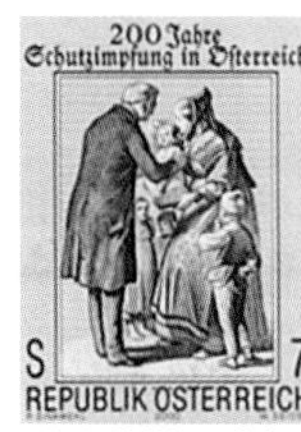
1218 Child receiving Vaccination

2000. Bicentenary of Vaccination in Austria.
2576 **1218** 7s. black and cinnamon 80 1·00

1219 Urania Building, Vienna

2000. 50th Anniv of Adult Education Association.
2577 **1219** 7s. brown, grey & gold 80 1·00

1220 The Nativity (altar piece, Ludesch Church)

2000. Christmas.
2578 **1220** 7s. multicoloured . . . 80 1·00

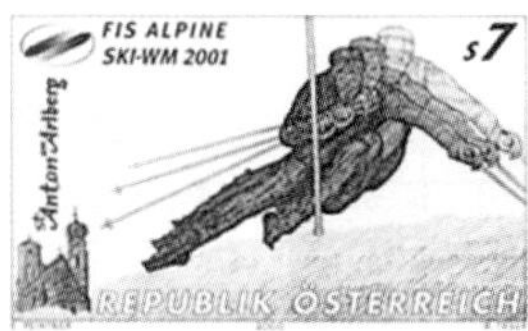
1221 Downhill Skier

2000. World Skiing Championship (2001), St. Anton am Arlberg.
2579 **1221** 7s. multicoloured . . . 80 1·10

1222 Pair of Mallards

2001. Hunting and the Environment. Protection of Wetlands.
2580 **1222** 7s. multicoloured . . . 80 1·10

2001. Folk Customs and Art (19th series). As T **1005**. Multicoloured.
2581 8s. Boat mill, Mureck, Styria . . . . 85 1·10

1223 Steam Locomotive No. 3

2001. Centenary of Zillertal Railway.
2582 **1223** 7s. multicoloured . . . 80 1·00

1224 Players and Club Emblem

2001. SV Casino Salzburg, National Football Champion.
2583 **1224** 7s. multicoloured . . . 80 1·00

1225 Rolf Rudiger

2001. *Confetti* (children's television programme).
2584 **1225** 7s. multicoloured . . . 80 1·00

1226 Monoplane and Airport

2001. 75th Anniv of Salzburg Airport.
2585 **1226** 14s. multicoloured . . . 1·50 1·50

1227 Baerenschuetz Gorge

2001. Natural Beauty Spots.
2586 **1227** 7s. multicoloured . . . 80 1·00

2001. Folk Customs and Art (20th series). As T **1005**. Multicoloured.
2587 7s. Lent season cloth from Eastern Tyrol . . . . . . 80 1·00

1228 Water Droplet

1230 Air Balloon

1229 Post Office Railway Car

2001. Europa. Water Resources.
2588 **1228** 15s. multicoloured . . . 1·75 1·60

2001. Stamp Day.
2589 **1229** 20s.+10s. mult . . . . 3·50 4·00

2001. Centenary of Austrian Flying Club.
2590 **1230** 7s. multicoloured . . . 80 40

1231 Refugee

2001. 50th Anniv of United Nations High Commissioner for Refugees.
2591 **1231** 21s. multicoloured . . . 4·00 2·10

1232 Kalte Rinne Viaduct

2001. U.N.E.S.C.O. World Heritage Site. The Semmering Railway.
2592 **1232** 35s. multicoloured . . . 4·00 5·00

1233 "Seppl" (mascot) (Michelle Schneeweiss)

2001. 7th International Hiking Olympics, Seefeld.
2593 **1233** 7s. multicoloured . . . 80 1·25

1234 Field Post Office at Famagusta

2001. Army Postal Services Abroad.
2594 **1234** 7s. multicoloured . . . 70 1·00

2001. Folk Customs and Art (21st series). As T **1005**. Multicoloured.
2595 7s. Rifle and Clubhouse, Preberschiessen, Salzburg (Rifleman's gathering) . . 80 1·00

1235 "Taurus" (Railway Engine)

2001. Conversion of East–West Railway to Four-tracked Railway.
2596 **1235** 7s. multicoloured . . . 80 1·00

1236 19th-century Theatrical Scene

2001. Birth Bicentenary of Johann Nestroy (playwright and actor).
2597 **1236** 7s. multicoloured . . . 80 1·00

1237 "The Continents" (detail Helmut Leherb)

2001. Austrian Modern Art.
2598 **1237** 7s. multicoloured . . . 80 1·00

1238 "False Friends" (Von Fuehrich)

2001. 125th Death Anniv of Joseph Ritter von Fuehrich (artist and engraver).
2599 **1238** 8s. deep green & green 85 1·10

1239 Pluviale (embroidered religious robe)

1240 Dobler

2001. Ancient Arts and Crafts (4th series).
2600 **1239** 10s. multicoloured . . . 1·25 1·50

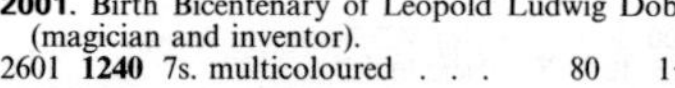
2001. Birth Bicentenary of Leopold Ludwig Dobler (magician and inventor).
2601 **1240** 7s. multicoloured . . . 80 1·00

1241 Dalmatik (religious vestment) (Carmelite Monastery, Silbergrasse, Vienna)

2001. Ancient Arts and Crafts (5th series).
2602 **1241** 7s. multicoloured . . . 80 1·00

1242 Building and Scientific Equipment

2001. 150th Anniv of the Central Institute for Meteorology and Geodynamics, Vienna.
2603 **1242** 12s. multicoloured . . . 1·50 1·75

1243 Cat

2001.
2604 **1243** 19s. multicoloured . . . 2·10 2·75

1244 Civil Servants

2001. Austrian World of Work (12th series). Civil Service.
2605 **1244** 7s. multicoloured . . . 80 1·00

1245 Figure of Infant Jesus

1246 House of the Basilisk, Vienna

2001. Christmas. Glass Shrine, Fitzmoos Church.
2606 **1245** 7s. multicoloured . . . 80 1·00

New Currency

2002. Tourism. Multicoloured.
2607 51c. Type **1246** 80 90
2608 58c. Wine cellars, Hadres, Lower Austria . . . . . 90 1·10
2609 73c. Alpine chalet, Salzburg 1·25 1·40
2610 87c. Alpach Valley, Tyrol 1·40 1·60
2611 €2.03 Heiligenkreuz, Lower Austria . . . . 3·00 3·50

1247 Stars, Map of Europe and €1 Coin

2002. Euro Currency.
2620 **1247** €3.27 multicoloured 4·75 4·50
No. 2620 is printed on the back under the gum with examples of Austrian schilling coins.

1248 Skiers and Olympic Rings

2002. Winter Olympic Games, Salt Lake City, U.S.A.
2621 **1248** 73c. multicoloured . . . 1·25 1·25

1249 Bouquet of Flowers

2002.
2622 **1249** 87c. multicoloured . . . 1·25 1·25

1250 Woman and Skyline

2002. Women's Day.
2623 **1250** 51c. multicoloured . . . 95 95

1251 Mel and Lucy

2002. "Philis" (children's stamp awareness programme) (1st issue).
2624 **1251** 58c. multicoloured . . . 75 75
See also Nos. 2629 and 2652.

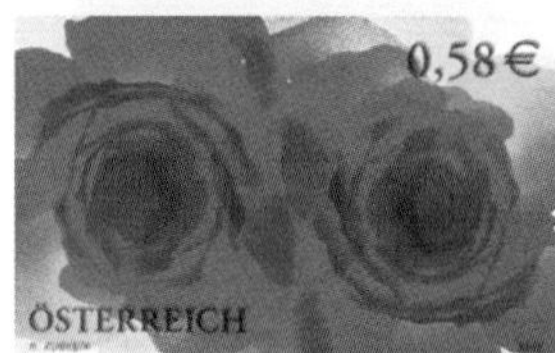
1252 Red Roses

2002. Greetings Stamp.
2625 **1252** 58c. multicoloured . . . 75 75

1253 Kubin

2002. 125th Birth Anniv of Alfred Kubin (artist).
2626 **1253** 87c. black and buff . . 1·25 1·25

1254 St. Elizabeth of Thuringia and Sick Man

2002. Caritas (Catholic charity organization).
2627 **1254** 51c. multicoloured . . . 90 90

1255 Tiger, Clown and Circus Tent

2002. Europa. The Circus.
2628 **1255** 87c. multicoloured . . . 1·25 70

1256 Sisko and Mauritius

2002. "Philis" (children's stamp awareness programme) (2nd issue).
2629 **1256** 58c. multicoloured . . . 80 45

1257 The Nativity

2002. 800th Anniv of Lilienfeld Abbey.
2630 **1257** €2.03 multicoloured 2·75 1·60

1258 Mimi

2002. *Confetti* (children's television programme).
2631 **1258** 51c. multicoloured . . . 70 40

1259 Railway Carriage, 1919

2002. Stamp Day.
2632 **1259** €1.60+80c. multicoloured . . . . 3·25 3·25

1260 Cheetah, Zebra and Orang-utan

2002. 250th Anniv of Schonbrunn Zoo. Mult.
2633 51c. Type **1260** 70 40
2634 58c. Gulls, flamingos and pelicans 80 45
2635 87c. Lion, turtle and crocodile . . . . 1·25 70
2636 €1.38 Elephant, birds and fish . . . . 1·90 1·10
Nos. 2633/6 were issued together, se-tenant, forming a composite design.

1261 Teddy Bears

2002. Centenary of the Teddy Bear.
2637 **1261** 51c. multicoloured . . . 70 40

1262 Chair No. 14 (Michael Thonet)

2002. 75th Anniv of "Design Austria" (design group)
2638 **1262** €1.38 multicoloured 1·90 1·00

1263 Crystal Cup

2002. Ancient Arts and Crafts.
2639 **1263** €1.60 multicoloured 2·10 1·25

1264 Museum Buildings

2002. Museumsquartier (MQ), Messepalast, Vienna.
2640 **1264** 58c. multicoloured . . . 75 45

1265 Figures supporting Emblem

2002. 50th Anniv of Union of Austrians Abroad.
2641 **1265** €2.47 multicoloured 3·25 2·00

1266 Clown Doctor

2002. "Rote Nasen" (Red Noses (charity)).
2642 **1266** 51c. multicoloured . . . 70 40

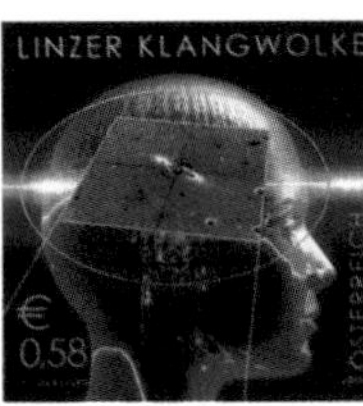

1267 Head

2002. Linzer Klangwolke (sound and light performance), Linz.
2643 **1267** 58c. multicoloured . . . 75 45

1268 Graf & Stift Typ 40/45

2002.
2644 **1268** 51c. multicoloured . . . 55 30

1269 Dog

2002.
2645 **1269** 51c. multicoloured . . . 55 30

1270 Steam Locomotive 109

2002.
2646 **1270** 51c. multicoloured . . . 55 30

1271 "Schutzenhaus" (Karl Goldammer)

2002. Austrian Modern Art.
2647 **1271** 51c. multicoloured . . . 55 30

1272 Lottery Ball

2002. 250th Anniv of Austrian Lottery. Sheet 72 × 90 mm.
MS2648 **1272** 87c. multicoloured 1·20 1·20

1273 Thayatal National Park

2002.
2649 **1273** 58c. multicoloured . . . 75 45

1274 Puch 175 SV

2002.
2650 **1274** 58c. multicoloured . . . 75 45

1275 "Eye"

2002. 75th Anniv of "Design Austria" (design group). Winning Entry in Design Competition.
2651 **1275** €1.38 multicoloured 1·80 1·80

1276 Edison and Gogo

2002. "Philis" (children's stamp awareness programme) (3rd issue).
2652 **1276** 58c. multicoloured . . . 75 45

1277 Crib Aureola, Thaur, Tyrol

2002. Christmas.
2653 **1277** 51c. multicoloured . . . 55 30

IMPERIAL JOURNAL STAMPS

J **18** J **21** Arms of Austria J **22** Arms of Austria

1853. Imperf.
J67 1k. blue . . . . 32·00 4·00
J15 2k. green . . . . £1600 65·00
J68 2k. brown . . . . 28·00 5·00
J32 4k. brown £425 £1100
The 2k. green has different corner ornaments.
For similar values in black or red, see Lombardy and Venetia Imperial Journal stamps, Nos. J22/4.

1890. Imperf.
J76 J **21** 1k. brown . . . . 9·50 1·50
J77 2k. green . . . . 8·50 2·00

1890. Perf.
J78 J **22** 25k. red . . . . 85·00 £170

NEWSPAPER STAMPS

N **2** Mercury N **8** Francis Joseph I N **11** Francis Joseph I

1851. Imperf.
N11b N **2** (0.6k.) blue . . . . . . £140 95·00
N12 (6k.) yellow £17000 £6500
N13 (6k.) red £39000 £44000
N14 (30k.) red . . . . . . 14·00 £10000

1858. Imperf.
N28 N **8** (1k.05) blue £550 £600
N29 (1k.05) lilac £750 £350

1861. Imperf.
N38 N **11** (1k.05) grey £170 £150

N **13** Arms of Austria AHN **17** Mercury N **19** Mercury

1863. Imperf.
N44 N **13** (1k.05) lilac 38·00 13·50

1867. Imperf.
AHN58b AHN **17** (1k.) lilac 40 30

1880. Imperf.
N69 N **19** ½k. green 6·50 1·10

N **31** Mercury
N **43** Mercury

1899. Imperf.
N122 N **31** 2h. blue 20 15
N123 6h. orange 2·10 2·00
N124 10h. brown 1·50 90
N125 20h. pink 1·50 1·90

1908. Imperf.
N207 N **43** 2h. blue 70 20
N208 6h. orange 4·50 50
N209 10h. red 4·50 40
N210 20h. brown 4·50 30

N **53** Mercury
N **54** Mercury

1916. Imperf.
N266 N **53** 2h. brown 10 15
N267 4h. green 35 90
N268 6h. blue 35 1·00
N269 10h. orange 45 1·10
N270 30h. red 35 95

1916. For Express. Perf.
N271 N **54** 2h. red on yellow 85 1·75
N272 5h. green on yellow 85 1·75

N **61** Mercury
N **68** Mercury

1917. For Express. Perf.
N294 N **61** 2h. red on yellow 25 30
N295 5h. green on yellow 25 30

1919. Optd **Deutschosterreich**. Imperf.
N318 N **53** 2h. brown 10 20
N319 4h. green 30 1·00
N320 6h. blue 25 1·00
N321 10h. orange 25 1·00
N322 30h. red 25 60

1919. For Express. Optd **Deutschosterreich**. Perf.
N334 N **61** 2h. red on yellow 15 30
N335 5h. green on yellow 15 30

1920. Imperf.
N365 N **68** 2h. violet 10 15
N366 4h. brown 10 25
N367 5h. slate 10 20
N368 6h. blue 10 20
N369 8h. green 10 45
N370 9h. bistre 10 15
N371 10h. red 10 15
N372 12h. blue 10 50
N373 15h. mauve 10 20
N374 18h. turquoise 10 30
N375 20h. orange 10 30
N376 30h. brown 10 20
N377 45h. green 10 45
N378 60h. red 10 20
N379 72h. brown 20 50
N380 90h. violet 25 75
N381 1k.20 red 25 85
N382 2k.40 green 25 85
N383 3k. grey 30 45

1921. For Express. No. N334 surch **50 50**.
N450 N **61** 50 on 2h. red on yell 15 25

N **78** Mercury
N **79** Posthorn and Arrow

1921. Imperf.
N452 N **78** 45h. grey 15 30
N453 75h. red 15 50
N454 1k.50 green 10 70
N455 1k.80 blue 10 80
N456 2k.25 brown 10 1·00
N457 3k. green 10 75
N458 6k. purple 10 90
N459 7k.50 brown 15 1·25

1921. For Express. Perf.
N460 N **79** 50h. lilac on yellow 10 2·40

POSTAGE DUE STAMPS

D **26**
D **44**

1894. Perf.
D 96 D **26** 1k. brown 2·75 1·00
D 97 2k. brown 3·00 2·00
D 98 3k. brown 3·75 95
D 99 5k. brown 3·75 50
D100 6k. brown 3·00 5·25
D101 7k. brown 1·50 5·25
D102 10k. brown 3·75 45
D103 20k. brown 1·50 5·25
D104 50k. brown 30·00 65·00

1899. As Type D **26**, but value in heller. Perf or imperf.
D126 D **26** 1h. brown 45 30
D127 2h. brown 60 20
D128 3h. brown 50 20
D129 4h. brown 65 15
D130 5h. brown 70 15
D131 6h. brown 60 20
D132 10h. brown 80 15
D133 12h. brown 90 60
D134 15h. brown 1·10 90
D135 20h. brown 1·40 30
D136 40h. brown 2·10 60
D137 100h. brown 4·75 2·10

1908. Perf.
D210 D **44** 1h. red 3·25 1·40
D211 2h. red 30 30
D212 4h. red 25 15
D213 6h. red 25 15
D214 10h. red 30 15
D215 14h. red 3·75 2·10
D216 20h. red 7·50 15
D217 25h. red 7·50 4·50
D218 30h. red 7·00 30
D219 50h. red 15·00 3·75
D220 100h. red 20·00 50
D221 5k. violet 60·00 11·00
D222 10k. violet £225 3·25

D **55**
D **56**

1916.
D273 D **55** 5h. red 10 10
D274 10h. red 10 10
D275 15h. red 10 10
D276 20h. red 10 10
D277 25h. red 30 75
D278 30h. red 25 25
D279 40h. red 10 35
D280 50h. red 1·00 1·90
D281 D **56** 1k. blue 25 20
D282 5k. blue 2·10 2·75
D283 10k. blue 2·50 1·25

1916. Nos. 189/90 optd **PORTO** or surch **15 15** also.
D284 1h. black 10 20
D285 15 on 2h. violet 25 40

1917. Unissued stamps as T **50** surch **PORTO** and value.
D286 **50** 10 on 24h. blue 1·50 50
D287 15 on 36h. violet 45 20
D288 20 on 54h. orange 35 35
D289 50 on 42h. brown 35 25
The above differ from Type **50** by showing a full-face portrait.

1919. Optd **Deutschosterreich**.
D323 D **55** 5h. red 20 20
D324 10h. red 20 25
D325 15h. red 35 50
D326 20h. red 30 40
D327 25h. red 8·75 15·00
D328 30h. red 30 35
D329 40h. red 40 65
D330 50h. red 45 1·25
D331 D **56** 1k. blue 5·50 11·00
D332 5k. blue 9·50 12·00
D333 10k. blue 10·50 3·75

D **69**
D **70**

1920. Imperf or perf (D **69**), perf (D **70**).
D384 D **69** 5h. pink 10 30
D385 10h. pink 10 25
D386 15h. pink 10 1·25
D387 20h. pink 10 30
D388 25h. pink 20 1·25
D389 30h. pink 10 30
D390 40h. pink 10 30
D391 50h. pink 10 30
D392 80h. pink 20 25
D393 D **70** 1k. blue 10 30
D394 1½k. blue 10 30
D395 2k. blue 10 40
D396 3k. blue 10 60
D397 4k. blue 15 1·00
D398 5k. blue 20 60
D399 8k. blue 10 75
D400 10k. blue 10 50
D401 20k. blue 45 1·25

1921. No. 343a surch **Nachmarke 7½ K**. Perf.
D451 **64** 7½k. on 15h. brown 10 10

D **83**
D **86**

1921.
D510 D **83** 1k. brown 15 25
D511 2k. brown 15 35
D512 4k. brown 15 65
D513 5k. brown 15 30
D514 7½k. brown 15 90
D515 – 10k. blue 15 35
D516 – 15k. blue 15 60
D517 – 20k. blue 15 60
D518 – 50k. blue 15 55
The 10k. to 50k. are larger (22 × 30 mm).

1922.
D526 D **83** 10k. turquoise 10 35
D527 15k. turquoise 10 65
D528 20k. turquoise 10 50
D529 25k. turquoise 10 1·10
D530 40k. turquoise 10 35
D531 50k. turquoise 10 1·10
D532 D **86** 100k. purple 10 20
D533 150k. purple 10 20
D534 200k. purple 10 20
D535 400k. purple 10 20
D536 600k. purple 20 55
D537 800k. purple 10 15
D538 1000k. purple 10 15
D539 D **86** 1200k. purple 1·40 3·00
D540 1500k. purple 15 25
D541 1800k. purple 2·50 7·00
D542 2000k. purple 50 90
D543 3000k. purple 9·00 16·00
D544 4000k. purple 7·25 15·00
D545 6000k. purple 9·00 23·00

D **94**
D **120**

1925.
D589 D **94** 1g. red 10 10
D590 2g. red 10 10
D591 3g. red 10 10
D592 4g. red 20 10
D593 5g. red 10 10
D594 6g. red 30 40
D595 8g. red 25 25
D596 10g. blue 25 10
D597 12g. blue 15 10
D598 14g. blue 15 10
D599 15g. blue 10 10
D600 16g. blue 30 25
D601 18g. blue 1·50 4·00
D602 20g. blue 25 10
D603 23g. blue 65 20
D604 24g. blue 2·75 10
D605 28g. blue 2·40 25
D606 30g. blue 70 15
D607 31g. blue 2·75 25
D608 35g. blue 3·00 15
D609 39g. blue 3·50 10
D610 40g. blue 2·25 2·25
D611 60g. blue 1·50 2·00
D612 – 1s. green 4·00 1·00
D613 – 2s. green 26·00 3·00
D614 – 5s. green £120 40·00
D615 – 10s. green 50·00 4·25
DESIGN: 1 to 10s. Horiz bands of colour.

1935.
D746 D **120** 1g. red 20 15
D747 2g. red 20 15
D748 3g. red 20 20
D749 5g. red 20 20
D750 – 10g. blue 20 10
D751 – 12g. blue 20 10
D752 – 15g. blue 20 55
D753 – 20g. blue 30 15
D754 – 24g. blue 50 10
D755 – 30g. blue 50 10
D756 – 39g. blue 75 10
D757 – 60g. blue 1·00 1·10
D758 – 1s. green 1·50 30
D759 – 2s. green 3·00 85
D760 – 5s. green 4·75 3·75
D761 – 10s. green 6·50 70
DESIGNS: 10 to 60g. As Type D **120** but with background of horizontal lines; 1 to 10s. As last, but with positions of figures, arms and inscriptions reversed.

D **143**
D **162**

1945.
D891 D **143** 1pf. red 10 15
D892 2pf. red 10 15
D893 3pf. red 10 15
D894 5pf. red 10 15
D895 10pf. red 10 15
D896 12pf. red 10 20
D897 20pf. red 10 20
D898 24pf. red 10 30
D899 30pf. red 10 65
D900 60pf. red 10 45
D901 1rm. violet 10 50
D902 2rm. violet 10 80
D903 5rm. violet 10 1·00
D904 10rm. violet 10 1·10

1946. Optd **PORTO**.
D956 **145** 3g. orange 10 15
D957 5g. green 10 15
D958 6g. purple 10 15
D959 8g. red 10 15
D960 10g. grey 10 20
D961 12g. brown 10 15
D962 15g. red 10 15
D963 20g. brown 10 15
D964 25g. blue 10 20
D965 30g. mauve 10 20
D966 40g. blue 10 25
D967 60g. green 10 25
D968 1s. violet 10 40
D969 2s. yellow 50 90
D970 5s. blue 45 70

1947.
D1035 D **162** 1g. brown 10 10
D1036 2g. brown 10 10
D1037 3g. brown 10 20
D1038 5g. brown 10 10
D1039 8g. brown 10 10
D1040 10g. brown 10 10
D1041 12g. brown 10 10
D1042 15g. brown 10 10
D1043 16g. brown 50 85
D1044 17g. brown 25 85
D1045 18g. brown 25 85
D1046 20g. brown 60 10
D1047 24g. brown 25 1·25
D1048 30g. brown 15 25
D1049 36g. brown 65 1·00
D1050 40g. brown 10 10
D1051 D **162** 42g. brown 95 1·40
D1052 48g. brown 75 1·40
D1053 50g. brown 70 25
D1054 60g. brown 20 30
D1055 70g. brown 20 25
D1056 80g. brown 4·00 2·10
D1057 1s. blue 20 10
D1058 1s.15 blue 3·00 30
D1059 1s.20 blue 3·50 1·50
D1060 2s. blue 30 20
D1061 5s. blue 40 30
D1062 10s. blue 50 30

D **184**
D **817**

1949.
D1178 D **184** 1g. red 20 15
D1179 2g. red 20 15
D1180 4g. red 45 45
D1181 5g. red 1·90 50
D1182 8g. red 2·40 1·90
D1183 10g. red 25 10
D1184 20g. red 25 10
D1185 30g. red 25 10
D1186 40g. red 25 10
D1187 50g. red 25 10
D1188 60g. red 10·50 45
D1189 63g. red 4·50 4·25
D1190 70g. red 25 10
D1191 80g. red 25 15
D1192 90g. red 45 35
D1193 1s. violet 50 15
D1194 1s.20 violet 50 20
D1195 1s.35 violet 30 20
D1196 1s.40 violet 50 40
D1197 1s.50 violet 50 15
D1198 1s.65 violet 50 35
D1199 1s.70 violet 50 40
D1200 2s. violet 75 20
D1201 2s.50 violet 50 20
D1202 3s. violet 50 20
D1203 4s. violet 85 60
D1204 5s. violet 1·10 35
D1205 10s. violet 1·25 25

1985.
D2074 D **817** 10g. yellow & black 10 10
D2075 20g. red and black 10 10
D2076 50g. orange & black 10 10
D2077 1s. blue and black 15 15
D2078 2s. brown & black 30 30
D2079 3s. violet and black 50 45
D2080 5s. yellow & black 85 75
D2081 10s. green & black 1·75 1·40

AUSTRIAN TERRITORIES ACQUIRED BY ITALY Pt. 2

Italian territory acquired from Austria at the close of the war of 1914–18, including Trentino and Trieste.

1918. 100 heller = 1 krone.
1918. 100 centesimi = 1 lira.
1919. 100 centesimi = 1 corona.

TRENTINO

1918. Stamps of Austria optd **Regno d'Italia Trentino 3 nov 1918.**

1 **49** 3h. purple 1·90 2·10
2 5h. green 1·50 1·50
3 6h. orange 30·00 25·00
4 10h. red 2·00 1·50
5 12h. green 85·00 80·00
6 **60** 15h. brown 2·50 2·50
7 20h. green 1·50 1·75
8 25h. blue 23·00 21·00
9 30h. violet 6·75 6·75
10 **51** 40h. green 32·00 32·00
11 50h. green 18·00 17·00
12 60h. blue 23·00 25·00
13 80h. brown 35·00 40·00
14 90h. red £850 £850
15 1k. red on yellow 35·00 38·00
16 **52** 2k. blue £180 £190
17 4k. green £1400 £1300
18 10k. violet £65000

1918. Stamps of Italy optd **Venezia Tridentina.**

19 **30** 1c. brown 40 1·25
20 **31** 2c. brown 40 1·25
21 **37** 5c. green 70 1·25
22 10c. red 70 1·25
23 **41** 20c. orange 1·10 1·90
24 **39** 40c. brown 35·00 35·00
25 **33** 45c. olive 17·00 24·00
26 **39** 50c. mauve 21·00 26·00
27 **34** 1l. brown and green 21·00 26·00

1919. Stamps of Italy surch **Venezia Tridentina** and value.

28 **37** 5h. on 5c. green 70 1·10
29 10h. on 10c. red 70 1·10
30 **41** 20h. on 20c. orange 70 1·10

VENEZIA GIULIA

For use in Trieste and territory, Gorizia and province, and in Istria.

1918. Stamps of Austria optd **Regno d'Italia Venezia Giulia 3. XI. 18.**

31 **49** 3h. purple 90 90
32 5h. green 90 90
33 6h. orange 1·10 1·10
34 10h. red 55 55
35 12h. green 1·10 1·10
36 **60** 15h. brown 55 55
37 20h. green 55 55
38 25h. blue 3·50 3·50
39 30h. purple 1·50 1·50
40 **51** 40h. green 40·00 60·00
41 50h. green 2·10 3·00
42 60h. blue 11·00 11·00
43 80h. brown 3·50 5·50
44 1k. red on yellow 3·50 6·75
45 **52** 2k. blue 85·00 £110
46 3k. red £140 £160
47 4k. green £210 £250
48 10k. violet £23000 £24000

1918. Stamps of Italy optd **Venezia Giulia.**

49 **30** 1c. brown 55 1·00
50 **31** 2c. brown 55 1·00
51 **37** 5c. green 55 55
52 10c. red 55 55
53 **41** 20c. orange 55 55
54 **39** 25c. blue 55 55
55 40c. brown 4·25 5·50
56 **33** 45c. green 75 1·25
57 **39** 50c. mauve 1·75 2·50
58 60c. red 27·00 30·00
59 **34** 1l. brown and green 14·00 14·00

1919. Stamps of Italy surch **Venezia Giulia** and value.

60 **37** 5h. on 5c. green 90 90
61 **41** 20h. on 20c. orange 70 70

EXPRESS LETTER STAMPS

1919. Express Letter stamp of Italy optd **Venezia Giulia.**

E60 E **35** 25c. red 21·00 23·00

POSTAGE DUE STAMPS

1918. Postage Due Stamps of Italy optd **Venezia Giulia.**

D60 D **12** 5c. mauve and orange 15 55
D61 10c. mauve & orange 15 55
D62 20c. mauve & orange 70 1·10
D63 30c. mauve & orange 1·50 1·90
D64 40c. mauve & orange 14·00 16·00
D65 50c. mauve & orange 35·00 45·00
D66 1l. mauve and blue £110 £120

GENERAL ISSUE

For use throughout the liberated area of Trentino, Venezia Giulia and Dalmatia.

1919. Stamps of Italy surch in new currency.

62 **30** 1ce. di cor on 1c. brown 90 90
64 **31** 2ce. di cor on 2c. brown 90 90
65 **37** 5ce. di cor on 5c. green 90 90
67 10ce. di cor on 10c. red 90 90
68 **41** 20ce. di cor on 20c. orange 90 90
70 **39** 25ce. di cor on 25c. blue 90 90
71 40ce. di cor on 40c. brown 90 90
72 **33** 45ce. di cor on 45c. green 90 90
73 **39** 50ce. di cor on 50c. mauve 90 90
74 60ce. di cor on 60c. red 90 1·50
75 **34** 1cor. on 1l. brown & green 90 1·50
76 una corona on 1l. brn & grn 2·00 5·50
82 5cor. on 5l. blue and red 21·00 25·00
83 10cor. on 10l. green & red 21·00 25·00

EXPRESS LETTER STAMPS

1919. Express Letter stamps of Italy surch in new currency.

E76 E **35** 25ce. di cor on 25c. red 70 1·10
E77 E **41** 30ce. di cor on 30c. red and blue 70 1·10

POSTAGE DUE STAMPS

1919. Postage Due stamps of Italy surch in new currency.

D76 D **12** 5ce. di cor on 5c. mauve and orange 40 90
D77 10ce. di cor. on 10c. mauve and orange 40 90
D78 20ce. di cor on 20c. mauve and orange 40 90
D79 30ce. di cor on 30c. mauve and orange 40 90
D80 40ce. di cor on 40c. mauve and orange 40 90
D81 50ce. di cor on 50c. mauve and orange 40 90
D82 una corona on 1l. mauve and blue 40 1·50
D86 1cor. on 1l. mve & blue 3·00 3·50
D83 due corona on 2l. mauve and blue 35·00 48·00
D87 2cor. on 2l. mve & blue 17·00 26·00
D84 cinque corona on 5l. mauve and blue 35·00 45·00
D88 5cor. on 5l. mve & blue 18·00 26·00

AUSTRO-HUNGARIAN MILITARY POST Pt. 2

A. GENERAL ISSUES

100 heller = 1 krone.

1915. Stamps of Bosnia and Herzegovina optd **K.U.K. FELDPOST.**

1 **25** 1h. olive 40 80
2 2h. blue 40 80
3 3h. lake 40 80
4 5h. green 40 40
5 6h. black 40 80
6 10h. red 25 45
7 12h. olive 40 1·00
8 20h. brown 50 75
9 25h. blue 50 1·00
10 30h. red 2·75 9·50
11 **26** 35h. green 1·90 7·00
12 40h. violet 1·90 7·00
13 45h. brown 1·90 7·00
14 **26** 50h. blue 1·90 7·00
15 60h. purple 50 4·00
16 72h. blue 2·00 7·13
17 **25** 1k. brown on cream 2·00 6·75
18 2k. indigo on blue 2·00 7·50
19 **26** 3k. red on green 21·00 60·00
20 5k. lilac on grey 18·00 55·00
21 10k. blue on grey £170 £375

2 Francis Joseph

1915.

22 **2** 1h. green 15 25
23 2h. blue 10 30
24 3h. red 15 25
25 5h. green 15 25
26 6h. black 15 35
27 10h. red 15 27
28 10h. blue 10 30
29 12h. green 15 40
30 15h. red 15 20
31 20h. brown 25 50
32 20h. green 25 60
33 25h. blue 15 30
34 30h. red 20 60
35 35h. green 25 85
36 40h. violet 25 85
37 45h. brown 25 85
38 50h. deep green 25 85
39 60h. purple 30 85
40 72h. blue 35 85
41 80h. brown 25 35
42 90h. red 65 1·90
43 – 1k. purple on cream 1·25 3·72
44 – 2k. green on blue 90 1·75
45 – 3k. red on green 70 1·00
46 – 4k. violet on grey 70 1·00
47 – 5k. violet on grey 21·00 25·00
48 – 10k. blue on grey 2·75 10·50

The kronen values are larger, with profile portrait.

1917. As 1917 issue of Bosnia, but inscr "K.u.K. FELDPOST".

49 1h. blue 90 20
50 2h. orange 90 20
51 3h. grey 90 20
52 5h. green 90 20
53 6h. violet 15 25
54 10h. brown 10 20
55 12h. blue 10 20
56 15h. red 15 20
57 20h. brown 15 20
58 25h. blue 20 45
59 30h. grey 15 20
60 40h. bistre 15 20
61 50h. green 10 20
62 60h. red 15 30
63 80h. blue 15 20
64 90h. purple 25 85
65 2k. red on buff 15 25
66 3k. green on blue 70 2·10
67 4k. red on green 14·50 26·00
68 10k. violet on grey 1·10 7·50

The kronen values are larger and the border is different.

1918. Imperial and Royal Welfare Fund. As 1918 issue of Bosnia, but inscr "K. UND K. FELDPOST".

69 **40** 10h. (+10h.) green 25 90
70 – 20h. (+10h.) red 25 90
71 **40** 45h. (+10h.) blue 25 90

NEWSPAPER STAMPS

N 4 Mercury

1916.

N49 N **4** 2h. blue 15 30
N50 6h. orange 35 1·40
N51 10h. red 60 1·40
N52 20h. brown 75 1·40

B. ISSUES FOR ITALY

100 centesimi = 1 lira.

1918. General Issue stamps of 1917 surch in figs and words.

1 2c. on 1h. blue 10 25
2 3c. on 2h. orange 10 25
3 4c. on 3h. grey 10 25
4 6c. on 5h. green 10 25
5 7c. on 6h. violet 10 25
6 11c. on 10h. brown 10 25
7 13c. on 12h. blue 10 25
8 16c. on 15h. red 10 25
9 22c. on 20h. brown 10 25
10 27c. on 25h. blue 30 65
11 32c. on 30h. grey 10 50
12 43c. on 40h. bistre 15 55
13 53c. on 50h. green 15 30
14 64c. on 60h. red 20 65
15 85c. on 80h. blue 15 35
16 95c. on 90h. purple 15 35
17 2l.11 on 2k. red on buff 25 55
18 3l.16 on 3k. green on blue 60 1·40
19 4l.22 on 4k. red on green 75 1·60

NEWSPAPER STAMPS

1918. Newspaper stamps of General Issue surch in figs and words.

N20 N **4** 3c. on 2h. blue 15 40
N21 7c. on 6h. orange 35 1·00
N22 11c. on 10h. red 35 95
N23 22c. on 20h. brown 30 95

1918. For Express. Newspaper stamps of Bosnia surch in figs and words.

N24 N **35** 3c. on 2h. red on yell 5·50 11·50
N25 6c. on 5h. green on yell 5·50 11·50

POSTAGE DUE STAMPS

1918. Postage Due stamps of Bosnia surch in figs and words.

D20 D **35** 6c. on 5h. red 3·50 5·50
D21 11c. on 10h. red 2·10 4·50
D22 16c. on 15h. red 80 2·25
D23 27c. on 25h. red 80 2·25
D24 32c. on 30h. red 80 2·25
D25 43c. on 40h. red 80 2·25
D26 53c. on 50h. red 80 2·25

C. ISSUES FOR MONTENEGRO

100 heller = 1 krone.

1917. Nos. 28 and 30 of General Issues optd **K.U.K. MILIT. VERWALTUNG MONTENEGRO.**

1 **2** 10h. blue 9·50 9·00
2 15h. red 11·50 9·00

D. ISSUES FOR RUMANIA

100 bani = 1 leu.

1917. General Issue stamps of 1917 optd **BANI** or **LEI.**

1 3b. grey 1·90 2·40
2 5b. green 1·90 2·00
3 6b. violet 1·90 1·90
4 10b. brown 15 75
5 12b. blue 1·10 1·50
6 15b. red 1·10 1·90
7 20b. brown 15 75
8 25b. blue 15 30
9 30b. grey 40 65
10 40b. bistre 15 65
11 50b. green 40 70
12 60b. red 40 70
13 80b. blue 15 45
14 90b. purple 40 65
15 2l. red on buff 50 90
16 3l. green on blue 65 1·10
17 4l. red on green 65 1·10

3 Charles I

1918.

18 **3** 3b. grey 15 70
19 5b. green 15 55
20 6b. violet 20 45
21 10b. brown 25 60
22 12b. blue 20 60
23 15b. red 20 50
24 20b. brown 20 45
25 25b. blue 20 45
26 30b. grey 20 42
27 40b. bistre 20 45
28 50b. green 25 60
29 60b. red 25 65
30 80b. blue 15 50
31 90b. purple 25 75
32 2l. red on buff 25 90
33 3l. green on blue 35 90
34 4l. red on green 40 1·00

E. ISSUES FOR SERBIA

100 heller = 1 krone.

1916. Stamps of Bosnia optd **SERBIEN.**

22 **25** 1h. olive 2·00 3·50
23 2h. blue 2·00 3·50
24 3h. lake 1·90 3·25
25 5h. green 25 75
26 6h. black 1·25 2·10
27 10h. red 25 70
28 12h. olive 1·25 2·10
29 20h. brown 65 1·40
30 25h. blue 65 1·25
31 30h. red 65 1·25
32 **26** 35h. green 65 1·25
33 40h. violet 65 1·25
34 45h. brown 65 1·25
35 50h. blue 65 1·25
36 60h. brown 65 1·25
37 72h. blue 65 1·25
38 **25** 1k. brown on cream 70 1·50
39 2k. indigo on blue 70 1·50
40 **26** 3k. red on green 70 1·60
42 10k. blue on grey 10·25 25·00

AUSTRO-HUNGARIAN POST OFFICES IN THE TURKISH EMPIRE Pt. 2

Various Austro-Hungarian P.O.s in the Turkish Empire. Such offices had closed by 15 December 1914 except for several in Albania which remained open until 1915.

A. LOMBARDY AND VENETIA CURRENCY

100 soldi = 1 florin.

1 2 3

1867.

1 **1** 2s. yellow 1·90 2·50
9 3s. green 1·25 23·00
10 5s. red 40 17·00
11 10s. blue 90 1·10
5 15s. brown 30 7·00
6 25s. lilac 25 35·00
7a **2** 30s. brown 1·40 50·00

1883.

14 **3** 2s. black and brown 20 £120
15 3s. black and green 1·25 28·00
16 5s. black and red 20 17·00
17 10s. black and blue 80 65
18 20s. black and grey 5·75 7·00
19 50s. black and mauve 1·25 17·00

B. TURKISH CURRENCY

40 paras = 1 piastre.

1886. Surch **10 PARA 10.**

21a **3** 10p. on 3s. green 40 8·00

1888. Nos. 71/75a of Austria surch.

22 **20** 10pa. on 3k. green 3·75 8·50
23 20pa. on 5k. red 55 7·50
24 1pi. on 10k. blue 65·00 1·00

25 2pi. on 20k. grey 2·00 3·50
26 5pi. on 50k. purple 2·00 14·00

1890. Stamps of Austria of 1890, the kreuzer values with lower figures of value removed, surch at foot.
27 **23** 8pa. on 2k. brown 15 40
28 10pa. on 3k. green 55 50
29 20pa. on 5k. red 30 45
30 1pi. on 10k. blue 40·00 15
31 2pi. on 20k. olive 7·25 25·00
32 5pi. on 50k. mauve 12·00 75·00
33 **24** 10pi. on 1g. blue 12·50 30·00
37 10pi. on 1g. lilac 10·75 25·00
34 20pi. on 2g. red 14·00 50·00
38 20pi. on 2g. green 40·00 80·00

1890. Stamps of Austria of 1891, with lower figures of value removed, surch at foot.
35 **25** 2pi. on 20k. green 4·75 1·40
36 5pi. on 50k. mauve 2·75 2·75

1900. Stamps of Austria of 1899, the heller values with lower figures of value removed, surch at foot.
46 **27** 10pa. on 5h. green 2·00 3·00
40 **28** 20pa. on 10h. red 5·75 1·00
48 1pi. on 25h. blue 1·40 50
49 **29** 2pi. on 50h. blue 3·00 5·75
43 **30** 5pi. on 1k. red 85 35
44 10pi. on 2k. lavender 2·10 2·75
45 20pi. on 4k. green 1·60 6·50

1903. Stamps of Austria of 1899, with all figures of value removed, surch at top and at foot.
55 **27** 10pa. green 55 1·50
56 **28** 20pa. red 1·25 80
57 30pa. mauve 65 3·25
58 1pi. blue 70 45
59 **29** 2pi. blue 75 80

11 Francis Joseph I

12 Francis Joseph I

1908. 60th Anniv of Emperor's Accession.
60 **11** 10pa. green on yellow 15 25
61 20pa. red on pink 25 25
62 30pa. brown on buff 35 90
63 60pa. purple on blue 55 3·50
70 1pi. ultramarine on blue 55 50
65 **12** 2pi. red on yellow 35 25
66 5pi. brown on grey 65 85
67 10pi. green on yellow 1·10 1·60
68 20pi. blue on grey 2·40 1·50

POSTAGE DUE STAMPS

1902. Postage Due stamps as Type D **32** of Austria, but with value in heller, surch with new value.
D50 D **32** 10pa. on 5h. green 1·40 2·75
D51 20pa. on 10h. green 1·50 3·25
D52 1pi. on 20h. green 1·90 4·00
D53 2pi. on 40h. green 1·75 3·75
D54 5pi. on 100h. green 2·10 3·50

D 13

1908.
D71 D **13** $\frac{1}{4}$pi. green 3·25 8·75
D72 $\frac{1}{2}$pi. green 1·90 6·50
D73 1pi. green 2·25 8·00
D74 1$\frac{1}{2}$pi. green 1·40 16·00
D75 2pi. green 2·25 17·00
D76 5pi. green 2·25 10·50
D77 10pi. green 16·00 £130
D78 20pi. green 12·50 £150
D79 30pi. green 18·00 15·00

C. FRENCH CURRENCY

100 centimes = 1 franc.

1903. Stamps of Austria surch **CENTIMES** or **FRANC**.
F1 **27** 5c. on 5h. green and black 1·50 5·25
F2 **28** 10c. on 10h. red and black (No. 143) 1·10 5·75
F3 25c. on 25h. blue and black (No. 145) 34·00 34·00
F4 **29** 50c. on 50h. blue and black 15·00 £225
F5 **30** 1f. on 1k. red 1·40 £150
F6 2f. on 2k. lilac 10·50 £375
F7 4f. on 4k. green 13·50 £600

1904. Stamps of Austria surch **CENTIMES**.
F14 **33** 5c. on 5h. green 2·25 8·25
F13 **28** 10c. on 10h. red and black (No. 160) 28·00 46·00
F10 25c. on 25h. blue and black (No. 176) 1·80 £150
F11 **35** 50c. on 50h. blue 75 £500

1906. Type of Austria surch **CENTIMES**.
F15 **28** 10c. on 10h. red (No. 184) 1·20 46·00
F16 15c. on 15h. violet and black (as No. 185) 90 42·00
No. F16 was not issued without the surch.

1908. 60th Anniv of Emperor's Accession. As T **11/12** but in centimes or franc.
F17 **11** 5c. green on yellow 20 1·10
F18 10c. red on pink 40 1·50
F19 15c. brown on buff 55 7·75
F20 25c. blue on blue 14·50 7·00
F21 **12** 50c. red on yellow 2·10 38·00
F22 1f. brown on grey 3·00 55·00

AZERBAIJAN Pt. 10

Formerly part of the Russian Empire. Became independent on 27 May 1918, following the Russian Revolution. Soviet troops invaded the country on 27 April 1920, and a Soviet Republic followed. From 1 October 1923 stamps of the Transcaucasian Federation were used but these were superseded by those of the Soviet Union in 1924.

With the dissolution of the Soviet Union in 1991, Azerbaijan once again became an independent state.

1919. 100 kopeks = 1 rouble.
1992. 100 qopik = 1 manat.

1 Standard-bearer

6 Famine Supplies

3 "Labour"

4 Petroleum Well

1919. Imperf. Various designs.
1 **1** 10k. multicoloured 40 50
2 – 20k. multicoloured 30 50
3 – 40k. olive, black and yellow 25 30
4 – 60k. orange, black & yellow 25 30
5 – 1r. blue, black and yellow 25 30
6 – 2r. red, black and yellow 25 30
7 – 5r. blue, black and yellow 25 40
8 – 10r. olive, black & yellow 50 75
9 – 25r. blue, black and red 50 1·00
10 – 50r. olive, black and red 75 1·50
DESIGNS—HORIZ: 40k. to 1r. Reaper; 2r. to 10r. Citadel, Baku; 25r., 50r. Temple of Eternal Fires.

1921. Imperf.
11 **3** 1r. green 30 40
12 **4** 2r. brown 30 40
13 – 5r. brown 30 40
14 – 10r. grey 50 50
15 – 25r. orange 30 40
16 – 50r. violet 30 70
17 – 100r. orange 30 70
18 – 150r. blue 30 40
19 – 250r. violet and buff 30 40
20 – 400r. blue 30 60
21 – 500r. black and lilac 30 60
22 – 1000r. red and blue 30 50
23 – 2000r. black and blue 30 50
24 – 3000r. brown and blue 30 60
25 – 5000r. green on olive 30 50
DESIGNS—HORIZ: 5r., 3000r. Bibi Eibatt Oilfield; 100r., 5000r. Goukasoff House (State Museum of Arts); 400r., 1000r. Hall of Judgment, Khan's Palace. VERT: 10r., 2000r. Minaret of Friday Mosque, Khan's Palace, Baku; 25r., 250r. Globe and Workers; 50r. Malden's Tower, Baku; 150r., 500r. Blacksmiths.

1921. Famine Relief. Imperf.
26 **6** 500r. blue 50 1·50
27 – 1000r. brown 85 2·50
DESIGN—VERT: 1000r. Starving family.
For stamps of the above issues surch with new values, see Stanley Gibbons Part 10 (Russia) Catalogue.

13 Azerbaijan Map and Flag

16 Maiden's Tower, Baku

1992. Independence.
83 **13** 35q. multicoloured 85 85

1992. Unissued stamp showing Caspian Sea surch **AZARBAYCAN** and new value.
84 25q. on 15k. multicoloured 20 20
85 35q. on 15k. multicoloured 30 30
86 50q. on 15k. multicoloured 50 50
87 1m.50 on 15k. multicoloured 1·40 1·40
88 2m.50 on 15k. multicoloured 2·25 2·25

1992. Dated "1992".
89 **16** 10q. green and black 10 10
90 20q. red and black 10 10
91 50q. yellow and black 10 10
92 1m.50 blue and black 50 50
See also Nos. 101/4.

17 Akhalteka Horse

1993. Horses. Multicoloured.
93 20q. Type **17** 10 10
94 30q. Kabarda horse 10 10
95 50q. Qarabair horse 10 10
96 1m. Don horse 10 10
97 2m.50 Yakut horse 30 30
98 5m. Orlov horse 55 55
99 10m. Diliboz horse 1·10 1·10

1993. Dated "1993"
101 **16** 50q. blue and black 10 10
102 1m. mauve and black 10 10
103 2m.50 yellow and black 10 10
104 5m. green and black 50 50

18 "Tulipa eichleri"

20 Map of Nakhichevan

19 Russian Sturgeon

1993. Flowers. Multicoloured.
105 25q. Type **18** 10 10
106 50q. "Puschkinia scilloides" 10 10
107 1m. "Iris elegantissima" 10 10
108 1m.50 "Iris acutiloba" 25 25
109 5m. "Tulipa florenskyii" 70 70
110 10m. "Iris reticulata" 1·25 1·25

1993. Fishes. Multicoloured.
112 25q. Type **19** 10 10
113 50q. Stellate sturgeon 10 10
114 1m. Iranian roach 20 20
115 1m.50 Caspian roach 25 25
116 5m. Caspian trout 55 55
117 10m. Black-backed shad 1·25 1·25

1993. 70th Birthday of President Heydar Aliev.
119 – 25m. black and red 1·10 1·10
120 **20** 25m. multicoloured 1·10 1·10
DESIGN: No. 119, President Aliev.

21 Government Building, Baku

22 Flags, and Dish Aerials on Maps

1993.
122 **21** 25q. black and yellow 10 10
123 30q. black and green 15 15
124 50q. black and blue 20 20
125 1m. black and red 40 40

1993. Azerbaijan–Iran Telecommunications Co-operation.
126 **22** 15q. multicoloured 70 70

23 National Colours and Islamic Crescent

24 State Arms

1994. National Day.
127 **23** 5m. multicoloured 40 40

1994.
128 **24** 8m. multicoloured 40 40

25 Sirvan Palace

26 Fuzuli

1994. Baku Architecture.
129 **25** 2m. red, silver and black 10 10
130 – 4m. green, silver and black 20 20
131 – 8m. blue, silver and black 45 45
DESIGNS: 4m. 15th-century tomb; 8m. Divan-Khana.

1994. 500th Birth Anniv (1992) of Mohammed ibn Suleiman Fuzuli (poet).
132 **26** 10m. multicoloured 25 25

1994. No. 126 surch **IRAN–AZERBAYGAN** and value.
133 **22** 2m. on 15q. multicoloured 10 10
134 20m. on 15q. multicoloured 30 30
135 25m. on 15q. multicoloured 50 50
136 50m. on 15q. multicoloured 1·00 1·00

1994. Nos. 122/5 surch.
137 **21** 5m. on 1m. black and red 20 20
138 10m. on 30q. black & grn 20 20
139 15m. on 30q. black & grn 20 20
140 20m. on 50q. black & blue 20 20
141 25m. on 1m. black & red 25 25
142 40m. on 50q. black & blue 30 30
143 50m. on 25q. black & yell 45 45
144 100m. on 25q. black & yell 95 95

29 Rasulzade

1994. 110th Birth Anniv of Mammed Amin Rasulzade (politician).
145 **29** 15m. brown, ochre & black 55 55

30 Mamedquluzade 32 Laumontite

31 Temple of the Fire Worshippers of Atashgah

1994. 125th Birth Anniv of Jalil Mamedquluzade (writer).
146 **30** 20m. black, gold and blue . . . 55 55

1994. 115th Anniv of Nobel Partnership to Exploit Black Sea Oil. Multicoloured.
147 15m. Type **31** 20 20
148 20m. Oil wells 25 25
149 25m. "Zoroastr" (first oil tanker in Caspian Sea) . . 40 40
150 50m. Nobel brothers and Petr Bilderling (partners) . . . 75 75

1994. Minerals. Multicoloured.
152 5m. Type **32** 20 20
153 10m. Epidot calcite 45 45
154 15m. Andradite 70 70
155 20m. Amethyst 95 95

33 Players

1994. World Cup Football Championship, U.S.A.
157 **33** 5m. multicoloured 10 10
158 – 10m. multicoloured 10 10
159 – 20m. multicoloured 20 20
160 – 25m. multicoloured 25 25
161 – 30m. multicoloured 30 30
162 – 50m. multicoloured 55 55
163 – 80m. multicoloured 70 70
DESIGNS: 10m. to 80m. Match scenes.

34 Posthorn

1994.
165 **34** 5m. red and black 10 10
166 10m. green and black . . . 10 10
167 20m. blue and black . . . 20 20
168 25m. yellow and black . . 20 20
169 40m. brown and black . . 25 25

35 Coelophysis and Segisaurus

1994. Prehistoric Animals. Multicoloured.
170 5m. Type **35** 10 10
171 10m. Pentaceratops and tyrannosaurids 10 10
172 20m. Segnosaurus and oviraptor 20 20
173 25m. Albertosaurus and corythosaurus 25 25
174 30m. Igaunodons 25 25
175 50m. Stegosaurus and allosaurus 40 40
176 80m. Tyrannosaurus and saurolophus 65 65

36 Nesting Grouse

1994. The Caucasian Black Grouse. Multicoloured.
178 50m. Type **36** 20 20
179 80m. Grouse on mountain . . 40 40
180 100m. Pair of grouse 55 55
181 120m. Grouse in spring meadow 90 90

1994. No. 84 further surch **400 M.**
182 400m. on 25q. on 15k. mult 35 35

38 "Kapitan Razhabov" (tug)

1994. Ships. Multicoloured.
183 50m. Type **38** 25 25
184 50m. "Azerbaijan" (ferry) . . 25 25
185 50m. "Merkuri 1" (ferry) . . 25 25
186 50m. "Tovuz" (container ship) 25 25
187 50m. "Ganzha" (tanker) . . 25 25
Nos. 183/7 were issued together, se-tenant, the backgrounds of which form a composite design of a map.

40 White-tailed Sea Eagle

1994. Birds of Prey. Multicoloured.
189 10m. Type **40** 25 25
190 15m. Imperial eagle 30 30
191 20m. Tawny eagle 45 45
192 25m. Lammergeier (vert) . . 50 50
193 50m. Saker falcon (vert) . . . 1·00 1·00
Nos. 190/1 are wrongly inscr "Aguila".

41 "Felis libica caudata"

1994. Wild Cats. Multicoloured.
195 10m. Type **41** 25 25
196 15m. Manul cat 30 30
197 20m. Lynx 45 45
198 25m. Leopard (horiz) 50 50
199 50m. Tiger (horiz) . . . . . 1·25 1·25

42 Ancient Greek and Modern Javelin Throwers

1994. Centenary of Int Olympic Committee. Mult.
201 100m. Type **42** 45 45
202 100m. Ancient Greek and modern discus throwers . . 45 45
203 100m. Baron Pierre de Coubertin (founder of modern games) and flame 45 45

1995. Nos. 89/92 and 101/4 surch.
204 **15** 250m. on 10q. green & blk 30 30
205 250m. on 20q. red & black 30 30
206 250m. on 50q. yell & blk 30 30
207 250m. on 1m.50 bl & blk 30 30
208 500m. on 50q. blue & blk 65 65
209 500m. on 1m. mve & blk 65 65
210 500m. on 2m.50 yellow and black 65 65
211 500m. on 5m. green & blk 65 65

44 Apollo

1995. Butterflies. Multicoloured.
212 10m. Type **44** 20 20
213 25m. "Zegris menestho" . . 30 30
214 50m. "Manduca atropos" . . 50 50
215 60m. "Pararge adrastoides" 70 70

45 Aleksei Urmanov (Russia) (gold, men's figure skating) 48 "Polyorchis karafutoensis"

1995. Winter Olympic Games, Lillehammer, Norway, Medal Winners. Multicoloured.
217 10m. Type **45** 10 10
218 25m. Nancy Kerrigan (U.S.A.) (silver, women's figure skating) 20 20
219 40m. Bonnie Blair (U.S.A.) (gold, women's 500m. speed skating) (horiz) . . . 25 25
220 50m. Takanori Kano (Japan) (gold, men's ski jumping) (horiz) 30 30
221 80m. Philip Laros (Canada) (silver, men's freestyle skiing) 50 50
222 100m. German team (gold, three-man bobsleigh) . . . 70 70

1995. Nos. 165/7 surch.
225 **34** 100m. on 5m. red & black 10 10
226 250m. on 10m. grn & blk 25 25
227 500m. on 20m. blue & blk 45 45

1995. Marine Animals. Multicoloured.
228 50m. "Loligo vulgaris" (horiz) 10 10
229 100m. "Orchistoma pileus" (horiz) 25 25
230 150m. "Pegea confoederata" (horiz) 40 40
231 250m. Type **48** 70 70
232 300m. "Agalma okeni" . . . 85 85

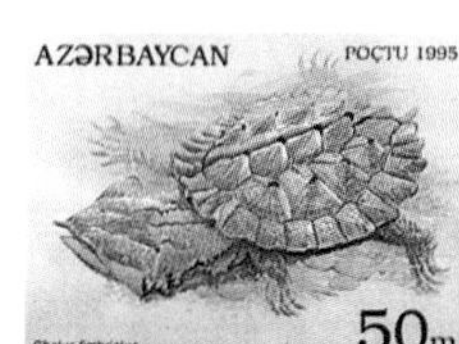

49 Matamata Turtle

1995. Tortoises and Turtles. Multicoloured.
234 50m. Type **49** 10 10
235 100m. Loggerhead turtle . . 25 25
236 150m. Leopard tortoise . . 40 40
237 250m. Indian star tortoise . . 70 70
238 300m. Hermann's tortoise . . 85 85

50 Uzeyir Hacibeyov (composer, 110th) 53 Charles's Hydrogen Balloon, 1783

1995. Birth Anniversaries.
240 **50** 250m. silver and black . . 40 40
241 – 400m. gold and black . . . 75 75
DESIGN: 400m. Vakhid (poet, centenary).

1995. Nos. 84/88 surch.
242 200m. on 2m.50 on 15k. mult 25 25
243 400m. on 25q. on 15k. mult 50 50
244 600m. on 35q. on 15k. mult 85 85
245 800m. on 50q. on 15k. mult 1·10 1·10
246 1000m. on 1m.50 on 15k. multicoloured . . . . . . 1·40 1·40

1995. Nos. 168/9 surch.
247 **34** 400m. on 25m. yell & blk 25 25
248 900m. on 40m. brn & blk 60 60

1995. History of Airships. Multicoloured.
249 100m. Type **53** 10 10
250 150m. Tissandier Brothers' electrically-powered airship, 1883 . . . . 25 25
251 250m. J.-B. Meusnier's elliptical balloon design, 1784 (horiz) 40 40
252 300m. Baldwin's dirigible airship, 1904 (horiz) . . . 50 50
253 400m. U.S. Navy dirigible airship, 1917 (horiz) . . . 60 60
254 500m. Pedal-powered airship, 1909 (horiz) 70 70
No. 249 is wrongly dated.

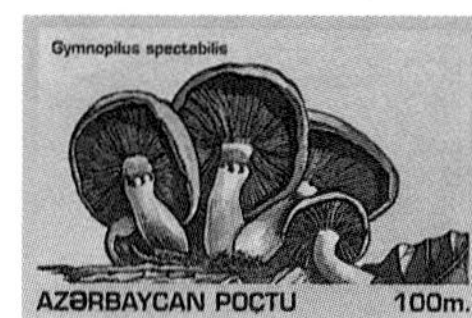

54 "Gymnopilus spectabilis"

1995. Fungi. Multicoloured.
256 100m. Type **54** 25 25
257 250m. Fly agaric 65 65
258 300m. Parasol mushroom . . 70 70
259 400m. "Hygrophorus spectosus" . . . . 1·00 1·00
The 250m. is wrongly inscr "agaris".

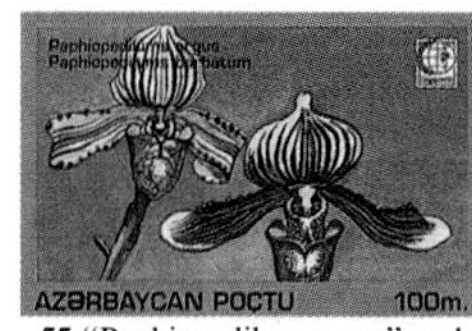

55 "Paphiopedilum argus" and "Paphiopedilum barbatum"

1995. "Singapore '95" International Stamp Exhibition. Orchids. Multicoloured.
261 100m. Type **55** 25 25
262 250m. "Maxillaria picta" . . 65 65
263 300m. "Laeliocattleya" . . . 70 70
264 400m. "Dendrobium nobile" 1·00 1·00

56 Pres. Aliev and U.N. Secretary-General Boutros Boutros Ghali

1995. 50th Anniv of U.N.O.
266 **56** 250m. multicoloured . . . 1·25 1·25

57 Players 58 American Bald Eagle

1995. World Cup Football Championship, France (1998). Multicoloured.
267 100m. Type **57** 20 20
268 150m. Dribbling 40 40
269 250m. Tackling 60 60
270 300m. Preparing to kick ball 65 65
271 400m. Contesting for ball . . 90 90

1995. Air.
273 **58** 2200m. multicoloured . . . 1·50 1·50

59 Persian 60 Horse

1995. Cats. Multicoloured
274 100m. Type **59** 10 10
275 150m. Chartreux 25 25
276 250m. Somali 30 30
277 300m. Longhair Scottish fold 45 45
278 400m. Cymric 50 50
279 500m. Turkish angora . . . 70 70

1995. Flora and Fauna. Multicoloured.
281 100m. Type **60** 10 10
282 200m. Grape hyacinths (vert) 20 20
283 250m. Beluga 25 25
284 300m. Golden eagle 30 30
285 400m. Tiger 30 30
286 500m. Georgian black grouse nesting 50 50
287 1000m. Georgian black grouse in meadow . . . . 1·00 1·00

61 Lennon and Signature

1995. 15th Death Anniv of John Lennon (entertainer).
288 **61** 500m. multicoloured . . . 55 55

62 Early Steam Locomotive, U.S.A.

1996. Railway Locomotives. Multicoloured.
289 100m. Type **62** 40 40
290 100m. New York Central Class J3 locomotive . . . 40 40
291 100m. Steam locomotive on bridge 40 40
292 100m. Steam locomotive No. 1959, Germany . . . 40 40
293 100m. Steam locomotive No. 4113, Germany . . . 40 40
294 100m. Steam locomotive, Italy 40 40
295 100m. Class 59 steam locomotive, Japan 40 40
296 100m. Class QJ steam locomotive, China 40 40
297 100m. Class Sn 23 steam locomotive, China 40 40

63 Operating Theatre and Topcubasov

1996. Birth Centenary of M. Topcubasov (surgeon).
299 **63** 300m. multicoloured . . . 65 65

64 Feast and Woman wearing Traditional Costume

1996. New Year.
300 **64** 250m. multicoloured . . . 65 65

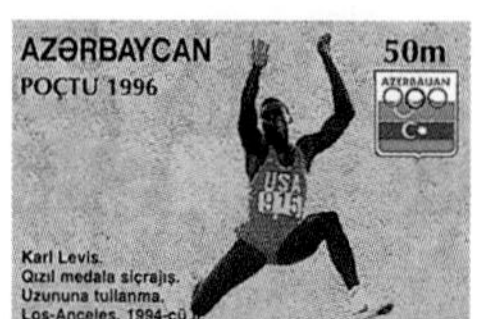

65 Carl Lewis (athletics, Los Angeles, 1984)

1996. Olympic Games, Atlanta. Previous Gold Medallists. Multicoloured.
301 50m. Type **65** (wrongly inscr "1994") 10 10
302 100m. Mohammed Ali (Cassius Clay) (boxing, Rome, 1960) 20 20
303 150m. Li Ning (gymnastics, Los Angeles, 1984) 40 40
304 200m. Said Aouita (5000m, Los Angeles, 1984) 50 50
305 250m. Olga Korbut (gymnastics, Munich, 1972) 65 65
306 300m. Nadia Comaneci (gymnastics, Montreal, 1976) 85 85
307 400m. Greg Louganis (diving, Los Angeles, 1984) . . . . 1·00 1·00

66 "Maral-Gol"

1996. 5th Death Anniv of G. Aliev (painter). Mult.
309 100m. "Reka Cura" 50 50
310 200m. Type **66** . . . . 1·00 1·00

67 Behbudov and Globe

1996. 7th Death Anniv of Resid Behbudov (singer).
311 **67** 100m. multicoloured . . . 65 65

68 Mammadaliev and Flasks
69 National Flag and Government Building

1996. 1st Death Anniv of Yusif Mammadaliev (scientist).
312 **68** 100m. multicoloured . . . 65 65

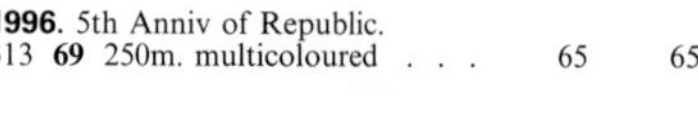

1996. 5th Anniv of Republic.
313 **69** 250m. multicoloured . . . 65 65

70 Dome of the Rock

1996. 3000th Anniv of Jerusalem. Multicoloured.
314 100m. Praying at the Wailing Wall 40 40
315 250m. Interior of church . . 1·00 1·00
316 300m. Type **70** . . . . 1·10 1·10

71 German Shepherd

1996. Dogs. Multicoloured.
318 50m. Type **71** 10 10
319 100m. Basset hounds 25 25
320 150m. Collies 35 35
321 200m. Bull terriers 50 50
322 300m. Boxers 70 70
323 400m. Cocker spaniels . . . 1·10 1·10

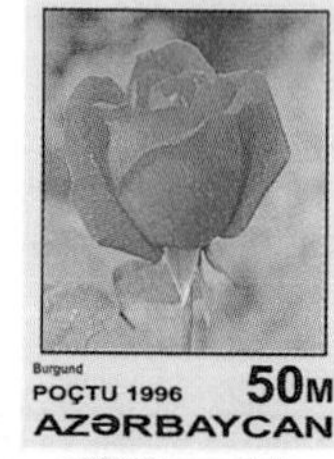

72 Shaft-tailed Whydah
73 "Burgundy"

1996. Birds. Multicoloured.
325 50m. Type **72** 10 10
326 100m. Blue-naped mousebird 25 25
327 150m. Asian black-headed oriole 35 35
328 200m. Golden oriole 50 50
329 300m. Common starling . . . 70 70
330 400m. Yellow-fronted canary 1·00 1·00

1996. Roses. Multicoloured.
332 50m. Type **73** 10 10
333 100m. "Virgo" 20 20
334 150m. "Rose Gaujard" . . . 30 30
335 200m. "Luna" 45 45
336 300m. "Lady Rose" 70 70
337 400m. "Landora" . . . . . 1·00 1·00

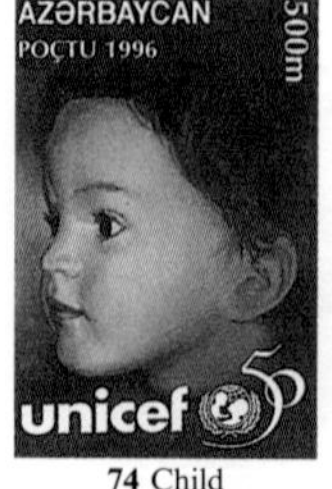

74 Child
75 Spain v. Bulgaria

1996. 50th Anniv of U.N.I.C.E.F.
339 **74** 500m. multicoloured . . . 1·00 1·00

1996. European Football Championship, England. Multicoloured.
340 100m. Type **75** 20 20
341 150m. Rumania v. France . . 30 30
342 200m. Czech Republic v. Germany 45 45
343 250m. England v. Switzerland 55 55
344 300m. Croatia v. Turkey . . 70 70
345 400m. Italy v. Russia . . . . 1·00 1·00

76 Chinese Junk

1996. Ships. Multicoloured.
347 100m. Type **76** 25 25
348 150m. "Danmark" (Danish full-rigged cadet ship) . . . 40 40
349 200m. "Nippon-Maru II" (Japanese cadet ship) . . . 45 45
350 250m. "Mircea" (Rumanian barque) 55 55
351 300m. "Kruzenshtern" (Russian cadet barque) . . 85 85
352 400m. "Ariadne" (German cadet schooner) . . . . . 1·10 1·10

77 Baxram Gur killing Dragon (fountain by A. Shulgin at Baku)
82 Dog

78 Nariman Narimanov (politician and writer)

1997.
354 **77** 100m. purple and black . . 55 55
356 250m. black and yellow . . 20 20
357 400m. black and red . . . 40 40
358 500m. black and green . . 45 45
359 1000m. black and blue . . 75 75

1997. Anniversaries. Multicoloured.
365 250m. Type **78** (125th birth anniv (1995)) 55 55
366 250m. Fatali Xoyskin (politician, 120th birth anniv (1995)) 55 55
367 250m. Aziz Mammed-Kerim ogli Aliyev (politician, birth centenary) 55 55
368 250m. Ilyas Afendiyev (writer, 1st death anniv) . . 55 55

1997. Red Cross. Various stamps optd **Red Cross** and cross. (a) Nos. 93/99.
370 20q. multicoloured 50 50
371 30q. multicoloured 50 50
372 50q. multicoloured 50 50
373 1m. multicoloured 75 75
374 2m.50 multicoloured 75 75
375 5m. multicoloured . . . . . 1·60 1·60
376 10m. multicoloured . . . . . 4·25 4·25

(b) Nos. 195/9.
378 10m. multicoloured 70 70
379 15m. multicoloured . . . . . 1·00 1·00
380 20m. multicoloured . . . . . 1·40 1·40
381 25m. multicoloured . . . . . 1·60 1·60
382 50m. multicoloured . . . . . 3·00 3·00

1997. 50th Anniv of Rotary Club International in Azerbaijan. Various stamps optd **50th Anniversary of the Rotary Club** and emblem. (a) Nos. 314/16.
384 100m. multicoloured 90 90
385 250m. multicoloured . . . . 3·00 3·00
386 300m. multicoloured . . . . 3·50 3·50

(b) Nos. 347/52.
388 100m. multicoloured 30 30
389 150m. multicoloured 55 55
390 200m. multicoloured 70 70
391 250m. multicoloured . . . . 1·00 1·00
392 300m. multicoloured . . . . 1·10 1·10
393 400m. multicoloured . . . . 1·40 1·40

1997. "The Town Band of Bremen" by the Brothers Grimm. Multicoloured.
395 250m. Type **82** . . . . 1·10 1·10
396 250m. Donkey and cat . . . 1·10 1·10
397 250m. Rooster . . . . 1·10 1·10
Nos. 395/7 were issued together, se-tenant, forming a composite design.

83 Seal Pup

1997. The Caspian Seal. Multicoloured.
399 250m. Type **83** 65 65
400 250m. Bull and mountain peak 65 65
401 250m. Bull and gull 65 65
402 250m. Cow (profile) 65 65
403 250m. Cow (full face) 65 65
404 250m. Young seal (three-quarter face) 65 65
Nos. 399/404 were issued together, se-tenant, forming a composite design.

84 Tanbur

1997. Traditional Musical Instruments. Mult.
406 250m. Type **84** 50 50
407 250m. Gaval (tambourine) . . 50 50
408 500m. Jang (harp) . . . . . 1·00 1·00

86 Sirvani

1997. 870th Birth Anniv (1996) of Xanqani Sirvani (poet).
410 **86** 250m. multicoloured . . . 90 90

87 Taza-pir Mosque, Baku

1997. Mosques. Multicoloured.
411 250m. Type **87** 70 70
412 250m. Momuna-Xatun Mosque, Nakhichevan . . 70 70
413 250m. Govharaga Mosque, Shusha 70 70

88 Rasulbekov and Baku T.V. Tower

90 Katarina Wit, East Germany

89 Italy, 1938

1997. 80th Birth Anniv of G. D. Rasulbekov (former Minister of Telecommunications).
414 **88** 250m. multicoloured . . . 65 65

1997. World Cup Football Championship, France (1998).
415 **89** 250m. black 55 55
416 – 250m. multicoloured . . . 55 55
417 – 250m. black 55 55
418 – 250m. multicoloured . . . 55 55
419 – 250m. multicoloured . . . 55 55
420 – 250m. multicoloured . . . 55 55
DESIGNS—World Champion Teams: No. 416, Argentina, 1986; 417, Uruguay, 1930 (wrongly inscr "1980"); 418, Brazil, 1994; 419, England, 1966; 420, West Germany, 1990.

1997. Winter Olympic Games, Nagano, Japan. Mult.
422 250m. Type **90** (figure skating gold medal, 1984 and 1988) 50 50
423 250m. Elvis Stoyko, Canada (figure skating silver medal, 1994) 50 50
424 250m. Midori Ito, Japan (figure skating silver medal, 1992) 50 50
425 250m. Azerbaijan flag and silhouettes of sports . . . 50 50
426 250m. Olympic torch and mountain 50 50
427 250m. Kristin Yamaguchi, U.S.A. (figure skating gold medal, 1992) 50 50
428 250m. John Curry, Great Britain (figure skating gold medal, 1976) 50 50
429 250m. Cen Lu, China (figure skating bronze medal, 1994) 50 50

91 Diana, Princess of Wales

1998. Diana, Princess of Wales Commem. Mult.
431 400m. Type **91** 40 40
432 400m. Wearing black polo-neck jumper 40 40

92 Aliyev and Mountain Landscape

1998. 90th Birth Anniv of Hasan Aliyev (ecologist).
433 **92** 500m. multicoloured . . . 65 65

95 Ashug Alesker (singer)

1998. Birth Anniversaries. Multicoloured.
436 250m. Type **95** (175th anniv) 65 65
437 250m. Magomedhuseyn Shakhriyar (poet, 90th anniv) 65 65
438 250m. Qara Qarayev (composer, 80th anniv) . . 65 65

96 Bul-Bul

1998. Birth Centenary of Bul-Bul (Murtuz Meshadirza ogli Mamedov) (singer).
439 **96** 500m. multicoloured . . . 75 75

97 Mickey and Minnie Mouse playing Chess

1998. World Rapid Chess Championship, Georgia. Multicoloured.
440 250m. Type **97** 40 40
441 500m. Mickey, Minnie, pawn and rook 70 70
442 500m. Goofy, bishop and knight 70 70
443 500m. Donald Duck, king and bishop 70 70
444 500m. Pluto, rook, pawn and clockwork pawn 70 70
445 500m. Minnie and queen . . 70 70
446 500m. Daisy Duck, bishop and king 70 70
447 500m. Goofy, Donald and pawn 70 70
448 500m. Mickey, queen and rook 70 70

98 Preparing Pastries

1998. Europa. National Festivals: New Year. Mult.
450 1000m. Type **98** 85 85
451 3000m. Acrobat and wrestlers 2·40 2·40

1999. "iBRA" International Stamp Exhibition, Nuremberg, Germany. Nos. 450/1 optd with exhibition emblem.
452 1000m. multicoloured 90 90
453 3000m. multicoloured . . . . 2·75 2·75

100 Greater Flamingo, Gizilagach National Park

101 14th-century Square Tower

1999. Europa. Parks and Gardens. Multicoloured.
454 1000m. Type **100** 90 90
455 3000m. Stag, Girkan National Park . . . . . . 2·75 2·75

1999. Towers at Mardakyan.
456 **101** 1000m. black and blue . . 50 50
457 – 3000m. black and red . . 1·40 1·40
DESIGN: 3000m. 13th-century round tower.

102 President Aliev and Flag

1999. 75th Anniv of Nakhichevan Autonomous Region. Multicoloured.
460 1000m. Type **102** 75 75
461 1000m. Map of Nakhichevan 75 75

103 Cabbarli

1999. Birth Centenary of Cafar Cabbarli (dramatist).
463 **103** 250m. multicoloured . . . 1·10 1·10

105 Flag, Pigeon and Emblem on Scroll

106 Caravanserai Inner Court and Maiden's Tower, Baku

1999. 125th Anniv of Universal Postal Union. Multicoloured.
465 250m. Type **105** 10 10
466 300m. Satellite, computer and emblem . . . . 2·00 2·00

1999. 19th-century Caravanserais. Multicoloured.
467 500m. Type **106** 95 95
468 500m. Camels outside caravanserai, Sheki 95 95

107 Anniversary Emblem

1999. 50th Anniv of Council of Europe.
469 **107** 1000m. multicoloured . . 1·00 1·00

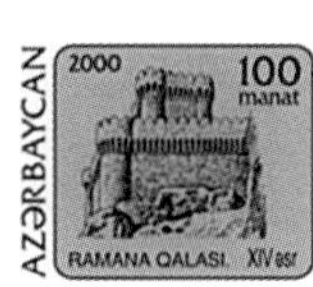

109 "Building Europe"

111 14th-century Square Tower, Ramana

2000. Europa.
471 **109** 1000m. multicoloured . . 90 90
472 3000m. multicoloured . . 2·75 2·75

2000. Towers of Mardakyan.
474 **111** 100m. black and orange 25 25
475 – 250m. black and green . . 55 55
DESIGN: 250m. 14th-century round tower, Nardaran.
See also Nos. 499/500.

112 Wrestling

2000. Olympic Games, Sydney. Multicoloured.
476 500m. Type **112** 65 65
477 500m. Weightlifting 65 65
478 500m. Boxing 65 65
479 500m. Relay 65 65

113 Duck flying

2000. The Ferruginous Duck. Multicoloured.
480 500m. Type **113** 45 45
481 500m. Ducks in water and standing on rocks 45 45
482 500m. Duck standing on rock and others swimming by grasses 45 45
483 500m. Ducks at sunset . . . 45 45

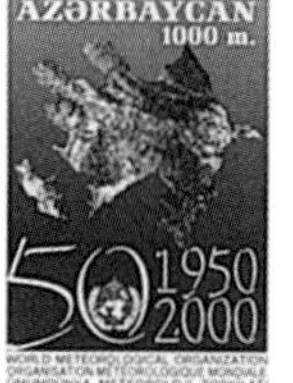

114 Satellite Picture of Azerbaijan and Emblem

117 Rasul-Rza

115 Quinces

2000. 50th Anniv of World Meteorological Organization.
484 **114** 1000m. multicoloured . . 65 65

2000. Fruits. Multicoloured.
485 500m. Type **115** 55 55
486 500m. Pomegranates (*Punica granatum*) 55 55
487 500m. Peaches (*Persica*) . . . 55 55
488 500m. Figs (*Ficus carica*) . . 55 55

2000. 90th Birth Anniv of Rasul-Rza (poet).
490 **117** 250m. multicoloured . . . 50 50

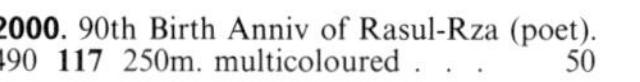

118 Levantine Viper

2000. Reptiles. Multicoloured.
491 500m. Type **118** 75 75
492 500m. Rock lizard (*Lacerta saxicola*) (wrongly inscr "Laserta saxcola") 75 75
493 500m. Ottoman viper (*Vipera xanthina*) 75 75
494 500m. Toad-headed agama (*Phrynocephalus mystaceus*) 75 75

119 Rahman

2000. 90th Birth Anniv of Sabit Rahman (writer).
496 **119** 1000m. multicoloured . . 45 45

120 Emblem

2000. U.N.E.S.C.O. International Year of Culture and Peace.
497 **120** 3000m. multicoloured . . 1·40 1·40

122 Seal, Lesser White-fronted Goose and Oil Rig

2001. Europa. Water Resources. The Caspian Sea. Multicoloured.
499 1000m. Type **122** 55 55
500 3000m. Sturgeon, crab and oil rig . . . . 1·60 1·60

123 Building and Flags

2001. Admission of Azerbaijan to Council of Europe.
501 **123** 1000m. multicoloured . . 55 55

2001. Towers of Sheki. As T **111**
502 100m. black and lilac 10 10
503 250m. black and yellow . . . 25 25
DESIGNS: 100m. 18th-century round tower; 250m. Ruin of 12th-century tower.

125 Tusi, Globe and Books

2001. 800th Birth Anniv of Nasraddin Tusi (mathematician and astronomer). Sheet 110 × 78 mm.
MS505 **125** 3000m. multicoloured 1·40 1·40

126 Handshake and Emblem

128 Short-eared Owl (*Asio flammeus*)

127 Yuri Gagarin, "Vostok 1" and Globe

2001. 10th Anniv of Union of Independent States.
506 **126** 1000m. multicoloured . . 45 45

2001. 40th Anniv of First Manned Space Flight. Sheet 83 × 56 mm.
MS507 **127** 3000m. multicoloured 1·40 1·40

2001. Owls. Multicoloured.
508 1000m. Type **128** 45 45
509 1000m. Tawny owl (*Strix aluco*) 45 45
510 1000m. Scops owl (*Otus scops*) 45 45
511 1000m. Long-eared owl (*Asio otus*) 45 45
512 1000m. Eagle owl on branch (*Bubo bubo*) 45 45
513 1000m. Little owl (*Athene noctua*) 45 45
MS514 91 × 68 mm. 1000 m. Eagle owl (*Bubo bubo*) in flight 45 45

129 Pres. Heydar Aliyev

2001. 10th Anniv of Independence.
515 **129** 5000m. multicoloured . . 2·25 2·25

130 Pres. Vladimir Putin and Pres. Heydar Aliyev

2001. Visit of President Putin to Azerbaijan.
516 **130** 1000m. multicoloured . . 45 45

131 Emblem and Athletes

2002. 10th Anniv of National Olympic Committee.
517 **131** 3000m. multicoloured . . 1·40 1·40

132 Circus Performers

2002. Europa. Circus. Multicoloured.
518 1000m. Type **132** 45 45
519 3000m. Equestrian juggler and trapeze artist . . . . 1·40 1·40

133 Presidents Heydar Aliyev and Jiang Zemin

2002. 10th Anniv of Azerbaijan--China Diplomatic Relations.
520 **133** 1000m. multicoloured . . 45 45

134 Molla Panah Vagif's Mausoleum, Susa

136 Emblem

2002. Towers of Karabakh.
521 **134** 100m. black and green . . 10 10
522 – 250m. black and cinnamon 10 10
DESIGNS: 250m. 19th-century mosque, Aghdam.

2002. 10th Anniv of Azermarka Stamp Company. No. 83 surch **Azermarka 1992--2002 1000m.**
523 **13** 1000m. on 35q. multicoloured 45 45

2002. 10th Anniv of New Azerbaijan Party.
524 **136** 3000m. multicoloured . . 1·40 1·40

137 African Monarch (*Danaus chrysippus*)

2002. Butterflies and Moths. Multicoloured.
525 1000m. Type **137** (inscr "Danais") 45 45
526 1000m. Southern swallowtail (*Papilio alexanor*) 45 45
527 1000m. *Thaleropis jonia* . . . 45 45
528 1000m. Red admiral (*Vanessa atalanta*) 45 45
529 1000m. *Argynnis alexandra* 45 45
530 1000m. *Brahmaea christoph* (moth) 45 45

138 Pres. Heydar Aliyev and Pope John Paul II

2002. Pope John Paul II's Visit to Azerbaijan. Sheet 80 × 65 mm.
MS531 **138** 1500m. multicoloured 55 55

139 Telegraph Machine, Building Facade and Emblem

2002. 70th Anniv of Baku Telegraph Office.
532 **139** 3000m. multicoloured . . 1·10 1·10

140 Gadjiyev and Piano

2002. 80th Birth Anniv of Ruaf Gadjiyev (composer).
533 **140** 5000m. multicoloured . . 1·90 1·90

141 Bearded Men with Swords, Black Pawns, White Pawn and White Rook

2002. European Junior Chess Championships, Baku. Showing chess board and views of Baku. Multicoloured.
534 1500m. Type **141** 55 55
535 1500m. Two knights on horseback 55 55
536 1500m. Two elephants . . . 55 55
537 1500m. Black rook, black pawn, bearded men with swords and fallen knight 55 55
Nos. 534/7 were issued together, se-tenant, forming a composite design showing a chess game and views of ancient Baku.

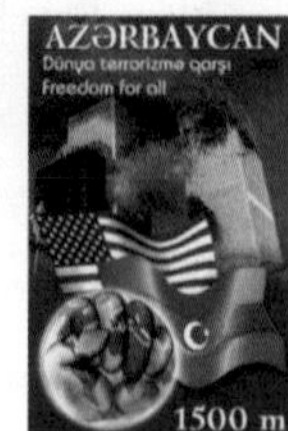

142 World Trade Centre, New York, U.S.A. and Azerbaijan Flags and Globe

2002. 1st Anniv of Attack on World Trade Centre, New York. Sheet 130 × 65 mm containing vert design as T **142**. Multicoloured.
MS538 1500m. × 3 Type **142** 1·60 1·60

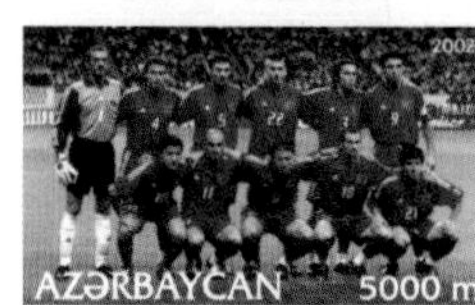

143 Turkish Football Team

2002. Football World Cup Championship, Japan and South Korea. Sheet 102 × 110 mm.
MS539 **143** 5000m. multicoloured 1·90 1·90

144 Dove, Woman, Flag and Emblems

145 Siamese Fighting Fish (*Betta splendens*)

2002. United Nations Development Fund for Women.
540 **144** 3000m. multicoloured . . 1·10 1·10

2002. Aquarium Fish. Multicoloured.
541 100m. Type **145** 10 10
542 100m. Blue discus (*Symphysodon aequifasciatus*) 10 10
543 100m. Freshwater angelfish (*Pterophyllum scalare*) . . . 10 10
544 100m. Black moor (*Carassius auratus auratus*) 10 10
545 100m. Boeseman's rainbowfish (*Melanotaenia boesemani*) 10 10
546 1000m. Firemouth cichlid (*Cichlasoma meeki*) 35 35

AZORES Pt. 9

A group of islands in the Atlantic Ocean.

1868. 1000 reis = 1 milreis.
1912. 100 centavos = 1 escudo.
2002. 100 cents = 1 euro.

NOTE. Except where otherwise stated, Nos. 1/393 are all stamps of Portugal optd **ACORES**.

1868. Curved value labels. Imperf.
1 **14** 5r. black £2250 £1500
2 10r. yellow £1000 £7500
3 20r. bistre £150 £130
4 50r. green £150 £130
5 80r. orange £170 £140
6 100r. purple £170 £140

1868. Curved value labels. Perf.
7 **14** 5r. black . . . . 55·00 55·00
9 10r. yellow . . . . 70·00 55·00
10 20r. bistre . . . . 55·00 50·00
11 25r. pink . . . . 55·00 8·50
12 50r. green £160 £150
13 80r. orange £160 £150
14 100r. lilac £160 £150
16 120r. blue . . . . £130 95·00
17 240r. lilac £475 £300

1871. Straight value labels.
38 **15** 5r. black . . . . 10·00 6·75
39 10r. yellow . . . . 22·00 13·00
73 10r. green . . . . 60·00 50·00
29 15r. brown . . . . 20·00 14·50
31 20r. bistre . . . . 22·00 20·00
109 20r. red . . . . £100 85·00
32 25r. pink . . . . 12·50 3·25
33 50r. green . . . . 65·00 32·00
54 50r. blue . . . . £110 65·00
101b 80r. orange . . . . 55·00 45·00
103 100r. mauve . . . . 45·00 40·00
25 120r. blue £120 £100
49 150r. blue £130 £120
104 150r. yellow . . . . 45·00 40·00
26 240r. lilac £650 £550
50 300r. lilac . . . . 65·00 45·00
94 1000r. black . . . . 90·00 85·00

1880.
58 **16** 5r. black . . . . 18·00 8·00
61 25r. grey . . . . 40·00 6·50
61b 25r. brown . . . . 40·00 6·50
60 **17** 25r. grey . . . . £100 32·00
67 **16** 50r. blue . . . . £120 29·00

1882.
136 **19** 5r. grey . . . . 10·50 4·00
125 10r. green . . . . 21·00 9·75
139 20r. red . . . . 22·00 13·00
126 25r. brown . . . . 14·50 3·00
141 25r. mauve . . . . 22·00 2·10
142 50r. blue . . . . 18·00 3·25
128 500r. black £120 £110
129 500r. mauve . . . . £100 70·00

1894. Prince Henry the Navigator.
143 **32** 5r. orange . . . . 2·25 2·25
144 10r. red . . . . 2·25 2·25
145 15r. brown . . . . 2·75 2·75
146 20r. lilac . . . . 3·00 3·00
147 25r. green . . . . 3·25 3·25
148 50r. blue . . . . 8·50 4·50
149 75r. red . . . . 15·00 6·50
150 80r. green . . . . 18·00 6·50
151 100r. brown on buff . . . 18·00 5·50
152 150r. red . . . . 26·00 12·50
153 300r. blue on buff . . . . 28·00 20·00
154 500r. purple . . . . 50·00 30·00
155 1000r. black on buff . . . £100 48·00

1895. St. Anthony of Padua.
156 **35** 2½r. black . . . . 2·10 1·00
157 – 5r. orange . . . . 6·50 2·00
158 – 10r. mauve . . . . 6·50 3·00
159 – 15r. brown . . . . 10·00 4·50

160 – 20r. grey 10·00 6·50
161 – 25r. purple and green 7·00 2·10
162 **37** 50r. brown and blue 22·00 10·00
163 75r. brown and red 32·00 28·00
164 80r. brown and green 35·00 32·00
165 100r. black and brown 35·00 28·00
166 – 150r. red and brown 65·00 70·00
167 – 200r. blue and brown 80·00 70·00
168 – 300r. black and brown £100 75·00
169 – 500r. brown & green £140 £100
170 – 1000r. lilac and green £200 £150

1898. Vasco da Gama stamps as Nos. 378/385 of Portugal but inscr "ACORES".
171 2½r. green 2·25 95
172 5r. red 2·25 1·10
173 10r. purple 4·50 2·10
174 25r. green 4·50 2·10
175 50r. blue 6·75 6·50
176 75r. brown 14·00 10·00
177 100r. brown 18·00 10·00
178 150r. bistre 27·00 20·00

1906. "King Carlos" key-type inscr "ACORES" and optd with letters **A**, **H** and **PD** in three of the corners.
179 S 2½r. grey 30 30
180 5r. orange 30 30
181 10r. green 30 30
182 20r. lilac 45 40
183 25r. red 45 30
184 50r. blue 3·75 3·50
185 75r. brown on yellow 1·25 90
186 100r. blue on blue 1·25 1·00
187 200r. purple on pink 1·25 1·00
188 300r. blue on pink 4·25 3·50
189 500r. black on blue 10·50 9·00

7 King Manoel

1910.
190 **7** 2½r. lilac 35 30
191 5r. black 40 35
192 10r. green 40 35
193 15r. brown 60 50
194 20r. red 85 70
195 25r. brown 40 35
196 50r. blue 2·00 1·00
197 75r. brown 2·00 1·00
198 80r. grey 2·00 2·00
199 100r. brown on green 3·25 2·50
200 200r. green on pink 3·25 2·50
201 300r. black on blue 2·00 2·00
202 500r. brown and olive 6·00 5·25
203 1000r. black and blue 14·00 12·00

1910. Optd **REPUBLICA**.
204 **7** 2½r. lilac 30 25
205 5r. black 25 25
206 10r. green 30 25
207 15r. brown 1·25 1·00
208b 20r. red 75 75
209 25r. brown 25 25
210a 50r. blue 1·00 75
211 75r. brown 1·00 65
212 80r. grey 1·00 65
213 100r. brown on green 80 60
214 200r. green on orange 80 60
215 300r. black on blue 2·40 1·60
216 500r. brown and green 2·75 2·25
217 1000r. black and blue 5·75 3·75

1911. Vasco da Gama stamps of Azores optd **REPUBLICA**, some surch also.
218 2½r. green 50 40
219 15r. on 5r. red 50 40
220 25r. green 50 40
221 50r. blue 1·50 1·00
222 75r. brown 1·25 1·10
223 80r. on 150r. brown 1·25 1·25
224 100r. brown 1·40 1·25
225 1000r. on 10r. purple 13·00 9·50

1911. Postage Due stamps optd or surch **REPUBLICA ACORES**.
226 D **48** 5r. black 95 85
227 10r. mauve 2·00 85
228 20r. orange 3·25 2·50
229 200r. brown on buff 14·50 12·50
230 300r. on 50r. grey 14·50 12·50
231 500r. on 100r. red on pink 14·50 12·50

1912. "Ceres" type.
250 **56** ¼c. brown 35 30
273 ¼c. black 40 20
252 1c. green 80 60
274 1c. brown 35 35
254 1½c. brown 80 60
275 1½c. green 40 40
256 2c. red 60 45
257 2c. orange 40 40
258 2½c. lilac 60 45
259 3c. red 40 40
278 3c. blue 30 30
260 3½c. green 40 40
261 4c. green 40 40
401 4c. orange 40 40
262 5c. blue 60 45
280 5c. brown 40 35
264 6c. purple 40 40
282 6c. brown 40 35
403 6c. red 25 25
265 7½c. brown 4·50 2·50
266 7½c. blue 1·25 1·10
267 8c. grey 60 45
283 8c. green 55 40
284 8c. orange 70 65
268 10c. brown 4·50 2·00
285 10c. red 80 40
286 12c. blue 1·75 1·25
287 12c. green 65 55
288 13½c. blue 1·75 1·25
249 14c. blue on yellow 1·60 1·25
269 15c. purple 80 45
289 15c. black 40 35
290 16c. blue 65 60
243 20c. brown on green 8·00 4·25
291 20c. brown 65 55
292 20c. green 80 65
293 20c. drab 55 40
294 24c. blue 60 35
295 25c. pink 45 40
244 30c. brown on pink 45·00 35·00
245 30c. brown on yellow 1·60 1·25
296 30c. brown 1·25 1·10
406 32c. green 1·75 1·25
298 36c. red 65 40
299 40c. blue 65 45
300 40c. brown 1·25 60
407 40c. green 1·00 50
408 48c. pink 2·50 2·00
246 50c. orange on orange 4·00 2·00
247 50c. orange on yellow 4·00 2·00
302 50c. yellow 1·25 1·00
410 50c. red 3·00 2·50
303 60c. blue 1·25 1·00
304 64c. blue 3·25 2·25
411 64c. red 3·00 2·50
305 75c. pink 3·25 2·50
412 75c. red 2·25 2·00
306 80c. purple 1·75 1·40
307 80c. lilac 1·75 1·25
413 80c. green 2·25 2·00
308 90c. blue 1·75 1·40
309 96c. red 4·75 2·25
248 1e. green on blue 4·50 3·75
310 1e. lilac 1·75 1·40
314 1e. purple 2·40 2·10
414 **56** 1e. red 28·00 20·00
311 1e.10 brown 1·90 1·40
312 1e.20 green 2·10 1·40
315 1e.20 buff 5·25 3·75
415 1e.25 blue 1·40 1·25
316 1e.50 purple 5·25 4·50
317 1e.50 lilac 5·25 4·50
400 1e.60 blue 2·50 1·10
313 2e. green 5·75 3·25
319 2e.40 green 48·00 32·00
320 3e. pink 55·00 32·00
321 3e.20 green 6·50 6·75
322 5e. green 12·00 6·75
323 10e. pink 32·00 19·00
324 20e. blue 75·00 50·00

1925. C. C. Branco Centenary.
325 **65** 2c. orange 20 20
326 3c. green 20 20
327 4c. blue 20 20
328 5c. red 20 20
329 – 10c. blue 20 20
330 – 16c. orange 25 25
331 **67** 25c. red 25 25
332 – 32c. green 40 40
333 **67** 40c. black and green 40 40
334 48c. purple 85 85
335 – 50c. green 85 70
336 – 64c. brown 85 70
337 – 75c. grey 85 70
338 **67** 80c. brown 85 70
339 – 96c. red 1·00 85
340 – 1e.50 blue on blue 1·00 85
341 **67** 1e.60 blue 1·10 1·00
342 – 2e. green on green 1·60 1·50
343 – 2e.40 red on orange 2·25 1·60
344 – 3e.20 black on green 3·00 3·00

1926. 1st Independence Issue.
345 **76** 2c. black and orange 30 30
346 – 3c. black and blue 30 30
347 **76** 4c. black and green 30 30
348 – 5c. black and brown 30 30
349 **76** 6c. black and orange 30 30
350 – 15c. black and green 55 55
351 **77** 20c. black and violet 55 55
352 – 25c. black and red 55 55
353 **77** 32c. black and green 55 55
354 – 40c. black and brown 55 55
355 – 50c. black and olive 1·10 1·10
356 – 75c. black and red 1·10 1·10
357 – 1e. black and violet 1·40 1·40
358 – 4e.50 black and green 4·75 4·75

1927. 2nd Independence Issue.
359 **80** 2c. black and brown 25 25
360 – 3c. black and blue 25 25
361 **80** 4c. black and orange 25 25
362 – 5c. black and brown 25 25
363 – 6c. black and brown 25 25
364 – 15c. black and brown 25 25
365 **80** 25c. black and grey 90 90
366 – 32c. black and green 90 90
367 – 40c. black and green 55 55
368 – 96c. black and red 2·25 2·25
369 – 1e.60 black and blue 2·25 2·25
370 – 4e.50 black and yellow 5·00 5·00

1928. 3rd Independence Issue.
371 – 2c. black and blue 25 25
372 **84** 3c. black and green 25 25
373 – 4c. black and red 25 25
374 – 5c. black and olive 25 25
375 – 6c. black and brown 25 25
376 **84** 15c. black and grey 45 45
377 – 16c. black and purple 55 55
378 – 25c. black and blue 55 55
379 – 32c. black and green 55 55
380 – 40c. black and brown 55 55
381 – 50c. black and red 1·10 1·10
382 **84** 80c. black and grey 1·10 1·10
383 – 96c. black and red 2·10 2·10
384 – 1e. black and mauve 2·10 2·10
385 – 1e.60 black and blue 2·10 2·10
386 – 4e.50 black and yellow 5·00 5·00

1929. "Ceres" type surch **ACORES** and new value.
387 **56** 4c. on 25c. pink 55 55
388 4c. on 60c. blue 1·00 1·00
389 10c. on 25c. pink 90 90
390 12c. on 25c. pink 90 90
391 15c. on 25c. pink 90 90
392 20c. on 25c. pink 1·60 1·60
393 40c. on 1e.10 brown 3·00 3·00

14 10r. Stamp of 1868

1980. 112th Anniv of First Azores Stamps.
416 **14** 6e.50 black, yellow & red 20 10
417 – 19e.50 blk, purple & blue 90 55
DESIGN: 19e.50, 100r. stamp of 1868.

15 Map of the Azores

1980. World Tourism Conference, Manila, Philippines. Multicoloured.
419 50c. Type **15** 10 10
420 1e. Church 10 10
421 5e. Windmill 40 10
422 6e.50 Traditional costume 50 10
423 8e. Coastal scene 80 35
424 30e. Coastal village 1·60 60

16 St. Peter's Cavalcade, Sao Miguel Island

1981. Europa. Folklore.
425 **16** 22e. multicoloured 1·25 65

17 Bulls attacking Spanish Soldiers

1981. 400th Anniv of Battle of Salga. Mult.
427 8e.50 Type **17** 45 10
428 33e.50 Friar Don Pedro leading attack 1·75 10

18 "Myosotis azorica"

1981. Regional Flowers. Multicoloured.
429 4e. Type **18** 15 10
430 7e. "Tolpis azorica" 25 15
431 8e.50 "Ranunculus azoricus" 35 15
432 10e. "Lactuca watsoniana" 50 10
433 12e.50 "Hypericum foliosum" 20 10
434 20e. "Platanthera micranta" 65 35
435 27e. "Vicia dennesiana" 1·25 60
436 30e. "Rubus hochstetterorum" 75 25
437 33e.50 "Azorina vidalii" 1·25 75
438 37e.50 "Vaccinium cylindraceum" 1·00 55
439 50e. "Laurus azorica" 1·50 75
440 100e. "Juniperus brevifolia" 2·10 80

19 Embarkation of the Heroes of Mindelo

20 Chapel of the Holy Ghost

1982. Europa. Multicoloured.
445 **19** 33e.50 multicoloured 1·75 70

1982. Regional Architecture. Multicoloured.
447 27e. Type **20** 1·10 60
448 33e.50 Chapel of the Holy Ghost (different) 1·60 85

21 Geothermal Power Station, Pico Vermeilho, Sao Miguel

1983. Europa.
449 **21** 37e.50 multicoloured 1·40 60

22 Flag of Azores

1983. Flag.
451 **22** 12e.50 multicoloured 70 10

23 Two "Holy Ghost" Jesters, Sao Miguel

1984. Traditional Costumes. Multicoloured.
452 16e. Type **23** 50 10
453 51e. Two women wearing Terceira cloak 1·90 1·10

23a Bridge

1984. Europa.
454 **23a** 51e. multicoloured 1·90 1·10

24 "Megabombus ruderatus"

1984. Insects (1st series). Multicoloured.
456 16e. Type **24** 30 10
457 35e. Large white (butterfly) 95 50
458 40e. "Chrysomela banksi" (leaf beetle) 1·40 50
459 51e. "Phlogophora interrupta" (moth) 1·50 80

1985. Insects (2nd series). As T **24**. Multicoloured.
460 20e. "Polyspilla polyspilla" (leaf beetle) 35 10
461 40e. "Sphaerophoria nigra" (hover fly) 95 40
462 46e. Clouded yellow (butterfly) 1·40 60
463 60e. Southern grayling (butterfly) 1·50 70

25 Drummer **26** Jeque

1985. Europa. Music Year.
464 **25** 60e. multicoloured . . . . 2·00 90

1985. Traditional Boats. Multicoloured.
466 40e. Type **26** . . . . 1·25 65
467 60e. Bote . . . . 1·75 75

27 Northern Bullfinch **28** Alto das Covas Fountain, Terceira

1986. Europa.
468 **27** 68e.50 multicoloured . . . 2·10 90

1986. Regional Architecture. Drinking Fountains. Multicoloured.
470 22e.50 Type **28** 50 10
471 52e.50 Faja de Baixo, Sao Miguel . . . . 1·60 1·40
472 68e.50 Portoes de S. Pedro, Terceira . . . . 2·40 95
473 100e. Agua d'Alto, Sao Miguel . . . . 3·00 80

29 Ox Cart, Santa Maria

1986. Traditional Carts. Multicoloured.
474 25e. Type **29** 50 10
475 75e. Ram cart, Sao Miguel 2·40 1·25

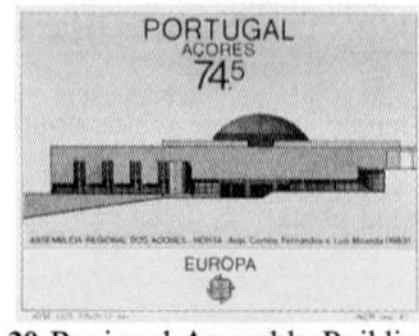

30 Regional Assembly Building (Correia Fernandes and Luis Miranda)

1987. Europa. Architecture.
476 **30** 74e.50 multicoloured . . . 2·10 95

31 Santa Cruz, Graciosa

1987. Windows and Balconies. Multicoloured.
478 51e. Type **31** . . . . 1·50 75
479 74e.50 Ribeira Grande, Sao Miguel . . . . 1·75 75

32 A. C. Read's Curtiss NC-4 Flying Boat, 1919

1987. Historic Airplane Landings in the Azores. Multicoloured.
480 25e. Type **32** 45 75
481 57e. E. F. Christiansen's Dornier Do-X flying boat, 1932 . . . . 1·60 10
482 74e.50 Italo Balbo's Savoia Marchetti S-55X flying boat, 1933 . . . . 2·40 90
483 125e. Charles Lindbergh's Lockheed 8 Sirius seaplane "Tingmissartoq", 1933 . . 2·50 1·25

33 19th-century Mule-drawn Omnibus

1988. Europa. Transport and Communications.
484 **33** 80e. multicoloured . . . . 2·00 75

34 Wood Pigeon

1988. Nature Protection. Birds (1st series). Mult.
486 27e. Type **34** 50 10
487 60e. Eurasian woodcock . . 1·60 80
488 80e. Roseate tern . . . . . . 1·75 80
489 100e. Common buzzard . . . 2·10 80
See also Nos. 492/5 and 500/3.

35 Azores Arms

1988. Coats-of-arms. Multicoloured.
490 55e. Type **35** . . . . 1·40 65
491 80e. Bettencourt family arms 1·75 85

1989. Nature Protection (2nd series). Goldcrest. As T **34**. Multicoloured.
492 30e. Goldcrest perched on branch 75 20
493 30e. Pair 75 20
494 30e. Goldcrest on nest . . . 75 20
495 30e. Goldcrest with outspread wings 75 20

36 Boy in Boat

1989. Europa. Children's Games and Toys.
496 **36** 80e. multicoloured . . . . 1·90 85

37 Pioneers

1989. 550th Anniv of Portuguese Settlement in Azores. Multicoloured.
498 29e. Type **37** 50 10
499 87e. Settler breaking land . . 2·00 1·00

1990. Nature Protection (3rd series). Northern Bullfinch. As T **34**. Multicoloured.
500 32e. Two bullfinches 95 25
501 32e. Bullfinch on branch . . 95 25
502 32e. Bullfinch landing on twig 95 25
503 32e. Bullfinch on nest 95 25

38 Vasco da Gama P.O.

1990. Europa. P.O. Buildings.
504 **38** 80e. multicoloured . . . . 1·40 70

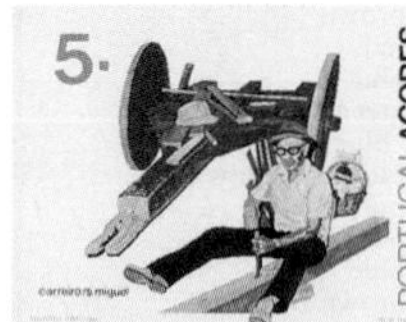

39 Cart Maker

1990. Traditional Occupations. Multicoloured.
506 5e. Type **39** 10 70
507 10e. Viol maker 10 10
508 32e. Potter 50 20
509 35e. Making roof tiles . . . 45 15
510 38e. Carpenter 45 20
511 60e. Tinsmith . . . . 1·40 60
512 65e. Laying pavement mosaics . . . . 1·00 55
513 70e. Quarrying . . . . 1·25 60
514 85e. Basket maker . . . . . 1·10 50
515 100e. Cooper . . . . 1·90 90
516 110e. Shaping stones . . . . 1·75 65
517 120e. Boat builders . . . . . 1·50 75

40 "Hermes" Spaceplane

1991. Europa. Europe in Space.
520 **40** 80e. multicoloured . . . . 1·40 80

41 "Helena" (schooner)

1991. Inter-island Transport. Multicoloured.
522 35e. Type **41** 45 10
523 60e. Beech Model 18 airplane, 1947 . . . . . . 90 40
524 80e. "Cruzeiro do Canal" (ferry), 1987 . . . . 1·40 70
525 110e. British Aerospace ATP airliner, 1991 . . . . . . 1·60 75

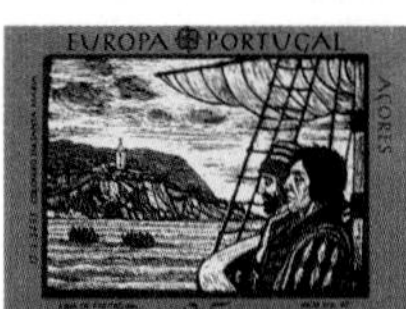

42 "Santa Maria" off Azores

1992. Europa. 500th Anniv of Discovery of America by Columbus.
526 **42** 85e. multicoloured . . . . 1·00 60

43 "Insulano" (steamer, 1868)

1992. The Empresa Insulana de Navegacao Shipping Fleet. Multicoloured.
527 38e. Type **43** 45 15
528 65e. "Carvalho Araujo" (ferry, 1930) 90 50
529 85e. "Funchal" (ferry, 1961) 1·10 60
530 120e. "Terceirense" (freighter, 1948) . . . . 1·50 65

44 Ox-mill

1993. Traditional Grinders. Multicoloured.
531 42e. Type **44** 45 20
532 130e. Hand-mill . . . . . . 1·75 85

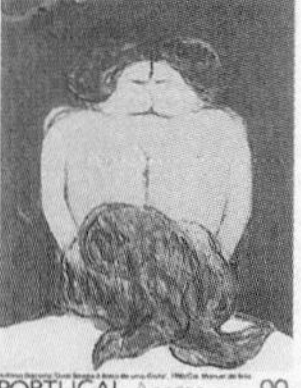

45 "Two Sirens at the Entrance of a Grotto" (Antonio Dacosta) **46** Main Entrance, Praia da Vitoria Church, Terceira

1993. Europa. Contemporary Art.
533 **45** 90e. multicoloured . . . . 1·25 60

1993. Doorways. Multicoloured.
535 42e. Type **46** 45 20
536 70e. South door, Praia da Vitoria Church 80 40
537 90e. Main door, Ponta Delgada Church, Sao Miguel . . . . 1·00 50
538 130e. South door, Ponta Delgada Church . . . . . 1·50 65

47 Floral Decoration, Our Lady of Sorrows, Caloura, Sao Miguel

1994. Tiles. Multicoloured.
539 40e. Type **47** 35 20
540 70e. Decoration of crosses, Our Lady of Sorrows, Caloura, Sao Miguel . . . 80 40
541 100e. "Adoration of the Wise Men", Our Lady of Hope Monastery, Ponta Delgada, Sao Miguel . . . . 1·10 55
542 150e. "St. Bras" (altar frontal), Our Lady of Anjos, Santa Maria . . . 1·50 75

48 Monkey and Explorer with Model Caravel **49** Doorway, St. Barbaras Church, Cedros, Faial

1994. Europa. Discoveries. Multicoloured.
543 **48** 100e. multicoloured . . . . 1·00 20

1994. Manoeline Architecture. Multicoloured.
545 45e. Type **49** 40 20
546 140e. Window, Ribeira Grande, Sao Miguel . . . 1·40 70

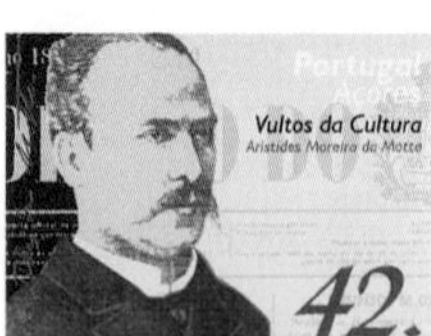

50 Aristides Moreira da Motta

1995. Centenary of Decree decentralizing Government of the Azores and Madeira Islands. Pro-autonomy activists. Multicoloured.
547 42e. Type **50** 40 20
548 130e. Gil Mont' Alverne de Sequeira . . . . 1·25 60

51 Santana Palace, Ponta Delgada

1995. Architecture of Sao Miguel. Multicoloured.
549 45e. Type **51** 40 20
550 80e. Chapel of Our Lady of the Victories, Furnas . . . 75 35
551 95e. Hospital, Ponta Delgada 90 35
552 135e. Ernesto do Canto's villa, Furnas . . . . 1·10 55

52 Contendas Lighthouse, Terceira (½-size illustration)

1996. Lighthouses. Multicoloured.
553 47e. Type **52** 35 20
554 78e. Molhe Lighthouse, Sao Miguel 80 40
555 98e. Arnel Lighthouse, Sao Miguel 90 50
556 140e. Santa Clara Lighthouse, Sao Miguel . . 1·25 60

53 Natalia Correia (poet)

1996. Europa. Famous Women.
558 **53** 98e. multicoloured 90 45

54 Bird eating Grapes (St. Peter's Church, Ponta Delgada)

1997. Gilded Wooden Altarpieces. Multicoloured.
560 49e. Type **54** 40 20
561 80e. Cherub (St. Peter of Alcantara Convent, Sao Roque) 72 30
562 100e. Cherub with wings (All Saints Church, Jesuit College, Ponta Delgada) 85 50
563 140e. Caryatid (St. Joseph's Church, Ponta Delgada) 1·25 65

55 Island of the Seven Cities

1997. Europa. Tales and Legends.
564 **55** 100e. multicoloured 95 45

56 Emperor and Empress and young Bulls (Festival of the Holy Spirit)

1998. Europa. National Festivals.
566 **56** 100e. multicoloured 85 45

57 Spotted Dolphin

1998. "Expo '98" World's Fair, Lisbon. Marine Life. Multicoloured.
568 50e. Type **57** 40 20
569 140e. Sperm whale (79 × 30 mm) . . . . . . 1·10 60

58 Mt. Pico Nature Reserve

1999. Europa. Parks and Gardens.
570 **58** 100e. multicoloured 80 40

59 "Emigrants" (Domingos Rebelo)

1999. Paintings. Multicoloured.
572 51e. Type **59** 40 20
573 95e. "Portrait of Vitorino Nemesio" (Antonio Dacosta) (vert) 75 40
574 100e. "Cattle loose on the Alto das Covas" (Ze van der Hagen Bretao) 80 40
575 140e. "Vila Franca Island" (Duarte Maia) . . . . . . 1·10 60

60 "Building Europe"

2000. Europa.
576 **60** 100e. multicoloured 80 40

61 Fishermen retrieving Mail Raft

2000. History of Mail Delivery in the Azores. Mult.
578 85e. Type **61** 65 35
579 140e. Zeppelin airship dropping mail sacks . . . 35 55

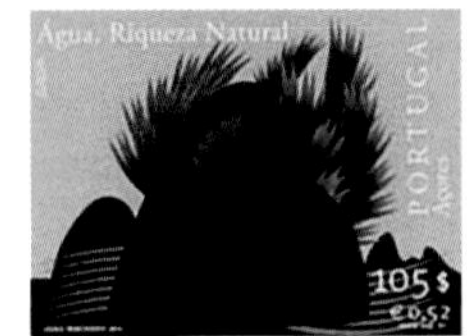

62 Coast Line

2001. Europa. Water Resources.
580 **62** 105e. multicoloured 80 40

63 Arch and Town

2001. U.N.E.S.C.O. World Heritage Site, Angra do Heroismo. Multicoloured.
582 53e. Type **63** 35 20
583 85e. Monument and town . . 65 35
584 140e. Balcony and view over town . . . . 1·10 55

64 Clown

2002. Europa. Circus.
586 **64** 54c. multicoloured 70 35
MS587 140 × 110 mm. No. 586 × 3 2·10 2·10

65 Faial Island, Azores

2002. Windmills. Multicoloured.
588 43c. Type **65** 55 30
589 54c. Onze-Lieve-Vrouw-Lombeek, Roosdaal . . . 70 35
Stamps of a similar design were issued by Belgium.

CHARITY TAX STAMPS

Used on certain days of the year as an additional postal tax on internal letters. The proceeds were devoted to public charities. If one was not affixed in addition to the ordinary postage, postage due stamps were used to collect the deficiency and the fine.

1911. No. 206 optd **ASSISTENCIA**.
C218a **7** 10r. green . . . . 1·10 75

1913. No. 252 optd **ASSISTENCIA**.
C250 **56** 1c. green . . . . 3·50 2·50

1915. For the Poor. Charity stamp of Portugal optd **ACORES**.
C251 C **58** 1c. red 45 30

1925. No. C251 surch **15 ctvs**.
C325 C **58** 15c. on 1c. red 80 55

1925. Portuguese Army in Flanders issue of Portugal optd **ACORES**.
C345 C **71** 10c. red 80 80
C346 10c. green 80 80
C347 10c. blue 80 80
C348 10c. brown 80 80

1925. As Marquis de Pombal issue of Portugal, inscr "ACORES".
C349 C **73** 20c. green 80 80
C350 – 20c. green 80 80
C351 C **75** 20c. green 80 80

NEWSPAPER STAMPS

1876. Stamps of Portugal optd **ACORES**.
N146 N **16** 2r. black . . . . . . 4·00 2·10
N150b N **17** 2½r. green . . . . . 4·00 1·25
N150a 2½r. brown . . . . . 4·00 1·25

PARCEL POST STAMPS

1921. Stamps of Portugal optd **ACORES**.
P325 P **59** 1c. brown 40 40
P326 2c. orange 40 40
P327 5c. brown 40 40
P328 10c. brown 55 40
P329 20c. blue 55 40
P330 40c. red 55 40
P331 50c. black 70 65
P332 60c. blue 70 65
P333 70c. brown . . . . . . 1·75 1·60
P334 80c. blue . . . . . . 1·75 1·60
P335 90c. violet . . . . . . 1·75 1·60
P336 1e. green . . . . . . 1·75 1·60
P337 2e. lilac . . . . . . 2·75 2·50
P338 3e. olive . . . . . . 5·00 2·50
P339 4e. blue . . . . . . 5·75 2·50
P340 5e. lilac . . . . . . 5·75 5·00
P341 10e. brown . . . . . 25·00 14·50

POSTAGE DUE STAMPS

Nos. D179/351 are stamps of Portugal overprinted **ACORES**.

1904.
D179 D **49** 5r. brown 90 80
D180 10r. orange 95 80
D181 20r. mauve . . . . . 1·60 1·25
D182 30r. green . . . . . 1·60 1·25
D183 40r. lilac . . . . . 2·50 1·75
D184 50r. red . . . . . . 4·25 3·00
D185 100r. blue . . . . . 5·50 4·50

1911. As last, optd **REPUBLICA**.
D218 D **49** 5r. brown 45 45
D219 10r. orange 45 45
D220 20r. mauve 65 55
D221 30r. green 65 55
D222 40r. lilac . . . . . 1·00 75
D223 50r. red . . . . . . 5·00 5·00
D224 100r. blue . . . . . 2·00 2·00

1918. Value in centavos.
D325 D **49** ½c. brown 50 50
D326 1c. orange 50 50
D327 2c. purple 50 50
D328 3c. green 50 50
D329 4c. lilac 50 50
D330 5c. red 50 50
D331 10c. blue 50 50

1922.
D332 D **49** ½c. green 30 30
D333 1c. green 35 35
D334 2c. green 35 35
D335 3c. green 60 35
D336 8c. green 60 35
D337 10c. green 60 35
D338 12c. green 60 35
D339 16c. green 60 35
D340 20c. green 60 35
D341 24c. green 60 35
D342 32c. green 60 35
D343 36c. green 60 35
D344 40c. green 60 35
D345 48c. green 60 35
D346 50c. green 60 35
D347 60c. green 60 35
D348 72c. green 60 35
D349 80c. green . . . . . . 3·50 2·75
D350 1e.20 green . . . . . 3·50 2·75

1925. Portuguese Army in Flanders.
D351 D **72** 20c. brown 80 65

1925. As Nos. C349/51, optd **MULTA**.
D352 D **73** 40c. green 80 80
D353 – 40c. green 80 80
D354 D **75** 40c. green 80 80

BADEN Pt. 7

In S.W. Germany. Formerly a Grand Duchy, now part of the German Federal Republic.

60 kreuzer = 1 gulden.

1

2

1851. Imperf.
1 **1** 1k. black on buff £250 £200
8 1k. black on white . . . . . £140 21·00
3 3k. black on yellow . . . . £120 12·00
9 3k. black on green . . . . . £140 5·25
10 3k. black on blue . . . . . £550 27·00
5 6k. black on green . . . . . £400 40·00
11 6k. black on orange . . . . £250 19·00
6 9k. black on red . . . . . . 75·00 19·00

1860. Shaded background behind Arms. Perf.
13 **2** 1k. black . . . . 70·00 19·00
16 3k. blue . . . . 75·00 14·00
17 6k. orange . . . . 90·00 55·00
22 6k. blue . . . . 95·00 60·00
19 9k. red £200 £150
25 9k. brown . . . . 75·00 60·00

1862. Uncoloured background behind Arms.
27 1k. black . . . . 40·00 10·00
28 3k. red . . . . 38·00 1·50
30 6k. blue . . . . 6·75 20·00
33 9k. brown . . . . 12·00 25·00
36 18k. green £350 £500
38 30k. orange . . . . 26·00 £1300

1868. "K R." instead of "KREUZER".
39 1k. green . . . . 3·50 4·00
41 3k. red . . . . 2·00 1·50
44 7k. blue . . . . 17·00 32·00

For issues of 1947 to 1964 see Germany: Allied Occupation (French Zone).

RURAL POSTAGE DUE STAMPS

D 4

1862.
D39 D **4** 1k. black on yellow . . . 3·75 £275
D40 3k. black on yellow . . . 2·00 95·00
D41 12k. black on yellow . . 30·00 £10000

BAGHDAD Pt. 1

A city in Iraq. Special stamps issued during British occupation in the War of 1914–18.

16 annas = 1 rupee.

1917. Various issues of Turkey surch **BAGHDAD IN BRITISH OCCUPATION** and new value in annas.

A. Pictorial issues of 1913.
1 **32** ¼a. on 2pa. red £110 £130
2 **34** ¼a. on 5pa. purple . . . . . 80·00 85·00
3 – ½a. on 10pa. green (No. 516) £550 £650
4 **31** ½a. on 10pa. green £950 £1100
5 – 1a. on 20pa. red (No. 504) £350 £375
6 – 2a. on 1pi. blue (No. 518) . . £140 £170

B. As last, but optd with small star.
7 – 1a. on 20pa. red £190 £225
8 – 2a. on 1pi. blue £3000 £3500

C. Postal Jubilee issue.
9 **60** ½a. on 10pa. red £375 £400
10b 1a. on 20pa. blue £800 £950
11b 2a. on 1pi. black & violet 80·00 90·00

D. Optd with Turkish letter "B".
12 **30** 2a. on 1pi. blue £325 £450

E. Optd with star and Arabic date within crescent.
13 **30** ½a. on 10pa. green . . . . 80·00 85·00
14 1a. on 20pa. red £350 £375
15 **23** 1a. on 20pa. red £375 £400
16 **21** 1a. on 20pa. red (No. N185) £3250 £4000

17 **30** 2a. on 1pi. blue . . . . . . 90·00 £110
18 **21** 2a. on 1pi. blue £150 £160

F. Optd as last, but with date between star and crescent.

19 **23** ½a. on 10pa. green . . . . 95·00 £100
20 **60** ½a. on 10pa. red £140 £150
21 **30** 1a. on 20pa. red . . . . . 90·00 £120
22 **28** 1a. on 20pa. red £350 £400
23 **15** 1a. on 10pa. on 20pa. red £170 £170
24 **30** 2a. on 1pi. blue £150 £160
25 **28** 2a. on 1pi. blue £1300 £1500

BAHAMAS Pt. 1

A group of islands in the Br. W. Indies, S.E. of Florida. Self-Government introduced on 7 January 1964. The islands became an independent member of the British Commonwealth on 10 July 1973.

1859. 12 pence = 1 shilling;
20 shillings = 1 pound.
1966. 100 cents = 1 dollar.

1 2 3

1859. Imperf.
2 **1** 1d. red . . . . 50·00 £1500

1860. Perf.
33 **1** 1d. red . . . . 50·00 15·00
26 **2** 4d. red . . . . £275 60·00
31 6d. violet . . . . £160 60·00
39b **3** 1s. green . . . . 8·00 7·00

1883. Surch **FOURPENCE**.
45 **2** 4d. on 6d. violet £550 £400

5 6 Queen's Staircase, Nassau

1884.
48 **5** 1d. red . . . . 7·00 2·50
52 2½d. blue . . . . 9·50 2·25
53 4d. yellow . . . . 9·50 4·00
54 6d. mauve . . . . 6·00 26·00
56 5s. green . . . . 65·00 75·00
57 £1 red £275 £225

1901.
111 **6** 1d. black and red . . . . 80 1·50
76a 3d. purple on buff . . . . 5·50 4·50
77 3d. black and brown . . . 2·00 2·25
59 5d. black and orange . . . 8·50 48·00
78 5d. black and mauve . . . 2·75 5·50
113 2s. black and blue . . . . 18·00 22·00
61 3s. black and green . . . . 35·00 60·00

7 8

1902.
71 **7** ½d. green . . . . 5·00 3·00
62 1d. red . . . . 1·50 2·50
63 2½d. blue . . . . 6·50 1·25
64 4d. yellow . . . . 15·00 55·00
66 6d. brown . . . . 3·50 19·00
67 1s. black and red . . . . . 20·00 48·00
69 5s. purple and blue . . . . 65·00 80·00
70 £1 green and black £250 £325

1912.
115 **8** ½d. green 50 40
116 1d. red . . . . 1·00 15
117 1½d. red . . . . 3·25 1·00
118 2d. grey . . . . 1·25 2·75
119 2½d. blue . . . . 1·00 2·75
120 3d. purple on yellow . . . . 6·50 16·00
121 4d. yellow . . . . 1·50 5·00
122 6d. brown . . . . 70 1·25
123 1s. black and red . . . . . 2·75 5·50
124 5s. purple and blue . . . . 35·00 65·00
125 £1 green and black £160 £300

1917. Optd **1.1.17.** and Red Cross.
90 **6** 1d. black and red . . . . . 40 2·00

1918. Optd **WAR TAX** in one line.
96 **8** ½d. green . . . . 1·75 1·75
97 1d. red . . . . 1·00 35
93 **6** 1d. black and red . . . . . 3·50 4·25
98 3d. purple on yellow . . . . 1·00 1·50
100 3d. black and brown . . . . 50 4·00
99 **8** 1s. black and red . . . . . 9·00 2·75

1919. Optd **WAR CHARITY 3.6.18.**
101 **6** 1d. black and red . . . . . 30 2·50

1919. Optd **WAR TAX** in two lines.
102 **8** ½d. green . . . . 30 1·25
103 1d. red . . . . 1·50 1·50
105 **6** 3d. black and brown . . . . 75 8·00
104 **8** 1s. black and red . . . . . 16·00 30·00

16 17 Seal of the Colony

1920. Peace Celebration.
106 **16** ½d. green . . . . 1·00 5·50
107 1d. red . . . . 2·75 1·00
108 2d. grey . . . . 2·75 7·50
109 3d. brown . . . . 2·75 9·00
110 1s. green . . . . 12·00 35·00

1930. Tercentenary of the Colony.
126 **17** 1d. black and red . . . . 2·00 2·75
127 3d. black and brown . . . 4·00 15·00
128 5d. black and violet . . . 4·00 15·00
129 2s. black and blue . . . . 18·00 45·00
130 3s. black and green . . . . 42·00 85·00

1931. As T **17**, but without dates at top.
131b 2s. black and blue . . . . . 7·00 3·50
132a 3s. black and green . . . . 7·50 2·25

1935. Silver Jubilee. As T **13** of Antigua.
141 1½d. blue and red . . . . . 1·00 2·75
142 2½d. brown and blue . . . . 5·00 9·00
143 6d. blue and olive . . . . . 7·00 13·00
144 1s. grey and purple . . . . . 7·00 9·00

19 Greater Flamingo (in flight)

1935.
145 **19** 8d. blue and red . . . . . 6·00 3·25

1937. Coronation. As T **2** of Aden.
146 ½d. green 15 15
147 1½d. brown 30 90
148 2½d. blue 50 90

20 King George VI 21 Sea Garden, Nassau

1938.
149 **20** ½d. green . . . . 70 1·25
149e ½d. purple . . . . 1·00 2·50
150 1d. red . . . . 8·50 3·75
150ab 1d. grey 60 70
151 1½d. brown . . . . 1·50 1·25
152 2d. grey . . . . 18·00 5·00
152b 2d. red . . . . 1·00 65
152c 2d. green . . . . 1·00 80
153 2½d. blue . . . . 3·25 1·50
153a 2½d. violet . . . . 1·25 1·25
154 3d. violet . . . . 16·00 3·75
154a 3d. blue . . . . 60 1·25
154b 3d. red . . . . 60 3·25
158 **21** 4d. blue and orange . . 1·00 1·00
159 – 6d. green and blue . . . 60 1·00
160 – 8d. blue and red . . . . 6·75 2·25
154c **20** 10d. orange . . . . 2·50 20
155c 1s. black and red . . . 11·00 75
156b 5s. purple and blue . . . 28·00 17·00
157a £1 green and black . . . 60·00 48·00

DESIGNS—As Type **21**: 6d. Fort Charlotte; 8d. Greater flamingos.

1940. Surch **3d.**
161 **20** 3d. on 2½d. blue . . . . . 1·50 1·50

1942. 450th Anniv of Landing of Columbus. Optd **1492 LANDFALL OF COLUMBUS 1942**.
162 **20** ½d. green 30 60
163 1d. grey 30 60
164 1½d. brown 40 60
165 2d. red 50 65
166 2½d. blue 50 65
167 3d. blue 30 65
168 **21** 4d. blue and orange . . . 40 90
169 – 6d. green & blue (No. 159) . . . . . . 40 1·75
170 – 8d. blue and red (No. 160) . . . . . . 1·00 70
171 **20** 1s. black and red . . . . 6·50 3·75
172a **17** 2s. black and blue . . . . 8·00 10·00
173 3s. black and green . . . 6·50 6·50
174a **20** 5s. purple and blue . . . 19·00 14·00
175a £1 green and black . . . 30·00 25·00

1946. Victory. As T **9** of Aden.
176 1½d. brown 10 50
177 3d. blue 10 50

26 Infant Welfare Clinic

1948. Tercentenary of Settlement of Island of Eleuthera. Inscr as in T **26**.
178 **26** ½d. orange 30 90
179 – 1d. olive 30 35
180 – 1½d. yellow 30 80
181 – 2d. red 30 40
182 – 2½d. brown 50 75
183 – 3d. blue . . . . 2·00 85
184 – 4d. black 60 70
185 – 6d. green . . . . 2·00 80
186 – 8d. violet 90 70
187 – 10d. red 70 35
188 – 1s. brown . . . . 1·50 50
189 – 2s. purple . . . . 4·00 8·50
190 – 3s. blue . . . . 8·50 8·50
191 – 5s. mauve . . . . 12·00 4·50
192 – 10s. grey . . . . 10·00 10·00
193 – £1 red . . . . 9·50 15·00

DESIGNS: 1d. Agriculture; 1½d. Sisal; 2d. Straw work; 2½d. Dairy; 3d. Fishing fleet; 4d. Island settlement; 6d. Tuna fishing; 8d. Paradise Beach; 10d. Modern hotels; 1s. Yacht racing; 2s. Water sports—skiing; 3s. Shipbuilding; 5s. Transportation; 10s. Salt production; £1 Parliament Buildings.

1948. Silver Wedding. As T **10/11** of Aden.
194 1½d. brown 20 25
195 £1 grey . . . . 32·00 32·00

1949. 75th Anniv of U.P.U. As T **20/23** of Antigua.
196 2½d. violet 35 50
197 3d. blue . . . . 2·25 2·50
198 6d. blue . . . . 55 2·25
199 1s. red 55 75

1953. Coronation. As T **13** of Aden.
200 6d. black and blue 60 50

42 Infant Welfare Clinic 43 Queen Elizabeth II

1954. Designs as Nos. 178/93 but with portrait of Queen Elizabeth II and without commemorative inscr as in T **42**.
201 **42** ½d. black and red . . . . 10 1·50
202 – 1d. olive and brown . . . 10 30
203 – 1½d. blue and black . . . 15 80
204 – 2d. brown and green . . . 15 30
205 – 3d. black and red . . . . 65 1·25
206 – 4d. turquoise and purple 30 30
207 – 5d. brown and blue . . . . 1·40 2·25
208 – 6d. blue and black . . . . 2·25 20
209 – 8d. black and lilac 70 40
210 – 10d. black and blue . . . 30 10
211 – 1s. blue and brown . . . . 1·50 10
212 – 2s. orange and black . . . 2·00 70
213 – 2s.6d. black and blue . . . 3·50 2·00
214 – 5s. green and orange . . . 18·00 75
215 – 10s. black and slate . . . 20·00 2·50
216 – £1 black and violet . . . . 20·00 6·50

DESIGNS: 1½d. Hatchet Bay, Eleuthera; 4d. Water sports—skiing; 5d. Dairy; 6d. Transportation; 2s. Sisal; 2s.6d. Shipbuilding; 5s. Tuna fishing. Other values the same as for the corresponding values in Nos. 178/93.

1959. Centenary of 1st Bahamas Postage Stamp.
217 **43** 1d. black and red 35 20
218 2d. black and green . . . 35 1·00
219 6d. black and blue 45 40
220 10d. black and brown . . . 50 1·00

44 Christ Church Cathedral

1962. Centenary of Nassau.
221 **44** 8d. green 45 55
222 – 10d. violet 45 25

DESIGN: 10d. Nassau Public Library.

1963. Freedom from Hunger. As T **28** of Aden.
223 8d. sepia 40 40

1963. Bahamas Talks. Nos. 209/10 optd **BAHAMAS TALKS 1962**.
224 8d. black and lilac 40 75
225 10d. black and blue 50 75

1963. Centenary of Red Cross. As T **33** of Antigua.
226 1d. red and black 50 50
227 10d. red and blue . . . . . 1·75 2·50

1964. New Constitution. Nos. 201/16 optd **NEW CONSTITUTION 1964**.
228 **42** ½d. black and red . . . . 15 1·50
229 – 1d. olive and brown . . . 15 15
230 – 1½d. blue and black . . . 70 1·50
231 – 2d. brown and green . . . 15 20
232 – 3d. black and red . . . . 1·75 1·75
233 – 4d. turquoise and purple 70 55
234 – 5d. brown and blue . . . . 70 1·50
235 – 6d. blue and black . . . . 2·50 30
236 – 8d. black and lilac 70 30
237 – 10d. black and blue . . . 30 15
238 – 1s. blue and brown . . . . 1·50 15
239 – 2s. brown and black . . . 2·00 1·75
240 – 2s.6d. black and blue . . . 3·00 2·75
241 – 5s. green and orange . . . 7·00 3·25
242 – 10s. black and slate . . . 7·00 5·50
243 – £1 black and violet . . . . 7·50 18·00

1964. 400th Birth Anniv of Shakespeare. As T **34** of Antigua.
244 6d. turquoise 20 10

1964. Olympic Games, Tokyo. No. 211 surch **8d.** and Olympic rings.
245 8d. on 1s. blue and brown . . 45 15

49 Colony's Badge

1965.
247 **49** ½d. multicoloured . . . . 15 1·75
248 – 1d. slate, blue and orange 30 1·00
249 – 1½d. red, green and brown 15 2·25
250 – 2d. slate, green and blue 15 10
251 – 3d. red, blue and purple 3·00 20
252 – 4d. green, blue and brown 4·00 2·50
253 – 6d. green, blue and red 50 10
254 – 8d. purple, blue & bronze 50 30
255 – 10d. brown, green and violet 25 10
256a – 1s. multicoloured 30 10
257 – 2s. brown, blue and green 1·00 1·25
258 – 2s.6d. olive, blue and red 2·50 3·00
259 – 5s. brown, blue and green 2·75 1·00
260 – 10s. red, blue and brown 16·00 3·50
261 – £1 brown, blue and red 17·00 9·00

DESIGNS: 1d. Out Island regatta; 1½d. Hospital; 2d. High School; 3d. Greater flamingo; 4d. R.M.S. "Queen Elizabeth"; 6d. "Development"; 8d. Yachting; 10d. Public square; 1s. Sea garden; 2s. Old cannons at Fort Charlotte; 2s.6d. Sikorsky S-38 flying boat, 1929, and Boeing 707 airliner; 5s. Williamson film project, 1914, and undersea post office, 1939; 10s. Queen or pink conch; £1 Columbus's flagship.

1965. Centenary of I.T.U. As T **36** of Antigua.
262 1d. green and orange 15 10
263 2s. purple and olive 65 45

1965. No. 254 surch **9d.**
264 9d. on 8d. purple, blue & bronze 30 15

1965. I.C.Y. As T **37** of Antigua.
265 ½d. purple and turquoise . . 10 1·10
266 1s. green and lavender . . . 30 40

1966. Churchill Commemoration. As T **38** of Antigua.
267 ½d. blue 10 40
268 2d. green 40 30
269 10d. brown 75 85
270 1s. violet . . . . 75 1·40

1966. Royal Visit. As T **39** of Antigua but inscr "to the Caribbean" omitted.
271 6d. black and blue 75 50
272 1s. black and mauve . . . . 1·25 1·25

1966. Decimal currency. Nos. 247/61 surch.
273 **49** 1c. on ½d. multicoloured 10 30
274 – 2c. on 1d. slate, blue and orange 75 30
275 – 3c. on 2d. slate, green and blue 10 10
276 – 4c. on 3d. red, blue and purple . . . . 2·00 20
277 – 5c. on 4d. green, blue and brown . . . . 2·00 3·00
278 – 8c. on 6d. green, blue and red 20 20
279 – 10c. on 8d. purple, blue and bronze 30 75
280 – 11c. on 1½d. red, green and brown 15 30
281 – 12c. on 10d. brown, green and violet 15 10
282 – 15c. on 1s. multicoloured 25 10

283 – 22c. on 2s. brown, blue and green . . . . 60 1·25
284 – 50c. on 2s.6d. olive, blue and red . . . . 1·00 1·40
285 – $1 on 5s. brown, blue and green . . . . 1·75 1·50
286 – $2 on 10s. red, blue and brown . . . . 7·50 4·50
287 – $3 on £1 brown, blue and red . . . . 7·50 4·50

1966. World Cup Football Championships. As T **36** of Antigua.
288 8c. multicoloured 25 15
289 15c. multicoloured 30 25

1966. Inauguration of W.H.O. Headquarters, Geneva. As T **41** of Antigua.
290 11c. black, green and blue . . 50 90
291 15c. black, purple and ochre 50 50

1966. 20th Anniv of U.N.E.S.C.O. As T **54/6** of Antigua.
292 3c. multicoloured 10 10
293 15c. yellow, violet and olive 35 20
294 $1 black, purple and orange 1·10 2·00

1967. As Nos. 247/51, 253/9 and 261 but values in decimal currency, and new designs for 5c. and $2.
295 **49** 1c. multicoloured . . . . . 10 3·00
296 – 2c. slate, blue and green . . 50 60
297 – 3c. slate, green and violet 10 10
298 – 4c. red, light blue and blue 4·25 50
299 – 5c. black, blue and purple 1·00 3·25
300 – 8c. green, blue and brown 25 10
301 – 10c. purple, blue and red 30 70
302 – 11c. red, green and blue . . 25 80
303 – 12c. brown, green and olive 25 10
304 – 15c. multicoloured 55 10
305 – 22c. brown, blue and red 70 65
306 – 50c. olive, blue and green 2·00 1·00
307 – $1 maroon, blue and purple . . . . 2·00 60
308 – $2 multicoloured . . . . . 13·00 3·00
309 – $3 brown, blue and purple 3·75 2·00
NEW DESIGNS: 5c. "Oceanic"; $2 Conch shell (different).

69 Bahamas Crest

1967. Diamond Jubilee of World Scouting. Mult.
310 3c. Type **69** 35 15
311 15c. Scout badge 40 15

71 Globe and Emblem

1968. Human Rights Year. Multicoloured.
312 3c. Type **71** 10 10
313 12c. Scales of Justice and emblem 20 10
314 $1 Bahamas Crest and emblem 70 80

74 Golf

1968. Tourism. Multicoloured.
315 5c. Type **74** . . . . 1·75 1·75
316 11c. Yachting . . . . 1·25 40
317 15c. Horse-racing . . . . . 1·75 45
318 50c. Water-skiing . . . . . 2·50 6·50

78 Racing Yacht and Olympic Monument

1968. Olympic Games, Mexico City.
319 **78** 5c. brown, yellow and green 40 75
320 – 11c. multicoloured 40 25
321 – 50c. multicoloured . . . . 60 1·75
322 **78** $1 grey, blue and violet . . 2·00 3·75
DESIGNS: 11c. Long jumping and Olympic Monument; 50c. Running and Olympic Monument.

81 Legislative Building

1968. 14th Commonwealth Parliamentary Conference. Multicoloured.
323 3c. Type **81** 10 30
324 10c. Bahamas Mace and Westminster Clock Tower (vert) 15 30
325 12c. Local straw market (vert) 15 25
326 15c. Horse-drawn surrey . . 20 35

85 Obverse and reverse of $100 Gold Coin

1968. Gold Coins commemorating the first General Election under the New Constitution.
327 **85** 3c. red on gold 40 40
328 – 12c. green on gold 45 50
329 – 15c. purple on gold 50 60
330 – $1 black on gold . . . . . 1·25 3·25
OBVERSE AND REVERSE OF: 12c. $50 gold coin; 15c. $20 gold coins; $1, $10 gold coin.

89 First Flight Postcard of 1919

1969. 50th Anniv of Bahamas Airmail Services.
331 **89** 12c. multicoloured 50 50
332 – 15c. multicoloured . . . . 60 1·75
DESIGN: 15c. Sikorsky S-38 flying boat of 1929.

91 Game-fishing Boats

1969. Tourism. One Millionth Visitor to Bahamas. Multicoloured.
333 3c. Type **91** 25 10
334 11c. Paradise Beach 35 15
335 12c. "Sunfish" sailing boats 35 15
336 15c. Rawson Square and parade 45 25
MS337 130 × 96 mm. Nos. 333/6 3·00 4·50

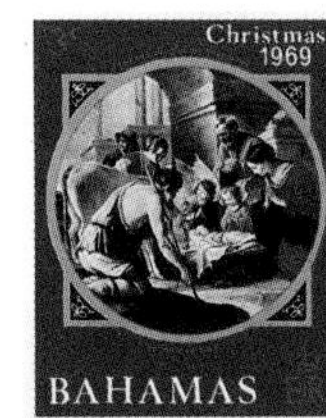

92 "The Adoration of the Shepherds" (Louis le Nain)

1969. Christmas. Multicoloured.
338 3c. Type **92** 10 20
339 11c. "The Adoration of the Shepherds" (Poussin) . . . 15 30
340 12c. "The Adoration of the Kings" (Gerard David) . . 15 20
341 15c. "The Adoration of the Kings" (Vincenzo Foppa) 20 65

93 Badge of Girl Guides

1970. Diamond Jubilee of Girl Guides' Association. Multicoloured.
342 3c. Type **93** 30 10
343 12c. Badge of Brownies . . . 45 20
344 15c. Badge of Rangers . . . 50 35

94 New U.P.U. Headquarters and Emblem

1970. New U.P.U. Headquarters Building.
345 **94** 3c. multicoloured 10 25
346 15c. multicoloured 20 50

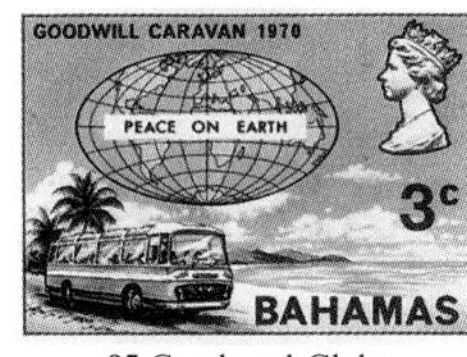

95 Coach and Globe

1970. "Goodwill Caravan". Multicoloured.
347 3c. Type **95** 75 20
348 11c. Diesel train and globe 1·50 60
349 12c. "Canberra" (liner), yacht and globe . . . . 1·50 60
350 15c. B.A.C. One Eleven airliner and globe . . . . 1·50 1·75
MS351 165 × 125 mm. Nos. 347/50 9·50 16·00

96 Nurse, Patients and Greater Flamingo

1970. Centenary of British Red Cross. Multicoloured.
352 3c. Type **96** 75 50
353 15c. Hospital and blue marlin 75 1·75

97 "The Nativity" (detail, Pittoni)

1970. Christmas. Multicoloured.
354 3c. Type **97** 15 15
355 11c. "The Holy Family" (detail, Anton Raphael Mengs) 20 25
356 12c. "The Adoration of the Shepherds" (detail, Giorgione) 20 20
357 15c. "The Adoration of the Shepherds" (detail, School of Seville) 30 75
MS358 114 × 140 mm. Nos. 354/7 1·40 3·50

98 International Airport

1971. Multicoloured.
359 1c. Type **98** 10 30
360 2c. Breadfruit 15 35
361 3c. Straw market 15 30
362 4c. Hawksbill turtle . . . . 1·75 9·50
363 5c. Nassau grouper 60 60
364 6c. As 4c. . . . . 45 1·25
365 7c. Hibiscus . . . . 2·00 4·50
366 8c. Yellow elder . . . . . . 60 1·50
367 10c. Bahamian sponge boat 55 30
368 11c. Greater flamingos . . . 2·50 3·25
369 12c. As 7c. . . . . 2·00 3·00
370 15c. Bonefish 55 55
466 16c. As 7c. 70 35
371 18c. Royal poinciana . . . 65 65
467a 21c. As 2c. . . . . 80 1·25
372 22c. As 18c. . . . . 2·75 14·00
468 25c. As 4c. 90 40
469 40c. As 10c. . . . . 5·50 75
470 50c. Post Office, Nassau . . 1·50 1·75
471 $1 Pineapple (vert) . . . . 1·50 2·50
399 $2 Crawfish (vert) . . . . . 1·50 6·00
473 $3 Junkanoo (vert) . . . . 2·00 9·00

99 Snowflake

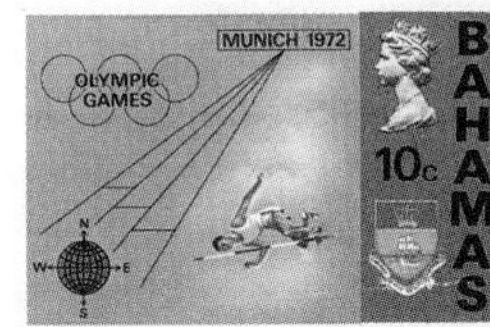

101 Shepherd

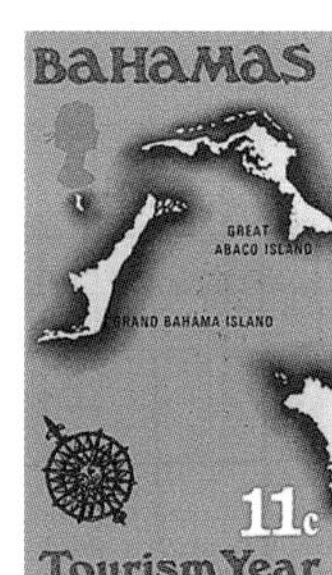

100 High Jumping

1971. Christmas.
377 **99** 3c. purple, orange and gold 10 10
378 – 11c. blue and gold 20 15
379 – 15c. multicoloured 20 20
380 – 18c. blue, ultram & gold 25 25
MS381 126 × 95 mm. Nos. 377/80 1·25 1·50
DESIGNS: 11c. "Peace on Earth" (doves); 15c. Arms of Bahamas and holly; 18c. Starlit lagoon

1972. Olympic Games, Munich. Multicoloured.
382 10c. Type **100** 35 60
383 11c. Cycling . . . . 1·50 75
384 15c. Running 60 75
385 18c. Sailing . . . . 95 1·25
MS386 127 × 95 mm. Nos. 382/5 3·25 3·00

1972. Christmas. Multicoloured.
387 3c. Type **101** 10 10
388 6c. Bells 10 10
389 15c. Holly and Cross 15 20
390 20c. Poinsettia 25 45
MS391 108 × 140 mm. Nos. 387/90 80 2·25

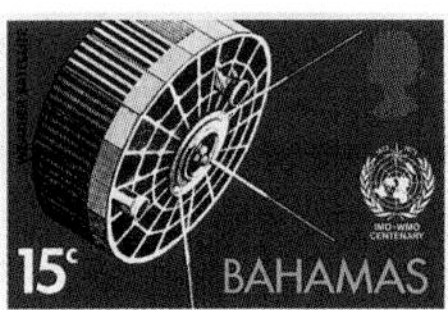

102 Northerly Bahama Islands

1972. Tourism Year of the Americas. Sheet 133 × 105 mm, containing T **102**.
MS392 11, 15, 18 and 50c. multicoloured . . . . 3·00 3·25
The four designs are printed, se-tenant in **MS**392, forming a composite map design of the Bahamas.

1972. Royal Silver Wedding. As T **52** of Ascension, but with mace and galleon in background.
393 11c. pink 15 15
394 18c. violet 15 20

104 Weather Satellite

1973. Centenary of I.M.O./W.M.O. Multicoloured.
410 15c. Type **104** 50 25
411 18c. Weather radar 60 35

105 C. A. Bain (national hero) **106** "The Virgin in Prayer" (Sassoferrato)

1973. Independence. Multicoloured.
412 3c. Type **105** 10 10
413 11c. Coat of arms 15 10
414 15c. Bahamas flag 20 15
415 $1 Governor-General, M. B. Butler 65 1·00
MS416 86 × 121 mm. Nos. 412/15 1·75 1·75

1973. Christmas. Multicoloured.
417 3c. Type **106** 10 10
418 11c. "Virgin and Child with St. John" (Filippino Lippi) 15 15
419 15c. "A Choir of Angels" (Simon Marmion) 15 15
420 18c. "The Two Trinities" (Murillo) 25 25
MS421 120 × 99 mm. Nos. 417/20 1·50 1·40

107 "Agriculture and Sciences"

1974. 25th Anniv of University of West Indies. Multicoloured.
422 15c. Type **107** 20 25
423 18c. "Arts, Engineering and General Studies" 25 30

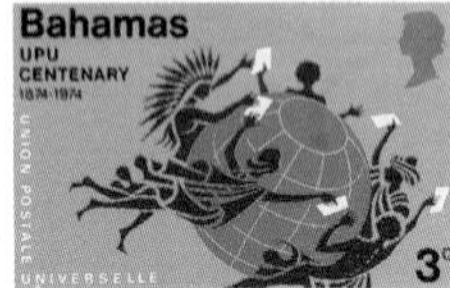

108 U.P.U. Monument, Berne

1974. Centenary of U.P.U.
424 **108** 3c. multicoloured 10 15
425 – 13c. multicoloured (vert) 20 25
426 – 14c. multicoloured 20 30
427 – 18c. multicoloured (vert) 25 40
MS428 128 × 95 mm. Nos. 424/7 80 1·60
DESIGNS—As Type **108** but showing different arrangements of the U.P.U. Monument.

109 Roseate Spoonbills

1974. 15th Anniv of Bahamas National Trust. Mult.
429 13c. Type **109** 1·40 85
430 14c. White-crowned pigeon 1·40 75
431 21c. White-tailed tropic birds 1·75 1·25
432 36c. Cuban amazon ("Bahamian parrot") 2·25 6·00
MS433 123 × 120 mm. Nos. 429/32 8·50 12·00

110 "The Holy Family" (Jacques de Stella)

1974. Christmas. Multicoloured.
434 8c. Type **110** 10 10
435 10c. "Madonna and Child" (16th-century Brescian School) 15 15
436 12c. "Virgin and Child with St. John the Baptist and St. Catherine" (Previtali) 15 15
437 21c. "Virgin and Child with Angels" (Previtali) 25 30
MS438 126 × 105 mm. Nos. 434/7 1·00 1·40

111 "Anteos maerula"

1975. Butterflies. Multicoloured.
439 3c. Type **111** 25 15
440 14c. "Eurema nicippe" 80 50
441 18c. "Papilio andraemon" 95 65
442 21c. "Euptoieta hegesia" 1·10 85
MS443 194 × 94 mm. Nos. 439/42 7·50 6·50

112 Sheep Husbandry

1975. Economic Diversification. Multicoloured.
444 3c. Type **112** 10 10
445 14c. Electric-reel fishing (vert) 20 15
446 18c. Farming 25 20
447 21c. Oil refinery (vert) 80 35
MS448 127 × 94 mm. Nos. 444/7 1·25 1·50

113 Rowena Rand (evangelist)

1975. International Women's Year.
449 **113** 14c. brown, lt blue & bl 20 50
450 – 18c. yellow, grn & brn 25 75
DESIGN: 18c. I.W.Y. symbol and harvest symbol.

114 "Adoration of the Shepherds" (Perugino)

1975. Christmas. Multicoloured.
451 3c. Type **114** 15 60
452 8c. "Adoration of the Magi" (Ghirlandaio) 20 10
453 18c. As 8c. 55 90
454 21c. Type **114** 60 95
MS455 142 × 107 mm. Nos. 451/4 2·25 4·00

115 Telephones, 1876 and 1976

1976. Centenary of Telephone. Multicoloured.
456 3c. Type **115** 20 50
457 16c. Radio-telephone link, Deleporte 40 50
458 21c. Alexander Graham Bell 50 65
459 25c. Satellite 60 1·00

116 Map of North America

1976. Bicentenary of American Revolution. Mult.
475 16c. Type **116** 30 30
476 $1 John Murray, Earl of Dunmore 1·50 1·75
MS477 127 × 100 mm. Nos. 476 × 4 6·00 7·50

117 Cycling **118** "Virgin and Child" (detail, Lippi)

1976. Olympic Games, Montreal.
478 **117** 8c. mauve, blue and light blue 1·25 20
479 – 16c. orange, brown and light blue 35 30
480 – 25c. blue, mauve and light blue 45 50
481 – 40c. brown, orange and blue 55 1·60
MS482 100 × 126 mm. Nos. 478/81 2·75 2·75
DESIGNS: 16c. Jumping; 25c. Sailing; 40c. Boxing.

1976. Christmas. Multicoloured.
483 3c. Type **118** 10 10
484 21c. "Adoration of the Shepherds" (School of Seville) 20 15
485 25c. "Adoration of the Kings" (detail, Foppa) 20 20
486 40c. "Virgin and Child" (detail, Vivarini) 35 40
MS487 107 × 127 mm. Nos. 483/6 1·00 2·00

119 Queen beneath Cloth of Gold Canopy

1977. Silver Jubilee. Multicoloured.
488 8c. Type **119** 10 10
489 16c. The Crowning 15 15
490 21c. Taking the Oath 15 15
491 40c. Queen with sceptre and orb 25 30
MS492 122 × 90 mm. Nos. 488/91 80 1·25

120 Featherduster

1977. Marine Life. Multicoloured.
493 3c. Type **120** 40 15
494 8c. Porkfish and cave 60 20
495 16c. Elkhorn coral 70 40
496 21c. Soft coral and sponge 80 55
MS497 119 × 93 mm. Nos. 493/6 2·75 4·50

121 Scouts around Campfire and Home-made Shower

1977. 6th Caribbean Scout Jamboree. Multicoloured.
498 16c. Type **121** 75 30
499 21c. Boating scenes 85 35

1977. Royal Visit. Nos. 488/91 optd **Royal Visit October 1977**.
500 8c. Type **119** 15 10
501 16c. The Crowning 20 15
502 21c. Taking the Oath 25 25
503 40c. Queen with sceptre and orb 30 40
MS504 122 × 90 mm. Nos. 500/3 1·25 1·50

123 Virgin and Child **124** Public Library, Nassau (Colonial)

1977. Christmas. Multicoloured.
505 3c. Type **123** 10 10
506 16c. The Magi 20 25
507 21c. Nativity scene 25 40
508 25c. The Magi and star 30 45
MS509 136 × 74 mm. Nos. 505/8 75 1·75

1978. Architectural Heritage.
510 **124** 3c. black and green 10 10
511 – 8c. black and blue 15 10
512 – 16c. black and mauve 20 20
513 – 18c. black and pink 25 30
MS514 91 × 91 mm. Nos. 510/13 70 1·60
DESIGNS: 8c. St. Matthew's Church (Gothic); 16c. Government House (Colonial); 18c. Hermitage, Cat Island (Spanish).

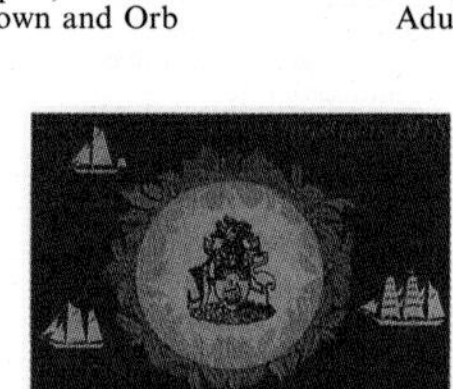

125 Sceptre, St. Edward's Crown and Orb **127** Child reaching for Adult

126 Coat of Arms within Wreath and Three Ships

1978. 25th Anniv of Coronation. Multicoloured.
515 16c. Type **125** 15 10
516 $1 Queen in Coronation regalia 50 65
MS517 147 × 96 mm. Nos. 515/16 1·25 1·00

1978. Christmas.
532 **126** 5c. gold, lake and red 15 10
533 – 21c. gold, deep blue and blue 30 25
MS534 95 × 95 mm. Nos. 532/3 1·50 5·00
DESIGN: 21c. Three angels with trumpets.

1979. International Year of the Child. Multicoloured.
535 5c. Type **127** 20 15
536 16c. Boys playing leapfrog 40 45
537 21c. Girls skipping 50 60
538 25c. Bricks with I.Y.C. emblem 50 75
MS539 101 × 125 mm. Nos. 535/8 1·40 3·00

128 Sir Rowland Hill and Penny Black

1979. Death Centenary of Sir Rowland Hill. Multicoloured.
540 10c. Type **128** 30 10
541 21c. Printing press, 1840, and 6d. stamp of 1862 40 30
542 25c. Great Britain 1856 6d. with "A 05" (Nassau) cancellation, and 1840 2d. Blue 40 50
543 40c. Early mailboat and 1d. stamp of 1859 45 70
MS544 115 × 80 mm. Nos. 540/3 2·00 3·00

129 Commemorative Plaque and Map of Bahamas

1979. 250th Anniv of Parliament. Multicoloured.
545 16c. Type **129** 35 10
546 21c. Parliament buildings 40 15
547 25c. Legislative Chamber 40 15
548 $1 Senate Chamber 80 1·00
MS549 116 × 89 mm. Nos. 545/8 1·75 3·75

130 Goombay Carnival Headdress **132** Virgin and Child

131 Landfall of Columbus, 1492

1979. Christmas.
550 **130** 5c. multicoloured 10 10
551 – 10c. multicoloured 15 10
552 – 16c. multicoloured 20 10
553 – 21c. multicoloured 20 20
554 – 25c. multicoloured 25 20
555 – 40c. multicoloured 30 45
MS556 50 × 88 mm. Nos. 550/5 2·00 3·00
DESIGNS: 10c. to 40c. Various Carnival costumes.

1980. Multicoloured.
557 1c. Type **131** . . . . . . 1·25 2·50
558 3c. Blackbeard the pirate . . 30 2·50
559 5c. Eleutheran Adventurers (Articles and Orders, 1647) 30 1·25
560 10c. Ceremonial mace 20 40
561 12c. The Loyalists, 1783–88 30 2·00
562 15c. Slave trading, Vendue House . . . . 5·50 1·25
563 16c. Wrecking in the 1800s 1·75 1·25
564 18c. Blockade running (American Civil War) . . . 2·00 2·50
565 21c. Bootlegging, 1919–29 . . 50 2·50
566 25c. Pineapple cultivation . . 40 2·50
567 40c. Sponge clipping . . . . 70 1·50
568 50c. Tourist development . . 75 1·50
569 $1 Modern agriculture . . . 75 4·25
570 $2 Modern air and sea transport . . . . 4·00 5·50
571 $3 Banking (Central Bank) 1·25 4·00
572 $5 Independence, 10 July 1973 . . . . 1·50 6·00

1980. Christmas. Straw-work. Multicoloured.
573 5c. Type **132** 10 10
574 21c. Three Kings 25 10
575 25c. Angel 25 15
576 $1 Christmas tree 75 85
MS577 168 × 105 mm. Nos. 573/6 1·25 2·25

133 Disabled Persons with Walking Stick

1981. International Year of Disabled People. Mult.
578 5c. Type **133** 10 10
579 $1 Disabled person in wheelchair . . . . 1·25 1·25
MS580 120 × 60 mm. Nos. 578/9 1·40 2·50

134 Grand Bahama Tracking Site

1981. Space Exploration. Multicoloured.
581 10c. Type **134** 30 15
582 20c. Satellite view of Bahamas (vert) 60 50
583 25c. Satelite view of Eleuthera 65 60
584 50c. Satellite view of Andros and New Province (vert) 1·00 1·25
MS585 115 × 99 mm. Nos. 581/4 2·25 2·25

135 Prince Charles and Lady Diana Spencer

1981. Royal Wedding. Multicoloured.
586 30c. Type **135** . . . . 1·50 30
587 $2 Prince Charles and Prime Minister Pindling . . . . 1·50 1·25
MS588 142 × 120 mm. Nos. 586/7 5·00 1·25

136 Bahamas Pintail ("Bahama Duck")

1981. Wildlife (1st series). Birds. Multicoloured.
589 5c. Type **136** . . . . 1·25 60
590 20c. Reddish egret . . . . . 2·00 60
591 25c. Brown booby . . . . . 2·00 65
592 $1 Black-billed whistling duck ("West Indian Tree Duck") 3·50 6·50
MS593 100 × 74 mm. Nos. 589/92 8·50 7·50
See also Nos. 626/30, 653/7 and 690/4.

1981. Commonwealth Finance Ministers' Meeting. Nos. 559/60, 566 and 568 optd **COMMONWEALTH FINANCE MINISTERS' MEETING 21–23 SEPTEMBER 1981**.
594 5c. Eleutheran Adventurers (Articles and Orders, 1647) 15 15
595 10c. Ceremonial mace 20 20
596 25c. Pineapple cultivation . . 50 60
597 50c. Tourist development . . 85 1·50

138 Poultry

1981. World Food Day. Multicoloured.
598 5c. Type **138** 20 10
599 20c. Sheep 35 35
600 30c. Lobsters 45 50
601 50c. Pigs . . . . 75 1·50
MS602 115 × 63 mm. Nos. 598/601 1·50 3·25

139 Father Christmas **141** Greater Flamingo (male)

140 Robert Koch

1981. Christmas. Multicoloured.
603 5c. Type **139** 45 75
604 5c. Mother and child 45 75
605 5c. St. Nicholas, Holland . . 45 75
606 25c. Lussibruden, Sweden . . 60 85
607 25c. Mother and child (different) 60 85
608 25c. King Wenceslas, Czechoslovakia 60 85
609 30c. Mother with child on knee 60 85
610 30c. Mother carrying child 60 85
611 $1 Christkindl Angel, Germany . . . . 1·00 1·50

1982. Centenary of Discovery of Tubercle Bacillus by Robert Koch.
612 **140** 5c. black, brown and lilac 70 40
613 – 16c. black, brown & orge 1·25 50
614 – 21c. multicoloured . . . . 1·40 55
615 – $1 multicoloured . . . . 3·00 6·50
MS616 94 × 97 mm. Nos. 612/15 6·00 7·50
DESIGNS: 16c. Stylised infected person; 21c. Early and modern microscopes; $1 Mantoux test.

1982. Greater Flamingos. Multicoloured.
617 25c. Type **141** . . . . 1·60 1·00
618 25c. Female . . . . 1·60 1·00
619 25c. Female with nestling . . 1·60 1·00
620 25c. Juvenile . . . . 1·60 1·00
621 25c. Immature bird . . . . . 1·60 1·00

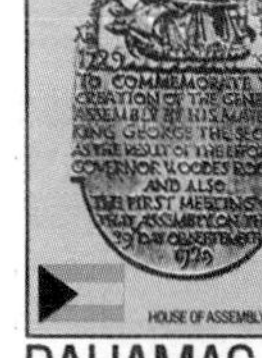

142 Lady Diana Spencer at Ascot, June, 1981 **143** House of Assembly Plaque

1982. 21st Birthday of Princess of Wales. Mult.
622 16c. Bahamas coat of arms 20 10
623 25c. Type **142** 45 15
624 40c. Bride and Earl Spencer arriving at St. Paul's . . . 60 20
625 $1 Formal portrait . . . . . 1·00 1·25

1982. Wildlife (2nd series). Mammals. As T **136**. Multicoloured.
626 10c. Buffy flower bat 80 15
627 16c. Bahamian hutia . . . . 1·00 25
628 21c. Common racoon . . . . 1·25 55
629 $1 Common dolphin . . . . 3·00 1·75
MS630 115 × 76 mm. Nos. 626/9 6·00 3·50

1982. 28th Commonwealth Parliamentary Association Conference. Multicoloured.
631 5c. Type **143** 15 10
632 25c. Association coat of arms 50 35
633 40c. Coat of arms 80 60
634 50c. House of Assembly . . . 1·10 75

144 Wesley Methodist Church, Baillou Hill Road

1982. Christmas. Churches. Multicoloured.
635 5c. Type **144** 10 20
636 12c. Centreville Seventh Day Adventist Church 15 20
637 15c. The Church of God of Prophecy, East Street . . . 15 30
638 21c. Bethel Baptist Church, Meeting Street 15 30
639 25c. St. Francis Xavier Catholic Church, Highbury Park 15 50
640 $1 Holy Cross Anglican Church, Highbury Park . . 60 3·00

145 Prime Minister Lyndon O. Pindling

1983. Commonwealth Day. Multicoloured.
641 5c. Type **145** 10 10
642 25c. Bahamian and Commonwealth flags . . . 50 40
643 35c. Map showing position of Bahamas 50 50
644 $1 Ocean liner . . . . 1·10 1·40

1983. Nos. 562/5 surch.
645 20c. on 15c. Slave trading, Vendue House 50 35
646 31c. on 21c. Bootlegging, 1919–29 . . . . 60 55
647 35c. on 16c. Wrecking in the 1800s 70 60
648 80c. on 18c. Blockade running (American Civil War) . . . . 80 1·40

147 Customs Officers and "Queen Elizabeth 2" (liner) **148** Raising the National Flag

1983. 30th Anniv of Customs Co-operation Council. Multicoloured.
649 31c. Type **147** . . . . 1·50 45
650 $1 Customs officers and Lockheed JetStar airliner 3·50 2·75

1983. 10th Anniv of Independence.
651 **148** $1 multicoloured . . . . 1·00 1·40
MS652 105 × 65 mm. No. 651 1·00 1·40

1983. Wildlife (3rd series). Butterflies. As T **136**.
653 5c. multicoloured . . . . . . 1·00 20
654 25c. multicoloured . . . . . 1·75 40
655 31c. black, yellow and red . . 1·75 55
656 50c. multicoloured . . . . . 2·00 85
MS657 120 × 80 mm. Nos. 653/6 5·50 6·00
DESIGNS: 5c. "Atalopedes carteri"; 25c. "Ascia monuste"; 31 c. "Phoebis agarithe"; 50c. "Dryas julia"

149 "Loyalist Dreams" **151** "Christmas Bells" (Monica Pinder)

150 Consolidated Catalina

1983. Bicentenary of Arrival of American Loyalists in the Bahamas. Multicoloured.
658 5c. Type **149** 10 10
659 31c. New Plymouth, Abaco (horiz) 30 50
660 35c. New Plymouth Hotel (horiz) 40 70
661 50c. "Island Hope" 45 90
MS662 111 × 76 mm. Nos. 658/61 1·25 2·50

1983. Air. Bicentenary of Manned Flight. Mult.
663 10c. Type **150** 55 15
664 25c. Avro Tudor IV 75 30
665 31c. Avro Lancastrian . . . 85 45
666 35c. Consolidated Commodore . . . . 1·00 50
For these stamps without the Manned Flight logo, see Nos. 699/702.

1983. Christmas. Children's Paintings. Multicoloured.
667 5c. Type **151** 15 10
668 20c. "Flamingo" (Cory Bullard) 35 30
669 25c. "Yellow Hibiscus with Christmas Candle" (Monique Bailey) 45 40
670 31c. "Santa goes-a-sailing" (Sabrina Seiler) (horiz) . . 55 45
671 35c. "Silhouette scene with Palm Trees" (James Blake) 60 50
672 50c. "Silhouette scene with Pelicans" (Erik Russell) (horiz) 70 70

152 1861 4d. Stamp **153** "Trent I" (paddle-steamer)

1984. 125th Anniv of First Bahamas Postage Stamp. Multicoloured.
673 5c. Type **152** 25 10
674 $1 1859 1d. stamp . . . . . 1·75 1·50

1984. 250th Anniv of "Lloyd's List" (newspaper). Multicoloured.
675 5c. Type **153** 50 10
676 31c. "Orinoco II" (mail ship), 1886 . . . . 1·00 60
677 35c. Cruise liners in Nassau harbour . . . . 1·10 75
678 50c. "Oropesa" (container ship) . . . . 1·40 1·60

154 Running

155 Bahamas and Caribbean Community Flags

1984. Olympic Games, Los Angeles.
679 **154** 5c. green, black and gold 15 20
680 – 25c. blue, black and gold 50 50
681 – 31c. red, black and gold 55 60
682 – $1 brown, black and gold 4·75 5·50
MS683 115 × 80 mm. Nos. 679/82 5·50 7·00
DESIGNS: 25c. Shot-putting; 31c. Boxing; $1 Basketball.

1984. 5th Conference of Caribbean Community Heads of Government.
684 **155** 50c. multicoloured . . . . 1·00 1·00

156 Bahama Woodstar

157 "The Holy Virgin with Jesus and Johannes" (19th-century porcelain plaque after Titian)

1984. 25th Anniv of National Trust. Multicoloured.
685 31c. Type **156** . . . . 3·25 3·25
686 31c. Belted kingfishers, greater flamingos and "Eleutherodactylus planirostris" (frog) . . . . 3·25 3·25
687 31c. Black-necked stilts, greater flamingos and "Phoebis sennae" (butterfly) . . . . 3·25 3·25
688 31c. "Urbanus proteus" (butterfly) and "Chelonia mydas" (turtle) . . . . . 3·25 3·25
689 31c. Osprey and greater flamingos . . . . 3·25 3·25
Nos. 685/9 were printed together in horiz strips of 5 forming a composite design.

1984. Wildlife (4th series). Reptiles and Amphibians. As T **136**.
690 5c. Allens' Cay iguana . . . 50 20
691 25c. Curly-tailed lizard . . . 1·25 60
692 35c. Greenhouse frog . . . . 1·50 85
693 50c. Atlantic green turtle . . 1·75 2·50
MS694 112 × 82 mm. Nos. 690/3 5·50 7·00

1984. Christmas. Religious Paintings. Multicoloured.
695 5c. Type **157** 30 10
696 31c. "Madonna with Child in Tropical Landscape" (aquarelle, Anais Colin) . . 80 60
697 35c. "The Holy Virgin with the Child" (miniature on ivory, Elena Caula) . . . . 1·00 65
MS698 116 × 76 mm. Nos. 695/7 1·90 3·50

1985. Air. As Nos. 663/6, but without Manned Flight logo.
699 10c. Type **150** 70 30
700 25c. Avro Tudor IV 85 40
701 31c. Avro Lancastrian . . . 85 55
702 35c. Consolidated Commodore . . . . 1·25 85

158 Brownie Emblem and Queen or Pink Conch

1985. International Youth Year. 75th Anniv of Girl Guide Movement. Multicoloured.
703 5c. Type **158** 60 50
704 25c. Tents and coconut palm 1·25 1·00
705 31c. Guide salute and greater flamingos . . . . 1·90 1·50
706 35c. Ranger emblem and marlin . . . . 1·90 1·50
MS707 95 × 74 mm. Nos. 703/6 5·50 7·50

159 Killdeer Plover

1985. Birth Bicent of John J. Audubon (ornithologist). Multicoloured.
708 5c. Type **159** . . . . 1·00 60
709 31c. Mourning dove (vert) . . 2·25 60
710 35c. "Mourning dove" (John J. Audubon) (vert) . . . . 2·25 65
711 $1 "Killdeer Plover" (John J. Audubon) . . . . 4·00 4·50

160 The Queen Mother at Christening of Peter Phillips, 1977

162 Queen Elizabeth II

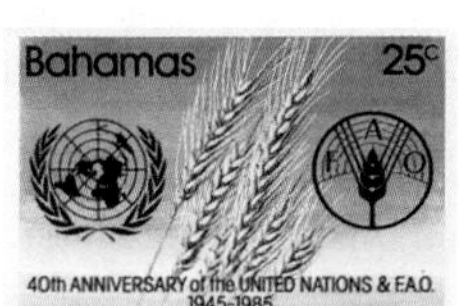

161 Ears of Wheat and Emblems

1985. Life and Times of Queen Elizabeth the Queen Mother. Multicoloured.
712 5c. Visiting Auckland, New Zealand, 1927 . . . . . . 35 20
713 25c. Type **160** 60 40
714 35c. The Queen Mother attending church 65 55
715 50c. With Prince Henry at his christening (from photo by Lord Snowdon) . . . . . 1·25 1·75
MS716 91 × 73 mm. $1.25, In horse-drawn carriage, Sark 2·75 1·90

1985. 40th Anniv of U.N.O. and F.A.O.
717 **161** 25c. multicoloured 85 60

1985. Commonwealth Heads of Government Meeting, Nassau. Multicoloured.
718 31c. Type **162** . . . . 2·50 3·25
719 35c. Bahamas Prime Minister's flag and Commonwealth emblem . . 2·50 3·25

163 "Grandma's Christmas Bouquet" (Alton Roland Lowe)

1985. Christmas. Paintings by Alton Roland Lowe. Multicoloured.
736 5c. Type **163** 60 40
737 25c. "Junkanoo Romeo and Juliet" (vert) . . . . 1·50 1·00
738 31c. "Bunce Gal" (vert) . . . 1·75 1·50
739 35c. "Home for Christmas" 1·75 2·75
MS740 110 × 68 mm. Nos. 736/9 2·75 3·25

1986. 60th Birthday of Queen Elizabeth II. As T **110** of Ascension. Multicoloured.
741 10c. Princess Elizabeth aged one, 1927 . . . . 15 15
742 25c. The Coronation, 1953 30 30
743 35c. Queen making speech at Commonwealth Banquet, Bahamas, 1985 . . . . . 35 40
744 40c. In Djakova, Yugoslavia, 1972 . . . . 35 45
745 $1 At Crown Agents Head Office, London, 1983 . . . 80 1·40

164 1980 1c. and 18c. Definitive Stamps

1986. "Ameripex '86" International Stamp Exn, Chicago.
746 **164** 5c. multicoloured 70 50
747 – 25c. multicoloured . . . . 1·60 50
748 – 31c. multicoloured . . . . 1·75 60
749 – 50c. multicoloured . . . . 2·50 4·00
750 – $1 black, green and blue 2·75 4·75
MS751 80 × 80 mm. No. 750 4·00 4·00
DESIGNS—HORIZ: (showing Bahamas stamps)—25c. 1969 50th Anniv of Bahamas Airmail Service pair; 31c. 1976 Bicentenary of American Revolution 16c., 50c. 1981 Space Exploration miniature sheet. VERT: $1 Statue of Liberty.
No. 750 also commemorates the Centenary of the Statue of Liberty.

1986. Royal Wedding. As T **112** of Ascension. Mult.
756 10c. Prince Andrew and Miss Sarah Ferguson 20 20
757 $1 Prince Andrew . . . . . 1·25 2·10

165 Rock Beauty (juvenile)

1986. Fishes. Multicoloured.
758A 5c. Type **165** 75 75
759A 10c. Stoplight parrotfish . . 80 1·00
760A 15c. Jackknife-fish . . . . 1·50 1·50
761A 20c. Flamefish . . . . . . 1·25 1·25
762A 25c. Peppermint basslet ("Swissguard basslet") . . 1·50 1·50
763A 30c. Spot-finned butterflyfish . . . . . . 1·10 1·50
764A 35c. Queen triggerfish . . . 1·10 2·50
765B 40c. Four-eyed butterflyfish 1·10 1·60
766A 45c. Royal gramma ("Fairy basslet") . . . . 1·50 1·25
767A 50c. Queen angelfish . . . 2·00 3·50
797 60c. Blue chromis . . . . . 2·25 5·00
769B $1 Spanish hogfish . . . . 2·75 3·00
799 $2 Harlequin bass . . . . . 3·00 7·50
771A $3 Black-barred soldierfish 6·00 7·00
772A $5 Cherub angelfish ("Pygmy angelfish") . . . 6·50 8·00
773A $10 Red hind . . . . . . 16·00 22·00

166 Christ Church Cathedral, Nassau, 1861

1986. 125th Anniv of City of Nassau. Diocese and Cathedral. Multicoloured.
774 10c. Type **166** 30 20
775 40c. Christ Church Cathedral, 1986 . . . . 70 80
MS776 75 × 100 mm. Nos. 774/5 3·50 5·50

167 Man and Boy looking at Crib

1986. Christmas. International Peace Year. Mult.
777 10c. Type **167** 35 20
778 40c. Mary and Joseph journeying to Bethlehem 85 75
779 45c. Children praying and Star of Bethlehem . . . . 95 1·00
780 50c. Children exchanging gifts 1·00 2·00
MS781 95 × 90 mm. Nos. 777/80 7·50 10·00

168 Great Isaac Lighthouse 169 Anne Bonney

1987. Lighthouses. Multicoloured.
782 10c. Type **168** . . . . 2·25 85
783 40c. Bird Rock lighthouse . . 4·25 1·75
784 45c. Castle Island lighthouse 4·25 2·00
785 $1 "Hole in the Wall" lighthouse . . . . 7·00 11·00

1987. Pirates and Privateers of the Caribbean. Multicoloured.
786 10c. Type **169** . . . . 2·50 1·25
787 40c. Edward Teach ("Blackbeard") . . . . . 4·50 3·50
788 45c. Captain Edward England . . . . 4·50 3·50
789 50c. Captain Woodes Rogers 5·00 5·50
MS790 75 × 95 mm. $1.25, Map of Bahamas and colonial coat of arms 9·00 4·25

170 Boeing 737

1987. Air. Aircraft. Multicoloured.
800 15c. Type **170** . . . . 2·25 1·50
801 40c. Boeing 757-200 . . . . 3·00 2·00
802 45c. Airbus Industrie A300 B4-200 . . . . 3·00 2·00
803 50c. Boeing 747-200 . . . . 3·00 3·25

171 "Norway" (liner) and Catamaran

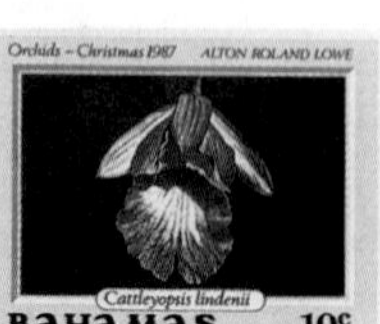

172 "Cattleyopsis lindenii"

1987. Tourist Transport. Multicoloured.
804 40c. Type **171** . . . . 2·00 2·00
805 40c. Liners and speedboat . . 2·00 2·00
806 40c. Game fishing boat and cruising yacht . . . . . . 2·00 2·00
807 40c. Game fishing boat and racing yachts . . . . . . 2·00 2·00
808 40c. Fishing boat and schooner . . . . 2·00 2·00
809 40c. Hawker Siddeley H.S.748 airliner . . . . . 2·00 2·00
810 40c. Boeing 737 and Boeing 727-200 airliners . . . . 2·00 2·00
811 40c. Beech 200 Super King Air aircraft and radio beacon . . . . 2·00 2·00
812 40c. Aircraft and Nassau control tower . . . . . . 2·00 2·00
813 40c. Helicopter and parked aircraft . . . . 2·00 2·00
Nos. 804/8 and 809/13 were each printed together, se-tenant, forming composite design.

1987. Christmas. Orchids. Multicoloured.
814 10c. Type **172** . . . . 1·75 60
815 40c. "Encyclia lucayana" . . 3·00 1·50
816 45c. "Encyclia hodgeana" . . 3·00 1·50
817 50c. "Encyclia lleidae" . . . 3·00 3·00
MS818 120 × 92 mm. Nos. 814/17 9·50 9·00

173 King Ferdinand and Queen Isabella of Spain

174 Whistling Ducks in Flight

1988. 500th Anniv (1992) of Discovery of America by Columbus (1st issue). Multicoloured.
819 10c. Type **173** 85 60
820 40c. Columbus before Talavera Committee . . . 1·75 1·75
821 45c. Lucayan village . . . . 1·90 1·90
822 50c. Lucayan potters . . . . 2·00 3·25
MS823 65 × 50 mm. $1.50, Map of Antilles, c. 1500 6·00 3·75
See also Nos. 844/8, 870/4, 908/12 and 933/7.

1988. Black-billed Whistling Duck. Multicoloured.
824 5c. Type **174** . . . . 2·25 1·75
825 10c. Whistling duck in reeds 2·25 1·75
826 20c. Pair with brood . . . . 4·00 2·75
827 45c. Pair wading . . . . . . 6·00 3·25

175 Grantstown Cabin, c.1820

177 "Oh Little Town of Bethlehem"

176 Olympic Flame, High Jumping, Hammer throwing, Basketball and Gymnastics

1988. 150th Anniv of Abolition of Slavery. Multicoloured.
828 10c. Type **175** 50 30
829 40c. Basket-making, Grantstown 1·25 95

1988. Olympic Games, Seoul. Designs taken from painting by James Martin. Multicoloured.
830 10c. Type **176** 90 50
831 40c. Athletics, archery, swimming, long jumping, weightlifting and boxing 90 60
832 45c. Javelin throwing, gymnastics, hurdling and shot put 90 60
833 $1 Athletics, hurdling, gymnastics and cycling 3·50 5·00
MS834 113 × 85 mm. Nos. 830/3 3·25 3·00

1988. 300th Anniv of Lloyd's of London. As T **123** of Ascension. Multicoloured.
835 10c. "Lloyd's List" of 1740 30 15
836 40c. Freeport Harbour (horiz) 1·50 60
837 45c. Space shuttle over Bahamas (horiz) 1·50 60
838 $1 "Yarmouth Castle" (freighter) on fire 2·50 1·90

1988. Christmas. Carols. Multicoloured.
839 10c. Type **177** 45 30
840 40c. "Little Donkey" 1·25 75
841 45c. "Silent Night" 1·25 90
842 50c. "Hark the Herald Angels Sing" 1·40 2·00
MS843 88 × 108 mm. Nos. 839/42 2·75 2·75

1989. 500th Anniv (1992) of Discovery of America by Columbus (2nd issue). As T **173**. Multicoloured.
844 10c. Columbus drawing chart 2·00 75
845 40c. Types of caravel 3·00 1·50
846 45c. Early navigational instruments 3·00 1·50
847 50c. Arawak artefacts 3·00 4·00
MS848 64 × 64 mm. $1.50, Caravel under construction (from 15th-cent "Nuremburg Chronicles") 2·50 2·50

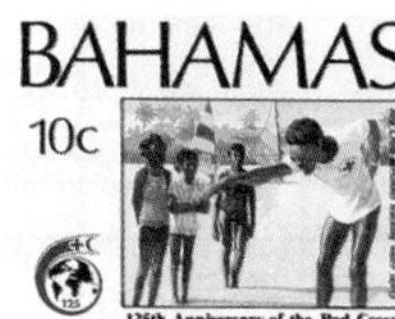

178 Cuban Emerald **179** Teaching Water Safety

1989. Hummingbirds. Multicoloured.
849 10c. Type **178** 1·75 1·25
850 40c. Ruby-throated hummingbird 3·00 2·00
851 45c. Bahama woodstar 3·00 2·00
852 50c. Rufous hummingbird 3·25 4·50

1989. 125th Anniv of Int Red Cross. Mult.
853 10c. Type **179** 1·50 40
854 $1 Henri Dunant (founder) and Battle of Solferino 3·50 3·75

1989. 20th Anniv of First Manned Landing on Moon. As T **126** of Ascension. Multicoloured.
855 10c. "Apollo 8" Communications Station, Grand Bahama 85 50
856 40c. Crew of "Apollo 8" (30 × 30 mm) 1·50 90
857 45c. "Apollo 8" emblem (30 × 30 mm) 1·50 90
858 $1 The Earth seen from "Apollo 8" 2·25 4·00
MS859 100 × 83 mm. $2 "Apollo 11" astronauts in training, Manned Spacecraft Centre, Houston 4·00 4·25

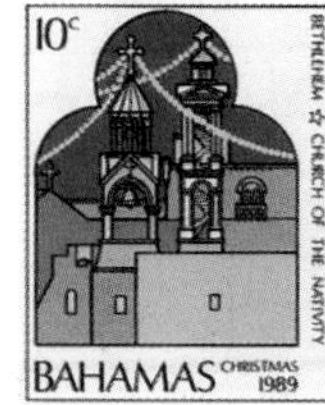

180 Church of the Nativity, Bethlehem

1989. Christmas. Churches of the Holy Land. Multicoloured.
860 10c. Type **180** 85 30
861 40c. Basilica of the Annunciation, Nazareth 1·75 70
862 45c. Tabgha Church, Galilee 1·75 70
863 $1 Church of the Holy Sepulchre, Jerusalem 3·25 5·00
MS864 92 × 109 mm. Nos. 860/3 7·50 8·00

181 1974 U.P.U. Centenary 13c. Stamp and Globe

1989. "World Stamp Expo '89" International Stamp Exhibition, Washington. Multicoloured.
865 10c. Type **181** 70 40
866 40c. New U.P.U. Headquarters Building 3c. and building 1·40 85
867 45c. 1986 "Ameripex '86" $1 and Capitol, Washington 1·40 90
868 $1 1949 75th anniv of U.P.U. 2½d. and Boeing 737 airliner 5·50 7·00
MS869 107 × 80 mm. $2 Map showing route of Columbus, 1492 (30 × 38 mm) 10·00 12·00

1990. 500th Anniv (1992) of Discovery of America by Columbus (3rd issue). As T **173**. Multicoloured.
870 10c. Launching caravel 1·75 80
871 40c. Provisional ship 2·75 2·00
872 45c. Shortening sail 2·75 2·00
873 50c. Lucayan fisherman 2·75 4·00
MS874 70 × 61 mm. $1.50, Departure of Columbus, 1492 5·50 7·00

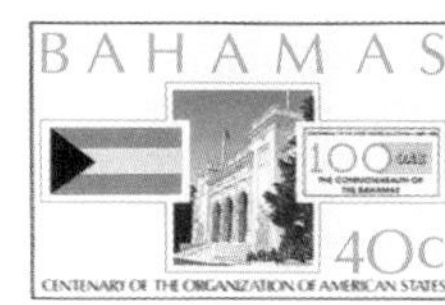

182 Bahamas Flag, O.A.S. Headquarters and Centenary Logo

1990. Centenary of Organization of American States.
875 **182** 40c. multicoloured 2·00 2·00

183 Supermarine Spitfire Mk I "Bahamas I"

1990. "Stamp World London 90" International Stamp Exhibition, London. Presentation Fighter Aircraft. Sheet 107 × 78 mm. containing T **183**. Multicoloured.
MS876 $1 Type **183**; $1 Hawker Hurricane Mk IIc "Bahamas V" 7·50 7·50

184 Teacher with Boy

1990. International Literacy Year. Multicoloured.
877 10c. Type **184** 1·00 50
878 40c. Three boys in class 1·75 1·25
879 50c. Teacher and children with books 1·75 4·75

1990. 90th Birthday of Queen Elizabeth the Queen Mother. As T **134** of Ascension.
880 40c. multicoloured 1·50 50
881 $1.50 black and ochre 2·75 4·00
DESIGNS—21 × 36 mm: 40c. "Queen Elizabeth 1938" (Sir Gerald Kelly); 29 × 37 mm: $1.50, Queen Elizabeth at garden party, France, 1938.

185 Cuban Amazon preening **186** The Annunciation

1990. Cuban Amazon ("Bahamian Parrot"). Mult.
882 10c. Type **185** 1·25 85
883 40c. Pair in flight 2·25 1·50
884 45c. Cuban amazon's head 2·25 1·50
885 50c. Perched on branch 2·50 3·75
MS886 73 × 63 mm. $1.50, Feeding on berries 8·00 8·50

1990. Christmas. Multicoloured.
887 10c. Type **186** 65 50
888 40c. The Nativity 1·25 70
889 45c. Angel appearing to Shepherds 1·25 70
890 $1 The Three Kings 3·00 5·50
MS891 94 × 110 mm. Nos. 887/90 9·00 9·50

187 Green-backed Heron ("Green Heron") **189** The Annunciation

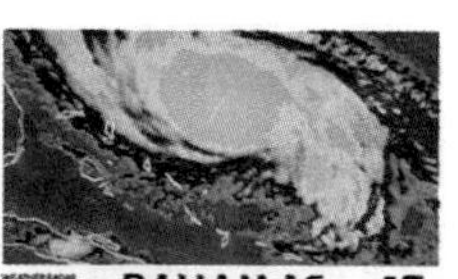

188 Radar Plot of Hurricane Hugo

1991. Birds. Multicoloured.
892 5c. Type **187** 85 1·25
893 10c. Turkey vulture 1·50 1·50
976 15c. Osprey 80 70
895 20c. Clapper rail 1·00 80
978 25c. Royal tern 60 70
979 30c. Key West quail dove 2·25 90
898 40c. Smooth-billed ani 1·75 55
899 45c. Burrowing owl 2·75 80
900 50c. Hairy woodpecker 2·25 80
983 55c. Mangrove cuckoo 2·00 80
902 60c. Bahama mockingbird 2·00 1·75
903 70c. Red-winged blackbird 2·00 1·75
904 $1 Thick-billed vireo 2·50 1·50
905 $2 Bahama yellowthroat 5·50 6·50
988 $5 Stripe-headed tanager 6·50 8·50
907 $10 Greater Antillean bullfinch 13·00 16·00

1991. 500th Anniv (1992) of Discovery of America by Columbus (4th issue). As T **173**. Multicoloured.
908 15c. Columbus navigating by stars 1·75 85
909 40c. Fleet in mid-Atlantic 2·50 2·25
910 55c. Lucayan family worshipping at night 2·50 2·50
911 60c. Map of First Voyage 3·25 5·00
MS912 56 × 61 mm. $1.50, "Pinta"'s look-out sighting land 6·00 7·00

1991. 65th Birthday of Queen Elizabeth II and 70th Birthday of Prince Philip. As T **139** of Ascension. Multicoloured.
913 15c. Prince Philip 1·00 1·50
914 $1 Queen Elizabeth II 1·75 2·00

1991. International Decade for Natural Disaster Reduction. Multicoloured.
915 15c. Type **188** 1·25 65
916 40c. Diagram of hurricane 1·75 1·50
917 55c. Flooding caused by Hurricane David, 1979 2·00 2·25
918 60c. U.S. Dept of Commerce weather reconnaissance Lockhead WP-3D Orion 2·75 4·00

1991. Christmas. Multicoloured.
919 15c. Type **189** 80 30
920 55c. Mary and Joseph travelling to Bethlehem 1·75 1·00
921 60c. Angel appearing to the shepherds 1·75 1·50
922 $1 Adoration of the kings 2·75 4·00
MS923 92 × 108 mm. Nos. 919/22 9·00 9·50

190 First Progressive Liberal Party Cabinet

1992. 25th Anniv of Majority Rule. Multicoloured.
924 15c. Type **190** 60 40
925 40c. Signing of Independence Constitution 1·40 1·10
926 55c. Prince of Wales handing over Constitutional Instrument (vert) 1·50 1·50
927 60c. First Bahamian Governor-General, Sir Milo Butler (vert) 1·75 3·00

1992. 40th Anniv of Queen Elizabeth II's Accession. As T **143** of Ascension. Multicoloured.
928 15c. Queen Elizabeth with bouquet 60 30
929 40c. Queen Elizabeth with flags 1·10 70
930 55c. Queen Elizabeth at display 1·10 90
931 60c. Three portraits of Queen Elizabeth 1·25 1·50
932 $1 Queen Elizabeth II 1·50 2·50

1992. 500th Anniv of Discovery of America by Columbus (5th issue). As T **173**. Multicoloured.
933 15c. Lucayans sighting fleet 1·75 1·00
934 40c. "Santa Maria" and dolphins 2·50 1·75
935 55c. Lucayan canoes approaching ships 2·50 2·25
936 60c. Columbus giving thanks for landfall 3·00 4·25
MS937 61 × 57 mm. $1.50, Children at Columbus Monument 3·50 5·00

191 Templeton, Galbraith and Hansberger Ltd Building

1992. 20th Anniv of Templeton Prize for Religion.
938 **191** 55c. multicoloured 1·50 1·75

192 Pole Vaulting **194** Mary visiting Elizabeth

193 Arid Landscape and Starving Child

1992. Olympic Games, Barcelona. Multicoloured.
939 15c. Type **192** 60 50
940 40c. Javelin 1·00 90
941 55c. Hurdling 1·10 1·25
942 60c. Basketball 5·50 5·00
MS943 70 × 50 mm. $2 Sailing 7·00 8·00

1992. International Conference on Nutrition, Rome. Multicoloured.
944 15c. Type **193** 1·25 75
945 55c. Seedling, cornfield and child 2·00 2·00

1992. 500th Anniv of Discovery of America by Columbus (6th issue). Sheet 65 × 65 mm, containing vert design as T **173**. Multicoloured.
MS946 $2 Columbus landing in Bahamas 6·50 7·50

1992. Christmas. Multicoloured.
947 15c. Type **194** 40 20
948 55c. The Nativity 1·10 1·00
949 60c. Angel and shepherds 1·25 1·50
950 70c. Wise Men and star 1·40 2·50
MS951 95 × 110 mm. Nos. 947/50 6·50 8·00

1992. Hurricane Relief. No. **MS**876 showing each stamp surch **HURRICANE RELIEF+$1**.
MS952 $1+$1 Type **183**; $1+$1 Hawker Hurricane Mk IIc "Bahamas V" 11·00 14·00

196 Flags of Bahamas and U.S.A. with Agricultural Worker

1993. 50th Anniv of The Contract (U.S.A.–Bahamas farm labour programme). Each including national flags. Multicoloured.

953 15c. Type **196** 1·75 70
954 55c. Onions 2·25 1·50
955 60c. Citrus fruit 2·50 2·50
956 70c. Apples 2·75 3·25

1993. 75th Anniv of Royal Air Force. As T **149** of Ascension. Multicoloured.

957 15c. Westland Wapiti IIA 1·50 85
958 40c. Gloster Gladiator I 2·00 1·00
959 55c. De Havilland Vampire F.3 2·25 1·75
960 70c. English Electric Lightning F.3 2·75 4·00
MS961 110 × 77 mm. 60c. Avro Shackleton M.R.2; 60c. Fairey Battle; 60c. Douglas Boston III; 60c. De Havilland D.H.9a 8·00 8·50

197 1978 Coronation Anniversary Stamps **198** "Lignum vitae" (national tree)

1993. 40th Anniv of Coronation. Multicoloured.

962 15c. Type **197** 70 50
963 55c. Two examples of 1953 Coronation stamp 1·75 1·75
964 60c. 1977 Silver Jubilee 8c. and 16c. stamps 1·75 2·00
965 70c. 1977 Silver Jubilee 21c. and 40c. stamps 2·00 2·75

1993. 20th Anniv of Independence. Mult.

966 15c. Type **198** 30 20
967 55c. Yellow elder (national flower) 90 90
968 60c. Blue marlin (national fish) 1·25 1·25
969 70c. Greater flamingo (national bird) 2·00 2·75

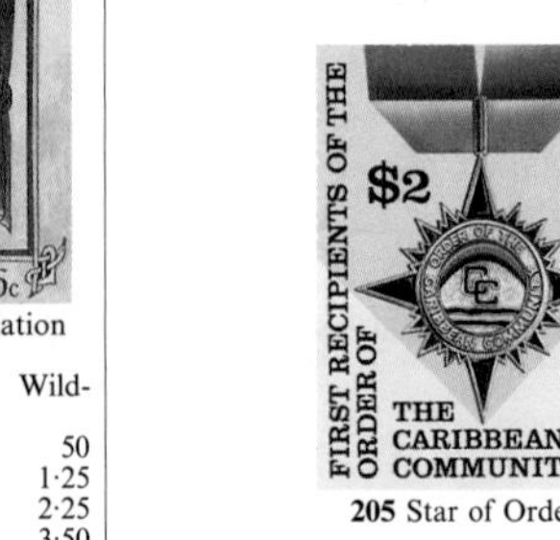

199 Cordia **200** The Annunciation

1993. Environment Protection (1st series). Wildflowers. Multicoloured.

970 15c. Type **199** 1·00 50
971 55c. Seaside morning glory 2·50 1·25
972 60c. Poinciana 2·75 2·25
973 70c. Spider lily 3·25 3·50

See also Nos. 1017/21, 1035/8, 1084/7, 1121/4, 1149/53 and 1193/6.

1993. Christmas. Multicoloured.

990 15c. Type **200** 1·00 50
991 55c. Angel and shepherds 2·75 1·75
992 60c. Holy Family 3·00 2·50
993 70c. Three Kings 3·25 3·50
MS994 86 × 106 mm. $1 Virgin Mary and Child 6·50 8·00

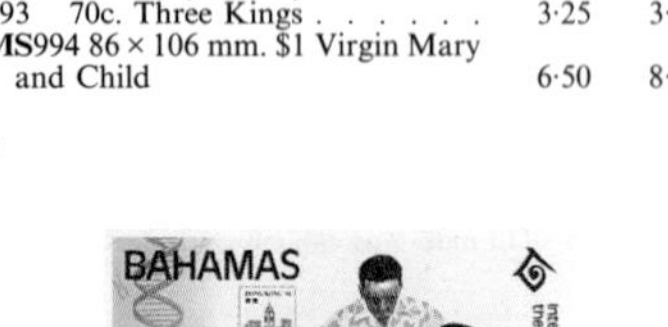

201 Family

1994. "Hong Kong '94" International Stamp Exhibition. International Year of the Family. Multicoloured.

995 15c. Type **201** 1·00 40
996 55c. Children doing homework 2·00 1·25
997 60c. Grandfather and grandson fishing 2·25 1·75
998 70c. Grandmother teaching grandchildren the Lord's Prayer 2·75 4·25

202 Flags of Bahamas and Great Britain

1994. Royal Visit. Multicoloured.

999 15c. Type **202** 1·00 50
1000 55c. Royal Yacht "Britannia" 2·25 1·75
1001 60c. Queen Elizabeth II 2·25 1·90
1002 70c. Queen Elizabeth and Prince Philip 2·25 3·50

203 Yachts

1994. 40th Anniv of National Family Island Regatta. Multicoloured.

1003 15c. Type **203** 80 40
1004 55c. Dinghies racing 1·75 1·25
1005 60c. Working boats 1·75 1·75
1006 70c. Sailing sloop 2·25 4·00
MS1007 76 × 54 mm. $2 Launching sloop (vert) 8·00 9·00

204 Logo and Bahamas 1968 Olympic Games Stamp

1994. Centenary of International Olympic Committee. Multicoloured.

1008 15c. Type **204** 1·25 50
1009 55c. 1976 Olympic Games stamps (vert) 2·25 1·25
1010 60c. 1984 Olympic Games stamps 2·25 2·25
1011 70c. 1992 Olympic Games stamps (vert) 2·50 3·50

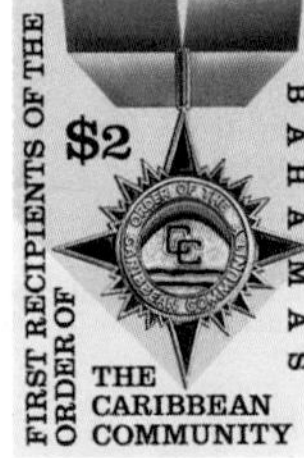

205 Star of Order

1994. First Recipients of Order of the Caribbean Community. Sheet 90 × 69 mm.

MS1012 **205** $2 multicoloured 5·50 6·50

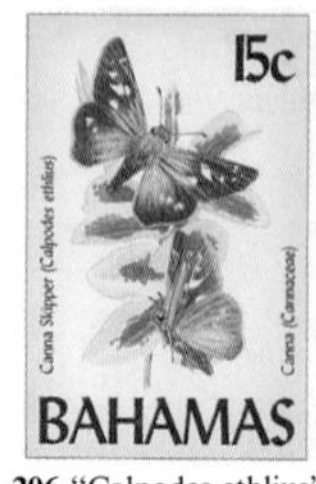

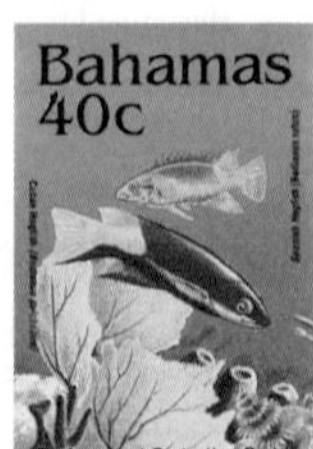

206 "Calpodes ethlius" and Canna **207** Spot-finned Hogfish and Spanish Hogfish

1994. Butterflies and Flowers. Multicoloured.

1013 15c. Type **206** 1·10 55
1014 55c. "Phoebis sennae" and cassia 2·00 1·50
1015 60c. "Anartia jatrophae" and passion flower 2·25 2·25
1016 70c. "Battus devilliersi" and calico flower 2·25 2·75

1994. Environment Protection (2nd series). Marine Life. Multicoloured.

1017 40c. Type **207** 1·00 1·25
1018 40c. Tomate and long-spined squirrelfish 1·00 1·25
1019 40c. French angelfish 1·00 1·25
1020 40c. Queen angelfish 1·00 1·25
1021 40c. Rock beauty 1·00 1·25
MS1022 57 × 55 mm. $2 Rock beauty, Queen angelfish and windsurfer 6·00 7·00

Nos. 1017/21 were printed together, se-tenant, with the backgrounds forming a composite design.

208 Angel

1994. Christmas. Multicoloured.

1023 15c. Type **208** 30 30
1024 55c. Holy Family 90 1·10
1025 60c. Shepherds 1·10 1·40
1026 70c. Wise Men 1·25 2·50
MS1027 73 × 85 mm. Jesus in manger 3·50 5·00

209 Lion and Emblem **210** Kirtlands Warbler on Nest

1995. 20th Anniv of the College of the Bahamas. Multicoloured.

1028 15c. Type **209** 30 30
1029 70c. Queen Elizabeth II and College building 1·25 1·75

1995. 50th Anniv of End of Second World War. As T **161** of Ascension. Multicoloured.

1030 15c. Bahamian infantry drilling 75 50
1031 55c. Consolidated PBY-5A Catalina flying boat 2·00 1·25
1032 60c. Bahamian women in naval operations room 2·00 2·25
1033 70c. Consolidated B-24 Liberator bomber 2·50 3·50
MS1034 75 × 85 mm. $2 Reverse of 1939–45 War Medal (vert) 3·00 4·00

1995. Environment Protection (3rd series). Endangered Species. Kirtland's Warbler. Mult.

1035 15c. Type **210** 55 75
1036 15c. Singing on branch 55 75
1037 25c. Feeding chicks 55 75
1038 25c. Catching insects 55 75
MS1039 73 × 67 mm. $2 On branch 6·50 8·00

No. **MS**1039 does not show the W.W.F. Panda emblem.

211 Eleuthera Cliffs

1995. Tourism. Multicoloured.

1040 15c. Type **211** 90 50
1041 55c. Clarence Town, Long Island 2·00 1·25
1042 60c. Albert Lowe Museum 2·25 2·25
1043 70c. Yachts 2·50 3·50

212 Pigs and Chick

1995. 50th Anniv of F.A.O. Multicoloured.

1044 15c. Type **212** 1·00 50
1045 55c. Seedling and hand holding seed 1·60 1·10
1046 60c. Family with fruit and vegetables 1·90 2·00
1047 70c. Fishes and crustaceans 2·75 3·50

213 Sikorsky S-55 Helicopter, Sinai, 1957

1995. 50th Anniv of United Nations. Multicoloured.

1048 15c. Type **213** 70 50
1049 55c. Ferret armoured car, Sinai, 1957 1·25 1·25
1050 60c. Fokker F.27 Friendship (airliner), Cambodia, 1991–93 1·50 1·75
1051 70c. Lockheed C-130 Hercules (transport) 1·60 2·25

214 St. Agnes Anglican Church

1995. Christmas. Churches. Multicoloured.

1052 15c. Type **214** 30 25
1053 55c. Church of God, East Street 90 90
1054 60c. Sacred Heart Roman Catholic Church 95 1·25
1055 70c. Salem Union Baptist Church 1·10 1·75

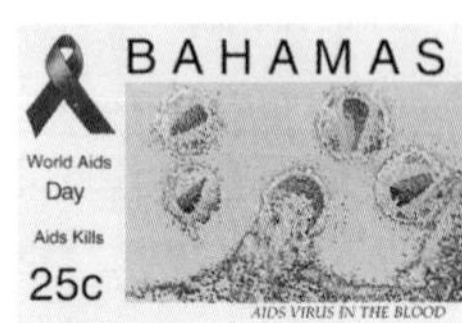

215 Microscopic View of AIDS Virus

1995. World AIDS Day. Multicoloured.

1056 25c. Type **215** 60 50
1057 70c. Research into AIDS 1·00 1·50

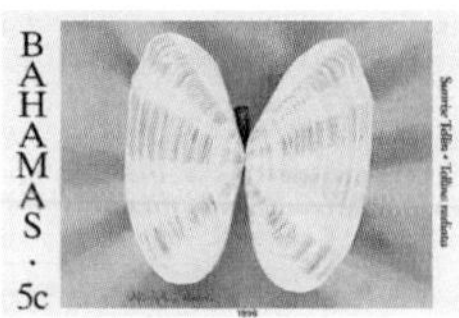

216 Sunrise Tellin

1996. Sea Shells. Multicoloured.

1098 5c. Type **216** 30 40
1099 10c. Queen conch 30 50
1100 15c. Angular triton 35 25
1101 20c. True tulip 40 35
1102 25c. Reticulated cowrie-helmet 50 40
1063 30c. Sand dollar 1·00 55
1103a 35c. As 30c. 75 55
1104 40c. Lace short-frond murex 75 60
1065 45c. Inflated sea biscuit 1·25 60
1106 50c. West Indian top shell 1·00 75
1067 55c. Spiny oyster 1·50 75
1108 60c. King helmet 1·25 90
1108a 65c. As 45c. 1·25 1·25
1109 70c. Lion's paw 1·25 1·25
1109a 80c. As 55c. 1·40 1·40
1110 $1 Crown cone 1·90 1·90
1111 $2 Atlantic partridge tun 4·00 4·00
1112 $5 Wide-mouthed purpura 8·00 8·50
1113 $10 Atlantic trumpet triton 15·00 17·00

217 East Goodwin Lightship with Marconi Apparatus on Mast

1996. Centenary of Radio. Multicoloured.

1074 15c. Type **217** 1·75 80
1075 55c. Newspaper headline concerning Dr. Crippen 2·25 1·25
1076 60c. "Philadelphia" (liner) and first readable transatlantic message 2·25 2·00
1077 70c. Guglielmo Marconi and "Elettra" (yacht) 2·75 3·50
MS1078 80 × 47 mm. $2 "Titanic" and "Carpathia" (liners) 5·50 7·50

218 Swimming **219** Green Anole

1996. Centenary of Modern Olympic Games. Multicoloured.

1079 15c. Type **218** 40 35
1080 55c. Running 90 90

1081 60c. Basketball . . . . . . 1·75 1·75
1082 70c. Long jumping . . . . 1·40 2·25
MS1083 73 × 86 mm. $2 Javelin throwing 3·00 4·00

1996. Environment Protection (4th series). Reptiles. Multicoloured.
1084 15c. Type **219** 55 50
1085 55c. Little Bahama bank boa . . . . 1·10 1·00
1086 60c. Inagua freshwater turtle 1·50 1·75
1087 70c. Acklins rock iguana . . 1·75 2·75
MS1088 85 × 105 mm. Nos. 1084/7 4·50 5·50

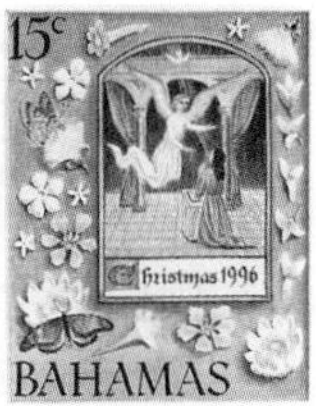

220 The Annunciation

221 Department of Archives Building

1996. Christmas. Multicoloured.
1089 15c. Type **220** 85 40
1090 55c. Joseph and Mary travelling to Bethlehem 2·00 1·00
1091 60c. Shepherds and angel . . 2·00 1·50
1092 70c. Adoration of the Magi 2·25 3·00
MS1093 70 × 87 mm. $2 Presentation in the Temple 3·00 3·75

1996. 25th Anniv of Archives Department.
1094 **221** 55c. multicoloured . . . 1·25 1·00
MS1095 83 × 54 mm. $2 multicoloured 4·25 5·50

1997. "HONG KONG '97" International Stamp Exhibition. Sheet 130 × 90 mm, containing design as No. 1070, but with "1997" imprint date. Multicoloured.
MS1096 $1 Crown cone 2·25 2·75

1997. Return of Hong Kong to China. Sheet 130 × 90 mm, containing design as No. 1069, but with "1997" imprint date.
MS1097 70c. Lion's paw 2·00 2·50

1997. Golden Wedding of Queen Elizabeth and Prince Philip. As T **173** of Ascension. Multicoloured.
1114 50c. Queen Elizabeth II in Bonn, 1992 . . . . 1·60 1·75
1115 50c. Prince Philip and Prince Charles at Trooping the Colour . . . . 1·60 1·75
1116 60c. Prince Philip . . . . . 1·60 1·75
1117 60c. Queen at Trooping the Colour . . . . 1·60 1·75
1118 70c. Queen Elizabeth and Prince Philip at polo, 1970 . . . . 1·75 2·00
1119 70c. Prince Charles playing polo . . . . 1·75 2·00
MS1120 110 × 70 mm. $2 Queen Elizabeth and Prince Philip in landau (horiz) 3·50 4·25

222 Underwater Scene

1997. Environment Protection (5th series). International Year of the Reefs.
1121 **222** 15c. multicoloured . . . 1·00 60
1122 – 55c. multicoloured . . . 2·00 1·00
1123 – 60c. multicoloured . . . 2·00 1·50
1124 – 70c. multicoloured . . . 2·25 2·75
DESIGNS: 55c. to 70c. Different children's paintings of underwater scenes.

223 Angel

223a Wearing Grey Jacket, 1988

1997. Christmas. Multicoloured.
1125 15c. Type **223** 85 40
1126 55c. Mary and Baby Jesus 1·40 80
1127 60c. Shepherd . . . . . . 1·60 1·10
1128 70c. King . . . . 1·90 2·75
MS1129 74 × 94 mm. $2 Baby Jesus wrapped in swaddling-bands. 4·75 5·00

1998. Diana, Princess of Wales Commemoration.
1130 **223a** 15c. multicoloured . . . 50 50
MS1131 145 × 70 mm. 15c. As No. 1130; 55c. Wearing striped jacket, 1983; 60c. In evening dress, 1983; 70c. Meeting crowds, 1993 2·50 2·75

1998. 80th Anniv of the Royal Air Force. As T **178** of Ascension. Multicoloured.
1132 15c. Handley Page Hyderabad 55 40
1133 55c. Hawker Demon . . . . 1·00 85
1134 60c. Gloster Meteor F.8 . . 1·10 1·25
1135 70c. Lockheed Neptune MR.1 . . . . 1·40 2·25
MS1136 110 × 76 mm. 50c. Sopwith Camel; 50c. Short 184 (seaplane); 50c. Supermarine Spitfire PR.19; 50c. North American Mitchell III 4·00 4·25

224 Newsletters

1998. 50th Anniv of Organization of American States. Multicoloured.
1137 15c. Type **224** 30 30
1138 55c. Headquarters building and flags, Washington . . 70 80

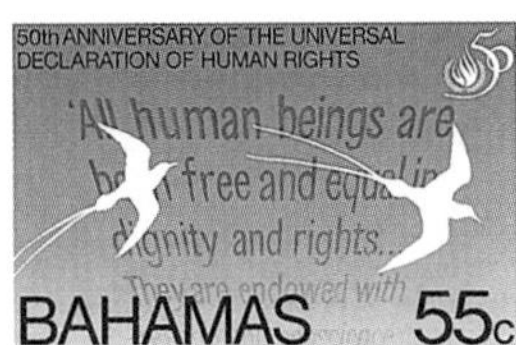

225 Start of Declaration and Birds

1998. 50th Anniv of Universal Declaration of Human Rights.
1139 **225** 55c. blue and black . . . 1·25 1·00

226 University Arms and Graduates

1998. 50th Anniv of University of the West Indies.
1140 **226** 55c. multicoloured . . . 1·25 1·00

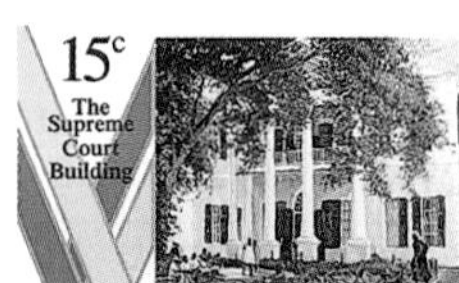

227 Supreme Court Building

1998. 25th Anniv of Independence. Multicoloured.
1141 15c. Type **227** 65 50
1142 55c. Nassau Library . . . . 1·25 1·00
1143 60c. Government House . . 1·40 1·40
1144 70c. Gregory Arch . . . . 1·60 2·25
MS1145 70 × 55 mm. $2 Island Regatta, George Town 3·00 4·00

228 "Disney Magic" (cruise liner) at Night

1998. Disney Cruise Line's Castaway Cay Holiday Development. Multicoloured.
1146 55c. Type **228** . . . . . . 1·25 1·25
1147 55c. "Disney Magic" by day 1·25 1·25

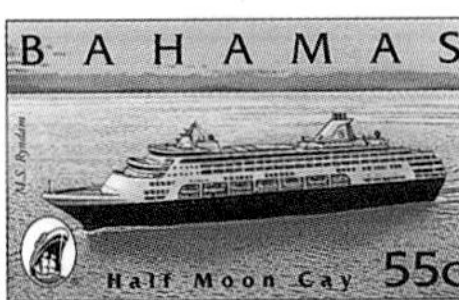

229 "Ryndam" (cruise liner)

1998. Holland America Line's Half Moon Cay Holiday Development.
1148 **229** 55c. multicoloured . . . 1·50 1·00

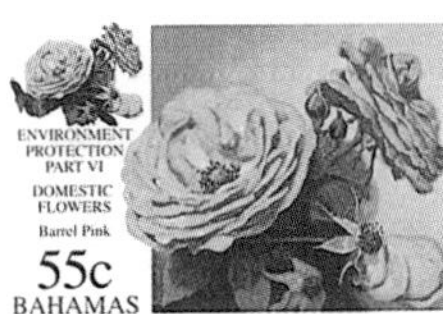

230 Barrel Pink Rose

1998. Environment Protection (6th series). Roses. Multicoloured.
1149 55c. Type **230** . . . . . . 1·00 1·25
1150 55c. Yellow cream . . . . . 1·00 1·25
1151 55c. Seven sisters . . . . . 1·00 1·25
1152 55c. Big red . . . . 1·00 1·25
1153 55c. Island beauty . . . . . 1·00 1·25
MS1154 100 × 70 mm. No. 1153 1·00 1·25

231 The Annunciation

1998. Christmas. Multicoloured.
1155 15c. Type **231** 50 30
1156 55c. Shepherds . . . . . . 1·00 70
1157 60c. Three Kings . . . . . 1·25 1·10
1158 70c. The Flight into Egypt 1·50 2·25
MS1159 87 × 67 mm. The Nativity 3·00 3·75

232 Killer Whale and other Marine Life

1998. International Year of the Ocean. Multicoloured.
1160 15c. Type **232** 65 50
1161 55c. Tropical fish 85 90

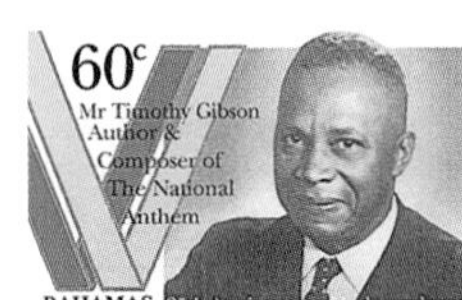

233 Timothy Gibson (composer)

1998. 25th Anniv of "March on Bahamaland" (national anthem).
1162 **233** 60c. multicoloured . . . 1·00 1·25

234 Head of Greater Flamingo and Chick

1999. 40th Anniv of National Trust (1st issue). Inagua National Park. Multicoloured.
1163 55c. Type **234** . . . . . . 1·00 1·25
1164 55c. Pair with two chicks . . 1·00 1·25
1165 55c. Greater flamingos asleep or stretching wings 1·00 1·25
1166 55c. Greater flamingos feeding . . . . 1·00 1·25
1167 55c. Greater flamingos in flight . . . . 1·00 1·25
Nos. 1163/7 were printed together, se-tenant, with the backgrounds forming a composite design.
See also Nos. 1173/7, 1198/1202 and 1207/11.

235 Arawak Indian Canoe

1999. "Australia '99" World Stamp Exhibition, Melbourne. Maritime History. Multicoloured.
1168 15c. Type **235** 30 30
1169 55c. "Santa Maria" (Columbus), 1492 . . . . 1·50 1·00
1170 60c. "Queen Anne's Revenge" (Blackbeard), 1716 . . . . 1·60 1·25
1171 70c. "The Banshee" (Confederate paddle-steamer) running blockade 1·75 2·25
MS1172 110 × 66 mm. $2 Firing on American ships, 1776 3·25 4·00

1999. 40th Anniv of National Trust (2nd issue). Exuma Cays Land and Sea Park. As T **234**. Mult.
1173 55c. Dolphin . . . . 1·00 1·25
1174 55c. Angelfish and parrotfish 1·00 1·25
1175 55c. Queen triggerfish . . . 1·00 1·25
1176 55c. Turtle . . . . 1·00 1·25
1177 55c. Lobster . . . . 1·00 1·25
Nos. 1173/7 were printed together, se-tenant, with the backgrounds forming a composite design.

236 Society Headquarters Building

1999. 40th Anniv of Bahamas Historical Society.
1178 **236** $1 multicoloured . . . . 1·50 2·00

1999. 30th Anniv of First Manned Landing on Moon. As T **186** of Ascension. Multicoloured.
1179 15c. Constructing ascent module 45 40
1180 65c. Diagram of command and service module . . . 1·25 1·25
1181 70c. Lunar module descending . . . . 1·25 1·60
1182 80c. Lunar module preparing to dock with service module . . . . . 1·25 1·90
MS1183 90 × 80 mm. $2 Earth as seen from Moon (circular, 40 mm diam) 3·25 4·00

1999. "Queen Elizabeth the Queen Mother's Century". As T **187** of Ascension. Multicoloured.
1184 15c. Visiting Herts Hospital, 1940 . . . . 50 35
1185 65c. With Princess Elizabeth, Hyde Park, 1944 . . . . 1·40 1·00
1886 70c. With Prince Andrew, 1997 . . . . 1·40 1·40
1887 80c. With Irish Guards' mascot, 1997 . . . . . . 1·40 2·00
MS1188 145 × 70 mm. $2 Lady Elizabeth Bowes-Lyon with her brother David, 1904, and England World Cup team celebrating, 1966. 3·25 4·00

237 "Delaware" (American mail ship), 1880

1999. 125th Anniv of U.P.U. Ships. Multicoloured.
1189 15c. Type **237** 85 50
1190 65c. "Atlantis" (liner), 1923 1·75 1·25
1191 70c. "Queen of Bermuda 2" (liner), 1937 . . . . . . 1·75 1·50
1192 80c. U.S.S. "Saufley" (destroyer), 1943 . . . . 2·00 2·25

238 "Turtle Pond" (Green Turtle)

1999. Environment Protection (7th series). Marine Life Paintings by Ricardo Knowles. Multicoloured.
1193 15c. Type **238** 50 35
1194 65c. "Turtle Cliff" (Loggerhead turtle) . . . 1·25 1·00
1195 70c. "Barracuda" . . . . . 1·40 1·40
1196 80c. "Coral Reef" . . . . . 1·50 2·00
MS1197 90 × 75 mm. $2 "Atlantic Bottle-nosed Dolphins" 3·00 4·00
The 65c. is inscribed "GREEN TURTLES" in error.

1999. 40th Anniv of National Trust (3rd issue). Birds. As T **234**. Multicoloured.
1198 65c. Bridled tern and white-tailed tropic bird . . . . 1·00 1·25
1199 65c. Louisiana heron . . . 1·00 1·25
1200 65c. Bahama woodstar . . . 1·00 1·25
1201 65c. Black-billed whistling duck . . . . 1·00 1·25
1202 65c. Cuban amazon . . . . 1·00 1·25
Nos. 1198/1202 were printed together, se-tenant, with the backgrounds forming a composite design.

239 Man on Elephant Float

1999. Christmas. Junkanoo Festival. Multicoloured.
1203 15c. Type **239** 50 30
1204 65c. Man in winged costume 1·00 1·00
1205 70c. Man in feathered mask 1·25 1·25
1206 80c. Man blowing conch shell . . . . 1·50 1·75

1999. 40th Anniv of National Trust (4th issue). Flora and Fauna. As T **234**. Multicoloured.
1207 65c. Foxglove . . . . . . 1·40 1·50
1208 65c. Vole . . . . 1·40 1·50
1209 65c. Cuban amazon . . . . 1·40 1·50
1210 65c. Lizard . . . . 1·40 1·50
1211 65c. Red hibiscus . . . . . 1·40 1·50
Nos. 1207/11 were printed together, se-tenant, with the backgrounds forming a composite design.

240 New Plymouth

2000. Historic Fishing Villages. Multicoloured.
1212 15c. Type **240** 65 40
1213 65c. Cherokee Sound . . . 1·50 1·00
1214 70c. Hope Town . . . . . 1·60 1·40
1215 80c. Spanish Wells . . . . 1·75 2·25

241 Gold Medal Winning Bahamas Women's Relay Team

2000. "The Golden Girls" winners of 4 × 100 metre Relay at I.A.A.F. World Track and Field Championship '99, Spain. Sheet 100 × 55 mm.
MS1216 **241** $2 multicoloured 3·00 3·50

242 Prickly Pear

2000. Medicinal Plants (1st series). Multicoloured.
1217 15c. Type **242** 35 30
1218 65c. Buttercup . . . . . . 1·25 1·25
1219 70c. Shepherd's needle . . . 1·25 1·40
1220 80c. Five fingers . . . . . 1·40 1·75
See also Nos. 1282/5.

243 Re-arming and Re-fuelling Spitfire

2000. "The Stamp Show 2000" International Stamp Exhibition, London. 60th Anniv of Battle of Britain. Multicoloured.
1221 15c. Type **243** 70 45
1222 65c. Sqdn. Ldr. Stanford-Tuck's Hurricane Mk I 1·40 1·40
1223 70c. Dogfight between Spitfires and Heinkel IIIs 1·60 1·75
1224 80c. Flight of Spitfires attacking . . . . 1·60 1·75
MS1225 90 × 70 mm. $2 Presentation Spitfire Bahamas 3·00 3·50

244 Teachers' and Salaried Workers' Co-operative Credit Union Building

2000. Co-operatives Movement in Bahamas. Sheet 90 × 50 mm.
MS1226 $2 multicoloured 2·75 3·00

245 Swimming

2000. Olympic Games, Sydney. Each inscribed with details of previous Bahamian participation. Mult.
1227 15c. Type **245** 50 30
1228 65c. Triple jump . . . . . 1·40 1·25
1229 70c. Women's 4 × 100 m relay . . . . . 1·40 1·40
1230 80c. Sailing . . . . 1·50 1·75

246 *Encyclia cochleata*

2000. Christmas. Orchids. Multicoloured.
1231 15c. Type **246** 55 30
1232 65c. *Encyclia plicata* . . . . 1·40 1·25
1233 70c. *Bletia purpurea* . . . . 1·60 1·60
1234 80c. *Encyclia gracilis* . . . . 1·75 1·90

247 Cuban Amazon and Primary School Class

2000. Bahamas Humane Society. Multicoloured.
1235 15c. Type **247** 65 45
1236 65c. Cat and Society stall 1·50 1·25
1237 70c. Dogs and veterinary surgery . . . . 1·75 1·50
1238 80c. Goat and animal rescue van . . . . 1·90 1·90

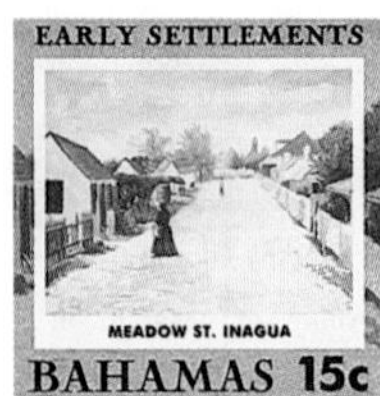

248 "Meadow Street, Inagua"

2001. Early Settlements. Paintings by Ricardo Knowles. Multicoloured.
1239 15c. Type **248** 40 30
1240 65c. "Bain Town" . . . . . 1·25 1·00
1241 70c. "Hope Town, Abaco" 1·40 1·40
1242 80c. "Blue Hills" . . . . . 1·50 1·75

249 Lynden Pindling presenting Independence Constitution, 1972

2001. Sir Lynden Pindling (former Prime Minister) Commemoration. Multicoloured.
1243 15c. Type **249** 35 25
1244 65c. Sir Lynden Pindling with Bahamas flag . . . 1·40 1·25

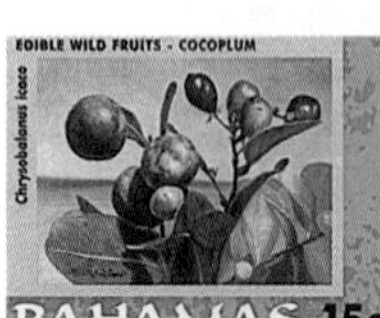

250 "Cocoaplum"

2001. Edible Wild Fruits. Paintings by Alton Roland Lowe. Multicoloured.
1245 15c. Type **250** 35 25
1246 65c. "Guana Berry" . . . . 1·25 1·10
1247 70c. "Mastic" . . . . 1·25 1·25
1248 80c. "Seagrape" . . . . . . 1·50 1·75

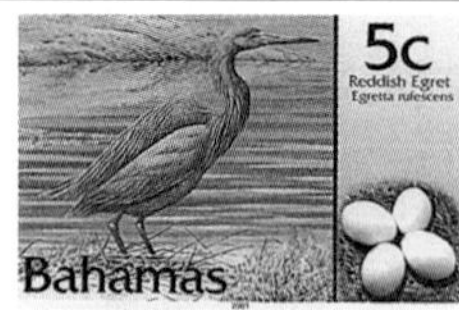

251 Reddish Egret

2001. Birds and their Eggs. Multicoloured.
1249 5c. Type **251** 10 15
1250 10c. American purple gallinule 15 20
1251 15c. Antillean nighthawk . . 20 25
1252 20c. Wilson's plover 25 30
1253 25c. Killdeer plover 30 35
1254 30c. Bahama woodstar . . . 40 45
1255 40c. Bahama swallow . . . 50 55
1256 50c. Bahama mockingbird 65 70
1257 60c. Black-cowled oriole . . 75 80
1258 65c. Great lizard cuckoo 85 90
1259 70c. Audubon's shearwater 90 95
1260 80c. Grey kingbird . . . . 1·00 1·10
1261 $1 Bananaquit . . . . . . 1·25 1·40
1262 $2 Yellow warbler . . . . 2·50 2·75
1263 $5 Greater Antillean bullfinch . . . . 6·50 6·75
1264 $10 Roseate spoonbill . . . 13·00 13·50

252 H.M.S. *Norfolk* (cruiser), 1933

2001. Royal Navy Ships connected to Bahamas. Multicoloured.
1265 15c. Type **252** 50 30
1266 25c. H.M.S. *Scarborough* (sloop), 1930s 65 50
1267 50c. H.M.S. *Bahamas* (frigate), 1944 . . . . . 1·00 1·00
1268 65c. H.M.S. *Battleaxe* (frigate), 1979 . . . . . 1·25 1·10
1269 70c. H.M.S. *Invincible* (aircraft carrier), 1997 . . 1·25 1·25
1270 80c. H.M.S. *Norfolk* (frigate), 2000 . . . . . 1·25 1·50

253 "Adoration of the Shepherds"

2001. Christmas. Paintings by Rubens. Mult.
1271 15c. Type **253** 35 25
1272 65c. "Adoration of the Magi" (with Van Dyck) 1·10 95
1273 70c. "Holy Virgin in Wreath of Flowers" (with Breughel) . . . . 1·25 1·25
1274 80c. "Holy Virgin adored by Angels" . . . . 1·25 1·50

2002. Golden Jubilee. As T **200** of Ascension.
1275 15c. black, green and gold 35 25
1276 65c. multicoloured . . . . . 1·10 95
1277 70c. multicoloured . . . . . 1·25 1·25
1278 80c. multicoloured . . . . . 1·25 1·50
MS1279 162 × 95 mm. Nos. 1275/8 and $2 multicoloured 3·00 3·50
DESIGNS—HORIZ: 15c. Princess Elizabeth; 65c. Queen Elizabeth in Bonn, 1992; 70c. Queen Elizabeth with Prince Edward, 1965; 80c. Queen Elizabeth at Sandringham, 1996. VERT (38 × 51 mm)—$2 Queen Elizabeth after Annigoni.

254 Avard Moncur (athlete)

2002. Award of BAAA Most Outstanding Male Athlete Title to Avard Moncur. Sheet 65 × 98 mm.
MS1280 **254** $2 multicoloured 2·50 2·60

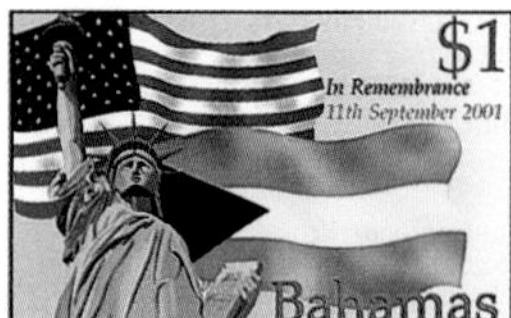

255 Statue of Liberty with U.S. and Bahamas Flags

2002. In Remembrance. Victims of Terrorist Attacks on U.S.A. (11 September 2001).
1281 **255** $1 multicoloured . . . . 1·25 1·40

2002. Medicinal Plants (2nd series). As T **242**. Multicoloured.
1282 15c. Wild sage 20 25
1283 65c. Seaside maho 85 90
1284 70c. Sea ox-eye 90 95
1285 80c. Mexican poppy . . . . 1·00 1·25

2002. Queen Elizabeth the Queen Mother Commemoration. As T **202** of Ascension.
1286 15c. brown, gold and purple 20 25
1287 65c. multicoloured 85 90
MS1288 145 × 70 mm. 70c. black and gold; 80c. multicoloured 1·90 2·00
DESIGNS: 15c. Queen Elizabeth at American Red Cross Club, London, 1944; 65c. Queen Mother at Remembrance Service, 1989; 70c. Queen Elizabeth, 1944; 80c. Queen Mother at Cheltenham Races, 2000.

256 Rice Bird and Rice

2002. Illustrations from *The Natural History of Carolina, Florida and the Bahama Islands* by Mark Catesby (1747). Multicoloured.
1289 15c. Type **256** 20 25
1290 25c. Alligator and red mangrove 30 35
1291 50c. Parrot fish 65 70
1292 65c. Ilathera duck and sea ox-eye 85 90
1293 70c. Flamingo and gorgonian coral 90 95
1294 80c. Crested bittern and inkberry . . . . 1·00 1·10

257 "While Shepherds watched their Flocks"

2002. Christmas. Scenes from Carols. Multicoloured.
1295 15c. Type **257** 20 25
1296 65c. "We Three Kings" . . 85 90
1297 70c. "Once in Royal David's City" 90 95
1298 80c. "I saw Three Ships" . . 1·00 1·10

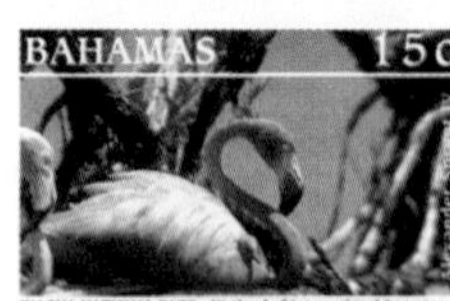

258 Flamingo on Nest

2003. Inagua National Park Wetlands. Flamingos. Multicoloured.
1299 15c. Type **258** 20 25
1300 25c. Flock of flamingos feeding 30 35
1301 50c. Group of flamingos . . 65 70
1302 65c. Group of flamingos walking 85 90
1303 70c. Flamingos taking-off 90 95
1304 80c. Flamingos in flight . . 1·00 1·10

259 Captain Edward Teach ("Blackbeard")

2003. Pirates. Multicoloured.
1305 15c. Type **259** 20 25
1306 25c. Captain "Calico Jack" Rackham 30 35
1307 50c. Anne Bonney 65 70

1308 65c. Captain Woodes Rogers . . . 85 90
1309 70c. Sir John Hawkins . . . 90 95
1310 80c. Captain Bartholomew Roberts ("Black Bart") 1·00 1·10

SPECIAL DELIVERY STAMPS

1916. Optd **SPECIAL DELIVERY**.
S2 **6** 5d. black and orange . . . . 45 6·50
S3 5d. black and mauve . . . . 30 2·50

BAHAWALPUR Pt. 1

A former Indian Feudatory state which joined Pakistan in 1947 and continued to use its own stamps until 1953.

12 pies = 1 anna, 16 annas = 1 rupee.

(1)

2 Amir Muhammad Bahawal Khan I Abbasi

1947. Nos. 265/8, 269a/77 and 259/62 of India optd with Type **1**.
1 **100a** 3p. slate . . . 19·00
2 ½a. purple . . . 19·00
3 9p. green . . . 19·00
4 1a. red . . . 19·00
5 **101** 1½a. violet . . . 19·00
6 2a. red . . . 19·00
7 3a. violet . . . 19·00
8 3½a. blue . . . 19·00
9 **102** 4a. brown . . . 19·00
10 6a. green . . . 19·00
11 8a. violet . . . 19·00
12 12a. lake . . . 19·00
13 – 14a. purple . . . 60·00
14 **93** 1r. grey and brown . . . 22·00
15 2r. purple and brown . . £1200
16 5r. green and blue . . . £1200
17 10r. purple and red . . . £1200

1948. Bicentenary Commemoration.
18 **2** ½a. black and red . . . . 2·25 2·50

4 H. H. the Amir of Bahawalpur

5 The Tombs of the Amirs

1948.
19 **4** 3p. black and blue . . . 1·50 19·00
20 ½a. black and red . . . 1·50 19·00
21 9p. black and green . . . 1·50 19·00
22 1a. black and red . . . 1·50 19·00
23 1½a. black and violet . . . 1·50 15·00
24 **5** 2a. green and red . . . 1·75 19·00
25 – 4a. orange and brown . . . 2·00 19·00
26 – 6a. violet and blue . . . 2·00 19·00
27 – 8a. red and violet . . . 2·00 19·00
28 – 12a. green and red . . . 2·25 28·00
29 – 1r. violet and brown . . . 19·00 40·00
35 – 1r. green and orange . . . 1·25 17·00
30 – 2r. green and red . . . 42·00 65·00
36 – 2r. black and red . . . 1·50 20·00
31 – 5r. black and violet . . . 42·00 80·00
37 – 5r. brown and blue . . . 1·60 38·00
32 – 10r. red and black . . . 32·00 95·00
38 – 10r. brown and green . . . 1·75 42·00
DESIGNS—HORIZ: 6a. Fort Derawar from the lake; 8a. Nur-Mahal Palace; 12a. Sadiq-Garh Palace. 46 × 32 mm: 10r. Three generations of Rulers. VERT (As Type **5**): 4a. Mosque in Sadiq-Garh; 1, 2, 5r. H.H. the Amir of Bahawalpur.

12 H.H. the Amir of Bahawalpur and Mohammed Ali Jinnah

1948. 1st Anniv of Union with Pakistan.
33 **12** 1½a. red and green . . . . 1·25 2·50

13 Soldiers of 1848 and 1948

14 Irrigation

1948. Centenary of Multan Campaign.
34 **13** 1½a. black and red . . . . 1·00 8·50

1949. Silver Jubilee of Accession of H.H. the Amir of Bahawalpur.
39 **14** 3p. black and blue . . . . 10 8·00
40 – ½a. black and orange . . . 10 8·00
41 – 9p. black and green . . . . 10 8·00
42 – 1a. black and red . . . . 10 8·00
DESIGNS: ½a. Wheat; 9p. Cotton; 1a. Sahiwal bull.

17 U.P.U. Monument, Berne

1949. 75th Anniv of U.P.U.
43 **17** 9p. black and green . . . . 20 1·25
44 1a. black and mauve . . . . 20 1·25
45 1½a. black and orange . . . 20 1·25
46 2½a. black and blue . . . . 20 1·25

OFFICIAL STAMPS

O 4 Eastern White Pelicans

1945. As Type O **4** with Arabic opt.
O1 – ½a. black and green . . . 3·25 13·00
O2 – 1a. black and red . . . . 3·75 6·50
O7 – 1a. black and brown . . . 35·00 50·00
O3 – 2a. black and violet . . . 3·25 10·00
O4 O **4** 4a. black and olive . . . 10·00 25·00
O5 – 8a. black and brown . . . 21·00 14·00
O6 – 1r. black and orange . . . 21·00 14·00
DESIGNS: ½a. Panjnad Weir; 1a. (No. O2), Camel and calf; 1a. (No. O7), Baggage camels; 2a. Blackbuck antelopes; 8a. Friday Mosque, Fort Derawar; 1r. Temple at Pattan Munara.

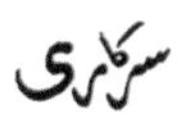

(O 8)

1945. Types as Nos. O1, etc., in new colours and without Arabic opt. (a) Surch as Type O **8**.
O11 ½a. on 8a. black and purple (as No. O5) . . . . 4·75 4·00
O12 1½a. on 5r. black and orange (as No. O6) . . . . 38·00 10·00
O13 1½a. on 2r. black and blue (as No. O1) . . . . £120 7·50
(b) Optd **SERVICE** and Arabic inscription.
O14 ½a. black and red (as No. O1) . . . . 1·25 11·00
O15 1a. black and red (as No. O2) . . . . 2·00 13·00
O16 2a. black and orange (as No. O3) . . . . 3·25 42·00

1945. As Type **4** but inscr "SERVICE" at left.
O17 3p. black and blue . . . . 3·25 7·50
O18 1½a. black and violet . . . . 19·00 7·50

O 11 Allied Banners

1946. Victory.
O19 O **11** 1½a. green and grey . . 2·75 3·50

1948. Stamps of 1948 with Arabic opt as in Type O **4**.
O20 **4** 3p. black and blue . . . . 80 11·00
O21 1a. black and red . . . . 80 10·00
O22 **5** 2a. green and red . . . . 80 11·00
O23 – 4a. orange and brown . . . 80 15·00
O24 – 1r. green and orange . . . 80 17·00
O25 – 2r. black and red . . . . 80 23·00
O26 – 5r. chocolate and blue . . . 80 38·00
O27 – 10r. brown and green . . . 80 38·00

1949. 75th Anniv of U.P.U. optd as in Type O **4**.
O28 **17** 9p. black and green . . . 15 4·50
O29 1a. black and mauve . . . 15 4·50
O30 1½a. black and orange . . 15 4·50
O31 2½a. black and blue . . . 15 4·50

BAHRAIN Pt. 1, Pt. 19

An archipelago in the Persian Gulf on the Arabian coast. An independent shaikhdom with Indian and later British postal administration. The latter was closed on 1 January 1966, when the Bahrain Post Office took over.

1933. 12 pies = 1 anna; 16 annas = 1 rupee.
1957. 100 naya paise = 1 rupee.

Stamps of India optd **BAHRAIN**.

1933. King George V.
1 **55** 3p. grey . . . 3·50 45
2 **56** ½a. green . . . 7·50 3·25
15 **79** ½a. green . . . 4·50 1·00
3 **80** 9p. green . . . 3·75 2·00
4 **57** 1a. brown . . . 7·00 2·50
16 **81** 1a. brown . . . 10·00 40
5 **82** 1a.3p. mauve . . . 7·00 1·00
6 **70** 2a. orange . . . 10·00 14·00
17 **59** 2a. orange . . . 40·00 7·50
7 **62** 3a. blue . . . 19·00 48·00
18 3a. red . . . 4·75 50
8 **83** 3a.6p. blue . . . 3·75 30
9 **71** 4a. green . . . 18·00 48·00
19 **63** 4a. olive . . . 4·75 40
10 **65** 8a. mauve . . . 6·00 30
11 **66** 12a. red . . . 7·50 1·25
12 **67** 1r. brown and green . . . 16·00 7·50
13 2r. red and orange . . . 28·00 35·00
14 5r. blue and violet . . . £120 £140

1938. King George VI.
20 **91** 3p. slate . . . 10·00 3·75
21 ½a. brown . . . 6·00 10
22 9p. green . . . 6·00 6·00
23 1a. red . . . 6·00 10
24 **92** 2a. red . . . 5·00 1·75
26 – 3a. green (No. 253) . . . 12·00 5·00
27 – 3a.6p. blue (No. 254) . . . 5·00 3·25
28 – 4a. brown (No. 255) . . . £120 70·00
30 – 8a. violet (No. 257) . . . £150 35·00
31 – 12a. red (No. 258) . . . £100 45·00
32 **93** 1r. slate and brown . . . 3·00 1·75
33 2r. purple and brown . . . 13·00 5·50
34 5r. green and blue . . . 15·00 13·00
35 10r. purple and red . . . 65·00 35·00
36w 15r. brown and green . . . 50·00 55·00
37 25r. slate and purple . . . £100 85·00

1942. King George VI.
38 **100a** 3p. slate . . . 2·25 1·25
39 ½a. mauve . . . 4·00 1·75
40 9p. green . . . 13·00 15·00
41 1a. red . . . 4·00 50
42 **101** 1a.3p. bistre . . . 8·00 17·00
43 1½a. violet . . . 4·75 4·50
44 2a. red . . . 5·50 1·50
45 3a. violet . . . 18·50 4·50
46 3½a. blue . . . 4·25 16·00
47 **102** 4a. brown . . . 2·75 1·50
48 6a. green . . . 13·00 9·00
49 8a. violet . . . 4·25 2·75
50 12a. purple . . . 7·00 4·00

Stamps of Great Britain surch **BAHRAIN** and new value in Indian currency.

1948. King George VI.
51 **128** ½a. on ½d. green . . . 50 1·25
71 ½a. on ½d. orange . . . 2·25 2·25
52 1a. on 1d. red . . . 50 1·50
72 1a. on 1d. blue . . . 2·75 20
53 1½a. on 1½d. brown . . . 50 2·00
73 1½a. on 1½d. green . . . 2·75 13·00
54 2a. on 2d. orange . . . 50 20
74 2a. on 2d. brown . . . 1·50 30
55 2½a. on 2½d. blue . . . 50 3·00
75 2½a. on 2½d. red . . . 2·75 13·00
56 3a. on 3d. violet . . . 50 10
76 **129** 4a. on 4d. blue . . . 2·75 1·50
57 6a. on 6d. purple . . . 50 10
58 **130** 1r. on 1s. brown . . . 1·25 10
59 **131** 2r. on 2s.6d. green . . . 5·50 4·75
60 5r. on 5s. red . . . 5·50 4·75
60a – 10r. on 10s. blue (No. 478a) . . . 65·00 48·00

1948. Silver Wedding.
61 **137** 2½a. on 2½d. blue . . . 1·00 70
62 **138** 15r. on £1 blue . . . 30·00 48·00

1948. Olympic Games.
63 **139** 2½a. on 2½d. blue . . . 70 2·75
64 **140** 3a. on 3d. violet . . . 80 2·75
65 – 6a. on 6d. purple . . . 1·50 2·75
66 – 1r. on 1s. brown . . . 1·75 2·75

1949. U.P.U.
67 **143** 2½a. on 2½d. blue . . . 40 2·25
68 **144** 3a. on 3d. violet . . . 60 2·75
69 – 6a. on 6d. purple . . . 50 3·00
70 – 1r. on 1s. brown . . . 1·25 2·00

1951. Pictorial stamps (Nos. 509/11).
77 **147** 2r. on 2s.6d. green . . . 23·00 8·00
78 – 5r. on 5s. red . . . 13·00 3·75
79 – 10r. on 10s. blue . . . 27·00 7·50

1952. Queen Elizabeth II.
97 **154** ½a. on ½d. orange . . . 10 15
81 1a. on 1d. blue . . . 10 10
82 1½a. on 1½d. green . . . 10 30
83 2a. on 2d. brown . . . 30 10
84 **155** 2½a. on 2½d. red . . . 20 1·75
85 3a. on 3d. lilac . . . 3·00 10
86 4a. on 4d. blue . . . 8·50 30
99 **157** 6a. on 6d. purple . . . 50 50
88 **160** 12a. on 1s.3d. green . . . 3·25 20
89 1r. on 1s.6d. blue . . . 3·25 10

1953. Coronation.
90 **161** 2½a. on 2½d. red . . . 1·25 75
91 – 4a. on 4d. blue . . . 2·25 4·75
92 **163** 12a. on 1s.3d. green . . . 3·25 4·25
93 – 1r. on 1s.6d. blue . . . 7·50 50

1955. Pictorial stamps (Nos. 595a/598a).
94 **166** 2r. on 2s.6d. brown . . . 5·50 2·00
95 – 5r. on 5s. red . . . 12·00 2·75
96 – 10r. on 10s. blue . . . 20·00 2·75

1957. Queen Elizabeth II.
102 **157** 1n.p. on 5d. brown . . . 10 10
103 **154** 3n.p. on ½d. orange . . . 30 2·25
104 6n.p. on 1d. blue . . . 30 2·25
105 9n.p. on 1½d. green . . . 30 2·50
106 12n.p. on 2d. pale brown . . . 30 60
107 **155** 15n.p. on 2½d. red . . . 30 15
108 20n.p. on 3d. lilac . . . 30 10
109 25n.p. on 4d. blue . . . 75 2·50
110 **157** 40n.p. on 6d. purple . . . 40 10
111 50n.p. on 9d. olive . . . 3·75 4·50
112 75n.p. on 1s.3d. green . . . 2·25 50

1957. World Scout Jubilee Jamboree.
113 **170** 15n.p. on 2½d. red . . . 25 35
114 **171** 25n.p. on 4d. blue . . . 30 35
115 – 75n.p. on 1s.3d. green . . . 40 45

16 Shaikh Sulman bin Hamed al-Khalifa

1960.
117 **16** 5n.p. blue . . . 10 10
118 15n.p. orange . . . 10 10
119 20n.p. violet . . . 10 10
120 30n.p. bistre . . . 10 10
121 40n.p. grey . . . 15 10
122 50n.p. green . . . 15 10
123 75n.p. brown . . . 30 15
124 – 1r. black . . . 2·00 30
125 – 2r. red . . . 3·00 2·25
126 – 5r. blue . . . 5·00 3·00
127 – 10r. green . . . 12·00 5·00
The rupee values are larger, 27 × 32½ mm.

18 Shaikh Isa bin Sulman al-Khalifa

19 Air Terminal, Muharraq

1964.
128 **18** 5n.p. blue . . . 10 10
129 15n.p. orange . . . 10 10
130 20n.p. violet . . . 10 10
131 30n.p. bistre . . . 10 10
132 40n.p. slate . . . 15 10
133 50n.p. green . . . 15 50
134 75n.p. brown . . . 25 10
135 **19** 1r. black . . . 8·50 2·25
136 2r. red . . . 9·00 2·25
137 – 5r. blue . . . 14·00 13·00
138 – 10r. myrtle . . . 14·00 13·00
DESIGN—As Type **19**: 5r., 10r. Deep water harbour.

21 Sheikh Isa bin Sulman al-Khalifa

22 Ruler and Bahrain Airport

1966.
139 **21** 5f. green . . . 10 10
140 10f. red . . . 15 15
141 15f. blue . . . 20 15
142 20f. purple . . . 20 15
143 **22** 30f. black and green . . . 25 15
144 40f. black and blue . . . 30 15

145 – 50f. black and red 55 25
146 – 75f. black and violet . . . 70 35
147 – 100f. blue and yellow . . . 2·00 90
148 – 200f. green and orange . . 8·00 1·90
149 – 500f. brown and yellow . . 6·75 3·25
150 – 1d. multicoloured . . . . 14·00 7·00

DESIGNS—As Type **22**: 50f., 75f. Ruler and Mina Sulman deep-water harbour. VERT (26½ × 42½ mm): 100f. Pearl-diving; 200f. Lanner falcon and horse-racing; 500f. Serving coffee, and ruler's palace. LARGER (37 × 52½ mm): 1d. Ruler, crest, date palm, horse, dhow, pearl necklace, mosque, coffee-pot and Bab-al-Bahrain (gateway).

23 Produce

24 W.H.O. Emblem and Map of Bahrain

1966. Trade Fair and Agricultural Show.
151 **23** 10f. turquoise and red . . 30 15
152 20f. lilac and green 65 35
153 40f. blue and brown . . . 1·40 50
154 200f. red and blue . . . . 6·50 3·75

1968. 20th Anniv of W.H.O.
155 **24** 20f. black and grey 60 45
156 40f. black and turquoise 2·00 1·10
157 150f. black and red . . . . 8·00 4·25

25 View of Isa Town

1968. Inauguration of Isa New Town. Mult.
158 50f. Type **25** . . . . 3·00 90
159 80f. Shopping centre . . . . 4·50 1·75
160 120f. Stadium . . . . 7·00 3·25
161 150f. Mosque . . . . 8·00 4·00

26 Symbol of Learning

1969. 50th Anniv of School Education in Bahrain.
162 **26** 40f. multicoloured . . . . 1·25 75
163 60f. multicoloured . . . . 2·40 1·25
164 150f. multicoloured . . . . 6·50 3·25

27 Dish Aerial and Map of Persian Gulf

1969. Opening of Satellite Earth Station, Ras Abu Jarjour. Multicoloured.
165 20f. Type **27** . . . . 2·00 50
166 40f. Dish aerial and palms (vert) . . . . 4·00 80
167 100f. Type **27** . . . . . . 9·00 3·25
168 150f. As 40f. . . . . 13·00 4·75

28 Arms, Map and Manama Municipality Building

1970. 2nd Arab Cities Organization Conf, Manama.
169 **28** 30f. multicoloured . . . . 1·25 1·25
170 150f. multicoloured . . . . 5·25 5·25

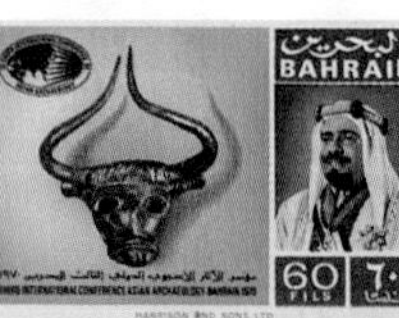

29 Copper Bull's Head, Barbar

1970. 3rd International Asian Archaeology Conference, Bahrain. Multicoloured.
171 60f. Type **29** . . . . 2·50 1·60
172 80f. Palace of Dilmun excavations . . . . 3·25 2·00
173 120f. Desert gravemounds . . 4·75 2·75
174 150f. Dilmun seal . . . . . 6·00 3·50

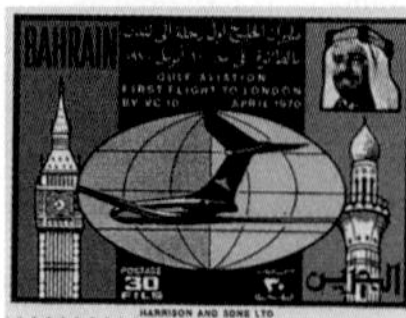

30 Vickers Super VC-10 Airliner, Big Ben, London, and Bahrain Minaret

1970. 1st Gulf Aviation Vickers Super VC-10 Flight, Doha–London.
175 **30** 30f. multicoloured . . . . 2·00 70
176 60f. multicoloured . . . . 4·50 1·50
177 120f. multicoloured . . . . 8·50 4·50

31 I.E.Y. Emblem and Open Book

1970. International Education Year. Multicoloured.
178 60f. Type **31** . . . . 1·75 1·40
179 120f. Emblem and Bahraini children . . . . 4·25 3·75

32 Allegory of Independence
34 Human Heart

33 Arab Dhow with Arab League and U.N. Emblems

1971. Independence Day and 10th Anniv of Ruler's Accession. Multicoloured.
180 30f. Type **32** . . . . 1·75 90
181 60f. Government House . . . 3·25 1·75
182 120f. Arms of Bahrain . . . 8·00 4·00
183 150f. Arms of Bahrain (gold background) . . . . 11·00 5·50

1972. Bahrain's Membership of Arab League and U.N. Multicoloured.
184 30f. Type **33** . . . . 3·00 95
185 60f. Type **33** . . . . 5·00 1·90
186 120f. Dhow sails (vert) . . . 6·00 4·00
187 150f. As 120f. . . . . 11·00 5·50

1972. World Health Day.
188 **34** 30f. multicoloured . . . . 2·00 2·00
189 60f. multicoloured . . . . 5·00 5·00

35 F.A.O. and U.N. Emblems

1973. 10th Anniv of World Food Programme.
190 **35** 30f. brown, red and green 2·75 2·75
191 60f. brown, lt brown & grn 5·00 5·00

36 "Races of the World"

1973. 25th Anniv of Declaration of Human Rights.
192 **36** 30f. blue, brown and black 2·00 1·00
193 60f. red, brown and black 3·50 2·50

38 Flour Mill

1973. National Day. "Progress in Bahrain". Mult.
195 30f. Type **38** . . . . 1·00 75
196 60f. Muharraq Airport . . . 2·50 1·00
197 120f. Sulmaniya Medical Centre . . . . 3·00 1·75
198 150f. Aluminium Smelter . . 3·50 3·00

39 U.P.U. Emblem within Letters

1974. Admission of Bahrain to U.P.U. Mult.
199 30f. Type **39** . . . . 1·50 55
200 60f. U.P.U. emblem on letters 2·50 90
201 120f. Ruler and emblem on dove with letter in beak (37 × 28 mm) . . . . . . 2·25 1·90
202 150f. As 120f. (37 × 28 mm) 3·25 2·75

40 Traffic Lights and Directing Hands

1974. International Traffic Day.
203 **40** 30f. multicoloured . . . . 1·75 1·60
204 60f. multicoloured . . . . 4·00 3·50

41 U.P.U. "Stamp" and Mail Transport

1974. Centenary of U.P.U.
205 **41** 30f. multicoloured 70 50
206 60f. multicoloured . . . . 1·25 90
207 120f. multicoloured . . . . 2·25 1·60
208 150f. multicoloured . . . . 2·75 1·90

42 Emblem and Sitra Power Station
43 Costume and Headdress

1974. National Day. Multicoloured.
209 30f. Type **42** 55 50
210 60f. Type **42** 95 85
211 120f. Emblem and Bahrain Dry Dock . . . . 2·50 2·00
212 150f. As 120f. . . . . 3·25 2·50

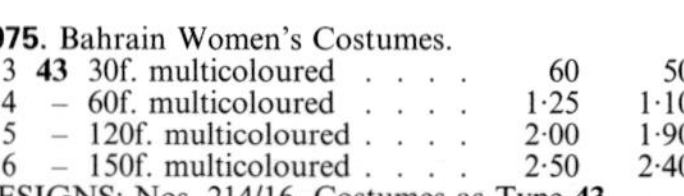

1975. Bahrain Women's Costumes.
213 **43** 30f. multicoloured 60 50
214 – 60f. multicoloured . . . . 1·25 1·10
215 – 120f. multicoloured . . . . 2·00 1·90
216 – 150f. multicoloured . . . . 2·50 2·40
DESIGNS: Nos. 214/16, Costumes as Type **43**.

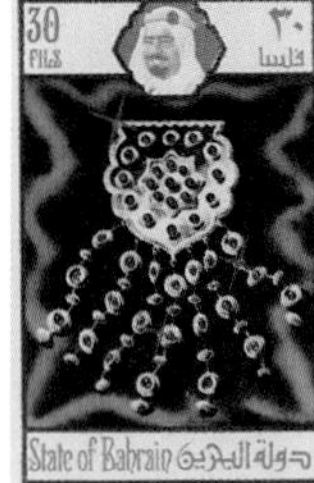

44 Jewelled Pendant
45 Women planting "Flower"

1975. Costume Jewellery. Multicoloured.
217 30f. Type **44** 60 50
218 60f. Gold crown . . . . . . 1·25 1·10
219 120f. Jewelled necklace . . . 2·00 1·90
220 150f. Gold necklace . . . . 2·50 2·40

1975. International Women's Year. Multicoloured.
221 30f. Type **45** . . . . 1·50 75
222 60f. Woman holding I.W.Y. emblem . . . . 3·00 1·75

46 Head of Horse

1975. Horses. Multicoloured.
223a 60f. Type **46** . . . . 4·00 4·00
223b 60f. Grey . . . . 4·00 4·00
223c 60f. Grey with foal (horiz) 4·00 4·00
223d 60f. Close-up of Arab with grey . . . . 4·00 4·00
223e 60f. Grey and herd of browns (horiz) . . . . . 4·00 4·00
223f 60f. Grey and brown (horiz) 4·00 4·00
223g 60f. Arabs riding horses (horiz) . . . . 4·00 4·00
223h 60f. Arab leading grey beside sea (horiz) . . . . 4·00 4·00

47 National Flag
48 Map of Bahrain within Cog and Laurel

1976.
224 **47** 5f. red, pink and blue . . 15 10
225 10f. red, pink & green . . 15 10
226 15f. red, pink & black . . 15 15
227 20f. red, pink & brown 15 15
227a **48** 25f. black and grey . . . 20 15
228 40f. black and blue . . . 20 15
228a 50f. green, black & olive 25 15
228b 60f. black and green . . . 30 20
229 80f. black and mauve . . 45 30
229b 100f. black and red . . . 55 45
230 150f. black and yellow . . 90 85
231 200f. black and yellow . . 1·10 1·00

49 Concorde Taking off

1976. 1st Commercial Flight of Concorde. Mult.
232 80f. Type **49** . . . . 2·25 2·00
233 80f. Concorde landing . . . 2·25 2·00
234 80f. Concorde en route . . . 2·25 2·00
235 80f. Concorde on runway . . 2·25 2·00

50 Soldier, Crest and Flag

52 Shaikh Isa bin Sulman al-Khalifa

51 King Khalid of Saudi Arabia and Shaikh of Bahrain with National Flags

1976. Defence Force Cadets' Day.

237 **50** 40f. multicoloured . . . . 1·40 1·25
238 80f. multicoloured . . . . 2·50 2·25

1976. Visit to Bahrain of King Khalid of Saudi Arabia.

239 **51** 40f. multicoloured . . . . 1·50 1·25
240 80f. multicoloured . . . . 3·00 2·50

1976.

241 **52** 300f. green and pale green 2·25 1·60
242 400f. purple and pink . . 3·00 2·25
243 500f. blue and pale blue 3·75 3·00
244 1d. black and grey . . . 7·50 4·75
244a 2d. violet and lilac . . . 15·00 11·00
244b 3d. brown and pink . . . 23·00 17·00

53 Ministry of Housing Emblem, Designs for Houses and Mosque

54 A.P.U. Emblem

1976. National Day.

245 **53** 40f. multicoloured . . . . 1·25 1·00
246 80f. multicoloured . . . . 2·75 1·75

1977. 25th Anniv of Arab Postal Union.

247 **54** 40f. multicoloured . . . . 1·25 1·00
248 80f. multicoloured . . . . 2·75 1·75

55 Dogs on Beach

1977. Saluki Dogs. Multicoloured.

249a 80f. Type **55** . . . . 2·40 2·40
249b 80f. Dog and dromedaries 2·40 2·40
249c 80f. Dog and antelope . . . 2·40 2·40
249d 80f. Dog on lawn of building . . . . 2·40 2·40
249e 80f. Head of dog . . . . . 2·40 2·40
249f 80f. Heads of two dogs . . 2·40 2·40
249g 80f. Dog in scrubland . . . 2·40 2·40
249h 80f. Dogs fighting . . . . . 2·40 2·40

56 Arab Students and Candle

1977. International Literacy Day.

250 **56** 40f. multicoloured . . . . 1·25 1·00
251 80f. multicoloured . . . . 2·75 1·75

57 Shipyard Installations and Arab Flags

1977. Inauguration of Arab Shipbuilding and Repair Yard Co.

252 **57** 40f. multicoloured . . . . 1·25 1·00
253 80f. multicoloured . . . . 2·75 1·75

58 Microwave Antenna

1978. 10th World Telecommunications Day.

254 **58** 40f. multicoloured . . . . 1·25 1·00
255 80f. silver, dp blue & blue 2·75 1·75

59 Child being helped to Walk

60 Boom Dhow

1979. International Year of the Child. Mult.

256 50f. Type **59** . . . . 1·00 80
257 100f. Hands protecting child 2·50 1·60

1979. Dhows. Multicoloured.

258 100f. Type **60** . . . . 2·60 2·40
259 100f. Baghla . . . . 2·60 2·40
260 100f. Shu'ai (horiz) . . . . 2·60 2·40
261 100f. Ghanja (horiz) . . . . 2·60 2·40
262 100f. Kotia . . . . 2·60 2·40
263 100f. Sambuk . . . . 2·60 2·40
264 100f. Jaliboot (horiz) . . . . 2·60 2·40
265 100f. Zarook (horiz) . . . . 2·60 2·40

61 Dome of Mosque, Mecca

1980. 1400th Anniv of Hejira.

266 **61** 50f. multicoloured 65 40
267 100f. multicoloured . . . . 1·60 1·25
268 150f. multicoloured . . . . 1·90 1·50
269 200f. multicoloured . . . . 2·50 2·00

62 Arab with Gyr Falcon

1980. Falconry. Multicoloured.

271 100f. Type **62** . . . . 2·75 1·60
272 100f. Arab looking at Lanner falcon on wrist . . . . . . 2·75 1·60
273 100f. Peregrine falcon resting with outstretched wings . . 2·75 1·60
274 100f. Peregrine falcon in flight . . . . 2·75 1·60
275 100f. Gyr falcon on pillar (with camels in background) (vert) . . . . 2·75 1·60
276 100f. Gyr falcon on pillar (closer view) (vert) . . . . 2·75 1·60
277 100f. Close-up of gyr falcon facing right (vert) . . . . 2·75 1·60
278 100f. Close-up of Lanner falcon full-face (vert) . . . 2·75 1·60

63 Map and I.Y.D.P. Emblem

1981. International Year for Disabled Persons.

279 **63** 50f. multicoloured . . . . 1·25 75
280 100f. multicoloured . . . . 2·25 1·75

64 Jubilee Emblem

1981. 50th Anniv of Electrical Power in Bahrain.

281 **64** 50f. multicoloured . . . . 1·25 75
282 100f. multicoloured . . . . 2·25 1·75

65 Carving

66 Mosque

1981. Handicrafts. Multicoloured.

283 50f. Type **65** 55 45
284 100f. Pottery . . . . 1·00 90
285 150f. Weaving . . . . 1·90 1·60
286 200f. Basket-making . . . . 2·25 2·10

1981. Mosques.

287 **66** 50f. multicoloured 70 55
288 – 100f. multicoloured . . . . 1·40 1·10
289 – 150f. multicoloured . . . . 2·00 1·75
290 – 200f. multicoloured . . . . 2·75 2·50

DESIGNS: 100f. to 200f. As Type **66** but showing different mosques.

67 Shaikh Isa bin Sulman al-Khalifa

69 Flags and Clasped Hands encircling Emblem

68 Dorcas Gazelle

1981. 20th Anniv of Coronation of Shaikh Isa bin Sulman al-Khalifa.

291 **67** 15f. gold, grey and mauve 25 20
292 50f. gold, grey and red . . 55 45
293 100f. gold, grey and brown 1·10 95
294 150f. gold, grey and blue 1·75 1·40
295 200f. gold, grey and blue 2·10 2·10

1982. Al-Areen Wildlife Park. Multicoloured.

296 100f. Goitred gazelle . . . . 1·75 1·75
297 100f. Type **68** . . . . . . 1·75 1·75
298 100f. Dhub lizard . . . . . 1·75 1·75
299 100f. Brown hares . . . . . 1·75 1·75
300 100f. Arabian oryx . . . . . 1·75 1·75
301 100f. Addax . . . . 1·75 1·75

1982. 3rd Supreme Council Session of Gulf Co-operation Council.

302 **69** 50f. multicoloured 65 50
303 – 100f. multicoloured . . . . 1·40 1·10

70 Madinat Hamad

1983. Opening of Madinat Hamad New Town. Multicoloured.

304 50f. Type **70** 65 50
305 100f. View of Madinat Hamad (different) . . . . 1·40 1·10

71 Shaikh Isa bin Sulman al-Khalifa

1983. Bicentenary of Al-Khalifa Dynasty. Mult.

306 100f. Type **71** 70 70
307 100f. Cartouche of Ali bin Khalifa al-Khalifa 70 70
308 100f. Isa bin Ali al-Khalifa 70 70
309 100f. Hamad bin Isa al-Khalifa 70 70
310 100f. Salman bin Hamad al-Khalifa 70 70
311 100f. Cartouche of Ahmed bin Mohammed al-Khalifa 70 70
312 100f. Cartouche of Salman bin Ahmed al-Khalifa . . . 70 70
313 100f. Cartouche of Abdullah bin Ahmed al-Khalifa . . . 70 70
314 100f. Cartouche of Mohammed bin Khalifa al-Khalifa 70 70

72 G.C.C. and Traffic and Licensing Directorate Emblems

1984. Gulf Co-operation Council Traffic Week.

316 **72** 15f. multicoloured 25 20
317 50f. multicoloured 80 40
318 100f. multicoloured . . . . 1·25 75

73 Hurdling

1984. Olympic Games, Los Angeles. Multicoloured.

319 15f. Type **73** 20 20
320 50f. Show-jumping 70 55
321 100f. Swimming . . . . . . 1·25 1·10
322 150f. Fencing . . . . 1·75 1·50
323 200f. Shooting . . . . 2·40 2·25

74 Manama and Emblem

1984. Centenary of Postal Services.

324 **74** 15f. multicoloured 35 20
325 50f. multicoloured . . . . 1·00 50
326 100f. multicoloured . . . . 1·75 95

75 Narrow-barred Spanish Mackerel

1985. Fishes. Multicoloured.

327 100f. Type **75** . . . . 1·40 1·00
328 100f. Crocodile needlefish (three fishes) . . . . 1·40 1·00
329 100f. Sombre sweetlips (fish swimming to left, blue and lilac background) . . . . 1·40 1·00
330 100f. White-spotted rabbitfish (two fishes, blue and lilac background) . . . . 1·40 1·00
331 100f. Grey mullet (two fishes, green and pink background) . . . . 1·40 1·00

332 100f. Two-banded seabream (green and grey background) . . . . 1·40 1·00
333 100f. River seabream (blue background) . . . . 1·40 1·00
334 100f. Malabar grouper (green background) . . . . 1·40 1·00
335 100f. Small-toothed emperor (pink anemone background) . . . . 1·40 1·00
336 100f. Golden trevally (fish swimming to right, blue and lilac background) . . . 1·40 1·00

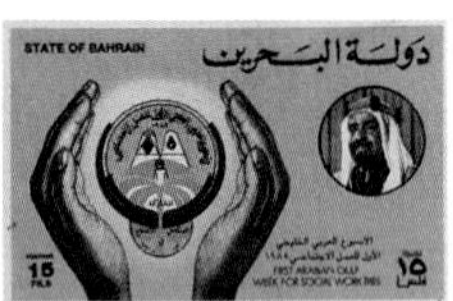

76 Hands cupping Emblem

1985. Arabian Gulf States Social Work Week.
337 **76** 15f. multicoloured 20 15
338 50f. multicoloured 60 40
339 100f. multicoloured . . . . 1·00 70

77 I.Y.Y. Emblem

1986. International Youth Year.
340 **77** 15f. multicoloured 20 15
341 50f. multicoloured 60 40
342 100f. multicoloured . . . . 1·00 70

78 Aerial View of Causeway

1986. Opening of Saudi–Bahrain Causeway. Mult.
343 15f. Type **78** 25 20
344 50f. Aerial view of island . . 60 40
345 100f. Aerial view of road bridge . . . . 1·00 70

79 Shaikh Isa bin Sulman al-Khalifa

1986. 25th Anniv of Accession of Shaikh Isa bin Sulman al-Khalifa.
346 **79** 15f. multicoloured 25 20
347 50f. multicoloured 60 40
348 100f. multicoloured . . . . 1·00 70

80 Emblem

1988. 40th Anniv of W.H.O.
350 **80** 50f. multicoloured 40 25
351 150f. multicoloured . . . . 1·25 90

81 Centre

1988. Opening of Ahmed al-Fateh Islamic Centre.
352 **81** 50f. multicoloured 40 25
353 150f. multicoloured . . . . 1·25 90

82 Running

1988. Olympic Games, Seoul. Multicoloured.
354 50f. Type **82** 30 20
355 80f. Dressage 60 40
356 150f. Fencing . . . . 1·10 80
357 200f. Football . . . . 1·90 1·40

83 Emblem in "1988"

1988. 9th Supreme Council Meeting of Gulf Co-operation Council.
358 **83** 50f. multicoloured 35 25
359 150f. multicoloured . . . . 1·25 90

84 Arab leading Camel

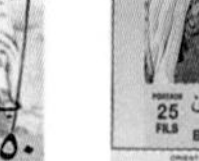

85 Shaikh Isa bin Sulman al-Khalifa

1989. Camels. Multicoloured.
360 150f. Type **84** . . . . 1·00 1·00
361 150f. Arab leading camel (different) . . . . 1·00 1·00
362 150f. Head of camel and pump-head . . . . . . 1·00 1·00
363 150f. Close-up of Arab on camel . . . . 1·00 1·00
364 150f. Arab riding camel . . . 1·00 1·00
365 150f. Two Arab camel-riders 1·00 1·00
366 150f. Head of camel and camel-rider (horiz) . . . . 1·00 1·00
367 150f. Camels at rest in camp (horiz) . . . . 1·00 1·00
368 150f. Camels with calf (horiz) 1·00 1·00
369 150f. Heads of three camels (horiz) . . . . 1·00 1·00
370 150f. Camel in scrubland (horiz) . . . . 1·00 1·00
371 150f. Arab on camel (horiz) 1·00 1·00

1989. Multicoloured, colour of frame given.
372 **85** 25f. green 20 10
373 40f. grey 30 10
374 50f. pink 30 10
375 60f. brown 40 15
376 75f. mauve 50 15
377 80f. green 50 15
378 100f. orange 70 25
379 120f. violet 80 25
380 150f. grey . . . . 1·00 35
381 200f. blue . . . . 1·25 45

86 Houbara Bustards

1990. The Houbara Bustard. Multicoloured.
383 150f. Type **86** . . . . 1·00 1·00
384 150f. Two bustards (facing each other) . . . . 1·00 1·00
385 150f. Chicks and eggs . . . . 1·00 1·00
386 150f. Adult and chick . . . . 1·00 1·00
387 150f. Adult (vert) . . . . . 1·00 1·00
388 150f. In flight . . . . 1·00 1·00
389 150f. Adult (facing right) . . 1·00 1·00
390 150f. Young bird (vert) . . . 1·00 1·00
391 150f. Adult (facing left) . . . 1·00 1·00
392 150f. Bird in display plumage 1·00 1·00
393 150f. Two bustards in display plumage . . . . 1·00 1·00
394 150f. Two bustards with bridge in background . . . 1·00 1·00

87 Anniversary Emblem

1990. 40th Anniv of Gulf Air.
395 **87** 50f. multicoloured 35 25
396 80f. multicoloured 55 35
397 150f. multicoloured . . . . 1·00 75
398 200f. multicoloured . . . . 1·40 95

88 Anniversary Emblem

1990. 50th Anniv of Bahrain Chamber of Commerce and Industry.
399 **88** 50f. multicoloured 30 20
400 80f. multicoloured 50 35
401 150f. multicoloured 95 65
402 200f. multicoloured . . . . 1·25 85

89 I.L.Y. Emblem

1990. International Literacy Year.
403 **89** 50f. multicoloured 30 20
404 80f. multicoloured 50 35
405 150f. multicoloured 95 65
406 200f. multicoloured . . . . 1·25 85

90 Crested Lark

1991. Birds. Multicoloured.
407 150f. Type **90** 90 90
408 150f. Hoopoe ("Upupa epops") 90 90
409 150f. White-cheeked bulbul ("Pycnonotus leucogenys") 90 90
410 150f. Turtle dove ("Streptopelia turtur") . . 90 90
411 150f. Collared dove ("Streptopelia decaocto") 90 90
412 150f. Common kestrel ("Falco tinnunculus") . . . 90 90
413 150f. House sparrow ("Passer domesticus") (horiz) . . . 90 90
414 150f. Great grey shrike ("Lanius excubitor") (horiz) 90 90
415 150f. Rose-ringed parakeet ("Psittacula krameri") . . 90 90

91 Shaikh Isa bin Sulman al-Khalifa

1991. 30th Anniv of Amir's Coronation.
416 **91** 50f. multicoloured 30 20
417 A 50f. multicoloured 30 20
418 **91** 80f. multicoloured 45 30
419 A 80f. multicoloured 45 30
420 **91** 150f. multicoloured 90 60
421 A 150f. multicoloured 90 60
422 **91** 200f. multicoloured . . . . 1·10 75
423 A 200f. multicoloured . . . . 1·10 75
DESIGN: A, The Amir and sunburst.

92 White Stork ("Ciconia ciconia")

1992. Migratory Birds. Multicoloured.
425 150f. Type **92** 80 80
426 150f. European bee eater ("Merops apiaster") . . . 80 80
427 150f. Common starling ("Sturnus vulgaris") . . . 80 80
428 150f. Grey hypocolius ("Hypocolius ampelinus") 80 80
429 150f. European cuckoo ("Cuculus canorus") . . . 80 80
430 150f. Mistle thrush ("Turdus viscivorus") 80 80
431 150f. European roller ("Coracias garrulus") . . . 80 80
432 150f. Eurasian goldfinch ("Carduelis carduelis") . . 80 80
433 150f. Red-backed shrike ("Lanius collurio") 80 80
434 150f. Redwing ("Turdus iliacus") (horiz) 80 80
435 150f. Pied wagtail ("Motacilla alba") (horiz) 80 80
436 150f. Golden oriole ("Oriolus oriolus") (horiz) 80 80
437 150f. European robin ("Erithacus rubecula") . . 80 80
438 150f. Nightingale ("Luscinia luscinia") 80 80
439 150f. Spotted flycatcher ("Muscicapa striata") . . . 80 80
440 150f. Barn swallow ("Hirundo rustica") . . . 80 80

93 Start of Race

1992. Horse-racing. Multicoloured.
441 150f. Type **93** 80 80
442 150f. Parading in paddock . . 80 80
443 150f. Galloping around bend 80 80
444 150f. Galloping past national flags 80 80
445 150f. Galloping past spectator stand 80 80
446 150f. Head-on view of horses 80 80
447 150f. Reaching winning post 80 80
448 150f. A black and a grey galloping 80 80

94 Show-jumping

1992. Olympic Games, Barcelona. Multicoloured.
449 50f. Type **94** 30 20
450 80f. Running 45 30
451 150f. Karate 85 55
452 200f. Cycling . . . . 1·10 75

95 Airport

1992. 60th Anniv of Bahrain International Airport.
453 **95** 50f. multicoloured 30 20
454 80f. multicoloured 45 30
455 150f. multicoloured 85 55
456 200f. multicoloured . . . . 1·10 75

96 Girl skipping

98 Artillery Gun Crew

97 Cable-cars and Pylons

1992. Children's Paintings. Multicoloured.
457 50f. Type **96** 30 20
458 80f. Women 45 30

459 150f. Women preparing food (horiz) 85 55
460 200f. Pearl divers (horiz) . . 1·40 75

1992. Expansion of Aluminium Industry. Mult.
461 50f. Type **97** 30 20
462 80f. Worker in aluminium plant 45 30
463 150f. Aerial view of aluminium plant 85 55
464 200f. Processed aluminium 1·10 75

1993. 25th Anniv of Bahrain Defence Force. Mult.
465 50f. Type **98** 25 15
466 80f. General Dynamics Fighting Falcon jet fighters, tanks and patrol boat . . . 40 25
467 150f. "Ahmed al Fatah" (missile corvette) (horiz) . . 75 50
468 200f. Fighting Falcon over Bahrain (horiz) . . . . . 1·00 65

99 Satellite View of Bahrain **100** Purple Heron

1993. World Meteorological Day. Multicoloured.
469 50f. Type **99** 30 20
470 150f. Satellite picture of world (horiz) 75 60
471 200f. Earth seen from space 1·25 85

1993. Water Birds. Multicoloured.
472 150f. Type **100** 90 90
473 150f. Moorhen ("Gallinula chloropus") 90 90
474 150f. Socotra cormorant ("Phalacrocorax nigrogularis") 90 90
475 150f. Crab plover ("Dromas ardeola") 90 90
476 150f. River kingfisher ("Alcedo atthis") 90 90
477 150f. Northern lapwing ("Vanellus vanellus") . . . 90 90
478 150f. Oystercatcher ("Haematopus ostralegus") (horiz) 90 90
479 150f. Black-crowned night heron ("Nycticorax nycticorax") 90 90
480 150f. Caspian tern ("Sterna caspia") (horiz) 90 90
481 150f. Ruddy turnstone ("Arenaria interpres") (horiz) 90 90
482 150f. Water rail ("Rallus aquaticus") (horiz) 90 90
483 150f. Mallard ("Anas platyrhyncos) (horiz) . . . 90 90
484 150f. Lesser black-backed gull ("Larus fuscus") (horiz) . . 90 90

101 Fawn

1993. The Goitered Gazelle. Multicoloured.
485 25f. Type **101** 15 10
486 50f. Doe walking 25 15
487 50f. Doe with ears pricked 25 15
488 150f. Male gazelle 75 60

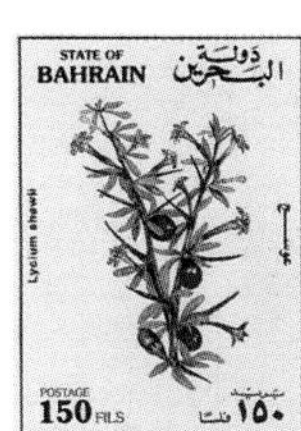
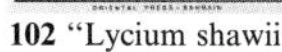

102 "Lycium shawii" **103** Children and Silhouettes of Parents' Heads

1993. Wild Flowers. Multicoloured.
489 150f. Type **102** 75 75
490 150f. "Alhagi maurorum" . . 75 75
491 150f. Caper-bush ("Caparis spinosa") 75 75
492 150f. "Cistanche phelypae" 75 75
493 150f. "Asphodelus tenuifolius" 75 75
494 150f. "Limonium axillare" . . 75 75
495 150f. "Cynomorium coccineum" 75 75
496 150f. "Calligonum polygonoides" 75 75

1994. International Year of the Family.
497 **103** 50f. multicoloured 20 15
498 80f. multicoloured 30 20
499 150f. multicoloured . . . 65 45
500 200f. multicoloured . . . 80 55

104 "Lepidochrysops arabicus" **105** Anniversary Emblem

1994. Butterflies. Multicoloured.
501 50f. Type **104** 20 20
502 50f. "Ypthima bolanica" . . 20 20
503 50f. Desert grass yellow ("Eurema brigitta") . . . 20 20
504 50f. "Precis limnoria" . . . 20 20
505 50f. Small tortoiseshell ("Aglais urticae") 20 20
506 50f. Protomedia ("Colotis protomedia") 20 20
507 50f. Clouded mother-of-pearl (Salamis anacardii") . . . 20 20
508 50f. "Byblia ilithyia" 20 20
509 150f. Swallowtail ("Papilio machaon") (horiz) 65 65
510 150f. Blue ("Agrodiaetus loewii") (horiz) 65 65
511 150f. Painted lady ("Vanessa cardui") (horiz) 65 65
512 150f. Chequered swallowtail ("Papilio demoleus") (horiz) 65 65
513 150f. Guineafowl ("Hamanumida daedalus") (horiz) 65 65
514 150f. "Funonia orithya" (horiz) 65 65
515 150f. "Funonia chorimine" (horiz) 65 65
516 150f. "Colias croceus" (horiz) 65 65

1994. 75th Anniv of International Red Cross and Red Crescent.
517 **105** 50f. multicoloured 20 15
518 80f. multicoloured 30 20
519 150f. multicoloured . . . 65 45
520 200f. multicoloured . . . 80 55

106 Goalkeeper

1994. World Cup Football Championship, U.S.A. Multicoloured.
521 50f. Type **106** 20 15
522 80f. Players 30 20
523 150f. Players' legs 65 45
524 200f. Player on ground . . . 80 55

107 Earth Station

1994. 25th Anniv of Ras Abu Jarjour Satellite Earth Station.
525 **107** 50f. multicoloured 20 15
526 80f. multicoloured 30 20
527 150f. multicoloured . . . 65 45
528 200f. multicoloured . . . 80 55

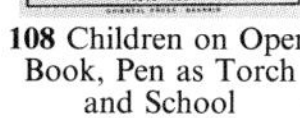

108 Children on Open Book, Pen as Torch and School **109** Dove with "Olive Branch" of Members' Flags

1994. 75th Anniv of Education in Bahrain.
529 **108** 50f. multicoloured 20 15
530 80f. multicoloured 30 20
531 150f. multicoloured . . . 65 45
532 200f. multicoloured . . . 80 55

1994. 15th Gulf Co-operation Council Supreme Council Session, Bahrain.
533 **109** 50f. multicoloured 20 15
534 80f. multicoloured 30 20
535 150f. multicoloured . . . 65 45
536 200f. multicoloured . . . 80 55

110 Date Palm Tree in Bloom

1995. The Date Palm.
537 80f. Type **110** 25 15
538 100f. Date palm with unripened dates 35 25
539 200f. Dates ripening 65 45
540 250f. Date palm trees with ripened dates 80 55

111 Campaign Emblem

1995. World Health Day. Anti-poliomyelitis Campaign.
542 **111** 80f. multicoloured 25 15
543 200f. multicoloured . . . 65 45
544 250f. multicoloured . . . 80 55

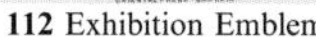
112 Exhibition Emblem **114** Headquarters, Cairo

113 Crops

1995. 1st National Industries Exhibition.
545 **112** 80f. multicoloured 25 15
546 200f. multicoloured . . . 65 45
547 250f. multicoloured . . . 80 55

1995. 50th Anniv of F.A.O. Multicoloured.
548 80f. Type **113** 25 15
549 200f. Field of crops 65 45
550 250f. Field of cabbages . . . 80 55

1995. 50th Anniv of Arab League.
551 **114** 80f. multicoloured 25 15
552 200f. multicoloured . . . 65 45
553 250f. multicoloured . . . 80 55

115 U.N. Headquarters and Map of Bahrain

1995. 50th Anniv of U.N.O.
554 **115** 80f. multicoloured 25 15
555 100f. multicoloured . . . 35 25
556 200f. multicoloured . . . 65 45
557 250f. multicoloured . . . 80 55

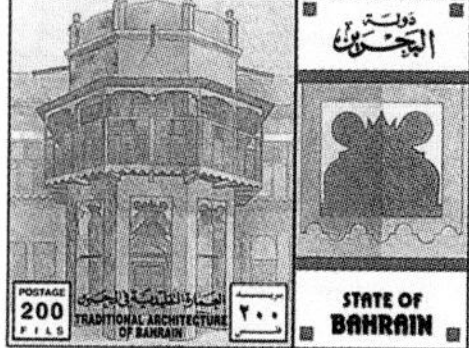
116 Tower

1995. Traditional Architecture. Multicoloured.
558 200f. Type **116** 65 65
559 200f. Balcony 65 65
560 200f. Doorway 65 65
561 200f. Multi-storied facade . . 65 65
562 200f. Entrance flanked by two windows 65 65
563 200f. Three arched windows 65 65

117 National Flag and Shaikh Isa Bin Sulman al-Khalifa **118** Bookcase and Open Book

1995. National Day.
564 **117** 80f. multicoloured 25 15
565 100f. multicoloured . . . 35 25
566 200f. multicoloured . . . 65 45
567 250f. multicoloured . . . 85 55

1996. 50th Anniv of Public Library.
568 **118** 80f. multicoloured 25 15
569 200f. multicoloured . . . 65 45
570 250f. multicoloured . . . 85 55

119 Divers on Dhow

1996. Pearl Diving. Multicoloured.
571 80f. Type **119** 40 15
572 100f. Divers 70 25
573 200f. Diver on sea-bed and dhow . . . . 1·00 45
574 250f. Diver with net 85 55

120 Globe, Ship and Olympic Rings

1996. Olympic Games, Atlanta.
576 **120** 80f. multicoloured 25 15
577 100f. multicoloured . . . 35 25
578 200f. multicoloured . . . 65 45
579 250f. multicoloured . . . 85 55

121 Interpol Emblem and Map, Arms and Flag of Bahrain

1996. 24th Anniv of Membership of International Criminal Police (Interpol).
580 **121** 80f. multicoloured 25 15
581 100f. multicoloured . . . 35 25
582 200f. multicoloured . . . 65 45
583 250f. multicoloured . . . 85 55

122 Anniversary Emblems in English and Arabic

1996. 25th Anniv of Aluminium Bahrain.

584	**122**	80f. multicoloured	25	15
585		100f. multicoloured	30	20
586		200f. multicoloured	65	45
587		250f. multicoloured	80	55

123 National Flag, Map and Shaikh Isa bin Sulman al-Khalifa

1996. 35th Anniv of Amir's Accession.

588	**123**	80f. multicoloured	25	15
589		100f. multicoloured	30	20
590		200f. multicoloured	65	45
591		250f. multicoloured	80	55

124 Tanker, Refinery and Storage Tanks

1997. 60th Anniv of Bahrain Refinery.

592	**124**	80f. multicoloured	25	20
593		200f. multicoloured	65	50
594		250f. multicoloured	85	70

125 Kuheilaan Weld umm Zorayr

1997. Arab Horses at Amiri Stud. Multicoloured.

595	200f. Musannaan (white horse), Al-Jellabieh and Rabdaan	65	65
596	200f. Type **125**	65	65
597	200f. Al-Jellaby	65	65
598	200f. Musannaan (brown horse)	65	65
599	200f. Kuheilaan Aladiyat	65	65
600	200f. Kuheilaan Aafas	65	65
601	200f. Al-Dhahma	65	65
602	200f. Mlolshaan	65	65
603	200f. Al-Kray	65	65
604	200f. Krush	65	65
605	200f. Al Hamdaany	65	65
606	200f. Hadhfaan	65	65
607	200f. Rabda	65	65
608	200f. Al-Suwaitieh	65	65
609	200f. Al-Obeyah	65	65
610	200f. Al-Shuwaimeh	65	65
611	200f. Al-Ma'anaghieh	65	65
612	200f. Al-Tuwaisah	65	65
613	200f. Wadhna	65	65
614	200f. Al-Saqlawieh	65	65
615	200f. Al-Shawafah	65	65

126 Championship Emblem

1997. 9th World Men's Junior Volleyball Championship.

616	**126**	80f. multicoloured	25	15
617		100f. multicoloured	30	20
618		200f. multicoloured	65	45
619		250f. multicoloured	80	55

127 Emblem

1997. 10th Anniv of Montreal Protocol (on reduction of use of chlorofluorocarbons).

620	**127**	80f. multicoloured	25	15
621		100f. multicoloured	30	20
622		200f. multicoloured	65	45
623		250f. multicoloured	80	55

128 Close-up of Support

1997. Inauguration of Shaikh Isa bin Salman Bridge between Manama and Muharraq. Multicoloured.

624	80f. Type **128**	25	15
625	200f. Distant view of middle section	65	45
626	250f. View of complete bridge (75 × 26 mm)	80	55

129 Complex at Night

1998. Inauguration of Urea Plant at Gulf Petrochemical Industries Co Complex. Mult.

628	80f. Type **129**	25	15
629	200f. Refining towers	65	45
630	250f. Aerial view of complex	80	55

130 Map of Bahrain and Anniversary Emblem

1998. 50th Anniv of W.H.O.

631	**130**	80f. multicoloured	25	15
632		200f. multicoloured	65	45
633		250f. multicoloured	80	55

131 Emblem

1998. World Cup Football Championship, France. Multicoloured.

634	80f. Type **131**	25	15
635	200f. Globes and football forming "98" (vert)	65	45
636	250f. Footballers and globe (vert)	80	55

132 Football

1998. 14th Arabian Gulf Cup Football Championship, Bahrain. Multicoloured.

637	80f. Type **132**	25	15
638	200f. Close-up of football	65	45
639	250f. As No. 638	85	55

133 Emblem and Koran

1999. Holy Koran Reading Competition.

640	**133**	100f. multicoloured	30	20
641		200f. multicoloured	65	45
642		250f. multicoloured	85	55

134 Shaikh Isa bin Sulman al-Khalifa and State Flag

1999. Shaikh Isa bin Sulman al-Khalifa Commemoration. Multicoloured.

643	100f. Type **134**	30	20
644	200f. Shaikh and map of Bahrain (41 × 31 mm)	65	45
645	250f. Shaikh, map of Bahrain and state flag	80	55

135 Emblem

1999. International Year of the Elderly. Mult.

647	100f. Type **135**	30	20
648	200f. Emblem and flame	65	45
649	250f. Emblem (different)	80	55

136 Emblem

1999. 10th Anniv of Bahrain Stock Exchange. Multicoloured.

650	100f. Type **136**	30	20
651	200f. Shaikh Isa bin Salman Bridge and emblem	65	40
652	250f. Globe and emblem	80	55

137 Shaikh Isa bin Salman and Shaikh Hamad bin Isa holding Flag

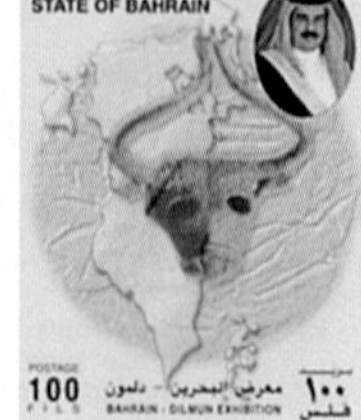

138 Map of Bahrain and Animal Skull

1999. National Day. Multicoloured.

653	100f. Type **137**	30	20
654	200f. Shaikh Hamad bin Isa and flag	65	40
655	250f. Shaikh Hamad bin Isa and globe	80	55

2000. Dilmun Exhibition. Multicoloured.

657	100f. Type **138**	35	25
658	200f. Map of Bahrain superimposed over animal skull	75	50
659	250f. Map of Bahrain and artefact	90	60

139 Map of Bahrain and Emblem

2000. 50th Anniv of Gulf Air. Multicoloured.

660	100f. Type **139**	35	25
661	200f. Map of Bahrain and emblem in circle	75	50
662	250f. Map of Bahrain, emblem and eagles	90	60

140 Emblem

2000. "Made in Bahrain 2000" Exhibition. Multicoloured.

663	100f. Type **140**	45	25
664	200f. Type **140**	75	50
665	250f. Oil refinery	90	60

141 Minarets and Fort

2000. Millennium. Multicoloured.

666	100f. Type **141**	45	25
667	100f. Dhows and factories	45	25
668	100f. Man harvesting dates	45	25
669	100f. Fort, globe and dish aerial	45	25
670	200f. Lake and bridge	75	50
671	200f. Modern building and woman	75	50
672	200f. Dhows, jug and wicker basket	75	50
673	200f. Horseman and falconer	75	50
674	250f. Pearl divers	90	60
675	250f. Opening clams	90	60
676	250f. Fishermen	90	60
677	250f. Man mending fishing nets	90	60

142 Emblem

2000. 21st Gulf Co-operation Council Supreme Council Session, Bahrain. Multicoloured.

678	100f. Type **142**	35	20
679	200f. Members' flags	70	40

143 Stained-glass Window

2001. 10th Anniv of Beit Al Qur'an (Islamic institution). Multicoloured.

680	100f. Type **143**	35	20
681	200f. Beit Al Qur'an by night	70	40
682	250f. Facade	90	55

144 Building

2001. 25th Anniv of Ministry of Housing and Agriculture. Multicoloured.

684	100f. Type **144**	35	20
685	150f. Sculpture and building	55	35
686	200f. Building viewed through arch	70	40
687	250f. Tall, arched building	90	55

145 Emblem and Stylized Figures

2001. International Year of Volunteers. Multicoloured.
688 100f. Type **145** 35 20
689 150f. Hands encircling emblem 55 35
690 200f. Star pattern and emblem 70 40
691 250f. Paper cut figures . . . 90 55

146 Emblem

2002. Arab Women's Day. Multicoloured.
692 100f. Type **146** 35 20
693 200f. Elliptical shapes and emblem 65 40
694 250f. Women (horiz) 80 45

147 Football and Emblem 148 Shaikh Hamad Bin Isa Al Khalifa

2002. World Cup Football Championship, Japan and South Korea. Sheet 124 × 64 mm containing T **147** and similar vert designs. Multicoloured.
MS695 100f. Type **147**; 200f. Earth, football and emblem; 250f. Football and white peaks 1·75 1·75

2002. Multicoloured, background colour given.
(a) Size 22 × 28 mm.
696 **148** 25f. brown 10 10
697 40f. purple 15 10
698 50f. grey 15 10
699 60f. blue 20 15
700 80f. blue 25 15
701 100f. orange 30 20
702 125f. mauve 40 25
703 150f. orange 45 25
704 200f. green 60 35
705 250f. pink 80 50
706 300f. brown . . . . . . 1·00 60
707 400f. green . . . . . . 1·25 75

2002. (b) 26 × 36 mm.
708 500f. mauve . . . . 1·60 95
709 1d. orange 30 20
710 2d. blue 60 35
711 3d. brown . . . . 1·00 60
MS712 246 × 162 mm. Nos. 696/711 9·25 9·50

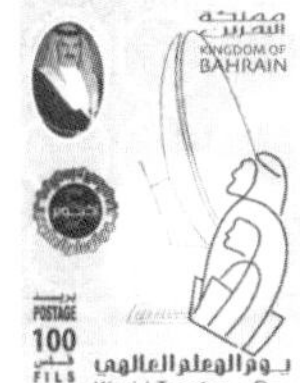

149 Stylized Teacher, Child and Symbols of Communication

2002. World Teacher's Day.
713 **149** 100f. multicoloured . . . 30 20
714 200f. multicoloured . . . 60 35

150 Emblem

2002. Parliamentary Election, 2002. Multicoloured.
715 100f. Type **150** 30
716 200f. Hand posting voting slip (vert) 60

151 Shaikh Hamad Bin Isa Al Khalifa and Flag

2002. National Day. Multicoloured.
717 100f. Type **151** 30
718 200f. Shaikh Hamad Bin Isa and flag (different) (vert) 60
719 250f. As No. 718 but with maroon background (vert) 80

WAR TAX STAMPS

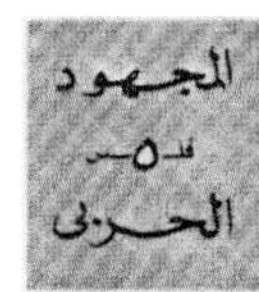

T **36** "War Effort" T **37** "War Effort"

1973.
T192 T **36** 5f. blue and cobalt . .

1973.
T194a T **37** 5f. blue . . . . 1·00 10

BAMRA Pt. 1

A state in India. Now uses Indian stamps.

12 pies = 1 anna; 16 annas = 1 rupee.

1 8

1888.
1 **1** ¼a. black on yellow £350
2 ½a. black on rose . . . . . . 70·00
3 1a. black on blue . . . . . . 48·00
4 2a. black on green . . . . . 70·00 £250
5 4a. black on yellow . . . . . 60·00 £250
6 8a. black on red . . . . . . 38·00

1890. Imperf.
10 **8** ¼a. black on red . . . . . . 1·75 2·25
11 ½a. black on green . . . . . 2·25 2·75
30 1a. black on yellow . . . . . 3·50 2·75
16 2a. black on red . . . . . . 3·75 4·25
19 4a. black on red . . . . . . 8·00 5·00
22 8a. black on red . . . . . . 12·00 15·00
25 1r. black on red . . . . . . 16·00 19·00

BANGLADESH Pt. 1

Formerly the Eastern wing of Pakistan. Following a landslide victory at the Pakistan General Election in December 1970 by the Awami League party the National Assembly was suspended. Unrest spread throughout the eastern province culminating in the intervention of India on the side of the East Bengalis. The new state became effective after the surrender of the Pakistan army in December 1971.

1971. 100 paisa = 1 rupee.
1972. 100 paisa = 1 taka.

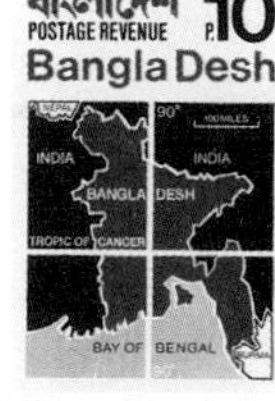

1 Map of Bangladesh 3 "Martyrdom"

1971.
1 **1** 10p. indigo, orange and blue 10 10
2 – 20p. multicoloured 10 10
3 – 50p. multicoloured 10 10
4 – 1r. multicoloured 10 10
5 – 2r. turquoise, blue and red . . 25 35
6 – 3r. light green, green and blue 30 55
7 – 5r. multicoloured . . . . . . 50 1·00
8 – 10r. gold, red and blue . . . . 1·00 2·00
DESIGNS: 20p. "Dacca University Massacre"; 50p. "75 Million People"; 1r. Flag of Independence; 2r. Ballot box; 3r. Broken chain; 5r. Shaikh Majibur Rahman; 10r. "Support Bangla Desh" and map.

1971. Liberation. Nos. 1 and 7/8 optd **BANGLADESH LIBERATED**.
9 10p. indigo, orange and blue 20 10
10 5r. multicoloured . . . . . . 2·00 2·50
11 10r. gold, red and blue . . . . 2·50 3·25

The remaining values of the original issue were also overprinted and placed on sale in Great Britian but were not issued in Bangladesh.

On 1 February 1972 the Agency placed on sale a further issue in the flag, map and Sheikh Mujib designs in new colours and new currency (100 paisa = 1 taka). This issue proved to be unacceptable to the Bangladesh authorities who declared them to be invalid for postal purposes, no supplies being sold within Bangladesh. The values comprise 1, 2, 3, 5, 7, 10, 15, 20, 25, 40, 50, 75p., 1, 2 and 5t.

1972. In Memory of the Martyrs.
12 **3** 20p. green and red 30 50

4 Flames of Independence 5 Doves of Peace

1972. 1st Anniv of Independence.
13 **4** 20p. lake and red 20 10
14 60p. blue and red 25 45
15 75p. violet and red 30 55

1972. Victory Day.
16 **5** 20p. multicoloured 25 10
17 60p. multicoloured 40 70
18 75p. multicoloured 45 70

6 "Homage to Martyrs" 7 Embroidered Quilt

8 Court of Justice 9 Flame Emblem

1973. In Memory of the Martyrs.
19 **6** 20p. multicoloured 15 10
20 60p. multicoloured 30 40
21 1t.35 multicoloured . . . . . 65 1·75

1973.
22 **7** 2p. black 10 80
23 – 3p. green 20 80
24 – 5p. brown 20 10
25 – 10p. black 20 10
26 – 20p. green 50 10
27 – 25p. mauve . . . . 3·00 10
28 – 50p. purple . . . . 2·00 30
29 – 60p. grey . . . . 1·00 75
30 – 75p. orange . . . . 1·00 75
31 – 90p. brown . . . . 1·25 1·50
32 **8** 1t. violet . . . . 5·00 30
33 – 2t. green . . . . 5·00 65
34 – 5t. blue . . . . 6·00 2·00
35 – 10t. pink . . . . 6·50 4·00
DESIGNS—As Type **7**: 3p. Jute field; 5p. Jack fruit; 10p. Bullocks ploughing; 20p. Rakta jaba (flower); 25p. Tiger; 60p. Bamboo grove; 75p. Plucking tea; 90p. Handicrafts. (28 × 22 mm): 50p. Hilsa (fish). As Type **8**. VERT: 2t. Date tree. HORIZ: 5t. Fishing boat; 10t. Sixty-dome mosque, Bagerhat.
See also Nos. 49/51a, 64/75 and 711.

1973. 25th Anniv of Declaration of Human Rights.
36 **9** 10p. multicoloured 10 10
37 1t.25 multicoloured 20 20

10 Family, Map and Graph 11 Copernicus and Heliocentric System

1974. First Population Census.
38 **10** 20p. multicoloured 10 10
39 25p. multicoloured 10 10
40 75p. multicoloured 20 20

1974. 500th Birth Anniv of Copernicus.
41 **11** 25p. orange, violet and black 10 10
42 75p. orange, green and black 25 50

12 U.N. H.Q. and Bangladesh Flag 13 U.P.U. Emblem

1974. Bangladesh's Admission to the U.N.
43 **12** 25p. multicoloured 10 10
44 1t. multicoloured 35 40

1974. Centenary of Universal Postal Union. Mult.
45 25p. Type **13** 10 10
46 1t.25 Mail runner 20 15
47 1t.75 Type **13** 20 25
48 5t. As 1t.25 . . . . 80 1·60

14 Courts of Justice

1974. As Nos. 32/5 with revised inscriptions.
49 **14** 1t. violet . . . . 1·50 10
50 – 2t. olive . . . . 2·00 1·75
51 – 5t. blue . . . . 7·00 70
51a – 10t. pink . . . . 15·00 12·00
For these designs redrawn to 32 × 20 mm or 20 × 32 mm, see Nos. 72/5 and, to 35 × 22 mm, see No. 711.

15 Tiger 16 Symbolic Family

1974. Wildlife Preservation. Multicoloured.
52 25p. Type **15** 70 10
53 50p. Tiger cub . . . . 1·00 70
54 2t. Tiger in stream . . . . . 1·75 3·50

1974. World Population Year. "Family Planning for All". Multicoloured.
55 25p. Type **16** 15 10
56 70p. Village family 25 50
57 1t.25 Heads of family (horiz) 40 1·10

17 Radar Antenna 19 Telephones of 1876 and 1976

18 Woman's Head

1975. Inauguration of Betbunia Satellite Earth Station.
58 **17** 25p. black, silver and red . . 10 10
59 1t. black, silver and blue . . 20 70

1975. International Women's Year.
60 **18** 50p. multicoloured 10 10
61 2t. multicoloured . . . . . 25 1·00

1976. As Nos. 24/31 and 49/51a but redrawn in smaller size.
64 – 5p. green 20 10
65 – 10p. black 20 10
66 – 20p. green 70 10
67 – 25p. mauve . . . . 3·25 10
68 – 50p. purple . . . . 3·25 10
69 – 60p. grey 40 20
70 – 75p. green . . . . 1·25 2·75
71 – 90p. brown 40 20
72 **14** 1t. violet . . . . 2·00 10
73 – 2t. green . . . . 7·50 10
74 – 5t. blue . . . . 3·25 2·75
75 – 10t. red . . . . 8·50 3·00

Nos. 64/71 are 23 × 18 mm (50p.) or 18 × 23 mm (others) and Nos. 72/75 are 20 × 32 mm (2t.) or 32 × 20 mm (others).

For the 10t. redrawn to 35 × 22 mm, see No. 711.

1976. Centenary of Telephone.
76 **19** 2t.25 multicoloured 25 20
77 – 5t. red, green and black . . 55 65
DESIGN: 5t. Alexander Graham Bell.

20 Eye and Nutriments

1976. Prevention of Blindness.
78 **20** 30p. multicoloured 50 10
79 2t.25 multicoloured . . . . 1·40 2·25

21 Liberty Bell

1976. Bicentenary of American Revolution. Mult.
80 30p. Type **21** 10 10
81 2t.25 Statue of Liberty 20 25
82 5t. "Mayflower" 55 50
83 10t. Mount Rushmore 55 80
MS84 167 × 95 mm. No. 83 . . . 1·50 3·00

22 Industry, Science, Agriculture and Education

23 Hurdling

1976. 25th Anniv of Colombo Plan.
85 **22** 30p. multicoloured 15 10
86 2t.25 multicoloured . . . . 35 1·00

1976. Olympic Games, Montreal. Multicoloured.
87 25p. Type **23** 10 10
88 30p. Running (horiz) 10 10
89 1t. Pole vaulting 15 10
90 2t.25 Swimming (horiz) . . . 30 45
91 3t.50 Gymnastics . . . . . . 55 1·25
92 5t. Football . . . . 1·00 2·00

24 The Blessing **25** Qazi Nazrul Islam (poet)

1977. Silver Jubilee. Multicoloured.
93 30p. Type **24** 10 10
94 2t.25 Queen Elizabeth II . . . 20 25
95 10t. Queen Elizabeth and Prince Philip 70 85
MS96 114 × 127 mm. Nos. 93/5 . . 80 1·50

1977. Qazi Nazrul Islam Commemoration.
97 **25** 40p. green and black . . . 10 10
98 – 2t.25 brown, red & lt brn . . 30 30
DESIGN—HORIZ: 2t.25, Head and shoulders portrait.

26 Bird with Letter

1977. 15th Anniv of Asian–Oceanic Postal Union.
99 **26** 30p. red, blue and grey . . 10 10
100 2t.25 red, blue and grey . . 20 25

27 Sloth Bear **28** Campfire and Tent

1977. Animals. Multicoloured.
101 40p. Type **27** 15 10
102 1t. Spotted deer 15 10
103 2t.25 Leopard (horiz) 30 20
104 3t.50 Gaur (horiz) 30 35
105 4t. Indian elephant (horiz) . . 80 50
106 5t. Tiger (horiz) 90 75

The Bengali numerals on the 40p. resemble "80", and that on the 4t. resembles "8".

1978. First National Scout Jamboree.
107 **28** 40p. red, blue and pale blue 30 10
108 – 3t.50 lilac, green and blue 1·25 30
109 – 5t. green, blue and red . . 1·40 45
DESIGNS—HORIZ: 3t.50, Scout stretcher-team. VERT: 5t. Scout salute.

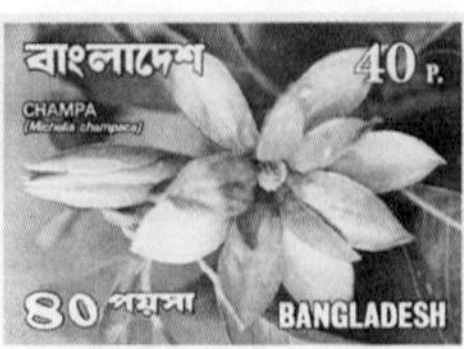

29 "Michelia champaca"

1978. Flowers. Multicoloured.
110 40p. Type **29** 20 10
111 1t. "Cassia fistula" 30 15
112 2t.25 "Delonix regia" 40 30
113 3t.50 "Nymphaea nouchali" . . 45 60
114 4t. "Butea monosperma" . . 45 80
115 5t. "Anthocephalus indicus" . 45 85

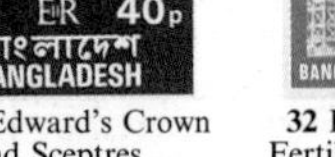

30 St. Edward's Crown and Sceptres **32** Fenchuganj Fertiliser Factory

31 Sir Alan Cobham's De Havilland D.H.50

1978. 25th Anniv of Coronation. Multicoloured.
116 40p. Type **30** 10 10
117 3t.50 Balcony scene 15 30
118 5t. Queen Elizabeth and Prince Philip 25 50
119 10t. Coronation portrait by Cecil Beaton 45 80
MS120 89 × 121 mm. Nos. 116/19 1·10 1·50

1978. 75th Anniv of Powered Flight.
121 **31** 40p. multicoloured 15 10
122 – 2t.25 brown and blue . . . 30 45
123 – 3t.50 brown and yellow . . 35 65
124 – 5t. multicoloured . . . . . 3·00 3·50
DESIGNS: 2t.25, Captain Hans Bertram's seaplane "Atlantis"; 3t.50, Wright brothers' Flyer III; 5t. Concorde.

1978.
125 – 5p. brown 10 10
126 **32** 10p. blue 10 10
127 – 15p. orange 10 10
128 – 20p. red 10 10
129 – 25p. blue 15 10
130 – 30p. green . . . . 2·25 10
131 – 40p. purple 30 10
132 – 50p. black . . . . 4·00 1·50
134 – 80p. brown 20 10
136 – 1t. violet . . . . 5·50 10
137 – 2t. blue . . . . 1·75 2·75
DESIGNS—HORIZ: 5p. Lalbag Fort; 25p. Jute on a boat; 40, 50p. Baitul Mukarram Mosque; 1t. Dotara (musical instrument); 2t. Karnaphuli Dam. VERT: 15p. Pineapple; 20p. Bangladesh gas; 30p. Banana tree; 80p. Mohastan Garh.

33 Tawaf-E-Ka'aba, Mecca **35** Moulana Abdul Hamid Khan Bhashani

34 Jasim Uddin

1978. Pilgrimage to Mecca. Multicoloured.
140 40p. Type **33** 20 10
141 3t. Pilgrims in Wuquf, Arafat (horiz) 60 45

1979. 3rd Death Anniv of Jasim Uddin (poet).
142 **34** 40p. multicoloured 20 50

1979. 3rd Death Anniv of Moulana Abdul Hamid Khan Bhashani (national leader).
143 **35** 40p. multicoloured 40 30

36 Sir Rowland Hill **37** Children with Hoops

1979. Death Centenary of Sir Rowland Hill.
144 **36** 40p. blue, red and light blue 10 10
145 – 3t.50 multicoloured 35 30
146 – 10t. multicoloured . . . . 80 1·00
MS147 176 × 96 mm. Nos. 144/6 2·00 2·75
DESIGNS: 3t.50, Sir Rowland Hill and first Bangladesh stamp; 10t. Sir Rowland Hill and Bangladesh U.P.U. stamp.

1979. International Year of the Child. Multicoloured.
148 40p. Type **37** 10 10
149 3t.50 Boy with kite 35 35
150 5t. Children jumping 50 50
MS151 170 × 120 mm. Nos. 148/50 1·50 2·75

38 Rotary International Emblem **40** A. K. Fazlul Huq

39 Canal Digging

1980. 75th Anniv of Rotary International.
152 **38** 40p. black, red and yellow 20 10
153 – 5t. gold and blue 65 45
DESIGN: 5t. Rotary emblem (different).

1980. Mass Participation in Canal Digging.
154 **39** 40p. multicoloured 40 30

1980. 18th Death Anniv of A. K. Fazlul Huq (national leader).
155 **40** 40p. multicoloured 30 30

41 Early Forms of Mail Transport

1980. "London 1980" International Stamp Exhibition. Multicoloured.
156 1t. Type **41** 15 10
157 10t. Modern forms of mail transport . . . . 1·25 90

42 Dome of the Rock **43** Outdoor Class

1980. Palestinian Welfare.
159 **42** 50p. lilac 70 30

1980. Education.
160 **43** 50p. multicoloured 40 30

44 Beach Scene

1980. World Tourism Conference, Manila. Mult.
161 50p. Type **44** 35 50
162 5t. Beach scene (different) . . 65 1·10
MS163 140 × 88 mm. Nos. 161/2 . 1·00 1·50

45 Mecca **46** Begum Roquiah

1980. Moslem Year 1400 A. H. Commemoration.
164 **45** 50p. multicoloured 20 20

1980. Birth Centenary of Begum Roquiah (campaigner for women's rights).
165 **46** 50p. multicoloured 10 10
166 2t. multicoloured 35 20

47 Spotted Deer and Scout Emblem

49 Queen Elizabeth the Queen Mother

1981. 5th Asia–Pacific and 2nd Bangladesh Scout Jamboree.
167 **47** 50p. multicoloured 40 15
168 5t. multicoloured . . . . . 1·25 2·00

1981. 2nd Population Census. Nos. 38/40 optd **2nd. CENSUS 1981**.
169 **10** 20p. multicoloured 10 10
170 25p. multicoloured 10 10
171 75p. multicoloured 20 30

1981. 80th Birthday of the Queen Mother.
172 **49** 1t. multicoloured 15 15
173 15t. multicoloured . . . . 1·75 2·50
MS174 95 × 73 mm. Nos. 172/3 2·40 2·50

50 Revolutionary with Flag and Sub-machine-gun

52 Kemal Ataturk in Civilian Dress

51 Bangladesh Village and Farm Scenes

1981. 10th Anniv of Independence. Mult.
175 50p. Type **50** 15 10
176 2t. Figures on map symbolizing Bangladesh life style 25 45

1981. U.N. Conference on Least Developed Countries, Paris.
177 **51** 50p. multicoloured 35 15

1981. Birth Centenary of Kemal Ataturk (Turkish statesman).
178 50p. Type **52** 45 30
179 1t. Kemal Ataturk in uniform 80 1·25

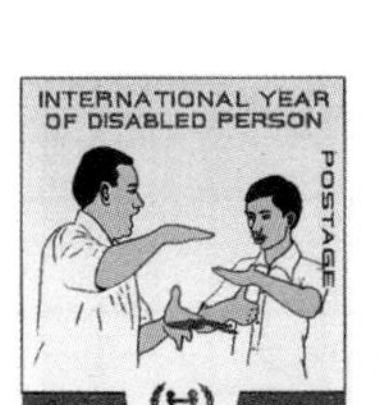

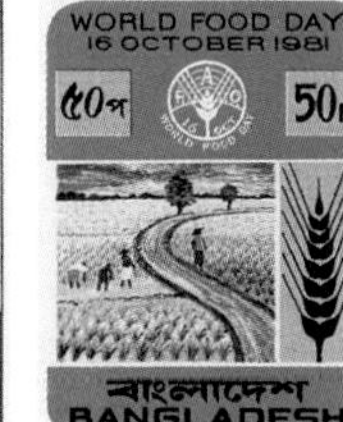

53 Deaf People using Sign Language

54 Farm Scene and Wheat Ear

1981. Int Year for Disabled Persons. Mult.
180 50p. Type **53** 40 20
181 2t. Disabled person writing (horiz) . . . . 85 2·25

1981. World Food Day.
182 **54** 50p. multicoloured 50 80

55 River Scene

56 Dr. M. Hussain

1982. 10th Anniv of Human Environment Conference.
183 **55** 50p. multicoloured 50 80

1982. 1st Death Anniv of Dr. Motahar Hussain (educationist).
184 **56** 50p. multicoloured 50 80

57 Knotted Rope surrounding Bengali "75"

1982. 75th Anniv of Boy Scout Movement and 125th Birth Anniv of Lord Baden-Powell. Multicoloured.
185 50p. Type **57** 75 30
186 2t. Lord Baden-Powell (vert) 2·25 4·25

সম্মিলিত
সশস্ত্র বাহিনী দিবস
২১ নভেম্বর,৮২

(58)

60 Metric Scales

59 Captain Mohiuddin Jahangir

1982. Armed Forces' Day. No. 175 optd with T **58**.
187 50p. Type **50** . . . . 2·75 2·75

1983. Heroes and Martyrs of the Liberation. Multicoloured, background colour of commemorative plaque given.
188 50p. Type **59** (orange) . . . 30 45
189 50p. Sepoy Hamidur Rahman (green) 30 45
190 50p. Sepoy Mohammed Mustafa Kamal (red) . . . 30 45
191 50p. Muhammed Ruhul Amin (yellow) 30 45
192 50p. Flt. Lt. M. Matiur Rahman (brown) 30 45
193 50p. Lance-Naik Munshi Abdur Rob (brown) . . . 30 45
194 50p. Lance-Naik Nur Mouhammad (green) . . . 30 45

1983. Introduction of Metric Weights and Measures. Multicoloured.
195 50p. Type **60** 40 30
196 2t. Weights, jug and tape measure (horiz) . . . . . 1·75 2·50

61 Dr. Robert Koch

63 Dr. Muhammed Shahidulla

62 Open Stage Theatre

1983. Centenary (1982) of Robert Koch's Discovery of Tubercle Bacillus. Multicoloured.
197 50p. Type **61** . . . . 1·00 40
198 1t. Microscope, slide and X-ray . . . . 2·25 3·25

1983. Commonwealth Day. Multicoloured.
199 1t. Type **62** 10 15
200 3t. Boat race 20 30
201 10t. Snake dance 50 90
202 15t. Picking tea . . . . . . 60 1·50

1983. Dr. Muhammed Shahidulla (Bengali scholar) Commemoration.
203 **63** 50p. multicoloured . . . . 75 1·00

64 Magpie Robin

1983. Birds of Bangladesh. Multicoloured.
204 50p. Type **64** . . . . 1·00 40
205 2t. White-throated kingfisher (vert) . . . . 1·50 2·25
206 3t.75 Lesser flame-backed woodpecker (vert) . . . . 1·50 2·75
207 5t. White-winged wood duck 1·75 3·25
MS208 165 × 110 mm. Nos. 240/7 (sold at 13t.) 6·50 13·00

65 "Macrobrachium rosenbergii"

1983. Marine Life. Multicoloured.
209 50p. Type **65** 60 30
210 2t. White pomfret . . . . . 1·00 1·50
211 3t.75 Rohu . . . . 1·10 1·75
212 5t. Climbing perch . . . . . 1·25 2·50
MS213 119 × 98 mm. Nos. 209/12 (sold at 13t.) 3·50 6·00

1983. Visit of Queen Elizabeth II. No. 95 optd **Nov. '83 Visit of Queen**.
214 10t. Queen Elizabeth and Prince Philip . . . . . . 4·25 5·50

67 Conference Hall, Dhaka

1983. 14th Islamic Foreign Ministers' Conference, Dhaka. Multicoloured.
215 50p. Type **67** 35 30
216 5t. Old Fort, Dhaka . . . . 1·25 2·75

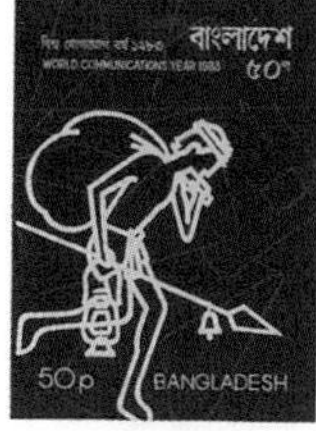

68 Early Mail Runner

69 Carrying Mail by Boat

1983. World Communications Year. Multicoloured.
217 50p. Type **68** 30 15
218 5t. Sailing ship, steam train and Boeing 707 airliner . . 2·00 1·50
219 10t. Mail runner and dish aerial (horiz) . . . . . . 2·75 4·00

1983. Postal Communications.
220 **69** 5p. blue 10 20
221 – 10p. purple 10 20
222 – 15p. blue 20 20
223 – 20p. black 50 20
224 – 25p. grey 20 20
225 – 30p. brown 20 20
226 – 50p. brown 50 10
227 – 1t. blue 50 10
228 – 2t. green 50 10
228a – 3t. brown . . . . 2·25 70
229 – 5t. purple . . . . 2·00 80

DESIGNS—HORIZ (22 × 17 mm): 10p. Counter, Dhaka G.P.O.; 15p. I.W.T.A. Terminal, Dhaka; 20p. Inside railway travelling post office; 30p. Emptying pillar box; 50p. Mobile post office van. (30 × 19 mm): 1t. Kamalapur Railway Station, Dhaka; 2t. Zia International Airport; 3t. Sorting mail by machine; 5t. Khulna G.P.O. VERT (17 × 22 mm): 25p. Delivering a letter.

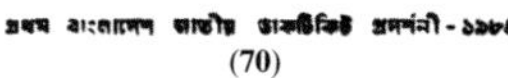

(70)

1984. 1st National Stamp Exhibition (1st issue). Nos. 161/2 optd with T **70** (5t.) or **First Bangladesh National Philatelic Exhibition—1984** (50p.)
230 **44** 50p. multicoloured . . . . 1·00 1·00
231 – 5t. multicoloured . . . . . 1·25 1·75

71 Girl with Stamp Album (⅔-size illustration)

1984. 1st National Stamp Exhibition (2nd issue). Multicoloured.
232 50p. Type **71** . . . . 65 1·25
233 7t.50 Boy with stamp album 1·10 1·75
MS234 98 × 117 mm. Nos. 232/3 (sold at 10t.) 3·00 4·00

72 Sarus Crane and Gavial

73 Eagle attacking Hen with Chicks

1984. Dhaka Zoo. Multicoloured.
235 1t. Type **72** . . . . 1·75 85
236 2t. Common peafowl and tiger . . . . 2·50 4·25

1984. Centenary of Postal Life Insurance. Mult.
237 1t. Type **73** 50 25
238 5t. Bangladesh family and postman's hand with insurance cheque . . . . . 1·50 2·00

খুলনাপেক্স—৮৪

74 Abbasuddin Ahmad

(75)

1984. Abbasuddin Ahmad (singer) Commemoration.
239 **74** 3t. multicoloured 70 70

1984. "Khulnapex-84" Stamp Exhibition. No. 86 optd with T **75**.
240 **22** 2t.25 multicoloured . . . . 1·00 1·50

76 Cycling

1984. Olympic Games, Los Angeles. Multicoloured.
241 1t. Type **76** . . . . 1·75 30
242 5t. Hockey . . . . 2·50 2·25
243 10t. Volleyball . . . . 2·75 4·00

77 Farmer with Rice and Sickle

1985. 9th Annual Meeting of Islamic Development Bank, Dhaka. Multicoloured.
244 1t. Type **77** 35 15
245 5t. Citizens of four races . . 1·25 2·00

78 Mother and Baby

80 Women working at Traditional Crafts

উপজেলা নির্বাচন ১৯৮৫

(79)

1985. Child Survival Campaign. Multicoloured.
246 1t. Type **78** 30 10
247 10t. Young child and growth graph . . . . 2·50 3·00

1985. Local Elections. Nos. 110/15 optd with T **79**.
248 40p. Type **29** 30 40
249 1t. "Cassia fistula" 30 30
250 2t.25 "Delonix regia" 50 65
251 3t.50 "Nymphaea nouchali" 60 85
252 4t. "Butea monosperma" . . 60 85
253 5t. "Anthocephalus indicus" 70 1·25

1985. U.N. Decade for Women. Multicoloured.
254 1t. Type **80** 25 10
255 10t. Women with microscope, computer terminal and in classroom . . . . 1·25 2·00

81 U.N. Building, New York, Peace Doves and Flags

1985. 40th Anniv of United Nations Organization and 11th Anniv of Bangladesh Membership. Multicoloured.
256 1t. Type **81** 10 10
257 10t. Map of world and Bangladesh flag . . . . . 80 1·10

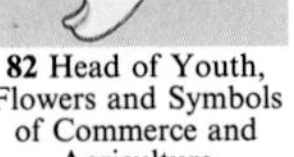

82 Head of Youth, Flowers and Symbols of Commerce and Agriculture

83 Emblem and Seven Doves

1985. International Youth Year. Multicoloured.
258 1t. Type **82** 10 10
259 5t. Head of youth, flowers and symbols of industry . . 40 60

1985. 1st Summit Meeting of South Asian Association for Regional Co-operation, Dhaka. Multicoloured.
260 1t. Type **83** 10 10
261 5t. Flags of member nations and lotus blossom 75 60

84 Zainul Abedin

তৃতীয় বাংলাদেশ
জাতীয় জাম্বুরী
১৯৮৫-৮৬

(85)

1985. 10th Death Anniv of Zainul Abedin (artist).
262 **84** 3t. multicoloured 75 30

1985. 3rd National Scout Jamboree. No. 109 optd with T **85**.
263 5t. green, blue and red . . . 2·50 3·25

86 "Fishing Net" (Safiuddin Ahmed)

1986. Bangladesh Paintings. Multicoloured.
264 1t. Type **86** 15 10
265 5t. "Happy Return" (Quamrul Hassan) 40 50
266 10t. "Levelling the Ploughed Field" (Zainul Abedin) . . 70 80

87 Two Players competing for Ball

1986. World Cup Football Championship, Mexico. Multicoloured.
267 1t. Type **87** 50 10
268 10t. Goalkeeper and ball in net . . . . 2·25 2·75
MS269 105 × 75 mm. 20t. Four players (60 × 44 mm) Imperf 5·50 5·50

88 General M. A. G. Osmani

90 Butterflies and Nuclear Explosion

1986. General M. A. G. Osmani (army commander-in-chief) Commemoration.
270 **88** 3t. multicoloured . . . . . 1·50 75

1986. South Asian Association for Regional Co-operation Seminar. No. 183 optd **SAARC SEMINAR '86**.
271 **55** 50p. multicoloured . . . . 2·25 3·00

1986. International Peace Year. Multicoloured.
272 1t. Type **90** 50 25
273 10t. Flowers and ruined buildings . . . . 2·75 3·75
MS274 109 × 80 mm. 20t. Peace dove and soldier 1·50 2·00

1987. Conference for Development. Nos. 152/3 optd **CONFERENCE FOR DEVELOPMENT '87**, No. 275 also surch **TK. 1.00**.
275 **38** 1t. on 40p. black, red and yellow 10 20
276 – 5t. gold and blue . . . . . 40 1·50

92 Demonstrators with Placards

1987. 35th Anniv of Bangla Language Movement. Multicoloured.
277 3t. Type **92** . . . . 1·25 2·00
278 3t. Martyrs' Memorial . . . 1·25 2·00
Nos. 277/8 were printed together, se-tenant, forming a composite design.

93 Nurse giving Injection

94 Pattern and Bengali Script

1987. World Health Day.
279 **93** 1t. black and blue . . . . 1·75 1·75
See also No 295.

1987. Bengali New Year Day. Multicoloured.
280 1t. Type **94** 10 10
281 10t. Bengali woman 40 60

95 Jute Shika

96 Ustad Ayet Ali Khan and Surbahar

1987. Export Products. Multicoloured.
282 1t. Type **95** 10 10
283 5t. Jute carpet (horiz) 30 35
284 10t. Cane table lamp 45 70

1987. 20th Death Anniv of Ustad Ayet Ali Khan (musician and composer).
285 **96** 5t. multicoloured . . . . . 1·25 60

97 Palanquin

1987. Transport. Multicoloured.
286 2t. Type **97** 20 15
287 3t. Bicycle rickshaw 40 20
288 5t. River steamer 80 35
289 7t. Express diesel train . . . 2·25 50
290 10t. Bullock cart 50 75

98 H. S. Suhrawardy

1987. Hossain Shadid Suhrawardy (politician) Commemoration.
291 **98** 3t. multicoloured 20 30

99 Villagers fleeing from Typhoon

1987. International Year of Shelter for the Homeless. Multicoloured.
292 5t. Type **99** 20 30
293 5t. Villagers and modern houses 20 30

100 President Ershad addressing Parliament

1987. 1st Anniv of Return to Democracy.
294 **100** 10t. multicoloured 40 60

1988. World Health Day. As T **93**.
295 25p. brown 30 20
DESIGN: 25p. Oral rehydration.

101 Woman planting Palm Saplings

1988. I.F.A.D. Seminar on Agricultural Loans for Rural Women. Multicoloured.
296 3t. Type **101** 15 20
297 5t. Village woman milking cow 20 40

102 Basketball

1988. Olympic Games, Seoul. Multicoloured.
298 5t. Type **102** 80 60
299 5t. Weightlifting 80 60
300 5t. Tennis 80 60
301 5t. Rifle-shooting 80 60
302 5t. Boxing 80 60

103 Interior of Shait Gumbaz Mosque, Bagerhat

1988. Historical Buildings. Multicoloured.
303 1t. Type **103** 25 10
304 4t. Paharpur Monastery . . . 40 15
305 5t. Kantanagar Temple, Dinajpur 40 15
306 10t. Lalbag Fort, Dhaka . . 55 30

104 Henri Dunant (founder), Red Cross and Crescent

105 Dr. Qudrat-i-Khuda in Laboratory

1988. 125th Anniv of International Red Cross and Red Crescent. Multicoloured.
307 5t. Type **104** 85 30
308 10t. Red Cross workers with patient . . . . 1·40 95

1988. Dr. Qudrat-i-Khuda (scientist) Commem.
309 **105** 5t. multicoloured 30 30

106 Wicket-keeper

107 Labourers, Factory and Technician

1988. Asia Cup Cricket. Multicoloured.
310 1t. Type **106** 80 90
311 5t. Batsman . . . . 1·00 1·00
312 10t. Bowler . . . . 1·75 1·40

1988. 32nd Meeting of Colombo Plan Consultative Committee, Dhaka.
313 **107** 3t. multicoloured 10 10
314 10t. multicoloured 40 45

108 Dhaka G.P.O. Building

1988. 25th Anniv of Dhaka G.P.O. Building. Multicoloured.
315 1t. Type **108** 15 10
316 5t. Post Office counter . . . 30 30

৫ম জাতীয় রোভার মুট
১৯৮৮-৮৯
(109)

1988. 5th National Rover Scout Moot. No. 168 optd with T **109**.
317 **47** 5t. multicoloured . . . . . 1·75 1·75

110 Bangladesh Airport

1989. Bangladesh Landmarks.
318 **110** 3t. black and blue . . . 10 10
318a – 4t. blue 10 15
710 – 5t. black and brown . . 10 15
320 – 10t. red . . . . 2·00 35
321 – 20t. multicoloured . . . 45 50
DESIGNS—VERT (22 × 33 mm): 5t. Curzon Hall. (19½ × 31½ mm): 10t. Fertiliser factory, Chittagong. HORIZ (33 × 23 mm): 4t. Chittagong port; 20t. Postal Academy, Rajshahi.

চতুর্থ দ্বিবার্ষিক এশীয়
চারুকলা প্রদর্শনী
বাংলাদেশ ১৯৮৯
(111)

1989. 4th Biennial Asian Art Exhibition. No. 266 optd with T **111**.
322 10t. "Levelling the Ploughed Field" (Zainul Abedin) . . 50 50

112 Irrigation Methods and Student with Telescope
113 Academy Logo

1989. 12th National Science and Technology Week.
323 **112** 10t. multicoloured 50 50

1989. 75th Anniv of Police Academy, Sardah.
324 **113** 10t. multicoloured 50 50

114 Rejoicing Crowds, Paris, 1789

1989. Bicentenary of French Revolution. Mult.
325 17t. Type **114** 70 75
326 17t. Storming the Bastille, 1789 . . . . 70 75
MS327 125 × 125 mm 5t. Men with pickaxes; 10t. "Liberty guiding the People" (detail) (Delacroix); 10t. Crowd with cannon. P 14 2·00 2·75
MS328 152 × 88 mm. 25t. Storming the Bastille. Imperf 2·00 2·75
The design of No. **MS**328 incorporates the three scenes featured on No. **MS**327.

115 Sowing and Harvesting

1989. 10th Anniv of Asia–Pacific Integrated Rural Development Centre. Multicoloured.
329 5t. Type **115** 45 45
330 10t. Rural activities 55 55
Nos. 329/30 were printed together, se-tenant, forming a composite design.

116 Helper and Child playing with Baby

1989. 40th Anniv of S.O.S. International Children's Village. Multicoloured.
331 1t. Type **116** 15 10
332 10t. Foster mother with children 55 55

117 U.N. Soldier on Watch
118 Festival Emblem

1989. 1st Anniv of Bangladesh Participation in U.N. Peace-keeping Force. Multicoloured.
333 4t. Type **117** 50 30
334 10t. Two soldiers checking positions . . . . 1·00 70

1989. 2nd Asian Poetry Festival, Dhaka.
335 **118** 2t. red, deep red and green 15 10
336 – 10t. multicoloured 60 65
DESIGN: 10t. Festival emblem and hall.

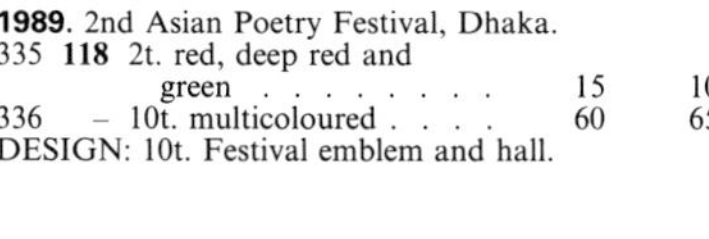

119 State Security Printing Press

1989. Inauguration of State Security Printing Press, Gazipur.
337 **119** 10t. multicoloured 65 65

120 Water Lilies and T.V. Emblem

1989. 25th Anniv of Bangladesh Television. Multicoloured.
338 5t. Type **120** 35 30
339 10t. Central emblem and water lilies 65 80

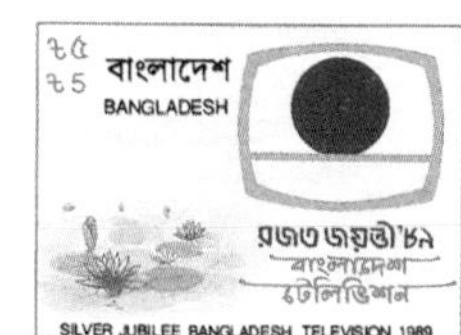

121 Gharial in Shallow Water

1990. Endangered Wildlife. Gharial. Multicoloured.
340 50p. Type **121** 80 45
341 2t. Gharial feeding . . . . . 1·00 60
342 4t. Gharials basking on sand bank . . . . 1·40 70
343 10t. Two gharials resting . . 1·75 95

122 Symbolic Family
124 Boy learning Alphabet

123 Justice S. M. Murshed

1990. Population Day.
344 **122** 6t. multicoloured 55 35

1990. 10th Death Anniv of Justice Syed Mahbub Murshed.
345 **123** 5t. multicoloured . . . . 1·50 50

1990. International Literacy Year. Multicoloured.
346 6t. Type **124** . . . . 1·00 50
347 10t. Boy teaching girl to write 1·50 1·00

125 Penny Black with "Stamp World London 90" Exhibition Emblem

127 Mango

126 Goalkeeper and Ball

1990. 150th Anniv of the Penny Black. Multicoloured.
348 7t. Type **125** . . . . 1·50 1·75
349 10t. Penny Black, 1983 World Communications Year stamp and Bengali mail runner . . . . 1·75 2·00

1990. World Cup Football Championship, Italy. Multicoloured.
350 8t. Type **126** . . . . 1·75 1·50
351 10t. Footballer with ball . . 2·00 1·75
MS352 104 × 79 mm. 25t. Colosseum, Rome, with football. Imperf 8·00 8·00

1990. Fruit. Multicoloured.
353 1t. Type **127** 30 10
354 2t. Guava 30 10
355 3t. Water melon 35 15
356 4t. Papaya 40 25
357 5t. Bread fruit 65 50
358 10t. Carambola . . . . . . 1·25 1·25

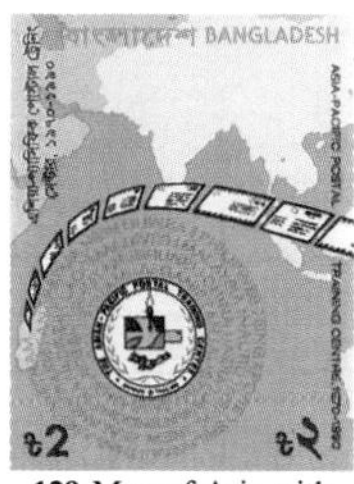

128 Man gathering Wheat

1990. U.N. Conference on Least Developed Countries, Paris.
359 **128** 10t. multicoloured . . . . 1·25 1·00

129 Map of Asia with Stream of Letters
131 Lalan Shah

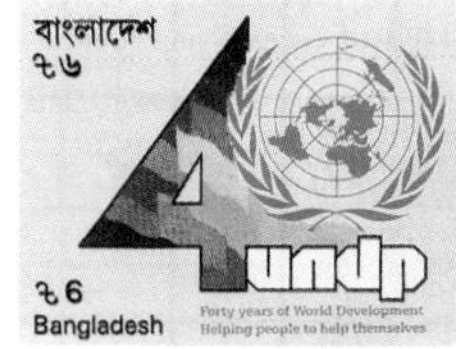

130 Canoe Racing

1990. 20th Anniv of Asia–Pacific Postal Training Centre. Multicoloured.
360 2t. Type **129** . . . . 1·25 1·25
361 6t. Map of Pacific with stream of letters . . . . . 1·25 1·25
Nos. 360/1 were printed together, se-tenant, forming a composite map design.

1990. Asian Games, Beijing. Multicoloured.
362 2t. Type **130** 70 20
363 4t. Kabaddi 85 25
364 8t. Wrestling . . . . 1·40 1·00
365 10t. Badminton . . . . . . 2·25 1·50

1990. 1st Death Anniv of Lalan Shah (poet).
366 **131** 6t. multicoloured . . . . 1·00 35

132 U.N. Logo and "40"

1990. 40th Anniv of United Nations Development Programme.
367 **132** 6t. multicoloured 80 35

133 Baby
134 "Danaus chrysippus"

1990. Immunization.
368 **133** 1t. green 10 10
369 2t. brown 10 10

1990. Butterflies. Multicoloured.
370 6t. Type **134** . . . . 1·60 1·60
371 6t. "Precis almana" . . . . . 1·60 1·60
372 10t. "Ixias pyrene" . . . . . 1·75 1·75
373 10t. "Danaus plexippus" . . 1·75 1·75

135 Drugs attacking Bangladesh

1991. U.N. Anti-drugs Decade. Multicoloured.
374 2t. Type **135** . . . . 1·00 50
375 4t. "Drug" snake around globe . . . . 1·25 1·25

136 Salimullah Hall

1991.
376 **136** 6t. blue and yellow . . . 15 20

137 Silhouetted People on Map
138 "Invincible Bangla" (statue)

1991. 3rd National Census.
382 **137** 4t. multicoloured . . . . 1·00 60

1991. 20th Anniv of Independence. Multicoloured.
383 4t. Type **138** 75 90
384 4t. "Freedom Fighter" (statue) 75 90
385 4t. Mujibnagar Memorial . . 75 90
386 4t. Eternal flame 75 90
387 4t. National Martyrs' Memorial 75 90
Nos. 383/7 were issued together, se-tenant, forming a composite design.

139 President Rahman Seated
141 Kaikobad

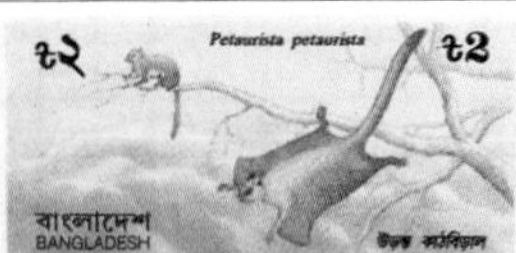

140 Red Giant Flying Squirrel

1991. 10th Death Anniv of President Ziaur Rahman. Multicoloured.
388 50p. Type **139** 20 15
389 2t. President Rahman's head in circular decoration . . . 80 1·10
MS390 146 × 75 mm. Nos. 388/9 (sold at 10t.) 1·25 2·00

1991. Endangered Species. Multicoloured.
391 2t. Type **140** . . . . 1·40 1·50
392 4t. Black-faced monkey (vert) 1·40 1·50
393 6t. Great Indian hornbill (vert) . . . . 1·40 1·50
394 10t. Armoured pangolin . . . 1·40 1·50

1991. 40th Death Anniv of Kaikobad (poet).
395 **141** 6t. multicoloured . . . . 1·00 60

142 Rabindranath Tagore and Temple

1991. 50th Death Anniv of Rabindranath Tagore (poet).
396 **142** 4t. multicoloured 70 55

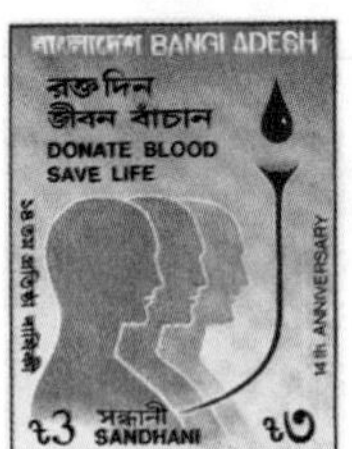

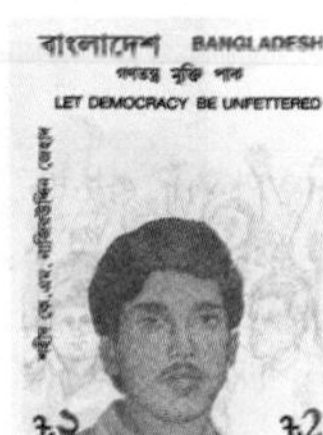

143 Voluntary Blood Programme

144 Shahid Naziruddin and Crowd

1991. 14th Anniv of "Sandhani" (medical students' association).
397 **143** 3t. black and red 75 50
398 – 5t. multicoloured . . . . 1·25 1·75
DESIGN: 5t. Blind man and eye.

1991. 1st Death Anniv of Shahid Naziruddin Jahad (democrat).
399 **144** 2t. black, green and brown 70 50

145 Shaheed Noor Hossain with Slogan on Chest

1991. 4th Death Anniv of Shaheed Noor Hossain (democrat).
400 **145** 2t. multicoloured 60 40

146 Bronze Stupa

1991. Archaeological Relics from Mainamati. Multicoloured.
401 4t. Type **146** . . . . 1·25 1·40
402 4t. Earthenware and bronze pitchers . . . . 1·25 1·40
403 4t. Remains of Salban Vihara Monastery . . . . 1·25 1·40
404 4t. Gold coins . . . . 1·25 1·40
405 4t. Terracotta plaque . . . . 1·25 1·40

147 Demostrators

1991. 1st Anniv of Mass Uprising.
406 **147** 4t. multicoloured . . . . 1·00 60

148 Munier Chowdhury

1991. 20th Anniv of Independence. Martyred Intellectuals (1st series). Each black and brown.
407 2t. Type **148** 35 35
408 2t. Ghyasuddin Ahmad . . . 35 35
409 2t. Rashidul Hasan 35 35
410 2t. Muhammad Anwar Pasha 35 35
411 2t. Dr. Muhammad Mortaza 35 35
412 2t. Shahid Saber 35 35
413 2t. Fazlur Rahman Khan . . 35 35
414 2t. Ranada Prasad Saha . . 35 35
415 2t. Adhyaksha Joges Chandra Ghose 35 35
416 2t. Santosh Chandra Bhattacharyya 35 35
417 2t. Dr. Gobinda Chandra Deb 35 35
418 2t. A. Muniruzzaman 35 35
419 2t. Mufazzal Haider Chaudhury 35 35
420 2t. Dr. Abdul Alim Choudhury 35 35
421 2t. Sirajuddin Hossain . . . 35 35
422 2t. Shahidulla Kaiser 35 35
423 2t. Altaf Mahmud 35 35
424 2t. Dr. Jyotirmay Guha Thakurta 35 35
425 2t. Dr. Muhammad Abul Khair 35 35
426 2t. Dr. Serajul Haque Khan 35 35
427 2t. Dr. Mohammad Fazle Rabbi 35 35
428 2t. Mir Abdul Quyyum . . . 35 35
429 2t. Golam Mostafa 35 35
430 2t. Dhirendranath Dutta . . 35 35
431 2t. S. Mannan 35 35
432 2t. Nizamuddin Ahmad . . . 35 35
433 2t. Abul Bashar Chowdhury 35 35
434 2t. Selina Parveen 35 35
435 2t. Dr. Abul Kalam Azad . . 35 35
436 2t. Saidul Hassan 35 35
See also Nos. 483/92, 525/40, 568/83, 620/35, 656/71, 691/706, 731/46 and 779/94.

149 "Penaeus monodon"

1991. Shrimps. Multicoloured.
437 6t. Type **149** . . . . 1·75 2·00
438 6t. "Metapenaeus monoceros" . . . . 1·75 2·00

150 Death of Raihan Jaglu

1992. 5th Death Anniv of Shaheed Mirze Abu Raihan Jaglu.
439 **150** 2t. multicoloured 80 50

151 Rural and Urban Scenes

152 Nawab Sirajuddaulah

1992. World Environment Day. Multicoloured.
440 4t. Type **151** 60 25
441 10t. World Environment Day logo (horiz) . . . . 1·40 2·00

1992. 235th Death Anniv of Nawab Sirajuddaulah of Bengal
442 **152** 10t. multicoloured . . . . 1·00 1·50

153 Syed Ismail Hossain Sirajee

1992. 61st Death Anniv of Syed Ismail Hossain Sirajee
443 **153** 4t. multicoloured 80 40

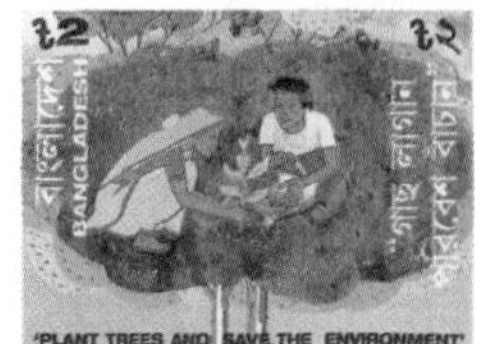

154 Couple planting Seedling

1992. Plant Week. Multicoloured.
444 2t. Type **154** 85 70
445 4t. Birds on tree (vert) . . . 1·25 70

155 Canoe Racing

1992. Olympic Games, Barcelona. Multicoloured.
446 4t. Type **155** . . . . 1·00 1·25
447 6t. Hands holding torch with Olympic rings . . . . . . 1·00 1·25
448 10t. Olympic rings and doves 1·00 1·25
449 10t. Olympic rings and multiracial handshake . . . 1·00 1·25

1992. "Banglapex '92", National Philatelic Exhibition (1st issue). No. 290 optd **Banglapex '92** in English and Bengali.
450 10t. Bullock cart . . . . . . 1·50 2·00
See also Nos. 452/3.

157 Masnad-e-Ala Isa Khan

1992. 393rd Death Anniv of Masnad-e-Ala Isa Khan.
451 **157** 4t. multicoloured 80 40

158 Ceremonial Elephant (19th-century ivory carving)

1992. "Banglapex '92" National Philatelic Exhibition (2nd issue). Multicoloured.
452 10t. Type **158** . . . . 1·25 1·75
453 10t. Victorian pillarbox between early and modern postmen . . . . 1·25 1·75
MS454 145 × 92 mm. Nos. 452/3. Imperf (sold at 25t.) 2·75 3·50

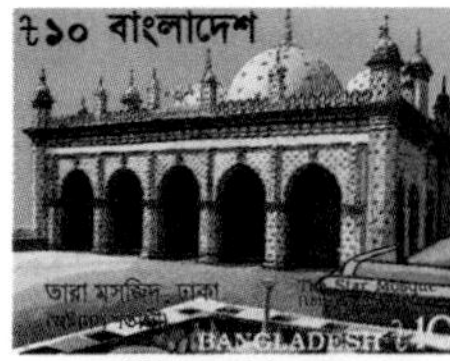

159 Star Mosque

1992. Star Mosque, Dhaka.
455 **159** 10t. mutlicoloured . . . . 1·50 1·50

160 Meer Nisar Ali Titumeer and Fort

1992. 161st Death Anniv of Meer Nisar Ali Titumeer.
456 **160** 10t. multicoloured . . . . 1·25 1·25

161 Terracotta Head and Seal

1992. Archaeological Relics from Mahasthangarh. Multicoloured.
457 10t. Type **161** . . . . 1·40 1·60
458 10t. Terracotta panel showing swan . . . . 1·40 1·60
459 10t. Terracotta statue of Surya . . . . 1·40 1·60
460 10t. Gupta stone column . . 1·40 1·60

162 Young Child and Food

1992. Int Conference on Nutrition, Rome.
461 **162** 4t. multicoloured 75 40

163 National Flags

164 Syed Abdus Samad

1992. 7th South Asian Association for Regional Co-operation Summit Conference, Dhaka. Mult.
462 6t. Type **163** 75 75
463 10t. S.A.A.R.C. emblem . . . 1·00 1·25

1993. Syed Abdus Samad (footballer) Commem.
464 **164** 2t. multicoloured . . . . 1·00 50

165 Haji Shariat Ullah

1993. Haji Shariat Ullah Commemoration.
465 **165** 2t. multicoloured 80 40

166 People digging Canal

1993. Irrigation Canals Construction Project. Mult.
466 2t. Type **166** 55 65
467 2t. Completed canal and paddy-fields 55 65

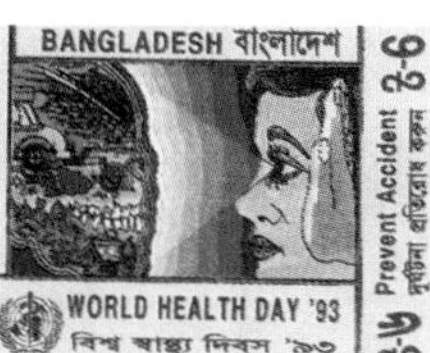

167 Accident Prevention

1993. World Health Day. Multicoloured.
468 6t. Type **167** . . . . 1·50 75
469 10t. Satellite photograph and symbols of trauma (vert) 1·75 2·00

168 National Images 169 Schoolchildren and Bengali Script

1993. 1400th Year of Bengali Solar Calendar.
470 **168** 2t. multicoloured 80 40

1993. Compulsory Primary Education. Mult.
471 2t. Type **169** 60 70
472 2t. Books and slate (horiz) 60 70

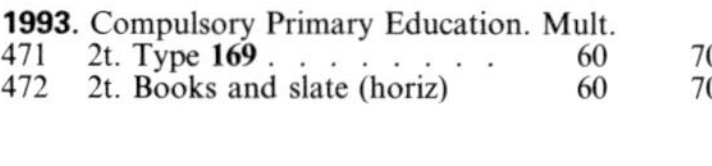

170 Nawab Sir Salimullah and Palace

1993. 122nd Birth Anniv of Nawab Sir Salimullah.
473 **170** 4t. multicoloured 85 40

171 Fish Production

1993. Fish Fortnight.
474 **171** 2t. multicoloured 40 40

172 Sunderban

1993. Natural Beauty of Bangladesh. Mult.
475 10t. Type **172** 70 90
476 10t. Kuakata beach 70 90
477 10t. Madhabkunda waterfall (vert) 70 90
478 10t. River Piyain, Jaflang (vert) 70 90
MS479 174×102 mm. Nos. 475/8. Imperf (sold at 50t.) 2·75 3·25

173 Exhibition Emblem 175 Burdwan House

174 Foy's Lake

1993. 6th Asian Art Biennale.
480 **173** 10t. multicoloured 60 80

1993. Tourism Month.
481 **174** 10t. multicoloured 70 90

1993. Foundation Day, Bangla Academy.
482 **175** 2t. brown and green . . . 60 40

1993. Martyred Intellectuals (2nd series). As T **148**. Each black and brown.
483 2t. Lt. Cdr. Moazzam Hussain 20 30
484 2t. Muhammad Habibur Rahman 20 30
485 2t. Khandoker Abu Taleb . . 20 30
486 2t. Moshiur Rahman 20 30
487 2t. Md. Abdul Muktadir . . 20 30
488 2t. Nutan Chandra Sinha . . 20 30
489 2t. Syed Nazmul Haque . . . 20 30
490 2t. Dr. Mohammed Amin Uddin 20 30
491 2t. Dr. Faizul Mohee 20 30
492 2t. Sukha Ranjan Somaddar 20 30

176 Throwing the Discus

1993. 6th South Asian Federation Games, Dhaka. Multicoloured.
493 2t. Type **176** 15 15
494 4t. Running (vert) 25 25

177 Tomb of Sultan Ghiyasuddin Azam Shah

1993. Muslim Monuments.
495 **177** 10t. multicoloured 60 80

178 Scouting Activities and Jamboree Emblem 179 Emblem and Mother giving Solution to Child

1994. 14th Asian–Pacific and 5th Bangladesh National Scout Jamboree.
496 **178** 2t. multicoloured 30 30

1994. 25th Anniv of Oral Rehydration.
497 **179** 2t. multicoloured 30 30

180 Interior of Chhota Sona Mosque, Nawabgonj

1994. Ancient Mosques. Multicoloured.
498 4t. Type **180** 30 20
499 6t. Exterior of Chhota Sona Mosque 40 50
500 6t. Exterior of Baba Adam's Mosque, Munshigonj . . . 40 50

181 Agricultural Workers and Emblem

1994. 75th Anniv of I.L.O. Multicoloured.
501 4t. Type **181** 25 20
502 10t. Worker turning cog (vert) . . . . 75 1·00

182 Priest releasing Peace Doves 184 Family, Globe and Logo

183 Scenes from Baishakhi Festival

1994. 1500th Year of Bengali Solar Calendar.
503 **182** 2t. multicoloured 25 25

1994. Folk Festivals. Multicoloured.
504 4t. Type **183** 25 25
505 4t. Scenes from Nabanna and Paush Parvana Festivals 25 25

1994. International Year of the Family.
506 **184** 10t. multicoloured . . . . 1·00 1·25

185 People planting Saplings 186 Player kicking Ball

1994. Tree Planting Campaign. Multicoloured.
507 4t. Type **185** 35 20
508 6t. Hands holding saplings 65 30

1994. World Cup Football Championship, U.S.A. Multicoloured.
509 20t. Type **186** . . . . 2·25 2·75
510 20t. Player heading ball . . . 2·25 2·75

187 Traffic on Bridge

1994. Inauguration of Jamuna Multi-purpose Bridge Project.
511 **187** 4t. multicoloured . . . . 1·00 30

188 Asian Black-headed Oriole 190 Nawab Faizunnessa Chowdhurani

189 Dr. Mohammad Ibrahim and Hospital

1994. Birds. Multicoloured.
512 4t. Type **188** 40 40
513 6t. Greater racquet-tailed drongo 60 80
514 6t. Indian tree pie 60 80
515 6t. Red junglefowl 60 80

1994. 5th Death Anniv of Dr. Mohammad Ibrahim (diabetes treatment pioneer).
517 **189** 2t. multicoloured 30 20

1994. 160th Birth Anniv of Nawab Faizunnessa Chowdhurani (social reformer).
518 **190** 2t. muticoloured 50 20

191 Boxing

1994. Asian Games, Hiroshima, Japan.
519 **191** 4t. multicoloured 75 30

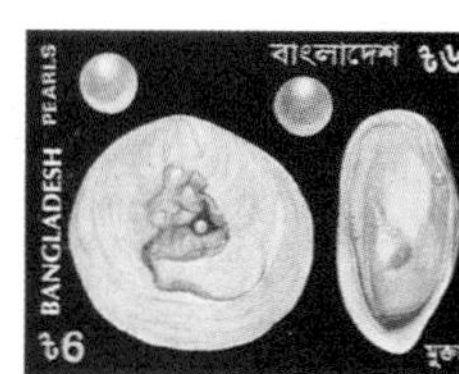

192 Pink and White Pearls with Windowpane Oysters

1994. Sea Shells. Multicoloured.
520 6t. Type **192** . . . . 95 1·10
521 6t. Tranquelous scallop and other shells . . . . 95 1·10
522 6t. Lister's conch, Asiatic Arabian cowrie, bladder moon and woodcock murex . . . . 95 1·10
523 6t. Spotted tun, spiny frog shell, spiral melongena and gibbous olive (vert) . . . . 95 1·10

193 Dr. Milon and Demonstrators

1994. 4th Death Anniv of Dr. Shamsul Alam Khan Milon (medical reformer).
524 **193** 2t. multicoloured 20 20

1994. Martyred Intellectuals (3rd series). As T **148**. Each black and brown.
525 2t. Dr. Harinath Dey 25 30
526 2t. Dr. A. F. Ziaur Rahman 25 30
527 2t. Mamun Mahmud 25 30
528 2t. Mohsin Ali Dewan . . . 25 30
529 2t. Dr. N. A. M. Jahangir . . 25 30
530 2t. Shah Abdul Majid . . . 25 30
531 2t. Muhammad Akhter . . . 25 30
532 2t. Meherunnesa 25 30
533 2t. Dr. Kasiruddin Talukder 25 30
534 2t. Fazlul Haque Choudhury 25 30
535 2t. Md. Shamsuzzaman . . . 25 30
536 2t. A. K. M. Shamsuddin . . 25 30
537 2t. Lt. Mohammad Anwarul Azim 25 30
538 2t. Nurul Amin Khan . . . 25 30
539 2t. Mohammad Sadeque . . 25 30
540 2t. Md. Araz Ali 25 30

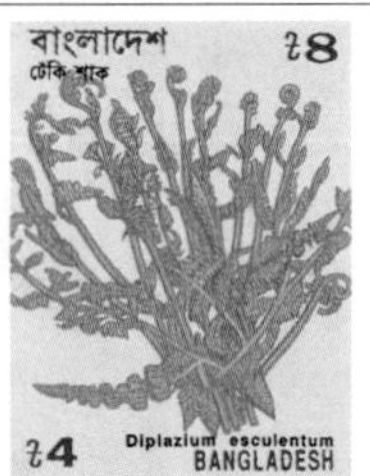
194 "Diplazium esculentum"

1995. Vegetables. Multicoloured.

541	4t. Type **194**	50	30
542	4t. "Momordica charantia"	50	30
543	6t. "Lagenaria siceraria"	70	55
544	6t. "Trichosanthes dioica"	70	55
545	10t. "Solanum melongena"	1·00	1·50
546	10t. "Cucurbita maxima" (horiz)	1·00	1·50

195 Sonargaon

1995. 20th Anniv of World Tourism Organization.
547 **195** 10t. multicoloured . . . . 1·50 1·50

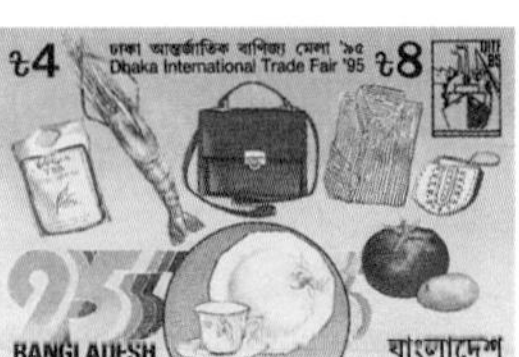
196 Exports

1995. Dhaka International Trade Fair '95. Mult.

548	4t. Type **196**	20	20
549	6t. Symbols of industry	45	65

197 Soldiers of Ramgarh Battalion (1795) and of Bangladesh Rifles (1995)

1995. Bicentenary of Bangladesh Rifles. Mult.

550	2t. Type **197**	60	35
551	4t. Riflemen on patrol	1·00	65

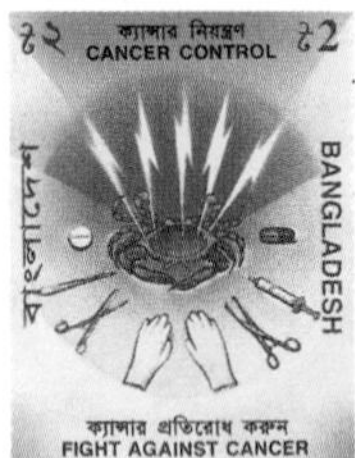
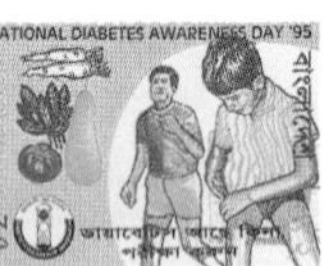
198 Surgical Equipment and Lightning attacking Crab (cancer)
199 Fresh Food and Boy injecting Insulin

1995. Campaign against Cancer.
552 **198** 2t. multicoloured 30 20

1995. National Diabetes Awareness Day.
553 **199** 2t. multicoloured 30 20

200 Munshi Mohammad Meherullah

1995. Munshi Mohammad Meherullah (Islamic educator) Commemoration.
554 **200** 2t. multicoloured 20 20

রাজশাহীপেক্স-৯৫
(201)

1995. "Rajshahipex '95" National Philatelic Exhibition. No. 499 optd with T **201**.
555 6t. Exterior of Chhota Sona Mosque . . . . 1·50 1·75

202 "Lagerstroemia speciosa"
203 Aspects of Farming

1995. Flowers. Multicoloured.

556	6t. Type **202**	65	65
557	6t. "Bombax ceiba" (horiz)	65	65
558	10t. "Passiflora incarnata"	90	1·00
559	10t. "Bauhinia purpurea"	90	1·00
560	10t. "Canna indica"	90	1·00
561	10t. "Gloriosa superba"	90	1·00

1995. 50th Anniv of F.A.O.
562 **203** 10t. multicoloured 55 75

204 Anniversary Emblem, Peace Dove and U.N. Headquarters

1995. 50th Anniv of United Nations. Multicoloured.

563	2t. Type **204**	20	20
564	10t. Peace doves circling dates and Globe	75	1·10
565	10t. Clasped hands and U.N. Headquarters	75	1·10

205 Diseased Lungs, Microscope, Family and Map

1995. 18th Eastern Regional Conference on Tuberculosis, Dhaka.
566 **205** 6t. multicoloured 85 65

206 Peace Doves, Emblem and National Flags

1995. 10th Anniv of South Asian Association for Regional Co-operation.
567 **206** 2t. multicoloured 60 20

1995. Martyred Intellectuals (4th series). As T **148**. Each black and brown.

568	2t. Abdul Ahad	15	20
569	2t. Lt. Col. Mohammad Qadir	15	20
570	2t. Mozammel Hoque Chowdhury	15	20
571	2t. Rafiqul Haider Chowdhury	15	20
572	2t. Dr. Azharul Haque	15	20
573	2t. A. K. Shamsuddin	15	20
574	2t. Anudwaipayan Bhattacharjee	15	20
575	2t. Lutfunnahar Helena	15	20
576	2t. Shaikh Habibur Rahman	15	20
577	2t. Major Naimul Islam	15	20
578	2t. Md. Shahidullah	15	20
579	2t. Ataur Rahman Khan Khadim	15	20
580	2t. A. B. M. Ashraful Islam Bhuiyan	15	20
581	2t. Dr. Md. Sadat Ali	15	20
582	2t. Sarafat Ali	15	20
583	2t. M. A. Sayeed	15	20

207 Aspects of COMDECA Projects

1995. 2nd Asia–Pacific Community Development Scout Camp.
584 **207** 2t. multicoloured 40 25

208 Volleyball Players

1995. Centenary of Volleyball.
585 **208** 6t. multicoloured 50 40

209 Man in Punjabi and Lungi

1995. Traditional Costumes. Multicoloured.

586	6t. Type **209**	65	65
587	6t. Woman in sari	65	65
588	10t. Christian bride and groom	1·00	1·00
589	10t. Muslim bride and groom	1·00	1·00
590	10t. Buddhist bride and groom (horiz)	1·00	1·00
591	10t. Hindu bride and groom (horiz)	1·00	1·00

210 Shaheed Amanullah Mohammad Asaduzzaman

1996. 27th Death Anniv of Shaheed Amanullah Mohammad Asaduzzaman (student leader).
592 **210** 2t. multicoloured 20 20

211 Bowler and Map

1996. World Cup Cricket Championship. Multicoloured.

593	4t. Type **211**	80	35
594	6t. Batsman and wicket keeper	1·00	60
595	10t. Match in progress (horiz)	1·25	1·75

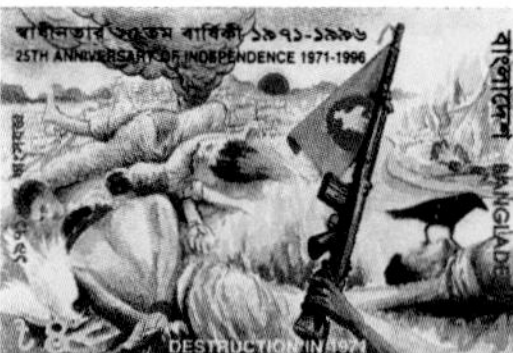
212 Liberation Struggle, 1971

1996. 25th Anniv of Independence. Multicoloured.

596	4t. Type **212**	40	50
597	4t. National Martyrs Memorial	40	50
598	4t. Education	40	50
599	4t. Health	40	50
600	4t. Communications	40	50
601	4t. Industry	40	50

213 Michael Madhusudan Dutt
214 Gymnastics

1996. Michael Madhusudan Dutt (poet) Commemoration.
602 **213** 4t. multicoloured 50 20

1996. Olympic Games, Atlanta. Multicoloured.

603	4t. Type **214**	25	20
604	6t. Judo	35	30
605	10t. Athletics (horiz)	40	50
606	10t. High jumping (horiz)	40	50
MS607	165 × 110 mm. Nos. 603/6 (sold at 40t.)	1·25	1·60

1996. 25th Anniv of Bangladesh Stamps. No. **MS**234 optd "**Silver Jubilee Bangladesh Postage Stamps 1971-96**" on sheet margin.
MS608 98 × 117 mm. Nos. 232/3 (sold at 10t.) 70 80

215 Bangabandhu Sheikh Mujibur Rahman

1996. 21st Death Anniv of Bangabandhu Sheikh Mujibur Rahman.
609 **215** 4t. multicoloured 20 20

216 Maulana Mohammad Akrum Khan

1996. 28th Death Anniv of Maulana Mohammad Akrum Khan.
610 **216** 4t. multicoloured 20 20

217 Ustad Alauddin Khan

1996. 24th Death Anniv of Ustad Alauddin Khan (musician).
611 **217** 4t. multicoloured 50 20

218 "Kingfisher" (Mayeesha Robbani)

1996. Children's Paintings. Multicoloured.
612 2t. Type **218** 35 25
613 4t. "River Crossing" (Iffat Panchlais) (horiz) 45 25

219 Syed Nazrul Islam

1996. 21st Death Anniv of Jail Martyrs. Multicoloured.
614 4t. Type **219** 20 30
615 4t. Tajuddin Ahmad 20 30
616 4t. M. Monsoor Ali 20 30
617 4t. A. H. M. Quamaruzzaman 20 30

220 Children receiving Medicine

1996. 50th Anniv of U.N.I.C.E.F. Multicoloured.
618 4t. Type **220** 35 20
619 10t. Mother and child . . . 50 75

1996. Martyred Intellectuals (5th series). As T **148**. Each black and brown.
620 2t. Dr. Jekrul Haque 25 25
621 2t. Munshi Kabiruddin Ahmed 25 25
622 2t. Md. Abdul Jabbar . . . 25 25
623 2t. Mohammad Amir 25 25
624 2t. A. K. M. Shamsul Huq Khan 25 25
625 2t. Dr. Siddique Ahmed . . . 25 25
626 2t. Dr. Soleman Khan . . . 25 25
627 2t. S. B. M. Mizanur Rahman 25 25
628 2t. Aminuddin 25 25
629 2t. Md. Nazrul Islam 25 25
630 2t. Zahirul Islam 25 25
631 2t. A. K. Lutfor Rahman . . 25 25
632 2t. Afsar Hossain 25 25
633 2t. Abul Hashem Mian . . . 25 25
634 2t. A. T. M. Alamgir 25 25
635 2t. Baser Ali 25 25

221 Celebrating Crowds

1996. 25th Anniv of Victory Day. Multicoloured.
636 4t. Type **221** 25 25
637 6t. Soldiers and statue (vert) 40 60

222 Paul P. Harris

1997. 50th Death Anniv of Paul Harris (founder of Rotary International).
638 **222** 4t. multicoloured 20 20

223 Shaikh Mujibur Rahman making Speech

1997. 25th Anniv of Shaikh Mujibur's Speech of 7 March (1996).
639 **223** 4t. multicoloured 20 20

224 Sheikh Mujibur Rahman
226 Heinrich von Stephan

225 Sheikh Mujibur Rahman and Crowd with Banners

1997. 77th Birth Anniv of Sheikh Mujibur Rahman (first President).
640 **224** 4t. multicoloured 30 20

1997. 25th Anniv (1996) of Independence.
641 **225** 4t. multicoloured 20 20

1997. Death Centenary of Heinrich von Stephan (founder of U.P.U.).
642 **226** 4t. multicoloured 30 20

227 Sheep

1997. Livestock. Multicoloured.
643 4t. Type **227** 45 45
644 4t. Goat 45 45
645 6t. Buffalo bull 65 65
646 6t. Cow 65 65

228 "Tilling the Field - 2" (S. Sultan)

1997. Bangladesh Paintings. Multicoloured.
647 6t. Type **228** 40 30
648 10t. "Three Women" (Quamrul Hassan) . . . . 60 1·00

229 Trophy, Flag and Cricket Ball

1997. 6th International Cricket Council Trophy Championship, Malaysia.
649 **229** 10t. multicoloured . . . . 1·50 1·25

230 Kusumba Mosque, Naogaon

1997. Historic Mosques. Multicoloured.
650 4t. Type **230** 40 20
651 6t. Atiya Mosque, Tangail . . 55 30
652 10t. Bagha Mosque, Rajshahi 90 1·25

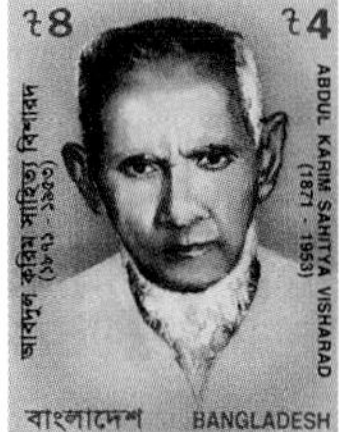

231 Adul Karim Sahitya Vishard
232 River Moot Emblem and Scouts standing on top of World

1997. 126th Birth Anniv of Abdul Karim Sahitya Vishard (scholar).
653 **231** 4t. multicoloured 20 20

1997. 9th Asia-Pacific and 7th Bangladesh Rover Moot, Lakkatura.
654 **232** 2t. multicoloured 40 20

233 Officers and Flag

1997. 25th Anniv of Armed Forces.
655 **233** 2t. multicoloured 75 40

1997. Martyred Intellectuals (6th series). As T **148**. Each black and brown.
656 2t. Dr. Shamsuddin Ahmed 55 55
657 2t. Mohammad Salimullah 55 55
658 2t. Mohiuddin Haider . . . 55 55
659 2t. Abdur Rahin 55 55
660 2t. Nitya Nanda Paul 55 55
661 2t. Abdel Jabber 55 55
662 2t. Dr. Humayun Kabir . . . 55 55
663 2t. Khaja Nizamuddin Bhuiyan 55 55
664 2t. Gulam Hossain 55 55
665 2t. Ali Karim 55 55
666 2t. Md. Moazzem Hossain 55 55
667 2t. Rafiqul Islam 55 55
668 2t. M. Nur Husain 55 55
669 2t. Captain Mahmood Hossain Akonda 55 55
670 2t. Abdul Wahab Talukder 55 55
671 2t. Dr. Hasimoy Hazra . . . 55 55

234 Mohammad Mansooruddin

1998. Professor Mohammad Mansooruddin (folklorist) Commemoration.
672 **234** 4t. multicoloured 85 30

235 Standard-bearer and Soldiers

1998. 50th Anniv of East Bengal Regiment.
673 **235** 2t. multicoloured 50 25

236 Bulbul Chowdhury

1998. Bulbul Chowdhury (traditional dancer) Commemoration.
674 **236** 4t. multicoloured 30 20

237 World Cup Trophy

1998. World Cup Football Championship, France.
675 6t. Type **237** 50 30
676 18t. Footballer and trophy 1·25 1·75

238 Eastern Approach Road, Bangabandhu Bridge

1998. Opening of Bangabandhu Bridge. Mult.
677 4t. Type **238** 45 20
678 6t. Western approach road 55 30
679 8t. Embankment 70 90
680 10t. Main span, Bangabandhu Bridge . . . 85 1·00

239 Diana, Princess of Wales

1998. Diana, Princess of Wales Commemoration. Multicoloured.
681 8t. Type **239** 75 60
682 18t. Wearing pearl choker . . 1·25 1·25
683 22t. Wearing pendant necklace . . . . 1·25 1·25

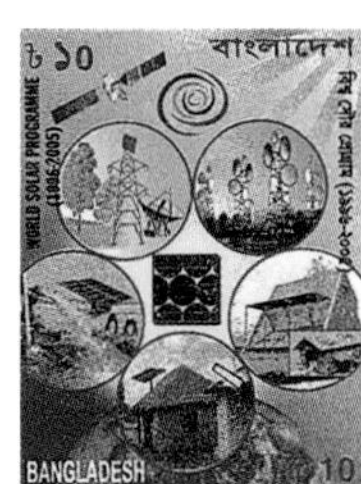

240 Means of collecting Solar Energy

1998. World Solar Energy Programme Summit.
684 **240** 10t. multicoloured 70 70

241 World Habitat Day Emblem and City Scene

1998. World Habitat Day.
685 **241** 4t. multicoloured 70 25

242 Farmworkers, Sunflower and "20"

1998. 20th Anniv of International Fund for Agricultural Development. Multicoloured.
686 6t. Type **242** 30 25
687 10t. Farmworker with baskets and harvested crops . . . 45 60

243 Batsman

1998. Wills International Cricket Cup, Dhaka.
688 **243** 6t. multicoloured . . . . 1·25 70

244 Begum Rokeya

1998. Begum Rokeya (campaigner for women's education) Commemoration.
689 **244** 4t. multicoloured 75 25

245 Anniversary Logo

1998. 50th Anniv of Universal Declaration of Human Rights.
690 **245** 10t. multicoloured 75 70

1998. Martyred Intellectuals (7th series). As T **148**. Each black and brown.
691 2t. Md. Khorshed Ali Sarker 30 30
692 2t. Abu Yakub Mahfuz Ali 30 30
693 2t. S. M. Nural Huda 30 30
694 2t. Nazmul Hoque Sarker . . 30 30
695 2t. Md. Taslim Uddin . . . 30 30
696 2t. Gulam Mostafa 30 30
697 2t. A. H. Nural Alam 30 30
698 2t. Timir Kanti Dev 30 30
699 2t. Altaf Hossain 30 30
700 2t. Aminul Hoque 30 30
701 2t. S. M. Fazlul Hoque . . . 30 30
702 2t. Mozammel Ali 30 30
703 2t. Syed Akbar Hossain . . . 30 30
704 2t. Sk. Abdus Salam 30 30
705 2t. Abdur Rahman 30 30
706 2t. Dr. Shyamal Kanti Lala 30 30

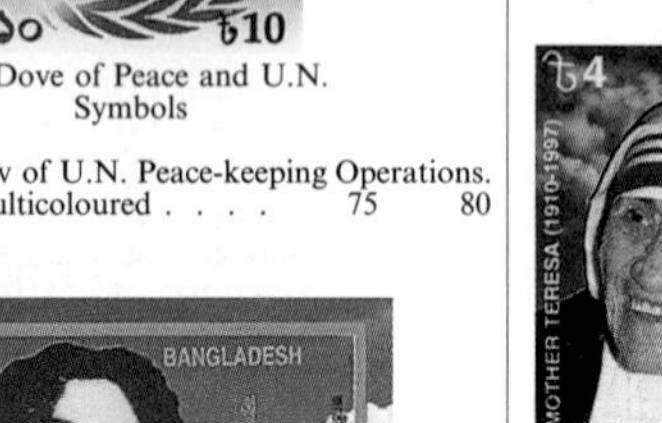

246 Dove of Peace and U.N. Symbols

1998. 50th Anniv of U.N. Peace-keeping Operations.
707 **246** 10t. multicoloured 75 80

247 Kazi Nazrul Islam

1998. Birth Centenary (1999) of Kazi Nazrul Islam (poet).
708 **247** 6t. multicoloured 70 40

248 Jamboree Emblem and Scout Activities

1999. 6th Bangladesh National Scout Jamboree.
709 **248** 2t. multicoloured 50 25

1999. As No. 75 but redrawn. Size 35 × 22 mm.
711 10t. red 20 25
No. 711 has been redrawn so that "SIXTY-DOME MOSQUE" appears above the face value at bottom right instead of below the main inscription at top left.

249 Surjya Sen and Demonstrators

1999. Surjya Sen (revolutionary) Commemoration.
715 **249** 4t. multicoloured 70 30

250 Dr. Fazlur Rahman Khan and Sears Tower

1999. 70th Birth Anniv of Dr. Fazlur Rahman Khan (architect).
716 **250** 4t. multicoloured 65 20

251 National Team Badges

1999. Cricket World Cup, England. Multicoloured.
717 8t. Type **251** . . . . 1·25 2·00
718 10t. Bangladesh cricket team badge and flag . . . . . . 1·50 1·25
MS719 139 × 89 mm. Nos. 717/18 (sold at 30t.) 2·75 3·25

252 Mother Teresa

253 Sheikh Mujibur Rahman, New York Skyline and Dove

1999. Mother Teresa Commemoration.
720 **252** 4t. multicoloured 70 30

1999. 25th Anniv of Bangladesh's Admission to U.N.
721 **253** 6t. multicoloured 70 35

254 Shaheed Mohammad Maizuddin

1999. 15th Death Anniv of Shaheed Mohammad Maizuddin (politician).
722 **254** 2t. multicoloured 50 30

255 Faces in Tree

1999. International Year of the Elderly.
723 **255** 6t. multicoloured 70 30

256 Shanty Town and Modern Buildings between Hands

1999. World Habitat Day.
724 **256** 4t. multicoloured 60 20

257 Mobile Post Office

1999. 125th Anniv of U.P.U. Multicoloured.
725 4t. Type **257** 60 50
726 4t. Postman on motorcycle 60 50
727 6t. Postal motor launch . . . 70 70
728 6t. Two Bangladesh airliners 70 70
MS729 141 × 90 mm. Nos. 725/8 (sold at 25t.) 2·00 2·25

258 Sir Jagadis Chandra Bose

1999. Sir Jagadis Chandra Bose (physicist and botanist) Commemoration.
730 **258** 4t. multicoloured 60 20

1999. Martyred Intellectuals (8th series). As T **148**. Each black and brown.
731 2t. Dr. Mohammad Shafi . . 25 25
732 2t. Maulana Kasimuddin Ahmed 25 25
733 2t. Quazi Ali Imam 25 25
734 2t. Sultanuddin Ahmed . . . 25 25
735 2t. A. S. M. Ershadullah . . 25 25
736 2t. Mohammad Fazlur Rahman 25 25
737 2t. Captain A. K. M. Farooq 25 25
738 2t. Md. Latafot Hossain Joarder 25 25
739 2t. Ram Ranjan Bhattacharjya 25 25
740 2t. Abani Mohan Dutta . . . 25 25
741 2t. Sunawar Ali 25 25
742 2t. Abdul Kader Miah . . . 25 25
743 2t. Major Rezaur Rahman 25 25
744 2t. Md. Shafiqul Anowar . . 25 25
745 2t. A. A. M. Mozammel Hoque 25 25
746 2t. Khandkar Abul Kashem 25 25

259 Bangladesh Flag and Monument

2000. New Millennium. Multicoloured.
747 4t. Type **259** 40 20
748 6t. Satellite, computer and dish aerial (vert) 60 70

260 Cub Scouts, Globe and Flag

2000. 5th Bangladesh Cub Camporee.
749 **260** 2t. multicoloured 30 20

261 Jibananada Das

2000. Death Centenary (1999) of Jibananada Das (poet).
750 **261** 4t. multicoloured 50 20

262 Dr. Muhammad Shamsuzzoha

2000. 30th Death Anniv (1999) of Dr. Muhammad Shamsuzzoha.
751 **262** 4t. multicoloured 50 20

263 Shafiur Rahman

2000. International Mother Language Day. Mult.
752 4t. Type **263** 40 40
753 4t. Abul Barkat 40 40
754 4t. Abdul Jabbar 40 40
755 4t. Rafiq Uddin Ahmad . . . 40 40

264 Meteorological Equipment

2000. 50th Anniv of World Meteorological Organization.
756 **264** 10t. multicoloured 80 80

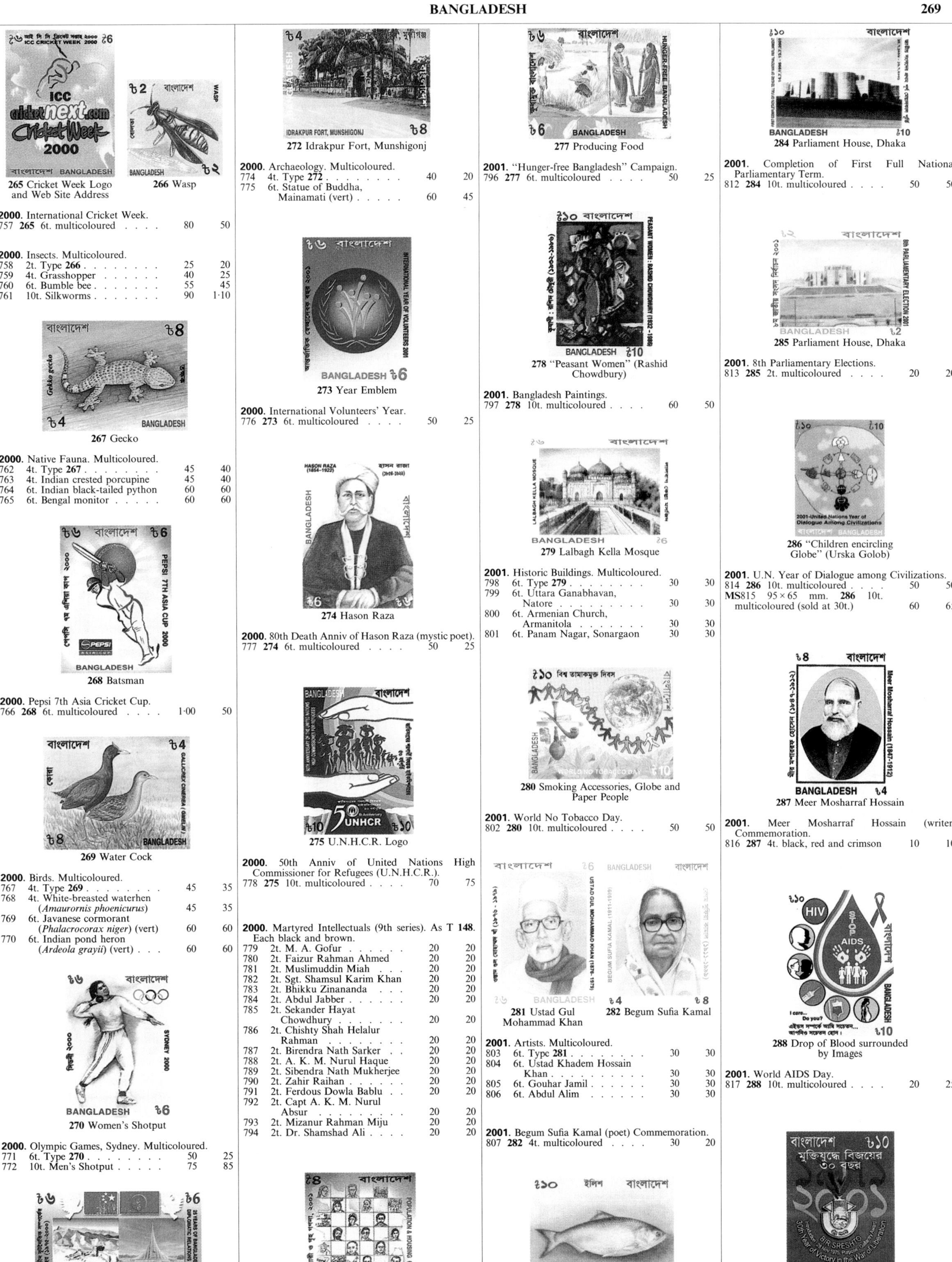

265 Cricket Week Logo and Web Site Address

266 Wasp

2000. International Cricket Week.
757 **265** 6t. multicoloured 80 50

2000. Insects. Multicoloured.
758 2t. Type **266** 25 20
759 4t. Grasshopper 40 25
760 6t. Bumble bee 55 45
761 10t. Silkworms . . . . 90 1·10

267 Gecko

2000. Native Fauna. Multicoloured.
762 4t. Type **267** 45 40
763 4t. Indian crested porcupine 45 40
764 6t. Indian black-tailed python 60 60
765 6t. Bengal monitor 60 60

268 Batsman

2000. Pepsi 7th Asia Cricket Cup.
766 **268** 6t. multicoloured . . . . 1·00 50

269 Water Cock

2000. Birds. Multicoloured.
767 4t. Type **269** 45 35
768 4t. White-breasted waterhen (*Amaurornis phoenicurus*) 45 35
769 6t. Javanese cormorant (*Phalacrocorax niger*) (vert) 60 60
770 6t. Indian pond heron (*Ardeola grayii*) (vert) . . . 60 60

270 Women's Shotput

2000. Olympic Games, Sydney. Multicoloured.
771 6t. Type **270** 50 25
772 10t. Men's Shotput 75 85

271 Clasped Hands, Landmarks and Flags

2000. 25th Anniv of Diplomatic Relations with People's Republic of China.
773 **271** 6t. multicoloured 50 25

272 Idrakpur Fort, Munshigonj

2000. Archaeology. Multicoloured.
774 4t. Type **272** 40 20
775 6t. Statue of Buddha, Mainamati (vert) 60 45

273 Year Emblem

2000. International Volunteers' Year.
776 **273** 6t. multicoloured 50 25

274 Hason Raza

2000. 80th Death Anniv of Hason Raza (mystic poet).
777 **274** 6t. multicoloured 50 25

275 U.N.H.C.R. Logo

2000. 50th Anniv of United Nations High Commissioner for Refugees (U.N.H.C.R.).
778 **275** 10t. multicoloured 70 75

2000. Martyred Intellectuals (9th series). As T **148**. Each black and brown.
779 2t. M. A. Gofur 20 20
780 2t. Faizur Rahman Ahmed 20 20
781 2t. Muslimuddin Miah . . . 20 20
782 2t. Sgt. Shamsul Karim Khan 20 20
783 2t. Bhikku Zinananda . . . 20 20
784 2t. Abdul Jabber 20 20
785 2t. Sekander Hayat Chowdhury 20 20
786 2t. Chishty Shah Helalur Rahman 20 20
787 2t. Birendra Nath Sarker . . 20 20
788 2t. A. K. M. Nurul Haque 20 20
789 2t. Sibendra Nath Mukherjee 20 20
790 2t. Zahir Raihan 20 20
791 2t. Ferdous Dowla Bablu . . 20 20
792 2t. Capt A. K. M. Nurul Absur 20 20
793 2t. Mizanur Rahman Miju 20 20
794 2t. Dr. Shamshad Ali 20 20

276 Map of Faces

2001. Population and Housing Census.
795 **276** 4t. multicoloured 50 20

277 Producing Food

2001. "Hunger-free Bangladesh" Campaign.
796 **277** 6t. multicoloured 50 25

278 "Peasant Women" (Rashid Chowdbury)

2001. Bangladesh Paintings.
797 **278** 10t. multicoloured 60 50

279 Lalbagh Kella Mosque

2001. Historic Buildings. Multicoloured.
798 6t. Type **279** 30 30
799 6t. Uttara Ganabhavan, Natore 30 30
800 6t. Armenian Church, Armanitola 30 30
801 6t. Panam Nagar, Sonargaon 30 30

280 Smoking Accessories, Globe and Paper People

2001. World No Tobacco Day.
802 **280** 10t. multicoloured 50 50

281 Ustad Gul Mohammad Khan

282 Begum Sufia Kamal

2001. Artists. Multicoloured.
803 6t. Type **281** 30 30
804 6t. Ustad Khadem Hossain Khan 30 30
805 6t. Gouhar Jamil 30 30
806 6t. Abdul Alim 30 30

2001. Begum Sufia Kamal (poet) Commemoration.
807 **282** 4t. multicoloured 30 20

283 Hilsa

2001. Fish. Multicoloured.
808 10t. Type **283** 40 50
809 10t. Tengra 40 50
810 10t. Punti 40 50
811 10t. Khalisa 40 50

284 Parliament House, Dhaka

2001. Completion of First Full National Parliamentary Term.
812 **284** 10t. multicoloured 50 50

285 Parliament House, Dhaka

2001. 8th Parliamentary Elections.
813 **285** 2t. multicoloured 20 20

286 "Children encircling Globe" (Urska Golob)

2001. U.N. Year of Dialogue among Civilizations.
814 **286** 10t. multicoloured 50 50
MS815 95×65 mm. **286** 10t. multicoloured (sold at 30t.) 60 65

287 Meer Mosharraf Hossain

2001. Meer Mosharraf Hossain (writer) Commemoration.
816 **287** 4t. black, red and crimson 10 10

288 Drop of Blood surrounded by Images

2001. World AIDS Day.
817 **288** 10t. multicoloured 20 25

289 Sreshto Medal

2001. 30th Anniv of Independence. Gallantry Medals. Multicoloured.
818 10t. Type **289** 20 25
819 10t. Uttom medal 20 25
820 10t. Bikram medal 20 25
821 10t. Protik medal 20 25

290 Publicity Poster

2002. 10th Asian Art Biennale, Dhaka.
822 **290** 10t. multicoloured 20 25

291 Letters from Bengali Alphabet

2002. 50th Anniv of Amar Ekushey (language movement). International Mother Language Day.
823 **291** 10t. black, gold and red 20 25
824 – 10t. black, gold and red 20 25
825 – 10t. black, gold and red 20 25
MS826 96 × 64 mm. 30t. multicoloured 60 65

DESIGNS—HORIZ: No. 824, Language Martyrs' Monument, Dhaka; 825, Letters from Bengali alphabet ("INTERNATIONAL MOTHER LANGUAGE DAY" inscr at right). VERT: No. **MS**826, Commemorative symbol of Martyrs' Monument.

292 Rokuon-Ji Temple, Japan

2002. 30th Anniv of Diplomatic Relations with Japan.
827 **292** 10t. multicoloured 20 25

293 Silhouetted Goats

2002. Goat Production.
828 **293** 2t. multicoloured 10 10

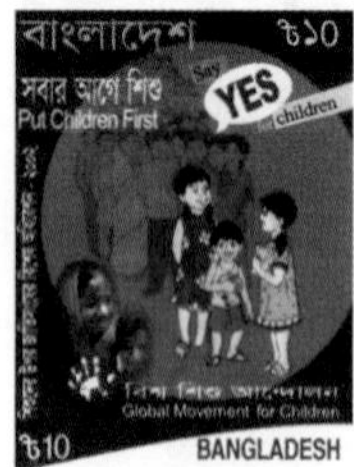

294 Children

2002. U.N. Special Session on Children.
829 **294** 10t. multicoloured 20 25

295 Mohammad Nasiruddin

2002. Mohammad Nasiruddin (journalist) Commemoration.
830 **295** 4t. black and brown 10 10

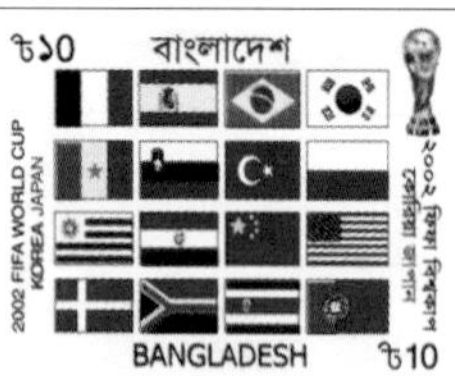

296 National Flags (trophy at top right)

2002. World Cup Football Championship, Japan and Korea. Multicoloured.
831 10t. Type **296** 20 25
832 10t. Pitch markings on world map 20 25
833 10t. National flags (trophy at top left) 20 25

297 Children tending Saplings

2002. National Tree Planting Campaign. Mult.
834 10t. Type **297** 20 25
835 10t. Citrus fruit 20 25
836 10t. Trees within leaf symbol (vert) 20 25

298 Children inside Symbolic House

2002. 30th Anniv of S.O.S. Children's Village in Bangladesh.
837 **298** 6t. multicoloured 15 20

299 Rural Family

2002. World Population Day.
838 **299** 6t. multicoloured 15 20

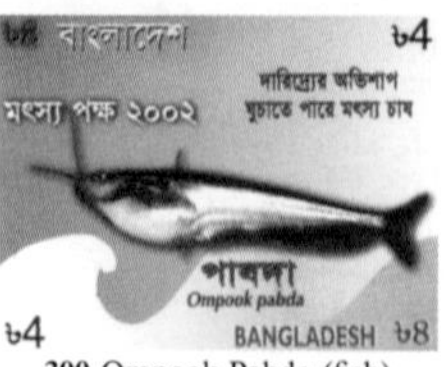

300 Ompook Pabda (fish)

2002. Fish. Multicoloured.
839 4t. Type **300** 10 10
840 4t. *Labeo gonius* 10 10

301 Bangladesh–U.K. Friendship Bridge, Bhairab

2002. Opening of Bangladesh–U.K. Friendship Bridge, Bhairab.
841 **301** 4t. multicoloured 10 10

302 Dhaka City Centre

2002. World Habitat Day.
842 **302** 4t. multicoloured 10 10

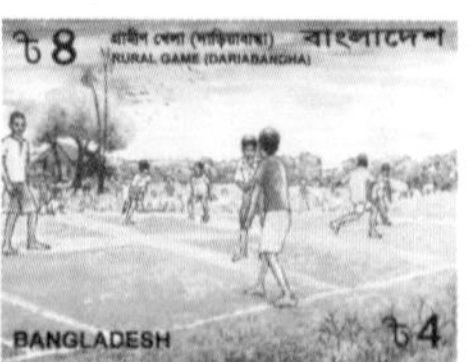

303 Dariabandha (Tag)

2002. Rural Games. Multicoloured.
843 4t. Type **303** 10 10
844 4t. Kanamachee (Blind-man's buff) 10 10

OFFICIAL STAMPS

1973. Nos. 22, etc. optd **SERVICE**.
O 1 **7** 2p. black 10 1·25
O 2 – 3p. green 10 1·25
O 3 – 5p. brown 20 10
O 4 – 10p. black 20 10
O 5 – 20p. green 1·50 10
O 6 – 25p. mauve 3·75 10
O 7 – 60p. grey 3·75 2·00
O 8 – 75p. orange 1·50 30
O 9 **8** 1t. violet 11·00 5·00
O10 – 5t. blue 5·00 8·00

1974. Nos. 49/51 optd **SERVICE**.
O11 **14** 1t. violet 4·50 50
O12 – 2t. olive 6·00 2·25
O13 – 5t. blue 11·00 11·00

1976. Nos. 64/70 and 72/4 optd **SERVICE**.
O14 – 5p. green 1·50 80
O15 – 10p. black 1·75 80
O16 – 20p. green 2·00 80
O17 – 25p. mauve 3·25 80
O18 – 50p. purple 3·25 50
O19 – 60p. grey 30 2·50
O20 – 75p. olive 30 3·25
O21 **14** 1t. blue 2·75 50
O22 – 2t. green 35 2·00
O23 – 5t. blue 30 2·00

1981. Nos. 125/37 optd **SERVICE**.
O24 – 5p. brown 1·50 2·25
O25 **32** 10p. blue 1·50 2·50
O26 – 15p. orange 1·50 2·25
O27 – 20p. red 1·50 2·25
O28 – 25p. blue 80 2·25
O29 – 30p. green 2·75 2·75
O30 – 40p. purple 2·75 2·00
O31 – 50p. black 30 10
O32 – 80p. brown 2·25 50
O33 – 1t. violet 30 10
O34 – 2t. blue 35 2·50

1983. Nos. 220/9, 318a and 710 (1989) optd **Service**.
O35 **69** 5p. blue 10 10
O36 – 10p. purple 10 10
O37 – 15p. blue 10 10
O38 – 20p. black 10 10
O39 – 25p. grey 10 10
O40 – 30p. brown 10 10
O41 – 50p. brown 10 10
O42 – 1 t. blue 75 10
O43 – 2t. green 10 10
O44 – 3t. black and blue 10 10
O45 – 4t. blue 10 15
O46 – 5t. purple 1·50 70

সার্ভিস (O 5) সার্ভিস (O 6) সার্ভিস (O 7)

1989. Nos. 227 and 710 (1989) optd with Type O **5**.
O47 1t. blue 20 10
O48 5t. black and brown 80 90

1990. Nos. 368/9 (Immunization) optd with Type O **6**.
O49 **133** 1t. green 10 10
O50 2t. brown 10 10

1992. No. 376 optd as Type O **6** but horiz.
O51 **136** 6t. blue and yellow 15 20

1995. No. 553 (National Diabetes Awareness Day) optd as Type O **6** but horiz.
O52 **199** 2t. multicoloured 70 70

1996. Nos. 221 and 223 optd with Type O **7**.
O53 10p. purple 20 20
O54 20p. black 30 30

1999. No. 710 optd as Type O **5** but vert.
O56 5t. black and brown 10 15

BARBADOS Pt. 1

An island in the Br. West Indies, E. of the Windward Islands, attained self-government on 16 October 1961 and achieved independence within the Commonwealth on 30 November 1966.

1852. 12 pence = 1 shilling;
20 shillings = 1 pound.
1950. 100 cents = 1 West Indian, later Barbados, dollar.

1 Britannia

2

1852. Imperf.
8 **1** (½d.) green £120 £200
10 (1d.) blue 30·00 60·00
4a (2d.) slate £225 £1200
5 (4d.) red 55·00 £275
11 **2** 6d. red £700 £120
12a 1s. black £200 75·00

1860. Perf.
21 **1** (½d.) green 15·00 11·00
24 (1d.) blue 30·00 3·50
25 (4d.) red 80·00 38·00
31 **2** 6d. red 80·00 20·00
33 6d. orange £100 28·00
35 1s. black 50·00 7·00

1873. Perf.
72 **2** ½d. green 10·00 50
74 1d. blue 55·00 65
63 3d. brown £325 £110
75 3d. mauve £100 6·00
76 4d. red £100 8·00
79 6d. yellow £110 1·00
81 1s. purple £130 3·25

3

4

1873.
64 **3** 5s. red £950 £300

1878. Half of No. 64 surch **1D**.
86 **3** 1d. on half 5s. red £4000 £600

1882.
90 **4** ½d. green 15·00 1·50
92 1d. red 17·00 1·00
93 2½d. blue 85·00 1·50
96 3d. purple 4·25 16·00
97 4d. grey £250 3·00
99 4d. brown 4·75 1·50
100 6d. brown 75·00 40·00
102 1s. brown 26·00 21·00
103 5s. bistre £150 £190

1892. Surch **HALF-PENNY**.
104 **4** ½d. on 4d. brown 2·25 4·00

6 Seal of Colony

7

1892.
105 **6** ¼d. grey and red 2·50 10
163 ¼d. brown 7·00 30
106 ½d. green 2·50 10
107 1d. red 4·75 10
108 2d. black and orange 8·00 75
166 2d. grey 7·50 9·50
139 2½d. blue 16·00 15
110 5d. olive 7·00 4·50
111 6d. mauve and red 16·00 2·00
168 6d. deep purple and purple 9·50 15·00
112 8d. orange and blue 4·00 22·00
113 10d. green and red 8·00 6·50
169 1s. black on green 9·50 14·00
114 2s.6d. black and orange 48·00 48·00
144 2s.6d. violet and green 42·00 95·00

1897. Diamond Jubilee.
116 **7** ¼d. grey and red 3·75 60
117 ½d. green 3·75 60
118 1d. red 3·75 60
119 2½d. blue 7·50 85
120 5d. brown 17·00 16·00
121 6d. mauve and red 23·00 22·00
122 8d. orange and blue 9·00 24·00
123 10d. green and red 48·00 55·00
124 2s.6d. black and orange 65·00 55·00

8 Nelson Monument

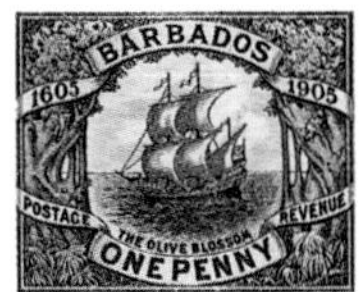

9 "Olive Blossom", 1650

1906. Death Centenary of Nelson.

145	8	¼d. black and grey	8·50	1·75
146		½d. black and green	9·50	15
147		1d. black and red	12·00	15
148		2d. black and yellow	1·75	4·50
149		2½d. black and blue	3·75	1·25
150		6d. black and mauve	18·00	25·00
151		1s. black and red	21·00	50·00

1906. Tercentenary of Annexation of Barbados.

152	9	1d. black, blue and green	10·00	25

1907. Surch **Kingston Relief Fund. 1d.**

153	6	1d. on 2d. black and orange	2·50	5·50

11

14

1912.

170	11	¼d. brown	1·50	1·50
171		½d. green	3·75	10
172		1d. red	8·50	10
173		2d. grey	2·75	14·00
174		2½d. blue	1·50	50
175		3d. purple on yellow	1·50	14·00
176		4d. red and black on yellow	1·50	17·00
177		6d. deep purple and purple	12·00	12·00

Larger type, with portrait at top centre.

178		1s. black on green	8·50	13·00
179		2s. blue and purple on blue	42·00	45·00
180		3s. violet and green	85·00	95·00

1916.

181	14	¼d. brown	75	40
182		½d. green	1·10	15
183a		1d. red	2·50	15
184		2d. grey	4·00	21·00
185		2½d. blue	3·50	2·25
186		3d. purple on yellow	2·25	6·00
187		4d. red on yellow	1·00	14·00
199		4d. black and red	80	3·75
188		6d. purple	3·50	4·00
189		1s. black on green	7·00	10·00
190		2s. purple on blue	16·00	7·50
191		3s. violet	48·00	£120
200		3s. green and violet	19·00	65·00

1917. Optd **WAR TAX**.

197	11	1d. red	50	15

16

18

1920. Victory. Inscr "VICTORY 1919".

201	16	¼d. black and brown	30	70
202		½d. black and green	1·00	15
203		1d. black and red	4·00	10
204		2d. black and grey	2·00	7·00
205		2½d. indigo and blue	2·75	17·00
206		3d. black and purple	3·00	6·00
207		4d. black and green	3·25	7·00
208		6d. black and orange	3·75	14·00
209	–	1s. black and green	10·00	27·00
210	–	2s. black and brown	26·00	38·00
211	–	3s. black and orange	30·00	45·00

The 1s. to 3s. show Victory full-face.

1921.

217	18	¼d. brown	25	10
219		½d. green	1·50	10
220		1d. red	80	10
221		2d. grey	1·75	20
222		2½d. blue	1·50	7·00
213		3d. purple on yellow	2·00	6·00
214		4d. red on yellow	1·75	14·00
225		6d. purple	3·50	5·50
215		1s. black on green	5·50	13·00
227		2s. purple on blue	10·00	19·00
228		3s. violet	14·00	55·00

19

21 Badge of the Colony

20 King Charles I and King George V

1925. Inscr "POSTAGE & REVENUE".

229	19	¼d. brown	25	10
230		½d. green	50	10
231		1d. red	50	10
231ba		1½d. orange	2·00	1·00
232		2d. grey	50	3·25
233		2½d. blue	50	80
234		3d. purple on yellow	1·00	45
235		4d. red on yellow	75	1·00
236		6d. purple	1·00	90
237		1s. black on green	2·00	6·50
238		2s. purple on blue	7·00	6·50
238a		2s.6d. red on blue	22·00	26·00
239		3s. violet	11·00	13·00

1927. Tercentenary of Settlement of Barbados.

240	20	1d. red	1·00	75

1935. Silver Jubilee. As T **13** of Antigua.

241		1d. blue and red	50	20
242		1½d. blue and grey	3·75	6·00
243		2½d. brown and blue	2·25	4·00
244		1s. grey and purple	17·00	18·00

1937. Coronation. As T **2** of Aden.

245		1d. red	30	15
246		1½d. brown	40	60
247		2½d. blue	70	50

1938. "POSTAGE & REVENUE" omitted.

248	21	½d. green	6·00	15
248c		½d. bistre	15	30
249a		1d. red	16·00	10
249c		1d. green	15	10
250		1½d. orange	15	40
250c		2d. purple	50	2·50
250d		2d. red	20	70
251		2½d. blue	50	60
252b		3d. brown	20	60
252c		3d. blue	20	1·75
253		4d. black	20	10
254		6d. violet	80	40
254a		8d. mauve	55	2·00
255a		1s. green	1·00	10
256		2s.6d. purple	7·00	1·50
256a		5s. blue	3·25	6·50

22 Kings Charles I, George VI, Assembly Chamber and Mace

1939. Tercentenary of General Assembly.

257	22	½d. green	2·50	80
258		1d. red	2·50	30
259		1½d. orange	2·50	60
260		2½d. blue	2·50	4·25
261		3d. brown	2·50	2·75

1946. Victory. As T **9** of Aden.

262		1½d. orange	15	15
263		3d. brown	15	15

1947. Surch **ONE PENNY**.

264	17	1d. on 2d. red	1·50	2·50

1948. Silver Wedding. As T **10/11** of Aden.

265		1½d. orange	30	10
266		5s. blue	10·00	7·00

1949. U.P.U. As T **20/23** of Antigua.

267		1½d. orange	30	50
268		3d. blue	1·75	2·75
269		4d. grey	35	2·25
270		1s. olive	35	60

24 Dover Fort

35 Seal of Barbados

1950.

271	24	1c. blue	30	2·50
272	–	2c. green	15	2·00
273	–	3c. brown and green	1·25	3·00
274	–	4c. red	15	40
275	–	6c. blue	15	2·25
276	–	8c. blue and purple	1·25	2·50
277	–	12c. blue and olive	1·00	1·00
278	–	24c. red and black	1·00	50
279	–	48c. violet	8·00	6·50
280	–	60c. green and lake	8·50	9·00
281	–	$1.20 red and olive	9·00	4·00
282	35	$2.40 black	16·00	17·00

DESIGNS—As Type **24**: HORIZ: 2c. Sugar cane breeding; 3c. Public buildings; 6c. Casting net; 8c. "Frances W. Smith" (schooner); 12c. Four-winged flyingfish; 24c. Old Main Guard Garrison; 60c. Careenage. VERT: 4c. Statue of Nelson; 48c. St. Michael's Cathedral; $1.20, Map and wireless mast.

1951. Inauguration of B.W.I. University College. As T **24/25** of Antigua.

283		3c. brown and blue	30	30
284		12c. blue and olive	55	1·75

36 King George VI and Stamp of 1852

1952. Centenary of Barbados Stamps.

285	36	3c. green and slate	20	40
286		4c. blue and red	20	1·00
287		12c. slate and green	20	1·00
288		24c. brown and sepia	20	55

37 Harbour Police

1953. As 1950 issue but with portrait or cypher (No. 301) of Queen Elizabeth II as in T **37**.

289	24	1c. blue	10	80
290	–	2c. orange and turquoise	15	50
291	–	3c. black and green	1·00	90
292	–	4c. black and orange	20	20
293	37	5c. blue and red	1·00	60
294	–	6c. brown	50	60
314	–	8c. black and blue	60	35
296	–	12c. blue and olive	1·00	10
297	–	24c. red and black	50	10
298	–	48c. violet	6·00	1·00
318	–	60c. green and purple	10·00	4·00
300	–	$1.20 red and olive	19·00	3·75
319	35	$2.40 black	1·25	1·75

1953. Coronation. As T **13** of Aden.

302		4c. black and orange	40	10

1958. British Caribbean Federation. As T **28** of Antigua.

303		3c. green	35	20
304		6c. blue	50	2·25
305		12c. red	50	30

38 Deep Water Harbour, Bridgetown

1961. Opening of Deep Water Harbour.

306	38	4c. black and orange	25	50
307		8c. black and blue	25	60
308		24c. red and black	25	60

39 Scout Badge and Map of Barbados

1962. Golden Jubilee of Barbados Boy Scout Association.

309	39	4c. black and orange	50	10
310		12c. blue and brown	80	15
311		$1.20 red and green	1·50	3·50

1965. Centenary of I.T.U. As T **36** of Antigua.

320		2c. lilac and red	20	40
321		48c. yellow and drab	45	1·00

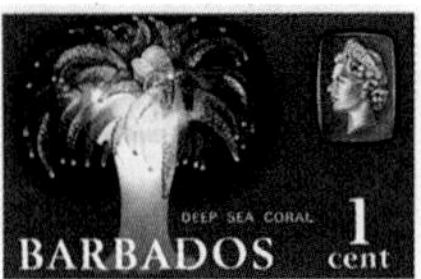

40 Deep Sea Coral

1965.

342	40	1c. black, pink and blue	10	20
323	–	2c. brown, yell & mve	20	15
324	–	3c. brown and orange	45	60
344	–	3c. brown and orange	30	2·75
325	–	4c. blue and green	15	10
326	–	5c. sepia, red and lilac	30	20
327	–	6c. multicoloured	45	20
328	–	8c. multicoloured	25	10
329	–	12c. multicoloured	35	10
330	–	15c. black, yellow and red	1·00	30
331	–	25c. blue and ochre	95	30
332	–	35c. red and green	1·50	15
333	–	50c. blue and green	2·00	40
334	–	$1 multicoloured	2·75	1·50
335	–	$2.50 multicoloured	2·75	3·25
355a	–	$5 multicoloured	13·00	8·00

DESIGNS—HORIZ: 2c. Lobster; 3c. (No. 324) Lined seahorse (wrongly inscribed "Hippocanpus"); 3c. (No. 344) (correctly inscribed "Hippocampus"); 4c. Sea urchin; 5c. Staghorn coral; 6c. Spot-finned butterflyfish; 8c. Rough file shell; 12c. Porcupinefish ("Balloon fish"); 15c Grey angel-fish; 25c. Brain coral; 35c. Brittle star; 50c. Four-winged flyingfish: $1 Queen or pink conch shell; $2.50, Fiddler crab. VERT: $5 Dolphin.

1966. Churchill Commemoration. As T **38** of Antigua.

336		1c. blue	10	2·25
337		4c. green	30	10
338		25c. brown	70	50
339		35c. violet	80	60

1966. Royal Visit. As T **39** of Antigua.

340		3c. black and blue	35	75
341		35c. black and mauve	1·40	1·00

54 Arms of Barbados

58 Policeman and Anchor

1966. Independence. Multicoloured.

356		4c. Type **54**	10	10
357		25c. Hilton Hotel (horiz)	15	10
358		35c. G. Sobers (Test cricketer)	1·50	65
359		50c. Pine Hill Dairy (horiz)	70	1·10

1967. 20th Anniv of U.N.E.S.C.O. As T **54/56** of Antigua.

360		4c. multicoloured	20	10
361		12c. yellow, violet and olive	45	50
362		25c. black, purple and orange	75	1·25

1967. Centenary of Harbour Police. Multicoloured.

363		4c. Type **58**	25	10
364		25c. Policeman and telescope	40	15
365		35c. "BPI" (police launch) (horiz)	45	15
366		50c. Policeman outside H.Q.	60	1·60

62 Governor-General Sir Winston Scott G.C.M.G

67 Radar Antenna

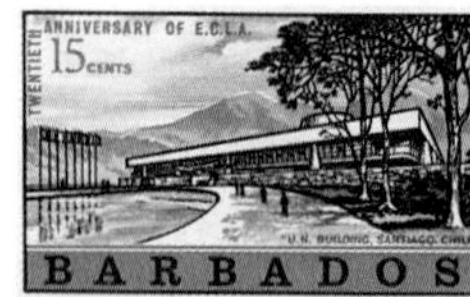

66 U.N. Building, Santiago, Chile

1967. 1st Anniv of Independence. Multicoloured.
367 4c. Type **62** 10 10
368 25c. Independence Arch (horiz) 20 10
369 35c. Treasury Building (horiz) 25 10
370 50c. Parliament Building (horiz) 35 90

1968. 20th Anniv of Economic Commission for Latin America.
371 **66** 15c. multicoloured 10 10

1968. World Meteorological Day. Multicoloured.
372 3c. Type **67** 10 10
373 25c. Meteorological Institute (horiz) 25 10
374 50c. Harp Gun and Coat of Arms 30 90

70 Lady Baden-Powell and Guide at Campfire

1968. Golden Jubilee of Girl Guiding in Barbados.
375 **70** 3c. blue, black and gold 20 60
376 – 25c. blue, black and gold 30 60
377 – 35c. yellow, black and gold 35 60
DESIGNS: 25c. Lady Baden-Powell and Pax Hill; 35c. Lady Baden-Powell and Guides' Badge.

73 Hands breaking Chain, and Human Rights Emblem

1968. Human Rights Year.
378 **73** 4c. violet, brown and green 10 20
379 – 25c. black, blue and yellow 10 25
380 – 35c. multicoloured 15 25
DESIGNS: 25c. Human Rights emblem and family enchained; 35c. Shadows of refugees beyond opening fence.

76 Racehorses in the Paddock

1969. Horse Racing. Multicoloured.
381 4c. Type **76** 25 15
382 25c. Starting-gate 25 15
383 35c. On the flat 30 15
384 50c. The winning-post 35 2·00
MS385 117 × 85 mm. Nos. 381/4 2·00 2·75

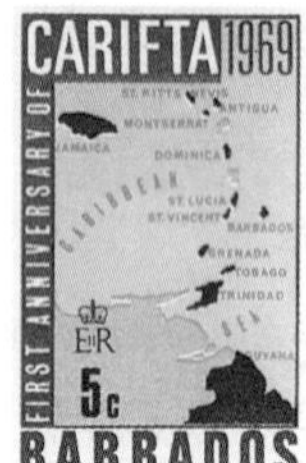

80 Map showing "CARIFTA" Countries

1969. 1st Anniv of "CARIFTA". Multicoloured.
386 5c. Type **80** 10 10
387 12c. "Strength in Unity" (horiz) 10 10
388 25c. Type **80** 10 10
389 50c. As 12c. 15 20

82 I.L.O. Emblem and "1919–1969"

1969. 50th Anniv of I.L.O.
390 **82** 4c. black, green and blue 10 10
391 25c. black, mauve and red 20 10

1969. No. 363 surch **ONE CENT**.
392 **58** 1c. on 4c. multicoloured 10 10

84 National Scout Badge

1969. Independence of Barbados Boy Scouts Association and 50th Anniv of Barbados Sea Scouts. Multicoloured.
393 5c. Type **84** 15 10
394 25c. Sea Scouts rowing 45 10
395 35c. Scouts around campfire 55 10
396 50c. Scouts and National Scout H.Q. 80 1·25
MS397 155 × 115 mm. Nos. 393/6 12·00 13·00

1970. No. 346 surch **4**.
398 4c. on 5c. sepia, red and lilac 10 10

89 Lion at Gun Hill

1970. Multicoloured.
399 1c. Type **89** 10 1·50
400 2c. Trafalgar Fountain 30 1·25
401 3c. Montefiore Drinking Fountain 10 1·00
402a 4c. St. James' Monument 30 10
403 5c. St. Ann's Fort 10 10
404 6c. Old Sugar Mill, Morgan Lewis 35 3·00
405 8c. The Cenotaph 10 10
406a 10c. South Point Lighthouse 1·25 15
407 12c. Barbados Museum (horiz) 1·50 10
408 15c. Sharon Moravian Church (horiz) 30 15
409 25c. George Washington House (horiz) 25 15
410 35c. Nicholas Abbey (horiz) 30 85
411 50c. Bowmanston Pumping Station (horiz) 40 1·00
412 $1 Queen Elizabeth Hospital (horiz) 70 2·50
413 $2.50 Suger Factory (horiz) 1·50 4·00
467 $5 Seawell International Airport (horiz) 4·00 5·50

105 Primary Schoolgirl

1970. 25th Anniv of U.N. Multicoloured.
415 4c. Type **105** 10 10
416 5c. Secondary schoolboy 10 10
417 25c. Technical student 35 10
418 50c. University building 55 1·50

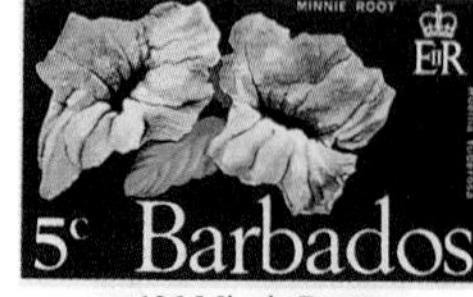

106 Minnie Root

1970. Flowers of Barbados. Multicoloured.
419 1c. Barbados Easter lily (vert) 10 2·00
420 5c. Type **106** 40 10
421 10c. Eyelash orchid 1·75 30
422 25c. Pride of Barbados (vert) 1·25 75
423 35c. Christmas hope 1·25 85
MS424 162 × 101 mm. Nos. 419/23. Imperf 2·00 5·50

107 "Via Dolorosa" Window, St. Margaret's Church, St. John

109 S. J. Prescod (politician)

108 "Sailfish" Dinghy

1971. Easter. Multicoloured.
425 4c. Type **107** 10 10
426 10c. "The Resurrection" (Benjamin West) 10 10
427 35c. Type **107** 15 10
428 50c. As 10c. 30 1·50

1971. Tourism. Multicoloured.
429 1c. Type **108** 10 40
430 5c. Tennis 40 10
431 12c. Horse-riding 60 10
432 25c. Water-skiing 40 20
433 50c. Scuba-diving 50 80

1971. Death Centenary of Samuel Jackman Prescod.
434 **109** 3c. multicoloured 10 15
435 35c. multicoloured 15 15

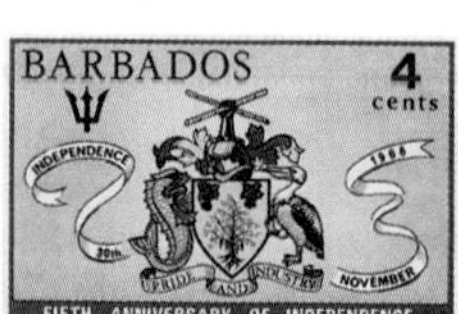

110 Arms of Barbados

1971. 5th Anniv of Independence. Multicoloured.
436 4c. Type **110** 20 10
437 15c. National flag and map 45 10
438 25c. Type **110** 45 10
439 50c. As 15c. 90 1·60

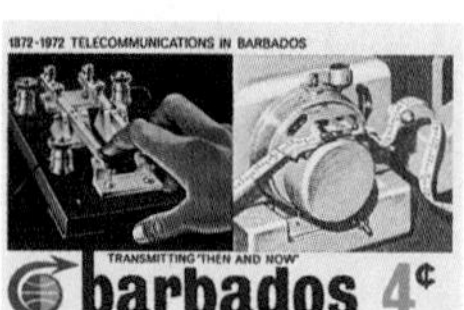

111 Transmitting "Then and Now"

1972. Centenary of Cable Link. Multicoloured.
440 4c. Type **111** 10 10
441 10c. Cable Ship "Stanley Angwin" 20 10
442 35c. Barbados Earth Station and "Intelsat 4" 35 20
443 50c. Mt. Misery and Tropospheric Scatter Station 50 1·75

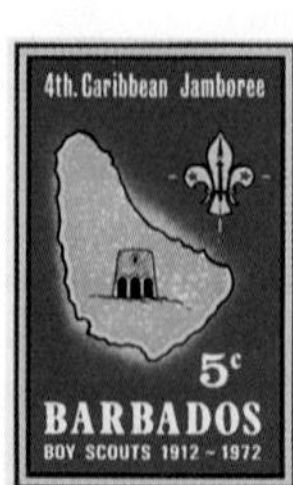

112 Map and Badge

1972. Diamond Jubilee of Scouts. Multicoloured.
444 5c. Type **112** 15 10
445 15c. Pioneers of scouting (horiz) 15 10
446 25c. Scouts (horiz) 30 15
447 50c. Flags (horiz) 60 1·00

113 Mobile Library

1972. Int Book Year. Multicoloured.
448 4c. Type **113** 20 10
449 15c. Visual-aids van 25 10
450 25c. Public library 25 10
451 $1 Codrington College 1·00 1·50

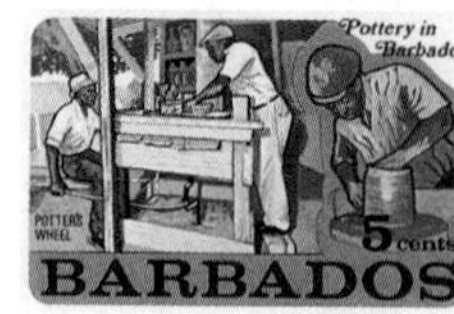

114 Potter's Wheel

1973. Pottery in Barbados. Multicoloured.
468 5c. Type **114** 10 10
469 15c. Kilns 20 10
470 25c. Finished products 25 10
471 $1 Market scene 90 1·10

115 First Flight, 1911

1973. Aviation.
472 **115** 5c. multicoloured 30 10
473 – 15c. multicoloured 90 10
474 – 25c. blue, blk & cobalt 1·25 20
475 – 50c. multicoloured 2·00 1·90
DESIGNS: 15c. De Havilland Cirrus Moth on first flight to Barbados, 1928; 25c. Lockheed Super Electra, 1939; 50c. Vickers Super VC-10 airliner, 1973.

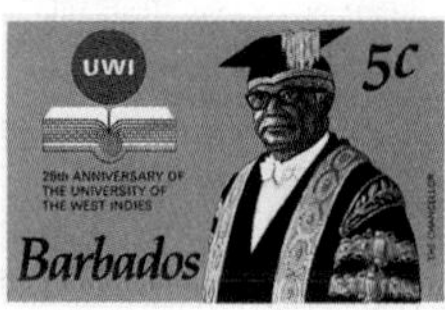

116 University Chancellor

1973. 25th Anniv of University of West Indies. Multicoloured.
476 5c. Type **116** 10 10
477 25c. Sherlock Hall 25 15
478 35c. Cave Hill Campus 30 25

1974. No. 462 surch **4c.**
479 4c. on 25c. multicoloured 15 15

118 Old Sail Boat

1974. Fishing Boats of Barbados. Multicoloured.
480 15c. Type **118** 30 15
481 35c. Rowing-boat 55 25
482 50c. Motor fishing-boat 70 70
483 $1 "Calamar" (fishing boat) 1·10 1·40
MS484 140 × 140 mm. Nos. 480/3 3·50 3·00

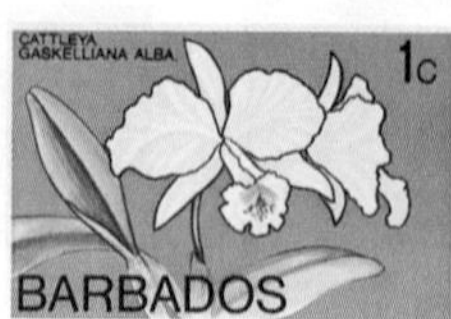

119 "Cattleya gaskelliana alba"

1974. Orchids. Multicoloured.
510 1c. Type **119** 15 1·25
511 2c. "Renanthera storiei" (vert) 15 1·25
512 3c. "Dendrobium" "Rose Marie" (vert) 15 1·00
488 4c. "Epidendrum ibaguense" (vert) 1·75 90
514 5c. "Schomburgkia humboldtii" (vert) 35 15
490 8c. "Oncidium ampliatum" (vert) 1·00 90
515 10c. "Arachnis maggie oei" (vert) 35 10
492 12c. "Dendrobium aggregatum" (vert) 45 2·75
517 15c. "Paphiopedilum puddle" (vert) 70 15
493b 20c. "Spathoglottis" "The Gold" 4·75 4·75
518 25c. "Epidendrum ciliare" (Eyelash) 70 10
550 35c. "Bletia patula" (vert) 2·00 1·75
519 45c. "Phalaenopsis schilleriana" "Sunset Glow" (vert) 60 15

496 50c. As 45c. (vert) . . . . . 5·50 4·50
497 $1 "Ascocenda" "Red Gem" (vert) . . . . . . 8·50 3·25
498 $2.50 "Brassolaeliocattleya" "Nugget" . . . . 3·50 7·00
499 $5 "Caularthron bicornutum" . . . . . . 3·50 6·00
500 $10 "Vanda" "Josephine Black" (vert) . . . . . . 4·00 13·00

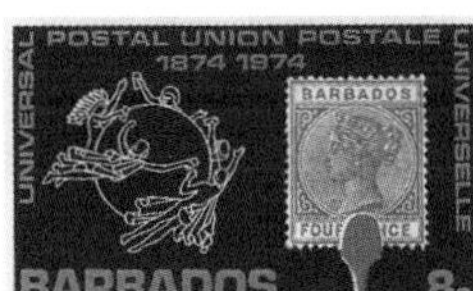

120 4d. Stamp of 1882, and U.P.U. Emblem

1974. Centenary of Universal Postal Union.
501 **120** 8c. mauve, orange & grn 10 10
502 – 35c. red, orge & brown 20 10
503 – 50c. ultram, bl & silver 25 35
504 – $1 blue, brown & black 55 1·00
MS505 126 × 101 mm. Nos. 501/4 1·50 2·25
DESIGNS: 35c. Letters encircling the globe; 50c. U.P.U. emblem and arms of Barbados; $1 Map of Barbados, sailing ship and Boeing 747 airliner.

121 Royal Yacht "Britannia"

1975. Royal Visit. Multicoloured.
506 8c. Type **121** 85 30
507 25c. Type **121** . . . . 1·40 30
508 35c. Sunset and palms . . . 60 35
509 $1 As 35c. . . . . 1·75 3·25

122 St. Michael's Cathedral

1975. 150th Anniv of Anglican Diocese. Mult.
526 5c. Type **122** 10 10
527 15c. Bishop Coleridge 15 10
528 50c. All Saints' Church . . . 45 50
529 $1 "Archangel Michael and Satan" (stained glass window, St. Michael's Cathedral, Bridgetown) . . 70 80

123 Pony Float

1975. Crop-over Festival. Multicoloured.
531 8c. Type **123** 10 10
532 25c. Man on stilts 10 10
533 35c. Maypole dancing . . . 15 10
534 50c. Cuban dancers 30 80
MS535 127 × 85 mm. Nos. 531/4 1·00 1·60

124 Barbados Coat of Arms

125 17th-Century Sailing Ship

1975. Coil Definitives.
536 **124** 5c. blue 15 80
537 25c. violet . . . . 25 1·10

1975. 350th Anniv of First Settlement. Multicoloured.
538 4c. Type **125** 50 20
539 10c. Bearded fig tree and fruit 30 15
540 25c. Ogilvy's 17th-century map . . . . 1·00 30
541 $1 Captain John Powell . . . 1·50 5·00
MS542 105 × 115 mm. Nos. 538/41 3·00 7·00

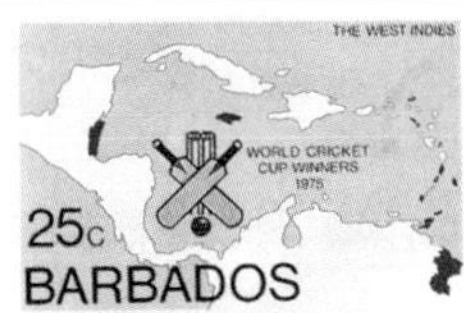

126 Map of Caribbean

1976. West Indian Victory in World Cricket Cup.
559 **126** 25c. multicoloured . . . . 1·00 1·00
560 – 45c. black and purple . . 1·00 2·00
DESIGN—VERT: 45c. The Prudential Cup.

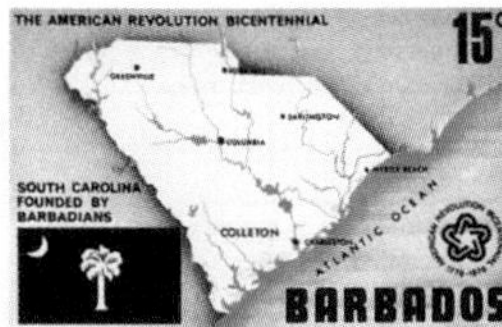

127 Flag and Map of South Carolina

1976. Bicentenary of American Revolution. Mult.
561 15c. Type **127** 45 15
562 25c. George Washington and map of Bridgetown 45 15
563 50c. Independence Declaration . . . . 60 1·00
564 $1 Prince Hall . . . . 75 3·00

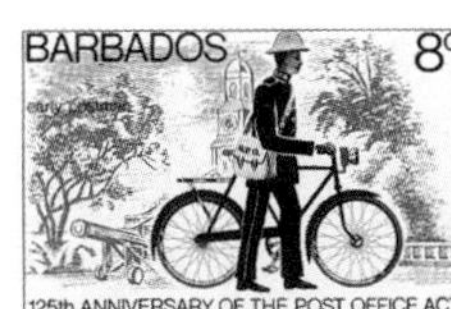

128 Early Postman

1976. 125th Anniv of Post Office Act. Multicoloured.
565 8c. Type **128** 10 10
566 35c. Modern postman . . . 25 10
567 50c. Early letter 30 75
568 $1 Delivery van . . . . . . 50 1·75

129 Coast Guard "Commander Marshall" and "T. T. Lewis" launches

1976. 10th Anniv of Independence. Multicoloured.
569 5c. Type **129** 30 20
570 15c. Reverse of currency note 30 10
571 25c. Barbados national anthem 30 20
572 $1 Independence Day parade 1·10 3·00
MS573 90 × 125 mm. Nos. 569/72 2·75 3·75

130 Arrival of Coronation Coach at Westminster Abbey

132 Maces of the House of Commons

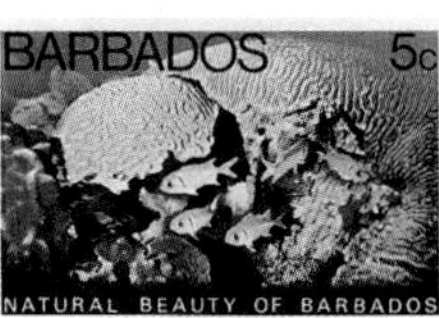

131 Underwater Park

1977. Silver Jubilee. Multicoloured.
574 15c. Queen knighting Garfield Sobers, 1975 . . . . 30 25
575 50c. Type **130** 30 40
576 $1 Queen entering Abbey . . 30 70

1977. Natural Beauty of Barbados. Multicoloured.
577 5c. Type **131** 15 10
578 35c. Royal palms (vert) . . . 30 10
579 50c. Underwater caves . . . 40 50
580 $1 Stalagmite in Harrison's Cave (vert) . . . . 70 1·10
MS581 138 × 92 mm. Nos. 577/80 2·25 2·75

1977. 13th Regional Conference of Commonwealth Parliamentary Association.
582 **132** 10c. orange, yellow & brn 10 10
583 – 25c. green, orge & dp grn 10 10
584 – 50c. multicoloured 20 20
585 – $1 blue, orange and dp bl 55 75
DESIGNS—VERT: 25c. Speaker's Chair; 50c. Senate Chamber. HORIZ: $1 Sam Lord's Castle.

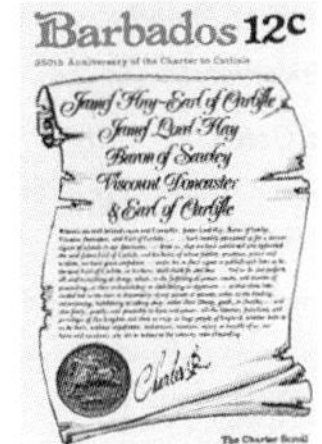

133 The Charter Scroll

135 Brown Pelican

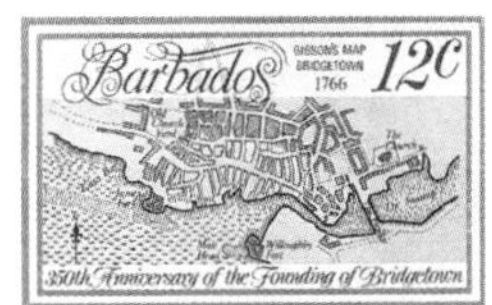

134 Gibson's Map of Bridgtown, 1766

1977. 350th Anniv of Granting of Charter to Earl of Carlisle. Multicoloured.
586 12c. Type **133** 15 10
587 25c. The earl receiving charter 15 10
588 45c. The earl and Charles I (horiz) 30 35
589 $1 Ligon's map, 1657 (horiz) 50 1·00

1977. Royal Visit. As Nos. 574/6 but inscr "SILVER JUBILEE ROYAL VISIT".
590 15c. Garfield Sobers being knighted, 1975 . . . . . . 60 50
591 50c. Type **130** 20 75
592 $1 Queen entering Abbey . . 30 1·25

1978. 350th Anniv of Founding of Bridgetown.
593 **134** 12c. multicoloured 15 10
594 – 25c. black, green & gold 15 10
595 – 45c. multicoloured 20 15
596 – $1 multicoloured 30 60
DESIGNS: 25c. "A Prospect of Bridgetown in Barbados" (engraving by S. Copens, 1695); 45c. "Trafalgar Square, Bridgetown" (drawing by J. M. Carter, 1835); $1 The Bridges, 1978.

1978. 25th Anniv of Coronation.
597 – 50c. olive, black & blue 25 50
598 – 50c. multicoloured 25 50
599 **135** 50c. olive, black & blue 25 50
DESIGNS: No. 597, Griffin of Edward III. No. 598, Queen Elizabeth II.

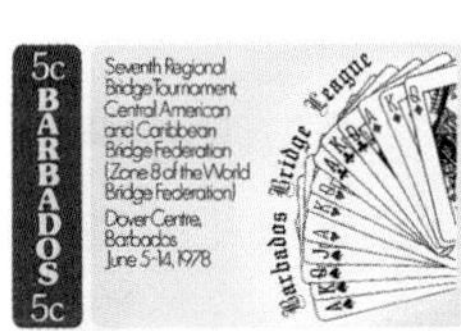

136 Barbados Bridge League Logo

1978. 7th Regional Bridge Tournament, Barbados. Multicoloured.
600 5c. Type **136** 10 10
601 10c. Emblem of World Bridge Federation 15 10
602 45c. Central American and Caribbean Bridge Federation emblem 25 10
603 $1 Playing cards on map of Caribbean 40 60
MS604 134 × 83 mm. Nos. 600/3 1·75 2·50

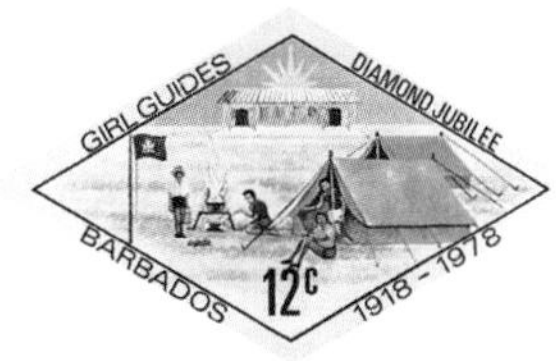

137 Camp Scene

1978. Diamond Jubilee of Guiding. Multicoloured.
605 12c. Type **137** 25 15
606 28c. Community work . . . 40 15
607 50c. Badge and "60" (vert) 55 30
608 $1 Guide badge (vert) . . . . 75 1·00

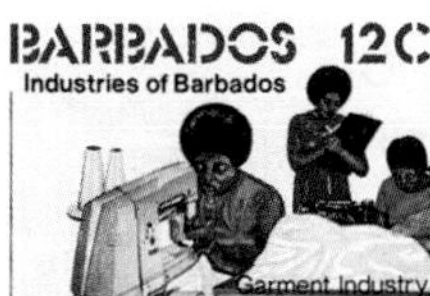

138 Garment Industry

1978. Industries of Barbados. Multicoloured.
609 12c. Type **138** 15 10
610 28c. Cooper (vert) 25 25
611 45c. Blacksmith (vert) 35 95
612 50c. Wrought iron working 40 95

139 "Forth" (early mail steamer)

1979. Ships. Multicoloured.
613 12c. Type **139** 35 10
614 25c. "Queen Elizabeth 2" in Deep Water Harbour . . . 55 15
615 50c. "Ra II" nearing Barbados . . . . 75 1·00
616 $1 Early mail paddle-steamer 1·00 2·50

140 1953 1c. Definitive Stamp

1979. Death Cent of Sir Rowland Hill. Mult.
617 12c. Type **140** 15 15
618 28c. 1975 350th anniv of first settlement 25c. commemorative (vert) . . . 20 30
619 45c. Penny Black with Maltese Cross postmark (vert) 30 45
MS620 137 × 90 mm. 50c. Unissued "Brittannia" blue 55 50

1979. St. Vincent Relief Fund. No. 495 surch **28c+4c ST. VINCENT RELIEF FUND.**
621 28c.+4c. on 35c. "Bletia patula" 50 60

142 Grassland Yellow Finch ("Grass Canary")

1979. Birds. Multicoloured.
622 1c. Type **142** . . . . 10 1·25
623 2c. Grey kingbird ("Rainbird") . . . . . . 10 1·25
624 5c. Lesser Antillean bullfinch ("Sparrow") . . 10 70
625 8c. Magnificent frigate bird ("Frigate Bird") . . . . 75 2·25
626 10c. Cattle egret 10 40
627 12c. Green-backed heron ("Green Gaulin") . . . . 50 1·50
627a 15c. Carib grackle ("Blackbird") . . . . . . 4·50 5·00
628 20c. Antillean crested hummingbird ("Humming Bird") 20 55
629 25c. Scaly-breasted ground dove ("Ground Dove") 20 60
630 28c. As 15c. . . . . 2·00 2·00
631 35c. Green-throated carib 70 70
631b 40c. Red-necked pigeon ("Ramier") . . . . 4·50 5·50
632 45c. Zenaida dove ("Wood Dove") . . . . 1·50 1·50
633 50c. As 40c. . . . . 1·50 2·00
633a 55c. American golden plover ("Black breasted Plover") 4·00 3·50
633b 60c. Bananaquit ("Yellow Breasted") . . . . 4·50 6·00
634 70c. As 60c. . . . . 2·00 3·50
635 $1 Caribbean elaenia ("Peer whistler") . . . . 2·00 1·50
636 $2.50 American redstart ("Christmas Bird") . . . 2·00 6·00
637 $5 Belted kingfisher ("Kingfisher") . . . . . 3·25 9·00
638 $10 Moorhen ("Red-seal Coot") . . . . 4·50 14·00

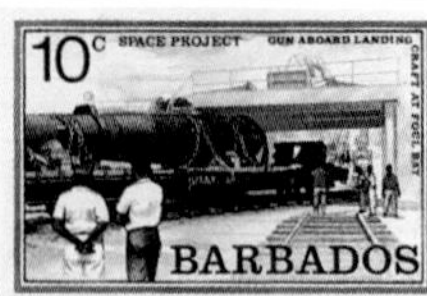

143 Unloading H.A.R.P. Gun on Railway Wagon at Foul Bay

1979. Space Projects Commemorations. Mult.

639	10c. Type **143**	15	10
640	12c. H.A.R.P. gun on railway wagon under tow (vert)	15	15
641	20c. Firing launcher (vert)	15	20
642	28c. Bath Earth Station and "Intelsat"	15	30
643	45c. "Intelsat" over Caribbean	25	50
644	50c. "Intelsat" over Atlantic (vert)	25	60
MS645	118 × 90 mm. $1 Lunar module descending on to Moon	1·00	80

144 Family

146 Private, Artillery Company, Barbados Volunteer Force, c.1909

145 Map of Barbados

1979. International Year of the Child. Multicoloured.

646	12c. Type **144**	10	10
647	28c. Ring of children and map of Barbados	15	15
648	45c. Child with teacher	20	20
649	50c. Children playing	20	20
650	$1 Children and kite	35	45

1980. 75th Anniv of Rotary International. Multicoloured.

651	12c. Type **145**	15	10
652	28c. Map of Caribbean	15	15
653	50c. Rotary anniversary emblem	20	35
654	$1 Paul P. Harris (founder)	30	95

1980. Barbados Regiment. Multicoloured.

655	12c. Type **146**	25	10
656	35c. Drum Major, Zouave uniform	35	15
657	50c. Sovereign's and Regimental Colours	40	30
658	$1 Barbados Regiment Women's Corps	55	70

147 Early Postman

1980. "London 1980" International Stamp Exhibition. Two sheets each 122 × 125 mm containing T **147** or similar vert design. Multicoloured.

MS659	(a) 28c. × 6, Type **147**. (b) 50c. × 6, Modern postwoman and Inspector Set of 2 sheets	1·00	1·25

148 Yellow-tailed Snapper

1980. Underwater Scenery. Multicoloured

660	12c. Type **148**	20	10
661	28c. Banded butterflyfish	35	15
662	50c. Male and female blue-headed wrasse and princess parrotfish	45	25
663	$1 French grunt and French angelfish	70	70
MS664	136 × 110 mm. Nos. 660/3	2·50	3·75

149 Bathsheba Railway Station

1981. Early Transport. Multicoloured.

665	12c. Type **149**	30	10
666	28c. Cab stand at The Green	20	15
667	45c. Animal-drawn tram	30	30
668	70c. Horse-drawn bus	45	60
669	$1 Railway Station, Fairchild Street	70	95

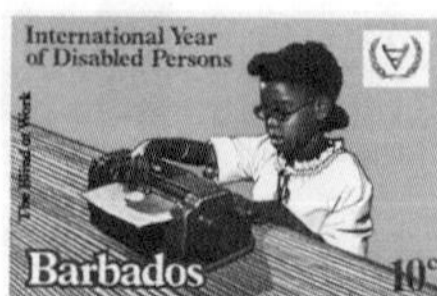

150 The Blind at Work

1981. Int Year for Disabled Persons. Mult.

670	10c. Type **150**	20	10
671	25c. Sign Language (vert)	25	15
672	45c. "Be alert to the white cane" (vert)	40	25
673	$2.50 Children at play	80	3·00

151 Prince Charles dressed for Polo

152 Landship Manoeuvre

1981. Royal Wedding. Multicoloured.

674	28c. Wedding bouquet from Barbados	15	10
675	50c. Type **151**	20	15
676	$2.50 Prince Charles and Lady Diana Spencer	55	1·25

1981. Carifesta (Caribbean Festival of Arts), Barbados. Multicoloured.

677	15c. Type **152**	15	15
678	20c. Yoruba dancers	15	20
679	40c. Tuk band	20	25
680	55c. Sculpture by Frank Collymore	25	35
681	$1 Harbour scene	50	75

1981. Nos. 630, 632 and 634 surch.

682	15c. on 28c. Carib grackle	30	15
683	40c. on 45c. Zenaida dove	30	35
684	60c. on 70c. Bananaquit	30	45

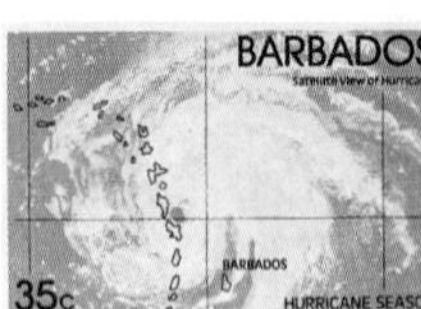

154 Satellite View of Hurricane

1981. Hurricane Season.

685	**154** 35c. black and blue	35	20
686	– 50c. multicoloured	45	35
687	– 60c. multicoloured	70	50
688	– $1 multicoloured	85	90

DESIGNS: 50c. Hurricane "Gladys" from "Apollo 7"; 60c. Police Department on hurricane watch; $1 McDonnell Banshee "hurricane chaser" aircraft.

155 Twin Falls

1981. Harrison's Cave. Multicoloured.

689	10c. Type **155**	10	10
690	20c. Stream in Rotunda Room	20	15
691	55c. Formations in Rotunda Room	25	30
692	$2.50 Cascade Pool	60	2·25

156 Black Belly Ram

1982. Black Belly Sheep. Multicoloured.

693	40c. Type **156**	15	20
694	50c. Black belly ewe	15	20
695	60c. Ewe with lambs	20	45
696	$1 Ram and ewe, with map of Barbados	35	1·50

157 Barbados Coat of Arms and Flag

1982. President Reagan's Visit. Multicoloured.

697	20c. Type **157**	40	1·25
698	20c. U.S.A. coat of arms and flag	40	1·25
699	55c. Type **157**	50	1·50
700	55c. As No. 698	50	1·50

158 Lighter

1982. Early Marine Transport. Multicoloured.

701	20c. Type **158**	20	15
702	35c. Rowing boat	35	25
703	55c. Speightstown schooner	50	40
704	$2.50 Inter-colonial schooner	1·75	2·50

159 Bride and Earl Spencer Proceeding up the Aisle

160 "To Help other People"

1982. 21st Birthday of Princess of Wales. Mult.

705	20c. Barbados coat of arms	20	15
706	60c. Princess at Llanelwedd, October, 1981	45	50
707	$1.20 Type **159**	75	1·10
708	$2.50 Formal portrait	1·25	1·90

1982. 75th Anniv of Boy Scout Movement. Mult.

709	15c. Type **160**	50	10
710	40c. "I Promise to do my Best" (horiz)	80	30
711	55c. "To do my Duty to God, the Queen and my Country" (horiz)	90	65
712	$1 National and Troop flags	1·40	1·75
MS713	119 × 93 mm. $1.50, The Scout Law	3·50	3·00

161 Arms of George Washington

1982. 250th Birth Anniv of George Washington. Multicoloured.

714	10c. Type **161**	10	10
715	55c. Washington House, Barbados	25	30
716	60c. Washington with troops	25	35
717	$2.50 Washington taking Oath	75	1·60

162 "Agraulis vanillae"

1983. Butterflies. Multicoloured.

718	20c. Type **162**	1·00	40
719	40c. "Danaus plexippus"	1·50	40
720	55c. "Hypolimnas misippus"	1·50	45
721	$2.50 "Hemiargus hanno"	3·25	3·75

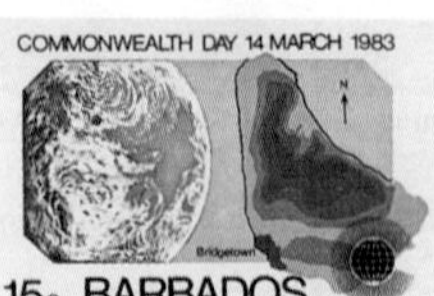

163 Map of Barbados and Satellite View

1983. Commonwealth Day. Multicoloured.

722	15c. Type **163**	20	10
723	40c. Tourist beach	25	20
724	60c. Sugar cane harvesting	35	40
725	$1 Cricket match	1·25	1·10

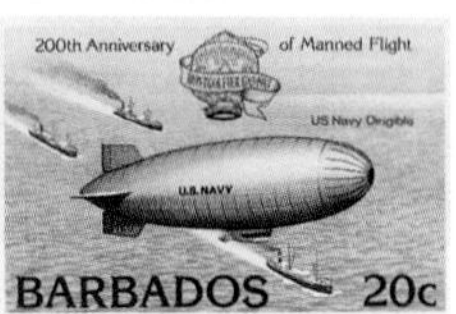

164 U.S. Navy "M" Class Airship M-20

1983. Bicentenary of Manned Flight.

726	20c. Type **164**	35	15
727	40c. Douglas DC-3	40	40
728	55c. Vickers Viscount 837	40	50
729	$1 Lockheed TriStar 500	65	2·50

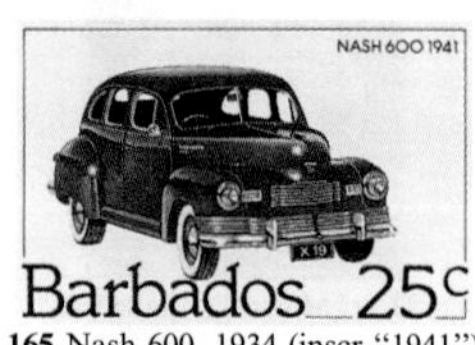

165 Nash 600, 1934 (inscr "1941")

1983. Classic Cars. Multicoloured.

730	25c. Type **165**	35	20
731	45c. Dodge D-8 coupe, 1938	40	30
732	75c. Ford Model A tourer, 1930	60	1·50
733	$2.50 Dodge Four tourer, 1918	1·25	4·50

166 Game in Progress

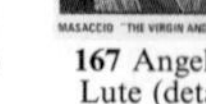
167 Angel playing Lute (detail "The Virgin and Child") (Masaccio)

1983. Table Tennis World Cup Competition. Multicoloured.

734	20c. Type **166**	25	20
735	65c. Map of Barbados	50	55
736	$1 World Table Tennis Cup	75	1·00

1983. Christmas. 50th Anniv of Barbados Museum.

737	**167** 10c. multicoloured	30	10
738	– 25c. multicoloured	60	20
739	– 45c. multicoloured	90	40
740	– 75c. black and gold	1·40	1·60
741	– $2.50 multicoloured	4·50	6·00
MS742	59 × 98 mm. $2 multicoloured	1·75	2·00

DESIGNS—HORIZ: 45c. "The Barbados Museum" (Richard Day); 75c. "St. Ann's Garrison" (W. S. Hedges); $2.50, Needham's Point, Carlisle Bay. VERT: 25c., $2 Different details from "The Virgin and Child" (Masaccio).

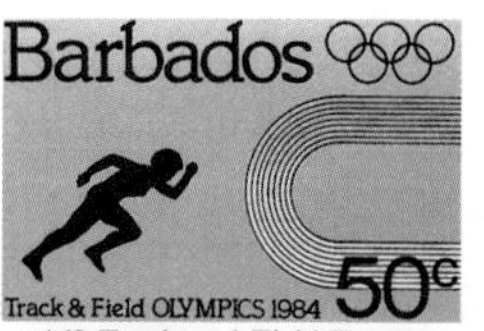

168 Track and Field Events

1984. Olympic Games, Los Angeles.
745 **168** 50c. green, black and brown 60 45
746 – 65c. orange, blk & brn . . 80 60
747 – 75c. blue, black & dp bl 1·00 85
748 – $1 brown, black and yellow . . . . 2·50 1·75
MS749 115 × 97 mm. Nos. 745/8 7·00 8·00
DESIGNS: 65c. Shooting; 75c. Sailing; $1 Cycling.

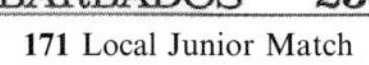

169 Global Coverage **171** Local Junior Match

170 U.P.U. 1943 3d. Stamp and Logo

1984. 250th Anniv of "Lloyd's List" (newspaper). Multicoloured.
750 45c. Type **169** 80 40
751 50c. Bridgetown harbour . . 90 50
752 75c. "Philosopher" (full-rigged ship), 1857 . . . . 1·40 1·25
753 $1 "Sea Princess" (liner), 1984 . . . . 1·40 1·60

1984. Universal Postal Union Congress, Hamburg. Sheet 90 × 75 mm.
MS754 **170** $2 multicoloured 2·50 2·50

1984. 60th Anniv of International Chess Federation. Multicoloured.
755 25c. Type **171** . . . . 1·50 30
756 45c. Staunton and 19th-century knights . . . 1·75 50
757 65c. Staunton queen and 18th-century queen from Macao . . . . 2·00 1·75
758 $2 Staunton and 17th-century rooks . . . . 3·75 6·50

172 Poinsettia **174** The Queen Mother at Docks

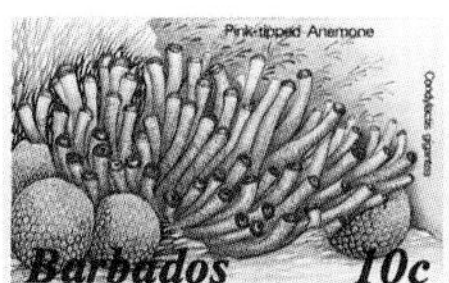

173 Pink-tipped Anemone

1984. Christmas. Flowers. Multicoloured.
759 50c. Type **172** . . . . 1·75 90
760 65c. Snow-on-the-Mountain 2·00 1·75
761 75c. Christmas Candle . . . 2·25 3·25
762 $1 Christmas Hope . . . . . 2·50 3·75

1985. Marine Life. Multicoloured.
794B 1c. Bristle worm . . . . . 30 2·50
795B 2c. Spotted trunkfish . . . 30 2·50
796A 5c. Coney . . . . 65 1·50
797B 10c. Type **173** 30 30
798B 20c. Christmas tree worm 30 40
799B 25c. Hermit crab 40 40
800A 35c. Animal flower . . . . 1·00 1·50
801B 40c. Vase sponge 50 50
802B 45c. Spotted moray 60 50
803B 50c. Ghost crab 60 60
804B 65c. Flamingo tongue snail 65 70
805B 75c. Sergeant major 70 75
806B $1 Caribbean warty anemone 85 85
807B $2.50 Green turtle . . . . 1·50 6·00
808B $5 Rock beauty (fish) . . . 2·00 8·00
809B $10 Elkhorn coral . . . . 3·25 8·00

1985. Life and Times of Queen Elizabeth the Queen Mother. Multicoloured.
779 25c. In the White Drawing Room, Buckingham Palace, 1930s 50 20
780 65c. With Lady Diana Spencer at Trooping the Colour, 1981 . . . . . . 2·00 80

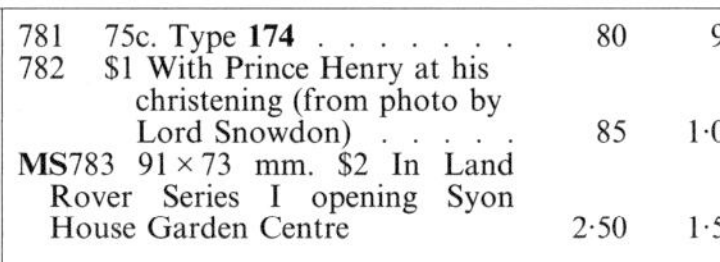
781 75c. Type **174** 80 90
782 $1 With Prince Henry at his christening (from photo by Lord Snowdon) . . . . . 85 1·00
MS783 91 × 73 mm. $2 In Land Rover Series I opening Syon House Garden Centre 2·50 1·50

175 Peregrine Falcon

1985. Birth Bicentenary of John J. Audubon (ornithologist). Designs showing original paintings. Multicoloured.
784 45c. Type **175** . . . . 2·25 80
785 65c. Prairie warbler (vert) . . 2·50 2·25
786 75c. Great blue heron (vert) 2·75 3·00
787 $1 Yellow warbler (vert) . . 3·00 4·00

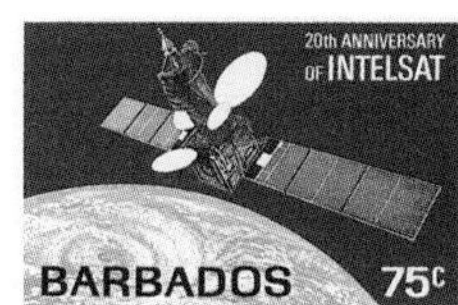

176 Intelsat Satellite orbiting Earth

1985. 20th Anniv of Intelsat Satellite System.
788 **176** 75c. multicoloured . . . . 1·00 70

177 Traffic Policeman

1985. 150th Anniv of Royal Barbados Police. Multicoloured.
789 25c. Type **177** 80 20
790 50c. Police band on bandstand . . . . 1·40 80
791 65c. Dog handler . . . . . . 1·60 1·40
792 $1 Mounted policeman in ceremonial uniform . . . . 1·75 2·00
MS793 85 × 60 mm. $2 Police Band on parade (horiz). 1·50 2·75

1986. 60th Birthday of Queen Elizabeth II. As T **110** of Ascension. Multicoloured.
810 25c. Princess Elizabeth aged two, 1928 . . . . 40 20
811 50c. At University College of West Indies, Jamaica, 1953 50 40
812 65c. With Duke of Edinburgh, Barbados, 1985 70 50
813 75c. At banquet in Sao Paulo, Brazil, 1968 . . . . 70 60
814 $2 At Crown Agents Head Office, London, 1983 . . . 1·10 1·50

178 Canadair DC-4M2 North Star of Trans-Canada Airlines

1986. "Expo '86" World Fair, Vancouver. Mult.
815 50c. Type **178** 75 50
816 $2.50 "Lady Nelson" (cargo liner) . . . . 2·00 2·50

1986. "Ameripex '86" International Stamp Exhibition, Chicago. As T **164** of Bahamas, showing Barbados stamps. Multicoloured.
817 45c. 1976 Bicentenary of American Revolution 25c. 70 35
818 50c. 1976 Bicentenary of American Revolution 50c. 80 55
819 65c. 1981 Hurricane Season $1 . . . . 90 1·00
820 $1 1982 Visit of President Reagan 55c. . . . . 1·00 1·75
MS821 90 × 80 mm. $2 Statue of Liberty and liner "Queen Elizabeth 2" 7·00 9·50
No. **MS**821 also commemorates the Centenary of the Statue of Liberty.

1986. Royal Wedding. As T **112** of Ascension. Multicoloured.
822 45c. Prince Andrew and Miss Sarah Ferguson 75 35
823 $1 Prince Andrew in midshipman's uniform . . 1·25 75

179 Transporting Electricity Poles, 1923 **180** "Alpinia purpurata" and Church Window

1986. 75th Anniv of Electricity in Barbados. Multicoloured.
824 10c. Type **179** 15 10
825 25c. Heathman Ladder, 1935 (vert) 25 20
826 65c. Transport fleet, 1941 . . 60 60
827 $2 Bucket truck, 1986 (vert) 1·60 2·00

1986. Christmas. Multicoloured.
828 25c. Type **180** 20 20
829 50c. "Anthurium andraeanum" 45 45
830 75c. "Heliconia rostrata" . . 75 80
831 $2 "Heliconia × psittacorum" 1·50 3·50

181 Shot Putting

1987. 10th Anniv of Special Olympics. Multicoloured.
832 15c. Type **181** 25 15
833 45c. Wheelchair racing . . . 45 30
834 65c. Long jumping 60 65
835 $2 Logo and slogan . . . . 1·25 2·50

182 Barn Swallow **183** Sea Scout saluting

1987. "Capex '87" International Stamp Exhibition, Toronto. Birds. Multicoloured.
836 25c. Type **182** . . . . 2·00 50
837 50c. Yellow warbler . . . . 2·25 1·75
838 65c. Audubon's shearwater 2·25 1·75
839 75c. Black-whiskered vireo 2·50 3·25
840 $1 Scarlet tanager . . . . . 2·75 4·00

1987. 75th Anniv of Scouting in Barbados. Multicoloured.
841 10c. Type **183** 20 10
842 25c. Scout jamboree 30 20
843 65c. Scout badges 65 45
844 $2 Scout band . . . . 1·60 1·75

184 Bridgetown Synagogue

1987. Restoration of Bridgetown Synagogue. Multicoloured.
845 50c. Type **184** . . . . 2·00 1·75
846 65c. Interior of Synagogue 2·25 2·25
847 75c. Ten Commandments (vert) . . . . 2·50 2·50
848 $1 Marble laver (vert) . . . 2·75 3·25

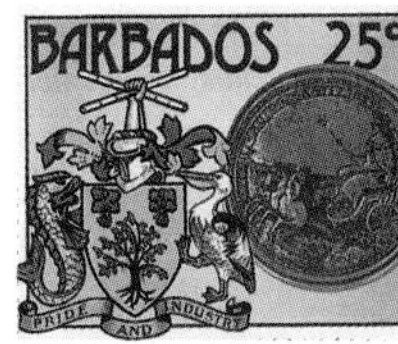

185 Arms and Colonial Seal

1987. 21st Anniv of Independence. Mult.
849 25c. Type **185** 40 20
850 45c. Flags of Barbados and Great Britain . . . . . . 1·00 35
851 65c. Silver dollar and one penny coins . . . . 1·00 55
852 $2 Colours of Barbados Regiment . . . . 2·50 2·75
MS853 94 × 56 mm. $1.50, Prime Minister E. W. Barrow (vert) 1·00 1·25

186 Herman C. Griffith

1988. West Indian Cricket. Each showing portrait, cricket equipment and early belt buckle. Multicoloured.
854 15c. E. A. (Manny) Martindale . . . . 2·50 75
855 45c. George Challenor . . . 3·25 75
856 50c. Type **186** . . . . 3·50 2·25
857 75c. Harold Austin . . . . . 3·75 3·50
858 $2 Frank Worrell . . . . . 4·50 11·00

187 "Kentropyx borckianus" **188** Cycling

1988. Lizards of Barbados. Multicoloured.
859 10c. Type **187** . . . . 1·75 50
860 50c. "Hemidactylus mabouia" 3·00 70
861 65c. "Anolis extremus" . . . 3·00 1·25
862 $2 "Gymnophthalmus underwoodii" . . . . . . 6·00 9·00

1988. Olympic Games, Seoul. Multicoloured.
863 25c. Type **188** . . . . 1·50 40
864 45c. Athletics 60 30
865 75c. Relay swimming 75 65
866 $2 Yachting . . . . 1·75 2·50
MS867 114 × 63 mm. Nos. 863/6 4·25 3·00

1988. 300th Anniv of Lloyd's of London. As T **123** of Ascension.
868 40c. multicoloured 55 30
869 50c. multicoloured 65 35
870 65c. multicoloured . . . . . 1·50 45
871 $2 blue and red . . . . . . 4·25 2·00
DESIGNS—VERT: 40c. Royal Exchange, 1774; $2 Sinking of "Titanic", 1912. HORIZ: 50c. Early sugar mill; 65c. "Author" (container ship).

189 Harry Bayley and Observatory

1988. 25th Anniv of Harry Bayley Observatory. Multicoloured.
872 25c. Type **189** 60 20
873 65c. Observatory with North Star and Southern Cross constellations . . . . . . 1·25 75
874 75c. Andromeda galaxy . . . 1·50 90
875 $2 Orion constellation . . . 2·75 4·75

190 L.I.A.T. Hawker Siddeley H.S.748

1989. 50th Anniv of Commercial Aviation in Barbados. Multicoloured.
876 25c. Type **190** . . . . 2·00 40
877 65c. Pan Am Douglas DC-8-62 . . . . 2·75 1·25
878 75c. British Airways Concorde at Grantley Adams Airport . . . . . 2·75 1·25
879 $2 Caribbean Air Cargo Boeing 707-351C . . . . . 4·50 7·00

191 Assembly Chamber

1989. 350th Anniv of Parliament.
880 **191** 25c. multicoloured 40 20
881 – 50c. multicoloured 60 35

882 – 75c. blue and black . . . 1·00 50
883 – $2.50 multicoloured . . . 2·50 2·25
DESIGNS: 50c. The Speaker; 75c. Parliament Buildings, c. 1882; $2.50, Queen Elizabeth II and Prince Philip in Parliament.

192 Brown Hare **193** Bread 'n Cheese

1989. Wildlife Preservation. Multicoloured.
884 10c. Type **192** 70 30
885 50c. Red-footed tortoise (horiz) . . . . 1·50 70
886 65c. Savanna ("Green") monkey . . . . 1·75 1·25
887 $2 "Bufo marinus" (toad) (horiz) . . . . 3·25 6·00
MS888 87 × 97 mm. $1 Small Indian mongoose 1·00 1·25

1989. 35th Commonwealth Parliamentary Conference. Square design as T **191**. Mult.
MS889 108 × 69 mm. $1 Barbados Mace 1·00 1·50

1989. Wild Plants. Multicoloured.
921 2c. Type **193** . . . . 40 1·50
891 5c. Scarlet cordia 50 90
892 10c. Columnar cactus . . . 50 30
893 20c. Spiderlily 50 30
925 25c. Rock balsam 55 20
895 30c. Hollyhock 70 25
895a 35c. Red sage . . . . 1·25 1·00
927 45c. Yellow shak-shak . . . 65 35
928 50c. Whitewood 70 40
898 55c. Bluebell . . . . 1·00 55
930 65c. Prickly sage 80 55
900 70c. Seaside samphire . . . 1·25 1·25
901 80c. Flat-hand dildo . . . . 1·75 1·40
901a 90c. Herringbone . . . . . 1·75 2·25
902 $1.10 Lent tree . . . . . . 1·50 2·25
934 $2.50 Rodwood . . . . . . 1·90 4·00
935 $5 Cowitch . . . . 3·25 6·00
936 $10 Maypole . . . . 6·50 9·00

194 Water Skiing **195** Barbados 1852 1d. Stamp

1989. "World Stamp Expo '89" International Stamp Exn., Washington. Watersports. Mult.
906 25c. Type **194** . . . . 1·25 40
907 50c. Yachting . . . . 2·25 1·00
908 65c. Scuba diving . . . . . 2·25 1·75
909 $2.50 Surfing . . . . 6·00 10·00

1990. 150th Anniv of the Penny Black and "Stamp World London '90" International Stamp Exn.
910 **195** 25c. green, black and yellow . . . . 1·25 40
911 – 50c. multicoloured . . . . 1·75 1·00
912 – 65c. multicoloured . . . . 1·75 1·50
913 – $2.50 multicoloured . . . 4·00 7·50
MS914 90 × 86 mm. 50c. multicoloured; 50c. multicoloured 1·75 2·25
DESIGNS: 50c. 1882 1d. Queen Victoria stamp; 65c. 1899 2d. stamp; $2.50, 1912 3d. stamp; miniature sheet, 50c. Great Britain Penny Black, 50c. Barbados "1906" Nelson Centenary 1s.

196 Bugler and Jockeys

1990. Horse Racing. Multicoloured.
915 25c. Type **196** 45 30
916 45c. Horse and jockey in parade ring 70 50
917 75c. At the finish 90 85
918 $2 Leading in the winner (vert) . . . . 2·50 4·50

1990. 90th Birthday of Queen Elizabeth the Queen Mother. As T **134** of Ascension.
919 75c. multicoloured 75 60
920 $2.50 black and green . . . . 2·25 3·00

DESIGNS—21 × 36 mm: 75c. Lady Elizabeth Bowes-Lyon, April 1923 (from painting by John Lander). 29 × 37 mm: $2.50, Lady Elizabeth Bowes-Lyon on her engagement, January 1923.

197 "Orthemis ferruginea" (dragonfly)

1990. Insects. Multicoloured.
937 50c. Type **197** . . . . 1·50 80
938 65c. "Ligyrus tumulosus" (beetle) . . . . 1·75 1·00
939 75c. "Neoconocephalus sp." (grasshopper) . . . . . . 2·00 1·25
940 $2 "Bostra maxwelli" (stick-insect) . . . . 3·50 5·50

1990. Visit of the Princess Royal. Nos. 925, 901 and 903 optd **VISIT OF HRH THE PRINCESS ROYAL OCTOBER 1990**.
941 25c. Rock balsam . . . . . 1·50 50
942 80c. Flat-hand dildo . . . . 2·75 2·00
943 $2.50 Rodwood . . . . . . 6·00 8·00

199 Star **201** Sorting Daily Catch

200 Adult Male Yellow Warbler

1990. Christmas. Multicoloured.
944 20c. Type **199** 65 20
945 50c. Figures from crib . . . 1·00 50
946 $1 Stained glass window . . 2·00 1·50
947 $2 Angel (statue) . . . . . . 3·00 5·50

1991. Endangered Species. Yellow Warbler. Multicoloured.
948 10c. Type **200** . . . . 1·40 80
949 20c. Pair feeding chicks in nest . . . . 2·00 80
950 45c. Female feeding chicks in nest . . . . 2·50 80
951 $1 Male with fledgeling . . . 4·00 5·25

1991. Fishing in Barbados. Multicoloured.
952 5c. Type **201** 50 50
953 50c. Line fishing (horiz) . . . 1·75 90
954 75c. Fish cleaning (horiz) . . 2·25 1·25
955 $2.50 Game fishing . . . . . 4·50 6·50

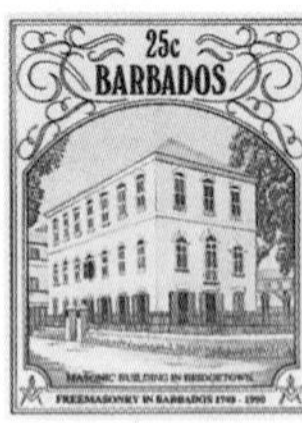

202 Masonic Building, Bridgetown

1991. 250th Anniv of Freemasonry in Barbados (1990).
956 **202** 25c. multicoloured . . . . 1·25 50
957 – 65c. multicoloured . . . . 2·00 1·25
958 – 75c. black, yellow & brn 2·00 1·25
959 – $2.50 multicoloured . . . 4·75 7·00
DESIGNS: 65c. Compass and square (masonic symbols); 75c. Royal Arch jewel; $2.50, Ceremonial apron, columns and badge.

203 "Battus polydamus"

1991. "Phila Nippon '91" International Stamp Exhibition, Tokyo. Butterflies. Multicoloured.
960 20c. Type **203** . . . . 1·00 40
961 50c. "Urbanus proteus" (vert) 1·50 65
962 65c. "Phoebis sennae" . . . 1·60 95
963 $2.50 "Junonia evarete" (vert) . . . . 4·00 6·00
MS964 87 × 86 mm. $4 "Vanessa cardui" 8·00 9·00

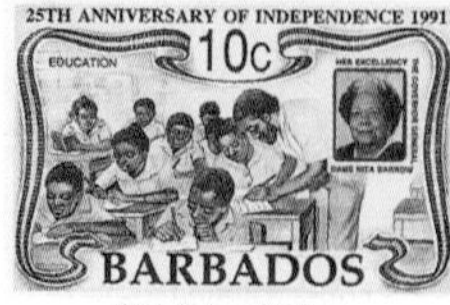

204 School Class

1991. 25th Anniv of Independence. Multicoloured.
965 10c. Type **204** 20 20
966 25c. Barbados Workers' Union Labour College . . 30 30
967 65c. Building a house 70 90
968 75c. Sugar cane harvesting 80 1·00
969 $1 Health clinic . . . . . . 1·00 2·00
MS970 123 × 97 mm. $2.50, Gordon Greenidge and Desmond Haynes (cricketers) (vert) 8·00 9·00

205 Jesus carrying Cross

1992. Easter. Multicoloured.
971 35c. Type **205** 80 30
972 70c. Crucifixion . . . . . . 1·40 90
973 90c. Descent from the Cross 1·50 1·25
974 $3 Risen Christ . . . . . . 4·00 6·50

206 Cannon Ball

1992. Conservation. Flowering Trees. Multicoloured.
975 10c. Type **206** 60 40
976 30c. Golden shower tree . . . 1·00 50
977 80c. Frangipani . . . . . . 2·25 2·50
978 $1.10 Flamboyant . . . . . 2·75 3·00

207 "Epidendrum" "Costa Rica"

1992. Orchids. Multicoloured.
979 55c. Type **207** 85 65
980 65c. "Cattleya guttaca" . . . 1·00 1·00
981 70c. "Laeliacattleya" "Splashing Around" . . . 1·00 1·00
982 $1.40 "Phalaenopsis" "Kathy Saegert" . . . . 1·60 3·00

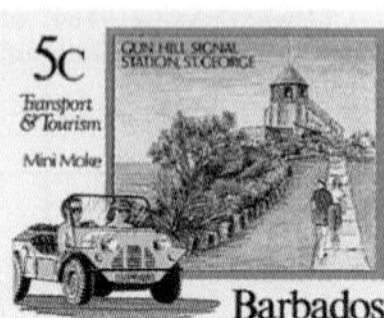

208 Mini Moke and Gun Hill Signal Station, St. George

1992. Transport and Tourism. Multicoloured.
983 5c. Type **208** 50 50
984 35c. Tour bus and Bathsheba Beach, St. Joseph . . . . 1·00 30
985 90c. B.W.I.A. McDonnell Douglas MD-83 over Grantley Adams Airport 2·50 2·25
986 $2 "Festivale" (liner) and Bridgetown harbour . . . 3·75 5·50

209 Barbados Gooseberry **212** Sailor's Shell-work Valentine and Carved Amerindian

211 18 pdr Culverin of 1625, Denmark Fort

1993. Cacti and Succulents. Multicoloured.
987 10c. Type **209** 55 30
988 35c. Night-blooming cereus 1·25 35
989 $1.40 Aloe . . . . 3·00 3·50
990 $2 Scrunchineel . . . . . . 3·50 5·50

1993. 75th Anniv of Royal Air Force. As T **149** of Ascension. Multicoloured.
991 10c. Hawker Hunter F.6 . . 65 40
992 30c. Handley Page Victor K2 1·00 40
993 70c. Hawker Typhoon IB . . 1·50 1·50
994 $3 Hawker Hurricane Mk I 3·50 5·50
MS995 110 × 77 mm. 50c. Armstrong Whitworth Siskin IIIA; 50c. Supermarine S6B; 50c. Supermarine Walrus Mk I; 50c. Hawker Hart 2·25 2·75

1993. 14th World Orchid Conference, Glasgow. Nos. 979/82 optd **WORLD ORCHID CONFERENCE 1993**.
996 55c. Type **207** . . . . 1·25 1·25
997 65c. "Cattleya guttaca" . . . 1·40 1·40
998 70c. "Laeliacattleya" "Splashing Around" . . . 1·40 1·40
999 $1.40 "Phalaenopsis" "Kathy Saegert" . . . . 2·25 3·50

1993. 17th-century English Cannon. Mult.
1000 5c. Type **211** 30 50
1001 45c. 6 pdr of 1649–60, St. Ann's Fort 85 50
1002 $1 9 pdr demi-culverin of 1691, The Main Guard 1·75 2·00
1003 $2.50 32 pdr demi–cannon of 1693–94, Charles Fort 2·75 4·50

1993. 60th Anniv of Barbados Museum. Mult.
1004 10c. Type **212** 50 50
1005 75c. "Barbados Mulatto Girl" (Agostino Brunias) 1·50 1·50
1006 90c. Morris Cup and soldier of West India Regiment, 1858 . . . . 2·00 2·25
1007 $1.10 Ogilby's map of Barbados, 1679, and Ashanti gold weights . . 2·25 2·75

213 Plesiosaurus **214** Cricket

1993. Prehistoric Aquatic Animals. Mult.
1008 90c. Type **213** . . . . . . 2·00 2·50
1009 90c. Ichthyosaurus . . . . 2·00 2·50
1010 90c. Elasmosaurus . . . . . 2·00 2·50
1011 90c. Mosasaurus . . . . . 2·00 2·50
1012 90c. Archelon . . . . 2·00 2·50
Nos. 1008/12 were printed together, se-tenant, with the background forming a composite design.

1994. Sports and Tourism. Multicoloured.
1013 10c. Type **214** . . . . . . 1·25 75
1014 35c. Rally driving . . . . . 1·40 50
1015 50c. Golf . . . . 2·25 1·50
1016 70c. Long distance running 1·75 2·25
1017 $1.40 Swimming . . . . . 2·00 3·25

215 Whimbrel

1994. "Hong Kong '94" Int Stamp Exhibition. Migratory Birds. Multicoloured.
1018 10c. Type **215** 50 50
1019 35c. Pacific golden plover ("American Golden Plover") 1·00 50
1020 70c. Ruddy turnstone 1·50 1·50
1021 $3 Louisiana heron ("Tricoloured Heron") 3·50 5·50

216 Bathsheba Beach and Logo

1994. 1st United Nations Conference of Small Island Developing States. Multicoloured.
1022 10c. Type **216** 20 15
1023 65c. Pico Tenneriffe 80 60
1024 90c. Ragged Point Lighthouse 2·25 1·75
1025 $2.50 Consett Bay 2·50 4·25

217 William Demas **219** Private, 2nd West India Regt, 1860

218 Dutch Flyut, 1695

1994. First Recipients of Order of the Caribbean Community. Multicoloured.
1026 70c. Type **217** 70 1·00
1027 70c. Sir Shridath Ramphal 70 1·00
1028 70c. Derek Walcott 70 1·00

1994. Ships. Multicoloured.
1075 5c. Type **218** 50 60
1076 10c. "Geestport" (freighter), 1994 75 40
1031B 25c. H.M.S. "Victory" (ship of the line), 1805 50 40
1078 30c. "Royal Viking Queen" (liner), 1994 50 30
1079 35c. H.M.S. "Barbados" (frigate), 1945 50 30
1080 45c. "Faraday" (cable ship), 1924 50 35
1081 50c. U.S.C.G. "Hamilton" (coastguard cutter), 1974 2·50 75
1082 65c. H.M.C.S. "Saguenay" (destroyer), 1939 75 70
1083 70c. "Inanda" (cargo liner), 1928 75 70
1084 80c. H.M.S. "Rodney" (battleship), 1944 75 70
1085 90c. U.S.S. "John F. Kennedy" (aircraft carrier), 1982 75 70
1086 $1.10 "William and John" (immigrant ship), 1627 1·00 1·00
1087 $5 U.S.C.G. "Champlain" (coastguard cutter), 1931 4·00 4·50
1042B $10 "Artist" (full-rigged ship), 1877 7·00 8·00

1995. Bicentenary of Formation of West India Regiment. Multicoloured.
1043 30c. Type **219** 55 35
1044 50c. Light Company private, 4th West India Regt, 1795 70 55
1045 70c. Drum Major, 3rd West India Regt, 1860 85 1·10
1046 $1 Privates in undress and working dress, 5th West India Regt, 1815 1·00 1·40
1047 $1.10 Troops from 1st and 2nd West India Regts in Review Order, 1874 1·25 1·75

1995. 50th Anniv of End of Second World War. As T **161** of Ascension. Multicoloured.
1048 10c. Barbadian Bren gun crew 60 50
1049 35c. Avro Type 683 Lancaster bomber 90 50
1050 55c. Supermarine Spitfire 1·25 75
1051 $2.50 "Davisian" (cargo liner) 3·00 4·50
MS1052 75 × 85 mm. $2 Reverse of 1939–45 War Medal (vert) 1·50 2·25

220 Member of 1st Barbados Combermere Scout Troop, 1912

1995. 300th Anniv of Combermere School. Mult.
1053 5c. Type **220** 25 40
1054 20c. Violin and sheet of music 45 30
1055 35c. Sir Frank Worrell (cricketer) (vert) 1·50 55
1056 $3 Painting by pupil 2·25 4·00
MS1057 174 × 105 mm. Nos. 1053/6 and 90c. 1981 Carifesta 55c. stamp. 4·00 4·75

1995. 50th Anniv of United Nations. As T **213** of Bahamas. Multicoloured.
1058 30c. Douglas C-124 Globemaster (transport), Korea, 1950–53 70 40
1059 45c. Royal Navy Sea King helicopter 1·00 50
1060 $1.40 Westland Wessex helicopter, Cyprus, 1964 1·50 2·00
1061 $2 Sud Aviation SA 341 Gazelle helicopter, Cyprus, 1964 1·50 2·50

221 Blue Beauty **223** Football

222 Magnifying Glass, Tweezers and 1896 Colony Seal ¼d. Stamp

1995. Water Lilies. Multicoloured.
1062 10c. Type **221** 35 30
1063 65c. White water lily 1·00 60
1064 70c. Sacred lotus 1·00 60
1065 $3 Water hyacinth 2·75 4·00

1996. Centenary of Barbados Philatelic Society. Each showing magnifying glass, tweezers and stamp. Multicoloured.
1066 10c. Type **222** 30 30
1067 55c. 1906 Tercentenary of Annexation 1d. 65 45
1068 $1.10 1920 Victory 1s. 1·25 1·40
1069 $1.40 1937 Coronation 2½d. 1·60 2·50

1996. Cent of Modern Olympic Games. Mult.
1070 20c. Type **223** 40 30
1071 30c. Relay running 45 30
1072 55c. Basketball 1·60 60
1073 $3 Rhythmic gymnastics 2·25 3·75
MS1074 68 × 89 mm. $2.50, "The Discus Thrower" (Myron) 2·00 3·25

224 Douglas DC-10 of Canadian Airlines

1996. "CAPEX '96" International Stamp Exhibition, Toronto. Aircraft. Multicoloured.
1089 10c. Type **224** 40 30
1090 90c. Boeing 767 of Air Canada 1·00 80
1091 $1 Airbus Industrie A320 of Air Canada 1·00 1·10
1092 $1.40 Boeing 767 of Canadian Airlines 1·40 2·50

225 Chattel House

1996. Chattel Houses.
1093 **225** 35c. multicoloured 40 25
1094 – 70c. multicoloured 70 60
1095 – $1.10 multicoloured 90 1·10
1096 – $2 multicoloured 1·60 2·75
DESIGNS: 70c. to $2, Different houses.

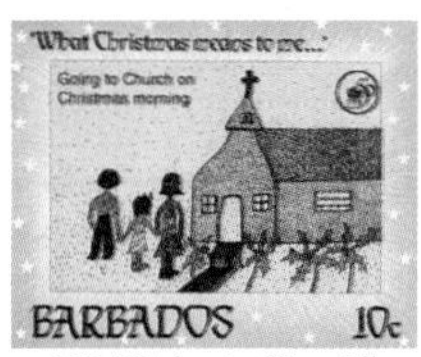

226 "Going to Church"

1996. Christmas. 50th Anniv of U.N.I.C.E.F. Children's Paintings. Multicoloured.
1097 10c. Type **226** 35 15
1098 30c. "The Tuk Band" 55 25
1099 55c. "Singing carols" 70 40
1100 $2.50 "Decorated house" 1·75 3·25

227 Doberman Pinscher

1997. "HONG KONG '97" International Stamp Exhibition. Dogs. Multicoloured.
1101 10c. Type **227** 65 40
1102 30c. German shepherd 1·25 40
1103 90c. Japanese akita 1·75 1·25
1104 $3 Irish red setter 3·75 6·00

228 Barbados Flag and State Arms

1997. Visit of President Clinton of U.S.A. Multicoloured.
1105 35c. Type **228** 50 65
1106 90c. American flag and arms 70 85

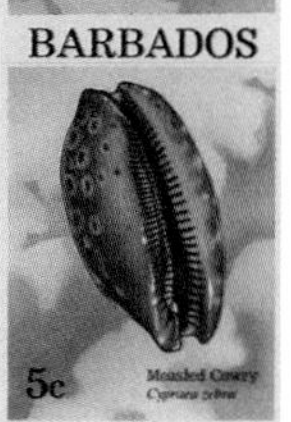

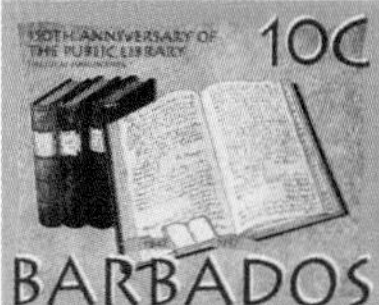

229 Measled Cowrie **230** Lucas Manuscripts

1997. Shells. Multicoloured.
1107 5c. Type **229** 25 30
1108 35c. Trumpet triton 60 25
1109 90c. Scotch bonnet 1·25 90
1110 $2 West Indian murex 1·75 2·75
MS1111 71 × 76 mm. $2.50, Underwater scene 2·25 3·00

1997. 150th Anniv of the Public Library Service. Multicoloured.
1112 10c. Type **230** 20 15
1113 30c. Librarian reading to children 40 25
1114 70c. Mobile library van 80 60
1115 $3 Man using computer 2·25 3·50

231 Barbados Cherry

1997. Local Fruits. Multicoloured.
1116 35c. Type **231** 35 30
1117 40c. Sugar apple 40 30
1118 $1.15 Soursop 95 1·00
1119 $1.70 Pawpaw 1·50 2·25

232 Arms of formaer British Caribbean Federation

1998. Birth Centenary of Sir Grantley Adams (statesman). Sheet 118 × 74 mm, containing T **232** and similar vert designs. Multicoloured.
MS1120 $1 Type **232**; $1 Sir Grantley Adams; $1 Flag of former British Caribbean Federation 3·25 3·50

1998. Diana, Princess of Wales Commemoration. Sheet 145 × 70 mm, containing vert designs as T **177** of Ascension. Multicoloured.
MS1121 $1.15, Wearing blue hat, 1985; $1.15, Wearing red jacket, 1981; $1.15, Wearing tiara, 1987; $1.15, Wearing black jacket 3·25 3·75

233 Environment Regeneration

1998. 50th Anniv of Organization of American States. Multicoloured.
1122 15c. Type **233** 20 15
1123 $1 Stilt dancing 70 70
1124 $2.50 Judge and figure of Justice 1·75 2·50

234 Frank Worrell Hall

1998. 50th Anniv of University of West Indies. Multicoloured.
1125 40c. Type **234** 30 30
1126 $1.15 Student graduating 1·00 1·25
1127 $1.40 50th anniversary plaque 1·25 2·00
1128 $1.75 Quadrangle 2·50 3·00

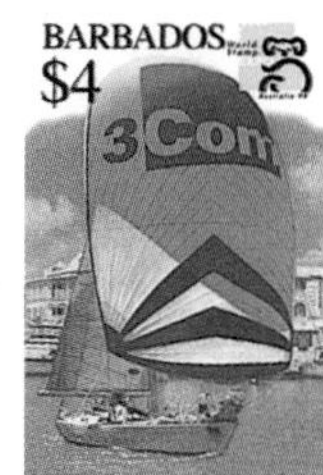

235 Catamaran **236** Racing Yacht

1998. Tourism. Multicoloured.
1129 10c. Type **235** 40 20
1130 45c. "Jolly Roger" (tourist schooner) (horiz) 85 35
1131 70c. "Atlantis" (tourist submarine) (horiz) 1·25 80
1132 $2 "Harbour Master" (ferry) 2·75 3·50

1999. "Australia '99" World Stamp Exhibition, Melbourne. Sheet 90 × 90 mm.
MS1133 **236** $4 multicoloured 3·00 4·00

237 Juvenile Piping Plover in Shallow Water

1999. Endangered Species. Piping Plover. Mult.
1134 10c. Type **237** 20 20
1135 45c. Female with eggs 55 55
1136 50c. Male and female with fledglings 55 65
1137 70c. Male in shallow water 65 85

1999. 30th Anniv of First Manned Landing on Moon. As T **186** of Ascension. Multicoloured.
1138 40c. Astronaut in training 45 30
1139 45c. 1st stage separation 45 35
1140 $1.15 Lunar landing module 1·25 1·00
1141 $1.40 Docking with service module 1·40 1·75
MS1142 90 × 80 mm. $2.50, Earth as seen from Moon (circular, 40 mm diam) 2·00 2·75

238 Hare running

1999. "China '99" International Stamp Exhibition, Beijing. Hares. Multicoloured.
1143 70c. Type **238** . . . . . . 1·10 1·10
1144 70c. Head of hare . . . . . 1·10 1·10
1145 70c. Baby hares suckling . . 1·10 1·10
1146 70c. Hares boxing . . . . . 1·10 1·10
1147 70c. Two leverets . . . . . 1·10 1·10
Nos. 1143/7 were printed together, se-tenant, forming a composite background design.

239 Horse-drawn Mail Cart

1999. 125th Anniv of U.P.U. Multicoloured.
1148 10c. Type **239** 45 20
1149 45c. Mail van 70 35
1150 $1.75 Sikorsky S42 flying boat . . . . 1·25 1·75
1151 $2 Computer and fax machine . . . . 1·25 2·00

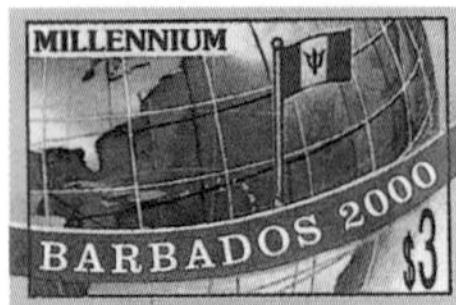

240 Globe and Barbados Flag

2000. New Millennium. Sheet 90 × 80 mm.
MS1152 **240** $3 multicoloured 3·00 3·50

241 Drax Hall House

2000. Pride of Barbados. Multicoloured.
1153 5c. Type **241** 10 10
1154 10c. Reaping sugar cane (vert) 10 15
1155 40c. Needham's Point Lighthouse (vert) 25 30
1156 45c. Port St. Charles . . . 30 35
1157 65c. Interior of Jewish synagogue 40 45
1158 70c. Bridgetown Port (I) 45 50
1158a 70c. Bridgetown Port (II) 45 50
1159 90c. Harrison's Cave . . . 60 65
1160 $1.15 Villa Nova . . . . . 75 ·80
1161 $1.40 Cricket at Kensington Oval 90 95
1162 $1.75 Sunbury House . . . 1·10 1·25
1163 $2 Bethel Methodist Church . . . . 1·25 1·40
1164 $3 Peacock, Barbados Wildlife Reserve (vert) 1·90 2·00
1165 $5 Royal Westmoreland Golf Course (vert) . . . 3·25 3·50
1166 $10 Grantley Adams International Airport . . 6·50 6·75
Two types of 50c. :
I. Central design reversed. The bows of three of the four liners shown point to the right.
II. Design corrected. The bows of three of the four liners point to the left.

242 Sir Conrad Hunte batting

2000. West Indies Cricket Tour and 100th Test Match at Lord's. Multicoloured.
1167 45c. Type **242** 60 35
1168 90c. Malcolm Marshall bowling . . . . 1·25 75
1169 $2 Sir Garfield Sobers batting . . . . 2·00 2·50
MS1170 121 × 104 mm. $2.50, Lord's Cricket Ground (horiz) 2·25 2·75

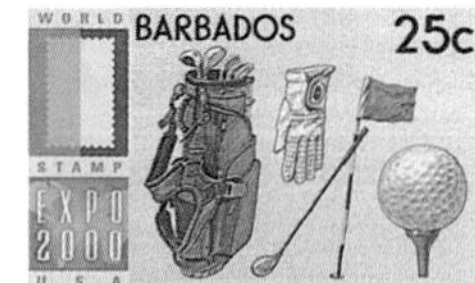

243 Golf Clubs, Flag and Ball on Tee Peg

2000. "EXPO 2000" World Stamp Exhibition, Anaheim, U.S.A. Golf. Multicoloured.
1171 25c. Type **243** 50 35
1172 40c. Golfer teeing off on top of giant ball 70 35
1173 $1.40 Golfer on green . . . 1·50 1·60
1174 $2 Golfer putting . . . . . 2·00 2·75

244 Bentley Mk VI Drophead Coupe, 1947

2000. Vintage Cars. Multicoloured.
1175 10c. Type **244** 25 15
1176 30c. Vanden Plas Princess Limousine, 1964 . . . . 50 25
1177 90c. Austin Atlantic, 1952 1·00 70
1178 $3 Bentley Special, 1950 . . 3·00 3·75

245 Thread Snake

2001. "HONG KONG 2001" Stamp Exhibition. Sheet 125 × 80 mm.
MS1179 **245** $3 multicoloured 3·00 3·50

246 Lizardfish

2001. Deep Sea Creatures. Multicoloured.
1180 45c. Type **246** 50 55
1181 45c. Golden-tailed moray . . 50 55
1182 45c. Black-barred soldierfish 50 55
1183 45c. Golden zoanthid . . . 50 55
1184 45c. Sponge brittle star . . 50 55
1185 45c. Magnificent feather duster 50 55
1186 45c. Bearded fireworm . . . 50 55
1187 45c. Lima shell 50 55
1188 45c. Yellow tube sponge . . 50 55

247 Octagonal, Fish and Butterfly Kites

2001. "Philanippon '01" International Stamp Exhibition, Tokyo. Kites. Multicoloured.
1189 10c. Type **247** 20 15
1190 65c. Hexagonal, bird and geometric kites 60 45
1191 $1.40 Policeman, Japanese and butterfly kites . . . . 1·40 1·50
1192 $1.75 Anti-drug, geisha and eagle kites . . . . 1·60 1·75

248 George Washington on the Quay, 1751

249 Shaggy Bear(Traditional Carnival Character)

2001. 250th Anniv of George Washington's Visit to Barbados. Multicoloured.
1193 45c. Type **248** 40 30
1194 50c. George Washington in Barbados 40 30
1195 $1.15 George Washington superimposed on Declaration of Independence, 1776 . . . 80 80
1196 $2.50 Needham's Point Fort, 1750 . . . . 1·50 2·00
MS1197 110 × 90 mm. $3 George Washington as President of U.S.A. 1·75 2·25

2001. 35th Anniv of Independence. Multicoloured.
1198 25c. Type **249** 25 20
1199 45c. Tuk band 40 30
1200 $1 Landship Dancers . . . 75 65
1201 $2 Guitar, saxophone and words of National Anthem . . . . 1·40 1·60

2002. Golden Jubilee. As T **200** of Ascension.
1202 10c. black, violet and gold 20 15
1203 70c. multicoloured 55 50
1204 $1 black, violet and gold . . 75 75
1205 $1.40 multicoloured . . . . 1·10 1·40
MS1206 162 × 95 mm. Nos. 1202/5 and $3 multicoloured 4·75 5·00
DESIGNS—HORIZ: 10c. Princess Elizabeth; 70c. Queen Elizabeth in cerise hat; $1 Queen Elizabeth wearing Imperial State Crown, Coronation, 1953; $1.40, Queen Elizabeth in purple feathered hat. VERT (38 × 51 mm)—$3 Queen Elizabeth after Annigoni.
Designs as Nos. 1202/5 in **MS**1206 omit the gold frame around each stamp and "Golden Jubilee 1952–2002" inscription.

250 1852 (½d.) Britannia Stamp and Map

2002. 150th Anniv of Inland Postal Service. Multicoloured.
1207 10c. Type **250** 20 15
1208 45c. Early twentieth-century postman delivering letter 45 35
1209 $1.15 *Esk* (mail steamer) . . 1·25 1·25
1210 $2 B.W.I.A. Tri-Star airliner 1·60 2·00

251 *Alpinia purpurata*

252 Drax Hall Windmill, St. George

2002. Flowers. Multicoloured.
1211 10c. Type **251** 10 10
1212 40c. *Heliconia caribaea* . . . 25 30
1213 $1.40 *Polianthes tuberosa* (horiz) 90 95
1214 $2.50 *Anthurium* (horiz) . . 1·60 1·75

2002. 375th Anniv of First Settlement.
1215 **252** 10c. brown, agate and blue 10 15
1216 – 45c. brown, agate and blue 30 35
1217 – $1.15 multicoloured . . 75 80
1218 – $3 multicoloured . . . . 1·90 2·00
DESIGNS: 45c. Donkey cart; $1.15, Cattle Mill ruins, Gibbons; $3, Morgan Lewis windmill, St. Andrew.

253 Traditional Christmas Fare

2002. Christmas. Multicoloured.
1219 45c. Type **253** 30 35
1220 $1.15 Christmas morning in the park 75 80
1221 $1.40 Nativity scene from float parade 90 95

254 AIDS Ribbon

2002. Centenary of Pan American Health Organization. Multicoloured.
1222 10c. Type **254** 10 15
1223 70c. Amateur athletes . . . 45 50
1224 $1.15 Sir George Alleyne (Director-General of P.A.H.O.) 75 80
1225 $2 Pregnant woman . . . . 1·25 1·40

POSTAGE DUE STAMPS

D 1

D 2

1934.
D1 **D 1** ½d. green . . . . 1·25 8·00
D2 1d. black . . . . 1·25 1·25
D3 3d. red . . . . 20·00 18·00

1950. Values in cents.
D4a **D 1** 1c. green . . . . 30 3·00
D8 2c. black . . . . 30 5·00
D9 6c. red . . . . 50 7·00

1976.
D14a **D 2** 1c. mauve and pink . . 10 10
D15a – 2c. blue and light blue 10 10
D16a – 5c. brown and yellow 10 15
D17a – 10c. blue and lilac . . . 15 20
D18a – 25c. deep green and green 20 30
D19 – $1 red and deep red . . 75 1·25
DESIGNS: Nos. D15/19 show different floral backgrounds.

BARBUDA Pt. 1

One of the Leeward Is., Br. W. Indies. Dependency of Antigua. Used stamps of Antigua and Leeward Is. concurrently. The issues from 1968 are also valid for use in Antigua. From 1971 to 1973 the stamps of Antigua were again used.

1922. 12 pence = 1 shilling;
20 shillings = 1 pound.
1951. 100 cents = 1 West Indian dollar.

1922. Stamps of Leeward Islands optd **BARBUDA**.
1 **11** ½d. green . . . . 1·50 9·00
2 1d. red . . . . 1·25 9·00
3 2d. grey . . . . 1·50 7·00
4 2½d. blue . . . . 1·25 7·50
9 3d. purple on yellow . . . . 1·75 12·00
5 6d. purple . . . . 2·00 18·00
10 1s. black on green . . . . 1·50 8·00
6 2s. purple and blue on blue 14·00 48·00
7 3s. green and violet . . . . 32·00 75·00
8 4s. black and red . . . . . 38·00 75·00
11 5s. green and red on yellow 65·00 £130

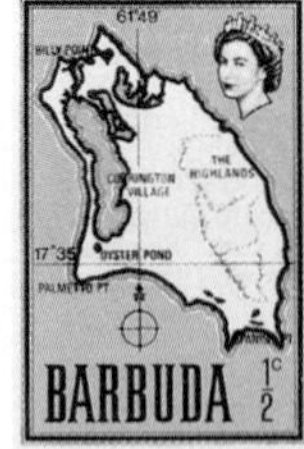

2 Map of Barbuda

3 Greater Amberjack

1968.
12 **2** ½c. brown, black and pink 20 1·25
13 1c. orange, black and flesh 30 10
14 2c. brown, red and rose . . 50 10
15 3c. brown, yellow and lemon 30 10
16 4c. black, green & lt green 70 1·25
17 5c. turquoise and black . . 30 10
18 6c. black, purple and lilac 40 1·25
19 10c. black, blue and cobalt 30 60
20 15c. black, green & turq . . 30 1·50
20a – 20c. multicoloured . . . . 1·50 2·00
21 **3** 25c. multicoloured 60 25
22 – 35c. multicoloured 80 25
23 – 50c. multicoloured 80 55
24 – 75c. multicoloured 80 80
25 – $1 multicoloured . . . . 85 2·00
26 – $2.50 multicoloured . . . 1·50 5·00
27 – $5 multicoloured . . . . 2·75 7·50
DESIGNS: As T **3**—20c. Great barracuda; 35c. French angelfish; 50c. Porkfish; 75c. Princess parrotfish; $1, Long-spined squirrelfish; $2.50, Bigeye; $5, Blue chromis.

10 Sprinting and Aztec Sun-stone

1968. Olympic Games. Mexico. Multicoloured.
28 25c. Type **10** 45 25
29 35c. High-jumping and Aztec statue 50 25
30 75c. Dinghy-racing and Aztec lion mask 55 45

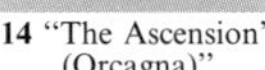

14 "The Ascension" (Orcagna)"
18 "Sistine Madonna" (Raphael)

15 Scout Enrolment Ceremony

1969. Easter Commemoration.
32 **14** 25c. black and blue 15 45
33 35c. black and red 15 50
34 75c. black and lilac 15 55

1969. 3rd Caribbean Scout Jamboree. Multicoloured.
35 25c. Type **15** 45 55
36 35c. Scouts around camp fire 60 65
37 75c. Sea Scouts rowing boat 75 85

1969. Christmas.
38 **18** ½c. multicoloured 10 10
39 25c. multicoloured 10 15
40 35c. multicoloured 10 20
41 35c. multicoloured 20 35

19 William I (1066–87)
21 "The Way to Calvary" (Ugolino)

1970. English Monarchs. Multicoloured.
42 35c. Type **19** 30 15
43 35c. William II (1087–1100) 10 15
44 35c. Henry I (1100–35) 10 15
45 35c. Stephen (1135–54) 10 15
46 35c. Henry II (1154–89) . . . 10 15
47 35c. Richard I (1189–99) . . . 10 15
48 35c. John (1199–1216) 10 15
49 35c. Henry III (1216–72) . . . 10 15
50 35c. Edward I (1272–1307) . . 10 15
51 35c. Edward II (1307–27) . . 10 15
52 35c. Edward III (1327–77) . . 10 15
53 35c. Richard II (1377–99) . . 10 15
54 35c. Henry IV (1399–1413) . . 10 15
55 35c. Henry V (1413–22) . . . 10 15
56 35c. Henry VI (1422–61) . . . 10 15
57 35c. Edward IV (1462–83) . . 10 15
58 35c. Edward V (April–June 1483) 10 15
59 35c. Richard III (1483–85) . . 10 15
60 35c. Henry VII (1485–1509) 10 15
61 35c. Henry VIII (1509–47) . . 10 15
62 35c. Edward VI (1547–53) . . 10 15
63 35c. Lady Jane Grey (1553) . . 10 15
64 35c. Mary I (1553–8) 10 15
65 35c. Elizabeth I (1558–1603) 10 15
66 35c. James I (1603–25) 10 15
67 35c. Charles I (1625–49) . . . 10 15
68 35c. Charles II (1649–1685) . . 10 15
69 35c. James II (1685–1688) . . 10 15
70 35c. William III (1689–1702) 10 15
71 35c. Mary II (1689–1694) . . 10 15
72 35c. Anne (1702–1714) 15 15
73 35c. George I (1714–1727) . . 15 15
74 35c. George II (1727–1760) . . 15 15
75 35c. George III (1760–1820) 15 15
76 35c. George IV (1820–1830) 15 15
77 35c. William IV (1830–1837) 15 60
78 35c. Victoria (1837–1901) . . . 15 60
See also Nos. 710/5.

1970. No. 12 surch **20c**.
79 **2** 20c. on ½c. brn, blk & pink 10 20

1970. Easter. Paintings. Multicoloured.
80 25c. Type **21** 15 30
81 35c. "The Deposition from the Cross" (Ugolino) 15 30
82 75c. Crucifix (The Master of St. Francis) 15 35

22 Oliver is introduced to Fagin ("Oliver Twist")

1970. Death Centenary of Charles Dickens. Mult.
83 20c. Type **22** 20 25
84 75c. Dickens and scene from "The Old Curiosity Shop" 45 65

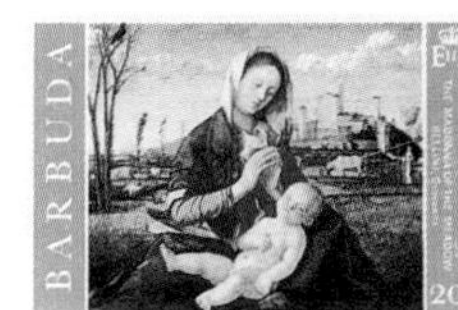

23 "Madonna of the Meadows" (G. Bellini)

1970. Christmas. Multicoloured.
85 20c. Type **23** 10 25
86 50c. "Madonna, Child and Angels" (from Wilton diptych) 15 30
87 75c. "The Nativity" (della Francesca) 15 35

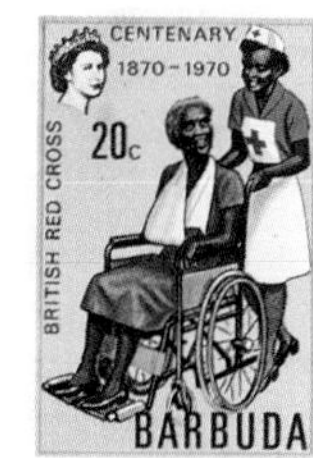

24 Nurse with Patient in Wheelchair
25 "Angel with Vases"

1970. Centenary of British Red Cross. Multicoloured.
88 20c. Type **24** 15 30
89 35c. Nurse giving patient magazines (horiz) 20 40
90 75c. Nurse and mother weighing baby (horiz) . . . 25 70

1971. Easter. "Mond" Crucifixion by Raphael. Multicoloured.
91 35c. Type **25** 15 75
92 50c. "Christ crucified" 15 85
93 75c. "Angel with vase" . . . 15 90

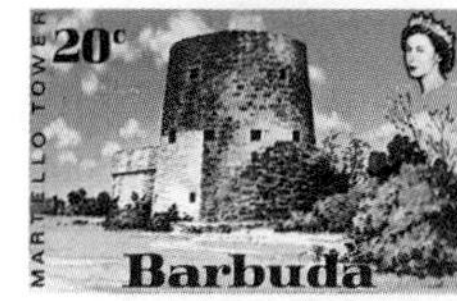

26 Martello Tower

1971. Tourism. Multicoloured.
94 20c. Type **26** 15 25
95 25c. "Sailfish" dinghy 25 30
96 50c. Hotel bungalows 25 35
97 75c. Government House and Mystery Stone 25 40

27 "The Granducal Madonna" (Raphael)

1971. Christmas. Multicoloured.
98 ½c. Type **27** 10 10
99 35c. "The Ansidei Madonna" (Raphael) 10 20
100 50c. "The Madonna and Child" (Botticelli) 15 25
101 75c. "The Madonna of the Trees" (Bellini) 15 30

Four stamps to commemorate the 500th Birth Anniv of Durer were prepared in late 1971, but their issue was not authorised by the Antigua Government.

1973. Royal Wedding. Nos. 370/1 of Antigua optd **BARBUDA** twice.
102 **106** 25c. multicoloured . . . . 3·25 2·00
103 $2 multicoloured . . . . 1·25 1·25

1973. Ships. Nos. 269/85 of Antigua optd **BARBUDA**.
116 **92** ½c. multicoloured 15 20
104 – 1c. multicoloured 15 30
105 – 2c. multicoloured 25 30
117 – 3c. multicoloured 25 25
106 – 4c. multicoloured 30 30
107 – 5c. multicoloured 40 40
108 – 6c. multicoloured 40 40
109 – 10c. multicoloured 45 45
118 – 15c. multicoloured 45 50
110 – 20c. multicoloured 55 60
111 – 25c. multicoloured 55 60
112 – 35c. multicoloured 55 70
113 – 50c. multicoloured 55 70
114 – 75c. multicoloured 55 70
119 – $1 multicoloured 55 70
115 – $2.50 multicoloured . . . 75 1·50
121 – $5 multicoloured . . . . . 1·10 2·50

1973. Military Uniforms. Nos. 353, 355 and 357 of Antigua optd **BARBUDA**.
122 ½c. multicoloured 10 10
123 20c. multicoloured 15 10
124 75c. multicoloured 40 15

1973. Carnival. Nos. 360/3 of Antigua optd **BARBUDA**.
126 20c. multicoloured 10 10
127 35c. multicoloured 10 10
128 75c. multicoloured 20 25
MS129 134 × 95 mm. Nos. 359/62 of Antigua 1·00 2·25

1973. Christmas. Nos. 364/69 of Antigua optd **BARBUDA**.
130 **105** 3c. multicoloured 10 10
131 – 5c. multicoloured 10 10
132 – 20c. multicoloured 10 10
133 – 35c. multicoloured 15 15
134 – $1 multicoloured 30 30
MS135 130 × 128 mm. Nos. 130/4 2·75 9·00

1973. Honeymoon Visit. Nos. 373/4 of Antigua additionally optd **BARBUDA**.
136 35c. multicoloured 30 20
137 $2 multicoloured 70 60

1974. University of West Indies. Nos. 376/9 of Antigua optd **BARBUDA**.
139 5c. multicoloured 10 10
140 20c. multicoloured 10 10
141 35c. multicoloured 15 15
142 75c. multicoloured 15 15

1974. Military Uniforms. Nos. 380/4 of Antigua optd **BARBUDA**.
143 ½c. multicoloured 10 10
144 10c. multicoloured 15 10
145 20c. multicoloured 25 10
146 35c. multicoloured 25 10
147 75c. multicoloured 45 25

1974. Centenary of U.P.U. (1st issue). Nos. 386/92 of Antigua optd with either a or b. (a) **BARBUDA 13 JULY 1992**.
148 ½c. multicoloured 10 10
150 1c. multicoloured 10 10
152 2c. multicoloured 20 15
154 5c. multicoloured 50 15
156 20c. multicoloured 40 70
158 35c. multicoloured . . . . . 80 1·50
160 $1 multicoloured . . . . . . 2·25 4·00

(b) **BARBUDA 15 SEPT. 1874 G.P.U.** ("General Postal Union").
149 ½c. multicoloured 10 10
151 1c. multicoloured 10 10
153 2c. multicoloured 20 15
155 5c. multicoloured 50 15
157 20c. multicoloured 40 70
159 35c. multicoloured . . . . . 80 1·50
161 $1 multicoloured . . . . . . 2·25 4·00
MS162 141 × 164 mm. No. **MS**393 of Antigua optd **BARBUDA** 3·50 6·00

1974. Antiguan Steel Bands. Nos. 394/98 of Antigua optd **BARBUDA**.
163 5c. deep red, red and black 10 10
164 20c. brown, lt brown & blk 10 10
165 35c. light green, green and black 10 10
166 75c. deep blue, blue and black 20 20
MS167 115 × 108 mm. Nos. 163/6 65 80

39 Footballers

1974. World Cup Football Championships (1st issue).
168 **39** 35c. multicoloured 10 10
169 – $1.20 multicoloured . . . 25 35
170 – $2.50 multicoloured . . . 35 50
MS171 70 × 128 mm. Nos. 168/70 85 90
DESIGNS: $1.20, $2.50, Footballers in action similar to Type **39**.

1974. World Cup Football Championships (2nd issue). Nos. 399/403 of Antigua optd **BARBUDA**.
172 **111** 5c. multicoloured 10 10
173 – 35c. multicoloured 20 10
174 – 75c. multicoloured 25 15
175 – $1 multicoloured 25 25
MS176 135 × 130 mm. Nos. 172/5 75 1·00

41 Ship Letter of 1833

1974. Cent of Universal Postal Union (2nd issue). Multicoloured.
177 35c. Type **41** 10 10
178 $1.20 Stamps and postmarks of 1922 . . . . 25 50
179 $2.50 Britten Norman Islander mailplane over map of Barbuda 35 75
MS180 128 × 97 mm. Nos. 177/9 1·00 2·00

42 Greater Amberjack

1974. Multicoloured.
181 ½c. Oleander, Rose Bay (vert) 10 40
182 1c. Blue petrea (vert) . . . 15 40
183 2c. Poinsettia (vert) 15 40
184 3c. Cassia tree (vert) 15 40
185 4c. Type **42** . . . . 1·60 40
186 5c. Holy Trinity School . . 15 15
187 6c. Snorkeling 15 30
188 10c. Pilgrim Holiness Church 15 20
189 15c. New Cottage Hospital 15 20
190 20c. Post Office and Treasury 15 20
191 25c. Island jetty and boats (vert) 30 30
192 35c. Martello Tower 30 30
193 50c. Warden's House . . . 30 30
194 75c. Britten Norman Islander aircraft . . . . . 1·75 1·00
195 $1 Tortoise 70 80
196 $2.50 Spiny lobster . . . . 80 1·75
197 $5 Magnificent frigate bird 3·50 2·50
197b $10 Hibiscus (vert) . . . . 1·50 4·50
The 50c. to $1 are 39 × 25 mm, $2.50 and $5 45 × 29 mm, $10 34 × 48 mm.

1974. Birth Centenary of Sir Winston Churchill (1st issue). Nos. 408/12 of Antigua optd **BARBUDA**.
198 **113** 5c. multicoloured 15 10
199 – 35c. multicoloured 25 15
200 – 75c. multicoloured 40 45
201 – $1 multicoloured 75 70
MS202 107 × 82 mm. Nos. 198/201 6·50 13·00

43 Churchill making Broadcast

1974. Birth Centenary of Sir Winston Churchill (2nd issue). Multicoloured.
203 5c. Type **43** 10 10
204 35c. Churchill and Chartwell 10 10
205 75c. Churchill painting . . . 20 20
206 $1 Churchill making "V" sign 25 30
MS207 146 × 95 mm. Nos. 203/6 75 2·50

1974. Christmas. Nos. 413/21 of Antigua optd **BARBUDA**.
208 **114** ½c. multicoloured 10 10
209 – 1c. multicoloured 10 10
210 – 2c. multicoloured 10 10
211 – 3c. multicoloured 10 10
212 – 5c. multicoloured 10 10
213 – 20c. multicoloured 10 10
214 – 35c. multicoloured 15 15
215 – 75c. multicoloured 30 30
MS216 139 × 126 mm. Nos. 208/15 80 1·40

1975. Nelson's Dockyard. Nos. 427/32 of Antigua optd **BARBUDA**.
217 **116** 5c. multicoloured 15 15
218 – 15c. multicoloured 40 25
219 – 35c. multicoloured 55 35

220 – 50c. multicoloured 60 50
221 – $1 multicoloured 65 80
MS222 130 × 134 mm. As Nos. 217/21, but larger format; 43 × 28 mm 1·75 2·75

45 Ships of the Line

1975. Sea Battles. Battle of the Saints, 1782. Mult.
223 35c. Type **45** 50 65
224 50c. H.M.S. "Ramillies" . . 50 75
225 75c. "Bonhomme Richard" (American frigate) firing broadside 60 90
226 95c. "L'Orient" (French ship of the line) burning . . . . 60 1·25

1975. "Apollo–Soyuz" Space Project. No. 197 optd **U.S.A.-U.S.S.R SPACE COOPERATION 1975** with **APOLLO** (No. 227) or **SOYUZ** (No. 228).
227 $5 multicoloured . . . . . . 3·25 6·00
228 $5 multicoloured . . . . . . 3·25 6·00

47 Officer, 65th Foot, 1763

1975. Military Uniforms. Multicoloured.
229 35c. Type **47** 60 60
230 50c. Grenadier, 27th Foot 1701–10 . . . . 75 75
231 75c. Officer, 21st Foot, 1793–6 . . . . 80 80
232 95c. Officer, Royal Regiment of Artillery, 1800 . . . . . 90 90

1975. 25th Anniv of United Nations. Nos. 203/6 optd **30TH ANNIVERSARY UNITED NATIONS 1945–1975.**
233 **43** 5c. multicoloured 10 10
234 – 35c. multicoloured 10 15
235 – 75c. multicoloured 15 20
236 – $1 multicoloured 20 30

1975. Christmas. Nos. 457/65 of Antigua optd **BARBUDA**.
237 **121** ½c. multicoloured 10 15
238 – 1c. multicoloured 10 15
239 – 2c. multicoloured 10 15
240 – 3c. multicoloured 10 15
241 – 5c. multicoloured 10 15
242 – 10c. multicoloured 10 15
243 – 35c. multicoloured 15 20
244 – $2 multicoloured . . . . 60 1·00
MS245 138 × 119 mm. Nos. 241/4 1·10 2·25

1975. World Cup Cricket Winners. Nos. 466/8 of Antigua optd **BARBUDA**.
246 **122** 5c. multicoloured . . . . 90 1·00
247 – 35c. multicoloured . . . . 1·75 2·00
248 – $2 multicoloured . . . . 3·25 4·25

51 Surrender of Cornwallis at Yorktown (Trumbull)

1976. Bicentenary of American Revolution.
249 **51** 15c. multicoloured 10 15
250 – 15c. multicoloured 10 15
251 – 15c. multicoloured 10 15
252 – 35c. multicoloured 10 15
253 – 35c. multicoloured 10 15
254 – 35c. multicoloured 10 15
255 – $1 multicoloured 15 25
256 – $1 multicoloured 15 25
257 – $1 multicoloured 15 25
258 – $2 multicoloured 25 40
259 – $2 multicoloured 25 40
260 – $2 multicoloured 25 40
MS261 140 × 70 mm. Nos. 249/54 and 255/60 (two sheets) 1·75 9·00

DESIGNS—As Type **51**: Nos. 249/51; 252/4, The Battle of Princeton; 255/7, Surrender of General Burgoyne at Saratoga; 258/60, Jefferson presenting Declaration of Independence.

Type **51** shows the left-hand stamp of the 15c. design.

52 Bananaquits

1976. Birds. Multicoloured.
262 35c. Type **52** 60 50
263 50c. Blue-hooded euphonia 60 60
264 75c. Royal tern 60 80
265 95c. Killdeer plover ("Killdeer") 65 85
266 $1.25 Shiney-headed cowbird ("Glossy Cowbird") . . . 70 1·00
267 $2 American purple gallinule ("Purple Gallinule") . . . 75 1·25

1976. Royal Visit to the U.S.A. Nos. 249/60 additionally inscr "H.M. QUEEN ELIZABETH ROYAL VISIT 6TH JULY 1976 H.R.H. DUKE OF EDINBURGH".
268 15c. multicoloured 10 15
269 15c. multicoloured 10 15
270 15c. multicoloured 10 15
271 35c. multicoloured 10 20
272 35c. multicoloured 10 20
273 35c. multicoloured 10 20
274 $1 multicoloured 15 50
275 $1 multicoloured 15 50
276 $1 multicoloured 15 50
277 $2 multicoloured 25 70
278 $2 multicoloured 25 70
279 $2 multicoloured 25 70
MS280 143 × 81 mm. Nos. 268/73 and 274/9 (two sheets) 2·00 9·00

1976. Christmas. Nos. 514/18 of Antigua optd **BARBUDA**.
281 **128** 8c. multicoloured 10 10
282 – 10c. multicoloured 10 10
283 – 15c. multicoloured 10 10
284 – 50c. multicoloured 15 15
285 – $1 multicoloured 25 30

1976. Olympic Games, Montreal. Nos. 495/502 of Antigua optd **BARBUDA**.
286 **125** ½c. brown, yellow and black 10 10
287 – 1c. violet and black . . . 10 10
288 – 2c. green and black . . . 10 10
289 – 15c. blue and black . . . 10 10
290 – 30c. brown, yellow & blk 10 10
291 – $1 orange, red and black 20 20
292 – $2 red and black 35 35
MS293 88 × 138 mm. Nos. 289/92 1·75 2·40

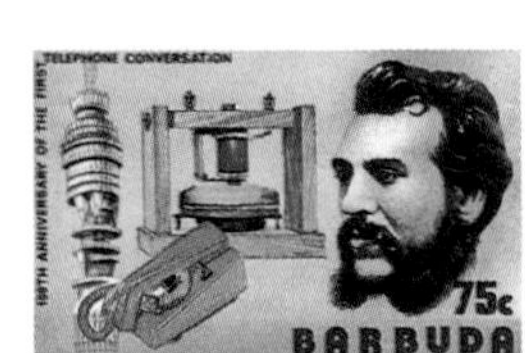

55 P.O. Tower, Telephones and Alexander Graham Bell

1977. Cent of First Telephone Transmission. Mult.
294 75c. Type **55** 15 35
295 $1.25 T.V. transmission by satellite 20 55
296 $2 Globe showing satellite transmission scheme . . . 30 75
MS297 96 × 144 mm. Nos. 294/6 70 2·00

56 St. Margaret's Church, Westminster

1977. Silver Jubilee (1st issue). Multicoloured.
298 75c. Type **56** 10 15
299 75c. Street decorations . . . 10 15
300 75c. Westminster Abbey . . 10 15
301 $1.25 Household Cavalry . . 15 20
302 $1.25 Coronation Coach . . 15 20
303 $1.25 Postillions 15 20
MS304 148 × 83 mm. As Nos. 298/303, but with silver borders. 75 1·50

Nos. 298/300 and 301/3 were printed together, se-tenant, forming composite designs.

See also Nos. 323/30 and 375/8.

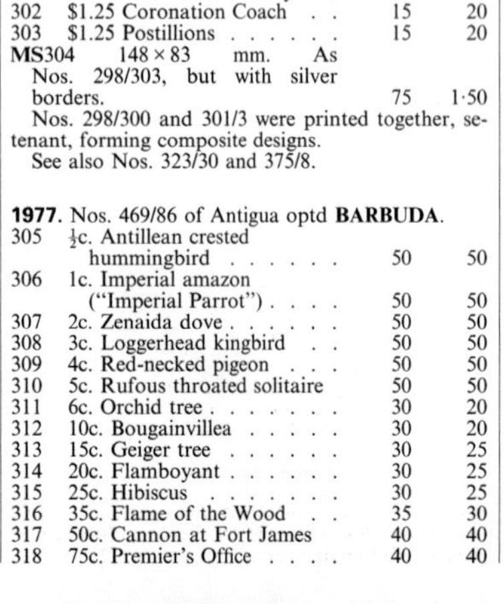

1977. Nos. 469/86 of Antigua optd **BARBUDA**.
305 ½c. Antillean crested hummingbird 50 50
306 1c. Imperial amazon ("Imperial Parrot") 50 50
307 2c. Zenaida dove 50 50
308 3c. Loggerhead kingbird . . 50 50
309 4c. Red-necked pigeon . . . 50 50
310 5c. Rufous throated solitaire 50 50
311 6c. Orchid tree 30 20
312 10c. Bougainvillea 30 20
313 15c. Geiger tree 30 25
314 20c. Flamboyant 30 25
315 25c. Hibiscus 30 25
316 35c. Flame of the Wood . . 35 30
317 50c. Cannon at Fort James 40 40
318 75c. Premier's Office 40 40

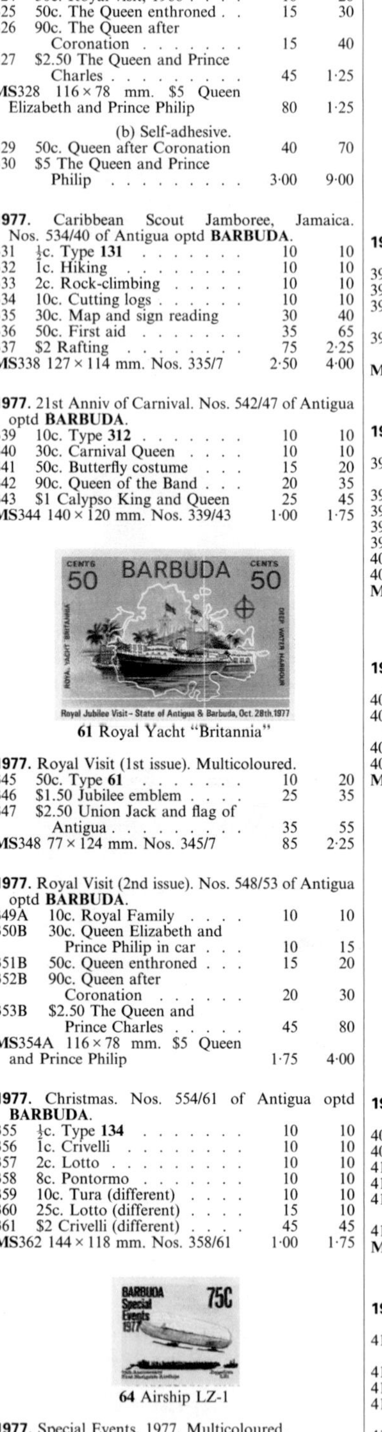

319 $1 Potworks Dam 50 60
320 $2.50 Irrigation scheme . . . 75 1·60
321 $5 Government House . . . 1·25 3·25
322 $10 Coolidge Airport . . . . 3·50 7·50

1977. Silver Jubilee (2nd issue). Nos. 526/31 of Antigua optd **BARBUDA**. (a) Ordinary gum.
323 10c. Royal Family 10 15
324 30c. Royal visit, 1966 . . . . 10 20
325 50c. The Queen enthroned . . 15 30
326 90c. The Queen after Coronation 15 40
327 $2.50 The Queen and Prince Charles . . . . 45 1·25
MS328 116 × 78 mm. $5 Queen Elizabeth and Prince Philip 80 1·25

(b) Self-adhesive.
329 50c. Queen after Coronation 40 70
330 $5 The Queen and Prince Philip . . . . 3·00 9·00

1977. Caribbean Scout Jamboree, Jamaica. Nos. 534/40 of Antigua optd **BARBUDA**.
331 ½c. Type **131** 10 10
332 1c. Hiking 10 10
333 2c. Rock-climbing 10 10
334 10c. Cutting logs 10 10
335 30c. Map and sign reading 30 40
336 50c. First aid 35 65
337 $2 Rafting . . . . 75 2·25
MS338 127 × 114 mm. Nos. 335/7 2·50 4·00

1977. 21st Anniv of Carnival. Nos. 542/47 of Antigua optd **BARBUDA**.
339 10c. Type **312** 10 10
340 30c. Carnival Queen 10 10
341 50c. Butterfly costume . . . 15 20
342 90c. Queen of the Band . . . 20 35
343 $1 Calypso King and Queen 25 45
MS344 140 × 120 mm. Nos. 339/43 1·00 1·75

61 Royal Yacht "Britannia"

1977. Royal Visit (1st issue). Multicoloured.
345 50c. Type **61** 10 20
346 $1.50 Jubilee emblem 25 35
347 $2.50 Union Jack and flag of Antigua 35 55
MS348 77 × 124 mm. Nos. 345/7 85 2·25

1977. Royal Visit (2nd issue). Nos. 548/53 of Antigua optd **BARBUDA**.
349A 10c. Royal Family 10 10
350B 30c. Queen Elizabeth and Prince Philip in car . . . 10 15
351B 50c. Queen enthroned . . . 15 20
352B 90c. Queen after Coronation 20 30
353B $2.50 The Queen and Prince Charles 45 80
MS354A 116 × 78 mm. $5 Queen and Prince Philip 1·75 4·00

1977. Christmas. Nos. 554/61 of Antigua optd **BARBUDA**.
355 ½c. Type **134** 10 10
356 1c. Crivelli 10 10
357 2c. Lotto 10 10
358 8c. Pontormo 10 10
359 10c. Tura (different) 10 10
360 25c. Lotto (different) 15 10
361 $2 Crivelli (different) 45 45
MS362 144 × 118 mm. Nos. 358/61 1·00 1·75

64 Airship LZ-1

1977. Special Events, 1977. Multicoloured.
363 75c. Type **64** 30 30
364 75c. German battleship and German Navy airship L-31 30 30
365 75c. "Graf Zeppelin" in hangar 30 30
366 75c. Gondola of military airship 30 30
367 95c. Sputnik 1 . . . . 35 35
368 95c. Vostok rocket 35 35
369 95c. Voskhod rocket 35 35
370 95c. Space walk 35 35
371 $1.25 Fuelling for flight . . . 40 45
372 $1.25 Leaving New York . . 40 45
373 $1.25 "Spirit of St. Louis" . . 40 45
374 $1.25 Welcome to England 40 45
375 $2 Lion of England 50 70
376 $2 Unicorn of Scotland . . . 50 70
377 $2 Yale of Beaufort 50 70
378 $2 Falcon of Plantagenets . . 50 70
379 $5 "Daniel in the Lion's Den" (Rubens) . . . . . 50 1·25
380 $5 Different detail of painting 50 1·25
381 $5 Different detail of painting 50 1·25
382 $5 Different detail of painting 50 1·25
MS383 132 × 156 mm. Nos. 362/82 6·00 17·00

EVENTS: 75c. 75th anniv of navigable airships; 95c. 20th anniv of U.S.S.R. space programme; $1.25, 50th anniv of Lindbergh's transatlantic flight; $2 Silver Jubilee of Queen Elizabeth II; $5 400th birth anniv of Rubens.

Nos. 379/82 form a composite design.

1978. 10th Anniv of Statehood. Nos. 562/7 of Antigua optd **BARBUDA**.
384 10c. Type **135** 10 10
385 15c. State flag 15 10
386 50c. Police band . . . . . . 1·25 70
387 90c. Premier V. C. Bird . . . 20 40
388 $2 State Coat of Arms . . . 40 80
MS389 122 × 99 mm. Nos. 385/88 6·50 3·50

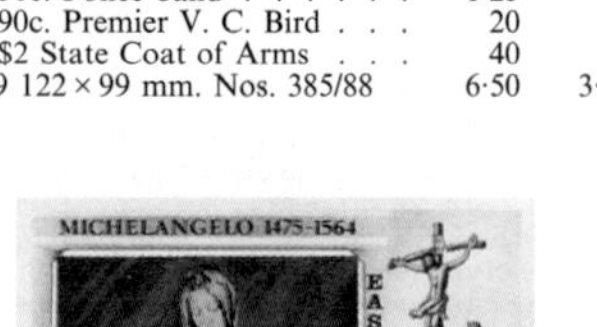

66 "Pieta" (sculpture) (detail)

1978. Easter. Paintings and Sculptures by Michelangelo. Multicoloured.
390 75c. Type **66** 15 15
391 95c. "The Holy Family" . . 15 20
392 $1.25 "Libyan sibyl" (from the Sistine Chapel) 15 35
393 $2 "The Flood" (from the Sistine Chapel) 20 45
MS394 117 × 85 mm. Nos. 390/3 1·60 2·00

1978. 75th Anniv of Powered Flight. Nos. 568/75 of Antigua optd **BARBUDA**.
395 ½c. Wright Glider No. III, 1902 . . . . 10 10
396 1c. Wright Flyer I, 1903 . . . 10 10
397 2c. Launch system and engine 10 10
398 10c. Orville Wright (vert) . . 10 10
399 50c. Wright Flyer III, 1905 25 20
400 90c. Wilbur Wright (vert) . . 35 25
401 $2 Wright Type B, 1910 . . . 60 45
MS402 90 × 75 mm. $2.50, Wright Flyer I on launch system 1·50 2·25

1978. Sailing Week. Nos. 576/80 of Antigua optd **BARBUDA**.
403 10c. Sunfish regatta 20 10
404 50c. Fishing and work boat race 40 25
405 90c. Curtain Bluff race . . . 55 35
406 $2 Power boat rally 85 75
MS407 110 × 77 mm. $2.50, Guadeloupe–Antigua race 1·25 1·60

68 St. Edward's Crown

1978. 25th Anniv of Coronation (1st issue). Multicoloured.
408 75c. Type **68** 15 20
409 75c. Imperial State Crown . . 15 20
410 $1.50 Queen Mary's Crown 20 30
411 $1.50 Queen Mother's Crown 20 30
412 $2.50 Queen Consort's Crown 35 50
413 $2.50 Queen Victoria's Crown 35 50
MS414 123 × 117 mm. Nos. 408/13 1·10 1·75

1978. 25th Anniv of Coronation (2nd issue). Nos. 581/5 of Antigua optd **BARBUDA**.
415 10c. Queen Elizabeth and Prince Philip 10 10
416 30c. The Crowning 10 10
417 50c. Coronation procession 10 15
418 90c. Queen seated in St. Edward's Chair 15 20
419 $2.50 Queen wearing Imperial State Crown 30 60
MS420 114 × 103 mm. $5 Queen Elizabeth and Prince Philip 1·00 1·50

1978. 25th Anniv of Coronation (3rd issue). As Nos. 587/9 of Antigua, additionally inscr "BARBUDA".
421 25c. Glass Coach 30 70
422 50c. Irish State Coach . . . 30 70
423 $5 Coronation Coach . . . . 1·00 2·25

1978. World Cup Football Championship, Argentina. Nos. 590/3 of Antigua optd **BARBUDA**.
424 10c. Player running with ball 10 10
425 15c. Players in front of goal 10 10
426 $3 Referee and player . . . . 1·00 1·25
MS427 126 × 88 mm. 25c. Player crouching with ball; 30c. Players heading ball; 50c. Players running with ball; $2 Goalkeeper diving 80 90

1978. Flowers. As Nos. 594/7 of Antigua optd **BARBUDA**.
428 25c. Petrea 15 20
429 50c. Sunflower 25 40

430 90c. Frangipani 35 45
431 $2 Passion flower 60 90
MS432 118 × 85 mm. $2.50, Hibiscus 1·00 1·50

1978. Christmas. As Nos. 599/601 of Antigua optd **BARBUDA**.
433 8c. "St. Ildefonso receiving the Chasuble from the Virgin" 10 10
434 25c. "The Flight of St. Barbara" 15 15
435 $2 "Madonna and Child, with St. Joseph, John the Baptist and Donor" . . . 60 1·25
MS436 170 × 113 mm. $4 "The Annuciation" 1·00 1·25

70 Black-barred Soldierfish

1978. Flora and Fauna. Multicoloured.
437 25c. Type **70** . . . . 75 1·50
438 50c. "Cynthia cardui" (butterfly) . . . . 1·25 2·25
439 75c. Dwarf poinciana . . . . 75 2·25
440 95c. "Heliconius charithonia" (butterfly) . . . . 1·50 2·50
441 $1.25 Bougainvillea . . . . . 1·00 2·50

71 Footballers and World Cup **72** Sir Rowland Hill

1978. Anniversaries and Events.
442 75c. Type **71** 30 30
443 95c. Wright Brothers and Flyer I (horiz) 30 40
444 $1.25 Balloon "Double Eagle II" and map of Atlantic (horiz) 40 45
445 $2 Prince Philip paying homage to the Queen . . . 40 60
MS446 122 × 90 mm. Nos. 442/5. Imperf 4·00 6·00
EVENTS: 75c. Argentina—Winners of World Cup Football Championship; 95c. 75th anniv of powered flight; $1.25, First Atlantic crossing by balloon; $2 25th anniv of Coronation.

1979. Death Centenary of Sir Rowland Hill (1st issue). Multicoloured.
447 75c. Type **72** 25 45
448 95c. Mail coach, 1840 (horiz) 25 50
449 $1.25 London's first pillar box, 1855 (horiz) 30 60
450 $2 Mail leaving St. Martin's Le Grand Post Office, London 45 85
MS451 129 × 104 mm. Nos. 447/50. Imperf 1·40 2·25

1979. Death Centenary of Sir Rowland Hill (2nd issue). Nos. 603/6 of Antigua optd **BARBUDA**.
452 25c. 1d. Stamp of 1863 . . . 15 15
453 50c. Penny Black 20 20
454 $1 Stage-coach and woman posting letter, c. 1840 . . . 35 30
455 $2 Modern mail transport . . 80 60
MS456 108 × 82 mm. $2.50, Sir Rowland Hill 75 80

1979. Easter. Works of Durer. Nos. 608/11 of Antigua optd **BARBUDA**.
457 10c. multicoloured 10 10
458 50c. multicoloured 20 20
459 $4 black, mauve and yellow 90 1·10
MS460 114 × 99 mm. $2.50, multicoloured 55 75

74 Passengers alighting from British Airways Boeing 747

1979. 30th Anniv of International Civil Aviation Organization. Multicoloured.
461 75c. Type **74** 25 50
462 95c. Air traffic control . . . 25 50
463 $1.25 Ground crew-man directing Douglas DC-8 on runway 25 50

1979. International Year of the Child (1st issue). Nos. 612/15 of Antigua optd **BARBUDA**.
464 25c. Yacht 20 15
465 50c. Rocket 30 25
466 90c. Car 40 35
467 $2 Toy train 60 80
MS468 80 × 112 mm. $5 Airplane 1·10 1·10

1979. Fishes. Nos. 617/21 of Antigua optd **BARBUDA**.
469 30c. Yellow jack 20 15
470 50c. Blue-finned tuna 25 20
471 90c. Sailfish 30 30
472 $3 Wahoo . . . . 65 1·10
MS473 122 × 75 mm. $2.50, Great barracuda 1·00 1·25

1979. Death Bicentenary of Captain Cook. Nos. 622/6 of Antigua optd **BARBUDA**.
474 25c. Cook's Birthplace, Marton 25 25
475 50c. H.M.S. "Endeavour" . . 70 35
476 90c. Marine chronometer . . 70 40
477 $3 Landing at Botany Bay 1·50 1·25
MS478 110 × 85 mm. $2.50, H.M.S. "Resolution" 1·25 1·50

77 "Virgin with the Pear"

1979. International Year of the Child (2nd issue). Paintings by Durer. Multicoloured.
479 25c. Type **77** 15 15
480 50c. "Virgin with the Pink" (detail) 20 25
481 75c. "Virgin with the Pear" (different detail) 25 30
482 $1.25 "Nativity" (detail) . . 25 40
MS483 86 × 118 mm. Nos. 479/82 1·00 1·75

1979. Christmas. Nos. 627/31 of Antigua optd **BARBUDA**.
484 8c. The Holy Family 10 10
485 25c. Mary and Jesus on donkey 15 10
486 50c. Shepherd looking at star 25 15
487 $4 The Three Kings 85 80
MS488 113 × 94 mm. $3 Angel with trumpet 80 1·10

1980. Olympic Games, Moscow. Nos. 632/6 of Antigua optd **BARBUDA**.
489 10c. Javelin 10 10
490 25c. Running 15 10
491 $1 Pole vault 35 20
492 $2 Hurdles 55 40
MS493 127 × 96 mm. $3 Boxing 70 1·10

1980. "London 1980" International Stamp Exhibition. Nos. 452/5 optd **LONDON 1980**.
494 25c. 1d. stamp of 1863 . . . 35 20
495 50c. Penny Black 45 40
496 $1 Stage-coach and woman posting letter, c. 1840 . . . 85 65
497 $2 Modern mail transport . . 2·75 1·50

80 "Apollo 11" Crew Badge

1980. 10th Anniv of "Apollo 11" Moon Landing. Multicoloured.
498 75c. Type **80** 35 25
499 95c. Plaque left on Moon . . 35 30
500 $1.25 Rejoining the mother-ship 65 50
501 $2 Lunar module 65 75
MS502 118 × 84 mm. Nos. 498/501 1·40 2·50

81 American Wigeon ("American Widgeon")

1980. Birds. Multicoloured.
503 1c. Type **81** 70 90
504 2c. Snowy plover 70 70
505 4c. Rose-breasted grosbeak 75 70
506 6c. Mangrove cuckoo 75 70
507 10c. Adelaide's warbler . . . 75 70
508 15c. Scaly-breasted thrasher 80 70
509 20c. Yellow-crowned night heron 80 70
510 25c. Bridled quail dove . . . 80 70
511 35c. Carib grackle 85 90
512 50c. Northern pintail 90 55
513 75c. Black-whispered vireo 1·00 55
514 $1 Blue-winged teal . . . . . 1·25 80
515 $1.50 Green-throated carib (vert) . . . . 1·50 80
516 $2 Red-necked pigeon (vert) 2·25 1·25
517 $2.50 Wied's crested flycatcher ("Stolid Flycatcher") (vert) . . . . 2·75 1·50
518 $5 Yellow-bellied sapsucker (vert) . . . . 4·00 3·50
519 $7.50 Caribbean elaenia (vert) 5·00 5·50
520 $10 Great egret (vert) . . . . 5·00 5·00

1980. Famous Works of Art. Nos. 651/8 of Antigua optd **BARBUDA**.
521 10c. "David" (statue, Donatello) 10 10
522 30c. "The Birth of Venus" (painting, Sandro Botticelli) 15 15
523 50c. "Reclining Couple" (sarcophagus), Cerveteri . . 15 20
524 90c. "The Garden of Earthly Delights" (painting, Hieronymus Bosch) . . . 20 25
525 $1 "Portinari Altarpiece" (painting, Hugo van der Goes) 20 25
526 $4 "Eleanora of Toledo and her Son Giovanni de'Medici" (painting, Agnolo Bronzino) 60 80
MS527 99 × 124 mm. $5 "The Holy Family" (painting, Rembrandt) 1·50 1·75

1980. 75th Anniv of Rotary International. Nos. 658/62 of Antigua optd **BARBUDA**.
528 30c. Rotary Headquarters . . 15 15
529 50c. Antigua Rotary banner 20 20
530 90c. Map of Antigua 25 25
531 $3 Paul P. Harris (founder) 65 65
MS532 102 × 77 mm. $5 Antigua flags and Rotary emblems 1·50 2·25

1980. 80th Birthday of the Queen Mother. Nos. 663/5 of Antigua optd **BARBUDA**.
533 10c. multicoloured 50 15
534 $2.50 multicoloured . . . . 1·25 1·50
MS535 68 × 88 mm. $3 multicoloured 2·25 1·75

1980. Birds. Nos. 666/70 of Antigua optd **BARBUDA**.
536 10c. Ringed kingfisher . . . 2·75 1·00
537 30c. Plain pigeon . . . . . . 3·25 1·10
538 $1 Green-throated carib . . . 4·25 2·75
539 $2 Black necked stilt . . . . 5·25 5·25
MS540 73 × 73 mm. $2.50, Roseate tern 4·50 2·75

1981. Sugar Cane Railway Locomotives. Nos. 681/5 of Antigua optd **BARBUDA**.
541 25c. Diesel locomotive No. 15 1·00 25
542 50c. Narrow-gauge steam locomotive . . . . 1·25 35
543 90c. Diesel locomotive Nos. 1 and 10 . . . . 1·75 45
544 $3 Steam locomotive hauling sugar cane . . . . 3·25 1·40
MS545 82 × 111 mm. $2.50, Antigua sugar factory, railway yard and sheds 1·50 1·75

84 Florence Nightingale

1981. Famous Women.
546 **84** 50c. multicoloured 15 30
547 – 90c. multicoloured 40 55
548 – $1 multicoloured 35 60
549 – $4 black, brown and lilac 50 1·75
DESIGNS: 90c. Marie Curie; $1 Amy Johnson; $4 Eleanor Roosevelt.

85 Goofy in Motor-boat

1981. Walt Disney Cartoon Characters. Mult.
550 10c. Type **85** 70 15
551 20c. Donald Duck reversing car into sea 85 20
552 25c. Mickey Mouse asking tug-boat to take on more than it can handle 90 30
553 30c. Porpoise turning tables on Goofy 90 35
554 35c. Goofy in sailing boat . . 90 35
555 40c. Mickey Mouse and boat being lifted out of water by fish . . . . 1·00 40
556 75c. Donald Duck fishing for flying-fish with butterfly net 1·25 60
557 $1 Minnie Mouse in brightly decorated sailing boat . . . 1·25 80
558 $2 Chip and Dale on floating ship-in-bottle . . . . . . 1·75 1·40
MS559 127 × 101 mm. $2.50, Donald Duck 4·00 3·00

1981. Birth Centenary of Picasso. Nos. 697/701 of Antigua optd with **BARBUDA**.
560 10c. "Pipes of Pan" 10 10
561 50c. "Seated Harlequin" . . 25 15
562 90c. "Paulo as Harlequin" . . 35 30
563 $4 "Mother and Child" . . . 90 1·00
MS564 115 × 140 mm. $5 "Three Musicians" (detail) 1·50 1·50

87/8 Buckingham Palace (½-size illustration)

1981. Royal Wedding (1st issue). Buildings. Each printed in black on either pink, green or lilac backgrounds.
565 $1 Type **87** 25 40
566 $1 Type **88** 25 40
567 $1.50 Caernarvon Castle (right) 30 50
568 $1.50 Caernarvon Castle (left) 30 50
569 $4 Highgrove House (right) 55 90
570 $4 Highgrove House (left) . . 55 90
MS571 75 × 90 mm. $5 black and yellow (St. Paul's Cathedral—26 × 32 mm) 80 1·25
Same prices for any background colour. The two versions of each value form composite designs.

1981. Royal Wedding (2nd issue). Nos. 702/5 of Antigua optd **BARBUDA**.
572 25c. Prince Charles and Lady Diana Spencer 15 15
573 50c. Glamis Castle 25 25
574 $4 Prince Charles skiing . . . 75 1·00
MS575 95 × 85 mm. $5 Glass coach 90 90

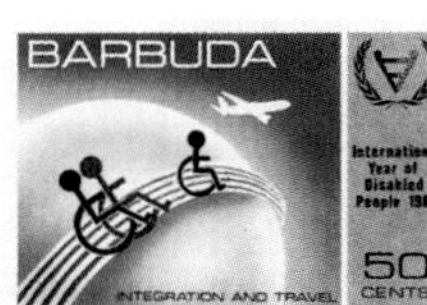

89 "Integration and Travel"

1981. International Year of Disabled Persons (1st issue).
576 **89** 50c. multicoloured 25 20
577 – 90c. black, orange and green 25 25
578 – $1 black, blue and green 30 30
579 – $4 black, yellow and brown 45 85
DESIGNS: 90c. Braille and sign language; $1 "Helping hands"; $4 "Mobility aids for disabled".
See also Nos. 603/6.

1981. Royal Wedding (3rd issue). Nos. 706/12 of Antigua optd **BARBUDA**.
580 25c. Prince of Wales at Investiture, 1969 . . . . . 40 60
581 25c. Prince Charles as baby, 1948 . . . . 40 60
582 $1 Prince Charles at R.A.F. College, Cranwell, 1971 . . 50 70
583 $1 Prince Charles attending Hill House School, 1956 50 70
584 $2 Prince Charles and Lady Diana Spencer 75 90

585 $2 Prince Charles at Trinity College, 1967 . . . . . . 75 90
586 $5 Prince Charles and Lady Diana . . . . 3·25 4·25

1981. Independence. No. 686/96 of Antigua additionally optd **BARBUDA**.
587 6c. Orchid tree 50 15
588 10c. Bougainvillea 55 15
589 20c. Flamboyant 70 20
590 25c. Hibiscus 80 25
591 35c. Flame of the wood . . . 90 30
592 50c. Cannon at Fort James 1·10 45
593 75c. Premier's Office . . . . 1·25 75
594 $1 Potworks Dam . . . . . 1·50 80
595 $2.50 Irrigation scheme, Diamond Estate . . . . . 2·50 2·75
596 $5 Government House and Gardens . . . . 2·75 3·75
597 $10 Coolidge International Airport . . . . 4·50 6·00

1981. 50th Anniv of Antigua Girl Guide Movement. Nos. 713/16 of Antigua optd **BARBUDA**.
598 10c. Irene Joshua (founder) 55 10
599 50c. Campfire sing-song . . . 1·25 30
600 90c. Sailing . . . . 1·75 45
601 $2.50 Animal tending . . . . 3·00 1·40

1981. International Year of Disabled Persons (2nd issue). Sport for the Disabled. Nos. 728/32 of Antigua optd **BARBUDA**.
603 10c. Swimming 15 15
604 50c. Discus throwing 20 25
605 90c. Archery 45 45
606 $2 Baseball . . . . 60 1·50
MS607 108 × 84 mm. $4 Basketball 2·00 1·75

1981. Christmas. Paintings. Nos. 723/7 of Antigua optd **BARBUDA**.
608 8c. "Holy Night" (Jacques Stella) 10 10
609 30c. "Mary with Child" (Julius Schnorr von Carolfeld) 20 20
610 $1 "Virgin and Child" (Alsono Cano) 40 40
611 $3 "Virgin and Child" (Lorenzo di Credi) . . . . 1·10 1·10
MS612 77 × 111 mm. $5 "Holy Family" (Pieter von Avon) 1·75 2·25

93 Princess of Wales

97 Vincenzo Lunardi's Balloon Flight, London, 1785

1982. Birth of Prince William of Wales (1st issue).
613 **93** $1 multicoloured 50 50
614 $2.50 multicoloured . . . 70 1·10
615 $5 multicoloured . . . . 1·25 1·75
MS616 88 × 108 mm. $4 multicoloured 2·00 2·10

1982. South Atlantic Fund. Nos. 580/6 surch **S. Atlantic Fund + 50c.**
617 25c.+50c. Prince of Wales at Investiture, 1969 . . . . . 30 40
618 25c.+50c. Prince Charles as baby, 1948 . . . . 30 40
619 $1+50c. Prince Charles at R.A.F. College, Cranwell, 1971 . . . . 50 65
620 $1+50c. Prince Charles attending Hill House School, 1956 . . . . . . 50 65
621 $2+50c. Prince Charles and Lady Diana Spencer . . . 75 90
622 $2+50c. Prince Charles at Trinity College, 1967 . . . 75 90
623 $5+50c. Prince Charles and Lady Diana Spencer . . . 3·00 3·50

1982. 21st Birthday of Princess of Wales (1st issue). As Nos. 613/16 but inscr "Twenty First Birthday Greetings to H.R.H. The Princess of Wales."
624 $1 multicoloured . . . . . . 1·50 45
625 $2.50 multicoloured . . . . 2·25 1·25
626 $5 multicoloured . . . . . . 3·00 2·40
MS627 88 × 108 mm. $4 multicoloured 2·75 2·25

1982. 21st Birthday of Princess of Wales (2nd issue). Nos. 748/51 of Antigua optd **BARBUDA MAIL**.
628 90c. Queen's House, Greenwich 80 45
629 $1 Prince and Princess of Wales . . . . 1·25 50
630 $4 Princess of Wales . . . . 3·00 1·50

1982. Birth of Prince William of Wales (2nd issue). Nos. 757/60 of Antigua further optd **BARBUDA MAIL**.
632 90c. Queen's House, Greenwich 70 45
633 $1 Prince and Princess of Wales . . . . 1·25 50
634 $4 Princess of Wales . . . . 3·25 2·00
MS635 102 × 75 mm. $5 Princess of Wales (different) 4·25 2·50

1982. Birth Centenary of Franklin D. Roosevelt and 250th Birth Anniv of George Washington. Nos. 761/8 of Antigua optd **BARBUDA MAIL**.
636 10c. Roosevelt in 1940 . . . 10 10
637 25c. Washington as blacksmith 15 15
638 45c. Churchill, Roosevelt and Stalin at Yalta Conference 1·25 25
639 60c. Washington crossing Delaware 20 25
640 $1 "Roosevelt Special" train 1·25 40
641 $3 Portrait of Roosevelt . . . 60 90
MS642 92 × 87 mm. $4 Roosevelt and wife 1·00 1·75
MS643 92 × 87 mm. $4 Portrait of Washington 1·00 1·75

1982. Christmas. Religious Paintings by Raphael. Nos. 769/73 of Antigua optd **BARBUDA MAIL**.
644 10c. "Annunciation" 10 10
645 30c. "Adoration of the Magi" 15 15
646 $1 "Presentation at the Temple" 40 40
647 $4 "Coronation of the Virgin" . . . . 1·00 1·00
MS648 95 × 142 mm. $5 "Marriage of the Virgin" 1·25 2·00

1983. 500th Birth Anniv of Raphael. Details from "Galatea" Fresco. Nos. 774/8 of Antigua optd **BARBUDA MAIL**.
649 45c. Tritons and dolphins . . 20 20
650 50c. Sea Nymph carried off by Triton 20 20
651 60c. Winged angel steering dolphins (horiz) 25 25
652 $4 Cupids shooting arrows 1·00 1·00
MS653 101 × 102 mm. $5 Galatea pulled along by dolphins 1·25 2·00

1983. Commonwealth Day. Nos. 779/82 of Antigua optd **BARBUDA MAIL**.
654 25c. Pineapple produce . . . 45 55
655 45c. Carnival 50 70
656 60c. Tourism . . . . 70 1·25
657 $3 Airport . . . . 2·00 3·50

1983. World Communications Year. Nos. 783/6 of Antigua optd **BARBUDA MAIL**.
658 15c. T.V. satellite coverage of Royal Wedding . . . . . 1·75 20
659 50c. Police communications 3·00 90
660 60c. House-to-diesel train telephone call . . . . . . 2·50 90
661 $3 Satellite earth station with planets Jupiter and Saturn 3·75 2·50
MS662 100 × 90 mm. $5 "Comsat" satellite over West Indies 2·25 2·50

1983. Bicent of Manned Flight (1st issue). Mult.
663 $1 Type **97** 25 35
664 $1.50 Montgolfier brothers' balloon flight, Paris, 1783 40 55
665 $2.50 Blanchard and Jeffries' Cross-Channel balloon flight, 1785 . . . . 60 90
MS666 111 × 111 mm. $5 Maiden flight of airship LZ-127 "Graf Zeppelin", 1928 2·00 2·75
See also Nos. 672/6.

1983. Whales. Nos. 788/93 of Antigua optd **BARBUDA MAIL**.
667 15c. Bottlenose dolphin . . . 1·25 40
668 50c. Finback whale . . . . . 4·00 1·60
669 60c. Bowhead whale . . . . 4·50 1·75
670 $3 Spectacled porpoise . . . 5·50 4·25
MS671 122 × 101 mm. $5 Narwhal 6·00 4·50

1983. Bicentenary of Manned Flight (2nd issue). Nos. 811/15 of Antigua optd **BARBUDA MAIL**.
672 30c. Dornier Do-X flying boat 85 35
673 50c. Supermarine S6B seaplane . . . . 1·10 60
674 60c. Curtiss Sparrowhawk biplane and airship U.S.S. "Akron" . . . . 1·25 70
675 $4 Hot-air balloon "Pro-Juventute" . . . . 4·50 4·00
MS676 80 × 105 mm. $5 Airship LZ-127 "Graf Zeppelin" 3·75 4·25

1983. Nos. 565/70 surch.
677 45c. on $1 Type **87** 25 45
678 45c. on $1 Type **88** 25 45
679 50c. on $1.45 Caernarvon Castle (right) 25 45
680 50c. on $1.45 Caernarvon Castle (left) 25 45
681 60c. on $4 Highgrove House (left) 25 45
682 60c. on $4 Highgrove House (right) 25 45

1983. Nos. 793/810 of Antigua optd **BARBUDA MAIL**.
683 1c. Cashew nut 10 10
684 2c. Passion fruit 15 10
685 3c. Mango 15 10
686 5c. Grapefruit 15 10
687 10c. Pawpaw 20 10
688 15c. Breadfruit 40 10
689 20c. Coconut 50 15
690 25c. Oleander 50 15
691 30c. Banana 55 20
692 40c. Pineapple 65 25
693 45c. Cordia 70 30
694 50c. Cassia 80 30
695 60c. Poui 80 30
696 $1 Frangipani . . . . 1·10 50
697 $2 Flamboyant . . . . . . 1·75 1·25
698 $2.50 Lemon . . . . 2·00 1·75
699 $5 Lignum vitae . . . . . . 3·00 2·75
700 $10 National flag and coat of arms . . . . 4·50 5·50

1983. Christmas. 500th Birth Anniv of Raphael. Nos. 816/20 of Antigua optd **BARBUDA MAIL**.
701 10c. multicoloured 10 10
702 30c. multicoloured 10 20
703 $1 multicoloured 30 50
704 $4 multicoloured . . . . . . 1·00 1·50
MS705 101 × 131 mm. $5 multicoloured 1·40 2·50

1983. Bicentenary (1984) of Methodist Church. Nos. 821/4 of Antigua optd **BARBUDA MAIL**.
706 15c. Type **181** 20 15
707 50c. Nathaniel Gilbert (founder in Antigua) . . . 30 25
708 60c. St. John Methodist Church steeple 30 30
709 $3 Ebenezer Methodist Church, St John's . . . . 80 1·00

100 Edward VII

1984. Members of British Royal Family. Mult.
710 $1 Type **100** . . . . 50 1·10
711 $1 George V . . . . 50 1·10
712 $1 George VI . . . . 50 1·10
713 $1 Elizabeth II . . . . 50 1·10
714 $1 Charles, Prince of Wales 50 1·10
715 $1 Prince William of Wales 50 1·10

1984. Olympic Games, Los Angeles (1st issue). Nos. 825/9 of Antigua optd **BARBUDA MAIL**.
716 25c. Discus 25 20
717 50c. Gymnastics 40 40
718 90c. Hurdling 50 60
719 $3 Cycling . . . . 2·75 1·50
MS720 82 × 67 mm. $5 Volleyball 2·75 3·25

1984. Ships. Nos. 830/4 of Antigua optd **BARBUDA MAIL**.
721 45c. "Booker Vanguard" (freighter) . . . . 1·50 45
722 50c. "Canberra" (liner) . . . 1·50 50
723 60c. Yachts . . . . 1·75 60
724 $4 "Fairwind" (cargo liner) 4·25 2·75
MS725 101 × 80 mm. $5 18th-century British man-o-war (vert) 4·50 4·25

1984. Universal Postal Union Congress, Hamburg. Nos. 835/8 of Antigua optd **BARBUDA MAIL**.
726 15c. Chenille 25 15
727 50c. Shell flower 30 30
728 60c. Anthurium 40 40
729 $3 Angels trumpet . . . . . 75 1·25
MS730 100 × 75 mm. $5 Crown of Thorns 2·00 2·50

101 Olympic Stadium, Athens, 1896

1984. Olympic Games, Los Angeles (2nd issue). Multicoloured.
731 $1.50 Type **101** 50 90
732 $2.50 Olympic stadium, Los Angeles, 1984 . . . . . . 70 1·50
733 $5 Athlete carrying Olympic torch . . . . 1·10 2·25
MS734 121 × 95 mm. No. 733 1·50 2·50

1984. Presidents of the United States of America. Nos. 856/63 of Antigua optd **BARBUDA MAIL**.
735 10c. Abraham Lincoln . . . 10 10
736 20c. Harry Truman 15 15
737 30c. Dwight Eisenhower . . 20 25
738 40c. Ronald Reagan 25 30
739 90c. Gettysburg Address, 1863 . . . . 40 55
740 $1.10 Formation of N.A.T.O., 1949 . . . . . 40 65
741 $1.50 Eisenhower during Second World War 45 70
742 $2 Reagan and Caribbean Basin Initiative . . . . . 50 1·00

1984. Abolition of Slavery. Nos. 864/8 of Antigua optd **BARBUDA MAIL**.
743 40c. View of Moravian Mission 30 30
744 50c. Antigua Courthouse, 1823 . . . . 40 40
745 60c. Planting sugar-cane, Monks Hill 45 45
746 $3 Boiling house, Delaps' Estate . . . . 1·40 1·40
MS747 95 × 70 mm. $5 Loading sugar, Willoughby Bay 2·00 2·50

1984. Songbirds. Nos. 869/74 of Antigua optd **BARBUDA MAIL**.
748 40c. Rufous-sided towhee . . 1·50 45
749 50c. Parula warbler . . . . . 1·60 50
750 60c. House wren . . . . . . 1·75 55
751 $2 Ruby-crowned kinglet . . 3·00 1·50
752 $3 Common flicker ("Yellow-shafted Flicker") . . . . . 3·50 2·25
MS753 76 × 76 mm. $5 Yellow-breasted chat 4·00 4·50

1984. 450th Death Anniv of Correggio (painter). Nos. 878/82 of Antigua optd **BARBUDA MAIL**.
754 25c. "The Virgin and Infant with Angels and Cherubs" 15 20
755 60c. "The Four Saints" . . . 40 45
756 90c. "St. Catherine" 50 55
757 $3 "The Campori Madonna" 1·25 1·75
MS758 90 × 60 mm. $5 "St. John the Baptist" 1·75 3·25

1984. "Ausipex" International Stamp Exibition Melbourne. Australian Sports. Nos. 875/7 of Antigua optd **BARBUDA MAIL**.
759 $1 Grass-skiing 50 60
760 $5 Australian Football . . . 2·00 3·00
MS761 108 × 78 mm. Boomerang-throwing 2·00 3·25

1984. 150th Birth Anniv of Edgar Degas (painter). Nos. 883/7 of Antigua optd **BARBUDA MAIL**.
762 15c. "The Blue Dancers" . . 10 10
763 50c. "The Pink Dancers" . . 30 40
764 70c. "Two Dancers" 45 55
765 $4 "Dancers at the Bar" . . 1·25 3·50
MS766 90 × 60 mm. $5 "The Folk Dancers" (40 × 27 mm) 1·75 2·75

1985. Famous People. Nos. 888/96 of Antigua optd **BARBUDA MAIL**.
767 60c. Winston Churchill . . . 3·75 1·75
768 60c. Mahatma Gandhi . . . 3·75 1·75
769 60c. John F. Kennedy . . . 3·75 1·75
770 60c. Mao Tse-tung . . . . 3·75 1·75
771 $1 Churchill with General De Gaulle, Paris, 1944 (horiz) 3·75 1·75
772 $1 Gandhi leaving London by train, 1931 (horiz) . . . 3·75 1·75
773 $1 Kennedy with Chancellor Adenauer and Mayor Brandt, Berlin, 1963 (horiz) 3·75 1·75
774 $1 Mao Tse-tung with Lin Piao, Peking, 1969 (horiz) 3·75 1·75
MS775 114 × 80 mm. $5 Flags of Great Britain, India, the United States and China 3·50 3·75

103 Lady Elizabeth Bowes-Lyon, 1907, and Camellias

104 Roseate Tern

1985. Life and Times of Queen Elizabeth the Queen Mother. Multicoloured.
776 15c. Type **103** 25 10
777 45c. Duchess of York, 1926, and "Elizabeth of Glamis" roses 30 25
778 50c. The Queen Mother after the Coronation, 1937 . . . 30 25
779 60c. In Garter robes, 1971, and dog roses 30 30
780 90c. Attending Royal Variety Show, 1967, and red Hibiscus 40 45
781 $1 The Queen Mother in 1982, and blue plumbago 65 1·10
782 $3 Receiving 82nd birthday gifts from children, and morning glory . . . . . . 90 1·60

1985. Birth Bicentenary of John J. Audubon (ornithologist) (1st issue). Designs showing original paintings. Multicoloured.
783 45c. Type **104** 25 30
784 50c. Mangrove cuckoo . . . 25 30
785 60c. Yellow-crowned night heron 30 40
786 $5 Brown pelican . . . . . 1·75 3·50
See also Nos. 794/7 and 914/17.

1985. Centenary (1986) of Statue of Liberty (1st issue). Nos. 907/13 of Antigua optd **BARBUDA MAIL**.
787 25c. Torch from statue in Madison Square Park, 1885 . . . . 20 20
788 30c. Statue of Liberty and scaffolding ("Restoration and Renewal") (vert) . . . 20 20
789 50c. Frederic Bartholdi (sculpture) supervising construction, 1876 . . . . 30 30
790 90c. Close-up of Statue . . . 55 55

791 $1 Statue and sailing ship ("Operation Sail", 1976) (vert) 60 60
792 $3 Dedication ceremony, 1886 (vert) . . . . 1·75 1·75
MS793 110 × 80 mm. $5 Port of New York 3·75 3·00
See also Nos. 987/96.

1985. Birth Bicentenary of John J. Audubon (ornithologist) (2nd issue). Nos. 924/8 of Antigua optd **BARBUDA MAIL**.
794 90c. Slavonian grebe ("Horned Grebe") . . . . 7·50 4·25
795 $1 British storm petrel ("Least Petrel") . . . . . 7·50 4·50
796 $1.50 Great blue heron . . . 8·50 6·50
797 $3 Double-crested cormorant (white phase) . . . . . . 12·00 11·00
MS798 103 × 72 mm. $5 White-tailed tropic bird (vert) 20·00 9·00

1985. Butterflies. Nos. 929/33 of Antigua optd **BARBUDA MAIL**.
799 25c. "Anaea cyanea" . . . . 4·00 1·25
800 60c. "Leodonta dysoni" . . . 6·00 2·00
801 90c. "Junea doraete" . . . . 7·00 2·50
802 $4 "Prepona pylene" . . . . 12·00 14·00
MS803 132 × 105 mm. $5 "Caervois gerdtrudtus" 15·00 8·50

1985. Centenary of Motorcycle. Nos. 919/23 of Antigua optd **BARBUDA MAIL**.
804 10c. Triumph 2hp "Jap", 1903 . . . . 40 10
805 30c. Indian "Arrow", 1949 70 20
806 60c. BMW "R100RS", 1976 1·10 40
807 $4 Harley Davidson "Model II", 1916 . . . . 3·50 2·75
MS808 90 × 93 mm. $5 Laverda "Jota", 1975 4·00 4·00

1985. 85th Birthday of Queen Elizabeth the Queen Mother. Nos. 776/82 optd **4TH AUG 1900–1985**.
809 15c. Type **103** 75 50
810 45c. Duchess of York, 1926 and "Elizabeth of Glamis" roses . . . . 1·10 60
811 50c. The Queen Mother after the Coronation, 1937 . . . 1·10 60
812 60c. In Garter robes, 1971, and dog roses . . . . . . 1·25 1·00
813 90c. Attending Royal Variey Show, 1967, and red hibiscus . . . . 1·25 1·25
814 $2 The Queen Mother in 1982, and blue plumbago 1·40 3·75
815 $3 Receiving 82nd birthday gifts from children, and morning glory . . . . . . 1·50 3·75

1985. Native American Artefacts. Nos. 914/18 of Antigua optd **BARBUDA MAIL**.
816 15c. Arawak pot sherd and Indians making clay utensils 15 10
817 50c. Arawak body design and Arawak Indians tattooing 25 25
818 60c. Head of the god "Yocahu" and Indians harvesting manioc 35 35
819 $3 Carib war club and Carib Indians going into battle 1·25 1·50
MS820 97 × 68 mm. $5 Taino Indians worshiping stone idol 2·00 3·00

1985. 40th Anniv of International Civil Aviation Organization. Nos. 934/8 of Antigua optd **BARBUDA MAIL**.
821 30c. Cessna Skyhawk . . . . 1·75 75
822 90c. Fokker D.VII . . . . . 2·75 1·25
823 $1.50 SPAD VII . . . . . . 3·25 4·00
824 $3 Boeing 747 . . . . 4·50 6·50
MS825 97 × 83 mm. De Havilland D.H.C.6 Twin Otter 3·25 3·50

1985. Life and Times of Queen Elizabeth the Queen Mother (2nd series). Nos. 946/9 of Antigua optd **BARBUDA MAIL**.
826 $1 The Queen Mother attending church . . . . . 5·00 2·50
827 $1.50 Watching children playing in London garden 6·00 3·00
828 $2.50 The Queen Mother in 1979 . . . . 7·00 3·50
MS829 56 × 85 mm. $5 With Prince Edward at Royal Wedding, 1981 17·00 11·00

1985. 850th Birth Anniv of Maimonides (physician philosopher and scholar). Nos. 939/40 of Antigua optd **BARBUDA MAIL**.
830 $2 green . . . . 4·50 3·75
MS831 70 × 84 mm. $5 brown 4·25 4·25

1985. Marine Life. Nos. 950/4 of Antigua optd **BARBUDA MAIL**.
832 15c. Magnificent frigate bird 5·50 1·00
833 45c. Brain coral . . . . . 5·50 80
834 60c. Cushion star . . . . . 5·50 1·25
835 $3 Spotted moray . . . . . 9·50 5·00
MS836 110 × 80 mm. $5 Elkhorn coral 14·00 6·50

1986. International Youth Year. Nos. 941/5 of Antigua optd **BARBUDA MAIL**.
837 25c. Young farmers with produce 15 15
838 50c. Hotel management trainees 25 30
839 60c. Girls with goat and boys with football ("Environment") 30 35
840 $3 Windsurfing ("Leisure") 1·50 1·60
MS841 102 × 72 mm. $5 Young people with Antiguan flag 2·75 3·25

1986. Royal Visit. Nos. 965/8 of Antigua optd **BARBUDA MAIL**.
842 60c. Flags of Great Britain and Antigua . . . . 1·50 35
843 $1 Queen Elizabeth II (vert) 1·50 55
844 $4 Royal Yacht "Britannia" 4·75 2·10
MS845 110 × 83 mm. $5 Map of Antigua 5·00 3·50

1986. 75th Anniv of Girl Guide Movement. Nos. 955/9 of Antigua optd **BARBUDA MAIL**.
846 15c. Girl Guides nursing . . 1·50 80
847 45c. Open-air Girl Guide meeting . . . . 2·75 1·75
848 60c. Lord and Lady Baden-Powell . . . . 2·75 2·50
849 $3 Girl Guides gathering flowers . . . . 7·50 9·50
MS850 67 × 96 mm. $5 Barn swallow (Nature study) 24·00 18·00

1986. 300th Birth Anniv of Johann Sebastian Bach (composer). Nos. 960/4 of Antigua optd **BARBUDA MAIL**.
851 25c. multicoloured . . . . . 2·75 70
852 50c. multicoloured . . . . . 3·00 1·40
853 $1 multicoloured . . . . . . 4·00 2·00
854 $3 multicoloured . . . . . . 7·00 8·00
MS855 104 × 73 mm. $5 black and grey 20·00 12·00

1986. Christmas. Religious Paintings. Nos. 985/8 of Antigua optd **BARBUDA MAIL**.
856 10c. "Madonna and Child" (De Landi) 40 30
857 25c. "Madonna and Child" (Berlinghiero) 80 50
858 60c. "The Nativity" (Fra Angelico) . . . . 1·50 1·00
859 $4 "Presentation in the Temple" (Giovanni di Paolo) . . . . 4·00 7·00
MS860 113 × 81 mm. $5 "The Nativity" (Antoniazzo Romano) 4·25 5·50

108 Queen Elizabeth II meeting Members of Legislature

1986. 60th Birthday of Queen Elizabeth II (1st issue). Multicoloured.
861 $1 Type **108** . . . . 50 1·00
862 $2 Queen with Headmistress of Liberta School . . . . 60 1·10
863 $2.50 Queen greeted by Governor-General of Antigua . . . . 60 1·25
MS864 95 × 75 mm. $5 Queen Elizabeth in 1928 and 1986 (33 × 27 mm) 5·50 8·00
See also Nos. 872/5.

109 Halley's Comet over Barbuda Beach

1986. Appearance of Halley's Comet (1st issue). Multicoloured.
865 $1 Type **109** . . . . 60 1·25
866 $2.50 Early telescope and dish aerial (vert) . . . . . 1·00 2·25
867 $5 Comet and world map . . 1·75 3·75
See also Nos. 886/9.

1986. 40th Anniv of United Nations Organization. Nos. 981/4 of Antigua optd **BARBUDA MAIL**.
868 40c. Benjamin Franklin and U.N. (New York) 1953 U.P.U. 5c. stamp . . . . 1·50 1·00
869 $1 George Washington Carver (agricultural chemist) and 1982 Nature Conservation 28c. stamp 2·25 2·25
870 $3 Charles Lindbergh (aviator) and 1978 I.C.A.O. 25c. stamp . . . . . . 4·00 5·00
MS871 101 × 77 mm. $5 Marc Chagell (artist) (vert) 11·00 12·00

1986. 60th Birthday of Queen Elizabeth II (2nd issue). Nos. 1005/8 of Antigua optd **BARBUDA MAIL**.
872 60c. black and yellow . . . . 2·50 1·25
873 $1 multicoloured . . . . . . 2·75 1·75
874 $4 muticoloured . . . . . . 4·25 4·25
MS875 120 × 85 mm. $5 black and brown 7·00 8·00

1986. World Cup Football Championship, Mexico. Nos. 995/9 of Antigua optd **BARBUDA MAIL**.
876 30c. Football, boots and trophy . . . . 3·25 1·00
877 60c. Goalkeeper (vert) . . . 4·50 2·00
878 $1 Referee blowing whistle (vert) . . . . 4·75 2·25
879 $4 Ball in net . . . . 9·00 7·00
MS880 87 × 76 mm. $5 Two players competing for ball 17·00 13·00

1986. "Ameripex '86" International Stamp Exhibition, Chicago. Famous American Trains. Nos. 1014/18 of Antigua optd **BARBUDA MAIL**.
881 25c. "Hiawatha" express . . 2·00 1·50
882 50c. "Grand Canyon" express 2·75 2·25
883 $1 "Powhattan Arrow" express . . . . 3·50 3·00
884 $3 "Empire State" express . . 6·00 7·00
MS885 117 × 87 mm. $5 Southern Pacific "Daylight" express 8·50 9·00

1986. Appearance of Halley's Comet (2nd issue). Nos. 1000/4 of Antigua optd **BARBUDA MAIL**.
886 5c. Edmond Halley and Old Greenwich Observatory . . 1·50 85
887 10c. Messerschmitt Me 163B Komet (fighter aircraft), 1944 . . . . 1·50 85
888 60c. Montezuma (Aztec Emperor) and Comet in 1517 (from "Historias de las Indias de Neuva Espana") . . . . 3·25 2·00
889 $4 Pocahontas saving Capt. John Smith and Comet in 1607 . . . . 10·00 7·50
MS890 101 × 70 mm. $5 Halley's Comet over English Harbour, Antigua 4·75 4·75

1986. Royal Wedding. Nos. 1019/22 of Antigua optd **BARBUDA MAIL**.
891 45c. Prince Andrew and Miss Sarah Ferguson 75 50
892 60c. Prince Andrew 90 65
893 $4 Prince Andrew with Prince Philip . . . . 3·50 4·00
MS894 88 × 88 mm. $5 Prince Andrew and Miss Sarah Ferguson (different) 7·00 7·50

1986. Sea Shells. Nos. 1023/7 of Antigua optd **BARBUDA MAIL**.
895 15c. Fly-specked cerith . . . 2·50 2·00
896 45c. Smooth Scotch bonnet 2·75 2·25
897 60c. West Indian crown conch . . . . 3·50 2·75
898 $3 Criboney murex . . . . . 8·00 12·00
MS899 109 × 75 mm. $5 Colourful Atlantic moon (horiz) 20·00 18·00

1986. Flowers. Nos. 1028/36 of Antigua optd **BARBUDA MAIL**.
900 10c. "Nymphaea ampla" (water lily) 20 30
901 15c. Queen of the night . . . 30 30
902 50c. Cup of gold 50 70
903 60c. Beach morning glory . . 55 70
904 70c. Golden trumpet 70 90
905 $1 Air plant 85 90
906 $3 Purple wreath . . . . . . 2·25 3·50
907 $4 Zephyr lily . . . . 2·75 3·75
MS908 Two sheets, each 102 × 72 mm. (a) $4 Dozakie. (b) $5 Four o'clock flower Set of 2 sheets 22·00 22·00

1986. Mushrooms. Nos. 1042/6 of Antigua optd **BARBUDA MAIL**.
909 10c. "Hygrocybe occidentalis var scarletina" 90 50
910 50c. "Trogia buccinalis" . . 3·25 1·75
911 $1 "Collybia subpruinosa" 4·75 2·75
912 $4 "Leucocoprinus brebissonii" . . . . . . 9·50 8·00
MS913 102 × 82 mm. $5 Pyrrhoglossum pyrrhum 22·00 13·00

1986. Birth Bicentenary of John J. Audubon (ornithologist) (3rd issue). Nos. 990/3 of Antigua optd **BARBUDA MAIL**.
914 60c. Mallard . . . . 5·00 2·50
915 90c. North American black duck ("Dusky Duck") . . 7·00 2·75
916 $1.50 American pintail ("Common Pintail") . . . 9·00 7·50
917 $3 American wigeon ("Wigeon") . . . . 13·00 12·00

1987. Local Boats. Nos. 1009/13 of Antigua optd **BARBUDA MAIL**.
918 30c. Tugboat . . . . 1·00 60
919 60c. Game fishing boat . . . 1·50 80
920 $1 Yacht . . . . 2·00 1·25
921 $4 Lugger with auxiliary sail 4·25 6·00
MS922 108 × 78 mm. $5 Boats under construction 17·00 15·00

1987. Centenary of First Benz Motor Car. Nos. 1052/60 of Antigua optd **BARBUDA MAIL**.
923 10c. Auburn "Speedster" (1933) 90 45
924 15c. Mercury "Sable" (1986) 1·00 50
925 50c. Cadillac (1959) . . . . 1·60 70
926 60c. Studebaker (1950) . . . 1·60 70
927 70c. Lagonda "V-12" (1939) 1·75 1·00
928 $1 Adler "Standard" (1930) 2·25 1·00
929 $3 DKW (1956) . . . . . . 3·00 3·75
930 $4 Mercedes "500K" (1936) 3·00 3·75
MS931 Two sheets, each 99 × 70 mm. (a) $5 Daimler (1896). (b) $5 Mercedes "Knight" (1921) Set of 2 sheets 19·00 15·00

1987. World Cup Football Championship Winners, Mexico. Nos. 1037/40 of Antigua optd **BARBUDA MAIL**.
932 30c. Football, boots and trophy . . . . 2·50 80
933 60c. Goalkeeper (vert) . . . 3·00 1·25
934 $1 Referee blowing whistle (vert) . . . . 3·50 2·00
935 $4 Ball in net . . . . 8·00 9·00

1987. America's Cup Yachting Championship. Nos. 1072/6 of Antigua optd **BARBUDA MAIL**.
936 30c. "Canada I" (1981) . . . 90 40
937 60c. "Gretel II" (1970) . . . 1·25 50
938 $1 "Sceptre" (1958) . . . . 1·60 80
939 $3 "Vigilant" (1893) . . . . 2·25 3·50
MS940 113 × 84 mm. $5 "Australia II" defeating "Liberty" (1983) (horiz) 4·00 4·50

1987. Marine Life. Nos. 1077/85 of Antigua optd **BARBUDA MAIL**.
941 15c. Bridled burrfish . . . . 4·00 80
942 30c. Common noddy ("Brown Noddy") . . . . 5·00 85
943 40c. Nassau grouper . . . . 4·50 1·00
944 50c. Laughing gull . . . . . 7·00 1·75
945 60c. French angelfish . . . . 7·00 1·50
946 $1 Porkfish . . . . 7·00 2·00
947 $2 Royal tern . . . . 13·00 8·00
948 $3 Sooty tern . . . . 13·00 9·00
MS949 Two sheets, each 120 × 94 mm. (a) $5 Banded butterflyfish. (b) $5 Brown booby Set of 2 sheets 35·00 17·00

1987. Milestones of Transportation. Nos. 1100/9 of Antigua optd **BARBUDA MAIL**.
950 10c. "Spirit of Australia" (fastest powerboat), 1978 2·00 75
951 15c. Werner von Siemens's electric locomotive, 1879 3·00 90
952 30c. U.S.S. "Triton" (first submerged circumnavigation), 1960 . . 3·00 90
953 50c. Trevithick's steam carriage (first passenger-carrying vehicle), 1801 . . 3·25 1·50
954 60c. U.S.S. "New Jersey" (battleship), 1942 . . . . 3·50 1·25
955 70c. Draisine bicycle, 1818 . . 3·75 1·75
956 90c. "United States" (liner) (holder of the Blue Riband), 1952 . . . . . . 4·00 1·75
957 $1.50 Cierva C.4 (first autogyro), 1923 . . . . . 4·00 4·50
958 $2 Curtiss NC-4 flying boat (first transatlantic flight), 1919 . . . . 5·50 6·00
959 $3 "Queen Elizabeth 2" (liner), 1969 . . . . 7·00 7·50

110 Shore Crab

1987. Marine Life. Multicoloured.
960 5c. Type **110** 10 20
961 10c. Sea cucumber 10 20
962 15c. Stop-light parrotfish . . 10 20
963 25c. Banded coral shrimp . . 15 20
964 35c. Spotted drum 15 20
965 60c. Thorny starfish 25 40
966 75c. Atlantic trumpet triton 30 60
967 90c. Feather star and yellow beaker sponge 30 65
968 $1 Blue gorgonian (vert) . . 30 65
969 $1.25 Slender filefish (vert) . . 40 85
970 $5 Barred hamlet (vert) . . . 70 4·00
971 $7.50 Royal gramma ("Fairy basslet") (vert) . . . . . 1·00 5·50
972 $10 Fire coral and banded butterflyfish (vert) . . . . 1·25 6·50

1987. Olympic Games, Seoul (1988). Nos. 1086/90 of Antigua optd **BARBUDA MAIL**.
973 10c. Handball 85 50
974 60c. Fencing . . . . 1·75 80
975 $1 Gymnastics . . . . 2·00 1·40
976 $3 Football . . . . 3·75 5·00
MS977 100 × 77 mm. $5 Boxing gloves 6·00 4·75

1987. Birth Centenary of Marc Chagall (artist). Nos. 1091/9 of Antigua optd **BARBUDA MAIL**.
978 10c. "The Profile" 10 20
979 30c. "Portrait of the Artist's Sister" 15 15
980 40c. "Bride with Fan" . . . 20 30
981 60c. "David in Profile" . . . 25 30
982 90c. "Fiancee with Bouquet" 40 50
983 $1 "Self Portrait with Brushes" 45 55

984 $3 "The Walk" . . . . . . 1·40 2·00
985 $4 "Three Candles" . . . . 1·75 2·25
MS986 Two sheets, each 110 × 95 mm. (a) $5 "Fall of Icarus" (104 × 89 mm). (b) $5 "Myth of Orpheus" (104 × 89 mm) Set of 2 sheets 4·50 5·50

1987. Centenary (1986) of Statue of Liberty (2nd issue). Nos. 1110/19 of Antigua optd **BARBUDA MAIL.**
987 15c. Lee Iacocoa at unveiling of restored statue 10 10
988 30c. Statue at sunset (side view) 15 15
989 45c. Aerial view of head . . 20 25
990 50c. Lee Iacocoa and torch 25 30
991 60c. Workmen inside head of statue (horiz) 25 30
992 90c. Restoration work (horiz) 40 50
993 $1 Head of statue 45 55
994 $2 Statue at sunset (front view) . . . . 90 1·40
995 $3 Inspecting restoration work (horiz) . . . . 1·40 2·00
996 $5 Statue at night . . . . . 2·25 3·00

1987. Entertainers. Nos. 1120/7 of Antigua optd **BARBUDA MAIL.**
997 15c. Grace Kelly . . . . . 1·75 70
998 30c. Marilyn Monroe . . . 3·75 1·25
999 45c. Orson Welles . . . . . 1·75 75
1000 50c. Judy Garland . . . . . 1·75 85
1001 60c. John Lennon . . . . . 7·00 1·75
1002 $1 Rock Hudson . . . . . 2·50 1·50
1003 $1 John Wayne . . . . . . 3·75 3·25
1004 $3 Elvis Presley . . . . . . 13·00 7·50

1987. "Capex '87" International Stamp Exhibition, Toronto. Reptiles and Amphibians. Nos. 1133/7 of Antigua optd **BARBUDA MAIL.**
1005 30c. Whistling frog . . . . 3·50 1·50
1006 60c. Croaking lizard . . . . 4·25 1·75
1007 $1 Antiguan anole . . . . . 5·00 2·00
1008 $3 Red-footed tortoise . . . 10·00 11·00
MS1009 106 × 76 mm. $5 Ground lizard 16·00 9·00

1988. Christmas. Religious Paintings. Nos. 1144/8 of Antigua optd **BARBUDA MAIL.**
1010 45c. "Madonna and Child" (Bernardo Daddi) . . . . 1·50 30
1011 60c. St. Joseph (detail, "The Nativity" (Sano di Pietro)) . . . . 1·60 55
1012 $1 Virgin Mary (detail, "The Nativity" (Sano di Pietro)) . . . . 1·75 1·00
1013 $4 "Music-making Angel" (Melozzo da Forli) . . . 4·25 6·50
MS1014 90 × 70 mm. $5 "The Flight into Egypt" (Sano di Pietro) 6·50 6·50

1988. Salvation Army's Community Service. Nos. 1163/71 of Antigua optd **BARBUDA MAIL.**
1015 25c. First aid at daycare centre, Antigua . . . . . 1·25 1·00
1016 30c. Giving penicillin injection, Indonesia . . . 1·25 1·00
1017 40c. Children at daycare centre, Bolivia . . . . . 1·25 1·00
1018 45c. Rehabilitation of the handicapped, India . . . 1·25 1·00
1019 50c. Training blind man, Kenya . . . . 1·75 1·50
1020 60c. Weighing baby, Ghana 1·75 1·50
1021 $1 Training typist, Zambia 2·25 2·25
1022 $2 Emergency food kitchen, Sri Lanka . . . . 2·75 3·50
MS1023 152 × 83 mm. $5 General Eva Burrows 20·00 20·00

1988. Bicentenary of U.S. Constitution. Nos. 1139/43 of Antigua optd **BARBUDA MAIL.**
1024 15c. House of Burgesses, Virginia ("Freedom of Speech") 10 15
1025 45c. State Seal, Connecticut 20 25
1026 60c. State Seal, Delaware . . 25 40
1027 $4 Gouverneur Morris (Pennsylvania delegate) (vert) . . . . 1·75 3·25
MS1028 105 × 75 mm. $5 Roger Sherman (Connecticut delegate) (vert) 2·75 3·25

1988. Royal Ruby Wedding. Nos. 1149/53 of Antigua optd **BARBUDA MAIL.**
1029 25c. brown, black and blue 1·75 40
1030 60c. multicoloured . . . . . 2·25 65
1031 $2 brown, black and green 4·50 2·50
1032 $3 multicoloured . . . . . 5·50 3·00
MS1033 102 × 77 mm. $5 multicoloured 10·00 6·00

1988. Birds of Antigua. Nos. 1154/62 of Antigua optd **BARBUDA MAIL.**
1034 10c. Great blue heron . . . 2·50 1·75
1035 15c. Ringed kingfisher (horiz) . . . . 2·75 1·75
1036 50c. Bananaquit (horiz) . . 3·50 1·75
1037 60c. American purple gallinule ("Purple Gallinule") (horiz) . . . . 3·50 1·75
1038 70c. Blue-hooded euphonia (horiz) . . . . 3·75 2·75
1039 $1 Brown-throated concure ("Caribbean Parakeet") 4·25 2·75
1040 $3 Troupial (horiz) . . . . 7·00 8·50
1041 $4 Purple-throated carib (horiz) . . . . 7·00 8·50
MS1042 Two sheets, each 115 × 86 mm. (a) $5 Greater flamingo. (b) $5 Brown pelican Set of 2 sheets 22·00 15·00

1988. 500th Anniv (1992) of Discovery of America by Columbus (1st issue). Nos. 1172/80 of Antigua optd **BARBUDA MAIL.**
1043 10c. Columbus's second fleet, 1493 . . . . 1·75 1·00
1044 30c. Painos Indian village and fleet . . . . 1·75 80
1045 45c. "Santa Mariagalante" (flagship) and Painos village . . . . 2·50 80
1046 60c. Painos Indians offering Columbus fruit and vegetables . . . . 1·75 85
1047 90c. Painos Indian and Columbus with scarlet macaw . . . . 3·75 1·75
1048 $1 Columbus landing on island . . . . 3·25 1·75
1049 $3 Spanish soldier and fleet 4·25 4·50
1050 $4 Fleet under sail . . . . 4·25 4·50
MS1051 Two sheets, each 110 × 80 mm. (a) $5 Queen Isabella's cross. (b) $5 Gold coin of Ferdinand and Isabella Set of 2 sheets 8·00 10·00
See also Nos. 1112/16, 1177/85, 1285/93, 1374/80 and 1381/2.

1988. 500th Birth Anniv of Titian. Nos. 1181/9 of Antigua optd **BARBUDA MAIL.**
1052 30c. "Bust of Christ" . . . 25 20
1053 40c. "Scourging of Christ" 30 25
1054 45c. "Madonna in Glory with Saints" 35 25
1055 50c. "The Averoldi Polyptych" (detail) . . . 35 30
1056 $1 "Christ Crowned with Thorns" 55 55
1057 $2 "Christ Mocked" . . . . 90 1·25
1058 $3 "Christ and Simon of Cyrene" . . . . 1·40 2·00
1059 $4 "Crucifixion with Virgin and Saints" . . . . . . 1·75 2·50
MS1060 Two sheets, each 110 × 95 mm. (a) $5 "Ecce Homo" (detail). (b) $5 "Noli me Tangere" (detail) Set of 2 sheets 5·00 6·50

1988. 16th World Scout Jamboree, Australia. Nos. 1128/32 of Antigua optd **BARBUDA MAIL.**
1061 10c. Scouts around campfire and red kangaroo . . . . 1·75 1·00
1062 60c. Scouts canoeing and blue-winged kookaburra 5·00 1·50
1063 $1 Scouts on assault course and ring-tailed rock wallaby . . . . 2·75 1·75
1064 $3 Field kitchen and koala 5·00 6·50
MS1065 103 × 78 mm. $5 Flags of Antigua, Australia and Scout Movement 2·75 3·50

1988. Sailing Week. Nos. 1190/4 of Antigua optd **BARBUDA MAIL.**
1066 30c. Two yachts rounding buoy 60 35
1067 60c. Three yachts . . . . . 1·00 70
1068 $1 British yacht under way 1·25 1·10
1069 $3 Three yachts (different) 2·25 2·75
MS1070 103 × 92 mm. $5 Two yachts 7·50 4·50

1988. Flowering Trees. Nos. 1213/21 of Antigua optd **BARBUDA MAIL.**
1071 10c. Jacaranda 10 10
1072 30c. Cordia 15 15
1073 50c. Orchid tree 20 25
1074 90c. Flamboyant 40 45
1075 $1 African tulip tree 45 50
1076 $2 Potato tree . . . . . . 80 1·25
1077 $3 Crepe myrtle . . . . . . 1·25 1·75
1078 $4 Pitch apple . . . . . . 1·60 2·25
MS1079 Two sheets, each 106 × 76 mm. (a) $5 Cassia. (b) $5 Chinaberry Set of 2 sheets 4·25 5·00

1988. Olympic Games, Seoul. Nos. 1222/6 of Antigua optd **BARBUDA MAIL.**
1080 40c. Gymnastics . . . . . 1·25 40
1081 60c. Weightlifting . . . . . 1·50 55
1082 $1 Water polo (horiz) . . . 1·75 1·00
1083 $3 Boxing (horiz) . . . . . 2·50 3·00
MS1084 114 × 80 mm. $5 Runner with Olympic torch 2·10 2·40

1988. Caribbean Butterflies. Nos. 1227/44 of Antigua optd **BARBUDA MAIL.**
1085 1c. "Danaus plexippus" . . 30 60
1086 2c. "Greta diaphanus" . . 30 60
1087 3c. "Calisto archebates" . . 40 60
1088 5c. "Hamadryas feronia" . . 40 60
1089 10c. "Mestra dorcas" . . . 50 50
1090 15c. "Hypolimnas misippus" 60 40
1091 20c. "Dione juno" 70 50
1092 25c. "Heliconius charithonia" 75 50
1093 30c. "Eurema pyro" . . . 85 50
1094 40c. "Papilio androgeus" 90 50
1095 45c. "Anteos maerula" . . 90 50
1096 50c. "Aphrissa orbis" . . . 1·10 75
1097 60c. "Astraptes xagua" . . 1·10 60
1098 $1 "Heliopetes arsalte" . . 1·40 1·00
1099 $2 "Polites baracoa" . . . 3·00 3·50
1100 $2.50 "Phocides pigmalion" 3·25 4·00
1101 $5 "Prepona amphitoe" . . 4·50 5·50
1102 $10 "Oarisma nanus" . . . 7·50 8·50
1102a $20 "Parides lycimenes" . . 12·00 13·00

1989. 25th Death Anniv of John F. Kennedy (American statesman). Nos. 1245/53 of Antigua optd **BARBUDA MAIL.**
1103 1c. President Kennedy and family 10 40
1104 2c. Kennedy commanding "PT109" 10 40
1105 3c. Funeral cortege 10 40
1106 4c. In motorcade, Mexico 10 40
1107 30c. As 1c. 75 40
1108 60c. As 4c. . . . . 1·75 55
1109 $1 As 3c. . . . . 1·90 1·50
1110 $4 As 2c. . . . . 5·50 7·00
MS1111 105 × 75 mm. $5 Kennedy taking presidential oath of office 3·75 5·00

1989. 500th Anniv (1992) of Discovery of America by Columbus (2nd issue). Pre-Columbian Arawak Society. Nos. 1267/71 of Antigua optd **BARBUDA MAIL.**
1112 $1.50 Arawak warriors . . . 2·75 3·25
1113 $1.50 Whip dancers . . . . 2·75 3·25
1114 $1.50 Whip dancers and chief with pineapple . . . 2·75 3·25
1115 $1.50 Family and camp fire 2·75 3·25
MS1116 71 × 84 mm. $6 Arawak chief 3·50 4·50

1989. 50th Anniv of First Jet Flight. Nos. 1272/80 of Antigua optd **BARBUDA MAIL.**
1117 10c. Hawker Siddeley Comet 4 airliner . . . . 2·50 1·25
1118 30c. Messerschmitt Me 262 fighter . . . . 3·00 1·25
1119 40c. Boeing 707 airliner . . 3·25 1·00
1120 60c. Canadair CL-13 Sabre fighter . . . . 3·75 1·00
1121 $1 Lockheed Starfighters . . 4·50 1·75
1122 $2 Douglas DC-10 airliner 5·50 5·00
1123 $3 Boeing 747-300/400 airliner . . . . 6·50 7·00
1124 $4 McDonnell Douglas Phantom II fighter . . . 6·50 7·00
MS1125 Two sheets, each 114 × 83 mm. (a) $7 Grumman F-14 Tomcat fighter. (b) $7 Concorde airliner Set of 2 sheets 38·00 26·00

1989. Caribbean Cruise Ships. Nos. 1281/9 of Antigua optd **BARBUDA MAIL.**
1126 25c. "Festivale" . . . . . . 2·50 1·00
1127 45c. "Southward" . . . . . 2·75 1·00
1128 50c. "Sagafjord" . . . . . 2·75 1·25
1129 60c. "Daphne" . . . . . . 3·00 1·25
1130 75c. "Cunard Countess" . . 3·00 2·75
1131 90c. "Song of America" . . 3·25 2·75
1132 $3 "Island Princess" . . . . 6·50 7·00
1133 $4 "Galileo" . . . . 6·50 7·00
MS1134 (a) 113 × 87 mm. $6 "Norway". (b) 111 × 82 mm. $6 "Oceanic" Set of 2 sheets 45·00 32·00

1989. Japanese Art. Paintings by Hiroshige. Nos. 1290/8 of Antigua optd **BARBUDA MAIL.**
1135 25c. "Fish swimming by Duck half-submerged in Stream" . . . . 2·25 70
1136 45c. "Crane and Wave" . . 2·75 70
1137 50c. "Sparrows and Morning Glories" . . . . 3·00 1·00
1138 60c. "Crested Blackbird and Flowering Cherry" . . . 3·00 1·00
1139 $1 "Great Knot sitting among Water Grass" . . 3·00 1·25
1140 $2 "Goose on a Bank of Water" . . . . 4·50 3·50
1141 $3 "Black Paradise Fly-catcher and Blossoms" . . 4·75 4·00
1142 $4 "Sleepy Owl perched on a Pine Branch" . . . . 5·50 4·50
MS1143 Two sheets, each 102 × 75 mm. (a) $5 "Bullfinch flying near a Clematis Branch". (b) $5 "Titmouse on a Cherry Branch" Set of 2 sheets 29·00 18·00

1989. World Cup Football Championship, Italy (1990). Nos. 1308/12 of Antigua optd **BARBUDA MAIL.**
1144 15c. Goalkeeper . . . . . . 1·60 50
1145 25c. Goalkeeper moving towards ball . . . . . . 1·60 50
1146 $1 Goalkeeper reaching for ball . . . . 3·00 1·75
1147 $4 Goalkeeper saving goal 5·50 7·00
MS1148 Two sheets, each 75 × 105 mm. (a) $5 Three players competing for ball (horiz). (b) $5 Ball and players' legs (horiz) Set of 2 sheets 24·00 24·00

1989. Christmas. Paintings by Raphael and Giotto. Nos. 1351/9 of Antigua optd **BARBUDA MAIL.**
1149 10c. "The Small Cowper Madonna" (Raphael) . . 15 20
1150 25c. "Madonna of the Goldfinch" (Raphael) . . 20 20
1151 30c. "The Alba Madonna" (Raphael) 20 20
1152 50c. Saint (detail, "Bologna Altarpiece") (Giotto) . . 35 30
1153 60c. Angel (detail, "Bologna Altarpiece") (Giotto) . . 45 45
1154 70c. Angel slaying serpent (detail, "Bologna Altarpiece") (Giotto) . . 50 50
1155 $4 Evangelist (detail, "Bologna Altarpiece") (Giotto) . . . . 2·25 3·50
1156 $5 "Madonna of Foligno" (Raphael) . . . . 2·50 3·50
MS1157 Two sheets, each 71 × 96 mm. (a) $5 "The Marriage of the Virgin" (detail) (Raphael). (b) $5 Madonna and Child (detail, "Bologna Altarpiece") (Giotto) Set of 2 sheets 10·00 12·00

1990. Fungi. Nos. 1313/21 of Antigua optd **BARBUDA MAIL.**
1158 10c. "Mycena pura" . . . . 1·75 75
1159 25c. Psathyrella turberculata" (vert) . . . 2·00 65
1160 50c. "Psilocybe cubenis" . . 2·50 1·00
1161 60c. "Leptonia caeruleocapitata" (vert) 2·50 1·00
1162 75c. "Xeromphalina tenuipes" (vert) . . . . . 2·50 1·40
1163 $1 "Chlorophyllum molybdites" (vert) . . . . 2·50 1·40
1164 $3 "Marasmius haematocephalus" . . . . 5·00 5·50
1165 $4 "Cantharellus cinnabarinus" . . . . . 5·00 5·50
MS1166 Two sheets, each 88 × 62 mm. (a) $6 "Leucopaxillus gracillimus" (vert). (b) $6 "Volvariella volvacea" Set of 2 sheets 35·00 22·00

1990. Local Fauna. Nos. 1322/6 optd **BARBUDA MAIL.**
1167 25c. Desmarest's hutia . . . 75 60
1168 45c. Caribbean monk seal 2·00 1·00
1169 60c. Mustache bat (vert) . . 1·50 1·00
1170 $4 American manatee (vert) 4·00 5·50
MS1171 113 × 87 mm. $5 West Indian giant rice rat 13·00 15·00

1990. 20th Anniv of First Manned Landing on Moon. Nos. 1346/50 optd **BARBUDA MAIL.**
1172 10c. Launch of "Apollo 11" 1·75 1·25
1173 45c. Aldrin on Moon . . . 3·00 80
1174 $1 Module "Eagle" over Moon (horiz) . . . . . . 4·25 2·25
1175 $4 Recovery of "Apollo 11" crew after splashdown (horiz) . . . . 8·00 10·00
MS1176 107 × 77 mm. $5 Astronaut Neil Armstrong 14·00 15·00

1990. 500th Anniv (1992) of Discovery of America by Columbus (3rd issue). New World Natural History – Marine Life. Nos. 1360/8 of Antigua optd **BARBUDA MAIL.**
1177 10c. Star-eyed hermit crab 1·25 1·25
1178 20c. Spiny lobster . . . . . 1·50 1·25
1179 25c. Magnificent banded fanworm . . . . 1·50 1·25
1180 45c. Cannonball jellyfish . . 2·00 75
1181 60c. Red-spiny sea star . . . 2·25 75
1182 $2 Peppermint shrimp . . . 3·50 3·75
1183 $3 Coral crab . . . . 3·75 4·50
1184 $4 Branching fire coral . . . 3·75 4·50
MS1185 Two sheets, each 101 × 69 mm. (a) $5 Common sea fan. (b) Portuguese man-o-war Set of 2 sheets 20·00 20·00

1990. "EXPO 90" International Gardens and Greenery Exhibition, Osaka. Orchids. Nos. 1369/77 of Antigua optd **BARBUDA MAIL.**
1186 15c. "Vanilla mexicana" . . 1·50 80
1187 45c. "Epidendrum ibaguense" . . . . 2·00 80
1188 50c. "Epidendrum secundum" . . . . 2·00 90
1189 60c. "Maxillaria conferta" 2·25 1·10
1190 $1 "Onicidium altissimum" 2·50 1·75
1191 $2 "Spiranthes lanceolata" 4·50 4·50
1192 $3 "Tonopsis utricularioides" . . . . . 5·00 5·50
1193 $5 "Epidendrum nocturnum" . . . . . . 6·50 7·50
MS1194 Two sheets, each 101 × 69 mm. (a) $6 "Octomeria graminifolia". (b) $6 "Rodriguezia lanceolata" Set of 2 sheets 27·00 18·00

1990. Reef Fishes. Nos. 1386/94 of Antigua optd **BARBUDA MAIL.**
1195 10c. Flamefish . . . . . . 1·75 1·25
1196 15c. Coney . . . . 1·75 1·25
1197 50c. Long-spined squirrelfish 2·50 1·10
1198 60c. Sergeant major . . . . 2·50 1·10
1199 $1 Yellow-tailed snapper . . 3·00 1·75
1200 $2 Rock beauty . . . . . . 5·00 5·00
1201 $3 Spanish hogfish . . . . 6·00 6·50
1202 $4 Striped parrotfish . . . . 6·00 6·50
MS1203 Two sheets, each 99 × 70 mm. (a) $5 Black-barred soldierfish. (b) $5 Four-eyed butterflyfish Set of 2 sheets 27·00 25·00

1990. 1st Anniv of Hurricane Hugo. Nos. 971/2 surch **1st Anniversary Hurricane Hugo 16th September, 1989-1990** and new value.
1204 $5 on $7.50 Fairy basslet (vert) . . . . 9·00 10·00
1205 $7.50 on $10 Fire coral and butterfly fish (vert) . . . 10·00 11·00

1990. 90th Birthday of Queen Elizabeth the Queen Mother. Nos. 1415/19 of Antigua optd **BARBUDA MAIL.**
1206 15c. multicoloured . . . . . 4·00 1·75
1207 35c. multicoloured . . . . . 7·00 1·50

1208 75c. multicoloured . . . . . 11·00 2·75
1209 $3 multicoloured . . . . . 20·00 13·00
MS1210 67 × 98 mm. $6 multicoloured 32·00 18·00

1990. Achievements in Space. Nos. 1395/414 of Antigua optd **BARBUDA MAIL.**
1211 45c. "Voyager 2" passing Saturn . . . . 2·50 2·00
1212 45c. "Pioneer 11" photographing Saturn . . 2·50 2·00
1213 45c. Astronaut in transporter . . . . 2·50 2·00
1214 45c. Space shuttle "Columbia" . . . . . . 2·50 2·00
1215 45c. "Apollo 10" command module on parachutes . . 2·50 2·00
1216 45c. "Skylab" space station 2·50 2·00
1217 45c. Astronaut Edward White in space . . . . . 2·50 2·00
1218 45c. "Apollo" spacecraft on joint mission . . . . . . 2·50 2·00
1219 45c. "Soyuz" spacecraft on joint mission . . . . . . 2·50 2·00
1220 45c. "Mariner 1" passing Venus . . . . 2·50 2·00
1221 45c. "Gemini 4" capsule . . 2·50 2·00
1222 45c. "Sputnik 1" . . . . . . 2·50 2·00
1223 45c. Hubble space telescope 2·50 2·00
1224 45c. North American X-15 rocket plane . . . . . . 2·50 2·00
1225 45c. Bell XS-1 airplane . . . 2·50 2·00
1226 45c. "Apollo 17" astronaut and lunar rock formation 2·50 2·00
1227 45c. Lunar rover . . . . . 2·50 2·00
1228 45c. "Apollo 14" lunar module . . . . 2·50 2·00
1229 45c. Astronaut Buzz Aldrin on Moon . . . . 2·50 2·00
1230 45c. Soviet "Lunokhod" lunar vehicle . . . . . . 2·50 2·00

1990. Christmas. Paintings by Renaissance Masters. Nos. 1457/65 of Antigua optd **BARBUDA MAIL.**
1231 25c. "Madonna and Child with Saints" (detail, Sebastiano del Piombo) 1·40 60
1232 30c. "Virgin and Child with Angels" (detail, Grunewald) (vert) . . . . 1·50 60
1233 40c. "The Holy Family and a Shepherd" (detail, Titian) . . . . 1·50 60
1234 60c. "Virgin and Child" (detail, Lippi) (vert) . . . 2·00 1·10
1235 $1 "Jesus, St. John and Two Angels" (Rubens) . . . . 2·75 1·50
1236 $2 "Adoration of the Shepherds" (detail, Vincenzo Catena) . . . . 3·75 4·25
1237 $4 "Adoration of the Magi" (detail, Giorgione) . . . . 5·50 6·50
1238 $5 "Virgin and Child adored by Warriors" (detail, Vincenzo Catena) . . . . 5·50 6·50
MS1239 Two sheets, each 71 × 101 mm. (a) $6 "Allegory of the Blessings of Jacob" (detail, Rubens) (vert). (b) $6 "Adoration of the Magi" (detail, Fra Angelico) (vert) Set of 2 sheets 17·00 19·00

1991. 150th Anniv of the Penny Black. Nos. 1378/81 of Antigua optd **BARBUDA MAIL.**
1240 45c. green . . . . 3·00 80
1241 60c. mauve . . . . 3·00 85
1242 $5 blue . . . . 10·00 11·00
MS1243 102 × 80 mm. $6 purple 12·00 12·00

1991. "Stamp World London 90" International Stamp Exhibition. Nos. 1382/4 of Antigua optd **BARBUDA MAIL.**
1244 50c. green and red . . . . 3·00 85
1245 75c. brown and red . . . . 3·00 1·25
1246 $4 blue and red . . . . . . 10·00 11·00
MS1247 104 × 81 mm. $6 black and red 12·00 12·00

119 Troupial

1991. Wild Birds. Multicoloured.
1248 60c. Type **119** . . . . . . 1·75 65
1249 $2 Adelaide's warbler ("Christmas Bird") . . . 3·00 2·50
1250 $4 Rose-breasted grosbeak 4·50 5·00
1251 $7 Wied's crested flycatcher ("Stolid Flycatcher") . . 6·50 9·00

1991. Olympic Games, Barcelona (1992). Nos. 1429/33 of Antigua optd **BARBUDA MAIL.**
1252 50c. Men's 20 kilometres walk . . . . 1·75 90
1253 75c. Triple jump . . . . . 2·00 1·00
1254 $1 Men's 10,000 metres . . 2·25 1·75
1255 $5 Javelin . . . . 7·50 9·50
MS1256 100 × 70 mm. $6 Athlete lighting Olympic flame at Los Angeles Olympics 11·00 12·00

1991. Birds. Nos. 1448/56 of Antigua optd **BARBUDA MAIL.**
1257 10c. Pearly-eyed thrasher . . 2·00 1·50
1258 25c. Purple-throated carib 2·75 80
1259 50c. Common yellowthroat 3·00 1·00
1260 60c. American kestrel . . . 3·00 1·10
1261 $1 Yellow-bellied sapsucker 3·25 1·75
1262 $2 American purple gallinule ("Purple Gallinule") . . . 4·50 4·75
1263 $3 Yellow-crowned night heron . . . . 5·00 6·50
1264 $4 Blue-hooded euphonia 5·00 6·50
MS1265 Two sheets, each 76 × 60 mm. (a) $6 Brown pelican. (b) Magnificent frigate bird Set of 2 sheets 24·00 21·00

1991. 350th Death Anniv of Rubens. Nos. 1466/74 of Antigua optd **BARBUDA MAIL.**
1266 25c. "Rape of the Daughters of Leucippus" (detail) . . 1·50 70
1267 45c. "Bacchanal" (detail) . . 1·75 70
1268 50c. "Rape of the Sabine Women" (detail) . . . . 1·75 75
1269 60c. "Battle of the Amazons" (detail) . . . . 1·90 85
1270 $1 "Rape of the Sabine Women" (different detail) 2·50 1·50
1271 $2 "Bacchanal" (different detail) . . . . 4·00 4·25
1272 $3 "Rape of the Sabine Women" (different detail) 5·50 6·50
1273 $4 "Bacchanal" (different detail) . . . . 5·50 6·50
MS1274 Two sheets, each 111 × 71 mm. (a) $6 "Rape of Hippodameia" (detail). (b) "Battle of the Amazons" (different detail) Set of 2 sheets 19·00 20·00

1991. 50th Anniv of Second World War. Nos. 1475/88 of Antigua optd **BARBUDA MAIL.**
1275 10c. U.S. troops cross into Germany, 1944 . . . . . 2·00 1·50
1276 15c. Axis surrender in North Africa, 1943 . . . . . . 2·50 1·50
1277 25c. U.S. tanks invade Kwalajalein, 1944 . . . . 2·75 1·10
1278 45c. Roosevelt and Churchill meet at Casablanca, 1943 5·00 1·50
1279 50c. Marshall Badoglio, Prime Minister of Italian anti-facist government, 1943 . . . . 2·75 1·50
1280 $1 Lord Mountbatten, Supreme Allied Commander South-east Asia, 1943 . . . . 7·00 3·00
1281 $2 Greek victory at Koritza, 1940 . . . . 7·50 7·50
1282 $4 Anglo-Soviet mutual assistance pact, 1941 . . . 8·50 8·50
1283 $5 Operation Torch landings, 1942 . . . . . 8·50 8·50
MS1284 Two sheets, each 108 × 80 mm. (a) $6 Japanese attack on Pearl Harbor, 1941. (b) $6 U.S.A.A.F. daylight raid on Schweinfurt, 1943 Set of 2 sheets 38·00 27·00

1991. 500th Anniv (1992) of Discovery of America by Columbus (4th issue). History of Exploration. Nos. 1503/11 of Antigua optd **BARBUDA MAIL.**
1285 10c. multicoloured . . . . . 1·25 1·00
1286 15c. multicoloured . . . . . 1·50 1·00
1287 45c. multicoloured . . . . . 2·00 80
1288 60c. multicoloured . . . . . 2·25 1·00
1289 $1 multicoloured . . . . . 3·00 1·75
1290 $2 multicoloured . . . . . 4·00 4·00
1291 $4 multicoloured . . . . . 6·50 7·00
1292 $5 multicoloured . . . . . 6·50 7·00
MS1293 Two sheets, each 106 × 76 mm. (a) $6 black and red. (b) $6 black and red Set of 2 sheets 22·00 20·00

1991. Butterflies. Nos. 1494/502 of Antigua optd **BARBUDA MAIL.**
1294 10c. "Heliconius charithonia" . . . . . . 2·00 1·50
1295 35c. "Marpesia petreus" . . 2·75 1·25
1296 50c. "Anartia amathea" . . 3·25 1·40
1297 75c. "Siproeta stelenes" . . 3·75 1·60
1298 $1 "Battus polydamas" . . 3·75 1·75
1299 $2 "Historis odius" . . . . 5·50 5·50
1300 $4 "Hypolimnas misippus" 7·50 8·00
1301 $5 "Hamadryas feronia" . . 7·50 8·00
MS1302 Two sheets. (a) 73 × 100 mm. $6 "Vanessa cardui" (caterpillar) (vert). (b) 100 × 73 mm. $6 "Danaus plexippus" (caterpillar) (vert) Set of 2 sheets 24·00 22·00

1991. 65th Birthday of Queen Elizabeth II. Nos. 1534/8 of Antigua optd **BARBUDA MAIL.**
1303 15c. Queen Elizabeth and Prince Philip in 1976 . . 2·50 85
1304 20c. The Queen and Prince Philip in Portugal, 1985 2·50 85
1305 $2 Queen Elizabeth II . . . 7·00 4·25
1306 $4 The Queen and Prince Philip at Ascot, 1986 . . 11·00 11·00
MS1307 68 × 90 mm. $4 The Queen at National Theatre, 1986 and Prince Philip 18·00 13·00

1991. 10th Wedding Anniv of Prince and Princess of Wales. Nos. 1539/43 of Antigua optd **BARBUDA MAIL.**
1308 10c. Prince and Princess of Wales at party, 1986 . . . 2·50 1·50
1309 40c. Separate portraits of Prince, Princess and sons 5·50 1·00
1310 $1 Prince Henry and Prince William . . . . 6·50 2·75
1311 $5 Princess Diana in Australia and Prince Charles in Hungary . . . 12·00 12·00
MS1312 68 × 90 mm. $4 Prince Charles in Hackney and Princess and sons in Majorca, 1987 18·00 13·00

1991. Christmas. Religious Paintings by Fra Angelico. Nos. 1595/1602 of Antigua optd **BARBUDA MAIL.**
1313 10c. "The Annunciation" . . 1·50 1·00
1314 30c. "Nativity" . . . . . . 2·00 70
1315 40c. "Adoration of the Magi" . . . . 2·00 70
1316 60c. "Presentation in the Temple" . . . . 2·50 70
1317 $1 "Circumcision" . . . . 3·25 1·60
1318 $3 "Flight into Egypt" . . . 5·50 6·00
1319 $4 "Massacre of the Innocents" . . . . 5·50 6·50
1320 $5 "Christ teaching in the Temple" . . . . 5·50 6·50

1992. Death Centenary (1990) of Vincent van Gogh (artist). Nos. 1512/24 of Antigua optd **BARBUDA MAIL.**
1321 5c. "Camille Roulin" . . . 1·10 1·10
1322 10c. "Armand Roulin" . . . 1·25 1·25
1323 15c. "Young Peasant Woman with Straw Hat sitting in the Wheat" . . 1·50 1·25
1324 25c. "Adeline Ravoux" . . . 1·50 1·25
1325 30c. "The Schoolboy" . . . 1·50 90
1326 40c. "Doctor Gachet" . . . 1·75 90
1327 50c. "Portrait of a Man" . . 1·75 1·25
1328 75c. "Two Children" . . . 2·75 1·75
1329 $2 "The Postman Joseph Roulin" . . . . 4·50 4·50
1330 $3 "The Seated Zouave" . . 5·00 5·50
1331 $4 "L'Arlesienne" . . . . . 5·50 6·50
1332 $5 "Self-Portrait, November/ December 1888" . . . . 5·50 6·50
MS1333 Three sheets, each 102 × 76 mm. (a) $5 "Farmhouse in Provence" (horiz). (b) $5 "Flowering Garden" (horiz). (c) $6 "The Bridge at Trinquetaille" (horiz). Imperf Set of 3 sheets 25·00 25·00

1992. Birth Centenary of Charles de Gaulle (French statesman). Nos. 1562/70 of Antigua optd **BARBUDA MAIL.**
1334 10c. Pres. De Gaulle and Kennedy, 1961 . . . . . 1·75 1·25
1335 15c. General De Gaulle with Pres. Roosevelt, 1945 (vert) . . . . 1·75 1·25
1336 45c. President De Gaulle with Chancellor Adenauer, 1962 (vert) . . 2·50 80
1337 60c. De Gaulle at Arc de Triomphe, Liberation of Paris, 1944 (vert) . . . . 2·75 1·00
1338 $1 General De Gaulle crossing the Rhine, 1945 3·25 1·75
1339 $2 General De Gaulle in Algiers, 1944 . . . . . 5·00 5·00
1340 $4 Presidents De Gaulle and Eisenhower, 1960 . . . . 7·00 8·50
1341 $5 De Gaulle returning from Germany, 1968 (vert) . . 7·00 8·50
MS1342 Two sheets. (a) 76 × 106 mm. $6 De Gaulle with crowd. (b) 106 × 76 mm. $6 De Gaulle and Churchill at Casablanca, 1943 Set of 2 sheets 26·00 23·00

1992. Easter. Religious Paintings. Nos. 1627/35 of Antigua optd **BARBUDA MAIL.**
1343 10c. "Supper at Emmaus" (Caravaggio) . . . . . . 1·25 1·00
1344 15c. "The Vision of St. Peter" (Zurbaran) . . 1·50 1·00
1345 30c. "Christ driving the Money-changers from the Temple" (Tiepolo) . . . . 1·75 70
1346 40c. "Martyrdom of St. Bartholomew" (detail) (Ribera) . . . . 1·75 70
1347 $1 "Christ driving the Money-changers from the Temple" (detail) (Tiepolo) 3·25 1·75
1348 $2 "Crucifixion" (detail) (Altdorfer) . . . . 4·50 4·50
1349 $4 "The Deposition" (detail) (Fra Angelico) . . . . . 6·50 7·50
1350 $5 "The Deposition" (different detail) (Fra Angelico) . . . . 6·50 7·50
MS1351 Two sheets. (a) 102 × 71 mm. $6 "The Last Supper" (detail) (Masip). (b) 71 × 102 mm. $6 "Crucifixion" (detail) (vert) (Altdorfer) Set of 2 sheets 22·00 22·00

1992. Anniversaries and Events. Nos. 1573/83 of Antigua optd **BARBUDA MAIL.**
1352 25c. Germans celebrating Reunification . . . . . . 1·00 70
1353 75c. Cubs erecting tent . . . 2·00 1·50
1354 $1.50 "Don Giovanni" and Mozart . . . . 7·00 3·25
1355 $2 Chariot driver and Gate at night . . . . 2·75 2·75
1356 $2 Lord Baden-Powell and members of the 3rd Antigua Methodist cub pack (vert) . . . . 2·75 2·75
1357 $2 Lilienthal's signature and glider "Flugzeug Nr. 5" 2·75 2·75
1358 $2.50 Driver in Class P36 steam locomotive (vert) 5·50 4·00
1359 $3 Statues from podium . . 3·00 4·00
1360 $3.50 Cubs and campfire . . 4·00 4·50
1361 $4 St. Peter's Cathedral, Salzburg . . . . 7·50 7·00
MS1362 Two sheets. (a) 100 × 72 mm. $4 Detail of chariot and helmet. (b) 89 × 117 mm. $5 Antiguan flag and Jamboree emblem (vert) Set of 2 sheets 21·00 22·00

1992. 50th Anniv of Japanese Attack on Pearl Harbor. Nos. 1585/94 of Antigua optd **BARBUDA MAIL.**
1364 $1 "Nimitz" class carrier and "Ticonderoga" class cruiser . . . . 3·75 2·75
1365 $1 Tourist launch . . . . . 3·75 2·75
1366 $1 U.S.S. "Arizona" memorial . . . . 3·75 2·75
1367 $1 Wreaths on water and aircraft . . . . 3·75 2·75
1368 $1 White tern . . . . 3·75 2·75
1369 $1 Japanese torpedo bombers over Pearl City 3·75 2·75
1370 $1 Zeros attacking . . . . 3·75 2·75
1371 $1 Battleship Row in flames 3·75 2·75
1372 $1 U.S.S. "Nevada" (battleship) underway . . 3·75 2·75
1373 $1 Zeros returning to carriers . . . . 3·75 2·75

1992. 500th Anniv of Discovery of America by Columbus (5th issue). World Columbian Stamp "Expo '92", Chicago. Nos. 1654/60 of Antigua optd **BARBUDA MAIL.**
1374 15c. Memorial cross and huts, San Salvador . . . 75 80
1375 30c. Martin Pinzon with telescope 90 90
1376 40c. Christopher Columbus 1·25 90
1377 $1 "Pinta" . . . . 3·75 2·50
1378 $2 "Nina" . . . . 5·00 5·00
1379 $4 "Santa Maria" . . . . . 7·50 8·50
MS1380 Two sheets, each 108 × 76 mm. (a) $6 Ship and map of West Indies. (b) $6 Sea monster Set of 2 sheets 22·00 23·00

1992. 500th Anniv of Discovery of America by Columbus (6th issue). Organization of East Caribbean States. Nos. 1670/1 of Antigua optd **BARBUDA MAIL.**
1381 $1 Columbus meeting Amerindians . . . . . . 2·50 1·50
1382 $2 Ships approaching island 6·50 4·75

1992. Postage Stamp Mega Event, New York. No. **MS**1690 of Antigua optd **BARBUDA MAIL.**
MS1383 $6 multicoloured 11·00 12·00

1992. 40th Anniv of Queen Elizabeth II's Accession. Nos. 1604/8 of Antigua optd **BARBUDA MAIL.**
1384 10c. Queen Elizabeth II and bird sanctuary . . . . . 3·50 1·75
1385 30c. Nelson's Dockyard . . 4·50 1·25
1386 $1 Ruins on Shirley Heights 6·00 2·75
1387 $5 Beach and palm trees . . 12·00 12·00
MS1388 Two sheets, each 75 × 98 mm. (a) $6 Beach. (b) $6 Hillside foliage Set of 2 sheets 30·00 22·00

1992. Prehistoric Animals. Nos. 1618/26 of Antigua optd **BARBUDA MAIL.**
1389 10c. Pteranodon . . . . . 2·00 1·50
1390 15c. Brachiosaurus . . . . 2·50 1·50
1391 30c. Tyrannosaurus Rex . . 3·00 1·25
1392 50c. Parasaurolophus . . . 3·00 1·50
1393 $1 Deinonychus (horiz) . . 3·75 2·25
1394 $2 Triceratops (horiz) . . . 6·00 5·00
1395 $4 Protoceratops hatching (horiz) . . . . 7·00 8·00
1396 $5 Stegosaurus (horiz) . . . 7·00 8·00
MS1397 Two sheets, each 100 × 70 mm. (a) $6 Apatosaurus (horiz). (b) $6 Allosaurus (horiz) Set of 2 sheets 25·00 21·00

1992. Christmas. Nos. 1691/9 of Antigua optd **BARBUDA MAIL.**
1398 10c. "Virgin and Child with Angels" (School of Piero della Francesca) . . . . . 1·75 75
1399 25c. "Madonna degli Alberelli" (Giovanni Bellini) . . . . 1·75 75
1400 30c. "Madonna and Child with St. Anthony Abbot and St. Sigismund" (Neroccio) . . . . 1·75 75
1401 40c. "Madonna and the Grand Duke" (Raphael) 2·00 75
1402 60c. "The Nativity" (Georges de la Tour) . . 2·25 75
1403 $1 "Holy Family" (Jacob Jordaens) . . . . 2·75 1·50

1404 $4 "Madonna and Child Enthroned" (Magaritone) 6·50 8·50
1405 $5 "Madonna and Child on a Curved Throne" (Byzantine school) 6·50 8·50
MS1406 Two sheets, each 76×102 mm. (a) $6 "Madonna and Child" (Domenco Ghirlando). (b) $6 "The Holy Family" (Pontormo) Set of 2 sheets 23·00 22·00

1993. Fungi. Nos. 1645/53 of Antigua optd **BARBUDA MAIL.**
1407 10c. "Amanita caesarea" 1·75 1·25
1408 15c. "Collybia fusipes" 2·00 1·25
1409 30c. "Boletus aereus" 2·25 1·50
1410 40c. "Laccaria amethystina" 2·25 1·50
1411 $1 "Russula virescens" 3·25 2·00
1412 $2 "Tricholoma equestre" ("Tricholoma auratum") 4·50 4·00
1413 $4 "Calocybe gambosa" 5·50 6·50
1414 $5 "Lentinus tigrinus" ("Panus tigrinus") 5·50 6·50
MS1415 Two sheets, each 100×70 mm. (a) $6 "Clavariadelphus truncatus". (b) $6 "Auricularia auricula-judae" Set of 2 sheets 24·00 21·00

1993. "Granada '92" International Stamp Exhibition, Spain. Spanish Paintings. Nos. 1636/44 of Antigua optd **BARBUDA MAIL.**
1416 10c. "The Miracle at the Well" (Alonzo Cano) 1·25 1·00
1417 15c. "The Poet Luis de Goingora y Argote" (Velazquez) 1·50 1·00
1418 30c. "The Painter Francisco Goya" (Vincente Lopez Portana) 1·75 1·00
1419 40c. "Maria de las Nieves Michaela Fourdinier" (Luis Paret y Alcazar) 1·75 1·00
1420 $1 "Carlos III eating before his Court" (Alcazar) (horiz) 3·00 2·25
1421 $2 "Rain Shower in Granada" (Antonio Munoz Degrain) (horiz) 4·75 4·75
1422 $4 "Sarah Bernhardt" (Santiago Ruisnol i Prats) 6·50 7·50
1423 $5 "The Hermitage Garden" (Joaquim Mir Trinxet) 6·50 7·50
MS1424 Two sheets, each 120×95 mm. (a) $6 "The Ascent of Monsieur Boucle's Montgolfier Balloon in the Gardens of Aranjuez" (Antonio Carnicero) (112×87 mm). (b) $6 "Olympus: Battle with the Giants" (Francisco Bayeu y Subias) (112×87 mm). Imperf Set of 2 sheets 17·00 18·00

1993. "Genova '92" International Thematic Stamp Exhibition. Hummingbirds and Plants. Nos. 1661/9 of Antigua optd **BARBUDA MAIL.**
1425 10c. Antillean crested hummingbird and wild plantain 2·00 1·50
1426 25c. Green mango and parrot's plantain 2·25 1·00
1427 45c. Purple-throated carib and lobster claws 2·50 1·25
1428 60c. Antillean mango and coral plant 2·75 1·50
1429 $1 Vervain hummingbird and cardinal's guard 3·25 2·25
1430 $2 Rufous-breasted hermit and heliconia 4·75 4·75
1431 $4 Blue-headed hummingbird and reed ginger 6·50 7·00
1432 $5 Green-throated carib and ornamental banana 6·50 7·00
MS1433 Two sheets, each 100×70 mm. (a) $6 Bee hummingbird and jungle flame. (b) $6 Western streamertail and bignonia Set of 2 sheets 25·00 19·00

1993. Inventors and Inventions. Nos. 1672/80 of Antigua optd **BARBUDA MAIL.**
1434 10c. Ts'ai Lun and paper 65 85
1435 25c. Igor Sikorsky and "Bolshoi Baltiskii" (first four-engined airplane) 2·25 80
1436 30c. Alexander Graham Bell and early telephone 1·25 80
1437 40c. Johannes Gutenberg and early printing press 1·25 80
1438 60c. James Watt and stationary steam engine 5·00 1·60
1439 $1 Anton van Leeuwenhoek and early microscope 3·50 2·25
1440 $4 Louis Braille and hands reading braille 6·00 7·00
1441 $5 Galileo and telescope 6·00 7·00
MS1442 Two sheets, each 100×71 mm. (a) $6 Edison and Latimer's phonograph. (b) $6 "Clermont" (first commercial paddle-steamer) Set of 2 sheets 16·00 17·00

1993. Anniversaries and Events. Nos. 900/14 of Antigua optd **BARBUDA MAIL.**
1443 10c. Russian cosmonauts 1·75 1·40
1444 40c. "Graf Zeppelin" (airship), 1929 3·00 1·00
1445 45c. Bishop Daniel Davis 80 70
1446 75c. Konrad Adenauer making speech 1·00 1·00
1447 $1 Bus Mosbacher and "Weatherly" (yacht) 2·25 1·75
1448 $1.50 Rain forest 2·50 2·50
1449 $2 Tiger 9·00 5·50
1450 $2 National flag, plant and emblem (horiz) 5·50 3·50
1451 $2 Members of Community Players company (horiz) 3·50 3·50
1452 $2.25 Women carrying pots 3·50 4·00
1453 $3 Lions Club emblem 3·75 4·25
1454 $4 Chinese rocket on launch tower 5·50 5·50
1455 $4 West German and N.A.T.O. flags 5·50 5·50
1456 $6 Hugo Eckener (airship pioneer) 6·50 7·00
MS1457 Four sheets, each 100×71 mm. (a) $6 Projected European space station. (b) $6 Airship LZ-129 "Hindenburg", 1936. (c) $6 Brandenburg Gate on German flag. (d) $6 "Danaus plexippus" (butterfly) Set of 4 sheets 38·00 32·00

1993. Flowers. Nos. 1733/41 of Antigua optd **BARBUDA MAIL.**
1458 15c. Cardinal's guard 1·75 1·25
1459 25c. Giant granadilla 1·90 1·10
1460 30c. Spider flower 2·00 1·25
1461 40c. Gold vine 2·25 1·40
1462 $1 Frangipani 3·50 2·25
1463 $2 Bougainvillea 4·50 4·50
1464 $4 Yellow oleander 6·00 7·00
1465 $5 Spicy jatropha 6·00 7·00
MS1466 Two sheets, each 100×70 mm. (a) $6 Bird lime tree. (b) $6 Fairy lily Set of 2 sheets 21·00 21·00

1993. World Bird Watch. Nos. 1248/51 optd **WORLD BIRDWATCH 9-10 OCTOBER 1993.**
1467 60c. Type **119** 4·00 1·75
1468 $2 Adelaide's warbler 7·00 4·50
1469 $4 Rose-breasted grosbeak 9·50 10·00
1470 $7 Wied's crested flycatcher 12·00 13·00

1993. Endangered Species. Nos. 1759/71 of Antigua optd **BARBUDA MAIL.**
1471 $1 St. Lucia amazon ("St. Lucia Parrot") 4·50 3·50
1472 $1 Cahow 4·50 3·50
1473 $1 Swallow-tailed kite 4·50 3·50
1474 $1 Everglade kite ("Everglades Kite") 4·50 3·50
1475 $1 Imperial amazon ("Imperial Parrot") 4·50 3·50
1476 $1 Humpback whale 4·50 3·50
1477 $1 Plain pigeon ("Puerto Rican Plain Pigeon") 4·50 3·50
1478 $1 St. Vincent amazon ("St. Vincent Parrot") 4·50 3·50
1479 $1 Puerto Rican amazon ("Puerto Rican Parrot") 4·50 3·50
1480 $1 Leatherback turtle 4·50 3·50
1481 $1 American crocodile 4·50 3·50
1482 $1 Hawksbill turtle 4·50 3·50
MS1483 Two sheets, each 100×70 mm. (a) $6 As No. 1476. (b) $6 West Indian manatee Set of 2 sheets. 28·00 26·00

1994. Bicentenary of the Louvre, Paris. Paintings by Peter Paul Rubens. Nos. 1742/9 and **MS**1758 of Antigua optd **BARBUDA MAIL.**
1484 $1 "The Destiny of Marie de' Medici" (upper detail) 3·25 3·00
1485 $1 "The Birth of Marie de' Medici" 3·25 3·00
1486 $1 "The Education of Marie de' Medici" 3·25 3·00
1487 $1 "The Destiny of Marie de' Medici" (lower detail) 3·25 3·00
1488 $1 "Henry VI receiving the Portrait of Marie" 3·25 3·00
1489 $1 "The Meeting of the King and Marie at Lyons" 3·25 3·00
1490 $1 "The Marriage by Proxy" 3·25 3·00
1491 $1 "The Birth of Louis XIII" 3·25 3·00
MS1492 70×100 mm. $6 "Helene Fourment with a Coach" (52×85 mm) 15·00 16·00

1994. World Cup Football Championship, 1994, U.S.A. (1st Issue). Nos. 1816/28 of Antigua optd **BARBUDA MAIL.**
1493 $2 Paul Gascoigne 3·50 2·50
1494 $2 David Platt 3·50 2·50
1495 $2 Martin Peters 3·50 2·50
1496 $2 John Barnes 3·50 2·50
1497 $2 Gary Lineker 3·50 2·50
1498 $2 Geoff Hurst 3·50 2·50
1499 $2 Bobby Charlton 3·50 2·50
1500 $2 Bryan Robson 3·50 2·50
1501 $2 Bobby Moore 3·50 2·50
1502 $2 Nobby Stiles 3·50 2·50
1503 $2 Gordon Banks 3·50 2·50
1504 $2 Peter Shilton 3·50 2·50
MS1505 Two sheets, each 135×109 mm. (a) $6 Bobby Moore holding World Cup. (b) $6 Gary Lineker and Bobby Robson Set of 2 sheets 21·00 17·00
See also Nos. 1573/9.

1994. Anniversaries and Events. Nos. 1829/38, 1840 and 1842/7 of Antigua optd **BARBUDA MAIL.**
1506 10c. Grand Inspector W.Heath 2·50 1·75
1507 15c. Rodnina and Oulanov (U.S.S.R.) (pairs figure skating) (horiz) 1·75 1·50
1508 30c. Present Masonic Hall, St. John's (horiz) 3·50 1·50
1509 30c. Willy Brandt with Helmut Schmidt and George Leber (horiz) 1·25 1·00
1510 30c. "Cat and Bird" (Picasso) (horiz) 1·25 1·00
1511 40c. Previous Masonic Hall, St. John's (horiz) 3·50 1·50
1512 40c. "Fish on a Newspaper" (Picasso) (horiz) 1·25 1·00
1513 40c. Early astronomical equipment 1·25 1·00
1514 40c. Prince Naruhito and engagement photographs (horiz) 1·25 1·00
1515 60c. Grand Inspector J.Jeffery 4·00 1·75
1516 $3 Masako Owada and engagement photographs (horiz) 3·00 4·00
1517 $4 Willy Brandt and protest march (horiz) 4·00 4·50
1518 $4 Galaxy 4·00 4·50
1519 $5 Alberto Tomba (Italy) (giant slalom) (horiz) 4·00 4·50
1520 $5 "Dying Bull" (Picasso) (horiz) 4·00 4·50
1521 $5 Pres. Clinton and family (horiz) 4·00 4·50
MS1522 Six sheets. (a) 106×75 mm. $5 Copernicus. (b) 106×75 mm. $6 Womens' 1500 metre speed skating medallists (horiz). (c) 106×75 mm. $6 Willy Brandt at Warsaw Ghetto Memorial (horiz). (d) 106×75 mm. $6 "Woman with a Dog" (detail) (Picasso) (horiz). (e) 106×75 mm. $6 Masako Owada. (f) 106×75 mm. $6 Pres. Clinton taking the Oath (42½×57 mm) Set of 2 sheets 40·00 40·00

1994. Aviation Anniversaries. Nos. 1848/55 of Antigua optd **BARBUDA MAIL.**
1523 30c. Hugo Eckener and Dr. W. Beckers with airship "Graf Zeppelin" over Lake George, New York 2·50 1·50
1524 40c. Chicago World's Fair from "Graf Zeppelin" 2·50 1·50
1525 40c. Gloster Whittle E28/39, 1941 2·50 1·50
1526 40c. George Washington writing balloon mail letter (vert) 2·50 1·50
1527 $4 Pres. Wilson and Curtiss "Jenny" 6·50 7·50
1528 $5 Airship LZ-129 "Hindenburg" over Ebbets Field baseball stadium, 1937 6·50 7·50
1529 $5 Gloster Meteor in dogfight 6·50 7·50
MS1530 Three sheets. (a) 86×105 mm. $6 Hugo Eckener (vert). (b) 105×86 mm. $6 Consolidated Catalina PBY-5 flying boat (57×42½ mm). (c) 105×86 mm. $6 Alexander Hamilton, Washington and John Jay watching Blanchard's balloon, 1793 (horiz) Set of 3 sheets 28·00 25·00

1994. Centenaries of Henry Ford's First Petrol Engine (Nos. 1531, 1533, 1533a) and Karl Benz's First Four-wheeled Car (others). Nos. 1856/60 of Antigua optd **BARBUDA MAIL.**
1531 30c. Lincoln Continental 2·00 1·25
1532 40c. Mercedes racing car, 1914 2·00 1·25
1533 $4 Ford "GT40", 1966 7·00 7·50
1534 $5 Mercedes Benz "gull-wing" coupe, 1954 7·00 7·50
MS1535 Two sheets. (a) 114×87 mm. $6 Ford's Mustang emblem. (b) 87×114 mm. $6 Germany 1936 12pf. Benz and U.S.A. 1968 12c. Ford stamps Set of 2 sheets 19·00 19·00

1994. Famous Paintings by Rembrandt and Matisse. Nos. 1881/9 of Antigua optd **BARBUDA MAIL.**
1536 15c. "Hannah and Samuel" (Rembrandt) 1·75 1·50
1537 15c. "Guitarist" (Matisse) 1·75 1·50
1538 30c. "The Jewish Bride" (Rembrandt) 2·00 1·10
1539 40c. "Jacob wrestling with the Angel" (Rembrandt) 2·00 1·10
1540 60c. "Interior with a Goldfish Bowl" (Matisse) 2·50 1·25
1541 $1 "Mlle. Yvonne Landsberg" (Matisse) 3·25 1·75
1542 $4 "The Toboggan" (Matisse) 6·50 7·50
1543 $5 "Moses with the Tablets of the Law" (Rembrandt) 6·50 7·50
MS1544 Two sheets. (a) 124×99 mm. $6 "The Blinding of Samson by the Philistines" (detail) (Rembrandt). (b) 99×124 mm. $6 "The Three Sisters" (detail) (Matisse) Set of 2 sheets 19·00 19·00

1994. "Polska '93" International Stamp Exhibition, Poznan. Nos. 1839, 1841 and **MS**1847f of Antigua optd **BARBUDA MAIL.**
1545 $1 "Woman Combing her Hair" (W. Slewinski) (horiz) 3·25 2·50
1546 $3 "Artist's Wife with Cat" (Konrad Kryzanowski) (horiz) 6·00 7·00
MS1547 70×100 mm. $6 "General Confusion" (S. I. Witkiewicz) 10·00 12·00

1994. Orchids. Nos. 1949/56 of Antigua optd **BARBUDA MAIL.**
1548 10c. "Spiranthes lanceolata" 2·00 1·50
1549 20c. "Ionopsis utricularioides" 3·00 1·50
1550 30c. "Tetramicra canaliculata" 3·25 1·25
1551 50c. "Oncidium picturatum" 3·75 1·50
1552 $1 "Epidendrum difforme" 4·50 2·25
1553 $2 "Epidendrum ciliare" 6·50 5·00
1554 $4 "Epidendrum ibaguense" 7·50 8·00
1555 $5 "Epidendrum nocturnum" 7·50 8·00
MS1556 Two sheets, each 100×73 mm. (a) $6 "Rodriguezia lanceolata". (b) $6 "Encyclia cochleata" Set of 2 sheets 26·00 25·00

1994. Centenary of Sierra Club (environmental protection society) (1992). Endangered Species. Nos. 1907/22 of Antigua optd **BARBUDA MAIL.**
1557 $1.50 Sumatran rhinoceros lying down 3·00 2·50
1558 $1.50 Sumatran rhinoceros feeding 3·00 2·50
1559 $1.50 Ring-tailed lemur on ground 3·00 2·50
1560 $1.50 Ring-tailed lemur on branch 3·00 2·50
1561 $1.50 Red-fronted brown lemur on branch 3·00 2·50
1562 $1.50 Head of red-fronted brown lemur 3·00 2·50
1563 $1.50 Head of red-fronted brown lemur in front of trunk 3·00 2·50
1564 $1.50 Sierra Club Centennial emblem 1·75 1·60
1565 $1.50 Head of bactrian camel 3·00 2·50
1566 $1.50 Bactrian camel 3·00 2·50
1567 $1.50 African elephant drinking 3·00 2·50
1568 $1.50 Head of African elephant 3·00 2·50
1569 $1.50 Leopard sitting upright 3·00 2·50
1570 $1.50 Leopard in grass (emblem at right) 3·00 2·50
1571 $1.50 Leopard in grass (emblem at left) 3·00 2·50
MS1572 Four sheets. (a) 100×70 mm. $1.50, Sumatran rhinoceros (horiz). (b) 70×100 mm. $1.50, Ring-tailed lemur (horiz). (C) 70×100 mm. $1.50, Bactrian camel (horiz) (d) 100×70 mm. $1.50, African elephant (horiz) Set of 4 sheets 11·00 11·00

1995. World Cup Football Championship, U.S.A. (2nd issue). Nos. 2039/45 of Antigua optd **BARBUDA MAIL.**
1573 15c. Hugo Sanchez (Mexico) 1·50 1·25
1574 35c. Jurgen Klinsmann (Germany) 2·00 1·25
1575 65c. Antiguan player 2·00 1·25
1576 $1.20 Cobi Jones (U.S.A.) 2·75 2·25
1577 $4 Roberto Baggio (Italy) 5·00 5·50
1578 $5 Bwalya Kalusha (Zambia) 5·00 5·50
MS1579 Two sheets. (a) 72×105 mm. $6 Maldive Islands player (vert). (b) 107×78 mm. $6 World Cup trophy (vert) Set of 2 sheets 15·00 14·00

1995. Christmas. Religious Paintings. Nos. 2058/66 of Antigua optd **BARBUDA MAIL.**
1580 15c. "Virgin and Child by the Fireside" (Robert Campin) 1·25 75
1581 35c. "The Reading Madonna" (Giorgione) 1·75 70
1582 40c. "Madonna and Child" (Giovanni Bellini) 1·75 70
1583 45c. "The Little Madonna" (Da Vinci) 1·75 70
1584 65c. "The Virgin and Child under the Apple Tree" (Lucas Cranach the Elder) 2·25 1·00
1585 75c. "Madonna and Child" (Master of the Female Half-lengths) 2·25 1·25
1586 $1.20 "An Allegory of the Church" (Alessandro Allori) 3·25 3·50
1587 $5 "Madonna and Child wreathed with Flowers" (Jacob Jordaens) 6·00 8·50
MS1588 Two sheets. (a) 123×88 mm. $6 "Madonna and Child with Commissioners" (detail) (Palma Vecchio). (b) 88×123 mm. $6 "The Virgin Enthroned with Child" (detail) (Bohemian master) Set of 2 sheets 15·00 15·00

1995. "Hong Kong '94" International Stamp Exhibition (1st issue). Nos. 1890/1 of Antigua optd **BARBUDA MAIL.**
1589 40c. Hong Kong 1981 $1 Fish stamp and sampans, Shau Kei Wan 1·75 1·75
1590 40c. Antigua 1990 $2 Reef fish stamp and sampans, Shau Kei Wan 1·75 1·75
See also Nos. 1591/6.

1995. "Hong Kong '94" International Stamp Exhibition (2nd issue). Nos. 1892/7 of Antigua optd **BARBUDA MAIL.**
1591 40c. Terracotta warriors 50 60
1592 40c. Cavalryman and horse 50 60
1593 40c. Warriors in armour 50 60
1594 40c. Painted bronze chariot and team 50 60

1595 40c. Pekingese dog 50 60
1596 40c. Warriors with horses 50 60

1995. Centenary of International Olympic Committee. Nos. 1990/2 of Antigua optd **BARBUDA MAIL**.
1597 50c. Edwin Moses (U.S.A.) (400 metres hurdles), 1984 75 75
1598 $1.50 Steffi Graf (Germany) (tennis), 1988 5·00 3·50
MS1599 79 × 110 mm. $6 Johann Olav Koss (Norway) (500, 1500 and 10,000 metre speed skating), 1994 6·00 7·00

1995. Dogs of the World. Chinese New Year ("Year of the Dog"). Nos. 1923/47 of Antigua optd **BARBUDA MAIL**.
1600 50c. West Highland white terrier 95 85
1601 50c. Beagle 95 85
1602 50c. Scottish terrier 95 85
1603 50c. Pekingese 95 85
1604 50c. Dachshund 95 85
1605 50c. Yorkshire terrier 95 85
1606 50c. Pomeranian 95 85
1607 50c. Poodle 95 85
1608 50c. Shetland sheepdog 95 85
1609 50c. Pug 95 85
1610 50c. Shih tzu 95 85
1611 50c. Chihuahua 95 85
1612 50c. Mastiff 95 85
1613 50c. Border collie 95 85
1614 50c. Samoyed 95 85
1615 50c. Airedale terrier 95 85
1616 50c. English setter 95 85
1617 50c. Rough collie 95 85
1618 50c. Newfoundland 95 85
1619 50c. Weimarana 95 85
1620 50c. English springer spaniel 95 85
1621 50c. Dalmatian 95 85
1622 50c. Boxer 95 85
1623 50c. Old English sheepdog 95 85
MS1624 Two sheets, each 93 × 58 mm. (a) $6 Welsh corgi. (b) $6 Labrador retriever Set of 2 sheets 18·00 16·00

1995. Centenary of First English Cricket Tour to the West Indies (1995). Nos. 1994/7 of Antigua optd **BARBUDA MAIL**.
1625 35c. Mike Atherton (England) and Wisden Trophy 2·00 1·00
1626 75c. Viv Richards (West Indies) (vert) 2·75 2·25
1627 $1.20 Richie Richardson (West Indies) and Wisden Trophy 3·50 3·50
MS1628 80 × 100 mm. $3 English team, 1895 (black and brown) 6·50 6·50

1995. "Philakorea '94" International Stamp Exhibition (1st issue). Nos. 1998/2009 of Antigua optd **BARBUDA MAIL**.
1629 40c. Entrance bridge, Songgwangsa Temple 1·00 80
1630 75c. Long-necked bottle 1·25 1·25
1631 75c. Punch'ong ware jar with floral decoration 1·25 1·25
1632 75c. Punch'ong ware jar with blue dragon pattern 1·25 1·25
1633 75c. Ewer in shape of bamboo shoot 1·25 1·25
1634 75c. Punch'ong ware green jar 1·25 1·25
1635 75c. Pear-shaped bottle 1·25 1·25
1636 75c. Porcelain jar with brown dragon pattern 1·25 1·25
1637 75c. Porcelain jar with floral pattern 1·25 1·25
1638 90c. Song-op Folk Village, Cheju 1·25 1·25
1639 $3 Port Sogwipo 3·00 3·50
MS1640 104 × 71 mm. $4 Ox herder playing flute (vert) 3·00 3·75

1995. 1st Recipients of Order of the Caribbean Community. Nos. 2046/8 of Antigua optd **BARBUDA MAIL**.
1641 65c. Sir Shridath Ramphal 50 55
1642 90c. William Demas 70 75
1643 $1.20 Derek Walcott 1·75 1·75

1995. 25th Anniv of First Moon Landing. Nos. 1977/89 of Antigua optd **BARBUDA MAIL**.
1644 $1.50 Edwin Aldrin (astronaut) 2·25 2·00
1645 $1.50 First lunar footprint 2·25 2·00
1646 $1.50 Neil Armstrong (astronaut) 2·25 2·00
1647 $1.50 Aldrin stepping onto Moon 2·25 2·00
1648 $1.50 Aldrin and equipment 2·25 2·00
1649 $1.50 Aldrin and U.S.A. flag 2·25 2·00
1650 $1.50 Aldrin at Tranquility Base 2·25 2·00
1651 $1.50 Moon plaque 2·25 2·00
1652 $1.50 "Eagle" leaving Moon 2·25 2·00
1653 $1.50 Command module in lunar orbit 2·25 2·00
1654 $1.50 First day cover of U.S.A. 1969 10c. First Man on Moon stamp 2·25 2·00
1655 $1.50 Pres. Nixon and astronauts 2·25 2·00
MS1656 72 × 102 mm. $6 Armstrong and Aldrin with postal official 12·00 12·00

1995. International Year of the Family. No. 1993 of Antigua optd **BARBUDA MAIL**.
1657 90c. Antiguan family 1·50 1·50

1995. 50th Anniv of D-Day. Nos. 2010/13 of Antigua optd **BARBUDA MAIL**.
1658 40c. Short S.25 Sunderland flying boat 2·00 1·00
1659 $2 Lockheed P-38 Lightning fighters attacking train 4·00 3·75
1660 $3 Martin B-26 Marauder bombers 5·00 4·50
MS1661 108 × 78 mm. $6 Hawker Typhoon fighter bomber 7·50 9·00

122 Queen Elizabeth the Queen Mother (95th birthday)

1995. Anniversaries. Multicoloured.
1662 $7.50 Type **122** 8·50 8·50
1663 $8 German bombers over St. Paul's Cathedral, London (horiz) (50th anniv of end of Second World War) 12·00 11·00
1664 $8 New York skyline with U.N. and national flags (horiz) (50th anniv of United Nations) 7·50 8·50

1995. Hurricane Relief. Nos. 1662/4 surch **HURRICANE RELIEF** and premium.
1665 $7.50+$1 Type **122** (90th birthday) 6·50 7·50
1666 $8+$1 German bombers over St. Paul's Cathedral, London (horiz) (50th anniv of end of Second World War) 6·50 7·50
1667 $8+$1 New York skyline with U.N. and national flags (horiz) (50th anniv of United Nations) 6·50 7·50

1996. Marine Life. Nos. 1967/76 of Antigua optd **BARBUDA MAIL**.
1668 50c. Bottlenose dolphin 90 85
1669 50c. Killer whale 90 85
1670 50c. Spinner dolphin 90 85
1671 50c. Oceanic sunfish 90 85
1672 50c. Caribbean reef shark and short fin pilot whale 90 85
1673 50c. Copper-banded butterflyfish 90 85
1674 50c. Mosaic moray 90 85
1675 50c. Clown triggerfish 90 85
1676 50c. Red lobster 90 85
MS1677 Two sheets, each 106 × 76 mm. (a) $6 Seahorse. (b) $6 Swordfish ("Blue Marlin") (horiz) Set of 2 sheets 11·00 12·00

1996. Christmas. Religious Paintings. Nos. 2267/73 of Antigua optd **BARBUDA MAIL**.
1678 15c. "Rest on the Flight into Egypt" (Paolo Veronese) 50 40
1679 35c. "Madonna and Child" (Van Dyck) 65 40
1680 65c. "Sacred Conversation Piece" (Veronese) 80 55
1681 75c. "Vision of St. Anthony" (Van Dyck) 90 60
1682 90c. "Virgin and Child" (Van Eyck) 1·10 75
1683 $6 "The Immaculate Conception" (Giovanni Tiepolo) 4·25 5·50
MS1684 Two sheets. (a) 101 × 127 mm. $5 "Christ appearing to his Mother" (detail) (Van der Weyden). (b) 127 × 101 mm. $6 "The Infant Jesus and the Young St. John" (Murillo) Set of 2 sheets 9·00 11·00

1996. Stars of Country and Western Music. Nos. 2014/38 of Antigua optd **BARBUDA MAIL**.
1685 75c. Travis Tritt 80 75
1686 75c. Dwight Yoakam 80 75
1687 75c. Billy Ray Cyrus 80 75
1688 75c. Alan Jackson 80 75
1689 75c. Garth Brooks 80 75
1690 75c. Vince Gill 80 75
1691 75c. Clint Black 80 75
1692 75c. Eddie Rabbit 80 75
1693 75c. Patsy Cline 80 75
1694 75c. Tanya Tucker 80 75
1695 75c. Dolly Parton 80 75
1696 75c. Anne Murray 80 75
1697 75c. Tammy Wynette 80 75
1698 75c. Loretta Lynn 80 75
1699 75c. Reba McEntire 80 75
1700 75c. Skeeter Davis 80 75
1701 75c. Hank Snow 80 75
1702 75c. Gene Autry 80 75
1703 75c. Jimmie Rodgers 80 75
1704 75c. Ernest Tubb 80 75
1705 75c. Eddy Arnold 80 75
1706 75c. Willie Nelson 80 75
1707 75c. Johnny Cash 80 75
1708 75c. George Jones 80 75
MS1709 Three sheets. (a) 100 × 70 mm. $6 Hank Williams Jr. (b) 100 × 70 mm. $6 Hank Williams Sr. (c) 70 × 100 mm. $6 Kitty Wells (horiz) Set of 3 sheets 15·00 15·00

1996. Birds. Nos. 2067/81 of Antigua optd **BARBUDA MAIL**.
1710 15c. Magnificent frigate bird 50 50
1711 25c. Antillean euphonia ("Blue-hooded Euphonia") 55 40
1712 35c. Eastern meadowlark ("Meadowlark") 60 50
1713 40c. Red-billed tropic bird 60 50
1714 45c. Greater flamingo 70 50
1715 60c. Yellow-faced grassquit 85 85
1716 65c. Yellow-billed cuckoo 90 90
1717 70c. Purple-throated carib 90 90
1718 75c. Bananaquit 90 90
1719 90c. Painted bunting 1·00 1·00
1720 $1.20 Red-legged honeycreeper 1·25 1·25
1721 $2 Northern jacana ("Jacana") 1·75 2·00
1722 $5 Greater Antillean bullfinch 3·50 3·75
1723 $10 Caribbean elaenia 6·00 7·00
1724 $20 Brown trembler ("Trembler") 11·00 13·00

1996. Birds. Nos. 2050, 2052 and 2054/7 of Antigua optd **BARBUDA MAIL**.
1725 15c. Bridled quail dove 85 60
1726 40c. Purple-throated carib (vert) 1·50 50
1727 $1 Broad-winged hawk ("Antigua Broad-winged Hawk") (vert) 2·25 1·50
1728 $4 Yellow warbler 3·75 5·50
MS1729 Two sheets. (a) 70 × 100 mm. $6 Female magnificent frigate bird (vert). (b) 100 × 70 mm. $6 Black-billed whistling duck ducklings Set of 2 sheets 10·50 10·50

1996. Prehistoric Animals. Nos. 2082/100 of Antigua optd **BARBUDA MAIL**.
1730 15c. Head of pachycephalosaurus 1·00 1·00
1731 20c. Head of afrovenator 1·00 1·00
1732 65c. Centrosaurus 1·00 1·00
1733 75c. Kronosaurus (horiz) 1·00 1·00
1734 75c. Ichthyosaurus (horiz) 1·00 1·00
1735 75c. Plesiosaurus (horiz) 1·00 1·00
1736 75c. Archelon (horiz) 1·00 1·00
1737 75c. Pair of tyrannosaurus (horiz) 1·00 1·00
1738 75c. Tyrannosaurus (horiz) 1·00 1·00
1739 75c. Parasaurolophus (horiz) 1·00 1·00
1740 75c. Pair of parasaurolophus (horiz) 1·00 1·00
1741 75c. Oviraptor (horiz) 1·00 1·00
1742 75c. Protoceratops with eggs (horiz) 1·00 1·00
1743 75c. Pteranodon and protoceratops (horiz) 1·00 1·00
1744 75c. Pair of protoceratops (horiz) 1·00 1·00
1745 90c. Pentaceratops drinking 1·50 1·50
1746 $1.20 Head of tarbosaurus 1·75 1·75
1747 $5 Head of styracosaurus 4·25 5·00
MS1748 Two sheets, each 101 × 70 mm. (a) $6 Head of Corythosaurus (horiz). (b) $6 Head of Carnotaurus (horiz) Set of 2 sheets 11·00 12·00

1996. Olympic Games, Atlanta (1st issue). Previous Gold Medal Winners. Nos. 2101/7 of Antigua optd **BARBUDA MAIL**.
1749 15c. Al Oerter (U.S.A.) (discus – 1956, 1960, 1964, 1968) 75 70
1750 20c. Greg Louganis (U.S.A.) (diving – 1984, 1988) 75 70
1751 65c. Naim Suleymanoglu (Turkey) (weightlifting – 1988) 1·25 70
1752 90c. Louise Ritter (U.S.A.) (high jump – 1988) 1·75 1·10
1753 $1.20 Nadia Comaneci (Rumania) (gymnastics – 1976) 2·50 1·90
1754 $5 Olga Bondarenko (Russia) (10,000 m – 1988) 4·50 6·00
MS1755 Two sheets, each 106 × 76 mm. (a) $6 United States crew (eight-oared shell – 1964). (b) $6 Lutz Hessilch (Germany) (cycling – 1988) (vert) Set of 2 sheets 8·50 9·00
See also Nos. 1922/44.

1996. 18th World Scout Jamboree, Netherlands. Tents. Nos. 2203/9 of Antigua optd **BARBUDA MAIL**.
1756 $1.20 The Explorer Tent 1·00 1·00
1757 $1.20 Camper tent 1·00 1·00
1758 $1.20 Wall tent 1·00 1·00
1759 $1.20 Trail tent 1·00 1·00
1760 $1.20 Miner's tent 1·00 1·00
1761 $1.20 Voyager tent 1·00 1·00
MS1762 Two sheets, each 76 × 106 mm. (a) $6 Scout and camp fire. (b) $6 Scout with back pack Set of 2 sheets 7·50 8·00

1996. Centenary of Nobel Prize Trust Fund. Nos. 2226/44 of Antigua optd **BARBUDA MAIL**.
1763 $1 Dag Hammarskjold (1961 Peace) 70 60
1764 $1 Georg Wittig (1979 Chemistry) 70 60
1765 $1 Wilhelm Ostwold (1909 Chemistry) 70 60
1766 $1 Robert Koch (1905 Medicine) 70 60
1767 $1 Karl Ziegler (1963 Chemistry) 70 60
1768 $1 Alexander Fleming (1945 Medicine) 70 60
1769 $1 Hermann Staudinger (1953 Chemistry) 70 60
1770 $1 Manfred Eigen (1967 Chemistry) 70 60
1771 $1 Arno Penzias (1978 Physics) 70 60
1772 $1 Shumal Agnon (1966 Literature) 70 60
1773 $1 Rudyard Kipling (1907 Literature) 70 60
1774 $1 Aleksandr Solzhenitsyn (1970 Literature) 70 60
1775 $1 Jack Steinburger (1988 Physics) 70 60
1776 $1 Andrei Sakharov (1975 Peace) 70 60
1777 $1 Otto Stern (1943 Physics) 70 60
1778 $1 John Steinbeck (1962 Literature) 70 60
1779 $1 Nadine Gordimer (1991 Literature) 70 60
1780 $1 William Faulkner (1949 Literature) 70 60
MS1781 Two sheets, each 100 × 70 mm. (a) $6 Elie Wiesel (1986 Peace) (vert). (b) $6 Dalai Lama (1989 Peace) (vert) Set of 2 sheets 8·50 9·00

1996. 70th Birthday of Queen Elizabeth II. Nos. 2355/8 of Antigua optd **BARBUDA MAIL**.
1782 $2 Queen Elizabeth II in blue dress 1·40 1·40
1783 $2 With bouquet 1·40 1·40
1784 $2 In Garter robes 1·40 1·40
MS1785 96 × 111 mm. $6 Wearing white dress 7·00 6·00

1997. Christmas. Religious Paintings by Filippo Lippi. Nos. 2377/83 of Antigua optd **BARBUDA MAIL**.
1786 60c. "Madonna Enthroned" 35 35
1787 90c. "Adoration of the Child and Saints" 55 55
1788 $1 "The Annunciation" 60 60
1789 $1.20 "Birth of the Virgin" 75 75
1790 $1.60 "Adoration of the Child" 90 90
1791 $1.75 "Madonna and Child" 1·00 1·00
MS1792 Two sheets, each 76 × 106 mm. (a) $6 "Madonna and Child" (different). (b) $6 "The Circumcision" Set of 2 sheets 8·00 8·50

1997. 50th Anniv of F.A.O. Nos. 2121/4 of Antigua optd **BARBUDA MAIL**.
1793 75c. Woman buying produce from market 80 80
1794 90c. Women shopping 90 90
1795 $1.20 Women talking 1·10 1·10
MS1796 100 × 70 mm. $6 Tractor 5·00 6·00

1997. 90th Anniv of Rotary International (1995). No. 2126 of Antigua optd **BARBUDA MAIL**.
1797 $5 Beach and rotary emblem 2·75 3·00
MS1798 74 × 104 mm. $6 National flag and emblem 3·25 3·75

1997. 50th Anniv of End of Second World War in Europe and the Pacific. Nos. 2108/16 and 2132/8 of Antigua optd **BARBUDA MAIL**.
1799 $1.20 Map of Berlin showing Russian advance 55 60
1800 $1.20 Russian tank and infantry 55 60
1801 $1.20 Street fighting in Berlin 55 60
1802 $1.20 German tank exploding 55 60
1803 $1.20 Russian air raid 55 60
1804 $1.20 German troops surrendering 55 60
1805 $1.20 Hoisting the Soviet flag on the Reichstag 55 60
1806 $1.20 Captured German standards 55 60
1807 $1.20 Gen. Chiang Kai-shek and Chinese guerrillas 55 60
1808 $1.20 Gen. Douglas MacArthur and beach landing 55 60
1809 $1.20 Gen. Claire Chennault and U.S. fighter aircraft 55 60
1810 $1.20 Brig. Orde Wingate and supply drop 55 60

1811 $1.20 Gen. Joseph Stilwell and U.S. supply plane . . 55 60
1812 $1.20 Field-Marshal Bill Slim and loading cow onto plane 55 60
MS1813 Two sheets, each 100 × 70 mm. (a) $3 Admiral Nimitz and aircraft carrier. (b) $6 Gen. Konev (vert) Set of 2 sheets 5·75 6·25

1997. Bees. Nos. 2172/6 of Antigua optd **BARBUDA MAIL.**

1814 90c. Mining bees 65 50
1815 $1.20 Solitary bee 80 80
1816 $1.65 Leaf-cutter bee . . . 1·10 1·25
1817 $1.75 Honey bees . . . . . 1·25 1·40
MS1818 110 × 80 mm. $6 Solitary mining bird 4·00 4·50

1997. Flowers. Nos. 2177/89 of Antigua optd **BARBUDA MAIL.**

1819 75c. Narcissus 55 60
1820 75c. Camellia 55 60
1821 75c. Iris 55 60
1822 75c. Tulip 55 60
1823 75c. Poppy 55 60
1824 75c. Peony 55 60
1825 75c. Magnolia 55 60
1826 75c. Oriental lily 55 60
1827 75c. Rose 55 60
1828 75c. Pansy 55 60
1829 75c. Hydrangea 55 60
1830 75c. Azaleas 55 60
MS1831 80 × 110 mm. $6 Calla lily 4·00 4·50

1997. Cats. Nos. 2190/202 of Antigua optd **BARBUDA MAIL.**

1832 45c. Somali 50 50
1833 45c. Persian and butterflies 50 50
1834 45c. Devon rex 50 50
1835 45c. Turkish angora 50 50
1836 45c. Himalayan 50 50
1837 45c. Maine coon 50 50
1838 45c. Ginger non-pedigree . . 50 50
1839 45c. American wirehair . . 50 50
1840 45c. British shorthair . . . 50 50
1841 45c. American curl 50 50
1842 45c. Black non-pedigree and butterfly 50 50
1843 45c. Birman 50 50
MS1844 104 × 74 mm. $6 Siberian kitten (vert) 5·00 5·00

1997. 95th Birthday of Queen Elizabeth the Queen Mother. Nos. 2127/31 of Antigua optd **BARBUDA MAIL.**

1845 $1.50 brown, lt brown & black . . . . 3·00 2·50
1846 $1.50 multicoloured . . . . 3·00 2·50
1847 $1.50 multicoloured . . . . 3·00 2·50
1848 $1.50 multicoloured . . . . 3·00 2·50
MS1849 102 × 27 mm. $6 multicoloured 6·00 5·00

1997. 50th Anniv of United Nations. Nos. 2117/18 of Antigua optd **BARBUDA MAIL.**

1850 75c. Signatures and Earl of Halifax 35 40
1851 90c. Virginia Gildersleeve 40 45
1852 $1.20 Harold Stassen . . . 55 60
MS1853 100 × 70 mm. $6 Pres. Franklin D. Roosevelt 3·50 4·00

1997. Trains of the World. Nos. 2210/25 of Antigua optd **BARBUDA MAIL.**

1854 35c. Trans-Gabon diesel-electric train 55 30
1855 65c. Canadian Pacific diesel-electric locomotive 60 40
1856 75c. Santa Fe Railway diesel-electric locomotive, U.S.A. 60 50
1857 90c. High Speed Train, Great Britain 60 60
1858 $1.20 TGV express train, France 60 70
1859 $1.20 Diesel-electric locomotive, Australia . . 60 70
1860 $1.20 Pendolino "ETR 450" electric train, Italy 60 70
1861 $1.20 Diesel-electric locomotive, Thailand . . 60 70
1862 $1.20 Pennslyvania Railroad Type 4 steam locomotive, U.S.A. 60 70
1863 $1.20 Beyer-Garratt steam locomotive, East African Railways 60 70
1864 $1.20 Natal Govt steam locomotive 60 70
1865 $1.20 Rail gun, American Civil War 60 70
1866 $1.20 Locomotive "Lion" (red livery), Great Britain 60 70
1867 $1.20 William Hedley's "Puffing Billy" (green livery), Great Britain . . 60 70
1868 $6 Amtrak high speed diesel locomotive, U.S.A. . . . 3·00 3·75
MS1869 Two sheets, each 110 × 80 mm. (a) $6 Locomotive "Iron Rooster", China (vert). (b) $6 "Indian-Pacific" diesel-electric locomotive, Australia (vert) Set of 2 sheets 8·00 8·50

1997. Golden Wedding of Queen Elizabeth II and Prince Philip (1st issue). Nos. 1662/3 optd **Golden Wedding of H.M. Queen Elizabeth II and Prince Philip 1947-1997.**

1870 $7.50 Type **122** . . . . . . 4·00 5·50
1871 $8 German bombers over St. Paul's Cathedral, London (horiz) . . . . . 5·50 6·00

See also Nos. 1925/30.

1997. Fungi. Nos. 2274/82 of Antigua optd **BARBUDA MAIL.**

1872 75c. "Hygrophoropsis aurantiaca" 55 55
1873 75c. "Hygrophorus bakerensis" 55 55
1874 75c. "Hygrophorus conicus" 55 55
1875 75c. "Hygrophorus miniatus" ("Hygrocybe miniata") 55 55
1876 75c. "Suillus brevipes" . . . 55 55
1877 75c. "Suillus luteus" 55 55
1878 75c. "Suillus granulatus" . . 55 55
1879 75c. "Suillus caerulescens" 55 55
MS1880 Two sheets, each 106 × 76 mm. (a) $6 "Conocybe filaris". (b) $6 "Hygrocybe flavescens" Set of 2 sheets 11·00 11·00

1997. Birds. Nos. 2140/64 of Antigua optd **BARBUDA MAIL.**

1881 75c. Purple-throated carib 45 50
1882 75c. Antillean crested hummingbird 45 50
1883 75c. Bananaquit 45 50
1884 75c. Mangrove cuckoo . . . 45 50
1885 75c. Troupial 45 50
1886 75c. Green-throated carib 45 50
1887 75c. Yellow warbler 45 50
1888 75c. Antillean euphonia ("Blue-hooded Euphonia") 45 50
1889 75c. Scaly-breasted thrasher 45 50
1890 75c. Burrowing owl 45 50
1891 75c. Carib grackle 45 50
1892 75c. Adelaide's warbler . . 45 50
1893 75c. Ring-necked duck . . . 45 50
1894 75c. Ruddy duck 45 50
1895 75c. Green-winged teal . . . 45 50
1896 75c. Wood duck 45 50
1897 75c. Hooded merganser . . 45 50
1898 75c. Lesser scaup 45 50
1899 75c. Black-billed whistling duck ("West Indian Tree Duck") 45 50
1900 75c. Fulvous whistling duck 45 50
1901 75c. Bahama pintail 45 50
1902 75c. Northern shoveler ("Shoveler") 45 50
1903 75c. Masked duck 45 50
1904 75c. American wigeon . . . 45 50
MS1905 Two sheets, each 104 × 74 mm. (a) $6 Head of purple gallinule. (b) $6 Heads of blue-winged teals Set of 2 sheets 6·00 7·00

1997. Sailing Ships. Nos. 2283/301 of Antigua optd **BARBUDA MAIL.**

1906 15c. H.M.S. "Resolution" (Cook) 40 40
1907 25c. "Mayflower" (Pilgrim Fathers) 40 30
1908 45c. "Santa Maria" (Columbus) 40 30
1909 75c. "Aemilia" (Dutch galleon) 40 45
1910 75c. "Sovereign of the Seas" (English galleon) 40 45
1911 90c. H.M.S. "Victory" (Nelson) 50 55
1912 $1.20 As No. 1909 . . . . 55 60
1913 $1.20 As No. 1910 . . . . 55 60
1914 $1.20 "Royal Louis" (French galleon) 55 60
1915 $1.20 H.M.S. "Royal George" (ship of the line) 55 60
1916 $1.20 "Le Protecteur" (French frigate) 55 60
1917 $1.20 As No. 1911 . . . . 55 60
1918 $1.50 As No. 1908 . . . . 70 75
1919 $1.50 "Victoria" (Magellan) 70 75
1920 $1.50 "Golden Hind" (Drake) 70 75
1921 $1.50 As No. 1907 . . . . 70 75
1922 $1.50 "Griffin" (La Salle) 70 75
1923 $1.50 As No. 1906 . . . . 70 75
MS1924 (a) 102 × 72 mm. $6 U.S.S. "Constitution" (frigate). (b) 98 × 67 mm. $6 "Grande Hermine" (Cartier) Set of 2 sheets 5·50 5·75

1997. Golden Wedding of Queen Elizabeth and Prince Philip (2nd issue). Nos. 2474/80 of Antigua optd **BARBUDA MAIL.**

1925 $1 Queen Elizabeth II . . . 1·50 1·50
1926 $1 Royal coat of arms . . . 1·50 1·50
1927 $1 Queen Elizabeth and Prince Philip at reception 1·50 1·50
1928 $1 Queen Elizabeth and Prince Philip in landau . . 1·50 1·50
1929 $1 Balmoral . . . . 1·50 1·50
1930 $1 Prince Philip . . . . . . 1·50 1·50
MS1931 100 × 71 mm. $6 Queen Elizabeth with Prince Philip in naval uniform 7·00 7·00

1997. Christmas. Religious Paintings. Nos. 2566/72 of Antigua optd **BARBUDA MAIL.**

1932 15c. "The Angel leaving Tobias and his Family" (Rembrandt) 50 35
1933 25c. "The Resurrection" (Martin Knoller) 55 35
1934 60c. "Astronomy" (Raphael) 75 50
1935 75c. "Music-making Angel" (Melozzo da Forli) . . . 80 55
1936 90c. "Amor" (Parmigianino) 90 70
1937 $1.20 "Madonna and Child with Saints" (Rosso Fiorentino) . . . . 1·10 1·40
MS1938 Two sheets, each 105 × 96 mm. (a) $6 "The Wedding of Tobias" (Gianantonio and Francesco Guardi) (horiz). (b) $6 "The Portinari Altarpiece" (Hugo van der Goes) (horiz) Set of 2 sheets 7·00 7·50

1998. Sea Birds. Nos. 2325/33 of Antigua optd **BARBUDA MAIL.**

1939 75c. Black skimmer 80 80
1940 75c. Black-capped petrel . . 80 80
1941 75c. Sooty tern 80 80
1942 75c. Royal tern 80 80
1943 75c. Pomarine skua ("Pomarine Jaegger") . . 80 80
1944 75c. White-tailed tropic bird 80 80
1945 75c. Northern gannet . . . 80 80
1946 75c. Laughing gull 80 80
MS1947 Two sheets, each 105 × 75 mm. (a) $5 Great frigate bird. (b) $6 Brown pelican Set of 2 sheets 7·00 7·50

1998. Centenary of Radio. Entertainers. Nos. 2372/6 of Antigua optd **BARBUDA MAIL.**

1948 65c. Kate Smith 45 45
1949 75c. Dinah Shore 50 50
1950 90c. Rudy Vallee 60 60
1951 $1.20 Bing Crosby 75 75
MS1952 72 × 104 mm. $6 Jo Stafford (28 × 42 mm) 3·50 4·00

1998. Olympic Games, Atlanta (2nd issue). Previous Medal Winners. Nos. 2302/23 of Antigua optd **BARBUDA MAIL.**

1953 65c. Florence Griffith Joyner (U.S.A.) (Gold – track, 1988) 60 60
1954 75c. Olympic Stadium, Seoul (1988) (horiz) 60 60
1955 90c. Allison Jolly and Lynne Jewell (U.S.A.) (Gold – yachting, 1988) (horiz) . . 60 60
1956 90c. Wolfgang Nordwig (Germany) (Gold – pole vaulting, 1972) 60 60
1957 90c. Shirley Strong (Great Britain) (Silver – 100 m hurdles, 1984) . . 60 60
1958 90c. Sergei Bubka (Russia) (Gold – pole vault, 1988) 60 60
1959 90c. Filbert Bayi (Tanzania) (Silver – 3000 m steeplechase, 1980) 60 60
1960 90c. Victor Saneyev (Russia) (Gold – triple jump, 1968, 1972, 1976) 60 60
1961 90c. Silke Renk (Germany) (Gold – javelin, 1992) . . 60 60
1962 90c. Daley Thompson (Great Britain) (Gold – decathlon, 1980, 1984) . . 60 60
1963 90c. Robert Richards (U.S.A.) (Gold – pole vault, 1952, 1956) 60 60
1964 90c. Parry O'Brien (U.S.A.) (Gold – shot put, 1952, 1956) 60 60
1965 90c. Ingrid Kramer (Germany) (Gold – Women's platform diving, 1960) 60 60
1966 90c. Kelly McCormick (U.S.A.) (Silver – Women's springboard diving, 1984) 60 60
1967 90c. Gary Tobian (U.S.A.) (Gold – Men's springboard diving, 1960) 60 60
1968 90c. Greg Louganis (U.S.A.) (Gold – Men's diving, 1984 and 1988) 60 60
1969 90c. Michelle Mitchell (U.S.A.) (Silver – Women's platform diving, 1984 and 1988) 60 60
1970 90c. Zhou Jihong (China) (Gold – Women's platform diving, 1984) . . 60 60
1971 90c. Wendy Wyland (U.S.A.) (Bronze – Women's platform diving, 1984) 60 60
1972 90c. Xu Yanmei (China) (Gold – Women's platform diving, 1988) . . 60 60
1973 90c. Fu Mingxia (China) (Gold – Women's platform diving, 1992) . . 60 60
1974 $1.20 2000 m tandem cycle race (horiz) . . . . 1·50 1·50
MS1975 Two sheets, each 106 × 76 mm. (a) $5 Bill Toomey (U.S.A.) (Gold – decathlon, 1968) (horiz). (b) $6 Mark Lenzi (U.S.A.) (Gold – Men's springboard diving, 1992) Set of 2 sheets 7·00 7·50

1998. World Cup Football Championship, France. Nos. 2525/39 of Antigua optd **BARBUDA MAIL.**

1976 60c. multicoloured 60 60
1977 75c. brown 60 60
1978 90c. multicoloured 65 65
1979 $1 brown 65 65
1980 $1 brown 65 65
1981 $1 brown 65 65
1982 $1 black 65 65
1983 $1 brown 65 65
1984 $1 brown 65 65
1985 $1 brown 65 65
1986 $1 brown 65 65
1987 $1.20 multicoloured 70 70
1988 $1.65 multicoloured 85 85
1989 $1.75 multicoloured 95 95
MS1990 Two sheets, each 102 × 127 mm. (a) $6 multicoloured. (b) $6 multicoloured Set of 2 sheets 7·00 7·50

1998. Cavalry through the Ages. Nos. 2359/63 of Antigua optd **BARBUDA MAIL.**

1991 60c. Ancient Egyptian cavalryman 60 60
1992 60c. 13th-century English knight 60 60
1993 60c. 16th-century Spanish lancer 60 60
1994 60c. 18th-century Chinese cavalryman 60 60
MS1995 100 × 70 mm. $6 19th-century French cuirassier (vert) 3·75 4·00

1998. 50th Anniv of U.N.I.C.E.F. Nos. 2364/7 of Antigua optd **BARBUDA MAIL.**

1996 75c. Girl in red sari 60 60
1997 90c. South American mother and child 70 70
1998 $1.20 Nurse with child . . . 80 80
MS1999 114 × 74 mm. $6 Chinese child 3·50 4·00

1998. 3000th Anniv of Jerusalem. Nos. 2368/71 of Antigua optd **BARBUDA MAIL.**

2000 75c. Tomb of Zachariah and "Verbascum sinuatum" 65 65
2001 90c. Pool of Siloam and "Hyacinthus orientalis" 75 75
2002 $1.20 Hurva Synagogue and "Ranunculus asiaticus" 1·10 1·10
MS2003 66 × 80 mm. $6 Model of Herod's Temple and "Cercis siliquastrum" 4·25 4·25

1998. Diana, Princess of Wales Commemoration. Nos. 2573/85 of Antigua optd **BARBUDA MAIL.**

2004 $1.65 Diana, Princess of Wales . . . . 1·00 1·00
2005 $1.65 Wearing hoop earrings (red and black) . . . . . 1·00 1·00
2006 $1.65 Carrying bouquet . . 1·00 1·00
2007 $1.65 Wearing floral hat . . 1·00 1·00
2008 $1.65 With Prince Harry . . 1·00 1·00
2009 $1.65 Wearing white jacket 1·00 1·00
2010 $1.65 In kitchen . . . . . . 1·00 1·00
2011 $1.65 Wearing black and white dress . . . . 1·00 1·00
2012 $1.65 Wearing hat (brown and black) . . . . 1·00 1·00
2013 $1.65 Wearing floral print dress (brown and black) 1·00 1·00
2014 $1.65 Dancing with John Travolta . . . . 1·00 1·00
2015 $1.65 Wearing white hat and jacket . . . . 1·00 1·00
MS2016 Two sheets, each 70 × 100 mm. (a) $6 Wearing red jumper. (b) $6 Wearing black dress for Papal audience (brown and black) Set of 2 sheets 7·00 7·50

1998. Broadway Musical Stars. Nos. 2384/93 of Antigua optd **BARBUDA MAIL.**

2017 $1 Robert Preston ("The Music Man") 65 65
2018 $1 Michael Crawford ("Phantom of the Opera") 65 65
2019 $1 Zero Mostel ("Fiddler on the Roof") 65 65
2020 $1 Patti Lupone ("Evita") 65 65
2021 $1 Raul Julia ("Threepenny Opera") 65 65
2022 $1 Mary Martin ("South Pacific") 65 65
2023 $1 Carol Channing ("Hello Dolly") 65 65
2024 $1 Yul Brynner ("The King and I") 65 65
2025 $1 Julie Andrews ("My Fair Lady") 65 65
MS2026 106 × 76 mm. $6 Mickey Rooney ("Sugar Babies") 3·50 4·00

1998. 20th Death Anniv of Charlie Chaplin (film star). Nos. 2404/13 of Antigua optd **BARBUDA MAIL.**

2027 $1 Charlie Chaplin as young man 65 65
2028 $1 Pulling face 65 65
2029 $1 Looking over shoulder 65 65
2030 $1 In cap 65 65

2031 $1 In front of star 65 65
2032 $1 In "The Great Dictator" 65 65
2033 $1 With movie camera and megaphone 65 65
2034 $1 Standing in front of camera lens 65 65
2035 $1 Putting on make-up 65 65
MS2036 76 × 106 mm. $6 Charlie Chaplin 3·75 4·00

1998. Butterflies. Nos. 2414/36 of Antigua optd **BARBUDA MAIL.**
2037 90c. "Charaxes porthos" 70 70
2038 $1.10 "Charaxes protoclea protoclea" 75 75
2039 $1.10 "Byblia ilithyia" 75 75
2040 $1.10 Black-headed tchagra (bird) 75 75
2041 $1.10 "Charaxes nobilis" 75 75
2042 $1.10 "Pseudacraea boisduvali trimeni" 75 75
2043 $1.10 "Charaxes smaragdalis" 75 75
2044 $1.10 "Charaxes lasti" 75 75
2045 $1.10 "Pseudacraea poggei" 75 75
2046 $1.10 "Graphium colonna" 75 75
2047 $1.10 Carmine bee eater (bird) 75 75
2048 $1.10 "Pseudacraea eurytus" 75 75
2049 $1.10 "Hypolimnas monteironis" 75 75
2050 $1.10 "Charaxes anticlea" 75 75
2051 $1.10 "Graphium leonidas" 75 75
2052 $1.10 "Graphium illyris" 75 75
2053 $1.10 "Nephronia argia" 75 75
2054 $1.10 "Graphium policenes" 75 75
2055 $1.10 "Papilio dardanus" 75 75
2056 $1.20 "Aethiopana honorius" 75 75
2057 $1.60 "Charaxes hadrianus" 1·00 1·00
2058 $1.75 "Precis westermanni" 1·10 1·10
MS2059 Three sheets, each 107 × 76 mm. (a) $6 "Charaxes lactincus" (horiz). (b) $6 "Eupheadra reophron". (c) "Euxantha tiberius") (horiz) Set of 3 sheets 10·00 11·00

1998. Christmas. Dogs. Nos. 2771/8 of Antigua optd **BARBUDA MAIL.**
2060 15c. Border collie 45 35
2061 25c. Dalmatian 55 35
2062 65c. Weimaraner 90 60
2063 75c. Scottish terrier 95 65
2064 90c. Long-haired dachshund 1·00 70
2065 $1.20 Golden retriever 1·25 1·10
2066 $2 Pekingese 1·75 2·25
MS2067 Two sheets, each 75 × 66 mm. (a) $6 Dalmatian. (b) $6 Jack Russell terrier Set of 2 sheets 8·00 8·00

1999. Lighthouses of the World. Nos. 2612/20 of Antigua optd **BARBUDA MAIL.**
2068 45c. Europa Point Lighthouse, Gibraltar 65 50
2069 65c. Tierra del Fuego, Argentina (horiz) 70 70
2070 75c. Point Loma, California, U.S.A. (horiz) 70 70
2071 90c. Groenpoint, Cape Town, South Africa 80 80
2072 $1 Youghal, Cork, Ireland 90 90
2073 $1.20 Launceston, Tasmania, Australia 1·00 1·00
2074 $1.65 Point Abino, Ontario, Canada (horiz) 1·25 1·25
2075 $1.75 Great Inagua, Bahamas (horiz) 1·25 1·25
MS2076 99 × 70 mm. $6 Cape Hatteras, North Carolina, U.S.A. 3·50 3·75

1999. Endangered Species. Nos. 2457/69 of Antigua optd **BARBUDA MAIL.**
2077 $1.20 Red bishop 80 85
2078 $1.20 Yellow baboon 80 85
2079 $1.20 Superb starling 80 85
2080 $1.20 Ratel 80 85
2081 $1.20 Hunting dog 80 85
2082 $1.20 Serval 80 85
2083 $1.65 Okapi 90 1·00
2084 $1.65 Giant forest squirrel 90 1·00
2085 $1.65 Lesser masked weaver 90 1·00
2086 $1.65 Small-spotted genet 90 1·00
2087 $1.65 Yellow-billed stork 90 1·00
2088 $1.65 Red-headed agama 90 1·00
MS2089 Three sheets, each 106 × 76 mm. (a) $6 South African crowned crane. (b) $6 Bat-eared fox. (c) $6 Malachite kingfisher Set of 3 sheets 9·00 10·00

1999. "Pacific 97" International Stamp Exhibition, San Francisco. Death Centenary of Heinrich von Stephan (founder of the U.P.U.). Nos. 2481/4 of Antigua optd **BARBUDA MAIL.**
2090 $1.75 blue 1·25 1·40
2091 $1.75 brown 1·25 1·40
2092 $1.75 mauve 1·25 1·40
MS2093 82 × 119 mm. $6 violet 3·00 3·25
DESIGNS: No. 2090, Kaiser Wilhelm I and Heinrich von Stephan; 2091, Von Stephan and Mercury; 2092, Carrier pigeon and loft; **MS**2093 Von Stephan and 15th-century Basel messenger.

1999. 175th Anniv of Brothers Grimm's Third Collection of Fairy Tales. *Cinderella*. Nos. 2485/8 of Antigua optd **BARBUDA MAIL.**
2094 $1.75 The Ugly Sisters and their Mother 1·25 1·40
2095 $1.75 Cinderella and her Fairy Godmother 1·25 1·40
2096 $1.75 Cinderella and the Prince 1·25 1·40
MS2097 124 × 96 mm. $6 Cinderella trying on slipper 3·00 3·25

1999. Orchids of the World. Nos. 2502/24 of Antigua optd **BARBUDA MAIL.**
2098 45c. *Odontoglossum cervantesii* 50 35
2099 65c. *Phalaenopsis* Medford Star 60 65
2100 75c. *Vanda* Motes Resplendent 65 65
2101 90c. *Odontonia* Debutante 70 70
2102 $1 *Iwanagaara* Apple Blossom 80 80
2103 $1.65 *Cattleya* Sophia Martin 1·10 1·25
2104 $1.65 Dogface Butterfly 1·10 1·25
2105 $1.65 *Laeliocattleya* Mini Purple 1·10 1·25
2106 $1.65 *Cymbidium* Showgirl 1·10 1·25
2107 $1.65 *Brassolaeliocattleya* Dorothy Bertsch 1·10 1·25
2108 $1.65 *Disa blackii* 1·10 1·25
2109 $1.65 *Paphiopedilum leeanum* 1·10 1·25
2110 $1.65 *Paphiopedilum macranthum* 1·10 1·25
2111 $1.65 *Brassocattleya* Angel Lace 1·10 1·25
2112 $1.65 *Saphrolae liocattleya* Precious Stones 1·10 1·25
2113 $1.65 Orange Theope Butterfly 1·10 1·25
2114 $1.65 *Promenaea xanthina* 1·10 1·25
2115 $1.65 *Lycasle macrobulbon* 1·10 1·25
2116 $1.65 *Amestella philippinensis* 1·10 1·25
2117 $1.65 *Masdevallia* Machu Picchu 1·10 1·25
2118 $1.65 *Phalaenopsis* Zuma Urchin 1·10 1·25
2119 $2 *Dendrobium victoria-reginae* 1·25 1·40
MS2120 Two sheets, each 76 × 106 mm. (a) $6 *Miltonia* Seine. (b) $6 *Paphiopedilum gratrixanum* Set of 2 sheets 6·00 6·25

1999. 50th Death Anniv of Paul Harris (founder of Rotary International). No. 2472/3 of Antigua optd **BARBUDA MAIL.**
2121 $1.65 Paul Harris and James Grant 1·40 1·60
MS2122 78 × 107 mm. $6 Group study exchange, New Zealand 3·00 3·25

1999. Royal Wedding. Nos. 2912/16 of Antigua optd **BARBOUDA MAIL.**
2123 $3 Sophie Rhys-Jones 1·50 1·75
2124 $3 Sophie and Prince Edward 1·50 1·75
2125 $3 Prince Edward 1·50 1·75
MS2126 108 × 78 mm. $6 Prince Edward with Sophie Rhys-Jones and Windsor Castle 3·75 3·75
All examples of Nos. 2123/5 show the incorrect country overprint as above.

1999. Fungi. Nos. 2489/501 of Antigua optd **BARBUDA MAIL.**
2127 45c. *Marasmius rotula* 50 35
2128 65c. *Cantharellus cibarius* 55 55
2129 70c. *Lepiota cristata* 60 60
2130 90c. *Auricularia mesenterica* 70 70
2131 $1 *Pholiota alnicola* 75 75
2132 $1.65 *Leccinum aurantiacum* 1·10 1·10
2133 $1.75 *Entoloma serrulatum* 1·10 1·10
2134 $1.75 *Panaeolus sphinctrinus* 1·10 1·10
2135 $1.75 *Volvariella bombycina* 1·10 1·10
2136 $1.75 *Conocybe percincta* 1·10 1·10
2137 $1.75 *Pluteus cervinus* 1·10 1·10
2138 $1.75 *Russula foetens* 1·10 1·10
MS2139 Two sheets, each 106 × 76 mm. (a) $6 *Amanita cothurnata*. (b) $6 *Panellus serotinus* Set of 2 sheets 6·00 6·25

1999. 1st Death Anniv of Diana, Princess of Wales. No. 2753 of Antigua optd **BARBUDA MAIL.**
2140 $1.20 Diana, Princess of Wales 75 75

1999. Railway Locomotives of the World. Nos. 2553/65 of Antigua optd **BARBUDA MAIL.**
2141 $1.65 Original drawing by Richard Trevithick, 1803 1·00 1·00
2142 $1.65 William Hedley's *Puffing Billy*, (1813–14) 1·00 1·00
2143 $1.65 Crampton locomotive of French Nord Railway, 1858 1·00 1·00
2144 $1.65 Lawrence Machine Shop locomotive, U.S.A., 1860 1·00 1·00
2145 $1.65 Natchez and Hamburg Railway steam locomotive *Mississippi*, U.S.A., 1834 1·00 1·00
2146 $1.65 Bury "Coppernob" locomotive, Furness Railway, 1846 1·00 1·00
2147 $1.65 David Joy's *Jenny Lind*, 1847 1·00 1·00
2148 $1.65 Schenectady Atlantic locomotive, U.S.A., 1899 1·00 1·00
2149 $1.65 Kitson Class 1800 tank locomotive, Japan, 1881 1·00 1·00
2150 $1.65 Pennsylvania Railroad express freight 1·00 1·00
2151 $1.65 Karl Golsdorf's 4 cylinder locomotive, Austria 1·00 1·00
2152 $1.65 Series "E" locomotive, Russia, 1930 1·00 1·00
MS2153 Two sheets, each 72 × 100 mm. (a) $6 George Stephenson's "Patentee" Type locomotive, 1843. (b) $6 Brunel's trestle bridge over River Lynher, Cornwall 6·50 7·00

1999. 175th Anniv of Cedar Hall Moravian Church. Nos. 2605/11 of Antigua optd **BARBUDA MAIL.**
2154 20c. First Church and Manse, 1822–40 25 25
2155 45c. Cedar Hall School, 1840 35 30
2156 75c. Hugh A. King, minister, 1945–53 50 45
2157 90c. Present Church building 55 50
2158 $1.20 Water tank, 1822 70 75
2159 $2 Former Manse, demolished 1978 1·00 1·25
MS2160 100 × 70 mm. $6 Present church building (different) (50 × 37 mm) 3·25 3·50

1999. Christmas. Religious Paintings. Nos. 2945/51 of Antigua optd **BARBUDA MAIL.**
2161 15c. multicoloured 20 20
2162 25c. black, stone and yellow 25 20
2163 45c. multicoloured 35 30
2164 60c. multicoloured 60 35
2165 $2 multicoloured 1·25 1·50
2166 $4 black, stone and yellow 2·00 2·50
MS2167 76 × 106 mm. $6 multicoloured 3·25 3·50

1999. Centenary of Thomas Oliver Robinson Memorial School. Nos. 2634/40 of Antigua optd **BARBUDA MAIL.**
2168 20c. green and black 20 20
2169 45c. multicoloured 35 30
2170 65c. green and black 50 40
2171 75c. multicoloured 55 50
2172 90c. multicoloured 60 60
2173 $1.20 brown, green and black 70 80
MS2174 106 × 76 mm. $6 brown 3·25 3·50

2000. Cats and Dogs. Nos. 2540/52 of Antigua optd **BARBUDA MAIL.**
2175 $1.65 Scottish fold kitten 1·00 1·00
2176 $1.65 Japanese bobtail 1·00 1·00
2177 $1.65 Tabby manx 1·00 1·00
2178 $1.65 Bicolor American shorthair 1·00 1·00
2179 $1.65 Sorel Abyssinian 1·00 1·00
2180 $1.65 Himalayan blue point 1·00 1·00
2181 $1.65 Dachshund 1·00 1·00
2182 $1.65 Staffordshire terrier 1·00 1·00
2183 $1.65 Shar-pei 1·00 1·00
2184 $1.65 Beagle 1·00 1·00
2185 $1.65 Norfolk terrier 1·00 1·00
2186 $1.65 Golden retriever 1·00 1·00
MS2187 Two sheets, each 107 × 77 mm. (a) $6 Red tabby (vert). (b) $6 Siberian husky (vert) 7·00 7·50

2000. Fishes. Nos. 2586/604 of Antigua optd **BARBUDA MAIL.**
2188 75c. Yellow damselfish 60 50
2189 90c. Barred hamlet 65 55
2190 $1 Yellow-tailed damselfish ("Jewelfish") 70 70
2191 $1.20 Blue-headed wrasse 80 80
2192 $1.50 Queen angelfish 1·00 1·00
2193 $1.65 Jackknife-fish 1·00 1·00
2194 $1.65 Spot-finned hogfish 1·00 1·00
2195 $1.65 Sergeant major 1·00 1·00
2196 $1.65 Neon goby 1·00 1·00
2197 $1.65 Jawfish 1·00 1·00
2198 $1.65 Flamefish 1·00 1·00
2199 $1.65 Rock beauty 1·00 1·00
2200 $1.65 Yellow-tailed snapper 1·00 1·00
2201 $1.65 Creole wrasse 1·00 1·00
2202 $1.65 Slender filefish 1·00 1·00
2203 $1.65 Long-spined squirrelfish 1·00 1·00
2204 $1.65 Royal gramma ("Fairy Basslet") 1·00 1·00
2205 $1.75 Queen triggerfish 1·10 1·10
MS2206 Two sheets, each 80 × 110 mm. (a) $6 Porkfish. (b) $6 Black-capped basslet 7·00 7·50

2000. Ships of the World. Nos. 2679/85 of Antigua optd **BARBUDA MAIL.**
2207 $1.75 *Savannah* (paddle-steamer) 1·10 1·10
2208 $1.75 Viking longship 1·10 1·10
2209 $1.75 Greek galley 1·10 1·10
2210 $1.75 Sailing clipper 1·10 1·10
2211 $1.75 Dhow 1·10 1·10
2212 $1.75 Fishing catboat 1·10 1·10
MS2213 Three sheets, each 100 × 70 mm. (a) $6 13th-century English warship (41 × 22 mm). (b) $6 Sailing dory (22 × 41 mm). (c) $6 Baltimore clipper (41 × 22 mm) 9·50 10·00

2000. Modern Aircraft. Nos. 2700/12 of Antigua optd **BARBUDA MAIL.**
2214 $1.65 Lockheed-Boeing General Dynamics Yf-22 1·00 1·00
2215 $1.65 Dassault-Breguet Rafale BO 1 1·00 1·00
2216 $1.65 MiG 29 1·00 1·00
2217 $1.65 Dassault-Breguet Mirage 2000D 1·00 1·00
2218 $1.65 Rockwell B-1B "Lancer" 1·00 1·00
2219 $1.65 McDonnell-Douglas C-17A 1·00 1·00
2220 $1.65 Space Shuttle 1·00 1·00
2221 $1.65 SAAB "Grippen" 1·00 1·00
2222 $1.65 Eurofighter EF-2000 1·00 1·00
2223 $1.65 Sukhoi SU 27 1·00 1·00
2224 $1.65 Northrop B-2 1·00 1·00
2225 $1.65 Lockheed F-117 "Nighthawk" 1·00 1·00
MS2226 Two sheets, each 110 × 85 mm. (a) $6 F18 Hornet. (b) $6 Sukhoi SU 35 7·00 7·50

BARWANI Pt. 1

A State of Central India. Now uses Indian stamps.

12 pies = 1 anna; 16 annas = 1 rupee.

1 Rana Ranjit Singh

2

1921.
5 **1** ¼a. green 19·00 60·00
19 ¼a. blue 1·00 11·00
37 B ¼a. black 3·00 28·00
18 ¼a. pink 1·50 12·00
4 ½a. blue 17·00 £130
29 ½a. green 2·75 12·00
10 **2** 1a. red 2·25 19·00
39 B 1a. brown 11·00 23·00
11 2a. purple 2·25 22·00
41 B 2a. red 23·00 90·00
31 4a. orange 60·00 £160
42Ba – 4a. green 12·00 38·00
DESIGN: 4 a. Another portrait of Rana Ranjit Singh.

4 Rana Devi Singh

5

1932.
32A **4** ¼a. slate 1·50 18·00
33A ½a. green 2·50 18·00
34A 1a. brown 2·75 17·00
35A 2a. purple 3·50 29·00
36A 4a. olive 6·00 32·00

1938.
43 **5** 1a. brown 28·00 50·00

BASUTOLAND Pt. 1

An African territory under British protection, N.E. of Cape Province. Self-Government introduced on 1 April 1965. Attained independence on 4 October 1966, when the country was renamed Lesotho.

1933. 12 pence = 1 shilling;
20 shillings = 1 pound.
1961. 100 cents = 1 rand.

1 King George V, Nile Crocodile and Mountains

1933.
1 **1** ½d. green 1·00 1·75
2 1d. red 75 1·25
3 2d. purple 1·00 80
4 3d. blue 75 1·25
5 4d. grey 2·00 7·00
6 6d. yellow 2·25 1·75
7 1s. orange 2·25 4·50
8 2s.6d. brown 21·00 45·00
9 5s. violet 48·00 65·00
10 10s. olive £120 £130

1935. Silver Jubilee. As T **13** of Antigua.
11 1d. blue and red 55 75
12 2d. blue and grey 65 1·25
13 3d. brown and blue 3·75 3·75
14 6d. grey and purple 3·75 3·75

1937. Coronation. As T **2** of Aden.
15 1d. red 35 70
16 2d. purple 50 85
17 3d. blue 60 85

1938. As T **1**, but portrait of King George VI.
18 ½d. green 30 1·25
19 1d. red 50 70
20 1½d. blue 40 50
21 2d. purple 30 60
22 3d. blue 30 1·25
23 4d. grey 1·50 3·50

24 6d. yellow 50 1·50
25 1s. orange 50 1·00
26 2s.6d. brown 8·50 8·50
27 5s. violet 22·00 9·50
28 10s. olive 23·00 17·00

1945. Victory. Stamps of South Africa optd **Basutoland**. Alternate stamps inscr in English or Afrikaans.
29 **55** 1d. brown and red 40 60
30 2d. blue and violet 40 50
31 3d. blue 40 70
Prices are for bi-lingual pairs.

5 King George VI and Queen Elizabeth

1947. Royal Visit.
32 – 1d. red 10 10
33 **5** 2d. green 10 10
34 – 3d. blue 10 10
35 – 1s. mauve 15 10
DESIGNS—VERT: 1d. King George VI. HORIZ: 3d. Queen Elizabeth II as Princess and Princess Margaret; 1s. The Royal Family.

1948. Silver Wedding. As T **10/11** of Aden.
36 1½d. blue 20 10
37 10s. green 30·00 27·00

1949. U.P.U. As T **20/23** of Antigua.
38 1½d. blue 20 1·25
39 3d. blue 1·75 2·00
40 6d. orange 1·00 2·25
41 1s. brown 50 1·00

1953. Coronation. As T **13** of Aden.
42 2d. black and purple 40 50

8 Qiloane

9 Mohair (Shearing Goats)

1954.
43 **8** ½d. black and sepia 10 10
44 – 1d. black and green 10 10
45 – 2d. blue and orange 60 10
46 – 3d. sage and red 80 30
47 – 4½d. indigo and blue 70 15
48 – 6d. brown and green 1·25 15
49 – 1s. bronze and purple 1·25 30
50 – 1s.3d. brown and turquoise 17·00 5·00
51 – 2s.6d. blue and red 15·00 7·50
52 – 5s. black and red 5·00 8·50
53 **9** 10s. black and purple 18·00 23·00
DESIGNS—HORIZ: 1d. Orange River; 2d. Mosuto horseman; 3d. Basuto household; 4½d. Maletsunyane Falls; 6d. Herd-boy playing lesiba; 1s. Pastoral scene; 1s.3d. De Havilland Comet 1 airplane over Lancers' Gap; 2s.6d. Old Fort, Leribe; 5s. Mission cave house.

1959. No. 45 Surch **½d.** and bar.
54 ½d. on 2d. blue and orange 10 15

20 "Chief Moshoeshoe I" (engraving by Delangle)

26 Basuto Household

1959. Inauguration of National Council.
55 **20** 3d. black and olive 30 10
56 – 1s. red and green 30 10
57 – 1s.3d. blue and orange 50 45
DESIGNS: 1s. Council house; 1s.3d. Mosuto horseman.

1961. Nos. 43/53 surch.
58 **8** ½c. on ½d. black and sepia 10 10
59 – 1c. on 1d. black and green 10 10
60 – 2c. on 2d. blue and orange 10 10
61 – 2½c. on 3d. green and red 10 10
62 – 3½c. on 4½d. indigo and blue 10 10
63 – 5c. on 6d. brown and green 10 10
64 – 10c. on 1s. green and purple 10 10
65 – 12½c. on 1s.3d. brown and turquoise 1·75 30
66 – 25c. on 2s.6d. blue and red 30 30
67a – 50c. on 5s. black and red 1·00 1·60
68b **9** 1r. on 10s. black and purple 9·50 11·00

1961. As 1954 but value in new currency as in T **26**.
69 **8** ½c. black and brown 10 20
70 – 1c. black and green (as 1d.) 10 40
71 – 2c. blue and orange (as 2d.) 50 1·40
86 **26** 2½c. green and red 15 15
73 – 3½c. indigo and blue (as 4½d.) 30 1·50
88 – 5c. brown and green (as 6d.) 30 40
75 – 10c. green and purple (as 1s.) 30 40
90 – 12½c. brown & grn (as 1s.3d.) 2·75 1·50
77 – 25c. blue and red (as 2s.6d.) 6·50 6·50
92 – 50c. black and red (as 5s.) 7·25 10·00
79 **9** 1r. black and purple 27·00 13·00

1963. Freedom from Hunger. As T **28** of Aden.
80 12½c. violet 40 15

1963. Centenary of Red Cross. As T **33** of Antigua.
81 2½c. red and black 20 10
82 12½c. red and blue 80 60

28 Mosotho Woman and Child

1965. New Constitution. Inscr "SELF GOVERNMENT 1965". Multicoloured.
94 2½c. Type **28** 20 10
95 3½c. Maseru border post 25 20
96 5c. Mountain scene 25 20
97 12½c. Legislative Buildings 45 70

1965. Centenary of I.T.U. As T **36** of Antigua.
98 1c. red and purple 15 10
99 20c. blue and brown 35 30

1965. I.C.Y. As T **37** of Antigua.
100 ½c. purple and turquoise 10 10
101 12½c. green and lavender 45 35

1966. Churchill Commemoration. As T **38** of Antigua.
102 1c. blue 15 30
103 2½c. green 35 10
104 10c. brown 45 30
105 22½c. violet 70 60

OFFICIAL STAMPS

1934. Nos. 1/3 and 6 optd **OFFICIAL**.
O1 **1** ½d. green £3500 £3500
O2 1d. red £1500 £1000
O3 2d. purple £900 £550
O4 6d. yellow £10000 £4750

POSTAGE DUE STAMPS

1933. As Type D **1** of Barbados.
D1b 1d. red 1·00 2·25
D2a 2d. violet 30 11·00

D **2**

1956.
D3 D **2** 1d. red 30 3·00
D4 2d. violet 30 5·00

1961. Surch.
D5 D **2** 1c. on 1d. red 10 35
D6 1c. on 2d. violet 10 35
D7 5c. on 2d. violet 15 45
D8 – 5c. on 2d. violet (No. D2a) 1·00 6·50

1964. As Type D **2**, but value in decimal currency.
D 9 1c. red 2·50 14·00
D10 5c. violet 2·50 14·00

For later issues see **LESOTHO**.

BATUM Pt. 1

Batum, a Russian port on the Black Sea, had been taken by Turkish troops during the First World War. Following the Armistice, British Forces occupied the town on 1 December 1918. Batum was handed over to the National Republic of Georgia on 7 July 1920.

100 kopeks = 1 rouble.

1 Aloe Tree

БАТУМ. ОБ.

Руб 10 Руб

(2)

1919. Imperf.
1 **1** 5k. green 6·50 12·00
2 10k. blue 6·50 12·00
3 50k. yellow 2·50 3·50
4 1r. brown 3·75 4·00
5 3r. violet 9·50 15·00
6 5r. brown 10·00 20·00

1919. Arms types of Russia surch as T **2**. Imperf (Nos. 7/8), perf (Nos. 9/10).
7 10r. on 1k. orange 45·00 55·00
8 10r. on 3k. red 19·00 24·00
9 10r. on 5k. purple £350 £350
10 10r. on 10 on 7k. blue £300 £300

1919. T **1** optd **BRITISH OCCUPATION**.
11 **1** 5k. green 12·00 12·00
12 10k. blue 12·00 12·00
13 25k. yellow 12·00 12·00
14 1r. blue 3·75 9·50
15 2r. pink 1·00 3·50
16 3r. violet 1·00 3·50
17 5r. brown 1·25 3·00
18 7r. red 4·25 6·50

1919. Arms types of Russia surch with Russian inscr, **BRITISH OCCUPATION** and new value.
19 10r. on 3k. red 15·00 19·00
20a 15r. on 1k. orange 40·00 45·00
29 25r. on 5k. purple 38·00 40·00
30a 25r. on 10 on 7k. blue 60·00 65·00
31a 25r. on 20 on 14k. red and blue 60·00 65·00
32a 25r. on 25k. purple and green 85·00 90·00
33 25r. on 50k. green and purple 60·00 65·00
21 50r. on 1k. orange £350 £400
34 50r. on 2k. green 90·00 95·00
35 50r. on 3k. red 90·00 95·00
36 50r. on 4k. red 80·00 85·00
37 50r. on 5k. purple 60·00 65·00
27 50r. on 10k. blue £1100 £1200
28 50r. on 15k. blue and brown £450 £550

1920. Romanov type of Russia surch with Russian inscr, **BRITISH OCCUPATION** and new value.
41 50r. on 4k. red 48·00 60·00

1920. Nos. 11, 13 and 3 surch with new value (50r. with **BRITISH OCCUPATION** also).
42 **1** 25r. on 5k. green 27·00 29·00
43 25r. on 25k. yellow 22·00 23·00
44a 50r. on 50k. yellow 13·00 14·00

1920. T **1** optd **BRITISH OCCUPATION**.
45 **1** 1r. brown 80 7·00
46 2r. blue 80 7·00
47 3r. pink 1·00 7·00
48 5r. black 80 7·00
49 7r. yellow 80 7·00
50 10r. green 70 7·00
51 15r. violet 1·25 8·50
52 25r. red 90 8·50
53 50r. blue 1·25 11·00

BAVARIA Pt. 7

In S. Germany. A kingdom till 1918, then a republic. Incorporated into Germany in 1920.

1849. 60 kreuzer = 1 gulden.
1874. 100 pfennig = 1 mark.

1

2 (Circle cut)

1849. Imperf.
1 **1** 1k. black £650 £1600

1849. Imperf. Circle cut by labels.
3 **2** 3k. blue 38·00 2·75
23 3k. red 38·00 4·50
7 6k. brown £5500 £170

1850. Imperf. As T **2**, but circle not cut.
8a **2** 1k. red 70·00 16·00
21 1k. yellow 50·00 17·00
11 6k. brown 40·00 2·25
25 6k. blue 50·00 7·00
16 9k. green 50·00 11·50
28 9k. brown 90·00 11·50
18 12k. red £100 £120
31 12k. green 75·00 50·00
19 18k. yellow £100 £180
32 18k. red £120 £375

3 **6** **8**

1867. Imperf.
34 **3** 1k. green 50·00 8·40
37 3k. red 1·75 46
39 6k. blue 35·00 17·00
41 6k. brown 65·00 38·00
43 7k. blue £325 9·00
46 9k. brown 40·00 27·00
48 12k. mauve £300 80·00
50 18k. red £110 £150
65 **6** 1m. mauve £550 65·00

1870. Perf.
51A **3** 1k. green 10·00 1·25
69 3k. red 70 3·50
55A 6k. brown 26·00 25·00
56A 7k. blue 2·40 2·10
59A 9k. brown 4·00 3·25
60A 10k. yellow 4·50 10·00
61A 12k. mauve £300 £950
63A 18k. red 8·00 10·00

1876. Perf.
120 **8** 2pf. grey 1·25 40
103 3pf. green 8·25 1·75
121 3pf. brown 15 20
122 5pf. green 15 20
107 5pf. mauve 14·50 1·25
123 10pf. red 30 20
124 20pf. blue 30 20
114 25pf. brown 25·00 5·25
125 25pf. orange 20 40
126 30pf. olive 35 60
127 40pf. yellow 35 70
86 50pf. red 40·00 4·50
117 50pf. brown 50·00 3·25
128 50pf. purple 25 85
129 80pf. mauve 1·75 2·75
100 **6** 1m. mauve 2·00 70
101a 2m. orange 3·00 3·75
136 3m. brown 6·75 28·00
137 5m. green 6·75 28·00

11

13 Prince Luitpold

1911. Prince Regent Luitpold's 90th Birthday.
138c **11** 3pf. brown on drab 20 20
139c 5pf. green on green 20 20
140d 10pf. red on buff 20 20
141b 20pf. blue on blue 1·75 40
142a 25pf. deep brown on buff 2·40 1·25
143a – 30pf. orange on buff 1·40 75
144a – 40pf. olive on buff 2·40 70
145a – 50pf. red on drab 2·25 1·40
146 – 60pf. green on buff 2·25 1·40
147a – 80pf. violet on drab 7·75 4·00
148a **13** 1m. brown on drab 2·25 1·00
149a 2m. green on green 2·25 6·00
150a 3m. red on buff 12·00 17·00
151 5m. blue on buff 17·00 22·00
152 10m. orange on yellow 27·00 40·00
153 20m. brown on yellow 17·00 19·00
The 30 pf. to 80 pf. values are similar to Type **11**, but larger.

14

1911. 25th Anniv of Regency of Prince Luitpold.
154 **14** 5pf. yellow, green & black 50 70
155 10pf. yellow, red & black 65 1·40

15 King Ludwig III

16

1914. Imperf or perf.
171A **15** 2pf. slate 15 70
172A 2½ on 2pf. slate 15 70
173A 3pf. brown 15 65
175A 5pf. green 15 65
176A 7½pf. green 15 70
178A 10pf. red 20 65
179A 15pf. red 20 65
181A 20pf. blue 20 90
183A 25pf. grey 30 70
184A 30pf. orange 30 70
185A 40pf. olive 30 70
186A 50pf. brown 25 70
187A 60pf. green 2·00 70
188A 80pf. violet 20 90
189A **16** 1m. brown 30 90
190A 2m. violet 40 1·60
191A 3m. red 55 3·75
192A – 5m. blue 80 7·00
193A – 10m. green 2·75 38·00
194A – 20m. brown 5·25 48·00
The 5, 10 and 20m. are larger.

1919. Peoples' State Issue. Overprinted **Volksstaat Bayern**. Imperf or perf.
195A **15** 3pf. brown 20 65
196A 5pf. green 25 65
197A 7½pf. green 25 65
198A 10pf. lake 25 65
199A 15pf. red 25 65
200A 20pf. blue 25 65

201A		25pf. grey	25	65
202A		30pf. orange	25	65
203A		35pf. orange	25	1·40
204A		40pf. olive	25	75
205A		50pf. brown	25	75
206A		60pf. turquoise	25	1·00
207A		75pf. brown	25	85
208A		80pf. violet	25	70
209A	16	1m. brown	25	90
210A		2m. violet	45	1·40
211A		3m. red	65	4·00
212A	–	5m. blue (No. 192)	1·40	10·50
213A	–	10m. green (No. 193)	1·75	21·00
214A	–	20m. brown (No. 194)	2·75	28·00

1919. 1st Free State Issue. Stamps of Germany (inscr "DEUTSCHES REICH") optd **Freistaat Bayern**.

215	24	2½pf. grey	30	55
216	10	3pf. brown	30	55
217		5pf. green	30	55
218	24	7½pf. orange	30	55
219	10	10pf. red	30	90
220	24	15pf. violet	30	70
221	10	20pf. blue	30	55
222		25pf. black & red on yell	30	1·25
223	24	35pf. brown	30	1·40
224	10	40pf. black and red	30	1·40
225		75pf. black and green	70	2·10
226		80pf. black & red on rose	70	2·50
227	12	1m. red	85	4·75
228	13	2m. blue	2·00	7·00
229	14	3m. black	2·00	11·00
230	15	5m. red and black	1·75	11·00

1919. 2nd Free State Issue. Stamps of Bavaria overprinted **Freistaat Bayern**. Imperf or perf.

231A	15	3pf. brown	15	1·10
232A		5pf. green	15	60
233A		7½pf. green	15	12·00
234A		10pf. lake	15	60
235A		15pf. red	15	60
236A		20pf. blue	15	60
237A		25pf. grey	15	1·10
238A		30pf. orange	15	2·00
239A		40pf. olive	15	11·50
240A		50pf. brown	15	1·40
241A		60pf. turquoise	30	11·50
242A		75pf. brown	55	11·50
243A		80pf. violet	30	2·75
244A	16	1m. brown	30	2·10
245A		2m. violet	40	4·25
246A		3m. red	55	6·00
247A	–	5m. blue (No. 192)	70	15·00
248A	–	10m. green (No. 193)	70	27·00
249A	–	20m. brown (No. 194)	3·00	55·00

1919. War Wounded. Surch **5 Pf. fur Kriegsbeschadigte Freistaat Bayern**. Perf.

250	15	10pf.+5pf. lake	45	1·90
251		15pf.+5pf. red	45	2·00
252		20pf.+5pf. blue	45	2·50

1920. Surch **Freistaat Bayern** and value. Imperf or perf.

253A	16	1m.25pf. on 1m. green	25	90
254A		1m.50pf. on 1m. orange	35	2·40
255A		2m.50pf. on 1m. slate	50	3·50

1920. No. 121 surch **20** in four corners.

256	8	20 on 3pf. brown	15	1·10

26

27

28

29 30

1920.

257	26	5pf. green	15	55
258		10pf. orange	15	55
259		15pf. red	15	55
260	27	20pf. violet	15	55
261		30pf. blue	15	1·50
262		40pf. brown	15	1·50
263	28	50pf. red	15	1·60
264		60pf. turquoise	15	1·90
265		75pf. red	15	2·40
266	29	1m. red and grey	55	2·40
267		1¼m. blue and brown	35	2·40
268		1½m. green and grey	35	2·75
269		2½m. black and grey	45	15·00
270	30	3m. blue	80	12·00
271		5m. orange	95	13·50
272		10m. green	1·75	18·00
273		20m. black	2·00	28·00

OFFICIAL STAMPS

O 18

1916.

O195	O 18	3pf. brown	15	35
O196		5pf. green	15	35
O197		7½pf. green on green	20	50
O198		7½pf. green	15·00	15
O199		10pf. red	15	15
O200		15pf. red on buff	15	15
O201		15pf. red	45	1·60
O202		20pf. blue on blue	1·10	2·00
O203		20pf. blue	40	15
O204		25pf. grey	50	15
O205		30pf. orange	15	15
O206		60pf. turquoise	45	50
O207		1m. purple on buff	1·25	2·00
O208		1m. purple	4·25	£450

1919. Optd **Volksstaat Bayern**.

O215	O 18	3pf. brown	20	5·25
O216		5pf. green	20	70
O217		7½pf. green	20	65
O218		10pf. red	20	65
O219		15pf. red	25	60
O220		20pf. blue	20	65
O221		25pf. grey	20	85
O222		30pf. orange	20	85
O223		35pf. orange	20	85
O224		50pf. olive	20	85
O225		60pf. turquoise	20	2·75
O226		75pf. brown	25	1·75
O227		1m. purple on buff	70	70
O228		1m. purple	3·00	£350

O 31 O 32 O 33

1920.

O274	O 31	5pf. green	15	2·50
O275		10pf. orange	15	2·50
O276		15pf. red	15	2·50
O277		20pf. violet	15	2·50
O278		30pf. blue	15	8·00
O279		40pf. brown	15	8·00
O280	O 32	50pf. red	15	20·00
O281		60pf. green	15	10·00
O282		70pf. lilac	15	23·00
O283		75pf. red	15	27·00
O284		80pf. blue	15	27·00
O285		90pf. olive	15	45·00
O286	O 33	1m. brown	15	35·00
O287		1¼m. green	15	50·00
O288		1½m. red	15	50·00
O289		2½m. blue	15	55·00
O290		3m. lake	55	80·00
O291		5m. green	4·75	90·00

POSTAGE DUE STAMPS

D 6

1862. Inscr "Bayer. Posttaxe" at top. Imperf.

D34	D 6	3k. black	£110	£325

1870. As Type D 6, but inscr "Bayr. Posttaxe" at top. Perf.

D65B	D 6	1k. black	10·50	£650
D66B		3k. black	10·50	£400

1876. Optd **Vom Empfanger zahlbar.**

D130a	8	2pf. grey	60	2·00
D131a		3pf. grey	40	1·40
D132a		5pf. grey	85	3·25
D133a		10pf. grey	55	70

1895. No. D131a surch **2** in each corner.

D134	8	2 on 3pf. grey	†	£40000

RAILWAY OFFICIALS' STAMPS

1908. Stamps of 1876 optd **E**.

R133	8	3pf. brown	1·75	3·50
R134		5pf. green	40	30
R135		10pf. red	40	15
R136		20pf. blue	70	70
R137		50pf. purple	7·75	7·00

BECHUANALAND Pt. 1

A colony and protectorate in Central S. Africa. British Bechuanaland (colony) was annexed to Cape of Good Hope in 1895. Internal Self-Government in the protectorate was introduced on 1 March 1965. Attained independence on 30 September 1966, when the country was renamed Botswana.

1885. 12 pence = 1 shilling;
20 shillings = 1 pound.
1961. 100 cents = 1 rand.

A. BRITISH BECHUANALAND

1885. Stamps of Cape of Good Hope ("Hope" seated) optd **British Bechuanaland**.

4	6	½d. black	7·00	11·00
38		1d. red	2·25	2·25
32		2d. bistre	3·25	2·25
2		3d. red	35·00	42·00
3		4d. blue	55·00	65·00
7		6d. purple	95·00	38·00
8		1s. green	£250	£150

1887. Stamp of Great Britain (Queen Victoria) optd **BRITISH BECHUANALAND**.

9	71	½d. red	1·25	1·25

3

4

1887.

10	3	1d. lilac and black	15·00	1·75
11a		2d. lilac and black	45·00	23·00
12		3d. lilac and black	3·50	5·50
13		4d. lilac and black	42·00	2·25
14		6d. lilac and black	55·00	2·50
15	4	1s. green and black	29·00	5·50
16		2s. green and black	50·00	35·00
17		2s.6d. green and black	60·00	60·00
18		5s. green and black	85·00	£150
19		10s. green and black	£170	£350
20	–	£1 lilac and black	£800	£700
21	–	£5 lilac and black	£2750	£1500

Nos. 20/1 are as Type **4** but larger, 23 × 39½ mm.

1888. Surch.

22	3	"1d." on 1d. lilac and black	7·50	6·50
23		"2d." on 2d. lilac and black	22·00	3·00
25		"4d." on 4d. lilac and black	£225	£325
26		"6d." on 6d. lilac and black	95·00	10·00
28	4	"1s." on 1s. green and black	£140	80·00

1888. Surch **ONE HALF PENNY** and bars.

29	3	½d. on 3d. lilac and black	£140	£150

1891. Stamps of Great Britain (Queen Victoria) optd **BRITISH BECHUANALAND**.

33	57	1d. lilac	6·00	1·50
34	73	2d. green and red	9·00	4·00
35	76	4d. green and brown	2·50	50
36	79	6d. purple on red	3·25	2·00
37	82	1s. green	13·00	16·00

B. BECHUANALAND PROTECTORATE

1888. No. 9 to 19 optd **Protectorate** or surch also.

40	71	½d. red	3·50	26·00
41	3	1d. on 1d. lilac and black	8·00	14·00
42		2d. on 2d. lilac and black	24·00	17·00
43		3d. on 3d. lilac and black	£130	£180
51		4d. on 4d. lilac and black	75·00	32·00
45		6d. on 6d. lilac and black	70·00	40·00
46	4	1s. green and black	80·00	50·00
47		2s. green and black	£600	£900
48		2s.6s. green and black	£500	£750
49		5s. green and black	£1200	£2000
50		10s. green and black	£3500	£5500

1889. Stamp of Cape of Good Hope ("Hope" seated) optd **Bechuanaland Protectorate**.

52	6	½d. black	2·75	38·00

1889. No. 9 surch **Protectorate Fourpence**.

53	71	4d. on ½d. red	20·00	3·50

1897. Stamp of Cape of Good Hope ("Hope" seated) optd **BRITISH BECHUANALAND**.

56	6	½d. green	2·50	9·50

1897. Queen Victoria stamps of Great Britain optd **BECHUANALAND PROTECTORATE**.

59	71	½d. red	1·00	2·25
60		½d. green	1·40	3·50
61	57	1d. lilac	4·00	75
62	73	2d. green and red	3·25	3·50
63	75	3d. purple on yellow	5·50	8·50
64	76	4d. green and brown	15·00	12·00
65	79	6d. purple on red	23·00	11·00

1904. King Edward VII stamps of Great Britain optd **BECHUANALAND PROTECTORATE**.

66	83	½d. turquoise	2·00	2·00
68		1d. red	7·50	30
69		2½d. blue	7·50	5·00
70	–	1s. green and red (No. 314)	35·00	£130

1912. King George V stamps of Great Britain optd **BECHUANALAND PROTECTORATE**.

73	105	½d. green	1·25	1·75
72	102	1d. red	2·00	60
92	104	1d. red	2·00	70
75	105	1½d. brown	2·75	3·00
93	106	2d. orange	1·75	1·00
78	104	2½d. blue	3·50	20·00
79	106	3d. violet	6·00	12·00
80		4d. grey	6·50	18·00
81	107	6d. purple	7·00	16·00
82	108	1s. brown	9·50	20·00
88	109	2s.6d. brown	85·00	£160
89		5s. red	£110	£275

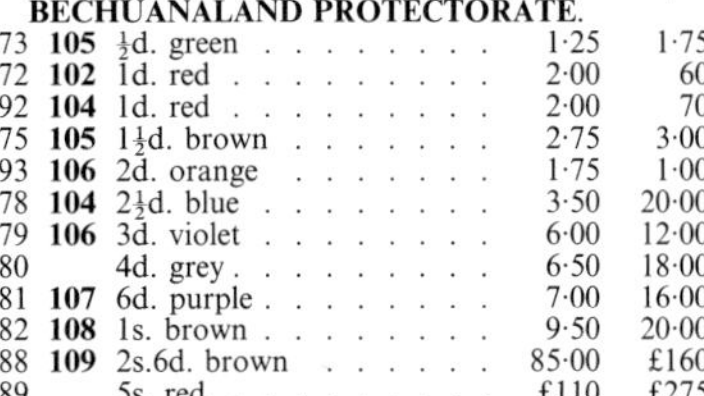

22 King George V, Baobab Tree and Cattle drinking

1932.

99	22	½d. green	1·00	30
100		1d. red	1·00	25
101		2d. brown	1·00	30
102		3d. blue	1·00	2·00
103		4d. orange	1·25	5·50
104		6d. purple	2·50	3·50
105		1s. black and olive	3·00	7·00
106		2s. black and orange	24·00	42·00
107		2s.6d. black and red	19·00	30·00
108		3s. black and purple	35·00	42·00
109		5s. black and blue	60·00	70·00
110		10s. black and brown	£120	£130

1935. Silver Jubilee. As T **13** of Antigua.

111		1d. blue and red	30	3·00
112		2d. blue and black	1·00	3·00
113		3d. brown and blue	2·50	3·00
114		6d. grey and purple	4·00	3·00

1937. Coronation. As T **2** of Aden.

115		1d. red	45	40
116		2d. brown	60	1·00
117		3d. blue	60	1·25

1938. As T **22**, but portrait of King George VI.

118		½d. green	2·00	2·25
119		1d. red	75	50
120a		1½d. blue	1·00	1·00
121		2d. brown	75	50
122		3d. blue	1·00	2·50
123		4d. orange	2·00	3·50
124a		6d. purple	4·00	2·50
125		1s. black and olive	4·00	4·75
126		2s.6d. black and red	14·00	14·00
127		5s. black and blue	30·00	17·00
128		10s. black and brown	14·00	21·00

1945. Victory. Stamps of South Africa optd **Bechuanaland**. Alternate stamps inscr in English or Afrikaans.

129	55	1d. brown and red	50	55
130		2d. blue and violet (No. 109)	50	1·00
131		3d. blue (No. 110)	50	1·00

Prices for bi-lingual pairs.

1947. Royal Visit. As Nos. 32/5 of Basutoland.

132		1d. red	10	10
133		2d. green	10	10
134		3d. blue	10	10
135		1s. mauve	10	10

1948. Silver Wedding. As T **10/11** of Aden.

136		1½d. blue	30	10
137		10s. grey	27·00	35·00

1949. U.P.U. As T **20/23** of Antigua.

138		1½d. blue	30	1·00
139		3d. blue	1·00	2·25
140		6d. mauve	45	1·25
141		1s. olive	45	1·25

1953. Coronation. As T **13** of Aden.

142		2d. black and brown	30	30

1955. As T **22** but portrait of Queen Elizabeth II, facing right.

143		½d. green	50	30
144		1d. red	80	10
145		2d. brown	1·25	30
146		3d. blue	3·00	70
146b		4d. orange	6·50	7·00
147		4½d. blue	1·50	35
148		6d. purple	1·25	60
149		1s. black and olive	1·25	80
150		1s.3d. black and lilac	14·00	9·50
151		2s.6d. black and red	10·00	9·50
152		5s. black and blue	15·00	6·50
153		10s. black and brown	27·00	15·00

26 Queen Victoria, Queen Elizabeth II and Landscape

28 African Golden Oriole ("Golden Oriole")

1960. 75th Anniv of Protectorate.

154	26	1d. sepia and black	40	50
155		3d. mauve and black	40	30
156		6d. blue and black	40	50

1961. Stamps of 1955 surch.

157		1c. on 1d. red	30	10
158		2c. on 2d. brown	20	10
159		2½c. on 2d. brown	30	10
160		2½c. on 3d. blue	2·00	4·00
161d		3½c. on 4d. orange	20	60

162a 5c. on 6d. purple 20 10
163 10c. on 1s. black and olive 20 10
164 12½c. on 1s.3d. black and lilac 65 20
165 25c. on 2s.6d. black and red 2·00 50
166 50c. on 5s. black and blue 3·00 2·00
167b 1r. on 10s. black and brown 7·00 4·50

1961.
168 **28** 1c. multicoloured 1·50 40
169 – 2c. orange, black and olive 2·00 2·75
170 – 2½c. multicoloured 1·75 10
171 – 3½c. multicoloured 2·00 2·00
172 – 5c. multicoloured 3·25 1·00
173 – 7½c. multicoloured 2·00 2·25
174 – 10c. multicoloured 2·00 60
175 – 12½c. multicoloured 18·00 5·50
176 – 20c. brown and drab 1·00 1·25
177 – 25c. sepia and lemon 1·50 1·00
178 – 35c. blue and orange 1·00 2·25
179 – 50c. sepia and olive 1·00 2·25
180 – 1r. black and brown 3·00 2·50
181 – 2r. brown and turquoise 18·00 9·00
DESIGNS—VERT: 2c. Hoopoe ("African Hoopoe"); 2½c. Scarlet-chested sunbird; 3½c. Yellow-rumped bishop ("Cape Widow-bird"); 5c. Swallow-tailed bee eater; 7½c. African grey hornbill ("Grey Hornbill"); 10c. Red-headed weaver; 12½c. Brown-hooded kingfisher; 20c. Woman musician; 35c. Woman grinding maize; 1r. Lion; 2r. Police camel patrol. HORIZ: 25c. Baobab tree; 50c. Bechuana ox.

1963. Freedom from Hunger. As T **28** of Aden.
182 12½c. green 30 15

1963. Centenary of Red Cross. As T **33** of Antigua.
183 2½c. red and black 20 10
184 12½c. red and blue 40 50

1964. 400th Birth Anniv of Shakespeare. As T **34** of Antigua.
185 12½c. brown 15 15

C. BECHUANALAND

42 Map and Gaberones Dam

1965. New Constitution.
186 **42** 2½c. red and gold 10 10
187 5c. blue and gold 15 40
188 12½c. brown and gold 20 40
189 25c. green and gold 20 55

1965. Centenary of I.T.U. As T **36** of Antigua.
190 2½c. red and yellow 20 10
191 12½c. mauve and brown 45 30

1965. I.C.Y. As T **37** of Antigua.
192 1c. purple and turquoise 10 10
193 12½c. green and lavender 60 55

1966. Churchill Commemoration. As T **38** of Antigua.
194 1c. blue 15 30
195 2½c. green 35 10
196 12½c. brown 70 30
197 20c. violet 75 50

43 Haslar Smoke Generator

1966. Bechuanaland Royal Pioneer Corps.
198 **43** 2½c. blue, red and green 25 10
199 – 5c. brown and blue 25 20
200 – 15c. blue, red and green 30 25
201 – 35c. multicoloured 30 80
DESIGNS: 5c. Bugler; 15c. Gun-site; 35c. Regimental cap badge.

POSTAGE DUE STAMPS

1926. Postage Due stamps of Great Britain optd **BECHUANALAND PROTECTORATE.**
D1 **D 1** ½d. green 4·50 70·00
D2 1d. red 4·50 50·00
D3 2d. black 6·00 85·00

D 3

1932.
D4 **D 3** ½d. green 6·00 40·00
D5a 1d. red 1·00 16·00
D6b 2d. violet 1·50 20·00

1961. Surch.
D7 **D 3** 1c. on 1d. red 25 50
D8 2c. on 2d. violet 25 1·50
D9 5c. on ½d. green 20 60

1961. As Type D 3 but value in decimal currency.
D10 1c. red 15 1·75
D11 2c. violet 15 1·75
D12 5c. green 30 2·00

For later issues see **BOTSWANA**.

BELARUS Pt. 10

Formerly a constituent republic of the Soviet Union, Belarus became independent in 1991.

100 kopeks = 1 rouble.

1 12th-century Cross

1992.
1 **1** 1r. multicoloured 15 15

2 Shyrma **3** Arms of Polotsk

1992. Birth Cent of R. R. Shyrma (composer).
2 **2** 20k. lt blue, blue and black 15 15

1992.
3 **3** 2r. multicoloured 15 15
See also Nos. 63 and 89/90.

4 Flag and Map (5)

1992.
4 **4** 5r. multicoloured 15 15
5 – 5r. black, yellow and red 15 15
DESIGN: No. 5, State arms.

1992. Millenary of Orthodox Church in Belarus. No. 1 optd with T **5**.
6 **1** 1r. multicoloured 15 15

6 Kamen Tower **7** State Arms

1992. Ancient Buildings and Monuments. Mult.
8 2r. Type **6** 10 10
9 2r. Calvinist church, Zaslavl 10 10
10 2r. St. Euphrosyne's church, Polotsk 10 10
11 2r. St. Boris Gleb church, Grodno (horiz) 10 10
12 2r. Mir castle (horiz) 10 10
13 2r. Nesvizh castle (horiz) 10 10

1992.
14 **7** 30k. blue 10 10
15 45k. green 10 10
16 50k. green 10 10
17 1r. brown 10 10
18 2r. brown 10 10
19 3r. yellow 10 10
20 5r. blue 15 15
21 10r. red 15 15
22 15r. violet 20 20
23 25r. green 20 20
24 50r. mauve 25 25
25 100r. red 25 25
26 150r. purple 25 25
27 200r. green 10 10
28 300r. red 15 15
29 600r. mauve 20 25
30 1000r. red 25 25
31 3000r. blue 50 50

8 Jug and Bowl

1992. Pottery. Multicoloured.
40 1r. Type **8** 10 10
41 1r. Vases and jug on jug tree 10 10
42 1r. Flagon 10 10
43 1r. Jugs 10 10

9 Chickens

1993. Corn Dollies. Multicoloured.
44 5r. Type **9** 10 10
45 10r. Woman and gunman (vert) 15 15
46 15r. Woman (vert) 25 25
47 25r. Man and woman (vert) 50 50

10 Harezki **11** Emblem

1993. Birth Centenary of M. I. Harezki (author).
48 **10** 50r. purple 15 15

1993. World Belarussian Congress, Minsk.
49 **11** 50r. red, gold and black 60 60

12 "Man Over Vitebsk"

1993. Europa. Contemporary Art. Paintings by Marc Chagall. Multicoloured.
50 1500r. Type **12** 2·25 2·25
51 1500r. "Promenade" (vert) 2·25 2·25

XVII ЗІМОВЫЯ
АЛІМПІЙСКІЯ
ГУЛЬНІ
ЛІЛЕХАМЕР,
НАРВЕГІЯ, 1994

1500
(13)

ЧЭМПІЯНАТ СВЕТУ
ПА ФУТБОЛУ,
ЗША, 1994

1500
(14)

1993. Sports Events. Nos. 4/5 variously surch.
(a) Winter Olympic Games, Lillehammer, Norway (1994). Surch **Winter Pre-Olympic Games Lillehammer, Norway 1500** (in capitals on No. 44) or in Cyrillic as T **13**.
53 **4** 1500r. on 5r. mult (in Cyrillic) 2·50 2·50
54 1500r. on 5r. mult (in English) 2·50 2·50
55 – 1500r. on 5r. black, yellow and red (in Cyrillic) 2·50 2·50
56 – 1500r. on 5r. black, yellow and red (in English) 2·50 2·50

(b) World Cup Football Championship, U.S.A. (1994). Surch **WORLD CUP USA 94 1500** or in Cyrillic as T **14**.
58 **4** 1500r. on 5r. mult (in Cyrillic) 2·50 2·50
59 1500r. on 5r. mult (in English) 2·50 2·50
60 – 1500r. on 5r. black, yellow and red (in Cyrillic) 2·50 2·50
61 – 1500r. on 5r. black, yellow and red (in English) 2·50 2·50

1993. Town Arms. As T **3**. Multicoloured.
63 25r. Minsk 15 15

15 St. Stanislav's Church, Mogilev

1993.
64 **15** 150r. multicoloured 40 40

16 Kastus Kalinowski (leader)

1993. 130th Anniv of Peasants' Uprising.
65 **16** 50r. multicoloured 20 20

17 Princess Ragneda **18** Statue of Budny

1993. 10th-century Rulers of Polotsk. Mult.
66 75r. Type **17** 30 30
67 75r. Prince Ragvalod and map 30 30

1993. 400th Death Anniv of Simon Budny (poet).
68 **18** 100r. multicoloured 50 50

19 Golden Eagle

1994. Birds in the Red Book. Multicoloured.
69 20r. Type **19** 10 10
70 40r. Mute swan ("Cygnus olor") 20 20
71 40r. River kingfisher ("Alcedo atthis") 20 20

1994. Nos. 14/16 surch.
72 **7** 15r. on 30k. blue 10 10
73 25r. on 45k. green 10 10
74 50r. on 50k. green 15 15
See also Nos. 86/8.

21 Map and Rocket Launchers (Liberation of Russia)

1994. 50th Anniv of Liberation. Multicoloured.
75 500r. Type **21** 10 10
76 500r. Map and airplanes (Ukraine) 10 10
77 500r. Map, tank and soldiers (Byelorussia) 10 10

22 Yasev Drazdovich and "Persecution"

1994. Artists and Paintings. Multicoloured.
78 300r. Type **22** 10 10
79 300r. Pyotr Sergievich and "The Path through Life" . . 10 10
80 300r. Ferdinand Rushchyts and "The Land" 10 10

23 Figure Skating **26** "Belarus"

25 Church, Synkavichai (16th-century)

1994. Winter Olympic Games, Lillehammer, Norway. Multicoloured.
81 1000r. Type **23** 15 15
82 1000r. Biathlon 15 15
83 1000r. Cross-country skiing . . 15 15
84 1000r. Speed skating 15 15
85 1000r. Ice hockey 15 15

1994. Birds in the Red Book. As Nos. 69/71 but values changed. Multicoloured.
86 300r. As Type **19** 10 10
87 400r. As No. 70 . . . . 10 10
88 400r. As No. 71 . . . . 10 10

1994. Town Arms. As T **3**. Multicoloured.
89 700r. Grodno 15 15
90 700r. Vitebsk 15 15

1994. Religious Buildings. Multicoloured.
91 700r. Type **25** 15 15
92 700r. Sts. Peter and Paul's Cathedral, Gomel (19th-century) 15 15

1994. 150th Birth Anniv of Ilya Repin (painter). Multicoloured.
93 1000r. Type **26** 15 15
94 1000r. Repin Museum 15 15
Nos. 93/4 were issued together, se-tenant, forming a composite design.

27 Tomasz Wojshezki and Battle Scene

1995. Bicentenary (1994) of Polish Insurrection. Multicoloured.
95 600r. Type **27** 10 10
96 600r. Jakub Jasinski 10 10
97 1000r. Mikhail Aginski . . . 15 15
98 1000r. Tadeusz Kosciuszko . . 15 15

28 Memorial **29** Aleksandr Stepanovich Popov (radio pioneer)

1995. 50th Anniv of End of Second World War. Multicoloured.
99 180r. Type **28** 10 10
100 600r. Clouds and memorial 10 10

1995. Centenary of First Radio Transmission (by Guglielmo Marconi).
101 **29** 600r. multicoloured 10 10

30 Obelisk to the Fallen of the Red Army, Minsk **31** Cherski

1995.
102 **30** 180r. bistre and red . . . 10 10
103 200r. green and bistre . . . 10 10
104 280r. green and blue . . . 15 15
107 600r. purple and bistre . . 15 15

1995. 150th Birth Anniv of Ivan Cherski (explorer).
115 **31** 600r. multicoloured 15 15

32 Motal **33** Head of Beaver

1995. Traditional Costumes (1st series). Mult.
116 180r. Type **32** 10 10
117 600r. Vaukavysk-Kamyanets 10 10
118 1200r. Pukhavits 20 20
See also Nos. 188/190 and 256/8.

1995. The Eurasian Beaver. Multicoloured.
119 300r. Type **33** 10 10
120 450r. Beaver gnawing branch 10 10
121 450r. Beaver (horiz) 10 10
122 800r. Beaver swimming . . . 15 15

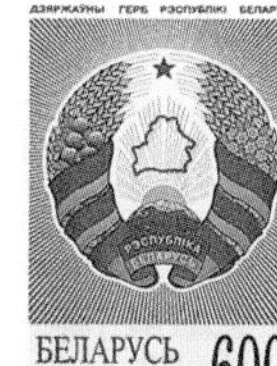

34 Writer and Script **35** Arms

1995. Writers' Day.
123 **34** 600r. multicoloured 15 15

1995. National Symbols. Multicoloured.
124 600r. Type **35** 15 15
125 600r. Flag over map and arms 15 15

36 Anniversary Emblem

1995. 50th Anniv of U.N.O.
126 **36** 600r. blue, black and gold 15 15

37 Mstislavl Church

1995. Churches. Multicoloured.
127 600r. Type **37** 15 15
128 600r. Kamai Church 15 15
See also Nos. 227/8.

1995
125 год
з дня нараджэння
(**38**)

1995. 125th Birth Anniv of Ferdinand Rushchyts (artist). No. 80 optd with T **38**.
129 300r. multicoloured 55 55

39 Sukhoi and Aircraft

1995. Birth Centenary of P. V. Sukhoi (aircraft designer).
130 **39** 600r. multicoloured 15 15

41 Leu Sapega (statesman)

1995. 17th-century Belarussians. Multicoloured.
132 600r. Type **41** 10 10
133 1200r. Kazimir Semyanovich (military scholar) 15 15
134 1800r. Simyaon Polatski (writer) 20 20

42 Lynx

1996. Mammals. Multicoloured.
135 1000r. Type **42** 10 10
136 2000r. Roe deer (vert) . . . 15 15
137 2000r. Brown bear 15 15
138 3000r. Elk (vert) 30 30
139 5000r. European bison . . . 55 55

1996. Nos. 17 and 23 optd with capital letter.
140 **7** B (200r.) on 1r. brown . . . 10 10
141 A (400r.) on 25r. green . . 10 10

44 Krapiva

1996. Birth Centenary of Kandrat Krapiva (writer).
142 **44** 1000r. multicoloured . . . 15 15

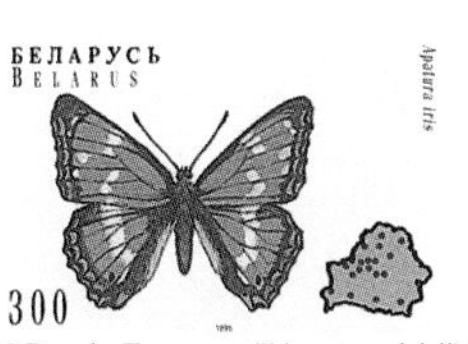

46 Purple Emperor ("Apatura iris")

1996. Butterflies and Moths. Multicoloured.
144 300r. Type **46** 45 45
145 300r. "Lopinga achine" . . . 45 45
146 300r. Scarlet tiger moth ("Callimorpha dominula") 45 45
147 300r. Clifden's nonpareil ("Catocala fraxini") . . . 45 45
148 300r. Swallowtail ("Papilio machaon") 45 45
149 300r. Apollo ("Parnassius apollo") 45 45
150 300r. "Ammobiota hebe" . . 45 45
151 300r. Palaeno sulphur yellow ("Colias palaeno") 45 45

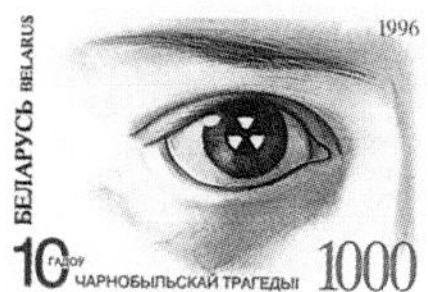

47 Radioactivity Symbol within Eye **48** State Arms

1996. 10th Anniv of Chernobyl Nuclear Disaster. Multicoloured.
153 1000r. Type **47** 15 15
154 1000r. Radioactivity symbol on diseased leaf 15 15
155 1000r. Radioactivity symbol on boarded-up window . . 15 15

1996. Arms and value in black, background colours given.
159 **48** 100r. blue 10 10
160 200r. grey 10 10
161 400r. brown 10 10
162 500r. green 10 10
163 600r. red 10 10
164 800r. blue 10 10
165 1000r. orange 10 10
166 1500r. mauve 10 10
167 1500r. blue 10 10
168 1800r. violet 10 10
169 2000r. green 10 10
170 2200r. mauve 10 10
171 2500r. blue 10 10
172 3000r. brown 15 15
173 3300r. yellow 15 15
174 5000r. blue 20 20
175 10000r. green 45 45
176 30000r. brown . . . . . . 1·25 1·25
177 50000r. purple . . . . . . 2·10 2·10

49 Russian and Belarussian Flags

1996. Russian–Belarussian Treaty.
182 **49** 1500r. multicoloured . . . 15 15

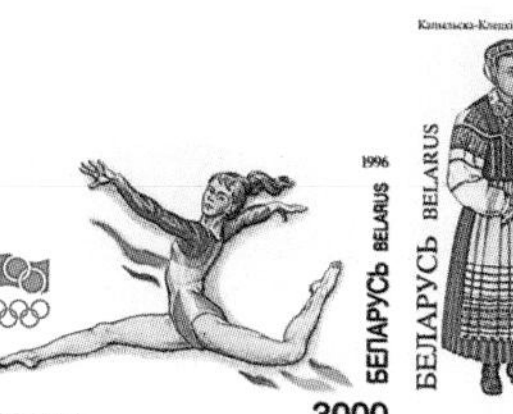

50 Gymnastics **51** Kapyl-Kletski

1996. Olympic Games, Atlanta. Multicoloured.
183 3000r. Type **50** 15 15
184 3000r. Throwing the discus 15 15
185 3000r. Weightlifting 15 15
186 3000r. Wrestling 15 15

1996. Traditional Costumes (2nd series). Mult.
188 1800r. Type **51** 10 10
189 2200r. David-Garadots Turau 10 10
190 3300r. Kobryn 15 15
See also Nos. 256/8.

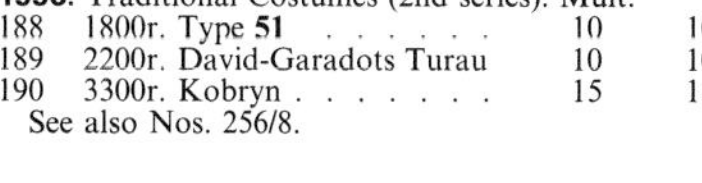

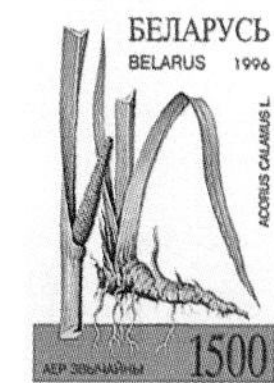

52 "Acorus calamus"

1996. Medicinal Plants. Multicoloured.
192 1500r. Type **52** 10 10
193 1500r. "Sanguisorba officinalis" 10 10
194 2200r. "Potentilla erecta" . . 10 10
195 3300r. "Frangula alnus" . . 15 15

53 Grey Heron ("Ardea cinerea")

1996. Birds. Multicoloured.
197 400r. Type **53** 25 25
198 400r. Black storks ("Ciconia nigra") 25 25
199 400r. Great cormorant ("Phalacrocorax carbo") 25 25
200 400r. White stork ("Ciconia ciconia") 25 25

201 400r. Black-headed gulls ("Larus ridibundus") . . . 25 25
202 400r. Common snipe ("Gallinago gallinago") . . 25 25
203 400r. White-winged black tern ("Chlidonias leucopterus") 25 25
204 400r. Penduline tit ("Remiz pendulinus") 25 25
205 400r. Eurasian bittern ("Botaurus stellaris") . . . 25 25
206 400r. Black coot ("Fulica atra") 25 25
207 400r. Little bittern ("Ixobrychus minutus") . . 25 25
208 400r. River kingfisher ("Alcedo atthis") 25 25
209 400r. Green-winged teals ("Anas crecca") 25 25
210 400r. Gadwalls ("Anas strepera") 25 25
211 400r. Northern pintails ("Anas acuta") 25 25
212 400r. Mallards ("Anas platyrhynchos") 25 25
213 400r. Greater scaups ("Aythya marila") 25 25
214 400r. Long-tailed duck ("Clangula hyemalis") . . 25 25
215 400r. Northern shovelers ("Anas clypeata") 25 25
216 400r. Garganeys ("Anas querquedula") 25 25
217 400r. European wigeon ("Anas penelope") 25 25
218 400r. Ferruginous ducks ("Aythya nyroca") 25 25
219 400r. Common goldeneyes ("Bucephala clangula") . . 25 25
220 400r. Goosander ("Mergus merganser") 25 25
221 400r. Smew ("Mergus albellus") 25 25
222 400r. Tufted duck ("Aythya fuligula") 25 25
223 400r. Red-breasted merganser ("Mergus serrator") . . . 25 25
224 400r. Common pochard ("Aythya ferina") 25 25

54 Title Page

55 Shchakatsikhin

1996. 400th Anniv of Publication of First Belarussian Grammar.
226 **54** 1500r. multicoloured . . . 10 10

1996. Churches. As T **37**. Multicoloured.
227 3300r. St. Nicholas's Church, Mogilev 10 10
228 3300r. Franciscan church, Pinsk 10 10

1996. Birth Centenary of Mikola Shchakatsikhin (artist).
229 **55** 2000r. multicoloured . . . 10 10

56 Old and New Telephones

1996. Cent of Telephone Service in Minsk.
230 **56** 2000r. multicoloured . . . 10 10

57 Lukashenka

1996. President Alyaksandr Rygoravich Lukashenka.
231 **57** 2500r. multicoloured . . . 10 10

58 Kiryla Turovski (12th-century Bishop of Turov)

59 Decorated Tree, Minsk

1996. Multicoloured.
232 3000r. Type **58** 15 15
233 3000r. Mikolaj Radziwill (16th-century Chancellor of Lithuania) 15 15
234 3000r. Mikola Gusovski (15th-16th century writer) 15 15

1996. New Year. Multicoloured.
235 1500r. Type **59** 10 10
236 2000r. Winter landscape (horiz) 10 10

60 "Paraskeva"

1996. Icons in National Museum, Minsk. Multicoloured.
237 3500r. Type **60** 15 15
238 3500r. "Illya" (17th-century) 15 15
239 3500r. "Three Holy Men" (Master of Sharashov) . . 15 15
240 3500r. "Madonna of Smolensk" 15 15

61 Zhukov

1997. Birth Cent of Marshal G. K. Zhukov.
242 **61** 2000r. black, gold and red 10 10

62 Theatre

1997. Kupala National Theatre, Minsk.
243 **62** 3500r. black and gold . . . 20 20

63 Byalnitsky-Birulya

1997. 125th Birth Anniv of W. K. Byalnitsky-Birulya (painter).
244 **63** 2000r. black and brown . . 10 10

(64)

1997. 105th Birth Anniv of R. R. Shyrma (composer). No. 2 surch with T **64**.
245 **2** 3500r. on 20k. light blue, blue and black 20 20

65 Salmon

1997. Fishes. Multicoloured.
246 2000r. Type **65** 10 10
247 3000r. Vimba 15 15
248 4500r. Barbel ("Barbus barbus") 20 20
249 4500r. European grayling ("Thymallus thymallus") 20 20

66 "SOS" on Globe

1997. International Conference on Developing Countries, Minsk. Multicoloured.
251 3000r. Type **66** 10 10
252 4500r. Protective hand over ecosystem 15 15

Nos. 251/2 were issued together, se-tenant, with intervening label showing the Conference emblem, the whole strip forming a composite design.

67 Emblem

69 Map, National Flag and Monument to the Fallen of Second World War, Minsk

1997. 50th Anniv of Belarussian Membership of Universal Postal Union.
253 **67** 3000r. multicoloured . . . 10 10

1997. No. 18 surch **100 1997**.
254 **7** 100r. on 2r. brown 10 10

1997. Independence Day.
255 **69** 3000r. multicoloured . . . 20 20

1997. Traditional Costumes (3rd series). As T **51**. Multicoloured.
256 2000r. Dzisensk 10 10
257 3000r. Navagrydsk 20 20
258 4500r. Bykhaisk 30 30

70 Page from Skorina Bible and Vilnius

1997. 480th Anniv of Printing in Belarus. Each red, black and grey.
259 3000r. Type **70** 20 20
260 3000r. Page from Skorina Bible and Prague 20 20
261 4000r. Franzisk Skorina and Polotsk 25 25
262 7500r. Skorina and Cracow 40 40

71 Jesuit College

1997. 900th Anniv of Pinsk.
263 **71** 3000r. multicoloured . . . 20 20

72 Books and Entrance

1997. 75th Anniv of National Library.
264 **72** 3000r. multicoloured . . . 20 20

73 Dark Glasses reflecting Hands reading Braille

1997. Cent of Schools for the Blind in Belarus.
265 **73** 3000r. multicoloured . . . 20 20

74 Child in Hand "Flower"

1997. World Children's Day.
266 **74** 3000r. multicoloured . . . 20 20

75 Red Ribbon and Crowd

1997. Red Ribbon AIDS Solidarity Campaign.
267 **75** 4000r. multicoloured . . . 20 20

76 Model 1221

1997. Belarussian Tractors. Multicoloured.
268 3300r. Type **76** 20 20
269 4400r. First Belarussian tractor, 1953 . . . . . . 25 25
270 7500r. Model 680 . . . . . 40 40
271 7500r. Model 952 . . . . . 40 40

(77)

1997. Restoration of Cross of St. Ephrosina of Polotsk. No. 1 surch with T **77**.
272 **1** 3000r. on 1r. multicoloured 20 20

78 St. Nicholas hang-gliding over Houses (New Year)

1997. Greetings Stamps. Multicoloured.
273 1400r. Type **78** 10 10
274 4400r. Procession of musicians (Christmas) . . . 25 25

79 Cross-country Skiing

1998. Winter Olympic Games, Nagano, Japan. Multicoloured.

No.	Type	Description		
275		2000r. Type **79**	15	15
276		3300r. Ice hockey	20	20
277		4400r. Biathlon	30	30
278		7500r. Freestyle skiing	55	55

80 Mashcherov

1998. 80th Birth Anniv of P. M. Mashcherov (writer).

No.	Type	Description		
279	**80**	2500r. multicoloured	15	15

81 MAZ-205 Lorry, 1947

1998. Tipper Trucks. Multicoloured.

No.	Type	Description		
280		1400r. Type **81**	10	10
281		2000r. MAZ-503, 1968	15	15
282		3000r. MAZ-5549, 1977	20	20
283		4400r. MAZ-5551, 1985	30	30
284		7500r. MAZ-5516, 1994	50	50

82 Entrance to Nyasvizh Castle

83 Mickiewicz

1998. Europa. National Festivals.

No.	Type	Description		
285	**82**	15000r. multicoloured	55	55

1998. Birth Bicentenary of Adam Mickiewicz (political writer).

No.	Type	Description		
286	**83**	8600r. multicoloured	35	35

(84)

85 Bluethroat

1998. 225th Anniv of Postal Service between Mogilov and St. Petersburg. No. 64 surch with T **84**.

No.	Type	Description		
287	**15**	8600r. on 150r. mult	35	35

1998. Birds. Multicoloured.

No.	Type	Description		
288		1500r. Type **85**	10	10
289		3200r. Penduline tit	15	15
290		3800r. Aquatic warbler	15	15
291		5300r. Savi's warbler	20	20
292		8600r. Azure tit	35	35

86 Watermill

87 Bulldozer Model 7821

1998.

No.	Type	Description		
293	**86**	100r. black and green	10	10
294	–	200r. black and brown	10	10
295	–	500r. black and blue	10	10
296	–	800r. black and violet	10	10
297	–	1000r. black and green	10	10
298	–	1000r. black and brown	10	10
299	–	2000r. black and blue	10	10
300	–	3000r. black and yellow	15	15
301	–	3200r. black and green	15	15
302	–	5000r. black and blue	25	25
303	–	5300r. black and yellow	25	25
304	–	10000r. black and orange	45	45
305	**86**	30000r. black and blue	40	40
306	–	50000r. black, orange and deep orange	60	60
308	–	100000r. black and mauve	1·40	1·40
309	–	500000r. black and brown	3·00	3·00

DESIGNS—VERT: 200, 50000r. Windmill; 500r. Stork; 800r. Cathedral of the Holy Trinity, Ishkold; 1000r. Bison; 1500, 3200r. Dulcimer; 2000r. Star; 3000, 5300r. Lute; 5000r. Church; 10000r. Flaming wheel; 500000r. Lyavoniha (folk dance). HORIZ: 100000r. Exhibition centre, Minsk.

1998. 50th Anniv of Belaz Truck Works. Mult.

No.	Type	Description		
310		1500r. Type **87**	10	10
311		3200r. Tipper Model 75131	15	15
312		3800r. Tipper Model 75303	15	15
313		5300r. Tipper Model 75483	20	20
314		8600r. Tipper Model 7555	35	35

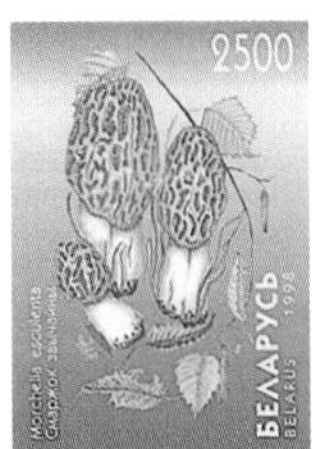

88 Common Morel

89 Lion's Head

1998. Fungi. Multicoloured.

No.	Type	Description		
315		2500r. Type **88**	10	10
316		3800r. "Morchella conica"	15	15
317		4600r. Shaggy parasol	20	20
318		5800r. Parasol mushroom	25	25
319		9400r. Shaggy ink cap	45	45

1998. Wood Sculptures. Multicoloured.

No.	Type	Description		
320		3400r. Type **89**	20	20
321		3800r. Archangel Michael	20	20
322		5800r. Prophet Zacharias	30	30
323		9400r. Madonna and Child	50	50

90 Emblem and Belarussian Stamps

1998. World Post Day.

No.	Type	Description		
324	**90**	5500r. multicoloured	30	30

91 "Kalozha" (V. K. Tsvirka)

1998. Paintings. Multicoloured.

No.	Type	Description		
325		3000r. Type **91**	20	20
326		3500r. "Hotel Lounge" (S. Yu. Zhukoiski)	20	20
327		5000r. "Winter Sleep" (V. K. Byalynitski-Birulya)	30	30
328		5500r. "Portrait of a Girl" (I. I. Alyashkevich) (vert)	30	30
329		10000r. "Portrait of an Unknown Woman" (I. F. Khrutski) (vert)	60	60

92 Anniversary Emblem

93 Girl, Rabbit and Fir Trees

1998. 50th Anniv of Universal Declaration of Human Rights.

No.	Type	Description		
330	**92**	7100r. multicoloured	35	35

1998. Christmas and New Year. Multicoloured.

No.	Type	Description		
331		5500r. Type **93**	30	30
332		5500r. Girl, rabbit and house	30	30

94 Pushkin and Adam Mickiewicz Monument, St. Petersburg (A. Anikeichyk)

1999. Birth Bicentenary of Aleksandr Pushkin (writer).

No.	Type	Description		
333	**94**	15300r. multicoloured	1·00	1·00

95 MAZ Model 8007 Truck and Excavator

1999. Minsk Truck and Military Works. Mult.

No.	Type	Description		
334		10000r. Type **95**	15	15
335		15000r. MAZ model 543M and Smerch rocket system	20	20
336		30000r. MAZ model 7907 crane	35	35
337		30000r. MAZ model 543M Rubezh missile launcher	35	35

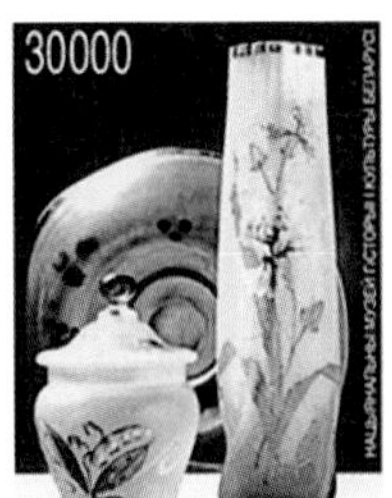

96 Dish, Jar and Vase

1999. Glasswork. Multicoloured.

No.	Type	Description		
339		30000r. Type **96**	40	40
340		30000r. Chalice	40	40
341		100000r. Oil lamp	1·40	1·40

(97)

1999. "iBRA '99" International Stamp Exhibition, Nuremberg. Nos. 69/71 surch with T **97**.

No.	Type	Description		
342		500000 on 20r. multicoloured (Type **19**)	10	10
343		500000 on 40r. multicoloured (No. 70)	35	35
344		500000 on 40r. multicoloured (No. 71)	35	35

98 Belavezhskaya Pushcha Reserve

1999. Europa. Parks and Gardens. Multicoloured.

No.	Type	Description		
345		150000r. Type **98**	55	55
346		150000r. Beaver in Byarezinski Reserve	55	55

99 Well

1999. Wooden Buildings. Multicoloured.

No.	Type	Description		
347		50000r. Type **99**	20	20
348		50000r. Public house	20	20
349		100000r. Windmill	40	40

100 "Portrait of Yu. M. Pen" (A. M. Brazer)

1999. Vitebsk Art School. Paintings. Multicoloured.

No.	Type	Description		
350		30000r. Type **100**	15	15
351		60000r. "St. Anthony's Church, Vitebsk" (S. B.Yudovin)	25	25
352		100000r. "Street in Vitebsk" (Yu. M. Pen)	30	30
353		100000r. "Kryvaya Street, Vitebsk" (M. P. Mikhalap) (horiz)	30	30

101 Karvat

1999. 3rd Death Anniv of Wing Commander Karvat.

No.	Type	Description		
355	**101**	25000r. multicoloured	10	10

102 Main Post Office, Minsk, 1954

1999. 125th Anniv of Universal Postal Union. Mult.

No.	Type	Description		
356		150000r. Type **102**	50	50
357		150000r. First post office in Minsk, 1800	50	50

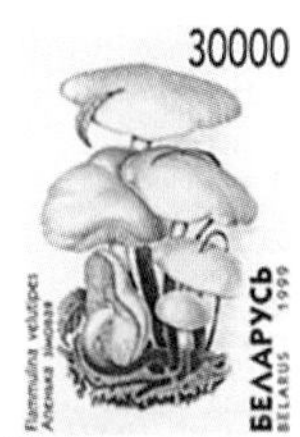

103 Golden Mushroom

1999. Fungi. Multicoloured.

No.	Type	Description		
358		30000r. Type **103**	10	10
359		50000r. Changeable agaric	15	15
360		75000r. *Lyophyllum connatum*	20	20
361		100000r. *Lyophyllum decastes*	30	30

104 East and West Belarussians Embracing

1999. 60th Anniv of Re-unification of Republic of Byelorussia.

No.	Type	Description		
363	**104**	29000r. multicoloured	10	10

105 MAZ MA3-6430, 1998

1999. Minsk Truck and Military Works. Lorries. Multicoloured.
364 51000r. Type **105** 15 15
365 86000r. Lorry Model MAZ MA3-4370 . . . . 30 30

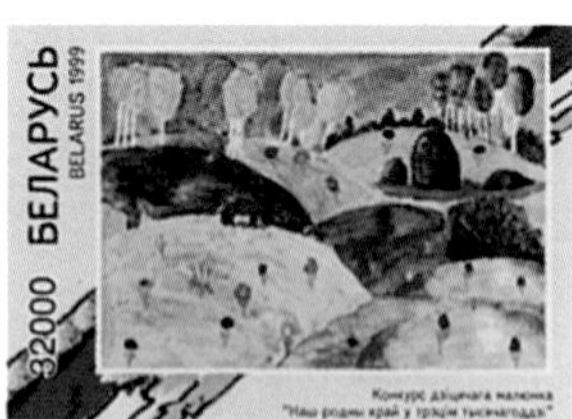
106 Landscape (Olya Smantser)

1999. Children's Painting Competition Winners. Mult.
366 32000r. Type **106** 10 10
367 59000r. Girl (Masha Dudarenko) (vert) 15 15

107 Teddybear in Snow (Mitya Kutas)

1999. Christmas and New Year. Children's Paintings. Multicoloured.
368 30000r. Type **107** 10 10
369 30000r. Children building snowman and ice-skating (Yulya Yakubovich) . . . 10 10

Currency Revaluation

108 Spasa-Praabrazhenskaya Church, Polatsk

110 Bison

2000. Birth Bimillenary of Jesus Christ. Mult.
370 50r. Type **108** 25 25
371 75r. St. Atsistratsiga Cathedral, Slutsk 40 40
372 100r. The Reverend Serafim Sarovskaga Church, Belaazersk 55 55

2000.
374 **110** 1r. black and green . . . 10 10
375 – 2r. black and blue 10 10
376 – 3r. black and yellow 10 10
377 – 5r. black and blue 10 10
378 – 10r. black and orange . . 10 10
380 – 20r. black and mauve . . 10 10
382 – 30r. black and green . . 15 15
383 – 50r. black and yellow . . 55 55
387 – 100r. black and mauve . . 1·00 1·10
DESIGNS—VERT: 2r. Star; 3r. Lyre; 5r. Synkovichy Church; 10r. Flaming wheel; 20r. Type **111**; 30r. Watermill; 50r. Windmill. HORIZ: 100r. Exhibition Centre.

111 Kryzhachok (folk dance)

112 Su-24 Bomber

2000. Self-adhesive.
391 **111** 20r. black and red 10 10

2000. 25th Death Anniv of Pavel Sukhoi (aircraft designer). Multicoloured.
392 50r. Type **112** 50 50
393 50r. Su-27 fighter 50 50
394 50r. Su-25 battle fighter . . . 50 50

113 Kupala Holiday

114 Stone-Curlew

2000.
396 **113** A black and blue 15 15
No. 396 was for Inland Letter Post rate.

2000. Birds in the Red Book. Multicoloured.
397 50r. Type **114** 25 25
398 50r. Smew (*Mergellus albellus*) 25 25
399 75r. Willow grouse 40 40
400 100r. Lesser spotted eagle (vert) 55 55

115 "The Partisan Madonna of Minsk" (M. Savitsky)

116 "Building Europe"

2000. 55th Anniv of End of Second World War.
401 **115** 100r. multicoloured . . . 55 55

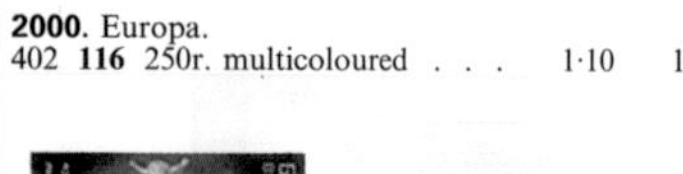

2000. Europa.
402 **116** 250r. multicoloured . . . 1·10 1·10

117 Scene from "Creation of the World"

118 Hands holding Lifebelt

2000. National Ballet Company.
403 **117** 100r. multicoloured . . . 55 55

2000. 50th Anniv of United Nations High Commission for Refugees.
405 **118** 50r. multicoloured 25 25

119 Head of Lynx

120 People wearing National Costumes

2000. Endangered Species. The Lynx. Multicoloured.
406 100r. Type **119** 55 55
407 100r. On branch 55 55
408 150r. Walking through woodland 80 80
409 150r. Adult and cub 80 80

2000. International Year of Culture.
410 **120** 100r. multicoloured . . . 55 55

121 Rings

2000. Olympic Games, Sydney. Multicoloured.
411 100r. Type **121** 55 55
412 100r. Kayaking 55 55
413 100r. Rhythmic gymnastics . . . 55 55

122 Amber

123 People around decorated Tree

2000. Minerals. Multicoloured.
415 200r. Type **122** . . . . . . 1·10 1·10
416 200r. Galit . . . . 1·10 1·10
417 200r. Flint . . . . 1·10 1·10
418 200r. Silvin . . . . 1·10 1·10

2000. New Year.
419 **123** 200r. multicoloured . . . 1·10 1·10

124 Nativity Scene

125 "Connection of Times" (Roman Zabello)

2000. Christmas.
420 **124** 100r. multicoloured . . . 55 55

2000. New Millennium. Children's Paintings. Multicoloured.
421 100r. Type **125** 55 55
422 100r. "Festival of Life" (Alena Emeliyanova) 55 55

BELGIAN CONGO Pt. 4

A Belgian colony in Central Africa. Became independent in July 1960. For later issues see Congo, Zaire, Democratic Republic of Congo, Katanga and South Kasai.

100 centimes = 1 franc.

INDEPENDENT STATE OF THE CONGO

The Independent State of the Congo was established in 1885, with King Leopold II of the Belgians as ruler.

1 Leopold II

5 Leopold II

1886. Various frames.
1 **1** 5c. green . . . . 8·25 14·50
2 10c. red . . . . 2·75 3·00
3 25c. blue . . . . 32·00 25·00
4 50c. green . . . . 5·50 6·50
5 5f. lilac £375 £190

1887. Surch **COLIS-POSTAUX Fr. 3.50.**
6 **1** 3f.50 on 5f. lilac £300 £600

1887.
7 **5** 5c. green 45 70
8 10c. red . . . . 1·00 85
9 25c. blue 90 90
10 50c. brown . . . . 40·00 14·50
11 50c. grey . . . . 2·25 11·50
12 5f. lilac £800 £300
13 5f. grey . . . . 90·00 75·00
14 10f. orange £350 £225

1887. Surch **COLIS-POSTAUX Fr. 3.50.**
15 **5** 3f.50 on 5f. violet £700 £400

1889. Surch **COLIS-POSTAUX Fr. 3.50** in frame.
16 **5** 3f.50 on 5f. violet £500 £275
17 3f.50 on 5f. grey . . . . . . £100 90·00

7 Port of Matadi

8 Stanley Falls

13 Oil Palms

14 Native Canoe

1894. Inscr "ETAT INDEPENDANT DU "CONGO".
18 **7** 5c. black and blue . . . . . 13·00 13·50
24 5c. black and brown . . . . 2·40 95
30 5c. black and green . . . . 1·25 35
19 **8** 10c. black and brown . . . 13·00 15·00
25 10c. black and blue . . . . 1·60 95
31 10c. black and red . . . . 2·40 50
26 **13** 15c. black and brown . . . 3·75 60
20 – 25c. black and orange . . . 3·25 1·90
32 – 25c. black and blue . . . 3·50 1·25
27 **14** 40c. black and green . . . . 4·75 2·10
21 – 50c. black and green . . . 1·75 1·00
33 – 50c. black and brown . . . 4·75 65
22 – 1f. black and violet . . . . 24·00 10·50
35 – 1f. black and red . . . . . £190 4·25
28 – 3f.50 black and red . . . . £120 70·00
23 – 5f. black and red . . . . . 38·00 19·00
29 – 10f. black and green . . . . £100 16·00
DESIGNS—HORIZ: 25c. Inkissi Falls; 50c. Railway Bridge over the M'pozo; 1f. African elephant hunt; 3f.50 Congo village; 10f. "Deliverance" (stern wheel paddle-steamer). VERT: 5f. Bangala Chief Morangi and wife.

BELGIAN CONGO

The Congo was annexed to Belgium in 1908 and was renamed the Belgian Congo.

1909. Nos. 23, 26/29 and 30/33 optd **CONGO BELGE.**
36A **7** 5c. black and green . . . 2·40 1·40
37A **8** 10c. black and red . . . . 3·00 1·40
38A **13** 15c. black and brown . . 5·00 2·50
49 – 25c. black and blue . . . 50 1·75
50 **14** 40c. black and green . . . 2·40 2·10
51 – 50c. black and brown . . 5·00 1·75
52 – 1f. black and red . . . . 24·00 3·50
53 – 3f.50 black and red . . . 24·00 14·50
54 – 5f. black and red . . . . 42·00 20·00
55b – 10f. black and green . . . 85·00 21·00

1909. As 1894 issue but inscr "CONGO BELGE".
56 **7** 5c. black and green 75 85
57 **8** 10c. black and red 60 65
58 **13** 15c. black and brown . . . 19·00 11·00
59 – 50c. black and bistre . . . . 3·25 2·75

1910. As 1894 issue but inscr "CONGO BELGE BELGISCH-CONGO" with values in French and Flemish.
60 **7** 5c. black and green 40 20
61 **8** 10c. black and red 50 15
62 **13** 15c. black and brown . . . 35 10
63 – 25c. black and blue . . . 1·40 25
64 **14** 40c. black and green . . . . 1·75 1·90
65 – 50c. black and bistre . . . . 3·00 1·60
66 – 1f. black and red . . . . . 4·50 2·10
68 – 3f. black and red . . . . . 21·00 12·50
67 – 5f. black and red . . . . . 20·00 19·00
69 – 10f. black and green . . . . 32·00 18·00

32 Port of Matadi

33 Stanley Falls

34 Inkissi Falls

1915. New types as **32** to **34** (with value in words at top) and other types as 1910 all inscr "CONGO BELGE" and "BELGISCH-CONGO".
70 **32** 5c. black and green 30 15
71 **33** 10c. black and red 45 35
72b **13** 15c. black and green . . . 55 35

73 **34** 25c. black and blue 1·00 25
74 **14** 40c. black and red 3·75 1·90
75 – 50c. black and red 7·00 1·50
76 – 1f. black and olive 2·75 65
77 – 5f. black and orange 1·90 1·00

1918. Types as before, surch with red cross and premium.
78 **32** 5c.+10c. blue and green 25 90
79 **33** 10c.+15c. blue and red 30 85
80 **13** 15c.+20c. blue and green 35 85
81 **34** 25c.+25c. blue 45 95
82 **14** 40c.+40c. blue and red 50 1·25
83 – 50c.+50c. blue and red 45 1·50
84 – 1f.+1f. blue and olive 2·25 2·50
85 – 5f.+5f. blue and orange 10·50 14·00
86 – 10f.+10f. blue and green 85·00 90·00

38 Congo Wharf

1920. Air.
87 **38** 50c. black and orange 40 10
88 – 1f. black and violet 40 10
89 – 2f. black and blue 65 35
90 – 5f. black and green 1·00 50
DESIGNS—HORIZ: 1f. District stores; 2f. Native canoes on beach. VERT: 5f. Provinicial prison.

1921. Stamps of 1910 surch.
91 **14** 5c. on 40c. black and green 30 95
92 – 10c. on 5c. black and green 30 35
93 – 15c. on 50c. black and olive 30 80
94 **13** 25c. on 15c. black & yellow 1·60 95
95 **8** 30c. on 10c. black and red 30 45
96 – 50c. on 25c. black and blue 1·50 55

1921. Stamps of 1910 optd **1921**.
97 1f. black and red 1·00 75
98 3f. black and red 2·50 2·50
99 5f. black and lake 7·00 7·50
100 10f. black and green 5·75 4·00

1922. Stamps of previous issues variously surch without bars.
101 – 5c. on 50c. black and lake (No. 75) 35 60
102 **32** 10c. on 5c. black and green (No. 70) 30 25
114 **8** 0.25 on 30c. on 10c. black and red (No. 95) 13·00 13·50
115 **33** 0.25 on 30c. on 10c. black and red (No. 104) 9·50 13·00
103 **14** 25c. on 40c. black and lake (No. 74) 2·00 30
104 **33** 30c. on 10c. black and red (No. 71) 25 30
105 **34** 50c. on 25c. black and blue (No. 73) 40 25

1922. Stamps of 1915 surch with new value and two bars through old values.
108 **32** 10c. on 5c. black & green 90 95
110 – 10c. on 1f. black & olive 1·00 1·40
112 **14** 25c. on 40c. black & lake 60 60
113 – 25c. on 5f. blk & orange 1·90 2·40

46 Wood Carver
56 Native Cattle

1923.
117 A 5c. yellow 15 10
118 B 10c. green 15 10
119 C 15c. brown 15 10
120 D 20c. olive 15 10
121 E 20c. green 15 10
122 F 25c. brown 15 10
123 **46** 30c. red 45 1·40
124 30c. olive 25 45
125 35c. green 3·00 1·90
126 D 40c. purple 20 10
142 **56** 45c. purple 45 25
127 G 50c. blue 25 30
128 50c. orange 35 10
143 **56** 60c. red 30 20
129 E 75c. orange 20 20
130 75c. blue 40 85
131 **46** 75c. red 60 15
132 H 1f. brown 30 20
133 1f. blue 30 10
134 1f. red 65 10
135 D 1f.25 blue 30 35
136 1f.50 blue 30 35
137 1f.75 blue 3·25 2·75
138 I 3f. brown 4·00 2·50
139 J 5f. grey 8·25 5·00
140 K 10f. black 20·00 9·00
DESIGNS: A, Ubangi woman; B, Baluba woman; C, Babuende woman; D, Ubangi man; E, Weaver; F, Basketmaker; G. Archer; H, Potter; I, Rubber worker; J, Palm oil; K, African elephant.

55 Native Canoe
58 H. M. Stanley

1925. Great War Colonial Memorial Fund. Inscr in French or in Flemish.
141a **55** 25c.+25c. black and red 45 2·25

1927. No. 136 surch **1.75**.
144 1.75 on 1f. 50 blue 45 35

1928. 50th Anniv of Stanley's Exploration of the Congo.
145 **58** 5c. olive 10 10
146 10c. violet 10 10
147 20c. red 10 10
148 35c. green 85 95
149 40c. brown 45 40
150 60c. sepia 45 20
151 1f. red 40 10
152 1f.60 grey 4·75 5·00
153 1f.75 blue 85 55
154 2f. brown 70 40
155 2f.75 purple 3·25 35
156 3f.50 red 1·10 55
157 5f. turquoise 65 45
158 10f. blue 85 45
159 20f. red 6·50 4·00

59 Nurse weighing Children
60 Doctor and Tent Surgery

1930. Congo Natives Protection Fund.
160 **59** 10c.+5c. red 60 1·50
161 – 20c.+10c. brown 80 1·90
162 **60** 35c.+15c. green 1·90 3·00
163 – 60c.+30c. purple 1·75 3·00
164 – 1f.+50c. red 3·50 4·50
165 – 1f.75+75c. blue 4·75 8·00
166 – 3f.50+1f.50 red 7·25 17·00
167 – 5f.+2f.50 brown 9·00 13·00
168 – 10f.+5f. black 11·00 18·00
DESIGNS—VERT: 20c. Missionary and child; 1f. Dispenser attending patients. HORIZ: 60c. View of local hospital; 1f.75, Nurses and patients; 3f.50, Nurse bathing baby; 5f. Operating theatre in local hospital; 10f. Children in school.

61 Native Kraal

1930. Air.
169 **61** 15f. black and sepia 4·25 1·75
170 – 30f. black and purple 5·75 3·75
DESIGN: 30f. Native porters.

1931. Surch.
171 40c. on 35c. grn (No. 148) 1·25 95
177 40c. on 35c. green (125) 3·50 8·00
178 50c. on 45c. purple (142) 1·90 1·25
172 1f.25 on 1f. red (151) 1·40 10
173 2f. on 1f.60 grey (152) 80 25
174 2f. on 1f.75 blue (153) 70 25
179 2f. on 1f.75 blue (137) 7·25 9·50
175 3f.25 on 2f.75 purple (155) 2·25 1·60
180 3f.25 on 3f. brown (138) 6·25 7·50
176 3f.25 on 3f.50 red (156) 4·25 6·00

67 Sankuru River
68 Flute Players

1931.
181 **67** 10c. brown 10 30
182 – 15c. grey 10 10
183 – 20c. mauve 15 35
184 – 25c. blue 35 10
185 **68** 40c. green 35 60
186 – 50c. violet 45 10
187 – 60c. purple 40 60
188 – 75c. red 40 15
189 – 1f. red 85 15
190 – 1f.25 brown 75 10
190b – 1f.50 black 1·00 65
191 – 2f. blue 1·00 30
191a – 2f.50 blue 1·25 1·00
192 – 3f.25 grey 1·25 1·25
193 – 4f. lilac 80 55
194 – 5f. purple 1·50 30
195 – 10f. orange 1·40 1·40
196 – 20f. sepia 2·40 2·10
DESIGNS—HORIZ: 15c., 25c. Native kraals (different views); 20c. Waterfall; 50c. Native musicians (seated); 1f.50, 2f., Riverside dwellings; 2f.50, 3f.25, Okapi; 4f. Canoes on river shore. VERT: 60c. Native musicians (standing); 75c. Mangbethu woman; 1f. Elephant transport; 1f.25., Native chief; 5f. Pressing out tapioca; 10f. Witch doctor; 20f. Woman carrying latex.

69 Fokker F.VIIb/3m over Congo
70 King Albert I

1934. Air
197 **69** 50c. black 60 65
198 1f. red 85 30
199 1f.50 green 70 15
200 3f. brown 30 20
201 4f.50 blue 90 10
202 5f. red 95 10
203 15f. purple 2·10 85
204 30f. red 2·50 2·40
205 50f. violet 7·00 2·25

1934. Death of King Albert.
206 **70** 1f.50 black 90 55

71 The Kings of Belgium

1935. 50th Anniv of Independent State of the Congo.
207 **71** 50c. green 1·10 1·10
208 1f.25 red 1·10 15
209 1f.50 purple 1·10 15
210 2f.40 orange 2·75 3·25
211 2f.50 blue 2·75 1·75
212 4f. violet 3·00 1·90
213 5f. brown 3·00 3·25

1936. Air. Surch **3.50F**.
214 **69** 3f.50 on 3f. brown 25 10

1936. King Albert Memorial Fund. Surch **+ 50 c**.
215 **71** 1f.50+50c. purple 2·75 6·75
216 2f.50+50c. blue 1·90 5·00

74 Queen Astrid and Congo Children
76 R. Molindi

1936. Queen Astrid Fund for Congo Children.
217 **74** 1f.25+5c. brown 70 1·25
218 1f.50+10c. red 80 1·75
219 2f.50+25c. blue 1·25 2·50

1938. Promotion of National Parks.
220 **76** 5c. black and violet 10 15
221 – 90c. brown and red 55 75
222 – 1f.50 black and purple 35 20
223 – 2f.40 brown and grey 20 30
224 – 2f.50 black and blue 40 40
225 – 4f.50 brown and green 80 65
DESIGNS—VERT: 90c. Bamboo-canes; 1f.50, R. Suza; 2f.40, R. Rutshuru. HORIZ: 2f.50, Mt. Karisimbi; 4f.50, Mitumba Forest.

77 Marabou Stork and Ruppels Griffon

1939. Leopoldville Zoological Gardens.
226 **77** 1f.+1f. purple 9·75 11·00
227 – 1f.25+1f.25 red 8·50 11·00
228 – 1f.50+1f.50 violet 9·50 11·00
229 – 4f.50+4f.50 green 7·50 11·00
230 – 5f.+5f. brown 9·50 11·00
DESIGNS: 1f.25, Kob; 1f.50, Young chimpanzees; 4f.50, Crocodiles; 5f. Lioness.

78 King Albert Memorial, Leopoldville
81 "Belgium Shall Rise Again"

1941.
231 **78** 10c. grey 1·25 1·40
232 15c. brown 25 20
233 25c. blue 75 35
234 50c. lilac 1·25 30
235 75c. pink 1·60 50
236 1f.25 brown 1·10 35
237 1f.75 orange 3·00 3·00
238 2f.50 red 1·60 15
239 2f.75 blue 1·75 60
240 5f. olive 3·75 2·75
241 10f. red 4·00 2·75

1941. Surch.
242 – 5c. on 1f.50 black & purple (No. 222) (postage) 15 1·10
243 **78** 75c. on 1f.75 orange 1·75 2·25
244 – 2f.50 on 2f.40 brown and grey (No. 223) 1·40 1·25
245 **69** 50c. on 1f.50 green (air) 90 80

1942. War Relief Fund.
246 **81** 10f.+40f. green 2·25 2·40
247 10f.+40f. blue 2·25 2·40

82 Oil Palms
84 Leopard

1942. (a) Inscr "BELGISCH CONGO BELGE".
248 **82** 5c. red 10 10
249 – 50f. black and blue 5·00 1·25
250 – 100f. black and red 8·75 1·60

(b) Inscr "CONGO BELGE BELGISCH CONGO", or vice versa.
251 **82** 10c. olive 10 10
252 15c. brown 10 20
253a 20c. blue 10 15
254 25c. purple 10 10
255a 30c. blue 20 10
256 50c. green 35 10
257 60c. brown 30 15
258 – 75c. black and violet 50 10
259a – 1f. black and brown 45 10
260 – 1f.25 black and red 45 10
261 **84** 1f.75 brown 1·10 50
262 2f. yellow 1·25 10
263a 2f.50 red 80 10
264 – 3f.50 olive 60 10
265 – 5f. orange 95 10
266a – 6f. blue 1·00 10
267a – 7f. black 1·00 10
268 – 10f. brown 85 10
269a – 20f. black and red 7·00 9·50
DESIGNS—As Type **82**: 75c. to 1f.25, Head of a native woman; 3f.50 to 10f. Askari sentry. As Type **84**: 20f. Okapi; 28 × 33 mm: 50 f. Head of woman; 100f. Askari sentry.

1944. Red Cross Fund. Surch **Au profit de la Croix Rouge Ten voordeele van het Roode Kruis** (or with French and Flemish reversed) and additional value.
269a **82** 50c.+50f. green 1·90 1·90
269b – 1f.25+100f. black and red (No. 260) 7·00 9·50
269c **84** 1f.75+100f. brown 7·00 9·50
269d – 3f.50+100f. green (No. 264) 7·00 9·50

87 Driving Slaves to Market
88 Leopold II

1947. 50th Anniv of Abolition of Slavery in Belgian Congo.
270 **87** 1f.25 brown 40 15
270a – 1f.50 violet 2·25 85
270b – 3f. brown 2·10 10
271 – 3f.50 blue 30 10
272 **88** 10f. orange 60 20
PORTRAITS–As Type **88**: 1f.50, Lavigerie. 3f. Dhanis. 3f.50, Lambermont.

89 Seated Figure

90 Railway Train and Map

1947. Native masks and carvings as T **89**.
273 **89** 10c. orange 10 10
274 A 15c. blue 10 10
275 B 20c. blue 10 10
276 C 25c. red 20 10
277 D 40c. purple 20 10
278 **89** 50c. brown 55 10
279 A 70c. green 10 20
280 B 75c. purple 25 10
281 C 1f. purple and orange . . 1·50 10
281a A 1f.20 brown and grey . . 85 60
282 D 1f.25 purple and green . . 35 20
282a E 1f.50 red and green . . . 17·00 4·50
282b B 1f.60 blue and grey . . . 1·10 70
283 **89** 2f. red and orange . . . 80 10
283a C 2f.40 green and turquoise 1·00 20
284 A 2f.50 green and brown . . 45 10
284a E 3f. indigo and blue . . . 5·00 10
285 B 3f.50 green and blue . . . 4·00 20
286 C 5f. purple and bistre . . . 1·75 10
287 D 6f. green and orange . . . 1·60 10
287a F 6f.50 brown and red . . . 2·40 10
287b D 8f. green and blue . . . 2·40 20
288 E 10f. brown and violet . . 12·50 10
289 F 20f. brown and red . . . 30 10
290 E 50f. black and brown . . 4·25 25
291 F 100f. black and red . . . 6·50 85
DESIGNS: A, Seated figure (different); B, Kneeling figure; C, Double mask; D, Mask; E, Mask with tassels; F, Mask with horns.

1948. 50th Anniv of Matadi–Leopoldville Railway.
292 **90** 2f.50 green and blue . . . 1·50 25

91 Globe and 19th-century Full-rigged Ship

92 Allegorical Figure and Map

1949. 75th Anniv of U.P.U.
293 **91** 4f. blue 55 70

1950. 50th Anniv of "Comite Special du Katanga" (Chartered Company).
294 **92** 3f. slate and blue . . . . . 1·90 1·25
295 6f.50 sepia and red . . . . 2·00 75

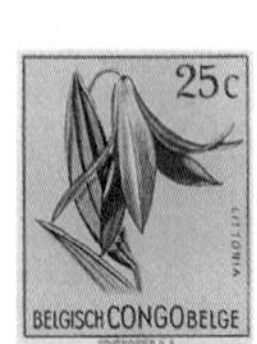
93 "Littonia"

94 St. Francis Xavier

1952. Flowers. Multicoloured.
296 10c. "Dissotis" 10 10
297 15c. "Protea" 10 10
298 20c. "Vellozia" 10 10
299 25c. Type **93** 10 10
300 40c. "Ipomoea" 25 10
301 50c. "Angraecum" 25 10
302 60c. "Euphorbia" 30 20
303 75c. "Ochna" 30 11
304 1f. "Hibiscus" 55 10
305 1f.25 "Protea" . . . . . . 1·60 1·40
306 1f.50 "Schizoglossum" . . . 45 10
307 2f. "Ansellia" . . . . . . 1·00 10
308 3f. "Costus" 95 10
309 4f. "Nymphaea" . . . . . 1·25 10
310 5f. "Thunbergia" . . . . . 1·60 10
311 6f.50 "Thonningia" . . . . 1·40 10
312 7f. "Gerbera" . . . . . . 1·60 10
313 8f. "Gloriosa" . . . . . . 2·75 30
314 10f. "Silene" . . . . . . 4·00 20
315 20f. "Aristolochia" . . . . 5·00 25
316 50f. "Eulophia" . . . . . . 12·50 1·00
317 100f. "Cryptosepalum" . . . 14·50 2·50
SIZES: Nos. 296/315, 21 × 25½ mm. Nos. 316/17, 22½ × 32½ mm.

1953. 400th Death Anniv of St. Francis Xavier.
318 **94** 1f.50c. black and blue . . 1·60 50

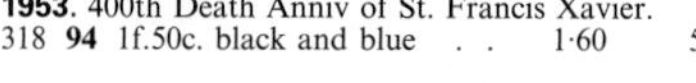

95 Lake Kivu

1953. Kivu Festival.
319 **95** 3f. black and red . . . . . 2·25 55
320 7f. brown and blue . . . . 2·50 30

96 Medallion

1954. 25th Anniv of Belgian Royal Colonial Institute. No. 322 has different frame.
321 **96** 4f.50 grey and blue 80 35
322 6f.50 brown and green . . 55 15

97 King Baudouin and Mountains

98 Badge and Map

1955. Inscr "CONGO BELGE . BELGISCH CONGO" or vice versa.
323 **97** 1f.50 black and red . . . . 9·00 1·90
324 – 3f. black and green . . . . 5·75 90
325 – 4f.50 black and blue . . . 5·75 90
326 – 6f.50 black & purple . . . 8·00 30
DESIGNS: 3f. Forest; 4f.50, River; 6f.50, Grassland.

1955. 5th Int Congress of African Tourism. Inscr in Flemish or French.
327 **98** 6f.50 blue . . . . 2·50 1·40

1956. Birth Bicentenary of Mozart. As T **316/17** of Belgium.
328 **316** 4f.50+1f.50 violet . . . . 4·75 5·00
329 **317** 6f.50+2f.50 blue . . . . . 7·00 6·50

99 Nurse with Children

101 Roan Antelope

100 Belgian Monarchs

1957. Red Cross Fund. Cross in red.
330 **99** 3f.+50c. blue . . . . . . 2·10 2·25
331 – 4f.50+50c. green . . . . . 2·40 2·40
332 – 6f.50+50c. brown . . . . 2·25 2·40
DESIGNS—HORIZ: 4f.50, Doctor inoculating patient; 6f.50, Nurse in tropical kit bandaging patient.

1958. 50th Anniv of Belgian Annexation of the Congo.
333 **100** 1f. red 40 10
334 1f.50 blue 45 10
335 3f. red 95 10
336 5f. green . . . . 1·60 60
337 6f.50 brown . . . . . . 1·40 25
338 10f. violet . . . . 1·40 55

1959. Wild Animals.
339 **101** 10c. brown, sepia & blue 10 40
340 – 20c. blue and red 10 70
341 – 40c. brown and blue . . . 25 85
342 – 50c. multicoloured 50 60
343 – 1f. black, green & brown 55 45
344 – 1f.50 black and yellow . . 80 40
345 – 2f. black, brown and red 1·00 55
346 – 3f. black, purple & slate 1·00 55
347 – 5f. brown, green & sepia 1·25 50
348 – 6f.50 brn, yellow & blue 1·10 55
349 – 8f. bistre, violet & brown 1·40 80
350 – 10f. multicoloured . . . . 1·50 1·25
DESIGNS—HORIZ: 20c. White rhinoceros; 50c. Demidoff's galago; 1f.50, African buffaloes; 3f. African elephants; 6f.50, Impala; 10f. Eland and common zebras. VERT: 40c. Giraffe; 1f. Gorilla; 2f. Eastern Black and White Colobus monkey; 5f. Okapis; 8f. Giant ground pangolin.

102 Madonna and Child

103 "African Resources"

1959. Christmas.
351 **102** 50c. brn, ochre & chestnut 15 20
352 1f. brown, violet & blue 10 15
353 2f. brown, blue and grey 20 25

1960. 10th Anniv of African Technical Co-operation Commission. Inscr in French or Flemish.
354 **103** 3f. orange and grey . . . 75 1·25

104 High Jumping

1960. Child Welfare Fund.
355 **104** 50c.+25c. blue and red . . 55 1·10
356 – 1f.50+50c. red & green . . 85 1·10
357 – 2f.+1f. green and red . . 90 1·25
358 – 3f.+1f.25 purple & bl . . 1·40 1·75
359 – 6f.50+3f.50 brn & red . . 1·60 2·25
DESIGNS: 1f.50, Hurdling; 2f. Football; 3f. Throwing the javelin; 6f.60, Throwing the discus.

POSTAGE DUE STAMPS

D 54

D 86

1923.
D141 **D 54** 5c. sepia 10 65
D142a 10c. red 10 60
D143 15c. violet 15 60
D144 30c. green 25 30
D145 50c. blue 35 45
D146 1f. grey 40 40

1943.
D270a **D 86** 10c. olive 30 75
D271a 20c. blue 25 70
D272a 50c. green 30 55
D273a 1f. brown 25 65
D274a 2f. orange 30 50

D 99

1957.
D330 **D 99** 10c. brown . . . . . 60 1·00
D331 20c. purple . . . . . 70 1·00
D332 50c. green . . . . . 1·00 1·00
D333 1f. blue . . . . . . 1·10 1·10
D334 2f. red . . . . . . 1·40 1·50
D335 4f. violet . . . . . 1·50 1·75
D336 6f. blue . . . . . . 1·90 2·00

For later issues see **CONGO (KINSHASA), ZAIRE REPUBLIC** and **DEMOCRATIC REPUBLIC OF CONGO**.

BELGIAN OCCUPATION OF GERMANY Pt. 7

Stamps used in German territory occupied by Belgian Forces at the end of the War of 1914/18, and including the districts of Eupen and Malmedy, now incorporated in Belgium.

100 centimes = 1 Belgian franc.

1919. Stamps of Belgium optd **ALLEMAGNE DUITSCHLAND**.
1 **51** 1c. orange 45 30
2 2c. brown 45 30
3 3c. grey . . . . 90 1·10
4 5c. green . . . . 1·00 65
5 10c. red . . . . 3·00 1·50
6 15c. violet . . . . 1·25 60
7 20c. purple . . . . 1·90 85
8 25c. blue . . . . 2·75 1·40
9 **63** 25c. blue . . . . 6·50 6·25
10 **52** 35c. black and brown . . . 2·50 85
11 – 40c. black and green . . . 3·00 1·50
12 – 50c. black and red . . . . 11·50 8·25
13 – 65c. black and red . . . . 4·00 6·50
14 **55** 1f. violet . . . . 30·00 19·00
15 – 2f. grey . . . . 90·00 45·00
16 – 5f. blue (FRANK, No. 194) 15·00 7·50
17 – 10f. sepia . . . . 90·00 55·00

1920. Stamps of Belgium surch **EUPEN & MALMEDY** and value.
18 **51** 5pf. on 5c. green 75 35
19 10pf. on 10c. red 90 45
20 15pf. on 15c. violet . . . . 1·10 60
21 20pf. on 20c. purple . . . . 1·25 85
22 30pf. on 25c. blue . . . . . 1·90 1·00
23 – 75pf. on 50c. black and red 28·00 18·00
24 **55** 1m.25 on 1f. violet . . . . 42·00 21·00

1920. Stamps of Belgium optd **Eupen**.
25 **51** 1c. orange 45 25
26 2c. brown 45 25
27 3c. grey 65 90
28 5c. green 75 65
29 10c. red . . . . 1·50 1·25
30 15c. violet . . . . 1·60 85
31 20c. purple . . . . 2·50 1·60
32 25c. blue . . . . 2·50 2·10
33 **63** 25c. blue . . . . 6·00 6·25
34 **52** 35c. black and brown . . . 2·50 1·40
35 – 40c. black and green . . . 3·00 1·90
36 – 50c. black and red . . . . 9·75 7·00
37 – 65c. black and red . . . . 4·25 6·75
38 **55** 1f. violet . . . . 30·00 17·00
39 – 2f. grey . . . . 60·00 42·00
40 – 5f. blue (FRANK, No. 194) 16·00 8·00
41 – 10f. sepia . . . . 80·00 50·00

1920. Stamps of Belgium optd **Malmedy**.
42 **51** 1c. orange 35 30
43 2c. brown 35 30
44 3c. grey 55 90
45 5c. green 80 65
46 10c. red . . . . 1·40 1·10
47 15c. violet . . . . 1·90 1·40
48 20c. purple . . . . 2·75 1·90
49 25c. blue . . . . 2·50 2·00
50 **63** 25c. blue . . . . 6·00 6·00
51 **52** 35c. black and brown . . . 2·40 1·75
52 – 40c. black and green . . . 2·75 1·90
53 – 50c. black and red . . . . 11·00 7·25
54 – 65c. black and red . . . . 4·25 6·75
55 **55** 1f. violet . . . . 30·00 15·00
56 – 2f. grey . . . . 65·00 42·00
57 – 5f. blue (FRANK, No. 194) 16·00 10·50
58 – 10f. sepia . . . . 85·00 55·00

POSTAGE DUE STAMPS

1920. Postage Due stamps of Belgium, 1919. (a) Optd **Eupen**.
D1 5c. green . . . . 1·40 1·10
D2 10c. red . . . . 2·40 1·40
D3 20c. green . . . . 7·25 5·75
D4 30c. blue . . . . 6·00 4·50
D5 50c. grey . . . . 24·00 16·50

(b) Optd **Malmedy**.
D 6 5c. green . . . . 2·40 1·10
D 7 10c. red . . . . 4·50 1·40
D 8 20c. green . . . . 24·00 16·00
D 9 30c. blue . . . . 9·25 5·75
D10 50c. grey . . . . 24·00 14·00

BELGIUM Pt. 4

An independent Kingdom of N.W. Europe.

1849. 100 centimes = 1 franc.
2002. 100 cents = 1 euro.

1 "Epaulettes"

3 "Medallions"

1849. Imperf.
1 **1** 10c. brown . . . . £1800 65·00
2a 20c. blue . . . . £1900 45·00

1861. Imperf.
12 **3** 1c. green £150 £100
13 10c. brown . . . . £325 6·00
14 20c. blue . . . . £350 6·00
15 40c. red . . . . £2750 55·00

1863. Perf.
24 **3** 1c. green . . . . 38·00 22·00
25 10c. brown . . . . 50·00 2·75
26 20c. blue . . . . 50·00 3·00
27 40c. red . . . . £325 21·00

5

8

10 "Small Lion"

1865. Various frames.
34 **5** 10c. grey . . . . £120 1·60
35 20c. blue . . . . £190 1·75
36 30c. brown . . . . £425 8·50

37 **8** 40c. red £500 15·00
38 **5** 1f. lilac £1300 75·00

1866.
43 **10** 1c. grey 32·00 10·50
44 2c. blue £110 70·00
45 5c. brown £140 65·00

11 **13** **14**

15 **20**

Types **13** to **20** and all later portraits to Type **38** are of Leopold II.

1869. Various frames.
46 **11** 1c. green 7·50 35
59a 2c. blue 15·00 2·00
60 5c. buff 38·00 80
49 8c. lilac 65·00 45·00
50 **13** 10c. green 26·00 50
51b **14** 20c. blue £100 1·00
62 **15** 25c. bistre 80·00 1·40
53a **13** 30c. buff 65·00 2·40
54b 40c. red 90·00 6·50
55a **15** 50c. grey £180 9·00
56 **13** 1f. mauve £325 14·50
57a **20** 5f. brown £1300 £1200

21 **25**

1883. Various frames.
63 **21** 10c. red 22·00 1·75
64 – 20c. grey £140 5·50
65 – 25c. blue £225 24·00
66 – 50c. violet £250 25·00

1884. Various frames.
67 **11** 1c. olive 13·00 55
68 1c. grey 3·25 30
69 2c. brown 11·00 1·50
70 5c. green 32·00 35
71 **25** 10c. red 9·00 25
72 – 20c. olive £140 1·10
73 – 25c. blue on red 11·50 60
74 – 35c. brown 12·50 2·25
75 – 50c. bistre 9·00 1·40
76 – 1f. brown on green £550 12·50
77 – 2f. lilac 60·00 28·00

32 **33** **34** Arms of Antwerp

1893.
78a **32** 1c. grey 65 30
79 2c. yellow 70 85
80 2c. brown 1·25 20
81 5c. green 3·75 30
82 **33** 10c. brown 1·50 20
83 10c. red 2·25 25
84 20c. olive 12·00 35
85 25c. blue 11·00 25
86a 35c. brown 17·00 1·50
87 50c. brown 40·00 9·50
88 50c. grey 45·00 1·50
89 1f. red on green 55 14·00
90 1f. orange 70·00 4·50
91 2f. mauve 75·00 45·00

The prices for the above and all following issues with the tablet are for stamps with the tablet attached. Without tablet, the prices will be about half those quoted.

See also Nos. 106/8.

1894. Antwerp Exhibition.
93 **34** 5c. green on red 5·25 2·50
94 10c. red on blue 2·50 1·75
95 25c. blue on red 95 80

35 St. Michael encountering Satan **36**

1896. Brussels Exhibition of 1897.
96 **35** 5c. violet 45 45
97 **36** 10c. red 7·50 2·75
98 10c. brown 20 25

37 **38** **40** St. Martin and the Beggar (from altarpiece by Van Dyck)

1905. Various frames.
99 **37** 10c. red 1·10 30
100 20c. olive 22·00 60
101 25c. blue 9·75 60
102 35c. purple 22·00 1·40
103 **38** 50c. grey 75·00 1·50
104 1f. orange £100 5·75
105 2f. mauve 65·00 13·50

1907. As T **32** but no scroll pattern between stamps and labels.
106 1c. grey 1·25 25
107 2c. red 14·00 5·50
108 5c. green 12·00 55

1910. Brussels Exhibition. A. Unshaded background. B. Shaded background. A.
109 **40** 1c. (+1c.) grey 85 90
110 2c. (+2c.) purple 7·50 7·00
111 5c. (+5c.) green 2·10 1·90
112 10c. (+5c.) red 2·10 1·90

B.
113 **40** 1c. (+1c.) green 2·10 1·90
114 2c. (+2c.) purple 5·25 5·00
115 5c. (+5c.) green 2·10 1·90
116 10c. (+5c.) red 2·10 1·90

1911. Nos. 109/16 optd **1911.**A.
117 **40** 1c. (+1c.) grey 20·00 15·00
118 2c. (+2c.) purple 80·00 50·00
119 5c. (+5c.) green 6·50 6·25
120 10c. (+5c.) red 6·50 6·25

B.
121 **40** 1c. (+1c.) green 30·00 23·00
122 2c. (+2c.) purple 38·00 21·00
123 5c. (+5c.) green 6·50 6·75
124 10c. (+5c.) red 6·50 6·75

1911. Charleroi Exhibition. Nos. 109/16 optd **CHARLEROI–1911.** A.
125 **40** 1c. (+1c.) grey 4·75 2·75
126 2c. (+2c.) purple 12·50 11·50
127 5c. (+5c.) green 7·50 7·75
128 10c. (+5c.) red 7·50 7·75

B.
129 **40** 1c. (+1c.) green 4·75 2·75
130 2c. (+2c.) purple 13·00 9·00
131 5c. (+5c.) green 7·50 6·25
132 10c. (+5c.) red 7·50 6·25

42 **43** **44**

45 Albert I **46** (Larger head)

1912.
133 **42** 1c. orange 10 15
134 **43** 2c. brown 20 20
135 **44** 5c. green 10 10
136 **45** 10c. red 55 40
137 20c. olive 12·50 4·00
138 35c. brown 50 45
139 40c. green 13·50 13·00
140 50c. grey 70 50
141 1f. orange 3·00 2·75
142 2f. violet 15·00 16·00
143 – 5f. purple 70·00 23·00

The 5f. is as Type **45** but larger (23 × 35 mm).

1912. Large head.
148 **46** 10c. red 10 15
145 20c. olive 25 30
150 25c. blue 20 25
147 40c. green 35 45

47 Merode Monument **48** Albert I

1914. Red Cross.
151 **47** 5c. (+5c.) red & green 2·25 3·00
152 10c. (+10c.) red & pink 3·75 4·75
153 20c. (+20c.) red & vio 40·00 42·00

1914. Red Cross.
154 **48** 5c. (+5c.) red and green 3·25 3·25
155 10c. (+10c.) red 40 30
156 20c. (+20c.) red & violet 9·50 9·75

49 Albert I

1915. Red Cross.
157 **49** 5c. (+5c.) red and green 6·25 2·40
158 10c. (+10c.) red and pink 18·00 10·50
159 20c. (+20c.) red & violet 32·00 14·50

51 Albert I **52** Cloth Hall, Ypres

55 Freeing of the Scheldt

1915.
170 **51** 1c. orange 20 15
171 2c. brown 15 15
179 3c. grey 30 20
172 5c. green 65 15
173 10c. red 90 15
174 15c. violet 1·00 20
187 20c. purple 1·90 25
176 25c. blue 45 30
188 **52** 35c. black and brown 45 20
189 – 40c. black and green 45 20
190 – 50c. black and red 4·00 20
191 **55** 1f. violet 28·00 65
192 – 2f. grey 18·00 1·50
193 – 5f. blue (FRANKEN) £250 £110
194 – 5f. blue (FRANK) 1·10 90
195 – 10f. brown 17·00 18·00

DESIGNS: As T **52**: 40c. Dinant; 50c. Louvain. As T **55**: 2f. Annexation of the Congo; 5f. King Albert at Furnes; 10f. The Kings of Belgium.

1918. Red Cross. Surch with new value and cross. Some colours changed.
222 **51** 1c.+1c. orange 25 25
223 2c.+2c. brown 35 35
224 5c.+5c. green 1·00 95
225 10c.+10c. red 2·10 1·90
226 15c.+15c. purple 4·50 4·25
227 20c.+20c. brown 9·25 8·00
228 25c.+25c. blue 18·00 17·00
229 **52** 35c.+35c. black & violet 9·00 8·50
230 – 40c.+40c. black & brown 9·00 8·50
231 – 50c.+50c. black and blue 9·00 8·50
232 **55** 1f.+1f. grey 28·00 32·00
233 – 2f.+2f. green 65·00 60·00
234 – 5f.+5f. brn (FRANKEN) £160 £140
235 – 10f.+10f. blue £500 4·25

63 "Perron" at Liege **64** Albert I

1919.
236a **63** 25c. blue 2·00 30

1919.
237 **64** 1c. brown 15 10
238 2c. olive 15 10
239 5c. green 25 25
240 10c. red 20 25
241 15c. violet 25 20
242 20c. sepia 1·00 1·00
243 25c. blue 1·50 1·25
244 35c. brown 1·90 1·40
245 40c. red 5·75 5·25
246 50c. brown 11·50 9·00
247 1f. orange 38·00 35·00
248 2f. purple £300 £275
249 5f. red 90·00 75·00
250 10f. red £110 £100

SIZES: 1c., 2c., 18½ × 21½ mm. 5c. to 2f., 22½ × 26½ mm. 5f., 10f., 27½ × 33 mm.

67 Discus thrower **68** Charioteer

1920. Olympic Games, Antwerp.
256 **67** 5c. (+5c.) green 1·75 1·40
257 **68** 10c. (+5c.) red 1·40 1·25
258 – 15c. (+5c.) brown 1·50 1·60

DESIGN—VERT: 15c. Runner.

73 Hotel de Ville, Termonde **76** Albert I

1920.
308b **73** 65c. black and purple 65 25

1921. Nos. 256/8 surch **20c. 20c.**
309 **67** 20c. on 5c. green 50 20
310 **68** 20c. on 10c. red 30 20
311 – 20c. on 15c. brown 50 25

1921.
313 **76** 50c. blue 25 10
314 75c. red 25 25
315 75c. blue 35 10
316 1f. sepia 50 10
317 1f. blue 30 15
318 2f. green 70 20
319 5f. purple 10·50 11·00
320 5f. brown 6·50 7·00
321 10f. red 7·25 5·25

1921. Surch **55c 55c.**
322 **73** 55c. on 65c. black & pur 2·00 35

80 **81** Albert I

1922. War Invalids Fund.
348 **80** 20c.+20c. brown 1·40 1·25

1922.
349 **81** 1c. orange 10 10
350 2c. olive 15 20
351 3c. brown 10 10
352 5c. slate 10 10
353 10c. green 10 10
354 15c. plum 10 10
355 20c. brown 15 10
356 25c. purple 15 20
357 25c. violet 45 10
358 30c. red 35 10
359 30c. mauve 25 10
360 35c. brown 30 30
361 35c. green 90 30
362 40c. red 35 15
363 50c. bistre 40 15
364 60c. olive 2·75 10
365 75c. violet 85 55
366 1f. yellow 40 35
367 1f. red 85 15
368 1f.25 blue 1·10 1·10
369 1f.50 blue 1·75 40
370 1f.75 blue 1·50 10
371 2f. blue 2·25 30
372 5f. green 25·00 1·40
373 10f. brown 60·00 7·75

83 Wounded Soldier

1923. War Invalids Fund.
374 **83** 20c.+20c. slate . . . . . . 1·60 1·90

87 Leopold I and Albert I

1925. 75th Anniv of 1st Belgian Stamps.
410 **87** 10c. green . . . . 6·50 6·50
411 15c. violet . . . . 3·00 3·00
412 20c. brown . . . . 3·00 3·00
413 25c. slate . . . . 3·00 3·00
414 30c. red . . . . 3·00 3·00
415 35c. blue . . . . 3·00 3·00
416 40c. sepia . . . . 3·00 3·00
417 50c. brown . . . . 3·00 3·00
418 75c. blue . . . . 3·00 3·00
419 1f. purple . . . . 5·50 5·75
420 2f. blue . . . . 3·50 4·00
421 5f. black . . . . 3·25 3·25
422 10f. red . . . . 6·50 5·75

88

90

1925. Anti-T.B. Fund.
423 **88** 15c.+5c. red and mauve . . 20 20
424 30c.+5c. red and grey . . . 20 15
425 1f.+10c. red and blue . . . 85 1·10

1926. Flood Relief. Type of 1922 surch **Inondations 30 c Watersnood**.
426 **81** 30c.+30c. green 70 75

1926. Flood Relief Fund. A. Shaded background. B. Solid background. A.
427 **90** 1f.+1f. blue . . . . 4·25 5·50

B.
428 **90** 1f.+1f. blue . . . . 1·00 1·10

91

92 Queen Elisabeth and King Albert

1926. War Tuberculosis Fund.
429 **91** 5c.+5c. brown 10 15
430 20c.+5c. brown 35 35
431 50c.+5c. violet 20 20
432 **92** 1f.50+25c. blue 55 55
433 5f.+1f. red . . . . 5·50 5·00

1927. Stamps of 1922 surch.
434 **81** 3c. on 2c. olive 10 10
435 10c. on 15c. plum 10 10
436 35c. on 40c. red 20 10
437 1f.75 on 1f.50 blue 90 65

94 Rowing Boat

1927. Anti-T.B. Fund.
438 **94** 25c.+10c. brown 85 75
439 35c.+10c. green 55 75
440 60c.+10c. violet 20 25
441 1f.75+25c. blue . . . . . 1·10 1·00
442 5f.+1f. purple . . . . . . 4·25 4·00

96 Ogives

97 Ruins of Orval Abbey

1928. Orval Abbey Restoration Fund. Inscr "ORVAL 1928" or "ORVAL".
461 **96** 5c.+5c. red and gold . . . 15 20
462 – 25c.+5c. violet and gold . . 30 35
463 – 35c.+10c. green 70 75
464 – 60c.+15c. brown 55 20
465 – 1f.75+25c. blue . . . . . 2·10 1·50
466 – 2f.+40c. purple . . . . . 14·00 14·00
467 – 3f.+1f. red . . . . 13·50 13·00
468 **97** 5f.+5f. lake . . . . 11·00 10·00
469 – 10f.+10f. sepia . . . . . . 11·00 10·00
DESIGNS—VERT: 35c., 2f. Cistercian monk stone-carving; 60c., 1f.75, 3f. Duchess Matilda retrieving her ring.

99 Mons Cathedral

101 Malines Cathedral

1928. Anti-T.B. Fund.
472 **99** 5c.+5c. red 20 20
473 – 25c.+15c. sepia 20 20
474 **101** 35c.+10c. green 85 90
475 – 60c.+15c. brown 25 35
476 – 1f.75+25c. violet . . . . 6·50 6·25
477 – 5f.+5f. purple . . . . . . 14·00 16·00
DESIGNS—As Type **99**: 25c. Tournai Cathedral. As Type **101**: 60c. Ghent Cathedral; 1f.75, St. Gudule Cathedral, Brussels; 5f. Louvain Library.

1929. Surch **BRUXELLES 1929 BRUSSEL 5 c** in frame.
478 **81** 5c. on 30c. mauve 15 10
479 5c. on 75c. violet 20 15
480 5c. on 1f.25c. blue 10 10
The above cancellation, whilst altering the original face value of the stamps, also constitutes a precancel, although stamps also come with additional ordinary postmark. The unused prices are for stamps with full gum and the used prices are for stamps without gum, with or without postmarks. We do not list precancels where there is no change in face value.

104 The Belgian Lion

105 Albert I

1929.
487 **104** 1c. orange 10 10
488 2c. green 35 45
489 3c. brown 10 10
490 5c. green 10 10
491 10c. bistre 10 10
492 20c. mauve 85 25
493 25c. red 30 10
494 35c. green 40 10
495 40c. purple 30 10
496 50c. blue 30 10
497 60c. mauve . . . . . . 1·60 20
498 70c. brown 90 10
499 75c. blue . . . . 1·40 10
500 75c. brown . . . . . . 4·75 10
501 **105** 10f. brown . . . . . . 13·50 3·25
502 20f. green . . . . . . 75·00 18·00
503a 50f. purple . . . . . . 22·00 13·00
504a 100f. red . . . . 16·00 17·00

1929. Laying of first Stone towards Restoration of Orval Abbey. Nos. 461/9 optd with crown over ornamental letter "L" and **19-8-29**.
543 5c.+5c. red and gold . . . . 60·00 55·00
544 25c.+5c. violet and gold . . . 60·00 55·00
545 35c.+10c. green . . . . . . 60·00 55·00
546 60c.+15c. brown . . . . . . 60·00 55·00
547 1f.75c.+25c. blue . . . . . . 60·00 55·00
548 2f.+40c. purple . . . . . . 60·00 55·00
549 3f.+1f. red . . . . 60·00 55·00
550 5f.+5f. lake . . . . 60·00 55·00
551 10f.+10f. sepia . . . . 60·00 55·00

109 Canal and Belfry, Bruges

1929. Anti-T.B. Fund.
552 – 5c.+5c. brown 20 25
553 – 25c.+15c. grey . . . . . 75 1·10
554 – 35c.+10c. green 70 75
555 – 60c.+15c. lake 30 35
556 – 1f.75+25c. blue . . . . . 4·50 5·00
557 **109** 5f.+5f. purple . . . . . . 22·00 22·00
DESIGNS—HORIZ: 5c. Waterfall at Coo; 35c. Menin Gate, Ypres; 60c. Promenade d'Orleans, Spa; 1f.75, "Aquitania" and "Dinteldyk" (liners), Antwerp Harbour. VERT: 25c. Bayard Rock, Dinant.

110 Paul Rubens

111 Zenobe Gramme

1930. Antwerp and Liege Exns.
558 **110** 35c. green 40 15
559 **111** 35c. green 40 15

112 Ostend

113 "Leopold II" by Jef Lempoels

1930. Air.
560 **112** 50c. blue 35 25
561 – 1f.50 brown (St. Hubert) 2·00 2·10
562 – 2f. green (Namur) . . . . 2·25 75
563 – 5f. red (Brussels) . . . . 1·50 95
564 – 5f. violet (Brussels) . . . 23·00 23·00

1930. Centenary of Independence.
565 – 60c. purple 30 20
566 **113** 1f. red . . . . 1·10 55
567 – 1f.75 blue . . . . 2·25 2·50
PORTRAITS: 60c. "Leopold I" by Lievin de Winne. 1f.75, King Albert I.

1930. I.L.O. Congress. Nos. 565/7 optd **B.I.T. OCT. 1930**.
569 60c. purple . . . . 1·75 1·90
570 1f. red . . . . 7·25 8·00
571 1f.75 blue . . . . 13·50 15·00

116 Wynendaele

117 Gaesbeek

1930. Anti-T.B. Fund.
572 – 10c.+5c. mauve 20 25
573 **116** 25c.+15c. sepia 55 60
574 – 40c.+10c. purple 60 70
575 – 70c.+15c. slate 45 55
576 – 1f.+25c. red . . . . . . 3·75 4·75
577 – 1f.75+25c. blue . . . . . 3·25 3·25
578 **117** 5f.+5f. green . . . . . . 26·00 29·00
DESIGNS: 10c. Bornhem; 40c. Beloeil; 70c. Oydonck, 1f. Ghent; 1f.75, Bouillon.

1931. Surch **2c**.
579 **104** 2c. on 3c. brown 10 20

1931. Surch **BELGIQUE 1931 BELGIE 10c**.
580 **104** 10c. on 60c. mauve . . . 40 20
See note below No. 480.

121 Albert I

123

1931.
582 **121** 75c. brown (18 × 22 mm) 1·10 10
583 1f. lake (21 × 23½ mm) . . 20 15
584 **123** 1f.25 black 50 35
585 1f.50 purple . . . . . . 1·10 35
586 1f.75 blue 50 10
587 2f. brown 75 15
588 2f.45 violet . . . . 2·10 30
589 2f.50 sepia . . . . 8·00 50
590 5f. green . . . . 22·00 85
591 10f. red . . . . 38·00 10·00
See also No. 654.

125 Queen Elisabeth

126 Reaper

127 Mercury

1931. Anti-Tuberculosis Fund.
593 **125** 10c.+5c. brown 25 25
594 25c.+15c. violet 90 55
595 50c.+10c. green 55 45
596 75c.+15c. sepia 45 20
597 1f.+25c. lake . . . . . . 6·00 5·75
598 1f.75+25c. blue . . . . . 4·75 3·50
599 5f.+5f. purple . . . . . . 45·00 45·00

1932. Surch **BELGIQUE 1932 BELGIE 10c**.
600 **104** 10c. on 40c. mauve . . . 2·50 25
601 10c. on 70c. brown . . . 2·50 20
See Note below No. 480.

1932.
602 **126** 2c. green 35 35
603 **127** 5c. red 10 10
604 **126** 10c. green 15 10
605 **127** 20c. lilac 65 15
606 **126** 25c. red 45 10
607 **127** 35c. green . . . . 1·90 10

129 Cardinal Mercier

132

1932. Cardinal Mercier Memorial Fund.
609 **129** 10c.+10c. purple 25 25
610 50c.+30c. mauve . . . . 1·50 1·60
611 75c.+25c. brown . . . . 1·10 1·40
612 1f.+2f. red . . . . 5·00 5·00
613 – 1f.75+75c. blue . . . . . 70·00 60·00
614 – 2f.50+2f.50 brown . . . . 70·00 60·00
615 – 3f.+4f.50 green . . . . . 70·00 60·00
616 – 5f.+20f. purple . . . . . 75·00 60·00
617 – 10f.+40f. red £130 £130
DESIGNS: 1f.75, 3f. Mercier protecting refugees at Malines; 2f.50, 5f. Mercier with busts of Aristotle and Thomas Aquinas; 10f. Mercier when Professor at Louvain University.

1932. Infantry Memorial.
618 **132** 75c.+3f.25 red . . . . . 50·00 50·00
619 1f.75+4f.25 blue . . . . . 50·00 50·00

133 Prof Piccard's Stratosphere Balloon "F.N.R.S.", 1931

134 Hulpe-Waterloo Sanatorium

1932. Scientific Research Fund.
621 **133** 75c. brown . . . . 2·00 25
622 1f.75 blue . . . . 11·00 95
623 2f.50 violet . . . . 13·50 55

1932. Anti-T.B. Fund.
624 **134** 10c.+5c. violet 25 25
625 25c.+15c. mauve . . . . 1·40 95
626 50c.+10c. red . . . . . . 1·40 55
627 75c.+15c. brown . . . . 1·00 25
628 1f.+25c. red . . . . . . 9·50 9·00
629 1f.75+25c. blue . . . . . 7·75 7·00
630 5f.+5f. green . . . . . . 70·00 70·00

1933. Lion type surch **BELGIQUE 1933 BELGIE 10c**.
631 **104** 10c. on 40c. mauve . . . 12·50 2·75
632 10c. on 70c. brown . . . 11·00 1·25
See note below No. 480.

135 The Transept

138 Anti-T.B. Symbol

1933. Orval Abbey Restoration Fund. Inscr "ORVAL".
633 – 5c.+5c. green . . . . . . 42·00 42·00
634 – 10c.+15c. green . . . . . 40·00 38·00
635 – 25c.+15c. brown . . . . 32·00 30·00
636 **135** 50c.+25c. lake . . . . . . 32·00 30·00
637 – 75c.+50c. green . . . . . 32·00 30·00
638 – 1f.+1f.25 lake . . . . . . 32·00 30·00
639 – 1f.25+1f.75 sepia . . . . 32·00 30·00
640 – 1f.75+2f.75 blue . . . . . 48·00 45·00
641 – 2f.+3f. mauve . . . . . . 48·00 45·00
642 – 2f.50+5f. brown . . . . . 48·00 45·00

643 – 5f.+20f. purple . . . . . 48·00 45·00
644 – 10f.+40f. blue £180 £170

DESIGNS—VERT: 10c. Abbey Ruins; 75c. Belfry, new abbey; 1f. Fountain, new abbey. HORIZ: 5c. The old abbey; 25c. Guests' Courtyard, new abbey; 1f.25, Cloister, new abbey; 1f.75, Foundation of Orval Abbey in 1131; 2f. Restoration of the abbey, XVI and XVII centuries; 2f.50, Orval Abbey, XVIII century; 5f. Prince Leopold laying foundation stone of new abbey; 10f. The Virgin Mary (30 × 45 mm).

1933. Anti-tuberculosis Fund.
646 **138** 10c.+5c. grey 55 45
647 25c.+15c. mauve . . . . 1·90 2·00
648 50c.+10c. brown . . . . 1·60 1·50
649 75c.+15c. sepia . . . . . 20·00 35
650 1f.+25c. red . . . . . . 9·75 11·50
651 1f.75+25c. blue . . . . . 14·00 16·00
652 5f.+5f. purple . . . . . . 95·00 £100

1934. Lion type surch **BELGIQUE 1934 BELGIE 10c.**
653 **104** 10c. on 40c. mauve . . . 11·00 1·25
See note below No. 480.

1934. King Albert's Mourning Stamp.
654 **121** 75c. black 20 10

140 Peter Benoit **141** Brussels Palace

1934. Benoit Centenary Memorial Fund.
658 **140** 75c.+25c. brown . . . . 4·50 4·00

1934. International Exhibition, Brussels.
659 – 35c. green 75 20
660 **141** 1f. red . . . . 1·40 30
661 – 1f.50 brown . . . . . . 3·75 80
662 – 1f.75 blue . . . . 4·00 20

DESIGNS: 35c. Congo Palace; 1f.50, Old Brussels; 1f.75, Grand Palace of the Belgian section.

142 King Leopold III **143** King Leopold III

1934. War Invalids' Fund. (a) Size 18 × 22 mm. (b) Size 21 × 24 mm. (i) Exhibition Issue.
663 **142** 75c.+25c. green (a) . . . 14·50 14·00
664 1f.+25c. purple (b) . . . 14·00 13·00

(ii) Ordinary postage stamps.
665 **142** 75c.+25c. purple (a) . . . 3·25 3·25
666 1f.+25c. red (b) . . . . . 5·50 5·00

1934.
667 **142** 70c. green 30 10
668 75c. brown 40 25
669 **143** 1f. red . . . . 3·00 30

144 Health Crusader

1934. Anti-tuberculosis Fund. Cross in red.
670 **144** 10c.+5c. black 20 25
671 25c.+15c. brown . . . . 2·00 2·10
672 50c.+10c. green . . . . . 1·25 1·40
673 75c.+15c. purple 70 65
674 1f.+25c. red . . . . . . 9·00 9·00
675 1f.75+25c. blue . . . . . 7·25 6·75
676 5f.+5f. purple . . . . . . 90·00 95·00

145 The Royal Children

1935. Queen Astrid's Appeal.
680 **145** 35c.+15c. green 75 85
681 70c.+30c. purple 75 80
682 1f.75+50c. blue . . . . . 3·25 3·50

146 "Mail-diligence" **151** Queen Astrid

1935. Brussels Int Exn.
683 **146** 10c.+10c. olive 35 45
684 25c.+25c. brown . . . . 1·75 1·75
685 35c.+25c. green . . . . . 2·50 2·50

1935. Air. Surch with new value twice.
686 **112** 1f. on 1f.50 brown . . . 35 45
687 4f. on 5f. red . . . . . . 7·00 6·50

1935. Death of Queen Astrid. Mourning Stamp.
713 **151** 70c.+5c. black 10 15

1935. Anti-tuberculosis Fund. Black borders.
714 **151** 10c.+5c. olive 10 15
715 25c.+15c. brown 20 25
716 35c.+5c. green 20 20
717 50c.+10c. mauve 30 30
718 1f. +25c. red 80 90
719 1f.75+25c. blue . . . . . 1·40 1·50
720 2f.45+55c. violet . . . . 2·40 2·75

152 State arms **153** **155** King Leopold III

1936.
727 **152** 2c. green 10 10
728 5c. orange 10 10
729 10c. olive 10 10
730 15c. blue 10 10
731 20c. violet 10 10
732 25c. red 10 10
733 25c. yellow 10 10
734 30c. brown 10 10
735 35c. green 10 10
736 40c. lilac 20 10
737 50c. blue 25 10
738 60c. grey 15 10
739 65c. mauve . . . . 1·75 15
740 70c. green 30 15
741 75c. mauve 50 15
742 80c. green . . . . 7·25 75
743 90c. violet 45 10
744 1f. brown 50 10

1936. Various frames. (a) Size 17½ × 22 mm.
745 **153** 70c. brown 25 10
746 75c. olive 25 10
747 1f. red 15 10

(b) Size 21 × 24 mm.
748 **153** 1f. red 30 10
749 1f.20 brown . . . . . . 1·60 20
750 1f.50 mauve 35 30
751 1f.75 blue 15 20
752 1f.75 red 20 10
753 2f. violet 95 95
754 2f.25 black 15 15
755 2f.50 red . . . . 5·50 40
756 3f.25 brown 25 20
757 5f. green . . . . 1·10 40

Nos. 746/7, 751/2, 754/5 and 757 are inscribed "BELGIE BELGIQUE".

1936.
760 **155** 1f.50 mauve 50 10
761 1f.75 blue 20 15
762 2f. violet 40 20
763 2f.25 violet 25 20
764 2f.45 black . . . . 32·00 55
765 2f.50 black . . . . 3·50 25
770 3f. brown . . . . 1·25 25
766 3f.25 brown 30 20
771 4f. blue . . . . 3·50 10
767 5f. green . . . . 2·00 40
772 6f. red . . . . 5·00 50
768 10f. purple 35 20
769 20f. red . . . . 1·10 30

See also No. 2775.

158 Prince Baudouin **159** Queen Astrid and Prince Baudouin

1936. Anti-tuberculosis Fund.
777 **158** 10c.+5c. brown 10 10
778 25c.+5c. violet 15 15
779 35c.+5c. green 15 10
780 50c.+5c. brown 25 25
781 70c.+5c. olive 15 15
782 1f.+25c. red . . . . . . 1·10 1·25
783 1f.75+25c. blue . . . . . 1·50 1·75
784 2f.45+2f.55 purple . . . . 3·50 4·25

1937. Stamp of 1929 surch **BELGIQUE 1937 BELGIE 10c.**
785 **104** 10c. on 40c. purple . . . 20 20
See note below No. 480.

1937. International Stamp Day.
786 **158** 2f.45c.+2f.55c. slate . . . 1·60 1·75

1937. Queen Astrid Public Utility Fund.
787 **159** 10c.+5c. purple 10 10
788 25c.+5c. olive 10 15
789 35c.+5c. green 10 15
790 50c.+5c. violet 20 25
791 70c.+5c. black 10 10
792 1f.+25c. red 90 95
793 1f.75c.+25c. blue . . . . 1·90 2·00
794 2f.45c.+1f.55c. brown . . 4·50 4·75

160 Queen Elisabeth **161** Princess Josephine Charlotte

1937. Eugene Ysaye Memorial Fund.
795 **160** 70c.+5c. black 20 25
796 1f.75+25c. blue 55 70

1937. Anti-tuberculosis Fund.
798 **161** 10c.+5c. green 15 10
799 25c.+5c. brown 20 20
800 35c.+5c. green 15 20
801 50c.+5c. olive 25 25
802 70c.+5c. purple 15 10
803 1f.+25c. red . . . . . . 1·10 1·10
804 1f.75+25c. blue . . . . . 85 1·10
805 2f.45+2f.55 purple . . . . 3·50 3·00

164 King Leopold

1938. Aeronautical Propaganda.
810 **164** 10c.+5c. purple 15 10
811 35c.+5c. green 25 25
812 70c.+5c. black 40 30
813 1f.75+25c. blue . . . . . 2·40 2·25
814 2f.45+2f.55 violet . . . . 35 3·50

165 Basilica of the Sacred Heart, Koekelberg

1938. Building (Completion) Fund.
815 **165** 10c.+5c. brown 10 15
816 – 35c.+5c. green 10 15
817 **165** 70c.+5c. grey 10 15
818 – 1f.+25c. red 45 40
819 **165** 1f.75+25c. blue 45 40
820 – 2f.45+2f.55 red . . . . . 3·25 3·00
821 – 5f.+5f. green . . . . . . 8·50 9·00

DESIGNS—HORIZ: 35c., 1f., 2f.45, Front view of Basilica. VERT: 5f. Interior view.

1938. Surch **2F50.**
823 **155** 2f.50 on 2f.45 black . . . 9·50 25

167 Exhibition Pavilion **170** Prince Albert of Liege

1938. International Exhibition, Liege (1939). Inscr "LIEGE 1939 LUIK".
824 – 35c. green 10 15
825 **167** 1f. red 25 20
826 – 1f.50 brown . . . . . . 1·25 45
827 – 1f.75 blue . . . . 1·25 10

DESIGNS—VERT: 35c. View of Liege. HORIZ: 1f.50, R. Meuse at Liege; 1f.75, Albert Canal and King Albert.

1938. Koekelberg Basilica Completion Fund. Surch.
828 – 40c. on 35c.+5c. green (No. 816) 40 50
829 **165** 75c. on 70c.+5c. grey . . 30 35
830 – 2f.50+2f.50 on 2f.45+2f.55 red (No. 820) . . . . . 5·50 5·00

1938. Anti-tuberculosis Fund.
831 **170** 10c.+5c. brown 10 15
832 30c.+5c. purple 10 15
833 40c.+5c. olive 10 15
834 75c.+5c. grey 10 15
835 1f.+25c. red 95 90
836 1f.75+25c. blue 95 85
837 2f.50+2f.50 green . . . . 4·25 4·25
838 5f.+5f. purple . . . . . . 8·50 8·50

171 King Leopold and Royal Children

1939. 5th Anniv of Int Red Cross Society.
839 – 10c.+5c. brown 10 10
840 – 30c.+5c. red 10 15
841 – 40c.+5c. olive 10 15
842 **171** 75c.+5c. black 20 20
843 – 1f.+25c. red . . . . . . 1·50 1·50
844 **171** 1f.75+25c. blue 95 90
845 – 2f.50+2f.50 violet . . . . 1·60 1·75
846 – 5f.+5f. green . . . . . . 5·00 5·25

DESIGNS—VERT: 10c. H. Dunant; 30c. Florence Nightingale; 40c. and 1f. Queen Elisabeth and Royal children; 2f.50, Queen Astrid. HORIZ: 5f. Queen Elisabeth and wounded soldier (larger).

173 Rubens's House (after engraving by Harrewijn) **175** Portrait by Memling

1939. Rubens's House Restoration Fund.
847 **173** 10c.+5c. brown 10 10
848 – 40c.+5c. purple 15 15
849 – 75c.+5c. green 25 30
850 – 1f.+25c. red . . . . . . 1·40 1·40
851 – 1f.50+25c. brown . . . . 1·75 1·75
852 – 1f.75+25c. blue . . . . . 2·75 2·75
853 – 2f.50+2f.50 purple . . . . 10·50 10·50
854 – 5f.+5f. grey . . . . . . 13·50 15·00

DESIGNS—As Type **173**: VERT: 40c. "Rubens's Sons, Albert and Nicholas"; 1f. "Helene Fourment (2nd wife) and Children"; 1f.50, "Rubens and Isabella Brant" (1st wife); 1f.75, Rubens (after engraving by Pontius); 2f.50, "Straw Hat" (Suzanne Fourment). HORIZ: 75c. Arcade of Rubens's house. 35 × 45 mm: 5f. "The Descent from the Cross".

1939. Exn of Memling's Paintings, Bruges.
855 **175** 75c.+75c. olive . . . . . 1·40 1·40

177 Orval Abbey Cloisters and Belfry **180** Thuin

1939. Orval Abbey Restoration Fund. Inscr "ORVAL".
861 – 75c.+75c. olive . . . . . 3·50 3·50
862 **177** 1f.+1f. red . . . . 1·25 1·25
863 – 1f.50+1f.50 brown . . . . 1·25 1·25
864 – 1f.75+1f.75 blue . . . . . 2·25 2·25
865 – 2f.50+2f.50 mauve . . . . 6·25 6·75
866 – 5f.+5f. purple . . . . . . 6·75 6·75

DESIGNS—As Type **177**: VERT: 75c. Monks in laboratory. HORIZ: 1f.50, Monks harvesting; 1f.75, Aerial view of Orval Abbey; 52½ × 35½ mm: 2f.50, Cardinal Van Roey, Statue of the Madonna and Abbot of Orval; 5f. Kings Albert and Leopold III and shrine.

1939. Anti-tuberculosis Fund. Belfries.
868 – 10c.+5c. olive 10 10
869 **180** 30c.+5c. brown 10 10
870 – 40c.+5c. purple 10 15
871 – 75c.+5c. grey 10 10
872 – 1f.+25c. red . . . . . . 95 1·10
873 – 1f.75+25c. blue 70 70
874 – 2f.50+2f.50 brown . . . . 7·25 7·25
875 – 5f.+5f. violet . . . . . . 8·50 8·25

DESIGNS—As Type **180**: 10c. Bruges; 40c. Lier; 75c. Mons. LARGER (21½ × 34 mm): 1f. Furnes; 1f.75, Namur; 2f.50, Alost; 5f. Tournai.

182 Arms of Mons **183** Painting

184 Monks studying Plans of Orval Abbey

1940. Winter Relief Fund.

901	**182**	10c.+5c. black, red and green	10	10
902	–	30c.+5c. multicoloured	10	10
903	–	40c.+10c. multicoloured	10	10
904	–	50c.+10c. multicoloured	10	10
905	–	75c.+15c. multicoloured	10	10
906	–	1f.+25c. multicoloured	35	35
907	–	1f.75c.+50c. mult	40	35
908	–	2f.50c.+2f.50c. olive, red and black	1·40	1·10
909	–	5f.+5f. multicoloured	1·60	1·25

DESIGNS: 30c. to 5f. Arms of Ghent, Arlon, Bruges, Namur, Hasselt, Brussels, Antwerp and Liege, respectively.

1941. Orval Abbey Restoration Fund.

935	**183**	10c.+15c. brown	35	35
936	–	30c.+30c. grey	35	35
937	–	40c.+60c. brown	35	35
938	–	50c.+65c. violet	35	35
939	–	75c.+1f. mauve	35	35
940	–	1f.+1f.50 red	35	35
941	**183**	1f.25+1f.75 green	35	35
942	–	1f.75+2f.50 blue	35	35
943	–	2f.+3f.50 mauve	35	35
944	–	2f.50+4f.50 brown	35	35
945	–	3f.+5f. green	35	35
946	**184**	5f.+10f. brown	1·40	1·10

DESIGNS—As Type **183**. 30c., 1f., 2f.50, Sculpture; 40c., 2f. Goldsmiths (Monks carrying candlesticks and cross); 50c., 1f.75, Stained glass (Monk at prayer); 75c., 3f. Sacred music.

1941. Surch.

955	**152**	10c. on 30c. brown	10	10
956		10c. on 40c. lilac	10	10
957	**153**	10c. on 70c. brown	10	10
958		50c. on 75c. olive	20	20
959	**155**	2f.25 on 2f.50 black	40	45

189 Maria Theresa **190** St. Martin, Dinant

1941. Soldiers' Families Relief Fund.

960	**189**	10c.+5c. black	10	10
961	–	35c.+5c. green	10	10
962	–	50c.+10c. brown	10	10
963	–	60c.+10c. violet	10	10
964	–	1f.+15c. red	10	10
965	–	1f.50+1f. mauve	20	20
966	–	1f.75+1f.75 blue	20	20
967	–	2f.25+2f.25 brown	20	25
968	–	3f.25+3f.25 brown	40	45
969	–	5f.+5f. green	65	70

PORTRAITS: 35c. to 5f. Charles of Lorraine, Margaret of Parma, Charles V, Johanna of Castile, Philip the Good, Margaret of Austria, Charles the Bold, Archduke Albert and Archduchess Isabella respectively.

1941. Winter Relief Fund. Statues.

970	**190**	10c.+5c. brown	15	10
971	–	35c.+5c. green	15	10
972	–	50c.+10c. violet	15	10
973	–	60c.+10c. brown	15	10
974	–	1f.+15c. red	15	10
975	**190**	1f.50+25c. green	25	25
976	–	1f.75+50c. blue	25	25
977	–	2f.25+2f.25 mauve	30	30
978	–	3f.25+3f.25 brown	30	30
979	–	5f.+5f. green	50	50

DESIGNS (Statues of St. Martin in churches)—As Type **190**: 35c., 1f. Lennick, St. Quentin; 50c., 3f. Beck, Limberg; 60c., 2f.25, Dave on the Meuse; 1f.75, Hal, Brabant. 35 × 50 mm: 5f. St. Trond.

193 Mercator **198** Prisoner writing Letter

1942. Anti-tuberculosis Fund. Portraits.

986	–	10c.+5c. brown	10	10
987	–	35c.+5c. green	10	10
988	–	50c.+10c. brown	10	10
989	–	60c.+10c. green	10	10
990	–	1f.+15c. red	10	10
991	**193**	1f.75+50c. blue	10	10
992	–	3f.25+3f.25 purple	15	10
993	–	5f.+5f. violet	20	20
994	–	10f.+30f. orange	1·10	1·10

SCIENTISTS—As T **193**: 10c. Bolland. 35c. Versale. 50c. S. Stevin. 60c. Van Helmont. 1f. Dodoens. 3f.25, Oertell. 5f. Juste Lipse. 25½ × 28½ mm: 10f. Plantin.

1942. Prisoners of War Fund.

1000	**198**	5f.+45f. grey	4·50	4·50

199 St. Martin **200** St. Martin sharing his cloak

1942. Winter Relief Fund.

1001	**199**	10c.+5c. orange	10	10
1002	–	35c.+5c. green	10	10
1003	–	50c.+10c. brown	10	10
1004	–	60c.+10c. black (horiz)	10	10
1005	–	1f.+15c. red	10	10
1006	–	1f.50+25c. green	20	25
1007	–	1f.75+50c. blue	20	25
1008	–	2f.25+2f.25 brn (horiz)	20	25
1009	–	3f.25+3f.25 purple (horiz)	35	40
1010	**200**	5f.+10f. brown	1·00	1·10
1011		10f.+20f. brown & vio	1·00	1·10
1012		10f.+20f. red & violet	90	1·00

201 Soldiers and Vision of Home

1943. Prisoners of War Relief Fund.

1013	**201**	1f.+30f. red	1·90	1·90
1014	–	1f.+30f. brown	1·50	1·60

DESIGN: No. 1014, Soldiers emptying parcel of books and vision of home.

202 Tiler

1943. Anti-tuberculosis Fund. Trades.

1015	**202**	10c.+5c. brown	10	10
1016	–	35c.+5c. green	10	10
1017	–	50c.+10c. brown	10	10
1018	–	60c.+10c. green	10	10
1019	–	1f.+15c. red	25	20
1020	–	1f.75+75c. blue	25	20
1021	–	3f.25+3f.25 purple	40	35
1022	–	5f.+25f. violet	75	65

DESIGNS: 35c. Blacksmith; 50c. Coppersmith; 60c. Gunsmith; 1f. Armourer; 1f.75, Goldsmith; 3f.25, Fishmonger; 5f. Clockmaker.

203 Ornamental Letter

204 Ornamental Letters (⅔-size illustration)

1943. Orval Abbey Restoration Fund. Designs showing single letters forming "ORVAL".

1023	**203**	50c.+1f. black	30	30
1024	–	60c.+1f.90 violet	20	20
1025	–	1f.+3f. red	20	20
1026	–	1f.75+5f.25 blue	20	20
1027	–	3f.25+16f.75 green	50	40
1028	**204**	5f.+30f. brown	85	65

205 St. Leonard's Church, Leon, and St. Martin

206 Church of Notre Dame, Hal, and St. Martin

207 St. Martin and River Scheldt

1943. Winter Relief Fund.

1029	**205**	10c.+5c. brown	10	10
1030	–	35c.+5c. green	10	10
1031	–	50c.+15c. green	10	10
1032	–	60c.+20c. purple	10	10
1033	–	1f.+1f. red	20	25
1034	–	1f.75+4f.25 blue	60	65
1035	–	3f.25+11f.75 mauve	90	85
1036	**206**	5f.+25f. blue	1·40	1·40
1037	**207**	10f.+30f. green	1·25	1·10
1038	–	10f.+30f. brown	1·25	1·10

DESIGNS: (Various churches and statues of St. Martin sharing his cloak). As Type **205**: HORIZ: 35c. Dion-le-Val; 50c. Alost; 60c. Liege; 3f.25, Loppem. VERT: 1f. Courtrai; 1f.75, Angre. As Type **207**: 10f. brown Meuse landscape.

208 "Daedalus and Icarus" **209** Jan van Eyck

1944. Red Cross.

1039	**208**	35c.+1f.65 green	25	25
1040	–	50c.+2f.50 grey	25	25
1041	–	60c.+3f.40 brown	25	45
1042	–	1f.+5f. red	35	40
1043	–	1f.75+8f.25 blue	30	35
1044	–	5f.+30f. brown	45	50

DESIGNS: 50c. "The Good Samaritan" (Jacob Jordsen); 60c. "Christ healing the Paralytic" (detail); 1f. "Madonna and Child"; 1f.75, "Self-portrait"; 5f. "St. Sebastian".

Nos. 1039 and 1041/4 depict paintings by Anthony van Dyck.

1944. Prisoners of War Relief Fund.

1045	**209**	10c.+15c. violet	20	20
1046	–	35c.+15c. green	20	20
1047	–	50c.+25c. brown	20	20
1048	–	60c.+40c. olive	20	30
1049	–	1f.+50c. red	20	25
1050	–	1f.75+4f.25 blue	20	30
1051	–	2f.25+8f.25 slate	50	50
1052	–	3f.25+11f.25 brown	25	30
1053	–	5f.+35f. grey	50	60

PORTRAITS: 35c. "Godefroid de Bouillon". 50c. "Jacob van Maerlant". 60c. "Jean Joses de Dinant". 1f. "Jacob van Artevelde". 1f.75, "Charles Joseph de Ligne". 2f.25, "Andre Gretry". 3f.25, "Jan Moretus-Plantin". 5f. "Ruusbroeck".

210 "Bayard and Four Sons of Aymon", Namur **211** Lion Rampant

1944. Anti-tuberculosis Fund. Provincial legendary types.

1054	**210**	10c.+5c. brown	10	10
1055	–	35c.+5c. green	10	10
1056	–	50c.+10c. violet	10	10
1057	–	60c.+10c. brown	10	10
1058	–	1f.+15c. red	10	10
1059	–	1f.75+5f.25 blue	10	20
1060	–	3f.25+11f.75 green	20	25
1061	–	5f.+25f. blue	25	35

DESIGNS—VERT: 35c. "Brabo severing the giant's hand", Antwerp; 60c. "Thyl Ulenspiegel" and "Nele", Flanders; 1f. "St. George and the Dragon", Hainaut; 1f.75, "Genevieve of Brabant, with the Child and the Hind", Brabant. HORIZ: 50c. "St. Hubert encounters the Hind with the Cross", Luxemburg; 3f.25, "Tchantches wrestling with the Saracen", Liege; 5f. "St. Gertrude rescuing the Knight with the cards", Limburg.

1944. Inscr "BELGIQUE-BELGIE" or "BELGIE-BELGIQUE".

1062A	**211**	5c. brown	10	10
1063A		10c. green	10	10
1064A		25c. blue	10	10
1065A		35c. brown	10	10
1066A		50c. green	10	10
1067B		75c. violet	10	20
1068B		1f. red	10	15
1069B		1f.25 brown	15	20
1070B		1f.50 orange	25	30
1071A		1f.75 blue	10	10
1072B		2f. blue	90	1·10
1073A		2f.75 mauve	10	10
1074B		3f. red	10	15
1075B		3f.50 grey	10	15
1076B		5f. brown	2·10	2·25
1077B		10f. black	45	45

1944. Overprinted with large V.

1078	**152**	2c. green	10	10
1079		15c. blue	10	10
1080		20c. violet	10	10
1081		60c. grey	10	10

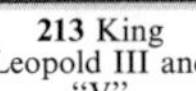

213 King Leopold III and "V" **214** War Victims

215 Rebuilding Homes

1944.

1082	**213**	1f. red	15	10
1083		1f.50 mauve	15	10
1084		1f.75 blue	25	40
1085		2f. violet	45	15
1086		2f.25 green	35	35
1087		3f.25 brown	20	10
1088		5f. green	75	15

1945. War Victims' Relief Fund.

1114	**214**	1f.+30f. red	75	65
1115	**215**	1¾f.+30f. blue	75	65

Nos. 1114/15 measure 50 × 35 mm.

1945. Post Office Employers' Relief Fund.

1119	**214**	1f.+9f. red	15	15
1120	**215**	1f.+9f. red	15	15

217 Resister

218 Group of Resisters

1945. Prisoners of War Relief Fund.
1121 **217** 10c.+15c. orange 10 10
1122 – 20c.+20c. violet 10 10
1123 – 60c.+25c. brown 10 10
1124 – 70c.+30c. green 10 10
1125 **217** 75c.+50c. brown 10 10
1126 – 1f.+75c. green 15 15
1127 – 1f.50+1f. red 15 15
1128 – 3f.50+3f.50 blue . . . . 1·00 80
1129 **218** 5f.+40f. brown . . . . . 1·50 90
DESIGNS—VERT: 20c., 1f. Father and child; 60c., 1f.50, Victim tied to stake. HORIZ: 70c., 3f.50, Rifleman.

219 West Flanders 222 Douglas DC-4

1945. Anti-tuberculosis Fund.
1130 **219** 10c.+15c. green 20 10
1131 – 20c.+20c. red 20 10
1132 – 60c.+25c. brown 20 10
1133 – 70c.+30c. green 20 10
1134 – 75c.+50c. brown 20 10
1135 – 1f.+75c. violet 20 10
1136 – 1f.50+1f. red 20 15
1137 – 3f.50+1f.50 blue 35 30
1138 – 5f.+45f. mauve . . . . . 2·50 2·00
ARMS DESIGNS—VERT: 20c. to 5f. Arms of Luxemburg, East Flanders, Namur, Limburg Hainaut, Antwerp, Liege and Brabant respectively.

1946. Air.
1165 **222** 6f. blue 30 20
1166 8f.50 red 45 40
1167 50f. green . . . . 3·75 65
1168 100f. grey . . . . 6·50 1·60

1946. Surch **-10%**, reducing the original value by 10%.
1171 **213** "-10%" on 1f.50 mauve 60 15
1172 "-10%" on 2f. violet . . 1·40 60
1173 "-10%" on 5f. green . . 1·25 15

224 "Marie Henriette" (paddle-steamer)

1946. Ostend–Dover Mail-boat Service Centenary.
1174a – 1f.35 blue 30 15
1175 **224** 2f.25 green 30 25
1176 – 3f.15 grey 25 25
DESIGNS—21½ × 18½ or 21 × 17 mm: 1f.35, "Prince Baudouin" (mail steamer). As T **224**: 3f.15, "Diamant" (paddle-steamer), formerly "Le Chemin de Fer".

225 Paratrooper

1946. Air. Bastogne Monument Fund.
1177 **225** 17f.50+62f.50 green . . . 1·00 75
1178 17f.50+62f.50 purple . . 1·00 75

226 Father Damien 227 E. Vandervelde

228 Francois Bovesse

1946. Belgian Patriots. (a) Father Damien.
1179 **226** 65c.+75c. blue . . . . . 1·40 95
1180 – 1f.35+2f. brown . . . . 1·40 85
1181 – 1f.75+18f. lake . . . . . 1·40 95
DESIGNS—HORIZ: 1f.35, Molokai Leper Colony. VERT: 1f.75, Damien's statue.

(b) Emile Vandervelde.
1182 **227** 65c.+75c. green . . . . 1·40 85
1183 – 1f.35+2f. blue . . . . . 1·40 85
1184 – 1f.75+18f. red . . . . . 1·40 95
DESIGNS—HORIZ: 1f.35, Vandervelde, miner, mother and child. VERT: 1f.75, Sower.

(c) Francois Bovesse.
1185 – 65c.+75c. violet . . . . 1·40 85
1186 **228** 1f.35+2f. brown . . . . 1·40 85
1187 – 1f.75+18f. red . . . . . 1·40 85
DESIGNS—VERT: 65c. Symbols of Patriotism and Learning; 1f.75, Draped memorial figures holding wreath and torch.

229 Pepin d'Herstal 230 Allegory of "Flight"

1946. War Victims' Relief Fund.
1188 **229** 75c.+25c. green 50 20
1189 – 1f.+50c. violet 50 35
1190 – 1f.50+1f. purple 65 35
1191 – 3f.50+1f.50 blue 80 50
1192 – 5f.+45f. mauve . . . . . 8·00 8·00
1194 – 5f.+45f. orange . . . . 8·25 8·00
DESIGNS: 1f. Charlemagne; 1f.50, Godfrey of Bouillon; 3f.50, Robert of Jerusalem; 5f. Baudouin of Constantinople.
See also Nos. 1207/11, 1258/9 and 1302/6.

1946. Air.
1193 **230** 2f.+8f. violet 40 40

231 Malines 232 Joseph Plateau

1946. Anti-tuberculosis Fund. No date.
1195 **231** 65c.+35c. red 50 25
1196 – 90c.+60c. olive 55 25
1197 – 1f.35+1f.15 green 55 30
1198 – 3f.15+1f.85 blue 75 35
1199 – 4f.50+45f.50 brown . . . 10·50 9·50
DESIGNS—(Arms and Industries): 90c. Dinant; 1f.35, Ostend; 3f.15, Verviers; 4f.50, Louvain.
See also Nos. 1212/16.

1947. Air. "Cipex" International Stamp Exhibition, New York. Nos. 1179/87 surch **LUCHTPOST POSTE AERIENNE** or **POSTE AERIENNE LUCHTPOST** and new value. (a) Father Damien.
1199a 1f.+2f. on 65c. +75c. blue 55 45
1199b 1f.+50+2f.50 on 1f.35+2f. brown 55 45
1199c 2f.+45f. on 1f.75+18f. red 55 45

(b) Emile Vandervelde.
1199d 1f.+2f. on 65c.+75c. green 55 45
1199e 1f.50+2f.50 on 1f.35+2f. blue 55 45
1199f 2f.+45f. on 1f.75+18f. red 55 45

(c) Francois Bovesse.
1199g 1f.+2f. on 65c.+75c. vio . . 55 45
1199h 1f.50+2f.50 on 1f.35+2f. brown 55 45
1199i 2f.+45f. on 1f.75+18f. red 55 45

1947. Int Film and Belgian Fine Arts Festival.
1200 **232** 3f.15 blue 65 20

233 Adrien de Gerlache 234 Explorers landing from "Belgica"

1947. 50th Anniv of Belgian Antarctic Expedition.
1201 **233** 1f.35 red 25 10
1202 **234** 2f.25 grey . . . . 2·50 60

1947. War Victims' Relief Fund. Mediaeval Princes as T **229**.
1207 65c.+35c. blue 85 45
1208 90c.+60c. green . . . . . 1·40 55
1209 1f.35+1f.15 red . . . . . 2·40 80
1210 3f.15+1f.85 blue . . . . . 2·50 95
1211 20f.+20f. purple . . . . . 60·00 30·00
DESIGNS: 65c. John II, Duke of Brabant; 90c. Philippe of Alsace; 1f.35, William the Good; 3f.15, Notger, Bishop of Liege; 20f. Philip the Noble.

1947. Anti-Tuberculosis Fund. Arms designs as T **231**, but dated "1947".
1212 65c.+35c. orange 35 35
1213 90c.+60c. purple 35 35
1214 1f.35+1f.15 brown 35 35
1215 3f.15+1f.85 blue . . . . . 1·75 65
1216 20f.+20f. green . . . . . . 16·00 12·00
DESIGNS (Arms and Industries): 65c. Nivelles; 90c. St. Truiden; 1f.35, Charleroi; 3f.15, St. Nicholas; 20f. Bouillon.

237 Chemical Industry 240 Textile Machinery

239 Antwerp Docks

1948. National Industries.
1217 **237** 60c. blue 15 15
1218 1f.20 brown . . . . . . 1·60 15
1219 – 1f.35 brown 15 15
1220 – 1f.75 green 35 15
1221 – 1f.75 red 25 25
1222 **239** 2f.25 grey . . . . 1·10 65
1223 – 2f.50 mauve . . . . . . 5·75 45
1224 **239** 3f. purple . . . . 9·50 35
1225 **240** 3f.15 blue . . . . 1·10 50
1226 4f. blue . . . . 8·00 35
1227 – 6f. blue . . . . 17·00 40
1228 – 6f.30 purple . . . . . . 2·25 4·25
DESIGNS—As Type **237**: 1f.35, 1f.75 green, Woman making lace; 1f.75 red, 2f.50, Agricultural produce. As Type **239**: 6f., 6f.30, Steel works.

242 St. Benedict and King Totila 243 St. Bega and Chevremont Castle

1948. Achel Abbey Fund. Inscr "ACHEL"
1232 **242** 65c.+65c. brown 65 45
1233 – 1f.35+1f.35 green 75 50
1234 – 3f.15+2f.85 blue . . . . 2·40 1·25
1235 – 10f.+10f. purple . . . . 8·50 7·00
DESIGNS—HORIZ: 1f.35, Achel Abbey. VERT: 3f.15, St. Benedict as Law-Giver; 10f. Death of St. Benedict.

1948. Chevremont Abbey Fund. Inscr "CHEVREMONT".
1236 **243** 65c.+65c. blue 60 45
1237 – 1f.35+1f.35 red 65 50
1238 – 3f.15+2f.85 blue . . . . 2·00 1·25
1239 – 10f.+10f. brown . . . . 8·25 6·25
DESIGNS—HORIZ: 1f.35, Chevremont Basilica and Convent. VERT: 3f.15, Madonna of Chevremont and Chapel; 10f. Monk and Madonna of Mt. Carmel.

244 Statue of Anseele 245 Ghent and E. Anseele

1948. Inauguration of Edward Anseele (Socialist Leader) Statue.
1245 **244** 65c.+35c. red . . . . . 1·75 1·00
1246 **245** 90c.+60c. grey . . . . . 2·40 1·50
1247 – 1f.35+1f.15 brn . . . . 1·50 1·00
1248 – 3f.15+1f.85 blue . . . . 5·00 3·25
DESIGNS: 1f.35, Statue and Ed. Anseele; 3f.15, Reverse side of statue.

247 "Liberty" 248 "Resistance"

1948. Antwerp and Liege Monuments Funds.
1253 **247** 10f.+10f. green . . . . . 30·00 15·00
1254 **248** 10f.+10f. brown . . . . 13·00 8·50

249 Cross of Lorraine

1948. Anti-tuberculosis Fund.
1255 **249** 20c.+5c. green 15 10
1256 1f.20+30c. purple . . . 70 35
1257 1f.75+25c. red 85 45
1258 – 4f.+3f.25 blue . . . . . 5·50 3·50
1259 – 20f.+20f. green . . . . . 30·00 21·00
DESIGNS—As Type **229**: 4f. Isabel of Austria; 20f. Albert, Archduke of Austria.

1949. Surch **1-1-49** at top, **31-XII-49** and value at bottom with posthorn in between. (a) Arms type.
1262 **152** 5c. on 15c. blue 10 10
1263 5c. on 30c. brown . . . 10 10
1264 5c. on 40c. lilac 10 10
1265 20c. on 70c. green . . . 10 10
1266 20c. on 75c. mauve . . . 10 10

(b) Anseele Statue.
1267 **244** 10c. on 65c.+35c. red . . 1·90 1·75
1268 **245** 40c. on 90c.+60c. grey 1·10 1·10
1269 – 80c. on 1f.35+1f.15 brown 50 45
1270 – 1f.20 on 3f.15+1f.85 blue 1·10 1·10

251 King Leopold I 253 St. Madeleine from "The Baptism of Christ"

252 Forms of Postal Transport

1949. Belgian Stamp Cent.
1271 **251** 90c. green (postage) . . 45 30
1272 1f.75 brown 25 15
1273 3f. red . . . . 5·25 2·50
1274 4f. blue . . . . 4·25 60
1275 **252** 50f. brown (air) . . . . 38·00 14·00

1949. Exhibition of Paintings by Gerard David, Bruges.
1276 **253** 1f.75 brown 55 20

255 Hemispheres and Allegorical Figure

1949. 75th Anniv of U.P.U.
1296 **255** 4f. blue . . . . 3·00 1·75

256 Guido Gezelle **257** Arnica

1949. 50th Death Anniv of Gezelle (poet).
1297 **256** 1f.75+75c. green . . . . 1·10 85

1949. Anti-tuberculosis and other Funds. (a) Flowers.
1298 **257** 20c.+5c. black, yellow and green 20 10
1299 – 65c.+10c. black, green and buff 85 45
1300 – 90c.+10c. black, blue and red . . . . 1·25 75
1301 – 1f.20+30c. mult . . . . 1·40 75
FLOWERS: 65c. Thistle. 90c. Periwinkle. 1f.20, Poppy.

(b) Portraits as T **229**.
1302 1f.75+25c. orange 55 25
1303 3f.+1f.50 red . . . . 7·00 5·00
1304 4f.+2f. blue . . . . 7·00 5·25
1305 6f.+3f. brown . . . . 13·50 7·50
1306 8f.+4f. green . . . . 15·00 9·25
PORTRAITS: 1f.75, Philip the Good. 3f. Charles V. 4f. Maria Christina. 6f. Charles of Lorraine. 8f. Maria Theresa.

260 Anglo-Belgian Monument, Hertain **261** Allegory of Saving

1950. Anglo-Belgian Union and other Funds.
1307 – 80c.+20c. green 80 40
1308 – 2f.50+50c. red . . . . 4·00 2·40
1309 **260** 4f.+2f. blue . . . . . . 5·75 4·50
DESIGNS—HORIZ: 80c. Arms of Great Britain and Belgium; 2f.50, British tanks at Tournai.

1950. National Savings Bank Centenary.
1310 **261** 1f.75 sepia 40 20

262 Hurdling **263** Sikorsky S-51 Helicopter and Douglas DC-4 leaving Melsbroeck

1950. European Athletic Championships. Inscr "HEYSEL 1950".
1311 **262** 20c.+5c. green 30 20
1312 – 90c.+10c. purple . . . . 2·75 1·40
1313 – 1f.75+25c. red . . . . . 4·50 1·40
1314 – 4f.+2f. blue . . . . . . 26·00 15·00
1315 – 8f.+4f. green . . . . . 28·00 18·00
DESIGNS—HORIZ: 1f.75, Relay racing. VERT: 90c. Javelin throwing; 4f. Pole vaulting; 8f. Sprinting.

1950. Air. Inauguration of Helicopter Airmail Services and Aeronautical Committee's Fund.
1317 **263** 7f.+3f. blue . . . . . . 6·50 4·00

265 Gentian **266** Sijsele Sanatorium

1950. Anti-tuberculosis and other Funds. Cross in red.
1326 **265** 20c.+5c. blue, green and purple 20 15
1327 – 65c.+10c. green and brown 80 40
1328 – 90c.+10c. light green and green . . . . 1·00 75
1329 – 1f.20+30c. blue, green and ultramarine . . . 1·25 75
1330 **266** 1f.75+25c. red . . . . . 1·50 1·00
1331 – 4f.+2f. blue . . . . . . 11·50 6·50
1332 – 8f.+4f. green . . . . . 19·00 13·50
DESIGNS—Flowers as Type **265**: 65c. Rushes; 90c. Foxglove; 1f.20, Sea lavender. Sanatoria as Type **266**: HORIZ: 4f. Jauche. VERT: 8f. Tombeek.

267 The Belgian Lion **268** "Science"

1951. (a) 17½ × 20½ mm.
1334 **267** 2c. brown 10 10
1335 3c. violet 10 10
1336 5c. lilac 15 15
1336a 5c. pink 10 10
1337 10c. orange 10 15
1338 15c. mauve 10 10
1333 20c. blue 10 10
1339 20c. red 10 15
1340 25c. green . . . . . . 1·75 45
1341 25c. blue 10 10
1342 30c. green 10 10
1343 40c. brown 10 15
1344a 50c. blue 15 25
1345 60c. mauve 10 10
1346 65c. purple . . . . . . 8·25 40
1347 75c. lilac 10 10
1348 80c. green 55 15
1349 90c. blue 85 30
1350 1f. red 10 15
1351 1f.50 grey 10 10
1353 2f. green 10 10
1354 2f.50 brown 10 10
1355 3f. mauve 10 10
1355a 4f. purple 15 10
1355b 4f.50 blue 25 10
1355c 5f. purple 25 10

(b) 20½ × 24½ mm.
1356 **267** 50c. blue 20 15
1357 60c. purple 70 55
1358a 1f. red 10 10

(c) Size 17½ × 22 mm.
1359 **267** 50c. blue 10 10
1360 1f. pink . . . . 1·40 65
1361 2f. green . . . . 3·50 20

1951. U.N.E.S.C.O. Fund. Inscr "UNESCO".
1365 **268** 80c.+20c. green . . . . 1·25 45
1366 – 2f.50+50c. brown . . . 7·25 4·75
1367 – 4f.+2f. blue . . . . . . 9·00 6·00
DESIGNS—HORIZ: 2f.50, "Education". VERT: 4f. "Peace".

269 Fairey Tipsy Belfair Trainer I

1951. Air. 50th Anniv of National Aero Club.
1368 – 6f. blue . . . . 19·00 30·00
1369 **269** 7f. red . . . . 19·00 30·00
DESIGN: 6f. Arsenal Air 100 glider.

1951. Air.
1370 – 6f. brown (glider) . . . 3·50 20
1371 **269** 7f. green . . . . 4·50 55

270 Monument **272** Queen Elisabeth

1951. Political Prisoners' National Monument Fund.
1372 **270** 1f.75+25c. brown . . . 1·75 45
1373 – 4f.+2f. blue . . . . . . 22·00 11·50
1374 – 8f.+4f. green . . . . . 22·00 13·00
DESIGNS—HORIZ: 4f. Breendonk Fort. VERT: 8f. Side view of monument.

1951. Queen Elisabeth Medical Foundation Fund.
1376 **272** 90c.+10c. grey . . . . . 2·75 60
1377 1f.75+25c. red . . . . . 3·75 1·25
1378 3f.+1f. green . . . . . 22·00 9·50
1379 4f.+2f. blue . . . . . . 21·00 10·00
1380 8f.+4f. sepia . . . . . 26·00 13·00

273 Lorraine Cross and Dragon **274** Beersel Castle

1951. Anti-tuberculosis and other Funds.
1381 **273** 20c.+5c. red 20 10
1382 65c.+10c. blue 35 15
1383 90c.+10c. brown 45 30
1384 1f.20+30c. violet 90 40
1385 **274** 1f.75+75c. brown . . . 3·00 1·00
1386 – 3f.+1f. green . . . . . 9·25 5·25
1387 – 4f.+2f. blue . . . . . . 11·00 7·00
1388 – 8f.+4f. black . . . . . 17·00 9·50
CASTLES—As Type **274**: VERT: 3f. Horst Castle. 8f. Veves Castle. HORIZ: 4f. Lavaux St. Anne Castle.
For stamps as Type **273** but dated "1952" see Nos. 1416/19 and for those dated "1953" see Nos. 1507/10.

276 Consecration of the Basilica

1952. 25th Anniv of Cardinalate of Primate of Belgium and Koekelberg Basilica Fund.
1389 – 1f.75+25c. brown . . . 95 35
1390 – 4f.+2f. blue . . . . . . 11·00 5·50
1391 **276** 8f.+4f. purple . . . . . 14·00 7·50
DESIGNS—24 × 35 mm: 1f.75, Interior of Koekelberg Basilica; 4f. Exterior of Koekelberg Basilica.

277 King Baudouin **278** King Baudouin

1952.
1393 **277** 1f.50 grey . . . . . . 1·10 15
1394 2f. red 35 15
1395 4f. blue . . . . 3·75 30
1396a **278** 50f. purple . . . . . . 2·75 25
1397a 100f. red . . . . 4·00 25

279 Francis of Taxis **281** A. Vermeylen

1952. 13th U.P.U. Congress, Brussels. Portraits of Members of the House of Thurn and Taxis.
1398 **279** 80c. green 10 15
1399 – 1f.75 orange 10 10
1400 – 2f. brown 40 20
1401 – 2f.50 red 95 30
1402 – 3f. olive 95 15
1403 – 4f. blue 95 10
1404 – 5f. brown . . . . 2·50 40
1405 – 5f.75 violet . . . . . 3·00 90
1406 – 8f. black . . . . 13·00 2·50
1407 – 10f. purple . . . . . . 18·00 6·25
1408 – 20f. grey . . . . 65·00 32·00
1409 – 40f.+10f. turquoise . . . £130 85·00
DESIGNS—VERT: 1f.75, John Baptist; 2f. Leonard; 2f.50, Lamoral; 3f. Leonard Francis; 4f. Lamoral Claud; 5f. Eugene Alexander; 5f.75, Anselm Francis; 8f. Alexander Ferdinand; 10f. Charles Anselm; 20f. Charles Alexander; 40f. Beaulieu Chateau.

1952. Culture Fund. Writers.
1410 **281** 65c.+30c. lilac . . . . 3·50 1·75
1411 – 80c.+40c. green . . . . 3·50 1·75
1412 – 90c.+45c. olive . . . . 3·50 1·75
1413 – 1f.75+75c. lake . . . . 6·25 3·50
1414 – 4f.+2f. blue . . . . . . 24·00 13·00
1415 – 8f.+4f. sepia . . . . . 25·00 14·00
PORTRAITS: 80c. K. van de Woestijne. 90c. C. de Coster. 1f.75, M. Maeterlinck. 4f. E. Verhaeren. 8f. H. Conscience.
A 4f. blue as No. 1414 and an 8f. lake as No. 1415 each se-tenant with a label showing a laurel wreath and bearing a premium "+ 9 fr." were put on sale by subscription only.

282 Arms, Malmedy **284** Dewe and Monument at Liege

1952. Anti-tuberculosis and other Funds. As T **273** but dated "1952" and designs as T **282**.
1416 **273** 20c.+5c. brown 10 10
1417 80c.+20c. green 55 30
1418 1f.20+30c. purple . . . 1·25 60
1419 1f.50+50c. olive . . . . 1·25 60
1420 **282** 2f.+75c. red . . . . . . 1·60 70
1421 – 3f.+1f.50 brown . . . . 15·00 10·00
1422 – 4f.+2f. blue . . . . . . 14·00 8·50
1423 – 8f.+4f. purple . . . . . 15·00 10·00
DESIGNS—HORIZ: 3f. Ruins, Burgreuland. VERT: 4f. Dam, Eupen; 8f. Saint and lion, St. Vith.

1953. Walthere Dewe Memorial Fund.
1435 **284** 2f.+1f. lake . . . . . . 2·00 1·10

285 Princess Josephine Charlotte **286** Fishing Boats "Marcel", "De Meeuw" and "Jacqueline Denise"

1953. Red Cross National Disaster Fund. Cross in red.
1436 **285** 80c.+20c. green . . . . 2·25 90
1437 1f.20+30c. brown . . . 1·90 80
1438 2f.+50c. lake . . . . . 1·90 80
1439 2f.50+50c. red . . . . . 12·00 7·00
1440 4f.+1f. blue . . . . . . 11·00 6·00
1441 5f.+2f. black . . . . . 12·00 6·25

1953. Tourist Propaganda and Cultural Funds.
1442 **286** 80c.+20c. green . . . . 1·60 65
1443 – 1f.20+30c. brown . . . 4·75 2·10
1444 – 2f.+50c. sepia . . . . . 4·75 2·10
1445 – 2f.50+50c. mauve . . . 12·50 5·50
1446 – 4f.+2f. blue . . . . . . 16·00 9·00
1447 – 8f.+4f. green . . . . . 19·00 11·00
DESIGNS—HORIZ: 1f.20, Bridge Bouillon; 2f. Antwerp. VERT: 2f.50, Namur; 4f. Ghent; 8f. Freyr Rocks and River Meuse.

289 King Baudouin **290**

1953. (a) 21 × 24½ mm.
1453 **289** 1f.50 black 15 10
1454 2f. red . . . . 6·25 10
1455 2f. green 25 10
2188 2f.50 brown 30 10
1457 3f. purple 25 10
1458 3f.50 green 75 10
1459 4f. blue . . . . 1·75 10
1460 4f.50 brown . . . . . 1·10 10
1462 5f. violet 85 10
1463 6f. mauve . . . . 1·75 10
1464 6f.50 grey . . . . . . 70·00 12·00
2189 7f. blue 35 25
1466 7f.50 brown . . . . . 65·00 14·50
1467 8f. blue 40 10
1468 8f.50 purple . . . . . 12·50 40
1469 9f. olive . . . . 70·00 1·25
1470 12f. turquoise 70 10
1471 30f. orange . . . . . . 7·50 35

(b) 17½ × 22 mm.
1472 **289** 1f.50 black 30 20
1473 2f.50 brown . . . . . 6·00 5·00
1474 3f. mauve 40 10
1475 3f.50 green 35 10
1476 4f.50 brown . . . . . 1·50 60

1953. European Child Welfare Fund.
1482 **290** 80c.+20c. green . . . . 3·75 2·10
1483 2f.50+1f. red . . . . . 21·00 14·00
1484 4f.+1f.50 blue . . . . . 24·00 16·00

293 Ernest Malvoz **296** King Albert Statue

1953. Anti-tuberculosis and other Funds. As T **273** but dated "1953" and portraits as T **293**.
1507 **273** 20c.+5c. blue 25 20
1508 80c.+20c. purple . . . . 1·10 45
1509 1f.20+30c. brown . . . 1·25 70
1510 1f.50+50c. slate . . . . 1·60 95
1511 **293** 2f.+75c. green . . . . . 2·00 1·25
1512 – 3f.+1f.50 red . . . . . 12·00 6·75
1513 – 4f.+2f. blue . . . . . . 14·00 8·00
1514 – 8f.+4f. brown . . . . . 16·00 9·25
PORTRAITS—VERT: 3f. Carlo Forlanini. 4f. Albert Calmette. HORIZ: 8f. Robert Koch.

1954. Surch **20c** and **I-I-54** at top, **31-XII-54** at bottom and bars in between.
1515 **267** 20c. on 65c. purple . . . 1·25 20
1516 20c. on 90c. blue . . . . 1·25 20
See note below No. 480.

1954. King Albert Memorial Fund.
1520 **296** 2f.+50c. brown . . . . 5·25 2·40
1521 – 4f.+2f. blue . . . . . . 19·00 10·50
1522 – 9f.+4f.50 black . . . . 18·00 10·50
DESIGNS—HORIZ: 4f. King Albert Memorial. VERT: 9f. Marche-les-Dames Rocks and medallion portrait.

298 Monument

299 Breendonk Camp and Fort

1954. Political Prisoners' National Monument Fund.
1531 **298** 2f.+1f. red . . . . . . 15·00 8·00
1532 **299** 4f.+2f. brown . . . . . 30·00 16·00
1533 – 9f.+4f.50 green . . . . . 35·00 19·00
DESIGN—VERT: 9f. As Type **298** but viewed from different angle.

300 Entrance to Beguinal House

1954. Beguinage of Bruges Restoration Fund.
1534 **300** 80c.+20c. green 80 50
1535 – 2f.+1f. red . . . . . . 9·00 5·50
1536 – 4f.+2f. violet . . . . . 12·50 7·00
1537 – 7f.+3f.50 purple . . . . 26·00 15·00
1538 – 8f.+4f. brown . . . . . 26·00 15·00
1539 – 9f.+4f.50 blue . . . . . 45·00 24·00
DESIGNS—HORIZ: 2f. River scene. VERT: 4f. Convent Buildings; 7f. Cloisters; 8f. Doorway; 9f. Statue of our Lady of the Vineyard (larger, 35 × 53 mm).

302 Map of Europe and Rotary Symbol

1954. 50th Anniv of Rotary International and 5th Regional Conference, Ostend.
1540 **302** 20c. red 10 10
1541 – 80c. green 25 20
1542 – 4f. blue . . . . 1·25 35
DESIGNS: 80c. Mermaid, "Mercury" and Rotary symbol; 4f. Rotary symbol and hemispheres.

303 Child

304 "The Blind Man and the Paralytic" (after Anto-Carte)

1954. Anti-T.B. and other Funds.
1543 **303** 20c.+5c. green 15 20
1544 80c.+20c. black 65 40
1545 1f.20+30c. brown . . . 1·40 1·00
1546 1f.50+50c. violet . . . . 2·75 1·60
1547 **304** 2f.+75c. red . . . . . . 4·25 2·75
1548 4f.+1f. blue . . . . . . 15·00 9·50

305 Begonia and the Rabot

1955. Ghent Flower Show.
1549 **305** 80c. red 35 20
1550 – 2f.50 sepia . . . . . . 5·25 1·90
1551 – 4f. lake . . . . 3·00 65
DESIGNS—VERT: 2f.50, Azaleas and Chateau des Comtes; 4f. Orchid and the "Three Towers".

306 "Homage to Charles V" (A. De Vriendt)

307 "Charles V" (Titian)

1955. Emperor Charles V Exhibition, Ghent.
1552 **306** 20c. red 15 10
1553 **307** 2f. green 70 10
1554 – 4f. blue . . . . 3·25 95
DESIGN—As Type **306**: 4f. "Abdication of Charles V" (L. Gallait).

308 Emile Verhaeren (after C. Montald)

309 "Textile Industry"

1955. Birth Centenary of Verhaeren (poet).
1555 **308** 20c. black 10 10

1955. 2nd Int Textile Exhibition, Brussels.
1556 **309** 2f. purple 75 20

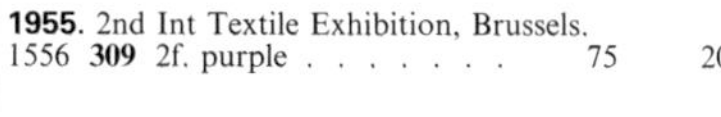

310 "The Foolish Virgin" (R. Wouters)

311 "The Departure of the Liege Volunteers in 1830" (Soubre)

1955. 3rd Biennial Sculpture Exn, Antwerp.
1557 **310** 1f.20 green 70 30
1558 2f. violet . . . . 1·25 15

1955. Liege Exn. 125th Anniv of 1830 Revolution.
1559 **311** 20c. green 10 10
1560 2f. brown 65 10

312 Ernest Solvay

1955. Cultural Fund. Scientists.
1561 **312** 20c.+5c. brown 15 20
1562 – 80c.+20c. violet 95 35
1563 – 1f.20+30c. blue . . . . 4·50 2·40
1564 – 2f.+50c. red . . . . . 4·00 2·10
1565 – 3f.+1f. green . . . . . 10·00 5·75
1566 – 4f.+2f. brown . . . . . 10·00 5·75
PORTRAITS—VERT: 80c. Jean-Jacques Dony. 2f. Leo H. Baekeland. 3f. Jean-Etienne Lenoir. HORIZ: 1f.20, Egide Walschaerts. 4f. Emile Fourcault and Emile Gobbe.

313 "The Joys of Spring" (E. Canneel)

314 E. Holboll (Danish postal official)

1955. Anti-T.B. and other Funds.
1567 **313** 20c.+5c. mauve 15 20
1568 80c.+20c. green 45 30
1569 1f.20+30c. brown . . . 2·00 85
1570 1f.50+50c. violet . . . . 1·60 70
1571 **314** 2f.+50c. red . . . . . 7·00 3·25
1572 – 4f.+2f. blue . . . . . 17·00 9·25
1573 – 8f.+4f. sepia . . . . . 18·00 9·75
PORTRAITS—As Type **314**: 4f. J. D. Rockefeller (philanthropist). 8f. Sir R. W. Philip (physician).

315 Blood Donors Emblem

316 Mozart when a Child

317 Queen Elisabeth and Mozart Sonata

1956. Blood Donors.
1574 **315** 2f. red 30 10

1956. Birth Bicentenary of Mozart. Inscr as in T **316**.
1575 – 80c.+20c. green 40 15
1576 **316** 2f.+1f. purple . . . . . 3·00 1·60
1577 **317** 4f.+2f. lilac . . . . . . 6·50 3·50
DESIGN—As Type **316**: 80c. Palace of Charles de Lorraine, Brussels.

318

319 Queen Elisabeth Medallion (Courtens)

1956. "Scaldis" Exhibitions in Tournai, Ghent and Antwerp.
1578 **318** 2f. blue 20 10

1956. 80th Birthday of Queen Elisabeth and Foundation Fund.
1579 **319** 80c.+20c. green 40 20
1580 2f.+1f. lake . . . . . . 2·75 1·40
1581 4f.+2f. sepia . . . . . . 3·50 2·40

320

321 Electric Train Type 122 and Railway Bridge

1956. Europa.
1582 **320** 2f. green . . . . 1·40 10
1583 4f. violet . . . . 6·50 30

1956. Electrification of Brussels–Luxembourg Railway Line.
1584 **321** 2f. blue 30 10

322 E. Anseele

1956. Birth Centenary of Anseele (statesman).
1588 **322** 20c. purple 10 10

323 Medieval Ship

324 Weighing a Baby

1956. Anti-tuberculosis and other Funds.
1589 **323** 20c.+5c. brown 10 10
1590 80c.+20c. green 50 25
1591 1f.20+30c. purple . . . 55 30
1592 1f.50+50c. slate 80 50
1593 **324** 2f.+50c. green . . . . . 1·40 95
1594 – 4f.+2f. purple . . . . . 3·75 5·75
1595 – 8f.+4f. red . . . . . . 10·00 7·00
DESIGNS—As Type **324**: HORIZ: 4f. X-ray examination. VERT: 8f. Convalescence and rehabilitation.

325 "Atomium" and Exhibition Emblem

327 Emperor Maximilian I, with Messenger

1957. Brussels International Exhibition.
1596 **325** 2f. red 15 10
1597 2f.50 green 25 20
1598 4f. violet 55 20
1599 5f. purple . . . . 1·00 35

1957. Stamp Day.
1603 **327** 2f. red 30 15

328 Charles Plisnier and Albrecht Rodenbach (writers)

1957. Cultural Fund. Belgian Celebrities.
1604 **328** 20c.+5c. violet 10 10
1605 – 80c.+20c. brown 30 15
1606 – 1f.20+30c. sepia 60 35
1607 – 2f.+50c. red . . . . . . 1·60 95
1608 – 3f.+1f. green . . . . . 2·00 1·75
1609 – 4f.+2f. blue . . . . . . 2·40 2·00
DESIGNS: 80c. Professors Emiel Vliebergh and Maurice Wilmotte; 1f.20, Paul Pastur and Julius Hoste; 2f. Lodewijk de Raet and Jules Destree (politicians); 3f. Constantin Meunier and Constant Permeke (artists); 4f. Lieven Gevaert and Edouard Empain (industrialists).

329 Sikorsky S-58 Helicopter

1957. Conveyance of 100,000th Passenger by Belgian Helicopter Service.
1610 **329** 4f. blue, green and grey 70 30

330 Steamer entering Zeebrugge Harbour

1957. 50th Anniv of Completion of Zeebrugge Harbour.
1611 **330** 2f. blue 30 10

331 King Leopold I entering Brussels (after Simonau)

332 Scout and Guide Badges

1957. 126th Anniv of Arrival of King Leopold I in Belgium.
1612 **331** 20c. green 15 10
1613 – 2f. mauve 40 10
DESIGN—HORIZ: 2f. King Leopold I at frontier (after Wappers).

1957. 50th Anniv of Boy Scout Movement and Birth Centenary of Lord Baden-Powell.
1614 **332** 80c. brown 25 15
1615 – 4f. green 95 40
DESIGN—VERT: 4f. Lord Baden-Powell.

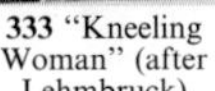

333 "Kneeling Woman" (after Lehmbruck) **334** "Agriculture and Industry"

1957. 4th Biennial Sculpture Exn, Antwerp.
1616 **333** 2f.50 green 75 55

1957. Europa.
1617 **334** 2f. purple 45 10
1618 4f. blue . . . . 1·10 35

335 Sledge-dog Team

1957. Belgian Antarctic Expedition, 1957–58.
1619 **335** 5f.+2f.50 orange, brown and grey . . . . . . 2·40 1·75

336 General Patton's Grave at Hamm **337** Adolphe Max

1957. General Patton Memorial Issue.
1621 **336** 1f.+50c. black . . . . . 1·25 55
1622 – 2f.50+50c. green . . . . 1·50 65
1623 – 3f.+1f. brown . . . . . 3·00 1·60
1624 – 5f.+2f.50 slate . . . . . 5·75 3·50
1625 – 6f.+3f. red . . . . . . 7·75 5·75
DESIGNS—HORIZ: 2f.50, Patton Memorial project at Bastogne; 3f. Gen. Patton decorating Brig.-General A. MacAuliffe; 6f. (51 × 35½ mm) Tanks in action. VERT: 5f. General Patton.

1957. 18th Death Anniv of Burgomaster Adolphe Max (patriot).
1626 **337** 2f.50+1f. blue 90 55

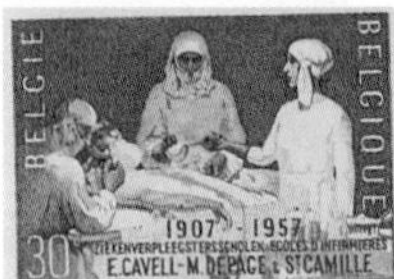

338 Queen Elisabeth with Doctors Depage and Debaisieux at a surgical operation

1957. 50th Anniv of "Edith Cavell-Marie Depage" and "St. Camille" Nursing Schools.
1627 **338** 30c. red 20 10

339 "Carnival Kings of Fosses" (Namur) **340** "Infanta Isabella with Crossbow" (Brussels)

1957. Anti-tuberculosis and other Funds. Provincial Legends.
1628 **339** 30c.+20c. pur & yell . . 20 15
1629 – 1f.+50c. sepia & blue . . 25 20
1630 – 1f.50+50c. grey & red . . 45 25
1631 – 2f.+1f. black & green . . 45 30
1632 **340** 2f.50+1f. grn & mve . . 1·50 90
1633 – 5f.+2f. black & blue . . 3·00 2·45
1634 – 6f.+2f.50 lake & red . . 3·50 3·25
DESIGNS: As Type **339**—HORIZ: 1f.50, "St. Remacle and the Wolf" (Liege). VERT: 1f. "Op Signoorken" (Antwerp); 2f. "The Long Man and the Pea Soup" (Limburg). As Type **340**—HORIZ: 6f. "Carnival Kings of Binche" (Hainaut). VERT: 5f. "The Virgin with the Inkwell" (West Flanders).

341 Posthorn and Postilion's Badges

1958. Postal Museum Day.
1635 **341** 2f.50 grey 20 10

342 Benelux Gate

1958. Inauguration of Brussels International Exhibition. Inscr as in T **342**.
1636 **342** 30c.+20c. sepia, brown and violet 10 10
1637 – 1f.+50c. purple, slate and green 10 10
1638 – 1f.50+50c. violet, turquoise and green 20 15
1639 – 2f.50+1f. red, blue and vermilion 30 20
1640 – 3f.+1f.50 blue, black and red 60 50
1641 – 5f.+3f. mauve, black and blue . . . . 1·00 90
DESIGNS—HORIZ: 1f. Civil Engineering Pavilion; 1f.50, Belgian Congo and Ruanda-Urundi Pavilion; 2f.50, "Belgium, 1900"; 3f. Atomium; 5f. (49 × 33½ mm) Telexpo Pavilion.

343 "Food and Agriculture Organization"

1958. United Nations Commemoration.
1642 – 50c. grey (postage) . . . 1·90 1·75
1643 **343** 1f. red 15 25
1644 – 1f.50 blue 20 20
1645 – 2f. purple 35 40
1646 – 2f.50 green 15 25
1647 – 3f. turquoise 40 40
1648 – 5f. mauve 20 25
1649 – 8f. brown 50 50
1650 – 11f. lilac . . . . 1·00 1·00
1651 – 20f. red . . . . 1·90 1·75

1652 – 5f. blue (air) 15 10
1653 – 6f. green 20 15
1654 – 7f.50 violet 20 15
1655 – 8f. sepia 25 25
1656 – 9f. red 35 40
1657 – 10f. brown 40 40
DESIGNS (Emblems and symbols)—HORIZ: 50c. I.L.O. 2f.50, U.N.E.S.C.O. 3f. U.N. Pavilion, Brussels Int Exn; 6f. World Meteorological Organization; 8f. (No. 1649), Int Monetary Fund; 8f. (No. 1655), General Agreement on Tariffs and Trade; 10f. Atomic Energy Agency; 11f. W.H.O. 20f. U.P.U. VERT: 1f.50, U.N.O. 2f. World Bank; 5f. (No. 1648), I.T.U. 5f. (No. 1652), I.C.A.O. 7f.50, Protection of Refugees; 9f. UNICEF.

344 Eugene Ysaye **345** "Europa"

1958. Birth Centenary of Ysaye (violinist).
1658 **344** 30c. blue and red 10 10

1958. Europa.
1659 **345** 2f.50 blue and red . . . 80 10
1660 5f. red and blue . . . . 1·50 30

346 "Marguerite Van Eyck" (after Jan Van Eyck)

1958. Cultural Relief Funds. Paintings as T **346**. Frames in brown and yellow.
1661 **346** 30c.+20c. myrtle 10 20
1662 – 1f.+50c. lake 55 35
1663 – 1f.+50+50c. blue 85 65
1664 – 2f.50+1f. sepia . . . . . 1·60 1·40
1665 – 3f.+1f.50 red . . . . . 2·10 1·75
1666 – 5f.+3f. blue . . . . . . 3·75 3·50
PAINTINGS—HORIZ: 1f. "Carrying the Cross" (Hieronymus Bosch). 3f. "The Rower" (James Ensor). VERT: 1f.50, "St. Donatien" (Jan Gossaert). 2f.50, Self-portrait (Lambert Lombard). 5f. "Henriette with the Large Hat" (Henri Evenepoel).

347 "Hoogstraten" **348** Pax—"Creche vivante"

1958. Anti-tuberculosis and other Funds. Provincial Legends.
1667 **347** 40c.+10c. blue & grn . . 10 15
1668 – 1f.+50c. sepia & yell . . 20 20
1669 – 1f.50+50c. pur & grn . . 40 20
1670 – 2f.+1f. brown & red . . 45 25
1671 **348** 2f.50+1f. red and green 1·40 75
1672 – 5f.+2f. purple & blue . . 3·00 2·75
1673 – 6f.+2f. blue & red . . . 3·50 3·25
DESIGNS: As Type **347**—VERT: 1f. "Jean de Nivelles"; 1f.50, "Jeu de Saint Evermare a Russon". HORIZ: 2f. "Les penitents de Furnes". As Type **348**—HORIZ: "Marches de l'Entre Sambre et Meuse". VERT: 6f. "Pax—Vierge".

349 "Human Rights" **350** "Europe of the Heart"

1958. 10th Anniv of Human Rights Declaration.
1674 **349** 2f.50 slate 25 10

1959. "Heart of Europe". Fund for Displaced Persons.
1675 **350** 1f.+50c. purple 25 20
1676 2f.50+1f. green 65 50
1677 5f.+2f.50 brown . . . . 1·10 85

351 J. B. de Taxis taking the oath at the hands of Charles V (after J.-E. Van den Bussche)

352 N.A.T.O. Emblem

1959. Stamp Day.
1680 **351** 2f.50 green 35 10

1959. 10th Anniv of N.A.T.O.
1681 **352** 2f.50 blue and red . . . 30 10
1682 5f. blue and green . . . 75 55
On the 5f. value the French and Flemish inscriptions are transposed.
For similar design but inscr "1969", see No. 2112.

353 "Blood Transfusion"

354 J. H. Dunant and battle scene at Solferino, 1859

1959. Red Cross Commem. Inscr "1859 1959".
1683 **353** 40c.+10c. red & grey . . 15 15
1684 1f.+50c. red & sepia . . 80 35
1685 1f.50+50c. red and lilac 1·75 1·10
1686 – 2f.50+1f. red & grn . . . 2·10 1·40
1687 – 3f.+1f.50 red and blue 3·75 2·45
1688 **354** 5f.+3f. red and sepia . . 6·75 4·00
DESIGN—As Type **353**—HORIZ: 2f.50, 3f. Red Cross and broken sword ("Aid for the wounded").

355 Philip the Good **356** Arms of Philip the Good

1959. Royal Library of Belgium Fund. Mult.
1689 40c.+10c. Type **355** 10 20
1690 1f.+50c. Charles the Bold 30 30
1691 1f.50+50c. Maximillian of Austria 95 45
1692 2f.50+1f. Philip the Fair . . 1·75 1·50
1693 3f.+1f.50 Charles V . . . . 2·40 2·25
1694 5f.+3f. Type **355** . . . . . 3·50 3·25

358 Town Hall, Oudenarde **359** Pope Adrian VI

1959. Oudenarde Town Hall Commem.
1699 **358** 2f.50 purple 25 10

1959. 500th Birth Anniv of Pope Adrian VI.
1700 **359** 2f.50 red 15 10
1701 5f. blue 30 30

360 "Europa" **361** Boeing 707

1959. Europa.
1702 **360** 2f.50 red 25 10
1703 5f. turquoise 45 35

1959. Inauguration of Boeing 707 Airliners by SABENA.
1704 **361** 6f. blue, grey and red . . 1·25 50

362 Antwerp fish (float) **363** Stavelot "Blancs Moussis" (carnival figures)

1959. Anti-tuberculosis and other Funds. Carnival scenes.
1705 **362** 40c.+10c. green, red and bistre 10 15
1706 – 1f.+50c. green, violet and olive 30 20
1707 – 2f.+50c. yellow, purple and brown 35 25
1708 **363** 2f.50+1f. blue, violet and grey 55 25
1709 – 3f.+1f. purple, yellow and grey . . . . . . 1·40 85
1710 – 6f.+2f. blue, red and olive . . . . 3·25 3·00
1711 – 7f.+3f. blk, yell, & bl . . 3·75 3·25
DESIGNS—As Type **362**—HORIZ: 1f. Mons dragon (float); 2f. Eupen and Malmedy clowns in chariot. As Type **363**—VERT: 3f. Ypres jester. HORIZ: 6f. Holy Family; 7f. Madonna and child.

364 Countess Alexandrine of Taxis (tapestry)

365 Indian Azalea

1960. Stamp Day.
1712 **364** 3f. blue 45 10

1960. Ghent Flower Show. Inscr as in T **365**.
1713 **365** 40c. red and purple . . . 10 10
1714 – 3f. yellow, red and green 45 10
1715 – 6f. red, green and blue 1·10 50
FLOWERS: 3f. Begonia. 6f. Anthurium and bromelia.

366 Refugee

367 "Labour" (after Meunier)

1960. World Refugee Year. Inscr as in T **366**.
1716 – 40c.+10c. purple 10 20
1717 **366** 3f.+1f.50 sepia 40 30
1718 – 6f.+3f. blue 95 80
DESIGNS: 40c. Child refugee; 6f. Woman refugee.

1960. 75th Anniv of Belgian Socialist Party. Inscr as in T **367**.
1720 **367** 40c. purple and red . . . 10 15
1721 – 3f. brown and red . . . 45 20
DESIGN—HORIZ: 3f. "Workers" (after Meunier).

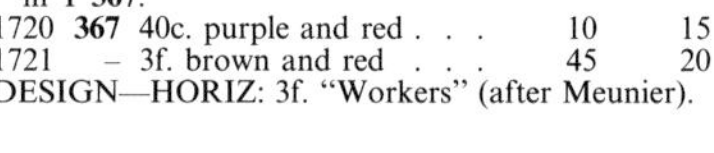

369 Parachutist on ground

1960. Parachuting. Designs bearing emblem of National Parachuting Club.
1726 – 40c.+10c. black & blue 20 20
1727 – 1f.+50c. black & blue . . 1·00 60
1728 – 2f.+50c. black, blue and green . . . . 2·10 1·25
1729 – 2f.50+1f. black, turquoise and green 3·50 2·25
1730 **369** 3f.+1f. black, blue and green . . . . 3·50 2·25
1731 6f.+2f. black, blue and green 3·75 3·00
DESIGNS—HORIZ: 40c., 1f., Parachutists dropping from Douglas DC-4 aircraft. VERT: 2f., 2f.50, Parachutists descending.

370 Ship's Officer and Helmsman

1960. Congo Independence.
1732 **370** 10c. red 10 10
1733 – 40c. red 10 10
1734 – 1f. purple 40 20
1735 – 2f. green 35 20
1736 – 2f.50 blue 50 20
1737 – 3f. blue 50 15
1738 – 6f. violet . . . . 1·50 60
1739 – 8f. brown . . . . 5·50 4·50
DESIGNS—As Type **370**: 40c. Doctor and nurses with patient; 1f. Tree-planting; 2f. Sculptors; 2f.50, Sport (putting the shot); 3f. Broadcasting from studio. (52 × 35½ mm): 6f. Children with doll; 8f. Child with globe.

371 Refugee Airlift

1960. Congo Refugees Relief Fund.
1740 **371** 40c.+10c. turquoise . . . 15 20
1741 – 3f.+1f.50 red . . . . . 1·75 1·10
1742 – 6f.+3f. violet . . . . . 3·25 2·75

DESIGNS—As Type **371**: 3f. Mother and child. 35 × 51½ mm: 6f. Boeing 707 airplane spanning map of aircraft route.

1960. Surch.
1743 **267** 15c. on 30c. green . . . 10 10
1744 15c. on 50c. blue 10 10
1745 20c. on 30c. green . . . 10 10

373 Conference Emblem

374 Young Stamp Collectors

1960. 1st Anniv of E.P.T. Conference.
1746 **373** 3f. lake 40 15
1747 6f. green 75 40

1960. "Philately for the Young" Propaganda.
1748 **374** 40c. black and bistre . . 10 10

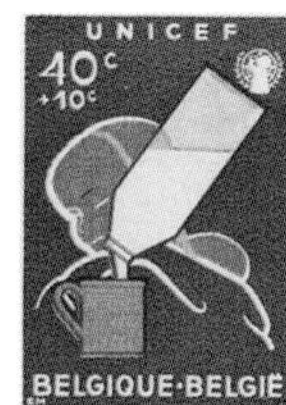

375 Pouring Milk for Child

376 Frere Orban (founder)

1960. United Nations Children's Fund.
1749 **375** 40c.+10c. yellow, green and brown 10 20
1750 – 1f.+50c. red, blue and drab 55 45
1751 – 2f.+50c. bistre, green and violet . . . . 1·25 1·10
1752 – 2f.50+1f. sepia, blue and red . . . . 1·75 1·25
1753 – 3f.+1f. violet, orange and turquoise . . . . . . 1·90 1·50
1754 – 6f.+2f. brown, green and blue . . . . 3·00 2·00
DESIGNS: 1f. Nurse embracing children; 2f. Child carrying clothes, and ambulance; 2f.50, Nurse weighing baby; 3f. Children with linked arms; 6f. Refugee worker and child.

1960. Centenary of Credit Communal (Co-operative Bank).
1755 **376** 10c. brown and yellow 10 10
1756 40c. brown and green . . 15 10
1757 1f.50 brown and violet 70 50
1758 3f. brown and red . . . 70 20

377 Tapestry

1960. Anti-T.B. and other Funds. Arts and Crafts.
1759 **377** 40c.+10c. ochre, brown and blue 10 20
1760 – 1f.+50c. blue, brown and indigo 65 55
1761 – 2f.+50c. green, black and brown . . . . 1·10 85
1762 – 2f.50+1f. yellow and brown . . . . 1·90 1·40
1763 – 3f.+1f. black, brown and blue . . . . 2·25 1·75
1764 – 6f.+2f. lemon and black 3·25 2·25
DESIGNS—VERT: 1f. Crystalware; 2f. Lace. HORIZ: 2f.50, Brassware; 3f. Diamond-cutting; 6f. Ceramics.

378 King Baudouin and Queen Fabiola

379 Nicolaus Rockox (after Van Dyck)

1960. Royal Wedding.
1765 **378** 40c. sepia and green . . 15 10
1766 3f. sepia and purple . . 55 10
1767 6f. sepia and blue . . . 1·75 40

1961. Surch in figs and **1961** at top, **1962** at bottom and bars in between.
1768 **267** 15c. on 30c. green . . . 60 10
1769 20c. on 30c. green . . . 1·60 10
See note below No. 480.

1961. 400th Birth Anniv of Nicolaus Rockox (Burgomaster of Antwerp).
1770 **379** 3f. black, bistre & brn 30 10

380 Seal of Jan Bode

381 K. Kats (playwright) and Father N. Pietkin (poet)

1961. Stamp Day.
1771 **380** 3f. sepia and brown . . 30 10

1961. Cultural Funds. Portrait in purple.
1772 40c.+10c. lake and pink . . 10 15
1773 1f.+50c. lake and brown . . 1·40 1·10
1774 2f.+50c. red and yellow . . 2·40 2·10
1775 2f.50+1f. myrtle and sage 2·40 2·10
1776 3f.+1f. blue and light blue 2·75 2·25
1777 6f.+2f. blue and lavender . . 3·50 2·75
PORTRAITS: 40c. Type **381**. 1f. A. Mockel and J. F. Willems (writers). 2f. J. van Rijswijck and X. Neujean (politicians). 2f.50, J. Demarteau (journalist) and A. van de Perre (politician). 3f. J. David (litterateur) and A. du Bois (writer). 6f. H. Vieuxtemps (violinist) and W. de Mol (composer).

382 White Rhinoceros

383 Cardinal A.P. de Granville (first Archbishop)

1961. Philanthropic Funds. Animals of Antwerp Zoo.
1778 40c.+10c. dp brown & brn 15 15
1779 1f.+50c. brown and green 70 65
1780 2f.+50c. sepia, red and black 1·25 85
1781 2f.50+1f. brown and red . . 1·25 95
1782 3f.+1f. brown and orange 1·50 1·10
1783 6f.+2f. ochre and blue . . 1·90 1·40
ANIMALS—VERT: 40c. Type **382**; 1f. Wild horse and foal, 2f. Okapi. HORIZ: 2f.50, Giraffe; 3f. Lesser panda; 6f. Elk.

1961. 400th Anniv of Archbishopric of Malines.
1784 **383** 40c.+10c. brown, red and purple 10 10
1785 – 3f.+1f.50 mult 55 35
1786 – 6f.+3f. bistre, violet and purple 90 80
DESIGNS: 3f. Cardinal's Arms; 6f. Symbols of Archbishopric and Malines.

385 "Interparliamentary Union"

1961. 50th Interparliamentary Union Conference, Brussels.
1791 **385** 3f. brown and turquoise 45 10
1792 6f. purple and red . . . 70 40

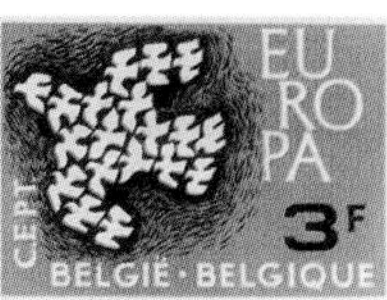

386 Doves

1961. Europa.
1793 **386** 3f. black and olive . . . 20 10
1794 6f. black and brown . . 40 25

387 Reactor BR 2, Mol

388 "The Mother and Child" (after Paulus)

1961. Euratom Commemoration.
1795 **387** 40c. green 10 10
1796 – 3f. mauve 15 10
1797 – 6f. blue 35 30
DESIGNS—VERT: 3f. Heart of reactor BR 3, Mol. HORIZ: 6f. View of reactor BR 3, Mol.

1961. Anti-T.B. and other Funds. Belgian paintings of mothers and children. Frames in gold.
1798 **388** 40c.+10c. sepia 10 15
1799 – 1f.+50c. blue 40 40
1800 – 2f.+50c. red 80 65
1801 – 2f.50+1f. lake 80 70
1802 – 3f.+1f. violet 75 65
1803 – 6f.+2f. myrtle 95 85
PAINTINGS: 1f. "Maternal Love" (Navez). 2f. "Maternity" (Permeke). 2f.50, "The Virgin and the Child" (Van der Weyden). 3f. "The Virgin with the Apple" (Memling), 6f. "The Myosotis Virgin" (Rubens).

389 Horta Museum

390 Male Castle

1962. Birth Cent of Victor Horta (architect).
1804 **389** 3f. brown 25 10

1962. Cultural and Patriotic Funds. Buildings.
1805 **390** 40c.+10c. green 10 10
1806 – 90c.+10c. mauve 20 20
1807 – 1f.+50c. lilac 40 30
1808 – 2f.+50c. violet 60 55
1809 – 2f.50+1f. brown 80 70
1810 – 3f.+1f. turquoise 90 80
1811 – 6f.+2f. red . . . . . . 1·50 1·25
BUILDINGS—HORIZ: 90c. Royal Library, Brussels. 1f. Collegiate Church, Soignies. 6f. Ypres Halls. VERT: 1f. Notre-Dame Basilica, Tongres. 2f.50, Notre-Dame Church, Hanswijk, Malines. 3f. St. Denis-en-Broqueroie Abbey.

391 16th-Century Postilion

392 G. Mercator (after F. Hogenberg)

1962. Stamp Day.
1812 **391** 3f. brown and green . . 25 10
See also No. 1997.

1962. 450th Birth Anniv of Mercator (geographer).
1813 **392** 3f. sepia 25 10

393 Brother A. M. Gochet (scholar)

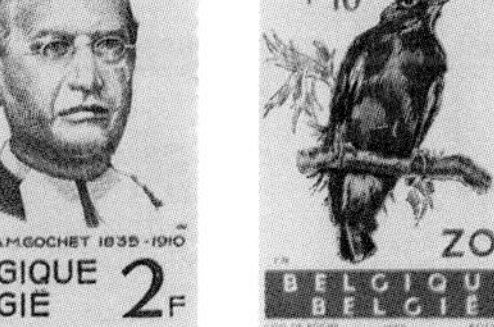

394 Guianan Cock of the Rock ("Coq de Roch, Rotshann")

1962. Gochet and Triest Commemoration.
1814 **393** 2f. blue 10 15
1815 – 3f. brown 25 15
PORTRAIT: 3f. Canon P.-J. Triest (benefactor of the aged).

1962. Philanthropic Funds. Birds of Antwerp Zoo. Birds, etc., in natural colours; colours of name panel and inscription given.
1816 **394** 40c.+10c. blue 10 20
1817 – 1f.+50c. blue and red . . 35 35
1818 – 2f.+50c. mauve & blk . . 60 60
1819 – 2f.50+1f. turq & red . . 75 80

1820 – 3f.+1f. brown & grn . . 90 1·00
1821 – 6f.+2f. blue and red . . 1·10 1·25
BIRDS: 1f. Red lory ("Rode Lori, Lori Rouge"); 2f. Green turaco ("Touracou du Senegal, Senegal Toerakoe"); 2f.50, Keel-billed toucan ("Kortbek Toecan, Toucan a Bec Court"); 3f. Greater bird of paradise ("Grand Paradijsier, Grosse Paradisvogel"); 6f. Congo peafowl ("Kongo Pauw, Paon du Congo").

395 Europa "Tree"

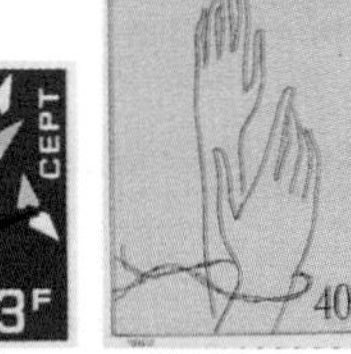
396 "Captive Hands" (after sculpture by Ianchelivici)

1962. Europa.
1822 **395** 3f. black, yellow & red 20 10
1823 6f. black, yellow & olive 40 35

1962. Concentration Camp Victims.
1824 **396** 40c. blue and black . . . 15 10

397 Reading Braille

398 "Adam" (after Michelangelo)

1962. Handicapped Children Relief Funds.
1825 **397** 40c.+10c. brown 10 20
1826 – 1f.+50c. red 30 40
1827 – 2f.+50c. mauve 75 80
1828 – 2f.50+1f. green 70 80
1829 – 3f.+1f. blue 75 75
1830 – 6f.+2f. sepia 65 90
DESIGNS—VERT: 1f. Girl solving puzzle; 2f.50, Crippled child with ball; 3f. Girl walking with crutches. HORIZ: 2f. Child with earphones; 6f. Crippled boys with football.

1962. "The Rights of Man".
1831 **398** 3f. sepia and green . . . 20 15
1832 6f. sepia and brown . . 40 35

399 Queen Louise-Marie

400 Menin Gate, Ypres

1962. Anti-tuberculosis and other Funds. Belgian Queens in green and gold.
1833 40c.+10c. Type **399** 10 10
1834 40c.+10c. As T **399** but inscr "ML" 10 10
1835 1f.+50c. Marie-Henriette . . 45 40
1836 2f.+1f. Elisabeth 80 75
1837 3f.+1f.50 Astrid . . . . . . 1·10 95
1838 8f.+2f.50 Fabiola . . . . . 1·25 1·10

1962. Ypres Millenary.
1839 **400** 1f.+50c. multicoloured 30 40

401 H. Pirenne

402 "Peace Bell"

1963. Birth Cent of Henri Pirenne (historian).
1841 **401** 3f. blue 30 10

1963. Cultural Funds and Installation of "Peace Bell" in Koekelberg Basilica. Bell in yellow; "PAX" in black.
1842 **402** 3f.+1f.50 green & bl . . 1·25 1·10
1843 6f.+3f. chestnut & brn 65 65

403 "The Sower" (after Brueghel)

404 17th-century Duel

1963. Freedom from Hunger.
1845 **403** 2f.+1f. brown, black and green 20 20
1846 – 3f.+1f. brown, black and purple 25 20
1847 – 6f.+2f. yellow, black and brown 40 40
PAINTINGS—HORIZ: 3f. "The Harvest" (Brueghel). VERT: 6f. "The Loaf" (Anto Carte).

1963. 350th Anniv of Royal Guild and Knights of St. Michael.
1848 **404** 1f. red and blue 10 10
1849 – 3f. violet and green . . . 20 10
1850 – 6f. multicoloured 40 30
DESIGNS—HORIZ: 3f. Modern fencing. VERT: 6f. Arms of the Guild.

405 19th-century Mail-coach

1963. Stamp Day.
1851 **405** 3f. black and ochre . . . 25 10
See also No. 1998.

406 Hotel des Postes, Paris, and Belgian 1c. Stamp of 1863

407 Child in Wheatfield

1963. Centenary of Paris Postal Conference.
1852 **406** 6f. sepia, mauve & grn 35 35

1963. "8th May" Peace Movement.
1853 **407** 3f. multicoloured 20 15
1854 6f. multicoloured 35 35

408 "Transport"

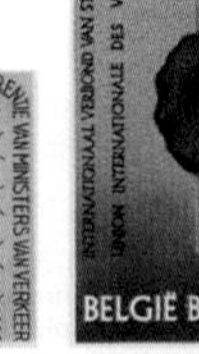
409 Town Seal

1963. European Transport Ministers' Conference, Brussels.
1855 **408** 6f. black and blue . . . 35 35

1963. Int Union of Towns Congress, Brussels.
1856 **409** 6f. multicoloured 35 35

410 Racing Cyclists

411 Sud Aviation SE 210 Caravelle

1963. Belgian Cycling Team's Participation in Olympic Games, Tokyo (1964).
1857 **410** 1f.+50c. multicoloured 10 25
1858 – 2f.+1f. multicoloured . . 10 25
1859 – 3f.+1f.50 mult 25 35
1860 – 6f.+3f. multicoloured . . 35 50
DESIGNS—HORIZ: 2f. Group of cyclists; 3f. Cyclists rounding bend. VERT: 6f. Cyclists being paced by motorcyclists.

1963. 40th Anniv of SABENA Airline.
1861 **411** 3f. black and turquoise 20 10

412 "Co-operation"

413 Princess Paola with Princess Astrid

1963. Europa.
1862 **412** 3f. black, brown & red 65 15
1863 6f. black, brown & blue 1·00 40
No. 1863 is inscr with "6 F" on the left, "BELGIE" at foot and "BELGIQUE" on right.

1963. Centenary of Red Cross and Belgian Red Cross Fund. Cross in red.
1864 – 40c.+10c. red & yell . . 10 10
1865 **413** 1f.+50c. grey & yellow 20 20
1866 – 2f.+50c. mauve & yell 25 25
1867 – 2f.50+1f. blue & yell . . 25 35
1868 – 3f.+1f. brown & yell . . 45 45
1869 – 3f.+1f. bronze & yell . . 1·45 2·00
1870 – 6f.+2f. green & yellow 1·10 1·25
DESIGNS—As T **413**: 40c. Prince Philippe; 2f. Princess Astrid; 2f.50, Princess Paola; 6f. Prince Albert; 46 × 35 mm: 3f. (2), Prince Albert and family.

414 J. Destree (writer)

1963. Jules Destree and H. Van de Velde Commems.
1871 **414** 1f. purple 10 10
1872 – 1f. green 10 10
DESIGN: No. 1872, H. Van de Velde (architect).

415 Bas-reliefs from Facade of Postal Cheques Office (after O. Jespars)

416 Balthasar Gerbier's Daughter

1963. 50th Anniv of Belgian Postal Cheques Office.
1873 **415** 50c. black, blue & red 10 15

1963. T.B. Relief and Other Funds. Rubens's Drawings. Background buff; inscr in black: designs colour given.
1874 **416** 50c.+10c. blue 10 10
1875 – 1f.+40c. red 20 20
1876 – 2f.+50c. violet 20 20
1877 – 2f.50+1f. green 45 40
1878 – 3f.+1f. brown 45 35
1879 – 6f.+2f. black 75 65
DRAWINGS—VERT: Rubens's children—1f. Nicolas (aged 2). 2f. Franz (aged 4). 2f.50, Nicolas (aged 6). 3f. Albert (aged 3). HORIZ: ($46\frac{1}{2} \times 35\frac{1}{2}$ mm): 6f. Infant Jesus, St. John and two angels.

417 Dr. G. Hansen and Laboratory

1964. Leprosy Relief Campaign.
1880 **417** 1f. black and brown . . 15 20
1881 – 2f. brown and black . . 20 25
1882 – 5f. black and brown . . 45 35
DESIGNS: 2f. Leprosy hospital; 5f. Father Damien.

418 A. Vesale (anatomist) with Model of Human Arm

419 Postilion

1964. Belgian Celebrities.
1884 **418** 50c. black and green . . 10 10
1885 – 1f. black and green . . . 15 20
1886 – 2f. black and green . . . 20 20
DESIGNS—HORIZ: 1f. J. Boulvin (engineer) and internal combustion engine; 2f. H. Jaspar (statesman) and medallion.

1964. Stamp Day.
1887 **419** 3f. grey 20 10

420 Admiral Lord Gambier and U.S. Ambassador J. Q. Adams after signing treaty (from painting by Sir A. Forestier)

1964. 150th Anniv of Signing of Treaty of Ghent.
1888 **420** 6f.+3f. blue 50 55

421 Arms of Ostend

422 Ida of Bure (Calvin's wife)

1964. Millenary of Ostend.
1889 **421** 3f. multicoloured 20 10

1964. "Protestantism in Belgium".
1890 – 1f.+50c. blue 15 20
1891 **422** 3f.+1f.50 red 20 25
1892 – 6f.+3f. brown 45 50
PORTRAITS: 1f. P. Marnix of St. Aldegonde (Burgomaster of Antwerp). 6f. J. Jordaens (painter).

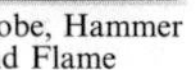
423 Globe, Hammer and Flame

424 Infantryman of 1918

1964. Centenary of Socialist International.
1893 **423** 50c. red and blue 10 10
1894 – 1f. red and blue 10 10
1895 – 2f. red and blue 15 25
DESIGNS: 1f. "SI" on Globe; 2f. Flames.

1964. 50th Anniv of German Invasion of Belgium. Multicoloured.
1896 1f.+50c. Type **424** 15 10
1897 2f.+1f. Colour sergeant of the Guides Regt, 1914 . . 15 20
1898 3f.+1f.50 Trumpeter of the Grenadiers & Drummers of the Infantry and Carabiniers, 1914 . . . . 25 30

425 Soldier at Bastogne

426 Europa "Flower"

1964. "Liberation–Resistance". Multicoloured
1899 3f.+1f. Type **425** 20 20
1900 6f.+3f. Soldier at estuary of the Scheldt 45 50

1964. Europa.
1901 **426** 3f. grey, red and green 20 10
1902 6f. blue, green and red 40 35

429 Pand Abbey, Ghent

1964. Pand Abbey Restoration Fund.
1905 **429** 2f.+1f. bl, turq & blk . . 20 25
1906 – 3f.+1f. brown, blue and purple 20 25
DESIGN: 3f. Waterside view of Abbey.

430 King Baudouin, Queen Juliana and Grand Duchess Charlotte

1964. 20th Anniv of "BENELUX".
1907 **430** 3f. purple, blue and olive . . . 30 10

431 "One of Charles I's Children" (Van Dyck)
432 "Diamonds"

1964. T.B. Relief and Other Funds. Paintings of Royalty.
1908 **431** 50c.+10c. purple 15 15
1909 – 1f.+40c. red 15 20
1910 – 2f.+1f. purple 20 25
1911 – 3f.+1f. grey 25 25
1912 – 4f.+2f. violet 30 35
1913 – 6f.+3f. violet 40 50
DESIGNS—VERT: 1f. "William of Orange and his fiancee, Marie" (Van Dyck); 2f. "Portrait of a Little Boy" (E. Quellin and Jan Fyt); 3f. "Alexander Farnese at the age of 12 Years" (A. Moro); 4f. "William II, Prince of Orange" (Van Dyck). HORIZ—LARGER (46 × 35 mm): 6f. "Two Children of Cornelis De Vos" (C. de Vos).

1965. "Diamantexpo" (Diamonds Exn) Antwerp.
1914 **432** 2f. multicoloured 20 20

433 "Textiles"
434 Vriesia

1965. "Textirama" (Textile Exn), Ghent.
1915 **433** 1f. black, red and blue . . . 10 10

1965. Ghent Flower Show. Inscr "FLORALIES GANTOISES", etc. Multicoloured.
1916 1f. Type **434** 10 20
1917 2f. Echinocactus 20 25
1918 3f. Stapelia 20 10

435 Paul Hymans
436 Rubens

1965. Birth Cent of Paul Hymans (statesman).
1919 **435** 1f. violet 10 10

1965. Centenary of General Savings and Pensions Funds. Painters.
1920 **436** 1f. sepia and mauve . . 20 10
1921 – 2f. sepia and turquoise . . 20 10
1922 – 3f. sepia and purple . . 15 10
1923 – 6f. sepia and red 30 25
1924 – 8f. sepia and blue . . . 45 40
PAINTERS: 2f. Franz Snyders. 3f. Adam van Noort. 6f. Anthony van Dyck. 8f. Jakob Jordaens.

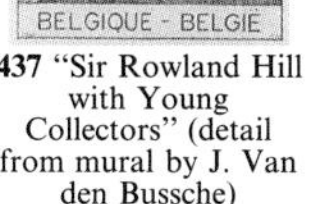

437 "Sir Rowland Hill with Young Collectors" (detail from mural by J. Van den Bussche)
438 19th-century Postmaster

1965. "Philately for the Young".
1925 **437** 50c. green 10 10

1965. Stamp Day.
1926 **438** 3f. green 20 10

439 Globe and Telephone

1965. Centenary of I.T.U.
1928 **439** 2f. black and purple . . 15 20

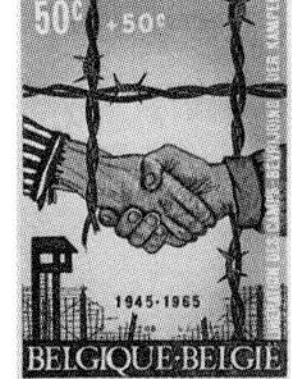

440 Handclasp
441 Abbey Staircase

1965. 20th Anniv of Liberation of Prison Camps.
1929 **440** 50c.+50c. purple, black and bistre 10 10
1930 – 1f.+50c. multicoloured 20 20
1931 – 3f.+1f.50 black, purple and green 25 25
1932 – 8f.+5f. multicoloured . . 75 75
DESIGNS—VERT: 1f. Hand reaching for barbed wire. HORIZ: 3f. Tank entering prison camp; 8f. Rose within broken wall.

1965. Affligem Abbey.
1933 **441** 1f. blue 10 10

442 St. Jean Berchmans, Birthplace and Residence
443 Toc H Lamp and Arms of Poperinge

1965. St. Jean Berchmans.
1934 **442** 2f. brown and purple . . 10 10

1965. 50th Anniv of Founding of Toc H Movement at Talbot House, Poperinge.
1935 **443** 3f. multicoloured 20 10

444 Maison Stoclet, Brussels
445 Tractor ploughing

1965. Josef Hoffman (architect) Commemoration.
1936 **444** 3f.+1f. grey and drab . . 20 25
1937 – 6f.+3f. brown 40 45
1938 – 8f.+4f. purple & drab . . 65 65
DESIGNS—Maison Stoclet: VERT: 6f. Entrance hall. HORIZ: 8f. Rear of building.

1965. 75th Anniv of Boerenbond (Belgian Farmers' Association). Multicoloured.
1939 50c. Type **445** 10 10
1940 3f. Horse-drawn plough . . 20 10

446 Europa "Sprig"

1965. Europa.
1941 **446** 1f. black and pink . . . 10 10
1942 3f. black and green . . . 20 10

447 Jackson's Chameleon

1965. Philanthropic Funds. Reptiles of Antwerp Zoo. Multicoloured.
1943 1f.+50c. Type **447** 10 20
1944 2f.+1f. Iguana 20 20
1945 3f.+1f.50 Nile lizard 25 30
1946 6f.+3f. Komodo lizard . . . 45 45

448 J. Lebeau (after A. Schollaert)
449 Leopold I (after 30c. and 1f. Stamps of 1865)

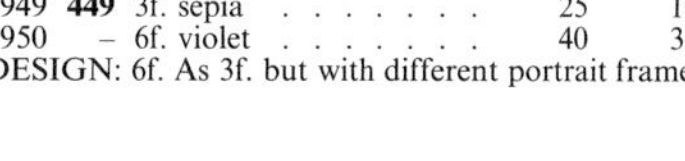

1965. Death Cent of Joseph Lebeau (statesman).
1948 **448** 1f. multicoloured 10 10

1965. Death Centenary of King Leopold I.
1949 **449** 3f. sepia 25 10
1950 – 6f. violet 40 35
DESIGN: 6f. As 3f. but with different portrait frame.

450 Huy
451 Guildhouse

1965. Tourist Publicity. Multicoloured.
1951 50c. Type **450** 10 10
1952 50c. Hoeilaart (vert) 10 10
See also Nos. 1995/6, 2025/6, 2083/4, 2102/3, 2123/4, 2159/60, 2240/1 and 2250/1.

1965. T.B. Relief and Other Funds. Public Buildings, Brussels.
1953 **451** 50c.+10c. blue 10 10
1954 – 1f.+40c. turquoise . . . 10 20
1955 – 2f.+1f. purple 20 20
1956 – 3f.+1f.50 violet 25 25
1957 – 10f.+4f.50 sepia and grey 70 70
BUILDINGS—HORIZ: 1f. Brewers' House; 2f. Builders' House; 3f. House of the Dukes of Brabant. VERT: (24½ × 44½ mm): 10f. Tower of Town Hall.

452 Queen Elisabeth (from medallion by A. Courtens)
453 "Peace on Earth"

1965. Queen Elisabeth Commem.
1958 **452** 3f. black 25 10

1966. 75th Anniv of "Rerum Novarum" (papal encyclical). Multicoloured.
1959 50c. Type **453** 10 10
1960 1f. "Building for Tomorrow" (family and new building) 10 10
1961 3f. Arms of Pope Paul VI (vert 24½ × 45 mm) . . . 10 10

454 Rural Postman
455 High Diving

1966. Stamp Day.
1964 **454** 3f. black, lilac & buff . . 25 10

1966. Swimming.
1965 **455** 60c.+40c. brown, green and blue 10 10
1966 – 10f.+4f. brown, purple and green 80 70
DESIGN: 10f. Diving from block.

456 Iguanodon Fossil (Royal Institute of Natural Sciences)
457 Eurochemic Symbol

1966. National Scientific Institutions.
1967 **456** 1f. black and green . . . 25 20
1968 – 2f. black, orge & cream 10 20
1969 – 2f. multicoloured 10 20
1970 – 3f. multicoloured 10 10
1971 – 3f. gold, black and red 10 10
1972 – 6f. multicoloured 25 25
1973 – 8f. multicoloured 45 45
DESIGNS—HORIZ: No. 1968, Kasai head (Royal Central African Museum); No. 1969, Snow crystals (Royal Meteorological Institute). VERT: No. 1970, "Scholar" (Royal Library); No. 1971, Seal (General Archives); No. 1972, Arend-Roland comet and telescope (Royal Observatory); No. 1973, Satellite and rocket (Space Aeronomy Inst.).

1966. European Chemical Plant, Mol.
1974 **457** 6f. black, red and drab 35 25

458 A. Kekule
460 Rik Wouters (self-portrait)

1966. Centenary of Professor August Kekule's Benzene Formula.
1975 **458** 3f. brown, black & blue 25 10

1966. 19th World I.P.T.T. Congress, Brussels. Optd **XIXe CONGRES IPTT** and emblem.
1976 **454** 3f. black, lilac and buff 25 10

1966. 50th Death Anniv of Rik Wouters (painter).
1977 **460** 60c. multicoloured . . . 10 10

461 Minorites Convent, Liege

1966. Cultural Series.
1978 **461** 60c.+40c. purple, blue and brown 10 20
1979 – 1f.+50c. blue, purple and turquoise 10 20
1980 – 2f.+1f. red, purple and brown 10 20
1981 – 10f.+4f.50 purple, turquoise and green 70 65
DESIGNS: 1f. Val-Dieu Abbey, Aubel; 2f. Huy and town seal; 10f. Statue of Ambiorix and castle, Tongres.

463 Europa "Ship"
464 Surveying

1966. Europa.
1989 **463** 3f. green 25 10
1990 6f. purple 45 35

1966. Antarctic Expeditions.
1991 **464** 1f.+50c. green 10 10
1992 – 3f.+1f.50 violet 25 25
1993 – 6f.+3f. red 45 50

DESIGNS: 3f. Commander A. de Gerlache and "Belgica" (polar barque); 6f. "Magga Dan" (Antarctic supply ship) and meteorological operations.

1966. Tourist Publicity. As T **450**. Multicoloured.
1995 2f. Bouillon 10 10
1996 2f. Lier (vert) 10 10

1966. 75th Anniv of Royal Federation of Belgian Philatelic Circles. Stamps similar to Nos. 1812 and 1851 but incorporating "1890 1996" and F.I.P. emblem.
1997 **391** 60c. purple and green 10 10
1998 **405** 3f. purple and ochre 10 10

466 Children with Hoops **467** Lions Emblem

1966. "Solidarity" (Child Welfare).
1999 – 1f.+1f. black & pink 10 10
2000 – 2f.+1f. black & green 10 10
2001 – 3f.+1f.50 black & lav 20 25
2002 **466** 6f.+3f. brown & flesh 40 40
2003 – 8f.+3f.50 brown & grn 50 50
DESIGNS—VERT: 1f. Boy with ball and dog; 2f. Girl with skipping-rope; 3f. Boy and girl blowing bubbles. HORIZ: 8f. Children and cat playing "Follow My Leader".

1967. Lions International.
2004 **467** 3f. sepia, blue and olive 25 10
2005 6f. sepia, violet and green 35 35

468 Part of Cleuter Pistol

1967. Arms Museum, Liege.
2006 **468** 2f. black, yellow & red 20 20

469 I.T.Y. Emblem

1967. International Tourist Year.
2007 **469** 6f. blue, red and black 40 25

471 Woodland and Trientalis (flowers), Hautes Fagnes

1967. Nature Conservation. Multicoloured.
2009 1f. Type **471** 10 20
2010 1f. Dunes and eryngium (flowers), Westhoek 10 20

472 Paul-Emile Janson (statesman) **473** 19th-century Postman

1967. Janson Commemoration.
2011 **472** 10f. blue 55 35

1967. Stamp Day.
2012 **473** 3f. purple and red 25 10

474 Cogwheels **475** Flax Plant and Shuttle

1967. Europa.
2013 **474** 3f. black, red and blue 25 10
2014 6f. black, yellow & green 45 35

1967. Belgian Linen Industry.
2015 **475** 6f. multicoloured 35 25

476 Kursaal in 19th Century

1967. 700th Anniv of Ostend's Rank as Town.
2016 **476** 2f. sepia, buff and blue 10 10

478 With F.I.T.C.E. Emblem **479** Robert Schuman (statesman)

1967. European Telecommunications Day. "Stamp Day" design of 1967 incorporating F.I.T.C.E. emblem as T **478** in green.
2021 **478** 10f. sepia and blue 55 35
"F.I.T.C.E." "Federation des Ingenieurs des Telecommunications de la Communaute Europeenne."

1967. Charity.
2022 **479** 2f.+1f. green 25 25
2023 – 5f.+2f. brown, yellow and black 40 40
2024 – 10f.+5f. multicoloured 70 75
DESIGNS—HORIZ: 5f. Kongolo Memorial, Gentinnes (Congo Martyrs). VERT: 10f. "Colonial Brotherhood" emblem (Colonial Troops Memorial).

1967. Tourist Publicity. As T **450**. Mult.
2025 1f. Ypres 10 10
2026 1f. Spontin 10 20

480 "Caesar Crossing the Rubicon" (Tournai Tapestry) **481** "Jester in Pulpit" (from Erasmus's "Praise of Folly")

1967. Charles Plisnier and Lodewijk de Raet Foundations.
2028 **480** 1f. multicoloured 10 10
2029 – 1f. multicoloured 10 10
DESIGN No. 2029, "Maximilian hunting boar" (Brussels tapestry).

1967. Cultural Series. "Erasmus and His Time".
2030 1f.+50c. multicoloured 10 10
2031 2f.+1f. multicoloured 20 25
2032 3f.+1f.50 multicoloured 25 25
2033 5f.+2f. black, red & carmine 35 40
2034 6f.+3f. multicoloured 45 45
DESIGNS—VERT: 1f. Type **481**. 2f. "Jester declaiming" (from Erasmus' "Praise of Folly"); 3f. Erasmus; 6f. Pierre Gilles ("Aegidius" from painting by Metzijs). HORIZ: 5f. "Sir Thomas More's Family" (Holbein).

482 "Princess Margaret of York" (from miniature) **483** Arms of Ghent University

1967. "British Week".
2035 **482** 6f. multicoloured 40 25

1967. Universities of Ghent and Liege. Mult.
2036 3f. Type **483** 25 10
2037 3f. Liege 25 10

485 Our Lady of Virga Jesse, Hasselt

1967. Christmas.
2039 **485** 1f. blue 10 10

486 "Children's Games" (section of Brueghel's painting)

1967. "Solidarity".
2040 **486** 1f.+50c. multicoloured 10 10
2041 – 2f.+50c. multicoloured 10 10
2042 – 3f.+1f. multicoloured 25 25
2043 – 6f.+3f. multicoloured 45 40
2044 – 10f.+4f. multicoloured 70 65
2045 – 13f.+6f. multicoloured 90 90
Nos. 2040/5 together form the complete painting.

487 Worker in Protective Hand **489** Army Postman (1916)

1968. Industrial Safety Campaign.
2046 **487** 3f. multicoloured 25 10

1968. Stamp Day.
2068 **489** 3f. purple, brown & blue 25 10

490 Belgian 1c. "Small Lion" Stamp of 1866 **491** Grammont and Seal of Baudouin VI

1968. Cent of State Printing Works, Malines.
2069 **490** 1f. olive 10 10

1968. "Historical Series". Multicoloured.
2070 2f. Type **491** 25 20
2071 3f. Theux-Franchimont Castle and battle emblems 25 10
2072 6f. Archaeological discoveries, Spiennes 40 25
2073 10f. Roman oil lamp and town crest, Wervik 55 40

492 Europa "Key" **493** Queen Elisabeth and Dr. Depage

1968. Europa.
2074 **492** 3f. gold, black & green 25 15
2075 6f. silver, black and red 45 35

1968. Belgian Red Cross Fund. Cross in red.
2076 **493** 6f.+3f. sepia, black and green 55 50
2077 – 10f.+5f. sepia, black and green 75 70
DESIGN: 10f. Queen Fabiola and baby.

494 Gymnastics **495** "Explosion"

1968. Olympic Games, Mexico. Multicoloured.
2078 1f.+50c. Type **494** 10 10
2079 2f.+1f. Weightlifting 10 20
2080 3f.+1f.50 Hurdling 20 20
2081 6f.+2f. Cycling 25 30
2082 13f.+5f. Sailing (vert 24½ × 45 mm) 45 70
Each design includes the Olympic "rings" and a Mexican cultural motif.

1968. Tourist Publicity. As Type **450**.
2083 2f. multicoloured 10 10
2084 2f. black, blue and green 10 10
DESIGNS: No. 2083, Farm-house and windmill, Bokrijk; No. 2084, Bath-house and fountain, Spa.

1968. Belgian Disasters. Victims Fund. Mult.
2085 10f.+5f. Type **495** 55 70
2086 12f.+5f. "Fire" 75 1·00
2087 13f.+5f. "Typhoon" 90 90

496 St. Laurent Abbey, Liege

1968. "National Interest".
2088 **496** 2f. black, bistre & blue 10 20
2089 – 3f. brown, grey & lt brn 25 10
2090 – 6f. black, blue & dp bl 35 20
2091 – 10f. multicoloured 65 35
DESIGNS: 3f. Church, Lissewege; 6f. "Mineral Seraing" and "Gand" (ore carriers), canal-lock, Zandvliet; 10f. Canal-lift, Ronquieres.

497 Undulate Triggerfish

1968. "Solidarity" and 125th Anniv of Antwerp Zoo. Designs showing fish. Multicoloured.
2092 1f.+50c. Type **497** 10 20
2093 3f.+1f.50 Ear-spotted angelfish 20 20
2094 6f.+3f. Lionfish 40 45
2095 10f.+5f. Diagonal butterflyfish 65 70

498 King Albert in Bruges (October, 1918) **499** Lighted Candle

1968. Patriotic Funds.
2096 **498** 1f.+50c. multicoloured 10 20
2097 – 3f.+1f.50 mult 20 25

2098 – 6f.+3f. multicoloured . . 40 45
2099 – 10f.+5f. multicoloured 65 70
DESIGNS—HORIZ: 3f. King Albert entering Brussels (November, 1918); 6f. King Albert in Liege (November, 1918). LARGER (46 × 35 mm): 10f. Tomb of the Unknown Soldier, Brussels.

1968. Christmas.
2100 **499** 1f. multicoloured 10 10

500 "Mineral Seraing" (ore carrier) in Ghent Canal

1968. Ghent Maritime Canal.
2101 **500** 6f. black brown, & blue 35 20

1969. Tourist Publicity. As Type **450**.
2102 1f. black, blue & pur (vert) 10 10
2103 1f. black, olive and blue . . 10 10
DESIGNS. No. 2102, Town Hall, Louvain; No. 2103, Valley of the Ourthe.

501 "Albert Magnis" (detail of wood carving by Quellin, Confessional, St. Paul's Church, Antwerp)

1969. St. Paul's Church, Antwerp, and Aulne Abbey Commemoration.
2104 **501** 2f. sepia 10 10
2105 – 3f. black and mauve . . 10 10
DESIGN: 3f. Aulne Abbey.

502 "The Travellers" (sculpture, Archaeological Museum, Arlon)
503 Broodjes Chapel, Antwerp

1969. 2,000th Anniv of Arlon.
2106 **502** 2f. purple 10 20

1969. "150 Years of Public Education in Antwerp".
2107 **503** 3f. black and grey . . . 25 10

504 Mail Train
505 Colonnade

1969. Stamp Day.
2108 **504** 3f. multicoloured 20 10

1969. Europa.
2109 **505** 3f. multicoloured 20 15
2110 6f. multicoloured 45 35

507 NATO Emblem
508 "The Builders" (F. Leger)

1969. 20th Anniv of N.A.T.O.
2112 **507** 6f. blue and brown . . . 35 35

1969. 50th Anniv of I.L.O.
2113 **508** 3f. multicoloured 25 10

509 "Houses" (I. Dimitrova)
510 Racing Cyclist

1969. U.N.I.C.E.F. "Philanthropy" Funds. Mult.
2114 1f.+50c. Type **509** 10 20
2115 3f.+1f.50 "My Art" (C. Patric) 25 25
2116 6f.+3f. "In the Sun" (H. Rejchlova) 45 40
2117 10f.+5f. "Out for a Walk" (P. Sporn) (horiz) 65 70

1969. World Championship Cycle Races, Zolder.
2118 **510** 6f. multicoloured 40 25

511 Mgr. V. Scheppers
512 National Colours

1969. Monseigneur Victor Scheppers (founder of "Brothers of Mechlin") Commemoration.
2119 **511** 6f.+3f. purple 50 50

1969. 25th Anniv of BENELUX Customs Union.
2120 **512** 3f. multicoloured 25 10

513 Pascali Rose and Annevoie Gardens

1969. Flowers and Gardens. Multicoloured.
2121 2f. Type **513** 10 10
2122 2f. Begonia and Lochristi Gardens 10 10

1969. Tourist Publicity. As Type **450**.
2123 2f. brown, red and blue . . 10 10
2124 2f. black, green and blue . . 10 10
DESIGNS: No. 2123, Veurne Furnes; No. 2124, Vielsalm.

514 "Feats of Arms" from "History of Alexander the Great" (Tournai, 15th century)
516 Wounded Soldier

515 Astronauts and Location of Moon Landing

1969. "Cultural Works" Tapestries. Mult.
2125 1f.+50c. Type **514** 10 20
2126 3f.+1f.50 "The Violinist" from "Festival" (David Teniers II, Oudenarde, c.1700) 35 30
2127 10f.+4f. "The Paralytic", from "The Acts of the Apostles" (Brussels, c.1517) 85 80

1969. 1st Man on the Moon.
2128 **515** 6f. sepia 40 25

1969. 50th Anniv of National War Invalids Works (O.N.I.G.).
2130 **516** 1f. green 10 10

517 "The Postman" (Daniella Sainteney)
519 Count H. Carton de Wiart (from painting by G. Geleyn)

518 John F. Kennedy Motorway Tunnel, Antwerp

1969. "Philately for the Young".
2131 **517** 1f. multicoloured 10 10

1969. Completion of Belgian Road-works. Mult.
2132 3f. Type **518** 25 10
2133 6f. Loncin flyover, Wallonie motorway 40 35

1969. Birth Centenary of Count Henry Carton de Wiart (statesman).
2134 **519** 6f. sepia 35 30

520 "Barbu d'Anvers" (Cockerel)

1969. "The Poultry-yard" (poultry-breeding).
2135 **520** 10f.+5f. multicoloured 90 85

521 "Le Denombrement de Bethleem" (detail, Brueghel)

1969. Christmas.
2136 **521** 1f.50 multicoloured . . . 10 10

522 Emblem, "Coin" and Machinery
523 Window, St. Waudru Church, Mons

1969. 50th Anniv of National Credit Society (S.N.C.I.).
2137 **522** 3f.50 brown and blue . . 25 10

1969. "Solidarity". Musicians in Stained-glass Windows. Multicoloured.
2138 1f.50+50c. Type **523** . . . 15 20
2139 3f.50+1f.50 's-Herenelderen Church 25 25
2140 7f.+3f. St. Jacques Church, Liege 55 60
2141 9f.+4f. Royal Museum of Art and History, Brussels 90 90
No. 2141 is larger, 36 × 52 mm.

524 Camellias
525 Beech Tree in National Botanical Gardens

1970. Ghent Flower Show. Multicoloured.
2142 1f.50 Type **524** 10 10
2143 2f.50 Water-lily 25 20
2144 3f.50 Azaleas 25 10

1970. Nature Conservation Year. Multicoloured.
2146 3f.50 Type **525** 25 10
2147 7f. Birch 35 30

526 Young "Postman"

1970. "Philately for the Young".
2148 **526** 1f.50 multicoloured . . . 10 10

527 New U.P.U. Headquarters Building

1970. New U.P.U. Headquarters Building.
2149 **527** 3f.50 green 25 10

528 "Flaming Sun"

1970. Europa.
2150 **528** 3f.50 cream, blk & lake 30 10
2151 7f. flesh, black and blue 45 35

529 Open-air Museum, Bokrijk
530 Clock-tower, Virton

1970. Cultural Works. Multicoloured.
2152 1f.50+50c. Type **529** . . . 10 20
2153 3f.50+1f.50 Relay Post-house, Courcelles 20 20
2154 7f.+3f. "The Reaper of Trevires" (bas-relief, Virton) 45 50
2155 9f.+4f. Open-air Museum, Middelheim, (Antwerp) 60 60

1970. Historic Towns of Virton and Zelzate.
2156 **530** 2f.50 violet and ochre . . 10 20
2157 – 2f.50 black and blue . . 10 10
DESIGN—HORIZ: No. 2157, "Skaustand" (freighter), canal bridge, Zelzate.

531 Co-operative Alliance Emblem

1970. 75th Anniv of Int Co-operative Alliance.
2158 **531** 7f. black and orange . . 35 20

1970. Tourist Publicity, As Type **450**.
2159 1f.50 green, blue and black 10 10
2160 1f.50 buff, blue & deep blue 10 10
DESIGNS—HORIZ: No. 2159, Kasterlee. VERT: No. 2160, Nivelles.

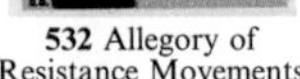

532 Allegory of Resistance Movements **533** King Baudouin

1970. 25th Anniv of Prisoner of War and Concentration Camps Liberation.
2161 **532** 3f.50+1f.50 black, red and green 25 20
2162 – 7f.+3f. black, red and mauve 45 50
DESIGN: 7f. Similar to Type **532**, but inscr "LIBERATION DES CAMPS", etc.

1970. King Baudouin's 40th Birthday.
2163 **533** 3f.50 brown 20 10
See also Nos. 2207/23c and 2335/9b.

534 Fair Emblem **535** U.N. Headquarters, New York

1970. 25th International Ghent Fair.
2164 **534** 1f.50 multicoloured . . . 10 10

1970. 25th Anniv of United Nations.
2165 **535** 7f. blue and black . . . 25 20

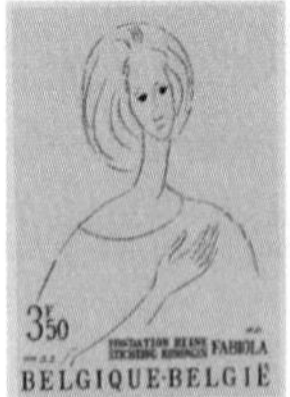

536 Queen Fabiola **537** Angler's Rod and Reel

1970. Queen Fabiola Foundation.
2166 **536** 3f.50 black and blue . . 20 10

1970. Sports. Multicoloured.
2167 3f.50+1f.50 Type **537** . . . 30 30
2168 9f.+4f. Hockey stick and ball 45 55

539 "The Mason" (sculpture by G. Minne) **541** "Madonna and Child" (Jan Gossaert)

540 Man, Woman and Hillside Town

1970. 50th Anniv of National Housing Society.
2170 **539** 3f.50 brown & yell . . . 10 10

1970. 25th Anniv of Belgian Social Security.
2171 **540** 2f.50 multicoloured . . . 10 10

1970. Christmas.
2172 **541** 1f.50 brown 10 10

542 C. Huysmans (statesman) **543** Arms of Eupen, Malmedy and St. Vith

1970. Cultural Works. Famous Belgians.
2173 **542** 1f.50+50c. brown and red 10 10
2174 – 3f.50+1f.50 brown and purple 20 15
2175 – 7f.+3f. brown & green 45 40
2176 – 9f.+4f. brown & blue . . 60 60
PORTRAITS: 3f.50, Cardinal J. Cardijn. 7f. Maria Baers (Catholic social worker). 9f. P. Pastur (social reformer).

1970. 50th Anniv of Annexation of Eupen, Malmedy and St. Vith.
2177 **543** 7f. brown and sepia . . 20 20

544 "The Uneasy Town" (detail, Paul Delvaux) **545** Telephone

1970. "Solidarity". Paintings. Multicoloured.
2178 3f.50+1f.50 Type **544** . . . 25 30
2179 7f.+3f. "The Memory" (Rene Magritte) 45 45

1971. Inaug of Automatic Telephone Service.
2183 **545** 1f.50 multicoloured . . . 10 10

546 "Auto" Car

547 Touring Club Badge

1971. 50th Brussels Motor Show.
2184 **546** 2f.50 black and red . . . 10 10

1971. 75th Anniv of Royal Touring Club of Belgium.
2185 **547** 3f.50 gold, red & blue 20 10

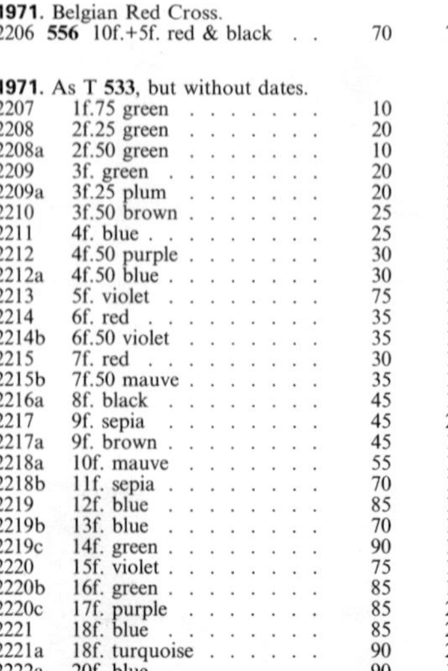

548 Tournai Cathedral **549** "The Letter-box" (T. Lobrichon)

1971. 800th Anniv of Tournai Cathedral.
2186 **548** 7f. blue 35 35

1971. "Philately for the Young".
2187 **549** 1f.50 brown 10 10

550 Notre-Dame Abbey, Marche-les-Dames

1971. Cultural Works.
2190 **550** 3f.50+1f.50 black, green and brown 25 30
2191 – 7f.+3f. black, red and yellow 45 45
DESIGN: 7f. Convent, Turnhout.

552 King Albert I, Jules Destree and Academy

1971. 50th Anniv of Royal Academy of French Language and Literature.
2201 **552** 7f. black and grey . . . 35 35

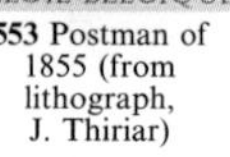

553 Postman of 1855 (from lithograph, J. Thiriar) **554** Europa Chain

1971. Stamp Day.
2202 **553** 3f.50 multicoloured . . . 20 10

1971. Europa.
2203 **554** 3f.50 brown and black 20 10
2204 7f. green and black . . . 30 30

555 Satellite Earth Station **556** Red Cross

1971. World Telecommunications Day.
2205 **555** 7f. multicoloured 35 25

1971. Belgian Red Cross.
2206 **556** 10f.+5f. red & black . . 70 70

1971. As T **533**, but without dates.
2207 1f.75 green 10 15
2208 2f.25 green 20 15
2208a 2f.50 green 10 10
2209 3f. green 20 10
2209a 3f.25 plum 20 10
2210 3f.50 brown 25 10
2211 4f. blue 25 10
2212 4f.50 purple 30 15
2212a 4f.50 blue 30 10
2213 5f. violet 75 10
2214 6f. red 35 10
2214b 6f.50 violet 35 10
2215 7f. red 30 10
2215b 7f.50 mauve 35 10
2216a 8f. black 45 10
2217 9f. sepia 45 20
2217a 9f. brown 45 10
2218a 10f. mauve 55 10
2218b 11f. sepia 70 10
2219 12f. blue 85 10
2219b 13f. blue 70 10
2219c 14f. green 90 10
2220 15f. violet 75 10
2220b 16f. green 85 10
2220c 17f. purple 85 20
2221 18f. blue 85 20
2221a 18f. turquoise 90 20
2222a 20f. blue 90 10
2222b 22f. black . . . . 1·25 1·10
2222c 22f. turquoise . . . . . . 1·25 25
2222d 25f. purple . . . . 1·25 25
2223a 30f. orange . . . . 1·60 10
2223b 35f. turquoise . . . . . . 1·75 25
2223c 40f. blue . . . . 2·00 20
2223d 45f. brown . . . . 2·50 40
See also Nos. 2335/9.

557 Scientist, Adelie Penguins and "Erika Dan" (polar vessel)

1971. 10th Anniv of Antarctic Treaty.
2230 **557** 10f. multicoloured . . . 50 50

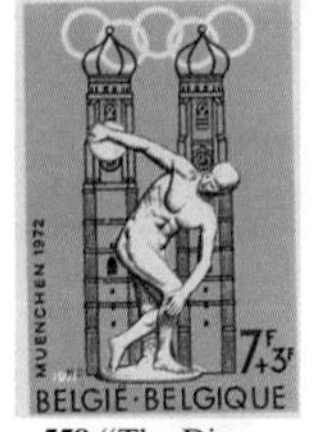

558 "The Discus thrower" and Munich Cathedral **559** G. Hubin (statesman)

1971. Olympic Games, Munich (1972) Publicity.
2231 **558** 7f.+3f. black & blue . . 45 45

1971. Georges Hubin Commemoration.
2232 **559** 1f.50 violet and black . . 10 10

560 Notre-Dame Abbey, Orval **561** Processional Giants, Ath

1971. 900th Anniv of Notre-Dame Abbey, Orval.
2233 **560** 2f.50 brown 10 10

1971. Historic Towns.
2234 **561** 2f.50 multicoloured . . . 10 10
2235 – 2f.50 brown 10 20
DESIGN—HORIZ: (46 × 35 mm): No. 2235, View of Ghent.

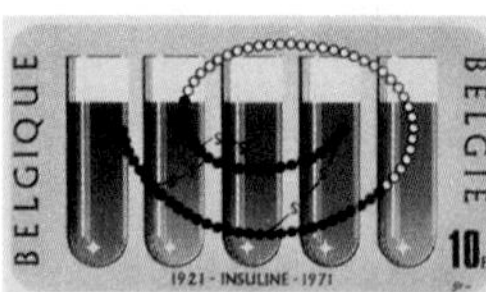

562 Test-tubes and Diagram

1971. 50th Anniv of Discovery of Insulin.
2236 **562** 10f. multicoloured . . . 55 40

563 Flemish Festival Emblem

1971. Cultural Works. Festivals. Multicoloured.
2237 3f.50+1f.50 Type **563** . . . 25 25
2238 7f.+3f. Walloon Festival emblem 55 60

564 Belgian Family and "50" **565** Dr. Jules Bordet (medical scientist)

1971. 50th Anniv of "League of Large Families".
2239 **564** 1f.50 multicoloured . . . 10 10

1971. Tourist Publicity. Designs similar to T **450**.
2240 2f.50 black, brown and blue 10 10
2241 2f.50 black, brown and blue 10 10
DESIGNS: No. 2240, St. Martin's Church, Alost; No. 2241, Town Hall and belfry, Mons.

1971. Belgian Celebrities.
2242 **565** 3f.50 green 25 10
2243 – 3f.50 brown 25 10
DESIGN: No. 2242, Type **565** (10th death anniv); No. 2243, "Stijn Streuvels" (Frank Lateur, writer, birth cent.).

566 Achaemenid Tomb, Buzpar

567 Elewijt Chateau

1971. 2500th Anniv of Persian Empire.
2244 **566** 7f. multicoloured 40 30

1971. "Belgica 72" Stamp Exhibition, Brussels (2nd issue).
2245 – 3f.50+1f.50 green 25 25
2246 **567** 7f.+3f. brown 55 50
2247 – 10f.+5f. blue 85 80
DESIGNS—HORIZ: (52 × 35½ mm): 3f. Attre Chateau; 10f. Royal Palace, Brussels.

568 F.I.B./V.B.N. Emblem

569 "The Flight into Egypt" (15th-century Dutch School)

1971. 25th Anniv of Federation of Belgian Industries.
2248 **568** 3f.50 gold, black & blue 25 10

1971. Christmas.
2249 **569** 1f.50 multicoloured . . . 10 10

1971. Tourist Publicity. Designs similar to T **450**.
2250 1f.50 blue and buff 10 10
2251 2f.50 blue and buff 20 10
DESIGNS—HORIZ: 1f.50, Town Hall, Malines. VERT: 2f.50, Basilica, St. Hubert.

570 "Actias luna"

1971. "Solidarity". Insects in Antwerp Zoo. Multicoloured.
2252 1f.50+50c. Type **570** . . . 10 10
2253 3f.50+1f.50 "Tabanus bromius" (horiz) 30 30
2254 7f.+3f. "Polistes gallicus" (horiz) 55 50
2255 9f.+4f. "Cicindela campestris" 65 65

572 Road Signs and Traffic Signals

573 Book Year Emblem

1972. 20th Anniv of "Via Secura" Road Safety Organization.
2263 **572** 3f.50 multicoloured . . . 25 10

1972. International Book Year.
2264 **573** 7f. blue, brown & black 40 30

574 Coins of Belgium and Luxembourg

576 "Auguste Vermeylen" (I. Opsomer)

1972. 50th Anniv of Belgo–Luxembourgeoise Economic Union.
2265 **574** 1f.50 silver, black and orange 10 10

1972. Birth Centenary of Auguste Vemeylen (writer).
2267 **576** 2f.50 multicoloured . . . 10 20

577 "Belgica 72" Emblem

578 Heart Emblem

1972. "Belgica 72" Stamp Exn., Brussels (3rd Issue).
2268 **577** 3f.50 purple, blue & brn 25 10

1972. World Heart Month.
2269 **578** 7f. multicoloured 40 25

579 Astronaut cancelling Letter on Moon

580 "Communications"

1972. Stamp Day.
2270 **579** 3f.50 multicoloured . . . 25 10

1972. Europa.
2271 **580** 3f.50 multicoloured . . . 30 10
2272 7f. multicoloured 50 40

581 Quill Pen and Newspaper

582 "UIC" on Coupled Wagons

1972. "Liberty of the Press". 50th Anniv of Belga News Agency and 25th Congress of International Federation of Newspaper Editors (F.I.E.J.).
2273 **581** 2f.50 multicoloured . . . 20 10

1972. 50th Anniv of Int Railways Union (U.I.C.).
2274 **582** 7f. multicoloured 35 25
See also No. P2266.

583 Couvin

584 Leopold I 10c. "Epaulettes" Stamp of 1849

1972. Tourist Publicity.
2275 **583** 2f.50 purple, blue & grn 20 25
2276 – 2f.50 brown and blue . . 20 25
DESIGN—VERT: No. 2276, Aldeneik Church, Maaseik.

1972. "Belgica 72" Stamp Exn, Brussels (4th issue).
2277 **584** 1f.50+50c. brown, black and gold 20 20
2278 – 2f.+1f. red, brown and gold 25 25
2279 – 2f.50+1f. red, brown and gold 30 25
2280 – 3f.50+1f.50 lilac, black and gold 35 35
2281 – 6f.+3f. violet, black and gold 45 45
2282 – 7f.+3f. red, black and gold 55 60
2283 – 10f.+5f. blue, black and gold 85 80
2284 – 15f.+7f.50 green, turquoise and gold . . 1·25 1·25
2285 – 20f.+10f. chestnut, brown and gold . . . 1·75 1·60
DESIGNS: 2f. Leopold I 40c. "Medallion" of 1849; 2f.50, Leopold II 10c. of 1883. 3f.50, Leopold II 50c. of 1883; 6f. Albert I; 2f. "Tin Hat" of 1919; 7f. Albert I 50f. of 1929; 10f. Albert I 1f.75 of 1931; 15f. Leopold III 5f. of 1936; 20f. Baudouin 3f.50 of 1970.

585 "Beatrice" (G. de Smet)

586 Emblem of Centre

1972. "Philately for the Young".
2287 **585** 3f. multicoloured 25 20

1972. Inauguration of William Lennox Epileptic Centre, Ottignies.
2288 **586** 10f.+5f. multicoloured 85 75

587 Dish Aerial and "Intelstat 4" Satellite

588 Frans Masereel (wood-carver and painter)

1972. Inaug of Satellite Earth Station, Lessive.
2289 **587** 3f.50 black, silver & bl 25 10

1972. Masereel Commem.
2290 **588** 4f.50 black and green . . 30 10

589 "Adoration of the Magi" (F. Timmermans)

590 "Empress Maria Theresa" (unknown artist)

1972. Christmas.
2291 **589** 3f.50 multicoloured . . . 25 10

1972. Bicentenary of Belgian Royal Academy of Sciences, Letters and Fine Arts.
2292 **590** 2f. multicoloured 25 10

591 Greylag Goose

592 "Fire"

1972. "Solidarity". Birds from Zwin Nature Reserve. Multicoloured.
2293 2f.+1f. Type **591** 25 25
2294 4f.50+2f. Northern lapwing 40 40
2295 8f.+4f. White stork 65 65
2296 9f.+4f.50 Common kestrel (horiz) 80 80

1973. Industrial Buildings Fire Protection Campaign.
2297 **592** 2f. multicoloured 10 10

593 W.M.O. Emblem and Meteorological Equipment

595 W.H.O. Emblem as Man's "Heart"

594 Bijloke Abbey and Museum, Ghent

1973. Centenary of World Meteorological Organization.
2298 **593** 9f. multicoloured 50 35

1973. Cultural Works. Religious Buildings.
2299 **594** 2f.+1f. green 20 25
2300 – 4f.50+2f. brown 35 35
2301 – 8f.+4f. red 60 60
2302 – 9f.+4f.50 blue 80 75
DESIGNS: 4f.50, Collegiate Church of St. Ursmer, Lobbes; 8f. Park Abbey, Heverlee; 9f. Floreffe Abbey.

1973. 25th Anniv of W.H.O.
2303 **595** 8f. black, yellow & red 40 30

596 Ball in Hands

1973. 1st World Basketball Championships for the Handicapped, Bruges.
2304 **596** 10f.+5f. multicoloured 85 80

597 Europa "Posthorn"

598 Thurn and Taxis Courier (17th-cent)

1973. Europa.
2305 **597** 4f.50 blue, yellow & brn 25 10
2306 8f. blue, yellow & green 45 35

1973. Stamp Day.
2307 **598** 4f.50 brown and red . . 25 10

599 Fair Emblem

600 Arrows encircling Globe

1973. 25th International Fair, Liege.
2308 **599** 4f.50 multicoloured . . . 25 10

1973. 5th World Telecommunications Day.
2309 **600** 3f.50 multicoloured . . . 20 10

601 "Sport" (poster for Ghent Exhibition, 1913)

1973. 60th Anniv of Workers' International Sports Organization.
2310 **601** 4f.50 multicoloured . . . 25 10

602 Douglas DC-10-30CF and De Havilland D.H.9

1973. 50th Anniv of SABENA.
2311 **602** 8f. black, blue and grey 45 40

603 Ernest Tips's Biplane, 1908

1973. 35th Anniv (1972) of "Les Vieilles Tiges de Belgique" (pioneer aviators' association).
2312 **603** 10f. black, blue & green 55 30

604 15th-Century Printing-press
605 "Woman Bathing" (fresco by Lemaire)

1973. Historical Events and Anniversaries.
2313 **604** 2f.+1f. blk, brn & red . . 25 25
2314 – 3f.50+1f.50 mult 25 25
2315 – 4f.50+2f. mult 35 35
2316 – 8f.+4f. multicoloured . . 65 65
2317 – 9f.+4f.50 mult 70 60
2318 – 10f.+5f. multicoloured 90 95
DESIGNS—VERT (As Type **604**): 2f. (500th anniv of first Belgian printed book, produced by Dirk Martens); 3f.50, Head of Amon (Queen Elisabeth Egyptological Foundation. 50th anniv.); 4f.50, "Portrait of a Young Girl" (Petrus Christus, 500th death anniv). HORIZ (36 × 25 mm): 8f. Gold coins of Hadrian and Marcus Aurelius (Discovery of Roman treasure at Luttre-Liberchies); (52 × 35 mm); 9f. "Members of the Great Council" (Coessaert) (Great Council of Malines, 500th anniv.). 10f. "Jong Jacob" (East Indiaman) (Ostend Merchant Company, 250th anniv).

1973. Thermal Treatment Year.
2319 **605** 4f.50 multicoloured . . . 25 10

606 Adolphe Sax and Tenor Saxophone
607 St. Nicholas Church, Eupen

1973. Belgian Musical Instrument Industry.
2320 **606** 9f. multicoloured 45 35

1973. Tourist Publicity.
2321 **607** 2f. multicoloured 10 20
See also Nos. 2328/9, 2368/70, 2394/5, 2452/5, 2508/11, 2535/8, 2573/6, 2595/6 and 2614.

608 "Little Charles" (Evenepoel)
609 J. B. Moens (philatelist) and Perforations

1973. "Philately for the Young".
2322 **608** 3f. multicoloured 25 20

1973. 50th Anniv of Belgian Stamp Dealers Association.
2323 **609** 10f. multicoloured . . . 55 40

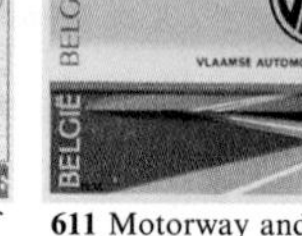

610 "Adoration of the Shepherds" (H. van der Goes)
611 Motorway and Emblem

1973. Christmas.
2324 **610** 4f. blue 30 20

1973. 50th Anniv of "Vlaamse Automobilistenbond" (VAB) (motoring organization).
2325 **611** 5f. multicoloured 30 10

612 L. Pierard (after sculpture by Ianchelevici)
613 Early Microphone

1973. 21st Death Anniv of Louis Pierard (politician and writer).
2326 **612** 4f. red and cream . . . 30 10

1973. 50th Anniv of Belgium Radio.
2327 **613** 4f. black and blue . . . 30 20

1973. Tourist Publicity. As T **607**.
2328 3f. grey, brown and blue . . 25 10
2329 4f. grey and green 30 25
DESIGNS—HORIZ: 3f. Town Hall, Leau; 4f. Chimay Castle.

614 F. Rops (self-portrait)
615 Jack of Diamonds

1973. 75th Death Anniv of Felicien Rops (artist and engraver).
2330 **614** 7f. black and brown . . 40 35

1973. "Solidarity". Old Playing Cards. Mult.
2331 5f.+2f.50 Type **615** 40 40
2332 5f.+2f.50 Jack of Spades . . 40 40
2333 5f.+2f.50 Queen of Hearts 40 40
2334 5f.+2f.50 King of Clubs . . 40 40

1973. As Nos. 2207/23 but smaller, 22 × 17 mm.
2335 **583** 3f. green . . . . 1·10 85
2336 4f. blue 20 25
2337 4f.50 blue 25 20
2338 5f. mauve 25 20
2338c 6f. red 35 10
2339 6f.50 violet 25 20
2339b 8f. grey 40 20

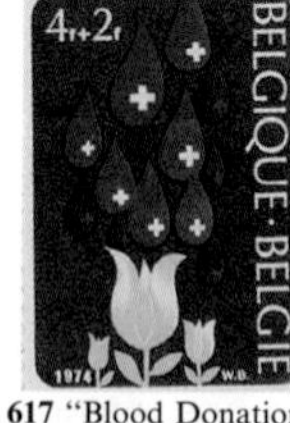

616 King Albert (Baron Opsomer)
617 "Blood Donation"

1974. 40th Death Anniv of King Albert I.
2340 **616** 4f. blue and black . . . 25 20

1974. Belgian Red Cross. Multicoloured.
2341 4f.+2f. Type **617** 35 35
2342 10f.+5f. "Traffic Lights" (Road Safety) 85 80

618 "Protection of the Environment"
619 "Armand Jamar" (Self-portrait)

1974. Robert Schuman Association for the Protection of the Environment.
2343 **618** 3f. multicoloured 25 10

1974. Belgian Cultural Celebrities. Multicoloured.
2344 4f.+2f. Type **619** 35 35
2345 5f.+2f.50 Tony Bergmann (author) and view of Lier 40 40
2346 7f.+3f.50 Henri Vieuxtemps (violinist) and view of Verviers 55 60
2347 10f.+5f. "James Ensor" (self-portrait with masks) (35 × 52 mm) 85 85

620 N.A.T.O. Emblem
621 Hubert Krains (Belgian postal administrator)

1974. 25th Anniv of North Atlantic Treaty Organization.
2348 **620** 10f. blue and light blue 55 35

1974. Stamp Day.
2349 **621** 5f. black and grey . . . 25 10

622 "Destroyed Town" (O. Zadkine)
623 Heads of Boy and Girl

1974. Europa. Sculptures.
2350 **622** 5f. black and red 40 10
2351 – 10f. black and blue . . . 75 45
DESIGN: 10f. "Solidarity" (G. Minne).

1974. 10th Lay Youth Festival.
2352 **623** 4f. multicoloured 25 25

625 New Planetarium, Brussels

1974. Historical Buildings.
2354 **625** 3f. brown and blue . . . 20 15
2355 – 4f. brown and red . . . 25 25
2356 – 5f. brown and green . . 35 15
2357 – 7f. brown and yellow . . 40 25
2358 – 10f. brown, orange & bl 55 30
DESIGNS—As T **625**. HORIZ: 4f. Pillory, Braine-le-Chateau. VERT: 10f. Belfry, Bruges. 45 × 25 mm: 5f. Ruins of Soleilmont Abbey; 7f. "Procession" (fountain sculpture, Ghent).

626 "BENELUX"

1974. 30th Anniv of Benelux Customs Union.
2359 **626** 5f. blue, green & lt blue 25 10

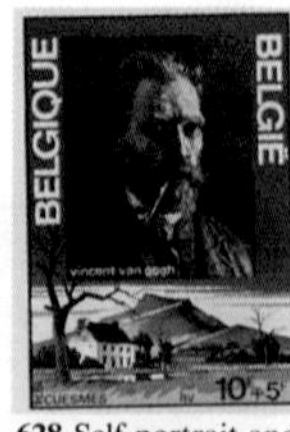

627 "Jan Vekemans at the Age of Five" (Cornelis de Vos)
628 Self-portrait and Van Gogh House, Cuesmes

1974. "Philately for the Young".
2360 **627** 3f. multicoloured 25 20

1974. Opening of Vincent Van Gogh House, Cuesmes.
2361 **628** 10f.+5f. multicoloured 85 70

629 Corporal Tresignies and Brule Bridge

1974. 60th Death Anniv of Corporal Leon Tresignies (war hero).
2362 **629** 4f. green and brown . . 25 20

630 Montgomery Blair and U.P.U. Emblem
631 Graph within Head

1974. Centenary of U.P.U.
2363 **630** 5f. black and green . . . 25 10
2364 – 10f. black and red . . . 50 40
DESIGN: 10f. H. von Stephan and U.P.U. Monument.

1974. 25th Anniv of Central Economic Council.
2365 **631** 7f. multicoloured 40 25

632 Rotary Emblem on Belgian Flag
633 Wild Boar

1974. 50th Anniv of Rotary Int in Belgium.
2366 **632** 10f. multicoloured . . . 55 30

1974. 40th Anniv of Granting of Colours to Ardennes Regiment of Chasseurs.
2367 **633** 3f. multicoloured 25 10

1974. Tourist Publicity. As T **607**.
2368 3f. brown and yellow . . . 25 20
2369 4f. green and blue 25 25
2370 4f. green and blue 25 25
DESIGNS—VERT: No. 2368, Aarschot. HORIZ: No. 2369, Meeting of three frontiers, Gemmenich; 2370, Nassogne.

634 "Angel" (detail, "The Mystic Lamb", Brothers Van Eyck)

635 Gentian

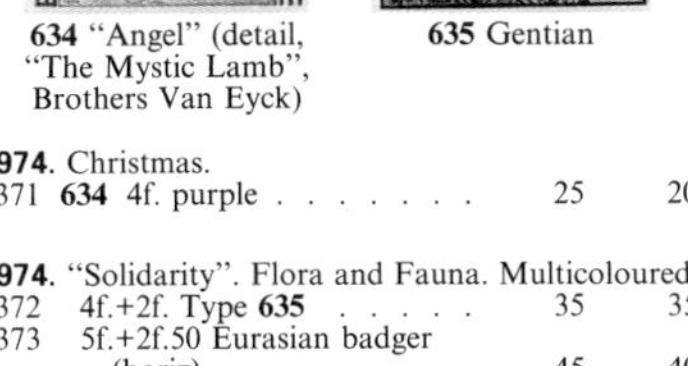

1974. Christmas.
2371 **634** 4f. purple 25 20

1974. "Solidarity". Flora and Fauna. Multicoloured.
2372 4f.+2f. Type **635** 35 35
2373 5f.+2f.50 Eurasian badger (horiz) 45 40
2374 7f.+3f.50 "Carabus auratus" (beetle) (horiz) 55 60
2375 10f.+5f. Spotted cat's-ear . . 85 85

636 Adolphe Quetelet (after J. Odevaere)

637 Exhibition Emblem

1974. Death Centenary of Adolphe Quetelet. (scientist).
2376 **636** 10f. black and brown . . 50 30

1975. "Themabelga" Stamp Exhibition, Brussels (1st issue).
2377 **637** 6f.50 orange, blk & grn 35 10
See also Nos. 2411/16.

638 "Neoregelia carolinae"

639 Student and Young Boy

1975. Ghent Flower Show. Multicoloured.
2378 4f.50 Type **638** 25 25
2379 5f. "Tussilago petasites" . . 35 15
2380 6f.50 "Azalea japonica" . . 35 10

1975. Cent of Charles Buls Normal School.
2381 **639** 4f.50 multicoloured . . . 25 15

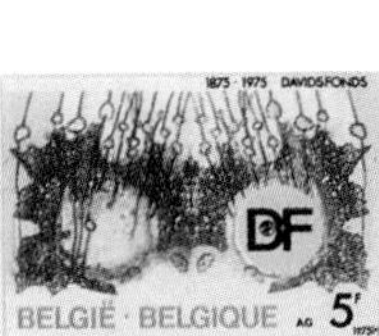

640 Foundation Emblem

641 King Albert I

1975. Centenary of Davids Foundation (Flemish cultural organisation).
2382 **640** 5f. multicoloured 25 10

1975. Birth Centenary of King Albert I.
2383 **641** 10f. black and purple . . 55 30

642 Pesaro Palace, Venice

643 "Postman of 1840" (J. Thiriar)

1975. Cultural Works.
2384 **642** 6f.50+2f.50 brown . . . 45 45
2385 – 10f.+4f.50 purple 80 70
2386 – 15f.+6f.50 blue . . . . . 1·10 1·00
DESIGNS—HORIZ: 10f. Sculpture Museum, St. Bavon Abbey, Ghent. VERT: 15f. "Virgin and Child" (Michelangelo, 500th Birth Anniv.)

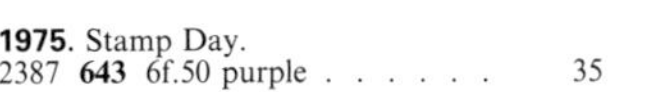

1975. Stamp Day.
2387 **643** 6f.50 purple 35 10

644 "An Apostle" (detail, "The Last Supper", Dirk Bouts)

645 Prisoners' Identification Emblems

1975. Europa. Paintings.
2388 **644** 6f.50 black, blue & grn 35 10
2389 – 10f. black, red & orange 70 40
DESIGN: 10f. "The Suppliant's Widow" (detail, "The Justice of Otho", Dirk Bouts).

1975. 30th Anniv of Concentration Camps' Liberation.
2390 **645** 4f.50 multicoloured . . . 25 10

646 St John's Hospice, Bruges

1975. European Architectural Heritage Year.
2391 **646** 4f.50 purple 25 10
2392 – 5f. green 35 20
2393 – 10f. blue 55 35
DESIGNS—VERT: 5f. St. Loup's Church, Namur. HORIZ: 10f. Martyrs Square, Brussels.

1975. Tourist Publicity. As T **607**.
2394 4f.50 brown, buff and red 25 10
2395 5f. multicoloured 25 10
DESIGN—VERT: 4f.50, Church, Dottignies. HORIZ: 5f. Market Square, Saint Truiden.

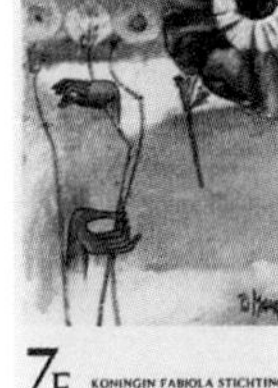

647 G. Ryckmans and L. Cerfaux (founders), and Louvain University Library

648 "Metamorphosis" (P. Mara)

1975. 25th Anniv of Louvain Colloquium Biblicum (Biblical Scholarship Association).
2396 **647** 10f. sepia and blue . . . 50 30

1975. Queen Fabiola Foundation for the Mentally Ill.
2397 **648** 7f. multicoloured 40 25

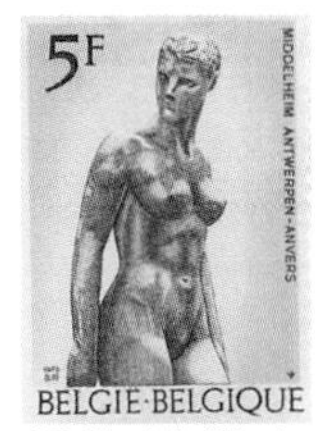

649 Marie Popelin (women's rights pioneer) and Palace of Justice

650 "Assia" (Charles Despiau)

1975. International Women's Year.
2398 **649** 6f.50 purple and green 40 10

1975. 25th Anniv of Middelheim Open-air Museum, Antwerp.
2399 **650** 5f. black and green . . . 25 15

651 Dr. Hemerijckx and Leprosy Hospital, Zaire

1975. Dr. Frans Hemerijckx (treatment of leprosy pioneer) Commemoration.
2400 **651** 20f.+10f. mult . . . . . 1·75 1·60

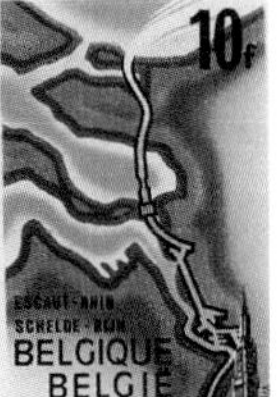

652 Canal Map

653 "Cornelia Vekemans at the Age of Seven" (Cornelis de Vos)

1975. Opening of Rhine–Scheldt Canal.
2401 **652** 10f. multicoloured . . . 50 35

1975. "Philately for the Young".
2402 **653** 4f.50 multicoloured . . . 25 20

654 National Bank and F. Orban (founder)

1975. 125th Anniv of Belgian National Bank.
2403 **654** 25f. multicoloured . . . 1·25 40

655 Edmond Thieffry (pilot) and "Princess Marie-Jose"

656 University Seal

1975. 50th Anniv of First Flight, Brussels–Kinshasa.
2404 **655** 7f. purple and black . . 40 20

1975. 550th Anniv of Louvain University.
2405 **656** 6f.50 black, green & bl 40 10

657 "Angels", (detail, "The Nativity", R. de le Pasture)

658 Emile Moyson (Flemish Leader)

1975. Christmas.
2406 **657** 5f. multicoloured 25 25

1975. "Solidarity".
2407 **658** 4f.50+2f. purple 35 35
2408 – 6f.50+3f. green 55 60
2409 – 10f.+5f. vio, blk & bl . . 85 80
2410 – 13f.+6f. multicoloured 1·10 1·00
DESIGNS—VERT: 6f.50, Dr. Augustin Snellaert (Flemish literature scholar); 13f. Detail of retable, St. Dymphne Church, Geel. HORIZ: 10f. Eye within hand, and Braille characters (150th anniv of introduction of Braille).

659 Cheese Seller

660 "African" Collector

1975. "Themabelga" International Thematic Stamp Exhibition, Brussels (2nd issue). Traditional Belgian Trades. Multicoloured.
2411 4f.50+1f.50 Type **659** . . . 35 35
2412 6f.50+3f. Potato seller . . . 50 50
2413 6f.50+3f. Basket-carrier . . 50 50
2414 10f.+5f. Prawn fisherman and pony (horiz) 80 70
2415 10f.+5f. Knife-grinder and cart (horiz) 80 70
2416 30f.+15f. Milk-woman with dog-cart (horiz) . . . . . 2·25 2·00

1976. Centenary of "Conservatoire Africain" (Charity Organization).
2417 **660** 10f.+5f. multicoloured 85 80

661 Owl Emblem and Flemish Buildings

662 Bicentennial Symbol

1976. 125th Anniv of Wilhems Foundation (Flemish cultural organization).
2418 **661** 5f. multicoloured 25 25

1976. Bicentenary of American Revolution.
2419 **662** 14f. multicoloured . . . 80 50

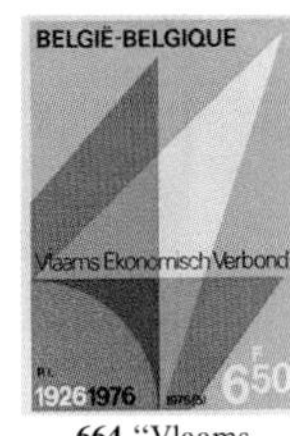

663 Cardinal Mercier

664 "Vlaams Ekonomisch Verbond"

1976. 50th Death Anniv of Cardinal Mercier.
2420 **663** 4f.50 purple 25 15

1976. 50th Anniv of Flemish Economic Federation.
2421 **664** 6f.50 multicoloured . . . 35 10

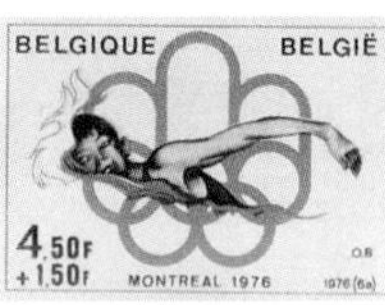

665 Swimming

1976. Olympic Games, Montreal. Multicoloured.
2422 4f.50+1f.50 Type **665** . . . 35 35
2423 5f.+2f. Running (vert) . . . 35 35
2424 6f.50+2f.50 Horse jumping 50 50

666 Money Centre Building, Brussels

1976. Stamp Day.
2425 **666** 6f.50 brown 35 10

667 Queen Elisabeth playing Violin

668 Basket-making

1976. 25th Anniv of Queen Elisabeth International Music Competitions.
2426 **667** 14f.+6f. red & black . . 1·00 1·00

1976. Europa. Traditional Crafts. Multicoloured.
2427 6f.50 Type **668** 40 10
2428 14f. Pottery (horiz) 85 40

669 Truck on Motorway

670 Queen Elisabeth

1976. 14th Congress of International Road Haulage Union, Brussels.
2429 **669** 14f. black, red & yellow 70 40

1976. Birth Centenary of Queen Elisabeth.
2430 **670** 14f. green 70 40

673 Ardennes Horses

1976. 50th Anniv of Ardennes Draught Horses Society.
2436 **673** 5f. multicoloured 35 25

675 "Madonna and Child" (detail)

1976. 400th Birth Anniv of Peter Paul Rubens (artist) (1st issue). Multicoloured.
2438 4f.50+1f.50 "Descent from the Cross" (detail) 45 45
2439 6f.50+3f. "Adoration of the Shepherds" (detail) (24½ × 35 mm) 55 60
2440 6f.50+3f. "Virgin of the Parrot" (detail) (24½ × 35 mm) 55 60
2441 10f.+5f. "Adoration of the Kings" (detail) (24½ × 35 mm) 95 90
2442 10f.+5f. "Last Communion of St. Francis" (detail) (24½ × 35 mm) 95 90
2443 30f.+15f. Type **675** . . . . 2·50 2·10
See also Nos. 2459 and 2497.

676 William the Silent, Prince of Orange

678 Underground Train

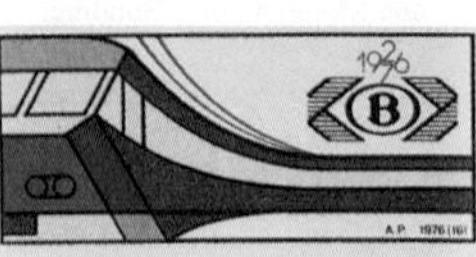

677 Modern Electric Train

1976. 400th Anniv of Pacification of Ghent.
2444 **676** 10f. green 55 25

1976. 50th Anniv of National Belgian Railway Company.
2445 **677** 6f.50 multicoloured . . . 40 10

1976. Opening of Brussels Metro (Underground) Service.
2446 **678** 6f.50 multicoloured . . . 40 10

679 "The Young Musician" (W. C. Duyster)

680 Charles Bernard (writer, birth cent)

1976. "Philately for the Young" and Young Musicians' Movement.
2447 **679** 4f.50 multicoloured . . . 45 10

1976. Cultural Anniversaries.
2448 **680** 5f. purple 25 25
2449 – 5f. red 25 25
2450 – 6f.50 brown 35 20
2451 – 6f.50 green 35 20

DESIGNS—VERT: No. 2449, Fernand Toussaint van Boelaere (writer, birth cent 1975); No. 2450, "St. Jerome in Mountain Landscape" (J. le Patinier) (25th anniv of Charles Plisnier Foundation). HORIZ: No. 2451, "Story of the Blind" (P. Brueghel) (25th anniv of "Vereniging voor Beschaafde Omgangstaal" (Dutch language organisation)).

1976. Tourist Publicity. As T **607**.
2452 4f.50 multicoloured 25 25
2453 4f.50 multicoloured 25 25
2454 5f. brown and blue 25 25
2455 5f. brown and olive 25 25
DESIGNS—HORIZ: No. 2452, Hunnegem Priory, Grammont; No. 2454, River Lys, Sint-Martens-Latem; No. 2455, Chateau. Ham-sur-Heure. VERT: No. 2453, Remouchamps Caves.

681 "Child with Impediment" (Velasquez)

682 "The Nativity" (detail, Master of Flemalle)

1976. National Association for Aid to the Mentally Handicapped.
2456 **681** 14f.+6f. multicoloured 1·00 1·00

1976. Christmas.
2457 **682** 5f. violet 35 25

683 Monogram

1977. 400th Birth Anniv of Peter Paul Rubens (2nd issue).
2459 **683** 6f.50 black and lilac . . 40 15

684 Belgian Lion

1977. (a) Size 17 × 20 mm.
2460 **684** 50c. brown 10 10
2461 65c. red 10 10
2462 1f. mauve 10 10
2463 1f.50 grey 10 10
2464a 2f. orange 10 10
2465 2f.50 green 25 20
2466 2f.75 blue 25 30
2467a 3f. violet 20 10
2468 4f. brown 25 10
2469 4f.50 blue 35 10
2470 5f. green 25 10
2471 6f. red 35 10
2472 7f. red 40 10
2473 8f. blue 40 10
2474 9f. orange 85 20

(b) 17 × 22 mm.
2475 **684** 1f. mauve 10 20
2476 2f. orange 35 20
2477 3f. violet 35 30

685 Dr. Albert Hustin (pioneer of blood transfusion)

686 "50 Years of F.A.B.I."

1977. Belgian Red Cross.
2478 **685** 6f.50+2f.50 red and black 55 50
2479 – 14f.+7f. red, blue and black . . . . 1·10 1·00
DESIGN: 14f.+7f. Knee joint and red cross (World Rheumatism Year).

1977. 50th Anniv of Federation of Belgian Engineers.
2480 **686** 6f.50 multicoloured . . . 40 10

687 Jules Bordet School, Brussels (bicent)

688 Gulls in Flight

1977. Cultural Anniversaries.
2481 **687** 4f.50+1f. mult 25 25
2482 – 4f.50+1f. mult 25 25
2483 – 5f.+2f. multicoloured . . 35 35
2484 – 6f.50+2f. mult 40 40
2485 – 6f.50+2f. red & black . . 40 40
2486 – 10f.+5 slate 75 75
DESIGNS—VERT: 24 × 37 mm: No. 2482, Marie-Therese College, Herve (bicentenary); 2483, Detail from "La Grande Pyramide Musicale" (E. Tytgat) (50th anniv of Brussels Philharmonic Society). 35 × 45 mm: No. 2486, Camille Lemonnier (75th anniv of Society of Belgian Authors writing in French). HORIZ: 35 × 24 mm: No. 2484, Lucien van Obbergh and stage scene (50th anniv of Union of Artists). 37 × 24 mm: No. 2485, Emblem of Humanist Society (25th anniv).

1977. 25th Anniv of District 112 of Lions International.
2487 **688** 14f. multicoloured . . . 85 35

689 Footballers

690 Pillar Box, 1852

1977. 30th International Youth Tournament of European Football Association.
2488 **689** 10f.+5f. multicoloured 85 80

1977. Stamp Day.
2489 **690** 6f.50 olive 45 10

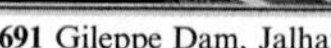

691 Gileppe Dam, Jalhay

692 "Mars and Mercury Association Emblem"

1977. Europa. Multicoloured.
2490 6f.50 Type **691** 40 20
2491 14f. The Yser, Nieuport . . 80 45

1977. 50th Anniv of Mars and Mercury Association of Reserve and Retired Officers.
2492 **692** 5f. green, black & brown 25 10

693 De Hornes Coat of Arms

694 "Self-Portrait"

1977. Historical Anniversaries.
2493 **693** 4f.50 lilac 25 20
2494 – 5f. red 25 20
2495 – 6f.50 brown 20 15
2496 – 14f. green . . . . 1·10 45
DESIGNS AND EVENTS—VERT: 4f.50, Type **693** (300th anniv of creation of principality of Overijse under Eugene-Maximilien de Hornes); 6f.50, Miniature (600th anniv of Froissart's "Chronicles"); 14f. "The Conversion of St. Hubert" (1250th death anniv). HORIZ: (45 × 24 mm): 5f. Detail from "Oxford Chest" (675th anniv of Battle of Golden Spurs).

1977. 400th Birth Anniv of Peter Paul Rubens (3rd issue).
2497 **694** 5f. multicoloured 35 20

695 "The Mystic Lamb" (detail, Brothers Van Eyck)

1977. 50th Anniv of International Federation of Library Associations and Congress, Brussels.
2499 **695** 10f. multicoloured . . . 55 25

696 Gymnast and Footballer

1977. Sports Events and Anniversaries.
2500 **696** 4f.50 red, black & grn 25 20
2501 – 6f.50 black, violet and brown 35 10
2502 – 10f. turquoise, black and salmon 55 35
2503 – 14f. green, blk & ochre 80 40
DESIGNS—VERT: 4f.50, Type **696** (50th anniv of Workers' Central Sports Association); 10f. Basketball (20th European Championships); 14f. Hockey (International Hockey Cup competition). HORIZ: 6f.50, Disabled fencers (Rehabilitation through sport).

697 Festival Emblem

1977. "Europalia '77" Festival.
2504 **697** 5f. multicoloured 25 10

699 "The Egg-seller" (Gustave de Smet)

700 "The Stamp Collectors" (detail, Constant Cap)

1977. Promoting Belgian Eggs.
2506 **699** 4f.50 black and ochre . . 25 20

1977. "Philately for the Young".
2507 **700** 4f.50 sepia 25 10

1977. Tourist Publicity. As **T607**.
2508 4f.50 multicoloured 25 20
2509 4f.50 black, blue and green 25 20
2510 5f. multicoloured 25 20
2511 5f. multicoloured 25 20
DESIGNS—VERT: No. 2508, Bailiff's House, Gembloux; No. 2509, St. Aldegone's Church. HORIZ: No. 2510, View of Liege and statue of Mother and Child; No. 2511, View and statue of St. Nicholas.

701 "Nativity" (detail, R. de la Pasture)

702 Albert-Edouard Janssen (financier)

1977. Christmas.
2512 **701** 5f. red 25 25

1977. "Solidarity".
2513 **702** 5f.+2f.50 black 40 40
2514 – 5f.+2f.50 red 40 40
2515 – 10f.+5f. purple 80 75
2516 – 10f.+5f. grey 80 75
DESIGNS: No. 2514, Joseph Wauters (politician); No. 2516, Jean Capart (egyptologist); No. 2515, August de Boeck (composer).

703 Distressed Girl (Deserted Children) **704** Railway Signal as Arrows on Map of Europe

1978. Philanthropic Works. Multicoloured.
2517 4f.50+1f.50 Type **703** . . . 35 30
2518 6f.+3f. Blood pressure measurement (World Hypertension Month) . . 45 45
2519 10f.+5f. De Mick Sanatorium, Brasschaat (Anti-tuberculosis) (horiz) 85 85

1978. "European Action". Multicoloured.
2520 10f. Type **704** (25th anniv of European Conference of Transport Ministers) . . . 55 25
2521 10f. European Parliament Building, Strasbourg (first direct elections) 55 25
2522 14f. Campidoglio Palace, Rome and map of EEC countries (20th anniv of Treaties of Rome) (horiz) 85 40
2523 14f. Paul Henri Spaak (Belgian Prime Minister) (horiz) 85 40

705 Grimbergen Abbey

1978. 850th Anniv of Premonstratensian Abbey, Grimbergen.
2524 **705** 4f.50 brown 40 25

706 Emblem **707** 5f. Stamp of 1878

1978. 175th Anniv of Ostend Chamber of Commerce and Industry.
2525 **706** 8f. multicoloured 40 10

1978. Stamp Day.
2526 **707** 8f. brown, blk & drab 40 10

708 Antwerp Cathedral **709** Theatre and Characters from "The Brussels Street Singer"

1978. Europa. Multicoloured.
2527 8f. Type **708** 45 20
2528 14f. Pont des Trous, Tournai (horiz) 90 50

1978. Cultural Anniversaries.
2529 **709** 6f.+3f. multicoloured . . 45 45
2530 – 6f.+3f. multicoloured . . 45 45
2531 – 8f.+4f. brown 60 60
2532 – 10f.+5f. brown 80 75
DESIGNS AND EVENTS: No. 2529, (Type **709**) (Royal Flemish Theatre Cent.); 2530, Arquebusier with standard, arms and Company Gallery, Vise (Royal Company of Crossbowmen of Vise 400th anniv); 2531, Karel van der Woestijne (poet) (birth cent); 2532, Don John of Austria (signing of Perpetual Edict, 400th anniv).

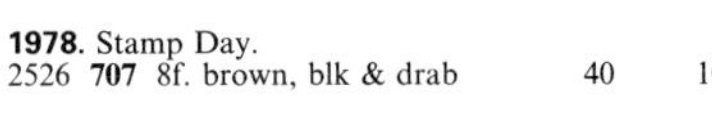

710 "Education" **711** "K.V.I."

1978. Teaching. Multicoloured.
2533 6f. Type **710** (Municipal education in Ghent, 150th anniv) 35 25
2534 8f. Paul Pastur Workers' University, Charleroi (75th anniv) 40 25

1978. Tourist Publicity. As T **607**.
2535 4f.50 sepia, buff and blue 25 25
2536 4f.50 multicoloured 25 25
2537 6f. multicoloured 35 25
2538 6f. multicoloured 35 25
DESIGNS—VERT: No. 2535, Jonathas House, Enghien. HORIZ: No. 2536, View of Wetteren and couple in local costume; 2537, Brussels tourist hostess; 2538, Carnival Prince and church tower.

1978. 50th Anniv of Royal Flemish Association of Engineers.
2539 **711** 8f. black and red 40 10

712 Young Stamp Collector **713** Mountain Scenery

1978. "Philately for the Young".
2540 **712** 4f.50 violet 25 20

1978. Olympic Games (1980) Preparation.
2541 **713** 6f.+2f.50 mult 45 40
2542 – 8f.+3f.50 green, brown and black 55 50
DESIGN: 8f. Kremlin Towers.

714 "The Nativity" (detail, Bethlehem Door, Notre Dame, Huy) **715** Tabernacle, Brussels Synagogue (centenary)

1978. Christmas.
2544 **714** 6f. black 35 25

1978. "Solidarity". Anniversaries.
2545 **715** 6f.+2f. brown, grey and black 45 40
2546 – 8f.+3f. multicoloured . . 65 55
2547 – 14f.+7f. multicoloured 1·10 1·00
DESIGNS—HORIZ: (36 × 24 mm): 8f. Dancing figures (Catholic Students Action, 50th anniv); 14f. Father Dominique-Georges Pire and African Village (Award of Nobel Peace Prize, 20th anniv).

716 Relief Workers giving First Aid **717** "Till Eulenspiegel" (legendary character)

1978. Belgian Red Cross. Multicoloured.
2548 8f.+3f. Type **716** 55 60
2549 16f.+8f. Skull smoking, bottle and syringe ("Excess kills") . . . . . 1·25 1·25

1979. 10th Anniv of Lay Action Centres.
2550 **717** 4f.50 multicoloured . . . 35 20

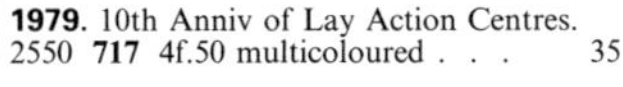

718 "European Dove" **719** Millenary Emblem

1979. 1st Direct Elections to European Assembly.
2551 **718** 8f. multicoloured 45 10

1979. Brussels Millenary (1st issue).
2552 **719** 4f.50 brown, blk & red 25 20
2553 8f. turquoise, blk & grn 65 10
See also Nos. 2559/62.

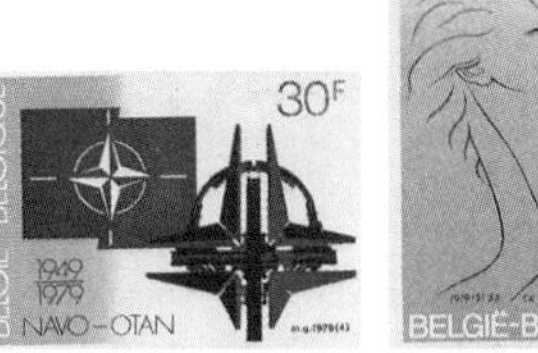

720 Sculpture at N.A.T.O. Headquarters and Emblem **721** Drawing of Monument

1979. 30th Anniv of North Atlantic Treaty Organization.
2554 **720** 30f. blue, gold and light blue . . . . 1·50 45

1979. 25th Anniv of Breendonk Monument.
2555 **721** 6f. orange and black . . 35 25

722 Railway Parcels Stamp, 1879

1979. Stamp Day.
2556 **722** 8f. multicoloured 40 10

723 Mail Coach and Renault R4 Post Van

1979. Europa. Multicoloured.
2557 8f. Type **723** 45 10
2558 14f. Semaphore posts, satellite and dish aerial . . 85 45

724 "Legend of Our Lady of Sablon" (detail of tapestry, Town Museum of Brussels) **725** Caduceus and Factory

1979. Brussels Millenary (2nd issue). Multicoloured.
2559 6f.+2f. Type **724** 40 40
2560 8f.+3f. Different detail of tapestry 50 55
2561 14f.+7f. "Legend of Our Lady of Sablon" (tapestry) . . . . 1·10 1·10
2562 20f.+10f. Different detail of tapestry . . . . 1·50 1·50
The tapestry shown on Nos. 2559/60 is from Brussels Town Museum and that on Nos. 2561/2 from the Royal Museum of Art and History.

1979. 175th Anniv of Verviers Chamber of Commerce.
2564 **725** 8f. multicoloured 40 10

726 "50" and Bank Emblem

1979. 50th Anniv of Professional Credit Bank.
2565 **726** 4f.50 blue and gold . . . 25 25

727 Bas-relief

1979. 50th Anniv of Chambers of Trade and Commerce.
2566 **727** 10f. crimson, orange and red 50 25

728 Cambre Abbey

1979. Cultural Anniversaries.
2567 **728** 6f.+2f. multicoloured . . 45 40
2568 – 8f.+3f. multicoloured . . 50 50
2569 – 14f.+7f. black, orange and green . . . . . . 1·10 1·00
2570 – 20f.+10f. brown, red and grey . . . . 1·50 1·50
DESIGNS: 6f. Type **728** (50th anniv of restoration); 8f. Beauvoorde Chateau; 14f. Barthelemy Dumortier (founder) and newspaper "Courrier de L'Escaut" (150th anniv); 20f. Crypt, shrine and Collegiate Church of St. Hermes, Renaix (850th anniv of consecration).

729 "Tintin" with Dog, Stamps and Magnifier

1979. "Philately for the Young".
2571 **729** 8f. multicoloured . . . . 2·00 40

730 Le Grand-Hornu

1979. Le Grand-Hornu Industrial Archaeological Site.
2572 **730** 10f.+5f. black & grey . . 85 80

1979. Tourist Publicity. As T **607**.
2573 5f. multicoloured 25 20
2574 5f. multicoloured 25 20
2575 6f. black, turquoise & green 35 25
2576 6f. multicoloured 35 25
DESIGNS—HORIZ: No. 2573, Royal African Museum, Tervuren, and hunters with hounds; 2575, St. John's Church, Poperinge, and statue of Virgin Mary. VERT: No. 2574, Belfry, Thuin, and men carrying religious image; 2576, St. Nicholas's Church and cattle market, Ciney.

731 Francois Auguste Gevaert **732** Madonna and Child, Foy-Notre-Dame Church

1979. Music. Each brown and ochre.
2577 5f. Type **731** (150th birth anniv) 25 25
2578 6f. Emmanuel Durlet . . . 35 25
2579 14f. Grand piano and string instruments (40th anniv of Queen Elisabeth Musical Chapel) 75 40

1979. Christmas.
2580 **732** 6f. black and blue . . . 35 25

733 H. Heyman (politician, birth centenary)   **734** "1830–1980"

1979. "Solidarity".
2581 **733** 8f.+3f. brown, green and black 55 50
2582 – 10f.+5f. multicoloured 75 65
2583 – 16f.+8f. black, green and yellow . . . . 1·25 1·25
DESIGNS—VERT: As Type **733**. 10f. War Invalids Organization medal (50th anniv). HORIZ: (44×24 mm): 16f. Child's head and International Year of the Child emblem.

1980. 150th Anniv of Independence (1st issue).
2584 **734** 9f. mauve & lt mauve . . 45 15
See also Nos. 2597/2601.

735 Frans Van Cauwelaert   **736** Spring Flowers

1980. Birth Centenary of Frans Van Cauwelaert (politician).
2585 **735** 5f. black 25 10

1980. Ghent Flower Show. Multicoloured.
2586 5f. Type **736** 25 25
2587 6f.50 Summer flowers . . . 35 30
2588 9f. Autumn flowers 45 10

737 Telephone and Diagram of Satellite Orbit

1980. 50th Anniv of Telegraph and Telephone Office.
2589 **737** 10f. multicoloured . . . 50 25

738 5f. Airmail Stamp of 1930

1980. Stamp Day.
2590 **738** 9f. multicoloured 50 10

739 St. Benedict of Nursia

1980. Europa. Multicoloured.
2591 9f. Type **739** 70 10
2592 14f. Marguerite of Austria 90 45

740 Ivo van Damme   **741** Palais de la Nation

1980. Ivo van Damme (athlete) Commemoration.
2593 **740** 20f.+10f. mult . . . . . 1·50 1·50

1980. 4th Interparliamentary Conference on European Co-operation and Security, Brussels.
2594 **741** 5f. blue, lilac and black 25 25

742 Golden Carriage, Mons

1980. Tourist Publicity. Multicoloured.
2595 6f.50 Type **742** 35 25
2596 6f.50 Damme 35 25

743 King Leopold I and Queen Louise-Marie

1980. 150th Anniv of Belgian Independence (2nd issue).
2597 **743** 6f.50+1f.50 pur & blk . . 45 40
2598 – 9f.+3f. blue & black . . 55 50
2599 – 14f.+6f. green & blk . . 1·10 1·00
2600 – 17f.+8f. orange. & blk 1·25 1·25
2601 – 25f.+10f. green & blk . . 1·75 1·75
DESIGNS: 9f. King Leopold II and Queen Marie-Henriette; 14f. King Albert I and Queen Elisabeth; 17f. King Leopold III and Queen Astrid; 25f. King Baudouin and Queen Fabiola.

744 King Baudouin   **745** "Brewer" (detail, Reliquary of St. Lambert)

1980. King Baudouin's 50th Birthday.
2603 **744** 9f. red 50 15

1980. Millenary of Liege. Multicoloured.
2604 9f.+3f. Type **745** 55 60
2605 17f.+6f. "The Miner" (sculpture by Constantin Meunier) (horiz) . . . . 1·25 1·25
2606 25f.+10f. "Seat of Wisdom" (Madonna, Collegiate Church of St. John, Liege) . . . . 2·00 1·90

746 Chiny

1980. Tourist Publicity.
2608 **746** 5f. multicoloured 30 25

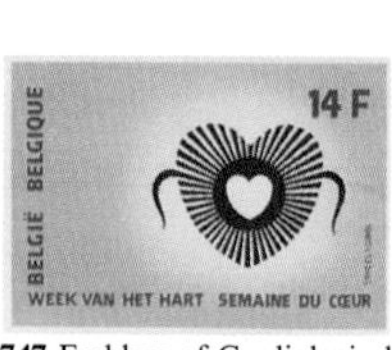

747 Emblem of Cardiological League of Belgium   **748** Rodenbach (statue at Roulers)

1980. Heart Week.
2609 **747** 14f. light blue, red and blue 70 40

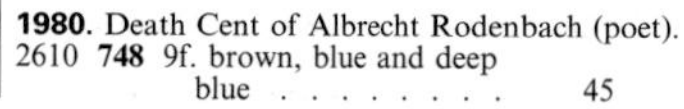

1980. Death Cent of Albrecht Rodenbach (poet).
2610 **748** 9f. brown, blue and deep blue 45 10

749 "Royal Procession" (children of Thyl Uylenspiegel Primary School)

1980. "Philately for the Young".
2611 **749** 5f. multicoloured 25 20

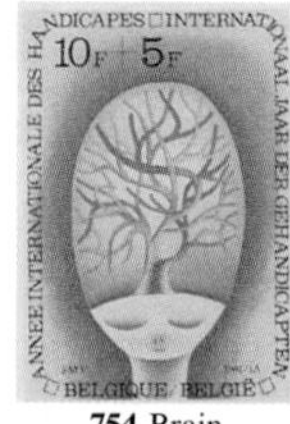

750 Emblem   **751** "Garland of Flowers and Nativity" (attr. D. Seghers)

1980. 50th Anniv of Belgian Broadcasting Corporation.
2612 **750** 10f. black and grey . . . 50 25

1980. Christmas.
2613 **751** 6f.50 multicoloured . . . 35 25

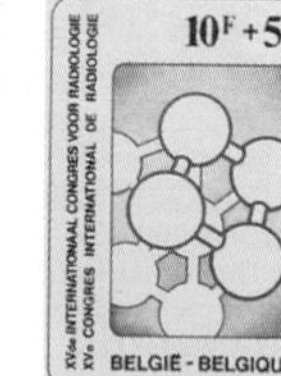

752 Gateway, Diest   **754** Brain

1980. Tourist Publicity.
2614 **752** 5f. multicoloured 25 20
See also Nos. 2648/51 and 2787/92.

1981. International Year of Disabled Persons. Multicoloured.
2637 10f.+5f. Type **754** 85 80
2638 25f.+10f. Eye . . . . 2·00 1·75

755 "Baron de Gerlache" (after F. J. Navez)   **756** Emblem of 15th International Radiology Convention

1981. Historical Anniversaries.
2639 **755** 6f. multicoloured 35 25
2640 – 9f. multicoloured 45 10
2641 – 50f. brown & yellow . . 2·50 65
DESIGNS—As T **755**: 6f. Type **755** (1st President of Chamber of Deputies) (150th anniv of Chamber); 9f. Baron de Stassart (1st President of Senate) (after F. J. Navez) (150th anniv of Senate). 35×51 mm: 50f. Statue of King Leopold I by Geefs (150th anniv of royal dynasty).

1981. Belgian Red Cross.
2642 **756** 10f.+5f. bl, blk & red . . 85 80
2643 – 25f.+10f. blue, red and black . . . . 2·00 1·75
DESIGN: 25f. Dove and globe symbolizing international emergency assistance.

757 Tchantches and Op-Signoorke (puppets)

1981. Europa. Multicoloured.
2644 9f. Type **757** 55 10
2645 14f. D'Artagnan and Woltje (puppets) 90 55

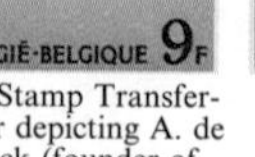

758 Stamp Transfer-roller depicting A. de Cock (founder of Postal Museum)   **759** Ovide Decroly

1981. Stamp Day.
2646 **758** 9f. multicoloured 45 10

1981. 110th Birth Anniv of Dr. Ovide Decroly (educational psychologist).
2647 **759** 35f.+15f. brown & bl . . 2·50 2·40

1981. Tourist Publicity. As T **752**. Multicoloured.
2648 6f. Statue of our Lady of Tongre 35 25
2649 6f. Egmont Castle, Zottegem 35 25
2650 6f.50 Dams on Eau d'Heure (horiz) 40 25
2651 6f.50 Tongerlo Abbey, Antwerp (horiz) 40 25

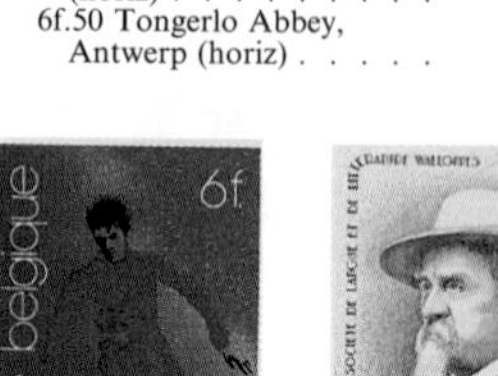

760 Footballer   **761** Edouard Remouchamps (Walloon dramatist)

1981. Cent of Royal Antwerp Football Club.
2652 **760** 6f. red, brown & black 40 25

1981. 125th Anniv of Society of Walloon Language and Literature.
2653 **761** 6f.50 brown and stone 35 25

762 French Horn

1981. Centenary of De Vredekring Band, Antwerp.
2654 **762** 6f.50 blue, mve & blk . . 35 25

763 Audit Office

1981. 150th Anniv of Audit Office.
2655 **763** 10f. purple 50 25

765 Tombs of Marie of Burgundy and Charles the Bold

1981. Relocation of Tombs of Marie of Burgundy and Charles the Bold in Notre-Dame Church, Bruges.
2657 **765** 50f. multicoloured . . . 2·50 65

766 Boy holding Globe in Tweezers   **767** King Baudouin

1981. "Philately for Youth".
2658 **766** 6f. multicoloured 35 25

1981.
2659 **767** 50f. light blue and blue 3·00 15
2660 65f. mauve and black . . 4·00 75
2661 100f. brown and blue . . 5·50 50

768 Max Waller (founder)

769 Nativity (miniature from "Missale ad usum d. Leodensis")

1981. Cultural Anniversaries.
2672 **768** 6f. multicoloured 35 15
2673 – 6f.50 multicoloured . . . 40 25
2674 – 9f. multicoloured . . . 45 10
2675 – 10f. multicoloured . . . 55 40
2676 – 14f. lt brn & brn 85 50
DESIGNS: 6f. Type **768** (centenary of literary review "La Jeune Belgique"); 6f.50," Liqueur Drinkers" (detail, Gustave van de Woestijne (inscr "Woestyne") (birth centenary); 9f. Fernand Severin (poet, 50th death anniv); 10f. Jan van Ruusbroec (mystic, 600th death anniv); 14f. Owl (La Pensee et les Hommes organization, 25th anniv).

1981. Christmas.
2677 **769** 6f.50 brown and black 35 25

770 Mounted Gendarme, 1832

771 Cellist and Royal Conservatory of Music, Brussels

1981. "Solidarity". Multicoloured.
2678 9f.+4f. Type **770** 70 65
2679 20f.+7f. Carabinier . . . . 1·40 1·25
2680 40f.+20f. Mounted Guide, 1843 . . . . 3·00 2·75

1982. 150th Anniversaries. Multicoloured.
2681 6f.50 Type **771** 35 25
2682 9f. Front of former Law Court, Brussels (anniv of judiciary) 45 10

772 Sectional View of Cyclotron

773 Billiards

1982. Science. Multicoloured.
2683 6f. Type **772** (Installation of cyclotron at National Radio-elements Institute, Fleurus) 35 25
2684 14f. Telescope and galaxy (Royal Observatory) . . . 70 40
2685 50f. Dr. Robert Koch and tubercle bacillus (centenary of discovery) 2·40 50

1982. Sports. Multicoloured.
2686 6f.+2f. Type **773** 70 70
2687 9f.+4f. Cycling 90 95
2688 10f.+5f. Football . . . . . 1·10 1·00
2689 50f.+14f. "Treaty of Rome" (yacht) . . . . 3·00 2·75

774 Joseph Lemaire (after Jean Maillard)

775 Voting (Universal Suffrage)

1982. Birth Centenary of Joseph Lemaire (Minister of State and social reformer).
2691 **774** 6f.50 multicoloured . . . 35 45

1982. Europa.
2692 **775** 10f. multicoloured . . . 70 25
2693 – 17f. green, black and grey . . . . 1·25 40
DESIGN: 17f. Portrait and signature of Emperor Joseph II (Edict of Toleration).

1982. Surch **1 F**.
2694 **684** 1f. on 5f. green 10 10

777 17th-century Postal Messenger

778 "Tower of Babel" (Brueghel the Elder)

1982. Stamp Day.
2695 **777** 10f. multicoloured . . . 50 10

1982. World Esperanto Congress, Antwerp.
2696 **778** 12f. multicoloured . . . 70 30

1982. Tourist Publicity. As T **752**.
2697 7f. blue and light blue . . . 45 25
2698 7f. black and green 45 25
2699 7f.50 brown and light brown 45 25
2700 7f.50 violet and lilac 45 25
2701 7f.50 black and grey 45 25
2702 7f.50 black and pink 45 25
DESIGNS—VERT: No. 2697, Gosselies Tower; 2698, Zwijveke Abbey, Termonde; 2701, Entrance gate, Grammont Abbey; 2702, Beveren pillory. HORIZ: No. 2699, Stavelot Abbey; 2700, Abbey ruins, Villers-la-Ville.

780 Louis Paul Boon (writer)

781 Abraham Hans

1982. Cultural Anniversaries.
2707 **780** 7f. black, red and grey 35 25
2708 – 10f. multicoloured . . . 45 10
2709 – 12f. multicoloured . . . 60 30
2710 – 17f. multicoloured . . . 90 40
DESIGNS: 7f. Type **780** (70th birth anniv); 10f. "Adoration of the Shepherds" (detail of Portinari retable) (Hugo van der Goes, 500th death anniv); 12f. Michel de Ghelderode (dramatist, 20th death anniv); 17f. "Motherhood" (Pierre Paulus, birth centenary (1981)).

1982. Birth Centenary of Abraham Hans (writer).
2711 **781** 17f. black, turquoise and blue 80 25

782 Children playing Football

1982. "Philately for the Young". Scout Year.
2712 **782** 7f. multicoloured 45 25

783 Masonic Emblems

784 Star over Village

1982. 150th Anniv of Belgium Grand Orient (Freemasonry Lodge).
2713 **783** 10f. yellow and black . . 55 10

1982. Christmas.
2714 **784** 10f.+1f. multicoloured 70 70

785 Cardinal Cardijn

1982. Birth Centenary of Cardinal Joseph Cardijn.
2715 **785** 10f. multicoloured . . . 55 10

786 King Baudouin

787 King Baudouin

1982.
2716 **786** 10f. blue 55 10
2717 11f. brown 70 10
2718 12f. green 90 10
2719 13f. red 85 10
2720 14f. black 85 10
2721 15f. red 90 30
2722 20f. blue . . . . 1·25 10
2723 22f. purple . . . . . . 2·25 95
2724 23f. green . . . . 2·10 45
2725 24f. grey . . . . 1·40 25
2726 25f. blue . . . . 1·50 20
2727 30f. brown . . . . . . 1·40 10
2728 40f. red . . . . 2·10 20
2729 **787** 50f. light brown, brown and black . . . . . . 3·50 20
2730 100f. blue, deep blue and black . . . . 9·00 25
2731 200f. light green, green and deep green . . . 18·00 80

788 St. Francis preaching to the Birds

789 Messenger handing Letter to King in the Field

1982. 800th Birth Anniv of St. Francis of Assisi.
2736 **788** 20f. multicoloured . . . 1·00 40

1982. "Belgica 82" Postal History Exhibition. Multicoloured.
2737 7f.+2f. Type **789** 45 45
2738 7f.50+2f.50 Messenger, Basel (vert) 55 60
2739 10f.+3f. Messenger, Nuremburg (vert) 70 70
2740 17f.+7f. Imperial courier, 1750 (vert) . . . . 1·25 1·25
2741 20f.+9f. Imperial courier, 1800 . . . . 1·50 1·50
2742 25f.+10f. Belgian postman, 1886 . . . . 1·75 1·60

790 Emblem

791 Horse Tram

1983. 50th Anniv of Caritas Catholica Belgica.
2744 **790** 10f.+2f. red and grey . . 70 70

1983. Trams. Multicoloured.
2745 7f.50 Type **791** 45 25
2746 10f. Electric tram 50 10
2747 50f. Tram with trolley (invented by K. van de Poele) . . . . 2·75 50

792 Mountaineer

793 Brussels Buildings, Open Periodicals and Globe

1983. Belgian Red Cross. Multicoloured.
2748 12f.+3f. Type **792** 80 80
2749 20f.+5f. Walker . . . . . . 1·25 1·10

1983. 24th International Periodical Press Federation World Congress, Brussels.
2750 **793** 20f. multicoloured . . . 1·00 30

794 Woman at Work

1983. Women.
2751 **794** 8f. multicoloured 45 25
2752 – 11f. multicoloured . . . 55 10
2753 – 20f. yellow, brown & bl 1·10 40
DESIGNS: 11f. Woman at home; 20f. Woman manager.

795 Graphic Representation of Midi Railway Station, Brussels

1983. Stamp Day. World Communications Year.
2754 **795** 11f. black, red and blue 55 20

796 Procession of the Holy Blood

1983. Procession of the Holy Blood, Bruges.
2755 **796** 8f. multicoloured 45 20

797 "The Man in the Street"

798 Hot-air Balloon over Town

1983. Europa. Paintings by Paul Delvaux. Mult.
2756 11f. Type **797** 80 20
2757 20f. "Night Trains" (horiz) 1·40 45

1983. Bicentenary of Manned Flight. Mult.
2758 11f. Type **798** 55 10
2759 22f. Hot-air balloon over countryside . . . . 1·25 40

799 Church of Our Lady, Hastiere

800 Milkmaid

1983. Tourist Publicity. Multicoloured.
2760 8f. Type **799** 55 25
2761 8f. Tumulus, Landen . . . 55 25
2762 8f. Park, Mouscron 55 25
2763 8f. Wijnendale Castle, Torhout 55 25

1983. Tineke Festival, Heule.
2764 **800** 8f. multicoloured 40 20

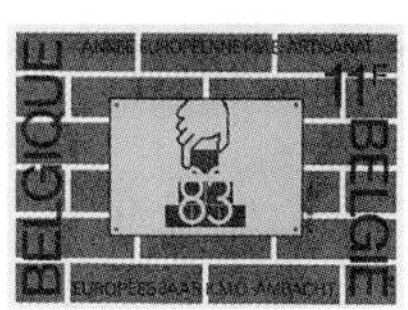

801 Plaque on Wall

802 Rainbow and Child

1983. European Small and Medium-sized Industries and Crafts Year.
2765 **801** 11f. yellow, black & red 55 10

1983. "Philately for the Young". 20th Anniv of Queen Fabiola Village No. 1 (for handicapped people).
2766 **802** 8f. multicoloured 50 20

803 Textiles

804 Conscience (after wood engraving by Nelly Degouy)

1983. Belgian Exports (1st series). Multicoloured.
2767 10f. Type **803** 50 25
2768 10f. Steel beams (metallurgy) 50 25
2769 10f. Diamonds 50 25
See also Nos. 2777/80.

1983. Death Centenary of Hendrik Conscience (writer).
2770 **804** 20f. black and green 1·10 25

805 "Madonna" (Jef Wauters)

806 2nd Foot Regiment

1983. Christmas.
2771 **805** 11f.+1f. multicoloured 70 65

1983. "Solidarity". Military Uniforms. Mult.
2772 8f.+2f. Type **806** 55 60
2773 11f.+2f. Lancer 90 85
2774 50f.+12f. Grenadier 3·25 3·00

1983. King Leopold III Commemoration.
2775 **155** 11f. black 70 10

807 Free University of Brussels

808 Albert I

1984. 150th Anniv of Free University of Brussels.
2776 **807** 11f. multicoloured 55 10

1984. Belgian Exports (2nd series). As T **803**. Multicoloured.
2777 11f. Retort and test tubes (chemicals) 55 25
2778 11f. Combine harvester (agricultural produce) 55 25
2779 11f. Ship, coach and electric commuter train (transport) 55 25
2780 11f. Atomic emblem and computer terminal (new technology) 55 25

1984. 50th Death Anniv of King Albert I.
2781 **808** 8f. black and stone 50 25

809 Judo

810 Releasing Doves

1984. Olympic Games, Los Angeles. Multicoloured.
2782 8f.+2f. Type **809** 55 50
2783 12f.+3f. Windsurfing (vert) 75 70

1984. 25th Anniv of Movement without a Name.
2785 **810** 12f. multicoloured 60 10

811 Clasped Hands

1984. 50th Anniv of National Lottery.
2786 **811** 12f.+3f. multicoloured 85 80

812 St. John Bosco with Children

813 Bridge

1984. 50th Anniv of Canonization of St. John Bosco (founder of Salesians).
2787 **812** 8f. multicoloured 40 10

1984. Europa. 25th Anniv of European Posts and Telecommunications Conference.
2788 **813** 12f. red and black 65 20
2789 22f. blue and black 1·40 30

814 Leopold II 1884 10c. Stamp

1984. Stamp Day.
2790 **814** 12f. multicoloured 65 10

815 Dove and Pencils

1984. 2nd European Parliament Elections.
2791 **815** 12f. multicoloured 65 10

816 Shako

817 Church of Our Lady of the Chapel, Brussels

1984. 150th Anniv of Royal Military School.
2792 **816** 22f. multicoloured 1·25 40

1984. Tourist Publicity. Multicoloured.
2793 10f. Type **817** 55 20
2794 10f. St. Martin's Church and lime tree, Montigny-le-Tilleul 55 20
2795 10f. Belfry and Town Hall, Tielt (vert) 55 20

818 "Curious Masks" (detail, James Ensor)

1984. Inaug of Brussels Modern Art Museum.
2796 **818** 8f.+2f. multicoloured 55 60
2797 – 12f.+3f. multicoloured 90 95
2798 – 22f.+5f. multicoloured 1·40 1·40
2799 – 50f.+13f. grn, bl & blk 3·25 3·00
DESIGNS: 12f. "The Empire of Lights" (detail, Rene Magritte); 22f. "The End" (detail, Jan Cox); 50f. "Rhythm No. 6" (Jo Delahaut).

819 Symbolic Design

820 Averbode Abbey

1984. 50th Anniv of Chirojeugd (Christian youth movement).
2800 **819** 10f. yellow, violet & bl 50 25

1984. Abbeys.
2801 **820** 8f. green and brown 35 20
2802 – 22f. brown & dp brown 1·10 30
2803 – 24f. green & light green 1·25 45
2804 – 50f. lilac and brown 2·50 60
DESIGNS—VERT: 22f. Chimay; 24f. Rochefort. HORIZ: 50f. Affligem.

821 Smurf as Postman

822 Child collecting Flowers

1984. "Philately for the Young".
2805 **821** 8f. multicoloured 1·25 40

1984. Children.
2806 10f.+2f. Type **822** 70 65
2807 12f.+3f. Children with globe 85 80
2808 15f.+3f. Child on merry-go-round 1·10 1·00

823 Meulemans

824 Three Kings

1984. Birth Cent of Arthur Meulemans (composer).
2809 **823** 12f. black and orange 65 10

1984. Christmas.
2810 **824** 12f.+1f. multicoloured 80 75

825 St. Norbert

826 "Virgin of Louvain" (attr. Jan Gossaert)

1985. 850th Death Anniv of St. Norbert.
2811 **825** 22f. brown & lt brown 1·25 40

1985. "Europalia 85 Espana" Festival.
2812 **826** 12f. multicoloured 65 20

827 Press Card in Hatband

828 Blood System as Tree

1985. Cent of Professional Journalists Association.
2814 **827** 9f. multicoloured 45 25

1985. Belgian Red Cross. Blood Donations.
2815 **828** 9f.+2f. multicoloured 70 70
2816 – 23f.+5f. red, blue and black 1·60 1·50
DESIGN: 23f. Two hearts.

829 "Sophrolaelio cattleya" "Burlingama"

830 Pope John Paul II

1985. Ghent Flower Festival. Orchids. Mult.
2817 12f. Type **829** 65 20
2818 12f. Phalaenopsis "Malibu" 65 20
2819 12f. Tapeu orchid ("Vanda coerulea") 65 20

1985. Visit of Pope John Paul II.
2820 **830** 12f. multicoloured 70 20

831 Rising Sun behind Chained Gates

1985. Centenary of Belgian Workers' Party.
2821 9f. Type **831** 50 30
2822 12f. Broken wall, flag and rising sun 65 20

832 Jean de Bast (engraver)

1985. Stamp Day.
2823 **832** 12f. blue 60 10

834 Class 18 Steam Locomotive, 1896

1985. Public Transport Year. Multicoloured.
2826 9f. Type **834** 55 25
2827 12f. Locomotive "Elephant", 1835 70 20
2828 23f. Class 23 tank engine, 1904 1·40 50
2829 24f. Class I Pacific locomotive, 1935 1·40 50

835 Cesar Franck and Score

1985. Europa. Music Year. Multicoloured.
2831 12f. Type **835** 70 20
2832 23f. Queen and king with viola dressed in music score (Queen Elisabeth International Music Competition) 1·40 40

836 Planned Canal Lock, Strepy-Thieu

837 Church of Our Lady's Assumption, Avernas-le-Bauduin

1985. Permanent International Navigation Congress Association Centenary Congress, Brussels. Multicoloured.
2833 23f. Type **836** 1·40 50
2834 23f. Aerial view of Zeebrugge harbour 1·40 50

1985. Tourist Publicity. Multicoloured.
2835 12f. Type **837** 70 25
2836 12f. Saint Martin's Church, Marcinelle (horiz) 70 25

2837 12f. Roman tower and Church of old beguinage, Tongres 70 25
2838 12f. House, Wachtebeke (horiz) 70 25

838 Queen Astrid

839 Baking Matton Tart, Grammont

1985. 50th Death Anniv of Queen Astrid.
2839 **838** 12f. lt brown & brown 85 10

1985. Traditional Customs. Multicoloured.
2840 12f. Type **839** 65 25
2841 24f. Young people dancing on trumpet filled with flowers (cent of Red Youths, St. Lambert Cultural Circle, Hermalle-sous-Argenteau) . . . . . 1·40 45

840 Dove and Concentration Camp

1985. 40th Anniv of Liberation. Multicoloured.
2842 9f. Type **840** 55 25
2843 23f. Battle of the Ardennes 1·40 50
2844 24f. Troops landing at Scheldt estuary . . . . . 1·40 50

841 Hawfinch ("Appelvink – Gros Bec")

842 Claes and Fictional Character

1985. Birds (1st series). Multicoloured.
2845 1f. Lesser spotted woodpecker ("Pic epeichette") 30 10
2846 2f. Eurasian tree sparrow ("Moineau friquet") . . 25 10
2847 3f. Type **841** 45 10
2847a 3f.50 European robin ("Rouge-gorge") 25 10
2848 4f. Bluethroat ("Gorge-bleue") 35 10
2848a 4f.50 Common stonechat ("Traquet patre") . . . 35 20
2849 5f. Eurasian nuthatch ("Sittelle torche-pot") . . 35 10
2850 6f. Northern bullfinch ("Bouvreuil") 55 10
2851 7f. Blue tit ("Mesange bleue") 55 20
2852 8f. River kingfisher ("Martin-pecheur") . . . 55 20
2853 9f. Eurasian goldfinch ("Chardonneret") . . . 90 10
2854 10f. Chaffinch ("Pinson") 60 20
See also Nos. 3073/86 and 3306/23.

1985. Birth Centenary of Ernest Claes (writer).
2855 **842** 9f. multicoloured 45 25

843 Youth

844 Trazegnies Castle

1985. "Philately for the Young". International Youth Year.
2856 **843** 9f. multicoloured 45 25

1985. "Solidarity". Castles. Multicoloured.
2857 9f.+2f. Type **844** 70 65
2858 12f.+3f. Laarne 85 80
2859 23f.+5f. Turnhout . . . . . 1·50 1·40
2860 50f.+12f. Colonster . . . . 3·00 3·00

845 Miniature from "Book of Hours of Duc de Berry"

1985. Christmas.
2861 **845** 12f.+1f. multicoloured 85 80

846 King Baudouin and Queen Fabiola

1985. Royal Silver Wedding.
2862 **846** 12f. grey, blue and deep blue 90 20

847 Map and 1886 25c. Stamp

848 Giants and Belfry, Alost

1986. Centenary of First Independent State of Congo Stamp.
2863 **847** 10f. blue, grey & dp blue 90 25

1986. Carnivals. Multicoloured.
2864 9f. Type **848** 45 25
2865 12f. Clown, Binche 70 20

849 Dove as Hand holding Olive Twig

850 Emblem

1986. International Peace Year.
2866 **849** 23f. multicoloured . . . 1·25 45

1986. 10th Anniv of King Baudouin Foundation.
2867 **850** 12f.+3f. blue, light blue and grey . . . . . . 1·25 1·10

851 Virgin Mary

1986. "The Mystic Lamb" (altarpiece, Brothers Van Eyck). Multicoloured.
2868 9f.+2f. Type **851** 70 65
2869 13f.+3f. Christ in Majesty 1·00 1·00
2870 24f.+6f. St. John the Baptist 1·75 1·60

852 Exhibits

1986. Stamp Day. 50th Anniv of Postal Museum, Brussels.
2872 **852** 13f. multicoloured . . . 70 10

853 Living and Dead Fish and Graph

854 Malinois Shepherd Dog

1986. Europa. Multicoloured.
2873 13f. Type **853** 70 20
2874 24f. Living and dead trees and graph . . . . 1·40 50

1986. Belgian Dogs. Multicoloured.
2875 9f. Type **854** 55 30
2876 13f. Tervuren shepherd dog 85 10
2877 24f. Groenendael cattle dog 1·40 50
2878 26f. Flanders cattle dog . . 1·60 50

855 St. Ludger Church, Zele

856 Boy, Broken Skateboard and Red Triangle

1986. Tourist Publicity.
2879 **855** 9f. brown and flesh . . . 50 25
2880 – 9f. red and pink 50 25
2881 – 13f. green & light green 75 25
2882 – 13f. black and green . . 75 25
2883 – 13f. blue and azure . . . 75 25
2884 – 13f. brown & lt brown 75 25
DESIGNS—VERT: No. 2880, Town Hall, Wavre; 2882, Chapel of Our Lady of the Dunes, Bredene. HORIZ: 2881, Water-mills, Zwalm; 2883, Chateau Licot, Viroinval; 2884, Chateau d'Eynebourg, La Calamine.

1986. "Philately for the Young". 25th International Festival of Humour, Knokke.
2885 **856** 9f. black, green & red . . 50 20

857 Constant Permeke (artist)

1986. Celebrities. Multicoloured.
2886 9f. Type **857** (birth centenary) 45 25
2887 13f. Michael Edmond de Selys-Longchamps (naturalist) 70 20
2888 24f. Felix Timmermans (writer) (birth cent) . . . 1·25 40
2889 26f. Maurice Careme (poet) 1·40 40

858 Academy Building, Ghent

1986. Centenary of Royal Academy for Dutch Language and Literature.
2890 **858** 9f. blue 45 25

859 Hops, Glass of Beer and Barley

1986. Belgian Beer.
2891 **859** 13f. multicoloured . . . 70 20

860 Symbols of Provinces and National Colours

1986. 150th Anniv of Provincial Councils.
2892 **860** 13f. multicoloured . . . 65 10

861 Lenoir Hydrocarbon Carriage, 1863

1986. "Solidarity". Cars. Multicoloured.
2893 9f.+2f. Type **861** 70 70
2894 13f.+3f. Pipe de Tourisme saloon, 1911 . . . . . . 1·10 1·00
2895 24f.+6f. Minerva 22 h.p. coupe, 1930 . . . . . . 2·00 1·90
2896 26f.+6f. FN 8 cylinder saloon, 1931 . . . . . . 2·00 1·90

862 Snow Scene

1986. Christmas.
2897 **862** 13f.+1f. multicoloured 90 90

863 Tree and "100"

1986. Centenaries. Multicoloured.
2898 9f. Type **863** (Textile Workers Christian Union) 70 30
2899 13f. Tree and "100" (Christian Unions) . . . 65 20

864 Corneel Heymans

865 Emblem

1987. Belgian Red Cross. Nobel Physiology and Medicine Prize Winners. Each black, red and stone.
2900 13f.+3f. Type **864** . . . . 1·10 1·00
2901 24f.+6f. Albert Claude . . . 2·00 1·75

1987. "Flanders Technology International" Fair.
2902 **865** 13f. multicoloured . . . 65 15

866 Bee Orchid

868 Jakob Wiener (engraver)

867 "Waiting" (detail of mural, Gustav Klimt)

1987. European Environment Year. Multicoloured.
2903 9f.+2f. Type **866** 85 85
2904 24f.+6f. Small horse-shoe bat . . . . 2·00 1·90
2905 26f.+6f. Peregrine falcon ("Slechtvalk–Faucan Pelerin") . . . . 2·00 2·00

1987. "Europalia 87 Austria" Festival.
2906 **867** 13f. multicoloured . . . 65 10

1987. Stamp Day.
2907 **868** 13f. deep green and green 65 10

869 Penitents' Procession, Furnes

870 Louvain-la-Neuve Church (Jean Cosse)

1987. Folklore Festivals. Multicoloured.
2908 9f. Type **869** 85 35
2909 13f. "John and Alice" (play), Wavre 70 10

1987. Europa. Architecture. Multicoloured.
2910 13f. Type **870** 85 20
2911 24f. St.-Maartensdal (Regional Housing Association tower block), Louvain (Braem, de Mol and Moerkerke) . . . . . 1·10 50

871 Statue of Gretry and Stage Set

872 Virelles Lake

1987. 20th Anniv of Wallonia Royal Opera.
2912 **871** 24f. multicoloured . . . 1·40 45

1987. Tourist Publicity. Multicoloured.
2913 13f. St. Christopher's Church, Racour 85 25
2914 13f. Type **872** 85 25
2915 13f. Heimolen windmill, Keerbergen 85 25
2916 13f. Boondael Chapel . . . 85 25
2917 13f. Statue of Jan Breydel and Pieter de Coninck, Bruges 85 25

873 Rowing

1987. Centenary of Royal Belgian Rowing Association (2918) and European Volleyball Championships (2919). Multicoloured.
2918 9f. Type **873** 45 30
2919 13f. Volleyball (27 × 37 mm) 70 20

874 Emblem

1987. Foreign Trade Year.
2920 **874** 13f. multicoloured . . . 65 10

875 "Leisure Time" (P. Paulus)

1987. Centenary of Belgian Social Law.
2921 **875** 26f. multicoloured . . . 1·40 45

876 Willy and Wanda (comic strip characters)

1987. "Philately for the Young".
2922 **876** 9f. multicoloured . . . . 1·60 30

878 Rixensart Castle

1987. "Solidarity". Castles. Multicoloured.
2928 9f.+2f. Type **878** 70 65
2929 13f.+3f. Westerlo 90 85
2930 26f.+5f. Fallais . . . . . . 2·00 1·90
2931 50f.+12f. Gaasbeek . . . . 3·50 3·25

879 "Madonna and Child" (Remi Lens)

880 Cross and Road

1987. Christmas.
2932 **879** 13f.+1f. multicoloured 90 90

1987. 50th Anniv of Yellow and White Cross (home nursing organization).
2933 **880** 9f.+2f. multicoloured . . 90 90

881 Newsprint ("Le Soir")

1987. Newspaper Centenaries.
2934 **881** 9f. multicoloured 45 25
2935 – 9f. black and brown . . . 45 25
DESIGN—VERT: No. 2935, Type characters ("Het Laatste Nieuws" (1988)).

882 Lighthouse, "Snipe" (trawler) and Horse Rider in Sea

883 "Flanders Alive" (cultural activities campaign)

1988. The Sea. Multicoloured.
2936 10f. Type **882** 60 55
2937 10f. "Asannot" (trawler) and people playing on beach 60 55
2938 10f. Cross-channel ferry, yacht and bathing huts . . 60 55
2939 10f. Container ship, spotted redshank and oystercatcher 60 55

Nos. 2936/9 were issued together, se-tenant, forming a composite design.

1988. Regional Innovations.
2940 **883** 13f. multicoloured . . . 70 20
2941 – 13f. black, yellow & red 70 20
DESIGN: No. 2941, "Operation Athena" emblem (technological advancement in Wallonia).

884 19th-century Postman (after James Thiriar)

885 "Bengale Triomphant"

1988. Stamp Day.
2942 **884** 13f. brown and cream 65 10

1988. Philatelic Promotion Fund. Illustrations from "60 Roses for a Queen" by Pierre-Joseph Redoute (1st series). Multicoloured.
2943 13f.+3f. Type **885** . . . . 1·25 1·25
2944 24f.+6f. "Centfeuille cristata" . . . . 2·00 1·90
See also Nos. 2979/80 and 3009/10.

886 Non-polluting Motor

1988. Europa. Transport and Communications. Multicoloured.
2946 13f. Dish aerial 90 20
2947 24f. Type **886** . . . . . . 1·40 60

887 Table Tennis

1988. Olympic Games, Seoul. Multicoloured.
2948 9f.+2f. Type **887** 90 90
2949 13f.+3f. Cycling . . . . . . 1·25 1·25

888 Amay Tower

889 Monnet

1988. Tourist Publicity.
2951 **888** 9f. black and brown . . 55 25
2952 – 9f. black and blue 55 25
2953 – 9f. black, green and pink 55 25
2954 – 13f. black and pink . . . 80 20
2955 – 13f. black and grey . . . 80 20
DESIGNS—VERT: No. 2952, Lady of Hanswijk Basilica, Malines; 2954, Old Town Hall and village pump, Peer. HORIZ: No. 2953, St. Sernin's Church, Waimes; 2955, Basilica of Our Lady of Bon Secours, Peruwelz.

1988. Birth Centenary of Jean Monnet (statesman).
2956 **889** 13f. black and cream . . 65 20

890 Tapestry (detail) and Academy Building

891 Antwerp Ethnographical Museum Exhibits

1988. 50th Annivs of Royal Belgian Academy of Medicine (2957) and Royal Belgian Academy of Sciences, Literature and Fine Arts (2958). Multicoloured.
2957 9f. Type **890** 45 25
2958 9f. Symbols of Academy and building 45 25

1988. Cultural Heritage. Multicoloured.
2959 9f. Type **891** 45 25
2960 13f. Tomb of Lord Gilles Othon and Jacqueline de Lalaing, St. Martin's Church, Trazegnies . . . 70 20
2961 24f. Organ, St. Bartholomew's Church, Geraardsbergen 1·40 55
2962 26f. St. Hadelin's reliquary, St. Martin's Church, Vise 1·75 45

892 Spirou (comic strip character) and Stamp

1988. "Philately for the Young". 50th Anniv of "Spirou" (comic).
2963 **892** 9f. multicoloured . . . . 1·40 35

893 Jacques Brel (songwriter)

1988. "Solidarity". Death Anniversaries. Mult.
2964 9f.+2f. Type **893** (10th) . . 1·25 1·25
2965 13f.+3f. Jef Denyn (carilloner) (47th) . . . . 1·25 1·25
2966 26f.+6f. Fr. Ferdinand Verbiest (astronomer) (300th) . . . . 2·00 1·90

894 "75"

1988. 75th Anniv of Belgian Giro Bank.
2967 **894** 13f. multicoloured . . . 70 20

895 Winter Scene

1988. Christmas.
2968 **895** 9f. multicoloured 50 35

896 Standard Bearer and Guards of Royal Mounted Escort

897 Wooden Press, 1600

1988. 50th Anniv of Royal Mounted Escort.
2969 **896** 13f. multicoloured . . . 70 20

1988. Printing Presses.
2970 **897** 9f. black, pink and blue 45 25
2971 – 24f. brown, pink and deep brown . . . . . 1·25 50
2972 – 26f. green, pink and light green . . . . 1·40 50
DESIGNS—VERT: 24f. 18th-cent Stanhope metal letterpress. HORIZ: 26f. 19th-cent Krause lithographic press.

898 "Crucifixion of Christ" (detail, Rogier van der Weyden)

1989. Belgian Red Cross. Paintings. Mult.
2973 9f.+2f. Type **898** 90 90
2974 13f.+3f. "Virgin and Child" (Gerard David) . . . . . 1·25 1·25
2975 24f.+6f. "The Good Samaritan" (detail, Denis van Alsloot) . . . . . . 2·00 1·90

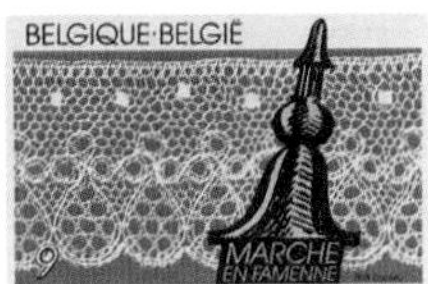

899 Marche en Famenne

1989. Lace-making Towns.
2976 **899** 9f. green, black & brown 55 35
2977 – 13f. blue, black & grey 70 25
2978 – 13f. red, black & grey . . 70 25
DESIGNS: No. 2977, Bruges; 2978, Brussels.

1989. Philatelic Promotion Fund. "60 Roses for a Queen" by Pierre-Joseph Redoute (2nd series). As T **885**. Multicoloured.
2979 13f.+5f. "Centfeuille unique melee de rouge" . . . . 1·25 1·25
2980 24f.+6f. "Bengale a grandes feuilles" . . . . 2·00 1·90

900 Post-chaise and Mail Coach

1989. Stamp Day.
2982 **900** 13f. yellow, black & brn 70 20

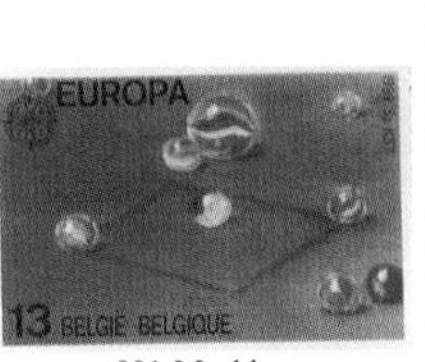

901 Marbles **902** Palette on Column

1989. Europa. Children's Games and Toys. Multicoloured.
2983 13f. Type **901** 90 25
2984 24f. Jumping-jack . . . . . 1·75 80

1989. 325th Anniv of Royal Academy of Fine Arts, Antwerp.
2985 **902** 13f. multicoloured . . . 75 20

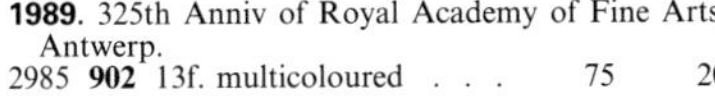

903 Brussels (½-size illustration)

1989. 3rd Direct Elections to European Parliament.
2986 **903** 13f. multicoloured . . . 75 25

904 Hand (detail, "Creation of Adam", Michelangelo) **905** St. Tillo's Church, Izegem

1989. Bicentenary of French Declaration of Rights of Man.
2987 **904** 13f. black, red and blue 75 25

1989. Tourist Publicity. Multicoloured.
2988 9f. Type **905** 55 35
2989 9f. Logne Castle, Ferrieres (vert) 55 35
2990 13f. Antoing Castle (vert) 85 25
2991 13f. St. Laurentius's Church, Lokeren (vert) 85 25

906 Mallard

1989. Ducks. Multicoloured.
2992 13f. Type **906** . . . . . . 1·10 50
2993 13f. Green-winged teal ("Sarcelle d'Hiver") . . . 1·10 50
2994 13f. Common shoveler ("Canard Souchet") . . . 1·10 50
2995 13f. Pintail ("Canard Pilet") 1·10 50

907 "Shogun Uesugi Shigefusa" (Kamakura period wood figure)

1989. "Europalia 89 Japan" Festival.
2996 **907** 24f. multicoloured . . . 1·40 45

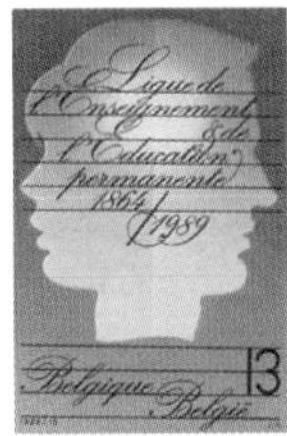

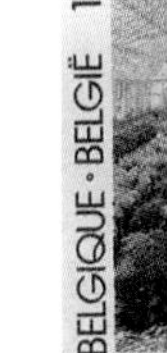

908 Profiles **909** Map

1989. 125th Anniv of League of Teaching and Permanent Education.
2997 **908** 13f. multicoloured . . . 70 15

1989. 150th Anniv of Division of Limburg between Netherlands and Belgium.
2998 **909** 13f. multicoloured . . . 70 15

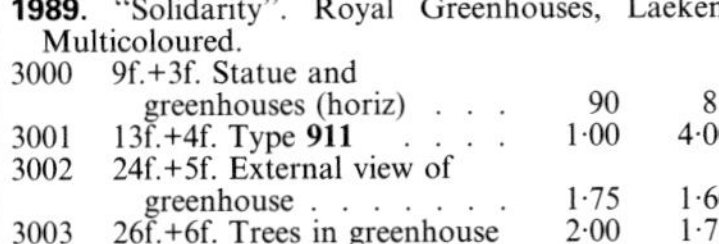

910 Nibbs (comic strip character) **911** Flower Beds in Greenhouse

1989. "Philately for the Young".
2999 **910** 9f. multicoloured . . . . 1·25 35

1989. "Solidarity". Royal Greenhouses, Laeken. Multicoloured.
3000 9f.+3f. Statue and greenhouses (horiz) . . . 90 85
3001 13f.+4f. Type **911** . . . . 1·00 4·00
3002 24f.+5f. External view of greenhouse . . . . 1·75 1·60
3003 26f.+6f. Trees in greenhouse 2·00 1·75

912 Treble Clef

1989. 50th Anniv of Queen Elisabeth Musical Chapel, Waterloo.
3004 **912** 24f.+6f. multicoloured 2·00 1·90

913 Army Musicians

1989. Christmas. Centenary of Salvation Army in Belgium.
3005 **913** 9f. multicoloured 50 20

914 Fr. Damien and Church **915** Fr. Daens

1989. Death Cent of Fr. Damien (missionary).
3006 **914** 24f. multicoloured . . . 1·75 45

1989. 150th Birth Anniv of Fr. Adolf Daens (social reformer).
3007 **915** 9f. turquoise and green 50 20

916 "Courier" (Albrecht Durer) **917** "Iris florentina"

1990. 500th Anniv of Regular European Postal Services.
3008 **916** 14f. chocolate, buff and brown 65 20

1990. Philatelic Promotion Fund. "60 Roses for a Queen" by Pierre-Joseph Redoute (3rd series). As T **885**. Multicoloured.
3009 14f.+7f. "Bengale Desprez" 1·40 1·25
3010 25f.+12f. "Bengale Philippe" 2·25 2·25

1990. Ghent Flower Show. Multicoloured.
3012 10f. Type **917** 55 35
3013 14f. "Cattleya harrisoniana" 85 20
3014 14f. "Lilium bulbiferum" . . 85 20

918 Emilienne Brunfaut (women's rights activist)

1990. International Women's Day.
3015 **918** 25f. red and black . . . 1·40 45

919 Special Olympics **921** "Postman Roulin" (Vincent van Gogh)

920 Water, Tap and Heart

1990. Sporting Events. Multicoloured.
3016 10f. Type **919** 55 25
3017 14f. Football (World Cup football championship, Italy) 85 15
3018 25f. Disabled pictogram and ball (Gold Cup wheelchair basketball championship, Bruges) . . . . 1·40 45

1990. 75th Anniv of Foundation of National Water Supply Society (predecessor of present water-supply companies).
3019 **920** 14f. multicoloured . . . 80 20

1990. Stamp Day.
3020 **921** 14f. multicoloured . . . 80 20

922 Worker and Crowd **923** Liege I Post Office

1990. Centenary of Labour Day.
3021 **922** 25f. brown, pink & black 1·40 50

1990. Europa. Post Office Buildings.
3022 – 14f. black and blue . . . 90 20
3023 **923** 25f. black and red . . . 2·00 50
DESIGN—HORIZ: 14f. Ostend I Post Office.

924 Monument of the Lys, Courtrai

1990. 50th Anniv of the 18 Days Campaign (resistance to German invasion).
3024 **924** 14f. black, yellow & red 85 20

925 Battle Scene (⅔-size illustration)

1990. 175th Anniv of Battle of Waterloo.
3026 **925** 25f. multicoloured . . . 1·60 1·25

926 Berendrecht Lock, Antwerp **927** King Baudouin

1990. Tourist Publicity. Multicoloured.
3027 10f. Type **926** 65 30
3028 10f. Procession of Bayard Steed, Termonde 65 30
3029 14f. St. Rolende's March, Gerpinnes (vert) 80 25
3030 14f. Lommel (1000th anniv) 80 25
3031 14f. St. Clement's Church, Watermael 80 25

1990.
3032 **927** 14f. multicoloured . . . 90 20

928 Eurasian Perch

1990. Fishes. Multicoloured.
3033 14f. Type **928** . . . . 1·75 60
3034 14f. Eurasian minnow ("Vairon") . . . . 1·75 60
3035 14f. European bitterling ("Bouviere") . . . . 1·75 60
3036 14f. Three-spined stickle-back ("Epinoche") . . . 1·75 60

929 Orchestra and Children (½-size illustration)

1990. "Solidarity". Multicoloured.
3037 10f.+2f. Type **929** (50th anniv of Jeunesses Musicales) . . . . 1·75 1·60
3038 14f.+3f. Count of Egmont (16th-century campaigner for religious tolerance) and Beethoven (composer of "Egmont" overture) . . 2·10 2·00
3039 25f.+6f. Jozef Cantre (sculptor) and sculptures (birth centenary) . . . . 2·75 2·50

930 Lucky Luke (comic strip character)

1990. "Philately for the Young".
3040 **930** 10f. multicoloured . . . 1·25 35

931 St. Bernard

1990. 900th Birth Anniv of St. Bernard (Abbot of Clairvaux and Church mediator).
3041 **931** 25f. black and flesh . . . 1·40 45

932 "Pepingen, Winter 1977" (Jozef Lucas)

1990. Christmas.
3042 **932** 10f. multicoloured . . . 55 25

933 "Self-portrait"

1990. 300th Death Anniv of David Teniers, the Younger (painter). Multicoloured.
3043 10f. Type **933** 55 25
3044 14f. "Dancers" 85 20
3045 25f. "Peasants playing Bowls outside Village Inn" . . . 1·40 45

934 King Baudouin and Queen Fabiola (photograph by Valeer Vanbeckbergen)

1990. Royal 30th Wedding Anniversary.
3046 **934** 50f.+15f. mult . . . . . 6·50 7·00

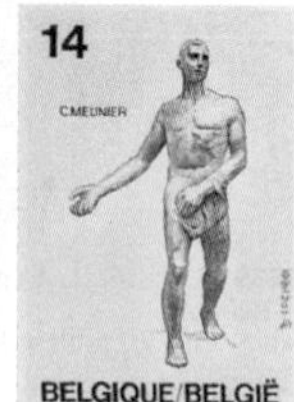

935 "Temptation of St. Anthony" (detail, Hieronymus Bosch)

936 "The Sower" (detail of "Monument to Labour", Brussels) (Constantin Meunier)

1991. Belgian Red Cross. Paintings. Mult.
3047 14f.+3f. Type **935** . . . . 2·10 1·90
3048 25f.+6f. "The Annunciation" (detail, Dirck Bouts) . . . . . . 3·00 3·00

1991. 19th-Century Sculpture.
3049 **936** 14f. black & cinnamon 85 25
3050 – 25f. black and blue . . . 1·40 45
DESIGN: 25f. Detail of Brabo Fountain, Antwerp (Jef Lambeaux).

937 Rhythmic Gymnastics (European Youth Olympic Days, Brussels)

1991. Sports Meetings.
3051 **937** 10f. grey, mauve & blk 55 25
3052 – 10f. grey, green & black 55 25
DESIGN: No. 3052, Korfball (Third World Championship, Belgium).

938 New Stamp Printing Office, Malines (Hugo van Hoecke)

1991. Stamp Day.
3053 **938** 14f. multicoloured . . . 80 20

939 Cogwheels

1991. Centenary of Liberal Trade Union.
3054 **939** 25f. blue, light blue and deep blue . . . . . . 1·40 50

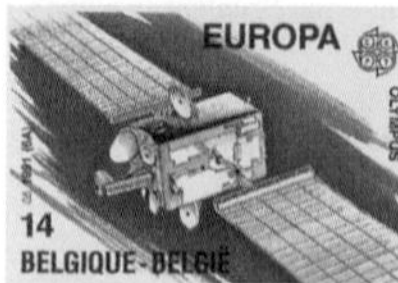

940 "Olympus 1" Communications Satellite

1991. Europa. Europe in Space. Multicoloured.
3055 14f. Type **940** . . . . . . 1·40 20
3056 25f. "Ariane 5" rocket carrying space shuttle "Hermes" . . . . 2·25 50

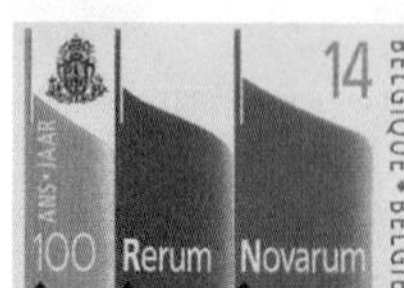

941 Leo XIII's Arms and Standard, and Christian Labour Movement Banners

1991. Centenary of "Rerum Novarum" (encyclical letter from Pope Leo XIII on workers' rights).
3057 **941** 14f. multicoloured . . . 80 20

942 "Isabella of Portugal and Philip the Good" (anon)

1991. "Europalia 91 Portugal" Festival.
3058 **942** 14f. multicoloured . . . 80 20

943 Neptune Grottoes, Couvin

1991. Tourist Publicity. Multicoloured.
3059 14f. Type **943** 80 20
3060 14f. Dieleghem Abbey, Jette 80 20
3061 14f. Niel Town Hall (vert) 80 20
3062 14f. Hautes Fagnes nature reserve 80 20
3063 14f. Giant Rolarius, Roeselare (vert) 80 20

944 King Baudouin (photograph by Dimitri Ardelean)

1991. 60th Birthday (1990) and 40th Anniv of Accession to Throne of King Baudouin.
3064 **944** 14f. multicoloured . . . 1·50 20

945 Academy Building, Caduceus and Leopold I

1991. 150th Anniv of Royal Academy of Medicine.
3065 **945** 10f. multicoloured . . . 55 25

946 "The English Coast at Dover"

948 Hands reaching through Bars

947 Death Cap

1991. 61st Death Anniv of Alfred Finch (painter and ceramic artist).
3066 **946** 25f. multicoloured . . . 1·40 50

1991. Fungi. Multicoloured.
3067 14f. Type **947** . . . . . . 1·50 65
3068 14f. The Blusher (inscr "Golmotte") . . . . . . 1·50 65
3069 14f. Flaky-stemmed witches' mushroom (inscr "Bolet a pied rouge") . . . . . . 1·50 65
3070 14f. "Hygrocybe persistens" (inscr "Hygrophore jaune conique") . . . . 1·50 65

1991. 30th Anniv of Amnesty International (3071) and 11th Anniv of Belgian Branch of Medecins sans Frontieres (3072). Multicoloured.
3071 25f. Type **948** . . . . . . 1·40 50
3072 25f. Doctor examining baby 1·40 55

1991. Birds (2nd series). As T **841**. Mult.
3073 50c. Goldcrest ("Roitelet Huppe") 10 10
3074 1f. Redpoll ("Sizerin Flamme") 15 10
3075 2f. Blackbird ("Merle Noir") 15 10
3076 3f. Reed bunting ("Bruant des Roseaux") 30 10
3077 4f. Pied wagtail ("Bergeronette Grise") 30 10
3078 5f. Barn swallow ("Hirondelle de Cheminee") 30 10
3079 5f.50 Jay ("Geai des Chenes") 40 20
3080 6f. White-throated dipper ("Cincle Plongeur") . . 40 20
3081 6f.50 Sedge-warbler ("Phragmite des Jones") 50 20
3082 7f. Golden oriole ("Loriot") 50 20
3083 8f. Great tit ("Mesange Charbonniere") 65 20
3084 9f. Song thrush ("Grive Musicienne") 65 20
3085 10f. Western greenfinch ("Verdier") 65 20
3086 11f. Winter wren ("Troglodyte Mignon") 85 20
3087 13f. House sparrow ("Moineau Domestique") 85 20
3088 14f. Willow warbler ("Pouillot Fitis") . . . . 1·10 20
3088a 16f. Bohemian waxwing ("Jaseur Boreal") . . . 1·10 20

949 Exhibition Emblem

1991. "Telecom 91" International Telecommunications Exhibition, Geneva.
3089 **949** 14f. multicoloured . . . 75 20

950 Blake and Mortimer in "The Yellow Mark" (Edgar P. Jacobs)

1991. "Philately for the Young". Comic Strips. Multicoloured.
3090 14f. Type **950** . . . . . . 1·50 70
3091 14f. Cori the ship boy in "The Ill-fated Voyage" (Bob de Moor) . . . . . 1·50 70
3092 14f. "Cities of the Fantastic" (Francois Schuiten) . . . . 1·50 70
3093 14f. "Boule and Bill" (Jean Roba) . . . . 1·50 70

951 Charles Dekeukeleire

1991. "Solidarity". Film Makers.
3094 **951** 10f.+2f. black, brown and green 90 85
3095 – 14f.+3f. black, orange and brown . . . . . 1·40 1·25
3096 – 25f.+6f. black, ochre and brown . . . . 2·25 2·25
DESIGNS: 14f. Jacques Ledoux; 25f. Jacques Feyder.

952 Printing Press forming "100" ("Gazet van Antwerpen")

1991. Newspaper Centenaries. Multicoloured.

3097 **952** 10f. black, lt grn & grn 55 25

3098 – 10f. yellow, blue & blk 55 25

DESIGN: No. 3098, Cancellation on "stamp" ("Het Volk").

953 "Our Lady rejoicing in the Child" (icon, Chevetogne Abbey)

955 Speed Skating

954 Mozart and Score

1991. Christmas.

3099 **953** 10f. multicoloured . . . 55 25

1991. Death Bicentenary of Wolfgang Amadeus Mozart (composer).

3100 **954** 25f. purple, bl & ultram 1·60 80

1992. Olympic Games, Albertville and Barcelona. Multicoloured.

3101 10f.+2f. Type **955** . . . . 1·00 1·00

3102 10f.+2f. Baseball . . . . . 1·00 1·10

3103 14f.+3f. Tennis (horiz) . . . 1·40 2·00

3104 25f.+6f. Clay-pigeon shooting . . . . 2·50 2·25

956 Fire Hose and Service Emblem

957 Flames and Silhouette of Man

1992. Fire Service.

3105 **956** 14f. multicoloured . . . 75 20

1992. The Resistance.

3106 **957** 14f. yellow, black & red 75 20

958 Tapestry and Carpet

959 Belgian Pavilion and Exhibition Emblem

1992. Prestige Occupations. Multicoloured.

3107 10f. Type **958** 55 25

3108 14f. Chef's hat and cutlery (10th anniv (1991) of Association of Belgian Master Chefs) 75 20

3109 27f. Diamond and "100" (centenary (1993) of Antwerp Diamond Club) 1·75 40

1992. "Expo '92" World's Fair, Seville.

3110 **959** 14f. multicoloured . . . 75 20

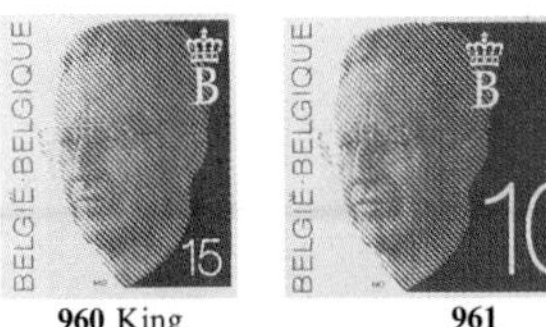

960 King Baudouin

961

1992.

3111 **960** 15f. red 75 10

3115 28f. green . . . . 1·75 50

3120 **961** 100f. green . . . . . . 5·50 65

962 Van Noten at Work

963 "White Magic No. VI"

1992. Stamp Day. 10th Death Anniv of Jean van Noten (stamp designer).

3124 **962** 15f. black and red . . . 80 20

1992. Original Art Designs for Stamps. Mult.

3125 15f. Type **963** 80 25

3126 15f. "Colours" (horiz) . . . 80 25

964 Compass Rose, Setting Sun and Harbour

1992. Europa. 500th Anniv of Discovery of America. Multicoloured.

3127 15f. Type **964** . . . . . . 1·40 25

3128 28f. Globe and astrolabe forming "500" . . . . . 2·75 65

965 Faces of Different Colours

1992. Anti-racism.

3129 **965** 15f. grey, black & pink 75 20

966 "The Hamlet" (Jacob Smits)

1992. Belgian Paintings in Orsay Museum, Paris. Multicoloured.

3130 11f. Type **966** 55 30

3131 15f. "The Bath" (Alfred Stevens) 90 20

3132 30f. "Man at the Helm" (Theo van Rysselberghe) 1·75 45

967 Proud Margaret

968 Mannekin-Pis, Brussels

1992. Folk Tales. Multicoloured.

3133 11f.+2f. Type **967** . . . . 1·25 1·10

3134 15f.+3f. Witches ("Les Macrales") . . . . 1·75 1·60

3135 28f.+6f. Reynard the fox . . 2·75 2·50

1992. Tourist Publicity. Multicoloured.

3136 15f. Type **968** 80 25

3137 15f. Former Landcommandery of Teutonic Order, Alden Biesen (now Flemish cultural centre) (horiz) . . 80 25

3138 15f. Andenne (1300th anniv) 80 25

3139 15f. Carnival revellers on Fools' Monday, Renaix (horiz) 80 25

3140 15f. Great Procession (religious festival), Tournai (horiz) 80 25

969 European Polecat

1992. Mammals. Multicoloured.

3141 15f. Type **969** . . . . . . 1·40 70

3142 15f. Eurasian red squirrel 1·40 70

3143 15f. Eurasian hedgehog . . 1·40 70

3144 15f. Common dormouse . . 1·40 70

970 Henri van der Noot, Jean van der Meersch and Jean Vonck

1992. 203rd Anniv of Brabant Revolution.

3145 **970** 15f. multicoloured . . . 80 20

971 Arms of Thurn and Taxis

972 Gaston Lagaffe (cartoon character)

1992. 500th Anniv of Mention of Thurn and Taxis Postal Services in Lille Account Books.

3146 **971** 15f. multicoloured . . . 80 20

1992. "Philately for the Young".

3147 **972** 15f. multicoloured . . . 1·10 20

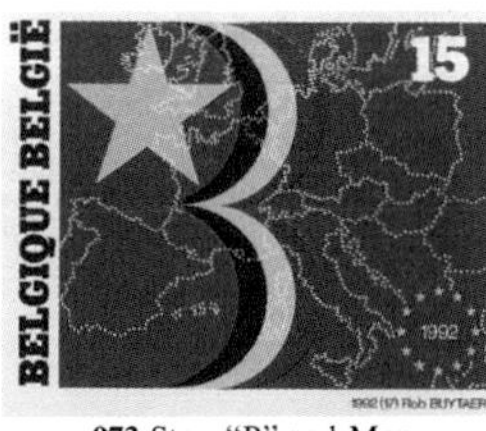

973 Star, "B" and Map

1992. European Single Market.

3148 **973** 15f. multicoloured . . . 80 20

974 Okapi

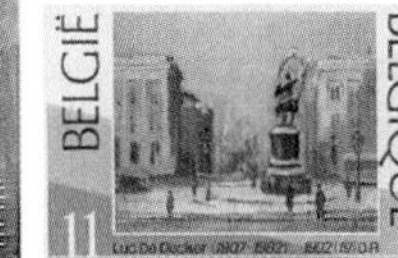

975 "Place Royale in Winter" (Luc de Decker)

1992. 150th Anniv of Antwerp Zoo. Mult.

3149 15f. Type **974** 80 25

3150 30f. Golden-headed tamarin 1·75 40

1992. Christmas.

3151 **975** 11f. multicoloured . . . 55 25

976 "Man with Pointed Hat" (Adriaen Brouwer)

1993. Belgian Red Cross. Paintings. Mult.

3152 15f.+3f. Type **976** . . . . 1·60 1·60

3153 28f.+7f. "Nereid and Triton" (Peter Paul Rubens) (horiz) . . . . . 3·25 3·25

977 Council of Leptines, 743

1993. Historical Events. Multicoloured.

3154 11f. Type **977** 55 30

3155 15f. Queen Beatrix and King Matthias I Corvinus of Hungary (detail of "Missale Romanum") (77 × 24 mm) 90 20

3156 30f. Battle scene (Battles of Neerwinden, 1673 and 1773) . . . . 1·75 40

978 Town Hall

1993. Antwerp, European City of Culture. Mult.

3158 15f. Panorama of Antwerp (76 × 24 mm) 90 20

3159 15f. Type **978** 90 20

3160 15f. "Study of Women's Heads and Male Torso" (Jacob Jordaens) 90 20

3161 15f. St. Job's altarpiece, Schoonbroek 90 20

3162 15f. "Angels" (stained glass window by Eugeen Yoors, Mother of God Chapel, Marie-Josee Institute, Elisabethville) (vert) . . . 90 20

979 1893 2f. Stamp

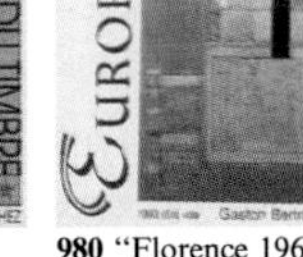

980 "Florence 1960" (Gaston Bertrand)

1993. Stamp Day.

3163 **979** 15f. multicoloured . . . 75 20

1993. Europa. Contemporary Art. Multicoloured.

3164 15f. Type **980** 70 20

3165 28f. "The Gig" (Constant Permeke) . . . . 1·50 55

981 Red Admiral ("Vanessa atalanta")

1993. Butterflies. Multicoloured.

3166 15f. Type **981** 75 30

3167 15f. Purple emperor ("Apatura iris") 75 30

3168 15f. Peacock ("Inachis io") 75 30

3169 15f. Small tortoiseshell ("Aglais urticae") 75 30

982 Knot

983 Mayan Warrior (statuette)

1993. 150th Anniv of Alumni of Free University of Brussels Association.
3170 **982** 15f. blue and black . . . 75 25

1993. "Europalia 93 Mexico" Festival.
3171 **983** 15f. multicoloured . . . 75 20

984 Ommegang, Brussels

1993. Folklore Festivals. Multicoloured.
3172 11f. Type **984** 65 30
3173 15f. Royale Moncrabeau, Namur 75 20
3174 28f. Stilt-walkers, Merchtem (vert) . . . . 1·40 50

985 La Hulpe Castle

1993. Tourist Publicity.
3175 **985** 15f. black and blue . . . 75 20
3176 – 15f. black and lilac . . . 75 20
3177 – 15f. black and grey . . . 75 20
3178 – 15f. black and pink . . . 75 20
3179 – 15f. black and green . . 75 20
DESIGNS—HORIZ: No. 3176, Cortewalle Castle, Beveren; 3177, Jehay Castle; 3179, Raeren Castle. VERT: No. 3178, Arenberg Castle, Heverlee.

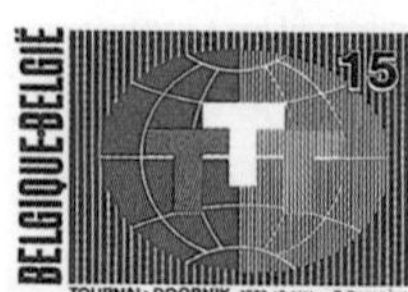

986 Emblem

1993. 2nd International Triennial Textile Exhibition, Tournai.
3180 **986** 15f. blue, red and black 75 20

987 Presidency Emblem

1993. Belgian Presidency of European Community Council.
3181 **987** 15f. multicoloured . . . 75 20

988 Magritte

989 King Baudouin

1993. 25th Death Anniv (1992) of Rene Magritte (artist).
3182 **988** 30f. multicoloured . . . 1·50 50

1993. King Baudouin Commemoration.
3183 **989** 15f. black and blue . . . 90 20

990 Red and White Cat

1993. Cats. Multicoloured.
3184 15f. Type **990** . . . . . . 1·00 50
3185 15f. Tabby and white cat standing on rock . . . . 1·00 50
3186 15f. Silver tabby lying on wall . . . . 1·00 50
3187 15f. Tortoiseshell and white cat sitting by gardening tools . . . . 1·00 50

991 Highlighted Cancer Cell

992 Frontispiece

1993. Anti-cancer Campaign.
3188 **991** 15f.+3f. multicoloured 1·40 1·25

1993. 450th Anniv of "De Humani Corporis Fabrica" (treatise on human anatomy) by Andreas Vesalius.
3189 **992** 15f. black, brown & red 75 20

993 Natacha (cartoon character)

1993. "Philately for the Young".
3190 **993** 15f. multicoloured . . . 1·00 25

994 Sun's Rays

995 "Madonna and Child" (statue, Our Lady of the Chapel, Brussels)

1993. 50th Anniv of Publication of "Le Faux Soir" (resistance newspaper).
3191 **994** 11f. multicoloured . . . 55 40

1993. Christmas.
3192 **995** 11f. multicoloured . . . 55 25

996 Child looking at Globe

1993. Children's Town Councils.
3193 **996** 15f. multicoloured . . . 80 20

997 King Albert II

998 King Albert II

1993.
3194 **997** 16f. multicoloured . . . 1·10 10
3195 16f. turquoise and blue 90 10
3196 20f. brown and stone . . 90 10
3197 30f. purple and mauve 1·25 20
3198 32f. orange and yellow 1·10 20
3199 40f. red and mauve . . . 2·00 20
3200 50f. myrtle and green . . 3·25 25
3201 **998** 100f. multicoloured . . . 4·50 35
3202 200f. multicoloured . . . 9·00 85

999 "Ma Toute Belle" (Serge Vandercam)

1000 Olympic Flames and Rings

1994. Painters' Designs. Multicoloured.
3210 16f. Type **999** 75 20
3211 16f. "The Malleable Darkness" (Octave Landuyt) (horiz) 75 20

1994. Sports. Multicoloured.
3212 16f.+3f. Type **1000** (cent of International Olympic Committee) . . . . . . 1·50 1·50
3213 16f.+3f. Footballers (World Cup Football Championship, U.S.A.) 1·50 1·50
3214 16f.+3f. Skater (Winter Olympic Games, Lillehammer, Norway) . . 1·50 1·50

1001 Hanriot HD-1

1002 Masthead of "Le Jour-Le Courrier" (centenary)

1994. Biplanes. Multicoloured.
3215 13f. Type **1001** 75 30
3216 15f. Spad XIII 90 25
3217 30f. Schrenck FBA.H flying boat . . . . 1·50 50
3218 32f. Stampe SV-4B . . . . 1·75 45

1994. Newspaper Anniversaries. Multicoloured.
3219 16f. Type **1002** 85 20
3220 16f. Masthead of "La Wallonie" (75th anniv) (horiz) 85 20

1003 "Fall of the Golden Calf" (detail, Fernand Allard l'Olivier)

1994. Centenary of Charter of Quaregnon (social charter).
3221 **1003** 16f. multicoloured . . . 85 20

1004 1912 5f. Stamp

1994. Stamp Day. 60th Death Anniv of King Albert I.
3222 **1004** 16f. purple, mauve & bl 85 20

1005 Reconciliation of Duke John I and Arnold, Squire of Wezemaal

1994. 700th Death Anniv of John I, Duke of Brabant. Illustrations from 15th-century "Brabantse Yeesten". Multicoloured.
3223 13f. Type **1005** 70 25
3224 16f. Tournament at wedding of his son John to Margaret of York, 1290 85 20
3225 30f. Battle of Woeringen (77 × 25 mm) . . . . . . 1·75 55

1006 Georges Lemaitre (formulator of expanding Universe and of "big bang" theory)

1008 St. Peter's Church, Bertem

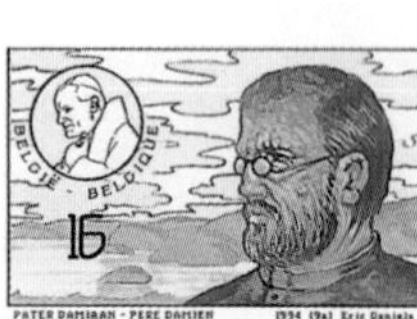

1007 Father Damien (missionary and leprosy worker)

1994. Europa. Discoveries and Inventions. Mult.
3226 16f. Type **1006** 70 20
3227 30f. Gerardus Mercator (inventor of Mercator projection in cartography) 1·50 50

1994. Visit of Pope John Paul II. Mult.
3228 16f. Type **1007** (beatification) 85 20
3229 16f. St. Mutien-Marie (5th anniv of canonization) . . 85 20

1994. Tourist Publicity. Multicoloured.
3230 16f. Type **1008** 85 20
3231 16f. St. Bavo's Church, Kanegem (vert) 85 20
3232 16f. Royal St. Mary's Church, Schaarbeek . . . 85 20
3233 16f. St. Gery's Church, Aubechies 85 20
3234 16f. Sts. Peter and Paul's Church, St.-Severin en Condroz (vert) 85 20

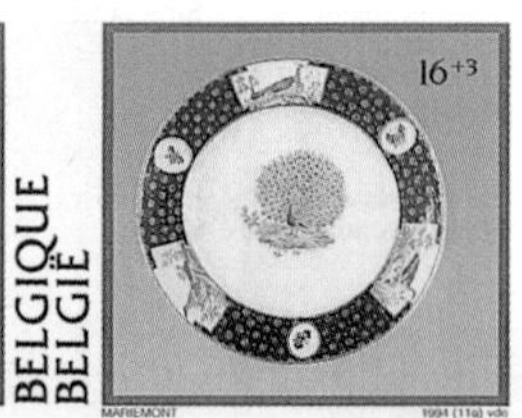

1009 Tournai Porcelain Plate from Duke of Orleans Service (Mariemont Museum)

1994. Museum Exhibits. Multicoloured.
3235 16f.+3f. Type **1009** . . . . 1·40 1·25
3236 16f.+3f. Etterbeek porcelain coffee cup and saucer (Louvain Municipal Museum) . . . . 1·40 1·25

1010 Guillame Lekeu (composer)

1994. Anniversaries. Multicoloured.
3238 16f. Type **1010** (death cent) 75 20
3239 16f. Detail of painting by Hans Memling (500th death anniv) 75 20

1011 Generals Crerar, Montgomery and Bradley and Allied Troops (½-size illustration)

1994. 50th Anniv of Liberation.
3240 **1011** 16f. multicoloured . . . 90 30

1012 Marsh Marigold ("Caltha palustris")

1994. Flowers. Multicoloured.

3241	16f. Type **1012**	1·10	55
3242	16f. White helleborine ("Cephalanthera damasonium")	1·10	55
3243	16f. Sea bindweed ("Calystegia soldanella")	1·10	55
3244	16f. Broad-leaved helleborine ("Epipactis helleborine")	1·10	55

1013 Cubitus (cartoon character) **1014** Simenon and Bridge of Arches, Liege

1994. "Philately for the Young".
3245 **1013** 16f. multicoloured . . . 70 25

1994. 5th Death Anniv of Georges Simenon (novelist).
3246 **1014** 16f. multicoloured . . . 70 20
The depiction of the bridge alludes to Simenon's first novel "Au Pont des Arches".

1015 Deaf Man and Butterfly

1994. "Solidarity".
3247 **1015** 16f.+3f. mult . . . . . 1·00 1·00

1016 Santa Claus on Rooftop

1994. Christmas.
3248 **1016** 13f. multicoloured . . . 70 25

1017 Field and Flax Knife (Flax Museum, Courtrai)

1995. Museums. Multicoloured.

3249	16f.+3f. Type **1017**	90	95
3250	16f.+3f. River and pump (Water and Fountain Museum, Genval)	90	95

The premium was for the promotion of philately.

1018 Emblem

1995. Anniversaries. Anniversary emblems.

3252	**1018**	16f. red, blue & black	85	20
3253	–	16f. multicoloured	85	20
3254	–	16f. multicoloured	85	20
3255	–	16f. red, black & brown	85	20

ANNIVERSARIES: No. 3252, 50th anniv of August Vermeylen Fund; 3253, Centenary of Touring Club of Belgium; 3254, Centenary of Federation of Belgian Enterprises; 3255, 50th anniv of Social Security in Belgium.

1019 "Hibiscus rosa-sinensis"

1995. Ghent Flower Show. Multicoloured.

3256	13f. Type **1019**	70	65
3257	16f. Azalea	90	20
3258	30f. Fuchsia	1·50	40

1020 Crossword Puzzle **1021** Frans de Troyer (promoter of thematic philately)

1995. Games and Pastimes. Multicoloured.

3259	13f. Type **1020**	70	20
3260	16f. King (chess piece)	85	25
3261	30f. Scrabble	1·50	40
3262	34f. Queen (playing cards)	1·75	65

1995. Post Day.
3263 **1021** 16f. black, stone & orge 85 20

1022 Watch Tower and Barbed Wire Fence

1995. Europa. Peace and Freedom. Mult.

3264	16f. Type **1022** (50th anniv of liberation of concentration camps)	1·40	20
3265	30f. Nuclear cloud (25th anniv of Non-Proliferation Treaty)	2·25	50

1023 Soldiers of the Irish Brigade and Memorial Cross

1995. 250th Anniv of Battle of Fontenoy.
3266 **1023** 16f. multicoloured . . . 90 20

1024 U.N. Emblem

1995. 50th Anniv of U.N.O.
3267 **1024** 16f. multicoloured . . . 85 20

1025 "Sauvagemont, Maransart" (Pierre Alechinsky)

1995. Artists' Philatelic Creations.

3268	**1025**	16f. red, black & yellow	85	20
3269	–	16f. multicoloured	85	20

DESIGN: No. 3269, "Telegram-style" (Pol Mara).

1026 Paul Cauchie (Brussels)

1995. Tourist Publicity. Art nouveau house facades by named architects. Multicoloured.

3270	16f. Type **1026**	85	20
3271	16f. Frans Smet-Verhas (Antwerp)	85	20
3272	16f. Paul Jaspar (Liege)	85	20

1027 Anniversary Emblem

1995. Cent of Royal Belgian Football Assn.
3273 **1027** 16f.+4f. mult . . . . . 1·10 1·00

1028 "Mercator" (Belgian cadet barque)

1995. Sailing Ships. Multicoloured.

3274	16f. Type **1028**	1·00	55
3275	16f. "Kruzenshern" (Russian cadet barque) (inscr "Kruzenstern")	1·00	55
3276	16f. "Sagres II" (Portuguese cadet barque)	1·00	55
3277	16f. "Amerigo Vespucci" (Italian cadet ship)	1·00	55

1029 Princess Astrid and Globe

1995. Red Cross. Multicoloured.

3278	16f.+3f. Type **1029** (Chairwoman)	1·00	90
3279	16f.+3f. Wilhelm Rontgen (discoverer of X-rays) and X-ray of hand	1·00	90
3280	16f.+3f. Louis Pasteur (chemist) and microscope	1·00	90

1030 1908 Minerva

1995. Motorcycles. Multicoloured.

3281	13f. Type **1030**	70	30
3282	16f. 1913 FN (vert)	85	20
3283	30f. 1929 La Mondiale	1·40	50
3284	32f. 1937 Gillet (vert)	1·60	45

1031 Sammy (cartoon character)

1995. "Philately for the Young".
3285 **1031** 16f. multicoloured . . . 1·00 20

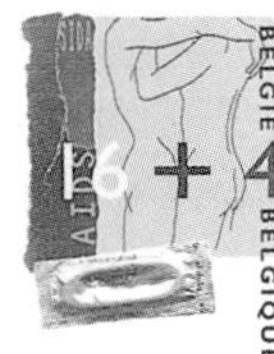
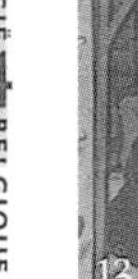

1032 Couple and Condom in Wrapper **1034** "Nativity" (from 15th-century breviary)

1033 King Albert II and Queen Paola (photograph by Christian Louis)

1995. "Solidarity". AIDS Awareness.
3286 **1032** 16f.+4f. mult . . . . . 1·00 90

1995. King's Day.
3287 **1033** 16f. multicoloured . . . 90 20

1995. Christmas.
3288 **1034** 13f. multicoloured . . . 15 15

1035 Puppets, Walloon Museum, Liege

1996. Museums. Multicoloured.

3289	16f.+4f. Type **1035**	1·00	1·00
3290	16f.+4f. National Gin Museum, Hasselt	1·00	1·00

The premium was used for the promotion of philately.

1036 "Emile Mayrisch" **1037** "LIBERALISME"

1996. 70th Death Anniv of Theo van Rysselberghe (painter). No value expressed.
3292 **1036** A (16f.) mult 20 20

1996. 150th Anniv of Liberal Party.
3293 **1037** 16f. dp blue, violet & bl 20 20

1038 Oscar Bonnevalle (stamp designer) and "Gelatenheid"

1996. Stamp Day.
3294 **1038** 16f. multicoloured . . . 20 20

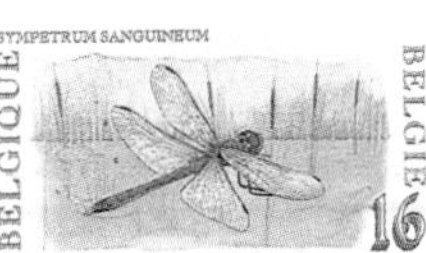

1039 Dragonfly ("Sympetrum sanguineum")

1996. 150th Anniv of Royal Institute of Natural Sciences of Belgium. Insects. Multicoloured.

3295	16f. Type **1039**	60	60
3296	16f. Buff-tailed bumble bee ("Bombus terrestris")	60	60

3297 16f. Stag beetle ("Lucanus cervus") 60 60
3298 16f. May beetle ("Melolontha melolontha") 60 60
3299 16f. European field cricket ("Gryllus campestris") . . 60 60
3300 16f. Seven-spotted ladybird ("Coccinella septempunctata") 60 60

1040 Yvonne Nevejean (rescuer of Jewish children)

1042 King Albert II

1996. Europa. Famous Women. Multicoloured.
3301 16f. Type **1040** 20 20
3302 30f. Marie Gevers (poet) . . 50 50

1996. Birds (3rd series). As T **841**. Mult.
3303 1f. Crested tit ("Mesange Huppee") 15 10
3304 2f. Redwing ("Grive mauvis") 20 10
3305 3f. Eurasian skylark ("Alouette des champs") 20 10
3306 4f. Pied flycatcher ("Gore-mouche noir") 30 10
3307 5f. Common starling ("Etourneau sansonnet") 20 10
3308 6f. Spruce siskin ("Tarin des aulnes") 20 20
3309 7f. Yellow wagtail ("Bergeronnette printaniere") 30 20
3310 7f.50 Great grey shrike ("Pie-Grienche Grise") . . 30 20
3311 9f. Green woodpecker ("Pic Vert") 35 20
3312 10f. Turtle dove ("Tourterelle des Bois") 30 20
3313 15f. Willow tit ("Mesange boreale") 65 20
3314 16f. Coal tit ("Mesange noire") 65 20
3315 21f. Fieldfare ("Grive Litorne") (horiz) 90 60
3316 150f. Black-billed magpie ("Pie bavarde") (35 × 25 mm) . . . . . . 6·25 75

1996. 62nd Birthday of King Albert II.
3327 **1042** 16f. multicoloured . . . 85 10

1043 Han sur Lesse Grottoes

1996. Tourist Publicity. Multicoloured.
3328 16f. Type **1043** 85 20
3329 16f. Statue of beguine, Begijnendijk (vert) 85 20

1044 Royal Palace

1996. Brussels, Heart of Europe. Mult.
3330 16f. Type **1044** 85 20
3331 16f. St. Hubert Royal Galleries 85 20
3332 16f. Le Petit Sablon, Egmont Palace (horiz) . . 85 20
3333 16f. Jubilee Park (horiz) . . 85 20

1045 1900 Germain 6CV Voiturette

1996. Cent of Motor Racing at Spa. Mult.
3334 16f. Type **1045** 85 25
3335 16f. 1925 Alfa Romeo P2 85 25
3336 16f. 1939 Mercedes Benz W154 . . . . 85 25
3337 16f. 1967 Ferrari 330P . . . 85 25

1046 Table Tennis

1996. Olympic Games, Atlanta. Mult.
3338 16f.+4f. Type **1046** 90 95
3339 16f.+4f. Swimming 90 95

1996.
3341 **1042** 16f. blue 70 15
3342 17f. blue 85 10
3343 18f. green 85 20
3344 19f. lilac 85 25
3344a 20f. brown 90 10
3345 25f. brown . . . . . 1·25 20
3346 28f. brown . . . . . 1·25 30
3347 32f. violet . . . . . . 1·40 25
3348 34f. blue . . . . . . 1·25 30
3349 36f. blue . . . . . . 1·50 30
3350 50f. green . . . . . . 2·25 30

1047 "The Straw Hat" (Peter Paul Rubens)

1048 Philip the Fair

1996. Paintings by Belgian Artists in the National Gallery, London. Multicoloured.
3351 14f. "St. Ivo" (Rogier van der Weyden) 70 30
3352 16f. Type **1047** 85 20
3353 30f. "Man in a Turban" (Jan van Eyck) . . . . . 1·50 45

1996. 500th Anniv of Marriage of Philip the Fair and Joanna of Castile and Procession into Brussels. Details of triptych by the Master of Affligem Abbey at Zierikzee Town Hall. Multicoloured.
3354 16f. Type **1048** 85 20
3355 16f. Joanna of Castile . . . 85 20

1049 Cloro (cartoon character)

1996. "Philately for the Young".
3356 **1049** 16f. multicoloured . . . 90 20

1050 Title of First Issue and Charles Letellier (founder)

1996. 150th Anniv of "Mons Almanac".
3357 **1050** 16f. black, yell & mve 85 20

1051 Arthur Grumiaux (violinist, 10th death anniv)

1996. Music and Literature Anniversaries.
3358 **1051** 16f. multicoloured . . . 85 20
3359 – 16f. multicoloured . . . 85 20
3360 – 16f. black and brown 85 20
3361 – 16f. multicoloured . . . 85 20

DESIGNS: No. 3359, Flor Peeters (organist, 10th death anniv); 3360, Christian Dotremont (poet, 5th death anniv); 3361, Paul van Ostaijen (writer, birth centenary) and cover drawing by Oscar Jespers for "Bezette Stad".

1052 Globe and Children of Different Races

1996. "Solidarity". 50th Anniv of U.N.I.C.E.F.
3362 **1052** 16f.+4f. mult 85 95

1054 Students

1997. Centenary of Catholic University, Mons.
3364 **1054** 17f. multicoloured . . . 85 20

1055 Barbed Wire and Buildings

1997. Museums. Multicoloured.
3365 17f.+4f. Type **1055** (Deportation and Resistance Museum, Dossin Barracks, Malines) 1·10 1·00
3366 17f.+4f. Foundryman pouring molten metal (Fourneau Saint-Michel Iron Museum) . . . . . 1·10 1·00

The premium was used for the promotion of philately.

1056 Deer and Landscape (½-size illustration)

1997. "Cantons of the East" (German-speaking Belgium).
3368 **1056** 17f. black and brown 85 25

1057 Marie Sasse

1997. Opera Singers. Multicoloured.
3369 17f. Type **1057** 85 20
3370 17f. Ernest van Dijck . . . 85 20
3371 17f. Hector Dufranne . . . 85 20
3372 17f. Clara Clairbert 85 20

1058 Soldier on Duty

1997. Belgian Involvement in United Nations Peacekeeping Forces.
3373 **1058** 17f. multicoloured . . . 85 20

1059 The Goat Riders

1997. Europa. Tales and Legends. Mult.
3374 17f. Type **1059** 90 20
3375 30f. Jean de Berneau . . . 1·50 50

1060 Spinoy working on Recess Plate

1997. Stamp Day. 4th Death Anniv of Constant Spinoy (engraver).
3376 **1060** 17f. brown, yell & blk 85 20

1061 "The Man in the Street" (detail)

1062 Flower Arrangement

1997. Birth Centenary of Paul Delvaux (artist). Multicoloured.
3377 15f. Type **1061** 70 30
3378 17f. "The Public Voice" (horiz) 85 20
3379 32f. "The Messenger of the Night" . . . . 1·50 55

1997. 2nd International Flower Show, Liege.
3380 **1062** 17f. multicoloured . . . 85 20

1063 Men's Judo

1997. Judo. Each black and red.
3381 17f.+4f. Type **1063** . . . . 1·10 1·00
3382 17f.+4f. Women's judo (showing female symbol) 1·10 1·00

1064 Queen Paola and Belvedere Villa

1997. 60th Birthday of Queen Paola.
3383 **1064** 17f. multicoloured . . . 90 20

1065 Jommeke, Flip and Filiberke (comic strip characters)

1997. "Philately for the Young".
3384 **1065** 17f. multicoloured . . . 90 20

1066 "Rosa damascena" "Coccinea"

1067 St. Martin's Cathedral, Hal

1997. Roses. Illustrations by Pierre-Joseph Redoute. Multicoloured.

3385	17f. Type **1066**	85	20
3386	17f. "Rosa sulfurea"	85	20
3387	17f. "Rosa centifolia"	85	20

1997. Tourist Publicity. Multicoloured.

3388	17f. Type **1067**	85	20
3389	17f. Notre-Dame Church, Laeken (horiz)	85	20
3390	17f. St. Martin's Cathedral, Liege	85	20

1068 Stonecutter

1997. Trades. Multicoloured.

3391	17f. Type **1068**	85	20
3392	17f. Bricklayer	85	20
3393	17f. Carpenter	60	10
3394	17f. Blacksmith	85	20

1069 Queen amidst Workers

1997. Centenary of Apimondia (International Apicultural Association) and 35th Congress, Antwerp. Bees. Multicoloured.

3395	17f. Type **1069**	85	50
3396	17f. Development of egg	85	50
3397	17f. Bees emerging from cells	85	50
3398	17f. Bee collecting nectar from flower	85	50
3399	17f. Bee fanning at hive entrance and worker arriving with nectar	85	50
3400	17f. Worker feeding drone	85	50

1070 "Belgica" (polar barque) ice-bound

1997. Cent of Belgian Antarctic Expedition.

3401	**1070** 17f. multicoloured	85	20

1071 Mask

1073 "Fairon" (Pierre Grahame)

1997. Centenary of Royal Central Africa Museum, Tervuren. Multicoloured.

3402	17f. Type **1071**	85	20
3403	17f. Museum (74 × 24 mm)	85	20
3404	34f. Statuette	1·75	60

1997. Christmas.

3408	**1073** 15f. multicoloured	70	25

1074 Disjointed Figure

1075 Azalea "Mrs. Haerens A"

1997. "Solidarity". Multiple Sclerosis.

3409	**1074** 17f.+4f. black & blue	90	90

1997. Willow Tit. As No. 3318 but horiz.

3410	15f. multicoloured	65	60

1997. Self-adhesive.

3411	**1075** (17f.) multicoloured	85	20

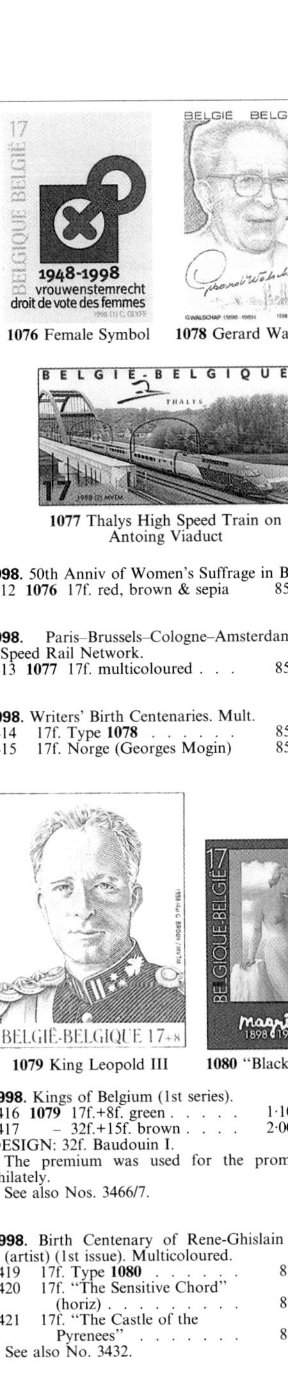

1076 Female Symbol **1078** Gerard Walschap

1077 Thalys High Speed Train on Antoing Viaduct

1998. 50th Anniv of Women's Suffrage in Belgium.

3412	**1076** 17f. red, brown & sepia	85	25

1998. Paris–Brussels–Cologne–Amsterdam High Speed Rail Network.

3413	**1077** 17f. multicoloured	85	25

1998. Writers' Birth Centenaries. Mult.

3414	17f. Type **1078**	85	25
3415	17f. Norge (Georges Mogin)	85	25

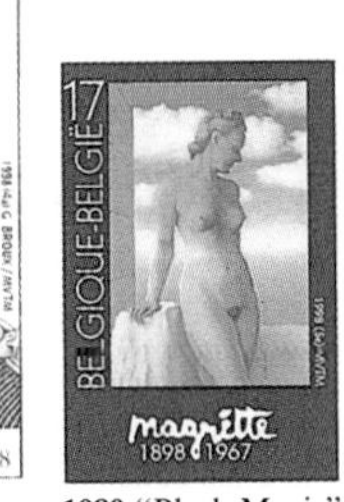

1079 King Leopold III **1080** "Black Magic"

1998. Kings of Belgium (1st series).

3416	**1079** 17f.+8f. green	1·10	1·10
3417	– 32f.+15f. brown	2·00	1·90

DESIGN: 32f. Baudouin I.

The premium was used for the promotion of philately.

See also Nos. 3466/7.

1998. Birth Centenary of Rene-Ghislain Magritte (artist) (1st issue). Multicoloured.

3419	17f. Type **1080**	85	25
3420	17f. "The Sensitive Chord" (horiz)	85	25
3421	17f. "The Castle of the Pyrenees"	85	25

See also No. 3432.

1081 "La Foire aux Amours" (Felicien Rops)

1998. Art Anniversaries. Multicoloured.

3422	17f. Type **1081** (death cent)	85	70
3423	17f. "Hospitality for the Strangers" (Gustave van de Woestijne) (bicentenary of Museum of Fine Arts, Ghent)	85	70
3424	17f. "Man with Beard" (self-portrait of Felix de Boeck, birth centenary)	85	70
3425	17f. "black writing mixed with colours..." (Karel Appel and Christian Dotremont) (50th anniv of Cobra art movement)	85	70

1082 Anniversary Emblem

1998. 75th Anniv of Belgian Postage Stamp Dealers' Association.

3426	**1082** 17f. multicoloured	85	25

1083 Avro RJ85 Airplane

1998. 75th Anniv of Sabena Airlines.

3427	**1083** 17f. multicoloured	85	40

1084 Fox

1998. Wildlife of the Ardennes. Mult.

3428	17f. Type **1084**	85	35
3429	17f. Red deer ("Cervus elaphus")	85	35
3430	17f. Wild boar ("Sus scrofa")	85	35
3431	17f. Roe deer ("Capreolus capreolus")	85	35

1085 "The Return" (Magritte)

1998. Birth Centenary of Rene-Ghislain Magritte (artist) (2nd issue).

3432	**1085** 17f. multicoloured	85	25

1086 Struyf **1088** Pelote

1087 Guitarist (Torhout and Werchter Festival)

1998. Stamp Day. 2nd Death Anniv of Edmond Struyf (founder of Pro-Post (organization for promotion of philately)).

3433	**1086** 17f. black, red & yellow	85	25

1998. Europa. National Festivals.

3434	**1087** 17f. violet and yellow	85	25
3435	– 17f. violet and mauve	85	25

DESIGN: No. 3435, Music conductor (Wallonie Festival).

1998. Sports. Multicoloured.

3436	17f.+4f. Type **1088**	90	85
3437	17f.+4f. Handball	90	85

1089 Emblem

1090 Marnix van Sint-Aldegonde

1998. European Heritage Days. Mult.

3439	17f. Type **1089**	70	35
3440	17f. Bourla Theatre, Antwerp	70	35
3441	17f. La Halle, Durbuy	70	35
3442	17f. Halletoren, Kortrijk	70	35
3443	17f. Louvain Town Hall	70	35
3444	17f. Perron, Liege	70	35
3445	17f. Royal Theatre, Namur	70	35
3446	17f. Aspremont-Lynden Castle, Rekem	70	35
3447	17f. Neo-Gothic kiosk, Saint Nicolas	70	35
3448	17f. Saint-Vincent's Chapel, Tournai	70	35
3449	17f. Villers-la-Ville Abbey	70	35
3450	17f. Saint-Gilles Town Hall	70	35

1998. 400th Death Anniv of Philips van Marnix van St. Aldegonde (writer).

3451	**1090** 17f. multicoloured	85	25

1091 Face

1998. Bicentenary of "Amis Philanthropes" (circle of free thinkers).

3452	**1091** 17f. black and blue	85	25

1092 Mniszech Palace

1998. Belgium Embassy, Warsaw, Poland.

3453	**1092** 17f. multicoloured	85	25

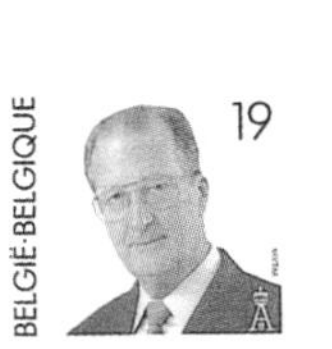

1093 King Albert II

1096 Chick Bill and Ric Hochet

1094 "The Eighth Day" (dir. Jaco van Dormael)

1998.

3454	**1093** 19f. lilac	85	25

No. 3454 was for use on direct mail by large companies.

1998. 25th Anniv of Brussels and Ghent Film Festivals. Multicoloured.

3455	17f. Type **1094**	85	25
3456	17f. "Daens" (dir. Stijn Coninx)	85	25

1998. "Philately for the Young". Comic Strip Characters.

3460	**1096** 17f. multicoloured	85	25

1097 "Youth and Space"

1998. 14th World Congress of Association of Space Explorers.

3461	**1097** 17f. multicoloured	85	25

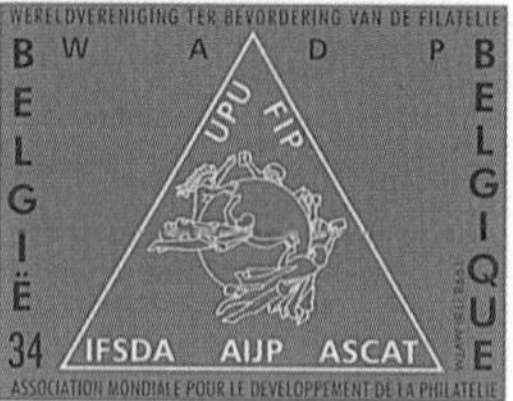

1098 Universal Postal Union Emblem

1998. World Post Day.
3462 **1098** 34f. blue & ultramarine 1·75 40

1099 "The Three Kings" (Michel Provost)

1998. Christmas. No value indicated.
3463 **1099** (17f.) multicoloured . . 85 25

1100 Detail of Triptych by Constant Dratz

1101 Blind Man with Guide Dog

1998. Cent of General Belgium Trade Union.
3464 **1100** 17f. multicoloured . . . 85 25

1998. "Solidarity". Guide Dogs for the Blind.
3465 **1101** 17f.+4f. multicoloured 1·00 1·00
The face value is embossed in Braille.

1999. Kings of Belgium (2nd series). As T **1079**.
3466 17f.+8f. deep green & green 1·10 1·10
3467 32f.+15f. black . . . . . . 2·00 2·00
KINGS: 17f. Albert I; 32f. Leopold II.
The premium was used for the promotion of philately.

1102 Candle ("Happy Birthday")

1103 Barn Owl

1999. Greetings stamps. No value expressed. Mult.
3469 (17f.) Type **1102** 75 40
3470 (17f.) Stork carrying heart ("Welcome" (new baby)) 75 40
3471 (17f.) Wristwatch ("Take your Time" (retirement)) 75 40
3472 (17f.) Four-leafed clover ("For your pleasure") . . 75 40
3473 (17f.) White doves ("Congratulations" (marriage)) 75 40
3474 (17f.) Arrow through heart ("I love you") 75 40
3475 (17f.) Woman with heart as head ("Happy Mother's Day") 75 40
3476 (17f.) Man with heart as head ("Happy Father's Day") 75 40

1999. Owls. Multicoloured.
3477 17f. Type **1103** 80 50
3478 17f. Little owl ("Athene noctua") 80 50
3479 17f. Tawny owl ("Strix aluco") 80 50
3480 17f. Long-eared owl ("Asio otus") 80 50

1104 Leopard Tank (Army)

1999. 50th Anniv of North Atlantic Treaty Organization. Multicoloured.
3481 17f. Type **1104** 80 25
3482 17f. General Dynamics F-16 jet fighters (Air Force) . . 80 25
3483 17f. "De Wandelaar" (frigate) (Navy) 80 25
3484 17f. Field hospital (Medical Service) 80 25
3485 17f. Display chart of military operations (General Staff) 80 25

1105 Envelopes and World Map

1999. 125th Anniv of U.P.U.
3486 **1105** 34f. multicoloured . . . 1·50 1·00

1106 De Bunt Nature Reserve, Hamme

1999. Europa. Parks and Gardens. Multicoloured.
3487 17f. Type **1106** 80 25
3488 17f. Harchies Marsh 80 25

1107 1849 10c. "Epaulettes" Stamp

1999. Stamp Day. 150th Anniv of First Belgian Postage Stamp. Multicoloured.
3489 17f. Type **1107** 80 25
3490 17f. 1849 20c."Epaulettes" stamp 80 25

1108 Racing

1999. Sport. Belgian Motor Cycling. Multicoloured.
3491 17f.+4f. Type **1108** . . . . 1·10 1·00
3492 17f.+4f. Trial (vert) . . . . 1·10 1·00

1109 "My Favourite Room"

1999. 50th Death Anniv of James Ensor (artist) (1st issue).
3494 **1109** 17f. mullticoloured . . 80 25
See also Nos. 3501/3.

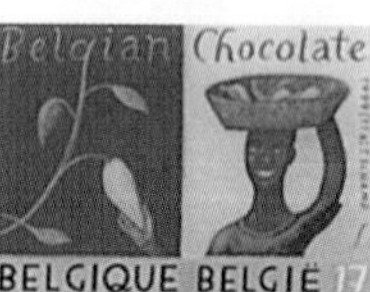

1110 Giant Family, Geraardsbergen

1111 Harvesting of Cocoa Beans

1999. Tourist Publicity. Multicoloured.
3495 17f. Type **1110** 80 25
3496 17f. Members of Confrerie de la Misericorde in Car d'Or procession, Mons (horiz) 80 25

1999. Belgian Chocolate. Multicoloured.
3497 17f. Type **1111** 80 25
3498 17f. Chocolate manufacture 80 25
3499 17f. Selling product 80 25

1112 Photographs of 1959 and 1999

1999. 40th Wedding Anniv of King Albert and Queen Paola.
3500 **1112** 17f. multicoloured . . . 90 25

1113 "Woman eating Oysters"

1999. 50th Death Anniv of James Ensor (artist) (2nd issue).
3501 **1113** 17f. multicoloured . . . 80 25
3502 – 30f. black, brown and grey . . . . 1·25 90
3503 – 32f. multicoloured . . . 1·60 85
DESIGNS—30f. "Triumph of Death"; 32f. "Old Lady with Masks".

1115 Henri la Fontaine (President of International Peace Bureau), 1913

1999. Belgian Winners of Nobel Peace Prize.
3509 **1115** 17f. red and gold . . . 80 20
3510 – 21f. blue and gold . . . 85 60
DESIGNS: 3510, Auguste Beernaert (Prime Minister 1884–94), 1909.

DENOMINATION. From No. 3511 Belgian stamps are denominated both in Belgian francs and in euros.

1116 King Albert II

1116a King Albert II

1999.
3511 **1116** 17f. multicoloured . . 80 10
3512 17f. blue 80 10
3513 19f. purple 85 15
3514 20f. brown 90 20
3515 25f. brown . . . . . 1·10 10
3516 30f. purple . . . . . 1·25 10
3517 32f. green . . . . . . 1·25 15
3518 34f. blue . . . . . . 1·50 20
3519 36f. brown . . . . . 1·50 10
3520 **1116a** 50f. blue . . . . . . 2·25 30
3521 200f. lilac . . . . . 8·00 30

1118 Geranium "Matador"

1119 Reindeer holding Glass of Champagne

1999. Flowers. No value expressed (geranium) or inscr "ZONE A PRIOR" (tulip). Multicoloured. Self-adhesive.
3526 (17f.) Type **1118** 85 25
3527 (21f.) Tulip (21 × 26 mm) . . 1·10 25
The geranium design was for use on inland letters up to 20g. and the tulip design for letters within the European Union up to 20g.

1999. Christmas.
3530 **1119** 17f. multicoloured . . . 80 25

1120 Child bandaging Teddy Bear

1999. "Solidarity". Red Cross. Multicoloured.
3531 17f.+4f. Type **1120** 90 85
3532 17f.+4f. Child and teddy bear cleaning teeth (vert) 90 85

1121 Prince Philippe and Mathilde d'Udekem d'Acoz

1999. Engagement of Prince Philippe and Mathilde d'Udekem d'Acoz.
3533 **1121** 17f. multicoloured 1·10 50

1123 Fireworks and Streamer forming "2000"

2000. New Year.
3536 **1123** 17f. multicoloured . . . 80 25

1124 Red-backed Shrike

1125 Brussels Skyline and Group of People

2000. Birds. Multicoloured.
3537 50c. Goldcrest ("Roitelet Huppe") 10 10
3538 1f. Red crossbill ("Beccroisé des Sapins") 10 10
3539 2f. Short-toed treecreeper ("Grimpereau des Jardins") 10 10
3540 3f. Meadow pipit ("Pipit Farlouse") 10 10
3541 5f. Brambling ("Pinson du Nord") 20 10
3542 7f.50 Great grey shrike ("Pie-Grieche Grise") . . 30 20
3543 8f. Great tit ("Mesange Charbonniere") 40 10
3544 10f. Wood warbler ("Pouillot Siffleur") . . . 40 10
3545 16f. Type **1124** 40 10
3546 16f. Common tern ("Sterne Pierregarin") 40 10
3547 21f. Fieldfare ("Grive Litorne") (horiz) 85 15
3548 150f. Black-billed magpie ("Pie Bavarde") (36 × 25 mm) . . . . . . 6·25 20

2000. Brussels, European City of Culture. Mult.
3555 17f. Type **1125** 80 30
3556 17f. Toots Tielmans (jazz musician), Anne Teresa de Keersmaeker (gymnast) and skyline 80 30
3557 17f. Airplane, train and skyline 80 30
Nos. 3555/7 were issued together, se-tenant, forming a composite design showing the Brussels skyline.

1126 Queen Astrid

2000. Queens of Belgium.

3558 **1126** 17f.+8f. green and deep green . . . . 1·10 1·10
3559 – 32f.+15f. brown and black . . . . 1·60 1·60

DESIGN: 32f. Queen Fabiola.

The premium was used for the promotion of philately.

See also Nos. 3615/16.

1127 Mathematical Formulae

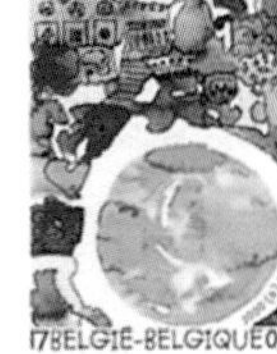

1128 Globe and Technology (Joachim Beckers)

2000. World Mathematics Year.

3561 **1127** 17f. multicoloured . . . 80 15

2000. "Stampin' the Future". Winning Entries in Children's International Painting Competition.

3562 **1128** 17f. multicoloured . . . 80 15

1129 "Charles V as Sovereign Master of the Order of the Golden Fleece" (anon)

2000. 500th Birth Anniv of Charles V, Holy Roman Emperor. Paintings of Charles V. Multicoloured.

3563 17f. Type **1129** 65 10
3564 21f. "Charles V" (Corneille de la Haye) 75 30

1130 Common Adder

2000. Amphibians and Reptiles. Multicoloured.

3566 17f. Type **1130** 80 20
3567 17f. Sand lizard (*Lacerta agilis*) (vert) 80 20
3568 17f. Common tree frog (*Hyla arborea*) (vert) . . . 80 20
3569 17f. Spotted salamander (*Salamander salamander*) 80 20

1131 Children flying Kites

2000. Red Cross and Red Crescent Movements.

3570 **1131** 17f.+4f. multicoloured 75 75

1132 Players Celebrating

2000. European Football Championship, Belgium and The Netherlands. Multicoloured. (a) With face value. Size 26 × 38 mm.

3571 17f. Type **1132** 60 10
3572 21f. Football 65 20

(b) Size 20 × 26 mm. Self-adhesive.

3573 (17f.) As Type **1132** 60 10

Nos. 3571/3 were printed together, se-tenant, with the backgrounds forming the composite design of a crowd of spectators and the Belgian flag.

1133 Cat and Rabbit reading Book

2000. Stamp Day. Winning Entry in Stamp Design Competition.

3574 **1133** 17f. black, blue and red 60 10

1134 Francois de Tassis (detail of tapestry)

1135 *Iris spuria*

2000. "Belgica 2001" Int Stamp Exhibition, Brussels, (1st issue).

3575 **1134** 17f. multicoloured . . . 60 20

See also Nos. 3629/33.

2000. Ghent Flower Show. Multicoloured.

3576 16f. Type **1135** 60 15
3577 17f. Rhododendron (horiz) 65 10
3578 21f. Begonia (horiz) 70 20

1136 Prince Philippe

2000. 2nd Anniv of Prince Philippe (cultural organization).

3579 **1136** 17f. brn, grey & sil . . 60 10

1137 Harpsichord

1139 "Building Europe"

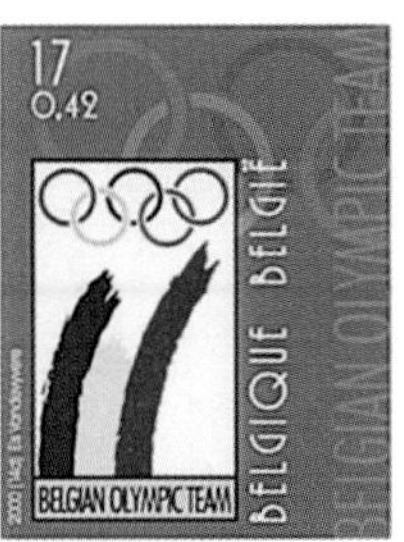

1138 Belgium Team Emblem and Olympic Rings

2000. 250th Death Anniv of Johann Sebastian Bach. No value expressed. Multicoloured.

3580 (17f.) Type **1137** 60 25
3581 (17f.) Violin 60 25
3582 (17f.) Two tenor lutes . . . 60 25
3583 (17f.) Treble viol 60 25
3584 (17f.) Three trumpets . . . 60 25
3585 (17f.) Bach . . . . 3·25 1·40

2000. Olympic Games, Sydney. Multicoloured.

3586 17f. Type **1138** 60 10
3587 17f.+4f. Tae-kwon-do . . . 70 70
3588 17f.+4f. Paralympic athlete (horiz) 70 70

2000. Europa.

3590 **1139** 21f. multicoloured . . . 70 15

1140 Flemish Beguinages

2000. U.N.E.S.C.O. World Heritage Sites in Belgium. Multicoloured.

3591 17f. Type **1140** 60 10
3592 17f. Grand-Place, Brussels 60 10
3393 17f. Four lifts, Centre Canal, Wallonia 50 10

1141 Baroque Organ, Norbertine Abbey Church, Grimbergen

2000. Tourism. Churches and Church Organs. Mult.

3594 17f. Type **1141** 60 15
3595 17f. St. Wandru Abbey, Mons 60 15
3596 17f. O.-L.-V. Hemelvaartkerk (former abbey church), Ninove . . 60 15
3597 17f. St. Peter's Church, Bastogne 60 15

1142 Red-backed Shrike ("Pie grieche ecorcheur")

1143 Marcel, Charlotte, Fanny and Konstantinopel

2000.

3598 **1142** 16f. multicoloured . . . 65 15
3599 – 17f. mult (51 × 21 mm) 70 20
3600 – 23f. lilac 85 20

DESIGNS: 17f. Francois de Tassis (detail of tapestry) and Belgica 2001 emblem; 23f. King Albert II.

2000. "Philately for the Young". Kiekeboe (cartoon series created by Robert Merhottein).

3601 **1143** 17f. multicoloured . . . 60 15

1144 "Springtime"

2000. Hainaut Flower Show.

3602 **1144** 17f. multicoloured . . . 60 15

1145 Pansies

1148 Postman

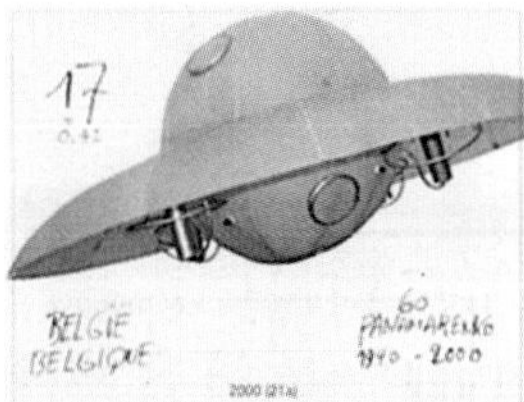

1147 "Bing of the Ferro Lusto X" (Panamarenko)

2000. Flowers. No value expressed. Self-adhesive.

3603 **1145** (17f.) multicoloured . . 60 15

2000. Modern Art. Multicoloured.

3608 17f. Type **1147** 60 15
3609 17f. "Construction" (Anne-Mie van Kerckhoven) (vert) 60 15
3610 17f. "Belgique eternelle" (Jacques Charlier) 60 15
3611 17f. "Les Belles de Nuit" (Marie Jo Lafontaine) . . 60 15

2000. Christmas.

3612 **1148** 17f. multicoloured . . . 60 15

1150 Stars

2000. New Year.

3614 **1150** 17f. gold, blue & blk 70 10

2001. Queens of Belgium. As T **1126**.

3615 17f.+8f. green & dp green 90 90
3616 32f.+15f. black and green 1·50 1·50

DESIGNS: 17f. Queen Elisabeth; 32f. Queen Marie-Henriette; 50f. Queen Louise-Marie.

The premium was used for the promotion of philately.

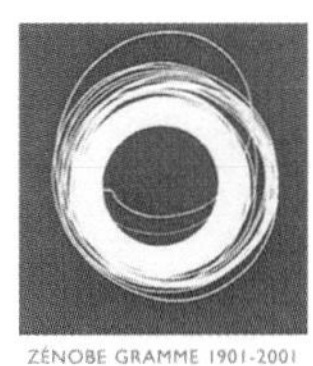

1151 Movement of a Dynamo

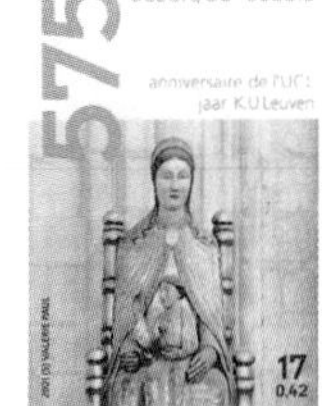

1152 Virgin and Child (statue)

2001. Death Centenary of Zenobe Gramme (physicist).

3619 **1151** 17f. black, red & black 60 10

2001. 575th Anniv of Louvain Catholic University.

3620 **1152** 17f. multicoloured . . . 60 10

2001. As T **998** but with face value expressed in francs and euros.

3621 100f. multicoloured . . . . 3·00 35

1153 Willem Elsschot (poet)

2001. Music and Literature.

3622 **1153** 17f. brown and black . . 60 10
3623 – 17f. grey and black . . 60 10

DESIGN: 17f. Albert Ayguesparse (poet).

1154 Boy washing Hands

2001. Europa. Water Resources.

3625 **1154** 21f. multicoloured . . . 70 20

1155 Type 12 Steam Locomotive

2001. 75th Anniv of National Railway Company. Multicoloured.

3626 17f. Type **1155** 60 15
3627 17f. Series 06 dual locomotive No. 671 . . . 60 15
3628 17f. Series 03 locomotive No. 328 . . . . 60 15

Nos. 3626/8 were issued together, se-tenant, forming a composite design.

1156 16th-century Postman on horseback

2001. "Belgica 2001" International Stamp Exhibition, Brussels (2nd issue). 500th Anniv of European Post. Multicoloured.

3629 17f. Type **1156** 70 20
3630 17f. 17th-century postman with walking staff (vert) 70 20
3631 17f. 18th-century postman and hand using quill (vert) 70 20
3632 17f. Steam locomotive and 19th-century postman (vert) 70 20
3633 17f. 20th-century forms of communication (vert) . . 70 20

1157 Hassan II Mosque, Casablanca

2001. Places of Worship. Multicoloured.

3635 17f. Type **1157** 60 10
3636 34f. Koekelberg Basilica . . 1·25 20

1158 "Winter Landscape with Skaters" (Pieter Bruegel the Elder)

2001. Art. Multicoloured.

3637 17f. Type **1158** 60 25
3638 17f. "Heads of Negros" (Peter Paul Rubens) . . . 60 25
3639 17f. "Sunday" (Frits van den Berghe) 60 25
3640 17f. "Mussels" (Marcel Broodthaers) 60 25

1159 Pottery Vase **1160** Luc Orient

2001. Chinese Pottery. Multicoloured.

3641 17f. Type **1159** 60 10
3642 34f. Teapot . . . . 1·25 20

2001. "Philately for the Young". Cartoon Characters.

3643 **1160** 17f. multicoloured . . . 60 10

1161 Cyclists (World Cycling Championship, Antwerp)

2001. Sports. Multicoloured.

3644 17f.+4f. Type **1161** 70 70
3645 17f.+4f. Gymnast (World Gymnastics Championships, Ghent) 70 70

1162 Emblem

2001. Belgian Presidency of European Union.

3646 **1162** 17f. multicoloured . . . 60 10

1163 Binche

2001. Town Hall Belfries.

3647 **1163** 17f. mauve and black 60 10
3648 – 17f. blue, mauve & blk 60 10

DESIGN: No. 3648, Diksmuide.

1164 Damme

2001. Large Farmhouses. Multicoloured.

3649 17f. Type **1164** 60 10
3650 17f. Beauvechain 60 10
3651 17f. Louvain 60 10
3652 17f. Honnelles 60 10
3653 17f. Hasselt 60 10

1165 Red Cross and Doctor

2001. Red Cross.

3654 **1165** 17f.+4f. multicoloured 65 65

1166 Stam and Pilou **1167** Ovide Decroly (educational psychologist) and Road Sign

2001. Stamp Day. No value expressed. Self-adhesive.

3655 **1166** (17f.) multicoloured . . 50 15

No. 3655 was for use on inland standard letters up to 20g.

2001. The Twentieth Century. Science and Technology. Sheet 166 × 200 mm. Multicoloured.

MS3656 17f. Type **1167**; 17f. Dandelion and windmills (alternative energy sources); 17f. Globe, signature and map (first solo non-stop crossing of North Atlantic by Charles Lindbergh); 17f. Man with head on lap (Sigmund Freud, founder of psychoanalysis); 17f. Astronaut and foot print on moon surface (Neil Armstrong, first man on the moon, 1969); 17f. Claude Levi-Strauss (anthropologist); 17f. DNA double helix and athletes (human genetic code); 1f. Pierre Teilhard de Chardin (theologian palaeontologist and philosopher); 17f. Max Weber (sociologist) and crowd; 17f. Albert Einstein (physicist) (Theory of Relativity); 17f. Knight and jacket of pills (discovery of Penicillin, 1928); 17f. Ilya Prigogine (theoretical chemist and clock face; 17f. Text and Roland Barthes (writer and critic); 17f. Simone de Beauvoir (feminist writer); 17f. Globe and technology highway (computer science); 17f. John Maynard Keynes (economist) and folded paper; 17f. Marc Bloch (historian) and photographs; 17f. Tools and Julius Robert Oppenheimer (nuclear physicist); 17f. Marie and Pierre Curie, discoverers of radioactivity, 1896); 17f. Caricature of Ludwig Josef Wittgenstein (philosopher) 10·50 10·50

1168 Nativity

2001. Christmas.

3657 **1168** 15f. multicoloured . . . 45 10

1169 Sunset

2001. Bereavement. No value expressed.

3658 **1169** (17f.) multicoloured . . 50 15

See also No. 3732.

1170 Daffodil **1171** Tintin

2001. Flowers. No value expressed. Self-adhesive.

(a) Without service indicator. Multicoloured.

3659 (17f.) Type **1170** 50 15

(b) Inscr "ZONE A PRIOR".

3660 (21f.) Tulip "Darwin" (vert) 65 20

No. 3659 was for use on inland letters up to 20g. and No. 3660 was for use on letters within the European Union up to 20g.

2001. 70th Anniv of Tintin in *Congo* (cartoon strip). Multicoloured.

3661 17f. Type **1171** 50 15
MS3662 123 × 88 mm. 34f. Tintin, Snowy and guide in car (48 × 37 mm) 1·10 1·10

New Currency 100 cents = 1 euro

1172 King Albert II

1173 King Albert II

2002.

3663 **1173** 7c. blue and red 10 10
3666 **1172** 42c. red 55 15
3667 47c. green 60 20
3668 **1173** 49c. red 65 20
3669 52c. blue 65 20
3670 59c. blue 75 25
3672 **1173** 79c. blue and red . . . 1·00 30

Nos. 3663, 3668 and 3672 are inscribed "PRIOR" at left.

1174 Female Tennis Player

2002. Centenary of Royal Belgian Tennis Federation. Multicoloured.

3675 42c. Type **1174** 55 15
3676 42c. Male tennis player . . 55 15

1175 Cyclist

2002. International Cycling Events held at Circuit Zolder. Multicoloured.

3677 42c. Type **1175** (World Cyclo-Cross Championships) 55 15
3678 42c. Cyclist with hand raised (Road Cycling Championships) 55 15

1176 Dinosaur

2002. Winning Entry in Children's Stamp Design Competition at "Belgica 2001".

3679 **1176** 42c.+10c. mult 70 70

The premium was used for the promotion of philately.

1177 Antwerp from River

2002. 150th Anniv of Antwerp University.

3680 **1177** 42c. blue and black . . 55 15

1178 Buildings and Architectural Drawing

2002. "Bruges 2002", European City of Culture. Multicoloured.

3681 42c. Type **1178** 55 15
3682 42c. Organ pipes and xylophone 55 15
3683 42c. Octopus 55 15

1179 16th-century Manuscript (poem, Anna Bijns)

2002. Women and Art. Multicoloured.
3684 42c. Type **1179** 55 15
3685 84c. Woman writing (painting, Anna Boch) (vert) . . . . 1·10 35

1180 Fountain Pen and Writing

2002. Stamp Day.
3686 **1180** 47c. multicoloured . . . 60 20

1181 Papillon

2002. Centenary of Flanders Canine Society. Multicoloured.
3687 42c. Type **1181** 55 15
3688 42c. Brussels griffon 55 15
3689 42c. Bloodhounds 55 15
3690 42c. Bouvier des Ardennes 55 15
3691 42c. Schipperke 55 15

1182 Stock Dove ("Pigeon Colombin-Holenduif")

1183 Big Top, Ringmaster, Seal and Clown

2002. Birds. Multicoloured.
3692 7c. Type **1182** 10 10
3698 25c. Oystercatcher ("Scholekster-Huitrier Pie") 30 10
3701 41c. Collared dove ("Touterelle Turque") . . 50 15
3702 57c. Black tern ("Guifette Noire") 75 20
3704 70c. Redshank ("Chevailer Gambette") 90 25
3705 €1 Wheatear ("Traquet Motteux") (38 × 27 mm) 1·25 40
3706 €2 Ringed plover ("Grand Gravelot") (38 × 27 mm) 2·50 75
3709 €5 Ruff ("Combattant Varie") (38 × 27 mm) . . 6·50 1·90

2002. Europa. Circus. Winning Entry in Children's Drawing Competition.
3710 **1183** 52c. multicoloured . . . 70 20

1184 Paramedic, Patient and Damaged Buildings

2002. Red Cross.
3711 **1184** 84c.+12c. multicoloured 1·25 1·25

1185 Abbey Buildings

2002. 850th Anniv of Leffe Abbey.
3712 **1185** 42c. multicoloured . . . 55 15

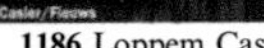

1186 Loppem Castle

2002. Tourism. Castles. Sheet 161 × 141 mm containing T **1186** and similar horiz designs showing castles. Multicoloured.
MS3713 42c. Type **1186**; 42c. Horst; 42c. Wissekerke; 42c. Chimay; 42c. Ecaussinnes-Lalaing; 42c. Reinhardstein; 42c. Modave; 42c. Ooidonk; 42c. Corroy-le-Chateau; 42c. Alden Biesen 5·00 5·00

1187 Show Jumping

2002. Horses. Designs showing equestrian events. Multicoloured.
3714 40c. Type **1187** 50 15
3715 42c. Carriage driving (vert) 55 15
MS3716 126 × 91 mm. 52c. Two Brabant draught horses' heads (Centenary of St. Paul's horse procession, Opwijk) (37 × 48 mm) 70 70

1188 Golden Spur and Battle Scene

1189 Onze-Lieve-Vrouw-Lombeek, Roosdaal

2002. 700th Anniv of Battle of the Golden Spurs (Flemish--French battle), Kortrijk. Multicoloured.
3717 42c. Type **1188** 55 15
3718 52c. Broel towers 55 15
MS3719 126 × 91 mm. 57c. Flemish and French soldiers, river and knight on horseback (48 × 38 mm) 70 20

2002. Windmills. Multicoloured.
3720 42c. Type **1189** 55 15
3721 52c. Faial Island, Azores, Portugal 70 20
Stamps of a similar design were issued by Portugal.

1190 Liedekerke Lacework and Statue of Lace-maker

2002. Lace-making. Multicoloured.
3722 42c. Type **1190** 55 15
3723 74c. Pag lacework . . . . . 1·00 1·00
Stamps of a similar design were issued by Croatia.

1191 Bakelandt, Red Zita and Stagecoach

2002. "Philately for the Young". Bakelandt (comic strip created by Hec Leemans).
3724 **1191** 42c. multicoloured . . . 55 15

1192 Teddy Bear

1193 Rey

2002. "The Rights of the Child".
3725 **1192** 42c. multicoloured . . . 55 15

2002. Birth Centenary of Jean Rey (politician).
3726 **1193** 52c. blue and cobalt . . 70 20

1194 Princess Elisabeth

1195 Church, Ice Cream Van and Family

2002. 1st Birthday of Princess Elisabeth. Multicoloured.
3727 49c. Type **1194** 65 20
3728 59c. Princess Elisabeth with parents (horiz) 75 25
MS3729 123 × 88 mm 84c. Princess Elisabeth (different) (59 × 38 mm) 1·10 1·10
No. 3727 was issued with a se-tenant label inscribed "PRIOR".

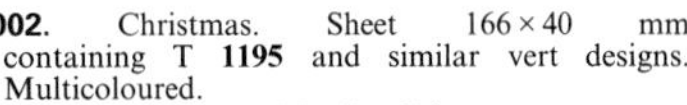

2002. Christmas. Sheet 166 × 40 mm containing T **1195** and similar vert designs. Multicoloured.
MS3730 41c. Type **1195**; 41c. Skier in snowy fir tree; 41c. Tobogganist and bird wearing hat; 41c. Skier wearing kilt; 41c. Skiers holding candles; 41c. Boy holding snowman- shaped ice cream; 41c. Children throwing snowballs; 41c. Children, snowman, and elderly man; 41c. Brazier, refreshment hut and people; 41c. Hut, robbers, cow and policeman 2·75 2·75

1196 Bricks

2002. The Twentieth Century. Society. Sheet 200 × 166 mm containing T **1196**.
MS3731 41c. purple, red and pink (Type **1196** (social housing)); 41c. deep purple, orange and purple ("MEI/MAI 68" and rubble (student protests)); 41c. slate, grey and green (telephone telecommunications)); 41c. red, orange and brown (slabs (gap between wealth and poverty)); 41c. brown, bistre and blue (broken crucifix (secularization of society)); 41c. multicoloured (towers of blocks (urbanization)); 41c. pink, violet and purple (combined female and male symbols (universal suffrage)); 41c. blue, orange and grey (enclosed circle (social security)); 41c. grey, green and bistre (schoolbag (equality in education)); 41c. grey, purple and deep purple (elderly man (ageing population)); 41c. blue, green and emerald ("E" (European Union)); 41c. chestnut, brown and yellow (stylized figure (declaration of Human Rights)); 41c. bistre, orange and light orange (pyramid of blocks (growth of consumer society)); 41c. blue, mauve and green (female symbol (feminism)); 41c. brown, sepia and light brown (mechanical arm (de-industrialization)); 41c. brown and green (dripping nozzle (oil crises)); 41c. multicoloured (vehicle (transportation)); 41c.lilac, brown and purple (sperm and egg (contraception)); 41c. green, red and grey (television (growth of television and radio)); 41c. pink, violet and blue (electric plug (increase in home appliances)) 10·50 10·50

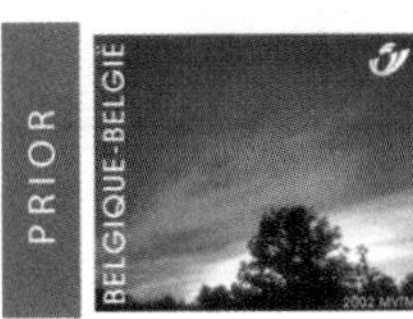

1197 Sunset

2002. Bereavement. No value expressed.
3732 **1197** (49c.) multicoloured . . 65 20

1198 Crocus

1199 Nero and Adhemar (cartoon characters)

2002. Flowers. No value expressed. Ordinary or self-adhesive gum.
3733 **1198** (49c.) multiicoloured . . 65 20
No. 3733 was for use on inland letters up to 50 g.

2003. 80th (2002) Birth Anniv of Marc Sleen (cartoonist). Multicoloured.
3735 49c. Type **1199** 65 20
MS3736 121 × 91 mm 82c. Nero and Marc Sleen (49 × 38 mm) 1·10 1·10

1200 Firefighters, Engine and Ladders

2003. Public Services (Nos. 3737/41) and St. Valentine (3742). Multicoloured.
3737 49c. Type **1200** 65 20
3738 49c. Traffic police men and policewoman 65 20
3739 49c. Civil defence workers mending flood defences 65 20
3740 49c. Elderly woman wearing breathing mask, hand holding syringe and theatre nurse 65 20
3741 49c. Postman riding bicycle and obtaining signature for parcel 65 20
3742 49c. Hearts escaping from birdcage 65 20

1201 Van de Velde and New House, Tervuren

2003. 140th Birth Anniv of Henry van de Velde (architect). Multicoloured.
3743 49c. Type **1201** 65 20
3744 59c. Van de Velde and Belgian pavilion, Paris International Exhibition, 1937 (vert) 75 25
3745 59c. Van de Velde and Book Tower, Central Library, Ghent University (vert) 75 25
MS3746 91 × 125 mm 84c. Woman and Art Nouveau newel post 1·10 1·10

1202 Bowls

2003. Traditional Sports. Multicoloured.
3747 49c. Type **1202** 65 20
3748 49c. Archery 65 20
MS3749 91 × 126 mm. 82c. Pigeon racing 1·10 1·10

1203 Berlioz

2003. Birth Bicentenary of Hector Berlioz (composer).
3750 **1203** 59c. multicoloured . . . 75 25

EXPRESS LETTER STAMPS

E 107 Ghent

1929.
E530 – 1f.75 blue 60 25
E531 E 107 2f.35 red 1·90 35
E581 – 2f.45 green 14·00 1·75
E532 – 3f.50 purple 11·50 6·00
E533 – 5f.25 olive 8·50 7·00
DESIGNS: 1f.75, Town Hall, Brussels; 2f.45, Eupen; 3f.50, Bishop's Palace, Liege; 5f.25, Antwerp Cathedral.

1932. No. E581 surch **2 Fr 50** and cross.
E608 2f.50 on 2f.45 green 12·00 1·50

MILITARY STAMPS

1967. As T **289** (Baudouin) but with letter "M" within oval at foot.
M2027 1f.50 green 20 15

1971. As No. 2207/8a and 2209a but with letter "M" within oval at foot.
M2224 1f.75 green 35 50
M2225 2f.25 green 35 45
M2226 2f.50 green 10 15
M2227 3f.25 plum 15 20

NEWSPAPER STAMPS

1928. Railway Parcels stamps of 1923 optd **JOURNAUX DAGBLADEN 1928**.
N443 P 84 10c. red 40 40
N444 20c. green 40 40
N445 40c. olive 40 40
N446 60c. orange 60 40
N447 70c. brown 60 40
N448 80c. violet 75 45
N449 90c. slate 6·50 2·40
N450 – 1f. blue 1·60 45
N451 – 2f. olive 3·25 3·00
N452 – 3f. red 3·25 60
N453 – 4f. red 3·25 60
N454 – 5f. violet 3·25 60
N455 – 6f. brown 4·50 1·50
N456 – 7f. orange 12·50 2·50
N457 – 8f. brown 8·50 1·00
N458 – 9f. purple 25·00 7·50
N459 – 10f. green 8·75 1·75
N460 – 20f. pink 25·00 9·25

1929. Railway Parcels stamps of 1923 optd **JOURNAUX DAGBLADEN** only.
N505 P 84 10c. red 70 30
N506 20c. green 40 40
N507 40c. olive 40 30
N508 60c. orange 60 40
N509 70c. brown 45 30
N510 80c. violet 75 65
N511 90c. slate 6·25 4·50
N512 – 1f. blue 1·10 40
N513 – 1f.10 brown 3·50 1·25
N514 – 1f.50 blue 3·50 1·25
N515 – 2f. olive 2·40 55
N516 – 2f.10 slate 10·50 7·50
N517 – 3f. red 2·40 50
N518 – 4f. red 2·40 50
N519 – 5f. violet 2·40 50
N520 – 6f. brown 5·50 1·10
N521 – 7f. orange 16·00 1·10
N522 – 8f. brown 10·50 1·10
N523 – 9f. purple 23·00 12·50
N524 – 10f. green 12·50 2·75
N525 – 20f. pink 30·00 10·00

PARCEL POST STAMPS

Stamps issued at Belgian Post Offices only.

1928. Optd **COLIS POSTAL POSTCOLLO**.
B470 81 4f. brown 4·75 1·25
B471 5f. bistre 4·75 1·25

B 106 G.P.O., Brussels

1929.
B526 B 106 3f. sepia 1·25 20
B527 4f. slate 1·25 20
B528 5f. red 1·25 20
B529 6f. purple 22·00 24·00

1933. Surch **X4 4X**.
B645 B 106 4f. on 6f. purple 23·00 25

POSTAGE DUE STAMPS

D 21 D 35

1870.
D63 D 21 10c. green 3·00 1·90
D64 20c. blue 42·00 3·00

1895.
D 96a D 35 5c. green 10 10
D 97 10c. brown 13·00 4·50
D101 10c. red 10 10
D 98a 20c. green 10 10
D102 30c. blue 20 15
D 99 50c. brown 19·00 4·00
D103 50c. grey 40 25
D100 1f. red 16·00 8·00
D104 1f. yellow 4·75 3·50

1919. As Type D **35**, but value in colour on white background.
D 251 D 35 5c. green 55 25
D 323 5c. grey 10 10
D 252 10c. red 1·00 30
D 324 10c. green 10 10
D 253 20c. green 5·50 1·00
D 325 20c. brown 10 10
D 254 30c. blue 2·75 35
D 326 30c. red 60 45
D 327 35c. green 20 10
D 328 40c. brown 15 10
D 330 50c. grey 15 10
D 329 50c. blue 2·75 35
D 331 60c. red 25 20
D1146 65c. green 4·75 2·75
D 332 70c. brown 25 10
D 333 80c. grey 25 10
D 334 1f. violet 40 15
D 335 1f. purple 45 20
D 336 1f.20 olive 55 20
D 337 1f.40 green 50 35
D 338 1f.50 olive 55 40
D1147 1f.60 mauve 9·25 5·25
D1148 1f.80 red 11·50 4·75
D 339 2f. mauve 55 15
D1149 2f.40 lavender 6·25 2·75
D1150 3f. red 1·40 45
D 340 3f.50 blue 55 15
D1151 4f. blue 7·00 40
D1152 5f. brown 2·40 25
D1153 7f. violet 2·40 1·50
D1154 8f. purple 7·50 8·00
D1155 10f. violet 3·50 2·50

D 218 D 462

1945. Inscr "A PAYER" at top and "TE BETALEN" at bottom, or vice versa.
D1130A D 218 10c. olive 10 10
D1131A 20c. blue 10 10
D1132A 30c. red 10 10
D1133A 40c. blue 10 10
D1134A 50c. green 10 10
D1135A 1f. brown 10 10
D1136A 2f. orange 10 10

1966.
D2812 D 462 1f. mauve 10 10
D2813 2f. green 10 10
D2814 3f. blue 20 20
D2815 4f. green 20 20
D1985ab 5f. purple 25 20
D2816 5f. lilac 25 25
D1986 6f. brown 70 20
D1987 7f. red 55 30
D2817 7f. orange 40 35
D2818 8f. grey 40 35
D2819 9f. red 40 40
D2820 10f. brown 40 40
D2821 20f. green 1·10 45
D1988 20f. green 80 80
D2822 On No. D1988 the "F" is outside the shield; on No. D2822 it is inside.

RAILWAY PARCELS STAMPS

In Belgium the parcels service is largely operated by the Belgian Railways for which the following stamps were issued.

Certain stamps under this heading were also on sale at post offices in connection with a "small parcels" service. These show a posthorn in the design except for Nos. P1116/18.

P 21

1879.
P63 P 21 10c. brown 75·00 4·75
P64 20c. blue £190 14·50
P65 25c. green £275 8·50
P66 50c. red £1300 8·00
P67 80c. yellow £1400 55·00
P68 1f. grey £190 12·50

P 22

1882.
P69 P 22 10c. brown 20·00 1·40
P73 15c. grey 8·00 7·00
P75 20c. blue 70·00 3·00
P77 25c. green 70·00 3·50
P78 50c. red 70·00 65
P81 80c. yellow 70·00 85
P84 80c. brown 65·00 70
P86 1f. grey £350 2·50
P87 1f. purple £400 3·50
P88 2f. buff £170 60·00

P 35

1895. Numerals in black except 1f. and 2f.
P 96 P 35 10c. brown 11·00 70
P 97 15c. slate 11·00 1·25
P 98 20c. blue 17·00 90
P 99 25c. green 17·00 1·25
P100 30c. orange 22·00 1·75
P101 40c. green 30·00 2·00
P102 50c. red 30·00 80
P103 60c. lilac 55·00 80
P104 70c. blue 55·00 1·25
P105 80c. yellow 55·00 1·25
P106 90c. red 85·00 1·75
P107 1f. purple £225 2·75
P108 2f. buff £275 13·00

P 37 Winged Railway Wheel

1902.
P109a P 35 10c. slate and brown 15 20
P110 15c. purple and slate 25 25
P111 20c. brown and blue 25 25
P112 25c. red and green 35 25
P113 30c. green and orange 25 30
P114 35c. green and brown 25 30
P115 40c. mauve and green 30 30
P116 50c. mauve and pink 25 20
P117 55c. blue and purple 35 30
P118 60c. red and lilac 25 20
P119 70c. red and blue 10 20
P120 80c. purple and yellow 10 20
P121 90c. green and red 20 20
P122 P 37 1f. orange and purple 20 20
P123 1f.10 black and red 20 20
P124 2f. green and bistre 25 20
P125 3f. blue and black 25 25
P126 4f. red and green 65 1·25
P127 5f. green and orange 40 70
P128 10f. purple and yellow 75 80

1915. Stamps of 1912–14 optd **CHEMINS DE FER SPOORWEGEN** and Winged Railway Wheel.
P160 44 5c. green £130
P161 46 10c. red £160
P162 20c. green £170
P163 25c. blue £170
P164 45 35c. brown £250
P165 46 40c. green £225
P166 45 50c. grey £225
P167 1f. orange £200
P168 2f. violet £1300
P169 – 5f. purple (No. 143) £2500

P 59 Winged Railway Wheel P 60 Steam Locomotive

1915.
P196 P 59 10c. blue 75 55
P197 15c. olive 1·25 1·40
P198 20c. red 1·10 90
P199 25c. brown 1·10 90
P200 30c. mauve 1·10 90
P201 35c. grey 1·10 75
P202 40c. orange 1·10 75
P203 50c. bistre 1·75 1·90
P204 55c. brown 1·50 85
P205 60c. lilac 2·00 2·10
P206 70c. green 1·00 75
P207 80c. brown 1·00 70
P208 90c. blue 1·50 90
P209 P 60 1f. grey 1·00 75
P210 1f.10 bl (FRANKEN) 22·00 25·00
P211 1f.10 blue (FRANK) 1·60 70
P212 2f. red 35·00 1·10
P213 3f. violet 35·00 1·10
P214 4f. green 38·00 2·40
P215 5f. brown 70·00 2·50
P216 10f. orange 75·00 2·50

P 69 Winged Railway Wheel P 70 Steam Train

1920.
P259 P 69 10c. green 1·40 70
P280 10c. red 30 25
P281 15c. green 40 25
P261 20c. red 1·40 70
P282 20c. green 55 30
P262 25c. brown 1·75 85
P283 25c. blue 50 25
P263 30c. mauve 24·00 23·00
P284 30c. brown 50 25
P285 35c. brown 50 35
P286 40c. orange 50 25
P265 50c. bistre 7·00 1·25
P287 50c. red 80 20
P266 55c. brown 7·50 6·00
P288 55c. yellow 4·25 4·00
P267 60c. purple 9·00 95
P289 60c. red 50 25
P290 70c. green 2·40 45
P269 80c. brown 42·00 1·50
P291 80c. violet 1·75 35
P270 90c. blue 10·00 1·00
P292 90c. yellow 29·00 26·00
P293 90c. purple 5·25 35
P271 P 70 1f. grey 75·00 1·10
P272 1f.10 blue 13·00 95
P273 1f.20 green 14·00 1·10
P274 1f.40 brown 14·00 1·10
P275 2f. red £110 1·10
P276 3f. mauve £120 80
P277 4f. green £120 1·25
P278 5f. brown £120 80
P279 10f. orange £120 90
On Nos. P271/9 the engine has one head lamp.

1920. Three head lamps on engine.
P294 P 70 1f. brown 5·25 25
P296 1f.10 blue 1·60 25
P297 1f.20 orange 2·10 25
P298 1f.40 yellow 13·00 2·50
P299 1f.60 green 27·00 60
P300 2f. red 26·00 25
P301 3f. red 26·00 25
P302 4f. green 26·00 25
P303 5f. violet 24·00 25
P304 10f. yellow £130 16·00
P305 10f. brown 30·00 25
P306 15f. red 30·00 25
P307 20f. blue £350 3·00

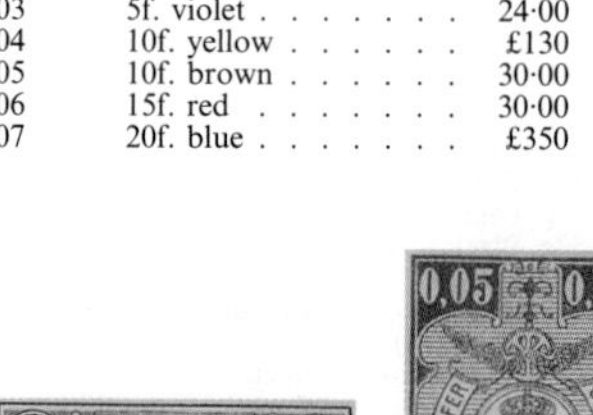

P 76 P 84

1921.
P312 P 76 2f. black 6·50 35
P313 3f. brown 60·00 35
P314 4f. green 38·00 35
P315 5f. red 38·00 35
P316 10f. brown 38·00 35
P317 15f. red 38·00 75
P318 20f. blue £110 1·75

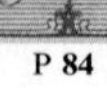

1923.
P375 P 84 5c. brown 20 20
P376 10c. red 10 10
P377 15c. blue 20 20
P378 20c. green 15 10
P379 30c. purple 15 10
P380 40c. olive 15 10
P381 50c. red 15 10
P382 60c. orange 15 10
P383 70c. brown 15 10
P384 80c. violet 15 10
P385 90c. slate 60 10

Similar type, but horiz.
P386 1f. blue 20 15
P388 1f.10 orange 1·50 45
P389 1f.50 green 1·50 35
P390 1f.70 brown 45 45
P391 1f.80 red 2·25 70
P392 2f. olive 20 20
P393 2f.10 green 3·75 75
P394 2f.40 violet 1·75 90
P395 2f.70 grey 26·00 85
P396 3f. red 20 15
P397 3f.30 brown 4·00 85
P398 4f. red 20 15
P399 5f. violet 55 15
P400 6f. brown 20 15
P401 7f. orange 30 15
P402 8f. brown 30 15
P403 9f. purple 1·25 15
P404 10f. green 50 10
P405 20f. pink 70 15
P406 30f. green 2·40 40

P407 40f. slate 35·00 95
P408 50f. bistre 4·00 45
See Nos. P876/7 and P911/34.

1924. No. P394 surch **2F30.**
P409 2f.30 on 2f.40 violet 2·25 40

P **139** Type 5 Steam locomotive "Goliath", 1930

P **149** Diesel Locomotive

1934.
P655 P **139** 3f. green 8·00 1·75
P656 4f. mauve 3·25 20
P657 5f. red 45·00 20

1935. Centenary of Belgian Railway.
P 89 P **149** 10c. red 35 20
P690 20c. violet 30 20
P691 30c. brown 40 20
P692 40c. blue 50 20
P693 50c. orange 50 15
P694 60c. green 45 15
P695 70c. blue 45 20
P696 80c. black 45 20
P697 90c. red 90 45
Horiz type. Locomotive "Le Belge", 1835.
P698 1f. purple 60 20
P699 2f. black 1·60 20
P700 3f. orange 2·10 20
P701 4f. purple 2·10 20
P702 5f. purple 3·25 20
P703 6f. green 4·50 20
P704 7f. violet 18·00 20
P705 8f. black 18·00 25
P706 9f. blue 20·00 20
P707 10f. red 20·00 20
P708 20f. green 35·00 25
P709 30f. violet £100 3·50
P710 40f. brown £100 35
P711 50f. red £140 3·25
P712 100f. blue £250 48·00

P **162** Winged Railway Wheel and Posthorn

1938.
P 806 P **162** 5f. on 3f.50 green 15·00 25
P 807 5f. on 4f.50 purple 10 10
P 808 6f. on 5f.50 red 30 10
P1162 8f. on 5f.50 brown 55 15
P1163 10f. on 5f.50 blue 70 10
P1164 12f. on 5f.50 violet 95 20

P **176** Seal of the International Railway Congress

1939. International Railway Congress, Brussels.
P856 P **176** 20c. brown 2·75 2·75
P857 50c. blue 2·75 2·75
P858 2f. red 2·75 2·75
P859 9f. green 2·75 2·75
P860 10f. purple 2·75 2·75

1939. Surch **M. 3Fr.**
P867 P **162** 3f. on 5f.50 red 45 30

1940. Optd **B** in oval and two vert bars.
P878 P **84** 10c. red 10 10
P879 20c. green 10 10
P880 30c. purple 10 10
P881 40c. olive 10 10
P882 50c. red 10 10
P883 60c. orange 45 50
P884 70c. brown 10 10
P885 80c. violet 10 10
P886 90c. slate 15 20
P887 1f. blue 10 15
P888 2f. olive 15 10
P889 3f. red 15 10
P890 4f. red 15 10
P891 5f. violet 15 10
P892 6f. brown 30 10
P893 7f. orange 30 10
P894 8f. brown 30 10
P895 9f. purple 30 10
P896 10f. green 30 10
P897 20f. pink 50 30
P898 30f. green 65 85
P899 40f. slate 1·60 2·10
P900 50f. bistre 90 1·10

1940. As Type P **84** but colours changed.
P911 P **84** 10c. olive 10 15
P912 20c. violet 10 15
P913 30c. red 10 15
P914 40c. blue 10 15
P915 50c. green 10 15
P916 60c. grey 10 15
P917 70c. green 10 15
P918 80c. orange 15 15
P919 90c. lilac 1·75 15
Similar design, but horizontal.
P920 1f. green 20 15
P921 2f. brown 25 15
P922 3f. grey 30 15
P923 4f. olive 35 15
P924 5f. lilac 45 15
P925 5f. black 65 25
P926 6f. red 60 25
P927 7f. violet 60 25
P928 8f. green 60 25
P929 9f. blue 75 25
P930 10f. mauve 75 25
P931 20f. blue 2·00 30
P932 30f. yellow 3·25 70
P933 40f. red 4·25 80
P934 50f. red 6·50 55
No. P925 was for use as a railway pacels tax stamp.

P **195** Engine Driver

P **216** Mercury

1942. Various designs.
P1090 P **195** 10c. grey 20 10
P1091 20c. violet 20 15
P1092 30c. red 20 20
P1093 40c. blue 20 10
P1094 50c. blue 20 15
P1095 60c. black 20 15
P1096 70c. green 40 25
P1097 80c. orange 30 25
P1098 90c. brown 35 25
P1099 – 1f. green 20 20
P1100 – 2f. purple 20 20
P1101 – 3f. black 90 30
P1102 – 4f. blue 20 20
P1103 – 5f. brown 20 20
P1104 – 6f. green 90 50
P1105 – 7f. violet 25 20
P1106 – 8f. red 25 20
P1107 – 9f. blue 45 20
P 996 – 9f.20 red 40 35
P1108 – 10f. red 2·10 45
P1109 – 10f. brown 1·50 40
P 997 P **195** 12f.30 green 40 25
P 998 – 14f.30 red 40 25
P1110 – 20f. green 70 25
P1111 – 30f. violet 80 25
P1112 – 40f. red 45 20
P1113 – 50f. blue 8·25 20
P 999 – 100f. blue 14·00 14·50
DESIGNS—As Type P **195**: 1f. to 9f.20, Platelayer; 10f. and 14f.30 to 50f. Railway porter; 24½ × 34½ mm: 100f. Electric train.
No. P1109 was for use as a railway parcels tax stamp.

1945. Inscribed "BELGIQUE-BELGIE" or vice-versa.
P1116A P **216** 3f. green 10 10
P1117A 5f. blue 10 10
P1118A 6f. red 10 10

P **224** Level Crossing

1947.
P1174 P **224** 100f. green 4·75 20

P **230** Archer

1947.
P1193 P **230** 8f. brown 70 30
P1194 10f. blue and black 70 15
P1195 12f. violet 1·10 25

1948. Surch.
P1229 P **230** 9f. on 8f. brown 75 20
P1230 11f. on 10f. blue and black 75 25
P1231 13f.50 on 12f. violet 1·10 20

P **246** "Parcel Post"

1948.
P1250 P **246** 9f. brown 5·75 20
P1251 11f. red 5·00 10
P1252 13f.50 black 8·50 10

P **254** Type 1 Locomotive, 1867 (dated 1862)

1949. Locomotives.
P1277 – ½f. brown 40 25
P1278 P **254** 1f. red 50 25
P1279 – 2f. blue 80 20
P1280 – 3f. red (1884) 1·90 20
P1281 – 4f. green (1901) 1·25 20
P1282 – 5f. red (1902) 1·25 20
P1283 – 6f. purple (1904) 1·90 20
P1284 – 7f. green (1905) 2·75 20
P1285 – 8f. blue (1906) 3·25 20
P1286 – 9f. brown (1909) 4·50 20
P1287 – 10f. olive (1910) 6·00 20
P1288 – 10f. black and red (1905) 5·50 1·40
P1289 – 20f. orange (1920) 15·00 20
P1290 – 30f. blue (1928) 22·00 20
P1291 – 40f. red (1930) 38·00 20
P1292 – 50f. mauve (1935) 19·00 20
P1293 – 100f. red (1939) 75·00 30
P1294 – 300f. violet (1951) £100 40
DESIGNS: 50c. Locomotive "Le Belge", 1835; 2f. Type 29 locomotive, 1875; 3f. Type 25 locomotive, 1884; 4f. Type 18 locomotive, 1901; 5f. Type 22 locomotive, 1902; 6f. Type 53 locomotive, 1904; 7f. Type 8 locomotive, 1905; 8f. Type 16 locomotive, 1906; 9f. Type 10 locomotive, 1909; 10f. (P1287) Type 36 locomotive, 1910; 10f. (P 1288) Type 38 locomotive, 1905; 20f. Type 38 locomotive, 1920; 30f. Type 48 locomotive, 1928; 40f. Type 5 locomotive, 1935; 50f. Type 1 Pacific locomotive, 1935; 100f. Type 12 locomotive, 1939; 300f. Two-car electric train, 1951.
The 300f. is larger (37½ × 25 mm).

1949. Electrification of Charleroi–Brussels Line. As Type P**254**.
P1296 60f. brown 19·00 20
DESIGN: 60f. Type 101 electric locomotive, 1945.

P **258** Loading Parcels

1950.
P1307 – 11f. orange 4·00 20
P1308 – 12f. purple 14·00 1·40
P1309 – 13f. green 4·75 15
P1310 – 15f. blue 12·00 20
P1311 P **258** 16f. grey 4·00 15
P1312 – 17f. brown 4·75 20
P1313 P **258** 18f. red 10·00 80
P1314 – 20f. orange 5·00 20
DESIGNS—HORIZ: 11, 12, 17f. Dispatch counter; 13, 15f. Sorting compartment.

P **271** Mercury

1951. 25th Anniv of National Belgian Railway Society.
P1375 P **271** 25f. blue 9·50 7·50

1953. Nos. P1307, P1310 and P1313 surch.
P1442 – 13f. on 15f. blue 48·00 3·25
P1443 – 17f. on 11f. orange 23·00 80
P1444 P **258** 20f. on 18f. red 12·50 2·00

P **288** Electric Train and Brussels Skyline

1953. Inauguration of Nord-Midi Junction.
P1451 P **288** 200f. green £180 70
P1452 200f. green & brown £190 2·40

P **291** Nord Station

P **292** Central Station

1953. Brussels Railway Stations.
P1485 P **291** 1f. ochre 20 10
P1486 2f. black 35 10
P1487 3f. green 40 10
P1488 4f. orange 60 10
P1489 5f. brown 2·00 15
P1490 – 5f. brown 8·00 15
P1491 P **291** 6f. purple 85 10
P1492 7f. green 85 10
P1493 8f. red 1·10 10
P1494 9f. blue 1·40 10
P1495 – 10f. green 1·90 10
P1496 – 10f. black 1·10 10
P1497 – 15f. red 10·50 40
P1498 – 20f. blue 3·00 10
P1498a – 20f. green 1·60 30
P1499 – 30f. purple 4·75 10
P1500 – 40f. mauve 6·25 10
P1501 – 50f. mauve 7·75 10
P1501a – 50f. blue 2·50 50
P1502 – 60f. violet 16·00 10
P1503 – 80f. purple 25·00 20
P1504 P **292** 100f. green 14·00 35
P1505 200f. blue 80·00 60
P1506 300f. mauve £140 1·10
DESIGNS—VERT: 5f. (P1490), 10f. (P1496), 15, 20f. (P1498a), 50f. (P1501a), Congress Station; 10f. (P1495), 20f. (P1498) to 50f. (P1501), Midi Station. HORIZ: 60, 80f. Chapelle Station.
Nos. P1490, P1496/7, P1498a and P1501a were for use as railway parcels tax stamps.

P **295** Electric Train Type 121 and Nord Station, Brussels

P **326** Mercury and Railway Winged Wheel

1953.
P1517 P **295** 13f. brown 16·00 20
P1518 18f. blue 16·00 20
P1519 21f. mauve 16·00 30

1956. Surch in figures.
P1585 P **295** 14f. on 13f. brown 5·50 15
P1586 19f. on 18f. blue 5·50 15
P1587 22f. on 21f. mauve 5·50 20

1957.
P1600 P **326** 14f. green 5·50 15
P1601 19f. sepia 5·50 15
P1602 22f. red 5·50 25

1959. Surch **20 F.**
P1678 P **326** 20f. on 19f. sepia 20·00 20
P1679 20f. on 22f. red 20·00 55

P **357** Brussels Nord Station, 1861–1954

1959.
P1695 P **357** 20f. olive 9·00 10
P1696 – 24f. red 3·50 20
P1697 – 26f. blue 3·50 1·75
P1698 – 28f. purple 3·50 1·10
DESIGNS—VERT: 24f. Brussels Midi station, 1869–1949. HORIZ: 26f. Antwerp Central station, 1905; 28f. Ghent St. Pieter's station.

P **368** Congress Seal, Type 202 Diesel and Type 125 Electric Locomotives

1960. 75th Anniv of Int Railway Congress Assn.
P1722 P **368** 20f. red 35·00 24·00
P1723 50f. blue 35·00 24·00

P1724 60f. purple . . . . . 35·00 24·00
P1725 70f. green . . . . . 35·00 24·00

1961. Nos. P1695/8 surch.
P1787 P **357** 24f. on 20f. olive . . 40·00 15
P1788 – 26f. on 24f. red . . . 3·50 15
P1789 – 28f. on 26f. blue . . 3·50 15
P1790 – 35f. on 28f. purple 3·50 15

P **477** Arlon Station

1967.
P2017 P **477** 25f. ochre . . . . . 6·75 25
P2018 30f. green . . . . . 2·00 25
P2019 35f. blue . . . . . 2·25 25
P2020 40f. red . . . . . . 19·00 25

P **488** Type 122 Electric Train

1968.
P2047 P **488** 1f. bistre 25 15
P2048 2f. green 25 15
P2049 3f. green 45 15
P2050 4f. orange 45 15
P2051 5f. brown 50 15
P2052 6f. plum 45 15
P2053 7f. green 50 15
P2054 8f. red 65 15
P2055 9f. blue . . . . . . 1·10 15
P2056 – 10f. green . . . . . 2·25 15
P2057 – 20f. blue . . . . . 1·75 15
P2058 – 30f. lilac . . . . . 4·00 15
P2059 – 40f. violet . . . . . 4·50 15
P2060 – 50f. purple . . . . 5·50 15
P2061 – 60f. violet . . . . . 7·00 20
P2062 – 70f. brown . . . . 7·50 20
P2063 – 80f. purple . . . . 5·50 20
P2063a – 90f. green . . . . . 5·00 25
P2064 – 100f. green . . . . 8·75 20
P2065 – 200f. violet . . . . 11·00 35
P2066 – 300f. mauve . . . . 20·00 1·10
P2067 – 500f. yellow . . . . 30·00 1·50
DESIGNS: 10f. to 40f. Type 126 electric train; 50, 60, 70, 80, 90f. Type 160 electric train; 100, 200, 300f. Type 205 diesel-electric train; 500f. Type 210 diesel-electric train.

1970. Surch.
P2180 P **477** 37f. on 25f. ochre . . 42·00 4·50
P2181 48f. on 35f. blue . . 4·25 3·50
P2182 53f. on 40f. red . . . 4·25 3·50

P **551** Ostend Station

1971. Figures of value in black.
P2192 P **551** 32f. ochre . . . . . 1·25 1·10
P2193 37f. grey . . . . . . 10·50 11·00
P2194 42f. blue . . . . . . 1·75 1·50
P2195 44f. mauve . . . . . 1·75 1·50
P2196 46f. violet . . . . . 2·00 1·50
P2197 50f. red . . . . . . 1·75 1·50
P2198 52f. brown . . . . . 10·50 11·00
P2199 54f. green . . . . . 5·25 4·00
P2200 61f. blue . . . . . . 2·40 2·00

1972. Nos. P2192/5 and P2198/200 surch in figures.
P2256 P **551** 34f. on 32f. ochre . . 1·90 80
P2257 40f. on 37f. grey . . 1·90 80
P2258 47f. on 44f. mauve 2·10 80
P2259 53f. on 42f. blue . . 2·75 80
P2260 56f. on 52f. brown 2·50 80
P2261 59f. on 54f. green . . 2·75 80
P2262 66f. on 61f. blue . . 3·00 70

P **575** Emblems within Bogie Wheels

1972. 50th Anniv of Int Railways Union (U.I.C.).
P2266 P **575** 100f. black, red and green . . . . . . 7·00 1·60
See also No. 2274.

P **624** Global Emblem

1974. 4th International Symposium of Railway Cybernetics, Washington.
P2353 P **624** 100f. black, red and yellow . . . . . . 4·25 1·25

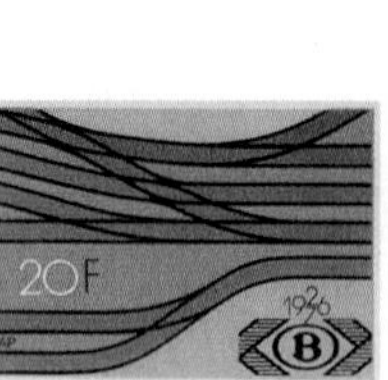

P **671** Railway Junction

P **698** Railway Station at Night

1976.
P2431 P **671** 20f. black, bl & lilac 95 75
P2432 50f. black, green and turquoise . . . . 1·75 75
P2433 100f. black & orange 3·25 1·00
P2434 150f. black, mauve and deep mauve 5·00 1·00

1977.
P2505 P **698** 1000f. mult . . . . . 42·00 14·00

P **753** Goods Wagon, Type 2216 A8

1980. Values in black.
P2615 P **753** 1f. ochre 15 15
P2616 2f. red 15 15
P2617 3f. blue 15 15
P2618 4f. blue 15 15
P2619 5f. brown 20 15
P2620 6f. orange 30 20
P2621 7f. violet 35 20
P2622 8f. black 35 20
P2623 9f. green 40 35
P2624 – 10f. brown 40 30
P2625 – 20f. blue . . . . . 1·00 35
P2626 – 30f. ochre . . . . . 1·75 30
P2627 – 40f. mauve . . . . . 2·10 30
P2628 – 50f. purple . . . . . 2·40 35
P2629 – 60f. olive . . . . . 2·75 35
P2630 – 70f. blue . . . . . 3·50 2·00
P2631 – 80f. purple . . . . . 4·00 60
P2632 – 90f. mauve . . . . . 4·50 2·10
P2633 – 100f. red . . . . . 5·00 85
P2634 – 200f. brown . . . . 9·75 1·25
P2635 – 300f. olive . . . . . 14·50 1·60
P2636 – 500f. purple . . . . 26·00 2·75
DESIGNS: 10f. to 40f. Packet wagon, Type 3614 A5; 50f. to 90f. Self-discharging wagon, Type 1000 D; 100f. to 500f. Tanker wagon, Type 2000 G.

P **833** Electric Train entering Station

1985. 150th Anniv of Belgian Railways. Paintings by P. Delvaux. Multicoloured.
P2824 250f. Type P **833** . . . . 12·50 5·00
P2825 500f. Electric trains in station . . . . 24·00 9·50

RAILWAY PARCEL TAX STAMPS

1940. As Nos. P399 and P404 but colours changed.
P876 P **84** 5f. brown 25 25
P877 10f. black . . . . . . 3·50 3·50

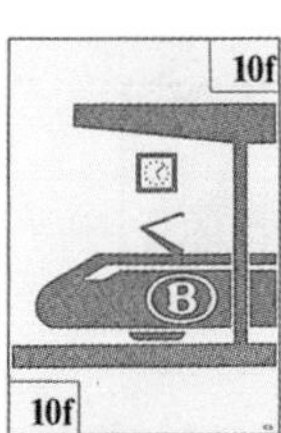

PD **779** Electric Locomotive at Station

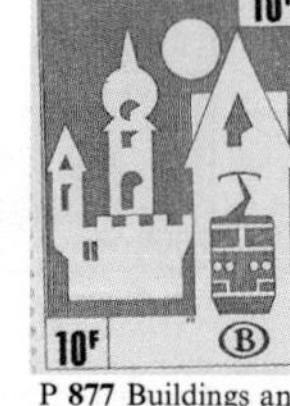

P **877** Buildings and Electric Locomotive

1982.
P2703 P **779** 10f. red & black . . 1·40 25
P2704 20f. green & blk . . 1·60 1·25
P2705 50f. brown & blk . . 3·00 55
P2706 100f. blue & blk . . 5·50 85

1987.
P2923 P **877** 10f. red 75 40
P2924 20f. green . . . . . 1·25 1·10
P2925 50f. brown . . . . . 3·50 1·25
P2926 100f. purple . . . . 6·25 2·50
P2927 150f. brown . . . . 9·50 2·75

RAILWAY OFFICIAL STAMPS

For use on the official mail of the Railway Company.

1929. Stamps of 1922 optd with winged wheel.
O481 **81** 5c. slate 25 20
O482 10c. green 30 25
O483 35c. green 35 25
O484 60c. olive 45 15
O485 1f.50 blue . . . . 15·00 7·00
O486 1f.75 blue . . . . 1·90 50

1929. Stamps of 1929 optd with winged wheel.
O534 **104** 5c. green 15 10
O535 10c. bistre 15 20
O536 25c. red . . . . 1·90 45
O537 35c. green 60 20
O538 40c. purple 60 20
O539 50c. blue 35 20
O540 60c. mauve . . . . . . 14·00 7·50
O541 70c. brown . . . . . . 4·00 95
O542 75c. blue . . . . 5·25 75

1932. Stamps of 1931–34 optd with winged wheel.
O620 **126** 10c. green 55 50
O677 **127** 35c. green . . . . . . 9·50 50
O678 **142** 70c. green . . . . . . 3·25 30
O679 **121** 75c. brown . . . . . . 1·60 35

1936. Stamps of 1936 optd with winged wheel.
O721 **152** 10c. olive 15 15
O722 35c. green 10 10
O723 40c. lilac 20 20
O724 50c. blue 40 45
O725 **153** 70c. brown . . . . . . 2·75 3·00
O726 75c. olive 45 25

1941. Optd **B** in oval frame.
O948 **152** 10c. green 15 15
O949 40c. lilac 15 15
O950 50c. blue 15 15
O951 **153** 1f. red (No. 747) . . . 15 10
O952a 1f. red (No. 748) . . . 10 15
O953 2f.25 black 35 35
O954 **155** 2f.25 violet 25 35

1942. Nos. O722, O725 and O726 surch.
O983 **152** 10c. on 35c. green . . . 10 10
O984 **153** 50c. on 70c. brown . . 10 15
O985 50c. on 75c. olive . . 10 15

O **221** O **283**

1946. Designs incorporating letter "B".
O1156 O **221** 10c. green 10 15
O1157 20c. violet . . . . . 2·40 70
O1158 50c. blue 10 10
O1159 65c. purple . . . . 3·00 75
O1160 75c. mauve 15 15
O1161 90c. violet . . . . . 3·50 25
O1240 – 1f.35 brn (as 1219) 1·75 45
O1241 – 1f.75 green (as 1220) 4·75 45
O1242 **239** 3f. purple . . . . . 21·00 6·50
O1243 **240** 3f.15 blue . . . . . 9·25 5·75
O1244 4f. blue . . . . . . 17·00 7·50

1952.
O1424 O **283** 10c. orange 30 10
O1425 20c. red . . . . . 2·75 55
O1426 30c. green . . . . 1·25 35
O1427 40c. brown 30 15
O1428 50c. blue 25 10
O1429 60c. mauve 55 20
O1430 65c. purple . . . . 24·00 17·00
O1431 80c. green . . . . 4·00 90
O1432 90c. blue . . . . . 6·00 85
O1433 1f. red 40 10
O1433a 1f.50 grey 10 10
O1434 2f.50 brown 20 10

1954. As T **289** (King Baudouin) but with letter "B" incorporated in design.
O1523 1f.50 black 30 20
O1524 2f. red . . . . 32·00 30
O1525 2f. green 35 20
O1526 2f.50 brown . . . . . . 26·00 50
O1527 3f. mauve . . . . 1·40 20
O1528 3f.50 green 65 20
O1529 4f. blue 80 25
O1530 6f. red . . . . 1·40 45

1971. As Nos. 2209/20 but with letter "B" incorporated in design.
O2224 3f. green 80 60
O2225 3f.50 brown 25 10
O2226 4f. blue 90 40
O2227 4f.50 purple 25 20
O2228 4f.50 blue 30 20
O2229 5f. violet 30 20
O2230 6f. red 30 10
O2231 6f.50 violet 35 20
O2232a 7f. red 30 15
O2233 8f. black 35 20
O2233a 9f. brown 40 10
O2234 10f. red 40 20
O2235 15f. violet 50 30
O2236 25f. purple . . . . 1·10 20
O2237 30f. brown . . . . 1·25 25

1977. As T **684** but with letter "B" incorporated in design.
O2455 50c. brown 10 10
O2456 1f. mauve 10 10
O2457 2f. orange 20 15
O2458 4f. brown 25 10
O2459 5f. green 25 25

BELIZE Pt. 1

British Honduras was renamed Belize on 1 June 1973 and the country became independent within the Commonwealth on 21 September 1981.

100 cents = 1 dollar.

1973. Nos. 256/66 and 277/8 of British Honduras optd **BELIZE** and two stars.
347 – ½c. multicoloured 10 20
348 **63** 1c. black, brown and yellow 10 20
349 – 2c. black, green and yellow 10 20
350 – 3c. black, brown and lilac 10 10
351 – 4c. multicoloured 10 20
352 – 5c. black and red 10 20
353 – 10c. multicoloured 15 15
354 – 15c. multicoloured 20 20
355 – 25c. multicoloured 35 35
356 – 50c. multicoloured 65 75
357 – $1 multicoloured 75 1·50
358 – $2 multicoloured 1·25 2·75
359 – $5 multicoloured 1·40 4·75

1973. Royal Wedding. As T **47** of Anguilla. Background colours given. Multicoloured.
360 26c. blue 15 10
361 50c. brown 15 20

82 Mozambique Mouthbrooder

1974. As Nos. 256/66 and 276/78 of British Honduras. Multicoloured.
362 ½c. Type **82** 10 50
363 1c. Spotted jewfish 10 30
364 2c. White-lipped peccary ("Waree") 10 30
365 3c. Misty grouper 10 10
366 4c. Collared anteater 10 30
367 5c. Bonefish 10 30
368 10c. Paca ("Gibnut") 15 15
369 15c. Dolphin 20 20
370 25c. Kinkajou ("Night Walker") 35 35
371 50c. Mutton snapper 60 70
372 $1 Tayra ("Bush Dog") 75 1·50
373 $2 Great barracuda 1·25 2·50
374 $5 Puma 1·50 5·50

83 Deer

1974. Mayan Artefacts (1st series). Pottery Motifs. Multicoloured.
375 3c. Type **83** 10 10
376 6c. Jaguar deity 10 10
377 16c. Sea monster 15 10
378 26c. Cormorant 25 10
379 50c. Scarlet macaw 40 40
See also Nos. 398/402.

84 "Parides arcas"

1974. Butterflies of Belize. Multicoloured.
380 ½c. Type **84** 90 4·00
381 1c. "Evenus regalis" 90 1·75
405 2c. "Colobura dirce" 50 70
406 3c. "Catonephele numilia" 1·25 70
407 4c. "Battus belus" 3·00 30
408 5c. "Callicore patelina" 3·25 30
386 10c. "Diaethria astala" 1·50 70
410 15c. "Nessaea aglaura" 75 70
388 16c. "Prepona pseudojoiceyi" 4·50 7·00
412 25c. "Papilio thoas" 6·50 40
390 26c. "Hamadryas arethusa" 2·50 4·25
413 35c. Type **84** 12·00 4·50
391 50c. "Panthiades bathildis" 2·75 65
392 $1 "Caligo uranus" 6·50 6·00
393 $2 "Heliconius sapho" 4·00 1·25
394 $5 "Eurytides philolaus" 5·50 6·00
395 $10 "Philaethria dido" 10·00 4·00

85 Churchill when Prime Minister, and Coronation Scene

1974. Birth Centenary of Sir Winston Churchill. Multicoloured.
396 50c. Type **85** 20 20
397 $1 Churchill in stetson, and Williamsburg Liberty Bell 30 30

86 The Actun Balam Vase

1975. Mayan Artefacts (2nd series). Multicoloured.
398 3c. Type **86** 10 10
399 6c. Seated figure 10 10
400 16c. Costumed priest 25 15
401 26c. Head with headdress 35 20
402 50c. Layman and priest 45 1·75

87 Musicians

1975. Christmas. Multicoloured.
435 6c. Type **87** 10 10
436 26c. Children and "crib" 20 10
437 50c. Dancer and drummers (vert) 30 55
438 $1 Family and map (vert) 55 1·60

88 William Wrigley Jr. and Chicle Tapping

1976. Bicent of American Revolution. Mult.
439 10c. Type **88** 10 10
440 35c. Charles Lindbergh 20 40
441 $1 J. L. Stephens (archaeologist) 50 1·50

89 Cycling

1976. Olympic Games, Montreal. Multicoloured.
442 35c. Type **89** 15 10
443 45c. Running 20 15
444 $1 Shooting 35 1·40

1976. No. 390 surch **20c.**
445 20c. on 26c. multicoloured 1·50 1·75

1976. West Indian Victory in World Cricket Cup. As Nos. 559/60 of Barbados.
446 35c. multicoloured 40 50
447 $1 black and purple 60 2·00

1976. No. 426 surch **5c.**
448 5c. on 15c. multicoloured 1·10 2·75

92 Queen and Bishops

1977. Silver Jubilee. Multicoloured.
449 10c. Royal Visit, 1975 10 10
450 35c. Queen and Rose Window 15 15
451 $2 Type **92** 45 90

93 Red-capped Manakin

94 Laboratory Workers

1977. Birds (1st series). Multicoloured.
452 8c. Type **93** 75 55
453 10c. Hooded oriole 90 30
454 25c. Blue-crowned motmot 1·25 55
455 35c. Slaty-breasted tinamou 1·50 75
456 45c. Ocellated turkey 1·75 1·25
457 $1 White hawk 3·00 5·50
MS458 110 × 133 mm. Nos. 452/7 8·25 11·00
See also Nos. 467/78, 488/94 and 561/7.

1977. 75th Anniv of Pan-American Health Organization. Multicoloured.
459 35c. Type **94** 20 20
460 $1 Mobile medical unit 40 65
MS461 126 × 95 mm. Nos. 459/60 85 1·40

1978. Nos. 386 and 413 optd **BELIZE DEFENCE FORCE 1ST JANUARY 1978.**
462 10c. "Diaethria astala" 75 1·00
463 35c. Type **84** 1·50 2·25

96 White Lion of Mortimer

97 "Russelia sarmentosa"

1978. 25th Anniv of Coronation.
464 **96** 75c. brown, red and silver 20 30
465 – 75c. multicoloured 20 30
466 – 75c. brown, red and silver 20 30
DESIGNS: No. 465, Queen Elizabeth II; 466, Jaguar (Maya god of Day and Night).

1978. Birds (2nd series). As T **93**. Multicoloured.
467 10c. White-capped parrot("White-crowned Parrot") 55 30
468 25c. Crimson-collared tanager 80 45
469 35c. Black-headed trogon ("Citreoline Trogon") 1·10 55
470 45c. American finfoot ("Sungrebe") 1·25 1·75
471 50c. Muscovy duck 1·40 2·50
472 $1 King vulture 2·00 6·50
473 111 × 133 mm. Nos. 467/72 8·00 11·00

1978. Christmas. Wild Flowers and Ferns. Mult.
474 10c. Type **97** 15 10
475 15c. "Lygodium polymorphum" 20 15
476 35c. "Heliconia aurantiaca" 20 20
477 45c. "Adiantum tetraphyllum" 20 40
478 50c. "Angelonia ciliaris" 35 50
479 $1 "Thelypteris obliterata" 50 1·25

98 Fairchild Monoplane of Internal Airmail Service, 1937

1979. Centenary of U.P.U. Membership. Mult.
480 5c. Type **98** 25 30
481 10c. "Heron H" (mail boat), 1949 25 10
482 35c. Internal mail service, 1920 (canoe) 25 20
483 45c. Steam Creek Railway mail, 1910 45 55
484 50c. Mounted mail courier, 1882 45 60
485 $1 "Eagle" (mail boat), 1856 80 2·50

1979. No. 413 surch **15c.**
487 **84** 15c. on 35c. multicoloured 2·25 1·75

1979. Birds (3rd series). As T **93**. Multicoloured.
488 10c. Boat-billed heron 65 30
489 25c. Grey-necked wood rail 90 30
490 35c. Lineated woodpecker 1·10 55
491 45c. Blue-grey tanager 1·25 70
492 50c. Laughing falcon 1·25 1·25
493 $1 Long-tailed hermit 1·60 4·00
MS494 113 × 136 mm. Nos. 488/93 4·75 6·00

101 Paslow Building, Belize G.P.O.

1979. 25th Anniv of Coronation. Multicoloured.
495 25c. Type **101** 1·50 10
496 50c. Houses of Parliament 2·00 10
497 75c. Coronation State Coach 2·50 15
498 $1 Queen on horseback (vert) 3·25 20
499 $2 Prince of Wales (vert) 3·25 35
500 $3 Queen and Duke of Edinburgh (vert) 3·25 35
501 $4 Portrait of Queen (vert) 3·25 40
502 $5 St. Edward's Crown (vert) 3·50 40
MS503 Two sheets, both 126 × 95 mm: (a) $5 Princess Anne on horseback at Montreal Olympics (vert); $10 Queen at Montreal Olympics (vert). (b) $15 As Type **101** Set of 2 sheets 22·00

102 Mortimer and Vaughan "Safety" Airplane, 1910

1979. Death Centenary of Sir Rowland Hill. 60th Anniv of I.C.A.O. (International Civil Aviation Organization), previously Int Commission for Air Navigation. Multicoloured.
504 4c. Type **102** 50 10
505 25c. Boeing 720 1·50 20
506 50c. Concorde 4·25 30
507 75c. Handley Page H.P.18 W.8b (1922) 2·00 30
508 $1 Avro Type F (1912) 2·00 30
509 $1.50 Samuel Cody's biplane (1910) 2·75 30
510 $2 A.V. Roe Triplane I (1909) 2·75 40
511 $3 Santos Dumont's biplane "14 bis" (1906) 2·75 45
512 $4 Wright Type A 3·00 65
MS513 Two sheets: (a) 115 × 95 mm. $5 Dunne D-5 (1910), $5 G.B. 1969 Concorde stamp; (b) 130 × 95 mm. $10 Boeing 720 (different) Set of 2 sheets 20·00

103 Handball

104 Olympic Torch

1979. Olympic Games, Moscow (1980). Mult.
514 25c. Type **103** 45 10
515 50c. Weightlifting 65 10
516 75c. Athletics 90 15
517 $1 Football 1·25 20
518 $2 Yachting 1·75 25
519 $3 Swimming 2·00 30
520 $4 Boxing 2·50 30
521 $5 Cycling 8·00 90
MS522 Two sheets: (a) 126 × 92 mm. $5 Athletics (different), $10 Boxing (different); (b) 92 × 126 mm. $15 As $5 Set of 2 sheets 16·00

1979. Winter Olympic Games, Lake Placid (1980). Multicoloured.
523 25c. Type **104** 20 10
524 50c. Giant slalom 45 15
525 75c. Figure-skating 65 15
526 $1 Downhill skiing 80 15
527 $2 Speed-skating 1·60 20
528 $3 Cross-country skiing 2·50 30
529 $4 Shooting 3·00 40
530 $5 Gold, Silver and Bronze medals 3·50 45
MS531 Two sheets: (a) 127 × 90 mm. $5 Lighting the Olympic Flame, $10 Gold, Silver and Bronze medals (different); (b) 90 × 127 mm. $15 Olympic Torch (different) Set of 2 sheets 20·00

105 Measled Cowrie

1980. Shells. Multicoloured.
532 1c. Type **105** 55 10
533 2c. Callico clam 70 10
534 3c. Altantic turkey wing (vert) 80 10
535 4c. Leafy jewel box (vert) . . 80 10
536 5c. Trochlear latirus 80 10
537 10c. Alphabet cone (vert) . . 1·00 10
538 15c. Cabrits murex (vert) . . 1·40 10
539 20c. Stiff pen shell . . . . . 1·50 10
540 25c. Little knobbed scallop (vert) . . . . 1·50 10
541 35c. Glory of the Atlantic cone (vert) . . . . 1·75 10
542 45c. Sunrise tellin (vert) . . . 2·00 10
543 50c. "Leucozonia nassa leucozonalis" . . . . . . 2·00 10
544 85c. Triangular typhis . . . 3·00 10
545 $1 Queen or pink conch (vert) . . . . 3·25 10
546 $2 Rooster-tail conch (vert) 5·00 30
547 $5 True tulip . . . . 7·50 50
548 $10 Star arene . . . . 9·50 90
MS549 Two sheets, each 125 × 90 mm. (a) Nos. 544 and 547. (b) Nos. 546 and 548 38·00 15·00

106 Girl and Flower Arrangement
108 Jabiru

1980. International Year of the Child (1st issue). Multicoloured.
550 25c. Type **106** 45 10
551 50c. Boy holding football . . 70 10
552 75c. Boy with butterfly . . . 1·00 10
553 $1 Girl holding doll . . . . 1·00 10
554 $1.50 Boy carrying basket of fruit . . . . 1·50 15
555 $2 Boy holding reticulated cowrie-helmet shell . . . . 1·75 20
556 $3 Girl holding posy . . . . 2·25 25
557 $4 Boy and girl wrapped in blanket . . . . 2·50 30
MS558 130 × 95 mm. $5 Three children of different races. $5 "Madonna with Cat" (A. Dürer) (each 35 × 53 mm). 8·50
MS559 111 × 151 mm. $10 Children and Christmas tree (73 × 110 mm). 8·50
See also Nos. 583/91.

1980. No. 412 surch **10c**.
560 10c. on 25c. "Papilio thoas" 75 1·00

1980. Birds (4th series). Multicoloured.
561 10c. Type **108** . . . . 6·50 2·75
562 25c. Barred antshrike . . . . 7·50 2·75
563 35c. Northern royal flycatcher ("Royal Flycatcher") . . . 7·50 2·75
564 45c. White-necked puffbird 7·50 3·00
565 50c. Ornate hawk-eagle . . . 7·50 3·00
566 $1 Golden-masked tanager 8·00 3·75
MS567 85 × 90 mm. $2 Type **108**, $3 As $1 32·00 18·00

109 Speed Skating
111 Witch in Sky

1980. Winter Olympic Games, Lake Placid. Medal Winners. Multicoloured.
568 25c. Type **109** 30 15
569 50c. Ice-hockey 50 15
570 75c. Figure-skating 60 15
571 $1 Alpine-skiing 85 15
572 $1.50 Giant slalom (women) 1·25 25
573 $2 Speed-skating (women) . . 1·50 30
574 $3 Cross-country skiing . . . 2·25 40
575 $5 Giant slalom . . . . . . 3·50 55
MS576 Two sheets: (a) 126 × 91 mm. $5 Type **109**; $10 Type **109**; (b) 91 × 126 mm. $10 As 75 c. Set of 2 sheets 16·00

1980. "ESPAMER" International Stamp Exhibition, Madrid. Nos. 560/5 optd **BELIZE ESPAMER '80 MADRID 3-12 OCT 1980** and emblem (Nos. 577/9) or surch also.
577 10c. Type **107** . . . . 6·50 2·50
578 25c. Barred antshrike . . . . 7·00 2·75
579 35c. Northern royal flycatcher 7·00 2·75
580 40c. on 45c. White-necked puffbird . . . . 7·50 3·00
581 40c. on 50c. Ornate hawk eagle . . . . 7·50 3·00
582 40c. on $1 Golden-masked tanager . . . . 8·00 3·00

1980. International Year of the Child (2nd issue). "Sleeping Beauty".
583 **111** 25c. multicoloured . . . . 1·50 15
584 – 40c. multicoloured . . . . 1·75 15
585 – 50c. multicoloured . . . . 2·00 15
586 – 75c. multicoloured . . . . 2·25 20
587 – $1 multicoloured . . . . 2·25 25
588 – $1.50 multicoloured . . . 2·75 40
589 – $3 multicoloured . . . . 3·75 50
590 – $4 multicoloured . . . . 3·75 55
MS591 Two sheets: (a) 82 × 110 mm. $8 "Paumgartner Altar-piece" (Dürer); (b) 110 × 82 mm. $5 Marriage ceremony, $5 Sleeping Beauty and Prince on horseback Set of 2 sheets 19·00
DESIGNS: 40c. to $4, Illustrations from the story.

112 H.M. Queen Elizabeth the Queen Mother

1980. 80th Birthday of H.M. Queen Elizabeth the Queen Mother.
592 **112** $1 multicoloured . . . . 2·25 50
MS593 82 × 110 mm, $5 As Type **112** (41 × 32 mm) 14·00 4·75

113 The Annunciation
115 Paul Harris (founder)

1980. Christmas. Multicoloured.
594 25c. Type **113** 65 10
595 50c. Bethlehem . . . . 1·25 10
596 75c. The Holy Family . . . 1·50 10
597 $1 The Nativity . . . . . . 1·60 10
598 $1.50 The Flight into Egypt 1·75 15
599 $2 Shepherds following the Star . . . . 2·00 20
600 $3 Virgin, Child and Angel 2·25 25
601 $4 Adoration of the Kings 2·25 30
MS602 Two sheets, each 82 × 111 mm: (a) $5 As $1: (b) $10 As $3 Set of 2 sheets 14·00

1981. "WIPA" International Stamp Exhibition, Vienna. Nos. 598 and 601 surch.
603 $1 on $1.50 The Flight into Egypt . . . . 7·00 1·60
604 $2 on $4 Adoration of the Kings . . . . 8·00 2·25
MS605 82 × 111 mm. $2 on $10 Virgin, Child and Angel 7·50 3·50

1981. 75th Anniv of Rotary International. Mult.
606 25c. Type **115** . . . . 1·75 25
607 50c. Emblems of Rotary activities . . . . 2·25 35
608 $1 75th Anniversary emblem 2·75 65
609 $1.50 Educational scholarship programme (horiz) . . . . 3·50 1·00
610 $2 "Project Hippocrates" . . 4·00 1·40
611 $3 Emblems . . . . 5·00 2·00
612 $5 Emblems and handshake (horiz) . . . . 6·00 3·25
MS613 Two sheets: (a) 95 × 130 mm. $10 As 50c. (b) 130 × 95 mm, $5 As $1, $10 As $2 Set of 2 sheets 29·00

116 Coat of Arms of Prince of Wales
118 Athletics

1981. Royal Wedding. Mult. (a) Size 22 × 38 mm.
614 50c. Type **116** 45 50
615 $1 Prince Charles in military uniform 80 90
616 $1.50 Royal couple . . . . . 1·25 1·50

(b) Size 25 × 42 mm, with gold borders.
617 50c. Type **116** 45 30
618 $1 As No. 615 . . . . 80 50
619 $1.50 As No. 616 . . . . . . 1·25 70
MS620 145 × 85 mm. $3 × 3 As Nos 614/16, but 30 × 47 mm. P 14 2·50 4·25

1981. No. 538 surch **10c**.
621 10c. on 15c. "Murex cabritii" 3·50 3·50

1981. History of the Olympics. Multicoloured.
622 85c. Type **118** . . . . 2·00 30
623 $1 Cycling . . . . 6·00 50
624 $1.50 Boxing . . . . 3·00 50
625 $2 1984 Games–Los Angeles and Sarajevo . . . . . . 3·75 50
626 $3 Baron de Coubertin . . . 4·50 60
627 $5 Olympic Flame . . . . . 5·50 70
MS628 Two sheets, each 175 × 123 mm: (a) $5 As $3, $10 As $5 (each 35 × 53 mm). P13½; (b) $15 As $2 (45 × 67 mm). P 14½. Set of 2 sheets 35·00

1981. Independence Commemoration (1st issue). Optd **Independence 21 Sept., 1981**. (a) On Nos. 532/44 and 546/8.
629 1c. Type **105** . . . . 1·00 10
630 2c. Callico clam . . . . . . 1·00 10
631 3c. Atlantic turkey wing (vert) . . . . 1·00 10
632 4c. Leafy jewel box (vert) . . 1·00 10
633 5c. Trochlear latirus . . . . 1·25 10
634 10c. Alphabet cone (vert) . . 1·50 10
635 15c. Cabrits murex (vert) . . 2·25 10
636 20c. Stiff pen shell . . . . . 2·25 15
637 25c. Little knobbed scallop (vert) . . . . 2·50 25
638 35c. Glory of the Atlantic cone . . . . 2·50 30
639 45c. Sunrise tellin (vert) . . . 3·00 40
640 50c. "Leucozonia nassa leucozonalis" . . . . . . 3·00 40
641 85c. Triangular typhis . . . 4·75 90
642 $2 Rooster-tail conch (vert) 9·00 2·50
643 $5 True tulip . . . . 11·00 5·50
644 $10 Star arene . . . . 13·00 9·50
MS645 Two sheets, each 126 × 91 mm; (a) Nos. 641 and 643; (b) Nos. 642 and 644 Set of 2 sheets 38·00

(b) On Nos. 606/12.
646 25c. Type **115** . . . . 2·25 25
647 50c. Emblems of Rotary activities . . . . 2·50 35
648 $1 75th Anniversary emblem 3·00 65
649 $1.50 Educational scholarship programme . . . . 3·75 1·25
650 $2 "Project Hippocrates" . . 4·50 1·60
651 $3 Emblems . . . . 5·50 2·50
652 $5 Emblems and hand-shake 7·00 3·75
MS653 Two sheets: (a) 95 × 130 mm. $10 As 50 c.; (b) 130 × 95 mm. $5 As $1, $10 As $2 Set of 2 sheets 38·00
See also Nos. 657/63.

1981. "ESPAMER" International Stamp Exhibition, Buenos Aires. No. 609 surch **$1 ESPAMER 81 BUENOS AIRES 13-22 NOV** and emblem.
654 $1 on $1.50 Educational scholarship programme . . 9·00 2·75
MS655 95 × 130 mm. $1 on $5 75th anniversary emblem, $1 on $10 "Project Hippocrates" 13·00 7·00

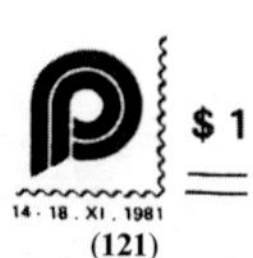

(121)

1981. "Philatelia 81" International Stamp Exhibition, Frankfurt. No. **MS**549 surch with T **121**.
MS656 Two sheets, each 125 × 90 mm: (a) $1 on 85 c. "Tripterotyphis triangularis", $1 on $5 "Fasciolaria tulipa"; (b) $1 on $2 "Strombus gallus", $1 on $10 "Arene cruentata" Set of 2 sheets 45·00

122 Black Orchid
123 Uruguayan Footballer

1981. Independence Commemoration (2nd issue). Multicoloured.
657 10c. Belize Coat of Arms (horiz) . . . . 2·00 20
658 35c. Map of Belize . . . . . 3·75 40
659 50c. Type **122** . . . . 8·00 1·00
660 85c. Baird's tapir (horiz) . . 2·50 1·00
661 $1 Mahogany tree . . . . . 2·50 1·10
662 $2 Keel-billed toucan (horiz) 12·00 3·75
MS663 130 × 98 mm. $5 As 10c. 10·00 5·00

1981. World Cup Football Championship, Spain (1st issue). Multicoloured.
664 10c. Type **123** . . . . 2·00 20
665 25c. Italian footballer . . . . 3·00 20
666 50c. German footballer . . . 3·75 40
667 $1 Brazilian footballer . . . 4·75 60
668 $1.50 Argentinian footballer 6·00 1·25
669 $2 English footballer . . . . 6·50 1·40
MS670 Two sheets: (a) 145 × 115 mm. $2 "SPAIN '82" logo; (b) 155 × 115 mm. $3 Footballer (46 × 76 mm) Set of 2 sheets 25·00 6·50
See also Nos. 721/7.

124 H.M.S. "Centurion" (frigate)

1981. Sailing Ships. Multicoloured.
671 10c. Type **124** . . . . 2·75 40
672 25c. "Madagascar" (1837) . . 4·00 50
673 35c. Brig "Whitby" (1838) . . 4·50 55
674 55c. "China" (1838) . . . . 5·00 85
675 85c. "Swiftsure" (1850) . . . 6·50 1·25
676 $2 "Windsor Castle" (1857) 9·00 2·75
MS677 110 × 87 mm. $5 Ships in battle 26·00 8·00

1982. "ESSEN '82" Int Stamp Exn, West Germany. Nos. 662 and 669 surch **$1 ESSEN 82**.
678 $1 on $2 Keel-billed toucan 9·00 2·50
679 $1 on $2 English footballer 9·00 2·50

126 Princess Diana

1982. 21st Birthday of Princess of Wales. (a) Size 22 × 38 mm.
680 **126** 50c. multicoloured . . . . 1·60 45
681 – $1 multicoloured . . . . 2·00 75
682 – $1.50 multicoloured . . . 2·00 1·50

(b) Size 25 × 43 mm.
683 **126** 50c. multicoloured . . . . 1·60 30
684 – $1 multicoloured . . . . 2·00 60
685 – $1.50 multicoloured . . . 2·00 1·10
MS686 145 × 85 mm. $3 × 3 As Nos. 680/2, but 30 × 47 mm. 2·75 3·00
DESIGNS: Portraits of Princess of Wales with different backgrounds.

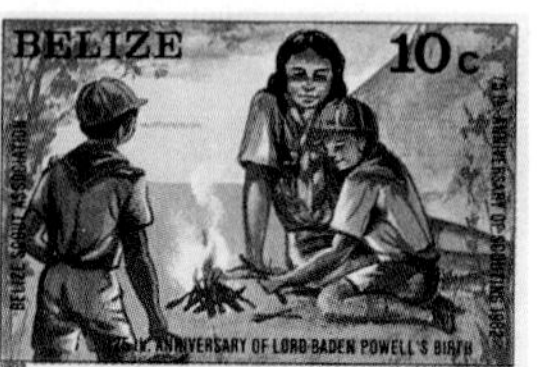

127 Lighting Campfire

1982. 125th Birth Anniv of Lord Baden-Powell. Multicoloured.
687 10c. Type **127** . . . . 1·75 20
668 25c. Bird watching . . . . . 4·50 30
689 35c. Three scouts, one playing guitar . . . . . . 2·75 30
690 50c. Hiking . . . . 3·00 55

691 85c. Scouts with flag . . . . 4·25 1·00
692 $2 Saluting . . . . 4·75 2·50
MS693 Two sheets: each 85 × 115 mm: (a) $2 Scout with flag; (b) $3 Portrait of Lord Baden-Powell Set of 2 sheets 26·00 11·00

128 "Gorgonia ventalina"

1982. 1st Anniv of Independence. Marine Life. Multicoloured.
694 10c. Type **128** . . . . 2·00 20
695 35c. "Carpiuis corallinus" . . 3·25 20
696 50c. "Plexaura flexuasa" . . 3·75 45
697 85c. "Candylactis gigantea" 4·00 60
698 $1 "Stenopus hispidus" . . . 5·00 90
699 $2 Sergeant major . . . . . 6·00 1·60
MS700 130 × 98 mm. $5 "Schyllarides aequinoclialis" 27·00 10·00

1982. "BELGICA 82" International Stamp Exhibition, Brussels. Nos. 687/92 optd **BELGICA 82 INT. YEAR OF THE CHILD SIR ROWLAND HILL 1795 1879 Picasso CENTENARY OF BIRTH** and emblems.
701 10c. Type **127** . . . . 2·25 30
702 25c. Bird watching . . . . . 5·00 75
703 35c. Three scouts, one playing guitar . . . . . . 3·50 1·00
704 50c. Hiking . . . . 3·75 1·50
705 85c. Scouts with flag . . . . 8·50 2·50
706 $2 Saluting . . . . 9·50 6·50

1982. Birth of Prince William of Wales (1st issue). Nos. 680/5 optd **BIRTH OF H.R.H. PRINCE WILLIAM ARTHUR PHILIP LOUIS 21ST JUNE 1982**. (a) Size 22 × 38 mm.
707 50c. multicoloured 45 45
708 $1 multicoloured 55 60
709 $1.50 multicoloured 75 85

(b) Size 25 × 43 mm.
710 50c. multicoloured 45 45
711 $1 multicoloured 55 60
712 $1.50 multicoloured 75 85

1982. Birth of Prince William of Wales (2nd issue). Nos. 614/19 optd **BIRTH OF H.R.H. PRINCE WILLIAM ARTHUR PHILIP LOUIS 21ST JUNE 1982**. (a) Size 22 × 38 mm.
714 50c. Type **116** . . . . 2·50 1·00
715 $1 Prince Charles in military uniform . . . . 5·00 2·00
716 $1.50 Royal couple . . . . . 7·50 3·00

(b) Size 25 × 42 mm.
717 50c. Type **116** 50 50
718 $1 As No. 715 . . . . 70 70
719 $1.50 As No. 716 . . . . . 1·10 1·10
MS720 145 × 85 mm. $3 × 3 As Nos. 714/16 but 30 × 47 mm 7·00 7·00

131 Scotland v New Zealand

1982. World Cup Football Championship, Spain (2nd issue). Multicoloured.
721 20c.+10c. Type **131** . . . . . 2·25 1·00
722 30c.+15c. Scotland v New Zealand (different) . . . . 2·25 1·00
723 40c.+20c. Kuwait v France 2·50 1·00
724 60c.+50c. Italy v Brazil . . . 3·00 1·40
725 $1+50c. France v Northern Ireland . . . . 3·50 1·60
726 $1.50+75c. Austria v Chile 4·25 2·00
MS727 Two sheets: (a) 91 × 137 mm. $1+50 c. Germany v Italy (50 × 70 mm); (b) 122 × 116 mm. $2+$1 England v France (50 × 70 mm) Set of 2 sheets 14·00 9·00

133 Belize Cathedral

1983. Visit of Pope John Paul II.
729 **133** 50c. multicoloured . . . . 2·25 1·25
MS730 135 × 110 mm. $2.50, Pope John Paul II (30 × 47 mm.) 20·00 7·00

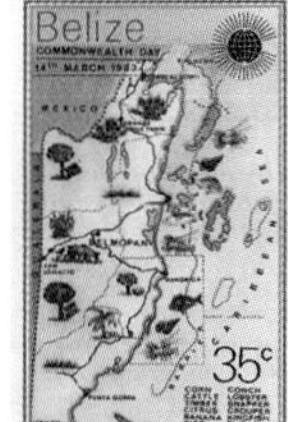

134 Map of Belize

1983. Commonwealth Day. Multicoloured.
731 35c. Type **134** 35 35
732 50c. "Maya Stella" from Lamanai Indian church (horiz) 40 50
733 85c. Supreme Court Building (horiz) 50 75
734 $2 University Centre, Belize (horiz) . . . . 85 2·25

1983. No. 658 surch **10c.**
735 10c. on 35c. Map of Belize

136 De Lana-Terzis "Aerial Ship", 1670

1983. Bicentenary of Manned Flight. Multicoloured.
736 10c. Type **136** . . . . 2·50 65
737 25c. De Gusmao's "La Passarole", 1709 . . . . . 3·25 70
738 50c. Guyton de Morveau's balloon with oars, 1784 . . 3·50 1·00
739 85c. Airship . . . . 4·25 1·25
740 $1 Airship "Clement Bayard" 4·50 1·60
741 $1.50 Beardmore airship R-34 5·00 3·25
MS742 Two sheets: (a) 125 × 84 mm. $3 Charles Green's balloon "Royal Vauxhall"; (b) 115 × 128 mm. $3 Montgolfier balloon, 1783 (vert) Set of 2 sheets 25·00 6·00

1983. Nos. 662 and 699 surch **$1.25**.
743 $1.25 on $2 Keel-billed toucan . . . . 11·00 10·00
744 $1.25 on $2 Sergeant major 6·00 8·00

1983. No. 541 surch **10c.**
746 10c. on 35c. Glory of the Atlantic cone . . . . . . 35·00

141 Altun Ha

1983. Maya Monuments. Multicoloured.
747 10c. Type **141** 10 10
748 15c. Xunantunich 10 10
749 75c. Cerros 30 40
750 $3 Lamanal . . . . 70 1·25
MS751 102 × 72 mm. $3 Xunantunich (different) 1·00 1·75

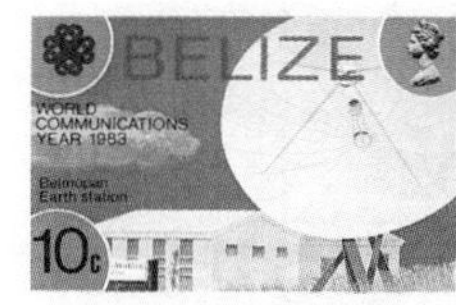

142 Belmopan Earth Station

1983. World Communications Year. Multicoloured.
752 10c. Type **142** 30 10
753 15c. "Telstar 2" 40 25
754 75c. U.P.U. logo . . . . . . 70 1·75
755 $2 M.V. "Heron H" mail service . . . . 1·25 4·50

143 Jaguar Cub

1983. The Jaguar. Multicoloured.
756 5c. Type **143** 30 75
757 10c. Adult jaguar 35 45
758 85c. Jaguar in river . . . . . 1·75 3·00
759 $1 Jaguar on rock . . . . . 2·00 3·25
MS760 102 × 72 mm. $3 Jaguar in tree (44 × 28 mm). P 13½ × 14 1·50 2·50

144 Pope John Paul II

1983. Christmas.
761 **144** 10c. multicoloured 25 10
762 15c. multicoloured 25 10
763 75c. multicoloured 50 60
764 $2 multicoloured . . . . 80 1·40
MS765 102 × 72 mm. $3 multi 1·50 3·75

145 Four-eyed Butterflyfish

1984. Marine Life from the Belize Coral Reef. Multicoloured.
766 1c. Type **145** . . . . 15 1·00
767 2c. Cushion star 20 80
768 3c. Flower coral 25 80
769 4c. Royal gramma ("Fairy basslet") 25 80
770 5c. Spanish hogfish 30 80
771 6c. Star-eyed hermit crab . . 30 1·00
772a 10c. Sea fans and fire sponge 35 35
773a 15c. Blue-headed wrasse . . 50 60
774a 25c. Blue-striped grunt . . . 70 80
775a 50c. Coral crab . . . . . . 1·00 1·75
776a 60c. Tube sponge . . . . . 1·00 1·75
777 75c. Brain coral . . . . . . 1·00 1·50
778 $1 Yellow-tailed snapper . . 1·00 1·25
779 $2 Common lettuce slug . . 1·25 65
780 $5 Three-spotted damselfish 1·50 80
781 $10 Rock beauty . . . . . 2·00 1·40

1984. Visit of the Archbishop of Canterbury. Nos. 772 and 775 optd **VISIT OF THE LORD ARCHBISHOP OF CANTERBURY 8th-11th MARCH 1984**.
782 10c. Sea fans and fire sponge 1·00 50
783 50c. Coral crab . . . . . . 1·75 1·75

147 Shooting

1984. Olympic Games, Los Angeles. Multicoloured. (a) As T **147**.
784 25c. Type **147** 30 25
785 75c. Boxing 50 70
786 $1 Marathon 60 90
787 $2 Cycling . . . . 2·50 2·50
MS788 101 × 72 mm. $3 Statue of discus thrower 1·60 2·75

(b) Similar designs to T **147** but Royal cypher replaced by Queen's Head.
789 5c. Marathon 20 80
790 20c. Sprinting 25 80
791 25c. Shot-putting 25 80
792 $2 Olympic torch . . . . . 35 1·10

148 British Honduras 1866 1s. Stamp

1984. "Ausipex" International Stamp Exhibition, Melbourne. Multicoloured.
793 15c. Type **148** 25 15
794 30c. British mail coach, 1784 35 25
795 65c. Sir Rowland Hill and Penny Black 65 65
796 75c. British Honduras railway locomotive, 1910 . . . . . 70 75
797 $2 Royal Exhibition Buildings, Melbourne (46 × 28 mm) . . . . . . 1·00 2·00
MS798 103 × 73 mm. $3 Australia 1932 Sydney Harbour Bridge 5s. and British Honduras 1866 1s. stamps (44 × 28 mm). P 13½ × 14 1·10 2·00

149 Prince Albert

150 White-fronted Amazon ("White-fronted Parrot")

1984. 500th Anniv (1985) of British Royal House of Tudor. Multicoloured.
799 50c. Type **149** 25 35
800 50c. Queen Victoria 25 35
801 75c. King George VI 30 45
802 75c. Queen Elizabeth the Queen Mother 30 45
803 $1 Princess of Wales 40 70
804 $1 Prince of Wales 40 70
MS805 147 × 97 mm. $1.50, Prince Philip; $1.50, Queen Elizabeth II 1·25 2·00

1984. Parrots. Multicoloured.
806 $1 Type **150** . . . . 1·75 2·00
807 $1 White-capped parrot (horiz) . . . . 1·75 2·00
808 $1 Mealy amazon ("Mealy Parrot") (horiz) . . . . 1·75 2·00
809 $1 Red-lored amazon ("Red-lored Parrot") . . . . . . 1·75 2·00
MS810 102 × 73 mm. $3 Scarlet macaw 3·25 3·75

Nos. 806/9 were issued together, se-tenant, forming a composite design.

151 Effigy Censer, 1450 (Santa Rita Site)

153 White-tailed Kite

152 Governor-General inspecting Girl Guides

1984. Maya Artefacts. Multicoloured.
811 25c. Type **151** 30 25
812 75c. Vase, 675 (Actun Chapat) 60 80
813 $1 Tripod vase, 500 (Santa Rita site) . . . . 65 1·00
814 $2 Sun god Kinich Ahau, 600 (Altun Ha site) . . . . . 90 2·50

1985. International Youth Year and 75th Anniv of Girl Guides Movement. Multicoloured.
815 25c. Type **152** 30 15
816 50c. Girl Guides camping . . 45 30
817 90c. Checking map on hike 60 45
818 $1.25 Students in laboratory 70 60
819 $2 Lady Baden-Powell (founder) 90 75

1985. Birth Bicentenary of John J. Audubon (ornithologist). Designs showing original paintings. Multicoloured.
820 10c. Type **153** 50 60
821 15c. Ruby-crowned kinglet ("Cuvier's Kinglet") (horiz) 50 60
822 25c. Painted bunting 60 60
822a 60c. As 25c. . . . . 18·00 8·50
823 75c. Belted kingfisher . . . 60 1·40
824 $1 Common cardinal ("Northern Cardinal") . . 60 2·25
825 $3 Long-billed curlew (horiz) . . . . 1·00 3·00
MS826 139 × 99 mm. $5 "John James Audubon" (John Syme) 2·50 2·00

154 The Queen Mother with Princess Elizabeth, 1928

1985. Life and Times of Queen Elizabeth the Queen Mother. Multicoloured.
827 10c. Type **154** 10 10
828 15c. The Queen Mother, 1980 10 10
829 75c. Waving to the crowd, 1982 . . . . 40 40
830 $5 Four generations of Royal Family at Prince William's Christening . . . . 1·50 2·75
MS831 Two sheets, each 138 × 98 mm. (a) $2 The Queen Mother with Prince Henry (from photo by Lord Snowdon) (38 × 50 mm): (b) $5 The Queen Mother, 1984 (38 × 50 mm) Set of 2 sheets 3·75 4·50

1985. Inauguration of New Government. Nos. 772/3 and 775 optd **INAUGURATION OF NEW GOVERNMENT – 21st. DECEMBER 1984.**
832 10c. Sea fans and fire sponge 1·25 60
833 15c. Blue-headed wrasse . . . 1·25 60
834 50c. Coral crab . . . . . . 1·75 3·25

156 British Honduras 1935 Silver Jubilee 25c. stamp and King George V with Queen Mary in Carriage (½-size illustration)

1985. 50th Anniv of First Commonwealth Omnibus Issue. Designs showing British Honduras/Belize stamps. Multicoloured.
835 50c. Type **156** 40 70
836 50c. 1937 Coronation 3c., and King George VI and Queen Elizabeth in Coronation robes 40 70
837 50c. 1946 Victory 3c. and Victory celebrations . . . 40 70
838 50c. 1948 Royal Silver Wedding 4c. and King George VI and Queen Elizabeth at Westminster Abbey service 40 70
839 50c. 1953 Coronation 4c. and Queen Elizabeth II in Coronation robes 40 70
840 50c. 1966 Churchill 25c., Sir Winston Churchill and fighter aircraft 40 70
841 50c. 1972 Royal Silver Wedding 50c. and 1948 Wedding photograph . . . 40 70
842 50c. 1973 Royal Wedding 50c. and Princess Anne and Capt. Mark Phillips at their Wedding 40 70
843 50c. 1977 Silver Jubilee $2 and Queen Elizabeth II during tour 40 70
844 50c. 1978 25th anniversary of Coronation 75c. and Imperial Crown 40 70
MS845 138 × 98 mm. $5 Queen Elizabeth in Coronation robes (38 × 50 mm) 4·00 4·00

157 Mounted Postboy and Early Letter to Belize

1985. 350th Anniv of British Post Office. Mult.
846 10c. Type **157** 40 25
847 15c. "Hinchinbrook II" (sailing packet) engaging "Grand Turk" (American privateer) 55 25
848 25c. "Duke of Marlborough II" (sailing packet) 70 30
849 75c. "Diana" (packet) . . . 1·25 1·50
850 $1 Falmouth packet ship . . 1·25 1·75
851 $3 "Conway" (mail paddle-steamer) . . . . 2·25 5·00

1985. Commonwealth Heads of Government Meeting, Nassau, Bahamas. Nos. 827/30 optd **COMMONWEALTH SUMMIT CONFERENCE, BAHAMAS 16th-22nd OCTOBER 1985.**
852 10c. Type **154** 30 30
853 15c. The Queen Mother, 1980 40 35
854 75c. Waving to the crowd, 1982 . . . . 80 80
855 $4 Four generations of Royal Family at Prince William's christening . . . . 2·00 3·75
MS856 Two sheets, each 138 × 98 mm. (a) $2 The Queen Mother with Prince Henry (from photo by Lord Snowdon) (38 × 50 mm): (b) $5 The Queen Mother, 1984 (38 × 50 mm) Set of 2 sheets 2·75 3·50

1985. 80th Anniv of Rotary International. Nos. 815/19 optd **80TH ANNIVERSARY OF ROTARY INTERNATIONAL.**
857 25c. Type **152** 60 40
858 50c. Girl Guides camping . . 1·00 75
859 90c. Checking map on hike 1·50 1·75
860 $1.25 Students in laboratory 2·00 2·50
861 $2 Lady Baden-Powell (founder) . . . . 2·50 3·25

160 Royal Standard and Belize Flag

1985. Royal Visit. Multicoloured.
862 25c. Type **160** 80 95
863 75c. Queen Elizabeth II . . . 1·25 2·00
864 $4 Royal Yacht "Britannia" (81 × 39 mm) . . . . . . 3·75 3·75
MS865 138 × 98 mm. $5 Queen Elizabeth II (38 × 50 mm). 4·25 4·75

161 Mountie in Canoe (Canada)

1985. Christmas. 30th Anniv of Disneyland, U.S.A. Designs showing dolls from "It's a Small World" exhibition. Multicoloured.
866 1c. Type **161** 10 15
867 2c. Indian chief and squaw (U.S.A.) 10 15
868 3c. Incas climbing Andes (South America) 10 15
869 4c. Africans beating drums (Africa) 10 15
870 5c. Snake-charmer and dancer (India and Far East) 10 15
871 6c. Boy and girl with donkey (Belize) 10 15
872 50c. Musician and dancer (Balkans) . . . . 1·50 1·50
873 $1.50 Boys with camel (Egypt and Saudi Arabia) . . . . 2·50 3·25
874 $3 Woman and girls playing with kite (Japan) . . . . . 3·25 4·50
MS875 127 × 102 mm. $4 Beefeater and castle (Great Britain). P 13½ × 14 4·75 7·00

1985. World Cup Football Championship, Mexico (1986) (1st issue). Nos. 835/44 optd **PRE "WORLD CUP FOOTBALL" MEXICO 1986** and trophy.
876 50c. Type **156** 65 80
877 50c. 1937 Coronation 3c., and King George VI and Queen Elizabeth in Coronation robes 65 80
878 50c. Victory 3c., and Victory celebrations 65 80
879 50c. 1948 Royal Silver Wedding 4c., and King George VI and Queen Elizabeth at Westminster Abbey service 65 80
880 50c. 1953 Coronation 4c., and Queen Elizabeth II in Coronation robes 65 80
881 50c. 1966 Churchill 25c., Sir Winston Churchill and fighter aircraft 65 80
882 50c. 1972 Royal Silver Wedding 50c. and 1948 wedding photograph . . . 65 80
883 50c. 1973 Royal Wedding 5c., and Princess Anne and Capt. Mark Phillips at their Wedding 65 80
884 50c. 1977 Silver Jubilee $2 and Queen Elizabeth II during tour 65 80
885 50c. 1978 25th anniv of Coronation 75c. and Imperial Crown 65 80
MS886 138 × 98 mm. $5 Queen Elizabeth II in Coronation robes 4·25 4·25
See also Nos. 936/40.

163 Indian Costume

165 Princess Elizabeth aged Three

164 Pope Pius X

1986. Costumes of Belize. Multicoloured.
887 5c. Type **163** 75 30
888 10c. Maya 80 30
889 15c. Garifuna . . . . 1·00 35
890 25c. Creole . . . . 1·25 35
891 50c. Chinese . . . . 1·75 1·25
892 75c. Lebanese . . . . 2·00 2·00
893 $1 European c. 1900 . . . . 2·00 2·50
894 $2 Latin . . . . 2·75 3·75
MS895 139 × 98 mm. Amerindian (38 × 50 mm.) 6·00 7·00

1986. Easter. 20th-century Popes. Multicoloured.
896 50c. Type **164** . . . . 1·10 1·40
897 50c. Benedict XV . . . . . . 1·10 1·40
898 50c. Pius XI . . . . 1·10 1·40
899 50c. Pius XII . . . . 1·10 1·40
900 50c. John XXIII . . . . . . 1·10 1·40
901 50c. Paul VI . . . . 1·10 1·40
902 50c. John Paul I . . . . . . 1·10 1·40
903 50c. John Paul II . . . . . . 1·10 1·40
MS904 147 × 92 mm. $4 Pope John Paul II preaching (vert). 9·00 9·00

1986. 60th Birthday of Queen Elizabeth II. Mult.
905 25c. Type **165** 30 55
906 50c. Queen wearing Imperial State Crown 50 75
907 75c. At Trooping the Colour 65 85
908 $3 Queen wearing diadem . . 1·25 2·25
MS909 147 × 93 mm. $4 Queen Elizabeth II (37 × 50 mm) 3·00 4·00

166 Halley's Comet and Japanese "Planet A" Spacecraft

1986. Appearance of Halley's Comet. Multicoloured.
910 10c. Type **166** 35 60
911 15c. Halley's Comet, 1910 . . 40 70
912 50c. Comet and European "Giotto" spacecraft 50 80
913 75c. Belize Weather Bureau 70 80
914 $1 Comet and U.S.A. space telescope . . . . 95 1·10
915 $2 Edmond Halley . . . . . 1·50 1·60
MS916 147 × 93 mm. $4 Computer enhanced photograph of Comet (37 × 50 mm) 5·50 7·00

167 George Washington

1986. United States Presidents. Multicoloured.
917 10c. Type **167** 35 60
918 20c. John Adams 35 65
916 30c. Thomas Jefferson . . . 40 70
920 50c. James Madison 50 70
921 $1.50 James Monroe . . . . 80 1·25
922 $2 John Quincy Adams . . . 1·00 1·50
MS923 147 × 93 mm. $4 George Washington (different) 3·50 4·75

168 Auguste Bartholdi (sculptor) and Statue's Head

1986. Centenary of Statue of Liberty. Multicoloured.
924 25c. Type **168** 40 65
925 50c. Statue's head at U.S. Centennial Celebration, Philadelphia, 1876 . . . . 55 85
926 75c. Unveiling ceremony, 1886 . . . . 55 90
927 $4 Statue of Liberty and flags of Belize and U.S.A. . . . 1·00 2·00
MS928 147 × 92 mm. $4 Statue of Liberty and New York skyline (37 × 50 mm.) 3·75 5·00

169 British Honduras 1866 1s. Stamp

1986. "Ameripex" International Stamp Exhibition, Chicago. Multicoloured.
929 10c. Type **169** 40 55
930 15c. 1981 Royal Wedding $1.50 stamps 55 75
931 50c. U.S.A. 1918 24c. airmail inverted centre error . . . 75 80
932 75c. U.S.S. "Constitution" (frigate) . . . . 75 1·10
933 $1 Liberty Bell . . . . . . 80 1·40
934 $2 White House . . . . . . 90 1·60
MS935 147 × 93 mm. $4 Capitol, Washington (37 × 50 mm) 3·25 4·00

170 English and Brazilian Players

1986. World Cup Football Championship, Mexico (2nd issue). Multicoloured.
936 25c. Type **170** . . . . 1·50 1·75
937 50c. Mexican player and Maya statues . . . . . . 1·75 2·00
938 75c. Two Belizean players . . 2·00 2·25
939 $3 Aztec stone calendar . . . 2·25 2·50
MS940 147 × 92 mm. $4 Flags of competing nations on two footballs (37 × 50 mm) 6·00 8·00

171 Miss Sarah Ferguson

1986. Royal Wedding. Multicoloured.
941 25c. Type **171** 65 40
942 75c. Prince Andrew . . . . . 1·00 90
943 $3 Prince Andrew and Miss Sarah Ferguson (92 × 41 mm) . . . . . . 1·75 2·75
MS944 155 × 106 mm. $1 Miss Sarah Ferguson (different). $3 Prince Andrew (different) 4·00 6·00

1986. World Cup Football Championship Winners, Mexico. Nos. 936/9 optd **ARGENTINA – WINNERS 1986.**
945 25c. Type **170** . . . . 1·50 1·75
946 50c. Mexican player and Maya statues . . . . . . 1·75 2·00
947 75c. Two Belizean players . . 2·00 2·25
948 $3 Aztec stone calendar . . . 3·00 3·25
MS949 147 × 92 mm. $4 Flags of competing nations on two footballs (37 × 50 mm) 6·50 8·50

1986. "Stockholmia '86" International Stamp Exhibition, Sweden. Nos. 929/34 optd **STOCKHOLMIA 86** and emblem.
950 10c. Type **169** 50 70
951 15c. 1981 Royal Wedding $1.50 stamp 65 85
952 50c. U.S.A. 1918 24c. airmail inverted centre error . . . 80 1·00

953 75c. U.S.S. "Constitution" 1·00 1·40
954 $1 Liberty Bell 1·25 1·50
955 $2 White House 1·60 1·75
MS956 147 × 93 mm. $4 Capitol, Washington (37 × 50 mm) 5·00 7·00

174 Amerindian Girl

1986. International Peace Year. Multicoloured.
957 25c. Type **174** 55 75
958 50c. European boy and girl 70 1·00
959 75c. Japanese girl 90 1·50
960 $3 Indian boy and European girl 1·50 2·50
MS961 132 × 106 mm. $4 As 25c. but vert (35 × 47 mm) 4·25 5·50

175 "Amanita lilloi" 176 Jose Carioca

1986. Fungi and Toucans. Multicoloured.
962 5c. Type **175** 1·25 1·00
963 10c. Keel-billed toucan 1·60 1·40
964 20c. "Boletellus cubensis" 1·75 1·50
965 25c. Collared aracari 1·75 1·50
966 75c. "Psilocybe caerulescens" 2·00 1·75
967 $1 Emerald toucanet 2·00 1·75
968 $1.25 Crimson-rumped toucanet ("Crimson-rumped Toucan") 2·25 2·00
969 $2 "Russula puiggarii" 2·25 2·25

1986. Christmas. Designs showing Walt Disney cartoon characters in scenes from "Saludos Amigos". Multicoloured.
970 2c. Type **176** 20 20
971 3c. Jose Carioca, Panchito and Donald Duck 20 20
972 4c. Daisy Duck as Rio Carnival dancer 20 20
973 5c. Mickey and Minnie Mouse as musician and dancer 20 20
974 6c. Jose Carioca using umbrella as flute 20 20
975 50c. Donald Duck and Panchito 1·00 1·75
976 65c. Joe Carioca and Donald Duck playing hide and seek 1·25 2·00
977 $1.35 Donald Duck playing maracas 2·00 3·00
978 $2 Goofy as matador 2·75 3·50
MS979 131 × 111 mm. $4 Donald Duck 7·00 9·00

177 Princess Elizabeth in Wedding Dress, 1947 179 "Mother and Child"

178 "America II", 1983

1987. Royal Ruby Wedding. Multicoloured.
980 25c. Type **177** 25 20
981 75c. Queen and Duke of Edinburgh, 1972 45 50
982 $1 Queen on her 60th birthday 50 60
983 $4 In Garter robes 1·00 2·00
MS984 171 × 112 mm. $6 Queen and Duke of Edinburgh (44 × 50 mm) 5·50 7·00

1987. America's Cup Yachting Championship. Multicoloured.
985 25c. Type **178** 30 25
986 75c. "Stars and Stripes", 1987 40 50
987 $1 "Australia II", 1983 50 60
988 $4 "White Crusader" 1·00 2·00
MS989 171 × 112 mm. $6 Sails of "Australia II" (44 × 50 mm) 4·50 7·00

1987. Wood Carvings by George Gabb. Mult.
990 25c. Type **179** 15 25
991 75c. "Standing Form" 35 50
992 $1 "Love-doves" 40 60
993 $4 "Depiction of Music" 1·10 2·00
MS994 173 × 114 mm. $6 "African Heritage" (44 × 50 mm) 3·50 5·50

180 Black-handed Spider Monkey

1987. Primates. Multicoloured.
995 25c. Type **180** 25 20
996 75c. Black howler monkey 40 55
997 $1 Spider monkeys with baby 45 65
998 $4 Two black howler monkeys 1·10 2·25
MS999 171 × 112 mm. $6 Young spider monkey (44 × 50 mm) 4·50 6·50

181 Guides on Parade

1987. 50th Anniv of Girl Guide Movement in Belize. Multicoloured.
1000 25c. Type **181** 45 20
1001 75c. Brownie camp 80 1·00
1002 $1 Guide camp 1·00 1·25
1003 $4 Olave, Lady Baden-Powell 3·00 5·00
MS1004 173 × 114 mm. $6 As $4 but vert (44 × 50 mm) 4·00 6·50

182 Indian Refugee Camp

1987. Int Year of Shelter for the Homeless. Mult.
1005 25c. Type **182** 50 25
1006 75c. Filipino family and slum 90 90
1007 $1 Family in Middle East shanty town 1·00 1·25
1008 $4 Building modern house in Belize 2·00 4·50

183 "Laelia euspatha"

1987. Christmas. Orchids. Illustrations from Sander's "Reichenbachia". Multicoloured.
1009 1c. Type **183** 85 85
1010 2c. "Cattleya citrina" 85 85
1011 3c. "Masdevallia backhousiana" 85 85
1012 4c. "Cypripedium tautzianum" 85 85
1013 5c. "Trichopilia suavis alba" 85 85
1014 6c. "Odontoglossum hebraicum" 85 85
1015 7c. "Cattleya trianaei schroederiana" 85 85
1016 10c. "Saccolabium giganteum" 85 85
1017 30c. "Cattleya warscewiczii" 1·00 1·00
1018 50c. "Chysis bractescens" 1·40 1·40
1019 70c. "Cattleya rochellensis" 1·60 1·60
1020 $1 "Laellia elegans schilleriana" 1·75 1·75
1021 $1.50 "Laelia anceps percivaliana" 1·90 1·90
1022 $3 "Laelia gouldiana" 2·50 2·50
MS1023 Two sheets, each 171 × 112 mm. (a) $3 "Odontoglossum roezlii" (40 × 47 mm). (b) $5 "Cattleya dowiana aurea" (40 × 47 mm) Set of 2 sheets 10·00 11·00

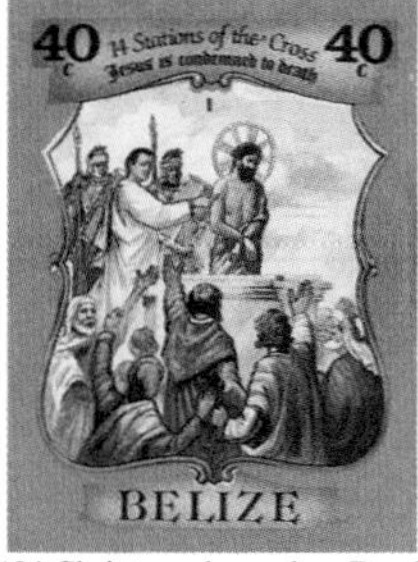

184 Christ condemned to Death

1988. Easter. The Stations of the Cross. Mult.
1024 40c. Type **184** 30 50
1025 40c. Christ carrying the Cross 30 50
1026 40c. Falling for the first time 30 50
1027 40c. Christ meets Mary 30 50
1028 40c. Simon of Cyrene helping to carry the Cross 30 50
1029 40c. Veronica wiping the face of Christ 30 50
1030 40c. Christ falling a second time 30 50
1031 40c. Consoling the women of Jerusalem 30 50
1032 40c. Falling for the third time 30 50
1033 40c. Christ being stripped 30 50
1034 40c. Christ nailed to the Cross 30 50
1035 40c. Dying on the Cross 30 50
1036 40c. Christ taken down from the Cross 30 50
1037 40c. Christ being laid in the sepulchre 30 50

185 Basketball

1988. Olympic Games, Seoul. Multicoloured.
1038 10c. Type **185** 1·75 55
1039 25c. Volleyball 1·00 30
1040 60c. Table tennis 1·00 60
1041 75c. Diving 1·00 70
1042 $1 Judo 1·10 1·00
1043 $2 Hockey 4·75 4·00
MS1044 76 × 106 mm. $3 Gymnastics 4·00 5·00

186 Public Health Nurse, c. 1912

1988. 125th Anniv of Int Red Cross. Mult.
1045 60c. Type **186** 2·50 1·25
1046 75c. "Aleda E. Lutz" (hospital ship) and ambulance launch, 1937 2·75 1·50
1047 $1 Ambulance at hospital tent, 1956 3·25 1·75
1048 $2 Auster ambulance plane, 1940 4·00 4·75

187 Collared Anteater ("Ants Bear")

1989. Small Animals of Belize. Multicoloured.
1049 10c. Paca ("Gibnut") 2·00 2·00
1050 25c. Four-eyed opossum (vert) 2·00 1·50
1051 50c. Type **187** 2·50 2·00
1052 60c. As 10c. 2·50 2·25
1053 75c. Red brocket 2·50 2·25
1054 $1 Collared peccary 4·00 6·00

1989. 20th Anniv of First Manned Landing on Moon. As T **126** of Ascension. Multicoloured.
1055 25c. Docking of "Apollo 9" modules 1·25 30
1056 50c. "Apollo 9" command service module in Space (30 × 30 mm) 1·75 75
1057 75c. "Apollo 9" emblem (30 × 30 mm) 2·00 1·25
1058 $1 "Apollo 9" lunar module in space 2·25 1·75
MS1059 83 × 100 mm. $5 "Apollo II" command service module undergoing test 8·00 8·50

1989. No. 771 surch **5c**.
1060 5c. on 6c. Star-eyed hermit crab 7·00 2·00

1989. "World Stamp Expo '89" International Stamp Exhibition, Washington. No. **MS**1059 optd **WORLD STAMP EXPO '89, United States Postal Service Nov 17—20 and Nov 24—Dec 3. 1989 Washington Convention Center Washington, DC** and emblem.
MS1061 83 × 100 mm. $5 "Apollo II" command service module undergoing tests 7·50 8·50

190 Wesley Church 191 White-winged Tanager and "Catonephele numilia"

1989. Christmas. Belize Churches.
1062 **190** 10c. black, pink and brown 20 10
1063 – 25c. black, lilac and mauve 25 20
1064 – 60c. black, turq & bl 50 70
1065 – 75c. black, grn & lt grn 65 90
1066 – $1 black, lt yell & yell 80 1·25
DESIGNS: 25c. Baptist Church; 60c. St. John's Anglican Cathedral; 75c. St. Andrew's Presbyterian Church; $1 Holy Redeemer Roman Catholic Cathedral.

1990. Birds and Butterflies. Multicoloured.
1067A 5c. Type **191** 60 60
1068B 10c. Keel-billed toucan and "Nessaea aglaura" 80 70
1069A 15c. Magnificent frigate bird and "Eurytides philolaus" 80 40
1070A 25c. Jabiru and "Heliconius sapho" 80 40
1071A 30c. Great blue heron and "Colobura dirce" 80 50
1072A 50c. Northern oriole and "Hamadryas arethusia" 1·00 60
1073A 60c. Scarlet macaw and "Evenus regalis" 1·25 70
1074A 75c. Red-legged honey-creeper and "Callicore patelina" 1·25 75
1075A $1 Spectacled owl and "Caligo uranus" 2·25 1·60
1076A $2 Green jay and "Philaethria dido" 2·75 3·50
1077A $5 Turkey vulture and "Battus belus" 4·50 6·00
1078A $10 Osprey and "Papilio thoas" 8·50 10·00

1990. First Belize Dollar Coin. No. 1075 optd **FIRST DOLLAR COIN 1990**.
1079 $1 Spectacled owl and "Caligo uranus" 4·25 2·75

193 Green Turtle

1990. Turtles. Multicoloured.
1080 10c. Type **193** 65 40
1081 25c. Hawksbill turtle 1·00 40
1082 60c. Saltwater loggerhead turtle 1·50 1·50
1083 75c. Freshwater loggerhead turtle 1·60 1·60
1084 $1 Bocatora turtle 2·00 2·00
1085 $2 Hicatee turtle 2·75 5·00

194 Fairey Battle

1990. 50th Anniv of the Battle of Britain. Multicoloured.
1086 10c. Type **194** 80 50
1087 25c. Bristol Type 152 Beaufort . . . . 1·40 50
1088 60c. Bristol Type 142 Blenheim Mk IV . . . . 2·00 2·00
1089 75c. Armstrong-Whitworth Whitley . . . . 2·00 2·00
1090 $1 Vickers-Armstrong Wellington Mk 1c . . . . 2·00 2·00
1091 $1 Handley Page Hampden 2·50 3·50

195 "Cattleya bowringiana"

1990. Christmas. Orchids. Multicoloured.
1092 25c. Type **195** 85 20
1093 50c. "Rhyncholaelia digbyana" . . . . 1·25 50
1094 60c. "Sobralia macrantha" 1·50 1·00
1095 75c. "Chysis bractescens" 1·50 1·00
1096 $1 "Vanilla planifolia" . . . 1·75 1·75
1097 $2 "Epidendrum polyanthum" . . . . . . 2·50 4·00

196 Common Iguana

1991. Reptiles and Mammals. Multicoloured.
1098 25c. Type **196** 80 35
1099 50c. Morelet's crocodile . . 1·25 90
1100 60c. American manatee . . 1·50 1·50
1101 75c. Boa constrictor . . . . 1·75 1·75
1102 $1 Baird's tapir . . . . . . 2·00 2·00
1103 $2 Jaguar . . . . 2·75 3·75

1991. 65th Birthday of Queen Elizabeth II and 70th Birthday of Prince Philip. As T **139** of Ascension. Multicoloured.
1104 $1 Queen Elizabeth II wearing tiara . . . . . . 1·00 1·40
1105 $1 Prince Philip wearing panama . . . . 1·00 1·40

197 Weather Radar

1991. International Decade for Natural Disaster Reduction.
1106 **197** 60c. multicoloured . . . 1·50 1·25
1107 – 75c. multicoloured . . . 1·60 1·40
1108 – $1 blue and black . . . 1·75 1·75
1109 – $2 multicoloured . . . . 2·50 3·25
DESIGNS: 75c. Weather station; $1 Floods in Belize after Hurricane Hattie, 1961; $2 Satellite image of Hurricane Gilbert.

198 Thomas Ramos and Demonstration

1991. 10th Anniv of Independence. Famous Belizeans (1st series). Multicoloured.
1110 25c. Type **198** 60 30
1111 60c. Sir Isaiah Morter and palm trees . . . . 1·25 1·50
1112 75c. Antonio Soberanis and political meeting . . . . 1·25 1·75
1113 $1 Santiago Ricalde and cutting sugar-cane . . . . 1·50 2·00
See also Nos. 1126/9 and 1148/51.

199 "Anansi the Spider"

1991. Christmas. Folklore. Multicoloured.
1114 25c. Type **199** . . . . . . 1·00 20
1115 60c. "Jack-o-Lantern" . . . 1·50 55
1116 60c. "Tata Duende" (vert) 1·75 1·25
1117 75c. "Xtabai" . . . . . . 1·75 1·25
1118 $1 "Warrie Massa" (vert) 2·00 1·75
1119 $2 "Old Heg" . . . . . . 3·00 5·50

200 "Gongora quinquenervis"

1992. Easter. Orchids. Multicoloured.
1120 25c. Type **200** 90 20
1121 50c. "Oncidium sphacelatum" . . . . . . 1·50 75
1122 60c. "Encyclia bratescens" 1·75 1·75
1123 75c. "Epidendrum ciliare" 1·75 1·75
1124 $1 "Psygmorchis pusilla" . . 2·00 2·25
1125 $2 "Galeandra batemanii" 2·75 4·50

1992. Famous Belizeans (2nd series). As T **198**, but inscr "EMINENT BELIZEANS" at top. Multicoloured.
1126 25c. Gwendolyn Lizarraga (politician) and High School 75 30
1127 60c. Rafael Fonseca (civil servant) and Government Offices, Belize . . . . . . 1·50 1·50
1128 75c. Vivian Seay (health worker) and nurses . . . 1·75 1·75
1129 $1 Samuel Haynes (U.N.I.A. worker) and words of National Anthem . . . . 2·00 2·25

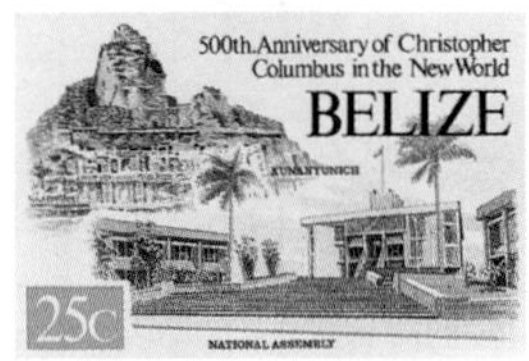

201 Xunantunich and National Assembly

1992. 500th Anniv of Discovery of America by Columbus. Mayan sites and modern buildings. Multicoloured.
1130 25c. Type **201** . . . . . . 1·00 25
1131 60c. Altun Ha and Supreme Court . . . . 1·50 1·00
1132 75c. Santa Rita and Tower Hill Sugar Factory . . . 1·60 1·25
1133 $5 Lamanai and Citrus Company works . . . . 8·00 11·00

202 Hashishi Pampi

1992. Christmas. Folklore. Multicoloured.
1134 25c. Type **202** 30 20
1135 60c. Cadejo 60 60
1136 $1 La Sucia (vert) . . . . . 90 1·00
1137 $5 Sisimito . . . . 4·00 6·50

1993. 75th Anniv of Royal Air Force. As T **149** of Ascension. Multicoloured.
1138 25c. Sud Aviation SA 330L Puma helicopter . . . . . 1·00 60
1139 50c. Hawker Siddeley Harrier GR3 . . . . . . 1·25 80
1140 60c. De Havilland DH98 Mosquito Mk XVIII . . 1·40 1·10
1141 75c. Avro Type 683 Lancaster . . . . 1·40 1·10
1142 $1 Consolidated Liberator I 1·60 1·40
1143 $3 Short Stirling Mk I . . . 3·25 5·50

203 "Lycaste aromatica"

1993. 14th World Orchid Conference, Glasgow. Multicoloured.
1144 25c. Type **203** 40 25
1145 60c. "Sobralia decora" . . . 75 80
1146 $1 "Maxillaria alba" . . . 1·00 1·10
1147 $2 "Brassavola nodosa" . . 1·75 2·75

1993. Famous Belizeans (3rd series). As T **198**, but inscr "EMINENT BELIZEANS" at top. Multicoloured.
1148 25c. Herbert Watkin Beaumont, Post Office and postmark 40 25
1149 60c. Dr. Selvyn Walford Young and score of National Anthem 75 85
1150 75c. Cleopatra White and health centre . . . . . . 90 1·25
1151 $1 Dr. Karl Heusner and early car . . . . 1·10 1·40

204 Boom and Chime Band

1993. Christmas. Local Customs. Mult.
1152 25c. Type **204** 60 20
1153 60c. John Canoe dance . . 1·25 75
1154 75c. Cortez dance . . . . . 1·25 80
1155 $2 Maya musical group . . 3·25 5·00

1994. "Hong Kong '94" International Stamp Exhibition. No. 1075 optd **HONG KONG '94** and emblem.
1156 $1 Spectacled owl and "Caligo uranus" . . . . 2·50 2·25

1994. Royal Visit. As T **202** of Bahamas. Mult.
1157 25c. Flags of Belize and Great Britain . . . . . . 1·00 35
1158 60c. Queen Elizabeth II in yellow coat and hat . . . 1·50 85
1159 75c. Queen Elizabeth in evening dress . . . . . . 1·75 1·00
1160 $1 Queen Elizabeth, Prince Philip and Yeomen of the Guard . . . . 2·00 1·75

205 "Lonchorhina aurita" (bat)

1994. Bats. Multicoloured.
1161 25c. Type **205** 35 20
1162 60c. "Vampyrodes caraccioli" 65 65
1163 75c. "Noctilio leporinus" . . 80 80
1164 $2 "Desmodus rotundus" 2·00 3·25

1994. 75th Anniv of I.L.O. No. 1074 surch **10c** and anniversary emblem.
1165 10c. on 75c. multicoloured 1·25 1·00

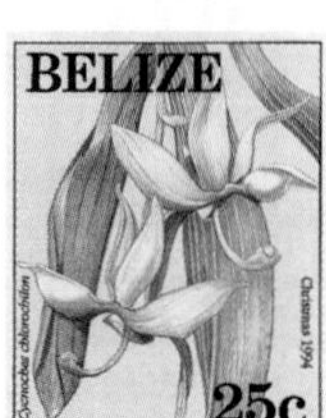

207 "Cycnoches chlorochilon"

1994. Christmas. Orchids. Multicoloured.
1166 25c. Type **207** 45 20
1167 60c. "Brassavola cucullata" 75 70
1168 75c. "Sobralia mucronata" 90 70
1169 $1 "Nidema boothii" . . . 1·10 1·25

208 Ground Beetle (**209**)

1995. Insects. Multicoloured.
1170A 5c. Type **208** 30 50
1171A 10c. Harlequin beetle . . . 30 50
1172A 15c. Giant water bug . . . 40 60
1173A 25c. Peanut-head bug . . 50 20
1174A 30c. Coconut weevil . . . 55 25
1175A 50c. Mantis 70 40
1176B 60c. Tarantula wasp . . . 80 50
1177B 75c. Rhinoceros beetle . . 85 60
1178B $1 Metallic wood borer . . 1·00 90
1179B $2 Dobson fly . . . . . . 2·50 3·00
1180B $5 Click beetle . . . . . 4·25 5·00
1181B $10 Long-horned beetle 7·00 8·50

1995. 50th Anniv of End of Second World War. As T **161** of Ascension. Multicoloured.
1182 25c. War memorial 30 25
1183 60c. Remembrance Day parade 75 80
1184 75c. British Honduras forestry unit . . . . . . 90 1·00
1185 $1 Vickers-Armstrong Wellington bomber . . . 1·10 1·40

1995. "Singapore '95" International Stamp Exhibition. Nos. 1166/9 optd with T **209**.
1186 25c. Type **207** 60 30
1187 60c. "Brassavola cucullata" 1·00 90
1188 75c. "Sobralia mucronata" 1·25 1·10
1189 $1 "Nidema boothii" . . . 1·50 1·75

1995. 50th Anniv of United Nations. As T **213** of Bahamas. Multicoloured.
1190 25c. M113-light reconnaisance vehicle . . 25 20
1191 60c. Sultan armoured command vehicle 60 65
1192 75c. Leyland-Daf 8 × 4 drop truck 75 80
1193 $2 Warrior infantry combat vehicle . . . . 1·50 2·50

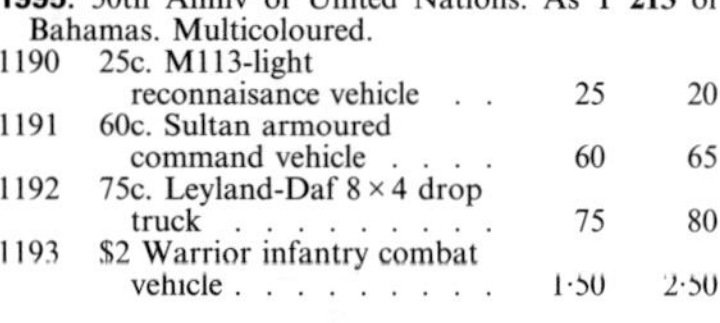

210 Male and Female Blue Ground Dove

1995. Christmas. Doves. Multicoloured.
1194 25c. Type **210** 35 20
1195 60c. White-fronted doves . . 70 70
1196 75c. Pair of ruddy ground doves 85 90
1197 $1 White-winged doves . . . 1·25 1·25

1996. "CHINA '96" 9th Asian International Stamp Exhibition, Peking. Nos. 1172, 1174/5 and 1179 optd **'96 CHINA** and emblem.
1198 15c. Giant water bug . . . 15 15
1199 30c. Coconut weevil 30 30
1200 50c. Mantis 45 50
1201 $2 Dobson fly . . . . . . 1·60 2·25

212 Unloading Banana Train, Commerce Bight Pier

1996. "CAPEX '96" International Stamp Exhibition, Toronto. Railways. Multicoloured.
1202 25c. Type **212** 75 30
1203 60c. Locomotive No. 1 Stann Creek station . . . 1·25 80
1204 75c. Locomotive No. 4 pulling mahogany log train . . . . 1·25 90
1205 $3 L.M.S. No. 5602 "British Honduras" locomotive . . 3·00 5·00

213 "Epidendrum stamfordianum"

214 Red Poll

1996. Christmas. Orchids. Multicoloured.
1206 25c. Type **213** 40 20
1207 60c. "Oncidium carthagenense" 70 70
1208 75c. "Oerstedella verrucosa" 80 90
1209 $1 "Coryanthes speciosa" 1·10 1·25

1997. "HONG KONG '97" International Stamp Exhibition. Chinese New Year ("Year of the Ox"). Cattle Breeds. Multicoloured.
1210 25c. Type **214** 60 25
1211 60c. Brahman 95 90
1212 75c. Longhorn 1·25 1·10
1213 $1 Charbray 1·40 1·60

215 Coral Snake

216 Adult Male Howler Monkey

1997. Snakes. Multicoloured.
1214 25c. Type **215** 35 20
1215 60c. Green vine snake 60 60
1216 75c. Yellow-jawed tommygoff 70 70
1217 $1 Speckled racer 85 1·00

1997. Endangered Species. Howler Monkey. Multicoloured.
1218 10c. Type **216** 20 15
1219 25c. Female feeding 30 20
1220 60c. Female with young 60 65
1221 75c. Juvenile monkey feeding 80 95

217 "Maxillaria elatior"

1997. Christmas. Orchids. Multicoloured.
1222 25c. Type **217** 25 20
1223 60c. "Dimmerandra emarginata" 50 50
1224 75c. "Macradenia brassavolae" 60 60
1225 $1 "Ornithocephalus gladiatus" 75 80

1998. Diana, Princess of Wales Commemoration. Sheet, 145 × 70 mm, containing vert designs as T **177** of Ascension. Multicoloured.
MS1226 $1 Wearing floral dress, 1988; $1 In evening dress, 1981; $1 Wearing pearl drop earrings, 1988; $1 Carrying bouquet, 1983 3·00 3·50

218 School Children using the Internet

1998. 50th Anniv of Organization of American States. Multicoloured.
1227 25c. Type **218** 25 20
1228 $1 Map of Central America 1·00 1·10

219 University Arms

1998. 50th Anniv of University of West Indies.
1229 **219** $1 multicoloured 1·00 1·00

220 Baymen Gun Flats

1998. Bicentenary of Battle of St. George's Cay. Multicoloured.
1230 10c. Boat moored at quayside (vert) 30 50
1231 10c. Three sentries and cannon (vert) 30 50
1232 10c. Cannon and rowing boats (vert) 30 50
1233 25c. Type **220** 60 25
1234 60c. Baymen sloops 80 80
1235 75c. British schooners 85 85
1236 $1 H.M.S. "Merlin" (sloop) 1·00 1·00
1237 $2 Spanish flagship 1·75 2·00

221 "Brassia maculata"

222 "Eucharis grandiflora"

1998. Christmas. Orchids. Multicoloured.
1238 25c. Type **221** 35 20
1239 60c. "Encyclia radiata" 50 40
1240 75c. "Stanhopea ecornuta" 50 55
1241 $1 "Isochilus carnosiflorus" 60 80

1999. Easter. Flowers. Multicoloured.
1242 10c. Type **222** 20 10
1243 25c. "Hippeastrum puniceum" 30 20
1244 60c. "Zephyranthes citrina" 50 50
1245 $1 "Hymenocallis littoralis" 60 80

223 Postman on Bicycle

1999. 125th Anniv of U.P.U. Multicoloured.
1246 25c. Type **223** 50 30
1247 60c. Postal truck 65 55
1248 75c. "Dee" (mail ship) 85 80
1249 $1 Modern airliner 1·00 1·25

224 "Holy Family with Jesus and St. John" (School of Rubens)

1999. Christmas. Religious Paintings. Multicoloured.
1250 25c. Type **224** 20 20
1251 60c. "Holy Family with St. John" (unknown artist) 50 45
1252 75c. "Madonna and Child with St. John and Angel" (unknown artist) 55 60
1253 $1 "Madonna with Child and St. John" (Andrea del Salerno) 75 75

225 Iguana

2000. Wildlife. Multicoloured.
1254 5c. Type **225** 10 10
1255 10c. Gibnut 10 10
1256 15c. Howler monkey 10 15
1257 25c. Collared anteater 20 25
1258 30c. Hawksbill turtle 20 25
1259 50c. Red brocket antelope 35 40
1260 60c. Jaguar 40 45
1261 75c. American manatee 55 60
1262 $1 Crocodile 70 75
1263 $2 Baird's tapir 1·40 1·50
1264 $5 Collared peccary 3·50 3·75
1265 $10 Boa constrictor 7·00 7·25

226 Mango

2000. Fruits. Multicoloured.
1266 25c. Type **226** 30 25
1267 60c. Cashew 55 50
1268 75c. Papaya 70 70
1269 $1 Banana 90 1·00

227 Meeting in Battlefield Park and Supreme Court, 1950

2000. 50th Anniv of People's United Party. Mult.
1270 10c. Type **227** 20 15
1271 25c. Voters queuing, 1954 30 25
1272 60c. Legislative Council and Mace, 1964 55 50
1273 75c. National Assembly Building (under construction and completed), Belmopan, 1967–70 70 70
1274 $1 Belizean flag in searchlights, Independence, 1981 1·25 1·40

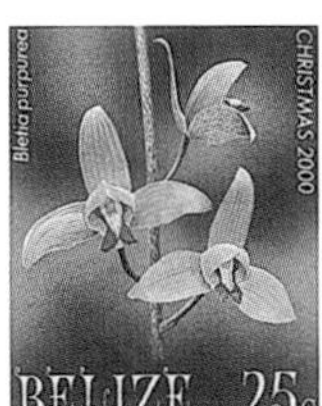

228 *Bletia purpurea*

2000. Christmas. Orchids. Multicoloured
1275 25c. Type **228** 30 25
1276 60c. *Cyrtopodium punctatum* 55 50
1277 75c. *Cycnoches egertonianum* 70 70
1278 $1 *Catasetum integerrimum* 90 1·00

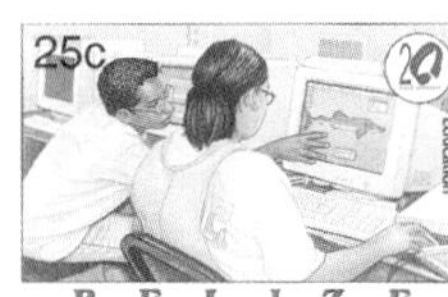

229 Children at Computers

2001. 20th Anniv of Independence. Multicoloured.
1279 25c. Type **229** 30 25
1280 60c. Shrimp farm 50 45
1281 75c. Privassion Cascade (vert) 65 60
1282 $2 Map of Belize (vert) 1·75 2·00

230 *Sobralia fragrans*

2001. Christmas. Orchids. Multicoloured.
1283 25c. Type **230** 30 25
1284 60c. *Encyclia cordigera* 55 50
1285 75c. *Maxillaria fulgens* 70 70
1286 $1 *Epidendrum nocturnum* 90 1·00

2002. Golden Jubilee. As T **200** of Ascension.
1287 25c. black, violet and gold 30 25
1288 60c. multicoloured 55 50
1289 75c. black, violet and gold 70 70
1290 $1 multicoloured 90 1·00
MS1291 162 × 95 mm. Nos. 1287/90 and $5 multicoloured 6·00 6·50
DESIGNS—Horiz: 25c. Princess Elizabeth in pantomime, Windsor, 1943; 60c. Queen Elizabeth in floral hat; 75c. Queen Elizabeth in garden with Prince Charles and Princess Anne, 1952; $1 Queen Elizabeth in South Africa, 1995. VERT (38 × 51 mm)—$5 Queen Elizabeth after Annigoni.

231 *Dichaea neglecta*

2002. Christmas. Orchids. Multicoloured.
1292 25c. Type **231** 15 25
1293 50c. *Epinendrum hawkesii* 30 35
1294 60c. *Encyclia belizensis* 40 45
1295 75c. *Eriopsis biloba* 50 55
1296 $1 *Harbenaria monorrhiza* 65 75
1297 $2 *Mormodes buccinator* 1·25 1·40

232 B.D.F. Emblem

2003. 25th Anniv of Belize Defence Force.
1298 **232** 25c. multicoloured 15 20

POSTAGE DUE STAMPS

D 2

1976.
D 6 **D 2** 1c. red and green 10 1·00
D 7 – 2c. purple and violet 15 1·00
D 8 – 5c. green and brown 20 1·25
D 9 – 15c. green and red 30 1·50
D10 – 25c. orange and green 40 1·75
DESIGNS: Nos. D7/10 as Type **D 2** but with different frames.

BENIN Pt. 6; Pt. 12

A French possession on the W. coast of Africa incorporated, in 1899, into the colony of Dahomey.

100 centimes = 1 franc.

A. FRENCH COLONY

1892. Stamps of French Colonies. "Commerce" type, optd **BENIN**.
1 J 1c. black on blue £120 £110
2 2c. brown on yellow £110 £100
3 4c. brown on grey 48·00 45·00
4 5c. green on light green 17·00 15·00
5 10c. black on lilac 60·00 60·00
6 15c. blue on light blue 35·00 13·00
7 20c. red on green £190 £170
8 25c. black on red 80·00 50·00
9 30c. brown on drab £140 £120
10 35c. black on orange £140 £120
11 40c. red on yellow £120 £110
12 75c. red on pink £250 £225
13 1f. green £275 £225

1892. Nos. 4 and 6 surch.
14 J 01 on 5c. green on lt green £220 £170
15 40 on 15c. blue on lt blue £130 70·00
16 75 on 15c. blue on lt blue £600 £400

1893. "Tablet" key-type inscr "GOLFE DE BENIN" in red (1, 5, 15, 25, 75c., 1f.) or blue (others).
17 D 1c. black on blue 1·90 4·00
18 2c. brown on buff 2·25 3·75
19 4c. brown on grey 2·00 4·00
20 5c. green on light green 5·50 7·00
21 10c. black on lilac 6·25 6·50
22 15c. blue 28·00 21·00
23 20c. red on green 8·00 9·25
24 25c. black on pink 27·00 14·50
25 30c. brown on drab 16·00 10·50
26 40c. red on yellow 2·50 4·25
27 50c. red on pink 2·25 3·75
28 75c. brown on orange 9·00 11·00
29 1f. green 55·00 55·00

1894. "Tablet" key-type inscr "BENIN" in red (1, 5, 15, 25, 75c., 1f.) or blue (others).
33 D 1c. black on blue 2·25 3·25
34 2c. brown on buff 2·50 4·00
35 4c. brown on grey 1·75 3·75
36 5c. green on light green 3·50 3·75
37 10c. black on lilac 4·50 4·25
38 15c. blue 9·00 2·25
39 20c. red on green 7·75 7·25
40 25c. black on pink 10·00 3·00
41 30c. brown on drab 4·00 6·00
42 40c. red on yellow 14·00 9·00
43 50c. red on pink 19·00 15·00

44 75c. brown on orange . . . 14·00 12·00
45 1f. green . . . . 4·25 5·00

POSTAGE DUE STAMPS

1894. Postage Due stamps of French Colonies optd **BENIN**. Imperf.
D46 U 5c. black . . . . £120 55·00
D47 10c. black . . . . £120 55·00
D48 20c. black . . . . £120 55·00
D49 30c. black . . . . £120 55·00

B. PEOPLE'S REPUBLIC

The Republic of Dahomey was renamed the People's Republic of Benin on 30 November 1975.

185 Celebrations

1976. Republic of Benin Proclamation. Mult.
603 50f. Type **185** 50 30
604 60f. President Kerekou making Proclamation . . . 70 30
605 100f. Benin arms and flag . . 1·25 65

186 Skiing

1976. Air. Winter Olympic Games, Innsbruck. Multicoloured.
606 60f. Type **186** 90 45
607 150f. Bobsleighing (vert) . . 1·60 95
608 300f. Figure-skating . . . . 3·50 2·00

1976. Various Dahomey stamps surch **POPULAIRE DU BENIN** and new value (609/11) or surch only (617/18).
617 **108** 50f. on 1f. multicoloured (postage) 50 25
618 – 60f. on 2f. multicoloured (No. 415) 60 35
609 – 135f. brown, purple and blue (No. 590) (air) . . 1·40 75
610 – 210f. on 300f. brown, red and blue (No. 591) . . 2·10 1·10
611 – 380f. on 500f. brown, red and green (No. 592) . . 3·75 1·90

188 Alexander Graham Bell, Early Telephone and Satellite

1976. Telephone Centenary.
612 **188** 200f. red, violet & brown 2·25 1·50

189 Basketball

1976. Air. Olympic Games, Montreal. Mult.
613 60f. Long jump (horiz) . . . 75 40
614 150f. Type **189** . . . . 1·50 90
615 200f. Hurdling (horiz) . . . 2·10 1·25

191 Scouts and Camp-fire

1976. African Scout Jamboree, Jos, Nigeria.
619 **191** 50f. purple, brown & blk 75 60
620 – 70f. brown, green & blk 1·25 70
DESIGN: 70f. "Comradeship".

192 Konrad Adenauer  **193** Benin 1c. Stamp, 1893, and Lion Cub

1976. Air. Birth Centenary of Konrad Adenauer (German statesman).
621 **192** 90f. slate, blue and red . . 1·25 50
622 – 250f. blue, red & lt blue 3·25 1·40
DESIGN—HORIZ: 250f. Adenauer and Cologne Cathedral.

1976. Air. "Juvarouen 76" Youth Stamp Exhibition, Rouen.
623 – 60f. blue and turquoise 1·00 40
624 **193** 210f. red, brown & olive 2·25 1·25
DESIGN—HORIZ: 60f. Dahomey 60f. Stamp of 1965, and children's silhouettes.

194 Blood Bank, Cotonou

1976. National Days of Blood Transfusion Service. Multicoloured.
625 5f. Type **194** 20 10
626 50f. Casualty and blood clinic 50 40
627 60f. Donor, patient and ambulance 90 50

195 Manioc  **196** "Apollo" Emblem and Rocket

1976. National Products Campaign Year. Mult.
628 20f. Type **195** 25 15
629 50f. Maize cultivation 60 25
630 60f. Cocoa trees 80 35
631 150f. Cotton plantation . . . 1·75 75

1976. Air. 5th Anniv of "Apollo 14" Space Mission.
632 **196** 130f. lake, brown & blue 1·25 65
633 – 270f. blue, turquoise & red . . . . 2·50 1·25
DESIGN: 270f. Landing on Moon.

197 Classroom  **198** Roan Antelope

1976. 3rd Anniv of Bariba Periodical "Kparo".
634 **197** 50f. multicoloured 75 40

1976. Mammals in Pendjari National Park. Multicoloured.
635 10f. Type **198** 40 30
636 30f. African buffalo 75 60
637 50f. Hippopotamus (horiz) 1·25 80
638 70f. Lion . . . . 1·50 1·00

199 "Freedom"  **200** "The Annunciation" (Master of Jativa)

1976. 1st Anniv of Proclamation of Republic. Multicoloured.
639 40f. Type **199** 45 25
640 150f. Maize cultivation . . . 1·40 75

1976. Air. Christmas. Multicoloured.
641 50f. Type **200** 65 30
642 60f. "The Nativity" (David) 75 40
643 270f. "Adoration of the Magi" (Dutch school) . . 3·00 1·60
644 300f. "The Flight into Egypt" (Fabriano) (horiz) . . . . 3·25 2·00

201 Table Tennis and Games Emblem

1976. West African University Games, Cotonou. Multicoloured.
645 10f. Type **201** 20 15
646 50f. Sports Hall, Cotonou . . 55 25

202 Loser with Ticket and Winner with Money

1977. Air. 10th Anniv of National Lottery.
647 **202** 50f. multicoloured 65 30

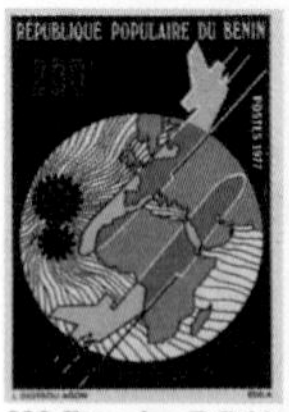

203 Douglas DC-10 crossing Globe  **205** Adder

204 Chateau Sassenage, Grenoble

1977. Europafrique.
648 **203** 200f. multicoloured . . . 2·25 2·00

1977. Air. 10th Anniv of International French Language Council.
649 **204** 200f. multicoloured . . . 1·90 95

1977. Reptiles and Domestic Animals. Mult.
650 2f. Type **205** 30 20
651 3f. Tortoise 30 20
652 5f. Zebus 50 30
653 10f. Cats 75 30

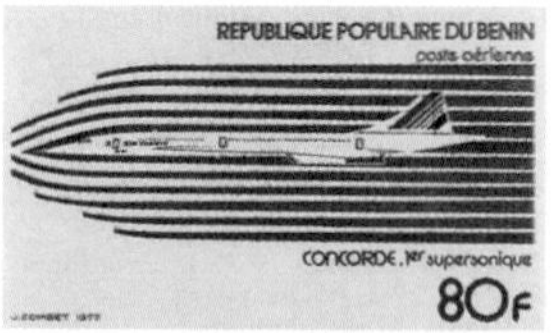

206 Concorde

1977. Air. Aviation.
654 **206** 80f. red and blue 80 45
655 – 150f. red, violet & green 1·75 80
656 – 300f. violet, red & mauve 2·50 1·60
657 – 500f. red, blue & green . . 5·00 2·75
DESIGNS: 150f. "Graf Zeppelin"; 300f. Charles Lindbergh and "Spirit of St. Louis"; 500f. Charles Nungesser and Francois Coli with "L'Oiseau".

207 Footballer heading Ball  **208** Rheumatic Patients

1977. Air. World Football Cup Eliminators. Multicoloured.
658 60f. Type **207** 65 25
659 200f. Goalkeeper and players 1·90 90

1977. World Rheumatism Year.
660 **208** 100f. multicoloured . . . 1·25 65

209 Karate  **210** Mao Tse-tung

1977. 2nd African Games, Lagos. Multicoloured.
661 90f. Type **209** 95 55
662 100f. Javelin (horiz) . . . . 1·10 70
663 150f. Hurdling . . . . 1·75 1·10

1977. 1st Death Anniv of Mao Tse-tung.
665 **210** 100f. multicoloured . . . 1·25 75

211 Sterilising Scalpels  **212** "Miss Haverfield" (Gainsborough)

1977. 150th Birth Anniv of Joseph Lister.
666 **211** 150f. grey, red & carmine 1·60 75
667 – 210f. olive, green & red 2·25 1·10
DESIGN: 210f. Lister and antiseptic spray.

1977. Air. Paintings.
668 **212** 100f. green and brown . . 1·25 40
669 – 150f. brown, bistre & red 1·90 90
670 – 200f. red and bistre . . . 2·50 1·25
DESIGNS: 150f. "Self-Portrait" (Rubens); 200f. "Study of an Old Man" (da Vinci).

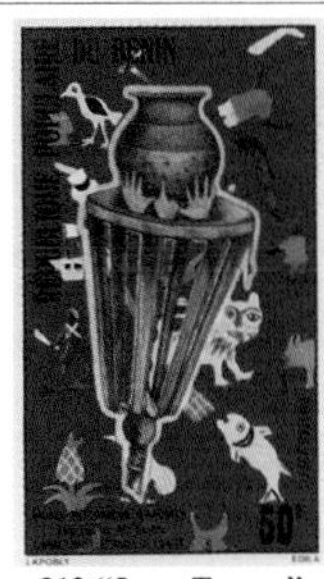

213 "Jarre Trouee" Emblem of King Ghezo (D'Abomey Museum)

214 Atacora Waterfall

1977. Historic Museums of Benin. Mult.

No.		Description	Unused	Used
671		50f. Type **213**	55	35
672		60f. Mask (Porto-Novo Museum) (horiz)	80	45
673		210f. D'Abomey Museum	2·10	1·10

1977. Tourism. Multicoloured.

No.		Description	Unused	Used
674		50f. Type **214**	50	30
675		60f. Stilt houses, Ganvie (horiz)	75	45
676		150f. Hut village, Savalou	1·90	95

1977. Air. 1st Commercial Concorde Flight. Paris–New York. No. 654 optd **1er VOL COMMERCIAL 22.11.77 PARIS NEW-YORK**.

No.		Description	Unused	Used
678	**206**	80f. red and blue	1·25	75

216 "Viking" on Mars ("Operation Viking", 1977)

1977. Air. Space Conquest Anniversaries.

No.		Description	Unused	Used
679	**216**	100f. brown, olive & red	90	50
680	–	150f. blue, turq & mve	1·40	75
681	–	200f. brown, blue & red	2·25	95
682	–	500f. blue, brn & olive	5·50	2·75

DESIGNS AND EVENTS: 150f. Sir Isaac Newton, apple and stars (250th death anniv); 200f. Komarov and "Soyuz 2" over Moon (10th death anniv); 500f. Space dog "Laika" and rocket (20th anniv of ascent into Space).

217 Monument, Red Flag Square, Cotonou

218 Mother and Child with Owl of Wisdom

1977. Air. 1st Anniv of Inauguration of Red Flag Square Monument.

No.		Description	Unused	Used
683	**217**	500f. multicoloured	5·00	2·25

1977. Fight against Witchcraft. Multicoloured.

No.		Description	Unused	Used
684		60f. Type **218**	80	50
685		150f. Felling the tree of sorcery	2·00	1·00

219 "Suzanne Fourment"

1977. Air. 400th Birth Anniv of Rubens.

No.		Description	Unused	Used
686	**219**	200f. brown, red & green	2·50	1·10
687	–	380f. orange and brown	4·50	2·00

DESIGN: 380f. "Albert Rubens".

220 Battle Scene

1978. "Victory over Imperialism".

No.		Description	Unused	Used
688	**220**	50f. multicoloured	80	40

221 Benin Houses and Map of Heads

223 Abdoulaye Issa

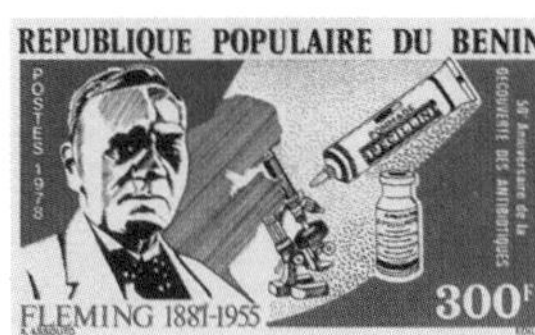

222 Sir Alexander Fleming, Microscope and Drugs

1978. General Population Census.

No.		Description	Unused	Used
689	**221**	50f. multicoloured	65	25

1978. 50th Anniv of Discovery of Antibiotics.

No.		Description	Unused	Used
690	**222**	300f. multicoloured	3·75	1·90

1978. 1st Death Anniv of Abdoulaye Issa.

No.		Description	Unused	Used
691	**223**	100f. multicoloured	90	45

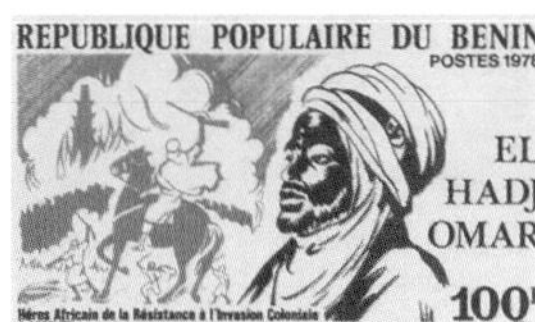

224 El Hadj Omar

1978. Heroes of Anti-colonial Resistance.

No.		Description	Unused	Used
692	–	90f. multicoloured	80	40
693	**224**	100f. green, grey & blue	95	55

DESIGN: 90f. Samory Toure.

225 "Communications"

1978. 10th World Telecommunications Day.

No.		Description	Unused	Used
694	**225**	100f. multicoloured	1·25	65

226 Footballer and Stadium

1978. World Cup Football Championship, Argentina. Multicoloured.

No.		Description	Unused	Used
695		200f. Type **226**	1·60	85
696		300f. Tackling (vert)	2·50	1·40
697		500f. Footballer and world map	4·50	2·10

1978. Argentina's Victory in World Cup Football Championship. Nos. 695/7 optd.

No.		Description	Unused	Used
699	**226**	200f. multicoloured	1·75	1·10
700	–	300f. multicoloured	2·50	1·75
701	–	500f. multicoloured	4·50	3·00

OPTS: 200f. **FINALE ARGENTINE: 3 HOLLANDE: 1**; 300f. **CHAMPION 1978 ARGENTINE**; 500f. **3e BRESIL 4e ITALIE**.

228 Map, Olympic Flag and Basketball Players

1978. 3rd African Games, Algiers. Multicoloured.

No.		Description	Unused	Used
703		50f. Type **228**	60	30
704		60f. African map and Volleyball	85	50
705		80f. Cyclists and map of Algeria	1·00	60

229 Martin Luther King

230 Bicycle Taxi (Oueme)

1978. 10th Anniv of Martin Luther King's Assassination.

No.		Description	Unused	Used
707	**229**	300f. multicoloured	2·75	1·50

1978. Benin Provinces. Multicoloured.

No.		Description	Unused	Used
708		50f. Type **230**	60	30
709		60f. Leather work (Borgou)	70	35
710		70f. Drums (Oueme)	90	45
711		100f. Calabash with burnt-work ornamentation (Zou)	1·25	50

231 "Stamps" and Magnifying Glass

1978. Philatelic Exhibition, Riccione, Italy.

No.		Description	Unused	Used
712	**231**	200f. multicoloured	1·90	95

232 Parthenon and Frieze showing Horsemen

1978. Air. U.N.E.S.C.O. Campaign for the Preservation of the Acropolis. Multicoloured.

No.		Description	Unused	Used
713		70f. Acropolis and Frieze showing Procession	70	30
714		250f. Type **232**	2·10	1·00
715		500f. The Parthenon (horiz)	4·25	1·90

235 Turkeys

236 Post Runner and Boeing 747

1978. Domestic Poultry. Multicoloured.

No.		Description	Unused	Used
722		10f. Type **235**	15	15
723		20f. Ducks	30	15
724		50f. Chickens	80	35
725		60f. Helmeted guineafowl	95	45

1978. Centenary of U.P.U. Paris Congress. Mult.

No.		Description	Unused	Used
726		50f. Messenger of the Dahomey Kings (horiz)	70	30
727		60f. Pirogue oarsman, boat and post car	80	35
728		90f. Type **236**	1·00	50

237 Red-breasted Merganser and Baden 1851 1k. Stamp

1978. Air. "Philexafrique" Exhibition, Libreville (Gabon) (1st issue) and International Stamp Fair, Essen, West Germany. Multicoloured.

No.		Description	Unused	Used
729		100f. Type **237**	2·50	1·25
730		100f. African Buffalo and Dahomey 1966 50f. African Pygmy Goose stamp	2·50	1·25

See also Nos. 747/8.

238 Raoul Follereau

1978. 1st Death Anniv of Raoul Follereau (leprosy pioneer).

No.		Description	Unused	Used
731	**238**	200f. multicoloured	1·50	75

239 Wilbur and Orville Wright and Wright Flyer 1

1978. Air. 75th Anniv of First Powered Flight.

No.		Description	Unused	Used
732	**239**	500f. blue, yellow & brn	5·00	2·25

240 I.Y.C. Emblem

241 Hydrangea

1979. International Year of the Child. Mult.

No.		Description	Unused	Used
733		10f. Type **240**	15	15
734		20f. Children in balloon	20	15
735		50f. Children dancing around globe	40	20

1979. Flowers. Multicoloured.

No.		Description	Unused	Used
736		20f. Type **241**	30	30
737		25f. Assangokan	35	30
738		30f. Geranium	50	40
739		40f. Water Lily (horiz)	65	40

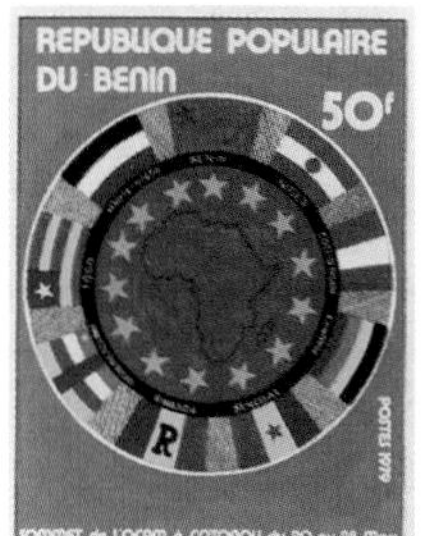

242 Flags around Map of Africa

1979. O.C.A.M. Summit Meeting, Cotonou (1st series). Multicoloured.
740 50f. Type **242** 50 30
741 60f. Flags and map of Benin 65 40
742 80f. O.C.A.M. flag and map of member countries 90 45
See also Nos. 754/6.

1979. Various stamps surch.
743 **205** 50f. on 2f. multicoloured (postage)
743a – 50f. on 3f. multicoloured (651)
743b – 50f. on 70f. brown, green and black (620)
744 **207** 50f. on 60f. mult (air)
745 **192** 50f. on 90f. blue, deep blue and red
746 – 50f. on 150f. mult (607)
747 **189** 50f. on 150f. mult

244 Antenna, Satellite and Wave Pattern

1979. World Telecommunications Day.
748 **244** 50f. multicoloured 65 30

245 Headquarters Building

1979. West African Savings Bank Building Opening.
749 **245** 50f. multicoloured 55 30

246 "Resolution" and "Discovery" in Karakakoa Bay, Hawaii

1979. Air. Death Bicentenary of Capt. James Cook.
750 **246** 20f. blue, green & brown 85 45
751 – 50f. brown, green & blue 1·00 60
DESIGN: 50f. Cook's death at Kowrowa.

247 Guelede Mask, Abomey Tapestry and Fiery-breasted Bush Shrike

1979. "Philexafrique" Stamp Exhibition, Gabon (2nd issue).
752 **247** 15f. multicoloured 75 20
753 – 50f. orange, yellow & turq 95 55
DESIGN: 50f. Lockheed Tristar 500, satellite, U.P.U. emblem and canoe post.

1979. Common African and Mauritian Organization Summit Conference, Cotonou (2nd issue). Nos. 740/2 optd **26 Au 28 Juin 1979**.
754 50f. Type **242** 55 30
755 60f. Map of Benin and flags of members 70 40
756 80f. OCAM flag and map showing member countries 90 45

249 Olympic Flame, Benin Flags and Pictograms

1979. Pre-Olympic Year. Multicoloured.
757 10f. Type **249** 20 15
758 50f. High jump 65 40

250 Roan Antelope

1979. Endangered Animals. Multicoloured.
759 5f. Type **250** 30 20
760 10f. Giraffes (vert) 40 30
761 20f. Chimpanzee 60 40
762 50f. African elephants (vert) 1·25 40

251 Emblem, Concorde and Map of Africa

252 Post Offices, Antenna, Telephone and Savings Book

1979. 20th Anniv of ASECNA (African Air Safety Organization). Multicoloured.
763 50f. Type **251** 40 20
764 60f. As No. 763 but emblem at bottom right and without dates 50 25

1979. 20th Anniv of Posts and Telecommunications Office. Multicoloured.
765 50f. Type **252** 60 40
766 60f. Collecting, sorting and delivering mail 85 50

253 Rotary Emblem, Symbols of Services and Globe

254 Copernicus and Planetary System

1980. 75th Anniv of Rotary International. Mult.
767 90f. Cotonou Rotary Club banner (vert) 75 40
768 200f. Type **253** 1·50 75

1980. 50th Anniv of Discovery of Planet Pluto. Multicoloured.
769 70f. Kepler and astrolabe 65 40
770 100f. Type **254** 90 50

255 Pharaonic Capital

1980. 20th Anniv of Nubian Monuments Preservation Campaign. Multicoloured.
771 50f. Type **255** 45 25
772 60f. Rameses II, Abu Simbel 55 40
773 150f. Temple, Abu Simbel (horiz) 1·25 75

256 Lenin in Library

1980. 110th Birth Anniv of Lenin. Mult.
774 50f. Lenin and globe 50 25
775 150f. Type **256** 1·60 65

257 Monument

1980. Martyrs Square, Cotonou.
776 **257** 50f. multicoloured 40 15
777 – 60f. multicoloured 50 20
778 – 70f. multicoloured 55 25
779 – 100f. multicoloured 80 30
DESIGNS—HORIZ: 60f. to 100f. Different views of the monument.

258 Farmer using Telephone

259 Assan

1980. World Telecommunications Day. Mult.
780 50f. Type **258** 40 25
781 60f. Telephone 50 25

1980. Traditional Musical Instruments. Mult.
782 5f. Type **259** 20 10
783 10f. Tinbo (horiz) 20 10
784 15f. Tam-tam sato 25 15
785 20f. Kora (horiz) 25 15
786 30f. Gangan (horiz) 60 35
787 50f. Sinhoun (horiz) 85 50

260 Monument

1980. King Gbehanzin Monument.
788 **260** 1000f. multicoloured 9·50 6·25

261 Dieudonne Costes, Maurice Bellonte and "Point d'Interrogation"

1980. 50th Anniv of First Paris–New York Non-stop Flight.
789 – 90f. red, lt blue & blue 1·00 50
790 **261** 100f. red, blue and flesh 1·25 60
DESIGN: 90f. Airplane "Point d'Interrogation" and scenes of New York and Paris.

262 "Lunokhod I"

1980. 10th Anniv of "Lunokhod I".
791 – 90f. brown, blue and violet (postage) 75 50
792 **262** 210f. purple, blue and yellow (air) 2·25 1·10
DESIGN (48 × 36 mm): 90f. Rocket and "Lunokhod I".

263 Show-jumping

1980. Olympic Games, Moscow. Multicoloured.
793 50f. Olympic Flame, running track, emblem and mascot Mischa the bear (horiz) 45 20
794 60f. Type **263** 50 30
795 70f. Judo (horiz) 70 40
796 200f. Olympic flag and globe surrounded by sports pictogram 1·50 75
797 300f. Weightlifting 2·50 1·25

264 O.C.A.M. Building

1980. Common African and Mauritian Organization Village, Cotonou. Multicoloured.
798 50f. Entrance to O.C.A.M. village 45 20
799 60f. View of village 50 20
800 70f. Type **264** 70 55

265 Dancers

1980. Agbadja Dance. Multicoloured.
801 30f. Type **265** 50 25
802 50f. Singer and musicians 75 40
803 60f. Dancers and musicians 85 50

266 Casting a Net

267 Philippines under Magnifying Glass

1980. Fishing. Multicoloured.
804 5f. Type **266** 10 10
805 10f. Fisherman with catch (vert) 25 15
806 15f. Line fishing 35 20
807 20f. Fisherman emptying eel-pot 40 20
808 50f. Hauling in a net 65 30
809 60f. Fish farm 1·25 40

1980. World Tourism Conference, Manila. Mult.
810 50f. Type **267** 55 25
811 60f. Conference flag on globe 70 25

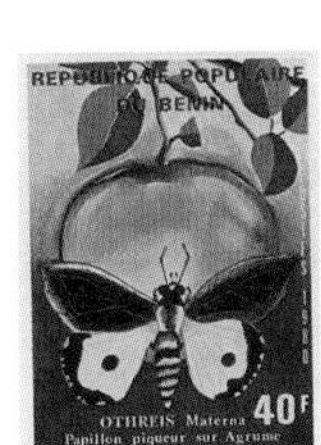
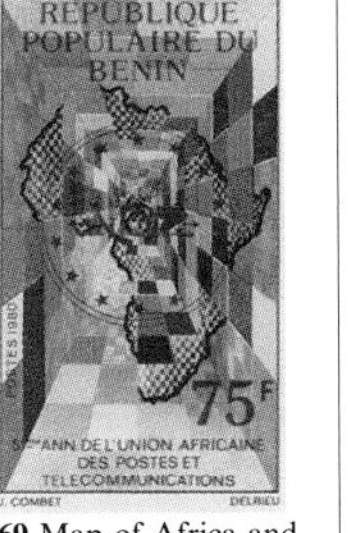

268 "Othreis materna" **269** Map of Africa and Posthorn

1980. Insects. Multicoloured.

812	40f. Type **268**	65	30
813	50f. "Othreis fullonia" (butterfly)	90	40
814	200f. "Oryctes" sp. (beetle)	2·75	1·25

1980. 5th Anniv of African Posts and Telecommunications.

815 **269**	75f. multicoloured	80	25

270 Hands freed from Chains **271** "Self-portrait"

1980. 30th Anniv of Signing of Human Rights Convention. Multicoloured.

816	30f. Type **270**	25	15
817	50f. African pushing through bars	45	20
818	60f. Figure holding Human Rights flame	55	20

1980. 90th Death Anniv of Van Gogh (artist). Multicoloured.

819	100f. Type **271**	1·75	80
820	300f. "The Postman Roulin"	4·25	2·10

272 Offenbach and Scene from "Orpheus in the Underworld"

1980. Death Centenary of Jacques Offenbach (composer).

821 **272**	50f. black, red and green	75	50
822 –	60f. blue, brown & dp brn	1·25	75

DESIGN: 60f. Offenbach and scene from "La Vie Parisienne".

273 Kepler and Astronomical Diagram

1980. 30th Death Anniv of Johannes Kepler (astronomer).

823 **273**	50f. red, blue and grey	55	25
824 –	60f. blue, black and green	70	25

DESIGN: 60f. Kepler, satellite and dish aerials.

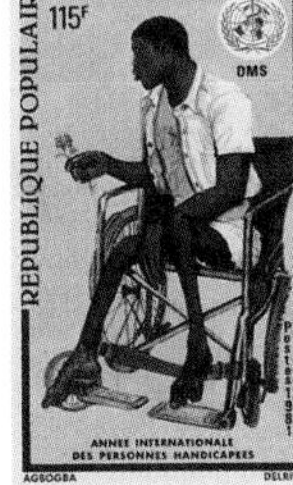

274 Footballers **275** Disabled Person holding Flower

1981. Air. World Cup Football Championship. Multicoloured.

825	200f. Football and globe	1·50	55
826	500f. Type **274**	3·75	1·60

1981. International Year of Disabled People.

827 **275**	115f. multicoloured	1·00	40

276 Yuri Gagarin

1981. 20th Anniv of First Man in Space.

828 **276**	500f. multicoloured	4·50	2·50

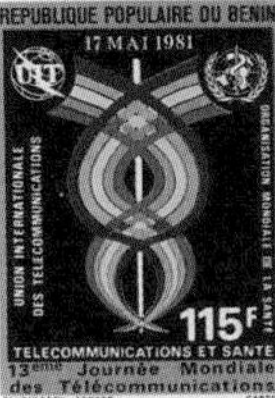

277 I.T.U. and W.H.O. Emblems and Ribbons forming Caduceus **278** Amaryllis

1981. World Telecommunications Day.

829 **277**	115f. multicoloured	90	40

1981. Flowers. Multicoloured.

830	10f. Type **278**	25	20
831	20f. "Eischornia crassipes"	40	30
832	80f. "Parkia biglobosa"	1·25	60

279 Hotel and Map

1981. Opening of Benin Sheraton Hotel.

833 **279**	100f. multicoloured	90	40

1981. Surch **50F**.

834 **216**	50f. on 100f. brown, green and red	45	20
835 **193**	50f. on 210f. red, brown and green	45	20

281 Prince Charles, Lady Diana Spencer and Tower Bridge

1981. Air. British Royal Wedding.

836 **281**	500f. multicoloured	3·75	1·75

282 Guinea Pig

1981. Domestic Animals. Multicoloured.

837	5f. Type **282**	25	20
838	60f. Cat	70	40
839	80f. Dogs	1·00	60

283 Heinrich von Stephan (founder of U.P.U.)

1981. World Universal Postal Union Day.

840 **283**	100f. slate and red	75	40

284 Heads, Quill, Paper Darts and U.P.U. Emblem

1981. International Letter Writing Week.

841 **284**	100f. blue and purple	75	40

285 "The Dance"

1981. Air. Birth Centenary of Pablo Picasso. Multicoloured.

842	300f. Type **285**	2·75	95
843	500f. "The Three Musicians"	4·75	1·60

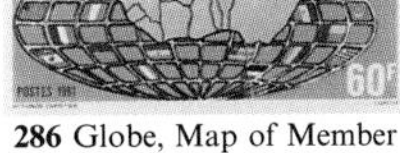

286 Globe, Map of Member Countries and Communication Symbols **287** St. Theodore Stratilates (tile painting)

1981. 5th Anniv of E.C.O.W.A.S. (Economic Community of West African States).

844 **286**	60f. multicoloured	65	25

1981. Air. 1300th Anniv of Bulgarian State.

845 **287**	100f. multicoloured	75	35

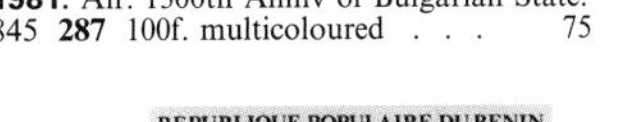

288 Tractor and Map

1981. 10th Anniv of West African Rice Development Association.

846 **288**	60f. multicoloured	65	25

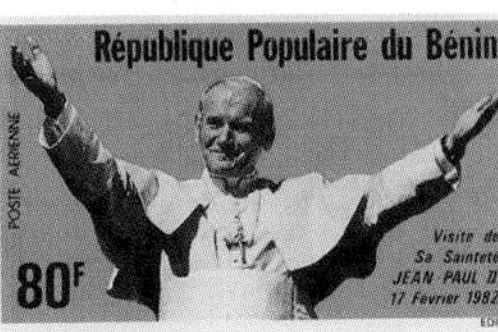

289 Pope John Paul II

1982. Air. Papal Visit.

847 **289**	80f. multicoloured	1·50	65

290 John Glenn

1982. Air. 20th Anniv of First United States Manned Space Flight.

848 **290**	500f. multicoloured	4·25	1·90

291 Dr. Robert Koch

1982. Centenary of Discovery of Tubercle Bacillus.

849 **291**	115f. multicoloured	1·25	45

292 Washington, U.S. Flag and Map

1982. 250th Birth Anniv of George Washington.

850 **292**	200f. multicoloured	1·90	75

1982. Red Cross. Surch **Croix Rouge 8 Mai 1982 60f.**

851 **266**	60f. on 5f. multicoloured	50	25

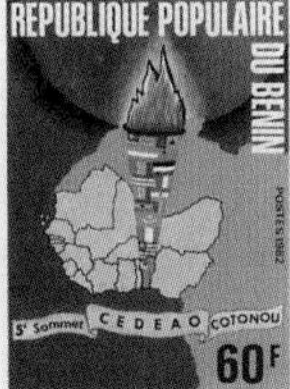

294 Map of Member Countries and Torch **295** Scouts round Campfire

1982. 5th Economic Community of West African States Summit, Cotonou.

852 **294**	60f. multicoloured	50	25

1982. Air. 75th Anniv of Boy Scout Movement.

853 **295**	105f. multicoloured	1·25	75

296 Footballers

1982. World Cup Football Championship, Spain. Multicoloured.

854	90f. Type **296**	75	40
855	300f. Leg with sock formed from flags of participating countries and globe/football	2·40	1·10

1982. African Posts and Telegraph Union. Surch **UAPT 1982 60f.**

856 **282**	60f. on 5f. multicoloured	65	30

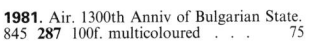

298 Stamp of Map of France and Magnifying Glass

1982. "Philexfrance 82" International Stamp Exhibition, Paris.
857 **298** 90f. multicoloured . . . . 1·00 50

1982. World Cup Football Championship Results. Nos. 854/5 optd.
858 90f. Type **296** . . . . 1·00 50
859 300f. Leg with flags of participating countries and football "globe" . . . . . 2·75 1·25
OVERPRINTS: 90f. **COUPE 82 ITALIE bat RFA 3-1**; 300f. **COUPE 82 1 ITALIE 2 RFA 3 POLOGNE**.

1982. Riccione Stamp Exhibition. Optd **RICCIONE 1982**.
860 **231** 200f. multicoloured . . . 1·50 65

301 Laughing Kookaburra ("Dacelo Gigas")

302 World Map and Satellite

1982. Birds. Multicoloured.
861 5f. Type **301** 30 20
862 10f. Bluethroat ("La Gorge Bleue") (horiz) 45 20
863 15f. Barn swallow ("L'Hirondelle") 45 20
864 20f. Woodland kingfisher ("Martin-Pecheur") and Village weaver ("Tisserin") 70 25
865 30f. Reed warbler ("La Rousserolle") (horiz) . . . 1·10 35
866 60f. Warbler sp. ("Faurette Commoune") (horiz) . . . 1·40 50
867 80f. Eagle owl ("Hibou Grand Doc") . . . . . . 2·50 95
868 100f. Sulphur-crested cockatoo ("Cacatoes") . . 3·00 1·25

1982. I.T.U. Delegates' Conference, Nairobi.
869 **302** 200f. turq, blue & blk . . 1·50 65

303 U.P.U. Emblem and Heads

1982. U.P.U. Day.
870 **303** 100f. green, blue & brown 90 40

305 "Claude Monet in his Studio"

1982. Air. 150th Birth Anniv of Edouard Manet (artist).
876 **305** 300f. multicoloured . . . 5·50 2·25

306 "Virgin and Child" (Grunewald)

1982. Air. Christmas. Multicoloured.
877 200f. Type **306** . . . . 2·25 1·10
878 300f. "Virgin and Child with Angels and Cherubins" (Correggio) . . . . 2·75 1·40

307 Pres. Mitterrand and Pres. Kerekou

1983. Visit of President Mitterrand.
879 **307** 90f. multicoloured . . . . 1·10 45

1983. Various stamps surch.
880 – 60f. on 50f. multicoloured (No. 798) (postage) . . 45 20
881 – 60f. on 70f. multicoloured (No. 778) 45 20
882 **279** 60f. on 100f. mult 45 25
883 – 75f. on 80f. multicoloured (No. 832) 75 40
884 – 75f. on 80f. multicoloured (No. 839) 75 40
885 **262** 75f. on 210f. red, blue and yellow (air) 65 35

309 "Tender Benin" (tug) and "Amazone" (oil rig)

1983. Seme Oilfield.
886 **309** 125f. multicoloured . . . 1·40 60

1983. Various stamps surch.
887 **267** 5f. on 50f. multicoloured 10 10
888 **284** 10f. on 100f. blue & pur 10 10
889 – 10f. on 200f. mult (No. 659) 10 10
890 – 15f. on 200f. red and bistre (No. 670) 10 10
891 – 15f. on 200f. mult (No. 796) 10 10
892 – 15f. on 210f. green, deep green and red (No. 667) 10 10
893 – 15f. on 270f. mult (No. 643) 10 10
894 **219** 20f. on 200f. brown, red and olive 20 10
895 – 25f. on 70f. mult (No. 795) 25 10
896 – 25f. on 210f. mult (No. 673) 20 10
897 – 25f. on 270f. blue, turq & red (No. 633) 20 10
898 – 25f. on 380f. brown and red (No. 687) 25 10
899 – 30f. on 200f. brown, blue and red (No. 681) . . . 30 20
900 **290** 40f. on 500f. mult 40 20
901 **282** 75f. on 5f. multicoloured 55 40
902 – 75f. on 100f. red, blue and pink (No. 790) 55 40
903 – 75f. on 150f. mult (No. 631) 55 40
904 – 75f. on 150f. violet, red and green (No. 655) . . 65 40
905 **211** 75f. on 150f. grey, orange and red 55 40
906 – 75f. on 150f. dp brown, brown & red (No. 669) 65 40

311 W.C.Y. Emblem

1983. World Communications Year.
907 **311** 185f. multicoloured . . . 1·50 65

312 Stamps of Benin and Thailand and World Map

1983. Air. "Bangkok 1983" International Stamp Exhibition.
908 **312** 300f. multicoloured . . . 2·50 1·25

313 Hand with Tweezers and Stamp

1983. "Riccione 83" Stamp Fair, San Marino.
909 **313** 500f. multicoloured . . . 3·75 1·60

314 First Aid

315 Carved Table and Chairs

1983. 20th Anniv of Benin Red Cross.
910 **314** 105f. multicoloured . . . 95 50

1983. Benin Woodwork. Multicoloured.
911 75f. Type **315** 65 25
912 90f. Rustic table and chairs 90 40
913 200f. Monkeys holding box 1·60 65

316 Boeing 747, World Map and U.P.U. Emblem

1983. U.P.U. Day.
914 **316** 125f. green, blue & brown 1·25 60

317 Egoun

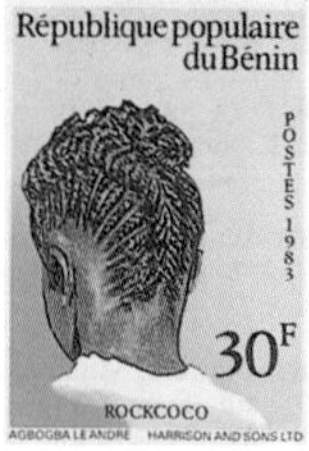

318 Rockcoco

1983. Religious Cults. Multicoloured.
915 75f. Type **317** 65 30
916 75f. Zangbeto 65 30

1983. Hair-styles. Multicoloured.
917 30f. Type **318** 25 20
918 75f. Serpent 65 40
919 90f. Songas 90 45

319 Alfred Nobel

1983. 150th Birth Anniv of Alfred Nobel.
920 **319** 300f. multicoloured . . . 2·75 1·50

320 "Madonna of Lorette" (Raphael)

1983. Air. Christmas.
921 **320** 200f. multicoloured . . . 1·90 95

1984. Various stamps surch.
922 – 5f. on 150f. mult (No. 685) (postage) . . 15 15
923 **316** 5f. on 125f. green, blue and brown . . . . . . 1·50 1·25
924 **292** 10f. on 200f. mult 15 15
925 – 10f. on 200f. mult (No. 913) 20 20
926 – 15f. on 300f. mult (No. 820) 20 20
927 – 25f. on 300f. mult (No. 644) 25 10
928 **276** 40f. on 500f. mult . . . . 1·00 90
929 **314** 75f. on 105f. mult 70 60
930 **275** 75f. on 115f. mult 70 45
931 **277** 75f. on 115f. mult 70 60
932 **291** 75f. on 115f. mult 70 60
933 **311** 75f. on 185f. mult 70 60
934 **302** 75f. on 200f. turquoise, blue and black 70 60
935 **320** 15f. on 200f. mult (air) . . 10 10
936 **285** 15f. on 300f. mult 10 10
937 **312** 25f. on 300f. mult 25 10
938 **281** 40f. on 500f. mult 30 25
939 **295** 75f. on 105f. mult . . . . 1·00 90
940 **306** 90f. on 200f. mult 70 45
941 **305** 90f. on 300f. mult 70 45

322 Flags, Agriculture and Symbol of Unity and Growth

323 U.P.U. Emblem and Magnifying Glass

1984. 25th Anniv of Council of Unity.
942 **322** 75f. multicoloured 65 25
943 90f. multicoloured 75 30

1984. 19th Universal Postal Union Congress, Hamburg.
944 **323** 90f. multicoloured . . . . 1·00 40

324 Abomey-Calavi Ground Station

325 Koumboro (Borgou)

1984. Inauguration of Abomey-Calavi Ground Station.
945 **324** 75f. multicoloured 65 40

1984. Traditional Costumes. Multicoloured.
946 5f. Type **325** 25 25
947 10f. Taka (Borgou) 35 30
948 20f. Toko (Atacora Province) 50 40

326 Olympic Mascot

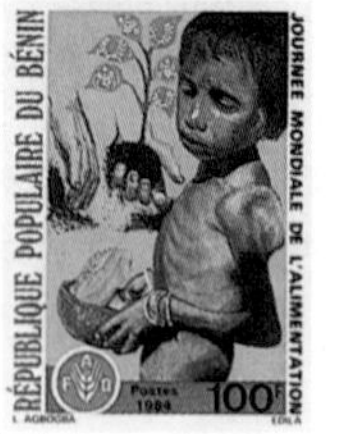

327 Plant and Starving Child

1984. Air. Olympic Games, Los Angeles.
949 **326** 300f. multicoloured . . . 2·50 1·25

1984. World Food Day.
950 **327** 100f. multicoloured . . . 75 35

328 Anatosaurus

1984. Prehistoric Animals. Multicoloured.
951 75f. Type **328** 90 50
952 90f. Brontosaurus . . . . . . 1·25 60

329 "Virgin and Child" (detail, Murillo)

1984. Air. Christmas.
953 **329** 500f. multicoloured . . . 4·25 1·90

1984. Various stamps surch.
954 **203** 75f. on 200f. mult (post) 1·50 1·25
955 **226** 75f. on 200f. mult . . . . 1·25 1·00
956 – 75f. on 300f. mult (No. 696) . . . . . . 1·25 1·00
957 **229** 75f. on 300f. mult 70 45
958 – 90f. on 300f. mult (No. 855) . . . . . . 1·25 1·00
959 – 90f. on 500f. mult (No. 697) . . . . . . 1·25 1·00
960 – 90f. on 500f. mult (No. 701) . . . . . . 1·25 1·00
961 **204** 75f. on 200f. mult (air) . . 55 40
962 – 75f. on 200f. mult (No. 825) . . . . . . 1·25 1·00
963 – 75f. on 300f. violet, red and mauve (No. 656) 1·50 1·25
964 – 75f. on 300f. mult (No. 878) 55 40
965 **239** 90f. on 500f. blue, yellow and brown . . . . . . 1·50 1·25
966 – 90f. on 500f. mult (No. 715) 70 40
967 – 90f. on 500f. mult (No. 843) 70 40

331 Sidon Merchant Ship (2nd century)

1984. Air. Ships.
968 **331** 90f. black, green & blue 1·10 60
969 – 125f. multicoloured . . . 1·75 90
DESIGN—VERT: 125f. Sail merchantman "Wavertree", 1895.

332 Emblem on Globe and Hands reaching for Cultural Symbols

333 Benin Arms

1985. 15th Anniv of Cultural and Technical Co-operation Agency.
970 **332** 300f. multicoloured . . . 2·25 95

1985. Air. Postal Convention between Benin and Sovereign Military Order of Malta. Multicoloured.
971 75f. Type **333** 60 25
972 75f. Arms of Sovereign Military Order 60 25

334 Soviet Flag, Soldier and Tank

335 Teke Dance, Borgou

1985. 40th Anniv of End of Second World War.
973 **334** 100f. multicoloured . . .

1985. Traditional Dances. Multicoloured.
974 75f. Type **335** 75 50
975 100f. Tipen ti dance, Atacora 1·10 60

1985. Various Dahomey Stamps optd **POPULAIRE DU BENIN** (985/6) or **REPUBLIQUE POPULAIRE DU BENIN** (others), Nos. 976/7 and 979/85 surch also.
976 **174** 15f. on 40f. mult (post) 20 10
977 **182** 25f. on 40f. brown, blue and violet (air) 20 10
978 **115** 40f. black, purple & bl 25 10
978a – 75f. on 85f. brown, blue and green (No. 468) 50 25
979 – 75f. on 85f. brown, blue and green (No. 482) 50 25
980 **135** 75f. on 100f. purple, violet and green . . . 50 25
981 – 75f. on 125f. green, blue and purple (No. 509) 50 25
982 **127** 90f. on 20f. brown, blue and green 65 40
983 – 90f. on 150f. purple, blue & brown (No. 456) . . 65 40
984 – 90f. on 200f. green, red and blue (No. 438) . . 65 40
985 – 90f. on 200f. mult (No. 563) 65 40
986 – 150f. mult (No. 562) . . 1·00 65

338 Oil Rig

1985. Air. "Philexafrique" International Stamp Exhibition, Lome, Togo (1st issue). Mult.
987 200f. Type **338** . . . . 2·50 1·75
988 200f. Footballers . . . . . . 2·40 1·50
See also Nos. 999/1000.

339 Emblem

1985. International Youth Year.
989 **339** 150f. multicoloured . . . 1·10 55

340 Football between Globes

1985. World Cup Football Championship, Mexico (1986) (1st issue).
990 **340** 200f. multicoloured . . . 1·50 80
See also No. 1015.

341 Boeing 727, Map and Emblem

1985. 25th Anniv of Aerial Navigation Security Agency for Africa and Malagasy.
991 **341** 150f. multicoloured . . . 1·25 90

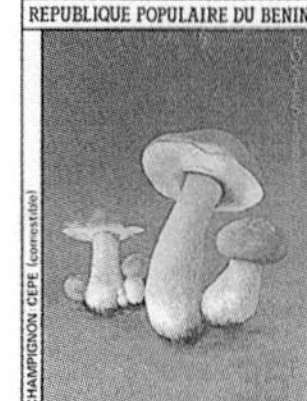

342 "Boletus edulis"

343 Audubon and Arctic Skua ("Labbe Parasite")

1985. Fungi. Multicoloured.
992 35f. Type **342** . . . . 1·60 60
993 40f. "Amanita phalloides" . . 2·10 1·10
994 100f. "Paxillus involutus" . . 4·75 2·10

1985. Birth Bicentenary of John J. Audubon (ornithologist). Multicoloured.
995 150f. Type **343** . . . . 2·00 1·10
996 300f. Audubon and oystercatcher ("Huitrier Pie") . . . . 4·50 2·40

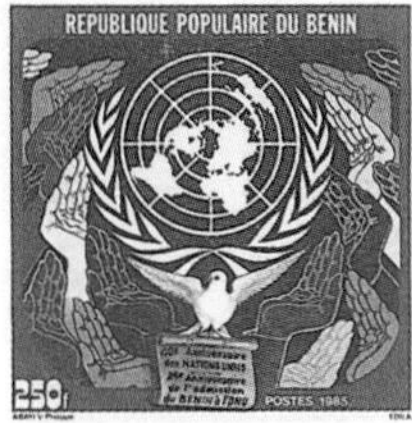

344 Emblem, Hands and Dove

1985. 40th Anniv of United Nations Organization and 25th Anniv of Benin's Membership.
997 **344** 250f. multicoloured . . . 1·90 90

345 Stamps and Globe

1985. "Italia '85" International Stamp Exhibition, Rome.
998 **345** 200f. multicoloured . . . 1·50 80

1985. "Philexafrique" International Stamp Exhibition, Lome, Togo (2nd issue). As Type **338**. Multicoloured.
999 250f. Forest and hand holding tools . . . . . . 2·50 1·60
1000 250f. Magnifying glass over judo stamp . . . . 2·50 1·60

1985. Various Dahomey stamps optd **Republique Populaire du Benin**. Nos. 1001/9 and 1011 surch also.
1001 – 75f. on 35f. mult (No. 596) (postage) . . 50 25
1002 – 90f. on 70f. multicoloured (No. 419) 70 35
1003 – 90f. on 140f. multicoloured (No. 446) 70 35
1004 **113** 100f. on 40f. red, brown and green 75 40
1005 – 150f. on 45f. multicoloured (No. 597) . . . . . . 1·10 65
1006 – 75f. on 70f. multicoloured (No. 342) (air) . . . . 6·50 6·50
1007 – 75f. on 100f. multicoloured (No. 251) . . . . . . 2·25 60
1008 **59** 75f. on 200f. mult . . . 2·25 60
1009 – 90f. on 250f. multicoloured (No. 272) . . . . . . 2·50 60
1010 **110** 100f. multicoloured . . . 45 40
1011 – 150f. on 500f. multicoloured (No. 252) . . . . . . 3·75 1·40
No. 1010 is surcharged on the unoverprinted unissued stamp subsequently issued as No. 422.

349 Church, Children playing and Nativity Scene

1985. Air. Christmas.
1012 **349** 500f. multicoloured . . . 4·00 1·60

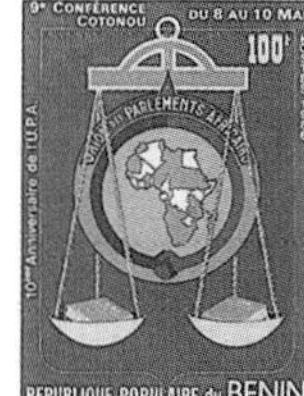

350 Emblem

1986. 10th Anniv of African Parliamentary Union and Ninth Conference, Cotonou.
1013 **350** 100f. multicoloured . . . 75 40

351 Halley, Comet and "Giotto" Space Probe

1986. Appearance of Halley's Comet.
1014 **351** 205f. multicoloured . . . 2·25 1·25

352 Footballers

1986. World Cup Football Championship, Mexico (2nd issue). Multicoloured.
1015 **352** 500f. Footballers . . . . 3·75 1·75

353 Dead and Healthy Trees

354 Amazone

1986. Anti-desertification Campaign.
1016 **353** 150f. multicoloured . . . 1·25 65

1986.
1017 **354** 100f. blue 65 20
1018 150f. purple 95 25

355 "Haemanthus"

356 "Inachis io", "Aglais urticae" and "Nymphalis antiopa"

1986. Flowers. Multicoloured.
1019 100f. Type **355** . . . . . . 1·10 75
1020 205f. "Hemerocallis" . . . 2·25 1·25

1986. Butterflies. Multicoloured.
1021 150f. Type **356** . . . . . . 1·75 1·10
1022 150f. "Anthocharis cardamines", "Papilio machaon" and "Cynthia cardui" . . . . 1·75 1·10

1986. Various stamps of Dahomey surch **Republique Populaire du Benin** and new value.
1024 – 150f. on 100f. mult (444) (postage) . . . . . .
1025 – 15f. on 85f. mult (600) (air) . . . .
1026 – 25f. on 200f. mult (432)
1027 **150** 25f. on 200f. deep green, violet and green . . .
1030 **175** 100f. purple, indigo & bl
1031 **128** 150f. on 100f. blue, violet and red . . . .

358 Statue and Buildings

359 Bust of King Behanzin

1986. Centenary of Statue of Liberty.
1032 **358** 250f. multicoloured . . . 2·25 1·00

1986. King Behanzin.
1033 **359** 440f. multicoloured . . . 3·75 1·90
For design in smaller size, see Nos. 1101/4.

360 Family with Crib, Church and Nativity Scene

1986. Air. Christmas.
1034 **360** 300f. multicoloured . . . 2·50 1·10

361 Rainbow and Douglas DC-10

1986. Air. 25th Anniv of Air Afrique.
1035 **361** 100f. multicoloured . . . 1·00 60

362 Emblem around Map in Cog

1987. Brazil Culture Week, Cotonou.
1036 **362** 150f. multicoloured . . . 1·75 70

363 Cotonou Centre for the Blind and Partially Sighted

1987. Rotary International 910 District Conference, Cotonou.
1037 **363** 300f. multicoloured . . . 2·50 1·10

1987. Various stamps of Dahomey optd **Republique Populaire du Benin**. Nos. 1038/9 and 1042/53 surch also.
1038 **129** 10f. on 65f. black, violet and red (postage) . . . . . .
1039 – 15f. on 100f. red, blue and green (434) . . .
1040 **98** 40f. green, blue and brown . . . .
1042 – 150f. on 200f. mult (560) . . . .
1043 **144** 10f. on 65f. black, yellow & purple (air)
1046 – 25f. on 150f. mult (487)
1047 – 30f. on 300f. mult (602)
1048 **140** 40f. on 15f. purple, green and blue . . .
1049 – 40f. on 100f. mult (453)
1051 – 50f. on 140f. mult (601)
1052 – 50f. on 500f. mult (252)
1053 – 70f. on 250f. mult (462)
1054 – 80f. mult (286) . . . .
1055 – 100f. mult (429) . . . .
1055a – 100f. mult (447) . . . .

365 De Dion-Bouton and Trepardoux Steam Tricycle and Ford Coupe

1987. Centenary of Motor Car. Multicoloured.
1058 150f. Type **365** . . . . . . 1·50 75
1059 300f. Daimler motor carriage, 1886 and Mercedes Benz W124 series saloon . . . . . . 2·75 1·50

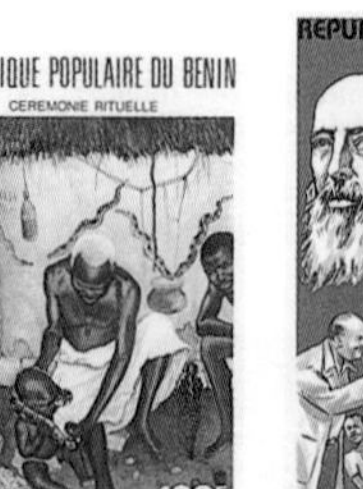

366 Baptism in the Python Temple

368 G. Hansen and R. Follereau (leprosy pioneers) and Patients

367 Shrimp

1987. Ritual Ceremonies.
1060 **366** 100f. multicoloured . . . 95 50

1987. Shellfish. Multicoloured.
1061 100f. Type **367** . . . . . . 1·10 60
1062 150f. Crab . . . . 1·40 90

1987. Anti-leprosy Campaign.
1063 **368** 200f. multicoloured . . . 1·90 95

369 Crop-spraying and Locusts

1987. Anti-locust Campaign.
1064 **369** 100f. multicoloured . . . 1·10 60

370 Fisherman and Farmer

1987. Air. 10th Anniv of International Agricultural Development Fund.
1065 **370** 500f. multicoloured . . . 3·75 1·90

371 Nativity Scene in Moon and Father Christmas giving Sweets to Crowd

1987. Christmas.
1066 **371** 150f. multicoloured . . . 1·25 75

372 Rally

375 Hands holding Pot Aloft

1988. 15th Anniv (1987) of Start of Benin Revolution.
1067 **372** 100f. multicoloured . . .

1988. Various stamps surch. (a) Stamps of Dahomey surch **Populaire du Benin** (1081c) or **Republique Populaire du Benin** (others).
1068 – 5f. on 3f. black and blue (173) (postage)
1069 – 20f. on 100f. mult (506)
1071 – 25f. on 100f. mult (576)
1073 – 50f. on 45f. mult (320)
1074 **178** 55f. on 200f. olive, brown and green . .
1075a 125f. on 100f. mult (557) . . . .
1076 **116** 10f. on 50f. black, orange and blue (air)
1077 **161** 15f. on 150f. red and black . . . .
1078 – 25f. on 100f. mult (526)
1079 **156** 25f. on 100f. blue, brown and violet . .
1079a **153** 40f. on 35f. mult . . .
1080 – 40f. on 100f. mult (495)
1081 **162** 40f. on 150f. red, brown and blue . . .
1081a **148** 100f. brown and green
1081b **181** 125f. on 75f. lilac, red and green . . . . .
1081c – 125f. on 150f. blue and purple (541) . . . .
1082 – 125f. on 250f. mult (491) . . . .
1082a – 125f. red and brown (540) . . . .
1083 – 190f. on 250f. brown, green and red (594)
1084 – 1000f. on 150f. multicoloured (545)

(b) No. 618 of Benin surch **Republique Populaire du Benin**.
1085 – 10f. on 60f. on 2f. mult . .

(c) Stamps of Benin surch only.
1086 **359** 125f. on 440f. mult (postage) . . . . . .
1087 **338** 125f. on 200f. mult (air)
1088 – 190f. on 250f. mult (999)
1089 – 190f. on 250f. mult (1000) . . . .

1988. 25th Anniv of Organization of African Unity.
1094 **375** 125f. multicoloured . . . 95 40

376 Resuscitation of Man pulled from River

1988. 125th Anniv of Red Cross Movement.
1095 **376** 200f. multicoloured . . . 1·50 1·00

377 King

378 Scout and Camp

1988. 20th Death Anniv of Martin Luther King (Civil Rights leader).
1096 **377** 200f. multicoloured . . . 1·50 75

1988. 1st Benin Scout Jamboree, Savalou.
1097 **378** 125f. multicoloured . . . 1·25 90

379 Healthy Family and Health Care

1988. 40th Anniv of W.H.O. and 10th Anniv of "Health for All by 2000" Declaration.
1098 **379** 175f. multicoloured . . . 1·25 65

380 Dugout Canoes and Houses

1988. Ganvie (lake village). Multicoloured.
1099 125f. Type **380** 95 50
1100 190f. Boatman and houses 1·60 75

1988. As T **359** but smaller (17 × 24 mm).
1101 **359** 40f. black 25 15
1102 125f. red 75 25
1103 190f. blue . . . . 1·25 25
1104 220f. green . . . . . . 1·50 40

381 Adoration of the Magi

1988. Air. Christmas.
1105 **381** 500f. multicoloured . . . 3·75 1·90

382 Offering to Hebiesso, God of Thunder

1988. Ritual Ceremony.
1106 **382** 125f. multicoloured . . . 95 50

383 Roseate Tern

1989. Endangered Animals. Roseate Tern. Mult.
1107 10f. Type **383** 25 15
1108 15f. Tern with fish 50 20
1109 50f. Tern on rocks . . . . 1·00 40
1110 125f. Tern flying . . . . . 2·50 85

384 Eiffel Tower

386 Tractor, Map and Pump

1989. Centenary of Eiffel Tower.
1111 **384** 190f. multicoloured . . . 1·60 1·00

1989. 30th Anniv of Agriculture Development Council.
1113 **386** 75f. multicoloured . . .

387 Symbols of Revolution and France 1950 National Relief Fund Stamps

1989. Bicentenary of French Revolution and "Philexfrance 89" International Stamp Exhibition, Paris.
1114 **387** 190f. multicoloured . . . 1·90 1·25

388 Burbot

1989. Fishes. Multicoloured.
1115 125f. Type **388** . . . . . . 1·50 75
1116 190f. Northern pike and Atlantic salmon . . . . . 2·25 1·25

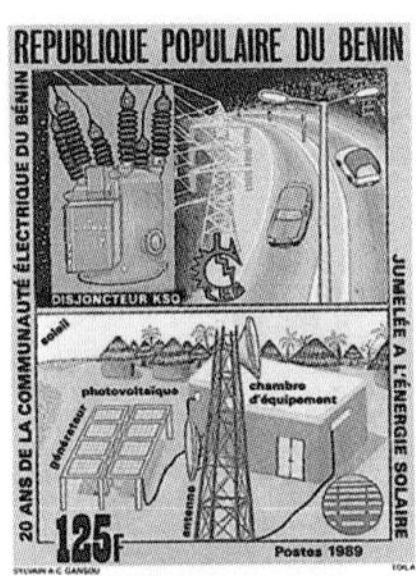
389 Circuit Breaker, Illuminated Road and Solar Energy Complex

1989. 20th Anniv of Benin Electricity Community.
1117 **389** 125f. multicoloured . . . 95 50

390 Lion within Wreath

1989. Death Centenary of King Glele.
1118 **390** 190f. multicoloured . . . 1·40 75

391 Nativity

1989. Christmas.
1119 **391** 200f. multicoloured . . . 1·50 90

392 Anniversary Emblem and Means of Communications

1990. Centenary of Postal and Telecommunications Ministry (1st issue).
1120 **392** 125f. multicoloured . . . 95 50
See also No. 1127.

393 Oranges

1990. Fruit and Flowers. Multicoloured.
1121 60f. Type **393** 45 30
1122 190f. Kaufmannia tulips (vert) . . . . 1·75 90
1123 250f. Cashew nuts (vert) . . 1·90 1·10

394 Launch of "Apollo 11" and Footprint on Moon

1990. 21st Anniv of First Manned Moon Landing.
1124 **394** 190f. multicoloured . . . 1·40 75

395 Footballers

1990. World Cup Football Championship, Italy. Multicoloured.
1125 125f. Type **395** . . . . . . 1·10 60
1126 190f. Mascot holding torch and pennant (vert) . . . 1·75 75

396 Balloons, Emblem and Means of Communication

398 De Gaulle

1990. Centenary of Postal and Telecommunications Ministry (2nd issue).
1127 **396** 150f. multicoloured . . . 1·10 55

1990. World Cup Finalists. No. 1125 optd **FINALE R.F.A.-ARGENTINE 1-0**.
1128 **395** 125f. multicoloured . . . 80 50

1990. Birth Centenary of Charles de Gaulle (French statesman) (1st issue).
1129 **398** 190f. multicoloured . . . 1·50 1·00
See also No. 1160.

399 "Galileo" Space Probe orbiting Jupiter

400 Nativity

1990. Space Exploration.
1130 **399** 100f. multicoloured . . . 75 50

1990. Christmas.
1131 **400** 200f. multicoloured . . . 1·50 1·00

401 Hands pointing to Scales of Justice

1990. National Conference of Active Forces.
1132 **401** 125f. multicoloured . . .

406 Different Cultures and Emblem

1991. African Tourism Year.
1150 **406** 190f. multicoloured . . . 1·50 1·00

407 Tennis Player

408 Flag and Arms

1991. Cent of French Open Tennis Championships.
1151 **407** 125f. multicoloured . . . 1·50 75

1991. 31st Anniv of Independence.
1152 **408** 125f. multicoloured . . . 1·50 75

1991. "Riccione 91" Stamp Fair. No. 1130 optd **"Riccione 91"**.
1153 **399** 100f. multicoloured . . . 1·00 60

410 Adoration of the Magi

1991. Christmas.
1154 **410** 125f. multicoloured . . . 95 40

411 Guelede Dancer

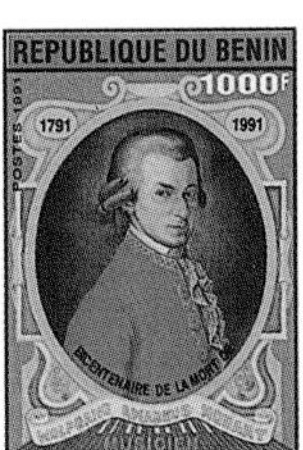
412 Mozart

1991.
1155 **411** 190f. multicoloured . . . 1·50 65

1991. Death Bicentenary of Wolfgang Amadeus Mozart (composer).
1156 **412** 1000f. multicoloured . . 8·00 5·00

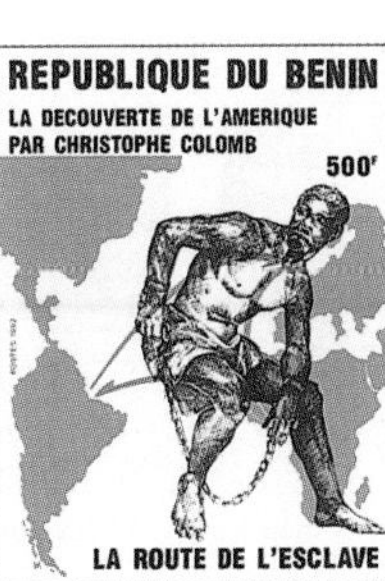
413 Slave in Chains and Route Map

1992. 500th Anniv of Discovery of America by Columbus.
1157 **413** 500f. black, brown & bl 3·75 2·50
1158 – 1000f. multicoloured . . 7·00 5·00
DESIGN—HORIZ: 1000f. Columbus landing at Guanahami, Bahamas.

1992. Birth Centenary (1990) of Charles de Gaulle (French statesman) (2nd issue). As No. 1129 but value changed.
1160 **398** 300f. multicoloured . . . 2·25 1·50

414 Child, Produce and Emblems

415 Pope John Paul II

1992. International Nutrition Conference, Rome.
1161 **414** 190f. multicoloured . . . 1·40 1·00

1993. Papal Visit.
1162 **415** 190f. multicoloured . . . 1·25 90

416 Emblem and Voodoo Culture

1993. "Ouidah 92" Voodoo Culture Festival.
1163 **416** 125f. multicoloured . . . 75 50

417 Well and Blue-throated Roller

1993. Possotome Artesian Well.
1164 **417** 125f. multicoloured . . . 75 50

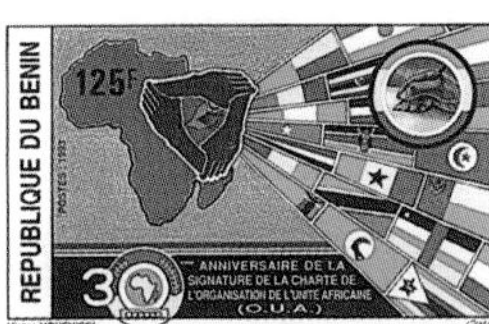
418 Map, Clasped Hands and Flags of Member Countries

1993. 30th Anniv of Organization of African Unity.
1165 **418** 125f. multicoloured . . . 70 40

419 John F. Kennedy (President of United States, 1961–63)

1993. Death Anniversaries. Multicoloured.
1166 190f. Type **419** (30th anniv) 85 45
1167 190f. Dr. Martin Luther King (American civil rights campaigner, 25th anniv) (vert) 85 45

1993. Stamps of Dahomey variously optd or surch.
(a) **REPUBLIQUE DU BENIN**.
1167a **139** 5f. multicoloured (postage) . . . . . .
1170 **108** 50f. on 1f. multicoloured (617)
1171 **113** 80f. on 40f. red, brown and green . . . . .
1173 135f. on 20f. black, green and red (190)
1175 135f. on 30f. black, brown and violet (472) . . . .
1177 **107** 135f. on 40f. mult . . .

1179 – 135f. on 60f. olive, red and purple (181)
1181 – 200f. on 100f. mult (322)
1186 – 15f. on 40f. mult (458) (air)
1190 **126** 100f. multicoloured
1190a **119** 125f. on 40f. mult
1191 – 125f. on 65f. red and blue (552)
1201 – 200f. on 250f. mult (569)

(b) **DU BENIN**.

1207 **60** 5f. on 1f. multicoloured (postage)
1208 – 10f. on 3f. black and blue (173)
1211 – 25f. multicoloured (441)
1220 – 135f. on 3f. mult (274)
1223 – 20f. on 200f. mult (451) (air)
1225 – 25f. on 85f. mult (600)
1227 **140** 30f. on 15f. purple, green and blue
1231 – 125f. on 70f. mult (383)
1235 – 150f. purple, blue and brown (456)
1236 – 150f. multicoloured (527)
1239 **150** 200f. green, violet and emerald
1242 – 200f. on 150f. mult (562)
1243 **179** 300f. multicoloured

(c) **BENIN**.

1257 – 25f. on 500f. brown, red and green (592) (air)
1258 – 30f. on 200f. mult (528)
1260a – 100f. brown, green and blue (522)
1261 **116** 125f. on 50f. black, orange and blue
1263a – 190f. on 200f. mult (478)
1266 – 300f. brn, red & bl (591)

422 Conference Emblem

1994. U.N.E.S.C.O. Conference on the Slave Route, Ouidah.

1275 **422** 300f. multicoloured . . . 75 40

423 World Map

1994. International Year of the Family.

1276 **423** 200f. multicoloured . . . 50 25

425 Water Polo

1995. Olympic Games, Atlanta (1996) (1st issue). Multicoloured.

1278 45f. Type **425** . . . 20 20
1279 50f. Throwing the javelin (vert) . . . 25 20
1280 75f. Weightlifting (vert) . . 35 25
1281 100f. Tennis (vert) . . . 50 40
1282 135f. Baseball (vert) . . . 60 50
1283 200f. Synchronised swimming (vert) . . . 90 70

See also Nos. 1347/52.

426 Paddle-steamer

1995. Ships. Multicoloured.

1285 40f. Type **426** . . . 20 20
1286 50f. "Charlotte" (paddle steamer) . . . 25 20
1287 75f. "Citta di Catania" (Italian liner) . . . 35 25
1288 100f. "Mountbatten" SR-N4 (hovercraft) . . . 50 40
1289 135f. "Queen Elizabeth 2" (liner) . . . 60 50
1290 200f. "Matsu-Nef" (Japanese nuclear-powered freighter) . . . 90 70

427 Chimpanzee

1995. Primates. Multicoloured.

1292 50f. Type **427** . . . 25 20
1293 75f. Mandrill . . . 35 30
1294 100f. Colobus . . . 50 40
1295 135f. Barbary ape . . . 70 50
1296 200f. Hamadryas baboon . . 1·00 75

428 Tabby Shorthair

1995. Cats. Multicoloured.

1298 40f. Type **428** . . . 20 20
1299 50f. Sorrel Abyssinian ("Ruddy red") . . . 25 20
1300 75f. White Persian long-hair 35 30
1301 100f. Seal colourpoint . . . 50 40
1302 135f. Tabby point . . . 60 50
1303 200f. Black shorthair . . . 90 70

429 German Shepherd

1995. Dogs. Multicoloured.

1305 40f. Type **429** . . . 20 20
1306 50f. Beagle . . . 25 20
1307 75f. Great dane . . . 35 30
1308 100f. Boxer . . . 50 40
1309 135f. Pointer . . . 60 50
1310 200f. Long-haired fox terrier 90 70

430 Arms **431** Lion

1995.

1312 **430** 135f. multicoloured . . . 35 20
1313 150f. multicoloured . . . 35 20
1314 200f. multicoloured . . . 50 25

See also Nos. 1458 and 1480/2.

1995. Mammals. Multicoloured.

1315 50f. Type **431** . . . 25 20
1316 75f. African buffalo . . . 35 30
1317 100f. Chimpanzee . . . 50 40
1318 135f. Impala . . . 70 50
1319 200f. Cape ground squirrel (horiz) . . . 1·00 75

432 Hawfinches **433** "Dracunculus vulgaris"

1995. Birds and their Young. Multicoloured.

1321 40f. Type **432** . . . 20 20
1322 50f. Spotted-necked doves 25 20
1323 75f. Peregrine falcons . . . 35 30
1324 100f. Blackburnian warblers 50 40
1325 135f. Black-headed gulls . . 60 50
1326 200f. Eastern white pelican 90 70

1995. Flowers. Multicoloured.

1327 40f. Type **433** . . . 20 20
1328 50f. Daffodil . . . 25 20
1329 75f. Amaryllis . . . 35 30
1330 100f. Water-lily . . . 50 40
1331 135f. "Chrysanthemum carinatum" . . . 60 50
1332 200f. Iris . . . 90 70

434 Lynx **435** "Angraecum sesquipedale"

1995. Big Cats and their Young. Mult.

1333 40f. Type **434** . . . 20 20
1334 50f. Pumas . . . 30 20
1335 75f. Cheetahs . . . 35 20
1336 100f. Leopards . . . 45 25
1337 135f. Tigers . . . 60 30
1338 200f. Lions . . . 85 40

1995. Orchids. Multicoloured.

1339 40f. Type **435** . . . 20 20
1340 50f. "Polystachya virginea" 25 20
1341 75f. "Disa uniflora" . . . 35 30
1342 100f. "Ansellia africana" . . 50 40
1343 135f. "Angraecum eichlerianum" . . . 60 50
1344 200f. "Jumellea confusa" . . 90 70

436 Emblem **437** Diving

1995. 6th Francophone Summit, Cotonou.

1345 **436** 150f. multicoloured . . . 35 20
1346 200f. multicoloured . . . 50 25

1996. Olympic Games, Atlanta (2nd issue). Multicoloured.

1347 40f. Type **437** . . . 20 20
1348 50f. Tennis . . . 25 20
1349 75f. Running . . . 35 30
1350 100f. Gymnastics . . . 50 40
1351 135f. Weightlifting . . . 60 50
1352 200f. Shooting . . . 90 70

438 Player with Ball

1996. World Cup Football Championship, France (1998) (1st issue).

1354 **438** 40f. multicoloured . . . 35 20
1355 – 50f. multicoloured . . . 35 20
1356 – 75f. multicoloured . . . 75 50
1357 – 100f. multicoloured . . . 90 60
1358 – 135f. multicoloured . . . 1·25 1·00
1359 – 200f. multicoloured . . . 1·90 1·50

DESIGNS: 50f. to 200f. Different players.

See also Nos. 1473/8.

439 Small Striped Swallowtail

1996. Butterflies. Multicoloured.

1361 40f. Type **439** . . . 35 20
1362 50f. Red admiral . . . 35 20
1363 75f. Common blue . . . 75 50
1364 100f. African monarch . . . 90 60
1365 135f. Painted lady . . . 1·25 1·00
1366 200f. "Argus celbulina orbitulus" . . . 1·90 1·50

440 Dancer

1996. "China '96" International Stamp Exhibition, Peking. Multicoloured.

1368 40f. Type **440** . . . 75 50
1369 50f. Exhibition emblem . . 1·00 75
1370 75f. Water-lily . . . 1·50 1·00
1371 100f. Temple of Heaven, Peking . . . 2·00 1·50

Nos. 1368/71 were issued together, se-tenant, forming a composite design.

441 Emblem

1996. 15th Convention of Lions Club International, Cotonou.

1457 **441** 100f. multicoloured . . . 75 50
1372 135f. multicoloured . . . 1·10 75
1373 150f. multicoloured . . . 1·10 75
1374 200f. multicoloured . . . 1·50 1·00

442 "Holy Family of Rouvre" (Raphael)

1996. Christmas. Multicoloured.

1375 40f. Type **442** . . . 35 20
1376 50f. "The Holy Family" (Raphael) . . . 35 20
1377 75f. "St. John the Baptist" (Bartolome Murillo) . . . 75 60
1378 100f. "The Virgin of the Scales" (Leonardo da Vinci) . . . 95 60
1379 135f. "The Virgin and Child" (Gerhard David) 1·25 1·00
1380 200f. "Adoration of the Magi" (Juan Mayno) . . 1·90 1·50

443 "Thermopylae" (clipper) (inscr "Thermopyles")

1996. Ships. Multicoloured.

1382 40f. Type **443** . . . 35 20
1383 50f. Barque . . . 35 20
1384 75f. "Nightingale" (full-rigged ship) . . . 75 50
1385 100f. Opium clipper . . . 90 60
1386 135f. "Torrens" (full-rigged ship) . . . 1·25 1·00
1387 200f. English tea clipper . . 1·90 1·50

444 Serval **445** Hurdler and Gold Medal

1996. Big Cats. Multicoloured.
1389 40f. Type **444** 35 20
1390 50f. Golden cat 35 20
1391 75f. Ocelot 75 50
1392 100f. Bobcat 90 60
1393 135f. Leopard cat . . . . . . 1·25 1·00
1394 200f. "Felis euptilura" . . . 1·95 1·50

1996. Centenary of Issue by Greece of First Olympic Stamps. Multicoloured.
1396 40f. Type **445** . . . . 1·00 50
1397 50f. Hurdler and Olympic flames . . . . 1·00 50
1398 75f. Pierre de Coubertin (founder of modern Olympics) and map showing south-west U.S.A. . . . . 1·25 60
1399 100f. Map showing south-east U.S.A. . . . . 1·50 75
Nos. 1396/9 were issued together, se-tenant, forming a composite design.

446 Running

447 "Parodia subterranea"

1996. "Olymphilex '96" Olympics and Sports Stamp Exhibition, Atlanta. Multicoloured.
1400 40f. Type **446** 35 20
1401 50f. Canoeing 35 20
1402 75f. Gymnastics 75 50
1403 100f. Football 90 60
1404 135f. Tennis . . . . 1·25 1·00
1405 200f. Baseball . . . . . . 1·90 1·50

1996. Flowering Cacti. Multicoloured.
1407 40f. Type **447** 35 20
1408 50f. "Astrophytum senile" 35 20
1409 75f. "Echinocereus melanocentrus" 75 50
1410 100f. "Turbinicarpus klinkerianus" 90 60
1411 135f. "Astrophytum capricorne" . . . . . . 1·25 1·00
1412 200f. "Nelloydia grandiflora" . . . . . . 1·90 1·50

448 Chestnut Horse

449 Longisquama

1996. Horses. Multicoloured.
1413 40f. Type **448** 35 20
1414 50f. Horse on hillside . . . 35 20
1415 75f. Foal by fence 75 50
1416 100f. Mother and foal . . . 95 60
1417 135f. Pair of horses . . . . 1·40 1·00
1418 200f. Grey horse (horiz) . . 2·00 1·50

1996. Prehistoric Animals. Multicoloured.
1419 40f. Type **449** 35 20
1420 50f. Dimorphodon 35 20
1421 75f. Dunkleosteus (horiz) . . 75 50
1422 100f. Eryops (horiz) 90 60
1423 135f. Peloneustes (horiz) . . 1·25 1·00
1424 200f. Deinonychus (horiz) 1·90 1·50

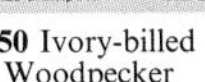

450 Ivory-billed Woodpecker

451 Golden Tops

1996. Birds. Multicoloured.
1425 40f. Type **450** 35 20
1426 50f. Grey-necked bald crow 35 20
1427 75f. Kakapo 75 50
1428 100f. Puerto Rican amazon 90 60
1429 135f. Japanese crested ibis 1·25 1·00
1430 200f. California condor . . 1·90 1·50

1996. Fungi. Multicoloured.
1432 40f. Type **451** 35 20
1433 50f. "Psilocybe zapotecorum" 35 20
1434 75f. "Psilocybe mexicana" 75 50
1435 100f. "Conocybe siligineoides" 90 60
1436 135f. "Psilocybe caerulescens mazatecorum" . . . . . 1·25 1·00
1437 200f. "Psilocybe caerulescens nigripes" . . . . 1·90 1·50

452 Impala

1996. Mammals. Multicoloured.
1439 40f. Type **452** 35 20
1440 50f. Waterbuck 35 20
1441 75f. African buffalo 75 50
1442 100f. Blue wildebeest . . . 90 60
1443 135f. Okapi . . . . 1·25 1·00
1444 200f. Greater kudu . . . . 1·90 1·40

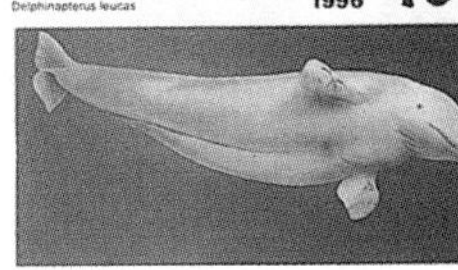

453 White Whale

1996. Marine Mammals. Multicoloured.
1445 40f. Type **453** 35 20
1446 50f. Bottle-nosed dolphin . . 35 20
1447 75f. Blue whale 75 50
1448 100f. "Eubalaena australis" 90 60
1449 135f. "Gramphidelphis griseus" . . . . 1·25 1·00
1450 200f. Killer whale . . . . . 1·90 1·40

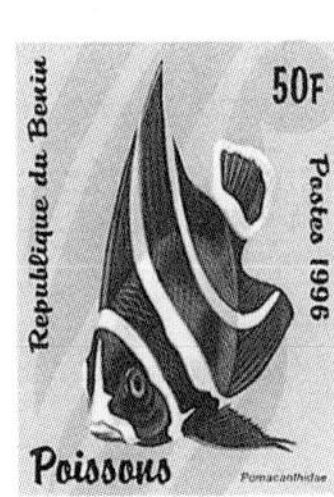

454 Grey Angelfish

455 Grenadier, Glassenapps Regiment

1996. Fishes. Multicoloured.
1451 50f. Type **454** 10 10
1452 75f. Sail-finned tang (horiz) 15 10
1453 100f. Golden trevally (horiz) 20 10
1454 135f. Pyramid butterflyfish (horiz) 25 15
1455 200f. Racoon butterflyfish (horiz) 40 20

1996. Arms. Dated "1996".
1458 **430** 100f. multicoloured . . . 95 40

1996. Stamps of Benin variously surch.
1469 **311** 15f. on 185f. mult (postage) . . . . . .
1470 **379** 25f. on 175f. mult . . .
1473 **359** 50f. on 220f. green (1104) . . . .
1479 **414** 150f. on 190f. mult . . .
1480 **415** 150f. on 190f. mult . . .
1484 **412** 250f. on 1000f. mult . . .
1494 **193** 40f. on 210f. red, brown and green (air) . . . .
1495 – 40f. on 210f. purple, blue and yellow (792) . . .
1499 – 150f. on 500f. red, ultramarine and green (657) . . . .

1996. Stamps of Dahomey variously optd or surch. (a) **Republique de Benin** (1510, 1516, 1519, 1522, 1526/9, 1535, 1544, 1556, 1558 and 1568) or **REPUBLIQUE DU BENIN** (others).
1510 – 35f. on 85f. brown, orange and green (493) (postage) . . . . .
1511 – 125f. on 100f. violet, red and black (510) . . .
1516 **85** 150f. on 30f. mult . . .
1519 **113** 150f. on 40f. red, brown and green . . . . . .
1522 – 150f. on 45f. mult (597)
1526 – 35f. on 100f. deep blue and blue (326) (air) . .
1527 – 35f. on 100f. on 200f. multicoloured (409) . .
1528 – 35f. on 125f. green, blue and light blue (553) . .
1529 – 35f. on 300f. brown, red and blue (591) . . . .
1535 – 150f. multicoloured (527)
1544 **112** 150f. on 40f. multicoloured . . . .
1556 – 150f. on 110f. mult (386)
1558 – 150f. on 120f. mult (404)
1568 – 200f. on 500f. mult (252)

(b) **DU BENIN**.
1578 35f. on 125f. brown and green (540) (air) . . .
1579 125f. on 65f. mult (465)
1580 **168** 135f. on 35f. mult . . .

(c) **BENIN** .
1587 **68** 150f. on 30f. mult (post)
1591 25f. on 85f. mult (600) (air) . . . .

1997. Military Uniforms. Multicoloured.
1600 135f. Type **455** 35 20
1601 150f. Officer, Von Groben's Regiment 35 20
1602 200f. Private, Dohna's Regiment 75 50
1603 270f. Artilleryman 90 60
1604 300f. Cavalry trooper . . . 1·25 1·00
1605 400f. Trooper, Mollendorf's Dragoons . . . . 1·90 1·40

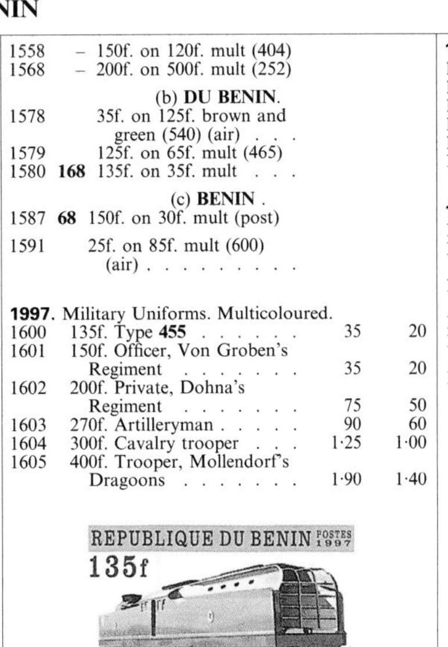

456 Reid Macleod Gas-turbine Locomotive, 1920

1997. Railway Locomotives. Multicoloured.
1607 135f. Type **456** 25 15
1608 150f. Class O5 steam locomotive, 1935, Germany 30 15
1609 200f. Locomotive "Silver Fox", Great Britain . . . 40 20
1610 270f. Class "Merchant Navy" locomotive, 1941, Great Britain 55 30
1611 300f. Diesel locomotive, 1960, Denmark 60 30
1612 400f. GM Type diesel locomotive, 1960 . . . . 80 40
No. 1607 is wrongly inscr "Reid Maclead 1920".

457 Footballer and Map

458 Arms

1997. World Cup Football Championship, France (1998) (2nd issue).
1614 **457** 135f. multicoloured . . . 35 20
1615 – 150f. multicoloured . . . 35 20
1616 – 200f. multicoloured . . . 75 50
1617 – 270f. multicoloured . . . 90 60
1618 – 300f. mult (horiz) . . . 1·25 1·00
1619 – 400f. mult (horiz) . . . 1·90 1·50
DESIGNS: 150f. to 400f. Each showing map of France and player.

1997. T **430** redrawn as T **458**. Dated "1997".
1621 **458** 135f. multicoloured . . . 40 25
1622 150f. multicoloured . . . 70 35
1623 200f. multicoloured . . . 90 50

459 Horse's Head

1997. Horses. Multicoloured.
1624 135f. Type **459** 40 25
1625 150f. Bay horse 55 35
1626 200f. Chestnut horse looking forward 70 45
1627 270f. Chestnut horse looking backwards 80 60
1628 300f. Black horse . . . . . 1·00 70
1629 400f. Profile of horse . . . 1·25 85

460 Irish Setter

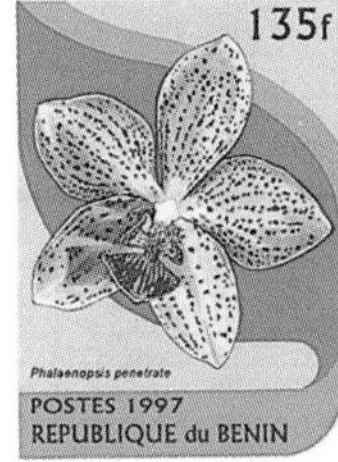

461 "Phalaenopsis penetrate"

1997. Dogs. Multicoloured.
1631 135f. Type **460** 40 25
1632 150f. Saluki 55 35
1633 200f. Dobermann pinscher 70 45
1634 270f. Siberian husky 80 60
1635 300f. Basenji . . . . 1·00 90
1636 400f. Boxer . . . . 1·25 85

1997. Orchids. Multicoloured.
1638 135f. Type **461** 40 25
1639 150f. "Phalaenopsis" "Golden Sands" 55 35
1640 200f. "Phalaenopsis" "Sun Spots" 70 45
1641 270f. "Phalaenopsis fuscata" 80 60
1642 300f. "Phalaenopsis christi floyd" . . . . 1·00 70
1643 400f. "Phalaenopsis cayanne" . . . . 1·25 85

462 Buick Model C Tourer, 1905

1997. Motor Cars. Multicoloured.
1645 135f. Type **462** 40 25
1646 150f. Ford model A tonneau, 1903 . . . . . 55 35
1647 200f. Stanley steamer tourer, 1913 . . . . 70 45
1648 270f. Stoddar-Dayton tourer, 1911 . . . . . . 80 60
1649 300f. Cadillac convertible sedan, 1934 . . . . . . 1·00 70
1650 400f. Cadillac convertible sedan, 1931 . . . . . . 1·25 85

463 Northern Bullfinch

1997. Birds. Multicoloured.
1652 135f. Type **463** 40 25
1653 150f. Spruce siskin 50 35
1654 200f. Ring ousel 70 50
1655 270f. Crested tit 90 70
1656 300f. Spotted nutcracker . . 1·00 75
1657 400f. Nightingale . . . . . 1·50 1·00

464 "Faucaria lupina"

1997. Cacti. Multicoloured.
1659 135f. Type **464** 40 25
1660 150f. "Conophytum bilobun" 50 35
1661 200f. "Lithops aucampiae" 70 50
1662 270f. "Lithops helmutii" . . 90 70
1663 300f. "Stapelia grandiflora" 1·00 75
1664 400f. "Lithops fulviceps" . . 1·50 1·00

465 Egyptian Merchant Ship

1997. Ancient Sailing Ships. Multicoloured.
1666 135f. Type **465** 45 30
1667 150f. Greek merchant ship 45 30
1668 200f. Phoenician galley . . . 75 50
1669 270f. Roman merchant ship 1·00 60
1670 300f. Norman knarr . . . . 1·10 70
1671 400f. Mediterranean sailing ship . . . . 1·50 90

466 Black-tipped Grouper

1997. Fishes. Multicoloured.

1673	135f. Type **466**	30	15
1674	150f. Cardinal fish	30	15
1675	200f. Indo-Pacific humpheaded parrotfish	45	25
1676	270f. Regal angelfish	60	30
1677	300f. Wrasse	65	35
1678	400f. Hawkfish	85	45

467 Emblem

1997. 10th Anniv of African Petroleum Producers' Association.

1680 **467**	135f. multicoloured	50	25
1681	200f. multicoloured	85	35
1682	300f. multicoloured	1·10	50
1683	500f. multicoloured	1·75	70

468 Caesar's Mushroom

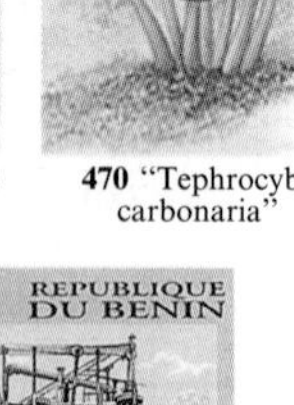

470 "Tephrocybe carbonaria"

469 "Puffing Billy", 1813

1997. Fungi. Multicoloured.

1684	135f. Type **468**	40	25
1685	150f. Slimy-banded cort	50	35
1686	200f. "Amanita bisporigera"	70	50
1687	270f. The blusher	90	70
1688	300f. Cracked green russula	1·00	75
1689	400f. Strangulated amanita	1·50	1·00

1997. Steam Railway Locomotives. Mult.

1691	135f. Type **469**	30	15
1692	150f. "Rocket", 1829	30	15
1693	200f. "Royal George", 1827	45	25
1694	270f. "Novelty", 1829	60	30
1695	300f. "Locomotion", 1825 (vert)	65	35
1696	400f. "Sans Pareil", 1829 (vert)	85	45

1998. Fungi. Multicoloured.

1698	135f. Type **470**	25	15
1699	150f. Butter mushroom	30	15
1700	200f. Oyster fungus	40	20
1701	270f. "Hohenbuehelia geogenia"	50	25
1702	300f. Bitter bolete	60	30
1703	400f. "Lepiota leucothites"	80	40

471 Philadelphia or "Double Deck", 1885

1998. Fire Engines. Multicoloured.

1705	135f. Type **471**	25	15
1706	150f. "Veteran", 1850	30	15
1707	200f. Merryweather, 1894	40	20
1708	270f. 19 th-century Hippomobile	50	25
1709	300f. Jeep "Willy", 1948	60	30
1710	400f. Chevrolet 6400	80	40

472 Uranite

1998. Minerals. Multicoloured.

1712	135f. Type **472**	25	15
1713	150f. Quartz	30	15
1714	200f. Aragonite	40	20
1715	270f. Malachite	50	25
1716	300f. Turquoise	60	30
1717	400f. Corundum	80	40

473 Locomotive

1998. Steam Railway Locomotives. Multicoloured.

1719	135f. Type **473**	25	15
1720	150f. Green locomotive	30	15
1721	200f. Brown locomotive	40	20
1722	270f. Lilac locomotive	50	25
1723	300f. Toledo Furnace Co No. 1	60	30
1724	400f. No. 1 "Helvetia"	80	40

474 Diana, Princess of Wales

1998. 1st Death Anniv of Diana, Princess of Wales. Multicoloured.

1726	135f. Type **474**	25	15
1727	150f. Wearing pink dress	25	15
1728	200f. Wearing beige jacket	35	20
1729	270f. Wearing white jacket with revers	50	25
1730	300f. Making speech	55	30
1731	400f. Wearing collarless single-breasted white jacket	70	35
1732	500f. Wearing red jacket	90	45
1733	600f. Wearing black jacket	1·10	55
1734	700f. Wearing double-breasted white jacket	1·25	65

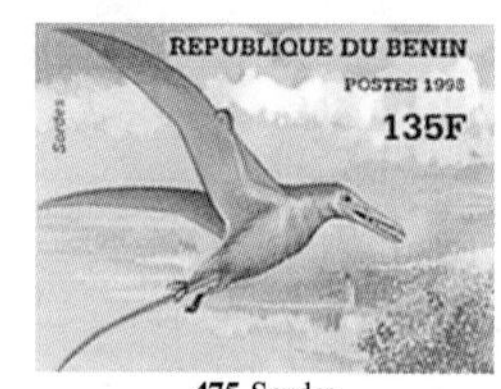

475 Sordes

1998. Prehistoric Animals. Multicoloured.

1735	135f. Type **475**	25	15
1736	150f. Scaphognatus	25	15
1737	200f. Dsungaripterus	35	20
1738	270f. Brontosaurus	50	25
1739	300f. Diplodocus	55	30
1740	400f. Coelurus and baryonyx	70	35
1741	500f. Kronosaurus and ichthyosaurus	90	45
1742	600f. Ceratosaurus	1·10	55
1743	700f. Yangchuansaurus	1·25	65

Nos. 1735/43 were issued together, se-tenant, forming a composite design.

476 Beagle

477 Abyssinian

1998. Dogs. Multicoloured.

1744	135f. Type **476**	25	15
1745	150f. Dalmatians	25	15
1746	200f. Dachshund	35	20
1747	270f. Cairn terrier	50	25
1748	300f. Shih-tzus	55	30
1749	400f. Pug	70	35

1998. Cats. Multicoloured.

1751	135f. Type **477**	25	15
1752	150f. Striped silver tabby	25	15
1753	200f. Siamese	35	20
1754	270f. Red tabby (horiz)	50	25
1755	300f. Wild cat (horiz)	55	30
1756	400f. Manx (horiz)	70	35

478 Bugatti 13 Torpedo, 1910

1998. Motor Cars. Multicoloured.

1758	135f. Type **478**	25	15
1759	150f. Clement voiturette, 1903	25	15
1760	200f. Stutz Bearcat speedster, 1914	35	20
1761	270f. Darracq phaeton, 1907	50	25
1762	300f. Napier delivery car, 1913	55	30
1763	400f. Pierce Arrow roadster, 1911	70	35

479 Apollo

1998. Butterflies. Multicoloured.

1765	135f. Type **479**	25	15
1766	150f. Orange-tip	25	15
1767	200f. Camberwell beauty	35	20
1768	250f. Speckled wood	40	20
1769	300f. Purple-edged copper	55	30
1770	400f. Chequered skipper	70	35

480 Gouldian Finch

1999. Birds. Multicoloured.

1772	135f. Type **480**	25	15
1773	150f. Saffron finch	25	15
1774	200f. Red-billed quelea	35	20
1775	270f. Golden bishop	50	25
1776	300f. Red-crested cardinal	55	30
1777	400f. Golden-breasted bunting	70	35

481 Boat, Ceylon

1999. Sailing Boats. Multicoloured.

1779	135f. Type **481**	25	15
1780	150f. Tanka-Tim, Canton, Macao	25	15
1781	200f. Sampan, Hong Kong	35	20
1782	270f. Outrigger sailing canoe, Polynesia	50	25
1783	300f. Junk, Japan	55	30
1784	400f. Dacca-Pulwar, Bengal	70	35

482 White Rhinoceros

1999. Mammals.

1786 **482**	50f. grey	10	10
1787 –	100f. violet	20	10
1788 –	135f. green	25	15
1789 –	135f. black	25	15
1790 –	150f. blue	25	15
1791 –	150f. green	25	15
1792 –	200f. blue	35	20
1793 –	200f. brown	35	20
1794 –	300f. brown	55	25
1795 –	300f. red	55	35
1796 –	400f. brown	70	35
1797 –	500f. brown	90	45

DESIGNS: No. 1787, Sable antelope; 1788, Warthog (*Phacochoerus aethiopicus*); 1789, Brown hyena (*Hyaena brunnea*); 1790, Eastern black-and-white colobus (*Colobus guereza*); 1791, Hippopotamus (*Hippopotamus amphibius*); 1792, Mountain zebra (*Equus zebra*); 1793, African buffalo (*Synceros caffer*) (wrongly inscr "Cyncerus"); 1794, Lion (*Panthera leo*); 1795, Cheetah (*Acinonyx jubatus*); 1796, Hunting dog; 1797, Potto.

483 Mikhail Tal

1999. Chess Players. Multicoloured.

1798	135f. Type **483**	25	15
1799	150f. Emanuel Lasker	25	15
1800	200f. Jose Raul Capablanca	35	20
1801	270f. Aleksandr Alekhine	50	25
1802	300f. Max Euwe	55	25
1803	400f. Mikhail Botvinnik	70	35

484 *Brassocattleya cliftonii*

1999. Orchids. Multicoloured.

1805	50f. Type **484**	10	10
1806	100f. Wilsonara	20	10
1807	150f. *Cypripedium paeony*	25	15
1808	300f. *Cymbidium babylon*	55	25
1809	400f. Cattleya	70	35
1810	500f. *Miltonia minx*	90	45

485 Royal Python

1999. Snakes. Multicoloured.

1812	135f. Type **485**	25	15
1813	150f. Royal python (different)	25	15
1814	200f. African rock python	35	20
1815	2000f. Head of African rock python	3·50	1·75

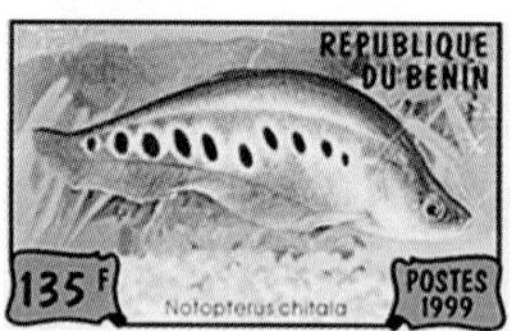

486 Clown Knifefish

1999. Fishes. Multicoloured.

1816	135f. Type **486**	25	15
1817	150f. Puntius filamentosus	25	15
1818	200f. *Epalzeorhynchos bicolor*	35	20
1819	270f. Spotted rasbora	50	25
1820	300f. Tigernander	55	25
1821	400f. Siamese fighting fish	70	35

487 A. Murdock's Steam Tricycle, 1786

1999. Steam-powered Vehicles. Multicoloured.

1823	135f. Type **487**	25	15
1824	150f. Richard Trevithick's locomotive, 1800	25	15
1825	200f. Trevithick's locomotive, 1803	35	20
1826	270f. John Blenkinsop's locomotive, 1811	50	25
1827	300f. Foster and Rastik's *Stourbridge Lion*, 1829	55	30
1828	400f. Peter Cooper's *Tom Thumb*, 1829	70	35

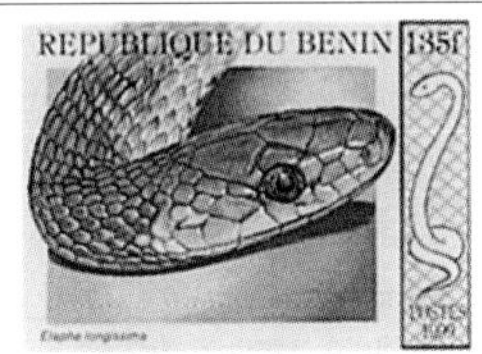
488 Aesculapian Snake

1999. Snakes. Multicoloured.
1830 135f. Type **488** 25 15
1831 150f. Common pine snake 25 15
1832 200f. Grass snake 35 20
1833 270f. Green whip snake . . 50 25
1834 300f. Jamaica boa 55 30
1835 400f. Diamond-back rattlesnake 70 35

489 Testing Chinese Lantern (14th-century)

1999. "China 1999" International Stamp Exhibition, Peking. Multicoloured.
1837 50f. Type **486** 10 10
1838 100f. Satellite launching centre, Jiuquan 20 10
1839 135f. DFH-3 communications satellite 25 15
1840 150f. Satellite launch 25 15
1841 200f. Launch of *Long March* (rocket) 35 20
1842 300f. *Yuan Wang* (passenger ferry) at sea 55 30
1843 400f. Dish aerial 70 35
1844 500f. Items of space post . . 90 45
Nos. 1837/44 were issued together, se-tenant, with the backgrounds forming a composite design of the Earth.

490 Cheetah

1999. Big Cats. Multicoloured.
1845 135f. Type **490** 25 15
1846 150f. Jaguar 25 15
1847 200f. Snow leopard 35 20
1848 270f. Leopard 50 25
1849 300f. Puma 55 25
1850 400f. Tiger 70 35

PARCEL POST STAMPS

1982. Optd or surch **Colis Postaux**.
P871 – 100f. multicoloured (No. 779) (postage) . . 75 40
P872 **256** 100f. on 150f. mult . . . 75 40
P873 – 300f. mult (No. 797) . . 2·25 1·10
P874 **260** 1000f. multicoloured . . 6·75 3·25
P875 **274** 5000f. on 500f. mult (air) 35·00 17·00

1988. No. 543 of Dahomey surch **Republique Populaire du Benin colis postaux**.
P1089 **174** 5f. on 40f. multicoloured (postage) . . . . . .
P1093 – 500f. on 200f. mult . . 3·00 1·90
P1092 – 300f. on 200f. blue, yellow & brown (air)

POSTAGE DUE STAMPS

D 233 Pineapples

1978. Fruits. Multicoloured.
D716 10f. Type **D 233** 30 30
D717 20f. Cashew nuts (vert) . . 50 40
D718 40f. Oranges 85 70
D719 50f. Breadfruit . . . . . . 1·10 80

D **234** Village Postman on Bicycle

1978. Rural Post.
D720 D **234** 60f. brown, grn & red 95 60
D721 – 80f. blue, brn & red 1·10 75
DESIGN: 80f. River village and postman in canoe.

BERGEDORF Pt. 7

A German city on the Elbe, governed by Hamburg and Lubeck until 1867 when it was purchased by the former. In 1868 became part of North German Confederation.

16 schilling = 1 Hamburg mark.

1

1861. Various sizes. Imperf.
1 **1** ½s. black on lilac £375
2 ½s. black on blue . . . . . . 35·00 £550
4 1s. black on white . . . . . . 35·00 £250
5 1½s. black on yellow . . . . . 15·00 £950
6 3s. black on red £550
7 3s. blue on red . . . . 18·00 £1200
8 4s. black on brown . . . . . 18·00 £1600

BERMUDA Pt. 1

A group of islands in the W. Atlantic, E. of N. Carolina. Usually regarded by collectors as part of the Br. W. Indies group, though this is not strictly correct.

1865. 12 pence = 1 shilling;
20 shillings = 1 pound.
1970. 100 cents = 1 dollar (U.S.).

9 Queen Victoria

13 Dry Dock

1865. Portrait. Various frames.
19 **9** ½d. stone . . . . 2·75 4·25
21a ½d. green . . . . 2·50 80
24a 1d. red . . . . 9·00 20
25 2d. blue . . . . 55·00 3·75
26a 2d. purple . . . . 3·50 1·50
27b 2½d. blue . . . . 5·00 40
10 3d. yellow . . . . £170 60·00
28 3d. grey . . . . 22·00 6·50
20 4d. red . . . . 17·00 1·75
28a 4d. brown . . . . 28·00 50·00
7 6d. mauve . . . . 90·00 55·00
11 1s. green . . . . 11·00 £120
29b 1s. brown . . . . 13·00 16·00

1874. Surch in words.
15 **9** 1d. on 2d. blue £700 £375
16 1d. on 3d. yellow £450 £350
17 1d. on 1s. green £500 £250
12 3d. on 1d. red £15000
14 3d. on 1s. green £1400 £650

1901. Surch **ONE FARTHING** and bar.
30 **9** ¼d. on 1s. grey . . . . 1·75 50

1902.
34 **13** ½d. brown and violet . . . 1·75 1·50
31 ½d. black and green . . . . 12·00 1·75
36 ½d. green . . . . 14·00 2·75
32 1d. brown and red . . . . 8·00 10
38 1d. red . . . . 19·00 10
39 2d. grey and orange . . . . 7·50 11·00
40 2½d. brown and blue . . . . 15·00 7·00
41 2½d. blue . . . . 12·00 6·50
33 3d. mauve and green . . . 3·00 2·00
42 4d. blue and brown . . . . 3·00 16·00

14 Badge of the Colony

15

1910.
44a **14** ¼d. brown . . . . 60 1·50
77 ½d. green . . . . 1·50 15
78d 1d. red . . . . 10·00 80
79b 1½d. brown . . . . 9·00 35
80 2d. grey . . . . 1·50 1·50
82b 2½d. blue . . . . 1·75 75
81a 2½d. green . . . . 1·75 1·50
84 3d. purple on yellow . . . 4·00 1·00
83 3d. blue . . . . 16·00 26·00
85 4d. red on yellow . . . . 2·00 1·00
86 6d. purple . . . . 1·00 80
51 1s. black on green . . . . 4·25 4·00
51b **15** 2s. purple and blue on blue 18·00 50·00
52 2s.6d. black and red on blue . . . . 29·00 80·00
52b 4s. black and red . . . . 60·00 £160
53d 5s. green and red on yellow 45·00 95·00
92 10s. green and red on green £130 £250
93 12s.6d. black and orange £250 £350
55 £1 purple and black on red £325 £550

1918. Optd **WAR TAX**.
56 **14** 1d. red . . . . 50 1·00

18

1920. Tercentenary of Representative Institutions. (a) 1st Issue.
59 **18** ¼d. brown . . . . 3·25 18·00
60 ½d. green . . . . 3·25 9·50
65 1d. red . . . . 3·75 30
61 2d. grey . . . . 13·00 40·00
66 2½d. blue . . . . 13·00 12·00
62 3d. purple on yellow . . . . 12·00 38·00
63 4d. black and red on yellow 12·00 35·00
67 6d. purple . . . . 26·00 70·00
64 1s. black on green . . . . . 16·00 48·00

19

(b) 2nd Issue.
74 **19** ¼d. brown . . . . 1·50 3·75
75 ½d. green . . . . 2·75 6·00
76 1d. red . . . . 2·50 35
68 2d. grey . . . . 5·50 28·00
69 2½d. blue . . . . 9·00 3·00
70 3d. purple on yellow . . . . 5·50 16·00
71 4d. red on yellow . . . . . 16·00 21·00
72 6d. purple . . . . 12·00 50·00
73 1s. black on green . . . . . 23·00 50·00

1935. Silver Jubilee. As T **13** of Antigua.
94 1d. blue and red 45 60
95 1½d. blue and grey . . . . . 70 2·25
96 2½d. brown and blue . . . . 1·40 1·00
97 1s. grey and purple . . . . . 15·00 24·00

20 Hamilton Harbour

22 "Lucie" (yacht)

1936.
98 **20** ½d. green 10 10
99 – 1d. black and red 30 30
100 – 1½d. black and brown . . . 1·00 50
101 **22** 2d. black and blue . . . . 5·00 2·00
102 – 2½d. blue . . . . 1·00 25
103 – 3d. black and red . . . . 2·75 1·40
104 – 6d. red and violet 80 10
105 – 1s. green . . . . 5·00 9·00
106 **20** 1s.6d. brown 50 10
DESIGNS—HORIZ: 1d., 1½d. South Shore, near Spanish Rock; 3d. Point House, Warwick Parish. VERT: 2½d., 1s. Grape Bay, Paget Parish; 6d. House at Par-la-Ville, Hamilton.
The 1d., 1½d., 2½d. and 1s. values include a portrait of King George V.

1937. Coronation. As T **2** of Aden.
107 1d. red 50 50
108 1½d. brown . . . . 60 1·50
109 2½d. blue . . . . 70 1·50

26 Ships in Hamilton Harbour

28 White-tailed Tropic Bird, Arms of Bermuda and Native Flower

1938.
110 **26** 1d. black and red 85 20
111b 1½d. blue and brown . . 2·25 50
112 **22** 2d. blue and brown . . . 45·00 8·50
112a 2d. blue and red . . . . 1·50 1·00
113 – 2½d. blue and deep blue 11·00 1·25
113b – 2½d. blue and black . . . 2·75 1·75
114 – 3d. black and red . . . . 18·00 2·75
114a – 3d. black and blue . . . 1·75 40
114c **28** 7½d. black, blue and green 5·00 2·75
115 – 1s. green . . . . 2·00 50
DESIGNS—VERT: 3d. St. David's Lighthouse. The 2½d. and 1s. are as 1935, but with King George VI portrait.

1938. As T **15**, but King George VI portrait.
116c 2s. purple and blue on blue 8·00 1·50
117d 2s.6d. black and red on blue 16·00 12·00
118f 5s. green and red on yellow 24·00 20·00
119e 10s. green and red on green 38·00 42·00
120b 12s.6d. grey and orange . . 95·00 50·00
121d £1 purple and black on red 50·00 75·00

1940. Surch **HALF PENNY**.
122 **26** ½d. on 1d. black and red 40 50

1946. Victory. As T **9** of Aden.
123 1½d. brown 15 15
124 3d. blue 15 15

1948. Silver Wedding. As T **10/11** of Aden.
125 1½d. brown 30 50
126 £1 red . . . . 40·00 48·00

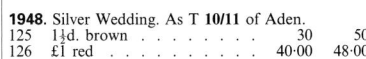

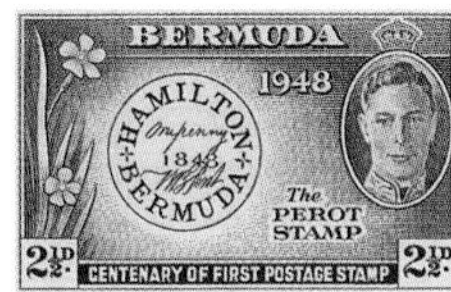
31 Postmaster Perot's Stamp

1949. Centenary of Postmaster Perot's Stamp.
127 **31** 2½d. blue and brown . . . 15 25
128 3d. black and blue 15 15
129 6d. violet and green . . . 15 15

1949. U.P.U. As T **20/23** of Antigua.
130 2½d. black . . . . 30 1·00
131 3d. blue . . . . 1·40 1·25
132 6d. purple 40 75
133 1s. green . . . . 40 1·00

1953. Coronation. As T **13** of Aden.
134 1½d. black and blue 60 30

34 Easter Lily

43 Hog Coin

1953.
135a – ½d. olive 40 60
136 – 1d. black and red . . . . 1·50 50
137 **34** 1½d. green 30 10
138 – 2d. blue and red 50 40
139 – 2½d. red . . . . 2·00 50
140 – 3d. purple 30 10
141 – 4d. black and blue . . . 30 75
142 – 4½d. green . . . . 1·50 1·00
143 – 6d. black and turquoise 5·50 60
156 – 6d. black and mauve . . 70 15
143a – 8d. black and red . . . . 2·50 30
143b – 9d. violet . . . . 8·00 2·50
144 – 1s. orange 50 15
145 – 1s.3d. blue . . . . 3·50 30
146 – 2s. brown . . . . 4·00 85
147 – 2s.6d. red . . . . 4·50 45
148 **43** 5s. red . . . . 19·00 85
149 – 10s. blue . . . . 13·00 5·00
150 – £1 multicoloured . . . . 25·00 21·00
DESIGNS—HORIZ: ½d. Easter lilies; 1d., 4d. Postmaster Perot's stamp; 2d. "Victory II" (racing dinghy); 2½d. Sir George Somers and "Sea Venture"; 3d., 1s.3d. Map of Bermuda; 4½d. 9d. "Sea Venture" (galleon), coin and Perot stamp; 6d. (No. 143), 8d. White-tailed tropic bird; 6d. (No. 156), Perot's Post Office; 1s. Early Bermuda coins; 2s. Arms of St. George's 10s. Obverse and reverse of hog coin; £1 Arms of Bermuda. VERT: 2s.6d. Warwick Fort.
No. 156 commemorates the restoration and reopening of Perot's Post Office.

1953. Royal Visit. As No. 143a but inscr "ROYAL VISIT 1953".
151 6d. black and turquoise . . . 50 20

1953. Three Power Talks. Nos. 140 and 145 optd **Three Power Talks December, 1953.**
152 3d. purple 10 10
153 1s.3d. blue 10 10

1956. 50th Anniv of United States-Bermuda Yacht Race. Nos. 143a and 145 optd **50TH ANNIVERSARY US – BERMUDA OCEAN RACE 1956.**
154 8d. black and red 20 45
155 1s.3d. blue 20 55

49 Arms of King James I and Queen Elizabeth II

1959. 350th Anniv of Settlement. Arms in red, yellow and blue. Frame colours given.
157 **49** 1½d. blue 25 10
158 3d. grey 30 50
159 4d. purple 35 55
160 8d. violet 35 15
161 9d. olive . . . . 35 1·25
162 1s.3d. brown 35 30

50 The Old Rectory, St George's, c.1730

1962.
163 **50** 1d. purple, black and orange 10 75
164 – 2d. multicoloured 75 35
165 – 3d. brown and blue 10 10
166 – 4d. brown and mauve . . . 20 40
167 – 5d. blue and red . . . . . 75 2·50
168 – 6d. blue, green & lt blue 30 30
169 – 8d. blue, green and orange 30 35
170 – 9d. blue and brown 30 60
197 – 10d. violet and ochre . . . 75 60
171 – 1s. multicoloured 30 10
172 – 1s.3d. lake, grey and bistre 75 15
173 – 1s.6d. violet and ochre . . 75 1·00
199 – 1s.6d. blue and red . . . . 2·25 50
200 – 2s. brown and orange . . . 2·25 75
175 – 2s.3d. sepia and green . . 1·00 6·50
176 – 2s.6d. sepia, green & yell 55 50
177 – 5s. purple and green . . . 1·25 1·50
178 – 10s. mauve, green and buff 4·50 7·00
179 – £1 black, olive and orange 14·00 14·00
DESIGNS: 2d. Church of St. Peter, St. George's; 3d. Government House, 1892; 4d. The Cathedral. Hamilton, 1894; 5d., 1s.6d. (No. 199) H.M. Dockyard, 1811; 6d. Perot's Post Office, 1848; 8d. G.P.O., Hamilton, 1869; 9d. Library, Par-la-Ville; 10d., 1s.6d. (No. 173) Bermuda cottage, c. 1705; 1s. Christ Church, Warwick, 1719; 1s.3d. City Hall, Hamilton, 1960; 2s. Town of St. George; 2s.3d. Bermuda house, c. 1710; 2s.6d. Bermuda house, early 18th century; 5s. Colonial Secretariat, 1833; 10s. Old Post Office, Somerset, 1890; £1 The House of Assembly, 1815.

1963. Freedom from Hunger. As T **28** of Aden.
180 1s.3d. sepia 60 40

1963. Centenary of Red Cross. As T **33** of Antigua.
181 3d. red and black 50 25
182 1s.3d. red and blue . . . . . 1·00 2·50

67 "Tsotsi in the Bundu" (Finn class yacht)

1964. Olympic Games, Tokyo.
183 **67** 3d. red, violet and blue . . 10 10

1965. Centenary of I.T.U. As T **36** of Antigua.
184 3d. blue and green 35 25
185 2s. yellow and blue . . . . . 65 1·25

68 Scout Badge and St. Edward's Crown

1965. 50th Anniv of Bermuda Boy Scouts Association.
186 **68** 2s. multicoloured 50 50

1965. I.C.Y. As T **37** of Antigua.
187 4d. purple and turquoise . . 50 20
188 2s.6d. green and lavender . . 75 80

1966. Churchill Commemoration. As T **38** of Antigua.
189 3d. blue 25 20
190 6d. green 50 70
191 10d. brown 70 75
192 1s.3d. violet . . . . 80 2·50

1966. World Cup Football Championship. As T **40** of Antigua.
193 10d. multicoloured 60 15
194 2s.6d. multicoloured 90 1 25

1966. 20th Anniv of U.N.E.S.C.O. As T **54/56** of Antigua.
201 4d. multicoloured 45 15
202 1s.3d. yellow, violet and olive 75 50
203 2s. black, purple and orange 1·00 1·10

69 G.P.O. Building

1967. Opening of New General Post Office.
204 **69** 3d. multicoloured 10 10
205 1s. multicoloured 10 10
206 1s.6d. multicoloured . . . 20 25
207 2s.6d. multicoloured . . . 20 70

70 "Mercury" (cable ship) and Chain Links

1967. Inauguration of Bermuda–Tortola Telephone Service. Multicoloured.
208 3d. Type **70** 15 10
209 1s. Map, telephone and microphone 25 10
210 1s.6d. Telecommunications media 25 25
211 2s.6d. "Mercury" (cable ship) and marine fauna 40 70

74 Human Rights Emblem and Doves

1968. Human Rights Year.
212 **74** 3d. indigo, blue and green 10 10
213 1s. brown, blue and light blue 10 10
214 1s.6d. black, blue and red 10 15
215 2s.6d. green, blue and yellow 15 25

75 Mace and Queen's Profile

1968. New Constitution.
216 **75** 3d. multicoloured 10 10
217 1s. multicoloured 10 10
218 – 1s.6d. yellow, black and blue 10 20
219 – 2s.6d. lilac, black and yellow 15 75
DESIGNS: 1s.6d., 2s.6d., Houses of Parliament, and House of Assembly, Bermuda.

77 Football, Athletics and Yachting

1968. Olympic Games, Mexico.
220 **77** 3d. multicoloured 15 10
221 1s. multicoloured 25 10
222 1s.6d. multicoloured . . . 50 30
223 2s.6d. multicoloured . . . 50 1·40

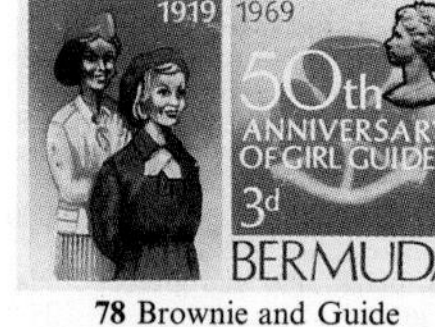
78 Brownie and Guide

1969. 50th Anniv of Girl Guides. Multicoloured.
224 3d. Type **78** 10 10
225 1s. Type **78** 20 10
226 1s.6d. Guides and Badge . . 25 40
227 2s.6d. As 1s.6d. . . . . . . 35 1·40

80 Emerald-studded Gold Cross and Seaweed

1969. Underwater Treasure. Multicoloured.
228 4d. Type **80** 20 10
229 1s.3d. Emerald-studded gold cross and sea-bed 35 15
230 2s. As Type **80** 45 90
231 2s.6d. As 1s.3d. . . . . . . 45 1·75

1970. Decimal Currency. Nos. 163/79 surch.
232 1c. on 1d. purple, black & orge . . . . 10 1·75
233 2c. on 2d. multicoloured . . 10 10
234 3c. on 3d. brown and blue 10 10
235 4c. on 4d. brown and mauve 10 10
236 5c. on 8d. blue, green & orge 15 2·00
237 6c. on 6d. blue, green & lt blue . . . . 15 1·25
238 9c. on 9d. blue and brown 30 2·50
239 10c. on 10d. violet and ochre 30 25
240 12c. on 1s. multicoloured . . 30 1·00
241 15c. on 1s.3d. lake, grey & bis . . . . 1·50 1·00
242 18c. on 1s.6d. blue and red 80 65
243 24c. on 2s. brown and orange 85 1·50
244 30c. on 2s.6d. sepia, grn & yell . . . . 1·00 2·75
245 36c. on 2s.3d. sepia and green 1·75 7·00
246 60c. on 5s. purple and green 2·25 3·75
247 $1.20 on 10s. mve, grn & buff . . . . 4·00 15·00
248 $2.40 on £1 black, ol & orge 5·50 19·00

83 Spathiphyllum

1970. Flowers. Multicoloured.
249 1c. Type **83** 10 20
250 2c. Bottlebrush 20 25
251 3c. Oleander (vert) 15 10
252 4c. Bermudiana 15 10
253 5c. Poinsettia 30 20
254 6c. Hibiscus 30 30
255 9c. Cereus 20 45
256 10c. Bougainvillea (vert) . . 20 15
257 12c. Jacaranda 80 60
258 15c. Passion flower . . . . 90 1·40
258a 17c. As 15c. . . . . 2·75 4·00
259 18c. Coralita . . . . 2·25 2·25
259a 20c. As 18c. . . . . 2·75 4·00
260 24c. Morning glory . . . . 1·50 4·25
260a 25c. As 24c. . . . . 2·75 4·50
261 30c. Tecoma . . . . 1·00 1·25
262 36c. Angel's trumpet . . . . 1·25 2·25
262a 40c. As 36c. . . . . 2·75 5·50
263 60c. Plumbago . . . . 1·75 1·75
263a $1 As 60c. . . . . 3·25 6·50
264 $1.20 Bird of paradise flower . . . . 2·25 3·00
264a $2 As $1.20 . . . . 5·50 8·50
265 $2.40 Chalice cup . . . . . 5·00 6·00
265a $3 As $2.40 . . . . 11·00 11·00

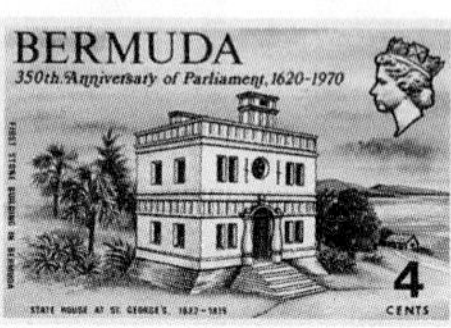
84 The State House, St. George's

1970. 350th Anniv of Bermuda Parliament. Multicoloured.
266 4c. Type **84** 10 10
267 15c. The Sessions House, Hamilton 25 20
268 18c. St. Peter's Church, St. George's 25 25
269 24c. Town Hall, Hamilton . . 35 60
MS270 131 × 95 mm. Nos. 266/9 1·10 1·25

85 Street Scene, St. George's

1971. "Keep Bermuda Beautiful". Multicoloured.
271 4c. Type **85** 20 10
272 15c. Horseshoe Bay 65 65
273 18c. Gibbs Hill Lighthouse 1·50 2·25
274 24c. Hamilton Harbour . . . 1·25 2·50

86 Building of the "Deliverance"

1971. Voyage of the "Deliverance". Multicoloured.
275 4c. Type **86** 60 20
276 15c. "Deliverance" and "Patience" at Jamestown (vert) . . . . 1·50 1·75
277 18c. Wreck of the "Sea Venture" (vert) . . . . . 1·50 2·25
278 24c. "Deliverance" and "Patience" on high seas . . 1·75 2·50

87 Green overlooking Ocean View

1971. Golfing in Bermuda. Multicoloured.
279 4c. Type **87** 70 10
280 15c. Golfers at Port Royal 1·25 65
281 18c. Castle Harbour . . . . 1·25 1·00
282 24c. Belmont . . . . 1·50 2·00

1971. Anglo-American Talks. Nos. 252, 258, 259 and 260 optd **HEATH-NIXON DECEMBER 1971**.
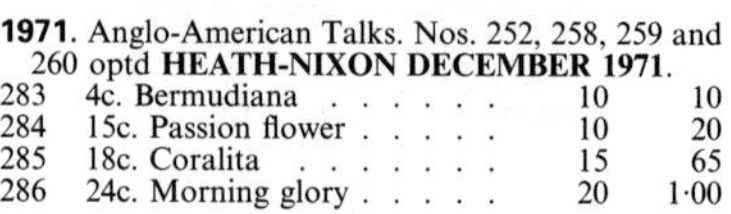
283 4c. Bermudiana 10 10
284 15c. Passion flower 10 20
285 18c. Coralita 15 65
286 24c. Morning glory . . . . . 20 1·00

89 Bonefish

1972. World Fishing Records. Multicoloured.
287 4c. Type **89** 30 10
288 15c. Wahoo 30 50
289 18c. Yellow-finned tuna . . . 35 75
290 24c. Greater amberjack . . . 40 1·25

1972. Silver Wedding. As T **52** of Ascension, but with "Admiralty Oar" and Mace in background.
291 4c. violet 15 10
292 15c. red 15 50

91 Palmetto

1973. Tree Planting Year. Multicoloured.
293 4c. Type **91** 25 10
294 15c. Olivewood bark 65 75
295 18c. Bermuda cedar . . . . 70 1·25
296 24c. Mahogany . . . . . . 75 1·60

1973. Royal Wedding. As T **47** of Anguilla, background colour given. Multicoloured.
297 15c. mauve 15 15
298 18c. blue 15 15

92 Bernard Park, Pembroke, 1973

1973. Centenary of Lawn Tennis. Multicoloured.

299	4c. Type **92**	30	10
300	15c. Clermont Court, 1873	50	65
301	18c. Leamington Spa Court, 1872	55	1·75
302	24c. Staten Island Courts, 1874	65	2·25

93 Weather Vane, City Hall

1974. 50th Anniv of Rotary in Bermuda. Mult.

320	5c. Type **93**	15	10
321	17c. St. Peter's Church, St. George's	45	35
322	20c. Somerset Bridge	50	1·50
323	25c. Map of Bermuda, 1626	60	2·25

94 Jack of Clubs and "good bridge hand"

1975. World Bridge Championships, Bermuda. Multicoloured.

324	5c. Type **94**	20	10
325	17c. Queen of Diamonds and Bermuda Bowl	35	50
326	20c. King of Hearts and Bermuda Bowl	40	1·75
327	25c. Ace of Spades and Bermuda Bowl	40	2·50

95 Queen Elizabeth II and the Duke of Edinburgh

1975. Royal Visit.

328 **95**	17c. multicoloured	60	65
329	20c. multicoloured	65	2·10

96 Short S.23 Flying Boat "Cavalier", 1937

1975. 50th Anniv of Air-mail Service to Bermuda. Multicoloured.

330	5c. Type **96**	40	10
331	17c. U.S. Navy airship "Los Angeles", 1925	1·25	85
332	20c. Lockheed Constellation, 1946	1·40	2·75
333	25c. Boeing 747-100, 1970	1·50	3·50
MS334	128 × 85 mm. Nos. 330/3	11·00	15·00

97 Supporters of American Army raiding Royal Magazine

1975. Bicentenary of Gunpowder Plot, St. George's. Multicoloured.

335	5c. Type **97**	15	10
336	17c. Setting off for raid	30	40
337	20c. Loading gunpowder aboard American ship	35	1·40
338	25c. Gunpowder on beach	35	1·50
MS339	165 × 138 mm. Nos. 335/8	2·25	7·00

98 Launching "Ready" (bathysphere)

1976. 50th Anniv of Bermuda Biological Station. Multicoloured.

357	5c. Type **98**	30	10
358	17c. View from the sea (horiz)	60	60
359	20c. H.M.S. "Challenger", 1873 (horiz)	65	2·25
360	25c. Beebe's Bathysphere descent, 1934	70	3·00

99 "Christian Radich" (cadet ship)

1976. Tall Ships Race. Multicoloured.

361	5c. Type **99**	75	20
362	12c. "Juan Sebastian de Elcano" (Spanish cadet schooner)	80	2·25
363	17c. "Eagle" (U.S. coastguard cadet ship)	80	1·50
364	20c. "Sir Winston Churchill" (cadet schooner)	80	1·75
365	40c. "Kruzenshtern" (Russian cadet barque)	1·00	2·75
366	$1 "Cutty Sark" trophy	1·25	7·00

100 Silver Trophy and Club Flags

1976. 75th Anniv of St. George's v. Somerset Cricket Cup Match. Multicoloured.

367	5c. Type **100**	30	10
368	17c. Badge and pavilion, St. George's Club	50	65
369	20c. Badge and pavilion, Somerset Club	65	2·75
370	25c. Somerset playing field	1·00	3·75

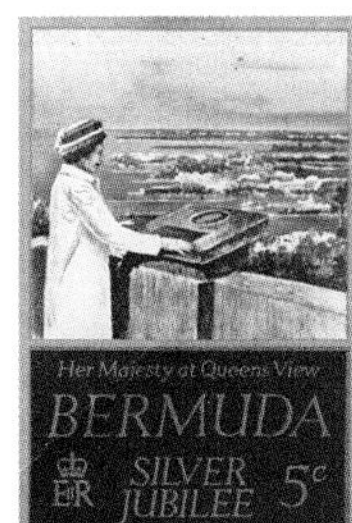

101 Royal Visit, 1975

1977. Silver Jubilee. Multicoloured.

371	5c. Type **101**	10	10
372	20c. St. Edward's Crown	15	20
373	$1 The Queen in Chair of Estate	40	1·25

102 Stockdale House, St. George's, 1784–1812

1977. Centenary of U.P.U. Membership. Mult.

374	5c. Type **102**	15	10
375	15c. Perot Post Office and stamp	25	50
376	17c. St. George's P.O. c. 1860	25	50
377	20c. Old G.P.O., Hamilton, c. 1935	30	60
378	40c. New G.P.O., Hamilton, 1967	45	1·10

103 17th-Century Ship approaching Castle Island

1977. Piloting. Multicoloured.

379	5c. Type **103**	50	10
380	15c. Pilot leaving ship, 1795	70	60
381	17c. Pilots rowing out to paddle-steamer	80	60
382	20c. Pilot gig and brig "Harvest Queen"	85	2·25
383	40c. Modern pilot cutter and R.M.S. "Queen Elizabeth 2"	1·60	3·75

104 Great Seal of Queen Elizabeth I

1978. 25th Anniv of Coronation. Multicoloured.

384	8c. Type **104**	10	10
385	50c. Great Seal of Queen Elizabeth II	30	30
386	$1 Queen Elizabeth II	60	75

105 White-tailed Tropic Bird

1978. Wildlife. Multicoloured.

387	3c. Type **105**	2·50	2·00
388	4c. White-eyed vireo	2·75	2·50
389	5c. Eastern bluebird	1·25	1·75
390	7c. Whistling frog	50	1·50
391	8c. Common cardinal ("Cardinal Redbird")	1·25	55
392	10c. Spiny lobster	20	10
393	12c. Land crab	30	70
394	15c. Lizard (Skink)	30	15
395	20c. Four-eyed butterflyfish	30	30
396	25c. Red hind	30	20
397	30c. "Danaus plexippus" (butterfly)	2·25	2·50
398	40c. Rock beauty	50	1·75
399	50c. Banded butterflyfish	55	1·50
400	$1 Blue angelfish	2·25	1·75
401	$2 Humpback whale	2·00	2·75
402	$3 Green turtle	2·50	3·00
403	$5 Cahow	5·50	6·00

106 Map by Sir George Somers, 1609

1979. Antique Maps. Multicoloured.

404	8c. Type **106**	15	10
405	15c. Map by John Seller, 1685	20	15
406	20c. Map by H. Moll, 1729–40 (vert)	25	25
407	25c. Map by Desbruslins, 1740	30	30
408	50c. Map by Speed, 1626	45	80

107 Policeman and Policewoman

1979. Centenary of Police Force. Multicoloured.

409	8c. Type **107**	30	10
410	20c. Policeman directing traffic (horiz)	50	55
411	25c. "Blue Heron" (police launch) (horiz)	60	65
412	50c. Police Morris Marina and motorcycle	80	1·50

108 1d. "Perot" Stamp of 1848 and 1840 Penny Black

1980. Death Cent of Sir Rowland Hill. Mult.

413	8c. Type **108**	20	10
414	20c. "Perot" and Sir Rowland Hill	30	25
415	25c. "Perot" and early letter	30	30
416	50c. "Perot" and "Paid 1" cancellation	35	70

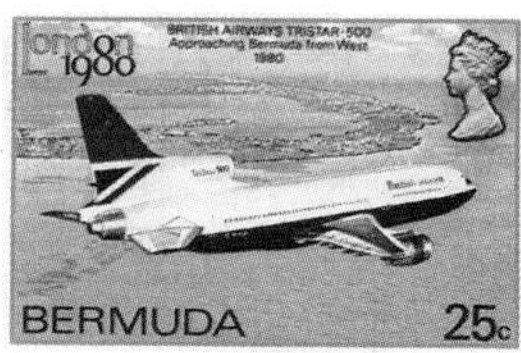

109 Lockheed TriStar 500 approaching Bermuda

1980. "London 1980" International Stamp Exhibition. Multicoloured.

417	25c. Type **109**	30	15
418	50c. "Orduna I" (liner) at Grassy Bay, 1926	45	35
419	$1 "Delta" (screw steamer) at St. George's Harbour, 1856	85	1·00
420	$2 "Lord Sidmouth" (sailing packet) in Old Ship Channel, St. George's	1·40	2·00

110 Gina Swainson ("Miss World 1979–80")

1980. "Miss World 1979–80" Commem. Mult.

421	8c. Type **110**	15	10
422	20c. Miss Swainson after crowning ceremony	20	20
423	50c. Miss Swainson on Peacock Throne	35	35
424	$1 Miss Swainson in Bermuda carriage	70	90

111 Queen Elizabeth the Queen Mother

1980. 80th Birthday of The Queen Mother.

425 **111**	25c. multicoloured	30	1·00

112 Bermuda from Satellite

1980. Commonwealth Finance Ministers Meeting. Muticoloured.

426	8c. Type **112**	10	10
427	20c. "Camden"	20	40
428	25c. Princess Hotel, Hamilton	20	50
429	50c. Government House	35	1·25

113 Kitchen, 18th-century

1981. Heritage Week. Multicoloured.
430 8c. Type **113** 15 10
431 25c. Gathering Easter lilies, 20th-century 30 35
432 30c. Fishing, 20th-century . . 40 50
433 40c. Stone cutting, 19th-century 40 80
434 50c. Onion shipping, 19th-century 65 90
435 $1 Privateering, 17th-century 1·25 2·50

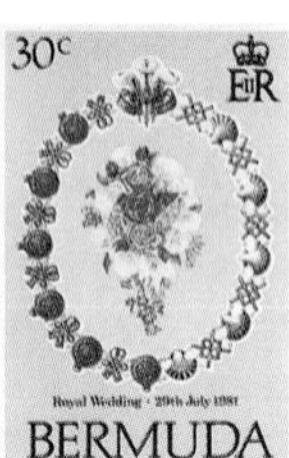

114 Wedding Bouquet from Bermuda
115 "Service", Hamilton

1981. Royal Wedding. Multicoloured.
436 30c. Type **114** 20 20
437 50c. Prince Charles as Royal Navy Commander 35 40
438 $1 Prince Charles and Lady Diana Spencer 55 80

1981. 25th Anniv of Duke of Edinburgh Award Scheme. Multicoloured.
439 10c. Type **115** 15 10
440 25c. "Outward Bound", Paget Island 20 20
441 30c. "Expedition", St. David's Island 20 30
442 $1 Duke of Edinburgh . . . 55 1·25

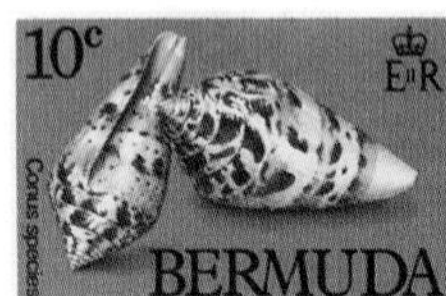

116 Lightbourne's Cone

1982. Sea Shells. Multicoloured.
443 10c. Type **116** 30 10
444 25c. Finlay's frog shell . . . 55 55
445 30c. Royal bonnet 60 60
446 $1 Lightbourne's murex . . . 1·75 3·25

117 Regimental Colours and Colour Party

1982. Bermuda Regiment. Multicoloured.
447 10c. Type **117** 65 10
448 25c. Queen's Birthday Parade 1·10 80
449 30c. Governor inspecting Guard of Honour . . . . 1·40 1·40
450 40c. Beating the Retreat . . . 1·50 1·75
451 50c. Ceremonial gunners . . . 1·50 2·00
452 $1 Guard of Honour, Royal visit, 1975 . . . . 2·25 3·50

118 Charles Fort
119 Arms of Sir Edwin Sandys

1982. Historic Bermuda Forts. Multicoloured.
453 10c. Type **118** 20 20
454 25c. Pembroks Fort 50 85
455 30c. Southampton Fort (horiz) . . . . 60 1·25
456 $1 Smiths Fort and Pagets Fort (horiz) . . . . 1·25 4·25

1983. Coat of Arms (1st series). Multicoloured.
457 10c. Type **119** 45 15
458 25c. Arms of the Bermuda Company . . . . 1·40 1·00
459 50c. Arms of William Herbert, Earl of Pembroke 2·25 3·50
460 $1 Arms of Sir George Somers . . . . 3·00 6·00
See also Nos. 482/5 and 499/502.

120 Early Fitted Dinghy
122 Joseph Stockdale

121 Curtiss N-9 Seaplane

1983. Fitted Dinghies. Multicoloured.
461 12c. Type **120** 45 15
462 30c. Modern dinghy inshore 60 75
463 40c. Early dinghy (different) 70 90
464 $1 Modern dinghy with red and white spinnaker . . . 1·40 3·25

1983. Bicentenary of Manned Flight. Multicoloured.
465 12c. Type **121** (First flight over Bermuda) 60 20
466 30c. Stinson Pilot Radio seaplane (First completed flight between U.S. and Bermuda) . . . . 1·25 1·25
467 40c. S.23 Flying boat "Cavalier" (First scheduled passenger flight) . . . . . 1·50 1·75
468 $1 U.S.N. "Los Angeles" (airship) moored to U.S.S. "Patoka" . . . . 2·75 5·50

1984. Bicentenary of Bermuda's First Newspaper and Postal Service. Multicoloured
469 12c. Type **122** 30 15
470 30c. "The Bermuda Gazette" 60 80
471 40c. Stockdale's postal service (horiz) . . . . 80 1·10
472 $1 "Lady Hammond" (mail boat) (horiz) . . . . 2·50 3·25

123 Sir Thomas Gates and Sir George Somers

1984. 375th Anniv of First Settlement. Mult.
473 12c. Type **123** 20 15
474 30c. Jamestown, Virginia . . 50 1·25
475 40c. Wreck of "Sea Venture" 90 1·25
476 $1 Fleet leaving Plymouth, Devon . . . . 2·00 6·00
MS477 130 × 73 mm. Nos. 474 and 476 3·75 9·00

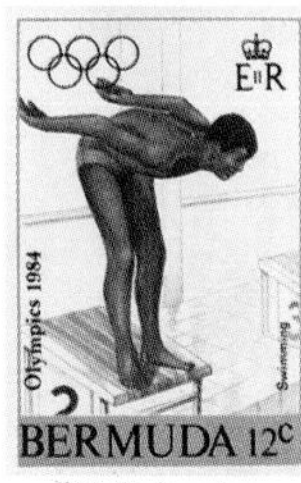

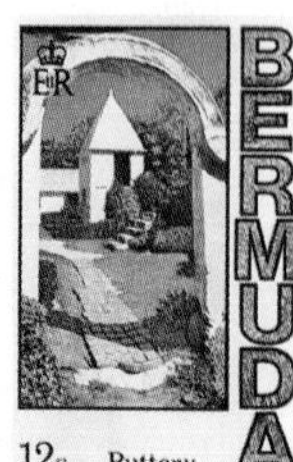

124 Swimming
125 Buttery

1984. Olympic Games, Los Angeles. Multicoloured.
478 12c. Type **124** 40 15
479 30c. Track and field events (horiz) 70 75
480 40c. Equestrian . . . . . . 1·25 1·25
481 $1 Sailing (horiz) . . . . . . 2·50 5·50

1984. Coat of Arms (2nd series). As T **119**. Mult.
482 12c. Arms of Henry Wriothesley, Earl of Southampton 50 15
483 30c. Arms of Sir Thomas Smith . . . . 1·00 85
484 40c. Arms of William Cavendish, Earl of Devonshire . . . . 1·25 1·50
485 $1 Town arms of St. George 2·75 4·50

1985. Bermuda Architecture. Multicoloured.
486 12c. Type **125** 35 15
487 30c. Limestone rooftops (horiz) 80 70
488 40c. Chimneys (horiz) . . . . 95 1·00
489 $1.50 Entrance archway . . . 3·00 3·75

126 Osprey
127 The Queen Mother with Grandchildren, 1980

1985. Birth Bicentenary of John J. Audubon (ornithologist). Designs showing original drawings. Multicoloured.
490 12c. Type **126** . . . . 2·00 65
491 30c. Yellow-crowned night heron . . . . 2·00 95
492 40c. Great egret (horiz) . . . 2·25 1·25
493 $1.50 Eastern bluebird ("Bluebird") . . . . 3·75 6·50

1985. Life and Times of Queen Elizabeth the Queen Mother. Multicoloured.
494 12c. Queen Consort, 1937 . . 35 15
495 30c. Type **127** 60 50
496 40c. At Clarence House on 83rd birthday 70 60
497 $1.50 With Prince Henry at his christening (from photo by Lord Snowdon) . . . . 2·00 2·75
MS498 91 × 73 mm. $1 With Prince Charles at 80th birthday celebrations 3·00 3·00

1985. Coats of Arms (3rd series). As T **119**. Mult.
499 12c. Hamilton 75 15
500 30c. Paget . . . . 1·40 80
501 40c. Warwick . . . . 1·60 1·40
502 $1.50 City of Hamilton . . . 3·75 4·50

128 Halley's Comet and Bermuda Archipelago

1985. Appearance of Halley's Comet. Multicoloured.
503 15c. Type **128** 85 25
504 40c. Halley's Comet, A.D. 684 (from Nuremberg Chronicles, 1493) . . . . . 1·60 1·75
505 50c. "Halley's Comet, 1531" (from Peter Apian woodcut, 1532) . . . . . 1·90 2·50
506 $1.50 "Halley's Comet, 1759" (Samuel Scott) . . . . . . 3·50 5·50

129 "Constellation" (schooner) (1943)

1986. Ships Wrecked on Bermuda. Multicoloured.
507A 3c. Type **129** . . . . 70 1·00
508A 5c. "Early Riser" (pilot boat), 1876 . . . . . . 20 20
509A 7c. "Madiana" (screw steamer), 1903 . . . . . 65 2·25
510A 10c. "Curlew" (sail/ steamer), 1856 . . . . . 30 30
511A 12c. "Warwick" (galleon), 1619 . . . . 60 80
512A 15c. H.M.S. "Vixen" (gun-boat), 1890 . . . . . . 40 60
512cA 18c. As 7c. . . . . 5·00 4·25
513A 20c. "San Pedro" (Spanish galleon), 1594 . . . . . 1·10 80
514A 25c. "Alert" (fishing sloop), 1877 . . . . . . 60 2·50
515A 40c. "North Carolina" (barque), 1880 . . . . . 65 1·25
516A 50c. "Mark Antonie" (Spanish privateer), 1777 1·50 2·75
517A 60c. "Mary Celestia" (Confederate paddle-steamer), 1864 . . . . . 1·50 1·75
517cA 70c. "Caesar" (brig), 1818 5·50 6·50
518B $1 "L'Herminie" (French frigate), 1839 . . . . . 1·50 1·60
519A $1.50 As 70c. . . . . . . 4·50 5·50
520B $2 "Lord Amherst" (transport), 1778 . . . . 2·50 4·50
521B $3 "Minerva" (sailing ship), 1849 . . . . . . 4·25 7·00
522A $5 "Caraquet" (cargo liner), 1923 . . . . . . 4·75 11·00
523A $8 H.M.S. "Pallas" (frigate), 1783 . . . . . 6·00 12·00

1986. 60th Birthday of Queen Elizabeth II. As T **110** of Ascension. Multicoloured.
524 15c. Princess Elizabeth aged three, 1929 . . . . 45 30
525 40c. With Earl of Rosebery at Oaks May Meeting, Epsom, 1954 . . . . . . 80 60
526 50c. With Duke of Edinburgh, Bermuda, 1975 80 75
527 60c. At British Embassy, Paris, 1972 . . . . 90 90
528 $1.50 At Crown Agents Head Office, London, 1983 . . . 2·00 2·50

1986. "Ameripex '86" International Stamp Exhibition, Chicago. As T **164** of Bahamas, showing Bermuda stamps. Multicoloured.
529 15c. 1984 375th Anniv of Settlement miniature sheet 1·50 30
530 40c. 1973 Lawn Tennis Centenary, 24c. . . . . . 2·25 70
531 50c. 1983 Bicentenary of Manned Flight 12c. . . . 2·25 1·00
532 $1 1976 Tall Ships Race 17c. 3·75 3·00
MS533 80 × 80 mm. $1.50, Statue of Liberty and "Monarch of Bermuda" 7·50 6·50
No. **MS**533 also commemorates the Centenary of the Statue of Liberty.

1986. 25th Anniv of World Wildlife Fund. No. 402 surch **90c**.
534 90c. on $3 Green turtle . . . 3·00 4·25

131 Train in Front Street, Hamilton, 1940

1987. Transport (1st series). Bermuda Railway. Multicoloured.
535 15c. Type **131** . . . . 2·00 25
536 40c. Train crossing Springfield Trestle . . . . 2·50 90
537 50c. "St. George Special" at Bailey's Bay Station . . . 2·50 1·50
538 $1.50 Boat train at St. George . . . . 4·00 3·50
See also Nos. 557/60, 574/7 and 624/9.

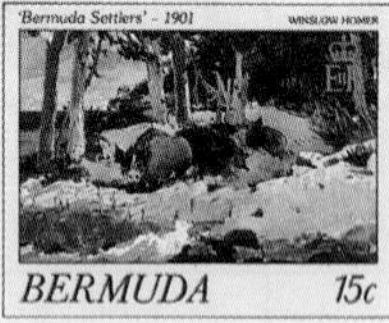

132 "Bermuda Settlers", 1901

1987. Bermuda Paintings (1st series). Works by Winslow Homer. Multicoloured.
539 15c. Type **132** 60 25
540 30c. "Bermuda", 1900 . . . 85 45
541 40c. "Bermuda Landscape", 1901 (buff frame) 95 55
544 40c. Type **132** . . . . 90 1·60
545 40c. As No. 540 . . . . . . 90 1·60
546 40c. As No. 541 (grey frame) 90 1·60
547 40c. As No. 542 . . . . . . 90 1·60
548 40c. As No. 543 . . . . . . 90 1·60
542 50c. "Inland Water", 1901 . . 1·10 70
543 $1.50 "Salt Kettle", 1899 . . 2·50 2·50
See also Nos. 607/10 and 630/3.

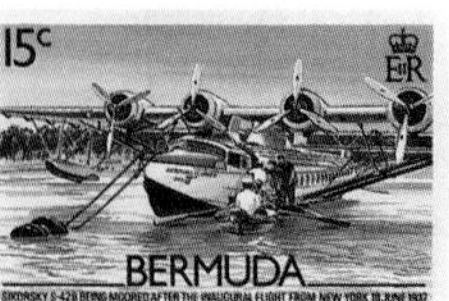

133 Sikorsky S-42B Flying Boat "Bermuda Clipper"

1987. 50th Anniv of Inauguration of Bermuda–U.S.A. Air Service. Multicoloured.
549 15c. Type **133** . . . . 2·00 15
550 40c. Short S.23 flying boat "Cavalier" . . . . 3·00 70
551 50c. "Bermuda Clipper" in flight over signpost . . . . 3·25 80
552 $1.50 "Cavalier" on apron and "Bermuda Clipper" in flight . . . . 6·00 4·00

134 19th-century Wagon carrying Telephone Poles

1987. Centenary of Bermuda Telephone Company. Multicoloured.

553	15c. Type **134**	75	15
554	40c. Early telephone exchange	1·40	60
555	50c. Early and modern telephones	1·75	70
556	$1.50 Communications satellite orbiting Earth	2·75	3·50

135 Mail Wagon, c. 1869

1988. Transport (2nd series). Horse-drawn Carts and Wagons. Multicoloured.

557	15c. Type **135**	25	15
558	40c. Open cart, c. 1823	55	55
559	50c. Closed cart, c. 1823	65	65
560	$1.50 Two-wheeled wagon, c. 1930	2·00	2·50

136 "Old Blush"

1988. Old Garden Roses (1st series). Multicoloured.

561	15c. Type **136**	85	25
562	30c. "Anna Olivier"	1·25	45
563	40c. "Rosa chinensis semperflorens" (vert)	1·40	85
564	50c. "Archduke Charles"	1·50	1·25
565	$1.50 "Rosa chinensis viridiflora" (vert)	3·00	5·00

See also Nos. 584/8 and, for designs with the royal cypher instead of the Queen's head, Nos. 589/98 and 683/6.

1988. 300th Anniv of Lloyd's of London. As T **123** of Ascension. Multicoloured.

566	18c. Loss of H.M.S. "Lutine" (frigate), 1799	85	25
567	50c. "Sentinel" (cable ship) (horiz)	1·60	65
568	60c. "Bermuda" (liner), Hamilton, 1931 (horiz)	£175	75
569	$2 Loss of H.M.S. "Valerian" (sloop) in hurricane, 1926	3·00	3·25

137 Devonshire Parish Militia, 1812

1988. Military Uniforms. Multicoloured.

570	18c. Type **137**	1·50	25
571	50c. 71 st (Highland) Regiment, 1831–34	2·00	1·10
572	60c. Cameron Highlanders, 1942	2·25	1·25
573	$2 Troop of horse, 1774	4·75	7·00

138 "Corona" (ferry)

1989. Transport (3rd series). Ferry Services. Mult.

574	18c. Type **138**	35	25
575	50c. Rowing boat ferry	75	65
576	60c. St. George's barge ferry	85	75
577	$2 "Laconia"	2·50	3·00

139 Morgan's Island

1989. 150 Years of Photography. Multicoloured.

578	18c. Type **139**	85	25
579	30c. Front Street, Hamilton	1·10	45
580	50c. Waterfront, Front Street, Hamilton	1·60	1·25
581	60c. Crow Lane from Hamilton Harbour	1·75	1·40
582	70c. Shipbuilding, Hamilton Harbour	1·90	2·75
583	$1 Dockyard	2·25	3·25

1989. Old Garden Roses (2nd series). As T **136**. Multicoloured.

584	18c. "Agrippina" (vert)	90	25
585	30c. "Smith's Parish" (vert)	1·25	60
586	50c. "Champney's Pink Cluster"	1·75	1·40
587	60c. "Rosette Delizy"	1·75	1·60
588	$1.50 "Rosa bracteata"	2·75	5·00

1989. Old Garden Roses (3rd series). Designs as Nos. 561/5 and 584/8, but with royal cypher at top left instead of Queen's head. Multicoloured.

589	50c. As No. 565 (vert)	1·60	2·00
590	50c. As No. 563 (vert)	1·60	2·00
591	50c. Type **136**	1·60	2·00
592	50c. As No. 562	1·60	2·00
593	50c. As No. 564	1·60	2·00
594	50c. As No. 585 (vert)	1·60	2·00
595	50c. As No. 584 (vert)	1·60	2·00
596	50c. As No. 586	1·60	2·00
597	50c. As No. 587	1·60	2·00
598	50c. As No. 588	1·60	2·00

140 Main Library, Hamilton

1989. 150th Anniv of Bermuda Library. Mult.

599	18c. Type **140**	60	25
600	50c. The Old Rectory, St. George's	1·25	65
601	60c. Somerset Library, Springfield	1·25	75
602	$2 Cabinet Building, Hamilton	3·25	3·25

141 1865 1d. Rose

1989. Commonwealth Postal Conference. Mult.

603 **141**	18c. grey, pink and red	1·50	25
604 –	50c. grey, blue & lt blue	2·00	75
605 –	60c. grey, purple and mauve	2·25	1·25
606 –	$2 grey, green and emerald	3·75	6·00

DESIGNS: 50c. 1866 2d. blue; 60c. 1865 6d. purple; $2 1865 1s. green.

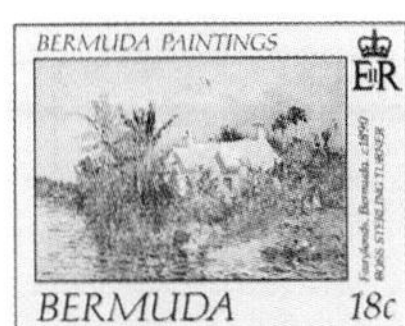

142 "Fairylands, c. 1890" (Ross Turner)

1990. Bermuda Paintings (2nd series). Multicoloured.

607	18c. Type **142**	75	25
608	50c. "Shinebone Alley, c. 1953" (Ogden Pleissner)	1·25	1·25
609	60c. "Salt Kettle, 1916" (Prosper Senat)	1·25	1·50
610	$2 "St. George's, 1934" (Jack Bush)	3·25	7·00

1990. "Stamp World London 90" International Stamp Exhibition. Nos. 603/6 optd **Stamp World London 90** and logo.

611	18c. grey, pink and red	1·25	25
612	50c. grey, blue and light blue	1·75	1·50
613	60c. grey, purple and mauve	2·00	1·75
614	$2 grey, green and emerald	3·50	7·00

1990. Nos. 511, 516 and 519 surch.

615	30c. on 12c. "Warwick" (galleon), (1619)	1·50	1·00
616	55c. on 50c. "Mark Antonie" (Spanish privateer), 1777	2·00	2·00
617	80c. on $1.50 "Caesar" (brig), 1818	2·50	4·00

145 The Halifax and Bermudas Cable Company Office, Hamilton

1990. Centenary of Cable and Wireless in Bermuda.

618 **145**	20c. brown and black	70	25
619 –	55c. brown and black	2·00	1·25
620 –	70c. multicoloured	2·00	2·75
621 –	$2 multicoloured	4·75	7·50

DESIGNS: 55c. "Westmeath" (cable ship), 1890; 70c. Wireless transmitter station, St. George's, 1928; $2 "Sir Eric Sharp" (cable ship).

1991. President Bush–Prime Minister Major Talks, Bermuda. Nos. 618/19 optd **BUSH-MAJOR 16 MARCH 1991**.

622 **145**	20c. brown and black	2·00	1·50
623 –	55c. brown and black	3·00	3·50

147 Two-seater Pony Cart, 1805

1991. Transport (4th series). Horse-drawn Carriages. Multicoloured.

624	20c. Type **147**	80	30
625	30c. Varnished rockaway, 1830	90	60
626	55c. Vis-a-Vis victoria, 1895	1·60	1·10
627	70c. Semi-formal phaeton, 1900	2·25	2·50
628	80c. Pony runabout, 1905	2·50	3·75
629	$1 Ladies phaeton, 1910	2·75	4·50

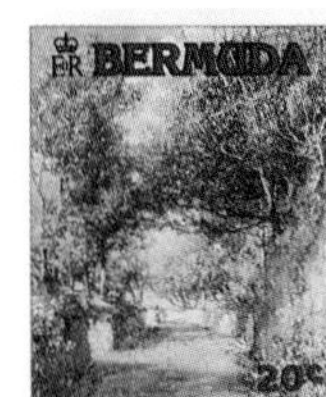

148 "Bermuda, 1916" (Prosper Senat)

1991. Bermuda Paintings (3rd series). Multicoloured.

630	20c. Type **148**	1·00	30
631	55c. "Bermuda Cottage" 1930 (Frank Allison) (horiz)	2·00	1·40
632	70c. "Old Maid's Lane", 1934 (Jack Bush)	2·50	3·25
633	$2 "St. George's", 1953 (Ogden Pleissner) (horiz)	5·00	8·50

1991. 65th Birthday of Queen Elizabeth II and 70th Birthday of Prince Philip. As T **139** of Ascension. Multicoloured.

634	55c. Prince Philip in tropical naval uniform	1·25	1·75
635	70c. Queen Elizabeth II in Bermuda	1·25	1·75

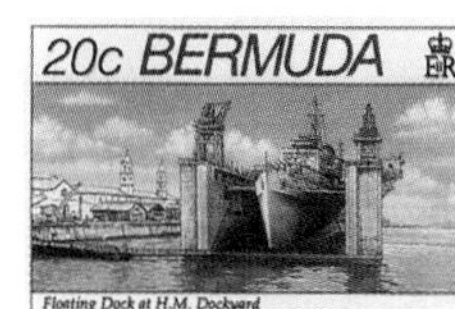

149 H.M.S. "Argonaut" (cruiser) in Floating Dock

1991. 50th Anniv of Second World War. Mult.

636	20c. Type **149**	1·50	40
637	55c. Kindley Airfield	2·25	1·40
638	70c. Boeing 314A flying boat and map of Atlantic route	2·75	3·50
639	$2 Censored trans-Atlantic mail	4·50	8·50

1992. 40th Anniv of Queen Elizabeth II's Accession. As T **143** of Ascension. Multicoloured.

640	20c. Old fort on beach	60	30
641	30c. Public gardens	75	55
642	55c. Cottage garden	1·25	90
643	70c. Beach and hotels	1·60	2·25
644	$1 Queen Elizabeth II	1·90	2·75

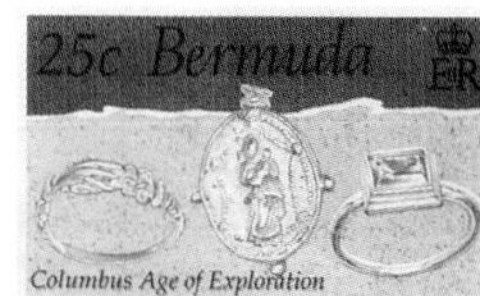

150 Rings and Medallion

1992. 500th Anniv of Discovery of America by Columbus. Spanish Artifacts. Multicoloured.

645	25c. Type **150**	1·25	35
646	35c. Ink wells	1·40	75
647	60c. Gold ornaments	2·25	2·00
648	75c. Bishop buttons and crucifix	2·50	3·25
649	85c. Earrings and pearl buttons	2·75	3·75
650	$1 Jug and bowls	3·00	4·25

151 "Wreck of 'Sea Venture' "

1992. Stained Glass Windows. Multicoloured.

651	25c. Type **151**	1·50	40
652	60c. "Birds in tree"	2·75	2·00
653	75c. "St. Francis feeding bird"	3·25	3·00
654	$2 "Shells"	7·00	10·00

152 German Shepherd

1992. 7th World Congress of Kennel Clubs. Mult.

655	25c. Type **152**	1·25	40
656	35c. Irish setter	1·50	70
657	60c. Whippet (vert)	2·25	2·25
658	75c. Border terrier (vert)	2·25	3·25
659	85c. Pomeranian (vert)	2·50	3·75
660	$1 Schipperke (vert)	2·50	4·25

153 Policeman, Cyclist and Cruise Liner

154 "Duchesse de Brabant" and Bee

1993. Tourism Posters by Adolph Treidler. Mult.

679	25c. Type **153**	2·25	80
680	60c. Seaside golf course	3·00	2·75
681	75c. Deserted beach	2·50	2·75
682	$2 Dancers in evening dress and cruise liner	4·50	7·00

1993. Garden Roses (4th series).

683 **154**	10c. multicoloured	60	1·00
684	25c. multicoloured	60	50
685	50c. multicoloured	1·40	2·00
686	60c. multicoloured	90	1·25

1993. 75th Anniv of Royal Air Force. As T **149** of Ascension. Multicoloured.

687	25c. Consolidated PBY-5 Catalina	85	35
688	60c. Supermarine Spitfire Mk IX	2·00	2·00
689	75c. Bristol Type 156 Beaufighter Mk X	2·25	2·25
690	$2 Handley Page Halifax Mk III	3·75	5·50

155 Hamilton from the Sea

1993. Bicentenary of Hamilton. Mult.

691	25c. Type **155**	1·00	35
692	60c. Waterfront	2·00	2·00
693	75c. Barrel warehouse	2·00	2·50
694	$2 Sailing ships off Hamilton	5·00	7·00

156 "Queen of Bermuda" (liner) at Hamilton

157 Queen Elizabeth II in Bermuda

1994. 75th Anniv of Furness Line's Bermuda Cruises. Adolphe Treidler Posters. Multicoloured.

695 25c. Type **156** 65 35
696 60c. "Monarch of Bermuda" entering port (horiz) . . . 1·50 1·60
697 75c. "Queen of Bermuda" and "Ocean Monarch" (liners) (horiz) . . . . . . 1·60 1·75
698 $2 Passengers on promenade deck at night . . . . . . 3·50 5·50

1994. Royal Visit. Multicoloured.

699 25c. Type **157** 85 35
700 60c. Queen Elizabeth and Prince Philip in open carriage . . . . 1·75 1·75
701 75c. Royal Yacht "Britannia" 3·50 3·00

158 Peach

1994. Flowering Fruits. Multicoloured.

792 5c. Type **158** 30 50
703A 7c. Fig 35 60
704A 10c. Calabash (vert) 35 35
795 15c. Natal plum 50 25
796 18c. Locust and wild honey 50 30
797 20c. Pomegranate 50 35
798 25c. Mulberry (vert) . . . 50 40
709A 35c. Grape (vert) 70 55
710A 55c. Orange (vert) . . . . 1·00 80
711A 60c. Surinam cherry . . . . 1·25 90
802 75c. Loquat . . . . 1·50 1·50
803 90c. Sugar apple . . . . . 1·75 1·75
804 $1 Prickly pear (vert) . . . 2·00 2·50
715A $2 Paw paw . . . . 3·50 3·50
716A $3 Bay grape . . . . 5·00 6·00
717A $5 Banana (vert) . . . . . 7·50 8·00
718A $8 Lemon . . . . 11·00 12·00

159 Nurse with Mother and Baby

1994. Centenary of Hospital Care. Multicoloured.

719 25c. Type **159** . . . . . . 1·00 35
720 60c. Patient on dialysis machine . . . . 2·00 1·90
721 75c. Casualty on emergency trolley . . . . 2·25 2·25
722 $2 Elderly patient in wheelchair with physiotherapists . . . . . 4·75 7·00

160 Gombey Dancers

1994. Cultural Heritage (1st series). Multicoloured.

723 25c. Type **160** 75 35
724 60c. Christmas carol singers 1·40 1·50
725 75c. Marching band . . . . 2·25 2·00
726 $2 National Dance Group performers . . . . 4·50 7·00

See also Nos. 731/4.

161 Bermuda 1970 Flower 1c. Stamps and 1c. Coin

162 Bermuda Coat of Arms

1995. 25th Anniv of Decimal Currency. Mult.

727 25c. Type **161** 45 35
728 60c. 1970 5c. stamps and coin 1·00 1·25
729 75c. 1970 10c. stamps and coin . . . . 1·25 1·75
730 $2 1970 25c. stamps and coin 3·50 5·00

1995. Cultural Heritage (2nd series). As T **160**. Multicoloured.

731 25c. Kite flying 55 35
732 60c. Majorettes . . . . . . 1·50 1·50
733 75c. Portuguese dancers . . . 1·75 2·00
734 $2 Floral float . . . . 3·75 6·00

1995. 375th Anniv of Bermuda Parliament.

735 **162** 25c. multicoloured 85 35
736 $1 multicoloured . . . . 1·90 2·50

For design as No. 736 but inscr "Commonwealth Finance Ministers Meeting", see No. 765.

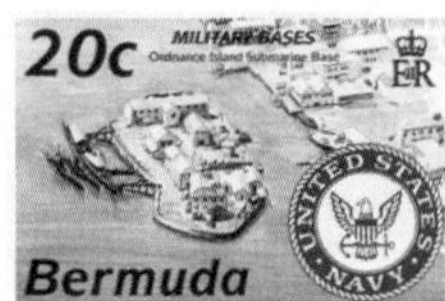

163 U.S. Navy Ordnance Island Submarine Base

1995. Military Bases. Multicoloured.

737 20c. Type **163** 50 50
738 25c. Royal Naval Dockyard 60 35
739 60c. U.S.A.F. Fort Bell and Kindley Field . . . . . 1·25 1·25
740 75c. R.A.F. Darrell's Island flying boat base . . . . 1·50 1·75
741 90c. U.S. Navy operating base . . . . 1·50 2·50
742 $1 Canadian Forces Communications Station, Daniel's Head . . . . . . 1·60 2·50

164 Triple Jump

1996. Olympic Games, Atlanta. Multicoloured.

743 25c. Type **164** 60 35
744 30c. Cycling . . . . 2·00 1·00
745 65c. Yachting . . . . 1·60 1·90
746 80c. Show jumping . . . . . 1·75 2·50

165 Jetty and Islets, Hamilton

1996. Panoramic Paintings of Hamilton (Nos. 747/51) and St. George's (Nos. 752/6) by E. J. Holland. Multicoloured.

747 60c. Type **165** . . . . 1·25 1·50
748 60c. End of island and buildings . . . . 1·25 1·50
749 60c. Yachts and hotel . . . . 1·25 1·50
750 60c. Islet, hotel and cathedral 1·25 1·50
751 60c. Cliff and houses by shore . . . . 1·25 1·50
752 60c. Islet and end of main island . . . . 1·25 1·50
753 60c. Yacht and houses on hillside . . . . 1·25 1·50
754 60c. Yacht and St. George's Hotel on hilltop . . . . . 1·25 1·50
755 60c. Shoreline and fishing boats . . . . 1·25 1·50
756 60c. Entrance to harbour channel . . . . 1·25 1·50

166 Somerset Express Mail Cart, c. 1900

1996. "CAPEX '96" International Stamp Exhibition, Toronto. Local Transport. Multicoloured.

757 25c. Type **166** 95 35
758 60c. Victoria carriage and railcar, 1930s . . . . . . 2·25 1·75
759 75c. First bus, 1946 . . . . 2·25 2·00
760 $2 Sightseeing bus, c. 1947 4·50 6·50

167 Hog Fish Beacon

1996. Lighthouses. Multicoloured.

761 30c. Type **167** . . . . 1·25 50
762 65c. Gibbs Hill Lighthouse 1·75 1·25
763 80c. St. David's Lighthouse 2·25 2·00
764 $2 North Rock Beacon . . . 3·75 6·00

See also Nos. 770/3.

1996. Commonwealth Finance Ministers' Meeting. As No. 736, but inscr "Commonwealth Finance Ministers Meeting" at top and with wider gold frame.

765 $1 multicoloured . . . . . . 2·00 2·50

168 Waterville

1996. Architectural Heritage. Multicoloured.

766 30c. Type **168** 80 45
767 65c. Bridge House . . . . . 1·25 1·50
768 80c. Fannie Fox's Cottage . . 1·60 2·00
769 $2.50 Palmetto House . . . . 3·75 6·50

1997. "HONG KONG '97" International Stamp Exhibition. Designs as Nos. 761/4, but incorporating "HONG KONG '97" logo and with some values changed.

770 30c. As Type **167** . . . . . 1·50 50
771 65c. Gibbs Hill Lighthouse 2·25 1·50
772 80c. St David's Lighthouse 2·50 2·00
773 $2.50 North Rock Beacon . . 5·00 7·50

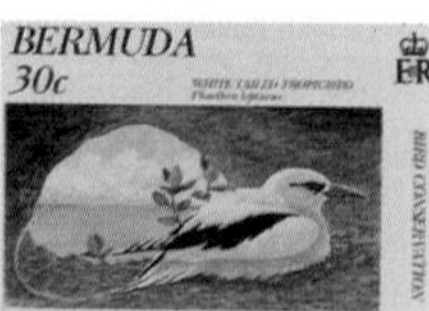

169 White-tailed Tropic Bird

1997. Bird Conservation. Multicoloured.

774 30c. Type **169** 60 50
775 60c. White-tailed tropic bird and chick (vert) . . . . . 1·25 1·25
776 80c. Cahow and chick (vert) 1·75 2·00
777 $2.50 Cahow . . . . 4·00 6·00

170 Queen Elizabeth II with Crowd

1997. Golden Wedding of Queen Elizabeth and Prince Philip. Multicoloured.

778 30c. Type **170** 50 40
779 $2 Queen Elizabeth and Prince Philip . . . . . . 3·00 4·25
MS780 90 × 56 mm. Nos. 778/9 3·50 4·25

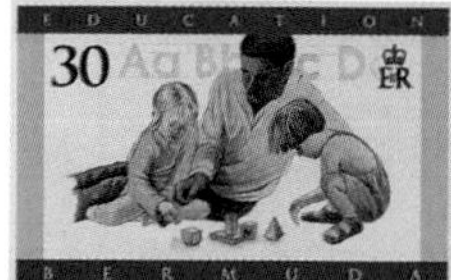

171 Father playing with Children

1997. Education. Multicoloured.

781 30c. Type **171** 50 40
782 40c. Teacher and children with map 60 55
783 60c. Boys holding sports trophy . . . . 85 1·25
784 65c. Pupils outside Berkeley Institute . . . . 90 1·25
785 80c. Scientific experiments . . 1·25 2·00
786 90c. New graduates . . . . . 1·40 2·50

1998. Diana, Princess of Wales Commemoration. Sheet, 145 × 170 mm, containing vert designs as T **177** of Ascension. Multicoloured.

MS787 30c. Wearing black hat, 1983; 40c. Wearing floral dress; 65c. Wearing blue evening dress, 1996; 80c. Carrying bouquets, 1993 (sold at $2.15 + 25c. charity premium) 3·50 4·00

172 "Fox's Cottage, St. Davids" (Ethel Tucker)

1998. Paintings by Catherine and Ethel Tucker. Multicoloured.

788 30c. Type **172** 90 40
789 40c. "East Side, Somerset" 1·10 70
790 65c. "Long Bay Road, Somerset" . . . . 1·75 1·25
791 $2 "Flatts Village" . . . . . 4·00 6·00

173 Horse and Carriage

1998. Hospitality in Bermuda. Multicoloured.

809 25c. Type **173** 70 35
810 30c. Golf club desk . . . . . 1·00 60
811 65c. Chambermaid preparing room . . . . 1·25 1·25
812 75c. Kitchen staff under training . . . . 1·25 1·60
813 80c. Waiter at beach hotel . . 1·50 1·75
814 90c. Nightclub bar . . . . . 1·50 2·50

174 "Agave attenuata"

1998. Centenary of Botanical Gardens. Multicoloured.

815 30c. Type **174** 85 40
816 65c. Bermuda palmetto tree 1·75 90
817 $1 Banyan tree . . . . . . 2·25 2·25
818 $2 Cedar tree . . . . 3·50 5·00

175 Lizard with Fairy Lights (Claire Critchley)

1998. Christmas. Children's Paintings. Mult.

819 25c. Type **175** 60 35
820 40c. "Christmas stairway" (Cameron Rowling) (horiz) 90 1·10

176 Shelly Bay

1999. Bermuda Beaches. Multicoloured.
821 30c. Type **176** 75 40
822 60c. Catherine's Bay . . . . 1·00 90
823 65c. Jobson's Cove . . . . . 1·10 1·00
824 $2 Warwick Long Bay . . . 3·25 4·50

177 Tracking Station

1999. 30th Anniv of First Manned Landing on Moon. Multicoloured.
825 30c. Type **177** 65 40
826 60c. Mission launch (vert) . . 1·00 90
827 75c. Aerial view of tracking station, Bermuda . . . . . 1·25 1·25
828 $2 Astronaut on Moon (vert) 3·00 4·25
MS829 90 × 80 mm. 65c. Earth as seen from Moon (circular, 40 mm diam) 1·50 2·00

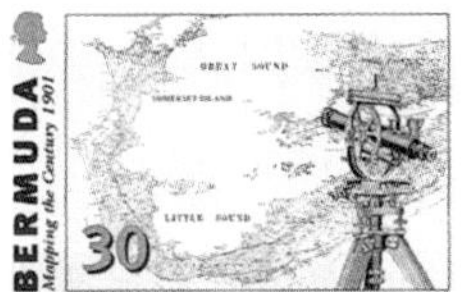
178 Theodolite and Map, 1901

1999. Centenary of First Digital Map of Bermuda.
830 **178** 30c. multicoloured 75 40
831 – 65c. black, stone & silver 1·40 1·25
832 – 80c. multicoloured . . . . 1·60 1·60
833 – $1 multicoloured . . . . 1·75 2·25
DESIGNS: 65c. Street map, 1901; 80c. Street plan and aerial photograph, 1999; $1 Satellite and Bermuda from Space, 1999.

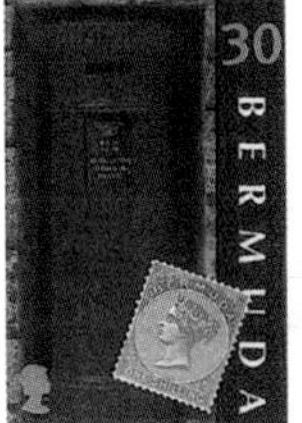
179 Victorian Pillar Box and Bermuda 1865 1s. Stamp

180 Sir Henry Tucker and Meeting of House of Assembly

1999. Bermuda Postal History. Multicoloured.
834 30c. Type **179** 65 40
835 75c. King George V pillar box and 1920 2s. stamp . . 1·40 1·25
836 95c. King George VI wall box and 1938 3d. stamp . . 1·60 2·00
837 $1 Queen Elizabeth II pillar box and 1953 Coronation 1½d. stamp . . . . 1·60 2·00

2000. Pioneers of Progress. Each brown, black and gold.
838 30c. Type **180** 60 80
839 30c. Gladys Morrell and suffragettes 60 80
840 30c. Dr. E. F. Gordon and workers 60 80

181 *Amerigo Vespucci* (full-rigged ship)

182 Prince William

2000. Tall Ships Race. Multicoloured.
841 30c. Type **181** 85 45
842 60c. *Europa* (barque) . . . . 1·25 1·25
843 80c. *Juan Sebastian de Elcano* (schooner) . . . . 1·40 1·75

2000. Royal Birthdays. Multicoloured.
844 35c. Type **182** 80 45
845 40c. Duke of York 85 50
846 50c. Princess Royal 90 70
847 70c. Princess Margaret . . . 1·10 1·60
848 $1 Queen Elizabeth the Queen Mother . . . . . . 1·60 2·25
MS849 169 × 90 mm. Nos. 884/8 4·50 5·00

183 Santa Claus with Smiling Vegetable (Meghan Jones)

2000. Christmas. Children's Paintings. Mult.
850 30c. Type **183** 60 45
851 45c. Christmas tree and presents (Carlita Lodge) . . 80 80

2001. Endangered Species. Bird Conservation. Designs as Nos. 774/7, but with different face values, inscriptions redrawn and WWF panda emblem added. Multicoloured.
852 15c. As Type **169** 55 60
853 15c. Cahow 55 60
854 20c. White-tailed tropic bird with chick (vert) 55 60
855 20c. Cahow with chick (vert) 55 60
MS856 200 × 190 mm. Nos. 852/5 each × 4 6·00 6·50
No. **MS**856 includes the "HONG KONG 2001" logo on the margin.

184 King's Castle

2001. Historic Buildings, St. George's. Multicoloured.
857 35c. Type **184** 75 55
858 50c. Bridge House 95 75
859 55c. Whitehall . . . . 1·00 80
860 70c. Fort Cunningham . . . 1·40 1·40
861 85c. St. Peter's Church . . . 1·60 2·00
862 95c. Water Street . . . . . . 1·75 2·25

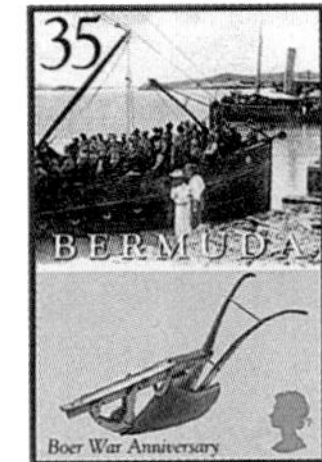
185 Boer Prisoners on Boat and Plough

2001. Centenary of Anglo-Boer War. Multicoloured.
863 35c. Type **185** 75 55
864 50c. Prisoners in shelter and boot 95 75
865 70c. Elderly Boer with children and jewellery . . . 1·40 1·40
866 95c. Bermuda residents and illustrated envelope of 1902 1·90 2·50

186 Girl touching Underwater Environment

2001. 75th Anniv of Bermuda Aquarium. Multicoloured.
867 35c. Type **186** 60 55
868 50c. Museum exhibits (horiz) 80 75
869 55c. Feeding giant tortoise (horiz) 85 80
870 70c. Aquarium building (horiz) . . . . 1·25 1·10
871 80c. Lesson from inside tank 1·25 1·50
872 95c. Turtle . . . . 1·50 1·75

187 "Fishing Boats" (Charles Lloyd Tucker)

2001. Paintings of Charles Lloyd Tucker. Multicoloured.
873 35c. Type **187** 70 55
874 70c. "Bandstand and City Hall, Hamilton" . . . . . 1·25 1·10
875 85c. "Hamilton Harbour" . . 1·50 1·50
876 $1 "Train in Front Street, Hamilton" 1 75 2 00

2002. Golden Jubilee. As T **200** of Ascension.
877 10c. black, violet and gold . . 50 50
878 35c. multicoloured . . . . . 1·25 1·10
879 70c. black, violet and gold . . 1·75 1·40
880 85c. multicoloured . . . . . 2·00 2·00
MS881 162 × 95 mm. Nos. 887/80 and $1 multicoloured 6·00 6·50
DESIGNS—HORIZ: 10c. Princess Elizabeth with corgi; 35c. Queen Elizabeth in evening dress, 1965; 70c. Queen Elizabeth in car, 1952; 85c. Queen Elizabeth on Merseyside, 1991. VERT (38 × 51 mm)—$2 Queen Elizabeth after Annigoni
Designs as Nos. 877/80 in No. **MS**881 omit the gold frame around each stamp and the "Golden Jubilee 1952–2002" inscription.

188 Fantasy Cave

2002. Caves. Multicoloured.
882 35c. Type **188** 70 55
883 70c. Crystal Cave . . . . . 1·25 1·10
884 80c. Prospero's Cave . . . . 1·40 1·40
885 $1 Cathedral Cave . . . . . 1·75 2·00

189 Fielder and Somerset Club Colours

190 Slit Worm-shell

2002. Centenary of Bermuda Cup Cricket Match. Multicoloured.
886 35c. Type **189** 45 50
887 35c. Batsman and wicketkeeper with St. George's Club colours 45 50
MS888 110 × 85 mm. $1 Batsman (48 × 31 mm) 1·25 1·25

2002. Queen Elizabeth the Queen Mother Commemoration. As T **202** of Ascension.
889 30c. brown, gold and purple 40 45
890 $1.25 multicoloured . . . . 1·60 1·75
MS891 145 × 70 mm. Nos. 889/90 2·00 2·10
DESIGNS: 30c. Duchess of York, 1923; $1.25, Queen Mother on her birthday, 1995.
Designs as Nos. 889/90 in No. **MS**891 omit the "1900-2002" inscription and the coloured frame.

2002. Shells. Multicoloured.
892 5c. Type **190** 10 10
893 10c. Netted olive 15 20
894 20c. Angular triton (horiz) . . 25 30
895 25c. Frog shell (horiz) . . . 30 35
896 30c. Colourful atlantic moon (horiz) 40 45
897 35c. Noble wentletrap 45 50
898 40c. Atlantic trumpet triton (horiz) 50 55
899 45c. Zigzag scallop 60 65
900 50c. Bermuda cone 65 70
901 75c. Very distorted distorsio (horiz) . . . . 95 1·00
902 80c. Purple sea snail (horiz) 1·00 1·10
903 90c. Flame helmet (horiz) . . 1·10 1·25
904 $1 Scotch bonnet (horiz) . . 1·60 2·75
905 $2 Gold mouth triton (horiz) 2·50 2·75
906 $3 Bermuda's slit shell (horiz) 3·75 4·00
907 $4 Reticulated cowrie-helmet (horiz) . . . . 5·25 5·50
908 $5 Dennison's morum (horiz) 6·50 6·75
909 $8 Sunrise tellin . . . . . . 10·50 11·00

191 Dove of Peace

192 Research Station and *Weatherbird II* (research ship)

2002. World Peace Day.
910 **191** 35c. multicoloured 45 50
911 – 70c. multicoloured 90 95
DESIGN: 70c. Dove.

2003. Centenary of Bermuda Biological Research Station. Multicoloured.
912 35c. Type **192** 45 50
913 70c. Spotfin butterflyfish (horiz) 90 95
914 85c. Collecting coral (horiz) 1·10 1·25
915 $1 Krill . . . . 1·25 1·40

EXPRESS LETTER STAMP

E 1 Queen Elizabeth II

1996.
E1 E **1** $22 orange and blue . . . 30·00 32·00

BHOPAL Pt. 1

A state of C. India. Now uses Indian stamps.

12 pies = 1 anna; 16 annas = 1 rupee.

3

4

1876. Imperf.
5 **3** ¼a. black . . . . 6·50 11·00
2 ½a. red . . . . 16·00 35·00

1878. Imperf or perf.
7 **4** ¼a. green . . . . 8·50 13·00
15 ¼a. red . . . . 5·00 2·00
8 ½a. red . . . . 5·50 11·00
9 ½a. brown . . . . 23·00 35·00

1881. As T **3**, but larger. Imperf or perf.
29 ¼a. black . . . . 1·75 1·25
37 ½a. red . . . . 1·40 3·00
46 ½a. black . . . . 1·00 1·50
30 1a. brown . . . . 1·50 3·75
31 2a. blue . . . . 1·25 1·50
32 4a. yellow . . . . 1·75 3·00

13

15

1884. Perf.
49 **13** ¼a. green . . . . 4·50 12·00
76 ¼a. black 85 85

1884. Imperf or perf.
64 **15** ¼a. green 50 45
65 ¼a. black 30 30
53 ½a. black . . . . 60 2·50
56 ½a. red . . . . 50 1·10

17

1890. Imperf or perf.
71 **17** 8a. greenish black . . . . . 19·00 19·00

19

20 State Arms

1902. Imperf.
90 **19** ¼a. red . . . . 70 3·50
91 ½a. black . . . . 70 4·25
92 1a. brown . . . . 1·40 5·00

94 2a. blue . . . . 4·50 19·00
96 4a. yellow . . . . 15·00 42·00
97 8a. lilac . . . . 40·00 £100
98 1r. red . . . . 60·00 £140

1908. Perf.
100 **20** 1a. green . . . . 3·50 3·50

OFFICIAL STAMPS

1908. As T **20** but inscr "H.H. BEGUM'S SERVICE" optd **SERVICE**.
O301 ½a. green . . . . 2·00 10
O302 1a. red . . . . 4·00 35
O307 2a. blue . . . . 3·00 40
O304 4a. brown . . . . 10·00 30

O 4

1930. Type O 4 optd **SERVICE**.
O309 O **4** ½a. green . . . . 8·50 1·25
O310 1a. red . . . . 9·50 15
O311 2a. blue . . . . 9·00 45
O312 4a. brown . . . . . . 8·50 80

1932. As T **20**, but inscr "POSTAGE" at left and "BHOPAL STATE" at right, optd **SERVICE**.
O313 ¼a. orange . . . . 2·50 50

1932. As T **20**, but inscr "POSTAGE" at left and "BHOPAL GOVT" at right, optd **SERVICE**.
O314 ½a. green . . . . 5·00 10
O315 1a. red . . . . 8·50 15
O316 2a. blue . . . . 8·50 45
O317 4a. brown . . . . 7·00 1·00

1935. Nos. O314, etc, surch.
O318 ¼a. on ½a. green . . . . . 22·00 13·00
O319 3p. on ½a. green . . . . . 2·75 3·25
O320 ¼a. on 2a. blue . . . . . . 23·00 16·00
O321 3p. on 2a. blue . . . . . . 4·00 3·50
O323 ¼a. on 4a. brown . . . . . 60·00 21·00
O325 3p. on 4a. brown . . . . . 2·50 3·00
O326 1a. on ½a. green . . . . . 3·50 1·50
O328 1a. on 2a. blue . . . . . . 70 1·25
O329 1a. on 4a. brown . . . . . 4·50 4·75

O 8

1935.
O330 O **8** 1a.3p. blue and red . . 3·50 50
O331 1a.6p. blue and red . . 1·75 50
O332 1a.6p. red . . . . . . 5·00 1·00
Nos. O331/2 are similar to Type O **8**, but inscr "BHOPAL STATE POSTAGE".

O 9

1936. Type O 9 optd **SERVICE**.
O333 O **9** ¼a. yellow 90 30
O335 1a. red . . . . 1·50 10

O **10** The Moti Mahal

1936. As Type O **4** optd **SERVICE**.
O336d O **10** ½a. purple and green 70 30
O337 – 2a. brown and blue 1·75 50
O338 – 2a. green and violet 8·00 30
O339 – 4a. blue and brown 3·50 50
O340 – 8a. purple and blue 4·50 1·50
O341 – 1r. blue and purple 16·00 6·50
DESIGNS: 2a. The Moti Masjid; 4a. Taj Mahal and Be-Nazir Palaces; 8a. Ahmadabad Palace; 1r. Rait Ghat.

Nos. O336 is inscr "BHOPAL GOVT" below the arms, other values have "BHOPAL STATE".

1940. Animal designs, as Type O **10** but inscr "SERVICE" in bottom panel.
O344 ¼a. blue (Tiger) . . . . . . 3·50 1·25
O345 1a. purple (Spotted deer) 18·00 1·75

1941. As Type O **8** but "SERVICE" inscr instead of optd.
O346 O **8** 1a.3p. green . . . . . 1·25 1·25

1944. Palaces as Type O **10** but smaller.
O347 ½a. green (Moti Mahal) . . 85 80
O348 2a. violet (Moti Masjid) 7·50 3·00
O348c 2a. purple (Moti Masjid) 2·00 3·00
O349 4a. brown (Be-Nazir) . . . 4·75 1·60
The 2a. and 4a. are inscr "BHOPAL STATE", and the other "BHOPAL GOVT".

O **14** Arms of Bhopal

1944.
O350 O **14** 3p. blue 65 60
O351b 9p. brown . . . . . . 2·00 3·00
O352 1a. purple . . . . . . 4·25 1·25
O352b 1a. violet . . . . . . 7·00 2·25
O353 1½a. red . . . . 1·25 60
O354 3a. yellow . . . . . . 9·00 10·00
O354d 3a. brown . . . . . . 85·00 75·00
O355 6a. red . . . . 13·00 38·00

1949. Surch **2 As.** and bars.
O356 O **14** 2a. on 1½a. red . . . . 2·50 6·00

1949. Surch **2 As.** and ornaments.
O357 O **14** 2a. on 1½a. red £650 £650

BHOR — Pt. 1

A state of W. India, Bombay district. Now uses Indian stamps.

12 pies = 1 anna; 16 annas = 1 rupee.

1

3 Pandit Shankar Rao

1879. Imperf.
1 **1** ½a. red . . . . 2·50 4·00

Similar to T **1**, but rectangular.
2 1a. red . . . . 4·50 6·00

1901. Imperf.
3 **3** ½a. red . . . . 12·00 32·00

BHUTAN — Pt. 21

An independent territory in treaty relations with India and bounded by India, Sikkim and Tibet.

100 chetrum = 1 ngultrum.

1 Postal Runner

2 "Uprooted Tree" Emblem and Crest of Bhutan

1962.
1 **1** 2ch. red and grey 10 10
2 – 3ch. red and blue 20 20
3 – 5ch. brown and green . . . . 1·00 1·00
4 – 15ch. yellow, black and red . . 10 10
5 **1** 33ch. green and violet 20 20
6 – 70ch. ultramarine and blue . . 60 60
7 – 1n.30 black and blue . . . . 1·25 1·25
DESIGNS—HORIZ: 3, 70ch. Archer. 5ch., 1n.30, Yak. 15ch. Map of Bhutan, Maharaja Druk Gyalpo and Paro Dzong (fortress and monastery).

1962. World Refugee Year.
8 **2** 1n. red and blue 45 45
9 2n. violet and green . . . . . 1·40 1·40

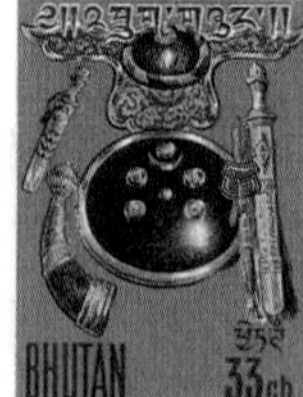

3 Accoutrements of Ancient Warrior

4 "Boy filling box" (with grain)

1962. Membership of Colombo Plan.
10 **3** 33ch. multicoloured 20 20
11 70ch. multicoloured 35 35
12 1n.30 red, brown & yellow 80 80

1963. Freedom from Hunger.
13 **4** 20ch. brown, blue & yellow 25 25
14 1n.50 purple, brown & blue 90 90

1964. Winter Olympic Games, Innsbruck, and Bhutanese Winter Sports Committee Fund. Nos. 10/12 surch **INNSBRUCK 1964 +50 ch**, Olympic rings and emblem.
15 **3** 33ch.+50ch. multicoloured . . 2·75 2·75
16 70ch.+50ch. multicoloured . . 2·75 2·75
17 1n.30+50ch. multicoloured 2·75 2·75

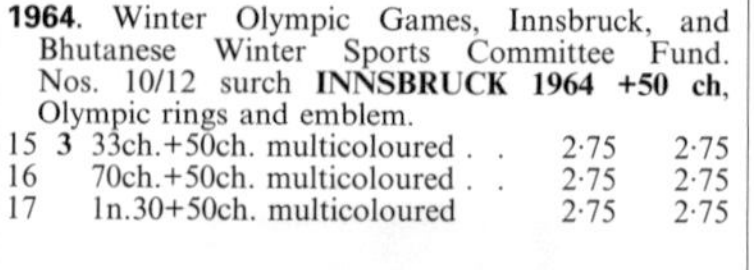

6 Dancer with upraised hands

1964. Bhutanese Dancers. Multicoloured.
18 2ch. Standing on one leg (vert) 10 10
19 3ch. Type **6** 10 10
20 5ch. With tambourine (vert) 10 10
21 20ch. As 2ch. 10 10
22 33ch. Type **6** 15 15
23 70ch. With sword 25 25
24 1n. With tasselled hat (vert) 55 55
25 1n.30 As 5ch. 70 70
26 2n. As 70ch. . . . . 1·25 1·25

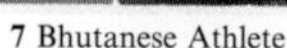

7 Bhutanese Athlete

9 Primula

8 Flags at Half-mast

1964. Olympic Games, Tokyo. Multicoloured.
27 2ch. Type **7** 10 10
28 5ch. Boxing 10 10
29 15ch. Type **7** 10 10
30 33ch. As 5ch. 15 15
31 1n. Archery 55 55
32 2n. Football 90 90
33 3n. As 1n. . . . . . 1·50 1·50

1964. Pres. Kennedy Commemoration.
34 **8** 33ch. multicoloured 20 20
35 1n. multicoloured 55 55
36 3n. multicoloured . . . . . 1·25 1·25

1965. Flowers. Multicoloured.
37 2ch. Type **9** 10 10
38 5ch. Gentian 10 10
39 15ch. Type **9** 10 10
40 33ch. As 5ch. 15 15
41 50ch. Rhododendron 20 20
42 75ch. Peony 30 30
43 1n. As 50ch. 30 30
44 2n. As 75ch. 70 70

1965. Churchill Commemoration. Optd **WINSTON CHURCHILL 1874 1965**.
45 **1** 33ch. green and violet . . . 15 15
46 **8** 1n. multicoloured 45 45
47 – 1n. multicoloured (No. 43) 45 45
48 – 2n. multicoloured (No. 44) 75 75
49 **8** 3n. multicoloured . . . . . 1·25 1·25

11 Pavilion and Skyscrapers

1965. New York World's Fair. Mult.
50 1ch. Type **11** 10 10
51 10ch. Buddha and Michelangelo's "Pieta" . . . 10 10
52 20ch. Bhutan houses and New York skyline 10 10
53 33ch. Bhutan and New York bridges 10 10
54 1n.50 Type **11** 55 55
55 2n. As 10ch. 90 90

1965. Surch.
56 **2** 5ch. on 1n. (No. 8) . . . . . 24·00 24·00
57 5ch. on 2n. (No. 9) . . . . . 27·00 27·00
58 – 10ch. on 70ch. (No. 23) . . . 6·75 6·75
59 – 10ch. on 2n. (No. 26) . . . . 6·75 6·75
60 – 15ch. on 70ch. (No. 6) . . . 5·00 5·00
61 – 15ch. on 1n.30 (No. 7) . . . 5·00 5·00
62 – 20ch. on 1n. (No. 24) . . . . 6·75 6·75
63 – 20ch. on 1n.30 (No. 25) . . . 6·75 6·75

13 "Telstar" and Portable Transmitter

1966. Centenary of I.T.U. Multicoloured.
64 35ch. Type **13** 20 20
65 2n. "Telstar" & morse key . . 65 65
66 3n. "Relay" and headphones 1·00 1·00

14 Asiatic Black Bear

1966. Animals. Multicoloured.
68 1ch. Type **14** 10 10
69 2ch. Snow leopard 10 10
70 4ch. Pygmy hog 10 10
71 8ch. Tiger 10 10
72 10ch. Dhole 10 10
73 75ch. As 8ch. 30 30
74 1n. Takin 30 30
75 1n.50 As 10ch. 45 45
76 2n. As 4ch. 80 80
77 3n. As 2ch. . . . . 1·00 1·00
78 4n. Type **14** . . . . 1·25 1·25
79 5n. As 1n. . . . . 1·60 1·60

15 Simtoke Dzong (fortress)

1966.
80 – 5c. brown 15 15
81 **15** 15ch. brown 15 15
82 20ch. green 20 20
DESIGN: 5ch. Rinpung Dzong (fortress).

16 King Jigme Dorji Wangchuck (obverse of 50n.p. coin)

1966. 40th Anniv of King Jigme Wangchuck's Accession (father of King Jigme Dorji Wangchuck). Circular designs, embossed on gold foil, backed with multicoloured patterned paper. Imperf. Sizes: (a) Diameter 38 mm; (b) Diameter 50 mm; (c) Diameter 63 mm. (i) 50n.p. Coin
83 **16** 10ch. green (a) 20 20
(ii) 1r. Coin
84 **16** 25ch. green (b) 25 25
(iii) 3r. Coin
85 **16** 50ch. green (c) 50 50
(iv) 1 sertum Coin
86 **16** 1n. red (a) 90 90
87 – 1n.30 red (a) . . . . 1·25 1·25
(v) 2 sertum Coin
88 **16** 2n. red (b) . . . . 1·75 1·75
89 – 3n. red (b) . . . . 2·75 2·75
(vi) 5 sertum Coin
90 **16** 4n. red (c) . . . . 3·75 3·75
91 – 5n. red (c) . . . . 4·50 4·50
Nos. 87, 89 and 91 show the reverse side of the coins (Symbol).

17 "Abominable Snowman"

1966. "Abominable Snowman". Various triangular designs.
92 **17** 1ch. multicoloured 10 10
93 – 2ch. multicoloured 10 10
94 – 3ch. multicoloured 10 10
95 – 4ch. multicoloured 10 10
96 – 5ch. multicoloured 10 10
97 – 15ch. multicoloured . . . 10 10
98 – 30ch. multicoloured . . . 10 10
99 – 40ch. multicoloured . . . 20 20
100 – 50ch. multicoloured . . . 20 20
101 – 1n.25 multicoloured . . . 35 35
102 – 2n.50 multicoloured . . . 70 70
103 – 3n. multicoloured 80 80
104 – 5n. multicoloured . . . . 1·40 1·40
105 – 6n. multicoloured . . . . 1·40 1·40
106 – 7n. multicoloured . . . . 1·75 1·75

1967. Air. Optd **AIR MAIL** and helicopter motif.
107 **6** 33ch. multicoloured . . . 10 10
108 – 50ch. mult (No. 41) . . . 15 15
109 – 70ch. mult (No. 23) . . . 20 20
110 – 75ch. mult (No. 42) . . . 25 25
111 – 1n. mult (No. 24) 30 30
112 – 1n.50 mult (No. 75) . . . 35 35
113 – 2n. mult (No. 76) 35 35
114 – 3n. mult (No. 77) 65 65
115 **14** 4n. multicoloured 90 90
116 – 5n. mult (No. 79) . . . . 1·40 1·40

20 "Lilium sherriffiae"

1967. Flowers. Multicoloured.
117 3ch. Type **20** 10 10
118 5ch. "Meconopsis" 10 10
119 7ch. "Rhododendron dhwoju" 10 10
120 10ch. "Pleione hookeriana" 10 10
121 50ch. Type **20** 20 20
122 1n. As 5ch. 35 35
123 2n.50 As 7ch. 90 90
124 4n. As 10ch. . . . . 1·40 1·40
125 5n. "Rhododendron giganteum" . . . . 1·75 1·75

21 Scouts planting Sapling

1967. Bhutanese Boy Scouts. Multicoloured.
126 5ch. Type **21** 10 10
127 10ch. Scouts preparing meal 10 10
128 15ch. Scout mountaineering 20 20
129 50ch. Type **21** 30 30
130 1n.25. As 10ch. 45 45
131 4n. As 15ch. . . . . 1·25 1·25

1967. World Fair, Montreal. Nos. 53/5 optd **expo67** and emblem.
133 – 33ch. multicoloured . . . 20 20
134 **11** 1n.50 multicoloured . . . 40 40
135 – 2n. multicoloured 55 55

23 Avro Lancaster Bomber

1967. Churchill and Battle of Britain Commemoration. Multicoloured.
137 45ch. Type **23** 25 25
138 2n. Supermarine Spitfire fighter 50 50
139 4n. Hawker Hurricane Mk IIC fighter . . . . . . 1·00 1·00

1967. World Scout Jamboree, Idaho. Nos. 126/31 optd **WORLD JAMBOREE IDAHO, U.S.A. AUG. 1-9/67.**
141 **21** 5ch. multicoloured 10 10
142 – 10ch. multicoloured . . . 10 10
143 – 15ch. multicoloured . . . 10 10
144 – 50ch. multicoloured . . . 30 30
145 – 1n.25 multicoloured . . . 55 55
146 – 4n. multicoloured . . . . 1·60 1·60

25 Painting

1967. Bhutan Girl Scouts. Multicoloured.
148 5ch. Type **25** 10 10
149 10ch. Playing musical instrument 10 10
150 15ch. Picking fruit 10 10
151 1n.50 Type **25** 30 30
152 2n.50 As 10ch. 45 45
153 5n. As 15ch. . . . . 1·10 1·10

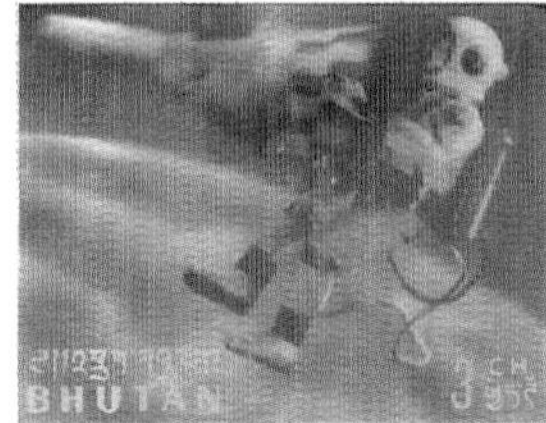

26 Astronaut in Space

1967. Space Achievements. With laminated prismatic-ribbed plastic surface. Multicoloured.
155 3ch. Type **26** (postage) . . . 15 15
156 5ch. Space vehicle and astronaut 15 15
157 7ch. Astronaut and landing vehicle 20 20
158 10ch. Three astronauts in space 30 30
159 15ch. Type **26** 35 35
160 30ch. As 5ch. 70 70
161 50ch. As 7ch. 90 90
162 1n.25 As 10ch. . . . . 2·75 2·75
163 2n.50 Type **26** (air) 90 90
164 4n. As 5ch. . . . . 1·40 1·40
165 5n. As 7ch. . . . . 2·25 2·25
166 9n. As 10ch. . . . . 3·25 3·25
The laminated plastic surface gives the stamps a three-dimensional effect.

27 Tashichho Dzong

1968.
168 **27** 10ch. purple and green . . 20 15

28 Elephant

1968. Mythological Creatures.
169 **28** 2ch. red, blue and brown (postage) 15 15
170 – 3ch. pink, blue & green . . 15 15
171 – 4ch. orange, green & blue 15 15
172 – 5ch. blue, yellow & pink 15 15
173 – 15ch. green, purple & blue 15 15
174 **28** 20ch. brown, blk & orge 15 15
175 – 30ch. yellow, black & blue 20 20
176 – 50ch. bistre, green & black 25 25
177 – 1n.25 black, green & red 25 25
178 – 2n. yellow, violet & black 35 35
179 **28** 1n.50 green, purple and yellow (air) 35 35
180 – 2n.50 red, black & blue . . 45 45
181 – 4n. orange, green & black 65 65
182 – 5n. brown, grey & orange 90 90
183 – 10n. violet, grey & black 1·75 1·75
DESIGNS: 3, 30ch., 2n.50, Garuda; 4, 50ch., 4n. Tiger; 5ch., 1n.25, 5n. Wind horse; 15ch., 2, 10n. Snow lion.

29 Tongsa Dzong

1968.
184 **29** 50ch. green 30 30
185 – 75ch. brown and blue . . . 35 35
186 – 1n. blue and violet 40 40
DESIGNS: 75ch. Daga Dzong; 1n. Lhuntsi Dzong.

30 Ward's Trogon

1968. Rare Birds.
187 2ch. Red-faced liocichla ("Crimson-winged Laughing Thrush") (horiz) (postage) 10 10
188 3ch. Type **30** 15 15
189 4ch. Burmese ("Grey") Peacock-pheasant (horiz) 20 20
190 5ch. Rufous-necked hornbill 25 25
191 15ch. Fire-tailed 'myzornis' ("Myzornis") (horiz) . . . 35 35
192 20ch. As No. 187 . . . . . 45 45
193 30ch. Type **30** 50 50
194 50ch. As No. 189 . . . . . 55 55
195 1n.25 As No. 190 . . . . . 75 75
196 2n. As No. 191 . . . . . . 1·25 1·25
197 1n.50 As No. 187 (air) . . . 85 85
198 2n.50 Type **30** . . . . 1·25 1·25
199 4n. As No. 189 . . . . . . 1·90 1·90
200 5n. As No. 190 . . . . . . 2·75 2·75
201 10n. As No. 191 . . . . . . 5·25 5·25

31 Mahatma Gandhi

1969. Birth Centenary of Mahatma Gandhi.
202 **31** 20ch. brown and blue . . . 45 45
203 2n. brown and yellow . . . 1·10 1·10

1970. Various stamps surch **5 CH** or **20 CH.**
(a) Freedom from Hunger (No. 14).
223 20ch. on 1n.50 purple, brown and blue . . . . 2·25 2·25
(b) Animals (Nos. 75/9).
224 20ch. on 1n.50 multicoloured 2·25 2·25
225 20ch. on 2n. multicoloured 2·25 2·25
204 20ch. on 3n. multicoloured 90 90
205 20ch. on 4n. multicoloured 90 90
206 20ch. on 5n. multicoloured 90 90
(c) Abominable Snowmen (Nos. 101/6).
226 20ch. on 1n.25 multicoloured 2·25 2·25
227 20ch. on 2n.50 multicoloured 2·25 2·25
207 20ch. on 3n. multicoloured 90 90
208 20ch. on 5n. multicoloured 90 90
209 20ch. on 6n. multicoloured 90 90
210 20ch. on 7n. multicoloured 90 90
(d) Flowers (Nos. 124/5).
211 20ch. on 4n. multicoloured 90 90
212 20ch. on 5n. multicoloured 90 90
(e) Boy Scouts (Nos. 130/1).
228 20ch. on 1n.25 multicoloured 2·25 2·25
213 20ch. on 4n. multicoloured 90 90
(f) Churchill (Nos. 138/9).
229 20ch. on 2n. multicoloured 2·25 2·25
230 20ch. on 4n. multicoloured 2·25 2·25
(g) 1968 Pheasants (Appendix).
231 20ch. on 2n. multicoloured 3·50 3·50
214 20ch. on 4n. multicoloured 2·00 2·00
232 20ch. on 7n. multicoloured 3·50 3·50
(h) Mythological Creatures (Nos. 175/80 and 182/3).
233 5ch. on 30ch. yellow, black and blue (postage) 70 70
234 5ch. on 50ch. bistre, green and black 70 70
235 5ch. on 1n.25 black, green and red 70 70
236 5ch. on 2n. yellow, vio & blk 70 70
215 20ch. on 2n. yellow, violet and black 90 90
237 5ch. on 1n.50 green, purple and brown (air) 70 70
238 5ch. on 2n.50 red, black and blue 70 70
216 20ch. on 5n. brown, grey and orange 90 90
217 20ch. on 10n. violet, grey and black 90 90
(i) Rare Birds (Nos. 193/201).
239 20ch. on 30ch. mult (postage) 3·50 3·50
240 20ch. on 50ch. multicoloured 3·50 3·50
241 20ch. on 1n. 25. multicoloured . . . . . . 3·50 3·50
218 20ch. on 2n. multicoloured 1·75 1·75
242 20ch. on 1n.50. mult (air) . . 3·50 3·50
219 20ch. on 2n.50. multicoloured 2·00 2·00
220 20ch. on 4n. multicoloured 2·00 2·00
221 20ch. on 5n. multicoloured 2·00 2·00
222 20ch. on 10n. multicoloured 2·00 2·00
(j) 1969 U.P.U. (Appendix).
243 20ch. on 1n.05. multicoloured 2·25 2·25
244 20ch. on 1n.40. multicoloured 2·25 2·25
245 20ch. on 4n. multicoloured 2·25 2·25
For stamps surcharged with 55 or 90ch. values, see Nos. 253/65 and for 25ch. surcharges see Nos. 385/410.

33 Wangdiphodrang Dzong and Bridge

34 Book Year Emblem

1971.
246 **33** 2ch. grey 10 10
247 3ch. mauve 10 10
248 4ch. violet 10 10
249 5ch. green 10 10
250 10ch. brown 10 10
251 15ch. blue 15 15
252 20ch. purple 20 20

1971. Various stamps surch **55 CH** or **90 CH.**
I. Dancers (Nos. 25/6).
253 55ch. on 1n.30 multicoloured 90 90
254 90ch. on 2n. multicoloured 90 90
II. Animals (Nos. 77/8).
255 55ch. on 3n. multicoloured 90 90
256 90ch. on 4n. multicoloured 90 90
III. Boy Scouts (No. 131).
257 90ch. on 4n. multicoloured 90 90
IV. 1968 Pheasants (Appendix).
258 55ch. on 5n. multicoloured 3·00 3·00
259 90ch. on 9n. multicoloured 3·00 3·00
V. Air. Mythological Creatures (No. 181).
260 55ch. on 4n. orange, green and black 55 55
VI. 1968 Mexico Olympics (Appendix).
261 90ch. on 1n.05 multicoloured 1·40 1·40
VII. Rare Birds (No. 196).
262 90ch. on 2n. multicoloured 3·00 3·00
VIII. 1969 U.P.U. (Appendix).
263 55ch. on 60ch. multicoloured 90 90
IX. 1970 New U.P.U. Headquarters (Appendix).
264 90ch. on 2n. 50 gold and red 7·50 7·50
X. 1971 Moon Vehicles (plastic-surfaced) (Appendix).
265 90ch. on 1n. 70 multicoloured 90 90

1972. International Book Year.
266 **34** 2ch. green and blue 15 15
267 3ch. brown and yellow . . 15 15
268 5ch. brown, orange & red 20 20
269 20ch. brown and blue . . . 15 15

35 Dochi

1972. Dogs. Multicoloured.
270 5ch. Apsoo standing on hind legs (vert) 10 10
271 10ch. Type **35** 10 10
272 15ch. Brown and white damci 15 15
273 25ch. Black and white damci 15 15
274 55ch. Apsoo lying down . . 20 20
275 8n. Two damci . . . . . . 1·60 1·60

36 King and Royal Crest

1974. Coronation of King Jigme Singye Wangchuck. Multicoloured.
277 10ch. Type **36** 10 10
278 25ch. Bhutan Flag 10 10
279 1n.25 Good Luck signs . . . 35 35
280 2n. Punakha Dzong 55 55
281 3n. Royal Crown 70 70

37 Mail Delivery by Horse

1974. Centenary of U.P.U. Multicoloured.
283 1ch. Type **37** (postage) . . . 10 10
284 2ch. Early and modern locomotives 10 10
285 3ch. "Hindoostan" (paddle-steamer) and "Iberia" (liner) 20 20
286 4ch. Vickers Vimy and Concorde aircraft 30 30
287 25ch. Mail runner and four-wheel drive 15 15
288 1n. As 25ch. (air) 30 30
289 1n.40 As 2ch. . . . . 1·50 1·50
290 2n. As 4ch. . . . . 1·50 1·50

38 Family and W.P.Y. Emblem

1974. World Population Year.
292 **38** 25ch. multicoloured . . . 10 10
293 50ch. multicoloured . . . 20 20
294 90ch. multicoloured . . . 35 35
295 2n.50 multicoloured . . . 80 80

39 Eastern Courtier

1975. Butterflies. Multicoloured.
297 1ch. Type **39** 10 10
298 2ch. Bamboo forester 10 10
299 3ch. Tailed labyrinth 10 10
300 4ch. Blue duchess 10 10
301 5ch. Cruiser 15 15
302 10ch. Bhutan glory 15 15
303 3n. Bi-coloured commodore 65 65
304 5n. Red-breasted jezebel . . . 1·40 1·40

40 King Jigme Singye Wangchuck

1976. King Jigme's 20th Birthday. Imperf.
(a) Diameter 39 mm.
306 **40** 15ch. green on gold . . . 10 10
307 1n. red on gold 30 30
308 – 1n.30 red on gold 35 35

(b) Diameter 50 mm.
309 **40** 25ch. green on gold . . . 10 10
310 2n. red on gold 45 45
311 – 3n. red on gold 70 70

(c) Diameter 63 mm.
312 **40** 90ch. green on gold . . . 25 25
313 4n. red on gold . . . . . 1·10 1·10
314 – 5n. red on gold . . . . . 1·25 1·25
DESIGN: 1n.30, 3, 5n. Decorative motif.

41 "Apollo"

1976. "Apollo"–"Soyuz" Space Link. Mult.
315 10n. Type **41** . . . . 2·40 2·40
316 10n. "Soyuz" . . . . 2·40 2·40

42 Jewellery

1976. Handicrafts and Craftsmen. Mult.
318 1ch. Type **42** 10 10
319 2ch. Coffee-pot, hand bell and sugar dish 10 10
320 3ch. Powder horns 10 10
321 4ch. Pendants and inlaid box 10 10
322 5ch. Painter 10 10
323 15ch. Silversmith 15 15
324 20ch. Wood carver with tools 15 15
325 1n.50 Textile printer 35 35
326 10n. Printer . . . . 2·75 2·75

43 "Rhododendron cinnabarinum"

45 Dragon Mask

44 Skiing

1976. Rhododendrons. Multicoloured.
328 1ch. Type **43** 10 10
329 2ch. "R. campanulatum" . . 10 10
330 3ch. "R. fortunei" 10 10
331 4ch. "R. arboreum" 10 10
332 5ch. "R. arboreum" (different) 10 10
333 1n. "R. falconeri" 35 35
334 3n. "R. hodgsonii" 70 70
335 5n. "R. keysii" . . . . . . 1·40 1·40

1976. Winter Olympic Games, Innsbruck. Mult.
337 1ch. Type **44** 10 10
338 2ch. Bobsleighing 10 10
339 3ch. Ice hockey 10 10
340 4ch. Cross-country skiing . . 10 10
341 5ch. Women's figure skating 10 10
342 2n. Downhill skiing 45 45
343 4n. Speed skating . . . . . 1·10 1·10
344 10n. Pairs figure skating . . . 2·40 2·40

1976. Ceremonial Masks. Laminated prismatic-ribbed plastic surface.
346 **45** 5ch. mult (postage) 15 15
347 – 10ch. multicoloured . . . 15 15
348 – 15ch. multicoloured . . . 20 20
349 – 20ch. multicoloured . . . 20 20
350 – 25ch. multicoloured . . . 20 20
351 – 30ch. multicoloured . . . 20 20
352 – 35ch. multicoloured . . . 20 20
353 – 1n. multicoloured (air) . . 35 35
354 – 2n. multicoloured 65 65
355 – 2n.50 multicoloured . . . 80 80
356 – 3n. multicoloured 90 90
DESIGNS: 10ch. to 3n. Similar Bhutanese masks.

46 Orchid

1976. Flowers. Multicoloured.
358 1ch. Type **46** 10 10
359 2ch. Orchid (different) . . . 10 10
360 3ch. Orchid (different) . . . 10 10
361 4ch. "Primula denticulata" 10 10
362 5ch. Arum 10 10
363 2n. Orchid (different) 40 40
364 4n. "Leguminosa" 70 70
365 6n. Rhododendron . . . . . 1·40 1·40

47 Double Carp Emblem

1976. 25th Anniv of Colombo Plan.
367 3ch. Type **47** 10 10
368 4ch. Vase emblem 10 10
369 5ch. Geometric design . . . 10 10
370 25ch. Design incorporating animal's face 30 30
371 1n.25 Ornamental design . . 35 35
372 2n. Floral design 70 70
373 2n.50 Carousel design 90 90
374 3n. Wheel design . . . . . . 1·10 1·10

48 Bandaranaike Conference Hall

1976. 5th Non-aligned Countries Summit Conference, Colombo.
375 **48** 1n.25 multicoloured . . . 35 35
376 2n.50 multicoloured . . . 70 70

49 Liberty Bell

1978. Anniversaries and Events. Mult.
377 20n. Type **49** (bicentenary of U.S. independence) . . . . 4·50 4·50
378 20n. Alexander Graham Bell early telephone (telephone centenary) . . . . 4·50 4·50
379 20n. Archer (Olympic Games, Montreal) . . . . 4·50 4·50
380 20n. Alfred Nobel (75th anniv of Nobel Prizes) . . 4·50 4·50
381 20n. "Spirit of St. Louis" (50th anniv of Lindbergh's transatlantic flight) . . . . 4·50 4·50
382 20n. Airship LZ3 (75th anniv of Zeppelin) . . . . 4·50 4·50
383 20n. Queen Elizabeth II (25th anniv of Coronation) . . . 4·50 4·50

1978. Provisionals. Various stamps surch **25 Ch** (385, 394) or **25 CH** (others). I. Girl Scouts (No. 153).
385 25ch. on 5n. mult (postage) 1·40 1·40

II. Air. 1968 Mythological Creatures (Nos. 181 and 183).
386 25ch. on 4n. orange, green and black . . . . 1·40 1·40
387 25ch. on 10n. violet, grey and black . . . . 1·40 1·40

III. 1971 Admission to U.N. (Appendix).
388 25ch. on 3n. mult (postage) 1·40 1·40
389 25ch. on 5n. mult (air) . . . 1·40 1·40
390 25ch. on 6n. multicoloured 1·40 1·40

IV. Boy Scouts Anniv (Appendix).
391 25ch. on 6n. multicoloured 1·40 1·40

V. 1972 Dogs (No. 275).
392 25ch. on 8n. multicoloured 1·40 1·40

VI. 1973 Dogs (Appendix).
393 25ch. on 4n. multicoloured 1·40 1·40

VII. 1973 "Indipex 73" (Appendix).
394 25ch. on 3n. mult (postage) 1·40 1·40
395 25ch. on 5n. mult (air) . . . 1·40 1·40
396 25ch. on 6n. multicoloured 1·40 1·40

VIII. U.P.U. (Nos. 289/90).
397 25ch. on 1n. 40 multicoloured 6·50 6·50
398 25ch. on 2n. multicoloured 1·50 1·50

IX. World Population Year (No. 295).
399 25ch. on 2n.50 multicoloured 1·40 1·40

X. Butterflies (Nos. 303/4).
400 25ch. on 3n. multicoloured 1·40 1·40
401 25ch. on 5n. multicoloured 1·40 1·40

XI. "Apollo"–"Soyuz" (Nos. 315/16).
402 25ch. on 10n. mult (315) . . 1·40 1·40
403 25ch. on 10n. mult (316) . . 1·40 1·40

XII. Handicrafts (No. 326).
404 25ch. on 10n. multicoloured 1·40 1·40

XIII. Rhododendrons (No. 335).
405 25ch. on 5n. multicoloured 1·40 1·40

XIV. Winter Olympics (Nos. 343/4).
406 25ch. on 4n. multicoloured 1·40 1·40
407 25ch. on 10n. multicoloured 1·40 1·40

XV. Flowers (Nos. 364/5).
408 25ch. on 4n. multicoloured 1·40 1·40
409 25ch. on 6n. multicoloured 1·40 1·40

XVI. Colombo Plan (No. 373).
410 25ch. on 2n.50 multicoloured 1·75 1·75

50 Mother and Child

1979. International Year of the Child. Mult.
411 2n. Type **50** 55 55
412 5n. Mother carrying two children . . . . 1·25 1·25
413 10n. Children at school . . . 2·25 2·25

51 Conference Emblem and Dove

1979. 6th Non-Aligned Countries Summit Conference, Havana. Multicoloured.
415 25ch. Type **51** 20 20
416 10n. Emblem and Bhutanese symbols . . . . 2·75 2·75

52 Dorji (rattle)

1979. Antiquities. Multicoloured.
417 5ch. Type **52** 10 10
418 10ch. Dilbu (hand bell) (vert) 10 10
419 15ch. Jadum (cylindrical pot) (vert) 10 10
420 25ch. Jamjee (teapot) 10 10
421 1n. Kem (cylindrical container) (vert) 20 20
422 1n.25 Jamjee (different) . . . 30 30
423 1n.70 Sangphor (ornamental vessel) (vert) 35 35
424 2n. Jamjee (different) (vert) 45 45

425 3n. Yangtho (pot with lid) (vert) . . . 65 65
426 4n. Battha (circular case) . . 90 90
427 5n. Chhap (ornamental flask) (vert) . . . 1·10 1·10

53 Rinpiang Dzong, Bhutan Stamp and Rowland Hill Statue

1980. Death Cent of Sir Rowland Hill. Mult.
428 1n. Type **53** . . . 15 15
429 2n. Dzong, Bhutan stamp and statue . . . 35 35
430 5n. Ounsti Dzong, Bhutan stamp and statue . . . 1·10 1·10
431 10n. Lingzi Dzong and British 1912 1d. stamp . . 2·25 2·25

54 Dungtse Lhakhang, Paro

55 St. Paul's Cathedral

1981. Monasteries. Multicoloured.
433 1n. Type **54** . . . 30 30
434 2n. Kich Lhakhang, Paro (horiz) . . . 65 65
435 2n.25 Kurjey Lhakhang (horiz) . . . 70 70
436 3n. Tangu, Thimphu (horiz) 90 90
437 4n. Cheri, Thimphu (horiz) 1·10 1·10
438 5n. Chorten, Kora (horiz) . . 1·40 1·40
439 7n. Tak-Tsang, Paro . . . 1·75 1·75

1981. Wedding of Prince of Wales. Multicoloured.
440 1n. Type **55** . . . 20 20
441 5n. Type **55** . . . 90 90
442 20n. Prince Charles and Lady Diana Spencer . . . 3·50 3·50
443 25n. As No. 442 . . . 4·75 4·75

56 Orange-bellied Leafbird ("Orange-billed Chiropsis")

57 Footballers

1982. Birds. Multicoloured.
445 2n. Type **56** . . . 85 85
446 3n. Himalayan monal pheasant ("Monal Pheasant") . . . 1·40 1·40
447 5n. Ward's trogon . . . 2·40 2·40
448 10n. Mrs. Gould's sunbird . . 4·25 4·25

1982. World Cup Football Championship, Spain.
450 **57** 1n. multicoloured . . . 15 15
451 – 2n. multicoloured . . . 35 35
452 – 3n. multicoloured . . . 45 45
453 – 20n. multicoloured . . . 3·50 3·50
DESIGNS: 2n. to 20n. Various football scenes.

58 St. James's Palace

59 Lord Baden-Powell (founder)

1982. 21st Birthday of Princess of Wales. Mult.
455 1n. Type **58** . . . 25 25
456 10n. Prince and Princess of Wales . . . 1·75 1·75
457 15n. Windsor Castle . . . 2·75 2·75
458 25n. Princess in wedding dress . . . 4·50 4·50

1982. 75th Anniv of Boy Scout Movement. Multicoloured.
460 3n. Type **59** . . . 45 45
461 5n. Scouts around campfire 90 90
462 15n. Map reading . . . 2·75 2·75
463 20n. Pitching tents . . . 3·50 3·50

60 Rama finds Mowgli

1982. "The Jungle Book" (cartoon film). Mult.
465 1ch. Type **60** . . . 10 10
466 2ch. Bagheera leading Mowgli to Man-village . . 10 10
467 3ch. Kaa planning attack on Bagheera and Mowgli . . 10 10
468 4ch. Mowgli and elephants 10 10
469 5ch. Mowgli and Baloo . . . 10 10
470 10ch. Mowgli and King Louie . . . 10 10
471 30ch. Kaa and Shere Khan 15 15
472 2n. Mowgli, Baloo and Bagheera . . . 45 45
473 20n. Mowgli carrying jug for girl . . . 4·75 4·75

1982. Birth of Prince William of Wales. Nos. 455/8 optd **ROYAL BABY 21.6.82.**
475 1n. multicoloured . . . 25 25
476 10n. multicoloured . . . 1·75 1·75
477 15n. multicoloured . . . 2·75 2·75
478 25n. multicoloured . . . 4·50 4·50

62 Washington surveying

1982. 250th Birth Anniv of George Washington and Birth Centenary of Franklin D. Roosevelt. Mult.
480 50ch. Type **62** . . . 10 10
481 1n. Roosevelt and Harvard University . . . 15 15
482 2n. Washington at Valley Forge . . . 35 35
483 3n. Roosevelt's mother and family . . . 55 55
484 4n. Washington at Battle of Monmouth . . . 70 70
485 5n. Roosevelt and the White House . . . 90 90
486 15n. Washington and Mount Vernon . . . 2·75 2·75
487 20n. Churchill, Roosevelt and Stalin at Yalta . . . 3·50 3·50

1983. "Druk Air" Bhutan Air Service. Various stamps optd **DRUK AIR** (491) or **Druk Air** (others), No. 489 surch also.
489 **42** 30ch. on 1n. multicoloued (postage) . . . 2·25 2·25
490 – 5n. multicoloured (Scouts, Appendix) . . . 2·25 2·25
491 – 8n. mult (No. 275) . . . 2·25 2·25
492 – 5n. mult ("Indipex 73", Appendix) (air) . . . 2·75 2·75
493 – 7n. mult (Munich Olympics, Appendix) . . 2·75 2·75

64 "Angelo Doni"

1983. 500th Birth Anniv of Raphael (artist). Multicoloured.
494 1n. Type **64** . . . 20 20
495 4n. "Maddalena Doni" . . . 70 70
496 5n. "Baldassare Castiglione" 90 90
497 20n. "Woman with Veil" . . 3·50 3·50

65 Ta-Gyad-Boom-Zu (the eight luck-bringing symbols)

1983. Religious Offerings. Multicoloured.
499 25ch. Type **65** . . . 10 10
500 50ch. Doeyun Nga (the five sensory symbols) . . . 15 15
501 2n. Norbu Chadun (the seven treasures) (47 × 41 mm) . . 55 55
502 3n. Wangpo Nga (the five sensory organs) . . . 80 80
503 8n. Sha Nga (the five kinds of flesh) . . . 1·75 1·75
504 9n. Men-Ra-Tor Sum (the sacrificial cake) (47 × 41 mm) . . . 2·00 2·00

66 Dornier Wal Flying Boat "Boreas"

1983. Bicentenary of Manned Flight. Mult.
506 50ch. Type **66** . . . 15 15
507 3n. Savoia-Marchetti S.66 flying boat . . . 65 65
508 10n. Hawker Osprey biplane 2·50 2·50
509 20n. Astra airship "Ville de Paris" . . . 4·50 4·50

67 Mickey Mouse as Caveman

68 Golden Langur

1984. World Communications Year. Mult.
511 4ch. Type **67** . . . 10 10
512 5ch. Goofy as printer . . . 10 10
513 10ch. Chip 'n' Dale with morse key . . . 10 10
514 20ch. Pluto talks to girlfriend on telephone . . . 10 10
515 25ch. Minnie Mouse pulling record from bulldog . . . 10 10
516 50ch. Morty and Ferdie with microphone and loudhailers . . . 15 15
517 1n. Huey, Dewey, and Louie listening to radio . . . 25 25
518 5n. Donald Duck watching television on buffalo . . . 1·00 1·00
519 20n. Daisy Duck with computers and abacus . . 4·00 4·00

1984. Endangered Species. Multicoloured.
521 50ch. Type **68** . . . 15 15
522 1n. Golden langur family in tree (horiz) . . . 25 25
523 2n. Male and female Golden langurs with young (horiz) 45 45
524 4n. Group of langurs . . . 1·00 1·00

69 Downhill Skiing

70 "Sans Pareil", 1829

1984. Winter Olympic Games, Sarajevo. Mult.
526 50ch. Type **69** . . . 10 10
527 1n. Cross-country skiing . . 20 20
528 3n. Speed skating . . . 65 65
529 20n. Four-man bobsleigh . . 3·75 3·75

1984. Railway Locomotives. Multicoloured.
531 50ch. Type **70** . . . 15 15
532 1n. "Planet", 1830 . . . 40 40
533 3n. "Experiment" 1832 . . . 90 90
534 4n. "Black Hawk", 1835 . . . 1·25 1·25
535 5n.50 "Jenny Lind", 1847 (horiz) . . . 1·50 1·50
536 8n. "Bavaria", 1851 (horiz) 2·40 2·40
537 10n. Great Northern locomotive No. 1, 1870 (horiz) . . . 2·75 2·75
538 25n. Steam locomotive Type 110, Prussia, 1880 (horiz) . . . 7·25 7·25

71 Riley Sprite Sports Car, 1936

1984. Cars. Multicoloured.
540 50ch. Type **71** . . . 10 10
541 1n. Lanchester Forty saloon, 1919 . . . 20 20
542 3n. Itala 35/45 racer, 1907 . . 55 55
543 4n. Morris Oxford (Bullnose) tourer, 1913 . . . 70 70
544 5n.50 Lagonda LG6 drophead coupe, 1939 . . 1·00 1·00
545 6n. Wolseley four seat tonneau, 1903 . . . 1·10 1·10
546 8n. Buick Super convertible, 1952 . . . 1·60 1·60
547 20n. Maybach Zeppelin limousine, 1933 . . . 3·75 3·75

72 Women's Archery

73 Domkhar Dzong

1984. Olympic Games, Los Angeles. Multicoloured.
549 15ch. Type **72** . . . 10 10
550 25ch. Men's archery . . . 10 10
551 2n. Table tennis . . . 35 35
552 2n.25 Basketball . . . 40 40
553 5n.50 Boxing . . . 1·00 1·00
554 6n. Running . . . 1·25 1·25
555 8n. Tennis . . . 1·60 1·60

1984. Monasteries.
557 **73** 10ch. blue . . . 10 10
558 – 25ch. red . . . 10 10
559 – 50ch. violet . . . 10 10
560 – 1n. brown . . . 15 15
561 – 2n. red . . . 35 35
562 – 5n. green . . . 95 95
DESIGNS: 25ch. Shemgang Dzong; 50ch. Chapcha Dzong; 1n. Tashigang Dzong; 2n. Pungthang Dzong; 5n. Dechhenphoda Dzong.

74 "Magician Mickey"

1984. 50th Anniv of Donald Duck. Scenes from films. Multicoloured.
563 4ch. Type **74** . . . 10 10
564 5ch. "Slide, Donald, Slide" 10 10
565 10ch. "Donald's Golf Game" 10 10
566 20ch. "Mr. Duck Steps Out" 10 10
567 25ch. "Lion Around" . . . 10 10
568 50ch. "Alpine Climbers" . . 15 15
569 1n. "Flying Jalopy" . . . 25 25
570 5n. "Frank Duck brings 'Em Back Alive" . . . 1·10 1·10
571 20n. "Good Scouts" . . . 4·25 4·25

1984. Various stamps surch. (a) World Cup Football Championship, Spain (Nos. 450/3).
573 5n. on 1n. multicoloured . . 1·25 1·25
574 5n. on 2n. multicoloured . . 1·25 1·25
575 5n. on 3n. multicoloured . . 1·25 1·25
576 5n. on 20n. multicoloured . . 1·25 1·25

(b) 21st Birthday of Princess of Wales (Nos. 455/8).
578 5n. on 1n. multicoloured . . 85 85
579 5n. on 10n. multicoloured . . 85 85
580 5n. on 15n. multicoloured . . 85 85
581 40n. on 25n. multicoloured 8·75 8·75

(c) Birth of Prince William of Wales (Nos. 475/8).
583 5n. on 1n. multicoloured . . 85 85
584 5n. on 10n. multicoloured . . 85 85
585 5n. on 15n. multicoloured . . 85 85
586 40n. on 25n. multicoloured 7·75 7·75

(d) Wedding of Prince of Wales (Nos. 440/3).
588 10n. on 1n. multicoloured . . 2·10 2·10
589 10n. on 5n. multicoloured . . 2·10 2·10

590 10n. on 20n. multicoloured 2·10 2·10
591 10n. on 25n. multicoloured 2·10 2·10

(e) 75th Anniv of Boy Scout Movement (Nos. 460/3).

593 10n. on 3n. multicoloured . . 2·10 2·10
594 10n. on 5n. multicoloured . . 2·10 2·10
595 10n. on 15n. multicoloured 2·10 2·10
596 10n. on 20n. multicoloured 2·10 2·10

76 Shinje Choegyel

77 Bhutan and U.N. Flags

1985. The Judgement of Death Mask Dance. Multicoloured.
598 5ch. Type **76** 10 10
599 35ch. Raksh Lango 15 15
600 50ch. Druelgo 15 15
601 2n.50 Pago 55 55
602 3n. Telgo 60 60
603 4n. Due Nakcung 70 70
604 5n. Lha Karpo . . . . . . 1·00 1·00
605 5n.50 Nyalbum . . . . . . 1·10 1·10
606 6n. Khimda Pelkyi . . . . . 1·25 1·25

1985. 40th Anniv of U.N.O.
608 **77** 50ch. multicoloured . . . 10 10
609 – 15n. multicoloured . . . . 2·10 2·10
610 – 20n. black and blue . . . 3·00 3·00
DESIGNS—VERT: 15n. U.N. building, New York. HORIZ: 20n. Veterans' War Memorial Building, San Francisco (venue of signing of charter, 1945).

78 Mickey Mouse tramping through Black Forest

1985. 150th Birth Anniv of Mark Twain (writer) and International Youth Year. Multicoloured.
612 50ch. Type **78** 15 15
613 2n. Mickey Mouse, Donald Duck and Goofy on steamboat trip on Lake Lucerne 40 40
614 5n. Mickey Mouse, Donald Duck and Goofy climbing Rigi-Kulm 80 80
615 9n. Mickey Mouse and Goofy rafting to Heidelberg on River Neckar . . . . 1·25 1·25
616 20n. Mickey Mouse leading Donald Duck on horse back up the Riffelberg . . 3·50 3·50
Nos. 612/16 show scenes from "A Tramp Abroad" (cartoon film of Twain novel).

79 Prince sees Rapunzel

1985. Birth Bicentenaries (1985 and 1986) of Grimm Brothers (folklorists). Multicoloured.
618 1n. Type **79** 15 15
619 4n. Rapunzel (Minnie Mouse) in tower 55 55
620 7n. Mother Gothel calling to Rapunzel to let down her hair 85 85
621 8n. Prince climbing tower using Rapunzel's hair . . . 1·25 1·25
622 15n. Prince proposing to Rapunzel . . . . 1·90 1·90

80 "Brewers Duck" (mallard)

1985. Birth Bicentenary of John J. Audubon (ornithologist). Audubon illustrations. Mult.
624 50ch. Type **80** 10 10
625 1n. "Willow Ptarmigan" (Willow/red Grouse) . . . 15 15
626 2n. "Mountain Plover" . . . 45 45
627 3n. "Red-throated Loon" (Red-throated Diver) . . . 70 70
628 4n. "Spruce Grouse" 85 85
629 5n. "Hooded Merganser" . . 1·10 1·10
630 15n. "Trumpeter Swan" (Whooper Swan) . . . . . 3·00 3·00
631 20n. Common goldeneye . . 4·00 4·00

81 Members' Flags around Buddhist Design

1985. South Asian Regional Co-operation Summit, Dhaka, Bangladesh.
634 **81** 50ch. multicoloured . . . 10 10
635 5n. multicoloured 80 80

82 Precious Wheel

85 Mandala of Phurpa (Ritual Dagger)

1986. The Precious Symbols. Multicoloured.
636 30ch. Type **82** 10 10
637 50ch. Precious Gem 15 15
638 1n.25 Precious Queen 15 15
639 2n. Precious Minister 30 30
640 4n. Precious Elephant 55 55
641 6n. Precious Horse 85 85
642 8n. Precious General . . . . 1·25 1·25

1986. Olympic Games Gold Medal Winners. Nos. 549/50 and 552/5 optd.
643 **72** 15ch. **GOLD HYANG SOON SEO SOUTH KOREA** 15 15
644 – 25ch. **GOLD DARRELL PACE USA** 15 15
645 – 2n.25 **GOLD MEDAL USA** 25 25
646 – 5n.50 **GOLD MARK BRELAND USA** . . . 80 80
647 – 6n. **GOLD DALEY THOMPSON ENGLAND** 85 85
648 – 8n. **GOLD STEFAN EDBERG SWEDEN** . . 1·25 1·25

1986. "Ameripex 86" International Stamp Exhibition, Chicago. Various stamps optd **AMERIPEX 86**.
653 8n. mult (No. 621) . . . . . 1·10 1·10
650 9n. mult (No. 615) . . . . . 1·25 1·25
654 15n. mult (No. 622) . . . . 2·00 2·00
651 20n. mult (No. 616) . . . . 3·00 3·00

1986. Kilkhor Mandalas of Mahayana Buddhism. Multicoloured.
656 10ch. Type **85** 10 10
657 25ch. Mandala of Amitayus in Wrathful Form 10 10
658 50ch. Mandala of Overpowering Deities . . . 15 15
659 75ch. Mandala of the Great Wrathful One 20 20
660 1n. Type **85** 20 20
661 3n. As 25ch. 50 50
662 5n. As 50ch. 75 75
663 7n. As 75ch. . . . . 1·00 1·00

1986. 75th Anniv of Girl Guides. Nos. 460/3 optd **75th ANNIVERSARY GIRL GUIDES**.
664 3n. multicoloured 45 45
665 5n. multicoloured 65 65
666 15n. multicoloured . . . . . 2·00 2·00
667 20n. multicoloured . . . . . 3·00 3·00

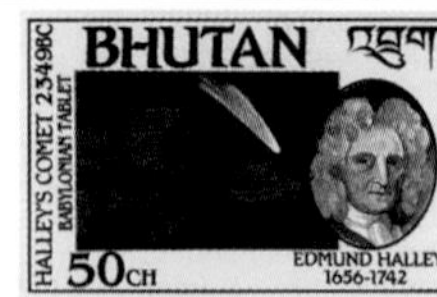

87 Babylonian Tablet and Comet over Noah's Ark

1986. Appearance of Halley's Comet. Mult.
669 50ch. Type **87** 15 15
670 1n. 17th-century print 15 15
671 2n. 1835 French silhouette . . 35 35
672 3n. Bayeux tapestry 50 50
673 4n. Woodblock from "Nuremburg Chronicle" 70 70
674 5n. Illustration of Revelation 6, 12–13 from 1160 Bible 85 85
675 15n. Comet in constellation of Cancer . . . . 2·25 2·25
676 20n. Decoration on Delft plate . . . . 3·25 3·25

88 Statue and "Libertad" (Argentine full-rigged cadet ship)

1986. Centenary of Statue of Liberty. Multicoloured.
678 50ch. Type **88** 15 15
679 1n. "Shalom" (Israeli liner) 15 15
680 2n. "Leonardo da Vinci" (Italian liner) 35 35
681 3n. "Mircea" (Rumanian cadet barque) 50 50
682 4n. "France" (French liner) 70 70
683 5n. S.S. "United States" (American liner) 85 85
684 15n. "Queen Elizabeth 2" (British liner) . . . . . . 2·25 2·25
685 20n. "Europa" (West German liner) . . . . . . 2·75 2·75
The descriptions of the ships on Nos. 678 and 681 were transposed in error.

89 "Santa Maria"

1987. 500th Anniv (1992) of Discovery of America by Columbus. Multicoloured.
687 20ch. Type **89** 30 30
688 25ch. Queen Isabella of Spain 15 15
689 50ch. Flying fish 60 40
690 1n. Columbus's coat of arms 25 25
691 2n. Christopher Columbus . . 45 45
692 3n. Columbus landing with Spanish soldiers 80 80

90 Canadian National Class "U1-f" Steam Locomotive No. 6060

1987. "Capex '87" International Stamp Exhibition, Toronto. Canadian Railways. Multicoloured.
695 50ch. Type **90** 20 20
696 1n. Via Rail "L.R.C." electric locomotive No. 6903 . . . 20 20
697 2n. Canadian National GM "GF30t" diesel locomotive No. 5341 . . . . 45 45
698 3n. Canadian National steam locomotive No. 6157 . . . 60 60
699 8n. Canadian Pacific steam locomotive No. 2727 . . . 1·60 1·60
700 10n. Via Express diesel locomotive No. 6524 . . . 2·00 2·00
701 15n. Canadian National "Turbotrain" . . . . . . 3·00 3·00
702 20n. Canadian Pacific diesel-electric locomotive No. 1414 . . . . 4·00 4·00

91 "Two Faces" (sculpture)

1987. Birth Centenary of Marc Chagall (artist). Multicoloured.
704 50ch. Type **91** 15 15
705 1n. "At the Barber's" 15 15
706 2n. "Old Jew with Torai" . . 35 35
707 3n. "Red Maternity" 50 50
708 4n. "Eve of Yom Kippur" . . 70 70
709 5n. "The Old Musician" . . 85 85
710 6n. "The Rabbi of Vitebsk" 85 85
711 7n. "Couple at Dusk" . . . 1·25 1·25
712 9n. "The Artistes" . . . . . 1·25 1·25
713 10n. "Moses breaking the Tablets" . . . . 1·50 1·50
714 12n. "Bouquet with Flying Lovers" . . . . 1·75 1·75
715 20n. "In the Sky of the Opera" . . . . 3·00 3·00

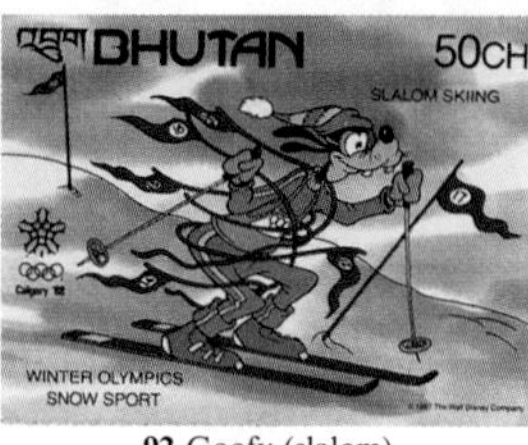

92 Goofy (slalom)

1988. Winter Olympic Games, Calgary. Mult.
717 50ch. Type **92** 15 15
718 1n. Donald Duck pushing Goofy at start (downhill skiing) 15 15
719 2n. Goofy in goal (ice hockey) 25 25
720 4n. Goofy (biathlon) 50 50
721 7n. Goofy and Donald Duck (speed skating) 85 85
722 8n. Minnie Mouse (figure skating) . . . . 1·00 1·00
723 9n. Minnie Mouse (free-style skating) . . . . 1·25 1·25
724 20n. Goofy and Mickey Mouse (two-man bobsleigh) . . . . 2·50 2·50

93 Stephenson's Railway Locomotive "Rocket", 1829

1988. Transport. Multicoloured.
726 50ch. Pullman "Pioneer" sleeper, 1985 . . . . 35 35
727 1n. Type **93** 35 35
728 2n. Pierre Lallement's "Velocipede", 1866 . . . . 25 25
729 3n. Benz "Patent Motor Wagon", 1866 . . . . . . 45 45
730 4n. Volkswagen Beetle . . . 60 60
731 5n. Mississippi paddle-steamers "Natchez" and "Robert E. Lee", 1870 . . 70 70
732 6n. American La France motor fire engine, 1910 . . 85 85
733 7n. Frigate U.S.S. "Constitution", 1797 (vert) 85 85
734 9n. Bell rocket belt, 1961 (vert) . . . . 1·25 1·25
735 10n. Trevithick's railway locomotive, 1804 . . . . . 2·25 2·25
No. 731 is wrongly inscribed "Natches" and No. 733 is wrongly dated "1787".

94 Dam and Pylon

1988. Chhukha Hydro-electric Project.
737 **94** 50ch. multicoloured . . . 15 15

1988. World Aids Day. Nos. 411/13 optd **WORLD AIDS DAY**.
738 **50** 2n. multicoloured 35 35
739 – 5n. multicoloured 95 95
740 – 10n. multicoloured . . . . 1·75 1·75

96 "Diana and Actaeon" (detail)

1989. 500th Birth Anniv of Titian (painter). Multicoloured.

741 50ch. "Gentleman with a Book" 15 15
742 1n. "Venus and Cupid, with a Lute Player" (detail) . . 15 15
743 2n. Type **96** 25 25
744 3n. "Cardinal Ippolito dei Medici" 45 45
745 4n. "Sleeping Venus" (detail) 50 50
746 5n. "Venus risen from the Waves" (detail) 80 80
747 6n. "Worship of Venus" (detail) 95 95
748 7n. "Fete Champetre" (detail) 85 85
749 10n. "Perseus and Andromeda" (detail) . . . 1·75 1·75
750 15n. "Danae" (detail) . . . . 2·10 2·10
751 20n. "Venus at the Mirror" 2·50 2·50
752 25n. "Venus and the Organ Player" (detail) . . . . . 3·25 3·25

97 Volleyball

1989. Olympic Games, Seoul (1988). Mult.

754 50ch. Gymnastics 15 15
755 1n. Judo 15 15
756 2n. Putting the shot 25 25
757 4n. Type **97** 50 50
758 7n. Basketball (vert) . . . . 1·00 1·00
759 8n. Football (vert) . . . . . 1·25 1·25
760 9n. High jumping (vert) . . . 1·50 1·50
761 20n. Running (vert) . . . . 3·00 3·00

1989. "Fukuoka '89" Asia-Pacific Exhibition. Nos. 598/606 optd **ASIA-PACIFIC EXPOSITION FUKUOKA '89**.

763 5ch. multicoloured 10 10
764 35ch. multicoloured 15 15
765 50ch. multicoloured 15 15
766 2n.50 multicoloured 25 25
767 3n. multicoloured 35 35
768 4n. multicoloured 45 45
769 5n. multicoloured 60 60
770 5n.50 multicoloured 75 75
771 6n. multicoloured 95 95

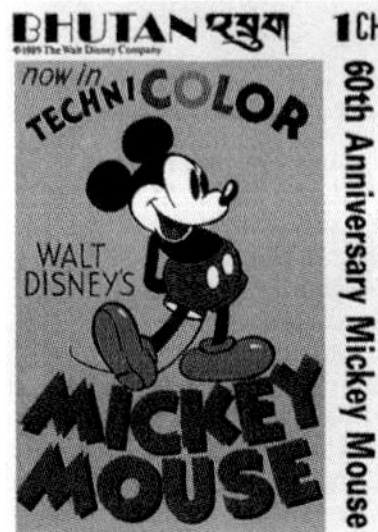

99 Mickey Mouse

1989. 60th Anniv of Mickey Mouse. Film Posters. Multicoloured.

772 1ch. Type **99** 10 10
773 2ch. "Barnyard Olympics" . . 15 15
774 3ch. "Society Dog Show" . . 15 15
775 4ch. "Fantasia" 15 15
776 5ch. "The Mad Dog" 15 15
777 10ch. "A Gentleman's Gentleman" 15 15
778 50ch. "Symphony hour" . . 15 15
779 10n. "The Moose Hunt" . . 1·25 1·25
780 15n. "Wild Waves" . . . . . 2·00 2·00
781 20n. "Mickey in Arabia" . . 2·50 2·50
782 25n. "Tugboat Mickey" . . . 3·25 3·25
783 30n. "Building a Building" 3·75 3·75

100 "Tricholoma pardalotum"

1989. Fungi. Multicoloured.

785 50ch. Type **100** 15 15
786 1n. "Suillus placidus" 25 15
787 2n. Royal boletus 30 25
788 3n. "Gomphidius glutinosus" 45 40
789 4n. Scarlet-stemmed boletus 60 50
790 5n. Elegant boletus 70 60
791 6n. "Boletus appendiculatus" 95 80
792 7n. Griping toadstool . . . . 1·00 85
793 10n. "Macrolepiota rhacodes" . . . . 1·60 1·40
794 15n. The blusher . . . . . . 2·40 2·10
795 20n. Death cap . . . . . . 3·25 2·75
796 25n. False death cap . . . . 4·00 3·50

101 "La Reale" (Spanish galley), 1680

1989. 30th Anniv of International Maritime Organization. Multicoloured.

798 50ch. Type **101** 15 15
799 1n. "Turtle" (submarine), 1776 . . . . 15 15
800 2n. "Charlotte Dundas" (steamship), 1802 . . . . . 25 25
801 3n. "Great Eastern" (paddle-steamer), 1858 . . . . . . 40 40
802 4n. H.M.S. "Warrior" (armoured ship), 1862 . . 50 50
803 5n. Mississippi river steamer, 1884 . . . . 80 80
804 6n. "Preussen" (full-rigged ship), 1902 . . . . 1·00 1·00
805 7n. U.S.S. "Arizona" (battleship), 1915 . . . . . 1·10 1·10
806 10n. "Bluenose" (fishing schooner), 1921 . . . . . 1·75 1·75
807 15n. Steam trawler, 1925 . . 1·75 1·75
808 20n. "Liberty" freighter, 1943 2·75 2·75
809 25n. "United States" (liner), 1952 . . . . 3·50 3·50

102 Nehru

103 Greater Flamed-backed Woodpecker

1989. Birth Centenary of Jawaharlal Nehru (Indian statesman).

811 **102** 1n. brown 15 15

No. 811 is erroneously inscribed "ch".

1989. Birds. Multicoloured.

812 50ch. Type **103** 15 15
813 1n. Black-naped blue monarch ("Black-naped Monarch") 15 15
814 2n. White-crested laughing thrush 25 20
815 3n. Blood pheasant 35 25
816 4n. Plum-headed ("Blossom-headed") parakeet 45 35
817 5n. Rosy minivet 60 45
818 6n. Chestnut-headed fulvetta ("Tit-Babbler") (horiz) . . 65 50
819 7n. Blue pitta (horiz) 80 60
820 10n. Black-naped oriole (horiz) . . . . 1·25 90
821 15n. Green magpie (horiz) . . 1·75 1·25
822 20n. Three-toed kingfisher ("Indian Three-toed Kingfisher")(horiz) . . . . 2·25 1·75
823 25n. Ibis bill (horiz) . . . . 3·00 2·25

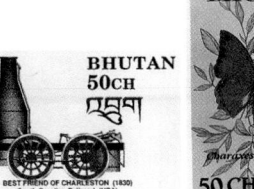

104 "Best Friend of Charleston", 1830, U.S.A.

105 "Charaxes harmodius"

1990. Steam Railway Locomotives. Mult.

825 50ch. Type **104** 15 15
826 1n. Class U locomotive, 1948, France 20 20
827 2n. Consolidation locomotive, 1866, U.S.A. 40 40
828 3n. Luggage engine, 1843, Great Britain 55 55
829 4n. Class 60-3 Shay locomotive No. 18, 1913, U.S.A. 75 75
830 5n. "John Bull", 1831, U.S.A. 80 80
831 6n. "Hercules", 1837, U.S.A. 85 85
832 7n. Locomotive No. 947, 1874, Great Britain 90 90
833 10n. "Illinois", 1852, U.S.A. 1·50 1·50

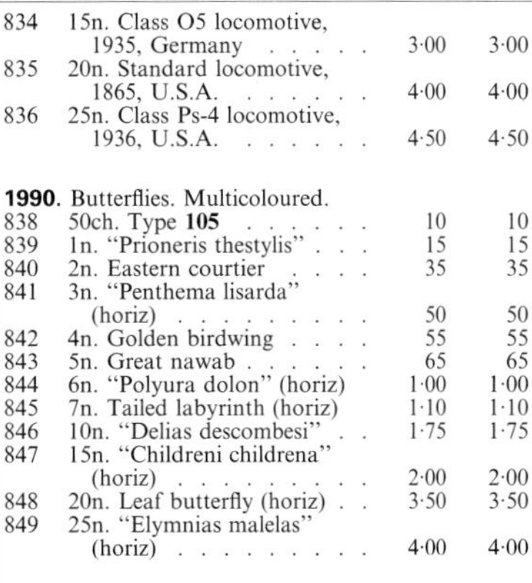

834 15n. Class O5 locomotive, 1935, Germany . . . . . 3·00 3·00
835 20n. Standard locomotive, 1865, U.S.A. . . . . . . 4·00 4·00
836 25n. Class Ps-4 locomotive, 1936, U.S.A. . . . . . . 4·50 4·50

1990. Butterflies. Multicoloured.

838 50ch. Type **105** 10 10
839 1n. "Prioneris thestylis" . . . 15 15
840 2n. Eastern courtier 35 35
841 3n. "Penthema lisarda" (horiz) 50 50
842 4n. Golden birdwing 55 55
843 5n. Great nawab 65 65
844 6n. "Polyura dolon" (horiz) 1·00 1·00
845 7n. Tailed labyrinth (horiz) 1·10 1·10
846 10n. "Delias descombesi" . . 1·75 1·75
847 15n. "Childreni childrena" (horiz) . . . . 2·00 2·00
848 20n. Leaf butterfly (horiz) . . 3·50 3·50
849 25n. "Elymnias malelas" (horiz) . . . . 4·00 4·00

106 "Renanthera monachica"

107 "Plum Estate, Kameido"

1990. "Expo '90" International Garden and Greenery Exposition, Osaka. Orchids. Mult.

851 10ch. Type **106** 15 15
852 50ch. "Vanda coerulea" . . . 15 15
853 1n. "Phalaenopsis violacea" 15 15
854 2n. "Dendrobium nobile" . . 35 35
855 5n. "Vandopsis lissochiloides" 85 85
856 6n. "Paphiopedilum rothschildianum" 95 95
857 7n. "Phalaenopsis schilleriana" . . . . 1·10 1·10
858 9n. "Paphiopedilum insigne" 1·40 1·40
859 10n. "Paphiopedilum bellatulum" . . . . 1·75 1·75
860 20n. "Doritis pulcherrima" 3·50 3·50
861 25n. "Cymbidium giganteum" 4·25 4·25
862 35n. "Phalaenopsis mariae" 5·75 5·75

1990. Death of Emperor Hirohito and Accession of Emperor Akihito of Japan. "100 Famous Views of Edo" by Ando Hiroshige. Multicoloured.

864 10ch. Type **107** 15 15
865 20ch. "Yatsumi Bridge" . . . 15 15
866 50ch. "Ayase River and Kanegafuchi" 15 15
867 75ch. "View of Shiba Coast" 15 15
868 1n. "Grandpa's Teahouse, Meguro" 15 15
869 2n. "Inside Kameido Tenjin Shrine" 30 30
870 6n. "Yoroi Ferry, Koami-cho" 75 75
871 7n. "Sakasai Ferry" 80 80
872 10n. "Fukagawa Lumberyards" . . . . . . 1·25 1·25
873 15n. "Suido Bridge and Surugadai" . . . . 2·00 2·00
874 20n. "Meguro Drum Bridge and Sunset Hill" . . . . . 3·50 3·50
875 25n. "Atagoshita and Yabu Lane" . . . . 4·25 4·25

108 Thimphu Post Office

1990.

877 **108** 1n. multicoloured 15 15

109 Giant Panda

1990. Mammals. Multicoloured.

878 50ch. Type **109** 10 10
879 1n. Giant panda in tree . . . 15 15
880 2n. Giant panda with cub . . 35 35
881 3n. Giant panda (horiz) . . . 50 50
882 4n. Giant panda eating (horiz) 50 50
883 5n. Tiger (horiz) 60 60
884 6n. Giant pandas pulling up bamboo (horiz) 80 80
885 7n. Giant panda and cub resting (horiz) 85 85
886 10n. Indian elephant (horiz) 1·40 1·40
887 15n. Giant panda beside fallen tree . . . . 1·90 1·90
888 20n. Indian muntjac (inscr "Barking deer") (horiz) . . 3·50 3·50
889 25n. Snow leopard (horiz) . . 4·25 4·25

110 Roim

1990. Religious Musical Instruments. Mult.

891 10ch. Dungchen (large trumpets) 10 10
892 20ch. Dungkar (Indian chank shell) 10 10
893 30ch. Type **110** 10 10
894 50ch. Tinchag (cup cymbals) 10 10
895 1n. Dradu and drilbu (pellet drum and hand bell) . . . 15 15
896 2n. Gya-ling (oboes) 25 25
897 2n.50 Nga (drum) 30 30
898 3n.50 Kang-dung (trumpets) 50 50

111 Penny Black and Bhutan 1962 2ch. Stamp

1990. "Stamp World London 90" International Stamp Exhibition. 150th Anniv of the Penny Black. Multicoloured.

900 50ch. Type **111** 10 10
901 1n. Oldenburg 1852 $\frac{1}{30}$th. stamp 15 15
902 2n. Bergedorf 1861 1½s. stamp 25 25
903 4n. German Democratic Republic 1949 50pf. stamp 45 45
904 5n. Brunswick 1852 1 sgr. stamp 60 60
905 6n. Basel 1845 2½r. stamp . . 65 65
906 8n. Geneva 1843 5c.+5c. stamp 85 85
907 10n. Zurich 1843 4r. stamp 1·10 1·10
908 15n. France 1849 20c. stamp 2·00 2·00
909 20n. Vatican City 1929 5c. stamp . . . . 2·40 2·40
910 25n. Israel 1948 3m. stamp 2·75 2·75
911 30n. Japan 1871 48m. stamp 3·50 3·50

Each value also depicts the Penny Black.
No. 901 is wrongly inscribed "Oldenberg".

112 Girls

113 Temple of Artemis, Ephesus

1990. South Asian Association for Regional Co-operation Girl Child Year. Multicoloured.

913 50ch. Type **112** 10 10
914 20n. Girl . . . . 2·50 2·50

1991. Wonders of the World. Designs featuring Walt Disney cartoon characters. Multicoloured.

915 1ch. Type **113** 10 10
916 2ch. Statue of Zeus, Olympia 10 10
917 3ch. Pyramids of Egypt . . . 10 10
918 4ch. Lighthouse of Alexandria, Egypt 10 10
919 5ch. Mausoleum, Halicarnassus 10 10
920 10ch. Colossus of Rhodes . . 10 10
921 50ch. Hanging Gardens of Babylon 10 10
922 5n. Mauna Loa Volcanoes, Hawaii (horiz) 65 65
923 6n. Carlsbad Caverns, New Mexico (horiz) 80 80
924 10n. Rainbow Bridge National Monument, Utah (horiz) . . . . 1·40 1·40
925 15n. Grand Canyon, Colorado (horiz) . . . . . 1·90 1·90
926 20n. Old Faithful, Yellowstone National Park, Wyoming (horiz) . . . . . 2·50 2·50

927 25n. Sequoia National Park, California (horiz) . . . . . 3·00 3·00
928 30n. Crater Lake and Wizard Island, Oregon (horiz) . . 3·50 3·50

114 "Atalanta and Meleager" (detail)

1991. 350th Death Anniv (1990) of Peter Paul Rubens (painter). Multicoloured.
930 10ch. Type **114** 10 10
931 50ch. "The Fall of Phaeton" (detail) 10 10
932 1n. "Feast of Venus Verticordia" (detail) . . . 15 15
933 2n. "Achilles slaying Hector" (detail) 25 25
934 3n. "Arachne punished by Minerva" (detail) 35 35
935 4n. "Jupiter receives Psyche on Olympus" (detail) . . . 45 45
936 5n. "Atalanta and Meleager" (different detail) 55 55
937 6n. "Atalanta and Meleager" (different detail) 70 70
938 7n. "Venus in Vulcan's Furnace" (detail) . . . . . 1·00 1·00
939 10n. "Atalanta and Meleager" (different detail) 1·25 1·25
940 20n. "Briseis returned to Achilles" (detail) . . . . . 2·50 2·50
941 30n. "Mars and Rhea Sylvia" (detail) . . . . 3·50 3·50

115 "Cottages, Reminiscence of the North"

1991. Death Centenary (1990) of Vincent van Gogh (painter). Multicoloured.
943 10ch. Type **115** 10 10
944 50ch. "Head of a Peasant Woman with Dark Cap" 10 10
945 1n. "Portrait of a Woman in Blue" 15 15
946 2n. "Head of an Old Woman with White Cap (the Midwife)" 35 35
947 8n. "Vase with Hollyhocks" 95 95
948 10n. "Portrait of a Man with a Skull Cap" . . . . . . 1·25 1·25
949 12n. "Agostina Segatori sitting in the Cafe du Tambourin" . . . . 1·40 1·40
950 15n. "Vase with Daisies and Anemones" . . . . 2·00 2·00
951 18n. "Fritillaries in a Copper Vase" . . . . 2·25 2·25
952 20n. "Woman sitting in the Grass" . . . . 2·50 2·50
953 25n. "On the Outskirts of Paris" (horiz) . . . . . . 3·25 3·25
954 30n. "Chrysanthemums and Wild Flowers in a Vase" 4·00 4·00

116 Winning Uruguay Team, 1930

1991. World Cup Football Championship. Mult.
956 50ch. Type **116** 10 10
957 1n. Italy, 1934 . . . . 15 15
958 2n. Italy, 1938 . . . . 25 25
959 3n. Uruguay, 1950 . . . . . 35 35
960 5n. West Germany, 1954 . . 60 60
961 10n. Brazil, 1958 . . . . . . 1·25 1·25
962 20n. Brazil, 1962 . . . . . . 2·50 2·50
963 25n. England, 1966 . . . . . 3·00 3·00
964 29n. Brazil, 1970 . . . . . . 4·00 4·00
965 30n. West Germany, 1974 . . 4·00 4·00
966 31n. Argentina, 1978 . . . . 4·00 4·00
967 32n. Italy, 1982 . . . . . . 4·00 4·00
968 33n. Argentina, 1986 . . . . 4·25 4·25
969 34n. West Germany, 1990 . . 4·25 4·25
970 35n. Stadium, Los Angeles (venue for 1994 World Cup) . . . . 4·25 4·25

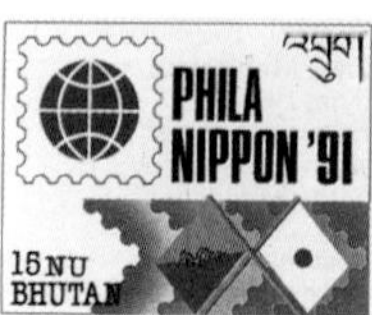

117 Bhutan and Japan State Flags

1991. "Phila Nippon '91" International Stamp Exhibition, Tokyo.
972 **117** 15n. multicoloured . . . 2·10 2·10

118 Teachers, Pupils and Hemisphere

1992. "Education for All by Year 2000".
973 **118** 1n. multicoloured 15 15

119 Hurdler

120 "Santa Maria"

1992. Olympic Games, Barcelona. Mult.
974 25n. Type **119** . . . . 3·00 3·00
975 25n. Body of hurdler . . . . 3·00 3·00
Nos. 974/5 were issued together, se-tenant, forming a composite design.

1992. 500th Anniv of Discovery of America by Columbus. Multicoloured.
977 15n. Type **120** . . . . 1·10 1·10
978 20n. Columbus . . . . . . 1·50 1·50

121 Brandenburg Gate and rejoicing Couple

1992. 2nd Anniv of Reunification of Germany.
980 **121** 25n. multicoloured . . . 1·75 1·75

122 British Aerospace BAe 146 and Post Van

1992. 30th Anniv of Bhutan Postal Organization. Multicoloured.
982 1n. Type **122** 20 20
983 3n. Rural letter courier . . . 25 25
984 5n. Emptying post box . . . 45 45

123 Industry and Agriculture

1992. 20th Anniv of Accession of King Jigme Singye Wangchuck. Multicoloured.
985 1n. Type **123** 10 10
986 5n. British Aerospace RJ70 of National Airline 35 35
987 10n. House with water-pump 70 70
988 15n. King Jigme Singye Wangchuk . . . . 1·00 1·00
Nos. 985/8 were issued together, se-tenant, each horizontal pair within the block forming a composite design.

124 Dragon

1992. International Volunteer Day.
990 **124** 1n.50 multicoloured . . . 15 15
991 9n. multicoloured 75 75
992 15n. multicoloured . . . 1·10 1·10

125 "Meconopsis grandis"

127 "The Love Letter" (Jean Honore Fragonard)

1993. Medicinal Flowers. Designs showing varieties of the Asiatic Poppy. Multicoloured.
993 1n.50 Type **125** 10 10
994 7n. "Meconopsis" sp. 50 50
995 10n. "Meconopsis wallichii" 70 70
996 12n. "Meconopsis horridula" 80 80
997 20n. "Meconopsis discigera" 1·40 1·40

1993. Paintings. Multicoloured.
1000 1ch. Type **127** (postage) . . 10 10
1001 2ch. "The Writer" (Vittore Carpaccio) 10 10
1002 3ch. "Mademoiselle Lavergne" (Jean Etienne Liotard) 10 10
1003 5ch. "Portrait of Erasmus" (Hans Holbein) 10 10
1004 10ch. "Woman writing a Letter" (Gerard Terborch) 10 10
1005 15ch. Type **127** 10 10
1006 25ch. As No. 1001 . . . . 10 10
1007 50ch. As No. 1002 . . . . 10 10
1008 60ch. As No. 1003 . . . . 10 10
1009 80ch. As No. 1004 . . . . 10 10
1010 1n. Type **127** 15 15
1011 1n.25 As No. 1001 . . . . 20 20
1012 2n. As No. 1002 (air) . . . 30 30
1013 3n. As No. 1003 . . . . . 40 40
1014 6n. As No. 1004 . . . . . 85 85

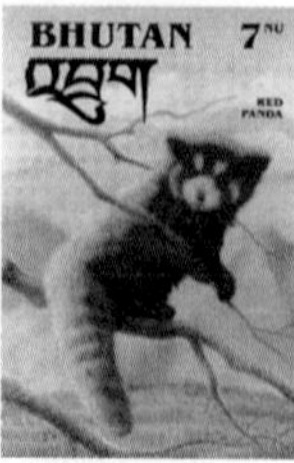

128 Lesser Panda

130 Namtheo-say

1993. Environmental Protection. Multicoloured.
1016 7n. Type **128** 45 45
1017 10n. One-horned rhinoceros 70 70
1018 15n. Black-necked crane and blue poppy . . . . 1·00 1·00
1019 20n. Takin . . . . 1·25 1·25
Nos. 1016/19 were issued together, se-tenant, forming a composite design.

1993. Door Gods. Multicoloured.
1021 1n.50 Type **130** 10 10
1022 5n. Pha-ke-po 40 40
1023 10n. Chen-mi Jang 80 80
1024 15n. Yul-khor-sung . . . . 1·25 1·25

131 "Rhododendron mucronatum"

132 Dog

1994. Flowers. Multicoloured.
1025 1n. Type **131** 10 10
1026 1n.50 "Anemone rupicola" 10 10
1027 2n. "Polemonium coeruleum" 15 15
1028 2n.50 "Rosa marophylla" 20 20
1029 4n. "Paraquilegia microphylla" 30 30
1030 5n. "Aquilegia nivalis" . . . 40 40
1031 6n. "Geranium wallichianum" 45 45
1032 7n. "Rhododendron campanulatum" (wrongly inscr "Rhodendron") . . 55 55
1033 9n. "Viola suavis" 70 70
1034 10n. "Cyananthus lobatus" 80 80

1994. New Year. Year of the Dog. "Hong Kong '94" International Stamp Exhibition.
1036 **132** 11n.50 multicoloured . . 90 90

133 Trophy and Mascot

1994. World Cup Football Championship, U.S.A.
1038 **133** 15n. multicoloured . . . 55 55

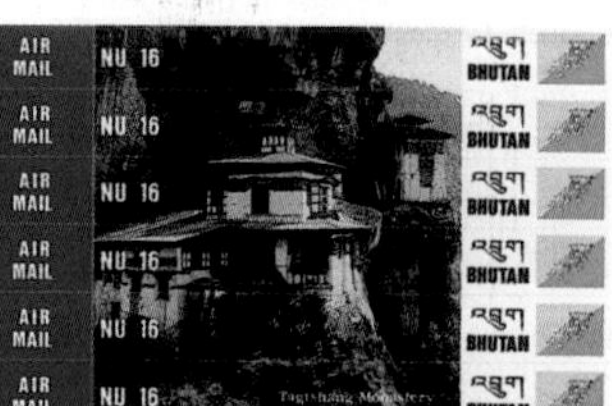

134 Tagtshang Monastery (½-size illustration)

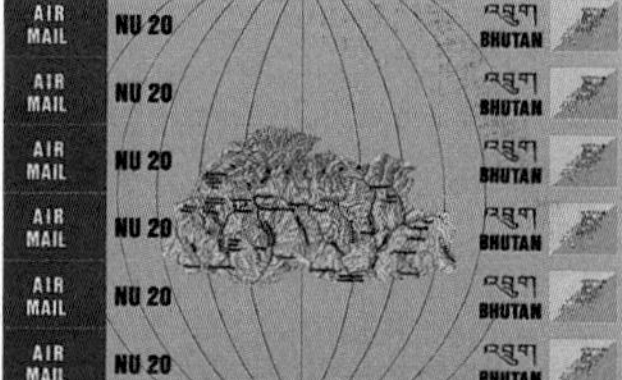

135 Relief Map of Bhutan (½-size illustration)

1994. Air. Self-adhesive.
1039 **134** 16n. multicoloured . . . 60 60
1040 **135** 20n. multicoloured . . . 75 75
The individual stamps are peeled directly from the card backing. Each card contains six different designs with the same face value forming the composite designs illustrated. Each stamp is a horizontal strip with a label indicating the main class of mail covered by the rate at the left, separated by a vertical line of rouletting. The outer edges of the cards are imperforate.

138 Horseman with raised Sword

1994. 350th Anniv of Victory over Tibet-Mongol Army. Multicoloured.
1043 15n. Type **138** 55 55
1044 15n. Archers and hand-to-hand sword fighting . . . 55 55
1045 15n. Horseman with insignia on helmet amongst infantry 55 55
1046 15n. Drummer, piper and troops 55 55
Nos. 1043/6 were issued together, se-tenant, forming a composite design of a battle scene and the Drugyel Dzong.

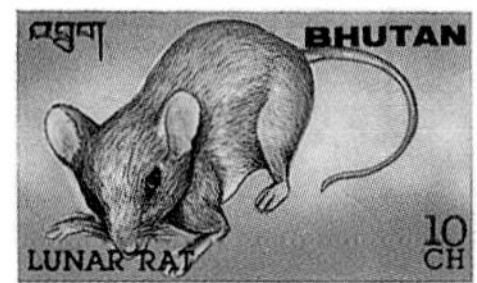

140 Lunar Rat

1995. New Year. Year of the Boar. Mult.

1048 10ch. Type **140** 10 10
1049 20ch. Lunar ox 10 10
1050 30ch. Lunar tiger 10 10
1051 40ch. Lunar rabbit 10 10
1052 1n. Lunar dragon 10 10
1053 2n. Lunar snake 10 10
1054 3n. Lunar horse 10 10
1055 4n. Lunar sheep 15 15
1056 5n. Lunar monkey 20 20
1057 7n. Lunar rooster 25 25
1058 8n. Lunar dog 30 30
1059 9n. Lunar boar 35 35

141 "Pleione praecox" **142** Human Resources Development

1995. Flowers. Multicoloured.

1061 9n. Type **141** 35 35
1062 10n. "Primula calderina" 35 35
1063 16n. "Primula whitei" 60 60
1064 18n. "Notholirion macrophyllum" 65 65

1995. 50th Anniv of U.N.O. Multicoloured.

1065 1n.50 Type **142** 10 10
1066 5n. Transport and Communications 20 20
1067 9n. Health and Population 35 35
1068 10n. Water and Sanitation 35 35
1069 11n.50 U.N. in Bhutan 45 45
1070 16n. Forestry and Environment 60 60
1071 18n. Peace and Security 65 65

143 Greater Pied Kingfisher ("Himalayan Pied Kingfisher") **144** Making Paper

1995. "Singapore '95" International Stamp Exhibition. Birds. Multicoloured.

1072 1n. Type **143** 10 10
1073 2n. Blyth's tragopan 10 10
1074 3n. Long-tailed minivets 10 10
1075 10n. Red junglefowl 35 35
1076 15n. Black-capped sibia 55 55
1077 20n. Red-billed chough 70 70

1995. Traditional Crafts. Multicoloured.

1079 1n. Type **144** 10 10
1080 2n. Religious painting 10 10
1081 3n. Clay sculpting 10 10
1082 10n. Weaving 35 35
1083 15n. Making boots 55 55
1084 20n. Carving wooden bowls 70 70

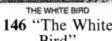

146 "The White Bird" **147** Blue Pansy

1996. Folk Tales. Multicoloured.

1087 1n. Type **146** 10 10
1088 2n. "Sing Sing Lhamo and the Moon" 10 10
1089 3n. "The Hoopoe" 10 10
1090 5n. "The Cloud Fairies" 20 20
1091 10n. "The Three Wishes" 35 35
1092 20n. "The Abominable Snowman" 70 70

1996. Butterflies. Multicoloured.

1094 2n. Type **147** 10 10
1095 3n. Blue peacock 10 10
1096 5n. Great mormon 20 20
1097 10n. Fritillary 35 35
1098 15n. Blue duke 55 55
1099 25n. Brown gorgon 90 90

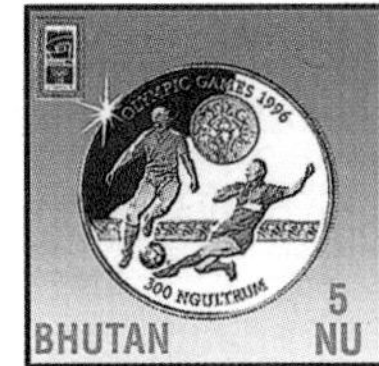

148 300n. Football Coin

1996. Olympic Games, Atlanta. Mult.

1101 5n. Type **148** 20 20
1102 7n. 300n. basketball coin 25 25
1103 10n. 5s. judo coin 35 35

149 Standard Goods Locomotive, India

1996. Trains. Multicoloured.

1105 20n. Type **149** 70 70
1106 20n. Diesel-electric locomotive, Finland 70 70
1107 20n. Shunting tank locomotive, Russia 70 70
1108 20n. Alco PA-1 diesel-electric locomotive, U.S.A. 70 70
1109 20n. Class C11 passenger tank locomotive, Japan 70 70
1110 20n. Settebello high speed electric train, Italy 70 70
1111 20n. Tank locomotive No. 191, Chile 70 70
1112 20n. Pacific locomotive, France 70 70
1113 20n. Steam locomotive No. 10, Norway 70 70
1114 20n. Atlantic express locomotive, Germany 70 70
1115 20n. Express steam locomotive, Belgium 70 70
1116 20n. Type 4 diesel-electric locomotive, Great Britain 70 70

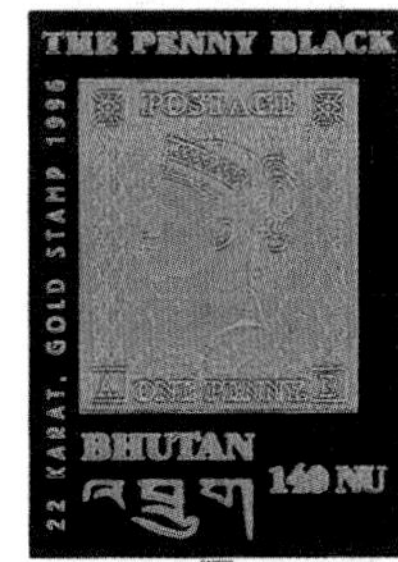

150 Penny Black

1996.

1118 **150** 140n. gold and black 4·25 4·25

151 Vegard Ulvang, Norway **152** Bee

1997. Winter Olympic Gold Medallists. Multicoloured. (a) Without frame.

1119 10n. Type **151** (30km. cross-country skiing, 1992) 30 30
1120 15n. Kristi Yamaguchi, U.S.A. (women's figure skating, 1992) 45 45
1121 25n. Markus Wasmeier, Germany (men's super giant slalom, 1994) 75 75
1122 30n. Georg Hackl, Germany (luge, 1992) 95 95

(b) As T **151** but with black frame around design.

1123 15n. Andreas Ostler, West Germany (two-man bobsleighing, 1952) 45 45
1124 15n. East German team (four-man bobsleighing, 1984) 45 45
1125 15n. Stein Eriksen, Norway (men's giant slalom, 1952) 45 45
1126 15n. Alberto Tomba, Italy (men's giant slalom, 1988) 45 45

1997. Insects and Arachnidae. Multicoloured.

1128 1ch. Type **152** 10 10
1129 2ch. "Neptunides polychromus" (beetle) 10 10
1130 3ch. "Conocephalus maculctus" (grasshopper) 10 10
1131 4ch. "Blattidae" sp. (beetle) 10 10
1132 5ch. Great diving beetle 10 10
1133 10ch. Hercules beetle 10 10
1134 15ch. Ladybird 10 10
1135 20ch. "Sarcophaga haemorrhoidalis" (fly) 10 10
1136 25ch. Stag beetle 10 10
1137 30ch. Caterpillar 10 10
1138 35ch. "Lycia hirtaria" (moth) 10 10
1139 40ch. "Clytarius pennatus" (beetle) 10 10
1140 45ch. "Ephemera denica" (mayfly) 10 10
1141 50ch. European field cricket 10 10
1142 60ch. Elephant hawk moth 10 10
1143 65ch. "Gerris" sp. (beetle) 10 10
1144 70ch. Banded agrion 10 10
1145 80ch. "Tachyta nana" (beetle) 10 10
1146 90ch. "Eurydema pulchra" (shieldbug) 10 10
1147 1n. "Hadrurus hirsutus" (scorpion) 10 10
1148 1n.50 "Vespa germanica" (wasp) 10 10
1149 2n. "Pyrops" sp. (beetle) 10 10
1150 2n.50 Praying mantis 10 10
1151 3n. "Araneus diadematus" (spider) 10 10
1152 3n.50 "Atrophaneura" sp. (butterfly) 10 10

153 Polar Bears

1997. "Hong Kong '97" International Stamp Exhibition. Multicoloured.

1154 10n. Type **153** 30 30
1155 10n. Koalas ("Phascolarctos cinereus") 30 30
1156 10n. Asiatic black bear ("Selenarctos thibetanus") 30 30
1157 10n. Lesser panda ("Ailurus fulgens") 30 30

154 Rat

1997. New Year. Year of the Ox. Multicoloured.

1159 1ch. Type **154** 10 10
1160 2ch. Ox 10 10
1161 3ch. Tiger 10 10
1162 4ch. Rabbit 10 10
1163 90ch. Monkey 10 10
1164 5n. Dragon 15 15
1165 6n. Snake 20 20
1166 7n. Horse 20 20
1167 8n. Ram 25 25
1168 10n. Cock 30 30
1169 11n. Dog 30 30
1170 12n. Boar 35 35

155 Lynx

1997. Endangered Species. Multicoloured.

1172 10n. Type **155** 30 30
1173 10n. Lesser ("Red") panda ("Ailurus fulgens") 30 30
1174 10n. Takin ("Budorcas taxicolor") 30 30
1175 10n. Forest musk deer ("Moschus chrysogaster") 30 30
1176 10n. Snow leopard ("Panthera uncia") 30 30
1177 10n. Golden langur ("Presbytis geei") 30 30
1178 10n. Tiger ("Panthera tigris") 30 30
1179 10n. Indian muntjac ("Muntiacus muntjak") 30 30
1180 10n. Bobak marmot ("Marmota bobak") 30 30
1181 10n. Dhole ("Cuon alpinis") running 30 30
1182 10n. Dhole walking 30 30
1183 10n. Mother dhole nursing cubs 30 30
1184 10n. Two dhole 30 30

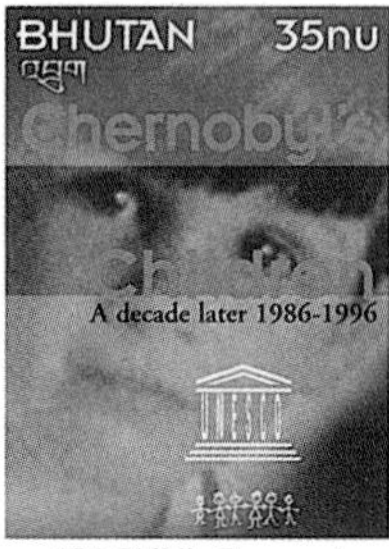

156 Child's Face and U.N.E.S.C.O. Emblem

1997. 10th Anniv of Chernobyl Nuclear Disaster.

1186 **156** 35n. multicoloured 1·00 1·00

157 Mount Huangshah, China

1997. 50th Anniv of U.N.E.S.C.O. World Heritage Sites. Multicoloured.

1187 10n. Type **157** 30 30
1188 10n. Statue of Emperor Qin, China 30 30
1189 10n. Imperial bronze dragon, China 30 30
1190 10n. Pyramids, Tikal National Park, Guatemala 30 30
1191 10n. Fountain, Evora, Portugal 30 30
1192 10n. Forest path, Shirakami-Sanchi, Japan 30 30
1193 10n. View from Eiffel Tower, Paris, France 30 30
1194 10n. Wooden walkway, Valley Below the Falls, Croatia 30 30
1195 15n. Bamberg Cathedral, Germany 45 45
1196 15n. Aerial view of Bamberg 45 45
1197 15n. St. Michael's Church, Hildesheim, Germany 45 45
1198 15n. Potsdam Palace, Germany 45 45
1199 15n. Church, Potsdam 45 45
1200 15n. Waterfront, Lubeck, Germany 45 45
1201 15n. Quedlinberg, Germany 45 45
1202 15n. Benedictine church, Lorsch, Germany 45 45

158 Turkish Angora **159** Stuart Pearce (England)

1997. Domestic Animals. Mult. (a) Cats.

1204 10n. Type **158** 30 30
1205 15n. Oriental shorthair 45 45
1206 15n. Japanese bobtail 45 45
1207 15n. Ceylon 45 45
1208 15n. Exotic 45 45
1209 15n. Rex 45 45
1210 15n. Ragdoll 45 45
1211 15n. Russian blue 45 45
1212 20n. British shorthair 55 55
1213 25n. Burmese 70 70

(b) Dogs.

1214 10n. Dalmatian 30 30
1215 15n. Siberian husky 45 45
1216 20n. Saluki 55 55
1217 20n. Dandie Dinmont terrier 55 55
1218 20n. Chinese crested 55 55

1219 20n. Norwich terrier 55 55
1220 20n. Basset hound 55 55
1221 20n. Cardigan Welsh corgi 55 55
1222 20n. French bulldog 55 55
1223 25n. Shar-Pei 70 70

Nos. 1206/11 and 1217/22 respectively were issued together, se-tenant, forming composite designs.

1997. World Cup Football Championship, France (1998). Black (Nos. 1225, 1231, 1235, 1237, 1241, 1243) or multicoloured (others).

1225 5n. Type **159** 15 15
1226 10n. Paul Gascoigne (England) 30 30
1227 10n. Diego Maradona (Argentina 1986) (horiz) 30 30
1228 10n. Carlos Alberto (Brazil 1970) (horiz) 30 30
1229 10n. Dunga (Brazil 1994) (horiz) 30 30
1230 10n. Bobby Moore (England 1966) (horiz) 30 30
1231 10n. Fritz Walter (West Germany 1954) (horiz) . . 30 30
1232 10n. Walter Matthaus (Germany 1990) (horiz) 30 30
1233 10n. Franz Beckenbauer (West Germany 1974) (horiz) 30 30
1234 10n. Daniel Passarella (Argentina 1978) (horiz) 30 30
1235 10n. Italy team, 1938 (horiz) 30 30
1236 10n. West Germany team, 1954 (horiz) 30 30
1237 10n. Uruguay team, 1958 (horiz) 30 30
1238 10n. England team, 1966 (horiz) 30 30
1239 10n. Argentina team, 1978 (horiz) 30 30
1240 10n. Brazil team, 1962 (horiz) 30 30
1241 10n. Italy team, 1934 (horiz) 30 30
1242 10n. Brazil team, 1970 (horiz) 30 30
1243 10n. Uruguay team, 1930 (horiz) 30 30
1244 10n. David Beckham (England) 45 45
1245 20n. Steve McManaman (England) 55 55
1246 25n. Tony Adams (England) 70 70
1247 30n. Paul Ince (England) . . 85 85

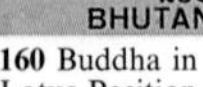

160 Buddha in Lotus Position

161 Jawaharlal Nehru and King Jigme Dorji Wangchuck

1997. "Indepex '97" International Stamp Exhibition, New Delhi. 50th Anniv of Independence of India. Multicoloured.

1249 3n. Type **160** 10 10
1250 7n. Mahatma Gandhi with hands together 20 20
1251 10n. Gandhi (three-quarter face portrait) 30 30
1252 15n. Buddha with feet on footstool 45 45

1997. Int Friendship between India and Bhutan.

1254 **161** 3n. black and pink . . . 10 10
1255 – 10n. multicoloured . . . 30 30

DESIGN: 10n. Prime Minister Rajiv Gandhi of India and King Jigme Singye Wangchuck.

162 Tiger

1998. New Year. Year of the Tiger.

1257 **162** 3n. multicoloured . . . 10 10

163 Safe Motherhood and Anniversary Emblems

1998. 50th Anniv of W.H.O.

1259 **163** 3n. multicoloured . . . 10 10
1260 10n. multicoloured . . . 30 30

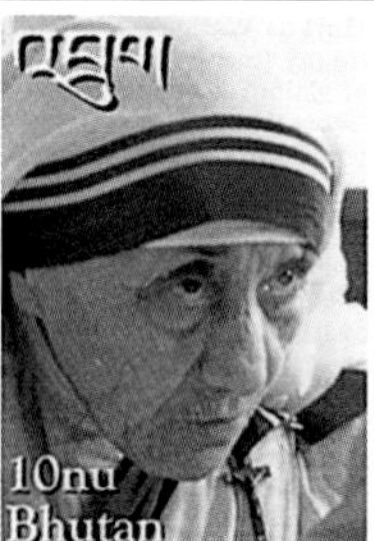

164 Mother Teresa

1998. Mother Teresa (founder of Missionaries of Charity) Commemoration. Multicoloured.

1262 10n. Type **164** 30 30
1263 10n. With Diana, Princess of Wales 30 30
1264 10n. Holding child 30 30
1265 10n. Holding baby 30 30
1266 10n. With Sisters 30 30
1267 10n. Smiling 30 30
1268 10n. Praying 30 30
1269 10n. With Pope John Paul II 30 30
1270 10n. Close-up of face . . . 30 30

165 Red-billed Chough

1998. Birds. Multicoloured.

1272 10ch. Type **165** 10 10
1273 30ch. Great Indian hornbill ("Great Hornbill") . . . 10 10
1274 50ch. Western Singing bush lark ("Singing Lark") . . 10 10
1275 70ch. Chestnut-flanked white-eye 10 10
1276 90ch. Magpie robin (wrongly inscr "Megpie-robin") 10 10
1277 1n. Mrs. Gould's sunbird . . 10 10
1278 2n. Long-tailed tailor bird ("Tailorbird") 10 10
1279 3n. Mallard ("Duck") . . . 10 10
1280 5n. Great spotted cuckoo ("Spotted Cuckoo") . . . 15 15
1281 7n. Severtzov's tit warbler ("Goldcrest") 20 20
1282 9n. Common mynah 25 25
1283 10n. Green cochoa 30 30

166 Rabbit

1999. New Year. Year of the Rabbit. Multicoloured.

1285 4n. Type **166** 10 10
1286 16n. Rabbit on hillock . . . 45 45

168 King Wangchuck

1999. 25th Anniv of Coronation of King Jigme Singye Wangchuck. Multicoloured.

1289 25n. Type **168** 75 75
1290 25n. Facing left (yellow background) 75 75
1291 25n. Facing forwards (orange background) . . 75 75
1292 25n. With arm raised (green background) 75 75

169 Early German Steam Locomotive

1999. Trains. Multicoloured.

1294 5n. Type **169** 15 15
1295 10n. Electric locomotive . . 30 30
1296 10n. "Hikari" express train, Japan 30 30
1297 10n. Steam locomotive, South Africa, 1953 . . . 30 30
1298 10n. Super Chief locomotive, U.S.A., 1946 30 30
1299 10n. Magleus Magnet train, Japan, 1991 . . . . . . 30 30
1300 10n. *Flying Scotsman*, Great Britain, 1992 . . . . . . 30 30
1301 10n. Kodama locomotive, Japan, 1958 . . . . . . 30 30
1302 10n. "Blue Train", South Africa, 1969 . . . . . . 30 30
1303 10n. Intercity train, Germany, 1960 . . . . . 30 30
1304 10n. ET 403 high speed electric locomotive, Germany, 1973 . . . . . 30 30
1305 10n. 4-4-0 steam locomotive, U.S.A., 1855 . . . . . . 30 30
1306 10n. Beyer-Garratt steam locomotive, South Africa, 1954 (wrongly inscr "BAYER GARRATT") 30 30
1307 10n. Settebello locomotive, Italy, 1953 . . . . . . 30 30
1308 15n. Pacific Class 01 steam locomotive, Germany . . 45 45
1309 15n. Neptune Express, Germany 45 45
1310 15n. 4-6-0 steam locomotive, Great Britain 45 45
1311 15n. Shovelnose Streamliner diesel locomotive, U.S.A. 45 45
1312 15n. Electric locomotive, Germany 45 45
1313 15n. Early steam locomotive, Germany . . 45 45
1314 15n. Union Pacific diesel locomotive, U.S.A. . . . 45 45
1315 15n. 1881 Borsig steam locomotive, Germany . . 45 45
1316 15n. Borsig 4-6-4 diesel locomotive, Germany . . 45 45
1317 15n. Diesel-electric locomotive, France . . . 45 45
1318 15n. Pennsylvania Railroad locomotive, U.S.A. . . . 45 45
1319 15n. Steam locomotive, Germany 45 45
1320 15n. Amtrak locomotive, U.S.A. 45 45
1321 15n. 2-2-2 steam locomotive, Great Britain 45 45
1322 15n. P class steam locomotive, Denmark . . 45 45
1323 15n. Electric locomotive, France 45 45
1324 15n. First Japanese locomotive 45 45
1325 15n. 2-8-2 steam locomotive, Germany 45 45
1326 20n. Steam locomotive . . . 45 45
1327 30n. Electric locomotive . . 45 45

170 "Festive Dancers"

1999. 150th Death Anniv of Katsushika Hokusai (artist). Multicoloured.

1329 15n. Type **170** 45 45
1330 15n. "Drawings of Women" (woman reading) 45 45
1331 15n. "Festive Dancers" (man wearing pointed hat) 45 45
1332 15n. "Festive Dancers" (man looking up) 45 45
1333 15n. "Drawings of Women" (woman sitting on ground) 45 45
1334 15n. "Festive Dancers" (woman) 45 45
1335 15n. "Suspension Bridge between Hida and Etchu" 45 45
1336 15n. "Drawings of Women" (woman dressing hair) . . 45 45
1337 15n. "Exotic Beauty" 45 45
1338 15n. "The Poet Nakamaro in China" 45 45
1339 15n. "Drawings of Women" (woman rolling up sleeve) 45 45
1340 15n. "Chinese Poet in Snow" 45 45
1341 15n. "Mount Fuji seen above Mist on the Tama River" (horiz) 45 45
1342 15n. "Mount Fuji seen from Shichirigahama" (horiz) 45 45
1343 15n. "Sea Life" (turtle) (horiz) 45 45
1344 15n. "Sea Life" (fish) (horiz) 45 45
1345 15n. "Mount Fuji reflected in a Lake" (horiz) 45 45
1346 15n. "Mount Fuji seen through the Piers of Mannenbashi" (horiz) . . 45 45

171 Tyrannosaurus Rex

1999. Prehistoric Animals. Multicoloured.

1348 10n. Type **171** 30 30
1349 10n. Dimorphodon 30 30
1350 10n. Diplodocus 30 30
1351 10n. Pterodaustro 30 30
1352 10n. Tyrannosaurus Rex (different) 30 30
1353 10n. Edmontosaurus 30 30
1354 10n. Apatosaurus 30 30
1355 10n. Deinonychus 30 30
1356 10n. Hypsilophodon 30 30
1357 10n. Oviraptor 30 30
1358 10n. Stegosaurus beside lake 30 30
1359 10n. Head of Triceratops . . 30 30
1360 10n. Pterodactylus and Brachiosaurus 30 30
1361 10n. Pteranodon 30 30
1362 10n. Anurognathus and Tyrannosaurus Rex . . . 30 30
1363 10n. Brachiosaurus 30 30
1364 10n. Corythosaurus 30 30
1365 10n. Iguanodon 30 30
1366 10n. Lesothosaurus 30 30
1367 10n. Allosaurus 30 30
1368 10n. Velociraptor 30 30
1369 10n. Triceratops in water . . 30 30
1370 10n. Stegosaurus in water 30 30
1371 10n. Compsognathus . . . 30 30
1372 20n. Moeritherium 60 60
1373 20n. Platybelodon 60 60
1374 20n. Woolly mammoth . . . 60 60
1375 20n. African elephant . . . 60 60
1376 20n. Deinonychus 60 60
1377 20n. Dimorphodon 60 60
1378 20n. Archaeopteryx 60 60
1379 20n. Common pheasant ("Ring-necked Pheasant") 60 60

Nos. 1348/59 and 1360/71 were issued together, se-tenant, with the backgrounds forming a composite design

172 Siberian Musk Deer

1999. "China '99" World Philatelic Exhibition, Peking. Animals. Multicoloured.

1381 20n. Type **172** 60 60
1382 20n. Takin (*Budorcas taxicolor*) 60 60
1383 20n. Bharal ("Blue sheep") (*Pseudois nayur*) (wrongly inscr "nayour") 60 60
1384 20n. Yak (*Bos gunniens*) . . 60 60
1385 20n. Common goral (*Nemorhaedus goral*) . . . 60 60

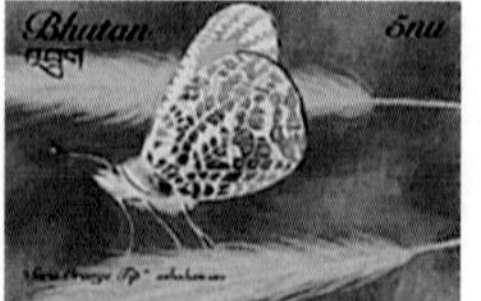

173 Sara Orange-tip

1999. Butterflies. Multicoloured.

1386 5n. Type **173** 15 15
1387 10n. Pipe-vine swallowtail 30 30
1388 15n. Longwings 45 45
1389 20n. Viceroy 60 60
1390 20n. Frosted skipper 60 60
1391 20n. Fiery skipper 60 60
1392 20n. Banded hairstreak . . 60 60
1393 20n. Cloudless ("Clouded") sulphur 60 60
1394 20n. Milbert's tortoiseshell 60 60
1395 20n. Eastern tailed blue . . 60 60
1396 20n. Jamaican kite ("Zebra") swallowtail . . 60 60
1397 20n. Colorado hairstreak . . 60 60
1398 20n. Pink-edged sulphur . . 60 60
1399 20n. Barred sulphur (wrongly inscr "Fairy Yellow") 60 60
1400 20n. Red-spotted purple . . 60 60
1401 20n. Aphrodite 60 60
1402 25n. Silver-spotted skipper (vert) 75 75
1403 30n. Great spangled fritillary (vert) 90 90
1404 35n. Little copper (vert) . . 1·00 1·00

Nos. 1390/95 and 1396/1401 were issued together, se-tenant, forming a composite design.

174 Chestnut-breasted Chlorophonia

1999. Birds. Multicoloured.
1406 15n. Type **174** 45 45
1407 15n. Yellow-faced amazon 45 45
1408 15n. White ibis 45 45
1409 15n. Parrotlet sp. ("Caique") 45 45
1410 15n. Green jay 45 45
1411 15n. Tufted coquette 45 45
1412 15n. Troupial 45 45
1413 15n. American purple gallinule ("Purple Gallinule") 45 45
1414 15n. Copper-rumped hummingbird 45 45
1415 15n. Great egret ("Common egret") 45 45
1416 15n. Rufous-browed pepper shrike 45 45
1417 15n. Glittering-throated emerald 45 45
1418 15n. Great kiskadee 45 45
1419 15n. Cuban green woodpecker 45 45
1420 15n. Scarlet ibis 45 45
1421 15n. Belted kingfisher . . . 45 45
1422 15n. Barred antshrike . . . 45 45
1423 15n. Brown-throated conure ("Caribbean Parakeet") 45 45
1424 15n. Rufous-tailed jacamar (vert) 45 45
1425 15n. Scarlet macaw (vert) . . 45 45
1426 15n. Channel-billed toucan (vert) 45 45
1427 15n. Louisiana heron ("Tricolored heron") (vert) 45 45
1428 15n. St. Vincent amazon ("St. Vincent Parrot") (vert) 45 45
1429 15n. Blue-crowned motmot (vert) 45 45
1430 15n. Horned screamer (vert) 45 45
1431 15n. Grey plover ("Black-billed Plover") (vert) 45 45
1432 15n. Eastern meadowlark ("Common meadowlark") (vert) 45 45

Nos. 1406/14, 1415/23 and 1424/32 were issued together, se-tenant, forming a composite design.

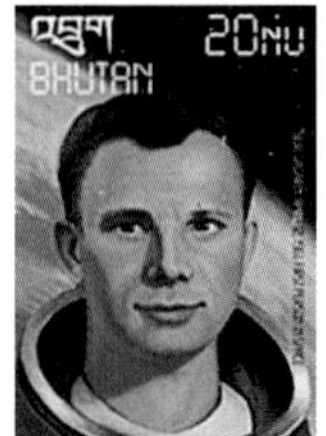

175 Yuri Gagarin (first person in space, 1961)

1999. 30th Anniv of First Manned Moon Landing. Multicoloured.
1434 20n. Type **175** 60 60
1435 20n. Alan Shepard (first American in space, 1961) 60 60
1436 20n. John Glenn (first American to orbit Earth, 1962) 60 60
1437 20n. Valentina Tereshkova (first woman in space, 1963) 60 60
1438 20n. Edward White (first American to walk in space, 1965) 60 60
1439 20n. Neil Armstrong (first person to set foot on Moon, 1969) 60 60
1440 20n. Neil Armstrong (wearing N.A.S.A. suit) 60 60
1441 20n. Michael Collins 60 60
1442 20n. Edwin (Buzz) Aldrin 60 60
1443 20n. *Columbia* (pointing upwards) 60 60
1444 20n. *Eagle* on lunar surface 60 60
1445 20n. Edwin Aldrin on lunar surface 60 60
1446 20n. N.A.S.A. X-15 rocket (1960) 60 60
1447 20n. Gemini 8 (1966) . . . 60 60
1448 20n. Saturn V rocket (1969) 60 60
1449 20n. *Columbia* (pointing downwards) 60 60
1450 20n. *Eagle* above Moon . . 60 60
1451 20n. Edwin Aldrin descending ladder 60 60

Nos. 1434/9, 1440/5 and 1446/51 were issued together, se-tenant, forming a composite design.

176 Tortoiseshell Cat

1999. Animals. Multicoloured.
1453 5n. Type **176** 15 15
1454 5n. Man watching blue and white cat 15 15
1455 5n. Girl and pet cat 15 15
1456 10n. Chinchilla golden longhair adult and kittens 30 30
1457 12n. Russian blue adult and kitten 35 35
1458 12n. Birman 35 35
1459 12n. Devon rex 35 35
1460 12n. Pewter longhair 35 35
1461 12n. Bombay 35 35
1462 12n. Sorrel somali 35 35
1463 12n. Red tabby manx . . . 35 35
1464 12n. Blue smoke longhair 35 35
1465 12n. Oriental tabby shorthair adult and kitten 35 35
1466 12n. Australian silky terrier 35 35
1467 12n. Samoyed 35 35
1468 12n. Basset bleu de Gascogne 35 35
1469 12n. Bernese mountain dog 35 35
1470 12n. Pug 35 35
1471 12n. Bergamasco 35 35
1472 12n. Basenji 35 35
1473 12n. Wetterhoun 35 35
1474 12n. Drever 35 35
1475 12n. Przewalski horse . . . 35 35
1476 12n. Shetland pony 35 35
1477 12n. Dutch gelderlander horse 35 35
1478 12n. Shire horse 35 35
1479 12n. Arab 35 35
1480 12n. Boulonnais 35 35
1481 12n. Falabella 35 35
1482 12n. Orlov trotter 35 35
1483 12n. Suffolk punch 35 35
1484 15n. Lipizzaner 45 45
1485 20n. Andalusian 60 60
1486 25n. Weimaraner (dog) . . . 60 60

177 Bharal

1999. Animals and Birds of the Himalayas. Multicoloured. (a) Animals.
1489 20n. Type **177** 60 60
1490 20n. Lynx 60 60
1491 20n. Rat snake 60 60
1492 20n. Indian elephant 60 60
1493 20n. Langur 60 60
1494 20n. Musk deer 60 60
1495 20n. Otter 60 60
1496 20n. Tibetan wolf 60 60
1497 20n. Himalayan black bear 60 60
1498 20n. Snow leopard 60 60
1499 20n. Flying squirrel 60 60
1500 20n. Red fox 60 60
1501 20n. Ibex 60 60
1502 20n. Takin 60 60
1503 20n. Agama lizard 60 60
1504 20n. Marmot 60 60
1505 20n. Red panda 60 60
1506 20n. Leopard cat 60 60

(b) Birds.
1508 20n. Red-crested pochard 60 60
1509 20n. Satyr tragopan 60 60
1510 20n. Lammergeier ("Lammergeier Vulture") 60 60
1511 20n. Kalij pheasant 60 60
1512 20n. Great Indian hornbill 60 60
1513 20n. White stork ("Stork") 60 60
1514 20n. Rufous-necked hornbill (wrongly inscr "Rofous") 60 60
1515 20n. Black drongo ("Drongo") 60 60
1516 20n. Himalayan monal pheasant 60 60
1517 20n. Black-necked crane . . 60 60
1518 20n. Little green bee-eater 60 60
1519 20n. Oriental ibis ("Ibis") 60 60
1520 20n. Crested lark 60 60
1521 20n. Ferruginous duck . . . 60 60
1522 20n. Blood pheasant 60 60
1523 20n. White-crested laughing thrush ("Laughing Thrush") 60 60
1524 20n. Golden eagle 60 60
1525 20n. Siberian rubythroat . . 60 60

178 Elephant, Monkey, Rabbit and Bird (Four Friends)

1999. Year 2000.
1527 **178** 10n. multicoloured . . . 30 30
1528 20n. multicoloured . . . 60 60

179 Elegant Stink Horn

1999. Fungi. Multicoloured.
1529 20n. Type **179** 60 60
1530 20n. *Pholiota squarrosoides* 60 60
1531 20n. Scaly inky cap (*Coprinus quadrifidus*) . . 60 60
1532 20n. Golden spindles (*Clavulinopsis fusiformis*) 60 60
1533 20n. *Spathularia velutipes* . . 60 60
1534 20n. *Ganoderma lucidum* . . . 60 60
1535 20n. *Microglossum rufum* . . 60 60
1536 20n. *Lactarius hygrophoroides* 60 60
1537 20n. *Lactarius speciosus complex* 60 60
1538 20n. *Calostoma cinnabarina* 60 60
1539 20n. *Clitocybe clavipes* . . . 60 60
1540 20n. *Microstoma floccosa* . . 60 60
1541 20n. Frost's bolete (*Boletus frostii*) 60 60
1542 20n. Common morel (*Morchella esculenta*) (wrongly inscr "estculenta") 60 60
1543 20n. *Hypomyces lactifluorum* 60 60
1544 20n. *Polyporus auricularius* 60 60
1545 20n. *Cantharellus lateritius* 60 60
1546 20n. *Volvariella pusilla* . . . 60 60

180 Green Dragon with Red Flames

2000. New Year. Year of the Dragon. Multicoloured.
1548 3n. Type **180** 10 10
1549 5n. Green dragon encircling moon 15 15
1550 8n. Dragon and symbols of Chinese zodiac 20 20
1552 12n. Brown dragon encircling moon 35 35

181 LZ-1 (first flight), 1900

2000. Centenary of First Zeppelin Flight. Multicoloured.
1554 25n. Type **181** 70 70
1555 25n. LZ-2, 1906 . . . . . . 70 70
1556 25n. LZ-3 over hills (first flight, 1906) 70 70
1557 25n. LZ-127 *Graf Zeppelin* (first flight, 1928) 70 70
1558 25n. LZ-129 *Hindenberg* (first flight, 1936) 70 70
1559 25n. LZ-130 *Graf Zeppelin II* (first flight, 1938) . . . 70 70
1560 25n. LZ-1 over hill with tree 70 70
1561 25n. LZ-2 over mountains 70 70
1562 25n. LZ-3 against sky . . . 70 70
1563 25n. LZ-4 (first flight, 1908) 70 70
1564 25n. LZ-5 (first flight, 1909) 70 70
1565 25n. LZ-6 (formation of Deutsche Liftschiffahrts Aktien Gesellschaft (DELAG) (world's first airline), 1909) 70 70
1566 25n. LZ-1 over grassy hills, 1900 . . . . 70 70
1567 25n. Z11 *Ersatz*, 1913 . . . 70 70
1568 25n. LZ-6 exiting hanger, 1909 . . . . 70 70
1569 25n. LZ-10 *Schwabein* first flight, 1911) 70 70
1570 25n. LZ-7 *Deutschland* (inscr "Ersatz Deutschland") . . 70 70
1571 25n. LZ-11 *Viktoria Luise* 70 70

182 Lunix III

2000. "WORLD STAMP EXPO 2000" International Stamp Exhibition, Anaheim, California. Space. Multicoloured.
1573 25n. Type **182** 70 70
1574 25n. Ranger 9 . . . . . . 70 70
1575 25n. Lunar Orbiter 70 70
1576 25n. Lunar Prospector spacecraft 70 70
1577 25n. *Apollo 11* spacecraft . . 70 70
1578 25n. Selen satellite 70 70
1579 25n. Space shuttle *Challenger* 70 70
1580 25n. North American X-15 experimental rocket aircraft 70 70
1581 25n. Space shuttle *Buran* . . 70 70
1582 25n. Hermes (experimental space plane) 70 70
1583 25n. X-33 Venturi Star (re-usable launch vehicle) . . 70 70
1584 25n. Hope (unmanned experimental spacecraft) 70 70
1585 25n. Victor Patsayev (cosmonaut) 70 70
1586 25n. Yladisloav Volkov (cosmonaut) 70 70
1587 25n. Georgi Dobrvolski (cosmonaut) 70 70
1588 25n. Virgil Grissom (astronaut) 70 70
1589 25n. Roger Chaffee (astronaut) 70 70
1590 25n. Edward White (astronaut) 70 70

183 Trashigang Dzong

2000. "EXPO 2000" World's Fair, Hanover, Germany (1st issue). Monasteries. Multicoloured.
1592 3n. Type **183** 10 10
1593 4n. Lhuentse Dzong 10 10
1594 6n. Gasa Dzong 15 15
1595 7n. Punakha Dzong 20 20
1596 10n. Trashichhoe Dzong . . . 30 30
1597 20n. Paro Dzong 55 55

184 Snow Leopard

2000. "EXPO 2000" World's Fair, Hanover, Germany (2nd issue). Wildlife. Multicoloured.
1599 10n. Type **184** 30 30
1600 10n. Common raven ("Raven") 30 30
1601 10n. Golden langur 30 30
1602 10n. Rhododendron 30 30
1603 10n. Black-necked crane . . 30 30
1604 10n. Blue poppy 30 30

185 Jesse Owens (U.S.A.) (Berlin, 1936)

2000. Olympic Games, Sydney. Multicoloured.
1605 20n. Type **185** 55 55
1606 20n. Kayaking (modern games) 55 55
1607 20n. Fulton County Stadium, Atlanta, Georgia (1996 games) 55 55
1608 20n. Ancient Greek athlete 55 55

186 G. and R. Stephenson's *Rocket* (first steam locomotive)

2000. 175th Anniv of Opening of Stockton and Darlington Railway. Multicoloured.
1609 50n. Type **186** 55 55
1610 50n. Steam locomotive (opening of London and Birmingham railway, 1828) 55 55
1611 50n. Northumbrian locomotive, 1825 . . . . 55 55

187 Laird Commercial (biplane), 1929

2000. Airplanes. Multicoloured.
1613 25n. Type **187** 70 70
1614 25n. Ryan B-5 Brougham, 1927 (wrongly inscr "Broughm") 70 70
1615 25n. Cessna AW, 1928 . . . 70 70
1616 25n. Travel Air 4000 biplane, 1927 . . . . . . 70 70
1617 25n. Fairchild F-71, 1927 . . 70 70
1618 25n. Command Aire biplane, 1928 . . . . . . 70 70
1619 25n. Waco YMF biplane, 1935 . . . . 70 70
1620 25n. Piper J-4 Cub Coupe, 1938 . . . . 70 70
1621 25n. Ryan ST-A, 1937 . . . 70 70
1622 25n. Spartan Executive, 1939 . . . . 70 70
1623 25n. Luscombe 8, 1939 . . . 70 70
1624 25n. Stinson SR5 Reliant seaplane, 1935 . . . . . 70 70
1625 25n. Cessna 195 seaplane, 1949 . . . . 70 70
1626 25n. Waco SRE biplane, 1940 . . . . 70 70
1627 25n. Erco Ercope, 1948 . . 70 70
1628 25n. Boeing Stearman biplane, 1941 . . . . . . 70 70
1629 25n. Beech Staggerwing biplane, 1944 . . . . . . 70 70
1630 25n. Republic Seabee, 1947 70 70

188 A Kind of Loving, 1962

190 Aquinas

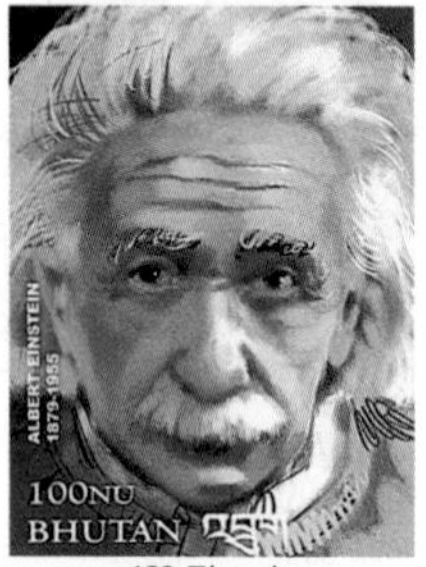

189 Einstein

2000. Berlin Film Festival. Winners of Golden Bear Award. Multicoloured.
1632 25n. Type **188** 65 65
1633 25n. *Bushido Zankoku Monogatari*, 1963 . . . . 65 65
1634 25n. *Hobson's Choice*, 1954 65 65
1635 25n. *El Lazarillo de Tormes*, 1960 . . . . 65 65
1636 25n. *In the Name of the Father*, 1997 . . . . . . 65 65
1637 25n. *Les Cousins*, 1959 . . . 65 65
MS1638 96 × 102 mm. 100n. *Die Ratten*, 1962 2·50 2·50

2000. Albert Einstein—*Time* Magazine Man of the Century. Sheet 113 × 83 mm.
MS1639 **189** 100n. multicoloured 2·50 2·50

2000. 775th Birth Anniv of Thomas Aquinas (Catholic philosopher and theologian). Sheet 136 × 76 mm.
MS1640 **190** 25n. × 4 multicoloured 2·50 2·50

191 Pierre de Coubertin

2000. New Millennium. Multicoloured. (a) Centenary of the Modern Olympic Games.
1641 25n. Type **191** (founder of modern games) 65 65
1642 25n. Hand holding baton (first modern Games, Athens, 1896) 65 65
1643 25n. Jesse Owen (Berlin, 1936) 65 65
1644 25n. Handprint and white dove (Munich, 1972) . . . 65 65
1645 25n. Sydney Opera House (Sydney, 2000) 65 65
1646 25n. Children wearing T-shirts (Greece, 2004) . . 65 65

(b) Breakthroughs in Modern Medicine.
1647 25n. Albert Calmette (bacteriologist, joint discoverer of B.C.G. vaccine) 65 65
1648 25n. Camillo Colgi and S. Ramon y Cajal (discovery of the neurone) 65 65
1649 25n. Alexander Fleming (bacteriologist, discoverer of penicillin) 65 65
1650 25n. Jonas Salk (virologist, developer of polio vaccine) 65 65
1651 25n. Christiaan Barnard (surgeon, performed first human heart transplant) 65 65
1652 25n. Luc Mantagnier (A.I.D.S. research) . . . 65 65

192 Paro Taktsang

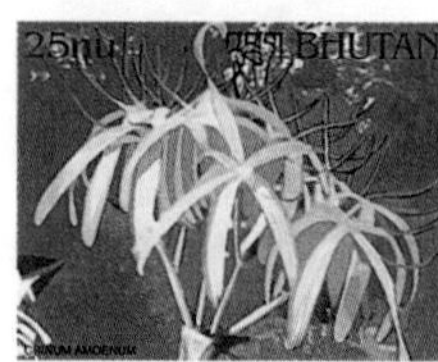

193 Christopher Columbus

2000. Sheet 86 × 49 mm.
MS1653 **192** multicoloured 2·50 2·50

2000. Explorers. Two sheets, each 66 × 83 mm. Multicoloured.
MS1654 (a) 100n. Type **193**; (b) 100n. Captain James Cook 5·00 5·00

194 *Crinum amoenum*

2000. Flowers of the Himalayan Mountains. Multicoloured.
1655 25n. Type **194** 65 65
1656 25n. *Beaumontia grandiflora* 65 65
1657 25n. *Trachelospermum lucidum* 65 65
1658 25n. *Curcuma aromatica* . . 65 65
1659 25n. *Barleria cristata* . . . 65 65
1660 25n. *Holmskioldia sanguinea* 65 65
1661 25n. *Meconopsis villosa* . . 65 65
1662 25n. *Salva hians* 65 65
1663 25n. *Caltha palustris* 65 65
1664 25n. *Anemone polyanthes* . . 65 65
1665 25n. *Cypripedium cordigerum* 65 65
1666 25n. *Cryptochilus luteus* . . 65 65
1667 25n. *Androsace globifera* . . 65 65
1668 25n. *Tanacetum atkinsonii* 65 65
1669 25n. *Aster stracheyi* 65 65
1670 25n. *Arenaria glanduligera* 65 65
1671 25n. *Sibbaldia purpurea* . . 65 65
1672 25n. *Saxifraga parnassifolia* 65 65
MS1673 Three sheets, each 68 × 98 mm. (a) 100n. *Dendrobium densiflorum* (vert); (b) 100n. *Rhododendron arboreum* (vert); (c) 100n. *Gypsophila cerastioides* 8·00 8·00

Nos. 1655/60, 1661/6 and 1667/72 respectively were issued together, se-tenant, forming a composite design.

195 "The Duke and Duchess of Osuna with their Children" (detail, Francisco de Goya)

2000. "Espana 2000" International Stamp Exhibition, Madrid. Prado Museum Exhibits. Multicoloured.
1674 25n. Type **195** 65 65
1675 25n. Young child (detail from "The Duke and Duchess of Osuna with their Children") 65 65
1676 25n. Duke (detail from "The Duke and Duchess of Osuna with their Children") 65 65
1677 25n. "Isidoro Maiquez" (Francisco de Goya) . . . 65 65
1678 25n. "Dona Juana Galarza de Goicoechea" (Francisco de Goya) . . . 65 65
1679 25n. "Ferdinand VII in an Encampment" (Francisco de Goya) 65 65
1680 25n. "Portrait of an Old Man" (Joos van Cleve) 65 65
1681 25n. "Mary Tudor" (Anthonis Mor) 65 65
1682 25n. "Portrait of a Man" (Jan van Scorel) 65 65
1683 25n. "The Court Jester Pejeron" (Anthonis Mor) 65 65
1684 25n. "Elizabeth of France" (Frans Pourbus the Younger) 65 65
1685 25n. "King James I" (Paul van Somer) 65 65
1686 25n. "The Empress Isabella of Portugal" (Titian) . . . 65 65
1687 25n. "Lucrecia di Baccio del Fede, the Painter's Wife" (Andrea del Sarto) . . . 65 65
1688 25n. "Self-Portrait" (Titian) 65 65
1689 25n. "Philip II" (Sofonisba Anguisciola) 65 65
1690 25n. "Portrait of a Doctor" (Lucia Anguisciola) . . . 65 65
1691 25n. "Anna of Austria" (Sofonisba Anguisciola) 65 65
MS1692 (a) 90 × 110 mm. 100n. Duchess and Duke (detail from "The Duke and Duchess of Osuna with their Children" (Francisco de Goya) (horiz); (b) 90 × 110 mm. 100n. "Charles V at Mühlberg" (Titian); (c) 110 × 90 mm. 100n. "The Relief of Genoa" (Antonio de Pereda) 8·00 8·00

196 Butterfly

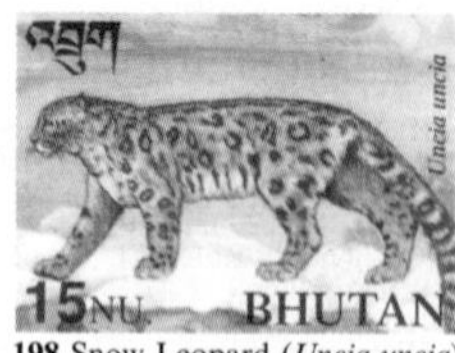

197 Snake

2000. "Indepex Asiana 2000" International Stamp Exhibition, Calcutta. Multicoloured.
1693 5n. Type **196** 15 15
1694 8n. Red jungle fowl 20 20
1695 10n. *Zinnia elegans* 25 25
1696 12n. Tiger 30 30
MS1697 144 × 84 mm. 15 n. Spotted deer (28 × 34 mm) 40 40

2001. New Year. Year of the Snake. Multicoloured.
1698 3n. Type **197** 10 10
1699 20n. Snake 55 55
MS1700 135 × 135 mm. 3, 10n. As Type **197**; 15, 20n. As No. 1699 1·25 1·25

198 Snow Leopard (*Uncia uncia*)

2001. "Hong Kong 2001" International Stamp Exhibition. Nature Protection. Sheet 195 × 138 mm containing T **198** and similar horiz designs. Multicoloured.
MS1701 15n. Type **198**; 15n. Rufous-necked hornbill (*Aceros nipalensis*); 15n. Black-necked crane (*Grus nigricollis*); 15n. Tiger (*Panthera tigris*) 1·60 1·60

199 Working in Fields

2001. International Year of Volunteers. Mult.
1702 3n. Type **199** 10 10
1703 4n. Planting crops 10 10
1704 10n. Children and bucket 25 25
1705 15n. Planting seeds and making compost 40 40
MS1706 170 × 120 mm. Nos. 1702/5 85 85

APPENDIX

The following stamps have either been issued in excess of postal needs or have not been available to the public in reasonable quantities at face value. Such stamps may later be given full listing if there is evidence of regular postal use.

1968.

Bhutan Pheasants, 1, 2, 4, 8, 15ch., 2, 4, 5, 7, 9n.

Winter Olympic Games, Grenoble. Optd on 1966 Abominable Snowmen issue. 40ch., 1n.25, 3, 6n.

Butterflies (plastic-surfaced). Postage 15. 50ch., 1n.25, 2n., Air 3, 4, 5, 6n.

Paintings (relief-printed). Postage 2, 4, 5, 10 45, 80ch., 1n.05, 1n.40, 2, 3, 4, 5n.; Air 1n.50, 2n.50, 6, 8n.

Olympic Games, Mexico. 5, 45, 60, 80ch., 1n.05, 2, 3, 5n.

Human Rights Year. Die-stamped surch on unissued "Coins". 15ch. on 50n.p., 33ch. on 1r., 9n. on 3r.75.

1969.

Flood Relief. Surch on 1968 Mexico Olympics issue. 5ch.+5ch., 80ch.+25ch., 2n.+50ch.

Fish (plastic-surfaced). Postage 15, 20, 30ch.; Air 5, 6, 7n.

Insects (plastic-surfaced). Postage 10, 75ch., 1n.25, 2n.; Air 3, 4, 5, 6n.

Admission of Bhutan to Universal Postal Union. 5, 10, 15, 45, 60ch., 1n.05, 1n.40, 4n.

5000 Years of Steel Industry. On steel foil. Postage 2, 5, 15, 45, 75ch., 1 n 50, 1n.75, 2n.; Air 3, 4, 5, 6n.

Birds (plastic-surfaced). Postage 15, 50ch., 1n.25, 2n.; Air 3, 4, 5, 6n.

Buddhist Prayer Banners. On silk rayon. 15, 75ch., 2, 5, 6n.

Moon Landing of "Apollo 11" (plastic-surfaced). Postage 3, 5, 15, 20, 25, 45, 50ch., 1n.75; Air 3, 4, 5, 6n.

1970.

Famous Paintings (plastic-surfaced). Postage 5, 10, 15ch., 2n.75; Air 3, 4, 5, 6n.

New U.P.U. Headquarters Building, Berne. 3, 10, 20ch., 2n.50.

Flower Paintings (relief-printed). Postage 2, 3, 5, 10, 15, 75ch., 1n., 1n.40; Air 80, 90ch., 1n.10, 1n.40, 1n.60, 1n.70, 3n., 3n.50.

Animals (plastic-surfaced). Postage 5, 10, 20, 25, 30, 40, 65, 75, 85ch.; Air 2, 3, 4, 5n.

Conquest of Space (plastic-surfaced). Postage 2, 5, 15, 25, 30, 50, 75ch., 1n.50; Air 2, 3, 6, 7n.

1971.

History of Sculpture (plastic-moulded). Postage 10, 75ch., 1n.25, 2n.; Air 3, 4, 5, 6n.

Moon Vehicles (plastic-surfaced). Postage 10ch., 1n.70; Air 2n.50, 4n.

History of the Motor Car (plastic-surfaced). Postage 2, 5, 10, 15, 20, 30, 60, 75, 85ch., 1n., 1n.20, 1n.55, 1n.80, 2n., 2n.50; Air 4, 6, 7, 9, 10n.

Bhutan's Admission to United Nations. Postage 5, 10, 20ch., 3 n; Air 2n.50, 5, 6n.

60th Anniv of Boy Scout Movement. 10, 20, 50, 75ch., 2, 6n.

World Refugee Year. Optd on 1971 United Nations issue. Postage 5, 10, 20ch., 3n.; Air 2n.50, 5, 6n.

1972.

Famous Paintings (relief-printed). Postage 15, 20, 90ch., 2n.50; Air 1n.70, 4n.60, 5n.40, 6n.

Famous Men (plastic-moulded). Postage 10, 15, 55ch.; Air 2, 6, 8n.

Olympic Games, Munich. Postage 10, 15, 20, 30, 45ch.; Air 35ch., 1n.35, 7n.

Space Flight of "Apollo 16" (plastic-surfaced). Postage 15, 20, 90ch., 2n.50; Air 1n.70, 4n.60, 5n.40, 6n.

1973.

Dogs. 2, 3, 15, 20, 30, 99ch., 2n.50, 4n.

Roses (on scent-impregnated paper). Postage 15, 25, 30ch., 3n.; Air 6, 7n.

Moon Landing of "Apollo 17" (plastic-surfaced). Postage 10, 15, 55ch. 2n.; Air 7n., 9n.

"Talking Stamps" (miniature records). Postage 10, 25ch., 1n.25, 7, 8n.; Air 3, 9n.

Death of King Jigme Dorji Wangchuck. Embossed on gold foil. Postage 10, 25ch., 3n.; Air 6, 8n.

Mushrooms. 15, 25, 30ch., 3, 6, 7n.

"Indipex 73" Stamp Exhibition, New Delhi. Postage 5, 10, 15, 25ch., 1n.25, 3n.; Air 5, 6n.

BIAFRA Pt. 1

The Eastern Region of Nigeria declared its Independence on 30 May 1967 as the Republic of Biafra. Nigerian military operations against the breakaway Republic commenced in July 1967.

The Biafran postal service continued to use Nigerian stamps when supplies of these became low. In July 1967 "Postage Paid" cachets were used pending the issue of Nos. 1/3.

12 pence = 1 shilling;
20 shillings = 1 pound.

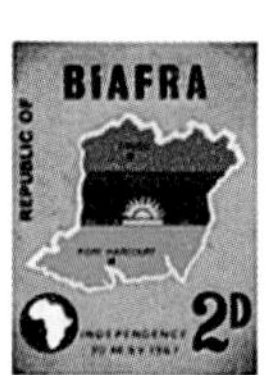

1 Map of Republic

5 Flag and Scientist

1968. Independence. Multicoloured.
1 2d. Type **1** 10 65
2 4d. Arms, flag and date of Independence 10 65
3 1s. Mother and child (17 × 22 mm) 15 1·75

1968. Nos. 172/5 and 177/85 of Nigeria optd **SOVEREIGN BIAFRA** and arms.
4 ½d. multicoloured (No. 172) 1·50 4·00
5 1d. multicoloured (No. 173) 1·50 6·00
6 1½d. multicoloured (No. 174) 7·00 12·00
7 2d. multicoloured (No. 175) 24·00 48·00
8 4d. multicoloured (No. 177) 17·00 48·00
9 6d. multicoloured (No. 178) 7·00 12·00
10 9d. blue and red (No. 179) 3·00 2·75
11 1s. multicoloured (No. 180) 60·00 £110
12 1s.3d. multicoloured (No. 181) 35·00 50·00
13 2s.6d. multicoloured (No. 182) 1·75 12·00
14 5s. multicoloured (No. 183) 2·25 11·00
15 10s. multicoloured (No. 184) 10·00 35·00
16 £1 multicoloured (No. 185) 10·00 35·00

The overprint on No. 15 does not include **SOVEREIGN**.

1968. 1st Anniv of Independence. Multicoloured.
17 4d. Type **5** 15 10
18 1s. Victim of atrocity 20 20
19 2s.6d. Nurse and refugees 45 3·00
20 5s. Biafran arms and banknote 60 3·50
21 10s. Orphaned child 1·00 4·00

16 Child in Chains, and Globe

17 Pope Paul VI, Africa, and Papal Arms

1969. 2nd Anniv of Independence. Multicoloured; frame colours given.
35 **16** 2d. orange 1·25 4·25
36 4d. red 1·25 4·25
37 1s. blue 1·75 7·00
38 2s.6d. green 2·00 14·00

1969. Visit of Pope Paul to Africa. Multicoloured; background colours given.
39 **17** 4d. orange 40 3·00
40 – 6d. blue 55 6·50
41 – 9d. green 75 8·50
42 – 3s. mauve 2·25 14·00

DESIGNS: Pope Paul VI, map of Africa and 6d. Arms of Vatican; 9d. St. Peter's Basilica; 3s. Statue of St. Peter.

BIJAWAR Pt. 1

A state of Central India. Now uses Indian stamps.

12 pies = 1 anna; 16 annas = 1 rupee.

1 Maharaja Sarwant Singh

2 Maharaja Sarwant Singh

1935.
6 **1** 3p. brown 4·00 3·50
2 6p. red 4·75 4·25
3 9p. violet 6·00 4·25
4 1a. blue 6·50 4·50
5 2a. green 6·50 4·75

1937.
11 **2** 4a. orange 10·00 65·00
12 6a. lemon 11·00 65·00
13 8a. green 12·00 80·00
14 12a. blue 12·00 80·00
15 1r. violet 32·00 £120

BOHEMIA AND MORAVIA Pt. 5

Following the proclamation of Slovak Independence on 14 March, 1939, the Czech provinces of Bohemia and Moravia became a German Protectorate. The area was liberated in 1945 and returned to Czechoslovakia.

100 haleru = 1 koruna.

1939. Stamps of Czechoslovakia optd **BOHMEN u. MAHREN CECHY a MORAVA**.
1 **34** 5h. blue 10 1·10
2 10h. brown 10 1·10
3 20h. red 20 1·10
4 25h. green 10 1·10
5 30h. purple 10 1·10
6 **59** 40h. blue 2·50 4·50
7 **77** 50h. green 25 1·10
8 **60a** 60h. violet 2·50 4·50
9 **61** 1k. purple (No. 348) 90 1·50
10 1k. purple (No. 395) 30 1·10
11 – 1k.20 purple (No. 354) 3·50 4·50
12 **64** 1k.50 red 3·50 4·50
13 – 1k.60 green (No. 355a) 2·50 4·50
14 – 2k. green (No. 356) 1·25 2·00
15 – 2k.50 blue (No. 357) 3·25 4·50
16 – 3k. brown (No. 358) 3·25 4·50
17 **65** 4k. violet 3·50 6·00
18 – 5k. green (No. 361) 3·50 9·00
19 – 10k. blue (No. 362) 4·25 13·50

2 Linden Leaves and Buds

3 Karluv Tyn Castle

5 Zlin

1939.
20 **2** 5h. blue 10 10
21 10h. brown 10 10
22 20h. red 10 10
23 25h. green 10 10
24 30h. purple 10 10
25 – 40h. blue 10 10
26 **3** 50h. green 10 10
27 – 60h. violet 10 10
28 – 1k. red 10 10
29 – 1k.20 purple 10 40
30 – 1k.50 red 10 10
31 – 2k. green 10 10
32 – 2k.50 blue 10 10
33 **5** 3k. mauve 10 10
34 – 4k. grey 10 10
35 – 5k. green 10 55
36 – 10k. blue 10 85
37 – 20k. brown 30 1·40

DESIGNS—As Type **3**: 40h. Svikov Castle; 60h. St. Barbara's Church, Kutna Hora; 1k. St. Vitus's Cathedral, Prague. As Type **5**—VERT: 1k.20, 1k.50, Brno Cathedral; 2k., 2k.50, Olomouc. HORIZ: 4k. Ironworks, Moravska-Ostrava; 5k., 10k., 20k. Karlsburg, Prague.

1940. As 1939 issue, but colours changed and new values.
38 **2** 30h. brown 10 10
39 40h. orange 10 15
40 50h. green 10 15
44 – 50h. green 10 10
41 **2** 60h. violet 10 10
42 80h. orange 10 15
45 – 80h. blue 10 20
43 **2** 1k. brown 10 10
46 – 1k.20 brown 10 25
47 – 1k.20 red 10 10
48 – 1k.50 pink 10 10
49 – 2k. green 10 10
50 – 2k. blue 10 10
51 – 2k.50 blue 10 10
52 – 3k. green 10 15
53 – 5k. green 10 10
54 – 6k. brown 10 25
55 – 8k. green 10 25
56 – 10k. blue 10 30
57 – 20k. brown 45 1·25

DESIGNS—As Type **3**: 50h. (No. 44), Neuhaus Castle; 80h. (No. 45), 3k. Pernstyn Castle; 1k.20 (No. 46), 2k.50, Brno Cathedral; 1k.20 (No. 47), St. Vitus's Cathedral, Prague; 1k.50 St. Barbara's Church, Kutna Hora; 2k. Pardubitz Castle. As Type **5**—HORIZ: 5k. Bridge at Beching; 6k. Samson Fountain, Budweis; 8k. Kremsier; 10k. Wallenstein Palace, Prague; 20k. Karlsburg, Prague.

6 Red Cross Nurse and Wounded Soldier

7 Patient in Hospital

1940. Red Cross Relief Fund.
58 **6** 60h.+40h. blue 20 1·00
59 1k.20+80h. plum 20 1·00

1941. Red Cross Relief Fund.
60 **7** 60h.+40h. blue 10 65
61 1k.20+80h. plum 10 75

8 Anton Dvorak

9 Harvesting

10 Blast-furnace, Pilsen

1941. Birth Centenary of Dvorak (composer).
62 **8** 60h. violet 10 70
63 1k.20 brown 25 70

1941. Prague Fair.
64 **9** 30h. brown 10 10
65 60h. green 10 10
66 **10** 1k.20 plum 10 25
67 2k.50 blue 10 30

11 "Stande- theater", Prague

12 Mozart

1941. 150th Death Anniv of Mozart.
68 **11** 30h.+30h. brown 10 25
69 60h.+60h. green 10 25
70 **12** 1k.20+1k.20 red 10 50
71 2k.50+2k.50 blue 10 70

(13)

1942. 3rd Anniv of German Occupation. Optd with T **13**.
72 1k.20 red (No. 47) 20 75
73 2k.50 blue (No. 51) 30 90

14 Adolf Hitler

15 Adolf Hitler

1942. Hitler's 53rd Birthday.
74 **14** 30h.+20h. brown 10 10
75 60h.+40h. green 10 10
76 1k.20+80h. purple 10 10
77 2k.50+1k.50 blue 10 40

1942. Various sizes.
78 **15** 10h. black 10 10
79 30h. brown 10 10
80 40h. blue 10 10
81 50h. green 10 10
82 60h. violet 10 10
83 80h. orange 10 10
84 1k. brown 10 10
85 1k.20 red 10 10
86 1k.50 red 10 10
87 1k.60 green 10 35
88 2k. blue 10 10
89 2k.40 brown 10 20
90 2k.50 blue 10 10
91 3k. olive 10 10
92 4k. purple 10 10
93 5k. green 10 10
94 6k. brown 10 10
95 8k. blue 10 10
96 10k. green 10 85
97 20k. violet 10 1·00
98 30k. red 20 1·50
99 50k. blue 25 3·00

SIZES—17½ × 21½ mm: 10h. to 80h.; 18½ × 21 mm: 1k. to 2k.40; 19 × 24 mm: 2k.50 to 8k.; 24 × 30 mm: 10k. to 50k.

16 Nurse and Patient

17 Mounted Postman

1942. Red Cross Relief Fund.
100 **16** 60h.+40h. blue 10 30
101 1k.20+80h. red 10 30

1943. Stamp Day.
102 **17** 60h. purple 10 08

18 Peter Parler

19 Adolf Hitler

1943. Winter Relief Fund.
103 – 60h.+40h. violet 10 10
104 **18** 1k.20+80h. red 10 10
105 – 2k.50+1k.50 blue 10 10

DESIGNS: 60h. Charles IV; 2k.50, King John of Luxembourg.

1943. Hitler's 54th Birthday.
106 **19** 60h.+1k.40 violet 10 20
107 1k.20+3k.80 red 10 25

20 Scene from "The Mastersingers of Nuremberg"

21 Richard Wagner

1943. 130th Birth Anniv of Wagner.
108 **20** 60h. violet 10 10
109 **21** 1k.20 red 10 10
110 – 2k.50 blue 10 10

DESIGN: 2k.50, Blacksmith scene from "Siegfried".

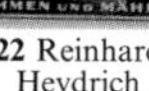
22 Reinhard Heydrich

23 Arms of Bohemia and Moravia and Red Cross

1943. 1st Death Anniv of Reinhard Heydrich (German Governor).
111 **22** 60h.+4k.40 black 10 50

1943. Red Cross Relief Fund.
112 **23** 1k.20+8k.80 blk & red 10 20

24 National Costumes

25 Arms of Bohemia and Moravia

1944. 5th Anniv of German Occupation.
113 **24** 1k.20+3k.80 red 10 10
114 **25** 4k.20+18k.80 brown 10 10
115 **24** 10k.+20k. blue 10 25

26 Adolf Hitler

27 Smetana

1944. Hitler's 55th Birthday.
116 **26** 60h.+1k.40 brown 10 10
117 1k.20+3k.80 green 10 25

1944. 600th Death Anniv of Bedrich Smetana (composer).
118 **27** 60h.+1k.40 green 10 20
119 1k.20+3k.80 red 10 25

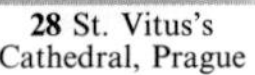
28 St. Vitus's Cathedral, Prague

29 Adolf Hitler

1944.
120 **28** 1k.50 purple 10 10
121 2k.50 violet 10 15

1944.
122 **29** 4k.20 green 10 40

NEWSPAPER STAMPS

N **6** Dove

N **19** Dove

1939. Imperf.
N38 N **6** 2h. brown 10 25
N39 5h. blue 10 25
N40 7h. red 10 25
N41 9h. green 10 25
N42 10h. red 10 25
N43 12h. blue 10 25
N44 20h. green 10 25
N45 50h. brown 10 40
N46 1k. green 10 65

1940. For bulk postings. No. N42 optd **GD-OT**.
N60 N **6** 10h. red 20 60

1943. Imperf.
N106 N **19** 2h. brown 10 10
N107 5h. blue 10 10
N108 7h. red 10 10
N109 9h. green 10 10
N110 10h. red 10 10
N111 12h. blue 10 10
N112 20h. green 10 10
N113 50h. brown 10 10
N114 1k. green 10 20

OFFICIAL STAMPS

O **7** Numeral and Laurel Wreath

O **19** Eagle and Numeral

1941.
O60 O **7** 30h. brown 10 10
O61 40h. blue 10 10
O62 50h. green 10 10
O63 60h. green 10 10
O64 80h. red 40 15
O65 1k. brown 15 10
O66 1k.20 red 15 10
O67 1k.50 purple 30 25
O68 2k. blue 30 10
O69 3k. green 30 10
O70 4k. purple 40 65
O71 5k. yellow . . . . 98 1·00

1943.
O106 O **19** 30h. brown 10 20
O107 40h. blue 10 20
O108 50h. green 10 20
O109 60h. violet 10 20
O110 80h. red 10 20
O111 1k. brown 10 20
O112 1k.20 red 10 10
O113 1k.50 brown 10 25
O114 2k. blue 10 25
O115 3k. green 10 25
O116 4k. purple 10 25
O117 5k. green 10 45

PERSONAL DELIVERY STAMPS

P **6**

1939.
P38 P **6** 50h. blue . . . . 40 1·10
P39 50h. red . . . . 65 1·25

POSTAGE DUE STAMPS

D **6**

1939.
D38 D **6** 5h. red 10 10
D39 10h. red 10 10
D40 20h. red 10 10
D41 30h. red 10 10
D42 40h. red 10 10
D43 50h. red 10 10
D44 60h. red 10 10
D45 80h. red 10 10
D46 1k. blue 10 25
D47 1k.20 blue 15 25
D48 2k. blue 40 85
D49 5k. blue 55 95
D50 10k. blue . . . . 70 1·40
D51 20k. blue . . . . 2·00 3·75

BOLIVAR Pt. 20

One of the states of the Granadine Confederation. A department of Colombia from 1886, now uses Colombian stamps.

1863. 100 centavos = 1 peso.

1

2

3

1863. Imperf.
1 **1** 10c. green £350 £275
2 10c. red . . . . 20·00 20·00
3 1p. red . . . . 10·00 10·00

1872. Various frames. Imperf.
4 **2** 5c. blue . . . . 5·00 5·50
5 **3** 10c. mauve . . . . 7·00 7·50
6 – 20c. green . . . . 15·00 16·00
7 – 80c. red . . . . 38·00 30·00

6 7 8

1874. Imperf.
8 **6** 5c. blue . . . . 12·00 7·50
9 **7** 5c. blue . . . . 6·00 5·00
10 **8** 10c. mauve . . . . 2·00 2·00

9 Simon Bolivar

10 Simon Bolivar

1879. Various frames. Dated "1879". White or blue paper. Perf.
14 **9** 5c. blue 20 20
12 10c. mauve 20 20
13 20c. red 25 20

1880. Various frames. Dated "1880". White or blue paper.
19 **9** 5c. blue 15 15
20 10c. mauve 25 25
21 20c. red 25 25
22 80c. green . . . . 2·00 2·00
23 1p. orange . . . . 2·75 2·75

1882.
30 **10** 5p. red and blue . . . . . 1·00 1·00
31 10p. blue and purple . . . . 1·00 1·00

11 Simon Bolivar

12 Simon Bolivar

1882. Various frames. Dated "1882".
32 **11** 5c. blue 20 20
33 10c. mauve 20 20
34 20c. red 25 35
35 80c. green 55 55
36 1p. orange 65 60

1883. Various frames. Dated "1883".
37 **11** 5c. blue 15 15
38 10c. mauve 20 20
39 20c. red 20 20
40 80c. green 45 55
41 1p. orange 55 80

1884. Various frames. Dated "1884".
42 **11** 5c. blue 40 40
43 10c. mauve 15 15
44 20c. red 15 15
45 80c. green 20 25
46 1p. orange 45 55

1885. Various frames. Dated "1885".
47 **11** 5c. blue 10 10
48 10c. mauve 10 10
49 20c. red 10 10
50 80c. green 20 25
51 1p. orange 55 35

1891.
56 **12** 1c. black 15 20
57 5c. orange 35 25
58 10c. red 55 55
59 20c. blue 65 65
60 50c. green 95 95
61 1p. violet 95 95

13 Simon Bolivar

1903. Various sizes and portraits. Imperf or perf. On paper of various colours.
63 **13** 50c. green 45 45
64 50c. blue 30 30
65 50c. violet . . . . 90 1·00
67 – 1p. red 50 50
68 – 1p. green 70 70
69 – 5p. red 35 35
70b – 10p. blue 50 50
71 – 10p. violet . . . . 2·50 2·50
PORTRAITS: 1p. Fernandez Madrid. 5p. Rodriguez Torices. 10p. Garcia de Toledo.

20 J. M. del Castillo 23

1904. Various portraits. Imperf or perf.
77 **20** 5c. black 15 15
78 – 10c. brown (M. Anguiano) . . 15 15
80 – 20c. red (P.G. Ribon) . . . 40 40

1904. Figures in various frames. Imperf.
81 **23** ½c. black 30 25
82 1c. blue (horiz) 50 50
83 2c. violet 75 70

ACKNOWLEDGMENT OF RECEIPT STAMPS

AR 19

AR 27

1903. Imperf. On paper of various colours.
AR75 AR **19** 20c. orange 60 60
AR76 20c. blue 50 50

1904. Imperf.
AR85 AR **27** 2c. red . . . . . . 1·00 1·00

LATE FEE STAMPS

L 18

1903. Imperf. On paper of various colours.
L73 L **18** 20c. red 30 30
L74 20c. violet 30 30

REGISTRATION STAMPS

1879. As T **9** but additionally inscr "CERTIFICADA".
R17 **9** 40c. brown 60 60

1880. As previous issue dated "1880".
R28 **9** 40c. brown 30 35

1882. As T **11**, but additionally inscr "CERTIFICADA". Dated as shown.
R52 **11** 40c. brown ("1882") . . . 25 40
R53 40c. brown ("1883") . . . 40 40
R54 40c. brown ("1884") . . . 15 15
R55 40c. brown ("1885") . . . 35 40

R 17

1903. Imperf. On paper of various colours.
R72 R **17** 20c. orange 50 50

R 26

1904. Imperf.
R84 R **26** 5c. black . . . . 2·00 2·00

BOLIVIA Pt. 20

A republic of Central South America.

1867. 100 centavos = 1 boliviano.
1963. 100 centavos = 1 peso boliviano ($b).
1987. 100 centavos = 1 boliviano.

1 Condor

4 (9 Stars)

1867. Imperf.
3a **1** 5c. green . . . . 2·40 3·00
10 5c. mauve . . . . £120 90·00
7 10c. brown . . . . £140 90·00
8 50c. yellow . . . . 12·50 19·00
11 50c. blue £200 £160
9 100c. blue . . . . 38·00 48·00
12 100c. green . . . . 90·00 85·00

1868. Nine stars below Arms. Perf.
32 **4** 5c. green . . . . 11·00 5·50
33 10c. red . . . . 16·00 5·50
34 50c. blue . . . . 28·00 16·00
35 100c. orange . . . . 28·00 17·00
36 500c. black £300 £225

1871. Eleven stars below Arms. Perf.
37 **4** 5c. green . . . . 6·25 4·00
38 10c. red . . . . 8·75 6·25
39 50c. blue . . . . 23·00 11·00
40 100c. orange . . . . 22·00 11·00
41 500c. black £1100 £1100

7

11

1878. Perf.
42 **7** 5c. blue . . . . 5·75 2·50
43 10c. orange . . . . 4·75 1·90
44 20c. green . . . . 14·00 2·40
45 50c. red . . . . 70·00 7·50

1887. Eleven stars below Arms. Roul.
46 **4** 1c. red . . . . 1·50 1·40
47 2c. violet . . . . 1·50 1·40
48 5c. blue . . . . 4·50 2·00
49 10c. orange . . . . 4·50 2·00

1890. Nine stars below Arms. Perf.
50 **4** 1c. red 90 50
58 2c. violet . . . . 2·75 1·40
52 5c. blue . . . . 2·50 50
53 10c. orange . . . . 4·00 60
54 20c. green . . . . 8·00 1·00
55 50c. red . . . . 4·00 1·00
56 100c. yellow . . . . 8·00 2·00

1893. Eleven stars below Arms. Perf.
59 **4** 5c. blue . . . . 3·75 1·40

1894.
63 **11** 1c. bistre 60 60
64 2c. red 60 60

65		5c. green	60	60
66		10c. brown	60	40
67		20c. blue	2·00	85
68		50c. red	4·75	1·25
69		100c. red	11·00	4·00

12 Frias **13**

1897.

77	**12**	1c. green	70	50
78	–	2c. red (Linares)	1·00	90
79	–	5c. green (Murillo)	1·40	40
80	–	10c. purple (Monteagudo)	1·60	40
81	–	20c. black and red (J. Ballivian)	3·00	70
82	–	50c. orange (Sucre)	3·00	1·40
83	–	1b. blue (Bolivar)	3·00	3·50
84	**13**	2b. multicoloured	23·00	30·00

18 Sucre **19** A. Ballivian **24**

1899.

92	**18**	1c. blue	1·40	40
93		2c. red	1·00	25
94		5c. green	3·75	85
95		5c. red	1·00	50
96		10c. orange	1·40	70
97		20c. red	1·75	30
98		50c. brown	3·75	1·40
99		1b. lilac	1·00	1·00

1901.

100	**19**	1c. red	35	15
101	–	2c. green (Camacho)	40	25
102	–	5c. red (Campero)	40	25
103	–	10c. blue (J. Ballivian)	1·00	15
104	–	20c. black and purple (Santa Cruz)	45	15
105	**24**	2b. brown	2·40	1·75

25 **26** Murillo

1909. Issued in La Paz. Centenary of Revolution of July, 1809. Centres in black.

110	**25**	5c. blue	5·50	3·00
111	**26**	10c. green	5·50	3·00
112	–	20c. orange (Lanza)	5·50	3·00
113	–	2b. red (Montes)	5·50	3·00

37 P. D. Murillo **F 8** Figure of Justice

1909. Centenary of Beginning of War of Independence, 1809–25.

115	–	1c. black and brown	25	15
116	–	2c. black and green	35	25
117	**37**	5c. black and red	35	10
118	–	10c. black and blue	35	10
119	–	20c. black and violet	40	25
120	–	50c. black and bistre	60	35
121	–	1b. black and brown	60	50
122	–	2b. black and brown	1·00	70

PORTRAITS: 1c. M. Betanzos. 2c. I. Warnes. 10c. B. Monteagudo. 20c. E. Arze. 50c. A. J. Sucre. 1b. S. Bolivar. 2b. M. Belgrano.

1910. Centenary of Liberation of Santa Cruz, Potosi and Cochabamba. Portraits as T **37**.

123		5c. black and green	25	10
124		10c. black and red	25	10
125		20c. black and blue	55	35

PORTRAITS: 5c. I. Warnes. 10c. M. Betanzos. 20c. E. Arze.

1911. Nos. 101 and 104 surch **5 Centavos 1911**.

127		5c. on 2c. green	40	20
128		5c. on 20c. black & purple	10·00	10·00

1912. Stamps similar to Type F **8** optd **CORREOS 1912**, or surch also.

130	F **8**	2c. green	40	25
131		5c. orange	35	35
132		10c. red	85	50
129		10c. on 1c. blue	35	15

1913. Portraits as 1901 and new types.

133	**19**	1c. pink	35	25
134	–	2c. red	35	20
135	–	5c. green	40	10
136	–	8c. yellow (Frias)	70	30
137	–	10c. grey	70	25
139	–	50c. purple (Sucre)	95	35
140	–	1b. blue (Bolivar)	1·40	85
141	**24**	2b. black	2·75	1·75

46 Monolith **47** Mt. Potosi

1916. Various sizes.

142	**46**	½c. brown	20	20
143	**47**	1c. green	25	15
144	–	2c. black and red	30	15
145	–	5c. blue	50	10
147	–	10c. blue and orange	85	10

DESIGNS—HORIZ: 2c. Lake Titicaca; 5c. Mt. Illimani; 10c. Parliament Building, La Paz.

51 **54** Morane Saulnier Type P Airplane

1919.

158a	**51**	1c. lake	15	10
158b		2c. violet	25	15
151		5c. green	35	10
152		10c. red	35	10
179		15c. blue	50	15
180		20c. blue	35	15
154		22c. blue	50	45
155		24c. violet	35	25
162		50c. orange	1·75	35
163		1b. brown	40	15
164		2b. brown	25	15

See also Nos. 194/206.

1923. Surch **Habilitada** and value.

165	**51**	5c. on 1c. lake	35	25
169		15c. on 10c. red	40	35
168		15c. on 22c. blue	40	35

1924. Air. Establishment of National Aviation School.

170	**54**	10c. black and red	30	25
171		15c. black and lake	1·10	70
172		25c. black and blue	55	35
173		50c. black and orange	1·10	70
174	–	1b. black and brown	1·10	1·00
175	–	2b. black and brown	2·25	2·00
176	–	5b. black and violet	3·50	3·25

Nos. 174/6 have a different view.

57 Andean Condor

1925. Centenary of Independence.

184	–	5c. red on green	50	25
185	–	10c. red on yellow	85	45
186	–	15c. red	35	10
187	**57**	25c. blue	2·00	50
188	–	50c. purple	35	10
189	–	1b. red	85	85
190	–	2b. yellow	1·25	1·25
191	–	5b. brown	1·40	1·40

DESIGNS—VERT: 5c. Torch of Freedom; 10c. Kantuta (national flower); 15c. Pres. B. Saavedra; 50c. Head of Liberty; 1b. Mounted archer; 5b. Marshal Sucre. HORIZ: 2b. Hermes.

1927. Surch **1927** and value.

192	**51**	5c. on 1c. lake	1·40	50
193		10c. on 24c. violet	1·40	85

1928.

194	**51**	2c. yellow	35	25
195		3c. pink	40	35
196		4c. red	40	35
197		20c. olive	60	25
198		25c. blue	60	35
199		30c. violet	60	50
200		40c. orange	1·00	85
201		50c. brown	1·00	50
202		1b. red	1·25	85
203		2b. purple	1·75	1·75
204		3b. green	1·75	1·60
205		4b. lake	2·75	2·40
206		5b. brown	3·25	2·75

1928. Optd **Octubre 1927** and star.

207	**51**	5c. green	25	15
208		10c. grey	35	15
209		15c. red	50	35

1928. Surch **15 cts. 1928**.

211	**51**	15c. on 20c. blue	5·50	5·50
213		15c. on 24c. violet	95	50
216		15c. on 50c. orange	70	40

66 "L.A.B." (Lloyd Aereo Boliviano) **68** Andean Condor

1928. Air.

217	**66**	15c. green	55	55
218		20c. blue	20	10
219		35c. red	35	35

1928.

221	**68**	5c. green	2·25	30
222	–	10c. blue	35	10
223	–	15c. red	35	10

DESIGNS: 10c. Pres. Siles; 15c. Map of Bolivia.

1930. Stamps of 1913 and 1916 surch **R. S. 21-4 1930** and value.

224	–	0.01c. on 2c. (No. 134)	70	70
225	–	0.03c. on 2c. (No. 144)	85	70
226	**46**	25c. on ½c. brown	70	50
227	–	25c. on 2c. (No. 144)	70	50

1930. Air. Optd **CORREO AEREO R. S. 6-V-1930** or surch **5 Cts**. also.

228	**54**	5c. on 10c. black & red	8·00	10·00
229		10c. black and red	8·00	10·00
231		15c. black and lake	8·00	10·00
232		25c. black and blue	8·00	10·00
233		50c. black and orange	8·00	10·00
235		1b. black and brown	£100	£100

1930. "Graf Zeppelin" Air stamps. Stamps of 1928 surch **Z 1930** and value.

241	**66**	1b.50 on 15c. green	20·00	27·00
242		3b. on 20c. blue	20·00	27·00
243		6b. on 35c. red	35·00	45·00

75 Junkers F-13 over Bullock Cart **77** Pres. Siles

78 Map of Bolivia **79** Marshal Sucre

1930. Air.

244	**75**	5c. violet	1·60	65
245	–	15c. red	1·60	65
246	–	20c. yellow	65	40
247	**75**	35c. green	65	15
248	–	50c. blue	65	15
249	**75**	1b. brown	65	20
250	–	2b. red	65	30
251	**75**	3b. grey	3·75	1·60

DESIGN: 15, 20, 50c., 2b. Junkers F-13 seaplane over river boat.

1930.

252	**77**	1c. brown	25	25
253	–	2c. green (Potosi)	85	35
254	–	5c. blue (Illimani)	85	15
255	–	10c. red (E. Abaroa)	85	15
256	**78**	15c. violet	70	15
257		35c. red	1·40	70
258		45c. orange	1·40	70
259	**79**	50c. slate	70	50
260	–	1b. brown (Bolivar)	35	35

80 Symbols of Revolution

1931. 1st Anniv of Revolution.

263	**80**	15c. red	1·40	35
264		50c. lilac	45	50

81

1932. Air.

265	**81**	5c. blue	45	50
266		10c. grey	50	25
267		15c. red	45	35
268		25c. orange	45	35
269		30c. green	40	35
270		50c. purple	40	35
271		1b. brown	40	35

1933. Surch **Habilitada D. S. 13-7-1933** and value.

273	**51**	5c. on 1b. red	40	20
274	**78**	15c. on 35c. red	20	20
275		15c. on 45c. orange	20	20
276	**51**	15c. on 50c. brown	85	15
277		25c. on 40c. orange	40	15

83 **84** M. Baptista

1933.

278	**83**	2c. green	25	15
279		5c. blue	15	10
280		10c. red	40	25
281		15c. violet	25	15
282		25c. blue	60	40

1935. Ex-President Baptista Commemoration.

283	**84**	15c. violet	50	20

85 Map of Bolivia **86** Fokker Super Universal

1935.

284	**85**	2c. blue	25	15
285		3c. yellow	25	15
286		5c. green	25	15
287		5c. red	25	15
288		10c. brown	25	15
289		15c. blue	25	15
290		15c. red	25	15
291		20c. green	25	15
292		25c. blue	35	15
293		30c. red	35	25
294		40c. orange	60	20
295		50c. violet	60	15
296		1b. yellow	60	40
297		2b. brown	60	40

1935. Air.

298	**86**	5c. brown	15	15
299		10c. green	15	15
300		20c. violet	15	15
301		30c. blue	15	15
302		50c. orange	35	15
303		1b. brown	35	30
304		1½b. yellow	1·00	15
305		2b. red	1·00	45
306		5b. green	1·25	45
307		10b. brown	2·10	85

1937. Surch **Comunicaciones D.S. 25-2-37** and value in figures.

308	**83**	5c. on 2c. green	20	20
310		15c. on 25c. blue	25	25
311		30c. on 25c. blue	40	40
312	**51**	45c. on 1b. brown	50	50
313		1b. on 2b. purple	60	60
314	**83**	2b. on 25c. blue	60	60
315	**80**	3b. on 50c. lilac	85	85
316		5b. on 50c. lilac	70	70

1937. Air. Surch **Correo Aereo D. S. 25-2-37** and value in figures.

321	**75**	5c. on 35c. green	35	35
322	**66**	20c. on 35c. red	40	25
323		50c. on 35c. red	75	40
324		1b. on 35c. red	90	50
325	**54**	2b. on 50c. black & orge	1·75	70
317	–	3b. on 50c. pur (No. 188)	90	35
318	–	4b. on 1b. red (No. 189)	75	70
319	**57**	5b. on 2b. orange	95	85
320		10b. on 5b. sepia (No. 191)	2·40	1·75
326	**54**	12b. on 10c. black & red	6·00	3·50
327		15b. on 10c. black & red	6·00	2·25

89 Native School **92** Junkers Ju52/3m over Cornfield

1938.

328 **89** 2c. red (postage) 10 10
329 – 10c. orange 15 10
330 – 15c. green 25 25
331 – 30c. yellow 40 35
332 – 45c. red 5·25 2·75
333 – 60c. violet 50 35
334 – 75c. blue 70 35
335 – 1b. brown 1·00 35
336 – 2b. buff 95 35

DESIGNS—VERT: 10c. Oil Wells; 15c. Industrial buildings; 30c. Pincers and torch; 75c. Indian and condor. HORIZ: 45c. Sucre-Camiri railway map; 60c. Natives and book; 1b. Machinery; 2b. Agriculture.

337 – 20c. red (air) 25 20
338 – 30c. grey 25 20
339 – 40c. yellow 25 20
340 **92** 50c. green 35 20
341 – 60c. blue 35 20
342 – 1b. red 50 50
343 – 2b. buff 1·25 20
344 – 3b. brown 90 20
345 – 5b. violet 6·00 1·25

DESIGNS—VERT: 20c. Mint, Potosi; 30c. Miner; 40c. Symbolical of women's suffrage; 1b. Pincers, torch and slogan; 3b. New Government emblem; 5b. Junkers aircraft over map of Bolivia. HORIZ: 60c. Airplane and monument; 2b. Airplane over river.

102 Llamas

103 Arms

1939.

346 **102** 2c. green 70 50
347 4c. brown 70 50
348 5c. mauve 70 35
349 – 10c. black 70 50
350 – 15c. green 70 55
351 – 20c. green 70 35
352 **103** 25c. yellow 60 25
353 – 30c. blue 60 35
354 – 40c. red 2·75 60
355 – 45c. black 2·50 60
356 – 60c. red 1·40 70
357 – 75c. slate 1·40 70
358 – 90c. orange 4·25 75
359 – 1b. blue 4·25 75
360 – 2b. red 5·50 75
361 – 3b. violet 6·50 1·00
362 – 4b. brown 4·00 1·40
363 – 5b. purple 5·00 1·60

DESIGNS—HORIZ: 10, 15, 20c. Vicuna; 60, 75c. Mountain viscacha; 90c., 1b. Toco toucan; 2, 3b. Andean condor; 4, 5b. Jaguar. VERT: 40, 45c. Cocoi herons.

107 Virgin of Copacabana

111 Workman

1939. Air. 2nd National Eucharistic Congress. Inscr "II° CONGRESO EUCARISTICO NACIONAL".

364 – 5c. violet 25 35
365 **107** 30c. green 20 20
366 – 45c. blue 60 20
367 – 60c. red 60 40
368 – 75c. red 45 40
369 – 90c. blue 30 25
370 – 2b. brown 50 25
371 – 4b. mauve 70 40
372 **107** 5b. blue 1·75 25
373 – 10b. yellow 3·50 25

DESIGNS—TRIANGULAR: 5c., 10b. Allegory of the Light of Religion. VERT: 45c., 4b. The "Sacred Heart of Jesus"; 75c., 90c. S. Anthony of Padua. HORIZ: 60c., 2b. Facade of St. Francis's Church, La Paz.

1939. Obligatory Tax. Workers' Home Building Fund.

374 **111** 5c. violet 35 10

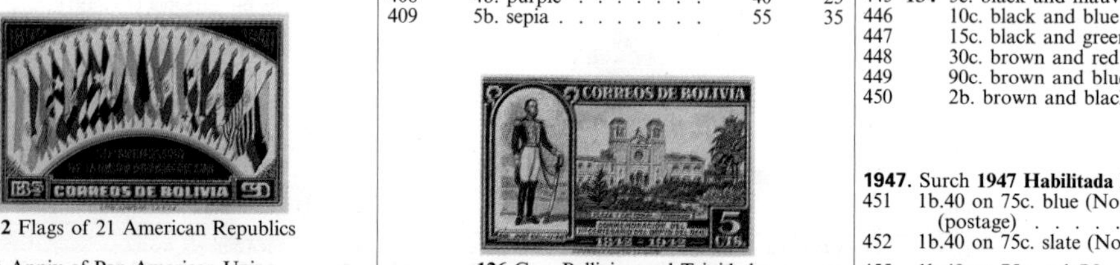

112 Flags of 21 American Republics

1940. 50th Anniv of Pan-American Union.

375 **112** 9b. red, blue & yellow 70 70

114 Urns of Murillo and Sagarnaga

117 Shadow of Aeroplane on Lake Titicaca

1941. 130th Death Anniv of P. D. Murillo (patriot).

376 – 10c. purple 10 10
377 **114** 15c. green 15 10
378 – 45c. red 15 15
379 – 1b.05 blue 35 15

DESIGNS—VERT: 10c. Murillo statue; 1b.05 Murillo portrait. HORIZ: 45c. "Murillo dreaming in Prison".

1941. Air.

380 **117** 10b. green 4·00 50
381 20b. blue 4·50 85
382 – 50b. mauve 9·25 1·75
383 – 100b. brown 18·00 6·00

DESIGN: 50, 100b. Andean condor over Mt. Illimani.

119 1867 and 1941 Issues

120 "Union is Strength"

1942. 1st Students' Philatelic Exn, La Paz.

384 **119** 5c. mauve 65 55
385 10c. orange 65 55
386 20c. green 1·10 60
387 40c. red 1·25 65
388 90c. blue 2·50 80
389 1b. violet 3·75 2·00
390 10b. brown 12·00 7·50

1942. Air. Chancellors' Meeting, Rio de Janeiro.

391 **120** 40c. red 35 25
392 50c. blue 35 25
393 1b. brown 40 35
394 5b. mauve 1·40 25
395 10b. purple 1·75 1·60

121 Mt. Potosi

122 Chaquiri Dam

1943. Mining Industry.

396 **121** 15c. brown 25 15
397 – 45c. blue 25 15
398 – 1b.25 purple 1·40 85
399 – 1b.50 green 35 25
400 – 2b. brown 1·40 85
401 **122** 2b.10 blue 50 40
402 – 3b. orange 2·50 90

DESIGNS—VERT: 45c. Quechisla (at foot of Mt. Choroloque); 1b.25, Miner Drilling. HORIZ: 1b.50, Dam; 2b. Truck Convoy; 3b. Entrance to Pulacayo Mine.

125 Gen. Ballivian leading Cavalry Charge

1943. Centenary of Battle of Ingavi.

403 **125** 2c. green 10 10
404 3c. orange 10 10
405 25c. purple 15 10
406 45c. blue 25 15
407 3b. red 25 15
408 4b. purple 40 25
409 5b. sepia 55 35

126 Gen. Ballivian and Trinidad Cathedral

1943. Centenary of Founding of El Beni. Centres in brown.

410 **126** 5c. green (postage) 10 10
411 10c. purple 15 15
412 30c. red 15 15
413 45c. blue 25 25
414 2b.10 orange 35 35

415 – 10. violet (air) 10 10
416 – 20c. green 15 10
417 – 30c. red 20 15
418 – 3b. blue 25 20
419 – 5b. black 60 35

DESIGN: Nos. 415/19, Gen. Ballivian and mule convoy crossing bridge below airplane.

127 Trans. "Honour-Work-Law/All for the Country"

129 Allegory of "Flight"

1944. Revolution of 20th December, 1943.

420 **127** 20c. orange (postage) 10 10
421 20c. green 10 10
422 90c. blue 10 10
423 90c. red 10 10
424 – 1b. purple 15 10
425 – 2b.40 brown 20 15

DESIGN—VERT: 1b., 2b.40, Clasped hands and flag.

426 **129** 40c. mauve (air) 10 10
427 – 1b. violet 15 10
428 – 1b.50 green 15 10
429 – 2b.50 blue 35 15

DESIGN—HORIZ: 1b.50, 2b.50, Lockheed 10 Electra airplane and sun.

131 Posthorn and Envelope

132 Douglas DC-2 and National Airways Route Map

1944. Obligatory Tax.

430 **131** 10c. red 1·00 25
432 10c. blue 1·00 25

Smaller Posthorn and Envelope.

469 10c. red 1·60 60
470 10c. yellow 1·40 60
471 10c. green 1·40 60
472 10c. brown 1·40 60

1945. Air. Panagra Airways, 10th Anniv of First La Paz–Tacna Flight.

433 **132** 10c. red 15 10
434 50c. orange 20 10
435 90c. green 30 10
436 5b. blue 45 15
437 20b. brown 1·40 45

133 Lloyd-Aereo Boliviano Air Routes

134 L. B. Vincenti and J. I. de Sanjines, Composers of National Anthem

1945. Air. 20th Anniv of First National Air Service.

438 **133** 20c. blue, orange & vio 10 10
439 30c. blue, orange & brn 10 10
440 50c. blue, orange & grn 10 10
441 90c. blue, orange & pur 10 10
442 2b. blue and orange 15 10
443 3b. blue, orange & red 20 15
444 4b. blue, orange & bistre 40 15

1946. Centenary of National Anthem.

445 **134** 5c. black and mauve 10 10
446 10c. black and blue 10 10
447 15c. black and green 10 10
448 30c. brown and red 15 15
449 90c. brown and blue 15 15
450 2b. brown and black 40 15

1947. Surch **1947 Habilitada Bs. 1.40**.

451 1b.40 on 75c. blue (No. 334) (postage) 15 10
452 1b.40 on 75c. slate (No. 357) 15 10
455 1b.40 on 75c. red (No. 368) (air) 15 10

136 Seizure of Government Palace

137 Mt. Iillimani

1947. Popular Revolution of 21 July 1946.

456 **136** 20c. green (postage) 10 10
457 50c. purple 10 10
458 1b.40 blue 10 10
459 3b.70 orange 15 10
460 4b. violet 25 15
461 10b. olive 30 30

462 **137** 1b. red (air) 10 10
463 1b.40 green 10 10
464 2b.50 blue 15 15
465 3b. orange 25 20
466 4b. mauve 35 20

138 Arms of Bolivia and Argentina

140 Cross and Child

1947. Meeting of Presidents of Bolivia and Argentina.

467 **138** 1b.40 orange (postage) 10 10
468 2b.90 blue (air) 25 25

1948. 3rd Inter-American Catholic Education Congress.

473 – 1b.40 bl & yell (postage) 35 10
474 **140** 2b. green and orange 50 15
475 – 3b. green and blue 55 20
476 – 5b. violet and orange 60 25
477 – 5b. brown and green 75 25

478 – 2b.50 orange & yell (air) 30 35
479 **140** 3b.70 red and buff 40 35
480 – 4b. mauve and blue 40 25
481 – 4b. blue and orange 40 15
482 – 13b.60 blue and green 50 25

DESIGNS: 1b.40, 2b.50, Christ the Redeemer, Monument; 3b., 4b. (No. 480), Don Bosco; 5b. (No. 476), 4b. (No. 481), Virgin of Copacabana; 5b. (No. 477), 13b.60, Pope Pius XII.

141 Map of S. America and Bolivian Auto Club Badge

142 Posthorn, Globe and Pres. G. Pacheco

1948. Pan-American Motor Race.

483 **141** 5b. blue & pink (postage) 1·00 20
484 10b. green & cream (air) 1·10 25

1950. 75th Anniv of U.P.U.

485 **142** 1b.40 blue (postage) 10 10
486 4b.20 red 10 10

487 1b.40 brown (air) 10 10
488 2b.50 orange 10 10
489 3b.30 purple 10 10

1950. Air. Surch **XV ANIVERSARIO PANAGRA 1935–1950** and value.

490 **132** 4b. on 10c. red 10 10
491 10b. on 20b. brown 25 20

1950. No. 379 surch **Bs. 2.- Habilitada D.S.6.VII.50.**

492 2b. on 1b.05 blue 15 10

145 Apparition at Potosi

146 Douglas DC-2

1950. 400th Anniv of Apparition at El Potosi.

493 **145** 20c. violet 10 10
494 30c. orange 10 10
495 50c. purple 10 10
496 1b. red 10 10
497 2b. blue 15 10
498 6b. brown 25 10

1950. Air. 25th Anniv of Lloyd Aereo Boliviano.

499 **146** 20c. orange 15 10
500 30c. violet 15 10

501		50c. green	15	10
502		1b. yellow	15	10
503		3b. blue	15	10
504		15b. red	50	15
505		50b. brown	1·40	40

1950. Air. Surch **Triunfo de la Democracia 24 de Sept. 49 Bs. 1.40.**

506	137	1b.40 on 3b. orange	15	15

148 U.N. Emblem and Globe

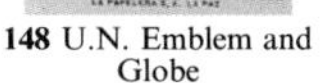

150 St. Francis Gate

149 Gate of the Sun, Tiahuanacu

1950. 5th Anniv of U.N.O.

507	148	60c. blue (postage)	70	10
508		2b. green	95	25
509		3b.60 red (air)	35	15
510		4b.70 brown	45	15

1951. 4th Centenary of Founding of La Paz. Centres in black.

511	149	20c. green (postage)	10	10
512	150	30c. orange	10	10
513	A	40c. brown	10	10
514	B	50c. red	10	10
515	C	1b. purple	10	10
516	D	1b.40 violet	15	15
517	E	2b. purple	15	15
518	F	3b. mauve	20	15
519	G	5b. red	25	15
520	H	10b. sepia	50	25
521	149	20c. red (air)	15	15
522	150	30c. violet	15	15
523	A	40c. slate	15	15
524	B	50c. green	15	15
525	C	1b. red	20	20
526	D	2b. orange	35	35
527	E	3b. blue	35	35
528	F	4b. red	40	40
529	G	5b. green	40	40
530	H	10b. brown	45	45

DESIGNS—HORIZ: As Type **149**: A, Camacho Avenue; B, Consistorial Palace; C, Legislative Palace; D, G.P.O. E, Arms; F, Pedro de la Casca authorizes plans of City; G, Founding the City; H, City Arms and Captain A. de Mendoza.

151 Tennis

1951. Sports. Centres in black.

531	–	20c. blue (postage)	15	10
532	151	50c. red	15	10
533	–	1b. purple	20	10
534	–	1b.40 yellow	20	15
535	–	2b. red	25	15
536	–	3b. brown	55	50
537	–	4b. blue	70	50
538	–	20c. violet (air)	25	10
539	–	30c. purple	35	10
540	–	50c. orange	50	10
541	–	1b. brown	50	10
542	–	2b.50 orange	70	40
543	–	3b. sepia	70	50
544	–	5b. red	1·40	1·00

DESIGNS—Postage: 20c. Boxing; 1b. Diving; 1b.40, Football; 2b. Skiing; 3b. Pelota; 4b. Cycling. Air: 20c. Horse-jumping; 30c. Basketball; 50c. Fencing; 1b. Hurdling; 2b.50, Javelin; 3b. Relay race; 5b. La Paz Stadium.

152 Andean Condor and Flag

1951. 100th National Flag Anniv. Flag in red, yellow and green.

545	152	2b. green	10	10
546		3b.50c. blue	10	10
547		5b. violet	15	15
548		7b.50c. grey	35	15
549		15b. red	40	25
550		30b. brown	85	50

153 Posthorn and Envelope

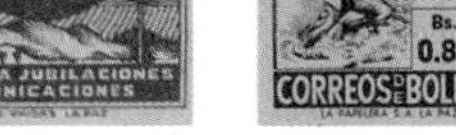
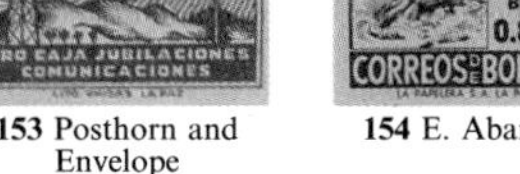

154 E. Abaroa

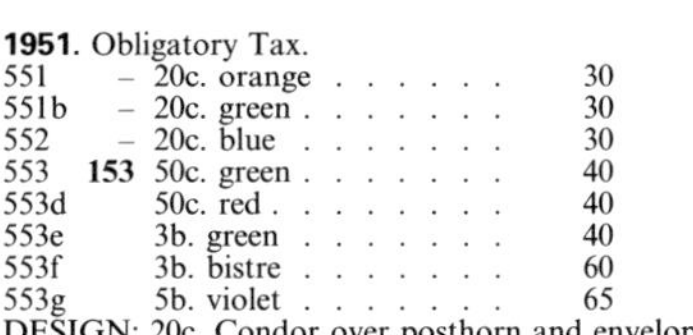

1951. Obligatory Tax.

551	–	20c. orange	30	15
551b	–	20c. green	30	15
552	–	20c. blue	30	15
553	153	50c. green	40	15
553d		50c. red	40	15
553e		3b. green	40	15
553f		3b. bistre	60	45
553g		5b. violet	65	15

DESIGN: 20c. Condor over posthorn and envelope.

1952. 73rd Death Anniv of Abaroa (patriot).

554	154	80c. red (postage)	10	10
555		1b. orange	10	10
556		2b. green	15	10
557		5b. blue	20	15
558		10b. mauve	35	15
559		20b. brown	70	40
560		70c. red (air)	10	10
561		2b. yellow	15	15
562		3b. green	15	15
563		5b. blue	15	15
564		50b. purple	70	50
565		100b. black	75	70

155 Isabella the Catholic

156 Columbus Lighthouse

1952. 500th Birth Anniv of Isabella the Catholic.

566	155	2b. blue (postage)	10	10
567		6b.30 red	25	15
568		50b. green (air)	40	25
569		100b. brown	45	35

1952. Columbus Memorial Lighthouse. On tinted papers.

570	156	2b. blue (postage)	20	15
571		5b. red	40	20
572		9b. green	65	35
573		2b. purple (air)	15	10
574		3b.70 turquoise	15	10
575		4b.40 orange	20	10
576		20b. brown	45	10

157 Miner

159 Revolutionaries

158 Villarroel, Paz Estenssoro and Siles Zuazo

1953. Nationalization of Mining Industry.

577	157	2b.50c. red	10	10
578		8b. violet	15	10

1953. 1st Anniv of Revolution of April 9th, 1952.

579	158	50c. mauve (postage)	10	10
580		1b. red	10	10
581		2b. blue	10	10
582		3b. green	10	10
583		4b. yellow	10	10
584		5b. violet	15	10
585		3b.70 brown (air)	15	15
590	159	6b. mauve	15	15
586	158	9b. red	15	15
587		10b. turquoise	15	15
588		16b. orange	15	15
591	159	22b.50 brown	25	20
589	158	40b. grey	40	15

1953. Obligatory Tax. No. 551b and similar stamp surch **50 cts.**

592		50c. on 20c. mauve	30	30
593		50c. on 20c. green	15	15

161

162 Ear of Wheat and Map

1954. Obligatory Tax.

594	161	1b. lake	25	10
595		1b. brown	25	10

1954. 1st National Agronomical Congress.

596	162	25b. blue	15	10
597		85b. brown	35	15

163 Pres. Paz Estenssoro embracing Indian

167 Derricks

166 Refinery

1954. Air. 3rd Inter-American Indigenous Congress.

598	163	20b. brown	10	10
599		100b. turquoise	25	10

1954. 1st Anniv of Agrarian Reform. As T **162**, but designs inscr "REFORMA AGRARIA".

600		5b. red (postage)	10	10
601		17b. turquoise	10	10
602		27b. mauve (air)	10	15
603		30b. orange	15	10
604		45b. purple	25	10
605		300b. green	70	25

DESIGNS—5b., 17b. Cow's head and map; 27b. to 300b. Indian peasant woman.

1955. Obligatory Tax. Nos. 553e and 553f surch **Bs. 5.—D. S. 21-IV-55.**

606	153	5b. on 3b. green	25	10
607		5b. on 3b. bistre	25	10

1955. Development of Petroleum Industry.

608	166	10b. blue (postage)	10	10
609		35b. red	10	10
610		40b. green	10	10
611		50b. purple	15	10
612		80b. brown	25	10
613	167	55b. blue (air)	10	10
614		70b. black	20	10
615		90b. green	30	10
616		500b. mauve	45	40
617		1000b. brown	85	75

168 Control Tower

169 Douglas DC-6B Aircraft

1957. Obligatory Tax. Airport Building Fund.

618	168	5b. blue	50	10
620		5b. red	50	10
619	169	10b. green	40	10
620b		20b. brown	55	25

DESIGNS: 5b. (No. 620), Douglas DC-6B over runway; 20b. Lockheed Constellation in flight.

1957. Currency revaluation. Founding of La Paz stamps of 1951 surch. Centres in black.

621	F	50b. on 3b. mauve (post)	10	10
622	E	100b. on 2b. purple	10	10
623	C	200b. on 1b. purple	15	10
624	D	300b. on 1b.40 violet	20	10
625	149	350b. on 20c. green	30	10
626	A	400b. on 40c. brown	30	10
627	150	600b. on 30c. orange	40	10
628	B	800b. on 50c. red	45	10
629	H	1000b. on 10b. sepia	45	15
630	G	2000b. on 5b. red	50	25
631	E	100b. on 3b. blue (air)	10	10
632	D	200b. on 2b. orange	10	10
633	F	500b. on 4b. red	15	10
634	C	600b. on 1b. red	15	10
635	149	700b. on 20c. red	30	15
636	A	800b. on 40c. slate	40	20
637	150	900b. on 30c. violet	45	10
638	B	1800b. on 50c. green	45	35
639	G	3000b. on 5b. green	70	30
640	H	5000b. on 10b. brown	1·10	50

172 Congress Buildings (Santiago de Chile and La Paz)

173 "Latin America" on Globe

1957. 7th Latin-America Economic Congress, La Paz.

641	172	150b. bl & grey (postage)	10	10
642		350b. grey and brown	20	10
643		550b. sepia and blue	25	10
644		750b. green and red	35	10
645		900b. brown and green	50	15
646	173	700b. violet & lilac (air)	15	10
647		1200b. brown	25	15
648		1350b. red and mauve	40	25
649		2700b. olive and turq	75	45
650		4000b. violet and blue	95	50

174 Steam Train and Presidents of Bolivia and Argentina

1957. Yacuiba-Santa Cruz Railway Inauguration.

651	174	50b. orange (postage)	55	45
652		350b. blue and light blue	1·75	60
653		1000b. brown & cinna	4·25	1·25
654		600b. purple & pink (air)	1·60	60
655		700b. violet and blue	3·00	1·25
656		900b. green	4·25	75

175 Presidents and Flags of Bolivia and Mexico

1960. Visit of Mexican President to Bolivia.

657	175	350b. olive (postage)	15	10
658		600b. brown	25	10
659		1,500b. sepia	50	15
660		400b. red (air)	25	10
661		800b. blue	45	20
662		2,000b. green	70	40

The President's visit to Bolivia did not take place.

176 Indians and Mt. Illimani

177 "Gate of the Sun", Tiahuanacu

1960. Tourist Publicity.

663	176	500b. bistre (postage)	30	10
664		1000b. blue	50	15
665		2000b. sepia	1·40	35
666		4000b. green	2·50	1·75
667	177	3000b. grey (air)	1·25	75
668		5000b. orange	1·90	75
669		10,000b. purple	3·00	1·75
670		15,000b. violet	4·25	3·00

178 Refugees

179 "Uprooted Tree"

1960. World Refugee Year.

671	178	50b. brown (postage)	10	10
672		350b. purple	15	10
673		400b. blue	15	10
674		1000b. sepia	50	15
675		3000b. green	70	70
676	179	600b. blue (air)	35	35
677		700b. brown	35	35
678		900b. turquoise	40	35
679		1800b. violet	40	35
680		2000b. black	45	40

180 Jaime Laredo (violinist) **181** Jaime Laredo (violinist)

1960. Jaime Laredo Commem.

681 **180** 100b. green (postage) . . 10 10
682 350b. lake 20 10
683 500b. blue 25 10
684 1000b. brown 35 15
685 1500b. violet 60 60
686 5000b. black . . . . . . 2·00 2·00

687 **181** 600b. plum (air) 50 25
688 700b. olive 50 35
689 800b. brown 50 35
690 900b. blue 70 35
691 1800b. turquoise . . . . 1·00 1·00
692 4000b. grey . . . . 2·00 70

182 Rotary Emblem and Nurse with Children **183**

1960. Founding of Children's Hospital by La Paz Rotary Club. Wheel in blue and yellow, foreground in yellow; background given.

693 **182** 350b. green (postage) . . 15 10
694 500b. sepia 25 10
695 600b. violet 35 10
696 1000b. grey 45 15

697 600b. brown (air) 45 25
698 1000b. olive 40 25
699 1800b. purple 70 70
700 5000b. black . . . . . . 2·00 80

1960. Air. Unissued stamp, surch as in T **183**.

701 **183** 1200b. on 10b. orange . . 2·75 1·75

184 Design from Gate of the Sun **185** Flags of Argentina and Bolivia

1960. Unissued Tiahuanacu Excavation stamps surch as in T **184**. Gold backgrounds.

702 50b. on ½c. red 30 20
703 100b. on 1c. red 35 15
704 200b. on 2c. black 50 15
705 300b. on 5c. green 25 15
706 350b. on 10c. green 25 50
707 400b. on 15c. blue 35 15
708 500b. on 20c. red 35 15
709 500b. on 50c. red 40 15
710 600b. on 22½c. green . . . 30 25
711 600b. on 60c. violet 40 35
712 700b. on 25c. violet 50 20
713 700b. on 1b. green 85 80
714 800b. on 30c. red 40 20
715 900b. on 40c. green 30 25
716 1000b. on 2b. blue 40 35
717 1800b. on 3b. grey . . . . 3·25 2·40
718 4000b. on 4b. grey . . . . 19·00 16·00
719 5000b. on 5b. grey . . . . 5·00 4·75

DESIGNS: Various gods, motifs and ornaments. SIZES: Nos. 702/6, As Type **184**. Nos. 707/17, As Type **184** but horiz. No. 718, 49 × 23 mm. No. 719, 50 × 52½ mm.

1961. Air. Visit of Pres. Frondizi of Argentina.

720 **185** 4000b. multicoloured . . 70 60
721 – 6000b. sepia and green . . 1·00 85

DESIGN: 6000b. Presidents of Argentina and Bolivia.

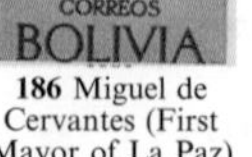
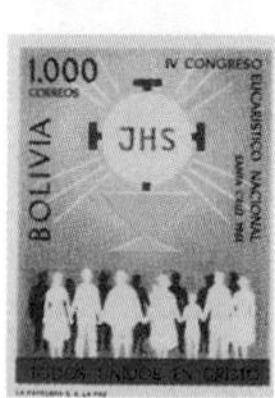

186 Miguel de Cervantes (First Mayor of La Paz) **187** "United in Christ"

1961. M. de Cervantes Commem and 4th Centenary of Santa Cruz de la Sierra (1500b.).

722 **186** 600b. violet and ochre (postage) 40 10
723 – 1500b. blue and orange 60 20
724 – 1400b. brown & green (air) 60 25

DESIGNS: 1400b. Portrait as Type **186** (diamond shape, 30½ × 30½ mm); 1500b. Nuflo de Chaves (vert: as Type **186**).

See also Nos. 755/6.

1962. 4th National Eucharistic Congress, Santa Cruz.

725 **187** 1000b. yellow, red and green (postage) 45 35
726 – 1400b. yellow, pink and brown (air) 45 35

DESIGN: 1400b. Virgin of Cotoca.

1962. Nos. 671/80 surch.

727 **178** 600b. on 50b. brown (postage) 25 15
728 900b. on 350b. purple . . 30 15
729 1000b. on 400b. blue . . 25 15
730 2000b. on 1000b. brown 25 30
731 3500b. on 3000b. green 45 45

732 **179** 1200b. on 600b. blue (air) 40 35
733 1300b. on 700b. brown 35 35
734 1400b. on 900b. green . . 40 35
735 2800b. on 1800b. violet 60 50
736 3000b. on 2000b. black 60 50

189 Hibiscus **190** Infantry

1962. Flowers in actual colours; background colours given.

737 **189** 200b. green (postage) . . 25 10
738 – 400b. brown 25 10
739 – 600b. deep blue 50 10
740 – 1000b. violet 85 20

741 – 100b. blue (air) 10 10
742 – 800b. green 40 15
743 – 1800b. violet 90 35
744 – 10,000b. deep blue . . . 4·50 2·25

FLOWERS: Nos. 738, 740 Orchids; 739, St. James' lily; 741/4, Types of Kantuta (national flowers).

1962. Armed Forces Commemoration.

745 **190** 400b. mult (postage) . . . 10 10
746 – 500b. multicoloured . . . 15 10
747 – 600b. multicoloured . . . 20 15
748 – 2000b. multicoloured . . 60 40

749 – 600b. mult (air) 35 15
750 – 1200b. multicoloured . . 45 20
751 – 2000b. multicoloured . . 65 35
752 – 5000b. multicoloured . . 1·75 85

DESIGNS: No. 746, Cavalry; 747, Artillery; 748, Engineers; 749, Parachutists and aircraft; 750, 752, "Overseas Flights" (Lockheed Super Electra airplane over oxen-cart); 751, "Aerial Survey" (Douglas DC-3 airplane photographing ground).

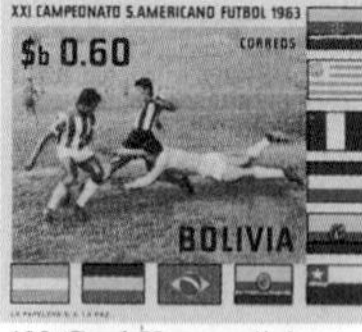

191 Campaign Emblem **192** Goal-Keeper diving to save Goal

1962. Malaria Eradication.

753 **191** 600b. yellow, violet and lilac (postage) 25 15
754 – 2000b. yellow, green and blue (air) 55 50

DESIGN: 2000b. As No. 753 but with laurel wreath and inscription encircling emblem.

1962. Spanish Discoverers. As T **186** but inscribed "1548–1962".

755 600b. mauve on blue (postage) 35 15
756 1200b. brown on yellow (air) 45 20

PORTRAITS: 600b. A. de Mendoza. 1200b. P. de la Gasca.

(Currency reform. 1000 (old) pesos = 1 (new) peso)

1963. 21st South American Football Championships, La Paz. Multicoloured.

757 **192** 60c. Type **192** (postage) 40 10
758 1p. Goalkeeper saving ball (vert) 60 15
759 1p.40 Andean condor on football (vert) (air) . . 2·40 1·50
760 1p.80 Ball in corner of net (vert) 70 70

193 Globe and Emblem **194** Alliance Emblem

1963. Freedom from Hunger.

761 **193** 60c. yellow, blue and indigo (postage) 25 10
762 – 1p.20 yellow, blue and myrtle (air) 50 50

DESIGN: 1p.20, Ear of wheat across Globe.

1963. Air. "Alliance for Progress".

763 **194** 1p.20 green, blue & bis 55 35

195 Oil Derrick

1963. 10th Anniv of Revolution (1962).

764 **195** 10c. grn & brn (postage) 10 10
765 – 60c. sepia and orange . . 30 10
766 – 1p. yellow, violet & green 35 15

767 – 1p.20 pink, brown and grey (air) 45 20
768 – 1p.40 green and ochre . . 55 25
769 – 2p.80 buff and slate . . . 70 50

DESIGNS: 60c. Map of Bolivia; 1p. Students; 1p.20, Ballot box and voters; 1p.40, Peasant breaking chain; 2p.80, Miners.

196 Flags of Argentina and Bolivia **197** Marshal Santa Cruz

1966. Death Centenary of Marshal Santa Cruz.

770 **196** 10c. mult (postage) . . . 10 10
771 60c. multicoloured 20 10
772 1p. multicoloured 35 15
773 2p. multicoloured 50 20

774 **197** 20c. blue (air) 10 10
775 60c. green 20 10
776 1p.20 brown 50 35
777 2p.80 black 65 40

198 Generals Barrientos and Ovando, Bolivian Map and Flag **199** Needy Children

1966. Co-Presidents Commemoration.

778 **198** 60c. mult (postage) . . . 20 10
779 1p. multicoloured 30 10

780 2p.80 mult (air) 95 70
781 10p. multicoloured . . . 1·10 35

1966. Aid for Poor Children.

783 **199** 30c. brown, sepia and ochre (postage) 15 10
784 – 1p.40 black & blue (air) 70 45

DESIGN: 1p.40, Mother and needy children.

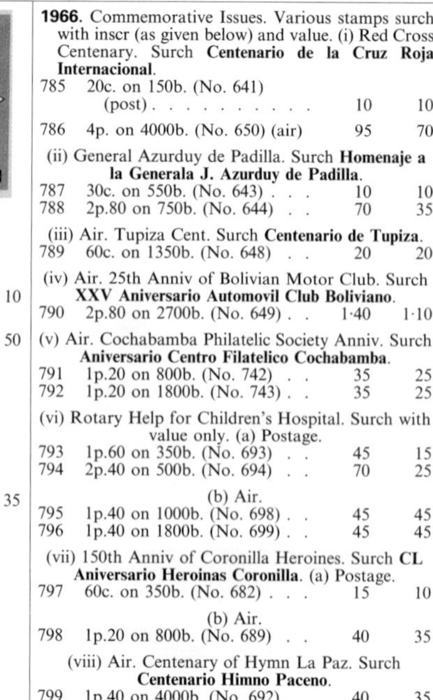

1966. Commemorative Issues. Various stamps surch with inscr (as given below) and value. (i) Red Cross Centenary. Surch **Centenario de la Cruz Roja Internacional**.

785 20c. on 150b. (No. 641) (post) 10 10
786 4p. on 4000b. (No. 650) (air) 95 70

(ii) General Azurduy de Padilla. Surch **Homenaje a la Generala J. Azurduy de Padilla**.

787 30c. on 550b. (No. 643) . . . 10 10
788 2p.80 on 750b. (No. 644) . . 70 35

(iii) Air. Tupiza Cent. Surch **Centenario de Tupiza**.

789 60c. on 1350b. (No. 648) . . 20 20

(iv) Air. 25th Anniv of Bolivian Motor Club. Surch **XXV Aniversario Automovil Club Boliviano**.

790 2p.80 on 2700b. (No. 649) . . 1·40 1·10

(v) Air. Cochabamba Philatelic Society Anniv. Surch **Aniversario Centro Filatelico Cochabamba**.

791 1p.20 on 800b. (No. 742) . . 35 25
792 1p.20 on 1800b. (No. 743) . . 35 25

(vi) Rotary Help for Children's Hospital. Surch with value only. (a) Postage.

793 1p.60 on 350b. (No. 693) . . 45 15
794 2p.40 on 500b. (No. 694) . . 70 25

(b) Air.

795 1p.40 on 1000b. (No. 698) . . 45 45
796 1p.40 on 1800b. (No. 699) . . 45 45

(vii) 150th Anniv of Coronilla Heroines. Surch **CL Aniversario Heroinas Coronilla**. (a) Postage.

797 60c. on 350b. (No. 682) . . . 15 10

(b) Air.

798 1p.20 on 800b. (No. 689) . . 40 35

(viii) Air. Centenary of Hymn La Paz. Surch **Centenario Himno Paceno**.

799 1p.40 on 4000b. (No. 692) . . 40 35

(ix) Air. 12th Anniv of Agrarian Reform. Surch **XII Aniversario Reforma Agraria**.

800 10c. on 27b. (No. 602) . . . 15 15

(x) Air. 25th Anniv of Chaco Peace Settlement. Surch **XXV Aniversario Paz del Chaco**.

801 10c. on 55b. (No. 613) . . . 15 15

All the following are surch on Revenue stamps. The design shows a beach scene with palms, size 27 × 21½mm.

(xi) Centenary of Rurrenabaque. Surch **Centenario de Rurrenabaque**.

802 1p. on 10b. brown 30 10

(xii) 25th Anniv of Busch Government. Surch **XXV Aniversario Gobierno Busch**.

803 20c. on 5b. red 10 10

(xiii) 20th Anniv of Villarroel Government. Surch **XX Aniversario Gob. Villarroel**.

804 60c. on 2b. green 15 10

(xiv) 25th Anniv of Pando Department. Surch **XXV Aniversario Dpto. Pando**. (a) Postage.

805 1p.60 on 50c. violet 45 15

(b) Air. Surch **Aereo** also.

806 1p.20 on 1b. blue 50 40

201 Sower **202** "Macheteros"

1967. 50th Anniv of Lions International. Mult.

807 **201** 70c. Type **201** (postage) 35 10
808 2p. Lions emblem and Inca obelisks (horiz) (air) 55 45

1968. 9th Congress of the U.P.A.E. (Postal Union of the Americas and Spain). Bolivian Folklore. Designs showing costumed figures. Multicoloured.

810 **202** 30c. Type **202** (postage) 10 10
811 60c. "Chunchos" 15 10
812 1p. "Wiphala" 25 15
813 2p. "Diablada" 50 20

814 1p.20 "Pujllay" (air) . . . 25 15
815 1p.40 "Ujusiris" 35 20
816 2p. "Morenada" 50 25
817 3p. "Auki-aukis" 85 50

203 Arms of Tarija **204** President G. Villarroel

1968. 150th Anniv of Battle of the Tablada (1817).
819 **203** 20c. mult (postage) . . . 10 10
820 30c. multicoloured 10 10
821 40c. multicoloured 15 10
822 60c. multicoloured 20 10
823 – 1p. multicoloured (air) . . 35 15
824 – 1p.20 multicoloured . . . 40 15
825 – 2p. multicoloured 70 35
826 – 4p. multicoloured 70 50
DESIGNS: Nos. 823/6, Moto Mendez.

1968. 400th Anniv of Cochabamba.
827 **204** 20c. brn & orge (postage) 15 10
828 30c. brown & turquoise 15 10
829 40c. brown and purple . . 15 10
830 50c. brown and green . . 15 10
831 1p. brown and bistre . . 35 10
832 – 1p.40 black & red (air) . . 35 25
833 – 3p. black and blue . . . 35 40
834 – 4p. black and red 50 50
835 – 5p. black and green . . . 60 40
836 – 10p. black and violet . . 1·10 75
DESIGN—HORIZ: 1p.40 to 10p. Similar portrait of President.

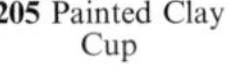

205 Painted Clay Cup **206** President J. F. Kennedy

1968. 20th Anniv of U.N.E.S.C.O. (1966).
837 **205** 20c. mult (postage) . . . 15 10
838 60c. multicoloured 40 25
839 1p.20 black & blue (air) 40 20
840 2p.80 black and green . . 45 45
DESIGNS: Nos. 839/40, U.N.E.S.C.O. emblem.

1968. 5th Death Anniv of John F. Kennedy (U.S. President).
841 **206** 10c. black & grn (postage) 15 10
842 4p. black and violet . . . 95 95
843 1p. black and green (air) 35 20
844 10p. black and red . . . 1·90 1·90

207 I.T.U. Emblem **208** Tennis Player

1968. Centenary (1965) of I.T.U.
846 **207** 10c. black grey and yellow (postage) 15 10
847 60c. black, orange & bistre 35 10
848 1p.20 black, grey and yellow (air) 30 10
849 1p.40 black, blue & brn 40 20

1968. South American Tennis Championships, La Paz.
850 **208** 10c. black, brown and grey (postage) 20 10
851 20c. black, brown & yell 20 10
852 30c. black, brown & blue 20 10
853 1p.40 black, brown and orange (air) 45 25
854 2p.80 black, brown & bl 50 50

209 Unofficial 1r. Stamp of 1863 **210** Rifle-shooting

1963. Stamp Centenary.
856 **209** 10c. brown, black and green (postage) 15 10
857 30c. brown, black & blue 15 10
858 2p. brown, black & drab 25 10
859 – 1p.40 green, black and yellow (air) 50 25
860 – 2p.80 green, blk & pink 70 50
861 – 3p. green, black & lilac 70 50
DESIGNS: Nos. 859/61 First Bolivian stamp.

1969. Olympic Games, Mexico (1968).
863 **210** 40c. black, red and orange (postage) 15 10
864 – 50c. black, red and green 15 10
865 – 60c. black, blue & green 25 10
866 – 1p.20 black, green and ochre (air) 40 15
867 – 2p.80 black, red & yell . . 85 35
868 – 5p. multicoloured . . . . 1·00 1·00
DESIGNS—HORIZ: 50c. Horse-jumping; 60c. Canoeing; 5p. Hurdling. VERT: 1p.20, Running; 2p.80, Throwing the discus.

211 F. D. Roosevelt **212** "Temensis laothoe violetta"

1969. Air. Franklin D. Roosevelt Commem.
870 **211** 5p. black, orange & brown . . . . 1·40 75

1970. Butterflies. Multicoloured.
871 5c. Type **212** (postage) . . . 35 35
872 10c. "Papilio crassus" 70 70
873 20c. "Catagramma cynosura" 70 70
874 30c. "Eunica eurota flora" . . 70 70
875 80c. "Ituna phenarete" . . . 70 70
876 1p. "Metamorpha dido wernichei" (air) 90 50
877 1p.80 "Heliconius felix" . . . 1·25 65
878 2p.80 "Morpho casica" . . . 1·75 1·75
879 3p. "Papilio yuracares" . . . 1·90 1·75
880 4p. "Heliconsus melitus" . . 2·50 2·00

213 Scout mountaineering **214** President A. Ovando and Revolutionaries

1970. Bolivian Scout Movement. Multicoloured.
882 **213** 5c. Type **213** (postage) . . 15 10
883 10c. Girl-scout planting shrub 15 10
884 50c. Scout laying bricks (air) 15 10
885 1p.20 Bolivian scout badge 35 15

1970. Obligatory Tax. Revolution and National Day.
886 **214** 20c. blk & red (postage) 25 15
887 30c. black & green (air) 25 15
DESIGN: 30c. Pres. Ovando, oil derricks and laurel sprig.

1970. "Exfilca 70" Stamp Exhibition, Caracas, Venezuela. No. 706 further surch **EXFILCA 70** and new value.
888 30c. on 350b. on 10c. . . . 15 10

1970. Provisionals. Various stamps surch.
889 **178** 60c. on 900b. on 350b. (postage) 30 10
890 – 1p.20 on 1500b. (No. 723) 50 15
891 **185** 1p.20 on 4000b. (air) . . 35 15

217 Pres. G. Busch and Oil Derrick **218** "Amaryllis escobar uriae"

1971. 32nd Death Anniv of President G. Busch and 25th Death Anniv of Pres. Villarroel.
892 **217** 20c. blk & lilac (postage) 35 10
893 – 30c. black and blue (air) 30 10
DESIGN: 30c. Pres. Villarroel and oil refinery.

1971. Bolivian Flora. Multicoloured.
894 30c. Type **218** (postage) . . . 15 10
895 40c. "Amaryllis evansae" . . 15 10
896 50c. "Amaryllis yungacensis" (vert) 20 15
897 2p. "Gymnocalycium chiquitanum" (vert) . . . 55 35
898 1p.20 "Amaryllis pseudopardina" (air) . . . 45 15
899 1p.40 "Rebutia kruegeri" (vert) 60 15
900 2p.80 "Lobivia pentlandii" 95 25
901 4p. "Rebutia tunariensis" (vert) . . . . 1·60 50

219 Sica Sica Cathedral **220** Pres. H. Banzer

1971. "Exfilima" Stamp Exhibition, Lima, Peru.
903 **219** 20c. multicoloured 15 10

1972. "Bolivia's Development".
904 **220** 1p.20 multicoloured . . . 35 15

221 Chiriwano de Achocalla Dance **222** "Virgin and Child" (B. Bitti)

1972. Folk Dances. Multicoloured.
905 20c. Type **221** (postage) . . . 10 10
906 40c. Rueda Chapaca 20 15
907 60c. Kena-Kena 30 15
908 1p. Waca Thokori 40 25
909 1p.20 Kusillo (air) 40 15
910 1p.40 Taquirari 45 15

1972. Bolivian Paintings. Multicoloured.
911 10c. "The Washerwoman" (M. P. Holguin) (postage) 10 10
912 50c. "Coronation of the Virgin" (G. M. Berrio) . . 20 10
913 70c. "Arquebusier" (anon.) 25 10
914 80c. "St. Peter of Alcantara" (M. P. Holguin) 25 15
915 1p. Type **222** 35 15
916 1p.40 "Chola Pacena" (G. de Rojas) (air) 40 10
917 1p.50 "Adoration of the Kings" (G. Gamarra) . . . 40 10
918 1p.60 "Pachamama Vision" (A. Borda) 40 10
919 2p. "Idol's Kiss" (G. de Rojas) 40 25

223 Tarija Cathedral

1972. "EXFILIBRA 72" Stamp Exhibition, Rio de Janeiro.
920 **223** 30c. multicoloured 15 10

224 National Arms

1972. Air.
921 **224** 4p. multicoloured 95 35

225 Santos Dumont and "14 bis"

1973. Air. Birth Centenary of Alberto Santos Dumont (aviation pioneer).
922 **225** 1p.40 black and yellow . . 1·25 45

226 "Echinocactus notocactus" **227** Power Station, Santa Isabel

1973. Cacti. Multicoloured.
923 20c. Type **226** (postage) . . . 10 10
924 40c. "Echinocactus lenninghaussii" 15 10
925 50c. "Mammillaria bocasana" 20 10
926 70c. "Echinocactus lenninghaussii" (different) 30 10
927 1p.20 "Mammillaria bocasana" (different) (air) 40 15
928 1p.90 "Opuntia cristata" . . 60 20
929 2p. "Echinocactus rebutia" 85 25

1973. Bolivian Development Multicoloured.
930 10c. Type **227** (postage) . . . 10 10
931 20c. Tin foundry 15 10
932 90c. Bismuth plant 40 10
933 1p. Gas plant 40 10
934 1p.40 Road bridge, Highways 1 and 4 (air) 50 15
935 2p. Inspection car crossing bridge, Al Beni . . . . . 8·00 2·50

228 "Cattleya nobilior" **229** Morane Saulnier Type P and Emblem

1974. Orchids. Multicoloured.
936 20c. Type **228** (postage) . . . 10 10
937 50c. "Zygopetalum bolivianum" 20 10
938 1p. "Huntleya melagris" . . 35 10
939 2p.50 "Cattleya luteola" (horiz) (air) 90 25
940 3p.80 "Stanhopaea" . . . . 1·00 35
941 4p. "Catasetum" (horiz) . . . 1·00 45
942 5p. "Maxillaria" . . . . . . 1·75 50

1974. Air. 50th Anniv of Bolivian Air Force. Multicoloured.
944 3p. Type **229** 75 50
945 3p.80 Douglas DC-3 crossing Andes . . . . 1·25 70
946 4p.50 Triplane trainer and Morane Saulnier Paris I aircraft . . . . 1·25 70
947 8p. Col. Rafael Pabon and biplane fighter . . . . . . 1·75 1·40
948 15p. Jet airliner on "50" . . 3·75 2·00

230 General Sucre (after J. Wallpher)

1974. 150th Anniv of Battle of Avacucho.
949 **230** 5p. multicoloured 75 55

231 U.P.U. and Exhibition Emblems

1974. Centenary of U.P.U. and Expo U.P.U. (Montevideo) and Prenfil U.P.U. (Buenos Aires) Stamp Exhibitions.
950 **231** 3p.50 green, black & bl 70 45

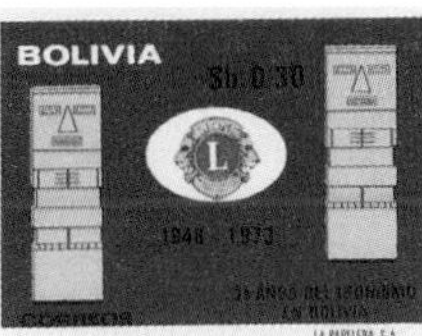

232 Lions Emblem and Steles

1975. 50th Anniv of Lions International in Bolivia.
951 **232** 30c. multicoloured 35 10

233 Exhibition Emblem

1975. "Espana 75" International Stamp Exhibition, Madrid.
952 **233** 4p.50 multicoloured . . . 55 35

234 Emblem of Meeting   235 Arms of Pando

1975. Cartagena Agreement. First Meeting of Postal Ministers, Quito, Ecuador.
953 **234** 2p.50 silver, violet & blk . . . 45 30

1975. 150th Anniv of Republic (1st issue). Provincial Arms. Multicoloured.
955 20c. Type **235** (postage) . . . 10 10
956 2p. Chuzuisaca 50 35
957 3p. Cochabamba 70 50
958 20c. Beni (air) 10 10
959 30c. Tarija 10 10
960 50c. Potosi 10 10
961 1p. Oruro . . . . 4·50 1·50
962 2p.50 Santa Cruz 50 50
963 3p. La Paz 70 50
See also Nos. 965/78.

236 Presidents Perez and Banzer   237 Pres. Victor Paz Estenssoro

1975. Air. Visit of Pres. Perez of Venezuela.
964 **236** 3p. multicoloured 75 55

1975. 150th Anniv of Republic (2nd issue).
965 30c. Type **237** (postage) . . 10 10
966 60c. Pres. Thomas Frias . . 15 10
966a 1p. Ismael Montes 20 10
967 2p.50 Aniceto Arce 50 25
968 7p. Bautista Saavedra . . . 95 35
969 10p. Jose Manuel Pando . . 1·40 50
970 15p. Jose Maria Linares . . 1·75 1·75
971 50p. Simon Bolivar . . . . 6·25 6·25
972 50c. Rene Barrientos Ortuno (air) 15 10
973 2p. Francisco B. O'Connor 50 25
973a 3p.80 Gualberto Villaroel 70 50
974 4p.20 German Busch . . . 70 70
975 4p.50 Pres. Hugo Banzer Suarez 70 70
976 20p. Jose Ballivian . . . . 2·50 1·40
977 30p. Pres. Andres de Santa Cruz . . . . 3·25 3·25
978 40p. Pres. Antonio Jose de Sucre . . . . 4·25 4·25
Nos. 965/70, 972/4 and 976/78 are smaller, 24 × 33 mm.

238 Laurel Wreath and L.A.B. Emblem   239 "EXFIVIA"

1975. Air. 50th Anniv of Lloyd-Aereo Boliviano (national airline). Multicoloured.
979 1p. Type **238** 15 10
980 1p.50 Douglas DC-9 and L.A.B. route map (horiz) 35 15
981 2p. Guillermo Kyllmann (founder) and Junkers F-13 aircraft (horiz) 45 25

1975. Obligatory Tax. As No. 893 but inscr "XXV ANIVERSARIO DE SU GOBIERNO".
982 30c. black and blue 30 10

1975. "Exfivia 75". Stamp Exhibition.
983 **239** 3p. multicoloured 70 35

240 U.P.U. Emblem

1975. Air. Centenary (1974) of U.P.U.
984 **240** 25p. multicoloured . . . 2·00 2·00

241 Chiang Kai-shek

1976. 1st Death Anniv of President Chiang Kai-shek.
985 **241** 2p.50 multicoloured . . . 60 25

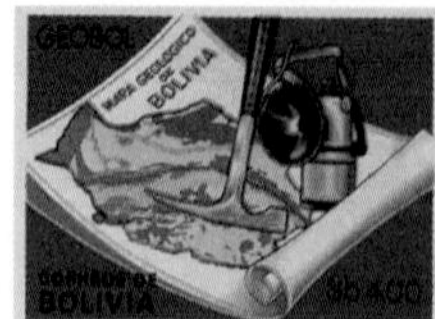

242 Geological Hammer, Lamp and Map

1976. Bolivian Geological Institute.
986 **242** 4p. multicoloured 55 55

243 Naval Insignia

1976. Navy Day.
987 **243** 50c. multicoloured 25 10

244 Douglas DC-10 and Divided Roundel

1976. 50th Anniv of Lufthansa Airline.
988 **244** 3p. multicoloured 90 35

245 Bolivian Boy Scout and Badge

1976. 60th Anniv of Bolivian Boy Scouts.
989 **245** 1p. multicoloured 50 20

246 Battle Scene   247 Brother Vicente Bernedo (missionary)

1976. Bicentenary of American Revolution.
990 **246** 4p.50 multicoloured . . . 95 45

1976. Brother Vincente Bernedo Commemoration.
992 **247** 1p.50 multicoloured . . . 35 15

248 Rainbow over La Paz, Police Handler with Dog   249 Bolivian Family

1976. 150th Anniv of Police Service.
993 **248** 2p.50 multicoloured . . . 40 25

1976. National Census.
994 **249** 2p.50 multicoloured . . . 55 35

250 Pedro Poveda (educator)

1976. Poveda Commemoration.
995 **250** 1p.50 multicoloured . . . 35 15

251 Arms, Bolivar and Sucre   252 "Numeral"

1976. International Bolivarian Societies Congress.
996 **251** 1p.50 multicoloured . . . 55 25

1976.
997 **252** 20c. brown 10 10
998 1p. blue 25 10
999 1p.50 green 40 10

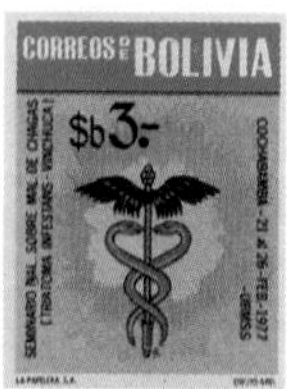
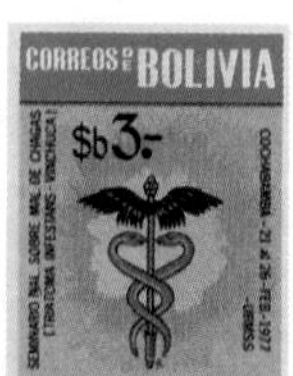

253 Boy and Girl   254 Caduceus

1977. Christmas 1976 and 50th Anniv of Inter-American Children's Institute.
1000 **253** 50c. multicoloured . . . 15 10

1977. National Seminar on "Chagas Disease".
1001 **254** 3p. multicoloured . . . 70 10

255 Court Buildings, La Paz   256 Tower and Map

1977. 150th Anniv of Bolivian Supreme Court. Multicoloured.
1002 2p.50 Type **255** 30 10
1003 4p. Dr. Manuel M. Urcullu, first President 45 10
1004 4p.50 Dr. Pantaleon Dalence, President, 1883–89 . . . . 50 10

1977. 90th Anniv of Oruro Club.
1005 **256** 3p. multicoloured . . . 50 15

257 Newspaper Mastheads   258 Games Poster

1977. Bolivian Newspapers. Multicoloured.
1006 1p.50 Type **257** 25 10
1007 2p.50 "Ultima Hora" and Alfredo Alexander (horiz) 35 10
1008 3p. "El Diaro" and Jose Carrasco (horiz) 45 15
1009 4p. "Los Tiempos" and Demetrio Canelas 50 15
1010 5p.50 "Presencia" 70 20

1977. 8th Bolivarian Games, La Paz.
1011 **258** 5p. multicoloured . . . 70 20

259 Tin Miner and Mining Corporation Emblem   260 Miners, Globe and Chemical Symbol for Tin

1977. 25th Anniv of Bolivian Mining Corporation.
1012 **259** 3p. multicoloured . . . 4·25 2·00

1977. International Tin Symposium, La Paz.
1013 **260** 6p. multicoloured . . . 55 30

261 Map of Bolivia and Radio Masts   263 "Eye", Compass, Key and Law Book

1977. 50th Anniv of Bolivian Radio.
1014 **261** 2p.50 multicoloured . . 35 10

1977. "Exfivia 77" Philatelic Exhibition, Cochabamba. No. 719 surch **EXFIVIA — 77 $b. 5.—**.
1015 5p. on 5,000b. on $b. 5 grey and gold 85 15

1978. 50th Anniv of Audit Department.
1016 **263** 5p. multicoloured . . . 45 15

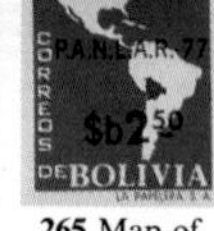

264 Aesculapius Staff and Map of Andean Countries   265 Map of the Americas   266 Mt. Illimani

1978. 5th Meeting of Andean Countries' Health Ministers.
1017 **264** 2p. orange and black . . 40 10

1978. World Rheumatism Year (1977).
1018 **265** 2p.50 blue and red . . . 35 15

1978.
1019 **266** 50c. green and blue . . . 10 10
1020 – 1p. yellow and brown . . 15 10
1021 – 1p.50 grey and red . . . 25 10
DESIGNS—HORIZ: 1p.50, Mt. Cerro de Potosi. VERT: 1p. Pre-Columbian monolith.

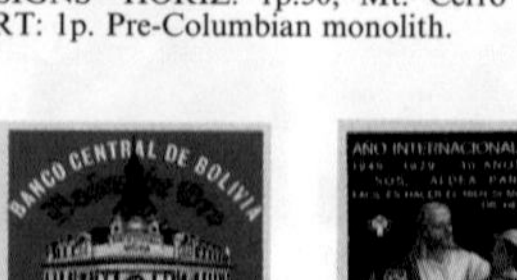

267 Central Bank   268 Jesus with Children

1978. 50th Anniv of Bank of Bolivia.
1022 **267** 7p. multicoloured . . . 70 25

1979. International Year of the Child.
1023 **268** 8p. multicoloured . . . 60 15

269 Antofagasta Cancellation

270 Antofagasta

1979. Centenary of Loss of Litoral Department to Chile.

1024	**269**	50c. brown and black	10	10
1025	–	1p. mauve and black	15	10
1026	–	1p.50 green and black	25	10
1027	**270**	5p.50 multicoloured	40	15
1028	–	6p.50 multicoloured	55	20
1029	–	7p. multicoloured	55	20
1030	–	8p. multicoloured	60	25
1031	–	10p. multicoloured	75	35

DESIGNS—HORIZ: 1p. La Chimba cancel; 1p.50, Mejillonos cancel. VERT: (As Type **270**). 6p.50, Woman in chains; 7p. Eduardo Arbaroa; 8p. Map of Department, 1876; 10p. Arms of Litoral.

271 Map and Radio Club Emblem

272 Runner and Games Emblem

1979. Radio Club of Bolivia.
1032 **271** 3p. multicoloured . . . 40 10

1979. 1st "Southern Cross" Games. Mult.
1033 6p.50 Type **272** 55 20
1034 10p. Gymnast 75 35

273 Bulgarian Stamp of 1879

274 "Exfilmar" Emblem

1979. "Philaserdica 79" Philatelic Exhibition, Sofia, Bulgaria.
1035 **273** 2p.50 black, yellow and light yellow 30 10

1979. "Exfilmar 79" Maritime Philatelic, Exhibition, La Paz.
1036 **274** 2p. blue, black and light blue 20 20

275 O.A.S. Emblem and Map

276 Franz Tamayo (lawyer)

1979. 9th Congress of Organization of American States, La Paz.
1037 **275** 6p. multicoloured . . . 50 20

1979. Anniversaries and Events.

1038	**276**	2p.80 light grey, black and grey	35	10
1039	–	5p. multicoloured	35	20
1040	–	5p. multicoloured	35	20
1041	–	6p. multicoloured	45	20
1042	–	9p.50 multicoloured	2·00	80

DESIGNS—VERT: 2p.80, Type **276** (birth centenary); 5p. (No. 1039) U.N. emblem and delegates (18th CEPAL Sessions, La Paz); 5p. (No. 1042), Gastroenterological laboratory (Japanese health co-operation); 6p. Radio mast (50th anniv of national radio). HORIZ: 9p.50, Puerto Suarez iron ore deposits.

277 500c. Stamp of 1871, Exhibition Emblem and Flag

1980. "Exfilmar" Bolivian Maritime Stamp Exhibition, La Paz.
1043 **277** 4p. multicoloured . . . 50 15

278 Juana Azurduy de Padilla

1980. Birth Bicentenary of Juana Azurduy de Padilla (Independence heroine).
1044 **278** 4p. multicoloured . . . 55 15

279 Jean Baptiste de la Salle (founder)

1980. 300th Anniv of Brothers of Christian Schools.
1045 **279** 9p. multicoloured . . . 75 30

280 "Victory in a Chariot", Emblem and Flags

1980. "Espamer 80" International Stamp Exhibition, Madrid.
1046 **280** 14p. multicoloured . . . 1·10 45

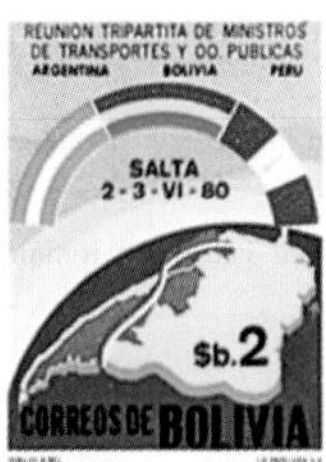
281 Flags over Map of South America

282 Diesel Locomotive

1980. Meeting of Public Works and Transport Ministers of Argentina, Bolivia and Peru.
1047 **281** 2p. multicoloured . . . 25 10

1980. Inauguration of Santa Cruz-Trinidad Railway, Third Section.
1048 **282** 3p. multicoloured . . . 90 50

283 Soldier and Citizen with Flag destroying Communism

284 Scarlet Macaw

1981. 1st Anniv of 17 July Revolution. Mult.

1049	1p. Type **283**	15	10
1050	3p. Flag shattering hammer and sickle on map	35	10
1051	40p. Flag on map of Bolivia showing provinces	3·25	85
1052	50p. Rejoicing crowd (horiz)	3·75	85

1981. Macaws. Multicoloured.

1053	4p. Type **284**	65	35
1054	7p. Green-winged macaw	1·00	50
1055	8p. Blue and yellow macaw	1·25	60
1056	9p. Red-fronted macaw	1·40	65
1057	10p. Yellow-collared macaw	1·40	65
1058	12p. Hyacinth macaw	1·90	90
1059	15p. Military macaw	1·50	1·10
1060	20p. Chestnut-fronted macaw	3·00	1·25

285 Virgin and Child receiving Flower

286 Emblem

1981. Christmas.
1061 **285** 1p. pink and red 15 10
1062 – 2p. light blue and blue 30 10
DESIGN: 2p. Child and star (horiz).
See also No. 1080.

1982. 22nd American Air Force Commanders' Conference, Buenos Aires.
1063 **286** 14p. multicoloured . . . 1·10 35

287 Cobija

288 Simon Bolivar

1982. 75th Anniv of Cobija City.
1064 **287** 28p. multicoloured . . . 30 20

1982. Birth Bicentenary of Simon Bolivar.
1065 **288** 18p. multicoloured . . . 35 25

289 Dish Antenna

290 Footballers

1982. World Communication Year.
1066 **289** 26p. multicoloured . . . 30 20

1982. World Cup Football Championship, Spain. Multicoloured.
1067 4p. Type **290** 20 10
1068 100p. "The Final Number" (Picasso) . . . . 1·25 65

291 Boy playing Football

1982. Bolivian Youth. Multicoloured.
1069 16p. Type **291** 20 20
1070 20p. Girl playing piano (horiz) 25 30

292 Harvesting

1982. China-Bolivian Agricultural Co-operation.
1071 **292** 30p. multicoloured . . . 50 20

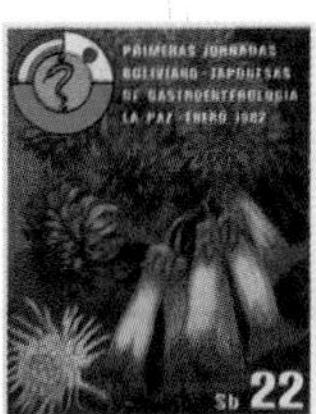
293 Flowers

1982. 1st Bolivian-Japanese Gastroenterological Days.
1072 **293** 22p. multicoloured . . . 25 20

294 Bolivian Stamps

295 Hernando Siles

1982. 10th Anniv of Bolivian Philatelic Federation.
1073 **294** 19p. multicoloured . . . 35 15

1982. Birth Centenary of Hernando Siles (former President).
1074 **295** 20p. buff and brown . . 40 20

296 Baden-Powell

297 "Liberty", Cochabamba

1982. 125th Birth Anniv of Lord Baden-Powell and 75th Anniv of Boy Scout Movement.
1075 **296** 5p. multicoloured . . . 15 10

1982. 25th Anniv of Cochabamba Philatelic Centre.
1076 **297** 3p. buff, black & blue 10 10

298 High Court, Cochabamba

299 Virgin of Copacabana

1982. 150th Anniv of High Court, Cochabamba.
1077 **298** 10p. black, red and bronze 25 10

1982. 400th Anniv of Enthronement of Virgin of Copacabana.
1078 **299** 13p. multicoloured . . . 30 15

300 Puerto Busch Naval Base

1982. Navy Day.
1079 **300** 14p. multicoloured . . . 60 20

1982. Christmas. Design as Type **285**, inscribed "NAVIDAD 1982".
1080 **285** 10p. grey and green . . 20 10

301 Footballer and Emblem

1983. 10th American Youth Football Championships.
1081 **301** 50p. multicoloured . . . 55 45

302 Sun Gate

1983. "Exfivia 83" Stamp Exhibition.
1082 **302** 150p. red 90 35

303 Presidents Figueiredo and Zuazo

1984. Visit of President of Brazil.
1083 **303** 150p. multicoloured . . 40 15

1984. Various stamps surch.
1084 **276** 40p. on 2p.80 light grey, black and grey 15 10
1085 – 60p. on 1p.50 green and black (1026) 15 10
1086 **265** 60p. on 2p.50 blue and red 15 10
1087 **274** 100p. on 2p. blue, black and light blue 30 15
1088 **174** 200p. on 350b. blue and light blue . . . . . . 2·25 90

1984. "Mladost 84" Youth Stamp Exn, Pleven, Bulgaria. No. 1035 surch.
1089 **273** 40p. on 2p.50 black, yellow and light yellow 15 10

306 "Simon Bolivar" (Mulato Gil de Quesada)

308 Pedestrian walking in Road

1984. Birth Bicentenary of Simon Bolivar. Mult.
1090 50p. Type **306** 15 10
1091 200p. "Simon Bolivar entering La Paz" (Carmen Baptista) 35 20

1984. Various stamps surch.
1092 **297** 500p. on 3p. buff, black and blue (postage) . . 45 30
1093 **290** 1000p. on 4p. mult . . . 90 65
1094 **285** 2000p. on 10p. grey and green . . . . 2·00 85
1095 **296** 5000p. on 5p. mult . . . 4·75 2·00
1096 – 10000p. on 3p.80 mult (No. 940) (air) . . . . 6·25 3·75

1984. Road Safety Campaign. Multicoloured.
1097 80p. Type **308** 10 10
1098 120p. Police motorcyclist and patrol car 10 10

309 "Mendezs Birthplace" (Jorge Campos)

310 Legs and Feet on Map and Bata Emblem

1984. Birth Bicentenary of Jose Eustaquio Mendez. Multicoloured.
1099 300p. Type **309** 15 10
1100 500p. "Battle of La Tablada" (M. Villegas) . . 20 10

1984. World Footwear Festival. Mult.
1101 100p. Type **310** 10 10
1102 200p. Legs and feet on map and Power emblem . . . 10 10
1103 600p. Football and globes (World Cup, Mexico, 1986) (horiz) 15 10

311 Inca Postal Runner

312 Vicuna

1985.
1104 **311** 11000p. blue 30 15

1985. Endangered Animals.
1105 **312** 23000p. brown and deep brown 35 15
1106 – 25000p. brown, blue and orange . . . . 1·00 20
1107 – 30000p. red and green 45 20
DESIGNS—VERT: 25000p. Andean condor; 30000p. Marsh deer.

313 National Work Education Service Emblem

314 Hand with Syringe, Victim in Droplet and Campaign Emblem

1985. International Professional Education Year.
1108 **313** 2000p. blue and red . . 10 10

1985. Anti-polio Campaign.
1109 **314** 20000p. blue and violet 30 15

315 Vicenta Juaristi Eguino

316 U.N. Emblem

1985. Birth Bicentenary of Vicenta Juaristi Eguino (Independence heroine).
1110 **315** 300000p. multicoloured 30 15

1985. 40th Anniv of U.N.O.
1111 **316** 1000000p. blue and gold 45 30

317 Emblem

318 Emblem, Envelope and Posthorn

1985. 75th Anniv of "The Strongest" Football Club.
1112 **317** 200000p. multicoloured 20 10

1986. Cent of Bolivian U.P.U. Membership.
1113 **318** 800000p. multicoloured 65 30

319 Bull and Rider

321 Football as Globes

1986. 300th Anniv of Trinidad City.
1114 **319** 1400000p. multicoloured 1·00 45

1986. No. 1108 surch.
1115 **313** 200000p. on 2000p. blue and red 15 10
1116 5000000p. on 2000p. blue and red . . . . . 3·50 1·60

1986. World Cup Football Championship, Mexico.
1117 **321** 300000p. red and black 25 10
1118 – 550000p. multicoloured 45 20
1119 – 1000000p. black and green (horiz) 80 40
1120 – 2500000p. green & yell 1·90 85
DESIGNS—VERT: 550000p. Pique (mascot); 2500000p. Trophy. HORIZ: 1000000p. Azteca Stadium, Mexico City.

322 Alfonso Subieta Viaduct

323 Envelope

1986. 25th Anniv of American Development Bank.
1121 **322** 400000p. blue 35 15

1986. 50th Anniv of Society of Postmen.
1122 **323** 2000000p. brown . . . . 1·60 70

324 Emblem and Dove

325 Emblem

1986. International Peace Year.
1123 **324** 200000p. green 15 10

1986. International Youth Year (1985).
1124 **325** 150000p. red 15 10
1125 500000p. green 45 30
1126 – 3000000p. multicoloured 2·10 1·00
DESIGNS: 3000000p. Child clutching trophy and flag (25th anniv of Enrique Happ Sports Club, Cochabamba).

326 Zampa (after F. Diaz de Ortega)

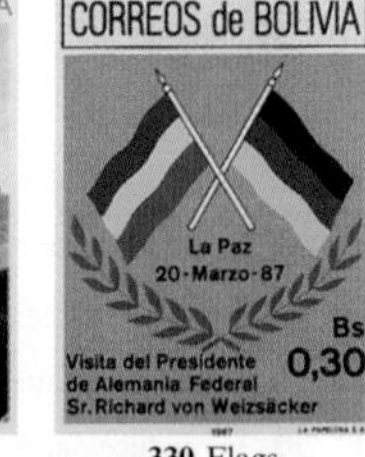

328 Refinery

327 1870 500c. Stamp

1986. 50th Death Anniv of Friar Jose Antonio Zampa.
1127 **326** 400000p. multicoloured 35 15

1986. 15th Anniv of Bolivian Philatelic Federation.
1128 **327** 600000p. brown 50 20

1986. 50th Anniv of National Petroleum Refining Corporation.
1129 **328** 1000000p. multicoloured 1·00 30

329 Demon Mask

330 Flags

1987. Centenary of 10th February Society, Oruro.
1130 **329** 20c. multicoloured . . . 10 10

1987. State Visit of President Richard von Weizsacker of German Federal Republic.
1131 **330** 30c. multicoloured . . . 15 15

331 National Arms

1987. Visit of King Juan Carlos of Spain.
1132 **331** 60c. multicoloured . . . 60 20

332 Andean ("Condor")

333 Modern View of Potosi

1987. Endangered Animals. Multicoloured.
1133 20c. Type **332** 35 25
1134 20c. Tapir 10 10
1135 30c. Vicuna (new-born) . . 15 15
1136 30c. Armadillo 15 15
1137 40c. Spectacled bear 25 20
1138 60c. Keel-billed toucans ("Tucan") . . . . 1·10 50

1987. "Exfivia 87" Stamp Exhibition, Potosi. Multicoloured.
1139 40c. Type **333** 25 20
1140 50c. 18th-century engraving of Potosi 30 25

334 "Nina" and Stern of "Santa Maria"

1987. "Espamer '87" Stamp Exhibition, La Coruna. Multicoloured.
1141 20c. Type **334** 30 15
1142 20c. "Pinta" and bow of "Santa Maria" 30 15
Nos. 1141/2 were printed together, se-tenant, forming a composite design.

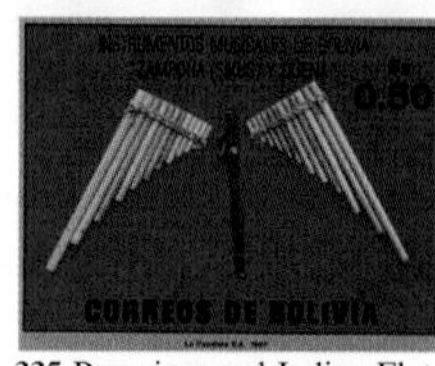
335 Pan-pipes and Indian Flute

1987. Musical Instruments. Multicoloured.
1143 50c. Type **335** 30 20
1144 1b. Indian guitars . . . . . 1·00 35

336 Carabuco Church

1988. Visit of Pope John Paul II. Mult.
1145 20c. Type **336** 10 10
1146 20c. Tihuanacu church . . . 10 10
1147 20c. Cathedral of the Kings, Beni 10 10
1148 30c. St. Joseph church, Chiquitos 15 15
1149 30c. St. Francis's church, Sucre 15 15
1150 40c. Cobija chapel (vert) . . 20 15
1151 50c. Cochabamba cathedral (vert) 25 20
1152 50c. Jayu Kcota church . . 25 20
1153 60c. St. Francis's Basilica, La Paz (vert) 30 25
1154 70c. Church of Jesus, Machaca 60 30
1155 70c. St. Lawrence's church, Potosi (vert) 60 30
1156 80c. Vallegrande church . . 70 35
1157 80c. Copacabana Virgin (vert) 70 35
1158 80c. "The Holy Family" (Peter Paul Rubens) (vert) 70 35
1159 1b.30 Concepcion church . . 1·10 55
1160 1b.30 Tarija cathedral (vert) 1·10 55
1161 1b.50 Pope and Arms of John Paul II and Bolivia 1·40 65

337 Handshake and Flags

1988. Visit of President Jose Sarney of Brazil.
1162 **337** 50c. multicoloured . . . 25 20

338 St. John Bosco

339 La Paz–Beni Steam Locomotive

1988. Death Centenary of St. John Bosco (founder of Salesian Brothers).
1163 **338** 30c. multicoloured . . . 15 15

1988. Centenary of Bolivian Railways.
1164 **339** 1b. multicoloured . . . 2·25 1·10

340 Aguirre

341 "Column of the Future" (Battle of Bahia Monument)

1988. Death Cent of Nataniel Aguirre (writer).
1165 **340** 1b. black and brown . . 80 35

1988. 50th Anniv of Pando Department. Mult.
1166 40c. Type **341** 15 10
1167 60c. Rubber production . . 50 20

342 Athlete

343 Mother Rosa Gattorno

1988. Olympic Games, Seoul.
1168 **342** 1b.50 multicoloured . . 1·25 55

1988. 88th Death Anniv of Mother Rosa Gattorno (Founder of the Daughters of St. Anne).
1169 **343** 80c. multicoloured . . . 70 30

344 Bernardino de Cardenas

345 Ministry Building

1988. 220th Death Anniv of Br. Bernardino de Cardenas (first Bishop of La Paz).
1170 **344** 70c. black and brown . . 60 25

1988. Ministry of Transport and Communications.
1171 **345** 2b. black, green & red 1·60 70

346 Arms

347 Rally Car

1988. 50th Anniv of Army Communications Corps.
1172 **346** 70c. multicoloured . . . 65 25

1988. 50th Anniv of Bolivian Automobile Club.
1173 **347** 1b.50 multicoloured . . 1·00 55

348 Microphone and Emblem

1989. 50th Anniv of Radio Fides.
1174 **348** 80c. multicoloured . . . 65 30

349 Obverse and Reverse of 1852 Gold Cuartillo

1989. Coins.
1175 **349** 1b. multicoloured . . . 80 35

350 "Bulgaria 89" Stamp Exhibition Emblem and Orchid

351 Birds

1989. Events and Plants. Multicoloured.
1176 50c. Type **350** 20 15
1177 60c. "Italia '90" World Cup football championship emblem and kantuta (national flower) (horiz) 50 20
1178 70c. "Albertville 1986" emblem and "Heliconia humilis" 55 25
1179 1b. Olympic Games, Barcelona emblem and "Hoffmanseggia" 80 35
1180 2b. Olympic Games, Seoul emblem and bromeliad . . 1·60 70

1989. Bicentenary of French Revolution.
1181 **351** 70c. multicoloured . . . 60 25

352 Clock Tower and Steam Locomotive

353 Federico Ahlfeld Waterfall, River Pauserna

1989. Centenary of Uyuni.
1182 **352** 30c. grey, black & blue 75 40

1989. Noel Kempff Mercado National Park. Multicoloured.
1183 1b.50 Type **353** . . . . . . 1·25 60
1184 3b. Pampas deer . . . . . 2·40 1·00

354 Making Metal Articles

1989. America. Tiahuanacu Culture. Mult.
1185 50c. Type **354** 20 15
1186 1b. Kalasasaya Temple . . 70 35

355 Dr. Carlos Perez and Jaime Zamora

356 Cobija Arch

1989. Meeting of Presidents of Bolivia and Venezuela.
1187 **355** 2b. multicoloured . . . 1·40 70

1989. World Heritage Site, Potosi. Mult.
1188 60c. Type **356** 50 15
1189 80c. Mint 60 20

357 "Andean Lake" (Arturo Borda)

1989. Christmas. Paintings. Multicoloured.
1190 40c. Type **357** 15 10
1191 60c. "Virgin of the Roses" (anon) 45 15
1192 80c. "Conquistador" (Jorge de la Reza) 55 20
1193 1b. "Native Harmony" (Juan Rimsa) 70 25
1194 1b.50 "Woman with Pitcher" (Cecilio Guzman de Rojas) . . . . 1·10 40
1195 2b. "Flower of Tenderness" (Gil Imana) . . . . . . 1·40 55

358 Foot crushing Syringe

359 Map of Americas

1990. Anti-drugs Campaign.
1196 **358** 80c. multicoloured . . . 60 20

1990. Centenary of Organization of American States.
1197 **359** 80c. blue and deep blue 55 20

360 Colonnade

361 Penny Black, Sir Rowland Hill and Bolivian 5c. Condor Stamp

1990. 450th Anniv of White City.
1198 **360** 1b.20 multicoloured . . 85 35

1990. 150th Anniv of the Penny Black.
1199 **361** 4b. multicoloured . . . 2·75 1·25

362 Giuseppe Meaza Stadium, Milan

363 Emblem

1990. World Cup Football Championship, Italy. Multicoloured.
1200 2b. Type **362** . . . . 1·40 55
1201 6b. Match scene . . . . . 4·00 1·50

1990. Cent of Bolivian Chamber of Commerce.
1202 **363** 50c. black, blue & gold 40 10

364 Satellite, Map and Globe

366 Chipaya Village, Oruro

365 Hall

1990. Telecommunications Development Year.
1203 **364** 70c. multicoloured . . . 50 15

1990. Centenary of Cochabamba Social Club.
1204 **365** 40c. multicoloured . . . 15 10

1990. America. Multicoloured.
1205 80c. Type **366** 50 15
1206 1b. Nevado Huayna, Cordillera Real (mountain) (vert) 65 20

367 Emblem

368 Trees and Mountains

1990. "Meeting of Two Worlds. United towards Progress". 500th Anniv (1992) of Discovery of America by Columbus.
1207 **367** 2b. multicoloured . . . 1·25 40

1990. 400th Anniv of Larecaja District.
1208 **368** 1b.20 multicoloured . . 70 25

369 Dove and German National Colours

370 Boys playing Football (Omar Espana)

1990. Unification of Germany.
1209 **369** 2b. multicoloured . . . 1·25 55

1990. Christmas. Rights of the Child.
1210 **370** 50c. multicoloured . . . 15 10

371 Arms of Bolivia and Ecuador

373 Andes

372 Flags and Andes

1990. Visit of Pres. Rodrigo Borja Cevallos of Ecuador.
1211 **371** 80c. multicoloured . . . 60 15

1990. 4th Andean Presidents' Council, La Paz.
1212 **372** 1b.50 multicoloured . . 90 30

1990. "Exfivia 90" National Stamp Exhibition.
1213 **373** 40c. blue 15 10

374 Arms of Bolivia and Mexico

376 Emblem

375 Emblem, Globe and Flags

1990. Visit of Pres. Carlos Salinas de Gortari of Mexico.
1214 **374** 60c. multicoloured . . . 50 15

1990. Express Mail Service.
1215 **375** 1b. multicoloured . . . 60 20

1991. 50th Anniv of Bolivian Radio Club.
1216 **376** 2b.40 multicoloured . . 1·40 50

377 Head of Bear 378 National Museum of Archaeology

1991. The Spectacled Bear. Multicoloured.
1217 30c. Type **377** 10 10
1218 30c. Bear on branch 10 10
1219 30c. Bear and cub at water's edge 10 10
1220 30c. Bear and cubs on branches 10 10

1991. "Espamer '91" Spain–Latin America Stamp Exhibition, Buenos Aires. Multicoloured.
1221 50c. Type **378** 15 10
1222 50c. National Art Museum 15 10
1223 1b. National Museum of Ethnography and Folklore 60 20

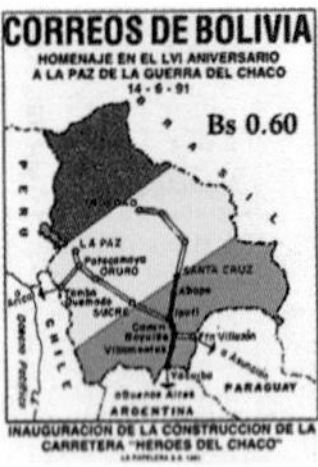

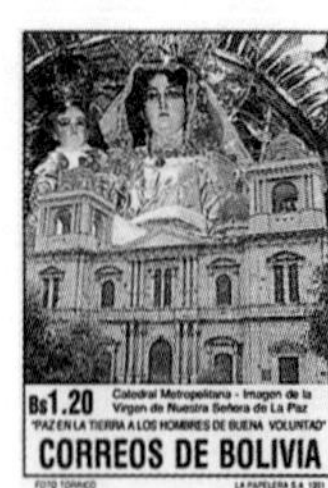

379 Map 380 Statue of Our Lady of La Paz and Cathedral

1991. 56th Anniv of Ending of Chaco War and Beginning of Construction of "Heroes of Chaco" Road.
1224 **379** 60c. multicoloured . . . 20 15

1991. La Paz Cathedral.
1225 **380** 1b.20 multicoloured . . 80 25

381 Presidents Lacalle and Paz Zamora

1991. Meeting of Uruguayan and Bolivian Presidents.
1226 **381** 1b. multicoloured . . . 60 20

382 Presidents Paz Zamora and Menem

1991. Meeting of Bolivian and Argentine Presidents.
1227 **382** 1b. multicoloured . . . 60 20

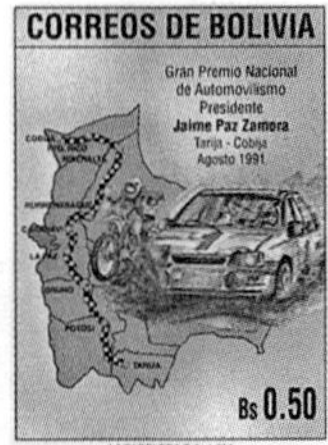

383 "Exfivia 83", "87" and "90" Stamps 385 Route Map, Motor Cycle and Rally Car

384 Presidents Fujimori and Paz Zamora

1991. 20th Anniv of Bolivian Philatelic Federation.
1228 **383** 70c. multicoloured . . . 45 10

1991. Presidential Summit of Bolivia and Peru.
1229 **384** 50c. multicoloured . . . 15 10

1991. Pres. Jaime Paz Zamora National Grand Prix Motor Rally, Tarija-Cobija.
1230 **385** 50c. multicoloured . . . 15 10

386 Data Retrieval Systems

1991. "Ecobol" Postal Security.
1231 **386** 1b.40 multicoloured . . 90 30

387 "First Discovery of Chuquiago" (Arturo Reque) 388 Stylized Figures and City Skyline

1991. America. Voyages of Discovery. Mult.
1232 60c. Type **387** 20 10
1233 1b.20 "Foundation of City of Our Lady of La Paz" (J. Rimsa) (vert) 80 30

1991. National Population and Housing Census.
1234 **388** 50c. multicoloured . . . 15 10

389 "Landscape" (Daniel Pena y Sarmiento)

1991. Christmas. Multicoloured.
1235 2b. Type **389** . . . . 1·00 40
1236 5b. "Fruit Seller" (Cecilio Guzman de Rojas) . . . 2·50 1·00
1237 15b. "Native Mother" (Crespo Gastelu) . . . . 7·50 3·00

390 Camp-site and Emblem

1992. 75th Anniv (1990) of Bolivian Scout Movement and Los Andes Jamboree, Cochabamba.
1238 **390** 1b.20 multicoloured . . 80 30

391 Simon Bolivar 392 Raising Flag

1992. "Exfilbo 92" National Stamp Exhibition, La Paz.
1239 **391** 1b.20 deep brown, brown and stone . . . 80 30

1992. Creation of Bolivian Free Zone in Ilo, Peru. Multicoloured.
1240 1b.20 Type **392** 65 30
1241 1b.50 Presidents Fujimori (Peru) and Paz Zamora (horiz) 80 30
1242 1b.80 Beach at Ilo (horiz) 95 35

393 Logotype of Pavilion

1992. "Expo '92" World's Fair, Seville, and "Granada '92" Int Stamp Exhibition. Mult.
1243 30c. Type **393** 10 10
1244 50c. Columbus's fleet . . . 30 10

394 Rotary International Emblem and Prize

1992. Rotary Club Miraflores District 4690 "Illimani de Oro" Prize.
1245 **394** 90c. gold, blue & black 30 20

395 School and Perez

1992. Birth Centenary of Elizardo Perez (founder of Ayllu School, Warisata).
1246 **395** 60c. blue, black & yellow 50 10

396 Government Palace

1992. U.N.E.S.C.O. World Heritage Site, Sucre.
1247 **396** 50c. multicoloured . . . 15 10

397 Mario Martinez Guzman 398 Front Page

1992. Olympic Games, Barcelona.
1248 **397** 1b.50 multicoloured . . 80 30

1992. 25th Anniv of "Los Tiempos" (newspaper).
1249 **398** 50c. multicoloured . . . 15 10

399 Canoeing 400 Columbus leaving Palos (after Bejarano)

1992. 1st International River Bermejo Canoeing Championship.
1250 **399** 1b.20 multicoloured . . 75 30

1992. America. 500th Anniv of Discovery of America by Columbus.
1251 **400** 60c. brown and black . . 20 10
1252 – 2b. multicoloured . . . 95 40
DESIGN—HORIZ: 2b. "Columbus meeting the Caribisis Tribe" (Luis Vergara).

401 Football Match 402 "Chenopodium quinoa"

1992. World Cup Football Championship, U.S.A. (1994).
1253 **401** 1b.20 multicoloured . . 1·25 30

1992. 50th Anniv of Interamerican Institute for Agricultural Co-operation.
1254 **402** 1b.20 multicoloured . . 80 30

403 University Arms and Minerals

1992. Cent of Oruro Technical University.
1255 **403** 50c. multicoloured . . . 15 10

404 Mascots

1992. 12th Bolivarian Games, Cochabamba and Santa Cruz (1st issue).
1256 **404** 2b. multicoloured . . . 1·00 40
See also No. 1271.

405 Cayman

1992. Ecology and Conservation. Multicoloured.
1257 20c. Type **405** 10 10
1258 50c. Spotted cavy 15 10
1259 1b. Chinchilla 30 20
1260 2b. Anteater . . . . 1·00 40
1261 3b. Jaguar . . . . 1·50 65
1262 4b. Long-tailed sylph ("Picaflor") (vert) . . . . 3·50 1·60
1263 5b. Piranhas . . . . 2·50 1·10
Each stamp also bears the emblem of an anniversary or event.

406 Battle Scene

1992. 150th Anniv of Battle of Ingavi.
1264 **406** 1b.20 brown and black 65 30

407 Man following Star in Boat

1992. Christmas. Multicoloured.
1265 1b.20 Type **407** 60 20
1266 2b.50 Star over church . . . 1·40 50
1267 6b. Infant in manger and church . . . . 3·00 1·25

408 Nicolas Copernicus (450th death anniv)

409 Mother Nazaria (after Victor Eusebio Choque)

1993. Astronomy.
1268 – 50c. multicoloured . . . 15 10
1269 **408** 2b. black . . . . 1·00 35
DESIGN—HORIZ: 50c. Santa Ana International Astronomical Observatory, Tarija (10th anniv (1992)).

1993. Beatification (1992) of Mother Nazaria Ignacia March Meza.
1270 **409** 60c. multicoloured . . . 40 10

410 Pictograms and Flags of Ecuador, Venezuela, Peru, Bolivia, Colombia and Panama

1993. 12th Bolivarian Games, Cochabamba and Santa Cruz (2nd issue).
1271 **410** 2b.30 multicoloured . . 1·10 35

411 Bolivia 1962 10000b. Kantuta and Brazil 90r. "Bull's Eye" Stamps

1993. 150th Anniv of First Brazilian Stamps.
1272 **411** 2b.30 multicoloured . . 1·10 35

412 "Morpho sp."

1993. Butterflies. Multicoloured.
1273 60c. Type **412** 40 10
1274 60c. "Archaeoprepona demophon" 40 10
1275 80c. "Papilio sp." 45 10
1276 80c. Orion ("Historis odius") 45 10
1277 80c. Mexican fritillary ("Euptoieta hegesia") . . 45 10
1278 1b.80 "Morpho deidamia" 1·10 30
1279 1b.80 Orange swallowtail ("Papilio thoas") . . . . 1·10 30
1280 1b.80 Monarch ("Danaus plexippus") . . . . 1·10 30
1281 2b.30 Scarlet emperor ("Anaea marthesia") . . . 1·25 35
1282 2b.30 "Caligo sp." . . . . . 1·25 35
1283 2b.30 "Rothschildia sp." . . 1·25 35
1284 2b.70 "Heliconius sp." . . . 1·50 45
1285 2b.70 "Marpesia corinna" 1·50 45
1286 2b.70 "Prepona chromus" 1·50 45
1287 3b.50 Rusty-tipped page ("Siproeta epaphus") . . 1·90 60
1288 3b.50 "Heliconius sp." . . . 1·90 60

413 "Eternal Father" (wood statuette, Gaspar de la Cueva)

414 "Virgin of Urkupina"

1993.
1289 **413** 1b.80 multicoloured . . 90 30

1993. 400th Anniv of Quillacollo.
1290 **414** 50c. multicoloured . . . 15 10

415 Student, Machinery and Emblem

1993. 50th Anniv (1992) of Pedro Domingo Murillo Technical College.
1291 **415** 60c. multicoloured . . . 15 10

416 Owl (painting, Chuquisaca)

417 Common Squirrel-monkeys

1993. Cave Art. Multicoloured.
1292 80c. Type **416** 20 10
1293 80c. Animals (painting, Cochabamba) 20 10
1294 80c. Geometric patterns (engraving, Chuquisaca) (vert) 20 10
1295 80c. Sun (engraving, Beni) (vert) 20 10
1296 80c. Llama (painting, Oruro) 20 10
1297 80c. Human figure (engraving, Potosi) . . . 20 10
1298 80c. Church and tower (painting, La Paz) (vert) 20 10
1299 80c. Warrior (engraving, Tarija) (vert) 20 10
1300 80c. Religious mask (engraving, Santa Cruz) (vert) 20 10

1993. America. Endangered Animals. Mult.
1301 80c. Type **417** 20 10
1302 2b.30 Ocelot . . . . 1·00 35

418 Emblems and Map

419 Yolanda Bedregal (poet)

1993. 90th Anniv (1992) of Pan-American Health Organization. Anti-AIDS Campaign.
1303 **418** 80c. multicoloured . . . 20 10

1993. Personalities. Each brown.
1304 50c. Type **419** 15 10
1305 70c. Simon Martinic (President of Cochabamba Philatelic Centre) 20 10
1306 90c. Eugenio von Boeck (politician and President of Bolivian Philatelic Federation) 25 15
1307 1b. Marina Nunez del Prado (sculptor) 25 15

420 "Virgin with Child and Saints" (anonymous)

421 Riberalta Square

1993. Christmas. Multicoloured.
1308 2b.30 "Adoration of the Shepherds" (Leonardo Flores) 95 35
1309 3b.50 Type **420** . . . . . 1·50 60
1310 6b. "Virgin of the Milk" (Melchor Perez de Holguin) . . . . 2·50 1·00

1994. Centenary of Riberalta.
1311 **421** 2b. multicoloured . . . 85 35

422 "Population and Our World" (Mayari Rodriguez)

1994. 2nd Prize-winning Design (6–8 year group) in United Nations Fund for Population Activities International Design Contest.
1312 **422** 2b.30 multicoloured . . 1·00 35

423 Sanchez de Lozada

424 Mascot

1994. Presidency of Gonzalo Sanchez de Lozada.
1313 **423** 2b. multicoloured . . . 85 35
1314 2b.30 multicoloured . . 1·00 35

1994. World Cup Football Championship, U.S.A. Multicoloured.
1315 80c. Type **424** 20 10
1316 1b.80 Bolivia v Uruguay . . 75 30
1317 2b.30 Bolivia v Venezuela 95 35
1318 2b.50 Bolivian team (left half) . . . . 1·00 35
1319 2b.50 Bolivian team (right half) . . . . 1·00 35
1320 2b.70 Bolivia v Ecuador . . 1·10 45
1321 3b.50 Bolivia v Brazil . . . 1·50 60
Nos. 1318/19 were issued together, se-tenant, forming a composite design.

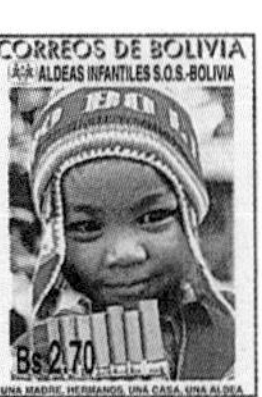

425 Child

427 "Buddleja coriacea"

426 St. Peter's Church and Mgr. Jorge Manrique Hurtado (Archbishop, 1967–87)

1994. S.O.S. Children's Villages.
1322 **425** 2b.70 multicoloured . . 1·10 45

1994. 50th Anniv (1993) of Archdiocese of La Paz. Multicoloured.
1323 1b.80 Type **426** 75 30
1324 2b. Church of the Sacred Heart of Mary and Mgr. Abel Antezana y Rojas (first Archbishop, 1943–67) (vert) 85 35
1325 3b.50 Santo Domingo Church and Mgr. Luis Sainz Hinojosa (Archbishop since 1987) (vert) . . . . 1·50 60

1994. Environmental Protection. Trees. Mult.
1326 60c. Type **427** 15 10
1327 1b.80 "Bertholletia exelsa" 50 30
1328 2b. "Schinus molle" (horiz) 80 35
1329 2b.70 "Polylepis racemosa" 1·00 45
1330 3b. "Tabebuia chrysantha" 1·25 50
1331 3b.50 "Erythrina falcata" (horiz) . . . . 1·40 60

428 Paz

429 Tramcar and Mail Van

1994. Dr. Victor Paz Estenssoro (former President).
1332 **428** 2b. multicoloured . . . 55 35

1994. America. Postal Transport. Mult.
1333 1b. Type **429** . . . . 2·25 1·50
1334 5b. Airplane and ox cart . . 1·25 80

430 Coral Tree

431 Diagram of Eclipse

1994. 300th Anniv of San Borja.
1335 **430** 1b.60 multicoloured . . 40 25

1994. Solar Eclipse.
1336 **431** 3b.50 multicoloured . . 1·40 60

432 1894 100c. Stamp

433 Col. Marzana and Soldiers

1994. Centenary of Arms Issue of 1894.
1337 **432** 1b.80 multicoloured . . 50 30

1994. 62nd Anniv of Defence of Fort Boqueron.
1338 **433** 80c. multicoloured . . . 20 10

434 "Delicate Flower of Tarija"

435 Emblem

1994. Christmas. Pastels of children by Maria Susana Castillo. Multicoloured.
1339 2b. Type **434** 55 35
1340 5b. "Child of the High Plateau" . . . . 1·75 40
1341 20b. "Shoot of the Bolivian East" . . . . 6·75 2·40

1994. Pan-American Scout Jamboree, Cochabamba.
1342 **435** 1b.80 multicoloured . . 50 30

436 Sucre

437 Santa Ana Cathedral

1995. Birth Bicentenary of General Antonio Jose de Sucre. Multicoloured.
1343 1b.80 Type **436** 50 30
1344 3b.50 Sucre and national colours 90 60

1995. Centenary (1994) of Yacuma Province, Beni Department.
1345 **437** 1b.90 multicoloured . . 80 35
1346 2b.90 multicoloured . . 1·10 50

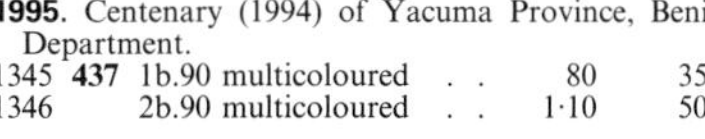

438 "Holy Virgin of Copacabana", Sanctuary and Franciscans

1995. Centenary of Franciscan Presence at Copacabana Sanctuary.
1347 **438** 60c. multicoloured . . . 15 10
1348 80c. multicoloured . . . 20 10

439 Anniversary Emblem

440 Paraguay and Bolivia Flags (Chaco Peace Treaty, 1938)

1995. 25th Anniv of Andean Development Corporation.
1349 **439** 2b.40 multicoloured . . 80 35

1995. Visit of President Juan Carlos Wasmosy of Paraguay and 169th Anniv (1994) of Republic of Bolivia.
1350 **440** 2b. multicoloured . . . 45 30

441 Montenegro

442 Digging Potatoes

1995. 50th Anniv of Publication of "Nationalism and Colonialism" by Carlos Montenegro.
1351 **441** 1b.20 black and pink . . 25 15

1995. 50th Anniv of F.A.O.
1352 **442** 1b. multicoloured . . . 20 10

443 Anniversary Emblem

1995. 50th Anniv of U.N.O.
1353 **443** 2b.90 dp blue, gold & bl 90 40

444 Andean Condor ("Condor")

1995. America. Endangered Species. Mult.
1354 5b. Type **444** . . . . 1·60 70
1355 5b. Llamas . . . . 1·60 70
Nos. 1354/5 were issued together, se-tenant, forming a composite design.

445 Airbus Industrie A320

447 Brewery Complex

446 Stone Head

1995. 50th Anniv (1994) of I.C.A.O.
1356 **445** 50c. multicoloured . . . 10 10

1995. Archaeology. Samaipata Temple, Florida. Multicoloured.
1357 1b. Type **446** 20 10
1358 1b.90 Stone head (different) 40 25
1359 2b. Excavation and stone head 45 30
1360 2b.40 Entrance and animal-shaped vessel 55 35
Nos. 1357/60 were issued together, se-tenant, forming a composite design.

1995. Centenary of Taquina Brewery.
1361 **447** 1b. multicoloured . . . 20 10

448 "The Annunciation" (Cima da Conegliano)

449 Jose de Sanjines (lyricist)

1995. Christmas. Multicoloured.
1362 1b.20 Type **448** 25 15
1363 3b. "The Nativity" (Hans Baldung) 90 40
1364 3b.50 "Adoration of the Wise Men" (altarpiece, Rogier van der Weyden) 1·10 50

1995. 150th Anniv of National Anthem. Mult.
1365 1b. Type **449** 20 10
1366 2b. Benedetto Vincenti (composer) 45 30
Nos. 1365/6 were issued together, se-tenant, forming a composite design.

450 Flats, Villarroel, Factories, Road and Railway

452 Summit Emblem

1996. 50th Anniv of Decree for Abolition of Enforced Amerindian Labour. Mult.
1367 1b.90 Type **450** . . . . . . 1·25 1·10
1368 2b.90 Pres. Gualberto Villarroel addressing Congress and freed workers . . . . 2·25 1·90
Nos. 1367/8 were issued together, se-tenant, forming a composite design.

1996. Various stamps surch.
1369 – 50c. on 3000000p. multicoloured (No. 1126) (postage) 10 10
1370 **265** 60c. on 2p.50 blue and red 10 10
1371 **313** 60c. on 5000000p. on 2000p. blue and red (No. 1116) 10 10
1372 **319** 60c. on 1400000p. mult 10 10
1373 1b. on 2500000p. green and yellow (No. 1120) 20 10
1374 **311** 1b.50 on 11000p. blue 30 20
1375 **312** 2b.50 on 23000p. brown and sepia 55 35
1376 **316** 3b. on 1000000p. blue and gold 65 40
1377 **272** 3b.50 on 6p.50 mult . . 80 50
1378 **279** 3b.50 on 9p. mult . . . 80 50
1379 **323** 3b.50 on 2000000p. brown 80 50
1380 **298** 20b. on 10p. black, purple and bronze . . 5·00 2·00
1381 **299** 20b. on 13p. mult . . . 5·00 2·00
1382 – 3b.80 on 3p.80 mult (No. 945) (air) 85 55
1383 – 20b. on 3p.80 mult (No. 973a) . . . . . 5·00 2·00

1996. 10th Rio Group Summit Meeting, Cochabamba. Multicoloured.
1384 2b.50 Type **452** 55 35
1385 3b.50 Rio Group emblem 80 50

453 Summit Emblem

454 Facade

1996. Summit of the Americas on Sustainable Development, Santa Cruz de la Sierra.
1386 **453** 2b.50 multicoloured . . 55 35
1387 5b. multicoloured . . . 1·10 70

1996. National Bank.
1388 **454** 50c. black and blue . . . 10 10

455 De Lemoine

456 Family

1996. 220th Birth Anniv of Jose Joaquin de Lemoine (first postal administrator).
1389 **455** 1b. brown and stone . . 20 10

1997. CARE (Co-operative for American Relief Everywhere). Multicoloured.
1390 60c. Type **456** (20th anniv in Bolivia) 10 10
1391 70c. Hands cradling globe (50th anniv) (vert) 15 10

457 Musicians playing Piccolo and Saxophone

458 Casa Dorada (cultural centre)

1997. 50th Anniv of National Symphony Orchestra. "Overture" by G. Rodo Boulanger. Multicoloured.
1392 1b.50 Type **457** 30 20
1393 2b. Musicians playing violin and cello 45 30
Nos. 1392/3 were issued together, se-tenant, forming a composite design of the complete painting.

1997. Tarija. Multicoloured.
1394 50c. Type **458** 10 10
1395 60c. Entre Rios Church and musician 10 10
1396 80c. Narrows of San Luis (horiz) 15 10
1397 1b. Memorial to the Fallen of the Chaco War (territorial dispute with Paraguay) (horiz) 20 10
1398 3b. Virgin and shrine of Chaguaya (horiz) 60 40
1399 20b. Birthplace and statue of Jose Eustaquio Mendez (Independence hero), San Lorenzo (horiz) . . . . . 4·75 1·90

459 La Glorieta, Sucre

1997. Chuquisaca. Multicoloured.
1400 60c. Type **459** 10 10
1401 1b. Government Palace, Sucre (vert) 20 10
1402 1b.50 Footprints and drawing of dinosaur . . . 30 20
1403 1b.50 Interior of House of Freedom 30 20
1404 2b. Man playing traditional wind instrument (vert) . . 40 25
1405 3b. Statue of Juana Azurduy de Padilla (Independence heroine) (vert) 60 40

460 Miners' Monument

1997. Oruro. Multicoloured.
1406 50c. Type **460** 35 25
1407 60c. Demon carnival mask 10 10
1408 1b. Vigin of the Cave (statue) 20 10
1409 1b.50 Sajama (volcano) (horiz) 30 20
1410 2b.50 Chipaya child and belfry 50 30
1411 3b. Moreno (Raul Shaw) (singer and musician) (horiz) 60 40

461 Pres. Gonzalo Sanchez de Lozada of Bolivia and Pres. Chirac

1997. Visit to Bolivia of President Jacques Chirac of France.
1412 **461** 4b. multicoloured . . . 80 50

462 Children playing (Pamela G. Villarroel)

463 St. John Bosco (founder)

1997. 50th Anniv of U.N.I.C.E.F. Children's Drawings. Multicoloured.
1413 50c. Type **462** 10 10
1414 90c. Boy leaping across clifftop (Lidia Acapa) . . 20 10
1415 1b. Children of different races on top of world (Gabriela Philco) 20 10
1416 2b.50 Children and swing (Jessica Grundy) 50 30

1997. Centenary of Salesian Brothers in Bolivia. Multicoloured.
1417 1b.50 Type **463** 30 20
1418 2b. Church and statue of Bosco with child 40 25

464 Chulumani

465 Emblem

1997. La Paz. Multicoloured.
1419 50c. Type **464** 10 10
1420 80c. Inca stone monolith . . 15 10
1421 1b.50 La Paz and Mt. Illimani 30 20
1422 2b. Gate of the Sun, Tiahuanaco (horiz) . . . 40 25
1423 2b.50 Dancers 50 30
1424 10b. "Virgin of Copacabana" and balsa raft on Lake Titicaca (horiz) . . . . 2·50 1·75

1997. Football Events. Multicoloured.
1425 3b. Type **465** (America Cup Latin-American Football Championship, Bolivia) 60 40
1426 5b. Eiffel Tower and trophy (World Cup Football Championship, France (1998) Eliminating Rounds) . . . . 1·00 65

466 Parliamentary Session and Building

467 Valley

1997. National Congress.
1427 **466** 1b. multicoloured . . . 20 10

1997. America. Traditional Costumes. Mult.
1428 5b. Type **467** . . . . 1·00 65
1429 15b. Eastern region . . . . 3·50 1·40

468 Members Flags and Southern Cross

469 "Virgin of the Hill" (anon)

1997. 6th Anniv of Mercosur (South American Common Market).
1430 **468** 3b. multicoloured . . . 60 40

1997. Christmas. Multicoloured.
1431 2b. Type **469** 40 25
1432 5b. "Virgin of the Milk" (anon) . . . . 1·00 65
1433 10b. "Holy Family" (Melchor Perez Holguin) 2·00 1·25

470 Diana, Princess of Wales

1997. Diana, Princess of Wales Commemoration. Multicoloured.
1434 2b. Type **470** 40 25
1435 3b. Diana, Princess of Wales beside minefield warning sign (horiz) 60 40

471 Presidents of Boliva and Spain

1998. State Visit of Prime Minister Jose Maria Aznar of Spain.
1436 **471** 6b. multicoloured . . . 2·00 80

472 Juan Munoz Reyes (President) and Medallion

473 Linked Arms and Globe

1998. 75th Anniv of Bolivian Engineers' Association.
1437 **472** 3b.50 multicoloured . . 60 40

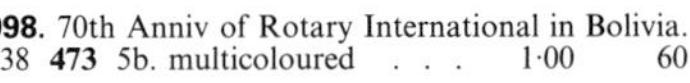

1998. 70th Anniv of Rotary International in Bolivia.
1438 **473** 5b. multicoloured . . . 1·00 60

474 Delivering Letter, 1998

475 Werner Guttentag Tichauer (35th anniv of his bibliography)

1998. America. The Postman. Multicoloured.
1439 3b. Type **474** 60 40
1440 4b. Postmen on parade, 1942 (horiz) 80 50

1998. Anniversaries.
1441 **475** 1b.50 brown 20 10
1442 – 2b. green 40 25
1443 – 3b.50 black 60 40
DESIGNS—VERT: 2b. Martin Cardenas Hermosa (botanist, birth centenary (1999)); 3b. Adrian Patino Carpio (composer, 47th death anniv).

476 Amazon Water-lily

1998. Beni. Multicoloured.
1444 50c. Type **476** 10 10
1445 1b. "Callandria" sp. 20 10
1446 1b.50 White tajibo tree (vert) 20 10
1447 3b.50 Ceremonial mask . . 60 40
1448 5b. European otter . . . . 1·00 60
1449 7b. King vulture ("Tropical Condor") . . . . 1·40 90

477 River Acre

1998. Pando. Multicoloured.
1450 50c. Type **477** 10 10
1451 1b. Pale-throated sloth (vert) 20 10
1452 1b.50 Arroyo Bahia (vert) 20 10
1453 4b. Boa constrictor 80 50
1454 5b. Capybara with young 1·00 60
1455 7b. Palm trees, Cobija (vert) 1·40 90

478 Rural Activities and First Lady

1998. America. Women. Multicoloured.
1456 1b.50 Type **478** 20 10
1457 2b. First Lady, girl at blackboard and woman using computer 40 25
Nos. 1456/7 were issued together, se-tenant, forming a composite design.

479 Town Arms and Church

1998. 450th Anniv of La Paz.
1458 **479** 2b. multicoloured . . . 40 25

480 Emblem

481 Magnifying Glass and 1998 7b. Stamp

1998. 50th Anniv of Organization of American States.
1459 **480** 3b.50 blue and yellow . . 60 40

1998. "Espamer 98" Stamp Exhibition, Buenos Aires and 25th Anniv of Bolivian Philatelic Federation.
1460 **481** 2b. multicoloured . . . 40 25

482 "People going to Church" (Kathia Lucuy Saenz)

1998. Christmas. Multicoloured.
1461 2b. Type **482** 40 25
1462 6b. Pope John Paul II (vert) 1·25 80
1463 7b. Pope John Paul II with Mother Teresa (vert) . . . 1·40 90

483 U.P.U. Monument, Berne

1999. 125th Anniv of Universal Postal Union.
1464 **483** 3b.50 multicoloured . . 70 45

484 Statue of Football Player

1999. 75th Anniv of Cochabamba Football Association.
1465 **484** 5b. multicoloured . . . 1·40 65

485 Red Cross Lorries at Earthquake Site

1999. 50th Anniv of Geneva Conventions.
1466 **485** 5b. multicoloured . . . 1·00 65

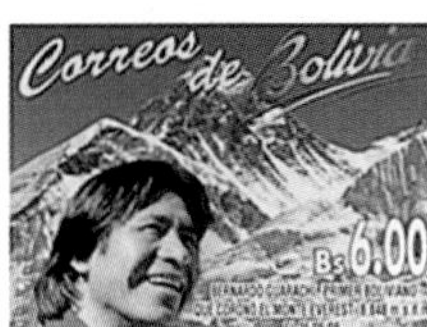

486 Bernardo Guarachi and Mt. Everest

1999. 1st Ascent (1998) of Mt. Everest by a Bolivian.
1467 **486** 6b. multicoloured . . . 1·25 85

487 Winners on Podium

1999. 30th Anniv of First Special Olympics. Multicoloured.
1468 2b. Type **487** 40 25
1469 2b.50 Athletes on race track and winners on podium 50 30

488 Golden Palace

1999. Centenary of Japanese Immigration to Bolivia. Multicoloured.
1470 3b. Type **488** 60 40
1471 6b. View over lake and flags (vert) . . . . 1·25 85

489 Children dancing

1999. Anti-drugs Campaign.
1472 **489** 3b.50 multicoloured . . 70 45

490 Route Map and Presidents Hugo Banzer Suarez of Bolivia and Fernando Cardoso of Brazil

1999. Inauguration of Gas Pipeline from Santa Cruz, Bolivia, to Campinas, Brazil. Multicoloured.
1473 3b. Type **490** 60 40
1474 6b. Presidents Hugo Banzer Suarez and Fernando Cardoso embracing . . . 1·25 85

491 Village Scene

493 International Lions Emblem

492 "Hacia la Gloria" (directed Rau Duran, Mario Camacho and Jose Jimenez)

1999. 50th Anniv of S.O.S. Children's Villages.
1475 **491** 3b.50 multicoloured . . 70 45

1999. Centenary of Motion Pictures in Bolivia. Multicoloured.
1476 50c. Type **492** 10 10
1477 50c. "Jonah and the Pink Whale" (dir. J. Carlos Valdivia) 10 10
1478 1b. "Wara Wara" (dir. Jose Velasco) 20 15
1479 1b. "Vuelve Sebastiana" (dir. Jorge Ruiz) 20 15
1480 3b. "The Chaco Campaign" (dir. Juan Penaranda, Jose Velasco and Mario Camacho) 60 40
1481 3b. "The Watershed" (dir. Jorge Ruiz) 60 40
1482 6b. "Yawar Mallku" (dir. Jorge Sanjines) . . . . . 1·25 85
1483 6b. "Mi Socio" (dir. Paolo Agazzi) . . . . 1·25 85

1999. 50th Anniv (1998) of La Paz Lions Club.
1485 **493** 3b.50 multicoloured . . 70 45

494 Mt. Tunari

1999. Cochabamba. Multicoloured.
1486 50c. Type **494** 10 10
1487 1b. Forest, Cochabamba Valley 20 15
1488 2b. Omereque vase and fertility goddess (vert) . . 40 25
1489 3b. Totora 60 40
1490 5b. Teofilo Vargas Candia (composer) and music score (vert) . . . . 1·00 65
1491 6b. "Christ of Harmony" (mountain-top statue) (vert) . . . . 1·25 85

495 Tarapaya Lagoon (Inca spa)

496 Globe with Children, Fish, Flower, Pencil, Heart and Stars

1999. Potosi. Multicoloured.
1492 50c. Type **495** 10 10
1493 1b. First republican coins, minted in 1827 (horiz) . . 20 10
1494 2b. Mt. Chorolque (horiz) 45 30
1495 3b. Green Lagoon (horiz) 65 40
1496 4b. "The Mestizo sitting on a Trunk" (Teofilo Loaiza) 90 60
1497 6b. Alfredo Dominguez Romeo (Tupiceno singer) 1·25 80

1999. America. A New Millennium without Arms. Multicoloured.
1498 3b.50 Type **496** 75 50
1499 3b.50 Globe emerging from flower 75 50

497 Children from S.O.S. Childrens Village

498 Ugarte

1999. Christmas. Multicoloured.
1500 2b. Type **497** 45 30
1501 6b. "The Birth of Jesus" (Gaspar Miguel de Berrios) (vert) . . . . . 1·25 80
1502 7b. "Our Family in the World" (Omar Medina) (vert) . . . . 1·50 1·00

2000. 5th Death Anniv of Victor Agustin Ugarte (football player).
1503 **498** 3b. grey, green and yellow 65 40

499 El Arenal Park

2000. Santa Cruz. Multicoloured.
1504 50c. Type **499** 10 10
1505 1b. Ox cart 20 10
1506 2b. Raul Otero Reiche, Gabriel Rene Moreno and Hernando Sanabria Fernandez (writers) . . . 45 30
1507 3b. Cotoca Virgin (statue) (vert) 65 40
1508 5b. Anthropomorphic vase (vert) . . . . 1·10 70
1509 6b. Bush dog . . . . 1·25 80

500 "The Village of Serinhaem in Brazil" (Frans Post)

2000. 500th Anniv of Discovery of Brazil.
1510 **500** 5b. multicoloured . . . 1·10 70

501 Granado

2000. Javier del Granado (poet) Commemoration.
1511 **501** 3b. grey, blue and red 65 40

502 Cyclists

503 Oriental Clay Figure

2000. "Double Copacabana" Cycle Race.
1512 **502** 1b. multicoloured . . . 20 10
1513 – 3b. multicoloured . . . 65 40
1514 – 5b. multicoloured . . . 1·10 70
1515 – 7b. multicoloured . . . 1·50 1·00
DESIGNS: 3b. to 7b. Various race scenes.

2000. National Archaeology Museum Exhibits. Each brown and gold.
1516 50c. Type **503** 10 10
1517 50c. Clay figure, Potosi . . 10 10
1518 70c. Oriental clay head, Beni 15 10
1519 90c. Clay vase, Tarija . . . 20 10
1520 1b. Clay head, Oruro . . . 20 10
1521 1b. Yampara clay urn . . . 20 10
1522 3b. Inca wood carving . . . 65 40
1523 5b. Oriental anthropomorphic vase . . 1·10 70
1524 20b. Tiwanaku clay mask 4·50 3·00

504 Male and Female Symbols in Red Vortex

2000. America. Anti-A.I.D.S. Campaign. Multicoloured.
1525 3b.50 Type **504** 75 45
1526 3b.50 Couple walking through wall 75 45

505 Soldier's Head and Bird on Laurel Wreath

2000. Centenary of Maximiliano Parades Military School.
1527 **505** 2b.50 multicoloured . . 55 35

506 "Self-portrait"

2000. Birth Centenary of Cecilio Guzman de Rojas (artist). Showing paintings. Multicoloured.
1528 1b. Type **506** 25 15
1529 2b.50 "Triumph of Nature" (horiz) 55 35
1530 5b. "Andina" . . . . 1·10 65
1531 6b. "Students' Quarrel" (horiz) . . . . 1·25 75

507 Crowd and Brandenburg Gate

2000. 50th Anniv of German Federal Republic.
1532 **507** 6b. multicoloured . . . 1·25 75

508 San Francisco Basilica, La Paz

509 Waterfall and Statue

2000. Holy Year 2000. Bolivian Episcopal Conference. Multicoloured.
1533 4b. Type **508** 90 55
1534 6b. Stalks of grain breaking through barbed-wire . . . 1·25 75

2000. New Millennium.
1535 **509** 5b. multicoloured . . . 1·10 65

510 Archangel Gabriel

511 Painting of John the Baptist and Emblem

2000. Christmas. Showing 17th-century paintings of Angels from Calamarca Church. Multicoloured.
1536 3b. Type **510** 65 40
1537 5b. Angel of Virtue . . . . 1·10 65
1538 10b. Angel with ear of corn 2·25 1·40

2000. 900th Anniv of Sovereign Military Order of St. John.
1539 **511** 6b. multicoloured . . . 1·25 75

512 Lobster Claw (*Heliconia rostrata*)

2001. Patriotic Symbols. Multicoloured.
1540 10b. Type **512** (designated national flower, 1990) . . 2·25 1·40
1541 20b. *Periphrangus dependens* (designated national flower 1924) . . . . . . 4·50 2·75
1542 30b. First Bolivian coat of arms (adopted 1825) . . . 6·50 4·00
1543 50b. Second Bolivian coat of arms (adopted 1826) . . . 11·00 6·50
1544 100b. Present day Bolivian coat of arms (adopted 1851) . . . . 20·00 12·00

513 Map and Stars of European Union and Map of Bolivia

2001. 25th Anniv of Co-operation between Bolivia and European Union.
1550 **513** 6b. multicoloured . . . 1·25 75

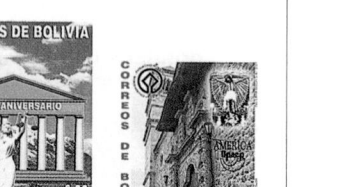

514 Statue of Justice, Lion and Portico

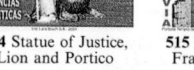

515 Temple of San Francisco, Potosi

2001. 171st Anniv of Faculty of Law and Political Sciences, Universidad de Mayor of San Andres, La Paz.
1551 **514** 6b. multicoloured . . . 1·00 60

2001. America. U.N.E.S.C.O. World Heritage Sites. Multicoloured.
1552 1b.50 Type **515** 25 15
1553 5b. "Fraile" and "Ponce" (monoliths) (horiz) . . . 80 50

516 Man carrying Envelopes up Stairs

518 Family

517 Devil's Molar (mountain)

2001. Philately. Each green.
1554 50c. Type **516** 10 10
1555 1b. Boy with six stamps . . 15 10
1556 1b.50 Man with glasses and stamp album 25 15
1557 2b. Child wearing hat, and three stamps 35 20
1558 2b.50 Humanized stamp lying in tray 40 25

2001.
1559 **517** 1b.50 multicoloured . . 25 15

2001. National Census. Multicoloured.
1560 1b. Type **518** 15 10
1561 1b.50 People surrounding wheelchair user 25 15
1562 1b.50 Aboriginal woman and people of different races 25 15
1563 2b.50 People of different races 40 25
1564 3b. Children 50 30

519 Silver Spot (*Dione juno*)

2001. Butterflies and Insects. Multicoloured.
1565 1b. Type **519** 15 10
1566 1b. *Orthoptera* sp. 15 10
1567 1b.50 Bamboo page (*Philaethria dido*) 25 15
1568 2b.50 Jewel butterfly (*Diaethria clymena*) (inscr "Diathria clymene") . . . 40 25
1569 2b.50 *Mantis religiosa* . . . 40 25
1570 3b. *Tropidacris latreillei* . . 50 30
1571 4b. Hercules beetle (*Dynastes hercules*) (inscr "Escarabajo Hercule") . . 65 40
1572 5b. *Arctiidae* sp. 80 50
1573 5b. *Acrocinus longimanus* . . 80 50
1574 5b. *Lucanidae* sp. 80 50
1575 6b. *Morpho godarti* . . . . 1·00 60
1576 6b. *Caligo idomeneus* ("inscr idomineus") . . . . . . 1·00 60

520 Map of Americas and Emblem

2001. 21st Inter-America Scout Conference, Cochabamba.
1577 **520** 3b.50 multicoloured . . 60 35

521 Woman and Emblem

522 St. Mary Magdalen

2001. Breast Cancer Prevention Campaign.
1578 **521** 1b.50 multicoloured . . 25 15

2001. Christmas. Showing sculptures by Gaspar of La Cueva from Convent of San Francisco, Potosi. Multicoloured.
1579 3b. Type **522** 25 15
1580 5b. St. Apolonia 80 50
1581 10b. St. Teresa of Avila . . 1·75 1·00

523 Portrait and Casa La Laertad, Sucre

2001. Joaquin Gantier Valda Commemoration.
1582 **523** 4b. multicoloured . . . 65 40

524 Flags and Hands enclosing Farmer, Mother, Child and Doctor

2001. 25th Anniv of Co-operation between Bolivia and Belgium.
1583 **524** 6b. multicoloured . . . 65 40

POSTAGE DUE STAMPS

D 81

D 93 "Youth"

1931.
D265 **D 81** 5c. blue 70 85
D266 10c. red 70 85
D267 15c. yellow . . . . . 1·00 85
D268 30c. green . . . . . 1·00 85
D269 40c. violet . . . . . 1·75 1·75
D270 50c. sepia . . . . . . 2·40 2·40

1938. Triangular designs.
D346 **D 93** 5c. red 50 50
D347 – 10c. green 50 50
D348 – 30c. blue 50 50
DESIGNS: 10c. Torch of Knowledge; 30c. Date and Symbol of 17 May 1936 Revolution.

BOPHUTHATSWANA Pt. 1

The republic of Bophuthatswana was established on 6 December 1977 as one of the "black homelands" constructed from the territory of the Republic of South Africa.

Although this independence did not receive international political recognition we are satisfied that the stamps had "de facto" acceptance as valid for the carriage of mail outside Bophuthatswana.

Bophuthatswana was formally re-incorporated into South Africa on 27 April 1994.

100 cents = 1 rand.

1 Hand releasing Dove

1977. Independence. Multicoloured.
1 4c. Type **1** 35 35
2 10c. Leopard (national emblem) 75 60
3 15c. Coat of arms . . . . . . 1·25 1·00
4 20c. National flag . . . . . . 1·50 1·40

2 African Buffalo

1977. Tribal Totems. Multicoloured.
5a 1c. Type **2** 20 15
6a 2c. Bush pig 20 15
7a 3c. Chacma baboon 20 15
8a 4c. Leopard 20 10
9a 5c. Crocodile 20 10
10 6c. Savanna monkey 20 10
11a 7c. Lion 30 15
12a 8c. Spotted hyena 20 15
13 9c. Cape porcupine 25 15
14 10c. Aardvark 25 10
15 15c. Tilapia (fish) 80 15
16 20c. Hunting dog 25 20
17 25c. Common duiker 40 30
18 30c. African elephant 60 35
19 50c. Python 70 40
20 1r. Hippopotamus . . . . . 1·40 1·00
21 2r. Greater kudu . . . . . . 1·50 2·25

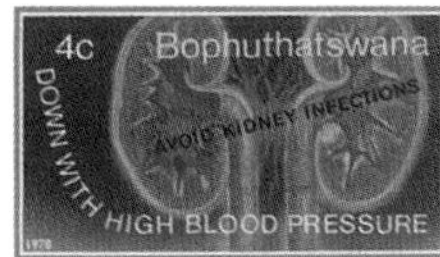

3 Infected Kidney

1978. World Hypertension Month. Multicoloured.
22 4c. Type **3** 50 25
23 10c. Heart and spoon of salt 70 70
24 15c. Spoon reflecting skull, knife and fork . . . . . . 1·25 1·25

4 Skull behind Steering Wheel of Car

1978. Road Safety. Multicoloured.
25 4c. Type **4** 70 40
26 10c. Child knocked off tricycle 90 80
27 15c. Pedestrian stepping in front of car . . . . 1·00 1·10
28 20c. Cyclist ignoring stop sign 1·40 1·75

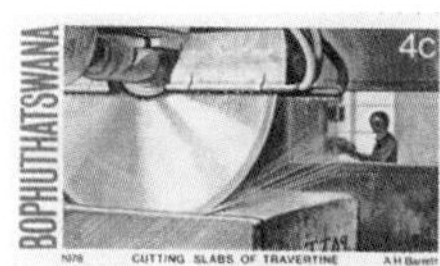

5 Cutting slabs of Travertine

1978. Semi-precious Stones. Multicoloured.
29 4c. Type **5** 65 25
30 10c. Polishing travertine . . . 1·25 85
31 15c. Sorting semi-precious stones . . . . 1·50 1·25
32 20c. Factory at Taung . . . . 2·25 1·60

6 Wright Flyer I

1978. 75th Anniv of First Powered Flight by Wright Brothers.
33 **6** 10c. black, blue and red . . . 1·00 1·00
34 – 15c. black, blue and red . . . 1·40 1·50
DESIGN: 15c. Orville and Wilbur Wright.

7 Pres. Lucas M. Mangope

9 Kallie Knoetze (South Africa)

8 Drying Germinated Wheat Sorghum

1978. 1st Anniv of Independence. Multicoloured.
35 4c. Type **7** 25 20
36 15c. Full face portrait of President 75 60

1978. Sorghum Beer-making. Multicoloured.
37 4c. Type **8** 25 20
38 15c. Cooking the ground grain 65 70
39 20c. Sieving the liquid 70 75
40 25c. Drinking the beer . . . . 80 1·00

1979. Knoetze–Tate Boxing Match. Multicoloured.
41 15c. Type **9** 75 75
42 15c. John Tate (U.S.A.) . . . 75 75

10 Emblem and Drawing of Local Fable (Hendrick Sebapo)

1979. International Year of the Child. Children's Drawings of Local Fables. Multicoloured.
43 4c. Type **10** 20 20
44 15c. Family with animals (Daisy Morapedi) 25 25
45 20c. Man's head and landscape (Peter Tladi) . . . 35 35
46 25c. Old man, boy and donkey (Hendrick Sebapo) 45 60

11 Miner and Molten Platinum

1979. Platinum Industry.
47 **11** 4c. multicoloured 25 10
48 – 15c. multicoloured 35 30
49 – 20c. multicoloured 45 45
50 – 25c. black and grey 60 65
DESIGNS: 15c. Platinum granules and industrial use; 20c. Telecommunications satellite; 25c. Jewellery.

12 Cattle

13 Cigarettes forming Cross

1979. Agriculture. Multicoloured.
51 5c. Type **12** 20 20
52 15c. Picking cotton 25 25
53 20c. Scientist examining maize 30 30
54 25c. Catch of fish 35 35

1979. Anti-smoking Campaign.
55 **13** 5c. multicoloured 40 20

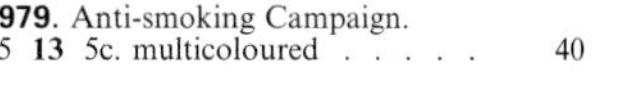

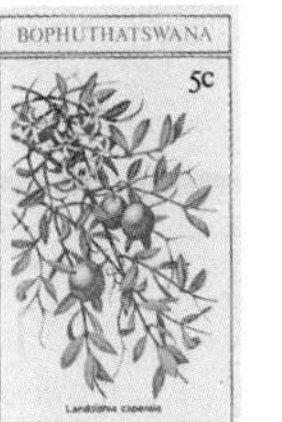

14 "Landolphia capensis"

15 Pied Babbler

1980. Edible Wild Fruits. Multicoloured.
56 5c. Type **14** 15 15
57 10c. "Vangueria infausta" . . 30 30
58 15c. "Bequaertiodendron magalismontanum" 40 40
59 20c. "Sclerocarya caffra" . . . 55 55

1980. Birds. Multicoloured.
60 5c. Type **15** 30 20
61 10c. Carmine bee eater . . . 40 35
62 15c. Shaft-tailed whydah . . . 60 60
63 20c. Brown parrot ("Meyer's Parrot") 70 65

16 Sun City Hotel

17 Deaf Child

1980. Tourism. Sun City. Multicoloured.
64 5c. Type **16** 10 15
65 10c. Gary Player Country Club 40 30
66 15c. Casino 45 50
67 20c. Extravaganza 50 70

1981. Int Year of Disabled Persons. Mult.
68 5c. Type **17** 15 10
69 15c. Blind child 30 20
70 20c. Archer in wheelchair . . 45 35
71 25c. Tuberculosis X-ray . . . 60 60

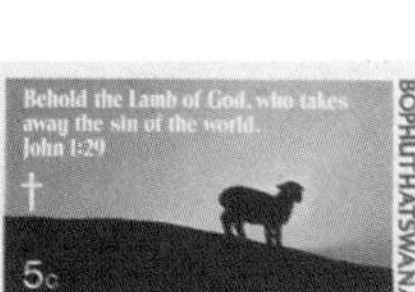

18 "Behold the Lamb of God …"

19 Siemens and Halske Wall Telephone, 1885

1981. Easter. Multicoloured.
72 5c. Type **18** 10 10
73 15c. Bread ("I am the bread of life") 25 25
74 20c. Shepherd ("I am the good shepherd") 35 35
75 25c. Wheatfield ("Unless a grain of wheat falls into the earth and dies …") 45 45

1981. History of the Telephone (1st series). Multicoloured.
76 5c. Type **19** 10 10
77 15c. Ericsson telephone, 1895 25 25
78 20c. Hasler telephone, 1900 . . 35 35
79 25c. Mix and Genest wall telephone, 1904 . . . . . . 45 45
See also Nos. 92/5, 108/11 and 146/9.

20 "Themeda triandra"

21 Boy Scout

1981. Indigenous Grasses (1st series). Multicoloured.
80 5c. Type **20** 10 10
81 15c. "Rhynchelytrum repens" 20 25
82 20c. "Eragrostis capensis" . . 20 30
83 25c. "Monocymbium ceresiiforme" 30 45
See also Nos. 116/19.

1982. 75th Anniv of Boy Scout Movement. Multicoloured.
84 5c. Type **21** 15 10
85 15c. Mafeking siege stamps . . 35 35
86 20c. Original cadet 40 40
87 25c. Lord Baden-Powell . . . 45 45

22 Jesus arriving at Bethany (John 12:1)

23 Ericsson Telephone, 1878

1982. Easter. Multicoloured.
88 15c. Type **22** 25 25
89 20c. Jesus sending disciples for donkey (Matthew 21:1,2) . . 30 30

90	25c. Disciples taking donkey (Mark 11:5,6)	40	40
91	30c. Disciples with donkey and foal (Matthew 21:7)	45	45

1982. History of the Telephone (2nd series). Multicoloured.

92	8c. Type **23**	15	10
93	15c. Ericsson telephone, 1885	20	20
94	20c. Ericsson telephone, 1893	20	20
95	25c. Siemens and Halske telephone, 1898	30	30

24 Old Parliament Building

1982. 5th Anniv of Independence. Multicoloured.

96	8c. Type **24**	10	10
97	15c. New government offices	20	20
98	20c. University, Mmabatho	25	25
99	25c. Civic Centre, Mmabatho	30	30

25 White Rhinoceros

1983. Pilanesberg Nature Reserve. Multicoloured.

100	8c. Type **25**	30	10
101	20c. Common zebras	40	30
102	25c. Sable antelope	40	35
103	40c. Hartebeest	60	60

26 Disciples bringing Donkeys to Jesus (Matthew 21:7)

1983. Easter. Palm Sunday. Multicoloured.

104	8c. Type **26**	10	10
105	20c. Jesus stroking colt (Mark 11:7)	30	30
106	25c. Jesus enters Jerusalem on donkey (Matthew 21:8)	35	35
107	40c. Crowd welcoming Jesus (Mark 11:9)	60	60

1983. History of the Telephone (3rd series). As T **19**. Multicoloured.

108	10c. A.T.M. table telephone c. 1920	15	10
109	20c. A/S Elektrisk wall telephone, c. 1900	30	30
110	25c. Ericsson wall telephone c. 1900	35	35
111	40c. Ericsson wall telephone c. 1900 (different)	60	60

27 Kori Bustard

1983. Birds of the Veld. Multicoloured.

112	10c. Type **27**	30	20
113	20c. Black bustard ("Black Korhaan")	45	45
114	25c. Crested bustard ("Red-crested Korhaan")	55	55
115	40c. Denhan's ("Stanley Bustard")	70	80

1984. Indigenous Grasses (2nd series). As T **20**. Multicoloured.

116	10c. "Panicum maximum"	15	10
117	20c. "Hyparrhenia dregeana"	20	20
118	25c. "Cenchrus ciliaris"	25	35
119	40c. "Urochloa brachyura"	50	70

28 Money-lenders in the Temple (Mark 11:11)

1984. Easter. Multicoloured.

120	10c. Type **28**	15	10
121	20c. Jesus driving the money-lenders from the Temple (Mark 11:15)	25	20
122	25c. Jesus and fig tree (Matthew 21:9)	35	35
123	40c. The withering of the fig tree (Matthew 21:9)	60	70

29 Car Upholstery, Ga-Rankuwa

1984. Industries. Multicoloured.

124	1c. Textile mill	10	10
125	2c. Sewing sacks, Selosesha	10	10
126	3c. Ceramic tiles, Babelegi	10	10
127	4c. Sheepskin car seat covers	10	10
128	5c. Crossbow manufacture	15	10
129	6c. Automobile parts, Babelegi	15	10
130	7c. Hosiery, Babelegi	15	10
131	8c. Specialised bicycle factory, Babelegi	30	10
132	9c. Lawn mower assembly line	30	15
133	10c. Dress factory, Thaba 'Nchu	20	10
134	11c. Molten platinum	60	20
135	12c. Type **29**	40	15
136	14c. Maize mill, Mafeking	50	15
137	15c. Plastic bags, Babelegi	25	15
137b	16c. Brick factory, Mmabatho	60	15
137c	18c. Cutlery manufacturing, Mogwase	60	15
138	20c. Men's clothing, Babelegi	25	15
138b	21c. Welding bus chassis	50	50
138c	21c. Fitting engine to bus chassis	50	50
138d	21c. Bus body construction	50	50
138e	21c. Spraying and finishing bus	50	50
138f	21c. Finished bus	50	50
139	25c. Chromium plating pram parts	30	20
140	30c. Spray painting metal beds	40	25
141	50c. Milk processing plant	50	40
142	1r. Modern printing works	60	75
143	2r. Industrial complex, Babelegi	1·00	2·50

1984. History of the Telephone (4th series). As T **19**. Multicoloured.

146	11c. Schuchhardt table telephone, 1905	15	10
147	20c. Siemens wall telephone, 1925	25	20
148	25c. Ericsson table telephone, 1900	30	30
149	30c. Oki table telephone, 1930	40	50

30 Yellow-throated Plated Lizard

31 Giving Oral Vaccine against Polio

1984. Lizards. Multicoloured.

150	11c. Type **30**	20	10
151	25c. Transvaal girdled lizard	30	30
152	30c. Ocellated sand lizard	35	40
153	45c. Bibron's thick-toed gecko	50	60

1985. Health. Multicoloured.

154	11c. Type **31**	35	10
155	25c. Vaccinating against measles	45	30
156	30c. Examining child for diphtheria	50	40
157	50c. Examining child for whooping cough	70	80

32 Chief Montshiwa of Barolong booRatshidi

34 "Faurea saligna" and planting Sapling

33 The Sick flock to Jesus in the Temple (Matthew, 21:41)

1985. Centenary of Mafeking.

158 **32**	11c. black, grey and orange	20	10
159 –	25c. black, grey and blue	40	30

DESIGN: 25c. Sir Charles Warren.

1985. Easter. Multicoloured.

160	12c. Type **33**	20	10
161	25c. Jesus cures the sick (Matthew 21:14)	30	20
162	30c. Children praising Jesus (Matthew 21:15)	35	30
163	50c. Community leaders discussing Jesus's acceptance of praise (Matthew 21:15, 16)	50	60

1985. Tree Conservation. Multicoloured.

164	12c. Type **34**	20	10
165	25c. "Boscia albitrunca" and kudu	25	20
166	30c. "Erythrina lysistemon" and mariqua sunbird	35	30
167	50c. "Bequaertiondendron magalismontanum" and bee	55	50

35 Jesus at Mary and Martha's, Bethany (John 12:2)

1986. Easter. Multicoloured.

168	12c. Type **35**	25	10
169	20c. Mary anointing Jesus's feet (John 12:3)	30	20
170	25c. Mary drying Jesus's feet with her hair (John 12:3)	35	25
171	30c. Disciple condemns Mary for anointing Jesus's head with oil (Matthew 26:7)	45	50

36 "Wesleyan Mission Station and Residence of Moroka, Chief of the Barolong, 1834" (C. D. Bell)

1986. Paintings of Thaba 'Nchu. Multicoloured.

172	14c. Type **36**	40	15
173	20c. "James Archbell's Congregation, 1834" (Charles Davidson Bell)	60	60
174	25c. "Mission Station at Thaba 'Nchu, 1850" (Thomas Baines)	65	80

37 Farmer using Tractor (agricultural development)

1986. Temisano Development Project. Mult.

175	14c. Type **37**	20	10
176	20c. Children at school (community development)	30	20
177	25c. Repairing engine (training)	35	30
178	30c. Grain elevator (secondary industries)	50	50

38 Stewardesses and Cessna Citation II

1986. "B.O.P." Airways. Multicoloured.

179	14c. Type **38**	25	10
180	20c. Passengers disembarking from Boeing 707	40	20
181	25c. Mmabatho International Airport	50	35
182	30c. Cessna Citation II	60	50

39 Netball

40 "Berkheya zeyheri"

1987. Sports. Multicoloured.

183	14c. Type **39**	20	15
184	20c. Tennis	30	30
185	25c. Football	30	30
186	30c. Athletics	45	50

1987. Wild Flowers. Multicoloured.

187	16c. Type **40**	25	15
188	20c. "Plumbago auriculata"	35	35
189	25c. "Pterodiscus speciosus"	35	35
190	30c. "Gazania krebsiana"	40	50

41 E. M. Mokgoko Farmer Training Centre

1987. Tertiary Education. Multicoloured.

191	16c. Type **41**	20	15
192	20c. Main lecture block, University of Bophuthatswana	30	35
193	25c. Manpower Centre	30	35
194	30c. Hotel Training School	30	50

42 Posts

1987. 10th Anniv of Independence. Communications. Multicoloured.

195	16c. Type **42**	25	15
196	30c. Telephone	35	35
197	40c. Radio	35	35
198	50c. Television	40	50

43 Jesus entering Jerusalem on Donkey (John 12:12–14)

1988. Easter. Multicoloured.

199	16c. Type **43**	25	15
200	30c. Judas negotiating with chief priests (Mark 14:10–11)	35	35
201	40c. Jesus washing the disciples' feet (John 13:5)	35	35
202	50c. Jesus handing bread to Judas (John 13:26)	40	50

44 Environment Education

1988. National Parks Board. Multicoloured.

203	16c. Type **44**	25	15
204	30c. Rhinoceros (Conservation)	40	40
205	40c. Catering workers	40	40
206	50c. Cheetahs (Tourism)	55	65

45 Sunflowers

1988. Crops. Multicoloured.

207	16c. Type **45**	25	15
208	30c. Peanuts	35	35

209 40c. Cotton 45 45
210 50c. Cabbages 60 60

46 Ngotwane Dam

1988. Dams. Multicoloured.
211 16c. Type **46** 30 20
212 30c. Groothoek Dam 50 50
213 40c. Sehujwane Dam 50 50
214 50c. Molatedi Dam 70 70

47 The Last Supper (Matthew 26: 26)

1989. Easter. Multicoloured.
215 16c. Type **47** 40 20
216 30c. Jesus praying in Garden of Gethsemane (Matthew 26:39) 60 55
217 40c. Judas kissing Jesus (Mark 14:45) 70 70
218 50c. Peter severing ear of High Priest's slave (John 18:10) 85 1·00

48 Cock (Thembi Atong) 49 Black-shouldered Kite

1989. Children's Art. Designs depicting winning entries in National Children's Day Art Competition.
219 18c. Type **48** 30 20
220 30c. Traditional thatched hut (Muhammad Mahri) 40 40
221 40c. Airplane, telephone wires and houses (Tshepo Mashokwi) 45 45
222 50c. City scene (Miles Brown) 50 60

1989. Birds of Prey. Paintings by Claude Finch-Davies. Multicoloured.
223 18c. Type **49** 1·10 30
224 30c. Pale chanting goshawk 1·25 75
225 40c. Lesser kestrel 1·50 1·10
226 50c. Short-toed eagle 1·60 1·50

50 Bilobial House

1989. Traditional Houses. Multicoloured.
227 18c. Type **50** 25 20
228 30c. House with courtyards at front and side 35 35
229 40c. House with conical roof 35 35
230 50c. House with rounded roof 40 50

51 Early Learning Schemes

1990. Community Services. Multicoloured.
231 18c. Type **51** 25 20
232 30c. Clinics 35 35
233 40c. Libraries 35 35
234 50c. Hospitals 40 45

52 Lesser Climbing Mouse

1990. Small Mammals. Multicoloured.
235 21c. Type **52** 30 20
236 30c. Zorilla 40 40
237 40c. Transvaal elephant shrew 60 60
238 50c. Large-toothed rock hyrax 80 85

53 Variegated Sandgrouse

1990. Sandgrouse. Paintings by Claude Finch-Davies. Multicoloured.
239 21c. Type **53** 90 30
240 35c. Double-banded sandgrouse 1·10 75
241 40c. Namaqua sandgrouse 1·10 90
242 50c. Yellow-throated sandgrouse 1·40 1·40

54 Basketry

1990. Traditional Crafts. Multicoloured.
243 21c. Type **54** 40 20
244 35c. Training 60 60
245 40c. Beer making 60 65
246 50c. Pottery 65 75

55 Sud Aviation Alouette II Helicopter 56 Wild Custard Apple

1990. Bophuthatswana Air Force. Multicoloured.
247 21c. Type **55** 1·10 1·10
248 21c. MBB-Kawasaki BK-117 helicopter 1·10 1·10
249 21c. Pilatus PC-7 turbo trainer 1·10 1·10
250 21c. Pilatus PC-6 1·10 1·10
251 21c. CASA C-212 Aviocar 1·10 1·10

1991. Edible Wild Fruit. Multicoloured.
252 21c. Type **56** 45 25
253 35c. Spine-leaved monkey orange 60 70
254 40c. Sycamore fig 65 75
255 50c. Kei apple 75 85

57 Arrest of Jesus (Mark 14:46)

1991. Easter. Multicoloured.
256 21c. Type **57** 45 25
257 35c. First trial by the Sanhedrin (Mark 14:53) 60 55
258 40c. Assault and derision of Jesus after sentence (Mark 14:65) 70 70
259 50c. Servant girl recognizing Peter (Mark 14:67) 75 90

58 Class 7A Locomotive No. 350, 1897 59 Caneiro Chart, 1502

1991. Steam Locomotives. Multicoloured.
260 25c. Class 6A locomotive No. 194, 1897, trucks and caboose (71 × 25 mm) 85 55
261 40c. Type **58** 1·10 85
262 50c. Double-boiler Class 6Z locomotives pulling Cecil Rhodes's funeral train (71 × 25 mm) 1·25 1·25
263 60c. Class 8 locomotive at Mafeking station, 1904 1·40 1·75

1991. Old Maps (1st series). Multicoloured.
264 25c. Type **59** 95 40
265 40c. Cantino Chart, 1502 1·40 95
266 50c. Giovanni Contarini's map, 1506 1·60 1·40
267 60c. Martin Waldseemuller's map, 1507 1·60 1·90

See also Nos. 268/71 and 297/300.

60 Fracanzano Map, 1508

1992. Old Maps (2nd series). Multicoloured.
268 27c. Type **60** 95 40
269 45c. Martin Waldseemuller's map (from edition of Ptolemy), 1513 1·40 95
270 65c. Section of Waldseemuller's woodcut "Carta Marina Navigatora Portugallan Navigationes", 1516 1·60 1·50
271 85c. Map from Laurent Fries's "Geographia", 1522 1·60 2·00

61 Delivery of Jesus to Pilate (Mark 15:1)

1992. Easter. Multicoloured.
272 27c. Type **61** 25 20
273 45c. Scourging of Jesus (Mark 15:15) 40 40
274 65c. Placing crown of thorns on Jesus's head (Mark 15: 17–18) 50 70
275 85c. Soldiers mocking Jesus (Mark 15:19) 60 90

62 Sweet Thorn

1992. Acacia Trees. Multicoloured.
276 35c. Type **62** 30 25
277 70c. Camel thorn 50 60
278 90c. Umbrella thorn 60 80
279 1r.05 Black thorn 70 1·00

63 View of Palace across Lake 64 Light Sussex

1992. The Lost City Complex, Sun City. Mult.
280 35c. Type **63** 35 45
281 35c. Palace facade 35 45
282 35c. Palace porte cochere 35 45
283 35c. Palace lobby 35 45
284 35c. Tusk Bar, Palace 35 45

1993. Chickens. Multicoloured.
285 35c. Type **64** 50 25
286 70c. Rhode Island red 75 60
287 90c. Brown leghorn 90 1·00
288 1r.05 White leghorn 1·10 1·40

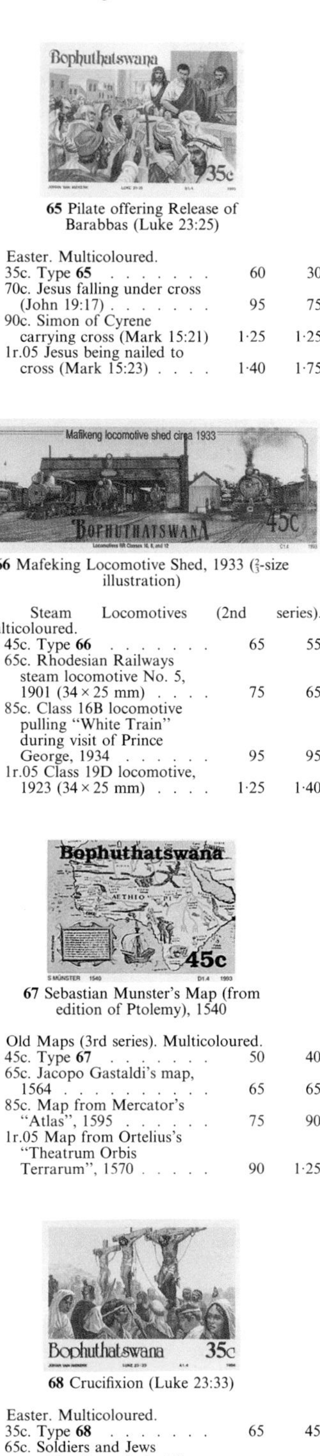

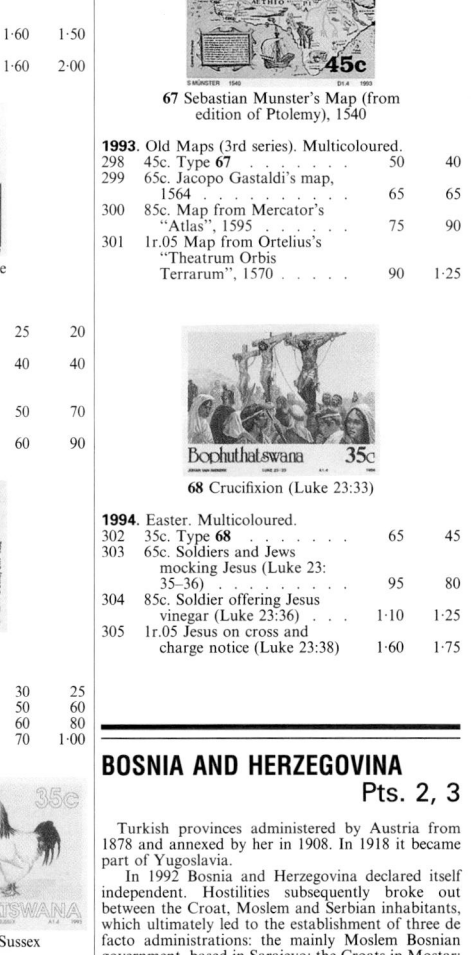

65 Pilate offering Release of Barabbas (Luke 23:25)

1993. Easter. Multicoloured.
289 35c. Type **65** 60 30
290 70c. Jesus falling under cross (John 19:17) 95 75
291 90c. Simon of Cyrene carrying cross (Mark 15:21) 1·25 1·25
292 1r.05 Jesus being nailed to cross (Mark 15:23) 1·40 1·75

66 Mafeking Locomotive Shed, 1933 (½-size illustration)

1993. Steam Locomotives (2nd series). Multicoloured.
293 45c. Type **66** 65 55
294 65c. Rhodesian Railways steam locomotive No. 5, 1901 (34 × 25 mm) 75 65
295 85c. Class 16B locomotive pulling "White Train" during visit of Prince George, 1934 95 95
296 1r.05 Class 19D locomotive, 1923 (34 × 25 mm) 1·25 1·40

67 Sebastian Munster's Map (from edition of Ptolemy), 1540

1993. Old Maps (3rd series). Multicoloured.
298 45c. Type **67** 50 40
299 65c. Jacopo Gastaldi's map, 1564 65 65
300 85c. Map from Mercator's "Atlas", 1595 75 90
301 1r.05 Map from Ortelius's "Theatrum Orbis Terrarum", 1570 90 1·25

68 Crucifixion (Luke 23:33)

1994. Easter. Multicoloured.
302 35c. Type **68** 65 45
303 65c. Soldiers and Jews mocking Jesus (Luke 23: 35–36) 95 80
304 85c. Soldier offering Jesus vinegar (Luke 23:36) 1·10 1·25
305 1r.05 Jesus on cross and charge notice (Luke 23:38) 1·60 1·75

BOSNIA AND HERZEGOVINA
Pts. 2, 3

Turkish provinces administered by Austria from 1878 and annexed by her in 1908. In 1918 it became part of Yugoslavia.

In 1992 Bosnia and Herzegovina declared itself independent. Hostilities subsequently broke out between the Croat, Moslem and Serbian inhabitants, which ultimately led to the establishment of three de facto administrations: the mainly Moslem Bosnian government, based in Sarajevo; the Croats in Mostar; and the Serbian Republic in Pale. Under the Dayton Agreement in November 1995 the Republic was split between a Moslem-Croat Federation and the Serbian Republic.

A. AUSTRO-HUNGARIAN MILITARY POST

1879. 100 kreuzer = 1 gulden.
1900. 100 heller = 1 krone.
1993. 100 paras = 1 dinar.
2002. 100 cents = 1 euro.

1 Value at top 2 Value at bottom

1879.

106 1 ½k. black . . . . 11·00 23·00
135 1k. grey . . . . 3·00 1·10
136 2k. yellow . . . . 1·90 50
137 3k. green . . . . 3·00 1·25
146 5k. red . . . . 4·00 55
139 10k. blue . . . . 4·00 75
140 15k. brown . . . . 3·25 3·75
141 20k. green . . . . 4·00 4·25
142 25k. purple . . . . 5·00 6·00

1900.

148 2 1h. black 20 15
149 2h. grey 20 15
151 3h. yellow 20 15
152 5h. green 15 10
154 6h. brown 30 15
155 10h. red 15 10
156 20h. pink . . . . £100 8·00
158 25h. blue 90 35
173 30h. brown . . . . £110 8·25
160 40h. orange . . . . £120 13·00
161 50h. purple 60 45

Larger stamps with value in each corner.

162 1k. red 80 50
163 2k. blue . . . . 1·40 1·50
164 5k. green . . . . 3·00 4·50

1901. Black figures of value.

177 2 20h. pink and black 60 45
178 30h. brown and black . . . 55 45
180 35h. blue and black . . . . 1·00 65
181 40h. orange and black . . . 70 65
182 45h. turquoise and black . . 80 70

4 View of Doboj

5 In the Carshija (business quarter) Sarajevo

1906.

186 4 1h. black 10 15
187 – 2h. violet 10 15
188 – 3h. yellow 10 15
189 – 5h. green 35 10
190 – 6h. brown 20 20
191 – 10h. red 40 10
192 – 20h. brown 65 20
193 – 25h. blue . . . . 1·40 90
194 – 30h. green . . . . 1·40 45
195 – 35h. green . . . . 1·40 45
196 – 40h. orange . . . . 1·40 45
197 – 45h. red . . . . 1·40 75
198 – 50h. brown . . . . 1·60 90
199 5 1k. red . . . . 4·75 3·00
200 – 2k. green . . . . 6·25 11·50
201 – 5k. blue . . . . 4·75 7·75

DESIGNS—As Type 4: 2h. Mostar; 3h. The old castle, Jajce; 5h. Naretva pass and Prenz Planina; 6h. Valley of the Rama; 10h. Valley of the Vrbas; 20h. Old Bridge, Mostar; 25h. The Begova Djamia (Bey's Mosque), Sarajevo; 30h. Post by beast of burden; 35h. Village and lake, Jezero; 40h. Mail wagon; 45h. Bazaar at Sarajevo; 50h. Post car. As Type 5: 2k. St. Luke's Campanile at Jajce; 5k. Emperor Francis Joseph I.

See also Nos. 359/61.

1910. 80th Birthday of Francis Joseph I. As stamps of 1906 but with date-label at foot.

343 1h. black 50 25
344 2h. violet 60 25
345 3h. yellow 60 25
346 5h. green 65 25
347 6h. brown 70 45
348 10h. red 65 15
349 20h. brown . . . . 1·60 1·40
350 25h. blue . . . . 3·00 2·50
351 30h. green . . . . 2·00 2·25
352 35h. green . . . . 2·75 2·25
353 40h. orange . . . . 3·00 2·25
354 45h. red . . . . 5·25 5·50
355 50h. brown . . . . 5·25 6·00
356 1k. red . . . . 5·25 6·25
357 2k. green . . . . 19·00 21·00
358 5k. blue . . . . 3·50 6·00

1912. As T 4 (new values and views).

359 12h. blue . . . . 4·50 5·00
360 60h. grey . . . . 3·25 4·25
361 72h. red . . . . 12·50 16·00

DESIGNS: 12h. Jajce; 60h. Konjica; 72h. Vishegrad.

25 Francis Joseph I 26 Francis Joseph I

1912. Various frames. Nos. 378/82 are larger (27 × 22 mm).

362 25 1h. olive 30 10
363 2h. blue 30 10
364 3h. lake 30 10
365 5h. green 30 10
366 6h. black 30 10
367 10h. red 30 10
368 12h. green 50 20
369 20h. brown . . . . 3·50 10
370 25h. blue . . . . 1·75 10
371 30h. red . . . . 1·75 10
372 26 35h. green . . . . 1·75 10
373 40h. violet . . . . 6·00 10
374 45h. brown . . . . 3·00 20
375 50h. blue . . . . 2·50 10
376 60h. brown . . . . 2·25 10
377 72h. blue . . . . 3·00 3·25
378 25 1k. brown on cream . . . 12·00 35
379 2k. blue on blue . . . . 7·25 50
380 26 3k. red on green . . . . 11·00 10·00
381 5k. lilac and grey . . . . 21·00 25·00
382 10k. blue on grey . . . . 65·00 95·00

1914. Nos. 189 and 191 surch **1914.** and new value.

383 7h. on 5h. green 40 40
384 12h. on 10h. red 40 40

1915. Nos. 189 and 191 surch **1915.** and new value.

385 7h. on 5h. green . . . . . . 9·00 9·00
386 12h. on 10h. red 30 40

1915. Surch **1915.** and new value.

387 25 7h. on 5h. green . . . . . 70 1·75
388 12h. on 10h. red . . . . . 1·50 1·75

1916. Surch **1916.** and new value.

389 25 7h. on 5h. green 60 60
390 12h. on 10h. red 60 65

31

1916. War Invalids' Fund.

391 31 5h. (+2h.) green 85 80
392 – 10h. (+2h.) purple . . . . 1·40 1·40

DESIGN: 10h. Blind soldier and girl.

See also Nos. 434/5.

33 Francis Joseph I 34 Francis Joseph I

1916.

393 33 3h. black 25 25
394 5h. olive 45 50
395 6h. violet 45 50
396 10h. bistre . . . . 2·00 2·25
397 12h. grey 45 60
398 15h. red 45 25
399 20h. brown 45 60
400 25h. blue 45 60
401 30h. green 45 60
402 40h. red 45 60
403 50h. green 45 60
404 60h. lake 45 60
405 80h. brown . . . . 1·40 40
406 90h. purple . . . . 1·60 80
407 34 2k. red on yellow . . . . 65 1·00
408 3k. green on blue . . . . 80 2·10
409 4k. red on green . . . . 5·50 10·00
410 10k. violet on grey . . . . 28·00 20·00

1917. War Widows' Fund. Optd **WITWEN-UND WAISENWOCHE 1917.**

411 33 10h. (+2h.) bistre 10 20
412 15h. (+2h.) pink 10 20

36 Design for Memorial Church, Sarajevo 39 Emperor Charles

1917. Assassination of Archduke Ferdinand. Fund for Memorial Church at Sarajevo.

413 36 10h. (+2h.) black 10 30
414 – 15h. (+2h.) red 10 30
415 – 40h. (+2h.) blue 10 30

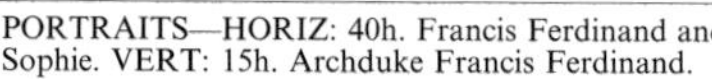

PORTRAITS—HORIZ: 40h. Francis Ferdinand and Sophie. VERT: 15h. Archduke Francis Ferdinand.

1917.

416 39 3h. grey 10 20
417 5h. olive 10 10
418 6h. violet 60 70
419 10h. brown 20 10
420 12h. blue 60 70
421 15h. red 10 10
422 20h. brown 10 10
423 25h. blue 90 65
424 30h. green 25 20
425 40h. bistre 25 20
426 50h. green 90 50
427 60h. red 90 45
428 80h. blue 20 25
429 90h. lilac . . . . 1·00 1·40
430 – 2k. red on yellow 60 35
431 – 3k. green on blue . . . . 15·00 16·00
432 – 4k. red on green . . . . 6·00 8·00
433 – 10k. violet on grey . . . . 4·00 6·25

The kronen values are larger (25 × 25 mm) and with different border.

1918. War Invalids' Fund.

434 – 10h. (+2h.) green (as No. 392) 60 70
435 31 15h. (+2h.) brown 60 70

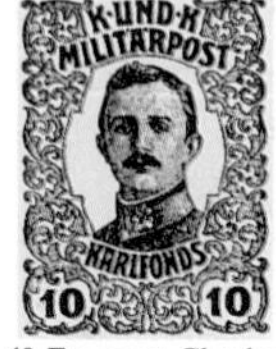

40 Emperor Charles

1918. Emperor's Welfare Fund.

436 40 10h. (+10h.) green 40 85
437 – 15h. (+10h.) brown 40 85
438 40 40h. (+10h.) purple 40 85

DESIGN—15h. Empress Zita.

1918. Optd **1918.**

439 – 2h. violet (No. 344) . . . . 50 1·00
440 25 2h. blue . . . . 50 1·10

NEWSPAPER STAMPS

N 27 Girl in Bosnian Costume N 35 Mercury

1913. Imperf.

N383 N 27 2h. blue 40 40
N384 6h. mauve . . . . . . 1·40 1·40
N385 10h. red . . . . 1·60 1·40
N386 20h. green . . . . . . 2·10 1·60

For these stamps perforated see Yugoslavia, Nos. 25 to 28.

1916. For Express.

N411 N 35 2h. red 25 25
N412 5h. green 45 45

POSTAGE DUE STAMPS

D 4 D 35

1904. Imperf. or perf.

D183 D 4 1h. black, red & yellow 30 10
D184 2h. black, red & yellow 30 15
D185 3h. black, red & yellow 30 10
D186 4h. black, red & yellow 30 10
D187 5h. black, red & yellow 1·40 10
D188 6h. black, red & yellow 25 10
D189 7h. black, red & yellow 2·25 3·25
D190 8h. black, red & yellow 2·25 1·50
D191 10h. black, red & yellow 50 10
D192 15h. black, red & yellow 40 10
D193 20h. black, red & yellow . . . . . . 3·00 25
D194 50h. black, red & yellow . . . . . . 1·10 30
D195 200h. black, red & grn 4·00 2·25

1916.

D411 D 35 2h. red . . . . 40 1·00
D412 4h. red 35 60
D413 5h. red 40 60
D414 6h. red 35 85
D415 10h. red 35 50
D416 15h. red . . . . 2·75 5·25
D417 20h. red 35 50
D418 25h. red . . . . 90 2·00
D419 30h. red . . . . 90 2·00
D420 40h. red . . . . . . 7·25 12·50
D421 50h. red . . . . . . 23·00 40·00
D422 1k. blue . . . . 2·50 5·25
D423 3k. blue . . . . 12·00 23·00

B. INDEPENDENT REPUBLIC

I. SARAJEVO GOVERNMENT

The following issues were used for postal purposes in those areas controlled by the Sarajevo government.

1993. 100 paras = 1 dinar.
1997. 100 fennig = 1 mark.

50 State Arms 51 Games Emblem

1993. Imperf.

450 50 100d. blue, lemon & yellow 10 10
451 500d. blue, yellow & pink 15 15
452 1000d. ultramarine, yellow and blue 25 25
453 5000d. blue, yellow & grn 75 75
454 10000d. blue, lemon & yell 1·50 1·50
455 20000d. blue, yellow & bis 3·00 3·00
456 50000d. blue, yellow & grey . . . . 7·50 7·50

1994. 10th Anniv of Winter Olympic Games, Sarajevo. Imperf.

457 51 50000d. black and orange 5·00 5·00

Currency Reform
10000 (old) dinars = 1 (new) dinar.

53 Facade 55 Postman and Globe

54 Historical Map, 10th–15th Centuries

1995. Sarajevo Head Post Office. Multicoloured.

460 10d. Type 53 . . . . 10 10
461 20d. Interior 15 15
462 30d. As No. 461 . . . . . 30 30
463 35d. Before conflict 35 35
464 50d. As No. 463 . . . . . 45 45
465 100d. Present day 90 90
466 200d. As No. 465 . . . . 1·75 1·75

1995. Bosnian History. Multicoloured.

467 35d. Type 54 . . . . 30 30
468 100d. 15th-century Bogomil tomb, Oplicici (vert) . . . 80 80
469 200d. Arms of Kotromanic Dynasty (14th-15th centuries) (vert) . . . . . 1·60 1·60
470 300d. Charter by Ban Kulin of Bosnia, 1189 . . . . . 2·50 2·00

1995. World Post Day.

471 55 100d. multicoloured . . . 95 95

56 Dove with Olive Branch

1995. Europa. Peace and Freedom.

472 56 200d. multicoloured . . . 1·75 1·75

57 Children and Buildings (A. Softic)

1995. Children's Week.
473 **57** 100d. multicoloured . . . 95 95

58 Tramcar, 1895

59 "Simphyandra hofmannii"

1995. Centenary of Sarajevo Electric Tram System.
474 **58** 200d. multicoloured . . . 1·75 1·75

1995. Flowers. Multicoloured.
475 100d. Type **59** 95 95
476 200d. Turk's-head lily . . . . 1·90 1·90

60 Dalmatian Barbel Gudgeon

1995. Fishes. Multicoloured.
477 100d. Type **60** 95 95
478 200d. Adriatic minnow . . . 1·90 1·90

61 Kozija Bridge, Sarajevo

1995. Bridges. Multicoloured.
479 20d. Type **61** 15 15
480 30d. Arslanagica Bridge, Trebinje 25 25
481 35d. Latinska Bridge, Sarajevo 35 35
482 50d. Old bridge, Mostar . . 45 45
483 100d. Visegrad 90 90

62 Visiting Friends

1995. Christmas. Multicoloured.
484 100d. Type **62** . . . . 1·00 1·00
485 200d. Madonna and Child (vert) . . . . 2·00 2·00

63 Queen Jelena of Bosnia and Tomb (600th death anniv)

1995. Multicoloured.
486 30d. Type **63** 20 20
487 35d. Husein Kapetan Gradascevic "Dragon of Bosnia" (leader of 1831 uprising against Turkey) 30 30
488 100d. Mirza Safvet Basagic (125th death anniv) (horiz) 95 95

64 Places of Worship and Graveyards

1995. Religious Pluralism.
489 **64** 35d. multicoloured 35 35

65 Stadium and Sports

1995. Destruction of Olympic Stadium, Sarajevo. Multicoloured.
490 35d. Type **65** 30 30
491 100d. Stadium ablaze (vert) 95 95

66 Bahrija Hadzic (opera singer)

67 Child's Handprint

1996. Europa. Famous Women. Multicoloured.
492 80d. Type **66** 75 75
493 120d. Nasiha Hadzic (children's writer and radio presenter) . . . . 1·10 1·10

1996. 50th Anniv of U.N.I.C.E.F. Multicoloured.
494 50d. Child stepping on landmine (P. Mirna and K. Princes) 65 65
495 150d. Type **67** . . . . 1·25 1·25

68 Bobovac Castle

69 Roofed Fountain and Extract from Holy Koran

1996.
496 **68** 35d. black, blue and violet 35 35

1996. Bairam Festival.
497 **69** 80d. multicoloured 75 75

70 Town Hall

1996. Centenary of Sarajevo Town Hall.
498 **70** 80d. multicoloured 75 75

71 Hands on Computer Keyboard and Title Page of "Bosanki Prijatelj"

1996. 150th Anniv of Journalists' Association.
499 **71** 100d. multicoloured . . . 95 95

72 Essen

1996. "Essen 96" International Stamp Fair, Essen.
500 **72** 200d. multicoloured . . . 1·75 1·75

73 Running

74 "Campanula hercegovina"

1996. Centenary of Modern Olympic Games and Olympic Games, Atlanta. Multicoloured.
501 30d. Type **73** 25 25
502 35d. Games emblem 30 30
503 80d. Torch bearer and Olympic flag 75 75
504 120d. Pierre de Coubertin (founder) . . . . 1·10 1·10

Nos. 501/4 were issued together, se-tenant, with the backgrounds forming a composite design of athletes.

1996. Flowers. Multicoloured.
505 30d. Type **74** 30 30
506 35d. "Iris bosniaca" 35 35

75 Barak

1996. Dogs. Multicoloured.
507 35d. Type **75** 35 35
508 80d. Tornjak 85 85

76 Globe, Telephone and Alexander Bell

1996. Anniversaries. Multicoloured.
509 80d. Type **76** (120th anniv of Bell's invention of telephone) 80 80
510 120d. 1910 50h. stamp (cent of post car in Bosnia and Herzegovina) . . . . . . 1·10 1·10

77 Charter with Seal

78 Hot-air Balloons

1996. Granting of Privileges to Dubrovnik by Ban Stepan II Kotromanic, 1333.
511 **77** 100d. multicoloured . . . 95 95

1996. SOS Children's Village, Sarajevo.
512 **78** 100d. multicoloured . . . 95 95

79 Muslim Costume of Bjelasnice

80 Bogomil Soldier

1996. Traditional Costumes. Multicoloured.
513 50d. Type **79** 40 40
514 80d. Croatian 75 75
515 100d. Muslim costume of Sarajevo . . . . 1·10 1·10

1996. Military Uniforms. Multicoloured.
516 35d. Type **80** 30 30
517 80d. Austro-Hungarian rifleman 75 75
518 100d. Turkish light cavalryman . . . . 1·10 1·10
519 120d. Medieval Bosnian king 1·25 1·25

81 Mosque

1996. Winter Festival, Sarajevo.
520 **81** 100d. multicoloured . . . 90 90

82 Map and State Arms

1996. Bosnia Day.
521 **82** 120d. multicoloured . . . 1·00 1·00

83 Crowd around Baby Jesus

1996. Christmas.
522 **83** 100d. multicoloured . . . 90 90

84 Pope John Paul II

85 Palaeolithic Rock Carving, Badanj

1996. Papal Visit.
523 **84** 500d. multicoloured . . . 4·00 4·00

1997. Archaeological Finds. Multicoloured.
524 35d. Type **85** 30 30
525 50d. Neolithic ceramic head, Butmir 40 40
526 80d. Bronze Age "birds" wagon, Glasinac 65 65

86 Ferhad Pasha Mosque, Banja Luka

87 "Clown" (Martina Nokto)

1997. Bairam Festival.
528 **86** 200d. multicoloured . . . 1·50 1·50

1997. Children's Week.
529 **87** 100d. multicoloured . . . 75 75

88 Komadina

89 Trojan Warriors and Map

1997. 72nd Death Anniv of Mujaga Komadina (developer and Mayor of Mostar).
530 **88** 100d. multicoloured . . . 75 75

1997. Europa. Tales and Legends. Mult.
531 100d. Type **89** (theory of Roberto Prays) 75 75
532 120d. Man on prayer-mat and castle ("The Miraculous Spring of Ajvatovica") 90 90

90 "Rainbow Warrior"

1997. 26th Anniv of Greenpeace (environmental organization). Designs showing the "Rainbow Warrior". Multicoloured.
533 35d. Type **90** 35 35
534 80d. inscr "Dorreboom" . . 80 65
535 100d. inscr "Beltra" . . . . 1·10 1·10
536 120d. inscr "Morgan" . . . 1·40 1·40

91 Open Air Cinema, Sarajevo

1997. 3rd International Film Festival, Sarajevo.
537 **91** 110d. multicoloured . . . 90 90

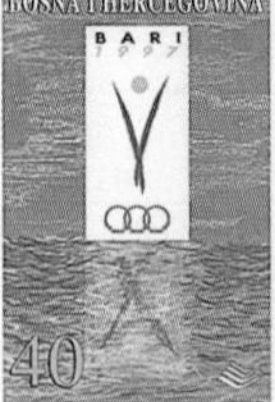

92 Games Emblem **93** Diagram of Electrons

1997. Mediterranean Games, Bari. Mult.
538 40d. Type **92** 35 35
539 130d. Boxing, basketball and kick boxing . . . . 1·10 1·10

1997. Anniversaries and Event. Mult.
540 40d. Type **93** (centenary of discovery of electrons) . . 35 35
541 110d. Vasco da Gama (navigator) and map (500th anniv of science of navigation) (vert) . . . . . 1·75 1·25
542 130d. Airmail envelope and airplane (Stamp Day) . . . 1·40 1·40
543 150d. Steam locomotive "Bosna" (125th anniv of railway in Bosnia and Herzegovina) . . . . . . 1·25 1·25

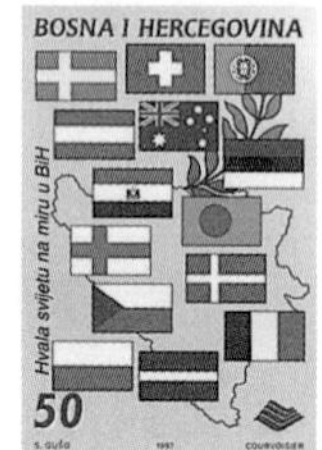

94 Vole **95** Map and Flags

1997. Flora and Fauna. Multicoloured.
544 40d. Type **94** 35 35
545 40d. "Oxytropis prenja" . . . 35 35
546 80d. Alpine newt 65 65
547 110d. "Dianthus freynii" . . 1·10 1·10

1997. International Peace Day. Mult.
548 50d. Type **95** 50 50
549 60d. Flags and right half of globe showing Europe and Africa 55 55
550 70d. Flags and left half of globe showing the Americas 60 60
551 110d. Map and flags (including U.S.A. and U.K.) . . . . 1·10 1·10
Nos. 548/51 were issued together, se-tenant, Nos. 549/50 forming a composite design.

96 House with Attic

1997. Architecture. Multicoloured.
552 40d. Type **96** 35 35
553 50d. Tiled stove and door . . 50 50
554 130d. Three-storey house . . 1·40 1·40

97 Sarajevo in 1697 and 1997

1997. 300th Anniv of Great Fire of Sarajevo.
555 **97** 110d. multicoloured . . . 1·10 1·10

98 Augustin Tin Ujevic

1997. Personalities. Multicoloured.
556 1m.30 Type **98** (lyricist and essayist) 90 90
557 2m. Zaim Imanovic (singer) (vert) . . . . 1·40 1·40

99 Sarajevo and Corps Emblem

1997. Contribution of Italian Pioneer Corps in Reconstruction of Sarajevo.
558 **99** 1m.40 multicoloured . . . 95 95

100 Diana, Princess of Wales, and Roses

1997. Diana, Princess of Wales, Commem.
559 **100** 2m.50 multicoloured . . . 1·90 1·90

101 "Gnijezdo" (Fikret Libovac)

1997. Art. Multicoloured.
560 35f. Type **101** 20 20
561 80f. "Sarajevo Library" (sculpture, Nusret Pasic) 55 55

102 Youth Builders Emblem attached to Route Map

1997. 50th Anniv of Samac-Sarajevo Railway.
562 **102** 35f. multicoloured 30 30

103 Nativity (icon) **105** Mosque Fountain

1997. Religious Events. Multicoloured.
563 50f. Type **103** (Orthodox Christmas) 35 35
564 1m.10 Wreath on door (Christmas) 80 80
565 1m.10 Pupils before teacher (14th-century miniature) (Haggadah) 80 80

1998. Bairam Festival.
567 **105** 1m. multicoloured 70 70

106 Zvornik

1998. Old Fortified Towns. Multicoloured.
568 35f. Type **106** 25 25
569 70f. Bihac 50 50
570 1m. Pocitelj 70 70
571 1m.20 Gradacac 85 85

107 Muradbegovic

1998. Birth Centenary of Ahmed Muradbegovic (dramatist and actor-director).
572 **107** 1m.50 multicoloured . . . 1·10 1·10

108 Branislav Djurdjev **109** White Storks

1998. Former Presidents of the University of Arts and Science. Multicoloured.
573 40f. Type **108** 30 30
574 70f. Alojz Benac 50 50
575 1m.30 Edhem Camo 95 95

1998. Endangered Species. The White Stork. Multicoloured.
576 70f. Type **109** 50 50
577 90f. Two storks flying 65 65
578 1m.10 Two adult storks on nest 80 80
579 1m.30 Adult stork with young 95 95

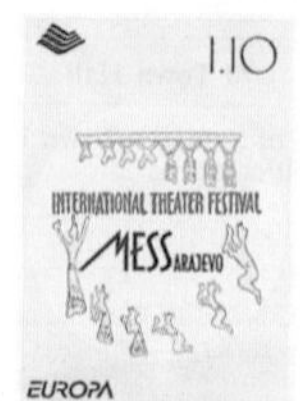

110 International Theatre Festival, Sarajevo

1998. Europa. National Festivals.
580 **110** 1m.10 multicoloured . . . 80 80

111 Footballs

1998. World Cup Football Championship, France. Multicoloured.
581 50f. Type **111** 35 35
582 1m. Map of Bosnia and ball 70 70
583 1m.50 Asim Ferhatovic Hase (footballer) . . . . 1·10 1·10

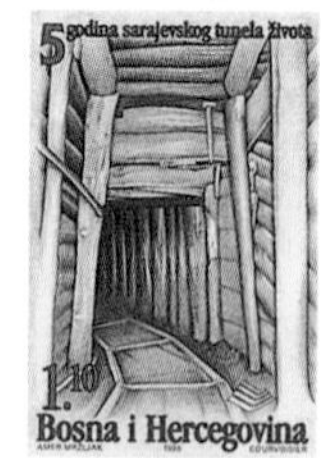

113 Common Morel **114** Tunnel

1998. Fungi. Multicoloured.
585 50f. Type **113** 35 35
586 80f. Chanterelle 55 55
587 1m.10 Edible mushroom . . 80 80
588 1m.35 Caesar's mushroom . . 95 95

1998. 5th Anniv of Sarajevo's Supply Tunnels.
589 **114** 1m.10 multicoloured . . . 80 80

115 Eiffel Tower and Underground Train

1998. Paris Metro.
590 **115** 2m. multicoloured . . . . 1·40 1·40

116 Henri Dunant (founder of Red Cross) **118** Travnik

1998. Anti-tuberculosis Week.
591 **116** 50f. multicoloured 35 35

1998. Old Towns.
593 **118** 5f. black and green . . . 10 10
597 – 38f. black and brown . . 25 25
DESIGN: 38f. Sarajevo.

119 Postal Workers in New Uniforms **120** Lutes

1998. World Post Day.
605 **119** 1m. multicoloured 70 70

1998. Musical Instruments.
606 **120** 80f. multicoloured 55 55

121 "The Creation of Adam" (detail of fresco on ceiling of Sistine Chapel, Michelangelo)

1998. World Disabled Day.
607 **121** 1m. multicoloured 70 70

122 Bjelasnica Mountain Range

1998.
608 **122** 1m. multicoloured 70 70

123 People

1998. 50th Anniv of Universal Declaration of Human Rights.
609 **123** 1m.35 multicoloured . . . 90 90

124 Christmas Tree (Lamija Pehilj)

1998. Christmas and New Year. Multicoloured.
610 1m. Type **124** 70 70
611 1m.50 Father Andeo Zvizdovic . . . . 1·00 1·00

125 Sarajevo University and "Proportion of Man" (Leonardo da Vinci)

127 Astronaut, Earth and Moon

126 Feral Rock Pigeons

1999. Anniversaries. Multicoloured.
612 40f. Type **125** (50th anniv) 25 25
613 40f. Sarajevo High School (120th anniv) (horiz) . . . 25 25

1999. Flora and Fauna. Multicoloured.
614 80f. Type **126** 55 55
615 1m.10 "Knautia sarajevensis" 75 75

1999. 30th Anniv of First Manned Moon Landing.
616 **127** 2m. multicoloured . . . .

128 Slapovi Une

1999. Europa. Parks and Gardens.
617 **128** 2m. multicoloured . . . . 1·40 1·40

129 Gorazde

1999.
618 **129** 40f. multicoloured 25 25

130 Children playing Football in Sun (Pranjkovic Nenad)

1999. Children's Week.
619 **130** 50f. multicoloured 35 35

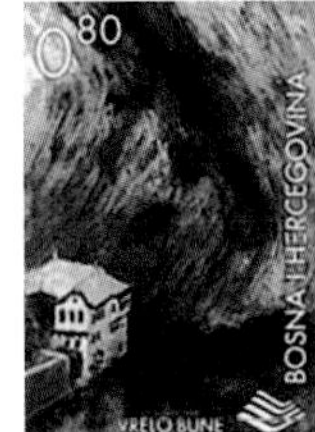
131 House

1999. World Environment Day.
620 **131** 80f. multicoloured 55 55

132 Church, Mosque and Emblem

1999. "Philexfrance 99" International Stamp Exhibition, Paris, France.
621 **132** 2m. multicoloured . . . . 1·40 1·40

133 Sarajevo on Stamp

1999. 120th Anniv of First Bosnia and Herzegovina Stamps.
622 **133** 1m. multicoloured 70 70

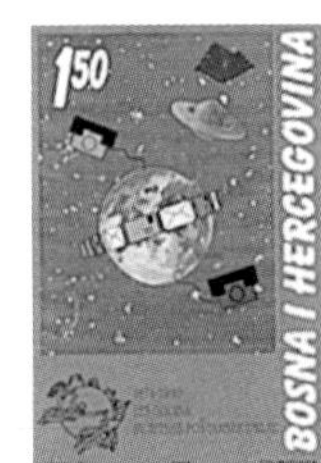
134 Letters encircling Globe and Telephones

1999. 125th Anniv of Universal Postal Union.
623 **134** 1m.50 multicoloured . . . 1·00 1·00

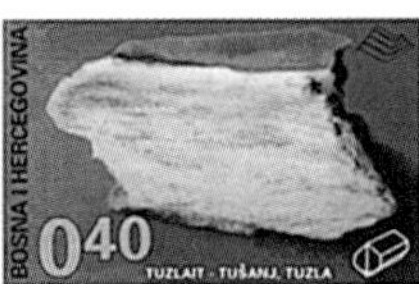
135 Tuzlait from Tuoanj

1999. Minerals. Multicoloured.
624 40f. Type **135** 20 20
625 60f. Siderit from Vitez . . . 40 40
626 1m.20 Hijelofan from Busovaca 80 80
627 1m.80 Quartz from Srebrenica (vert) . . . . . 1·25 1·25

136 Dove and Cathedral

137 Kursum Medresa, Sarajevo, 1537 (site of library)

1999. Southern Europe Stability Pact, Sarajevo.
628 **136** 2m. multicoloured . . . . 1·40 1·40

1999. Gazi-Husref Library. Multicoloured.
629 1m. Type **137** 70 70
630 1m.10 Miniature from Hval Codex, 1404 . . . . 75 75

138 Koran, 1550

1999.
631 **138** 1m.50 multicoloured . . . 1·00 1·00

139 X-Ray and Thermal Image of Hands

1999. Centenary of Radiology in Bosnia and Herzegovina.
632 **139** 90f. multicoloured 60 60

140 Kresevljakovic

1999. 40th Death Anniv of Hamdija Kresvljakovic (historian).
633 **140** 1m.30 multicoloured . . . 90 90

141 Chess Emblems and Stars

1999. 15th European Chess Clubs Championship Final, Bugojno.
634 **141** 1m.10 multicoloured . . . 75 75

142 Twipsy (exhibition mascot)

1999. "Expo 2000" World's Fair, Hanover, Germany.
635 **142** 1m. multicoloured 60 60

143 Painting (Afan Ramic)

1999.
636 **143** 1m.20 multicoloured . . . 75 75

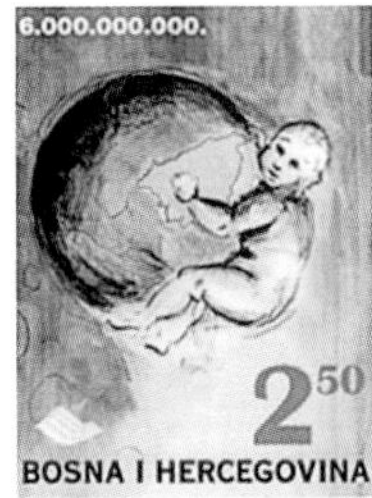
144 Globe and Baby

1999. Birth of World's Six Billionth Inhabitant in Sarajevo.
637 **144** 2m.50 multicoloured . . . 1·50 1·50

146 Philharmonic Orchestra Building, Sarajevo

147 Woman

1999. International Music Festival, Sarajevo.
639 **146** 40f. black and red 25 25
640 – 1m.10 multicoloured . . . 65 65
DESIGN: 1m.10, Festival poster

2000. Bairam Festival.
641 **147** 1m.10 multicoloured . . . 65 65

149 Spaho

150 Morse Apparatus

2000. 60th (1999) Death Anniv of Mehmed Spaho (politician).
643 **149** 1m. multicoloured 60 60

2000. 50th Anniv of Amateur Radio in Bosnia and Herzegovina.
644 **150** 1m.50 multicoloured . . . 95 95

151 Illuminated Manuscript

2000. 50th Anniv of Institute of Oriental Studies, Sarajevo University.
645 **151** 2m. multicoloured . . . . 1·25 1·25

152 Boracko River

2000. 15th Anniv of Emerald River Nature Protection Organization. Multicoloured.
646 40f. Type **152** 25 25
647 1m. Figure of woman and river (vert) 60 60

154 Griffon Vulture

2000. Birds. Multicoloured.
649 1m. Type **154** 60 60
650 1m.50 White spoonbill . . . 95 95

155 "Building Europe"

2000. Europa.
651 **155** 2m. multicoloured . . . . 1·25 1·25

156 Count Ferdinand von Zeppelin and LZ-1

2000. Centenary of 1st Zeppelin Flight.
652 **156** 1m.50 multicoloured . . . 95 95

157 Zenica

2000. Towns. Multicoloured.
653 50f. Type **157** 35 35
654 1m. Mostar 65 65
655 1m.10 Bihac 75 75
656 1m.50 Tuzla (vert) . . . . . 1·00 1·00

158 Millennium

2000. New Millennium. Sheet 100 × 72 mm containing T **158** and similar multicoloured design.
MS657 80f. Type **158**; 1m.20, Millennium (57 × 57 mm) 80 80

159 Vranduk

2000. Towns. Multicoloured.
658 1m.30 Type **159** 90 90
659 1m.50 Franciscan Abbey, Kraljeva Sutjeska . . . . 1·00 1·00

160 Tom Sawyer, Huckleberry Finn (characters) and Twain

2000. *The Adventures of Tom Sawyer* (children's book by Mark Twain).
660 **160** 1m.50 multicoloured . . . 1·00 1·00

161 People walking (Ismet Mujezinovic)

2000. Paintings. Multicoloured.
661 60f. Type **161** 40 40
662 80f. Trees (Ivo Seremet) . . . 55 55

162 Children and Globe

2000. International Children's Week.
663 **162** 1m.60 multicoloured . . . 1·10 1·10

163 Refugees

2000. 50th Anniv of United Nations Commissioner for Refugees.
664 **163** 1m. multicoloured 65 65

II. CROATIAN POSTS

Issues made by the Croat administration in Mostar.

1993. 100 paras = 1 Croatian dinar.
1994. 100 lipa = 1 kuna.

C **1** Statue and Church C **2** Silvije Kranjcevic (poet)

1993. Sanctuary of Our Lady Queen of Peace Shrine, Medugorje.
C1 C **1** 2000d. multicoloured . . . 50 50

1993. Multicoloured.
C2 200d. Type C **2** 10 10
C3 500d. Jajce 15 15
C4 1000d. Mostar (horiz) 20 20

C **3** Medieval Gravestone C **4** "Madonna of the Grand Duke" (Raphael)

1993. 250th Anniv of Census in Bosnia and Herzegovina.
C5 C **3** 100d. multicoloured . . . 10 10

1993. Christmas.
C6 C **4** 6000d. multicoloured . . . 1·25 1·25

C **5** "Uplands in Bloom"

1993. Europa. Contemporary Art. Paintings by Gabrijel Jurkic. Multicoloured.
C7 3500d. Type C **5** . . . . . . 1·75 1·75
C8 5000d. "Wild Poppy" . . . . 2·25 2·25

C **6** Kravica Waterfall

1993.
C9 C **6** 3000d. multicoloured . . . 60 60

C **7** Hrvoje (from "Hrvoje's Missal" by Butko)

1993. 577th Death Anniv of Hrvoje Vukcic Hrvatinic, Duke of Split, Viceroy of Dalmatia and Croatia and Grand Duke of Bosnia.
C10 C **7** 1500d. multicoloured . . 30 30

C **8** Plehan Monastery

1993.
C11 C **8** 2200d. multicoloured . . 45 45

C **9** Arms C **11** "Campanula hercegovina"

C **10** Bronze Cross, Rama-Scit (Mile Blazevic)

1994. Proclamation (August 1993) of Croatian Community of Herceg Bosna.
C12 C **9** 10000d. multicoloured . . 2·00 2·00

1994.
C13 C **10** 2k.80 multicoloured . . 55 55

1994. Flora and Fauna. Multicoloured.
C14 3k.80 Type C **11** 75 75
C15 4k. Mountain dog 80 80

C **12** Hutova Swamp

1994.
C16 C **12** 80l. multicoloured . . . 20 20

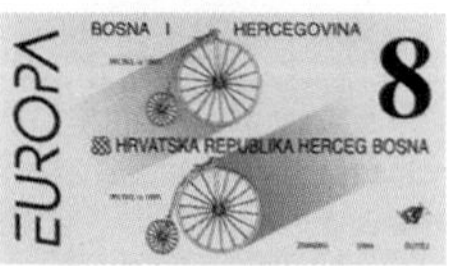

C **13** Penny Farthing Bicycles

1994. Europa. Discoveries and Inventions. Mult.
C17 8k. Type C **13** . . . . 1·50 1·50
C18 10k. Mercedes cars, 1901 . . 2·00 2·00

C **14** Views of Town and Fortress

1994. 550th Anniv of First Written Record of Ljubuski.
C19 C **14** 1k. multicoloured . . . 20 20

C **15** Hospital and Christ C **16** Anniversary Emblem

1994. 2nd Anniv of Dr. Nikolic Franciscan Hospital, Nova Bila.
C20 C **15** 5k. multicoloured . . . 1·00 1·00

1995. 50th Anniv of U.N.O. Self-adhesive. Rouletted.
C21 C **16** 1k.50 blue, red & black 30 30

C **17** Crib

1995. Christmas.
C22 C **17** 5k.40 multicoloured . . 1·10 1·10

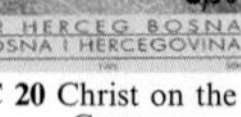

C **18** Franciscan Monastery, Kraljeva Sutjeska C **19** Srebrenica

1995.
C23 C **18** 3k. multicoloured . . . 60 60

1995. Towns. Multicoloured.
C24 2k. Type C **19** 40 40
C25 4k. Franciscan Monastery, Mostar 80 80

C **20** Christ on the Cross C **21** Statue and Church

1995. Europa. Peace and Freedom.
C26 C **20** 6k.50 multicoloured . . 1·25 1·25

1996. 15th Anniv of Sanctuary of Our Lady Queen of Peace Shrine, Medugorje.
C27 C **21** 10k. multicoloured . . . 2·00 2·00

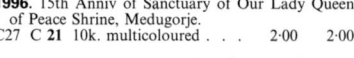

C **22** Queen Katarina Kosaca Kotromanic C **23** Monastery

1996. Europa. Famous Women.
C28 C **22** 2k.40 multicoloured . . 50 50

1996. 150th Anniv of Franciscan Monastery and Church, Siroki Brijeg.
C29 C **23** 1k.40 multicoloured . . 30 30

C **24** Virgin Mary C **26** "Madonna and Child" (anon)

1996. Self-adhesive. Rouletted.
C30 C **24** 2k. mult (postage) . . . 40 40
C31 9k. multicoloured (air) 1·75 1·75

1996. "Taipeh '96" International Stamp Exn. Nos. C30/1 surch **1.10** and emblem.
C32 C **24** 1k.10 on 2k. mult (postage) 20 20
C33 1k.10 on 9k. mult (air) 20 20

1996. Christmas.
C34 C **26** 2k.20 multicoloured . . 45 45

C **27** St. George and the Dragon C **28** Pope John Paul II

1997. Europa. Tales and Legends. Mult.
C35 2k. Type C **27** 40 40
C36 5k. Zeus as bull and Europa (39 × 34 mm) . . . . . . 1·00 1·00

1997. Papal Visit.
C37 C **28** 3k.60 multicoloured . . 70 70

C 29 Chapel, Samatorje, Gorica

C 30 Purple Heron

1997.
C39 C **29** 1k.40 multicoloured . . 25 25

1997. Flora and Fauna. Multicoloured.
C40 1k. Type C **30** 20 20
C41 2k.40 "Symphyandra hofmannii" (orchid) . . . 45 45

C 31 "Birth of Christ" (fresco, Giotto)

1997. Christmas.
C42 C **31** 1k.40 multicoloured . . 25 25

C 32 Cats

1998. Europa. Animated Film Festival.
C43 C **32** 6k.50 multicoloured . . 1·10 1·10

C 33 Seal

C 35 "Sibiraea croatica"

C 34 Livno

1998. 550th Anniv of Herzegovina.
C44 C **33** 2k.30 red, black and gold 40 40

1998. 1100th Anniv of Livno.
C45 C **34** 1k.20 multicoloured . . 20 20

1998.
C46 C **35** 1k.40 multicoloured . . 25 25

C 36 Griffon Vulture

C 37 Adoration of the Wise Men

1998.
C47 C **36** 2k.40 multicoloured . . 40 40

1998. Christmas.
C48 C **37** 5k.40 multicoloured . . 90 90

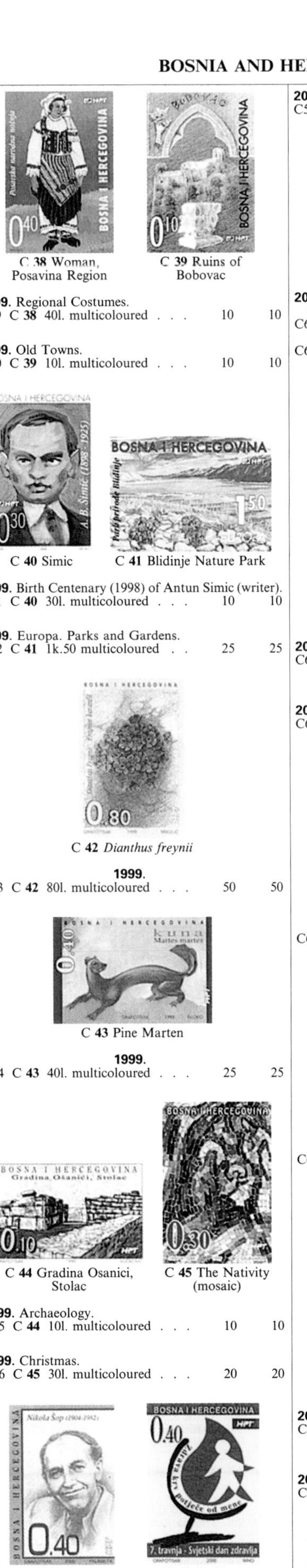

C 38 Woman, Posavina Region

C 39 Ruins of Bobovac

1999. Regional Costumes.
C49 C **38** 40l. multicoloured . . . 10 10

1999. Old Towns.
C50 C **39** 10l. multicoloured . . . 10 10

C 40 Simic

C 41 Blidinje Nature Park

1999. Birth Centenary (1998) of Antun Simic (writer).
C51 C **40** 30l. multicoloured . . . 10 10

1999. Europa. Parks and Gardens.
C52 C **41** 1k.50 multicoloured . . 25 25

C 42 *Dianthus freynii*

1999.
C53 C **42** 80l. multicoloured . . . 50 50

C 43 Pine Marten

1999.
C54 C **43** 40l. multicoloured . . . 25 25

C 44 Gradina Osanici, Stolac

C 45 The Nativity (mosaic)

1999. Archaeology.
C55 C **44** 10l. multicoloured . . . 10 10

1999. Christmas.
C56 C **45** 30l. multicoloured . . . 20 20

C 46 Sop

C 47 Emblem

2000. 96th Birth Anniv of Nikola Sop (poet).
C57 C **46** 40l. multicoloured . . . 25 25

2000. World Health Day.
C58 C **47** 40l. multicoloured . . . 25 25

C 48 Ceramic Doves

2000. Europa.
C59 C **48** 1k.80 multicoloured . . 30 30

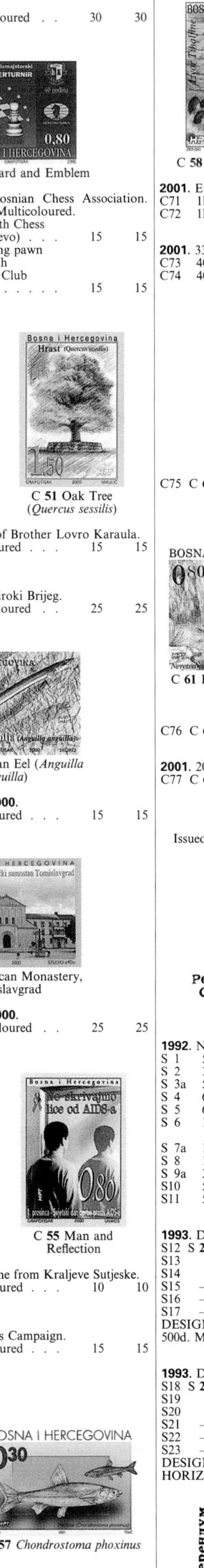

C 49 Chess Board and Emblem

2000. 40th Anniv of Bosnian Chess Association. Chess Events in 2000. Multicoloured.
C60 80l. Type C **49** (30th Chess Olympiad, Sarajevo) . . . 15 15
C61 80l. Octopus holding pawn and emblem (16th European Chess Club Cup, Neum) 15 15

C 50 Brother Karaula

C 51 Oak Tree (*Quercus sessilis*)

2000. Birth Bicentenary of Brother Lovro Karaula.
C62 C **50** 80l. multicoloured . . . 15 15

2000. Chestnut Oak of Siroki Brijeg.
C63 C **51** 1k.50 multicoloured . . 25 25

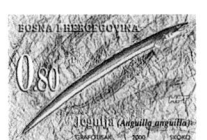

C 52 European Eel (*Anguilla anguilla*)

2000.
C64 C **52** 80l. multicoloured . . . 15 15

C 53 Franciscan Monastery, Tomislavgrad

2000.
C65 C **53** 1k.50 multicoloured . . 25 25

C 54 Woman and Patterned Cloth

C 55 Man and Reflection

2000. Traditional Costume from Kraljeve Sutjeske.
C66 C **54** 40l. multicoloured . . . 10 10

2000. A.I.D.S. Awareness Campaign.
C67 C **55** 80l. multicoloured . . . 15 15

C 56 Nativity

C 57 *Chondrostoma phoxinus*

2000. Christmas.
C68 C **56** 40l. multicoloured . . . 10 10

2001. Fishes. Multicoloured.
C69 30l. Type C **57** 10 10
C70 1k.50 *Salmo marmoratus* . . 25 25

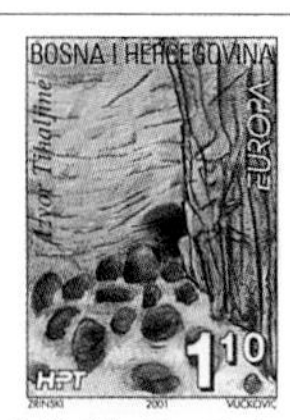

C 58 Tihaljina Spring

C 59 Petar Zrinski

2001. Europa. Water Resources. Multicoloured.
C71 1k.10 Type C **58** 20 20
C72 1k.80 Pliva Waterfall 30 30

2001. 330th Death Anniversaries. Multicoloured.
C73 40l. Type C **59** 10 10
C74 40l. Fran Krsto Frankopan 10 10

C 60 16th-century Galley Ship

2001.
C75 C **60** 1k.80 multicoloured . . 30 30

C 61 Boat, Neretva River Valley

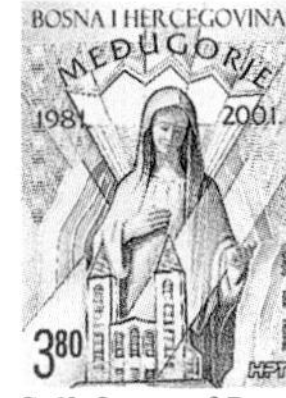

C 62 Queen of Peace of Medugorje

2001.
C76 C **61** 80l. multicoloured . . . 15 15

2001. 20th Anniv of Medugorje. Sheet 90 × 65 mm.
C77 C **62** 3k.80 multicoloured . . 65 65

III. REPUBLIKA SRPSKA

Issued by the Serb administration based in Pale.

100 paras = 1 dinar.
1998. 100 fennig = 1 mark.

30
Република
Српска
(S 1)

S 2 Stringed Instrument

1992. Nos. 2587/98 of Yugoslavia surch as Type S **1**.
S 1 5d. on 10p. violet and green 10 10
S 2 30d. on 3d. blue and red . . 60·00 60·00
S 3a 50d. on 40p. green & purple 50 50
S 4 60d. on 20p. red and yellow 60 60
S 5 60d. on 30p. green & orange 60 60
S 6 100d. on 1d. blue and purple . . . . 1·00 1·00
S 7a 100d. on 2d. blue and red 1·00 1·00
S 8 100d. on 3d. blue and red 1·00 1·00
S 9a 300d. on 5d. ultram & blue 3·00 3·00
S10 500d. on 50p. green & violet 5·00 5·00
S11 500d. on 60p. mauve & red 5·00 5·00

1993. Dated "1992".
S12 S **2** 10d. black and yellow . . 10 10
S13 20d. black and blue . . . 25 25
S14 30d. black and pink . . . 35 35
S15 – 50d. black and red . . . 60 60
S16 – 100d. black and red . . . 1·25 1·25
S17 – 500d. black and blue . . . 6·25 6·25
DESIGNS—VERT: 50, 100d. Coat of arms. HORIZ: 500d. Monastery.

1993. Dated "1993".
S18 S **2** 5000d. black and lilac . . 10 10
S19 6000d. black and yellow 15 15
S20 10000d. black and blue . . 25 25
S21 – 20000d. black and red . . 55 55
S22 – 30000d. black and red . . 85 85
S23 – 50000d. black and lilac . . 1·40 1·40
DESIGNS—VERT: 20000, 30000d. Coat of arms. HORIZ: 50000d. Monastery.

референдум
15-16. 05. '93.
7500
(S 3)

S 4 Symbol of St. John the Evangelist

1993. Referendum. Nos. S15/16 surch as Type S **3**.
S24 7500d. on 50d. black and red 60 60
S25 7500d. on 100d. black and red 60 60
S26 9000d. on 50d. black and red 80 80

1993. No value expressed.
S27 S **4** A red 40 40
No. S27 was sold at the rate for internal letters.

Currency Reform

S **5** Icon of St. Stefan

1994. Republic Day.
S28 S **5** 1d. multicoloured 4·00 4·00

S **6** King Petar I

1994. 150th Birth Anniv of King Petar I of Serbia.
S29 S **6** 80p. sepia and brown 2·50 2·50

S **7** Banja Luka

1994. 500th Anniv of Banja Luka.
S30 S **7** 1d.20 multicoloured 2·00 2·50

1994. Issued at Doboj. Surch with letter. (a) On Nos. S13/16.
S31 S **2** A on 20d. black and blue
S32 R on 20d. black and blue
S33 R on 30d. black and pink
S34 – R on 50d. black and red
S35 – R on 100d. black and red

(b) On Nos. S18/19 and S21/2.
S36 S **2** R on 5000d. black and lilac
S37 R on 6000d. black and yellow
S38 – A on 20000d. black and red
S39 – R on 20000d. black and red
S40 – R on 30000d. black and red
Set of 10 65·00

Stamps surcharged "A" were sold at the current rate for internal letters and those surcharged "R" at the rate for internal registered letters. The "R" on No. S32 is reversed.

S **9** "Madonna and Child" (icon)

1994. Cajnicka Church.
S41 S **9** 1d. multicoloured 2·00 2·00

1994. Nos. S18/20 and S23 surch (Nos. 542/3 with letter).
S42 S **2** A on 5000d. black & lilac 1·10 1·10
S43 R on 6000d. black & yell 1·10 1·10
S44 40p. on 10000d. blk & bl 1·10 1·10
S45 – 2d. on 50000d. black and lilac 1·10 1·10

No. S42 was sold at the current rate for internal letters and No. S43, which shows the surcharge as the cyrillic letter resembling "P", at the rate for internal registered letters.

S **11** Tavna Monastery

1994. Monasteries. Multicoloured.
S46 60p. Type S **11** 2·00 2·00
S47 1d. Mostanica (horiz) 2·00 2·00
S48 1d.20 Zitomislic 2·25 2·25

S **12** "Aquilegia dinarica"

S **14** Relay Station, Mt. Kozara

1996. Nature Protection. Multicoloured.
S49 1d.20 Type S **12** 1·25 1·25
S50 1d.20 "Edraianthus niveus" (plant) 1·25 1·25
S51 1d.20 Shore lark 1·25 1·25
S52 1d.20 "Dinaromys bogdanovi" (dormouse) 1·25 1·25

1996. Nos. S14/16, S19 and S22 surch.
S53 S **2** 70p. on 30d. black and pink 30 30
S54 – 1d. on 100d. black & red 40 40
S55 – 2d. on 30000d. blk & red 80 80
S56 – 3d. on 50d. black and red 1·25 1·25
S57 S **2** 5d. on 6000d. black and yellow 2·25 2·25

1996.
S58 S **14** A green and bistre
S59 – R purple and brown
S60 – 1d.20 violet and blue
S61 – 2d. lilac and mauve
S62 – 5d. purple and blue
S63 – 10d. brown and sepia
Set of 6 6·50 6·50

DESIGNS—VERT: R, Kraljica relay station, Mt. Ozren; 2d. Relay station, Mt. Romanija; 5d. Stolice relay station, Mt. Maljevica. HORIZ: 1d.20, Bridge over river Drina at Srbinje; 10d. Bridge at Visegrad.

No. S58 was sold at the current rate for an internal letter and No. S59 at the rate for an internal registered letter.

S **15** Orthodox Church, Bascarsiji

1997.
S64 S **15** 2d.50 multicoloured 1·00 1·00

S **16** Pupin

S **17** "Primula kitaibeliana"

1997. 62nd Death Anniv of Michael Pupin (physicist and inventor).
S65 S **16** 2d.50 multicoloured 1·00 1·00

1997. Flowers. Multicoloured.
S66 3d.20 Type S **17** 85 85
S67 3d.20 "Pedicularis hoermanniana" 85 85
S68 3d.20 "Knautia sarajevensis" 85 85
S69 3d.20 "Oxytropis campestris" 85 85

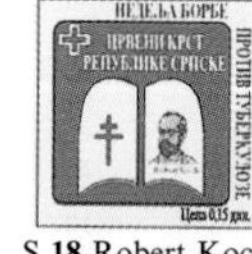

S **18** Robert Koch

S **19** Branko Copic

1997. Obligatory Tax. Anti-tuberculosis Week. Self-adhesive
S70 S **18** 15f. red and blue 10 10

1997. Writers. Each mauve and yellow.
S71 A (60p.) Type S **19** 25 25
S72 R (90p.) Jovan Ducic 35 35
S73 1d.50 Mesa Selimovic 35 35
S74 3d. Aleksa Santic 85 85
S75 5d. Petar Kocic 1·25 1·25
S76 10d. Ivo Andric 2·50 2·50

S **20** European Otter

S **21** Two Queens

1997. Nature Protection. Multicoloured.
S77 2d.50 Type S **20** 50 50
S78 4d.50 Roe deer 1·10 1·10
S79 6d.50 Brown bear 1·75 1·75

1997. Europa. Tales and Legends. Multicoloured.
S80 2d.50 Type S **21** 1·00 1·00
S81 6d.50 Prince on horseback 2·50 2·50

S **22** Diana, Princess of Wales

1998. Diana, Princess of Wales Commemoration.
S82 S **22** 3d.50 multicoloured ("DIANA" in Roman alphabet) 1·25 1·25
S83 3d.50 multicoloured ("DIANA" in Cyrillic alphabet) 1·25 1·25

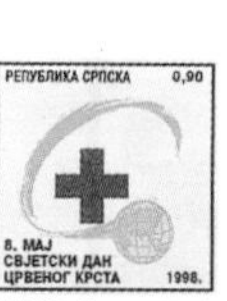

S **23** Cross and Globe

S **24** Brazil

1998. Obligatory Tax. Red Cross. Self-adhesive.
S84 S **23** 90f. red, blue and ultram 60 60

1998. World Cup Football Championship, France. Showing flags and players of countries in final rounds. Multicoloured.
S 85 90f. Type S **24** 60 60
S 86 90f. Morocco 60 60
S 87 90f. Norway 60 60
S 88 90f. Scotland 60 60
S 89 90f. Italy 60 60
S 90 90f. Chile 60 60
S 91 90f. Austria 60 60
S 92 90f. Cameroun 60 60
S 93 90f. France 60 60
S 94 90f. Saudi Arabia 60 60
S 95 90f. Denmark 60 60
S 96 90f. South Africa 60 60
S 97 90f. Spain 60 60
S 98 90f. Nigeria 60 60
S 99 90f. Paraguay 60 60
S100 90f. Bulgaria 60 60
S101 90f. Netherlands 60 60
S102 90f. Belgium 60 60
S103 90f. Mexico 60 60
S104 90f. South Korea 60 60
S105 90f. Germany 60 60
S106 90f. United States of America 60 60
S107 90f. Yugoslavia 60 60
S108 90f. Iran 60 60
S109 90f. Rumania 60 60
S110 90f. England (U.K. flag) 60 60
S111 90f. Tunisia 60 60
S112 90f. Colombia 60 60
S113 90f. Argentina 60 60
S114 90f. Jamaica 60 60
S115 90f. Croatia 60 60
S116 90f. Japan 60 60

S **25** Couple and Musical Instrument

1998. Europa. National Festivals. Multicoloured.
S117 7m.50 Type S **25** 5·00 5·00
S118 7m.50 Couple from Neretva and musical instrument 5·00 5·00

S **26** Family walking in Countryside

1998. Obligatory Tax. Anti-tuberculosis Week.
S119 S **26** 75f. multicoloured 50 50

S **27** St. Pantelejmon

S **28** Bijelijna

1998. 800th Anniv of Hilandar Monastery. Icons. Multicoloured.
S120 50f. Type S **27** 35 35
S121 70f. Jesus Christ 45 45
S122 1m.70 St. Nikola 1·10 1·10
S123 2m. St. John of Rila 1·40 1·40

1999. Towns. Multicoloured. (a) With face value.
S124 15f. Type S **28** 10 10
S125 20f. Sokolac 15 15
S126 75f. Prijedor 50 50
S127 2m. Brcko 1·40 1·40
S128 4m.50 Zvornik 3·00 3·00
S129 10m. Doboj 6·75 6·75

(b) Face value expressed by letter.
S130 A (50f.) Banja Luka 35 35
S131 R (1m.) Trebinje 70 70

No. S130 was sold at the current rate for an internal letter and No. S131 at the rate for an internal registered letter.

S **29** Airliner over Lake

1999. Founding of Air Srpska (state airline). Multicoloured.
S132 50f. Type S **29** 35 35
S133 50f. Airliner above clouds 35 35
S134 75f. Airliner over beach 50 50
S135 1m.50 Airliner over lake (different) 1·00 1·00

S **30** Table Tennis Ball as Globe

1999. International Table Tennis Championships, Belgrade. Multicoloured.
S136 1m. Type S **30** 70 70
S137 2m. Table tennis table, bat and ball 1·40 1·40

S **31** Kozara National Park

S **32** Open Hands

1999. Europa. National Parks. Multicoloured.
S138 1m.50 Type S **31** 1·00 1·00
S139 2m. Perucica National Park 1·40 1·40

1999. Obligatory Tax. Red Cross.
S140 S **32** 10f. multicoloured 10 10

S 33 Manuscript

1999. 780th Anniv of Bosnia and Herzegovina Archbishopric (S142, S144/8) and 480th Anniv of Garazole Printing Works (S141, S143). Mult.

S141 50f. Type **S 33** 30 30
S142 50f. Dobrun Monastery . . 30 30
S143 50f. "G" 30 30
S144 50f. Zhitomislib Monastery 30 30
S145 50f. Gomionitsa Monastery 30 30
S146 50f. Madonna and Child with angels and prophets (icon, 1578) 30 30
S147 50f. St. Nicolas (icon) . . . 30 30
S148 50f. Wise Men (icon) . . . 30 30

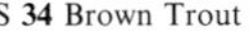

S 34 Brown Trout S 35 Lunar Module on Moon's Surface

1999. Fishes. Multicoloured.

S149 50f. Type **S 34** 30 30
S150 50f. Lake trout (*Salmo trutta morpha lacustris*) 30 30
S151 75f. Huchen 45 45
S152 1m. European grayling . . . 65 65

1999. 30th Anniv of First Manned Landing on Moon. Multicoloured.

S153 1m. Type **S 35** 65 65
S154 2m. Astronaut on Moon . . 1·25 1·25

S 36 Pencil and Emblem

1999. 125th Anniv of Universal Postal Union. Mult.

S155 75f. Type **S 36** 45 45
S156 1m.25 Earth and emblem 75 75

BOTSWANA Pt. 1

Formerly Bechuanaland Protectorate, attained independence on 30 September 1966, and changed its name to Botswana.

1966. 100 cents = 1 rand.
1976. 100 thebe = 1 pula.

47 National Assembly Building

1966. Independence. Multicoloured.

202 2½c. Type **47** 15 10
203 5c. Abattoir, Lobatsi 20 10
204 15c. National Airways Douglas DC-3 . . . . . . 65 20
205 35c. State House, Gaberones 40 30

1966. Nos. 168/81 of Bechuanaland optd **REPUBLIC OF BOTSWANA**.

206 **28** 1c. multicoloured 25 10
207 – 2c. orange, black and olive 30 1·25
208 – 2½c. multicoloured 30 10
209 – 3½c. multicoloured 50 20
210 – 5c. multicoloured . . . . . 50 1·50
211 – 7½c. multicoloured . . . . 50 1·75
212 – 10c. multicoloured 70 20
213 – 12½c. multicoloured . . . . 2·00 2·75
214 – 20c. brown and drab . . . 30 1·00
215 – 25c. sepia and lemon . . . 30 2·00
216 – 35c. blue and orange . . . 40 2·25
217 – 50c. sepia and olive 30 70
218 – 1r. black and brown . . . 40 1·25
219 – 2r. brown and turquoise 75 2·50

52 Golden Oriole

1967. Multicoloured.

220 1c. Type **52** 30 15
221 2c. Hoopoe ("African Hoopese") 40 70
222 3c. Groundscraper thrush . . 55 10
223 4c. Cordon-bleu ("Blue Waxbill") 55 10
224 5c. Secretary bird 55 10
225 7c. Southern yellow-billed hornbill ("Yellow-billed Hornbill") 60 90
226 10c. Burchell's gonolek ("Crimson-breasted Strike") 60 15
227 15c. Malachite kingfisher . . 7·00 3·00
228 20c. African fish eagle ("Fish Eagle") . . . . 7·00 2·00
229 25c. Go-away bird ("Grey Loerie") . . . . 4·00 1·50
230 35c. Scimitar-bill . . . . . . 6·00 2·25
231 50c. Comb duck ("Knob-Billed Duck") . . . . . . 2·75 2·75
232 1r. Levaillant's barbet ("Crested Barbet") . . . . 5·00 3·50
233 2r. Didric cuckoo ("Diederick Cuckoo") . . . . 7·00 16·00

66 Students and University

1967. 1st Conferment of University Degrees.

234 **66** 3c. sepia, blue and orange 10 10
235 7c. sepia, blue and turquoise 10 10
236 15c. sepia, blue and red . . 10 10
237 35c. sepia, blue and violet 20 20

67 Bushbuck

1967. Chobe Game Reserve. Multicoloured.

238 3c. Type **67** 10 20
239 7c. Sable Antelope 15 30
240 35c. Fishing on the Chobe River . . . . 80 1·10

70 Arms of Botswana and Human Rights Emblem

1968. Human Rights Year.

241 **70** 3c. multicoloured 10 10
242 – 15c. multicoloured 25 45
243 – 25c. multicoloured 25 60

The designs of Nos. 242/3 are similar, but are arranged differently.

73 Eland and Giraffe Rock Paintings, Tsodilo Hills

1968. Opening of National Museum and Art Gallery. Multicoloured.

244 3c. Type **73** 20 20
245 7c. Girl wearing ceremonial beads (31 × 48 mm) 25 40
246 10c. "Baobab Trees" (Thomas Baines) 25 30
247 15c. National Museum and art gallery (72 × 19 mm) . . 40 1·50
MS248 132 × 82 mm. Nos. 244/7 1·00 2·25

77 African Family, and Star over Village

1968. Christmas.

249 **77** 1c. multicoloured 10 10
250 2c. multicoloured 10 10
251 5c. multicoloured 10 10
252 25c. multicoloured 15 50

78 Scout, Lion and Badge in frame

1969. 22nd World Scout Conference, Helsinki. Mult.

253 3c. Type **78** 30 30
254 15c. Scouts cooking over open fire (vert) . . . . . . 35 1·00
255 25c. Scouts around camp fire 35 1·00

81 Woman, Child and Christmas Star 82 Diamond Treatment Plant, Orapa

1969. Christmas.

256 **81** 1c. blue and brown 10 10
257 2c. olive and brown . . . 10 10
258 4c. yellow and brown . . . 10 10
259 35c. brown and violet . . . 20 20
MS260 86 × 128 mm. Nos. 256/9 70 1·10

1970. Developing Botswana. Multicoloured.

261 3c. Type **82** 70 20
262 7c. Copper-nickel mining . . 95 20
263 10c. Copper-nickel mine, Selebi-Pikwe (horiz) . . . 1·25 15
264 35c. Orapa Diamond mine and diamonds (horiz) . . . 2·75 1·25

83 Mr. Micawber ("David Copperfield")

1970. Death Centenary of Charles Dickens. Mult.

265 3c. Type **83** 20 10
266 7c. Scrooge ("A Christmas Carol") 25 10
267 15c. Fagin ("Oliver Twist") . 45 40
268 25c. Bill Sykes ("Oliver Twist") 70 60
MS269 114 × 81 mm. Nos. 265/8 2·75 3·75

84 U.N. Building and Emblem

1970. 25th Anniv of United Nations.

270 **84** 15c. blue, brown and silver 70 30

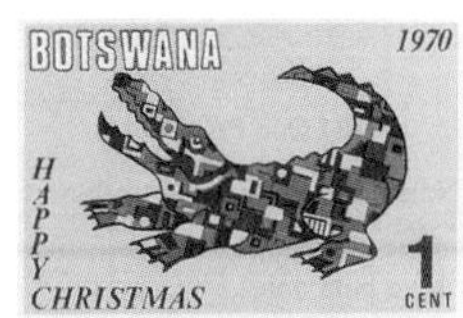

85 Crocodile

1970. Christmas. Multicoloured.

271 1c. Type **85** 10 10
272 2c. Giraffe 10 10
273 7c. Elephant 15 15
274 25c. Rhinoceros 60 80
MS275 128 × 90 mm. Nos. 271/4 1·00 3·00

86 Sorghum

1971. Important Crops. Multicoloured.

276 3c. Type **86** 15 10
277 7c. Millet 20 10
278 10c. Maize 20 10
279 35c. Groundnuts 70 80

87 Map and Head of Cow 88 King bringing Gift of Gold

1971. 5th Anniv of Independence.

280 **87** 3c. black, brown and green 10 10
281 – 4c. black, light blue and blue 10 10
282 – 7c. black and orange . . . 20 15
283 – 10c. multicololured 20 15
284 – 20c. multicoloured . . . . 55 2·00

DESIGNS: 4c. Map and cogs; 7c. Map and common zebra; 10c. Map and sorghum stalk crossed by tusk; 20c. Arms and map of Botswana.

1971. Christmas. Multicoloured.

285 2c. Type **88** 10 10
286 3c. King bringing frankincense 10 10
287 7c. King bringing myrrh . . 10 10
288 20c. Three Kings behold the star 35 65
MS289 85 × 128 mm. Nos. 285/8 1·00 3·50

89 Orion 90 Postmark and Map

1972. "Night Sky".

290 **89** 3c. blue, black and red . . 75 30
291 – 7c. blue, black and yellow 1·10 80
292 – 10c. green, black and orange . . . . 1·25 85
293 – 20c. blue, black and green 1·75 3·25

CONSTELLATIONS: 7c. The Scorpion; 10c. The Centaur; 20c. The Cross.

1972. Mafeking-Gubulawayo Runner Post. Mult.

294 3c. Type **90** 30 10
295 4c. Bechuanaland stamp and map 30 35
296 7c. Runners and map 45 50
297 20c. Mafeking postmark and map . . . . 1·10 1·50
MS298 84 × 216 mm. Nos. 294/7 vertically se-tenant, forming a composite map design 11·00 15·00

For these designs with changed inscription see Nos. 652/5.

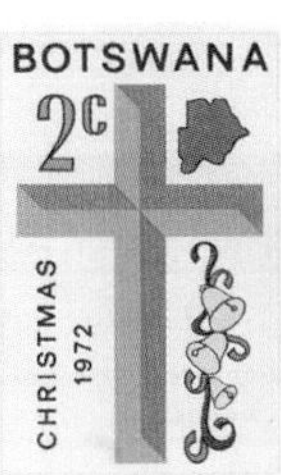

91 Cross, Map and Bells 92 Thor

1972. Christmas. Each with Cross and Map. Mult.

299 2c. Type **91** 10 75
300 3c. Cross, map and candle . . 10 10
301 7c. Cross, map and Christmas tree 15 25
302 20c. Cross, map, star and holly 40 85
MS303 96 × 119 mm. Nos. 299/302 1·25 3·25

1973. Centenary of I.M.O./W.M.O. Norse Myths. Multicoloured.

304 3c. Type **92** 20 10
305 4c. Sun God's chariot (horiz) 25 15

306 7c. Ymir, the frost giant . . 30 15
307 20c. Odin and Sleipnir (horiz) 75 70

93 Livingstone and River Scene

1973. Death Centenary of Dr. Livingstone. Mult.
308 3c. Type **93** 20 10
309 20c. Livingstone meeting Stanley 90 90

94 Donkey and Foal at Village Trough

1973. Christmas. Multicoloured.
310 3c. Type **94** 10 10
311 4c. Shepherd and flock (horiz) 10 10
312 7c. Mother and Child 10 10
313 20c. Kgotla meeting (horiz) 40 85

95 Gaborone Campus

1974. 10th Anniv of University of Botswana, Lesotho and Swaziland. Multicoloured.
314 3c. Type **95** 10 10
315 7c. Kwaluseni Campus . . . 10 10
316 20c. Roma Campus 15 20
317 35c. Map and flags of the three countries 20 35

96 Methods of Mail Transport

1974. Centenary of U.P.U. Multicoloured.
318 2c. Type **96** 55 35
319 3c. Post Office, Palapye, circa 1889 . . . . 55 35
320 7c. Bechuanaland Police Camel Post, circa 1900 . . 95 70
321 20c. Hawker Siddeley H.S.748 and De Havilland D.H.9 mail planes of 1920 and 1974 . . . . 2·75 2·50

97 Amethyst

1974. Botswana Minerals. Multicoloured.
322 1c. Type **97** . . . . 60 1·75
323 2c. Agate-"Botswana Pink" 60 1·75
324 3c. Quartz 65 80
325 4c. Copper nickel 70 60
326 5c. Moss agate . . . . 70 1·00
327 7c. Agate 80 60
328 10c. Stilbite . . . . 1·60 65
329 15c. Moshaneng banded marble . . . . 2·00 3·75
330 20c. Gem diamonds . . . . 4·00 4·25
331 25c. Chrysotile . . . . 5·00 2·50
332 35c. Jasper . . . . 5·00 5·00
333 50c. Moss quartz . . . . . . 4·50 7·00
334 1r. Citrine . . . . 7·50 10·00
335 2r. Chalcopyrite . . . . . . 20·00 20·00

98 "Stapelia variegata" **99** President Sir Seretse Khama

1974. Christmas. Multicoloured.
336 2c. Type **98** 20 40
337 7c. "Hibiscus lunarifolius" . . 40 20
338 15c. "Ceratotheca triloba" . . 60 1·00
339 20c. "Nerine laticoma" . . . 70 1·25
MS340 85 × 130 mm. Nos. 336/9 2·00 4·25

1975. 10th Anniv of Self-Government.
341 **99** 4c. multicoloured 10 10
342 10c. multicoloured 15 10
343 20c. multicoloured 25 25
344 35c. multicoloured 45 50
MS345 93 × 130 mm. Nos. 341/4 1·00 1·50

100 Ostrich

1975. Rock Paintings, Tsodilo Hills. Multicoloured.
346 4c. Type **100** 60 10
347 10c. White rhinoceros . . . . 1·00 10
348 25c. Spotted hyena . . . . . 2·00 55
349 35c. Scorpion . . . . 2·00 1·10
MS350 150 × 150 mm. Nos. 346/9 11·00 7·50

101 Map of British Bechuanaland, 1885 **102** "Aloe marlothii"

1975. Anniversaries. Multicoloured.
351 6c. Type **101** 30 20
352 10c. Chief Khama, 1875 . . . 40 15
353 25c. Chiefs Sebele, Bathoen and Khama, 1895 (horiz) 80 75
EVENTS: 6c.90th anniv of Protectorate; 10c. Centenary of Khama's accession; 25c.80th anniv of Chiefs' visit to London.

1975. Christmas. Aloes. Multicoloured.
354 3c. Type **102** 20 10
355 10c. "Aloe lutescens" 40 20
356 15c. "Aloe zebrina" . . . . 60 1·50
357 25c. "Aloe littoralis" . . . . 75 2·50

103 Drum

1976. Traditional Musical Instruments. Mult.
358 4c. Type **103** 15 10
359 10c. Hand piano 20 10
360 15c. Segankuru (violin) . . . 25 50
361 25c. Kudu signal horn . . . 30 1·25

104 One Pula Note

1976. 1st National Currency. Multicoloured.
362 4c. Type **104** 15 10
363 10c. Two pula note 20 10
364 15c. Five pula note 35 20
365 25c. Ten pula note 45 45
MS366 163 × 107 mm. Nos. 362/5 1·00 3·50

1976. Nos. 322/35 surch in new currency.
367 1t. on 1c. multicoloured . . . 2·00 70
368 2t. on 2c. multicoloured . . . 2·00 1·75
369 3t. on 3c. multicoloured . . . 1·50 60
370 4t. on 4c. multicoloured . . . 2·50 40
371 5t. on 5c. multicoloured . . . 2·50 40
372 7t. on 7c. multicoloured . . . 1·25 2·75
373 10t. on 10c. multicoloured . . 1·25 80
374 15t. on 15c. multicoloured . . 4·25 3·25
375 20t. on 20c. multicoloured . . 7·50 80
376 25t. on 25c. multicoloured . . 5·00 1·25
377 35t. on 35c. multicoloured . . 4·50 5·00
378 50t. on 50c. multicoloured . . 7·00 9·00
379 1p. on 1r. multicoloured . . 8·00 9·50
380 2p. on 2r. multicoloured . . 11·00 11·00

106 Botswana Cattle

1976. 10th Anniv of Independence. Multicoloured.
381 4t. Type **106** 15 10
382 10t. Antelope, Okavango Delta (vert) 20 10
383 15t. School and pupils . . . 20 40
384 25t. Rural weaving (vert) . . 20 50
385 35t. Miner (vert) 75 85

107 "Colophospermum mopane"

1976. Christmas. Trees. Multicoloured.
386 3t. Type **107** 15 10
387 4t. "Baikiaea plurijuga" . . . 15 10
388 10t. "Sterculia rogersii" . . . 20 10
389 25t. "Acacia nilotica" . . . 45 50
390 40t. "Kigelia africana" . . . 75 1·25

108 Coronation Coach

1977. Silver Jubilee. Multicoloured.
391 4t. The Queen and Sir Seretse Khama 10 10
392 25t. Type **108** 20 15
393 40t. The Recognition 35 90

109 African Clawless Otter

1977. Diminishing Species. Multicoloured.
394 3t. Type **109** . . . . 3·50 40
395 4t. Serval . . . . 3·50 40
396 10t. Bat-eared fox . . . . . 4·25 40
397 25t. Temminck's ground pangolin . . . . 10·00 2·00
398 40t. Brown hyena . . . . . 12·00 7·50

110 Cwihaba Caves

1977. Historical Monuments. Multicoloured.
399 4t. Type **110** 20 10
400 5t. Khama Memorial 20 10
401 15t. Green's Tree 30 40
402 20t. Mmajojo Ruins 30 45
403 25t. Ancient morabaraba board 30 50
404 35t. Matsieng's footprint . . . 40 60
MS405 154 × 105 mm. Nos. 399/404 2·50 3·25

111 "Hypoxis nitida" **112** Black Bustard

1977. Christmas. Lilies. Multicoloured.
406 3t. Type **111** 15 10
407 5t. "Haemanthus magnificus" 15 10
408 10t. "Boophane disticha" . . 20 10
409 25t. "Vellozia retinervis" . . 40 55
410 40t. "Ammocharis coranica" 55 1·25

1978. Birds. Multicoloured.
411 1t. Type **112** . . . . 70 1·25
412 2t. Marabou stork . . . . . 90 1·25
413 3t. Green wood hoopoe ("Red Billed Hoopoe") . . 70 85
414 4t. Carmine bee eater . . . . 90 1·00
415 5t. African jacana 70 40
416 7t. African paradise flycatcher ("Paradise Flycatcher) . . 1·00 3·00
417 10t. Bennett's woodpecker . . 2·00 60
418 15t. Red bishop . . . . . . 1·50 3·00
419 20t. Crowned plover . . . . 1·75 2·00
420 25t. Giant kingfisher . . . . 70 3·00
421 30t. White-faced whistling duck ("White-faced Duck") 70 70
422 35t. Green-backed heron . . 70 3·25
423 45t. Black-headed heron . . . 1·00 3·00
424 50t. Spotted eagle owl . . . 5·00 4·50
425 1p. Gabar goshawk . . . . 2·50 4·50
426 2p. Martial eagle . . . . . . 3·00 8·00
427 5p. Saddle-bill stork . . . . 6·50 16·00

113 Tawana making Kaross

1978. Okavango Delta. Multicoloured.
428 4t. Type **113** 10 10
429 5t. Tribe localities 10 10
430 15t. Bushman collecting roots 25 40
431 20t. Herero woman milking 35 55
432 25t. Yei poling "mokoro" (canoe) 40 60
433 35t. Mbukushu fishing . . . 45 1·50
MS434 150 × 98 mm. Nos. 428/33 1·50 3·75

114 "Caralluma lutea" **115** Sip Well

1978. Christmas. Flowers. Multicoloured.
435 5t. Type **114** 35 10
436 10t. "Hoodia lugardii" . . . 50 15
437 15t. "Ipomoea transvaalensis" 90 55
438 25t. "Ansellia gigantea" . . . 1·10 70

1979. Water Development. Multicoloured.
439 3t. Type **115** 10 10
440 5t. Watering pit 10 10
441 10t. Hand dug well 15 10
442 22t. Windmill 20 30
443 50t. Modern drilling rig . . . 40 55

116 Pottery

1979. Handicrafts. Multicoloured.
444 5t. Type **116** 10 10
445 10t. Clay modelling 10 10
446 25t. Basketry 20 25
447 40t. Beadwork 40 50
MS448 123 × 96 mm. Nos. 444/7 1·00 2·50

117 British Bechuanaland 1885 1d. Stamp and Sir Rowland Hill

1979. Death Centenary of Sir Rowland Hill. Mult.
449 5t. Type **117** 20 10
450 25t. Bechuanaland Protectorate 1932 2d. stamp 45 50
451 45t. 1967 Hoopoe 2c. definitive stamp . . . . . 55 1·25

118 Children Playing

1979. International Year of the Child. Multicoloured.
452 5t. Type **118** 20 10
453 10t. Child playing with doll (vert) 30 20

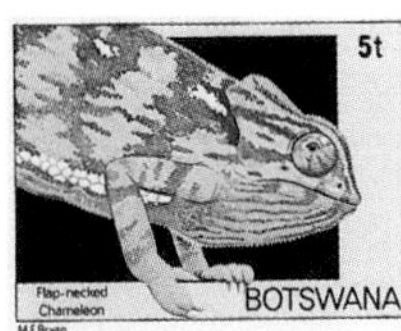

119 "Ximenia caffra" **120** Flap-necked Chameleon

1979. Christmas. Flowers. Multicoloured.
454 5t. Type **119** 10 10
455 10t. "Sclerocarya caffra" 20 20
456 15t. "Hexalobus monopetalus" 35 35
457 25t. "Ficus soldanella" 45 45

1980. Reptiles. Multicoloured.
458 5t. Type **120** 30 10
459 10t. Leopard tortoise 30 15
460 25t. Puff adder 50 65
461 40t. White-throated monitor 60 2·50

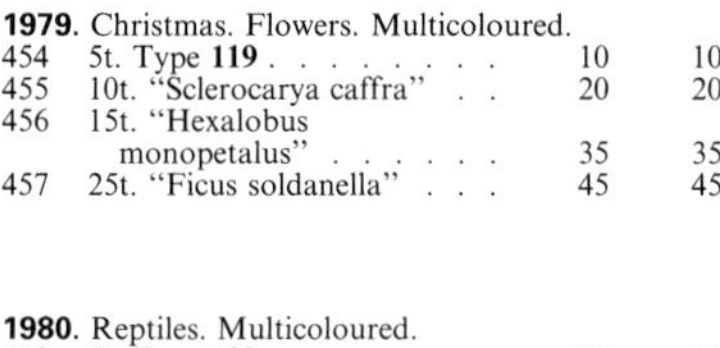

121 Rock Breaking

1980. Early Mining. Multicoloured.
462 5t. Type **121** 25 15
463 10t. Ore hoisting 30 15
464 15t. Ore transport 70 60
465 20t. Ore crushing 75 70
466 25t. Smelting 80 90
467 35t. Tool and products 1·00 1·40

122 "Chiwele and the Giant"

1980. Folktales. Multicoloured.
468 5t. Type **122** 10 10
469 10t. "Kgori is not deceived" (vert) 15 10
470 30t. "Nyambi's wife and Crocodile" (vert) 45 45
471 45t. "Clever Hare" (horiz) 60 60
The 10t. and 30t. are 28 × 37 mm and the 45t. 44 × 27 mm.

123 Game watching, Makgadikgadi Pans

1980. World Tourism Conference, Manila.
472 **123** 5t. multicoloured 45 20

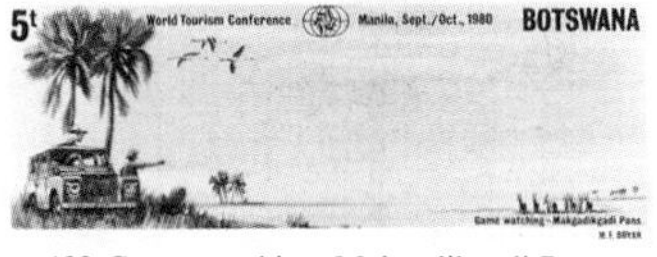

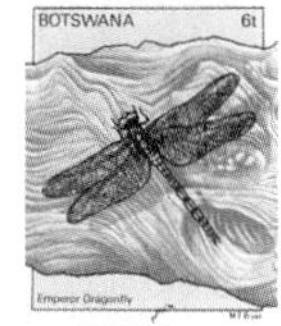

124 "Acacia gerrardii" **126** "Anax imperator" (dragonfly)

125 Heinrich von Stephan and Botswana 3d. and 3c. U.P.U. Stamps

1980. Christmas. Multicoloured.
473 6t. Type **124** 10 10
474 1t. "Acacia nilotica" 20 10
475 25t. "Acacia erubescens" 45 30
476 40t. "Dichrostachys cinerea" 70 70

1981. 150th Birth Anniv of Heinrich von Stephan (founder of Universal Postal Union). Multicoloured.
477 6t. Type **125** 75 30
478 20t.6d. and 7c. U.P.U. stamps 1·75 2·25

1981. Insects. Multicoloured.
479 6t. Type **126** 15 10
480 7t. "Sphodromantis gastrica" (mantid) 15 20
481 10t. "Zonocerus elegans" (grasshopper) 15 20
482 20t. "Kheper nigroaeneus" (beetle) 25 50
483 30t. "Papilio demodocus" (butterfly) 35 70
484 45t. "Acanthocampa belina" (moth larva) 40 1·10
MS485 180 × 89 mm. Nos. 479/84 3·00 7·50

127 Camphill Community Rankoromane, Otse

1981. International Year for Disabled Persons. Multicoloured.
486 6t. Type **127** 20 10
487 20t. Resource Centre for the Blind, Mochudi 55 35
488 30t. Tlamelong Rehabilitation Centre, Tlokweng 75 45

128 Woman reading Letter

1981. Literacy Programme. Multicoloured.
489 6t. Type **128** 20 10
490 7t. Man filling in form 20 15
491 20t. Boy reading newspaper 60 35
492 30t. Child being taught to read 80 45

129 Sir Seretse Khama and Building

1981. 1st Death Anniv of Sir Seretse Khama (former President). Multicoloured.
493 6t. Type **129** 15 10
494 10t. Seretse Khama and building (different) 25 15
495 30t. Seretse Khama and Botswana flag 40 45
496 45t. Seretse Khama and building (different) 55 70

1981. Nos. 417 and 422 surch.
497 25t. on 35t. Green-backed heron 3·50 2·00
498 30t. on 10t. Bennett's woodpecker 3·50 2·00

131 Traditional Ploughing

1981. Cattle Industry. Multicoloured.
499 6t. Type **131** 10 10
500 20t. Agricultural show 30 50
501 30t. Botswana Meat Commission 35 60
502 45t. Vaccine Institute, Botswana 50 1·00

132 "Nymphaea caerulea"

1981. Christmas. Flowers. Multicoloured.
503 6t. Type **132** 20 10
504 10t. "Nymphoides indica" 25 10
505 25t. "Nymphaea lotus" 60 90
506 40t. "Ottelia kunenensis" 80 2·25

133 "Cattle Post Scene" (Boitumelo Golaakwena)

1982. Children's Art. Multicoloured.
507 6t. Type **133** 40 10
508 10t. "Kgotla Meeting" (Reginald Klinck) 50 15
509 30t. "Village Water Supply" (Keronmemang Matswiri) 1·75 1·25
510 45t. "With the Crops" (Kennedy Balemoge) 1·75 2·75

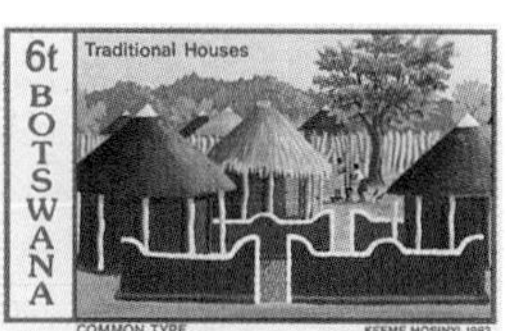

134 Common Type

1982. Traditional House. Multicoloured.
511 6t. Type **134** 40 15
512 10t. Kgatleng type 50 15
513 30t. North Eastern type 2·00 1·10
514 45t. Sarwa type 2·00 3·00

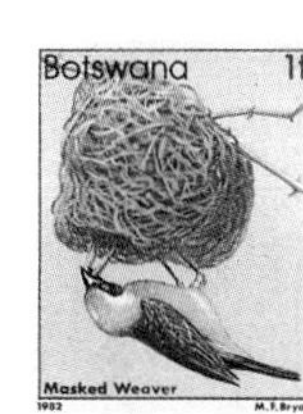

135 African Masked Weaver **136** "Coprinus comatus"

1982. Birds. Multicoloured.
515 1t. Type **135** 80 1·50
516 2t. Miombo double-collared sunbird ("Lesser double-collared Sunbird") 90 1·60
517 3t. Red-throated bee eater 1·00 1·60
518 4t. Ostrich 1·00 1·60
519 5t. Grey-headed gull 1·00 1·60
520 6t. African pygmy ("Pygmy Goose") 1·00 40
521 7t. Cattle egret 1·00 15
522 8t. Lanner falcon 2·50 1·50
523 10t. Yellow-billed stork 1·00 20
524 15t. Red-billed pintail ("Red-billed Teal") (horiz) 2·75 25
525 20t. Barn owl (horiz) 5·50 3·50
526 25t. Hammerkop ("Hammerkop") (horiz) 3·25 70
527 30t. South African stilt ("Stilt") (horiz) 3·75 90
528 35t. Blacksmith plover (horiz) 3·75 80
529 45t. Senegal wattled plover ("Watted Plover") (horiz) 3·75 1·75
530 50t. Helmeted guineafowl ("Crowned Guineafowl") (horiz) 4·75 2·50
531 1p. Cape vulture (horiz) 9·00 12·00
532 2p. Augur buzzard (horiz) 11·00 16·00

1982. Christmas. Fungi. Multicoloured.
533 7t. Type **136** 2·25 20
534 15t. "Lactarius deliciosus" 3·50 65
535 35t. "Amanita pantherina" 5·50 2·00
536 50t. "Boletus edulis" 7·00 7·00

137 President Quett Masire

1983. Commonwealth Day. Multicoloured.
537 7t. Type **137** 10 10
538 15t. Native dancers 15 20
539 35t. Melbourne conference centre 45 55
540 45t. Meeting of Heads of State, Melbourne 55 80

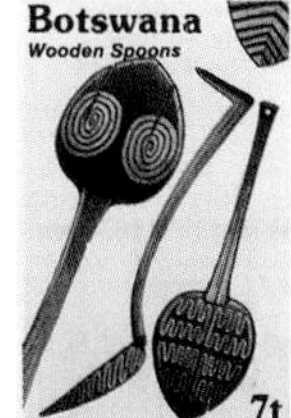

138 Wattled Crane **139** Wooden Spoons

1983. Endangered Species. Multicoloured.
541 7t. Type **138** 3·00 55
542 15t. "Aloe lutescens" 2·50 80
543 35t. Roan antelope 3·00 3·25
544 50t. Ivory palm 3·50 6·00

1983. Traditional Artifacts. Multicoloured.
545 7t. Type **139** 25 10
546 15t. Personal ornaments 45 30
547 35t. Ox-hide milk bag 75 65
548 50t. Decorated knives 1·00 1·10
MS549 115 × 102 mm. Nos. 545 × 8 4·25 5·00

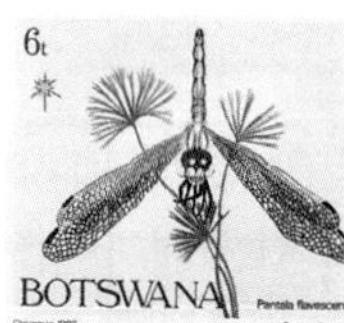

140 "Pantala flavescens"

1983. Christmas. Dragonflies. Multicoloured.
550 6t. Type **140** 85 10
551 15t. "Anax imperator" 1·75 50
552 25t. "Trithemis arteriosa" 2·00 85
553 45t. "Chlorolestes elegans" 2·75 4·50

141 Sorting Diamonds **142** Riding Cattle

1984. Mining Industry. Multicoloured.
554 7t. Type **141** 2·00 50
555 15t. Lime kiln 2·00 75
556 35t. Copper-nickel smelter plant (vert) 3·25 3·25
557 60t. Stockpiled coal (vert) 3·75 9·00

1984. Traditional Transport. Multicoloured.
558 7t. Type **142** 20 10
559 25t. Sledge 65 60
560 35t. Wagon 85 1·50
561 50t. Two-wheeled donkey cart 1·25 4·00

143 Avro 504 Aircraft **144** "Papilio demodocus"

1984. 40th Anniv of International Civil Aviation Organization. Multicoloured.
562 7t. Type **143** 75 20
563 10t. Westland Wessex trimotor 1·00 35
564 15t. Junkers Ju 52/3m 1·40 95
565 25t. De Havilland Dominie 2·00 1·75
566 35t. Douglas DC-3 "Wenala" 2·25 3·50
567 50t. Fokker Friendship 2·50 6·50

1984. Christmas. Butterflies. Multicoloured.
568 7t. Type **144** 2·00 30
569 25t. "Byblia anvatara" 2·25 1·50
570 35t. "Danaus chrysippus" 3·50 3·00
571 50t. "Graphium taboranus" 4·75 10·00
No. 570 is incorrectly inscr "Hypolimnas misippus".

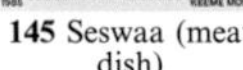

145 Seswaa (meat dish)

146 1885 British Bechuanaland Overprint on Cape of Good Hope ½d.

1985. 5th Anniv of Southern African Development Co-ordination Conference. Traditional Foods. Multicoloured.
572 7t. Type **145** 40 10
573 15t. Bogobe (cereal porridge) 65 35
574 25t. Madila (soured coagulated cow's milk) . . 90 55
575 50t. Phane (caterpillars) . . . 1·50 1·75
MS576 117 × 103 mm. Nos. 572/5 6·00 9·00

1985. Centenary of First Bechuanaland Stamps.
577 **146** 7t. black, grey and red . . 1·00 20
578 – 15t. black, brown yell . . 1·75 50
579 – 25t. black and red . . . . 2·25 80
580 – 35t. black, blue and gold 2·50 2·00
581 – 50t. multicoloured . . . . 2·75 3·25
DESIGNS—VERT: 15t. 1897 Bechuanaland Protectorate overprint on G.B. 3d.; 25t. Bechuanaland Protectorate 1932 1d. definitive. HORIZ: 35t. Bechuanaland 1965 Internal Self-Government 5c.; 50t. Botswana 1966 Independence 2½c.

147 Bechuanaland Border Police, 1885–95

1985. Centenary of Botswana Police. Multicoloured.
582 7t. Type **147** . . . . 2·00 50
583 10t. Bechuanaland Mounted Police, 1895–1902 . . . . 2·25 50
584 25t. Bechuanaland Protectorate Police, 1903–66 . . . . 3·25 2·00
585 50t. Botswana Police, from 1966 . . . . 4·50 6·00

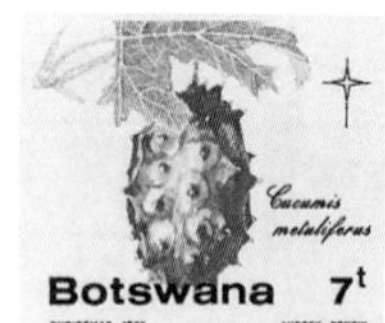

148 "Cucumis metuliferus"

1985. Christmas. Edible Wild Cucumbers. Mult.
586 7t. Type **148** . . . . 1·00 10
587 15t. "Acanthosicyos naudinianus" . . . . . . 2·00 70
588 25t. "Coccinia sessifolia" . . 2·75 1·25
589 50t. "Momordica balsamina" 4·50 8·50

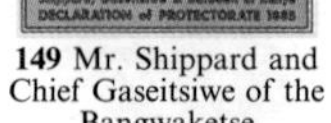

149 Mr. Shippard and Chief Gaseitsiwe of the Bangwaketse

150 Halley's Comet over Serowe

1985. Centenary of Declaration of Bechuanaland Protectorate. Multicoloured.
590 7t. Type **149** 35 10
591 15t. Sir Charles Warren and Chief Sechele of the Bakwena 70 45
592 25t. Revd. Mackenzie and Chief Khama of the Bamangwato . . . . . . 1·25 85
593 50t. Map showing Protectorate . . . . 2·75 2·75
MS594 130 × 133 mm. Nos. 590/3 10·00 12·00

1986. Appearance of Halley's Comet. Multicoloured.
595 7t. Type **150** 80 15
596 15t. Comet over Bobonong at sunset . . . . 1·50 70
597 35t. Comet over Gomare at dawn . . . . 2·00 1·50
598 50t. Comet over Thamaga and Letlhakeng . . . . . 2·25 3·50

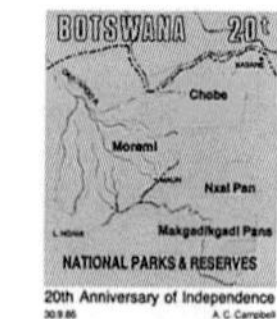

151 Milk Bag

152 Map showing National Parks and Reserves

1986. Traditional Milk Containers. Multicoloured.
599 8t. Type **151** 15 10
600 15t. Clay pot and calabashes 25 30
601 35t. Wooden milk bucket . . 50 65
602 50t. Milk churn . . . . . . 70 1·10

1986. 20th Anniv of Independence. Sheet 100 × 120 mm. Multicoloured.
MS603 20t. Type **152**; 20t. Morupule power station; 20t. Cattle breeding in Kgalagadi; 20t. National Assembly Building 3·25 2·25

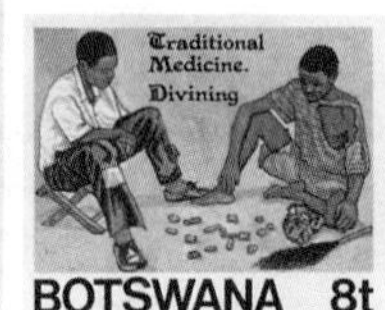

153 "Ludwigia stogonifera"

154 Divining

1986. Christmas. Flowers of Okavango. Mult.
604 8t. Type **153** . . . . 1·25 10
605 15t. "Sopubia mannii" . . . 2·25 1·10
606 35t. "Commelina diffusa" . . 3·50 3·00
607 50t. "Hibiscus diversifolius" 4·00 11·00

1987. Traditional Medicine. Multicoloured.
608 8t. Type **154** 80 10
609 15t. Lightning prevention . . 1·50 80
610 35t. Rain making . . . . . 2·25 2·50
611 50t. Blood letting . . . . . 2·75 7·50

1987. Nos. 520, 523 and 530 surch.
612 3t. on 6t. African pygmy goose . . . . 2·00 60
613 5t. on 10t. Yellow-billed stork 2·00 60
614 20t. on 50t. Helmeted guineafowl (horiz) . . . . 4·00 1·40

156 Oral Rehydration Therapy

157 Cape Fox

1987. U.N.I.C.E.F. Child Survival Campaign. Multicoloured.
615 8t. Type **156** 35 10
616 15t. Growth monitoring . . . 60 55
617 35t. Immunization . . . . . 1·25 2·00
618 50t. Breast feeding . . . . . 1·50 4·50

1987. Animals of Botswana. Multicoloured.
619 1t. Type **157** 10 70
620 2t. Lechwe . . . . 50 1·25
621 3t. Zebra 15 70
622 4t. Duiker . . . . 15 1·50
623 5t. Banded mongoose . . . . 20 1·50
624 6t. Rusty-spotted genet . . . 20 1·50
625 8t. Hedgehog 30 10
626 10t. Scrub hare 30 10
627 12t. Hippopotamus . . . . . 2·50 3·00
628 15t. Suricate . . . . 2·00 1·75
629 20t. Caracal 70 65
630 25t. Steenbok . . . . 70 1·50
631 30t. Gemsbok . . . . 1·25 1·50
632 35t. Square-lipped rhinoceros 1·50 1·50
633 40t. Mountain reedbuck . . . 1·40 1·50
634 50t. Rock dassie . . . . . . 90 1·75
635 1p. Giraffe . . . . 2·50 3·75
636 2p. Tsessebe . . . . 2·50 4·75
637 3p. Side-striped jackal . . . 3·75 7·00
638 5p. Hartebeest . . . . 6·00 11·00

158 "Cyperus articulatus"

159 Planting Seeds with Digging Stick

1987. Christmas. Grasses and Sedges of Okavango. Multicoloured.
639 8t. Type **158** 40 10
640 15t. Broomgrass 60 40
641 30t. "Cyperus alopurcides" 1·25 75
642 1p. Bulrush sedge . . . . . 2·50 5·00
MS643 88 × 99 mm. Nos. 639/42 4·25 4·75

1988. Early Cultivation. Multicoloured.
644 8t. Type **159** 40 10
645 15t. Using iron hoe 60 35
646 35t. Wooden ox-drawn plough . . . . 1·00 1·00
647 50t. Villagers working in lesotlas communal field . . 1·40 2·00

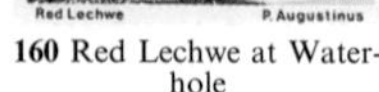
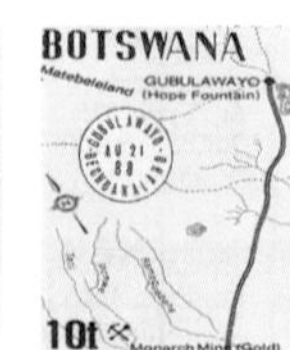

160 Red Lechwe at Water-hole

161 Gubulawayo Postmark and Route Southwards to Tati

1988. Red Lechwe. Multicoloured.
648 10t. Type **160** 90 15
649 15t. Red lechwe and early morning sun . . . . 1·75 65
650 35t. Female and calf . . . . 2·50 1·75
651 75t. Herd on the move . . . 3·75 8·00

1988. Cent of Mafeking–Gubalawayo Runner Post. Designs as Nos. 294/7, but redrawn smaller with changed inscriptions as in T **161**. Multicoloured.
652 10t. Type **161** 35 10
653 15t. Bechuanaland 1888 6d. on 6d. stamp and route from Tati southwards . . . 55 30
654 30t. Runners and twin routes south from Shoshong . . . 95 75
655 60t. Mafeking postmark and routes to Bechuanaland and Transvaal . . . . . 1·60 2·75
MS656 81 × 151 mm. Nos. 652/5 vertically se-tenant, forming a composite map design 6·00 6·50

162 Pope John Paul II and Outline Map of Botswana

163 National Museum and Art Gallery, Gaborone

1988. Visit of Pope John Paul II. Multicoloured.
657 10t. Type **162** . . . . . . 1·50 20
658 15t. Pope John Paul II . . . 1·75 30
659 30t. Pope giving blessing and outline map . . . . . . 2·25 70
660 80t. Pope John Paul II (different) . . . . 3·00 2·75

1988. 20th Anniv of National Museum and Art Gallery, Gaborone. Multicoloured.
661 8t. Type **163** 15 10
662 15t. Pottery 20 25
663 30t. Blacksmith's buffalo bellows 35 40
664 60c. Children and land rover mobile museum van . . . 70 1·00

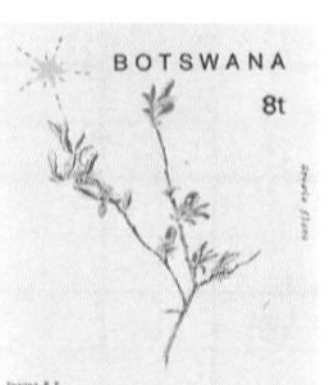

164 "Grewia flava"

165 Basket Granary

1988. Flowering Plants of South-eastern Botswana. Multicoloured.
665 8t. Type **164** 20 10
666 15t. "Cienfuegosia digitata" 30 25
667 40t. "Solanum seaforthianum" 60 55
668 75t. "Carissa bispinosa" . . . 1·00 1·40

1989. Traditional Grain Storage. Multicoloured.
669 8t. Type **165** 65 10
670 15t. Large letlole granary . . 1·00 40
671 30t. Pot granary . . . . . . 1·60 60
672 60t. Two types of serala . . . 2·25 2·25

166 Female with Eggs

1989. Slaty Egret. Multicoloured.
673 8t. Type **166** 55 15
674 15t. Chicks in nest 75 40
675 30t. In flight . . . . 1·00 75
676 60t. Pair building nest . . . 1·40 1·60
MS677 119 × 89 mm. Nos. 673/6 3·25 2·75

167 "My Work at Home" (Ephraim Seeletso)

1989. Children's Paintings. Multicoloured.
678 10t. Type **167** 35 10
679 15t. "My Favourite Game" (hopscotch) (Neelma Bhatia) (vert) 50 35
680 30t. "My Favourite Toy" (clay animals) (Thabo Habana) 75 70
681 1p. "My School Day" (Thabo Olesitse) . . . . . 2·00 3·25

168 "Eulophia angolensis"

171 Telephone Engineer

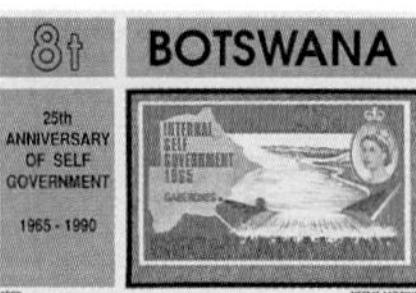

169 Bechuanaland 1965 New Constitution 25c. Stamp (25th anniv of Self-Government)

1989. Christmas. Orchids. Multicoloured.
682 8t. Type **168** 70 10
683 15t. "Eulophia hereroensis" 1·25 60
684 30t. "Eulophia speciosa" . . 1·75 1·00
685 60t. "Eulophia petersii" . . . 2·50 6·50

1990. Anniversaries.
686 **169** 8t. multicoloured 70 15
687 – 15t. multicoloured 75 50
688 – 30t. multicoloured . . . . 2·75 1·60
689 – 60t. black, blue and yellow . . . . 3·25 6·00
DESIGNS: 15t. Casting vote in ballot box (25th anniv of First Elections); 30t. Outline map and flags of Southern Africa Development Co-ordination Conference countries (10th anniv); 60t. Penny Black (150th anniv of first postage stamp).

1990. Nos. 619, 624 and 627 surch.
690 10t. on 1t. Type **157** 45 20
691 20t. on 6t. Rusty-spotted genet 60 80
692 50t. on 12t. Hippopotamus 2·00 3·25

1990. "Stamp World London 90" International Stamp Exhibition. Multicoloured.
693 8t. Type **171** 35 10
694 15t. Transmission pylon . . . 65 40
695 30t. Public telephone . . . . 1·00 75
696 2p. Testing circuit board . . 3·00 6·50

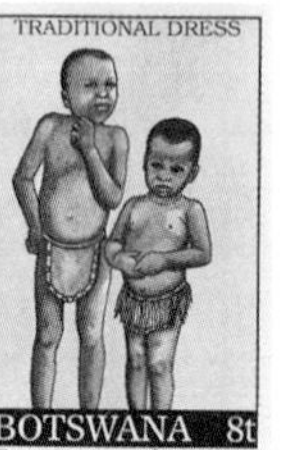

172 Young Children

173 "Acacia nigrescens"

1990. Traditional Dress. Multicoloured.
697 8t. Type **172** 35 10
698 15t. Young woman 65 40

699 30t. Adult man . . . . . . 1·00 70
700 2p. Adult woman . . . . . 3·00 6·50
MS701 104 × 150 mm. Nos. 697/700 4·50 6·50

1990. Christmas. Flowering Trees. Multicoloured.
702 8t. Type **173** 50 10
703 15t. "Peltophorum africanum" 85 35
704 30t. "Burkea africana" . . . 1·50 75
705 2p. "Pterocarpus angolensis" 3·50 7·00

174 Children running in front of Hatchback

1990. 1st National Road Safety Day. Multicoloured.
706 8t. Type **174** . . . . 2·00 30
707 15t. Careless overtaking . . . 2·50 1·00
708 30t. Cattle on road . . . . . 3·25 2·75

175 Cattle **176** Children

1991. Rock Paintings. Multicoloured.
709 8t. Type **175** . . . . 1·75 40
710 15t. Cattle, drying frames and tree . . . . 2·25 85
711 30t. Animal hides . . . . . 2·75 1·50
712 2p. Family herding cattle . . 4·75 8·50

1991. National Census. Multicoloured.
713 8t. Type **176** 90 20
714a 15t. Village . . . . 1·50 55
715 30t. School . . . . 1·75 90
716 2p. Hospital . . . . 6·00 8·50

177 Tourists viewing Elephants

1991. African Tourism Year. Okavango Delta. Mult.
717 8t. Type **177** . . . . 1·50 70
718 15t. Crocodiles basking on river bank . . . . 1·75 90
719 35t. Fish eagles and De Havilland D.H.C.7 Dash Seven aircraft . . . . . . 3·50 3·25
720 2p. Okavango wildlife (26 × 44 mm) . . . . . . 5·50 8·50

178 "Harpagophytum procumbens" **179** "Cacosternum boettgeri"

1991. Christmas. Seed Pods. Multicoloured.
721 8t. Type **178** 60 10
722 15t. "Tylosema esculentum" 1·00 40
723 30t. "Abrus precatorius" . . 1·75 80
724 2p. "Kigelia africana" . . . 4·00 7·50

1992. Nos. 621, 624 and 627 surch.
725 8t. on 12t. Hippopotamus . . 1·00 70
726 10t. on 12t. Hippopotamus 1·00 70
727 25t. on 6t. Rusty-spotted genet . . . . 1·25 1·50
728 40t. on 3t. Zebra . . . . . . 2·25 3·50

1992. Climbing Frogs. Multicoloured.
729 8t. Type **179** 45 30
730 10t. "Hyperolius marmoratus angolensis" (vert) 45 30
731 40t. "Bufo fenoulheti" . . . 1·40 1·50
732 1p. "Hyperolius sp." (vert) 2·00 4·75

180 Air-conditioned Carriages

1992. Deluxe Railway Service. Multicoloured.
733 10t. Type **180** . . . . 1·25 40
734 25t. Diesel locomotive No. BD001 (vert) . . . . . . 2·00 80
735 40t. Carriage interior (vert) 2·25 1·25
736 2p. Diesel locomotive No. BD028 . . . . 3·50 7·00
MS737 127 × 127 mm. Nos. 733/6 9·50 9·50

181 Cheetah **182** Boxing

1992. Animals. Multicoloured.
738 1t. Type **181** . . . . 30 1·50
739 2t. Spring hare . . . . 30 1·50
740 4t. Blackfooted cat . . . . . 40 1·50
741 5t. Striped mouse . . . . . 40 1·25
742 10t. Oribi 45 10
743 12t. Pangolin . . . . 75 2·00
744 15t. Aardwolf 75 40
745 20t. Warthog 75 40
746 25t. Ground squirrel 75 20
747 35t. Honey badger . . . . . 1·00 30
748 40t. Common mole rat . . . 1·00 30
749 45t. Wild dog . . . . 1·00 30
750 50t. Water mongoose . . . . 1·00 35
751 80t. Klipspringer . . . . . . 1·75 1·75
752 1p. Lesser bushbaby . . . . 1·75 1·75
753 2p. Bushveld elephant shrew 2·50 3·50
754 5p. Zorilla . . . . 4·25 6·50
755 10p. Vervet monkey . . . . 6·50 9·50

1992. Olympic Games, Barcelona. Multicoloured.
756 10t. Type **182** 60 10
757 50t. Running . . . . 1·50 50
758 1p. Boxing (different) . . . . 2·00 2·50
759 2p. Running (different) . . . 2·50 4·50
MS760 87 × 117 mm. Nos. 756/9 4·50 7·00

183 "Adiantum incisum" **184** Helping Blind Person (Lions Club International)

1992. Christmas. Ferns. Multicoloured.
761 10t. Type **183** 40 10
762 25t. "Actiniopteris radiata" 70 35
763 40t. "Ceratopteris cornuta" 1·00 55
764 1p.50 "Pellaea calomelanos" 3·00 6·00

1993. Charitable Organizations in Botswana. Mult.
765 10t. Type **184** 80 20
766 15t. Nurse carrying child (Red Cross Society) (horiz) 90 40
767 25t. Woman watering seedling (Ecumenical Decade) 90 50
768 35t. Deaf children (Round Table) (horiz) . . . . . . 1·25 1·50
769 40t. Crowd of people (Rotary International) . . . . . . 1·25 1·75
770 50t. Hands at prayer (Botswana Christian Council) (horiz) . . . . . 1·50 2·50

185 Bechuanaland Railways Class "6" Locomotive No. 1 **186** Long-crested Eagle

1993. Railway Centenary. Multicoloured.
771 10t. Type **185** 75 40
772 40t. Class "19" locomotive No. 317 . . . . 1·40 75
773 50t. Class "12" locomotive No. 256 . . . . 1·40 90
774 1p.50 Class "7" locomotive No. 71 . . . . 2·00 4·50
MS775 190 × 100 mm. Nos. 771/4 4·50 5·00

1993. Endangered Eagles. Multicoloured.
776 10t. Type **186** 55 35
777 25t. Short-toed eagle ("Snake eagle") . . . . 1·00 65
778 50t. Bateleur ("Bateleur Eagle") . . . . 1·40 1·75
779 1p.50 Secretary bird . . . . 2·50 5·00

187 "Aloe zebrina"

1993. Christmas. Flora. Multicoloured.
780 12t. Type **187** 40 10
781 25t. "Croton megalobotrys" 60 25
782 50t. "Boophane disticha" . . 85 70
783 1p. "Euphoria davyi" . . . . 1·25 3·00

188 Boy with String Puppet

1994. Traditional Toys. Multicoloured.
784 10t. Type **188** 20 10
785 40t. Boys with clay cattle . . 45 30
786 50t. Boy with spinner 50 50
787 1p. Girls playing in make-believe houses . . . . . . 1·10 2·50

189 Interior of Control Tower, Gaborone Airport

1994. 50th Anniv of I.C.A.O. Multicoloured.
788 10t. Type **189** 40 10
789 25t. Crash fire tender 55 30
790 40t. Loading supplies onto airliner (vert) 75 75
791 50t. Control tower, Gaborone (vert) . . . . 80 1·50

1994. No. 743 surch **10t.**
792 10t. on 12t. Pangolin . . . . 4·00 75

191 Lesser Flamingos at Sua Pan **192** "Ziziphus mucronata"

1994. Environment Protection. Makgadikgadi Pans. Multicoloured.
793 10t. Type **191** 75 40
794 35t. Baobab trees (horiz) . . 50 40
795 50t. Zebra and palm trees . . 65 80
796 2p. Map of area (horiz) . . . 2·50 4·50

1994. Christmas. Edible Fruits. Multicoloured.
797 10t. Type **192** 25 10
798 25t. "Strychnos cocculoides" 40 30
799 40t. "Bauhinia petersiana" 60 70
800 50t. "Schinziphyton rautonenii" . . . . 70 1·10

193 Fisherman with Bow and Arrow **194** Boys watering Horses (F.A.O.)

1995. Traditional Fishing. Multicoloured.
801 15t. Type **193** 35 20
802 40t. Men in canoe and boy with fishing rod 60 40
803 65t. Fisherman with net . . . 80 75
804 80t. Fisherman with basket fish trap . . . . 1·00 1·60

1995. 50th Anniv of United Nations. Multicoloured.
805 20t. Type **194** 20 10
806 50t. Schoolchildren queueing for soup (W.F.P.) 35 30
807 80t. Policeman conducting census (U.N.D.P.) 60 80
808 1p. Weighing baby (U.N.I.C.E.F.) . . . . . . 70 1·50

195 Brown Hyena

1995. Endangered Species. Brown Hyena. Mult.
809 20t. Type **195** 45 60
810 50t. Pair of hyenas 65 75
811 80t. Hyena stealing ostrich eggs . . . . 1·10 1·50
812 1p. Adult hyena and cubs . . 1·25 2·00

196 "Adenia glauca" **198** Spears

1995. Christmas. Plants. Multicoloured.
813 20t. Type **196** 35 10
814 50t. "Pterodiscus ngamicus" 60 30
815 80t. "Sesamothamnus lugardii" . . . . 1·00 1·00
816 1p. "Fockea multiflora" . . . 1·10 1·75

1996. Nos. 738/40 surch.
817 20t. on 2t. Spring hare . . . 50 30
818 30t. on 1t. Type **181** 60 30
819 70t. on 4t. Blackfooted cat 1·25 2·00

1996. Traditional Weapons. Multicoloured.
820 20t. Type **198** 20 10
821 50t. Axes 35 30
822 80t. Shield and knobkerries 55 65
823 1p. Knives and sheaths . . . 60 1·25

199 Child with Basic Radio **200** Olympic Flame, Rings and Wreath

1996. Centenary of Radio. Multicoloured.
824 20t. Type **199** 25 10
825 50t. Radio Botswana's mobile transmitter 40 30
826 80t. Police radio control . . . 60 70
827 1p. Listening to radio . . . . 70 1·40

1996. Centenary of Modern Olympic Games. Mult.
828 20t. Type **200** 25 10
829 50t. Pierre de Coubertin (founder of modern Olympics) 40 30
830 80t. Map of Botswana with flags and athletes 75 75
831 1p. Ruins of ancient stadium at Olympia . . . . 75 1·40

201 Family Planning Class (Botswana Family Welfare Association) **202** "Adansonia digitata" Leaf and Blossom

1996. Local Charities. Multicoloured.
832 20t. Type **201** 20 10
833 30t. Blind workers (Pudulogong Rehabilitation Centre) 20 15
834 50t. Collecting seeds (Forestry Association of Botswana) 30 30
835 70t. Secretarial class (Y.W.C.A.) 40 70
836 80t. Children's day centre (Botswana Council of Women) 50 75
837 1p. Children's village, Tlokweng (S.O.S. Children's village) . . . . 60 1·25

1996. Christmas. Parts of Life Cycle for "Adansonia digitata". Multicoloured.
838 20t. Type **202** 25 10
839 50t. Fruit 40 25

840 80t. Tree in leaf 60 75
841 1p. Tree with bare branches 70 1·40

203 Tati Hotel

204 Steam Locomotive, Bechuanaland Railway, 1897

1997. Francistown Centenary. Multicoloured.
842 20t. Type **203** 15 10
843 50t. Railway Station 55 35
844 80t. Company Manager's House 60 75
845 1p. Monarch Mine . . . . . 80 1·40

1997. Railway Centenary. Multicoloured.
846 35t. Type **204** 30 20
847 50t. Elephants crossing railway line 50 35
848 80t. First locomotive in Bechuanaland, 1897 . . . 60 45
849 1p. Beyer-Garratt type steam locomotive No. 352 . . . 65 65
850 2p. Diesel locomotive No. BD339 . . . . 90 1·50
851 2p.50 Fantuzzi container stacker . . . . 1·00 1·75

205 Pel's Fishing Owl

206 "Combretum zeyheri"

1997. Birds. Multicoloured.
852 5t. Type **205** 30 50
853 10t. African harrier hawk ("Gymnogene") (horiz) . . 30 30
854 15t. Brown parrot ("Meyer's Parrot") 30 30
855 20t. Harlequin quail (horiz) 40 30
856 25t. Mariqua sunbird ("Marico Sunbird") (horiz) 40 30
857 30t. Kurrichane thrush (horiz) 50 30
858 40t. Paradise sparrow ("Redheaded Finch") . . . 50 30
859 50t. Red-billed buffalo weaver ("Buffalo Weaver") 60 40
860 60t. Sacred ibis (horiz) . . . 70 60
861 70t. Cape shoveler (horiz) . . 70 70
862 80t. Black-throated honeyguide ("Greater Honeyguide") (horiz) . . . 70 70
863 1p. Woodland kingfisher (horiz) 80 80
864 1p.25 Purple heron . . . . . 90 1·00
865 1p.50 Yelllow-billed oxpecker (horiz) . . . . 90 1·10
866 2p. Shaft-tailed whydah . . . 1·00 1·25
867 2p.50 White stork . . . . . 1·00 1·25
868 5p. Ovampo sparrow hawk ("Sparrowhawk") . . . . 1·75 2·00
869 10p. Spotted crake . . . . . 2·75 3·50
No. 861 is inscribed "Shoveller" in error.

1997. Golden Wedding of Queen Elizabeth and Prince Philip. As T **173** of Ascension. Multicoloured.
870 35t. Prince Philip with carriage 20 55
871 35t. Queen Elizabeth with binoculars 20 55
872 2p. Queen Elizabeth with horse team . . . . 90 1·50
873 2p. Prince Philip and horse 90 1·50
874 2p.50 Queen Elizabeth and Prince Philip . . . . . . 1·10 1·50
875 2p.50 Princess Anne and Prince Edward . . . . . . 1·10 1·50
MS876 110 × 70 mm. 10p. Queen Elizabeth and Prince Philip in landau (horiz) 4·00 5·00

1997. Christmas. Plants. Multicoloured.
877 35t. Type **206** 35 10
878 1p. "Combretum apiculatum" 90 35
879 2p. "Combretum molle" . . 1·60 1·60
880 2p.50 "Combretum imberbe" 1·75 2·00

207 Baobab Trees

1998. Tourism (1st series). Multicoloured.
881 35t. Type **207** 25 15
882 1p. Crocodile 50 40
883 2p. Stalactites (vert) . . . . 85 1·10
884 2p.50 Tourists and rock paintings (vert) . . . . . 1·10 1·60
See also Nos. 899/902.

1998. Diana, Princess of Wales Commemoration. As T **223a** of Bahamas. Multicoloured.
885 35t. Princess Diana, 1990 . . 25 15
886 1p. In green hat, 1992 . . . 40 35
887 2p. In white blouse, 1993 . . 75 1·10
888 2p.50 With crowd, Cambridge, 1993 . . . . . 90 1·50
MS889 145 × 70 mm. As Nos. 885/8, but each with a face value of 2p.50 3·75 4·50

208 "Village Life" (tapestry)

209 "Ficus ingens"

1998. Botswana Weavers. Multicoloured.
890 35t. Type **208** 30 15
891 55t. Weaver dyeing threads 35 20
892 1p. "African wildlife" (tapestry) 90 65
893 2p. Weaver at loom . . . . 1·10 1·60
MS894 68 × 58 mm. 2p.50, "Elephants" (tapestry) (horiz) 1·50 2·00

1998. Christmas. Plants. Multicoloured.
895 35t. Type **209** 35 10
896 55t. "Ficus pygmaea" 50 20
897 1p. "Ficus abutilifolia" . . . 85 55
898 2p.50 "Ficus sycomorus" . . 1·60 2·25

1999. Tourism (2nd series). As T **207**. Multicoloured.
899 35t. Rock painting of men and cattle 35 10
900 55t. Expedition at Salt Pan 40 20
901 1p. Rock painting of elephant and antelope (vert) 65 55
902 2p. Tourists under Baobab tree (vert) . . . . 80 1·50

210 Road Map

1999. Southern African Development Community Day. Sheet 77 × 84 mm.
MS903 **210** 5p. multicoloured 2·25 2·50

211 Modern Post Office

1999. 125th Anniv of Universal Postal Union.
904 **211** 2p. multicoloured . . . . 1·25 1·25

212 Mpule Kwelagobe winning contest

1999. Mpule Kwelagobe ("Miss Universe 1999"). Multicoloured.
905 35t. Type **212** 25 10
906 1p. In traditional dress (horiz) 60 30
907 2p. In traditional dancing costume with lion . . . 1·00 60
908 2p.50 Wearing "Botswana" sash (horiz) . . . . 1·10 75
909 15p. With leopard in background (horiz) . . . . 6·00 8·00
MS910 175 × 80 mm. Nos. 905/9 8·50 9·50

213 Saddle-bill Stork and Limpopo River

2000. Scenic Rivers. Multicoloured.
911 35t. Type **213** 25 10
912 1p. Hippopotamuses in water lilies (vert) 50 30
913 2p. African skimmer and makoro (dugout canoe) . . 85 1·00
914 2p.50 African elephant at sunset, Chobe River (vert) 1·00 1·40

214 Mopane Moth

2000. Moths. Multicoloured.
915 35t. Type **214** 15 10
916 70t. Wild silk moth 25 20
917 1p. Crimson speckled footman ("Tiger Moth") 35 30
918 2p. African lunar moth . . . 65 60
919 15p. Speckled emperor moth 4·75 7·00
MS920 175 × 135 mm. Nos. 915/19 5·50 6·00
No. **MS**920 is in the shape of a moth.

215 Mother reading Medicine Label with Child ("Protect Your Children")

2000. United Nations Literacy Decade. Mult.
921 35t. Type **215** 15 10
922 70t. Adult literacy class ("Never Too Old To Learn") 25 20
923 2p. Man smoking next to petrol pump ("Be Aware Of Danger") 65 75
924 2p.50 Man at Automatic Teller Machine ("Be Independent") . . . . . . 85 1·25

216 Pres. Sir Seretse Khama

217 Doctor giving Eye Test

2000. Chiefs and Presidents.
925 **216** 35t. black, red and gold 20 10
926 – 1p. multicoloured 35 25
927 – 2p. multicoloured 65 75
928 – 2p.50 multicoloured . . . 80 1·25
DESIGNS—HORIZ (60 × 40 mm): 35t. Chiefs Sebele I of Bakwena, Bathoen I of Bangwaketse and Khama III of Bangato, 1895. VERT (as T **216**): 2p. Pres. Sir Ketumile Masire; 2p.50, Pres. Festus Mogae.

2000. Airborne Medical Service. Multicoloured.
929 35t. Type **217** 25 10
930 1p. Medical team and family 55 30
931 2p. Aircraft over canoes . . . 1·00 1·00
932 2p.50 Donkeys and mule cart on airstrip . . . . 1·25 1·50

218 Hippopotamus

2000. Wetlands (1st series). Okavango Delta. Mult.
933 35t. Type **218** 25 15
934 1p. Tiger fish and tilapia . . 45 30
935 1p.75 Painted reed frog and wattled crane (vert) . . . . 90 1·00

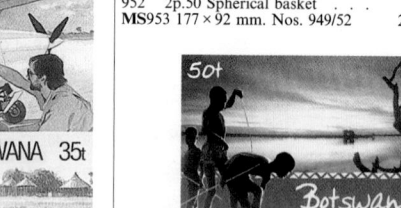

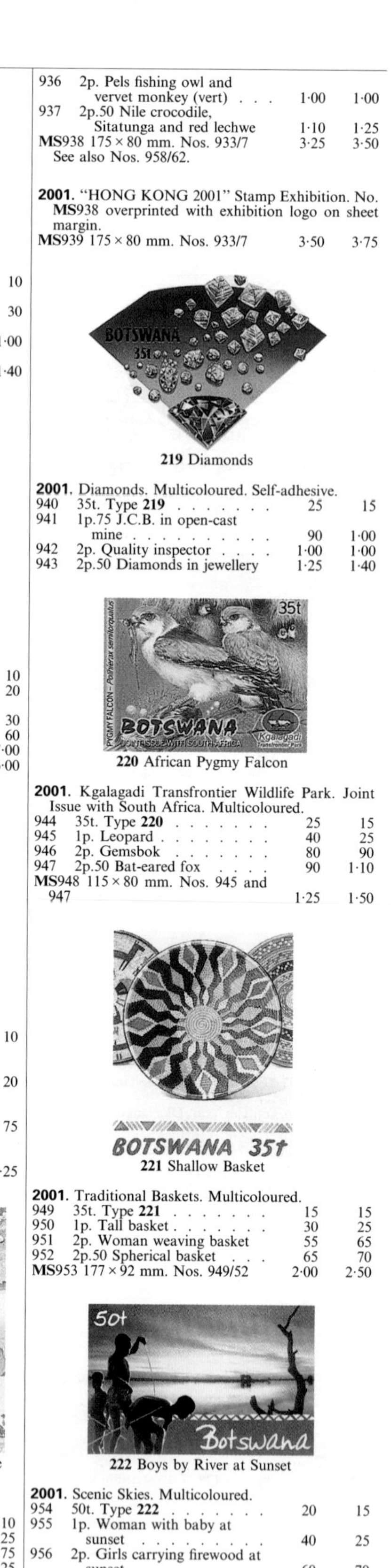

936 2p. Pels fishing owl and vervet monkey (vert) . . . 1·00 1·00
937 2p.50 Nile crocodile, Sitatunga and red lechwe 1·10 1·25
MS938 175 × 80 mm. Nos. 933/7 3·25 3·50
See also Nos. 958/62.

2001. "HONG KONG 2001" Stamp Exhibition. No. **MS**938 overprinted with exhibition logo on sheet margin.
MS939 175 × 80 mm. Nos. 933/7 3·50 3·75

219 Diamonds

2001. Diamonds. Multicoloured. Self-adhesive.
940 35t. Type **219** 25 15
941 1p.75 J.C.B. in open-cast mine . . . . 90 1·00
942 2p. Quality inspector . . . . 1·00 1·00
943 2p.50 Diamonds in jewellery 1·25 1·40

220 African Pygmy Falcon

2001. Kgalagadi Transfrontier Wildlife Park. Joint Issue with South Africa. Multicoloured.
944 35t. Type **220** 25 15
945 1p. Leopard 40 25
946 2p. Gemsbok 80 90
947 2p.50 Bat-eared fox . . . . 90 1·10
MS948 115 × 80 mm. Nos. 945 and 947 1·25 1·50

221 Shallow Basket

2001. Traditional Baskets. Multicoloured.
949 35t. Type **221** 15 15
950 1p. Tall basket 30 25
951 2p. Woman weaving basket 55 65
952 2p.50 Spherical basket . . . 65 70
MS953 177 × 92 mm. Nos. 949/52 2·00 2·50

222 Boys by River at Sunset

2001. Scenic Skies. Multicoloured.
954 50t. Type **222** 20 15
955 1p. Woman with baby at sunset 40 25
956 2p. Girls carrying firewood at sunset 60 70
957 10p. Traditional village at sunset near huts . . . . . 2·25 2·75

2001. Wetlands (2nd series). Chobe River. As T **218**. Multicoloured.
958 50t. Water monitor and carmine bee-eater 25 15
959 1p.75 Buffalo 50 50
960 2p. Savanna baboons (vert) 60 70
961 2p.50 Lion (vert) 70 80
962 3p. African elephants in river 90 1·00
MS963 175 × 80 mm. Nos. 958/62 2·75 3·00

223 Black Mamba

2002. Snakes. Multicoloured.
964 50t. Type **223** 25 15
965 1p.75 Spitting cobra (vert) . . 55 45
966 2p.50 Puff adder 65 70
967 3p. Boomslang (vert) 80 90

224 Mbukushu Pots

2002. Botswana Pottery. Multicoloured.
968 50t. Type **224** 10 10
969 2p. Sekgatla pots 45 50
970 2p.50 Setswana pots 55 55
971 3p. Kalanga pots 65 70

225 Queen Elizabeth in Evening Dress and Commonwealth Emblem

2002. Golden Jubilee. Multicoloured.
972 55t. Type **225** 10 15
973 2p.75 Queen Elizabeth with bouquet (vert) 60 65

226 Tree Squirrel

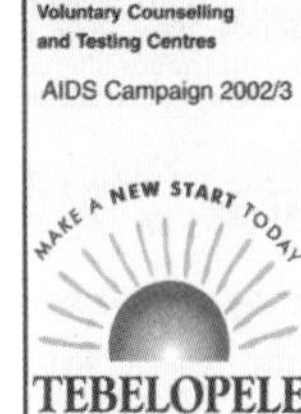

227 Tebelopele (counselling and testing centres) Symbol

2002. Mammals. Multicoloured.
974 5t. Type **226** 10 10
975 10t. Black-backed jackal . . 10 10
976 20t. African wild cat 10 10
977 30t. Slender mongoose (horiz) 10 10
978 40t. African civet (horiz) . . 10 10
979 55t. Elephant 10 15
980 90t. Reedbuck 20 25
981 1p. Kudu 20 25
982 1p.45 Waterbuck 35 40
983 1p.95 Sable (horiz) 45 50
984 2p.20 Sitatunga (horiz) . . . 50 55
985 2p.75 Porcupine (horiz) . . . 60 65
986 3p.30 Serval (horiz) 70 75
987 4p. Antbear (horiz) 90 95
988 5p. Bushpig (horiz) . . . . . 1·10 1·25
989 15p. Chakma baboon . . . . 3·25 3·50

2002. AIDS Awareness. Multicoloured.
990 55t. Type **227** 10 15
991 1p.10 AIDS ribbon and mother and baby badge . . 20 25
992 2p.75 Hands and male gender symbol 60 65
993 3p.30 Orphans with foster parent 70 75

2002. Wetlands (3rd series). The Makgadikgadi Pans. As T **218**. Multicoloured.
994 55t. Aardwolf 10 15
995 1p.10 Blue wildebeest and zebra 20 25
996 2p.50 Zebra (vert) 55 60
997 2p.75 Flamingo (vert) 60 65
998 3p.30 Pelican in flight 70 75
MS999 175 × 80 mm. Nos. 994/8 2·25 2·40

POSTAGE DUE STAMPS

1967. Nos. D10/12 of Bechuanaland optd **REPUBLIC OF BOTSWANA**.
D13 **D 1** 1c. red . . . . 15 1·75
D14 2c. violet . . . . 15 1·75
D15 5c. green . . . . 20 1·75

D 5 African Elephant

D 6 Common Zebra

1971.
D16 **D 5** 1c. red . . . . 1·10 3·25
D17 2c. violet . . . . 1·40 3·50
D18 6c. brown . . . . 1·75 5·50
D19 14c. green . . . . 2·00 7·50

1977.
D25a **D 6** 1t. black and red . . . 30 1·00
D26a 2t. black and green . . 30 1·00
D27a 4t. black and red . . . 30 1·00
D28a 10t. black and blue . . 30 1·00
D29a 16t. black and brown . . 35 1·25

BOYACA Pt. 20

One of the states of the Granadine Confederation. A Department of Colombia from 1886, now uses Colombian stamps.

100 centavos = 1 peso.

1 Mendoza Perez

1899. Imperf or perf.
1 **1** 5c. green . . . . 60 1·50

2

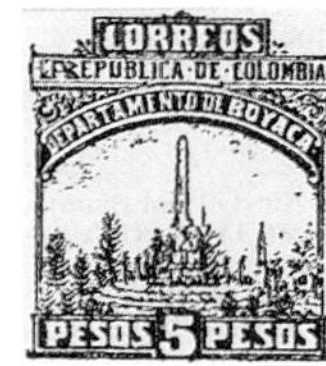

6 Battle of Boyaca Monument

1903. Imperf or perf.
3 **2** 10c. grey 15 15
4 10c. blue 60 60
12 – 10c. orange 20 15
5 **2** 20c. brown 20 20
5a 20c. lake 25 25
6 – 50c. turquoise 15 15
8 – 1p. red 20 15
9 – 1p. red . . . . 1·40 1·40
10 **6** 5p. black on red 50 35
11 – 10p. black on buff 50 40
DESIGNS—As Type **2**: 10c. orange, Building; 50c. Gen. Pinzon; 1p. Figure of value. As Type **6**: 10p. Pres. Marroquin.

BRAZIL Pt. 20

A country in the N.E. of S. America. Portuguese settlement, 1500. Kingdom, 1815. Empire, 1822. Republic from 1889.

1843. 1000 reis = 1 milreis.
1942. 100 centavos = 1 cruzeiro.
1986. 100 centavos = 1 cruzado.
1990. 100 centavos = 1 cruzeiro.
1994. 100 centavos = 1 real.

1 "Bull's Eye"

1843. Imperf.
4 **1** 30r. black £2250 £375
5 60r. black £600 £200
6 90r. black £2250 £950

2 **3** **4**

1844. Imperf.
10 **2** 10r. black . . . . £120 24·00
11 30r. black . . . . £150 35·00
12 60r. black . . . . £120 24·00
13 90r. black £900 £140
14 180r. black £3750 £1100
15 300r. black £4750 £1400
16 600r. black £4500 £1600

1850. Imperf.
17 **3** 10r. black . . . . 30·00 26·00
18 20r. black . . . . 90·00 £110
19 30r. black . . . . 12·00 3·50
20 60r. black . . . . 12·00 2·50
21 90r. black . . . . 95·00 12·00
22 180r. black . . . . £120 55·00
23 300r. black . . . . £350 70·00
24 600r. black . . . . £450 80·00

1854. Imperf.
25 **3** 10r. blue . . . . 12·00 9·00
26 30r. blue . . . . 35·00 55·00
27 **4** 280r. red . . . . £120 85·00
28 430r. yellow £190 £120

5

6

17 Emperor Dom Pedro II

1866. Various frames, but in T **5** the Emperor has a dark beard. Perf or roul.
43 **5** 10r. red . . . . 9·00 5·25
44a **6** 20r. purple . . . . 12·00 3·00
45 **5** 50r. blue . . . . 20·00 1·75
46a 80r. purple . . . . 55·00 4·75
47a 100r. green . . . . 20·00 1·25
55 **6** 200r. black . . . . 48·00 4·75
67 **17** 300r. green and orange . . 90·00 24·00
56 **5** 500r. orange . . . . £160 24·00

12

13

1878. Various frames, but in T **13** the Emperor's beard is white. Roulette.
57 **12** 10r. red . . . . 9·00 3·00
58 **13** 20r. mauve . . . . 12·00 2·40
59 **12** 50r. blue . . . . 18·00 1·75
60 80r. red . . . . 20·00 9·50
61 100r. green . . . . 20·00 1·25
62 200r. black . . . . £110 15·00
63 260r. brown . . . . 60·00 20·00
64 300r. brown . . . . 60·00 6·00
65 700r. red . . . . £130 80·00
66 1000r. grey . . . . £140 35·00

21

27 Pedro II

1881. Various frames. Perf.
71 **21** 10r. black . . . . 12·00 26·00
72 10r. orange . . . . 3·00 1·75
73 50r. blue . . . . 30·00 3·00
74 100r. olive . . . . 50·00 3·00
77 100r. lilac . . . . £175 1·75
75a 200r. red . . . . 42·00 3·50
No. 77 is inscr "CORREIO".

1884.
81 **27** 100r. lilac . . . . £175 3·50

25

26

29

30 Southern Cross

31 **32**

33 Entrance to Bay of Rio de Janeiro

35 Southern Cross

1884.
78 **25** 20r. green . . . . 24·00 3·50
80 **26** 50r. blue . . . . 20·00 5·25
83 **29** 100r. lilac . . . . 48·00 1·75
84 **30** 300r. blue . . . . £200 26·00
85a **31** 500r. olive . . . . £110 12·00
86 **32** 700r. lilac . . . . 75·00 £125
87 **33** 1000r. blue £225 £125

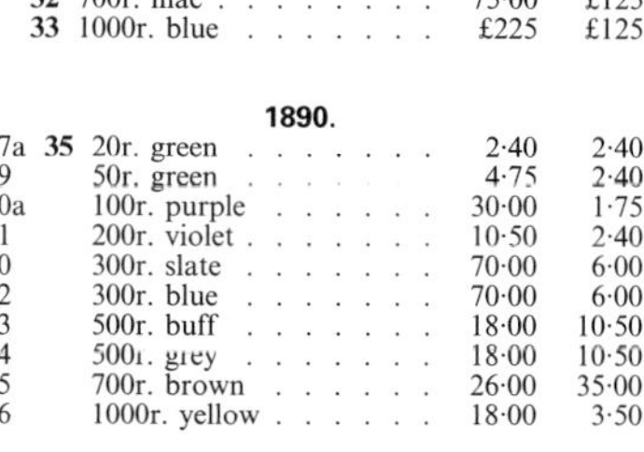
1890.
97a **35** 20r. green . . . . 2·40 2·40
89 50r. green . . . . 4·75 2·40
110a 100r. purple . . . . . . 30·00 1·75
91 200r. violet . . . . . . 10·50 2·40
100 300r. slate . . . . . . 70·00 6·00
92 300r. blue . . . . 70·00 6·00
93 500r. buff . . . . 18·00 10·50
94 500r. grey . . . . 18·00 10·50
95 700r. brown . . . . . . 26·00 35·00
96 1000r. yellow . . . . . . 18·00 3·50

37 Head of Liberty

38 Head of Liberty

1891.
111d **37** 100r. red and blue . . . 35·00 1·75

1893.

114 **38** 100r. red . . . . 70·00 1·75

39 Sugar-loaf Mountain

41 Head of Liberty

43 Head of Mercury

1894.
124 **39** 10r. blue and red . . . . 1·90 60
125 20r. blue and orange . . . 90 45
126 50r. blue . . . . 5·25 3·50
232 50r. green . . . . 9·00 3·75
127 **41** 100r. black and red . . . 3·50 40
239 100r. red . . . . 18·00 35
128 200r. black and orange . . 90 35
234 200r. blue . . . . 10·50 35
129 300r. black and green . . 14·00 60
153 500r. black and blue . . 26·00 1·75
131a 700r. black and mauve . . 14·50 1·75
132 **43** 1000r. mauve and green 55·00 1·75
133 2000r. purple and grey . . 55·00 12·00

1897. As T **39** but inscr "REIS REIS" instead of "DEZ REIS".
165a 10r. blue and red . . . . . 1·60 60

1898. Newspaper stamps of 1889 surch **1898** between value twice in figures.
168 **N 34** 100r. on 50r. orange . . 1·90 55·00
169 200r. on 100r. mauve . . 3·50 95
170 300r. on 200r. black . . 3·50 95
171 500r. on 300r. red . . . 5·25 4·00
173 700r. on 500r. green . . 7·00 1·75
172 700r. on 500r. orange 7·00 18·00
174 1000r. on 700r. orange 35·00 35·00
175 1000r. on 700r. blue . . 25·00 18·00
176 2000r. on 1000r. orange 25·00 18·00
177 2000r. on 1000r. brown 19·00 7·00

1898. Newspaper stamp of 1890 surch **200** over **1898**.
180 **N 37** 200r. on 100r. mauve . . 14·00 9·00

1898. Newspaper stamps of 1890 surch **1898** over new value.
182 **N 38** 20r. on 10r. blue . . . . 1·75 3·50
183 50r. on 20r. green . . . 9·00 10·50
184 100r. on 50r. green . . . 18·00 21·00

1899. Postage stamps of 1890 surch **1899** over new value.
194 **35** 50r. on 20r. green . . . . 1·75 3·50
195 100r. on 50r. green . . . 1·75 3·50
196 300r. on 200r. violet . . . 9·00 18·00
190b 500r. on 300r. slate . . . 55·00 12·50
190 500r. on 300r. blue . . . 55·00 12·50
191 700r. on 500r. buff . . . 35·00 10·50
192a 1,000r. on 700r. brown 25·00 10·50
193 2,000r. on 1,000r. yellow 35·00 5·25

50 Discovery of Brazil

52 Emancipation of Slaves

1900. 400th Anniv of Discovery of Brazil.
226 **50** 100r. red . . . . 7·00 3·50
227 – 200r. green and yellow . . 7·00 3·50
228 **52** 500r. blue . . . . 7·00 3·50
229 – 700r. green . . . . 7·00 3·50
DESIGNS—HORIZ: 200r. Declaration of Independence. VERT: 700r. Allegory of Republic.

56 Pan-American Congress

1906.
259a 56 100r. red 42·00 26·00
259b 200r. blue 90·00 8·75

57 Aristides Lobo 61 Liberty

1906.
260 57 10r. grey 90 20
261 – 20r. violet 90 20
262 – 50r. green 90 20
264 – 100r. red 1·75 20
265 – 200r. blue 1·75 20
267 – 300r. brown 3·50 60
268 – 400r. olive 26·00 1·75
269 – 500r. violet 5·25 60
272 – 600r. olive 2·75 90
273 – 700r. brown 5·25 2·75
274 61 1000r. red 28·00 90
275 – 1000r. green 3·50 35
276 – 1000r. grey 19·00 60
277 61 2000r. green 18·00 60
278 2000r. blue 9·00 90
279 5000r. pink 7·00 1·75
280 – 5000r. brown 55·00 10·50
281 – 10000r. brown 7·00 1·75
PORTRAITS: 20r. B. Constant. 50r. A. Cabral. 100r. Wandenkolk. 200r. D. da Fonseca. 300r. F. Peixoto. 400r., 600r. P. de Moraes. 500r. C. Salles. 700r., 5000r. (No. 280) R. Alves. 1000r. (Nos. 275/6) B. do Rio Branco. 10000r. N. Pecanha.

64 King Carlos and Pres. Affonso Penna and Emblems of Portuguese-Brazilian Amity
65 Emblems of Peace, Commerce and Industry

1908. Centenary of Opening of Brazilian Ports to Foreign Commerce.
282 64 100r. red 14·50 1·75

1908. National Exhibition, Rio de Janeiro.
283 65 100r. red 45·00 2·40

66 Bonifacio, San Martin, Hidalgo, Washington, O'Higgins, Bolivar
67 Cape Frio

1909. Pan-American Congress, Rio de Janeiro.
284 66 200r. blue 14·50 1·25

1915. 300th Anniv of Discovery of Cape Frio.
285 67 100r. turquoise on yellow 7·00 5·25

69 Bay of Guajara

1916. 300th Anniv of City of Belem.
286 69 100r. red 12·50 5·00

70 Revolutionary Flag

1917. Centenary of Pernambuco Revolution.
287 70 100r. blue 18·00 9·00

71 Liberty 72 Liberty 74 Inscr "BRAZIL"

1918. Various frames.
288 71 10r. brown 60 35
289 20r. violet 60 35
290 25r. grey 60 35
291 50r. green 1·75 60
292 72 100r. red 1·75 35
293 200r. blue 7·00 45
294 300r. orange 19·00 3·50
295 500r. purple 19·00 3·50
296 600r. orange 2·75 8·75
297 74 1000r. blue 7·00 35
298 2000r. brown 26·00 7·00
299 5000r. lilac 7·00 7·00
300 10,000r. red 9·00 1·00

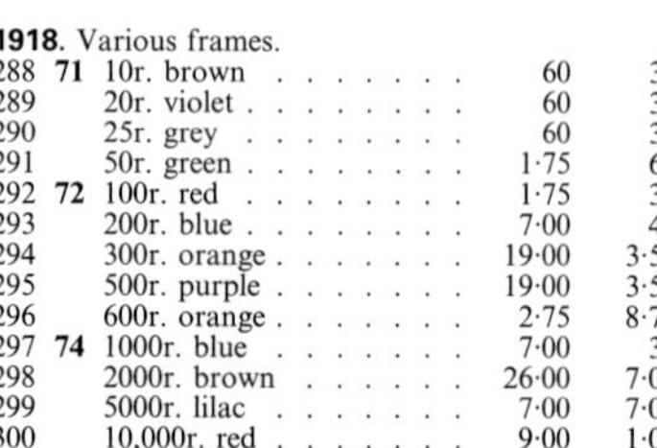

77 Steam Locomotive 78 "Industry" 79 "Agriculture"

80 "Aviation" 81 Mercury 82 "Shipping"

1920. T 74 inscr "BRASIL".
317 77 10r. purple 60 60
387 80 10r. brown 35 35
318 77 20r. grey 60 60
388 80 20r. violet 35 35
389 78 25r. purple 35 1·10
354 79 40r. brown 60 60
306 78 50r. green 1·25 60
355 50r. brown 60 60
390 80 50r. purple 35 35
391 50r. green 35 35
308 79 80r. green 20 3·50
309 80 100r. red 3·50 60
392 100r. orange 60 35
367 100r. green 1·25 60
420 100r. yellow 1·75 35
311 150r. violet 1·75 60
312 200r. blue 5·25 60
330 200r. red 1·25 60
383 200r. green 4·75 60
405 81 300r. grey 60 35
394 300r. green 1·50 35
333 300r. red 1·25 35
406 400r. blue 1·50 35
335 400r. orange 1·25 3·50
407 500r. brown 1·75 35
385 500r. blue 2·40 60
397 600r. brown 9·00 30
422 600r. orange 5·25 35
341 82 600r. orange 1·75 60
409 81 700r. violet 3·50 35
342 82 1000r. purple 3·50 35
410 81 1000r. blue 9·00 35
362c 74 2000r. blue 10·50 1·25
411 2000r. violet 10·50 1·25
363a 5000r. brown 21·00 1·25
364 10000r. purple 21·00 1·75

93 King Albert and Pres. Pessoa

1920. Visit of King of the Belgians.
431 93 100r. red 70 50

94 Declaration of Ypiranga 97 Brazilian Army entering Bahia

1922. Centenary of Independence.
432 94 100r. blue 5·25 90
433 – 200r. red 10·50 60
434 – 300r. green 10·50 60
DESIGNS: 200r. Dom Pedro I and J. Bonifacio; 300r. National Exn. and Pres. Pessoa.

1923. Centenary of Capture of Bahia from the Portuguese.
435 97 200r. red 12·00 7·00

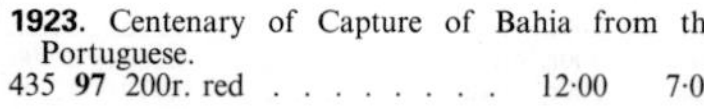

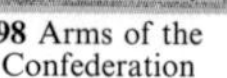
98 Arms of the Confederation 99 Ruy Barbosa

1924. Centenary of Confederation of the Equator.
436 98 200r. multicoloured 3·50 1·90

1927.
438b 99 1000r. red 2·40 1·25

100 "Justice"

1927. Centenary of Law Courses.
439 100 100r. blue 1·75 60
440 – 200r. red 1·25 35
DESIGN: 200r. Map and Balances.

1928. Air. Official stamps of 1913, Type O 67, surch **SERVICO AEREO** and new value. Centres in black.
441 50r. on 10r. grey 35 35
442 200r. on 1000r. brown 2·40 4·50
443 200r. on 2000r. brown 1·25 9·50
444 200r. on 5000r. bistre 1·50 1·25
445 300r. on 500r. yellow 1·50 1·90
446 300r. on 600r. purple 90 65
447 500r. on 50r. grey 1·50 65
448 1000r. on 20r. olive 1·25 35
449 2000r. on 100r. red 2·25 1·50
450 2000r. on 200r. blue 3·00 1·60
451 2000r. on 10,000r. black 2·25 65
452 5000r. on 20,000r. blue 8·75 3·75
453 5000r. on 50,000r. green 8·75 3·75
454 5000r. on 100,000r. red 24·00 30·00
455 10,000r. on 500,000r. brown 24·00 24·00
456 10,000r. on 1,000,000r. sepia 24·00 24·00

104 Liberty holding Coffee Leaves 106 Ruy Barbosa

1928. Bicent of Introduction of the Coffee Plant.
457 104 100r. green 3·50 2·40
458 200r. red 1·75 1·25
459 300r. black 10·50 60

1928. Official stamps of 1919 surch.
460 O 77 700r. on 500r. orange 9·00 9·00
461 1000r. on 100r. red 5·25 60
462 2000r. on 200r. blue 7·00 1·25
463 5000r. on 50r. green 7·00 1·75
464 10,000r. on 10r. brown 25·00 1·75

1929.
465 106 5000r. blue 21·00 1·25

108 Santos Dumonts Airship "Ballon No. 6" 109 Santos Dumont

1929. Air.
469 – 50r. green 15 10
470 108 200r. red 1·50 15
471 – 300r. blue 2·00 15
472 – 500r. purple 2·40 15
473 – 1000r. brown 7·00 25
479 – 2000r. green 12·00 1·25
480 – 5000r. red 14·50 1·40
481 109 10,000r. grey 14·50 3·00
DESIGNS: 50r. De Gusmao's monument; 300r. A. Severo's airship "Pax"; 500r. Santos Dumont's biplane "14 bis"; 1000r. R. de Barros's flying boat "Jahu"; 2000r. De Gusmao; 5000r. A. Severo.

110 112

1930. Air.
486 110 3000r. violet 1·75 1·75

1930. 4th Pan-American Architectural Congress.
487 – 100r. turquoise 3·50 3·50
488 112 200r. grey 6·00 2·40
489 – 300r. red 8·25 3·50
DESIGNS: 100r. Sun rays inscr "ARCHITECTOS"; 300r. Architrave and Southern Cross.

113 G. Vargas and J. Pessoa – "Redemption of Brazil" 114 O. Aranha – "What is the matter?"

1931. Charity. Revolution of 3 October 1930.
490 113 10r.+10r. blue 15 12·00
491 20r.+20r. brown 15 9·00
492 114 50r.+50r. green, red and yellow 15 15
493 113 100r.+50r. orange 1·25 60
494 200r.+100r. green 60 60
495 – 300r.+150r. mult 60 60
496 113 400r.+200r. red 1·75 1·75
497 500r.+250r. blue 1·25 90
498 600r.+300r. purple 90 18·00
499 700r.+350r. mult 1·25 90
500 1$+500r. green, red and yellow 3·50 60
501 – 2$+1$ grey and red 12·00 1·25
502 – 5$+2$ 500r. black & red 24·00 12·00
503 – 10$+5$ green & yellow 60·00 18·00
DESIGNS: 300r., 700r. as Type **113**, but portraits in circles and frames altered. Milreis values as Type **114** with different portraits and frames.

1931. No. 333 surch **1931 200 Reis**.
507 81 200r. on 300r. red 60 35

1931. Zeppelin Air Stamps. Surch **ZEPPELIN** and value.
508 108 2$500 on 200r. red (No. 470) 35·00 35·00
511 106 3$500 on 5000r. blue (No. 468b) 25·00 25·00
509 – 5$000 on 300r. blue (No. 471) 45·00 45·00
512 74 7$000 on 10,000r. red (No. 364) 28·00 28·00

1931. Air. No. 486 surch **2.500 REIS**.
510 110 2500r. on 3000r. violet 26·00 26·00

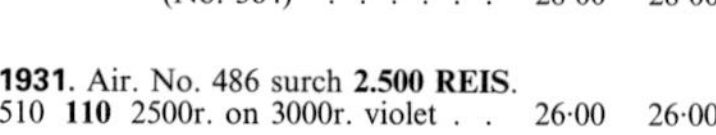

121 Brazil

1932. 400th Anniv of Colonization of Sao Vicente.
513 121 20r. purple 35 35
514 – 100r. black 90 90
515 – 200r. violet 1·75 35
516 – 600r. brown 3·00 2·75
517 – 700r. blue 3·50 3·00
DESIGNS: 100r. Natives; 200r. M. Afonso de Souza; 600r. King John III of Portugal; 700r. Founding of Sao Vicente.

125 Soldier and Flag 130 "Justice"

1932. Sao Paulo Revolutionary Government issue.
518 – 100r. brown 1·25 3·50
519 125 200r. red 60 1·25
520 – 300r. green 2·40 7·00
521 – 400r. blue 5·25 9·00
522 – 500r. sepia 7·00 9·00
523 – 600r. red 7·00 9·00
524 125 700r. violet 3·50 9·00
525 – 1000r. orange 2·40 9·00
526 – 2000r. brown 21·00 35·00
527 – 5000r. green 26·00 60·00
528 130 10,000r. purple 30·00 70·00
DESIGNS—As Type **125**: 100, 500r. Map of Brazil; 300r., 600r. Symbolical of freedom, etc., 400, 1000r. Soldier in tin helmet. As Type **130**: 2000r. "LEX" and sword; 5000r. "Justice" and soldiers with bayonets.

131 Campo Bello Square and memorial. Vassouras

1933. Centenary of Vassouras.
529 131 200r. red 1·25 1·25

132 Flag and Dornier Wal Flying Boat

1933. Air.
532 **132** 3500r. blue, green & yell 1·75 1·75

1933. Surch **200 REIS**.
536 **81** 200r. on 300r. red 60 60

134 Flag of the Race

1933. 441st Anniv of Departure of Columbus from Polos.
537 **134** 200r. red 1·75 1·25

135 Christian Symbols
137 Faith and Energy
136 From Santos Dumont Statue, St. Cloud

1933. 1st Eucharistic Congress, Sao Salvador.
538 **135** 200r. red 70 40

1933. Obligatory Tax for Airport Fund.
539 **136** 100r. purple 60 10

1933.
540 **137** 200r. red 60 35
543 200r. violet 1·25 35

138 "Republic" and Flags
139 Santos Dumont Statue, St. Cloud

1933. Visit of Pres. Justo of Argentina.
545 **138** 200r. blue 65 60
546 400r. green 1·75 1·75
547 600r. red 5·25 7·00
548 1000r. violet 7·00 5·25

1934. 1st National Aviation Congress, Sao Paulo.
549 **139** 200r. blue 1·25 70

140 Exhibition Building

1934. 7th International Sample Fair, Rio de Janeiro.
550 **140** 200r. brown 65 65
551 400r. red 3·50 3·50
552 700r. blue 3·50 3·00
553 1000r. orange 7·00 1·75

141 Brazilian Stamp of 1844

1934. National Philatelic Exhibition, Rio. Imperf.
555 **141** 200r.+100r. purple 1·25 3·00
556 300r.+100r. red 1·25 3·00
557 700r.+100r. blue 6·00 24·00
558 1000r.+100r. black 6·00 24·00

142 Christ of Mt. Corcovado
143 Jose de Anchieta

1934. Visit of Cardinal Pacelli.
559 **142** 300r. red 3·00 3·00
560 700r. blue 12·00 12·00

1934. 400th Anniv of Founding of Sao Paulo by Anchieta.
561 **143** 200r. brown 1·25 1·25
562 300r. violet 1·25 60
563 700c. blue 3·00 3·50
564 1000r. green 5·25 2·40

145 "Brazil" and "Uruguay"
146 Town of Igarassu

1935. Visit of President Terra of Uruguay.
565 – 200r. orange 65 60
566 **145** 300r. yellow 1·25 1·75
567 700r. blue 8·75 15·00
568 – 1000r. violet 18·00 10·50
DESIGN—HORIZ: 200, 1000r. Female figures as in Type **145** and bridge.

1935. 400th Anniv of Founding of Pernambuco.
569 **146** 200r. brown and red 1·75 1·25
570 300r. olive and violet 1·75 90

147 Nurse and Patient

1935. 3rd Pan-American Red Cross Conference.
571 **147** 200r.+100r. violet 3·00 3·00
572 300r.+100r. brown 3·00 3·00
573 700r.+100r. blue 15·00 13·00

149 Gen. da Silva

1935. Cent of Farroupilha "Ragged Revolution".
574 – 200r. black 1·75 1·25
575 – 300r. red 1·25 65
576 **149** 700r. blue 4·00 10·50
577 – 1000r. violet 5·25 5·25
DESIGNS: 200, 300r. Mounted Gaucho; 1000r. Marshal Caxias.

151 Gavea

1935. Children's Day.
578 **151** 300r. violet and brown 2·40 1·60
579 300r. turquoise and black 2·40 1·60
580 300r. blue and green 2·40 1·60
581 300r. black and red 2·40 1·60

152 Federal District Coat of Arms

1935. 8th International Fair.
582 **152** 200r. blue 3·50 3·50

153 Coutinho's ship "Gloria", 1535

1935. 400th Anniv of Colonization of State of Espirito Santo.
583 **153** 300r. red 6·00 3·00
584 – 700r. blue 9·00 6·00
DESIGN—VERT: 700r. Arms of Coutinho.

154a Viscount Cairu
155 Cameta

1936. Death Centenary of Cairu.
585 **154a** 1200r. violet 14·00 9·00

1936. Tercentenary of Founding of Cameta.
586 **155** 200r. buff 2·40 2·40
587 500r. green 2·40 1·25

156 Coin Press
157 Scales of "Justice"

1936. Numismatic Congress, Sao Paulo.
588 **156** 300r. brown 1·75 1·75

1936. 1st National Juridical Congress, Rio.
589 **157** 300r. red 1·25 1·25

158 A. Carlos Gomes

159 "Il Guarany"

1936. Birth Centenary of C. Gomes (composer).
590 **158** 300r. red 1·25 1·25
591 300r. brown 1·25 1·25
592 **159** 700r. blue 3·50 1·75
593 700r. buff 4·75 3·00

1936. 9th International Sample Fair, Rio. As T **152** with inscription and date altered.
594 **152** 200r. red 1·75 1·25

160 Congress Seal
161 Botafogo Bay

1936. 2nd National Eucharistic Congress, Belo Horizonte.
595 **160** 300r. multicoloured 1·75 1·25

1937. Birth Centenary of Dr. Francisco Pereira Passos.
596 **161** 700r. blue 1·25 1·25
597 700r. black 1·25 1·25

162 Esperanto Star and National Flags

1937. 9th Brazilian Esperanto Congress, Rio de Janeiro.
598 **162** 300r. green 1·75 1·25

163 Bay of Rio de Janeiro

1937. 2nd S. American Radio Conference.
599 **163** 300r. black and orange 1·25 1·25
600 700r. brown and blue 3·00 1·75

164 Globe

1937. Golden Jubilee of Esperanto.
601 **164** 300r. green 1·75 1·25

166 Iguazu Falls

1937. Tourist Propaganda.
602 – 200r. blue and brown 1·25 1·25
603 – 300r. green and orange 1·25 1·25
604 **166** 1000r. brown and sepia 3·50 2·40
605 – 2000r. red and green 15·00 16·00
606 **166** 5000r. green and black 30·00 30·00
607 – 10,000r. blue and red 60·00 60·00
DESIGNS—HORIZ: 200, 2000r. Monroe Palace, Rio. VERT: 300, 10,000r. Botanical Gardens, Rio.

168 J. Da Silva Paes
169 Eagle and Shield

1937. Bicent of Founding of Rio Grande do Sul.
608 **168** 300r. blue 1·25 60

1937. 150th Anniv of U.S. Constitution.
609 **169** 400r. blue 1·25 60

170 Coffee
171 "Grito" Memorial

1938. Coffee Propaganda.
610 **170** 1200r. multicoloured 7·00 60

1938. Commemoration of Abortive Proclamation of Republic.
611 **171** 400r. brown 1·25 60

172 Arms of Olinda

1938. 4th Centenary of Olinda.
612 **172** 400r. violet 1·25 60

173 Couto de Magalhaes 174 National Archives

1938. Birth Centenary of De Magalhaes.
613 **173** 400r. green 90 60

1938. Centenary of Founding of National Archives.
614 **174** 400r. brown 90 60

175 Rio de Janeiro 176 Santos

1939.
615 **175** 1200r. purple . . . . . . 2·40 15

1939. Centenary of Santos City.
616 **176** 400r. blue 65 60

177 Chalice-vine and Cup-of-gold Blossoms 178 Seal of Congress

1939. 1st S. American Botanical Congress, Rio.
617 **177** 400r. green . . . . 1·25 60

1939. 3rd National Eucharistic Congress, Recife.
618 **178** 400r. red 65 60

179 Duke of Caxias 180 Washington

1939. Soldiers' Day.
619 **179** 400r. blue 65 60

1939. New York World's Fair. Inscr "FEIRA MUNDIAL DE NOVA YORK".
620 **180** 400r. orange 50 25
621 – 800r. green 30 15
633 – 1m. violet . . . . 3·00 3·00
622 – 1200r. red 60 15
623 – 1600r. blue 60 25
634 – 5m. red . . . . 12·00 12·00
635 – 10m. slate . . . . 12·00 6·00
DESIGNS—HORIZ: 1200r. Grover Cleveland. VERT: 800r. Dom Pedro II; 1m. Water lily; 1600r. Statue of Liberty, Rio de Janeiro; 5m. Bust of Pres. Vargas; 10m. Relief map of Brazil.

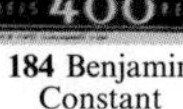

184 Benjamin Constant 188 Child and Southern Cross

1939. 50th Anniv of Constitution.
624 **184** 400r. green 90 60
625 – 800r. black 60 60
626 – 1200r. brown . . . . . . 1·50 60
DESIGNS—VERT: 800r. Marshal da Fonseca. HORIZ: 1200r. Marshal da Fonseca and Pres. Vargas.

1940. Child Welfare.
627 – 100r.+100r. violet 60 60
628 – 200r.+100r. blue . . . . 1·00 95
629 **188** 400r.+200r. olive 70 60
630 – 1200r.+400r. red . . . . 3·00 1·60
DESIGNS: 100r. Three Wise Men; 200r. Angel and Child; 1200r. Mother and Child.

189 Roosevelt, Vargas and American Continents 190 Map of Brazil

1940. 50th Anniv of Pan-American Union.
631 **189** 400r. blue 90 65

1940. 9th National Geographical Congress, Florianopolis.
632 **190** 400r. red 60 60

1940. Birth Centenary of Machado de Assis (poet and novelist). As T **173** but portrait of de Assis, dated "1839–1939".
636 400r. black 50 50

193 Two Workers 195 Brazilian Flags and Head of Liberty

194 Acclaiming King John IV of Portugal

1940. Bicentenary of Colonization of Porto Alegre.
637 **193** 400r. green 65 60

1940. Centenaries of Portugal (1140–1640-1940) (1st issue).
638 **194** 1200r. grey . . . . 3·50 60
See also Nos. 642/5.

1940. 10th Anniv of Govt. of President Vargas.
639 **195** 400r. purple 50 50

196 Date of Fifth Census 197 Globe showing Spotlight on Brazil

1941. 5th General Census.
640 **196** 400r. blue & red (postage) 30 10
641 **197** 1200r. brown (air) . . . . 5·25 90

199 Father Antonio Vieira 202 Father Jose Anchieta

1941. Centenaries of Portugal (2nd issue).
642 – 200r. pink 15 10
643 **199** 400r. blue 15 10
644 – 800r. violet 20 10
645 – 5400r. green . . . . . . 2·40 90
DESIGNS—VERT: 200r. Alfonso Henriques; 800r. Governor-Gen. Benevides. HORIZ: 5,400r. Carmona and Vargas.

1941. 400th Anniv of Order of Jesuits.
646 **202** 1m. violet . . . . 1·25 70

205 Oil Wells 210 Count of Porto Alegre

1941. Value in reis.
647 **205** 10r. orange 10 10
648 20r. olive 10 10
649 50r. brown 10 10
650 100r. turquoise 15 10
651 – 200r. brown 60 35
652 – 300r. red 15 10
653 – 400r. blue 20 10
654 – 500r. red 15 10
655 – 600r. violet . . . . 1·75 35
656 – 700r. red 60 35
657 – 1000r. grey . . . . 3·50 35
658 – 1200r. blue . . . . 5·25 35
659 – 2000r. purple . . . . . . 7·00 35
660 – 5000r. blue . . . . 9·00 60
661 **210** 10,000r. red . . . . . . 18·00 60
662 – 20,000r. brown . . . . . 16·00 60
663 – 50m. red . . . . 26·00 26·00
664 – 100m. blue . . . . 1·25 7·00
DESIGNS: 200r. to 500r. Wheat harvesting machinery; 600r. to 1200r. Smelting works; 2000r. "Commerce"; 5000r. Marshal F. Peixoto; 20,000r. Admiral Maurity; 50m. "Armed Forces"; 100m. Pres. Vargas.
For stamps with values in centavos and cruzeiros see Nos. 751, etc.

213 Amador Bueno 214 Brazilian Air Force Emblem

1941. 300th Anniv of Amador Bueno as King of Sao Paulo.
665 **213** 400r. black 55 35

1941. Aviation Week.
666 **214** 5400r. green . . . . . . 5·25 2·40

1941. Air. 4th Anniv of President Vargas's New Constitution. Optd **AEREO "10 Nov." 937-941**.
667 5400r. green (No. 645) . . . 5·25 1·75

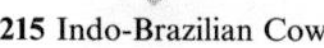

215 Indo-Brazilian Cow 216 Bernardino de Campos

1942. 2nd Agriculture and Cattle Show, Uberaba.
668a **215** 200r. blue 90 60
669a 400r. brown 90 60

1942. Birth Centenaries of B. de Campos and P. de Morais (lawyers and statesmen).
670 **216** 1000r. red . . . . 3·50 95
671 – 1200r. blue . . . . 9·00 65
PORTRAIT: 1200r. Prudente de Morais.

217 Torch of Learning 218 Map of Brazil showing Goiania

1942. 8th National Education Congress, Goiania.
672 **217** 400r. brown 45 25

1942. Founding of Goiania City.
673 **218** 400r. violet 45 25

219 Congressional Seal 221 Tributaries of R. Amazon

1942. 4th National Eucharistic Congress, Sao Paulo.
674 **219** 400r. brown 60 40

1942. Air. 5th Anniv of President Vargas's New Constitution. No. 645 surch **AEREO "10 Nov." 937-942** and value.
675 5cr.40 on 5400r. green . . . 4·75 2·40

1943. 400th Anniv of Discovery of River Amazon.
676 **221** 40c. brown 90 60

222 Early Brazilian Stamp 223 Memorial Tablet

1943. Centenary of Petropolis.
677 **222** 40c. violet . . . . 1·25 60

1943. Air. Visit of Pres. Morinigo of Paraguay.
678 **223** 1cr.20 blue . . . . 4·75 1·25

224 Map of S. America showing Brazil and Bolivia

1943. Air. Visit of President Penaranda of Bolivia.
679 **224** 1cr.20 multicoloured . . . 3·50 90

225 "Bulls-eye" 226

1943. Centenary of 1st Brazilian Postage Stamps.
(a) Postage. Imperf.
680 **225** 30c. black . . . . 1·75 90
681 60c. black . . . . 2·40 60
682 90c. black . . . . 1·25 90

(b) Air. Perf.
683 **226** 1cr. black and yellow . . 3·50 1·25
684 2cr. black and green . . . 4·75 1·25
685 5cr. black and red . . . . 6·00 1·75

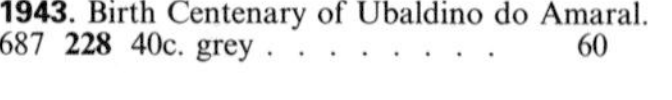

227 Book of the Law 228 Ubaldino do Amaral

1943. Air. Inter-American Advocates Conference.
686 **227** 1cr.20 red and brown . . 2·40 60

1943. Birth Centenary of Ubaldino do Amaral.
687 **228** 40c. grey 60 20

229 Indo-Brazilian Cow

1943. 9th Cattle Show, Bahia.
688 **229** 40c. brown . . . . 1·50 50

230 Justice and Seal 231 Santa Casa de Misericordia Hospital

1943. Centenary of Institute of Brazilian Lawyers.
689 **230** 2cr. red . . . . 3·50 1·75

1943. 400th Anniv of Santa Casa de Misericordia de Santos.
690 **231** 1cr. blue . . . . 1·25 60

232 Barbosa Rodrigues **233** Pedro Americo

1943. Birth Centenary of B. Rodrigues (botanist).
691 **232** 40c. green 40 15

1943. Birth Cent of Americo (artist and author).
692 **233** 40c. brown 90 20

1944. Air. No. 629 surch. **AEREO** and value.
693 **188** 20c. on 400r.+200r. . . . 1·75 90
694 40c. on 400r.+200r. . . . 3·50 90
695 60c. on 400r.+200r. . . . 5·25 60
696 1cr. on 400r.+200r. . . . 5·25 90
697 1cr.20 on 400r.+200r. . . 10·50 60

235 Gen. Carneiro and Defenders of Lapa **236** Baron do Rio Branco

1944. 50th Anniv of Siege of Lapa.
698 **235** 1cr.20c. red . . . . 1·75 60

1944. Inauguration of Monument to Baron do Rio Branco.
699 **236** 1cr. blue . . . . 1·50 60

237 Duke of Caxias **238** Emblems of Y.M.C.A.

1944. Centenary of Pacification of Revolutionary Uprising of 1842.
700 **237** 1cr.20 green and yellow 1·75 60

1944. Centenary of Y.M.C.A.
701 **238** 40c. blue, red and yellow 90 20

239 Rio Grande Chamber of Commerce **240** "Bartolomeo de Gusmao and the Aerostat" (Bernardino de Souza Pereira)

1944. Centenary of Founding of Rio Grande Chamber of Commerce.
702 **239** 40c. brown 90 25

1944. Air. Air Week.
703 **240** 1cr.20 red . . . . 1·25 15

241 Ribeiro de Andrada

1945. Death Cent of M. de Andrada (statesman).
704 **241** 40c. blue 90 15

242 Meeting between Caxias and Canabarro

1945. Cent of Pacification of Rio Grande do Sul.
705 **242** 40c. blue 90 15

244 L. L. Zamenhof **247** Baron do Rio Branco (statesman)

1945. 10th Brazilian Esperanto Congress, Rio de Janeiro.
706 – 40c. green (postage) . . . 90 60
707 **244** 1cr.20 brown (air) . . . . 1·25 60
DESIGN: 40c. Woman and map.

1945. Birth Centenary of Baron do Rio Branco.
708 – 40c. blue (postage) . . . 60 15
709 – 1cr.20 purple (air) . . . . 1·25 50
710 **247** 5cr. purple . . . . 4·75 60
DESIGNS—HORIZ: 40c. Bookplate. VERT: 1cr.20, S. America.

248 "Glory"

250 "Co-operation"

1945. Victory of Allied Nations in Europe. Roul.
711 – 20c. violet 50 10
712 **248** 40c. red 50 10
713 – 1cr. orange . . . . 1·75 60
714 – 2cr. blue . . . . 1·75 90
715 **250** 5cr. green . . . . 3·50 1·25
SYMBOLICAL DESIGNS—VERT: 20c. Tranquility (inscr "SAUDADE"). HORIZ: 1cr. "Victory" (inscr "VITORIA"); 2cr. "Peace" (inscr "PAZ").

251 F. M. da Silva **252** Bahia Institute

1945. 150th Birth Anniv of Francisco Manoel da Silva (composer of Brazilian National Anthem).
716 **251** 40c. red . . . . 1·25 60

1945. 50th Anniv of Founding of Bahia Institute of Geography and History.
717 **252** 40c. blue . . . . 1·75 15

253 Shoulder Flash **255** "V" Sign and Flashes

1945. Return of Brazilian Expeditionary Force.
718 **253** 20c. blue, red and green 50 15
719 – 40c. multicoloured 50 15
720 – 1cr. multicoloured . . . . 2·40 50
721 – 2cr. multicoloured . . . . 3·50 1·25
722 **255** 5cr. multicoloured . . . . 6·00 1·25
DESIGNS (embodying shoulder flashes) As Type **253**: 40c. B.E.F. flash. As Type **255**. HORIZ: 1cr. U.S.A. flag; 2cr. Brazilian flag.

256 Wireless Mast and Map **257** Admiral Saldanha da Gama

1945. 3rd Inter-American Radio Communication Conference.
723 **256** 1cr.20 black . . . . . . 1·25 15

1946. Birth Centenary of Admiral S. da Gama.
724 **257** 40c. grey . . . . 90 1·25

258 Princess Isabel d'Orleans-Braganza **261** P.O., Rio de Janeiro

260 Lockheed Super Electra over Bay of Rio de Janiero

1946. Birth Centenary of Princess Isabel d'Orleans-Braganza.
725 **258** 40c. black . . . . 90 1·75

1946. 5th Postal Union. Congress of the Americas and Spain.
726 – 40c. orange and black . . 50 15
727 **260** 1cr.30 orange and green 90 60
728 1cr.70 orange and red . . 1·25 90
729 **261** 2cr. blue and slate . . . . 1·75 50
730 **260** 2cr.20 orange and blue . . 1·25 90
731 **261** 5cr. blue and brown . . . 4·75 1·25
732 10cr. blue and violet . . . 6·00 90
DESIGN (25 × 37 mm): 40c. Post-horn, V and envelope.

262 Proposed Columbus Lighthouse **263** "Liberty"

1946. Construction of Columbus Lighthouse, Dominican Republic.
733 **262** 5cr. blue . . . . 9·00 2·50

1946. New Constitution.
734 **263** 40c. grey 10 10

264 Orchid

1946. 4th National Exn of Orchids, Rio de Janeiro.
735 **264** 40c. blue, red and yellow 65 10

265 Gen. A. E. Gomes Carneiro **266** Academy of Arts

1946. Birth Cent of Gen. A. E. Gomes Carneiro.
736 **265** 40c. green 35 10

1946. 50th Anniv of Brazilian Academy of Arts.
737 **266** 40c. blue 35 10

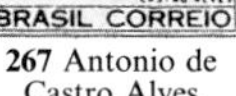

267 Antonio de Castro Alves **268** Pres. Gonzalez

1947. Birth Centenary of Castro Alves (poet).
738 **267** 40c. turquoise 35 10

1947. Visit of Chilean President.
739 **268** 40c. brown 35 10

269 "Peace and Security" **270** "Dove of Peace"

1947. Inter-American Defence Conference, Rio de Janeiro.
740 **269** 1cr.20 blue (postage) . . . 90 10
741 **270** 2cr.20 green (air) . . . . 1·25 50

271 Pres. Truman, Map of S. America and Statue of Liberty

1947. Visit of President Truman.
742 **271** 40c. blue 50 10

272 Pres. Enrico Gaspar Dutra **273** Woman and Child

1947. Commemorating Pres. Dutra.
743 **272** 20c. green 10 10
744 40c. red 15 10
745 1cr.20 blue 50 10

1947. Children's Week. 1st Brazilian Infant Welfare Convention and Paediatrics.
747 **273** 40c. blue 50 10

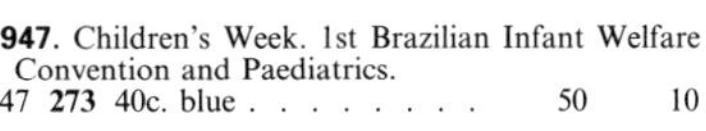

274 Icarus

1947. Obligatory Tax. "Week of the Wing" Aviation Fund.
748 **274** 40c.+10c. orange 50 10

275 Santos Dumont Monument, St. Cloud, France

276 Arms of Belo Horizonte

1947. Air. Homage to Santos Dumont (aviation pioneer).
749 **275** 1cr.20c. brown & green 1·25 50

1947. 50th Anniv of Founding of City of Belo Horizonte.
750 **276** 1cr.20c. red 65 10

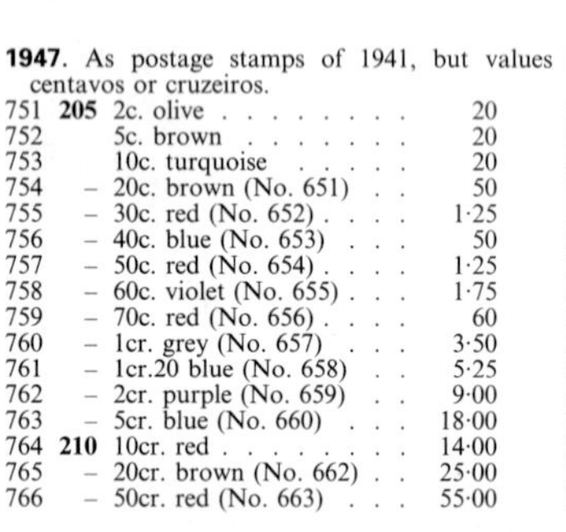

1947. As postage stamps of 1941, but values in centavos or cruzeiros.
751 **205** 2c. olive 20 10
752 5c. brown 20 10
753 10c. turquoise 20 10
754 – 20c. brown (No. 651) . . 50 10
755 – 30c. red (No. 652) . . . . 1·25 10
756 – 40c. blue (No. 653) . . . 50 10
757 – 50c. red (No. 654) . . . . 1·25 10
758 – 60c. violet (No. 655) . . . 1·75 10
759 – 70c. red (No. 656) 60 10
760 – 1cr. grey (No. 657) . . . 3·50 10
761 – 1cr.20 blue (No. 658) . . 5·25 10
762 – 2cr. purple (No. 659) . . 9·00 10
763 – 5cr. blue (No. 660) . . . 18·00 10
764 **210** 10cr. red . . . . 14·00 10
765 – 20cr. brown (No. 662) . . 25·00 10
766 – 50cr. red (No. 663) . . . 55·00 10

277 Rio de Janeiro and Rotary Emblem

278 Globe

279 Quitandinha Hotel

1948. Air. 39th Rotary Congress Rio de Janeiro.
769 **277** 1cr.20 red . . . . 1·25 50
770 3cr.80 violet . . . . . . 3·50 60

1948. International Industrial and Commercial Exhibition, Quitandinha.
771 **278** 40c. grn & mve (postage) 15 10
772 **279** 1cr.20 brown (air) 50 15
773 3cr.80 violet . . . . . . 1·75 15

280 Arms of Paranagua

281 Girl Reading

1948. Tercentenary of Founding of Paranagua.
774 **280** 5cr. brown . . . . 4·75 1·25

1948. National Children's Campaign.
775 **281** 40c. green 15 35

282 Three Muses (after Henrique Bernardelli)

1948. Air. Centenary of National School of Music.
776 **282** 1cr.20 blue . . . . 1·25 10

283 President Berres

1948. Air. Visit of Uruguayan President.
777 **283** 1cr.70 blue 50 10

284 Merino Ram

1948. Air. International Livestock Show, Bage.
778 **284** 1cr.20 orange . . . . . . 1·75 50

285 Congress Seal

286 "Tiradentes" (trans. "Tooth-puller")

1948. Air. 5th National Eucharistic Congress, Porto Alegre.
779 **285** 1cr.20 purple 50 10

1948. Birth Bicentenary of A. J. J. da Silva Xavier (patriot).
780 **286** 40c. orange 10 10

287 Crab and Globe

288 Adult Student

1948. Anti-cancer Campaign.
781 **287** 40c. purple 50 60

1949. Campaign for Adult Education.
782 **288** 60c. purple 50 10

289 Battle of Guararapes

1949. 300th Anniv of 2nd Battle of Guararapes.
783 **289** 60c. blue (postage) . . . 2·40 50
784 – 1cr.20 pink (air) . . . . . 4·75 1·75
DESIGN: 1cr.20, View of Guararapes.

290 St. Francis of Paula Church

291 Father Nobrega

1949. Bicentenary of Ouro Fino.
785 **290** 60c. brown 50 10

1949. 4th Centenary of Founding of Bahia.
(a) Postage. Imperf.
786 **291** 60c. violet 50 10
(b) Air. Perf.
787 **292** 1cr.20 blue . . . . 1·25 15

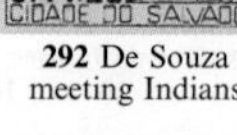

292 De Souza meeting Indians

293 Franklin D. Roosevelt

1949. Air. Homage to Franklin D. Roosevelt. Imperf.
788 **293** 3cr.80 blue . . . . 2·40 1·75

294 Douglas DC-3 and Air Force Badge

1949. Homage to Brazilian Air Force. Imperf.
789 **294** 60c. violet 50 10

295 Joaquim Nabuco

296 "Revelation"

1949. Air. Birth Centenary of J. Nabuco (lawyer and author).
790 **295** 3cr.80 purple . . . . . . 2·40 10

1949. 1st Sacerdotal Vocational Congress, Bahia.
791 **296** 60c. purple 50 10

297 Globe

1949. 75th Anniv of U.P.U.
792 **297** 1cr.50 blue 90 10

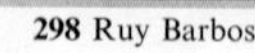

298 Ruy Barbosa

299 Cardinal Arcoverde

1949. Birth Cent of Ruy Barbosa (statesman).
793 **298** 1cr.20 red . . . . 1·25 15

1950. Birth Cent of Cardinal Joaquim Arcoverde.
794 **299** 60c. pink 50 10

300 "Agriculture and Industry"

301 Virgin of the Globe

1950. 75th Anniv of Arrival of Italian Immigrants.
795 **300** 60c. red 60 10

1950. Centenary of Establishment of Daughters of Charity of St. Vincent de Paul.
796 **301** 60c. blue and black . . . 50 10

302 Globe and Footballers

303 Stadium

1950. 4th World Football Championship, Rio de Janeiro.
797 **302** 60c. grey & bl (postage) 1·25 15
798 **303** 1cr.20 orange and blue (air) . . . . 1·60 50
799 – 5cr.80 yellow, green and blue . . . . 7·00 60
DESIGN—VERT: 5cr.80 Linesman and flag.

304 Three Heads, Map and Graph

305 Line of People and Map

1950. 6th Brazilian Census, 1950.
800 **304** 60c. red (postage) 50 10
801 **305** 1cr.20 brown (air) . . . . 1·25 10

306 Oswaldo Cruz

307 Blumenau and Itajai River

1950. 5th International Microbiological Congress. Rio de Janeiro.
802 **306** 60c. brown 50 10

1950. Centenary of Founding of Blumenau.
803 **307** 60c. pink 50 10

308 Government Offices

309 Arms

1950. Centenary of Amazon Province.
804 **308** 60c. red 60 10

1950. Centenary of Juiz de Fora City.
805 **309** 60c. red 60 10

310 P.O. Building, Recife

1951. Inauguration of Head Post Office, Pernambuco Province.
806 **310** 60c. red 50 10
807 1cr.20 red 60 10

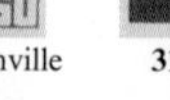

311 Arms of Joinville

312 S. Romero

1951. Centenary of Founding of Joinville.
808 **311** 60c. brown 60 10

1951. Birth Centenary of Sylvio Romero (poet).
809 **312** 60c. brown 60 10

313 De La Salle
314 Heart and Flowers

1951. Birth Tricentenary of Jean-Baptiste de la Salle (educational reformer).
810 **313** 60c. blue 65 10

1951. Mothers' Day.
811 **314** 60c. purple 90 50

315 J. Caetano and Stage
316 O. A. Derby

1951. 1st Brazilian Theatrical Congress.
812 **315** 60c. blue 50 10

1951. Birth Centenary of Derby (geologist).
813 **316** 2cr. slate 65 35

317 Crucifix and Congregation
318 E. P. Martins and Map

1951. 4th Inter-American Catholic Education Congress, Rio de Janeiro.
814 **317** 60c. brown and buff . . . 65 10

1951. 29th Anniv of First Rio–New York Flight.
815 **318** 3cr.80 brown & lemon . . 3·25 50

319 Penha Convent
320 Santos Dumont and Boys with Model Aircraft

1951. 400th Anniv of Founding of Vitoria.
816 **319** 60c. brown and buff . . . 65 10

1951. "Week of the Wing" and 50th Anniv of Santos Dumont's Flight over Paris.
817 **320** 60c. brn & orge (postage) 65 15
818 – 3cr.80 violet (air) . . . . 1·90 20
DESIGN: 3cr.80, "Ballon No. 6" airship over Eiffel Tower.

321 Wheat Harvesters
322 Bible and Map

1951. Wheat Festival, Bage.
819 **321** 60c. green and grey . . . 50 50

1951. Bible Day.
820 **322** 1cr.20 brown . . . . . . 1·25 35

323 Isabella the Catholic
324 Henrique Oswald

1952. 500th Birth Anniv of Isabella the Catholic.
821 **323** 3cr.80 blue . . . . 1·90 50

1952. Birth Centenary of Oswald (composer).
822 **324** 60c. brown 65 10

325 Map and Symbol of Labour
326 Dr. L. Cardoso

1952. 5th Conf of American Members of I.L.O.
823 **325** 1cr.50 red 65 10

1952. Birth Centenary of Cardoso (scientist) and 4th Brazilian Homoeopathic Congress, Porto Alegre.
824 **326** 60c. blue 50 15

327 Gen. da Fonseca
328 L. de Albuquerque

1952. Centenary of Telegraphs in Brazil.
825 **327** 2cr.40 red 65 15
826 – 5cr. blue . . . . 3·50 15
827 – 10cr. turquoise . . . . . 3·50 15
PORTRAITS—VERT: 5cr. Baron de Capanema. 10cr. E. de Queiros.

1952. Bicentenary of Mato Grosso City.
828 **328** 1cr.20 violet 65 10

329 Olympic Flame and Athletes
330 Councillor J. A. Saraiva

1952. 50th Anniv of Fluminense Football Club.
829 **329** 1cr.20 blue . . . . 1·25 60

1952. 100th Anniv of Terezina City.
830 **330** 60c. mauve 65 10

331 Emperor Dom Pedro II
332 Globe, Staff and Rio de Janeiro Bay

1952. Stamp Day and 2nd Philatelic Exhibition, Sao Paulo.
831 **331** 60c. black and blue . . . 65 10

1952. 2nd American Congress of Industrial Medicine.
832 **332** 3cr.80 green and brown 1·60 60

333 Dove, Globe and Flags

1952. United Nations Day.
833 **333** 3cr.80 blue . . . . 2·40 50

334 Compasses and Modern Buildings, Sao Paulo
335 D. A. Feijo (Statesman)

1952. City Planning Day.
834 **334** 60c. yellow, green & blue 50 10

1952. Homage to D. A. Feijo.
835 **335** 60c. brown 60 10

336 Father Damien

1952. Obligatory Tax. Leprosy Research Fund.
836 **336** 10c. brown 50 15
837 10c. green 15 10

337 R. Bernardelli

1952. Birth Centenary of Bernardelli (sculptor).
838 **337** 60c. blue 65 10

338 Arms of Sao Paulo and Settler
339 "Expansion"

1953. 400th Anniv of Sao Paulo (1st issue).
839 **338** 1cr.20 black and brown 1·75 50
840 – 2cr. green and yellow . . 3·50 50
841 – 2cr.80 brown and orange 1·90 15
842 **339** 3cr.80 brown and green 1·90 15
843 5cr.80 blue and green . . 1·50 15
DESIGNS—VERT: (Inscr as Type **339**): 2cr. Coffee blossom and berries; 2cr.80, Monk planting tree.
See also Nos. 875/9.

340
341 J. Ramalho

1953. 6th Brazilian Accountancy Congress, Port Alegre.
844 **340** 1cr.20 brown 95 10

1953. 4th Centenary of Santo Andre.
845 **341** 60c. blue 10 10

342 A. Reis and Plan of Belo Horizonte
343 "Almirante Saldanha" (cadet ship)

1953. Birth Centenary of A. Reis (engineer).
846 **342** 1cr.20 brown 15 10

1953. 4th Voyage of Circumnavigation by Training Ship "Almirante Saldanha".
847 **343** 1cr.50 blue 90 20

344 Viscount de Itaborahy
345 Lamp and Rio-Petropolis Highway

1953. Centenary of Bank of Brazil.
848 **344** 1cr.20 violet 15 10

1953. 10th Int Nursing Congress, Petropolis.
849 **345** 1cr.20 grey 15 10

346 Bay of Rio de Janeiro

1953. 4th World Conference of Young Baptists.
850 **346** 3cr.80c. turquoise 95 10

347 Ministry of Health and Education
348 Arms and Map

1953. Stamp Day and 1st National Philatelic Exhibition of Education, Rio de Janeiro.
851 **347** 1cr.20 turquoise 15 10

1953. Centenary of Jau City.
852 **348** 1cr.20 violet 15 10

349 Maria Quiteria de Jesus
350 Pres. Odria

1953. Death Centenary of Maria Quiteria de Jesus.
853 **349** 60c. blue 10 10

1953. Visit of President of Peru.
854 **350** 1cr.40 purple 15 10

351 Caxias leading Troops
352 Quill-pen and Map

1953. 150th Birth Anniv of Duke of Caxias.
855 **351** 60c. turquoise 35 15
856 – 1cr.20 purple 50 15
857 – 1cr.70 blue 50 15
858 – 3cr.80 brown . . . . . . 1·60 15
859 – 5cr.80 violet 85 15
DESIGNS: 1cr.20, Tomb; 1cr.70, 5cr.80, Portrait of Caxias; 3cr.80, Coat of arms.

1953. 5th National Congress of Journalists, Curitiba.
860 **352** 60c. blue 10 10

353 H. Hora **354** President Somoza

1953. Birth Centenary of H. Hora (painter).
861 **353** 60c. purple and orange . . 35 10

1953. Visit of President Somoza of Nicaragua.
862 **354** 1cr.40 purple 20 15

355 A. de Saint-Hilaire **356** J. do Patrocinio and "Spirit of Emancipation" (after R. Amoedo)

1953. Death Centenary of A. de Saint-Hilaire (explorer and botanist).
863 **355** 1cr.20 lake 20 10

1953. Death Centenary of J. do Patrocinio (slavery abolitionist).
864 **356** 60c. slate 10 10

357 Clock Tower, Crato **358** C. de Abreu

1953. Centenary of Crato City.
865 **357** 60c. green 15 10

1953. Birth Centenary of Abreu (historian).
866 **358** 60c. blue 20 10
867 5cr. violet . . . . 1·90 20

359 "Justice" **360** Harvesting

1953. 50th Anniv of Treaty of Petropolis.
868 **359** 60c. blue 15 10
869 1cr.20 purple 15 10

1953. 3rd National Wheat Festival, Erechim.
870 **360** 60c. turquoise 15 10

361 Teacher and Pupils **362** Porters with Trays of Coffee Beans

1953. 1st National Congress of Elementary Schoolteachers, Salvador.
871 **361** 60c. red 15 10

1953. Centenary of State of Parana.
872a – 2cr. brown and black . . 1·75 60
873 **362** 5cr. orange and black . . 2·40 60
DESIGN: 2cr. Portrait of Z. de Gois e Vasconcellos.

363 A. de Gusmao **364** Growth of Sao Paulo

365 Sao Paulo and Arms

1954. Death Bicent of Gusmao (statesman).
874 **363** 1cr.20 purple 50 10

1954. 400th Anniv of Sao Paulo (2nd issue).
875 **364** 1cr.20 brown . . . . . . 1·25 90
876 – 2cr. mauve . . . . 1·90 65
877 – 2cr.80 violet . . . . . . 3·00 55
878 **365** 3cr.80 green . . . . . . 3·00 55
879 5cr.80 red . . . . 3·00 55
DESIGNS—VERT: 2cr. Priest, pioneer and Indian; 2cr.80, J. de Anchieta.

366 J. F. Vieira, A. V. de Negreiros, A. F. Camarao and H. Dias

1954. 300th Anniv of Recovery from the Dutch of Pernambuco.
880 **366** 1cr.20 blue 50 10

367 Sao Paulo and Allegorical Figure

1954. 10th International Congress of Scientific Organization, Sao Paulo.
881 **367** 1cr.50 purple 15 10

368 Grapes and Winejar **369** Immigrants' Monument

1954. Grape Festival, Rio Grande do Sul.
882 **368** 40c. lake 15 10

1954. Immigrants' Monument, Caxias do Sul.
883 **369** 60c. violet 15 10

370 "Baronesa", 1852 (first locomotive used in Brazil) **371** Pres. Chamoun

1954. Centenary of Brazilian Railways.
884 **370** 40c. red . . . . 1·25 40

1954. Visit of President of Lebanon.
885 **371** 1cr.50 lake 20 10

372 Sao Jose College, Rio de Janeiro **373** Vel Marcelino Champagnat

1954. 50th Anniv of Marists in Brazil.
886 **372** 60c. violet 20 15
887 **373** 1cr.20 blue 20 15

374 Apolonia Pinto **375** Admiral Tamandare

1954. Birth Centenary of Apolonia Pinto (actress).
888 **374** 1cr.20 green 10 10

1954. Portraits.
889 **375** 2c. blue 15 15
890 5c. red 15 10
891 10c. green 15 10
892 – 20c. red 20 10
893 – 30c. slate 55 10
894 – 40c. red . . . . 1·25 10
895 – 50c. lilac . . . . 1·75 10
896 – 60c. turquoise 55 10
897 – 90c. salmon . . . . . . 1·50 15
904a – 1cr. brown . . . . . . 1·25 50
899 – 1cr.50 blue 25 10
904b – 2cr. green . . . . 1·75 50
904c – 5cr. purple . . . . . . 5·25 10
902 – 10cr. green . . . . . . 2·75 10
903 – 20cr. red . . . . 3·50 30
904 – 50cr. blue . . . . 10·50 10
PORTRAITS—20, 30, 40c. O. Cruz; 50c. to 90c. J. Murtinho; 1cr., 1cr.50, 2cr. Duke of Caxias; 5, 10cr., R. Barbosa; 20, 50cr. J. Bonifacio.

376 Boy Scout **377** B. Fernandes

1954. International Scout Encampment, Sao Paulo.
905 **376** 1cr.20 blue 95 15

1954. Tercentenary of Sorocaba City.
906 **377** 60c. red 10 10

378 Cardinal Piazza **379** Virgin and Map

1954. Visit of Cardinal Piazza (Papal Legate).
907 **378** 4cr.20 red 95 10

1954. Marian Year. Inscr "ANO MARIANO".
908 **379** 60c. lake 55 10
909 – 1cr.20 blue 65 10
DESIGN: 1cr.20, Virgin and globe.
No. 909 also commemorates the Centenary of the Proclamation of the Dogma of the Immaculate Conception.

380 Benjamin Constant and Braille Book

1954. Cent of Education for the Blind in Brazil.
910 **380** 60c. green 15 10

381 River Battle of Riachuelo **382** Admiral Barroso

1954. 150th Birth Anniv of Admiral Barroso.
911 **381** 40c. brown 90 15
912 **382** 60c. violet 25 10

383 S. Hahnemann (physician) **384** Nisia Floresta (suffragist)

1954. 1st World Congress of Homoeopathy.
913 **383** 2cr.70 green 95 10

1954. Removal of Ashes of Nisia Floresta (suffragist) from France to Brazil.
914 **384** 60c. mauve 10 10

385 Ears of Wheat **386** Globe and Basketball Player

1954. 4th Wheat Festival, Carazinho.
915 **385** 60c. olive 15 10

1954. 2nd World Basketball Championship.
916 **386** 1cr.40 red 95 15

387 Girl, Torch and Spring Flowers **388** Father Bento

1954. 6th Spring Games.
917 **387** 60c. brown 50 10

1954. Obligatory Tax. Leprosy Research Fund.
918 **388** 10c. blue 15 10
919 10c. mauve 15 10
919a 10c. salmon 15 10
919b 10c. green 15 10
919c 10c. lilac 15 10
919d 10c. brown 15 10
919e 10c. slate 15 10
919f 2cr. lake 15 10
919g 2cr. lilac 15 10
919h 2cr. orange 15 10
See also Nos. 1239/40.

389 Sao Francisco Power Station

1955. Inauguration of Sao Francisco Hydro-electric Station
920 **389** 60c. orange 15 10

390 Itutinga Power Plant

1955. Inaug of Itutinga Hydro-electric Station.
921 **390** 40c. blue 15 10

391 Rotary Symbol and Rio Bay **392** Aviation Symbols

1955. 50th Anniv of Rotary International.
922 **391** 2cr.70 green and black . . 2·40 10

1955. 3rd Aeronautical Congress, Sao Paulo.
923 **392** 60c. grey and black . . . 15 10

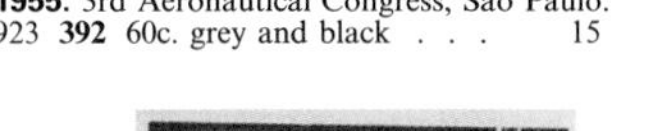

393 Fausto Cardoso Palace

1955. Centenary of Aracaiu.
924 **393** 40c. brown 10 10

394 Arms of Botucatu

1955. Centenary of Botucatu.
925 **394** 60c. brown 10 10
926 1cr.20 green 15 10

395 Young Athletes **396** Marshal da Fonseca

1955. 5th Children's Games, Rio de Janeiro.
927 **395** 60c. brown 50 10

1955. Birth Centenary of Marshal da Fonseca.
928 **396** 60c. violet 10 10

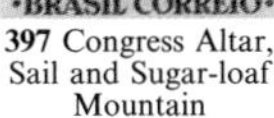

397 Congress Altar, Sail and Sugar-loaf Mountain **398** Cardinal Masella

1955. 36th International Eucharistic Congress.
929 **397** 1cr.40 green 10 10
930 – 2cr.70 lake (St. Pascoal) 90 90

1955. Visit of Cardinal Masella (Papal Legate) to Eucharistic Congress.
931 **398** 4cr.20 blue . . . . 1·75 15

399 Gymnasts

1955. 7th Spring Games.
932 **399** 60c. mauve 20 10

400 Monteiro Lobato **401** A. Lutz

1955. Honouring M. Lobato (author).
933 **400** 40c. green 10 10

1955. Birth Cent of Lutz (public health pioneer).
934 **401** 60c. green 15 10

402 Lt.-Col. T. C. Vilagran Cabrita **403** Salto Grande Dam

1955. Centenary of 1st Battalion of Engineers.
935 **402** 60c. blue 15 10

1956. Salto Grande Dam.
936 **403** 60c. red 15 10

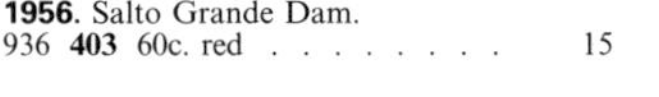

404 **405** Arms of Mococa

1956. 18th International Geographical Congress, Rio de Janeiro.
937 **404** 1cr.20 blue 50 10

1956. Centenary of Mococa, Sao Paulo.
938 **405** 60c. red 35 10

406 Girls Running **407** Douglas DC-3 and Map

1956. 6th Children's Games.
939 **406** 2cr.50 blue 65 10

1956. 25th Anniv of National Air Mail.
940 **407** 3cr.30 blue 95 10

408 Rescue Work

1956. Centenary of Firemen's Corps, Rio de Janeiro.
941 **408** 2cr.50 red 90 35

409 Franca Cathedral **410** Open book with Inscription and Map

1956. Centenary of City of Franca.
942 **409** 2cr.50 blue 60 10

1956. 50th Anniv of Arrival of Marist Brothers in N. Brazil.
943 **410** 2cr.50 blue (postage) . . . 50 10
944 – 3cr.30 purple (air) 15 10
DESIGN—VERT: 3cr.30, Father J. B. Marcelino Champagnat.

411 Hurdler **412** Forest and Map of Brazil

1956. 8th Spring Games.
945 **411** 2cr.50 red . . . . 1·25 35

1956. Afforestation Campaign.
946 **412** 2cr.50 green 50 10

413 Baron da Bocaina and Express Letter **414** Commemorative Stamp from Panama

1956. Birth Centenary of Baron da Bocaina.
947 **413** 2cr.50 brown 50 10

1956. Pan-American Congress. Panama.
948 **414** 3cr.30 black and green . . 95 15

415 Santos Dumont's Biplane "14 bis"

1956. Air. Alberto Santos Dumont (aviation pioneer) Commemoration.
949 **415** 3cr. green . . . . 1·60 40
950 3cr.30 blue 20 10
951 4cr. purple . . . . 1·25 10
952 6cr.50 brown 20 10
953 11cr.50 orange . . . . . 2·50 30

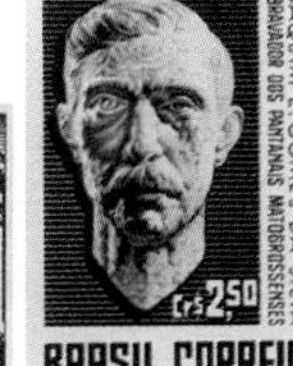

416 Volta Redonda Steel Mill, and Molten Steel **417** J. E. Gomes da Silva (civil engineer)

1957. Nat Steel Company's Expansion Campaign.
955 **416** 2cr.50 brown 40 10

1957. Birth Cententary of Gomes da Silva.
956 **417** 2cr.50 green 50 10

418 Allan Kardec, Code and Globe

1957. Centenary of Spiritualism Code.
957 **418** 2cr.50 brown 15 10

419 Young Gymnast **420** Gen. Craveiro Lopes

1957. 7th Children's Games.
958 **419** 2cr.50 lake . . . . 1·25 10

1957. Visit of President of Portugal.
959 **420** 6cr.50 blue 95 10

421 Stamp of 1932 **422** Lord Baden-Powell

1957. 25th Anniv of Sao Paulo Revolutionary Government.
960 **421** 2cr.50 red 60 10

1957. Air. Birth Centenary of Lord Baden-Powell.
961 **422** 3cr.30 lake 95 10

423 Convent of Santo Antonio

1957. 300th Anniv of Emancipation of Santo Antonio Province.
962 **423** 2cr.50 purple 15 10

424 Volleyball **425** Basketball

1957. 9th Spring Games.
963 **424** 2cr.50 brown . . . . . . 1·25 10

1957. 2nd Women's World Basketball Championships.
964 **425** 3cr.30 green and brown 1·25 10

426 U.N. Emblem, Map of Suez Canal and Soldier

1957. Air. United Nations Day.
965 **426** 5cr.30 blue 15 30

427 Count of Pinhal (founder), Arms and Locomotive **428** Auguste Comte (philosopher)

1957. Centenary of City of San Carlos.
966 **427** 2cr.50 red 90 30

1957. Death Centenary of Comte.
967 **428** 2cr.50 brown 50 10

429 Sarapui Radio Station

1957. Inauguration of Sarapui Radio Station.
968 **429** 2cr.50 myrtle 50 10

430 Admiral Tamandare (founder) and "Almirante Tamandare" (cruiser)

431 Coffee Beans and Emblem

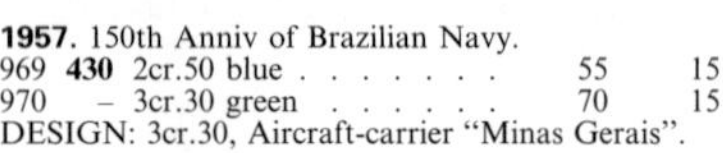

1957. 150th Anniv of Brazilian Navy.
969 **430** 2cr.50 blue 55 15
970 – 3cr.30 green 70 15
DESIGN: 3cr.30, Aircraft-carrier "Minas Gerais".

1957. Centenary of City of Ribeirao Preto.
971 **431** 2cr.50 red 60 10

432 King John VI of Portugal and Sail Merchantman

1958. 150th Anniv of Opening of Ports to Foreign Trade.
972 **432** 2cr.50 purple 60 10

433 Bugler

434 Locomotive "Baronesa", 1852, and Dom Pedro II Station, Rio de Janeiro

1958. 150th Anniv of Corps of Brazilian Marines.
973 **433** 2cr.50 red 50 10

1958. Centenary of Central Brazil Railway.
974 **434** 2cr.50 brown 85 20

435 High Court Building

436 Brazilian Pavilion

1958. 150th Anniv of Military High Courts.
975 **435** 2cr.50 green 15 10

1958. Brussels International Exhibition.
976 **436** 2cr.50 blue 10 10

437 Marshal C. M. da Silva Ronden

438 Jumping

1958. Rondon Commem and "Day of the Indian".
977 **437** 2cr.50 purple 15 10

1958. 8th Children's Games, Rio de Janeiro.
978 **438** 2cr.50 red 50 10

439 Hydro-electric Station

1958. Inaug of Salto Grande Hydro-electric Station.
979 **439** 2cr.50 purple 15 10

440 National Printing Works

441 Marshal Osorio

1958. 150th Anniv of National Printing Works.
980 **440** 2cr.50 brown 10 10

1958. 150th Birth Anniv of Marshal Osorio.
981 **441** 2cr.50 violet 10 10

442 Pres. Morales of Honduras

443 Botanical Gardens, Rio de Janeiro

1958. Visit of President of Honduras.
982 **442** 6cr.50 green . . . . . . 3·50 90

1958. 150th Anniv of Botanical Gardens, Rio de Janeiro.
983 **443** 2cr.50 green 10 10

444 Hoe, Rice and Cotton

445 Prophet Joel

1958. 50th Anniv of Japanese Immigration.
984 **444** 2cr.50 red 10 10

1958. Bicentenary of Basilica of the Good Jesus, Matosinhos.
985 **445** 2cr.50 blue 35 10

446 Brazil on Globe

1958. Int Investments Conf, Belo Horizonte.
986 **446** 2cr.50 brown 10 10

447 Tiradentes Palace, Rio de Janeiro

448 J. B. Brandao (statesman)

1958. 47th Inter-Parliamentary Union Conf.
987 **447** 2cr.50 brown 10 10

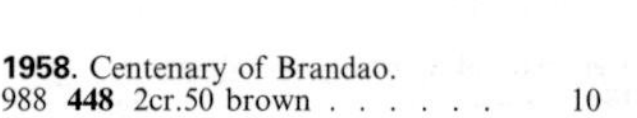

1958. Centenary of Brandao.
988 **448** 2cr.50 brown 10 10

449 Dawn Palace, Brasilia

1958. Construction of Presidential Palace.
989 **449** 2cr.50 blue 10 10

450 Freighters

1958. Govt Aid for Brazilian Merchant Navy.
990 **450** 2cr.50 blue 55 10

451 J. C. da Silva

452 Pres. Gronchi

1958. Birth Centenary of Da Silva (author).
991 **451** 2cr.50 brown 10 10

1958. Visit of President of Italy.
992 **452** 7cr. blue . . . . 1·75 10

453 Archers

454 Old People within Hour-glass

1958. 10th Spring Games, Rio de Janeiro.
993 **453** 2cr.50 orange 90 10

1958. Old People's Day.
994 **454** 2cr.50 lake 15 10

455 Machado de Assis (writer)

456 Pres. Vargas with oily Hand

1958. 50th Death Anniv of Machado de Assis.
995 **455** 2cr.50 brown 10 10

1958. 5th Anniv of State Petroleum Law.
996 **456** 2cr.50 blue 10 10

457 Globe showing Brazil and the Americas

458 Gen. L. Sodre

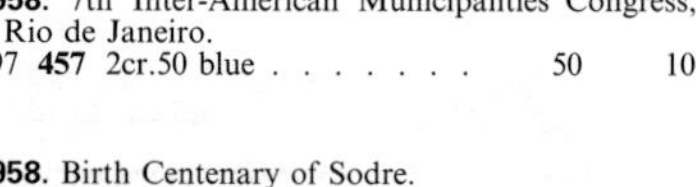

1958. 7th Inter-American Municipalities Congress, Rio de Janeiro.
997 **457** 2cr.50 blue 50 10

1958. Birth Centenary of Sodre.
998 **458** 3cr.30 green 10 10

459 U.N. Emblem

460 Footballer

1958. 10th Anniv of Human Rights Declaration.
999 **459** 2cr.50 blue 10 10

1959. World Football Cup Victory, 1958.
1000 **460** 3cr.30 brown & green . . 95 10

461 Map and Railway Line

462 Pres. Sukarno

1959. Centenary of Opening of Patos-Campina Grande Railway.
1001 **461** 2cr.50 brown 30 15

1959. Visit of President of Indonesia.
1002 **462** 2cr.50 blue 10 10

463 Basketball Player

464 King John VI of Portugal

1959. Air. World Basketball Championships 1959.
1003 **463** 3cr.30 brown & blue . . 90 10

1959.
1004 **464** 2cr.50 red 15 10

465 Polo Players

1959. Children's Games.
1005 **465** 2cr.50 brown 20 10

466 Dockside Scene

467 Church Organ, Diamantina

1959. Rehabilitation of National Ports Law.
1006 **466** 2cr.50 green 15 10

1959. Bicent of Carmelite Order in Brazil.
1007 **467** 3cr.30 lake 10 10

468 Dom J. S. de Souza (First Archbishop)

469 Sugar-loaf Mountain and Road

1959. Birth Cent of Archbishop of Diamantina.
1008 **468** 2cr.50 brown 10 10

1959. 11th International Roads Congress.
1009 **469** 3cr.30 blue and green . . 15 10

470 Londrina and Parana **471** Putting the Shot

1959. 25th Anniv of Londrina.
1010 **470** 2cr.50 green 10 10

1959. Spring Games.
1011 **471** 2cr.50 mauve 65 10

472 Daedalus **473** Globe and "Snipe" Class Yachts

1959. Air. Aviation Week.
1012 **472** 3cr.30 blue 10 10

1959. World Sailing Championships, Porto Alegre.
1013 **473** 6cr.50 green 10 10

474 Lusignan Cross and Arms of Salvador, Bahia **475** Gunpowder Factory

1959. 4th International Brazilian–Portuguese Study Conference, Bahia University.
1014 **474** 6cr.50 blue 10 10

1959. 50th Anniv of President Vargas Gunpowder Factory.
1015 **475** 3cr.30 brown 10 10

476 **477** Sud Aviation Caravelle

1959. Thanksgiving Day.
1016 **476** 2cr.50 blue 50 10

1959. Air. Inauguration of "Caravelle" Airliners by Brazilian National Airlines.
1017 **477** 6cr.50 blue 15 10

478 Burning Bush

1959. Centenary of Presbyterian Work in Brazil.
1018 **478** 3cr.30 green 10 10

479 P. da Silva and "Schistosoma mansoni"

1959. 50th Anniv of Discovery and Identification of "Schistosoma mansoni" (fluke).
1019 **479** 2cr.50 purple 50 10

480 L. de Matos and Church **481** Pres. Lopez Mateos of Mexico

1960. Birth Centenary of Luiz de Matos (Christian evangelist).
1020 **480** 3cr.30 brown 10 10

1960. Air. Visit of Mexican President.
1021 **481** 6cr.50 brown 10 10

482 Pres. Eisenhower **483** Dr. L. Zamenhof

1960. Air. Visit of United States President.
1022 **482** 6cr.50 brown 15 10

1960. Birth Centenary of Zamenhof (inventor of Esperanto).
1023 **483** 6cr.50 green 35 10

484 Adel Pinto (engineer) **485** "Care of Refugees"

1960. Birth Centenary of Adel Pinto.
1024 **484** 11cr.50 red 25 10

1960. Air. World Refugee Year.
1025 **485** 6cr.50 blue 20 10

486 Plan of Brasilia

1960. Inauguration of Brasilia as Capital.
1026 – 2cr.50 green (postage) . . 15 10
1027 – 3cr.30 violet (air) 10 10
1028 – 4cr. blue . . . . 1·25 10
1029 – 6cr.50 mauve 10 10
1030 **486** 11cr.50 brown 15 10
DESIGNS—Outlines representing: HORIZ: 2cr.50, President's Palace of the Plateau; 3cr.30, Parliament Buildings; 4cr. Cathedral. VERT: 6cr.50, Tower.

487 Congress Emblem

1960. Air. 7th Nat Eucharistic Congress, Curitiba.
1032 **487** 3cr.30 mauve 10 10

488 Congress Emblem, Sugar-loaf Mountain and Cross **489** Boy Scout

1960. Air. 10th Baptist World Alliance Congress, Rio de Janeiro.
1033 **488** 6cr.50 blue 10 10

1960. Air. 50th Anniv of Scouting in Brazil.
1034 **489** 3cr.30 orange 10 10

490 "Agriculture" **491** Caravel

1960. Cent of Brazilian Ministry of Agriculture.
1035 **490** 2cr.50 brown 15 10

1960. Air. 5th Death Centenary of Prince Henry the Navigator.
1036 **491** 6cr.50 black 30 10

492 P. de Frontin **493** Locomotive Piston Gear

1960. Birth Cent of Paulo de Frontin (engineer).
1037 **492** 2cr.50 orange 10 10

1960. 10th Pan-American Railways Congress.
1038 **493** 2cr.50 blue 35 10

494 Athlete **495**

1960. 12th Spring Games.
1039 **494** 2cr.50 turquoise 15 10

1960. World Volleyball Championships.
1040 **495** 11cr. blue 60 10

496 Maria Bueno in play

1960. Air. Maria Bueno's Wimbledon Tennis Victories, 1959–60.
1041 **496** 6cr. brown 15 10

497 Exhibition Emblem

1960. International Industrial and Commercial Exhibition, Rio de Janeiro.
1042 **497** 2cr.50 brown & yellow 10 10

498 War Memorial, Rio de Janeiro **499** Pylon and Map

1960. Air. Return of Ashes of World War II Heroes from Italy.
1043 **498** 3cr.30 lake 15 10

1961. Air. Inauguration of Tres Marias Hydro-electric Station.
1044 **499** 3cr.30 mauve 15 10

500 Emperor Haile Selassie **501** Sacred Book and Map of Brazil

1961. Visit of Emperor of Ethiopia.
1045 **500** 2cr.50 brown 10 10

1961. 50th Anniv of Sacre-Coeur de Marie College.
1046 **501** 2cr.50 blue 15 10

502 Map of Guanabara State **503** Arms of Academy

1961. Promulgation of Guanabara Constitution.
1047 **502** 7cr.50 brown 60 10

1961. 150th Anniv of Agulhas Negras Military Academy.
1048 **503** 2cr.50 green 20 10
1049 – 3cr.30 red 10 10
DESIGN: 3cr.30, Military cap and sabre.

504 "Spanning the Atlantic Ocean" **505** View of Ouro Preto

1961. Visit of Foreign Minister to Senegal.
1050 **504** 27cr. blue 95 10

1961. 250th Anniv of Ouro Preto.
1051 **505** 1cr. orange 35 10

506 Arsenal, Rio de Janeiro **507** Coffee Plant

1961. 150th Anniv of Rio de Janeiro Arsenal.
1052 **506** 5cr. brown 45 10

1961. Int Coffee Convention, Rio de Janeiro.
1053 **507** 20cr. brown . . . . . . 2·40 10

508 Tagore **509** 280r. Stamp of 1861 and Map of France

1960. Birth Cent of Rabindranath Tagore (poet).
1054 **508** 10cr. mauve 90 10

1961. "Goat's Eyes" Stamp Centenary.
1055 **509** 10cr. red . . . . 1·25 10
1056 – 20cr. orange . . . . . . 3·75 10
DESIGN: 20cr. 430r. stamp and map of the Netherlands.

510 Cloudburst  **511** Pinnacle, Rope and Haversack

1962. World Meteorological Day.
1057 **510** 10cr. brown . . . . . . 1·25 10

1962. 50th Anniv of 1st Ascent of "Finger of God" Mountain.
1058 **511** 8cr. green 10 10

512 Dr. G. Vianna and parasites

1962. 50th Anniv of Vianna's Cure for Leishman's Disease.
1059 **512** 8cr. blue 20 10

513 Campaign Emblem  **514** Henrique Dias (patriot)

1962. Air. Malaria Eradication.
1060 **513** 21cr. blue 10 10

1962. 300th Death Anniv of Dias.
1061 **514** 10cr. purple 15 10

515 Metric Measure  **516** "Snipe" Sailing-boats

1962. Cent of Brazil's Adoption of Metric System.
1062 **515** 100cr. red . . . . 1·25 10

1962. 13th "Snipe" Class Sailing Championships, Rio de Janeiro.
1063 **516** 8cr. turquoise 20 10

517 J. Mesquita and Newspaper "O Estado de Sao Paulo"

1962. Birth Centenary of Mesquita (journalist and founder of "O Estado de Sao Paulo").
1064 **517** 8cr. bistre . . . . 1·25 10

518 Empress Leopoldina  **519** Brasilia

1962. 140th Anniv of Independence.
1065 **518** 8cr. mauve 15 10

1962. 51st Interparliamentary Conference, Brasilia.
1066 **519** 10cr. orange 40 10

520 Foundry Ladle  **521** U.P.A.E. Emblem

1962. Inauguration of "Usiminas" (national iron and steel foundry).
1067 **520** 8cr. orange 10 10

1962. 50th Anniv of Postal Union of the Americas and Spain.
1068 **521** 8cr. mauve 10 10

522 Emblems of Industry  **523** Q. Bocaiuva

1962. 10th Anniv of National Bank.
1069 **522** 10cr. turquoise 15 10

1962. 50th Death Anniv of Bocaiuva (journalist and patriot).
1070 **523** 8cr. brown 10 10

524 Footballer

1962. Brazil's Victory in World Football Championships, 1962.
1071 **524** 10cr. turquoise . . . . . 1·25 10

525 Carrier Pigeon  **526** Dr. S. Neiva (first Brazilian P.M.G.)

1962. Tercentenary of Brazilian Posts.
1072 **525** 8cr. multicoloured . . . 10 10

1963.
1073 **526** 8cr. violet 50 10
1073a – 30cr. turquoise (Euclides da Cunha) 4·75 10
1073b – 50cr. brown (Prof. A. Moreira da Costa Lima) . . . . 3·50 10
1073c – 100cr. blue (G. Dias) 1·75 10
1073d – 200cr. red (Tiradentes) 7·00 10
1073e – 500cr. brown (Emperor Pedro I) . . . . . . 35·00 20
1073f – 1000cr. blue (Emperor Pedro II) . . . . . . 90·00 60

527 Rockets and "Dish" Aerial  **528** Cross

1963. Int Aeronautics and Space Exn, Sao Paulo.
1074 **527** 21cr. blue 60 10

1963. Ecumenical Council, Vatican City.
1075 **528** 8cr. purple 10 10

529 "abc" Symbol  **530** Basketball

1963. National Education Week.
1076 **529** 8cr. blue 10 10

1963. 4th World Basketball Championships.
1077 **530** 8cr. mauve 50 10

531 Torch Emblem

1963. 4th Pan-American Games, Sao Paulo.
1078 **531** 10cr. red 65 10

532 "OEA" and Map  **533** J. B. de Andrada e Silva

1963. 15th Anniv of Organization of American States.
1079 **532** 10cr. orange 50 10

1963. Birth Bicentenary of Jose B. de Andrada e Silva ("Father of Independence")
1080 **533** 8cr. bistre 10 10

534 Campaign Emblem

1963. Freedom from Hunger.
1081 **534** 10cr. blue 50 10

535 Centenary Emblem  **536** J. Caetano

1963. Red Cross Centenary.
1082 **535** 8cr. red and yellow . . . 20 10

1963. Death Centenary of Joao Caetano (actor).
1083 **536** 8cr. black 10 10

537 "Atomic" Development  **538** Throwing the Hammer

1963. 1st Anniv of National Nuclear Energy Commission.
1084 **537** 10cr. mauve 50 10

1963. International Students' Games, Porto Alegre.
1085 **538** 10cr. black and grey . . 65 10

539 Pres. Tito  **540** Cross and Map

1963. Visit of President Tito of Yugoslavia.
1086 **539** 80cr. drab . . . . 2·40 10

1963. 8th Int Leprology Congress, Rio de Janeiro.
1087 **540** 8cr. turquoise 10 10

541 Petroleum Installations  **543** A. Borges de Medeiros

542 "Jogos da Primavera"

1963. 10th Anniv of National Petroleum Industry.
1088 **541** 8cr. green 10 10

1963. Spring Games.
1089 **542** 8cr. yellow 10 10

1963. Birth Centenary of A. Borges de Medeiros (politician).
1090 **543** 8cr. brown 10 10

544 Bridge of Sao Joao del Rey  **546** Viscount de Maua

545 Dr. A. Alvim

1963. 250th Anniv of Sao Joao del Rey.
1091 **544** 8cr. blue 10 10

1963. Birth Cent of Dr. Alvaro Alvim (scientist).
1092 **545** 8cr. slate 10 10

1963. 150th Birth Anniv of Viscount de Maua (builder of Santos–Jundiai Railway).
1093 **546** 8cr. mauve 45 20

547 Cactus **548** C. Netto

1964. 10th Anniv of North-East Bank.
1094 **547** 8cr. green 10 10

1964. Birth Centenary of Coelho Netto (author).
1095 **548** 8cr. violet 10 10

549 L. Muller **550** Child with Spoon

1964. Birth Cent of Lauro Muller (patriot).
1096 **549** 8cr. red 10 10

1964. Schoolchildren's Nourishment Week.
1097 **550** 8cr. yellow and brown 10 10

551 "Chalice" (carved rock), Vila Velha, Parana **552** A. Kardec (author)

1964. Tourism.
1098 **551** 80cr. red 65 10

1964. Cent of Spiritual Code, "O Evangelho".
1099 **552** 30cr. green 95 10

553 Pres. Lubke **554** Pope John XXIII

1964. Visit of Pres. Lubke of West Germany.
1100 **553** 100cr. brown . . . . . 1·25 10

1964. Pope John Commemoration.
1101 **554** 20cr. lake 60 35

555 Pres. Senghor

1964. Visit of Pres. Senghor of Senegal.
1102 **555** 20cr. sepia 15 10

556 "Visit Rio de Janeiro"

1964. 400th Anniv (1965) of Rio de Janeiro.
1103 **556** 15cr. blue and orange . . 25 10
1104 30cr. red and blue . . . 65 10
1105 – 30cr. black and blue . . 1·60 40
1106 – 35cr. black and orange 15 10
1107 – 100cr. brn & grn on yell 65 10
1108 – 200cr. red and green . . 6·00 10
DESIGNS: As Type **556**—HORIZ: 30cr. (No. 1105), Tramway viaduct; 200cr. Copacabana Beach. VERT: 35cr. Estacio de Sa's statue; 100cr. Church of Our Lady of the Rock. SMALLER (24½ × 37 mm): 30cr. (No. 1104), Statue of St. Sebastian.

558 Pres. De Gaulle **559** Pres. Kennedy

1964. Visit of Pres. De Gaulle.
1110 **558** 100cr. brown 95 10

1964. Pres. Kennedy Commemoration.
1111 **559** 100cr. black 15 15

560 Nahum (statue)

1964. 150th Death Anniv of A. F. Lisboa (sculptor).
1112 **560** 10cr. black 30 10

561 Cross and Sword **562** V. Brazil (scientist)

1965. 1st Anniv of Democratic Revolution.
1113 **561** 120cr. grey 15 10

1965. Birth Cent of Vital Brazil.
1114 **562** 120cr. orange . . . . . 1·25 10

563 Shah of Iran **564** Marshal Rondon and Map

1965. Visit of Shah of Iran.
1115 **563** 120cr. red 65 10

1965. Birth Cent of Marshal C. M. da S. Rondon.
1116 **564** 30cr. purple 50 10

565 Lions Emblem **566** I.T.U. Emblem and Symbols

1965. Brazilian Lions Clubs National Convention, Rio de Janeiro.
1117 **565** 35cr. black and lilac . . 15 10

1965. I.T.U. Centenary.
1118 **566** 120cr. green and yellow 65 10

567 E. Pessoa **568** Barrosos Statue

1965. Birth Centenary of Epitacio Pessoa.
1119 **567** 35cr. slate 10 10

1965. Centenary of Naval Battle of Riachuelo.
1120 **568** 30cr. blue 15 10

569 Author and Heroine **570** Sir Winston Churchill

1965. Centenary of Publication of Jose de Alencar's "Iracema".
1121 **569** 30cr. purple 15 10

1965. Churchill Commemoration.
1122 **570** 200cr. slate . . . . . . 1·25 10

571 Scout Badge and Emblem of Rio's 400th Anniv **572** I.C.Y. Emblem

1965. 1st Pan-American Scout Jamboree, Rio de Janeiro.
1123 **571** 30r. multicoloured . . . 1·10 10

1965. International Co-operation Year.
1124 **572** 120cr. black and blue . . 1·25 10

573 L. Correia **574** Exhibition Emblem

1965. Birth Centenary of Leoncia Correia (poet).
1125 **573** 35cr. green 10 10

1965. Sao Paulo Biennale (Art Exn).
1126 **574** 30cr. red 10 10

575 President Saragat **576** Grand Duke and Duchess of Luxembourg

1965. Visit of President of Italy.
1127 **575** 100cr. green on pink . . 15 10

1965. Visit of Grand Duke and Duchess of Luxembourg.
1128 **576** 100cr. brown 15 10

577 Curtiss Fledgling on Map **578** O.E.A. Emblem

1965. Aviation Week and 3rd Philatelic Exn.
1129 **577** 35cr. blue 15 10

1965. Inter-American Conference, Rio de Janeiro.
1130 **578** 100cr. black and blue . . 45 10

579 King Baudouin and Queen Fabiola **580** Coffee Beans

1965. Visit of King and Queen of the Belgians.
1131 **579** 100cr. slate 50 10

1965. Brazilian Coffee.
1132 **580** 30cr. brown on cream 65 10

581 F. A. Varnhagen **583** Sister and Globe

582 Emblem and Map

1965. Air. 150th Birth Anniv of Francisco Varnhagen (historian).
1133 **581** 45cr. brown 15 10

1966. Air. 5th Anniv of "Alliance for Progress".
1134 **582** 120cr. blue & turquoise 95 10

1966. Air. Centenary of Dorothean Sisters Educational Work in Brazil.
1135 **583** 35cr. violet 10 10

584 Loading Ore at Quayside **585** "Steel"

1966. Inauguration of Rio Doce Iron-ore Terminal Tubarao, Espirito Santo.
1136 **584** 110cr. black and bistre 50 10

1966. Silver Jubilee of National Steel Company.
1137 **585** 30cr. black on orange . . 35 10

586 Prof. Rocha Lima

587 Battle Scene

1966. 50th Anniv of Professor Lima's Discovery of the Characteristics of "Rickettsia prowazeki" (cause of typhus fever).
1138 **586** 30cr. turquoise 65 10

1966. Centenary of Battle of Tuiuti.
1139 **587** 30cr. green 65 10

588 "The Sacred Face"

589 Mariz e Barros

1966. Air. "Concilio Vaticano II".
1140 **588** 45cr. brown 35 35

1966. Air. Death Centenary of Commander Mariz e Barros.
1141 **589** 35cr. brown 15 10

590 Decade Symbol

591 Pres. Shazar

1966. International Hydrological Decade.
1142 **590** 100cr. blue and brown 65 10

1966. Visit of President Shazar of Israel.
1143 **591** 100cr. blue 95 10

592 "Youth"

593 Imperial Academy of Fine Arts

1966. Air. Birth Centenary of Eliseu Visconti (painter).
1144 **592** 120cr. brown . . . . . 1·90 10

1966. 150th Anniv of French Art Mission's Arrival in Brazil.
1145 **593** 100cr. brown . . . . . 1·75 10

594 Military Service Emblem

595 R. Dario

1966. New Military Service Law.
1146 **594** 30cr. blue and yellow . . 15 10

1966. 50th Death Anniv of Ruben Dario (Nicaraguan poet).
1148 **595** 100cr. purple 65 10

596 Santarem Candlestick

597 Arms of Santa Cruz do Sul

1966. Centenary of Goeldi Museum.
1149 **596** 30cr. brown on salmon 15 10

1966. 1st National Tobacco Exn, Santa Cruz.
1150 **597** 30cr. green 15 10

598 U.N.E.S.C.O. Emblem

599 Capt. A. C. Pinto and Map

1966. 20th Anniv of U.N.E.S.C.O.
1151 **598** 120cr. black . . . . . . 1·25 35

1966. Bicentenary of Arrival of Captain A. C. Pinto.
1153 **599** 30cr. red 15 10

600 Lusignan Cross and Southern Cross

601 Madonna and Child

1966. "Lubrapex 1966" Stamp Exn, Rio de Janeiro.
1154 **600** 100cr. green 95 10

1966. Christmas.
1155 **601** 30cr. green 20 10
1156 – 35cr. blue and orange . . 20 15
1157 – 150cr. pink and blue . . 3·50 3·50
DESIGN—DIAMOND(34 × 34 mm). 35cr. Madonna and child (different). VERT (46 × 103 mm). 150cr. As 35cr. inscr "Pax Hominibus" but not "Brazil Correio".

602 Arms of Laguna

1967. Centenary of Laguna Postal and Telegraphic Agency.
1158 **602** 60cr. sepia 10 10

603 Grota Funda Viaduct and 1866 Viaduct

1967. Centenary of Santos–Jundiai Railway.
1159 **603** 50cr. orange . . . . . . 1·40 30

604 Polish Cross and "Black Madonna"

1967. Polish Millennium.
1160 **604** 50cr. red, blue & yellow 50 10

605 Research Rocket

606 Anita Garibaldi

1967. World Meteorological Day.
1161 **605** 50cr. black and blue . . 95 10

1967.

1162 – 1c. blue 10 10
1163 – 2c. red 10 10
1164 – 3c. green 15 10
1165 **606** 5c. black 15 10
1166 – 6c. brown 15 10
1167 – 10c. green . . . . 1·40 10
PORTRAITS: 1c. Mother Angelica. 2c. Marilia de Dirceu. 3c. Dr. R. Lobato. 6c. Ana Neri. 10c. Darci Vargas.

607 "VARIG 40 Years"

608 Lions Emblem and Globes

1967. 40th Anniv of Varig Airlines.
1171 **607** 6c. black and blue . . . 15 10

1967. 50th Anniv of Lions International.
1172 **608** 6c. green 25 10

609 "Madonna and Child"

610 Prince Akihito and Princess Michiko

1967. Mothers' Day.
1174 **609** 5c. violet 10 10

1967. Visit of Crown Prince and Princess of Japan.
1176 **610** 10c. black and red . . . 15 10

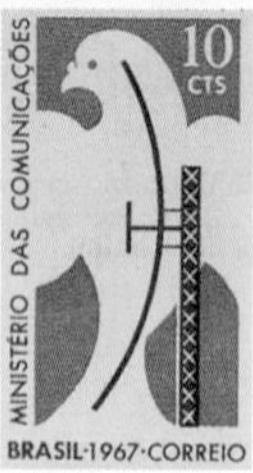

611 Radar Aerial and Pigeon

612 Brother Vicente do Salvador

1967. Inaug of Communications Ministry, Brasilia.
1177 **611** 10c. black and mauve . . 15 10

1967. 400th Birth Anniv of Brother Vicente do Salvador (founder of Franciscan Brotherhood, Rio de Janeiro).
1178 **612** 5c. brown 15 10

613 Emblem and Members

614 Mobius Symbol

1967. National 4-S ("4-H") Clubs Day.
1179 **613** 5c. green and black . . . 15 10

1967. 6th Brazilian Mathematical Congress. Rio de Janeiro.
1180 **614** 5c. black and blue . . . 15 10

615 Dorado (fish) and "Waves"

1967. Bicentenary of Piracicaba.
1181 **615** 5c. black and blue . . . 20 10

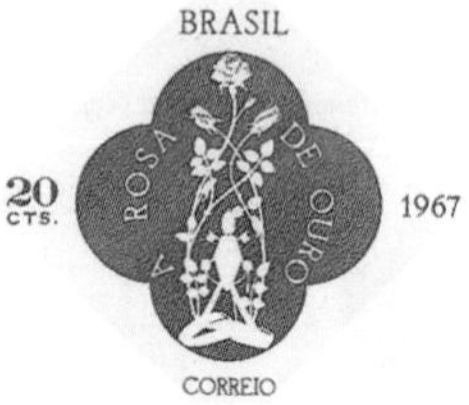

616 Papal Arms and "Golden Rose"

1967. Pope Paul's "Golden Rose" Offering to Our Lady of Fatima.
1182 **616** 20c. mauve and yellow 1·25 35

617 General A. de Sampaio

1967. Gen. Sampaio Commem.
1183 **617** 5c. blue 15 10

618 King Olav of Norway

619 Sun and Rio de Janeiro

1967. Visit of King Olav.
1184 **618** 10c. brown 15 10

1967. Meeting of International Monetary Fund, Rio de Janeiro.
1185 **619** 10c. black and red . . . 15 10

620 N. Pecanha (statesman)

621 Our Lady of the Apparition and Basilica

1967. Birth Centenary of Nilo Pecanha.
1186 **620** 5c. purple 10 10

1967. 250th Anniv of Discovery of Statue of Our Lady of the Apparition.
1187 **621** 5c. blue and ochre . . . 15 10

622 "Song Bird"

623 Balloon, Rocket and Airplane

1967. International Song Festival.
1189 **622** 20c. multicoloured . . . 55 35

1967. Aviation Week.
1190 **623** 10c. blue 60 10

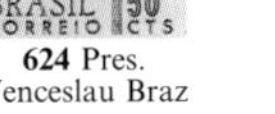

624 Pres. Venceslau Braz

625 Rio Carnival

1967.
1192 – 10c. blue 35 10
1193 – 20c. brown . . . . . . 1·75 10
1195 **624** 50c. black . . . . 12·00 10
1198 – 1cr. purple . . . . . . 18·00 10
1199 – 2cr. green . . . . 3·75 10
Portraits of Brazilian Presidents: 10c. Arthur Bernardes. 20c. Campos Salles. 1cr. Washington Luiz. 2cr. Castello Branco.

1967. International Tourist Year.
1200 **625** 10c. multicoloured . . . 15 10

626 Sailor, Anchor and "Almirante Tamandare" (cruiser)

627 Christmas Decorations

1967. Navy Week.
1202 **626** 10c. blue 30 15

1967. Christmas.
1203 **627** 5c. multicoloured 15 10

628 O. Bilac (poet), Aircraft, Tank and Aircraft carrier "Minas Gerais"

629 J. Rodrigues de Carvalho

1967. Reservists Day.
1204 **628** 5c. blue and yellow . . . 60 15

1967. Birth Centenary of Jose Rodriques de Carvalho (jurist and writer).
1205 **629** 10c. green 10 10

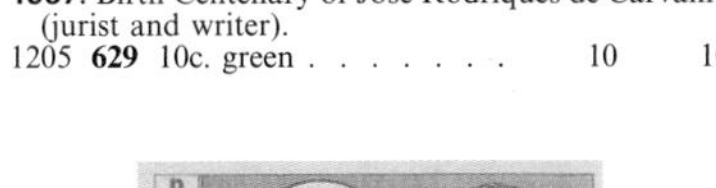

630 O. Rangel

1968. Birth Cent of Orlando Rangel (chemist).
1206 **630** 5c. black and blue . . . 15 10

631 Madonna and Diver

632 Map of Free Zone

1968. 250th Anniv of Paranagua Underwater Exploration.
1207 **631** 10c. green and slate . . 20 10

1968. Manaus Free Zone.
1208 **632** 10c. red, green and yellow 15 10

633 Human Rights Emblem

634 Paul Harris

1968. 20th Anniv of Declaration of Human Rights.
1209 **633** 10c. red and blue 10 10

GUM. All the following issues to No. 1425 are without gum, except where otherwise stated.

1968. Birth Centenary of Paul Harris (founder of Rotary International).
1210 **634** 20c. brown and green . . 1·25 60

635 College Arms

1968. Centenary of St. Luiz College. With gum.
1211 **635** 10c. gold, blue and red 25 10

636 Cabral and his Fleet, 1500

1968. 500th Birth Anniv of Pedro Cabral (discoverer of Brazil).
1212 **636** 10c. multicoloured . . . 30 15
1213 – 20c. multicoloured . . . 90 60
DESIGN: 20c. "The First Mass" (C. Portinari).

637 "Maternity" (after H. Bernardeli)

1968. Mother's Day.
1214 **637** 5c. multicoloured 20 15

638 Harpy Eagle

1968. 150th Anniv of National Museum. With gum.
1215 **638** 20c. black and blue . . . 2·50 60

639 Women of Brazil and Japan

1968. Inaug of "VARIG" Brazil–Japan Air Service.
1216 **639** 10c. multicoloured . . . 25 15

640 Horse-racing

1968. Centenary of Brazilian Jockey Club.
1217 **640** 10c. multicoloured . . . 20 10

641 Musician Wren

1968. Birds.
1218 – 10c. multicoloured . . . 50 25
1219 **641** 20c. brown, green & bl 1·50 25
1220 – 50c. multicoloured . . . 1·90 40
DESIGNS—VERT: 10c. Red-crested cardinal; 50c. Royal flycatcher.

642 Ancient Post-box

643 Marshal E. Luiz Mallet

1968. Stamp Day. With gum.
1221 **642** 5c. black, green & yellow 10 10

1968. Mallet Commemoration. With gum.
1222 **643** 10c. lilac 10 10

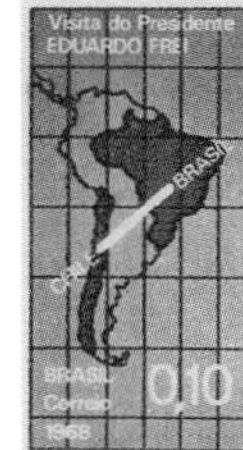

644 Map of South America

645 Lyceum Badge

1968. Visit of Chilean President. With gum.
1223 **644** 10c. orange 10 10

1968. Centenary of Portuguese Literacy Lyceum (High School). With gum.
1224 **645** 5c. green and pink . . . 10 10

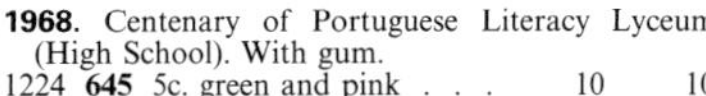

646 Map and Telex Tape

1968. "Telex Service for 25th City (Curitiba)". With gum.
1225 **646** 20c. green and yellow . . 55 35

647 "Cock" shaped as Treble Clef

648 Soldiers on Medallion

1968. 3rd Int Song Festival, Rio de Janeiro.
1226 **647** 6c. multicoloured 25 15

1968. 8th American Armed Forces Conference
1227 **648** 5c. black and blue . . . 15 10

649 "Petrobras" Refinery

650 Boy walking towards Rising Sun

1968. 15th Anniv of National Petroleum Industry.
1228 **649** 6c. multicoloured 50 15

1968. U.N.I.C.E.F.
1229 **650** 5c. black and blue . . . 20 15
1230 – 10c. black, red & blue 20 15
1231 – 20c. multicoloured . . . 50 15
DESIGNS—HORIZ: 10c. Hand protecting child. VERT: 20c. Young girl in plaits.

651 Children with Books

1968. Book Week.
1232 **651** 5c. multicoloured 15 10

652 W.H.O. Emblem and Flags

1968. 20th Anniv of W.H.O.
1233 **652** 20c. multicoloured . . . 30 15

653 J. B. Debret (painter)

1968. Birth Bicentenary of Jean Baptiste Debret (1st issue).
1234 **653** 10c. black and yellow . . 20 10
See Nos. 1273/4.

654 Queen Elizabeth II

1968. State Visit of Queen Elizabeth II.
1235 **654** 70c. multicoloured . . . 1·50 90

655 Brazilian Flag

656 F. Braga and part of "Hymn of National Flag"

1968. Brazilian Flag Day.
1236 **655** 10c. multicoloured . . . 20 15

1968. Birth Cent of Francisco Braga (composer).
1237 **656** 5c. purple 25 10

657 Clasped Hands

1968. Blood Donors' Day.
1238 **657** 5c. red, black and blue 15 10

1968. Obligatory Tax. Leprosy Research Fund. Revalued currency. With gum.
1239 **388** 5c. green . . . . 5·25 1·25
1240 5c. red . . . . 2·40 60

658 Steam Locomotive No. 1 "Maria Fumaca", 1868

1968. Centenary of Sao Paulo Railway.
1241 **658** 5c. multicoloured . . . . 2·50 2·50

659 Angelus Bell

660 F.A.V. Caldas Jr

1968. Christmas. Multicoloured.
1242 5c. Type **659** 15 10
1243 6c. Father Christmas giving present 15 10

1968. Birth Centenary of Francisco Caldas Junior (founder of "Correio do Povo" newspaper).
1244 **660** 10c. black, pink & red 15 10

661 Reservists Emblem and Memorial

1968. Reservists' Day. With gum.
1245 **661** 5c. green and brown . . 15 10

662 Dish Aerial

663 Viscount do Rio Branco

1969. Inaug of Satellite Communications System.
1246 **662** 30c. black and blue . . . 90 60

1969. 150th Birth Anniv of Viscount do Rio Branco.
1247 **663** 5c. sepia and drab . . . 15 10

664 St. Gabriel

1969. St. Gabriel's Day (Patron Saint of Telecommunications).
1248 **664** 5c. multicoloured 15 10

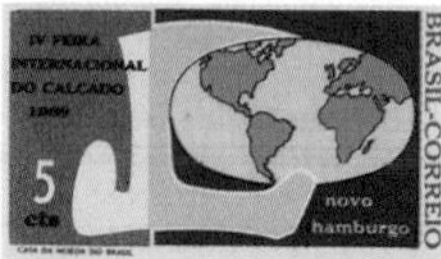

665 Shoemaker's Last and Globe

1969. 4th Int Shoe Fair, Novo, Hamburgo.
1249 **665** 5c. multicoloured 15 10

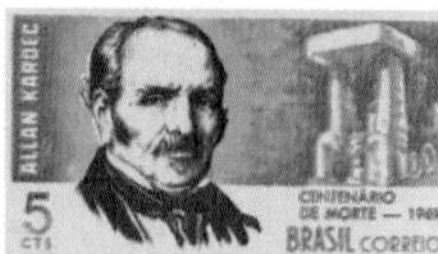

666 Kardec and Monument

1969. Death Centenary of "Allan Kardec" (Professor H. Rivail) (French educationalist and spiritualist).
1250 **666** 5c. brown and green . . 15 10

667 Men of Three Races and Arms of Cuiaba

1969. 250th Anniv of Cuiaba (capital of Mato Grosso state).
1251 **667** 5c. multicoloured 10 10

668 Mint and Banknote Pattern

1969. Opening of New State Mint Printing Works.
1252 **668** 5c. bistre and orange . . 20 15

669 Society Emblem and Stamps

1969. 50th Anniv of Sao Paulo Philatelic Society.
1253 **669** 5c. multicoloured 10 10

670 "Our Lady of Santana" (statue)

1969. Mothers' Day.
1254 **670** 5c. multicoloured 20 15

671 I.L.O. Emblem

1969. 50th Anniv of I.L.O. With gum.
1255 **671** 5c. gold and red 10 10

672 Diving Platform and Swimming Pool

673 "Mother and Child at Window" (after Di Cavalcanti)

1969. 40th Anniv of Cearense Water Sports Club, Fortaleza.
1256 **672** 20c. black, green & brn 40 15

1969. 10th Art Exhibition Biennale, Sao Paulo. Multicoloured.
1257 10c. Type **673** 60 15
1258 20c. Modern sculpture (F. Leirner) 90 30
1259 50c. "Sunset in Brasilia" (D. di Prete) . . . . 1·75 1·25
1260 1cr. "Angelfish" (A. Martins) . . . . . . 1·75 80
No. 1258 is square, size 33 × 33 mm and Nos. 1259/60 vertical, size 33 × 53mm.

674 Freshwater Angelfish

675 I. O. Teles de Manezes (founder)

1969. A.C.A.P.I. Fish Preservation and Development Campaign.
1261 **674** 20c. multicoloured . . . 45 15

1969. Centenary of Spiritualist Press. With gum.
1263 **675** 50c. green and orange 1·50 90

676 Postman delivering Letter

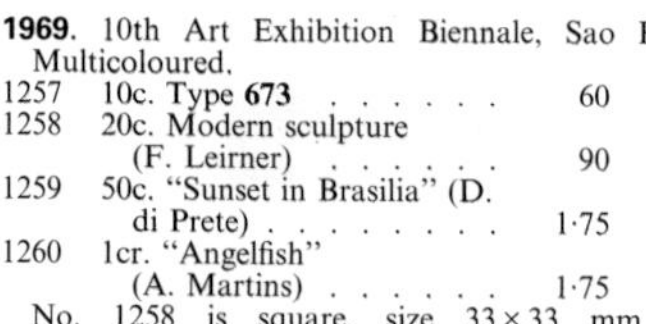

677 General Fragoso

1969. Stamp Day. With gum.
1264 **676** 30c. blue . . . . 1·25 60

1969. Birth Centenary of General Tasso Fragoso. With gum.
1265 **677** 20c. green 90 60

678 Map of Army Bases

1969. Army Week. Multicoloured.
1266 10c. Type **678** 25 15
1267 20c. Monument and railway bridge (39 × 22 mm) . . . 1·75 60

679 Jupia Dam

1969. Inauguration of Jupia Dam.
1268 **679** 20c. multicoloured . . . 55 55

680 Mahatma Gandhi and Spinning-wheel

1969. Birth Centenary of Mahatma Gandhi.
1269 **680** 20c. black and yellow . . 1·25 60

681 Alberto Santos Dumont, "Ballon No. 6", Eiffel Tower and Moon Landing

1969. 1st Man on the Moon and Santos Dumont's Flight (1906). Commemoration.
1270 **681** 50c. multicoloured . . . 1·75 1·25

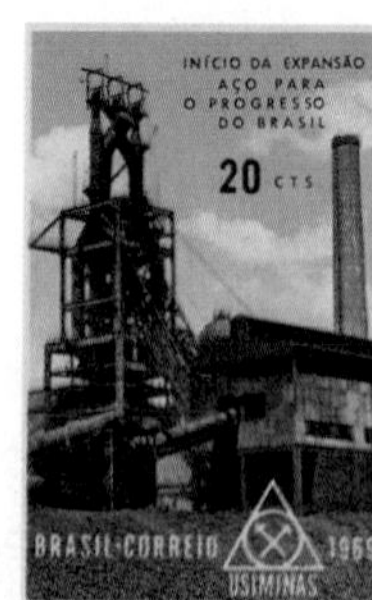

682 Smelting Plant

1969. Expansion of USIMINAS Steel Consortium.
1271 **682** 20c. multicoloured . . . 55 15

683 Steel Furnace

685 Exhibition Emblem

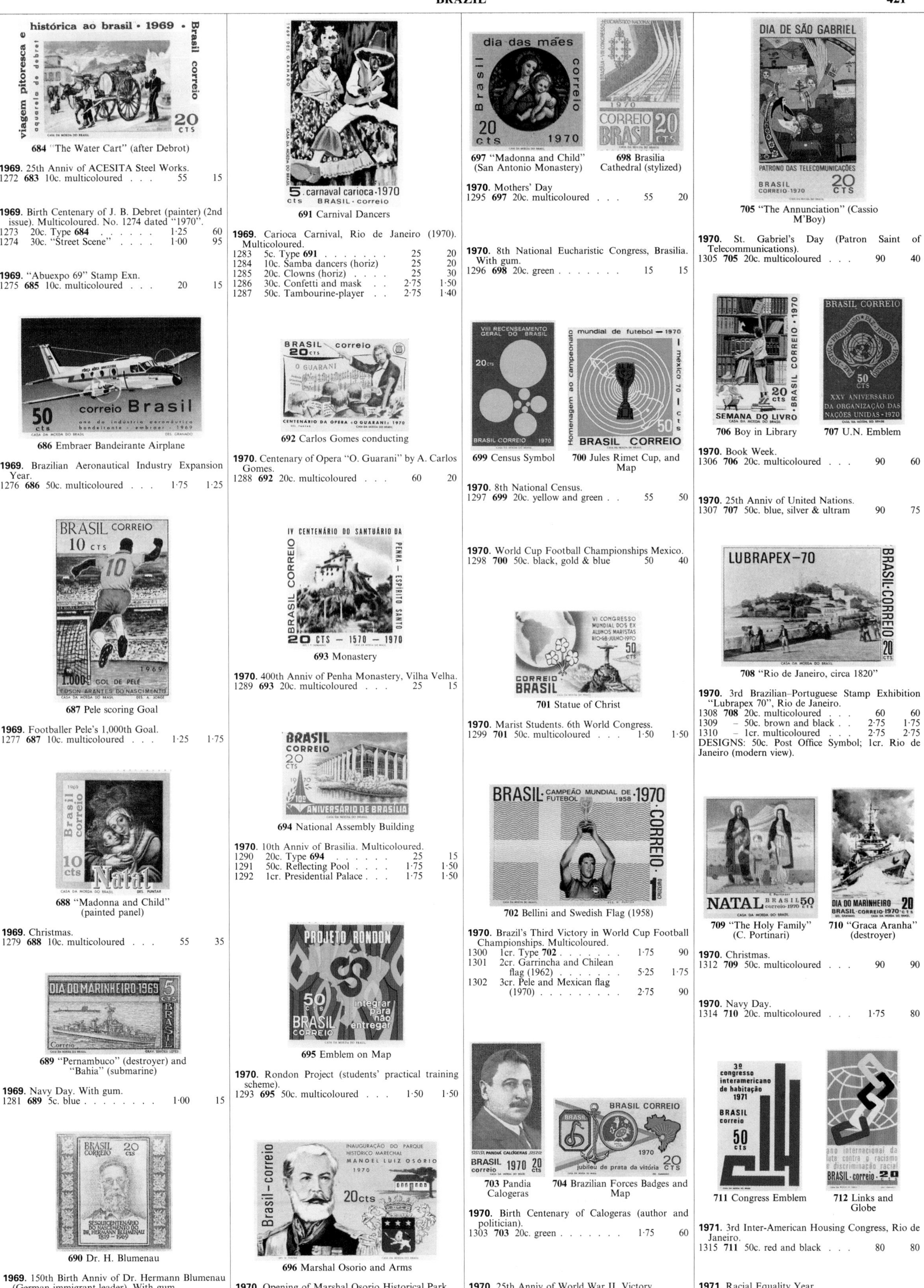

684 "The Water Cart" (after Debrot)

1969. 25th Anniv of ACESITA Steel Works.
1272 **683** 10c. multicoloured . . . 55 15

1969. Birth Centenary of J. B. Debret (painter) (2nd issue). Multicoloured. No. 1274 dated "1970".
1273 20c. Type **684** . . . . . . 1·25 60
1274 30c. "Street Scene" . . . . 1·00 95

1969. "Abuexpo 69" Stamp Exn.
1275 **685** 10c. multicoloured . . . 20 15

686 Embraer Bandeirante Airplane

1969. Brazilian Aeronautical Industry Expansion Year.
1276 **686** 50c. multicoloured . . . 1·75 1·25

687 Pele scoring Goal

1969. Footballer Pele's 1,000th Goal.
1277 **687** 10c. multicoloured . . . 1·25 1·75

688 "Madonna and Child" (painted panel)

1969. Christmas.
1279 **688** 10c. multicoloured . . . 55 35

689 "Pernambuco" (destroyer) and "Bahia" (submarine)

1969. Navy Day. With gum.
1281 **689** 5c. blue . . . . 1·00 15

690 Dr. H. Blumenau

1969. 150th Birth Anniv of Dr. Hermann Blumenau (German immigrant leader). With gum.
1282 **690** 20c. green 60 60

691 Carnival Dancers

1969. Carioca Carnival, Rio de Janeiro (1970). Multicoloured.
1283 5c. Type **691** 25 20
1284 10c. Samba dancers (horiz) 25 20
1285 20c. Clowns (horiz) 25 30
1286 30c. Confetti and mask . . 2·75 1·50
1287 50c. Tambourine-player . . 2·75 1·40

692 Carlos Gomes conducting

1970. Centenary of Opera "O. Guarani" by A. Carlos Gomes.
1288 **692** 20c. multicoloured . . . 60 20

693 Monastery

1970. 400th Anniv of Penha Monastery, Vilha Velha.
1289 **693** 20c. multicoloured . . . 25 15

694 National Assembly Building

1970. 10th Anniv of Brasilia. Multicoloured.
1290 20c. Type **694** 25 15
1291 50c. Reflecting Pool . . . . 1·75 1·50
1292 1cr. Presidential Palace . . . 1·75 1·50

695 Emblem on Map

1970. Rondon Project (students' practical training scheme).
1293 **695** 50c. multicoloured . . . 1·50 1·50

696 Marshal Osorio and Arms

1970. Opening of Marshal Osorio Historical Park.
1294 **696** 20c. multicoloured . . . 1·25 45

697 "Madonna and Child" (San Antonio Monastery)

698 Brasilia Cathedral (stylized)

1970. Mothers' Day
1295 **697** 20c. multicoloured . . . 55 20

1970. 8th National Eucharistic Congress, Brasilia. With gum.
1296 **698** 20c. green 15 15

699 Census Symbol

700 Jules Rimet Cup, and Map

1970. 8th National Census.
1297 **699** 20c. yellow and green . . 55 50

1970. World Cup Football Championships Mexico.
1298 **700** 50c. black, gold & blue 50 40

701 Statue of Christ

1970. Marist Students. 6th World Congress.
1299 **701** 50c. multicoloured . . . 1·50 1·50

702 Bellini and Swedish Flag (1958)

1970. Brazil's Third Victory in World Cup Football Championships. Multicoloured.
1300 1cr. Type **702** . . . . 1·75 90
1301 2cr. Garrincha and Chilean flag (1962) . . . . . . 5·25 1·75
1302 3cr. Pele and Mexican flag (1970) . . . . 2·75 90

703 Pandia Calogeras

704 Brazilian Forces Badges and Map

1970. Birth Centenary of Calogeras (author and politician).
1303 **703** 20c. green . . . . 1·75 60

1970. 25th Anniv of World War II. Victory.
1304 **704** 20c. multicoloured . . . 50 15

705 "The Annunciation" (Cassio M'Boy)

1970. St. Gabriel's Day (Patron Saint of Telecommunications).
1305 **705** 20c. multicoloured . . . 90 40

706 Boy in Library

707 U.N. Emblem

1970. Book Week.
1306 **706** 20c. multicoloured . . . 90 60

1970. 25th Anniv of United Nations.
1307 **707** 50c. blue, silver & ultram 90 75

708 "Rio de Janeiro, circa 1820"

1970. 3rd Brazilian–Portuguese Stamp Exhibition "Lubrapex 70", Rio de Janeiro.
1308 **708** 20c. multicoloured . . . 60 60
1309 – 50c. brown and black . . 2·75 1·75
1310 – 1cr. multicoloured . . . 2·75 2·75
DESIGNS: 50c. Post Office Symbol; 1cr. Rio de Janeiro (modern view).

709 "The Holy Family" (C. Portinari)

710 "Graca Aranha" (destroyer)

1970. Christmas.
1312 **709** 50c. multicoloured . . . 90 90

1970. Navy Day.
1314 **710** 20c. multicoloured . . . 1·75 80

711 Congress Emblem

712 Links and Globe

1971. 3rd Inter-American Housing Congress, Rio de Janeiro.
1315 **711** 50c. red and black . . . 80 80

1971. Racial Equality Year.
1316 **712** 20c. multicoloured . . . 60 30

713 "Morpho melacheilus"

1971. Butterflies. Multicoloured.
1317 20c. Type **713** . . . . . . 1·25 35
1318 1cr. "Papilio thoas brasiliensis" . . . . . . 6·00 2·40

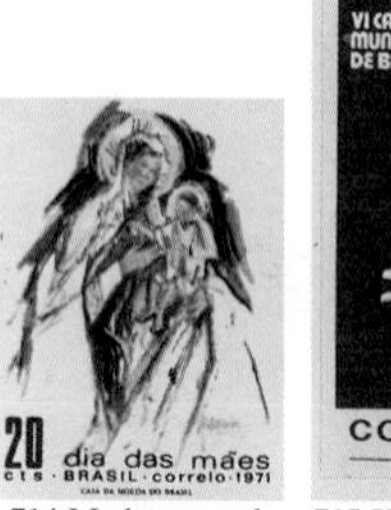

714 Madonna and Child

715 Hands reaching for Ball

1971. Mothers' Day.
1319 **714** 20c. multicoloured . . . 60 15

1971. 6th Women's Basketball World Championships.
1320 **715** 70c. multicoloured . . . 1·25 95

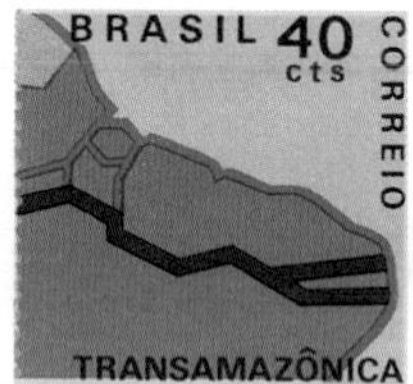

716 Eastern Part of Highway Map

1971. Trans-Amazon Highway Project. Mult.
1321 40c. Type **716** . . . . . . 6·25 3·75
1322 1cr. Western part of Highway Map . . . . . 6·25 5·25
Nos. 1321/2 were issued together se-tenant, forming a composite design.

717 "Head of Man" (V. M. Lima)

1971. Stamp Day. Multicoloured.
1323 40c. Type **717** . . . . . . 1·25 45
1324 1cr. "Arab Violinist" (Pedro Americo) . . . . 3·00 1·25

718 General Caxias and Map

719 Anita Garibaldi

1971. Army Week.
1325 **718** 20c. red and green . . . 50 15

1971. 150th Birth Anniv of Anita Garibaldi.
1326 **719** 20c. multicoloured . . . 20 15

720 Xavante and Santos Dumont's Biplane "14 bis"

1971. 1st Flight of Embraer Xavante Jet Fighter.
1327 **720** 40c. multicoloured . . . 1·25 45

721 Flags of Central American Republics

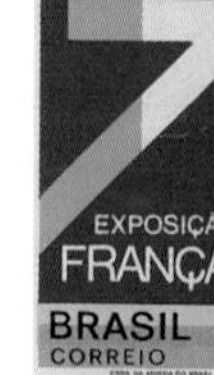

722 Exhibition Emblem

1971. 150th Anniv of Central American Republics' Independence.
1328 **721** 40c. multicoloured . . . 80 40

1971. "Franca 71" Industrial, Technical and Scientific Exhibition, Sao Paulo.
1329 **722** 1cr.30 multicoloured . . 1·25 90

723 "The Black Mother" (L. de Albuquerque)

724 Archangel Gabriel

1971. Centenary of Slaves Emancipation Law.
1330 **723** 40c. multicoloured . . . 40 20

1971. St. Gabriel's Day (Patron Saint of Communications).
1331 **724** 40c. multicoloured . . . 45 50

725 "Couple on Bridge" (Marisa da Silva Chaves)

1971. Children's Day. Multicoloured.
1332 35c. Type **725** 35 30
1333 45c. "Couple on Riverbank" (Mary Rosa e Silva) . . . 90 30
1334 60c. "Girl in Hat" (Teresa A. P. Ferreira) 35 30

726 "Laelia purpurata Werkhauserii superba"

727 Eunice Weaver

1971. Brazilian Orchids.
1335 **726** 40c. multicoloured . . . 1·50 50

1971. Obligatory Tax. Leprosy Research Fund.
1336 **727** 10c. green . . . . 1·25 65
1337 10c. purple 55 15

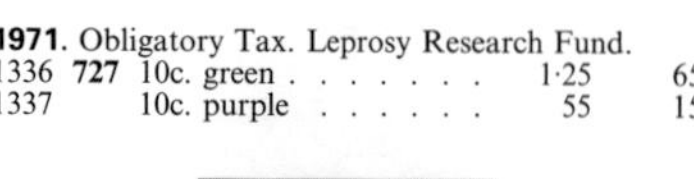

728 "25 Senac"

1971. 25th Annivs of SENAC (apprenticeship scheme) and SESC (workers' social service).
1338 **728** 20c. blue and black . . . 90 60
1339 – 40c. orange and black 90 60
DESIGN: 40c. As Type **728**, but inscribed "25 SESC".

729 "Parati" (gunboat)

1971. Navy Day.
1340 **729** 20c. multicoloured . . . 2·00 50

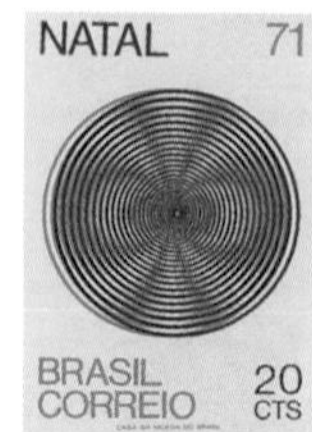

730 Cruciform Symbol

731 Washing Bomfim Church

1971. Christmas.
1341 **730** 20c. lilac, red and blue 30 15
1342 75c. black on silver . . . 55 1·75
1343 1cr.30 multicoloured . . 2·40 1·50

1972. Tourism. Multicoloured.
1344 20c. Type **731** . . . . . . 1·75 90
1345 40c. Cogwheel and grapes (Grape Festival, Rio Grande do Sul) . . . . . 1·75 20
1346 75c. Nazareth Festival procession, Belem . . . . 1·75 1·75
1347 1cr.30 Street scene (Winter Festival of Ouro Preto) 3·50 1·75

732 Pres. Lanusse

1972. Visit of President Lanusse of Argentina.
1348 **732** 40c. multicoloured . . . 90 75

733 Presidents Castello Branco, Costa e Silva and Medici

734 Post Office Symbol

1972. 8th Anniv of 1964 Revolution.
1349 **733** 20c. multicoloured . . . 40 30

1972.
1350 **734** 20c. brown . . . . . . 1·50 10

735 Pres. Tomas

1972. Visit of Pres. Tomas of Portugal.
1351 **735** 75c. multicoloured . . . 1·25 95

736 Exploratory Borehole (C.P.R.M.)

1972. Mineral Resources. Multicoloured.
1352 20c. Type **736** 60 15
1353 40c. Oil rig (PETROBRAS) (vert) . . . . 2·75 50
1354 75c. Power station and dam (ELECTROBRAS) . . . 95 1·25
1355 1cr.30 Iron ore production (Vale do Rio Doce Co.) 3·25 1·25

738 Postman and Map (Post Office)

1972. Communications. Multicoloured.
1357 35c. Type **738** 90 20
1358 45c. Microwave Transmitter (Telecommunications) (vert) 90 90
1359 60c. Symbol and diagram of Amazon microwave system 90 70
1360 70c. Worker and route map (Amazon Basin development) . . . . . . 1·25 70

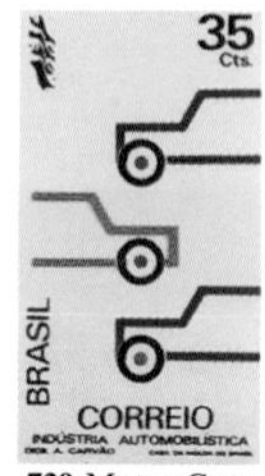

739 Motor Cars

740 Footballer (Independence Cup Championships)

1972. Major Industries.
1361 **739** 35c. orange, red & black 45 25
1362 – 45c. multicoloured . . . 45 40
1363 – 70c. multicoloured . . . 45 25
DESIGNS—HORIZ: 45c. Three hulls (Shipbuilding); 70c. Metal Blocks (Iron and Steel Industry).

1972. "Sports and Pastimes".
1364 **740** 20c. black and brown . . 40 15
1365 – 75c. black and red . . . 1·25 1·50
1366 – 1cr.30 black and blue . . 2·00 1·50
DESIGNS: 75c. Treble clef in open mouth ("Popular Music"); 1cr.30, Hand grasping plastic ("Plastic Arts").

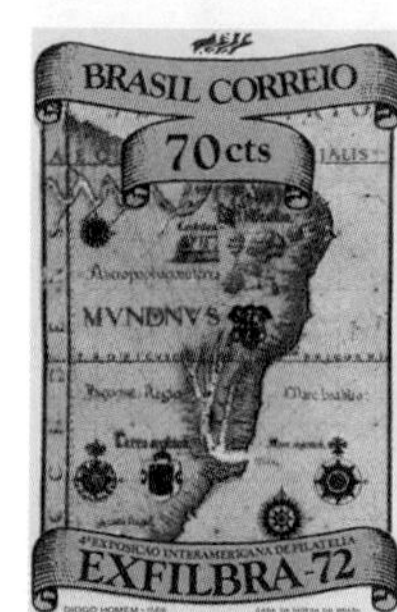

741 Diego Homem's Map of Brazil, 1568

1972. "EXFILBRA 72" 4th International Stamp Exhibition, Rio de Janeiro. Multicoloured.
1367 70c. Type **741** 60 35
1368 1cr. Nicolau Visscher's Map of Americas, c. 1652 . . . 5·25 60
1369 2cr. Lopo Homem's World Map, 1519 . . . . 2·40 90

742 Figurehead, Sao Francisco River

743 "Institution of Brazilian Flag"

1972. Brazilian Folklore. Multicoloured.
1371 45c. Type **742** 45 15
1372 60c. Fandango, Rio Grande do Sul 75 75
1373 75c. Capoeira (game), Bahia 30 15
1374 1cr.15 Karaja statuette . . . 30 25
1375 1cr.30 "Bumba-Meu-Boi" (folk play) . . . . . . 2·50 1·10

1972. 150th Anniv of Independence.
1376 **743** 30c. green and yellow . . 1·75 1·00
1377 – 70c. mauve and pink . . 75 30
1378 – 1cr. red and brown . . . 4·00 85
1379 – 2cr. black and brown . . 2·40 85
1380 – 3cr.50 black and grey . . 4·00 2·40
DESIGNS—HORIZ: 70c. "Proclamation of Emperor Pedro I" (lithograph after Debret); 2cr. Commemorative gold coin of Pedro I; 3cr.50, Declaration of Ypiranga monument. VERT: 1cr. "Emperor Pedro I" (H. J. da Silva).

744 Numeral and P.T.T. Symbol

747 Writing Hand and People ("Mobral" Literacy Campaign)

745 Scroll

1972.

1383 **744** 5c. orange 30 10
1384 10c. brown 40 10
1394 15c. blue 15 10
1385 20c. blue . . . . 2·40 10
1396 25c. brown 15 10
1386 30c. red . . . . 1·50 10
1387 40c. green 15 10
1388 50c. green . . . . 1·50 10
1398 70c. purple 60 10
1389 **745** 1cr. purple 60 10
1390 2cr. blue . . . . 1·75 10
1391 4cr. orange and lilac . . 3·50 35
1392 5cr. brown, cinnamon and red . . . . 3·50 10
1393 10cr. green, brown & blk 7·00 35

Nos. 1392/3 have a background of multiple P.T.T. symbols.

1972. Social Development. Multicoloured.
1412 10c. Type **747** 20 20
1413 20c. Graph and people (National Census Cent) 50 40
1414 1cr. House in hand (Pension Fund system) . . . . . 9·00 20
1415 2cr. Workers and factory (Gross National Product) 1·25 45

748 Legislative Building, Brasilia

1972. National Congress Building, Brasilia.
1416 **748** 1cr. black, orange & bl 9·00 4·50

749 Pottery Crib

750 Farm-worker and Pension Book (Rural Social Security Scheme)

1972. Christmas.
1417 **749** 20c. black and brown . . 40 20

1972. Government Services.
1418 **750** 10c. black, orange & bl 25 20
1419 – 10c. multicoloured . . . 90 90
1420 – 70c. black, brown & red 4·50 2·00
1421 – 2cr. multicoloured . . . 5·50 2·50

DESIGNS—VERT: 70c. Dr. Oswald Cruz, public health pioneer (birth cent.). HORIZ: 10c. (No. 1419), Children and traffic lights (Transport system development); 2cr. Bull, fish and produce (Agricultural exports).

751 Brazilian Expeditionary Force Monument

1972. Armed Forces' Day.
1422 **751** 10c. black, purple & brn 1·40 85
1423 – 30c. multicoloured . . . 2·00 85
1424 – 30c. multicoloured . . . 1·40 85
1425 – 30c. black, brn & lilac 1·40 85

DESIGNS: No. 1423, Sail-training ship (Navy); No. 1424, Trooper (Army); No. 1425, Dassault Mirage IIIC jet fighter (Air Force).

GUM. All the following issues are with gum, except where otherwise stated.

752 Emblem and Cogwheels

1973. 50th Anniv of Rotary in Brazil.
1426 **752** 1cr. blue, lt blue & yell 1·75 1·00

753 Swimming

1973. Sporting Events.
1427 **753** 40c. brown and blue . . 25 20
1428 – 40c. red and green . . . 2·75 55
1429 – 40c. brown and purple 90 45

DESIGNS AND EVENTSHORIZ: No. 1427, ("Latin Cup" Swimming Championships); No. 1428, Gymnast (Olympic Festival of Gymnastics, Rio de Janeiro). VERT: No. 1429, Volleyball player (Internation Volleyball Championships, Rio de Janeiro).

754 Paraguayan Flag

1973. Visit of Pres. Stroessner of Paraguay.
1430 **754** 70c. multicoloured . . . 1·40 80

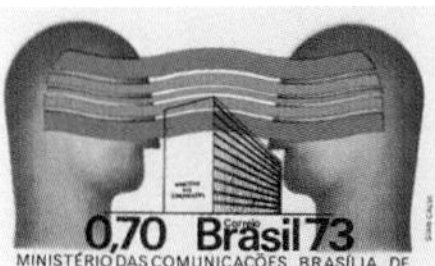

755 "Communications"

1973. Inauguration of Ministry of Communications Building, Brasilia.
1431 **755** 70c. multicoloured . . . 90 50

756 Neptune and Map

1973. Inauguration of "Bracan I" Underwater Cable, Recife to Canary Islands.
1432 **756** 1cr. multicoloured . . . 4·25 2·40

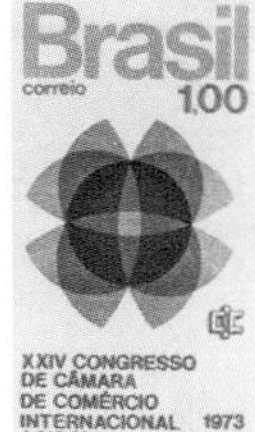

757 Congress Emblem

758 Swallow-tailed Manakin and "Acacia decurrens"

1973. 24th Int Chamber of Commerce Congress.
1433 **757** 1cr. purple and orange 4·25 2·40

1973. Tropical Birds and Plants. Mult.
1434 20c. Type **758** 65 30
1435 20c. Troupial and "Cereus peruvianus" 65 30
1436 20c. Brazilian ruby and "Tecoma umbellata" . . 65 30

759 "Tourism"

760 "Caboclo" Festival Cart

1973. National Tourism Year.
1437 **759** 70c. multicoloured . . . 60 30

1973. Anniversaries. Multicoloured.
1438 20c. Type **760** 90 30
1439 20c. Araribioa (Indian chief) 90 30
1440 20c. Convention delegates 90 30
1441 20c. "The Graciosa Road" 90 30

EVENTS: No. 1438, 150th anniv of Liberation Day; 1439, 400th anniv of Niteroi; 1440, Cent of Itu Convention; 1441, Cent of Nhundiaquara highway.

761 "Institute of Space Research"

1973. Scientific Research Institute. Mult.
1442 20c. Type **761** 50 25
1443 70c. "Federal Engineering School", Itajuba . . . . 1·50 50
1444 1cr. "Institute for Pure and Applied Mechanics" . . . 2·00 45

762 Santos Dumont and Biplane "14 bis"

1973. Birth Centenary of Alberto Santos Dumont (aviation pioneer).
1445 **762** 20c. brown, grn & lt grn 50 20
1446 – 70c. brown, red & yellow 1·25 1·25
1447 – 2cr. brown, ultram & bl 1·60 1·25

DESIGNS: 70c. Airship "Ballon No. 6"; 2cr. Monoplane No. 20 "Demoiselle".

763 Map of the World

1973. Stamp Day.
1448 **763** 40c. black and red . . . 1·90 1·25
1449 – 40c. black and red . . . 1·90 1·25

The design of No. 1449 differs from Type **763** in that the red portion is to the top and right, instead of to the top and left.

764 G. Dias

766 Festival Banner

1973. 150th Birth Anniv of Goncalves Dias (poet).
1450 **764** 40c. black and violet . . 60 30

See also Nos. 1459 and 1477.

1973. National Folklore Festival.
1452 **766** 40c. multicoloured . . . 60 20

767 Masonic Emblems

1973. 150th Anniv of Masonic Grand Orient Lodge of Brazil.
1453 **767** 1cr. blue . . . . 2·00 95

768 Fire Protection

1973. National Protection Campaign. Mult.
1454 40c. Type **768** 60 20
1455 40c. Cross and cornice (cultural protection) . . . 60 20
1456 40c. Winged emblem (protection in flight) . . . 60 20
1457 40c. Leaf (protection of nature) 60 20

1973. Birth Centenary of St. Theresa of Lisieux. As T **764**.
1459 2cr. brown and orange . . . 2·75 1·40

DESIGN: Portrait of St. Theresa.

770 M. Lobato and "Emilia"

1973. Monteiro Lobato's Children's Stories. Multicoloured.
1460 40c. Type **770** 50 50
1461 40c. "Aunt Nastasia" . . . 50 50
1462 40c. "Nazarinho", "Pedrinho" and "Quindim" 50 50
1463 40c. "Visconde de Sabugosa" 50 50
1464 40c. "Dona Benta" 50 50

771 Father J. M. Nunes Garcia

1973. "The Baroque Age". Multicoloured.
1465 40c. Wood carving, Church of St. Francia, Bahia . . 60 50
1466 40c. "Prophet Isaiah" (detail, sculpture by Aleijadinho) 60 50
1467 70c. Type **771** . . . . . . 1·75 1·75
1468 1cr. Portal, Church of Conceicao da Praia . . . 5·25 2·75
1469 2cr. "Glorification of Holy Virgin", ceiling, St. Francis Assisi Church, Ouro Preto . . . . 4·25 2·75

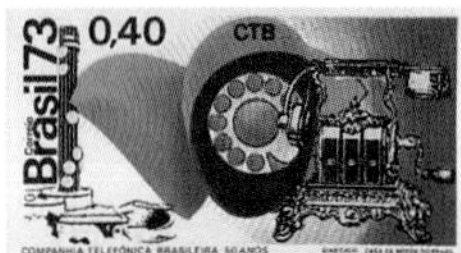

772 Early Telephone and Modern Instruments

1973. 50th Anniv of Brazilian Telephone Company.
1470 **772** 40c. multicoloured . . . 35 15

773 "Angel" (J. Kopke)

1973. Christmas.
1471 **773** 40c. multicoloured . . . 25 10

774 "Gailora" (river steamboat)

1973. Brazilian Boats. Multicoloured.
1472 40c. Type **774** 70 50
1473 70c. "Regatao" (river trading boat) . . . . . . 1·40 1·75
1474 1cr. "Jangada" (coastal raft) 4·75 2·40
1475 2cr. "Saveiro" (passenger boat) . . . . 4·75 2·40

775 Scales of Justice

1973. Judiciary Power.
1476 **775** 40c. violet and mauve . . 30 15

1973. Birth Centenary of Placido de Castro. As T **764**.
1477 40c. black and red 55 20
DESIGN: Portrait of Castro.

776 Scarlet Ibis and "Victoria Regia" Lilies
777 Saci Perere (goblin)

1973. Brazilian Flora and Fauna. Mult.
1478 40c. Type **776** . . . . . . 1·00 50
1479 70c. Jaguar and Indian tulip 4·75 45
1480 1cr. Scarlet macaw and palm . . . . 8·50 3·75
1481 2cr. Greater rhea and mulunga plant . . . . . 8·50 3·75

1974. Brazilian Folk Tales. Multicoloured.
1482 40c. Type **777** 35 15
1483 80c. Zumbi (warrior) . . . 90 40
1484 1cr. Chico Rei (African king) . . . . 1·25 20
1485 1cr.30 Little black boy of the pasture (32 × 33 mm) 2·40 80
1486 2cr.50 Iara, queen of the waters (32 × 33 mm) . . . 9·00 4·25

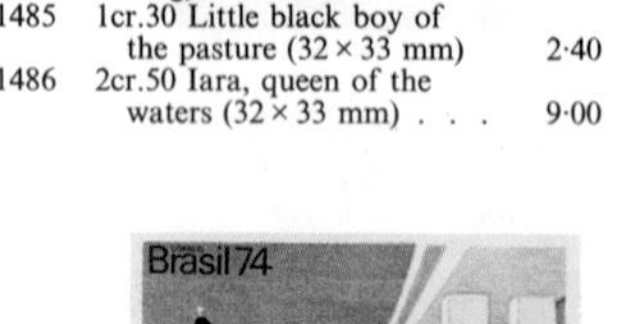

778 View of Bridge

1974. Inauguration of President Costa e Silva (Rio de Janeiro–Niteroi) Bridge.
1487 **778** 40c. multicoloured . . . 35 20

779 "Press"

1974. Brazilian Communications Pioneers.
1488 **779** 40c. red, blue & bistre 30 15
1489 – 40c. brown, blue & bistre 25 15
1490 – 40c. blue, pink & brown 30 15
DESIGNS AND EVENTS: No. 1488, Birth bicentenary of Hipolito da Costa (founder of newspaper "Correio Brasiliense", 1808); 1489, "Radio waves" (Edgar R. Pinto, founder of Radio Sociedade do Rio de Janeiro, 1923); 1490, "Television screen" (F. de Assis Chateaubriand, founder of first T.V. station, Sao Paulo, 1950).

780 "Construction"

1974. 10th Anniv of March Revolution.
1491 **780** 40c. multicoloured . . . 25 20

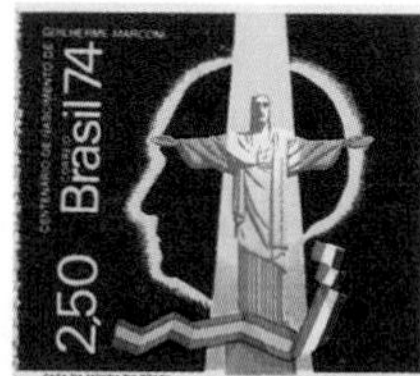

781 Christ of the Andes

1974. Birth Cent of G. Marconi (radio pioneer).
1492 **781** 2cr.50 multicoloured . . 7·00 3·50

782 Heads of Three Races

1974. Ethnical Origins and Immigration. Mult.
1493 40c. Type **782** 25 20
1494 40c. Heads of many races 10 20
1495 2cr.50 German immigration 3·75 1·25
1496 2cr.50 Italian immigration 9·00 1·25
1497 2cr.50 Japanese immigration 2·75 1·25

783 Artwork and Stamp-printing Press

1974. State Mint.
1498 **783** 80c. multicoloured . . . 95 20

784 Sete Cidades National Park

1974. Tourism. Multicoloured.
1499 40c. Type **784** 60 25
1500 80c. Ruins of church of St. Michael of the Missions 60 25

786 Caraca College

1974. Bicentenary of Caraca College.
1502 **786** 40c. multicoloured . . . 20 15

787 Wave Pattern

1974. 3rd Brazilian Telecommunications Congress, Brasilia.
1503 **787** 40c. black and blue . . . 15 15

788 Fernao Dias Paes

1974. 300th Anniv of Paes Expedition.
1504 **788** 20c. multicoloured . . . 15 15

1974. Visit of President Alvarez of Mexico. As T **754**. Multicoloured.
1505 80c. Mexican Flag . . . . . 1·75 1·25

789 Flags and Crowd in Stadium
791 Pederneiras (after J. Carlos)

1974. World Cup Football Championships, West Germany (2nd issue).
1506 **789** 40c. multicoloured . . . 50 50

1974. Birth Centenary of Raul Pederneiras (lawyer, author and artist).
1508 **791** 40c. black & yell on brn 20 20

792 Emblem and Seascape

1974. 13th Int Union of Building Societies and Savings Associations Congress, Rio de Janeiro.
1509 **792** 1cr.30 multicoloured . . 75 60

794 "UPU" on World Map

1974. Centenary of U.P.U.
1511 **794** 2cr.50 black and blue . . 7·00 3·50

795 Aruak Hammock

1974. "Popular Culture".
1512 **795** 50c. purple 75 30
1513 – 50c. light blue and blue 1·25 30
1514 – 50c. brown, red & yellow 40 30
1515 – 50c. brown and yellow 50 30
DESIGNS—SQUARE: No. 1513, Bilro Lace. VERT: (24 × 37 mm), No. 1514, Guitar player (folk literature); 1515, Horseman (statuette by Vitalino).

796 Coffee Beans

1974. Bicentenary of City of Campinas.
1516 **796** 50c. multicoloured . . . 90 50

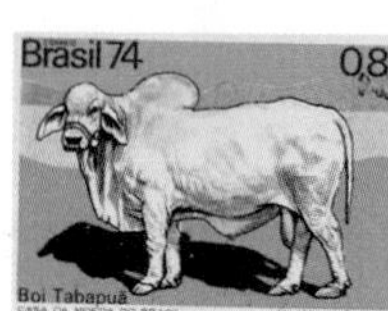

797 Hornless Tabapua

1974. Domestic Animals. Multicoloured.
1517 80c. Type **797** 95 60
1518 1cr.30 Creole horse 90 70
1519 2cr.50 Brazilian mastiff . . 9·00 1·75

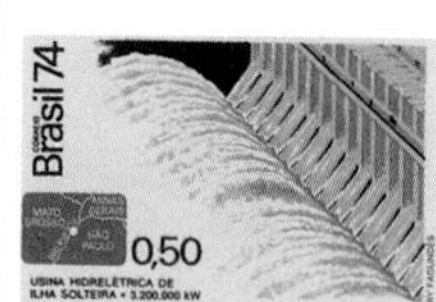

798 Ilha Solteira Dam
799 Herald Angel

1974. Ilha Solteira Hydro-electric Power Project.
1520 **798** 50c. brown, grey & yell 65 20

1974. Christmas.
1521 **799** 50c. multicoloured . . . 30 15

800 "The Girls" (Carlos Reis)
802 Athlete

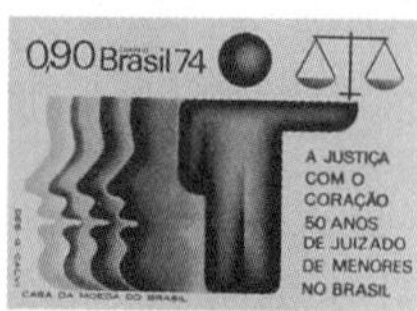

801 "Justice for Juveniles"

1974. "Lubrapex 74" Stamp Exhibition, Sao Paulo (2nd issue).
1522 **800** 1cr.30 multicoloured . . 40 25

1974. 50th Anniv of Brazilian Juvenile Court.
1523 **801** 90c. multicoloured . . . 20 20

1974. 50th Anniv of Sao Silvestre Long-distance Race.
1524 **802** 3cr.30 multicoloured . . 90 55

803 Mounted Newsvendor and Newspaper Masthead

1975. Cent of Newspaper "O Estado de S. Paulo".
1525 **803** 50c. multicoloured . . . 60 30

804 Industrial Complex, Sao Paulo

1975. Economic Resources.
1526 **804** 50c. yellow and blue . . 95 25
1527 – 1cr.40 yellow & brown 60 60
1528 – 4cr.50 yellow & black . . 3·00 25
DESIGNS: 1cr.40 Rubber industry, Acre; 4cr.50, Manganese industry, Amapa.

805 Santa Cruz Fortress, Rio de Janeiro

1975. Colonial Forts. Each brown on yellow.
1529 50c. Type **805** 10 15
1530 50c. Reis Magos Fort, Rio Grande do Norte 30 15
1531 50c. Monte Serrat Fort, Bahia 50 15
1532 90c. Nossa Senhora dos Remedios Fort, Fernando de Noronha 10 25

806 "Palafita" House, Amazonas

1975. Brazilian Architecture. Multicoloured.

No.	Type	Description	Mint	Used
1533		50c. Modern Architecture, Brasilia	1·50	1·50
1534		50c. Modern Architecture, Brasilia (yellow line at left)	16·00	8·00
1535		1cr. Type **806**	30	15
1536		1cr.40 Indian hut, Rondonia (yellow line at left)	3·00	3·00
1537		1cr.40 As No. 1536 but yellow line at right	55	60
1538		3cr.30 "Enxaimel" house, Santa Catarina (yellow line at right)	95	95
1539		3cr.30 As No. 1538 but yellow line at left	4·25	4·25

807 Oscar ("Astronotus ocellatus")

1975. Freshwater Fishes. Multicoloured.

No.	Type	Description	Mint	Used
1540		50c. Type **807**	1·40	25
1541		50c. South American pufferfish ("Colomesus psitacus")	55	35
1542		50c. Tail-spot livebearer ("Phallocerus caudimaculatus")	55	40
1543		50c. Red discus ("Symphysodon discus")	85	35

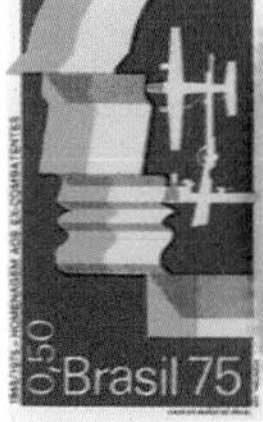

808 Flags forming Serviceman's Head

809 Brazilian Pines

1975. Honouring Ex-Servicemen of Second World War.

No.	Type	Description	Mint	Used
1544	**808**	50c. multicoloured	25	15

1975. Fauna and Flora Preservation. Mult.

No.	Type	Description	Mint	Used
1545		70c. Type **809**	1·60	20
1546		1cr. Giant otter (vert)	1·00	40
1547		3cr.30 Marsh cayman	95	40

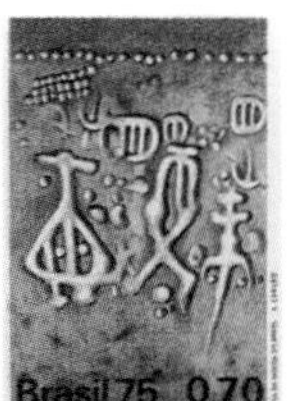

810 Inga Carved Stone, from Paraiba

811 Statue of the Virgin Mary

1975. Archaeology. Multicoloured.

No.	Type	Description	Mint	Used
1548		70c. Type **810**	95	20
1549		1cr. Marajoara pot from Para	25	20
1550		1cr. Fossilized garfish from Ceara (horiz)	30	20

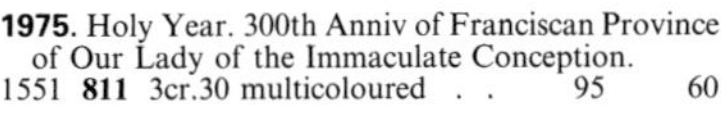
1975. Holy Year. 300th Anniv of Franciscan Province of Our Lady of the Immaculate Conception.

No.	Type	Description	Mint	Used
1551	**811**	3cr.30 multicoloured	95	60

812 Ministry of Communications Building, Rio de Janeiro

813 "Congada" Sword Dance, Minas Gerais

1975. Stamp Day.

No.	Type	Description	Mint	Used
1552	**812**	70c. red	45	15

1975. Folk Dances. Multicoloured.

No.	Type	Description	Mint	Used
1553		70c. Type **813**	25	30
1554		70c. "Frevo" umbrella dance, Pernambuco	25	30
1555		70c. "Warrior" dance, Alagoas	25	30

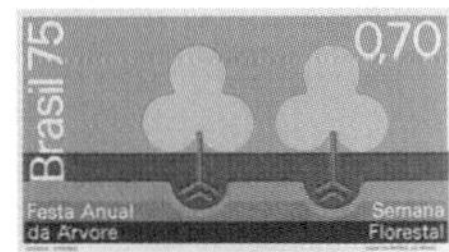

814 Stylized Trees

1975. Tree Festival.

No.	Type	Description	Mint	Used
1556	**814**	70c. multicoloured	25	10

815 Dish Aerial and Globe

816 Woman holding Globe

1975. Inauguration of Tangua Satellite Telecommunications Station.

No.	Type	Description	Mint	Used
1557	**815**	3cr.30 multicoloured	90	60

1975. International Women's Year.

No.	Type	Description	Mint	Used
1558	**816**	3cr.30 multicoloured	1·25	45

817 Tile, Balcony Rail and Memorial Column, Alcantara

1975. Historic Towns. Multicoloured.

No.	Type	Description	Mint	Used
1559		70c. Type **817**	40	25
1560		70c. Belfry, weather vane and jug, Goias (26 × 38 mm)	40	25
1561		70c. Sao Francisco Convent, Sao Cristovao (40 × 22 mm)	40	25

818 Crowd welcoming Walking Book

1975. Day of the Book.

No.	Type	Description	Mint	Used
1562	**818**	70c. multicoloured	20	15

819 ASTA Emblem and Arrows

1975. 45th American Society of Travel Agents Congress.

No.	Type	Description	Mint	Used
1563	**819**	70c. multicoloured	20	15

820 Two Angels

821 Aerial, and Map of America

1975. Christmas.

No.	Type	Description	Mint	Used
1564	**820**	70c. brown and red	15	10

1975. 2nd International Telecommunications Conference, Rio de Janeiro.

No.	Type	Description	Mint	Used
1565	**821**	5cr.20 multicoloured	3·50	1·75

822 Friar Nicodemus

823 People in front of Cross

1975. Obligatory Tax. Leprosy Research Fund.

No.	Type	Description	Mint	Used
1566	**822**	10c. brown	20	10

1975. Thanksgiving Day.

No.	Type	Description	Mint	Used
1567	**823**	70c. turquoise and blue	30	25

824 Emperor Pedro II in Naval Uniform (after P. P. da Silva Manuel)

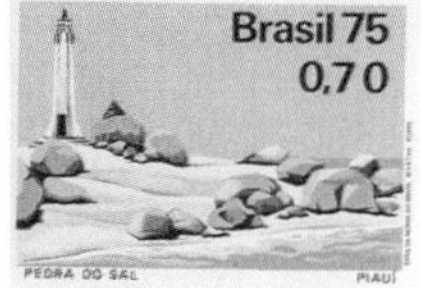

825 Sal Stone Beach, Piaui

1975. 150th Birth Anniv of Emperor Pedro II.

No.	Type	Description	Mint	Used
1568	**824**	70c. brown	40	20

1975. Tourism. Multicoloured.

No.	Type	Description	Mint	Used
1569		70c. Type **825**	30	20
1570		70c. Guarapari Beach, Espirito Santo	30	20
1571		70c. Torres Cliffs Rio Grande do Sul	30	20

826 Triple Jump

1975. 7th Pan-American Games, Santo Domingo, Dominican Republic.

No.	Type	Description	Mint	Used
1572	**826**	1cr.60 turquoise & black	20	20

827 U.N. Emblem and H.Q. Building, New York

1975. 30th Anniv of United Nations.

No.	Type	Description	Mint	Used
1573	**827**	1cr.30 violet on blue	15	15

828 Light Bulbs and House

1976. "Preservation of Fuel Resources". Mult.

No.	Type	Description	Mint	Used
1574		70c. Type **828**	25	10
1575		70c. Drops of petrol and car	25	10

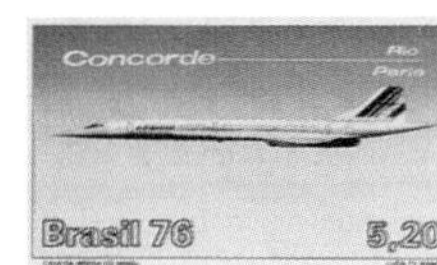

829 Concorde

1976. Concorde's First Commercial Flight, Paris–Rio de Janeiro.

No.	Type	Description	Mint	Used
1576	**829**	5cr.20 black and grey	1·10	40

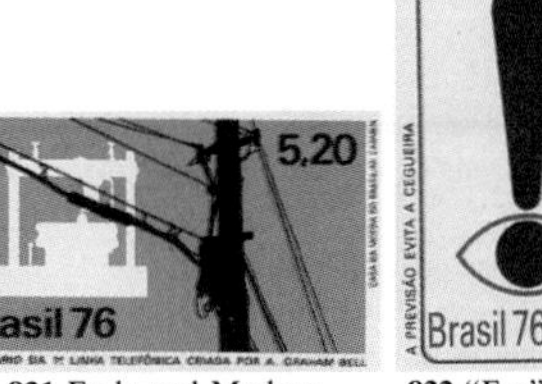

831 Early and Modern Telephone Equipment

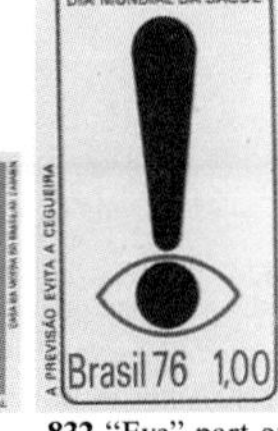

832 "Eye"-part of Exclamation Mark

1976. Telephone Centenary.

No.	Type	Description	Mint	Used
1578	**831**	5cr.20 black & orange	1·25	1·25

1976. World Health Day.

No.	Type	Description	Mint	Used
1579	**832**	1cr. red, brown & violet	30	50

833 Kaiapo Body-painting

834 Itamaraty Palace, Brasilia

1976. Brazil's Indigenous Culture. Mult.

No.	Type	Description	Mint	Used
1580		1cr. Type **833**	20	10
1581		1cr. Bakairi ceremonial mask	20	10
1582		1cr. Karaja feather head-dress	20	10

1976. Diplomats' Day.

No.	Type	Description	Mint	Used
1583	**834**	1cr. multicoloured	35	60

835 "The Sprinkler" (3D composition by J. Tarcisio)

836 Basketball

1976. Modern Brazilian Art. Multicoloured.

No.	Type	Description	Mint	Used
1584		1cr. Type **835**	15	10
1585		1cr. "Beribboned Fingers" (P. Checcacci) (horiz)	15	10

1976. Olympic Games, Montreal.

No.	Type	Description	Mint	Used
1586	**836**	1cr. black and green	10	10
1587	–	1cr.40 black and blue	25	10
1588	–	5cr.20 black and orange	1·25	1·25

DESIGNS: 1cr.40, Olympic yachts; 5cr.20, Judo.

837 Golden Lion-Tamarin

838 Cine Camera on Screen

1976. Nature Protection. Multicoloured.

No.	Type	Description	Mint	Used
1589		1cr. Type **837**	25	20
1590		1cr. Orchid ("Acacallis cyanea")	25	30

1976. Brazilian Cinematograph Industry.

No.	Type	Description	Mint	Used
1591	**838**	1cr. multicoloured	20	10

839 Ox-cart Driver

1976.

No.	Type	Description	Mint	Used
1592	**839**	10c. red	10	10
1593	–	15c. brown	25	10
1594	–	20c. blue	20	10
1595	–	30c. red	20	10
1596	–	40c. orange	20	10
1597a	–	50c. brown	25	10
1598	–	70c. black	15	10
1599	–	80c. green	1·75	10
1600a	–	1cr. black	20	10
1601	–	1cr.10 purple	20	10
1602	–	1cr.30 red	20	10
1603a	–	1cr.80 violet	20	10
1604a	–	2cr. brown	1·50	10
1605	–	2cr.50 brown	25	10
1605a	–	3cr.20 blue	25	10
1606a	–	5cr. lilac	95	10
1607	–	7cr. violet	6·00	10
1608a	–	10cr. green	95	10
1609	–	15cr. green	1·75	10
1610	–	20cr. blue	1·75	10
1611	–	21cr. purple	1·25	10
1612	–	27cr. brown	1·40	10

DESIGNS—HORIZ: 20c. Pirogue fisherman; 40c. Cowboy; 3cr.20, Sao Francisco boatman; 27cr. Muleteer. VERT: 15c. Bahia woman; 30c. Rubber gatherer; 50c. Gaucho; 70c. Women breaking Babacu chestnuts; 80c. Gold-washer; 1cr. Banana gatherer; 1cr.10, Grape harvester; 1cr.30, Coffee harvester; 1cr.80, Carnauba cutter; 2cr. Potter; 2cr.50, Basket maker; 5cr. Sugar-cane cutter; 7cr. Salt worker; 10cr. Fisherman; 15cr. Coconut vendor; 20cr. Lace maker; 21cr. Ramie cutter.

840 Neon Tetra ("Paracheirodon innesi")

1976. Brazilian Freshwater Fishes. Mult.

1613		1cr. Type **840**	50	45
1614		1cr. Splash tetra ("Copeina arnold")	50	45
1615		1cr. Prochilodus ("Prochilodus insignis")	50	45
1616		1cr. Spotted pike cichlid ("Crenicichla lepidota")	50	45
1617		1cr. Bottle-nosed catfish ("Ageneiosus sp.") . . .	50	45
1618		1cr. Reticulated corydoras ("Corydoras reticulatus")	50	45

841 Santa Marta Lighthouse **842** Postage Stamps as Magic Carpet

1976. 300th Anniv of Laguna.

1619	**841**	1cr. blue	40	15

1976. Stamp Day.

1620	**842**	1cr. multicoloured . . .	15	10

843 Oil Lamp and Profile

1976. 50th Anniv of Brazilian Nursing Assn.

1621	**843**	1cr. multicoloured . . .	20	10

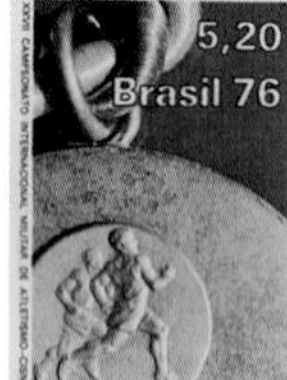

844 Puppet Soldier **845** Winner's Medal

1976. Mamulengo Puppet Theatre. Mult.

1622		1cr. Type **844**	20	15
1623		1cr.30 Puppet girl	20	15
1624		1cr.60 Finger puppets (horiz)	20	15

1976. 27th International Military Athletics Championships, Rio de Janeiro.

1625	**845**	5cr.20 multicoloured . .	45	20

846 Family within "House" **847** Rotten Tree

1976. SESC and SENAC National Organizations for Appenticeship and Welfare.

1626	**846**	1cr. blue	15	10

1976. Conservation of the Environment.

1627	**847**	1cr. multicoloured . . .	15	10

848 Electron Orbits and Atomic Agency Emblem

1976. 20th International Atomic Energy Conference, Rio de Janeiro.

1628	**848**	5cr.20 multicoloured . .	45	25

849 Underground Train **851** School Building

850 St. Francis

1976. Inauguration of Sao Paulo Underground Railway.

1629	**849**	1cr.60 multicoloured . .	45	25

1976. 750th Death Anniv of St. Francis of Assisi.

1630	**850**	5cr.20 multicoloured . .	45	20

1976. Centenary of Ouro Preto Mining School.

1631	**851**	1cr. violet	25	30

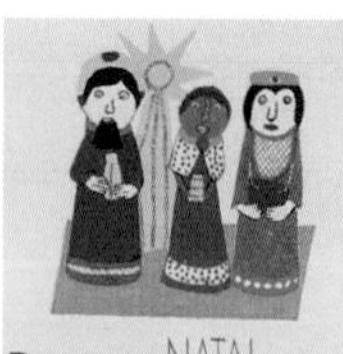

852 "Three Kings" (J. A. da Silva)

1976. Christmas. Multicoloured.

1632		80c. Type **852**	30	20
1633		80c. "Father Christmas" (T. Onivaldo Cogo) . . .	30	20
1634		80c. "Nativity Scene" (R. Yabe)	30	20
1635		80c. "Angels" (E. Folchini)	30	20
1636		80c. "Nativity" (A.L. Cintra)	30	20

854 "Our Lady of Monte Serrat" (Friar A. da Piedade)

1976. Brazilian Sculpture. Multicoloured.

1638		80c. Type **854**	15	10
1639		5cr. "St. Joseph" (unknown artist) (25 × 37 mm) . . .	40	20
1640		5cr.60 "The Dance" (J. Bernardelli) (square)	45	20
1641		6cr.50 "The Caravel" (B. Giorgi) (As 5cr.) . . .	35	20

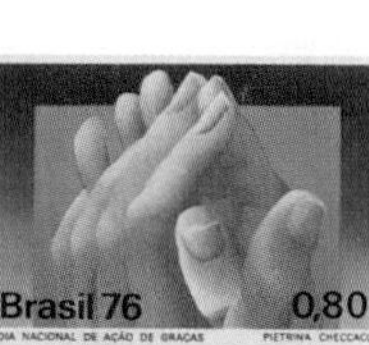

855 Hands in Prayer **856** Sailor of 1840

1976. Thanksgiving Day.

1642	**855**	80c. multicoloured . . .	15	10

1976. Brazilian Navy Commemoration. Mult.

1643		80c. Type **856**	20	10
1644		2cr. Marine of 1808	25	15

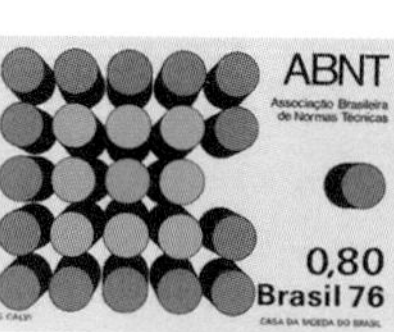

857 "Natural Resources" **858** "Wheel of Life" (wood-carving, G. T. de Oliveira)

1976. Brazilian Bureau of Standards.

1645	**857**	80c. multicoloured . . .	15	10

1977. 2nd World Black and African Festival of Arts and Culture, Lagos (Nigeria). Multicoloured.

1646		5cr. Type **858**	50	20
1647		5cr.60 "The Beggar" (wood-carving, A. dos Santos)	50	20
1648		6cr.50 Benin pectoral mask	90	20

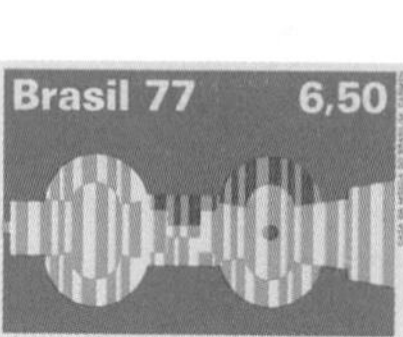

859 Airport Layout **860** Seminar Emblem

1977. Inauguration of Operation of International Airport, Rio de Janeiro.

1649	**859**	6c.50 multicoloured . . .	85	25

1977. 6th InterAmerican Budget Seminar.

1650	**860**	1cr.10 turq, bl & stone	20	10

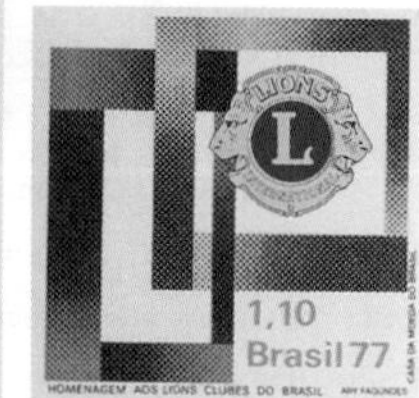

861 Salicylic Acid Crystals **862** Emblem of Lions Clubs

1977. World Rheumatism Year.

1651	**861**	1cr.10 multicoloured . .	20	10

1977. 25th Anniv of Brazilian Lions Clubs.

1652	**862**	1cr.10 multicoloured . .	20	10

863 H. Villa-Lobos and Music

1977. Brazilian Composers. Multicoloured.

1653		1cr.10 Type **863**	25	10
1654		1cr.10 Chiquinha Gonzaga and guitar	25	10
1655		1cr.10 Noel Rosa and guitar	25	10

864 Rural and Urban Workers **865** Memorial, Porto Seguro

1977. Industrial Protection and Safety. Mult.

1656		1cr.10 Type **864**	15	10
1657		1cr.10 Laboratory vessels . .	15	10

1977. Centenary of U.P.U. Membership. Views of Porto Seguro. Multicoloured.

1658		1cr.10 Type **865**	15	10
1659		5cr. Beach	1·25	20
1660		5cr.60 Old houses	55	20
1661		6cr.50 Post Office	50	25

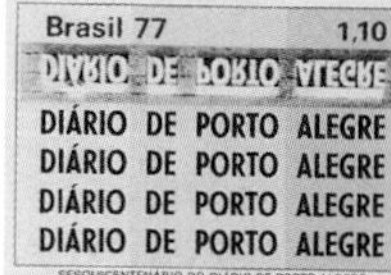

866 Newspaper Title in Linotype and Print

1977. 150th Anniv of Brazilian Newspaper "Diario de Porto Allegre".

1662	**866**	1cr.10 black & purple . .	15	10

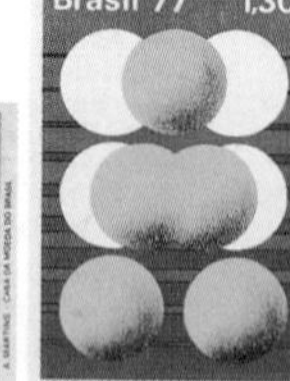

867 Blue Whale **868** "Cell System"

1977. Fauna Preservation.

1663	**867**	1cr.30 multicoloured . .	55	15

1977. 25th Anniv of National Economic Development Bank.

1664	**868**	1cr.30 multicoloured . .	15	10

869 Locomotive leaving Tunnel **870** Goliath Conch

1977. Centenary of Rio de Janeiro–Sao Paulo Railway.

1665	**869**	1c.30 black	60	25

1977. Brazilian Molluscs, Multicoloured.

1666		1cr.30 Type **870**	30	15
1667		1cr.30 Thin-bladed murex ("Murex tenuivaricosus")	30	15
1668		1cr.30 Helmet vase ("Vasum cassiforme")	30	15

871 Caduceus **872** Masonic Symbols

1977. 3rd International Congress of Odontology.

1669	**871**	1cr.30 brown, bis & orge	20	10

1977. 50th Anniv of Brazilian Grand Masonic Lodge.

1670	**872**	1cr.30 blue, dp bl & blk	25	10

873 "Sailboat" **874** Law Proclamation

1977. Stamp Day.

1671	**873**	1cr.30 multicoloured . .	15	10

1977. 150th Anniv of Juridical Courses.

1672	**874**	1cr.30 multicoloured . .	15	10

875 "Cavalhada" (horsemen)   **876** Doubloon

1977. Folklore. Multicoloured.
1673 1cr.30 Type **875** 20 10
1674 1cr.30 Horseman with flag 20 10
1675 1cr.30 Jousting (horiz) . . . 20 10

1977. Brazilian Colonial Coins. Multicoloured.
1676 1cr.30 Type **876** 20 10
1677 1cr.30 Pataca 20 10
1678 1cr.30 Vintem 20 10

877 Toy Windmill   **878** "Neoregelia carolinae"

1977. National Day.
1679 **877** 1cr.30 multicoloured . . 15 10

1977. Nature Conservation.
1680 **878** 1cr.30 multicoloured . . 20 10

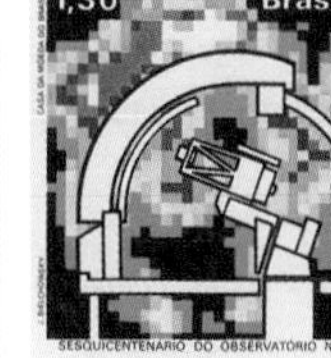

879 Pen, Pencil and Writing   **880** Observatory and Electrochromograph of Supernova

1977. 150th Anniv of Official Elementary Schooling.
1681 **879** 1cr.30 multicoloured . . 15 10

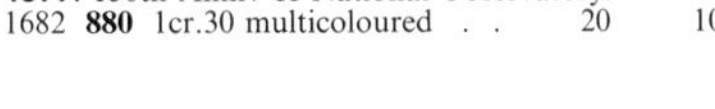

1977. 150th Anniv of National Observatory.
1682 **880** 1cr.30 multicoloured . . 20 10

881 Airship "Pax"   **882** Text from "O Guarani" and Ceci

1977. Aviation Anniversaries. Multicoloured.
1683 1cr.30 Type **881** 20 10
1684 1cr.30 Savoia Marchetti flying boat "Jahu" . . . 20 10

ANNIVERSARIES: No. 1683, 75th anniv of "Pax" flight; 1684, 50th anniv of "Jahu" South Atlantic crossing.

1977. Day of the Book and Jose de Alencar Commemoration.
1685 **882** 1cr.30 multicoloured . . 15 10

883 Radio Waves   **884** Nativity (in carved gourd)

1977. Amateur Radio Operators' Day.
1686 **883** 1cr.30 multicoloured . . 15 10

1977. Christmas. Multicoloured.
1687 1cr.30 Type **884** 15 10
1688 2cr. The Annunciation . . . 25 10
1689 5cr. Nativity 55 15

885 Emerald   **886** Angel holding Cornucopia

1977. "Portucale 77" Thematic Stamp Exhibition. Multicoloured.
1690 1cr.30 Type **885** 20 10
1691 1cr.30 Topaz 20 10
1692 1cr.30 Aquamarine 20 10

1977. Thanksgiving Day.
1693 **886** 1cr.30 multicoloured . . 15 10

887 Curtiss Fledgling Douglas DC-3 and Badge (National Airmail Service)

1977. National Integration. Multicoloured.
1694 1cr.30 Type **887** 30 10
1695 1cr.30 Amazon River naval patrol boat and badge (Amazon Fleet) 50 10
1696 1cr.30 Train crossing bridge and badges (Engineering Corps and Railway Battalion) 75 25

888 Douglas DC-10 and Varig Airline Emblems

1977. 50th Anniv of Varig State Airline.
1697 **888** 1cr.30 black, lt bl & bl 15 10

889 Sts. Cosmus and Damian Church, Igaracu   **890** Woman with Wheat Sheaf

1977. Regional Architecture, Churches. Mult.
1698 2cr.70 Type **889** 20 10
1699 7cr.50 St. Bento Monastery Church, Rio de Janeiro 60 25
1700 8cr.50 St. Francis Assisi Church, Ouro Preto . . . 65 25
1701 9cr.50 St. Anthony Convent Church, Joao Pessoa . . 80 30

1977. Diplomats' Day.
1702 **890** 1cr.30 multicoloured . . 15 10

891 Scene from "Fosca" and Carlos Gomes (composer)   **892** Foot kicking Ball

1978. Bicentenary of La Scala Opera House, Milan, and Carlos Gomes Commemoration.
1703 **891** 1cr.80 multicoloured . . 30 10

1978. World Cup Football Championship, Argentina. Multicoloured.
1704 1cr.80 Type **892** 20 10
1705 1cr.80 Ball in net 20 10
1706 1cr.80 Stylized player with cup 20 10

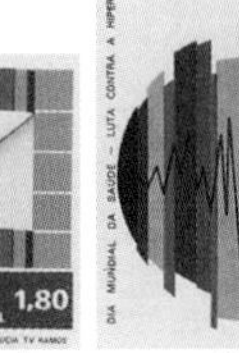

893 "Postal Efficiency"   **894** Electrocardiogram

1978. Postal Staff College.
1707 **893** 1cr.80 multicoloured . . 15 10

1978. World Hypertension Month.
1708 **894** 1cr.80 multicoloured . . 20 10

895 World Map and Antenna   **896** Saffron Finch

1978. World Telecommunications Day.
1709 **895** 1cr.80 multicoloured . . 15 10

1978. Birds. Multicoloured.
1710 7cr.50 Type **896** . . . . . . 1·25 50
1711 8cr.50 Banded cotinga . . . 1·60 60
1712 9cr.50 Seven-coloured tanager . . . . 1·90 85

897 "Discussing the Opening Speech" (G. Mondin)

1978. 85th Anniv of Union Court of Audit.
1713 **897** 1cr.80 multicoloured . . 15 10

898 Post and Telegraph Headquarters, Brasilia

1978. Opening of Post and Telegraph Headquarters.
1714 **898** 1cr.80 multicoloured . . 15 10

899 President Geisel   **900** Savoia Marchetti S-64 and Map

1978. President Geisel Commemoration.
1716 **899** 1cr.80 olive 20 10

1978. 50th Anniv of South Atlantic Flight by del Prete and Ferrarin.
1717 **900** 1cr.80 multicoloured . . 25 10

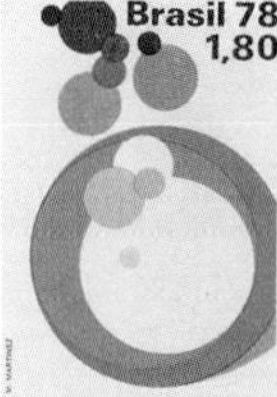

901 "Smallpox"   **902** 10r. Pedro II "White Beard" Stamp of 1878

1978. Global Eradication of Smallpox.
1718 **901** 1cr.80 multicoloured . . 20 10

1978. Stamp Day.
1719 **902** 1cr.80 multicoloured . . 15 10

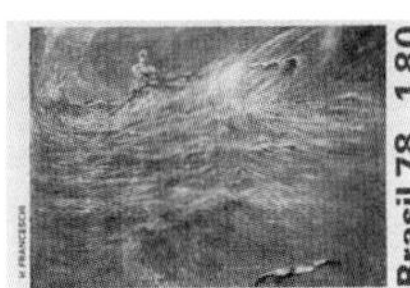

903 "Jangadeiros"

1978. Birth Centenary of Helios Seelinger (painter).
1720 **903** 1cr.80 multicoloured . . 15 10

904 Musicians with Violas

1978. Folk Musicians. Multicoloured.
1721 1cr.80 Type **904** 20 10
1722 1cr.80 Two fife players . . . 20 10
1723 1cr.80 Berimbau players . . 20 10

905 Children playing Football

1978. National Week.
1724 **905** 1cr.80 multicoloured . . 20 10

906 Patio de Colegio Church

1978. Restoration of Patio de Colegio Church, Sao Paulo.
1725 **906** 1cr.80 brown 15 10

907 "Justice" (A. Ceschiatti)

1978. 150th Anniv of Federal Supreme Court.
1726 **907** 1cr.80 black and bistre 15 10

908 Ipe (flowering tree)

1978. Environment Protection. Iguacu Falls National Park. Multicoloured.
1727 1cr.80 Type **908** 25 10
1728 1cr.80 Iguacu Falls 25 10

909 Stages of "Intelsat" Assembly

1978. 3rd Assembly. Users of "Intelsat" Telecommunications Satellite.
1729 **909** 1cr.80 multicoloured . . 15 10

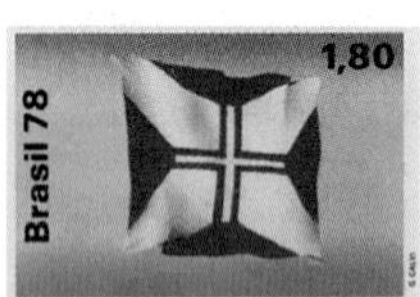
910 Flag of the Order of Christ

1978. "Lubrapex 78" Stamp Exhibition. Flags. Multicoloured.
1730 1cr.80 Type **910** 60 30
1731 1cr.80 Principality of Brazil 60 30
1732 1cr.80 United Kingdom of Brazil 60 30
1733 8cr.50 Empire of Brazil . . 60 30
1734 8cr.50 National Flag of Brazil 60 30

911 Postal Tramcar

1978. 18th U.P.U. Congress, Rio de Janeiro.
1735 **911** 1cr.80 brown, blk & bl 1·10 1·00
1736 – 1cr.80 brown, blk & bl 60 60
1737 – 1cr.80 grey, blk & rose 60 60
1738 – 7cr.50 grey, blk & rose 2·00 1·10
1739 – 8cr.50 brown, blk & grn 1·00 60
1740 – 9cr.50 brown, blk & grn 1·00 60
DESIGNS: No. 1736, Post container truck; 1737, Post van, 1914; 1738, Travelling post office; 1739, Mail coach; 1740, Mule caravan.

912 Gaucho

913 "Morro de Santo Antonio" (Nicolas Antoine Taunay)

1978. Day of the Book and J. Guimaraes Rosa Commemoration.
1741 **912** 1cr.80 multicoloured . . 20 10

1978. Landscape Paintings. Multicoloured.
1742 1cr.80 Type **913** 20 10
1743 1cr.80 "View of Pernambuco" (Frans Post) 20 10
1744 1cr.80 "Morro de Castelo" (Victor Meirelles) 20 10
1745 1cr.80 "Landscape at Sabara" (Alberto da Veiga Guignard) 20 10

914 Angel with Lute

915 "Thanksgiving"

1978. Christmas. Multicoloured.
1746 1cr.80 Type **914** 15 10
1747 1cr.80 Angel with lyre . . . 15 10
1748 1cr.80 Angel with trumpet 15 10

1978. Thanksgiving Day.
1749 **915** 1cr.80 ochre, blk & red 15 10

916 Red Cross Services

1978. 70th Anniv of Brazilian Red Cross.
1750 **916** 1cr.80 red and black . . 15 10

917 Peace Theatre, Belem

918 Underground Trains

1978. Brazilian Theatres. Multicoloured.
1751 10cr.50 Type **917** 50 15
1752 12cr. Jose de Alencar Theatre, Fortaleza 55 20
1753 12cr.50 Rio de Janeiro Municipal Theatre 60 20

1979. Inauguration of Rio de Janeiro Underground Railway.
1754 **918** 2cr.50 multicoloured . . 50 10

919 Old and New Post Offices

1979. 10th Anniv of Post & Telegraph Department and 18th U.P.U. Congress (2nd issue). Multicoloured.
1755 2cr.50 Type **919** 25 15
1756 2cr.50 Mail boxes 25 15
1757 2cr.50 Mail sorting 25 15
1758 2cr.50 Mail planes 25 15
1759 2cr.50 Telegraph and telex machines 25 15
1760 2cr.50 Postmen 25 15

920 "O'Day 23" Class Yacht

1979. "Brasiliana 79" 3rd World Thematic Stamp Exhibition (1st issue). Multicoloured.
1761 2cr.50 Type **920** 25 10
1762 10cr.50 "Penguin" class dinghy 55 20
1763 12cr. "Hobie Cat" class catamaran 55 20
1764 12cr.50 "Snipe" class dinghy 55 25
See Nos. 1773/6 and 1785/90.

921 Joao Bolinha (characters from children's story)

1979. Children's Book Day.
1765 **921** 2cr.50 multicoloured . . 20 10

922 "Victoria amazonica"

1979. 18th U.P.U. Congress (3rd issue). Amazon National Park. Multicoloured.
1766 10cr.50 Type **922** 60 20
1767 12cr. Amazon manatee . . . 65 25
1768 12cr.50 Tortoise 70 25

923 Bank Emblem

1979. 25th Anniv of Northeast Bank of Brazil.
1769 **923** 2cr.50 multicoloured . . 15 10

924 Physicians and Patient (15th cent woodcut)

1979. 150th Anniv of National Academy of Medicine.
1770 **924** 2cr.50 yellow and black 15 10

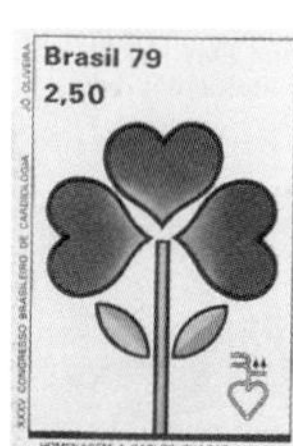
925 Clover with Hearts as Leaves

1979. 35th Brazilian Cardiology Congress.
1771 **925** 2cr.50 multicoloured . . 15 10

927 "Cithaerias aurora"

1979. "Brasiliana 79" (2nd issue). Butterflies. Multicoloured.
1773 2cr.50 Type **927** 30 15
1774 10cr.50 "Evenus regalis" . . 90 25
1775 12cr. "Caligo eurilochus" . . 1·00 35
1776 12cr.50 "Diaethria clymena janeira" . . . . 1·10 40

928 Embraer Xingu

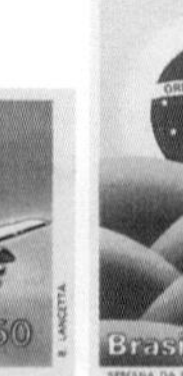
929 Globe illuminating Land

1979. 10th Anniv of Brazilian Aeronautical Industry.
1777 **928** 2cr.50 dp blue and blue 15 10

1979. National Week.
1778 **929** 3cr.20 blue, green & yell 15 10

930 Our Lady Aparecida

931 Envelope and Transport

1979. 75th Anniv of Coronation of Our Lady Aparecida.
1779 **930** 2cr.50 multicoloured . . 15 10

1979. 18th U.P.U. Congress, Rio de Janeiro (4th issue). Multicoloured.
1780 2cr.50 Type **931** 75 30
1781 2cr.50 Post Office emblems 20 10
1782 10cr.50 Globe 35 20
1783 12cr. Flags of Brazil and U.P.U 40 20
1784 12cr.50 U.P.U. emblem . . 40 20

932 "Igreja da Gloria"

933 Pyramid Fountain, Rio de Janeiro

1979. "Brasiliana 79" Third World Thematic Stamp Exhibition (3rd issue). Paintings by Leandro Joaquim. Multicoloured.
1785 2cr.50 Type **932** 15 10
1786 12cr. "Fishing on Guanabara Bay" 35 20
1787 12cr.50 "Boqueirao Lake and Carioca Arches" . . 45 25

1979. "Brasiliana 79" (4th issue). 1st International Exhibition of Classical Philately. Fountains.
1788 **933** 2cr.50 black, grn & emer 10 10
1789 – 10cr.50 black, turq & bl 35 20
1790 – 12cr. black, red and pink 40 25
DESIGNS—VERT: 12cr. Boa Vista, Recife. HORIZ: 10cr.50, Marilia Fountain, Ouro Preto.

934 World Map

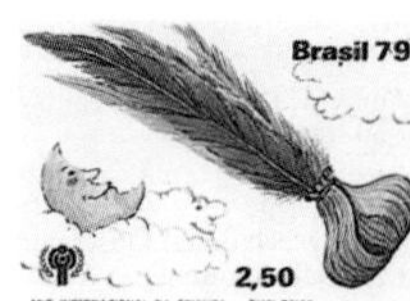
935 "UPU" and Emblem

1979. 3rd World Telecommunications Exhibition, Geneva.
1791 **934** 2cr.50 multicoloured . . 15 10

1979. U.P.U. Day.
1792 **935** 2cr.50 multicoloured . . 15 10
1793 10cr.50 multicoloured . . 35 15
1794 12cr. multicoloured . . . 35 15
1795 12cr.50 multicoloured . . 35 20

936 "Peteca" (shuttlecock)

1979. International Year of the Child. Mult.
1796 2cr.50 Type **936** 20 10
1797 3cr.20 Spinning top 20 10
1798 3cr.20 Jumping Jack 20 10
1799 3cr.20 Rag doll 20 10

937 "The Birth of Jesus"

1979. Christmas. Tiles from the Church of Our Lady of Health and Glory, Salvador. Multicoloured.
1800 3cr.20 Type **937** 15 10
1801 3cr.20 "Adoration of the Kings" 15 10
1802 3cr.20 "The Boy Jesus among the Doctors" . . . 15 10

939 Woman with Wheat

940 Steel Mill

1979. Thanksgiving Day.
1804 **939** 3cr.20 multicoloured . . 15 10

1979. 25th Anniv of Cosipa Steel Works, Sao Paulo.
1805 **940** 3cr.20 multicoloured . . 15 10

941 Plant within Raindrop

942 Coal Trucks

1980. Energy Conservation. Multicoloured.
1806 3cr.20 Type **941** 25 10
1807 17cr.+7cr. Sun and lightbulb 35 10
1808 20cr.+8cr. Windmill and lightbulb 90 55
1809 21cr.+9cr. Dam and lightbulb . . . . 1·50 30

1980. Coal Industry.
1810 **942** 4cr. black, orge & red 65 30

943 Coconuts

1980.
1811 **943** 2cr. brown 15 10
1812 – 3cr. red 15 10
1813 – 4cr. orange 15 10
1814 – 5cr. violet 15 10
1815 – 7cr. orange 35 10
1816 – 10cr. green 15 10
1817 – 12cr. green 10 10
1818 – 15cr. brown 15 10
1819 – 17cr. red 35 10
1820 – 20cr. brown 15 10
1821 – 24cr. orange 90 10
1822 – 30cr. black 90 10
1823 – 34cr. brown . . . . . 5·25 1·25
1824 – 38cr. red . . . . . . 3·50 50
1825 – 42cr. green . . . . . 7·00 1·25
1825a – 45cr. brown 10 10
1826 – 50cr. orange 20 10
1826a – 57cr. brown . . . . . 2·40 60
1826b – 65cr. purple 15 10
1827 – 66cr. violet . . . . . 5·25 1·25
1827a – 80cr. red 90 45
1828 – 100cr. brown 55 10
1828a – 120cr. blue 20 10
1829 – 140cr. red . . . . . 7·00 60
1829a – 150cr. green 20 10
1830 – 200cr. green . . . . . 1·75 10
1830a – 300cr. purple . . . . . 2·40 10
1831 – 500cr. brown . . . . . 2·40 10
1832 – 800cr. green . . . . . 1·75 10
1833 – 1000cr. olive . . . . . 1·75 10
1834 – 2000cr. orange . . . . . 2·40 10

DESIGNS: 3cr. Mangoes; 4cr. Corn; 5cr. Onions; 7cr. Oranges; 10cr. Passion fruit; 12cr. Pineapple; 15cr. Bananas; 17cr. Guarana; 20cr. Sugar cane; 24cr. Bee and honeycomb; 30cr. Silkworm and mulberry; 34cr. Cocoa beans; 38cr. Coffee; 42cr. Soya bean; 45cr. Manioc; 50cr. Wheat; 57cr. Peanuts; 65cr. Rubber; 66cr. Grapes; 80cr. Brazil nuts; 100cr. Cashews; 120cr. Rice; 140cr. Tomatoes; 150cr. Eucalyptus; 200cr. Castor-oil bean; 300cr. Parana pine; 500cr. Cotton; 800cr. Carnauba palm; 1000cr. Babassu palm; 2000cr. Sunflower.

944 Banknote with Development Symbols

1980. 21st Inter-American Bank of Development Directors' Annual Assembly Meeting, Rio de Janeiro.
1836 **944** 4cr. blue, brown & blk 15 10

945 Tapirape Mask

1980. Indian Art. Ritual Masks. Mult.
1837 4cr. Type **945** 20 10
1838 4cr. Tukuna mask (vert) . . 20 10
1839 4cr. Kanela mask (vert) . . 20 10

946 Geometric Head

947 Duke of Caxias (after Miranda Junior)

1980. 30th Anniv of Brazilian Television.
1840 **946** 4cr. multicoloured . . . 15 10

1980. Death Centenary of Duke de Caxias (General and statesman).
1841 **947** 4cr. multicoloured . . . 15 10

948 "The Labourer" (Candido Portinari)

1980. Art in Brazilian Museums. Mult.
1842 24cr. Type **948** 75 25
1843 28cr. "Mademoiselle Pogany" (statuette, Constantin Brancusi) . . 75 25
1844 30cr. "The Glass of Water" (A. de Figueiredo) 95 30

MUSEUMS. 24cr. Sao Paulo Museum of Art. 28cr. Rio de Janeiro Museum of Modern Art. 30cr. Rio de Janeiro Museum of Fine Art.

949 "Graf Zeppelin" flying through "50"

1980. 50th Annivs of "Graf Zeppelin" and First South Atlantic Air Mail Flight.
1845 **949** 4cr. black, blue & violet 20 15
1846 – 4cr. multicoloured . . . 20 15

DESIGN: No. 1846, Latecoere seaplane "Comte de la Vaulx".

951 Pope John Paul II and Fortaleza Cathedral

952 Shooting

1980. Papal Visit and 10th National Eucharistic Congress. Pope John Paul II and cathedrals. Multicoloured.
1848 4cr. Type **951** 25 15
1849 4cr. St. Peter's, Rome (horiz) 25 15
1850 24cr. Apericida (horiz) . . . 65 40
1851 28cr. Rio de Janeiro (horiz) 65 20
1852 30cr. Brasilia (horiz) . . . . 1·50 25

1980. Olympic Games, Moscow. Mult.
1853 4cr. Type **952** 20 10
1854 4cr. Cycling 20 10
1855 4cr. Rowing 20 10

953 Classroom

1980. Rondon Project (voluntary student work in rural areas).
1856 **953** 4cr. multicoloured . . . 20 10

954 Helen Keller and Anne Sullivan

956 Houses and Microscope

1980. Birth Centenary of Helen Keller, and 4th Brazilian Congress on Prevention of Blindness, Belo Horizonte.
1857 **954** 4cr. multicoloured . . . 20 10

1980. National Health Day. Campaign against Chagas Disease (barber bug fever).
1859 **956** 4cr. multicoloured . . . 20 10

957 Communications Equipment

1980. 15th Anniv of National Telecommunications System.
1860 **957** 5cr. stone, blue & green 20 10

959 "Cattleya amethystoglossa"

960 Vinaceous Amazon

1980. "Espamer 80" International Stamp Exhibition, Madrid. Orchids. Multicoloured.
1862 5cr. Type **959** 30 10
1863 5cr. "Laelia cinnabarina" 30 10
1864 24cr. "Zygopetalum crinitum" . . . . 1·75 35
1865 28cr. "Laelia tenebrosa" . . 1·75 40

1980. "Lubrapex 80" Portuguese–Brazilian Stamp Exhibition, Lisbon. Parrots. Multicoloured.
1866 5cr. Type **960** 60 40
1867 5cr. Red-tailed amazon . . 60 40
1868 28cr. Red-spectacled amazon 3·00 1·00
1869 28cr. Brown backed parrotlet . . . . 3·00 1·00

961 Captain Rodrigo (fictional character)

962 Flight into Egypt

1980. Book Day and Erico Verissimo (writer). Commemoration.
1870 **961** 5cr. multicoloured . . . 20 10

1980. Christmas.
1871 **962** 5cr. multicoloured . . . 20 10

963 Wave-form

1980. Inauguration of Telecommunications Centre for Research and Development, Campanas City.
1872 **963** 5cr. multicoloured . . . 20 10

964 Carvalho Viaduct, Paranagua–Curitiba Railway Line

1980. Centenary of Engineering Club.
1873 **964** 5cr. multicoloured . . . 45 25

965 Postal Chessboard

966 Sun and Wheat

1980. Postal Chess.
1874 **965** 5cr. multicoloured . . . 55 20

1980. Thanksgiving Day.
1875 **966** 5cr. multicoloured . . . 20 15

967 Father Anchieta writing Poem in Sand

1980. Beatification of Father Jose de Anchieta.
1876 **967** 5cr. multicoloured . . . 20 10

968 Christ on the Mount of Olives

1980. 250th Birth Anniv of Antonio Lisboa (Aleijadinho) (sculptor). Wood sculptures of Christ's head. Multicoloured.
1877 5cr. Type **968** 30 30
1878 5cr. The Arrest in the Garden 30 30
1879 5cr. Flagellation 30 30
1880 5cr. Wearing Crown of Thorns 30 30
1881 5cr. Carrying the cross . . . 30 30
1882 5cr. Crucifixion 30 30

969 Agricultural Produce

1981. Agricultural Development. Mult.
1883 30cr. Type **969** . . . . . . 1·25 25
1884 35cr. Shopping 80 30
1885 40cr. Exporting 80 30

970 Scout sitting by Camp Fire

1981. 4th Pan-American Jamboree. Multicoloured.
1886 5cr. Type **970** 25 10
1887 5cr. Troop cooking 25 10
1888 5cr. Scout with totem pole . . 25 10

973 Lima Barreto and Rio de Janeiro Street Scene

1981. Birth Centenary of Lima Barreto (author).
1891 **973** 7cr. multicoloured . . . 60 25

974 Tupi-Guarani Ceramic Funeral Urn

1981. Artefacts from Brazilian Museums. Mult.
1892 7cr. Type **974** (Archaeology and Popular Arts Museum, Paranagua) . . 20 15
1893 7cr. Marajoara "tanga" ceramic loincloth (Emilio Goeldi Museum, Para) . . 20 15
1894 7cr. Maraca tribe funeral urn (National Museum, Rio de Janeiro) 20 15

975 Ruby-topaz Hummingbird

1981. Hummingbirds. Multicoloured.
1895 7cr. Type **975** . . . . 1·00 25
1896 7cr. Horned sungem . . . . 1·00 25
1897 7cr. Frilled coquette . . . . 1·00 25
1898 7cr. Planalto hermit . . . . 1·00 25

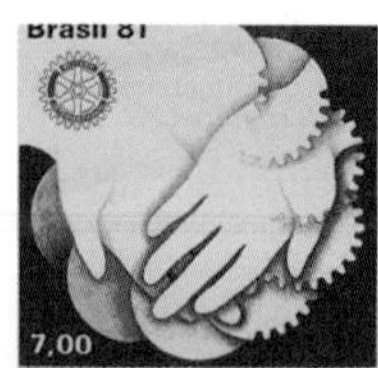

976 Hands and Cogwheels

1981. 72nd Int Rotary Convention, Sao Paulo.
1899 **976** 7cr. red and black . . . 15 10
1900 – 35cr. multicoloured . . . 1·50 60
DESIGN: 35cr. Head and cogwheels.

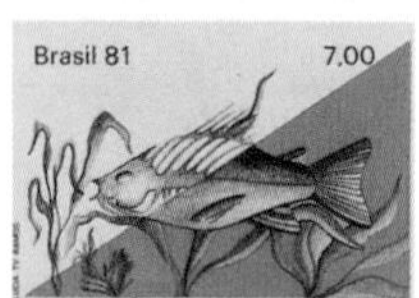

977 "Protection of the Water"

1981. Environment Protection. Multicoloured.
1901 7cr. Type **977** 25 15
1902 7cr. "Protection of the forests" 25 15
1903 7cr. "Protection of the air" 25 15
1904 7cr. "Protection of the soil" 25 15

978 Curtiss Fledgling

1981. 50th Anniv of National Air Mail Service.
1905 **978** 7cr. multicoloured . . . 20 10

979 Locomotive "Colonel Church" and Map of Railway

1981. 50th Anniv of Madeira–Mamore Railway Nationalization.
1906 **979** 7cr. multicoloured . . . 55 30

980 Esperanto Star and Arches of Alvorada Governmental Palace, Brasilia

1981. 66th World Esperanto Congress, Brasilia.
1907 **980** 7cr. green, grey & black 15 10

981 Pedro II and 50r. "Small Head" Stamp

1981. Cent of Pedro II "Small Head" Stamps.
1908 **981** 50cr. brown, blk & bl . . 1·10 25
1909 – 55cr. mauve and green 1·10 25
1910 – 60cr. blue, black & orge 95 30
DESIGNS: 55cr. Pedro II and 100r. "Small Head" stamp; 60r. Pedro II and 200r. "Small Head" stamp.

982 Military Institute of Engineering

1981. 50th Anniv of Military Institute of Engineering.
1911 **982** 12cr. multicoloured . . . 15 10

983 Caboclinhos Folkdance

1981. Festivities. Multicoloured.
1912 50cr. Type **983** 90 15
1913 55cr. Marujada folk festival 90 15
1914 60cr. Resado parade 90 20

984 Sun and Erect, Drooping, and Supported Flowers

1981. International Year of Disabled Persons.
1915 **984** 12cr. multicoloured . . . 20 10

985 "Dalechampia caperoniodes" **986** Image of Our Lady of Nazareth

1981. Flowers of the Central Plateau. Multicoloured.
1916 12cr. Type **985** 20 15
1917 12cr. "Palicourea rigida" . . 20 15
1918 12cr. "Eremanthus sphaerocephalus"(vert) . . 20 15
1919 12cr. "Cassia clausseni" (vert) 20 15

1981. Festival of Our Lady of Nazareth, Belem.
1920 **986** 12cr. multicoloured . . . 15 10

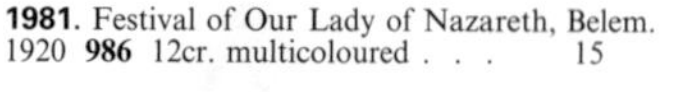

987 Christ the Redeemer Monument **988** Farmhands seeding the Land

1981. 50th Anniv of Christ the Redeemer Monument, Rio de Janeiro.
1921 **987** 12cr. multicoloured . . . 15 10

1981. World Food Day.
1922 **988** 12cr. multicoloured . . . 15 10

989 Santos Dumont and Biplane "14 bis" landing at Paris

1981. 75th Anniv of Santos Dumont's First Powered Flight.
1923 **989** 60cr. multicoloured . . . 75 20

990 Friar Santos Rita Durao, Title Page and Scene from "Caramuru"

1981. Book Day and Bicentenary of Publication of Epic Poem "Caramuru".
1924 **990** 12cr. multicoloured . . . 15 10

991 Crib, Juazeiro de Norte (Cica)

1981. Christmas. Various designs showing Cribs. Multicoloured.
1925 12cr. Type **991** 15 10
1926 50cr. Caruaru (Vitalino Filho) 75 15
1927 55cr. Sao Jose dos Campos (Eugenia) (vert) 75 15
1928 60cr. Taubate (Candida) (vert) . . . . 1·10 20

992 Alagoas

1981. State Flags (1st series). Multicoloured.
1929 12cr. Type **992** 50 50
1930 12cr. Bahia 50 50
1931 12cr. Federal District . . . 50 50
1932 12cr. Pernambuco 50 50
1933 12cr. Sergipe 50 50
See also Nos. 1988/92, 2051/5, 2113/17, 2204/7 and 3043/4.

993 Girls with Wheat **994** Heads and Symbols of Occupations

1981. Thanksgiving Day.
1934 **993** 12cr. multicoloured . . . 15 10

1981. 50th Anniv of Ministry of Labour.
1935 **994** 12cr. multicoloured . . . 15 10

995 Federal Engineering School, Itajuba

1981. Birth Centenary of Theodomiro Carneiro Santiago (founder of Federal Engineering School).
1936 **995** 15cr. green and mauve 15 10

996 Musician of Police Military Band and Headquarters **997** Army Library "Ex Libris"

1981. 150th Anniv of Sao Paulo Military Police. Multicoloured.
1937 12cr. Type **996** 25 10
1938 12cr. Lancers of Ninth of July Regiment, Mounted Police 25 10

1981. Centenary of Army Library.
1939 **997** 12cr. multicoloured . . . 15 10

999 Brigadier Eduardo Gomes

1982. Brigadier Eduardo Gomes Commem.
1941 **999** 12cr. blue and black . . 15 10

1000 Lage, Coal Trucks, "Ita" freighter and HL-1 Airplane

1981. Birth Cent of Henrique Lage (industrialist)
1942 **1000** 17cr. multicoloured . . 1·60 45

1001 Tackle **1002** Microscope, Bacillus and Lung

1982. World Cup Football Championship, Spain. Multicoloured.
1943 75cr. Type **1001** . . . . . . 1·75 50
1944 80cr. Kicking ball . . . . . 1·75 50
1945 85cr. Goalkeeper . . . . . 1·75 50

1982. Centenary of Robert Koch's Discovery of Tubercle Bacillus. Multicoloured.
1947 90cr. Type **1002** . . . . . . 4·25 1·75
1948 100cr. Flasks, tablets, syringe, bacillus and lung 4·25 1·75

1004 Oil Rig Workers

1982. Birth Centenary of Monteiro Lobato (writer).
1950 **1004** 17cr. multicoloured . . 20 10

1005 St. Vincent de Paul

1982. 400th Birth Anniv of St. Vincent de Paul.
1951 **1005** 17cr. multicoloured . . 15 10

1006 Fifth Fall

1982. Guaira's Seven Falls. Multicoloured.
1952 17cr. Type **1006** 20 10
1953 21cr. Seventh fall 25 10

1007 Envelope, Telephone, Antenna and Postcode

1982. 15th Anniv of Ministry of Communications.
1954 **1007** 21cr. multicoloured . . 15 10

1008 The Old Arsenal (National Historical Museum)

1982. 50th Anniv of Museology Course.
1955 **1008** 17cr. black and pink . . 15 10

1009 Cogwheels and Ore Mountains

1982. 40th Anniv of Vale do Rio Doce Company.
1956 **1009** 17cr. multicoloured . . 15 10

1010 Martim Afonso de Souza proclaiming Sao Vicente a Town

1982. 450th Anniv of Sao Vicente.
1957 **1010** 17cr. multicoloured . . 15 10

1011 Giant Anteater

1982. Animals. Multicoloured.
1958 17cr. Type **1011** 40 10
1959 21cr. Maned wolf 90 15
1960 30cr. Pampas deer . . . . . 1·75 25

1012 Film and "Golden Palm"

1014 Church of Our Lady of O, Sabara

1982. 20th Anniv of "Golden Palm" Film Award to "The Given World".
1961 **1012** 17cr. multicoloured . . 20 10

1982. Baroque-style Architecture in Minas Gerais. Multicoloured.
1963 17cr. Type **1014** 55 10
1964 17cr. Church of Our Lady of Carmo, Mariana (horiz) 55 10
1965 17cr. Church of Our Lady of Rosary, Diamantina (horiz) 55 10

1015 St. Francis of Assisi

1016 "Large Head" Stamp of 1882

1982. 800th Birth Anniv of St. Francis of Assisi.
1966 **1015** 21cr. multicoloured . . 15 10

1982. Centenary of Pedro II "Large Head" Stamps.
1967 **1016** 21cr. yellow, brn & blk 15 10

1017 Amazon River and Hands holding Seedling, Screw and Coin

1982. Manaus Free Trade Zone.
1968 **1017** 75cr. multicoloured . . 95 20

1019 Xango

1982. Orixas Religious Costumes. Mult.
1970 20cr. Type **1019** 20 10
1971 20cr. Iemanja 20 10
1972 20cr. Oxumare 20 10

1020 XII Florin

1982. 10th Anniv of Brazilian Central Bank Values Museum. Multicoloured.
1973 25cr. Type **1020** 20 10
1974 25cr. Pedro I Coronation piece 20 10

1021 "Ipiranga Cry" (Dom Pedro proclaiming independence)

1022 St. Theresa of Jesus

1982. Independence Week.
1975 **1021** 25cr. multicoloured . . 20 10

1982. 400th Death Anniv of St. Theresa of Jesus.
1976 **1022** 85cr. multicoloured . . 2·40 50

1023 Musical Instrument Maker

1024 Embraer Tucano Trainers

1982. "Lubrapex 82" Brazilian–Portuguese Stamp Exhibition, Curitiba. The Paranaense Fandango. Multicoloured.
1977 75cr. Type **1023** . . . . . . 1·75 50
1978 80cr. Dancers . . . . 1·75 50
1979 85cr. Musicians . . . . . . 1·75 50

1982. Aeronautical Industry Day.
1981 **1024** 24cr. multicoloured . . 20 25

1025 Bastos Tigre and Verse from "Saudade"

1982. Day of the Book and Birth Centenary of Bastos Tigre (poet).
1982 **1025** 24cr. multicoloured . . 15 10

1026 Telephone Dial on Map of Brazil

1982. 10th Anniv of Telebras (Brazilian Telecommunications Corporation).
1983 **1026** 24cr. multicoloured . . 15 10

1027 "Nativity" (C.S. Miyaba)

1982. Christmas. Children's Paintings. Mult.
1984 24cr. Type **1027** . . . . . . 1·25 10
1985 24cr. "Choir of Angels" (N. N. Aleluia) . . . . . 1·25 10
1986 30cr. "Holy Family" (F. T. Filho) . . . . 1·25 15
1987 30cr. "Nativity with Angel" (N. Arand) . . . . 1·25 15

1982. State Flags (2nd series). As T **992**. Mult.
1988 24cr. Ceara . . . . 1·75 60
1989 24cr. Espirito Santo . . . . 1·75 60
1990 24cr. Paraiba . . . . 1·75 60
1991 24cr. Rio Grande do Norte 1·75 60
1992 24cr. Rondonia . . . . . . 1·75 60

1028 "Germination"

1029 "Efeta" (S. Tempel)

1982. Thanksgiving Day.
1993 **1028** 24cr. multicoloured . . 50 10

1982. The Hard of Hearing.
1994 **1029** 24cr. multicoloured . . 15 10

1030 "Benjamin Constant" (cadet ship)

1982. Bicentenary of Naval Academy. Mult.
1995 24cr. Type **1030** 85 25
1996 24cr. "Almirante Saldanha" (cadet ship) 85 25
1997 24cr. "Brasil" (training frigate) 85 25

1032 Samba Parade Drummers

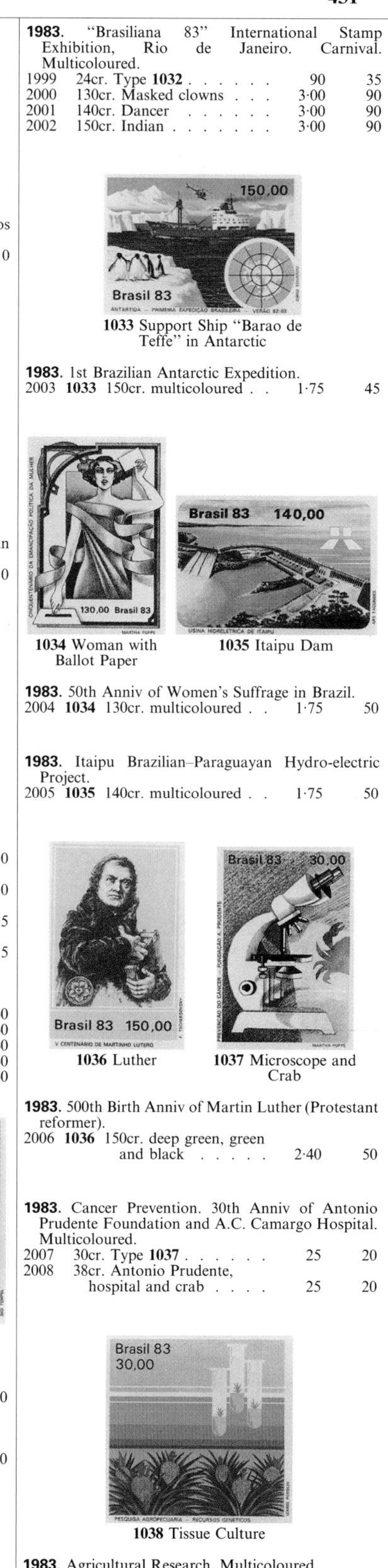

1983. "Brasiliana 83" International Stamp Exhibition, Rio de Janeiro. Carnival. Multicoloured.
1999 24cr. Type **1032** 90 35
2000 130cr. Masked clowns . . . 3·00 90
2001 140cr. Dancer . . . . . . 3·00 90
2002 150cr. Indian . . . . 3·00 90

1033 Support Ship "Barao de Teffe" in Antarctic

1983. 1st Brazilian Antarctic Expedition.
2003 **1033** 150cr. multicoloured . . 1·75 45

1034 Woman with Ballot Paper

1035 Itaipu Dam

1983. 50th Anniv of Women's Suffrage in Brazil.
2004 **1034** 130cr. multicoloured . . 1·75 50

1983. Itaipu Brazilian–Paraguayan Hydro-electric Project.
2005 **1035** 140cr. multicoloured . . 1·75 50

1036 Luther

1037 Microscope and Crab

1983. 500th Birth Anniv of Martin Luther (Protestant reformer).
2006 **1036** 150cr. deep green, green and black . . . . . 2·40 50

1983. Cancer Prevention. 30th Anniv of Antonio Prudente Foundation and A.C. Camargo Hospital. Multicoloured.
2007 30cr. Type **1037** 25 20
2008 38cr. Antonio Prudente, hospital and crab 25 20

1038 Tissue Culture

1983. Agricultural Research. Multicoloured.
2009 30cr. Type **1038** 20 10
2010 30cr. Brazilian wild chestnut tree 20 10
2011 38cr. Tropical soya beans 20 10

1039 Friar Rogerio Neuhaus before Altar

1040 Council Emblem and World Map

1983. Cent of Ordination of Friar Rogerio Neuhaus.
2012 **1039** 30cr. multicoloured . . 20 10

1983. 30th Anniv of Customs Co-operation Council.
2013 **1040** 30cr. multicoloured . . 20 10

1041 Satellite

1983. World Communications Year.
2014 **1041** 250cr. multicoloured . . 3·50 1·25

1042 Toco Toucan

1983. Toucans. Multicoloured.
2015 30cr. Type **1042** 90 20
2016 185cr. Red-billed toucan . . 3·00 85
2017 205cr. Red-breasted toucan 3·00 90
2018 215cr. Channel-billed toucan 3·00 1·10

1044 Baldwin Locomotive No. 1, 1881 **1045** Basketball Players

1983. Locomotives. Multicoloured.
2020 30cr. Type **1044** 55 30
2021 30cr. Hohenzollern locomotive No. 980, 1875 55 30
2022 38cr. Locomotive No. 1 "Maria Fumaca", 1868 55 30

1983. 9th Women's World Basketball Championship, Sao Paulo.
2023 30cr. Type **1045** 25 10
2024 30cr. Basketball players (different) 25 10

1046 Bolivar (after Tito Salas)

1983. Birth Bicentenary of Simon Bolivar.
2025 **1046** 30cr. multicoloured . . 20 10

1047 Boy with Kite and Boy waiting for Polio Vaccination **1048** Minerva and Computer Punched Tape

1983. Polio and Measles Vaccination Campaign. Multicoloured.
2026 30cr. Type **1047** 30 10
2027 30cr. Girl on bicycle and girl receiving measles vaccination 30 10

1983. 20th Anniv of Post-graduate Master's Programmes in Engineering.
2028 **1048** 30cr. light brown, blue and brown 20 10

1049 30r. "Bulls Eye" Stamp and Rio de Janeiro Bay

1983. "Brasiliana 83" International Stamp Exhibition, Rio de Janeiro. 140th Anniv of "Bull's Eye" Stamps.
2029 **1049** 185cr. black and blue 1·50 90
2030 – 205cr. black and blue 1·50 90
2031 – 215cr. black and violet 1·50 90
DESIGNS: Nos. 2030/1, As Type **1049** but showing 60r. and 90r. "Bull's Eye" stamp respectively.

1052 Embraer EMB-120

1983. Brazilian Aeronautics Industry.
2035 **1052** 30cr. multicoloured . . 25 10

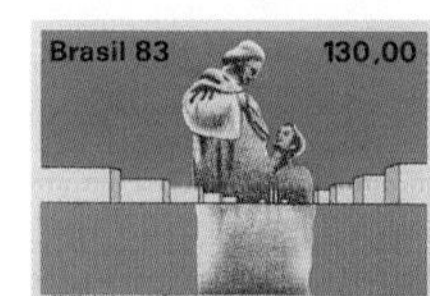

1053 Bosco and State Departments Esplanade, Brasilia

1983. Dom Bosco's Dream of Brazil.
2036 **1053** 130cr. multicoloured . . 75 10

1054 "Council of State decides on Independence" (detail, Georgina de Albuquerque)

1983. National Week.
2037 **1054** 50cr. multicoloured . . 15 10

1055 Iron and Steel Production

1983. 10th Anniv of Siderbras (Brazilian Steel Corporation).
2038 **1055** 45cr. multicoloured . . 15 10

1056 "Pilosocereus gounellei"

1983. Cacti. Multicoloured.
2039 45cr. Type **1056** 95 10
2040 45cr. "Melocactus bahiensis" 95 10
2041 57cr. "Cereus jamacari" . . 95 10

1057 Monstrance **1058** Mouth and Wheat

1983. 50th Anniv of National Eucharistic Congress.
2042 **1057** 45cr. multicoloured . . 15 10

1983. 20th Anniv of World Food Programme. Fishery Resources. Multicoloured.
2043 45cr. Type **1058** 20 15
2044 57cr. Fish and fishing pirogue 80 15

1060 "Our Lady of Angels" (wood, Franisco Xavier de Brito)

1983. Christmas. Statues of the Madonna. Multicoloured.
2046 45cr. Type **1060** 90 10
2047 315cr. "Our Lady of Birth" 2·75 90
2048 335cr. "Our Lady of Joy" (fired clay, Agostinho de Jesus) . . . . 2·75 90
2049 345cr. "Our Lady of Presentation" . . . . . . 2·75 90

1061 Moraes and Map of Italian Campaign

1983. Birth Centenary of Marshal Mascarenhas de Moraes.
2050 **1061** 45cr. pink, green & pur 20 15

1983. State Flags (3rd series). As Type **992**. Multicoloured.
2051 45cr. Amazonas 90 55
2052 45cr. Goias 90 55
2053 45cr. Rio de Janeiro 90 55
2054 45cr. Mato Grosso do Sul 90 55
2055 45cr. Parana 90 55

1062 Praying Figure and Wheat

1983. Thanksgiving Day.
2056 **1062** 45cr. multicoloured . . 15 10

1063 Friar Vincente Borgard **1064** Montgolfier Balloon

1983. Obligatory Tax. Anti-leprosy Week.
2057 **1063** 10cr. brown . . . . . 2·75 90

1983. Bicentenary of Manned Flight.
2058 **1064** 345cr. multicoloured . . 4·25 2·40

1065 Indian, Portuguese Navigator and Negro

1984. 50th Anniv of Publication of "Masters and Slaves" by Gilberto Freyre.
2059 **1065** 45cr. multicoloured . . 60 10

1066 Crystal Palace

1984. Centenary of Crystal Palace, Petropolis.
2060 **1066** 45cr. multicoloured . . 25 10

1068 "Don Afonso" (sail/steam warship) and Figurehead

1984. Cent of Naval Oceanographic Museum.
2062 **1068** 620cr. multicoloured . . 1·25 35

1069 Manacled Hands and Beached Fishing Pirogue

1984. Centenary of Abolition of Slavery in Ceara and Amazonas. Multicoloured.
2063 585cr. Type **1069** . . . . . 1·75 90
2064 610cr. Emancipated slave . . 1·75 90

1071 Long Jumping

1984. Olympic Games, Los Angeles. Mult.
2066 65cr. Type **1071** 90 50
2067 65cr. 100 metres 90 50
2068 65cr. Relay 90 50
2069 585cr. Pole vaulting 90 75
2070 610cr. High jumping 90 75
2071 620cr. Hurdling 90 75

1072 Oil Rigs and Blast Furnace **1073** Pedro Alvares Cabral

1984. Birth Cent (1983) of Getulio Vargas (President 1930–45 and 1951–54). Multicoloured.
2072 65cr. Type **1072** 15 10
2073 65cr. Ballot boxes and symbols of professions and trades 15 10
2074 65cr. Sugar refinery and electricity pylons 15 10

1984. "Espana 84" International Stamp Exhibition, Madrid. Explorers. Multicoloured.
2075 65cr. Type **1073** 15 10
2076 61cr. Christopher Columbus . . . . 1·75 20

1074 Heads and Map of Americas

1075 Chinese Painting

1984. 8th Pan-American Surety Association General Assembly.
2077 **1074** 65cr. multicoloured . . 15 10

1984. "Lubrapex 84" Brazilian-Portuguese Stamp Exhibition, Lisbon.
2078 **1075** 65cr. multicoloured . . 15 10
2079 – 585cr. multicoloured . . 90 50
2080 – 610cr. multicoloured . . 90 50
2081 – 620cr. multicoloured . . 90 50
DESIGNS: 585 to 620cr. Chinese paintings from Mariana Cathedral.

1077 Marsh Deer and Great Egret

1984. Mato Grosso Flood Plain. Multicoloured.
2083 65cr. Type **1077** 80 50
2084 65cr. Jaguar, capybara and roseate spoonbill 80 50
2085 80cr. Alligator, jabiru and red-cowled cardinals . . . 85 55

1078 "The First Letter Sent from Brazil" (Guido Mondin)

1079 Route Map and Dornier Wal Flying Boat

1984. 1st Anniv of Postal Union of the Americas and Spain H.Q., Montevideo, Uruguay.
2086 **1078** 65cr. multicoloured . . 40 15

1984. 50th Anniv of First Trans-Oceanic Air Route. Multicoloured.
2087 610cr. Type **1079** . . . . . 1·60 50
2088 620cr. Support ship "Westfalen" and Dornier Wal . . . . 2·00 45

1080 Mother and Baby

1081 Murrah Buffaloes

1984. Wildlife Preservation. Woolley Spider Monkey. Multicoloured.
2089 65cr. Type **1080** 50 10
2090 80cr. Monkey in tree . . . 25 10

1984. Marajo Island Water Buffaloes. Designs showing different races. Multicoloured.
2091 65cr. Type **1081** 40 30
2092 65cr. Carabao buffaloes . . 40 30
2093 65cr. Mediterranean buffaloes 30 25
Nos. 2091/3 were issued together, se-tenant, forming a composite design.

1082 Headquarters, Salvador

1984. 150th Anniv of Economic Bank.
2094 **1082** 65cr. multicoloured . . 15 10

1083 Da Luz Station, Sao Paulo

1085 Roof protecting Couple

1984. Preservation of Historic Railway Stations. Multicoloured.
2095 65cr. Type **1083** . . . . . . 1·00 35
2096 65cr. Japeri station Rio de Janeiro . . . . 1·00 35
2097 80cr. Sao Joao del Rei station, Minas Gerais . . 1·00 35

1984. 20th Anniv of National Housing Bank.
2099 **1085** 65cr. multicoloured . . 10 10

1086 "Pedro I" (Solano Peixoto Machado)

1984. National Week. Designs showing children's paintings. Multicoloured.
2100 100cr. Type **1086** 15 10
2101 100cr. Girl painting word "BRASIL" (Juruce Maria Klein) 15 10
2102 100cr. Children of different races under rainbow (Priscela Barreto da Fonseca Bara) 15 10
2103 100cr. Caravels (Carlos Peixoto Mangueira) . . . 15 10

1087 Headquarters, Mercury and Cogwheel

1984. 150th Anniv of Rio de Janeiro Commercial Association.
2104 **1087** 100cr. multicoloured . . 15 10

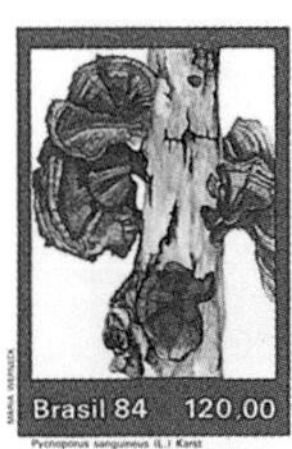

1088 Pedro I

1984. 150th Death Anniv of Emperor Pedro I.
2105 **1088** 1000cr. multicoloured 3·50 1·75

1089 "Pycnoporus sanguineus"

1090 Child stepping from Open Book

1984. Fungi. Multicoloured.
2106 120cr. Type **1089** 40 15
2107 1050cr. "Calvatia" sp. . . . 2·75 60
2108 1080cr. "Pleurotus" sp. (horiz) . . . . 2·75 60

1984. Book Day. Children's Literature.
2109 **1090** 120cr. multicoloured . . 20 10

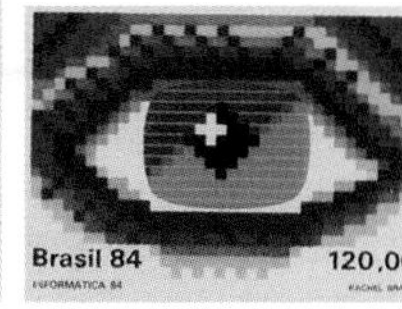

1091 New State Mint and 17th-century Minter

1092 Computer Image of Eye

1984. Inauguration of New State Mint, Santa Cruz, Rio de Janeiro.
2110 **1091** 120cr. blue & deep blue 15 10

1984. "Informatica 84" 17th National Information Congress and 4th International Informatics Fair, Rio de Janeiro.
2111 **1092** 120cr. multicoloured . . 15 10

1093 Sculpture by Bruno Giorgi and Flags

1094 Brasilia Cathedral and Wheat

1984. 14th General Assembly of Organization of American States, Brasilia.
2112 **1093** 120cr. multicoloured . . 15 10

1984. State Flags (4th series). As T **992**.
2113 120cr. red, black & buff . . 90 50
2114 120cr. multicoloured 90 50
2115 120cr. multicoloured 90 50
2116 120cr. multicoloured 90 50
2117 120cr. multicoloured 90 50
DESIGNS: No. 2113, Minas Gerais; 2114, Mato Grosso; 2115, Piaui; 2116, Maranhao; 2117, Santa Catarina.

1984. Thanksgiving Day.
2118 **1094** 120cr. multicoloured . . 15 10

1095 Father Bento Dias Pacheco

1096 "Nativity" (Djanira da Mota e Silva)

1984. Obligatory Tax. Anti-leprosy Week.
2119 **1095** 30cr. blue 50 10
See also Nos. 2208, 2263 and 2291.

1984. Christmas. Paintings from Federal Savings Bank collection. Multicoloured.
2120 120cr. Type **1096** 15 10
2121 120cr. "Virgin and Child" (Glauco Rodrigues) . . . 75 25
2122 1050cr. "Flight into Egypt" (Paul Garfunkel) . . . . 2·75 50
2123 1080cr. "Nativity" (Emiliano Augusto di Cavalcanti) . . 2·75 50

1097 Airbus Industrie A300

1984. 40th Anniv of I.C.A.O.
2124 **1097** 120cr. multicoloured . . 15 10

1098 Symbols of Agriculture and Industry on Hat

1984. 25th Anniv of North-east Development Office.
2125 **1098** 120cr. multicoloured . . 15 10

1099 "Virgin of Safe Journeys Church" (detail)

1985. 77th Death Anniv of Emilio Rouede (artist).
2126 **1099** 120cr. multicoloured . . 20 10

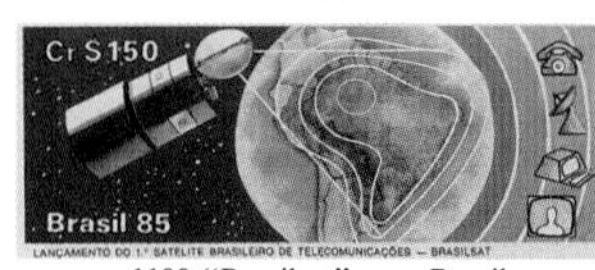

1100 "Brasilsat" over Brazil

1985. Launch of "Brasilsat" (first Brazilian telecommunications satellite).
2127 **1100** 150cr. multicoloured . . 25 10

1101 Electric Trains and Plan of Port Alegre Station

1985. Inauguration of Metropolitan Surface Railway, Recife and Porto Alegre.
2128 **1101** 200cr. multicoloured . . 60 20

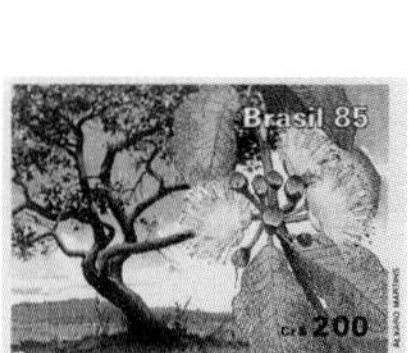

1102 Butternut Tree

1103 Parachutist

1985. Opening of Botanical Gardens, Brasilia.
2129 **1102** 200cr. multicoloured . . 20 10

1985. 40th Anniv of Military Parachuting.
2130 **1103** 200cr. multicoloured . . 20 10

1104 Map, Temperature Graph and Weather Scenes

1985. National Climate Programme.
2131 **1104** 500cr. multicoloured . . 20 10

1105 Campolina

1107 "Polyvolume" (Mary Vieira)

1106 Ouro Preto

1985. Brazilian Horses. Multicoloured.
2132 1000cr. Type **1105** . . . . . 1·25 15
2133 1500cr. Marajoara . . . . . 1·25 15
2134 1500cr. Mangalarga pacer 1·25 15

1985. U.N.E.S.C.O. World Heritage Sites. Multicoloured.
2135 220cr. Type **1106** 15 10
2136 220cr. Sao Miguel das Missoes 15 10
2137 220cr. Olinda 15 10

1985. 40th Anniv of Rio-Branco Institute (diplomatic training academy).
2138 **1107** 220cr. multicoloured . . 10 10

1108 National Theatre

1985. 25th Anniv of Brasilia. Multicoloured.
2139 220cr. Type **1108** 10 10
2140 220cr. Catetinho (home of former President Juscelino Keubitschek) and memorial 10 15

1109 Rondon and Morse Telegraph

1110 Fontoura and Pharmaceutical Equipment

1985. 120th Birth Anniv of Marshal Candido Mariano da Silva Rondon (military engineer and explorer).

2141	**1109**	220cr. multicoloured . .	10	10

1985. Birth Centenary of Candido Fontoura (pharmacist).

2142	**1110**	220cr. multicoloured . .	15	10

1111 Lizards

1112 Numeral

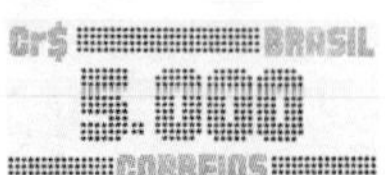

1113 Numeral

1985. Rock Paintings. Multicoloured.

2143	300cr. Type **1111**	10	10
2144	300cr. Deer	10	10
2145	2000cr. Various animals . .	75	15

1985.

2147	**1112**	50cr. red	10	10
2148		100cr. purple	10	10
2149		150cr. lilac	10	10
2150		200cr. blue	10	10
2151		220cr. green	50	10
2152		300cr. blue	10	10
2153		500cr. black	10	10
2154	**1113**	1000cr. brown	10	10
2155		2000cr. green	15	10
2156		3000cr. lilac	15	10
2157		5000cr. brown	1·75	10

1114 Common Noddies

1985. National Marine Park, Abrolhos. Mult.

2168	220cr. Type **1114**	55	35
2169	220cr. Magnificent frigate birds and blue-faced booby	55	35
2170	220cr. Blue-faced boobies and red-billed tropic bird	55	35
2171	2000cr. Grey plovers	2·75	65

1115 Breast-feeding

1116 Bell 47J Ranger Helicopter rescuing Man, "Brasil" (corvette) and Diver

1985. United Nations Children's Fund Child Survival Campaign. Multicoloured.

2172	220cr. Type **1115**	15	10
2173	220cr. Growth chart and oral rehydration	15	10

1985. International Sea Search and Rescue Convention, Rio de Janeiro.

2174	**1116**	220cr. multicoloured . .	1·00	30

1118 Children holding Hands

1119 Hands holding Host

1985. International Youth Year.

2176	**1118**	220cr. multicoloured . .	15	10

1985. 11th Nat Eucharistic Congress, Aparecida.

2177	**1119**	2000cr. multicoloured	75	50

1120 Scene from "Mineiro Blood", Camera and Mauro

1985. 60th Anniv of Humberto Mauro's Cataguases Cycle of Films.

2178	**1120**	300cr. multicoloured . .	15	10

1121 Escola e Sacro Museum

1122 Inconfidencia Museum, Ouro Preto

1985. 400th Anniv of Paraiba State.

2179	**1121**	330cr. multicoloured . .	15	10

1985. Museums. Multicoloured.

2180	300cr. Type **1122**	15	10
2181	300cr. Historical and Diplomatic Museum Itamaraty	15	10

1123 "Cabano" (Guido Mondin)

1124 Aeritalia/Aermacchi AM-X Fighter

1985. 150th Anniv of Cabanagem Insurrection, Belem City.

2182	**1123**	330cr. multicoloured . .	15	10

1985. AM-X (military airplane) Project.

2183	**1124**	330cr. multicoloured . .	15	10

1125 Captain and Crossbowman (early 16th century)

1985. Military Dress. Multicoloured.

2184	300cr. Type **1125**	15	10
2185	300cr. Arquebusier and sergeant (late 16th cent)	15	10
2186	300cr. Musketeer and pikeman (early 17th century)	15	10
2187	300cr. Mulatto fusilier and pikeman with scimitar (early 17th century) . . .	15	10

1126 "Farroupilha Rebels" (Guido Mondin)

1985. 150th Anniv of Farroupilha Revolution.

2188	**1126**	330cr. multicoloured . .	15	10

1127 Itaimbezinho Canyon

1985. Aparados da Serra National Park. Mult.

2189	3100cr. Type **1127**	95	15
2190	3320cr. Mountain range . .	95	15
2191	3480cr. Pine forest	95	15

1128 Neves and Brasilia Buildings

1985. Tancredo Neves (President-elect) Commem.

2192	**1128**	330cr. black & orange	15	10

1129 "FEB" on Envelope

1985. 40th Anniv (1984) of Brazilian Expeditionary Force Postal Service.

2193	**1129**	500cr. multicoloured . .	15	10

1130 "Especuladora", 1835

1985. 150th Anniv of Rio de Janeiro–Niteroi Ferry Service. Multicoloured.

2194	500cr. Type **1130**	70	20
2195	500cr. "Segunda", 1862 . .	70	20
2196	500cr. "Terceira", 1911 . .	70	20
2197	500cr. "Urca", 1981	70	20

1131 Muniz M-7

1985. 50th Anniv of Muniz M-7 Biplane's Maiden Flight.

2198	**1131**	500cr. multicoloured . .	30	15

1132 Dove Emblem and Stylized Flags

1133 Front Page of First Edition

1985. 40th Anniv of U.N.O.

2199	**1132**	500cr. multicoloured . .	15	10

1985. 160th Anniv of "Pernambuco Daily News".

2200	**1133**	500cr. multicoloured . .	15	10

1134 Adoration

1135 Child holding Wheat

1985. Christmas. Multicoloured.

2201	500cr. Type **1134**	15	10
2202	500cr. Adoration of the Magi	15	10
2203	500cr. Flight into Egypt . .	15	10

1985. State Flags (5th series). As T **992**. Mult.

2204	500cr. Para	15	10
2205	500cr. Rio Grande do Sul	15	10
2206	500cr. Acre	15	10
2207	500cr. Sao Paulo	15	10

1985. Obligatory Tax. Anti-leprosy Week.

2208	**1095**	100cr. red	25	25

1985. Thanksgiving Day.

2209	**1135**	500cr. multicoloured . .	10	10

1136 Transport, Mined Ore and Trees

1985. Carajas Development Programme.

2210	**1136**	500cr. multicoloured . .	20	10

1137 Gusmao and Balloons

1985. 300th Birth Anniv of Bartolomeu Lourenco de Gusmao (inventor).

2211	**1137**	500cr. multicoloured . .	10	10

1138 "The Trees"

1985. Birth Centenary of Antonio Francisco da Costa e Silva (poet).

2212	**1138**	500cr. multicoloured . .	10	10

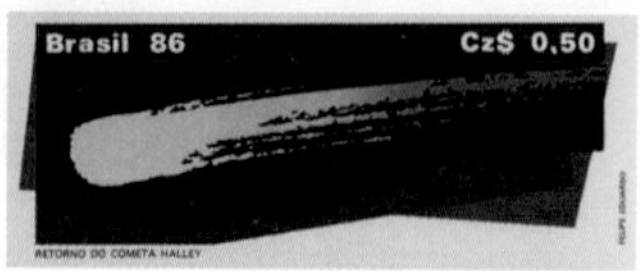

1140 Comet

1986. Appearance of Halley's Comet.

2214	**1140**	50c. multicoloured . . .	35	15

1141 Flags and Station

1142 Symbols of Industry, Agriculture and Commerce

1986. 2nd Anniv of Commander Ferraz Antarctic Station.

2215	**1141**	50c. multicoloured . . .	10	15

1986. Labour Day.

2216	**1142**	50c. multicoloured . . .	10	10

1143 "Maternity" **1144** Broken Chain Links as Birds

1986. 50th Death Anniv of Henrique Bernardelli (artist).
2217 **1143** 50c. multicoloured . . . 10 10

1986. 25th Anniv of Amnesty International.
2218 **1144** 50c. multicoloured . . . 10 10

1145 "Pyrrhopyge ruficauda"

1986. Butterflies. Multicoloured.
2219 50c. Type **1145** 85 30
2220 50c. "Pierriballia mandela molione" 85 30
2221 50c. "Prepona eugenes diluta" 85 30

1146 Gomes Peri, and Score of "O Guarani" **1147** Man in Safety Harness

1986. 150th Birth Anniv of Antonio Carlos Gomes (composer).
2222 **1146** 50c. multicoloured . . . 15 10

1986. Prevention of Industrial Accidents.
2223 **1147** 50c. multicoloured . . . 15 10

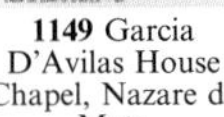

1149 Garcia D'Avilas House Chapel, Nazare de Mata **1150** Kubitschek and Alvorada Palace

1986.

2225	**1149**	10c. green	10	10
2226	–	20c. blue	10	10
2228	–	50c. orange	55	10
2230	–	1cz. brown	10	10
2231	–	2cz. red	10	10
2233	–	5cz. green	10	10
2235	–	10cz. blue	10	10
2236	–	20cz. red	10	10
2238	–	50cz. orange	15	15
2240	–	100cz. green	30	25
2241	–	200cz. blue	10	30
2242	–	500cz. brown	50	10

DESIGNS—HORIZ: 20c. Church of Our Lady of the Assumptiom, Anchieta; 50c. Reis Magos Fortress, Natal; 1cz. Pelourinho, Alcantara; 2cz. St. Francis's Monastery, Olinda; 5cz. St. Anthony's Chapel, Sao Roque; 10cz. St Lawrence of the Indians Church, Niteroi; 20cz. Principe da Beira Fortress, Costa Marques, Rondobua; 100cz. Church of Our Lady of Sorrows, Campanha; 200cz. Counting House, Ouro Preto; 500cz. Customs building, Belem. VERT: 50cz. Church of the Good Jesus, Matasinhos.

1986. 10th Death Anniv of Juscelino Kubitschek (President 1956–61).
2244 **1150** 50c. multicoloured . . . 25 10

1151 Mangabeira and Itamaraty Palace, Rio de Janeiro

1986. Birth Cent of Octavio Mangabeira (politician).
2245 **1151** 50c. multicoloured . . . 10 10

1152 Congress Emblem and Sao Paulo **1153** Microphone and Radio Waves

1986. 8th World Gastroenterology Congress, Sao Paulo.
2246 **1152** 50c. multicoloured . . . 10 10

1986. 50th Annivs. of National Radio and Education and Culture Ministry Radio.
2247 **1153** 50c. multicoloured . . . 10 10

1154 "Peace" (detail, Candido Portinari) **1155** "Urera mitis"

1986. International Peace Year.
2248 **1154** 50c. multicoloured . . . 10 10

1986. Flowers. Multicoloured.
2249 50c. Type **1155** 15 10
2250 6cz.50 "Couroupita guyanensis" 85 20
2251 6cz.90 Mountain ebony (horiz) 90 20

1156 Simoes Filho and Newspaper **1157** Title Page of Gregorio de Matto's MS

1986. Birth Centenary of Ernesto Simoes Filho (politician and founder of "A Tarde").
2252 **1156** 50c. multicoloured . . . 10 10

1986. Book Day. Poets' Birth Anniversaries.
2253 **1157** 50c. brown & lt brown 10 10
2254 – 50c. green and red . . . 10 10
DESIGNS: No. 2253, Type **1157** (350th anniv); 2254, Manuel Bandeira and last verse of "I'll Return to Pasargada" (centenary).

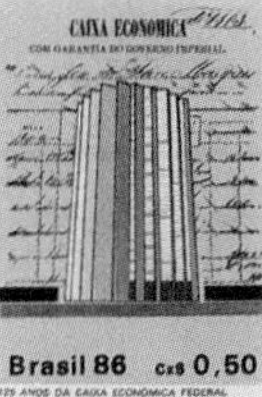

1158 Head Office, Brasilia **1159** Birds around Baby lying in Nest

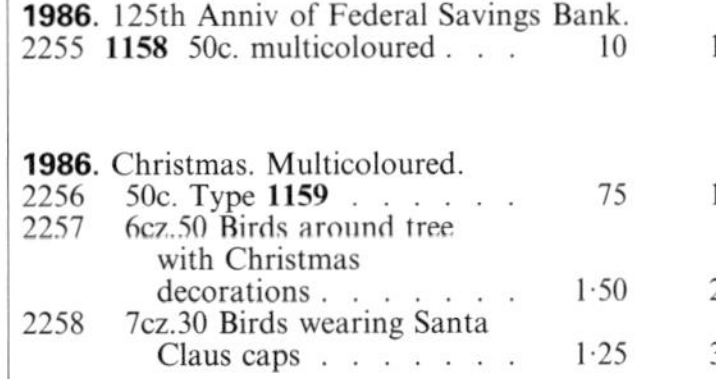

1986. 125th Anniv of Federal Savings Bank.
2255 **1158** 50c. multicoloured . . . 10 10

1986. Christmas. Multicoloured.
2256 50c. Type **1159** 75 15
2257 6cz.50 Birds around tree with Christmas decorations . . . . 1·50 25
2258 7cz.30 Birds wearing Santa Claus caps . . . . 1·25 30

1160 Rocha on Strip of Film **1161** "History of Empress Porcina"

1986. 5th Death Anniv of Glauber Rocha (film producer).
2259 **1160** 50c. multicoloured . . . 10 10

1986. "Lubrapex 86" Brazilian–Portuguese Stamp Exhibition, Rio de Janeiro. Design showing scenes from Cordel Literature. Multicoloured.
2260 6cz.90 Type **1161** 55 40
2261 6cz.90 "Romance of the Mysterious Peacock" . . 55 40

1986. Obligatory Tax. Anti-leprosy Week.
2263 **1095** 10c. brown 10 10

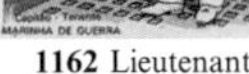

1162 Lieutenant Commander, 1930 **1163** "Graf Zeppelin" over Hangar

1986. Military Uniforms. Multicoloured.
2264 50c. Type **1162** 60 10
2265 50c. Military Aviation flight lieutenant, 1930 . . . . . 10 10

1986. 50th Anniv of Bartolomeu de Gusmao Airport, Santa Cruz.
2266 **1163** 1cz. multicoloured . . . 10 10

1164 Museum

1987. 50th Anniv of National Fine Arts Museum, Rio de Janeiro.
2267 **1164** 1cz. multicoloured . . . 10 10

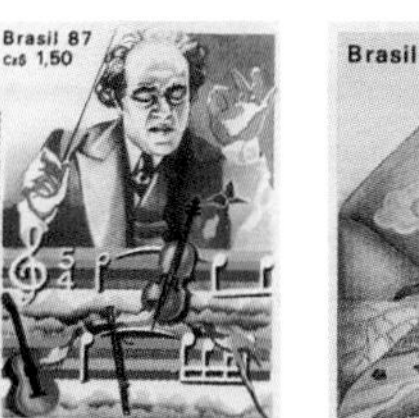

1165 Villa-Lobos conducting and Musical Motifs **1167** Landscape on Open Envelope (Rural Post Office Network)

1166 Flag, Lockheed Hercules Aircraft and Antarctic Landscape

1987. Birth Cent of Heitor Villa-Lobos (composer).
2268 **1165** 1cz.50 multicoloured . . 30 10

1987. Air Force Participation in Brazilian Antarctic Programme.
2269 **1166** 1cz. multicoloured . . . 90 20

1987. Special Mail Services. Multicoloured.
2270 1cz. Type **1167** 10 10
2271 1cz. Satchel and globe (International Express Mail Service) 10 10

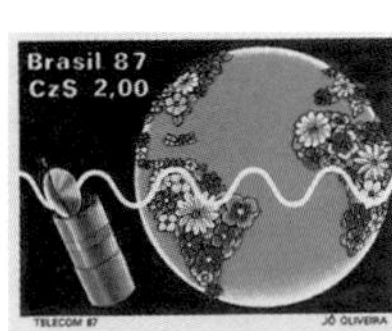

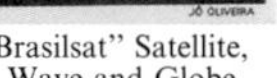

1168 "Brasilsat" Satellite, Radio Wave and Globe **1169** Modern Pentathlon

1987. "Telecom 87" World Telecommunications Exhibition, Geneva.
2272 **1168** 2cz. multicoloured . . . 10 10

1987. 10th Pan-American Games, Indianapolis, U.S.A.
2273 **1169** 18cz. multicoloured . . 1·75 50

1170 Hawksbill Turtle

1987. Endangered Animals. Multicoloured.
2274 2cz. Type **1170** 60 35
2275 2cz. Right whale 60 35

1171 Old and New Court Buildings and Symbol of Justice **1172** Arms

1987. 40th Anniv of Federal Appeal Court.
2276 **1171** 2cz. multicoloured . . . 10 10

1987. Centenary of Military Club.
2277 **1172** 3cz. multicoloured . . . 10 10

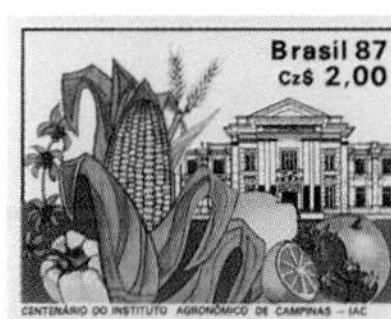

1173 Institute and Foodstuffs

1987. Centenary of Agronomic Institute, Campinas.
2278 **1173** 2cz. multicoloured . . . 10 10

1174 "Fulgora servillei"

1987. 50th Anniv of Brazilian Entomology Society. Multicoloured.
2279 3cz. Type **1174** 60 35
2280 3cz. "Zoolea lopiceps" . . . 60 35

1175 Features of Northern and North-east Regions
1176 Main Tower

1987. National Tourism Year. Multicoloured.
2281 3cz. Type **1175** 50 15
2282 3cz. Features of mid-west, south-east and south regions 10 10

1987. 150th Anniv of Royal Portuguese Reading Cabinet, Rio de Janeiro.
2283 **1176** 30cz. green and red . . 25 20

1177 International Sport Club (1975, 1976, 1979)

1987. Brazilian Football Championship Gold Cup Winners (1st series). Designs showing footballers and Club emblems.
2284 **1177** 3cz. red, black & yellow 35 10
2285 – 3cz. red, yellow & black 35 10
2286 – 3cz. multicoloured . . . 35 10
2287 – 3cz. red, black & yellow 35 10
DESIGNS: No. 2285, Sao Paulo Football Club (1977, 1986); 2286, Guarani Football Club (1978); 2287, Regatas do Flamengo Club (1980, 1982, 1983).
See also Nos. 2322/5, 2398 and 2408.

1178 St. Francis's Church and Tiled Column

1987. 400th Anniv of St. Francis's Monastery, Salvador.
2288 **1178** 4cz. multicoloured . . . 10 10

1179 Almeida and Scenes from "A Bagaceira"

1987. Birth Centenary of Jose Americo de Almeida (writer).
2289 **1179** 4cz. multicoloured . . . 10 10

1180 Barra do Picao

1987. 450th Anniv of Recife.
2290 **1180** 5cz. multicoloured . . . 30 10

1987. Obligatory Tax. Anti-leprosy Week.
2291 **1095** 30cz. green 15 15

1181 Rainbow, Dove and Open Hands

1182 Angels

1987. Thanksgiving Day.
2292 **1181** 5cz. multicoloured . . . 10 10

1987. Christmas. Multicoloured.
2293 6cz. Type **1182** 10 10
2294 6cz. Dancers on stage . . . 10 10
2295 6cz. Shepherd playing flute 10 10

1183 Bernardo Pereira de Vasconcelos (founder) and Pedro II

1987. 150th Anniv of Pedro II School, Rio de Janeiro.
2296 **1183** 6cz. yellow, blk & red 10 10

1184 "Cattleya guttata"

1987. 50th Anniv of Brazilian Orchid Growers Society. Multicoloured.
2297 6cz. Type **1184** 50 10
2298 6cz. "Laelia lobata" 50 10

1185 Statue and Fatima Basilica, Portugal

1987. Marian Year. Visit to Brazil of Statue of Our Lady of Fatima.
2299 **1185** 50cz. multicoloured . . 90 60

1186 Sousa, Indians and Fauna

1987. 400th Anniv of "Descriptive Treaties of Brazil" by Gabriel Soares de Sousa.
2300 **1186** 7cz. multicoloured . . . 40 15

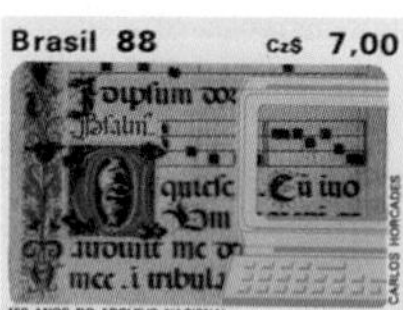

1187 Page from Book of Gregorian Chants and Computer Terminal

1988. 150th Anniv of National Archives.
2301 **1187** 7cz. multicoloured . . . 10 10

1188 National Colours, Caravel and Modern Ship

1988. 180th Anniv of Opening of Brazilian Ports to Free Trade.
2302 **1188** 7cz. multicoloured . . . 10 10

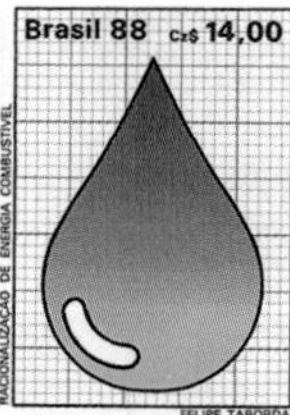

1190 Petrol Droplet

1192 Bonifacio and Emblems of his Life

1988. Energy Conservation. Multicoloured.
2304 14cz. Type **1190** 10 10
2305 14cz. Flash of electricity . . 10 10

1988. 150th Death Anniv of Jose Bonifacio de Andrada e Silva (scientist, writer and "Patriarch of the Independence").
2307 **1192** 20cz. multicoloured . . 10 10

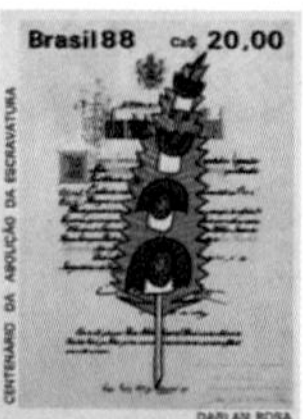

1193 Quill Pen on Page of Aurea Law

1988. Centenary of Abolition of Slavery. Mult.
2308 20cz. Type **1193** 10 10
2309 50cz. Norris map of Africa, 1773, slave ship and plan of trading routes 20 10

1194 Church of the Good Jesus of Matosinhos

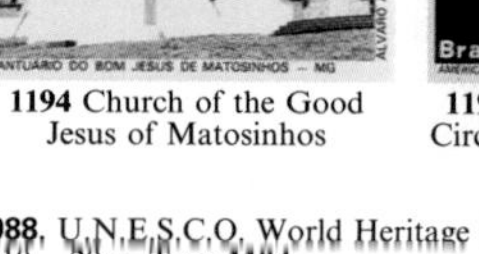

1195 Concentric Circles on Map of Americas

1988. U.N.E.S.C.O. World Heritage Sites. Mult.
2310 20cz. Type **1194** 10 10
2311 50cz. Brasilia 15 15
2312 100cz. Pelourinho, Salvador 15 15

1988. "Americas Telecom 88" Telecommunications Exhibition, Rio de Janeiro.
2313 **1195** 50cz. multicoloured . . 15 15

1196 "Kasato Maru" (first immigrant ship) and Japanese Family

1197 Postal Authority Emblem

1988. 80th Anniv of Japanese Immigration into Brazil.
2314 **1196** 100cz. multicoloured . . 55 25

1988. No value expressed.
2315 **1197** (–) blue 80 10
No. 2315 was valid for use at the current first class inland letter rate. It could not be used to pay postage to foreign countries.

1198 Judo
1199 Giant Anteater

1988. Olympic Games, Seoul.
2316 **1198** 20cz. multicoloured . . 80 10

1988. Endangered Mammals. Multicoloured.
2317 20cz. Type **1199** 50 10
2318 50cz. Thin-spined porcupine 60 15
2319 100cz. Bush dog . . . . . 1·25 25

1201 Industrial Symbols

1988. 50th Anniv of National Confederation of Industry.
2321 **1201** 50cz. multicoloured . . 15 15

1988. Brazilian Football Championship Gold Cup Winners (2nd series). As T **1177**. Multicoloured.
2322 50cz. Sport Club do Recife (1987) 40 15
2323 50cz. Coritiba Football Club (1985) 40 15
2324 100cz. Gremio Football Porto Alegrense (1981) . . 55 25
2325 200cz. Fluminense Football Club (1984) 75 40

1203 Raul Pompeia and Lines from "O Ateneu"

1988. Book Day. Centenaries of Publication of "O Ateneu" and "Verses". Multicoloured.
2327 50cz. Type **1203** 15 15
2328 100cz. Olavo Bilac and lines from "Verses" 30 25

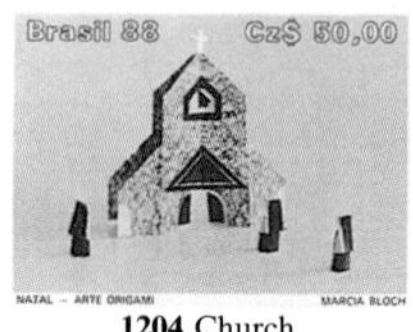

1204 Church

1205 Father Santiago Uchoa

1988. Christmas. Origami by Marcia Bloch. Multicoloured.
2329 50cz. Type **1204** 15 15
2330 100cz. Nativity 30 25
2331 200cz. Santa Claus and parcels 55 45

1988. Obligatory Tax. Anti-leprosy Week.
2332 **1205** 1cz.30 brown 50 10
See also Nos. 2614 and 2686.

1206 Mate and Rodeo Rider

1988. "Abrafex" Argentine–Brazilian Stamp Exhibition, Buenos Aires.
2333 **1206** 400cz. multicoloured . . 2·25 1·10

1207 Hatchetfish ("Gasteropelecus sp.")

1988. Freshwater Fishes. Multicoloured.
2334 55cz. Type **1207** 30 30
2335 55cz. Black arawana ("Osteoglossum ferreira") 30 30
2336 55cz. Green moenkhausia ("Moenkhausia sp.") . . 30 30
2337 55cz. Pearlfish ("Xavantei") 30 30
2338 55cz. Armoured bristlemouth catfish ("Ancistrus hoplogenys") 30 30
2339 55cz. Emerald catfish ("Brochis splendens") . . 30 30

1209 Dish Aerials

1210 "Four Arts"

1988. 10th Anniv of Ansat 10 (first Brazilian dish aerial), Macapa.
2341 **1209** 70cz. multicoloured . . 20 15

1988. Establishment of National Foundation of Scenic Arts.
2342 **1210** 70cz. multicoloured . . 20 15

1211 Court Building

1989. 380th Anniv of Bahia Court of Justice.
2343 **1211** 25c. multicoloured . . . 10 10

1212 Library Building and Detail of Main Door

1989. Public Library Year. 178th Anniv of First Public Library, Bahia.
2344 **1212** 25c. multicoloured . . . 10 10

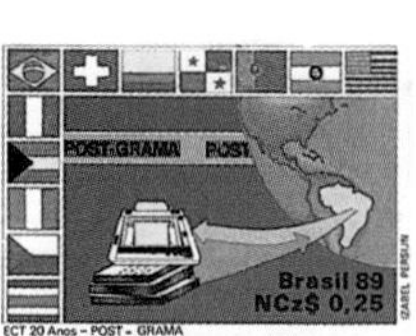

1213 Facsimile Machine **1215** Emblem

1989. 20th Anniv of Post and Telegraph Department. Postal Services. Multicoloured.
2345 25c. Type **1213** 10 10
2346 25c. Hand holding parcel (Express Mail Service) . . 10 10
2347 25c. Airbus Industrie 300 airplane on runway (SEDEX express parcel service) 10 10
2348 25c. Putting coin in savings box (CEF postal savings) 10 10

1989. "Our Nature" Programme.
2350 **1215** 25c. multicoloured . . . 10 10

1216 Hand reaching for Symbol of Freedom

1989. Bicentenary of Inconfidencia Mineira (independence movement). Multicoloured.
2351 30c. Type **1216** 10 10
2352 30c. Man's profile and colonial buildings 10 10
2353 40c. Baroque buildings in disarray 10 10

1217 School

1989. Cent of Rio de Janeiro Military School.
2354 **1217** 50c. multicoloured . . . 10 10

1218 "Pavonia alnifolia"

1989. Endangered Plants. Multicoloured.
2355 50c. Type **1218** 90 10
2356 1cz. "Worsleya rayneri" (vert) 90 10
2357 1cz.50 "Heliconia farinosa" (vert) . . . . 1·10 10

1219 Barreto and Pedro II Square, Recife Law School **1220** "Quiabentia zehntneri"

1989. 150th Birth Anniv of Tobias Barreto (writer).
2358 **1219** 50c. multicoloured . . . 10 10

1989. Flowers. Currency expressed as "NCz $". Multicoloured.
2359 10c. "Dichorisandra" sp. . . 10 10
2360 20c. Type **1220** 10 10
2361 50c. "Bougainvillea glabra" 10 10
2363 1cz. "Impatiens" sp. 50 10
2364 3cz. "Chorisia crispiflora" (vert) 10 15
2366 5cz. "Hibiscus trilineatus" 10 10
See also Nos. 2413/24.

1221 Shooting of "Revistinha"

1989. 20th Anniv of TV Cultura.
2371 **1221** 50c. multicoloured . . . 10 10

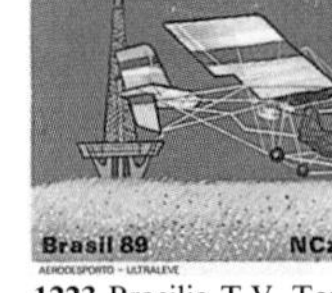

1222 Postal Authority Emblem **1223** Brasilia T.V. Tower and Microlight

1989. No value expressed.
2372 **1222** (–) blue and orange . . 80 10
No. 2372 was sold at the current rate for first class internal postage.

1989. Aerosports and 80th Anniv of Santos Dumont's Flight in "Demoiselle". Mult.
2373 50c. Type **1223** 50 10
2374 1cz.50 Eiffel Tower and "Demoiselle" 60 10

1225 Tourmaline

1989. Precious Stones. Multicoloured.
2376 50c. Type **1225** 10 10
2377 1cz.50 Amethyst 15 10

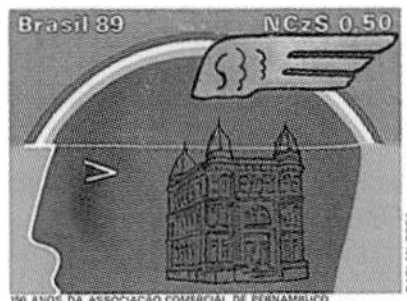

1226 Rainbow and Association H.Q. Mercury

1989. 150th Anniv of Pernambuco Trade Assn.
2379 **1226** 50c. multicoloured . . . 10 10

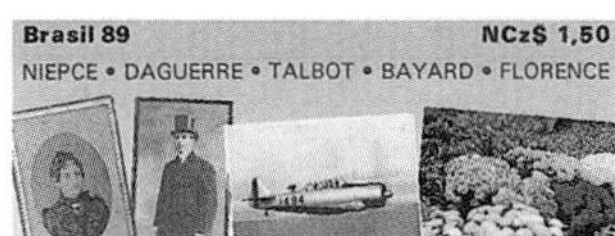

1228 Pioneers' Names and 19th-century to Modern Photographs

1989. International Photography Year.
2380 **1228** 1cz.50 multicoloured . . 15 10

1229 Power Station

1989. Centenary of Marmelos-o Power Station (first South American hydro-electric power station).
2381 **1229** 50c. multicoloured . . . 10 10

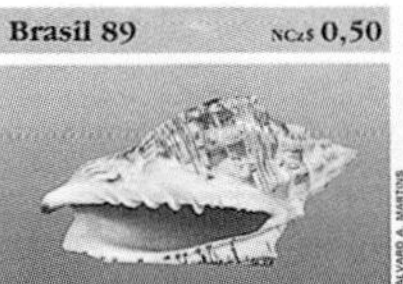

1230 Hebrew Volute **1231** Muiraquita

1989. Molluscs. Multicoloured.
2382 50c. Type **1230** 50 10
2383 1cz. Matthew's morum . . . 55 15
2384 1cz.50 Travasso's ancilla . . 60 20

1989. America. Pre-Columbian Artefacts. Mult.
2385 1cz. Type **1231** 80 10
2386 4cz. Caryatid vase (horiz) 80 10

1233 Casimiro de Abreu **1234** Postal Authority Emblem

1989. Book Day. Writers' Birth Annivs. Mult.
2388 1cz. Type **1233** (150th anniv) 10 10
2389 1cz. Machado de Assis (150th anniv) 10 10
2390 1cz. Cora Coralina (cent) . . 10 10

1989. No value expressed. Burelage in second colour.
2391 **1234** (–) red and orange . . 3·25 35
No. 2391 was sold at the current rate for first class international postage.

1235 Police Emblem

1989. 25th Anniv of Federal Police Department.
2392 **1235** 1cz. multicoloured . . . 10 10

1237 Angel **1238** Candle Flame as Dove

1989. Christmas. Multicoloured.
2394 70c. Type **1237** 10 10
2395 1cz. Nativity 10 10

1989. Thanksgiving Day.
2396 **1238** 1cz. multicoloured . . . 10 10

1239 Fr. Damien de Veuster **1240** "The Yellow Man"

1989. Obligatory Tax. Anti-leprosy Week.
2397 **1239** 2c. red 10 10
See also Nos. 2458, 2509 and 2565.

1989. Football Clubs. As T **1177**. Multicoloured.
2398 50c. Bahia Sports Club . . 10 10

1989. Birth Cent of Anita Malfatti (painter).
2399 **1240** 1cz. multicoloured . . . 10 10

1241 Archive and Proclamation by Bento Goncalves

1990. Cent of Bahia State Public Archive.
2400 **1241** 2cz. multicoloured . . . 20 15

1242 "Mimosa caesalpiniifolia"

1990. 40th Anniv of Brazilian Botanical Society. Multicoloured.
2401 2cz. Type **1242** 10 10
2402 13cz. "Caesalpinia echinata" 10 10

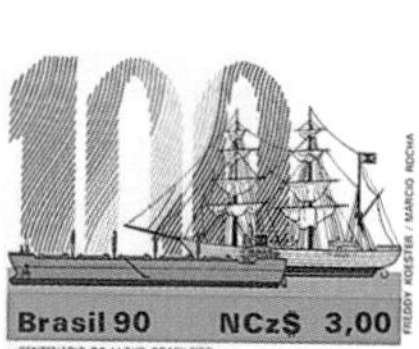

1243 Cathedral of St. John the Baptist, Santa Cruz do Sul **1244** Sailing Barque and Modern Container Ship

1990. Churches. Multicoloured.
2403 2cz. Type **1243** 10 10
2404 3cz. Our Lady of Victory Church, Oeiras (horiz) . . 10 10
2405 5cz. Our Lady of the Rosary Church, Ouro Preto . . . 10 10

1990. Cent of Lloyd Brasileiro Navigation Company.
2406 **1244** 3cz. multicoloured . . . 30 10

1990. Brazilian Football Clubs As T **1177**. Multicoloured.
2408 10cz. Vasco da Gama Regatas Club 15 10

1246 Collor and Newspaper Mastheads **1247** Sarney

1990. Birth Cent of Lindolfo Collor (journalist).
2409 **1246** 20cz. multicoloured . . 25 20

1990. Tribute to Jose Sarney (retiring President).
2410 **1247** 20cz. blue 25 20

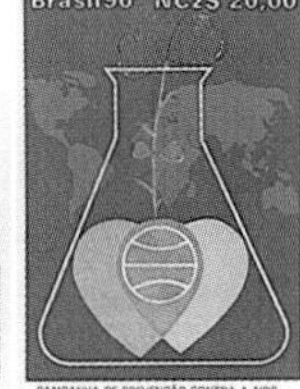

1248 Gold Coin, Anniversary Emblem and Bank Headquarters, Brasilia **1249** Hearts sprouting in Flask

1990. 25th Anniv of Brazil Central Bank.
2411 **1248** 20cr. multicoloured . . 25 20

1990. World Health Day. Anti-AIDS Campaign.
2412 **1249** 20cr. multicoloured . . 25 20

1990. Flowers. As T **1220** but with currency expressed as "Cr$".
2413 1cr. "Impatiens sp" . . . 10 10
2414 2cr. "Chorisia crispiflora" (vert) 10 10
2415 5cr. "Hibiscus trilineatus" 10 10
2417 10cr. "Tibouchina granulosa" (vert) 15 10
2418 20cr. "Cassia micranthera" (vert) 25 20
2420 50cr. "Clitoria fairchildiana" (vert) . . 30 10
2421 50cr. "Tibouchina mutabilis" (vert) 75 65
2422 100cr. "Erythrina crista-galli" (vert) 65 10

2423 200cr. "Jacaranda mimosifolia" (vert) . . . 65 10
2424 500cr. "Caesalpinia peltophoroides" (vert) 65 15
2424a 1000cr. "Pachira aquatica" (vert) 15 10
2424b 2000cr. "Hibiscus pernambucensis" (vert) 25 20
2424c 5000cr. "Triplaris surinamensis" (vert) . . 90 30
2424d 10000cr. "Tabebuia heptaphylia" (vert) . . . 65 10
2424e 20000cr. "Erythrina speciosa" (vert) 65 10

1250 Amazon Post Launch

1990. River Post Network.
2425 **1250** 20cr. multicoloured . . 55 25

1253 Lorry and Coach

1990. 22nd World Congress of Int Road Transport Union, Rio de Janeiro. Multicoloured.
2428 20cr. Type **1253** . . . . . . 1·00 55
2429 80cr. Van and motor car . . 1·25 55
Nos. 2428/29 were printed together, se-tenant, forming a composite design.

1254 Imperial Crown (Imperial Museum, Petropolis)

1990. Museum 50th Anniversaries. Multicoloured.
2430 20cr. Type **1254** 25 20
2431 20cr. "Our Lady of the Immaculate Conception" (woodcarving) (Missionary Museum, Sao Miguel das Missoes) . . . 25 20

1990. Creation of State of Tocantins. As T **992**, showing state flag.
2432 20cr. yellow, blue and black 25 20

1255 Service Building, Hildebrand Theodolite and Map of Rio de Janeiro

1990. Centenary of Army Geographic Service.
2433 **1255** 20cr. multicoloured . . 25 20

1256 Adhemar Gonzaga (producer)

1990. Brazilian Film Industry. Each maroon and purple.
2434 25cr. Type **1256** 80 25
2435 25cr. Carmen Miranda (actress) 80 25
2436 25cr. Carmen Santos (actress) 80 25
2437 25cr. Oscarito (actor) . . . 80 25

1257 Aerial View of House 1258 Ball and Net

1990. 5th Anniv of France–Brazil House, Rio de Janeiro.
2438 **1257** 50cr. multicoloured . . 60 10

1990. 12th World Men's Volleyball Championship, Brazil.
2439 **1258** 10cr. multicoloured . . 55 10

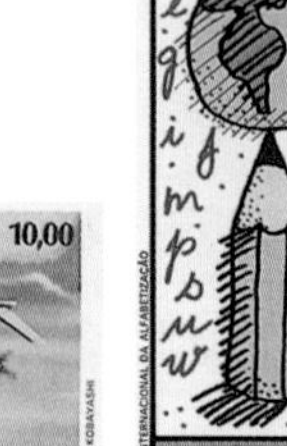

1259 Embraer/FMA Vector 1260 Globe, Pencil and Alphabet

1990. Aeronautics Industry.
2440 **1259** 10cr. multicoloured . . 15 10

1990. International Literacy Year.
2441 **1260** 10cr. multicoloured . . 15 10

1261 Institute

1990. Cent of Granbery Institute, Juiz de Fora.
2442 **1261** 13cr. multicoloured . . 15 10

1262 Map, Track and Diesel Locomotive

1990. 18th Pan-American Railways Congress, Rio de Janeiro.
2443 **1262** 95cr. multicoloured . . 1·50 1·50

1263 Satellite and Computer Communication

1990. 25th Anniv of Embratel (Telecommunications Enterprise).
2444 **1263** 13cr. multicoloured . . 15 10

1264 "Bathers" (Alfredo Ceschiatti)

1990. "Lubrapex 90" Brazilian–Portuguese Stamp Exhibition, Brasilia. Brasilia Sculptures. Mult.
2445 25cr. Type **1264** 30 25
2446 25cr. "Warriors" (Bruno Giorgi) 30 25
2447 100cr. "St. John" (Ceschiatti) . . . . 1·40 50
2448 100cr. "Justice" (Ceschiatti) 1·40 50

1265 "Bromelia antiacantha"

1990. America. 500th Anniv of Discovery of America by Columbus. Praia do Sul Nature Reserve. Multicoloured.
2450 15cr. Type **1265** 90 10
2451 105cr. Wooded shoreline of Lagoa do Sul . . . . . . 1·25 50
Nos. 2450/1 were printed together, se-tenant, forming a composite design.

1266 Oswald de Andrade (birth centenary) and Illustration from "Anthropophagic Manifesto"

1990. Book Day. Anniversaries. Mult.
2452 15cr. Type **1266** 15 10
2453 15cr. Guilherme de Almeida (birth cent) and illustration of "Greek Songs" 15 10
2454 15cr. National Library (180th anniv) and illuminated book 15 10

1267 Emblem and Tribunal Offices, Brasilia

1990. Centenary of National Accounts Tribunal.
2455 **1267** 15cr. multicoloured . . 15 10

1268 National Congress Building 1269 Fingers touching across Map of Americas

1990. Christmas. Brasilia Lights. Mult.
2456 15cr. Type **1268** 15 10
2457 15cr. Television Tower . . . 15 10

1990. Obligatory Tax. Anti-Leprosy Week. As No. 2397 but value and colour changed.
2458 **1239** 50c. blue 10 10

1990. Centenary of Organization of American States.
2459 **1269** 15cr. multicoloured . . 15 10

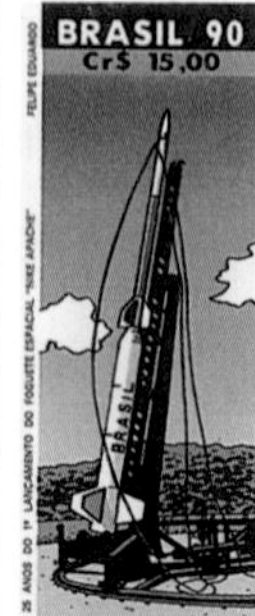

1270 "Nike Apache" Rocket on Launch Pad 1271 Sao Cristovao City

1990. 25th Anniv of Launch of "Nike Apache" Rocket.
2460 **1270** 15cr. multicoloured . . 15 10

1990. 400th Anniv of Colonization of Sergipe State.
2461 **1271** 15cr. multicoloured . . 15 10

1272 Gymnasts

1991. World Congress on Physical Education, Sports and Recreation, Foz do Iguacu.
2462 **1272** 17cr. multicoloured . . 20 15

1273 Cazuza

1991. "Rock in Rio" Concert. Multicoloured.
2463 25cr. Type **1273** 60 60
2464 185cr. Raul Seixas 80 80
Nos. 2463/4 were printed together, se-tenant, forming a composite design.

1274 Aeritalia/Aermacchi AM-X and Republic Thunderbolt

1991. 50th Anniv of Aeronautics Ministry.
2465 **1274** 17cr. multicoloured . . 20 15

1275 Effigies of Day Woman and Midnight Man, Olinda 1276 Antarctic Wildlife

1991. Carnival. Multicoloured.
2466 25cr. Type **1275** 10 10
2467 30cr. Electric trio on truck, Salvador 10 10
2468 280cr. Samba dancers, Rio de Janeiro 80 45

1991. Visit of President Collor to Antarctica.
2469 **1276** 300cr. multicoloured . . 3·25 2·00

1277 Hang-gliders

1991. 8th World Free Flight Championships, Governador Valadares.
2470 **1277** 36cr. multicoloured . . 15 10

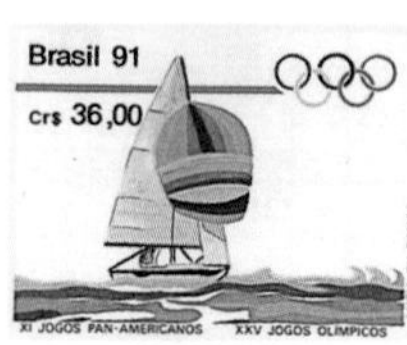
1278 Yachting

1991. 11th Pan-American Games, Cuba, and Olympic Games, Barcelona (1992). Mult.
2471 36cr. Type **1278** 30 10
2472 36cr. Rowing 10 10
2473 300cr. Swimming 85 75

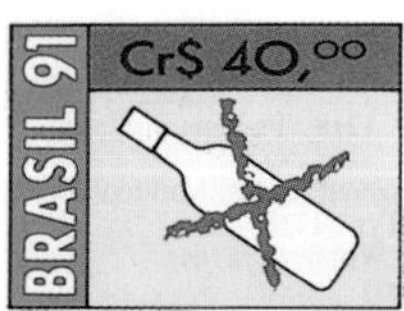
1279 Cross over Bottle (alcoholism)

1991. Anti-addiction Campaign. Mult.
2474 40cr. Type **1279** 10 10
2475 40cr. Cross over cigarette (smoking) 10 10
2476 40cr. Cross over syringe (drug abuse) 10 10

1280 Old and Present Offices and Mastheads

1281 Yanomami Youth in Ceremonial Paint

1991. Cent of "Jornal do Brasil" (newspaper).
2477 **1280** 40cr. multicoloured . . 10 10

1991. Indian Culture. The Yanomami. Mult.
2478 40cr. Type **1281** 10 10
2479 400cr. Hunter (horiz) . . . 80 70

1282 Orinoco Goose

1991. United Nations Conference on Environment and Development.
2480 **1282** 45cr. multicoloured . . 55 30

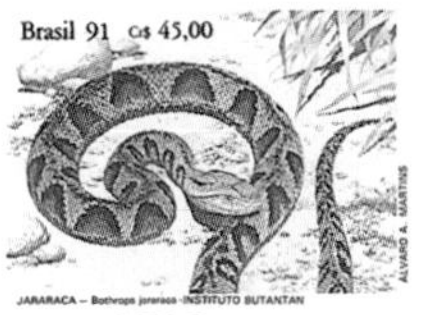

1283 Jararaca

1284 National Flag

1991. 90th Anniv of Butantan Institute (2481/2) and 173rd Anniv of National Museum (others). Multicoloured.
2481 45cr. Type **1283** 35 10
2482 45cr. Green tree boa 35 10
2483 45cr. Theropoda (dinosaurs) 35 10
2484 350cr. Sauropoda (dinosaurs) . . . . 1·25 60

1991. No value expressed.
2485 **1284** (–) multicoloured . . . 80 10

1285 Early Steam Pump and Santos City 6th Fire Group's Headquarters

1991. Fire Fighting.
2486 **1285** 45cr. multicoloured . . 10 10

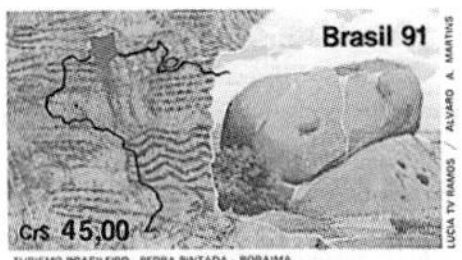

1286 Pedra Pintada, Boa Vista, Roraima

1991. Tourism. Centenaries of Boa Vista (1990) and Teresopolis. Multicoloured.
2487 45cr. Type **1286** 10 10
2488 350cr. God's Finger, Teresopolis, Rio de Janeiro 70 60

1287 Welder, "Justice" and Farmer

1991. 50th Anniv of Labour Justice Legal System.
2489 **1287** 45cr. multicoloured . . 10 10

1288 Folklore Characters, Singers and Mota

1991. 5th International Festival of Folklore and Birth Centenary of Leonardo Mota (folklorist).
2490 **1288** 45cr. red, ochre & black 10 10

1289 Jose Basilio da Gama (poet)

1290 Pope John Paul II

1991. Writers' Birth Anniversaries. Mult.
2491 45cr. Type **1289** (250th anniv) 10 10
2492 50cr. Luis Nicolau Fagundes Varela (poet, 150th anniv) 10 10
2493 50cr. Jackson de Figueiredo (essayist and philosopher, centenary) 10 10

1991. Papal Visit and 12th National Eucharistic Congress, Natal. Multicoloured.
2494 50cr. Type **1290** 60 50
2495 400cr. Congress emblem . . 90 70
Nos. 2494/5 were issued together, se-tenant, forming a composite design.

1291 "The Constitutional Commitment" (Aurelio de Figueiredo)

1292 Exhibition Emblem and dish Aerial

1991. Centenary of 1891 Constitution.
2496 **1291** 50cr. multicoloured . . 10 10

1991. "Telecom 91" International Telecommunications Exhibition, Geneva.
2497 **1292** 50cr. multicoloured . . 10 10

1293 Ferdinand Magellan

1294 White-vented Violetear and "Cattleya warneri"

1991. America. Voyages of Discovery. Mult.
2498 50cr. Type **1293** 15 10
2499 400cr. Francisco de Orellana on River Amazon . . . . 1·25 75

1991. "Brapex 91" National Stamp Exhibition, Vitoria. Humming Birds and Orchids in Mata Atlantica Forest. Multicoloured.
2500 50cr. Type **1294** 60 15
2501 65cr. Glittering-bellied emerald and "Rodriguezia venusta" 80 35
2502 65cr. Brazilian ruby and "Zygopetalum intermedium" 80 35

1295 "Self-portrait III"

1296 Agricultural Projects

1991. Birth Cent of Lasar Segall (artist).
2504 **1295** 400cr. multicoloured . . 80 30

1991. Centenary of Bureau of Agriculture and Provision, Sao Paulo.
2505 **1296** 70cr. multicoloured . . 20 10

1297 Dr. Manuel Ferraz de Campos Salles (President, 1898–1902)

1298 Madonna and Child

1991. 150th Birth Anniversaries. Mult.
2506 70cr. Type **1297** 10 10
2507 90cr. Dr. Prudente de Moraes (President, 1894–98) and Catete Palace, Rio de Janeiro (former Executive Headquarters) 10 10
Nos. 2506/7 were issued together, se-tenant, forming a composite design.

1991. Christmas.
2508 **1298** 70cr. multicoloured . . 10 10

1991. Obligatory Tax. Anti-leprosy Week.
2509 **1239** 3cr. green 35 10

1299 Hand holding Prayer Book

1991. Thanksgiving Day.
2510 **1299** 70cr. multicoloured . . 10 10

1301 Policeman in Historic Uniform and Tobias de Aguiar Battalion Building, Sao Paulo

1302 First Baptist Church, Niteroi (centenary)

1991. Military Police.
2512 **1301** 80cr. multicoloured . . 10 10

1992. Church Anniversaries. Multicoloured.
2513 250cr. Type **1302** 20 15
2514 250cr. Presbyterian Cathedral, Rio de Janeiro (130th anniv) 20 15

1303 Afranio Costa (silver, free pistol)

1992. Olympic Games, Barcelona (1st issue). 1920 Olympics Shooting Medal Winners. Multicoloured.
2515 300cr. Type **1303** 55 20
2516 2500cr. Guilherme Paraense (gold, 30 m revolver) . . 1·75 60
See also No. 2526.

1304 Old and Modern Views of Port

1992. Centenary of Port of Santos.
2517 **1304** 300cr. multicoloured . . 50 20

1305 White-tailed Tropic Birds

1992. 2nd United Nations Conference on Environment and Development, Rio de Janeiro (1st issue). Multicoloured.
2518 400cr. Type **1305** 75 60
2519 2500cr. Spinner dolphins . . 2·00 1·90
See also Nos. 2532/5, 2536/8, 2539/42 and 2543/6.

1306 Ipe

1307 Hunting using Boleadeira

1992. No value expressed.
2520 **1306** (–) multicoloured . . . 1·25 10
No. 2520 was valid for use at the second class inland letter rate.

1992. "Abrafex '92" Argentinian–Brazilian Stamp Exhibition, Porto Alegre. Multicoloured.
2521 250cr. Type **1307** 35 35
2522 250cr. Traditional folk dancing 20 15
2523 250cr. Horse and cart . . . 20 15
2524 1000cr. Rounding-up cattle 85 75

1308 Sportsmen on Globe

1992. Olympic Games, Barcelona (2nd issue).
2526 **1308** 300cr. multicoloured . . 20 15

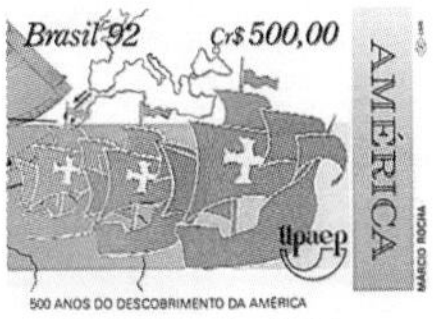

1310 Columbus's Fleet

1992. America. 500th Anniv of Discovery of America by Columbus. Multicoloured.
2528 500cr. Type **1310** 75 25
2529 3500cr. Columbus, route map and quadrant . . . 75 60
Nos. 2528/9 were issued together, se-tenant, forming a composite design.

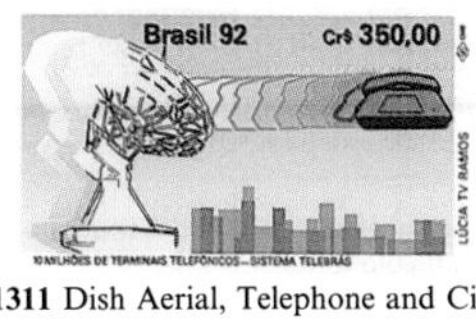

1311 Dish Aerial, Telephone and City

1992. Installation of 10,000,000th Telephone Line in Brazil.
2530 **1311** 350cr. multicoloured . . 15 10

1313 Hercule Florence (botanist)

1992. 2nd U.N. Conference on Environment and Development (2nd issue). 170th Anniv of Langsdorff Expedition. Multicoloured.

2532 500cr. Type **1313** 20 15
2533 500cr. Aime-Adrien Taunay (ethnographer) and Amerindians 20 15
2534 500cr. Johann Moritz Rugendas (zoologist) . . 20 15
2535 3000cr. Gregory Ivanovich Langsdorff and route map 60 60

1314 Urban and Rural Symbols

1992. 2nd U.N. Conference on Environment and Development (3rd issue). Multicoloured.

2536 450cr. Type **1314** 20 15
2537 450cr. Flags of Sweden (host of first conference) and Brazil around globe . . . 20 15
2538 3000cr. Globe, map, flora and fauna 60 30

1315 Monica sitting by Waterfall

1992. 2nd U.N. Conference on Environment and Development (4th issue). Ecology. Designs showing cartoon characters. Multicoloured.

2539 500cr. Type **1315** 20 15
2540 500cr. Cebolinha in canoe 20 15
2541 500cr. Cascao photographing wildlife . . 20 15
2542 500cr. Magali picking wild fruit 20 15

Nos. 2539/42 were issued together, se-tenant, forming a composite design.

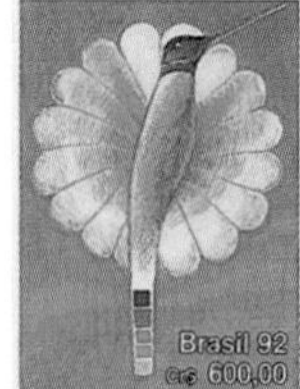
1316 "Nidularium innocentii" **1317** Humming-bird's Wings forming Flower

1992. 2nd U.N. Conference on Environment and Development (5th issue). 3rd Anniv of Margaret Mee Brazilian Botanical Foundation. Flower paintings by Margaret Mee. Multicoloured.

2543 600cr. Type **1316** 25 20
2544 600cr. "Canistrum exiguum" 25 20
2545 700cr. "Nidularium rubens" 25 20
2546 700cr. "Canistrum cyathiforme" 25 20

1992. National Diabetes Day.

2547 **1317** 600cr. multicoloured . . 20 15

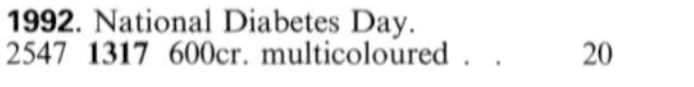

1318 Training Tower and First Manual Pump **1319** Animals, Cave Paintings and Map of Piaui State

1992. Centenary of Joinville Volunteer Fire Service.

2548 **1318** 550cr. multicoloured . . 20 15

1992. 13th Anniv of Capivara Mountain National Park. Multicoloured.

2549 550cr. Type **1319** 20 15
2550 550cr. Canyons and map of Brazil 20 15

Nos. 2549/50 were issued together, se-tenant, forming a composite design.

1320 Projects within Flask **1322** Santa Cruz Fortress, Anhatomirim Island

1321 Students at Work

1992. 24th Anniv of Financing Agency for Studies and Projects.

2551 **1320** 550cr. multicoloured . . 1·25 40

1992. 50th Anniv of National Industrial Training Service.

2552 **1321** 650cr. multicoloured . . 15 10

1992. Santa Catarina Fortresses. Multicoloured.

2553 650cr. Type **1322** 15 10
2554 3000cr. Santo Antonio Fort, Ratones Grande island . . 65 60

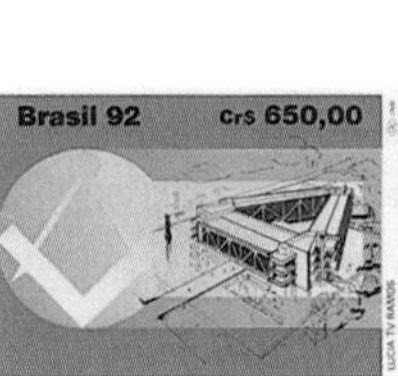

1323 Masonic Emblem and Palace, Brasilia **1324** Profiles of Child and Man forming Hourglass

1992. 170th Anniv of Grande Oriente (Federation of Brazil's Freemasonry Lodges).

2555 **1323** 650cr. multicoloured . . 10 10

1992. 50th Anniv of Brazilian Legion of Assistance.

2556 **1324** 650cr. multicoloured . . 10 10

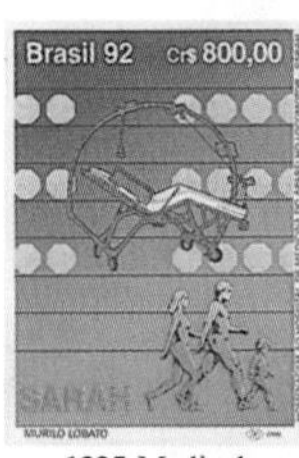

1325 Medical Equipment and Patients **1326** Menotti del Picchia

1992. Sarah Locomotor Hospital, Brasilia.

2557 **1325** 800cr. multicoloured . . 10 10

1992. Book Day. Writers' Birth Centenaries. Multicoloured.

2558 900cr. Type **1326** 10 10
2559 900cr. Graciliano Ramos . . 10 10
2560 1000cr. Assis Chateaubriand (journalist) (horiz) 15 10

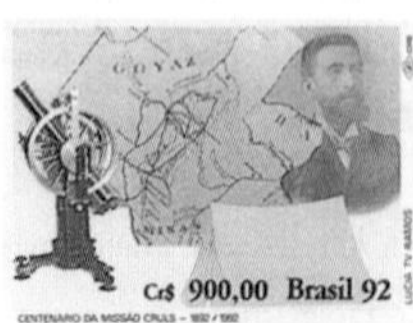

1327 Meridian Circle, Map, Cruls and Tent

1992. Centenary of Luiz Cruls's Exploration of Central Plateau.

2561 **1327** 900cr. multicoloured . . 10 10

1328 Productivity Graph on Flag

1992. 2nd Anniv of Brazilian Quality and Productivity Programme.

2562 **1328** 1200cr. multicoloured 15 10

1330 Father Christmas

1992. Christmas. No value expressed.

2564 **1330** (–) multicoloured . . . 90 10

1992. Obligatory Tax. Anti-leprosy Week.

2565 **1239** 30cr. brown 35 10

1331 Sister Dulce, Patients and Lacerda Lift, Salvador

1993. Sister Dulce (founder of Santo Antonio Hospital and Simoes Filho Educational Centre) Commemoration.

2566 **1331** 3500cr. multicoloured 20 20

1333 Tube Station, Pine Trees and Church of the Third Order of St. Francis of Assisi and Stigmata

1993. 300th Anniv of Curitiba.

2568 **1333** 4500cr. multicoloured 25 20

1334 Heart dripping Blood onto Flowers **1335** "Night with the Geniuses of Study and Love"

1993. Health and Preservation of Life. Mult.

2569 4500cr. Type **1334** (blood donation) 20 20
2570 4500cr. Crab attacking healthy cell (anti-cancer campaign) 20 20
2571 4500cr. Rainbow, head and encephalogram (mental health) 20 20

1993. 150th Birth Anniv of Pedro Americo (painter). Multicoloured.

2572 5500cr. Type **1335** 20 20
2573 36000cr. "David and Abizag" (horiz) 30 20
2574 36000cr. "A Carioca" . . . 30 20

1336 Flag **1337** "Dynastes hercules"

1993. No value expressed. Self-adhesive. Die-cut.

2575 **1336** (–) blue, yellow & grn 1·75 20

No. 2575 was valid for use at the current first class inland letter rate. It could not be used to pay postage to foreign countries.

1993. World Environment Day. Beetles. Mult.

2576 8000cr. Type **1337** 30 25
2577 55000cr. "Batus barbicornis" 90 25

1338 Map, Flags and Discussion Themes

1993. 3rd Iberian–American Summit Conference, Salvador.

2578 **1338** 12000cr. multicoloured 25 20

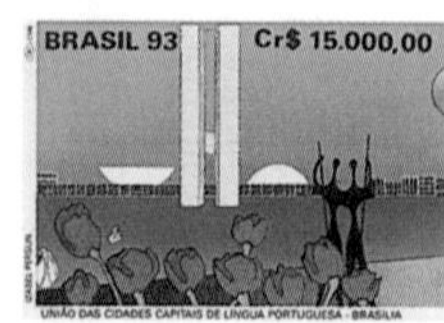

1339 Lake, Congress Building and "Os Candangos" (statue), Brasilia

1993. Union of Portuguese-speaking Capital Cities. Multicoloured.

2579 15000cr. Type **1339** 30 25
2580 71000cr. Copacabana beach and "Christ the Redeemer" (statue), Rio de Janeiro 30 25

Nos. 2579/80 were issued together, se-tenant, forming a composite design.

1340 30r. "Bulls Eye" Stamp

1993. 150th Anniv of First Brazilian Stamps (1st issue) and "Brasiliana 93" International Stamp Exhibition, Rio de Janeiro. Each black, red and yellow.

2581 30000cr. Type **1340** 90 50
2582 60000cr.60r. "Bull's Eye" stamp 90 50
2583 90000cr.90r. "Bull's Eye" stamp 90 50

See also Nos. 2585/8.

1341 Cebolinha designing Stamp

1993. 150th Anniv of First Brazilian Stamps (2nd issue). No value expressed. Cartoon characters. Multicoloured.

2585 (–) Type **1341** 90 15
2586 (–) Cascao as King and 30r. "Bull's Eye" stamp . . . 90 15
2587 (–) Monica writing letter and 60r. "Bull's Eye" stamp 90 15
2588 (–) Magali receiving letter and 90r. "Bull's Eye" stamp 90 15

Nos. 2585/8 were issued together, se-tenant, forming a composite design.

Nos. 2585/8 were valid for use at the current first class inland letter rate. They could not be used to pay postage to other countries.

1342 Imperial Palace (former postal H.Q.), Rio de Janeiro **1344** Forest Mound and Tools

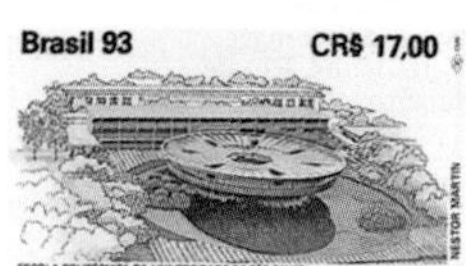

1343 Polytechnic School, Sao Paulo University

1993. 330th Anniv of Postal Service. Mult.

2589 20000cr. Type **1342** 40 35
2590 20000cr. Petropolis post office 40 35

2591 20000cr. Main post office, Rio de Janeiro 40 35
2592 20000cr. Niteroi post office 40 35

Currency Reform
1 (new) cruzeiro real = 1000 (old) cruzeiros.

1993. Engineering Schools. Multicoloured.
2593 17cr. Type **1343** (centenary, 1994) 30 25
2594 17cr. Old and new engineering schools, Rio de Janeiro Federal University (bicent, 1992) 30 25

1993. Preservation of Archaeological Sites. Mult.
2595 17cr. Type **1344** 20 15
2596 17cr. Coastal mound, shells and tools 20 15

1345 Guimaraes and National Congress

1993. Ulysses Guimaraes (politician).
2597 **1346** 22cr. Multicoloured. . . 25 20

1346 Hands holding Candles and Rope around Statue

1347 Hyacinth Macaw, Glaucous Macaw and Indigo Macaw

1993. Bicentenary of Procession of "Virgin of Nazareth", Belem.
2598 **1346** 22cr. multicoloured . . 25 20

1993. America. Endangered Macaws. Mult.
2599 22cr. Type **1347** 25 20
2600 130cr. Spix's macaw . . . . 1·10 90

1348 Vinicius de Moraes

1349 Liberty

1993. Composers' Anniversaries. Mult.
2601 22cr. Type **1348** (80th birth anniv) 25 20
2602 22cr. Alfredo da Rocha Vianna (pseud. Pixinguinha) and score of "Carinhoso" (20th death anniv) 25 20

1993. No value expressed.
2603 **1349** (–) blue, turq & yell . . 1·75 45
No. 2603 was sold at the current rate for first class international postage.

1350 Mario de Andrade

1351 Knot

1993. Book Day. Writers' Birth Centenaries. Multicoloured.
2604 30cr. Type **1350** 30 25
2605 30cr. Alceu Amoroso Lima (pseud. Tristao de Athayde) 30 25
2606 30cr. Gilka Machado (poet) 30 25

1993. 40th Anniv of Brazil–Portugal Consultation and Friendship Treaty.
2607 **1351** 30cr. multicoloured . . 30 25

1352 Nho-Quim

1993. 2nd International Comic Strip Biennial. No value expressed. Multicoloured.
2608 (–) Type **1352** 90 30
2609 (–) Benjamin (Louneiro) . . 60 25
2610 (–) Lamparina 60 25
2611 (–) Reco-Reco, Bolao and Azeitona (Luiz Sa) . . . 60 25
See note below Nos. 2585/8.

1353 Diagram and "Tamoio" (submarine)

1993. Launch of First Brazilian-built Submarine.
2612 **1353** 240cr. multicoloured . . 1·10 70

1354 Nativity

1993. Christmas. No value expressed.
2613 **1354** (–) multicoloured . . . 80 25
See note below Nos. 2585/8.

1993. Obligatory Tax. Anti-leprosy Week.
2614 **1205** 50c. blue 20 15

1355 Republic P-47 Thunderbolt Fighters over Tarquinia Camp, Italy

1356 Flag

1993. 50th Anniv of Formation of 1st Fighter Group, Brazilian Expeditionary Force.
2615 **1355** 42cr. multicoloured . . 60 25

1994. No value expressed. Self-adhesive. Imperf.
2616 **1356** (–) blue, yellow & green 60 30
See note below Nos. 2585/8.

1357 Foundation of Republican Memory, Convent and Cloisters

1994. 340th Anniv of Convent of Merces (now Cultural Centre), Sao Luis.
2617 **1357** 58cr. multicoloured . . 40 35

1358 "Mae Menininha"

1994. Birth Centenary of Mae Menininha do Gantois (Escolastica Maria da Conceiao Nazare).
2618 **1358** 80cr. multicoloured . . 20 20

1359 Olympic Rings and Rower

1360 Blue and White Swallow

1994. Centenaries of International Olympic Committee and Rowing Federation, Rio Grande do Sul. No value expressed.
2619 **1359** (–) multicoloured . . . 1·75 90
See note below No. 2603.

1994. Birds. Multicoloured.
2620 10cr. Type **1360** 10 10
2621 20cr. Roadside hawk . . . 10 10
2622 50cr. Rufous-bellied thrush 10 10
2623 100cr. Ruddy ground dove 15 10
2624 200cr. Southern lapwing . . 30 25
2625 500cr. Rufous-collared sparrow 80 70
See after Nos. 2649/61.

1361 Map and Prince Henry

1994. 600th Birth Anniv of Prince Henry the Navigator.
2626 **1361** 635cr. multicoloured . . 1·75 90

1362 Bicycle

1994. America. Postal Vehicles. Mult.
2627 110cr. Type **1362** 15 10
2628 635cr. Motor cycle . . . . 1·75 20

1363 Statue, Grain Store and Chapel of Help, Juazeiro do Norte

1994. 150th Anniv of Birth of Father Cicero Romao Batista. With service indicator.
2629 **1363** (–) multicoloured . . . 60 15
See note below Nos. 2585/8.

1364 Sabin and Children

1994. 1st Death Anniv of Albert Sabin (developer of oral polio vaccine).
2630 **1364** 160cr. multicoloured . . 25 20

1365 Castello Branco and Brasilia

1994. Carlos Castello Branco (journalist).
2631 **1365** 160cr. multicoloured . . 25 20

1366 "Euterpe oleracea"

1367 "Brazil"

1994. Birth Bicentenary of Karl Friedrich Phillip von Martius (botanist). With service indicator. Multicoloured. (a) Inscr "1. PORTE NACIONAL".
2632 (–) Type **1366** 85 15
2633 (–) "Jacaranda paucifoliolata" 85 15

(b) Inscr "1. PORTE INTERNACIONAL TAXE PERCUE".
2634 (–) "Barbacenia tomentosa" 1·50 30
Nos. 2632/3 were for use at the current first class inland letter rate and Nos. 2634 for first class international postage.

1994. With service indicator. (a) Size 21 × 28mm. Self-adhesive. Rouletted. (i) PRINTED MATTER. Inscr "1. PORTE IMPRESSO CATEGORIA II".
2635 **1367** (–) blue 10 10

(ii) INLAND POSTAGE. Inscr "3. PORTE NACIONAL".
2636 **1367** (3rd) red 30 20

(b) INLAND POSTAGE. Inscr "PORTE NACIONAL". Size 26 × 35mm.
2637 **1367** (4th) green 40 30
2638 (5th) red 75 30
Nos. 2635/8 were valid for internal use in the category described.

1368 Brazilian Player wearing "100"

1994. Centenary of Football in Brazil and World Cup Football Championship, U.S.A. With service indicator.
2639 **1368** (–) multicoloured . . . 2·40 90
See note below No. 2603.

1369 Emperor Tamarin ("Saguinus imperator")

1371 Pencils Crossing over Fingerprint

1994. Endangered Mammals. With service indicator. Multicoloured.
2640 (–) Type **1369** 60 15
2641 (–) Bare-faced tamarin ("Saguinus bicolor") . . . 60 15
2642 (–) Golden lion tamarin ("Leontopithecus rosalia") 60 15
See note below Nos. 2585/8.

1994. 10 Year Education Plan. With service indicator. Multicoloured.
2644 (–) Type **1371** (literacy campaign) 60 15
2645 (–) PRONAICA pencil and school (National Programme of Integral Care to Children and Teenagers) 60 15
2646 (–) Lecture scene and graph (increase in qualified teachers) 60 15
2647 (–) Pencil and "lecturers" on television (distance learning by video) 60 15
See note below Nos. 2585/8.

1994. Birds. As T **1360** but with value expressed as "R$". Multicoloured.
2649 1c. Type **1360** 10 10
2650 2c. As No. 2621 . . . . . 10 10
2652 5c. As No. 2622 . . . . . 10 10
2654 10c. As No. 2623 . . . . . 15 10
2655 15c. Saffron finch 20 15
2656 20c. As No. 2624 . . . . . 30 25
2657 22c. Fork-tailed fly-catcher 30 25
2658 50c. As No. 2625 . . . . . 75 65
2661 1r. Rufous hornero . . . . 1·50 1·25

1373 Edgard Santos (founder of Bahia University)

1374 "Petrobras X" (drilling platform), Campos Basin. Rio de Janeiro

1994. Anniversaries. With service indicator. Multicoloured.
2662 (–) Type **1373** (birth centenary) 20 15
2663 (–) Oswaldo Aranha (politician, birth centenary) 20 15
2664 (–) Otto Lara Resende (author and journalist, 2nd death anniv) 20 15
See note below Nos. 2585/8.

1994. 40th Anniv of Petrobras (state oil company).
2665 **1374** 12c. multicoloured . . . 40 15

1375 17th century Coin Production

1376 Loaf of Bread

1994. 300th Anniv of Brazilian Mint.
2666 **1375** 12c. multicoloured . . . 20 15

1994. Campaign against Famine and Misery. With service indicator.
2667 **1376** (–) multicoloured . . . 20 15
2668 – (–) black and blue . . . 20 15
DESIGN: No. 2668, Fish.
See note below Nos. 2585/8.

1377 Writing with Quill and Scales of Justice

1994. 150th Anniv of Brazilian Lawyers Institute.
2669 **1377** 12c. multicoloured . . . 20 15

1378 Family within Heart

1994. International Year of the Family.
2670 **1378** 84c. multicoloured . . . 1·25 60

1379 Hospital, White Stork and Babies forming "1000000"

1994. Centenary of Sao Paulo Maternity Hospital. Its Millionth Birth.
2671 **1379** 12c. multicoloured . . . 20 15

1380 Celestino performing and "Maternal Heart" (record sleeve)

1994. Birth Centenary of Vicente Celestino (singer).
2672 **1380** 12c. multicoloured . . . 20 15

1381 Fernando de Azevedo (educationist)

1994. Writers' Birth Anniversaries. Mult.
2673 12c. Type **1381** (cent) . . . 20 15
2674 12c. Tomas Antonio Gonzaga (poet, 250th) . . 20 15

1382 "Joao and Maria" (Hansel and Gretel)

1994. Centenary of Publication of "Fairy Tales" by Alberto Figueiredo Pimentel (first Brazilian children's book). Multicoloured.
2675 12c. Type **1382** 20 15
2676 12c. "Dona Baratinha" (Little Mrs Cockroach) 20 15
2677 84c. "Puss in Boots" . . . 1·25 1·10
2678 84c. "Tom Thumb" . . . . 1·25 1·10

1383 St. Clare, St. Damian's Convent and Statue of St. Francis

1994. 800th Birth Anniv of St. Clare of Assisi (founder of order of Poor Clares).
2679 **1383** 12c. multicoloured . . . 20 15

1384 Racing Car and Brazilian Flag

1994. Ayrton Senna (racing driver) Commemoration. Multicoloured.
2680 12c. Type **1384** 90 60
2681 12c. Senna and crowd waving farewell 90 60
2682 84c. Brazilian and chequered flags, racing cars and Senna giving victory salute . . . . 1·75 60
Nos. 2680/2 were issued together, se-tenant, forming a composite design.

1385 Books and Globe

1994. Centenary of Historical and Geographical Institute, Sao Paulo.
2683 **1385** 12c. multicoloured . . . 20 15

1386 Adoniran Barbosa and "11 o'Clock Train"

1994. Composers. Multicoloured.
2684 12c. Type **1386** 20 15
2685 12c. Score of "The Sea" (Dorival Caymmi) 20 15

1994. Obligatory Tax. Anti-Leprosy Week.
2686 **1205** 1c. purple 10 10

1387 Maggot wearing Santa Claus Hat in Apple

1994. Christmas. Multicoloured.
2687 12c. Type **1387** 20 15
2688 12c. Carol singers 20 15
2689 12c. Boy smoking pipe and letter in boot 20 15
2690 84c. Boy wearing saucepan on head and Santa Claus cloak 90 60

1389 Pasteur

1995. Death Centenary of Louis Pasteur (chemist).
2692 **1389** 84c. multicoloured . . . 1·10 30

1390 Duke of Caxias and Soldiers

1391 Pres. Franco

1995. 150th Anniv of Peace of Ponche Verde (pacification of Farroupilha Revolution) (2693) and 50th Anniv of Battle of Monte Castello (2694). Multicoloured.
2693 12c. Type **1390** 15 10
2694 12c. Soldier, Brazilian flag and battle scene 15 10

1995. Itamar Franco (President 1992–94).
2695 **1391** 12c. multicoloured . . . 15 10

1392 Meal before Child

1393 Alexandre de Gusmao (diplomat)

1995. 50th Anniv of F.A.O.
2696 **1392** 84c. multicoloured . . . 1·10 30

1995. Birth Anniversaries. Multicoloured.
2697 12c. Type **1393** (300th anniv) 15 10
2698 12c. Visconde (Viscount) de Jequitinhonha (lawyer, bicent (1994)) 15 10
2699 15c. Barao (Baron) do Rio Branco (diplomat, 150th anniv) 20 15

1394 Guglielmo Marconi and his Transmitter

1995. Centenary of First Radio Transmission.
2700 **1394** 84c. multicoloured . . . 1·10 30

1395 Ipe-amarelo and Cherry Blossom

1396 Solitary Tinamou ("Tinamus solitarius")

1995. Centenary of Brazil–Japan Friendship Treaty.
2701 **1395** 84c. multicoloured . . . 1·10 30

1995. Birds. Multicoloured.
2702 12c. Type **1396** 15 10
2703 12c. Razor-billed curassow ("Mitu mitu") 15 10

1397 St. John's Party, Campina Grande

1995. June Festivals. Multicoloured.
2704 12c. Type **1397** 15 10
2705 12c. Country wedding, Caruaru 15 10

1398 St. Antony holding Child Jesus (painting, Vieira Lusitano)

1995. 800th Birth Anniv of St. Antony of Padua.
2706 **1398** 84c. multicoloured . . . 1·10 30

1400 Laurel and "Republic"

1401 Player, Net and Anniversary Emblem

1995. 1st Anniv of Real Currency.
2708 **1400** 12c. brown, green & blk 15 10

1995. Centenary of Volleyball.
2709 **1401** 15c. multicoloured . . . 20 15

1402 "Angaturama limai"

1995. 14th Brazilian Palaeontology Society Congress, Uberaba. Dinosaurs. Multicoloured.
2710 15c. Type **1402** 20 10
2711 1r.50 Titanosaurus . . . . 2·00 1·75

1403 Crash Test Dummies in Car

1995. Road Safety Campaign. Multicoloured.
2712 12c. Type **1403** 15 10
2713 71c. Car crashing into glass of whisky 95 85

1404 "Calathea burle-marxii"

1405 Paratroopers

1995. "Singapore '95" International Stamp Exhibition. 10th Anniv of Donation to Nation by Roberto Burle Marx of his Botanical Collection. Multicoloured.
2714 15c. Type **1404** 20 15
2715 15c. "Vellozia burle-marxii" 20 15
2716 1r.50 "Heliconia aemygdiana" . . . . . . 2·00 1·75

1995. 50th Anniv of Parachutist Infantry Brigade.
2717 **1405** 15c. multicoloured . . . 20 15

1406 Paulista Museum and "Fernao Dias Paes Leme" (statue, Luigi Brizzolara)

1995. Centenary of Paulista Museum of the University of Sao Paulo.
2718 **1406** 15c. multicoloured . . . 20 15

1407 Olinda **1408** Scarlet Ibis and Stoat catching Fish

1995. Lighthouses. Multicoloured.
2719 15c. Type **1407** 35 25
2720 15c. Sao Joao 35 25
2721 15c. Santo Antonio da Barra 35 25

1995. "Lubrapex 95" Brazilian–Portuguese Stamp Exhibition, Sao Paulo. Fauna of the Tiete River Valley. Multicoloured.
2722 15c. Type **1408** 30 15
2723 84c. Great egret flying over canoe . . . . 1·10 95

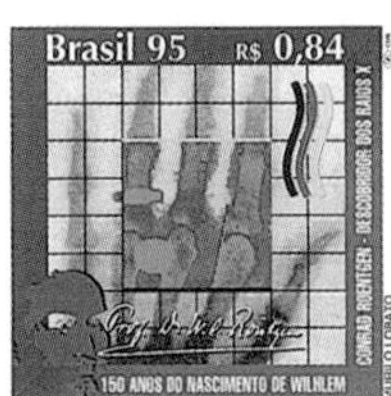

1409 X-Ray of Hand

1995. 150th Birth Anniv of Wilhelm Rontgen and Centenary of his Discovery of X-Rays.
2725 **1409** 84c. multicoloured . . . 1·10 30

1410 Arms and Crowd

1995. Centenary of Flamengo Regatta Club.
2726 **1410** 15c. multicoloured . . . 20 15

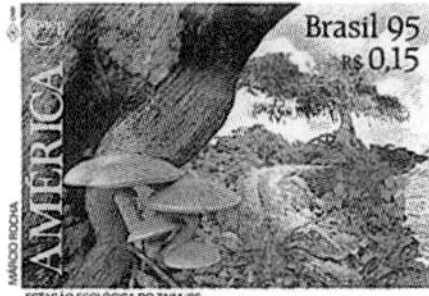

1411 Fungi and Alligator

1995. America. Environmental Protection. Mult.
2727 15c. Type **1411** 20 15
2728 84c. Black-necked swans on lake . . . . 1·10 95
Nos. 2727/8 were issued together, se-tenant, forming a composite design.

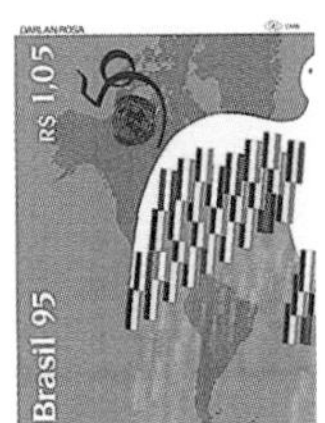

1412 Dove over World Map (left detail) **1413** Jose Maria Eca de Queiroz

1995. 50th Anniv of U.N.O. Multicoloured.
2729 1r.05 Type **1412** . . . . . 1·40 1·25
2730 1r.05 Dove over world map (right detail) . . . . . . 1·40 1·25
Nos. 2729/30 were issued together, se-tenant, forming a composite design.

1995. Book Day. Writers' Anniversaries. Mult.
2731 15c. Type **1413** (150th birth) 20 15
2732 15c. Rubem Braga (5th death) 20 15
2733 23c. Carlos Drummond de Andrade (8th death) . . . 30 25

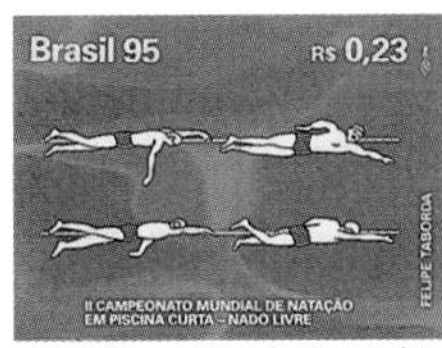

1415 Front Crawl (Freestyle)

1995. 11th World Short-course Swimming Championships, Rio de Janeiro. Multicoloured.
2735 23c. Type **1415** 30 25
2736 23c. Backstroke 30 25
2737 23c. Butterfly 30 25
2738 23c. Breaststroke 30 25
Nos. 2735/8 were issued together, se-tenant, forming a composite design of a swimming pool.

1416 Cherub

1995. Christmas. Multicoloured.
2739 15c. Type **1416** 20 15
2740 23c. Cherub (different) . . . 30 25
Nos. 2739/40 were issued together, se-tenant, forming a composite design.

1417 Flag, Former Headquarters and "Manequinho" (statue)

1995. Centenary (1994) of Botafogo Football and Regatta Club.
2741 **1417** 15c. multicoloured . . . 20 15

1418 Computer, Mouse and Masthead

1995. 170th Anniv of "Diario de Pernambuco" (newspaper)
2742 **1418** 23c. multicoloured . . . 30 25

1420 Prestes Maia and Sao Paulo

1996. Birth Centenary of Francisco Prestes Maia (Mayor of Sao Paulo).
2744 **1420** 18c. multicoloured . . . 20 15

1421 Bornhausen and Santa Catarina

1996. Birth Centenary of Irineu Bornhausen (Governor of State of Santa Catarina).
2745 **1421** 27c. multicoloured . . . 35 30

1422 "Ouro Preto Landscape" (Alberto da Veiga Guignard) **1423** Doll

1996. Artists' Birth Centenaries. Mult.
2746 15c. Type **1422** 20 15
2747 15c. "Boat with Little Flags and Birds" (Alfredo Volpi) 20 15

1996. 50th Anniv of United Nations Children's Fund. Campaign against Sexual Abuse.
2748 **1423** 23c. multicoloured . . . 30 25

1424 Anniversary Emblem **1426** Pantanal

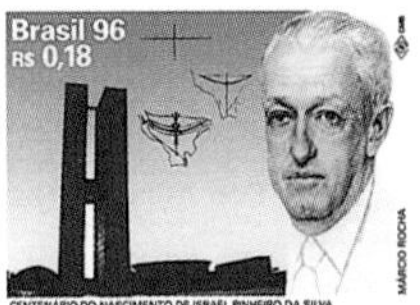

1425 Pinheiro da Silva and National Congress

1996. 500th Anniv (2000) of Discovery of Brazil by the Portuguese.
2749 **1424** 1r.05 multicoloured . . 1·25 1·10

1996. Birth Centenary of Israel Pinheiro da Silva (politician).
2750 **1425** 18c. multicoloured . . . 20 15

1996. Tourism. Multicoloured. Self-adhesive. Imperf (backing paper rouletted).
2751 23c. Amazon River 30 25
2752 23c. Type **1426** 30 25
2753 23c. Jangada raft 30 25
2754 23c. "The Sugarloaf", Guanabara Bay 30 25
2755 23c. Iguazu Falls 30 25

1427 Crimson Topaz

1996. "Espamer 96" Spanish and Latin-American Stamp Exhibition, Seville, Spain. Hummingbirds. Multicoloured.
2756 15c. Type **1427** 20 15
2757 1r.05 Black-breasted plover-crest . . . . 1·25 1·10
2758 1r.15 Swallow-tailed hummingbird . . . . . . 1·40 1·25

1428 Marathon Runners

1996. Cent of Modern Olympic Games. Mult.
2759 18c. Type **1428** 20 15
2760 23c. Gymnastics 30 25
2761 1r.05 Swimming . . . . . . 1·25 1·10
2762 1r.05 Beach volleyball . . . 1·25 1·10

1430 Dish Aerial, Satellite over Earth and Sports

1996. "Americas Telecom 96" International Telecommunications Exn, Rio de Janeiro.
2764 **1430** 1r.05 multicoloured . . 1·25 25

1432 Addict and Drugs

1996. Anti-drug Abuse Campaign.
2766 **1432** 27c. multicoloured . . . 35 30

1433 Coloured Pencils **1435** Gomes and Peace Theatre

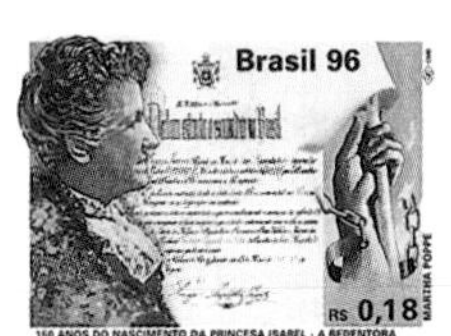

1434 Princess Isabel and Aurea Law

1996. Education Year.
2767 **1433** 23c. multicoloured . . . 30 25

1996. 150th Birth Anniv of Princess Isabel the Redeemer.
2768 **1434** 18c. multicoloured . . . 20 15
The Aurea Law abolished slavery in Brazil.

1996. Death Centenary of Carlos Gomes (opera composer).
2769 **1435** 50c. multicoloured . . . 60 50

1436 "Cattleya eldorado"

1996. 15th International Orchid Conference, Rio de Janeiro. Multicoloured.
2770 15c. Type **1436** 20 15
2771 15c. "Cattleya loddigesii" 20 15
2772 15c. "Promenaea stapellioides" 20 15

1437 Melania and Maximino and Virgin Mary

1996. 150th Anniv of Apparition of Our Lady at La Salette, France.
2773 **1437** 1r. multicoloured . . . 1·25 1·10

1439 "Marilyn Monroe" (Andy Warhol)

1996. 23rd International Biennale, Sao Paulo. Paintings. Multicoloured.
2775 55c. Type **1439** 60 50
2776 55c. "The Scream" (Edvard Munch) 60 50
2777 55c. "Mirror for the red Room" (Louise Bourgeois) 60 50
2778 55c. "Lent" (Pablo Picasso) 60 50

1440 Emblem

1996. Defenders of Nature (environmental organization).
2779 **1440** 10r. multicoloured . . . 11·00 9·50

1441 Vaqueiro **1442** Poinsettia and Lighted Candle

1996. America. Traditional Costumes. Mult.
2780 50c. Type **1441** 60 50
2781 1r. Baiana (seller of beancakes) . . . . 1·25 1·10

1996. Christmas.
2782 **1442** (–) multicoloured . . . 20 15
See second note below No. 2588.

1443 "Melindrosa" (cover of 1931 "O Cruzeiro" magazine) **1444** Ipiranga Monument

1996. 46th Death Anniv of Jose Carlos (caricaturist).
2783 **1443** (–) multicoloured . . . 20 15
See second note below No. 2588.

1996. Tourism. Multicoloured. Self-adhesive. Imperf (backing paper rouletted).
2784 (–) Type **1444** 15 10
2785 (–) Hercilio Luz Bridge . . 15 10
2786 (–) National Congress building 15 10
2787 (–) Pelourinho 15 10
2788 (–) Ver-o-Peso market . . . 15 10
Nos. 2784/8 were valid for use at the current first stage inland letter rate.

1445 Campaign Emblem and Guanabara Bay

1997. Bid by Rio de Janeiro for 2004 Olympic Games.
2789 **1445** (–) multicoloured . . . 60 50
No. 2789 was valid for use at the current first stage international letter rate.

1446 Postman and Letter Recipients

1997. America. The Postman.
2790 **1446** (–) multicoloured . . . 15 10
No. 2790 was valid for use at the current first stage inland letter rate.

1447 Alves, Flogging and Salvador Harbour

1997. 150th Birth Anniv of Antonio de Castro Alves (poet).
2791 **1447** 15c. multicoloured . . . 30 10

1448 Tamandare (after Miranda Junior) and "Rescue of 'Ocean Monarch by 'Don Afonso " (Samuel Walters)

1997. Death Centenary of Marquis of Tamandare (naval reformer).
2792 **1448** 23c. multicoloured . . . 40 20

1449 "Joy. Joy"

1997. Winning Entry in "Art on Stamps" Competition.
2793 **1449** 15c. multicoloured . . . 15 10

1450 Globe in Glass of Water **1451** Embraer EMB-145

1997. World Water Day.
2794 **1450** 1r.05 multicoloured . . 1·10 95

1997. Brazilian Aircraft. Multicoloured. Self-adhesive. Imperf (backing paper rouletted).
2795 15c. Type **1451** 15 10
2796 15c. Aeritalia/Aermacchi AM-X jet fighter 15 10
2797 15c. Embraer EMB-312 H Super Tucano 15 10
2798 15c. Embraer EMB-120 Brasilia 15 10
2799 15c. Embraer EMB-312 Tucano trainer 15 10

1452 Red Ribbon inside Condom **1454** Emblem

1997. Family Health Association (A.S.F.) Anti-AIDS Campaign.
2810 **1452** 23c. multicoloured . . . 25 20

1997. 500th Anniv (2000) of Discovery of Brazil by the Portuguese.
2812 **1454** 1r.05 multicoloured . . 1·10 95

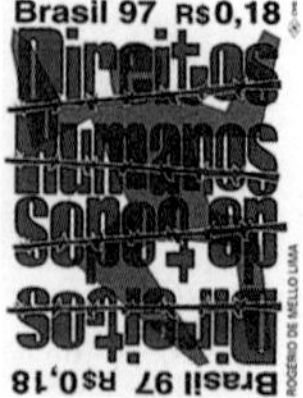

1455 Pixinguinha **1457** Inscription

1997. Birth Centenary of Pixinguinha (musician).
2813 **1455** 15c. multicoloured . . . 15 10

1997. "Human Rights, Rights of All".
2815 **1457** 18c. black and red . . . 20 15

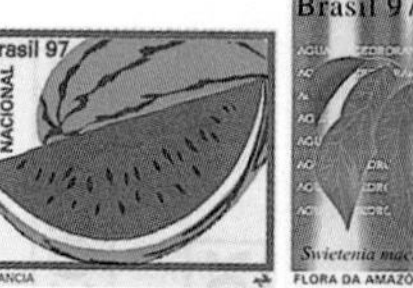

1459 Melon **1460** Mahogany ("Swietenia macropylla")

1997. Fruits. Self-adhesive. (a) Imperf (backing paper rouletted). (i) With service indicator.
2817 **1459** (–) red and green . . . 20 15

(ii) With face values.
2818 – 1c. yellow, orange & grn 10 10
2819 – 2c. yellow, brown & blk . . 10 10
2820 – 5c. orange, yellow & blk 10 10
2821 – 10c. yellow, brown & grn 10 10
2822 – 20c. yellow, red & green 20 15

(b) Die-cut wavy edge.
2823 – 1c. yellow, orange & grn 10 10
2826 – 10c. yellow, brown & grn 10 10
2828 – 20c. lt green, grn & blk . . 20 15
2829 – 22c. red, purple & green 20 15
2830 – 27c. orange, brown and green 55 50
2831 – 40c. multicoloured 40 35
2832 – 50c. multicoloured 30 25
2833 – 51c. green, lt grn & brn . . 50 45
2834 – 80c. red, green & yellow 80 70
2835 – 82c. lt grn, grn & dp grn 80 70
2836 – 1r. red, green & yellow . . 1·00 90
DESIGNS—HORIZ: Nos. 2818, 2823, Oranges; 2819, Bananas; 2820, Mango. VERT: Nos. 2821, 2826, Pineapple; 2822, Cashew nuts; 2828, Sugar-apple; 2829, Grapes; 2830, Cupuacu; 2831, Soursop; 2832, Suriname cherry ("Pitanga"); 2833, Coconut; 2834, Apples; 2835, Limes; 2836, Strawberries.
No. 2817 was valid for use at the current first stage inland letter rate.

1997. World Environment Day. Amazon Flora and Fauna. Multicoloured.
2836 27c. Type **1460** 30 25
2837 27c. Arapaima (55 × 22 mm) 30 25

1461 Antonio Vieira in Pulpit

1997. Death Anniversaries of Missionaries to Brazil. Multicoloured.
2838 1r.05 Type **1461** (300th) . . 1·10 95
2839 1r.05 Indian children and Jose de Auchieta (400th) 1·10 95

1462 Parnaiba Delta and Sculpture (Mestre Dezinho) **1463** Blue-black Grassquit

1997. Tourism. With service indicator. Mult.
2840 (–) Type **1462** . . . . . . 1·25 1·10
2841 (–) Lencois Maranhenses National Park and costume . . . . 1·25 1·10
Nos. 2840/1 were valid for use at the current rate for first class international postage.

1997. Birds. Multicoloured. Self-adhesive. Imperf (backing paper rouletted). (a) With service indicator.
2842 (–) Type **1463** 20 15

(b) With face value.
2843 22c. Social flycatcher ("Vermilion-crowned Flycatcher") 20 15
No. 2842 was valid for use at the current first stage inland letter rate.

1464 Academy

1998. Cent of Brazilian Literature Academy.
2850 **1464** 22c. multicoloured . . . 20 15

1465 "Gipsies" (Di Cavalcanti)

1997. Birth Centenary of Emiliano di Cavalcanti (artist).
2851 **1465** 31c. multicoloured . . . 30 25

1466 Pope John Paul II, "Christ the Redeemer" and Family

1997. 2nd World Meeting of Pope with Families, Rio de Janeiro.
2852 **1466** 1r.20 multicoloured . . 1·25 1·10

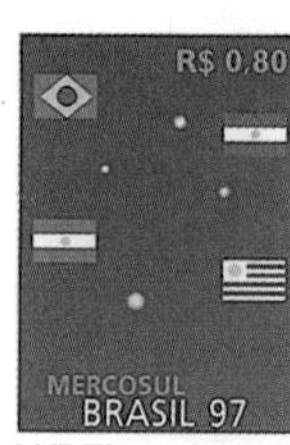

1467 Flags of Member Countries **1468** Antonio Conselheiro (religious leader)

1997. Mercosur (South American Common Market).
2853 **1467** 80c. multicoloured . . . 80 70

1997. Centenary of End of Canudos War.
2854 **1468** 22c. multicoloured . . . 20 15

1469 Mercosur Members starred on Map of South America

1997. 25th Anniv of Telebras.
2855 **1469** 80c. multicoloured . . . 80 70

1470 Lorenzo Fernandez and Score of "Sonata Breve"

1997. Composers' Birth Centenaries. Each black and gold.
2856 22c. Type **1470** 20 15
2857 22c. Francisco Mignone and score of "Second Brazilian Fantasia" 20 15

1471 "Our Good Mother" and Blackboard with Marist Motto

1997. Centenary of Marist Brothers in Brazil.

2858	**1471**	22c. multicoloured . . .	20	15

1472 Angel playing Trumpet

1473 "Equality" (Gian Calvi)

1997. Christmas.

2859	**1472**	22c. multicoloured . . .	20	15

1997. Children and Citizenship. Multicoloured.

2860	22c.+8c. Type **1473**	30	25
2861	22c.+8c. "Love and Tenderness" (Alcy Linares)	30	25
2862	22c.+8c. "Admission to School" (Ziraldo)	30	25
2863	22c.+8c. "Healthy Pregnancy" (Claudio Martins)	30	25
2864	22c.+8c. "Being Happy" (Cica Fittipaldi)	30	25
2865	22c.+8c. "Work for Parents, School for Children" (Roger Mello)	30	25
2866	22c.+8c. "Breast-feeding" (Angela Lago)	30	25
2867	22c.+8c. "Civil Registration" (Mauricio de Sousa)	30	25
2868	22c.+8c. "Integration of the Handicapped" (Nelson Cruz)	30	25
2869	22c.+8c. "Presence of Parents during Illness" (Eliardo Franca)	30	25
2870	22c.+8c. "Quality of Teaching" (Graca Lima)	30	25
2871	22c.+8c. "Safe Delivery" (Eva Furnari)	30	25
2872	22c.+8c. "Family and Community Life" (Gerson Conforti)	30	25
2873	22c.+8c. "Music playing" (Ana Raquel)	30	25
2874	22c.+8c. "Respect and Dignity" (Helena Alexandrino)	30	25
2875	22c.+8c. "Summary of Children's Statute" (Darlan Rosa)	30	25

1474 Children and Globe

1997. Education and Citizenship.

2876	**1474**	31c. blue and yellow . .	30	25

1475 Belo Horizonte at Night

1476 Outline Map and Books (Education)

1997. Centenary of Belo Horizonte.

2877	**1475**	31c. multicoloured . . .	30	25

1997. Citizens' Rights. Mult. Self-adhesive.

2878	22c. Type **1476**	20	15
2879	22c. Map and hand holding labour card (work) . . .	20	15
2880	22c. Map and fruit (agriculture)	20	15
2881	22c. Map and stethoscope (health)	20	15
2882	22c. Clapper-board and paint brush (culture) . . .	20	15

1477 Alexandrite

1998. Minerals. Multicoloured.

2883	22c. Type **1477**	15	10
2884	22c. Chrysoberyl cat's-eye	15	10
2885	22c. Indicolite	15	10

1478 Elis Regina (singer)

1998. America. Famous Women. Multicoloured.

2886	22c. Type **1478**	15	10
2887	22c. Clementina de Jesus (singer)	15	10
2888	22c. Dulcina de Moraes (actress)	15	10
2889	22c. Clarice Lispector (writer)	15	10

1479 Pupils

1998. Education. Multicoloured.

2890	31c. Type **1479** (universal schooling)	20	15
2891	31c. Teacher (teacher appraisal)	20	15

Nos. 2390/1 were issued together, se-tenant, forming a composite design of a classroom.

1480 Cruze Sousa

1998. Death Centenary of Joao da Cruze Sousa (poet).

2892	**1480**	36c. multicoloured . . .	20	15

1481 Map, 1519

1998. 500th Anniv (2000) of Discovery of Brazil by the Portuguese. Multicoloured.

2893	1r.05 Type **1481**	65	55
2894	1r.05 Galleon	1·10	90

Nos. 2893/4 were issued together, se-tenant, forming a composite design.

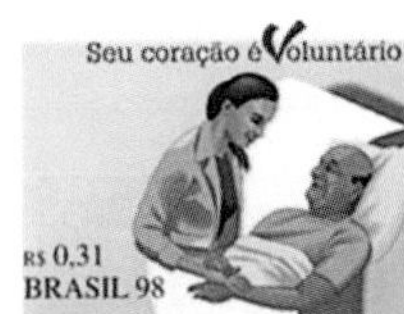

1482 Woman Caring for Elderly Man

1998. Voluntary Work. Multicoloured.

2895	31c. Type **1482**	20	15
2896	31c. Woman caring for child	20	15
2897	31c. Fighting forest fire . .	20	15
2898	31c. Adult's and child's hands	20	15

Nos. 2895/8 were issued together, se-tenant, forming a composite design.

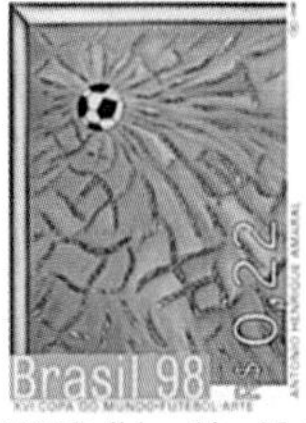

1483 Clown

1485 Ball breaking Net (Antonio Henrique Amaral)

1484 Turtle

1998. Circus. Multicoloured.

2899	31c. Type **1483**	20	15
2900	31c. Clown resting on stick	20	15
2901	31c. Clown (left half) and outside of Big Top . . .	20	15
2902	31c. Clown (right half) and inside of Big Top	20	15

Nos. 2899/2902 were issued together, se-tenant, forming a composite design.

1998. Expo '98 World's Fair, Lisbon. International Year of the Ocean. Multicoloured.

2903	31c. Type **1484**	20	15
2904	31c. Tail of whale	20	15
2905	31c. Barracuda	20	15
2906	31c. Jellyfish and fishes . .	20	15
2907	31c. Diver and school of fishes	20	15
2908	31c. Two dolphins	20	15
2909	31c. Angelfish (brown spotted fish)	20	15
2910	31c. Two whales	20	15
2911	31c. Two long-nosed butterflyfishes (with black stripe across eye)	20	15
2912	31c. Sea perch (red and yellow fish)	20	15
2913	31c. Manatee	20	15
2914	31c. Seabream (blue, yellow and white fish)	20	15
2915	31c. Emperor angelfish and coral	20	15
2916	31c. School of snappers (blue and yellow striped fishes)	20	15
2917	31c. Flying gurnard	20	15
2918	31c. Manta ray	20	15
2919	31c. Two butterflyfishes (black and green fishes)	20	15
2920	31c. Pipefish	20	15
2921	31c. Moray eel	20	15
2922	31c. Angelfish (blue, yellow and black) and coral . . .	20	15
2923	31c. Red and yellow fish, starfish and coral	20	15
2924	31c. Crab and coral	20	15
2925	31c. Snapper and coral . . .	20	15
2926	31c. Seahorse and coral . .	20	15

Nos. 2903/26 were issued together, se-tenant, forming a composite design.

1998. World Cup Football Championship, France. Designs depicting football art by named artists. Multicoloured.

2927	22c. Type **1485**	15	10
2928	22c. Aldemir Martins . . .	15	10
2929	22c. Glauco Rodrigues . . .	15	10
2930	22c. Marcia Grostein . . .	15	10
2931	22c. Claudio Tozzi	15	10
2932	22c. Zelio Alves Pinto . . .	15	10
2933	22c. Guto Lacaz	15	10
2934	22c. Antonio Peticov . . .	15	10
2935	22c. Cildo Meireles	15	10
2936	22c. Mauricio Nogueira Lima	15	10
2937	22c. Roberto Magalhaes . .	15	10
2938	22c. Luiz Zerbine	15	10
2939	22c. Maciej Babinski (horiz)	15	10
2940	22c. Wesley Duke Lee (horiz)	15	10
2941	22c. Joao Camara (horiz)	15	10
2942	22c. Jose Zaragoza (horiz)	15	10
2943	22c. Mario Gruber (horiz)	15	10
2944	22c. Nelson Leirner (horiz)	15	10
2945	22c. Carlos Vergara (horiz)	15	10
2946	22c. Tomoshige Kusuno (horiz)	15	10
2947	22c. Gregorio Gruber (horiz)	15	10
2948	22c. Jose Roberto Aguilar (horiz)	15	10
2949	22c. Ivald Granato (horiz)	15	10
2950	22c. Leda Catunda (horiz)	15	10

1486 Bean Casserole and Vegetables

1998. Cultural Dishes.

2951	**1486**	31c. multicoloured . . .	20	15

1487 "Araucaria angustifolia"

1998. Environmental Protection. Multicoloured.

2952	22c. Type **1487**	15	10
2953	22c. Azure jay ("Cyanocorax caeruleus")	15	10

Nos. 2952/3 were issued together, se-tenant, forming a composite design.

1488 "Tapajo"

1998. Launching of Submarine "Tapajo".

2954	**1488**	51c. multicoloured . . .	60	35

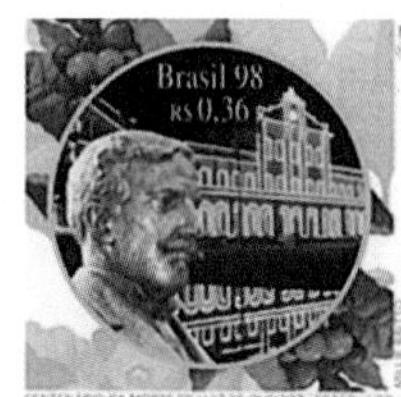

1489 Bust of Queiroz and College Building

1998. Death Centenary of Luiz de Queiroz (founder of Agricultural College, Piracicaba).

2955	**1489**	36c. multicoloured . . .	20	15

1490 Statue of St. Benedict and Monastery

1998. 400th Anniv of St. Benedict's Monastery, Sao Paulo.

2956	**1490**	22c. multicoloured . . .	15	10

1491 Santos-Dumont and his First Balloon "Brasil"

1998. Aviation. Aircraft Designs by Alberto Santos-Dumont (aviator). Multicoloured.

2957	31c. Type **1491**	20	15
2958	31c. Santos-Dumont and Dirigible "No.1"	20	15

1492 Early Film of Guanabara Bay

1998. Centenary (1997) of Brazilian Cinema. Multicoloured.

2959	31c. Type **1492**	20	15
2960	31c. Taciana Reis (actress) in "Limite" (dir. Mario Peixoto, 1912)	20	15
2961	31c. Grande Otela and Oscarito in "A Dupla do Barulho" (dir. Carlos Manga, 1953) (inscr "Chanchada")	20	15
2962	31c. Mazzaropi (actor) and film titles (Vera Cruz film company)	20	15
2963	31c. Glauber Rocha (director) ("New Cinema")	20	15
2964	31c. Titles of prize-winning films, 1962–98	20	15

1493 Andrade, Entrance to St. Antony's Church (Tiradentes) and Church of Our Lady of the Rosary (Ouro Preto)

1998. Birth Centenary of Rodrigo Melo Franco de Andrade (founder of Federal Institution for Preservation of the National Historic and Artistic Patrimony).
2965 **1493** 51c. multicoloured . . . 30 25

1494 Cascudo and Folk Characters

1998. Birth Centenary of Luis da Camara Cascudo (writer).
2966 **1494** 22c. multicoloured . . . 15 10

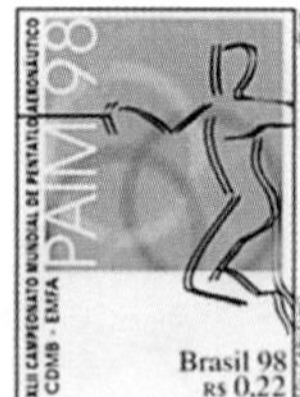

1495 Fencing

1998. 42nd World Aeronautical Pentathlon Championships, Natal. Multicoloured.
2967 22c. Type **1495** 15 10
2968 22c. Running 15 10
2969 22c. Swimming 15 10
2970 22c. Shooting 15 10
2971 22c. Basketball 15 10

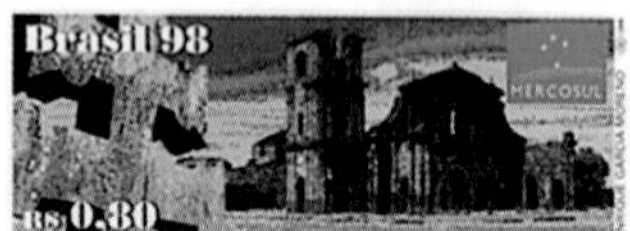

1496 Missionary Cross and St. Michael of the Missions Church

1998. Mercosur. Missions.
2972 **1496** 80c. multicoloured . . . 50 45

1497 Untitled Work (Jose Leonilson) (Biennale emblem)

1998. 24th Art Biennale, Sao Paulo. Paintings. Mult.
2973 31c. Type **1497** 20 15
2974 31c. "Tapuia Dance" (Albert von Eckhout) . . 20 15
2975 31c. "The Schoolboy" (Vincent van Gogh) (vert) 20 15
2976 31c. "Portrait of Michel Leiris" (Francis Bacon) (vert) 20 15
2977 31c. "The King's Museum" (Rene Magritte) (vert) . . 20 15
2978 31c. "Urutu" (Tarsila do Amaral) 20 15
2979 31c. "Facade with Arcs, Circle and Fascia" (Alfredo Volpi) (vert) . . 20 15
2980 31c. "The Raft of the Medusa" (Asger Jorn) . . 20 15

1498 "Citizenship" (Erika Albuquerque)

1998. Child and Citizenship.
2981 **1498** 22c. multicoloured . . . 15 10

1499 Mail Coach and "Postilhao da America" (brigantine)

1998. Bicentenary of Reorganization of Maritime Mail Service between Portugal and Brazil.
2982 **1499** 1r.20 multicoloured . . 1·10 90

1500 "D. Pedro I" (Simplicio Rodrigues da Sa), Crown and Sceptre

1501 Mangoes and Glasses of Juice

1998. Birth Bicentenary of Emperor Pedro I.
2983 **1500** 22c. multicoloured . . . 15 10

1998. Frisco (fruit juice) Publicity Campaign. Self-adhesive.
2984 **1501** 36c. multicoloured . . . 20 15

1502 "Solanum lycocarpum"

1998. Cerrado Flowers. Multicoloured.
2985 31c. Type **1502** 20 15
2986 31c. "Cattleya walkeriana" 20 15
2987 31c. "Kielmeyera coriacea" 20 15

1503 Mother Teresa (founder of Missionaries of Charity)

1998. Peace and Fraternity. Multicoloured.
2988 31c. Type **1503** 20 15
2989 31c. Friar Galvao (first Brazilian to be beatified, 1998) 20 15
2990 31c. Betinho (Herbert Jose de Souza) 20 15
2991 31c. Friar Damiao 20 15
Nos. 2988/91 were issued together, se-tenant, forming a central composite design of the Earth.

1504 Sergio Motta and Headquarters, Brasilia

1998. 1st Anniv of National Telecommunications Agency.
2992 **1504** 31c. multicoloured . . . 20 15
Motta was Minister of Communications when the agency was established.

1505 Tiles and Church of Our Lady of Fatima, Brasilia

1998. Christmas.
2993 **1505** 22c. multicoloured . . . 15 10

1506 Moxoto Goat **1507** Man casting Winged Shadow

1998. Domestic Animals. Mult. Self-adhesive.
2994 22c. Type **1506** 15 10
2995 22c. North-eastern donkey 15 10
2996 22c. Junqueira ox 15 10
2997 22c. Brazilian terrier (vert) 15 10
2998 22c. Brazilian shorthair (vert) 15 10

1998. 50th Anniv of Universal Declaration of Human Rights.
2999 **1507** 1r.20 multicoloured . . 75 65

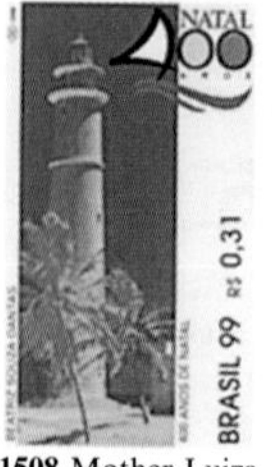

1508 Mother Luiza Lighthouse, Natal **1510** Stamp Vending Machines of 1940s and 1998

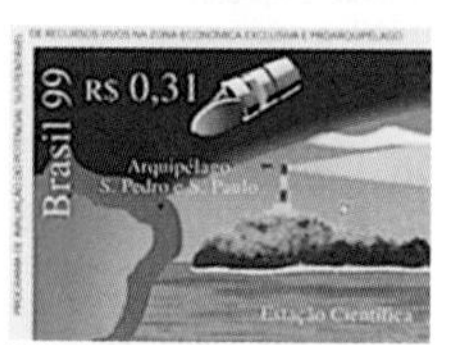

1509 Extent of Economic Zone, Satellite and Belmonte Lighthouse

1999. 400th Annivs of Natal (1999) and of Wise Men's Fortress (1998). Multicoloured.
3000 31c. Type **1508** 20 15
3001 31c. Wise Men's Fortress, Natal (horiz) 20 15

1999. Evaluation Programme of Sustainable Potential of Living Resources in the Exclusive Economic Zone (REVIZEE). Multicoloured.
3002 31c. Type **1509** (Sao Pedro and Sao Paulo Archipelago Research Programme) 20 15
3003 31c. Blue-faced booby on buoy 20 15
3004 31c. "Riobaldo" (research ship) 20 15
3005 31c. Turtle 20 15
3006 31c. Dolphin 20 15
3007 31c. Diver 20 15
Nos. 3002/7 were issued together, se-tenant, forming a composite design.
No. 3004 includes the emblem of "Australia 99" International Stamp Exhibition, Melbourne.

1999. 125th Anniv of Universal Postal Union. Multicoloured.
3008 31c. Type **1510** 20 15
3009 31c. Postal products vending machines of 1906 and 1998 . . . . 20 15
3010 31c. Postboxes of 1870 and 1973 . . . . 20 15
3011 31c. Brazilian Quality and Productivity Programme silver award to Rio Grande postal region, 1998 . . . . 20 15
Nos. 3008/11 were issued together, se-tenant, forming a composite design of the U.P.U. emblem.

1511 Lacerda Lift, Barra Lighthouse and Church of Our Lady of the Rosary

1999. 450th Anniv of Salvador.
3012 **1511** 1r.05 multicoloured . . 65 55

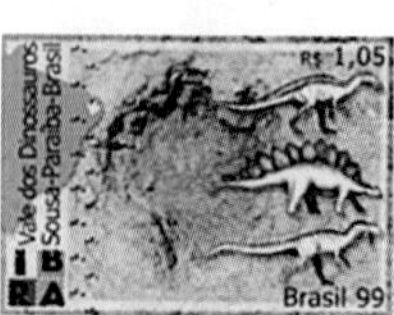

1512 Footprint, Iguanodon, Stegosaurus and Allosaurus

1999. "iBRA 99" International Stamp Exhibition, Nuremberg, Germany. Valley of the Dinosaurs, Sousa.
3013 **1512** 1r.05 multicoloured . . 65 55

1513 Fortress

1999. 415th Anniv of St. Amaro of Barra Grande Fortress, Guaruja.
3014 **1513** 22c. multicoloured . . . 15 10

1515 Camouflaged Airplane, Emblem, Dove and Globe

1999. 30th Anniv of 6th Air Transportation Squadron.
3016 **1515** 51c. multicoloured . . . 30 25

1516 Banner and Revellers **1519** Santos-Dumont and Ballon No.3

1518 Symbols of Computer Science, Chemistry, Engineering, Metallurgy and Geology

1999. Feast of the Holy Spirit, Planaltina.
3017 **1516** 22c. multicoloured . . . 15 10

1999. Centenary of Institute for Technological Research, Sao Paulo.
3019 **1518** 36c. multicoloured . . . 20 15

1999. Centenary of Flight of Alberto Santos-Dumont's Airship Ballon No.3.
3020 **1519** 1r.20 multicoloured . . 75 70

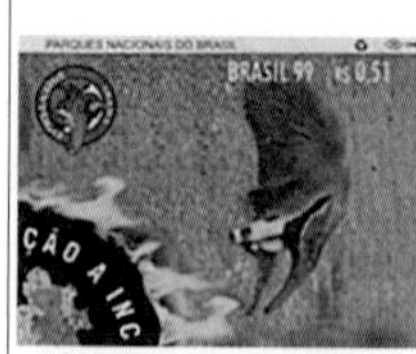

1520 Anteater and Emblem **1522** Stitched Heart

1999. National Campaign for Prevention and Combat of Forest Fires (PREVFOGO). Mult. Self-adhesive.
3021 51c. Type **1520** 35 30
3022 51c. Flower and IBAMA emblem 35 30
3023 51c. Leaf and IBAMA emblem 35 30
3024 51c. Burnt tree trunk and PREVFOGO emblem . . 35 30
Nos. 3021/4 were issued together, se-tenant, forming a composite design of a map and flames.
Nos. 3021/4 are also impregnated with the scent of burnt wood.

1999. 20th Anniv of Political Amnesty in Brazil.
3026 **1522** 22c. multicoloured . . . 15 10

1523 Joaquim Nabuco (politician)

1999. 150th Birth Anniversaries. Multicoloured.
3027 22c. Type **1523** 15 10
3028 31c. Rui Barbosa (politician) 20 15

1524 Dorado

1999. "China '99" International Stamp Exhibition, Peking. Fishes. Multicoloured.

3029	22c. Type **1524**	15	10
3030	31c. *Brycon microlepis*	20	15
3031	36c. *Acestrorhynchus pantaneiro*	25	20
3032	51c. Tetra "*Hyphessobrycon eques*"	35	30
3033	80c. *Rineloricaria* sp.	55	45
3034	90c. *Leporinus macrocephalus*	65	55
3035	1r.05 *Abramites* sp.	75	65
3036	1r.20 Bristle-mouthed catfish	85	75

Nos. 3029/36 were issued together, se-tenant, with the backgrounds forming a composite design.

No. 3036 also includes a hologram of the exhibition emblem.

1525 Open Book and Flags of Member Countries

1999. Mercosur. The Book.

3037	**1525** 80c. multicoloured	55	45

1526 Aguas Emendadas Ecological Station

1999. Water Resources. Multicoloured.

3038	31c. Type **1526**	20	15
3039	31c. House and jetty	20	15
3040	31c. Cedro Dam	20	15
3041	31c. Oros Dam	20	15

Nos. 3038/41 were issued together, se-tenant, forming a composite design of a whirlpool.

1527 "Ex Libris" (Eliseu Visconti)

1999. National Library, Rio de Janeiro.

3042	**1527** 22c. multicoloured	15	10

1999. State Flags (6th series). As T **992**.

3043	31c. Amapa	20	15
3044	36c. Roraima	25	20

1528 Piano and Woman

1999. 5th Death Anniv of Antonio Carlos Jobim (composer).

3045	**1528** 31c. multicoloured	20	15

1529 The Annunciation

1999. Christmas. Birth Bimillenary of Jesus Christ. Multicoloured.

3046	22c. Type **1529**	15	10
3047	22c. Adoration of the Magi	15	10
3048	22c. Presentation of Jesus in the Temple	15	10
3049	22c. Baptism of Jesus by John the Baptist	15	10
3050	22c. Jesus and the Twelve Apostles	15	10
3051	22c. Death and resurrection of Jesus	15	10

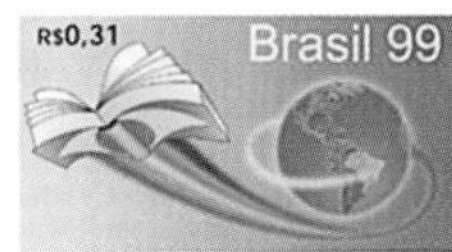

1530 Open Book and Globe

1999. New Middle School Education Programme.

3052	**1530** 31c. multicoloured	20	15

1531 Itamaraty Palace, Rio de Janeiro

1999. Centenary of Installation of Ministry of Foreign Relations Headquarters in Itamaraty Palace, Rio de Janeiro.

3053	**1531** 1r.05 brown and stone	75	65

1532 Buildings and Trees (Milena Karoline Ribeiro Reis)

2000. "Stampin the Future". Winning Entries in Children's International Painting Competition. Mult.

3054	22c.+8c. Type **1532**	20	15
3055	22c.+8c. Globe, sun, trees, children and whale (Caio Ferreira Guimaraes de Oliveira)	20	15
3056	22c.+8c. Woman with globe on dress (Clarissa Cazane)	20	15
3057	22c.+8c. Children hugging globe (Jonas Sampaio de Freitas)	20	15

1533 "2000"

2000. New Millennium.

3058	**1533** 90c. multicoloured	65	55

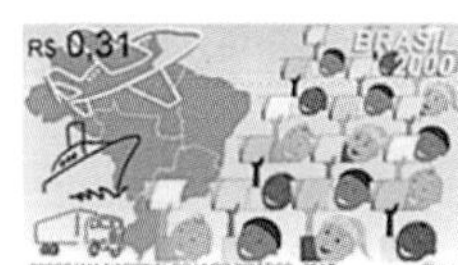

1534 Map of South America and Children holding Books

2000. National School Book Programme.

3059	**1534** 31c. multicoloured	20	15

1535 Ada Rogato

2000. Women Aviators. Multicoloured.

3060	22c. Type **1535**	15	10
3061	22c. Thereza de Marzo	15	10
3062	22c. Anesia Pinheiro	15	10

1536 Moqueca Capixaba

2000. Cultural Dishes. Multicoloured.

3063	1r.05 Type **1536**	75	65
3064	1r.05 Moqueca baiana	75	65

1537 Freyre and Institute Facade

2000. Birth Centenary of Gilberto Freyre (writer).

3065	**1537** 36c. multicoloured	25	15

1538 Painting and Emblem

2000. 500th Anniv of the Discovery of Brazil.

3066	**1538** 51c. multicoloured	30	25

1539 Natives

2000. 500th Anniv of the Discovery of Brazil. Multicoloured.

3067	31c. Type **1539**	15	10
3068	31c. Natives watching ships	15	10
3069	31c. Sailors in rigging	15	10
3070	31c. Ships sails and natives	15	10

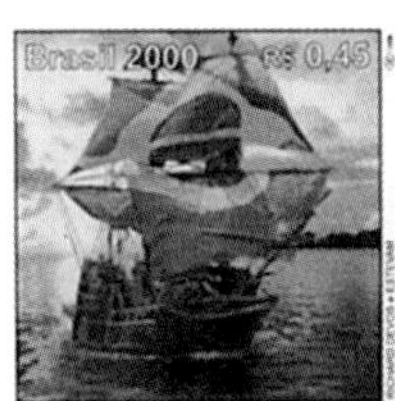

1540 Sailing Ship and Brazilian Flag

2000. 500th Anniv of the Discovery of Brazil. Multicoloured.

3071	45c. Type **1540**	25	10
3072	45c. Man dressed in red suit, pineapple and telephone dial	25	10
3073	45c. Red-spectacled amazon and silhouettes of sailing ships	25	10
3074	45c. Four babies	25	10
3075	45c. Go-kart, Formula 1 racing car and Ayrton Senna	25	10
3076	45c. Sloth, Toco toucan, crocodile, penguin and tiger	25	10
3077	45c. Outline of Brazil and compass roses	25	10
3078	45c. Peace dove	25	10
3079	45c. Child with decorated face	25	10
3080	45c. "500" emblem	25	10
3081	45c. Man wearing feather headdress	25	10
3082	45c. Man in boat, sails and town (Nataly M. N. Moriya)	25	10
3083	45c. Wristwatch, balloon, Alberto Santos-Dumont and his biplane *14 bis*	25	10
3084	45c. Sailing ship and document (first report of discovery)	25	10
3085	45c. Jules Rimet Cup and World Cup trophies, player, football and year dates (Brazilian victories in World Cup Football Championship)	25	10
3086	45c. Hand writing, street lights and fireworks	25	10
3087	45c. Banners and Brazilian flag forming cow	25	10
3088	45c. Golden conure perched on branch	25	10
3089	45c. Bakairi masks	25	10
3090	45c. Globe, ship and emblem	25	10

1541 Globe and Map of Brazil

2000. 2nd Anniv of BrazilTradeNet (business information web site).

3091	**1541** 27c. multicoloured	10	10

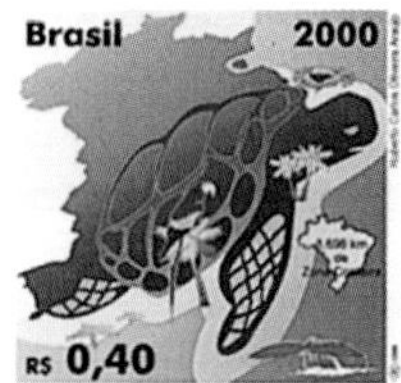

1542 Turtle, Scarlet Macaw and Map

2000. National Coastal Management Programme (G.E.R.C.O.).

3092	**1542** 40c. multicoloured	20	10

1544 Cruz, Students and Building Facade

2000. Centenary of the Oswaldo Cruz Foundation (medical research institution).

3094	**1544** 40c. multicoloured	20	10

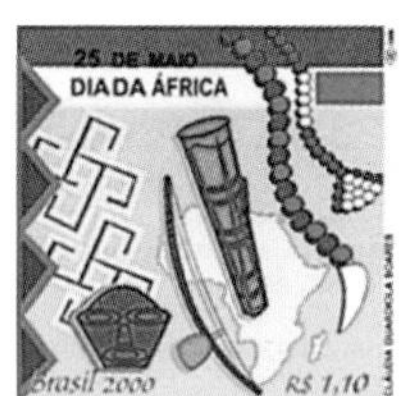

1545 Mask, Musical Instruments and Jewellery

2000. Africa Day.

3095	**1545** 1r.10 multicoloured	60	20

1546 Klink in Rowing Boat and Portion of Globe showing Route

2000. Voyages by Amyr Klink (navigator). Multicoloured.

3096	1r. Type **1546** (first South Atlantic crossing by rowing boat (1984))	55	30
3097	1r. *Paratii* (polar sailing boat) in Antarctica and portion of globe showing route (first single-handed circumnavigation of Antarctica (1999))	55	30

Nos. 3096/7 were issued together, se-tenant, forming a composite design.

1547 Flag, Buildings, Map and City Arms

2000. 150th Anniv of Juiz de Fora.

3098	**1547** 60c. multicoloured	35	20

1548 Hang Gliding

2000. Outdoor Pursuits. Multicoloured. Self-adhesive.

3099	27c. Type **1548**	10	10
3100	27c. Surfing	10	10
3101	40c. Rock climbing	20	10
3102	40c. Skateboarding	20	10

1549 Forest

2000. Environmental Protection. Multicoloured.
3103 40c. Type **1549** 20 10
3104 40c. Oncilla standing on branch in forest 20 10
3105 40c. Vegetation, adult oncilla and head of kitten 20 10
3106 40c. Vegetation, adult oncilla and body of kitten 20 10
Nos. 3103/6 were issued together, se-tenant, forming a composite design.

1550 *Cisne Branco* (full-rigged cadet ship)

2000. Brazilian Navy. Cadet Ships. Multicoloured.
3107 27c. Type **1550** 10 10
3108 27c. *Brasil* (cadet frigate) . . 10 10

1553 Teixeira, Carneiro Ribeiro Education Center, Salvador and Pupils

2000. Birth Centenary of Anisio Teixeira (education reformer).
3111 **1553** 45c. multicoloured . . . 25 10

1554 Child walking to School

2000. 10th Anniv of the Children and Teenagers Statute (3112) and 15th Anniv of National Movement of Street Boys and Girls (3113). Multicoloured.
3112 27c. Type **1554** 10 10
3113 40c. Rainbow with girl and boy holding star 20 10

1555 Capanema

2000. Birth Centenary of Gustavo Capanema Filho (politician).
3114 **1555** 60c. multicoloured . . . 40 20

1556 Television and Hand writing in Notebook

2000. 5th Anniv of Telecourse 2000 (educational television programme).
3115 **1556** 27c. multicoloured . . . 20 10

1557 Campos

2000. Birth Centenary of Milton Campos (politician and lawyer).
3116 **1557** 1r. multicoloured . . . 70 40

1558 Hand protecting Globe

2000. World Day for Protection of the Ozone Layer.
3117 **1558** 1r.45 multicoloured . . 1·00 60

1559 Archery

2000. Olympic Games, Sydney. Multicoloured.
3118 40c. Type **1559** 30 15
3119 40c. Beach volleyball . . . 30 15
3120 40c. Boxing 30 15
3121 40c. Football 30 15
3122 40c. Canoeing 30 15
3123 40c. Handball 30 15
3124 40c. Diving 30 15
3125 40c. Rhythmic gymnastics 30 15
3126 40c. Badminton 30 15
3127 40c. Swimming 30 15
3128 40c. Hurdling 30 15
3129 40c. Pentathlon 30 15
3130 40c. Basketball 30 15
3131 40c. Tennis 30 15
3132 40c. Marathon 30 15
3133 40c. High-jump 30 15
3134 40c. Long-distance running 30 15
3135 40c. Triple jump 30 15
3136 40c. Triathlon 30 15
3137 40c. Sailing 30 15
3138 40c. Pommel horse (gymnastics) 30 15
3139 40c. Weightlifting 30 15
3140 40c. Discus 30 15
3141 40c. Rings (gymnastics) . . 30 15
3142 40c. Athletics 30 15
3143 40c. Javelin 30 15
3144 40c. Artistic gymnastics . . 30 15
3145 40c. Hockey 30 15
3146 40c. Volleyball 30 15
3147 40c. Synchronized swimming 30 15
3148 40c. Judo 30 15
3149 40c. Wrestling 30 15
3150 40c. Cycling 30 15
3151 40c. Rowing 30 15
3152 40c. Parallel bars (gymnastics) 30 15
3153 40c. Horse riding 30 15
3154 40c. Pole vault 30 15
3155 40c. Fencing 30 15
3156 40c. Rifle shooting 30 15
3157 40c. Taekwondo 30 15

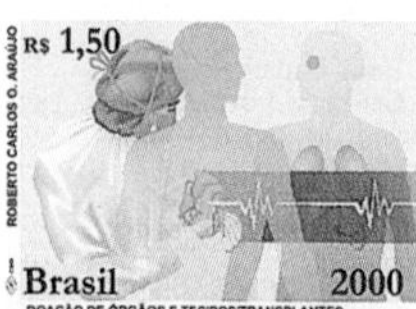

1560 Surgeon and Electrocardiogram Graph

2000. Organ Donation. Multicoloured.
3158 1r.50 Type **1560** . . . . . 1·10 65
3159 1r.50 Hands holding heart 1·10 65
Nos. 3158/9 were issued together, se-tenant, each pair forming a composite design.

1561 Brazilian Clovis Mask

2000. Brazil--China Joint Issue. 25th Anniv of Diplomatic Relations between Brazil and China. Multicoloured.
3160 27c. Type **1561** 20 10
3161 27c. Chinese Monkey King puppet 20 10

1562 Chico Landi and Ferrari 125 Formula 1 Racing Car

2000. Motor Racing Personalities. Multicoloured.
3162 1r.30 Type **1562** 90 50
3163 1r.45 Ayrton Senna and Formula 1 racing car . . 1·00 60

1563 Embraer EMB 145 AEW

1565 Conductor's Baton and Music Score

1564 Hand reaching for Star

2000. Brazilian Aircraft. Multicoloured. Self-adhesive.
3164 27c. Type **1563** 20 10
3165 27c. Super Tucano 20 10
3166 27c. Embraer AMX-T . . . 20 10
3167 27c. Embraer ERJ 135 . . . 20 10
3168 27c. Embraer ERJ 170 . . . 20 10
3169 27c. Embraer ERJ 145 . . . 20 10
3170 27c. Embraer ERJ 190 . . . 20 10
3171 27c. Embraer EMB 145 RS/ MP 20 10
3172 27c. Embraer ERJ 140 . . . 20 10
3173 27c. Embraer EMB 120 . . 20 10

2000. Christmas. Multicoloured.
3174 27c. Type **1564** 20 10
3175 27c. Mary and Jesus 20 10
3176 27c. Family and fishes . . . 20 10
3177 27c. Jesus pointing to his heart 20 10
3178 27c. Trees, Globe and open hand 20 10
3179 27c. Jesus and Globe . . . 20 10
Nos. 3174/5, 3176/7 and 3178/9 respectively were issued together, se-tenant, forming a composite design.

2000. Light and Sound Shows.
3180 **1565** 1r.30 multicoloured . . 90 50

1566 Maps and Baron Rio Branco

2000. Centenary of Arbitration Ruling setting Boundary between Brazil and French Guiana.
3181 **1566** 40c. multicoloured . . . 30 15

1567 Three Wise Men, Chalice and Dove

2001. New Millennium. Multicoloured.
3182 40c. Type **1567** 30 15
3183 1r.30 Star of David, Menorah, scroll and stone tablets 90 50
3184 1r.30 Minaret, dome and Holy Kaaba 90 50
MS3185 68 × 113 mm. As Nos. 3182/4 2·10 1·25
No. **MS**3185 also has a barcode at the bottom of the sheet, separated from the miniature sheet by a line of rouletting

1568 Map of Americas, Flags, Emblems and Waterfall

2001. 11th Pan American Scout Jamboree, Foz do Iguacu. Multicoloured.
3186 1r.10 Type **1568** 80 45
3187 1r.10 Waterfall, canoeists and emblems 80 45
Nos. 3186/7 were issued together, se-tenant, forming a composite design.

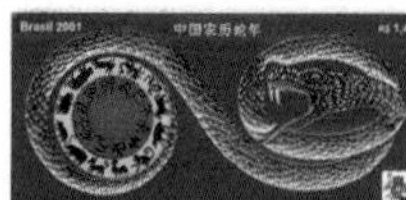
1569 Snake and Chinese Zodiac (½-size illustration)

2001. "HONG KONG 2001" Stamp Exihibition. New Year. Year of the Snake.
3188 **1569** 1r.45 multicoloured . . 1·00 60

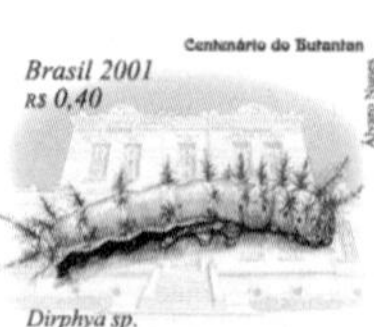

1570 *Dirphya* sp. and Institute

2001. Centenary of Butantan Institute (vaccine research centre), Sao Paulo. Venomous Animals. Sheet 115 × 155 mm containing T **1570** and similar horiz designs showing Institute building. Multicoloured.
3189 40c. Type **1570** 30 15
3190 40c. Puss caterpillar (*Megalopyge* sp.) 30 15
3191 40c. *Phoneutria* sp. 30 15
3192 40c. Brown scorpion (*Tityus bahiensis*) 30 15
3193 40c. Brazilian rattle snake (*Crotalus durissus*) 30 15
3194 40c. Coral snake (*Micrurus corallinus*) 30 15
3195 40c. Bushmaster (*Lachesis muta*) 30 15
3196 40c. Jararaca (*Bothrops jacaraca*) 30 15

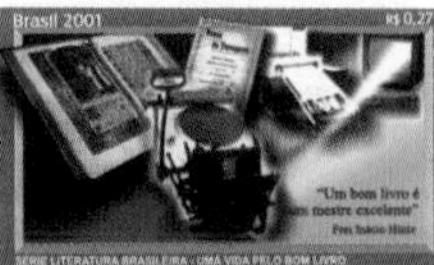

1571 Old and Modern Printing Methods

2001. Publishing.
3197 **1571** 27c. multicoloured . . . 20 10

1572 Airplane, World Map and Ship

2001. Exports.
3198 **1572** 1r.30 multicoloured . . 90 50

1573 Books and Library Facade

2001. 190th Anniv of National Library, Rio de Janeiro.
3199 **1573** 27c. multicoloured . . . 20 10

1574 Man, Microscope and Emblem

2001. Brazilian Council for Scientific and Technological Development (CNPq).
3200 **1574** 40c. blue 30 15

1575 Footballer and Emblem

1576 Children

2001. 89th Anniv of Santos Football Club.
3201 **1575** 1r. multicoloured . . . 70 40

2001. International Decade for a Culture of Peace.
3202 **1576** 1r.10 multicoloured . . 80 45

1577 Mendes and Halfeld Street

2001. Birth Centenary of Muriles Mendes (poet).

3203	**1577**	40c. multicoloured	30	15

1578 Building Facade and View of Town

2001. Centenary of Minas Gerais Trade Association.

3204	**1578**	40c. multicoloured	30	15

1579 Sunflower and No-Smoking Signs

2001. World No-Smoking Day.

3205	**1579**	40c. multicoloured	30	15

1580 Do Rego and Illustrations from his Novels

2001. Birth Centenary of Jose Lins do Rego (writer).

3206	**1580**	60c. multicoloured	40	20

1581 Hyacinth Macaw (*Anodorhynchus hyacinthinus*)

2001. Birds. Sheet 106 × 149 mm containing T **1581** and similar vert designs. Multicoloured.

MS3207	1r.30 Type **1581**; 1r.30 Sun conure (*Aratinga solititialis auricapilla*); 1r.30 Blue-throated conure (*Pyrrhura cruentata*); 1r.30 Yellow-faced amazon (*Amazona xanthops*)	2·10	2·10

1582 Sobrinho

2001. 1st Death Anniv of Alexandre Jose Barbosa Lima Sobrinho (journalist).

3208	**1582**	40c. multicoloured	15	10

1583 Jericoacoara Beach, Ceara

2001. Beaches. Multicoloured.

3209	40c. Type **1c583**	15	10
3210	40c. Ponta Negra beach, Rio Grande do Norte	15	10
3211	40c. Rosa beach, Santa Catarina	15	10

1584 Romi-Isetta, 1959 (½-size illustration)

2001. Cars. Sheet 159 × 115 mm containing T **1584** and similar horiz designs. Multicoloured.

MS3212	1r.10 Type **1584**; 1r.10 DKW-Vemag, 1965; 1r.10 Renault Gordini, 1962; 1r.10 Fusca-Volkswagen 1200, 1959; 1r.10 Simca Chambord, 1964; 1r.10 Aero Willys, 1961	2·75	2·75

1585 Sayao

2001. Birth Centenary of Bernado Sayao (politician and construction pioneer).

3213	**1585**	60c. multicoloured	25	15

EXPRESS STAMP

1930. Surch **1000 REIS EXPRESSO** and bars.

E490	**66**	1000r. on 200r. blue	5·25	2·40

NEWSPAPER STAMPS

N 34

N 37

1889. Roul.

N88	**N 34**	10r. orange	3·50	3·50
N89		20r. orange	9·00	9·00
N90		50r. orange	15·00	7·00
N91		100r. orange	6·00	3·50
N92		200r. orange	3·50	1·75
N93		300r. orange	4·00	1·75
N94		500r. orange	30·00	9·00
N95		700r. orange	4·75	15·00
N96		1000r. orange	4·75	15·00

1889. Roul.

N 97	**N 34**	10r. green	1·75	60
N 98		20r. green	1·75	60
N 99		50r. buff	2·40	1·25
N100a		100r. mauve	4·75	1·75
N101		200r. black	4·00	1·75
N102		300r. red	18·00	15·00
N103		500r. green	70·00	90·00
N104		700r. blue	38·00	60·00
N105		1000r. brown	18·00	45·00

1890. Perf.

N111	**N 37**	10r. blue	18·00	15·00
N112		20r. green	55·00	21·00
N113		100r. mauve	18·00	18·00

N 38 Southern Cross and Sugar-loaf Mountain

1890. Perf.

N119	**N 38**	10r. blue	2·40	1·75
N123a		20r. green	7·00	4·00
N127		50r. green	18·00	15·00

OFFICIAL STAMPS

O 64 Pres. Affonso Penna

O 67 Pres. Hermes de Fonseca

O 77 Pres. Wenceslao Braz

1906. Various frames.

O282	**O 64**	10r. green & orange	90	10
O283		20r. green & orange	1·25	10
O284		50r. green & orange	1·75	10
O285		100r. green & orange	90	10
O286		200r. green & orange	1·25	35
O287		300r. green & orange	3·50	60
O288		400r. green & orange	7·00	3·00
O289		500r. green & orange	3·50	1·75
O290		700r. green & orange	4·75	4·00
O291		1000r. green & orange	4·75	1·25
O292		2000r. green & orange	5·25	2·40
O293		5000r. green & orange	10·50	1·75
O294		10000r. green & orange	10·50	1·40

1913. Various frames.

O295	**O 67**	10r. black and grey	20	60
O296		20r. black and olive	20	60
O297		50r. black and grey	25	60
O298		100r. black and red	90	35
O299		200r. black and blue	1·25	35
O300		500r. black & yellow	3·00	60
O301		600r. black & purple	3·50	3·00
O302		1000r. black & brown	4·00	1·75
O303		2000r. black & brown	7·00	2·40
O304		5000r. black & bistre	9·00	3·50
O305		10000r. black	15·00	7·00
O306		20000r. black & blue	27·00	27·00
O307		50000r. black & green	48·00	48·00
O308		100000r. black & red	£140	£140
O309		500000r. black & brn	£200	£200
O310		1000000r. black & brn	£225	£225

1919.

O311	**O 77**	10r. brown	25	3·50
O312		50r. green	90	1·25
O313		100r. red	1·75	60
O314		200r. blue	2·40	60
O315		500r. orange	9·00	18·00

POSTAGE DUE STAMPS

D 34

D 45

D 64

1889. Roul.

D88	**D 34**	10r. red	3·50	1·25
D89		20r. red	5·25	2·40
D90		50r. red	7·00	4·75
D91		100r. red	3·50	1·75
D92		200r. red	70·00	21·00
D93		300r. red	10·50	10·50
D94		500r. red	9·00	9·00
D95		700r. red	16·00	18·00
D96		1000r. red	16·00	14·00

1890. Roul.

D 97	**D 34**	10r. orange	60	35
D 98		20r. blue	60	35
D 99		50r. olive	1·25	35
D100		200r. red	7·00	1·25
D101		300r. green	3·50	1·75
D102		500r. grey	4·75	3·50
D103		700r. violet	5·25	10·50
D104		1000r. purple	7·00	7·00

1895. Perf.

D172	**D 45**	10r. blue	1·75	1·25
D173		20r. green	9·00	7·00
D174		50r. green	14·00	9·00
D175		100r. red	7·00	2·40
D176b		200r. lilac	7·00	1·75
D177a		300r. blue	3·00	2·40
D178		2000r. brown	18·00	18·00

1906.

D282	**D 64**	10r. slate	35	35
D283		20r. violet	35	35
D284		50r. green	40	35
D285		100r. red	1·25	60
D286		200r. blue	90	40
D287		300r. grey	60	1·25
D288		400r. green	1·25	50
D289		500r. lilac	30·00	30·00
D290		600r. purple	1·25	2·40
D291		700r. brown	26·00	26·00
D292		1000r. red	3·00	3·50
D293		2000r. green	4·75	5·25
D294		5000r. brown	1·25	38·00

D 77

1919.

D345	**D 77**	5r. brown	40	40
D403		10r. mauve	35	35
D365		20r. olive	40	40
D404		20r. black	40	35
D405		50r. green	45	45
D375		100r. red	60	60
D407		200r. blue	1·75	60
D408		400r. brown	1·25	1·25
D401		600r. violet	60	60
D350		600r. orange	1·25	1·25
D409		1000r. turquoise	60	60
D439		2000r. brown	1·25	1·25
D411		5000r. blue	85	85

BREMEN Pt. 7

A free city of the Hanseatic League, situated on the R. Weser in northern Germany. Joined the North German Confederation in 1868.

72 grote = 1 thaler (internal).
22 grote = 10 silbergroschen (overseas mail).

1

2

3

1855. Imperf.

1	**1**	3g. black on blue	£170	£250

1856. Imperf.

3	**2**	5g. black on red	£140	£250
4		7g. black on yellow	£190	£550
5	**3**	5sg. green	£100	£200

4

5

1861. Zigzag roulette or perf.

17	**4**	2g. orange	60·00	£225
19	**1**	3g. black on blue	65·00	£275
20	**2**	5g. black on red	£100	£225
21		7g. black on yellow	£120	£3250
22	**5**	10g. black	£170	£900
24	**3**	5sg. green	£150	£150

BRITISH ANTARCTIC TERRITORY Pt. 1

Constituted in 1962 comprising territories south of latitude 60°S., from the former Falkland Island Dependencies.

1963. 12 pence = 1 shilling;
20 shillings = 1 pound.
1971. 100 (new) pence = 1 pound.

1 M.V. "Kista Dan"

1963.

1	**1**	½d. blue	1·25	1·75
2	–	1d. brown	1·25	80
3	–	1½d. red and purple	1·25	1·50
4	–	2d. purple	1·25	80
5	–	2½d. myrtle	3·25	1·25
6	–	3d. turquoise	3·75	1·50
7	–	4d. sepia	2·75	1·50
8	–	6d. olive and blue	4·75	2·25
9	–	9d. green	3·50	2·00
10	–	1s. turquoise	3·75	1·00
11	–	2s. violet and brown	20·00	10·00
12	–	2s.6d. blue	20·00	11·00
13	–	5s. orange and red	21·00	15·00
14	–	10s. blue and green	45·00	26·00
15	–	£1 black and blue	48·00	48·00
15a	–	£1 red and black	£120	£120

DESIGNS: 1d. Manhauling; 1½d. Muskeg (tractor); 2d. Skiing; 2½d. De Havilland D.H.C.2 Beaver (aircraft); 3d. R.R.S. "John Biscoe II"; 4d. Camp scene; 6d. H.M.S. "Protector"; 9d. Sledging; 1s. De Havilland D.H.C.3 Otter (aircraft); 2s. Huskies; 2s.6d. Westland Whirlwind helicopter; 5s. Snocat (tractor); 10s. R.R.S. "Shackleton"; £1 (No. 15), Antarctic map; £1 (No. 15a), H.M.S. "Endurance I".

1966. Churchill Commemoration. As T **38** of Antigua.

16	½d. blue	80	3·25
17	1d. green	3·00	3·25
18	1s. brown	21·00	6·50
19	2s. violet	24·00	7·00

17 Lemaire Channel and Icebergs

1969. 25th Anniv of Continuous Scientific Work.

20	**17**	3½d. black, blue and ultram	3·50	3·00
21	–	6d. multicoloured	1·25	2·50
22	–	1s. black, blue and red	1·25	2·00
23	–	2s. black, orange and turquoise	1·25	3·00

DESIGNS: 6d. Radio Sonde balloon; 1s. Muskeg pulling tent equipment; 2s. Surveyors with theodolite.

1971. Decimal Currency. Nos. 1/14 surch.

24	½p. on ½d. blue	60	3·00
25	1p. on 1d. brown	1·00	90
26	1½p. on 1½d. red and purple	1·25	75
27	2p. on 2d. purple	1·25	40
28	2½p. on 2½d. green	3·00	2·25
29	3p. on 3d. blue	2·50	75
30	4p. on 4d. brown	2·25	75
31	5p. on 6d. green and blue	4·75	3·50
32	6p. on 9d. green	16·00	8·00
33	7½p. on 1s. blue	19·00	8·50
34	10p. on 2s. violet and brown	20·00	14·00
35	15p. on 2s.6d. blue	20·00	15·00
36	25p. on 5s. orange and red	24·00	17·00
37	50p. on 10s. blue and green	42·00	30·00

19 Setting up Camp, Graham Land

21 James Cook and H.M.S. "Resolution"

1971. 10th Anniv of Antarctic Treaty. Muticoloured.

38	1½p. Type **19**	6·00	5·50
39	4p. Snow petrels	16·00	8·00
40	5p. Weddell seals	9·50	8·00
41	10p. Adelie penguins	22·00	9·00

Nos. 38/41 each include Antarctic map and Queen Elizabeth in their design.

1972. Royal Silver Wedding. As T **52** of Ascension, but with Kerguelen fur seals and Emperor penguins in background.

42	5p. brown	3·00	3·00
43	10p. green	3·00	3·00

1973. Multicoloured.

64a	½p. Type **21**	75	2·50
65	1p. Thaddeus von Bellingshausen and "Vostok"	60	2·25
66	1½p. James Weddell and "Jane"	60	2·25
47	2p. John Biscoe and "Tula"	2·50	1·75
48	2½p. J. S. C. Dumont d'Urville and "L'Astrolabe"	1·50	1·75
49	3p. James Clark Ross and H.M.S. "Erebus"	95	1·75
50	4p. C. A. Larsen and "Jason"	95	1·75
51	5p. Adrien de Gerlache and "Belgica"	1·00	1·75
52	6p. Otto Nordenskjold and "Antarctic"	1·25	1·75
53	7½p. W. S. Bruce and "Scotia"	1·50	2·25
74a	10p. Jean-Baptiste Charcot and "Pourquoi Pas?"	50	3·00
75	15p. Ernest Shackleton and "Endurance"	1·25	2·25
76	25p. Hubert Wilkins and Lockheed Vega "San Francisco"	1·25	1·50
77b	50p. Lincoln Ellsworth and Northrop Gamma "Polar Star"	85	2·75
78	£1 John Rymill and "Penola"	2·75	2·00

The 25p. and 50p. show aircraft; the rest show ships.

1973. Royal Wedding. As T **47** of Anguilla. Background colour given. Multicoloured.

59	5p. brown	40	20
60	15p. blue	70	30

22 Churchill and Churchill Peninsula, B.A.T.

1974. Birth Centenary of Sir Winston Churchill. Multicoloured.

61	5p. Type **22**	1·50	1·75
62	15p. Churchill and "Trepassey"	1·75	2·25

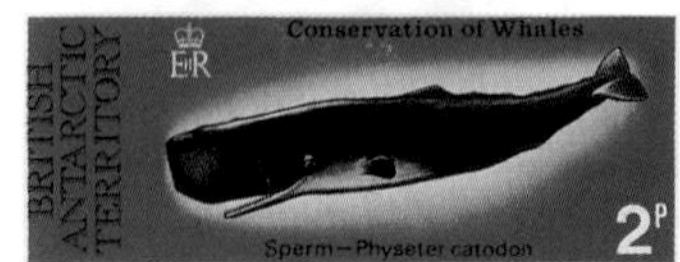

23 Sperm Whale

1977. Whale Conservation. Multicoloured.

79	2p. Type **23**	6·50	4·00
80	8p. Fin whale	7·50	4·50
81	11p. Humpback whale	8·00	4·50
82	25p. Blue whale	8·50	6·00

24 The Queen before Taking the Oath

1977. Silver Jubilee. Multicoloured.

83	6p. Prince Philip's visit, 1956/7	70	40
84	11p. The Coronation Oath	80	50
85	33p. Type **24**	1·25	65

25 Emperor Penguin

1978. 25th Anniv of Coronation.

86	– 25p. green, deep green and silver	80	1·00
87	– 25p. multicoloured	80	1·00
88 **25**	25p. green, deep green and silver	80	1·00

DESIGNS: No. 86, Black Bull of Clarence; 87, Queen Elizabeth II.

26 Macaroni Penguins

1979. Penguins. Multicoloured.

89	3p. Type **26**	11·00	11·00
90	8p. Gentoo penguins	3·00	3·00
91	11p. Adelie penguins	3·50	3·50
92	25p. Emperor penguins	4·50	4·50

27 Sir John Barrow and "Tula"

1980. 150th Anniv of Royal Geographical Society. Former Presidents. Multicoloured.

93	3p. Type **27**	20	15
94	7p. Sir Clement Markham and "Discovery"	20	25
95	11p. Lord Curzon and whaleboat "James Caird"	25	30
96	15p. Sir William Goodenough	30	35
97	22p. Sir James Wordie	35	55
98	30p. Sir Raymond Priestley	40	65

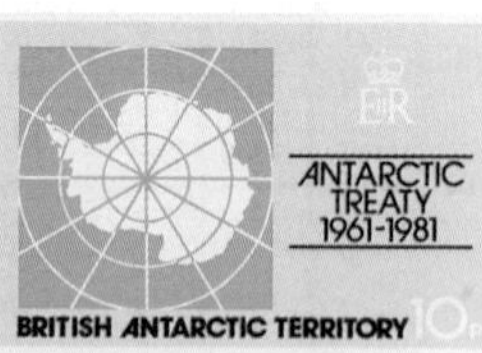

28 Map of Antarctic

1981. 20th Anniv of Antarctic Treaty.

99 **28**	10p. black, blue and light blue	40	80
100	– 13p. black, blue and green	45	90
101	– 25p. black, blue and mauve	55	1·00
102	– 26p. black, brown and red	55	1·00

DESIGNS: 13p. Conservation research ("scientific co-operation"); 25p. Satellite image mapping ("technical co-operation"); 26p. Global geophysics ("scientific co-operation").

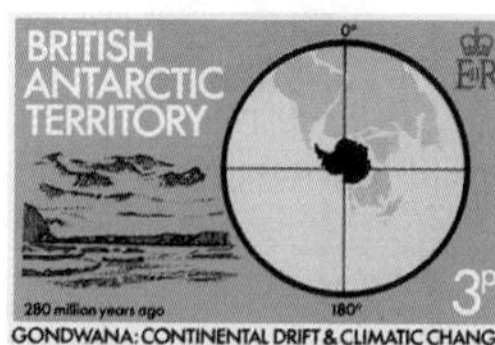

29 Map of Gondwana 280 million years ago and Contemporary Landscape Scene

1982. Gondwana – Continental Drift and Climatic Change. Maps of Gondwana showing position of continents, and contemporary landscapes. Mult.

103	3p. Type **29**	25	40
104	6p. 260 million years ago	30	50
105	10p. 230 million years ago	35	60
106	13p. 175 million years ago	45	70
107	25p. 50 million years ago	55	75
108	26p. Present day	55	75

30 British Antarctic Territory Coat of Arms

1982. 21st Birthday of Princess of Wales. Multicoloured.

109	5p. Type **30**	20	30
110	17p. Princess of Wales (detail of painting by Bryan Organ)	45	60
111	37p. Wedding ceremony	70	90
112	50p. Formal portrait	1·10	1·25

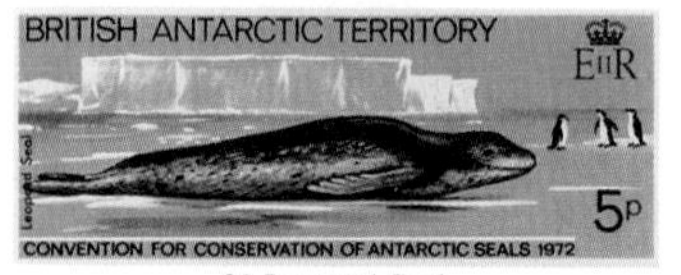

31 Leopard Seal

1983. 10th Anniv of Antarctic Seal Conservation Convention. Multicoloured.

113	5p. Type **31**	30	35
114	10p. Weddell seals	35	40
115	13p. Southern elephant seals	40	45
116	17p. Kerguelen fur seals	40	55
117	25p. Ross seals	40	65
118	34p. Crabeater seals	50	85

32 De Havilland Twin Otter 200/300

1983. Bicentenary of Manned Flight. Multicoloured.

119	5p. Type **32**	25	30
120	13p. De Havilland D.H.C.3 Otter	40	45
121	17p. Consolidated PBY-5A Canso amphibian	55	60
122	50p. Lockheed Vega "San Francisco"	1·10	1·25

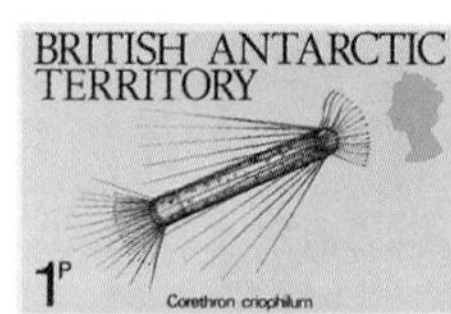

33 "Corethron criophilum"

1984. Marine Life. Multicoloured.

123	1p. Type **33**	60	1·75
124	2p. "Desmonema gaudichaudi"	65	1·75
125	3p. "Tomopteris carpenteri"	65	1·75
126	4p. "Pareuchaeta antarctica"	70	1·75
127	5p. "Antarctomysis maxima"	70	1·75
128	6p. "Antarcturus signiensis"	70	1·75
129	7p. "Serolis cornuta"	70	1·75
130	8p. "Parathemisto gaudichaudii"	70	1·75
131	9p. "Bovallia gigantea"	70	1·75
132	10p. "Euphausia superba"	70	1·75
133	15p. "Colossendeis australis"	70	1·75
134	20p. "Todarodes sagittatus"	75	1·75
135	25p. Antarctic rockcod	80	1·75
136	50p. Black-finned icefish	1·25	2·00
137	£1 Crabeater seal	1·75	2·50
138	£3 Antarctic marine food chain	5·00	6·50

34 M.Y. "Penola" in Stella Creek

1985. 50th Anniv of British Graham Land Expedition. Multicoloured.

139	7p. Type **34**	40	75
140	22p. Northern Base, Winter Island	70	1·40
141	27p. De Havilland Fox Moth at Southern Base, Barry Island	80	1·60
142	54p. Dog Team, near Ablation Point, George VI Sound	1·50	2·25

35 Robert McCormick and South Polar Skua

36 Dr. Edmond Halley

1985. Early Naturalists. Multicoloured.

143	7p. Type **35**	1·25	1·50
144	22p. Sir Joseph Dalton Hooker and "Deschampsia antarctica"	1·75	2·75
145	27p. Jean Rene C. Quoy and hourglass dolphin	1·90	2·75
146	54p. James Weddell and Weddell seal	2·75	4·00

1986. Appearance of Halley's Comet. Multicoloured.

147	7p. Type **36**	1·00	1·25
148	22p. Halley Station, Antarctica	1·75	2·25
149	27p. "Halley's Comet, 1531" (from Peter Apian woodcut, 1532)	2·00	2·50
150	44p. "Giotto" spacecraft	3·50	4·50

37 Snow Crystal

38 Captain Scott, 1904

1986. 50th Anniv of International Glaciological Society. Snow Crystals.

151 **37**	10p. light blue and blue	60	75
152	– 24p. green and deep green	90	1·40
153	– 29p. mauve and deep mauve	1·00	1·50
154	– 58p. blue and violet	1·40	2·50

1987. 75th Anniv of Captain Scott's Arrival at South Pole. Multicoloured.

155	10p. Type **38**	85	95
156	24p. Hut Point and "Discovery" Ross Island, 1902–4	1·40	2·00
157	29p. Cape Evans Hut, 1911–13	1·75	2·25
158	58p. Scott's expedition at South Pole, 1912	2·25	3·00

39 I.G.Y. Logo

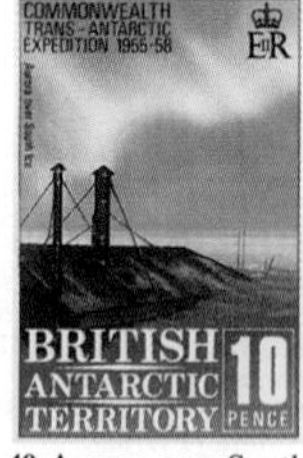

40 Aurora over South Ice Plateau Station

1987. 30th Anniv of International Geophysical Year.

159 **39**	10p. black and green	30	75
160	– 24p. multicoloured	60	1·40
161	– 29p. multicoloured	75	1·75
162	– 58p. multicoloured	1·40	2·50

DESIGNS: 24p. Port Lockroy; 29p. Argentine Islands; 58p. Halley Bay.

1988. 30th Anniv of Commonwealth Trans-Antarctic Expedition. Multicoloured.

163	10p. Type **40**	30	65
164	24p. "Otter" aircraft at Theron Mountains	60	1·25
165	29p. Seismic ice-depth sounding	70	1·50
166	58p. "Sno-cat" over crevasse	1·25	2·25

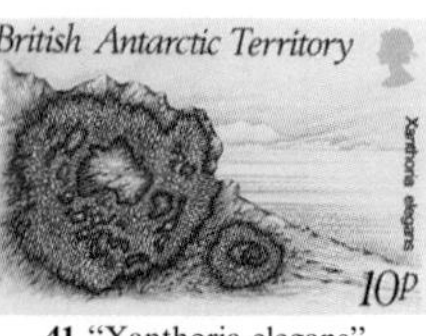

41 "Xanthoria elegans"

1989. Lichens. Multicoloured.

167	10p. Type **41**	90	1·00
168	24p. "Usnea aurantiaco-atra"	1·60	2·00
169	29p. "Cladonia chlorophaea"	1·75	2·25
170	58p. "Umbilicaria antarctica"	2·50	3·25

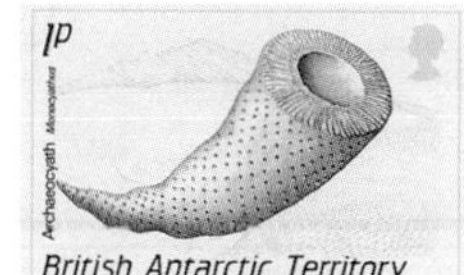

42 "Monocyathus" (archaecocyath)

1990. Fossils. Multicoloured.

171 1p. Type **42** . . . . 85 1·25
172 2p. "Lingulella" (brachiopod) 85 1·25
173 3p. "Triplagnoslus" (trilobite) 85 1·25
174 4p. "Lyriaspis" (trilobite) . . 1·00 1·25
175 5p. "Glossopteris" leaf (gymnosperm) . . . . . . 1·00 1·25
176 6p. "Gonatosorus" (fern) . . 1·00 1·40
177 7p. "Belemnopsis aucklandica" (belemnite) 1·00 1·40
178 8p. "Sanmartinoceras africanum insignicostatum" (ammonite) . . . . . . 1·00 1·40
179 9p. "Pinna antarctica" (mussel) . . . . 1·00 1·40
180 10p. "Aucellina andina" (mussel) . . . . 1·00 1·40
181 20p. "Pterotrigonia malagninoi" (mussel) . . . 1·50 2·00
182 25p. "Perissoptera" (conch shell) . . . . 1·50 2·00
183 50p. "Ainoceras sp." (ammonite) . . . . . . 2·00 3·00
184 £1 "Gunnarites zinsmeisteri" (ammonite) . . . . . . 3·50 4·50
185 £4 "Hoploparia" (crayfish) 7·00 8·00

1990. 90th Birthday of Queen Elizabeth the Queen Mother. As T **134** of Ascension.

186 26p. multicoloured . . . . . 1·75 2·75
187 £1 black and brown . . . . 3·75 4·75

DESIGNS: 29 × 36 mm: 26p. Wedding of Prince Albert and Lady Elizabeth Bowes-Lyon, 1923. 29 × 37 mm: £1 The Royal Family, 1940.

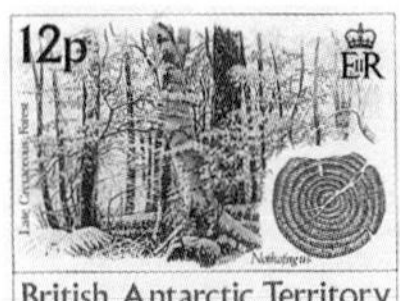

43 Late Cretaceous Forest and Southern Beech Fossil

1991. Age of the Dinosaurs. Multicoloured.

188 12p. Type **43** . . . . 1·25 1·25
189 26p. Hypsilophodont dinosaurs and skull . . . . 2·00 2·25
190 31p. Frilled sharks and tooth 2·25 2·50
191 62p. Mosasaur, plesiosaur, and mosasaur vertebra . . 3·50 4·00

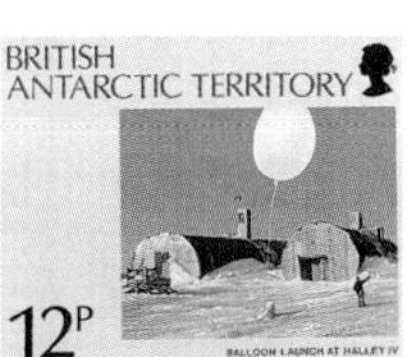

44 Launching Meteorological Balloon, Halley IV Station

1991. Discovery of Antarctic Ozone Hole. Mult.

192 12p. Type **44** . . . . 90 1·50
193 26p. Measuring ozone with Dobson spectrophotometer 1·60 2·50
194 31p. Satellite map showing ozone hole . . . . 1·75 2·75
195 62p. Lockheed ER-2 aircraft and graph of chlorine monoxide and ozone levels 3·00 4·00

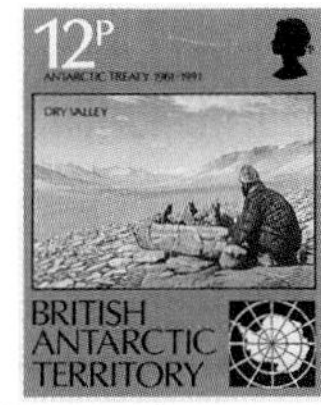

45 Researching Dry Valley

1991. 30th Anniv of Antarctic Treaty.

196 **45** 12p. multicoloured 90 90
197 – 26p. multicoloured . . . . 1·60 1·75
198 – 31p. black and green . . . 1·75 1·90
199 – 62p. multicoloured . . . . 3·00 3·25

DESIGNS: 26p. Relief map of ice sheet; 31p. BIOMASS logo; 62p. Ross seal.

46 "H.M.S. 'Erebus' and H.M.S. 'Terror' in the Antarctic" (J. Carmichael)

1991. Maiden Voyage of "James Clark Ross" (research ship). Multicoloured.

200 12p. Type **46** . . . . 90 1·50
201 26p. Launch of "James Clark Ross" . . . . 1·60 2·50
202 31p. "James Clark Ross" in Antarctica . . . . 1·75 2·75
203 62p. Scientific research . . . 3·00 3·75

1991. Birth Bicentenary of Michael Faraday (scientist). Nos. 200/3 additionally inscr "200th Anniversary M. Faraday 1791–1867".

204 12p. Type **46** . . . . 90 1·50
205 26p. Launch of "James Clark Ross" . . . . 1·60 2·50
206 31p. "James Clark Ross" in Antarctica . . . . 1·75 2·75
207 62p. Scientific research . . . 3·00 4·00

47 Ross Seals

1992. Endangered Species. Seals and Penguins. Multicoloured.

208 4p. Type **47** . . . . 80 1·25
209 5p. Adelie penguins . . . . 80 1·25
210 7p. Weddell seal with pup . . 80 1·25
211 29p. Emperor penguins with chicks . . . . 2·00 2·25
212 34p. Crabeater seals with pup 1·75 2·25
213 68p. Bearded penguins ("Chinstrap Penguin") with young . . . . 2·25 2·75

48 Sun Pillar at Faraday

1992. Lower Atmospheric Phenomena. Mult.

214 14p. Type **48** . . . . 80 1·50
215 29p. Halo over iceberg . . . 1·40 1·60
216 34p. Lee Wave cloud . . . . 1·75 2·00
217 68p. Nacreous clouds . . . . 2·75 3·25

49 "Fitzroy" (mail and supply ship)

1993. Antarctic Ships. Multicoloured.

218 1p. Type **49** . . . . 70 1·25
219 2p. "William Scoresby" (research ship) . . . . . . 80 1·25
220 3p. "Eagle" (sealer) . . . . 90 1·25
221 4p. "Trepassey" (supply ship) 90 1·25
222 5p. "John Biscoe I" (research ship) . . . . 90 1·25
223 10p. "Norsel" (supply ship) 1·25 1·50
224 20p. H.M.S. "Protector" (ice patrol ship) . . . . 1·50 1·75
225 30p. "Oluf Sven" (supply ship) . . . . 1·75 2·00
226 50p. "John Biscoe II" and "Shackleton" (research ships) . . . . 2·00 2·25
227 £1 "Tottan" (supply ship) . . 3·00 3·50
228 £3 "Perla Dan" (supply ship) 7·00 8·00
229 £5 H.M.S. "Endurance I" (ice patrol ship) . . . . . 10·00 11·00

1994. "Hong Kong '94", International Stamp Exhibition. Nos. 240/5 optd **HONG KONG '94** and emblem.

230 15p. Type **51** . . . . 95 1·00
231 24p. De Havilland Turbo Beaver III aircraft . . . . 1·40 1·75
232 31p. De Havilland Otter aircraft and dog team . . . 1·60 1·90
233 36p. De Havilland Twin Otter 200/300 aircraft and dog team . . . . 1·75 2·00
234 62p. De Havilland Dash Seven aircraft over landing strip, Rothera Point . . . 2·50 2·75
235 72p. De Havilland Dash Seven aircraft on runway 2·50 2·75

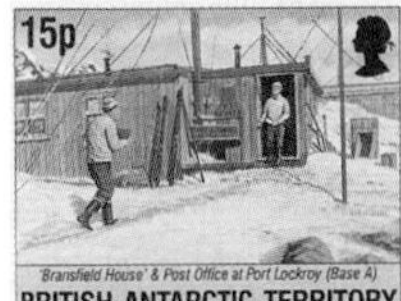

50 Bransfield House Post Office, Port Lockroy

1994. 50th Anniv of Operation Tabarin. Multicoloured.

236 15p. Type **50** . . . . 90 1·00
237 31p. Survey team, Hope Bay 1·40 1·60
238 36p. Dog team, Hope Bay . . 2·25 1·75
239 72p. "Fitzroy" (supply ship) and H.M.S. "William Scoresby" (minesweeper) 3·00 3·25

51 Huskies and Sledge

1994. Forms of Transportation. Multicoloured.

240 15p. Type **51** 60 70
241 24p. De Havilland Turbo Beaver III aircraft 80 90
242 31p. De Havilland Otter aircraft and dog team . . . 90 1·00
243 36p. De Havilland Twin Otter 200/300 aircaft and dog team . . . . 1·00 1·25
244 62p. De Havilland Dash Seven aircraft over landing strip, Rothera Point . . . 1·90 2·50
245 72p. De Havilland Dash Seven aircraft on runway 2·00 2·75

52 Capt. James Cook and H.M.S. "Resolution"

1994. Antarctic Heritage Fund. Multicoloured.

246 17p.+3p. Type **52** . . . . . 1·75 1·90
247 35p.+15p. Sir James Clark Ross with H.M.S. "Erebus" and H.M.S. "Terror" . . . . 2·00 2·25
248 40p.+10p. Capt. Robert Falcon Scott and interior of hut . . . . 2·00 2·25
249 76p.+4p. Sir Ernest Shackleton and "Endurance" . . . . . . 2·75 3·00

53 Pair of Crabeater Seals

1994. Antarctic Food Chain. Multicoloured.

250 35p. Type **53** . . . . 1·25 1·50
251 35p. Blue whale . . . . . . 1·25 1·50
252 35p. Wandering albatross . . 1·25 1·50
253 35p. Mackerel icefish . . . . 1·25 1·50
254 35p. Krill . . . . 1·25 1·50
255 35p. Seven star flying squid 1·25 1·50

54 Hauberg Mountains

1995. Geological Structures. Multicoloured.

256 17p. Type **54** 75 75
257 35p. Arrowsmith Peninsula 1·50 1·50
258 40p. Colbert Mountains . . . 1·75 1·75
259 76p. Succession Cliffs . . . . 2·50 2·50

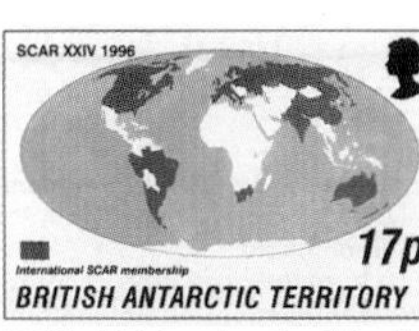

55 World Map showing Member Countries

1996. 24th Meeting of Scientific Committee on Antarctic Research. Multicoloured.

260 17p. Type **55** . . . . 1·00 1·00
261 35p. Scientist analysing ice samples . . . . 1·75 1·75
262 40p. Releasing balloon . . . 2·00 2·00
263 76p. Antarctic research ship catching marine life . . . . 2·75 2·75
MS264 100 × 90 mm. £1 S.C.A.R. logo 4·00 4·25

56 Killer Whales

1996. Whales. Multicoloured.

265 17p. Type **56** 70 60
266 35p. Sperm whales . . . . . 1·25 1·10
267 40p. Minke whales . . . . . 1·50 1·40
268 76p. Blue whale and calf . . 2·25 2·00
MS269 105 × 82 mm. £1 Humpback whale 2·50 2·75

1996. 70th Birthday of Queen Elizabeth II. As T **165** of Ascension, each incorporating a different photograph of the Queen. Mult.

270 17p. At premiere of "Chaplin", Leicester Square, 1992 . . . . . . 1·00 70
271 35p. At Buckingham Palace dinner, 1991 . . . . 1·50 1·25
272 40p. In Aberdeen, 1993 . . . 1·75 1·50
273 76p. At Royal Military School of Music, 1990 . . 2·25 2·25

1997. "HONG KONG '97" International Stamp Exhibition. Sheet 130 × 90 mm, containing design as No. 226. Multicoloured.

MS274 50p. "John Biscoe II" and "Shackleton" (research ships) 1·40 1·40

1997. Return of Hong Kong to China. Sheet 130 × 90 mm containing design as No. 227, but with "1997" imprint date.

MS275 £1 "Tottan" 2·75 3·00

57 Chinstrap Penguins sledging

58 Chart of South Shetland Islands (Swedish South Polar Expedition, 1902–3)

1997. Christmas. Multicoloured.

276 17p. Type **57** . . . . 1·00 75
277 35p. Emperor penguins carol singing . . . . 1·60 1·40
278 40p. Adelie penguins throwing snowballs . . . . 1·75 1·60
279 76p. Gentoo penguins ice-skating . . . . 2·25 2·75

1998. Diana, Princess of Wales Commemoration. Sheet 145 × 70 mm, containing vert designs as T **177** of Ascension. Multicoloured.

MS280 35p. Wearing sunglasses; 35p. Wearing round-necked white blouse, 1993; 35p. Wearing white blouse and jacket, 1990; 35p. Wearing green jacket, 1992 (sold at £1.40+20p. charity premium) 3·75 3·75

1998. History of Mapping in Antarctica. Multicoloured.

281 16p. Type **58** . . . . 1·00 75
282 30p. Map of Antarctic Peninsula (1949) . . . . . 1·60 1·25
283 35p. Map of AntarcticPeninsula (1964) 1·75 1·40
284 40p. Map of Antarctic Peninsula from Landsat (1981) . . . . 1·75 1·50
285 65p. Map of Antarctic Peninsula from satellite (1995) . . . . 2·25 2·25

59 Antarctic Explorer and H.M.S. "Erebus", 1843

1998. Antarctic Clothing. Multicoloured.

286 30p. Type **59** . . . . 1·00 80
287 35p. Explorer with dog, and "Discovery I", 1900 . . . 1·25 90

288	40p. Surveyor, and "Fitzroy", 1943	1·25	1·25
289	65p. Scientist with Adelie penguins, and "James Clark Ross", 1998	2·00	2·00

60 Snowy Sheathbill

1998. Antarctic Birds. Multicoloured.

290	1p. Type **60**	10	10
291	2p. Dove prion ("Antarctic Prion")	10	10
292	5p. Adelie penguin	10	10
293	10p. Emperor penguin	20	25
294	20p. Antarctic tern	40	45
295	30p. Black-bellied storm petrel	60	65
296	35p. Southern fulmar ("Antarctic Fulmar")	70	75
297	40p. Blue-eyed cormorant ("Blue-eyed Shag")	80	85
298	50p. South polar skua ("McCormick's Skua")	1·00	1·10
299	£1 Southern black-backed gull ("Kelp Gull")	2·00	2·10
300	£3 Wilson's storm petrel	6·00	6·25
301	£5 Antactic skua ("Brown Skua")	10·00	10·50

61 Mackerel Icefish

1999. Fish of the Southern Ocean. Multicoloured.

302	10p. Type **61**	40	35
303	20p. Blenny rockcod ("Toothfish")	65	55
304	25p. Borch	75	65
305	50p. Marbled rockcod ("Marbled notothen")	1·40	1·25
306	80p. Bernacchi's rockcod ("Bernach")	1·90	1·75

62 Map showing Crustal Microplates of West Antarctica

1999. British Antarctic Survey Discoveries. Mult.

307	15p. Type **62**	85	70
308	30p. Testing lead levels in ice	1·10	90
309	35p. Decolopodid sea spider (Gigantism in marine invertebrates) (horiz)	1·25	1·00
310	40p. Scientist operating Dobson Spectrophotometer for testing ozone layer (horiz)	1·40	1·10
311	70p. Radar antenna (aurora electric field research) (horiz)	1·60	1·25

63 Wreck of "Endurance"

2000. Shackleton's Trans-Antarctic Expedition, 1914–17, Commemoration. Multicoloured.

312	35p. Type **63**	1·50	1·25
313	40p. Ocean Camp on ice	1·50	1·25
314	65p. Launching "James Caird" from Elephant Island	2·00	2·50

64 Route of Commonwealth Trans-Antarctic Expedition, 1955–58

2000. "Heroic Age of Antarctica" (1st series). Commonwealth Trans-Antarctic Expedition, 1955–8. Multicoloured.

315	37p. Type **64**	1·25	1·40
316	37p. Expedition at South Pole, 1958	1·25	1·40
317	37p. *Magga Dan* (Antarctic supply ship)	1·25	1·40
318	37p. "Sno-cat" repair camp	1·25	1·40
319	37p. "Sno-cat" over crevasse	1·25	1·40
320	37p. Seismic explosion	1·25	1·40

See also Nos. 333/8 and 351/6.

65 *Bransfield* unloading "Sno-cat", Halley

2000. Survey Ships. Multicoloured.

321	20p. Type **65**	80	80
322	33p. *Ernest Shackelton* unloading supplies into *Tula*	1·10	1·10
323	37p. *Bransfield* in the ice (horiz)	1·25	1·25
324	43p. *Ernest Shackelton* with helicopter (horiz)	1·60	1·60

66 Iceberg and Opening Bars

2000. Composition of *Antarctic Symphony* by Sir Peter Maxwell Davies. Multicoloured.

325	37p. Type **66**	1·25	1·25
326	37p. Stern of *James Clark Ross* and pack ice	1·25	1·25
327	43p. Aircraft and camp on Jones Ice Self	1·40	1·40
328	43p. Frozen sea	1·40	1·40

67 Tourists at Port Lockroy

2001. Restoration of Port Lockroy Base. Multicoloured.

329	33p. Type **67**	90	90
330	37p. Port Lockroy and cruise ship	1·00	1·00
331	43p. Port Lockroy huts in 1945	1·25	1·25
332	65p. Interior of Port Lockroy laboratory in 1945	1·75	2·00

68 Map of Ross Sea Area

2001. "Heroic Age of Antarctica" (2nd series). Captain Scott's 1901–04 Expedition. Multicoloured.

333	33p. Type **68**	90	90
334	37p. Captain Robert F. Scott	1·00	1·00
335	43p. First Antarctic balloon ascent, 1902 (horiz)	1·25	1·25
336	65p. "Emperor Penguin chick" (drawing by Edward Wilson)	1·75	1·75
337	70p. Shackleton, Scott and Wilson and most southerly camp, 1902 (horiz)	1·75	1·75
338	80p. *Discovery I* trapped in ice off Hut Point (horiz)	1·90	1·90

2002. Golden Jubilee. As T **200** of Ascension.

339	20p. black, mauve and gold	70	70
340	37p. multicoloured	1·00	1·00
341	43p. black, mauve and gold	1·25	1·25
342	50p multicoloured	1·50	1·50
MS343	162 × 95 mm. Nos. 339/42 and 50p. multicoloured	5·00	5·50

DESIGNS—HORIZ: 20p. Princess Elizabeth and Princess Margaret making radio broadcast, 1940; 37p. Queen Elizabeth in Garter robes, 1998; 43p. Queen Elizabeth at Balmoral, 1952; 50p. Queen Elizabeth in London, 1996. VERT (38 × 51 mm)—50p. Queen Elizabeth after Annigoni.

Designs as Nos. 339/42 in No. **MS**343 omit the gold frame around each stamp and the "Golden Jubilee 1952–2002" inscription.

2002. Queen Elizabeth the Queen Mother Commemoration. As T **202** of Ascension.

344	40p. black, gold and purple	80	85
345	45p. multicoloured	90	95
MS346	145 × 70 mm. 70p. black and gold; 95p. multicoloured	1·25	1·40

DESIGNS: 40p. Lady Elizabeth Bowes-Lyon, 1913; 45p. Queen Mother on her birthday, 1996; 70p. Queen Elizabeth at niece's wedding, London, 1951; 95p. Queen Mother at Cheltenham Races, 1999.

Designs in No. **MS**346 omit the "1900–2002" inscription and the coloured frame.

69 Satellite and Antarctica

2002. 20th Anniv of Commission for Conservation of Antarctic Marine Living Resources (CCAMLR). Multicoloured.

347	37p. Type **69**	75	80
348	37p. Trawler and wandering albatross	75	80
349	37p. Icefish, toothfish and crabeater seal	75	80
350	37p. Krill and phytoplankton	75	80

2002. "Heroic Age of Antarctica" (3rd series). Scottish National Antarctic Expedition, 1902–04. As T **68** but horiz. Multicoloured.

351	30p. Map of Weddell Sea	60	65
352	40p. Piper Gilbert Kerr and emperor penguin (horiz)	80	85
353	45p. *Scotia* (expedition ship)	90	95
354	70p. Weather station and meteorologist (horiz)	1·40	1·50
355	95p. William Speirs Bruce	1·75	2·00
356	£1 Omond House, Laurie Island (horiz)	2·00	2·25

BRITISH COLUMBIA AND VANCOUVER ISLAND Pt. 1

Former British colonies, now a Western province of the Dominion of Canada, whose stamps are now used.

1860. 12 pence = 1 shilling;
20 shillings = 1 pound.
1865. 100 cents = 1 dollar.

1

1860. Imperf or perf.

2	1	2½d. pink	£350	£180

VANCOUVER ISLAND

2

1865. Imperf or perf. Various frames.

13	2	5c. red	£275	£150
14	–	10c. blue	£225	£140

BRITISH COLUMBIA

4 Emblems of United Kingdom

1865.

21	4	3d. blue	85·00	65·00

1868. Surch in words or figures and words.

28	4	2c. brown	£120	£120
29		5c. red	£150	£130
24		10c. red	£600	£475
31		25c. yellow	£150	£130
26		50c. mauve	£475	£425
27		$1 green	£800	£850

BRITISH COMMONWEALTH OCCUPATION OF JAPAN Pt. 1

Stamps used by British Commonwealth Occupation Forces, 1946–49.

12 pence = 1 shilling;
20 shillings = 1 pound.

1946. Stamps of Australia optd **B.C.O.F. JAPAN 1946.**

J1	27	½d. orange	3·50	5·00
J2	46	1d. purple	2·75	2·75
J3	31	3d. brown	2·25	2·25
J4	–	6d. brown (No. 189a)	15·00	9·00
J5	–	1s. green (No. 191)	15·00	12·00
J6	1	2s. red	42·00	48·00
J7	38	5s. red	95·00	£120

BRITISH EAST AFRICA Pt. 1

Now incorporated in Kenya and Uganda.

16 annas = 100 cents = 1 rupee.

1890. Stamps of Great Britain (1881) surch **BRITISH EAST AFRICA COMPANY** and value in annas.

1	57	½a. on 1d. lilac	£275	£200
2	73	1a. on 2d. green and red	£450	£275
3	78	4a. on 5d. purple and blue	£475	£300

3 Arms of the Company

11

1890. Nos. 16/19 are larger (24 × 25 mm).

4b	3	½a. brown	70	4·50
5		1a. green	4·50	5·50
6		2a. red	2·75	4·00
7c		2½a. black on yellow	4·50	5·00
8a		3a. black on red	2·00	6·00
9		4a. brown	2·50	6·00
11a		4½a. purple	2·50	16·00
29		5a. black on blue	1·25	10·00
30		7½a. black	1·25	15·00
12		8a. blue	5·50	9·50
13		8a. grey	£275	£225
14		1r. red	6·00	9·00
15		1r. grey	£225	£225
16	–	2r. red	14·00	28·00
17	–	3r. purple	8·50	40·00
18	–	4r. blue	12·00	40·00
19	–	5r. green	30·00	70·00

1891. With handstamped or pen surcharges. Initialled in black.

20	3	½a. on 2a. red	£4500	£850
31		½a. on 3a. black on red	£425	50·00
32		1a. on 3a. black on red	£5000	£2500
26		1a. on 4a. brown	£4000	£1400

1894. Surch in words and figures.

27	3	5a. on 8a. blue	65·00	85·00
28		7½a. on 1r. red	65·00	85·00

1895. Optd **BRITISH EAST AFRICA.**

33	3	½a. brown	70·00	42·00
34		1a. green	£140	£100
35		2a. red	£180	95·00
36		2½a. black on yellow	£180	55·00
37		3a. black on red	80·00	48·00
38		4a. brown	45·00	35·00
39		4½a. purple	£200	£100
40		5a. black on blue	£200	£130
41		7½a. black	£120	80·00
42		8a. blue	95·00	75·00
43		1r. red	55·00	50·00
44	–	2r. red	£425	£200
45	–	3r. purple	£225	£120
46	–	4r. blue	£180	£160
47	–	5r. green	£425	£250

1895. Surch with large 2½.

48	3	2½a. on 4½a. purple	£160	75·00

1895. Stamps of India (Queen Victoria) optd **British East Africa.**

49	23	½a. turquoise	6·50	5·50
50	–	1a. purple	5·50	6·00
51	–	1½a. brown	4·00	4·00
52	–	2a. blue	5·00	3·00
53	–	2a.6p. green	6·50	2·50
54	–	3a. orange	10·00	11·00
55a	–	4a. green (No. 96)	28·00	24·00
56	–	6a. brown (No. 80)	32·00	48·00
57c	–	8a. mauve	28·00	50·00
58	–	12a. purple on red	22·00	30·00
59	–	1r. grey (No. 101)	85·00	65·00
60	37	1r. green and red	42·00	£110
61	38	2r. red and orange	90·00	£140

62		3r. brown and green	90·00	£140
63		5r. blue and violet	£110	£150

1895. No. 51 surch with small **2½**.

64		2½ on 1½a. brown	85·00	42·00

1896.

65	11	½a. green	2·50	80
66		1a. red	5·50	40
67		2a. brown	4·00	4·25
68		2½a. blue	7·50	1·75
69		3a. grey	3·25	6·50
70		4a. green	6·00	3·50
71		4½a. yellow	7·50	16·00
72		5a. brown	7·50	4·25
73		7½a. mauve	5·00	22·00
74		8a. grey	4·00	5·50
75		1r. blue	48·00	23·00
76		2r. orange	70·00	25·00
77		3r. violet	65·00	30·00
78		4r. red	55·00	70·00
79		5r. brown	55·00	40·00

1897. Stamps of Zanzibar, 1896, optd **British East Africa**.

80	13	½a. green and red	55·00	45·00
81		1a. blue and red	95·00	90·00
82		2a. brown and red	38·00	21·00
83		4½a. orange and red	50·00	30·00
84		5a. brown and red	55·00	35·00
85		7½a. mauve and red	50·00	35·00

1897. As last, surch **2½**.

86	13	2½ on 1a. blue and red	£100	60·00
89		2½ on 3a. grey and red	£100	50·00

1897. As Type **11**, but larger.

92a		1r. blue	60·00	30·00
93		2r. orange	80·00	80·00
94		3r. violet	95·00	£110
95		4r. red	£300	£350
96		5r. brown	£225	£300
97		10r. brown	£300	£325
98		20r. green	£600	£1400
99		50r. mauve	£1600	£6000

BRITISH FORCES IN EGYPT Pt. 1

SPECIAL SEALS AND STAMPS FOR THE USE OF BRITISH FORCES IN EGYPT

A. SEALS

A 1

1932. (a) Inscr "POSTAL SEAL".

A1	A 1	1p. blue and red	85·00	3·50

(b) Inscr "LETTER SEAL".

A2	A 1	1p. blue and red	27·00	85

A 2

1932. Christmas Seals.

A3	A 2	3m. black on blue	48·00	70·00
A4		3m. lake	7·50	50·00
A5		3m. blue	7·00	26·00
A6a		3m. red	7·50	19·00

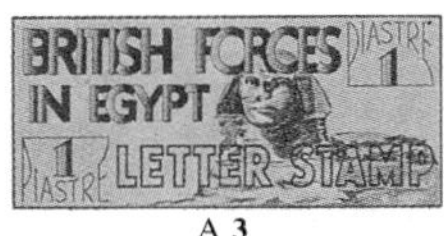

A 3

1934.

A9	A 3	1p. red	2·25	3·00
A8		1p. green	4·00	4·00

1935. Silver Jubilee. Optd **JUBILEE COMMEMORATION 1935**.

A10	A 3	1p. blue	£200	£180

1935. Provisional Christmas Seal. Surch **Xmas 1935 3 Milliemes**.

A11	A 3	3m. on 1p. red	16·00	70·00

B. POSTAGE STAMPS

A 6 King Fuad I

A 7 King Farouk

1936.

A12	A 6	3m. green	1·00	1·00
A13		10m. red	3·50	10

1939.

A14	A 7	3m. green	3·25	3·75
A15		10m. red	4·25	10

BRITISH GUIANA Pt. 1

Situated on the N.E. coast of S. America. A British colony granted full internal self-government in August 1951. Attained independence on 26 May 1966, when the country was renamed Guyana.

100 cents = 1 dollar.

1

1850. Imperf.

1	1	2c. black on red	—	£70000
2		4c. black on orange	£28000	£4250
4		8c. black on green	£16000	£3250
5		12c. black on blue	£5500	£2000

Prices are for used stamps cut round. Stamps cut square are worth much more.

2

3 Seal of the Colony

1852. Imperf.

9	2	1c. black on magenta	£8500	£4250
10		4c. black on blue	£11000	£6000

1853. Imperf.

12	3	1c. red	£2750	£1000
20		4c. blue	£950	£375

6

1856. Imperf.

23	6	1c. black on magenta	†	—
24		4c. black on magenta	†	£6000
25		4c. black on blue	£20000	£8500

7

9

1860. Perf.

29	7	1c. red	£1300	£200
40		1c. brown	£325	95·00
85		1c. black	10·00	4·25
87		2c. orange	25·00	3·25
89		4c. blue	80·00	13·00
92	9	6c. blue	£120	30·00
95	7	8c. red	£120	24·00
98		12c. lilac	£160	14·00
99		12c. grey	£160	16·00
64		24c. green	£170	50·00
79	9	24c. green	£150	90·00
82		48c. red	£225	50·00

The prices quoted for Nos. 29/82 are for fine copies with four margins. Medium specimens can be supplied at much lower rates.

10

16

1862. Various borders. Roul.

116	10	1c. black on red	£2500	£475
119		2c. black on yellow	£2500	£325
122		4c. black on blue	£2750	£600

The above prices are for stamps signed in the centre by the Postmaster. Unsigned stamps are worth considerably less.

1876.

126	16	1c. grey	2·75	1·40
171		2c. orange	22·00	15
172		4c. blue	90·00	5·00
173		6c. brown	5·00	6·50
174		8c. red	90·00	40
131		12c. violet	50·00	1·25
132		24c. green	60·00	3·00
133		48c. brown	£110	27·00
134		96c. olive	£475	£250

1878. Optd with thick horiz or horiz and vert bars.

(a) On postage stamps.

137	16	1c. on 6c. brown	38·00	£110
141	9	1c. on 6c. blue	£160	75·00

(b) On official stamps of 1875 and 1877.

138	7	1c. black	£200	70·00
139	16	1c. grey	£160	55·00
140		2c. orange	£300	65·00
144		4c. blue	£275	£100
145		6c. brown	£400	95·00
146	7	8c. red	£1700	£275
148	16	8c. red	£325	£100

1881. Surch with figure. Old value barred out in ink.

(a) On postage stamps.

152	9	"1" on 48c. red	45·00	5·00
149	16	"1" on 96c. olive	3·50	6·00
150		"2" on 96c. olive	4·50	11·00

(b) On stamps optd **OFFICIAL**.

153	7	"1" on 12c. lilac	£120	70·00
154	16	"1" on 48c. brown	£140	90·00
155		"2" on 12c. violet	70·00	27·00
157		"2" on 24c. green	80·00	45·00

26

30

1882.

162	26	1c. black on red	45·00	28·00
165		2c. black on yellow	75·00	42·00

Each stamp is perforated with the word "SPECIMEN".

1888. T **16** without value in bottom tablet, surch **INLAND REVENUE** and value.

175	16	1c. purple	1·25	20
176		2c. purple	1·25	30
177		3c. purple	1·00	20
178		4c. purple	8·00	30
179		6c. purple	8·00	3·75
180		8c. purple	1·50	30
181		10c. purple	6·00	2·50
182		20c. purple	20·00	11·00
183		40c. purple	21·00	20·00
184		72c. purple	40·00	50·00
185		$1 green	£425	£475
186		$2 green	£200	£225
187		$3 green	£140	£160
188		$4 green	£450	£550
189		$5 green	£275	£275

1889. No. 176 surch with additional **2**.

192	16	"2" on 2c. purple	1·75	15

1889.

193	30	1c. purple and grey	3·50	1·75
213		1c. green	75	10
194		2c. purple and orange	2·00	10
234		2c. purple and red	3·25	30
241a		2c. purple & black on red	3·50	10
253a		2c. red	8·50	10
195		4c. purple and blue	4·50	1·75
254		4c. brown and purple	2·25	60
214		5c. blue	2·75	10
243a		5c. purple & blue on blue	3·50	6·50
198		6c. purple and brown	7·00	11·00
236		6c. black and blue	6·50	11·00
256		6c. grey and black	13·00	7·00
199		8c. purple and red	12·00	1·25
215		8c. purple and black	2·75	1·10
200a		12c. purple and mauve	8·50	2·25
257		12c. orange and purple	4·00	4·00
246a		24c. purple and green	3·75	4·50
202		48c. purple and red	16·00	9·00
247a		48c. grey and brown	14·00	20·00
248a		60c. green and red	14·00	85·00
203		72c. purple and brown	28·00	38·00
205		96c. purple and red	65·00	70·00
250		96c. black & red on yellow	35·00	45·00

1890. Nos. 185/8 surch **ONE CENT**.

207	16	1 cent on $1 green	1·25	35
208		1 cent on $2 green	2·00	60
209		1 cent on $3 green	2·00	1·25
210		1 cent on $4 green	2·00	7·00

32 Mount Roraima

33 Kaieteur Falls

37

1898. Jubilee.

216	32	1c. black and red	5·00	75
217	33	2c. brown and blue	25·00	2·50
219	32	5c. green and brown	48·00	3·75
220	33	10c. black and red	25·00	20·00
221	32	15c. brown and blue	30·00	16·00

1899. Nos. 219/21 surch **TWO CENTS**.

222	32	2c. on 5c. green and brown	3·25	2·00
223	33	2c. on 10c. black and red	2·25	2·25
224	32	2c. on 15c. brown and blue	1·50	1·25

1905. T **30** but inscr "REVENUE", optd **POSTAGE AND REVENUE**.

251	30	$2.40 green and violet	£160	£275

1913.

259a	37	1c. green	2·25	25
260		2c. red	1·25	10
274		2c. violet	2·50	10
261b		4c. brown and purple	3·75	25
262		5c. blue	1·75	1·00
263		6c. grey and black	2·75	1·00
276		6c. blue	3·00	30
264		12c. orange and violet	1·25	1·00
278		24c. purple and green	2·00	4·50
279		48c. grey and purple	9·50	3·50
280		60c. green and red	10·00	48·00
281		72c. purple and brown	22·00	55·00
269a		96c. black and red on yellow	18·00	45·00

1918. Optd **WAR TAX**.

271	37	2c. red	1·25	15

39 Ploughing a Rice Field

40 Indian shooting Fish

41 Kaieteur Falls

42 Public Buildings, Georgetown

1931. Centenary of County Union.

283	39	1c. green	2·50	1·25
284	40	2c. brown	2·00	10
285	41	4c. red	1·75	45
286	42	6c. blue	2·25	2·75
287	41	$1 violet	23·00	48·00

43 Ploughing a Rice Field

44 Gold Mining

53 South America

1934.

288	43	1c. green	60	80
289	40	2c. brown	1·50	70
290	44	3c. red	30	10
291	41	4c. violet	2·00	1·75
292	–	6c. blue	2·75	3·50
293	–	12c. orange	20	20
294	–	24c. purple	3·50	6·00
295	–	48c. black	7·00	8·50
296	41	50c. green	10·00	17·00
297	–	60c. brown	26·00	27·00
298	–	72c. purple	1·25	2·25
299	–	96c. black	20·00	30·00
300	–	$1 violet	32·00	30·00

DESIGNS—HORIZ: 6c. Shooting logs over falls; 12c. Stabroek Market; 24c. Sugar canes in punts; 48c. Forest road; 60c. Victoria Regia lilies; 72c. Mount Roraima; $1 Botanical Gardens. VERT: 96c. Sir Walter Raleigh and his son.

The 2c., 4c. and 50c. are without the dates shown in Types **40/44** and the 12, 48, 72 and 96c. have no portrait.

1935. Silver Jubilee. As T **13** of Antigua.
301 2c. blue and grey 20 10
302 6c. brown and blue 1·00 1·75
303 12c. green and blue 4·00 8·00
304 24c. grey and purple 5·50 8·00

1937. Coronation. As T **2** of Aden.
305 2c. brown 15 10
306 4c. grey 50 30
307 6c. blue 60 1·00

1938. Designs as for same values of 1934 issue (except where indicated) but with portrait of King George VI (as in T **53**) where portrait of King George V previously appeared.
308a **43** 1c. green 30 10
309a – 2c. violet (As 4c.) 30 10
310b **53** 4c. red and black 50 15
311 – 6c. blue (As 2c.) 40 10
312a – 24c. green 1·25 10
313 – 36c. violet (As 4c.) 2·00 20
314 – 48c. orange 60 50
315 – 60c. brown (As 6c.) 11·00 4·00
316 – 96c. purple 2·50 2·75
317 – $1 violet 11·00 35
318 – $2 purple (As 72c.) 4·50 15·00
319 – $3 brown 27·00 25·00
DESIGN—HORIZ: $3 Victoria Regia lilies.

1946. Victory. As T **9** of Aden.
320 3c. red 10 20
321 6c. blue 30 50

1948. Silver Wedding. As T **10/11** of Aden.
322 3c. red 10 40
323 $3 brown 12·00 23·00

1949. U.P.U. As T **20/23** of Antigua.
324 4c. red 10 20
325 6c. blue 1·00 65
326 12c. orange 15 45
327 24c. green 15 60

1951. Inauguration of B.W.I. University College. As T **24/25** of Antigua.
328 3c. black and red 30 30
329 6c. black and blue 30 60

1953. Coronation. As T **13** of Aden.
330 4c. black and red 20 10

55 G.P.O., Georgetown

1954.
331 **55** 1c. black 10 10
332 – 2c. myrtle 10 10
333 – 3c. olive and brown 3·50 20
334 – 4c. violet 50 10
335 – 5c. red and black 30 10
336 – 6c. green 50 10
337 – 8c. blue 20 20
338a – 12c. black and brown 20 10
360 – 24c. black and orange 4·00 10
361 – 36c. red and black 60 60
341a – 48c. blue and brown 50 60
342 – 72c. red and green 12·00 2·75
364 – $1 multicoloured 7·00 90
344 – $2 mauve 18·00 6·00
345 – $5 blue and black 16·00 22·00
DESIGNS—HORIZ: 2c. Botanical Gardens; 3c. Victoria Regia lilies; 5c. Map of Caribbean; 6c. Rice combine-harvester; 8c. Sugar cane entering factory; 24c. Bauxite mining; 36c. Mount Roraima; $1 Channel-billed toucan; $2 Dredging gold. VERT: 4c. Amerindian shooting fish; 12c. Felling greenheart; 48c. Kaieteur Falls; 72c. Arapaima (fish); $5 Arms of British Guiana.

70

1961. History and Culture Week.
346 **70** 5c. sepia and red 20 10
347 6c. sepia and green 20 15
348 30c. sepia and orange 45 45

1963. Freedom from Hunger. As T **28** of Aden.
349 20c. violet 30 10

1963. Centenary of Red Cross. As T **33** of Antigua.
350 5c. red and black 20 20
351 20c. red and blue 55 35

71 Weightlifting

1964. Olympic Games, Tokyo.
367 **71** 5c. orange 10 10
368 8c. blue 15 35
369 25c. mauve 25 40

1965. Centenary of I.T.U. As T **36** of Antigua.
370 5c. green and olive 10 15
371 25c. blue and mauve 20 15

1965. I.C.Y. As T **37** of Antigua.
372 5c. purple and turquoise 15 10
373 25c. green and lavender 30 20

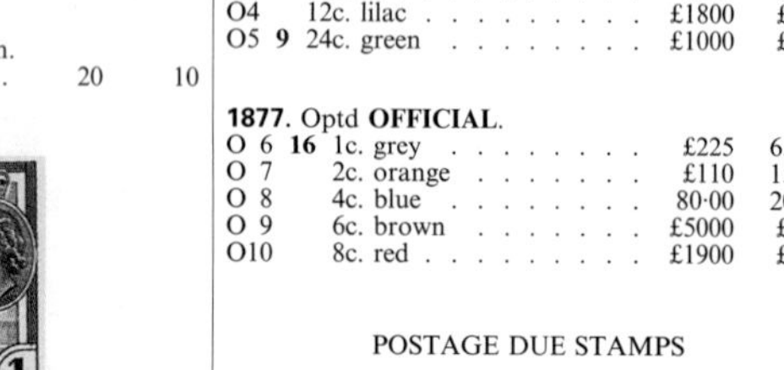

72 St George's Cathedral, Georgetown

1966. Churchill Commemoration.
374 **72** 5c. black, red and gold 50 10
375 25c. black, blue and gold 1·75 50

1966. Royal Visit. As T **39** of Antigua.
376 3c. black and blue 50 15
377 25c. black and mauve 1·50 60

OFFICIAL STAMPS

1875. Optd **OFFICIAL**.
O1 **7** 1c. black 50·00 18·00
O2 2c. orange £180 14·00
O3 8c. red £325 £120
O4 12c. lilac £1800 £500
O5 **9** 24c. green £1000 £225

1877. Optd **OFFICIAL**.
O 6 **16** 1c. grey £225 65·00
O 7 2c. orange £110 15·00
O 8 4c. blue 80·00 20·00
O 9 6c. brown £5000 £600
O10 8c. red £1900 £450

POSTAGE DUE STAMPS

1940. As Type D **1** of Barbados, but inscr "BRITISH GUIANA".
D1a 1c. green 1·50 12·00
D2a 2c. black 1·50 3·50
D3 4c. blue 30 9·00
D4 12c. red 28·00 4·00

For later issues see **GUYANA**.

BRITISH HONDURAS Pt. 1

A British colony on the East coast of Central America. Self-government was granted on 1 January 1964. The country was renamed Belize from 1 June 1973.

1866. 12 pence = 1 shilling;
20 shillings = 1 pound.
1888. 100 cents = 1 dollar.

1

8

1866.
17 **1** 1d. blue 42·00 13·00
18 1d. red 23·00 13·00
13 3d. brown £130 17·00
20 4d. mauve 75·00 4·75
9 6d. red £250 38·00
21 6d. yellow £275 £190
16 1s. green £200 11·00
22 1s. grey £250 £160

1888. Surch as **2 CENTS**.
36 **1** 1c. on 1d. green 80 1·50
37 2c. on 1d. red 60 2·25
25 2c. on 6d. red £120 £100
38 3c. on 3d. brown 3·25 1·40
39 6c. on 3d. blue 2·75 15·00
40 10c. on 4d. mauve 11·00 50
41 20c. on 6d. yellow 12·00 14·00
42 50c. on 1s. grey 29·00 80·00

1888. No. 42 surch **TWO**.
35 **1** "TWO" on 50c. on 1s. grey 48·00 95·00

1891. No. 40 surch **6** and bar.
44 **1** 6c. on 10c. on 4d. mauve 1·25 1·50

1891. Nos. 38 and 39 surch.
49 **1** "FIVE" on 3c. on 3d. brown 1·25 1·40
50 "15" on 6c. on 3d. blue 13·00 26·00

1891.
51 **8** 1c. green 2·50 1·25
52 2c. red 2·50 20
53 3c. brown 6·50 4·00
54 5c. blue 12·00 75
55 5c. black and blue on blue 16·00 2·50
56 6c. blue 6·50 2·00
57 10c. mauve and green (A) 10·00 8·50
58 10c. purple and green (B) 11·00 7·50
59a 12c. mauve and green 2·50 2·00
60 24c. yellow and blue 5·50 14·00
61 25c. brown and green 70·00 £120
62 50c. green and red 24·00 55·00
63 $1 green and red 70·00 £120
64 $2 green and blue 95·00 £150
65 $5 green and black £275 £350
NOTE: 10c. (A) inscr "POSTAGE POSTAGE"; (B) inscr "POSTAGE & REVENUE".

1899. Optd **REVENUE**.
66 **8** 5c. blue 12·00 2·50
67 10c. mauve and green 4·00 16·00
68 25c. brown and green 2·75 35·00
69 **1** 50c. on 1s. grey £150 £300

14

16

1902.
84a **14** 1c. green 1·00 2·00
85a 2c. purple and black on red 75 20
96 2c. red 12·00 10
86 5c. black and blue on blue 1·75 20
97 5c. blue 1·75 10
87 10c. purple and green 5·00 11·00
83 20c. purple 6·00 17·00
89 25c. purple and orange 7·00 48·00
100 25c. black on green 3·00 45·00
90 50c. green and red 15·00 70·00
91 $1 green and red 50·00 75·00
92 $2 green and blue 90·00 £150
93 $5 green and black £225 £275

1913.
101 **16** 1c. green 3·75 1·50
102 2c. red 3·50 1·00
103 3c. orange 80 20
104 5c. blue 2·00 85
105 10c. purple and green 3·00 6·50
106 25c. black on green 1·25 12·00
107 50c. purple and blue on blue 11·00 15·00
108 $1 black and red 19·00 48·00
109 $2 purple and green 65·00 80·00
110 $5 purple and black on red £200 £225

1915. Optd with pattern of wavy lines.
111a **16** 1c. green 50 13·00
112 2c. red 3·50 50
113 5c. blue 30 6·00

1916. Optd **WAR**.
114 **16** 1c. green (No. 111a) 10 1·25
119 1c. green (No. 101) 10 30
120 3c. orange (No. 103) 70 1·75

21

1921. Peace.
121 **21** 2c. red 3·25 50

As last, but without word "PEACE"
123 4c. grey 7·00 50

22

24 Maya figures

1922.
126 **22** 1c. green 5·00 6·50
127 2c. brown 1·50 1·50
128 2c. red 2·50 1·50
129 3c. orange 16·00 4·00
130 4c. grey 7·00 85
131 5c. blue 1·50 55
132 10c. purple and olive 1·25 30
133 25c. black on green 1·25 8·50
134 50c. purple and blue on blue 4·75 16·00
136 $1 black and red 8·00 23·00
137 $2 green and purple 32·00 80·00
125 $5 purple and black on red £200 £225

1932. Optd **BELIZE RELIEF FUND PLUS** and value.
138 **22** 1c.+1c. green 80 7·50
139 2c.+2c. red 85 7·50
140 3c.+3c. orange 90 18·00
141 4c.+4c. grey 11·00 22·00
142 5c.+5c. blue 6·50 14·00

1935. Silver Jubilee. As T **13** of Antigua.
143 3c. blue and black 2·00 50
144 4c. green and blue 2·00 3·50
145 5c. brown and blue 2·00 1·50
146 25c. grey and purple 4·00 4·00

1937. Coronation. As T **2** of Aden.
147 3c. orange 30 30
148 4c. grey 70 30
149 5c. blue 80 1·60

1938.
150 **24** 1c. purple and green 10 1·50
151 – 2c. black and red 20 1·00
152 – 3c. purple and brown 30 80
153 – 4c. black and green 30 70
154 – 5c. purple and blue 1·25 70
155 – 10c. green and brown 1·25 60
156 – 15c. brown and blue 2·75 70
157 – 25c. blue and green 2·75 1·25
158 – 50c. black and purple 11·00 3·50
159 – $1 red and olive 21·00 10·00
160 – $2 blue and purple 28·00 17·00
161 – $5 red and brown 29·00 24·00
DESIGNS—VERT: 2c. Chicle tapping; 3c. Cohune palm; $1 Court House, Belize; $2 Mahogany felling; $5 Arms of Colony. HORIZ: 4c. Local products; 5c. Grapefruit; 10c. Mahogany logs in river; 15c. Sergeant's Cay; 25c. Dorey; 50c. Chicle industry.

1946. Victory. As T **9** of Aden.
162 3c. brown 10 10
163 5c. blue 10 10

1948. Silver Wedding. As T **10** and **11** of Aden.
164 4c. green 15 20
165 $5 brown 16·00 42·00

36 Island of Saint George's Cay

1949. 150th Anniv of Battle of Saint George's Cay.
166 **36** 1c. blue and green 10 75
167 3c. blue and brown 10 1·25
168 4c. olive and violet 10 75
169 – 5c. brown and blue 90 20
170 – 10c. green and brown 80 30
171 – 15c. green and blue 80 30
DESIGNS: 5, 10 and 15c. H.M.S. "Merlin".

1949. U.P.U. As T **20/23** of Antigua.
172 4c. green 30 30
173 5c. blue 1·25 50
174 10c. brown 30 2·50
175 25c. blue 35 50

1951. Inauguration of B.W.I. University College. As T **24/25** of Antigua.
176 3c. violet and brown 45 1·50
177 10c. green and brown 45 30

1953. Coronation. As T **13** of Aden.
178 4c. black and green 40 30

39 Baird's Tapir **49** Mountain Orchid

1953.
179 – 1c. green and black 10 40
180a **39** 2c. brown and black 50 10
181a – 3c. lilac and mauve 10 10
182 – 4c. brown and green 50 30
183 – 5c. olive and red 10 10
184 – 10c. slate and blue 10 10
185 – 15c. green and violet 15 10
186 – 25c. blue and brown 6·00 2·50
187 – 50c. brown and purple 8·50 1·75
188 – $1 slate and brown 5·50 5·00
189 – $2 red and grey 6·50 4·50
190 **49** $5 purple and slate 48·00 17·00
DESIGNS—HORIZ: 1c. Arms of British Honduras; 3c. Mace and Legislative Council Chamber; 4c. Pine industry; 5c. Spiny lobster; 10c. Stanley Field Airport; 15c. Maya frieze, Xunantunich; 25c. "Morpho peleides" (butterfly); $1 Nine-banded armadillo; $2 Hawkesworth Bridge. VERT: 50c. Maya indian.

50 "Belize from Fort George, 1842" (C. J. Hullmandel)

1960. Post Office Centenary.
191 **50** 2c. green . . . . 30 1·25
192 – 10c. red 30 10
193 – 15c. blue 35 35
DESIGNS: 10c. Public seals, 1860 and 1960; 15c. Tamarind tree, Newtown Barracks.

1961. New Constitution. Stamps of 1953 optd **NEW CONSTITUTION 1960.**
194 **39** 2c. brown and black . . . 25 20
195 – 3c. lilac and mauve 30 20
196 – 10c. slate and blue 30 10
197 – 15c. green and violet . . . 30 20

1962. Hurricane Hattie Relief Fund. Stamps of 1953 optd **HURRICANE HATTIE**.
198 1c. green and black 10 65
199 10c. slate and blue 30 10
200 25c. blue and brown . . . . 1·40 80
201 50c. brown and purple . . . 50 1·00

55 Great Curassow

1962. Birds in natural colours; portrait and inscr in black; background colours given.
239 **55** 1c. yellow 10 50
240 – 2c. grey . . . . 30 1·00
204 – 3c. green . . . . 2·50 3·00
241 – 4c. grey . . . . 1·75 2·00
242 – 5c. buff 40 10
243 – 10c. stone 40 10
244 – 15c. stone 40 10
209 – 25c. slate . . . . 4·50 30
210 – 50c. grey . . . . 6·00 35
211 – $1 blue . . . . 9·00 1·00
212 – $2 stone . . . . 14·00 3·00
213 – $5 grey . . . . 25·00 16·00
BIRDS: 2c. Red-legged honeycreeper; 3c. Northern jacana ("American Jacana"); 4c. Great kiskadee; 5c. Scarlet-rumped tanager; 10c. Scarlet macaw; 15c. Slaty-tailed trogon ("Massena Trogon"); 25c. Red-footed booby; 50c. Keel-billed toucan; $1 Magnificent frigate bird; $2 Rufous-tailed jacamar; $5 Montezuma oropendola.

1963. Freedom from Hunger. As T **28** of Aden.
214 22c. green 30 15

1963. Centenary of Red Cross. As T **33** of Antigua.
215 4c. red and black 20 65
216 22c. red and blue 40 95

1964. New Constitution. Nos. 202, 204, 205, 207 and 209 optd **SELF GOVERNMENT 1964**.
217 **55** 1c. yellow 10 30
218 – 3c. green 45 30
219 – 4c. pale grey 45 30
220 – 10c. stone 45 10
221 – 25c. slate 55 30

1965. Centenary of I.T.U. As T **36** of Antigua.
222 2c. red and green 10 10
223 50c. yellow and purple . . . 35 25

1965. I.C.Y. As T **37** of Antigua.
224 1c. purple and turquoise . . 10 15
225 22c. green and lavender . . . 20 15

1966. Churchill Commemoration. As T **38** of Antigua.
226 1c. blue 10 40
227 4c. green 30 10
228 22c. brown 55 10
229 25c. violet 65 45

1966. Dedication of new Capital Site. Nos. 202, 204/5 207 and 209 optd **DEDICATION OF SITE NEW CAPITAL 9th OCTOBER 1965**.
230 **55** 1c. yellow 10 40
231 – 3c. green 45 40
232 – 4c. grey 45 40
233 – 10c. stone 45 10
234 – 25c. slate 55 35

58 Citrus Grove

1966. Stamp Centenary. Multicoloured
235 5c. Type **58** 10 10
236 10c. Half Moon Cay 10 10
237 22c. Hidden Valley Falls . . 10 10
238 25c. Maya ruins, Xunantunich 15 45

59 Sailfish

1967. International Tourist Year.
246 **59** 5c. blue, black and yellow 15 30
247 – 10c. brown, black and red 15 10
248 – 22c. orange, black and green 30 10
249 – 25c. blue, black and yellow 30 60
DESIGNS: 10c. Red brocket; 22c. Jaguar; 25c. Atlantic tarpon.

60 "Schomburgkia tibicinis"

61 Monument Belizean Patriots

1968. 20th Anniv of Economic Commission for Latin America. Orchids. Multicoloured.
250 5c. Type **60** 20 15
251 10c. "Maxillaria tenuifolia" 25 10
252 22c. "Bletia purpurea" . . . 30 10
253 25c. "Sobralia macrantha" 40 20

1968. Human Rights Year. Multicoloured.
254 22c. Type **61** 15 10
255 50c. Monument at site of new capital 15 20

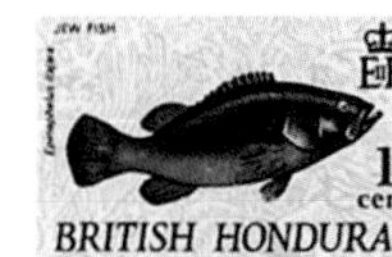

63 Spotted Jewfish

1968. Wildlife.
276 – ½c. multicoloured and blue 10 10
277 – ½c. multicoloured and yellow . . . . 2·50 1·00
256 **63** 1c. black, brown and yellow 20 10
257 – 2c. black, green and yellow 10 10
258 – 3c. black, brown and lilac 20 10
259 – 4c. multicoloured 15 95
260 – 5c. black and red 15 95
261 – 10c. multicoloured 15 10
262 – 15c. multicoloured . . . . 1·00 20
263 – 25c. multicoloured 30 20
264 – 50c. multicoloured . . . . 70 1·25
265 – $1 multicoloured . . . . . 2·50 1·25
266 – $2 multicoloured . . . . . 2·50 2·00
278 – $5 multicoloured . . . . . 5·00 12·00
DESIGNS: ½c. (Nos. 276 and 277) Mozambique mouthbrooder ("Crana"); 2c. White-lipped peccary; 3c. Misty grouper; 4c. Collared anteater; 5c. Bonefish; 10c. Paca; 15c. Dolphin; 25c. Kinkajou; 50c. Mutton snapper; $1 Tayra; $2 Great barracuda; $5 Puma.

64 "Rhyncholaelia digbyana"

65 Ziricote Tree

1969. Orchids of Belize (1st series). Multicoloured.
268 5c. Type **64** 50 20
269 10c. "Cattleya bowringiana" 55 15
270 22c. "Lycaste cochleatum" 85 15
271 25c. "Coryanthes speciosum" 1·10 1·10
See also Nos. 287/90.

1969. Indigenous Hardwoods (1st series). Mult.
272 5c. Type **65** 10 20
273 10c. Rosewood 10 10
274 22c. Mayflower 20 10
275 25c. Mahogany 20 45
See also Nos. 291/4, 315/18 and 333/7.

66 "The Virgin and Child" (Bellini)

69 Santa Maria

1969. Christmas. Paintings. Multicoloured.
279 5c. Type **66** 10 10
280 15c. Type **66** 10 10
281 22c. "The Adoration of the Magi" (Veronese) 10 10
282 25c. As No. 281 . . . . . . 10 20

1970. Population Census. Nos. 260/3 optd **POPULATION CENSUS 1970**.
283 5c. multicoloured 10 10
284 10c. multicoloured 15 10
285 15c. multicoloured 20 10
286 25c. multicoloured 20 15

1970. Orchids of Belize (2nd series). As T **64**. Mult.
287 5c. Black orchid 35 15
288 15c. White butterfly orchid 50 10
289 22c. Swan orchid 70 10
290 25c. Butterfly orchid 70 40

1970. Indigenous Hardwoods (2nd series). Mult.
291 5c. Type **69** 25 10
292 15c. Nargusta 40 10
293 22c. Cedar 45 10
294 25c. Sapodilla 45 35

70 "The Nativity" (A. Hughes)

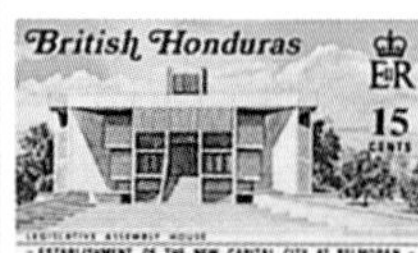

71 Legislative Assembly House

1970. Christmas. Multicoloured.
295 ½c. Type **70** 10 10
296 5c. "The Mystic Nativity" (Botticelli) 10 10
297 10c. Type **70** 10 10
298 15c. As 5c. 20 10
299 22c. Type **70** 25 10
300 50c. As 5c. 40 85

1971. Establishment of New Capital, Belmopan. Multicoloured.
301 5c. Old capital, Belize 10 10
302 10c. Government Plaza . . . 10 10
303 15c. Type **71** 10 10
304 22c. Magistrates' Court . . . 15 10
305 25c. Police H.Q 15 15
306 50c. New G.P.O 25 40
The 5c. and 10c. are larger, 60 × 22 mm.

72 "Tabebuia chrysantha"

1971. Easter. Flowers. Multicoloured.
307 ½c. Type **72** 10 10
308 5c. "Hymenocallis littoralis" 10 10
309 10c. "Hippeastrum equestre" 10 10
310 15c. Type **72** 20 10
311 22c. As 5c. 20 10
312 25c. As 10c. 20 30

1971. Racial Equality Year. Nos. 261 and 264 optd **RACIAL EQUALITY YEAR–1971**.
313 10c. multicoloured 25 10
314 50c. multicoloured 55 20

74 Tubroos

76 "Petrae volubis"

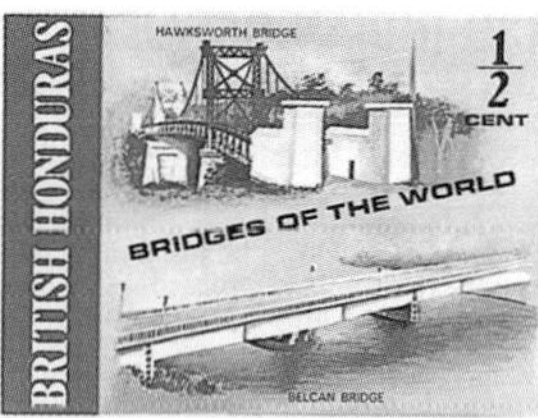

75 Hawksworth and Belcan Bridges

1971. Indigenous Hardwoods (3rd series). Mult.
315 5c. Type **74** 60 10
316 15c. Yemeri 80 30
317 26c. Billywebb . . . . 1·10 35
318 50c. Logwood . . . . 1·75 4·25
MS319 96 × 171 mm. Nos. 315/18 3·50 7·00

1971. Bridges of the World. Multicoloured.
320 ½c. Type **75** 10 20
321 5c. Narrows Bridge, N.Y. and Quebec Bridge 30 15
322 26c. London Bridge (1871) and reconstructed, Arizona (1971) 80 15
323 50c. Belize Mexican Bridge and Swing Bridge . . . . 1·00 1·25

1972. Easter. Wild Flowers. Multicoloured.
324 6c. Type **76** 15 10
325 15c. Yemeri 25 30
326 26c. Mayflower 50 45
327 50c. Tiger's Claw . . . . . . 80 1·40

77 Seated Figure

78 Banak

1972. Mayan Artefacts. Multicoloured.
328 3c. Type **77** 25 10
329 6c. Priest in "dancing" pose 25 10
330 16c. Sun God's head (horiz) 50 15
331 26c. Priest and Sun God . . 70 20
332 50c. Full-front figure . . . . 1·40 3·75

1972. Indigenous Hardwoods (4th series). Mult.
333 3c. Type **78** 25 10
334 5c. Quamwood 25 10
335 16c. Waika Chewstick . . . 55 15
336 26c. Mamee-Apple 75 25
337 50c. My Lady . . . . 1·60 3·25

1972. Royal Silver Wedding. As T **52** of Ascension, but with Orchids of Belize in background.
341 26c. green 25 10
342 50c. violet 40 65

80 Baron Bliss Day

1973. Festivals of Belize. Multicoloured.
343 3c. Type **80** 15 10
344 10c. Labour Day 15 10
345 26c. Carib Settlement Day . . 30 10
346 50c. Pan American Day . . . 50 85

POSTAGE DUE STAMPS

D 1

1923.
D1 **D 1** 1c. black . . . . 2·25 13·00
D4 2c. black . . . . 2·75 5·50
D5 4c. black . . . . 90 6·00

For later issues see **BELIZE**.

BRITISH INDIAN OCEAN TERRITORY Pt. 1

A Crown Colony, established 8 November 1965, comprising the Chagos Archipelago (previously administered by Mauritius) and Aldabra, Farquhar and Desroches, previously administered by Seychelles to which country they were returned on 29 June 1976.

The Chagos Archipelago has no indigenous population, but stamps were provided from 1990 for use by civilian workers at the U.S. Navy base on Diego Garcia.

1968. 100 cents = 1 rupee.
1990. 100 pence = 1 pound.

1968. Nos 196/200, 202/4 and 206/12 of Seychelles optd **B.I.O.T.**

1 **24** 5c. multicoloured 1·00 1·25
2 – 10c. multicoloured 10 15
3 – 15c. multicoloured 10 15
4 – 20c. multicoloured 15 15
5 – 25c. multicoloured 15 15
6 – 40c. multicoloured 20 20
7 – 45c. multicoloured 20 30
8 – 50c. multicoloured 20 30
9 – 75c. multicoloured 60 35
10 – 1r. multicoloured 70 35
11 – 1r.50 multicoloured 1·75 1·50
12 – 2r.25 multicoloured 3·00 3·75
13 – 3r.50 multicoloured 3·00 4·50
14 – 5r. multicoloured 10·00 7·50
15 – 10r. multicoloured 20·00 20·00

2 Lascar

1968. Marine Life. Multicoloured.

16 5c. Type **2** 70 2·00
17 10c. Smooth hammerhead (vert) 30 1·25
18 15c. Tiger shark 30 1·50
19 20c. Spotted eagle ray ("Bat ray") 30 1·00
20 25c. Yellow-finned butterflyfish and ear-spot angelfish (vert) 80 1·00
20a 30c. Robber crab 3·50 2·75
21 40c. Blue-finned trevalley ("Caranx") 70 40
22 45c. Crocodile needlefish ("Garfish") (vert) 2·25 2·50
23 50c. Pickhandle barracuda 70 30
23a 60c. Spotted pebble crab 3·50 3·25
24 75c. Indian Ocean steep-headed parrotfish 2·50 2·75
24a 85c. Rainbow runner ("Dorade") 4·50 3·50
25 1r. Giant hermit crab 1·50 35
26 1r.50 Parrotfish ("Humphead") 2·50 3·00
27 2r.25 Yellow-edged lyre-tail andAredate grouper ("Rock cod") 12·00 10·00
28 3r.50 Black marlin 4·00 3·75
29 5r. black, green and blue (Whale shark) (vert) 11·00 9·00
30 10r. Lionfish 9·00 8·00

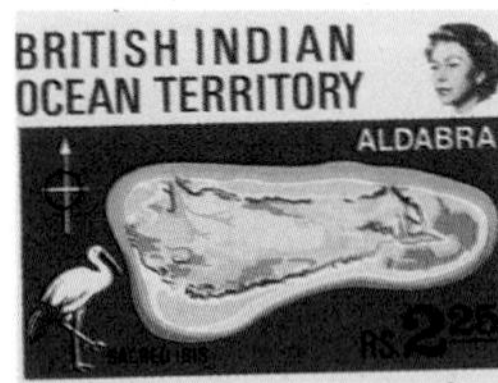

3 Sacred Ibis and Aldabra Coral Atoll

1969. Coral Atolls

31 **3** 2r.25 multicoloured 1·75 1·00

4 Outrigger Canoe

1969. Ships of the Islands. Multicoloured.

32 45c. Type **4** 65 75
33 75c. Pirogue 65 80
34 1r. M.V. "Nordvaer" 70 90
35 1r.50 "Isle of Farquhar" 80 1·00

5 Giant Land Tortoise

1971. Aldabra Nature Reserve. Multicoloured.

36 45c. Type **5** 2·50 2·50
37 75c. Aldabra lily 3·00 2·50
38 1r. Aldabra tree snail 3·50 2·75
39 1r.50 Western reef heron ("Dimorphic Egrets") 12·00 10·00

6 Arms of Royal Society and White-throated Rail

1971. Opening of Royal Society Research Station, Aldabra.

40 **6** 3r.50 multicoloured 15·00 8·50

7 Staghorn Coral

1972. Coral. Multicoloured.

41 40c. Type **7** 3·50 4·00
42 60c. Brain coral 4·00 4·25
43 1r. Mushroom coral 4·00 4·25
44 1r.75 Organ pipe coral 5·00 6·50

1972. Royal Silver Wedding. As T **52** of Ascension, but with White-throated rail and Sacred ibis in background.

45 95c. green 50 40
46 1r.50 violet 50 40

9 "Christ on the Cross"

10 Upsidedown Jellyfish

1973. Easter. Multicoloured.

47 45c. Type **9** 20 40
48 75c. "Joseph and Nicodemus burying Jesus" 30 55
49 1r. Type **9** 30 60
50 1r.50 As 75c. 30 70
MS51 126 × 110 mm. Nos. 47/50 1·00 4·00

1973. Wildlife (1st series). Multicoloured.

53 50c. Type **10** 3·50 3·00
54 1r. "Hypolimnas misippus" and "Belenois aldabrensis" (butterflies) 4·00 3·00
55 1r.50 "Nephila madagascariensis" (spider) 4·25 3·00

See also Nos. 58/61, 77/80 and 86/9.

11 M.V. "Nordvaer"

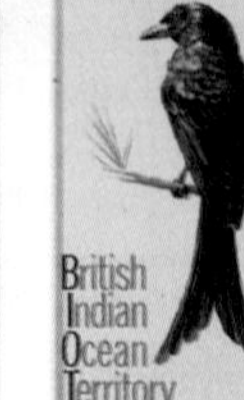

13 Aldabra Drongo

12 Red-cloud Auger and Subulat Auger

1974. 5th Anniv of "Nordvaer" Travelling Post Office. Multicoloured.

56 85c. Type **11** 85 75
57 2r.50 "Nordvaer" off shore 1·40 1·25

1974. Wildlife (2nd series). Shells. Multicoloured.

58 45c. Type **12** 2·25 1·25
59 75c. Great green turban 2·50 1·50
60 1r. Strawberry drupe 2·75 1·75
61 1r.50 Bull-mouth helmet 3·00 2·00

1975. Birds. Multicoloured.

62 5c. Type **13** 1·25 2·75
63 10c. Black coucal ("Malagasy Coucal") 1·25 2·75
64 20c. Mascarene fody ("Red-Headed Forest Foddy") 1·25 2·75
65 25c. White tern 1·25 2·75
66 30c. Crested tern 1·25 2·75
67 40c. Brown booby 1·25 2·75
68 50c. Common noddy ("Noddy Tern") (horiz) 1·25 3·00
69 60c. Grey heron 1·25 3·00
70 65c. Blue-faced booby (horiz) 1·25 3·00
71 95c. Madagascar white eye ("Malagasy White-eye") (horiz) 1·25 3·00
72 1r. Green-backed heron (horiz) 1·25 3·00
73 1r.75 Lesser frigate bird (horiz) 2·00 5·50
74 3r.50 White-tailed tropic bird (horiz) 2·75 5·50
75 5r. Souimanga sunbird (horiz) 4·00 5·00
76 10r. Madagascar turtle dove ("Malagasy Turtle Dove") (horiz) 8·00 9·00

14 "Grewia salicifolia"

1975. Wildlife (3rd series). Seashore Plants. Multicoloured.

77 50c. Type **14** 50 1·25
78 65c. "Cassia aldabrensis" 55 1·40
79 1r. "Hypoestes aldabrensis" 65 1·50
80 1r.60 "Euphorbia pyrifolia" 80 1·60

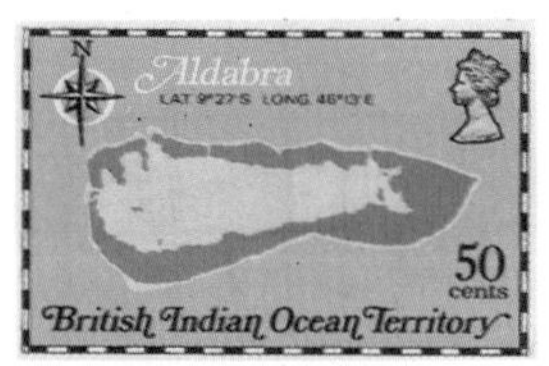

15 Map of Aldabra

1975. 10th Anniv of Territory. Maps. Multicoloured.

81 50c. Type **15** 80 65
82 1r. Desroches 95 85
83 1r.50 Farquhar 1·10 1·00
84 2r. Diego Garcia 1·25 1·25
MS85 147 × 147 mm. Nos. 81/4 7·00 14·00

16 "Utetheisa pulchella" (moth)

1976. Wildlife (4th series). Multicoloured.

86 65c. Type **16** 60 1·10
87 1r.20 "Dysdercus fasciatus" (bug) 75 1·25
88 1r.50 "Sphex torridus" (wasp) 80 1·40
89 2r. "Oryctes rhinoceros" (beetle) 85 1·40

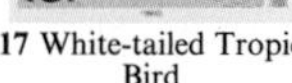

17 White-tailed Tropic Bird

19 Territory Flag

18 1974 Wildlife 1r.50 Stamp

1990. Birds. Multicoloured.

90 15p. Type **17** 1·10 2·00
91 20p. Madagascar turtle dove ("Turtle Dove") 1·25 2·00
92 24p. Great frigate bird ("Greater Frigate") 1·40 2·00
93 30p. Green-backed heron ("Little Green Heron") 1·50 2·25
94 34p. Great sand plover ("Greater Sand Plover") 1·60 2·25
95 41p. Crab plover 1·75 2·50
96 45p. Crested tern 2·50 2·50
97 54p. Lesser crested tern 2·25 2·75
98 62p. White tern ("Fairy Tern") 2·25 2·75
99 71p. Red-footed booby 2·25 3·00
100 80p. Common mynah ("Indian Mynah") 2·50 3·25
101 £1 Madagascar red fody ("Madagascar Fody") 2·75 3·50

1990. "Stamp World London 90" International Stamp Exhibition. Multicoloured.

102 15p. Type **18** 3·25 3·00
103 20p. 1976 Wildlife 2r. stamp 3·50 3·25
104 34p. 1975 Diego Garcia map 2r. stamp 5·50 5·00
105 54p. 1969 "Nordvaer" 1r. stamp 7·50 7·00

1990. 90th Birthday of Queen Elizabeth the Queen Mother. As T **34** of Ascension.

106 24p. multicoloured 3·50 3·50
107 £1 black and ochre 6·50 6·50

DESIGNS—21 × 36 mm: Lady Elizabeth Bowes-Lyon, 1923. 29 × 37 mm: £1 Queen Elizabeth and her daughters, 1940.

1990. 25th Anniv of British Indian Ocean Territory. Multicoloured.

108 20p. Type **19** 4·00 4·50
109 24p. Coat of arms 4·00 4·50
MS110 63 × 99 mm. £1 map of Chagos Archipelago 9·50 11·00

20 Postman emptying Pillar Box

1991. British Indian Ocean Territory Administration. Multicoloured.

111 20p. Type **20** 2·00 2·50
112 24p. Commissioner inspecting guard of Royal Marines 2·25 2·50
113 34p. Policeman outside station 4·00 4·50
114 54p. Customs officers boarding yacht 5·50 6·00

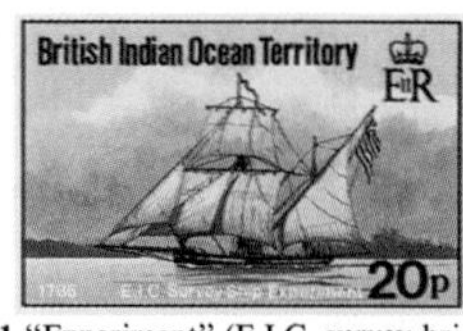

21 "Experiment" (E.I.C. survey brig), 1786

1991. Visiting Ships. Multicoloured.

115 20p. Type **21** 2·75 3·00
116 24p. "Pickering" (American brig), 1819 3·00 3·25
117 34p. "Emden" (German cruiser), 1914 4·00 4·25
118 54p. H.M.S. "Edinburgh" (destroyer), 1988 5·00 5·50

1992. 40th Anniv of Queen Elizabeth II's Accession. As T **143** of Ascension. Multicoloured.

119 15p. Catholic chapel, Diego Garcia 1·25 1·25
120 20p. Planter's house, Diego Garcia 1·40 1·40
121 24p. Railway tracks on wharf, Diego Garcia 3·00 2·00
122 34p. Three portraits of Queen Elizabeth 2·50 2·25
123 54p. Queen Elizabeth II 2·50 2·50

22 R.A.F. Consolidated PBY-5 Catalina (flying boat)

1992. Visiting Aircraft. Multicoloured.

124 20p. Type **22** 2·00 2·50
125 24p. R.A.F. Hawker Siddeley Nimrod M.R.2 (maritime reconnaissance aircraft) 2·25 2·50
126 34p. Lockheed P-3 Orion (transport aircraft) 2·75 3·25
127 54p. U.S.A.A.F. Boeing B-52 Stratofortress (heavy bomber) 3·50 4·50

23 "The Mystical Marriage of St. Catherine" (Correggio)

1992. Christmas. Religious Paintings. Mult.
128 5p. Type **23** 70 80
129 24p. "Madonna" (anon) 1·50 1·60
130 34p. "Madonna" (anon) (different) 1·75 2·25
131 54p. "The Birth of Jesus" (Kaspar Jele) 2·50 3·50

24 Coconut Crab and Rock

1993. Endangered Species. Coconut Crab. Mult.
132 10p. Type **24** 1·25 1·25
133 10p. Crab on beach 1·25 1·25
134 10p. Two crabs 1·25 1·25
135 15p. Crab climbing coconut tree 1·50 1·50

1993. 75th Anniv of Royal Air Force. As T **149** of Ascension. Multicoloured.
136 20p. Vickers Virginia Mk X 1·25 1·50
137 24p. Bristol Bulldog IIA 1·40 1·50
138 34p. Short S.25 Sunderland Mk III 1·75 2·00
139 54p. Bristol Blenheim Mk IV 2·75 3·25
MS140 110 × 77 mm. 20p. Douglas DC-3 Dakota; 20p. Gloster G.41 Javelin; 20p. Blackburn Beverley C1; 20p. Vickers VC-10 7·50 8·00

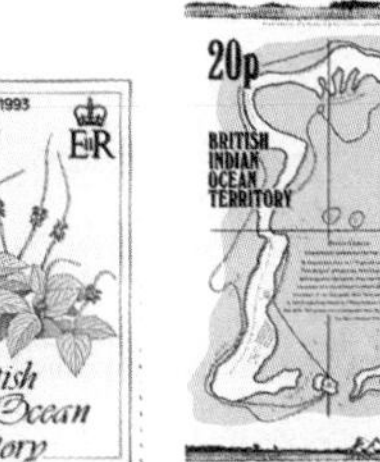

25 "Stachytarpheta urticifolia" 26 Forrest's Map of Diego Garcia, 1778

1993. Christmas. Flowers. Multicoloured.
141 20p. Type **25** 1·25 1·50
142 24p. "Ipomea pes-caprae" 1·25 1·50
143 34p. "Sida pusilla" 1·50 2·25
144 54p. "Catharanthus roseus" 2·50 3·00

1994. "Hong Kong '94" International Stamp Exhibition. Nos. 92 and 101 optd **HONG KONG '94** and emblem.
145 24p. Great frigate bird ("Greater Frigate") 2·00 1·75
146 £1 Madagascar red fody ("Madagascar Fody") 3·50 5·50

1994. 18th-century Maps. Each black and blue.
147 20p. Type **26** 90 1·50
148 24p. Blair's plan of Diego Garcia harbour, 1786–87 1·00 1·60
149 34p. Blair's chart of Chagos Archipelago, 1786–87 1·10 1·75
150 44p. Plan of part of Diego Garcia, 1774 1·40 1·90
151 54p. Fontaine's plan of Diego Garcia, 1770 1·60 2·00

27 "Junonia villida"

1994. Butterflies. Multicoloured.
152 24p. Type **27** 1·75 1·75
153 30p. "Petrelaea dana" 2·25 2·50
154 56p. "Hypolimnas misippus" 3·75 4·00

28 Short-tailed Nurse Sharks

1994. Sharks. Multicoloured.
155 15p. Type **28** 1·50 1·50
156 20p. Silver-tipped sharks 1·50 1·50
157 24p. Black-finned reef shark 1·50 1·50
158 30p. Oceanic white-tipped sharks 1·75 1·75
159 35p. Black-tipped shark 2·00 2·00
160 41p. Smooth hammerhead 2·00 2·00
161 46p. Sickle-finned lemon shark 2·00 2·00
162 55p. White-tipped reef shark 2·25 2·50
163 65p. Tiger sharks 2·25 2·50
164 74p. Indian sand tiger 2·50 3·00
165 80p. Great hammerhead 2·50 3·00
166 £1 Great white shark 2·50 3·25

1995. 50th Anniv of End of Second World War. As T **161** of Ascension. Multicoloured.
167 20p. Military cemetery 1·50 1·75
168 24p. Rusty 6-inch naval gun at Cannon Point 1·75 1·75
169 30p. Short S.25 Sunderland flying boat 2·00 2·25
170 56p. H.M.I.S. "Clive"(sloop) 3·00 3·75
MS171 75 × 85 mm. £1 Reverse of 1939–45 War Medal (vert) 2·50 3·00

29 Dolphin (fish)

1995. Gamefish. Multicoloured.
172 20p. Type **29** 1·50 1·60
173 24p. Sailfish 1·60 1·60
174 30p. Wahoo 2·25 2·50
175 56p. Striped marlin 3·25 3·75

30 "Terebra crenulata"

1996. Sea Shells. Multicoloured.
176 20p. Type **30** 1·25 1·50
177 24p. "Bursa bufonia" 1·25 1·50
178 30p. "Nassarius papillosus" 1·75 2·00
179 56p. "Lopha cristagalli" 3·00 3·25

1996. 70th Birthday of Queen Elizabeth II. As T **165** of Ascension, each incorporating a different photograph of the Queen. Multicoloured.
180 20p. View of lagoon from south 75 1·00
181 24p. Manager's House, Peros Banhos 80 1·00
182 30p. Wireless hut, Peros Banhos 1·00 1·40
183 56p. Sunset 1·50 2·00
MS184 64 × 66 mm. £1 Queen Elizabeth II 2·50 3·50

31 Loggerhead Turtle

1996. Turtles. Multicoloured.
185 20p. Type **31** 1·00 1·25
186 24p. Leatherback turtle 1·10 1·25
187 30p. Hawksbill turtle 1·40 1·60
188 56p. Green turtle 2·00 2·50

32 Commissioner's Representative (naval officer)

1996. Uniforms. Multicoloured.
189 20p. Type **32** 1·00 1·10
190 24p. Royal Marine officer 1·10 1·10
191 30p. Royal Marine in battle-dress 1·50 1·75
192 56p. Police officers 2·25 2·75

1997. "HONG KONG '97" International Stamp Exhibition. Sheet 130 × 90 mm, containing design as No. 163. Multicoloured.
MS193 65p. Tiger sharks 2·00 2·50

1997. Return of Hong Kong to China. Sheet 130 × 90 mm, containing design as No. 164, but with "1997" imprint date.
MS194 74p. Indian sand tiger 2·75 3·50

1997. Golden Wedding of Queen Elizabeth and Prince Philip. As T **173** of Ascension. Mult.
195 20p. Queen Elizabeth at Bristol, 1994 1·25 1·50
196 20p. Prince Philip competing in Royal Windsor Horse Show, 1996 1·25 1·50
197 24p. Queen Elizabeth in phaeton, Trooping the Colour, 1987 1·25 1·50
198 24p. Prince Philip 1·25 1·50
199 30p. Queen Elizabeth and Prince Philip with Land Rover 1·25 1·50
200 30p. Queen Elizabeth at Balmoral 1·25 1·50
MS201 110 × 71 mm. £1.50, Queen Elizabeth and Prince Philip in landau (horiz) 6·00 6·50
Nos. 195/6, 197/8 and 199/20 respectively were printed together, se-tenant, with the backgrounds forming a compsite design.

33 H.M.S. "Richmond" (frigate) and H.M.S. "Beaver" (frigate)

1997. Exercise Ocean Wave. Multicoloured.
202 24p. Type **33** 1·00 1·25
203 24p. H.M.S. "Illustrious" (aircraft carrier) launching aircraft 1·00 1·25
204 24p. H.M.S. "Beaver" 1·00 1·25
205 24p. Royal Yacht "Britannia", R.F.A. "Sir Percival" and H.M.S. "Beaver" 1·00 1·25
206 24p. Royal Yacht "Britannia" 1·00 1·25
207 24p. H.M.S. "Richmond", H.M.S. "Beaver" and H.M.S. "Gloucester" (destroyer) 1·00 1·25
208 24p. H.M.S. "Richmond" 1·00 1·25
209 24p. Aerial view of H.M.S. "Illustrious" 1·00 1·25
210 24p. H.M.S. "Gloucester" (wrongly inscr "Sheffield") 1·00 1·25
211 24p. H.M.S. "Trenchant" (submarine) and R.F.A. "Diligence" 1·00 1·25
212 24p. R.F.A. "Fort George" replenishing H.M.S. "Illustrious" and H.M.S. "Gloucester" 1·00 1·25
213 24p. Aerial view of H.M.S. "Richmond", H.M.S. "Beaver" and H.M.S. "Gloucester" 1·00 1·25

1998. Diana, Princess of Wales Commemoration. Sheet 145 × 70 mm, containing vert designs as T **177** of Ascension. Multicoloured.
MS214 26p. Wearing patterned jacket, 1993; 26p. Wearing heart-shaped earrings, 1988; 34p. Wearing cream jacket, 1993; 60p. Wearing blue blouse, 1982 (sold at £1.46 + 20p. charity premium) 3·25 4·00

1998. 80th Anniv of the Royal Air Force. As T **178** of Ascension. Multicoloured.
215 26p. Blackburn Iris 1·00 1·10
216 34p. Gloster Gamecock 1·25 1·40
217 60p. North American Sabre F.4 2·25 2·50
218 80p. Avro Lincoln 2·75 3·00
MS219 110 × 77 mm. 34p. Sopwith Baby (seaplane); 34p. Martinsyde Elephant; 34p. De Havilland Tiger Moth; 34p. North American Mustang III 5·00 6·00

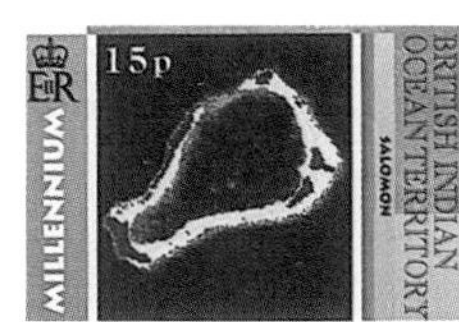

34 Bryde's Whale

1998. International Year of the Ocean. Multicoloured.
220 26p. Type **34** 1·10 1·25
221 26p. Striped dolphin 1·10 1·25
222 34p. Pilot whale 1·10 1·25
223 34p. Spinner dolphin 1·10 1·25

35 "Westminster" (East Indiaman), 1837

1999. Ships. Multicoloured.
224 2p. Type **35** 10 10
225 15p. "Sao Cristovao" (Spanish galleon), 1589 30 35
226 20p. "Sea Witch" (U.S. clipper), 1849 40 45
227 26p. H.M.S. "Royal George" (ship of the line), 1778 55 60
228 34p. "Cutty Sark" (clipper), 1883 70 75
229 60p. "Mentor" (East Indiaman), 1789 1·25 1·40
230 80p. H.M.S. "Trinculo" (brig), 1809 1·60 1·70
231 £1 "Enterprise" (paddle-steamer), 1825 2·00 2·10
232 £1.15 "Confiance" (French privateer), 1800 2·25 2·40
233 £2 "Kent" (East Indiaman), 1820 4·00 4·25

36 Cutty Sark (clipper)

1999. "Australia '99" World Stamp Exhibition, Melbourne. Sheet 150 × 75 mm, containing T **36** and similar horiz design. Multicoloured.
MS234 60p. Type **36**; 60p. "Thermopylae" (clipper) 2·75 3·75

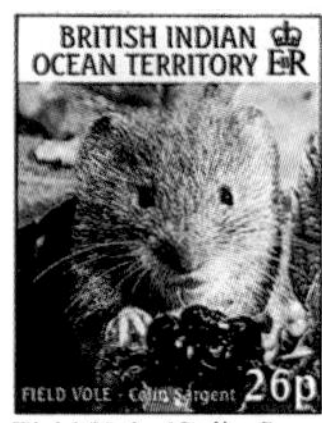

37 Field Vole (Colin Sargent)

2000. "The Stamp Show 2000", International Stamp Exhibition, London. "Shoot a Stamp" Competition Winners. Sheet 150 × 100 mm, containing T **37** and similar vert designs. Multicoloured.
MS235 26p. Type **37**; 34p. Atlantic puffin (P. J. Royal); 55p. Red fox (Jim Wilson); £1 European robin ("Robin") (Harry Smith) 5·00 6·00

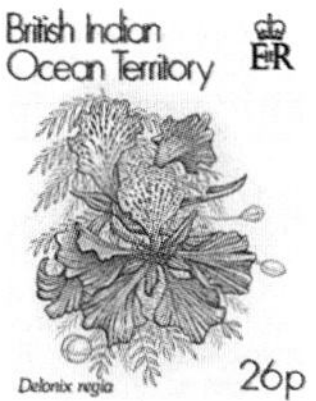

38 Satellite Image of Salomon Island

2000. New Millennium. Satellite Images of Islands. Multicoloured.
236 15p. Type **38** 80 90
237 20p. Egmont 90 1·00
238 60p. Blenheim Reef 1·75 2·00
239 80p. Diego Garcia 2·00 2·25

39 Queen Elizabeth the Queen Mother 40 *Delonix regia*

2000. Queen Elizabeth the Queen Mother's 100th Birthday. Multicoloured.
240 26p. Type **39** . . . . 90 1·00
241 34p. Wearing green hat and outfit . . . . 1·00 1·25
MS242 113 × 88 mm. 55p. In blue hat and outfit 4·00 4·50

2000. Christmas Flowers. Multicoloured.
243 26p. Type **40** . . . . 90 1·00
244 34p. *Barringtonia asiatica* . . 1·10 1·25
245 60p. *Zephyranthes rosea* . . . 1·90 2·25

2000. "HONG KONG 2001" Stamp Exhibition. Sheet 150 × 90 mm, containing T **41** and similar design showing butterfly. Multicoloured.
MS246 26p. Type **41**; 34p. "Junonia villida chagoensis" 1·75 2·00

42 H.M.S. *Turbulent*

2001. Centenary of Royal Navy Submarine Service. Multicoloured (except Nos. 248 and 250).
247 26p. Type **42** 80 90
248 26p. H.M.S. *Churchill* (grey and black) 80 90
249 34p. H.M.S. *Resolution* . . . 1·10 1·25
250 34p. H.M.S. *Vanguard* . . . 1·10 1·25
251 60p. H.M.S. *Otter* (73 × 27 mm) . . . . . . 1·75 2·00
252 60p. H.M.S. *Oberon* (73 × 27 mm) (grey and black) . . . . 1·75 2·00

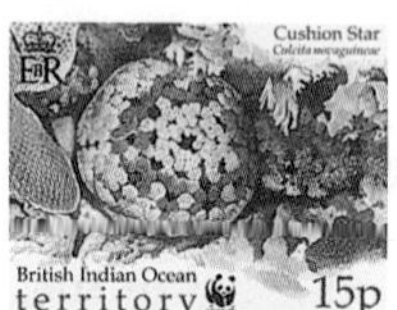

43 Cushion Star

2001. Endangered Species. Seastars. Multicoloured.
253 15p. Type **43** 50 60
254 26p. Azure sea star 70 80
255 34p. Crown-of-Thorns . . . 90 1·00
256 56p. Banded bubble star . . 1·40 1·60

44 *Scadoxus multiflora*

2001. Plants (1st series). Flowers. Multicoloured.
257 26p. Type **44** 70 80
258 34p. *Striga asiatica* 90 95
MS259 173 × 78 mm. Nos. 257/8 and 10p. "Catharanthus roseus" (horiz); 60p. "Argusia argentea" (horiz); 70p. "Euphorbia cyathophora" (horiz) 4·75 5·00
In No. **MS**259 the 60p. is inscribed "argentia" in error.

45 Crab Plovers on Beach

2001. Birdlife World Bird Festival. Crab Plovers. Sheet 175 × 80 mm, containing T **45** and similar multicoloured designs.
MS260 50p. Type **45**; 50p. Crab plover catching crab (vert); 50p. Head of crab plover (vert); 50p. Crab plovers in flight; 50p. Crab plover standing on one leg 5·50 6·00

2002. Golden Jubilee. As T **200** of Ascension.
261 10p. brown, blue and gold . . 40 50
262 25p. multicoloured 70 80
263 35p. black, blue and gold . . 1·00 1·10
264 55p. multicoloured . . . . . 1·40 1·60
MS265 162 × 95 mm. Nos. 261/4 and 75p. multicoloured 6·00 6·50
DESIGNS—HORIZ: 10p. Princess Elizabeth in pantomime, Windsor, 1943; 25p. Queen Elizabeth in floral hat, 1967; 35p. Princess Elizabeth and Prince Philip on their engagement, 1947; 55p. Queen Elizabeth in evening dress. VERT (38 × 51 mm)—75p. Queen Elizabeth after Annigoni.
Designs as Nos. 261/4 in No. **MS**265 omit the gold frame around each stamp and the "Golden Jubilee 1952–2002" inscription.

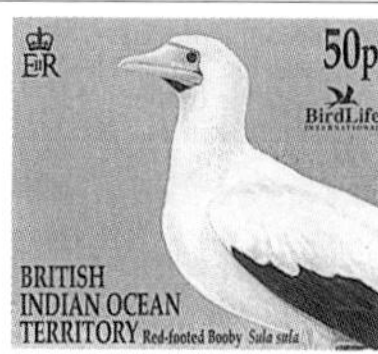

46 Adult Red-footed Booby

2002. Birdlife International. Red-footed Booby. Sheet 175 × 80 mm, containing T **46** and similar multicoloured designs.
MS266 50p. Type **46**; 50p. Head of dark morph red-footed booby; 50p. Adult bird in flight (vert); 50p. Dark morph on nest (vert); 50p. Fledgling on nest 2·50 2·75

2002. Queen Elizabeth the Queen Mother Commemoration. As T **202** of Ascension.
267 26p. brown, gold and purple 55 60
268 £1 multicoloured . . . . . . 2·00 2·10
MS269 145 × 70 mm. £1 black and gold; £1 multicoloured 4·00 4·25
DESIGNS: 26p. Lady Elizabeth Bowes-Lyon, 1921; £1 (No. 268) Queen Mother, 1986; £1 brownish black and gold (No. **MS**269) Queen Elizabeth at garden party, 1951; £1 multicoloured (No. **MS**269) Queen Mother at Cheltenham Races, 1994.
Designs in No. **MS**269 omit the "1900--2002" inscription and the coloured frame.

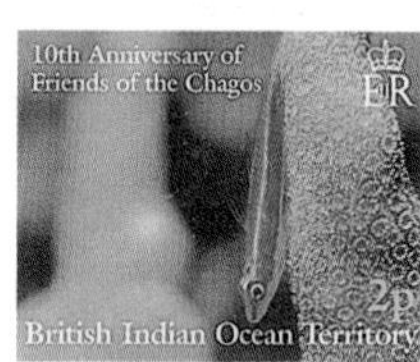

47 Microgoby

2002. 10th Anniv of Friends of Chagos (conservation association). Reef Fish. Mult.
270 2p. Type **47** 10 10
271 15p. Angel fish 30 35
272 26p. Surgeonfish 55 60
273 34p. Trunkfish 70 75
274 58p. Soldierfish . . . . . . 1·25 1·40
275 £1 Chagos anemonefish . . . 2·00 2·10

48 *Halgerda tesselata*

2003. Sea Slugs. Multicoloured.
276 2p. Type **48** 10 10
277 15p. *Notodoris minor* 30 35
278 26p. *Nembrotha lineolata* . . 50 55
279 50p. *Chromodoris quadricolor* 1·00 1·25
280 76p. *Glossodoris cincta* . . . 1·50 1·75
281 £1.10 *Chromodoris cf leopardus* . . . . 2·25 2·40

PARCEL POST STAMPS

2002. 10th Anniv of Friends of Chagos (conservation association). Reef Fish. Sheet 115 × 95 mm, containing horiz design as T **47**. Multicoloured.
PMS1 £1.90 Parrotfish . . . . . 3·75 4·00

BRITISH LEVANT Pt. 1

Stamps used at British post offices in the Turkish Empire. These offices closed in 1914. The stamps were again in use after 1918, during the British Occupation of Turkey.

Stamps of Great Britain surcharged or overprinted

A. BRITISH POST OFFICES IN TURKISH EMPIRE

I. TURKISH CURRENCY.

40 paras = 1 piastre.

1885. Queen Victoria stamps surch in **PARAS** or **PIASTRES**.
7 **71** 40pa. on ½d. red £425 £100
1 **64** 40pa. on 2½d. lilac . . . . 90·00 1·25
4 **74** 40pa. on 2½d. purple on blue . . . . 3·25 10
2 **62** 80pa. on 5d. green . . . . £180 9·50
5 **78** 80pa. on 5d. purple & blue 15·00 30
6 **81** 4pi. on 10d. purple and red 42·00 8·00
3a **58** 12pi. on 2s.6d. lilac . . . . 45·00 22·00

1902. King Edward VII stamps surch in **PARAS** or **PIASTRES**.
29 – 30pa. on 1½d. purple & grn 6·50 55
8 **83** 40pa. on 2½d. blue . . . . 13·00 10
9 – 80pa. on 5d. purple and blue . . . . 6·00 2·50
13 **83** 1pi. on 2½d. blue . . . . . 11·00 10
30 – 2pi. on 5d. purple and blue 9·50 1·50
10 – 4pi. on 10d. purple and red 10·00 4·00
21 – 5pi. on 1s. green and red . . 4·25 9·00
11 – 12pi. on 2s.6d. purple . . . 35·00 35·00
12 – 24pi. on 5s. red . . . . . . 32·00 40·00

1906. Surch **1 Piastre**.
15 – 1pi. on 2d. green and red . . £1300 £600

1909. King Edward VII stamps surch in **PIASTRE PARAS**.
17 – 1pi. 10pa. on 3d. pur on yell 12·00 32·00
18 – 1pi. 30pa. on 4d. grn & brn 5·00 17·00
19 – 1pi. 30pa. on 4d. orange . . 17·00 55·00
20 **83** 2pi. 20pa. on 6d. purple . . 18·00 55·00

1910. King Edward VII stamps surch in **PIASTRES**.
22 – 1¼pi. on 3d. purple on yellow . . . . 50 1·00
23 – 1¾pi. on 4d. orange 50 60
24 **83** 2½pi. on 6d. purple . . . . 1·40 65

1913. King George V stamps surch.
41 **105** 30pa. on ½d. green . . . 75 12·00
35 30pa. on 1½d. brown . . 3·50 14·00
36a **104** 1pi. on 2½d. blue . . . . 4·50 15
37 **106** 1¼pi. on 3d. violet . . . . 4·75 4·25
42 **104** 1½pi. on 1d. red . . . . . 1·50 1·25
38 **106** 1¾pi. on 4d. grey-green . . 3·00 6·00
43 **104** 3¾pi. on 2½d. blue . . . . 1·25 25
39 **108** 4pi. on 10d. blue . . . . 7·50 18·00
44 **106** 4½pi. on 3d. violet . . . . 2·00 3·75
40 **108** 5pi. on 1s. brown . . . . 40·00 60·00
45 **107** 7½pi. on 5d. brown . . . 50 10
46 **108** 15pi. on 10d. blue 70 15
47 18¾pi. on 1s. brown . . . 4·25 4·25
48 **109** 45pi. on 2s.6d. brown . . 20·00 45·00
49 90pi. on 5s. red . . . . 25·00 30·00
50 180pi. on 10s. blue . . . 45·00 40·00

II. BRITISH CURRENCY

1905. King Edward VII stamps optd **LEVANT**.
L 1 **83** ½d. green . . . . 8·50 15
L 2 1d. red . . . . 6·50 15
L 3 – 1½d. purple and green . . 4·50 1·75
L 4a – 2d. green and red . . . . 3·00 7·00
L 5 **83** 2½d. blue . . . . 8·50 20·00
L 6 – 3d. purple and yellow . . 6·00 12·00
L 7 – 4d. green and brown . . . 8·50 38·00
L 8 – 5d. purple and blue . . . 16·00 28·00
L 9 **83** 6d. purple . . . . 12·00 25·00
L10 1s. green and red . . . . 35·00 48·00

1911. King George V stamps optd **LEVANT**.
L12 **98** ½d. green . . . . 1·00 1·25
L14 **101** ½d. green 75 20
L16 **105** ½d. green . . . . 30 1·00
L13 **99** 1d. red . . . . 50 4·50
L15 **102** 1d. red . . . . 50 1·60
L17 **104** 1d. red . . . . 30 4·50
L18 **106** 2d. orange . . . . 1·25 28·00
L19 3d. violet . . . . 7·50 10·00
L20 4d. green . . . . 5·00 13·00
L21 **107** 5d. brown . . . . 12·00 28·00
L22a 6d. purple . . . . 26·00 8·50
L23 **108** 1s. brown . . . . 13·00 8·50
L24 **109** 2s.6d. brown . . . . . 38·00 90·00

B. BRITISH FIELD OFFICE IN SALONICA

1916. King George V stamps of Great Britain optd **Levant**.
S1 **105** ½d. green . . . . 40·00 £190
S2 **104** 1d. red . . . . 40·00 £180
S3 **106** 2d. orange £130 £325
S4 3d. violet . . . . 95·00 £325
S5 4d. green £130 £325
S6 **107** 6d. purple . . . . 75·00 £275
S7 **108** 9d. black £275 £500
S8 1s. brown £225 £450
The above stamps were optd at Salonica during the war of 1914–18.

BRITISH OCCUPATION OF ITALIAN COLONIES Pt. 1

Issues for use in Italian colonies occupied by British Forces. Middle East Forces overprints were used in Cyrenaica, Dodecanese Islands, Eritrea, Italian Somaliland and Tripolitania.

MIDDLE EAST FORCES

12 pence = 1 shilling;
20 shillings = 1 pound.

1942. Stamps of Great Britain optd **M.E.F.**
M11 **128** 1d. red . . . . 1·50 10
M12 2d. orange . . . . . . 1·50 1·25
M13 2½d. blue 50 10
M 4 3d. violet 50 10
M 5 **129** 5d. brown 50 15
M16 6d. purple 40 10
M17 **130** 9d. olive 85 10
M18 1s. brown 50 10
M19 **131** 2s.6d. green . . . . . . 7·00 1·00
M20 5s. red . . . . 12·00 17·00
M21 10s. blue (No. 478a) . . 15·00 10·00
PRICES. Our prices for Nos. M1/21 in used condition are for stamps with identifiable postmarks of the territories in which they were issued. These stamps were also used in the United Kingdom with official sanction, from the summer of 1950 onwards, and with U.K. postmarks are worth about 25 per cent less.

POSTAGE DUE STAMPS

1942. Postage Due stamps of Great Britain optd **M.E.F.**
MD1 **D 1** ½d. green . . . . 30 11·00
MD2 1d. red . . . . 30 1·75
MD3 2d. black . . . . 1·25 1·25
MD4 3d. violet . . . . 50 4·25
MD5 1s. blue . . . . 3·25 11·00

CYRENAICA

10 milliemes = 1 piastre;
100 piastres = 1 Egyptian pound.

24 Mounted Warrior

25 Mounted Warrior

1950.
136 **24** 1m. brown . . . . 1·50 3·25
137 2m. red . . . . 1·75 3·25
138 3m. yellow . . . . 1·75 3·50
139 4m. green . . . . 1·75 3·25
140 5m. grey . . . . 1·75 2·00
141 8m. orange . . . . 1·75 1·75
142 10m. violet . . . . 1·75 1·50
143 12m. red . . . . 1·75 1·25
144 20m. blue . . . . 1·75 1·25
145 **25** 50m. blue and brown . . . 3·00 3·25
146 100m. red and black . . . 7·50 9·00
147 200m. violet and blue . . . 12·00 25·00
148 500m. yellow and green . . 42·00 65·00

POSTAGE DUE STAMPS

D 26

1950.
D149 **D 26** 2m. brown . . . . . . 43·00 93·00
D150 4m. green . . . . . . 45·00 95·00
D151 8m. red . . . . 45·00 £100
D152 10m. orange . . . . . 45·00 £100
D153 20m. yellow . . . . . 45·00 £110
D154 40m. blue . . . . . . 45·00 £130
D155 100m. brown . . . . 45·00 £140

ERITREA

100 cents = 1 shilling.

BRITISH MILITARY ADMINISTRATION

1948. Stamps of Great Britain surch **B.M.A. ERITREA** and value in cents or shillings.
E 1 **128** 5c. on ½d. green 70 65
E 2 10c. on 1d. red . . . . 75 2·50
E 3 20c. on 2d. orange . . . 50 2·25
E 4 25c. on 2½d. blue . . . 70 60
E 5 30c. on 3d. violet . . . 1·25 4·50
E 6 **129** 40c. on 5d. brown . . . 50 4·25
E 7 50c. on 6d. purple . . . 50 1·00
E 7a **130** 65c. on 8d. red . . . . 7·00 2·00
E 8 75c. on 9d. olive 70 75
E 9 1s. on 1s. brown 70 50
E10 **131** 2s.50 on 2s.6d. green . . 8·00 10·00
E11 5s. on 5s. red . . . . . 8·00 16·00
E12 – 10s. on 10s. blue (No. 478a) . . . . . 22·00 22·00

BRITISH ADMINISTRATION

1950. Stamps of Great Britain surch **B.A. ERITREA** and value in cents or shillings.
E13 **128** 5c. on ½d. green . . . . 85 8·00
E26 5c. on ½d. orange . . . 30 75
E14 10c. on 1d. red . . . . 30 3·00
E27 10c. on 1d. blue 30 75
E15 20c. on 2d. orange . . . 30 80
E28 20c. on 2d. brown . . . 30 30
E16 25c. on 2½d. blue . . . 30 60
E29 25c. on 2½d. red . . . 30 30
E17 **128** 30c. on 3d. violet . . . . 30 2·25
E18 **129** 40c. on 5d. brown . . . 50 1·75
E19 50c. on 6d. purple . . . 30 20
E20 **130** 65c. on 8d. red . . . . . 1·75 1·50
E21 75c. on 9d. olive 30 25
E22 1s. on 1s. brown 30 15
E23 **131** 2s.50 on 2s.6d. green . . 6·00 4·75
E24 5s. on 5s. red . . . . . 6·50 12·00
E25 – 10s. on 10s. blue (No. 478a) . . . . . 60·00 55·00

1951. Nos. 509/11 of Great Britain surch **B.A. ERITREA** and value in cents and shillings.
E30 **147** 2s.50 on 2s.6d. green . . 10·00 23·00
E31 – 5s. on 5s. red . . . . . 21·00 23·00
E32 – 10s. on 10s. blue . . . 22·00 23·00

POSTAGE DUE STAMPS

1948. Postage Due stamps of Great Britain surch **B.M.A ERITREA** and new value in cents and shillings.
ED1 **D 1** 5c. on ½d. green . . . . 9·50 22·00
ED2 10c. on 1d. red . . . . 9·50 24·00
ED3 20c. on 2d. black . . . 7·00 16·00

ED4 30c. on 3d. violet . . . 9·50 15·00
ED5 1s. on 1s. blue . . . . . 17·00 29·00

1950. Postage Due stamps of Great Britain surch **B.A. ERITREA** and new value in cents or shillings.
ED 6 **D 1** 5c. on ½d. green . . . 11·00 48·00
ED 7 10c. on 1d. red . . . . 9·00 15·00
ED 8 20c. on 2d. black . . . 9·50 13·00
ED 9 30c. on 3d. violet . . . 11·00 20·00
ED10 1s. on 1s. blue . . . . 15·00 22·00

SOMALIA

BRITISH OCCUPATION

1943. Stamps of Great Britain optd **E.A.F.** (East African Forces).
S1 **128** 1d. red 60 60
S2 2d. orange . . . . 1·50 1·25
S3 2½d. blue . . . . 50 3·50
S4 3d. violet 70 15
S5 **129** 5d. brown 70 40
S6 6d. purple . . . . 50 1·25
S7 **130** 9d. olive . . . . 80 2·25
S8 1s. brown . . . . 1·75 15
S9 **131** 2s.6d. green . . . . . . 8·50 6·50

PRICES. Our prices for Nos. S1/9 in used condition are for stamps with identifiable postmarks of the territories in which they were issued. These stamps were also used in the United Kingdom with official sanction, from the summer of 1950, and with U.K. postmarks are worth about 25 per cent less.

BRITISH MILITARY ADMINISTRATION

1948. Stamps of Great Britain surch **B.M.A. SOMALIA** and new value in cents and shillings.
S10 **128** 5c. on ½d. green . . . . 1·25 1·75
S11 15c. on 1½d. brown . . . 1·75 15·00
S12 20c. on 2d. orange . . . 3·00 4·00
S13 25c. on 2½d. blue . . . . 2·25 4·50
S14 30c. on 3d. violet . . . . 2·25 9·00
S15 **129** 40c. on 5d. brown . . . . 1·25 20
S16 50c. on 6d. purple . . . . 50 2·00
S17 **130** 75c. on 9d. olive . . . . 2·00 18·00
S18 1s. on 1s. brown . . . . 1·25 20
S19 **131** 2s.50 on 2s.6d. green . . 4·25 25·00
S20 5s. on 5s. red . . . . . . 9·50 40·00

BRITISH ADMINISTRATION

1950. Stamps of Great Britain surch **B.A. SOMALIA** and value in cents and shillings.
S21 **128** 5c. on ½d. green . . . . 20 3·00
S22 15c. on 1½d. brown . . . 75 17·00
S23 20c. on 2d. orange . . . 75 7·00
S24 25c. on 2½d. blue . . . . 50 7·00
S25 30c. on 3d. violet . . . . 1·25 4·50
S26 **129** 40c. on 5d. brown . . . . 55 1·00
S27 50c. on 6d. purple . . . . 50 1·00
S28 **130** 75c. on 9d. olive . . . . 2·00 7·00
S29 1s. on 1s. brown . . . . 60 1·50
S30 **131** 2s.50 on 2s.6d. green . . 4·00 24·00
S31 5s. on 5s. red . . . . . . 11·00 95·00

TRIPOLITANIA

BRITISH MILITARY ADMINISTRATION

1948. Stamps of Great Britain surch **B.M.A. TRIPOLITANIA** and value in **M.A.L.** (Military Administration lire).
T 1 **128** 1l. on ½d. green . . . . . 50 1·50
T 2 2l. on 1d. red 30 15
T 3 3l. on 1½d. brown 30 50
T 4 4l. on 2d. orange 30 50
T 5 5l. on 2½d. blue 30 20
T 6 6l. on 3d. violet 30 40
T 7 **129** 10l. on 5d. brown 30 15
T 8 12l. on 6d. purple 30 20
T 9 **130** 18l. on 9d. olive 80 65
T10 24l. on 1s. brown . . . . 70 1·25
T11 **131** 60l. on 2s.6d. green . . . 3·50 7·50
T12 120l. on 5s. red . . . . . 15·00 17·00
T13 240l. on 10s. blue (No. 478a) . . . . . . 22·00 95·00

BRITISH ADMINISTRATION

1950. As Nos. T1/13 but surch **B.A. TRIPOLITANIA** and value in **M.A.L.**
T14 **128** 1l. on ½d. green . . . . . 2·50 12·00
T27 1l. on ½d. orange . . . . 20 6·00
T15 2l. on 1d. red . . . . . 2·25 40
T28 2l. on 1d. blue 20 90
T16 3l. on 1½d. brown . . . . 75 11·00
T29 3l. on 1½d. green . . . . 30 8·00
T17 4l. on 2d. orange . . . . 70 4·50
T30 4l. on 2d. brown . . . . 20 1·25
T18 5l. on 2½d. blue 50 70
T31 5l. on 2½d. red . . . . . 30 7·50
T19 6l. on 3d. violet . . . . . 1·50 3·25
T20 **129** 10l. on 5d. brown . . . . 30 4·00
T21 12l. on 6d. purple . . . . 1·75 50
T22 **130** 18l. on 9d. olive . . . . 2·00 2·50
T23 24l. on 1s. brown . . . . 2·00 3·50
T24 **131** 60l. on 2s.6d. green . . . 5·50 12·00
T25 120l. on 5s. red . . . . . 19·00 22·00
T26 – 240l. on 10s. blue (No. 478a) . . . . . . 32·00 65·00

1951. Nos. 509/11 of Great Britain surch **B.A. TRIPOLITANIA** and value in **M.A.L.**
T32 **147** 60l. on 2s.6d. green . . . 5·50 25·00
T33 – 120l. on 5s. red . . . . . 9·00 27·00
T34 – 240l. on 10s. blue . . . . 38·00 48·00

POSTAGE DUE STAMPS

1948. Postage Due stamps of Great Britain surch **B.M.A. TRIPOLITANIA** and value in **M.A.L.**
TD1 **D 1** 1l. on ½d. green . . . . 5·50 48·00
TD2 2l. on 1d. red . . . . . 2·50 30·00
TD3 4l. on 2d. black . . . . 7·50 30·00
TD4 6l. on 3d. violet . . . . 7·50 21·00
TD5 24l. on 1s. blue . . . . 28·00 £100

1950. As Nos. TD1/5 but surch **B.A. TRIPOLITANIA** and value in **M.A.L.**
TD 6 **D 1** 1l. on ½d. green . . . . 12·00 80·00
TD 7 2l. on 1d. red . . . . 2·50 27·00
TD 8 4l. on 2d. black . . . . 3·50 32·00
TD 9 6l. on 3d. violet . . . . 18·00 60·00
TD10 24l. on 1s. blue . . . . 48·00 £140

BRITISH POSTAL AGENCIES IN EASTERN ARABIA Pt. 1

British stamps surcharged for use in parts of the Persian Gulf.

The stamps were used in Muscat from 1 April 1948 to 29 April 1966; in Dubai from 1 April 1948 to 6 January 1961; In Qatar: Doha from August 1950, Umm Said from February 1956 to 31 March 1957; and in Abu Dhabi from 30 March 1963 (Das Island from December 1960) to 29 March 1964.

Nos. 21/2 were placed on sale in Kuwait Post Offices in 1951 and from February to November 1953 due to shortages of stamps with "KUWAIT" overprint. Isolated examples of other values can be found commercially used from Bahrain and Kuwait.

1948. 12 pies = 1 anna; 16 annas = 1 rupee.
1957. 100 naya paise = 1 rupee.

Stamps of Great Britain surch in Indian currency.

1948. King George VI.
16 **128** ½a. on ½d. green . . . . . 2·75 6·50
35 ½a. on ½d. orange . . . . 50 9·00
17 1a. on 1d. red . . . . . . 3·00 30
36 1a. on 1d. blue . . . . . 30 7·50
18 1½a. on 1½d. brown . . . . 8·00 2·50
37 1½a. on 1½d. green . . . . 8·00 23·00
19 2a. on 2d. orange . . . . 2·00 3·00
38 2a. on 2d. brown . . . . . 30 8·50
20 2½a. on 2½d. blue . . . . 3·50 5·50
39 2½a. on 2½d. red . . . . . 30 16·00
21 3a. on 3d. violet . . . . . 3·50 10
40 **129** 4a. on 4d. blue . . . . . 30 3·50
22 6a. on 6d. purple . . . . . 3·50 10
23 **130** 1r. on 1s. brown . . . . . 4·00 50
24 **131** 2r. on 2s.6d. green . . . . 9·50 35·00

1948. Royal Silver Wedding.
25 **137** 2½a. on 2½d. blue . . . . 2·00 2·50
26 **138** 15r. on £1 blue . . . . . 23·00 35·00

1948. Olympic Games.
27 **139** 2½a. on 2½d. blue . . . . 35 2·25
28 **140** 3a. on 3d. violet . . . . . 45 2·25
29 – 6a. on 6d. purple . . . . . 45 2·50
30 – 1r. on 1s. brown . . . . . 1·25 2·50

1949. 75th Anniv of U.P.U.
31 **143** 2½a. on 2½d. blue . . . . 50 2·75
32 **144** 3a. on 3d. violet . . . . . 50 2·75
33 – 6a. on 6d. purple . . . . . 50 2·25
34 – 1r. on 1s. brown . . . . . 2·00 3·25

1951. Pictorial.
41 **147** 2r. on 2s.6d. green . . . . 26·00 7·00

1952. Queen Elizabeth.
42 **154** ½a. on ½d. orange . . . . 10 2·25
43 1a. on 1d. blue . . . . . 10 2·25
44 1½a. on 1½d. green . . . . 10 2·25
45 2a. on 2d. brown 10 10
46 **155** 2½a. on 2½d. red 10 10
47 3a. on 3d. lilac . . . . . 20 1·25
48 4a. on 4d. blue . . . . . 75 4·00
49 **157** 6a. on 6d. purple 35 10
50 **160** 12a. on 1s.3d. green . . . 2·75 30
51 1r. on 1s.6d. blue . . . . 2·25 10

1953. Coronation.
52 **161** 2½a. on 2½d. red . . . . . 1·75 1·75
53 – 4a. on 4d. blue . . . . . 1·75 1·00
54 **163** 12a. on 1s.3d. green . . . 2·25 1·00
55 – 1r. on 1s.6d. blue . . . . 2·50 50

1955. Pictorials.
56 **166** 2r. on 2s.6d. brown . . . 6·50 70
57 – 5r. on 5s. red . . . . . . 10·00 2·25

1957. Value in naye paise. Queen Elizabeth II stamps surch **NP** twice (once only on 75n.p.) and value.
79 **157** 1n.p. on 5d. brown 10 20
80 **154** 3n.p. on ½d. orange 55 80
81 5n.p. on 1d. blue . . . . . 1·25 1·75
67 6n.p. on 1d. blue . . . . . 20 2·50
68 9n.p. on 1½d. green . . . . 20 2·00
83 10n.p. on 1½d. green . . . 1·00 2·25
69 12n.p. on 2d. brown . . . 30 2·00
85 **155** 15n.p. on 2½d. red 25 10
71 20n.p. on 3d. lilac 20 10
72 25n.p. on 4d. blue . . . . 70 3·50
87 30n.p. on 4½d. brown . . . 40 50
73 **157** 40n.p. on 6d. purple . . . 30 10
89 **158** 50n.p. on 9d. olive . . . . 1·00 2·00
75 **160** 75n.p. on 1s.3d. green . . 2·00 35

1957. World Scout Jubilee Jamboree.
76 **170** 15n.p. on 2½d. red 25 85
77 **171** 25n.p. on 4d. blue 30 85
78 – 75n.p. on 3d. green 35 85

BRITISH POST OFFICES IN CHINA Pt. 1

Stamps for use in Wei Hai Wei, and the neighbouring islands, leased to Great Britain from 1898 to 1 October 1930, when they were returned to China. The stamps were also used in the Treaty Ports from 1917 until 1922.

100 cents = 1 dollar.

1917. Stamps of Hong Kong (King George V) optd **CHINA**.
1 **24** 1c. brown . . . . 3·00 1·50
2 2c. green . . . . 4·00 30
3 4c. red . . . . 3·75 30
4 6c. orange . . . . 4·00 60
5 8c. grey . . . . 10·00 1·25
6 10c. blue . . . . 9·50 30
7 12c. purple on yellow . . . 7·50 2·50
8 20c. purple and olive . . . 11·00 60
9 25c. purple . . . . 7·50 15·00
11 30c. purple and orange . . 26·00 5·00
12b 50c. black on green . . . . 26·00 5·50
13 $1 purple and blue on blue 65·00 2·50
14 $2 red and black . . . . . £190 50·00
15 $3 green and purple . . . £400 £170
16 $5 green and red on green £350 £225
17 $10 purple and black on red £850 £425

BRITISH POST OFFICES IN CRETE Pt. 1

40 paras = 1 piastre.

B 1 B 2

1898.
B1 **B 1** 20pa. violet £425 £225

1898.
B2 **B 2** 10pa. blue . . . . 8·00 18·00
B4 10pa. brown . . . . . . 8·00 24·00
B3 20pa. green . . . . 13·00 16·00
B5 20pa. red . . . . 18·00 15·00

BRITISH POST OFFICES IN SIAM Pt. 1

Used at Bangkok.

100 cents = 1 dollar.

1882. Stamps of Straits Settlements optd **B** on issue of 1867.
1 **19** 32c. on 2a. yellow £35000

On issues of 1867 to 1883.
14 **5** 2c. brown £475 £350
13 **9** 2c. on 32c. red (No. 60) . . £2500 £2750
15 **5** 2c. red . . . . 55·00 45·00
16 4c. red £500 £300
17 4c. brown . . . . 75·00 70·00
4 **18** 5c. brown £275 £300
18 **5** 5c. blue £225 £160
5 **5** 6c. lilac £200 £110
20 8c. orange . . . . £140 65·00
21 **19** 10c. grey . . . . £150 85·00
8 **5** 12c. blue £900 £475
22 12c. purple £275 £150
9 24c. green £700 £150
10 **8** 30c. red £30000 £20000
11 **9** 96c. grey £5000 £2750

BRITISH VIRGIN ISLANDS Pt. 1

A group of the Leeward Islands, Br. W. Indies. Used general issues for Leeward Islands concurrently with Virgin Islands stamps until 1 July 1956. A Crown Colony.

1951. 100 cents = 1 West Indian dollar.
1962. 100 cents = 1 U.S. dollar.

1 St. Ursula 2

3 4

1866.
1 **1** 1d. green . . . . 45·00 60·00
16 **3** 4d. red . . . . 40·00 60·00
7 **2** 6d. red . . . . 60·00 90·00
11 **4** 1s. black and red £225 £300
No. 11 has a double-lined frame.

1867. With heavy coloured border.
18 **4** 1s. black and red . . . . . . 50·00 60·00

6 8

1880.
26 **6** ½d. yellow . . . . 85·00 80·00
27 ½d. green . . . . 4·50 8·50
24 1d. green . . . . 65·00 85·00
29 1d. red . . . . 25·00 28·00
25 2½d. brown . . . . 90·00 £120
31 2½d. blue . . . . 2·75 14·00

1887.
32 **1** 1d. red . . . . 2·25 7·00
35 **3** 4d. brown . . . . 35·00 65·00
39 **2** 6d. violet . . . . 13·00 42·00
41 **4** 1s. brown . . . . 45·00 70·00

1888. No. 18 surch **4D.**
42 **4** 4d. on 1s. black and red . . £120 £150

1899.
43 **8** ½d. green . . . . 1·50 55
44 1d. red . . . . 2·75 3·00
45 2½d. blue . . . . 12·00 3·25
46 4d. brown . . . . 4·00 18·00
47 6d. violet . . . . 4·50 3·50
48 7d. green . . . . 8·00 7·00
49 1s. yellow . . . . 22·00 35·00
50 5s. blue . . . . 70·00 85·00

9 11

1904.
54 **9** ½d. purple and green 75 40
55 1d. purple and red . . . . . 2·50 35
56 2d. purple and brown . . . . 6·00 4·50
57 2½d. purple and blue . . . . 2·00 2·00
58 3d. purple and black . . . . 3·50 3·00
59 6d. purple and brown . . . . 2·75 3·00
60 1s. green and red . . . . . 4·00 5·00
61 2s.6d. green and black . . . 23·00 55·00
62 5s. green and blue . . . . . 48·00 65·00

1913.
69 **11** ½d. green . . . . 1·50 3·75
70 1d. red . . . . 2·25 14·00
71 2d. grey . . . . 4·00 23·00
72 2½d. blue . . . . 5·50 9·00
73 3d. purple on yellow . . . . 2·75 6·50
74 6d. purple . . . . 5·00 11·00
75 1s. black on green . . . . . 3·25 9·00
76 2s.6d. black and red on blue 48·00 50·00
77 5s. green and red on yellow 35·00 £110

1917. Optd **WAR STAMP**.
78c **11** 1d. red . . . . 30 3·75
79a 3d. purple on yellow . . . . 3·00 11·00

14 15 King George VI and Badge of Colony

1922.
86 **14** ½d. green . . . . 85 2·75
87 1d. red 60 60
88 1d. violet . . . . 1·00 3·50
91 1½d. red . . . . 1·75 2·00
92 2d. grey . . . . 1·00 6·00
95 2½d. blue . . . . 2·50 3·50
94 2½d. orange . . . . 1·25 1·50
96 3d. purple on yellow . . . . 2·25 11·00
97 5d. purple and olive . . . . 5·50 45·00
98 6d. purple . . . . 1·50 6·50
83 1s. black on green . . . . . 75 14·00

No.	Description	Unused	Used
84	2s.6d. black and red on blue	5·50	11·00
101	5s. green and red on yellow	19·00	70·00

1935. Silver Jubilee. As T **13** of Antigua.

No.	Description	Unused	Used
103	1d. blue and red	1·25	3·75
104	1½d. blue and grey	1·25	3·50
105	2½d. brown and blue	1·50	3·50
106	1s. grey and purple	7·00	17·00

1937. Coronation. As T **2** of Aden.

No.	Description	Unused	Used
107	1d. red	20	1·25
108	1½d. brown	50	2·50
109	2½d. blue	50	1·00

1938.

No.	Description	Unused	Used
110a **15**	½d. green	30	1·00
111a	1d. red	30	60
112a	1½d. brown	1·00	1·00
113a	2d. grey	1·00	90
114a	2½d. blue	70	2·50
115a	3d. orange	70	80
116a	6d. mauve	2·00	80
117a	1s. brown	1·50	70
118a	2s.6d. brown	15·00	3·00
119a	5s. red	13·00	4·00
120	10s. blue	6·00	8·00
121	£1 black	8·00	20·00

1946. Victory. As T **9** of Aden.

No.	Description	Unused	Used
122	1½d. brown	10	10
123	3d. orange	10	20

1949. Silver Wedding. As T **10/11** of Aden.

No.	Description	Unused	Used
124	2½d. blue	10	10
125	£1 grey	13·00	16·00

1949. 75th Anniv of U.P.U. As T **20/23** of Antigua.

No.	Description	Unused	Used
126	2½d. blue	30	45
127	3d. orange	1·00	2·25
128	6d. mauve	30	40
129	1s. olive	30	40

1951. Inauguration of B.W.I. University College. As T **24/25** of Antigua.

No.	Description	Unused	Used
130	3c. black and red	40	1·50
131	12c. black and violet	60	1·50

16 Map

1951. Restoration of Legislative Council.

No.	Description	Unused	Used
132 **16**	6c. orange	30	1·00
133	12c. purple	30	50
134	24c. olive	30	50
135	$1.20 red	1·00	1·00

18 Map of Jost Van Dyke

1952.

No.	Description	Unused	Used
136 –	1c. black	80	1·50
137 **18**	2c. green	70	30
138 –	3c. black and brown	80	1·25
139 –	4c. red	70	1·25
140 –	5c. red and black	1·50	50
141 –	8c. blue	70	1·25
142 –	12c. violet	80	1·40
143 –	24c. brown	70	50
144 –	60c. green and blue	4·00	11·00
145 –	$1.20 black and blue	4·75	12·00
146 –	$2.40 green and brown	11·00	16·00
147 –	$4.80 blue and red	12·00	16·00

DESIGNS—VERT: 1c. Sombrero lighthouse; 24c. Badge of Presidency. HORIZ—VIEWS: 3c. Sheep industry; 5c. Cattle industry; 60c. Dead Man's Chest (Is); $1.20, Sir Francis Drake Channel; $2.40, Road Town. HORIZ—MAPS: 4c. Anegada Island; 8c. Virgin Gorda Island; 12c. Tortola Island; $4.80, Virgin Islands.

1953. Coronation. As T **13** of Aden.

No.	Description	Unused	Used
148	2c. black and green	30	1·00

29 Map of Tortola

30 Brown Pelican

1956.

No.	Description	Unused	Used
149 **29**	½c. black and purple	40	20
150 –	1c. turquoise and slate	1·50	75
151 –	2c. red and black	30	10
152 –	3c. blue and olive	30	30
153 –	4c. brown and turquoise	70	30
154 –	5c. black	50	10
155 –	8c. orange and blue	1·75	40
156 –	12c. blue and red	3·50	75
157 –	24c. green and brown	1·00	65
158 –	60c. blue and orange	8·00	8·00
159 –	$1.20 green and red	2·00	8·00
160 **30**	$2.40 yellow and purple	38·00	13·00
161 –	$4.80 sepia and turquoise	38·00	13·00

DESIGNS—HORIZ: As Type **13**: 1c. Virgin Islands sloop; 2c. Nelthrop Red Poll bull; 3c. Road Harbour; 4c. Mountain travel; 5c. Badge of the Presidency; 8c. Beach scene; 12c. Boat launching; 24c. White cedar tree; 60c. Skipjack tuna ("Bonito"); $1.20, Treasury Square Coronation celebrations. As Type **30**: $4.80, Magnificent frigate bird ("Man-o'-War Bird").

1962. New Currency. Nos. 149/53, 155/61 surch in U.S. Currency.

No.	Description	Unused	Used
162 **29**	1c. on ½c. black and purple	30	10
163 –	2c. on 1c. turq & vio	1·50	10
164 –	3c. on 2c. red and black	50	10
165 –	4c. on 3c. blue and olive	30	10
166 –	5c. on 4c. brown & turq	30	10
167 –	8c. on 8c. orange and blue	30	10
168 –	10c. on 12c. blue and red	1·50	10
169 –	12c. on 24c. green & brn	30	10
170 –	25c. on 60c. blue and orange	2·50	45
171 –	70c. on $1.20 green and red	35	45
172 **30**	$1.40 on $2.40 yellow and purple	9·00	3·75
173 –	$2.80 on $4.80 sepia & turq	9·00	3·75

1963. Freedom from Hunger. As T **28** of Aden.

No.	Description	Unused	Used
174	25c. violet	20	10

1963. Centenary of Red Cross. As T **33** of Antigua.

No.	Description	Unused	Used
175	2c. red and black	15	20
176	25c. red and blue	50	20

1964. 400th Birth Anniv of Shakespeare. As T **34** of Antigua.

No.	Description	Unused	Used
177	10c. blue	20	10

43 Skipjack Tuna

44 Map of Tortola

1964.

No.	Description	Unused	Used
178 **43**	1c. blue and olive	30	1·50
179 –	2c. olive and red	15	30
180	3c. sepia and turquoise	3·25	1·25
181 –	4c. black and red	80	2·00
182 –	5c. black and green	1·00	2·00
183 –	6c. black and orange	30	85
184 –	8c. black and mauve	30	50
185 –	10c. lake and lilac	1·75	30
186 –	12c. green and blue	2·00	2·50
187 –	15c. green and black	35	2·50
188 –	25c. green and purple	11·00	1·75
189 **44**	70c. black and brown	3·75	6·00
190 –	$1 green and brown	3·00	2·00
191 –	$1.40 blue and red	24·00	9·00
192 –	$2.80 black and purple	24·00	9·00

DESIGNS—HORIZ (As Type **43**): 2c. Soper's Hole; 3c. Brown pelican; 4c. Dead Man's Chest; 5c. Road Harbour; 6c. Fallen Jerusalem; 8c. The Baths, Virgin Gorda; 10c. Map of Virgiin Islands; 12c. "Youth of Tortola" (Tortola–St Thomas ferry); 15c. The Towers, Tortola; 25c. Beef Island Airfield. VERT (As Type **44**): $1 Virgin Gorda: $1.40, Yachts at anchor. (27½ × 37½ mm): $2.80, Badge of the Colony.

1965. Centenary of I.T.U. As T **36** of Antigua.

No.	Description	Unused	Used
193	4c. yellow and turquoise	20	10
194	25c. blue and buff	45	20

1965. I.C.Y. As T **37** of Antigua.

No.	Description	Unused	Used
195	1c. purple and turquoise	10	15
196	25c. green and lavender	30	15

1966. Churchill Commemoration. As T **38** of Antigua.

No.	Description	Unused	Used
197	1c. blue	10	30
198	2c. green	15	30
199	10c. brown	30	10
200	25c. violet	60	25

1966. Royal Visit. As T **39** of Antigua.

No.	Description	Unused	Used
201	4c. black and blue	40	10
202	70c. black and mauve	1·40	45

58 "Atrato I" (paddle-steamer), 1866

1966. Stamp Centenary. Multicoloured.

No.	Description	Unused	Used
203	5c. Type **58**	35	10
204	10c. 1d. and 6d. stamps of 1866	35	10
205	25c. Mail transport, Beef Island, and 6d. stamp of 1866	55	10
206	60c. Landing mail at Roadtown, 1866 and 1d. stamp of 1866	1·00	2·50

1966. Nos. 189 and 191/2 surch.

No.	Description	Unused	Used
207 **44**	50c. on 70c. blk & brn	1·25	90
208 –	$1.50 on $1.40 blue and red	2·25	2·00
209 –	$3 on $2.80 black and purple	2·25	2·75

1966. 20th Anniv of U.N.E.S.C.O. As T **54/6** of Antigua.

No.	Description	Unused	Used
210	2c. multicoloured	10	10
211	12c. yellow, violet and olive	20	10
212	60c. black, purple and orange	50	45

63 Map of Virgin Islands

1967. New Constitution.

No.	Description	Unused	Used
213 **63**	2c. multicoloured	10	10
214	10c. multicoloured	15	10
215	25c. multicoloured	15	10
216	$1 multicoloured	55	40

64 "Mercury" (cable ship) and Bermuda–Tortola Link

1967. Inauguration of Bermuda–Tortola Telephone Service. Multicoloured.

No.	Description	Unused	Used
217	4c. Type **64**	20	10
218	10c. Chalwell Telecommunications Station	20	10
219	50c. "Mercury" (cable ship)	50	30

67 Blue Marlin

1968. Game Fishing. Multicoloured.

No.	Description	Unused	Used
220	2c. Type **67**	10	65
221	10c. Cobia	25	10
222	25c. Wahoo	55	10
223	40c. Fishing launch and map	85	75

1968. Human Rights Year. Nos. 185 and 188 optd **1968 INTERNATIONAL YEAR FOR HUMAN RIGHTS.**

No.	Description	Unused	Used
224	10c. lake and lilac	20	10
225	25c. green and purple	30	40

72 Dr. Martin Luther King, Bible, Sword and Armour Gauntlet

1968. Martin Luther King Commemoration.

No.	Description	Unused	Used
226 **72**	4c. multicoloured	25	20
227	25c. multicoloured	40	40

73 De Havilland Twin Otter 100

1968. Opening of Beef Island Airport Extension. Multicoloured.

No.	Description	Unused	Used
228	2c. Type **73**	15	70
229	10c. Hawker Siddeley H.S.748 airliner	20	10
230	25c. De Havilland Heron 2 airplane	40	10
231	$1 Royal Engineers' cap badge	50	2·00

77 Long John Silver and Jim Hawkins

1969. 75th Death Anniv of Robert Louis Stevenson. Scenes from "Treasure Island".

No.	Description	Unused	Used
232 **77**	4c. blue, yellow and red	20	15
233 –	10c. multicoloured	20	10
234 –	40c. brown, black and blue	25	30
235 –	$1 multicoloured	45	1·00

DESIGNS—HORIZ: 10c. Jim Hawkins escaping from the pirates; $1 Treasure trove. VERT: 40c. The fight with Israel Hands.

82 Yachts in Road Harbour, Tortola

1969. Tourism. Multicoloured.

No.	Description	Unused	Used
236	2c. Tourist and yellow-finned grouper (fish)	15	50
237	10c. Type **82**	30	10
238	20c. Sun-bathing at Virgin Gorda National Park	40	20
239	$1 Tourist and Pipe Organ cactus at Virgin Gorda	90	1·50

Nos. 236 and 239 are vert.

85 Carib Canoe

1970.

No.	Description	Unused	Used
240 **85**	½c. buff, brown and sepia	10	1·25
241 –	1c. blue and green	15	30
242 –	2c. orange, brown and slate	40	1·00
243 –	3c. red, blue and sepia	30	1·25
244 –	4c. turquoise, blue & brn	30	50
245 –	5c. green, pink and black	30	10
246 –	6c. violet, mauve and green	40	2·00
247 –	8c. green, yellow and sepia	50	3·50
248 –	10c. blue and brown	50	15
249 –	12c. yellow, red and brown	65	1·50
250 –	15c. green, orange and brown	6·00	85
251 –	25c. green, blue and purple	4·00	1·75
252 –	50c. mauve, green and brown	2·75	1·50
253 –	$1 salmon, green and brown	3·00	3·75
254 –	$2 buff, slate and grey	7·00	7·00
255 –	$3 ochre, blue and sepia	2·75	4·50
256 –	$5 violet and grey	2·75	5·00

DESIGNS: 1c. "Santa Maria" (Columbus's flagship); 2c. "Elizabeth Bonaventure" (Drake's flagship); 3c. Dutch buccaneer, c. 1660; 4c. "Thetis", 1827 (after etching by E. W. Cooke); 5c. Henry Morgan's ship (17th-century); 6c. H.M.S. "Boreas" (Captain Nelson, 1784); 8c. H.M.S. "Eclair", 1804; 10c. H.M.S. "Formidable", 1782; 12c. H.M.S. "Nymph", 1778; 15c. "Windsor Castle" (sailing packet) engaging "Jeune Richard" (French brig), 1807; 25c. H.M.S. "Astrea", 1808; 50c. Wreck of R.M.S. "Rhone", 1867; $1 Tortola sloop; $2 H.M.S. "Frobisher"; $3 "Booker Viking" (cargo liner), 1967; $5 Hydrofoil "Sun Arrow".

102 "A Tale of Two Cities"

1970. Death Centenary of Charles Dickens.

No.	Description	Unused	Used
257 **102**	5c. black, red and grey	10	40
258 –	10c. black, blue and green	20	10
259 –	25c. black, green and yellow	30	25

DESIGNS: 10c. "Oliver Twist"; 25c. "Great Expectations".

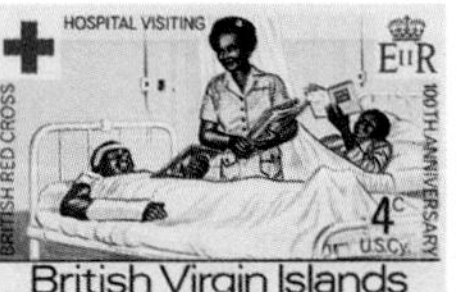

103 Hospital Visit

1970. Centenary of British Red Cross. Multicoloured.

260	4c. Type **103**	20	10
261	10c. First Aid class	20	10
262	25c. Red Cross and coat of arms	50	55

104 Mary Read

1970. Pirates. Multicoloured.

263	½c. Type **104**	10	15
264	10c. George Lowther	30	10
265	30c. Edward Teach (Blackbeard)	60	25
266	60c. Henry Morgan	80	1·00

105 Children and "UNICEF"

1971. 25th Anniv of U.N.I.C.E.F.

267	**105** 15c. multicoloured	10	10
268	30c. multicoloured	20	25

1972. Royal Visit of Princess Margaret. Nos 244 and 251 optd **VISIT OF H.R.H. THE PRINCESS MARGARET 1972 1972.**

269	4c. blue, light blue and brown	20	15
270	25c. green, blue and plum	30	45

107 Seaman of 1800 **110** J. C. Lettsom

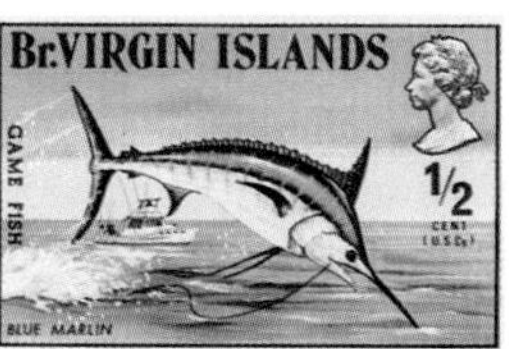

109 Blue Marlin

1972. "Interpex" Stamp Exhibition, New York. Naval Uniforms. Multicoloured.

271	½c. Type **107**	10	40
272	10c. Boatswain, 1787–1807	35	10
273	30c. Captain, 1795–1812	85	55
274	60c. Admiral, 1787–95	1·50	2·50

1972. Royal Silver Wedding. As T **52** of Ascension, but with sailfish and "Sir Winston Churchill" (cadet schooner) in background.

275	15c. blue	25	15
276	25c. blue	25	15

1972. Game Fish. Multicoloured.

277	½c. Type **109**	10	90
278	½c. Wahoo	15	90
279	15c. Yellow-finned tuna ("Allison tuna")	65	25
280	25c. White marlin	75	30
281	50c. Sailfish	1·25	1·50
282	$1 Dolphin	2·00	2·75
MS283	194 × 158 mm. Nos. 277/82	8·50	8·50

1973. "Interpex 1973" (Quakers). Multicoloured.

284	½c. Type **110**	10	15
285	10c. Lettsom House (horiz)	15	10
286	15c. Dr. W. Thornton	20	10
287	30c. Dr. Thornton and Capitol, Washington (horiz)	25	20
288	$1 William Penn (horiz)	60	1·10

111 Green-throated Carib and Antillean Crested Hummingbird

1973. First Issue of Coinage. Coins and local scenery. Multicoloured.

289	1c. Type **111**	10	30
290	5c. "Zenaida Dove" (5c. coin)	60	10
291	10c. "Ringed Kingfisher" (10c. coin)	75	10
292	25c. "Mangrove Cuckoo" (25c. coin)	95	15
293	50c. "Brown Pelican" (50c. coin)	1·10	1·00
294	$1 "Magnificent Frigate-bird ($1 coin)	1·40	2·00

1973. Royal Wedding. As T **47** of Anguilla. Multicoloured. Background colours given.

301	5c. brown	10	10
302	50c. blue	20	20

112 "Virgin and Child" (Pintoricchio) **113** Crest of the "Canopus" (French)

1973. Christmas. Multicoloured.

303	½c. Type **112**	10	10
304	3c. "Virgin and Child" (Lorenzo di Credi)	10	10
305	25c. "Virgin and Child" (Crivelli)	15	10
306	50c. "Virgin and Child with St. John" (Luini)	30	40

1974. "Interpex 1974". Naval Crests. Multicoloured.

307	5c. Type **113**	15	10
308	18c. U.S.S. "Saginaw"	25	25
309	25c. H.M.S. "Rothesay"	25	30
310	50c. H.M.C.S. "Ottawa"	45	60
MS311	196 × 128 mm. Nos. 307/10	1·25	4·00

114 Christopher Columbus

1974. Historical Figures.

312	**114** 5c. orange and black	20	10
313	– 10c. blue and black	20	10
314	– 25c. violet and black	25	25
315	– 40c. brown and deep brown	45	75
MS316	84 × 119 mm. Nos. 312/15	1·00	2·25

PORTRAITS: 10c. Sir Walter Raleigh; 25c. Sir Martin Frobisher; 40c. Sir Francis Drake.

115 Atlantic Trumpet Triton

1974. Seashells. Multicoloured.

317	5c. Type **115**	30	15
318	18c. West Indian murex	50	30
319	25c. Bleeding tooth	60	35
320	75c. Virgin Islands latirus	1·25	2·00
MS321	146 × 95 mm. Nos. 317/20	3·00	6·00

116 Churchill and St. Mary, Aldermanbury, London

1974. Birth Centenary of Sir Winston Churchill. Multicoloured.

322	10c. Type **116**	15	10
323	50c. St. Mary, Fulton, Missouri	35	50
MS324	141 × 108 mm. Nos. 322/3	80	1·40

117 H.M.S. "Boreas"

1975. "Interpex 1975" Stamp Exhibition, New York. Ships' Figure-heads. Multicoloured.

325	5c. Type **117**	20	10
326	18c. "Golden Hind"	40	15
327	40c. H.M.S. "Superb"	50	25
328	85c. H.M.S. "Formidable"	1·00	1·50
MS329	192 × 127 mm. Nos. 325/8	1·75	7·50

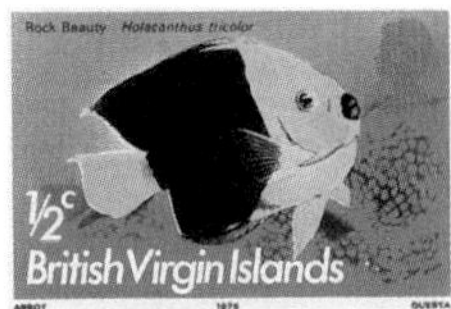

118 Rock Beauty

1975. Fishes. Multicoloured.

330	½c. Type **118**	15	50
331	1c. Long-spined squirrelfish	40	2·50
332	3c. Queen triggerfish	1·00	2·50
333	5c. Blue angelfish	30	20
334	8c. Stoplight parrotfish	30	25
335	10c. Queen angelfish	30	25
336	12c. Nassau grouper	40	30
337	13c. Blue tang	40	30
338	15c. Sergeant major	40	35
339	18c. Spotted jewfish	80	1·25
340	20c. Bluehead wrasse	60	80
341	25c. Grey angelfish	1·00	60
342	60c. Glass-eyed snapper	1·25	2·25
343	$1 Blue chromis	1·75	1·75
344	$2.50 French angelfish	2·00	4·50
345	$3 Queen parrotfish	2·50	4·50
346	$5 Four-eyed butterflyfish	2·75	6·00

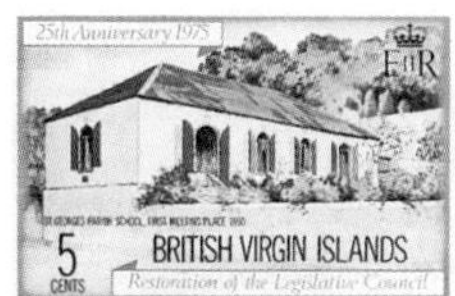

119 St. George's Parish School (first meeting-place, 1950)

1975. 25th Anniv of Restoration of Legislative Council. Multicoloured.

347	5c. Type **119**	10	10
348	25c. Legislative Council Building	20	10
349	40c. Mace and gavel	25	15
350	75c. Commemorative scroll	35	65

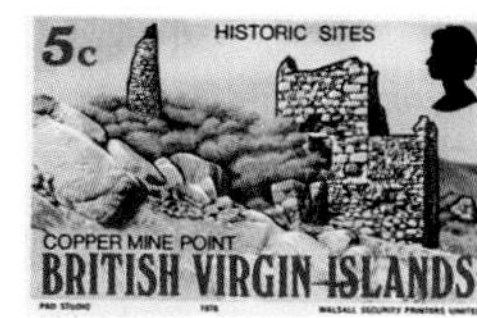

120 Copper Mine Point

1976. Historic Sites. Multicoloured.

351	5c. Type **120**	10	10
352	18c. Pleasant Valley	20	10
353	50c. Callwood Distillery	40	30
354	75c. The Dungeon	60	65

121 Massachusetts Brig "Hazard"

1976. Bicentenary of American Revolution. Mult.

355	8c. Type **121**	30	15
356	22c. American privateer "Spy"	45	20
357	40c. "Raleigh" (American frigate)	55	60
358	75c. Frigate "Alliance" and H.M.S. "Trepassy"	80	1·25
MS359	114 × 89 mm. Nos. 355/8	3·50	11·00

122 Government House, Tortola

1976. 5th Anniv of Friendship Day with U.S. Virgin Islands. Multicoloured.

360	8c. Type **122**	10	10
361	15c. Government House, St. Croix (vert)	10	10
362	30c. Flags (vert)	15	10
363	75c. Government seals	30	40

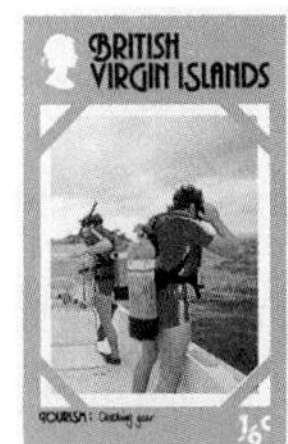

123 Royal Visit, 1966 **125** Divers checking Equipment

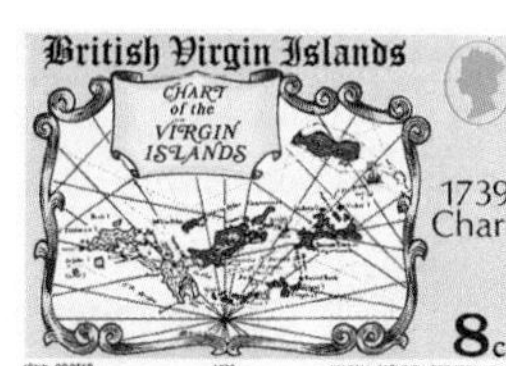

124 Chart of 1739

1977. Silver Jubilee. Multicoloured.

364	8c. Type **123**	10	10
365	30c. The Holy Bible	15	15
366	60c. Presentation of Holy Bible	25	40

1977. 18th-century Maps. Multicoloured.

367	8c. Type **124**	40	10
368	22c. French map, 1758	55	30
369	30c. Map from English and Danish surveys, 1775	65	65
370	75c. Map of 1779	85	1·50

1977. Royal Visit. As Nos. 364/6 inscr "SILVER JUBILEE ROYAL VISIT".

371	5c. Type **123**	10	10
372	25c. The Holy Bible	20	10
373	50c. Presentation of Holy Bible	35	25

1978. Tourism. Multicoloured.

374	½c. Type **125**	10	10
375	5c. Cup coral on wreck of "Rhone"	20	10
376	8c. Sponge formation on wreck of "Rhone"	25	10
377	22c. Cup coral and sponges	45	15
378	30c. Sponges inside cave	60	20
379	75c. Marine life	90	85

126 Fire Coral **127** Iguana

1978. Corals. Multicoloured.

380	8c. Type **126**	25	15
381	15c. Staghorn coral	40	30
382	40c. Brain coral	75	85
383	75c. Elkhorn coral	1·50	1·60

1978. 25th Anniv of Coronation.

384	– 50c. brown, green and silver	20	40
385	– 50c. multicoloured	20	40
386	**127** 50c. brown, green and silver	20	40

DESIGNS: No. 384, Plantagenet Falcon; 385, Queen Elizabeth II.

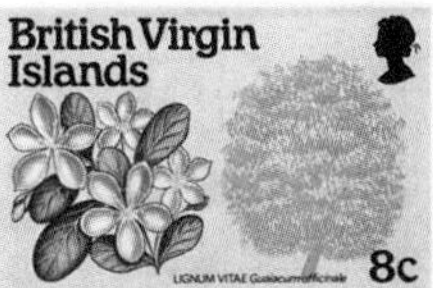

128 Lignum Vitae

1978. Flowering Trees. Multicoloured.

387	8c. Type **128**	15	10
388	22c. Ginger Thomas	20	15
389	40c. Dog almond	30	20
390	75c. White cedar	45	70
MS391	131 × 95 mm. Nos. 387/90	1·00	3·00

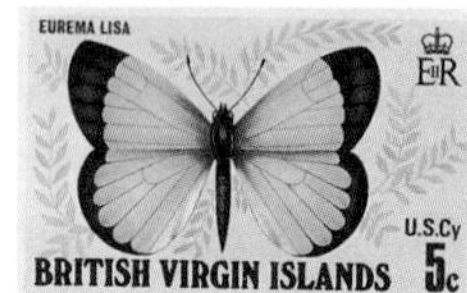

129 "Eurema lisa"

1978. Butterflies. Multicoloured.

392	5c. Type **129**	25	10
393	22c. "Agraulis vanillae"	40	20
394	30c. "Heliconius charithonia"	1·10	30
395	75c. "Hemiargus hanno"	1·40	1·25
MS396	159 × 113 mm. No. 392 × 6 and No. 393 × 3	2·50	5·50

130 Spiny Lobster

1978. Wildlife Conservation. Multicoloured.

397	5c. Type **130**	15	10
398	15c. Large iguana (vert)	25	10
399	22c. Hawksbill turtle	40	15
400	75c. Black coral (vert)	75	90
MS401	130 × 153 mm. Nos. 397/400	2·25	3·75

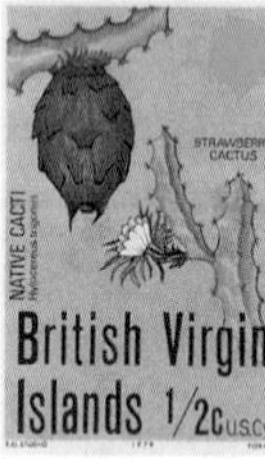

131 Strawberry Cactus **132** West Indian Girl

1979. Native Cacti. Multicoloured.

402	½c. Type **131**	10	10
403	5c. Snowy cactus	15	10
404	13c. Barrel cactus	20	20
405	22c. Tree cactus	25	35
406	30c. Prickly pear	30	40
407	75c. Dildo cactus	40	1·00

1979. International Year of the Child. Multicoloured.

408	5c. Type **132**	10	10
409	10c. African boy	10	10
410	13c. Asian girl	10	10
411	$1 European boy	50	85
MS412	91 × 114 mm. Nos. 408/11	70	1·50

133 1956 Road Harbour 3c. Definitive Stamp **134** Pencil Urchin

1979. Death Centenary of Sir Rowland Hill.

413 **133**	5c. dp blue, blue & green	10	10
414 –	13c. blue and mauve	10	10
415 –	75c. blue and purple	45	50
MS416	37 × 91 mm. $1 blue and red	70	1·25

DESIGNS (39 × 27 mm)—13c. 1880 2½d. red-brown; 75c. Great Britain 1910 unissued 2d. Tyrian plum. (40 × 28 mm)—$1 1867 1s. "Missing Virgin" error.

1979. Marine Life. Multicoloured.

417	½c. Calcified algae	40	2·50
418	1c. Purple-tipped sea anemone	55	2·50
419	3c. Common starfish	1·00	2·50
420	5c. Type **134**	1·00	1·75
421	8c. Atlantic trumpet triton	1·25	1·75
422	10c. Christmas tree worms	30	1·00
423a	13c. Flamingo tongue snail	1·50	75
424	15c. Spider crab	40	1·00
425	18c. Sea squirts	2·00	3·75
426	20c. True tulip	55	1·50
427	25c. Rooster-tail conch	1·25	3·75
428	30c. West Indian fighting conch	2·00	1·50
429	60c. Mangrove crab	1·50	2·50
430	$1 Coral polyps	1·50	4·00
431	$2.50 Peppermint shrimp	1·50	4·00
432	$3 West Indian murex	1·50	4·50
433	$5 Carpet anemone	2·00	5·50

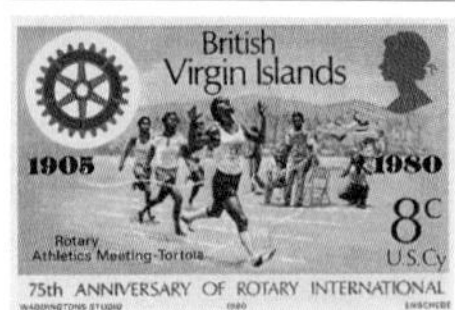

135 Rotary Athletics Meeting, Tortola

1980. 75th Anniv of Rotary International. Mult.

434	8c. Type **135**	10	10
435	22c. Paul P. Harris (founder)	15	10
436	60c. Mount Saga, Tortola ("Creation of National Park")	30	40
437	$1 Rotary anniversary emblem	55	75
MS438	149 × 148 mm. Nos. 434/7	1·00	3·50

136 Brown Booby **138** Sir Francis Drake

1980. "London 1980" International Stamp Exhibition. Birds. Multicoloured.

439	20c. Type **136**	20	20
440	25c. Magnificent frigate bird	25	25
441	50c. White-tailed tropic bird	40	40
442	75c. Brown pelican	55	55
MS443	152 × 130 mm. Nos. 439/42	1·25	2·25

1980. Caribbean Commonwealth Parliamentary Association Meeting, Tortola. Nos. 414/15 optd **CARIBBEAN COMMONWEALTH PARLIAMENTARY ASSOCIATION MEETING TORTOLA 11 19 JULY 1980.**

444	13c. blue and red	15	10
445	75c. deep blue and blue	40	40

1980. Sir Francis Drake Commemoration. Mult.

446	8c. Type **138**	50	10
447	15c. Queen Elizabeth I	70	15
448	30c. Drake receiving knighthood	90	30
449	75c. "Golden Hind" and coat of arms	1·75	1·25
MS450	171 × 121 mm. Nos. 446/9	3·75	6·50

139 Jost Van Dyke

1980. Island Profiles. Multicoloured

451	2c. Type **139**	10	10
452	5c. Peter Island	10	10
453	13c. Virgin Gorda	15	10
454	22c. Anegada	20	10
455	30c. Norman Island	25	15
456	$1 Tortola	70	1·00
MS457	95 × 88 mm. No. 456	85	1·50

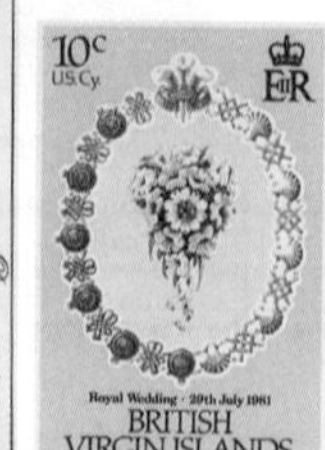

140 Dancing Lady **141** Wedding Bouquet from British Virgin Islands

1981. Flowers. Multicoloured.

458	5c. Type **140**	10	10
459	20c. Love in the mist	15	15
460	22c. "Pitcairnia angustifolia"	15	15
461	75c. Dutchman's pipe	35	65
462	$1 Maiden apple	35	80

1981. Royal Wedding. Multicoloured.

463	10c. Type **141**	10	10
464	35c. Prince Charles and Queen Elizabeth the Queen Mother in Garter robes	20	15
465	$1.25 Prince Charles and Lady Diana Spencer	60	80

142 Stamp Collecting **144** Detail from "The Adoration of the Shepherds" (Rubens)

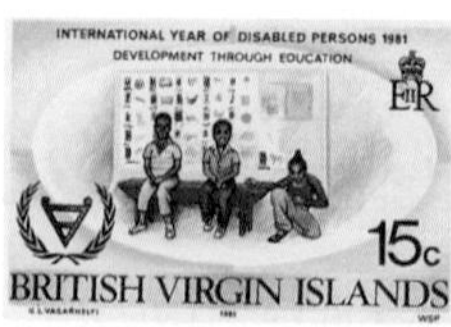

143 "Development through Education"

1981. 25th Anniv of Duke of Edinburgh Award Scheme. Multicoloured.

466	10c. Type **142**	10	10
467	15c. Athletics	10	10
468	50c. Camping	25	25
469	$1 Duke of Edinburgh	40	45

1981. International Year for Disabled Persons. Multicoloured.

470	15c. Type **143**	15	15
471	20c. Fort Charlotte Children's Centre	15	20
472	30c. "Developing cultural awareness"	20	30
473	$1 Fort Charlotte Children's Centre (different)	60	1·25

1981. Christmas.

474 **144**	5c. multicoloured	15	10
475 –	15c. multicoloured	25	10
476 –	30c. multicoloured	45	15
477 –	$1 multicoloured	1·10	1·10
MS478	117 × 90 mm. 50c. multicoloured (horiz)	1·75	85

DESIGNS: 15c. to $1 Further details from "The Adoration of the Shepherds" by Rubens.

145 Green-throated Caribs and Erythrina **147** Princess at Victoria and Albert Museum, November, 1981

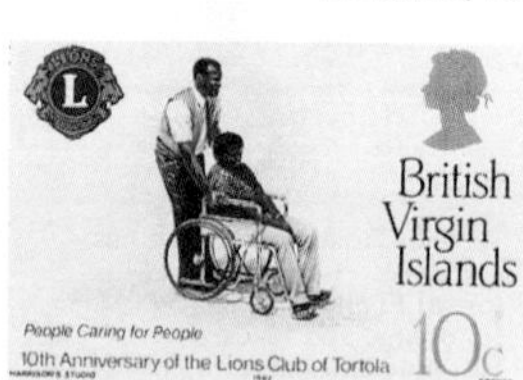

146 "People caring for People"

1982. Hummingbirds. Multicoloured.

479	15c. Type **145**	50	15
480	30c. Green-throated carib and bougainvillea	60	45
481	35c. Antillean crested hummingbirds and "granadilla passiflora"	70	55
482	$1.25 Antillean crested hummingbirds and hibiscus	1·75	3·00

1982. 10th Anniv of Lions Club of Tortola. Mult.

483	10c. Type **146**	15	10
484	20c. Tortola Headquarters	20	15
485	30c. "We Serve"	25	15
486	$1.50 "Lions" symbol	60	1·00
MS487	124 × 102 mm. Nos. 483/6	1·75	4·25

1982. 21st Birthday of Princess of Wales. Mult.

488	10c. British Virgin Islands coat of arms	15	10
489	35c. Type **147**	30	15
490	50c. Bride and groom proceeding into Vestry	45	35
491	$1.50 Formal portrait	1·10	1·10

148 Douglas DC-3

1982. 10th Anniv of Air BVI. Multicoloured.

492	10c. Type **148**	45	15
493	15c. Britten Norman Islander	60	20
494	60c. Hawker Siddeley H.S.748	1·10	75
495	75c. Runway scene	1·25	90

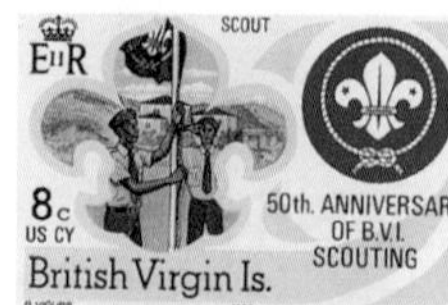

149 Scouts raising Flag

1982. 75th Anniv of Boy Scout Movement and 50th Anniv of Scouting in B.V.I. Multicoloured.

496	8c. Type **149**	20	10
497	20c. Cub Scout	30	25
498	50c. Sea Scout	40	55
499	$1 First camp, Brownsea Island, and portrait of Lord Baden-Powell	70	1·50

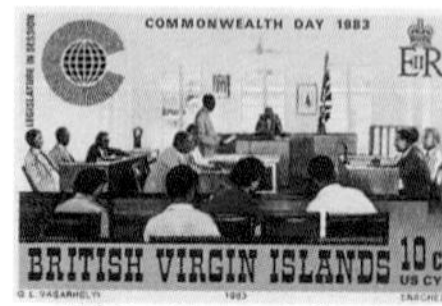

150 Legislature in Session

1983. Commonwealth Day. Multicoloured.

500	10c. Type **150**	10	10
501	30c. Tourism	25	20
502	35c. Satellite view of Earth showing Virgin Islands	25	25
503	75c. B.V.I. and Commonwealth flags	70	90

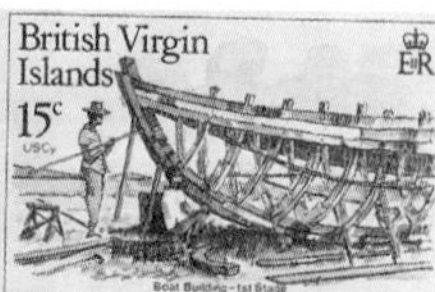

151 Florence Nightingale **152** Frame Construction

1983. Nursing Week. Multicoloured.

504	10c. Type **151**	50	15
505	30c. Staff nurse and assistant nurse	90	45
506	60c. Public Health nurses testing blood pressure (horiz)	1·75	1·25
507	75c. Peebles Hospital (horiz)	1·90	1·75

1983. Traditional Boat-building. Multicoloured.

508	15c. Type **152**	25	25
509	25c. Planking	30	45
510	50c. Launching	50	80
511	$1 Maiden voyage	65	1·75
MS512	127 × 101 mm. Nos. 508/11	2·00	3·75

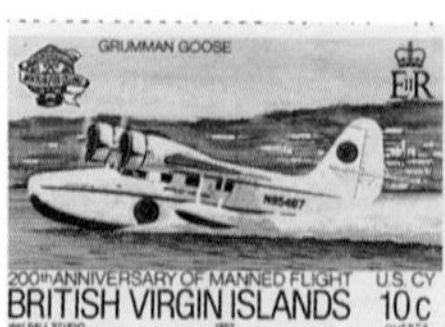

153 Grumman Goose Amphibian

1983. Bicentenary of Manned Flight. Multicoloured.

513	10c. Type **153**	20	15
514	30c. Riley Turbo Skyliner	45	45
515	60c. Embraer Bandeirante	65	85
516	$1.25 Hawker Siddeley H.S.748	90	1·60

154 "Madonna and Child with the Infant Baptist" **156** Port Purcell

155 Local Tournament

1983. Christmas. 500th Birth Anniv of Raphael. Multicoloured.
517 8c. Type **154** 10 10
518 15c. "La Belle Jardiniere" . . 20 15
519 50c. "Madonna del Granduca" 50 60
520 $1 "The Terranuova Madonna" . . . . 90 1·10
MS521 108 × 101 mm. Nos. 517/20 2·75 3·75

1984. 60th Anniv of International Chess Federation. Multicoloured.
522 10c. Type **155** . . . . 1·00 40
523 35c. Staunton king, rook and pawn (vert) . . . . 2·00 1·50
524 75c. Karpov's winning position against Jakobsen in 1980 Olympiad (vert) . . 3·75 4·25
525 $1 B.V.I. Gold Medal won by Bill Hook at 1980 Chess Olympiad . . . . 4·25 5·50

1984. 250th Anniv of "Lloyd's List" (newspaper). Multicoloured.
526 15c. Type **156** 25 30
527 25c. Boeing 747-100 . . . . 45 50
528 50c. Wreck of "Rhone" (mail steamer), 1867 . . . . . . 90 95
529 $1 "Booker Viking" (cargo liner) . . . . 1·50 1·60

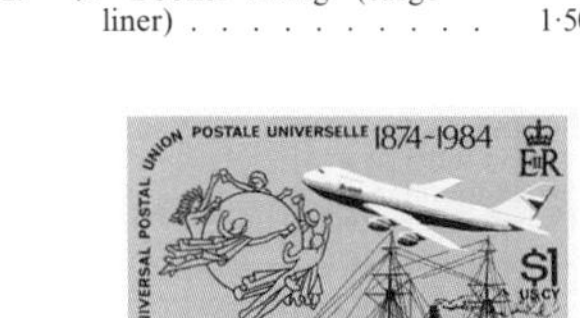

157 Mail Ship "Boyne", Boeing 747-100 and U.P.U. Logo

1984. Universal Postal Union Congress, Hamburg. Sheet 90 × 69 mm.
MS530 **157** $1 blue and black 2·25 2·50

158 Running

1984. Olympic Games, Los Angeles. Multicoloured.
531 15c. Type **158** 40 40
532 15c. Runner 40 40
533 20c. Wind-surfing 45 45
534 20c. Surfer 45 45
535 30c. Sailing 65 65
536 30c. Yacht 65 65

159 Steel Band

1984. 150th Anniv of Abolition of Slavery. Mult.
538 10c. Type **159** 30 35
539 10c. Dancing girls 30 35
540 10c. Men in traditional costumes 30 35
541 10c. Girl in traditional costumes 30 35
542 10c. Festival Queen 30 35
543 30c. Green and yellow dinghies 45 50
544 30c. Blue and red dinghies . . 45 50
545 30c. White and blue dinghies 45 50
546 30c. Red and yellow dinghies 45 50
547 30c. Blue and white dinghies 45 50
DESIGNS: Various aspects of Emancipation Festival. Nos. 543/7 form a composite design, the sail colours of the dinghies being described.

160 Sloop

1984. Boats. Multicoloured.
548 10c. Type **160** 40 20
549 35c. Fishing boat 80 65
550 60c. Schooner . . . . 1·10 1·25
551 75c. Cargo boat . . . . . . 1·10 1·60
MS552 125 × 90 mm. Nos. 548/51 2·00 4·00

161 One Cent Coin and Aerial View

1985. New Coinage. Coins and Local Scenery. Multicoloured.
553 1c. Type **161** 10 10
554 5c. Five cent coin and boulders on beach 10 10
555 10c. Ten cent coin and scuba diving 20 20
556 25c. Twenty-five cent coin and yachts 45 50
557 50c. Fifty cent coin and jetty 90 1·25
558 $1 One dollar coin and beach at night . . . . 1·75 2·25
MS559 103 × 159 mm. Nos. 553/8 3·00 7·00

162 Red-billed Tropic Bird

163 The Queen Mother at Festival of Remembrance

1985. Birds of the British Virgin Islands. Multicoloured.
560 1c. Type **162** . . . . 70 2·00
561 2c. Yellow-crowned night heron ("Night Gaulin") . . 70 2·00
562 5c. Mangrove cuckoo ("Rain Bird") . . . . 1·00 1·75
563 8c. Northern mockingbird ("Mockingbird") . . . . . 1·00 2·50
564 10c. Grey kingbird ("Chinchary") . . . . . . 1·00 40
565 12c. Red-necked pigeon ("Wild Pigeon") . . . . . 1·75 1·25
649 15c. Least bittern ("Bittlin") 2·25 1·25
567 18c. Smooth-billed ani ("Black Witch") . . . . . 2·25 2·75
651 20c. Clapper rail ("Pond Shakey") . . . . 2·25 1·25
652 25c. American kestrel ("Killy-killy") . . . . 2·25 1·25
570 30c. Pearly-eyed thrasher ("Thrushie") . . . . 2·25 1·40
654 35c. Bridled quail dove ("Marmi Dove") . . . . . 2·25 1·25
572 40c. Green-backed heron ("Little Gaulin") . . . . . 2·50 1·75
573 50c. Scaly-breasted ground dove ("Ground Dove") . . 2·75 3·00
574 60c. Little blue heron ("Blue Gaulin") . . . . 3·00 4·25
658 $1 Audubon's shearwater ("Pimleco") . . . . 3·75 4·50
576 $2 Blue-faced booby ("White Booby") . . . . 4·50 7·50
577 $3 Cattle egret ("Cow Bird") 5·50 9·50
578 $5 Zenaida dove ("Turtle Dove") . . . . 7·50 12·00

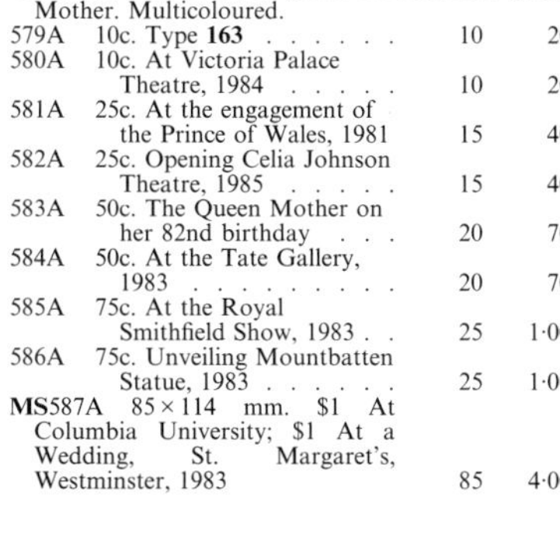

1985. Life and Times of Queen Elizabeth the Queen Mother. Multicoloured.
579A 10c. Type **163** 10 20
580A 10c. At Victoria Palace Theatre, 1984 . . . . . 10 20
581A 25c. At the engagement of the Prince of Wales, 1981 15 40
582A 25c. Opening Celia Johnson Theatre, 1985 . . . . . 15 40
583A 50c. The Queen Mother on her 82nd birthday . . . 20 70
584A 50c. At the Tate Gallery, 1983 . . . . 20 70
585A 75c. At the Royal Smithfield Show, 1983 . . 25 1·00
586A 75c. Unveiling Mountbatten Statue, 1983 . . . . . . 25 1·00
MS587A 85 × 114 mm. $1 At Columbia University; $1 At a Wedding, St. Margaret's, Westminster, 1983 85 4·00

164 Seaside Sparrow

165 S.V. "Flying Cloud"

1985. Birth Bicentenary of John J. Audubon (ornithologist). Designs showing original paintings. Multicoloured.
588 5c. Type **164** 30 20
589 30c. Passenger pigeon 40 70
590 50c. Yellow-breasted chat . . 45 1·75
591 $1 American kestrel . . . . 50 2·75

1986. Visiting Cruise Ships. Multicoloured.
592 35c. Type **165** 80 85
593 50c. M.V. "Newport Clipper" 1·10 1·50
594 75c. M.V. "Cunard Countess" . . . . 1·10 2·50
595 $1 M.V. "Sea Goddess" . . . 1·25 3·00

1986. Inaugural Flight of Miami–Beef Island Air Service. Nos 581/2 and 585/6 optd **MIAMI B.V.I. INAUGURAL FLIGHT**.
596A 25c. At the engagement of the Prince of Wales, 1981 40 50
597A 25c. Opening Celia Johnson Theatre, 1985 . . . . . 40 50
598A 75c. At the Royal Smithfield Show, 1983 . . 1·25 1·50
599A 75c. Unveiling Mountbatten statue, 1983 . . . . . . 1·25 1·50

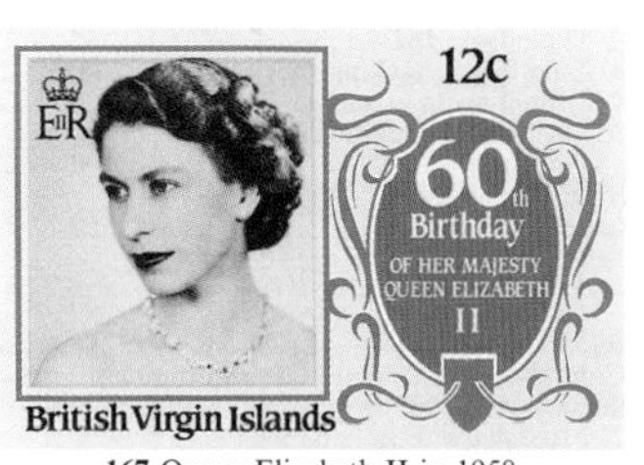

167 Queen Elizabeth II in 1958

1986. 60th Birthday of Queen Elizabeth II. Multicoloured.
600 12c. Type **167** 15 20
601 35c. At a Maundy Service . . 20 45
602 $1.50 Queen Elizabeth . . . 45 1·75
603 $2 During a visit to Canberra, 1982 (vert) . . . 60 2·25
MS604 85 × 115 mm. $3 Queen with bouquet 3·50 6·00

168 Miss Sarah Ferguson

1986. Royal Wedding. Multicoloured.
605 35c. Type **168** 30 70
606 35c. Prince Andrew and Miss Sarah Ferguson 30 70
607 $1 Prince Andrew in morning dress (horiz) . . . . 50 1·25
608 $1 Miss Sarah Ferguson (different) (horiz) . . . . . 50 1·25
MS609 115 × 85 mm. $4 Duke and Duchess of York in carriage after wedding (horiz) 2·50 6·00

169 Harvesting Sugar Cane

1986. History of Rum Making. Multicoloured.
610 12c. Type **169** 80 20
611 40c. Bringing sugar cane to mill . . . . 1·50 1·25
612 60c. Rum distillery . . . . . 2·00 3·25
613 $1 Delivering barrels of rum to ship . . . . 4·25 4·75
MS614 115 × 84 mm. $2 Royal Navy rum issue 6·50 8·50

170 "Sentinel"

1986. 20th Anniv of Cable and Wireless Caribbean Headquarters, Tortola. Cable Ships. Multicoloured.
615 35c. Type **170** 60 80
616 35c. "Retriever" (1961) . . . 60 80
617 60c. "Cable Enterprise" (1964) . . . . 75 1·50
618 60c. "Mercury" (1962) . . . 75 1·50
619 75c. "Recorder" (1955) . . . 75 1·75
620 75c. "Pacific Guardian" (1984) . . . . 75 1·75
621 $1 "Great Eastern" (1860's) 80 2·00
622 $1 "Cable Venture" (1977) 80 2·00
MS623 Four sheets, each 102 × 131 mm. (a) 40c. × 2 As 35c. (b) 50c. × 2 As 60c. (c) 80c. × 2 As 75c. (d) $1.50 × 2 As $1
Set of 4 sheets 5·00 12·00

1986. Centenary of Statue of Liberty. T **17** and similar vert views of Statue in separate miniature sheets. Multicoloured.
MS624 Nine sheets, each 85 × 115 mm. 50c.; 75c.; 90c.; $1; $1.25; $1.50; $1.75; $2; $2.50
Set of 9 sheets 7·00 13·00

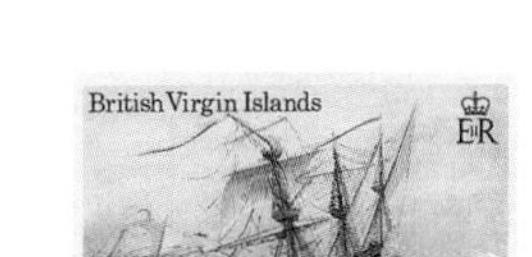

172 18th-century Spanish Galleon

1987. Shipwrecks. Multicoloured
625 12c. Type **172** . . . . 2·00 55
626 35c. H.M.S. "Astrea" (frigate), 1808 . . . . . . 3·25 1·40
627 75c. "Rhone" (mail steamer), 1867 . . . . 4·75 4·50
628 $1.50 "Captain Rokos" (freighter), 1929 . . . . . 7·00 9·00
MS629 85 × 65 mm. $1.50, "Volvart", 1819 14·00 14·00

173 Outline Map and Flag of Montserrat

174 Spider Lily

1987. 11th Meeting of Organization of Eastern Caribbean States. Each showing map and flag. Multicoloured.
630 10c. Type **173** 70 70
631 15c. Grenada 80 75
632 20c. Dominica 85 80
633 25c. St. Kitts-Nevis . . . . . 90 1·00
634 35c. St. Vincent and Grenadines . . . . 1·40 1·00
635 50c. British Virgin Islands . . 2·00 2·50
636 75c. Antigua and Barbuda . . 2·25 3·25
637 $1 St. Lucia . . . . 2·75 3·50

1987. Opening of Botanical Gardens. Multicoloured.
638 12c. Type **174** 80 35
639 35c. Barrel cactus . . . . . 1·75 1·00
640 $1 Wild plantain . . . . . . 2·75 3·25
641 $1.50 Little butterfly orchid 8·00 8·50
MS642 139 × 104 mm. $2.50, White cedar 3·75 6·00

175 Early Mail Packet and 1867 1s. Stamp

1987. Bicentenary of Postal Services. Multicoloured.
662 10c. Type **175** . . . . 1·75 80
663 20c. Map and 1899 1d. stamp 2·25 1·25
664 35c. Road Town Post Office and Customs House, c. 1913, and 1847 4d. stamp . . . . 2·50 1·75
665 $1.50 Piper Apache mail plane and 1964 25c. definitive . . . . 7·50 11·00
MS666 70 × 60 mm. $2.50, Mail ship, 1880's, and 1880 1d. 6·00 10·00

1988. 500th Birth Anniv of Titian (artist). As T **238** of Antigua. Multicoloured.
667 10c. "Salome" 55 55
668 12c. "Man with the Glove" 60 60
669 20c. "Fabrizio Salvaresio" . . 80 80
670 25c. "Daughter of Roberto Strozzi" 90 90
671 40c. "Pope Julius II" . . . . 1·40 2·00
672 50c. "Bishop Ludovico Beccadelli" . . . . 1·60 2·00

673 60c. "King Philip II" . . . . 1·75 2·50
674 $1 "Empress Isabella of Portugal" . . . . 2·25 2·75
MS675 Two sheets, each 110 × 95 mm. (a) $2 "Emperor Charles V at Muhlberg" (detail). (b) $2 "Pope Paul III and his Grandsons" (detail) Set of 2 sheets 12·00 14·00

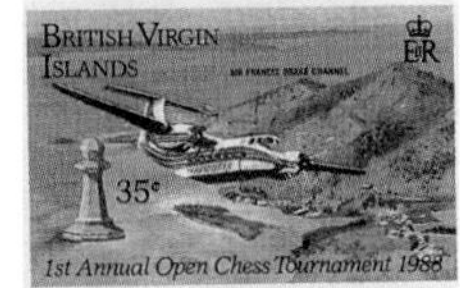

176 De Havilland D.H.C.5 over Sir Francis Drake Channel and Staunton Pawn

1988. 1st British Virgin Islands Open Chess Tournament. Multicoloured.
676 35c. Type **176** . . . . 6·00 1·75
677 $1 Jose Capablanca (former World Champion) and Staunton king . . . . . . 10·00 8·50
MS678 109 × 81 mm. $2 Chess match 9·00 11·00

177 Hurdling

1988. Olympic Games, Seoul. Multicoloured.
679 12c. Type **177** 35 25
680 20c. Windsurfing 60 45
681 75c. Basketball . . . . 3·75 3·25
682 $1 Tennis . . . . 3·75 3·75
MS683 71 × 102 mm. $2 Athletics 3·00 4·50

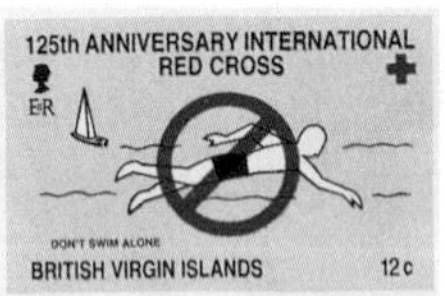

178 Swimmer ("Don't Swim Alone")

1988. 125th Anniv of International Red Cross
684 **178** 12c. black, red and blue 1·00 40
685 – 30c. black, red and blue 1·75 80
686 – 60c. black, red and blue 3·00 3·00
687 – $1 black, red and blue . . 3·50 4·00
MS688 68 × 96 mm. 50c. × 4 black and red 5·00 6·50
DESIGNS—HORIZ: 30c. Swimmers ("No swimming during electrical storms"); 60c. Beach picnic ("Don't eat before swimming"); $1 Boat and equipment ("Proper equipment for boating"). VERT: 50c. × 4 Recovery position, clearing airway, mouth-to-mouth resuscitation, cardiac massage.

179 Princess Alexandra

180 Brown Pelican in Flight

1988. Visit of Princess Alexandra. Designs showing different portraits.
689 **179** 40c. multicoloured . . . . 1·75 75
690 – $1.50 multicoloured . . . 3·75 4·75
MS691 102 × 98 mm. $2 multicoloured 5·00 6·50

1988. Wildlife (1st series). Aquatic Birds. Mult.
692 10c. Type **180** . . . . 1·60 50
693 12c. Brown pelican perched on post . . . . 1·60 55
694 15c. Brown pelican . . . . . 1·75 1·10
695 35c. Brown pelican swallowing fish . . . . . 2·75 3·00
MS696 106 × 76 mm. $2 Common shoveler (horiz) 8·50 9·00
No. **MS**696 is without the W.W.F. logo.

181 Anegada Rock Iguana

1988. Wildlife (2nd series). Endangered Species. Multicoloured.
697 20c. Type **181** . . . . 1·25 75
698 40c. Virgin Gorda dwarf gecko . . . . 1·50 1·40
699 60c. Hawksbill turtle . . . . 2·50 3·50
700 $1 Humpback whale . . . . 7·00 8·00
MS701 106 × 77 mm. $2 Trunk turtle (vert) 5·50 7·50

182 Yachts at Start

1989. Spring Regatta. Multicoloured.
702 12c. Type **182** 45 40
703 40c. Yacht tacking (horiz) . . 1·00 1·00
704 75c. Yachts at sunset . . . . 1·60 2·50
705 $1 Yachts rounding buoy (horiz) . . . . 2·00 2·75
MS706 83 × 69 mm. $2 Yacht under full sail 5·50 6·50

1989. 500th Anniv (1992) of Discovery of America by Columbus (1st issue). Pre-Columbian Arawak Society. As T **247** of Antigua. Multicoloured.
707 10c. Arawak in hammock . . 70 45
708 20c. Making fire . . . . . . 1·00 50
709 25c. Making implements . . 1·00 60
710 $1.50 Arawak family . . . . 4·50 7·00
MS711 85 × 70 mm. $2 Religious ceremony 7·00 9·00
See also Nos. 741/5, 793/7 and 818/26.

183 "Apollo II" Emblem

1989. 20th Anniv of First Manned Landing on the Moon. Multicoloured.
712 15c. Type **183** . . . . 1·00 60
713 30c. Edwin Aldrin deploying scientific experiments . . . 2·00 1·00
714 65c. Aldrin and U.S. flag on Moon . . . . 2·75 3·75
715 $1 "Apollo II" capsule after splashdown . . . . 3·75 4·00
MS716 102 × 77 mm. $2 Neil Armstrong (38 × 50 mm) 7·00 8·50

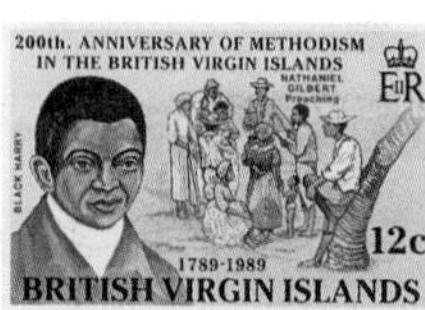

184 Black Harry and Nathaniel Gilbert preaching to Slaves

1989. Bicentenary of Methodist Church in British Virgin Islands. Multicoloured
717 12c. Type **184** . . . . 1·00 50
718 25c. Methodist school exercise book . . . . . . 1·40 75
719 35c. East End Methodist Church, 1810 . . . . . . 1·60 85
720 $1.25 Reverend John Wesley (founder of Methodism) and church youth choir . . 3·25 6·50
MS721 100 × 69 mm. $2 Dr. Thomas Cole 4·75 8·50

185 Player tackling

1989. World Cup Football Championships, Italy, 1990. Multicoloured.
722 5c. Type **185** 80 80
723 10c. Player dribbling ball . . 80 80
724 20c. Two players chasing ball 1·50 80
725 $1.75 Goalkeeper diving for ball . . . . 7·00 7·50
MS726 100 × 70 mm. $2 British Virgin Islands team captain 8·50 11·00

186 Princess Alexandra and Sunset House

1990. "Stamp World London 90" International Stamp Exhibition. Royal Visitors. Multicoloured.
727 50c. Type **186** . . . . 2·50 2·75
728 50c. Princess Margaret and Government House . . . . 2·50 2·75
729 50c. Hon. Angus Ogilvy and Little Dix Bay Hotel . . . 2·50 2·75
730 50c. Princess Diana with Princes William and Henry and Necker Island Resort 2·50 2·75
MS731 89 × 80 mm. $2 Royal Yacht "Britannia" 8·50 8·50

187 Audubon's Shearwater

1990. Birds. Multicoloured.
732 5c. Type **187** 80 90
733 12c. Red-necked pigeon . . . 1·25 40
734 20c. Moorhen ("Common Gallinule") . . . . 1·50 50
735 25c. Green-backed heron ("Green Heron") . . . . . 1·50 50
736 40c. Yellow warbler . . . . 1·75 1·25
737 60c. Smooth-billed ani . . . 2·00 2·50
738 $1 Antillean crested hummingbird . . . . . . 2·00 3·00
739 $1.25 Black-faced grassquit 2·00 4·00
MS740 Two sheets, each 98 × 70 mm. (a) $2 Royal tern egg (vert) (b) $2 Red-billed tropicbird egg (vert) Set of 2 sheets 8·50 7·00

1990. 500th Anniv (1992) of Discovery of America by Columbus (2nd issue). New World Natural History–Fishes. As T **260** of Antigua. Mult.
741 10c. Blue tang (horiz) . . . . 1·25 60
742 35c. Glass-eyed snapper (horiz) . . . . 2·25 70
743 50c. Slippery dick (horiz) . . 2·75 3·25
744 $1 Porkfish (horiz) . . . . . 4·25 4·50
MS745 100 × 70 mm. $2 Yellow-tailed snapper 5·00 6·00

188 Queen Elizabeth the Queen Mother

189 Footballers

1990. 90th Birthday of Queen Elizabeth the Queen Mother.
746 **188** 12c. multicoloured 50 25
747 – 25c. multicoloured 90 55
748 – 60c. multicoloured . . . . 1·75 2·25
749 – $1 multicoloured . . . . 2·00 2·50
MS750 75 × 75 mm. $2 multicoloured 2·75 2·75
DESIGNS: 25, 60c., $2 Recent photographs.

1990. World Cup Football Championships, Italy.
751 **189** 12c. multicoloured 60 40
752 – 20c. multicoloured 90 50
753 – 50c. multicoloured . . . . 1·75 2·00
754 – $1.25 multicoloured . . . 2·50 3·75
MS755 91 × 76 mm. $2 multicoloured 4·50 4·50
DESIGNS: 20, 50c., $2, Footballers.

190 Judo

1990. Olympic Games, Barcelona (1992). Mult.
756 12c. Type **190** . . . . 1·00 45
757 40c. Yachting . . . . 1·75 1·40
758 60c. Hurdling . . . . 2·25 3·25
759 $1 Show jumping . . . . . 3·50 4·00
MS760 78 × 105 mm. $2 Windsurfing 4·50 4·00

191 Tree-fern, Sage Mountain National Park

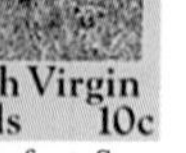

192 Haiti Haiti

1991. 30th Anniv of National Parks Trust. Multicoloured.
761 10c. Type **191** 70 80
762 25c. Coppermine ruins, Virgin Gorda (horiz) . . . 1·00 80
763 35c. Ruined windmill, Mt. Healthy . . . . 1·25 80
764 $2 The Baths (rock formation), Virgin Gorda (horiz) . . . . 7·00 9·00

1991. Flowers. Multicoloured.
765 1c. Type **192** . . . . 20 1·00
766 2c. Lobster claw . . . . . . 20 1·00
767 5c. Frangipani . . . . 20 1·00
887 10c. Autograph tree . . . . 50 1·10
769 12c. Yellow allamanda . . . 40 30
889 15c. Lantana 65 40
771 20c. Jerusalem thorn 50 30
772 25c. Turk's cap 55 40
892 30c. Swamp immortelle . . . 70 50
893 35c. White cedar 85 55
775 40c. Mahoe tree 75 65
895 45c. Pinguin 95 80
896 50c. Christmas orchid . . . . 2·25 1·75
778 70c. Lignum vitae . . . . . 1·10 2·00
779 $1 African tulip tree . . . . 1·25 2·00
899 $2 Beach morning glory . . . 3·00 4·75
781 $3 Organ pipe cactus . . . . 4·00 6·50
901 $5 Tall ground orchid . . . 8·50 12·00
783 $10 Ground orchid . . . . . 14·00 17·00

193 "Phoebis sennae"

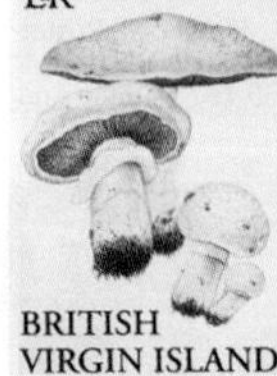

194 "Agaricus bisporus"

1991. Butterflies. Multicoloured.
784 5c. Type **193** 70 90
785 10c. "Dryas iulia" 80 90
786 15c. "Junonia evarete" . . . 1·00 75
787 20c. "Dione vanillae" . . . . 1·10 80
788 25c. "Battus polydamus" . . 1·25 1·00
789 30c. "Eurema lisa" . . . . . 1·40 1·00
790 35c. "Heliconius charitonius" 1·50 1·10
791 $1.50 "Siproeta stelenes" . . 3·50 5·50
MS792 Two sheets. (a) 77 × 117 mm. $2 "Danaus plexippus" (horiz). (b) 117 × 77 mm. $2 "Biblis hyperia" (horiz) Set of 2 sheets 14·00 15·00

1991. 500th Anniv (1992) of Discovery of America by Columbus (3rd issue). History of Exploration. As T **277** of Antigua. Multicoloured.
793 12c. multicoloured . . . . . 1·25 50
794 50c. multicoloured . . . . . 2·25 2·00
795 75c. multicoloured . . . . . 3·00 2·75
796 $1 multicoloured . . . . . . 3·50 3·50
MS797 105 × 76 mm. $2 black and orange 6·50 7·50
DESIGNS—HORIZ: 12c. "Vitoria" in Pacific (Magellan 1519–21); 50c. La Salle on the Mississippi, 1682; 75c. John Cabot landing in Nova Scotia, 1497–98; $1 Cartier discovering the St. Lawrence, 1534. VERT: $2 "Santa Maria" (woodcut).

1991. Death Centenary (1990) of Vincent Van Gogh (artist). As T **278** of Antigua. Multicoloured.
798 15c. "Cottage with Decrepit Barn and Stooping Woman" (horiz) . . . . . 1·25 50
799 30c. "Paul Gauguin's Armchair" . . . . 1·75 80
800 75c. "Breton Women" (horiz) 3·00 3·00
801 $1 "Vase with Red Gladioli" 3·50 3·50
MS802 103 × 81 mm. $2 "Dance Hall in Arles" (detail) (horiz) 8·50 10·00

1991. Christmas. Religious Paintings by Quinten Massys. As T **291** of Antigua. Multicoloured.
803 15c. "The Virgin and Child Enthroned" (detail) . . . . 1·25 25
804 30c. "The Virgin and Child Enthroned" (different detail) . . . . 2·00 50

805 60c. "Adoration of the Magi" (detail) . . . . 3·50 3·75
806 $1 "Virgin in Adoration" . . 3·75 4·00
MS807 Two sheets, each 102 × 127 mm. (a) $2 "The Virgin standing with Angels". (b) $2 "The Adoration of the Magi" Set of 2 sheets 12·00 14·00

1992. Fungi. Multicoloured.
808 12c. Type **194** . . . . 1·50 55
809 30c. "Lentinula edodes" (horiz) . . . . 2·25 85
810 45c. "Hygocybe acutoconica" 2·25 1·00
811 $1 "Gymnopilus chrysopellus" (horiz) . . . 4·00 6·00
MS812 94 × 68 mm. $2 "Pleurotous ostreatus" (horiz) 9·00 11·00

1992. 40th Anniv of Queen Elizabeth II's Accession. As T **288** of Antigua. Multicoloured.
813 12c. Little Dix Bay, Virgin Gorda 85 30
814 25c. Deadchest Bay, Peter Island . . . . 1·75 90
815 60c. Pond Bay, Virgin Gorda 2·25 2·25
816 $1 Cane Garden Bay, Tortola 2·50 2·75
MS817 75 × 97 mm. $2 Long Bay, Beef Island 7·00 7·50

195 Queen Isabella of Spain

196 Basketball

1992. 500th Anniv of Discovery of America by Columbus (4th issue). Multicoloured.
818 10c. Type **195** 80 75
819 15c. Fleet of Columbus (horiz) . . . . 1·40 90
820 20c. Arms awarded to Columbus . . . . 1·40 90
821 30c. Landing Monument, Watling Island and Columbus's signature (horiz) . . . . 1·40 1·00
822 45c. Christopher Columbus 1·90 1·40
823 50c. Landing in New World and Spanish royal standard (horiz) . . . . 1·90 1·90
824 70c. Convent at La Rabida 2·25 3·25
825 $1.50 Replica of "Santa Maria" and Caribbean Pavilion, New York World's Fair (horiz) . . . 3·50 4·75
MS826 Two sheets. (a) 116 × 86 mm. $2 Ships of second voyage at Virgin, Gorda (horiz). (b) 86 × 116 mm. $2 De la Cosa's map of New World (horiz) Set of 2 sheets 8·00 12·00

1992. Olympic Games, Barcelona. Multicoloured.
827 15c. Type **196** . . . . 2·50 75
828 30c. Tennis . . . . 2·50 90
829 60c. Volleyball . . . . 2·75 3·00
830 $1 Football . . . . 3·00 3·75
MS831 100 × 70 mm. $2 Olympic flame 8·00 9·50

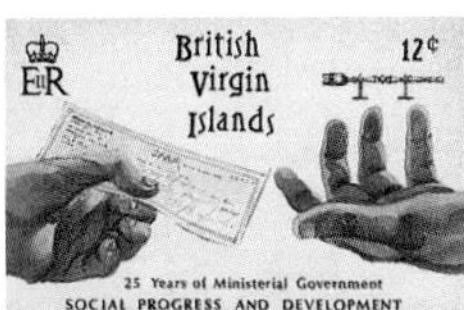

197 Issuing Social Security Cheque

1993. 25th Anniv of Ministerial Government. Multicoloured.
832 12c. Type **197** 40 40
833 15c. Map of British Virgin Islands . . . . 1·25 70
834 45c. Administration building 80 70
835 $1.30 International currency abbreviations . . . . . . 2·25 4·25

198 Cruising Yacht and Swimmers, The Baths, Virgin Gorda

1993. Tourism. Multicoloured.
836 15c. Type **198** . . . . 1·50 50
837 30c. Cruising yacht under sail (vert) . . . . 1·75 60
838 60c. Scuba diving . . . . . 2·50 2·75
839 $1 Cruising yacht at anchor and snorklers (vert) . . . . 2·75 3·25
MS840 79 × 108 mm. $1 "Promenade" (trimaran) (vert); $1 Scuba diving (different) (vert) 7·50 8·50

1993. 40th Anniv of Coronation. As T **307** of Antigua.
841 12c. multicoloured . . . . . 90 1·25
842 45c. multicoloured . . . . . 1·25 1·50
843 60c. grey and black . . . . . 1·40 1·75
844 $1 multicoloured . . . . . . 1·60 1·90
DESIGNS: 12c. Queen Elizabeth II at Coronation (photograph by Cecil Beaton); 45c. Orb; 60c. Queen with Prince Philip, Queen Mother and Princess Margaret, 1953; $1 Queen Elizabeth II on official visit.

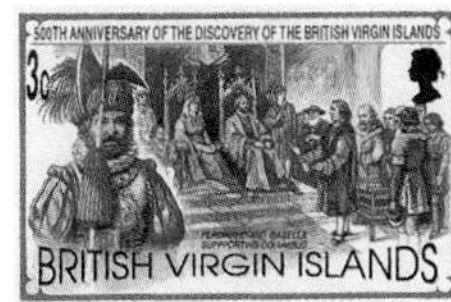

200 Columbus with King Ferdinand and Queen Isabella

1993. 500th Anniv of Discovery of Virgin Islands by Columbus. Multicoloured.
846 3c. Type **200** 15 40
847 12c. Columbus's ship leaving port 40 40
848 15c. Blessing the fleet 45 45
849 25c. Arms and flag of B.V.I. 60 60
850 30c. Columbus and "Santa Maria" 70 70
851 45c. Ships of second voyage 95 95
852 60c. Columbus in ship's boat 1·50 2·25
853 $1 Landing of Columbus . . 2·00 2·50
MS854 Two sheets, each 120 × 80 mm. (a) $2 Amerindians sighting fleet. (b) $2 Christopher Columbus and ships Set of 2 sheets 8·00 9·00

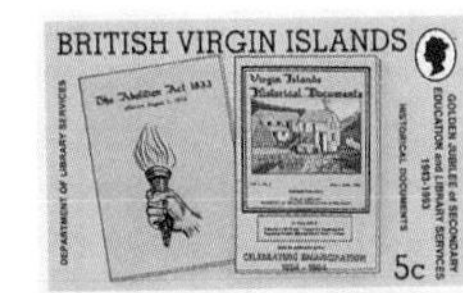

201 Library Services Publications

1993. 50th Anniv of Secondary Education and Library Services. Multicoloured.
855 5c. Type **201** 50 80
856 10c. Secondary school sports 1·00 90
857 15c. Stanley Nibbs (school teacher) (vert) 70 60
858 20c. Mobile library . . . . . 1·00 70
859 30c. Dr. Norwell Harrigan (adminstrator and lecturer) (vert) . . . . 1·00 70
860 35c. Children in library . . . 1·10 70
861 70c. Commemorative inscription on book . . . 2·00 3·25
862 $1 B.V.I. High School . . . 2·25 3·25

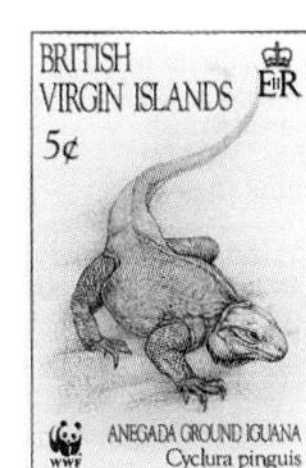

202 Anegada Ground Iguana

1994. Endangered Species. Anegada Ground Iguana.
863 **202** 5c. multicoloured 70 70
864 – 10c. multicoloured 70 70
865 – 15c. multicoloured 80 60
866 – 45c. multicoloured . . . . 1·25 1·25
MS867 106 × 77 mm. $2 multicoloured 3·00 4·00
DESIGNS: 10c. to $2 Different iguanas.
No. **MS**867 does not carry the W.W.F. Panda emblem.

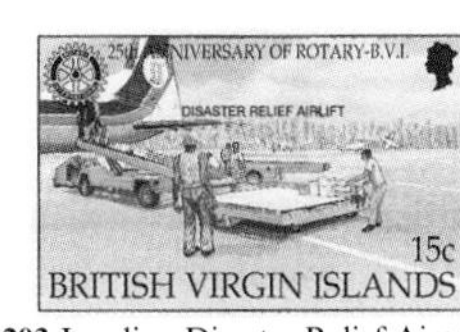

203 Loading Disaster Relief Aircraft

1994. Centenary of Rotary International in B.V.I. Multicoloured.
868 15c. Type **203** 35 35
869 45c. Training children in marine safety 85 85
870 50c. Donated operating table 90 1·00
871 90c. Paul Harris (founder) and emblem . . . . 1·60 2·50

1994. 25th Anniv of First Manned Moon Landing. As T **326** of Antigua. Multicoloured.
872 50c. Anniversary logo . . . . 2·00 2·25
873 50c. Lunar landing training vehicle . . . . 2·00 2·25
874 50c. Launch of "Apollo 11" 2·00 2·25
875 50c. Lunar module "Eagle" in flight . . . . 2·00 2·25
876 50c. Moon's surface . . . . 2·00 2·25
877 50c. Neil Armstrong (astronaut) taking first step 2·00 2·25
MS878 106 × 76 mm. $2 Signatures and mission logo 9·00 9·50

204 Argentina v. Netherlands, 1978

205 Pair of Juvenile Greater Flamingos

1994. World Cup Football Championship, U.S.A. Previous Winners. Multicoloured.
879 15c. Type **204** . . . . 1·25 50
880 35c. Italy v. West Germany, 1982 . . . . 2·00 70
881 50c. Argentina v. West Germany, 1986 . . . . . 2·75 2·25
882 $1.30 West Germany v. Argentina, 1990 . . . . . 4·50 6·50
MS883 74 × 101 mm. $2 U.S. flag and World Cup trophy (horiz) 8·50 9·50

1995. 50th Anniv of United Nations. As T **213** of Bahamas. Multicoloured.
903 15c. Peugeot P4 all-purpose field cars 45 40
904 30c. Foden medium road tanker 75 60
905 45c. SISU all-terrain vehicle 1·00 90
906 $2 Westland Lynx AH7 helicopter . . . . 3·75 5·50

1995. Anegada Flamingos Restoration Project. Multicoloured.
907 15c. Type **205** 75 50
908 20c. Pair of adults 75 55
909 60c. Adult feeding . . . . . 1·25 1·75
910 $1.45 Adult feeding chick . . 2·25 3·50
MS911 80 × 70 mm. $2 Chicks 3·50 5·00

206 "Tortola House with Christmas Tree" (Maureen Walters)

1995. Christmas. Children's Paintings. Mult.
912 12c. Type **206** . . . . 1·25 30
913 50c. "Father Christmas in Rowing Boat" (Collin Collins) . . . . 2·50 1·40
914 70c. "Christmas Tree and Gifts" (Clare Wassell) . . 2·75 2·75
915 $1.30 "Peace Dove" (Nicholas Scott) . . . . . 3·75 5·00

207 Seine Fishing

1996. Island Profiles (1st series). Jost Van Dyke. Multicoloured.
916 15c. Type **207** . . . . 1·25 40
917 35c. Sandy Spit . . . . . . 1·50 55
918 90c. Map . . . . 3·50 3·50
919 $1.50 Foxy's Regatta . . . . 3·75 5·00
See also Nos. 1003/6 and 1105/10.

1996. 70th Birthday of Queen Elizabeth II. As T **165** of Ascension, each incorporating a different photograph of the Queen. Multicoloured.
920 10c. Government House, Tortola 30 20
921 30c. Legislative Council Building 65 55
922 45c. Liner in Road Harbour 1·50 70
923 $1.50 Map of British Virgin Islands . . . . 3·25 5·00
MS924 63 × 65 mm. $2 Queen Elizabeth II 3·00 3·75

208 Hurdling

1996. Centenary of Modern Olympic Games. Multicoloured.
925 20c. Type **208** 45 30
926 35c. Volley ball 70 60
927 50c. Swimming . . . . . . 1·10 1·75
928 $1 Yachting . . . . 2·00 2·75

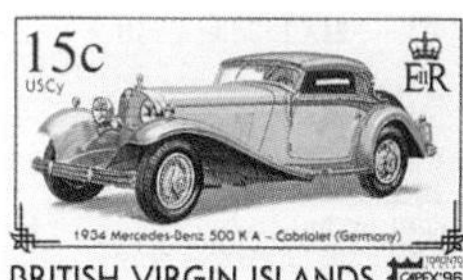

209 Mercedes-Benz "500 K A", 1934

1996. "CAPEX '96" International Stamp Exhibition, Toronto. Early Motor Cars. Multicoloured.
929 15c. Type **209** 45 30
930 40c. Citroen "12", 1934 . . . 1·00 70
931 60c. Cadillac "V-8 Sport Phaeton", 1932 . . . . . 1·25 1·75
932 $1.35 Rolls Royce "Phantom II", 1934 . . . . 2·75 4·00
MS933 79 × 62 mm. $2 Ford "Sport Coupe", 1932 3·25 4·25

210 Children with Computer

1996. 50th Anniv of U.N.I.C.E.F. Multicoloured.
934 10c. Type **210** 40 40
935 15c. Carnival costume . . . 50 50
936 30c. Children on Scales of Justice 80 80
937 45c. Children on beach . . . 1·25 1·25

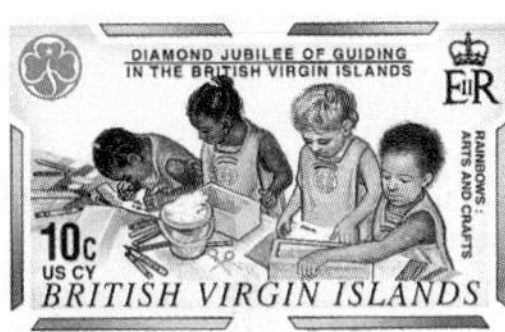

211 Young Rainbows in Art Class

1996. 75th Anniv of Guiding in the British Virgin Islands. Multicoloured.
938 10c. Type **211** 20 20
939 15c. Brownies serving meals 30 25
940 30c. Guides around campfire 50 45
941 45c. Rangers on parade . . . 65 60
942 $2 Lady Baden-Powell . . . 2·75 4·00

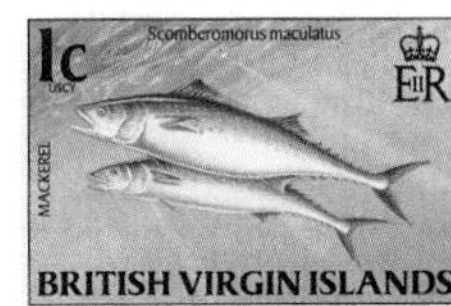

212 Spanish Mackerel

1997. Game Fishes. Multicoloured.
943 1c. Type **212** 10 10
944 10c. Wahoo 15 20
945 15c. Great barracuda 20 25
946 20c. Tarpon 25 30
947 25c. Tiger shark 30 35
948 35c. Sailfish 45 50
949 40c. Dolphin 50 55
950 50c. Black-finned tuna . . . 65 70
951 60c. Yellow-finned tuna . . . 75 80
952 75c. King mackerel ("Kingfish") . . . . 95 1·00
953 $1.50 White marlin . . . . . 1·90 2·00
954 $1.85 Amberjack . . . . . . 2·40 2·50
955 $2 Atlantic bonito . . . . . 2·50 2·75
956 $5 Bonefish . . . . 6·50 6·75
957 $10 Blue marlin . . . . . . 13·00 13·50

1997. "HONG KONG '97" International Stamp Exhibition. Sheet 130 × 90 mm, containing design as No. 953, but with "1997" imprint date. Mult.
MS958 $1.50, White marlin 2·25 2·75

1997. Golden Wedding of Queen Elizabeth and Prince Philip. As T **173** of Ascension. Multicoloured.
959 30c. Prince Philip with horse 70 1·00
960 30c. Queen Elizabeth at Windsor, 1989 . . . . . . 70 1·00
961 45c. Queen in phaeton, Trooping the Colour . . . 90 1·25
962 45c. Prince Philip in Scots Guards uniform . . . . . 90 1·25

963 70c. Queen Elizabeth and Prince Philip at the Derby, 1993 . . . . 1·25 1·60
964 70c. Prince Charles playing polo, Mexico, 1993 . . . . 1·25 1·60
MS965 110 × 70 mm. $2 Queen Elizabeth and Prince Philip in landau (horiz) 3·25 4·00

213 Fiddler Crab

1997. Crabs. Multicoloured.
966 12c. Type **213** 55 50
967 15c. Coral crab 60 50
968 35c. Blue crab 85 60
969 $1 Giant hermit crab . . . . 1·75 2·75
MS970 76 × 67 mm. $2 Arrow crab 3·50 4·50

214 "Psychilis macconnelliae"

1997. Orchids of the World. Multicoloured.
971 20c. Type **214** 70 85
972 50c. "Tolumnia prionochila" 1·00 1·10
973 60c. "Tetramicra canaliculata" . . . . . . 1·00 1·40
974 75c. "Liparis elata" . . . . 1·10 1·40
MS975 59 × 79 mm. $2 "Dendrobium crumenatum" (vert) 3·25 4·25

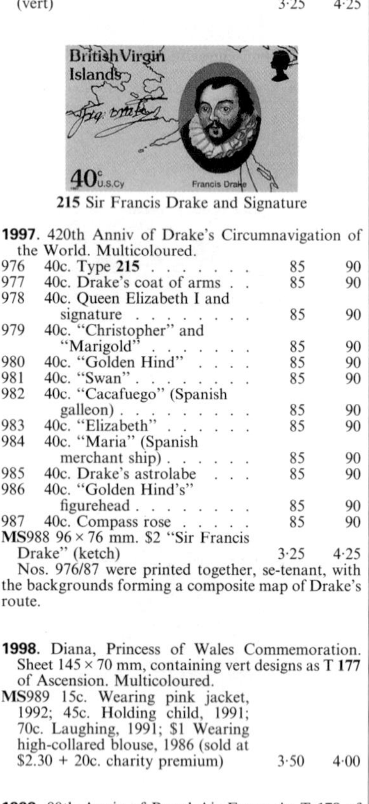

215 Sir Francis Drake and Signature

1997. 420th Anniv of Drake's Circumnavigation of the World. Multicoloured.
976 40c. Type **215** 85 90
977 40c. Drake's coat of arms . . 85 90
978 40c. Queen Elizabeth I and signature 85 90
979 40c. "Christopher" and "Marigold" 85 90
980 40c. "Golden Hind" 85 90
981 40c. "Swan" 85 90
982 40c. "Cacafuego" (Spanish galleon) 85 90
983 40c. "Elizabeth" 85 90
984 40c. "Maria" (Spanish merchant ship) 85 90
985 40c. Drake's astrolabe . . . 85 90
986 40c. "Golden Hind's" figurehead 85 90
987 40c. Compass rose 85 90
MS988 96 × 76 mm. $2 "Sir Francis Drake" (ketch) 3·25 4·25

Nos. 976/87 were printed together, se-tenant, with the backgrounds forming a composite map of Drake's route.

1998. Diana, Princess of Wales Commemoration. Sheet 145 × 70 mm, containing vert designs as T **177** of Ascension. Multicoloured.
MS989 15c. Wearing pink jacket, 1992; 45c. Holding child, 1991; 70c. Laughing, 1991; $1 Wearing high-collared blouse, 1986 (sold at $2.30 + 20c. charity premium) 3·50 4·00

1998. 80th Anniv of Royal Air Force. As T **178** of Ascension. Multicoloured.
990 20c. Fairey IIIF (seaplane) 60 40
991 35c. Supermarine Scapa (flying boat) 85 50
992 50c. Westland Sea King H.A.R.3 (helicopter) . . . 1·40 1·10
993 $1.50 BAe Harrier GR7 . . . 2·50 3·25
MS994 110 × 77 mm. 75c. Curtiss H.16 (flying boat); 75c. Curtiss JN-4A; 75c. Bell Airacobra; 75c. Boulton-Paul Defiant 6·50 7·00

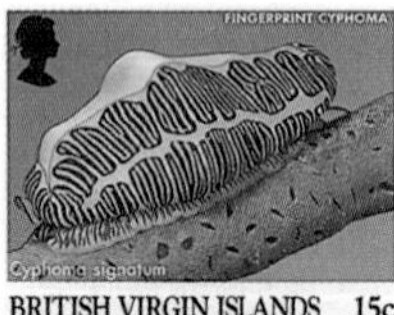

216 Fingerprint Cyphoma

1998. Marine Life. Multicoloured.
995 15c. Type **216** 70 40
996 30c. Long-spined sea urchin 90 55
997 45c. Split crown feather duster worm . . . . 1·25 70
998 $1 Upside down jelly . . . . 2·00 2·75
MS999 77 × 56 mm. $2 Giant anemone 4·75 5·00

217 "Carnival Reveller" (Rebecca Peck)

1998. Festival. Children's Paintings. Multicoloured.
1000 30c. Type **217** 75 50
1001 45c. "Leader of a Troupe" (Jehiah Maduro) 90 65
1002 $1.30 "Steel Pans" (Rebecca McKenzie) (horiz) . . . . 2·50 3·25

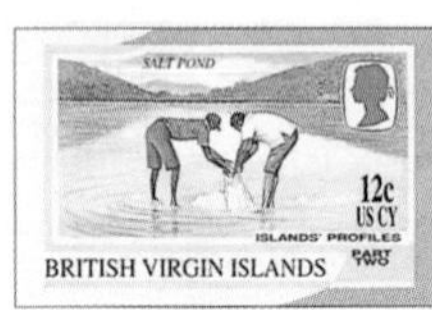

218 Salt Pond

1998. Island Profiles (2nd series). Salt Island. Multicoloured.
1003 12c. Type **218** 65 50
1004 30c. Wreck of "Rhone" (mail steamer) . . . . . 1·00 55
1005 70c. Traditional house . . . 1·25 1·60
1006 $1.45 Salt Island from the air . . . . 2·25 3·00
MS1007 118 × 78 mm. $2 Collecting salt 3·50 4·25

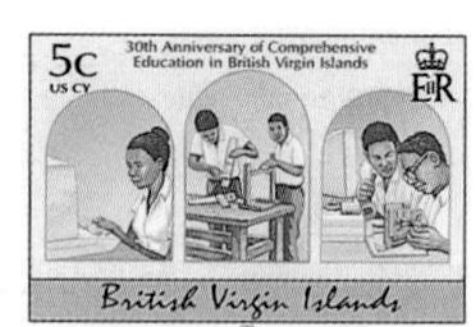

219 Business Studies, Woodwork and Technology Students

1998. Anniversaries. Multicoloured.
1008 5c. Type **219** 25 50
1009 15c. Comprehensive school band 45 30
1010 30c. Chapel, Mona Campus, Jamaica 60 40
1011 45c. Anniversary plaque and University arms 75 60
1012 50c. Dr. John Coakley Lettsom and map of Little Jost Van Dyke . . . . . 1·00 1·10
1013 $1 The Medical Society of London building and arms . . . . 1·60 2·25

EVENTS: 5, 15c. 30th anniv of Comprehensive Education in B.V.I.; 30, 45c. 50th anniv of University of West Indies; 50c., $1 250th anniv of Medical Society of London.

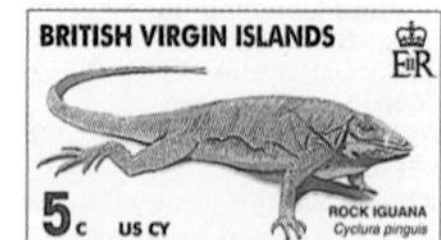

220 Rock Iguana

1999. Lizards. Multicoloured.
1014 5c. Type **220** 30 40
1015 35c. Pygmy gecko 85 45
1016 60c. Slippery back skink . . 1·50 1·00
1017 $1.50 Wood slave gecko . . 2·25 3·00
MS1018 100 × 70 mm. 75c. Doctor lizard; 75c. Yellow-bellied lizard; 75c. Man lizard; 75c. Ground lizard 4·50 5·50

1999. Royal Wedding. As T **185** of Ascension. Multicoloured.
1019 20c. Photographs of Prince Edward and Miss Sophie Rhys-Jones . . . . 1·00 40
1020 $3 Engagement photograph 4·75 6·00

1999. 30th Anniv of First Manned Landing on Moon. As T **186** of Ascension. Multicoloured.
1021 10c. "Apollo 11" on launch pad 45 35
1022 40c. Firing of second stage rockets . . . . 1·00 65
1023 50c. Lunar module on Moon . . . . 1·10 85
1024 $2 Astronauts transfer to command module . . . . 3·00 4·00
MS1025 90 × 80 mm. $2.50, Earth as seen from moon (circular, 40 mm diam) 3·75 4·50

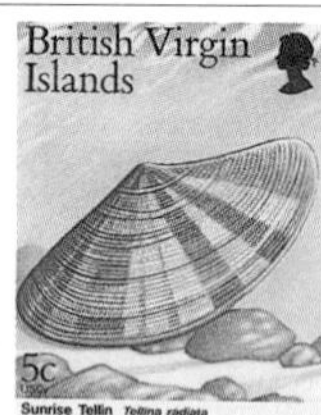

221 Sunrise Tellin

1999. Sea Shells. Multicoloured.
1026A 5c. Type **221** 45 55
1027A 10c. King helmet 45 55
1028A 25c. Measle cowrie 65 75
1029A 35c. West Indian top shell 75 85
1030A 75c. Zigzag scallop . . . . 1·00 1·25
1031A $1 West Indian fighting conch . . . . 1·25 1·50

Nos. 1026A/31A were printed together, se-tenant, with the backgrounds forming a composite design.

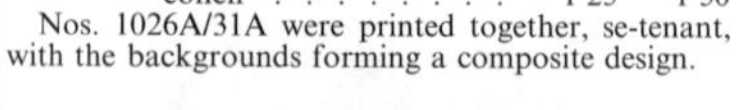

222 Zion Hill Methodist Church

1999. Christmas. Church Buildings. Multicoloured.
1032 20c. Type **222** 45 35
1033 35c. Seventh Day Adventist Church, Fat Hogs Bay, 1982 . . . . 60 45
1034 50c. Ruins of St. Phillip's Anglican Church, Kingstown . . . . 85 1·00
1035 $1 St. William's Catholic Church, Road Town . . . 1·60 2·25

223 King Henry VII **224** Duchess of York, 1920s

2000. "Stamp Show 2000" International Stamp Exhibition, London. Kings and Queens of England. Multicoloured.
1036 60c. Type **223** . . . . . . 1·10 1·25
1037 60c. Lady Jane Grey . . . . 1·10 1·25
1038 60c. King Charles I . . . . 1·10 1·25
1039 60c. King William III . . . 1·10 1·25
1040 60c. King George III . . . 1·10 1·25
1041 60c. King Edward VII . . . 1·10 1·25

2000. 18th Birthday of Prince William. As T **191** of Ascension. Multicoloured.
1042 20c. Prince William as baby (horiz) 60 35
1043 40c. Prince William playing with ball, 1984 . . . . . 90 60
1044 50c. Skiing in British Columbia, 1998 . . . . . 1·25 1·00
1045 $1 In evening dress, 1997 (horiz) . . . . 2·00 2·50
MS1046 175 × 95 mm. 60c. Prince William in 1999 (horiz) and Nos. 1042/5 6·00 6·00

2000. 100th Birthday of Queen Elizabeth the Queen Mother. Multicoloured.
1047 15c. Type **224** 50 25
1048 35c. As Queen Mother in 1957 . . . . 1·00 55
1049 70c. In evening dress, 1970 1·50 1·50
1050 $1.50 With family on 99th birthday . . . . 2·50 3·25

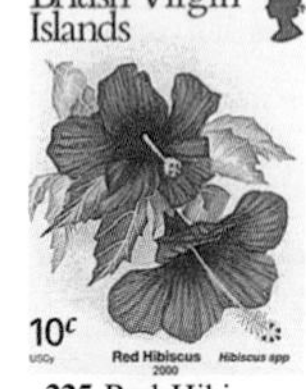

225 Red Hibiscus

2000. Flowers. Multicoloured.
1051 10c. Type **225** 30 30
1052 15c. Pink oleander 35 30
1053 35c. Yellow bell 75 55
1054 50c. Yellow and white frangipani . . . . 1·00 75
1055 75c. Flamboyant . . . . . 1·50 2·00
1056 $2 Bougainvillea . . . . . 3·25 4·00

226 Sunday Morning Well (Site of Emancipation Proclamation)

2000. New Millennium. Multicoloured.
1057 5c. Type **226** 15 25
1058 20c. Nurse Mary Louise Davies M.B.E. 45 35
1059 30c. Cheyney University, U.S.A. 60 45
1060 45c. Enid Leona Scatliffe (former chief education officer) 80 70
1061 50c. H. Lavity Stoutt Community College . . . 90 1·00
1062 $1 Sir J. Olva Georges . . . 1·60 2·00
MS1063 69 × 59 mm. $2 Private Samuel Hodge's Victoria Cross (vert) 3·25 3·75

227 Dr. Q. William Osborne and Arnando Scatliffe

2000. 50th Anniv of Restoration of Legislative Council. Multicoloured.
1064 10c. Type **227** 25 30
1065 15c. H. Robinson O'Neal and A. Austin Henley . . 35 30
1066 20c. Wilfred W. Smith and John C. Brudenell-Bruce 45 35
1067 35c. Howard R. Penn and I. G. Fonseca 65 55
1068 50c. Carlton L. de Castro and Theodolph H. Faulkner 90 90
1069 60c. Willard W. Wheatley (Chief Minister, 1971–79) 1·25 1·40
1070 $1 H. Lavity Stoutt (Chief Minister, 1967–71, 1979–83 and 1986–95) . . . . 1·60 2·00

2001. "HONG KONG 2001" Stamp Exhibition. Sheet 150 × 90 mm, containing T **228** and similar horiz design showing dove. Multicoloured.
MS1071 50c. Type **41**; 50c. Bar-tailed cuckoo dove 2·00 2·25

229 H.M.S. *Wistaria* (sloop), 1923–30

2001. Royal Navy Ships connected to British Virgin Islands (1st series). Multicoloured.
1072 35c. Type **229** 65 55
1073 50c. H.M.S. *Dundee* (sloop), 1933 . . . . 85 75
1074 60c. H.M.S. *Eurydice* (frigate), 1787 . . . . . 1·00 1·00
1075 75c. H.M.S. *Pegasus* (frigate), 1787 . . . . . 1·25 1·40
1076 $1 H.M.S. *Astrea* (frigate), 1807 . . . . 1·60 1·75
1077 $1.50 Royal Yacht *Britannia*, 1966 . . . . . 2·50 2·75

See also Nos. 1101/4.

230 Fridtjof Nansen (Peace Prize, 1922)

2001. Centenary of Nobel Prize. Multicoloured.
1078 10c. Type **230** 40 30
1079 20c. Albert Einstein (Physics Prize,1921) 45 35
1080 25c. Sir Arthur Lewis (Economic Sciences Prize, 1979) 45 40
1081 40c. Saint-John Perse (Literature Prize, 1960) . . 65 60
1082 70c. Mother Teresa (Peace Prize, 1979) . . . . . . 1·75 1·75
1083 $2 Christian Lous Lange (Peace Prize, 1921) . . . 3·00 3·50

2002. Golden Jubilee. As T **200** of Ascension.
1084 15c. brown, mauve and gold 50 25
1085 50c. multicoloured 90 75

1086 60c. multicoloured . . . . . 1·00 1·00
1087 75c. multicoloured . . . . . 1·25 1·50
MS1088 162 × 95 mm. Nos. 1084/7 and $1 multicoloured 4·75 5·25

DESIGNS—HORIZ: 15c. Princess Elizabeth in A.T.S. uniform, changing wheel; 50c. Queen Elizabeth in fur hat, 1977; 60c. Queen Elizabeth carrying bouquet; 75c. Queen Elizabeth at banquet, Prague, 1996. VERT (38 × 51 mm)—$1 Queen Elizabeth after Annigoni.

Designs as Nos. 1084/7 in No. **MS**1088 omit the gold frame around each stamp and the "Golden Jubilee 1952–2002" inscription.

231 Estuarine Crocodile

2002. Reptiles. Multicoloured.
1089 5c. Type **231** 10 10
1090 20c. Reticulated python . . 25 30
1091 30c. Komodo dragon . . . 40 45
1092 40c. Boa constrictor 50 55
1093 $1 Dwarf caiman . . . . . 1·25 1·40
1094 $2 *Sphaerodactylus parthenopion* (gecko) . . . 2·50 2·75
MS1095 89 × 68 mm. $1.50, Head of *Sphaerodactylus parthenopion* on finger 1·90 2·00

2002. Queen Elizabeth the Queen Mother Commemoration. As T **202** of Ascension.
1096 20c. brown, gold and purple 25 30
1097 60c. multicoloured 75 80
1098 $2 black, gold and purple 2·50 2·75
1099 $3 multicoloured . . . . . 3·75 4·00
MS1100 145 × 70 mm. Nos. 1098/9 6·25 6·75

DESIGNS—20c. Duchess of York, 1920s; 60c. Queen Mother at Somerset House, 2000; $2 Lady Elizabeth Bowes-Lyon, 1920; $3 Queen Mother inspecting guard of honour.

Designs as Nos. 1098/9 in No. **MS**1100 omit the "1900–2002" inscription and the coloured frame.

2002. Royal Navy Ships connected to British Virgin Islands (2nd series). As T **229**. Multicoloured.
1101 20c. H.M.S. Invincible (ship of the line) re-capturing H.M.S. *Argo* (frigate), 1783 . . . . 25 30
1102 35c. H.M.S. *Boreas* and H.M.S. *Solebay* (sailing frigates) 45 50
1103 50c. H.M.S. *Coventry* (frigate) 65 70
1104 $3 H.M.S. *Argyll* (frigate) 3·75 4·00

2002. Island Profiles (3rd series). Virgin Gorda. As T **218**. Multicoloured.
1105 5c. Spring Bay 10 10
1106 40c. Devils Bay 50 55
1107 60c. The Baths 75 80
1108 75c. St. Thomas Bay . . . 95 1·00
1109 $1 Savannah and Pond Bay 1·25 1·40
1110 $2 Trunk Bay . . . . . . 2·50 2·75

232 Young West Indian Whistling Duck and Nest

2002. Birdlife International. West Indian Whistling Duck. Multicoloured.
1111 10c. Type **232** 15 20
1112 35c. Adult bird on rock (vert) 45 50
1113 40c. Adult bird landing on water (vert) 50 55
1114 70c. Two adult birds 90 95
MS1115 175 × 80 mm. Nos. 1111/14 and $2 Head of duck 4·50 4·75

233 200 Metres Race

2003. Anniversaries and Events. Multicoloured.
1116 10c. Type **233** 15 20
1117 10c. Indoor cycling 15 20
1118 35c. Laser class dinghy racing 45 50
1119 35c. Women's long-jumping 45 50
1120 50c. Bareboat class yachts 65 70
1121 50c. Racing cruiser class yachts 65 70
1122 $1.35 Carlos and Esme Downing (founders) . . . 1·75 1·90
1123 $1.35 Copies of newspaper and anniversary logo . . 1·75 1·90

ANNIVERSARIES and EVENTS: 10c. Commonwealth Games, 2002; 35c. 20th anniv of British Virgin Islands' admission to Olympic Games; 50c. 30th anniv of Spring Regatta; $1.35, 40th anniv of *The Island Sun* (newspaper).

OFFICIAL STAMPS

1985. Nos. 418/21 and 423/33 optd **OFFICIAL**.
O 1 1c. Purple-tipped sea anemone . . . . 30 1·25
O 2 3c. Common starfish . . . . 45 1·25
O 3 5c. Type **134** 45 45
O 4 8c. Triton's trumpet (shell) 55 60
O 5 13c. Flamingo tongue snail 80 75
O 6 15c. Spider crab 85 70
O 7 18c. Sea squirts . . . . . . 90 1·75
O 8 20c. True tulip (shell) . . . 90 80
O 9 25c. Rooster tail conch (shell) . . . . 1·25 2·00
O10 30c. Fighting conch (shell) 1·40 1·00
O11 60c. Mangrove crab . . . . 2·00 2·50
O12 $1 Coral polyps . . . . . . 3·00 3·75
O13 $2.50 Peppermint shrimp . . 4·50 9·00
O14 $3 West Indian murex (shell) 5·50 10·00
O15 $5 Carpet anemone . . . . 7·50 10·00

1986. Nos. 560/78 optd **OFFICIAL**.
O16 1c. Type **162** . . . . 40 1·25
O17 2c. Yellow-crowned night heron . . . . 40 1·25
O18 5c. Mangrove cuckoo . . . 55 1·25
O19 8c. Northern mockingbird 55 1·75
O20 10c. Grey kingbird . . . . . 70 1·25
O21 12c. Red-necked pigeon . . 70 40
O22 15c. Least bittern 70 40
O23 18c. Smooth-billed ani . . . 70 75
O24 20c. Clipper rail . . . . . . 1·00 1·00
O25 25c. American kestrel . . . 1·00 1·00
O26 30c. Pearly-eyed thrasher . . 1·25 1·00
O27 35c. Bridled quail dove . . . 1·25 1·00
O28 40c. Green-backed heron . . 1·25 1·00
O29 50c. Scaly-breasted ground dove . . . . 1·40 1·75
O30 60c. Little blue heron . . . 1·50 2·50
O31 $1 Audubon's shearwater . . 2·25 3·50
O32 $2 Blue-faced booby . . . . 2·50 4·00
O33 $3 Cattle egret . . . . . . 6·00 7·00
O34 $5 Zenaida dove . . . . . . 6·50 7·50

1991. Nos. 767/8, 771, 773/9 and 781 optd **OFFICIAL**.
O35 5c. Frangipani . . . . . . 45 1·00
O36 10c. Autograph tree . . . . 45 1·00
O37 20c. Jerusalem thorn 55 55
O38 30c. Swamp immortelle . . . 70 55
O39 35c. White cedar 70 55
O40 40c. Mahoe tree 80 70
O41 45c. Pinguin 80 75
O42 50c. Christmas orchid . . . 1·50 90
O43 70c. Lignum vitae . . . . . 1·50 2·25
O44 $1 African tulip tree . . . . 1·50 2·50
O45 $3 Organ pipe cactus . . . . 4·00 6·50

BRUNEI Pt. 1

A Sultanate on the North Coast of Borneo.

100 cents = 1 dollar.

1 Star and Local Scene

1895.
1 **1** ½c. brown . . . . 3·00 20·00
2 1c. brown . . . . 3·25 15·00
3 2c. black . . . . 4·00 15·00
4 3c. blue . . . . 3·75 14·00
5 5c. green . . . . 6·50 16·00
6 8c. purple . . . . 6·50 27·00
7 10c. red . . . . 8·00 27·00
8 25c. green . . . . 65·00 80·00
9 50c. green . . . . 18·00 95·00
10 $1 green . . . . 20·00 £110

1906. Stamps of Labuan optd **BRUNEI.** or surch also.
11 **18** 1c. black and purple . . . . 29·00 55·00
12 2c. on 3c. black and brown 2·75 9·50
13 2c. on 8c. black and orange 27·00 80·00
14 3c. black and brown . . . . 28·00 85·00
15 4c. on 12c. black and yellow 3·75 5·00
16 5c. on 16c. green and brown 45·00 75·00
17 8c. black and orange . . . 9·00 32·00
18 10c. on 16c. green and brown . . . . 6·50 22·00
19 25c. on 16c. green and brown £100 £120
20 30c. on 16c. green and brown £100 £120
21 50c. on 16c. green and brown £100 £120
22 $1 on 8c. black and orange £100 £120

5 View on Brunei River

1907.
23 **5** 1c. black and green . . . . . 2·25 11·00
24 2c. black and red . . . . . 2·50 4·50
25 3c. black and brown . . . . 10·00 22·00
26 4c. black and mauve . . . . 7·50 10·00
27 5c. black and blue . . . . 50·00 90·00
28 8c. black and orange . . . . 7·50 23·00
29 10c. black and green . . . . 4·50 6·00
30 25c. blue and brown . . . . 32·00 48·00
31 30c. violet and black . . . . 23·00 22·00
32 50c. green and brown . . . . 15·00 22·00
33 $1 red and grey . . . . . . 60·00 90·00

1908.
35 **5** 1c. green . . . . 60 2·00
60 1c. black . . . . 1·00 75
79 1c. brown . . . . 50 2·00
36 2c. black and brown . . . . 3·25 1·25
61 2c. brown . . . . 90 6·50
62 2c. green . . . . 1·50 1·00
80 2c. grey . . . . 60 4·00
37 3c. red . . . . 3·50 1·25
63 3c. green . . . . 80 6·50
64 4c. purple . . . . 1·50 1·25
65 4c. orange . . . . 2·00 1·00
40 5c. black and orange . . . . 7·00 7·00
82 5c. orange . . . . 80 1·25
67 5c. grey . . . . 13·00 12·00
68 5c. brown . . . . 12·00 70
41 8c. blue and indigo . . . . 7·00 11·00
71 8c. blue . . . . 6·00 5·00
72 8c. black . . . . 12·00 75
84 8c. red . . . . 40 1·00
42 10c. purple on yellow . . . . 2·00 1·75
85 10c. violet 70 30
86 15c. blue . . . . 1·50 70
87 25c. purple . . . . 2·25 1·00
44 30c. purple and yellow . . . 9·00 12·00
88 30c. black and orange . . . 1·50 1·00
77 50c. black on green . . . . 7·50 15·00
89 50c. black . . . . 3·00 80
46 $1 black and red on blue . . 21·00 48·00
90 $1 black and red . . . . . 6·50 75
47 $5 red on green £120 £190
91 $5 green and orange . . . . 16·00 17·00
92 $10 black and purple . . . . 60·00 30·00
48 $25 black on red £475 £850

1922. Optd **MALAYA- BORNEO EXHIBITION. 1922.**
51 **5** 1c. green . . . . 4·00 26·00
52 2c. black and brown . . . . 4·50 30·00
53 3c. red . . . . 6·00 40·00
54 4c. red . . . . 8·50 48·00
55 5c. orange . . . . 12·00 55·00
56 10c. purple on yellow . . . . 6·50 55·00
57 25c. lilac . . . . 14·00 80·00
58 50c. black on green . . . . 45·00 £150
59 $1 black and red on blue . . 70·00 £190

7 Native Houses, Water Village

1924.
81 **7** 3c. green . . . . 1·00 5·00
83 6c. black . . . . 1·00 4·00
70 6c. red . . . . 3·75 11·00
74 12c. blue . . . . 4·50 9·00

8 Sultan Ahmed Tajudin and Water Village

1949. Silver Jubilee of H.H. the Sultan.
93 **8** 8c. black and red . . . . . 70 1·00
94 25c. purple and orange . . . 70 1·40
95 50c. black and blue . . . . 70 1·40

1949. 75th Anniv of U.P.U. As T **20/23** of Antigua.
96 8c. red . . . . 1·00 1·25
97 15c. blue . . . . 3·50 1·50
98 25c. mauve . . . . 1·00 1·50
99 50c. black . . . . 1·00 1·25

9 Sultan Omar Ali Saifuddin

1952. Dollar values as T **8**, but with arms instead of portrait inset.
100 **9** 1c. black 10 50
101 2c. black and orange . . . 10 50
102 3c. black and brown 10 30
103 4c. black and green 10 20
104 6c. black and grey 30 10
123 8c. black and red 60 10
106 10c. black and sepia 15 10
125 12c. black and violet . . . . 1·50 10
126 15c. black and blue 55 10
109 25c. black and purple . . . 2·50 10
110 50c. black and blue . . . . 1·75 10
111 $1 black and green (horiz) 1·50 1·40
112 $2 black and red (horiz) . . 4·50 2·50
113 $5 black and purple (horiz) 14·00 7·00

11 Brunei Mosque and Sultan Omar

1958. Opening of the Brunei Mosque.
114 **11** 8c. black and green 20 65
115 15c. black and red 25 15
116 35c. black and lilac 30 90

12 "Protein Foods"

1963. Freedom from Hunger.
117 **12** 12c. sepia . . . . 2·75 1·00

13 I.T.U. Emblem

1965. Centenary of I.T.U.
132 **13** 4c. mauve and brown . . . 35 10
133 75c. yellow and green . . . 1·00 75

14 I.C.Y. Emblem

1965. International Co-operation Year.
134 **14** 4c. purple and turquoise 20 10
135 15c. green and lavender . . 55 35

15 Sir Winston Churchill and St. Paul's Cathedral in Wartime

1966. Churchill Commemoration. Designs in black, red and gold and with backgrounds in colours given.
136 **15** 3c. blue 30 20
137 10c. green . . . . 1·50 20
138 15c. brown . . . . 1·75 35
139 75c. violet . . . . 4·25 2·25

16 Footballer's Legs, Ball and Jules Rimet Cup

1966. World Cup Football Championships.
140 **16** 4c. multicoloured 20 15
141 75c. multicoloured 80 60

17 W.H.O. Building

1966. Inauguration of W.H.O. Headquarters, Geneva.
142 **17** 12c. black, green and blue . . . 40 65
143 25c. black, purple and ochre . . . . 60 1·25

18 "Education"

1966. 20th Anniv of U.N.E.S.C.O.
144 **18** 4c. multicoloured 35 10
145 – 15c. yellow, violet and olive 75 50
146 – 75c. black, purple and orange . . . . 2·50 6·00
DESIGNS: 15c. "Science"; 75c. "Culture".

21 Religious Headquarters Building

1967. 1400th Anniv of Revelation of the Koran.
147 **21** 4c. multicoloured 10 10
148 10c. multicoloured 15 10
149 – 25c. multicoloured 20 30
150 – 50c. multicoloured . . . . 35 1·50
Nos. 149/50 have sprigs of laurel flanking the main design (which has a smaller circle) in place of flagpoles.

22 Sultan of Brunei, Mosque and Flags

1968. Installation of Y.T.M. Seri Paduka Duli Pengiran Temenggong. Multicoloured.
151 4c. Type **22** 15 60
152 12c. Sultan of Brunei, Mosque and Flags (different) (horiz) . . . . . 40 1·25
153 25c. Type **22** . . . . 55 1·75

23 Sultan of Brunei **24** Sultan of Brunei

1968. Birthday of Sultan.
154 **23** 4c. multicoloured 10 35
155 12c. multicoloured 20 60
156 25c. multicoloured . . . . 30 1·00

1968. Coronation of Sultan of Brunei.
157 4c. multicoloured 15 25
158 12c. multicoloured 25 50
159 25c. multicoloured 40 75

25 New Building and Sultan's Portrait

1968. Opening of Hall of Language and Literature Bureau. Multicoloured.
160 10c. Type **25** . . . . 20 1·75
161 15c. New Building and Sultan's portrait (48½ × 22 mm) 20 35
162 30c. As 15c. 45 90

27 Human Rights Emblem and struggling Man

1968. Human Rights Year.
163 **27** 12c. black, yellow and green 10 20
164 25c. black, yellow and blue 15 25
165 75c. black, yellow and purple . . . . 45 1·75

28 Sultan of Brunei and W.H.O. Emblem

1968. 20th Anniv of World Health Organization.
166 **28** 4c. yellow, black and blue 30 30
167 15c. yellow, black and violet 55 65
168 25c. yellow, black and olive 65 1·25

29 Deep Sea Oil-Rig, Sultan of Brunei and inset portrait of Pengiran Di-Gadong

1969. Installation (9th May, 1968) of Pengiran Shar-bandar as Y.T.M. Seri Paduka Duli Pengiran Di-Gadong Sahibol Mal.
169 **29** 12c. multicoloured 85 50
170 40c. multicoloured . . . . 1·25 2·00
171 50c. multicoloured . . . . 1·25 2·00

30 Aerial View of Parliament Buildings

1969. Opening of Royal Audience Hall and Legislative Council Chamber.
172 **30** 12c. multicoloured 20 25
173 25c. multicoloured 30 45
174 – 50c. red and violet . . . . 60 2·00
DESIGN: 50c. Elevation of new buildings.

32 Youth Centre and Sultan's Portrait

1969. Opening of New Youth Centre.
175 **32** 6c. multicoloured . . . . . 20 1·00
176 10c. multicoloured 25 10
177 30c. multicoloured . . . . 70 1·00

33 Soldier, Sultan and Badge **34** Badge, and Officer in Full-dress Uniform

1971. 10th Anniv of Royal Brunei Malay Regiment. Multicoloured.
178 10c. Type **33** 80 30
179 15c. Bell 205 Iroquois helicopter, Sultan and badge (horiz) . . . . . . 1·75 70
180 75c. "Pahlawan" (patrol boat), Sultan and badge (horiz) . . . . 3·25 7·00

1971. 50th Anniv of Royal Brunei Police Force. Multicoloured.
181 10c. Type **34** 50 30
182 15c. Badge and Patrol Constable 60 90
183 50c. Badge and Traffic Constable . . . . 1·10 6·00

35 Perdana Wazir, Sultan of Brunei and View of Water Village

1971. Installation of the Yang Teramat Mulia as the Perdana Wazir.
184 **35** 15c. multicoloured 40 50
185 – 25c. multicoloured . . . . 70 1·00
186 – 50c. multicoloured . . . . 1·40 5·00
Nos. 185/6 show various views of Brunei Town.

36 Pottery

1972. Opening of Brunei Museum. Mult.
187 10c. Type **36** 30 10
188 12c. Straw-work 40 20
189 15c. Leather-work 45 20
190 25c. Gold-work . . . . . . 1·25 1·25
191 50c. Museum Building (58 × 21 mm) . . . . . . 2·25 5·50

37 Modern Building, Queen Elizabeth and Sultan of Brunei

1972. Royal Visit. Each design with portrait of Queen and Sultan. Multicoloured.
192 10c. Type **37** 70 20
193 15c. Native houses 95 55
194 25c. Mosque . . . . 2·00 1·60
195 50c. Royal Assembly Hall . . 3·75 7·00

38 Secretariat Building

1972. Renaming of Brunei Town as Bandar Seri Begawan.
196 **38** 10c. multicoloured 20 15
197 – 15c. green, yellow and black 25 15
198 – 25c. blue, yellow and black 45 50
199 – 50c. red, blue and black . . 75 2·25
VIEWS: 15c. Darul Hana Palace; 25c. Old Brunei Town; 50c. Town and Water Village.

39 Blackburn Beverley C1 parachuting Supplies

1972. Opening of R.A.F. Museum, Hendon. Multicoloured.
200 25c. Type **39** . . . . 1·75 1·25
201 75c. Blackburn Beverley C1 landing . . . . 3·25 4·75

1972. Royal Silver Wedding. As T **52** of Ascension, but with girl with traditional flower-pot, and boy with bowl and pipe in background.
210 12c. red 10 10
211 75c. green 20 50

41 Interpol H.Q., Paris

1973. 50th Anniv of Interpol.
212 **41** 25c. green, purple and black . . . . 1·50 1·25
213 – 50c. blue, ultram & red . . 1·50 1·25
DESIGN: 50c. Different view of the H.Q.

42 Sultan, Princess Anne and Captain Phillips

1973. Royal Wedding.
214 **42** 25c. multicoloured 15 10
215 50c. multicoloured 15 25

43 Churchill Painting **44** Sultan Sir Hassanal Bolkiah Mu'izzaddin Waddaulah

1973. Opening of Churchill Memorial Building. Multicoloured.
216 12c. Type **43** 10 20
217 50c. Churchill statue . . . . 30 1·40

1975. Multicoloured. Background colours given.
218 **44** 4c. green 20 20
219 5c. blue 20 30
220 6c. green . . . . 3·25 5·00
221 10c. lilac 30 10
222 15c. brown . . . . 2·00 10
223 20c. stone 30 20
224 25c. green 40 15
225 30c. blue 40 15
226 35c. grey 40 20
227 40c. purple 40 20
228 50c. brown 40 20
229 75c. green . . . . 60 3·50
256 $1 orange . . . . 1·50 3·50
231 $2 yellow . . . . 2·25 11·00
232 $5 silver . . . . 3·00 18·00
233 $10 gold . . . . 5·00 30·00

45 Aerial View of Airport

1974. Inauguration of Brunei International Airport. Multicoloured.
234 50c. Type **45** . . . . 1·25 1·00
235 75c. Sultan in Army uniform, and airport (48 × 36 mm) 1·50 1·50

46 U.P.U. Emblem and Sultan

1974. Centenary of Universal Postal Union.
236 **46** 12c. multicoloured 20 20
237 50c. multicoloured . . . . 40 1·40
238 75c. multicoloured . . . . 50 1·75

47 Sir Winston Churchill

1974. Birth Centenary of Sir Winston Churchill.
239 **47** 12c. black, blue and gold 25 20
240 – 75c. black, green and gold 45 1·40
DESIGN: 75c. Churchill smoking cigar (profile).

48 Boeing 737 and R.B.A. Crest

1975. Inauguration of Royal Brunei Airlines. Mult.
241 12c. Type **48** . . . . 1·00 25
242 35c. Boeing 737 over Bandar Seri Begawan Mosque . . 1·75 1·25
243 75c. Boeing 737 in flight . . 2·50 2·50

1976. Surch **10 sen**.
263 **44** 10c. on 6c. brown . . . . 1·75 1·75

50 Royal Coat of Arms

51 The Moment of Crowning

1977. Silver Jubilee. Multicoloured.
264 10c. Type **50** 15 15
265 20c. Imperial State Crown . . 20 20
266 75c. Queen Elizabeth (portrait by Annigoni) . . 45 60

1978. 25th Anniv of Coronation. Multicoloured.
267 10c. Type **51** 15 10
268 20c. Queen in Coronation regalia 20 20
269 75c. Queen's departure from Abbey 55 80

52 Royal Crest

53 Human Rights Emblem and Struggling Man

1978. 10th Anniv of Coronation of Sultan.
270 **52** 10c. black, red and yellow 20 10
271 – 20c. multicoloured 40 25
272 – 75c. multicoloured . . . . 1·10 3·00
MS273 182 × 77 mm. Nos. 270/2 12·00 16·00
DESIGNS: 20c. Coronation; 75c. Sultan's Crown.

1978. Human Rights Year.
274 **53** 10c. black, yellow and red 15 10
275 20c. black, yellow and violet 20 35
276 75c. black, yellow and bistre . . . . 40 2·50
Type **53** is similar to the design used for the previous Human Rights issue in 1968.

54 Smiling Children

1979. International Year of the Child.
277 **54** 10c. multicoloured 20 10
278 – $1 black and green . . . . 80 2·50
DESIGN: $1 I.Y.C. emblem.

55 Earth Satellite Station

1979. Telisai Earth Satellite Station. Multicoloured.
279 10c. Type **55** 20 15
280 20c. Satellite and antenna . . 30 40
281 75c. Television camera, telex machine and telephone . . 60 2·75

56 Hegira Symbol

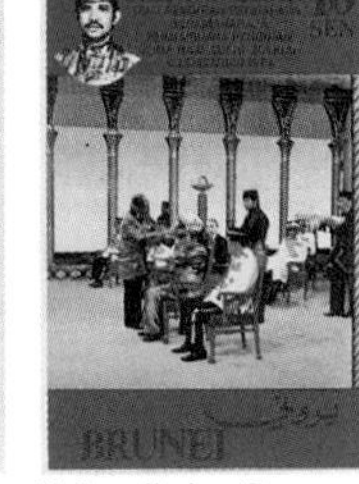

57 Installation Ceremony

1979. Moslem Year 1400 A.H. Commemoration.
282 **56** 10c. black, yellow and green 10 15
283 20c. black, yellow and blue 15 30
284 75c. black, yellow and lilac 45 2·00
MS285 178 × 200 mm. Nos. 282/4 3·00 6·50

1980. 1st Anniv of Prince Sufri Bolkiah's Installation as First Wazir. Multicoloured. Blue borders.
286 10c. Type **57** 15 10
287 75c. Prince Sufri . . . . . . 85 2·00

1980. 1st Anniv of Prince Jefri Bolkiah's Installation as Second Wazir. Designs similar to T **57**. Multicoloured. Green borders.
288 10c. Installation ceremony . . 15 10
289 75c. Prince Jefri . . . . . . 85 2·25

58 Royal Umbrella and Sash

59 I.T.U. and W.H.O. Emblems

1981. Royal Regalia (1st series). Multicoloured.
290 10c. Type **58** 20 15
291 15c. Sword and Shield . . . 35 25
292 20c. Lance and Sheath . . . 40 40
293 30c. Betel Leaf Container . . 60 1·25
294 50c. Coronation Crown (39 × 22 mm) . . . . . . 1·25 4·50
MS295 98 × 142 mm. Nos. 290/4 3·75 6·50
See Nos. 298/303, 314/19 and 320/5.

1981. World Telecommunications and Health Day.
296 **59** 10c. black and red 50 25
297 75c. black, blue and violet 2·25 4·50

60 Shield and Broadsword

61 Prince Charles as Colonel of the Welsh Guards

1981. Royal Regalia (2nd series). Multicoloured.
298 10c. Type **60** 10 10
299 15c. Blunderbuss and Pouch 20 20
300 20c. Crossed Lances and Sash 30 30
301 30c. Sword, Shield and Sash 40 75
302 50c. Forked Lance . . . . . 60 2·50
303 75c. Royal Drum (29 × 45 mm) . . . . . . 80 4·00

1981. Royal Wedding. Multicoloured.
304 10c. Wedding bouquet from Brunei 15 15
305 $1 Type **61** . . . . 35 1·50
306 $2 Prince Charles and Lady Diana Spencer . . . . . . 50 2·50

62 Fishing

63 Blind Man and Braille Alphabet

1981. World Food Day. Multicoloured.
307 10c. Type **62** 50 15
308 $1 Farm produce and machinery . . . . 4·50 7·00

1981. International Year for Disabled Persons. Multicoloured.
309 10c. Type **63** 65 20
310 20c. Deaf people and sign language . . . . 1·50 80
311 75c. Disabled person and wheelchairs . . . . 3·00 6·75

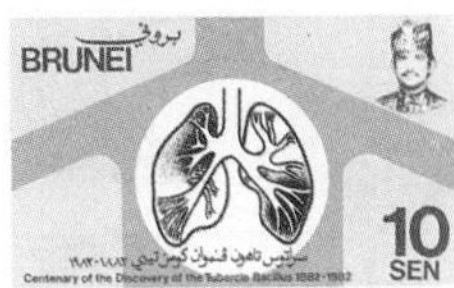

64 Drawing of Infected Lungs

1982. Centenary of Robert Koch's Discovery of Tubercle Bacillus. Multicoloured.
312 10c. Type **64** 50 25
313 75c. Magnified tubercle bacillus and microscope . . 3·00 5·00

1982. Royal Regalia (3rd series). As T **60**. Mult.
314 10c. Ceremonial Ornament 10 10
315 15c. Silver Betel Caddy . . . 20 20
316 20c. Traditional Flowerpot 25 30
317 30c. Solitary Candle 50 90
318 50c. Golden Pipe . . . . . . 70 2·50
319 75c. Royal Chin Support (28 × 45 mm) . . . . . . 90 4·00

1982. Royal Regalia (4th series). As T **60**. Mult.
320 10c. Royal Mace 25 10
321 15c. Ceremonial Shield and Spears 35 30
322 20c. Embroidered Ornament 45 40
323 30c. Golden-tasseled Cushion 75 1·50
324 50c. Ceremonial Dagger and Sheath . . . . 1·25 3·50
325 75c. Religious Mace (28 × 45 mm) . . . . . . 1·60 4·50

65 Brunei Flag

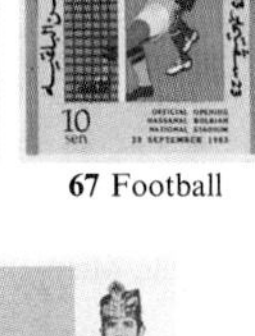

67 Football

66 "Postal Service"

1983. Commonwealth Day.
326 **65** 10c. multicoloured 15 70
327 – 20c. blue, black and buff 20 80
328 – 75c. blue, black and green 45 1·25
329 – $2 blue, black and yellow 1·10 1·75
DESIGNS: 20c. Brunei Mosque; 75c. Machinery; $2 Sultan of Brunei.

1983. World Communications Year.
330 **66** 10c. multicoloured 15 10
331 – 75c. yellow, brown and black 60 75
332 – $2 multicoloured . . . . . 1·75 2·25
DESIGNS: 75c. "Telephone Service"; $2 "Communications".

1983. Official Opening of the National Hassanal Bolkiah Stadium. Multicoloured.
333 10c. Type **67** 55 15
334 75c. Athletics . . . . 2·25 1·50
335 $1 View of stadium (44 × 27 mm) . . . . . . 2·75 4·00

68 Fishermen and Crustacea

1983. Fishery Resources. Multicoloured.
336 10c. Type **68** . . . . 1·00 15
337 50c. Fishermen with net . . . 3·00 1·50
338 75c. Fishing trawler . . . . 3·25 3·25
339 $1 Fishing with hook and tackle . . . . 3·50 4·00

69 Royal Assembly Hall

1984. Independence.
340 **69** 10c. brown and orange . . 20 10
341 – 20c. pink and red 30 20
342 – 35c. pink and purple . . . 60 60
343 – 50c. light blue and blue . . 1·75 1·25
344 – 75c. light green and green 1·75 2·00
345 – $1 grey and brown . . . . 2·00 2·50
346 – $3 multicoloured . . . . . 7·00 10·00
MS347 150 × 120 mm. Nos. 340/6 9·50 15·00
MS348 Two sheets, each 150 × 120 mm, containing 4 stamps (34 × 69 mm). (a) 25c. × 4 grey-black and new blue (Signing of the Brunei Constitution). (b) 25c. × 4 multicoloured (Signing of Brunei–U.K. Friendship Agreement) Set of 2 sheets 1·75 3·50
DESIGNS—34 × 25 mm: 20c. Government Secretariat Building; 35c. New Supreme Court; 50c. Natural gas well; 75c. Omar Ali Saifuddin Mosque; $1 Sultan's Palace. 68 × 24 mm: $3 Brunei flag and map of South-East Asia.

70 Natural Forests and Enrichment Planting

1984. Forestry Resources. Multicoloured.
349 10c. Type **70** . . . . 1·00 25
350 50c. Forests and water resources . . . . 2·50 2·25
351 75c. Recreation forests . . . 3·25 4·50
352 $1 Forests and wildlife . . . 4·75 6·00

71 Sultan Omar Saiffuddin 50c. Stamp of 1952

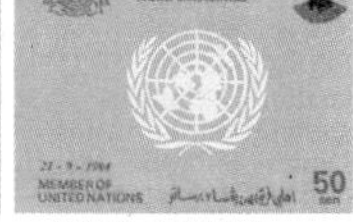

72 United Nations Emblem

1984. "Philakorea" International Stamp Exhibition, Seoul. Multicoloured.
353 10c. Type **71** 50 15
354 75c. Brunei River view 10c.stamp of 1907 . . . . 1·50 2·25
355 $2 Star and view ½c. stamp of 1895 . . . . 2·50 6·50
MS356 Three sheets, 117 × 100 mm, each containing one stamp as Nos. 353/5 Set of 3 sheets 3·75 6·50

1985. Admission of Brunei to World Organizations (1st issue).
357 **72** 50c. black, gold and blue 50 70
358 – 50c. multicoloured 50 70
359 – 50c. multicoloured 50 70
360 – 50c. multicoloured 50 70
MS361 110 × 151 mm. Nos. 357/60 2·25 3·00
DESIGNS: No. 358, Islamic Conference Organization logo; 359, Commonwealth logo; 360, A.S.E.A.N. emblem.
See also Nos. 383/7.

73 Young People and Brunei Flag

1985. International Youth Year. Multicoloured.
362 10c. Type **73** . . . . 1·25 20
363 75c. Young people at work . . . 5·00 7·00
364 $1 Young people serving the community . . . . 6·00 7·50

74 Palestinian Emblem

1985. International Palestinian Solidarity Day.
365 **74** 10c. multicoloured . . . . 1·75 20
366 50c. multicoloured . . . . 4·00 1·50
367 $1 multicoloured . . . . . 4·75 3·00

75 Early and Modern Scout Uniforms

76 Sultan Sir Hassanal Bolkiah Mu'izzaddin Waddaulah

1985. National Scout Jamboree. Multicoloured.
368 10c. Type **75** 60 10
369 20c. Scout on tower signalling with flag 90 40
370 $2 Jamboree emblem . . . . 2·75 3·25

1985.
371 **76** 10c. multicoloured 30 10
372 15c. multicoloured 30 10
373 20c. multicoloured 40 10
374 25c. multicoloured 40 15
375 35c. multicoloured 55 20
376 40c. multicoloured 60 25
377 50c. multicoloured 70 35
378 75c. multicoloured 90 50
379 $1 multicoloured . . . . . 1·25 70
380 $2 multicoloured . . . . . 2·25 1·75
381 $5 multicoloured . . . . . 4·25 5·00
382 $10 multicoloured . . . . 8·00 11·00
Nos. 379/82 are larger, size 32 × 39 mm.

1986. Admission of Brunei to World Organizations (2nd issue). As T **72**.
383 50c. black, gold and green . . 50 60
384 50c. black, gold and mauve . . 50 60
385 50c. black, gold and red . . . 50 60
386 50c. black, gold and blue . . 50 60
MS387 105 × 155 mm. Nos. 383/6 1·50 3·50
DESIGNS: No. 383, World Meteorological Organization emblem; 384, International Telecommunication Union emblem; 385, Universal Postal Union emblem; 386, International Civil Aviation Organization emblem.

78 Soldiers on Assault Course and Bell 205 Iroquois Helicopter

1986. 25th Anniv of Brunei Armed Forces. Multicoloured.
388 10c. Type **78** . . . . 3·50 3·50
389 20c. Operating computer . . 3·75 3·75
390 50c. Anti-aircraft missile, MBB-Bolkow Bo 150L helicopter and missile boat 4·75 4·75
391 75c. Army, commanders and parade . . . . 5·00 5·00
Nos. 388/91 were printed together, se-tenant, forming a composite design.

79 Tunggul Charok Buritan, Alam Bernaga (Alam Besar), Pisang-Pisang and Sandaran

80 Stylized Peace Doves

1986. Royal Ensigns (1st series).
392 **79** 10c. black, yellow and red 30 10
393 – 75c. multicoloured . . . . 1·10 1·10
394 – $2 black, yellow and green 2·25 2·75
DESIGNS: 75c. Ula-Ula Besar, Sumbu Layang and Payong Haram; $2 Panji-Panji, Chogan Istiadat (Chogan Di-Raja) and Chogan Ugama.

1986. Royal Ensigns (2nd series). As T **79**.
395 10c. multicoloured 30 10
396 75c. black, red and yellow . . 1·10 1·10
397 $2 multicoloured . . . . . . 2·25 2·75
DESIGNS: 10c. Dadap, Tunggul Kawan, Ambal, Payong Ubor-Ubor, Sapu-Sapu Ayeng and Rawai Lidah; 75c. Payong Tinggi and Payong Ubor-Ubor Tiga Ringkat; $2 Lambang Duli Yang Maha Mulia and Mahligai.

1986. International Peace Year. Multicoloured.
398 50c. Type **80** 75 75
399 75c. Stylized hands and "1986" . . . . 1·00 1·10
400 $1 International Peace Year emblem and arms of Brunei . . . . 1·25 1·50

81 Drug Addict in Cage and Syringe (poster by Othman bin Ramboh)

82 Cannon ("badil")

1987. National Anti-drug Campaign. Children's Posters. Multicoloured.
401 10c. Type **81** . . . . 1·00 35
402 75c. Drug addict and noose (Arman bin Mohd. Zaman) 2·50 4·00
403 $1 Blindfolded drug addict and noose (Abidin bin Hj. Rashid) . . . . 3·00 5·00

1987. Brassware (1st series). Multicoloured.
404 50c. Type **82** 50 50
405 50c. Lamp ("pelita") 50 50
406 50c. Betel container ("langguai") 50 50
407 50c. Water jug ("kiri") . . . 50 50
See also Nos. 434/7.

83 Map showing Member Countries

1987. 20th Anniv of Association of South East Asian Nations. Multicoloured.
408 20c. Type **83** 35 20
409 50c. Dates and figures "20" 60 50
410 $1 Flags of member states . . 1·25 1·25

84 Brunei Citizens

1987. 25th Anniv (1986) of Language and Literature Bureau. Multicoloured.
411 10c. Type **84** 30 30
412 50c. Flame emblem and hands holding open book 60 060
413 $2 Scenes of village life . . . 1·50 1·50
Nos. 411/13 were printed together, se-tenant, forming a composite design taken from a mural.

85 "Artocarpus odoratissima"

1987. Local Fruits (1st series). Multicoloured.
414 50c. Type **85** 45 55
415 50c. "Canarium odontophyllum mig" . . . 45 55
416 50c. "Litsea garciae" 45 55
417 50c. "Mangifera foetida lour" 45 55
See also Nos. 421/4, 459/62, 480/2 and 525/8.

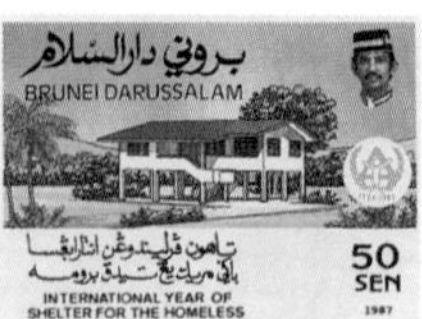

86 Modern House

1987. International Year of Shelter for the Homeless.
418 **86** 50c. multicoloured 40 50
419 – 75c. multicoloured 55 65
420 – $1 multicoloured 80 90
DESIGNS: 75c., $1 Modern Brunei housing projects.

1988. Local Fruits (2nd series). As T **85**. Mult.
421 50c. "Durio spp" . . . . . 85 1·10
422 50c. "Durio oxleyanus" . . . 85 1·10
423 50c. "Durio graveolens" (blue background) . . . . 85 1·10
424 50c. "Durio graveolens" (white background) . . . . 85 1·10

87 Wooden Lathe

89 Sultan reading Proclamation

88 Patterned Cloth

1988. Opening of Malay Technology Museum. Multicoloured.
425 10c. Type **87** 15 10
426 75c. Crushing sugar cane . . 55 70
427 $1 Bird scarer 70 85

1988. Handwoven Material (1st series). Mult.
428 10c. Type **88** 10 10
429 20c. Jong Sarat cloth 15 15
430 25c. Si Pugut cloth 20 25
431 40c. Si Pugut Bunga Berlapis cloth 30 35
432 75c. Si Lobang Bangsi Bunga Belitang Kipas cloth . . . 55 80
MS433 105 × 204 mm. Nos. 428/32 2·25 4·00
See also Nos. 442/7.

1988. Brassware (2nd series). As T **82**. Multicoloured.
434 50c. Lidded two-handled pot ("periok") 40 50
435 50c. Candlestick ("lampong") 40 50
436 50c. Shallow circular dish with stand ("gangsa") . . . 40 50
437 50c. Repousse box with lid ("celapa") 40 50

1988. 20th Anniv of Sultan's Coronation. Mult.
438 20c. Type **89** 20 15
439 75c. Sultan reading from Koran 70 60
440 $2 In Coronation robes (26 × 63 mm) . . . . . . 1·75 1·60
MS441 164 × 125 mm. Nos. 438/40 2·10 2·50

1988. Handwoven Material (2nd series). As T **88**. Multicoloured.
442 10c. Beragi cloth 15 10
443 20c. Bertabur cloth 20 20
444 25c. Sukma Indra cloth . . . 25 35
445 40c. Si Pugut Bunga cloth . . 40 75
446 75c. Beragi Si Lobang Bangsi Bunga Cendera Kesuma cloth . . . . 75 1·40
MS447 150 × 204 mm. Nos. 442/6 3·00 4·00

90 Malaria-carrying Mosquito

1988. 40th Anniv of W.H.O. Multicoloured.
448 25c. Type **90** . . . . 1·10 30
449 35c. Man with insecticide spray and sample on slide 1·25 45
450 $2 Microscope and magnified malaria cells . . . . 3·00 2·00

91 Sultan and Council of Ministers

1989. 5th Anniv of National Day. Mult.
451 20c. Type **91** 15 10
452 30c. Guard of honour . . . 20 15
453 60c. Firework display (27 × 55 mm) 45 40
454 $2 Congregation in mosque 1·50 1·75
MS455 164 × 124 mm. Nos. 451/4 2·25 2·75

92 Dove escaping from Cage

1989. "Freedom of Palestine". Multicoloured.
456 20c. Type **92** 40 20
457 75c. Map and Palestinian flag 1·50 1·00
458 $1 Dome of the Rock, Jerusalem . . . . 2·25 1·40

1989. Local Fruits (3rd series). As T **85**. Mult.
459 60c. "Daemonorops fissa" . . 2·00 2·25
460 60c. "Eleiodoxa conferta" . . 2·00 2·25
461 60c. "Salacca zalacca" . . . 2·00 2·25
462 60c. "Calamus ornatus" . . . 2·00 2·25

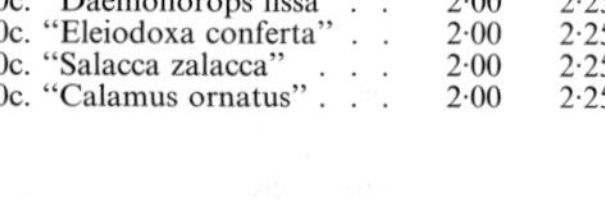

93 Oil Pump

1989. 60th Anniv of Brunei Oil and Gas Industry. Multicoloured.
463 20c. Type **93** . . . . 1·75 30
464 60c. Loading tanker . . . . 3·00 2·25
465 90c. Oil well at sunset . . . 3·25 3·00
466 $1 Pipe laying . . . . 3·50 3·00
467 $2 Oil terminal . . . . . . 6·50 8·00

94 Museum Building and Exhibits

1990. 25th Anniv of Brunei Museum. Multicoloured.
468 30c. Type **94** . . . . 1·50 70
469 60c. Official opening, 1965 2·25 2·25
470 $1 Brunei Museum . . . . . 3·00 3·50

95 Letters from Malay Alphabet

1990. International Literacy Year. Multicoloured.
471 15c. Type **95** 80 40
472 90c. English alphabet . . . . 3·50 4·00
473 $1 Literacy Year emblem and letters . . . . 3·50 4·00

96 Tarsier in Tree — 97 Symbolic Family

1990. Endangered Species. Western Tarsier. Multicoloured.
474 20c. Western Tarsier on branch 1·25 45
475 60c. Western Tarsier feeding 2·50 3·00
476 90c. Type **96** 3·50 4·25

1990. Worldwide Campaign against AIDS. Multicoloured.
477 20c. Type **97** 2·00 60
478 30c. Sources of infection 2·75 2·00
479 90c. "AIDS" headstone surrounded by skulls 6·75 7·50

1990. Local Fruits (4th series). As T **85**. Mult.
480 60c. "Willoughbea sp." (brown fruit) 2·75 3·50
481 60c. Ripe "Willoughbea sp." (yellow fruit) 2·75 3·50
482 60c. "Willoughbea angustifolia" 2·75 3·50

98 Proboscis Monkey on Ground

1991. Endangered Species. Proboscis Monkey. Multicoloured.
483 15c. Type **98** 1·50 60
484 20c. Head of monkey 1·60 70
485 50c. Monkey sitting on branch 3·00 3·25
486 60c. Female monkey with baby climbing tree 3·25 3·75

99 Junior School Classes

1991. Teachers' Day. Multicoloured.
487 60c. Type **99** 2·25 2·50
488 90c. Secondary school class 2·75 3·50

100 Young Brunei Beauty

1991. Fishes. Brunei Beauty. Multicoloured
489 30c. Type **100** 1·50 85
490 60c. Female fish 2·50 3·75
491 $1 Male fish 3·00 4·25

101 Graduate with Family — 102 Symbolic Heart and Trace

1991. Happy Family Campaign. Multicoloured.
492 20c. Type **101** 70 50
493 60c. Mothers with children 1·75 2·00
494 90c. Family 2·00 3·25

1992. World Health Day.
495 **102** 20c. multicoloured 1·50 50
496 – 50c. multicoloured 3·00 2·50
497 – 75c. multicoloured 4·25 5·00
DESIGNS: 50c., 70c. (48 × 27 mm) Heart and heartbeat trace.

103 Map of Cable System

1992. Launching of Singapore–Borneo–Philippines Fibre Optic Submarine Cable System. Mult.
498 20c. Type **103** 2·00 50
499 30c. Diagram of Brunei connection 2·00 1·50
500 90c. Submarine cable 4·25 5·00

104 Modern Sculptures

1992. Visit A.S.E.A.N. Year. Multicoloured.
501 20c. Type **104** 1·75 2·00
502 60c. Traditional martial arts 2·00 2·50
503 $1 Modern sculptures (different) 2·25 2·75
Nos. 501/3 were printed together, se-tenant, the backgrounds forming a composite design.

105 "A.S.E.A.N. 25" and Logo — 106 Sultan in Procession

1992. 25th Anniv of A.S.E.A.N (Association of South East Asian Nations). Multicoloured.
504 20c. Type **105** 1·25 65
505 60c. Headquarters building 2·75 2·75
506 90c. National landmarks 3·50 4·25

1992. 25th Anniv of Sultan's Accession. Mult.
507 25c. Type **106** 1·25 1·40
508 25c. Brunei International Airport 1·25 1·40
509 25c. Sultan's Palace 1·25 1·40
510 25c. Docks and Brunei University 1·25 1·40
511 25c. Mosque 1·25 1·40
Nos. 507/11 were printed together, se-tenant, forming a composite design.

107 Crested Wood Partridge — 108 National Flag and "10"

1992. Birds (1st series). Multicoloured.
512 30c. Type **107** 75 50
513 60c. Asiatic paradise flycatcher ("Asian Paradise Flycatcher") 1·60 2·25
514 $1 Great argus pheasant 1·90 3·00
See also Nos. 515/17, 518/20, 575/7 and 602/5.

1993. Birds (2nd series). As T **107**. Multicoloured.
515 30c. Long-tailed parakeet 1·00 50
516 60c. Magpie robin 2·00 2·25
517 $1 Blue-crowned hanging parrot ("Malay Lorikeet") 2·50 3·00

1993. Birds (3rd series). As T **107**. Multicoloured.
518 30c. Chesnut-breasted malkoha 1·25 50
519 60c. White-rumped shama 2·25 2·50
520 $1 Black and red broadbill (vert) 3·00 3·50

1994. 10th Anniv of National Day. Multicoloured.
521 10c. Type **108** 60 80
522 20c. Symbolic hands 70 85
523 30c. Previous National Day symbols 85 95
524 60c. Coat of arms 1·10 1·40

1994. Local Fruits (5th issue). As T **85**, but each 36 × 26 mm. Multicoloured.
525 60c. "Nephelium mutabile" 85 1·40
526 60c. "Nephelium xerospermoides" 85 1·40
527 60c. "Nephelium spp" 85 1·40
528 60c. "Nephelium macrophyllum" 85 1·40

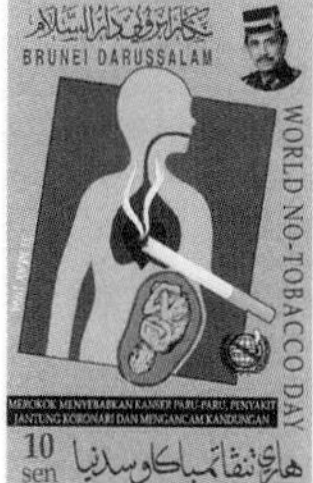

109 Cigarette burning Heart and Deformed Baby in Womb — 110 Raja Isteri (wife of Sultan in Guide uniform)

1994. World No Tobacco Day. Multicoloured.
529 10c. Type **109** 25 20
530 15c. Symbols of smoking over crowd of people 25 20
531 $2 Globe crushing cigarettes 2·75 4·00

1994. 40th Anniv of Brunei Girl Guides' Association. Multicoloured.
532 40c. Type **110** 1·10 1·40
533 40c. Guide receiving award 1·10 1·40
534 40c. Guide reading 1·10 1·40
535 40c. Group of guides 1·10 1·40
536 40c. Guides erecting tent 1·10 1·40

111 Turbo-prop Airliner on Runway

1994. 20th Anniv of Royal Brunei Airlines. Multicoloured.
537 10c. Type **111** 55 20
538 20c. Jet airliner on runway 85 35
539 $1 Jet airliner in the air 2·00 3·25

112 Malay Family

1994. International Day against Drug Abuse and Trafficking. Multicoloured.
540 20c. Type **112** 70 1·25
541 60c. Chinese family 1·10 1·60
542 $1 Doctor, police officers and members of youth organizations 1·50 1·90
Nos. 540/2 were printed together, se-tenant, forming a composite design.

113 Aerial View of City, 1970

1995. 25th Anniv of Bandar Seri Begawan. Mult.
543 30c. Type **113** 80 45
544 50c. City in 1980 1·25 1·25
545 $1 City in 1990 2·00 2·75

114 United Nations General Assembly — 115 Students in Laboratory

1995. 50th Anniv of United Nations. Multicoloured.
546 20c. Type **114** 40 25
547 60c. Security Council in session 75 80
548 90c. United Nations Building, New York (27 × 44 mm) 1·25 2·00

1995. 10th Anniv of University of Brunei. Mult.
549 30c. Type **115** 45 35
550 50c. University building 70 70
551 90c. Sultan visiting University 1·25 2·00

116 Police Officers — 117 Telephones

1996. 75th Anniv of Royal Brunei Police Force. Multicoloured.
552 25c. Type **116** 75 40
553 50c. Aspects of police work 1·10 1·10
554 75c. Sultan inspecting parade 1·75 2·50

1996. World Telecommunications Day. Children's Paintings. Multicoloured.
555 20c. Type **117** 50 30
556 35c. Telephone dial and aspects of telecommunications 65 45
557 $1 Globe and aspects of telecommunications 2·00 2·75

118 Sultan and Crowd — 119 Sultan Hassanal Bolkiah Mu'izzaddin Waddaulah

1996. 50th Birthday of Sultan Hassanal Bolkiah Mu'izzaddin Waddaulah. Multicoloured.
558 50c. Type **118** 75 1·10
559 50c. Sultan in ceremonial dress 75 1·10
560 50c. Sultan receiving dignitaries at mosque 75 1·10
561 50c. Sultan with subjects 75 1·10
MS562 152 × 100 mm. $1 Sultan in ceremonial dress (different) 1·75 2·50

1996.
563 **119** 10c. multicoloured 10 15
564 15c. multicoloured 10 15
565 20c. multicoloured 15 20
566 30c. multicoloured 20 25
567 50c. multicoloured 35 40
568 60c. multicoloured 45 50
569 75c. multicoloured 55 60
570 90c. multicoloured 65 70
571 – $1 multicoloured 70 75
572 – $2 multicoloured 1·40 1·50
573 – $5 multicoloured 3·50 3·75
574 – $10 multicoloured 7·25 7·50
DESIGN—27 × 39 mm: $1 to $10 Sultan in ceremonial robes.

121 Black-naped Tern

1996. Birds (4th series). Sea Birds. Multicoloured.
575 20c. Type **121** 65 40
576 30c. Roseate tern 65 50
577 $1 Bridled tern . . . . . . 1·50 2·50
No. 576 is inscr "ROSLATE TERN" in error.

122 "Acanthus ebracteatus"

1997. Mangrove Flowers. Multicoloured.
578 20c. Type **122** 35 25
579 30c. "Lumnitzera littorea" . . 45 35
580 $1 "Nypa fruticans" . . . . 1·25 2·00

123 "Heterocentrotus mammillatus"

1997. Marine Life. Multicoloured.
581 60c. Type **123** 60 85
582 60c. "Linckia laevigata" (starfish) 60 85
583 60c. "Oxycomanthus bennetti" (plant) 60 85
584 60c. "Bohadschia argus" (sea slug) 60 85

124 Children and Sign Language

1998. Asian and Pacific Decade of Disabled Persons, 1993–2002. Multicoloured.
585 20c. Type **124** 30 25
586 50c. Woman typing and firework display 60 70
587 $1 Disabled athletes . . . . 1·00 1·60

125 Sultan performing Ceremonial Duties

1998. 30th Anniv of Coronation of Sultan Hassanal Bolkiah Mu'izzaddin Waddaulah. Multicoloured.
588 60c. Type **125** 60 50
589 90c. Sultan on Coronation throne . . . . 90 1·25
590 $1 Coronation parade . . . 1·00 1·25
MS591 150 × 180 mm. Nos. 588/90 2·50 3·00

126 A.S.E.A.N. Architecture and Transport

127 Crown Prince at Desk

1998. 30th Anniv of Association of South-east Asian Nations. Multicoloured.
592 30c. Type **126** 70 70
593 30c. Map of Brunei and city scenes 70 70
594 30c. Flags of member nations 70 70

1998. Proclamation of Prince Al-Muhtadee Billah as Crown Prince. Multicoloured.
595 $1 Type **127** . . . . 1·00 1·00
596 $2 Crown Prince in military uniform . . . . 1·75 2·50
597 $3 Crown Prince's emblem 2·25 3·50
MS598 175 × 153 mm. Nos. 595/7. 5·50 7·00

128 Koran, Civil Servants and Handshake

129 Blue-eared Kingfisher

1998. 5th Anniv of Civil Service Day. Multicoloured.
599 30c. Type **128** 40 30
600 60c. Symbols of progress . . 65 65
601 90c. Civil servants at work 95 1·25

1998. Birds (5th series). Kingfishers. Multicoloured.
602 20c. Type **129** 60 50
603 30c. River kingfisher ("Common Kingfisher") . . 70 50
604 60c. White-collared kingfisher 1·00 85
605 $1 Stork-billed kingfisher . . 1·25 1·60

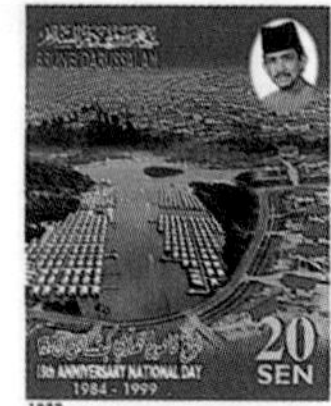

130 Water Village, Bandar Seri Begawan

1999. 15th Anniv of National Day. Multicoloured.
606 20c. Type **130** 30 20
607 60c. Modern telecommunications and air travel 80 80
608 90c. Aspects of modern Brunei . . . . 1·25 1·50
MS609 118 × 85 mm. Nos. 606/8 1·50 2·25

131 Rifle-shooting

132 Clasped Hands and Globe

1999. 20th South-east Asia Games, Brunei. Mult.
610 20c. Type **131** 40 45
611 20c. Golf and tennis 40 45
612 20c. Boxing and judo 40 45
613 20c. Squash and table tennis 40 45
614 20c. Swimming and canoe racing 40 45
615 20c. Hockey and cycling . . 40 45
616 20c. Basketball and football 40 45
617 20c. High jumping, shot putting and running . . . 40 45
618 20c. Snooker 40 45
619 20c. Bowling 40 45
MS620 110 × 73 mm. $1 Various sports . . . . 1·60 2·40

1999. 125th Anniv of Universal Postal Union. Multicoloured.
621 20c. Type **132** 40 20
622 30c. "125" and logos 50 25
623 75c. Aspects of postal service 1·10 1·40

133 Modern Building and Children using Computer

134 Sultan Mohamed Jemal-ul-Alam and Traditional Buildings, 1901–20

2000. New Millennium. Multicoloured.
624 20c. Type **133** 35 40
625 20c. Royal Palace, tree and people using computer . . 35 40
626 20c. Aerial view of mosque and factory 35 40
627 20c. Plan of Parterre Gardens 35 40
628 20c. Container ships and airliner 35 40
629 20c. Satellite dish aerials . . 35 40
MS630 221 × 121 mm. Nos. 624/9 1·40 1·75
Nos. 624/9 were printed together, se-tenant, with the backgrounds forming a composite design.

2000. Brunei in the 20th Century. Multicoloured.
631 30c. Type **134** 45 50
632 30c. Sultan Ahmed Tajudin, oil well and Brunei police, 1921–40 . . . . 45 50
633 30c. Signing of the Constitution and Brunei Mosque, 1941–60 . . . . 45 50
634 30c. Oil installation, satellite dish, Royal Brunei Airlines and bank note, 1961–80 . . 45 50
635 30c. Sultan on throne, international organisation emblems and crowd with trophy, 1981–99 . . . . . 45 50

135 Sultan Hashim Jalil-ul-Alam, 1885–1906

2000. The Sultans of Brunei. Multicoloured.
636 60c. Type **135** 80 90
637 60c. Sultan Mohamed Jemal-ul-Alam, 1906–24 . . . . 80 90
638 60c. Sultan Ahmed Tajudin, 1924–50 . . . . 80 90
639 60c. Sultan Omar Ali Saifuddin, 1950–67 . . . . 80 90
640 60c. Sultan Hassanal Bolkiah, 1967 . . . . 80 90
MS641 190 × 99 mm. Nos. 636/40 3·00 3·50

136 *Rafflesia pricei*

2000. Local Flowers. Multicoloured.
642 30c. Type **136** 45 30
643 50c. *Rhizanthes lowi* 70 70
644 60c. *Nepenthes rafflesiana* . . 80 80

137 Information Technology

2000. Asia–Pacific Economic Cooperation. Heads of Government Meeting. Multicoloured.
645 20c. Type **137** 40 30
646 30c. Small and medium businesses 50 35
647 60c. Tourism 80 85
MS648 150 × 108 mm. Nos. 645/7 1·50 2·00

138 Green Turtle

2000. Turtles. Multicoloured.
649 30c. Type **138** 50 55
650 30c. Hawksbill turtle 50 55
651 30c. Olive Ridley turtle . . . 50 55

139 Tourist Canoe on River

2001. "Visit Brunei Year" (1st series). Multicoloured.
652 20c. Type **139** 50 35
653 30c. Traditional water village 60 40
654 60c. Carved building facade 1·00 1·00
See also Nos. 669/72.

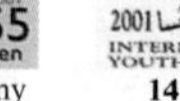

140 Sultan in Army Uniform

141 First Aid Demonstration

2001. 55th Birthday of Sultan Hassanal Bolkiah Muizzaddin Waddaulah. Multicoloured.
655 55c. Type **140** 70 75
656 55c. Sultan in Air Force uniform 70 75
657 55c. Sultan in traditional dress 70 75
658 55c. Sultan in Army camouflage jacket 70 75
659 55c. Sultan in Navy uniform 70 75
MS660 100 × 75 mm. 55c. Sultan and Bandar Seri Begawan (40 × 71 mm) 70 80

2001. International Youth Camp. Multicoloured.
661 30c. Type **141** 50 55
662 30c. Brunei guides and tent demonstration 50 55
663 30c. Scouts with cooking pot 50 55
MS664 110 × 77 mm. Nos. 661/3 1·40 1·60
Nos. 661/3 were printed together, se-tenant, forming a composite design.

142 Islamic Regalia

2001. 1st Islamic International Exhibition, Brunei. Multicoloured.
665 20c. Type **142** 30 40
666 20c. Exhibition centre . . . 30 40
667 20c. Computer communications 30 40
668 20c. Opening ceremony . . . 30 40

143 Forest Walkway

2001. Visit Brunei (2nd series). Multicoloured.
669 20c. Type **143** 30 40
670 20c. Waterfall 30 40
671 20c. Jerudong Theme Park 30 40
672 20c. Footbridges across lake 30 40

144 "Children encircling Globe" (Urska Golob)

2001. U.N. Year of Dialogue among Civilisations. Multicoloured.

673		30c. Type **144**	40	50
674		30c. Quotation marks illustrated with faces	40	50
675		30c. Cubist portrait and Japanese girl	40	50
676		30c. Coloured leaves	40	50

145 Male and Female Bulwer's Pheasants

2001. Endangered Species. Bulwer's Pheasant. Mult.

677		30c. Type **145**	40	50
678		30c. Male pheasant	40	50
679		30c. Female pheasant with chicks	40	50
680		30c. Female pheasant	40	50

146 Early and Modern Telephone Systems
147 50th Anniversary Logo

2002. 50th Anniv of Department of Telecommunications (JTB). Multicoloured.

681		50c. Type **146**	35	40
682		50c. JTB Golden Jubilee emblem	35	40
683		50c. Computer networks	35	40

2002. 50th Anniv of Survey Department. Mult.

684		50c. Type **147**	35	40
685		50c. Survey Department Offices	35	40
686		50c. Theodolite and thermal map	35	40

148 Modern Housing, Water Village

2002. 10th Anniv of Yayasan Sultan Haji Hassanal Bolkiah Foundation. Multicoloured.

687		10c. Type **148**	10	10
688		10c. Mosque and interior	10	10
689		10c. School and computer class	10	10
690		10c. University of Brunei	10	10

149 Anti-Corruption Bureau Headquarters

2002. 20th Anniv of Anti-Corruption Bureau. Multicoloured.

691		20c. Type **149**	15	20
692		20c. Skyscrapers and mosque	15	20
693		20c. Anti-Corruption Bureau posters	15	20

JAPANESE OCCUPATION OF BRUNEI

These stamps were valid throughout British Borneo (i.e. in Brunei, Labuan, North Borneo and Sarawak).

100 cents = 1 dollar.

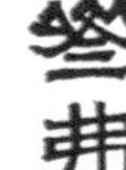

(**1**) ("Imperial Japanese Government")
(**2**) ("Imperial Japanese Postal Service $3")

1942. Stamps of Brunei optd with T **1**.

J 1	**5**	1c. black	6·50	23·00
J 2		2c. green	50·00	£110
J 3		2c. orange	3·75	9·00
J 4		3c. green	28·00	75·00
J 5		4c. orange	3·00	13·00
J 6		5c. brown	3·00	13·00
J 7	**7**	6c. grey	40·00	£200
J 8		6c. red	£550	£550
J 9	**5**	8c. black	£650	£850
J10	**7**	8c. red	4·25	12·00
J11	**5**	10c. purple on yellow	8·50	26·00
J12	**7**	12c. blue	25·00	26·00
J13		15c. blue	14·00	26·00
J14	**5**	25c. lilac	25·00	50·00
J15		30c. purple and orange	95·00	£180
J16		50c. black on green	38·00	60·00
J17		$1 black and red on blue	55·00	70·00
J18		$5 red on green	£850	£1900
J19		$25 black on red	£900	£1900

1944. No. J1 surch with T **2**.

J20	**5**	$3 on 1c. black	£6000	£5500

BRUNSWICK — Pt. 7

Formerly a duchy of N. Germany. Joined North German Confederation in 1868.

30 silbergroschen = 1 thaler.

1

1852. Imperf.

1	**1**	1sg. red	£4500	£250
2		2sg. blue	£2750	£200
3		3sg. red	£2750	£200

1853. Imperf.

4	**1**	¼gg. black on brown	£650	£225
5		⅓gg. black	£120	£300
15		½sg. black on green	20·00	£200
7		1sg. black on buff	£325	55·00
8		2sg. black on blue	£325	55·00
11		3sg. black on red	£375	70·00

3 **4**

1857. Imperf

12	**3**	4/4gg. black on brown	35·00	85·00

1864. Rouletted

22	**1**	⅓gg. black	£400	£1800
23		½sg. black on green	£180	£2500
24		1sg. black on yellow	£2500	£1300
25		1sg. yellow	£325	£120
26		2sg. black on blue	£325	£300
27		3sg. pink	£650	£425

1865. Roul.

28	**4**	⅓g. black	24·00	£325
29		1g. red	2·00	40·00
32		2g. blue	6·75	£100
34		3g. brown	5·75	£130

BUENOS AIRES — Pt. 20

A province of the Argentine Republic. Issued its own stamps from 1858 to 1862.

8 reales = 1 peso.

1 Paddle Steamer
2 Head of Liberty

1858. Imperf.

P13	**1**	4r. brown	£100	80·00
P17		1 (IN) p. brown	£125	80·00
P20		1 (IN) p. blue	65·00	50·00
P25		1 (TO) p. blue	£150	£100
P 1		2p. blue	90·00	50·00
P 4		3p. green	£450	£250
P 7		4p. red	£1500	£900
P10		5p. yellow	£1500	£900

1859. Imperf.

P37	**2**	4r. green on blue	90·00	50·00
P38		1p. blue	12·00	7·50
P45		1p. red	60·00	30·00
P43		2p. red	£120	80·00
P48		2p. blue	£120	45·00

BULGARIA Pt. 3

Formerly a Turkish province; a principality under Turkish suzerainty from 1878 to 1908, when an independent kingdom was proclaimed. A People's Republic since 1946.

1879. 100 centimes = 1 franc.
1881. 100 stotinki = 1 lev.

1 Large Lion

2 Large Lion

1879. Value in centimes and franc.

No.	Type	Description	Unused	Used
1	1	5c. black and yellow	85·00	25·00
3		10c. black and green	£375	75·00
5		25c. black and purple	£200	20·00
7		50c. black and blue	£350	80·00
8		1f. black and red	50·00	22·00

1881. Value in stotinki.

No.	Type	Description	Unused	Used
10	2	3s. red and grey	17·00	3·50
11		5s. black and yellow	17·00	3·50
14		10s. black and green	85·00	10·00
15		15s. red and green	85·00	10·00
18		25s. black and purple	£400	50·00
19		30s. blue and brown	17·00	10·00

See also No. 275/9.

A

B

C

D

1882.

No.	Type	Description	Unused	Used
46	2	1s. violet (Type A)	12·50	5·00
48		1s. violet (Type C)	85	20
47		2s. green (Type B)	11·50	3·75
49		2s. green (Type D)	85	20
21		3s. orange and yellow	85	35
23		5s. green	6·75	75
26		10s. red	8·50	75
28		15s. purple and mauve	6·75	50
31		25s. blue	6·75	90
33		30s. lilac and green	7·00	85
34		50s. blue and red	7·00	1·00
50		1l. black and red	30·00	4·00

1884. Surch with large figure of value.

No.	Type	Description	Unused	Used
38	2	3 on 10s. red	45·00	35·00
43		5 on 30s. blue and brown	45·00	40·00
45		15 on 25s. blue	65·00	50·00
40		50 on 1f. black and red	£300	£190

7

11 Arms of Bulgaria

13 Cherry wood Cannon used against the Turks

1889.

No.	Type	Description	Unused	Used
85	7	1s. mauve	10	10
88		2s. grey	45	20
89		3s. brown	15	10
90		5s. green	15	10
94		10s. red	50	10
96		15s. orange	35	10
100		25s. blue	50	10
58		30s. brown	4·00	10
59		50s. green	50	10
60		1l. red	45	40
83		2l. red and pink	1·60	1·40
84		3l. black and buff	3·25	2·75

1892. Surch **15**.

No.	Type	Description	Unused	Used
61	7	15 on 30s. brown	8·50	70

1895. Surch **01**.

No.	Type	Description	Unused	Used
74	2a	01 on 2s. green (No. 49)	65	15

1896. Baptism of Prince Boris.

No.	Type	Description	Unused	Used
78	11	1s. green	35	15
79		5s. blue	35	15
81		15s. violet	45	15
82		25s. red	4·00	30

1901. Surch in figures.

No.	Type	Description	Unused	Used
101	7	5 on 3s. brown	1·60	70
103		10 on 50s. green	1·60	90

1901. 25th Anniv of Uprising against Turkey.

No.	Type	Description	Unused	Used
104	13	5s. red	1·00	85
105		15s. green	1·00	85

14 Prince Ferdinand

16 Fighting at Shipka Pass

1901.

No.	Type	Description	Unused	Used
106	14	1s. black and purple	10	10
107		2s. blue and green	20	10
108		3s. black and orange	20	10
109		5s. brown and green	1·00	10
110		10s. brown and red	1·25	10
113		15s. black and lake	65	10
114		25s. black and blue	65	10
116		30s. black and brown	18·00	50
117		50s. brown and blue	1·00	15
118		1l. green and red	2·00	15
120		2l. black and red	3·75	50
123		3l. red and grey	4·50	85

1902. 25th Anniv of Battle of Shipka Pass.

No.	Type	Description	Unused	Used
124	16	5s. red	1·25	50
125		10s. green	1·25	50
126		15s. blue	4·50	1·75

1903. Surch.

No.	Type	Description	Unused	Used
140	15	5 on 15s. black and red	1·25	75
141		10 on 15s. black and red	2·50	40
143		25 on 30s. black & brown	7·50	90

18 Ferdinand I in 1887 and 1907

1907. 20th Anniv of Prince Ferdinand's Accession.

No.	Type	Description	Unused	Used
132	18	5s. green	7·00	90
134		10s. brown	12·50	90
137		25s. blue	24·00	1·90

1909. Optd **1909**.

No.	Type	Description	Unused	Used
146	7	1s. mauve	1·00	45
149		5s. green	1·00	45

1909. Surch **1909** and new value.

No.	Type	Description	Unused	Used
151	7	5 on 30s. brown	1·50	35
153		10 on 15s. orange	11·50	50
156		10 on 50s. green	1·50	55

1910. Surch **1910** and new value.

No.	Type	Description	Unused	Used
157	14	1 on 3s. black and orange	3·50	75
158		5 on 15s. black and lake	1·00	60

23 King Asen Tower

24 Tsar in General's Uniform

25 Veliko Turnovo

1911.

No.	Type	Description	Unused	Used
159	23	1s. green	10	10
182a		1s. slate	10	10
160	24	2s. black and red	10	10
161	25	3s. black and lake	1·50	25
162	–	5s. black and green	60	10
181	–	5s. purple and green	1·25	10
163	–	10s. black and red	55	10
181a	–	10s. sepia and brown	10	10
164	–	15s. bistre	7·50	30
183	–	15s. olive	1·00	30
165	–	25s. black and blue	30	10
166	–	30s. black and blue	2·75	15
182	–	30s. brown and olive	1·00	30
167	–	50s. black and yellow	16·00	15
168	–	1l. brown	4·25	15
169	–	2l. black and purple	1·00	60
170	–	3l. black and violet	9·00	2·75

DESIGNS—VERT: 5, 10, 25s., 1l. Portraits of Tsar Ferdinand. HORIZ: 15s. R. Isker; 30s. Rila Monastery; 50s. Tsars and Princes (after Ya. Veshin); 2l. Monastery of the Holy Trinity, Veliko Turnovo; 3l. Varna.

See also Nos. 229/30 and 236/7.

35 Tsar Ferdinand

1912. Tsar's Silver Jubilee

No.	Type	Description	Unused	Used
171	35	5s. grey	2·25	65
172		10s. red	3·50	1·25
173		25s. blue	4·50	1·90

ОСВОБ. ВОЙНА
1912-1913
(36) "War of Liberation" 1912–13

3
СТОТИНКИ
(37a)

1913. Victory over Turks. Stamps of 1911 optd as T **36**.

No.	Type	Description	Unused	Used
174	23	1s. green	25	10
175	24	2s. black and red	25	10
176	25	3s. black and lake	90	40
177	–	5s. black and green	25	10
178	–	10s. black and red	30	10
179	–	15s. bistre	2·75	75
180	–	25s. black and blue	1·75	40

1915. No. 165 surch **10 CT.** and bar.

No.	Type	Description	Unused	Used
180a	–	10s. on 25s. blk & blue	45	10

1916. Red Cross Fund. Surch with T **37a**.

No.	Type	Description	Unused	Used
185	7	3s. on 1s. mauve	5·00	5·75

45 Veles

46 Bulgarian Ploughman

38

39 Bulgarian Peasant

1917. Liberation of Macedonia.

No.	Type	Description	Unused	Used
193	45	1s. grey	10	10
194	46	1s. green	10	10
195	–	5s. green	10	10
186	38	5s. green	45	20
187	39	15s. grey	15	15
188	–	25s. blue	15	15
189	–	30s. orange	15	20
190	–	50s. violet	45	30
191	–	2l. brown	50	30
192	–	3l. red	75	45

DESIGNS—As Type **45**: 5s. Monastery of St. John, Ohrid. As Type **38**: 25s. Soldier and Mt. Sonichka; 50s. Ohrid and Lake. As Type **39**: 30s. Nish. 2l. Demir Kapija; 3l. Gevgeli.

48 Tsar Ferdinand

1918. 30th Anniv of Tsar's Accession.

No.	Type	Description	Unused	Used
196	48	1s. slate	10	10
197		2s. brown	10	10
198		3s. blue	25	20
199		10s. red	25	20

49 Parliament Building

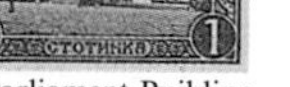
50 King Boris III

1919.

No.	Type	Description	Unused	Used
201	49	1s. black	10	10
202		2s. olive	10	10

1919. 1st Anniv of Enthronement of King Boris III.

No.	Type	Description	Unused	Used
203	50	3s. red	10	10
204		5s. green	10	10
205		10s. red	10	10
206		15s. violet	10	10
207		25s. blue	10	10
208		30s. brown	10	10
209		50s. brown	10	10

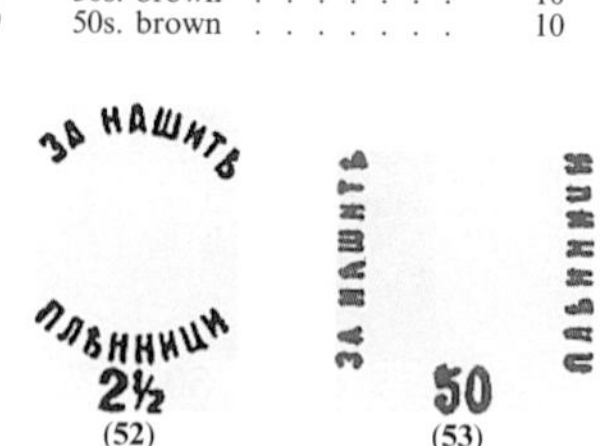
(52) (53)

1920. Prisoners of War Fund. Surch as T **52/53**.

No.	Type	Description	Unused	Used
210	49	1 on 2s. olive	10	10
211	50	2½ on 5s. green	10	10
212		5 on 10s. red	10	10
213		7½ on 15s. violet	10	10
214		12½ on 25s. blue	10	10
215		15 on 30s. brown	10	10
216		25 on 50s. brown	10	10
217	–	50 on 1l. brown (No. 168)	10	10
218	–	1 on 2l. brown (No. 191)	15	15
219	–	1½ on 3l. red (No. 192)	30	35

54 Vazov's Birthplace at Sopot and Cherry-wood Cannon

55 "The Bear-fighter", character from "Under the Yoke"

1920. 70th Birth Anniv of Ivan Vazov (writer).

No.	Type	Description	Unused	Used
220	54	30s. red	10	10
221	55	50s. green	10	10
222	–	1l. sepia	20	15
223	–	2l. brown	60	40
224	–	3l. violet	75	60
225	–	5l. blue	95	75

DESIGNS—HORIZ: 1l. Ivan Vazov in 1870 and 1920; 3l. Vazov's Houses in Plovdiv and Sofia. VERT: 2l. Vazov; 5l. Father Paisii Khilendarski (historian).

59 Aleksandr Nevski Cathedral, Sofia

62 King Boris III

1921.

No.	Type	Description	Unused	Used
226	59	10s. violet	10	10
227	–	20s. green	10	10
228	62	25s. blue	10	10
229	25	50s. orange	75	20
230		50s. blue	8·50	2·50
231	–	75s. violet	10	10
232	–	75s. blue	20	10
233	62	1l. red	15	10
234		1l. blue	10	10
235	–	2l. brown	25	10
236	–	3l. purple	45	10
237	–	5l. blue	2·00	30
238	62	10l. red	6·75	2·25

DESIGNS—HORIZ: 20s. Alexander II "The Liberator" Monument, Sofia; 75s. Shipka Pass Monastery; 5l. Rila Monastery. VERT: 2l. Harvester; 3l. King Asen Tower.

66 Tsar Ferdinand and Map

68 Mt. Shar

1921.

No.	Type	Description	Unused	Used
239	66	10s. red	10	10
240	–	10s. red	10	10
241	68	10s. red	10	10
242	–	10s. mauve	15	10
243	–	20s. blue	45	10

DESIGNS—VERT: No. 240, Tsar Ferdinand. HORIZ: No. 242, Bridge over Vardar, at Skopje; 243, St. Clement's Monastery, Ohrid.

71 Bourchier in Bulgarian Costume

72 J. D. Bourchier

73 Rila Monastery, Bourchier's Resting-place

1921. James Bourchier ("Times" Correspondent) Commemoration.

244	**71**	10s. red	10	10
245		20s. orange	10	10
246	**72**	30s. grey	10	10
247		50s. lilac	10	10
248		1l. purple	20	10
249	**73**	1½l. green	20	20
250		2l. green	20	10
251		3l. blue	45	20
252		5l. red	75	30

1924. Surch.

253	**49**	10s. on 1s. black	10	10
254	D **37**	10s. on 20s. orange	10	10
255		20s. on 5s. green	5·00	5·00
256		20s. on 10s. violet	1·40	1·40
257		20s. on 30s. orange	10	10
258	**50**	1l. on 5s. green	15	10
259	**25**	3l. on 50s. blue	1·10	40
260	**62**	6l. on 1l. red	50	30

77

78

79 King Boris III

81 Aleksandr Nevski Cathedral, Sofia

82 Harvesters

83 Proposed Rest-home, Verona

1925.

261	**77**	10s. blue & red on rose	10	10
262		15s. orange & red on blue	10	10
263		30s. buff and black	10	10
264	**78**	50s. brown on green	15	10
265	**79**	1l. olive	35	10
266		1l. green	50	10
267	**81**	2l. green and buff	85	10
267a	**79**	2l. brown	40	10
268	**82**	4l. red and yellow	75	10

1925. Sunday Delivery Stamps.

268b	**83**	1l. black on green	2·75	15
268c		1l. brown	2·50	15
268d		1l. orange	3·50	15
268e		1l. pink	3·50	15
268f		1l. violet on red	3·50	15
268g	–	2l. green	40	15
268h	–	2l. violet	40	20
268i	–	5l. blue	3·75	45
268j	–	5l. red	4·00	45

DESIGN: 2, 5l., Proposed Sanatorium, Bankya.

85 St. Nedelya's Cathedral, Sofia after Bomb Outrage

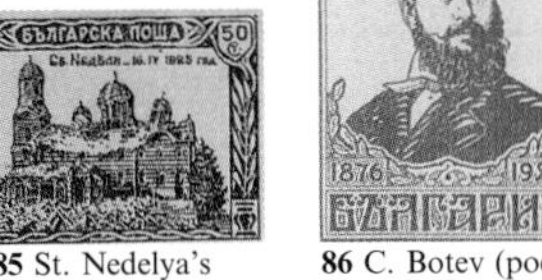

86 C. Botev (poet)

1926.

269	**85**	50s. black	10	10

1926. Botev Commemoration.

270	**86**	1l. green	30	15
271		2l. blue	65	15
272		4l. red	65	50

87

89 King Boris III

90 Saint Clement of Ohrid

1926.

273	**87**	6l. olive and blue	75	20
274		10l. brown and sepia	3·00	75

1927. As T **2** in new colours.

275		10s. red and green	10	10
276		15s. black and yellow	15	10
277		30s. slate and buff	10	10
278		30s. blue and buff	15	10
279		50s. black and red	15	10

1927. Air. Various stamps optd with Albatros biplane and No. 281 surch **1l** also.

281	**87**	1l. on 6l. green and blue	1·60	1·60
282	**79**	2l. brown	1·60	1·60
283	**82**	4l. red and yellow	2·75	2·00
284	**87**	10l. orange and brown	50·00	30·00

1928.

285	**89**	1l. green	75	10
286		2l. brown	1·25	10

1929. 50th Anniv of Liberation of Bulgaria and Millenary of Tsar Simeon.

287	**90**	10s. violet	15	10
288	–	15a. purple	15	10
289	–	30s. red	15	10
290	–	50s. green	25	10
291	–	1l. red	70	10
292	–	2l. blue	95	15
293	–	3l. green	2·10	50
294	–	4l. brown	3·00	25
295	–	5l. brown	95	55
296	–	6l. blue	2·75	1·25

PORTRAITS—23½ × 33½ mm: 15s. Konstantin Miladinov (poet and folklorist); 1l. Father Paisii Khilendarski (historian); 2l. Tsar Simeon; 4l. Vasil Levski (revolutionary); 5l. Georgi Benkovski (revolutionary); 6l. Tsar Alexander II of Russia, "The Liberator". 19 × 28½ mm: 30s. Georgi Rakovski (writer). 19 × 26 mm: 3l. Lyuben Karavelov (journalist).

98 Convalescent Home, Varna

1930. Sunday Delivery stamps.

297	**98**	1l. green and purple	5·00	15
298		1l. yellow and green	50	15
299		1l. brown and red	50	15

99

101 King Boris III

1930. Wedding of King Boris and Princess Giovanna of Italy.

300	**99**	1l. green	20	20
301	–	2l. purple	35	20
302	**99**	4l. red	35	30
303	–	6l. blue	45	35

DESIGN: 2, 6l. Portraits in separate ovals.

1931.

304a	**101**	1l. green (A)	15	10
305		2l. red (A)	50	10
306		4l. orange (A)	30	10
308a		4l. orange (B)	70	10
307		6l. blue (A)	35	10
308b		6l. blue (B)	70	10
308c		7l. blue (B)	25	20
308d		10l. slate (B)	10·00	55
308		12l. brown (A)	45	10
308e		14l. brown (B)	35	20
308f	–	20l. brown & pur (B)	85	60

(A) Without coloured frame-lines at top and bottom; (B) with frame-lines.

The 20l. is 24½ × 33½ mm.

103 Gymnastics

1831. Balkan Olympic Games.

309	**103**	1l. green	60	60
326		1l. turquoise	2·25	1·75
310	–	2l. red	1·10	60
327	–	2l. blue	3·00	1·75
311	–	4l. red	1·75	75
328	–	4l. purple	4·00	1·75
312	–	6l. green	4·75	1·50
329	–	6l. red	8·00	3·50
313	–	10l. red	10·00	5·00
330	–	10l. brown	45·00	20·00
314	–	12l. blue	45·00	10·50
331	–	12l. red	75·00	40·00
315	–	50l. brown	35·00	30·00
332	–	50l. red	£225	£200

DESIGNS—VERT (23 × 28 mm): 2l. Footballer; 4l. Horse-riding. As Type **103**—HORIZ: 6l. Fencing; 10l. Cycling. VERT: 12l. Diving; 50l. Spirit of Victory.

108

109 Rila Monastery

1931. Air.

316	**108**	1l. green	25	10
316a		1l. purple	10	10
317		2l. purple	25	10
317a		2l. green	15	10
318		6l. blue	35	20
318a		6l. red	40	20
319		12l. red	60	25
319a		12l. blue	50	30
320		20l. violet	60	40
321		30l. orange	1·25	75
322		50l. brown	1·50	95

1932. Air.

323	**109**	18l. green	55·00	40·00
324		24l. red	50·00	35·00
325		28l. blue	35·00	24·00

1934. Surch **2**.

333	**101**	2 on 3l. olive	3·75	35

111 Defending the Pass

113 Convalescent Home, Troyan

1934. Unveiling of Shipka Pass Memorial.

334	**111**	1l. green	45	50
340		1l. green	45	50
335	–	2l. red	45	20
341	–	2l. orange	45	20
336	–	3l. brown	1·50	1·50
342	–	3l. yellow	1·50	1·50
337	–	4l. red	1·25	40
343	–	4l. red	1·25	40
338	–	7l. blue	2·25	1·75
344	–	7l. light blue	2·25	1·75
339	–	14l. purple	7·50	7·50
345	–	14l. bistre	7·50	7·50

DESIGNS—VERT: 2l. Shipka Memorial; 3, 7l. Veteran standard-bearer; 14l. Widow showing memorial to orphans. HORIZ: 4l. Bulgarian veteran.

1935. Sunday Delivery stamps.

346	**113**	1l. red and brown	45	10
347		1l. blue and green	45	10
348	–	5l. blue and red	1·75	60

DESIGN: 5l. Convalescent Home, Bakya.

114 Capt. Georgi Mamarchef

115 Aleksandr Nevski Cathedral, Sofia

1935. Centenary of Turnovo Insurrection.

349	–	1l. blue	85	35
350	**114**	2l. purple	85	60

DESIGN: 1l. Velcho Atanasov Dzhamdzhiyata.

1935. 5th Balkan Football Tournament.

351	–	1l. green	1·60	1·50
352	**115**	2l. grey	3·00	2·50
353	–	4l. red	5·50	4·00
354	–	7l. blue	12·50	9·00
355	–	14l. orange	10·00	8·00
356	–	50l. brown	£140	£150

DESIGNS—HORIZ: 1l. Match in progress at Yunak Stadium, Sofia; 4l. Footballers. VERT: 7l. Herald and Balkan map; 14l. Footballer and trophy; 50l. Trophy.

116 Girl Gymnast

117 Janos Hunyadi

1935. 8th Bulgarian Gymnastic Tournament. Dated "12–14. VII. 1935".

357	–	1l. green	1·75	2·00
358	–	2l. blue	2·50	2·00
359	**116**	4l. red	6·00	5·00
360	–	7l. blue	6·50	6·50
361	–	14l. brown	6·50	7·00
362	–	50l. orange	90·00	£100

DESIGNS—VERT: 1l. Parallel bars; 2l. Male gymnast in uniform; 7l. Pole vault; 50l. Athlete and lion. HORIZ: 14l. Yunak Stadium, Sofia.

1935. Unveiling of Monument to Ladislas III of Poland at Varna. Inscr "WARNEN CZYK(A)", etc.

363	**117**	1l. orange	75	45
364	–	2l. red	2·25	60
365	–	4l. red	9·00	4·50
366	–	7l. blue	1·75	1·40
367	–	14l. green	1·75	1·10

DESIGNS—VERT: 2l. King Ladislas of Hungary enthroned (22 × 32 mm); 7l. King Ladislas in armour (20 × 31 mm). HORIZ: 4l. Varna Memorial (33 × 24 mm); 14l. Battle scene (30 × 25 mm).

118 Dimitur

119

120

1935. 67th Death Anniv of Khadzhi Dimitur (revolutionary).

368	–	1l. green	1·75	55
369	**118**	2l. brown	2·25	1·10
370	–	4l. red	5·00	3·25
371	–	7l. blue	6·50	5·00
372	–	14l. orange	6·50	6·00

DESIGNS—VERT: 1l. Dimitur's monument at Sliven; 7l. Revolutionary group (dated 1868). HORIZ: 4l. Dimitur and Stefan Karadzha (revolutionary); 14l. Dimitur's birthplace at Sliven.

1936.

373	**119**	10s. red	10	10
373a		15s. green	10	10
374	**120**	30s. red	10	10
374a		30s. brown	10	10
374b		30s. blue	10	10
375		50s. blue	10	10
375a		50s. red	10	10
375b		50s. green	10	10

121 Nesebur

122 St. Cyril and St. Methodius

1936. Slav Geographical and Ethnographical Congress, Sofia.

376	–	1l. violet	1·00	1·50
377	–	2l. blue	1·00	1·25
378	**121**	7l. blue	3·25	2·50

DESIGNS—25 × 34 mm: 1l. Meteorological Bureau, Mt. Musala; 23 × 34 mm: 2l. Peasant girl.

1937. Millenary of Introduction of Cyrillic Alphabet and Slavonic Liturgy.

379	**122**	1l. green	35	15
380		2l. purple	35	15
381	–	4l. red	45	15
382	**122**	7l. blue	1·50	1·10
383	–	14l. red	1·50	1·25

DESIGN: 4., 14l. The Saints Preaching.

124 Princess Marie Louise

125 King Boris III

1937.

No.	Type	Description	Unused	Used
384	124	1l. green	35	10
385		2l. red	40	15
386		4l. red	40	20

1937. 19th Anniv of Accession.

No.	Type	Description	Unused	Used
387	125	2l. red	30	30

126 Harvesting

129 Prince Simeon

1938. Agricultural Products.

No.	Type	Description	Unused	Used
388	126	10s. orange	10	10
389		10s. red	10	10
390	–	15s. red	30	10
391	–	15s. purple	30	10
392	–	30s. brown	15	10
393	–	30s. brown	15	10
394	–	50s. blue	55	10
395	–	50s. black	55	10
396	–	1l. green	60	10
397	–	1l. green	60	10
398	–	2l. red	55	10
399	–	2l. brown	55	10
400	–	3l. purple	1·10	35
401	–	3l. purple	1·10	35
402	–	4l. brown	70	20
403	–	4l. purple	70	20
404	–	7l. violet	1·40	55
405	–	7l. blue	1·40	55
406	–	14l. brown	2·25	1·40
407	–	14l. brown	2·25	1·40

DESIGNS—VERT: 15s. Sunflower; 30s. Wheat; 50s. Chickens and eggs; 1l. Grapes; 3l. Strawberries; 4l. Girl carrying grapes; 7l. Roses; 14l. Tobacco leaves. HORIZ: 2l. "Attar of Roses".

1938. 1st Birthday of Heir Apparent.

No.	Type	Description	Unused	Used
408	129	1l. green	10	10
409		2l. red	15	10
410	–	4l. red	20	10
411	129	7l. blue	80	35
412	–	14l. brown	80	35

DESIGN: 4, 14l. Another portrait.

131 King Boris III

132 First Locomotive in Bulgaria, 1866

1938. 20th Anniv of King's Accession. Portraits of King in various uniforms.

No.	Type	Description	Unused	Used
413	131	1l. green	10	10
414	–	2l. red	75	10
415	–	4l. brown	10	10
416	–	7l. blue	30	30
417	–	14l. mauve	30	30

1939. 50th Anniv of Bulgarian State Railways. Locomotive types dated "1888–1938".

No.	Type	Description	Unused	Used
418	132	1l. green	55	50
419	–	2l. brown	70	50
420	–	4l. orange	2·00	80
421	–	7l. blue	7·25	6·50

DESIGNS: 2l. Class 01 steam locomotive; 4l. Train crossing viaduct; 7l. King Boris as engine-driver.

133 P.O. Emblem

135 Gymnast

1939. 60th Anniv of Bulgarian P.O. Inscr "1879 1939".

No.	Type	Description	Unused	Used
422	133	1l. green	15	10
423	–	2l. red (G.P.O., Sofia)	20	10

1939. Yunak Gymnastic Society's Rally, Sofia.

No.	Type	Description	Unused	Used
424	135	1l. green	25	15
425	–	2l. red	25	15
426	–	4l. brown	40	15
427	–	7l. blue	1·40	60
428	–	14l. mauve	6·00	4·50

DESIGNS: 2l. Yunak badge; 4l. "The Discus-thrower" (statue by Miron); 7l. Rhythmic dancer; 14l. Athlete holding weight aloft.

Наводнението
1939
1+1
лева

(**136**) ("Inundation 1939")

1939. Sevlievo and Turnovo Floods Relief Fund. Surch as T **136** and value.

No.	Type	Description	Unused	Used
429	39	1l.+1l. on 15s. grey	15	15
430	73	2l.+1l. on 1½l. olive	15	15
431		4l.+2l. on 2l. green	20	20
432		7l.+4l. on 3l. blue	55	55
433		14l.+7l. on 5l. red	1·10	1·10

137 Mail Plane

138 King Boris III

1940. Air.

No.	Type	Description	Unused	Used
434	137	1l. green	15	10
435	–	2l. red	2·10	10
436	–	4l. orange	20	10
437	–	6l. blue	25	15
438	–	10l. brown	3·75	1·25
439	–	12l. brown	1·00	35
440		16l. violet	1·10	55
441	–	19l. blue	1·25	75
442	–	30l. mauve	1·90	1·10
443	–	45l. violet	4·75	2·25
444	–	70l. red	5·00	2·75
445	–	100l. blue	12·00	8·00

DESIGNS—VERT: Aircraft over: King Asen's Tower (2l.), Bachovo Monastery (4l.), Aleksandr Nevski Cathedral, Sofia (45l.), Shipka Pass Memorial (70l.); 10l. Airplane, mail train and express motor cycle; 30l. Airplane and swallow; 100l. Airplane and Royal cypher. HORIZ: 6l. Loading mails at aerodrome. Aircraft over: Sofia Palace (12l.), Mt. El Tepe (16l.), Rila Lakes and mountains (19l.).

1940.

No.	Type	Description	Unused	Used
445a	138	1l. green	15	10
446		2l. red	30	10

139 First Bulgarian Postage Stamp

1940. Cent of 1st Adhesive Postage Stamp.

No.	Type	Description	Unused	Used
447	139	10l. olive	1·50	1·25
448	–	20l. blue	1·50	1·25

DESIGN: 20l. has scroll dated "1840–1940".

140 Grapes

142 King Boris III

141 Ploughing

1940.

No.	Type	Description	Unused	Used
449	140	10s. orange	10	10
450	–	15s. blue	10	10
451	141	30s. brown	10	10
452	–	50s. violet	10	10
452a	–	50s. green	10	10
453	142	1l. green	10	10
454		2l. red	10	10
455		4l. orange	10	10
456		6l. violet	20	10
457		7l. blue	25	10
458		10l. green	25	10

DESIGNS—VERT: 15s. Beehive. HORIZ: 50s. Shepherd and flock.

143 Peasant Couple and King Boris

144 King Boris and Map of Dobrudja

1940. Recovery of Dobrudja from Rumania. Designs incorporating miniature portrait of King Boris.

No.	Type	Description	Unused	Used
464	143	1l. green	15	10
465	–	2l. red	15	10
466	144	4l. brown	15	10
467		7l. blue	55	30

DESIGN—VERT: 2l. Bulgarian flags and wheat-field.

145 Bee-keeping

1940. Agricultural Scenes.

No.	Type	Description	Unused	Used
468	–	10s. purple	10	10
469	–	10s. blue	10	10
470	–	15s. green	10	10
471	–	15s. olive	10	10
472	145	30s. orange	10	10
473		30s. green	10	10
474	–	50s. violet	10	10
475	–	50s. purple	10	10
476	–	3l. brown	55	10
477	–	3l. black	60	40
478	–	5l. brown	1·25	50
479	–	5l. blue	75	40

DESIGNS: 10s. Threshing; 15s. Ploughing with oxen; 50s. Picking apples; 3l. Shepherd; 5l. Cattle.

146 Pencko Slaveikov (poet)

147 St. Ivan Rilski

1940. National Relief.

No.	Type	Description	Unused	Used
480	146	1l. green	10	10
481	–	2l. red	15	10
482	147	3l. brown	15	10
483	–	4l. orange	15	10
484	–	7l. blue	1·00	75
485	–	10l. brown	2·00	75

DESIGNS: 2l. Bishop Sofronii of Vratsa; 4l. Marin Drinov (historian); 7l. Chernorisets Khratur (monk); 10l. Kolo Ficheto (writer).

148 Johannes Gutenberg

149 Nikola Karastoyanov

1940. 500th Anniv of Invention of Printing and Centenary of Bulgarian Printing.

No.	Type	Description	Unused	Used
486	148	1l. green	15	10
487	149	2l. brown	15	10

150 Botev

151 Arrival in Koslodui

1941. 65th Death Anniv of Khristo Botev (poet and revolutionary).

No.	Type	Description	Unused	Used
488	150	1l. green	10	10
489	151	2l. red	15	10
490	–	3l. brown	55	35

DESIGN—VERT: 3l. Botev Memorial Cross.

152 National History Museum

1941. Buildings in Sofia.

No.	Type	Description	Unused	Used
491	152	14l. brown	95	60
492	–	20l. green	35	15
493	–	50l. blue	1·75	1·25

DESIGNS: 20l. Tsarita Icanna Workers' Hospital; 50l. National Bank.

153 Thasos Island

154 Ohrid

1941. Reacquisition of Macedonia.

No.	Type	Description	Unused	Used
494	–	1l. green	10	10
495	153	2l. orange	10	10
496	–	2l. red	10	10
497	–	4l. brown	15	10
498	154	7l. blue	45	30

DESIGNS—VERT: 1l. Macedonian girl. HORIZ: 2l. (No. 496) King Boris and map dated "1941"; 4l. Poganovski Monastery.

155 Children on Beach

1942. Sunday Delivery. Inscr as in T **155**.

No.	Type	Description	Unused	Used
499	–	1l. green	10	10
500	155	2l. orange	10	10
501	–	5l. blue	30	25

DESIGNS: 1l. St. Konstantin Sanatorium, Varna; 5l. Sun-bathing terrace, Bankya.

156 Bugler at Camp

157 Folk Dancers

1942. "Work and Joy". Inscr as at foot of T **157**.

No.	Type	Description	Unused	Used
502	–	1l. green	10	10
503	–	2l. red	15	10
504	–	4l. black	15	10
505	156	7l. blue	20	10
506	157	14l. brown	35	20

DESIGNS—VERT: 1l. Guitarist and accordion player; 2l. Camp orchestra; 4l. Hoisting the flag.

158 Wounded Soldier

159 Queen visiting Wounded

1942. War Invalids. Inscr as T **158/9**.

No.	Type	Description	Unused	Used
507	158	1l. green	10	10
508	–	2l. red	10	10
509	–	4l. orange	10	10
510	–	7l. blue	10	10
511	–	14l. brown	10	10
512	159	20l. black	30	10

DESIGNS—HORIZ: 2l. Soldier and family; 4l. First aid on battlefield; 7l. Widow and orphans at grave; 14l. Unknown Soldiers Memorial.

160 Khan Kubrat (ruled 595–642)

161 King Boris III

1942. Historical series.

No.	Type	Description	Unused	Used
513	160	10s. black	10	10
514	–	15s. blue	10	10
515	–	30s. mauve	10	10
516	–	50s. blue	10	10
517	–	1l. green	10	10
518	–	2l. red	10	10
519	–	3l. brown	10	10
520	–	4l. orange	10	10
521	–	5l. green	15	10
522	–	7l. blue	15	10
523	–	10l. black	15	10
524	–	14l. olive	15	10
525	–	20l. brown	50	20
526	–	30l. black	90	30

DESIGNS: 15s. Cavalry charge (Khan as parukh, 680–701); 30s. Equestrian statue of Khan Krum (803–814); 50s. Baptism of King Boris I; 1l. St. Naum's School; 2l. King Boris crowns his son, Tsar Simeon; 3l. Golden Era of Bulgarian literature; 4l. Trial of Bogomil Vasilii; 5l. Proclamation of Second Bulgarian Empire; 7l. Ivan Asen II (1214–81) at Tebizond; 10l. Expulsion of Eutimil Patriarch of Turnovo; 14l. Wandering minstrels; 20l. Father Paisii Khilendarski (historian); 30l. Shipka Pass Memorial.

1944. King Boris Mourning Issue. Portraits dated "1894–1943". Perf or imperf.

No.	Type	Description	Unused	Used
527	161	1l. olive	10	10
528	–	2l. brown	15	15
529	–	4l. brown	15	15

530 – 5l. violet 35 35
531 – 7l. blue 35 35

163 King Simeon II

ВСИЧКО
ЗА
ФРОНТА
(164)

1944.
532 **163** 3l. orange 10 10

1945. "All for the Front". Parcel Post stamps optd as T **164** or surch also.
533 P **163** 1l. red 10 10
534 4l. on 1l. red 10 10
535 7l. purple 10 10
536 20l. brown 15 10
537 30l. purple 15 10
538 50l. orange 40 20
539 100l. blue 70 45

1945. Air. Optd with airplane or surch also.
540 **142** 1l. green 10 10
541 4l. orange 15 10
542 P **163** 10l. on 100l. yellow 30 15
543 45l. on 100l. yellow 35 15
544 75l. on 100l. yellow 55 30
545 100l. yellow 85 40
Nos. 540/1 are perf; the rest imperf.

167

1945. Slav Congress. Perf or imperf.
546 **167** 4l. red 10 10
547 10l. blue 10 10
548 50l. red 30 30

СЪБИРАЙТЕ
ВСЪКАКВИ
ПАРЦАЛИ
(**168**) "Collect All Rags"

СЪБИРАЙТЕ
СТАРО
ЖЕЛЪЗО
(**169**) "Collect Old Iron"

СЪБИРАЙТЕ
ХАРТИЕНИ
ОТПАДЪЦИ
(**170**) "Collect Wastepaper"

1945. Salvage Campaign. Nos. 457/9 optd with T **168/70**.
549 **142** 1l. green 15 10
550 2l. red 50 10
551 4l. orange 30 10
Prices are the same for these stamps with any one of the overprints illustrated.

171 Lion Rampant

172

1945. Lion Rampant, in various frames.
552 – 30s. green 10 10
553 – 50s. blue 10 10
554 **171** 1l. green 10 10
555 – 2l. brown 10 10
556 – 4l. blue 10 10
557 – 5l. violet 10 10
558 **172** 9l. grey 10 10
559 – 10l. blue 10 10
560 – 15l. brown 20 10
561 – 20l. black 20 10
562 – 20l. red 20 10

173 Chain-breaker

174 "VE Day"

1945. Liberty Loan. Imperf.
563 **173** 50l. orange 15 10
564 50l. lake 15 10
565 – 100l. blue 20 10
566 – 100l. brown 20 10
567 – 150l. red 45 20
568 – 150l. green 45 20
569 – 200l. olive 75 60
570 – 200l. blue 75 60
DESIGNS: 100l. Hand holding coin; 150l. Water-mill; 200l. Coin and symbols of industry and agriculture.

1945. "Victory in Europe".
571 **174** 10l. green and brown 10 10
572 50l. green and red 30 10

175

176

1945. 1st Anniv of Fatherland Front Coalition.
573 **175** 1l. olive 10 10
574 4l. blue 10 10
575 5l. mauve 10 10
576 **176** 10l. blue 10 10
577 20l. red 15 10
578 **175** 50l. green 30 20
579 100l. brown 50 30

177 Refugee Children

178 Red Cross Train

1946. Red Cross. Cross in red.
580 **177** 2l. olive 10 10
645d 2l. brown 10 10
581 – 4l. violet 10 10
645e – 4l. black 10 10
582 **177** 10l. purple 10 10
645f 10l. green 15 10
583 – 20l. dark blue 15 10
645g – 20l. light blue 25 15
584 – 30l. brown 15 15
645h – 30l. green 35 25
585 **178** 35l. black 2·25 1·50
645i 35l. green 1·75 1·10
586 – 50l. purple 35 25
645j – 50l. lake 70 45
587 **178** 100l. brown 4·25 2·75
645k 100l. blue 3·50 2·00
DESIGNS—HORIZ: 4l., 20l. Soldier on stretcher. VERT: 30l., 50l. Nurse and wounded soldier.

179 Postal Savings Emblem

180 Savings Bank-Note

1946. 50th Anniv of Savings Bank.
588 **179** 4l. red 40 25
589 **180** 10l. olive 15 10
590 – 20l. blue 15 10
591 – 50l. black 60 55
DESIGNS—VERT: 20l. Child filling money-box; 50l. Postal Savings Bank.

181 Arms of Russia and Bulgaria and Spray of Oak

182 Lion Rampant

1946. Bulgo-Russian Congress.
592 **181** 4l. red 7·00 7·00
593 4l. orange 10 10
594 20l. blue 7·00 7·00
595 20l. green 20 20

1946. Stamp Day. Imperf.
596 **182** 20l. blue 40 30

183

190

1946. Air. Inscr "PAR AVION".
597 **183** 1l. purple 15 10
598 2l. grey 15 10
599 – 4l. black 30 15
600 – 6l. blue 40 30
601 – 10l. green 10 10
602 – 12l. brown 10 10
603 – 16l. purple 10 10
604 – 19l. red 10 10
605 – 30l. orange 15 10
606 – 45l. green 45 15
607 – 75l. brown 55 15
608 **190** 100l. red 1·10 25
609 – 100l. grey 1·10 25
DESIGNS—23 × 18 mm: 4l. Bird carrying envelope; 100l. (No. 609), Airplane. 18 × 23 mm: 6l. Airplane and envelope; 10, 12, 19l. Wings and posthorn; 16l. Wings and envelope; 30l. Airplane; 45, 75l. Dove and posthorn.

192 Stamboliiski

193 Flags of Albania, Bulgaria, Yugoslavia and Rumania

1946. 25th Death Anniv of Aleksandur Stamboliiski (Prime Minister 1919–23).
610 **192** 100l. orange 7·00 7·00

1946. Balkan Games.
611 **193** 100l. brown 1·40 1·40

196 Artillery

195 Junkers Ju87B "Stuka" Dive Bombers

1946. Military and Air Services.
612 – 2l. red 10 10
613 – 4l. grey 10 10
614 **196** 5l. red 10 10
615 **195** 6l. brown 10 10
616 – 9l. mauve 10 10
617 – 10l. violet 10 10
618 – 20l. blue 35 15
619 – 30l. orange 35 15
620 – 40l. olive 40 20
621 – 50l. green 50 50
622 – 60l. brown 75 50
DESIGNS—HORIZ: 2, 20l. Grenade thrower and machine-gunner; 9l. Building pontoon-bridge; 10, 30l. Cavalry charge; 40l. Supply column; 50l. Motor convoy; 60l. Tanks. VERT: 4l. Grenade thrower.

203 St. Ivan Rilski

208 "New Republic"

1946. Death Millenary of St. Ivan Rilski.
623 **203** 1l. brown 10 10
624 – 4l. sepia 10 10
625 – 10l. green 25 10
626 – 20l. blue 30 10
627 – 50l. red 1·25 55
DESIGNS—HORIZ: 4l. Rila Monastery; 10l. Monastery entrance; 50l. Cloistered courtyard. VERT: 20l. Aerial view of Monastery.

1946. Referendum.
628 **208** 4l. red 10 10
629 20l. blue 10 10
630 50l. brown 25 15

209 Assault

210 Ambuscade

1946. Partisan Activities.
631 **209** 1l. purple 10 10
632 **210** 4l. green 10 10
633 – 5l. brown 10 10
634 **210** 10l. red 10 10
635 **209** 20l. blue 30 10
636 – 30l. brown 30 15
637 – 50l. black 40 25
DESIGNS—VERT: 5l., 50l. Partisan riflemen; 30l. Partisan leader.

211 Nurse and Children

212a Partisans

1947. Winter Relief.
638 **211** 1l. violet 10 10
639 – 4l. red 10 10
640 – 9l. olive 10 10
641 **211** 10l. grey 10 10
642 – 20l. blue 15 10
643 – 30l. brown 15 10
644 – 40l. red 30 25
645 **211** 50l. green 50 35
DESIGNS: 4l., 9l. Child carrying gifts; 20l., 40l. Hungry child; 30l. Destitute mother and child.

1947. Anti-fascists of 1923, 1941 and 1944 Commem.
645a – 10l. brown and orange 40 40
645b **212a** 20l. dp blue & lt blue 40 40
645c – 70l. brown and red 35·00 35·00
DESIGNS—HORIZ: 10l. Group of fighters; 70l. Soldier addressing crowd.

213 Olive Branch

214 Dove of Peace

1947. Peace.
646 **213** 4l. olive 10 10
647 **214** 10l. brown 10 10
648 20l. blue 20 15
"BULGARIA" is in Roman characters on the 20l.

215 "U.S.A." and "Bulgaria"

1947. Air. Stamp Day and New York International Philatelic Exhibition.
649 **215** 70l.+30l. brown 1·75 2·00

216 Esperanto Emblem and Map of Bulgaria

1947. 30th Esperanto Jubilee Congress, Sofia.
650 **216** 20l.+10l. purple & green 75 50

217 G.P.O., Sofia

218 National Theatre, Sofia

219 Parliament Building

220 President's Palace

221 G.P.O., Sofia

1947. Government Buildings. (a) T **217**.
651 1l. green 10 10

(b) T **218**.
652 50s. green 10 10
653 2l. red 10 10

654 4l. blue 10 10
655 9l. red 25 10

(c) T **219**.

656 50s. green 10 10
657 2l. blue 10 10
658 4l. blue 10 10
659 20l. blue 85 30

(d) T **220**.

660 1l. green 10 10

(e) T **221**.

661 1l. green 10 10
662 2l. red 10 10
663 4l. blue 10 10

222 Hydro-electric Power Station and Dam

223 Emblem of Industry

1947. Reconstruction.
664 **222** 4l. green 15 15
665 – 9l. brown (Miner) 15 15
666 **223** 20l. blue 25 25
667 – 40l. green (Motor plough) 85 85

224 Exhibition Building

225 Former Residence of the French Poet Lamartine

226 Rose and Grapes

227 Airplane over City

1947. Plovdiv Fair. (a) Postage.
668 **224** 4l. red 10 10
669 **225** 9l. red 10 10
670 **226** 20l. blue 25 15

(b) Air. Imperf.

671 **227** 40l. green . . . . 1·10 1·00

228 Cycle Racing

229 Basketball

231 V. E. Aprilov

1947. Balkan Games.
672 **228** 2l. lilac 40 20
673 **229** 4l. green 40 20
674 – 9l. brown . . . . 1·10 40
675 – 20l. blue . . . . 1·25 50
676 – 60l. red . . . . 3·00 2·00
DESIGNS—VERT: 9l. Chess; 20l. Football; 60l. Balkan flags.

1947. Death Cent of Vasil Aprilov (educationist).
678 – 4l. red 15 10
677 **231** 40l. blue 35 25
DESIGN: 4l. Another portrait of Aprilov.

233 Postman

235 Geno Kirov

1947. Postal Employees' Relief Fund.
679 **233** 4l.+2l. olive 10 10
680 – 10l.+5l. red 20 20
681 – 20l.+10l. blue 25 25
682 – 40l.+20l. brown . . . . 1·00 1·00
DESIGNS: 10l. Linesman; 20l. Telephonists; 40l. Wireless masts.

1947. Theatrical Artists' Benevolent Fund.
683 **235** 50s. brown 10 10
684 – 1l. green 10 10
685 – 2l. green 10 10
686 – 3l. blue 10 10
687 – 4l. red 10 10
688 – 5l. purple 10 10
689 – 9l.+5l. blue 15 15
690 – 10l.+6l. red 20 20
691 – 15l.+7l. violet 25 25
692 – 20l.+15l. blue 50 25
693 – 30l.+20l. purple . . . . 1·00 85
PORTRAITS: 1l. Zlotina Nedeva; 2l. Ivan Popov; 3l. Atanas Kirchev; 4l. Elena Snezhina; 5l. Stoyan Buchvarov; 9l. Khristo Ganchev; 10l. Adriana Budevska; 15l. Vasil Kirkov; 20l. Save Orgnyanov; 30l. Krustyn Sarafov.

236 "Rodina" (freighter)

1947. National Shipping Revival.
694 **236** 50l. blue . . . . 1·25 35

237 Worker and Flag

238 Worker and Globe

1948. 2nd General Workers' Union Congress.
695 **237** 4l. blue (postage) 15 10
696 **238** 60l. brown (air) 65 50

239

240

1948. Leisure and Culture.
697 **239** 4l. red 15 10
698 **240** 20l. blue 25 15
699 – 40l. green 40 20
700 – 60l. brown 65 40
DESIGNS—VERT: 40l. Workers' musical interlude; 60l. Sports girl.

241 Kikola Vaptsarov

242 Petlyakov Pe-2 Bomber over Baldwin's Tower

1948. Poets.
701 **241** 4l. red on cream 10 10
702 – 9l. brown on cream . . . 15 10
703 – 15l. purple on cream . . . 15 15
704 – 20l. blue on cream . . . 20 15
705 – 45l. green on cream . . . 65 75
PORTRAITS: 9l. Peya Yavorov; 15l. Khristo Smirnenski; 20l. Ivan Vazov; 45l. Petko Slaveikov.

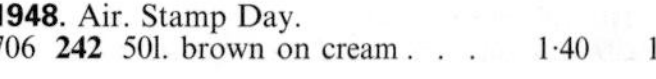

1948. Air. Stamp Day.
706 **242** 50l. brown on cream . . . 1·40 1·10

243 Soldier

244 Peasants and Soldiers

1948. Soviet Army Monument.
707 **243** 4l. red on cream 10 10
708 **244** 10l. green on cream . . . 15 10
709 – 20l. blue on cream . . . 25 15
710 – 60l. olive on cream . . . 75 45
DESIGNS—HORIZ: 20l. Soldiers of 1878 and 1944. VERT: 60l. Stalin and Spassky Tower, Kremlin.

245 Bath, Gorna Banya

246 Lion Emblem

1948. Bulgarian Health Resorts.
711 **245** 2l. red 10 10
712 – 3l. orange 10 10
713 – 4l. blue 15 10
717 – 5l. brown 15 10
714 – 10l. purple 25 10
718 – 15l. olive 35 10
715 **245** 20l. blue . . . . 1·00 15
716 – 20l. blue . . . . 1·50 15
DESIGNS: 3, 10l. Bath, Bankya; 4, 20l. (No. 716), Mineral bath, Sofia; 5, 15l. Malyovitsa Peak.

1948.

719 **246** 50s. orange 10 10
719a 50s. brown 10 10
720 1l. green 10 10
721 9l. black 15 10

247 Dimitur Blagoev

248 Youths marching

1948. 25th Anniv of September Uprising.
722 **247** 4l. brown 10 10
723 – 9l. orange 10 10
724 – 20l. blue 40 25
725 **248** 60l. brown . . . . 1·00 75
DESIGNS—VERT: 9l. Gabrit Genov. HORIZ: 20l. Bishop Andrei Monument.

249 Khristo Smirnenski

250 Miner

1948. 500th Birth Anniv of Smirnenski (poet and revolutionary).
726 **249** 4l. blue 10 10
727 16l. brown 15 10

1948.

728 **250** 4l. blue 75 25

251 Battle of Grivitsa

1948. Treaty of Friendship with Rumania.
729 **251** 20l. blue (postage) 20 10
730 – 40l. black (air) 25 15
731 – 100l. mauve 95 85
DESIGNS: 40l. Parliament Buildings in Sofia and Bucharest; 100l. Projected Danube Bridge.

252 Botev's House, Kalofer

253 Botev

1948. Birth Centenary of Khristo Botev (poet and revolutionary).
732 **252** 1l. green 10 10
733 **253** 4l. brown 15 10
734 4l. purple 15 10
735 – 9l. violet 40 10
736 – 15l. brown 20 10
737a – 20l. blue 20 10
738 – 40l. brown 45 20
739 – 50l. black 65 30
DESIGNS—HORIZ: 9l. River paddle-steamer "Radetski"; 15l. Village of Kalofer; 40l. Botev's mother and verse of poem. VERT: 20l. Botev in uniform; 50l. Quill, pistol and laurel wreath.

254 Lenin

255 Road Construction

1949. 25th Death Anniv of Lenin. Inscr "1924–1949".
740 **254** 4l. brown 15 10
741 – 20l. red 40 25
DESIGN—(27 × 37 mm): 20l. Lenin as an orator.

1949. National Youth Movement.
742 **255** 4l. red 20 10
743 – 5l. brown . . . . 1·10 40
744 – 9l. green . . . . 2·25 30
745 – 10l. violet 50 20
746 – 20l. blue 85 45
747 – 40l. brown . . . . . . 1·75 1·00
DESIGNS—HORIZ: 5l. Tunnel construction; 9l. Class 10 steam locomotive; 10l. Textile workers; 20l. Girl driving tractor; 40l. Workers in lorry.

256 Lisunov Li-2 over Pleven Mausoleum

1949. Air. 7th Philatelic Congress, Pleven.
748 **256** 50l. bistre . . . . 4·50 3·75

257 G. Dimitrov

258 G. Dimitrov

1949. Death of Georgi Dimitrov (Prime Minister 1946–49).
749 **257** 4l. red 15 10
750 **258** 20l. blue . . . . 1·00 25

259 Hydro-electric Power Station

260 Symbols of Agriculture and Industry

1949. Five Year Industrial and Agricultural Plan.
751 **259** 4l. olive (postage) 15 10
752 – 9l. red 25 15
753 – 15l. violet 40 20
754 – 20l. blue . . . . 1·25 40
755 **260** 50l. brown (air) . . . . . 2·75 1·50
DESIGNS—VERT: 9l. Cement works; 15l. Tractors in garage. HORIZ: 20l. Tractors in field.

261 Javelin and Grenade Throwing **262** Motor-cyclist and Tractor

1949. Physical Culture Campaign.
756 **261** 4l. red 30 15
757 – 9l. olive . . . . 1·40 50
758 **262** 20l. blue . . . . 2·00 1·00
759 – 50l. red . . . . 5·00 2·75
DESIGNS—HORIZ: 9l. Hurdling and leaping barbed-wire. VERT: 50l. Two athletes marching.

263 Globe **265** Guardsman with Dog

264 Guardsman and Peasant

1949. Air. 75th Anniv of Universal Postal Union.
760 **263** 50l. blue . . . . 2·40 1·10

1949. Frontier Guards.
761 **264** 4l. brown (postage) . . . 15 15
762 – 20l. blue . . . . 1·00 75
763 **265** 60l. green (air) . . . . . 2·75 2·75
DESIGN—VERT: 20l. Guardsman on coast.

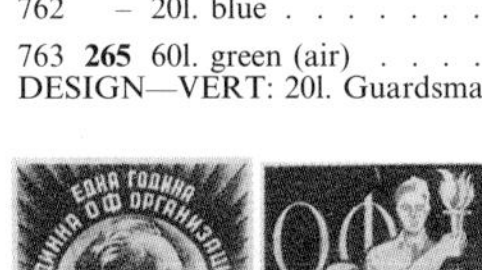

266 Georgi Dimitrov (Prime Minister 1946–49) **267** "Unanimity" **268** Zosif Stalin

1949. Fatherland Front.
764 **266** 4l. brown 15 10
765 **267** 9l. violet 20 10
766 – 20l. blue 30 20
767 – 50l. red . . . . 1·00 1·00
DESIGNS: 20l. Man and woman with wheelbarrow and spade; 50l. Young people marching with banners.

1949. 70th Birthday of Stalin.
768 **268** 4l. orange 25 10
769 – 40l. red 90 70
DESIGN—VERT: (25 × 37 mm): 40l. Stalin as an orator.

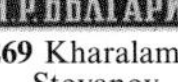

269 Kharalampi Stoyanov **270** Strikers and Train

1950. 30th Anniv of Railway Strike.
770 **269** 4l. brown 15 10
771 **270** 20l. blue . . . . 1·10 40
772 – 60l. olive . . . . 2·25 1·25
DESIGN—VERT: 60l. Two workers and flag.

271 Miner **272** Class 48 Steam Shunting Locomotive

1950.
773 **271** 1l. olive 10 10
773a 1l. violet 15 10
774 **272** 2l. black . . . . 3·00 40
774a 2l. brown . . . . 2·50 25
775 – 3l. blue 45 10
776a – 4l. green 40 10
777 – 5l. red 40 10
778 – 9l. grey 20 10
779 – 10l. purple 25 10
780 – 15l. red 45 15
781 – 20l. blue 80 45
DESIGNS—VERT: 3l. Ship under construction; 10l. Power station; 15l., 20l. Woman in factory. HORIZ: 4l. Tractor; 5l., 9l. Threshing machines.

273 Kolarov

1950. Death of Vasil Kolarov (Prime Minister 1949–50). Inscr "1877–1950".
782 **273** 4l. brown 10 10
783 – 20l. blue 40 35
DESIGN—(27½ × 39½ mm): 20l. Portrait as Type **273**, but different frame.

274 Starislas Dospevski (self-portrait) **274a** "In the Field" (Khristo Storclev)

1950. Painters and paintings.
784 **274** 1l. green 30 15
785 – 4l. orange . . . . 1·60 25
786 – 9l. brown . . . . 2·10 25
787 **274a** 15l. brown . . . . . . 2·90 70
788 20l. blue . . . . 4·75 2·00
789 – 40l. brown . . . . . . 5·50 2·75
790 – 60l. orange . . . . . . 6·25 4·00
DESIGNS—VERT: 4l. King Kaloyan and Desislava; 9l. Nikolai Pavlovich; 40l. Statue of Debeyanov (Ivan Lazarov); 60l. "Peasant" (Vladimir Dimitrov the Master).

275 Ivan Vazov and Birthplace, Sopot **276a** G. Dimitrov (statesman)

1950. Birth Centenary of Ivan Vazov (poet).
791 **275** 4l. olive 15 10

1950. 1st Death Anniv of Georgi Dimitrov.
792 – 50s. brown (postage) . . 15 10
793 – 50s. green 15 10
794 **276a** 1l. brown 20 10
795 – 2l. slate 20 10
796 – 4l. purple 75 20
797 – 9l. red . . . . 1·25 40
798 – 10l. red . . . . 1·90 85
799 – 15l. grey . . . . 1·90 85
800 – 20l. blue . . . . 3·00 1·75
801 – 40l. brown (air) . . . . 5·50 3·25
DESIGNS—HORIZ: 50s. green, Dimitrov and birthplace, Kovachevtsi; 2l. Dimitrov's house, Sofia; 15l. Dimitrov signing new constitution; 20l. Dimitrov; 40l. Mausoleum. VERT: 50s. brown, 4, 9, 10l. Dimitrov in various poses.

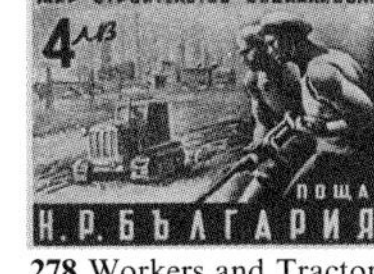

277 Runners **278** Workers and Tractor

1950.
802 **277** 4l. green 65 25
803 – 9l. brown (Cycling) . . . 85 40
804 – 20l. blue (Putting the shot) . . . . 1·10 85
805 – 40l. purple (Volleyball) . . 2·40 2·10

1950. 2nd National Peace Congress.
806 **278** 4l. red 10 10
807 – 20l. blue 40 25
DESIGN—VERT: 20l. Stalin on flag and three heads.

278b **279** Children on Beach

1950. Arms designs.
807a – 2l. brown 10 10
807b – 3l. red 10 10
807c **278b** 5l. red 10 10
807d – 9l. blue 20 10
Although inscribed "OFFICIAL MAIL", the above were issued as regular postage stamps.

1950. Sunday Delivery.
808 – 1l. green (Sanatorium) . . 15 10
809 **279** 2l. red 20 10
810 – 5l. orange (Sunbathing) . . 40 15
811 **279** 10l. blue 80 35

280 Molotov, Kolarov, Stalin and Dimitrov **281** Russian and Bulgarian Girls

1950. 2nd Anniv of Soviet–Bulgarian Treaty of Friendship.
812 **280** 4l. brown 10 10
813 – 9l. red 15 10
814 **281** 20l. blue 30 25
815 – 50l. green . . . . 2·00 75
DESIGNS—VERT: 9l. Spassky Tower and flags; 50l. Freighter and tractor.

282 Marshal Tolbukhin **284** A. S. Popov **286** Georgi Kirkov

1950. Honouring Marshal Tolbukhin.
816 **282** 4l. mauve 15 10
817 – 20l. blue . . . . 1·00 30
DESIGN—HORIZ: 20l. Bulgarians greeting Tolbukhin.

1951. 45th Death Anniv of Aleksandr Popov (radio pioneer).
818 **284** 4l. brown 25 15
819 20l. blue 85 30

1951. Anti-fascist Heroes.
823 – 1l. mauve 15 10
824 – 2l. plum 20 10
825 **286** 4l. red 20 10
826 – 9l. brown 60 40
827 – 15l. olive . . . . 1·75 70
828 – 20l. blue . . . . 1·75 1·00
829 – 50l. grey . . . . 4·25 1·50
PORTRAITS: 1l. Chankova, Adalbert Antonov-Malchika, Sasho Dimitrov and Lilyana Dimitrova; 2l. Stanke Dimitrov; 9l. Anton Ivanov; 15l. Mikhailov; 20l. Georgi Dimitrov at Leipzig; 50l. Nocho Ivanov and Acram Stoyahov.

285 First Bulgarian Truck **289** Embroidery

1951. National Occupations. (a) As T **285**.
820 – 1l. violet (Tractor) 15 10
821 – 2l. green (Steam-roller) . . 20 10
822 **285** 4l. brown 25 10

(b) As T **289**.
830 – 1l. brown (Tractor) . . . 15 10
831 – 2l. violet (Steam-roller) . . 15 10
832 – 4l. brown (Truck) 45 40
833 **289** 9l. violet 85 30
834 – 15l. purple (Carpets) . . . 1·50 1·00
835 – 20l. blue (Roses and Tobacco) . . . . . . 3·25 1·50
836 – 40l. green (Fruit) . . . . 5·00 2·10
The 9l. and 20l. are vert, the remainder horiz.

290 Turkish Attack

1951. 75th Anniv of April Uprising.
837 **290** 1l. brown 50 15
838 – 4l. green 50 15
839 – 9l. purple 85 45
840 – 20l. blue . . . . 1·25 80
841 – 40l. lake . . . . 1·90 1·50
DESIGNS—HORIZ: 4l. Proclamation of Uprising; 9l. Cannon and cavalry; 20l. Patriots in 1876 and 1944; 40l. Georgi Benkovsky and Georgi Dimitrov.

291 Dimitur Blagoev as Orator

1951. 60th Anniv of First Bulgarian Social Democratic Party Congress, Buzludzha.
842 **291** 1l. violet 20 10
843 4l. green 40 15
844 9l. purple . . . . 1·10 80

292 Babies in Creche

1951. Children's Day.
845 **292** 1l. brown 20 10
846 – 4l. purple 50 15
847 – 9l. green . . . . 1·00 35
848 – 20l. blue . . . . 2·00 1·25
DESIGNS: 4l. Children building models; 9l. Girl and children's play ground; 20l. Boy bugler and children marching.

293 Workers **294** Labour medal (Obverse) **295** Labour medal (Reverse)

1951. 3rd General Workers' Union Congress.
849 **293** 1l. black 10 10
850 – 4l. brown 15 10
DESIGN inscr "16 XII 1951"; 4l. Georgi Dimitrov and Valdo Chervenkov (Prime minister).

1952. Order of Labour.
851 **294** 1l. red 10 10
852 **295** 1l. brown 10 10
853 **294** 4l. green 10 10
854 **295** 4l. green 10 10
855 **294** 9l. violet 35 15
856 **295** 9l. blue 35 15

296 Vasil Kolarov Dam **297** G. Dimitrov and Chemical Works

1952.
857 **296** 4s. green 15 10
858 12s. violet 20 10
859 16s. brown 25 10
860 44s. red 60 10
861 80s. blue . . . . 3·00 25

1952. 70th Birth Anniv of Georgi Dimitrov (statesman). Dated "1882–1952".
862 **297** 16s. brown 40 20
863 – 44s. brown . . . . . . 1·00 35
864 – 80s. blue . . . . 1·75 1·00
DESIGNS—HORIZ: 44s. Georgi Dimitrov (Prime minister 1946–49) and Prime minister Vulko Chervenkov. VERT: 80s. Full-face portrait of Georgi Dimitrov.

298 Republika Power Station

299 N. Vaptsarov (revolutionary)

1952.

866 **298** 16s. sepia 40 10
867 44s. purple . . . . 1·25 15

1952. 10th Death Anniv of Nikola Vaptsarov (poet and revolutionary).

869 **299** 16s. lake 30 25
870 – 44s. brown . . . . 1·10 90
871 – 80s. sepia . . . . 2·10 90

PORTRAITS: 44s. Facing bayonets; 80s. Full-face.

300 Congress Delegates

1952. 40th Anniv of First Workers' Social Democratic Youth League Congress.

872 **300** 2s. lake 15 10
873 – 16s. violet 25 10
874 – 44s. green . . . . 1·50 65
875 – 80s. sepia . . . . 1·90 1·40

DESIGNS: 16s. Young partisans; 44s. Factory and guards; 80s. Dimitrov addressing young workers.

301 Attack on Winter Palace, St. Petersburg

1952. 35th Anniv of Russian Revolution. Dated "1917 1952".

876 **301** 4s. lake 10 10
877 – 8s. green 15 10
878 – 16s. blue 15 10
879 – 44s. sepia 50 20
880 – 80s. olive . . . . 1·25 40

DESIGNS: 8s. Volga–Don canal; 16s. Dove and globe; 44s. Lenin and Stalin; 80s. Lenin, Stalin and Himlay hydro-electric station.

302

303 Vintagers and Grapes

1952. Wood Carvings depicting National Products.

881 – 2s. brown 10 10
882 – 8s. green 10 10
883 – 12s. brown 20 10
884 – 16s. purple 45 10
885 **302** 28s. green 85 15
886 – 44s. brown 90 15
887 **303** 80s. blue . . . . 1·50 15
888 1l. violet . . . . 3·25 30
889 4l. red . . . . 4·25 1·90

DESIGNS—VERT: 2s. Numeral in carved frame. HORIZ: 8s. Gift-offering to idol; 12s. Birds and grapes; 16s. Rose-gathering; 44s. "Attar of Roses".

304 V. Levski

1953. 80th Anniv of Execution of Vasil Levski (revolutionary).

890 **304** 16s. brown on cream . . 15 10
891 – 44s. brown on cream . . 30 15

DESIGN: 44s. Levski addressing crowd.

305 Russian Army Crossing R. Danube

306 Mother and Children

1953. 75th Anniv of Liberation from Turkey.

892 **305** 8s. blue 30 10
893 – 16s. brown 25 10
894 – 44s. green 55 20
895 – 80s. lake . . . . 1·60 1·00
896 – 1l. black . . . . 2·00 1·60

DESIGNS—VERT: 16s. Battle of Shipka Pass. HORIZ: 44s. Peasants welcoming Russian soldiers; 80s. Bulgarians and Russians embracing; 1l. Shipka Pass memorial and Dimitrovgrad.

1953. International Women's Day.

897 **306** 16s. blue 15 10
898 16s. green 15 10

307 Karl Marx

308 May Day Parade

1953. 70th Death Anniv of Karl Marx.

899 **307** 16s. blue 15 15
900 – 44s. brown 40 25

DESIGN—VERT: 44s. Book "Das Kapital".

1953. Labour Day.

901 **308** 16s. red 20 10

309 Stalin

310 Goce Delcev (Macedonian revolutionary)

1953. Death of Stalin.

902 **309** 16s. brown 25 10
903 16s. black 25 15

1953. 50th Anniv of Ilinden–Preobrazhenie Rising.

904 **310** 16s. brown 10 10
905 – 44s. violet 40 25
906 – 1l. purple 55 30

DESIGNS. 44s. Insurgents and flag facing left. HORIZ: 1l. Insurgents and flag facing right.

311 Soldier and Insurgents

312 Dimitur Blagoev

1953. Army Day.

907 **311** 16s. red 25 10
908 – 44s. blue 65 15

DESIGN: 44s. Soldier, factories and combine-harvester.

1953. 50th Anniv of Bulgarian Workers' Social Democratic Party.

909 **312** 16s. brown 30 15
910 – 44s. red 65 20

DESIGN: 44s. Dimitrov and Blagoev.

313 Georgi Dimitrov and Vasil Kolarov

314 Railway Viaduct

1953. 30th Anniv of September Uprising.

911 **313** 8s. black 25 10
912 – 16s. brown 25 10
913 – 44s. red 80 30

DESIGNS: 16s. Insurgent and flag; 44s. Crowd of Insurgents.

1953. Bulgarian–Russian Friendship.

914 **314** 8s. blue 50 35
915 – 16s. slate 10 10
916 – 44s. brown 30 15
917 – 80s. orange 90 30

DESIGNS—HORIZ: 16s. Welder and industrial plant; 80s. Combine-harvester. VERT: 44s. Iron foundry.

315 Dog Rose

316 Vasil Kolarov Library

1953. Medicinal Flowers.

918 – 2s. blue 10 10
919 – 4s. orange 10 10
920 – 8s. turquoise 15 10
921 **315** 12s. green 15 10
922 – 12s. red 15 10
923 – 16s. blue 25 10
924 – 16s. brown 25 10
925 – 20s. red 50 10
926 – 28s. green 50 15
927 – 40s. blue 55 25
928 – 44s. brown 75 25
929 – 80s. brown . . . . 1·50 55
930 – 1l. brown . . . . 4·00 1·00
931 – 2l. purple . . . . 6·75 2·50

FLOWERS: 2s. Deadly nightshade; 4s. Thorn-apple; 8s. Sage; 16s. Great yellow gentian; 20s. Opium poppy; 28s. Peppermint; 40s. Bear-berry; 44s. Coltsfoot; 80s. Primula; 1l. Dandelion; 2l. Foxglove.

1953. 75th Anniv of Kolarov Library, Sofia.

932 **316** 44s. brown 30 15

317 Singer and Musician

318 Airplane over Mountains

1953. Amateur Theatricals.

933 **317** 16s. brown 15 10
934 – 44s. green 40 20

DESIGN: 44s. Folk-dancers.

1954. Air.

935 **318** 8s. green 10 10
936 – 12s. lake 10 10
937 – 16s. brown 15 10
938 – 20s. salmon 15 10
939 – 28s. blue 20 10
940 – 44s. purple 25 10
941 – 60s. brown 45 10
942 – 80s. green 75 25
943 – 1l. green . . . . 2·25 50
944 – 4l. blue . . . . 4·50 1·75

DESIGNS—VERT: 12s. Exhibition buildings, Plovdiv; 80s. Tirnovo; 4l. Partisans' Monument. HORIZ: 16s. Seaside promenade, Varna; 20s. Combine-harvester in cornfield; 28s. Rila Monastery; 44s. Studena hydro-electric barrage; 60s. Dimitrovgrad; 1l. Sofia University and equestrian statue.

319 Lenin and Stalin

320 Dimitur Blagoev and Crowd

1954. 30th Death Anniv of Lenin.

945 **319** 16s. brown 15 10
946 – 44s. lake 30 10
947 – 80s. blue 70 20
948 – 1l. green 95 75

DESIGNS—VERT: 44s. Lenin statue; 80s. Lenin–Stalin Mausoleum and Kremlin; 1l. Lenin.

1954. 30th Death Anniv of Blagoev.

949 **320** 16s. brown 15 10
950 – 44s. sepia 40 15

DESIGN: 44s. Blagoev writing at desk.

321 Dimitrov Speaking

322 Class 10 Steam Locomotive

1954. 5th Death Anniv of Dimitrov.

951 **321** 44s. lake 20 15
952 – 80s. brown 75 20

DESIGN—HORIZ: 80s. Dimitrov and blast-furnace.

1954. Railway Workers' Day.

953 **322** 44s. turquoise . . . . . . 1·90 20
954 44s. black . . . . 1·90 20

323 Miner Operating Machinery

324 Marching Soldiers

1954. Miners' Day.

955 **323** 44s. green 25 15

1954. 10th Anniv of Fatherland Front Government.

956 **324** 12s. lake 10 10
957 – 16s. red 10 10
958 – 28s. slate 20 10
959 – 44s. brown 25 10
960 – 80s. blue 70 30
961 – 1l. green . . . . 1·00 30

DESIGNS—VERT: 16s. Soldier and parents; 80s. Girl and boy pioneers; 1l. Dimitrov. HORIZ: 28s. Industrial plant; 44s. Dimitrov and workers.

325 Academy Building

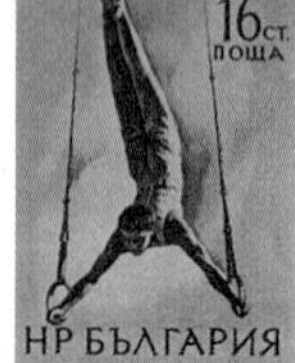

326 Gymnast

1954. 85th Anniv of Academy of Sciences.

962 **325** 80s. black . . . . 1·00 50

1954. Sports. Cream paper.

963 **326** 16s. green . . . . 1·50 20
964 – 44s. red . . . . 1·50 65
965 – 80s. brown . . . . 2·50 1·00
966 – 2l. blue . . . . 4·75 3·25

DESIGNS—VERT: 44s. Wrestlers; 2l. Ski-jumper. HORIZ: 80s. Horse-jumper.

327 Velingrad Rest Home

1954. 50th Anniv of Trade Union Movement.

967 **327** 16s. green 15 10
968 – 44s. red 15 15
969 – 80s. blue 85 30

DESIGNS—VERT: 44s. Foundryman. HORIZ: 80s. Georgi Dimitrov, Dimitur Blagoev and Georgi Kirkov.

328 Geese

329 Communist Party Building

1955.

970 **328** 2s. green 10 10
971 – 4s. olive 20 10
972 – 12s. brown 35 10
973 – 16s. brown 60 10
974 – 28s. blue 30 10
975 **329** 44s. red . . . . 10·50 20
976 – 80s. brown 70 20
977 – 1l. green . . . . 1·75 30

DESIGNS: 4s. Rooster and hens; 12s. Sow and piglets; 16s. Ewe and lambs; 28s. Telephone exchange; 80s. Flats; 1l. Cellulose factory.

330 Mill Girl

332 Rejoicing Crowds

1955. International Women's Day.

978 **330** 12s. brown 10 10
979 – 16s. green 20 10
980 – 44s. blue 75 10
981 – 44s. red 75 10

DESIGNS—HORIZ: 16s. Girl feeding cattle. VERT: 44s. Mother and baby.

1955. As Nos. 820 and 822 surch **16 CT.**

981a – 16s. on 1l. violet 20 10
982 **285** 16s. on 4l. brown . . . 75 10

1955. Labour Day.

983 **332** 16s. red 15 10
984 – 44s. blue 50 10

DESIGN: 44s. Three workers and globe.

333 St. Cyril and St. Methodius **334** Sergei Rumyantsev

1955. 1100th Anniv of 1st Bulgarian Literature. On cream paper.

985	333	4s. blue	10	10
986	–	8s. olive	10	10
987	–	16s. black	15	10
988	–	28s. red	25	15
989	–	44s. brown	45	20
990	–	80s. red	1·00	80
991	–	2l. black	2·50	1·60

DESIGNS: 8s. Monk writing; 16s. Early printing press; 28s. Khristo Botev (poet); 44s. Ivan Vazov (poet and novelist); 80s. Dimitur Blagoev (writer and editor) and books; 2l. Dimitur Blagoev Polygraphic Complex, Sofia.

1955. 30th Death Annivs of Bulgarian Poets. On cream paper.

992	334	12s. brown	30	10
993	–	16s. brown	40	10
994	–	44s. green	60	25

DESIGNS: 16s. Khristo Yusenov; 44s. Geo Milev.

335 F. Engels and Book **336** Mother and Children

1955. 60th Death Anniv of Engels.

995	335	44s. brown on cream	55	20

1955. World Mothers' Congress, Lausanne.

996	336	44s. lake on cream	35	10

337 "Youth of the World" **338** Main Entrance in 1892

1955. 5th World Youth Festival, Warsaw.

997	337	44s. blue on cream	30	15

1955. 16th International Fair, Plovdiv.

998	338	4s. brown on cream	10	10
999	–	16s. red on cream	10	10
1000	–	44s. green on cream	20	15
1001	–	80s. cream	85	20

DESIGNS—VERT: 16s. Sculptured group; 80s. Fair poster. HORIZ: 44s. Fruit.

339 Friedrich Schiller (dramatist) (150th death anniv) **340** Industrial Plant

1955. Cultural Annivs. Writers. On cream paper.

1002	339	16s. brown	30	15
1003	–	44s. red	75	15
1004	–	60s. blue	85	15
1005	–	80s. black	1·25	15
1006	–	1l. purple	2·50	1·00
1007	–	2l. olive	3·25	2·00

PORTRAITS: 44s. Adam Mickiewicz (poet, death centenary); 60s. Hans Christian Andersen (150th birth anniv); 80s. Baron de Montesquieu (philosopher, death bicentenary); 1l. Miguel de Cervantes (350th anniv of publication of "Don Quixote"); 2l. Walt Whitman (poet) (centenary of publication of "Leaves of Grass").

1955. Bulgarian–Russian Friendship. On cream paper.

1008	340	2s. slate	10	10
1009	–	4s. blue	10	10
1010	–	16s. green	55	25
1011	–	44s. brown	35	10
1012	–	80s. green	70	15
1013	–	1l. black	90	30

DESIGNS—HORIZ: 4s. Dam; 16s. Friendship railway bridge over River Danube between Ruse and Giurgiu (Rumania). VERT: 44s. Monument; 80s. Ivan-Michurin (botanist); 1l. Vladimir Mayakovsky (writer).

341 Emblem **342** Quinces

1956. Centenary of Library Reading Rooms. On cream paper.

1014	341	12s. red	10	10
1015	–	16s. brown	10	10
1016	–	44s. myrtle	50	20

DESIGNS: 16s. K. Pshourka writing; 44s. B. Kiro reading.

1956. Fruits.

1017	342	4s. red	1·40	10
1017a		4s. green	15	10
1018	–	8s. green (Pears)	60	15
1018a	–	8s. brown (Pears)	15	10
1019	–	16s. dark red (Apples)	1·25	15
1019a	–	16s. red (Apples)	35	10
1020	–	44s. violet (Grapes)	1·40	30
1020a	–	44s. ochre (Grapes)	70	20

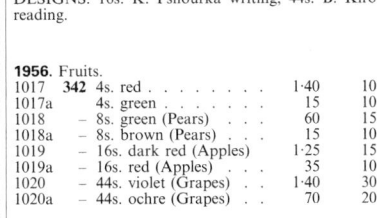

343 Artillerymen

1956. 80th Anniv of April Uprising.

1021	343	16s. brown	25	20
1022	–	44s. green (Cavalry charge)	30	25

344 Blagoev and Birthplace at Zagovichane

1956. Birth Centenary of Dimitur Blagoev (socialist writer).

1023	344	44s. turquoise	30	15

345 Cherries **346** Football

1956. Fruits.

1024	345	2s. lake	15	10
1025	–	12s. blue (Plums)	20	10
1026	–	28s. buff (Greengages)	35	10
1027	–	80s. red (Strawberries)	1·00	35

1956. Olympic Games.

1028	–	4s. blue	40	15
1029	–	12s. red	55	10
1030	–	16s. brown	60	10
1031	346	44s. green	1·10	30
1032	–	80s. brown	1·60	1·00
1033	–	1l. lake	2·40	1·40

DESIGNS—VERT: 4s. Gymnastics; 12s. Throwing the discus; 80s. Basketball. HORIZ: 16s. Pole vaulting; 1l. Boxing.

347 Tobacco and Rose **348** Gliders

1956. 17th International Fair, Plovdiv.

1034	347	44s. red	60	35
1035		44s. green	60	35

1956. Air. 30th Anniv of Gliding Club.

1036	–	44s. blue	30	15
1037	–	60s. violet	55	20
1038	348	80s. green	80	25

DESIGNS: 44s. Launching glider; 60s. Glider over hangar.

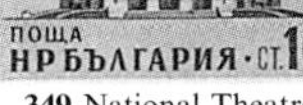

349 National Theatre **350** Wolfgang Mozart (composer, birth bicent)

1956. Centenary of National Theatre.

1039	349	16s. brown	15	10
1040	–	44s. turquoise	40	15

DESIGN: 44s. Dobri Voinikov and Sava Dobroplodni (dramatist).

1956. Cultural Anniversaries.

1041	–	16s. olive	20	10
1042	–	20s. brown	25	10
1043	350	40s. red	50	10
1044	–	44s. brown	40	15
1045	–	60s. slate	65	15
1046	–	80s. brown	75	15
1047	–	1l. green	1·25	60
1048	–	2l. green	2·40	1·25

PORTRAITS: 16s. Benjamin Franklin (journalist and statesman, 150th birth anniv); 20s. Rembrandt (artist, 350th birth anniv); 44s. Heinrich Heine (poet, death centenary); 60s. George Bernard Shaw (dramatist, birth centenary); 80s. Fyodor Dostoevsky (novelist, 75th death anniv); 1l. Henrik Ibsen (dramatist, 50th death anniv); 2l. Pierre Curie (physicist, 50th death anniv).

351 Cyclists **352** Woman with Microscope

1957. Tour of Egypt Cycle Race.

1049	351	80s. brown	90	30
1050		80s. turquoise	90	30

1957. International Women's Day. Inscr as in T **352**.

1051	352	12s. blue	10	10
1052	–	16s. brown	15	10
1053	–	44s. green	35	15

DESIGNS: 16s. Woman and children; 44s. Woman feeding poultry.

353 "New Times"

1957. 60th Anniv of "New Times" (book).

1054	353	16s. red	20	10

354 Lisunov Li-2 Airliner

1957. Air. 10th Anniv of Bulgarian Airways.

1055	354	80s. blue	1·00	30

355 St. Cyril and St. Methodius **356** Basketball

1957. Centenary of Canonization of Saints Cyril and Methodius (founders of Cyrillic alphabet).

1056	355	44s. olive and buff	85	20

1957. 10th European Basketball Championships.

1057	356	44s. green	1·60	30

357 Girl in National Costume **358** G. Dimitrov

1957. 6th World Youth Festival, Moscow.

1058	357	44s. blue	50	15

1957. 75th Birth Anniv of Georgi Dimitrov (statesman).

1059	358	44s. red	1·00	15

359 V. Levski

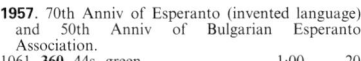

1957. 120th Birth Anniv of Vasil Levski (revolutionary).

1060	359	44s. green	85	15

360 View of Turnovo and Ludwig Zamenhof (inventor)

1957. 70th Anniv of Esperanto (invented language) and 50th Anniv of Bulgarian Esperanto Association.

1061	360	44s. green	1·00	20

361 Soldiers in Battle **362** Woman Planting Tree

1957. 80th Anniv of Liberation from Turkey.

1062	–	16s. green	20	10
1063	361	44s. brown	55	15

DESIGN: 16s. Old and young soldiers.

1957. Reafforestation Campaign.

1064	362	2s. green	10	10
1065	–	12s. brown	10	10
1066	–	16s. blue	10	10
1067	–	44s. turquoise	40	10
1068	–	80s. green	85	25

DESIGNS—HORIZ: 12s. Red deer in forest; 16s. Dam and trees; 44s. Polikarpov Po-2 biplane over forest; 80s. Trees and cornfield.

363 Two Hemispheres

1957. 4th World T.U.C., Leipzig.

1069	363	44s. blue	45	15

364 Lenin

1957. 40th Anniv of Russian Revolution. Inscr "1917–1957".

1070	364	12s. brown	30	10
1071	–	16s. turquoise	1·10	10
1072	–	44s. blue	1·10	30
1073	–	60s. red	1·75	25
1074	–	80s. green	2·75	50

DESIGNS: 16s. Cruiser "Aurora"; 44s. Dove of Peace over Europe; 60s. Revolutionaries; 80s. Oil refinery.

365 Youth and Girl

366 Partisans

1957. 10th Anniv of Dimitrov National Youth Movement.
1075 **365** 16s. red 15 10

1957. 15th Anniv of Fatherland Front.
1076 **366** 16s. brown 15 10

367 Mikhail Glinka (composer, death centenary)

368 Hotel Vasil, Kolarov

1957. Cultural Celebrities.
1077 **367** 12s. brown 30 10
1078 – 16s. green 30 10
1079 – 40s. blue . . . . 1·00 25
1080 – 44s. brown . . . . . . 1·10 25
1081 – 60s. brown . . . . . . 1·25 50
1082 – 80s. purple . . . . . . 3·25 2·10
DESIGNS: 16s. Ion Comenius (educationist) (300th anniv of publication of "Didoetica Opera Omria"); 40s. Carl Linnaeus (botanist, 250th birth anniv); 44s. William Blake (writer, birth bicent); 60s. Carlo Goldoni (dramatist, 250th birth anniv); 80s. Auguste Comte (philosopher, death centenary).

1958. Holiday Resorts.
1083 – 4s. blue 10 10
1084 8s. brown 10 10
1085 – 12s. green 10 10
1086 **368** 16s. green 15 10
1087 – 44s. turquoise 30 15
1088 – 60s. blue 40 15
1089 – 80s. brown 50 25
1090 – 1l. brown 60 25
DESIGNS—HORIZ: 4s. Skis and Pirin Mts; 8s. Old house in Koprivshtita; 12s. Hostel at Yelingrad; 44s. Hotel at Momin-Prokhod; 60s. Seaside hotel and peninsula, Nesebur; 80s. Beach scene, Varna; 1l. Modern hotels, Varna.

369 Brown Hare

371 Wrestlers

370 Marx and Lenin

1958. Forest Animals.
1091 **369** 2s. deep green & green 15 10
1092 – 12s. brown and green . . 40 10
1093 – 16s. brown and green . . 50 15
1094 – 44s. brown and blue . . 75 15
1095 – 80s. brown and ochre . . 1·00 40
1096 – 1l. brown and blue . . . 2·25 70
DESIGNS—VERT: 12s. Roe doe. HORIZ: 16s. Red deer; 44s. Chamois; 80s. Brown bear; 1l. Wild boar.

1958. 7th Bulgarian Communist Party Congress. Inscr as in T **370**.
1097 **370** 12s. brown 30 10
1098 – 16s. red 60 15
1099 – 44s. blue . . . . 1·25 15
DESIGNS: 16s. Workers marching with banners; 44s. Lenin blast furnaces.

1958. Wrestling Championships.
1100 **371** 60s. lake . . . . 1·75 1·00
1101 80s. sepia . . . . 2·00 1·25

372 Chessmen and "Oval Chessboard"

1958. 5th World Students' Team Chess Championship, Varna.
1102 **372** 80s. green . . . . 7·50 7·50

373 Russian Pavilion

1958. 18th International Fair, Plovdiv.
1103 **373** 44s. red 45 25

374 Swimmer

1958. Bulgarian Students' Games.
1104 **374** 16s. blue 15 10
1105 – 28s. brown 30 15
1106 – 44s. green 50 15
DESIGNS: 28s. Dancer; 44s. Volleyball players at net.

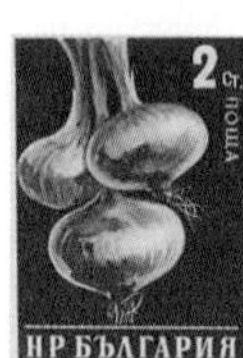

375 Onions

376 Insurgent with Rifle

1958. "Agricultural Propaganda".
1107 **375** 2s. brown 10 10
1108 – 12s. lake (Garlic) 10 10
1109 – 16s. myrtle (Peppers) . . 15 10
1110 – 44s. red (Tomatoes) . . 20 10
1111 – 80s. green (Cucumbers) 55 20
1112 – 1l. violet (Aubergines) 1·10 20

1958. 35th Anniv of September Uprising.
1113 **376** 16s. orange 15 10
1114 – 44s. lake 40 20
DESIGN—HORIZ: 44s. Insurgent helping wounded comrade.

377 Conference Emblem

1958. 1st World Trade Union's Young Workers' Conference, Prague.
1115 **377** 44s. blue 65 45

378 Exhibition Emblem

1958. Brussels International Exhibition.
1116 **378** 1l. blue and black . . . 10·50 8·50

379 Sputnik over Globe

380 Running

1958. Air. I.G.Y.
1117 **379** 80s. turquoise . . . . . 6·00 3·25

1958. Balkan Games. Inscr "1958".
1118 **380** 16s. brown 60 15
1119 – 44s. olive 70 20
1120 – 60s. blue . . . . 1·10 25
1121 – 80s. green . . . . 1·75 65
1122 – 4l. lake . . . . 9·25 6·75
DESIGNS—HORIZ: 44s. Throwing the javelin; 60s. High-jumping; 80s. Hurdling. VERT: 4l. Putting the shot.

381 Young Gardeners

382 Smirnenski

1958. 4th Dimitrov National Youth Movement Congress. Inscr as in T **381**.
1123 **381** 8s. green 10 10
1124 – 12s. brown 10 10
1125 – 16s. purple 15 10
1126 – 40s. blue 30 15
1127 – 44s. red 75 25
DESIGNS—HORIZ: 12s. Farm girl with cattle; 40s. Youth with wheel-barrow. VERT: 16s. Youth with pickaxe and girl with spade; 44s. Communist Party Building.

1958. 60th Birth Anniv of Khristo Smirnenski (poet and revolutionary).
1128 **382** 16s. red 15 15

383 First Cosmic Rockets

384 Footballers

1959. Air. Launching of First Cosmic Rocket.
1129 **383** 2l. brown and blue . . . 8·50 8·50

1959. Youth Football Games, Sofia.
1130 **384** 2l. brown on cream . . . 2·40 1·75

385 U.N.E.S.C.O. Headquarters, Paris

1959. Inauguration of U.N.E.S.C.O. Headquarters Building.
1131 **385** 2l. purple on cream . . . 2·40 1·90

386 Skier

388 Military Telegraph Linesman

1959. 40 Years of Skiing in Bulgaria.
1132 **386** 1l. blue on cream . . . 1·50 85

1959. No. 1110 surch **45 CT**.
1133 45s. on 44s. red . . . . . . 1·00 15

1959. 80th Anniv of 1st Bulgarian Postage Stamps.
1134 **388** 12s. yellow and green . . 15 10
1135 – 16s. mauve and purple 35 10
1136 – 60s. yellow and brown 85 25
1137 – 80s. salmon and red . . 95 25
1138 – 1l. blue . . . . 1·10 50
1139 – 2l. brown . . . . 3·50 1·90
DESIGNS—HORIZ: 16s. 19th-century mail-coach; 80s. Early postal car; 2l. Striking railway workers. VERT: 60s. Bulgarian 1879 stamp; 1l. Radio tower.

389 Great Tits

390 Cotton-picking

1959. Birds.
1140 **389** 2s. slate and yellow . . . 15 10
1141 – 8s. green and brown . . 20 15
1142 – 16s. sepia and brown . . 70 35
1143 – 45s. myrtle and brown 1·10 50
1144 – 60s. grey and blue . . . 2·75 75
1145 – 80s. drab and turquoise 4·25 70
DESIGNS—HORIZ: 8s. Hoopoe; 60s. Rock partridge; 80s. European cuckoo. VERT: 16s. Great spotted woodpecker; 45s. Grey partridge.

1959. Five Year Plan.
1146 – 2s. brown 10 10
1147 – 4s. bistre 20 10
1148 **390** 5s. green 20 10
1149 – 10s. brown 20 10
1150 – 12s. brown 15 10
1151 – 15s. mauve 20 10
1152 – 16s. violet 20 10
1153 – 20s. orange 30 10
1154 – 25s. blue 25 10
1155 – 28s. green 35 10
1156 – 40s. blue 45 10
1157 – 45s. brown 35 15
1158 – 60s. red 60 20
1159 – 80s. olive . . . . 1·25 20
1160 – 1l. lake 90 20
1161 – 1l.25 blue . . . . . . 2·25 75
1162 – 2l. red . . . . 1·25 35
DESIGNS—HORIZ: 2s. Children at play; 10s. Dairymaid milking cow; 16s. Industrial plant; 20s. Combine-harvester; 40s. Hydro-electric barrage; 60s. Furnaceman; 1l.25, Machinist. VERT: 4s. Woman doctor examining child; 12s. Tobacco harvesting; 15s. Machinist; 25s. Power linesman; 28s. Tending sunflowers; 45s. Miner; 80s. Fruit-picker; 1l. Workers with symbols of agriculture and industry; 2l. Worker with banner.

391 Patriots

392 Piper

1959. 300th Anniv of Batak.
1163 **391** 16s. brown 25 10

1959. Spartacist Games. Inscr "1958–1959".
1164 **392** 4s. olive on cream . . . 20 10
1165 – 12s. red on yellow . . . 20 10
1166 – 16s. lake on salmon . . 20 15
1167 – 20s. blue on blue 30 15
1168 – 80s. green on green . . . 90 35
1169 – 1l. brown on orange . . 1·25 60
DESIGNS—VERT: 12s. Gymnastics; 1l. Urn. HORIZ: 16s. Girls exercising with hoops; 20s. Dancers leaping; 80s. Ballet dancers.

393 Soldiers in Lorry

1959. 15th Anniv of Fatherland Front Government.
1170 **393** 12s. blue and red 10 10
1171 – 16s. black and red . . . 10 10
1172 – 45s. blue and red 20 10
1173 – 60s. green and red . . . 25 20
1174 – 80s. brown and red . . . 45 25
1175 – 1l.25 brown and red . . 95 45
DESIGNS—HORIZ: 16s. Partisans meeting Red Army soldiers; 45s. Blast furnaces; 60s. Tanks; 80s. Combine-harvester in cornfield. VERT: 1l.25, Pioneers with banner.

394 Footballer

1959. 50th Anniv of Football in Bulgaria.
1176 **394** 1l.25 green on yellow . . 6·75 5·00

395 Tupolev Tu-104A Jetliner and Statue of Liberty

396 Globe and Letter

1959. Air. Visit of Nikita Khrushchev (Russian Prime Minister) to U.S.A.
1177 **395** 1l. pink and blue . . . . 3·00 2·75

1959. International Correspondence Week.
1178 **396** 45s. black and green . . 60 15
1179 – 1l.25 red, black & blue 85 25
DESIGN: 1l.25, Pigeon and letter.

397 Parachutist **398** N. Vaptsarov

1960. 3rd Voluntary Defence Congress.
1180 **397** 1l.25 cream & turquoise 2·40 1·10

1960. 50th Birth Anniv of Nikola Vaptsarov (poet and revolutionary).
1181 **398** 80s. brown and green . . 45 15

399 Dr. L. Zamenhof **400**

1960. Birth Centenary of Dr. Ludwig Zamenhof (inventor of Esperanto).
1182 **399** 1l.25 green & lt green . . 1·40 85

1960. 50th Anniv of State Opera.
1183 **400** 80s. black and green . . 85 25
1184 – 1l.25 black and red . . . 1·25 30
DESIGN: 1l.25, Lyre.

401 Track of Trajectory of "Lunik 3" around the Moon

1960. Flight of "Lunik 3".
1185 **401** 1l.25 green, yellow & bl 7·00 5·00

402 Skier

1960. Winter Olympic Games.
1186 **402** 2l. brown, blue & black 1·60 1·00

403 Vela Blagoeva **404** Lenin

1960. 50th Anniv of International Women's Day. Inscr "1910–1960".
1187 **403** 16s. brown and pink . . 10 10
1188 – 28s. olive and yellow . . 15 10
1189 – 45s. green and olive . . 20 10
1190 – 60s. blue and light blue 30 15
1191 – 80s. brown and red . . . 35 15
1192 – 1l.25 olive and ochre . . 70 30
PORTRAITS: 28s. Anna Maimunkowa; 45s. Vela Piskova; 60s. Rosa Luxemburg; 80s. Clara Zetkin; 1l.25, Nadezhda Krupskaya.

1960. 90th Birth Anniv of Lenin.
1193 **404** 16s. flesh and brown . . 1·25 25
1194 – 45s. black and pink . . . 2·00 30
DESIGN: 45s. "Lenin at Smolny" (writing in chair).

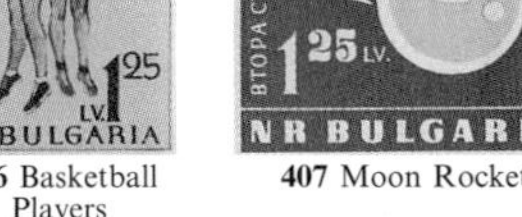

406 Basketball Players **407** Moon Rocket

1960. 7th European Women's Basketball Championships.
1195 **406** 1l.25 black and yellow 1·50 45

1960. Air. Landing of Russian Rocket on Moon.
1196 **407** 1l.25 black, yellow & bl 8·25 5·00

408 Parachutist **409** "Gentiana lutea"

1960. World Parachuting Championships, 1960.
1197 **408** 16s. blue and lilac . . . 60 55
1198 – 1l.25 red and blue . . . 2·75 85
DESIGN: 1l.25, Parachutes descending.

1960. Flowers.
1199 **409** 2s. orange, grn & drab 15 10
1200 – 5s. red, green and yellow 20 10
1201 – 25s. orge, grn & salmon 60 10
1202 – 45s. mauve, grn & lilac 75 15
1203 – 60s. red, green and buff 1·25 15
1204 – 80s. blue, green & drab 1·50 65
FLOWERS: 5s. "Tulipa rhodopea"; 25s. "Lilium jankae"; 45s. "Rhododendron ponticum"; 60s. "Cypripedium calceolus"; 80s. "Haberlea rhodopenis".

410 Football

1960. Olympic Games.
1205 **410** 8s. pink and brown . . . 10 10
1206 – 12s. pink and violet . . 15 10
1207 – 16s. pink & turquoise . . 25 15
1208 – 45s. pink and purple . . 50 15
1209 – 80s. pink and blue . . . 75 30
1210 – 2l. pink and green . . . 1·60 55
DESIGNS: 12s. Wrestling; 16s. Weightlifting; 45s. Gymnastics; 80s. Canoeing; 2l. Running.

411 Racing Cyclists

1960. Tour of Bulgaria Cycle Race.
1211 **411** 1l. black, yellow & red 1·75 1·10

412 Globes

1960. 15th Anniv of W.F.T.U.
1212 **412** 1l.25 cobalt and blue . . 60 30

413 Popov **414** Y. Veshin

1960. Birth Centenary of Alexsandr Popov (Russian radio pioneer).
1213 **413** 90s. black and blue . . . 1·10 30

1960. Birth Centenary of Yavoslav Veshin (painter).
1214 **414** 1l. olive and yellow . . . 5·00 2·40

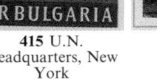

415 U.N. Headquarters, New York **416** Boyana Church

1961. 15th Anniv of U.N.O.
1215 **415** 1l. cream and brown . . 2·00 1·50

1961. 700th Anniv of Boyana Murals (1959).
1216 **416** 60s. black, emer & grn 1·00 15
1217 – 80s. grn, cream & orange 1·25 25
1218 – 1l.25 red, cream & green 2·00 65
DESIGNS (Frescoes of): 80s. Theodor Tiron; 1l.25, Desislava.

417 Cosmic Rocket and Dogs Belda and Strelka

1961. Russian Cosmic Rocket Flight of August, 1960.
1219 **417** 1l.25 blue and red . . . 8·50 6·00

419 Pleven Costume **420** Clock Tower, Vratsa

1961. Provincial Costumes.
1220 – 12s. yellow, green & orge 15 10
1221 **419** 16s. brown, buff & lilac 15 10
1222 – 28s. red, black, & green 25 10
1223 – 45s. blue and red 40 15
1224 – 60s. yellow, blue & turq 70 20
1225 – 80s. red, green & yellow 90 30
COSTUMES: 12s. Kyustendil; 28s. Sliven; 45s. Sofia; 60s. Rhodope; 80c. Karnobat.

1961. Museums and Monuments. Values and star in red.
1226 **420** 8s. green 10 10
1227 – 12s. violet 10 10
1228 – 16s. brown 15 10
1229 – 20s. blue 20 10
1230 – 28s. turquoise 25 15
1231 – 40s. brown 30 10
1232 – 45s. olive 35 15
1233 – 60s. slate 65 15
1234 – 80s. brown 85 20
1235 – 1l. turquoise . . . . . 1·25 45
DESIGNS—As Type **420**. VERT: 12s. Clock Tower, Bansko; 20s. "Agushev" building, Mogilitsa (Smolensk). HORIZ: 28s. Oslekoff House, Koprivshtitsa; 40s. Pasha's House, Melnik. SQUARE (27 × 27 mm): 16s. Wine jug; 45s. Lion (bas-relief); 60s. "Horseman of Madara"; 80s. Fresco, Bachkovo Monastery; 1l. Coin of Tsar Konstantin-Asen (13th cent).

421 Dalmatian Pelican **422** "Communications and Transport"

1961. Birds.
1236 – 2s. turquoise, blk & red 10 10
1237 **421** 4s. orange, blk & grn . . 15 10
1238 – 16s. orange, brn & grn 15 10
1239 – 80s. yellow, brn & turq 1·75 30
1240 – 1l. yellow, sepia and blue 1·75 75
1241 – 2l. yellow, brown & blue 2·75 80
DESIGNS: 2s. White capercaillie; 16s. Common pheasant; 80s. Great bustard; 1l. Lammergeier; 2l. Hazel grouse.

1961. 50th Anniv of Transport Workers' Union.
1242 **422** 80s. green and black . . 85 20

423 Gagarin and Rocket

1961. World's First Manned Space Flight.
1243 **423** 4l. turquoise, blk & red 5·00 3·25

424 Shevchenko (Ukrainian poet)

1961. Death Centenary of Taras Shevchenko.
1244 **424** 1l. brown and green . . 4·75 2·40

425 Throwing the Discus

1961. World Students' Games. Values and inscr in black.
1245 – 4s. blue 10 10
1246 – 5s. red 20 10
1247 – 16s. olive 30 10
1248 **425** 45s. blue 45 20
1249 – 1l.25 brown . . . . . . 1·00 35
1250 – 2l. mauve . . . . 1·25 80
DESIGNS—VERT: 4s. Water polo; 2l. Basketball. HORIZ: 5s. Tennis; 16s. Fencing; 1l.25, Sports Palace, Sofia.

426 Short-snouted Seahorse **427** "Space" Dogs

1961. Black Sea Fauna.
1251 – 2s. sepia and green . . . 10 10
1252 – 12s. pink and blue . . . 25 10
1253 – 16s. violet and blue . . . 40 10
1254 **426** 45s. brown and blue . . 1·40 50
1255 – 1l. blue and green . . . 2·75 1·00
1256 – 1l.25 brown and blue . . 4·00 1·50
DESIGNS—HORIZ: 2s. Mediterranean monk seal; 12s. Lung jellyfish; 16s. Common dolphins; 1l. Stellate sturgeons; 1l.25, Thorn-backed ray.

1961. Air. Space Exploration.
1257 **427** 2l. slate and purple . . . 4·00 3·00
1258 – 2l. blue, yellow & orange 8·25 5·00
DESIGN: No. 1258, "Venus" rocket in flight (24 × 41½ mm).

428 Dimitur Blagoev as Orator

1961. 70th Anniv of First Bulgarian Social Democratic Party Congress, Buzludzha.
1259 **428** 45s. red and cream . . . 25 15
1260 80s. blue and pink . . . 40 15
1261 2l. sepia and green . . . 1·40 45

429 Hotel

1961. Tourist issue. Inscr in black; designs green. Background colours given.
1262 **429** 4s. green 10 10
1263 – 12s. blue (Hikers) . . . 10 10
1264 – 16s. green (Tents) . . . 10 10
1265 – 1l.25 bistre (Climber) . . 85 15
Nos. 1263/5 are vert.

430 "The Golden Girl"

1961. Bulgarian Fables.
1266 **430** 2s. multicoloured 15 10
1267 – 8s. grey, black & purple 20 10
1268 – 12s. pink, black & green 25 10
1269 – 16s. multicoloured . . . 85 20

1270 – 45s. multicoloured . . . 1·50 30
1271 – 80s. multicoloured . . . 2·00 45
DESIGNS: 8s. Man and woman ("The Living Water"); 12s. Archer and dragon ("The Golden Apple"); 16s. Horseman ("Krali Marko", national hero); 45s. Female archer on stag ("Samovila-Vila", fairy); 80s. "Tom Thumb" and cockerel.

431 Major Titov in Space-suit

432 "Amanita caesarea"

1961. Air. 2nd Russian Manned Space Flight.
1272 **431** 75s. flesh, blue & olive 3·50 2·50
1273 – 1l.25 pink, bl & violet 4·50 3·75
DESIGN: 1l.25, "Vostok-2" in flight.

1961. Mushrooms.
1274 **432** 2s. red, bistre & black 10 10
1275 – 4s. brown, grn & blk . . 15 10
1276 – 12s. brown, bistre & blk 20 10
1277 – 16s. brown, mve & blk 20 10
1278 – 45s. multicoloured . . . 40 15
1279 – 80s. orange, sepia & blk 75 25
1280 – 1l.25 lav, brn & blk . . 90 45
1281 – 2l. brown, bistre & black 1·75 80
MUSHROOMS: 4s. "Psalliota silvatica"; 12s. "Boletus elegans"; 16s. "Boletus edulis"; 45s. "Lactarius deliciosus"; 80s. "Lepiota procera"; 1l.25, "Pleurotus ostreatus"; 2l. "Armillariella mellea".

433 Dimitur and Konstantin Miladinov (authors)

436 Isker River

1961. Publication Centenary of "Bulgarian Popular Songs".
1282 **433** 1l.25 black and olive . . 1·00 30

(Currency revaluation)

1962. Surch. (A) Surch in one line; (B) in two lines.
1283 1s. on 10s. brown (1149) . . 10 10
1284 1s. on 12s. brown (1150) . . 10 10
1285 2s. on 15s. mauve (1151) . . 10 10
1286 2s. on 16s. violet (1152) . . 10 10
1287 2s. on 20s. orange (1153) (A) 10 10
1288 2s. on 20s. orange (1153) (B) 25 10
1289 3s. on 25s. blue (1154) . . . 20 10
1290 3s. on 28s. green (1155) . . 20 10
1291 5s. on 44s. green (1087) . . 25 10
1292 5s. on 44s. red (1110) . . . 25 10
1293 5s. on 45s. brown (1157) . . 25 10
1294 10s. on 1l. red (1160) . . . 45 15
1295 20s. on 2l. red (1162) . . . 75 40
1296 40s. on 4l. red (889) . . . . 2·00 75

1962. Air.
1297 **436** 1s. blue and violet . . . 10 10
1298 – 2s. blue and pink 30 10
1299 – 3s. brown and chestnut 20 10
1300 – 10s. black and bistre . . 60 15
1301 – 40s. black and green . . 2·00 45
DESIGNS: 2s. Yacht at Varna; 3s. Melnik; 10s. Turnovo; 40s. Pirin Mountains.

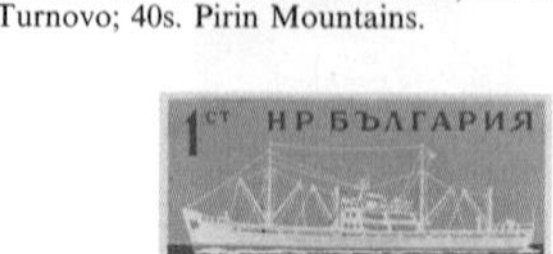

437 Freighter "Varna"

1962. Bulgarian Merchant Navy.
1302 **437** 1s. green and blue . . . 10 10
1303 – 5s. light blue and green 60 10
1304 – 20s. violet and blue . . . 1·75 35
SHIPS: 5s. Tanker "Komsomols"; 20s. Liner "Georgi Dimitrov".

438 Rila Mountains

1962. Views.
1305 **438** 1s. turquoise 10 10
1306 – 2s. blue 10 10
1307 – 6s. turquoise 60 10
1308 – 8s. purple 80 20
1309 – 13s. green 65 15
1310 – 1l. deep green . . . . . 5·25 40
VIEWS: 2s. Pirin Mts; 6s. Fishing boats, Nesebur; 8s. Danube shipping; 13s. Viden Castle; 1l. Rhodope Mts.

439 Georgi Dimitrov as Typesetter

440 Pink Roses

1962. 80th Anniv of State Printing Office.
1311 **439** 2s. red, black & yellow 10 10
1312 – 13s. black, orange & yell 75 15
DESIGN: 13s. Emblem of Printing Office.

1962. Bulgarian Roses. T **440** and similar designs.
1313 1s. pink, green and violet . . 10 10
1314 2s. red, green and buff . . . 10 10
1315 3s. red, green and blue . . . 25 10
1316 4s. yellow, turquoise & grn 35 10
1317 5s. pink, green and blue . . 65 20
1318 6s. red, green and turquoise 80 40
1319 8s. red, green and yellow . . 2·75 65
1320 13s. yellow, green and blue 4·75 1·10

441 "The World United against Malaria"

1962. Malaria Eradication.
1321 **441** 5s. yellow, black & brn 60 15
1322 – 20s. yellow, green & blk 1·40 60
DESIGN: 20s. Campaign emblem.

442 Lenin and Front Page of "Pravda"

1962. 50th Anniv of "Pravda" Newspaper.
1323 **442** 5s. blue, red and black 90 25

443 Text-book and Blackboard

444 Footballer

1962. Bulgarian Teachers' Congress.
1324 **443** 5s. black, yellow & blue 15 10

1962. World Football Championship, Chile.
1325 **444** 13s. brown, green & blk 1·10 35

445 Dimitrov

1962. 80th Birth Anniv of Georgi Dimitrov (Prime Minister 1946–49).
1326 **445** 2s. green 15 10
1327 5s. blue 75 35

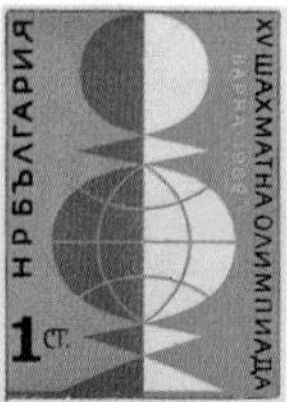

446 Bishop

448 Festival Emblem

1962. 15th Chess Olympiad, Varna. Inscr "1962". Inscr in black.
1328 **446** 1s. green and grey . . . 15 10
1329 – 2s. bistre and grey . . . 15 10
1330 – 3s. purple and grey . . . 15 10
1331 – 13s. orange and grey . . 1·50 40
1332 – 20s. blue and grey . . . 2·00 70
CHESS PIECES: 2s. Rook; 3s. Queen; 14s. Knight; 20s. Pawn.

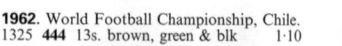

XXXV КОНГРЕС
1962
13 =
(447)

1962. 35th Esperanto Congress, Burgas. Surch as T **447**.
1333 **360** 13s. on 44s. green . . . 4·75 3·00

1962. World Youth Festival, Helsinki. Inscr "1962".
1334 **448** 5s. blue, pink and green 20 10
1335 – 13s. blue, purple & grey 50 20
DESIGN: 13s. Girl and emblem.

449 Ilyushin Il-18 Airliner

1962. Air. 13th Anniv of TABSO Airline.
1336 **449** 13s. blue, ultram & blk 1·25 20

450 Apollo

1962. Butterflies and Moths. Multicoloured.
1337 1s. Type **450** 10 10
1338 2s. Eastern festoon 15 10
1339 3s. Meleager's blue 20 10
1340 4s. Camberwell beauty . . . 25 10
1341 5s. Crimson underwing . . 30 10
1342 6s. Hebe tiger moth 85 15
1343 10s. Danube clouded . . . 3·00 60
1344 13s. Cardinal . . . . 2·75 90

451 K. E. Tsiolkovsky (scientist)

1962. Air. 13th International Astronautics Congress. Inscr "1962".
1345 **451** 5s. drab and green . . . 4·00 1·50
1346 – 13s. blue and yellow . . 2·00 75
DESIGN: 13s. Moon rocket.

452 Combine Harvester

1962. 8th Bulgarian Communist Party Congress.
1347 **452** 1s. olive and turquoise 10 10
1348 – 2s. turquoise and blue 15 30
1349 – 3s. brown and red . . . 20 10
1350 – 13s. sepia, red & purple 1·00 30
DESIGNS: 2s. Electric train; 3s. Steel furnace; 13s. Blagoev and Dimitrov.

453 Cover of "History of Bulgaria"

1962. Bicentenary of Paisii Khilendarski's "History of Bulgaria".
1351 **453** 2s. black and olive . . . 10 10
1352 – 5s. sepia and brown . . 25 10
DESIGN—HORIZ: 5s. Father Paisii at work on book.

454 Andrian Nikolaev and "Vostok 3"

1962. Air. 1st "Team" Manned Space Flight.
1353 **454** 1s. olive, blue and black 15 10
1354 – 2s. olive, green & black 30 15
1355 – 40s. pink, turquoise & blk . . . . 3·25 2·10
DESIGNS: 2s. Pavel Ropovich and "Vostok 4"; 40s. "Vostoks 3" and "4" in flight.

455 Parachutist

456 Aleko Konstantinov

1963.
1356 – 1s. lake 10 10
1357 – 1s. brown 10 10
1358 – 1s. turquoise 10 10
1359 – 1s. green 10 10
1360 **455** 1s. blue 10 10
DESIGNS—VERT: No. 1356, State crest. HORIZ: No. 1357, Sofia University; 1358, "Vasil Levski" Stadium, Sofia; 1359, "The Camels" (archway), Hisar.

1963. Birth Cent of Konstantinov (author).
1361 **456** 5s. green and red 20 10

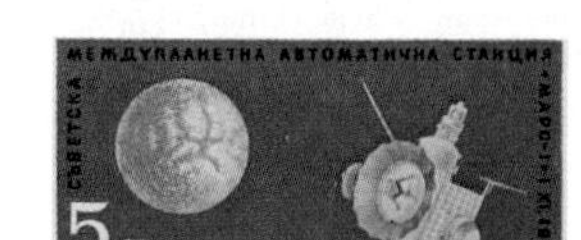

457 Mars and "Mars 1" Space Probe

1963. Air. Launching of Soviet Space Station "Mars 1".
1362 **457** 5s. multicoloured 70 30
1363 – 13s. turquoise, red & blk 1·40 75
DESIGN: 13s. Release of probe from rocket.

458 Orpheus Restaurant, "Sunny Beach"

459 V. Levski

1963. Black Sea Coast Resorts.
1364 **458** 1s. blue 10 10
1365a – 2s. red 80 15
1366 – 3s. bistre 25 10
1367 – 5s. purple 45 10
1368 – 13s. turquoise . . . . . 1·25 15
1369 – 20s. green . . . . . . 1·75 30
VIEWS "Sunny Beach": 5s. The Dunes Restaurant; 20s. Hotel. "Golden Sands"; 2s., 3s., 13s. Various hotels.

1963. 90th Anniv of Execution of Vasil Levski (revolutionary).
1370 **459** 13s. blue and yellow . . 75 30

460 Dimitrov, Boy and Girl

461 Eurasian Red Squirrel

1963. 10th Dimitrov Communist Youth League Congress, Sofia.
1371 **460** 2s. brown, red & black 15 10
1372 – 13s. brown, turq & blk 45 20
DESIGN: 13s. Girl and youth holding book and hammer aloft.

1963. Woodland Animals.
1373 **461** 1s. brown, red and green on turquoise 10 10
1374 – 2s. blk, red & grn on yell 15 10
1375 – 3s. sep, red & ol on drab 10 10
1376 – 5s. brown, red and blue on violet 60 10
1377 – 13s. black, red and brown on pink . . . 2·25 25
1378 – 20s. sepia, red and blue on blue . . . . . . 3·50 40
ANIMALS—HORIZ: 2s. East European hedgehog; 3s. Marbled polecat; 5s. Beech marten; 13s. Eurasian badger. VERT: 20s. European otter.

462 Wrestling

1963. 15th International Open Wrestling Championships, Sofia.
1379 **462** 5s. bistre and black . . . 20 15
1380 – 20s. brown and black . . 1·25 30
DESIGN—HORIZ: 20s. As Type **462** but different hold.

463 Congress Emblem and Allegory

1963. World Women's Congress, Moscow.
1381 **463** 20s. blue and black . . . 1·00 25

464 Esperanto Star and Sofia Arms
465 Rocket, Globe and Moon

1963. 48th World Esperanto Congress, Sofia.
1382 **464** 13s. multicoloured . . . 1·00 25

1963. Launching of Soviet Moon Rocket "Luna 4". Inscr "2.IV.1963".
1383 **465** 1s. blue 10 10
1384 – 2s. purple 10 10
1385 – 3s. turquoise 15 10
DESIGNS: 2s. Tracking equipment; 3s. Sputniks.

466 Valery Bykovsky in Spacesuit

1963. Air. 2nd "Team" Manned Space Flights. Inscr "14.VI.1963".
1386 **466** 1s. turquoise and lilac 10 10
1387 – 2s. brown and yellow . . 15 10
1388 – 5s. red and light red . . 25 10
1389 – 20s.+10s. grn & lt bl . . 2·10 80
DESIGNS: 2s. Valentina Tereshkova in spacesuit; 5s. Globe; 20s. Bykovsky and Tereshkova.

1963. Europa Fair, Riccione. Nos. 1314/5 and 1318 (Roses) optd **MOSTRA EUROPEISTICA.1963 RICCIONE** and sailing boat motif or additionally surch.
1390 2s. red, green and buff . . . 30 15
1391 5s. on 3s. red, green and blue 40 15
1392 13s. on 6s. red, green & turq 1·40 40

468 Relay-racing

1963. Balkan Games. Flags in red, yellow, blue, green and black.
1393 **468** 1s. green 10 10
1394 – 2s. violet 15 10
1395 – 3s. turquoise 20 10
1396 – 5s. red 50 20
1397 – 13s. brown . . . . . . 3·00 2·25
DESIGNS: 2s. Throwing the hammer; 3s. Long jumping; 5s. High jumping; 13s. Throwing the discus. Each design includes the flags of the competing countries.

469 Slavonic Scroll
470 Insurgents

1963. 5th International Slav Congress, Sofia.
1398 **469** 5s. red, yellow & dp grn 20 10

1963. 40th Anniv of September Uprising.
1399 **470** 2s. black and red 15 10

471 "Aquilegia aurea"
472 Khristo Smirnenski

1963. Nature Protection. Flowers in natural colours; background colours given.
1400 **471** 1s. turquoise 10 10
1401 – 2s. olive 10 10
1402 – 3s. yellow 20 10
1403 – 5s. blue 40 10
1404 – 6s. purple 45 15
1405 – 8s. light grey 65 15
1406 – 10s. mauve . . . . . . 1·75 25
1407 – 13s. olive . . . . 2·75 45
FLOWERS: 2s. Edelweiss; 3s. "Primula deorum"; 5s. White water-lily; 6s. Tulip; 8s. "Viola delphinantha"; 10s. Alpine clematis; 13s. "Anemone narcissiflora".

1963. 65th Birth Anniv of Smirnenski (poet and revolutionary).
1408 **472** 13s. black and lilac . . . 75 15

473 Chariot Horses (wall-painting)
474 Hemispheres and Centenary Emblem

1963. Thracian Tombs, Kazanilk.
1409 **473** 1s. red, yellow and grey 10 10
1410 – 2s. violet, yellow & grey 15 10
1411 – 3s. turquoise, yell & grey 20 10
1412 – 5s. brown, yellow & grn 25 10
1413 – 13s. black, yellow & grn 60 15
1414 – 20s. red, yellow & green 1·40 55
DESIGNS (wall paintings on tombs): 2s. Chariot race; 3s. Flautists; 5s. Tray-bearer; 13s. Funeral feast; 20s. Seated woman.

1964. Centenary of Red Cross.
1415 **474** 1s. yellow, red & black 10 10
1416 – 2s. blue, red and black 10 10
1417 – 3s. multicoloured 10 10
1418 – 5s. turq, red & black . . 25 10
1419 – 13s. black, red & orange 85 25
DESIGNS: 2s. Blood donation; 3s. Bandaging wrist; 5s. Nurse; 13s. Henri Dunant.

475 Speed-skating

1964. Winter Olympic Games, Innsbruck.
1420 **475** 1s. indigo, brown & blue 10 10
1421 – 2s. olive, mauve & black 10 10
1422 – 3s. green, brown & blk 15 10
1423 – 5s. multicoloured 25 15
1424 – 10s. orange, blk & grey 85 20
1425 – 13s. mauve, violet & blk 1·00 25
DESIGNS: 2s. Figure skating; 3s. Cross-country skiing; 5s. Ski jumping. Ice hockey—10s. Goalkeeper; 13s. Players.

476 Head (2nd cent)

1964. 2500 Years of Bulgarian Art. Borders in grey.
1426 **476** 1s. turquoise and red . . 10 10
1427 – 2s. sepia and red 10 10
1428 – 3s. bistre and red . . . 10 10
1429 – 5s. blue and red 25 10
1430 – 6s. brown and red . . . 35 10
1431 – 8s. brown and red . . . 50 15
1432 – 10s. olive and red . . . 60 15
1433 – 13s. olive and red . . . 1·10 25
DESIGNS: 2s. Horseman (1st to 4th cent); 3s. Jug (19th cent); 5s. Buckle (19th cent); 6s. Pot (19th cent); 8s. Angel (17th cent); 10s. Animals (8th to 10th cent); 13s. Peasant woman (20th cent).

477 "The Unborn Maid"

1964. Folk Tales. Multicoloured.
1434 1s. Type **477** 10 10
1435 2s. "Grandfather's Glove" 10 10
1436 3s. "The Big Turnip" . . . 10 10
1437 5s. "The Wolf and the Seven Kids" 25 10
1438 8s. "Cunning Peter" 40 15
1439 13s. "The Loaf of Corn" . . 1·25 30

478 Turkish Lacewing ("Ascalaphus ottomanus")

1964. Insects.
1440 **478** 1s. black, yellow & brn 10 10
1441 – 2s. black, ochre & turq 15 10
1442 – 3s. green, black & drab 20 10
1443 – 5s. violet, black & green 65 10
1444 – 13s. brown, black & vio 1·40 25
1445 – 20s. yellow, black & bl 2·50 40
DESIGNS—VERT: 2s. Thread lacewing fly ("Nemoptera coa"); 5s. Alpine longhorn beetle ("Rosalia alpina"); 13s. Cockchafer ("Anisoplia austriaca"). HORIZ: 3s. Cricket ("Saga natalia"); 20s. Hunting wasp ("Scolia flavitrons").

479 Football

1964. 50th Anniv of Levski Physical Culture Association.
1446 2s. Type **479** 15 10
1447 13s. Handball 95 30

480 Title Page and Petar Beron (author)

1964. 40th Anniv of First Bulgarian Primer.
1448 **480** 20s. black and brown . . 2·00 2·00

481 Stephenson's "Rocket", 1829

1964. Railway Transport. Multicoloured.
1449 1s. Type **481** 10 10
1450 2s. Class 05 steam locomotive 15 10
1451 3s. German V.320.001 diesel locomotive 25 10
1452 5s. Electric locomotive . . . 45 10
1453 8s. Class 05 steam locomotive and train on bridge 70 15
1454 13s. Class E41 electric train emerging from tunnel . . 1·10 25

482 Alsatian
(483)

1964. Dogs. Multicoloured.
1455 1s. Type **482** 10 10
1456 2s. Setter 20 10
1457 3s. Poodle 25 10
1458 4s. Pomeranian 30 10
1459 5s. St. Bernard 40 15
1460 6s. Fox terrier 85 15
1461 10s. Pointer . . . . 3·00 55
1462 13s. Dachshund . . . . . . 3·50 1·40

1964. Air. International Cosmic Exhibition, Riccione. No. 1386 surch with T **483** and No. 1387 surch as T **483**, but in Italian.
1463 **466** 10s. on 1s. turquoise and lilac 50 20
1464 – 20s. on 2s. brown & yell 1·00 30

484 Partisans and Flag

1964. 20th Anniv of Fatherland. Front Government. Flag in red.
1465 **484** 1s. blue and light blue 10 10
1466 – 2s. olive and bistre . . . 10 10
1467 – 3s. lake and mauve . . . 10 10
1468 – 4s. violet and lavender 15 10
1469 – 5s. brown and orange . . 20 10
1470 – 6s. blue and light blue 30 10
1471 – 8s. green and light green 70 10
1472 – 13s. brown and salmon 1·00 50
DESIGNS: 2s. Greeting Soviet troops; 3s. Soviet aid—arrival of goods; 4s. Industrial plant, Kremikovtsi; 5s. Combine-harvester; 6s. "Peace" campaigners; 8s. Soldier of National Guard; 3s. Blagoev and Dimitrov. All with flag as Type **484**.

(485)
486 Transport

1964. 21st Int Fair, Plovdiv. Surch with T **485**.
1473 20s. on 44s. ochre (No. 1020a) . . . . . . 1·90 35

1964. 1st National Stamp Exn, Sofia.
1474 **486** 20s. blue . . . . 2·75 1·00

487 Gymnastics
488 Vratsata

1964. Olympic Games, Tokyo. Rings and values in red.
1475 **487** 1s. green and light green 10 10
1476 – 2s. blue and lavender . . 10 10
1477 – 3s. blue and turquoise 15 10
1478 – 5s. violet and red 15 10
1479 – 13s. blue and light blue 1·00 15
1480 – 20s. green and buff . . . 1·40 25
DESIGNS: 2s. Long-jump; 3s. Swimmer on starting block; 5s. Football; 13s. Volleyball; 20s. Wrestling.

1964. Landscapes.
1481 **488** 1s. green 10 10
1482 – 2s. brown 10 10
1483 – 3s. blue 15 10
1484 – 4s. brown 20 10
1485 – 5s. green 30 10
1486 – 6s. violet 40 10
DESIGNS: 2s. The Ritli; 3s. Maliovitsa; 4s. Broken Rocks; 5s. Erkyupria; 6s. Rhodope mountain pass.

489 Paper and Cellulose Factory, Bukovtsi

1964. Air. Industrial Buildings.
1487 **489** 8s. turquoise 25 10
1488 – 10s. purple 35 10

1489 – 13s. violet 40 10
1490 – 20s. blue . . . . 1·00 15
1491 – 40s. green . . . . 1·90 60
DESIGNS: 10s. Metal works, Plovdiv; 13s. Metallurgical works, Kremikovtzi; 20s. Petrol refinery, Burgas; 40s. Fertiliser factory, Stara-Zagora.

490 Rila Monastery

1964. Philatelic Exn for Franco–Bulgarian Amity.
1492 **490** 5s. black and drab . . . 30 15
1493 – 13s. black and blue . . . 1·10 30
DESIGN: 13s. Notre-Dame, Paris (inscr in French).

491 500-year-old Walnut **492**

1964. Ancient Trees. Values and inscr in black.
1494 **491** 1s. brown 10 10
1495 – 2s. purple 10 10
1496 – 3s. sepia 15 10
1497 – 4s. blue 15 10
1498 – 10s. green 45 20
1499 – 13s. olive 80 25
TREES: 2s. Plane (1000 yrs.); 3s. Plane (600 yrs.); 4s. Poplar (800 yrs.); 10s. Oak (800 yrs.); 13s. Fir (1200 yrs.).

1964. 8th Congress of Int Union of Students, Sofia.
1500 **492** 13s. black and blue . . . 80 15

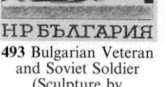

493 Bulgarian Veteran and Soviet Soldier (Sculpture by T. Zlatarev) **494** "Gold Medal"

1965. 30 Years of Bulgarian–Russian Friendship.
1501 **493** 2s. red and black 20 10

1965. Olympic Games, Tokyo (1964).
1502 **494** 20s. black, gold & brown 1·00 30

495 Vladimir Komarov

1965. Flight of "Voskhod 1". Multicoloured.
1503 1s. Type **495** 10 10
1504 2s. Konstantin Feoktistov 10 10
1505 5s. Boris Yegorov 15 10
1506 13s. The three astronauts . . 85 15
1507 20s. "Voskhod 1" . . . . . 1·40 25

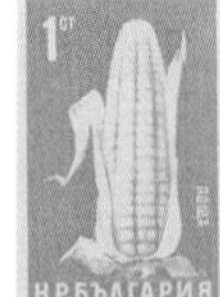

496 Corn-cob **497** "Victory against Fascism"

1965. Agricultural Products.
1508 **496** 1s. yellow 10 10
1509 – 2s. green 10 10
1510 – 3s. orange 15 10
1511 – 4s. olive 20 10
1512 – 5s. red 30 10
1513 – 10s. blue 55 20
1514 – 13s. bistre . . . . 1·25 25
DESIGNS: 2s. Ears of Wheat; 3s. Sunflowers; 4s. Sugar beet; 5s. Clover; 10s. Cotton; 13s. Tobacco.

1965. 20th Anniv of "Victory of 9 May, 1945".
1515 **497** 5s. black, bistre & grey 15 10
1516 – 13s. blue, black & grey 40 20
DESIGN: 13s. Globes on dove ("Peace").

498 Northern Bullfinch **499** Transport, Globe and Whale

1965. Song Birds. Multicoloured.
1517 1s. Type **498** 10 10
1518 2s. Golden oriole 15 10
1519 3s. Rock thrush 20 10
1520 5s. Barn swallows 60 10
1521 8s. European roller 95 15
1522 10s. Eurasian goldfinch . . 3·75 25
1523 13s. Rose-coloured starling 3·75 55
1524 20s. Nightingale . . . . . . 4·00 1·25

1965. 4th International Transport Conf, Sofia.
1525 **499** 13s. multicoloured . . . 1·10 30

500 I.C.Y. Emblem **501** I.T.U. Emblem and Symbols

1965. International Co-operation Year.
1526 **500** 20s. orange, olive & blk 90 25

1965. Centenary of I.T.U.
1527 **501** 20s. yellow, green & bl 1·25 30

502 Pavel Belyaev and Aleksei Leonov

1965. "Voskhod 2" Space Flight.
1528 **502** 2s. purple, grn & drab 30 10
1529 – 20s. multicoloured . . . 3·00 1·10
DESIGN: 20s. Leonov on space.

503 Common Stingray **504** Marx and Lenin

1965. Fishes. Borders in grey.
1530 **503** 1s. gold, black & orange 10 10
1531 – 2s. silver, indigo & blue 10 10
1532 – 3s. gold, black & green 20 10
1533 – 5s. gold, black and red 25 10
1534 – 10s. silver, blue & turq 1·50 25
1535 – 13s. gold, black & brown 1·75 45
FISHES: 2s. Atlantic bonito; 3s. Brown scorpionfish; 5s. Tub gurnard; 10s. Mediterranean horse-mackerel; 13s. Black Sea turbot.

1965. Organization of Socialist Countries' Postal Ministers' Conference, Peking.
1536 **504** 13s. brown and red . . . 1·10 20

505 Film and Screen **506** Quinces

1965. Balkan Film Festival. Varna.
1537 **505** 13s. black, silver & blue 85 20

1965. Fruits.
1538 **506** 1s. orange 10 10
1539 – 2s. olive (Grapes) . . . 10 10
1540 – 3s. bistre (Pears) 10 10
1541 – 4s. orange (Plums) . . . 15 10
1542 – 5s. red (Strawberries) . . 30 10
1543 – 6s. brown (Walnuts) . . 50 15

507 Ballerina **508** Dove, Emblem and Map

1965. Ballet Competitions, Varna.
1544 **507** 5s. black and mauve . . 85 30

1965. "Balkanphila" Stamp Exhibition, Varna.
1545 **508** 1s. silver, blue & yellow 10 10
1546 – 2s. silver, violet & yellow 10 10
1547 – 3s. gold, green & yellow 15 10
1548 – 13s. gold, red & yellow 1·00 85
1549 – 20s. brown, blue & silver 1·40 1·00
DESIGNS: 2s. Yacht emblem; 3s. Stylised fish and flowers; 13s. Stylised sun, planet and rocket. LARGER (45 × 25½ mm): 20s. Cosmonauts Pavel Belyaev and Aleksei Leonov.

509 Escapers in Boat **511** Gymnast

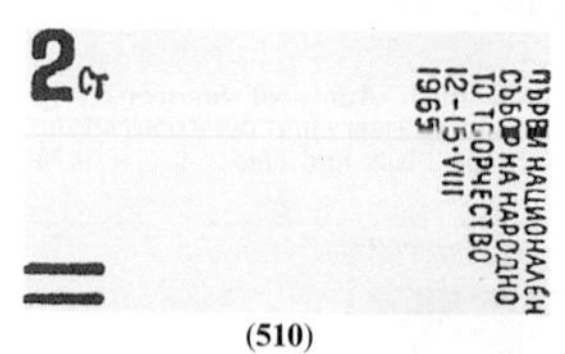
(510)

1965. 40th Anniv of Political Prisoners' Escape from "Bolshevik Island".
1551 **509** 2s. black and slate . . . 20 15

1965. National Folklore Competition. No. 1084 surch with T **510**.
1552 2s. on 8s. brown . . . . . 1·75 1·40

1965. Balkan Games.
1553 **511** 1s. black and red 10 10
1554 – 2s. purple and black . . 10 10
1555 – 3s. purple, black & red 10 10
1556 – 5s. brown, black & red 25 10
1557 – 10s. purple, black & mve 1·25 20
1558 – 13s. purple and black . . 1·00 25
DESIGNS: 2s. Gymnastics on bars; 3s. Weight-lifting; 5s. Rally car and building; 10s. Basketball; 13s. Rally car and map.

512 Dressage

1965. Horsemanship.
1559 **512** 1s. plum, black & blue 10 10
1560 – 2s. brown, black & ochre 10 10
1561 – 3s. red, black and purple 15 10
1562 – 5s. brown and green . . 55 10
1563 – 10s. brown, blk & grey 2·00 25
1564 – 13s. brown, grn & buff 2·10 35
DESIGNS: 5s. Horse-racing. Others, Horse-jumping (various).

513 Young Pioneers

1965. Dimitrov Septembrist Pioneers Organization.
1566 **513** 1s. green and turquoise 10 10
1567 – 2s. mauve and violet . . 10 10
1568 – 3s. bistre and olive . . . 10 10
1569 – 5s. ochre and blue . . . 15 10
1570 – 8s. orange and brown . . 50 15
1571 – 13s. violet and red . . . 95 30
DESIGNS: 2s. Admitting recruit; 3s. Camp bugler; 5s. Flying model airplane; 8s. Girls singing; 13s. Young athlete.

514 Junkers Ju 52/3m over Turnovo **515** Women of N. and S. Bulgaria

1965. Bulgarian Civil Aviation. Multicoloured.
1572 1s. Type **514** 10 10
1573 2s. Ilyushin Il-14M over Plovdiv 10 10
1574 3s. Mil Mi-4 helicopter over Dimitrovgrad 15 10
1575 5s. Tupolev Tu-104A over Ruse 35 10
1576 13s. Ilyushin Il-18 over Varna . . . . 1·40 20
1577 20s. Tupolev Tu-114 over Sofia . . . . 1·75 50

1965. 80th Anniv of Union of North and South Bulgaria.
1578 **515** 13s. black and green . . 85 30

516 I.Q.S.Y. Emblem and Earth's Radiation Zones **517** "Spring Greetings"

1965. International Quiet Sun Year.
1579 **516** 1s. yellow, green & blue 10 10
1580 – 2s. multicoloured 10 10
1581 – 13s. multicoloured . . . 90 20
DESIGNS (I.Q.S.Y. emblem and): 2s. Sun and solar flares; 13s. Total eclipse of the Sun.

1966. "Spring". National Folklore.
1582 **517** 1s. mauve, blue & drab 10 10
1583 – 2s. red, black and drab 10 10
1584 – 3s. violet, red and grey 10 10
1585 – 5s. red, violet and black 15 10
1586 – 8s. purple, brown & mve 35 15
1587 – 13s. mauve, black & bl 70 20
DESIGNS: 2s. Drummer; 3s. "Birds" (stylised); 5s. Folk dancer; 8s. Vase of flowers; 13s. Bagpiper.

518 Byala Bridge

1966. Ancient Monuments.
1588 **518** 1s. turquoise 10 10
1589 – 1s. green 10 10
1590 – 2s. green 10 10
1591 – 2s. purple 10 10
1592 – 8s. brown 40 15
1593 – 13s. blue 65 25
DESIGNS: No. 1589, Svilengrand Bridge; 1590, Fountain, Samokov; 1591, Ruins of Matochina Castle, Khaskovo; 1592, Cherven Castle, Ruse; 1593, Cafe, Bozhentsi, Gabrovo.

519 "Christ" (from fresco Boyana Church)

1966. "2,500 Years of Culture". Multicoloured.
1594 1s. Type **519** . . . . 5·50 4·25
1595 2s. "Destruction of the Idols" (from fresco, Boyana Church) (horiz) 30 15
1596 3s. Bachkovo Monastery . . 50 20
1597 4s. Zemen Monastery (horiz) 50 20
1598 5s. John the Baptist Church, Nesebur 60 30
1599 13s. "Nativity" (icon, Aleksandr Nevski Cathedral, Sofia) . . . . 1·10 85
1600 20s. "Virgin and Child" (icon, Archaeological Museum, Sofia) . . . . . 1·75 1·00

520 "The First Gunshot" at Koprivshtitsa

1966. 90th Anniv of April Uprising.

No.	Type	Description	Unused	Used
1601	**520**	1s. black, brown & gold	10	10
1602	–	2s. black, red and gold	10	10
1603	–	3s. black, green & gold	10	10
1604	–	5s. black, blue & gold	15	10
1605	–	10s. black, purple & gold	60	15
1606	–	13s. black, violet & gold	60	20

DESIGNS: 2s. Georgi Benkovski and Todor Kableskov; 3s. "Showing the Flag" at Panagyurishte; 5s. Vasil Petleshkov and Tsanko Dyustabanov; 10s. Landing of Khristo Botev's detachment at Kozlodui; 13s. Panyot Volov and Zlarion Dragostinov.

522 W.H.O. Building

1966. Inaug of W.H.O. Headquarters, Geneva.

No.	Type	Description	Unused	Used
1608	**522**	13s. blue and silver	1·00	20

523 Worker

1966. 6th Trades Union Congress, Sofia

No.	Type	Description	Unused	Used
1609	**523**	20s. black and pink	1·10	20

524 Indian Elephant

525 Boy and Girl holding Banners

1966. Sofia Zoo Animals. Multicoloured.

No.	Type	Description	Unused	Used
1610		1s. Type **524**	10	10
1611		2s. Tiger	10	10
1612		3s. Chimpanzee	15	10
1613		4s. Ibex	20	10
1614		5s. Polar bear	50	15
1615		8s. Lion	65	25
1616		13s. American bison	2·50	45
1617		20s. Eastern grey kangaroo	3·00	70

1966. 3rd Congress of Bulgarian Sports Federation.

No.	Type	Description	Unused	Used
1618	**525**	13s. blue, orge & cobalt	45	20

526 "Radetski" and Pioneer

1966. 90th Anniv of Khristo Botev's Seizure of River Paddle-steamer "Radetski".

No.	Type	Description	Unused	Used
1619	**526**	2s. multicoloured	20	10

527 Standard-bearer Simov-Kuruto

529 U.N.E.S.C.O. Emblem

528 Federation Emblem

1966. 90th Death Anniv of Nikola Simov-Kuruto (hero of the Uprising against Turkey).

No.	Type	Description	Unused	Used
1620	**527**	5s. multicoloured	30	10

1966. 7th Int Youth Federation Assembly, Sofia.

No.	Type	Description	Unused	Used
1621	**528**	13s. blue and black	65	15

1966. 20th Anniv of U.N.E.S.C.O.

No.	Type	Description	Unused	Used
1622	**529**	20s. ochre, red & black	85	30

530 Footballer with Ball

1966. World Cup Football Championships, London. Showing players in action. Borders in grey.

No.	Type	Description	Unused	Used
1623	**530**	1s. black and brown	10	10
1624	–	2s. black and red	10	10
1625	–	5s. black and bistre	20	10
1626	–	13s. black and blue	65	15
1627	–	20s. black and blue	1·00	30

532 Wrestling

1966. 3rd Int Wrestling Championships, Sofia.

No.	Type	Description	Unused	Used
1629	**532**	13s. sepia, green & brn	45	20

533 Throwing the Javelin

1966. 3rd Republican Spartakiade.

No.	Type	Description	Unused	Used
1630	**533**	2s. green, red & yellow	10	10
1631	–	13s. green, red & yellow	65	25

DESIGN: 13s. Running.

534 Map of Balkans, Globe and U.N.E.S.C.O. Emblem

1966. Int Balkan Studies Congress, Sofia.

No.	Type	Description	Unused	Used
1632	**534**	13s. green, pink & blue	65	15

535 Children with Construction Toy

1966. Children's Day.

No.	Type	Description	Unused	Used
1633	**535**	1s. black, yellow & red	10	10
1634	–	2s. black, brown & grn	10	10
1635	–	3s. black, yellow & blue	15	10
1636	–	13s. black, mauve & bl	1·00	25

DESIGNS: 2s. Rabbit and Teddy Bear; 3s. Children as astronauts; 13s. Children with gardening equipment.

536 Yuri Gagarin and "Vostok 1"

1966. Russian Space Exploration.

No.	Type	Description	Unused	Used
1637	**536**	1s. slate and grey	10	10
1638	–	2s. purple and grey	10	10
1639	–	3s. brown and grey	10	10
1640	–	5s. lake and grey	20	10
1641	–	8s. blue and grey	25	15
1642	–	13s. turquoise and grey	80	25
1643	–	20s.+10s. vio & grey	1·75	55

DESIGNS: 2s. German Titov and "Vostok 2"; 3s. Andrian Nikolaev, Povel Popovich and "Vostok 3" and "4"; 5s. Valentina Tereshkova, Vallery Bykovsky and "Vostok 5" and "6"; 8s. Vladimir Komarov, Boris Yegorov, Konstantin Feoktistov and "Voskhod 1"; 13s. Povel Belyaev, Aleksei Leonov and "Voskhod 2"; 20s. Gagarin, Leonov and Tereshkova.

537 St. Clement (14th-cent wood-carving)

538 Metodi Shatorov

1966. 1050th Death Anniv of St. Clement of Ohrid.

No.	Type	Description	Unused	Used
1645	**537**	5s. brown, red & drab	65	15

1966. Anti-fascist Fighters. Frames in gold; value in black.

No.	Type	Description	Unused	Used
1646	**538**	2s. violet and red	10	10
1647	–	3s. brown and mauve	10	10
1648	–	5s. blue and red	15	10
1649	–	10s. brown and orange	35	15
1650	–	13s. brown and red	70	15

PORTRAITS: 3s. Vladno Trichkov; 5s. Vulcho Ivanov; 10s. Rasko Daskalov; 13s. Gen. Vladimir Zaimov.

539 Georgi Dimitrov (statesman)

541 Bansko Hotel

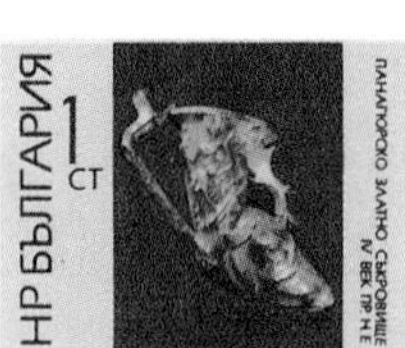

540 Deer's Head Vessel

1966. 9th Bulgarian Communist Party Congress, Sofia.

No.	Type	Description	Unused	Used
1651	**539**	2s. black and red	20	10
1652	–	20s. black, red and grey	1·10	20

DESIGN: 20s. Furnaceman and steelworks.

1966. The Gold Treasures of Panagyurishte. Multicoloured.

No.	Type	Description	Unused	Used
1653		1s. Type **540**	10	10
1654		2s. Amazon	20	10
1655		3s. Ram	25	10
1656		5s. Plate	30	10
1657		6s. Venus	35	10
1658		8s. Roe-buck	1·10	15
1659		10s. Amazon (different)	1·25	15
1660		13s. Amphora	1·40	30
1661		20s. Goat	2·00	65

Except for the 5s. and 13s. the designs show vessels with animal heads.

1966. Tourist Resorts.

No.	Type	Description	Unused	Used
1662	**541**	1s. blue	10	10
1663	–	2s. green (Belogradchik)	10	10
1664	–	2s. lake (Tryavna)	10	10
1665	–	20s. pur (Malovitsa, Rila)	70	15

542 Christmas Tree

1966. New Year. Multicoloured.

No.	Type	Description	Unused	Used
1666		2s. Type **542**	10	10
1667		13s. Money-box	45	15

543 Percho Slaveikov (poet)

544 Dahlias

1966. Cultural Celebrities.

No.	Type	Description	Unused	Used
1668	**543**	1s. bistre, blue & orange	10	10
1669	–	2s. brown, orge & grey	10	10
1670	–	3s. blue, bistre & orange	10	10
1671	–	5s. purple, drab & orge	10	10
1672	–	8s. grey, purple & blue	50	15
1673	–	13s. violet, blue & purple	65	25

CELEBRITIES. Writers (with pen emblem): 2s. Dimcho Debelyanov (poet); 3s. Petko Todorov. Painters (with brush emblem): 5s. Dimitur Dobrovich; 8s. Ivan Murkvichka; 13s. Iliya Beshkov.

1966. Flowers. Multicoloured.

No.	Type	Description	Unused	Used
1674		1s. Type **544**	10	10
1675		1s. Clematis	10	10
1676		2s. Poet's narcissus	15	10
1677		2s. Foxgloves	15	10
1678		3s. Snowdrops	25	10
1679		5s. Petunias	25	10
1680		13s. Tiger lilies	1·00	25
1681		20s. Canterbury bells	1·40	35

545 Common Pheasant

1967. Hunting. Multicoloured.

No.	Type	Description	Unused	Used
1682		1s. Type **545**	40	10
1683		2s. Chukar partridge	40	10
1684		3s. Grey partridge	30	10
1685		5s. Brown hare	75	10
1686		8s. Roe deer	2·00	20
1687		13s. Red deer	2·25	40

546 "Philately"

547 6th-cent B.C. Coin of Thrace

1967. 10th Bulgarian Philatelic Federation Congress, Sofia.

No.	Type	Description	Unused	Used
1688	**546**	10s. yellow, black & grn	1·60	1·00

1967. Ancient Bulgarian Coins. Coins in silver on black background except 13s. (gold on black). Frame colours given.

No.	Type	Description	Unused	Used
1689	**547**	1s. brown	10	10
1690	–	2s. purple	10	10
1691	–	3s. green	15	10
1692	–	5s. brown	25	10
1693	–	13s. turquoise	1·40	40
1694	–	20s. violet	1·90	75

COINS—SQUARE: 2s. 2nd-cent B.C. Macedonian tetradrachm; 3s. 2nd-cent B.C. Odessos (Varna) tetradrachm; 5s. 4th-cent B.C. Macedonian coin of Philip II. HORIZ: (38 × 25 mm): 13s. Obverse and reverse of 4th cent B.C. coin of King Sevt (Thrace); 20s. Obverse and reverse of 5th-cent B.C. coin of Apollonia (Sozopol).

548 Partisans listening to radio

1967. 25th Anniv of Fatherland Front. Mult.

No.	Type	Description	Unused	Used
1695		1s. Type **548**	10	10
1696		20s. Dimitrov speaking at rally	75	25

549 Nikola Kofardzhiev

550 "Cultural Development"

1967. Anti-fascist Fighters.
1697 **549** 1s. red, black & blue . . 10 10
1698 – 2s. green, black & blue 10 10
1699 – 5s. brown, black & blue 15 10
1700 – 10s. blue, black & lilac 30 10
1701 – 13s. purple, black & grey 55 15
PORTRAITS: 2s. Petko Napetov; 5s. Petko Petkov; 10s. Emil Markov; 13s. Traicho Kostov.

1967. 1st Cultural Conference, Sofia.
1702 **550** 13s. yellow, grn & gold 80 15

551 Angora Kitten

1967. Cats. Multicoloured.
1703 1s. Type **551** 10 10
1704 2s. Siamese (horiz) 20 10
1705 3s. Abyssinian 25 10
1706 5s. European black and white . . . . 1·25 10
1707 13s. Persian (horiz) . . . . 1·50 25
1708 20s. European tabby . . . . 2·25 90

552 "Golden Sands" Resort

1967. International Tourist Year. Multicoloured.
1709 13s. Type **552** 35 15
1710 20s. Pamporovo 80 20
1711 40s. Old Church, Nesebur 1·60 50

553 Scene from Iliev's Opera "The Master of Boyana"

1967. 3rd International Young Opera Singers' Competition, Sofia.
1712 **553** 5s. red, blue and grey . . 20 10
1713 – 13s. red, blue and grey 60 15
DESIGN—VERT: 13s. "Vocal Art" (song-bird on piano-keys).

554 G. Kirkov

1967. Birth Cent of Georgi Kirkov (patriot).
1714 **554** 2s. bistre and red . . . 15 10

555 Roses and Distillery

1967. Economic Achievements. Multicoloured.
1715 1s. Type **555** 10 10
1716 1s. Chick and incubator . . 10 10
1717 2s. Cucumber and glass-houses 10 10
1718 2s. Lamb and farm building 10 10
1719 3s. Sunflower and oil-extraction plant 10 10
1720 4s. Pigs and piggery 15 10
1721 5s. Hops and vines 15 10
1722 6s. Grain and irrigation canals 20 10
1723 8s. Grapes and "Bulgar" tractor 20 10
1724 10s. Apples and tree 35 10
1725 13s. Honey bees and honey 60 15
1726 20s. Honey bee on flower, and hives . . . . 1·10 25

556 D.K.M.S. Emblem

557 Map and Spassky Tower, Moscow Kremlin

1967. 11th Anniv of Dimitrov Communist Youth League.
1727 **556** 13s. black, red and blue 70 15

1967. 50th Anniv of October Revolution.
1728 **557** 1s. multicoloured 10 10
1729 – 2s. olive and purple . . 10 10
1730 – 3s. violet and purple . . 10 10
1731 – 5s. red and purple . . . 15 10
1732 – 13s. blue and purple . . 30 15
1733 – 20s. blue and purple . . 1·00 20
DESIGNS: 2s. Lenin directing revolutionaries; 3s. Revolutionaries; 5s. Marx, Engels and Lenin; 13s. Soviet oil refinery; 20s. "Molniya" satellite and Moon (Soviet space research).

558 Scenic "Fish" and Rod

560 Bogdan Peak, Sredna Mts

559 Cross-country Skiing

1967. 7th World Angling Championships, Varna.
1734 **558** 10s. multicoloured . . . 40 15

1967. Winter Olympic Games, Grenoble (1968).
1735 **559** 1s. black, red & turq . . 10 10
1736 – 2s. black, bistre & blue 10 10
1737 – 3s. black, blue & purple 10 10
1738 – 5s. black, yellow & grn 15 10
1739 – 13s. black, buff & blue 1·00 15
1740 – 20s.+10s. mult . . . . . 1·90 50
DESIGNS: 2s. Ski jumping; 3s. Biathlon; 5s. Ice hockey; 13s. Ice skating (pairs); 20s. Men's slalom.

1967. Tourism. Mountain Peaks.
1742 **560** 1s. green and yellow . . 10 10
1743 – 2s. sepia and blue . . . 10 10
1744 – 3s. indigo and blue . . . 10 10
1745 – 5s. green and blue . . . 15 10
1746 – 10s. brown and blue . . 30 10
1747 – 13s. black and blue . . . 40 15
1748 – 20s. blue and purple . . 70 25
DESIGNS—HORIZ: 2s. Cherni Vruh, Vitosha; 5s. Persenk, Rhodopes; 10s. Botev, Stara-Planina; 20s. Vikhren, Pirin. VERT: 3s. Ruen, Osogovska Planina; 13s. Musala, Rila.

561 G. Rakovski

1967. Death Cent of G. Rakovski (revolutionary).
1749 **561** 13s. black and green . . 45 15

562 Yuri Gagarin, Valentina Tereshkova and Aleksei Leonov

1967. Space Exploration. Multicoloured.
1750 1s. Type **562** 10 10
1751 2s. John Glenn and Edward White 15 10
1752 5s. "Molniya 1" 25 10
1753 10s. "Gemini 6" and "7" . . 65 15
1754 13s. "Luna 13" 85 15
1755 20s. "Gemini 10" docking with "Agena" . . . . . 1·10 35

563 Railway Bridge over Yantra River

1967. Views of Turnovo (ancient capital).
1756 **563** 1s. black, drab and blue 15 10
1757 – 2s. multicoloured 10 10
1758 – 3s. multicoloured 10 10
1759 – 5s. black, slate and red 65 20
1760 – 13s. multicoloured . . . 65 15
1761 – 20s. black, orange & lav 1·00 25
DESIGNS: 2s. Hadji Nikola's Inn; 3s. Houses on hillside; 5s. Town and river; 13s. "House of the Monkeys"; 20s. Gurko street.

564 "The Ruchenitsa" (folk dance, from painting by Murkvichka)

1967. Belgian–Bulgarian "Painting and Philately" Exhibition, Brussels.
1762 **564** 20s. green and gold . . . 1·90 1·50

565 "The Shepherd" (Zlatko Boyadzhiev)

1967. Paintings in the National Gallery, Sofia. Multicoloured.
1763 1s. Type **565** 10 10
1764 2s. "The Wedding" (Vladimir Dimitrov) (vert) 10 10
1765 3s. "The Partisans" Ilya Petrov (55 × 35 mm) . . . 20 10
1766 5s. "Anastasia Penchovich" (Nikolai Pavlovich) (vert) 85 15
1767 13s. "Self-portrait" (Zakharii Zograf) (vert) 1·50 50
1768 20s. "Old Town of Plovdiv" (Tsanko Lavrenov) . . . 2·00 1·00

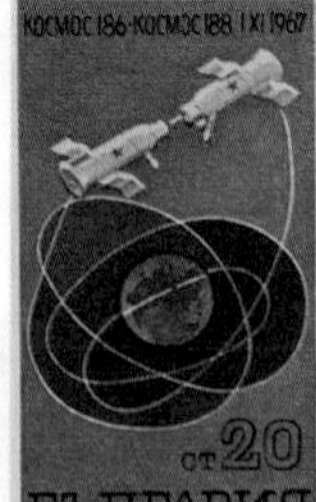

566 Linked Satellites "Cosmos 186" and "188"

1968. "Cosmic Activities". Multicoloured.
1770 20s. Type **566** . . . . . . 1·00 25
1771 40s. "Venus 4" and orbital diagram (horiz) . . . . . 1·90 50

567 "Crossing the Danube" (Orenburgski)

1968. 90th Anniv of Liberation from Turkey. Paintings. Inscr and frames in black and gold; centre colours below.
1772 **567** 1s. green 25 10
1773 – 2s. blue 10 10
1774 – 3s. brown 15 10
1775 – 13s. blue 60 25
1776 – 20s. turquoise . . . . . 1·00 40
DESIGNS—VERT: 2s. "Flag of Samara" (Veschin); 13s. "Battle of Orlovo Gnezdo" (Popov). HORIZ: 3s. "Battle of Pleven" (Orenburgski); 20s. "Greeting Russian Soldiers" (Goudienov).

568 Karl Marx

569 Gorky

1968. 150th Birth Anniv of Karl Marx.
1777 **568** 13s. grey, red & black 65 15

1968. Birth Cent of Maksim Gorky (writer).
1778 **569** 13s. green, orange & blk 65 15

570 Dancers

1968. 9th World Youth and Students' Festival. Sofia. Multicoloured.
1779 2s. Type **570** 10 10
1780 5s. Running 10 10
1781 13s. "Doves" 75 10
1782 20s. "Youth" (symbolic design) 85 25
1783 40s. Bulgarian 5c. stamp of 1879 under magnifier and Globe . . . . 1·50 55

571 "Campanula alpina"

572 "The Unknown Hero" (Ran Bosilek)

1968. Wild Flowers. Multicoloured.
1784 1s. Type **571** 10 10
1785 2s. Trumpet gentian 10 10
1786 3s. "Crocus veluchensis" . . 15 10
1787 5s. Siberian iris 20 10
1788 10s. Dog's-tooth violet . . . 30 10
1789 13s. House leek . . . . . . 1·00 15
1790 20s. Burning bush . . . . . 1·40 30

1968. Bulgarian–Danish Stamp Exhibition. Fairy Tales. Multicoloured.
1791 13s. Type **572** 45 20
1792 20s. "The Witch and the Young Men" (Hans Andersen) 55 35

573 Memorial Temple, Shipka

574 Copper Rolling-mill, Medet

1968. Bulgarian–West Berlin Stamp Exn.
1793 **573** 13s. multicoloured . . . 1·00 35

1968. Air.
1794 **574** 1l. red . . . . 2·75 35

575 Lake Smolyan

576 Gymnastics

1968.
1795 **575** 1s. green 10 10
1796 – 2s. myrtle 10 10
1797 – 3s. sepia 10 10

No.	Type	Description	Unused	Used
1798	–	8s. green	25	10
1799	–	10s. brown	65	10
1800	–	13s. olive	45	15
1801	–	40s. blue	1·25	35
1802	–	2l. brown	6·00	1·40

DESIGNS: 2s. River Ropotamo; 3s. Lomnitza Gorge, Erma River; 8s. River Isker; 10s. Cruise ship "Die Fregatte"; 13s. Cape Kaliakra, 40s. Sozopol, 2l. Mountain road, Kamchia River.

1968. Olympic Games, Mexico.

No.	Type	Description	Unused	Used
1803	**576**	1s. black and red	10	10
1804	–	2s. black, brown & grey	10	10
1805	–	3s. black and mauve	15	10
1806	–	10s. black, yell & turq	50	10
1807	–	13s. black, pink & blue	1·00	20
1808	–	20s.+10s. grey, pk & bl	1·75	40

DESIGNS: 2s. Horse-jumping; 3s. Fencing; 10s. Boxing; 13s. Throwing the discus; 20s. Rowing.

577 Dimitur on Mt. Buzludzha, 1868

1968. Centenary of Exploits of Khadzhi Dimitur and Stefan Karadzha (revolutionaries).

No.	Type	Description	Unused	Used
1810	**577**	2s. brown and silver	15	10
1811	–	13s. green and gold	35	15

DESIGN: 13s. Dimitur and Karadzha.

578 Human Rights Emblem

579 Cinereous Black Vulture

1968. Human Rights Year.

No.	Type	Description	Unused	Used
1812	**578**	20s. gold and blue	1·00	15

1968. 80th Anniv of Sofia Zoo.

No.	Type	Description	Unused	Used
1813	**579**	1s. black, brown & blue	50	10
1814	–	2s. black, yellow & brn	50	10
1815	–	3s. black and green	30	10
1816	–	5s. black, yellow & red	50	10
1817	–	13s. black, bistre & grn	1·60	15
1818	–	20s. black, green & blue	2·50	55

DESIGNS: 2s. South African crowned crane; 3s. Common zebra; 5s. Leopard; 13s. Python; 20s. Crocodile.

580 Battle Scene

1968. 280th Anniv of Chiprovtsi Rising.

No.	Type	Description	Unused	Used
1819	**580**	13s. multicoloured	80	15

581 Caterpillar-hunter

582 Flying Swans

1968. Insects.

No.	Type	Description	Unused	Used
1820	**581**	1s. green	15	10
1821	–	1s. brown	15	10
1822	–	1s. blue	15	10
1823	–	1s. brown	15	10
1824	–	1s. purple	35	10

DESIGNS—VERT: No. 1821, Stag beetle ("Lucanus cervus"); 1822, "Procerus scabrosus" (ground beetle). HORIZ: No. 1823, European rhinoceros beetle ("Oryctes nasicornis"); 1824, "Perisomena caecigena" (moth).

1968. "Co-operation with Scandinavia".

No.	Type	Description	Unused	Used
1825	–	2s. ochre and green	1·25	1·25
1826	**582**	5s. blue, grey & black	1·25	1·25
1827	–	13s. purple and maroon	1·25	1·25
1828	–	20s. grey and violet	1·25	1·25

DESIGNS: 2s. Wooden flask; 13s. Rose; 20s. "Viking ship".

583 Congress Building and Emblem

1968. International Dental Congress, Varna.

No.	Type	Description	Unused	Used
1829	**583**	20s. gold, green and red	85	15

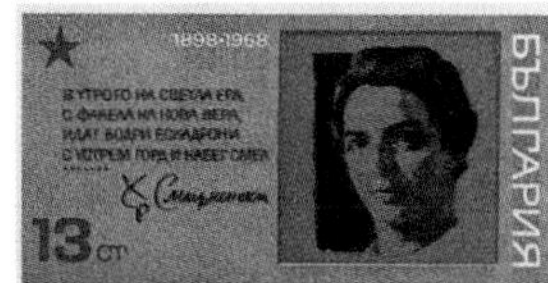

584 Smirnenski and Verse from "Red Squadrons"

1968. 70th Birth Anniv of Khristo Smirnenski (poet).

No.	Type	Description	Unused	Used
1830	**584**	13s. black, orange & gold	45	15

585 Dove with Letter

1968. National Stamp Exhibition, Sofia and 75th Anniv of "National Philately".

No.	Type	Description	Unused	Used
1831	**585**	20s. green	1·10	85

586 Dalmatian Pelican

1968. Srebirna Wildlife Reservation. Birds. Mult.

No.	Type	Description	Unused	Used
1832		1s. Type **586**	10	10
1833		2s. Little egret	15	10
1834		3s. Great crested grebe	20	10
1835		5s. Common tern	50	15
1836		13s. White spoonbill	1·50	50
1837		20s. Glossy ibis	2·75	85

587 Silistra Costume

1968. Provincial Costumes. Multicoloured.

No.	Type	Description	Unused	Used
1838		1s. Type **587**	10	10
1839		2s. Lovech	10	10
1840		3s. Yamboi	15	10
1841		13s. Chirpan	45	10
1842		20s. Razgrad	1·00	25
1843		40s. Ikhtiman	2·00	50

588 "St. Arsenius" (icon)

1968. Rila Monastery. Icons and murals. Mult.

No.	Type	Description	Unused	Used
1844		1s. Type **588**	10	10
1845		2s. "Carrying St. Ivan Rilski's Relics" (horiz)	10	10
1846		3s. "St. Michael torments the Rich Man's Soul"	15	10
1847		13s. "St. Ivan Rilski"	1·00	15
1848		20s. "Prophet Joel"	1·40	30
1849		40s. "St. George"	2·40	1·00

589 "Matricaria chamomilla"

1968. Medicinal Plants. Multicoloured.

No.	Type	Description	Unused	Used
1851		1s. Type **589**	10	10
1852		1s. "Mespilus oxyacantha"	10	10
1853		2s. Lily of the valley	10	10
1854		3s. Deadly nightshade	10	10
1855		5s. Common mallow	15	10
1856		10s. Yellow peasant's eye	25	10
1857		13s. Common poppy	50	15
1858		20s. Wild thyme	1·00	25

590 Silkworms and Spindles

1969. Silk Industry. Multicoloured.

No.	Type	Description	Unused	Used
1859		1s. Type **590**	10	10
1860		2s. Worm, cocoons and pattern	10	10
1861		3s. Cocoons and spinning wheel	10	10
1862		5s. Cocoons and pattern	15	10
1863		13s. Moth, cocoon and spindles	40	15
1864		20s. Moth, eggs and shuttle	85	25

591 "Death of Ivan Asen"

592 "Saints Cyril and Methodius" (mural, Troyan Monastery)

1969. Manasses Chronicle (1st series). Mult.

No.	Type	Description	Unused	Used
1865		1s. Type **591**	10	10
1866		2s. "Emperor Nicephorus invading Bulgaria"	10	10
1867		3s. "Khan Krum's Feast"	15	10
1868		13s. "Prince Sviatoslav invading Bulgaria"	85	15
1869		20s. "The Russian invasion"	1·10	25
1870		40s. "Jesus Christ, Tsar Ivan Alexander and Constantine Manasses"	2·10	75

See also Nos. 1911/16.

1969. Saints Cyril and Methodius Commem.

No.	Type	Description	Unused	Used
1871	**592**	28s. multicoloured	1·40	45

593 Galleon

594 Posthorn Emblem

1969. Air. "SOFIA 1969" International Stamp Exhibition. Transport. Multicoloured.

No.	Type	Description	Unused	Used
1872		1s. Type **593**	10	10
1873		2s. Mail coach	10	10
1874		3s. Steam locomotive	20	10
1875		5s. Early motor-car	15	10
1876		10s. Montgolfier's balloon and Henri Giffard's steam-powered dirigible airship	20	10
1877		13s. Early flying machines	30	15
1878		20s. Modern aircraft	85	25
1879		40s. Rocket and planets	1·50	50

1969. 90th Anniv of Bulgarian Postal Services.

No.	Type	Description	Unused	Used
1881	**594**	2s. yellow and green	10	10
1882	–	13s. multicoloured	65	10
1883	–	20s. blue	85	25

DESIGNS: 13s. Bulgarian Stamps of 1879 and 1946; 20s. Post Office workers' strike, 1919.

595 I.L.O. Emblem

596 "Fox" and "Rabbit"

1969. 50th Anniv of I.L.O.

No.	Type	Description	Unused	Used
1884	**595**	13s. black and green	35	15

1969. Children's Book Week.

No.	Type	Description	Unused	Used
1885	**596**	1s. black, orange & grn	10	10
1886	–	2s. black, blue and red	10	10
1887	–	13s. black, olive & blue	65	15

DESIGNS: 2s. Boy with "hedgehog" and "squirrel"; 13s. "The Singing Lesson".

597 Hand with Seedling

1969. "10,000,000 Hectares of New Forests".

No.	Type	Description	Unused	Used
1888	**597**	2s. black, green & purple	15	10

598 "St. George" (14th Century)

1969. Religious Art. Multicoloured.

No.	Type	Description	Unused	Used
1889		1s. Type **598**	10	10
1890		2s. "The Virgin and St. John Bogoslov" (14th century)	10	10
1891		3s. "Archangel Michael" (17th century)	15	10
1892		5s. "Three Saints" (17th century)	25	10
1893		8s. "Jesus Christ" (17th century)	30	10
1894		13s. "St. George and St. Dimitr" (19th century)	75	15
1895		20s. "Christ the Universal" (19th century)	1·10	15
1896		60s. "The Forty Martyrs" (19th century)	3·25	90
1897		80s. "The Transfiguration" (19th century)	4·00	1·60

599 Roman Coin

600 St. George and the Dragon

1969. "SOFIA 1969" International Stamp Exhibition. "Sofia Through the Ages".

No.	Type	Description	Unused	Used
1899	**599**	1s. silver, blue and gold	10	10
1900	–	2s. silver, green & gold	10	10
1901	–	3s. silver, lake and gold	10	10
1902	–	4s. silver, violet & gold	15	10
1903	–	5s. silver, purple & gold	15	10
1904	–	13s. silver, green & gold	50	15
1905	–	20s. silver, blue & gold	1·00	15
1906	–	40s. silver, red & gold	2·00	35

DESIGNS: 2s. Roman coin showing Temple of Aesculapius; 3s. Church of St. Sophia; 4s. Boyana Church; 5s. Parliament Building; 13s. National Theatre; 20s. Aleksandr Nevski Cathedral; 40s. Sofia University.

1969. Int Philatelic Federation Congress, Sofia.

No.	Type	Description	Unused	Used
1908	**600**	40s. black, orange & sil	2·00	75

601 St. Cyril

1969. 1,100th Death Anniv of St. Cyril.

1909 **601** 2s. green & red on silver 15 10
1910 – 28s. blue & red on silver 1·40 35

DESIGN: 28s. St. Cyril and procession.

1969. Manasses Chronicle (2nd series). Designs as T **591**, but all horiz. Multicoloured.

1911 1s. "Nebuchadnezzar II and Balthasar of Babylon, Cyrus and Darius of Persia" 10 10
1912 2s. "Cambyses, Gyges and Darius of Persia" 10 10
1913 5s. "Prophet David and Tsar Ivan Alexander" 15 10
1914 13s. "Rout of the Byzantine Army, 811" 85 15
1915 20s. "Christening of Khan Boris" 1·60 20
1916 60s. "Tsar Simeon's attack on Constantinople" 3·25 1·10

602 Partisans

1969. 25th Anniv of Fatherland Front Government.

1917 **602** 1s. lilac, red and black 10 10
1918 – 2s. brown, red & black 10 10
1919 – 3s. green, red and black 10 10
1920 – 5s. brown, red & black 20 10
1921 – 13s. blue, red & black 30 10
1922 – 20s. multicoloured 75 20

DESIGNS: 2s. Combine-harvester; 3s. Dam; 5s. Folk singers; 13s. Petroleum refinery; 20s. Lenin, Dimitrov and flags.

603 Gymnastics

1969. 3rd Republican Spartakiad. Multicoloured.

1923 2s. Type **603** 10 10
1924 20s. Wrestling 85 25

604 "Construction" and soldier

605 T. Tserkovski

1969. 25th Anniv of Army Engineers.

1925 **604** 6s. black and blue 15 10

1969. Birth Cent of Tsanke Tserkovski (poet).

1926 **605** 13s. multicoloured 35 15

606 "Woman" (Roman Statue)

607 Skipping-rope Exercise

1969. 1,800th Anniv of Silistra.

1927 **606** 2s. grey, blue and silver 15 10
1928 – 13s. brown, grn & silver 75 15

DESIGN—HORIZ: 13s. "Wolf" (bronze statue).

1969. World Gymnastics Competition, Varna.

1929 **607** 1s. grey, blue and green 10 10
1930 – 2s. grey and blue 10 10
1931 – 3s. grey, green and emerald 10 10
1932 – 5s. grey, purple and red 10 10
1933 – 13s.+5s. grey, bl & red 85 25
1934 – 20s.+10s. grey, green and yellow 1·40 40

DESIGNS: 2s. Hoop exercise (pair); 3s. Hoop exercise (solo); 5s. Ball exercise (pair); 13s. Ball exercise (solo); 20s. Solo gymnast.

608 Marin Drinov (founder)

1969. Cent of Bulgarian Academy of Sciences.

1935 **608** 20s. black and red 45 15

609 "Neophit Rilski" (Zakharii Zograf)

1969. Paintings in National Gallery, Sofia. Mult.

1936 1s. Type **609** 10 10
1937 2s. "German's Mother" (Vasil Stoilov) 10 10
1938 3s. "Workers' Family" (Neuko Balkanski) (horiz) 20 10
1939 4s. "Woman Dressing" (Ivan Nenov) 30 10
1940 5s. "Portrait of a Woman" (Nikolai Pavlovich) 30 10
1941 13s. "Krustyn Sarafov as Falstaff" (Dechko Uzunov) 85 15
1942 20s. "Artist's Wife" (N. Mikhailov) (horiz) 1·00 25
1943 20s. "Worker's Lunch" (Stoyan Sotirov) (horiz) 1·10 30
1944 40s. "Self-portrait" (Tseno Todorov) (horiz) 1·60 80

610 Pavel Banya

1969. Sanatoria.

1945 **610** 2s. blue 10 10
1946 – 5s. blue 10 10
1947 – 6s. green 20 10
1948 – 20s. green 55 15

SANATORIA: 5s. Khisar; 6s. Kotel; 20s. Narechen Polyclinic.

611 Deep-sea Trawler

1969. Ocean Fisheries.

1949 **611** 1s. grey and blue 30 10
1950 – 1s. green and black 10 10
1951 – 2s. violet and black 10 10
1952 – 3s. blue and black 10 10
1953 – 5s. mauve and black 20 10
1954 – 10s. grey and black 1·00 15
1955 – 13s. flesh, orange & blk 1·50 25
1956 – 20s. brown, ochre & blk 2·00 35

DESIGNS: 1s. (No. 1950), Cape hake; 2s. Atlantic horse-mackerel; 3s. South African pilchard; 5s. Large-eyed dentex; 10s. Chub mackerel; 13s. Senegal croaker; 20s. Vadigo.

612 Trapeze Act

613 V. Kubasov, Georgi Shonin and "Soyuz 6"

1969. Circus. Multicoloured.

1957 1s. Type **612** 10 10
1958 2s. Acrobats 10 10
1959 3s. Balancing act with hoops 10 10
1960 5s. Juggler, and bear on cycle 10 10
1961 13s. Equestrian act 40 15
1962 20s. Clowns 1·00 35

1970. Space Flights of "Soyuz 6, 7 and 8".

1963 **613** 1s. multicoloured 10 10
1964 – 2s. multicoloured 10 10
1965 – 3s. multicoloured 15 10
1966 – 28s. pink and blue 1·40 30

DESIGNS: 2s. Viktor Gorbacko, Vladislav Volkov, Anatoly Filipchenko and "Soyuz 7"; 3s. Aleksei Elseev, Vladimir Shatalov and "Soyuz 8"; 28s. Three "Soyuz" spacecraft in orbit.

614 Khan Asparerch and "Old-Bulgars" crossing the Danube, 679

1970. History of Bulgaria. Multicoloured.

1967 1s. Type **614** 10 10
1968 2s. Khan Krum and defeat of Emperor Nicephorus, 811 10 10
1969 3s. Conversion of Khan Boris I to Christianity, 865 15 10
1970 5s. Tsar Simeon and Battle of Akhelo, 917 20 10
1971 8s. Tsar Samuel and defeat of Byzantines, 976 20 10
1972 10s. Tsar Kaloyan and victory over Emperor Baldwin, 1205 30 15
1973 13s. Tsar Ivan Assen II and defeat of Komnine of Epirus, 1230 85 15
1974 20s. Coronation of Tsar Ivailo, 1277 1·40 25

615 Bulgarian Pavilion

1970. "Expo 70" World's Fair, Osaka, Japan (1st issue).

1975 **615** 20s. silver, yellow & brn 1·40 85

See Nos. 2009/12.

616 Footballers

1970. World Football Cup, Mexico.

1976 **616** 1s. multicoloured 10 10
1977 – 2s. multicoloured 10 10
1978 – 3s. multicoloured 15 10
1979 – 5s. multicoloured 20 10
1980 – 20s. multicoloured 1·25 35
1981 – 40s. multicoloured 2·40 60

DESIGNS: 2s. to 40s. Various football scenes.

617 Lenin

618 "Tephrocactus Alexanderi v. bruchi"

1970. Birth Cent of Lenin. Multicoloured.

1983 2s. Type **617** 10 10
1984 13s. Full-face portrait 40 15
1985 20s. Lenin writing 75 25

1970. Flowering Cacti. Multicoloured.

1986 1s. Type **618** 10 10
1987 2s. "Opuntia drummondii" 15 10
1988 3s. "Hatiora cilindrica" 20 10
1989 5s. "Gymnocalycium vatteri" 25 10
1990 8s. "Helianthо cereus grandiflorus" 40 20
1991 10s. "Neochilenia andreaeana" 1·75 25
1992 13s. "Peireskia vargasii v. longispina" 1·90 30
1993 20s. "Neobesseya rosiflora" 2·50 45

619 Rose

620 Union Badge

1970. Bulgarian Roses.

1994 **619** 1s. multicoloured 10 10
1995 – 2s. multicoloured 15 10
1996 – 3s. multicoloured 25 10
1997 – 4s. multicoloured 30 10
1998 – 5s. multicoloured 35 10
1999 – 13s. multicoloured 55 10
2000 – 20s. multicoloured 1·60 45
2001 – 28s. multicoloured 2·75 85

DESIGNS: 2s. to 28s. Various roses.

1970. 70th Anniv of Agricultural Union.

2002 **620** 20s. black, gold and red 1·00 25

621 Gold Bowl

1970. Gold Treasures of Thrace.

2003 **621** 1s. black, blue and gold 10 10
2004 – 2s. black, lilac and gold 10 10
2005 – 3s. black, red and gold 15 10
2006 – 5s. black, green & gold 20 10
2007 – 13s. black, orge & gold 1·00 15
2008 – 20s. black, violet & gold 1·50 30

DESIGNS: 2s. Three small bowls; 3s. Plain lid; 5s. Pear shaped ornaments; 13s. Large lid with pattern; 20s. Vase.

622 Rose and Woman with Baskets of Produce

1970. "Expo 70" World's Fair, Osaka, Japan (2nd issue). Multicoloured.

2009 1s. Type **622** 10 10
2010 2s. Three Dancers 10 10
2011 3s. Girl in National costume 10 10
2012 28s. Dancing couples 1·25 35

623 U.N. Emblem

1970. 25th Anniv of United Nations.

2014 **623** 20s. gold and blue 85 15

624 I. Vasov

1970. 120th Birth Anniv of Ivan Vasov (poet).

2015 **624** 13s. blue 45 15

625 Edelweiss Sanatorium, Borovets

1970. Health Resorts.

2016 **625** 1s. green 10 10
2017 – 2s. olive 10 10
2018 – 4s. blue 20 10
2019 – 8s. blue 30 10
2020 – 10s. blue 35 10

DESIGNS: 2s. Panorama Hotel, Pamporovo; 4s. Yachts, Albena; 8s. Harbour scene, Rousalka; 10s. Shtastlivetsa Hotel, Mt. Vitosha.

626 Hungarian Retriever

1970. Dogs. Multicoloured.
2021 1s. Type **626** 15 10
2022 2s. Retriever (vert) 20 10
2023 3s. Great Dane (vert) . . . 30 10
2024 4s. Boxer (vert) 40 10
2025 5s. Cocker spaniel (vert) . . 50 10
2026 13s. Dobermann pinscher (vert) . . . . 1·25 25
2027 20s. Scottish terrier (vert) . . 2·25 50
2028 28s. Russian hound . . . . 2·75 75

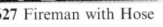

627 Fireman with Hose **628** Congress Emblem

1970. Fire Protection.
2029 **627** 1s. grey, yellow & black 10 10
2030 – 3s. red, grey and black 15 10
DESIGN. 3s. Fire-engine.

1970. 7th World Sociological Congress, Varna.
2031 **628** 13s. multicoloured . . . 50 15

629 Two Male Players **630** Cyclists

1970. World Volleyball Championships.
2032 **629** 2s. black and brown . . 10 10
2033 – 2s. orange, black & blue 15 10
2034 – 20s. yellow, black & grn 1·00 20
2035 – 20s. multicoloured . . . 1·00 20
DESIGNS: No. 2033, Two female players; 2034, Male player; 2035, Female player.

1970. 20th Round-Bulgaria Cycle Race.
2036 **630** 20s. mauve, yellow & grn 75 20

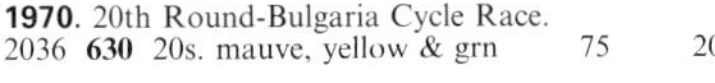

631 Enrico Caruso and Scene from "II Pagliacci"

1970. Opera Singers. Multicoloured.
2037 1s. Type **631** 10 10
2038 2s. Khristina Morfova and "The Bartered Bride" . . 10 10
2039 3s. Petur Raichev and "Tosca" 10 10
2040 10s. Tsvetana Tabakova and "The Flying Dutchman" 40 20
2041 13s. Katya Popova and "The Masters of Nuremberg" 45 10
2042 20s. Fyodor Chaliapin and "Boris Godunov" . . . . 1·75 40

632 Beethoven

1970. Birth Bicentenary of Ludwig von Beethoven (composer).
2043 **632** 28s. blue and purple . . 3·00 50

633 Ivan Asen II Coin

1970. Bulgarian Coins of the 14th century. Multicoloured.
2044 1s. Type **633** 10 10
2045 2s. Theodor Svetoslav . . . 10 10
2046 3s. Mikhail Shishman . . . 10 10
2047 13s. Ivan Alexander and Mikhail Asen 45 10
2048 20s. Ivan Sratsimir . . . . 1·00 15
2049 28s. Ivan Shishman (initials) 1·25 20

635 Engels **636** Snow Crystal

1970. 150th Birth Anniv of Friedrich Engels.
2051 **635** 13s. brown and red . . . 60 15

1970. New Year.
2052 **636** 2s. multicoloured 15 10

638 "Girl's Head" (Zheko Spiridonov)

1971. Modern Bulgarian Sculpture.
2054 **638** 1s. violet and gold . . . 10 10
2055 – 2s. green and gold . . . 35 10
2056 – 3s. brown and gold . . . 10 10
2057 – 13s. green and gold . . . 45 15
2058 – 20s. red and gold . . . 1·10 20
2059 – 28s. brown and gold . . 1·50 45
SCULPTURES: 2s. "Third Class Carriage" (Ivan Funev); 3s. "Elin Pelin" (Marko Markov); 13s. "Nina" (Andrei Nikolov); 20s. "Kneeling Woman" (Yavorov monument, Ivan Lazarov); 28s. "Engineer" (Ivan Funev).

639 Birds and Flowers

1971. Spring.
2061 **639** 1s. multicoloured 10 10
2062 – 2s. multicoloured 10 10
2063 – 3s. multicoloured 10 10
2064 – 5s. multicoloured 10 10
2065 – 13s. multicoloured . . . 25 10
2066 – 20s. multicoloured . . . 1·00 20
DESIGNS: 2s. to 20s. Various designs of birds and flowers similar to Type **639**.

640 "Khan Asparuch crossing Danube" (Boris Angelushev)

1971. Bulgarian History. Paintings. Mult.
2067 2s. Type **640** 10 10
2068 3s. "Ivajlo in Turnovo" (Ilya Petrov) 15 10
2069 5s. "Cavalry Charge, Benkovski" (P. Morosov) 50 10
2070 8s. "Gen. Gzrko entering Sofia, 1878" (D. Gyudzhenov) 85 10
2071 28s. "Greeting Red Army" (Stefan Venev) . . . . . 4·25 1·50

641 Running

1971. 2nd European Indoor Track and Field Championships. Multicoloured.
2073 2s. Type **641** 15 10
2074 20s. Putting the shot . . . . 1·60 25

642 School Building

1971. Foundation of First Bulgarian Secondary School, Bolgrad.
2075 **642** 2s. green, brown & sil 10 10
2076 – 20s. violet, brown & sil 95 20
DESIGN: 20s. Dimitur Mutev, Prince Bogoridi and Sava Radulov (founders).

643 Communards

1971. Centenary of Paris Commune.
2077 **643** 20s. black and red . . . 65 25

644 Georgi Dimitrov challenging Hermann Goering

1971. 20th Anniv of "Federation Internationale des Resistants".
2078 **644** 2s. multicoloured 15 10
2079 13s. multicoloured . . . 1·10 20

646 G. Rakovski **647** Worker and Banner ("People's Progress")

1971. 150th Birth Anniv of Georgi Rakovski (politician and Revolutionary).
2081 **646** 13s. brown, cream & grn 35 15

1971. 10th Bulgarian Communist Party Congress. Multicoloured.
2082 1s. Type **647** 10 10
2083 2s. Symbols of "Technical Progress" (horiz) 10 10
2084 12s. Men clasping hands ("Bulgarian-Soviet Friendship") 75 10

648 Pipkov and Music

1971. Birth Centenary of Panaiot Pipokov.
2085 **648** 13s. black, green & silver 60 20

649 "Three Races" **650** Mammoth

1971. Racial Equality Year.
2086 **649** 13s. multicoloured . . . 45 15

1971. Prehistoric Animals. Multicoloured.
2087 1s. Type **650** 10 10
2088 2s. Bear (vert) 10 10
2089 3s. Hipparion 15 10
2090 13s. Mastodon 90 15
2091 20s. Dinotherium (vert) . . 1·40 25
2092 28s. Sabre-toothed tiger . . 1·90 35

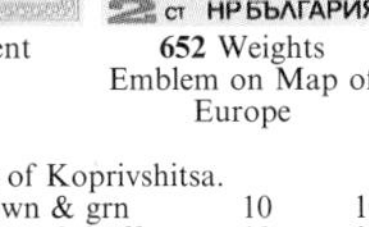

651 Facade of Ancient Building **652** Weights Emblem on Map of Europe

1971. Ancient Buildings of Koprivshitsa.
2093 **651** 1s. green, brown & grn 10 10
2094 – 2s. brown, green & buff 10 10
2095 – 6s. violet, brown & blue 20 10
2096 – 13s. red, blue & orange 65 25
DESIGNS: 1s. to 13s. Different facades.

1971. 30th European Weightlifting Championships, Sofia. Multicoloured.
2097 2s. Type **652** 10 10
2098 13s. Figures supporting weights . . . . 1·25 20

653 Frontier Guard and Dog **654** Tweezers, Magnifying Glass and "Stamp"

1971. 25th Anniv of Frontier Guards.
2099 **653** 2s. olive, green & turq 10 10

1971. 9th Congress of Bulgarian Philatelic Federation.
2100 **654** 20s.+10s. brown, black and red . . . . 1·50 50

655 Congress Meeting (sculpture)

1971. 80th Anniv of Bulgarian Social Democratic Party Congress, Buzludzha.
2101 **655** 2s. green, cream and red 15 10

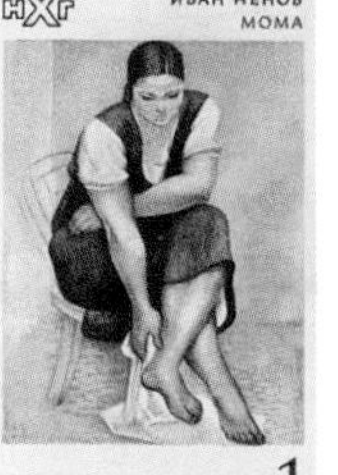

656 "Mother" (Ivan Nenov) **657** Factory Botevgrad

1971. Paintings from the National Art Gallery (1st series). Multicoloured.

2102	1s. Type **656**	10	10
2103	2s. "Lazorova" (Stefan Ivanov)	10	10
2104	3s. "Portrait of Yu. Kh." (Kiril Tsonev)	15	10
2105	13s. "Portrait of a Lady" (Dechko Uzunov)	75	15
2106	30s. "Young Woman from Kalotina" (Vladimir Dimitrov)	1·10	35
2107	40s. "Goryanin" (Stryan Venev)	2·00	60

See also Nos. 2145/50.

1971. Industrial Buildings.

2108	**657** 1s. violet	10	10
2109	– 2s. red	10	10
2110	– 10s. violet	20	10
2111	– 13s. red	25	10
2112	– 40s. brown	1·10	10

DESIGNS—VERT: 2s. Petro-chemical plant, Pleven. HORIZ: 10s. Chemical works, Vratsa; 13s. "Maritsa-Istok" plant, Dimitrovgrad; 40s. Electronics factory, Sofia.

658 Free Style Wrestling

1971. European Wrestling Championships, Sofia.

2113	**658** 2s. green, black and blue	10	10
2114	– 13s. black, red and blue	75	20

DESIGN: 13s. Greco-Roman wrestling.

659 Posthorn Emblem

1971. Organization of Socialist Countries' Postal Administrations Congress.

2115	**659** 20s. gold and green	65	25

660 Entwined Ribbons

1971. 7th European Biochemical Congress, Varna.

2116	**660** 13s. red, brown & black	65	25

661 "New Republic" Statue

1971. 25th Anniv of People's Republic.

2117	**661** 2s. red, yellow and gold	10	10
2118	– 13s. green, red and gold	50	20

DESIGN: 13s. Bulgarian flag.

662 Cross-country Skiing

1971. Winter Olympic Games, Sapporo, Japan. Multicoloured.

2119	1s. Type **662**	10	10
2120	2s. Downhill skiing	10	10
2121	3s. Ski jumping	15	10
2122	4s. Figure skating	15	10
2123	13s. Ice hockey	85	75
2124	28s. Slalom skiing	1·50	40

663 Brigade Members

664 U.N.E.S.C.O. Emblem and Wreath

1971. 25th Anniv of Youth Brigades Movement.

2126	**663** 2s. blue	15	10

1971. 25th Anniv of U.N.E.S.C.O.

2127	**664** 20s. multicoloured	75	25

665 "The Footballer"

1971. Paintings by Kiril Tsonev. Multicoloured.

2128	1s. Type **665**	10	10
2129	2s. "Landscape" (horiz)	10	10
2130	3s. Self-portrait	15	10
2131	13s. "Lilies"	75	10
2132	20s. "Woodland Scene" (horiz)	1·10	30
2133	40s. "Portrait of a Young Woman"	2·00	40

666 "Salyut" Space-station

1971. Space Flights of "Salyut" and "Soyuz 11". Multicoloured.

2134	2s. Type **666**	10	10
2135	13s. "Soyuz 11"	40	15
2136	40s. "Salyut" and "Soyuz 11" joined together	1·90	45

667 "Vikhren" (ore carrier)

1972. "One Million Tons of Bulgarian Shipping".

2138	**667** 18s. lilac, red and black	1·25	20

668 Goce Delcev

1972. Birth Centenaries of Macedonian Revolutionaries.

2139	**668** 2s. black and red	10	10
2140	– 5s. black and green	10	10
2141	– 13s. black and yellow	45	15

PATRIOTS: 5s. Jan Sandanski (1972); 13s. Dume Gruev (1971).

669 Gymnast with Ball

1972. World Gymnastics Championships, Havana (Cuba). Multicoloured.

2142	13s. Type **669**	85	15
2143	18s. Gymnast with hoop	1·00	25

1972. Paintings in Bulgarian National Gallery (2nd series). As T **656** but horiz. Multicoloured.

2145	1s. "Melnik" (Petur Mladenov)	10	10
2146	2s. "Ploughman" (Pencho Georgiev)	10	10
2147	3s. "By the Death-bed" (Aleksandur Zhendov)	15	10
2148	13s. "Family" (Vladimir Dimitrov)	75	15
2149	20s. "Family" (Neuko Balkanski)	1·25	25
2150	40s. "Father Paisii" (Koyu Denchev)	2·00	40

670 Bulgarian Worker

671 "Singing Harvesters"

1972. 7th Bulgarian Trade Unions Congress.

2151	**670** 13s. multicoloured	35	15

1972. 90th Birth Anniv of Vladimir Dimitrov, the Master (painter). Multicoloured.

2152	1s. Type **671**	10	10
2153	2s. "Farm Worker"	10	10
2154	3s. "Women Cultivators" (horiz)	10	10
2155	13s. "Peasant Girl" (horiz)	75	10
2156	20s. "My Mother"	1·10	30
2157	40s. Self-portrait	2·00	40

672 Heart and Tree Emblem

673 St. Mark's Cathedral

1972. World Heart Month.

2158	**672** 13s. multicoloured	1·10	50

1972. U.N.E.S.C.O. "Save Venice" Campaign.

2159	**673** 2s. green, turquoise & bl	10	10
2160	– 13s. brown, violet & grn	70	20

DESIGN: 13s. Doge's Palace.

674 Dimitrov at Typesetting Desk

1972. 90th Birth Anniv of Georgi Dimitrov (statesman). Multicoloured.

2161	1s. Type **674**	10	10
2162	2s. Dimitrov leading uprising of 1923	10	10
2163	3s. Dimitrov at Leipzig Trial	10	10
2164	5s. Dimitrov addressing workers	15	10
2165	13s. Dimitrov with Bulgarian crowd	40	15
2166	18s. Addressing young people	1·00	15
2167	28s. Dimitrov with children	1·40	20
2168	40s. Dimitrov's mausoleum	2·00	25
2169	80s. Portrait head (green and gold)	5·75	60
2173	80s. As No. 2169	10·00	10·00

No. 2173 has the centre in red and gold, and is imperforate.

675 "Lamp of Learning" and Quotation

1972. 250th Birth Anniv of Father Paisii Khilendurski (historian).

2171	**675** 2s. brown, green & gold	15	10
2172	– 13s. brown, grn & gold	75	20

DESIGN: 13s. Paisii writing.

676 Canoeing

1972. Olympic Games, Munich. Multicoloured.

2174	1s. Type **676**	10	10
2175	2s. Gymnastics	10	10
2176	3s. Swimming	10	10
2177	13s. Volleyball	35	10
2178	18s. Hurdling	85	25
2179	40s. Wrestling	1·50	45

677 Angel Kunchev

1972. Death Cent of Angel Kunchev (patriot).

2181	**677** 2s. mauve, gold & purple	10	10

678 "Golden Sands"

1972. Black Sea Resorts. Hotels. Multicoloured.

2182	1s. Type **678**	10	10
2183	2s. Druzhba	10	10
2184	3s. "Sunny Beach"	10	10
2185	13s. Primorsko	25	10
2186	28s. Rusalka	80	25
2187	40s. Albena	1·25	30

679 Canoeing (Bronze Medal)

1972. Bulgarian Medal Winners, Olympic Games, Munich. Multicoloured.

2188	1s. Type **679**	10	10
2189	2s. Long jumping (Silver Medal)	15	10
2190	3s. Boxing (Gold Medal)	15	10
2191	18s. Wrestling (Gold Medal)	1·00	30
2192	40s. Weightlifting (Gold Medal)	1·60	40

680 Subi Dimitrov

682 "Lilium rhodopaeum"

681 Commemorative Text

1972. Resistance Heroes. Multicoloured.

2193	1s. Type **680**	10	10
2194	2s. Tsvyatko Radoinov	10	10
2195	3s. Iordan Lyutibrodski	10	10
2196	5s. Mito Ganev	10	10
2197	13s. Nedelcho Nikolov	35	10

1972. 50th Anniv of U.S.S.R.

2198	**681** 13s. red, yellow & gold	50	15

1972. Protected Flowers. Multicoloured.

2199	1s. Type **682**	10	10
2200	2s. Marsh gentian	10	10
2201	3s. Sea lily	15	10
2202	4s. Globe flower	20	10
2203	18s. "Primula frondosa"	70	20

2204 23s. Pale pasque flower . . . 1·00 30
2205 40s. "Fritillaria stribrnyi" 2·00 50

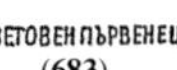

(683)

684 Dobri Chintulov

1972. "Bulgaria, World Weightlifting Champions". No. 2192 optd with T **683**.
2206 40s. multicoloured . . . . . 1·75 50

1972. 150th Birth Anniv of Dobri Chintulov (poet).
2207 **684** 2s. multicoloured 10 10

685 Forehead Ornament (19th-century)

686 Divers with Cameras

1972. Antique Ornaments.
2208 **685** 1s. black and brown . . 10 10
2209 – 2s. black and green . . . 10 10
2210 – 3s. black and blue . . . 10 10
2211 – 8s. black and red 20 10
2212 – 23s. black and brown . . 60 10
2213 – 40s. black and violet . . 1·25 20
DESIGNS: 2s. Belt-buckle (19th-century); 3s. Amulet (18th-century); 8s. Pendant (18th-century); 23s. Earrings (14th-century); 40s. Necklace (18th-century).

1973. Underwater Research in the Black Sea.
2214 **686** 1s. black, yellow & blue 10 10
2215 – 2s. black, yellow & blue 20 10
2216 – 18s. black, yellow & blue 90 25
2217 – 40s. black, yellow & blue 1·10 20
DESIGNS—HORIZ: 2s. Divers with underwater research vessel "Shelf 1". VERT: 18s. Diver and "NIV 100" diving bell; 40s. Lifting balloon.

687 "The Hanging of Vasil Levski" (Boris Angelushev)

688 Elhovo Mask

1973. Death Cent of Vasil Levski (patriot).
2219 **687** 2s. green and red 10 10
2220 – 20s. brown, cream & grn 1·50 40
DESIGN: 20s. "Vasil Levski" (Georgi Danchov).

1973. Kukeris' Festival Masks. Mult.
2221 1a. Type **688** 10 10
2222 2s. Breznik 10 10
2223 3s. Khisar 10 10
2224 13s. Radomir 40 15
2225 20s. Karnobat 50 25
2226 40s. Pernik . . . . 4·50 2·75

689 Copernicus

690 Vietnamese "Girl"

1973. 500th Birth Anniv of Copernicus.
2227 **689** 28s. purple, black & brn 1·50 50

1973. Vietnam Peace Treaty.
2229 **690** 18s. multicoloured . . . 20 10

691 Common Poppy

692 C. Botev (after T. Todorov)

1973. Wild Flowers. Multicoloured.
2231 1s. Type **691** 10 10
2232 2s. Ox-eye daisy 10 10
2233 3s. Peony 15 10
2234 13s. Cornflower 40 15
2235 18s. Corn cockle . . . . . 4·75 2·25
2236 28s. Meadow buttercup . . 1·25 65

1973. 125th Birth Anniv of Khristo Botev (poet and revolutionary).
2237 **692** 2s. yellow, brown & grn 10 10
2238 18s. grn, lt grn & bronze 80 65

693 Asen Khalachev and Insurgents

1973. 50th Anniv of June Uprising.
2239 **693** 1s. black, red and gold 10 10
2240 – 2s. black, orange & gold 10 10
DESIGN: 2s. "Wounded Worker" (illustration by Boris Angelushev to the poem "September" by Geo Milev).

694 Stamboliiski (from sculpture by A. Nikolov)

1973. 50th Death Anniv of Aleksandur Stamboliiski (Prime Minister 1919–23).
2241 **694** 18s. lt brn, brn & orge 40 20
2242 18s. orange . . . . . . 4·50 3·25

695 Muskrat

1973. Bulgarian Fauna. Multicoloured.
2243 1s. Type **695** 10 10
2244 2s. Racoon-dog 10 10
2245 3s. Mouflon (vert) 20 10
2246 12s. Fallow deer (vert) . . . 50 25
2247 18s. European bison . . . . 3·25 1·50
2248 40s. Elk . . . . 2·00 55

696 Turnovo

698 Congress Emblem

697 Insurgents on the March (Boris Angelushev)

1973. Air. Tourism. Views of Bulgarian Towns and Cities. Multicoloured.
2249 2s. Type **696** 10 10
2250 13s. Rusalka 30 10
2251 20s. Plovdiv . . . . 2·10 1·75
2252 28s. Sofia 80 50

1973. 50th Anniv of September Uprising.
2253 **697** 2s. multicoloured 10 10
2254 – 5s. violet, pink & red . . 75 35
2255 – 13s. multicoloured . . . 15 10
2256 – 18s. olive, cream & red 45 25
DESIGNS—HORIZ: 5s. "Armed Train" (Boris Angelushev). VERT: 13s. Patriotic poster by N. Mirchev. HORIZ: 18s. Georgi Dimitrov and Vasil Kolarov.

1973. 8th World Trade Union Congress, Varna.
2257 **698** 2s. multicoloured 10 10

699 "Sun" Emblem and Olympic Rings

700 "Prince Kaloyan"

1973. Olympic Congress, Varna. Multicoloured.
2258 13s. Type **699** 40 20
2259 28s. Lion Emblem of Bulgarian Olympic Committee (vert) 70 40

1973. Fresco Portraits, Boyana Church. Mult.
2261 1s. Type **700** 10 10
2262 2s. "Desislava" 30 10
2263 3s. "Saint" 20 10
2264 5s. "St. Eustratius" 25 10
2265 10s. "Tsar Constantine-Asen" 60 10
2266 13s. "Deacon Laurentius" 80 10
2267 18s. "Virgin Mary" . . . . 1·25 30
2268 20s. "St. Ephraim" . . . . 1·50 40
2269 28s. "Jesus Christ" . . . . 5·00 1·00

701 Smirnenski and Cavalry Charge

1973. 75th Birth Anniv of Khristo Smirnenski (poet and revolutionary).
2271 **701** 1s. blue, red and gold . . 10 10
2272 2s. blue, red and gold . . 10 10

702 Human Rights Emblem

704 "Finn" One-man Dinghy

703 Tsar Todor Svetoslav meeting the Byzantine Embassy, 1307

1973. 25th Anniv of Declaration of Human Rights.
2273 **702** 13s. gold, red and blue 15 10

1973. Bulgarian History. Multicoloured.
2274 1s. Type **703** 10 10
2275 2s. Tsar Mikhail Shishman in battle against Byzantines, 1328 . . . . 10 10
2276 3s. Battle of Rosokastro, 1332 and Tsar Ivan Aleksandur 10 10
2277 4s. Defence of Turnovo, 1393 and Patriarch Evtimii 10 10
2278 5s. Tsar Ivan Shisman's attack on the Turks . . . 10 10
2279 13s. Momchil attacks Turkish ships at Umur, 1344 . . . . 15 10
2280 18s. Meeting of Tsar Ivan Sratsimir and Crusaders, 1396 . . . . 25 10
2281 28s. Embassy of Empress Anne of Savoy meets Boyars Balik, Teodor and Dobrotitsa 75 30

1973. Sailing. Various Yachts. Multicoloured.
2282 1s. Type **704** 10 10
2283 2s. "Flying Dutchman" two-man dinghy 10 10
2284 3s. "Soling" yacht 15 10
2285 13s. "Tempest" dinghy . . . 60 35
2286 20s. "470" two-man dinghy 80 65
2287 40s. "Tornado" catamaran 3·25 1·50

705 "Balchik" (Bercho Obreshkov)

1973. 25th Anniv of National Art Gallery, Sofia and 150th Birth Anniv of Stanislav Dospevski (painter). Multicoloured.
2288 1s. Type **705** 10 10
2289 2s. "Mother and Child" (Stryan Venev) 10 10
2290 3s. "Rest" (Tsenko Boyadzhiev) 10 10
2291 13s. "Vase with Flowers" (Siruk Skitnik) (vert) . . . 20 10
2292 18s. "Mary Kuneva" (Iliya Petrov) (vert) 30 10
2293 40s. "Winter in Plovdiv" (Zlatyn Boyadzhiev) (vert) 1·10 50

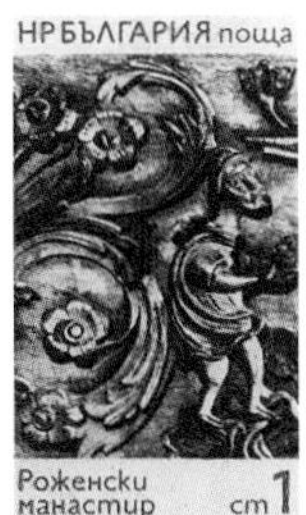

707 Old Testament Scene (Wood-carving)

1974. Wood-Carvings from Rozhen Monastery.
2296 **707** 1s. dk brn, cream & brn 10 10
2297 – 2s. dk brn, cream & brn 10 10
2298 – 3s. dk brn, cream & brn 10 10
2299 – 5s. olive, cream & green 10 10
2300 – 8s. olive, cream & green 10 10
2301 – 13s. brown, cream and chestnut 25 15
2302 – 28s. brown, cream and chestnut 40 15
DESIGNS: Nos. 2296/8, "Passover Table"; 2299/2300, "Abraham and the Angel"; 2301/2, "The Expulsion from Eden".
Nos. 2296/8, 2299/300 and 2301/2 form three composite designs.

708 "Lenin" (N. Mirchev)

1974. 50th Death Anniv of Lenin. Mult.
2303 2s. Type **708** 10 10
2304 18s. "Lenin with Workers" (W. A. Serov) 20 10

709 "Blagoev addressing Meeting" (G. Kovachev)

1974. 50th Death Anniv of D. Blagoev (founder of Bulgarian Social Democratic Party).
2305 **709** 2s. multicoloured 10 10

710 Sheep

1974. Domestic Animals.
2306 **710** 1s. brown, buff & green 10 10
2307 – 2s. purple, violet & red 10 10
2308 – 3s. brown, pink & green 10 10
2309 – 5s. brown, buff & blue 10 10
2310 – 13s. black, blue and brown 15 10
2311 – 20s. brown, pink & blue 1·10 25
DESIGNS: 2s. Goat; 3s. Pig; 5s. Cow; 13s. Buffalo; 20s. Horse.

711 Social Economic Integration Emblem

1974. 25th Anniv of Council for Mutual Economic Aid.
2312 **711** 13s. multicoloured . . . 20 10

712 Footballers

1974. World Cup Football Championship.
2313 **712** 1s. multicoloured 10 10
2314 – 2s. multicoloured 10 10
2315 – 3s. multicoloured 10 10
2316 – 13s. multicoloured . . . 25 10
2317 – 28s. multicoloured . . . 50 10
2318 – 40s. multicoloured . . . 2·00 75
DESIGNS: Nos. 2314/18, Various designs similar to Type **712**.

713 Folk-singers

714 "Cosmic Research" (Penko Barnbov)

1974. Amateur Arts and Sports Festival. Multicoloured.
2320 1s. Type **713** 10 10
2321 2s. Folk-dancers 10 10
2322 3s. Piper and drummer . . . 10 10
2323 5s. Wrestling 10 10
2324 13s. Athletics . . . . 1·00 50
2325 18s. Gymnastics . . . . . . 1·60 20

1974. "Mladost '74" Youth Stamp Exhibition, Sofia. Multicoloured.
2326 1s. Type **714** 10 10
2327 2s. "Salt Production" (Mariana Bliznakaa) . . . 20 10
2328 3s. "Fire-dancer" (Detelina Lalova) 10 10
2329 28s. "Friendship Train" (Vanya Boyanova) . . . 3·00 1·75

715 Motor-cars

1974. World Automobile Federation's Spring Congress, Sofia.
2331 **715** 13s. multicoloured . . . 20 10

716 Period Architecture

1974. U.N.E.S.C.O. Executive Council's 94th Session, Varna.
2332 **716** 18s. multicoloured . . . 15 10

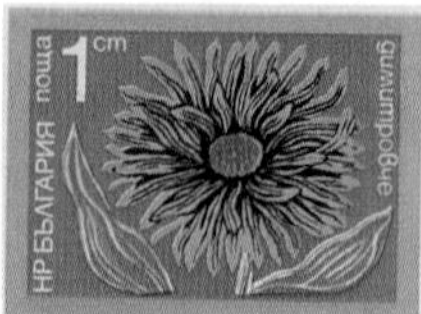

717 Chinese Aster

1974. Bulgarian Flowers. Multicoloured.
2333 1s. Type **717** 10 10
2334 2s. Mallow 10 10
2335 3s. Columbine 10 10
2336 18s. Tulip 40 10
2337 20s. Marigold 50 20
2338 28s. Pansy . . . . 1·60 50

718 19th Century Post-boy

1974. Centenary of U.P.U.
2340 **718** 2s. violet & blk on orge 10 10
2341 – 18s. green & blk on orge 25 10
DESIGN: 18s. First Bulgarian mail-coach.

719 Young Pioneer and Komsomol Girl

720 Communist Soldiers with Flag

1974. 30th Anniv of Dimitrov's Septembrist Pioneers Organization. Multicoloured.
2343 1s. Type **719** 10 10
2344 2s. Pioneer with doves . . . 10 10

1974. 30th Anniv of Fatherland Front Government. Multicoloured.
2346 1s. Type **720** 10 10
2347 2s. "Soviet Liberators" . . . 10 10
2348 5s. "Industrialisation" . . . 10 10
2349 13s. "Modern Agriculture" 10 10
2350 18s. "Science and Technology" 25 15

722 Gymnast on Beam

724 Envelope with Arrow pointing to Postal Code

1974. 18th World Gymnastic Championships, Varna. Multicoloured.
2352 2s. Type **722** 10 10
2353 13s. Gymnast on horse . . . 40 15

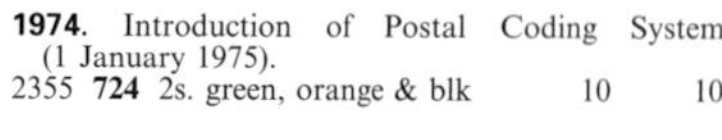
1974. Introduction of Postal Coding System (1 January 1975).
2355 **724** 2s. green, orange & blk 10 10

725 "Sourovachka" (twig decorated with coloured ribbons)

1974. New Year.
2356 **725** 2s. multicoloured 10 10

726 Icon of St. Theodor Stratilar

727 Apricot

1974. Bulgarian History.
2357 **726** 1s. multicoloured 10 10
2358 – 2s. grey, mauve & black 10 10
2359 – 3s. grey, blue and black 10 10
2360 – 5s. grey, lilac and black 10 10
2361 – 8s. black, buff and brown 10 10
2362 – 13s. grey, green & black 15 10
2363 – 18s. black, gold & red 20 10
2364 – 28s. grey, blue & black 75 50
DESIGNS: 2s. Bronze medallion; 3s. Carved capital; 5s. Silver bowl of Sivin Jupan; 8s. Clay goblet; 13s. Lioness (torso); 18s. Gold tray; 28s. Double-headed eagle.

1975. Fruit-tree Blossoms. Multicoloured.
2365 1s. Type **727** 10 10
2366 2s. Apple 10 10
2367 3s. Cherry 10 10
2368 19s. Pear 25 10
2369 28s. Peach 50 15

730 Star and Arrow

731 "Weights and Measures"

1975. 30th Anniv of "Victory in Europe" Day.
2372 **730** 2s. red, black & brown 10 10
2373 – 13s. black, brown & bl 20 10
DESIGNS: 13s. Peace dove and broken sword.

1975. Centenary of Metre Convention.
2374 **731** 13s. violet, black & silver 10 10

732 Tree and open Book

1975. 50th Anniv of Forestry School.
2375 **732** 2s. multicoloured 10 10

733 Michelangelo

734 Festival Emblem

1975. 500th Birth Anniv of Michelangelo.
2376 **733** 2s. purple and blue . . . 10 10
2377 – 13s. violet and purple . . 15 10
2378 – 18s. brown and green . . 20 10
DESIGNS—HORIZ: Sculptures from Giuliano de Medici's tomb: 13s. "Night"; 18s. "Day".

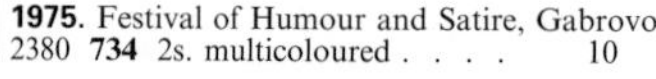
1975. Festival of Humour and Satire, Gabrovo.
2380 **734** 2s. multicoloured 10 10

735 Women's Head and Emblem

1975. International Women's Year.
2381 **735** 13s. multicoloured . . . 10 10

736 Vasil and Sava Kokareshkov

1975. "Young Martyrs to Fascism".
2382 **736** 1s. black, green & gold 10 10
2383 – 2s. black, mauve & gold 10 10
2384 – 5s. black, red and gold 10 10
2385 – 13s. black, blue & gold 20 10
DESIGNS—HORIZ: 2s. Mitko Palauzov and Ivan Vasilev; 5s. Nikola Nakev and Stefcho Kraichev; 13s. Ivanka Pashkolouva and Detelina Mincheva.

737 "Mother feeding Child" (Jean Millet)

738 Gabrovo Costume

1975. World Graphics Exhibition, Sofia. Celebrated Drawings and Engravings. Multicoloured.
2386 1s. Type **737** 10 10
2387 2s. "Mourning a Dead Daughter" (Goya) 10 10
2388 3s. "The Reunion" (Iliya Beshkov) 10 10
2389 13s. "Seated Nude" (Auguste Renoir) 10 10
2390 20s. "Man in a Fur Hat" (Rembrandt) 10 10
2391 40s. "The Dream" (Horore Daumier) (horiz) 70 20

1975. Women's Regional Costumes. Mult.
2393 2s. Type **738** 10 10
2394 3s. Trun costume 10 10
2395 5s. Vidin costume 10 10
2396 13s. Goce Delcev costume 15 10
2397 18s. Ruse costume 40 15

739 "Bird" (manuscript illumination)

740 Ivan Vasov

1975. Original Bulgarian Manuscripts. Mult.
2398 1s. Type **739** 10 10
2399 2s. "Head" 10 10
2400 3s. Abstract design 10 10
2401 8s. "Pointing finger" 10 10
2402 13s. "Imaginary creature" 10 10
2403 18s. Abstract design 40 15

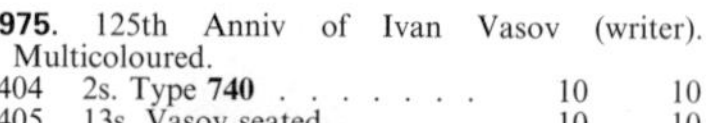
1975. 125th Anniv of Ivan Vasov (writer). Multicoloured.
2404 2s. Type **740** 10 10
2405 13s. Vasov seated 10 10

741 "Soyuz" and Aleksei Leonov

1975. "Apollo"–"Soyuz" Space Link. Mult.
2406 13s. Type **741** 30 10
2407 18s. "Apollo" and Thomas Stafford 50 10
2408 28s. Linking manoeuvre . . 1·50 20

742 Ryukyu Sailing Boat, Map and Emblems

1975. International Exposition, Okinawa.
2410 **742** 13s. multicoloured . . . 30 10

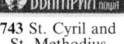

743 St. Cyril and St. Methodius **744** Footballer

1975. "Balkanphila V" Stamp Exhibition, Sofia.
2411 **743** 2s. brown, lt brn & red 10 10
2412 – 13s. brown, lt brn & grn 10 10
DESIGN: 13s. St. Constantine and St. Helene.

1975. 8th Inter-Toto (Football Pools) Congress, Varna.
2414 **744** 2s. multicoloured 10 10

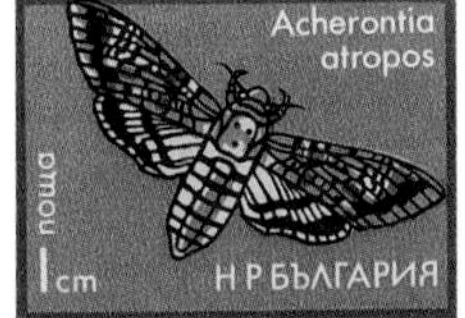

745 Deaths-head Hawk Moth

1975. Hawk Moths. Multicoloured.
2415 1s. Type **745** 10 10
2416 2s. Oleander hawk moth . . 10 10
2417 3s. Eyed hawk moth 15 10
2418 10s. Mediterranean hawk moth 25 20
2419 13s. Elephant hawk moth 50 25
2420 18s. Broad-bordered bee hawk moth . . . . 1·10 40

746 U.N. Emblem **747** Map of Europe on Peace Dove

1975. 30th Anniv of U.N.O.
2421 **746** 13s. red, brown & black 10 10

1975. European Security and Co-operation Conference, Helsinki.
2422 **747** 18s. lilac, blue & yellow 40 20

748 D. Khristov

1975. Birth Cent of Dobri Khristov (composer).
2423 **748** 5s. brown, yellow & grn 10 10

749 Constantine's Rebellion against the Turks

1975. Bulgarian History. Multicoloured.
2424 1s. Type **749** 10 10
2425 2s. Vladislav III's campaign 10 10
2426 3s. Battle of Turnovo . . . 10 10
2427 10s. Battle of Chiprovtsi . . 10 10
2428 13s. 17 th-century partisans 25 10
2429 18s. Return of banished peasants 40 25

750 "First Aid"

1975. 90th Anniv of Bulgarian Red Cross.
2430 **750** 2s. brown, black and red 10 10
2431 – 13s. green, black and red 25 10
DESIGN: 13s. "Peace and international Co-operation".

751 Ethnographical Museum, Plovdiv

1975. European Architectural Heritage Year.
2432 **751** 80s. brown, yellow & grn 1·75 1·75

752 Christmas Lanterns

1975. Christmas and New Year. Multicoloured.
2433 2s. Type **752** 10 10
2434 13s. Stylized peace dove . . 10 10

753 Egyptian Galley

1975. Historic Ships (1st series). Multicoloured.
2435 1s. Type **753** 10 10
2436 2s. Phoenician galley . . . 10 10
2437 3s. Greek trireme 10 10
2438 5s. Roman galley 10 10
2439 13s. "Mora" (Norman ship) 50 25
2440 18s. Venetian galley 90 35
See also Nos. 2597/2602, 2864/9, 3286/91 and 3372/7.

754 Modern Articulated Tramcar

1976. 75th Anniv of Sofia Tramways. Mult.
2441 2s. Type **754** 30 15
2442 13s. Early 20th-century tramcar . . . . 1·10 50

755 Skiing

1976. Winter Olympic Games, Innsbruck. Mult.
2443 1s. Type **755** 10 10
2444 2s. Cross-country skiing (vert) 10 10
2445 2s. Ski jumping 10 10
2446 13s. Biathlon (vert) 20 15
2447 18s. Ice hockey (vert) . . . 40 25
2448 18s. Speed skating (vert) . . 1·00 30

756 Stylized Bird

1976. 11th Bulgarian Communists Party Congress. Multicoloured.
2450 2s. Type **756** 10 10
2451 5s. "1956–1976, Fulfilment of the Five Year Plans" 10 10
2452 13s. Hammer and Sickle . . 10 10

757 Alexander Graham Bell and early Telephone

1976. Telephone Centenary.
2454 **757** 18s. lt brown, brn & pur 20 10

758 Mute Swan

1976. Waterfowl. Multicoloured.
2455 1s. Type **758** 20 10
2456 2s. Ruddy shelduck 25 10
2457 3s. Common shelduck . . . 40 15
2458 5s. Garganey 60 20
2459 13s. Mallard . . . . 1·25 30
2460 18s. Red-crested pochard . . 1·75 80

759 Guerillas' Briefing

1976. Cent of April Uprising (1st issue). Mult.
2461 1s. Type **759** 10 10
2462 2s. Peasants' briefing . . . 10 10
2463 5s. Krishina, horse and guard 10 10
2464 13s. Rebels with cannon . . 20 10
See also Nos. 2529/33.

760 Kozlodui Atomic Energy Centre

1976. Modern Industrial Installations.
2465 **760** 5s. green 10 10
2466 – 8s. red 10 10
2467 – 10s. green 10 10
2468 – 13s. violet 10 10
2469 – 20s. green 15 10
DESIGNS: 8s. Bobaudol plant; 10s. Sviloza chemical works; 13s. Devaya chemical works; 20s. Sestvitro dam.

761 Guard with Patrol-dog

1976. 30th Anniv of Frontier Guards. Mult.
2470 2s. Type **761** 10 10
2471 13s. Mounted guards . . . 10 10

762 Worker with Spade **763** Botev

1976. 30th Anniv of Youth Brigades Movement.
2472 **762** 2s. multicoloured 10 10

1976. Death Cent of Khristo Botev (poet).
2473 **763** 13s. green and brown . . 10 10

764 "Martyrs of First Congress" (relief) **765** Dimitur Blagoev

1976. 85th Anniv of 1st Bulgarian Social Democratic Party Congress, Buzludzha. Multicoloured.
2474 2s. Type **764** 10 10
2475 5s. Modern memorial, Buzludzha Peak 10 10

1976. 120th Birth Anniv of Dimitur Blagoev (founder of Bulgarian Social Democratic Party).
2476 **765** 13s. black, red and gold 10 10

767 Children Playing

1976. Child Welfare.
2478 **767** 1s. multicoloured 10 10
2479 – 2s. multicoloured 10 10
2480 – 5s. multicoloured 10 10
2481 – 23s. multicoloured . . . 25 20
DESIGNS: 2s. Girls with pram and boy on rocking horse; 5s. Playing ball; 23s. Dancing.

768 Wrestling

1976. Olympic Games, Montreal. Multicoloured.
2482 1s. Type **768** 10 10
2483 2s. Boxing (vert) 10 10
2484 3s. Weight-lifting (vert) . . 10 10
2485 13s. Canoeing (vert) 20 10
2486 18s. Gymnastics (vert) . . . 30 15
2487 28s. Diving (vert) 45 20
2488 40s. Athletics (vert) 65 30

769 Belt Buckle, Vidin **772** Fish on line

770 "Partisans at Night" (Petrov)

1976. Thracian Art (8th–4th Centuries B.C.). Mult.

2490	1s. Type **769**	10	10
2491	2s. Brooch, Durzhanitsa	10	10
2492	3s. Mirror handle, Chukarka	10	10
2493	5s. Helmet cheek guard, Gurlo	10	10
2494	13s. Gold decoration, Orizovo	10	10
2495	18s. Decorated horse-harness, Brezovo	15	15
2496	20s. Greave, Mogilanska Mogila	20	15
2497	28s. Pendant, Bukovtsi	25	25

1976. Paintings by Iliya Petrov and Tsanko Lavrenov from the National Gallery. Multicoloured.

2498	2s. Type **770**	10	10
2499	5s. "Kurshum-Khan" (Lavrenov)	10	10
2500	13s. "Seated Woman" (Petrov)	15	10
2501	18s. "Boy seated in chair" (Petrov) (vert)	25	10
2502	28s. "Old Plovdiv" (Lavrenov) (vert)	40	15

1976. World Sports Fishing Congress, Varna.
2505 **772** 5s. multicoloured 10 10

773 "The Pianist" **774** St. Theodor

1976. 75th Birth Anniv of Alex Jhendov (caricaturist).

2506	**773**	2s. dp grn, cream & grn	10	10
2507	–	5s. dp violet, vio & lilac	10	10
2508	–	13s. black, pink & red	20	10

DESIGNS: 5s. "Trick or Treat"; 13s. "The Leader".

1976. Zemen Monastery. Frescoes. Multicoloured.

2509	2s. Type **774**	10	10
2510	3s. St. Paul and Apostle	10	10
2511	5s. St. Joachim	10	10
2512	13s. Prophet Melchisadek	10	10
2513	19s. St. Porphyrus	15	10
2514	28s. Queen Doya	25	15

775 Legal Document **776** Horse Chestnut

1976. 25th Anniv of State Archives.
2516 **775** 5s. multicoloured 10 10

1976. Plants. Multicoloured.

2517	1s. Type **776**	10	10
2518	2s. Shrubby cinquefoil	10	10
2519	5s. Holly	15	10
2520	8s. Yew	15	10
2521	13s. "Daphne pontica"	30	15
2522	23s. Judas tree	75	30

777 Cloud over Sun

1976. Protection of the Environment. Mult.

2523	2s. Cloud over tree	10	10
2524	18s. Type **777**	20	10

778 Dimitur Polyanov

1976. Birth Cent of Dimitur Polyanov (poet).
2525 **778** 2s. lilac and orange . . . 10 10

779 Congress Emblem

1976. 33rd Bulgarian People's Agrarian Union Congress. Multicoloured.

2526	2s. Type **779**	10	10
2527	13s. Flags	10	10

781 "Khristo Botev" (Zlatyu Boyadzhiev)

1976. Centenary of April Uprising (2nd issue). Multicoloured.

2529	1s. Type **781**	10	10
2530	2s. "Partisan carrying Cherrywood Cannon" (Iliya Petrov)	10	10
2531	3s. "Necklace of Immortality" (Dechko Uzunov)	10	10
2532	13s. "April 1876" (Georgi Popov)	10	15
2533	18s. "Partisans" (Stoyan Venev)	25	20

782 Tobacco Workers

1976. 70th Birth Anniv of Veselin Staikov (artist). Multicoloured.

2535	1s. Type **782**	10	10
2536	2s. "Melnik"	10	10
2537	13s. "Boat Builders"	20	10

783 "Snowflake"

1976. New Year.
2538 **783** 2s. multicoloured 10 10

784 Zakhari Stojanov

1976. 125th Birth Anniv of Zakhari Stojanov (writer).
2539 **784** 2s. brown, red and gold 10 10

785 Bronze Coin of Septimus Severus

1977. Roman Coins struck in Serdica. Mult.

2540	1s. Type **785**	10	10
2541	2s. Bronze coin of Caracalla	10	10
2542	13s. Bronze coin of Caracalla (diff.)	10	10
2543	18s. Bronze coin of Caracalla (diff.)	15	15
2544	23s. Copper coin of Diocletian	25	20

786 Championships Emblem **787** Congress Emblem

1977. World Ski-orienteering Championships.
2545 **786** 13s. blue, red & ultram 20 10

1977. 5th Congress of Bulgarian Tourist Associations.
2546 **787** 2s. multicoloured 10 10

788 "Symphyandra wanneri" **789** V. Kolarov

1977. Mountain Flowers. Multicoloured.

2547	1s. Type **788**	10	10
2548	2s. "Petcovia orphanidea"	10	10
2549	3s. "Campanula lanatre"	10	10
2550	13s. "Campanula scutellata"	15	10
2551	43s. Nettle-leaved bellflower	60	40

1977. Birth Centenary of Vasil Kolarov (Prime Minister 1949–50).
2552 **789** 2s. grey, black & blue . . 10 10

790 Congress Emblem **791** Joint

1977. 8th Bulgarian Trade Unions Congress.
2553 **790** 2s. multicoloured 10 10

1977. World Rheumatism Year.
2554 **791** 23s. multicoloured . . . 20 10

792 Wrestling

1977. World University Games, Sofia. Mult.

2555	2s. Type **792**	10	10
2556	13s. Running	20	10
2557	23s. Handball	40	15
2558	43s. Gymnastics	70	25

793 Ivan Vazov National Theatre **794** Congress Emblem

1977. Buildings in Sofia. Pale brown backgrounds.

2559	**793**	12s. red	10	10
2560	–	13s. brown	10	10
2561	–	23s. blue	15	10
2562	–	30s. green	20	10
2563	–	80s. violet	60	25
2564	–	1l. brown	80	80

DESIGNS: 13s. Party Building; 23s. People's Army Building; 30s. Clement of Ohrid University; 80s. National Art Gallery; 1l. National Assembly Building.

1977. 13th Dimitrov Communist Youth League Congress.
2565 **794** 2s. red, green and gold 10 10

795 "St. Nicholas" Nesebur

1977. Bulgarian Icons. Multicoloured.

2566	1s. Type **795**	10	10
2567	2s. "Old Testament Trinity", Sofia	10	10
2568	3s. "The Royal Gates", Veliko Turnovo	10	10
2569	5s. "Deisis", Nesebur	10	10
2570	13s. "St. Nicholas", Elena	10	10
2571	23s. "The Presentation of the Blessed Virgin", Rila Monastery	30	10
2572	35s. "The Virgin Mary with Infant", Varna	40	15
2573	40s. "St. Demetrius on Horseback", Provadya	50	20

796 Wolf

1977. Wild Animals. Multicoloured.

2575	1s. Type **796**	10	10
2576	2s. Red fox	10	10
2577	10s. Weasel	20	10
2578	13s. Wild cat	35	15
2579	23s. Golden jackal	60	25

797 Congress Emblem **798** "Crafty Peter riding a Donkey" (drawing by Iliya Beshkov)

1977. 3rd Bulgarian Culture Congress.
2580 **797** 13s. multicoloured . . . 10 10

1977. 11th Festival of Humour and Satire, Gabrovo.
2581 **798** 2s. multicoloured 10 10

799 Congress Emblem

1977. 8th Congress of the Popular Front, Sofia.
2582 **799** 2s. multicoloured 10 10

800 Newspaper Masthead

1977. Centenary of Bulgarian Daily Press.
2583 **800** 2s. multicoloured 10 10

802 Conference Emblem

1977. International Writers Conference, Sofia.
2585 **802** 23s. blue, lt blue & grn 75 40

803 Map of Europe

1977. 21st Congress of European Organization for Quality Control, Varna.
2586 **803** 23s. multicoloured . . . 25 10

804 Basketball **805** Weightlifter

1977. Women's European Basketball Championships.
2587 **804** 23s. multicoloured . . . 40 10

1977. World Junior Weightlifting Championships.
2588 **805** 13s. multicoloured . . . 30 10

806 Georgi Dimitrov

1977. 95th Birth Anniv of Georgi Dimitrov (statesman).
2589 **806** 13s. brown and red . . . 15 10

807 Tail Section of Tupolev Tu-154

1977. Air. 30th Anniv of Bulgarian Airline "Balkanair".
2590 **807** 35s. multicoloured . . . 75 25

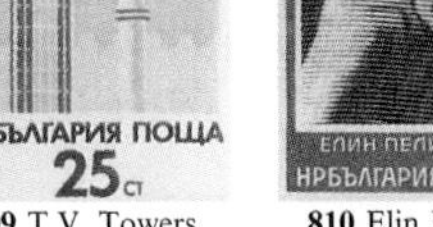
809 T.V. Towers, Berlin and Sofia **810** Elin Pelin alias Dimitur Stoyanov (writer)

1977. "Sozphilex 77" Stamp Exhibition, East Berlin.
2592 **809** 25s. blue and deep blue 40 10

1977. Writers and Painters.
2593 **810** 2s. brown and gold . . . 10 10
2594 – 5s. olive and gold . . . 10 10
2595 – 13s. red and gold . . . 10 10
2596 – 23s. blue and gold . . . 20 15

DESIGNS: 5s. Peyu Yavorov (poet); 13s. Boris Angelushev (painter and illustrator); 23s. Iseno Todorov (painter).

1977. Historic Ships (2nd series). As T **753**. Multicoloured.
2597 1s. Hansa Kogge 10 10
2598 2s. "Santa Maria" 10 10
2599 3s. Drake's "Golden Hind" 10 10
2600 12s. Carrack "Santa Catherina" 30 10
2601 13s. "La Couronne" (French galleon) 35 15
2602 43s. Mediterranean galley 1·10 40

811 Women Canoeists

1977. World Canoe Championships.
2603 **811** 2s. blue and yellow . . . 10 10
2604 – 23s. blue and turquoise 30 10
DESIGN: 23s. Men canoeists.

812 Balloon over Plovdiv **813** Presidents Zhivkov and Brezhnev

1977. Air. 85th Anniv "Panair". International Aviation Exhibition, Plovdiv.
2605 **812** 25s. orange, yell & brn 85 20

1977. Soviet–Bulgarian Friendship.
2606 **813** 18s. brown, red & gold 10 10

814 Conference Building

1977. 64th International Parliamentary Conference, Sofia.
2607 **814** 23s. green, pink and red 15 10

815 Newspaper Mastheads **816** "The Union of Earth and Water"

1977. 50th Anniv of Official Newspaper "Rabotnichesko Delo" (Workers' Press).
2608 **815** 2s. red, green and grey 10 10

1977. 400th Birth Anniv of Rubens. Mult.
2609 13s. Type **816** 25 10
2610 23s. "Venus and Adonis" (detail) 45 20
2611 40s. "Amorous Shepherd" (detail) 90 30

817 Cossack with Bulgarian Child (Angelushev) **818** Albena, Black Sea

1977. Centenary of Liberation from Turkey. (1978). Posters.
2613 **817** 2s. multicoloured 10 10
2614 – 13s. green, blue & red 10 10
2615 – 23s. blue, red & green 20 15
2616 – 25s. multicoloured . . . 20 15
DESIGNS: 13s. Bugler (Cheklarov); 23s. Mars (god of war) and Russian soldiers (Petrov); 25s. Flag of Russian Imperial Army.

1977. Tourism.
2617 **818** 35s. blue, turq & brn . . 75 20
2618 – 43s. yellow, grn & blue 75 20
DESIGN: 43s. Rila Monastery.

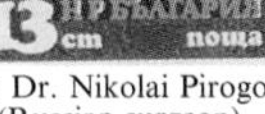

819 Dr. Nikolai Pirogov (Russian surgeon) **821** Soviet Emblems and Decree

820 Space walking

1977. Cent of Dr. Pirogov's Visit to Bulgaria.
2619 **819** 13s. brown, buff & grn 10 10

1977. Air. 20th Anniv of First Artificial Satellite. Multicoloured.
2620 12s. Type **820** 20 10
2621 25s. Space probe over Mars 40 10
2622 35s. Space probe "Venus-4" over Venus 55 10

1977. 60th Anniv of Russian Revolution.
2623 **821** 2s. red, black & stone . . 10 10
2624 – 13s. red and purple . . . 10 10
2625 – 23s. red and violet . . . 15 10
DESIGNS: 13s. Lenin; 23s. "1977" as flame.

822 Diesel Train on Bridge

1977. 50th Anniv of Transport, Bridges and Highways Organization.
2626 **822** 13s. yellow, green & olive 65 15

1977. 150th Birth Anniv of Petko Ratshev Slaveikov (poet). As T **810**.
2627 8s. brown and gold 10 10

824 Decorative Initials of New Year Greeting

1977. New Year. Multicoloured.
2628 2s. Type **824** 10 10
2629 13s. "Fireworks" 10 10

825 Footballer

1978. World Cup Football Championship, Argentina. Multicoloured.
2630 13s. Type **825** 20 10
2631 23s. Shooting the ball . . . 35 10

826 Baba Vida Fortress, Vidin

1978. Air. "The Danube – European River". Mult.
2633 25s. Type **826** 45 20
2634 35s. Friendship Bridge . . . 1·25 1·25

827 Television Mast, Moscow **829** Red Cross in Laurel Wreath

1978. 20th Anniv of Organization of Socialist Postal Administrations (O.S.S.).
2635 **827** 13s. multicoloured . . . 10 10

1978. Centenary of Bulgarian Red Cross.
2637 **829** 25s. red, brown & blue 50 10

830 "XXX" formed from Bulgarian and Russian National Colours

1978. 30th Anniv of Bulgarian–Soviet Friendship.
2638 **830** 2s. multicoloured 10 10

831 Leo Tolstoy (Russian writer) **832** Nikolai Roerich (artist)

1978. Famous Personalities.
2639 **831** 2s. green and yellow . . 10 10
2640 – 5s. brown and bistre . . 10 10
2641 – 13s. green and mauve . . 10 10
2642 – 23s. brown and grey . . 15 15
2643 – 25s. brown and green . . 15 15
2644 – 35s. violet and blue . . . 25 20
DESIGNS: 5s. Fyodor Dostoevsky (Russian writer); 13s. Ivan Turgenev (Russian writer); 23s. Vassily Vereshchagin (Russian artist); 25s. Giuseppe Garibaldi (Italian patriot); 35s. Victor Hugo (French writer).

1978. Nikolai Roerich Exhibition, Sofia.
2645 **832** 8s. brown, green & red 10 10

833 Bulgarian Flag and Red Star

1978. Communist Party National Conference, Sofia.
2646 **833** 2s. multicoloured 10 10

834 Goddess **835** "Spirit of Nature"

1978. "Philaserdica 79" International Stamp Exhibition (1st issue). Ancient Ceramics. Mult.
2647 2s. Type **834** 10 10
2648 5s. Mask with beard 10 10
2649 13s. Decorated vase 25 10
2650 23s. Vase with scallop design 45 15
2651 35s. Head of Silenus 60 20
2652 53s. Cockerel . . . . 1·25 30
See also Nos. 2674/9, 2714/18, 2721/5 and 2753/4.

1978. Birth Cent of Andrei Nikolov (sculptor).
2653 **835** 13s. blue, mauve & vio 10 10

836 Heart and Arrows

1978. World Hypertension Month.
2654 **836** 23s. red, orange & grey 20 10

837 "Kor Karoli" and Map of Route

1978. Georgi Georgiev's World Voyage.
2655 **837** 23s. blue, mauve & grn 55 25

838 Doves

1978. 11th World Youth and Students' Festival, Havana.
2656 **838** 13s. multicoloured . . . 10 10

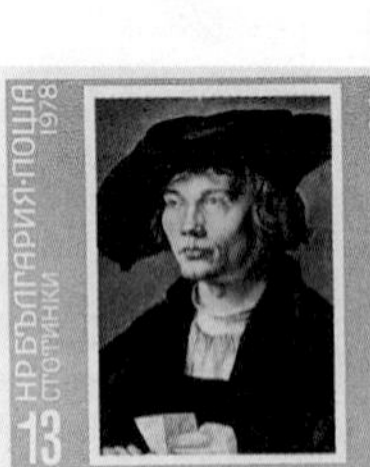

839 "Portrait of a Young Man" (Durer) **840** "Fritillaria stribrnyi"

1978. Paintings. Multicoloured.
2657 13s. Type **839** 10 10
2658 23s. "Bathsheba at the Fountain" (Rubens) . . . 20 10
2659 25s. "Signor de Moret" (Hans Holbein the Younger) 20 10
2660 35s. "Self portrait with Saskia" (Rembrandt) . . 30 10
2661 43s. "Lady in Mourning" (Tintoretto) 40 15
2662 60s. "Old Man with a Beard" (Rembrandt) . . . 45 20
2663 80s. "Man in Armour" (Van Dyck) 60 25

1978. Flowers. Multicoloured.
2664 1s. Type **840** 10 10
2665 2s. "Fritillaria drenovskyi" 10 10
2666 3s. "Lilium rhodopaeum" 10 10
2667 13s. "Tulipa urumoffii" . . 25 10
2668 23s. "Lilium jankae" . . . 40 15
2669 43s. "Tulipa rhodopaea" . . 70 30

841 Varna

1978. 63rd Esperanto Congress, Varna.
2670 **841** 13s. orange, red & green 10 10

842 Delcev

1978. 75th Death Anniv of Goce Delcev (Macedonian revolutionary).
2671 **842** 13s. multicoloured . . . 10 10

843 Freedom Fighters

1978. 75th Anniv of Ilinden-Preobrazhenie Rising.
2672 **843** 5s. black and red 10 10

845 "Market" (Noiden Petkov)

1978. "Philaserdica 79" International Stamp Exhibition (2nd issue). Paintings of Sofia. Multicoloured.
2674 2s. Type **845** 10 10
2675 5s. "View of Sofia" (Euril Stoichev) 10 10
2676 13s. "View of Sofia" (Boris Ivanov) . . . . 1·10 20
2677 23s. "Tolbukhin Boulevard" (Nikola Tanev) 20 10
2678 35s. "National Theatre" (Nikola Petrov) 25 10
2679 53s. "Market" (Anton Mitov) 35 15

846 Black Woodpecker **848** "Elka 55" Computer

1978. Woodpeckers. Multicoloured.
2680 1s. Type **846** 15 10
2681 2s. Syrian woodpecker . . . 15 10
2682 3s. Three-toed woodpecker 20 10
2683 13s. Middle-spotted woodpecker 70 30
2684 23s. Lesser spotted woodpecker . . . . . . 1·25 50
2685 43s. Green woodpecker . . 2·25 1·00

1978. Plovdiv International Fair.
2687 **848** 2s. multicoloured 10 10

849 "September 1923" (Boris Angelushev)

1978. 55th Anniv of September Uprising.
2688 **849** 2s. red and brown . . . 10 10

850 Khristo Danov

1978. 150th Birth Anniv of Khristo Danov (first Bulgarian publisher).
2689 **850** 2s. orange and lake . . . 10 10

851 "The People of Vladaya" (Todor Panayotov)

1978. 60th Anniv of Vladaya Mutiny.
2690 **851** 2s. lilac, brown and red 10 10

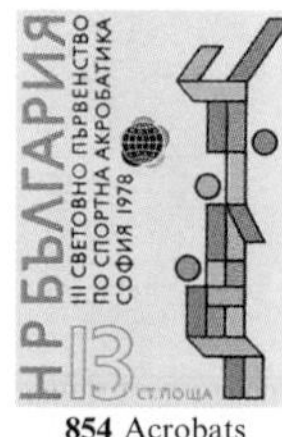

852 Hands supporting Rainbow **854** Acrobats

1978. International Anti-apartheid Year.
2691 **852** 13s. multicoloured . . . 10 10

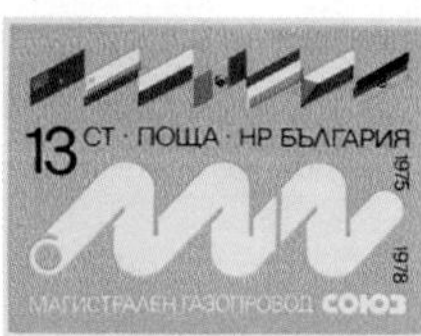

853 Pipeline and Flags

1978. Inauguration of Orenburg–U.S.S.R. Natural Gas Pipeline.
2692 **853** 13s. multicoloured . . . 10 10

1978. 3rd World Sports Acrobatics Championships, Sofia.
2693 **854** 13s. multicoloured . . . 25 10

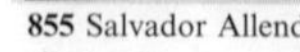

855 Salvador Allende **856** Human Rights Emblem

1978. 70th Birth Anniv of Salvador Allende (Chilean politician).
2694 **855** 13s. brown and red . . . 10 10

1978. 30th Anniv of Declaration of Human Rights.
2695 **856** 23s. yellow, red & blue 40 10

857 "Levski and Matei Mitkaloto" (Kalina Taseva) **858** Tourist Home, Plovdiv

1978. History of Bulgaria. Paintings. Multicoloured.
2696 1s. Type **857** 10 10
2697 2s. "Give Strength to my Arm" (Zlatyu Boyadzhiev) 10 10
2698 3s. "Rumena Voevoda" (Nikola Mirchev) (horiz) 10 10
2699 13s. "Kolya Ficheto" (Elza Goeva) 20 15
2700 23s. "A Family of the National Revival Period" (Naiden Petkov) 35 25

1978. European Architectural Heritage. Mult.
2701 43s. Type **858** 30 15
2702 43s. Tower of the Prince, Rila Monastery 30 15

859 "Geroi Plevny" and Route Map

1978. Opening of the Varna–Ilichovsk Ferry Service.
2703 **859** 13s. blue, red & green 70 10

860 Mosaic Bird (Santa Sofia Church)

1978. "Bulgaria 78" National Stamp Exhibition, Sofia.
2704 **860** 5s. multicoloured 15 10

861 Monument to St. Clement of Ohrid (university patron) (Lyubemir Dalcher) **862** Nikola Karastoyanov

1978. 90th Anniv of Sofia University.
2705 **861** 2s. lilac, black & green 10 10

1978. Birth Bicentenary of Nikola Karastoyanov (first Bulgarian printer).
2706 **862** 2s. brn, yell & chestnut 10 10

863 Initial from 13th Century Bible Manuscript

1978. Centenary of Cyril and Methodius People's Library. Multicoloured.
2707 2s. Type **863** 10 10
2708 13s. Monk writing (from a 1567 manuscript) 10 10
2709 23s. Decorated page from 16th-century manuscript Bible 15 10

864 Ballet Dancers

1978. 50th Anniv of Bulgarian Ballet.
2711 **864** 13s. green, mauve & lav 15 10

865 Tree of Birds

1978. New Year. Multicoloured.

2712 2s. Type **865** 10 10
2713 13s. Posthorn 10 10

866 1961 Communist Congress Stamp

1978. "Philaserdica 79" International Stamp Exhibition (3rd issue) and Bulgarian Stamp Centenary (1st issue).

2714 – 2s. red and green 10 10
2715 – 13s. claret and blue . . . 20 10
2716 – 23s. green and mauve . . 35 15
2717 **866** 35s. grey and blue . . . 50 20
2718 – 53s. green and red . . . 75 30

DESIGNS—HORIZ: 2s. 1901 "Cherrywood Cannon" stamp; 13s. 1946 "New Republic" stamp; 23s. 1957 Canonisation of St. Cyril and St. Methodius stamp. VERT: 53s. 1962 Dimitrov stamp.

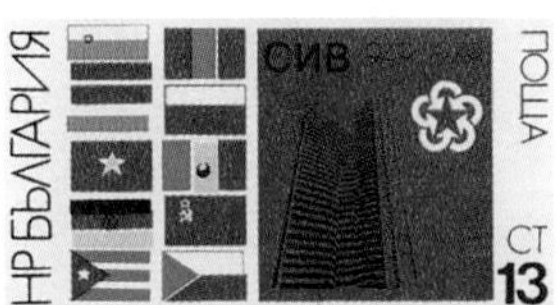

867 Council Building, Moscow and Flags

1979. 30th Anniv of Council of Mutual Economic Aid.

2720 **867** 13s. multicoloured . . . 10 10

1979. "Philaserdica 79" Int Stamp Exn (4th issue) and Bulgarian Stamp Cent (2nd issue). As Nos. 2714/18 but inscr "1979" and colours changed.

2721 – 2s. red and blue 10 10
2722 – 13s. claret and green . . 20 10
2723 – 23s. green, yellow & red 35 15
2724 **866** 35s. grey and red 50 20
2725 – 53s. brown and violet . . 75 30

868 National Bank 868a

1979. Centenary of Bulgarian National Bank.

2726 **868** 2s. grey and yellow . . . 10 10

1979. Coil stamps.

2726a **868a** 2s. blue 10 10
2726b 5s. red 10 10

The 5s. is as T **868a** but different pattern.

869 Stamboliiski 870 Child's Head as Flower

1979. Birth Centenary of Alexandur Stamboliiski (Prime Minister 1919–23).

2727 **869** 2s. brown and yellow . . 10 10

1979. International Year of the Child.

2728 **870** 23s. multicoloured . . . 20 10

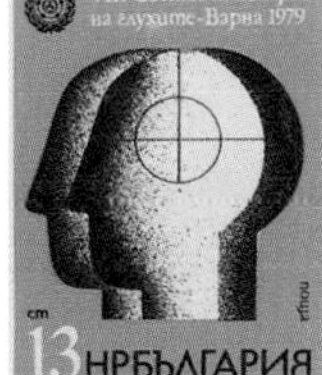

871 Profiles 872 "75" and Emblem

1979. 8th World Congress for the Deaf, Varna.

2729 **871** 13s. green and blue . . . 10 10

1979. 75th Anniv of Bulgarian Trade Unions.

2730 **872** 2s. green and orange . . 10 10

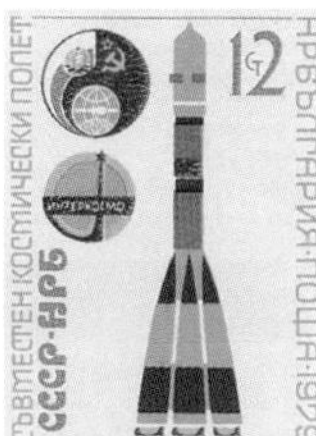

874 Rocket 876 Running

875 Carrier Pigeon and Tupolev Tu-154 Jet

1979. Soviet–Bulgarian Space Flight. Multicoloured.

2732 2s. Georgi Ivanov (horiz) . . 10 10
2733 12s. Type **874** 10 10
2734 13s. Nikolai Rukavishnikov and Ivanov (horiz) . . . 10 10
2735 25s. Link-up with "Salyut" space station (horiz) . . . 20 15
2736 35s. Capsule descending by parachute 30 20

1979. Centenary of Bulgarian Post and Telegraph Services. Multicoloured.

2738 2s. Type **875** 10 10
2739 5s. Old and new telephones 10 10
2740 13s. Morse key and teleprinter 10 10
2741 23s. Old radio transmitter and aerials 20 15
2742 35s. T.V. tower and satellite 30 20

1979. Olympic Games, Moscow (1980) (1st issue). Athletics. Multicoloured.

2744 2s. Type **876** 10 10
2745 13s. Pole vault (horiz) . . . 15 10
2746 25s. Discus 30 10
2747 35s. Hurdles (horiz) 40 15
2748 43s. High jump (horiz) . . . 50 20
2749 1l. Long jump . . . . . . 1·10 45

See also Nos. 2773/78, 2803/8, 2816/21, 2834/9 and 2851/6.

879 Hotel Vitosha-New Otani

1979. "Philaserdica 79" International Stamp Exhibition, Sofia (5th issue) and Bulgaria Day.

2753 **879** 2s. pink and blue 10 10

880 "Good Morning, Little Brother" (illus by Kukuliev of folktale)

1979. "Philaserdica 79" International Stamp Exhibition, Sofia (6th issue) and Bulgarian–Russian Friendship Day.

2754 **880** 2s. multicoloured 10 10

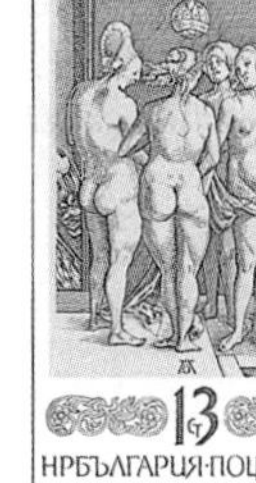

882 "Man on Donkey" (Boris Angelushev) 883 "Four Women"

1979. 12th Festival of Humour and Satire, Grabovo.

2756 **882** 2s. multicoloured 10 10

1979. 450th Death Anniv of Albrecht Durer (artist). Multicoloured.

2757 13s. Type **883** 20 10
2758 23s. "Three Peasants Talking" 55 20
2759 25s. "The Cook and his Wife" 40 20
2760 35s. "Portrait of Eobanus Hessus" 55 15

884 Clocktower, Byala Cherkva 885 Petko Todorov (birth centenary)

1979. Air. Clocktowers (1st series). Mult.

2762 13s. Type **884** 10 10
2763 23s. Botevgrad 20 10
2764 25s. Pazardzhik 25 10
2765 35s. Gabrovo 35 15
2766 53s. Tryavna 50 20

See also Nos. 2891/5.

1979. Bulgarian Writers.

2767 **885** 2s. black, brown & yell 10 10
2768 – 2s. green and yellow . . 10 10
2769 – 2s. red and yellow . . . 10 10

DESIGNS: No. 2768, Dimitur Dimov (70th birth anniv); 2769, Stefan Kostov (birth cent).

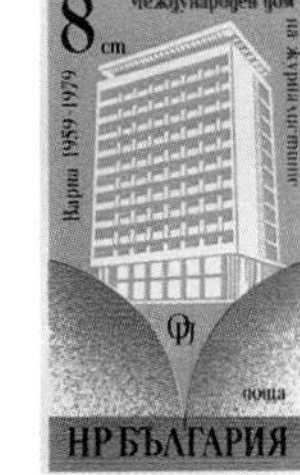

886 Congress Emblem 887 House of Journalists, Varna

1979. 18th Congress of International Theatrical Institute, Sofia.

2770 **886** 13s. cobalt, blue & black 10 10

1979. 20th Anniv of House of Journalists (holiday home), Varna.

2771 **887** 8s. orange, black & blue 10 10

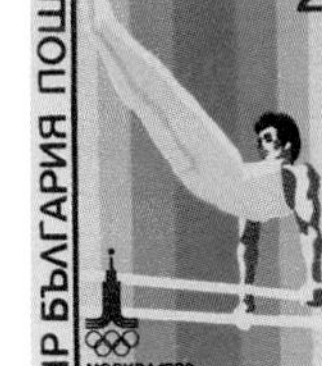

888 Children of Different Races 889 Parallel Bars

1979. "Banners for Peace" Children's Meeting, Sofia.

2772 **888** 2s. multicoloured 10 10

1979. Olympic Games, Moscow (1980) (2nd issue). Gymnastics. Multicoloured.

2773 2s. Type **889** 10 10
2774 13s. Horse exercise (horiz) 15 10
2775 25s. Rings exercise 30 10
2776 35s. Beam exercise 40 15
2777 43s. Uneven bars 50 20
2778 1l. Floor exercise . . . . . 1·10 45

890 "Virgin and Child" (Nesebur)

1979. Icons of the Virgin and Child. Mult.

2780 13s. Type **890** 10 10
2781 23s. Nesebur (diff) 25 10
2782 35s. Sozopol 40 10
2783 43s. Sozopol (diff) 50 15
2784 53s. Samokov 70 20

891 Anton Bezenshek 892 Mountaineer

1979. Centenary of Bulgarian Stenography.

2785 **891** 2s. yellow and grey . . . 10 10

1979. 50th Anniv of Bulgarian Alpine Club.

2786 **892** 2s. multicoloured 10 10

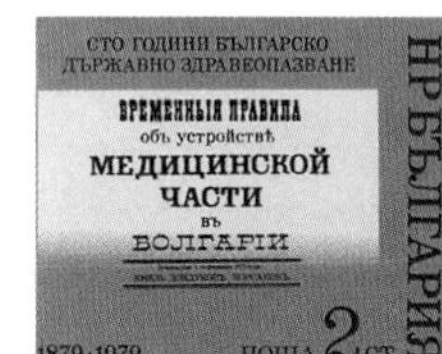

893 Commemorative Inscription

1979. Centenary of Bulgarian Public Health Services.

2787 **893** 2s. black, silver & green 10 10

894 Rocket and Flowers 896 Games Emblem

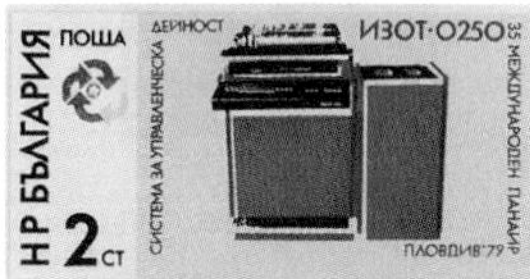

895 "IZOT–0250" Computer

1979. 35th Anniv of Fatherland Front Government. Multicoloured.

2788 2s. Type **894** 10 10
2789 5s. Russian and Bulgarian flags 10 10
2790 13s. "35" in national colours 10 10

1979. 35th Plovdiv Fair.

2791 **895** 2s. multicoloured 10 10

1979. World University Games, Mexico.

2792 **896** 5s. red, yellow and blue 10 10

897 Footballer

1979. 50th Anniv of DFS Lokomotiv Football Team.

2793 **897** 2s. red and black 40 10

898 Lyuben Karavelov **899** Cross-country Skiing

1979. Death Centenary of Lyuben Karavelov (newspaper editor and President of Bulgarian Revolutionary Committee).

2794	**898**	2s. green and blue	10	10

1979. Winter Olympic Games, Lake Placid (1980).

2795	**899**	2s. red, purple and black	10	10
2796	–	13s. orange, blue & blk	10	10
2797	–	23s. turquoise, blue and black	20	10
2798	–	43s. purple, turq & blk	40	20

DESIGNS: 13s. Speed skating; 23s. Skiing; 43s. Luge.

900 "Woman from Thrace" **901** Canoeing (Canadian pairs)

1979. 80th Birth Anniv of Dechko Uzunov (artist). Multicoloured.

2800	12s. "Figure in Red"	10	10
2801	13s. Type **900**	10	10
2802	23s. "Composition II"	20	10

1979. Olympic Games, Moscow (1980) (3rd issue). Water Sports. Multicoloured.

2803	2s. Type **901**	10	10
2804	13s. Swimming (freestyle)	15	10
2805	25s. Swimming (backstroke) (horiz)	30	10
2806	35s. Kayak (horiz)	40	15
2807	43s. Diving	50	20
2808	1l. Springboard diving	1·10	45

902 Nikola Vaptsarov

1979. 70th Birth Anniv of Nikola Vaptsarov (writer).

2810	**902**	2s. pink and red	10	10

903 "Dawn in Plovdiv" (Ioan Leviev)

1979. History of Bulgaria. Paintings. Mult.

2811	2s. "The First Socialists" (Boyan Petrov) (horiz)	10	10
2812	13s. "Dimitur Blagoev as Editor of "Rabotnik" (Dimitur Gyvdzhenov) (horiz)	10	10
2813	25s. "Workers' Party March" (Stoyan Sotirov) (horiz)	20	15
2814	35s. Type **903**	30	20

904 Doves in a Girl's Hair

1979. New Year.

2815	**904**	13s. multicoloured	10	10

905 Shooting **906** Procession with Relics of Saints

1979. Olympic Games, Moscow (1980) (4th issue). Multicoloured.

2816	2s. Type **905**	10	10
2817	13s. Judo (horiz)	15	10
2818	25s. Wrestling (horiz)	30	10
2819	35s. Archery	40	15
2820	43s. Fencing (horiz)	50	20
2821	1l. Fencing (different)	1·10	45

1979. Frescoes of Saints Cyril and Methodius in St. Clement's Basilica, Rome. Multicoloured.

2823	2s. Type **906**	10	10
2824	13s. Cyril and Methodius received by Pope Adrian II	10	10
2825	23s. Burial of Cyril the Philosopher	15	15
2826	25s. St. Cyril	20	15
2827	35s. St. Methodius	25	20

907 Television Screen showing Emblem **908** Puppet of Krali Marko (national hero)

1979. 25th Anniv of Bulgarian Television.

2828	**907**	5s. blue and deep blue	10	10

1980. 50th Anniv of International Puppet Theatre Organization (U.N.I.M.A.).

2829	**908**	2s. multicoloured	10	10

909 Thracian Rider (3rd-cent votive tablet) **910** "Meeting of Lenin and Dimitrov" (Aleksandur Poplilov)

1980. Centenary of National Archaeological Museum, Sofia.

2830	**909**	2s. brown, gold & purple	10	10
2831	–	13s. brown, gold & grn	10	10

DESIGN: 13s. Grave stele of Deines (5th–6th cent).

1980. 110th Birth Anniv of Lenin.

2832	**910**	13s. multicoloured	10	10

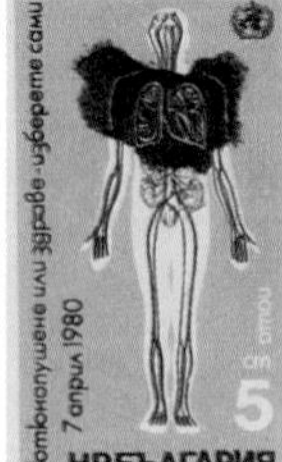
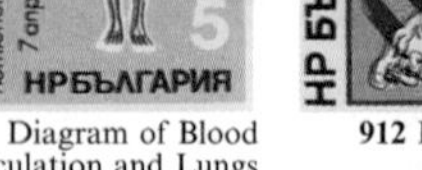
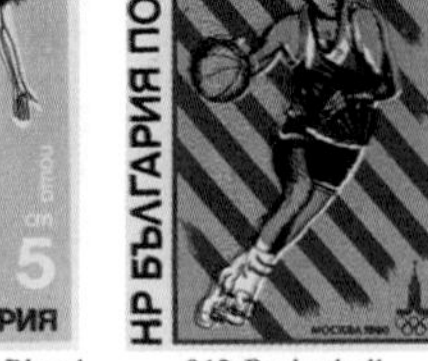

911 Diagram of Blood Circulation and Lungs obscured by Smoke **912** Basketball

1980. World Health Day. Anti-smoking Campaign.

2833	**911**	5s. multicoloured	10	10

1980. Olympic Games, Moscow (5th issue). Multicoloured.

2834	2s. Type **912**	10	10
2835	13s. Football	15	10
2836	25s. Hockey	30	10
2837	35s. Cycling	40	15
2838	43s. Handball	50	20
2839	1l. Volleyball	1·10	45

914 Penyo Penev **915** Penny Black

1980. 50th Birth Anniv of Penyo Penev (poet).

2842	**914**	5s. brown, red & turq	10	10

1980. "London 1980" International Stamp Exhibition.

2843	**915**	25s. black and red	75	25

916 Dimitur Khv. Chorbadzhuski-Chudomir (self-portrait)

1980. 90th Birth Anniv of Dimitur Khv. Chorbadzhusk-Chudomir (artist).

2844	**916**	5s. pink, brown & turq	10	10
2845	–	13s. black, blue & turq	10	10

DESIGN: 13s. "Our People".

917 Nikolai Gyaurov **918** Soviet Soldiers raising Flag on Berlin Reichstag

1980. 50th Birth Anniv of Nikolai Gyaurov (opera singer).

2846	**917**	5s. yellow, brown & grn	10	10

1980. 35th Anniv of "Victory in Europe" Day.

2847	**918**	5s. gold, brown & black	10	10
2848	–	13s. gold, brown & black	10	10

DESIGN: 13s. Soviet Army memorial, Berlin–Treptow.

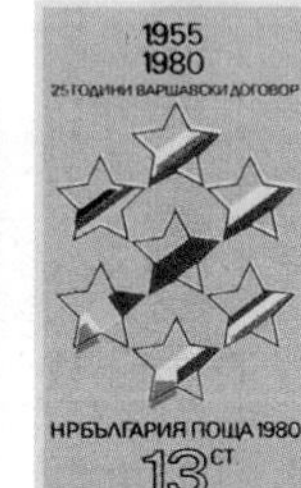

919 Open Book and Sun **920** Stars representing Member Countries

1980. 75th Anniv Bulgarian Teachers' Union.

2849	**919**	5s. purple and yellow	10	10

1980. 25th Anniv of Warsaw Pact.

2850	**920**	13s. multicoloured	10	10

921 Greek Girl with Olympic Flame **922** Ballerina

1980. Olympic Games, Moscow (6th issue). Multicoloured.

2851	2s. Type **921**	10	10
2852	13s. Spartacus monument, Sandanski	15	10
2853	25s. Liberation monument, Sofia (detail)	30	10
2854	35s. Liberation monument, Plovdiv	40	15
2855	43s. Liberation monument, Shipka Pass	50	20
2856	1l. Liberation monument, Ruse	1·10	45

1980. 10th International Ballet Competition, Varna.

2858	**922**	13s. multicoloured	10	10

923 Europa Hotel, Sofia

1980. Hotels. Multicoloured.

2859	23s. Type **923**	20	10
2860	23s. Bulgaria Hotel, Burgas (vert)	20	10
2861	23s. Plovdiv Hotel, Plovdiv	20	10
2862	23s. Riga Hotel, Ruse (vert)	20	10
2863	23s. Varna Hotel, Prazhba	20	10

1980. Historic Ships (3rd series). As T **753**. Multicoloured.

2864	5s. Hansa kogge "Jesus of Lubeck"	10	10
2865	8s. Roman galley	20	10
2866	13s. Galleon "Eagle"	25	10
2867	23s. "Mayflower"	40	15
2868	35s. Maltese galleon	55	25
2869	53s. Galleon "Royal Louis"	1·10	40

924 Parachute Descent

1980. 15th World Parachute Championships, Kazanluk. Multicoloured.

2870	13s. Type **924**	10	10
2871	25s. Parachutist in free fall	20	10

925 Clown and Children

1980. 1st Anniv of "Banners for Peace" Children's Meeting. Multicoloured.

2872	3s. Type **925**	10	10
2873	5s. "Cosmonauts in Spaceship" (vert)	10	10
2874	8s. "Picnic"	10	10
2875	13s. "Children with Ices"	10	10
2876	25s. "Children with Cat" (vert)	20	10
2877	35s. "Crowd"	1·10	40
2878	43s. "Banners for Peace" monument (vert)	40	20

926 Assembly Emblem 927 Iordan Iovkov

1980. Assembly of Peoples' Parliament for Peace, Sofia.
2879 **926** 25s. multicoloured . . . 15 10

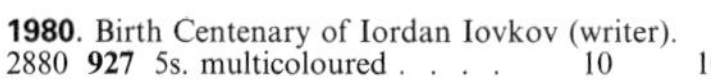

1980. Birth Centenary of Iordan Iovkov (writer).
2880 **927** 5s. multicoloured 10 10

928 Yakovlev Yak-24 Helicopter, Missile Launcher and Tank

1980. Bulgarian Armed Forces. Multicoloured.
2881 3s. Type **928** 15 10
2882 5s. Mikoyan Gurevich MiG-21 bomber, radar antennae and missile transporter 25 10
2883 8s. Mil Mi-24 helicopter, missile boat and landing ship "Ropucha" 60 15

929 Computer

1980. 36th Plovdiv Fair.
2884 **929** 5s. multicoloured 10 10

930 "Virgin and Child with St. Anne"

1980. Paintings by Leonardo da Vinci. Mult.
2885 5s. Type **930** 10 10
2886 8s. Angel (detail, "The Annunciation") 10 10
2887 13s. Virgin (detail, "The Annunciation") 10 10
2888 25s. "Adoration of the Kings" (detail) 20 15
2889 35s. "Woman with Ermine" 30 20

1980. Air. Clocktowers (2nd series). As T **884**. Multicoloured.
2891 13s. **Byala** 10 10
2892 23s. **Razgrad** 20 10
2893 25s. Karnobat 25 10
2894 35s. **Sevlievo** 35 15
2895 53s. Berkovitsa 50 20

931 "Parodia saint-pieana"

1980. Cacti. Multicoloured.
2896 5s. Type **931** 10 10
2897 13s. "Echinopsis bridgesii" 25 10
2898 25s. "Echinocereus purpureus" 50 10
2899 35s. "Opuntia bispinosa" . . 65 15
2900 53s. "Mamillopsis senilis" 90 20

933 Wild Horse

1980. Horses. Multicoloured.
2902 3s. Type **933** 20 10
2903 5s. Tarpan 25 10
2904 13s. Arabian 40 10
2905 23s. Anglo-Arabian 60 15
2906 35s. Draught horse . . . . 1·00 20

934 Vasil Stoin

1980. Birth Centenary of Vasil Stoin (collector of folk songs).
2907 **934** 5s. violet, yellow & gold 10 10

935 Armorial Lion 936 Red Star

1980. New Year. 1300th Anniv of Bulgarian State. Multicoloured.
2908 5s. Type **935** 10 10
2909 13s. Dish and dates "681–1981" 10 10

1980. 12th Bulgarian Communist Party Congress (1st issue).
2910 **936** 5s. yellow and red . . . 10 10
See also Nos. 2920/2.

937 Cross-country Skier

1981. World Ski-racing Championship, Velingrad.
2911 **937** 43s. orange, blue & blk 40 10

938 Midland Hawthorn ("Crataegus oxpacantha") 939 Skier

1981. Useful Plants. Multicoloured.
2912 3s. Type **938** 10 10
2913 5s. Perforate St. John's wort ("Hypericum perforatum") 10 10
2914 13s. Elder ("Sambucus nigra") 20 10
2915 25s. Dewberry ("Rubus caesius") 40 15
2916 35s. Lime ("Tilia argentea") 50 20
2917 43s. Dog rose ("Rosa canina") 75 25

1981. Alpine Skiing World Championships, Borovets.
2918 **939** 43s. yellow, black & blue 40 10

940 Nuclear Traces

1981. 25th Anniv of Nuclear Research Institute, Dubna, U.S.S.R.
2919 **940** 13s. black and silver . . 10 10

941 "XII" formed from Flag

1981. 12th Bulgarian Communist Party Congress (2nd issue).
2920 **941** 5s. multicoloured 10 10
2921 – 13s. red, black and blue 10 10
2922 – 23s. red, black and blue 10 10
DESIGNS: 13s. Stars; 23s. Computer tape.

942 Palace of Culture

1981. Opening of Palace of Culture, Sofia.
2924 **942** 5s. dp green, grn & red 10 10

943 "Self-portrait"

1981. 170th Birth Anniv (1980) of Zakharu Zograf (artist). Multicoloured.
2925 5s. Type **943** 10 10
2926 13s. "Portrait of Khristionia Zografska" 10 10
2927 23s. "The Transfiguration" (icon from Preobrazhenie Monastery) 20 10
2928 25s. "Doomsday" (detail) (horiz) 25 15
2929 35s. "Doomsday" (detail – different) (horiz) 40 20

944 Squacco Heron

1981. Birds. Multicoloured.
2930 5s. Type **944** 20 10
2931 8s. Eurasian bittern 40 15
2932 13s. Cattle egret 70 20
2933 25s. Great egret . . . . . . 1·25 50
2934 53s. Black stork . . . . . . 2·50 1·00

945 Liner "Georgi Dimitrov"

1981. Centenary of Bulgarian Shipbuilding. Mult.
2935 35s. Type **945** . . . . . . 1·00 30
2936 43s. Freighter "Petimata of RMS" . . . . 1·40 40
2937 53s. Tanker "Khan Asparuch" . . . . 2·00 70

946 Hofburg Palace, Vienna

1981. "WIPA 1981" International Stamp Exhibition, Vienna.
2938 **946** 35s. crimson, red & green 20 10

947 "XXXIV"

1981. 34th Bulgarian People's Agrarian Union Congress.
2939 **947** 5s. multicoloured 10 10
2940 – 8s. orange, black & blue 10 10
2941 – 13s. multicoloured . . . 10 10
DESIGNS: 8s. Flags; 13s. Bulgarian Communist Party and Agrarian Union flags.

948 Wild Cat

1981. International Hunting Exhibition, Plovdiv.
2942 **948** 5s. stone, black & brown 15 10
2943 – 13s. black, brn & stone 40 15
2944 – 23s. brown, blk & orge 60 20
2945 – 25s. black, brown & mve 70 40
2946 – 35s. lt brown, blk & brn 95 35
2947 – 53s. brown, blk & grn 1·50 50
DESIGNS: 13s. Wild boar; 23s. Mouflon; 25s. Chamois; 35s. Roe deer; 53s. Fallow deer.

949 "Crafty Peter" (sculpture, Georgi Chapkanov) 950 Bulgarian Arms and U.N.E.S.C.O. Emblem

1981. Festival of Humour and Satire, Gabrovo.
2949 **949** 5s. multicoloured 10 10

1981. 25th Anniv of U.N.E.S.C.O. Membership.
2950 **950** 13s. multicoloured . . . 10 10

951 Deutsche Flugzeugwerke D.F.W. C.V. Biplane

1981. Air. Aircraft. Multicoloured.
2951 5s. Type **951** 10 10
2952 12s. LAS-7 monoplane . . . 35 15
2953 25s. LAS-8 monoplane . . . 70 30
2954 35s. DAR-1 biplane 85 45
2955 45s. DAR-3 biplane . . . . 1·25 55
2956 55s. DAR-9 biplane . . . . 1·75 70

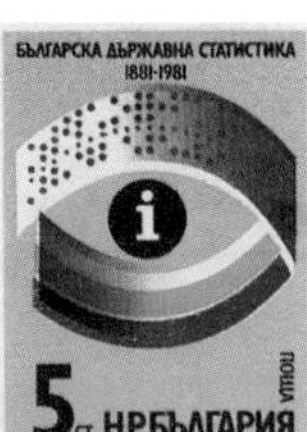
952 "Eye"

1981. Centenary of State Statistical Office.
2957 **952** 5s. multicoloured 10 10

953 Veliko Tirnovo Hotel

1981. Hotels.
2958 **953** 23s. multicoloured . . . 15 10

954 "Flying Figure"

1981. 90th Anniv of First Bulgarian Social Democratic Party Congress, Buzludzha. Sculptures by Velichko Minekov.
2959 **954** 5s. blue, black and green 10 10
2960 – 13s. brown, blk & orge 10 10
DESIGN: 13s. "Advancing Female".

955 Animal-shaped Dish

1981. Golden Treasure of Old St. Nicholas. Multicoloured.
2961 5s. Type **955** 10 10
2962 13s. Jug with decorated neck 10 10
2963 23s. Jug with loop pattern 20 10
2964 25s. Jug with bird pattern 25 10
2965 35s. Decorated vase 35 15
2966 53s. Decorated dish 50 25

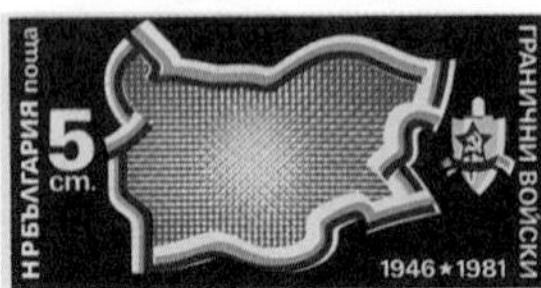

956 Badge and Map of Bulgaria

1981. 35th Anniv of Frontier Guards.
2967 **956** 5s. multicoloured 10 10

957 Saints Cyril and Methodius (9th century)

1981. 1300th Anniv of Bulgarian State.
2968 – 5s. green and grey 10 10
2969 **957** 5s. brown and yellow 10 10
2970 – 8s. violet and lilac 10 10
2971 – 12s. mauve and purple 10 10
2972 – 13s. purple and brown 10 10
2973 – 13s. green and black 10 10
2974 – 16s. green & deep green 15 10
2975 – 23s. black and blue 20 10
2976 – 25s. green and light green 20 10
2977 – 35s. brown and light brown 30 15
2978 – 41s. red and pink 35 20
2979 – 43s. red and pink 35 20
2980 – 53s. dp brown and brown 40 25
2981 – 55s. dp green and green 40 25
DESIGNS: No. 2968, Madara horsemen (8th century); 2970, Plan of Round Church at Veliki Preslav (10th century); 2971, Four Evangelists of King Ivan, 1356; 2972, Column of Ivan Asen II (13th century); 2973, Manasiev Chronicle (14th century); 2974, Rising of April 1876; 2975, Arrival of Russian liberation troops; 2976, Foundation ceremony of Bulgarian Social Democratic Party, 1891; 2977, Rising of September 1923; 2978, Formation of Fatherland Front Government, 9 September 1944; 2979, Bulgarian Communist Party Congress, 1948; 2980, 10th Communist Party Congress, 1971; 2981, Kremikovski metallurgical combine.

958 Volleyball Players **959** "Pegasus" (bronze sculpture)

1981. European Volleyball Championships.
2983 **958** 13s. red, blue and black 10 10

1981. Day of the Word.
2984 **959** 5s. green 10 10

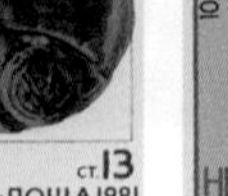

960 Loaf of Bread **961** Mask

1981. World Food Day.
2985 **960** 13s. brown, black & grn 10 10

1981. Cent of Bulgarian Professional Theatre.
2986 **961** 5s. multicoloured 10 10

962 Examples of Bulgarian Art

1981. Cultural Heritage Day.
2987 **962** 13s. green and brown 10 10

963 Footballer

1981. World Cup Football Championship, Spain (1982). Multicoloured.
2988 5s. Type **963** 10 10
2989 13s. Heading ball 25 10
2990 43s. Saving a goal 70 25
2991 53s. Running with ball 90 35

964 Dove encircled by Barbed Wire

1981. Anti-apartheid Campaign.
2992 **964** 5s. red, black and yellow 10 10

965 "Mother" (Lilyann Ruseva)

1981. 35th Anniv of U.N.I.C.E.F. Various designs showing mother and child paintings by named artists. Multicoloured.
2994 53s. Type **965** 50 20
2995 53s. "Bulgarian Madonna" (Vasil Stoilov) 50 20
2996 53s. "Village Madonna" (Ivan Milev) 50 20
2997 53s. "Mother" (Vladimir Dimitrov) 50 20

966 8th century Ceramic from Pliska

1981. New Year. Multicoloured.
2998 5s. Armorial lion 10 10
2999 13s. Type **966** 10 10

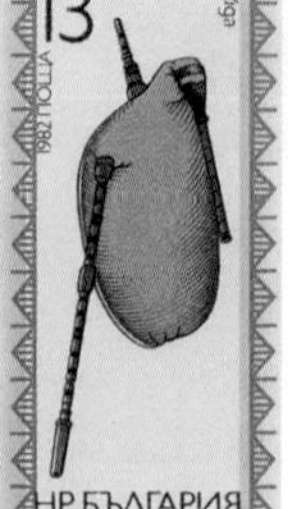

967 Bagpipes **968** Open Book

1982. Musical Instruments. Multicoloured.
3000 13s. Type **967** 10 10
3001 25s. Single and double flutes 20 10
3002 30s. Rebec 25 10
3003 35s. Flute and pipe 30 15
3004 44s. Mandolin 40 15

1982. 125th Anniv of Public Libraries.
3005 **968** 5s. green 10 10

969 "Sofia Plains"

1982. Birth Centenary of Nikola Petrov (artist).
3006 5s. Type **969** 10 10
3007 13s. "Girl Embroidering" 10 10
3008 30s. "Fields of Peshtera" 25 10

971 "Peasant Woman"

1982. Birth Centenary of Valadimir Dimitrov (artist). Multicoloured.
3010 5s. Figures in a landscape (horiz) 10 10
3011 8s. Town and harbour (horiz) 10 10
3012 13s. Town scene (horiz) 10 10
3013 25s. "Reapers" 20 10
3014 30s. Woman and child 20 15
3015 35s. Type **971** 25 15

972 Georgi Dimitrov

1982. 9th Bulgarian Trade Unions Congress, Sofia.
3017 **972** 5s. lt brn, dp brn & brn 10 10
3018 – 5s. brown and blue 10 10
DESIGN: No. 3018, Palace of Culture, Sofia.

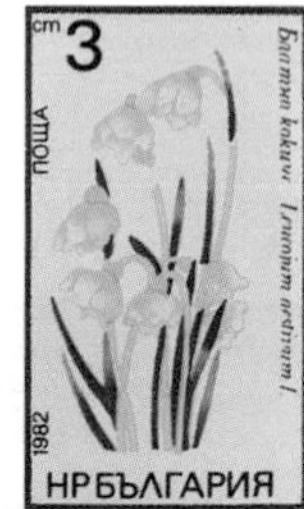

973 Summer Snowflake

1982. Medicinal Plants. Multicoloured.
3019 3s. Type **973** 10 10
3020 5s. Chicory 10 10
3021 8s. Rosebay willowherb 20 10
3022 13s. Solomon's seal 25 10
3023 25s. Sweet violet 50 15
3024 35s. "Ficaria verna" 50 25

974 Russian Space Station

1982. 25th Anniv of First Soviet Artificial Satellite.
3025 **974** 13s. multicoloured 10 10

976 Dimitrov and Congress Emblem

1982. 14th Dimitrov Communist Youth League Congress, Sofia.
3027 **976** 5s. blue, red & yellow 10 10

977 First French and Bulgarian Stamps

1982. "Philexfrance 82" International Stamp Exhibition, Paris.
3028 **977** 42s. multicoloured 75 25

978 Abstract with Birds **980** Georgi Dimitrov

1982. Alafrangi Frescoes from 19th-century Houses.
3029 **978** 5s. multicoloured 10 10
3030 – 13s. multicoloured 10 10
3031 – 25s. multicoloured 20 10
3032 – 30s. multicoloured 20 10
3033 – 42s. multicoloured 30 15
3034 – 60s. multicoloured 45 25
DESIGNS: 13s. to 60s. Various flower and bird patterns.

During 1982 sets were issued for World Cup Football Championship, Spain (5, 13, 30s.), Tenth Anniv of First European Security and Co-operation Conference (5, 13, 25, 30s.), World Cup Results (5, 13, 30s.) and 10th Anniv (1983) of European Security and Co-operation Conference, Helsinki (5, 13, 25, 30s.). Supplies and distribution of these stamps were restricted and it is understood they were not available at face value.

1982. 9th Fatherland Front Congress, Sofia.
3036 **980** 5s. multicoloured 10 10

981 Airplane

1982. 35th Anniv of Balkanair (state airline).
3037 **981** 42s. blue, green & red 65 30

982 Atomic Bomb Mushroom-cloud
983 Lyudmila Zhivkova

1982. Nuclear Disarmament Campaign.
3038 **982** 13s. multicoloured . . . 10 10

1982. 40th Birth Anniv of Lyudmila Zhivkova (founder of "Banners for Peace" Children's Meetings).
3039 **983** 5s. multicoloured 10 10
3040 13s. multicoloured . . . 10 10

984 Emblem

1982. 10th Anniv of U.N. Environment Programme.
3042 **984** 13s. green and blue . . . 10 10

985 Wave Pattern

1982. 5th Bulgarian Painters' Association Congress.
3043 **985** 5s. multicoloured 10 10

986 Child Musicians

1982. 2nd "Banners for Peace" Children's Meeting (1st issue). Children's Paintings. Multicoloured.
3044 3s. Type **986** 10 10
3045 5s. Children skating 10 10
3046 8s. Adults, children and flowers 10 10
3047 13s. Children with flags . . 20 15
See also Nos. 3057/62.

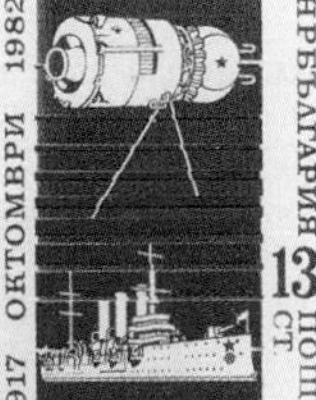
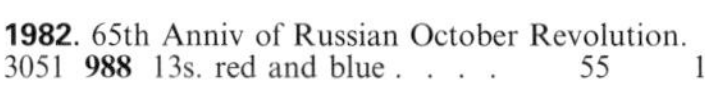
987 Moscow Park Hotel, Sofia
988 Cruiser "Aurora" and Satellite

1982. Hotels. Multicoloured.
3049 32s. Type **987** 20 10
3050 32s. Black Sea Hotel, Varna 20 10

1982. 65th Anniv of Russian October Revolution.
3051 **988** 13s. red and blue 55 10

989 Hammer and Sickle

1982. 60th Anniv of U.S.S.R.
3052 **989** 13s. red, gold & violet 10 10

990 "The Piano"

1982. Birth Cent of Pablo Picasso (artist). Mult.
3053 13s. Type **990** 20 10
3054 30s. "Portrait of Jacqueline" 55 10
3055 42s. "Maternity" 75 10

991 Boy and Girl

1982. 2nd "Banners for Peace" Children's Meeting (2nd issue). Multicoloured.
3057 3s. Type **991** 10 10
3058 5s. Market place 10 10
3059 8s. Children in fancy dress (vert) 10 10
3060 13s. Chickens (vert) 15 10
3061 25s. Interlocking heads . . . 25 15
3062 30s. Lion 30 20

992 Lions

1982. New Year. Multicoloured.
3064 5s. Type **992** 10 10
3065 13s. Decorated letters . . . 10 10

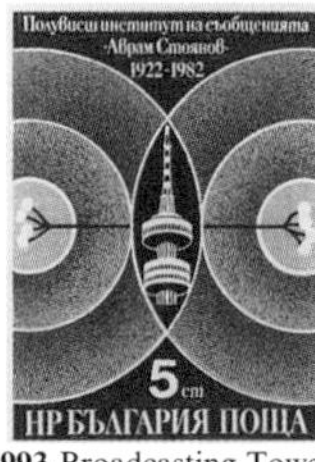

993 Broadcasting Tower
994 Dr. Robert Koch

1982. 60th Anniv of Avram Stoyanov Broadcasting Institute.
3066 **993** 5s. blue 10 10

1982. Cent of Discovery of Tubercle Bacillus.
3067 **994** 25s. brown and green . . 15 10

995 Simon Bolivar
996 Vasil Levski

1982. Birth Anniversaries.
3068 **995** 30s. green and grey . . . 20 10
3069 – 30s. yellow and brown 20 10
DESIGN: No. 3068, Type **995** (bicent); 3069, Rabindranath Tagore (philosopher, 120th anniv).

1983. 110th Death Anniv of Vasil Levski (revolutionary).
3070 **996** 5s. brown & green . . . 10 10

997 Skier

1983. "Universiade 83" University Games, Sofia.
3071 **997** 30s. multicoloured . . . 20 10

998 Northern Pike

1983. Freshwater Fishes. Multicoloured.
3072 3s. Type **998** 10 10
3073 5s. Beluga sturgeon 10 10
3074 13s. Chub 10 10
3075 25s. Zander 20 10
3076 30s. Wels 25 15
3077 42s. Brown trout 35 20

999 Karl Marx

1983. Death Centenary of Karl Marx.
3078 **999** 13s. red, purple & yellow 10 10

1000 Hasek and Illustrations from "The Good Soldier Schweik"

1983. Birth Centenary of Jaroslav Hasek (Czech writer).
3079 **1000** 13s. brown, grey & grn 10 10

1001 Martin Luther

1983. 500th Birth Anniv of Martin Luther (Protestant reformer).
3080 **1001** 13s. grey, black & brn 10 10

1002 Figures forming Initials

1983. 55th Anniv of Young Workers' Union.
3081 **1002** 5s. red, black & orange 10 10

1003 Khaskovo Costume
1004 Old Man feeding a Chicken

1983. Folk Costumes. Multicoloured.
3082 5s. Type **1003** 10 10
3083 8s. Pernik 10 10
3084 13s. Burgas 10 10
3085 25s. Tolbukhin 15 15
3086 30s. Blagoevgrad 20 15
3087 42s. Topolovgrad 30 25

1983. 6th International Festival of Humour and Satire, Gabrovo.
3088 **1004** 5s. multicoloured . . . 10 10

During 1983 sets were issued for European Security and Co-operation Conference, Budapest (5, 13, 25, 30s.), Olympic Games, Los Angeles (5, 13, 30, 42s.), Winter Olympic Games, Sarajevo (horiz designs, 5, 13, 30, 42s.) and European Security and Co-operation Conference, Madrid (5, 13, 30, 42s.). Supplies and distribution of these stamps were restricted, and it is understood they were not available at face value.

1005 Smirnenski

1983. 85th Birth Anniv of Khristo Smirnenski (poet).
3089 **1005** 5s. red, brown & yellow 10 10

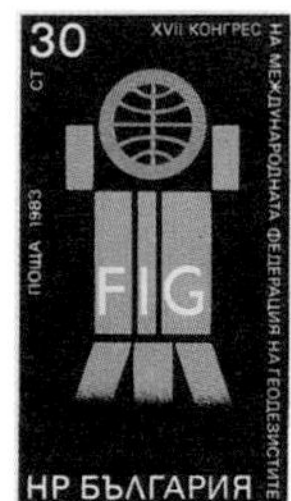

1006 Emblem

1983. 17th Int Geodesy Federation Congress.
3090 **1006** 30s. green, blue & yell 15 10

1007 Stylized Houses

1983. "Interarch 83" World Architecture Biennale, Sofia.
3091 **1007** 30s. multicoloured . . . 15 10

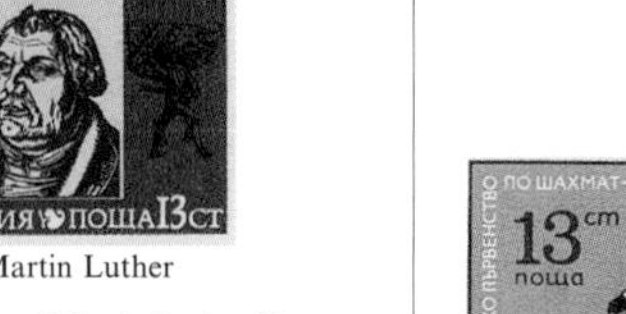

1008 Staunton Chessmen on Map of Europe
1011 Television Mast, Tolbukhin

1983. 8th European Chess Team Championship, Plovdiv.
3092 **1008** 13s. multicoloured . . . 20 10

1983. Air. World Communications Year.
3095 **1011** 5s. blue and red 10 10
3096 – 13s. mauve and red . . 15 10
3097 – 30s. yellow and red . . 20 10
DESIGNS: 13s. Postwoman; 30s. Radio tower, Mount Botev.

1012 Lenin addressing Congress

1983. 80th Anniv of 2nd Russian Social Democratic Workers' Party Congress.
3098 **1012** 5s. pur, dp pur & yell 10 10

1013 Pistol and Dagger on Book

1983. 80th Anniv of Ilinden-Preobrazhenie Rising.
3099 **1013** 5s. yellow and green . . 10 10

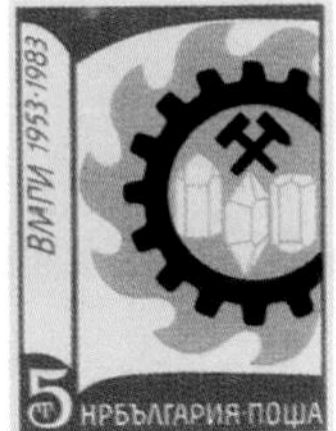

1014 Crystals and Hammers within Gearwheels

1983. 30th Anniv of Mining and Geology Institute, Sofia.
3100 **1014** 5s. grey, purple & blue . . . 10 10

1015 Georgi Dimitrov and Revolution Scenes

1983. 60th Anniv of September Uprising. Mult.
3101 5s. Type **1015** 10 10
3102 13s. Wreath and revolution scenes 10 10

1016 Animated Drawings **1017** Angora

1983. 3rd Animated Film Festival, Varna.
3103 **1016** 5s. multicoloured . . . 10 10

1983. Cats. Multicoloured.
3104 5s. Type **1017** 15 10
3105 13s. Siamese 35 10
3106 20s. Abyssinian (vert) . . . 50 10
3107 25s. European 60 15
3108 30s. Persian (vert) 75 15
3109 42s. Khmer . . . . 1·00 20

1018 Richard Trevithick's Locomotive, 1803

1983. Locomotives (1st series). Multicoloured.
3110 5s. Type **1018** 20 10
3111 13s. John Blenkinsop's rack locomotive "Prince Royal", 1810 . . . . . . 30 10
3112 42s. William Hedley's "Puffing Billy", 1813–14 2·25 50
3113 60s. Stephenson locomotive "Adler", 1835, Germany 3·75 75
See also Nos. 3159/63.

1020 Mask and Laurel as Lyre **1021** Ioan Kukuzel

1983. 75th Anniv of National Opera, Sofia.
3115 **1020** 5s. red, black & gold 10 10

1983. Bulgarian Composers.
3116 **1021** 5s. yellow, brown & grn 10 10
3117 – 8s. yellow, brown & red 10 10
3118 – 13s. yellow, brown and green 10 10
3119 – 20s. yellow, brown & bl 15 10
3120 – 25s. yellow, brn & grey 20 15
3121 – 30s. yell, dp brn & brn 25 20
DESIGNS: 8s. Georgi Atanasov; 13s. Petko Stainov; 20s. Veselin Stoyanov; 25s. Lyubomir Pipkov; 30s. Pancho Vladigerov.

1022 Snowflake

1983. New Year.
3122 **1022** 5s. green, blue & gold 10 10

1023 "Angelo Donni"

1983. 500th Birth Anniv of Raphael (artist). Multicoloured.
3123 5s. Type **1023** 10 10
3124 13s. "Portrait of a Cardinal" 10 10
3125 30s. "Baldassare Castiglioni" 25 15
3126 42s. "Woman with a Veil" 35 25

1024 Eurasian Common Shrew

1983. Protected Mammals. Multicoloured.
3128 12s. Type **1024** 45 20
3129 13s. Greater horseshoe bat 55 20
3130 20s. Common long-eared bat 85 30
3131 30s. Forest dormouse . . . 1·00 40
3132 42s. Fat dormouse . . . . 1·50 60

1025 Karavelov

1984. 150th Birth Anniv of Lyuben Karavelov (poet).
3133 **1025** 5s. blue, bistre & brn 10 10

During 1984 sets were issued for European Confidence- and Security-building Measures and Disarmament Conference, Stockholm (5, 13, 30, 42s.) and Winter Olympic Games, Sarajevo (vert designs, 5, 13, 30, 42s.). Supplies and distribution of these stamps were restricted and it is understood that they were not available at face value.

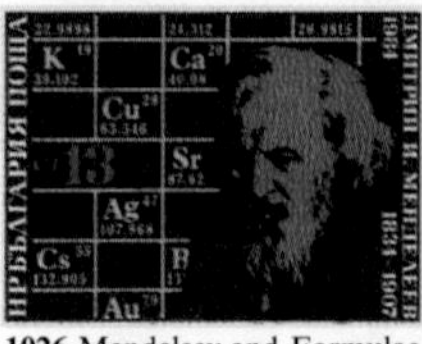

1026 Mendeleev and Formulae

1984. 150th Birth Anniv of Dmitry Mendeleev (chemist).
3134 **1026** 13s. multicoloured . . . 10 10

1027 Bulk Carrier "Gen. Vl. Zaimov"

1984. Ships. Multicoloured.
3135 5s. Type **1027** 20 10
3136 13s. Tanker "Mesta" . . . 45 10
3137 25s. Tanker "Veleka" . . . 85 20
3138 32s. Train ferry "Geroite na Odesa" 95 45
3139 42s. Bulk carrier "Rozhen" 1·40 55

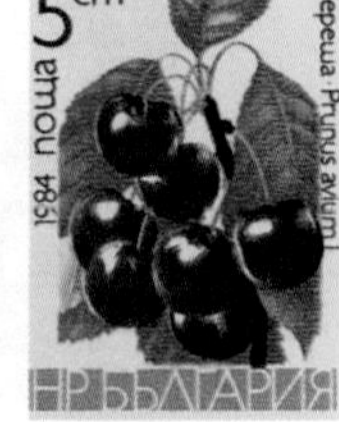

1029 Pigeon with Letter over Globe **1030** Wild Cherries

1984. "Mladost '84" Youth Stamp Exhibition, Pleven (1st issue).
3141 **1029** 5s. multicoloured . . . 15 10
See also Nos. 3171/2.

1984. Fruits. Multicoloured.
3142 5s. Type **1030** 10 10
3143 8s. Wild strawberries . . . 20 10
3144 13s. Dewberries 30 10
3145 20s. Raspberries 40 10
3146 42s. Medlars 75 20

1031 "Vitosha Conference" (K. Buyukliiski and P. Petrov)

1984. 60th Anniv of Bulgarian Communist Party Conference, Vitosha.
3147 **1031** 5s. purple, brn & red 10 10

1033 Athletes and Doves **1034** Mt. Everest

1984. 6th Republican Spartakiad.
3149 **1033** 13s. multicoloured . . . 10 10

1984. Bulgarian Expedition to Mt. Everest.
3150 **1034** 5s. multicoloured . . . 10 10

1036 Drummer

1984. 6th Amateur Performers Festival.
3152 **1036** 5s. multicoloured . . . 10 10

1037 Seal

1984. 50 Years of Bulgarian–U.S.S.R. Diplomatic Relations.
3153 **1037** 13s. multicoloured . . . 10 10

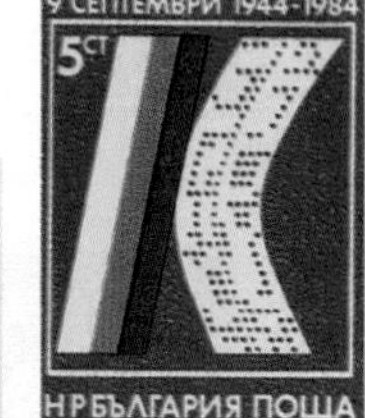

1038 Feral Rock Pigeon **1039** Production Quality Emblem

1984. Pigeons and Doves. Multicoloured.
3154 5s. Type **1038** 20 10
3155 13s. Stock pigeon 55 15
3156 20s. Wood pigeon 80 25
3157 30s. Turtle dove . . . . . . 1·25 45
3158 42s. Domestic pigeon . . . 1·60 60

1984. Locomotives (2nd series). As T **1018**. Multicoloured.
3159 13s. "Best Friend of Charleston", 1830, U.S.A. 30 10
3160 25s. "Saxonia", 1836, Saxony 55 10
3161 30s. "Lafayette", 1837, U.S.A. 65 15
3162 42s. "Borsig", 1841, Germany . . . . . . 1·25 20
3163 60s. "Philadelphia", 1843, U.S.A. . . . . 1·90 30

1984. 40th Anniv of Fatherland Front Government.
3164 **1039** 5s. red, lt green & green 10 10
3165 – 20s. red and violet . . . 10 10
3166 – 30s. red and blue . . . 15 10
DESIGNS: 20s. Monument to Soviet Army, Sofia; 30s. Figure nine and star.

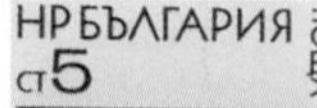

1040 "Boy with Harmonica" **1041** Mausoleum of Russian Soldiers

1984. Paintings by Nenko Balkanski. Multicoloured.
3167 5s. Type **1040** 10 10
3168 30s. "Window in Paris" . . 15 10
3169 42s. "Portrait of Two Women" (horiz) 20 10

1984. "Mladost '84" Youth Stamp Exhibition, Pleven (2nd issue).
3171 **1041** 5s. multicoloured . . . 10 10
3172 – 13s. black, grn & red 10 10
DESIGN: 13s. Panorama building.

1042 Pioneers saluting

1984. 40th Anniv of Dimitrov Septembrist Pioneers Organization.
3173 **1042** 5s. multicoloured . . . 10 10

1043 Vaptsarov (after D. Nikolov)

1984. 75th Birth Anniv of Nikola I. Vaptsarov (poet).
3174 **1043** 5s. yellow and red . . . 10 10

1044 Goalkeeper saving Goal

1984. 75th Anniv of Bulgarian Football.
3175 **1044** 42s. multicoloured . . . 50 15

1046 Devil's Bridge, R. Arda

1984. Bridges. Multicoloured.
3177 5s. Type **1046** 10 10
3178 13s. Kolo Ficheto Bridge, Byala 25 10
3179 30s. Asparukhov Bridge, Varna 50 20
3180 42s. Bebresh Bridge, Botevgrad 70 30

1047 Olympic Emblem

1984. 90th Anniv of International Olympic Committee.
3181 **1047** 13s. multicoloured . . . 10 10

1049 Dalmatian Pelican with Chicks **1050** Anton Ivanov

1984. Wildlife Protection. Dalmatian Pelican.
3183 **1049** 5s. multicoloured . . . 40 15
3184 – 13s. lav, blk & brn . . 90 25
3185 – 20s. multicoloured . . . 1·75 40
3186 – 32s. multicoloured . . . 2·50 75
DESIGNS: 13s. Two pelicans; 20s. Pelican on water; 32s. Pelican in flight.

1984. Birth Cent of Anton Ivanov (revolutionary).
3187 **1050** 5s. yell, brn & red . . . 10 10

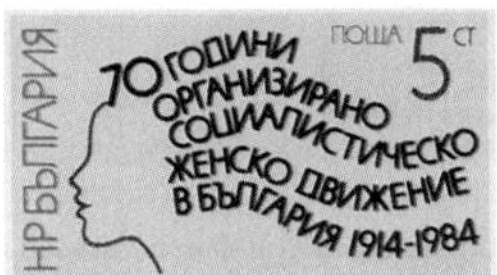

1051 Girl's Profile with Text as Hair

1984. 70th Anniv of Bulgarian Women's Socialist Movement.
3188 **1051** 5s. multicoloured . . . 10 10

1052 Snezhanka Television Tower

1984. Television Towers.
3189 **1052** 5s. blue, green & mve 10 10
3190 – 1l. brown, mauve & bis 75 20
DESIGN: 1l. Orelek television tower.

1053 Birds and Posthorns

1984. New Year. Multicoloured.
3191 5s. Type **1053** 10 10
3192 13s. Decorative pattern . . 10 10

1054 "September Nights"

1984. 80th Birth Anniv of Stoyan Venev (artist). Multicoloured.
3193 5s. Type **1054** 10 10
3194 30s. "Man with Three Orders" 10 10
3195 42s. "The Hero" 15 10

1055 Peacock (butterfly) **1056** Augusto Sandino

1984. Butterflies. Multicoloured.
3196 13s. Type **1055** 30 10
3197 25s. Swallowtail 50 20
3198 30s. Great banded grayling 60 25
3199 42s. Orange-tip 90 40
3200 60s. Red admiral . . . . . 1·25 60

1984. 50th Death Anniv of Augusto Sandino (Nicaraguan revolutionary).
3202 **1056** 13s. black, red & yell 10 10

1057 Tupolev Tu-154 Jetliner

1984. 40th Anniv of I.C.A.O.
3203 **1057** 42s. multicoloured . . . 90 35

1058 "The Three Graces" (detail)

1984. 500th Birth Anniv (1983) of Raphael (artist) (2nd issue). Multicoloured.
3204 5s. Type **1058** 10 10
3205 13s. "Cupid and the Three Graces" (detail) 15 10
3206 30s. "Original Sin" (detail) 35 15
3207 42s. "La Fornarina" 50 20

1059 "Sofia"

1984. Maiden Voyage of Danube Cruise Ship "Sofia".
3209 **1059** 13s. dp blue, blue & yell 90 10

1060 Eastern Hog-nosed Skunk

1985. Mammals.
3210 **1060** 13s. black, blue & orge 25 10
3211 – 25s. black, brown & grn 45 20
3212 – 30s. black, brown & yell 65 20
3213 – 42s. multicoloured . . . 1·00 25
3214 – 60s. multicoloured . . . 1·25 40
DESIGNS: 25s. Banded linsang; 30s. Zorilla; 42s. Banded palm civet; 60s. Broad-striped galidia.

1061 Nikolai Liliev

1985. Birth Centenary of Nikolai Liliev (poet).
3215 **1061** 30s. lt brn, brn & gold 15 10

1062 Tsvyatko Radoinov

1985. 90th Birth Anniv of Tsvyatko Radoinov (resistance fighter).
3216 **1062** 5s. brown and red . . . 10 10

1063 Asen Zlatarov **1066** Olive Branch and Sword Blade

1985. Birth Cent. of Asen Zlatarov (biochemist).
3217 **1063** 5s. purple, yellow & grn 10 10

1985. 30th Anniv of Warsaw Pact.
3220 **1066** 13s. multicoloured . . . 20 10

1067 Bach **1069** St. Methodius

1068 Girl with Birds

1985. Composers.
3221 **1067** 42s. blue and red . . . 1·00 25
3222 – 42s. violet and green . . 1·00 25
3223 – 42s. yellow, brn & orge 1·00 25
3224 – 42s. yellow, brn & red 1·00 25
3225 – 42s. yellow, grn & blue 1·00 25
3226 – 42s. yellow, red & grn 1·00 25
DESIGNS: No. 3222, Mozart; 3223, Tchaikovsky; 3224, Modest Petrovich Musorgsky; 3225, Giuseppe Verdi; 3226, Filip Kutev.

1985. 3rd "Banners for Peace" Children's Meeting, Sofia. Multicoloured.
3227 5s. Type **1068** 10 10
3228 8s. Children painting . . . 10 10
3229 13s. Girl among flowers . . . 10 10
3230 20s. Children at market stall 15 10
3231 25s. Circle of children . . . 20 15
3232 30s. Nurse 20 15

1985. 1100th Death Anniv of St. Methodius.
3234 **1069** 13s. multicoloured . . . 10 10

1070 Soldiers and Nazi Flags

1985. 40th Anniv of V.E. ("Victory in Europe") Day. Multicoloured.
3235 5s. Type **1070** 10 10
3236 13s. 11th Infantry parade, Sofia 15 10
3237 30s. Soviet soldier with orphan 40 10

1071 Woman carrying Child and Man on Donkey

1985. 7th International Festival of Humour and Satire, Gabrovo.
3239 **1071** 13s. black, yell & red 10 10

1072 Profiles and Flowers

1985. International Youth Year.
3240 **1072** 13s. multicoloured . . . 20 10

1073 Ivan Vazov

1985. 135th Birth Anniv of Ivan Vazov (poet).
3241 **1073** 5s. brown and stone . . 10 10

1074 Monument to Unknown Soldiers and City Arms

1985. Millenary of Khaskovo.
3242 **1074** 5s. multicoloured . . . 10 10

1075 Festival Emblem **1077** Vasil E. Aprilov (founder)

1076 Indira Gandhi

1985. 12th World Youth and Students' Festival, Moscow.
3243 **1075** 13s. multicoloured . . . 10 10

1985. Indira Gandhi (Indian Prime Minister) Commemoration.
3244 **1076** 30s. brown, orge & yell 20 10

1985. 150th Anniv of New Bulgarian School, Gabrovo.
3245 **1077** 5s. blue, purple & grn 10 10

1078 Congress Emblem

1985. 36th International Shorthand and Typing Federation Congress ("Intersteno"), Sofia.
3246 **1078** 13s. multicoloured . . . 10 10

1079 Alexandr Nevski Cathedral, Sofia

1985. Sixth General Assembly of World Tourism Organization, Sofia.
3247 **1079** 42s. green, blue & orge 30 15

1080 State Arms and U.N. Flag **1081** Rosa "Trakijka"

1985. 40th Anniv of U.N.O. (3248) and 30th Anniv of Bulgaria's Membership (3249). Multicoloured.
3248 13s. Dove around U.N. emblem 10 10
3249 13s. Type **1080** 10 10

1985. Roses. Multicoloured.
3250 5s. "Rosa damascena" . . . 10 10
3251 13s. Type **1081** 20 10
3252 20s. "Radiman" 30 10
3253 30s. "Marista" 45 15
3254 42s. "Valentina" 60 25
3255 60s. "Maria" 85 40

1082 Peace Dove

1985. 10th Anniv of European Security and Co-operation Conference, Helsinki.
3256 **1082** 13s. multicoloured . . . 10 10

1083 Water Polo

1985. European Swimming Championships, Sofia. Multicoloured.
3257 5s. Butterfly stroke (horiz) 10 10
3258 13s. Type **1083** 20 10
3259 42s. Diving 60 15
3260 60s. Synchronized swimming (horiz) 85 20

1084 Edelweiss

1985. 90th Anniv of Bulgarian Tourist Organization.
3261 **1084** 5s. multicoloured . . . 10 10

1085 State Arms **1086** Footballers

1985. Cent of Union of E. Roumelia and Bulgaria.
3262 **1085** 5s. black, orge & green 10 10

1985. World Cup Football Championship, Mexico (1986) (1st issue).
3263 **1086** 5s. multicoloured . . . 10 10
3264 – 13s. multicoloured . . . 20 10
3265 – 30s. multicoloured . . . 45 15
3266 – 42s. multicoloured . . . 60 20
DESIGNS: 13s. to 42s. Various footballers.
See also Nos. 3346/51.

1087 Computer Picture of Boy

1985. International Young Inventors' Exhibition, Plovdiv. Multicoloured.
3268 5s. Type **1087** 10 10
3269 13s. Computer picture of youth 10 10
3270 30s. Computer picture of cosmonaut 20 10

1088 St. John's Church, Nesebur

1985. 40th Anniv of U.N.E.S.C.O. Mult.
3271 5s. Type **1088** 10 10
3272 13s. Rila Monastery 10 10
3273 35s. Soldier (fresco, Ivanovo Rock Church) 25 10
3274 42s. Archangel Gabriel (fresco, Boyana Church) 30 15
3275 60s. Thracian woman (fresco, Kazanlak tomb) 50 20

1090 Colosseum, Rome **1091** "Gladiolus"

1985. "Italia '85" International Stamp Exhibition, Rome.
3278 **1090** 42s. multicoloured . . . 25 10

1985. Flowers.
3279 **1091** 5s. pink and red . . . 10 10
3280 – 5s. blue and light blue 10 10
3281 – 5s. lt violet & violet . . 10 10
3282 – 8s. light blue and blue 15 10
3283 – 8s. orange and red . . 15 10
3284 – 32s. orange and brown 50 30
DESIGNS: No. 3280, Garden iris; 3281, Dwarf morning glory; 3282, Morning glory; 3283, "Anemone coronaria"; 3284, Golden-rayed lily.

1985. Historic Ships (4th series). As T **753**. Multicoloured.
3286 5s. 17th-century Dutch fly 15 10
3287 12s. "Sovereign of the Seas" (English galleon) 30 10
3288 20s. Mediterranean polacca 55 20
3289 25s. "Prince Royal" (English warship) 60 25
3290 42s. Xebec 80 40
3291 60s. 17th-century English warship . . . . 1·25 60

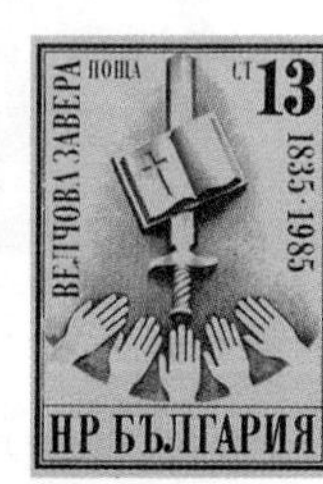

1094 Bacho Kiro **1095** Hands, Sword and Bible

1985. Revolutionaries.
3293 **1094** 5s. light brown, brown and blue 10 10
3294 – 5s. green, purple & brown 10 10
DESIGN: No. 3294, Georgi S. Rakovski

1985. 150th Anniv of Turnovo Uprising.
3295 **1095** 13s. brown, blue & pur 10 10

1096 "1185 Revolution" (G. Bogdanov)

1985. 800th Anniv of Liberation from Byzantine Empire. Multicoloured.
3296 5s. Type **1096** 10 10
3297 13s. "1185 Revolution" (Al. Terziev) 10 10
3298 30s. "Battle of Klakotnitsa, 1230" (B. Grigorov and M. Ganovski) 20 15
3299 42s. "Veliko Turnovo" (Ts. Lavrenov) 30 20

1098 Emblem and Globe

1985. International Development Programme for Posts and Telecommunications.
3302 **1098** 13s. multicoloured . . . 10 10

1099 Popov

1985. 70th Birth Anniv of Anton Popov (revolutionary).
3303 **1099** 5s. red 10 10

1100 Doves around Snowflake

1985. New Year. Multicoloured.
3304 5s. Type **1100** 10 10
3305 13s. Circle of stylized doves 10 10

1101 Pointer and Chukar Partridge

1985. Hunting Dogs. Multicoloured.
3306 5s. Type **1101** 50 20
3307 8s. Irish setter and common pochard 65 20
3308 13s. English setter and mallard 85 20
3309 20s. Cocker spaniel and Eurasian woodcock . . . 1·25 30
3310 25s. German pointer and rabbit 25 20
3311 30s. Bulgarian bloodhound and boar 30 20
3312 42s. Dachshund and fox . . 4·25 1·10

1102 Person in Wheelchair and Runners

1985. International Year of Disabled Persons (1984).
3313 **1102** 5s. multicoloured . . . 10 10

1103 Georgi Dimitrov (statesman)

1985. 50th Anniv of 7th Communist International Congress, Moscow.
3314 **1103** 13s. red 10 10

1104 Emblem within "40"

1986. 40th Anniv of U.N.I.C.E.F.
3315 **1104** 13s. blue, gold & black 10 10

1105 Blagoev **1106** Hands and Dove within Laurel Wreath

1986. 130th Birth Anniv of Dimitur Blagoev (founder of Bulgarian Social Democratic Party).
3316 **1105** 5s. purple and orange 10 10

1986. International Peace Year.
3317 **1106** 5s. multicoloured . . . 10 10

1107 "Dactylorhiza romana"

1986. Orchids. Multicoloured.
3318 5s. Type **1107** 10 10
3319 13s. "Epipactis palustris" . . 20 10
3320 30s. "Ophrys cornuta" . . . 40 10
3321 32s. "Limodorum abrotivum" 40 15
3322 42s. "Cypripedium calceolus" 55 20
3323 60s. "Orchis papilionacea" 1·40 25

1108 Angora Rabbit

1986. Rabbits.
3324 – 5s. grey, black & brown 10 10
3325 **1108** 25s. red and black . . . 35 10
3326 – 30s. brown, yell & blk 40 10
3327 – 32s. orange and black 40 15
3328 – 42s. red and black . . . 55 15
3329 – 60s. blue and black . . 1·50 25
DESIGNS: 5s. French grey; 30s. English lop-eared; 32s. Belgian; 42s. English spotted; 60s. Dutch black and white rabbit.

1109 Front Page and Ivan Bogorov

1986. 140th Anniv of "Bulgarian Eagle".
3330 **1109** 5s. multicoloured . . . 10 10

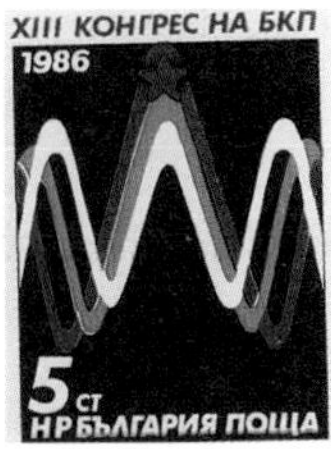

1111 Bashev
1112 Wave Pattern

1986. 50th Birth Anniv (1985) of Vladimir Bashev (poet).
3332 **1111** 5s. blue & light blue . . 10 10

1986. 13th Bulgarian Communist Party Congress.
3333 **1112** 5s. blue, green and red 10 10
3334 – 8s. blue and red 10 10
3335 – 13s. blue, red & lt blue 10 10
DESIGNS: 8s. Printed circuit as tail of shooting star; 13s. Computer picture of man.

1114 Monument, Panagyurishte
1116 Stylized Ear of Wheat

1986. 110th Anniv of April Uprising.
3338 **1114** 5s. black, stone and green 10 10
3339 – 13s. black, stone & red 10 10
DESIGN: 13s. Statue of Khristo Botev, Vratsa.

1986. 35th Bulgarian People's Agrarian Union Congress.
3341 **1116** 5s. gold, orange & blk 10 10
3342 – 8s. gold, blue and black 10 10
3343 – 13s. multicoloured . . . 10 10
DESIGNS: 8s. Stylized ear of wheat on globe; 13s. Flags.

1117 Transport Systems
1118 Emblem

1986. Socialist Countries' Transport Ministers Conference.
3344 **1117** 13s. multicoloured . . . 30 10

1986. 17th International Book Fair, Sofia.
3345 **1118** 13s. grey, red and black 10 10

1119 Player with Ball

1986. World Cup Football Championship, Mexico (2nd issue). Multicoloured.
3346 5s. Type **1119** 20 10
3347 13s. Player tackling (horiz) 30 10
3348 20s. Player heading ball (horiz) 50 15
3349 30s. Player kicking ball (horiz) 75 20
3350 42s. Goalkeeper (horiz) . . 90 40
3351 60s. Player with trophy . . 1·25 40

1120 Square Brooch

1986. Treasures of Preslav. Multicoloured.
3353 5s. Type **1120** 10 10
3354 13s. Pendant (vert) 10 10
3355 20s. Wheel-shaped pendant 15 10
3356 30s. Breast plate decorated with birds and chalice . . 20 10
3357 42s. Pear-shaped pendant (vert) 25 15
3358 60s. Enamelled cockerel on gold base 40 25

1121 Fencers with Sabres

1986. World Fencing Championships, Sofia. Mult.
3359 5s. Type **1121** 10 10
3360 13s. Fencers 10 10
3361 25s. Fencers with rapiers . . 20 10

1122 Stockholm Town Hall

1986. "Stockholmia 86" International Stamp Exn.
3362 **1122** 42s. brn, red & dp red 60 25

1124 Arms and Parliament Building, Sofia

1986. 40th Anniv of People's Republic.
3364 **1124** 5s. green, red & lt grn 10 10

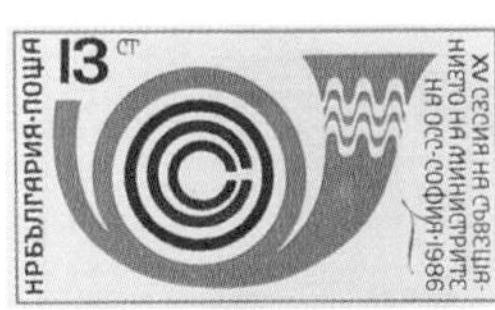

1125 Posthorn

1986. 15th Organization of Socialist Countries' Postal Administrations Session, Sofia.
3365 **1125** 13s. multicoloured . . . 10 10

1126 "All Pull Together"
1127 Dove and Book as Pen Nib

1986. 40th Anniv of Voluntary Brigades.
3366 **1126** 5s. multicoloured . . . 10 10

1986. 10th International Journalists Association Congress, Sofia.
3367 **1127** 13s. blue & deep blue 10 10

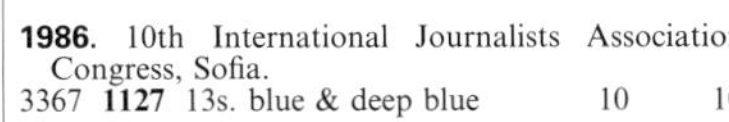

1128 Wrestlers

1986. 75th Anniv of Levski-Spartak Sports Club.
3368 **1128** 5s. multicoloured . . . 10 10

1129 Saints Cyril and Methodius with Disciples (fresco)

1986. 1100th Anniv of Arrival in Bulgaria of Pupils of Saints Cyril and Methodius.
3369 **1129** 13s. brown and buff . . 15 10

1130 Old and Modern Telephones

1986. Centenary of Telephone in Bulgaria.
3370 **1130** 5s. multicoloured . . . 10 10

1131 Weightlifter

1986. World Weightlifting Championships, Sofia.
3371 **1131** 13s. multicoloured . . . 15 10

1986. Historic Ships (5th series). 18th-century ships. As T **753**. Multicoloured.
3372 5s. "King of Prussia" . . . 15 10
3373 13s. Indiaman 30 10
3374 25s. Xebec 55 25
3375 30s. "Sv. Paul" 70 30
3376 32s. Topsail schooner . . . 70 30
3377 42s. "Victory" 90 35

1133 Silver Jug decorated with Seated Woman

1986. 14th Congress of Bulgarian Philatelic Federation and 60th Anniv of International Philatelic Federation. Repousse work found at Rogozen.
3379 **1133** 10s. grey, black & bl 15 15
3380 – 10s. green, blk & red 15 15
DESIGN: No. 3380, Silver jug decorated with sphinx.

1134 Doves between Pine Branches

1986. New Year.
3381 **1134** 5s. red, green and blue 10 10
3382 – 13s. mauve, blue & vio 15 10
DESIGN: 13s. Fireworks and snowflakes.

1135 Earphones as "60" on Globe

1986. 60th Anniv of Bulgarian Amateur Radio.
3383 **1135** 13s. multicoloured . . . 10 10

1137 Gen. Augusto Sandino and Flag

1988. 25th Anniv of Sandinista National Liberation Front of Nicaragua.
3385 **1137** 13s. multicoloured . . . 15 10

1138 Dimitur and Konstantin Miladinov (authors)
1139 Pencho Slaveikov (poet)

1986. 125th Anniv of "Bulgarian Popular Songs".
3386 **1138** 10s. blue, brn & red . . 15 10

1986. Writers' Birth Annivs. Multicoloured.
3387 5s. Type **1139** (125th anniv) 10 10
3388 5s. Stoyan Mikhailovski (130th anniv) 10 10
3389 8s. Nikola Atanasov (dramatist) (centenary) . . 10 10
3390 8s. Ran Bosilek (children's author) (centenary) . . . 10 10

1140 Raiko Daskalov
1141 "Girl with Fruit"

1986. Birth Cent of Raiko Daskalov (politician).
3391 **1140** 5s. brown 10 10

1986. 500th Birth Anniv of Titian (painter). Multicoloured.
3392 5s. Type **1141** 10 10
3393 13s. "Flora" 20 10
3394 20s. "Lucretia and Tarquin" 30 10
3395 30s. Caiphas and Mary Magdalene 50 15
3396 32s. "Toilette of Venus" (detail) 50 15
3397 42s. "Self-portrait" . . . . 1·10 20

1142 Fiat, 1905

1986. Racing Cars.
3399 **1142** 5s. brown, red & black 10 10
3400 – 10s. red, orange & blk 20 10
3401 – 25s. green, red & black 45 20
3402 – 32s. brown, red & blk 60 20
3403 – 40s. violet, red & black 70 25
3404 – 42s. grey, black and red 1·25 25
DESIGNS: 10s. Bugatti, 1928; 25s. Mercedes, 1936; 32s. Ferrari, 1952; 40s. Lotus, 1985; 42s. Maclaren, 1986.

1143 Steam Locomotive

1987. 120th Anniv of Ruse–Varna Railway.
3405 **1143** 5s. multicoloured . . . 20 10

1144 Debelyanov

1987. Birth Cent of Dimcho Debelyanov (poet).
3406 **1144** 5s. dp blue, yellow & bl 10 10

1145 Lazarus Ludwig Zamenhof (inventor)

1987. Centenary of Esperanto (invented language).

3407	**1145**	13s. blue, yellow & grn	15	10

1146 The Blusher **1147** Worker

1987. Edible Fungi. Multicoloured.

3408	5s. Type **1146**	10	10
3409	20s. Royal boletus	35	15
3410	30s. Red-capped scaber stalk	60	30
3411	32s. Shaggy ink cap	70	30
3412	40s. Bare-toothed russula	90	35
3413	60s. Chanterelle	1·25	75

1987. 10th Trade Unions Congress, Sofia.

3414	**1147**	5s. violet and red	10	10

1148 Silver-gilt Plate with Design of Hercules and Auge

1987. Treasure of Rogozen. Multicoloured.

3415	5s. Type **1148**	10	10
3416	8s. Silver-gilt jug with design of lioness attacking stag	10	10
3417	20s. Silver-gilt plate with quatrefoil design	15	10
3418	30s. Silver-gilt jug with design of horse rider	25	15
3419	32s. Silver-gilt pot with palm design	30	15
3420	42s. Silver jug with chariot and horses design	50	20

1150 Wrestlers **1152** "X" and Flags

1151 Totem Pole

1987. 30th European Freestyle Wrestling Championships, Turnovo.

3422	**1150**	5s. lilac, red and violet	10	10
3423	–	13s. dp blue, red & blue	15	10

DESIGNS: 13st. Wrestlers (different).

1987. "Capex '87" International Stamp Exhibition, Toronto.

3424	**1151**	42s. multicoloured	60	20

1987. 10th Fatherland Front Congress.

3425	**1152**	5s. green, orange & bl	10	10

1153 Georgi Dimitrov and Profiles

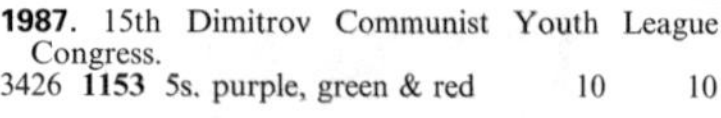
1987. 15th Dimitrov Communist Youth League Congress.

3426	**1153**	5s. purple, green & red	10	10

1154 Mask **1156** Mariya Gigova

1155 Mastheads

1987. 8th International Festival of Humour and Satire, Gabrovo.

3427	**1154**	13s. multicoloured	15	10

1987. 60th Anniv of "Rabotnichesko Delo" (newspaper).

3428	**1155**	5s. red and black	10	10

1987. 13th World Rhythmic Gymnastics Championships, Varna.

3429	**1156**	5s. blue and yellow	10	10
3430	–	8s. red and yellow	10	10
3431	–	13s. blue and stone	15	10
3432	–	25s. red and yellow	30	10
3433	–	30s. black and yellow	30	10
3434	–	42s. mauve and yellow	45	20

DESIGNS: 8s. Iliana Raeva; 13s. Aneliya Ralenkova; 25s. Dilyana Georgieva; 30s. Liliya Ignatova; 42s. Bianka Panova.

1157 Man breaking Chains around Globe and Kolarov

1987. 110th Birth Anniv of Vasil Kolarov (Prime Minister 1949–50).

3436	**1157**	5s. multicoloured	10	10

1158 Stela Blagoeva **1160** Roe Deer

1159 Levski

1987. Birth Centenary of Stela Blagoeva.

3437	**1158**	5s. brown and pink	10	10

1987. 150th Birth Anniv of Vasil Levski (revolutionary).

3438	**1159**	5s. brown and green	10	10
3439	–	13s. green and brown	15	10

DESIGN: 13s. Levski and Bulgarian Revolutionary Central Committee emblem.

1987. Stags. Multicoloured.

3440	5s. Type **1160**	10	10
3441	10s. Elk (horiz)	15	10
3442	32s. Fallow deer	50	20
3443	40s. Sika deer	60	20
3444	42s. Red deer (horiz)	60	20
3445	60s. Reindeer	90	30

1161 Barbed Wire as Dove

1987. International Namibia Day.

3446	**1161**	13s. black, red & orge	15	10

1162 Kirkov **1163** "Phacelia tanacetifolia"

1987. 120th Birth Anniv of Georgi Kirkov (pseudonym Maistora) (politician).

3447	**1162**	5s. red and pink	10	10

1987. Flowers. Multicoloured.

3448	5s. Type **1163**	10	10
3449	10s. Sunflower	15	10
3450	30s. False acacia	45	20
3451	32s. Dutch lavender	50	20
3452	42s. Small-leaved lime	60	20
3453	60s. "Onobrychis sativa"	90	30

1164 Mil Mi-8 Helicopter, Tupolev Tu-154 and Antonov An-12 Aircraft

1987. 40th Anniv of Balkanair.

3454	**1164**	25s. multicoloured	70	30

1165 1879 5c. Stamp

1987. "Bulgaria '89" International Stamp Exhibition, Sofia (1st issue).

3455	**1165**	13s. multicoloured	20	10

See also Nos. 3569, 3579/82 and 3602/5.

1166 Copenhagen Town Hall **1167** "Portrait of Girl" (Stefan Ivanov)

1987. "Hafnia '87" International Stamp Exhibition, Copenhagen.

3456	**1166**	42s. multicoloured	50	20

1987. Paintings in Sofia National Gallery. Mult.

3457	5s. Type **1167**	10	10
3458	8s. "Woman carrying Grapes" (Bencho Obreshkov)	10	10
3459	20s. "Portrait of a Woman wearing a Straw Hat" (David Perez)	30	10
3460	25s. "Women listening to Marimba" (Kiril Tsonev)	40	15
3461	32s. "Boy with Harmonica" (Nenko Balkanski)	50	15
3462	60s. "Rumyana" (Vasil Stoilov)	90	20

1168 Battle Scene

1987. 75th Anniv of Balkan War.

3463	**1168**	5s. black, stone and red	10	10

1169 Emblem

1987. 30th Anniv of International Atomic Energy Agency.

3464	**1169**	13s. blue, green and red	15	10

1170 Mastheads

1987. 95th Anniv of "Rabotnik", 90th Anniv of "Rabotnicheski Vestnik" and 60th Anniv of "Rabotnichesko Delo" (newspapers).

3465	**1170**	5s. red, blue and gold	10	10

1171 Winter Wren **1174** Biathlon

1173 Lenin and Revolutionary

1987. Birds. Multicoloured.

3466	5s. Type **1171**	10	10
3467	13s. Yellowhammer	30	15
3468	20s. Eurasian nuthatch	40	20
3469	30s. Blackbird	60	35
3470	42s. Hawfinch	90	40
3471	60s. White-throated dipper	1·25	60

1987. 70th Anniv of Russian Revolution.

3473	**1173**	5s. purple and red	10	10
3474	–	13s. blue and red	15	10

DESIGN: 13s. Lenin and cosmonaut.

1987. Winter Olympic Games, Calgary. Mult.

3475	5s. Type **1174**	10	10
3476	13s. Slalom	20	10
3477	30s. Figure skating (women's)	45	10
3478	42s. Four-man bobsleigh	65	15

1175 "Socfilex" Emblem within Folk-design Ornament

1987. New Year. Multicoloured.

3480	5s. Type **1175**	10	10
3481	13s. Emblem within flower ornament	15	10

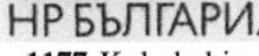

1177 Kabakchiev **1178** "Scilla bythynica"

1988. 110th Birth Anniv of Khristo Kabakchiev (Communist Party official).
3483 **1177** 5s. multicoloured . . . 10 10

1988. Marsh Flowers. Multicoloured.
3484 5s. Type **1178** 10 10
3485 10s. "Geum rhodopaeum" 15 10
3486 13s. "Caltha polypetala" . . 20 10
3487 25s. Fringed water-lily . . . 35 15
3488 30s. "Cortusa matthioli" . . 40 20
3489 42s. Water soldier 60 25

1179 Commander on Horseback

1988. 110th Anniv of Liberation from Turkey. Multicoloured.
3490 5s. Type **1179** 10 10
3491 13s. Soldiers 15 10

1180 Emblem

1988. Public Sector Workers' 8th International Congress, Sofia.
3492 **1180** 13s. multicoloured . . . 15 10

1181 "Yantra", 1888

1988. Centenary of State Railways. Locomotives. Multicoloured.
3493 5s. Type **1181** 20 10
3494 13s. "Khristo Botev", 1905 30 10
3495 25s. Steam locomotive No. 807, 1918 . . . . . 40 15
3496 32s. Class 46 steam locomotive, 1943 . . . . 55 20
3497 42s. Diesel locomotive, 1964 90 25
3498 60s. Electric locomotive, 1979 . . . . 1·25 40

1182 Ivan Nedyalkov (Shablin) **1183** Traikov

1988. Post Office Anti-fascist Heroes.
3499 **1182** 5s. light brown and brown 10 10
3500 – 8s. grey and blue . . . 10 10
3501 – 10s. green and olive . . 10 10
3502 – 13s. pink and red . . . 15 10
DESIGNS: 8s. Delcho Spasov; 10s. Nikola Ganchev (Gudzho); 13s. Ganka Rasheva (Boika).

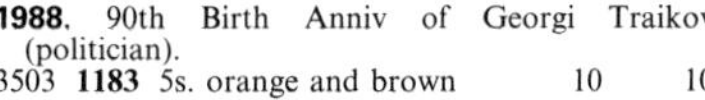

1988. 90th Birth Anniv of Georgi Traikov (politician).
3503 **1183** 5s. orange and brown 10 10

1184 Red Cross, Red Crescent and Globe **1185** Girl

1988. 125th Anniv of International Red Cross.
3504 **1184** 13s. multicoloured . . . 20 10

1988. 4th "Banners for Peace" Children's Meeting, Sofia. Children's paintings. Multicoloured.
3505 5s. Type **1185** 10 10
3506 8s. Artist at work 10 10
3507 13s. Circus (horiz) 20 10
3508 20s. Kite flying (horiz) . . . 30 15
3509 32s. Accordion player . . . 45 20
3510 42s. Cosmonaut 60 25

1186 Marx

1988. 170th Birth Anniv of Karl Marx.
3512 **1186** 13s. red, black & yellow 15 10

1187 Herring Gull **1189** "Soyuz TM" Spacecraft, Flags and Globe

1188 African Elephant

1988. Birds. Multicoloured.
3513 5s. Type **1187** 25 10
3514 5s. White stork 25 10
3515 8s. Grey heron 45 15
3516 8s. Carrion crow 45 15
3517 10s. Northern goshawk . . 60 20
3518 42s. Eagle owl . . . . . . 1·25 30

1988. Centenary of Sofia Zoo. Multicoloured.
3519 5s. Type **1188** 10 10
3520 13s. White rhinoceros . . . 20 10
3521 25s. Hunting dog 35 15
3522 30s. Eastern white pelican 70 30
3523 32s. Abyssinian ground hornbill 75 35
3524 42s. Snowy owl . . . . . . 1·75 55

1988. 2nd Soviet–Bulgarian Space Flight. Mult.
3525 5s. Type **1189** 10 10
3526 13s. Rocket on globe . . . 20 10

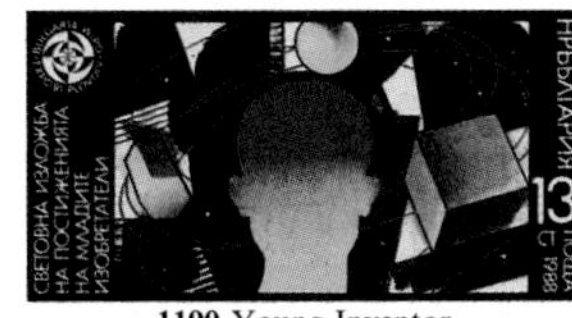

1190 Young Inventor

1988. International Young Inventors' Exhibition, Plovdiv.
3527 **1190** 13s. multicoloured . . . 20 10

1191 1856 Handstamp of Russian Duchy of Finland

1988. "Finlandia '88" International Stamp Exhibition, Helsinki.
3528 **1191** 30s. blue and red . . . 40 20

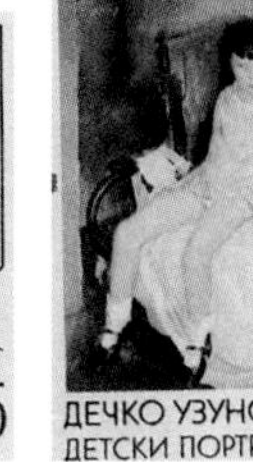

1192 Player taking Corner Kick **1193** "Portrait of Child"

1988. 8th European Football Championship, West Germany. Multicoloured.
3529 5s. Type **1192** 10 10
3530 13s. Goalkeeper and player 20 10
3531 30s. Referee and player . . 40 20
3532 42s. Player with trophy . . 60 25

1988. 2nd Death Anniv of Dechko Uzunov (painter). Multicoloured.
3534 5s. Type **1193** 10 10
3535 13s. "Portrait of Mariya Vasileva" 20 10
3536 30s. "Self-portrait" 40 20

1195 "St. John" **1196** High Jumping

1988. Icons from Kurdzhali. Multicoloured.
3538 5s. Type **1195** 10 10
3539 8s. "St. George and Dragon" 10 10

1988. Olympic Games, Seoul. Multicoloured.
3540 5s. Type **1196** 10 10
3541 13s. Weightlifting 20 10
3542 30s. Wrestling 40 20
3543 42s. Gymnastics 60 25

1197 Dimitur and Karadzha

1988. 120th Death Anniv of Khadzhi Dimitur and Stefan Karadzha (revolutionaries).
3545 **1197** 5s. green, black & brn 10 10

1198 Magazines

1988. 30th Anniv of "Problems of Peace and Socialism" (magazine).
3546 **1198** 13s. multicoloured . . . 15 10

1199 "The Dead Tree" (Roland Udo)

1988. Paintings in Lyudmila Zhivkova Art Gallery. Multicoloured.
3547 30s. Type **1199** 45 15
3548 30s. "Algiers Harbour" (Albert Marque) 45 15
3549 30s. "Portrait of Hermine David" (Jule Pasquin) . . 45 15
3550 30s. "Madonna and Child with two Saints" (Giovanni Rosso) 45 15

1200 University Building

1988. Centenary of St. Clement of Ohrid University, Sofia.
3551 **1200** 5s. black, yellow & grn 10 10

1201 Czechoslovakia 1918 Stamp Design

1988. "Praga '88" International Stamp Exhibition, Prague.
3552 **1201** 25s. red and blue . . . 35 15

1202 Korea 1884 5m. Stamp

1988. "Olymphilex '88" Olympic Stamps Exhibition, Seoul.
3553 **1202** 62s. red and green . . . 90 40

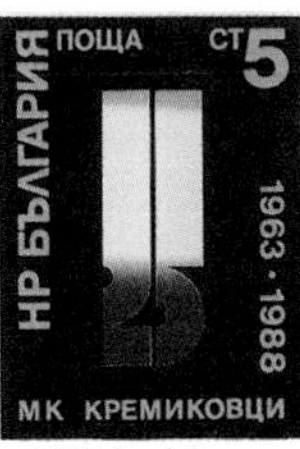

1203 Anniversary Emblem **1204** Parliament Building, Sofia, and Map

1988. 25th Anniv of Kremikovtsi Steel Mills.
3554 **1203** 5s. violet, red and blue 10 10

1988. 80th Interparliamentary Conference, Sofia.
3555 **1204** 13s. blue and red . . . 15 10

1205 Chalice, Glinena

1988. Kurdzhali Culture. Multicoloured.
3556 5s. Type **1205** 10 10
3557 8s. Part of ruined fortifications, Perperikon (vert) 10 10

1206 Soldiers

1988. 300th Anniv of Chiprovtsi Rising.
3558 **1206** 5s. multicoloured . . . 10 10

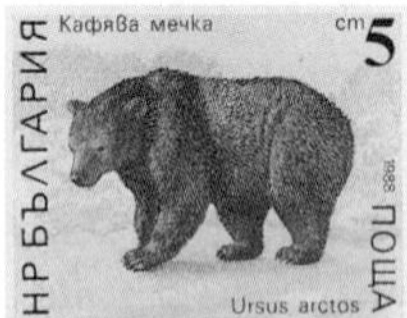

1207 Brown Bear

1988. Bears. Multicoloured.
3559 5s. Type **1207** 10 10
3560 8s. Polar bear 10 10
3561 13s. Sloth bear 25 10
3562 20s. Sun bear 35 15
3563 32s. Asiatic black bear . . . 50 20
3564 42s. Spectacled bear 65 25

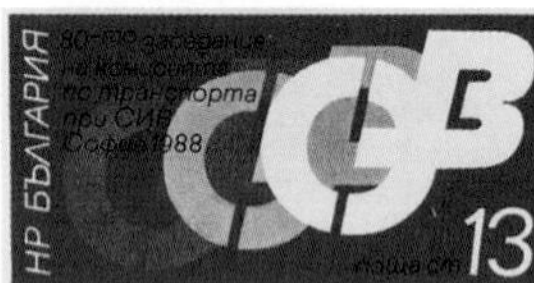

1208 Emblem

1988. 80th Council of Mutual Economic Aid Transport Commission Meeting, Sofia.
3565 **1208** 13s. red and black . . . 15 10

1209 Emblem

1988. World Ecoforum.
3566 **1209** 20s. multicoloured . . . 25 10

1210 Amphitheatre, Plovdiv

1988. "Plovdiv '88" National Stamp Exhibition.
3567 **1210** 5s. multicoloured . . . 10 10

1211 Transmission Towers

1988. 25th Anniv of Radio and Television.
3568 **1211** 5s. green, blue & brown 10 10

1212 1879 5c. Stamp

1988. "Bulgaria '89" International Stamp Exhibition (2nd issue).
3569 **1212** 42s. orange, blk & mve 60 25

1214 Children and Cars

1988. Road Safety Campaign.
3571 **1214** 5s. multicoloured . . . 10 10

1215 Rila Hotel, Borovets

1988. Hotels. Multicoloured.
3572 5s. Type **1215** 10 10
3573 8s. Pirin Hotel, Bansko . . 10 10
3574 13s. Shtastlivetsa Hotel, Vitosha 15 10
3575 30s. Perelik Hotel, Pamporovo 40 15

1216 Tree Decoration

1988. New Year. Multicoloured.
3576 5s. Type **1216** 10 10
3577 13s. "Bulgaria '89" emblem, tree and decorations . . . 15 10

1218 Mail Coach

1988. "Bulgaria '89" International Stamp Exhibition, Sofia (3rd issue). Mail Transport. Multicoloured.
3579 25s. Type **1218** 35 15
3580 25s. Paddle-steamer 35 15
3581 25s. Lorry 35 15
3582 25s. Biplane 45 15

1219 India 1947 1½a. Independence Stamp

1989. "India 89" International Stamp Exhibition, New Delhi.
3583 **1219** 62s. green and orange 1·40 60

1220 France 1850 10c. Ceres Stamp

1989. "Philexfrance '89" International Stamp Exhibition, Paris.
3584 **1220** 42s. brown and blue . . 90 40

1222 Don Quixote (sculpture, House of Humour and Satire)

1223 "Ramonda serbica"

1989. International Festival of Humour and Satire, Gabrovo.
3586 **1222** 13s. multicoloured . . . 20 10

1989. Flowers. Multicoloured.
3587 5s. Type **1223** 10 10
3588 10s. "Paeonia maskula" . . 15 10
3589 25s. "Viola perinensis" . . . 35 30
3590 30s. "Dracunculus vulgaris" 45 40
3591 42s. "Tulipa splendens" . . 60 55
3592 60s. "Rindera umbellata" 90 80

1224 Common Noctule Bat

1989. Bats. Multicoloured.
3593 5s. Type **1224** 10 10
3594 13s. Greater horseshoe bat 25 10
3595 30s. Large mouse-eared bat 65 20
3596 42s. Particoloured frosted bat 95 25

1225 Stamboliiski

1989. 110th Birth Anniv of Aleksandur Stamboliiski (Prime Minister 1919–23).
3597 **1225** 5s. black and orange . . 10 10

1227 Young Inventor

1989. International Young Inventors' Exhibition, Plovdiv.
3599 **1227** 5s. multicoloured . . . 10 10

1228 Stanke Dimitrov-Marek (Party activist)

1229 "John the Baptist" (Toma Vishanov)

1989. Birth Centenaries.
3600 **1228** 5s. red and black . . . 10 10
3601 – 5s. red and black . . . 10 10
DESIGN: No. 3601, Petko Yenev (revolutionary).

1989. "Bulgaria '89" International Stamp Exhibition, Sofia (4th issue). Icons. Multicoloured.
3602 30s. Type **1229** 45 15
3603 30s. "St. Dimitur" (Ivan Terziev) 45 15
3604 30s. "Archangel Michael" (Dimitur Molerov) . . . 45 15
3605 30s. "Madonna and Child" (Toma Vishanov) 45 15

1230 Fax Machine and Woman reading letter

1989. 110th Anniv of Bulgarian Post and Telegraph Services. Multicoloured.
3606 5s. Type **1230** 10 10
3607 8s. Telex machine and old telegraph machine 10 10
3608 35s. Modern and old telephones 40 15
3609 42s. Dish aerial and old radio 50 20

1232 A. P. Aleksandrov, A. Ya. Solovov and V. P. Savinikh

1989. Air. "Soyuz TM5" Soviet-Bulgarian Space Flight.
3611 **1232** 13s. multicoloured . . . 20 10

1233 Party Programme

1234 Sofronii Vrachanski (250th anniv)

1989. 70th Anniv of First Bulgarian Communist Party Congress, Sofia.
3612 **1233** 5s. blk, red & dp red 10 10

1989. Writers' Birth Anniversaries.
3613 **1234** 5s. green, brown & blk 10 10
3614 – 5s. green, brown & blk 10 10
DESIGN: No. 3614, Iliya Bluskov (150th anniv).

1235 Birds

1989. Bicentenary of French Revolution. Each black, red and blue.
3615 13s. Type **1235** 20 10
3616 30s. Jean-Paul Marat . . . 40 15
3617 42s. Robespierre 50 20

1236 Gymnastics

1989. 7th Friendly Armies Summer Spartakiad. Multicoloured.
3618 5s. Type **1236** 10 10
3619 13s. Show jumping 20 10
3620 30s. Long jumping 40 15
3621 42s. Shooting 50 20

1237 Aprilov

1238 Zagorchinov

1989. Birth Bicent of Vasil Aprilov (educationist).
3622 **1237** 8s. lt blue, blue & blk 10 10

1989. Birth Centenary of Stoyan Zagorchinov (writer).
3623 **1238** 10s. turq, brown & blk 15 10

1239 Woman in Kayak

1989. Canoeing and Kayak Championships, Plovdiv. Multicoloured.
3624 13s. Type **1239** 20 10
3625 30s. Man in kayak 45 15

1240 Felix Nadar taking Photograph from his Balloon "Le Geant" (1863) and Airship "Graf Zeppelin" over Alexsandr Nevski Cathedral, Sofia

1989. 150th Anniv of Photography.
3626 **1240** 42s. black, stone & yell . . . 80 30

1241 Lammergeier and Lynx

1989. Centenary of Natural History Museum.
3627 **1241** 13s. multicoloured . . . 1·00 20

1242 Soldiers **1243** Lyubomir Dardzhikov

1989. 45th Anniv of Fatherland Front Government. Multicoloured.
3628 5s. Type **1242** 10 10
3629 8s. Welcoming officers . . . 10 10
3630 13s. Crowd of youths . . . 15 10

1989. 48th Death Anniversaries of Post Office War Heroes. Multicoloured.
3631 5s. Type **1243** 10 10
3632 8s. Ivan Bankov Dobrev . . 10 10
3633 13s. Nestor Antonov . . . 10 10

1244 Yasenov **1246** Nehru

1245 Lorry leaving Weighbridge

1989. Birth Cent of Khisto Yasenov (writer).
3634 **1244** 8s. grey, brown & blk . . . 10 10

1989. 21st Transport Congress, Sofia.
3635 **1245** 42s. blue & deep blue . . . 50 20

1989. Birth Centenary of Jawaharlal Nehru (Indian statesman).
3636 **1246** 13s. yellow, brn & blk . . . 15 10

1248 Javelin Sand Boa

1989. Snakes. Multicoloured.
3638 5s. Type **1248** 10 10
3639 10s. Aesculapian snake . . . 10 10
3640 25s. Leopard snake 35 10
3641 30s. Four-lined rat snake . . 45 15
3642 42s. Cat snake 60 25
3643 60s. Whip snake 90 40

1249 Tiger and Balloon of Flags **1251** Goalkeeper saving Ball

1989. Young Inventors' Exhibition, Plovdiv.
3644 **1249** 13s. multicoloured . . . 15 10

1989. World Cup Football Championship, Italy (1990) (1st issue). Multicoloured.
3646 5s. Type **1251** 15 10
3647 13s. Player tackling 25 15
3648 30s. Player heading ball . . 65 30
3649 42s. Player kicking ball . . 90 40
See also Nos. 3675/8.

1252 Gliders

1989. 82nd International Airsports Federation General Conference, Varna. Aerial Sports. Mult.
3651 5s. Type **1252** 10 10
3652 13s. Hang gliding 20 15
3653 30s. Parachutist landing . . 40 20
3654 42s. Free falling parachutist . . 60 30

1253 Children on Road Crossing

1989. Road Safety.
3655 **1253** 5s. multicoloured . . . 10 10

1254 Santa Claus's Sleigh **1255** European Shorthair

1989. New Year. Multicoloured.
3656 5s. Type **1254** 10 10
3657 13s. Snowman 15 10

1989. Cats.
3658 **1255** 5s. black and yellow . . 15 10
3659 – 5s. black and grey . . . 15 10
3660 – 8s. black and yellow . . 20 10
3661 – 10s. black & brown . . 25 15
3662 – 10s. black and blue . . 25 15
3663 – 13s. black and red . . . 40 20
DESIGNS—HORIZ: No. 3659, Persian; 3660, European shorthair (different); 3662, Persian (different). VERT: No. 3661, Persian (different); 3663, Siamese.

1256 Christopher Columbus and "Santa Maria"

1990. Navigators and their Ships. Multicoloured.
3664 5s. Type **1256** 20 10
3665 8s. Vasco da Gama and "Sao Gabriel" 20 10
3666 13s. Ferdinand Magellan and "Vitoria" 35 10
3667 32s. Francis Drake and "Golden Hind" 45 20
3668 42s. Henry Hudson and "Discoverie" 65 25
3669 60s. James Cook and H.M.S. "Endeavour" . . 90 25

1257 Banner

1990. Centenary of Esperanto (invented language) in Bulgaria.
3670 **1257** 10s. stone, green & blk . . . 10 10

1258 "Portrait of Madeleine Rono" (Maurice Brianchon)

1990. Paintings. Multicoloured.
3671 30s. Type **1258** 45 20
3672 30s. "Still Life" (Suzanne Valadon) 45 20
3673 30s. "Portrait of a Woman" (Moise Kisling) 45 20
3674 30s. "Portrait of a Woman" (Giovanni Boltraffio) . . 45 20

1259 Players

1990. World Cup Football Championship, Italy.
3675 **1259** 5s. multicoloured . . . 10 10
3676 – 13s. multicoloured . . . 15 10
3677 – 30s. multicoloured . . . 45 20
3678 – 42s. multicoloured . . . 70 30
DESIGNS: 13 to 42s. Various match scenes.

1260 Bavaria 1849 1k. Stamp

1990. "Essen 90" International Stamp Fair.
3680 **1260** 42s. black and red . . . 70 40

1262 "100" and Rainbow

1990. Centenary of Co-operative Farming.
3682 **1262** 5s. multicoloured . . . 10 10

1263 "Elderly Couple at Rest"

1990. Birth Centenary of Dimitur Chorbadzhiiski-Chudomir (artist).
3683 **1263** 5s. multicoloured . . . 10 10

1264 Map

1990. Centenary of Labour Day.
3684 **1264** 10s. multicoloured . . . 15 10

1265 Emblem

1990. 125th Anniv of I.T.U.
3685 **1265** 20s. blue, red & black . . . 25 15

1266 Belgium 1849 10c. "Epaulettes" Stamp

1990. "Belgica 90" International Stamp Exhibition, Brussels.
3686 **1266** 30s. brown and green . . . 50 35

1267 Lamartine and his House

1990. Birth Bicentenary of Alphonse de Lamartine (poet).
3687 **1267** 20s. multicoloured . . . 25 15

1268 Brontosaurus

1990. Prehistoric Animals. Multicoloured.
3688 5s. Type **1268** 10 10
3689 8s. Stegosaurus 15 10
3690 13s. Edaphosaurus 20 10
3691 25s. Rhamphorhynchus . . 50 20
3692 32s. Protoceratops 65 30
3693 42s. Triceratops 90 40

1269 Swimming

1990. Olympic Games, Barcelona (1992) (1st issue). Multicoloured.
3694 5s. Type **1269** 10 10
3695 13s. Handball 20 10
3696 30s. Hurdling 50 25
3697 42s. Cycling 75 35
See also Nos. 3840/3.

1270 Southern Festoon

1990. Butterflies and Moths. Multicoloured.
3699 5s. Type **1270** 10 10
3700 10s. Jersey tiger moth . . . 15 10
3701 20s. Willow-herb hawk moth . 20 10
3702 30s. Striped hawk moth . . 50 20
3703 42s. "Thecla betulae" . . . 70 30
3704 60s. Cynthia's fritillary . . . 1·00 60

1271 Airbus Industrie A310 Jetliner

1990. Aircraft. Multicoloured.
3705 5s. Type **1271** 10 10
3706 10s. Tupolev Tu-204 . . . . 15 10
3707 25s. Concorde 40 20
3708 30s. Douglas DC-9 . . . . 45 25
3709 42s. Ilyushin Il-86 . . . . 60 35
3710 60s. Boeing 747-300/400 . . 90 55
No. 3705 is wrongly inscribed Airbus "A300".

1272 Iosif I **1274** Putting the Shot

1273 Road and U.N. Emblem within Triangles

1990. 150th Birth Anniv of Exarch Iosif I.
3711 **1272** 5s. mauve, black & grn 10 10

1990. International Road Safety Year.
3712 **1273** 5s. multicoloured . . . 10 10

1990. "Olymphilex '90" Olympic Stamps Exhibition, Varna. Multicoloured.
3713 5s. Type **1274** 10 10
3714 13s. Throwing the discus . . 20 10
3715 42s. Throwing the hammer 70 35
3716 60s. Throwing the javelin . . 95 55

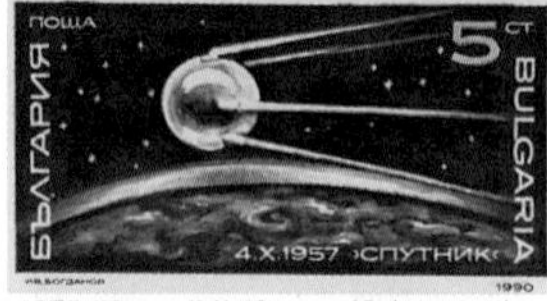

1275 "Sputnik" (first artificial satellite, 1957)

1990. Space Research. Multicoloured.
3717 5s. Type **1275** 10 10
3718 8s. "Vostok" and Yuri Gagarin (first manned flight, 1961) 10 10
3719 10s. Aleksei Leonov spacewalking from "Voskhod 2" (first spacewalk, 1965) 15 10
3720 20s. "Soyuz"–"Apollo" link, 1975 . . . . 30 15
3721 42s. Space shuttle "Columbia", 1981 . . . . 65 30
3722 60s. Space probe "Galileo" 90 45

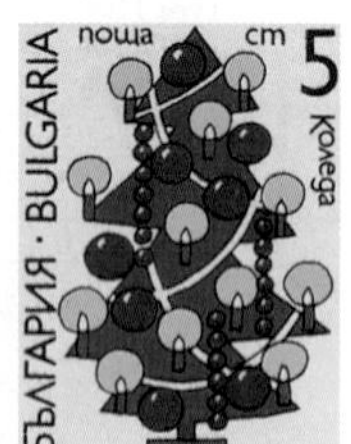

1276 St. Clement of Ohrid **1277** Tree

1990. 1150th Birth Anniv of St. Clement of Ohrid.
3724 **1276** 5s. brown, black & grn 10 10

1990. Christmas. Multicoloured.
3725 5s. Type **1277** 10 10
3726 20s. Father Christmas . . . 15 10

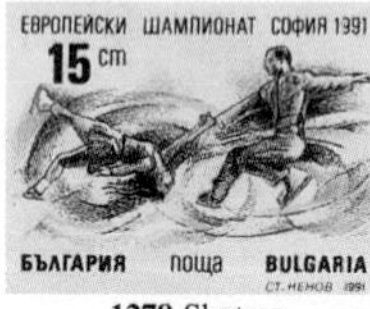

1278 Skaters

1991. European Figure Skating Championships, Sofia.
3727 **1278** 15s. multicoloured . . . 20 10

1279 Chicken **1281** "Good Day" (Paul Gauguin)

1280 Death Cap

1991. Farm Animals.
3728 – 20s. brown and black 10 10
3729 – 25s. blue and black . . 10 10
3730 **1279** 30s. brown and black 10 10
3731 – 40s. brown and black 15 10
3732 – 62s. green and black . . 25 10
3733 – 86s. red and black . . . 30 10
3734 – 95s. mauve and black 35 10
3735 – 1l. brown and black . . 40 15
3736 – 2l. green and black . . 60 25
3737 – 5l. violet and black . . 1·50 75
3738 – 10l. blue and black . . 1·75 75
DESIGNS: 20s. Sheep; 25s. Goose; 40s. Horse; 62, 95s. Billy goat; 86s. Sow; 1l. Donkey; 2l. Bull; 5l. Common turkey; 10l. Cow.

1991. Fungi. Multicoloured.
3746 5s. Type **1280** 10 10
3747 10s. "Amanita verna" . . . 25 10
3748 20s. Panther cap 60 15
3749 32s. Fly agaric 90 15
3750 42s. Beefsteak morel . . . . 1·25 35
3751 60s. Satan's mushroom . . 1·90 60

1991. Paintings. Multicoloured.
3752 20s. Type **1281** 10 10
3753 43s. "Madame Dobini" (Edgar Degas) 10 10
3754 62s. "Peasant Woman" (Camille Pissarro) 30 15
3755 67s. "Woman with Black hair" (Edouard Manet) 40 15
3756 80s. "Blue Vase" (Paul Cezanne) 50 20
3757 2l. "Madame Samari" (Pierre Auguste Renoir) 1·10 50

1282 Map

1991. 700th Anniv of Swiss Confederation.
3759 **1282** 62s. red and violet . . . 40 10

1283 Postman on Bicycle, Envelopes and Paper

1991. 100 Years of Philatelic Publications in Bulgaria.
3760 **1283** 30s. multicoloured . . . 10 10

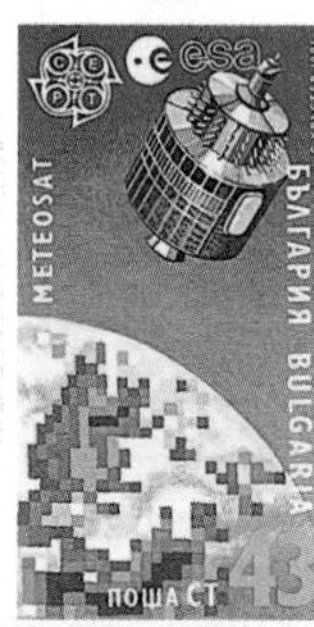

1284 "Meteosat" Weather Satellite

1991. Europa. Europe in Space. Multicoloured.
3761 43s. Type **1284** 10 10
3762 62s. "Ariane" rocket 40 10

1285 Przewalski's Horse

1991. Horses. Multicoloured.
3763 5s. Type **1285** 10 10
3764 10s. Tarpan 10 10
3765 25s. Black arab 15 10
3766 35s. White arab 20 15
3767 42s. Shetland pony 40 15
3768 60s. Draught horse 70 20

1286 "Expo '91"

1991. "Expo '91" Exhibition, Plovdiv.
3769 **1286** 30s. multicoloured . . . 10 10

1287 Mozart

1991. Death Bicentenary of Wolfgang Amadeus Mozart (composer).
3770 **1287** 62s. multicoloured . . . 40 10

1288 Astronaut and Rear of Space Shuttle "Columbia"

1991. Space Shuttles. Multicoloured.
3771 12s. Type **1288** 10 10
3772 32s. Satellite and "Challenger" 10 10
3773 50s. "Discovery" and satellite 30 10
3774 86s. Satellite and "Atlantis" (vert) 40 20
3775 1l.50 Launch of "Buran" (vert) 75 30
3776 2l. Satellite and "Atlantis" (vert) . . . . 1·10 40

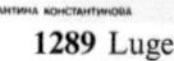

1289 Luge **1291** Japanese Chin

1290 Sheraton Hotel Balkan, Sofia

1991. Winter Olympic Games, Albertville (1992). Multicoloured.
3778 30s. Type **1289** 10 10
3779 43s. Skiing 20 10
3780 67s. Ski jumping 30 10
3781 2l. Biathlon 80 30

1991.
3783 **1290** 62s. multicoloured . . . 20 10

1991. Dogs. Multicoloured.
3784 30s. Type **1291** 10 10
3785 43s. Chihuahua 10 10
3786 62s. Miniature pinscher . . 20 10
3787 80s. Yorkshire terrier . . . 40 10
3788 1l. Mexican hairless 50 15
3789 3l. Pug . . . . 1·50 45

1292 Arms

1991. "Philatelia '91" Stamp Fair, Cologne.
3790 **1292** 86s. multicoloured . . . 50 10

1294 Japan 1871 48mon "Dragon" Stamp

1991. "Phila Nippon '91" International Stamp Exhibition, Tokyo.
3792 **1294** 62s. black, brown & bl 20 10

1295 Early Steam Locomotive and Tender

1991. 125th Anniv of the Railway in Bulgaria. Multicoloured.
3793 30s. Type **1295** 30 10
3794 30s. Early six-wheeled carriage 30 10

1296 Ball ascending to Basket **1297** "Christ carrying the Cross"

1991. Centenary of Basketball. Multicoloured.
3795 43s. Type **1296** 10 10
3796 62s. Ball level with basket mouth 10 10
3797 90s. Ball entering basket . . 40 10
3798 1l. Ball in basket 40 15

1991. 450th Birth Anniv of El Greco (painter). Multicoloured.
3799 43s. Type **1297** 10 10
3800 50s. "Holy Family with St. Anna" 10 10
3801 60s. "St. John of the Cross and St. John the Evangelist" 15 10
3802 62s. "St. Andrew and St. Francis" 15 10
3803 1l. "Holy Family with Magdalene" 35 15
3804 2l. "Cardinal Fernando Nino de Guevara" . . . 85 30

1298 Snowman, Moon, Candle, Bell and Heart

1991. Christmas. Multicoloured.
3806 30s. Type **1298** 10 10
3807 62s. Star, clover, angel, house and Christmas tree 10 10

1299 Small Pasque Flower

1991. Medicinal Plants. Multicoloured.

3808	30s.(+15s.) Pale pasque flower	10	10
3809	40s. Type **1299**	10	10
3810	55s. "Pulsatilla halleri"	15	10
3811	60s. "Aquilegia nigricans"	15	10
3812	1l. Sea buckthorn	35	15
3813	2l. Blackcurrant	85	30

No. 3808 includes a se-tenant premium-carrying label for 15s. inscribed "ACTION 2000. For Environment Protection".

1300 Greenland Seals

1991. Marine Mammals. Multicoloured.

3814	30s. Type **1300**	10	10
3815	43s. Killer whales	10	10
3816	62s. Walruses	15	10
3817	68s. Bottle-nosed dolphins	15	10
3818	1l. Mediterranean monk seals	35	15
3819	2l. Common porpoises	85	30

1301 Synagogue

1992. 500th Anniv of Jewish Settlement in Bulgaria.

3820	**1301** 1l. multicoloured	30	10

1302 Rossini, "The Barber of Seville" and Figaro

1992. Birth Bicentenary of Gioacchino Rossini (composer).

3821	**1302** 50s. multicoloured	10	10

1303 Plan of Fair

1992. Centenary of Plovdiv Fair.

3822	**1303** 1l. black and stone	20	10

1304 Volvo "740"

1992. Motor Cars. Multicoloured.

3823	30s. Type **1304**	10	10
3824	45s. Ford "Escort"	10	10
3825	50s. Fiat "Croma"	15	10
3826	50s. Mercedes Benz "600"	15	10
3827	1l. Peugeot "605"	35	15
3828	2l. B.M.W. "316"	85	30

1305 Amerigo Vespucci

1992. Explorers. Multicoloured.

3829	50s. Type **1305**	20	10
3830	50s. Francisco de Orellana	20	10
3831	1l. Ferdinand Magellan	40	10
3832	1l. Jimenez de Quesada	40	10
3833	2l. Sir Francis Drake	85	35
3834	3l. Pedro de Valdivia	1·25	50

1306 Granada

1992. "Granada '92" Int Stamp Exhibition.

3836	**1306** 62s. multicoloured	25	10

1307 "Santa Maria"

1992. Europa. 500th Anniv of Discovery of America by Columbus. Multicoloured.

3837	1l. Type **1307**	50	20
3838	2l. Christopher Columbus	1·00	40

Nos. 3837/8 were issued together, se-tenant, forming a composite design.

1308 House

1992. S.O.S. Children's Village.

3839	**1308** 1l. multicoloured	40	10

1309 Long Jumping

1992. Olympic Games, Barcelona (2nd issue). Multicoloured.

3840	50s. Type **1309**	15	10
3841	50s. Swimming	15	10
3842	1l. High jumping	40	15
3843	3l. Gymnastics	1·25	50

1310 1902 Laurin and Klement Motor Cycle

1992. Motor Cycles. Multicoloured.

3845	30s. Type **1310**	10	10
3846	50s. 1928 Puch "200 Luxus"	10	10
3847	50s. 1931 Norton "CS 1"	10	10
3848	70s. 1950 Harley Davidson	15	10
3849	1l. 1986 Gilera "SP 01"	35	15
3850	2l. 1990 BMW "K 1"	85	30

1311 Genoa

1992. "Genova '92" International Thematic Stamp Exhibition.

3851	**1311** 1l. multicoloured	40	10

1312 Grasshopper **1313** Silhouette of Head on Town Plan

1992. Insects. Multicoloured.

3852	1l. Four-spotted libellula	10	10
3853	2l. "Raphidia notata"	20	10
3854	3l. Type **1312**	40	10
3855	4l. Stag beetle	50	10
3856	5l. Fire bug	75	10
3857	7l. Ant	1·40	25
3858	20l. Wasp	3·00	1·25
3859	50l. Praying mantis	7·50	3·00

1992. 50th Anniv of Institute of Architecture and Building.

3862	**1313** 1l. red and black	35	10

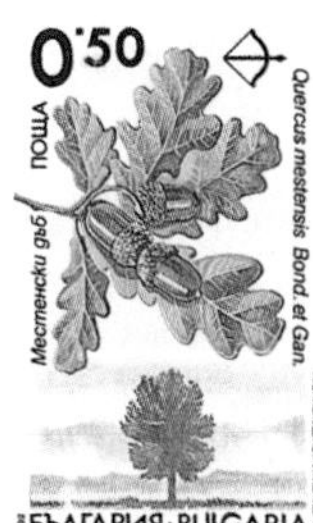

1314 Oak

1992. Trees. Multicoloured.

3863	50s. Type **1314**	10	10
3864	50s. Horse chestnut	10	10
3865	1l. Oak	40	10
3866	1l. Macedonian pine	40	10
3867	2l. Maple	80	20
3868	3l. Pear	1·25	35

1315 Embroidered Flower

1992. Centenary of Folk Museum, Sofia.

3869	**1315** 1l. multicoloured	35	10

1316 "Bulgaria" (freighter)

1992. Centenary of National Shipping Fleet. Multicoloured.

3870	30s. Type **1316**	10	10
3871	50s. "Kastor" (tanker)	20	10
3872	1l. "Geroite na Sebastopol" (train ferry)	65	25
3873	2l. "Aleko Konstantinov" (tanker)	65	25
3874	2l. "Bulgaria" (tanker)	85	40
3875	3l. "Varna" (container ship)	1·40	55

1317 Council Emblem

1992. Admission to Council of Europe.

3876	**1317** 7l. multicoloured	2·75	1·00

1319 "Santa Claus" (Ani Bacheva)

1992. Christmas. Children's Drawings. Mult.

3878	1l. Type **1319**	35	10
3879	7l. "Madonna and Child" (Georgi Petkov)	2·25	75

1320 Leopard **1322** Tengmalm's Owl

1321 Cricket

1992. Big Cats. Multicoloured.

3880	50s. Type **1320**	15	10
3881	50s. Cheetah	15	10
3882	1l. Jaguar	40	40
3883	2l. Puma	80	30
3884	2l. Tiger	80	30
3885	3l. Lion	1·25	45

1992. Sport. Multicoloured.

3886	50s. Type **1321**	10	10
3887	50s. Baseball	10	10
3888	1l. Pony and trap racing	40	10
3889	1l. Polo	40	10
3890	2l. Hockey	80	15
3891	3l. American football	1·25	40

1992. Owls. Multicoloured.

3892	30s. Type **1322**	15	10
3893	50s. Tawny owl (horiz)	15	10
3894	1l. Long-eared owl	40	20
3895	2l. Short-eared owl	80	35
3896	2l. Eurasian scops owl (horiz)	80	35
3897	3l. Barn owl	1·25	55

1323 "Khan Kubrat" (Dimitur Gyudzhenov)

1992. Historical Paintings. Multicoloured.

3898	50s. Type **1323**	15	10
3899	1l. "Khan Asparukh (Nikolai Pavlovich)	40	15
3900	2l. "Khan Terval at Tsarigrad" (Dimitur Panchev)	80	30
3901	3l. "Prince Boris" (Nikolai Pavlovich)	1·25	45

1324 Sculpted Head **1325** Shooting

1993. Centenary of National Archaeological Museum, Sofia.

3903	**1324** 1l. multicoloured	40	10

1993. "Borovets '93" Biathlon Championship. Multicoloured.

3904	1l. Type **1325**	40	15
3905	7l. Cross-country skiing	3·00	1·25

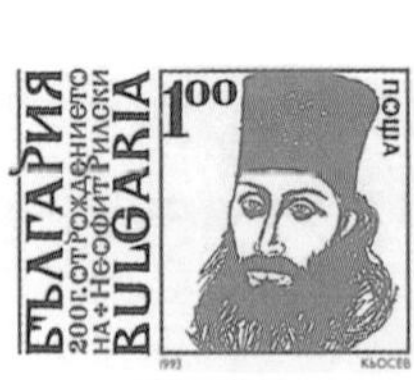
1326 Rilski

1327 "Morning" (sculpture, Georgi Chapkunov)

1993. Birth Bicentenary of Neofit Rilski (compiler of Bulgarian grammar and dictionary).
3906 **1326** 1l. bistre and red . . . 40 15

1993. Europa. Contemporary Art. Multicoloured.
3907 3l. Type **1327** 60 25
3908 8l. "Composition" (D. Buyukliiski) . . . . . 1·60 65

1328 Veil-tailed Goldfish

1993. Fishes. Multicoloured.
3909 1l. Type **1328** 15 10
3910 2l. Yucatan sail-finned molly 25 10
3911 3l. Two-striped lyretail . . . 50 15
3912 3l. Freshwater angelfish . . 50 15
3913 4l. Red discus 75 30
3914 8l. Pearl gourami . . . . . 1·50 55

1329 Apple

1330 Monteverdi

1993. Fruits. Multicoloured.
3915 1l. Type **1329** 15 10
3916 2l. Peach 25 10
3917 2l. Pear 25 10
3918 3l. Quince 50 15
3919 5l. Pomegranate 80 25
3920 7l. Fig . . . . 1·40 50

1993. 350th Death Anniv of Claudio Monteverdi (composer).
3921 **1330** 1l. green, yellow & red 20 10

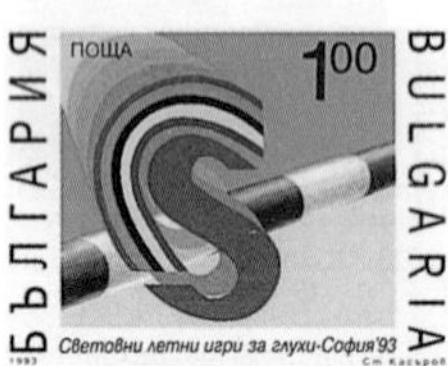
1331 High Jumping

1993. Int Games for the Deaf, Sofia. Mult.
3922 1l. Type **1331** 20 10
3923 2l. Swimming 40 10
3924 3l. Cycling 50 20
3925 4l. Tennis 70 25

1333 Prince Alexander

1334 Tchaikovsky

1993. Death Centenary of Prince Alexander I.
3928 **1333** 3l. multicoloured . . . 50 20

1993. Death Centenary of Pyotr Tchaikovsky (composer).
3929 **1334** 3l. multicoloured . . . 50 20

1335 Crossbow

1336 Newton

1993. Weapons. Multicoloured.
3930 1l. Type **1335** 15 10
3931 2l. 18th-century flintlock pistol 25 10
3932 3l. Revolver 50 15
3933 3l. Luger pistol 50 15
3934 5l. Mauser rifle 80 30
3935 7l. Kalashnikov assault rifle 1·40 55

1993. 350th Birth Anniv of Sir Isaac Newton (mathematician).
3936 **1336** 1l. multicoloured . . . 15 10

1337 "100" on Stamps and Globe

1993. Centenary of Bulgarian Philately.
3937 **1337** 1l. multicoloured . . . 25 10

1338 "Ecology" in Cyrillic Script

1993. Ecology. Multicoloured.
3938 1l. Type **1338** 15 10
3939 7l. "Ecology" in English . . 1·00 40

1339 Mallard

1993. Hunting. Multicoloured.
3940 1l. Type **1339** 20 10
3941 1l. Common pheasant . . . 20 10
3942 2l. Red fox 25 15
3943 3l. Roe deer 50 20
3944 6l. European brown hare . . 1·00 40
3945 8l. Wild boar . . . . . . 1·50 55

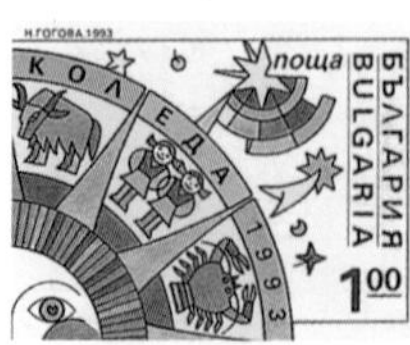
1340 "Taurus", "Gemini" and "Cancer"

1341 Sofia Costume

1993. Christmas. Signs of the Zodiac. Mult.
3946 1l. Type **1340** 15 10
3947 1l. "Leo", "Virgo" and "Libra" 15 10
3948 7l. "Aquarius", "Pisces" and "Aries" . . . . 1·00 40
3949 7l. "Scorpio", "Sagittarius" and "Capricorn" . . . . 1·00 40

Nos. 3946/7 and 3948/9 were each issued together, se-tenant; when placed together the four stamps form a composite design.

1993. Costumes. Multicoloured.
3950 1l. Type **1341** 15 10
3951 1l. Plovdiv 15 10
3952 2l. Belograd 25 15
3953 3l. Oryakhovo 35 20
3954 3l. Shumen 35 20
3955 8l. Kurdzhali . . . . . . 1·25 55

1342 Freestyle Skiing

1343 "Self-portrait" and "Tsar Simeon"

1994. Winter Olympic Games, Lillehammer, Norway. Multicoloured.
3956 1l. Type **1342** 15 10
3957 2l. Speed skating 25 10
3958 3l. Two-man luge 50 15
3959 4l. Ice hockey 75 30

1994. Death Centenary of Nikolai Pavlovich (artist).
3961 **1343** 3l. multicoloured . . . 20 10

1344 Plesiosaurus

1994. Prehistoric Animals. Multicoloured.
3962 2l. Type **1344** 35 10
3963 3l. Archaeopteryx 50 20
3964 3l. Iguanodon 50 15
3965 4l. Edmontonia 70 25
3966 5l. Styracosaurus 85 35
3967 7l. Tyrannosaurus . . . . . 1·00 40

1345 Players (Chile, 1962)

1994. World Cup Football Championship, U.S.A. Multicoloured.
3968 3l. Type **1345** 45 10
3969 6l. Players (England, 1966) 90 30
3970 7l. Goalkeeper making save (Mexico, 1970) . . . . . 1·00 40
3971 9l. Player kicking (West Germany, 1974) . . . . . 1·25 50

1346 Photoelectric Analysis (Georgi Nadzhakov)

1994. Europa. Discoveries. Multicoloured.
3973 3l. Type **1346** 40 10
3974 15l. Cardiogram and heart (Prof. Ivan Mitev) . . . . 2·00 75

1347 Khristov

1994. 80th Birth Anniv of Boris Khristov (actor).
3975 **1347** 3l. multicoloured . . . 25 10

1348 Sleeping Hamster

1349 Space Shuttle, Satellite and Dish Aerial

1994. The Common Hamster. Multicoloured.
3976 3l. Type **1348** 45 10
3977 7l. Hamster looking out of burrow . . . . 1·00 40
3978 10l. Hamster sitting up in grass . . . . 1·25 50
3979 15l. Hamster approaching berry . . . . 2·00 75

1994. North Atlantic Co-operation Council (North Atlantic Treaty Organization and Warsaw Pact members).
3980 **1349** 3l. multicoloured . . . 25 10

1350 Baron Pierre de Coubertin (founder of modern games)

1351 "Christ Pantocrator"

1994. Cent of International Olympic Committee.
3981 **1350** 3l. multicoloured . . . 50 20

1994. Icons. Multicoloured.
3982 2l. Type **1351** 30 10
3983 3l. "Raising of Lazarus" . . 45 10
3984 5l. "Passion of Christ" . . . 75 25
3985 7l. "Archangel Michael" . . 1·00 40
3986 8l. "Sts. Cyril and Methodius" . . . . . . 1·10 50
3987 15l. "Madonna Enthroned" 2·00 75

1352 Vechernik

1994. Christmas. Breads. Multicoloured.
3988 3l. Type **1352** 40 10
3989 15l. Bogovitsa . . . . . . 2·00 75

1353 "Golden Showers"

1994. Roses. Multicoloured.
3990 2l. Type **1353** 30 10
3991 3l. "Caen Peace Monument" 45 10
3992 5l. "Theresa of Lisieux" . . 75 25
3993 7l. "Zambra 93" . . . . . 1·00 40
3994 10l. "Gustave Courbet" . . 1·60 50
3995 15l. "Honore de Balzac . . 2·25 75

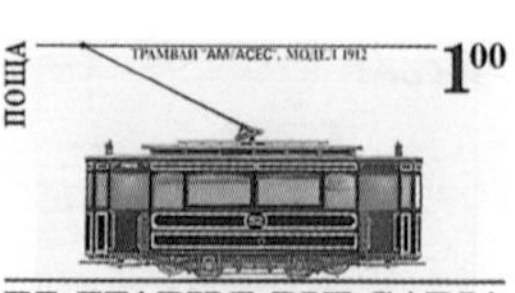
1355 "AM/ASES", 1912

1994. Trams. Multicoloured.
3997 1l. Type **1355** 15 10
3998 2l. "AM/ASES", 1928 . . . 35 15
3999 3l. "M.A.N./AEG", 1931 . . 50 20
4000 5l. "D.T.O.", 1942 . . . . 80 35
4001 8l. Republika, 1951 . . . . 1·75 65
4002 10l. Kosmonavt articulated tramcar set, 1961 . . . . 1·90 80

1356 Petleshkov and Flag

1995. 150th Birth Anniv of Vasil Petleshkov (leader of 1876 April uprising).
4003 **1356** 3l. multicoloured . . . 40 15

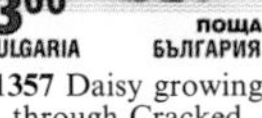
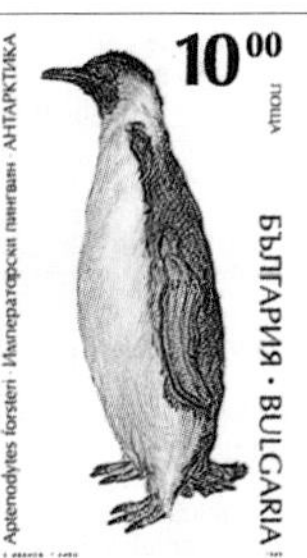

1357 Daisy growing through Cracked Helmet

1360 Emperor Penguin

1995. Europa. Peace and Freedom. Mult.
4004 3l. Type **1357** 40 15
4005 15l. Dove with olive branch on rifle barrel . . . . . . 1·90 75

1995. Antarctic Animals. Multicoloured.
4008 1l. Shrimp (horiz) 15 10
4009 2l. Ice fish (horiz) 30 10
4010 3l. Sperm whale (horiz) . . 45 20
4011 5l. Weddell's seal (horiz) . . 70 30
4012 8l. South polar skua (horiz) 1·10 45
4013 10l. Type **1360** . . . . . . 1·40 55

1361 Stambolov

1995. Death Cent of Stefan Stambolov (politician).
4014 **1361** 3l. multicoloured . . . 40 15

1362 Pole Vaulting

1995. Olympic Games, Atlanta (1996) (1st issue). Multicoloured.
4015 3l. Type **1362** 45 10
4016 7l. High jumping . . . . . 1·00 40
4017 10l. Long jumping . . . . . 1·40 55
4018 15l. Triple jumping . . . . 2·10 85
See also Nos. 4083/6.

1363 Pea

1365 "Ivan Nikolov-Zograf"

1364 "100"

1995. Food Plants. Multicoloured.
4019 2l. Type **1363** 30 10
4020 3l. Chickpea 40 15
4021 3l. Soya bean 40 15
4022 4l. Spinach 55 20
4023 5l. Peanut 70 30
4024 15l. Lentil . . . . 2·10 85

1995. Centenary of Organized Tourism.
4025 **1364** 1l. multicoloured . . . 40 15

1995. Birth Centenary of Vasil Zakhariev (painter).
4026 **1365** 2l. multicoloured . . . 30 10
4027 – 3l. multicoloured . . . 40 15
4028 – 5l. black, brown & grn 70 30
4029 – 10l. multicoloured . . . 1·40 55
DESIGNS: 3l. "Rila Monastery"; 5l. "Self-portrait"; 10l. "Raspberry Collectors".

1366 "Dove-Hands" holding Globe

1995. 50th Anniv of U.N.O.
4030 **1366** 3l. multicoloured . . . 40 15

1367 Polikarpov Po-2 Biplane

1995. Aircraft. Multicoloured.
4031 3l. Type **1367** 45 20
4032 5l. Lisunov Li-2 airliner . . 70 30
4033 7l. Junkers Ju 52 . . . . . 1·00 40
4034 10l. Focke Wulf Fw 58 . . 1·40 55

1368 Charlie Chaplin and Mickey Mouse

1995. Centenary of Motion Pictures. Mult.
4035 2l. Type **1368** 30 10
4036 3l. Marilyn Monroe and Marlene Dietrich 45 20
4037 5l. Nikolai Cherkasov and Humphrey Bogart 70 30
4038 8l. Sophia Loren and Liza Minelli . . . . 1·10 45
4039 10l. Gerard Philipe and Toshiro Mifune . . . . . 1·40 55
4040 15l. Katya Paskaleva and Nevena Kokanova . . . 2·10 85

1369 Agate

1995. Minerals. Multicoloured.
4041 1l. Type **1369** 15 10
4042 2l. Sphalerite 30 10
4043 5l. Calcite 70 30
4044 7l. Quartz . . . . 1·00 40
4045 8l. Pyromorphite . . . . . 1·10 45
4046 10l. Almandine . . . . . . 1·40 55

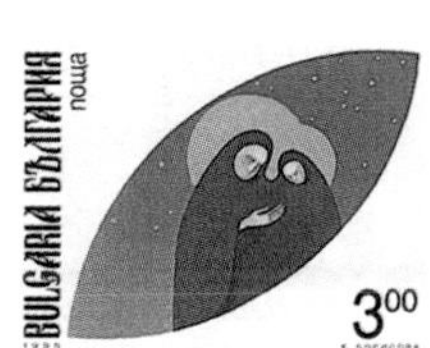

1370 Mary and Joseph

1995. Christmas. Multicoloured.
4047 3l. Type **1370** 40 15
4048 15l. Three wise men approaching stable . . . 1·90 75

1371 "Polynesian Woman with Fruit"

1996. Birth Centenary of Kiril Tsonev (painter).
4049 **1371** 3l. multicoloured . . . 30 10

1372 Luther (after Lucas Cranach the elder)

1996. 450th Death Anniv of Martin Luther (Protestant reformer).
4050 **1372** 3l. multicoloured . . . 30 10

1373 Preobrazhenie

1374 Bulgarian National Bank

1996. Monasteries.
4051 **1373** 3l. green 20 10
4052 – 5l. red 35 15
4053 – 10l. blue 70 30
4054 – 20l. orange . . . . . 1·40 55
4055 – 25l. brown . . . . . . 1·75 70
4056 – 40l. purple . . . . . . 2·75 1·10
DESIGNS: 5l. Arapov; 10l. Dryanovo; 20l. Bachkov; 25l. Troyan; 40l. Zograf.

1996. 5th Anniv of European Reconstruction and Development Bank.
4063 **1374** 7l. green, red and blue 45 20
4064 – 30l. blue, red & purple 1·90 75
DESIGN: 30l. Palace of Culture, Sofia.

1375 Yew

1996. Conifers. Multicoloured.
4065 5l. Type **1375** 35 15
4066 8l. Silver fir 60 25
4067 10l. Norway spruce 70 30
4068 20l. Scots pine . . . . . . 1·40 55
4069 25l. "Pinus heldreichii" . . 1·75 70
4070 40l. Juniper . . . . 3·00 1·25

1376 Battle Scene and Mourning Women

1377 Modern Officer's Parade Uniform

1996. 120th Anniversaries. Multicoloured.
4071 10l. Type **1376** (April uprising) 65 25
4072 40l. Khristo Botev and script (poet, death anniv) (horiz) . . . . 2·50 1·00

1996. Military Uniforms. Multicoloured.
4073 5l. Type **1377** 35 15
4074 8l. Second World War combat uniform 60 25
4075 10l. Balkan War uniform . . 70 30
4076 20l. Guard officer's ceremonial uniform . . . 1·40 55
4077 25l. Serbo-Bulgarian War officer's uniform . . . . 1·75 70
4078 40l. Russo-Turkish War soldier's uniform . . . . 3·00 1·75

1378 Monument

1996. 50th Anniv of the Republic.
4079 **1378** 10l. multicoloured . . . 70 30

1379 Elisaveta Bagryana (poet)

1996. Europa. Famous Women. Multicoloured.
4080 10l. Type **1379** 65 25
4081 40l. Katya Popova (opera singer) . . . . 2·50 1·00

1381 Nikola Stanchev (wrestling, Melbourne 1956)

1382 "The Letter" (detail)

1996. Olympic Games, Atlanta (2nd issue). Bulgarian Medal Winners. Multicoloured.
4083 5l. Type **1381** 20 10
4084 8l. Boris Georgiev (boxing, Helsinki 1952) 35 10
4085 10l. Ivanka Khristova (putting the shot, Montreal 1976) 40 15
4086 25l. Z. Iordanova and S. Otsetova (double sculls, Montreal 1976) . . . . . 1·00 40

1996. 250th Birth Anniv of Francisco Goya (painter). Multicoloured.
4088 5l. Detail of fresco 20 10
4089 8l. Type **1382** 35 10
4090 26l. "3rd of May 1808 in Madrid" (detail) . . . . 1·10 45
4091 40l. "Neighbours on a Balcony" (detail) . . . . 1·75 70

1383 Water Flea

1996. Aquatic Life. Multicoloured.
4093 5l. Type **1383** 20 10
4094 10l. Common water louse 45 15
4095 12l. European river crayfish 50 20
4096 25l. Prawn . . . . 1·10 45
4097 30l. "Cumella limicola" . . 1·25 50
4098 40l. Mediterranean shore crab . . . . 1·75 70

1385 Tryavna

1996. Houses.
4100 **1385** 10l. brown and stone 30 10
4101 – 15l. red and yellow . . 45 15
4102 – 30l. green and yellow 90 35
4103 – 50l. violet and mauve 1·50 60
4104 – 60l. green and lt green 1·75 70
4105 – 100l. ultramarine & bl 3·00 1·25
DESIGNS: 15l. Nesebur; 30l. Tryavna (different); 50l. Koprivshtitsa; 60l. Plovdiv; 100l. Koprivshtitsa (different).

1386 "Philadelphia", 1836

1996. Steam Locomotives. Multicoloured.
4106 5l. Type **1386** 15 10
4107 10l. "Jenny Lind", 1847 . . 30 10
4108 12l. "Liverpool", 1848 . . . 35 15
4109 26l. "Anglet", 1876 . . . . 80 30

1387 Anniversary Emblem and Academy

1996. Centenary of National Arts Academy.
4110 **1387** 15l. black and yellow 40 15

1388 Sword and Miniature from "Chronicle of Ivan Skilitsa"

1996. 1100th Anniv of Tsar Simeon's Victory over the Turks. Multicoloured.
4111 10l. Type **1388** 25 10
4112 40l. Dagger and right-hand detail of miniature . . . . 1·00 40
Nos. 4111/12 were issued together, se-tenant, forming a composite design.

1389 Fishes and Diver (Dilyana Lokmadzhieva)

1996. 50th Anniv of U.N.I.C.E.F. Children's Paintings. Multicoloured.
4113 7l. Type **1389** 20 10
4114 15l. Circus (Velislava Dimitrova) 40 15
4115 20l. Man and artist's pallet (Miglena Nikolova) . . . 55 20
4116 60l. Family meal (Darena Dencheva) . . . . 1·60 65

1390 Christmas Tree **1391** "Zograf Monastery"

1996. Christmas. Multicoloured.
4117 15l. Type **1390** 40 15
4118 60l. Star over basilica and Christmas tree . . . . . 1·50 60

1996. Birth Centenary of Tsanko Lavrenov (painter).
4119 **1391** 15l. multicoloured . . . 40 15

1392 Pointer

1997. Puppies. Multicoloured.
4120 5l. Type **1392** 15 10
4121 7l. Chow chow 20 10
4122 25l. Carakachan dog 70 30
4123 50l. Basset hound . . . . . 1·40 55

1393 Bell

1997. 150th Birth Anniv of Alexander Graham Bell (telephone pioneer).
4124 **1393** 30l. multicoloured . . . 50 20

1394 Man drinking **1395** Lady March (symbol of spring)

1997. Birth Centenary of Ivan Milev (painter). Murals from Kazaluk. Multicoloured.
4125 5l. Type **1394** 10 10
4126 15l. Woman praying 25 10
4127 30l. Reaper 45 20
4128 60l. Mother and child . . . 90 35

1997. Europa. Tales and Legends. Mult.
4129 120l. Type **1395** 25 10
4130 600l. St. George (national symbol) 85 35

1396 Kisimov in Character

1997. Birth Cent of Konstantin Kisimov (actor).
4131 **1396** 120l. multicoloured . . 20 10

1397 Von Stephan **1398** Old Town, Nesebur

1997. Death Centenary of Heinrich von Stephan (founder of U.P.U.).
4132 **1397** 60l. multicoloured . . . 10 10

1997. Historic Sights.
4133 **1398** 80l. brown and black 10 10
4134 – 200l. violet and black 15 10
4135 – 300l. yellow and black 20 10
4136 – 500l. green and black 25 10
4137 – 600l. yellow and black 35 15
4138 – 1000l. orange and black 55 20
DESIGNS: 200l. Sculpture, Ivanovski Church; 300l. Christ (detail of icon), Boyana Church; 500l. Horseman (stone relief), Madara; 600l. Figure of woman (carving from sarcophagus), Sveshary; 1000l. Tomb decoration, Kazanlak.

1399 Gaetano Donizetti

1997. Composers' Anniversaries. Multicoloured.
4139 120l. Type **1399** (birth bicentenary) 20 10
4140 120l. Franz Schubert (birth bicentenary) 20 10
4141 120l. Felix Mendelssohn-Bartholdy (150th death anniv) 20 10
4142 120l. Johannes Brahms (death centenary) 20 10

1400 "Trifolium rubens"

1997. Flowers in the Red Book. Multicoloured.
4143 80l. Type **1400** 15 10
4144 100l. "Tulipa hageri" . . . 25 10
4145 120l. "Inula spiraeifolia" . . 45 20
4146 200l. Thin-leafed peony . . . 60 25

1401 Anniversary Emblem **1402** Georgiev

1997. 50th Anniv of Civil Aviation.
4147 **1401** 120l. multicoloured . . 20 10

1997. Death Centenary of Evlogii Georgiev.
4148 **1402** 120l. multicoloured . . 20 10

1403 Show Jumping and Running

1997. World Modern Pentathlon Championship, Sofia. Multicoloured.
4149 60l. Type **1403** 10 10
4150 80l. Fencing and swimming 15 10
4151 100l. Running and fencing 25 10
4152 120l. Shooting and swimming 40 15
4153 200l. Show jumping and shooting 60 25

1405 D 2500 M Boat Engine

1997. Centenary of Diesel Engine. Multicoloured.
4155 80l. Type **1405** 10 10
4156 100l. D 2900 T tractor engine 15 10
4157 120l. D 3900 A truck engine 25 10
4158 200l. D 2500 K fork-lift truck engine 35 15

1406 Goddess with Mural Crown

1997. 43rd General Assembly of Atlantic Club, Sofia.
4159 **1406** 120l. mve, bl & ultram 25 10
4160 – 120l. grn, bl & ultram 25 10
4161 – 120l. brn, bl & ultram 25 10
4162 – 120l. vio, bl & ultram 25 10
DESIGNS: No. 4160, Eagle on globe; 4161, Venue; 4162, Venue (different).

1407 Cervantes and Don Quixote with Sancho

1997. 450th Birth Anniv of Miguel de Cervantes (writer).
4163 **1407** 120l. multicoloured . . 30 10

1408 Raztsvetnikov

1997. Birth Centenary of Asen Raztsvetnikov (writer and translator).
4164 **1408** 120l. multicoloured . . 30 10

1409 Fragment of Tombstone

1997. Millenary of Coronation of Tsar Samuel. Multicoloured.
4165 120l. Type **1409** 20 10
4166 600l. Tsar Samuel and knights in battle . . . . 1·10 45

1410 Star and Houses forming Christmas Tree

1997. Christmas. Multicoloured.
4167 120l. Type **1410** 15 10
4168 600l. Stable with Christmas tree roof . . . . 1·00 40

1411 Speed Skating

1997. Winter Olympic Games, Nagano, Japan (1998). Multicoloured.
4169 60l. Type **1411** 10 10
4170 80l. Skiing 15 10
4171 120l. Shooting (biathlon) . . 25 10
4172 600l. Ice skating . . . . . 1·25 50

1413 State Arms

1997.
4174 **1413** 120l. multicoloured . . 20 10

1414 Botev (after B. Petrov) **1415** Brecht

1998. 150th Birth and 120th Death (1996) Anniv of Khristo Botev (poet and revolutionary).
4175 **1414** 120l. multicoloured . . 20 10

1998. Birth Cent of Bertolt Brecht (playwright).
4176 **1415** 120l. multicoloured . . 20 10

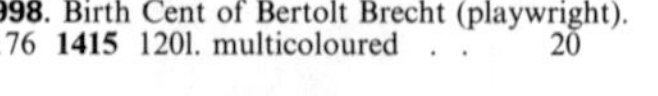

1416 Arrows

1998. Cent of Bulgarian Telegraph Agency.
4177 **1416** 120l. multicoloured . . 20 10

1417 Barn Swallow at Window

1998. 120th Birth Anniv of Aleksandur Bozhinov (children's illustrator). Multicoloured.
4178 120l. Type **1417** 25 10
4179 120l. Blackbird with backpack on branch . . . 25 10
4180 120l. Father Frost and children 25 10
4181 120l. Maiden Rositsa in field holding hands up to rain 25 10

1418 Tsar Alexander II

1419 Christ ascending and Hare pulling Cart of Eggs

1998. 120th Anniv of Liberation from Turkey. Multicoloured.
4182 120l. Type **1418** 15 10
4183 600l. Independence monument, Ruse . . . . 1·00 40

1998. Easter.
4184 **1419** 120l. multicoloured . . 20 10

1420 Torch Bearer

1998. 75th Anniv of Bulgarian Olympic Committee.
4185 **1420** 120l. multicoloured . . 20 10

1421 Map of Participating Countries

1998. Phare International Programme for Telecommunications and Post.
4186 **1421** 120l. multicoloured . . 20 10

1422 Girls in Folk Costumes

1998. Europa. National Festivals. Multicoloured.
4187 120l. Type **1422** 20 10
4188 600l. Boys wearing dance masks . . . . 1·00 40

(1423)

1424 "Dante and Virgil in Hell"

1998. Winning of Gold Medal in 15km Biathlon by Ekaterina Dafovska at Winter Olympic Games, Nagano. No. 4171 optd with T **1423**.
4189 120l. multicoloured 15 10

1998. Birth Bicentenary of Eugene Delacroix (artist).
4190 **1424** 120l. multicoloured . . 15 10

1425 Footballer and Club Badge

1426 European Tabby

1998. 50th Anniv of TsSKA Football Club.
4191 **1425** 120l. multicoloured . . 15 10

1998. Cats. Multicoloured.
4192 60l. Type **1426** 10 10
4193 80l. Siamese 15 10
4194 120l. Exotic shorthair . . 25 10
4195 600l. Birman . . . . 1·10 45

1427 "Oh, You are Jealous!"

1998. 150th Birth Anniv of Paul Gauguin (artist).
4196 **1427** 120l. multicoloured . . 15 10

1428 Khilendarski-Bozveli

1998. 150th Death Anniv of Neofit Khilendarski-Bozveli (priest and writer).
4197 **1428** 120l. multicoloured . . 15 10

1429 Tackling

1998. World Cup Football Championship, France. Multicoloured.
4198 60l. Type **1429** 10 10
4199 180l. Players competing for ball 15 10
4200 120l. Players and ball . . . 25 10
4201 600l. Goalkeeper . . . . . 1·10 40

1430 A. Aleksandrov

1998. 10th Anniv of Second Soviet–Bulgarian Space Flight.
4203 **1430** 120l. multicoloured . . 15 10

1431 Vasco da Gama

1998. "Expo '98" World's Fair, Lisbon. 500th Anniv of Vasco da Gama's Voyage to India. Multicoloured.
4204 600l. Type **1431** 80 30
4205 600l. "Sao Gabriel" (Vasco da Gama's ship) . . . . 1·00 40
Nos. 4204/5 were issued together, se-tenant, forming a composite design.

1432 Focke Wolf FW 61, 1937

1998. Helicopters. Multicoloured.
4206 80l. Type **1432** 10 10
4207 100l. Sikorsky R-4, 1943 . . 10 10
4208 120l. Mil Mi-V12, 1970 . . 15 10
4209 200l. McDonnell-Douglas MD-900, 1995 . . . . . 35 10

1434 Talev

1998. Birth Centenary of Dimitur Talev (writer).
4211 **1434** 180l. multicoloured . . 20 10

1435 Aleksandur Malinov (Prime Minister, 1931)

1436 "Limenitis redukta" and "Ligularia sibirica"

1998. 90th Anniv of Independence.
4212 **1435** 180l. black, blue & yell 25 10

1998. Butterflies and Flowers. Multicoloured.
4213 60l. Type **1436** 10 10
4214 180l. Painted lady and "Anthemis macrantha" 25 10
4215 200l. Red admiral and "Trachelium jacquinii" . . 25 10
4216 600l. "Anthocharis gruneri" and "Geranium tuberosum" 95 40

1437 Smirnenski

1998. Birth Cent of Khristo Smirnenski (writer).
4217 **1437** 180l. multicoloured . . 25 10

1438 Silhouette of Man

1998. 50th Anniv of Universal Declaration of Human Rights.
4218 **1438** 180l. multicoloured . . 25 10

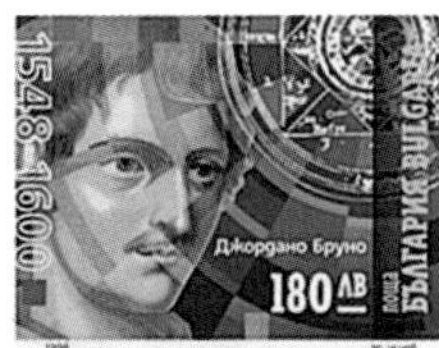

1439 Bruno

1998. 450th Birth Anniv of Giordano Bruno (scholar).
4219 **1439** 180l. multicoloured . . 25 10

1440 Man diving through Heart ("I Love You")

1998. Greetings Stamps. Multicoloured.
4220 180l. Type **1440** 25 10
4221 180l. Making wine (holiday) (vert) 25 10
4222 180l. Man in chalice (birthday) (vert) 25 10
4223 180l. Waiter serving wine (name day) (vert) 25 10

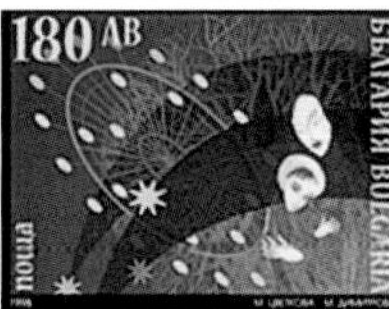

1441 Madonna and Child

1998. Christmas.
4224 **1441** 180l. multicoloured . . 25 10

1442 Geshov

1999. 150th Birth Anniv of Ivan Evstratiev Geshov (politician).
4225 **1442** 180l. multicoloured . . 25 10

1443 National Assembly Building, Sofia

1999. 120th Anniv of Third Bulgarian State. Mult.
4226 180l. Type **1443** 25 10
4227 180l. Council of Ministers 25 10
4228 180l. Statue of Justice (Supreme Court of Appeal) 25 10
4229 180l. Coins (National Bank) 25 10
4230 180l. Army 25 10
4231 180l. Lion emblem of Sofia and lamp post 25 10

1444 Georgi Karakashev (stage designer) and Set of "Kismet"

1999. Birth Centenaries. Multicoloured.
4232 180l. Type **1444** 25 10
4233 200l. Bencho Obreshkov (artist) and "Lodki" . . . 25 10
4234 300l. Score and Asen Naidenov (conductor of Sofia Opera) 35 15
4235 600l. Pancho Vladigerov (composer) and score of "Vardar" 75 30

1446 Sun and Emblem

1999. 50th Anniv of North Atlantic Treaty Organization.
4237 **1446** 180l. multicoloured . . 25 10

1447 Decorated Eggs

1999. Easter.
4238 **1447** 180l. multicoloured . . 25 10

1448 Red-crested Pochard and Ropotamo Reserve

1999. Europa. Parks and Gardens. Multicoloured.
4239 180l. Type **1448** 25 10
4240 600l. Central Balkan National Park 75 30

1449 Albrecht Durer (self-portrait) and Nuremberg

1999. "iBRA '99" International Stamp Exhibition, Nuremberg, Germany.
4241 **1449** 600l. multicoloured . . 75 30

1450 Anniversary Emblem

1999. 50th Anniv of Council of Europe.
4242 **1450** 180l. multicoloured . . 25 10

1451 Honore de Balzac (novelist)

1999. Birth Anniversaries. Multicoloured.
4243 180l. Type **1451** (bicentenary) 25 10
4244 200l. Johann Wolfgang von Goethe (poet and playwright) (250th anniv) 25 10
4245 300l. Aleksandr Pushkin (poet) (bicentenary) . . . 35 15
4246 600l. Diego de Silva Velazquez (painter) (400th anniv) 75 30

1452 Penny Farthing

1999. Bicycles. Multicoloured.
4247 180l. Type **1452** 25 10
4248 200l. Road racing bicycles 25 10
4249 300l. Track racing bicycles 35 15
4250 600l. Mountain bike 75 30

1454 Sopot Monastery Fountain

1456 Cracked Green Russula

1999. Fountains.
4252 **1454** 1st. light brown 10 10
4254 – 8st. green and black . . 10 10
4255 – 10st. deep brown . . . 10 10
4257 – 18st. light blue 10 10
4258 – 20st. bright blue . . . 10 10
4260 – 60st. brown and black 85 60
DESIGNS: 8st. Peacock Fountain, Karlovo; 10st. Peev Fountain, Kopivshtitsa; 18st. Sandanski Fountain; 20st. Eagle Owl Fountain, Karlovo; 60st. Fountain, Sokolski Monastery.

1999. Fungi. Multicoloured.
4266 10st. Type **1456** 10 10
4267 18st. Field mushroom . . . 25 20
4268 20st. "Hygrophorus russula" 30 20
4269 60st. Wood blewit 85 60

1458 Four-leaved Clover

1460 Lesser Grey Shrike

1999. Centenary of Organized Peasant Movement.
4271 **1458** 18st. multicoloured . . 25 20

1999. Song Birds and their Eggs. Multicoloured.
4273 8st. Type **1460** 10 10
4274 18st. Mistle thrush 25 20
4275 20st. Dunnock 30 20
4276 60st. Ortolan bunting . . . 85 60

1461 Greek Tortoise

1999. Reptiles. Multicoloured.
4277 10st. Type **1461** 10 10
4278 18st. Swamp turtle 30 20
4279 30st. Hermann's tortoise . . 35 25
4280 60st. Caspian turtle 85 60

1462 Boxing (16 medals)

1999. Bulgarian Olympic Medal Winning Sports. Multicoloured.
4281 10st. Type **1462** 10 10
4282 20st. High jumping (17 medals) 30 20
4283 30st. Weightlifting (31 medals) 35 25
4284 60st. Wrestling (60 medals) 85 60

1463 Police Light and Emblem

1999. 10th European Police Conference.
4285 **1463** 18st. multicoloured . . 20 10

1464 Jug

1465 Virgin and Child

1999. Gold Artefacts from Panagyurishte.
4286 **1464** 2st. brown and green 10 10
4287 – 3st. brown and green 10 10
4288 – 5st. brown and blue . . 10 10
4289 – 30st. brown and violet 20 10
4290 – 1l. brown and red . . . 90 35
DESIGNS: 3st. Human figures around top of drinking horn; 5st. Bottom of chamois-shaped drinking horn; 30st. Decorated handle and spout; 1l. Head-shaped jug.

1999. Christmas. Religious Icons. Multicoloured.
4291 18st. Type **1465** 15 10
4292 60st. Jesus Christ 85 30

1466 Scout beside Fire

1999. Scouts. Multicoloured.
4293 10st. Type **1466** 10 10
4294 18st. Scout helping child . . 15 10
4295 30st. Scout saluting 30 10
4296 60st. Girl and boy scouts . . 85 30

1467 Emblem

1999. "Expo 2005" World's Fair, Aichi, Japan.
4297 **1467** 18st. multicoloured . . 20 10

1468 Emblem and Flag

2000. Bulgarian Membership of European Union.
4298 **1468** 18st. multicoloured . . 10 10

1470 Peter Beron and Scientific Instruments

2000. Birth Anniversaries. Multicoloured.
4300 10st. Type **1470** (scientist, bicentenary) 10 10
4301 20st. Zakhari Stoyanov (writer, 150th anniv) . . . 15 10
4302 50st. Kolyo Ficheto (architect, bicentenary) . . 30 10

1471 Madonna and Child with Circuit Board

2000. Europa. Multicoloured.
4303 18st. Type **1471** 10 10
4304 60st. Madonna and Child (Leonardo da Vinci) with circuit board 40 10

1472 Judo

2000. Olympic Games, Sydney. Multicoloured.
4305 10st. Type **1472** 10 10
4306 18st. Tennis 10 10
4307 20st. Pistol shooting 15 10
4308 60st. Long jump 40 10

1473 *Puss in Boots* (Charles Perrault)

2000. Children's Fairytales. Multicoloured.
4309 18st. Type **1473** 10 10
4310 18st. *Little Red Riding Hood* (Brothers Grimm) 10 10
4311 18st. *Thumbelina* (Hans Christian Andersen) . . . 10 10

1474 "Friends" (detail) (Assen Vasiliev)

2000. Artists Birth Centenaries. Art. Multicoloured.
4312 18st. Type **1474** 10 10
4313 18st. "All Soul's Day" (detail) (Pencho Georgiev) 10 10
4314 18st. "Veliko Tunovo" (detail) (Ivan Khristov) 10 10
4315 18st. "At the Fountain" (sculpture) (detail) (Ivan Funev) 10 10

1475 Roman Mosaic (detail), Stara Zagora

2000. "EXPO 2000" World's Fair, Hanover, Germany.
4316 **1475** 60st. multicoloured . . 40 10

1476 Johannes Gutenberg (inventor of printing) and Printed Characters

2000. Anniversaries. Multicoloured.
4317 10st. Type **1476** (600th birth anniv) 10 10
4318 18st. Johann Sebastian Bach (composer, 250th death anniv) 10 10
4319 20st. Guy de Maupassant (writer, 150th birth anniv) 15 10
4320 60st. Antoine de Saint-Exupery (writer and aviator, birth centenary) 40 10

1477 *La Jeune* (Lebardy-Juillot airship) and Eiffel Tower, 1903

1480 St. Atanasii Church, Startsevo

1478 Vazov and Text

2000. Centenary of First Zeppelin Flight. Airship Development. Multicoloured.
4321 10st. Type **1477** 10 10
4322 18st. LZ-13 *Hansa* (Zeppelin airship) over Cologne . . 10 10
4323 20st. N-1 *Norge* over Rome 15 10
4324 60st. *Graf Zeppelin* over Sofia 40 10

2000. 150th Birth Anniv of Ivan Vazov (writer).
4325 **1478** 18st. multicoloured . . 10 10

2000. Churches.
4327 **1480** 22st. black and blue . . 15 10
4328 – 24st. black and mauve 15 10
4329 – 50st. black and yellow 30 10
4330 – 65st. black and green 40 10
4331 – 3l. black and orange 2·00 40
4332 – 5l. black and rose . . 3·00 80

DESIGNS: 24st. St. Clement of Orhid, Sofia; 50st. Mary of the Ascension, Sofia; 65st. St. Nedelya, Nedelino; 3l. Mary of the Ascension, Sofia (different), Sofia; 5l. Mary of the Ascension, Pamporovo.

1481 Ibex (*Capra ibex*)

2000. Animals. Multicoloured.

4333		10st. Type **1481**	10	10
4334		22st. Argali (*Ovis ammon*)	15	10
4335		30st. European bison (*Bison bonasus*)	20	10
4336		65st. Yak (*Bos grunniens*)	40	10

1482 Field Gladiolus (*Gladiolus segetum*) 1484 Order of Gallantry, 1880

1483 Crowd and Emblem

2000. Spring Flowers. Multicoloured.

4337		10st. Type **1482**	10	10
4338		22st. Liverwort (*Hepatica nobilis*)	15	10
4339		30st. Pheasant's eye (*Adonis vernalis*)	20	10
4340		65st. Peacock anemone (*Anemone pavonina*)	40	10

2000. 50th Anniv of European Convention on Human Rights.

4341	**1483**	65st. multicoloured	40	10

2000. Medals. Multicoloured.

4342		12st. Type **1484**	10	10
4343		22st. Order of St. Aleksandu, 1882	15	10
4344		30st. Order of Merit, 1891	20	10
4345		65st. Order of Cyril and Methodius, 1909	40	10

1485 Prince Boris-Mihail

2000. Bimillenary of Christianity. Multicoloured.

4346		22st. Type **1485**	15	10
4347		22st. St. Sofroni Vrachanski	15	10
4348		65st. Mary and Child (detail)	40	10
4349		65st. Antim I	40	10

1486 Seal

2000. 120th Anniv of Supreme Audit Office.

4350	**1486**	22st. multicoloured	15	10

1487 Microchip, Planets and "The Proportions of Man" (Leonardo DaVinci)

2001. New Millennium.

4351	**1487**	22st. multicoloured	15	10

1488 Tram

2001. Centenary of the Electrification of Bulgarian Transport. Multicoloured.

4352		22st. Type **1488**	15	10
4353		65st. Train carriages	45	10

1489 Muscat Grapes and Evsinograd Palace

2001. Viticulture. Multicoloured.

4354		12st. Type **1489**	10	10
4355		22st. Gumza grapes and Baba Vida Fortress	15	10
4356		30st. Shiroka Melnishka Loza grapes and Melnik Winery	20	10
4357		65st. Mavrud grapes and Asenova Krepost Fortress	45	10

1490 "@" and Microcircuits

2001. Information Technology. Sheet 82 x 95 mm containing T **1490** and similar horiz design. Multicoloured.

MS4358		Type **1490**; 65st. John Atanasoff (computer pioneer) and ABC	45	45

1491 Southern Europe and Emblem

2001. 10th Anniv of the Atlantic Club of Bulgaria. Sheet 87 × 87 mm.

MS4359		multicoloured	45	45

1492 Eagle and Lakes, Rila

2001. Europa. Water Resources. Multicoloured.

4360		22st. Type **1492**	15	10
4361		65st. Cave and waterfall, Rhodope	45	10

1493 Building, Bridge and Kableschkov

2001. 125th Anniv of the April Uprising and 150th Birth Anniv of Todor Kableschkov (revolutionary leader).

4362	**1493**	22st. multicoloured	15	10

1494 Juvenile Egyptian Vulture in Flight

2001. Endangered Species. Egyptian Vulture (*Neophron percnopterus*). Multicoloured.

4363		12st. Type **1494**	10	10
4364		22st. Juvenile landing	15	10
4365		30st. Adult and chick	20	10
4366		65st. Adult and eggs	45	10

1495 Georgi (Gundy) Asparuchov (footballer)

2001. Sportsmen. Multicoloured.

4367		22st. Type **1495**	15	10
4368		30st. Dancho (Dan) Kolev (wrestler)	20	10
4369		65st. Gen. Krum Lekarski (equestrian)	45	10

1496 Rainbow and People

2001. 50th Anniv United Nations High Commissioner for Refugees.

4370	**1496**	65st. multicoloured	45	10

1497 Alexander Zhendov

2001. Artists Birth Centenaries. Multicoloured.

4371		22st. Type **1497**	15	10
4372		65st. Ilya Beshkov	45	10

EXPRESS STAMPS

E 137 Express Delivery Van

1939.

E429	–	5l. blue	50	25
E430	E 137	6l. brown	30	25
E431	–	7l. brown	40	30
E432	E 137	8l. red	65	30
E433	–	20l. red	1·25	65

DESIGNS—VERT: 5l., 20l. Bicycle messenger; 7l. Motor-cyclist and sidecar.

OFFICIAL STAMPS

O 158 O 177

1942.

O507	O 158	10s. green	10	10
O508		30s. orange	10	10
O509		50s. brown	10	10
O510	–	1l. blue	10	10
O511	–	2l. green	10	10
O534		2l. red	20	10
O512	–	3l. mauve	10	10
O513	–	4l. pink	10	10
O514	–	5l. red	10	10

The 1l. to 5l. are larger (19 × 23 mm).

1945. Arms designs. Imperf or perf.

O580	–	1l. mauve	10	10
O581	O 177	2l. green	10	10
O582	–	3l. brown	10	10
O583	–	4l. blue	10	10
O584	–	5l. red	10	10

PARCEL POST STAMPS

P 153 Weighing Machine P 154 Loading Motor Lorry

1941.

P494	P 153	1l. green	10	10
P495	A	2l. red	30	10
P496	P 154	3l. brown	10	10
P497	B	4l. orange	10	10
P498	P 153	5l. blue	10	10
P506		5l. green	10	10
P499	B	6l. purple	10	10
P507		6l. brown	10	10
P500	P 153	7l. blue	10	10
P508		7l. sepia	10	10
P501	P 154	8l. turquoise	10	10
P509		8l. green	10	10
P502	A	9l. olive	50	15
P503	B	10l. orange	15	10
P504	P 154	20l. violet	35	10
P505	A	30l. black	1·60	15

DESIGNS—HORIZ: A, Loading mall coach; B, Motor-cycle combination.

P 163

1944. Imperf.

P532	P 163	1l. red	10	10
P533		3l. green	10	10
P534		5l. green	10	10
P535		7l. mauve	10	10
P536		10l. blue	10	10
P537		20l. brown	10	10
P538		30l. purple	10	10
P539		50l. orange	35	10
P540		100l. blue	60	25

POSTAGE DUE STAMPS

D 7 D 12 D 16

1884. Perf.

D75	D 7	5s. orange	17·00	2·50
D54		25s. lake	7·50	2·50
D55		50s. blue	3·50	2·50

1886. Imperf.

D50	D 7	5s. orange	£150	8·50
D51		25s. lake	£250	7·50
D52a		50s. blue	8·00	6·50

1893. Surch with bar and **30**.

D78d	D 7	30s. on 50s. blue (perf)	13·50	5·00
D79		30s. on 50s. blue (imperf)	10·00	4·00

1896. Perf.

D83	D 12	5s. orange	6·75	1·25
D84		10s. violet	4·25	1·60
D85		30s. green	3·15	1·00

1901.

D124	D 16	5s. red	35	20
D125		10s. green	70	25
D126		20s. blue	5·00	25
D127		30s. red	50	30
D128		50s. orange	7·50	4·50

D 37

D 110

1915.

D200 D 37 5s. green 15 10
D240 10s. violet 10 10
D202 20s. red 15 10
D241 20s. orange 10 10
D203a 30s. red 15 10
D242 50s. blue 10 10
D243 1l. green 10 10
D244 2l. red 10 10
D245 3l. brown 20 10

1932.

D326 D 110 1l. bistre 50 40
D327 2l. red 50 40
D328 6l. purple . . . . . 1·50 60

D 111

D 112

D 293

1933.

D333 D 111 20s. sepia 10 10
D334 40s. blue 10 10
D335 80s. red 10 10
D336 D 112 1l. brown 40 40
D337 2l. olive 50 50
D338 6l. violet 30 30
D339 14l. blue 40 40

1947. As Type D **112**, but larger (18 × 24 mm).
D646 1l. brown 10 10
D647 2l. red 10 10
D648 8l. orange 15 10
D649 20l. blue 35 15

1951.

D849 D 293 1l. brown 10 10
D850 2l. purple 10 10
D851 8l. orange 40 30
D852 20l. blue . . . . . . 1·10 90

BULGARIAN OCCUPATION OF RUMANIA Pt. 3

(DOBRUJA DISTRICT)

100 stotinki = 1 leva.

(1)

1916. Bulgarian stamps of 1911 optd with T **1**.
1 23 1s. grey 10 10
2 – 5s. brown and green . . . . 1·50 1·25
3 – 10s. sepia and brown 15 10
4 – 25s. black and blue 15 10

BUNDI Pt. 1

A state of Rajasthan, India. Now uses Indian stamps.

12 pies = 1 anna; 16 annas = 1 rupee.

3 Native Dagger

11 Raja protecting Sacred Cows

1894. Imperf.
12 3 ¼a. grey . . . . 3·50 3·50
13 1a. red . . . . 2·50 2·50
14 2a. green . . . . 7·50 11·00
8 4a. green . . . . 48·00 70·00
15 8a. red . . . . 9·00 12·00
16a 1r. yellow on blue . . . . . 12·00 20·00

1898. As T **3**, but with dagger point to left.
17a 3 4a. green . . . . 11·00 16·00

1914. Roul or perf.
26 11 ¼a. blue . . . . 1·90 4·25
38 ½a. black . . . . 1·50 4·50
28 1a. red . . . . 3·25 10·00
20a 2a. green . . . . 3·25 9·00
30 2½a. yellow . . . . 5·50 22·00
31 3a. brown . . . . 5·50 32·00
32 4a. green . . . . 3·50 35·00
33 6a. blue . . . . 12·00 80·00
42 8a. orange . . . . 9·00 55·00
43 10a. olive . . . . 16·00 80·00
44 12a. green . . . . 11·00 85·00
25 1r. lilac . . . . 22·00 90·00
46 2r. brown and black . . . 65·00 £225
47 3r. blue and brown . . . . 95·00 £275
48 4r. green and red £200 £350
49 5r. red and green £225 £375

20

21 Maharao Rajah Bahadur Singh

1941. Perf.
79 20 3p. blue . . . . 2·00 3·25
80 6p. blue . . . . 3·50 5·50
81 1a. red . . . . 4·00 7·00
82 2a. brown . . . . 6·00 15·00
83 4a. green . . . . 12·00 42·00
84 8a. green . . . . 14·00 £150
85 1r. blue . . . . 35·00 £225

1947.

86 21 ¼a. green . . . . 1·75 30·00
87 ½a. violet . . . . 1·75 28·00
88 1a. green . . . . 1·75 27·00
89 – 2a. red . . . . 1·75 55·00
90 – 4a. orange . . . . 1·75 80·00
91 – 8a. blue . . . . 2·00
92 – 1r. brown . . . . 15·00
DESIGNS: 2, 4a. Rajah in Indian dress; 8a., 1r. View of Bundi.

OFFICIAL STAMPS

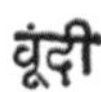

सरविस
(O 1)

1915. Optd as Type O **1**.
O 6A ¼a. blue . . . . 1·60
O16A ½a. black . . . . 7·50
O 8A 1a. red . . . . 4·00
O18A 2a. green . . . . 5·00
O 2A 2½a. yellow . . . . 2·75
O 3A 3a. brown . . . . 3·00
O19A 4a. green . . . . 9·00
O11A 6a. blue . . . . 13·00
O20A 8a. orange . . . . 15·00
O21A 10a. olive . . . . 48·00
O22A 12a. green . . . . 40·00
O 5A 1r. lilac . . . . 45·00
O24A 2r. brown and black . . . £375
O25A 3r. blue and brown £350
O26A 4r green and red £300
O27A 5r. red and green £325

1915. Optd **BUNDI SERVICE**.
O 6 B 11 ¼a. blue . . . . 1·75
O16 B ½a. black . . . . 3·00
O 8bB 1a. red . . . . 12·00
O18 B 2a. green . . . . 15·00
O 2 B 2½a. yellow . . . . . . 15·00
O 3 B 3a. brown . . . . 21·00
O19 B 4a. green . . . . 65·00
O11 B 6a. blue £200
O20 B 8a. orange . . . . 25·00
O21 B 10a. olive . . . . 75·00
O22 B 12a. green . . . . 90·00
O 5 B 1r. lilac . . . . 42·00
O24 B 2r. brown and black . . £180
O25 B 3r. blue and brown . . . £200
O26 B 4r. green and red . . . £300
O27 B 5r. red and green . . . £325
Prices for Nos. O2/27 are for unused examples. Used examples are generally worth a small premium over the prices quoted.

1941. Optd **SERVICE**.
O53 20 3p. blue . . . . 5·50 11·00
O54 6p. blue . . . . 13·00 11·00
O55 1a. red . . . . 13·00 8·00
O56 2a. brown . . . . 11·00 9·00
O57 4a. green . . . . 32·00 80·00
O58 20 8a. green £130 £400
O59 1r. blue £150 £425

For later issues see **RAJASTHAN**.

BURKINA FASO Pt. 12

A country in W. Africa, formerly known as Upper Volta. The name was changed in August 1984.

100 centimes = 1 franc.

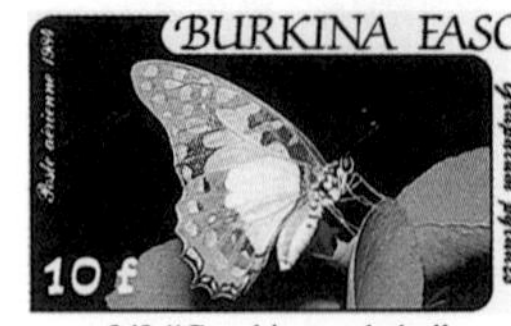

249 "Graphium pylades"

1984. Air. Butterflies. Multicoloured.
738 10f. Type **249** 10 10
739 120f. "Hyploimnas misippus" 65 40
740 400f. "Danaus chrysippus" 2·10 1·50
741 450f. "Papilio demodocus" 2·40 1·60

250 Soldier with Gun

253 Footballers and Statue

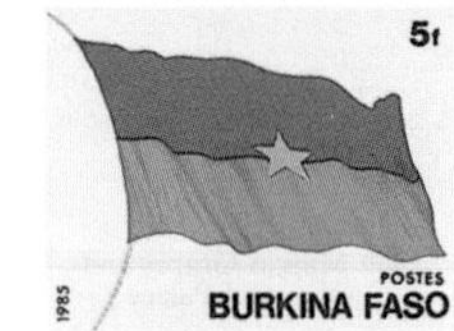

252 National Flag

1984. 1st Anniv of Captain Thomas Sankara's Presidency. Multicoloured.
742 90f. Type **250** 40 25
743 120f. Capt. Sankara and crowd 50 35

1984. Aid for the Sahel. No. 682 of Upper Volta optd **BURKINA FASO Aide au Sahel 84**.
743a 100f. multicoloured 20 15

1985. Nos. 716/21 of Upper Volta optd **BURKINA FASO**.
744 25f. Type **246** (postage) . . . 15 10
745 185f. "Pterocarpus lucens" 80 65
746 200f. "Phlebopus colossus sudanicus" . . . . 1·50 85
747 250f. "Cosmos sulphureus" 1·10 90
748 300f. "Trametes versicolor" (air) . . . . 1·75 1·25
749 400f. "Ganoderma lucidum" 2·25 1·75

1985. National Symbols. Multicoloured.
750 5f. Type **252** (postage) . . . 10 10
751 15f. National arms (vert) . . 10 10
752 90f. Maps of Africa and Burkina Faso 40 25
753 120f. Type **252** (air) 50 35
754 150f. As No. 751 . . . . . . 65 50
755 185f. As No. 752 . . . . . . 80 65

1985. World Cup Football Championship, Mexico.
756 253 25f. mult. (postage) . . . 15 10
757 – 45f. multicoloured 20 15
758 – 90f. multicoloured 40 25
759 – 100f. multicoloured (air) 45 30
760 – 150f. multicoloured . . . 65 50
761 – 200f. mult (horiz) 90 75
762 – 250f. mult (horiz) . . . . 1·10 90
DESIGNS: 45f. to 250f. Mexican statues and various footballing scenes.

254 Children playing and Boy

1985. Air "Philexafrique" International Stamp Exhibition, Lome, Togo (1st issue). Multicoloured.
764 200f. Type **254** 90 75
765 200f. Solar panels, transmission mast, windmill, dish aerial and tree 90 75
See also Nos. 839/40.

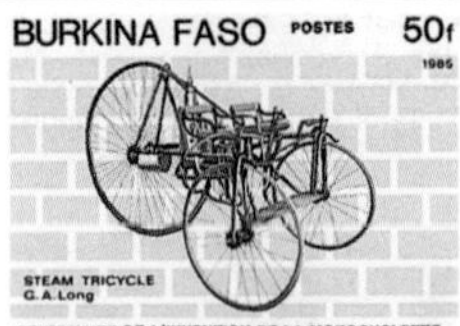

255 G. A. Long's Steam Tricycle

1985. Centenary of Motor Cycle. Multicoloured.
766 50f. Type **255** (postage) . . . 20 15
767 75f. Pope 30 20
768 80f. Manet 35 25
769 100f. Ducati (air) 45 30
770 150f. Jawa 65 50
771 200f. Honda 90 75
772 250f. B.M.W. . . . . 1·10 90

256 "Chamaeleon dilepis"

1985. Reptiles and Amphibians. Multicoloured.
773 5f. Type **256** (postage) . . . 10 10
774 15f. "Agama stellio" 10 10
775 33f. "Lacerta lepida" (horiz) 15 10
776 85f. "Hiperolius marmoratus" (horiz) 35 25
777 100f. "Echis leucogaster" (horiz) (air) 45 30
778 150f. "Kinixys erosa" (horiz) 65 50
779 250f. "Python regius" (horiz) 1·10 90

257 Benz "Victoria", 1893

1985. Motor Cars and Aircraft. Multicoloured.
780 5f. Type **257** (postage) . . . 10 10
781 25f. Peugeot "174", 1927 . . 15 10
782 45f. Bleriot XI airplane . . . 40 15
783 50f. Breguet 14T biplane . . . 40 15
784 500f. Bugatti "Napoleon T41 Royale" (air) . . . . . . 2·75 2·25
785 500f. Airbus Industrie A300 2·75 2·25
786 600f. Mercedes-Benz "540 K", 1938 . . . . 3·00 2·50
787 600f. Airbus Industrie A300 3·00 2·50

258 Wood Duck

1985. Birth Bicentenary of John J. Audubon (ornithologist). Multicoloured.
789 60f. Type **258** (postage) . . . 40 25
790 100f. Northern mockingbird 80 40
791 300f. Northern oriole . . . . 2·25 75
792 400f. White-breasted nuthatch 2·50 1·75
793 500f. Common flicker (air) 3·50 2·40
794 600f. Rough-legged buzzard 3·75 2·75

259 Young Lady Elizabeth Bowes-Lyon on Pony

1985. 85th Birthday of Queen Elizabeth the Queen Mother. Multicoloured.
796 75f. Type **259** (postage) . . . 30 20
797 85f. Marriage of Lady Elizabeth Bowes-Lyon and Albert, Duke of York . . 35 25

798 500f. Duke and Duchess of York with Princess Elizabeth (air) . . . . . . 2·25 1·90
799 600f. Royal family in Coronation robes . . . . 2·50 2·25

260 Gaucho on Piebald Horse

1985. "Argentina '85" International Stamp Exhibition, Buenos Aires. Horses. Multicoloured.
801 25f. Type **260** (postage) . . . 15 10
802 45f. Gaucho on horse 20 15
803 90f. Rodeo rider 45 30
804 100f. Rider hunting gazelle (air) 45 30
805 150f. Horses and gauchos at camp fire 65 50
806 200f. Horse and man sitting on steps 90 75
807 250f. Riding contest . . . . 1·10 90

261 Electric Locomotive No. 105-30 and Tank Wagon

1985. Trains. Multicoloured.
809 50f. Type **261** (postage) . . . 50 10
810 75f. Diesel shunting locomotive 65 15
811 80f. Diesel passenger locomotive 70 20
812 100f. Diesel railcar (air) . . . 90 20
813 150f. Diesel locomotive No. 6093 . . . . 1·25 35
814 200f. Diesel railcar No. 105 1·60 50
815 250f. Diesel locomotive pulling passenger train . . 2·40 70

262 Pot (Tikare) **263** "Pholiota mutabilis"

1985. Handicrafts. Multicoloured.
816 10f. Type **262** (postage) . . . 10 10
817 40f. Pot with lid decorated with birds (P. Bazega) . . 20 15
818 90f. Bronze statuette of mother with child (Ouagadougou) 40 25
819 120f. Bronze statuette of drummer (Ouagadougou) (air) 50 35

1985. Fungi. Multicoloured.
820 15f. Type **263** (postage) . . . 15 10
821 20f. "Hypholoma (nematoloma) fasciculare" 20 10
822 30f. "Ixocomus granulatus" 25 10
823 60f. "Agaricus campestris" 50 20
824 80f. "Trachypus scaber" . . 70 40
825 250f. "Marasmius scorodonius" . . . . . . 2·25 1·40
826 150f. "Armillaria mellea" (air) . . . . 1·10 60

264 "Virgin and Child"

1985. "Italia '85" International Stamp Exhibition, Rome. Paintings by Botticelli.
827 25f. Type **264** (postage) . . . 15 10
828 45f. "Portrait of an Unknown Man" 20 15
829 90f. "Mars and Venus" . . . 50 30
830 100f. "Birth of Venus" (air) 55 40
831 150f. "Allegory of Calumny" 75 60
832 200f. "Pallas and the Centaur" 90 75
833 250f. "Allegory of Spring" 1·10 90

265 Sikorsky S-55 Helicopter

1985. Red Cross. Multicoloured.
835 40f. Type **265** (postage) . . . 30 15
836 85f. Ambulance 35 25
837 150f. Henri Dunant (founder) (vert) (air) 65 50
838 250f. Nurse attending patient (vert) . . . . 1·10 90

266 Transport and Communications (development)

1985. Air. "Philexafrique" International Stamp Exhibition, Lome, Togo (2nd issue). Mult.
839 250f. Type **266** . . . . 3·75 1·50
840 250f. Youth activities (youth) 1·10 90

267 Girls drumming and clapping

1986. Dodo Carnival. Multicoloured.
841 20f. Type **267** 10 10
842 25f. Masked lion dancers . . 15 10
843 40f. Masked stick dancers and drummers 20 15
844 45f. Stick dancers with elaborate headdresses . . . 20 15
845 90f. Masked elephant dancer 40 25
846 90f. Animal dancers 40 25

268 Mother breast-feeding Baby

1986. Child Survival Campaign.
847 **268** 90f. multicoloured 40 25

269 Couple carrying Rail

1986. Railway Construction. Multicoloured.
848 90f. Type **269** (postage) . . . 70 15
849 120f. Laying tracks 85 25
850 185f. Workers waving to passing train . . . . . . 1·60 60
851 500f. "Inauguration of First German Railway" (Heim) (air) . . . . 4·00 1·75

No. 851 commemorates the 150th anniv of German railways.

270 Columbus before King of Portugal, and "Nina" **271** Village and First Aid Post

1986. 480th Death Anniv of Christopher Columbus (explorer). Multicoloured.
853 250f. Type **270** (postage) . . 1·60 90
854 300f. "Santa Maria" and Columbus with astrolabe 2·00 1·00
855 400f. Columbus imprisoned and "Santa Maria" . . . . 2·60 1·50
856 450f. Landing at San Salvador and "Pinta" (air) 3·25 1·60

1986. "Health For All by Year 2000". Mult.
858 90f. Type **271** 40 25
859 100f. Man receiving first aid (26 × 36 mm) 40 25
860 120f. People queuing for vaccinations (26 × 36 mm) 50 35

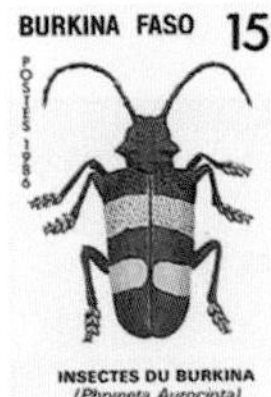

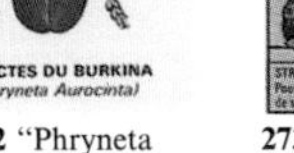

272 "Phryneta aurocinta" **273** Woman feeding Child and Fresh Foods

1986. Insects. Multicoloured.
861 15f. Type **272** 10 10
862 20f. "Sternocera interrupta" 10 10
863 40f. "Prosoprocera lactator" 35 15
864 45f. "Gonimbrasia hecate" 40 15
865 85f. "Charaxes epijasius" . . 70 50

1986. Gobi Health Strategy. Multicoloured.
866 30f. Type **273** 15 10
867 60f. Ingredients of oral rehydration therapy . . . 25 15
868 90f. Mother holding child for vaccination 40 25
869 120f. Doctor weighing child 50 35

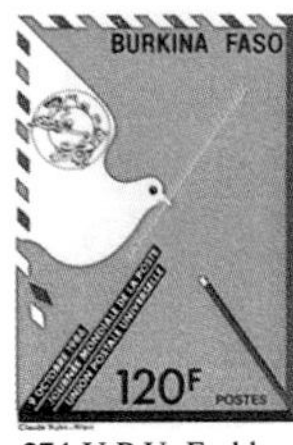

274 U.P.U. Emblem on Dove **275** Emblem

1986. World Post Day.
870 **274** 120f. multicoloured . . . 50 35

1986. International Peace Year.
871 **275** 90f. blue 40 25

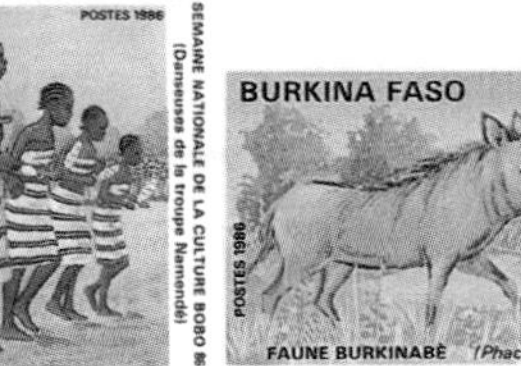

276 Namende Dancers **277** Warthog

1986. National Bobo Culture Week. Mult.
872 10f. Type **276** 10 10
873 25f. Mouhoun dancers . . . 10 10
874 90f. Houet dancer 40 25
875 105f. Seno musicians 40 25
876 120f. Ganzourgou dancers . . 50 35

1986. Wildlife. Multicoloured.
877 50f. Type **277** 20 15
878 65f. Spotted hyena 25 15
879 90f. Antelope 40 25
880 100f. Red-fronted gazelle . . 40 25
881 120f. Harnessed antelope . . 50 35
882 145f. Hartebeest 60 45
883 500f. Kob . . . . 2·00 1·50

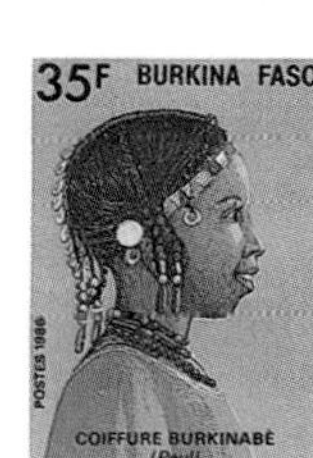

278 Peul **279** Charlie Chaplin within Film Frame (10th death anniv)

1986. Traditional Hairstyles. Multicoloured.
884 35f. Type **278** 25 15
885 75f. Dafing 30 20
886 90f. Peul (different) 55 30
887 120f. Mossi 60 35
888 185f. Peul (different) . . . . 1·00 80

1987. 10th Fespaco Film Festival.
889 – 90f. mauve, black & brn 40 25
890 – 120f. multicoloured . . . 50 35
891 **279** 185f. multicoloured . . . 75 60

DESIGNS: 90f. Camera on map in film frame; 120f. Cameraman and soundman (60th anniv of first talking film "The Jazz Singer").

280 Woman trimming Rug **281** "Calotripis procera"

1987. International Women's Day.
892 **280** 90f. multicoloured 40 25

1987. Flowers. Multicoloured.
893 70f. Type **281** 30 20
894 75f. "Acacia seyal" 30 20
895 85f. "Parkia biglobosa" . . . 35 25
896 90f. "Sterospernum kunthianum" 40 25
897 100f. "Dichrostachys cinerea" 40 25
898 300f. "Combretum paniculatum" . . . . . . 1·25 1·00

282 High Jumping

1987. Olympic Games, Seoul (1988). 50th Death Anniv of Pierre de Coubertin (founder of modern Olympic Games). Multicoloured.
899 75f. Type **282** 30 20
900 85f. Tennis (vert) 35 25
901 90f. Ski jumping 40 25
902 100f. Football 40 25
903 145f. Running 60 45
904 350f. Pierre de Coubertin and tennis game (vert) . . . . 1·50 1·25

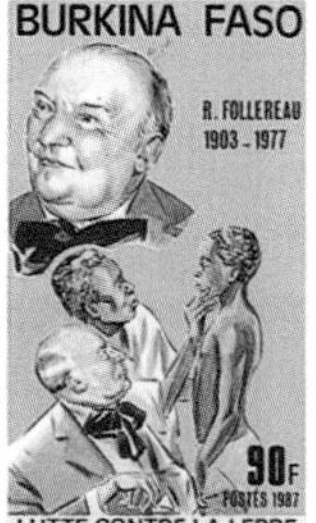

283 Follereau and Doctor treating Patient **285** Globe in Envelope

284 Woman sweeping

1987. Anti-leprosy Campaign. 10th Death Anniv of Raoul Follereau (pioneer). Multicoloured.
905 90f. Type **283** 40 25
906 100f. Laboratory technicians 40 25

907 120f. Gerhard Hansen (discoverer of bacillus) . . 50 35
908 300f. Follereau kissing patient 1·25 1·00

1987. World Environment Day. Multicoloured.
909 90f. Type **284** 40 25
910 145f. Emblem 60 45

1987. World Post Day.
911 **285** 90f. multicoloured 35 25

286 Luthuli and Open Book

1987. Anti-Apartheid Campaign. 20th Death Anniv of Albert John Luthuli (anti-apartheid campaigner). Multicoloured.
912 90f. Barbed wire and apartheid victims 35 25
913 100f. Type **286** 40 25

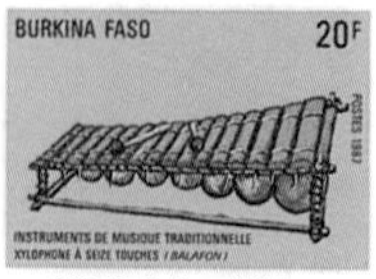

287 Dagari
288 Balafon (16 key xylophone)

1987. Traditional Costumes. Multicoloured.
914 10f. Type **287** 10 10
915 30f. Peul 15 10
916 90f. Mossi (female) 35 25
917 200f. Senoufo 80 60
918 500f. Mossi (male) . . . . . 1·90 1·40

1987. Traditional Music Instruments. Multicoloured.
919 20f. Type **288** 10 10
920 25f. Kunde en more (3 stringed lute) (vert) 10 10
921 35f. Tiahoun en bwaba (zither) 15 10
922 90f. Jembe en dioula (conical drum) 35 25
923 1000f. Bendre en more (calabash drum) (vert) . . 3·75 2·40

289 Dwellings

1987. International Year of Shelter for the Homeless.
924 **289** 90f. multicoloured 35 25

290 Small Industrial Units
291 People with Candles

1987. Five Year Plan for Popular Development. Multicoloured.
925 40f. Type **290** 15 10
926 55f. Management of dams . . 20 15
927 60f. Village community building primary school . . 25 15
928 90f. Bus (Transport and communications) 35 25
929 100f. National education: literacy campaign 40 25
930 120f. Intensive cattle farming 45 30

1988. 40th Anniv of W.H.O.
931 **291** 120f. multicoloured . . . 45 30

292 Exhibition Emblem and Games Mascot
293 Houet "Sparrow Hawk" Mask

1988. Olympic Games, Seoul, and "Olymphilex '88" Olympic Stamps Exhibition, Rome (932). Multicoloured.
932 30f. Type **292** 15 10
933 160f. Olympic flame (vert) . . 60 45
934 175f. Football 65 45
935 235f. Volleyball (vert) 90 65
936 450f. Basketball (vert) . . . 1·75 1·25

1988. Masks. Multicoloured.
938 10f. Type **293** 10 10
939 20f. Ouillo "Young Girls" mask 10 10
940 30f. Houet "Hartebeest" mask 15 10
941 40f. Mouhoun "Blacksmith" mask 15 10
942 120f. Ouri "Nanny" mask . . 45 30
943 175f. Ouri "Bat" mask (horiz) 65 45

294 Kieriba Jug
295 Envelopes forming Map

1988. Handicrafts. Multicoloured.
944 5f. Type **294** 10 10
945 15f. Mossi basket (horiz) . . 10 10
946 25f. Gurunsi chair (horiz) . . 10 10
947 30f. Bissa basket (horiz) . . . 15 10
948 45f. Ouagadougou hide box (horiz) 15 10
949 85f. Ouagadougou bronze statuette 35 20
950 120f. Ouagadougou hide travelling bag (horiz) . . . 45 30

1988. World Post Day.
951 **295** 120f. blue, black & yellow 45 30

296 White-collared Kingfisher

1988. Aquatic Wildlife. Multicoloured.
952 70f. Type **296** . . . . 1·25 40
953 100f. Elephantfish . . . . . 1·00 35
954 120f. Frog 55 30
955 160f. White-faced whistling duck . . . . 2·50 1·00

297 Mohammed Ali Jinnah (first Pakistan Governor-General)
298 Shepherds adoring Child

1988. Death Anniversaries. Multicoloured.
956 80f. Type **297** (40th anniv) (postage) 30 20
957 120f. Mahatma Gandhi (Indian human rights activist, 40th anniv) . . . 45 30
958 160f. John Fitzgerald Kennedy (U.S. President, 25th anniv) 60 45
959 235f. Martin Luther King (human rights activist, 20th anniv) (air) 90 65

1988. Christmas. Stained Glass Windows. Mult.
960 120f. Type **298** 45 30
961 160f. Wise men presenting gifts to Child 60 45
962 450f. Virgin and Child . . . 1·75 1·25
963 1000f. Flight into Egypt . . . 3·75 2·75

299 Satellite and Globe
300 W.H.O. and Aids Emblems

1989. 20th Anniv of FESPACO Film Festival. Multicoloured.
964 75f. Type **299** (postage) . . . 30 20
965 500f. Ababacar Samb Makharam (air) . . . . . 1·90 1·40
966 500f. Jean Michel Tchissoukou . . . . 1·90 1·40
967 500f. Paulin Soumanou Vieyra . . . . 1·90 1·40

1989. Campaign against AIDS.
969 **300** 120f. multicoloured . . . 45 30

301 "Oath of the Tennis Court" (Jacques Louis David) (½-size illustration)

1989. Air. "Philexfrance 89" International Stamp Exhibition, Paris, and Bicentenary of French Revolution. Multicoloured.
970 150f. Type **301** 60 45
971 200f. "Storming of the Bastille" (Thevenin) . . . 75 50
972 600f. "Rouget de Lisle singing La Marseillaise" (Pils) . . . . 2·25 1·60

302 Map and Tractor

1989. 30th Anniv of Council of Unity.
973 **302** 75f. multicoloured 30 20

303 "Striga generioides"
304 Sahel Dog

1989. Parasitic Plants. Multicoloured.
974 20f. Type **303** 10 10
975 50f. "Striga hermonthica" . . 20 15
976 235f. "Striga aspera" 90 65
977 450f. "Alectra vogelii" . . . 1·75 1·25

1989. Dogs. Multicoloured.
978 35f. Type **304** 10 10
979 50f. Young dog 20 15
980 60f. Hunting dog 20 15
981 350f. Guard dog . . . . . . 1·50 1·00

305 Statue
307 Pilgrims at Shrine of Our Lady of Yagma

1989. Solidarity with Palestinian People.
982 **305** 120f. multicoloured . . . 45 30

1989. Nos. 647/9 of Upper Volta optd **BURKINA FASO**.
983 **229** 90f. multicoloured 35 20
984 120f. multicoloured . . . 50 35
985 170f. multicoloured . . . 70 50

1990. Visit of Pope John Paul II. Multicoloured.
986 120f. Type **307** 50 35
987 160f. Pope and crowd 65 45

308 Mail Steamer, Globe and Penny Black
309 Goalkeeper catching Ball

1990. 150th Anniv of Penny Black and "Stamp World London 90" International Stamp Exhibition.
988 **308** 120f. multicoloured . . . 90 45

1990. World Cup Football Championship, Italy. Multicoloured.
990 30f. Type **309** 15 10
991 150f. Footballers 60 45

310 "Cantharellus cibarius"
311 Open Book

1990. Fungi. Multicoloured.
993 10f. Type **310** 10 10
994 15f. "Psalliota bispora" . . . 15 10
995 60f. "Amanita caesarea" . . 75 35
996 190f. "Boletus badius" . . . 2·40 1·25

1990. International Literacy Year.
998 **311** 40f. multicoloured 15 10
999 130f. multicoloured . . . 50 35

312 Maps, Emblem and Native Artefacts
313 De Gaulle

1990. 2nd International Salon of Arts and Crafts, Ouagadougou. Multicoloured.
1000 35f. Type **312** 15 10
1001 45f. Pottery (horiz) 20 15
1002 270f. Cane chair . . . . . 1·10 75

1990. Birth Centenary of Charles de Gaulle (French statesman).
1003 **313** 200f. multicoloured . . . 80 55

314 Quartz
315 Hand Holding Cigarette, Syringe and Tablets

1991. Rocks. Multicoloured.
1004 20f. Type **314** 10 10
1005 50f. Granite 20 15
1006 280f. Amphibolite . . . . . 1·10 75

1991. Anti-drugs Campaign.
1007 **315** 130f. multicoloured . . . 50 35

316 Film and Landscape

318 Traditional Hairstyle

317 Morse and Key

1991. 12th "Fespaco 91" Pan-African Cinema and Television Festival. Multicoloured.
1008 **316** 150f. multicoloured . . . 60 40

1991. Birth Bicentenary of Samuel Morse (inventor of signalling system).
1010 **317** 200f. multicoloured . . . 80 55

1991.
1011 **318** 5f. multicoloured 10 10
1012 10f. multicoloured . . . 10 10
1013 25f. multicoloured . . . 10 10
1014 50f. multicoloured . . . 10 10
1018 130f. multicoloured . . . 30 20
1019 150f. multicoloured . . . 60 40
1020 200f. multicoloured . . . 80 55
1021 330f. multicoloured . . . 80 55

319 "Grewia tenax"

320 Warba

1991. Flowers. Multicoloured.
1025 5f. Type **319** 10 10
1026 15f. "Hymenocardia acide" 10 10
1027 60f. "Cassia sieberiana" (vert) 25 20
1028 100f. "Adenium obesum" 40 30
1029 300f. "Mitragyna inermis" 1·25 85

1991. Dance Costumes. Multicoloured.
1030 75f. Type **320** 40 25
1031 130f. Wiskamba 65 40
1032 280f. Pa-Zenin . . . . . . 1·40 85

321 Pillar Box and Globe

322 Cake Tin

1991. World Post Day.
1033 **321** 130f. multicoloured . . . 50 35

1992. Cooking Utensils.
1034 45f. Type **322** 40 20
1035 130f. Cooking pot (vert) . . 1·00 70
1036 310f. Pestle and mortar (vert) . . . . 1·50 1·00
1037 500f. Ladle and bowl . . . 2·40 1·60

323 Yousouf Fofana

325 Child and Cardiograph

324 Disabled Man at Potter's Wheel

1992. African Nations Cup Football Championship, Senegal. Multicoloured.
1038 50f. Type **323** 25 20
1039 100f. Francois-Jules Bocande 50 35

1992. U.N. Decade of the Handicapped.
1041 **324** 100f. multicoloured . . . 50 35

1992. World Health Day. "Health in Rhythm with the Heart".
1042 **325** 330f. multicoloured . . . 1·60 1·10

326 Columbus and "Santa Maria"

1992. "Genova '92" International Thematic Stamp Exhibition and 500th Anniv of Discovery of America by Columbus. Multicoloured.
1043 50f. Type **326** 25 20
1044 150f. Amerindians watching Columbus's fleet off San Salvador 75 55

327 "Dysdercus voelkeri" (fire bug) on Cotton Boll

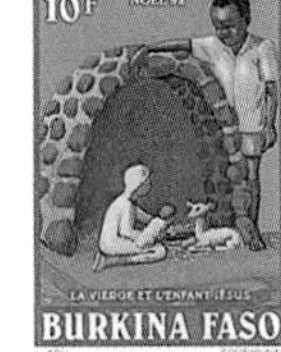

328 Crib

1992. Insects. Multicoloured.
1046 20f. Type **327** 10 10
1047 40f. "Rhizopertha dominica" (beetle) on leaf 20 15
1048 85f. "Orthetrum microstigma" (dragonfly) on stem 40 30
1049 500f. Honey bee on flower 2·40 1·60

1992. Christmas. Multicoloured.
1050 10f. Type **328** 10 10
1051 130f. Children decorating crib 60 40
1052 1000f. Boy with Christmas card . . . . 4·50 3·00

329 Film Makers' Monument

330 Yellow-billed Stork

1993. 13th "Fespaco" Pan-African Film Festival, Ouagadougou. Multicoloured.
1053 250f. Type **329** . . . . . . 1·10 75
1054 750f. Douta Seck (comedian) (horiz) . . . . 3·50 2·40

1993. Birds. Multicoloured.
1055 100f. Type **330** 95 60
1056 200f. Marabou stork . . . . 1·75 1·40
1057 500f. Saddle-bill stork . . . 4·50 2·75

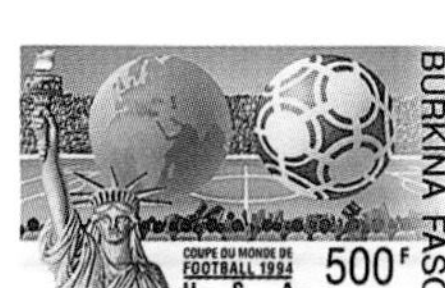

331 Statue of Liberty, Globe and Ball

1993. World Cup Football Championship, U.S.A. (1994). Multicoloured.
1059 500f. Type **331** . . . . . . 2·25 1·50
1060 1000f. Players, map of world and U.S. flag . . . . . . 4·50 3·00

332 Peterbilt Canadian Hauler and Diesel Locomotive Type BB 852, France

333 "Saba senegalensis"

1993. Centenary of Invention of Diesel Engine.
1061 **332** 1000f. multicoloured . . 5·75 3·00

1993. Wild Fruits. Multicoloured.
1062 150f. Type **333** 70 50
1063 300f. Karite (horiz) . . . . 1·40 95
1064 600f. Baobab . . . . 2·75 1·90

334 Flowers, "Stamps" and Sights of Paris

1993. 1st European Stamp Salon, Flower Gardens, Paris (1994). Multicoloured.
1065 400f. Type **334** 95 65
1066 650f. "Stamps", sights of Paris, daffodils and irises 1·50 1·00

335 Peulh Copper Hair Ornament

1993. Jewellery. Multicoloured.
1067 200f. Type **335** 50 35
1068 250f. Mossi agate necklace (vert) 60 40
1069 500f. Gourounsi copper bracelet . . . . 1·25 85

336 Gazelle

1993. The Red-fronted Gazelle. Multicoloured.
1070 30f. Type **336** 10 10
1071 40f. Two gazelle 10 10
1072 60f. Two gazelle (different) 15 10
1073 100f. Gazelle 25 20

337 Woodland Kingfisher

1994. Kingfishers.
1075 600f. Type **337** . . . . . . 1·50 1·00
1076 1200f. Striped kingfisher . . 3·00 2·00

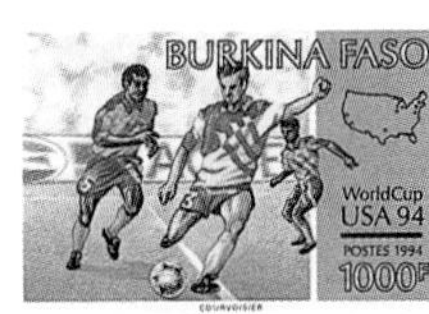

338 Players

1994. World Cup Football Championship, United States. Multicoloured.
1078 1000f. Type **338** . . . . . 2·40 1·60
1079 1800f. Goalkeeper saving ball . . . . 4·25 3·00

339 Dog with Puppy

1994. 1st European Stamp Salon, Flower Gardens, Paris, France.
1081 **339** 1500f. multicoloured . . 3·75 2·50

340 Astronaut planting Flag on Moon

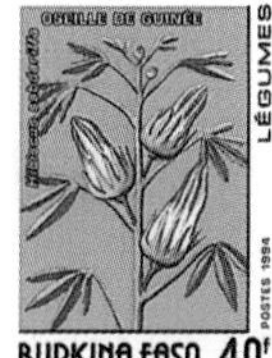

341 Guinea Sorrel

1994. 25th Anniv of First Manned Moon Landing. Multicoloured.
1083 750f. Type **340** . . . . . . 1·75 1·25
1084 750f. Landing module on Moon . . . . 1·75 1·25
Nos. 1083/4 were issued together, se-tenant, forming a composite design.

1994. Vegetables. Multicoloured.
1085 40f. Type **341** 10 10
1086 45f. Aubergine 10 10
1087 75f. Aubergine 20 15
1088 100f. Okra 25 20

342 Pig

343 Pierre de Coubertin (founder) and Anniversary Emblem

1994. Domestic Animals. Multicoloured.
1089 150f. Type **342** 35 25
1090 1000f. Goat (vert) . . . . . 2·40 1·60
1091 1500f. Sheep . . . . 3·75 2·50

1994. Centenary of Int Olympic Committee.
1092 **343** 320f. multicoloured . . . 80 55

344 Donkey Rider

345 Crocodile

1995. 20th Anniv of World Tourism Organization. Multicoloured.
1093 150f. Type **344** 40 30
1094 350f. Bobo-Dioulasso railway station (horiz) . . 90 60
1095 450f. Great Mosque, Bani (horiz) . . . . 1·10 75
1096 650f. Roan antelope and map (horiz) . . . . . . 1·60 1·10

1995. Multicoloured, colour of frame given.
1097 **345** 10f. brown 10 10
1098 20f. mauve 10 10
1099 25f. brown 10 10
1100 30f. green 10 10
1101 40f. purple 10 10
1102 50f. grey 15 10
1103 75f. purple 20 15
1104 100f. brown 20 15
1105 150f. green 40 30
1106 175f. blue 45 30
1107 250f. brown 65 45
1108 400f. green . . . . . . 1·00 70

346 "Rabi" (dir. Gaston Kabore)

1995. "Fespaco 95" Pan-African Film Festival and Centenary of Motion Pictures. Multicoloured.
1109 150f. Type **346** 40 30
1110 250f. "Tila" (Idrissa Ouedraogo) 65 45

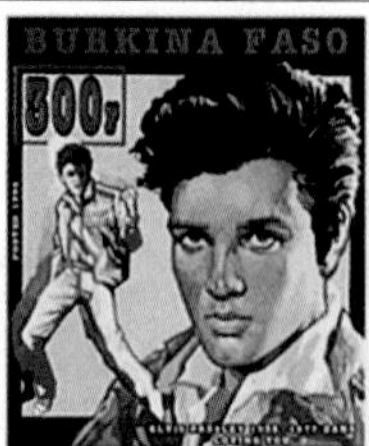
347 Elvis Presley in "Loving You"

1995. Entertainers. Multicoloured.

1111	300f. Type **347**	75	50
1112	400f. Marilyn Monroe	1·00	70
1113	500f. Elvis Presley in "Jailhouse Rock"	1·25	85
1114	650f. Marilyn Monroe in "Asphalt Jungle"	1·60	1·10
1115	750f. Marilyn Monroe in "Niagara"	1·90	1·40
1116	1000f. Elvis Presley in "Blue Hawaii"	2·50	1·75

348 Common Gonolek

1995. Birds. Multicoloured.

1118	450f. Type **348**	1·10	75
1119	600f. Red-cheeked cordon-bleu	1·50	1·10
1120	750f. Golden bishop	1·90	1·40

349 Hissing Sand Snake

1995. Reptiles. Multicoloured.

1122	450f. Type **349**	1·10	75
1123	500f. Sand python	1·25	85
1124	1500f. Tortoise	4·00	2·75

350 Basketball

1995. Olympic Games, Atlanta (1996). Mult.

1125	150f. Type **350**	40	30
1126	250f. Baseball	65	45
1127	650f. Tennis	1·60	1·10
1128	750f. Table tennis	1·90	1·40

351 Juan Manuel Fangio (racing driver)

1995. Sportsmen. Multicoloured.

1130	300f. Type **351**	75	50
1131	400f. Andre Agassi (tennis player)	1·00	70
1132	500f. Ayrton Senna (racing driver)	1·25	85
1133	1000f. Michael Schumacher (racing driver)	2·50	1·75

352 Children and Christmas Tree

1995. Christmas. Multicoloured.

1135	150f. Type **352**	40	30
1136	450f. Grotto, Yagma	1·10	75
1137	500f. Flight into Egypt	1·25	85
1138	1000f. Adoration of the Wise Men	2·50	1·75

353 Headquarters Building, New York

1995. 50th Anniv of United Nations. Multicoloured.

1139	500f. Type **353**	1·25	85
1140	1000f. Village council under tree with superimposed U.N. emblem (vert)	2·50	1·75

354 Mossi Type

1995. Traditional Houses. Multicoloured.

1141	70f. Type **354**	20	15
1142	100f. Kassena type	25	15
1143	200f. Roro type	50	35
1144	250f. Peulh type	65	45

APPENDIX

The following stamps have either been issued in excess of postal needs or have not been available to the public in reasonable quantities at face value. Such stamps may later be given full listing if there is evidence of regular postal use.

1985.

85th Birthday of Queen Elizabeth the Queen Mother. 1500f.

BURMA Pt. 1, Pt. 21

A territory in the east of India, which was granted independence by the British in 1948. From May 1990 it was known as Myanmar.

1937. 12 pies = 1 anna; 16 annas = 1 rupee.
1953. 100 pyas = 1 kyat.

1937. Stamps of India (King George V) optd **BURMA**.

1	**55**	3p. grey	60	10
2	**79**	½a. green	1·00	10
3	**80**	9p. green	1·00	10
4	**81**	1a. brown	75	10
5	**59**	2a. red	75	10
6	**61**	2½a. orange	60	10
7	**62**	3a. red	1·00	30
8	**83**	3½a. blue	2·00	10
9	**63**	4a. olive	1·00	10
10	**64**	6a. bistre	75	35
11	**65**	8a. mauve	1·50	10
12	**66**	12a. red	3·75	1·25
13	**67**	1r. brown and green	20·00	3·00
14		2r. red and orange	28·00	10·00
15		5r. blue and violet	38·00	17·00
16		10r. green and red	85·00	60·00
17		15r. blue and olive	£300	£125
18		25r. orange and blue	£600	£300

2 King George VI and "Chinthes"

3 King George VI and "Nagas"

4 "Karaweik" (royal barge)

8 King George VI and Peacock

1938. King George VI.

18a	**2**	1p. orange	3·00	1·00
19		3p. violet	20	70
20		6p. blue	20	10
21		9p. green	1·00	80
22	**3**	1a. brown	20	10
23		1½a. green	20	1·00
24		2a. red	45	10
25	**4**	2a.6p. red	14·00	1·25
26	–	3a. mauve	14·00	2·00
27	–	3a.6p. blue	1·25	4·25
28	**3**	4a. blue	60	10
29	–	8a. green	5·00	30
30	**8**	1r. purple and blue	5·00	20
31		2r. brown and purple	16·00	1·75
32	–	5r. violet and red	48·00	24·00
33	–	10r. brown and green	55·00	50·00

DESIGNS—HORIZ: As Type **4**: 3a. Burma teak; 3a.6p. Burma rice; 8a. River Irrawaddy. VERT: As Type **3**: 5, 10r. King George VI and "Nats".

1940. Cent of First Adhesive Postage Stamp. Surch **COMMEMORATION POSTAGE STAMP 6th MAY 1840 ONE ANNA 1A** and value in native characters.

34	**4**	1a. on 2a.6p. red	3·75	1·75

For Japanese issues see "Japanese Occupation of Burma".

1945. British Military Administration. Stamps of 1938 optd **MILY ADMN**.

35	**2**	1p. orange	10	10
36		3p. violet	10	60
37		6p. blue	10	30
38		9p. green	30	75
39	**3**	1a. brown	10	10
40		1½a. green	10	15
41		2a. red	10	15
42	**4**	2a.6p. red	2·00	70
43	–	3a. mauve	1·50	20
44	–	3a.6p. blue	10	70
45	**3**	4a. blue	10	60
46	–	8a. green	10	70
47	**8**	1r. purple and blue	40	50
48		2r. brown and purple	40	1·25
49	–	5r. violet and red	40	1·25
50	–	10r. brown and green	40	1·25

1946. British Civil Administration. As 1938, but colours changed.

51	**2**	3p. brown	10	1·75
52		6p. violet	10	30
53		9p. green	15	2·25
54	**3**	1a. blue	15	20
55		1½a. orange	15	10
56		2a. red	15	40
57	**4**	2a.6p. blue	2·75	3·75
57a	–	3a. blue	6·50	3·75
57b	–	3a. 6p. black and blue	50	1·75
58	**3**	4a. purple	50	30
59	–	8a. mauve	1·75	2·75
60	**8**	1r. violet and mauve	1·25	65
61		2r. brown and orange	6·00	3·00
62	–	5r. green and brown	6·00	15·00
63	–	10r. red and violet	8·50	19·00

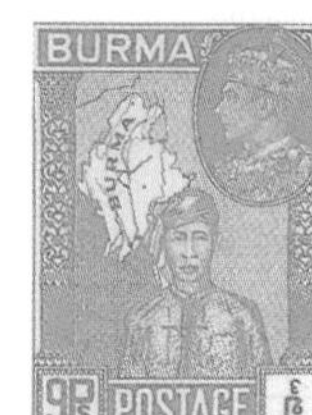
14 Burman

ကြားဖြတ်
အစိုးရ။
(18 Trans. "Interim Government")

1946. Victory.

64	**14**	9p. green	20	20
65	–	1½a. violet (Burmese woman)	20	10
66	–	2a. red (Chinthe)	20	10
67	–	3a.6p. (Elephant)	50	20

1947. Stamps of 1946 opt with T **18** or with larger opt on large stamps.

68	**2**	3p. brown	70	70
69		6p. violet	10	30
70		9p. green	10	30
71	**3**	1a. blue	10	30
72		1½a. orange	1·00	10
73		2a. red	30	15
74	**4**	2a.6p. blue	1·75	1·00
75	–	3a. blue	2·50	1·75
76	–	3a.6p. black and blue	50	2·00
77	**3**	4a. purple	1·75	30
78	–	8a. mauve	1·75	1·50
79	**8**	1r. violet and mauve	4·25	65
80		2r. brown and orange	4·50	3·50
81	–	5r. green and brown	4·50	4·00
82	–	10r. red and violet	3·25	4·00

20 Gen. Aung San, Chinthe and Map of Burma

21 Martyrs' Memorial

1948. Independence Day.

83	**20**	½a. green	10	10
84		1a. pink	10	10
85		2a. red	15	15
86		3½a. blue	20	15
87		8a. brown	25	25

1948. 1st Anniv of Murder of Aung San and his Ministers.

88	**21**	3p. blue	10	10
89		6p. green	10	10
90		9p. red	10	10
91		1a. violet	10	10
92		2a. mauve	10	10
93		3½a. green	15	15
94		4a. brown	15	15
95		8a. red	20	15
96		12a. purple	25	20
97		1r. green	35	20
98		2r. blue	60	40
99		5r. brown	1·90	1·10

22 Playing Cane-ball

25 Bell, Mingun Pagoda

27 Transplanting Rice

28 Lion Throne

1949. 1st Anniv of Independence.

100	**22**	3p. blue	95	25
120		3p. orange	65	25
101	–	6p. green	10	10
121	–	6p. purple	10	10
102	–	9p. red	10	10
122	–	9p. blue	10	10
103	**25**	1a. red	15	10
123		1a. blue	10	10
104	–	2a. orange	45	10
124	–	2a. green	40	20
105	**27**	2a.6p. mauve	20	15
125		2a.6p. green	20	15
106	–	3a. violet	20	15
126	–	3a. red	20	15
107	–	3a.6p. green	25	15
127	–	3a.6p. orange	25	15
108	–	4a. brown	25	15
128	–	4a. red	25	15
109	–	8a. red	35	15
129	–	8a. blue	25	20
110	**28**	1r. green	50	15
130		1r. violet	50	35
111		2r. blue	1·25	40
131		2r. green	85	75
112		5r. brown	2·50	1·25
132		5r. blue	2·25	2·25
113		10r. orange	4·25	1·90
133		10r. blue	5·50	4·25

DESIGNS—As Type **22**: 6p. Dancer; 9p. Girl playing saunggaut (string instrument); 2a. Hintha (legendary bird). As Type **25**: 4a. Elephant hauling log. As Type **27**: 3a. Girl weaving; 3a.6p. Royal Palace; 8a. Ploughing paddy field with oxen.

See also Nos. 137/50.

29 U.P.U. Monument, Berne

30 Independence Monument, Rangoon, and Map

1949. 75th Anniv of U.P.U.

114	**29**	2a. orange	15	15
115		3½a. green	20	15
116		6a. violet	25	25
117		8a. red	40	25
118		12½a. blue	70	40
119		1r. green	90	50

1953. 5th Anniv of Independence.

134	**30**	14p. green (22 × 18 mm)	20	10
135		20p. red (36½ × 26½ mm)	25	15
136		25p. blue (36½ × 26½ mm)	35	20

1954. New Currency. As 1949 issue but values in pyas and kyats.

137	**22**	1p. orange	65	10
138	–	2p. purple (as 6p.)	10	10
139	–	3p. blue (as 9p.)	10	10
140	**25**	5p. blue	10	10
141	**27**	10p. green	10	10
142	–	15p. green (as 2a.)	25	10
143	–	20p. red (as 3a.)	15	10
144	–	25p. orange (as 3a.6p.)	15	10
145	–	30p. red (as 4a.)	25	15
146	–	50p. blue (as 8a.)	25	15
147	**28**	1k. violet	75	25
148		2k. green	1·25	35
149		5k. blue	3·75	70
150		10k. blue	6·50	1·25

31 Sangiti Mahapasana Rock Cave in Grounds of Kaba-Aye Pagoda

1954. 6th Buddhist Council, Rangoon.
151 – 10p. blue 10 10
152 – 15p. purple 15 15
153 **31** 35p. brown 25 20
154 – 50p. green 40 25
155 – 1k. red 90 50
156 – 2k. violet . . . . 1·40 1·00
DESIGNS: 10p. Rock caves and Songha of Cambodia; 15p. Buddhist priests and Kuthodaw Pagoda, Mandalay; 50p. Rock cave and Songha of Thailand; 1k. Rock cave and Songha of Ceylon; 2k. Rock cave and Songha of Laos.

32 Fifth Buddhist Council Monuments

1956. Buddha Jayanti.
157 **32** 20p. green and blue . . . 20 15
158 – 40p. green and blue . . . 25 20
159 – 60p. yellow and green . . . 45 35
160 – 1k.25 blue and yellow . . . 85 70
DESIGNS: 40p. Thatbyinnyu Pagoda, Pagan; 60p. Shwedagan Pagoda, Rangoon; 1k.25, Sangiti Mahapasana Rock Cave and Kaba-Aye Pagoda, Rangoon (venue of 6th Buddhist Council).

မြို့မန္တလာ-နှစ်တရာ
၁၂၂၁-၁၃၂၁
15 P ၁၅ပြား

(33) ("Mandalay Town—100 Years/ 1221–1321")

1959. Centenary of Mandalay. No. 144 surch with T **33** and Nos. 147/8 with two-line opt only.
161 – 15p. on 25p. orange . . . 15 20
162 **28** 1k. violet 70 60
163 2k. green . . . . 1·50 1·25

1961. No. 134 surch as right-hand characters in third line of T **33**.
164 **30** 15p. on 14p. green 60 25

35 Torch-bearer in Rangoon

1961. 2nd South-East Asia Peninsula Games, Rangoon.
165 **35** 15p. blue and red 20 10
166 – 25p. green and brown . . . 25 15
167 – 50p. mauve and blue . . . 50 25
168 – 1k. yellow and green . . . 95 75
DESIGNS—VERT: 25p. Contestants; 50p. Women sprinting in Aung San Stadium, Rangoon. HORIZ: 1k. Contestants.

36 Children at Play

1961. 15th Anniv of U.N.I.C.E.F.
169 **36** 15p. red and pink 30 10

37 Flag and Map

အလုပ်သမားနေ့
၁၉၆၃

(39)

1963. 1st Anniv of Military Coup by General Ne Win.
170 **37** 15p. red 30 20

1963. Freedom from Hunger. Nos. 141 and 146 optd **FREEDOM FROM HUNGER**.
171 **27** 10p. green 40 35
172 – 50p. blue 75 65

1963. Labour Day. No. 143 optd with T **39**.
173 20p. red 35 20

40 White-browed Fantail

41 I.T.U. Emblem and Symbols

1964. Burmese Birds (1st series).
174 **40** 1p. black 15 15
175 2p. red 20 15
176 3p. green 20 15
177 – 5p. blue 25 20
178 – 10p. brown 25 20
179 – 15p. green 25 20
180 – 20p. brown and red . . . 45 25
181 – 25p. brown and yellow . . 45 25
182 – 50p. blue and red 85 30
183 – 1k. blue, yellow & grey . . 2·40 70
184 – 2k. blue, green and red . . 4·75 1·75
185 – 5k. multicoloured . . . . 9·75 4·50
BIRDS—22 × 26 mm: 5 to 15p. Indian roller. 27 × 37 mm: 25p. Crested serpent eagle. 50p. Sarus crane. 1k. Indian pied hornbill. 5k. Green peafowl. 35½ × 25 mm: 20p. Red-whiskered bulbul. 37 × 27 mm: 2k. Kalij pheasant.
See also Nos. 195/206.

1965. Centenary of I.T.U.
186 **41** 20p. mauve 15 15
187 50p. green (34 × 24½ mm) 40 40

42 I.C.Y. Emblem

43 Harvesting

1965. International Co-operation Year.
188 **42** 5p. blue 10 10
189 10p. brown 20 10
190 15p. olive 25 10

1966. Peasants' Day
191 **43** 15p. multicoloured 25 15

44 Cogwheel and Hammer

45 Aung San and Agricultural Cultivation

1967. May Day.
192 **44** 15p. yellow, black & blue 25 20

1968. 20th Anniv of Independence.
193 **45** 15p. multicoloured 25 20

46 Burma Pearls

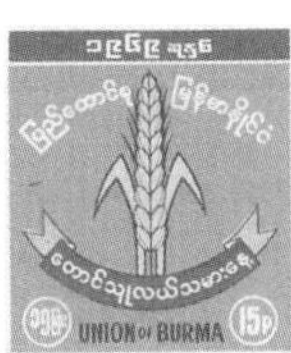

47 Spike of Paddy

1968. Burmese Gems, Jades and Pearls Emporium, Rangoon.
194 **46** 15p. ultram, blue & yell . . 40 15

1968. Burmese Birds (2nd series). Designs and colours as Nos. 174/85 but formats and sizes changed.
195 **40** 1p. black 15 15
196 2p. red 15 15
197 3p. green 20 15
198 – 5p. blue 20 15
199 – 10p. brown 20 15
200 – 15p. yellow 25 20
201 – 20p. brown and red . . . 25 20
202 – 25p. brown and yellow . . 30 25
203 – 50p. blue and red 55 45
204 – 1k. blue, yellow & grey . . 1·60 45
205 – 2k. blue, green and red . . 4·50 1·10
206 – 5k. multicoloured . . . . 9·50 4·50
NEW SIZES—21 × 17 mm: 1, 2, 3p. 39 × 21 mm: 20p., 2k. 23 × 28 mm: 5, 10, 15p. 21 × 39 mm: 25, 50p., 1, 5k.

1969. Peasants' Day.
218 **47** 15p. yellow, blue & green 25 10

48 I.L.O. Emblem

49 Football

1969. 50th Anniv of I.L.O.
219 **48** 15p. gold and green . . . 15 10
220 50p. gold and red 40 25

1969. 5th South-East Asian Peninsula Games, Rangoon.
221 **49** 15p. multicoloured 20 10
222 – 25p. multicoloured 25 15
223 – 50p. multicoloured 50 20
224 – 1k. black, green & blue . . 95 50
DESIGNS—HORIZ: 25p. Running. VERT: 50p. Weightlifting; 1k. Volleyball.

50 Marchers with Independence, Resistance and Union Flags

1970. 25th Anniv of Burmese Armed Forces.
225 **50** 15p. multicoloured 20 15

51 "Peace and Progress"

1970. 25th Anniv of United Nations.
226 **51** 15p. multicoloured 25 20

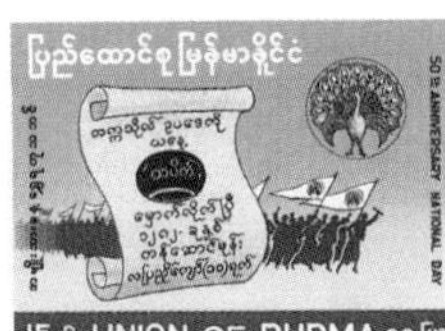

52 Boycott Declaration and Marchers

1970. National Day and 50th Anniv of University Boycott. Multicoloured.
227 15p. Type **52** 10 10
228 25p. Students on boycott march 20 10
229 50p. Banner and demonstrators 40 20

53 Burmese Workers

1971. 1st Burmese Socialist Programme Party Congress. Multicoloured.
230 5p. Type **53** 10 10
231 15p. Burmese races and flags 15 10
232 25p. Hands holding scroll . . 25 15
233 50p. Party flag 50 30

54 Child drinking Milk

1971. 25th Anniv of U.N.I.C.E.F. Multicoloured.
235 15p. Type **54** 25 15
236 50p. Marionettes 55 40

55 Aung San and Independence Monument, Panglong

1972. 25th Anniv of Independence. Multicoloured.
237 15p. Type **55** 10 10
238 50p. Aung San and Burmese in national costumes . . . 25 20
239 1k. Flag and map (vert) . . . 60 40

56 Burmese and Stars

1972. 10th Anniv of Revolutionary Council.
240 **56** 15p. multicoloured 20 10

57 Human Heart

59 Casting Vote

58 Ethnic Groups

1972. World Health Day.
241 **57** 15p. red, black & yellow 20 15

1973. National Census.
242 **58** 15p. multicoloured 20 10

1973. National Constitutional Referendum.
243 **59** 5p. red and black 15 10
244 – 10p. multicoloured 15 10
245 – 15p. multicoloured 15 10
DESIGNS—HORIZ: 10p. Voter supporting map. VERT: 15p. Burmese with ballot papers.

60 Open-air Meeting

1974. Opening of 1st Pyithu Hluttaw (People's Assembly). Multicoloured.
246 15p. Burmese flags, 1752–1974 (80 × 26 mm) 20 15
247 50p. Type **60** 40 25
248 1k. Burmese badge 80 55

61 U.P.U. Emblem and Carrier Pigeon

1974. Centenary of Universal Postal Union. Mult.
249 15p. Type **61** 15 10
250 20p. Woman reading letter (vert) 20 10
251 50p. U.P.U. emblem on "stamps" (vert) 45 20
252 1k. Stylized doll (vert) . . . 75 35
253 2k. Postman delivering letter to family . . . . 1·75 75

62 Kachin Couple

63 Bamar Couple

1974. Burmese Costumes. Inscr "SOCIALIST REPUBLIC OF THE UNION OF BURMA".

No.	Type	Description	Unused	Used
254	62	1p. mauve	10	10
255		3p. brown and mauve	10	10
256		5p. violet and mauve	10	10
257		10p. blue	10	10
258		15p. green and light green	10	10
259	63	20p. black, brown & blue	15	10
260	–	50p. violet, brown & ochre	40	15
261	–	1k. violet, mauve & black	1·10	60
262	–	5k. multicoloured	4·00	2·25

DESIGNS—As Type **62**: 3p. Kayah girl; 5p. Kayin couple and bronze drum; 15p. Chin couple. As Type **63**: 50p. Mon woman; 1k. Rakhine woman; 5k. Musician.

For 15, 50p. and 1k. stamps in these designs, but inscr "UNION OF BURMA", see Nos. 309/11.

64 Woman on Globe and I.W.Y. Emblem

1975. International Women's Year

No.	Type	Description	Unused	Used
263	64	50p. black and green	30	20
264	–	2k. black and blue	1·25	95

DESIGN—VERT: 2k. Globe on flower and I.W.Y. emblem.

65 Burmese and Flag

66 Emblem and Burmese Learning Alphabet

1976. Constitution Day.

No.	Type	Description	Unused	Used
265	65	20p. black and blue	15	10
266	–	50p. brown and blue	35	30
267	–	1k. multicoloured	1·00	60

DESIGNS—As Type **65**: 50p. Burmese with banners and flag. 57 × 21 mm: 1k. Map of Burma, Burmese and flag.

1976. International Literacy Year.

No.	Type	Description	Unused	Used
268	66	10p. brown and red	10	10
269	–	15p. turquoise, grn & blk	10	10
270	–	50p. blue, orange & black	40	20
271	–	1k. multicoloured	75	50

DESIGNS—HORIZ: 15p. Abacus and open books. 50p. Emblem. VERT: 1k. Emblem, open book and globe.

67 Early Train and Ox-cart

1977. Centenary of Railway.

No.	Type	Description	Unused	Used
272	–	15p. green, black & mauve	5·25	1·10
273	67	20p. multicoloured	1·75	40
274	–	25p. multicoloured	2·75	60
275	–	50p. multicoloured	3·50	1·00
276	–	1k. multicoloured	7·75	1·90

DESIGNS—26 × 17 mm: 15p. Early steam locomotive. As Type **67**—HORIZ: 25p. Diesel locomotive DD1517, steam train and railway station; 50p. Ava railway bridge over River Irrawaddy. VERT: Diesel train emerging from tunnel.

68 Karaweik Hall

1978.

No.	Type	Description	Unused	Used
277	68	50p. brown	35	25
278	–	1k. multicoloured	95	60

DESIGN—79½ × 25 mm: 1k. Side view of Karaweik Hall.

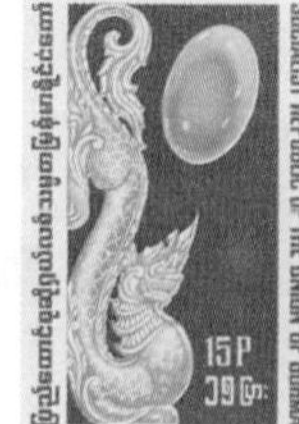

69 Jade Naga and Gem

1979. 16th Gem Emporium.

No.	Type	Description	Unused	Used
279	69	15p. green and turquoise	15	10
280	–	20p. blue, yellow & mauve	35	15
281	–	50p. blue, brown & green	65	40
282	–	1k. multicoloured	1·25	70

DESIGNS—As T **69**: 20p. Hintha (legendary bird) holding pearl in beak; 50p. Hand holding pearl and amethyst pendant. 55 × 20 mm: 1k. Gold jewel-studded dragon.

70 "Intelsat IV" Satellite over Burma

1979. Introduction of Satellite Communications System.

No.	Type	Description	Unused	Used
283	70	25p. multicoloured	25	15

71 I.Y.C. Emblem on Map of Burma

72 Weather Balloon

1979. International Year of the Child.

No.	Type	Description	Unused	Used
284	71	25p. orange and blue	35	25
285		50p. red and violet	65	40

1980. World Meteorological Day.

No.	Type	Description	Unused	Used
286	72	25p. blue, yellow & black	25	15
287	–	50p. green, black and red	50	35

DESIGN: 50p. Meteorological satellite and W.M.O. emblem.

73 Weightlifting

1980. Olympic Games, Moscow.

No.	Type	Description	Unused	Used
288	73	20p. green, orange & blk	20	10
289	–	50p. black, orange and red	45	25
290	–	1k. black, orange and blue	90	50

DESIGNS: 50p. Boxing; 1k. Football.

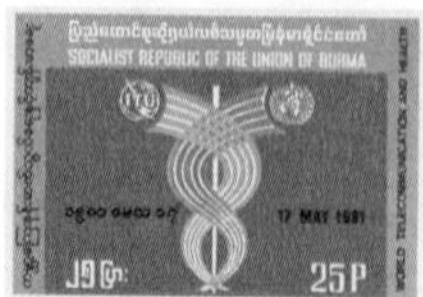

74 I.T.U. and W.H.O. Emblems with Ribbons forming Caduceus

1981. World Telecommunications Day.

No.	Type	Description	Unused	Used
291	74	25p. orange and black	20	10

75 Livestock and Vegetables

1981. World Food Day. Multicoloured.

No.	Type	Description	Unused	Used
292		25p. Type 75	35	10
293		50p. Farm produce and farmer holding wheat	55	20
294		1k. Globe and stylized bird	75	45

76 Athletes and Person in Wheelchair

1981. International Year of Disabled Persons.

No.	Type	Description	Unused	Used
295	76	25p. multicoloured	25	15

77 Telephone, Satellite and Antenna

1983. World Communications Year.

No.	Type	Description	Unused	Used
296	77	15p. blue and black	10	10
297		25p. mauve and black	30	15
298		50p. green, black and red	50	35
299		1k. brown, black & green	1·25	70

78 Fish and Globe

1983. World Food Day.

No.	Type	Description	Unused	Used
300	78	15p. yellow, blue & black	15	10
301		25p. orange, green & black	25	15
302		50p. green, yellow & black	60	60
303		1k. blue, yellow and black	1·75	1·40

79 Globe and Log

1984. World Food Day.

No.	Type	Description	Unused	Used
304	79	15p. blue, yellow & black	10	10
305		25p. violet, yellow & black	15	10
306		50p. green, pink and black	50	40
307		1k. mauve, yellow & black	1·00	90

80 Potted Plant

1985. International Youth Year.

No.	Type	Description	Unused	Used
308	80	15p. multicoloured	25	20

1989. As Nos. 258/9 and 260/1 but inscr "UNION OF BURMA".

No.	Type	Description	Unused	Used
309	62	15p. dp green & green	25	20
309a	–	20p. black, brown & blue	5·00	
310	–	50p. violet and brown	50	30
311	–	1k. violet, mauve & black	85	65

OFFICIAL STAMPS

1937. Stamps of India (King George V) optd **BURMA SERVICE**.

No.	Type	Description	Unused	Used
O 1	55	3p. grey	2·00	10
O 2	79	½a. green	8·50	10
O 3	80	9p. green	4·50	30
O 4	81	1a. brown	5·00	10
O 5	59	2a. red	9·00	35
O 6	61	2½a. orange	4·50	2·00
O 7	63	4a. olive	5·00	10
O 8	64	6a. bistre	4·25	7·50
O 9	65	8a. mauve	4·00	80
O10	66	12a. red	4·00	5·00
O11	67	1r. brown and green	15·00	4·00
O12		2r. red and orange	35·00	38·00
O13		5r. blue and violet	95·00	48·00
O14		10r. green and red	£275	£130

1939. Stamps of 1938 optd **SERVICE**.

No.	Type	Description	Unused	Used
O15	2	3p. violet	15	20
O16		6p. blue	15	20
O17		9p. green	4·00	3·25
O18	3	1a. brown	15	15
O19		1½a. green	3·50	1·75
O20		2a. red	1·25	20
O21	4	2a.6p. red	15·00	13·00
O22	3	4a. blue	4·50	45
O23	–	8a. green (No. 29)	15·00	4·00
O24	8	1r. purple and blue	25·00	5·50
O25		2r. brown and purple	30·00	15·00
O26	–	5r. violet and red (No. 32)	25·00	29·00
O27	–	10r. brown and green (No. 33)	£120	38 00

1946. Stamps of 1946 optd **SERVICE**.

No.	Type	Description	Unused	Used
O28	2	3p. brown	1·75	3·25
O29		6p. violet	1·75	2·25
O30		9p. green	30	3·25
O31	3	1a. blue	20	2·00
O32		1½a. orange	20	20
O33		2a. red	20	2·00
O34	4	2a.6p. blue	1·60	6·00
O35	3	4a. purple	20	70
O36	–	8a. mauve (No. 59)	3·00	3·50
O37	8	1r. violet and mauve	60	4·00
O38		2r. brown and orange	7·50	42·00
O39	–	5r. green and brown (No. 62)	9·00	48·00
O40	–	10r. red and violet (No. 63)	17·00	55·00

1947. Interim Government. Nos. O28 etc., optd with T **18** or with large overprint on larger stamps.

No.	Type	Description	Unused	Used
O41	2	3p. brown	30	40
O42		6p. violet	1·75	10
O43		9p. green	2·50	90
O44	3	1a. blue	2·75	80
O45		1½a. orange	5·00	30
O46		2a. red	2·75	15
O47	4	2a.6p. blue	26·00	12·00
O48	3	4a. purple	11·00	40
O49	–	8a. mauve	10·00	4·00
O50	8	1r. violet and mauve	14·00	2·25
O51		2r. brown and orange	14·00	20·00
O52	–	5r. green and brown	14·00	20·00
O53	–	10r. red and violet	14·00	30·00

အစိုးရကိစ္စ

(O 29) (size of opt varies)

1949. 1st Anniv of Independence. Nos. 100/4 and 107/113 optd as Type O **29**.

No.	Type	Description	Unused	Used
O114	22	3p. blue	40	10
O115	–	6p. green	10	15
O116	–	9p. red	10	15
O117	25	1a. red	10	15
O118	–	2a. orange	15	15
O119	–	3a.6p. green	15	15
O120	–	4a. brown	15	15
O121	–	8a. red	15	15
O122	28	1r. green	40	25
O123		2r. blue	65	45
O124		5r. brown	2·25	1·50
O125		10r. orange	5·00	3·75

1954. Nos. 137/40 and 142/50 optd as Type O **29**.

No.	Type	Description	Unused	Used
O151	22	1p. orange	10	10
O152	–	2p. purple	10	10
O153	–	3p. blue	10	10
O154	25	5p. blue	10	10
O155	–	15p. green	10	10
O156	–	20p. red	15	10
O157	–	25p. orange	15	10
O158	–	30p. red	15	10
O159	–	50p. blue	25	20
O160	28	1k. violet	45	20
O161		2k. green	1·25	35
O162		5k. blue	2·50	90
O163		10k. blue	6·00	2·50

1964. No. 139 optd **Service**.

No.	Type	Description	Unused	Used
O174	–	3p. blue	9·50	6·50

1965. Nos. 174/7 and 179/85 optd as Type O **29**.

No.	Type	Description	Unused	Used
O196	40	1p. black	20	15
O197		2p. red	30	25
O198		3p. green	30	25
O199	–	5p. blue	35	30
O200	–	15p. green	35	30
O201	–	20p. brown and red	65	60
O202	–	25p. brown and yellow	70	65
O203	–	50p. blue and red	1·25	80
O204	–	1k. blue, yellow & grey	3·50	1·90
O205	–	2k. blue, green & red	4·75	1·75
O206	–	5k. multicoloured	14·00	12·00

1968. Nos. 195/8 and 200/6 optd as Type O **29**.

No.	Type	Description	Unused	Used
O207		1p. black	20	15
O208		2p. red	25	20
O209		3p. green	30	25
O210		5p. blue	30	25
O211		15p. green	30	25
O212		20p. brown and red	40	30
O213		25p. brown and yellow	30	25
O214		50p. blue and red	30	25
O215		1k. blue, yellow and grey	1·75	45
O216		2k. blue, green and red	3·50	1·10
O217		5k. multicoloured	5·00	4·50

For later issues see **MYANMAR**.

JAPANESE OCCUPATION OF BURMA

1942. 12 pies = 1 anna; 16 annas = 1 rupee.
1942. 100 cents = 1 rupee.

(1)

(3)

Note.—There are various types of the Peacock overprint. Our prices, as usual in this Catalogue, are for the cheapest type.

1942. Postage stamps of Burma of 1937 (India types) optd as T **1**.
J22 **55** 3p. grey . . . . 3·25 19·00
J23 **80** 9p. green . . . . 23·00 65·00
J24 **59** 2a. red £100 £180
J 2 **83** 3½a. blue . . . . 55·00

1942. Official stamp of Burma of 1937 (India type) optd as T **1**.
J3 **64** 6a. bistre . . . . 75·00

1942. Postage stamps of Burma, 1938, optd as T **1** or with T **3** (rupee values).
J25 **1** 1p. orange £190 £300
J12 3p. violet . . . . 18·00 70·00
J27 6p. blue . . . . 25·00 50·00
J14 9p. green . . . . 20·00 65·00
J29 **3** 1a. brown . . . . 9·00 40·00
J30 1½a. green . . . . 21·00 65·00
J16 2a. red . . . . 20·00 80·00
J17 4a. blue . . . . 38·00 £100
J18 **8** 1r. purple and blue £275
J19 2r. brown and purple . . . £160

1942. Official stamps of Burma of 1939 optd with T **1**.
J 7 **1** 3p. violet . . . . 25·00 85·00
J 8 6p. blue . . . . 17·00 16·00
J 9 **3** 1a. brown . . . . 17·00 15·00
J35 1½a. green £170 £300
J10 2a. red . . . . 23·00 95·00
J11 4a. blue . . . . 23·00 75·00

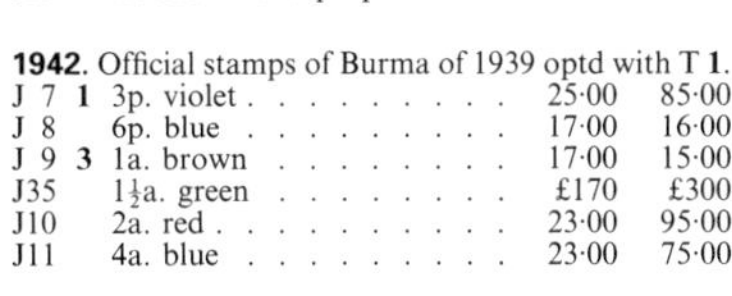

(**6a**) ("Yon Thon" = "Office Use")

1942. Official stamp of Burma of 1939 optd with T **6a**.
J44 8a. green (No. O23) . . . . 90·00

7

8 Farmer

1942. Yano Seal.
J45 **7** (1a.) red . . . . 38·00 65·00

1942.
J46 **8** 1a. red . . . . 16·00 16·00

1942. Stamps of Japan surch in annas or rupees.
J47 – ¼a. on 1s. brown (No. 314) 27·00 32·00
J48 **83** ¼a. on 2s. red . . . . . . 32·00 35·00
J49 – ¾ a on 3s. green (No. 316) 60·00 65·00
J50 – 1a. on 5s. purple (No. 396) 48·00 45·00
J51 – 3a. on 7s. green (No. 320) 90·00 £100
J52 – 4a. on 4s. green (No. 317) 45·00 48·00
J53 – 8a. on 8s. violet (No. 321) £150 £150
J54 – 1r. on 10s. red (No. 322) 18·00 24·00
J55 – 2r. on 20s. blue (No. 325) 50·00 50·00
J56 – 5r. on 30s. blue (No. 327) 12·00 27·00

1942. No. 386 of Japan commemorating the fall of Singapore, surch in figures.
J56g – 4a. on 4s.+2s. green and red £150 £160

1942. Handstamped **5 C.**
J57 **5** 5c. on 1a. red (No. J46) . . 13·00 17·00

1942. Nos. J47/53 with anna surcharges obliterated, and handstamped with new values in figures.
J58 – 1c. on ¼a. on 1s. brown . . 48·00 48·00
J59 **84** 2c. on ¼a. on 2s. red . . . 45·00 50·00
J60 – 3c. on ¾a. on 3s. green . . 50·00 50·00
J61 – 5c. on 1a. on 5s. red . . . 65·00 65·00
J62 – 10c. on 3a. on 7s. green . . £110 £100
J63 – 15c. on 4a. on 4s. green . . 35·00 38·00
J64 – 20c. on 8a. on 8s. violet . . £450 £400

1942. Stamps of Japan surch in cents.
J65 – 1c. on 1s. brown (No. 314) 22·00 20·00
J66 **83** 2c. on 2s. red . . . . . . 45·00 32·00
J67 – 3c. on 3s. green (No. 316) 55·00 48·00
J68 – 5c. on 5s. purple (No. 396) 60·00 45·00
J69 – 10c. on 7s. green (No. 320) 75·00 60·00
J70 – 15c. on 4s. green (No. 317) 17·00 20·00
J71 – 20c. on 8s. violet (No. 321) £160 85·00

14 Burma State Crest

15 Farmer

1943. Perf or imperf.
J72 **14** 5c. red . . . . 18·00 22·00

1943.
J73a **15** 1c. orange . . . . 2·00 4·50
J74 2c. green . . . . 60 1·00
J75 3c. blue . . . . 2·50 1·00
J77 5c. red . . . . 2·75 1·75
J78 10c. brown . . . . 5·00 4·25
J79 15c. mauve . . . . 30 1·75
J80 20c. lilac 30 80
J81 30c. green . . . . 30 1·00

16 Soldier carving word "Independence"

17 Rejoicing Peasant

18 Boy with National Flag

1943. Independence Day. Perf or roul.
J85 **16** 1c. orange . . . . 1·00 1·75
J86 **17** 3c. blue . . . . 2·00 2·25
J87 **18** 5c. red . . . . 1·75 2·25

19 Burmese Woman

20 Elephant carrying Log

21 Watch Tower Mandalay

1943.
J88 **19** 1c. orange . . . . 28·00 15·00
J89 2c. green . . . . 50 2·00
J90 3c. violet . . . . 50 2·25
J91 **20** 5c. red 55 60
J92 10c. blue . . . . 1·50 1·10
J93 15c. orange . . . . 75 2·75
J94 20c. green . . . . 75 1·75
J95 30c. brown . . . . 75 1·75
J96 **21** 1r. orange . . . . 30 2·00
J97 2r. violet . . . . 30 2·25

22 Bullock Cart

23 Shan Woman

1943. Shan States issue.
J 98 **22** 1c. brown . . . . 27·00 35·00
J 99 2c. green . . . . 27·00 35·00
J100 3c. violet . . . . 3·75 10·00
J101 5c. blue . . . . 2·00 5·50
J102 **23** 10c. blue . . . . 13·00 17·00
J103 20c. red . . . . 28·00 17·00
J104 30c. brown . . . . 17·00 45·00

ဗမာနိုင်ငံတော်

၂၀ ဆင့်။

(**24** "Burma State" and value)

1944. Optd with T **24**.
J105 **22** 1c. brown . . . . 3·50 6·00
J106 2c. green . . . . 50 2·50
J107 3c. violet . . . . 2·25 7·00
J108 5c. blue . . . . 1·00 1·50
J109 **23** 10c. blue . . . . 3·25 2·00
J110 20c. red . . . . 50 1·50
J111 30c. brown . . . . 50 1·75

BURUNDI Pt. 12

Once part of the Belgian territory, Ruanda-Urundi. Independent on 1 July 1962, when a monarchy was established. After a revolution in 1967 Burundi became a republic.

100 centimes = 1 franc.

1962. Stamps of Ruanda-Urundi optd **Royaume du Burundi** and bar or surch also. (a) Flowers. (Nos. 178, etc.).
1 25c. multicoloured 25 20
2 40c. multicoloured 25 20
3 60c. multicoloured 35 35
4 1f.25 multicoloured . . . . . . 16·00 16·00
5 1f.50 multicoloured 60 60
6 5f. multicoloured . . . . . . 1·10 90
7 7f. multicoloured . . . . . . 1·75 1·40
8 10f. multicoloured . . . . . . 2·50 2·25

(b) Animals (Nos. 203/14).
9 10c. black, red and brown . . 10 10
10 20c. black and green 10 10
11 40c. black, olive and mauve 10 10
12 50c. brown, yellow & green 10 10
13 1f. black, blue and brown . . 10 10
14 1f.50 black and orange . . . 10 10
15 2f. black, brown and turq . . 10 10
16 3f. black, red and brown . . 10 10
17 3f.50 on 3f. black, red & brn 10 10
18a 4f. on 10f. multicoloured . . 20 20
19 5f. multicoloured 20 20
20 6f.50 brown, yellow and red 20 20
21 8f. black, mauve and blue . . 35 25
23 10f. multicoloured 50 30

(c) Animals (Nos. 229/30).
24 **25** 20f. multicoloured . . . . . 1·60 60
25 – 50f. multicoloured . . . . . 1·90 1·10

10 King Mwambutsa IV and Royal Drummers

1962. Independence. Inscr "1.7.1962".
26 **10** 50c. sepia and lake 10 10
27 A 1f. green, red & deep green 10 10
28 B 2f. sepia and olive 10 10
29 **10** 3f. sepia and red 10 10
30 A 4f. green, red and blue . . 15 10
31 B 8f. sepia and violet 30 15
32 **10** 10f. sepia and green 40 15
33 A 20f. green, red and sepia . . 45 20
34 B 50f. sepia and mauve . . . 1·25 45
DESIGNS—VERT: A, Burundi flag and arms. HORIZ: B, King and outline map of Burundi.

1962. Dag Hammarskjold Commem. No. 222 of Ruanda-Urundi surch **HOMMAGE A DAG HAMMARSKJOLD ROYAUME DU BURUNDI** and new value. U.N. emblem and wavy pattern at foot. Inscr in French or Flemish.
35 3f.50 on 3f. salmon and blue 35 35
36 6f.50 on 3f. salmon and blue 65 45
37 10f. on 3f. salmon and blue . . 1·25 1·10

1962. Malaria Eradication. As Nos. 31 and 34 but colours changed and with campaign emblem superimposed on map.
38 B 8f. sepia, turquoise & bistre 55 35
39 50f. sepia, turquoise & olive 1·40 35

12 Prince Louis Rwagasore

13 "Sowing"

1963. Prince Rwagasore Memorial and Stadium Fund.
40 **12** 50c.+25c. violet 10 10
41 – 1f.+50c. blue and orange . . 10 10
42 – 1f.50+75c. vio & bistre . . . 10 10
43 **12** 3f.50+1f.50 mauve 20 10
44 – 5f.+2f. blue and pink . . . 20 10
45 – 6f.50+3f. violet & olive . . 25 10
DESIGNS—HORIZ: 1f., 5f. Prince and stadium; 1f.50, 6f.50 Prince and memorial.

1963. Freedom from Hunger.
46 **13** 4f. purple and olive 15 15
47 8f. purple and olive 20 15
48 15f. purple and green 35 15

1963. "Peaceful Uses of Outer Space" Nos. 28 and 34 optd **UTILISATIONS PACIFIQUES DE L'ESPACE** around globe encircled by rocket.
49 B 2f. sepia and olive . . . . . 2·25 2·25
50 50f. sepia and mauve . . . . 3·50 3·50

1963. 1st Anniv of Independence. Nos. 30/3 but with colours changed and optd **Premier Anniversaire**.
51 A 4f. green, red and olive . . 20 10
52 B 8f. sepia and orange 30 10
53 **10** 10f. sepia and mauve . . . 40 20
54 A 20f. green, red and grey . . 90 30

1963. Nos. 27 and 33 surch.
55 A 6f.50 on 1f. green, red and deep green 55 10
56 15f. on 20f. grn, red & sepia 85 35

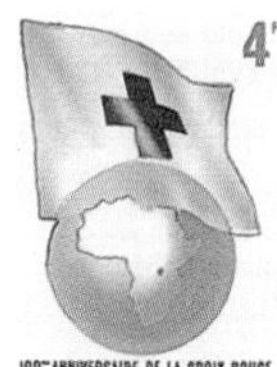

17 Globe and Red Cross Flag

1963. Centenary of Red Cross.
57 **17** 4f. green, red and grey . . . 20 10
58 8f. brown, red and grey . . 40 20
59 10f. blue, red and grey . . . 50 20
60 20f. violet, red and grey . . 1·10 40

IMPERF STAMPS. Many Burundi stamps from No. 61 onwards exist imperf from limited printings and/or miniature sheets.

18 "1962" and U.N.E.S.C.O. Emblem

1963. 1st Anniv of Admission to U.N.O. Emblems and values in black.
61 **18** 4f. olive and yellow 15 10
62 – 8f. blue and lilac 25 10
63 – 10f. violet and blue 40 10
64 – 20f. green and yellow . . . 65 20
65 – 50f. brown and ochre . . . 1·75 35
EMBLEMS: 8f. I.T.U.; 10f. W.M.O.; 20f. U.P.U.; 50f. F.A.O.

19 U.N.E.S.C.O. Emblem and Scales of Justice

1963. 15th Anniv of Declaration of Human Rights.
66 **19** 50c. blk, blue and pink . . 10 10
67 – 1f.50 black, blue & orange 10 10
68 – 3f.50 black, green & brown 15 10
69 – 6f.50 black, green and lilac 25 10
70 – 10f. black, bistre and blue 40 15
71 – 20f. multicoloured 70 25
DESIGNS: 3f.50, 6f.50, Scroll; 10f., 20f. Lincoln.

20 Ice-hockey

22 Burundi Dancer

21 Hippopotamus

1964. Winter Olympic Games, Innsbruck.
72 **20** 50c. black, gold and olive 15 10
73 – 3f.50 black, gold & brown 20 10
74 – 6f.50 black, gold and grey 45 20
75 – 10f. black, gold and grey 90 35
76 – 20f. black, gold and bistre 2·10 65
DESIGNS: 3f.50, Figure-skating; 6f.50, Olympic flame; 10f. Speed-skating; 20f. Skiing (slalom).

1964. Burundi Animals. Multicoloured. (i) Postage. (a) Size as T **21**.
77 50c. Impala 10 10
78 1f. Type **21** 10 10
79 1f.50 Giraffe 10 10
80 2f. African buffalo 20 10
81 3f. Common zebra 20 10
82 3f.50 Waterbuck 20 10

(b) Size 16 × 42½ mm or 42½ × 26 mm.
83 4f. Impala 25 10
84 5f. Hippopotamus 30 10
85 6f.50 Common zebra 30 10
86 8f. African buffalo 55 20
87 10f. Giraffe 60 20
88 15f. Waterbuck 85 30

(c) Size 53½ × 33½ mm.
89 20f. Cheetah 1·50 40
90 50f. African elephant 4·00 65
91 100f. Lion 6·50 1·10

(ii) Air. Inscr "POSTE AERIENNE" and optd with gold border. (a) Size 26 × 42½ mm or 42½ × 26 mm.
92 6f. Common zebra 35 10
93 8f. African buffalo 60 10
94 10f. Impala 70 10
95 14f. Hippopotamus 85 15
96 15f. Waterbuck 1·40 35

(b) Size 53½ × 33½ mm.
97 20f. Cheetah 1·75 40
98 50f. African elephant 4·00 90
The impala, giraffe and waterbuck stamps are all vert. designs, and the remainder are horiz.

1964. World's Fair, New York (1st series). Gold backgrounds.
99 **22** 50c. multicoloured 10 10
100 – 1f. multicoloured 10 10
101 – 4f. multicoloured 15 10
102 – 6f.50 multicoloured 20 10
103 – 10f. multicoloured 40 15
104 – 15f. multicoloured 70 20
105 – 20f. multicoloured 90 30
DESIGNS: 1f. to 20f. Various dancers and drummers as Type **22**.
See also Nos. 175/81.

23 Pope Paul and King Mwambutsa IV

1964. Canonization of 22 African Martyrs. Inscriptions in gold.
106 **23** 50c. lake and blue 15 10
107 – 1f. blue and purple 15 10
108 – 4f. sepia and mauve 25 10
109 – 8f. brown and red 40 15
110 – 14f. brown and turquoise 40 20
111 **23** 20f. green and red 65 40
DESIGNS—VERT: 1f., 8f. Group of martyrs. HORIZ: 4f., 14f., Pope John XXIII and King Mwambutsa IV.

24 Putting the Shot

1964. Olympic Games, Tokyo. Inscr "TOKYO 1964". Multicoloured.
112 50c. Type **24** 10 10
113 1f. Throwing the discus 10 10
114 3f. Swimming (horiz) 10 10
115 4f. Relay-racing 10 10
116 6f.50 Throwing the javelin 30 20
117 8f. Hurdling (horiz) 35 20
118 10f. Long-jumping (horiz) 40 20
119 14f. High-diving 55 20
120 18f. High-jumping (horiz) 65 35
121 20f. Gymnastics (horiz) 85 35

25 Scientist, Map and Emblem

1965. Anti-T.B. Campaign. Country name, values and Lorraine Cross in red.
122 **25** 2f.+50c. sepia and drab 10 10
123 4f.+1f.50 green & pink 25 10
124 5f.+2f.50 violet & buff 30 15
125 8f.+3f. blue and grey 40 20
126 10f.+5f. red and green 55 30

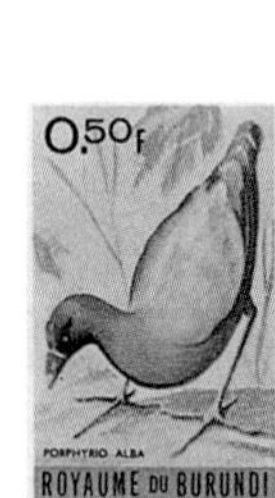

26 Purple Swamphen

27 "Relay" Satellite and Telegraph Key

1965. Birds. Multicoloured. (i) Postage. (a) Size as T **26**.
127 50c. Type **26** 10 10
128 1f. Little bee eater 10 10
129 1f.50 Secretary bird 10 10
130 2f. Painted stork 20 10
131 3f. Congo peafowl 25 10
132 3f.50 African darter 30 10

(b) Size 26 × 42½ mm.
133 4f. Type **26** 40 10
134 5f. Little bee eater 50 15
135 6f.50 Secretary bird 60 15
136 8f. Painted stork 60 15
137 10f. Congo peafowl 70 15
138 15f. African darter 85 25

(c) Size 33½ × 53 mm.
139 20f. Saddle-bill stork 1·25 25
140 50f. Abyssinian ground hornbill 2·40 50
141 100f. South African crowned crane 4·00 90

(ii) Air. Inscr "POSTE AERIENNE". Optd with gold border. (a) Size 26 × 42½ mm.
142 6f. Secretary bird 50 10
143 8f. African darter 60 15
144 10f. Congo peafowl 70 15
145 14f. Little bee eater 75 20
146 15f. Painted stork 85 20

(b) Size 33½ × 53 mm.
147 20f. Saddle-bill stork 1·25 30
148 50f. Abyssinian ground hornbill 2·25 80
149 75f. Martial eagle 2·50 1·00
150 130f. Lesser flamingo 4·75 1·60

1965. Centenary of I.T.U. Multicoloured.
151 1f. Type **27** 10 10
152 3f. "Telstar 1" and hand telephone 10 10
153 4f. "Lunik 3" and wall telephone 10 10
154 6f.50 Weather satellite and tracking station 15 10
155 8f. "Telstar 2" and headphones 15 15
156 10f. "Sputnik" and radar scanner 20 15
157 14f. "Syncom" and aerial 30 20
158 20f. "Pioneer 5" space probe and radio aerial 35 30

28 Arms (reverse of 10f. coin)

1965. 1st Independence Anniv Gold Coinage Commem. Circular designs on gold foil, backed with multicoloured patterned paper. Imperf. (i) Postage. (a) 10f. coin. Diameter 1½ in.
159 **28** 2f.+50c. red & yellow 15 15
160 – 4f.+50c. blue & red 20 20

(b) 25f. coin. Diameter 1¾ in.
161 **28** 6f.+50c. orange & grey 50 30
162 – 8f.+50c. blue & purple 60 60

(c) 50f. coin. Diameter 2¼ in.
163 **28** 12f.+50c. green & purple 60 60
164 – 15f.+50c. green & lilac 65 65

(d) 100f. coin. Diameter 2⅝ in.
165 **28** 25f.+50c. blue and flesh 1·25 1·25
166 – 40f.+50c. mauve & brn 1·75 1·75

(ii) Air. (a) 10f. coin. Diameter 1½ in.
167 **28** 3f.+1f. violet & lavender 30 30
168 – 5f.+1f. red & turquoise 40 40

(b) 25f. coin. Diameter 1¾ in.
169 **28** 11f.+1f. purple & yellow 60 60
170 – 14f.+1f. green and red 60 60

(c) 50f. coin. Diameter 2¼ in.
171 **28** 20f.+1f. black and blue 85 85
172 – 30f.+1f. red and orange 1·10 1·10

(d) 100f. coin. Diameter 2⅝ in.
173 **28** 50f.+1f. violet and blue 1·25 1·25
174 – 100f.+1f. purple & mve 3·00 3·00
DESIGNS: The 4, 5, 8, 14, 15, 30, 40 and 100f. each show the obverse side of the coin (King Mwambutsa IV).

1965. Worlds Fair, New York (2nd series). As Nos. 99/105, but with silver backgrounds.
175 **22** 50c. multicoloured 10 10
176 – 1f. multicoloured 10 10
177 – 4f. multicoloured 15 10
178 – 6f.50 multicoloured 25 10
179 – 10f. multicoloured 45 20
180 – 15f. multicoloured 55 30
181 – 20f. multicoloured 70 35

29 Globe and I.C.Y. Emblem

1965. International Co-operation Year. Mult.
182 1f. Type **29** 10 10
183 4f. Map of Africa and cogwheel emblem of U.N. Science and Technology Conference 15 10
184 8f. Map of South-East Asia and Colombo Plan emblem 20 10
185 10f. Globe and U.N. emblem 25 10
186 18f. Map of Americas and "Alliance for Progress" emblem 40 10
187 25f. Map of Europe and C.E.P.T. emblems 60 30
188 40f. Space map and satellite (U.N.—"Peaceful Uses of Outer Space") 1·00 50

30 Prince Rwagasore and Memorial

1966. Prince Rwagasore and Pres. Kennedy Commemoration.
189 **30** 4f.+1f. brown and blue 20 10
190 – 10f.+1f. blue, brn & grn 30 10
191 – 20f.+2f. green and lilac 65 15
192 – 40f.+2f. brown & green 75 30
DESIGNS—HORIZ: 10f. Prince Rwagasore and Pres. Kennedy; 20f. Pres. Kennedy and memorial library. VERT: 40f. King Mwambutsa at Pres. Kennedy's grave.

31 Protea

1966. Flowers. Multicoloured. (i) Postage. (a) Size as T **31**.
194 50c. Type **31** 15 10
195 1f. Crossandra 15 10
196 1f.50 Ansellia 15 10
197 2f. Thunbergia 15 10
198 3f. Schizoglossum 25 10
199 3f.50 Dissotis 25 10

(b) Size 41 × 41 mm.
200 4f. Type **31** 25 10
201 5f. Crossandra 35 10
202 6f.50 Ansellia 45 10
203 8f. Thunbergia 65 10
204 10f. Schizoglossum 70 10
205 15f. Dissotis 85 10

(c) Size 50 × 50 mm.
206 20f. Type **31** 1·10 15
207 50f. Gazania 2·50 35
208 100f. Hibiscus 4·00 55
209 150f. Markhamia 6·25 75

(ii) Air. (a) Size 41 × 41 mm.
210 6f. Dissotis 25 15
211 8f. Crossandra 35 15
212 10f. Ansellia 35 15
213 14f. Thunbergia 40 15
214 15f. Schizoglossum 40 15

(b) Size 50 × 50 mm.
215 20f. Gazania 65 20
216 50f. Type **31** 1·75 40
217 75f. Hibiscus 2·50 1·00
218 130f. Markhamia 3·75 1·40

1967. Various stamps optd. (i) Nos. 127, etc. (Birds) optd **REPUBLIQUE DU BURUNDI** and bar. (a) Postage.
221 50c. multicoloured 1·60 25
222 1f.50 multicoloured 35 25
223 3f.50 multicoloured 45 35
224 5f. multicoloured 60 45
225 6f.50 multicoloured 60 65
226 8f. multicoloured 70 80
227 10f. multicoloured 80 80
228 15f. multicoloured 1·10 1·25
229 20f. multicoloured 2·75 1·75
230 50f. multicoloured 5·25 3·75
231 100f. multicoloured 8·50 7·00

(b) Air.
232 6f. multicoloured 55 25
233 8f. multicoloured 70 40
234 10f. multicoloured 85 65
235 14f. multicoloured 1·10 65
236 15f. multicoloured 1·25 80
237 20f. multicoloured 1·75 95
238 50f. multicoloured 6·25 2·75
239 75f. multicoloured 8·50 3·50
240 130f. multicoloured 12·00 5·75

(ii) Nos. 194, etc. (Flowers) optd as Nos. 221, etc., but with two bars. (a) Postage.
241 50c. multicoloured 15 15
242 1f. multicoloured 15 15
243 1f.50 multicoloured 15 15
244 2f. multicoloured 15 15
245 3f. multicoloured 20 15
246 3f.50 multicoloured 30 15
247 4f. multicoloured 1·90 15
248 5f. multicoloured 50 20
249 6f.50 multicoloured 45 30
250 8f. multicoloured 45 30
251 10f. multicoloured 60 40
252 15f. multicoloured 75 45
253 50f. multicoloured 3·75 65
254 100f. multicoloured 9·00 2·50
255 150f. multicoloured 8·50 9·25

(b) Air.
256 6f. multicoloured 20 15
257 8f. multicoloured 30 15
258 10f. multicoloured 35 15
259 14f. multicoloured 45 30
260 15f. multicoloured 55 30
261 20f. multicoloured 1·75 40
262 50f. multicoloured 3·75 65
263 75f. multicoloured 5·75 90
264 130f. multicoloured 5·75 1·50

35 Sir Winston Churchill and St. Paul's Cathedral

1967. Churchill Commemoration.
265 **35** 4f.+1f. multicoloured 30 10
266 – 15f.+2f. multicoloured 50 25
267 – 20f.+3f. multicoloured 60 35
DESIGNS (Churchill and): 15f. Tower of London; 20f. Big Ben and Boadicea statue, Westminster.

36 Egyptian Mouthbrooder

1967. Fishes. Multicoloured. (a) Postage. (i) Size as T **36**.
269 50c. Type **36** 15 20
270 1f. Spotted climbing-perch 15 20
271 1f.50 Six-banded lyretail 15 20
272 2f. Congo tetra 15 20
273 3f. Jewel cichlid 15 20
274 3f.50 Spotted mouthbrooder 15 20

(ii) Size 53½ × 27 mm.
275 4f. Type **36** 50 20
276 5f. As 1f. 50 20
277 6f.50. As 1f.50 65 20
278 8f. As 2f. 65 20

279 10f. As 3f. . . . . 1·00 20
280 15f. As 3f.50 . . . . 1·10 20

(iii) Size 63½ × 31½ mm.

281 20f. Type **36** . . . . 1·90 30
282 50f. Dusky snakehead . . . 3·50 50
283 100f. Red-tailed notho . . . 7·50 75
284 150f. African tetra . . . . . 7·50 1·10

(b) Air. (i) Size 50 × 23 mm.

285 6f. Type **36** 30 20
286 8f. As 1f. 45 20
287 10f. As 1f.50 . . . . 55 20
288 14f. As 2f. 65 20
289 15f. As 3f. 80 20

(ii) Size 59 × 27 mm.

290 20f. As 3f.50 . . . . 95 20
291 50f. As 50f. (No. 282) . . . . 4·75 30
292 75f. As 100f. . . . . 6·00 50
293 130f. As 150f. . . . . 11·00 1·00

37 Baule Ancestral Figures

1967. "African Art". Multicoloured.

294 50c. Type **37** (postage) . . . 10 10
295 1f. "Master of Buli's" carved seat 10 10
296 1f.50 Karumba antelope's head 10 10
297 2f. Bobo buffalo's head . . . 10 10
298 4f. Guma-Goffa funeral figures 15 10
299 10f. Bakoutou "spirit" (carving) (air) 30 20
300 14f. Bamum sultan's throne 40 20
301 17f. Bebin bronze head . . . 45 20
302 24f. Statue of 109th Bakouba king 55 30
303 26f. Burundi basketwork and lances 60 35

1967. 50th Anniv of Lions International. Nos. 265/7 optd **1917 1967** and emblem.

304 4f.+1f. multicoloured 50 20
305 15f.+2f. multicoloured . . . 80 35
306 20f.+3f. multicoloured . . . 95 35

39 Lord Baden-Powell (founder)

1967. 60th Anniv of Scout Movement and World Scout Jamboree, Idaho.

308 50c. Scouts climbing (postage) 20 10
309 1f. Scouts preparing meal . . 20 10
310 1f.50 Type **39** 20 10
311 2f. Two scouts 20 10
312 4f. Giving first aid 30 10
313 10f. As 50c. (air) 60 15
314 14f. As 1f. 70 15
315 17f. Type **39** 85 15
316 24f. As 2f. . . . . 1·10 35
317 26f. As 4f. . . . . 1·25 40

40 "The Gleaners" (Millet)

1967. World Fair, Montreal. Multicoloured.

318 4f. Type **40** 15 10
319 8f. "The Water-carrier of Seville" (Velasquez) 15 10
320 14f. "The Triumph of Neptune and Amphitrite" (Poussin) 35 15
321 18f. "Acrobat with a ball" (Picasso) 35 15
322 25f. "Margaret van Eyck" (Van Eyck) 95 25
323 40f. "St. Peter denying Christ" (Rembrandt) . . . 1·10 50

41 Boeing 707

1967. Air. Opening of Bujumbura Airport. Aircraft and inscr in black and silver.

325 **41** 10f. green 40 10
326 – 14f. yellow 65 20
327 – 17f. blue 95 20
328 – 26f. purple . . . . 1·60 30

AIRCRAFT: 14f. Boeing 727 over lakes. 17f. Vickers Super VC-10 over lake. 26f. Boeing 727 over Bujumbura Airport.

42 Pres. Micombero and Flag

1967. 1st Anniv of Republic. Multicoloured.

329 5f. Type **42** 25 10
330 14f. Memorial and Arms . . 35 15
331 20f. View of Bujumbura and Arms 50 20
332 30f. "Place de la Revolution" and President Micombero 90 30

43 "The Adoration of the Shepherds" (J. B. Mayno)

1967. Christmas. Religious Paintings. Mult.

333 1f. Type **43** 10 10
334 4f. "The Holy Family" (A. van Dyck) 15 10
335 14f. "The Nativity" (Maitre de Moulins) 40 20
336 26f. "Madonna and Child" (C. Crivelli) 75 30

45 Downhill Skiing

1968. Winter Olympic Games, Grenoble. Mult.

339 5f. Type **45** 20 10
340 10f. Ice-hockey 25 10
341 14f. Figure-skating 40 10
342 17f. Bobsleighing 50 10
343 26f. Ski-jumping 65 10
344 40f. Speed-skating . . . . . 1·10 25
345 60f. Olympic torch . . . . . 1·75 30

46 "Portrait of a Young Man" (Botticelli)

1968. Famous Paintings. Multicoloured.

347 1f.50 Type **46** (postage) . . . 10 10
348 2f. "La Maja Vestida" (Goya) (horiz) 10 10
349 4f. "The Lacemaker" (Vermeer) 15 10
350 17f. "Woman and Cat" (Renoir) (air) 40 20
351 24f. "The Jewish Bride" (Rembrandt) (horiz) . . . 55 30
352 26f. "Pope Innocent X" (Velasquez) 80 40

47 Module landing on Moon

1968. Space Exploration. Multicoloured.

353 4f. Type **47** (postage) 20 10
354 6f. Russian cosmonaut in Space 30 10
355 8f. Weather satellite 30 10
356 10f. American astronaut in Space 45 15
357 14f. Type **47** (air) 40 15
358 18f. As 6f. 50 15
359 25f. As 8f. 80 25
360 40f. As 10f. . . . . 1·10 40

48 "Salamis aethiops"

1968. Butterflies. Multicoloured. (a) Postage. (i) Size 30½ × 34 mm.

362 50c. Type **48** 15 15
363 1f. "Graphium ridleyanus" . . 20 15
364 1f.50 "Cymothoe" 25 15
365 2f. "Charaxes eupale" . . . 35 15
366 3f. "Papilio bromius" 40 15
367 3f.50 "Teracolus annae" . . . 50 15

(ii) Size 34 × 38 mm.

368 4f. Type **48** 50 15
369 5f. As 1f. 50 15
370 6f.50 As 1f.50 . . . . 60 15
371 8f. As 2f. 90 20
372 10f. As 3f. . . . . 1·10 20
373 15f. As 3f.50 . . . . 1·40 25

(iii) Size 41 × 46 mm.

374 20f. Type **48** . . . . 2·50 30
375 50f. "Papilio zenobia" . . . 4·50 75
376 100f. "Danais chrysippus" . . 8·25 1·25
377 150f. "Salamis temora" . . . 14·00 2·10

(b) Air. With gold frames. (i) Size 33 × 37 mm.

378 6f. As 3f.50 . . . . 50 15
379 8f. As 1f. 55 15
380 10f. As 1f.50 . . . . 60 15
381 14f. As 2f. 70 20
382 15f. As 3f. . . . . 1·00 20

(ii) Size 39 × 44 mm.

383 20f. As 50f. (No. 375) . . . . 2·40 25
384 50f. Type **48** . . . . 5·50 50
385 75f. As 100f. . . . . 6·75 90
386 130f. As 150f. . . . . 12·50 1·10

49 "Woman by the Manzanares" (Goya)

1968. International Letter-writing Week. Mult.

387 4f. Type **49** (postage) 25 10
388 7f. "Reading a Letter" (De Hooch) 35 10
389 11f. "Woman reading a Letter" (Terborch) 40 10
390 14f. "Man writing a Letter" (Metsu) 45 10
391 17f. "The Letter" (Fragonard) (air) 60 10
392 26f. "Young Woman reading Letter" (Vermeer) 80 20
393 40f. "Folding a Letter" (Vigee-Lebrun) 90 25
394 50f. "Mademoiselle Lavergne" (Liotard) . . . 95 35

50 Football

1968. Olympic Games, Mexico. Multicoloured.

396 4f. Type **50** (postage) 25 10
397 7f. Basketball 30 10
398 13f. High jumping 35 10
399 24f. Relay racing 55 20
400 40f. Throwing the javelin . . 1·25 40
401 10f. Putting the shot (air) . . 25 15
402 17f. Running 45 15
403 26f. Throwing the hammer . . 70 25
404 50f. Hurdling . . . . 1·40 45
405 75f. Long jumping . . . . . 2·25 60

51 "Virgin and Child" (Lippi)

1968. Christmas. Paintings. Multicoloured.

407 3f. Type **51** (postage) 20 10
408 5f. "The Magnificat" (Botticelli) 25 10
409 6f. "Virgin and Child" (Durer) 40 10
410 11f. "Virgin and Child" (Raphael) 40 10
411 10f. "Madonna" (Correggio) (air) 25 10
412 14f. "The Nativity" (Baroccio) 35 15
413 17f. "The Holy Family" (El Greco) 55 20
414 26f. "Adoration of the Magi" (Maino) 75 35

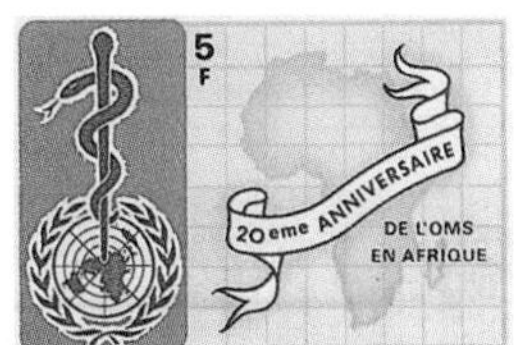

52 W.H.O. Emblem and Map

1969. 20th Anniv of World Health Organization Operation in Africa.

416 **52** 5f. multicoloured 15 10
417 6f. multicoloured 20 10
418 11f. multicoloured 25 15

53 Hand holding Flame

1969. Air. Human Rights Year.
419 **53** 10f. multicoloured 35 10
420 14f. multicoloured 45 10
421 26f. multicoloured 65 25

1969. Space Flight of "Apollo 8". Nos. 407/14 optd ***VOL DE NOEL APOLLO 8*** and space module.
422 3f. multicoloured (postage) 15 10
423 5f. multicoloured 25 10
424 6f. multicoloured 40 10
425 11f. multicoloured 50 20
426 10f. multicoloured (air) . . . 30 15
427 14f. multicoloured 35 20
428 17f. multicoloured 55 25
429 26f. multicoloured 70 35

55 Map showing African Members

1969. 5th Anniv of Yaounde Agreement between Common Market Countries and African-Malagasy Economic Community. Multicoloured.
430 5f. Type **55** 20 10
431 14f. Ploughing with tractor 40 15
432 17f. Teacher and pupil . . . 55 20
433 26f. Maps of Africa and Europe (horiz) 75 25

56 "Resurrection" (Isenmann)

1969. Easter. Multicoloured.
434 11f. Type **56** 30 10
435 14f. "Resurrection" (Caron) 40 15
436 17f. "Noli me Tangere" (Schongauer) 45 20
437 26f. "Resurrection" (El Greco) 75 30

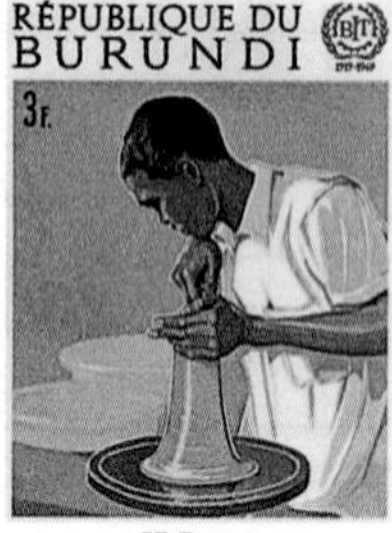

57 Potter

1969. 50th Anniv of I.L.O. Multicoloured.
439 3f. Type **57** 10 10
440 5f. Farm workers 10 10
441 7f. Foundry worker 25 10
442 10f. Harvester 25 15

58 Nurse and Patient

1969. 50th Anniv of League of Red Cross Societies. Multicoloured.
443 4f.+1f. Type **58** (postage) . . 15 10
444 7f.+1f. Stretcher bearers . . . 35 10
445 11f.+1f. Operating theatre . . 50 15
446 17f.+1f. Blood bank 60 25
447 26f.+3f. Laboratory (air) . . 75 25
448 40f.+3f. Red Cross truck in African village . . . . . . 1·10 45
449 50f.+3f. Nurse and woman patient . . . . 1·60 50

59 Steel Works

1969. 5th Anniv of African Development Bank. Multicoloured.
451 10f. Type **59** 30 30
452 17f. Broadcaster 50 50
453 30f. Language laboratory . . 70 70
454 50f. Tractor and harrow . . 1·25 1·25

60 Pope Paul VI

1969. 1st Papal Visit to Africa. Multicoloured.
456 3f.+2f. Type **60** 15 10
457 5f.+2f. Pope Paul and map of Africa (horiz) 30 10
458 10f.+2f. Pope Paul and African flags (horiz) . . . 30 10
459 14f.+2f. Pope Paul and the Vatican (horiz) 55 10
460 17f.+2f. Type **60** 60 10
461 40f.+2f. Pope Paul and Uganda Martyrs (horiz) . . 1·25 30
462 50f.+2f. Pope Paul enthroned (horiz) . . . . 1·60 35

61 "Girl reading Letter" (Vermeer)

1969. International Letter-writing Week. Mult.
464 4f. Type **61** 15 10
465 7f. "Graziella" (Renoir) . . . 20 10
466 14f. "Woman writing a Letter" (Terborch) 30 10
467 26f. "Galileo" (unknown painter) 55 15
468 40f. "Beethoven" (unknown painter) . . . . 1·10 35

62 Blast-off

63 "Adoration of the Magi" (detail, Rubens)

1969. 1st Man on the Moon. Multicoloured.
470 4f. Type **62** (postage) 30 10
471 6f.50 Rocket in Space 40 10
472 7f. Separation of lunar module 50 10
473 14f. Module landing on Moon 80 15
474 17f. Command module in orbit . . . . 1·10 25
475 26f. Astronaut descending ladder (air) . . . . 1·25 20
476 40f. Astronaut on Moon's surface . . . . 2·00 25
477 50f. Module in sea . . . . . 3·00 45

1969. Christmas. Multicoloured.
479 5f. Type **63** (postage) 15 10
480 6f. "Virgin and Child with St. John" (Romano) . . . 15 10
481 10f. "Madonna of the Magnificat" (Botticelli) . . 40 15
482 17f. "Virgin and Child" (Garofalo) (horiz) (air) . . 60 15
483 26f. "Madonna and Child" (Negretti) (horiz) 80 20
484 50f. "Virgin and Child" (Barbarelli) (horiz) . . . . 1·60 35

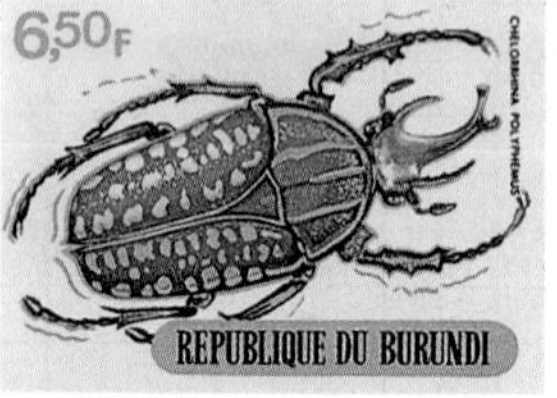

64 "Chelorrhina polyphemus"

1970. Beetles. Multicoloured. (a) Postage. (i) Size 39 × 28 mm.
486 50c. "Sternotomis bohemani" 20 10
487 1f. "Tetralobus flabellicornis" 20 10
488 1f.50 Type **64** 20 10
489 2f. "Brachytritus hieroglyphicus" 20 10
490 3f. "Goliathus goliathus" . . 20 10
491 3f.50 "Homoderus mellyi" . . 30 10

(ii) Size 46 × 32 mm.
492 4f. As 50c. 45 10
493 5f. As 1f. 65 10
494 6f. Type **64** 65 10
495 8f. As 2f. 65 10
496 10f. As 3f. 70 10
497 15f. As 3f.50 . . . . 1·10 15

(iii) Size 62 × 36 mm.
498 20f. As 50c. . . . . 1·50 30
499 50f. "Stephanorrhina guttata" 4·00 40
500 100f. "Phyllocnema viridocostata" . . . . . . 6·75 85
501 150f. "Mecynorrhina oberthueri" . . . . 8·25 1·60

(b) Air. (i) Size 46 × 32 mm.
502 6f. As 3f.50 . . . . 35 10
503 8f. As 1f. 45 10
504 10f. Type **64** 60 15
505 14f. As 2f. 70 15
506 15f. As 3f. 75 20

(ii) Size 52 × 36 mm.
507 20f. As 50f. (No. 499) . . . . 1·25 25
508 50f. As 50c. . . . . 4·00 35
509 75f. As 100f. . . . . 5·00 55
510 130f. As 150f. . . . . 8·00 80

65 "Jesus Condemned to Death"

1970. Easter. "The Stations of the Cross" (Carredano). Multicoloured.
511 1f. Type **65** (postage) 10 10
512 1f.50 "Carrying the Cross" 10 10
513 2f. "Jesus falls for the First Time" 10 10
514 3f. "Jesus meets His Mother" 10 10
515 3f.50 "Simon of Cyrene takes the Cross" 15 10
516 4f. "Veronica wipes the face of Christ" 15 10
517 5f. "Jesus falls for the Second Time" 15 10
518 8f. "The Women of Jerusalem" (air) 20 10
519 10f. "Jesus falls for the Third Time" 25 15
520 14f. "Christ stripped" 30 25
521 15f. "Jesus nailed to the Cross" 40 25
522 18f. "The Crucifixion" . . . 40 30
523 20f. "Descent from the Cross" 50 30
524 50f. "Christ laid in the Tomb" . . . . 1·25 45

66 Japanese Parade

1970. World Fair, Osaka, Japan (EXPO '70). Multicoloured.
526 4f. Type **66** 15 10
527 6f.50 Exhibition site from the air 75 15
528 7f. African pavilions 20 10
529 14f. Pagoda (vert) 30 10
530 26f. Recording pavilion and pool 60 15
531 40f. Tower of the Sun (vert) 1·00 30
532 50f. National flags (vert) . . 1·25 35

67 Burundi Cow

1970. Source of the Nile. Multicoloured.
534 7f. Any design (postage) . . 95 30
535 14f. Any design (air) . . . . 1·25 30

Nos. 534 and 535 were each issued in se-tenant sheets of 18 stamps as Type **67**, showing map sections, animals and birds, forming a map of the Nile from Cairo to Burundi.

68 Common Redstart

1970. Birds. Multicoloured. (a) Postage. Size 44 × 33 mm or 33 × 44 mm.
536 2f. Great grey shrike (vert) 25 10
537 2f. Common starling (vert) 25 10
538 2f. Yellow wagtail (vert) . . 25 10
539 2f. Sand martin (vert) 25 10
540 3f. Winter wren 60 10
541 3f. Firecrest 60 10
542 3f. Eurasian sky lark 60 10
543 3f. Crested lark 60 10
544 3f.50 Woodchat shrike (vert) 65 10
545 3f.50 Rock thrush (vert) . . . 65 10
546 3f.50 Black redstarts (vert) . . 65 10
547 3f.50 Ring ousel (vert) . . . 65 10
548 4f. Type **68** 95 10
549 4f. Dunnock 95 10
550 4f. Grey wagtail 95 10
551 4f. Meadow pipit 95 10
552 5f. Hoopoe (vert) . . . . . 1·25 15
553 5f. Pied flycatcher (vert) . . . 1·25 15
554 5f. Great reed warbler (vert) 1·25 15
555 5f. River kingfisher (vert) . . 1·25 15
556 6f.50 House martin . . . . . 1·40 20
557 6f.50 Sedge warbler . . . . . 1·40 20
558 6f.50 Fieldfare . . . . 1·40 20
559 6f.50 Golden oriole . . . . . 1·40 20

(b) Air. Size 52 × 44 mm or 44 × 52 mm.
560 8f. As No. 536 . . . . 1·50 20
561 8f. As No. 537 . . . . 1·50 20
562 8f. As No. 538 . . . . 1·50 20
563 8f. As No. 539 . . . . 1·50 20
564 10f. As No. 540 . . . . . . 1·75 25
565 10f. As No. 541 . . . . . . 1·75 25
566 10f. As No. 542 . . . . . . 1·75 25
567 10f. As No. 543 . . . . . . 1·75 25
568 14f. As No. 544 . . . . . . 1·75 25
569 14f. As No. 545 . . . . . . 1·75 25
570 14f. As No. 546 . . . . . . 1·75 25
571 14f. As No. 547 . . . . . . 1·75 25
572 20f. Type **68** . . . . 2·10 30
573 20f. As No. 549 . . . . . . 2·10 30
574 20f. As No. 550 . . . . . . 2·10 30
575 20f. As No. 551 . . . . . . 2·10 30
576 30f. As No. 552 . . . . . . 2·25 30
577 30f. As No. 553 . . . . . . 2·25 30
578 30f. As No. 554 . . . . . . 2·25 30
579 30f. As No. 555 . . . . . . 2·25 30
580 50f. As No. 556 . . . . . . 3·75 30
581 50f. As No. 557 . . . . . . 3·75 30
582 50f. As No. 558 . . . . . . 3·75 30
583 50f. As No. 559 . . . . . . 3·75 30

69 Library

1970. International Educational Year. Mult.
584 3f. Type **69** 10 10
585 5f. Examination 15 10
586 7f. Experiments in the laboratory 25 10
587 10f. Students with electron microscope 30 10

70 United Nations Building, New York

1970. Air. 25th Anniv of United Nations. Mult.
588 7f. Type **70** 25 10
589 11f. Security Council in session 30 10
590 26f. Paul VI and U Thant 70 20
591 40f. U.N. and National flags 1·00 30

71 Pres. Micombero and Wife

1970. 4th Anniv of Republic.
593 4f. Type **71** 10 10
594 7f. Pres. Micombero and flag 25 10
595 11f. Revolution Memorial 35 15

72 King Baudouin and Queen Fabiola

1970. Air. Visit of King and Queen of the Belgians. Each brown, purple and gold.
597 6f. Type **72** 65 15
598 20f. Pres. Micombero and King Baudouin 1·50 40
599 40f. Pres. Micombero in evening dress 3·00 70

73 "Adoration of the Magi" (Durer)

1970. Christmas. Multicoloured.
601 6f.50+1f. Type **73** (postage) 50 15
602 11f.+1f. "The Virgin of the Eucharist" (Botticelli) 60 25
603 20f.+1f. "The Holy Family" (El Greco) 90 30
604 14f.+3f. "The Adoration of the Magi" (Velasquez) (air) 50 25
605 26f.+3f. "The Holy Family" (Van Cleve) 85 40
606 40f.+3f. "Virgin and Child" (Van der Weyden) 1·40 60

74 Lenin in Discussion

76 "The Resurrection" (Il Sodoma)

75 Lion

1970. Birth Cent of Lenin. Each brown and gold.
608 3f.50 Type **74** 20 15
609 5f. Lenin addressing Soviet 30 15
610 6f.50 Lenin with soldier and sailor 40 15
611 15f. Lenin speaking to crowd 60 25
612 50f. Lenin 2·00 55

1971. African Animals (1st series). Multicoloured. (a) Postage. Size 38 × 38 mm.
613 1f. Type **75** 35 10
614 1f. African buffalo 35 10
615 1f. Hippopotamus 35 10
616 1f. Giraffe 35 10
617 2f. Topi 50 15
618 2f. Black rhinoceros 50 15
619 2f. Common zebra 50 15
620 2f. Leopard 50 15
621 3f. Grant's gazelle 85 25
622 3f. Cheetah 85 25
623 3f. African white-backed vultures 85 25
624 3f. Okapi 85 25
625 5f. Chimpanzee 1·00 25
626 5f. African elephant 1·00 25
627 5f. Spotted hyena 1·00 25
628 5f. Gemsbok 1·00 25
629 6f. Gorilla 1·40 25
630 6f. Blue wildebeest 1·40 25
631 6f. Warthog 1·40 25
632 6f. Hunting dog 1·40 25
633 11f. Sable antelope 2·25 30
634 11f. Caracal 2·25 30
635 11f. Ostriches 2·25 30
636 11f. Bongo 2·25 30

(b) Air. Size 44 × 44 mm.
637 10f. Type **75** 70 35
638 10f. As No. 614 70 35
639 10f. As No. 615 70 35
640 10f. As No. 616 70 35
641 14f. As No. 617 80 40
642 14f. As No. 618 80 40
643 14f. As No. 619 80 40
644 14f. As No. 620 80 40
645 17f. As No. 621 90 40
646 17f. As No. 622 90 40
647 17f. As No. 623 90 40
648 17f. As No. 624 90 40
649 24f. As No. 625 1·50 55
650 24f. As No. 626 1·50 55
651 24f. As No. 627 1·50 55
652 24f. As No. 628 1·50 55
653 26f. As No. 629 1·50 55
654 26f. As No. 630 1·50 55
655 26f. As No. 631 1·50 55
656 26f. As No. 632 1·50 55
657 31f. As No. 633 1·60 70
658 31f. As No. 634 1·60 70
659 31f. As No. 635 1·60 70
660 31f. As No. 636 1·60 70

See also Nos. 1028/75, 1178/1225 and 1385/97.

1971. Easter. Multicoloured.
661 3f. Type **76** (postage) 15 10
662 6f. "The Resurrection" (Del Castagno) 30 10
663 11f. "Noli Me Tangere" (Correggio) 45 15
664 14f. "The Resurrection" (Borrassa) (air) 50 20
665 17f. "The Resurrection" (Della Francesca) 65 20
666 26f. "The Resurrection" (Pleydenwyurff) 85 30

1971. Air. United Nations Campaigns. Nos. 637/48 optd or surch. (a) Optd **LUTTE CONTRE LE RACISME ET LA DISCRIMINATION RACIALE** and Racial Equality Year emblem.
668 10f. multicoloured 90 15
669 10f. multicoloured 90 15
670 10f. multicoloured 90 15
671 10f. multicoloured 90 15

(b) Surch **LUTTE CONTRE L'ANALPHABETISME**, U.N.E.S.C.O. emblem and premium (Campaign against Illiteracy).
672 14f.+2f. multicoloured 1·40 25
673 14f.+2f. multicoloured 1·40 25
674 14f.+2f. multicoloured 1·40 25
675 14f.+2f. multicoloured 1·40 25

(c) Surch **AIDE INTERNATIONALE AUX REFUGIES**, emblem and premium (Int Help for Refugees).
676 17f.+1f. multicoloured 2·25 40
677 17f.+1f. multicoloured 2·25 40
678 17f.+1f. multicoloured 2·25 40
679 17f.+1f. multicoloured 2·25 40

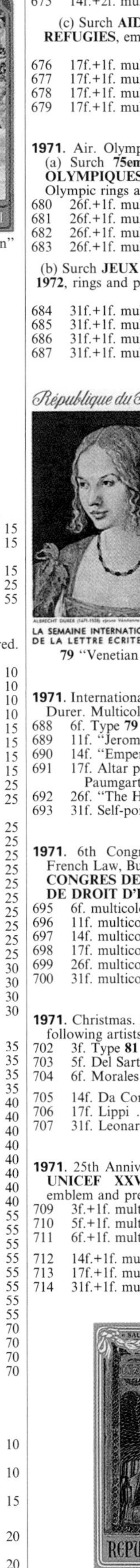

1971. Air. Olympic Commems. Nos. 653/56 surch. (a) Surch **75eme ANNIVERSAIRE DES JEUX OLYMPIQUES MODERNES (1896–1971)**, Olympic rings and premium.
680 26f.+1f. multicoloured 1·25 35
681 26f.+1f. multicoloured 1·25 35
682 26f.+1f. multicoloured 1·25 35
683 26f.+1f. multicoloured 1·25 35

(b) Surch **JEUX PRE-OLYMPIQUES MUNICH 1972**, rings and premium (Olympic Games, Munich (1972)).
684 31f.+1f. multicoloured 2·25 1·10
685 31f.+1f. multicoloured 2·25 1·10
686 31f.+1f. multicoloured 2·25 1·10
687 31f.+1f. multicoloured 2·25 1·10

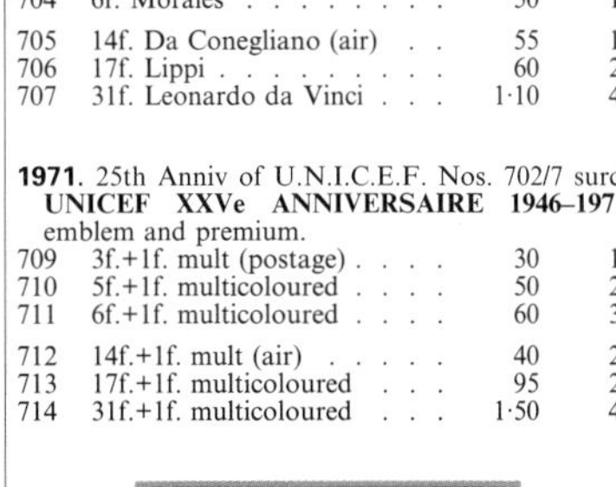

79 "Venetian Girl" **81** "The Virgin and Child" (Il Perugino)

1971. International Letter-writing Week. Paintings by Durer. Multicoloured.
688 6f. Type **79** 30 30
689 11f. "Jerome Holzschuhers" 35 35
690 14f. "Emperor Maximilian" 40 40
691 17f. Altar painting, Paumgartner 65 65
692 26f. "The Halle Madonna" 80 80
693 31f. Self-portrait 1·00 1·00

1971. 6th Congress of International Institute of French Law, Bujumbura. Nos. 668/693 optd **VIeme CONGRES DE L'INSTITUT INTERNATIONAL DE DROIT D'EXPRESSION FRANCAISE**.
695 6f. multicoloured 30 10
696 11f. multicoloured 35 10
697 14f. multicoloured 45 20
698 17f. multicoloured 65 20
699 26f. multicoloured 75 25
700 31f. multicoloured 1·00 25

1971. Christmas. Paintings of "Virgin and Child" by following artists. Multicoloured.
702 3f. Type **81** (postage) 15 10
703 5f. Del Sarto 25 10
704 6f. Morales 50 10
705 14f. Da Conegliano (air) 55 15
706 17f. Lippi 60 20
707 31f. Leonardo da Vinci 1·10 45

1971. 25th Anniv of U.N.I.C.E.F. Nos. 702/7 surch **UNICEF XXVe ANNIVERSAIRE 1946–1971**, emblem and premium.
709 3f.+1f. mult (postage) 30 10
710 5f.+1f. multicoloured 50 20
711 6f.+1f. multicoloured 60 30
712 14f.+1f. mult (air) 40 20
713 17f.+1f. multicoloured 95 25
714 31f.+1f. multicoloured 1·50 45

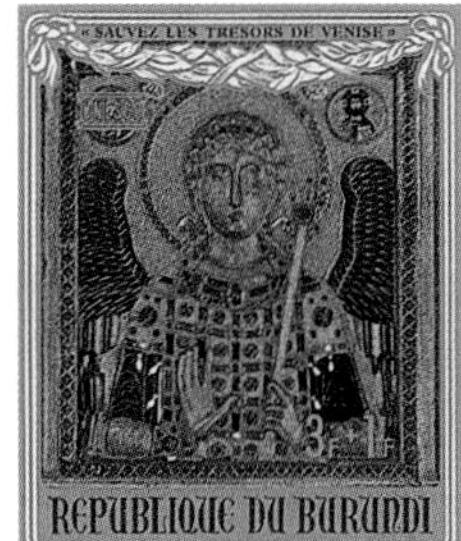

83 "Archangel Michael" (icon, St. Mark's)

1971. U.N.E.S.C.O. "Save Venice" Campaign. Multicoloured.
716 3f.+1f. Type **83** (postage) 25 10
717 5f.+1f. "La Polenta" (Longhi) 35 15
718 6f.+1f. "Gossip" (Longhi) 35 15
719 11f.+1f. "Diana's Bath" (Pittoni) 45 25
720 10f.+1f. Casa d'Oro (air) 45 10
721 17f.+1f. Doge's Palace 65 15
722 24f.+1f. St. John and St. Paul Church 90 25
723 31f.+1f. "Doge's Palace and Piazzetta" (Canaletto) 2·00 40

84 "Lunar Orbiter"

1972. Conquest of Space. Multicoloured.
725 6f. Type **84** 15 15
726 11f. "Vostok" spaceship 40 15
727 14f. "Luna 1" 45 30
728 17f. First Man on Moon 65 30
729 26f. "Soyuz 11" space flight 80 40
730 40f. "Lunar Rover" 1·60 95

85 Slalom skiing

1972. Winter Olympic Games, Sapporo, Japan. Multicoloured.
732 5f. Type **85** 15 10
733 6f. Pair skating 20 10
734 11f. Figure-skating 35 10
735 14f. Ski-jumping 35 20
736 17f. Ice-hockey 50 20
737 24f. Speed skating 60 25
738 26f. Ski-bobbing 60 25
739 31f. Downhill skiing 75 25
740 50f. Bobsleighing 1·50 35

86 "Ecce Homo" (Metzys)

1972. Easter. Paintings. Multicoloured.
742 3f.50 Type **86** 20 10
743 6f.50 "The Crucifixion" (Rubens) 30 10
744 10f. "The Descent from the Cross" (Portormo) 40 10
745 18f. "Pieta" (Gallegos) 70 15
746 27f. "The Trinity" (El Greco) 1·40 30

87 Gymnastics

1972. Olympic Games. Munich. Multicoloured.
748 5f. Type **87** (postage) 20 10
749 6f. Throwing the javelin 20 10
750 11f. Fencing 35 15
751 14f. Cycling 50 20
752 17f. Pole-vaulting 75 20
753 24f. Weightlifting (air) 65 25
754 26f. Hurdling 90 25
755 31f. Throwing the discus 1·40 40
756 40f. Football 1·50 50

88 Prince Rwagasore, Pres. Micombero and Drummers

1972. 10th Anniv of Independence. Multicoloured.

758	5f. Type **88** (postage)	15	10
759	7f. Rwagasore, Micombero and map	25	10
760	13f. Pres. Micombero and Burundi flag	40	15
761	15f. Type **65** (air)	30	15
762	18f. As 7f.	35	15
763	27f. As 13f.	60	30

89 "Madonna and Child" (A. Solario)

1972. Christmas. "Madonna and Child" paintings by artists given below. Multicoloured.

765	5f. Type **89** (postage)	30	10
766	10f. Raphael	50	10
767	15f. Botticelli	75	15
768	18f. S. Mainardi (air)	50	15
769	27f. H. Memling	1·00	25
770	40f. Lotto	1·50	40

90 "Platycoryne crocea"

1972. Orchids. Multicoloured.

772	50c. Type **90** (postage)	30	15
773	1f. "Cattleya trianaei"	30	15
774	2f. "Eulophia cucullata"	30	15
775	3f. "Cymbidium hamsey"	30	15
776	4f. "Thelymitra pauciflora"	30	15
777	5f. "Miltassia"	30	15
778	6f. "Miltonia"	1·25	15
779	7f. Type **90**	1·25	15
780	8f. As 1f.	1·40	15
781	9f. As 2f.	1·40	20
782	10f. As 3f.	1·90	20
783	13f. As 4f. (air)	1·25	15
784	14f. As 5f.	1·25	15
785	15f. As 6f.	1·60	20
786	18f. Type **90**	1·60	20
787	20f. As 1f.	1·60	25
788	27f. As 2f.	2·75	30
789	36f. As 3f.	4·50	40

Nos. 779/89 are size 53 × 53 mm.

1972. Christmas Charity. Nos. 765/770 surch.

790	5f.+1f. mult (postage)	35	15
791	10f.+1f. multicoloured	65	20
792	15f.+1f. multicoloured	75	25
793	18f.+1f. multicoloured (air)	60	20
794	27f.+1f. multicoloured	90	25
795	40f.+1f. multicoloured	1·50	45

92 H. M. Stanley

1973. Centenary of Stanley/Livingstone African Exploration. Multicoloured.

797	5f. Type **92** (postage)	20	10
798	7f. Expedition bearers	25	10
799	13f. Stanley directing foray	45	15
800	15f. Dr. Livingstone (air)	35	20
801	18f. Stanley meets Livingstone	55	20
802	27f. Stanley conferring with Livingstone	1·00	30

93 "The Scourging" (Caravaggio)

1973. Easter. Multicoloured.

804	5f. Type **93** (postage)	15	10
805	7f. "Crucifixion" (Van der Weyden)	25	10
806	13f. "The Deposition" (Raphael)	50	15
807	15f. "Christ bound to the Pillar" (Guido Reni) (air)	45	25
808	18f. "Crucifixion" (M. Grunewald)	70	25
809	27f. "The Descent from the Cross" (Caravaggio)	1·10	30

94 Interpol Emblem

1973. 50th Anniv of Interpol. Multicoloured.

811	5f. Type **94** (postage)	25	10
812	10f. Burundi flag	40	10
813	18f. Interpol H.Q., Paris	60	15
814	27f. As 5f. (air)	75	25
815	40f. As 10f.	1·25	35

95 Capricorn, Aquarius and Pisces

1973. 500th Birth Anniv of Copernicus.

816 **95**	3f. gold, red and black (postage)	20	10
817 –	3f. gold, red and black	20	10
818 –	3f. gold, red and black	20	10
819 –	3f. gold, red and black	20	10
820 –	5f. multicoloured	30	10
821 –	5f. multicoloured	30	10
822 –	5f. multicoloured	30	10
823 –	5f. multicoloured	30	10
824 –	7f. multicoloured	40	10
825 –	7f. multicoloured	40	10
826 –	7f. multicoloured	40	10
827 –	7f. multicoloured	40	10
828 –	13f. multicoloured	60	10
829 –	13f. multicoloured	60	10
830 –	13f. multicoloured	60	10
831 –	13f. multicoloured	60	10
832 –	15f. multicoloured (air)	40	15
833 –	15f. multicoloured	40	15
834 –	15f. multicoloured	40	15
835 –	15f. multicoloured	40	15
836 –	18f. multicoloured	55	15
837 –	18f. multicoloured	55	15
838 –	18f. multicoloured	55	15
839 –	18f. multicoloured	55	15
840 –	27f. multicoloured	95	25
841 –	27f. multicoloured	95	25
842 –	27f. multicoloured	95	25
843 –	27f. multicoloured	95	25
844 –	36f. multicoloured	2·10	40
845 –	36f. multicoloured	2·10	40
846 –	36f. multicoloured	2·10	40
847 –	36f. multicoloured	2·10	40

DESIGNS: No. 816, Type **95**; 817, Aries, Taurus and Gemini; 818, Cancer, Leo and Virgo; 819, Libra, Scorpio and Sagittarius; 820/23, Greek and Roman Gods; 824/7, Ptolemy and Ptolemaic System; 828/31, Copernicus and Solar System; 823/5, Copernicus, Earth, Pluto and Jupiter; 836/39, Copernicus, Venus, Saturn and Mars; 840/43, Copernicus, Uranus, Neptune and Mercury; 844/7, Earth and spacecraft.

The four designs of each value were issued se-tenant in blocks of four within the sheet, forming composite designs.

96 "Protea cynaroides"

1973. Flora and Butterflies. Multicoloured.

849	1f. Type **96** (postage)	70	15
850	1f. "Precis octavia"	70	15
851	1f. "Epiphora bauhiniae"	70	15
852	1f. "Gazania longiscapa"	70	15
853	2f. "Kniphofia" – "Royal Standard"	70	15
854	2f. "Cymothoe coccinata hew"	1·00	20
855	2f. "Nudaurelia zambesina"	1·00	20
856	2f. "Freesia refracta"	1·00	15
857	3f. "Calotis eupompe"	1·00	20
858	3f. Narcissus	1·00	15
859	3f. "Cineraria hybrida"	1·00	15
860	3f. "Cyrestis camillus"	1·00	20
861	5f. "Iris tingitana"	1·40	15
862	5f. "Papilio demodocus"	2·10	20
863	5f. "Catopsilia avelaneda"	2·10	20
864	5f. "Nerine sarniensis"	1·40	15
865	6f. "Hypolimnas dexithea"	2·10	20
866	6f. "Zantedeschia tropicalis"	1·40	15
867	6f. "Sandersonia aurantiaca"	1·40	15
868	6f. "Drurya antimachus"	2·10	20
869	11f. "Nymphaea capensis"	1·75	20
870	11f. "Pandoriana pandora"	2·75	25
871	11f. "Precis orythia"	2·75	25
872	11f. "Pelargonium domesticum"–"Aztec"	1·75	20
873	10f. Type **96** (air)	50	10
874	10f. As No. 850	90	10
875	10f. As No. 851	90	10
876	10f. As No. 852	50	10
877	14f. As No. 853	60	10
878	14f. As No. 854	1·00	20
879	14f. As No. 855	1·00	20
880	14f. As No. 856	40	15
881	17f. As No. 857	1·25	25
882	17f. As No. 858	90	20
883	17f. As No. 859	90	20
884	17f. As No. 860	1·25	25
885	24f. As No. 861	1·40	25
886	24f. As No. 862	1·75	30
887	24f. As No. 863	1·75	30
888	24f. As No. 864	1·10	25
889	26f. As No. 865	1·75	30
890	26f. As No. 866	1·10	30
891	26f. As No. 867	1·10	30
892	26f. As No. 868	1·75	30
893	31f. As No. 869	1·25	35
894	31f. As No. 870	1·90	45
895	31f. As No. 871	1·90	45
896	31f. As No. 872	1·25	35

Nos. 849, 852/3, 856, 858/9, 861, 864, 866/7, 869, 872, 876/7, 880, 882/3, 885, 888, 890/1, 893 and 896 depict flora and the remainder butterflies.

The four designs of each value were issued se-tenant in blocks of four within the sheet, forming composite designs.

97 "Virgin and Child" (G. Bellini)

1973. Christmas. Various paintings of "The Virgin and Child" by artists listed below. Multicoloured.

897	5f. Type **97** (postage)	45	10
898	10f. Van Eyck	55	15
899	15f. G. A. Boltraffio	75	20
900	18f. Raphael (air)	35	10
901	27f. P. Perugino	1·10	30
902	40f. Titian	1·60	40

1973. Christmas Charity. Nos. 897/902 surch.

904 **97**	5f.+1f. mult (postage)	50	15
905 –	10f.+1f. multicoloured	80	20
906 –	15f.+1f. multicoloured	95	25
907 –	18f.+1f. mult (air)	70	15
908 –	27f.+1f. multicoloured	1·10	35
909 –	40f.+1f. multicoloured	1·60	50

98 "The Pieta" (Veronese)

1974. Easter. Religious Paintings. Multicoloured.

911	5f. Type **98**	15	10
912	10f. "The Virgin and St. John" (Van der Weyden)	30	15
913	18f. "The Crucifixion" (Van der Weyden)	60	20
914	27f. "The Entombment" (Titian)	85	30
915	40f. "The Pieta" (El Greco)	2·10	50

99 Egyptian Mouthbrooder ("Haplochromis multicolor")

1974. Fishes. Multicoloured.

917	1f. Type **99** (postage)	55	10
918	1f. Spotted mouthbrooder ("Tropheus duboisi")	55	10
919	1f. Freshwater butterfly-fish ("Pantodon buchholzi")	55	10
920	1f. Six-banded distichodus ("Distichodus sexfasciatus")	55	10
921	2f. Rainbow krib ("Pelmatochromis kribensis")	55	10
922	2f. African leaf-fish ("Polycentropsis abbreviata")	55	10
923	2f. Three-lined tetra ("Nannaethiops tritaeniatus")	55	10
924	2f. Jewel cichlid ("Hemichromis bimaculatus")	55	10
925	3f. Spotted climbing-perch ("Ctenopoma acutirostre")	55	10
926	3f. African mouthbrooder ("Tilapia melanopleura")	55	10
927	3f. Angel squeaker ("Synodontis angelicus")	55	10
928	3f. Two-striped lyretail ("Aphyosemion bivittatum")	55	10
929	5f. Diamond fingerfish ("Monodactylus argenteus")	90	10
930	5f. Regal angelfish ("Pygoplites diacanthus")	90	10
931	5f. Moorish idol ("Zanclus canescens")	90	10
932	5f. Peacock hind ("Cephalopholis argus") and surgeonfish	90	10
933	6f. Bigeye ("Priacanthus arenatus")	2·75	10
934	6f. Rainbow parrotfish ("Scarus guacamaia") and French angelfish	2·75	10
935	6f. French angelfish ("Pomacanthus arcuatus")	2·75	10
936	6f. John dory ("Zeus faber")	2·75	10
937	11f. Scribbled cowfish ("Lactophrys quadricornis")	3·00	20
938	11f. Ocean surgeonfish ("Acanthurus bahianus")	3·00	20
939	11f. Queen triggerfish ("Balistes vetula")	3·00	20
940	11f. Queen angelfish ("Holocanthus ciliaris")	3·00	20
941	10f. Type **99** (air)	45	10
942	10f. As No. 918	45	10
943	10f. As No. 919	45	10
944	10f. As No. 920	45	10
945	14f. As No. 921	95	10
946	14f. As No. 922	95	10
947	14f. As No. 923	95	10
948	14f. As No. 924	95	10
949	17f. As No. 925	95	10
950	17f. As No. 926	95	10
951	17f. As No. 927	95	10
952	17f. As No. 928	95	10
953	24f. As No. 929	2·10	10
954	24f. As No. 930	2·10	10
955	24f. As No. 931	2·10	10
956	24f. As No. 932	2·10	10
957	26f. As No. 933	3·00	20
958	26f. As No. 934	3·00	20
959	26f. As No. 935	3·00	20
960	26f. As No. 936	3·00	20
961	31f. As No. 937	3·75	30
962	31f. As No. 938	3·75	30
963	31f. As No. 939	3·75	30
964	31f. As No. 940	3·75	30

The four designs of each value are arranged together in se-tenant blocks of four within the sheet, forming composite designs.

100 Footballers and World Cup Trophy

1974. World Cup Football Championships.
965 **100** 5f. mult (postage) 25 10
966 – 6f. multicoloured 30 10
967 – 11f. multicoloured 40 20
968 – 14f. multicoloured 50 25
969 – 17f. multicoloured 55 25
970 – 20f. multicoloured (air) 70 35
971 – 26f. multicoloured 90 45
972 – 40f. multicoloured 1·40 60
DESIGNS: Nos. 966/72, Football scenes as Type **100**.

101 Burundi Flag

1974. Centenary of U.P.U. Multicoloured.
974 6f. Type **101** (postage) 20 10
975 6f. Burundi P.T.T. Building 20 10
976 11f. Postmen carrying letters 30 10
977 11f. Postmen carrying letters 30 10
978 14f. U.P.U. Monument 1·25 70
979 14f. Mail transport 1·25 70
980 17f. Burundi on map 55 10
981 17f. Dove and letter 55 10
982 24f. Type **101** (air) 80 20
983 24f. As No. 975 80 20
984 26f. As No. 976 1·10 30
985 26f. As No. 977 1·10 30
986 31f. As No. 978 2·75 1·10
987 31f. As No. 979 2·75 1·10
988 40f. As No. 980 3·50 45
989 40f. As No. 981 3·50 45
The two designs in each denomination were arranged together in se-tenant pairs within the sheet, each pair forming a composite design.

102 "St. Ildefonse writing a letter" (El Greco)

1974. International Letter-writing Week. Mult.
991 6f. Type **102** 30 15
992 11f. "Lady sealing a letter" (Chardin) 50 20
993 14f. "Titus at desk" (Rembrandt) 55 30
994 17f. "The Love-letter" (Vermeer) 60 30
995 26f. "The Merchant G. Gisze" (Holbein) 65 50
996 31f. "A. Lenoir" (David) 90 55

103 "Virgin and Child". (Van Orley)

1974. Christmas. Showing "Virgin and Child" paintings by artists named. Multicoloured.
998 5f. Type **103** (postage) 25 10
999 10f. Hans Memling 45 15
1000 15f. Botticelli 1·00 20
1001 18f. Hans Memling (different) (air) 35 20
1002 27f. F. Lippi 1·10 35
1003 40f. L. di Gredi 1·50 45

1974. Christmas Charity. Nos. 998/1003 surch.
1005 **103** 5f.+1f. mult (postage) 30 10
1006 – 10f.+1f. multicoloured 40 25
1007 – 15f.+1f. multicoloured 1·10 30
1008 – 18f.+1f. mult (air) 55 20
1009 – 27f.+1f. multicoloured 85 35
1010 – 40f.+1f. multicoloured 1·60 45

104 "Apollo" Spacecraft with Docking Tunnel

1975. "Apollo–Soyuz" Space Project.
1012 26f. Type **104** (postage) 45 30
1013 26f. Leonov and Kubasov 45 30
1014 26f. "Soyuz" Spacecraft 45 30
1015 26f. Slayton, Brand and Stafford 45 30
1016 31f. "Soyuz" launch 55 40
1017 31f. "Apollo" and "Soyuz" spacecraft 55 40
1018 31f. "Apollo" third stage separation 55 40
1019 31f. Slayton, Brand, Stafford, Leonov and Kubasov 55 40
1020 27f. Type **104** (air) 60 45
1021 27f. As No. 1012 60 45
1022 27f. As No. 1013 60 45
1023 27f. As No. 1014 60 45
1024 40f. As No. 1015 80 60
1025 40f. As No. 1016 80 60
1026 40f. As No. 1017 80 60
1027 40f. As No. 1018 80 60
The four designs in each value were issued together in se-tenant blocks of four within the sheet.

105 Addax

1975. African Animals (2nd series). Multicoloured.
1028 1f. Type **105** (postage) 40 15
1029 1f. Roan antelope 40 15
1030 1f. Nyala 40 15
1031 1f. White rhinoceros 40 15
1032 2f. Mandrill 40 15
1033 2f. Eland 40 15
1034 2f. Salt's dik-dik 40 15
1035 2f. Thomson's gazelles 40 15
1036 3f. African claw-less otter 55 15
1037 3f. Bohar reedbuck 55 15
1038 3f. African civet 55 15
1039 3f. African buffalo 55 15
1040 5f. Black wildebeest 55 15
1041 5f. African asses 55 15
1042 5f. Angolan black and white colobus 55 15
1043 5f. Gerenuk 55 15
1044 6f. Addra gazelle 95 20
1045 6f. Black-backed jackal 95 20
1046 6f. Sitatungas 95 20
1047 6f. Banded duiker 95 20
1048 11f. Fennec fox 1·40 20
1049 11f. Lesser kudus 1·40 20
1050 11f. Blesbok 1·40 20
1051 11f. Serval 1·40 20
1052 10f. Type **105** (air) 60 10
1053 10f. As No. 1029 60 10
1054 10f. As No. 1030 60 10
1055 10f. As No. 1031 60 10
1056 14f. As No. 1032 70 15
1057 14f. As No. 1033 70 15
1058 14f. As No. 1034 70 15
1059 14f. As No. 1035 70 15
1060 17f. As No. 1036 1·10 15
1061 17f. As No. 1037 1·10 15
1062 17f. As No. 1038 1·10 15
1063 17f. As No. 1039 1·10 15
1064 24f. As No. 1040 1·75 20
1065 24f. As No. 1041 1·75 20
1066 24f. As No. 1042 1·75 20
1067 24f. As No. 1043 1·75 20
1068 26f. As No. 1044 1·90 20
1069 26f. As No. 1045 1·90 20
1070 26f. As No. 1046 1·90 20
1071 26f. As No. 1047 1·90 20
1072 31f. As No. 1048 2·25 25
1073 31f. As No. 1049 2·25 25
1074 31f. As No. 1050 2·25 25
1075 31f. As No. 1051 2·25 25
The four designs in each value were issued together in horiz. se-tenant strips within the sheet, forming composite designs.

1975. Air. International Women's Year. Nos. 1052/9 optd **ANNEE INTERNATIONALE DE LA FEMME**.
1076 **105** 10f. multicoloured 80 50
1077 – 10f. multicoloured 80 50
1078 – 10f. multicoloured 80 50
1079 – 10f. multicoloured 80 50
1080 – 14f. multicoloured 1·40 60
1081 – 14f. multicoloured 1·40 60
1082 – 14f. multicoloured 1·40 60
1083 – 14f. multicoloured 1·40 60

1975. Air. 30th Anniv of United Nations. Nos. 1068/75 optd **30eme ANNIVERSAIRE DES NATIONS UNIES**.
1084 26f. multicoloured 1·40 1·25
1085 26f. multicoloured 1·40 1·25
1086 26f. multicoloured 1·40 1·25
1087 26f. multicoloured 1·40 1·25
1088 31f. multicoloured 2·25 2·00
1089 31f. multicoloured 2·25 2·00
1090 31f. multicoloured 2·25 2·00
1091 31f. multicoloured 2·25 2·00

108 "Jonah"

1975. Christmas. 500th Birth Anniv of Michaelangelo. Multicoloured.
1092 5f. Type **108** (postage) 25 10
1093 5f. "Libyan Sibyl" 25 10
1094 13f. "Daniel" 90 10
1095 13f. "Cumaean Sybil" 90 10
1096 27f. "Isaiah" 1·25 15
1097 27f. "Delphic Sybil" (different) 1·25 15
1098 18f. "Zachariah" (air) 90 10
1099 18f. "Joel" 90 10
1100 31f. "Erythraean Sybil" 1·60 30
1101 31f. "Ezekiel" 1·60 30
1102 40f. "Persian Sybil" 2·00 35
1103 40f. "Jeremiah" 2·00 35

1975. Christmas Charity. Nos. 1092/1103 surch **+1F**.
1105 **108** 5f.+1f. mult (postage) 45 10
1106 – 5f.+1f. multicoloured 45 10
1107 – 13f.+1f. multicoloured 75 10
1108 – 13f.+1f. multicoloured 75 10
1109 – 27f.+1f. multicoloured 1·25 15
1110 – 27f.+1f. multicoloured 1·25 15
1111 – 18f.+1f. mult (air) 1·00 10
1112 – 18f.+1f. multicoloured 1·00 10
1113 – 31f.+1f. multicoloured 1·60 30
1114 – 31f.+1f. multicoloured 1·60 30
1115 – 40f.+1f. multicoloured 1·90 35
1116 – 40f.+1f. multicoloured 1·90 35

110 Speed Skating

111 Basketball

1976. Winter Olympic Games, Innsbruck. Mult.
1118 17f. Type **110** (postage) 45 20
1119 24f. Figure-skating 50 20
1120 26f. Two-man bobsleigh 60 20
1121 31f. Cross-country skiing 70 30
1122 18f. Ski-jumping (air) 40 25
1123 36f. Skiing (slalom) 1·50 40
1124 50f. Ice-hockey 1·60 60

1976. Olympic Games, Montreal. Multicoloured.
1126 14f. Type **111** (postage) 40 30
1127 14f. Pole-vaulting 40 30
1128 17f. Running 60 45
1129 17f. Football 60 45
1130 28f. As No. 1127 90 65
1131 28f. As No. 1128 90 65
1132 40f. As No. 1129 1·50 1·10
1133 40f. Type **111** 1·50 1·10
1134 27f. Hurdling (air) 90 65
1135 27f. High-jumping (horiz) 90 65
1136 31f. Gymnastics (horiz) 1·25 90
1137 31f. As No. 1134 (horiz) 1·25 90
1138 50f. As No. 1135 (horiz) 1·90 1·40
1139 50f. As No. 1136 (horiz) 1·90 1·40

112 "Battle of Bunker Hill" (detail, John Trumbull)

113 "Virgin and Child" (Dirk Bouts)

1976. Air. Bicent of American Revolution. Mult.
1141 18f. Type **112** 55 15
1142 18f. As Type **112** 55 15
1143 26f. Franklin, Jefferson and John Adams 75 25
1144 26f. As No. 1143 75 25
1145 36f. "Signing of Declaration of Independence" (Trumbull) 1·25 35
1146 36f. As No. 1145 1·25 35
The two designs of each value form composite pictures. Type **112** is the left-hand portion of the painting.

1976. Christmas. Multicoloured.
1148 5f. Type **113** (postage) 35 10
1149 13f. "Virgin of the Trees" (Bellini) 65 10
1150 27f. "Virgin and Child" (C. Crivelli) 1·00 25
1151 18f. "Virgin and Child" with St. Anne" (Leonardo) (air) 80 30
1152 31f. "Holy Family with Lamb" (Raphael) 1·10 60
1153 40f. "Virgin with Basket" (Correggio) 1·60 70

1976. Christmas Charity. Nos. 1148/53 surch **+1F**.
1155 **113** 5f.+1f. mult (postage) 25 10
1156 – 13f.+1f. multicoloured 70 30
1157 – 27f.+1f. multicoloured 1·10 50
1158 – 18f.+1f. mult (air) 60 30
1159 – 31f.+1f. multicoloured 1·00 45
1160 – 40f.+1f. multicoloured 1·90 65

115 "The Ascent of Calvary" (Rubens)

1977. Easter. 400th Birth Anniv of Peter Paul Rubens. Multicoloured.
1162 10f. Type **115** 35 25
1163 21f. "Christ Crucified" 95 70
1164 27f. "The Descent from the Cross" 1·10 80
1165 35f. "The Deposition" 1·50 1·10

116 Alexander Graham Bell

117 Kobs

1977. Telephone Centenary and World Telecommunications Day. Multicoloured.
1167 10f. Type **116** (postage) 25 15
1168 10f. Satellite, Globe and telephones 25 15
1169 17f. Switchboard operator and wall telephone 45 30
1170 17f. Satellite transmitting to Earth 45 30
1171 26f. A. G. Bell and first telephone 80 60
1172 26f. Satellites circling Globe, and videophone 80 60
1173 18f. Type **116** (air) 40 30
1174 18f. As No. 1172 40 30
1175 36f. As No. 1169 1·10 80
1176 36f. As No. 1168 1·10 80

1977. African Animals (3rd series). Multicoloured.
1178 2f. Type **117** (postage) 75 20
1179 2f. Marabou storks 75 20
1180 2f. Blue wildebeest 75 20
1181 2f. Bush pig 75 20
1182 5f. Grevy's zebras 85 20
1183 5f. Whale-headed stork 85 20
1184 5f. Striped hyenas 85 20
1185 5f. Pygmy chimpanzee 85 20
1186 8f. Greater flamingoes 95 20
1187 8f. Nile crocodiles 95 20
1188 8f. Green tree snake 95 20
1189 8f. Greater kudus 95 20
1190 11f. Large-toothed rock hyrax 1·00 20
1191 11f. Cobra 1·00 20
1192 11f. Golden jackals 1·00 20
1193 11f. Verreaux eagles 1·00 20
1194 21f. Ratel 1·25 30
1195 21f. Bushbuck 1·25 30
1196 21f. Secretary bird 1·25 30
1197 21f. Klipspringer 1·25 30
1198 27f. Bat-eared fox 1·60 30
1199 27f. African elephants 1·60 30
1200 27f. Vulturine guineafowl 1·60 30
1201 27f. Impalas 1·60 30
1202 9f. Type **117** (air) 60 25
1203 9f. As No. 1179 60 25
1204 9f. As No. 1180 60 25
1205 9f. As No. 1181 60 25
1206 13f. As No. 1182 85 30
1207 13f. As No. 1183 85 30
1208 13f. As No. 1184 85 30

1209	13f. As No. 1185	85	30
1210	30f. As No. 1186	1·25	50
1211	30f. As No. 1187	1·25	50
1212	30f. As No. 1188	1·25	50
1213	30f. As No. 1189	1·25	50
1214	35f. As No. 1190	1·40	60
1215	35f. As No. 1191	1·40	60
1216	35f. As No. 1192	1·40	60
1217	35f. As No. 1193	1·40	60
1218	54f. As No. 1194	2·40	70
1219	54f. As No. 1195	2·40	70
1220	54f. As No. 1196	2·40	70
1221	54f. As No. 1197	2·40	70
1222	70f. As No. 1198	3·25	85
1223	70f. As No. 1199	3·25	85
1224	70f. As No. 1200	3·25	85
1225	70f. As No. 1201	3·25	85

The four designs in each value were issued together se-tenant in horizontal strips within the sheet, forming composite designs.

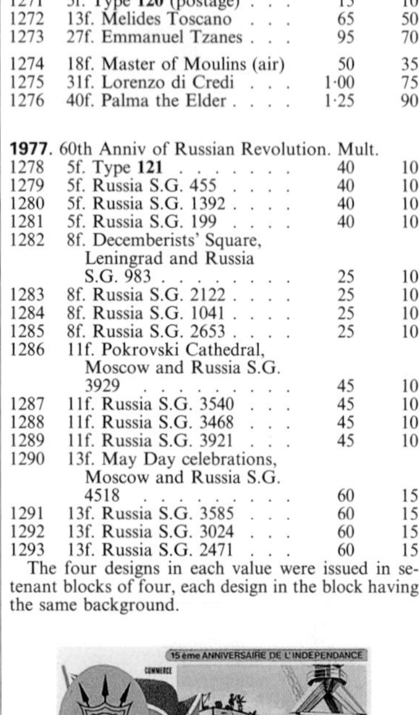

118 "The Man of Iron" (Grimm) **119** U.N. General Assembly and U.N. 3c. Stamp, 1954

1977. Fairy Tales. Multicoloured.

1226	5f. Type **118**	20	10
1227	5f. "Snow White and Rose Red" (Grimm)	20	10
1228	5f. "The Goose Girl" (Grimm)	20	10
1229	5f. "The Two Wanderers" (Grimm)	20	10
1230	11f. "The Hermit and the Bear" (Aesop)	60	10
1231	11f. "The Fox and the Stork" (Aesop)	60	10
1232	11f. "The Litigious Cats" (Aesop)	60	10
1233	11f. "The Blind and the Lame" (Aesop)	60	10
1234	14f. "The Ice Maiden" (Andersen)	70	10
1235	14f. "The Old House" (Andersen)	70	10
1236	14f. "The Princess and the Pea" (Andersen)	70	10
1237	14f. "The Elder Tree Mother" (Andersen)	70	10
1238	17f. "Hen with the Golden Eggs" (La Fontaine)	80	15
1239	17f. "The Wolf Turned Shepherd" (La Fontaine)	80	15
1240	17f. "The Oyster and Litigants" (La Fontaine)	80	15
1241	17f. "The Wolf and the Lamb" (La Fontaine)	80	15
1242	26f. "Jack and the Beanstalk" (traditional)	1·60	25
1243	26f. "Alice in Wonderland) (Lewis Carroll)	1·60	25
1244	26f. "Three Heads in the Well" (traditional)	1·60	25
1245	26f. "Tales of Mother Goose" (traditional)	1·60	25

1977. 25th Anniv of United Nations Postal Administration. Multicoloured.

1246	8f. Type **119** (postage)	40	30
1247	8f. U.N. 4c. stamp, 1957	40	30
1248	8f. U.N. 3c. stamp, 1954 (FAO)	40	30
1249	8f. U.N. 1½ c. stamp, 1951	40	30
1250	10f. Security Council and U.N. 8c. red, 1954	50	35
1251	10f. U.N. 8c. green, 1956	50	35
1252	10f. U.N. 8c. black, 1955	50	35
1253	10f. U.N. 7c. stamp, 1959	50	35
1254	21f. Meeting hall and U.N. 3c. grey, 1956	80	60
1255	21f. U.N. 8c. stamp, 1956	80	60
1256	21f. U.N. 3c. brown, 1953	80	60
1257	21f. U.N. 3c. green, 1952	80	60
1258	24f. Building by night and U.N. 4c. red, 1957 (air)	80	60
1259	24f. U.N. 8c. brn & grn, 1960	80	60
1260	24f. U.N. 8c. green, 1955	80	60
1261	24f. U.N. 8c. red, 1955	80	60
1262	27f. Aerial view of U.N. 8c. red, 1957	90	65
1263	27f. U.N. 3c. stamp, 1953	90	65
1264	27f. U.N. 8c. green, 1954	90	65
1265	27f. U.N. 8c. brown, 1956	90	65
1266	35f. U.N. Building by day and U.N. 5c. stamp, 1959	1·40	1·00
1267	35f. U.N. 3c. stamp, 1962	1·40	1·00
1268	35f. U.N. 3c. bl & pur, 1951	1·40	1·00
1269	35f. U.N. 1c. stamp, 1951	1·40	1·00

The four designs in each value were issued together in se-tenant blocks of four, each design in the block having the same background.

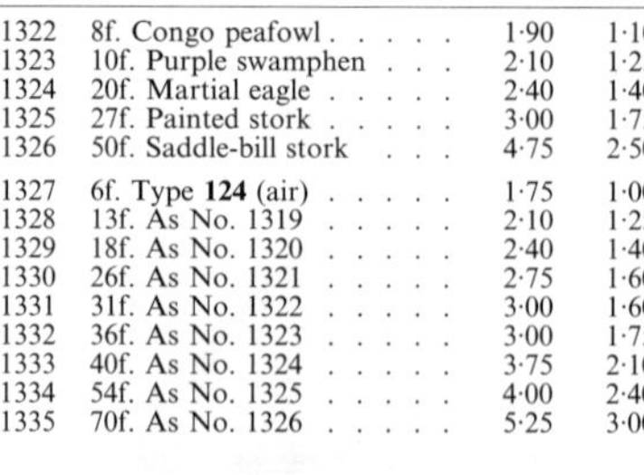

120 "Virgin and Child" (Jean Lambardos) **121** Cruiser "Aurora" and Russian 5r. Stamp, 1922

1977. Christmas. Paintings of Virgin and Child by artists named. Multicoloured.

1271	5f. Type **120** (postage)	15	10
1272	13f. Melides Toscano	65	50
1273	27f. Emmanuel Tzanes	95	70
1274	18f. Master of Moulins (air)	50	35
1275	31f. Lorenzo di Credi	1·00	75
1276	40f. Palma the Elder	1·25	90

1977. 60th Anniv of Russian Revolution. Mult.

1278	5f. Type **121**	40	10
1279	5f. Russia S.G. 455	40	10
1280	5f. Russia S.G. 1392	40	10
1281	5f. Russia S.G. 199	40	10
1282	8f. Decemberists' Square, Leningrad and Russia S.G. 983	25	10
1283	8f. Russia S.G. 2122	25	10
1284	8f. Russia S.G. 1041	25	10
1285	8f. Russia S.G. 2653	25	10
1286	11f. Pokrovski Cathedral, Moscow and Russia S.G. 3929	45	10
1287	11f. Russia S.G. 3540	45	10
1288	11f. Russia S.G. 3468	45	10
1289	11f. Russia S.G. 3921	45	10
1290	13f. May Day celebrations, Moscow and Russia S.G. 4518	60	15
1291	13f. Russia S.G. 3585	60	15
1292	13f. Russia S.G. 3024	60	15
1293	13f. Russia S.G. 2471	60	15

The four designs in each value were issued in se-tenant blocks of four, each design in the block having the same background.

122 Tanker Unloading (Commerce)

1977. 15th Anniv of Independence. Mult.

1294	1f. Type **122**	20	15
1295	5f. Assembling electric armatures (Economy)	20	15
1296	11f. Native dancers (Tourism)	30	20
1297	14f. Picking coffee (Agriculture)	45	30
1298	17f. National Palace, Bujumbura	55	40

1977. Christmas Charity. Nos. 1271/6 surch **+1F.**

1299	**120** 5f.+1f. mult (postage)	30	15
1300	– 13f.+1f. multicoloured	65	20
1301	– 27f.+1f. multicoloured	95	45
1302	– 18f.+1f. mult (air)	65	25
1303	– 31f.+1f. multicoloured	1·00	45
1304	– 40f.+1f. multicoloured	1·60	60

123 "Madonna and Child" (Solario) **124** Abyssinian Ground Hornbill

1979. Christmas (1978). Paintings of Virgin and Child by named artists. Multicoloured.

1306	13f. Rubens	85	85
1307	17f. Type **123**	90	90
1308	27f. Tiepolo	1·40	1·40
1309	31f. Gerard David	1·60	1·60
1310	40f. Bellini	2·00	2·00

1979. Christmas Charity. Nos. 1306/10 surch **+1F.**

1312	– 13f.+1f. multicoloured	85	85
1313	**123** 17f.+1f. multicoloured	90	90
1314	– 27f.+1f. multicoloured	1·40	1·40
1315	– 31f.+1f. multicoloured	1·60	1·60
1316	– 40f.+1f. multicoloured	2·00	2·00

1979. Birds. Multicoloured.

1318	1f. Type **124** (postage)	1·10	60
1319	2f. African darter	1·10	60
1320	3f. Little bee eater	1·10	60
1321	5f. Lesser flamingo	1·50	80
1322	8f. Congo peafowl	1·90	1·10
1323	10f. Purple swamphen	2·10	1·25
1324	20f. Martial eagle	2·40	1·40
1325	27f. Painted stork	3·00	1·75
1326	50f. Saddle-bill stork	4·75	2·50
1327	6f. Type **124** (air)	1·75	1·00
1328	13f. As No. 1319	2·10	1·25
1329	18f. As No. 1320	2·40	1·40
1330	26f. As No. 1321	2·75	1·60
1331	31f. As No. 1322	3·00	1·60
1332	36f. As No. 1323	3·00	1·75
1333	40f. As No. 1324	3·75	2·10
1334	54f. As No. 1325	4·00	2·40
1335	70f. As No. 1326	5·25	3·00

125 Mother and Child

1979. International Year of the Child. Mult.

1336	10f. Type **125**	90	90
1337	20f. Baby	1·40	1·40
1338	27f. Child with doll	1·50	1·50
1339	50f. S.O.S. village, Gitega	2·00	2·00

126 "Virgin and Child" (Raffaellino Del Garbo) **127** Sir Rowland Hill and Penny Black

1979. Christmas. "Virgin and Child" paintings by named artists. Multicoloured.

1341	20f. Type **126**	90	90
1342	27f. Giovanni Penni	1·10	1·10
1343	31f. Giulio Romano	1·25	1·25
1344	50f. Detail of "Adoration of the Shepherds" (Jacopo Bassano)	1·75	1·75

1979. Death Centenary of Sir Rowland Hill. Mult.

1346	20f. Type **127**	80	80
1347	27f. German East Africa 25p. stamp and Ruanda-Urundi 5c. stamp	95	95
1348	31f. Burundi 1f.25 and 50f. stamps of 1962	1·10	1·10
1349	40f. 4f. (1962) and 14f. (1969) stamps of Burundi	1·25	1·25
1350	60f. Heinrich von Stephan (founder of U.P.U.) and Burundi 14f. U.P.U. stamps of 1974	6·75	3·00

1979. Christmas Charity. Nos. 1341/4 additionally inscr with premium.

1352	20f.+1f. multicoloured	65	65
1353	27f.+1f. multicoloured	1·40	1·40
1354	31f.+1f. multicoloured	1·60	1·60
1355	50f.+1f. multicoloured	2·10	2·10

1980. As Nos. 1318/19 and 1321/3 but new values.

(a) With copper frames.

1356a	5f. Abyssinian ground hornbill		
1356b	10f. African darter		
1356c	40f. Lesser flamingo		
1356d	45f. Congo peafowl		
1356e	50f. Purple swamphen		

(b) With grey-green frames.

1356f	5f. As No. 1356a		
1356g	10f. As No. 1356b		
1356h	40f. As No. 1356c		
1356i	45f. As No. 1356d		
1356j	50f. As No. 1356e		

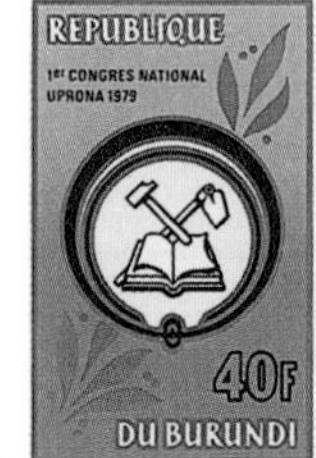

128 Approaching Hurdle (110 m Hurdles, Thomas Munkelt) **130** Congress Emblem

129 "The Virgin and Child" (Sebastiano Mainardi)

1980. Olympic Medal Winners. Multicoloured.

1357	20f. Type **128**	95	95
1358	20f. Jumping hurdle	95	95
1359	20f. Completing jump	95	95
1360	30f. Discus—beginning to throw	1·40	1·40
1361	30f. Continuing throw	1·40	1·40
1362	30f. Releasing discus	1·40	1·40
1363	40f. Football—running for goal (Czechoslovakia)	1·50	1·50
1364	40f. Kicking ball	1·50	1·50
1365	40f. Saving ball	1·50	1·50

1980. Christmas. Multicoloured.

1367	10f. Type **129**	90	90
1368	30f. "Doni Tondo" (Michelangelo)	1·50	1·50
1369	40f. "The Virgin and Child" (Piero di Cosimo)	2·10	2·10
1370	45f. "The Holy Family" (Fra Bartolomeo)	2·25	2·25

1980. 1st National Party Congress, Uprona.

1372	**130** 10f. multicoloured	30	30
1373	40f. multicoloured	1·50	1·50
1374	45f. multicoloured	1·60	1·60

1981. Christmas Charity. Nos. 1367/70 additionally inscr with premium.

1376	10f.+1f. multicoloured	75	75
1377	30f.+1f. multicoloured	1·75	1·75
1378	40f.+1f. multicoloured	2·25	2·25
1379	50f.+1f. multicoloured	2·50	2·50

131 Kepler and Dish Aerial

1981. 350th Death Anniv of Johannes Kepler (astronomer). First Earth Satellite Station in Burundi. Multicoloured.

1381	10f. Type **131**	60	60
1382	40f. Satellite and antenna	1·50	1·50
1383	45f. Satellite (different) and antenna	1·90	1·90

132 Giraffes

1982. African Animals (4th series). Multicoloured.

1385	2f. Lion	4·75	2·10
1386	3f. Type **132**	4·75	2·10
1387	5f. Black rhinoceros	4·75	2·10
1388	10f. African buffalo	15·00	6·75
1389	20f. African elephant	23·00	11·50
1390	25f. Hippopotamus	26·00	12·50
1391	30f. Common zebra	30·00	14·50
1392	50f. Warthog	55·00	26·00
1393	60f. Eland	70·00	32·00
1394	65f. Black-backed jackal	85·00	40·00
1395	70f. Cheetah	95·00	45·00
1396	75f. Blue Wildebeest	£100	48·00
1397	85f. Spotted hyena	£120	60·00

1983. Animal Protection Year. Nos. 1385/97 optd with World Wildlife Fund Emblem.

1398	2f. Type **131**	5·00	4·25
1399	3f. Giraffe	5·00	4·25
1400	5f. Black rhinoceros	5·00	4·25
1401	10f. African buffalo	14·00	13·00
1402	20f. African elephant	23·00	20·00
1403	25f. Hippopotamus	26·00	24·00
1404	30f. Common zebra	28·00	25·00
1405	50f. Warthog	55·00	48·00
1406	60f. Eland	70·00	60·00
1407	65f. Jackal ("Canis mesomelas")	80·00	75·00
1408	70f. Cheetah	95·00	80·00
1409	75f. Blue wildebeest	£100	90·00
1410	85f. Spotted Hyena	£120	£110

133 Flag and National Party Emblem

1983. 20th Anniv (1982) of Independence. Multicoloured.
1411 10f. Type **133** 65 65
1412 25f. Flag and arms . . . . 1·00 1·00
1413 30f. Flag and map of Africa 1·10 1·10
1414 50f. Flag and emblem . . . 1·50 1·50
1415 65f. Flag and President Bagaza . . . . 2·00 2·00

134 "Virgin and Child" (Lucas Signorelli)

1983. Christmas. Multicoloured.
1416 10f. Type **134** . . . . . . 1·10 1·10
1417 25f. E. Murillo . . . . . . 1·50 1·50
1418 30f. Carlo Crivelli . . . . . 1·75 1·75
1419 50f. Nicolas Poussin . . . . 2·40 2·40
DESIGNS: Virgin and Child paintings by named artists.

1983. Christmas Charity. Nos. 1416/19 additionally inscr with premium.
1421 10f.+1f. multicoloured . . . 1·10 1·10
1422 25f.+1f. multicoloured . . . 1·50 1·50
1423 30f.+1f. multicoloured . . . 1·75 1·75
1424 50f.+1f. multicoloured . . . 2·40 2·40

135 "Papilio zalmoxis"

1984. Butterflies. Multicoloured.
1426 5f. Type **135** . . . . 2·00 85
1427 5f. "Cymothoe coccinata" 2·00 85
1428 10f. "Papilio antimachus" 4·75 2·10
1429 10f. "Asterope pechueli" . . 4·75 2·10
1430 30f. "Bebearia mardania" 9·25 4·00
1431 30f. "Papilio hesperus" . . 9·25 4·00
1432 35f. "Euphaedra perseis" . . 12·00 5·25
1433 35f. "Euphaedra neophron" 12·00 5·25
1434 65f. "Pseudacraea striata" 22·00 9·75
1435 65f. "Euphaedra imperialis" 22·00 9·75

136 Stamps of German East Africa and Belgian Occupation

1984. 19th U.P.U. Congress, Hamburg. Mult.
1436 10f. Type **136** 65 65
1437 30f. 1962 Burundi overprinted stamps . . . . 1·10 1·10
1438 35f. 1969 14f. Letter-writing Week and 1982 30f. Zebra stamps . . . . 1·25 1·25
1439 65f. Heinrich von Stephan (founder of U.P.U.) and 1974 14f. U.P.U. Centenary stamps . . . . 18·00 11·50

137 Jesse Owens (runner)

1984. Olympic Games, Los Angeles. Mult.
1441 10f. Type **137** . . . . 1·10 1·10
1442 30f. Rafer Johnson (discus thrower) . . . . 1·60 1·60
1443 35f. Bob Beamon (long jumper) . . . . 1·75 1·75
1444 65f. K. Keino (sprinter) . . 2·25 2·25

138 "Virgin and Child" (Botticelli)

1984. Christmas. Multicoloured.
1446 10f. "Rest on the Flight into Egypt" (Murillo) 30 30
1447 25f. "Virgin and Child" (R. del Garbo) . . . . 1·10 1·10
1448 30f. Type **138** . . . . 1·60 1·60
1449 50f. "Adoration of the Shepherds" (J. Bassano) 2·00 2·00

1984. Christmas Charity. As Nos. 1446/49 but with additional premium.
1451 10f.+1f. multicoloured . . . 30 30
1452 25f.+1f. multicoloured . . . 1·10 1·10
1453 30f.+1f. multicoloured . . . 1·60 1·60
1454 50f.+1f. multicoloured . . . 2·00 2·00

139 Thunbergia

140 Bombs as Flats

1986. Flowers. Multicoloured.
1456 2f. Type **139** (postage) . . . 1·40 80
1457 3f. African violets . . . . . 1·40 80
1458 5f. "Clivia" . . . . 1·40 80
1459 10f. "Cassia" . . . . 1·40 80
1460 20f. Bird of Paradise flower 2·50 1·60
1461 35f. "Gloriosa" . . . . . . 4·50 3·00

1462 70f. Type **139** (air) . . . . 2·50 2·10
1463 75f. As No. 1457 . . . . . 2·75 2·25
1464 80f. As No. 1458 . . . . . 2·75 2·40
1465 85f. As No. 1459 . . . . . 3·25 2·75
1466 100f. As No. 1460 . . . . . 3·50 2·75
1467 150f. As No. 1461 . . . . . 6·00 5·00

1987. International Peace Year (1986). Mult.
1468 10f. Type **140** 20 20
1469 20f. Molecular diagrams as flower 40 40
1470 30f. Clasped hands across globe . . . . 1·10 1·10
1471 40f. Chicks in split globe . . 1·25 1·25

141 Map, Airplane and Emblem

1987. 10th Anniv of Great Lakes Countries Economic Community. Multicoloured.
1473 5f. Type **141** 55 55
1474 10f. Map, ear of wheat, cogwheel and emblem . . 65 65
1475 15f. Map, factory and emblem 75 75
1476 25f. Map, electricity pylons and emblem . . . . . . 1·60 1·60
1477 35f. Map, flags and emblem 2·25 2·25

142 Leaves and Sticks Shelter

1988. International Year of Shelter for the Homeless (1987). Multicoloured.
1479 10f. Type **142** 55 55
1480 20f. People living in concrete pipes 70 70
1481 80f. Boys mixing mortar . . 1·50 1·50
1482 150f. Boys with model house 3·00 3·00

143 Skull between Cigarettes

144 Pope John Paul II

1989. Anti-smoking Campaign. Multicoloured.
1484 5f. Type **143** 70 70
1485 20f. Cigarettes, lungs and skull . . . . 1·40 1·40
1486 80f. Cigarettes piercing skull 2·25 2·25

1989. Various stamps surch.
1487b 20f. on 3f. mult (No. 1457) 70 70
1487c 80f. on 30f. mult (No. 1430) . . . . . . 2·00 2·00
1487d 80f. on 30f. mult (No. 1431) . . . . . . 2·00 2·00
1487e 80f. on 35f. mult (No. 1432) . . . . . . 2·00 2·00
1487f 80f. on 35f. mult (No. 1433) . . . . . . 2·00 2·00
1487g 85f. on 65f. mult (No. 1435) . . . . . .

1990. Papal Visit.
1488 **144** 5f. multicoloured 45 45
1489 10f. multicoloured . . . 45 45
1490 20f. multicoloured . . . 70 70
1491 30f. multicoloured . . . 70 70
1492 50f. multicoloured . . . 1·40 1·40
1493 80f. multicoloured . . . 2·00 2·00

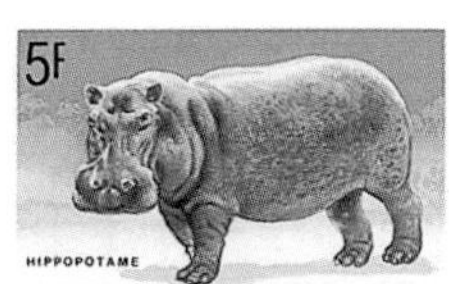

145 Hippopotamus

1991. Animals. Multicoloured.
1495 5f. Type **145** . . . . 1·10 75
1496 10f. Hen and cockerel . . . 1·10 75
1497 20f. Lion . . . . 1·10 75
1498 30f. Elephant . . . . 1·10 1·10
1499 50f. Helmet guineafowl ("Pintade") . . . . 3·00 2·25
1500 80f. Crocodile . . . . 4·50 3·25

146 Drummer

147 "Impatiens petersiana"

1992. Traditional Dancing. Multicoloured.
1502 15f. Type **146** 25 25
1503 30f. Men dancing 40 40
1504 115f. Group of drummers (horiz) . . . . 1·90 1·90
1505 200f. Men dancing in fields (horiz) . . . . 3·25 3·25

1992. Flowers. Multicoloured.
1507 15f. Type **147** 90 65
1508 20f. "Lachenalia aloides" "Nelsonii" 90 65
1509 30f. Egyptian lotus . . . . 1·40 1·00
1510 50f. Kaffir lily . . . . . . 3·00 2·25

148 Pigtail Macaque

1992. Air. Animals. Multicoloured.
1512 100f. Type **148** . . . . . . 2·40 1·75
1513 115f. Grevy's zebra . . . . 2·75 2·10
1514 200f. Ox . . . . 4·00 3·00
1515 220f. Eastern white pelican 5·00 3·75

149 People holding Hands and Flag

1992. 30th Anniv of Independence. Multicoloured.
1517 30f. Type **149** 20 20
1518 85f. State flag 80 80
1519 110f. Independence monument (vert) . . . . 1·10 1·10
1520 115f. As No. 1518 . . . . . 1·10 1·10
1521 120f. Map (vert) . . . . . 1·40 1·40
1522 140f. Type **149** . . . . . . 1·50 1·50
1523 200f. As No. 1519 . . . . . 2·10 2·10
1524 250f. As No. 1521 . . . . . 2·75 2·75

150 "Russula ingens"

1992. Fungi. Multicoloured.
1525 10f. Type **150** 15 15
1526 15f. "Russula brunneorigida" 20 20
1527 20f. "Amanita zambiana" 25 30
1528 30f. "Russula subfistulosa" 40 45
1529 75f. "Russula meleagris" . . 90 95
1530 85f. As No. 1529 . . . . . 1·00 1·10
1531 100f. "Russula immaculata" 1·25 1·25
1532 110f. Type **150** . . . . . . 1·40 1·40
1533 115f. As No. 1526 . . . . . 1·40 1·40
1534 120f. "Russula sejuncta" . . 1·40 1·60
1535 130f. As No. 1534 . . . . . 1·50 1·60
1536 250f. "Afroboletus luteolus" 3·00 3·25

151 Columbus's Fleet, Treasure and Globes

1992. 500th Anniv of Discovery of America by Columbus. Multicoloured.
1541 200f. Type **151** . . . . . . 2·00 2·00
1542 400f. American produce, globes and Columbus's fleet . . . . 4·25 4·25

152 Serval

1992. The Serval. Multicoloured.
1543 30f. Type **152** 60 50
1544 130f. Pair sitting and crouching . . . . 2·40 2·00
1545 200f. Pair, one standing over the other . . . . 3·75 3·00
1546 220f. Heads of pair . . . . 4·00 3·50

153 Running

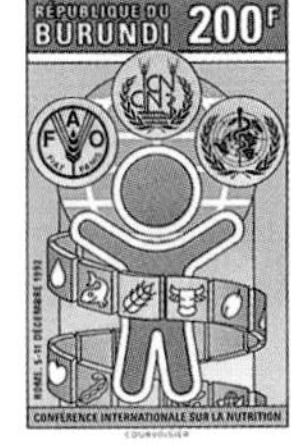

154 Emblems

1992. Olympic Games, Barcelona. Multicoloured.
1547 130f. Type **153** . . . . . . 1·50 1·50
1548 500f. Hurdling . . . . . . 5·25 5·25

1992. International Nutrition Conference, Rome. Multicoloured.
1549 200f. Type **154** . . . . . . 2·00 2·00
1550 220f. Woman's face made from vegetables (G. Arcimbolo) . . . . . 2·40 2·40

155 Horsemen

156 Flags of Member Countries and European Community Emblem

1992. Christmas. Details of "Adoration of the Magi" by Gentile da Fabriano. Multicoloured.

No.	Type	Description	Unused	Used
1551		100f. Type **155**	90	90
1552		130f. Three Kings	1·10	1·10
1553		250f. Holy family	2·50	2·50

1993. European Single Market. Multicoloured.

No.	Type	Description	Unused	Used
1555		130f. Type **156**	1·25	1·25
1556		500f. Europe shaking hands with Africa	5·00	5·00

157 Indonongo

1993. Musical Instruments. Multicoloured.

No.	Type	Description	Unused	Used
1557		200f. Type **157**	2·00	2·00
1558		220f. Ingoma (drum)	2·25	2·25
1559		250f. Ikembe (xylophone)	2·50	2·50
1560		300f. Umuduri (musical bow)	3·25	3·25

158 Broad Blue-banded Swallowtail

159 Players, Stadium, United States Flag and Statue of Liberty

1993. Butterflies. Multicoloured.

No.	Type	Description	Unused	Used
1561		130f. Type **158**	1·50	1·25
1562		200f. Green charaxes	2·40	2·10
1563		250f. Migratory glider	3·00	2·50
1564		300f. Red swallowtail	3·75	3·50

1993. World Cup Football Championship, U.S.A. (1994). Multicoloured.

No.	Type	Description	Unused	Used
1566		130f. Type **159**	1·25	1·25
1567		200f. Players, stadium, United States flag and Golden Gate Bridge	2·50	2·50

160 Cattle

161 Woman with Baby and Two Men

1993. Domestic Animals. Multicoloured.

No.	Type	Description	Unused	Used
1568		100f. Type **160**	1·00	1·00
1569		120f. Sheep	1·10	1·10
1570		130f. Pigs	1·25	1·25
1571		250f. Goats	2·50	2·50

1993. Christmas. Each orange and black.

No.	Type	Description	Unused	Used
1572		100f. Type **161**	1·25	1·25
1573		130f. Nativity	1·50	1·50
1574		250f. Woman with baby and three men	3·00	3·00

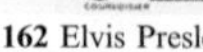
162 Elvis Presley

163 "The Discus Thrower" (statue)

1994. Entertainers. Multicoloured.

No.	Type	Description	Unused	Used
1576		60f. Type **162**	30	30
1577		115f. Mick Jagger	55	55
1578		120f. John Lennon	60	60
1579		200f. Michael Jackson	1·00	1·00

1994. Cent of International Olympic Committee.

No.	Type	Description	Unused	Used
1581	**163**	150f. multicoloured	75	75

164 Pres. Buyoya handing over Baton of Power to Pres. Ndadaye

165 Madonna, China

1994. 1st Anniv of First Multi-party Elections in Burundi. Multicoloured.

No.	Type	Description	Unused	Used
1582		30f.+10f. Type **164**	20	20
1583		110f.+10f. Pres. Ndadaye (first elected President) giving inauguration speech	60	60
1584		115f.+10f. Arms on map	60	60
1585		120f.+10f. Warrior on map	65	65

1994. Christmas. Multicoloured.

No.	Type	Description	Unused	Used
1586		115f. Type **165**	55	55
1587		120f. Madonna, Japan	60	60
1588		250f. Black Virgin, Poland	1·25	1·25

166 Emblem and Earth

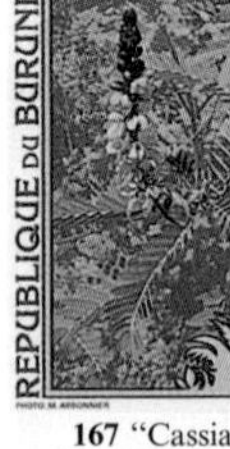
167 "Cassia didymobotrya"

1995. 50th Anniversaries. Multicoloured.

No.	Type	Description	Unused	Used
1590		115f. Type **166** (F.A.O.)	55	55
1591		120f. U.N.O. emblems and dove	60	60

1995. Flowers. Multicoloured.

No.	Type	Description	Unused	Used
1592		15f. Type **167**	15	15
1593		20f. "Mitragyna rubrostipulosa"	15	15
1594		30f. "Phytolacca dodecandra"	25	20
1595		85f. "Acanthus pubescens"	65	60
1596		100f. "Bulbophyllum comatum"	80	75
1597		110f. "Angraecum evrardianum"	90	80
1598		115f. "Eulophia burundiensis"	90	80
1599		120f. "Habenaria adolphii"	1·00	90

168 Otraca Bus

169 Boy with Panga

1995. Transport. Multicoloured.

No.	Type	Description	Unused	Used
1600		30f. Type **168**	15	15
1601		115f. Transintra lorry	65	65
1602		120f. Lake ferry	90	70
1603		250f. Air Burundi airplane	1·40	1·40

1995. Christmas. Multicoloured.

No.	Type	Description	Unused	Used
1604		100f. Type **169**	55	55
1605		130f. Boy with sheaf of wheat	75	75
1606		250f. Mother and children	1·40	1·40

170 Venuste Niyongabo

1996. Olympic Games, Atlanta. Runners. Mult.

No.	Type	Description	Unused	Used
1608		130f. Type **170** (5000 m gold medal winner)	40	40
1609		500f. Arthemon Hatungimana	1·50	1·50

171 Hadada Ibis

1996. Birds. Multicoloured.

No.	Type	Description	Unused	Used
1610		15f. Type **171**	25	25
1611		20f. Egyptian goose	25	25
1612		30f. African fish eagle	25	25
1613		120f. Goliath heron	75	75
1614		165f. South African crowned crane	1·00	1·00
1615		220f. African jacana	1·40	1·40

172 Marlier's Julie

1996. Fishes of Lake Tanganyika. Multicoloured.

No.	Type	Description	Unused	Used
1616		30f. Type **172**	25	20
1617		115f. "Cyphotilapia frontosa"	75	60
1618		120f. "Lamprologus brichardi"	75	60
1619		250f. Stone squeaker	1·50	1·25

173 Children

1998. 50th Anniv of S.O.S Children's Villages. Multicoloured.

No.	Type	Description	Unused	Used
1621		100f. Type **173**	25	25
1622		250f. Flags, "50" and children waving	65	65
1623		270f. Children dancing around flag	70	70

174 Madonna and Child

175 Diana, Princess of Wales

1999. Christmas (1996–98). Multicoloured.

No.	Type	Description	Unused	Used
1624		100f. Type **174** (1996)	25	25
1625		130f. Madonna and Child (different) (1997)	30	30
1626		250f. Madonna and Child (different) (1998)	65	65

1999. 2nd Death Anniv of Diana, Princess of Wales.

No.	Type	Description	Unused	Used
1628	**175**	100f. multicoloured	20	20
1629		250f. multicoloured	20	20
1630		300f. multicoloured	50	50

176 Danny Kaye (entertainer) holding African Baby

2000. New Millennium. "A World Free from Hunger".

No.	Type	Description	Unused	Used
1631	**176**	350f. multicoloured	60	60

BUSHIRE Pt. 1

An Iranian seaport. Stamps issued during the British occupation in the 1914–18 War.

20 chahis = 1 kran, 10 krans = 1 toman.

1915. Portrait stamps of Iran (1911) optd **BUSHIRE Under British Occupation.**

No.	Type	Description	Unused	Used
1	**57**	1ch. orange and green	40·00	42·00
2		2ch. brown and red	40·00	38·00
3		3ch. green and grey	48·00	55·00
4		5ch. red and brown	£300	£300
5		6ch. lake and green	38·00	26·00
6		9ch. lilac and brown	38·00	42·00
7		10ch. brown and red	40·00	42·00
8		12ch. blue and green	48·00	50·00
9		24ch. green and purple	80·00	55·00
10		1kr. red and blue	75·00	29·00
11		2kr. red and green	£200	£160
12		3kr. black and lilac	£170	£180
13		5kr. blue and red	£120	£100
14		10kr. red and brown	£100	95·00

1915. Coronation issue of Iran optd **BUSHIRE Under British Occupation.**

No.	Type	Description	Unused	Used
15	**66**	1ch. blue and red	£350	£350
16		2ch. red and blue	£6500	£7000
17		3ch. green	£425	£425
18		5ch. red	£5500	£5500
19		6ch. red and green	£4200	£4500
20		9ch. violet and brown	£600	£650
21		10ch. brown and green	£900	£950
22		12ch. blue	£1100	£1200
23		24ch. black and brown	£425	£425
24	**67**	1kr. black, brown and silver	£425	£450
25		2kr. red, blue and silver	£375	£400
26		3kr. black, lilac and silver	£500	£500
27		5kr. slate, brown and silver	£475	£500
28	–	1t. black, violet and gold	£425	£475
29	–	3t. red, lake and gold	£3000	£3000

BUSSAHIR (BASHAHR) Pt. 1

A state in the Punjab, India. Now uses Indian stamps.

12 pies = 1 anna; 16 annas = 1 rupee.

1

1895. Various frames. Imperf, perf or roul.

No.	Type	Description	Unused	Used
9	**1**	¼a. pink	48·00	85·00
10		½a. grey	19·00	95·00
11		1a. red	20·00	75·00
12		2a. yellow	29·00	80·00
13		4a. violet	20·00	85·00
14		8a. brown	21·00	90·00
15		12a. green	60·00	£110
16		1r. blue	35·00	90·00

1896. Similar types, but inscriptions on white ground and inscr "POSTAGE" instead of "STAMP".

No.	Type	Description	Unused	Used
27	**1**	¼a. violet	16·00	14·00
37		¼a. red	3·25	8·00
25		½a. blue	6·50	14·00
26		1a. olive	13·00	30·00
32		1a. red	3·75	11·00
41		2a. yellow	35·00	60·00
36		4a. red	40·00	90·00

CAICOS ISLANDS Pt. 1

Separate issues for these islands, part of the Turks and Caicos Islands group, appeared from 1981 to 1985.

100 cents = 1 dollar.

1981. Nos. 514, 518, 520, 523 and 525/7 of Turks and Caicos Islands optd **CAICOS ISLANDS**.

No.	Type	Description	Unused	Used
1		1c. Indigo hamlet	15	15
2		5c. Spanish grunt	20	20
3		8c. Four-eyed butterflyfish	20	20
4		20c. Queen angelfish	35	30
5		50c. Royal gramma ("Fairy Basslet")	50	1·00

6 $1 Fin-spot wrasse . . . . . . 70 1·75
7 $2 Stoplight parrotfish . . . . 1·40 3·25

1981. Royal Wedding. Nos. 653/6 of Turks and Caicos Islands optd. (A) **Caicos Islands**.
8A 35c. Prince Charles and Lady Diana Spencer . . . 20 25
9A 65c. Kensington Palace . . . 30 40
10A 90c. Prince Charles as Colonel of the Welsh Guards 40 50

(B) **CAICOS ISLANDS**.
8B 35c. Prince Charles and Lady Diana Spencer 30 70
9B 65c. Kensington Palace . . . 40 1·00
10B 90c. Prince Charles as Colonel of the Welsh Guards . . . . 50 1·50

1981. Royal Wedding. As Nos. 657/9 of Turks and Caicos Islands, but each inscr "Caicos Islands". Mult. Self-adhesive.
12 20c. Lady Diana Spencer . . . 30 40
13 $1 Prince Charles . . . . . . 80 1·25
14 $2 Prince Charles and Lady Diana Spencer . . . . . . 4·00 5·50

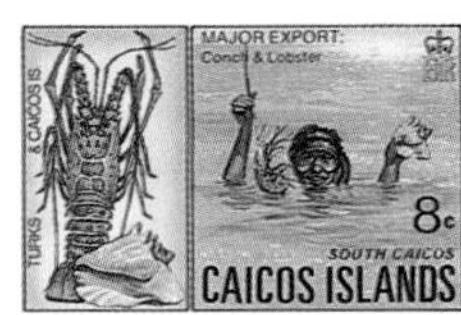

4 Queen or Pink Conch and Lobster Fishing, South Caicos

1983. Multicoloured.
15 8c. Type **4** . . . . 1·25 75
16 10c. Hawksbill turtle, East Caicos . . . . 1·50 90
17 20c. Arawak Indians and idol, Middle Caicos . . . . . . 1·50 90
18 35c. Boat-building, North Caicos . . . . 1·75 1·25
19 50c. Marine biologist at work, Pine Cay . . . . 2·50 1·75
20 95c. Boeing 707 airliner at new airport, Providenciales . . . 4·75 3·00
21 $1.10 Columbus's "Pinta", West Caicos . . . . 4·75 3·00
22 $2 Fort George Cay . . . . . 3·50 4·50
23 $3 Pirates Anne Bonny and Calico Jack at Parrot Cay 6·00 4·75

5 Goofy and Patch

1983. Christmas. Multicoloured.
30 1c. Type **5** 10 20
31 1c. Chip and Dale 10 20
32 2c. Morty 10 20
33 2c. Morty and Ferdie 10 20
34 3c. Goofy and Louie 10 20
35 3c. Donald Duck, Huey, Dewey and Louie 10 20
36 50c. Uncle Scrooge . . . . . 3·50 2·75
37 70c. Mickey Mouse and Ferdie 3·75 3·25
38 $1.10 Pinocchio, Jiminy Cricket and Figaro . . . . 4·50 4·25
MS39 126 × 101 mm. $2 Morty and Ferdie 3·75 3·50

6 "Leda and the Swan"

7 High Jumping

1984. 500th Birth Anniv of Raphael. Mult.
40 35c. Type **6** 75 50
41 50c. "Study of Apollo for Parnassus" . . . . 1·00 70
42 95c. "Study of two figures for the battle of Ostia" . . . . 2·00 1·25
43 $1.10 "Study for the Madonna of the Goldfinch" . . . . . 2·00 1·50
MS44 71 × 100 mm. $2.50, "The Garvagh Madonna" 3·00 3·25

1984. Olympic Games, Los Angeles.
45 **7** 4c. multicoloured 15 10
46 – 25c. multicoloured 30 20
47 – 65c. black, deep blue and blue . . . . 1·50 50
48 – $1.10 multicoloured . . . . 1·25 85
MS49 105 × 75 mm. $2 multicoloured 2·25 3·00
DESIGNS—VERT: 25c. Archery; 65c. Cycling; $1.10, Football. HORIZ: $2.50, Show jumping.

8 Horace Horsecollar and Clarabelle Cow

1984. Easter. Walt Disney Cartoon Characters. Multicoloured.
50 35c. Type **8** . . . . 1·25 60
51 45c. Mickey and Minnie Mouse, and Chip . . . . . 1·40 75
52 75c. Gyro Gearloose, Chip 'n Dale . . . . 1·75 1·25
53 85c. Mickey Mouse, Chip 'n Dale . . . . 1·75 1·40
MS54 127 × 101 mm. $2.20, Donald Duck 5·50 3·75

1984. Universal Postal Union Congress Hamburg. Nos. 20/1 optd **UNIVERSAL POSTAL UNION 1874–1984** and emblem.
55 95c. Boeing 707 airliner at new airport, Providenciales . . . 1·00 1·25
56 $1.10 Columbus's "Pinta", West Caicos . . . . 1·25 1·50

1984. "Ausipex" International Stamp Exhibition, Melbourne. No. 22 optd **AUSIPEX 1984**.
57 $2 Fort George Cay . . . . . 2·40 2·50

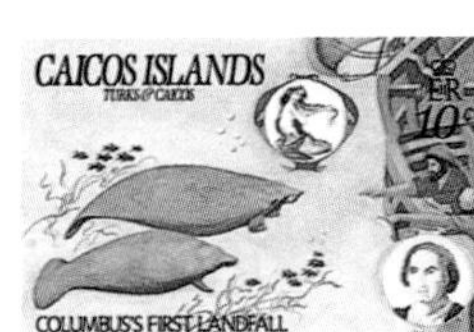

11 Seamen sighting American Manatees

1984. 492nd Anniv of Columbus's First Landfall. Multicoloured.
58 10c. Type **11** 90 65
59 70c. Columbus's fleet . . . . 3·50 3·00
60 $1 First landing in the West Indies . . . . 4·00 3·50
MS61 99 × 69 mm. $2 Fleet of Columbus (different) 2·75 3·00

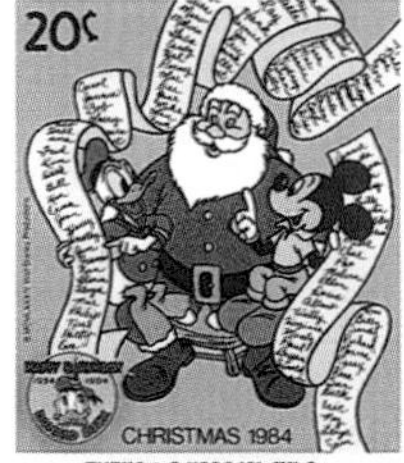

12 Donald Duck and Mickey Mouse with Father Christmas

1984. Christmas. Walt Disney Cartoon Characters. Multicoloured.
62 20c. Type **12** . . . . 1·25 85
63 35c. Donald Duck opening refrigerator . . . . 1·60 1·00
64 50c. Mickey Mouse, Donald Duck and toy train . . . . 2·25 1·75
65 75c. Donald Duck and parcels 2·75 2·50
66 $1.10 Donald Duck and carol singers . . . . 3·00 3·00
MS67 127 × 102 mm. $2 Donald Duck as Christmas tree 3·75 4·00

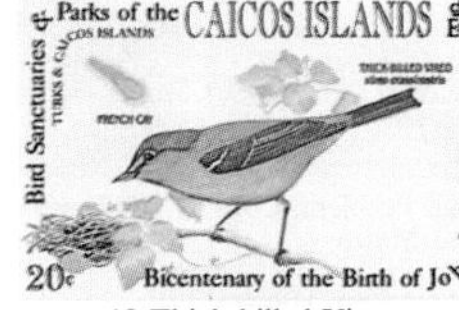

13 Thick-billed Vireo

1985. Birth Bicentenary of John J. Audubon (ornithologist). Multicoloured.
68 20c. Type **13** . . . . 1·75 60
69 35c. Black-faced grassquit . . 2·00 85
70 50c. Pearly-eyed thrasher . . . 2·25 1·25
71 $1 Greater Antillean bullfinch 2·75 2·00
MS72 100 × 70 mm. $2 Striped-headed tanager 3·50 3·50

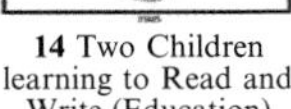
14 Two Children learning to Read and Write (Education)

16 The Queen Mother visiting Foundation for the Disabled, Leatherhead

15 Douglas DC-3 on Ground

1985. International Youth Year. 40th Anniv of United Nations. Multicoloured.
73 16c. Type **14** 20 25
74 35c. Two children on playground swings (Health) 50 55
75 70c. Boy and girl (Love) . . . 1·00 1·10
76 90c. Three children (Peace) . . 1·25 1·40
MS77 101 × 71 mm. $2 Child, dove carrying ears of wheat and map of the Americas 2·75 3·00

1985. 40th Anniv of International Civil Aviation Organization. Multicoloured.
78 35c. Type **15** . . . . 2·75 55
79 75c. Convair CV 440 Metropolitan . . . . 3·75 1·40
80 90c. Britten Norman Islander 3·75 1·60
MS81 100 × 70 mm. $2.20, Hand-gliding over the Caicos Islands 3·00 3·25

1985. Life and Times of Queen Elizabeth the Queen Mother. Multicoloured.
82 35c. Type **16** . . . . 1·10 55
83 65c. With Princess Anne (horiz) . . . . 1·60 95
84 95c. At Epsom, 1961 . . . . 1·90 1·60
MS85 56 × 85 mm. $2 Visiting Royal Hospital, Chelsea 4·25 3·00

1985. 150th Birth Anniv of Mark Twain (author). Designs as T **118** of Anguilla, showing Walt Disney cartoon characters in scenes from "Tom Sawyer, Detective". Multicoloured.
86 8c. Huckleberry Finn (Goofy) and Tom Sawyer (Mickey Mouse) reading reward notice 60 20
87 35c. Huck and Tom meeting Jake Dunlap . . . . 1·75 65
88 95c. Huck and Tom spying on Jubiter Dunlap . . . . . . 3·25 2·00
89 $1.10 Huck and Tom with hound (Pluto) . . . . . . 3·25 2·25
MS90 127 × 101 mm. Tom unmasking Jubiter Dunlap 4·75 4·25

1985. Birth Bicentenaries of Grimm Brothers (folklorists). Designs as T **119** of Anguilla, showing Walt Disney cartoon characters in scenes from "Six Soldiers of Fortune". Multicoloured.
91 16c. The Soldier (Donald Duck) with his meagre pay 1·50 30
92 25c. The Soldier meeting the Strong Man (Horace Horsecollar) . . . . 1·75 45
93 65c. The Soldier meeting the Marksman (Mickey Mouse) 3·25 1·25
94 $1.35 The Fast Runner (Goofy) winning the race against the Princess (Daisy Duck) . . . . 4·00 2·25
MS95 126 × 101 mm. $2 The Soldier and the Strong Man with sack of gold 4·75 4·00

CAMBODIA Pt. 21

A kingdom in south-east Asia.

From 1887 Cambodia was part of the Union of Indo-China. In 1949 it became an Associated State of the French Union, in 1953 it attained sovereign independence and in 1955 it left the Union.

Following the introduction of a republican constitution in 1970 the name of the country was changed to Khmer Republic and in 1975 to Kampuchea.

In 1989 it reverted to the name of Cambodia. Under a new constitution in 1993 it became a parliamentary monarchy.

1951. 100 cents = 1 piastre.
1955. 100 cents = 1 riel.

1 "Apsara" or Dancing Nymph

2 Throne Room, Phnom-Penh

3 King Norodom Sihanouk

5 "Kinnari"

1951.
1 **1** 10c. green and deep green . . 85 85
2 20c. brown and red 70 55
3 30c. blue and violet 70 55
4 40c. blue and ultramarine . . 70 55
5 **2** 50c. green and deep green . . 60 55
6 **3** 80c. green and blue 85 90
7 **2** 1p. violet and blue . . . . . 1·25 1·10
8 **3** 1p.10 red and lake . . . . . 1·40 1·10
9 **3** 1p.50 red and lake . . . . . 1·75 1·25
10 **2** 1p.50 blue and indigo . . . . 1·60 1·25
11 **3** 1p.50 brown and chocolate 1·60 1·25
12 1p.90 blue and indigo . . . . 2·75 2·25
13 **2** 2p. brown and red . . . . . 2·75 1·50
14 **3** 3p. brown and red . . . . . 3·25 2·75
15 **1** 5p. violet and blue . . . . . 12·00 5·25
16 **2** 10p. blue and violet . . . . 24·00 12·00
17 **3** 15p. violet and deep violet . . 30·00 18·00

1952. Students' Aid Fund. Surch **AIDE A L'ETUDIANT** and premium.
18 **3** 1p.10+40c. red and lake . . . 3·75 4·00
19 1p.90+60c. blue & indigo . . 3·75 4·00
20 3p.+1p. brown and red . . . 3·75 4·00
21 **1** 5p.+2p. violet and blue . . . 3·75 4·00

1953. Air.
22 **5** 50c. green 85 80
23 3p. red 95 85
24 3p.30 violet . . . . 1·40 1·25
25 4p. blue and brown . . . . . 1·60 1·50
26 5p.10 ochre, red and brown 2·75 2·25
27 6p.50 purple and brown . . . 2·75 2·75
28 9p. green and mauve . . . . 3·75 4·00
29 11p.50 multicoloured . . . . 8·00 6·50
30 30p. ochre, brown and green 15·00 11·00

6 Arms of Cambodia

7 "Postal Transport"

1954.
31 – 10c. red 30 30
32 – 20c. green 30 20
33 – 30c. blue 30 20
34 – 40c. violet 30 20
35 – 50c. purple 30 20
36 – 70c. brown 40 30
37 – 1p. violet 50 30
38 – 1p.50 red 50 30
39 **6** 2p. red 50 50
40 2p.50 green 80 70
41 **7** 2p.50 green . . . . 1·75 1·25
42 **6** 3p. blue . . . . 1·50 1·40
43 **7** 4p. sepia . . . . 2·50 2·50
44 **6** 4p.50 violet . . . . 1·90 1·40
45 **7** 5p. red . . . . 3·50 2·50
46 **6** 6p. brown . . . . 2·25 1·90
47 **7** 10p. violet . . . . 3·75 2·25
48 15p. blue . . . . 4·25 2·75
49 – 20p. blue . . . . 8·25 5·50
50 – 30p. green . . . . 13·00 9·75
DESIGNS—VERT: 10c. to 50c. View of Phnom Daun Penah. HORIZ: 70c. 1, 1p.50, 20, 30p. East Gate, Temple of Angkor.

8 King Norodom Suramarit **9** King and Queen of Cambodia

1955.
51 – 50c. blue 25 25
52 **8** 50c. violet 25 25
53 1r. red 40 25
54 2r. blue 45 40
55 – 2r.50 brown 60 50
56 – 4r. green 90 80
57 – 6r. lake 1·40 1·10
58 **8** 7r. brown 1·75 1·25
59 – 15r. lilac 2·75 2·10
60 **8** 20r. green 4·00 3·00
PORTRAIT: Nos. 51, 55/7 and 59, Queen Kossamak.
For stamps as Nos. 58 and 60, but with black border, see Nos. 101/2.

1955. Coronation (1st issue).
61 **9** 1r.50 sepia and brown 55 35
62 2r. black and blue 55 35
63 3r. red and orange 70 55
64 5r. black and green 1·10 90
65 10r. purple and violet 1·90 1·10
See Nos. 66/71.

10 King Norodom Suramarit **11** Prince Sihanouk, Flags and Globe

1956. Coronation (2nd issue).
66 **10** 2r. red 1·50 1·50
67 – 3r. blue 2·10 2·10
68 – 5r. green 4·00 4·00
69 **10** 10r. green 7·75 7·75
70 30r. violet 18·00 18·00
71 – 50r. purple 35·00 35·00
PORTRAIT—VERT: 3, 5, 50r. Queen of Cambodia.

1957. 1st Anniv of Admission of Cambodia to U.N.O.
72 **11** 2r. red, blue and green 1·00 70
73 4r.50 blue 1·00 70
74 8r.50 red 1·00 70

12 **13** Mythological Bird

1957. 2,500th Anniv of Buddhism. (a) With premiums.
75 **12** 1r.50+50c. bis, red & bl 1·25 1·25
76 6r.50+1r.50 bis, red & pur 2·00 2·00
77 8r.+2r. bistre, red & blue 3·25 3·25
(b) Colours changed and premiums omitted.
78 **12** 1r.50 red 85 85
79 6r.50 violet 1·00 1·00
80 8r. green 1·00 1·00

1957. Air.
81 **13** 50c. lake 30 15
82 1r. green 40 20
83 4r. blue 1·40 95
84 50r. red 6·00 5·50
85 100r. red, green and blue 10·50 7·75

14 King Ang Duong **15** King Norodom I

1958. King Ang Duong Commemoration.
86 **14** 1r.50 brown and violet 35 35
87 5r. bistre and black 45 45
88 10r. sepia and purple 90 90

1958. King Norodom I Commemoration.
89 **15** 2r. brown and blue 30 30
90 6r. green and orange 45 45
91 15r. brown and green 90 90

16 Children

1959. Children's World Friendship.
92 **16** 20c. purple 25 25
93 50c. blue 40 40
94 80c. red 90 90

1959. Red Cross Fund. Nos. 92/4 surch with red cross and premium.
95 **16** 20c.+20c. purple 25 25
96 50c.+30c. blue 50 50
97 80c.+50c. red 95 95

18 Prince Sihanouk, Plan of Port and Freighter **19** Sacred Plough in Procession

1960. Inauguration of Sihanoukville Port.
98 **18** 2r. sepia and red 50 50
99 5r. brown and blue 50 50
100 20r. blue and violet 1·75 1·75

1960. King Norodom Suramarit Mourning issue. Nos. 58 and 60 reissued with black border.
101 **8** 7r. brown and black 3·00 3·00
102 20r. green and black 3·00 3·00

1960. Festival of the Sacred Furrow.
103 **19** 1r. purple 40 40
104 2r. brown 50 50
105 3r. green 75 75

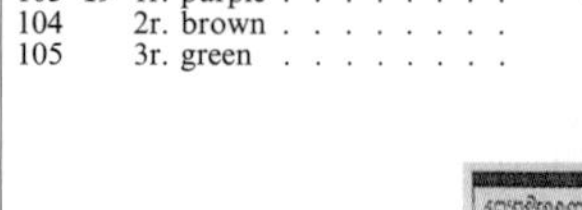

20 Child and Book ("Education") **21** Flag and Dove of Peace

1960. "Works of the Five Year Plan".
106 **20** 2r. brown, blue and green 35 25
107 – 3r. green and brown 45 30
108 – 4r. violet, green and pink 45 35
109 – 6r. brown, orange & green 55 45
110 – 10r. blue, green and bistre 1·25 85
111 – 25r. red and lake 2·75 2·40
DESIGNS—HORIZ: 3r. Chhouksar Barrage ("Irrigation"); 6r. Carpenter and huts ("Construction"); 10r. Rice-field ("Agriculture"). VERT: 4r. Industrial scene and books ("National balance-sheet"); 25r. Anointing children ("Child welfare").

1961. Peace. Flag in red and blue.
112 **21** 1r.50 green and brown 35 35
113 5r. red 50 50
114 7r. blue and green 65 65

23 Frangipani **24** "Rama" (from temple door, Baphoun)

1961. Cambodian Flowers.
115 **23** 2r. yellow, green & mauve 45 45
116 – 5r. mauve, green and blue 70 70
117 – 10r. red, green and blue 2·00 2·00
FLOWERS: 5r. Oleander. 10r. Amaryllis.

1961. Cambodian Soldiers Commemoration.
118 **24** 1r. mauve 40 25
118a 2r. blue 2·50 1·50
119 3r. green 50 35
120 6r. orange 70 45

25 Prince Norodom Sihanouk and Independence Monument

1961. Independence Monument.
121 **25** 2r. green (postage) 65 50
122 4r. sepia 65 50
123 7r. multicoloured (air) 60 50
124 30r. red, blue and green 2·00 1·60
125 50r. multicoloured 3·00 2·75

1961. 6th World Buddhist Conference. Optd **VIe CONFERENCE MONDIALE BOUDDHIQUE 12-11-1961**.
126 **6** 2p.50 (2r.50) green 50 50
127 4p.50 (4r.50) violet 70 70

27 Power Station (Czech Aid) **28** Campaign Emblem

1962. Foreign Aid Programme.
128 **27** 2r. lake and red 25 15
129 – 3r. brown, green and blue 30 15
130 – 4r. brown, red and blue 30 15
131 – 5r. purple and green 40 35
132 – 6r. brown and blue 80 50
DESIGNS: 3r. Motorway (American Aid); 4r. Textile Factory (Chinese Aid); 5r. Friendship Hospital (Soviet Aid); 6r. Airport (French Aid).

1962. Malaria Eradication.
133 **28** 2r. purple and brown 35 20
134 4r. green and brown 40 40
135 6r. violet and bistre 50 35

29 Curucmas

1962. Cambodian Fruits (1st issue).
136 **29** 2r. yellow and brown 45 40
137 – 4r. green and turquoise 65 45
138 – 6r. red, green and blue 80 60
FRUITS: 4r. Lychees. 6r. Mangosteens.

1962. Cambodian Fruits (2nd issue).
139 2r. brown and green 40 30
140 5r. green and brown 55 40
141 9r. brown and green 70 45
DESIGNS—VERT: 2r. Pineapples. 5r. Sugar-cane. 9r. "Bread" trees.

1962. Surch.
142 **16** 50c. on 80c. red 60 35
150 – 3r. on 2r.50 brn (No. 55) 45 40

1962. Inauguration of Independence Monument. Surch **INAUGURATION DU MONUMENT** and new value.
143 **25** 3r. on 2r. green (postage) 50 30
144 12r. on 7r. mult (air) 1·40 1·00

32 Campaign Emblem, Corn and Maize **33** Temple Preah Vihear

1963. Freedom from Hunger.
145 **32** 3r. chestnut, brown & blue 50 40
146 6r. chestnut, brown & blue 50 40

1963. Reunification of Preah Vihear Temple with Cambodia.
147 **33** 3r. brown, purple & green 30 20
148 6r. green, orange and blue 50 40
149 15r. brown, blue & green 80 65

35 Kep sur Mer

1963. Cambodian Resorts. Multicoloured.
151 3r. Koh Tonsay (vert) 35 25
152 7r. Popokvil (waterfall) (vert) 50 30
153 20r. Type **35** 1·60 70

1963. Red Cross Centenary. Surch **1863 1963 CENTENAIRE DE LA CROIX-ROUGE** and premium.
154 **28** 4r.+40c. green & brown 60 60
155 6r.+60c. violet & bistre 95 95

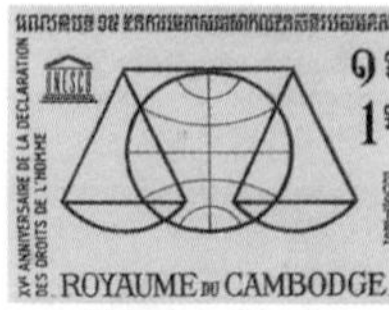

37 Scales of Justice

1963. 15th Anniv of Declaration of Human Rights.
156 **37** 1r. green, red and blue 30 30
157 3r. red, blue and green 50 50
158 12r. blue, green and red 95 95

38 Kouprey **39** Black-billed Magpie

1964. Wild Animal Protection.
159 **38** 50c. brown, green & chest 40 25
160 3r. brown, chestnut & grn 55 35
161 6r. brown, blue and green 85 55

1964. Birds.
162 **39** 3r. blue, green and indigo 65 40
163 – 6r. orange, purple & blue 1·00 65
164 – 12r. green and purple 1·90 95
BIRDS: 6r. River kingfisher. 12r. Grey heron.

40 "Hanuman" **42** Airline Emblem

1964. Air.
165 **40** 5r. mauve, brown & blue 60 40
166 10r. bistre, mauve & green 95 40
167 20r. bistre, violet and blue 1·60 75
168 40r. bistre, blue and red 3·50 1·50
169 80r. orange, green & purple 5·75 3·75

1964. Air Olympic Games, Tokyo. Surch **JEUX OLYMPIQUES TOKYO-1964**, Olympic rings and value.
170 **40** 3r. on 5r. mve, brn and bl 55 40
171 6r. on 10r. bis, mve & grn 85 60
172 9r. on 20r. bistre, vio & bl 95 70
173 12r. on 40r. bis, bl & red 1·90 1·10

1964. 8th Anniv of Royal Air Cambodia.
174 **42** 1r.50 red and violet 20 15
175 3r. red and blue 30 20
176 7r.50 red and blue 75 45

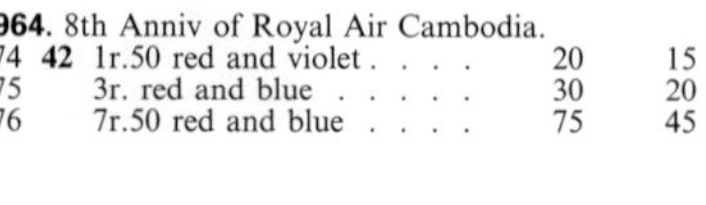

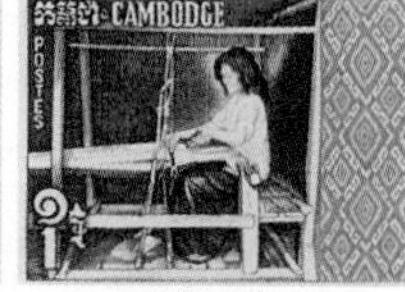

43 Prince Norodom Sihanouk **44** Weaving

1964. 10th Anniv of Foundation of Sangkum (Popular Socialist Community).

177	43	2r. violet	25	20
178		3r. brown	35	30
179		10r. blue	70	55

1965. Native Handicrafts.

180	44	1r. violet, brown & bistre	25	25
181	–	3r. brown, green & purple	45	35
182	–	5r. red, purple and green	75	50

DESIGNS: 3r. Engraving. 5r. Basket-making.

1965. Indo-Chinese People's Conference. Nos. 178/9 optd **CONFERENCE DES PEUPLES INDOCHINOIS**.

183	43	3r. brown	40	35
184		10r. blue	60	45

46 I.T.U. Emblem and Symbols **47** Cotton

1965. Centenary of I.T.U.

185	46	3r. bistre and green	35	30
186		4r. blue and red	45	30
187		10r. purple and violet	70	60

1965. Industrial Plants. Multicoloured.

188	1r.50 Type **47**	30	20
189	3r. Groundnuts	45	25
190	7r.50 Coconut palms	70	50

48 Preah Ko

1966. Cambodian Temples.

191	48	3r. green, turquoise & brn	50	30
192	–	5r. brown, green & purple	60	40
193	–	7r. brown, green & ochre	80	50
194	–	9r. purple, green and blue	1·25	70
195	–	12r. red, green & verm	1·90	1·40

TEMPLES: 5r. Baksei Chamkrong, 7r. Banteay Srei, 9r. Angkor Vat. 12r. Bayon.

49 W.H.O. Building **50** Tree-planting

1966. Inaug of W.H.O. Headquarters, Geneva.

196	49	2r. multicoloured	30	15
197		3r. multicoloured	35	25
198		5r. multicoloured	55	35

1966. Tree Day.

199	50	1r. brown, green & dp brn	20	15
200		3r. brown, green & orange	35	25
201		7r. brown, green and grey	60	40

51 U.N.E.S.C.O. Emblem **52** Stadium

1966. 20th Anniv of U.N.E.S.C.O.

202	51	3r. multicoloured	35	25
203		7r. multicoloured	45	35

1966. "Ganefo" Games, Phnom Penh.

204	52	3r. blue	25	20
205	–	4r. green	35	25
206	–	7r. red	50	40
207	–	10r. brown	70	60

DESIGNS: 4r., 7r., 10r. Various bas-reliefs of ancient sports from Angkor Vat.

53 Wild Boar **56** Ballet Dancer

1967. Fauna.

208	53	3r. black, green and blue	60	25
209	–	5r. multicoloured	75	30
210	–	7r. multicoloured	1·10	50

FAUNA—VERT: 5r. Hog-deer. HORIZ: 7r. Indian elephant.

1967. International Tourist Year. Nos. 191/2, 194/5 and 149 optd **ANNEE INTERNATIONALE DU TOURISME 1967**.

211	48	3r. green, turquoise & brn	45	35
212		5r. brown, green & purple	55	35
213	–	9r. purple, green and blue	65	55
214	–	12r. red, green & verm	90	70
215	33	15r. brown, blue & green	1·10	90

1967. Millenary of Banteay Srei Temple. No. 193 optd **MILLENAIRE DE BANTEAY SREI 967–1967**.

216	7r. brown, green and ochre	50	35

1967. Cambodian Royal Ballet. Designs showing ballet dancers.

217	56	1r. orange	25	20
218	–	3r. blue	40	30
219	–	5r. blue	50	35
220	–	7r. red	60	45
221	–	10r. multicoloured	1·10	60

1967. Int Literacy Day. Surch **Journee Internationale de l'Alphabetisation 8-9-67** and new value.

222	37	6r. on 12r. blue, grn & red	50	35
223	15	7r. on 15r. brown & green	60	40

58 Decade Emblem **59** Royal University of Kompong-Cham

1967. International Hydrological Decade.

224	58	1r. orange, blue and black	20	15
225		6r. orange, blue and violet	40	30
226		10r. orange, lt green & grn	65	45

1968. Cambodian Universities and Institutes.

227	59	4r. purple, blue & brown	30	20
228	–	6r. brown, green and blue	45	35
229	–	9r. brown, green and blue	65	40

DESIGNS: 6r. "Khmero-Soviet Friendship" Higher Technical Institute; 9r. Sangkum Reaster Niyum University Centre.

60 Doctor tending child

1968. 20th Anniv of W.H.O.

230	60	3r. blue	30	20
231	–	7r. blue	40	35

DESIGN: 7r. Man using insecticide.

61 Stadium

1968. Olympic Games, Mexico.

232	61	1r. brown, green and red	25	20
233	–	2r. brown, red and blue	35	20
234	–	3r. brown, blue and purple	40	25
235	–	5r. violet	45	30
236	–	7r.50 brown, green & red	55	40

DESIGNS—HORIZ: 2r. Wrestling; 3r. Cycling. VERT: 5r. Boxing; 7r.50, Runner with torch.

62 Stretcher-party

1968. Cambodian Red Cross Fortnight.

237	62	3r. red, green and blue	40	25

63 Prince Norodom Sihanouk

1968. 15th Anniv of Independence.

238	63	7r. violet, green and blue	35	35
239	–	8r. brown, green and blue	45	45

DESIGN: 8r. Soldiers wading through stream.

64 Human Rights Emblem and Prince Norodom Sihanouk

1968. Human Rights Year.

240	64	3r. blue	30	20
241		5r. purple	35	20
242		7r. black, orange & green	65	30

65 I.L.O. Emblem

1969. 50th Anniv of I.L.O.

243	65	3r. blue	25	15
244		6r. red	40	20
245		9r. green	60	35

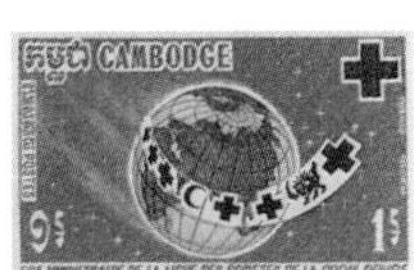

66 Red Cross Emblems around Globe

1969. 50th Anniv of League of Red Cross Societies.

246	66	1r. multicoloured	25	15
247		3r. multicoloured	30	20
248		10r. multicoloured	65	35

67 Golden Birdwing

1969. Butterflies.

249	67	3r. black, yellow & violet	1·00	45
250	–	4r. black, green & verm	1·00	50
251	–	8r. black, orange & green	1·50	90

DESIGNS: 4r. Tailed jay. 8r. Orange tiger.

68 Diesel Train and Route Map

1969. Opening of Phnom Penh–Sihanoukville Railway.

252	68	3r. multicoloured	1·25	90
253	–	6r. brown, green & green	1·50	1·10
254	–	8r. black	2·75	1·75
255	–	9r. blue, turquoise & grn	2·75	1·75

DESIGNS: 6r. Phnom Penh Station; 8r. Diesel locomotive and Kampor Station; 9r. Steam locomotive at Sihanoukville Station.

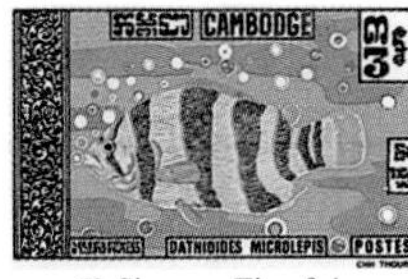

69 Siamese Tigerfish

1970. Fishes. Multicoloured.

256	3r. Type **69**	50	30
257	7r. Marbled sleeper	1·25	75
258	9r. Chevron snakehead	1·90	90

70 Vat Tepthidaram **71** Dish Aerial and Open Book

1970. Buddhist Monasteries in Cambodia. Mult.

259	2r. Type **70**	20	15
260	3r. Vat Maniratanaram (horiz)	25	15
261	6r. Vat Patumavati (horiz)	45	20
262	8r. Vat Unnalom (horiz)	55	40

1970. World Telecommunications Day.

263	71	3r. multicoloured	20	10
264		4r. multicoloured	30	15
265		9r. multicoloured	50	30

72 New Headquarters Building

1970. Opening of New U.P.U. Headquarters Building, Berne.

266	72	1r. multicoloured	20	10
267		3r. multicoloured	25	15
268		4r. multicoloured	40	25
269		10r. multicoloured	65	35

73 "Nelumbium speciosum"

1970. Aquatic Plants. Multicoloured.

270	3r. Type **73**	60	15
271	4r. "Eichhornia crassipes"	85	20
272	13r. "Nymphea lotus"	1·50	50

74 "Banteay-srei" (bas-relief)

1970. World Meteorological Day.

273	74	3r. red and green	20	10
274		4r. red, green and blue	30	15
275		7r. green, blue and black	40	20

75 Rocket, Dove and Globe

1970. 25th Anniv of United Nations.

276	75	3r. multicoloured	20	15
277		5r. multicoloured	40	20
278		10r. multicoloured	60	40

76 I.E.Y. Emblem

1970. International Education Year.

279	76	1r. blue	15	10
280		3r. purple	20	15
281		8r. green	45	20

77 Samdech Chuon Nath

1971. 2nd Death Anniv of Samdech Chuon-Nath (Khmer language scholar).
282 **77** 3r. multicoloured 15 15
283 8r. multicoloured 45 20
284 9r. multicoloured 55 30

For issues between 1971 and 1989 see under KHMER REPUBLIC and KAMPUCHEA in volume 3.

203 17th-century Coach

1989. Coaches. Multicoloured.
1020 2r. Type **203** 10 10
1021 3r. Paris–Lyon coach, 1720 20 10
1022 5r. Mail coach, 1793 . . . . 30 10
1023 10r. Light mail coach, 1805 65 20
1024 15r. Royal mail coach . . . 1·00 30
1025 20r. Russian mail coach . . 1·25 40
1026 35r. Paris–Lille coupe, 1837 (vert) . . . . 2·40 70

204 "Papilio zagreus"

1989. "Brasiliana 89" International Stamp Exhibition, Rio de Janeiro. Butterflies. Multicoloured.
1028 2r. Type **204** 10 10
1029 3r. "Morpho catenarius" . . 20 10
1030 5r. "Morpho aega" 30 10
1031 10r. "Callithea sapphira" ("wrongly inscr "saphhira") 65 20
1032 15r. "Catagramma sorana" 1·00 30
1033 20r. "Pierella nereis" . . . 1·25 40
1034 35r. "Papilio brasiliensis" 2·40 70

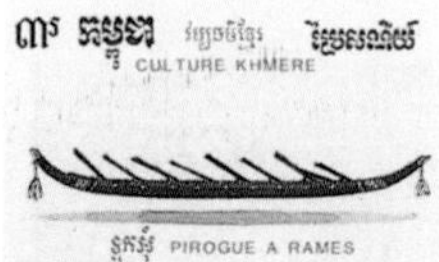

205 Pirogue

1989. Khmer Culture. Multicoloured.
1036 3r. Type **205** 30 10
1037 12r. Pirogue (two sets of oars) . . . . 1·00 30
1038 30r. Pirogue with cabin . . 2·50 70

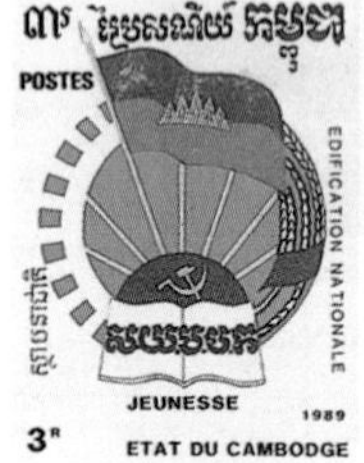

206 Youth

207 Goalkeeper

1989. National Development. Multicoloured.
1039 3r. Type **206** 25 10
1040 12r. Trade unions emblem (horiz) 90 30
1041 30r. National Front emblem (horiz) . . . . 2·40 70

1990. World Cup Football Championship, Italy. Multicoloured.
1042 2r. Type **207** 10 10
1043 3r. Dribbling ball 20 10
1044 5r. Controlling ball with thigh 30 10
1045 10r. Running with ball . . . 65 20
1046 15r. Shooting . . . . 1·00 30
1047 20r. Tackling . . . . 1·25 40
1048 35r. Tackling (different) . . 2·40 70

208 Two-horse Postal Van

1990. "Stamp World London 90" International Stamp Exhibition. Royal Mail Horse-drawn Transport. Multicoloured.
1050 2r. Type **208** 10 10
1051 3r. One-horse cart 20 10
1052 5r. Rural post office cart . . 30 10
1053 10r. Rural post office van 65 20
1054 15r. Local post office van 1·00 30
1055 20r. Parcel-post cart . . . . 1·25 40
1056 35r. Two-horse wagon . . . 2·40 70

209 Rice Grains

210 Shooting

1990. Cultivation of Rice. Multicoloured.
1058 3r. Type **209** 25 10
1059 12r. Transporting rice (horiz) 90 30
1060 30r. Threshing rice . . . . 2·40 70

1990. Olympic Games, Barcelona (1992) (1st issue). Multicoloured.
1061 2r. Type **210** 10 10
1062 3r. Putting the shot 20 10
1063 5r. Weightlifting 30 10
1064 10r. Boxing 65 20
1065 15r. Pole vaulting . . . . 1·00 30
1066 20r. Basketball . . . . . . 1·25 40
1067 35r. Fencing . . . . 2·40 70
See also Nos. 1163/9, 1208/12 and 1241/5.

211 Four-man Bobsleighing

1990. Winter Olympic Games, Albertville (1992) (1st issue). Multicoloured.
1069 2r. Type **211** 10 10
1070 3r. Speed skating 20 10
1071 5r. Figure skating 30 10
1072 10r. Ice hockey 65 20
1073 15r. Biathlon . . . . 1·00 30
1074 20r. Lugeing . . . . 1·25 40
1075 35r. Ski jumping . . . . . 2·40 70
See also Nos. 1152/8.

212 Facade of Banteay Srei

1990. Khmer Culture. Multicoloured.
1077 3r. Type **212** 25 10
1078 12r. Ox-carts (12th-century relief) 90 30
1079 30r. Banon ruins (36 × 21 mm) . . . . . . 2·40 70

213 "Zizina oxleyi"

1990. "New Zealand 1990" International Stamp Exhibition, Auckland. Butterflies. Multicoloured.
1080 2r. Type **213** 10 10
1081 3r. "Cupha prosope" . . . 10 10
1082 5r. "Heteronympha merope" 25 10
1083 10r. "Dodonidia helmsi" . . 50 15
1084 15r. "Argirophenga antipodum" 90 30
1085 20r. "Tysonotis danis" . . . 1·40 45
1086 35r. "Pyrameis gonnarilla" 2·10 70

214 "Vostok"

1990. Spacecraft. Multicoloured.
1088 2r. Type **214** 15 10
1089 3r. "Soyuz" 20 10
1090 5r. Satellite 35 10
1091 10r. "Luna 10" 75 25
1092 15r. "Mars 1" . . . . . . 1·10 40
1093 20r. "Venus 3" . . . . . . 1·50 50
1094 35r. "Mir" space station . . 2·50 95

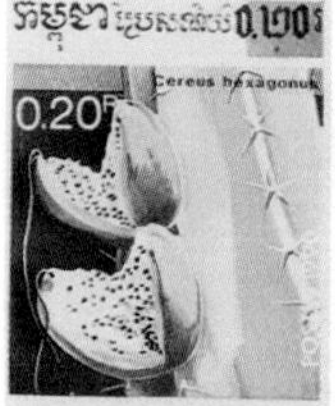

215 Poodle

1990. Dogs. Multicoloured.
1096 20c. Type **215** 10 10
1097 80c. Shetland sheepdog . . 10 10
1098 3r. Samoyede 25 10
1099 6r. Springer spaniel 50 15
1100 10r. Wire-haired fox terrier 90 30
1101 15r. Afghan hound . . . . 1·40 45
1102 25r. Dalmatian . . . . . . 2·10 70

216 "Cereus hexagonus"

217 Learning to Write

1990. Cacti. Multicoloured.
1104 20c. Type **216** 10 10
1105 80c. "Arthrocereus rondonianus" 10 10
1106 3r. "Matucana multicolor" 25 10
1107 6r. "Hildewintera aureispina" 50 15
1108 10r. "Opuntia retrosa" . . . 90 30
1109 15r. "Erdisia tenuicula" . . 1·40 45
1110 25r. "Mamillaria yaquensis" 2·10 70

1990. International Literacy Year.
1111 **217** 3r. black and blue . . . 25 10
1112 12r. black and yellow . . 95 30
1113 30r. black and pink . . . 2·50 70

218 English Nef, 1200

1990. Ships. Multicoloured.
1114 20c. Type **218** 10 10
1115 80c. 16th-century Spanish galleon 15 10
1116 3r. Dutch jacht, 1627 . . . 30 10
1117 6r. "La Couronne" (French galleon), 1638 . . . . . . 55 15
1118 10r. Dumont d'Urville's ship "L'Astrolabe", 1826 . . . 95 30
1119 15r. "Louisiane" (steamer), 1864 . . . . 1·50 45
1120 25r. Clipper, 1900 (vert) . . 2·25 70
No. 1118 is wrongly inscribed "d'Uville".

219 Phnom-Penh–Kampong Som Railway

1990. National Development. Multicoloured.
1122 3r. Type **219** . . . . 2·75 30
1123 12r. Port, Kampong Som 95 30
1124 30r. Fishing boats, Kampong Som . . . . . 3·00 70

220 Sacre-Coeur de Montmartre and White Bishop

221 Columbus

1990. "Paris '90" World Chess Championship, Paris. Multicoloured.
1125 2r. Type **220** 15 10
1126 3r. "The Horse Trainer" (statue) and white knight 25 10
1127 5r. "Victory of Samothrace" (statue) and white queen 40 10
1128 10r. Azay-le-Rideau Chateau and white rook 80 25
1129 15r. "The Dance" (statue) and white pawn . . . . . 1·25 40
1130 20r. Eiffel Tower and white king . . . . 1·60 50
1131 35r. Arc de Triomphe and black chessmen . . . . . 2·75 95

1990. 500th Anniv (1992) of Discovery of America by Columbus (1st issue). Multicoloured.
1133 2r. Type **221** 15 10
1134 3r. Queen Isabella's jewel-chest 20 10
1135 5r. Queen Isabella the Catholic 35 10
1136 10r. "Santa Maria" (flagship) . . . . 1·40 25
1137 15r. Juan de la Cosa . . . . 1·10 40
1138 20r. Monument to Columbus . . . . 1·50 50
1139 35r. Devin Pyramid, Yucatan . . . . 2·50 95
See also Nos. 1186/92.

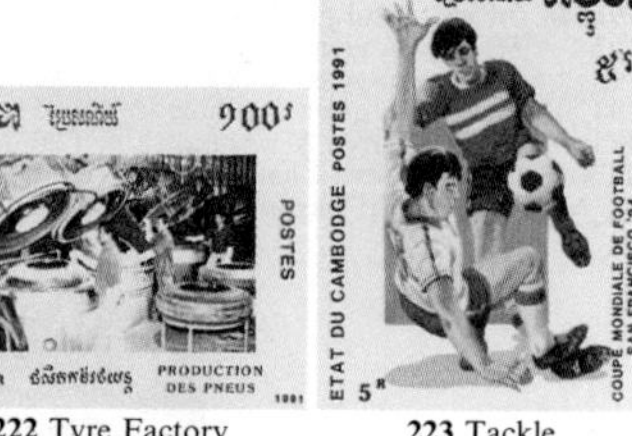

222 Tyre Factory **223** Tackle

1991. National Festival. Multicoloured.
1141 100r. Type **222** 55 25
1142 300r. Rural hospital . . . . 1·60 75
1143 500r. Freshwater fishing (27 × 40 mm) . . . . . . 2·75 1·25

1991. World Cup Football Championship, U.S.A. (1994) (1st issue).
1144 **223** 5r. multicoloured 10 10
1145 – 25r. multicoloured . . . 10 10
1146 – 70r. multicoloured . . . 30 10
1147 – 100r. multicoloured . . . 40 15
1148 – 200r. multicoloured . . . 85 25
1149 – 400r. multicoloured . . . 1·60 45
1150 – 1000r. multicoloured . . 4·25 1·25
DESIGNS: 25r. to 1000r. Different footballing scenes.
See also Nos. 1220/4, 1317/21 and 1381/5.

224 Speed Skating

1991. Winter Olympic Games, Albertville (1992) (2nd issue). Multicoloured.
1152 5r. Type **224** 10 10
1153 25r. Slalom skiing 10 10
1154 70r. Ice hockey 30 10
1155 100r. Bobsleighing 40 15
1156 200r. Freestyle skiing . . . 85 25
1157 400r. Ice skating . . . . . 1·60 45
1158 1000r. Downhill skiing . . . 4·25 1·25

225 "Torso of Vishnu Reclining" (11th cent)

1991. Sculpture. Multicoloured.

1160 100r. "Garuda" (Koh Ker, 10th century) . . . 55 25

1161 300r. Type **225** . . . 1·60 75

1162 500r. "Reclining Nandin" (7th century) . . . 2·75 1·25

226 Pole Vaulting

1991. Olympic Games, Barcelona (1992) (2nd issue). Multicoloured.

1163 5r. Type **226** . . . 10 10

1164 25r. Table tennis . . . 10 10

1165 70r. Running . . . 30 10

1166 100r. Wrestling . . . 40 15

1167 200r. Gymnastics (bars) . . . 85 25

1168 400r. Tennis . . . 1·60 45

1169 1000r. Boxing . . . 4·25 1·25

227 Douglas DC-10-30

1991. Airplanes. Multicoloured.

1171 5r. Type **227** . . . 10 10

1172 25r. McDonnell Douglas MD-11 . . . 10 10

1173 70r. Ilyushin Il-96-300 . . . 30 10

1174 100r. Airbus Industrie A310 . . . 40 15

1175 200r. Yakovlev Yak-42 . . . 85 25

1176 400r. Tupolev Tu-154 . . . 1·60 45

1177 1000r. Douglas DC-9 . . . 4·25 1·25

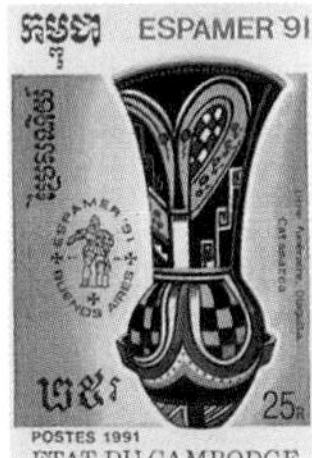

228 Diaguita Funerary Urn, Catamarca

1991. "Espamer '91" Iberia–Latin America Stamp Exhibition, Buenos Aires. Multicoloured.

1178 5r. Bareales glass pot, Catamarca (horiz) . . . 10 10

1179 25r. Type **228** . . . 10 10

1180 70r. Quiroga urn, Tucuman . . . 30 10

1181 100r. Round glass pot, Santiago del Estero (horiz) . . . 40 15

1182 200r. Pitcher, Santiago del Estero (horiz) . . . 85 25

1183 400r. Diaguita funerary urn, Tucuman . . . 1·60 45

1184 1000r. Bareales funerary urn, Catamarca (horiz) . . 4·25 1·25

229 "Pinta"

1991. 500th Anniv (1992) of Discovery of America by Columbus (2nd issue). Each brown, stone and black.

1186 5r. Type **229** . . . 30 10

1187 25r. "Nina" . . . 35 10

1188 70r. "Santa Maria" . . . 75 20

1189 100r. Landing at Guanahani, 1492 (horiz) 1·00 25

1190 200r. Meeting of two cultures (horiz) . . . 85 25

1191 400r. La Navidad (first European settlement in America) (horiz) . . . 3·00 75

1192 1000r. Amerindian village (horiz) . . . 4·25 1·25

230 "Neptis pryeri"

1991. "Phila Nippon '91" International Stamp Exhibition, Tokyo. Butterflies. Multicoloured.

1194 5r. Type **230** . . . 10 10

1195 25r. "Papilio xuthus" . . . 10 10

1196 70r. Common map butterfly 30 10

1197 100r. "Argynnis anadiomene" . . . 40 15

1198 200r. "Lethe marginalis" . . 85 25

1199 400r. "Artopoetes pryeri" 1·60 45

1200 1000r. African monarch . . 4·25 1·25

231 Coastal Fishing Port

1991. National Development. Food Industry. Multicoloured.

1202 100r. Type **231** . . . 80 25

1203 300r. Preparing palm sugar (29 × 40 mm) . . . 1·60 75

1204 500r. Picking peppers . . . 2·75 1·25

232 Chakdomuk Costumes

233 Wrestling

1992. National Festival. Traditional Costumes. Multicoloured.

1205 150r. Type **232** . . . 55 30

1206 350r. Longvek . . . 1·25 70

1207 1000r. Angkor . . . 3·50 1·25

1992. Olympic Games, Barcelona (3rd issue). Multicoloured.

1208 5r. Type **233** . . . 10 10

1209 15r. Football . . . 10 10

1210 80r. Weightlifting . . . 20 10

1211 400r. Archery . . . 1·10 35

1212 1500r. Gymnastics . . . 4·25 1·40

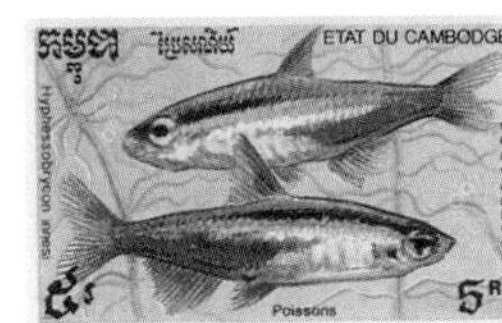

234 Neon Tetra

1992. Fishes. Multicoloured.

1214 5r. Type **234** . . . 10 10

1215 15r. Siamese fighting fish . . 15 10

1216 80r. Kaiser tetra . . . 25 10

1217 400r. Dwarf gourami . . . 1·50 50

1218 1500r. Port hoplo . . . 5·25 2·25

235 Germany v. Columbia

236 Monument

1992. World Cup Football Championship, U.S.A. (1994) (2nd issue). Multicoloured.

1220 5r. Type **235** . . . 10 10

1221 15r. Netherlands player (horiz) . . . 10 10

1222 80r. Uruguay v. C.I.S. (ex-Soviet states) . . . 20 10

1223 400r. Cameroun v. Yugoslavia . . . 1·10 35

1224 1500r. Italy v. Sweden . . . 4·25 1·40

1992. Khmer Culture. 19th-century Architecture. Multicoloured.

1226 150r. Type **236** . . . 55 30

1227 350r. Stupa . . . 1·25 70

1228 1000r. Mandapa library . . 3·50 1·25

237 Motor Car

1992. 540th Birth Anniv (1992) of Leonardo da Vinci (artist and inventor). Multicoloured.

1229 5r. Type **237** . . . 10 10

1230 15r. Container ship . . . 30 10

1231 80r. Helicopter . . . 20 10

1232 400r. Scuba diver . . . 1·10 35

1233 1500r. Parachutists (vert) . . 4·25 1·40

238 Juan de la Cierva and Autogyro

1992. "Expo '92" World's Fair, Seville. Inventors. Multicoloured.

1235 5r. Type **238** . . . 10 10

1236 15r. Thomas Edison and electric light bulb . . . 10 10

1237 80r. Samuel Morse and Morse telegraph . . . 20 10

1238 400r. Narciso Monturiol and "Ictineo" (early submarine) . . . 2·75 50

1239 1500r. Alexander Graham Bell and early telephone 4·25 1·40

239 Weightlifting

1992. Olympic Games, Barcelona (4th issue). Multicoloured.

1241 5r. Type **239** . . . 10 10

1242 15r. Boxing . . . 10 10

1243 80r. Basketball . . . 20 10

1244 400r. Running . . . 1·00 35

1245 1500r. Water polo . . . 4·00 1·40

240 Palm Trees

1992. Environmental Protection. Multicoloured.

1247 5r. Couple on riverside . . . 10 10

1248 15r. Pagoda . . . 10 10

1249 80r. Type **240** . . . 20 10

1250 400r. Boy riding water buffalo . . . 1·00 35

1251 1500r. Swimming in river . . 4·00 1·40

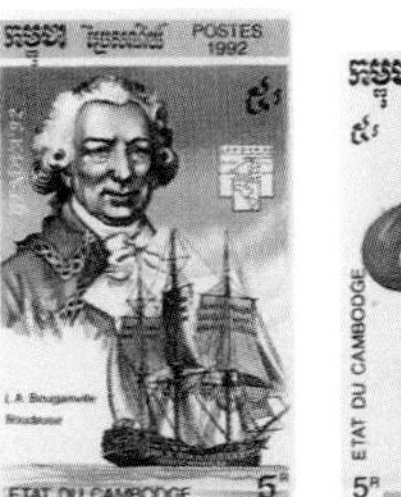

241 Louis de Bougainville and "La Boudeuse"

242 "Albatrellus confluens"

1992. "Genova '92" International Thematic Stamp Exhibition, Genoa. Multicoloured.

1253 5r. Type **241** . . . 10 10

1254 15r. James Cook and H.M.S. "Endeavour" . . 15 10

1255 80r. Charles Darwin and H.M.S. "Beagle" . . . 25 10

1256 400r. Jacques Cousteau and "Calypso" . . . 1·10 35

1257 1500r. "Kon Tiki" (replica of balsa raft) . . . 4·25 1·40

1992. Fungi. Multicoloured.

1259 5r. Type **242** . . . 10 10

1260 15r. Scarlet-stemmed boletus 10 10

1261 80r. Verdigris agaric . . . 30 10

1262 400r. "Telamonia armillata" 1·50 60

1263 1500r. Goaty smell cortinarius . . . 6·00 2·00

243 Bellanca Pacemaker Seaplane, 1930

1992. Aircraft. Multicoloured.

1264 5r. Type **243** . . . 10 10

1265 15r. Canadair CL-215 fire-fighting amphibian, 1965 10 10

1266 80r. Grumman G-21 Goose amphibian, 1937 . . . 20 10

1267 400r. Grumman SA-6 Sealand flying boat, 1947 95 30

1268 1500r. Short S.23 Empire "C" Class flying boat, 1936 . . . 3·75 1·00

244 Dish Aerial

1992. National Development. Multicoloured.

1270 150r. Type **244** . . . 40 20

1271 350r. Dish aerial, flags and satellite . . . 90 45

1272 1000r. Hotel Cambodiana 2·25 1·10

245 Sociological Institute

1993. National Festival. Multicoloured.

1273 50r. Type **245** . . . 15 10

1274 450r. Motel Cambodiana . . 1·00 50

1275 1000r. Theatre, Bassac . . . 2·25 1·10

246 Bottle-nosed Dolphin and Submarine

1993. Wildlife and Technology. Multicoloured.

1276 150r. Type **246** . . . 55 10

1277 200r. Supersonic jet airplane and peregrine falcon . . . 60 10

1278 250r. Eurasian beaver and dam . . . 75 15

1279 500r. Satellite and natterer's bat . . . 2·25 30

1280 900r. Rufous humming-bird and helicopter . . . 3·50 70

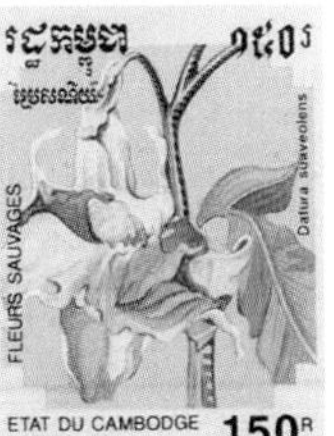

247 "Datura suaveolens"

1993. Wild Flowers. Multicoloured.

1281 150r. Type **247** . . . 40 10

1282 200r. "Convolvulus tricolor" 50 10

1283 250r. "Hippeastrum" hybrid 65 15

1284 500r. "Camellia" hybrid . . 1·25 30

1285 900r. "Lilium speciosum" 2·25 55

248 Vihear Temple

1993. Khmer Culture. Multicoloured.
1287 50r. Sculpture of ox 15 10
1288 450r. Type **248** . . . . . . 1·10 20
1289 1000r. Offering to Buddha 2·50 55

249 Philippine Flying Lemur

1993. Animals. Multicoloured.
1290 150r. Type **249** 40 10
1291 200r. Red giant flying squirrel 50 10
1292 250r. Fringed gecko 65 15
1293 500r. Wallace's flying frog 1·25 30
1294 900r. Flying lizard . . . . . 2·25 55

250 "Symbrenthia hypselis"

1993. "Brasiliana '93" International Stamp Exhibition, Rio de Janeiro. Butterflies. Mult.
1295 250r. Type **250** 65 15
1296 350r. "Sithon nedymond" 90 20
1297 600r. "Geitoneura minyas" 1·50 35
1298 800r. "Argyreus hyperbius" 2·00 50
1299 1000r. "Argyrophenga antipodum" . . . . . . 2·50 60

251 Armed Cambodians reporting to U.N. Base

253 Santos-Dumont, Eiffel Tower and "Ballon No. 6", 1901

252 Venetian Felucca

1993. United Nations Transitional Authority in Cambodia Pacification Programme. Each black and blue.
1301 150r. Type **251** 40 10
1302 200r. Military camp 50 10
1303 250r. Surrender of arms . . 65 15
1304 500r. Vocational training . . 1·25 30
1305 900r. Liberation . . . . . . 2·25 50

1993. Sailing Ships. Multicoloured.
1307 150r. Type **252** 40 10
1308 200r. Phoenician galley . . 50 10
1309 250r. Egyptian merchantman 65 15
1310 500r. Genoese merchantman 1·25 30
1311 900r. English merchantman 2·25 50

1993. 120th Birth Anniv of Alberto Santos-Dumont (aviator). Multicoloured.
1312 150r. Type **253** 40 10
1313 200r. "14 bis" (biplane), 1906 (horiz) 50 10
1314 250r. "Demoiselle" (monoplane), 1909 (horiz) 65 15
1315 500r. Embraer EMB-201 A (horiz) . . . . 1·25 30
1316 900r. Embraer EMB-111 (horiz) . . . . 2·25 50

254 Footballer

1993. World Cup Football Championship, U.S.A. (1994) (3rd issue).
1317 **254** 250r. multicoloured . . . 65 10
1318 – 350r. multicoloured . . . 90 15
1319 – 600r. multicoloured . . . 1·50 30
1320 – 800r. multicoloured . . . 2·00 40
1321 – 1000r. mult (vert) . . . 2·50 50
DESIGNS: 350r. to 1000r. Various footballing scenes.

255 European Wigeon

1993. "Bangkok 1993" International Stamp Exhibition, Thailand. Ducks. Multicoloured.
1323 250r. Type **255** 65 10
1324 350r. Baikal teal 90 15
1325 600r. Mandarin . . . . . . 1·50 30
1326 800r. Wood duck . . . . . . 2·00 40
1327 1000r. Harlequin duck . . . 2·50 50

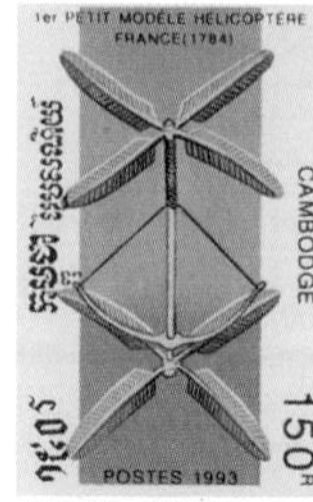
256 First Helicopter Model, France, 1784

257 "Cnaphalocrocis medinalis"

1993. Vertical Take-off Aircraft. Multicoloured.
1329 150r. Type **256** 40 10
1330 200r. Model of steam helicopter, 1863 . . . . . 50 10
1331 250r. New York–Atlanta–Miami autogyro flight, 1927 (horiz) 65 10
1332 500r. Sikorsky helicopter, 1943 (horiz) . . . . . . 1·25 20
1333 900r. French vertical take-off jet . . . . 2·25 40

1993. National Development. Harmful Insects. Multicoloured.
1335 50r. Type **257** 10 10
1336 450r. Brown leaf-hopper . . 1·10 15
1337 500r. "Scirpophaga incertulas" . . . . 1·25 20
1338 1000r. Stalk-eyed fly . . . . 2·50 40

258 Ministry of Posts and Telecommunications

1993. 40th Anniv of Independence.
1340 **258** 300r. multicoloured . . . 75 15
1341 – 500r. multicoloured . . . 1·25 20
1342 – 700r. blue, red & black 1·75 30
DESIGNS—VERT: 500r. Independence monument. HORIZ: 700r. National flag.

259 Boy with Pony

260 Figure Skating

1993. Figurines by M. J. Hummel. Multicoloured.
1343 50r. Type **259** 10 10
1344 100r. Girl and pram 25 10
1345 150r. Girl bathing doll . . . 40 10
1346 200r. Girl holding doll . . . 50 10
1347 250r. Boys playing 65 10
1348 300r. Girls pulling boy in cart 75 15
1349 350r. Girls playing ring-o-roses 90 15
1350 600r. Boys with stick and drum . . . . 1·50 25

1994. Winter Olympic Games, Lillehammer, Norway. Multicoloured.
1351 150r. Type **260** 40 10
1352 250r. Two-man luge (horiz) 65 10
1353 400r. Skiing (horiz) . . . . 1·00 15
1354 700r. Biathlon (horiz) . . . 1·75 30
1355 1000r. Speed skating . . . . 2·50 40

261 Opel, 1924

1994. Motor Cars. Multicoloured.
1357 150r. Type **261** 40 10
1358 200r. Mercedes, 1901 . . . 50 10
1359 250r. Ford Model "T", 1927 65 10
1360 500r. Rolls Royce, 1907 . . 1·25 20
1361 900r. Hutton, 1908 . . . . 2·25 35

262 Gymnastics

263 Siva and Uma (10th century, Banteay Srei)

1994. Olympic Games, Atlanta (1996) (1st issue). Multicoloured.
1363 150r. Type **262** 40 10
1364 200r. Football 50 10
1365 250r. Throwing the javelin 65 10
1366 300r. Canoeing 75 15
1367 600r. Running . . . . . . 1·50 25
1368 1000r. Diving (horiz) . . . 2·50 40
See also Nos. 1437/41 and 1495/1500.

1994. Khmer Culture. Statues. Multicoloured.
1370 300r. Type **263** 75 15
1371 500r. Vishnu (6th cent, Tvol Dai-Buon) . . . . 1·25 20
1372 700r. King Jayavarman VII (12th–13th century, Krol Romeas Angkor) . . . . 1·75 30

264 Olympic Flag

1994. Centenary of International Olympic Committee. Multicoloured.
1373 100r. Type **264** 30 10
1374 300r. Flag and torch 90 15
1375 600r. Flag and Pierre de Coubertin (reviver of modern Olympic Games) 1·75 25

265 Mesonyx

1994. Prehistoric Animals. Multicoloured.
1376 150r. Type **265** 40 10
1377 250r. Doedicurus 65 10
1378 400r. Mylodon . . . . . . 1·00 15
1379 700r. Uintatherium . . . . 1·75 30
1380 1000r. Hyrachyus . . . . . 2·50 40

266 Players

267 "Soldiers in Combat"

1994. World Cup Football Championship, U.S.A. (4th issue).
1381 **266** 150r. multicoloured . . . 40 10
1382 – 250r. multicoloured . . . 65 10
1383 – 400r. multicoloured . . . 1·00 15
1384 – 700r. multicoloured . . . 1·75 30
1385 – 1000r. multicoloured . . 2·50 40
DESIGNS: 250r. to 1000r. Different footballing scenes.

1994. Tourism. Statues in Public Gardens. Mult.
1387 300r. "Stag and Hind" . . . 75 15
1388 500r. Type **267** . . . . . . 1·25 20
1389 700r. "Lions" . . . . 1·75 30

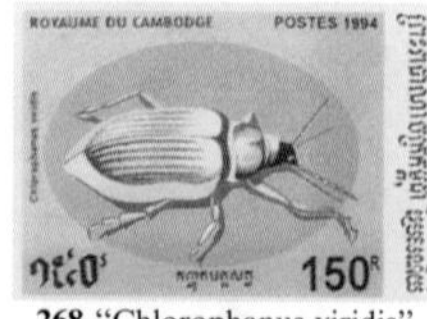
268 "Chlorophanus viridis"

1994. Beetles. Multicoloured.
1390 150r. Type **268** 40 10
1391 200r. "Chrysochroa fulgidissima" 50 10
1392 250r. "Lytta vesicatoria" . . 65 10
1393 500r. "Purpuricenus kaehleri" . . . . 1·25 20
1394 900r. Herculese beetle . . . 2·25 25

269 Halley's Diving-bell, 1690

1994. Submarines. Multicoloured.
1396 150r. Type **269** 40 10
1397 200r. "Gimnote", 1886 (horiz) 50 10
1398 250r. "Peral" (Spain), 1888 (horiz) 65 10
1399 500r. "Nautilus" (first nuclear-powered submarine), 1954 (horiz) 1·25 20
1400 900r. "Trieste" (bathyscaphe), 1953 (horiz) . . . . 2·25 35

270 Francois-Andre Philidor, 1795

1994. Chess Champions. Multicoloured.
1402 150r. Type **270** 40 10
1403 200r. Mahe de la Bourdonnais, 1821 . . . 50 10
1404 250r. Karl Anderssen, 1851 65 10
1405 500r. Paul Morphy, 1858 . . 1·25 20
1406 900r. Wilhelm Steinitz, 1866 2·25 35

271 Sikorsky S-42 Flying Boat

1994. Aircraft. Multicoloured.
1408 150r. Type **271** 40 10
1409 200r. Vought-Sikorsky VS-300A helicopter prototype 50 10
1410 250r. Sikorsky S-37 biplane 65 10
1411 500r. Sikorsky S-35 biplane 1·25 20
1412 900r. Sikorsky S-43 amphibian . . . . 2·25 35

272 Penduline Tit

1994. Birds. Multicoloured.

1414	150r. Type **272**	40	10
1415	250r. Bearded reedling	65	10
1416	400r. Little bunting	1·00	15
1417	700r. Cirl bunting	1·75	30
1418	1000r. Goldcrest	2·50	40

273 Postal Service Float

1994. National Independence Festival. Mult.

1420	300r. Type **273**	80	15
1421	500r. Soldiers marching	1·40	25
1422	700r. Women's army units on parade	2·00	35

274 Chruoi Changwar Bridge

1994. National Development. Multicoloured.

1423	300r. Type **274**	80	15
1424	500r. Olympique Commercial Centre	1·40	25
1425	700r. Sakyamony Chedei Temple	2·00	35

275 Psittacosaurus

1995. Prehistoric Animals. Multicoloured.

1426	100r. Type **275**	30	10
1427	200r. Protoceratops	90	10
1428	300r. Montanoceraptors	1·00	15
1429	400r. Centrosaurus	1·40	20
1430	700r. Styracosaurus	2·25	35
1431	800r. Triceratops	2·50	40

276 Orange-tip

278 Death Cap

277 Swimming

1995. Butterflies. Multicoloured.

1432	100r. Type **276**	30	10
1433	200r. Scarce swallowtail	1·50	10
1434	300r. Dark green fritillary	2·00	15
1435	600r. Red admiral	2·50	30
1436	800r. Peacock	3·00	40

1995. Olympic Games, Atlanta (1996) (2nd issue). Multicoloured.

1437	100r. Type **277**	30	10
1438	200r. Callisthenics (vert)	1·50	10
1439	400r. Basketball (vert)	2·00	20
1440	800r. Football (vert)	2·50	40
1441	1000r. Cycling (vert)	3·00	45

1995. Fungi. Multicoloured.

1443	100r. Type **278**	40	15
1444	200r. Chanterelle	75	20
1445	300r. Honey fungus	1·00	30
1446	600r. Field mushroom	2·10	60
1447	800r. Fly agaric	3·00	80

279 Kneeling Ascetic

281 Black-capped Lory

280 Gaur

1995. Khmer Culture. Statues. Multicoloured.

1448	300r. Type **279**	1·00	15
1449	500r. Parasurama	1·75	25
1450	700r. Shiva	3·00	35

1995. Protected Animals. Multicoloured.

1451	300r. Type **280**	80	15
1452	500r. Kouprey (vert)	1·75	25
1453	700r. Saurus crane (vert)	3·00	35

1995. Parrot Family. Multicoloured.

1454	100r. Type **281**	40	15
1455	200r. Princess parrot	80	15
1456	400r. Eclectus parrot	1·50	30
1457	800r. Scarlet macaw	3·00	65
1458	1000r. Budgerigar	3·50	70

282 Bird (sculpture)

1995. Tourism. Public Gardens. Multicoloured.

1460	300r. Type **282**	80	15
1461	500r. Water feature	1·50	25
1462	700r. Mythical figures (sculpture)	2·75	35

283 Richard Trevithick's Locomotive, 1804

1995. Steam Locomotives. Multicoloured.

1463	100r. Type **283**	30	25
1464	200r. G. and R. Stephenson's "Rocket", 1829	70	55
1465	300r. George Stephenson's "Locomotion", 1825	1·00	85
1466	600r. "Lafayette", 1837	2·00	1·75
1467	800r. "Best Friend of Charleston", 1830	2·40	2·25

284 Bristol Type 142 Blenheim Mk II Bomber

1995. Second World War Planes. Multicoloured.

1469	100r. Type **284**	40	10
1470	200r. North American B-25B Mitchell bomber (horiz)	90	20
1471	300r. Avro Type 652 Anson Mk I general purpose plane (horiz)	1·25	30
1472	600r. Avro Manchester bomber (horiz)	2·00	55
1473	800r. Consolidated B-24 Liberator bomber (horiz)	2·50	70

285 Gathering Crops

1995. 50th Anniv of F.A.O. Multicoloured.

1475	300r. Type **285**	1·00	30
1476	500r. Transplanting crops	1·75	50
1477	700r. Paddy field	2·75	80

286 Bridge

1995. 50th Anniv of U.N.O. Preah Kunlorng Bridge. Multicoloured.

1478	300r. Type **286**	1·10	25
1479	500r. People on bridge	2·00	45
1480	700r. Closer view of bridge	2·50	60

287 Queen Monineath

1995. National Independence. Multicoloured.

1481	700r. Type **287**	3·00	80
1482	800r. King Norodom Sihanouk	3·50	90

288 Pennant Coralfish

1995. Fishes. Multicoloured.

1483	100r. Type **288**	30	15
1484	200r. Copper-banded butterflyfish	70	25
1485	400r. Crown anemonefish	1·25	45
1486	800r. Palette surgeonfish	2·50	85
1487	1000r. Queen angelfish	3·00	1·10

289 Post Office Building

1995. Cent of Head Post Office, Phnom Penh.

1489	**289**	300r. multicoloured	1·25	25
1490		500r. multicoloured	1·75	40
1491		700r. multicoloured	2·50	60

290 Independence Monument

1995. 40th Anniv of Admission of Cambodia to United Nations Organization. Multicoloured.

1492	300r. Type **290**	1·25	25
1493	400r. Angkor Wat	1·75	35
1494	800r. U.N. emblem and national flag (vert)	2·50	70

291 Tennis

292 Kep State Chalet

1996. Olympic Games, Atlanta (3rd issue). Mult.

1495	100r. Type **291**	25	10
1496	200r. Volleyball	60	15
1497	300r. Football	1·00	20
1498	500r. Running	1·40	35
1499	900r. Baseball	2·40	70
1500	1000r. Basketball	2·50	75

1996.

1502	**292**	50r. blue and black	10	10
1503	–	100r. red and black	30	10
1504	–	200r. yellow and black	40	10
1505	–	500r. blue and black	1·00	20
1506	–	800r. mauve and black	1·40	35
1507	–	1000r. yellow and black	1·75	50
1508	–	1500r. green and black	3·00	75

DESIGNS—HORIZ: 100r. Power station; 200r. Wheelchair; 500r. Handicapped basketball team; 1000r. Kep beach; 1500r. Serpent Island. VERT: 800r. Man making crutches.

293 European Wild Cat

1996. Wild Cats. Multicoloured.

1509	100r. "Felis libyca" (vert)	40	10
1510	200r. Type **293**	75	15
1511	300r. Caracal	1·00	20
1512	500r. Geoffroy's cat	1·75	35
1513	900r. Black-footed cat	2·75	70
1514	1000r. Flat-headed cat	3·00	75

294 Player dribbling Ball

295 Tusmukh

1996. World Cup Football Championship, France (1998) (1st issue). Multicoloured.

1515	**294**	100r. multicoloured	55	10
1516	–	200r. multicoloured	75	15
1517	–	300r. multicoloured	1·10	20
1518	–	500r. multicoloured	1·75	35
1519	–	900r. multicoloured	3·00	70
1520	–	1000r. mult (horiz)	3·25	75

DESIGNS: 200r. to 1000r. Different players.

See also Nos. 1613/18 and 1726/31.

1996. Khmer Culture. Multicoloured.

1522	100r. Type **295**	30	10
1523	300r. Ream Iso	75	15
1524	900r. Isei	1·25	30

296 Pacific Steam Locomotive No. 620, Finland

1996. Railway Locomotives. Multicoloured.

1525	100r. Type **296**	20	10
1526	200r. GNR steam locomotive No. 261, Great Britain	25	15
1527	300r. Steam tank locomotive, 1930	65	20
1528	500r. Steam tank locomotive No. 1362, 1914	90	30
1529	900r. LMS Turbomotive No. 6202, 1930, Great Britain	1·25	40
1530	1000r. Locomotive "Snake", 1884, New Zealand	1·60	55

297 White-rumped Shama

1996. Birds. Multicoloured.

1532	100r. Type **297**	15	10
1533	200r. Pekin robin	20	10
1534	300r. Varied tit	50	15
1535	500r. Black-naped oriole	70	20
1536	900r. Japanese bush warbler	1·00	30
1537	1000r. Blue and white flycatcher	1·25	40

298 Rhythmic Gymnastics

1996. "Olymphilex '96" Olympic Stamps Exhibition, Atlanta, U.S.A. Multicoloured.

1538	100r. Type **298**	30	10
1539	200r. Judo	40	10
1540	300r. High jumping	75	15
1541	500r. Wrestling	1·00	20
1542	900r. Weightlifting	1·50	30
1543	1000r. Football	2·50	40

299 Douglas M-2, 1926

1996. Biplanes. Multicoloured.

1545	100r. Type **299**	30	10
1546	200r. Pitcairn PS-5 Mailwing, 1926	50	10
1547	300r. Boeing 40-B, 1928	75	15
1548	500r. Potez 25, 1925	1·50	20
1549	900r. Stearman C-3MB, 1927	2·25	30
1550	1000r. De Havilland D.H.4, 1918	2·75	40

300 Aspara **302** Jose Raul Capablanca (1921–27)

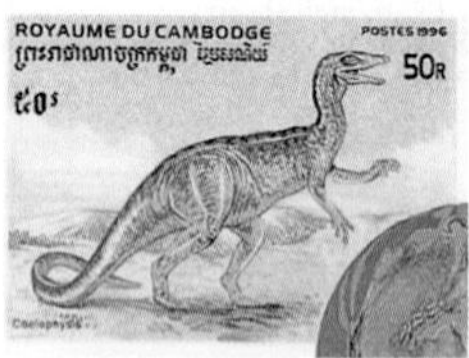

301 Coelophysis

1996. Tonle Bati Temple Ruins.

1552	**300**	50r. black and yellow	25	10
1553	–	100r. black and blue	35	10
1554	–	200r. black and brown	50	10
1555	–	500r. black and blue	1·50	20
1556	–	800r. black and green	1·75	25
1557	–	1000r. black and green	2·75	30
1558	–	1500r. black and bistre	3·00	35

DESIGNS—VERT: 100r. Aspara (different); 200r. Aspara (different); 800r. Taprum Temple; 1000r. Grandmother Peou Temple. HORIZ: 500r. Reliefs on wall; 1500r. Overall view of Tonle Bati.

1996. Prehistoric Animals. Multicoloured.

1559	50r. Type **301**	30	10
1560	100r. Euparkeria	40	10
1561	150r. Plateosaurus	50	10
1562	200r. Herrerasaurus	75	10
1563	250r. Dilophosaurus	1·00	10
1564	300r. Tuojiangosaurus	1·50	10
1565	350r. Camarasaurus	1·75	10
1566	400r. Ceratosaurus	2·00	10
1567	500r. Espinosaurio	2·25	15
1568	700r. Ouranosaurus	2·50	25
1569	800r. Avimimus	3·25	30
1570	1200r. Deinonychus	3·50	35

Nos. 1559/62, 1563/6 and 1567/70 respectively were issued together, se-tenant, each sheetlet containing a composite design of a globe.

1996. World Chess Champions. Multicoloured.

1571	100r. Type **302**	15	10
1572	200r. Aleksandr Alekhine (1927–35, 1937–46)	20	10
1573	300r. Vasily Vasilevich Smyslov (1957–58)	50	15
1574	500r. Mikhail Nekhemyevich Tal (1960–61)	70	20
1575	900r. Robert Fischer (1972–75)	1·00	30
1576	1000r. Anatoly Karpov (1975–85)	1·25	40

303 Brown Bear

1996. Mammals and their Young. Multicoloured.

1578	100r. Type **303**	15	10
1579	200r. Lion	20	10
1580	300r. Malayan tapir	75	15
1581	500r. Bactrian camel	1·00	20
1582	900r. Ibex (vert)	1·25	30
1583	1000r. Californian sealion (vert)	1·50	40

304 Rough Collie

1996. Dogs. Multicoloured.

1584	200r. Type **304**	35	10
1585	300r. Labrador retriever	75	15
1586	500r. Dobermann pinscher	1·00	20
1587	900r. German shepherd	1·50	30
1588	1000r. Boxer	1·75	40

305 Chinese Junk

1996. Ships. Multicoloured.

1589	200r. Type **305**	50	15
1590	300r. Phoenician warship, 1500–1000 B.C.	75	20
1591	500r. Roman war galley, 264–241 B.C.	1·00	25
1592	900r. 19th-century full-rigged ship	1·25	35
1593	1000r. "Sirius" (paddle-steamer), 1838	1·50	45

306 Silver Pagoda, Phnom Penh

1996. 45th Anniv of Cambodian Membership of Universal Postal Union.

1595	**306**	200r. multicoloured	50	10
1596		400r. multicoloured	1·00	15
1597		900r. multicoloured	2·00	30

307 Environmental Vessel and Helicopter

1996. 25th Anniv of Greenpeace (environmental organization). Multicoloured.

1598	200r. Type **307**	70	10
1599	300r. Float-helicopter hovering over motor launch	2·00	15
1600	500r. Helicopter on deck and motor launches	2·50	20
1601	900r. Helicopter with two barrels suspended beneath	3·50	30

308 Ox

1996. New Year. Year of the Ox. Details of painting by Han Huang. Multicoloured.

1603	500r. Type **308**	80	20
1604	500r. Ox with head turned to right (upright horns)	80	20
1605	500r. Brown and white ox with head up ("handlebar" horns)	80	20
1606	500r. Ox with head in bush ("ram's" horns)	80	20

309 Dam, Phnom Kaun Sat

1996. 10th International United Nations Volunteers Day. Multicoloured.

1607	100r. Type **309**	35	10
1608	500r. Canal, O Angkrung	1·25	20
1609	900r. Canal, Chrey Krem	2·25	30

310 Architect's Model of Reservoir

1996. 43rd Anniv of Independence. Water Management. Multicoloured.

1610	100r. Type **310**	35	10
1611	500r. Reservoir	1·25	20
1612	900r. Reservoir (different)	2·25	30

311 Players

1997. World Cup Football Championship, France (1998) (2nd issue).

1613	**311**	100r. multicoloured	50	10
1614	–	200r. multicoloured	75	10
1615	–	300r. multicoloured	1·00	10
1616	–	500r. multicoloured	1·40	10
1617	–	900r. multicoloured	2·50	20
1618	–	1000r. multicoloured	2·50	20

DESIGNS: 200r. to 1000r. Different footballing scenes.

312 Two Elephants

1997. The Indian Elephant. Multicoloured.

1620	300r. Type **312**	30	10
1621	500r. Group of three	60	10
1622	900r. Elephants fighting	1·10	20
1623	1000r. Adult and calf	1·25	20

314 Horse-drawn Water Pump, 1731 **315** Statue on Plinth

1997. Fire Engines. Multicoloured.

1630	200r. Type **314**	15	10
1631	500r. Putnam horse-drawn water pump, 1863	35	10
1632	900r. Merryweather horse-drawn engine, 1894	60	20
1633	1000r. Shand Mason Co horse-drawn water pump, 1901	65	20
1634	1500r. Maxin Motor Co automatic pump, 1949	95	30
1635	4000r. Merryweather exhaust pump, 1950	3·25	90

1997. Angkor Wat.

1637	**315**	300r. black and red	20	10
1638	–	300r. black and blue	20	10
1639	–	800r. black and green	55	15
1640	–	1500r. black & brown	1·25	30
1641	–	1700r. black & orange	1·40	35
1642	–	2500r. black and blue	2·00	55
1643	–	3000r. black & green	2·50	75

DESIGNS—VERT: No. 1638, Statue in wall recess; 1639, Walled courtyard; 1640, Decorative panel with two figures. HORIZ: No. 1641, Rectangular gateway; 1642, Statues and arched gateway; 1643, Stupa and ruins.

316 Steller's Eider

1997. Aquatic Birds. Multicoloured.

1644	200r. Type **316**	15	10
1645	500r. Egyptian goose	35	10
1646	900r. American wigeon	60	20
1647	1000r. Falcated teal	65	20
1648	1500r. Surf scoter	95	30
1649	4000r. Blue-winged teal	2·75	90

317 Von Stephan **318** Main Entrance

1997. Death Centenary of Heinrich von Stephan (founder of U.P.U.).

1651	**317**	500r. blue & dp blue	35	10
1652		1500r. green and olive	1·25	30
1653		2000r. yellow & green	1·75	45

1997. Khmer Culture. Banteay Srei Temple. Multicoloured.

1654	500r. Type **318**	35	10
1655	1500r. Main and side entrances	1·25	30
1656	2000r. Courtyard	1·75	45

319 Birman

1997. Cats. Multicoloured.

1657	200r. Type **319**	15	10
1658	500r. Exotic shorthair	35	10
1659	900r. Persian	60	20
1660	1000r. Turkish van	65	20
1661	1500r. American shorthair	95	30
1662	4000r. Scottish fold	2·75	90

320 No. 488

1997. Steam Railway Locomotives. Multicoloured.
1664 200r. Type **320** 15 10
1665 500r. "Frederick Smith" . . 35 10
1666 900r. No. 3131 . . . . . . 60 20
1667 1000r. London Transport No. L44, Great Britain 65 20
1668 1500r. LNER No. 1711, Great Britain . . . . . . 1·25 30
1669 4000r. No. 60523 "Chateau du Soleil" . . . . 3·25 90

321 Shar-pei

1997. Dogs. Multicoloured.
1671 200r. Type **321** 15 10
1672 500r. Chin-chin 35 10
1673 900r. Pekingese 60 20
1674 1000r. Chow-chow (vert) . . 65 20
1675 1500r. Pug (vert) . . . . . 1·25 30
1676 4000r. Akita (vert) . . . . 3·25 90

322 Qunalom Temple

1997. 30th Anniv of Association of South East Asian Nations. Multicoloured.
1678 500r. Type **322** 35 10
1679 1500r. Royal Palace . . . . 1·25 30
1680 2000r. National Museum . . 1·75 45

323 15th-century Caravelle

1997. Sailing Ships. Multicoloured.
1681 200r. Type **323** 20 10
1682 500r. Spanish galleon . . . 50 15
1683 900r. "Great Harry" (British galleon) 90 25
1684 1000r. "La Couronne" (French galleon) . . . . 1·00 25
1685 1500r. 18th-century East Indiaman . . . . 1·40 35
1686 4000r. 19th-century clipper 4·25 1·00

324 Public Garden **325** Satan's Mushroom

1997. Public Gardens (Nos. 1688/91) and Tuk Chha Canal (others).
1688 **324** 300r. green and black . . 20 10
1689 – 300r. red and black . . . 20 10
1690 – 800r. yellow and black 55 15
1691 – 1500r. orange and black 95 30
1692 – 1700r. pink and black . . 1·10 35
1693 – 2500r. blue and black . . 1·75 55
1694 – 3000r. blue and black . . 2·25 75
DESIGNS—HORIZ: 300r. Statue at intersection of paths; 300r. Hedging in triangular bed; 1500r. Tree and statue of lion; 1700r. View along canal; 2500r. View across canal; 3000r. Closed lock gates. VERT: 800r. Mounted bowl.

1997. Fungi. Multicoloured.
1695 200r. Type **325** 15 10
1696 500r. "Amanita regalis" . . 35 10
1697 900r. "Morchella semilibera" 60 20
1698 1000r. "Gomphus clavatus" 65 20
1699 1500r. "Hygrophorus hypothejus" . . . . . . 2·25 75
1700 4000r. "Albatrellus confluens" . . . . 2·75 90

326 Peaceful Fightingfish ("Betta imbellis") and Siamese Fightingfish ("Betta splendens")

1997. Fishes. Multicoloured.
1702 200r. Type **326** 15 10
1703 500r. Banded gourami . . . 35 10
1704 900r. Rosy barbs 60 20
1705 1000r. Paradise fish 65 20
1706 1500r. "Epalzeorhynchos frenatus" . . . . 2·25 75
1707 4000r. "Capoeta tetrazona" 2·75 90

327 Kampot Post Office

1997. 44th Anniv of Independence. Multicoloured.
1709 1000r. Type **327** 65 20
1710 3000r. Prey Veng Post Office 2·25 75

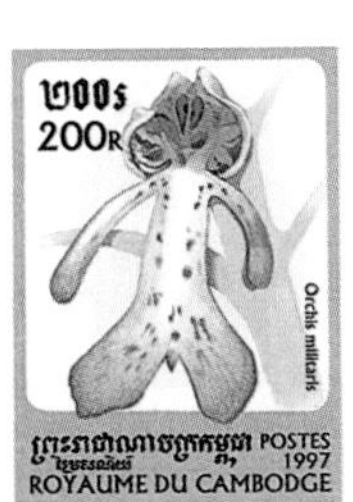

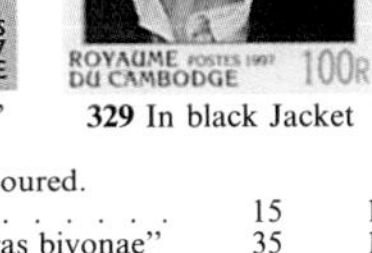

328 "Orchis militaris" **329** In black Jacket

1997. Orchids. Multicoloured.
1711 200r. Type **328** 15 10
1712 500r. "Orchiaceras bivonae" 35 10
1713 900r. "Orchiaceras spuria" 60 20
1714 1000r. "Gymnadenia conopsea" 65 20
1715 1500r. "Serapias neglecta" 2·25 30
1716 4000r. "Pseudorhiza bruniana" . . . . 2·75 90

1997. Diana, Princess of Wales Commemoration. Multicoloured.
1718 100r. Type **329** 10 10
1719 200r. In black dress 15 10
1720 300r. In blue jacket 15 10
1721 500r. Close-up of Princess in visor 35 10
1722 1000r. In mine-protection clothing 65 20
1723 1500r. With Elizabeth Dole 95 30
1724 2000r. Holding landmine . . 1·75 60
1725 2500r. With Mother Teresa and Sisters of Charity . . 2·10 70

330 Player with Ball **331** Suorprat Gateway

1998. World Cup Football Championship, France (3rd issue).
1726 **330** 200r. multicoloured . . . 10 10
1727 – 500r. multicoloured . . . 35 10
1728 – 900r. multicoloured . . . 60 20
1729 – 1000r. multicoloured . . 65 20
1730 – 1500r. multicoloured . . 95 30
1731 – 4000r. multicoloured . . 2·75 90
DESIGNS: 500r. to 4000r. Different footballing scenes.

1998. Temple Ruins.
1733 **331** 300r. orange and black 15 10
1734 – 500r. pink and black . . 25 10
1735 – 1200r. orange and black 70 20
1736 – 1500r. orange and black 95 30
1737 – 1700r. blue and black . . 1·00 30
1738 – 2000r. green and black 1·25 40
1739 – 3000r. lilac and black . . 2·10 70
DESIGNS—HORIZ: No. 1734, Kumlung wall; 1735, Bapuon entrance; 1737, Prerup; 1738, Preah Khan. VERT: No. 1736, Palilai; 1739, Bayon.

332 Tiger Cub **334** Rottweiler

333 Oakland, Antioch and Eastern Electric Locomotive No. 105

1998. New Year. Year of the Tiger. Multicoloured.
1740 200r. Type **332** 10 10
1741 500r. Tiger and cubs 35 15
1742 990r. Tiger on alert 60 20
1743 1000r. Tiger washing itself (horiz) 65 20
1744 1500r. Tiger lying in grass (horiz) 95 30
1745 4000r. Tiger snarling (horiz) 2·75 90

1998. Railway Locomotives. Multicoloured.
1747 200r. Type **333** 10 10
1748 500r. New York, Westchester and electric locomotive No. 1 . . . . 35 15
1749 900r. Spokane and Inland electric locomotive No. MII 60 20
1750 1000r. International Railway electric locomotive 65 20
1751 1500r. British Columbia Electric Railway locomotive No. 823 . . . 90 30
1752 4000r. Southern Pacific electric locomotive No. 200 . . . . 2·75 90

1998. Dogs. Multicoloured.
1754 200r. Type **334** 10 10
1755 500r. Beauceron 35 15
1756 900r. Boxer 60 20
1757 1000r. Siberian husky . . . 65 20
1758 1500r. Welsh Pembroke corgi 90 30
1759 4000r. Basset hound . . . . 2·75 90

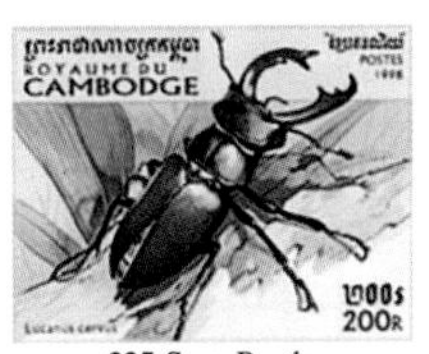

335 Stag Beetle

1998. Beetles. Multicoloured.
1761 200r. Type **335** 10 10
1762 500r. "Carabus auronitens" (ground beetle) 35 15
1763 900r. Alpine longhorn beetle 60 20
1764 1000r. "Geotrupes" (dor beetle) 65 20
1765 1500r. "Megasoma elephas" 90 30
1766 4000r. "Chalcosoma" . . . 2·75 90

336 Prerup Temple

1998. Khmer Culture. Multicoloured.
1768 500r. Type **336** 30 10
1769 1500r. Bayon Temple . . . 90 30
1770 2000r. Angkor Vat . . . . 1·40 45

337 Cutter

1998. Ships. Multicoloured.
1771 200r. Type **337** 10 10
1772 500r. "Britannia" (mail paddle-steamer, 1840) . . 35 10
1773 900r. Viking longship, Gokstad 60 20
1774 1000r. "Great Britain" (steam/sail) 65 20
1775 1500r. Medieval coasting nau 90 30
1776 4000r. Full-rigged ship (inscr "Fregate") . . . . 2·75 90

338 Scottish Fold

1998. Domestic Cats. Multicoloured.
1778 200r. Type **338** 10 10
1779 500r. Ragdoll 35 10
1780 900r. Cymric 60 20
1781 1000r. Devon rex 65 20
1782 1500r. American curl . . . 90 30
1783 4000r. Sphinx . . . . 2·75 90

339 "Petasites japonica"

1998. Flowers. Multicoloured.
1785 200r. Type **339** 10 10
1786 500r. "Gentiana triflora" . . 35 10
1787 900r. "Doronicum cordatum" 60 20
1788 1000r. "Scabiosa japonica" 65 20
1789 1500r. "Magnolia sieboldii" 90 30
1790 4000r. "Erythronium japonica" . . . . 2·75 90

340 "Baptism of Christ" (Gerard David)

1998. "Italia 98" International Stamp Exhibition, Milan. Paintings. Multicoloured.
1792 200r. Type **340** 10 10
1793 500r. "Madonna of Martin van Niuwenhoven" (Hans Memling) 35 10
1794 900r. "Baptism of Christ" (Hendrich Holtzius) . . . 60 20
1795 1000r. "Christ with the Cross" (Luis de Morales) 65 20
1796 1500r. "Elias in the Desert" (Dirk Bouts) 90 30
1797 4000r. "The Virgin" (Petrus Christus) . . . . 2·75 90
There are errors of spelling in some of the inscriptions.

341 "Phyciodes tharos"

1998. Butterflies. Multicoloured.
1799 200r. Type **341** 10 10
1800 500r. "Pararge megera" . . 35 10
1801 900r. Monarch 60 20
1802 1000r. Apollo 65 20
1803 1500r. Swallowtail 90 30
1804 4000r. "Eumenis semele" . . 2·75 90

342 Post Box, 1997

1998. World Post Day. Multicoloured.
1806 1000r. Type **342** 65 20
1807 3000r. Wall-mounted post box, 1951 . . . . 2·00 65

343 Big-Headed Turtle

1998. Tortoise and Turtles. Multicoloured.
1808 200r. Type **343** 10 10
1809 500r. Green turtle 35 10
1810 900r. American soft-shelled turtle 60 20
1811 1000r. Hawksbill turtle . . . 65 20
1812 1500r. Aldabra tortoise . . 90 30
1813 4000r. Leatherback sea turtle . . . . 2·75 90

344 Bayon Dance

1998. 45th Anniv of Independence. Multicoloured.
1815 500r. Type **344** 35 10
1816 1500r. Bayon dance (different) 90 30
1817 2000r. Bayon dance (different) . . . . 1·25 40

345 Cheetah

1998. Big Cats. Multicoloured.
1818 200r. Type **345** 10 10
1819 500r. Snow leopard 35 10
1820 900r. Ocelot 60 30
1821 1000r. Leopard 65 20
1822 1500r. Serval 90 30
1823 4000r. Jaguar . . . . 2·75 90

346 Rabbit

1999. New Year. Year of the Rabbit. Multicoloured. Showing rabbits.
1825 200r. Type **346** 10 10
1826 500r. Facing left 35 10
1827 900r. Sitting in bush . . . 60 30
1828 1000r. Sitting on rock . . . 65 30
1829 1500r. Sitting upright . . . 90 30
1830 4000r. Head looking out from grass (vert) . . . . 2·75 90

347 Foster and Rastik's "Stourbridge Lion", 1829, U.S.A.

1999. Steam Railway Locomotives. Multicoloured.
1832 200r. Type **347** 10 10
1833 500r. "Atlantic", 1832 . . . 30 10
1834 900r. No. O35, 1934 . . . 60 20
1835 1000r. Daniel Gooch's "Iron Duke", 1847, Great Britain 65 20
1836 1500r. "4-6-0" 90 30
1837 4000r. "4-4-2" . . . . . . 2·75 90

348 Aquamarine **349** Alsatian

1999. Minerals. Multicoloured.
1839 200r. Type **348** 10 10
1840 500r. Cat's eye 30 10
1841 900r. Malachite 60 20
1842 1000r. Emerald 65 20
1843 1500r. Turquoise 90 30
1844 4000r. Ruby . . . . 2·75 90

1999. Dogs. Multicoloured.
1846 200r. Type **349** 10 10
1847 500r. Shih tzu (horiz) . . . 30 10
1848 900r. Tibetan spaniel (horiz) 60 20
1849 1000r. Ainu-ken 65 20
1850 1500r. Lhassa apso (horiz) 90 30
1851 4000r. Tibetan terrier (horiz) 2·75 90

350 La Rapide, 1881

1999. Cars. Multicoloured.
1853 200r. Type **350** 10 10
1854 500r. Car designed by Frank Duryea, 1895 . . . . . 30 10
1855 900r. Car designed by Marius Barbarou, 1898 60 20
1856 1000r. Panhard, 1898 . . . 65 20
1857 1500r. Mercedes-Benz "Tonneau", 1901 . . . . 90 30
1858 4000r. Ford, 1915 . . . . . 2·75 90

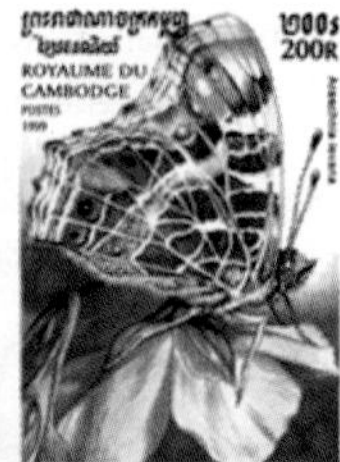

351 Ragdoll **353** *Araschnia levana*

352 Dragon Bridge

1999. Cats. Multicoloured.
1860 200r. Type **351** 10 10
1861 500r. Russian blue 20 10
1862 900r. Bombay 50 15
1863 1000r. Siamese 50 15
1864 1500r. Oriental shorthair . . 80 25
1865 4000r. Somali . . . . 2·60 85

1999. Khmer Culture. Multicoloured.
1867 500r. Type **352** 20 10
1868 1500r. Temple of 100 Columns, Kratie 80 25
1869 2000r. Krapum Chhouk, Kratie . . . . 1·25 40

1999. Butterflies. Multicoloured.
1870 200r. Type **353** 10 10
1871 500r. Painted lady (horiz) 20 10
1872 900r. *Clossiana euphrosyne* 50 15
1873 1000r. *Coenonympha hero* 50 15
1874 1500r. Apollo (horiz) . . . 80 25
1875 4000r. *Plebejus argus* . . . 2·60 85

354 Saurornitholestes

1999. Prehistoric Animals. Multicoloured.
1877 200r. Type **354** 10 10
1878 500r. Prenocephale 20 10
1879 900r. Wuerhosaurus 50 15
1880 1000r. Muttaburrasaurus . . 50 15
1881 1500r. Shantungosaurus . . 80 25
1882 4000r. Microceratops . . . 2·60 85

355 *Flabellina affinis* **357** Prasat Neak Poan

356 "Flowers in a Vase" (Henri Fantin-Latour)

1999. Molluscs. Multicoloured.
1884 200r. Type **355** 10 10
1885 500r. *Octopus macropus* . . 20 10
1886 900r. *Helix hortensis* 50 15
1887 1000r. *Lima hians* 50 15
1888 1500r. *Arion empiricorum* . . 80 25
1889 4000r. Swan mussel . . . . 2·60 85

1999. "Philexfrance 99" International Stamp Exhibition, Paris. Paintings. Multicoloured.
1891 200r. Type **356** 10 10
1892 500r. "Fruit" (Paul Cezanne) 20 10
1893 900r. "Table and Chairs" (Andre Derain) 50 15
1894 1000r. "Vase on a Table" (Henri Matisse) 50 15
1895 1500r. "Tulips and Marquerites" (Othon Friesz) 80 25
1896 4000r. "Still Life with Tapestry" (Matisse) . . . 2·60 85

1999. Temples.
1898 **357** 100r. blue and black . . 10 10
1899 – 300r. red and black . . . 10 10
1900 – 500r. grn & blk (vert) . . 20 10
1901 – 1400r. green and black 75 25
1902 – 1600r. mauve and black 80 25
1903 – 1800r. vio & blk (vert) 1·10 35
1904 – 1900r. brown and black 1·25 40

DESIGNS: 300r. Statue, Neak Poan; 500r. Banteay Srey; 1400r. Banteay Samre; 1600r. Banteay Srey; 1800r. Bas-relief, Angkor Vat; 1900r. Brasat Takeo.

358 Pagoda, Tongzhou **359** *Cymbidium insigne*

1999. "China 1999" International Stamp Exhibition, Peking. Multicoloured.
1905 200r. Type **358** 10 10
1906 500r. Pagoda, Tianning Temple 20 10
1907 900r. Pagoda, Summer Palace 50 15
1908 900r. Pagoda, Blue Cloud Temple 50 15
1909 1000r. White pagoda, Bei Hai 50 15
1910 1000r. Pagoda, Scented Hill 50 15
1911 1500r. Pagoda, Yunju Temple 85 25
1912 4000r. White pagoda, Miaoying Temple . . . . 2·60 85

1999. Orchids. Multicoloured.
1913 200r. Type **359** 10 10
1914 500r. *Papilionanthe teres* . . 20 10
1915 900r. *Panisea uniflora* . . . 50 15
1916 1000r. *Euanthe sanderiana* 50 15
1917 1500r. *Dendrobium trigonopus* 80 25
1918 4000r. *Vanda coerulea* . . . 2·60 85

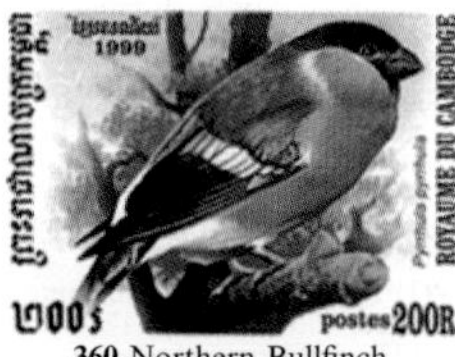

360 Northern Bullfinch

1999. Birds. Multicoloured.
1920 200r. Type **360** 10 10
1921 500r. Hawfinch 20 10
1922 900r. Western greenfinch . . 50 15
1923 1000r. Yellow warbler . . . 50 15
1924 1500r. Great grey shrike . . 85 25
1925 4000r. Blue tit . . . . . . 2·60 85

361 Emblem

1999. 46th Anniv of Independence. Multicoloured.
1927 500r. Type **361** 20 10
1928 1500r. People with symbols of transport and industry 85 25
1929 2000r. People queueing to vote . . . . 1·25 40

362 Tiger Barbs

1999. Fishes. Multicoloured.
1930 200r. Type **362** 10 10
1931 500r. Rainbow shark minnow 20 10
1932 900r. Clown rasbora 50 15
1933 1000r. Orange-spotted cichlid 50 15
1934 1500r. Crescent betta . . . 85 25
1935 4000r. Honey gourami . . . 2·60 85

363 Harpy Eagle

1999. Birds of Prey. Multicoloured.
1937 200r. Type **363** 10 10
1938 500r. Bateleur (vert) 20 10
1939 900r. Egyptian vulture (vert) 50 15
1940 1000r. Peregrine falcon (vert) 50 15
1941 1500r. Red-tailed hawk (vert) 85 25
1942 4000r. American bald eagle 2·60 85

364 Mail Carriage and Globe

1999. 125th Anniv of Universal Postal Union.
1944 **364** 1600r. multicoloured . . 90 30

365 Giant Panda

1999. Mammals. Multicoloured.
1945 200r. Type **365** 10 10
1946 500r. Yak 20 10
1947 900r. Chinese water deer . . 50 10
1948 1000r. Eurasian water shrew (horiz) 50 10
1949 1500r. European otter (horiz) 85 25
1950 4000r. Tiger (horiz) . . . . 2·60 85

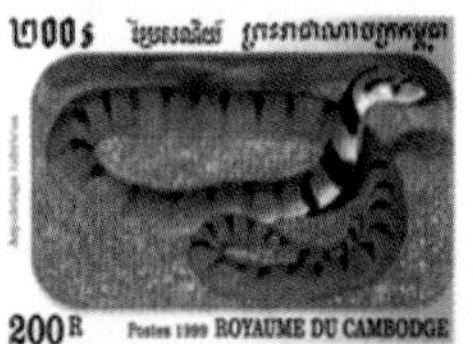

366 Coral Snake

1999. Snakes. Multicoloured.
1952 200r. Type **366** 10 10
1953 500r. Rainbow boa 20 10
1954 900r. Yellow anaconda . . . 50 10
1955 1000r. Southern ring-necked snake 50 10
1956 1500r. Harlequin snake . . 85 25
1957 4000r. Eastern tiger snake 2·60 85

367 Dragon

2000. New Year. Year of the Dragon.
1959 **367** 200r. multicoloured . . . 10 10
1960 – 500r. red, buff and black 25 10
1961 – 900r. multicoloured . . . 55 15
1962 – 1000r. multicoloured . . 60 20
1963 – 1500r. multicoloured . . 90 30
1964 – 4000r. multicoloured . . 2·75 80
MS1965 86 × 110 mm. 4500r. multicoloured 3·00 90
DESIGNS: 500r. Dragon enclosed in circle; 900r. Green dragon with red flames; 1000r. Heraldic dragon; 1500r. Red dragon with blue extremities; 4000r. Blue dragon with yellow flames; 4500r. Dragon's head (32 × 40 mm).

368 Iguanodon (½-size illustration)

2000. Dinosaurs. Multicoloured.
1966 200r. Type **368** 10 10
1967 500r. Euoplocepalus 25 10
1968 900r. Diplosaurus 55 15
1969 1000r. Diplodocus 60 20
1970 1500r. Stegoceras 90 30
1971 4000r. Stegosaurus . . . . 2·75 80
MS1972 110 × 85 mm. 4500r. Brachiosaurus (32 × 40 mm) 3·00 90

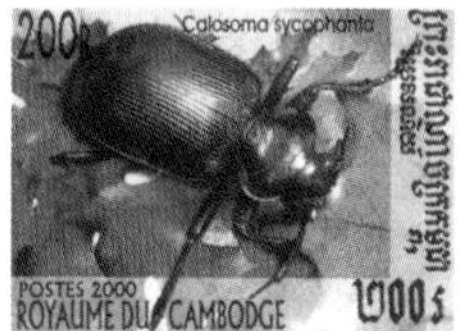
369 Ground Beetle (*Calosoma sycophanta*)

2000. Insects. Multicoloured.
1973 200r. Type **369** 10 10
1974 500r. European rhinoceros beetle (*Oryctes nasicornis*) 25 10
1975 900r. *Diochrysa fastuosa* . . 55 15
1976 1000r. *Blaps gigas* 60 20
1977 1500r. Green tiger beetle (*Cincindela campestris*) . . 90 30
1978 4000r. *Cissistes cephalotes* 2·75 1·60
MS1979 107 × 85 mm. 4500r. Scarab beetle (*Scarabaeus aegyptiorum*) (40 × 32 mm) 3·00 90

370 Box Turtle (*Cuora amboinensis*)

2000. "Bangkok 2000" International Stamp Exhibition. Turtles and Tortoise. Multicoloured.
1980 200r. Type **370** 10 10
1981 500r. Yellow box turtle (*Cuora flavomarginata*) . . 25 10
1982 900r. Black-breasted leaf turtle (*Geoemyda spengleri*) (horiz) 55 15
1983 1000r. Impressed tortoise (*Manouria (Geochelone) impressa*) (horiz) 60 20
1984 1500r. Reeves' turtle (*Chinemys reevesi*) (horiz) 90 30
1985 4000r. Spiny turtle (*Heosemys spinosa*) (horiz) 2·75 1·60
MS1986 111 × 86 mm. 4500r. Annadal's turtle (*Hieremys annandalei*) (horiz) (40 × 32 mm) 3·00 90

371 Ox-cart carrying Rice

2000. Rice Cultivation.
1987 **371** 100r. green and black . . 10 10
1988 – 300r. blue and black . . 10 10
1989 – 500r. mauve and black 25 10
1990 – 1400r. blue and black . . 95 30
1991 – 1600r. brown and black 1·00 30
1992 – 1900r. brown and black 1·25 35
1993 – 2200r. red and black . . 1·40 40
DESIGNS: 300r. Harrowing; 500r. Threshing; 1400r. Winnowing; 1600r. Planting; 1900r. Ploughing; 2200r. Binding sheaves.

372 *Jules Petiet* Steam Locomotive

2000. Locomotives. "WIPA 2000" International Stamp Exhibition, Vienna (**MS**2000). Multicoloured.
1994 200r. Type **372** 10 10
1995 500r. *Longue Chaudiere* steam locomotive, 1891 25 10
1996 900r. *Glehn du Busquet* steam locomotive, 1891 55 15
1997 1000r. *Le Grand Chocolats* steam locomotive 60 20
1998 1500r. *Le Pendule Francais* diesel locomotive 90 30
1999 4000r. TGV 001 locomotive, 1976 . . . . 2·75 1·60
MS2000 110 × 86 mm. 4500r. "Le Shuttle" in tunnel (80 × 32 mm) 3·00 90

373 Fly Agaric (*Amanita muscaria*)

2000. Fungi. Multicoloured.
2001 200r. Type **373** 10 10
2002 500r. Panther cap (*Amanita pantherina*) 25 10
2003 900r. *Clitocybe olearia* . . . 55 15
2004 1000r. *Lactarius scrobiculatus* 60 20
2005 1500r. *Scleroderma vulgare* 90 30
2006 4000r. *Amanita verna* . . . 2·75 1·60
MS2007 110 × 86 mm. 4500r. Death cap (*Amanita phalloides*) (32 × 40 mm) 3·00 90

374 *Betta unimaculata* and *Betta pugnax* (½-size illustration)

2000. Fighting Fish. Multicoloured.
2008 200r. Type **374** 10 10
2009 500r. *Betta macrostoma* and *Betta taeniata* 25 10
2010 900r. *Betta foerschi* and *Betta imbellis* 55 15
2011 1000r. *Betta tessyae* and *Betta picta* 60 20
2012 1500r. *Betta edithae* and *Betta bellica* 90 30
2013 4000r. *Betta smaragdina* . . 2·75 1·60
MS2014 110 × 85 mm. 4500r. Siamese fighting fish (*Betta splendens*) (40 × 32 mm) 3·00 90

375 Woman in Arched Alcove (stone carving)

2000. Khmer Cultural Heritage. Each brown and black.
2015 500r. Type **375** 20 10
2016 1000r. Woman in flowered head-dress in rectangula bas-relief 60 20
2017 2000r. Woman with right arm raised in arche bas-relief . . . . 1·75 55

EXPRESS MAIL STAMPS

E 313 Bohemian Waxwing

1997. Birds. Multicoloured.
E1624 600r. Type **E 313** . . . . 1·00 30
E1625 900r. Great grey shrike . . 1·40 45
E1626 1000r. Eurasian tree sparrow . . . . 1·75 55
E1627 2000r. Black redstart . . . 3·50 1·10
E1628 2500r. Reed bunting . . . 4·50 1·50
E1629 3000r. Ortolan bunting . . 5·25 1·75

POSTAGE DUE STAMPS

D 13

1957.
D81 **D 13** 10c. red, blue & black 20 20
D82 50c. red, blue & black 40 40
D83 1r. red, blue & black 55 55
D84 3r. red, blue & black 70 70
D85 5r. red, blue & black 1·40 1·40

CAMEROON Pt. 1

12 pence = 1 shilling;
20 shillings = 1 pound.

Former German colony occupied by British and French troops during 1914–16. The territory was divided between them and the two areas were administered under League of Nations mandates from 1922, converted into United Nations trusteeships in 1946.

The British section was administered as part of Nigeria until 1960, when a plebiscite was held. The northern area voted to join Nigeria and the southern part joined the newly-independent Cameroun Republic (formerly the French trust territory). In November 1995 this republic joined the Commonwealth.

I. CAMEROONS EXPEDITIONARY FORCE

1915. "Yacht" key-types of German Kamerun surch **C.E.F.** and value in English currency.
B 1 N ½d. on 3pf. brown . . . . 13·00 30·00
B 2 ½d. on 5pf. green . . . . . 3·25 9·50
B 3 1d. on 10pf. red . . . . . 1·25 9·50
B 4 2d. on 20pf. blue . . . . . 3·50 20·00
B 5 2½d. on 25pf. black and red on yellow . . . . 12·00 45·00
B 6 3d. on 30pf. black and orange on buff . . . . . 12·00 45·00
B 7 4d. on 40pf. black and red 12·00 45·00
B 8 6d. on 50pf. black and purple on buff . . . . . 12·00 45·00
B 9 8d. on 80pf. black and red on rose . . . . 12·00 45·00
B10 O 1s. on 1m. red £160 £650
B11 2s. on 2m. blue £160 £650
B12 3s. on 3m. black £160 £650
B13 5s. on 5m. red and black £190 £700

II. CAMEROONS TRUST TERRITORY

Issue used in the British trusteeship from October 1960 until June 1961 in the northern area and until September 1961 in the southern area, when they joined with Nigeria and the Cameroun Republic respectively.

1960. Stamps of Nigeria of 1953 optd **CAMEROONS U.K.T.T.**
T1 **18** ½d. black and orange . . 10 1·25
T2 – 1d. black and green . . . 10 70
T3 – 1½d. green 10 20
T4c – 2d. grey 10 40
T5 – 3d. black and lilac . . . 15 10
T6 – 4d. black and blue . . . 10 1·25
T7 – 6d. brown and black . . 30 20
T8 – 1s. black and purple . . . 15 10
T9 **26** 2s.6d. black and green . . 1·10 80
T10 – 5s. black and orange . . 1·60 3·50
T11 – 10s. black and brown . . 2·50 6·50
T12 **29** £1 black and violet . . . 8·50 20·00

III. REPUBLIC OF CAMEROON

The Republic of Cameroon joined the Commonwealth on 1 November 1995 and issues from that date will be listed below, when examples and information have been received.

CAMEROUN Pt. 7; Pt. 6; Pt. 12

Territory in western Africa which became a German Protectorate in 1884. During 1914–16 it was occupied by Allied troops and in 1922 Britain and France were granted separate United Nations mandates.

In 1960 the French trust territory became an independent republic and, following a plebiscite, in September 1961 the southern part of the area under British control joined the Cameroun Republic. In November 1995 the republic joined the Commonwealth.

A. GERMAN COLONY OF KAMERUN

100 pfennig = 1 mark.

1897. Stamps of Germany optd **Kamerun**.
K1a **8** 3pf. brown . . . . 7·00 13·00
K2 5pf. green . . . . 4·00 5·00
K3 **9** 10pf. red . . . . 4·00 5·00
K4 20pf. blue . . . . 3·50 6·25
K5 25pf. orange . . . . 18·00 29·00
K6a 50pf. brown . . . . 13·00 22·00

1900. "Yacht" key-types inscr "KAMERUN".
K 7 N 3pf. brown . . . . 95 1·25
K21 5pf. green 55 95
K22 10pf. red 45 45
K10 20pf. blue . . . . 20·00 1·60
K11 25pf. black & red on yell 1·25 4·25
K12 30pf. black & orge on buff 1·40 3·25
K13 40pf. black and red . . . 1·40 3·25
K14 50pf. black & pur on buff 1·75 4·00
K15 80pf. black & red on rose 2·25 8·25
K16 O 1m. red . . . . 48·00 48·00
K17 2m. blue . . . . 5·50 42·00
K18 3m. black . . . . 5·00 80·00
K19 5m. red and black £100 £400

B. FRENCH ADMINISTRATION OF CAMEROUN

100 centimes = 1 franc.

1915. Stamps of Gabon with inscription "AFRIQUE EQUATORIALE-GABON" optd **Corps Expeditionnaire Franco-Anglais CAMEROUN**.
1 **7** 1c. brown and orange . . . . 60·00 32·00
2 2c. black and brown £120 £120
3 4c. violet and blue £120 £120
4 5c. olive and green . . . . . 27·00 23·00
5 10c. red and lake (on No. 37 of Gabon) . . . . . . 25·00 16·00
6 20c. brown and violet £120 £130
7 **8** 25c. brown and blue . . . . 48·00 32·00
8 30c. red and grey £120 £120
9 35c. green and violet . . . . 50·00 32·00
10 40c. blue and brown £120 £120
11 45c. violet and red £120 £120
12 50c. grey and green £120 £120
13 75c. brown and orange . . . £180 £130
14 **9** 1f. yellow and brown £180 £130
15 2f. brown and red £200 £170

1916. Optd **Occupation Francaise du Cameroun**.
(a) On stamps of Middle Congo.
16 **1** 1c. olive and brown . . . . 65·00 65·00
17 2c. violet and brown . . . . 75·00 65·00
18 4c. blue and brown . . . . 75·00 65·00
19 5c. green and blue . . . . . 32·00 25·00
20 **2** 35c. brown and blue . . . . 85·00 65·00
21 45c. violet and orange . . . 70·00 60·00

(b) On stamps of French Congo
22 **6** 15c. violet and green . . . . 75·00 70·00
23 **8** 20c. green and red . . . . . £110 75·00
24 30c. red and yellow . . . . . 70·00 60·00
25 40c. brown and green . . . . 70·00 60·00
26 50c. violet and lilac . . . . . 75·00 55·00
27 75c. purple and orange . . . 80·00 55·00
28 – 1f. drab and grey (48) . . . £100 80·00
29 – 2f. red and brown (49) . . . £120 80·00

1916. Stamps of Middle Congo optd **CAMEROUN Occupation Francaise**.
30 **1** 1c. olive and brown . . . . 10 2·40
31 2c. violet and brown . . . . 10 2·40
32 4c. blue and brown . . . . 10 2·40
33 5c. green and blue . . . . . 60 1·90
34 10c. red and blue . . . . . 50 2·40
34a 15c. purple and red . . . . 2·50 2·75
35 20c. brown and blue . . . . 1·25 2·75
36 **2** 25c. blue and green . . . . 1·00 1·25
37 30c. pink and green . . . . 2·00 2·40
38 35c. brown and blue . . . . 1·75 2·75
39 40c. green and brown . . . . 1·40 3·25
40 45c. violet and orange . . . 2·25 3·25
41 50c. green and orange . . . 2·50 3·25
42 75c. brown and blue . . . . 2·50 3·25

43 **3** 1f. green and violet . . . . 1·75 3·00
44 2f. violet and green . . . . 6·50 9·50
45 5f. blue and pink . . . . . 8·25 14·00

1921. Stamps of Middle Congo (colours changed) optd **CAMEROUN**.
46 **1** 1c. orange and green . . . . 10 2·75
47 2c. red and brown . . . . . 10 2·75
48 4c. green and grey . . . . . 20 2·75
49 5c. orange and red . . . . . 20 2·50
50 10c. light green and green . . 30 2·75
51 15c. orange and blue . . . . 80 3·00
52 20c. grey and purple . . . . 1·40 3·00
53 **2** 25c. orange and grey . . . . 1·40 1·90
54 30c. red and carmine . . . . 1·75 3·00
55 35c. blue and grey . . . . . 1·50 3·00
56 40c. orange and green . . . 1·75 3·00
57 45c. red and brown . . . . . 1·75 3·00
58 50c. ultramarine and blue . . 1·00 2·75
59 75c. green and purple . . . . 1·00 3·00
60 **3** 1f. orange and grey . . . . . 3·75 4·00
61 2f. red and green . . . . . 7·00 9·00
62 5f. grey and red . . . . . . 6·50 14·00

1924. Stamps of 1921 surch.
63 **1** 25c. on 15c. orange & blue 55 3·00
64 **3** 25c. on 2f. red and green . . 1·50 3·00
65 25c. on 5f. grey and red . . . 1·25 3·50
66 **2** "65" on 45c. red and brown 1·10 4·00
67 "85" on 75c. green & red . . 2·25 4·25

5 Cattle fording River

1925.
68 **5** 1c. mauve and olive . . . 10 1·75
69 2c. green & red on green 10 1·75
70 4c. black and blue . . . . 30 2·00
71 5c. mauve and yellow . . 35 40
72 10c. orange & pur on yell 90 50
73 15c. green . . . . 1·90 2·75
88 15c. red and lilac . . . . 55 2·50
74 **A** 20c. brown and olive . . . 1·60 3·00
89 20c. green . . . . 80 2·50
90 20c. brown and red . . . 20 25
75 25c. black and green . . . 55 25
76 30c. red and green . . . . 45 1·00
91 30c. green and olive . . . 50 1·40
77 35c. black and brown . . 1·25 3·00
91a 35c. green . . . . 2·50 3·00
78 40c. violet and orange . . 2·75 3·25
79 45c. red . . . . 40 3·00
92 45c. brown and mauve . . 3·25 3·50
80 50c. red and green . . . . 2·25 40
93 55c. red and blue . . . . 2·75 3·75
81 60c. black and mauve . . 2·50 2·75
94 60c. red . . . . 1·50 2·75
82 65c. brown and blue . . . 2·25 40
83 75c. blue . . . . 60 2·75
95 75c. mauve and brown . . 50 1·25
95a 80c. brown and red . . . 90 3·50
84 85c. blue and red . . . . 80 2·50
96 90c. red . . . . 2·50 3·00
85 **B** 1f. brown and blue . . . 55 3·00
97 1f. blue . . . . 75 1·40
98 1f. mauve and brown . . 1·00 2·25
99 1f. brown and green . . . 2·50 1·75
100 1f.10 brown and red . . . 2·75 6·00
100a 1f.25 blue and brown . . 7·75 6·00
101 1f.50 blue . . . . 2·50 75
101a 1f.75 red and brown . . . 95 1·90
101b 1f.75 blue . . . . 7·00 7·00
86 2f. orange and olive . . . 3·00 60
102 3f. mauve and brown . . 4·75 3·75
87 5f. black & brown on bl 3·75 60
103 10f. mauve and orange . . 9·50 9·00
104 20f. green and red . . . . 20·00 16·00
DESIGNS—VERT: A, Tapping rubber-trees. HORIZ: B, Liana suspension bridge.

1926. Surch with new value.
105 **B** 1f.25 on 1f. blue . . . . . 60 2·75

1931. "Colonial Exhibition" key-types inscribed "CAMEROUN".
106 **E** 40c. green . . . . 4·25 4·50
107 **F** 50c. mauve . . . . 4·75 5·00
108 **G** 90c. orange . . . . 4·75 5·25
109 **H** 1f.50 blue . . . . 6·25 5·25

14 Sailing Ships

1937. Paris International Exhibition. Inscr "EXPOSITION INTERNATIONALE PARIS 1937".
110 – 20c. violet . . . . 2·25 4·00
111 **14** 30c. green . . . . 2·25 3·50
112 – 40c. red . . . . 1·10 3·75
113 – 50c. brown & deep brown 1·90 3·25
114 – 90c. red . . . . 1·25 4·00
115 – 1f.50 blue . . . . 1·50 3·75
DESIGNS—VERT: 20c. Allegory of Commerce; 50c. Allegory of Agriculture. HORIZ: 40c. Berber, Negress and Annamite; 90c. France extends torch of Civilization; 1f.50, Diane de Poitiers.

19 Pierre and Marie Curie

1938. International Anti-cancer Fund.
116 **19** 1f.75+50c. blue . . . . . 6·00 14·00

20

21 Lamido Woman

1939. New York World's Fair.
117 **20** 1f.25 red . . . . 2·00 3·25
118 2f.25 blue . . . . 2·00 3·50

1939.
119 **21** 2c. black . . . . 20 2·50
120 3c. mauve . . . . 15 2·00
121 4c. blue . . . . 65 2·50
122 5c. brown . . . . 45 2·50
123 10c. green . . . . 45 2·25
124 15c. red . . . . 70 2·75
125 20c. purple . . . . 55 2·75
126 **A** 25c. black . . . . 1·10 2·75
127 30c. orange . . . . 35 3·00
128 40c. blue . . . . 50 3·00
129 45c. green . . . . 1·40 4·50
130 50c. brown . . . . 70 3·00
131 60c. blue . . . . 1·10 3·25
132 70c. purple . . . . 2·25 4·25
133 **B** 80c. blue . . . . 1·25 4·50
134 90c. blue . . . . 2·75 2·00
135 1f. red . . . . 2·50 3·00
135a 1f. brown . . . . 1·75 2·25
136 1f.25 red . . . . 3·75 7·00
137 1f.40 orange . . . . . . 1·90 3·25
138 1f.50 brown . . . . 90 1·60
139 1f.60 brown . . . . 2·25 4·25
140 1f.75 blue . . . . 1·40 2·75
141 2f. green . . . . 1·50 1·25
142 2f.25 blue . . . . 1·90 2·75
143 2f.50 purple . . . . . . 2·00 2·75
144 3f. violet . . . . 1·25 2·25
145 **C** 5f. brown . . . . 1·75 3·00
146 10f. purple . . . . 1·50 3·75
147 20f. green . . . . 3·50 5·00
DESIGNS—VERT: A, Banyo Waterfall; C, African boatman. HORIZ: B, African elephants.

25 Storming the Bastille

1939. 150th Anniv of Revolution.
148 **25** 45c.+25c. green . . . . . 6·25 11·50
149 70c.+30c. brown . . . . . 4·75 11·50
150 90c.+35c. orange . . . . . 5·50 13·00
151 1f.25+1f. red . . . . . . 5·50 16·00
152 2f.25+2f. blue . . . . . . 8·75 20·00

1940. Adherence to General de Gaulle. Optd **CAMEROUN FRANCAIS 27-8-40**.
153 **21** 2c. black . . . . 1·10 60
154 3c. mauve . . . . 85 1·00
155 4c. blue 65 45
156 5c. brown . . . . 3·75 4·00
157 10c. green 80 25
158 15c. red . . . . 1·25 2·75
159 20c. purple . . . . 12·00 10·50
160 **A** 25c. black . . . . 1·00 70
161 30c. orange . . . . 9·75 10·50
162 40c. blue . . . . 3·25 1·40
163 45c. green . . . . 2·00 1·10
164 – 50c. red & green (No. 80) 80 45
165 **A** 60c. blue . . . . 3·75 4·50
166 70c. purple . . . . 1·75 75
167 **B** 80c. blue . . . . 4·75 1·75
168 90c. blue 75 30
169 **20** 1f.25 red . . . . 3·75 1·40
170 **B** 1f.25 red 80 85
171 1f.40 orange . . . . . . 1·50 1·10
172 1f.50 brown 75 50
173 1f.60 brown . . . . 1·50 85
174 1f.75 blue . . . . 1·50 1·10
175 **20** 2f.25 blue . . . . 3·75 1·50
176 **B** 2f.25 blue 70 60
177 2f.50 purple 55 40
178 – 5f. black and brown on blue (No. 87) . . . . 17·00 6·25
179 **C** 5f. brown . . . . 16·00 6·00
180 – 10f. mve & orge (No. 103) 30·00 6·50
181 **C** 10f. purple . . . . 55·00 45·00
182 – 20f. green & red (No. 104) 50·00 13·00
183 **C** 20f. green £140 £180

1940. War Relief Fund. Nos. 100a, 101a and 86 surch **OEUVRES DE GUERRE** and premium.
184 1f.25+2f. blue and brown . . 19·00 22·00
185 1f.75+3f. red and brown . . 19·00 22·00
186 2f.+5f. orange and olive . . . 16·00 16·00

1940. Spitfire Fund. Nos. 126, 129, 131/2 surch **+5 Frs. SPITFIRE**.
187 **A** 25c.+5f. black . . . . . . 95·00 £100
188 45c.+5f. green £110 £100
189 60c.+5f. blue £110 £110
190 70c.+5f. purple £100 £110

1941. Spitfire Fund. Surch **SPITFIRE +10 fr. General de GAULLE**.
190a **20** 1f.25+10f. red £100 £100
190b 2f.25+10f. blue £100 £100

29b Sikorsky S-43 over Map

29c Sikorsky S-43 Amphibian

1941. Air.
190c **29b** 25c. red . . . . 90 3·00
190d 50c. green . . . . . . 50 3·00
190e 1f. purple . . . . . . 1·75 3·00
190f **29c** 2f. olive . . . . 65 2·75
190g 3f. brown . . . . . . 90 2·75
190h 4f. blue . . . . 55 1·75
190i 6f. myrtle . . . . . . 70 2·75
190j 7f. purple . . . . . . 55 2·75
190k 12f. orange . . . . . . 5·50 6·75
190l 20f. red . . . . 3·00 3·50
190m – 50f. blue . . . . 3·25 3·75
DESIGN: 50f. Latecoere 631 flying boat over harbour.

1941. Laquintinie Hospital Fund. Surch **+10 Frs. AMBULANCE LAQUINTINIE**.
191 **20** 1f.25+10f. red . . . . . . 32·00 28·00
192 2f.25+10f. blue . . . . . . 32·00 28·00

31 Cross of Lorraine, Sword and Shield

32 Fairey FC-1

1942. Free French Issue.
193 **31** 5c. brown (postage) . . . 10 1·25
194 10c. blue 10 15
195 25c. green 10 40
196 30c. red 10 40
197 40c. green 10 30
198 80c. purple 10 35
199 1f. mauve 35 15
200 1f.50 red 40 15
201 2f. black 45 15
202 2f.50 blue 45 30
203 4f. violet 20 30
204 5f. yellow 40 25
205 10f. brown 30 45
206 20f. green 55 65
207 **32** 1f. orange (air) . . . . . 1·50 2·75
208 1f.50 red . . . . 1·90 2·75
209 5f. purple . . . . 80 2·75
210 10f. black . . . . 45 3·00
211 25f. blue . . . . 1·75 3·00
212 50f. green . . . . 2·25 3·00
213 100f. red . . . . 2·00 2·75

1943. Surch **Valmy +100 frs.**
213a – 1f.25+100f. blue and brown (No. 100a) . . . 16·00 32·00
213b **20** 1f.25+100f. red . . . . . 10·00 32·00
213c – 1f.25+100f. red (No. 136) 21·00 32·00
213d – 1f.50+100f. brown (No. 138) . . . . . 19·00 32·00
213e **20** 2f.25+100f. blue . . . . 12·00 32·00

33

34 Felix Eboue

1944. Mutual Aid and Red Cross Funds.
214 **33** 5f.+20f. red . . . . 80 4·50

1945. Surch.
215 **31** 50c. on 5c. brown . . . . 1·40 2·75
216 60c. on 5c. brown . . . . 60 3·00
217 70c. on 5c. brown 75 30
218 1f.20 on 5c. brown . . . . 1·10 30
219 2f.40 on 25c. green . . . . 1·25 1·00
220 3f. on 25c. green . . . . 1·00 1·25
221 4f.50 on 25c. green . . . . 1·60 3·50
222 15f. on 2f.50 blue . . . . 1·75 3·50

1945.
223 **34** 2f. black . . . . 20 1·75
224 25f. green . . . . 1·25 3·00

35 "Victory"

1946. Air. Victory.
225 **35** 8f. purple . . . . 25 2·00

36 Chad

1946. Air. From Chad to the Rhine. Inscr "DU TCHAD AU RHIN".
226 **36** 5f. blue . . . . 2·00 3·50
227 – 10f. purple . . . . 1·40 3·50
228 – 15f. red . . . . 1·75 3·25
229 – 20f. blue . . . . 1·75 3·50
230 – 25f. brown . . . . 2·25 3·50
231 – 50f. black . . . . 1·25 3·75
DESIGNS: 10f. Koufra; 15f. Mareth; 20f. Normandy; 25f. Paris; 50f. Strasbourg.

37 Zebu and Herdsman

45 Aeroplane, African and Mask

1946.
232 **37** 10c. green (postage) . . . 15 60
233 30c. orange . . . . 15 2·00
234 40c. blue . . . . 15 2·75
235 – 50c. sepia . . . . 55 1·40
236 – 60c. purple . . . . 15 2·25
237 – 80c. brown . . . . 30 2·75
238 – 1f. orange 40 15
239 – 1f.20 green . . . . 35 3·00
240 – 1f.50 red . . . . 1·10 1·10
241 – 2f. black 35 10
242 – 3f. red . . . . 1·50 10
243 – 3f.60 red . . . . 1·25 3·00
244 – 4f. blue 85 15
245 – 5f. red . . . . 1·75 15
246 – 6f. blue . . . . 1·50 15
247 – 10f. green . . . . 1·25 15
248 – 15f. blue . . . . 1·25 15
249 – 20f. green . . . . 1·50 25
250 – 25f. black . . . . 1·50 60
251 – 50f. green (air) . . . . . 1·75 75
252 – 100f. brown . . . . 2·25 2·25
253 **45** 200f. olive . . . . 4·25 4·75
DESIGNS—VERT: 50c. to 80c. Tikar women; 1f. to 1f.50, Africans carrying bananas; 2f. to 4f. Bowman; 5f. to 10f. Lamido horsemen; 15f. to 25f. Native head. HORIZ: 50f. Birds over mountains; 100f. African horsemen and Dewoitine D-333 trimotor airplane.

46 People of Five Races, Lockheed Constellation Airplane and Globe

1949. Air. 75th Anniv of U.P.U.
254 **46** 25f. multicoloured . . . . 2·50 6·00

47 Doctor and Patient

1950. Colonial Welfare Fund.
255 **47** 10f.+2f. green & turq . . . 4·50 7·75

48 Military Medal

49 Porters Carrying Bananas

50 Transporting Logs

1952. Military Medal Centenary.
256 **48** 15f. red, yellow and green 4·50 5·00

1953.
257 **49** 8f. violet, orange and purple (postage) 35 10
258 15f. brown, yellow & red 1·50 35
259 – 40f. brown, pink & choc 1·25 30
260 **50** 50f. ol, brn & sep (air) . . 2·50 65
261 – 100f. sepia, brown & turq 5·75 1·10
262 – 200f. brown, blue & grn 8·25 7·25
262a – 500f. indigo, blue and lilac . . . . 16·00 14·50
DESIGNS—As Type **49**: 40f. Woman gathering coffee. As Type **50**: HORIZ: 100f. Airplane over giraffes; 200f. Freighters, Douala Port. VERT: 500f. Sud Ouest Corse II over Piton d'Humsiki.

51 Edea Barrage

1953. Air. Opening of Edea Barrage.
263 **51** 15f. blue, lake and brown 2·75 1·50

52 "D-Day"

1954. Air. 10th Anniv of Liberation.
264 **52** 15f. green and turquoise 4·00 4·00

53 Dr. Jamot and Students

1954. Air. 75th Birthday of Dr. Jamot (physician).
265 **53** 15f. brown, blue & green 4·50 4·00

54 Native Cattle

1956. Economic and Social Development Fund. Inscr "F.I.D.E.S.".
266 **54** 5f. brown and sepia . . . 30 25
267 – 15f. turq, blue & black . . 1·25 25
268 – 20f. turquoise and blue . . 1·10 30
269 – 25f. blue . . . . 1·50 35
DESIGNS: 15f. R. Wouri bridge; 20f. Technical education; 25f. Mobile medical unit.

55 Coffee

1956.
270 **55** 15f. vermilion and red . . 40 15

56 Woman, Child and Flag

57 "Human Rights"

1958. 1st Anniv of First Cameroun Govt.
271 **56** 20f. multicoloured 35 25

1958. 30th Anniv of Declaration of Human Rights.
272 **57** 20f. brown and red . . . . 75 2·75

58 "Randia malleifera"

1958. Tropical Flora.
273 **58** 20f. multicoloured . . . . 1·50 45

59 Loading Bananas on Ship at Douala

60 Prime Minister A. Ahidjo

1959.
274 **59** 20f. multicoloured 65 45
275 – 25f. green, brn & pur . . . 60 40
DESIGN—VERT: 25f. Bunch of bananas and native bearers in jungle path.

C. INDEPENDENT REPUBLIC

1960. Proclamation of Independence. Inscr "1 ER JANVIER 1960".
276 – 20f. multicoloured 55 15
277 **60** 25f. green, bistre & black 55 15
DESIGN: 20f. Cameroun flag and map.

61 "Uprooted Tree"

62 C.C.T.A. Emblem

1960. World Refugee Year.
278 **61** 30f. green, blue and brown 1·00 50

1960. 10th Anniv of African Technical Co-operation Commission.
279 **62** 50f. black and purple . . . 1·10 60

63 Map and Flag

64 U.N. Headquarters, Emblem and Cameroun Flag

1961. Red Cross Fund. Flag in green, red and yellow; cross in red; background colours given.
280 **63** 20f.+5f. green and red . . 70 70
281 25f.+10f. red and green . . 95 95
282 30f.+15f. red and green . . 1·75 1·75

1961. Admission to U.N.O. Flag in green, red and yellow; emblem in blue, buildings and inscr in colours given.
283 **64** 15f. brown and green . . . 45 30
284 25f. green and blue 55 30
285 85f. purple, blue and red 2·10 1·10

1961. Surch **REPUBLIQUE FEDERALE** and value in Sterling currency.
286 – ½d. on 1f. orange (238) (postage) 35 25
287 – 1d. on 2f. black (241) . . 45 30
288 **54** 1½d. on 5f. brown & sepia 50 40
289 – 2d. on 10f. green (247) . . 95 50
290 – 3d. on 15f. turquoise, indigo and black (267) 1·25 35
291 – 4d. on 15f. vermilion and red (270) . . . . . . 1·10 85
292 – 6d. on 20f. mult (274) . . 2·25 1·25
293 **60** 1s. on 25f. grn, bis & blk 2·75 2·00
294a **61** 2s.6d. on 30f. green, blue and brown . . . . . . 4·75 4·75
295a – 5s. on 100r. sepia, brown and turquoise (264) (air) . . . . 9·00 9·00
296a – 10s. on 200f. brown, blue and green (265) . . . . 18·00 18·00
297a – £1 on 500f. indigo, blue and lilac (253a) . . . . 30·00 30·00
The above were for use in the former British Cameroon Trust Territory pending the introduction of the Cameroun franc.

66 Pres. Ahidjo and Prime Minister Foncha

1962. Reunification. (a) T **66**.
298 20f. brown and violet . . . . 16·00 14·00
299 25f. brown and green . . . . 16·00 14·00
300 60f. green and red . . . . . 16·00 14·00

(b) T **66** surch in Sterling currency.
301 3d. on 20f. brown & violet
302 6d. on 25f. brown and green
303 2s.6d. on 60f. green and red
Set of 3 . . . . £375 £375

68 Lions International Badge, Doctor and Leper

1962. World Leprosy Day. Lions International Relief Fund.
304 **68** 20f.+5f. purple & brown 60 60
305 25f.+10f. purple & blue . . 70 70
306 50f.+15f. purple & green 1·40 1·40

69 European, African and Boeing 707 Airliners

1962. Air. Foundation of "Air Afrique" Airline.
307 **69** 25f. purple, violet & grn 65 40

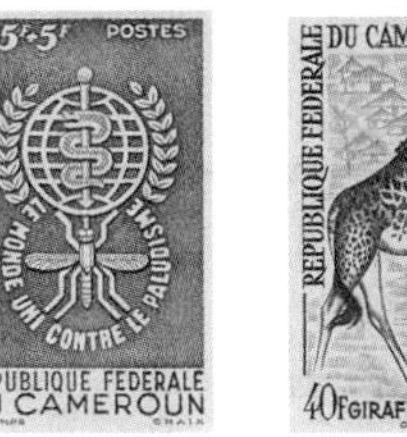
70 Campaign Emblem

71 Giraffes and Waza Camp

1962. Malaria Eradication.
308 **70** 25f.+5f. mauve 65 60

1962. (a) Postage. Animals.
309 A 50c. sepia, blue & turquoise 10 10
310 B 1f. black, turquoise & orge 10 10
311 C 1f.50 brown, sage & blk . . 10 10
312 D 2f. black, blue and green 15 10
313 C 3f. brown, orange & purple 15 10
314 B 4f. sepia, green & turq . . 20 10
315 D 5f. purple, green & brown 20 10
316 A 6f. sepia, blue and lemon 30 15
317 E 8f. blue, red and green . . 65 45
318 F 10f. black, orange & blue 50 15
319 A 15f. brown, blue & turq . . 65 35
320 **71** 20f. brown and grey . . . 85 35
321 F 25f. brown, yellow & grn 2·10 85
322 E 30f. black, blue & brown 2·50 90
323 **71** 40f. lake and green . . . . 4·75 1·40

(b) Air.
324 – 50f. brown, myrtle & blue 90 40
325 – 100f. multicoloured . . . . 2·75 85
326 – 200f. black, brn & turq . . 8·50 2·10
327 – 500f. buff, purple and blue 9·50 3·00
DESIGNS—HORIZ: As Type **71**: A, Moustached monkey; B, African elephant and Ntem Falls; C, Kob, Dschang; D, Hippopotamus, Hippo Camp; E, African manatee, Lake Ossa; F, Buffalo, Batoun Region. (48 × 27 mm): 50f. Cocotiers Hotel, Douala; 100f. "Cymothoe sangaris" (butterfly); 200f. Ostriches; 500f. Kapsikis, Mokolo (landscape).

72 Union Flag

1962. 1st Anniv of Union of African and Malagasy States. Flag in green, red and gold.
328 **72** 30f. brown . . . . 1·40 65

73 Map and View

74 "The School Under the Tree"

1962. 1st Anniv of Reunification.
329 **73** 9f. bistre, violet & brown 30 20
330 18f. red, green and blue . . 40 30
331 – 20f. bistre, blue and purple 45 30
332 – 25f. orange, sepia & blue 45 35
333 – 50f. blue, sepia and red . . 1·25 80
DESIGNS: 20f., 25f. Sunrise over Cameroun; 50f. Commemorative scroll.

1962. Literacy and Popular Education Plan.
334 **74** 20f. red, yellow and green 65 35

75 Globe and "Telstar"

1963. 1st Trans-Atlantic Television Satellite Link.
335 **75** 1f. ol, vio & blue (postage) 10 10
336 2f. lake, green and blue . . 15 15
337 3f. olive, purple and green 20 20
338 25f. blue and green 85 85
339 100f. brown and green (air) (48 × 27 mm) . . . . . 1·90 1·10

76 Globe and Emblem

77 VHF Station, Mt. Bankolo, Yaounde

1963. Freedom from Hunger.
340 **76** 18f.+5f. blue, brn & grn . . 70 40
341 25f.+5f. green & brown . . 85 45

1963. Inauguration of Doala–Yaounde VHF Radio Service.
342 **77** 15f. mult (postage) 35 30
343 – 20f. multicoloured 45 35
344 – 100f. multicoloured (air) 1·90 1·10
DESIGNS: 20f. Aerials and control panel; 100f. Edea relay station (26 × 44 mm).

78 "Centre regional ..."

80 Pres. Ahidjo

1963. Inauguration of U.N.E.S.C.O. Regional Schoolbooks Production Centre, Yaounde.
345 **78** 20f. red, black and green . . . 35 20
346 25f. red, black and orange . . . 40 20
347 100f. red, black and gold . . . 1·50 85

1963. Air. African and Malagasian Posts and Telecommunications Union. As T **18** of Central African Republic.
348 85f. multicoloured . . . . . 1·60 1·10

1963. 2nd Anniv of Reunification. Multicoloured.
349 9f. Type **80** 30 20
350 18f. Map and flag 40 20
351 20f. Type **80** 45 30

1963. Air. Inauguration of "DC-8" Service. As T **11** of Congo Republic.
352 50f. multicoloured 90 45

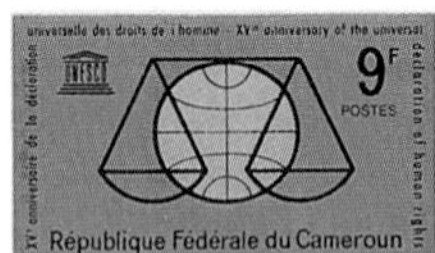

82 Globe and Scales of Justice

1963. 15th Anniv of Declaration of Human Rights.
353 **82** 9f. brown, black and blue . . . 35 15
354 18f. red, black and green . . . 40 20
355 25f. green, black & red . . 50 30
356 75f. blue, black & yellow . . 1·60 65

83 Lion

1964. Waza National Park.
357 **83** 10f. bistre green & brown . . 1·25 35
358 25f. bistre and green . . . 2·40 80

84 Football Stadium, Yaounde

1964. Tropics Cup. Inscr as in T **84**.
359 **84** 10f. brown, turquoise & grn 35 20
360 – 18f. green, red and violet . . 40 30
361 – 30f. blue, brown and black . . 70 40
DESIGNS: 18f. Sports Equipment; 30f. Stadium Entrance. Yaounde.

85 Palace of Justice, Yaounde

1964. 1st Anniv of European–African Economic Convention. Multicoloured.
362 15f. Type **85** . . . . 1·25 55
363 40f. Sun, moon and economic emblems (vert) . . . . . . 2·10 1·10

86 Olympic Flame and Hurdling

1964. Olympic Games, Toyko.
364 **86** 9f. red, blk & grn (postage) . . 1·75 1·40
365 – 10f. brown, violet and red . . 1·90 1·40
366 – 300f. turquoise, brown and red (air) . . . . 7·75 4·25
DESIGNS—VERT: 10f. Running. HORIZ: 300f. Wrestling.

87 Ntem Falls

88 Co-operation

1964. Folklore and Tourism.
367 – 9f. red, blue & grn (postage) 45 20
368 – 18f. blue, brown and red . . 55 35
369 **87** 20f. drab, green and red . . 65 35
370 – 25f. red, brown & orange . . 1·40 55
371 – 50f. brown, grn & bl (air) . . 90 55
372 – 250f. sepia, grn & brn . . 9·75 3·25
DESIGNS—As Type **87**. VERT: 9f. Bamileke dance costume; 18f. Bamenda dance mask. HORIZ: 25f. Fulani horseman. LARGER (43 × 27½ mm): 50f. View of Kribi and Longji; 250f. Black rhinoceros.

1964. French, African and Malagasy Co-operation.
373 **88** 18f. brown, green and blue . . 1·25 75
374 30f. brown, turq & brn . . 2·50 1·00

89 Pres. Kennedy

1964. Air. Pres. Kennedy Commem.
375 **89** 100f. sepia, grn & apple . . 2·00 2·00

90 Inscription recording laying of First Rail

1965. Opening of Mbanga–Kumba Railway.
376 **90** 12f. indigo, green and blue . . 1·00 60
377 – 20f. yellow, green and red . . 2·75 1·25
DESIGN—HORIZ: (36 × 22 mm): 20f. Series BB500 diesel locomotive.

91 Abraham Lincoln

1965. Air. Death Centenary of Abraham Lincoln.
378 **91** 100f. multicoloured . . . . 2·00 1·40

92 Ambulance and First Aid Post

1965. Cameroun Red Cross.
379 **92** 25f. yellow, green and red . . 50 30
380 – 50f. brown, red and grey . . 1·25 45
DESIGN—VERT: 50f. Nurse and child.

93 "Syncom" and I.T.U. Emblem

1965. Air. Centenary of I.T.U.
381 **93** 70f. black, blue and red . . 1·40 70

94 Churchill giving "V" Sign

95 "Map" Savings Bank

1965. Air. Churchill Commem. Multicoloured.
382 12f. Type **94** . . . . 1·00 55
383 18f. Churchill, oak spray and cruiser "De Grasse" . . . 1·40 60

1965. Federal Postal Savings Bank.
384 **95** 9f. yellow, red and green . . 30 15
385 – 15f. brown, green & blue . . 40 20
386 – 20f. brown, chest & turq . . 45 30
DESIGNS—HORIZ: (48 × 27 mm): 15f. Savings Bank building. VERT: (27 × 48 mm): 20f. "Cocoa-bean" savings bank.

96 Africa Cup and Players

1965. Winning of Africa Cup by Oryx Football Club.
387 **96** 9f. brown, yellow and red . . 55 35
388 20f. blue, yellow and red . . 1·40 45

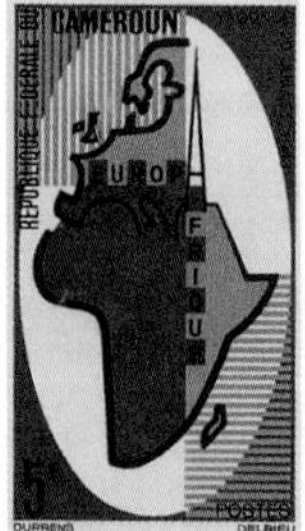

97 Map of Europe and Africa

98 U.P.U. Monument, Berne and Doves

1965. "Europafrique".
389 **97** 5f. red, lilac and black . . 20 15
390 – 40f. multicoloured 90 60
DESIGN: 40f. Yaounde Conference.

1965. 5th Anniv of Admission to U.P.U.
391 **98** 30f. purple and red 60 45

99 I.C.Y. Emblem

1965. International Co-operation Year.
392 **99** 10f. red & blue (postage) . . 35 30
393 100f. blue and red (air) . . 1·60 90

100 Pres. Ahidjo and Government House

1965. Re-election of Pres. Ahidjo. Multicoloured.
394 9f. Pres. Ahidjo wearing hat, and Government House (vert) 20 10
395 18f. Type **100** 35 15
396 20f. As 9f. 45 20
397 25f. Type **100** 55 30

101 Musgum Huts, Pouss

1965. Folklore and Tourism.
398 **101** 9f. green, brown and red (postage) 35 15
399 – 18f. brown, green & blue . . 50 30
400 – 20f. brown and blue . . . 70 30
401 – 25f. grey, lake and green . . 95 30
402 – 50f. brown, blue and green (48 × 27 mm) (air) . . 2·00 80
DESIGNS—HORIZ: 18f. Great Calao's dance (N. Cameroons); 25f. National Tourist office, Yaounde; 50f. Racing pirogue on Sanaga River, Edea. VERT: 20f. Sultan's palace gate Foumban.

102 "Vostok 6"

1966. Air. Spacecraft.
403 **102** 50f. green and red 80 45
404 – 100f. blue and purple . . 2·00 85
405 – 200f. violet and blue . . . 3·50 2·10
406 – 500f. blue and indigo . . 8·50 4·25
DESIGNS: 100f. "Gemini 4", and White in space; 200f. "Gemini 5"; 500f. "Gemini 6" and "Gemini 7" making rendezvous.

103 Mountain's Hotel, Buea

1966. Cameroun Hotels.
407 **103** 9f. bistre, green and red (postage) 30 15
408 – 20f. black, green & blue . . 35 20
409 – 35f. red, brown & green . . 60 40
410 **103** 18f. black, grn & bl (air) . . 35 20
411 – 25f. indigo, red and blue . . 55 20
412 – 50f. brown, orange & grn . . 5·25 3·00
413 – 60f. brown, green & blue . . 1·40 55
414 – 85f. blue, red and green . . 1·75 65
415 – 100f. purple, blue & grn . . 2·40 95
416 – 150f. orange, brn & blue . . 3·25 1·60
HOTELS—HORIZ: 20f. Deputies, Yaounde. 25f. Akwa Palace, Douala. 35f. Dschang. 50f. Terminus, Yaounde. 60f. Imperial, Yaounde. 85f. Independence, Yaounde. 150f. Huts, Waza Camp. VERT: 100f. Hunting Lodge, Mora.

104 Foumban Bas-relief

1966. World Festival of Negro Arts, Dakar
417 **104** 9f. black and red 55 15
418 – 18f. purple, brn and grn . . 55 30
419 – 20f. brown, blue & violet . . 80 30
420 – 25f. brown and plum . . 90 30
DESIGNS—VERT: 18f. Ekoi mask; 20f. Bamileke statue. HORIZ: 25f. Bamoun stool.

105 W.H.O. Headquarters, Geneva

106 "Phaeomeria magnifica"

1966. U.N. Agency Buildings.
421 **105** 50f. lake, blue and yellow . . 90 50
422 – 50f. yellow, blue & green . . 90 50
DESIGN: No. 422, I.T.U. Headquarters, Geneva.

1966. Flowers. Multicoloured. (a) Postage. Size as T **106**.
423 9f. Type **106** 45 15
424 15f. "Strelitzia reginae" . . . 65 15
425 18f. "Hibiscus schizopetalus x rosa-sinensis" 55 20
426 20f. "Antigonon leptopus" . . 55 15

(b) Air. Size 26 × 45½ mm.
427 25f. "Hibiscus mutabilis" ("Caprice des dames") . . 80 20
428 50f. "Delonix regia" . . . . 1·40 30
429 100f. "Bougainvillea glabra" . . 2·50 50
430 200f. "Thevetia peruviana" . . 3·75 1·50
431 250f. "Hippeastrum equestre" . . 4·50 1·90
For stamps as Type **106** but showing fruits, see Nos. 463/71.

107 Mobile Gendarmerie

1966. Air. Cameroun Armed Forces.
432 **107** 20f. blue, brown & plum 45 20
433 – 25f. green, violet & brown 45 20
434 – 60f. indigo, green & blue 1·60 80
435 – 100f. blue, red & purple 2·40 95
DESIGNS: 25f. Paratrooper; 60f. Gunboat "Vigilant"; 100f. Dassault MD-315 Flamant airplane.

108 Wembley Stadium

1966. Air. World Cup Football Championships.
436 **108** 50f. green, blue and red 1·40 45
437 – 200f. red, blue and green 3·75 2·10
DESIGN: 200f. Footballers.

109 Douglas DC-8F Jet Trader and "Air Afrique" Emblem

1966. Air. Inauguration of DC-8 Air Service.
438 **109** 25f. grey, black & purple 60 35

110 U.N. General Assembly

1966. 6th Anniv of Admission to U.N.
439 **110** 50f. purple, green & blue 65 20
440 – 100f. blue, brown & green 1·40 65
DESIGN—VERT: 100f. Africans encircling U.N. emblem within figure "6".

111 1st Minister's Residency, Buea (side view)

1966. 5th Anniv of Cameroun's Reunification. Multicoloured.
441 9f. Type **111** 30 15
442 18f. Prime Minister's Residency, Yaounde (front view) 40 20
443 20f. As 18f. but side view 45 30
444 25f. As Type **111** but front view 55 30

112 Learning to Write

1966. 20th Anniv of U.N.E.S.C.O. and U.N.I.C.E.F.
445 **112** 50f. brown, purple & blue 90 45
446 – 50f. black, blue & purple 90 45
DESIGN: No. 446. Cameroun children.

113 Buea Cathedral

1966. Air. Religious Buildings.
447 **113** 18f. purple, blue & green 35 20
448 – 25f. violet, brown & green 45 20
449 – 30f. lake, green & purple 55 30
450 – 60f. green, red & turquoise 1·10 50
BUILDINGS: 25f. Yaounde Cathedral. 30f. Orthodox Church, Yaounde. 60f. Garoua Mosque.

114 Proclamation

1967. 7th Anniv of Independence.
451 **114** 20f. red, green & yellow 1·90 1·10

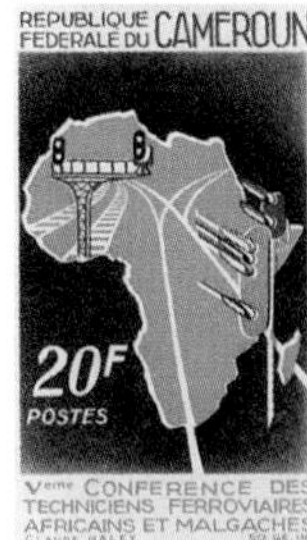

115 Map of Africa, Railway Lines and Signals

117 Aircraft and I.C.A.O. Emblem

116 Lions Emblem and Jungle

1967. 5th African and Malagasy Railway Technicians Conference, Yaounde. Multicoloured.
452 20f. Type **115** 2·00 1·00
453 20f. Map of Africa and diesel train 3·25 1·25

1967. 50th Anniv of Lions International. Mult.
454 50f. Type **116** 80 45
455 100f. Lions emblem and palms 1·75 95

1967. International Civil Aviation Organization.
456 **117** 50f. multicoloured 90 45

118 Dove and I.A.E.A. Emblem

1967. International Atomic Energy Agency.
457 **118** 50f. blue and green 90 45

119 Rotary Banner and Emblem

1967. 10th Anniv of Cameroun Branch, Rotary Int.
458 **119** 25f. red, gold and blue 80 45

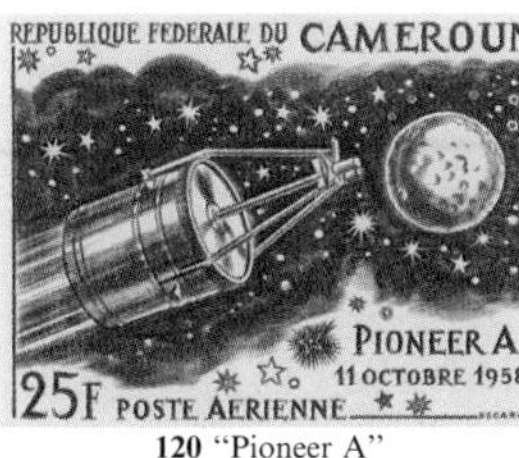

120 "Pioneer A"

1967. Air. "Conquest of the Moon".
459 **120** 25f. green, brown & blue 40 20
460 – 50f. violet, purple & grn 85 35
461 – 100f. purple, brown & bl 2·00 85
462 – 250f. purple, grey and brown 4·50 2·50
DESIGNS: 50f. "Ranger 6"; 100f. "Luna 9"; 250f. "Luna 10".

121 Grapefruit

122 Sanaga Waterfalls

1967. Fruits. Multicoloured.
463 1f. Type **121** 10 10
464 2f. Papaw 10 10
465 3f. Custard-apple 15 15
466 4f. Breadfruit 15 15
467 5f. Coconut 30 15
468 6f. Mango 35 15
469 8f. Avocado 65 30
470 10f. Pineapple 1·10 40
471 30f. Bananas 3·00 1·25

1967. International Tourist Year.
472 **122** 30f. multicoloured 55 30

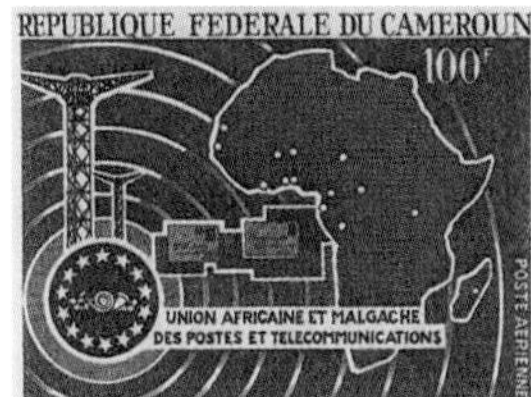

123 Map, Letters and Pylons

1967. Air. 5th Anniv of African and Malagasy Posts and Telecommunications Union (U.A.M.P.T.).
473 **123** 100f. pur, lake & turq 2·00 85

124 Harvesting Coconuts (carved box)

125 Crossed Skis

1967. Cameroun Art.
474 **124** 10f. brown, red and blue 30 15
475 – 20f. brown, green & yell 45 30
476 – 30f. brown, red & green 65 30
477 – 100f. brown, red & grn 2·00 70
DESIGNS (Carved boxes): 20f. Lion-hunting; 30f. Harvesting coconuts (different); 100f. Carved chest.

1967. Air. Winter Olympic Games, Grenoble.
478 **125** 30f. brown and blue 1·40 65

126 Cameroun Exhibit

1967. Air. World Fair, Montreal.
479 **126** 50f. brown, chest & pur 90 35
480 – 100f. brown, purple & grn 2·75 95
481 – 200f. green, purple & brn 3·75 1·90
DESIGNS: 100f. Totem poles; 200f. African pavilion.

For No. 481 optd **PREMIER HOMME SUR LA LUNE 20 JUILLET 1969/FIRST MAN LANDING ON MOON 20 JULY 1969** see note below Nos. 512/17.

127 Chancellor Adenauer and Cologne Cathedral

128 Arms of the Republic

1967. Air. Adenauer Commem. Multicoloured.
482 30f. Type **127** 80 30
483 70f. Adenauer and Chancellor's residence, Bonn 1·75 55

1968. 8th Anniv of Independence.
484 **128** 30f. multicoloured 65 35

129 Pres. Ahidjo and King Faisal of Saudi Arabia

1968. Air. Pres. Ahidjo's Pilgrimage to Mecca and Visit to the Vatican. Multicoloured.
485 30f. Type **129** 65 35
486 60f. Pope Paul VI greeting Pres. Ahidjo 1·60 55

130 "Explorer VI" (televised picture of Earth)

1968. Air. Telecommunications Satellites.
487 **130** 20f. grey, red and blue 40 20
488 – 30f. blue, indigo and red 55 30
489 – 40f. green, red & plum 80 40
DESIGNS: 30f. "Molnya"; 40f. "Molnya" (televised picture of Earth).

131 Douala Port

1968. Air. Five-year Development Plan.
490 – 20f. blue, red and green 35 20
491 – 30f. blue, green & brown 4·25 1·75
492 – 30f. blue, brown & green 65 30
493 – 40f. brown, green & turq 65 30
494 **131** 60f. purple, indigo & blue 1·75 70
DESIGNS—VERT: 20f. Steel forge; 30f. (No. 491), "Transcamerounais" express train leaving tunnel; 30f. (No. 492), Tea-harvesting; 40f. Rubber-tapping.

132 Spiny Lobster

1968. Fishes and Crustaceans.
495 **132** 5f. green, brown & violet 15 15
496 – 10f. slate, brown & blue 20 15
497 – 15f. brown, chest & pur 60 15
498 – 20f. brown and blue 70 15
499 – 25f. blue, brown and green 80 45
500 – 30f. brown, blue and red 1·00 45
501 – 40f. blue, brown & orge 1·40 55
502 – 50f. red, slate and green 2·00 65
503 – 55f. purple, brown & blue 2·75 1·10
504 – 60f. blue, purple & green 4·25 1·40
FISHES AND CRUSTACEANS—HORIZ: 10f. Freshwater crayfish. 15f. Nile mouthbrooder. 20f. Sole. 25f. Northern pike. 30f. Swimming crab. 55f. Dusky snakehead. 60f. Capitaine threadfin. VERT: 40f. African spadefish. 50f. Prawn.

133 Refinery and Tanker

1968. Inauguration of Petroleum Refinery, Port Gentil, Gabon.
505 **133** 30f. multicoloured . . . . 1·00 40

134 Boxing

1968. Air. Olympic Games, Mexico.
506 **134** 30f. brown, green & emer 60 30
507 – 50f. brown, red & green 1·25 50
508 – 60f. brown, blue & green 1·50 55
DESIGNS: 50f. Long-jumping; 60f. Gymnastics.

135 Human Rights Emblem

1968. Human Rights Year.
510 **135** 15f. blue & orge (postage) 45 20
511 30f. green & purple (air) 55 35

136 Mahatma Gandhi and Map of India

137 "The Letter" (A. Cambon)

1968. Air. "Apostles of Peace".
512 **136** 30f. black, yellow & blue 45 30
513 – 30f. black and blue . . . 45 30
514 – 40f. black and pink . . . 65 55
515 – 60f. black and lilac . . . 90 65
516 – 70f. black, buff & buff . . 1·25 80
517 – 70f. black and green . . . 1·25 80
PORTRAITS: No. 513, Martin Luther King. No. 514, J. F. Kennedy. No. 515, R. F. Kennedy. No. 516, Gandhi (full-face). No. 517, Martin Luther King (half-length).

During 1969, Nos. 481 and 512/17 were issued optd **PREMIER HOMME SUR LA LUNE 20 JUILLET 1969/FIRST MAN LANDING ON MOON 20 JULY 1969** in very limited quantities.

1968. Air. "Philexafrique" Stamp Exhibition, Abidjan (in 1969). (1st issue).
519 **137** 100f. multicoloured . . . 3·00 2·40

138 Wouri Bridge and 1f. stamp of 1925

1969. Air. "Philexafrique" Stamp Exhibition, Abidjan, Ivory Coast (2nd issue).
520 **138** 50f. blue, olive and green 1·50 1·10

139 President Ahidjo

1969. 9th Anniv of Independence.
521 **139** 30f. multicoloured 65 25

140 Vat of Chocolate

1969. Chocolate Industry Development.
522 **140** 15f. blue, brown and red 30 20
523 – 30f. brown, choc & grn 55 30
524 – 50f. red, green & bistre 80 35
DESIGNS—HORIZ: 30f. Chocolate factory. VERT: 50f. Making confectionery.

141 "Caladium bicolor"

142 Reproduction Symbol

1969. Air. 3rd Int Flower Show, Paris. Mult.
525 30f. Type **141** 65 45
526 50f. "Aristolochia elegans" 1·40 65
527 100f. "Gloriosa simplex" . . 3·00 1·40

1969. Abbia Arts and Folklore.
528 **142** 5f. purple, turq & blue . . 20 15
529 – 10f. orange, olive & blue 30 15
530 – 15f. indigo, red & blue . . 40 20
531 – 30f. green, brown & blue 60 30
532 – 70f. red, green and blue 1·50 70
DESIGNS—HORIZ: 10f. "Two Toucans"; 30f. "Vulture attacking Monkey". VERT: 15f. Forest Symbol; 70f. Oliphant-player.

143 Post Office, Douala

1969. Air. New Post Office Buildings.
533 **143** 30f. brown, blue & green 40 20
534 – 50f. red, slate & turquoise 65 35
535 – 100f. brown and turquoise 1·40 65
DESIGNS: 50f. G.P.O., Buea; 100f. G.P.O., Bafoussam.

144 "Coronation of Napoleon" (David)

1969. Air. Birth Bicent of Napoleon Bonaparte.
536 **144** 30f. multicoloured 90 55
537 – 1,000f. gold . . . . . . 35·00
DESIGN: 1,000f. "Napoleon crossing the Alps". No. 537 is embossed on gold foil.

145 Kumba Station

146 Bank Emblem

1969. Opening of Mbanga–Kumba Railway. Mult.
538 30f. Type **145** . . . . 1·00 75
539 50f. Diesel train on bridge over River Mungo (vert) 3·25 1·50

1969. 5th Anniv of African Development Bank.
540 **146** 30f. brown, green & vio 60 30

1969. Air. Negro Writers. Portrait designs as T **136**.
541 15f. brown and blue 40 20
542 30f. brown and purple . . . 50 20
543 30f. brown and yellow . . . 50 20
544 50f. brown and green 70 40
545 50f. brown and agate 70 40
546 100f. brown and yellow . . . 1·75 1·10
DESIGNS—VERT: No. 541, Dr. P. Mars (Haiti); No. 542, W. Dubois (U.S.A.); No. 543, A. Cesaire (Martinique); No. 544, M. Garvey (Jamaica); No. 545, L. Hughes (U.S.A.); No. 546, R. Maran (Martinique).

148 I.L.O. Emblem

1969. Air. 50th Anniv of I.L.O.
548 **148** 30f. black and turquoise 55 30
549 50f. black and mauve . . 90 40

149 Astronauts and "Apollo 11" in Sea

1969. Air. 1st Man on the Moon. Multicoloured.
550 200f. Type **149** . . . . 3·25 1·75
551 500f. Astronaut and module on Moon . . . . 7·75 3·50

150 Airplane, Map and Airport

1969. 10th Anniv of Aerial Navigation Security Agency for Africa and Madagascar (ASECNA).
552 **150** 100f. green . . . . 1·50 70

151 President Ahidjo, Arms and Map

1970. Air. 10th Anniv of Independence.
553 **151** 1,000f. gold & mult . . . 21·00
No. 553 is embossed on gold foil.

152 Mont Febe Hotel, Yaounde

1970. Air. Tourism.
554 **152** 30f. grey, green & brn . . 60 30

153 Lenin

154 "Lantana camara"

1970. Air. Birth Centenary of Lenin.
555 **153** 50f. brown and yellow . . 1·40 35

1970. African Climbing Plants. Multicoloured.
556 15f. Type **154** (postage) . . . 35 15
557 30f. "Passiflora quadrangularis" 80 20
558 50f. "Cleome speciosa" (air) 1·40 55
559 100f. "Mussaenda erythrophylla" . . . . . . 2·50 1·40

155 Lions' Emblem and Map of Africa

1970. Air. 13th Congress of Lions International District 403, Yaounde.
560 **155** 100f. multicoloured . . . 1·90 80

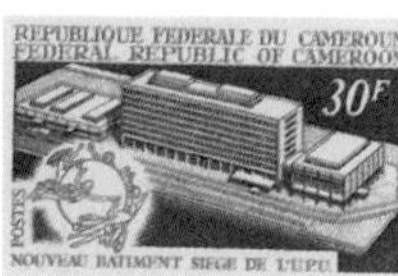

156 New U.P.U. H.Q.

1970. New U.P.U. Headquarters Building, Berne.
561 **156** 30f. green, violet & blue 55 20
562 50f. blue, red and grey . . 80 30

157 U.N. Emblem and Stylized Doves

1970. Air. 25th Anniv of United Nations.
563 **157** 30f. brown and orange . . 65 30
564 – 50f. indigo and blue . . . 90 40
DESIGN—VERT: 50f. U.N. emblem and stylized dove.

158 Fermenting Vats

1970. Brewing Industry.
565 **158** 15f. brown, green & grey 35 20
566 – 30f. red, brown and blue 65 30
DESIGN: 30f. Storage tanks.

159 Japanese Pavilion

1970. Air. Expo 70.
567 **159** 50f. blue, red and green 90 45
568 – 100f. red, blue and green 1·90 80
569 – 150f. brown, slate & blue 3·00 1·50
DESIGNS—VERT: 100f. Expo Emblem and Map of Japan. HORIZ: 150f. Australian Pavilion.

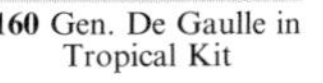

160 Gen. De Gaulle in Tropical Kit

162 Dancers

161 Aztec Stadium, Mexico City

1970. Air. "Homage to General De Gaulle".
570 **160** 100f. brown, blue & grn 2·50 1·60
571 – 200f. blue, green & brn 4·50 2·25
DESIGN: 200f. Gen. De Gaulle in military uniform.
Nos. 570/1 were issued together as a triptych, separated by a stamp-size label showing maps of France and Cameroun.

1970. Air. World Cup Football Championships, Mexico. Multicoloured.
572 50f. Type **161** 80 40
573 100f. Mexican team . . . . 1·75 1·00
574 200f. Pele and Brazilian team with World Cup (vert) . . 3·00 1·40

1970. Ozila Dancers.
575 **162** 30f. red, orange & grn . . 70 35
576 50f. red, brown & scar . . 1·90 80

163 Doll in National Costume

164 Beethoven (after Stieler)

1970. Cameroun Dolls.
577 **163** 10f. green, black & red . . 45 35
578 15f. red, green & yellow 55 45
579 30f. brown, green & blk 1·50 55

1970. Air. Birth Bicent of Beethoven.
580 **164** 250f. multicoloured . . . 3·75 1·90

1970. Air. Rembrandt Paintings. As T **144**. Mult.
581 70f. "Christ at Emmaus" . . 1·40 45
582 150f. "The Anatomy Lesson" 2·50 95

166 "Industry and Agriculture"

167 Bust of Dickens

1970. "Europafrique" Economic Community.
583 **166** 30f. multicoloured 60 30

1970. Air. Death Centenary of Charles Dickens.
584 **167** 40f. brown and red . . . 65 30
585 – 50f. multicoloured 80 35
586 – 100f. multicoloured . . . 1·40 90
DESIGNS: 50f. Characters from David Copperfield; 100f. Dickens writing.

1971. Air. De Gaulle Memorial Issue. Nos. 570/1 optd **IN MEMORIAM 1890-1970**.
587 **160** 100f. brown, blue & grn 2·50 1·40
588 – 200f. blue, green & brn 4·50 2·00

169 University Buildings

1971. Inauguration of Federal University, Yaounde.
589 **169** 50f. green, blue & brown 65 30

170 Presidents Ahidjo and Pompidou

1971. Visit of Pres. Pompidou of France.
590 **170** 30f. multicoloured 90 55

171 "Cameroun Youth"

1971. 5th National Youth Festival.
591 **171** 30f. multicoloured 55 30

172 Timber Yard, Douala

1971. Air. Industrial Expansion.
592 **172** 40f. brown, green & red 40 20
593 – 70f. brown, green and blue 90 40
594 – 100f. red, blue & green . . 1·50 50
DESIGNS—VERT: 70f. "Alucam" aluminium plant, Edea. HORIZ: 100f. Mbakaou Dam.

173 "Gerbera hybrida"

174 "World Races"

1971. Flowers. Multicoloured.
595 20f. Type **173** 45 35
596 40f. "Opuntia polyantha" . . 1·00 45
597 50f. "Hemerocallis hybrida" 1·40 55
For similar designs inscr "United Republic of Cameroon" etc., see Nos. 648/52.

1971. Racial Equality Year. Multicoloured.
598 20f. Type **174** 35 15
599 30f. Hands of four races clasping globe 50 20

175 Crowned Cranes, Camp de Waza

1971. Landscapes.
600 **175** 10f. blue, red and green 1·00 30
601 – 20f. red, brown & green 40 25
602 – 30f. green, blue & brown 55 25
DESIGNS: 20f. African pirogue; 30f. Sanaga River.

176 Relay-racing

1971. Air. 75th Anniv of Modern Olympic Games.
603 **176** 30f. blue, red and brown 45 30
604 – 50f. purple and blue . . . 65 30
605 – 100f. black, green & red 1·40 55
DESIGNS—VERT: 50f. Olympic runner with torch. HORIZ: 100f. Throwing the discus.

177 "Villalba" (deep-sea trawler)

1971. Air. Fishing Industry.
606 **177** 30f. brown, green & blue 65 45
607 – 40f. purple, blue & green 80 45
608 – 70f. brown, red and blue 1·75 65
609 – 150f. multicoloured . . . 3·75 1·75
DESIGNS: 40f. Traditional fishing method, Northern Cameroun; 70f. Fish quay, Douala; 150f. Shrimp-boats, Douala.

178 Peace Palace, The Hague

1971. 25th Anniv of International Court of Justice, The Hague.
610 **178** 50f. brown, blue & green 65 30

179 1916 French Occupation 20c. and 1914–18 War Memorial, Yaounde

1971. Air. "Philatecam 71" Stamp Exhibition, Yaounde (1st issue).
611 **179** 20f. brown, ochre & grn 35 20
612 – 25f. brown, green & blue 40 20
613 – 40f. green, grey & brown 65 20
614 – 50f. multicoloured 85 35
615 – 100f. green, brown & orge 2·00 65
DESIGNS: 25f. 1954 15f. Jamot stamp and memorial; 40f. 1965 25f. Tourist Office stamp and public buildings, Yaounde; 50f. German stamp and Imperial German postal emblem; 100f. 1915 Expeditionary Force optd, error, and Expeditionary Force memorial.
See also No. 620.

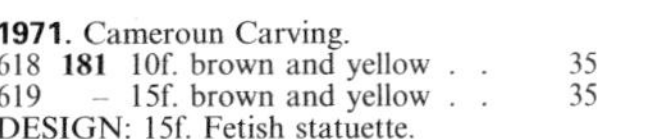

180 Rope Bridge

181 Bamoun Horseman (carving)

1971. "Rural Life". Multicoloured.
616 40f. Type **180** 70 20
617 45f. Local market (horiz) . . 85 30

1971. Cameroun Carving.
618 **181** 10f. brown and yellow . . 35 15
619 – 15f. brown and yellow . . 35 20
DESIGN: 15f. Fetish statuette.

182 Pres. Ahidjo, Flag and "Reunification" Road

1971. Air. "Philatecam 71" Stamp Exhibition, Yaounde (2nd issue).
620 **182** 250f. multicoloured . . . 5·25 3·75

183 Satellite and Globe

1971. Pan-African Telecommunications Network.
621 **183** 40f. multicoloured 55 35

184 U.A.M.P.T. Headquarters, Brazzaville and Carved Stool

1971. Air. 10th Anniv of African and Malagasy Posts and Telecommunications Union.
622 **184** 100f. multicoloured . . . 1·40 65

185 Children acclaiming Emblem

1971. 25th Anniv of U.N.I.C.E.F.
623 **185** 40f. purple, blue & slate 60 20
624 – 50f. red, green and blue 70 35
DESIGN—VERT: 50f. Ear of Wheat and Emblem.

186 "The Annunciation" (Fra Angelico)

1971. Air. Christmas. Paintings. Multicoloured.
625 40f. Type **186** 45 15
626 45f. "Virgin and Child" (Del Sarto) 55 30
627 150f. "The Holy Family with the Lamb" (detail Raphael) (vert) . . . . 2·75 95

187 Cabin, South-Central Region

1972. Traditional Cameroun Houses. Mult.
628 10f. Type **187** 20 15
629 15f. Adamaoua round house 35 20

188 Airline Emblem

1972. Air. Cameroun Airlines' Inaugural Flight.
630 **188** 50f. multicoloured 55 20

189 Giraffe and Palm Tree

190 Africa Cup

1972. Festival of Youth. Multicoloured.
631 2f. Type **189** 15 10
632 5f. Domestic scene 15 10
633 10f. Blacksmith (horiz) . . . 20 15
634 15f. Women 20 15

1972. African Football Cup Championships. Mult.
635 20f. Type **190** 45 20
636 40f. Players with ball (horiz) 65 35
637 45f. Team captains . . . . . 1·10 35

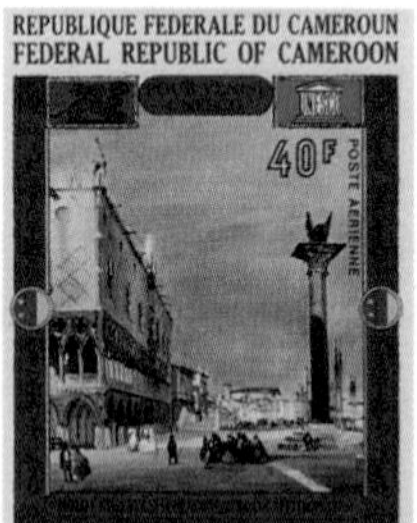

191 "St. Mark's Square and Doge's Palace" (detail-Caffi)

1972. Air. U.N.E.S.C.O. "Save Venice" Campaign. Multicoloured.
638 40f. Type **191** 55 30
639 100f. "Regatta on the Grand Canal" (detail – Canaletto) 1·75 55
640 200f. "Regatta on the Grand Canal" (detail – Canaletto) (different) . . . . 3·50 1·40

192 Assembly Building, Yaounde

1972. 110th Session of Inter-Parliamentary Council, Yaounde.
641 **192** 40f. multicoloured 55 30

193 Horseman, North Cameroun

1972. Traditional Life and Folklore. Mult.
642 15f. Type **193** 30 15
643 20f. Bororo woman (vert) . . 35 15
644 40f. Wouri River and Mt. Cameroun . . . . 1·40 45

194 Pataiev, Dobrovolsky and Volkov

1972. Air. "Soyuz 11" Cosmonauts. Memorial Issue.
645 **194** 50f. multicoloured 65 35

195 U.N. Building, New York, Gate of Heavenly Peace, Peking and Chinese Flag

1972. Air. Admission of Chinese People's Republic to U.N.
646 **195** 50f. multicoloured 55 20

196 Chemistry Laboratory, Federal University

1972. Pres. Ahidjo Prize.
647 **196** 40f. red, green & purple 55 35

1972. Flowers. As T **173**, but inscr "UNITED REPUBLIC OF CAMEROON", etc. Mult.
648 40f. "Solanum macranthum" 55 20
649 40f. "Kaempferia aethiopica" 65 20
650 45f. "Hoya carnosa" 65 35
651 45f. "Cassia alata" 65 20
652 50f. "Crinum sanderianum" 90 35

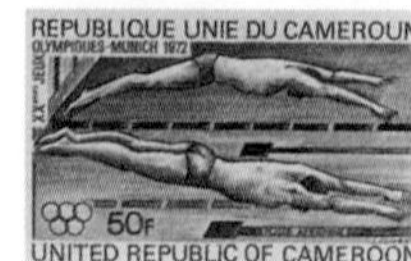

197 Swimming

1972. Air. Olympic Games, Munich.
653 **197** 50f. green, brown & lake 80 35
654 – 50f. brown, blue and sepia 80 35
655 – 200f. lake, grey & purple 3·25 1·40
DESIGNS—HORIZ: No. 655, Horse-jumping. VERT: No. 654, Boxing.

198 "Charaxes ameliae"

201 Great Blue Turacos

1972. Butterflies. Multicoloured.
657 40f. Type **198** . . . . 2·00 55
658 45f. "Papiliotynderaeus" . . 2·50 1·10

1972. No. 471 surch.
659 40f. on 30f. multicoloured . . 60 40

1972. Air. Olympic Gold Medal Winners. Nos. 653/5 optd as listed below.
660 50f. green, brown and red . . 80 35
661 50f. brown, blue and sepia 80 35
662 200f. lake, grey and purple 3·25 1·40
OVERPRINTS: No. 660, **NATATION MARK SPITZ 7 MEDAILLES D'OR**. No. 661, **SUPER-WELTER KOTTYSCH MEDAILLE D'OR**. No. 662, **CONCOURS COMPLET MEADE MEDAILLE D'OR**.

1972. Birds. Multicoloured.
663 10f. Type **201** . . . . 1·00 50
664 45f. Red-faced lovebirds (horiz) . . . . 2·25 1·00

202 "The Virgin with Angels" (Cimabue)

203 St. Theresa

1972. Air. Christmas. Multicoloured.
665 45f. Type **202** 80 35
666 140f. "The Madonna of the Rose Arbour" (S. Lochner) 2·25 1·25

1973. Air. Birth Centenary of St. Theresa of Lisieux.
667 **203** 45f. blue, brown & violet 55 20
668 – 100f. mauve, brown, & bl 1·40 55
DESIGN: 100f. Lisieux Basilica.

204 Emperor Haile Selassie and "Africa Hall", Addis Ababa

1973. Air. 80th Birthday of Emperor Haile Selassie of Ethiopia.
669 **204** 45f. multicoloured 60 35

205 Cotton Cultivation, North Cameroun

207 Human Hearts

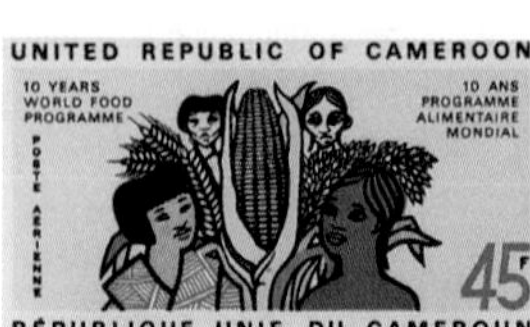

206 "Food for All"

1973. 3rd Five Year Plan. Multicoloured.
670 5f. Type **205** 10 10
671 10f. Cacao pods, South-central region . . . 10 10
672 15f. Forestry, South-eastern area 20 10
673 20f. Coffee plant, West Cameroun 45 15
674 45f. Tea-picking, West Cameroun 95 30

1973. Air. 10th Anniv of World Food Programme.
675 **206** 45f. multicoloured 60 35

1973. Air. 25th Anniv of W.H.O.
676 **207** 50f. red and blue 60 30

208 Pres. Ahidjo, Map, Flag and Cameroun Stamp

1973. 1st Anniv of United Republic. Mult.
677 10f. Type **208** (postage) . . . 45 20
678 20f. Pres. Ahidjo, proclamation and stamp 65 35
679 45f. Pres. Ahidjo, map of Cameroun rivers and stamp (air) 55 20
680 70f. Significant dates on Cameroun flag 80 50

209 Mask

210 Dr. G. A. Hansen

1973. Bamoun Masks.
681 **209** 5f. black, brown & green 10 10
682 – 10f. brown, black & purple 20 10
683 – 45f. brown, black & red 55 30
684 – 100f. brown, black & blue 1·40 55
DESIGNS: 10f., 45f., 100f., as Type **209**, but different masks.

1973. Centenary of Hansen's Identification of Leprosy Bacillus.
685 **210** 45f. blue, lt blue & brown 55 30

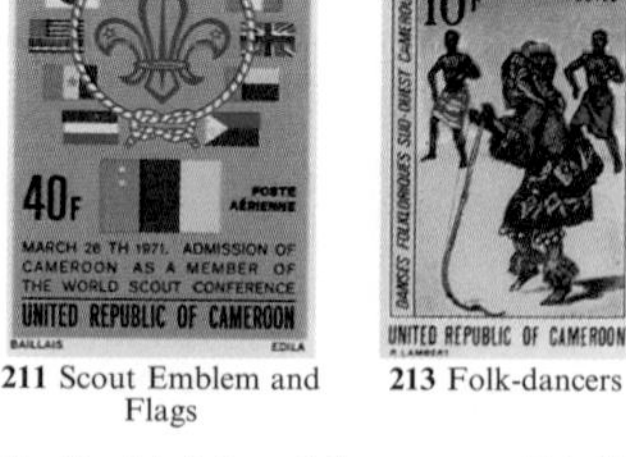

211 Scout Emblem and Flags

213 Folk-dancers

1973. Air. Admission of Cameroun to 24th World Scout Conference.
686 **211** 40f. multicoloured 50 30
687 45f. multicoloured 60 35
688 100f. multicoloured . . . 1·40 60

1973. African Solidarity "Drought Relief". No. 670 surch **100F. SECHERESSE SOLIDARITE AFRICAINE.**
689 **205** 100f. on 5f. multicoloured 1·25 90

1973. Folklore Dances of South-west Cameroun. Multicoloured.
690 10f. Type **213** 15 10
691 25f. Dancer in plumed hat . . 45 15
692 45f. Dancers with "totem" 80 30

214 W.M.O. Emblem

1973. Centenary of W.M.O.
693 **214** 45f. blue and green . . . 55 30

215 Garoua Party H.Q. Building

1973. 7th Anniv of Cameroun National Union.
694 **215** 40f. multicoloured 55 30

216 Crane with Letter and Telecommunications Emblem

1973. 12th Anniv of U.A.M.P.T.
695 **216** 100f. blue, lt blue & green 1·40 55

217 African Mask and Old Town Hall, Brussels

218 Avocado

1973. Air. African Fortnight, Brussels.
696 **217** 40f. brown and purple . . 55 30

1973. Cameroun Fruits. Multicoloured.
697 10f. Type **218** 30 15
698 20f. Mango 35 15
699 45f. Plum 85 20
700 50f. Custard-apple . . . . . 1·25 35

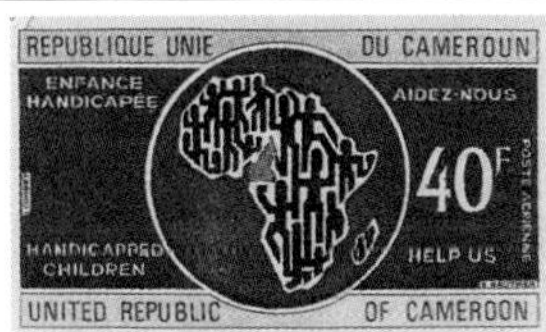

219 Map of Africa

1973. Air. Aid for Handicapped Children.
701 **219** 40f. red, brown & green . . . 55 35

220 Kirdi Village

1973. Cameroun Villages.
702 **220** 15f. black, green & brown . . 20 15
703 – 45f. brown, red & orange . . 50 30
704 – 50f. black, green & orange . . 70 35
DESIGNS: 45f. Mabas village. 50f. Fishing village.

221 Earth Station

1973. Air. Inauguration of Satellite Earth Station, Zamengoe.
705 **221** 100f. brown, blue & grn . . 1·10 55

222 "The Madonna with Chancellor Rolin" (Van Eyck)

223 Handclasp on Map of Africa

1973. Air. Christmas. Multicoloured.
706 45f. Type **222** 80 40
707 140f. "The Nativity" (Federico Fiori–Il Barocci) . . 2·25 1·50

1974. 10th Anniv of Organization of African Unity.
708 **223** 40f. blue, red and green . . 40 20
709 45f. green, blue and red . . 50 20

224 Mill-worker

1974. C.I.C.A.M. Industrial Complex.
710 **224** 45f. brown, green & red . . 55 20

225 Bilinga Carved Panel (detail)

1974. Cameroun Art.
711 **225** 10f. brown and green . . 20 15
712 – 40f. brown and red . . . 50 20
713 – 45f. red and blue 70 30
DESIGNS: 40f. Tubinga carving (detail); 45f. Acajou Ngollon carved panel (detail).

1974. No. 469 surch.

714 40f. on 8f. multicoloured . . 60 30

227 Cameroun Cow

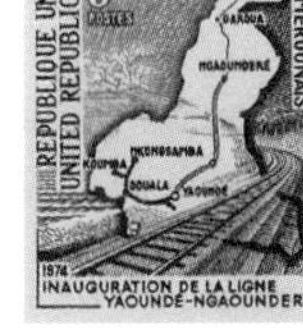

228 Route-map and Track

1974. Cattle-raising in North Cameroun. Mult.
715 40f. Type **227** (postage) . . . 65 30
716 45f. Cattle in pen (air) . . . 65 35

1974. Trans-Cameroun Railway. Inauguration of Yaounde–Ngaoundere Line.
717 **228** 5f. brown, blue & green . . 70 55
718 – 20f. brown, blue & violet . 1·25 75
719 – 40f. red, blue & green . . 2·00 1·25
720 – 100f. green, blue & brown . 3·75 2·10
DESIGNS—HORIZ: 20f. Laying track; 100f. Railway bridge over Djerem River. VERT: 40f. Welding rails.

229 Sir Winston Churchill

1974. Air. Birth Cent of Sir Winston Churchill.
721 **229** 100f. black, red & blue . . 1·10 55

230 Footballer and City Crests

1974. Air. World Cup Football Championships.
722 **230** 45f. orange, slate & grey . . 55 20
723 – 100f. orange, slate & grey . 1·00 50
724 – 200f. blue, orange & blk . 2·00 1·25
DESIGNS: 100f. Goalkeeper and city crests; 200f. World Cup.

1974. Air. West Germany's Victory in World Cup Football Championships. Nos. 722/4 optd **7th JULY 1974 R.F.A. 2 HOLLANDE 1 7 JUILLET 1974.**
725 **230** 45f. orange, slate & grey . . 55 20
726 – 100f. orange, slate & grey . 1·25 50
727 – 200f. blue, orange & blk . 2·40 1·50

232 U.P.U. Emblem and Hands with Letters

1974. Centenary of Universal Postal Union.
728 **232** 40f. red, blue and green (postage) 65 35
729 – 100f. green, vio & bl (air) 1·40 65
730 – 200f. green, red and blue . 2·25 1·40
DESIGNS: 100f. Cameroun U.P.U. headquarters stamps of 1970; 200f. Cameroun U.P.U. 75th anniv stamps of 1949.

233 Copernicus and Solar System

1974. Air. 500th Birth Anniv (1973) of Copernicus.
731 **233** 250f. blue, red & brown . . 3·50 2·25

234 Modern Chess Pieces

1974. Air. Chess Olympics, Nice.
732 **234** 100f. multicoloured . . . 2·75 1·10

235 African Mask and "Arphila" Emblem

1974. Air. "Arphila 75" Stamp Exhibition, Paris.
733 **235** 50f. brown and red . . . 45 30

236 African Leaders, U.D.E.A.C. H.Q. and Flags

1974. 10th Anniv of Central African Customs and Economics Union.
734 **236** 40f. mult (postage) . . . 55 30
735 – 100f. multicoloured (air) . 1·40 50
DESIGN: 100f. Similar to Type **236**.

1974. No. 717 surch **100F 10 DECEMBRE 1974**.
736 **228** 100f. on 5f. brn, bl & grn . 2·00 1·50

238 "Apollo" Emblem, Astronaut, Module and Astronaut's Boots

1974. Air. 5th Anniv of 1st Landing on Moon.
737 **238** 200f. brown, red & blue . . 2·75 1·40

1974. Christmas. As T **222**. Multicoloured.
738 40f. "Virgin of Autumn" (15th-century sculpture) . . 60 35
739 45f. "Virgin and Child" (Luis de Morales) 80 45

239 De Gaulle and Eboue

1975. Air. 30th Anniv of Felix Eboue ("Free French" leader).
740 **239** 45f. multicoloured . . . . 1·40 55
741 200f. multicoloured . . . 4·50 2·50

240 "Celosia cristata"

242 Afo Akom Statue

241 Fish and Fishing-boat

1975. Flowers of North Cameroun. Mult.
742 5f. Type **240** 15 10
743 40f. "Costus spectabilis" . . 60 20
744 45f. "Mussaenda erythrophylla" 80 30

1975. Offshore Fishing.
745 **241** 40f. brown, blue & choc . . 95 30
746 – 45f. brown, bistre & blue . 1·25 45
DESIGN: 45f. Fishing-boat and fish in net.

1975.

747 **242** 40f. multicoloured 45 20
748 45f. multicoloured 55 35
749 200f. multicoloured . . . 2·10 1·50

243 "Polypore" (fungus)

245 Presbyterian Church, Elat

244 View of Building

1975. Natural History. Multicoloured.
750 15f. Type **243** . . . . 3·25 1·25
751 40f. "Nymphalis Chrysalis" . 2·00 55

1975. Inaug of New Ministry of Posts Building.
752 **244** 40f. blue, green & brown . . 45 15
753 45f. brown, green & blue . . 65 35

1975. Churches and Mosque.
754 **245** 40f. brown, blue & black . . 35 15
755 – 40f. brown, blue & slate . . 35 15
756 – 45f. brown, green & blk . . 45 20
DESIGNS: No. 755, Foumban Mosque; No. 756, Catholic Church, Ngaoundere.

246 Marquis de Lafayette (after Chappel) and Naval Battle

247 Harvesting Maize

1975. Air. Bicent (1976) of American Revolution.
757 **246** 100f. blue, turq & brn . . 1·75 85
758 – 140f. blue, brown & green . 1·90 90
759 – 500f. green, brown & blue . 6·00 1·25
DESIGNS: 140f. George Washington (after Stuart) and Continental Infantry (after Ogden); 500f. Benjamin Franklin (after Peale and Nee) and Boston.

1975. "Green Revolution". Multicoloured.
760 40f. Type **247** 45 15
761 40f. Ploughing with oxen (horiz) 40 20

248 "The Burning Bush" (N. Froment)

1975. Air. Christmas. Multicoloured.
762 50f. Type **248** 55 45
763 500f. "Adoration of the Magi" (Gentile da Fabriano) (horiz) . . . . . 6·50 4·75

249 Tracking Aerial

1976. Inauguration of Satellite Monitoring Station, Zamengoe. Multicoloured.
764 40f. Type **249** 35 15
765 100f. Close-up of tracking aerial (vert) 65 40

250 Porcelain Rose **252** Masked Dancer

251 Concorde

1976. Flowers. Multicoloured.
766 40f. Type **250** 55 15
767 50f. Flower of North Cameroun 85 20

1976. Air. Concorde's First Commercial Flight, Paris to Rio de Janeiro.
768 **251** 500f. multicoloured . . . 4·50 2·40

1976. Cameroun Dances. Multicoloured.
770 40f. Type **252** (postage) . . . 55 35
771 50f. Drummers and two dancers (air) 45 20
772 100f. Female dancer 90 35

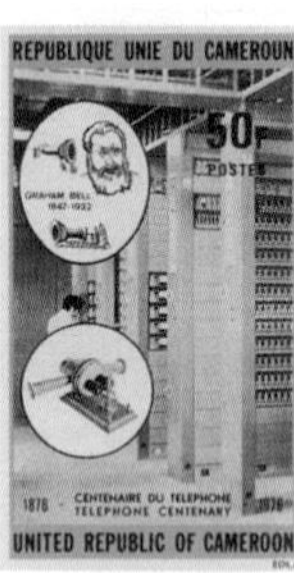

253 Telephone Exchange **255** Dr. Adenauer and Cologne Cathedral

254 Young Men Building House

1976. Air. Telephone Centenary.
773 **253** 50f. multicoloured 40 30

1976. 10th Anniv of National Youth Day. Multicoloured.
774 40f. Type **254** 30 15
775 45f. Gathering palm leaves 40 15

1976. Birth Centenary of Dr. Konrad Adenauer (Statesman).
776 **255** 100f. multicoloured . . . 65 35

256 "Adoration of the Shepherds" (Charles Le Brun)

1976. Air. Christmas.
777 30f. Type **256** 45 15
778 60f. "Adoration of the Magi" (Rubens) 55 30
779 70f. "Virgin and Child" (Bellini) 80 40
780 500f. "The New-born" (G. de la Tour) . . . . 5·75 3·50

257 Pres. Ahidjo and Douala Party H.Q.

1976. 10th Anniv of Cameroun National Union. Multicoloured.
782 50f. Type **257** 35 15
783 50f. Pres. Ahidjo and Yaounde Party H.Q. . . . 35 15

258 Bamoun Copper Pipe **259** Crowned Cranes ("Crown-Cranes")

1977. 2nd World Festival of Negro Arts, Nigeria. Multicoloured.
784 50f. Type **258** (postage) . . . 55 30
785 60f. Traditional chief on throne (sculpture) (air) . . 85 35

1977. Cameroun Birds. Multicoloured.
786 30f. Ostrich . . . . 2·75 65
787 50f. Type **259** . . . . 2·75 95

260 "Christ on the Cross" (Issenheim Altarpiece, Mathias Grunewald)

1977. Air. Easter. Multicoloured.
788 50f. Type **260** 65 30
789 125f. "Christ on the Cross" (Veslasquez) (vert) . . . . 1·40 55
790 150f. "The Entombment" (Titian) . . . . 2·25 85

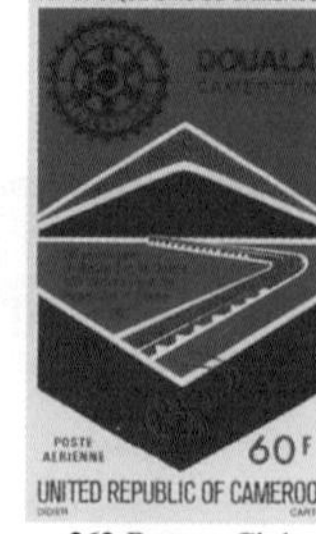

261 Lions Club Emblem **262** Rotary Club Emblem, Mountain and Road

1977. Air. 19th Congress of Douala Lions Club.
792 **261** 250f. multicoloured . . . 3·25 2·00

1977. Air. 20th Anniv of Douala Rotary Club.
793 **262** 60f. red and blue 50 30

263 Jean Mermoz and Seaplane "Comte de la Vaulx"

1977. Air. History of Aviation.
794 **263** 50f. blue, orange & brown 65 35
795 – 60f. purple and orange . . 70 45
796 – 80f. lake and blue 85 45
797 – 100f. green and yellow . . 1·40 65
798 – 300f. blue, red & purple 4·50 2·40
799 – 500f. purple, grn & plum 6·50 3·75
DESIGNS—VERT: 60f. Antoine de Saint-Exupery and Latecoere 2b. HORIZ: 80f. Maryse Bastie and Caudron C-635 Simoun; 100f. Sikorski S-43 amphibian (1st airmail, Marignane–Douala, 1937); 300f. Concorde; 500f. Charles Lindbergh and "Spirit of St. Louis".

1977. Air. 10th Anniv of International French Language Council. As T **204** of Benin.
801 70f. multicoloured 55 30

264 Cameroun 40f. and Basle 2½r. Stamps

1977. "Jufilex" Stamp Exhibition, Berne.
802 **264** 50f. multicoloured 65 35
803 – 70f. green, black & brown 90 45
804 – 100f. multicoloured . . . 1·90 65
DESIGNS: 70f. Zurich 4r. and Kamerun 1m. stamps; 100f. Geneva 5+5c. and Cameroun 20f. stamps.

265 Stafford and "Apollo" Rocket

1977. U.S.A.–U.S.S.R. Space Co-operation. Mult.
805 40f. Type **265** (postage) . . . 35 15
806 60f. Leonov and "Soyuz" rocket 45 20
807 100f. Brand and "Apollo" space vehicle (air) 65 35
808 250f. "Apollo–Soyuz" link-up 2·00 1·10
809 350f. Kubasov and "Soyuz" vehicle . . . . 2·75 1·40

266 Luge Sledging

1977. Winter Olympics. Innsbruck. Multicoloured.
811 40f. Type **266** (postage) . . . 30 15
812 50f. Ski-jumping 40 15
813 140f. Ski-marathon (air) . . . 90 45
814 200f. Ice-hockey . . . . . . 1·40 65
815 350f. Figure-skating . . . . 2·75 1·10

1977. Palestinian Welfare. No. 765 optd **Au bien-etre des familles des martyrs et des combattants pour la liberte de la Palestine. To the Welfare of the families of martyrs and freedom fighters of Palestine.**
817 100f. multicoloured 65 45

268 Mao Tse-tung and Great Wall of China

1977. 1st Death Anniv of Mao Tse-tung.
818 **268** 100f. brown and green . . 1·50 65

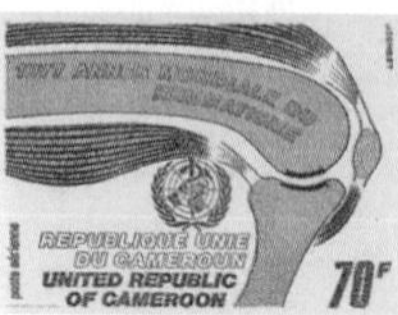

269 Knee Joint

1977. Air. World Rheumatism Year.
819 **269** 70f. brown, red & blue . . 55 20

1977. Air. 1st Paris–New York Commercial Flight of Concorde. Nos. 798 and 768 optd **PREMIER VOL PARIS-NEW YORK FIRST FLIGHT PARIS-NEW YORK 22 nov. 1977 — 22nd Nov. 1977.**
820 – 300f. blue, red & purple 2·75 1·40
821 **251** 500f. multicoloured . . . 4·25 2·25

271 "The Nativity" (Albrecht Altdorfer)

1977. Christmas. Multicoloured.
822 30f. Type **271** (postage) . . . 40 15
823 50f. "Madonna of the Grand Duke" (Raphael) 70 30
824 60f. "Virgin and Child with Four Saints" (Bellini) (horiz) (air) 80 30
825 400f. "Adoration of the Shepherds" (G. de la Tour) (horiz) . . . . 4·50 2·25

272 Club Flag and Rotary Emblem **273** Pres. Ahidjo, Flag and Map

1978. 20th Anniv of Yaounde Rotary Club.
826 **272** 50f. multicoloured 60 30

1978. New Cameroun Flag. Multicoloured.
827 50f. Type **273** (postage) . . . 55 20
828 60f. President, Flag and arms (air) 30 20

274 "Cardioglossa escalerae"

1978. Cameroun Frogs. Multicoloured.
829 50f. Type **274** (postage) . . . 50 35
830 60f. "Cardioglossa elegans" 1·00 45
831 100f. "Cardioglossa trifasciata" (air) . . . . . 1·25 35

275 "L'Arlesienne" (Van Gogh)

1978. Air. Paintings. Multicoloured.
832 200f. Type **275** . . . . 3·00 1·40
833 200f. "Deposition of Christ" (Durer) . . . . 2·25 65

276 Raoul Follereau and Leprosy Distribution Map

1978. Air. World Leprosy Day.
834 **276** 100f. multicoloured . . . 80 45

277 Capt. Cook and the Siege of Quebec

1978. Air. 250th Birth Anniv of Capt. James Cook.
835 **277** 100f. green, blue & lilac 1·40 55
836 – 250f. brown, red and lilac 3·25 1·40
DESIGN: 250f. Capt. Cook, H.M.S. "Adventure" and H.M.S. "Resolution".

278 Footballers

1978. Air. World Cup Football Championship, Argentina. Multicoloured.
837 100f. Argentinian Team (horiz) 70 35
838 200f. Type **278** . . . . 1·50 65
839 1000f. Football illuminating globe . . . . 9·00 4·50

279 Jules Verne and scene from "From the Earth to the Moon"

1978. 150th Birth Anniv of Jules Verne (novelist). Multicoloured.
840 250f. Type **279** (postage) . . 1·90 55
841 400f. Portrait and "20,000 Leagues under the Sea" (horiz) (air) . . . . 3·25 1·40

280 "Hypolimnas salmacis"

1978. Butterflies. Multicoloured.
842 20f. Type **280** 35 20
843 25f. "Euxanthe trajanus" . . 35 20
844 30f. "Euphaedra cyparissa" 45 20

281 Planting Trees

282 Carved Bamoun Drum

1978. Protection against Saharan Encroachment.
845 **281** 10f. multicoloured 15 10
846 15f. multicoloured 20 10

1978. Musical Instruments. Multicoloured.
847 50f. Type **282** (postage) . . . 35 20
848 60f. Gueguerou (horiz) . . . 50 30
849 100f. Mvet Zither (air) . . . 80 35

283 Presidents of Cameroun and France with Independence Monument, Douala

1978. Visit of President Giscard d'Estaing.
850 **283** 60f. multicoloured 85 40

284 African, Human Rights Charter and Emblem

1979. 30th Anniv of Declaration of Human Rights.
851 **284** 5f. mult (postage) 15 10
852 500f. multicoloured (air) 5·25 2·50
See also No. 1070.

285 Lions Emblem and Map of Cameroun

286 Globe, Emblem and Waving Children

1979. Air. Lions International Congress.
853 **285** 60f. multicoloured 60 30

1979. International Year of the Child.
854 **286** 50f. multicoloured 55 20

287 Penny Black, Rowland Hill and German Cameroun 10pf. Stamp

1979. Air. Death Cent of Sir Rowland Hill.
855 **287** 100f. black, red & turq . . 1·10 45

288 Black Rhinoceros

289 "Telecom 79"

1979. Endangered Animals (1st series). Mult.
856 50f. Type **288** 65 30
857 60f. Giraffe (vert) 80 45
858 60f. Gorilla 80 35
859 100f. African elephant (vert) 2·75 1·00
860 100f. Leopard . . . . 1·75 75
See also Nos. 891/2, 904/6, 975/7, 939/40 and 1007/8.

1979. Air. 3rd World Telecommunications Exhibition, Geneva.
861 **289** 100f. orange, blue & grey 90 45

290 Pope John Paul II

291 Dr. Jamot, Map and "Glossina palpalis"

1979. Air. Popes.
862 **290** 100f. blue, violet & grn 1·90 55
863 – 100f. brown, red & green 1·90 55
864 – 100f. chestnut, olive & grn 1·90 55
DESIGNS: No. 863, Pope John Paul I. No. 864, Pope Paul VI.

1979. Birth Centenary of Dr. Eugene Jamot (discoverer of sleeping sickness cure).
865 **291** 50f. brown, blue and red 60 30

292 "The Annunciation" (Fra Filippo Lippi)

1979. Christmas. Multicoloured.
866 10f. Type **292** 10 10
867 50f. "Rest during the Flight into Egypt" (Antwerp Master) 35 10
868 60f. "The Nativity" (Kalkar) 50 15
869 60f. "The Flight into Egypt" (Kalkar) 50 15
870 100f. "The Nativity" (Boticelli) . . . . 1·25 35

293 "Double Eagle II" and Balloonists

1979. Air. 1st Atlantic Crossing by Balloon. Multicoloured.
871 500f. Type **293** . . . . 4·50 1·40
872 500f. "Double Eagle II" over Atlantic and balloonists in basket . . . . 4·50 1·40

294 "Piper capense"

1979. Medicinal Plants. Multicoloured.
873 50f. Type **294** 65 15
874 60f. "Pteridium aquilinum" 70 20

295 Pres. Ahidjo, Map, Independence Stamp and Arms

1980. 20th Anniv of Independence.
875 **295** 50f. multicoloured 45 20

296 Congress Building

1980. 3rd Ordinary Congress of Cameroun National Union, Bafoussam.
876 **296** 50f. multicoloured 45 20

297 Globe

1980. 75th Anniv of Rotary International. Mult.
877 200f. Type **297** . . . . 2·00 65
878 200f. Map of Cameroun . . 2·00 65

298 Voacanga Fruit and Seeds

299 "Dissotis perkinsiae"

1980. Medicinal Plants. Multicoloured.
880 50f. Type **298** 45 10
881 60f. Voacanga tree 45 15
882 100f. Voacanga flowers . . . 80 20

1980. Flowers. Multicoloured.
883 50f. Type **299** 45 10
884 60f. "Brillantaisia" sp. . . . 65 15
885 100f. "Clerodendron splendens" . . . . 1·40 20

300 Ka'aba, Mecca

1980. 1350th Anniv of Mohammed's Occupation of Mecca.
886 **300** 50f. multicoloured 65 35

301 Ice Skating

1980. Air. Olympic Games, Moscow and Lake Placid.
887 – 100f. brown and ochre . . 65 30
888 **301** 150f. brown and blue . . 1·00 45
889 – 200f. brown and green . . 1·75 55
890 – 300f. brown and red . . . 2·25 95
DESIGNS: 100f. Running; 200f. Throwing the Javelin; 300f. Wrestling.

302 Crocodile

1980. Endangered Animals (2nd series). Mult.
891 200f. Type **302** . . . . 2·50 55
892 300f. Kob . . . . 3·25 90

303 Bororo Girls and Roumsiki Peak

1980. Tourism. Multicoloured.
893 50f. Type **303** 40 15
894 60f. Dschang tourist centre 45 20

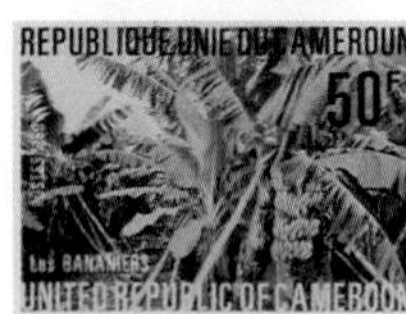

304 Banana Trees

1981. Bertona Agricultural Research Station. Multicoloured.
895 50f. Type **304** 45 10
896 60f. Cattle in watering hole 55 15

305 Girl on Crutches

1981. Int Year of Disabled People. Multicoloured.
897 60f. Type **305** 40 20
898 150f. Boy in wheelchair . . . 1·00 50

306 Camair Headquarters, Douala

1981. 10th Anniv of Cameroun Airlines. Mult.
899 100f. Type **306** 65 20
900 200f. Boeing 747 "Mount Cameroun" . . . . 1·60 45
901 300f. Douala International Airport . . . . 2·50 65

307 Presentation African Club Champions Cup
308 African Buffalo

1981. Football Victories of Cameroun Clubs. Multicoloured.
902 60f. Type **307** 65 35
903 60f. Cup presentation (African Cup Winner's Cup) 65 35

1981. Endangered Animals (3rd series). Mult.
904 50f. Type **308** 65 20
905 50f. Cameroun tortoise . . . 65 20
906 100f. Long-tailed pangolin . . 1·40 35

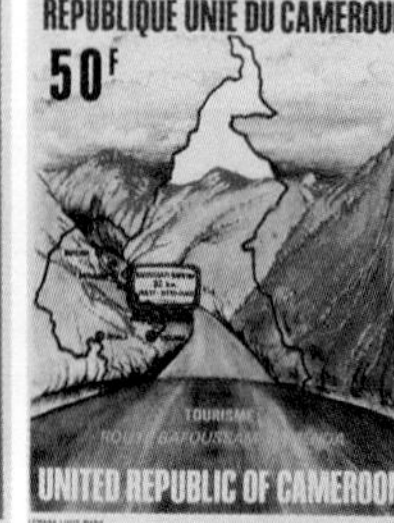

309 Prince Charles, Lady Diana Spencer and St. Paul's Cathedral
310 Bafoussam–Bamenda Road

1981. Wedding of Prince of Wales. Multicoloured.
907 500f. Type **309** . . . . 3·75 1·75
908 500f. Prince Charles, Lady Diana and Royal Coach 3·75 1·75

1981. Tourism.
910 **310** 50f. multicoloured 45 15

311 Yuri Gagarin and "Vostok 1"

1981. 20th Anniv of 1st Men in Space. Mult.
911 500f. Type **311** . . . . 4·50 1·40
912 500f. Alan Shepard and "Freedom 7" . . . . . . 4·50 1·40

312 "Cam Iroko" (freighter) in Harbour

1981. Cameroun Shipping Lines.
913 **312** 60f. multicoloured 65 30

313 Scout Salute and Badge within Knotted Rope, and National Flag

1981. Air. 4th African Scouting Conference, Abidjan. Multicoloured.
914 100f. Type **313** 55 30
915 500f. Saluting Girl Guide . . 3·75 1·40

314 Unity Monument

1981. 20th Anniv of Reunification.
916 **314** 50f. multicoloured 45 20

315 "L'Estaque" (Cezanne)

1981. Air. Paintings. Multicoloured.
917 500f. Type **315** . . . . 5·25 1·50
918 500f. "Guernica" (detail) (Picasso) . . . . 5·25 1·50

316 "Virgin and Child" (detail of San Zeno altarpiece, Mantegna)

1981. Air. Christmas. Paintings. Multicoloured.
919 50f. "Virgin and Child" (detail, "The Burning Bush") (Nicholas Froment) 30 10
920 60f. Type **316** 45 15
921 400f. "The Flight into Egypt" (Giotto) (horiz) . . . . . 3·00 1·25

317 "Voacanga thouarsii"

1981. Medicinal Plants. Multicoloured.
923 60f. Type **317** 55 15
924 70f. "Cassia alata" 65 20

318 "Descent from the Cross" (detail, Giotto)

1982. Easter. Paintings. Multicoloured.
925 100f. "Christ in the Garden of Olives" (Eugene Delacroix) 65 20
926 200f. Type **318** . . . . 1·40 45
927 250f. "Pieta in the Countryside" (Bellini) . . . 2·00 55

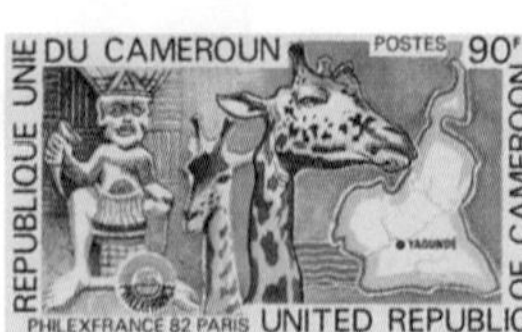

319 Carving, Giraffes and Map

1982. "Philexfrance 82" International Stamp Exhibition, Paris.
928 **319** 90f. multicoloured 80 20

320 Clay Water Jug

1982. Local Handicrafts. Multicoloured.
929 60f. Python-skin handbag . . 45 15
930 70f. Type **320** 55 20

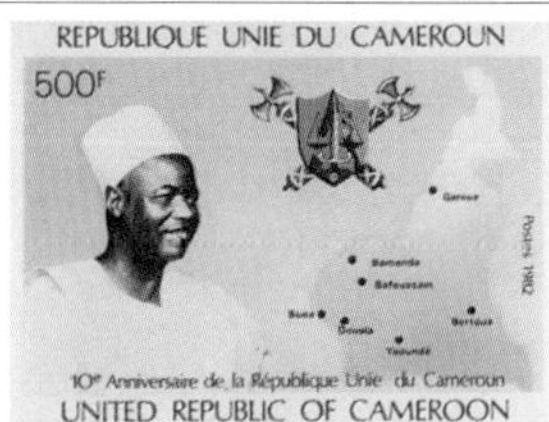

321 Pres. Ahidjo, Map and Arms

1982. 10th Anniv of United Republic.
931 **321** 500f. multicoloured . . . 4·50 1·40

322 Douala Town Hall

1982. Town Halls. Multicoloured.
932 40f. Type **322** 35 10
933 60f. Yaounde town hall . . . 45 15
See also No. 1139.

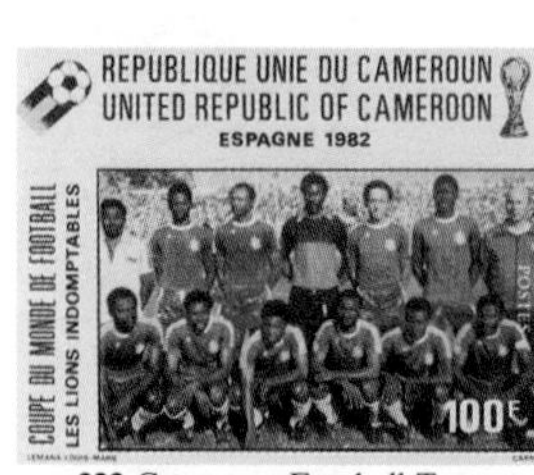

323 Cameroun Football Team

1982. World Cup Football Championship, Spain. Multicoloured.
934 100f. Type **323** . . . . 1·40 35
935 200f. Cameroun and Algerian teams . . . . 2·50 55
936 300f. Nkono Thomas, Cameroun goalkeeper . . . 3·75 80
937 400f. Cameroun team (different) . . . . 5·25 1·40

324 Bongo
325 Cameroun Mountain Francolin ("Perdrix")

1982. Endangered Animals (4th series). Mult.
939 200f. Type **324** . . . . 2·40 85
940 300f. Black colobus . . . . . 3·50 1·40

1982. Birds. Multicoloured.
941 10f. Type **325** 60 35
942 15f. Red-eyed dove ("Tourterelle") 70 50
943 20f. Barn swallow ("Hirondelle") . . . . . . 1·00 90
See also No. 1071.

326 Scouts round Campfire

1982. 75th Anniv of Boy Scout Movement. Multicoloured.
944 200f. Type **326** . . . . 2·00 55
945 400f. Lord Baden-Powell . . 3·50 1·40

327 I.T.U. Emblem
328 Nyasoso Chapel

1982. I.T.U. Delegates' Conference, Nairobi.
946 **327** 70f. multicoloured 55 20

1982. 25th Anniv of Presbyterian Church. Multicoloured.
947 45f. Buea Chapel 40 15
948 60f. Type **328** 50 20

329 World Cup, Footballers and Globe

1982. World Cup Football Championship Result.
949 **329** 500f. multicoloured . . . 4·50 1·90
950 1000f. multicoloured . . . 8·50 3·25

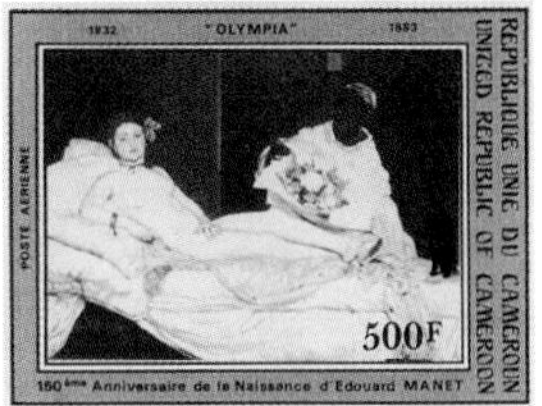

330 "Olympia" (Edouard Manet)

1982. Air. Artists' Anniversaries. Multicoloured.
951 500f. Type **330** (150th birth anniv) . . . . 4·50 1·75
952 500f. "Still-life" (Georges Braque, birth centenary) 4·50 1·75

331 Council Headquarters, Brussels

333 Pres. Kennedy

332 Yaounde University Hospital

1983. 30th Anniv of Customs Co-operation Council. Multicoloured.
953 250f. Type **331** . . . . 1·90 1·10
954 250f. Council emblem . . . . 1·90 1·10

1983. Second Yaounde Medical Days.
955 **332** 60f. multicoloured 55 15
956 70f. multicoloured 65 20

1983. Air. 20th Death Anniv of John F. Kennedy (U.S. President).
957 **333** 500f. multicoloured . . . 4·50 2·00

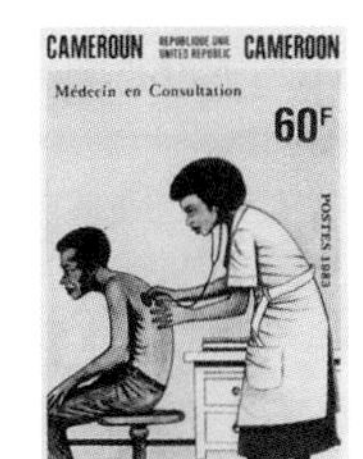

334 Woman Doctor

335 Lions Emblem and Map

1983. Cameroun Women. Multicoloured.
958 60f. Type **334** 55 20
959 70f. Woman lawyer 55 20

1983. Air. District 403 of Lions International Convention, Douala.
960 **335** 70f. multicoloured 45 20
961 150f. multicoloured . . . 1·25 55

336 Bafoussam Town Hall

1983. Town Halls. Multicoloured.
962 60f. Type **336** 45 15
963 70f. Garoua town hall . . . 55 20

337 President Biya and National Flag

1983. 11th Anniv of United Republic. Mult.
964 60f. Type **337** 45 15
965 70f. Pres. Biya and national arms 55 20

338 Container Ship and Buoy

1983. 25th Anniv of I.M.O.
966 **338** 500f. multicoloured . . . 5·00 2·00

339 Martial Eagle ("L'Aigle Martial")

340 Bread Mask ("Wery-Nwen-Nto")

1983. Birds. Multicoloured.
967 25f. Type **339** . . . . 1·60 40
968 30f. Rufous-breasted sparrow hawk ("L'Epervier") . . . 2·25 90
969 50f. Purple heron ("Le Heron Pourpre") . . . . 4·50 1·25
See also Nos. 1157 and 1169.

1983. Cameroun Artists. Multicoloured.
970 60f. Type **340** 55 15
971 70f. Basket with lid ("Chechia Bamoun") . . . 65 20

341 Mobile Rural Post Office

1983. World Communications Year. Multicoloured.
972 90f. Type **341** 65 20
973 150f. Radio operator with morse key . . . . 1·40 35
974 250f. Tom-tom drums . . . 2·40 55

342 African Civet

1983. Endangered Animals (5th series). Mult.
975 200f. Type **342** . . . . 2·40 65
976 200f. Gorilla . . . . 2·40 65
977 350f. Guinea-pig (vert) . . . 3·75 1·25
See also No. 1170.

343 "Jeanne d'Aragon" (Raphael)

1983. Air. Paintings. Multicoloured.
978 500f. Type **343** . . . . 4·50 1·75
979 500f. "Massacre of Scio" (Delacroix) . . . . 4·50 1·75

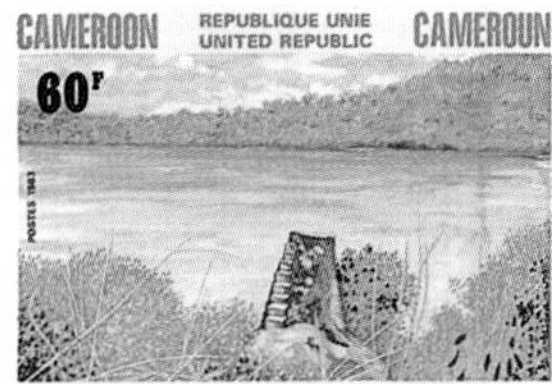

344 Lake Tizon

1983. Landscapes. Multicoloured.
980 60f. Type **344** 45 15
981 70f. Mount Cameroun in eruption 55 15

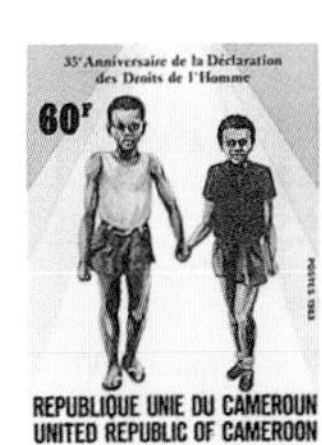

345 Boy and Girl holding Hands
346 Christmas Tree

1983. 35th Anniv of Declaration of Human Rights.
982 **345** 60f. multicoloured 45 15
983 70f. multicoloured 55 15

1983. Christmas. Multicoloured.
984 60f. Type **346** 35 15
985 200f. Stained-glass window, Yaounde Cathedral . . . . 1·40 55
986 500f. Statue of angel, Reims Cathedral . . . . 3·75 1·40
987 500f. "The Rest on the Flight into Egypt" (Philipp Otto Runge) (horiz) . . . . . . 3·75 1·40

348 "Pieta" (G. Hernandez)

1984. Air. Easter. Multicoloured.
992 200f. Type **348** . . . . 1·75 55
993 500f. "Martyrdom of St. John the Evangelist" (C. le Brun) . . . . 4·00 2·00

349 Urban Council Building, Bamenda

1984. Town Halls. Multicoloured.
995 60f. Type **349** 45 15
996 70f. Mbalmayo 55 20

350 High Jump

351 Running with Ball

1984. Air. Olympic Games, Los Angeles. Mult.
997 100f. Type **350** 65 30
998 150f. Volleyball . . . . . . 1·25 45
999 250f. Basketball . . . . . . 2·00 65
1000 500f. Cycling . . . . 3·75 1·40

1984. Air. European Football Championship. Multicoloured.
1001 250f. Type **351** . . . . . . 2·00 65
1002 250f. Heading ball . . . . . 2·00 65
1003 500f. Tackle . . . . 3·75 1·40

352 Catholic Church, Zoetele

1984. Churches. Multicoloured.
1005 60f. Type **352** 45 15
1006 70f. Marie Gocker Protestant Church, Yaounde 55 20

353 Antelope

1984. Endangered Animals (6th series). Mult.
1007 250f. Type **353** . . . . . . 2·50 1·10
1008 250f. Wild boar . . . . . . 2·50 1·10

354 Pres. Biya and Arms

1984. Air. President's Oath-taking Ceremony.
(a) Inscr in French.
1009 **354** 60f. multicoloured . . . 40 15
1010 70f. multicoloured . . . 45 15
1011 200f. multicoloured . . . 1·40 40

(b) Inscr in English.
1012 **354** 60f. multicoloured . . . 40 15
1013 70f. multicoloured . . . 45 15
1014 200f. multicoloured . . . 1·40 40

355 "Diana Bathing" (Watteau)

1984. Air. Anniversaries. Multicoloured.
1015 500f. Type **355** (300th birth anniv) (wrongly inscr "1624") . . . . 4·75 1·40
1016 500f. Diderot (encyclopaedist, death bicentenary) . . . . . . 4·75 1·40

1984. Air. Olympic Games Medal Winners. Nos. 997/1000 optd.
1017 100f. **MOEGENBURG (R.F.A.) 11-08-84** 65 35
1018 150f. **U.S.A. 11-08-84** . . . 1·25 50

1019 250f. **YOUGOSLAVIE 9-08-84** . . . . 2·00 1·10
1020 500f. **GORSKI (U.S.A.) 3-08-84** . . . . 3·75 1·90

357 Nightingale ("Le Rossignol") **358** Neil Armstrong

1984. Birds. Multicoloured.
1021 60f. Type **357** . . . . 2·00 70
1022 60f. Ruppell's griffon ("Le Vautour") . . . . 2·00 70
See also No. 1158.

1984. Air. 15th Anniv of 1st Man on the Moon. Multicoloured.
1023 500f. Type **358** . . . . . . 4·50 1·75
1024 500f. Launching of "Apollo 12" . . . . . . 4·50 1·75

359 Maize and Young Plants

1984. Agro-pastoral Fair. Bamenda. Mult.
1025 60f. Type **359** 45 15
1026 70f. Zebus 55 20
1027 300f. Potatoes . . . . . . 2·50 85

360 Anniversary Emblem **362** Balafons (xylophone)

361 Wrestling

1984. 40th Anniv of I.C.A.O.
1028 – 200f. multicoloured . . . 1·40 55
1029 **360** 200f. blue & deep blue 1·40 55
1030 – 300f. multicoloured . . . 2·40 85
1031 – 300f. multicoloured . . . 3·00 1·40
DESIGNS: No. 1028, "Icarus" (Hans Herni); 1030, Cameroun Airlines Boeing 737; 1031, "Solar Princess" (Sadiou Diouf).

1985. "Olymphilex '85" International Thematic Stamps Exhibition, Lausanne.
1032 **361** 150f. multicoloured . . . 1·40 55

1985. Musical Instruments. Multicoloured.
1033 60f. Type **362** 45 10
1034 70f. Mvet (stringed instrument) 55 15
1035 100f. Flute . . . . 1·10 20

363 Intelcam Headquarters, Yaounde

1985. 20th Anniv of Int Telecommunications Satellite Consortium.
1036 – 125f. black, orange & bl 1·40 45
1037 **363** 200f. multicoloured . . . 1·75 50
DESIGN: 125f. "Intelsat V" satellite.

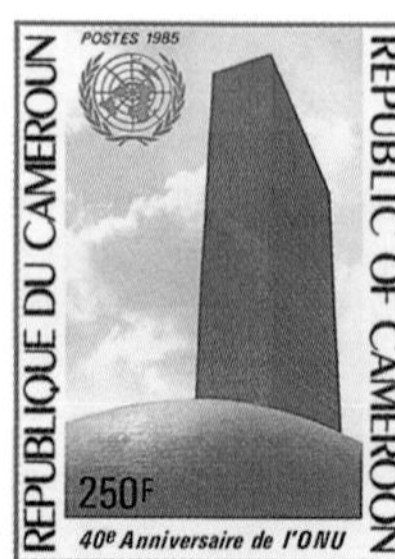

365 U.N. Emblem and Headquarters

1985. 40th Anniv of U.N.O.
1038 **365** 250f. multicoloured . . . 2·40 65
1039 500f. multicoloured . . . 4·50 1·40

366 French and Cameroun Flags and Presidents

1985. President Mitterrand of France's Visit to Cameroun. (a) Inscr "Mitterand" in error.
1040 **366** 60f. multicoloured . . .
1041 70f. multicoloured . . .

(b) Inscr corrected to "Mitterrand".
1041a **366** 60f. multicoloured . . . 55 30
1041b 70f. multicoloured . . . 65 30

367 U.N.I.C.E.F. Emblem

1985. Child Survival Campaign.
1042 **367** 60f. black, blue & yell 45 15
1043 – 300f. multicoloured . . . 2·40 80
DESIGN: Doctor inoculating babies.

368 Lake Barumbi, Kumba

1985. Landscapes. Multicoloured.
1044 60f. Type **368** 55 10
1045 70f. Pygmy village, Bonando 55 15
1046 150f. River Cameroun . . . 1·40 35

369 Ebolowa Town Hall

1985. Town Halls. Multicoloured.
1047 60f. Type **369** 45 15
1048 60f. Ngaoundere town hall 45 15

370 Pope John Paul II **371** Porcupine

1985. Papal Visit to Cameroun. Multicoloured.
1049 60f. Type **370** 60 30
1050 70f. Pope John Paul II holding crucifix 80 30
1051 200f. Pres. Biya and Pope John Paul II . . . . . . 2·25 1·25

1985. Animals. Multicoloured.
1053 125f. Type **371** . . . . . . 1·25 35
1054 200f. Squirrel . . . . 1·75 55
1055 350f. Greater cane rat . . . 2·75 90

372 Wooden Mask **373** "Tomb of Henri Claude d'Harcourt" (detail)

1985. Cameroun Art (1st series). Multicoloured.
1056 60f. Type **372** 45 15
1057 70f. Wooden mask (different) 55 20
1058 100f. Men using pestle and mortar (wooden bas-relief) 80 30
See also Nos. 1081/3.

1985. Air. Death Anniversaries. Multicoloured.
1059 500f. Type **373** (bicentenary Jean Baptiste Pigalle (sculptor)) . . . . 4·75 1·40
1060 500f. Louis Pasteur (bacteriologist, 90th anniv) (after Edelfelt) . . 4·75 1·40

374 Yellow-casqued Hornbill ("Le Toucan") **375** Child's Toys

1985. Birds. Multicoloured.
1061 140f. Type **374** . . . . . . 2·10 70
1062 150f. Cock . . . . 1·75 60
1063 200f. European robins ("Le Rouge-gorge") . . . . . 3·25 1·10
See also No. 1156.

1985. Air. Christmas. Multicoloured.
1064 250f. Type **375** . . . . . . 1·90 65
1065 300f. Akono church . . . . 2·25 80
1066 400f. Christmas crib . . . . 2·75 1·10
1067 500f. "The Virgin of the Blue Diadem" (Raphael) 4·50 1·40

377 "Virgin Mary" (Pierre Prud'hon)

1986. Easter. Multicoloured.
1072 210f. Type **377** . . . . . . 1·40 65
1073 350f. "Stoning of St. Stephen" (Van Scorel) 2·50 1·25

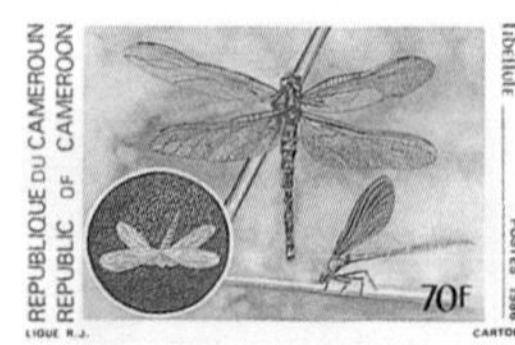

378 "Anax sp."

1986. Insects. Multicoloured.
1074 70f. Type **378** 60 40
1075 70f. Bee on flower (vert) . . 60 40
1076 100f. Grasshopper 90 55

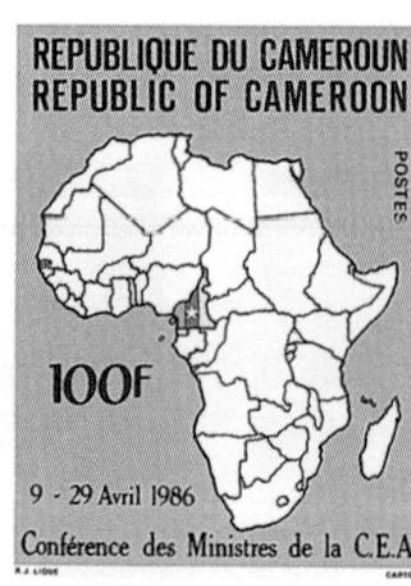

379 Map of Africa

1986. Economic Commission for Africa Ministers' Conference. Multicoloured.
1077 100f. Type **379** 80 45
1078 175f. Members' flags . . . . 1·40 65

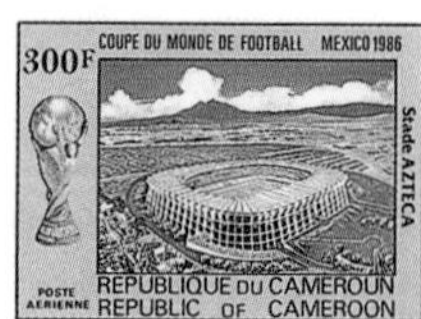

380 Azteca Stadium

1986. Air. World Cup Football Championship, Mexico. Multicoloured.
1079 300f. Type **380** . . . . . . 2·25 1·10
1080 400f. Mexico team . . . . 3·00 1·40

1986. Cameroun Art (2nd series). As T **372**. Multicoloured.
1081 70f. Copper Statuette . . . 45 15
1082 100f. Wooden ash-tray . . . 70 20
1083 130f. Wooden horseman . . 1·40 35

381 Queen Elizabeth

1986. 60th Birthday of Queen Elizabeth II. Multicoloured.
1084 100f. Type **381** 80 35
1085 175f. Queen and President Biya . . . . 1·40 55
1086 210f. Queen Elizabeth (different) . . . . 1·75 80

1986. 25th Anniv of American Peace Corps in Cameroun.
1068 **376** 70f. multicoloured . . . 55 20
1069 100f. multicoloured . . . 80 35

1986. As Nos. 851 and 941 but inscr "Republique du Cameroun/Republic of Cameroon".
1070 **284** 5f. multicoloured 10 10
1071 **325** 10f. multicoloured . . . 80 40

382 President Biya

1986. 1st Anniv of Cameroun Republic Democratic Party. Multicoloured.
1087 70f. Type **382** 50 20
1088 70f. Bamenda Party headquarters (horiz) . . . 50 20
1089 100f. President Biya making speech 65 30

383 Argentine Team 384 Mask Dancer with Sword

1986. Air. World Cup Football Championship Winners.
1090 **383** 250f. multicoloured . . . 2·50 1·10

1986. Traditional Dances of North-west Kwem. Multicoloured.
1091 100f. Type **384** 70 45
1092 130f. Mask dancer with rattle . . . . 1·25 55

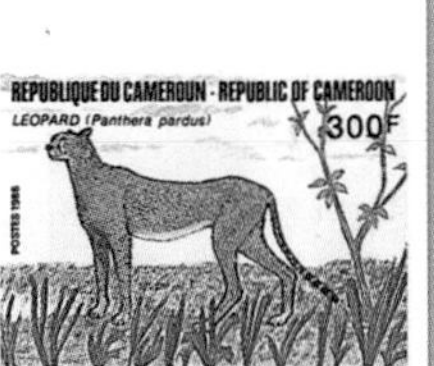

385 Cheetah 386 Bishop Desmond Tutu (Nobel Peace Prize Winner)

1986. Endangered Animals (7th series). Mult.
1093 300f. Type **385** . . . . . . 2·50 1·40
1094 300f. Varan . . . . 2·50 1·40

1986. International Peace Year. Multicoloured.
1095 175f. Type **386** . . . . . . 1·40 55
1096 200f. Type **386** . . . . . . 1·75 65
1097 250f. I.P.Y. and U.N. emblems . . . . 2·00 1·10

387 Pierre Curie (physicist)

1986. Air. Death Anniversaries. Multicoloured.
1098 500f. Type **387** (80th anniv) 5·25 2·25
1099 500f. Jean Mermoz and "Arc en Ciel" (aviation pioneer, 50th anniv) . . . 5·25 2·25

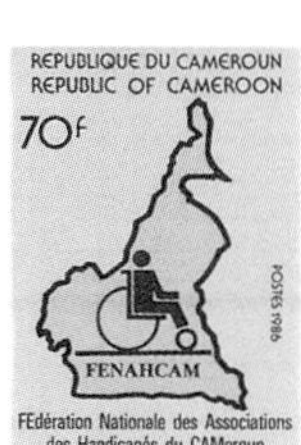

388 Emblem 389 Man holding Syringe and National Flag "Umbrella" over Woman and Child

1986. National Federation of Cameroun Handicapped Associations.
1100 **388** 70f. yellow and red . . . 50 20

1986. African Vaccination Year.
1101 70f. Type **389** 50 15
1102 100f. Flag behind woman holding child being immunised 65 30

390 Trees on Map 391 Loading Palm Nuts onto Trailer at Dibombari

1986. National Tree Day.
1103 70f. Type **390** 50 15
1104 100f. Hands holding clump of earth and seedling . . 65 30

1986. Agricultural Development. Multicoloured.
1105 70f. Type **391** 50 20
1106 70f. Payment for produce harvested 50 20
1107 200f. Pineapple plantation 1·40 65

392 "Antestiopsis lineaticollis intricata"

1987. Harmful Insects. Multicoloured.
1108 70f. Type **392** 70 45
1109 100f. "Distantiella theobroma" 85 55

393 Millet

1987. Agricultural Show, Maroua. Multicoloured.
1110 70f. Type **393** 50 30
1111 100f. Cotton 65 40
1112 150f. Cattle . . . . 1·25 55

394 Shot-putting

1987. 4th All-Africa Games, Kenya. Mult.
1113 100f. Type **394** 65 35
1114 140f. Pole-vaulting . . . . 1·25 45

395 Drill Baboon

1988. Endangered Mammals. Drill Baboon. Multicoloured.
1115 30f. Type **395** 30 15
1116 40f. Adult baboons 35 15
1117 70f. Young baboon 60 35
1118 100f. Mother with baby . . 1·10 55

396 National Assembly Building

1989. Centenary of Interparliamentary Union.
1119 **396** 50f. multicoloured . . . 35 15

397 Cameroun and Argentine Players

1990. World Cup Football Championship, Italy. Multicoloured.
1120 200f. Type **397** . . . . . . 1·50 55
1121 250f. Cameroun player and match scene . . . . . . 2·00 1·10
1122 250f. Cameroun winning goal . . . . 2·00 1·10
1123 300f. Cameroun first eleven 2·25 1·40

1990. Nos. 1062 and 1093 surch.
1125 – 20f. on 150f. mult . . . 15 10
1126 **385** 70f. on 300f. mult . . . 45 20

399 Milla and Match Scene

1990. Roger Milla, 4th Best Player in World Cup.
1127 **399** 500f. multicoloured . . . 3·75 2·50

400 Anniversary Emblem

1990. 40th Anniv of United Nations Development Programme.
1129 **400** 50f. multicoloured . . . 35 20

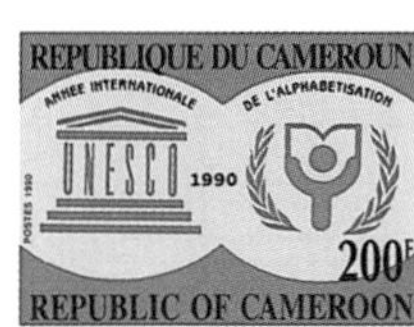

401 U.N.E.S.C.O. and I.L.Y. Emblems

1990. International Literacy Year.
1130 **401** 200f. black, lt blue & bl 1·40 55

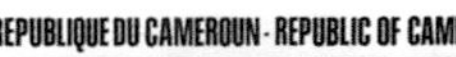

402 Arms and Pres. Paul Biya

1991. 30th Anniv (1990) of Independence. Multicoloured.
1131 150f. Type **402** . . . . . . 1·40 55
1132 1000f. Flag, city and 1960 20f. Independence stamp 7·75 3·75

403 Treating Cacao Plantation

1991. Unissued stamps (for Ebolowa Agricultural Show) with bars over inscr and surch **125F**. Multicoloured.
1134 125f. on 70f. Type **403** . . .
1135 125f. on 100f. Sheep . . . .
The stamps without surcharge were sold only by the Paris agency.

405 Snake on National Colours and Map

1991. Anti-AIDS Campaign. Multicoloured.
1137 15f. Type **405** 10 10
1138 25f. Youth pushing back "AIDS" in French and English (horiz) 15 10
See also Nos. 1171/2.

1991. As No. 932 but inscr "Republic du Cameroun / Republic of Cameroun".
1139 **322** 40f. multicoloured . . . 30 15

406 Oribi

1991. Sovereign Military Order of Malta Child Survival Project. Antelopes. Multicoloured.
1140 125f.+10f. Type **406** . . . . 1·25 95
1141 250f.+20f. Waterbucks . . . 2·25 2·25

407 Serle's Bush Shrike ("La Pie Grieche du Mont-kupe") 408 African Elephant

1991. Birds. Multicoloured.
1143 70f. Type **407** 60 45
1144 70f. Grey-necked bald crow ("Le Picathartes Chauve") (horiz) 60 45
1145 300f. As No. 1144 . . . . . . 2·50 1·50
1146 350f. Type **407** . . . . . . 3·00 1·75

1991. Animals. Multicoloured.
1148 125f. Type **408** . . . . . . 1·10 55
1149 250f. Buffalo . . . . 2·00 1·40

409 Mvolye Church

1991. Centenary (1990) of Catholic Church in Cameroun. Multicoloured.
1151 125f. Type **409** . . . . . . 1·10 55
1152 250f. Akono church . . . . 2·00 1·40

410 Emblems

1991. 7th African Group Meeting of Int Savings Banks Institute, Yaounde.
1154 **410** 250f. multicoloured . . . 2·00 1·10

1992. Birds. As previous designs but with values changed. Multicoloured.
1156 125f. As No. 1063 . . . . . 1·40 50
1157 200f. As No. 968 . . . . . 1·60 60
1158 350f. Type **357** . . . . . . 2·75 1·50

411 Columbus's Fleet — 412 Mbappe Lepe (footballer)

1992. 500th Anniv of Discovery of America by Columbus. Multicoloured.

1159	125f. Type **411**	1·40	50
1160	250f. Columbus kneeling on beach	2·10	1·40
1161	400f. Meeting Amerindians	3·00	1·90
1162	500f. Fleet crossing the Atlantic	4·75	3·00

1992. Cameroun Football. Multicoloured.

1163	125f. Type **412**	1·10	40
1164	250f. League emblem	2·10	1·40
1165	400f. National Football Federation emblem (horiz)	3·00	1·90
1166	500f. Ahmadou Ahidjo Stadium, Yaounde (horiz)	4·25	4·75

See also Nos. 1173/5.

413 Crocodile

1993. Endangered Animals. Mult. Self-adhesive.

1167	125f. Type **413**	1·00	65
1168	250f. Kob (vert)	2·00	1·40

1993. As Nos. 967 and 975 but inscr "REPUBLIQUE DU CAMEROUN REPUBLIC OF CAMEROON" and with values changed.

1169 **339**	370f. multicoloured	2·50	1·60
1170 **342**	410f. multicoloured	3·25	2·00

1993. Anti-AIDS Campaign. As Nos. 1137/8 but values changed. Multicoloured.

1171	100f. Type **405**	80	55
1172	175f. As No. 1138	1·40	80

1993. As Nos. 1163/5 but values changed.

1173	10f. As No. 1165	10	10
1174	25f. As No. 1164	10	10
1175	50f. Type **412**	15	10

414 President Biya holding Football and Lion (national team mascot)

1994. World Cup Football Championship, United States. Multicoloured.

1176	125f. Type **414**	50	40
1177	250f. Emblem, lion, player and map of Cameroun	90	65
1178	450f. Players, ball showing world map, national flag and trophy	1·75	1·25
1179	500f. Eagle and lion supporting ball	1·90	1·50

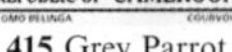

415 Grey Parrot — 417 Anniversary Emblem and Dove carrying Branch

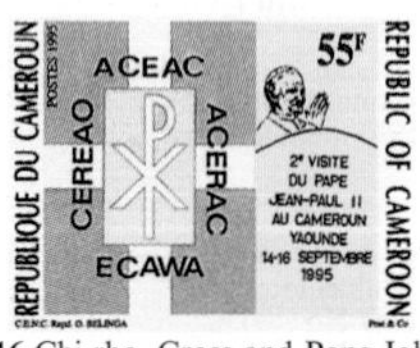

416 Chi-rho, Cross and Pope John Paul II

1995.

1181 **415**	125f. multicoloured	50	35

1995. 2nd Papal Visit.

1182 **416**	55f. black, pink & yell	25	20
1183	– 125f. multicoloured	50	35

DESIGN: 125f. Pope and open book.

1995. 50th Anniv of U.N.O. Multicoloured.

1184	200f. Type **417**	55	40
1185	250f. Anniversary emblem and figures joining hands	65	45

Cameroun joined the Commonwealth on 1 November 1995.

MILITARY FRANK STAMP

M 78 Arms and Crossed Swords

1963. No value indicated.

M1 M 78	(–) lake	3·25	3·25

POSTAGE DUE STAMPS

D 8 Felling Mahogany Tree — D 25 African Idols

1925.

D 88 D 8	2c. black and blue	10	2·00
D 89	4c. purple and olive	10	1·60
D 90	5c. black and lilac	20	1·90
D 91	10c. black and red	45	2·75
D 92	15c. black and grey	85	2·50
D 93	20c. black and olive	1·75	2·75
D 94	25c. black and yellow	80	3·25
D 95	30c. orange and blue	1·60	3·50
D 96	50c. black and brown	1·25	3·50
D 97	60c. red and green	1·40	4·00
D 98	1f. green & red on grn	1·25	95
D 99	2f. mauve and red	1·90	5·75
D100	3f. blue and brown	4·25	7·75

1939.

D148 D 25	5c. purple	10	2·50
D149	10c. blue	20	3·00
D150	15c. red	10	8·50
D151	20c. brown	20	2·50
D152	30c. blue	20	1·90
D153	50c. green	25	2·75
D154	60c. purple	25	2·75
D155	1f. violet	45	1·75
D156	2f. orange	40	3·00
D157	3f. blue	50	3·50

D 46

1947.

D254 D 46	10c. red	10	2·75
D255	30c. orange	10	2·75
D256	50c. black	10	2·75
D257	1f. red	15	2·75
D258	2f. green	1·75	3·00
D259	3f. mauve	2·00	3·25
D260	4f. blue	2·00	2·75
D261	5f. brown	1·75	3·00
D262	10f. blue	1·75	1·60
D263	20f. sepia	1·90	4·00

D 77 "Hibiscus rosa sinensis"

1963. Flowers. Multicoloured.

D342	50c. Type D **77**	10	10
D343	50c. "Erythrine"	10	10
D344	1f. "Plumeria lutea"	10	10
D345	1f. "Ipomoea sp."	10	10
D346	1f.50 "Grinum sp."	10	10
D347	1f.50 "Hoodia gordonii"	10	10
D348	2f. "Ochna"	10	10
D349	2f. "Gloriosa"	10	10
D350	5f. "Costus spectabilis"	15	15
D351	5f. "Bougainvillea spectabilis"	15	15
D352	10f. "Delonix regia"	40	40
D353	10f. "Haemanthus"	40	40
D354	20f. "Titanopsis"	1·25	1·25
D355	20f. "Ophthalmophyllum"	1·25	1·25
D356	40f. "Zingiberacee"	1·75	1·75
D357	40f. "Amorphophalus"	1·75	1·75

CANADA Pt. 1

A British dominion consisting of the former province of Canada with British Columbia, New Brunswick, Newfoundland, Nova Scotia and Prince Edward Island.

1851. 12 pence = 1 shilling (Canadian).
1859. 100 cents = 1 dollar.

COLONY OF CANADA

1 Beaver — 2 Prince Albert

3 — 4

5 — 6 Jacques Cartier

1851. Imperf.

17 **4**	½d. red	£700	£400
5 **1**	3d. red	£1100	£160
2 **2**	6d. purple	£16000	£900
12 **5**	7½d. green	£7000	£1500
14 **6**	10d. blue	£6500	£1100
4 **3**	12d. black	£75000	£40000

1858. Perf.

25 **4**	½d. red	£1900	£600
26 **1**	3d. red	£2500	£300
27a **2**	6d. purple	£7000	£2250

1859. Values in cents. Perf.

29 **4**	1c. red	£225	27·00
44	2c. red	£400	£140
31 **1**	5c. red	£250	11·00
38 **2**	10c. purple	£800	42·00
36	10c. brown	£750	42·00
40 **5**	12½c. green	£600	40·00
42 **6**	17c. blue	£800	60·00

DOMINION OF CANADA

13 — 14

1868. Various frames.

54 **13**	½c. black	55·00	50·00
55 **14**	1c. brown	£300	40·00
56a	1c. yellow	£650	60·00
57	2c. green	£325	28·00
49	3c. red	£650	23·00
63	5c. green	£700	65·00
59b	6c. brown	£650	38·00
60	12½c. blue	£475	40·00
70	15c. purple	65·00	17·00
69	15c. blue	£140	29·00

27 — 21 — 28

1870. Various frames.

101 **27**	½c. black	10·00	6·50
75 **21**	1c. yellow	25·00	1·00
104	2c. green	35·00	1·75
105	3c. red	30·00	80
106	5c. grey	65·00	1·75
107	6c. brown	32·00	8·50
117 –	8c. grey	90·00	4·25
120 –	8c. purple	75·00	4·25
111 **21**	10c. pink	£170	23·00

On 8c. head is to left.

1893.

115 **28**	20c. red	£160	42·00
116	50c. blue	£225	24·00

30 — 31

1897. Jubilee.

121 **30**	½c. black	48·00	48·00
122	1c. orange	10·00	4·50
124	2c. green	15·00	9·00
126	3c. red	12·00	2·25
128	5c. blue	40·00	14·00
129	6c. brown	85·00	85·00
130	8c. violet	32·00	29·00
131	10c. purple	50·00	42·00
132	15c. slate	85·00	85·00
133	20c. red	85·00	85·00
134	50c. blue	£120	95·00
136	$1 red	£425	£425
137	$2 violet	£700	£350
138	$3 bistre	£850	£700
139	$4 violet	£800	£600
140	$5 green	£800	£600

1897. Maple-leaves in four corners.

141 **31**	½c. black	6·00	4·75
143	1c. green	18·00	90
144	2c. violet	18·00	1·50
145	3c. red	24·00	50
146	5c. blue	60·00	2·75
147	6c. brown	55·00	22·00
148	8c. orange	75·00	7·00
149	10c. purple	£130	55·00

1898. As T **31** but figures in lower corners.

150	½c. black	3·25	1·10
151	1c. green	22·00	40
154	2c. purple	22·00	30
155	2c. red	30·00	30
156	3c. red	45·00	1·00
157	5c. blue	95·00	1·75
159	6c. brown	85·00	50·00
160	7c. yellow	55·00	13·00
162	8c. orange	£100	26·00
163	10c. purple	£160	14·00
165	20c. green	£300	48·00

33 — 35 King Edward VII

1898. Imperial Penny Postage.

168 **33**	2c. black, red and blue	25·00	4·75

1899. Surch **2 CENTS**.

171	2c. on 3c. red (No. 145)	12·00	8·00
172	2c. on 3c. red (No. 156)	17·00	4·25

1903.

175 **35**	1c. green	21·00	50
176	2c. red	20·00	50
178	5c. blue	70·00	2·50
180	7c. olive	55·00	2·75
182	10c. purple	£110	11·00
185	20c. olive	£200	23·00
187	50c. violet	£350	85·00

36 King George V and Queen Mary, when Prince and Princess of Wales — 44

1908. Tercentenary of Quebec. Dated "1608 1908".

188 **36**	½c. brown	3·50	3·50
189 –	1c. green	13·00	2·75
190 –	2c. red	18·00	1·00
191 –	5c. blue	45·00	20·00
192 –	7c. olive	50·00	40·00
193 –	10c. violet	55·00	45·00
194 –	15c. orange	80·00	70·00
195 –	20c. brown	£100	85·00

DESIGNS: 1c. Cartier and Champlain; 2c. King Edward VII and Queen Alexandra; 5c. Champlain's House in Quebec; 7c. Generals Montcalm and Wolfe; 10c. Quebec in 1700; 15c. Champlain's departure for the West; 20c. Cartier's arrival before Quebec.

1912.

196 **44**	1c. green	5·50	50
200	2c. red	4·50	50
205	3c. brown	5·00	50
205b	5c. blue	60·00	75
209	7c. yellow	20·00	3·00
210	10c. purple	90·00	2·75

212 20c. olive 29·00 1·50
215 50c. brown 48·00 3·75
See also Nos. 246/55.

1915. Optd **WAR TAX** diagonally.
225 **44** 5c. blue £110 £190
226 20c. olive 55·00 95·00
227 50c. brown £110 £150

46 **47**

1915.
228 **46** 1c. green 8·00 50
229 2c. red 12·00 70

1916.
233 **47** 2c.+1c. red 22·00 1·25
239 2c.+1c. brown 4·00 50

48 Quebec Conference, 1864, from painting "The Fathers of the Confederation" by Robert Harris

1917. 50th Anniv of Confederation.
244 **48** 3c. brown 18·00 1·75

1922.
246 **44** 1c. yellow 2·50 60
247 2c. green 2·25 10
248 3c. red 3·75 10
249 4c. yellow 8·00 3·50
250 5c. violet 5·00 1·75
251 7c. brown 12·00 7·00
252 8c. blue 19·00 10·00
253 10c. blue 20·00 3·25
254 10c. brown 18·00 3·00
255 $1 orange 50·00 8·00

1926. Surch **2 CENTS** in one line.
264 **44** 2c. on 3c. red 42·00 50·00

1926. Surch **2 CENTS** in two lines.
265 **44** 2c. on 3c. red 16·00 21·00

51 Sir J. A. Macdonald
52 "The Fathers of the Confederation"

1927. 60th Anniv of Confederation. I. Commemoration Issue. Dated "1867–1927".
266 **51** 1c. orange 2·50 1·50
267 **52** 2c. green 2·25 30
268 – 3c. red 7·00 5·00
269 – 5c. violet 3·25 3·50
270 – 12c. blue 24·00 5·00
DESIGNS—HORIZ: As Type **52**: 3c. Parliament Buildings, Ottawa; 12c. Map of Canada, 1867–1927. VERT: As Type **51**: 5c. Sir W. Laurier.

56 Darcy McGee
57 Sir W. Laurier and Sir J. A. Macdonald

II. Historical Issue.
271 **56** 5c. violet 3·00 2·50
272 **57** 12c. green 16·00 4·50
273 – 20c. red 17·00 12·00
DESIGN—As Type **57**: 20c. R. Baldwin and L. H. Lafontaine.

59

1928. Air.
274 **59** 5c. brown 6·00 3·50

60 King George V
61 Mount Hurd and Indian Totem Poles

1928.
275 **60** 1c. orange 2·75 60
276 2c. green 1·25 20
277 3c. red 17·00 15·00
278 4c. yellow 13·00 6·50
279 5c. violet 6·50 3·25
280 8c. blue 7·50 4·75
281 **61** 10c. green 8·50 1·25
282 – 12c. black 22·00 10·00
283 – 20c. red 27·00 12·00
284 – 50c. blue £100 38·00
285 – $1 olive £110 65·00
DESIGNS—HORIZ: 12c. Quebec Bridge; 20c. Harvesting with horses; 50c. "Bluenose" (fishing schooner); $1 Parliament Buildings, Ottawa.

66
67 Parliamentary Library, Ottawa
68 The Old Citadel, Quebec

1930.
288 **66** 1c. orange 1·75 1·00
289 1c. green 1·50 10
290 2c. green 1·75 10
291 2c. red 70 1·00
292b 2c. brown 1·25 10
293 3c. red 90 10
294 4c. yellow 6·50 4·50
295 5c. violet 2·75 4·50
296 5c. blue 5·50 20
297 8c. blue 11·00 16·00
298 8c. red 7·50 5·50
299 **67** 10c. olive 15·00 1·00
300 **68** 12c. black 14·00 5·50
325 13c. violet 32·00 2·25
301 – 20c. red 22·00 1·00
302 – 50c. blue 80·00 17·00
303 – $1 olive 95·00 23·00
DESIGNS—HORIZ: 20c. Harvesting with tractor; 50c. Acadian Memorial Church, Grand Pre, Nova Scotia; $1 Mount Edith Cavell.

72 Mercury and Western Hemisphere
73 Sir Georges Etienne Cartier

1930. Air.
310 **72** 5c. brown 19·00 18·00

1931.
312 **73** 10c. green 5·50 20

1932. Air. Surch **6** and bars.
313 **59** 6c. on 5c. brown 3·00 2·50

1932. Surch **3** between bars.
314a **66** 3c. on 2c. red 1·00 60

76 King George V
77 Duke of Windsor when Prince of Wales
78 Allegory of British Empire
80 King George V

1932. Ottawa Conference. (a) Postage.
315 **76** 3c. red 70 80
316 **77** 5c. blue 9·00 5·00
317 **78** 13c. green 9·50 6·00

(b) Air. Surch **6 6 OTTAWA CONFERENCE 1932**.
318 **72** 6c. on 5c. brown 10·00 12·00

1932.
319 **80** 1c. green 60 10
320 2c. brown 70 10
321b 3c. red 85 10
322 4c. brown 35·00 9·00
323 5c. blue 10·00 10
324 8c. orange 23·00 4·25

81 Parliament Buildings, Ottawa

1933. U.P.U. Congress (Preliminary Meeting).
329 **81** 5c. blue 6·00 3·00

1933. Optd **WORLD'S GRAIN EXHIBITION & CONFERENCE REGINA 1933**.
330 – 20c. red (No. 295) 16·00 7·00

83 S.S. "Royal William" (after S. Skillett)

1933. Cent of 1st Transatlantic Steamboat Crossing.
331 **83** 5c. blue 9·50 3·00

84 Jacques Cartier approaching Land

1934. 4th-century of Discovery of Canada.
332 **84** 3c. blue 2·50 1·50

85 U.E.L. Statue, Hamilton

1934. 150th Anniv of Arrival of United Empire Loyalists.
333 **85** 10c. olive 8·50 5·00

86 Seal of New Brunswick

1934. 150th Anniv of New Brunswick.
334 **86** 2c. brown 1·50 2·25

87 Queen Elizabeth II when Princess
88 King George VI when Duke of York
89 King George V and Queen Mary

1935. Silver Jubilee. Dated "1910–1935".
335 **87** 1c. green 55 60
336 **88** 2c. brown 60 60
337 **89** 3c. red 1·75 60
338 – 5c. blue 5·50 6·00
339 – 10c. green 3·25 4·00
340 – 13c. blue 6·50 6·00
DESIGNS—VERT: 5c. Duke of Windsor when Prince of Wales. HORIZ: 10c. Windsor Castle; 13c. Royal Yacht "Britannia".

93 King George V
94 Royal Canadian Mounted Policeman

1935.
341 **93** 1c. green 1·00 10
342 2c. brown 1·00 10
343 3c. red 1·00 10
344 4c. yellow 3·00 1·75
345 5c. blue 2·50 10
346 8c. orange 3·50 3·50
347 **94** 10c. red 6·50 50
348 – 13c. violet 6·50 65
349 – 20c. green 17·00 70
350 – 50c. violet 25·00 4·75
351 – $1 blue 40·00 11·00
DESIGNS—HORIZ: 13c. Confederation, Charlottetown, 1864; 20c. Niagara Falls; 50c. Parliament Buildings, Victoria, B.C.; $1 Champlain Monument, Quebec.

99 Daedalus

1935. Air.
355 **99** 6c. brown 3·00 1·00

100 King George VI and Queen Elizabeth

1937. Coronation.
356 **100** 3c. red 1·00 50

101 King George VI
102 Memorial Chamber Parliament Buildings, Ottawa
104 Fort Garry Gate, Winnipeg

1937.
357 **101** 1c. green 1·50 10
358 2c. brown 1·75 10
359 3c. red 1·75 10
360 4c. yellow 4·00 1·75
361 5c. blue 4·00 10
362 8c. orange 3·75 1·75
363 **102** 10c. red 5·00 10
364 – 13c. blue 15·00 1·25
365 **104** 20c. brown 22·00 80
366 – 50c. green 45·00 8·50
367 – $1 violet 60·00 9·00
DESIGNS—HORIZ: 13c. Halifax Harbour; 50c. Vancouver Harbour; $1 Chateau de Ramezay, Montreal.

107 Fairchild 45-80 Sekani Seaplane over "Distributor" on Mackenzie River

1938. Air.
371 **107** 6c. blue 11·00 70

108 Queen Elizabeth II when Princess and Princess Margaret

1939. Royal Visit.

372 **108** 1c. black and green . . . 1·75 10
373 – 2c. black and brown . . . 60 50
374 – 3c. black and red 60 10

DESIGNS—HORIZ: 3c. King George VI and Queen Elizabeth. VERT: 2c. National War Memorial, Ottawa.

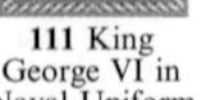

111 King George VI in Naval Uniform

112 King George VI in Military Uniform

114 Grain Elevator

115 Farm Scene

121 Air Training Camp

1942. War Effort.

375 **111** 1c. green (postage) . . . 1·50 10
376 **112** 2c. brown . . . . 1·75 10
377 – 3c. red . . . . 1·25 60
378 – 3c. purple 90 10
379 **114** 4c. grey . . . . 5·50 1·00
380 **112** 4c. red 70 10
381 **111** 5c. blue . . . . 3·00 10
382 **115** 8c. sepia . . . . 5·50 75
383 – 10c. brown . . . . . . 5·50 10
384 – 13c. green . . . . . . 6·50 6·50
385 – 14c. green . . . . . . 16·00 1·00
386 – 20c. brown . . . . . . 14·00 35
387 – 50c. violet . . . . . . 26·00 3·25
388 – $1 blue . . . . 42·00 6·00

399 **121** 6c. blue (air) . . . . . . 18·00 5·50
400 7c. blue . . . . 3·00 10

DESIGNS—As Type **112**: 3c. King George VI. As Type **121**. VERT: 10c. Parliament Buildings. HORIZ: 13, 14c. Ram tank; 20c. Corvette; 50c. Munitions factory; $1 H.M.S. "Cossack" (destroyer).

122 Ontario Farm Scene

1946. Re-conversion to Peace.

401 **122** 8c. brown (postage) . . . 1·25 2·00
402 – 10c. green . . . . . . 1·75 10
403 – 14c. brown . . . . . . 4·00 1·00
404 – 20c. grey . . . . 3·00 10
405 – 50c. green . . . . . . 17·00 3·00
406 – $1 purple . . . . . . 27·00 3·00

407 – 7c. blue (air) . . . . . . 4·00 10

DESIGNS: 10c. Great Bear Lake; 14c. St. Maurice River power station; 20c. Combine harvester; 50c. Lumbering in British Columbia; $1 "Abegweit" (train ferry); 7c. Canada geese in flight.

129 Alexander Graham Bell and "Fame"

130 "Canadian Citizenship"

1947. Birth Centenary of Graham Bell (inventor of the telephone).

408 **129** 4c. blue 15 10

1947. Advent of Canadian Citizenship and 80th Anniv of Confederation.

409 **130** 4c. blue 10 10

131 Queen Elizabeth II when Princess

132 Queen Victoria. Parliament Building, Ottawa, and King George VI

1948. Princess Elizabeth's Wedding.

410 **131** 4c. blue 10 10

1948. Centenary of Responsible Government.

411 **132** 4c. grey 10 10

133 Cabot's Ship "Matthew"

1949. Entry of Newfoundland into Canadian Confederation.

412 **133** 4c. green 30 10

134 "Founding of Halifax, 1749" (after C. W. Jeffries)

135 King George VI

1949. Halifax Bicentenary.

413 **134** 4c. violet 30 10

1949. Portraits of King George VI.

414 **135** 1c. green 10 10
415 – 2c. brown 70 35
415a – 2c. green 50 10
416 – 3c. purple 30 10
417 – 4c. red 20 10
418 – 5c. blue . . . . 2·00 10

1950. As Nos. 414 and 416/18 but without "POSTES POSTAGE".

424 1c. green 10 50
425 2c. brown . . . . 10 1·50
426 3c. purple 10 65
427 4c. red 10 20
428 5c. blue . . . . 30 1·25

142 Drying Furs

141 Oil Wells in Alberta

145 Mackenzie King

1950.

432 **142** 10c. purple . . . . 1·75 10
441 – 20c. grey . . . . 1·50 10
431 **141** 50c. green . . . . 6·00 1·00
433 – $1 blue . . . . 38·00 5·00

DESIGNS: 20c. Forestry products; $1 Fisherman.

1951. Canadian Prime Ministers.

434 – 3c. green (Borden) 10 50
444 – 3c. purple (Abbott) . . . 15 20
435 **145** 4c. red 10 10
445 – 4c. red (A. Mackenzie) . . 20 10
475 – 4c. violet (Thompson) . . 15 20
483 – 4c. violet (Bennett) . . . 10 20
476 – 5c. blue (Bowell) 15 10
484 – 5c. blue (Tupper) 10 10

146 Mail Trains, 1851 and 1951

149 Reproduction of 3d., 1851

1951. Centenary of First Canadian Postage Stamp. Dated "1851 1951".

436 **146** 4c. black 35 10
437 – 5c. violet . . . . 65 1·75
438 – 7c. blue . . . . 35 1·00
439 **149** 15c. red . . . . 1·40 10

DESIGNS—As Type **146**: 5c. "City of Toronto" and S.S. "Prince George"; 7c. Mail coach and Canadair DC-4M North Star airplane.

150 Queen Elizabeth II when Princess and Duke of Edinburgh

1951. Royal Visit.

440 **150** 4c. violet 10 10

152 Red Cross Emblem

1952. 18th Int Red Cross Conf, Toronto.

442 **152** 4c. red and blue 15 10

153 Canada Goose

1952.

443 **153** 7c. blue 75 10

165 Eskimo Hunter

164 Northern Gannet

160 Textile Industry

154 Pacific Coast Indian House and Totem Pole

1953.

477 **165** 10c. brown 30 10
474 **164** 15c. black . . . . 1·00 10
488 – 20c. green 55 10
489 – 25c. red 55 10
462 **160** 50c. green . . . . 1·25 10
446 **154** $1 black . . . . 3·75 20

DESIGNS (As Type **160**)—HORIZ: 20c. Pulp and paper industry. VERT: 25c. Chemical industry.

155 Polar Bear

158 Queen Elizabeth II

1953. National Wild Life Week.

447 **155** 2c. blue 10 10
448 – 3c. sepia (Elk) 10 40
449 – 4c. slate (American bighorn) 15 10

1953.

450 **158** 1c. brown 10 10
451 2c. green 15 10
452 3c. red 15 15
453 4c. violet 20 10
454 5c. blue 20 10

159 Queen Elizabeth II

161

1953. Coronation.

461 **159** 4c. violet 10 10

1954.

463 **161** 1c. brown 10 10
464 2c. green 20 10
465 3c. red 70 10
466 4c. violet 30 10
467 5c. blue 30 10
468 6c. orange . . . . 1·00 45

1954. National Wild Life Week. As T **155**.

472 4c. slate (Walrus) 35 10
473 5c. blue (American beaver) 35 10

166 Musk-ox

168 Dove and Torch

167 Whooping Cranes

1955. National Wild Life Week.

478 **166** 4c. violet 30 10
479 **167** 5c. blue . . . . 1·00 20

1955. 10th Anniv of I.C.A.O.

480 **168** 5c. blue 20 20

169 Pioneer Settlers

1955. 50th Anniv of Alberta and Saskatchewan Provinces.

481 **169** 5c. blue 15 20

170 Scout Badge and Globe

1955. 8th World Scout Jamboree.

482 **170** 5c. brown and green . . . 20 10

173 Ice-hockey Players

1956. Ice-hockey Commemoration.

485 **173** 5c. blue 20 20

1956. National Wild Life Week. As T **155**.

486 4c. violet (Reindeer) 20 15
487 5c. blue (Mountain goat) . . 20 10

178

179 Fishing

1956. Fire Prevention Week.

490 **178** 5c. red and black 30 10

1957. Outdoor Recreation.

491 **179** 5c. blue 25 10
492 – 5c. blue 25 10
493 – 5c. blue 25 10
494 – 5c. blue 25 10

DESIGNS: No. 492, Swimming; 493, Hunting; 494, Skiing.

183 White-billed Diver

1957. National Wild Life Week.

495 **183** 5c. black 50 20

184 Thompson with Sextant, and North American Map — **185** Parliament Buildings, Ottawa

1957. Death Cent of David Thompson (explorer).
496 **184** 5c. blue 15 30

1957. 14th U.P.U. Congress, Ottawa.
497 **185** 5c. slate 15 10
498 – 15c. slate . . . . 55 1·75
DESIGNS—HORIZ (33½ × 22 mm): 15c. Globe within posthorn.

187 Miner — **188** Queen Elizabeth II and Duke of Edinburgh

1957. Mining Industry.
499 **187** 5c. black 35 10

1957. Royal Visit.
500 **188** 5c. black 30 10

189 "A Free Press" — **190** Microscope

1958. The Canadian Press.
501 **189** 5c. black 15 40

1958. International Geophysical Year.
502 **190** 5c. blue 20 10

191 Miner panning for Gold

1958. Centenary of British Columbia.
503 **191** 5c. turquoise 20 10

192 La Verendrye statue

1958. La Verendrye (explorer) Commemoration.
504 **192** 5c. blue 15 10

193 Samuel de Champlain and Heights of Quebec — **194** Nurse

1958. 350th Anniv of Founding of Quebec by Samuel de Champlain.
505 **193** 5c. brown and green . . . 30 10

1958. National Health.
506 **194** 5c. purple 30 10

195 "Petroleum 1858–1958" — **196** Speaker's Chair and Mace

1958. Centenary of Canadian Oil Industry.
507 **195** 5c. red and olive 30 10

1958. Bicentenary of First Elected Assembly.
508 **196** 5c. slate 30 10

197 John McCurdy's Biplane "Silver Dart" — **198** Globe showing N.A.T.O. Countries

1959. 50th Anniv of First Flight of the "Silver Dart" in Canada.
509 **197** 5c. black and blue 30 10

1959. 10th Anniv of N.A.T.O.
510 **198** 5c. blue 40 10

199 — **200** Queen Elizabeth II

1959. "Associated Country Women of the World" Commemoration.
511 **199** 5c. black and olive . . . 15 10

1959. Royal Visit.
512 **200** 5c. red 30 10

201 Maple Leaf linked with American Eagle

1959. Opening of St. Lawrence Seaway.
513 **201** 5c. blue and red 20 10

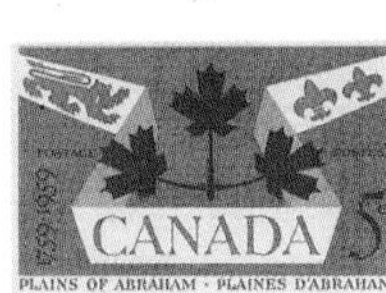

202 Maple Leaves — **203** Girl Guides Badge

1959. Bicentenary of Battle of Quebec.
514 **202** 5c. green and red 30 10

1960. Golden Jubilee of Canadian Girl Guides Movement.
515 **203** 5c. blue and brown . . . 20 10

204 Dollard des Ormeaux — **205** Surveyor, Bulldozer and Compass Rose

1960. Tercent of Battle of Long Sault.
516 **204** 5c. blue and brown . . . 20 10

1961. Northern Development.
517 **205** 5c. green and red 15 10

206 E. Pauline Johnson — **207** Arthur Meighen (statesman)

1961. Birth Centenary of E. Pauline Johnson (Mohawk poetess).
518 **206** 5c. green and red 15 10

1961. Arthur Meighen Commemoration.
519 **207** 5c. blue 15 10

208 Engineers and Dam

1961. Colombo Plan.
520 **208** 5c. brown and blue . . . 30 10

209 "Resources for Tomorrow" — **210** "Education"

1961. Natural Resources.
521 **209** 5c. green and brown . . . 15 10

1962. Education Year.
522 **210** 5c. black and brown . . . 15 10

211 Lord Selkirk and Farmer — **212** Talon bestowing Gifts on Married Couple

1962. 150th Anniv of Red River Settlement.
523 **211** 5c. brown and green . . . 20 10

1962. Jean Talon Commemoration.
524 **212** 5c. blue 20 10

213 British Columbia and Vancouver Island 2½d. Stamp of 1860, and Parliament Buildings, B.C. — **214** Highway (map version) and Provincial Arms

1962. Centenary of Victoria, B.C.
525 **213** 5c. red and black 30 10

1962. Opening of Trans-Canada Highway.
526 **214** 5c. black and brown . . . 15 10

215 Queen Elizabeth II and Wheat (agriculture) Symbol — **216** Sir Casimir Gzowski

1962. Different symbols in top left corner.
527 **215** 1c. brown 10 10
528 – 2c. green 15 10
529 – 3c. violet 15 10
530 – 4c. red 15 10
531 – 5c. blue 15 10
SYMBOLS: 1c. Crystals (Mining); 2c. Tree (Forestry); 3c. Fish (Fisheries); 4c. Electricity pylon (Industrial power); 5c. Wheat (Agriculture).

1963. 150th Birth Anniv of Sir Casimir Gzowski (engineer).
535 **216** 5c. purple 10 10

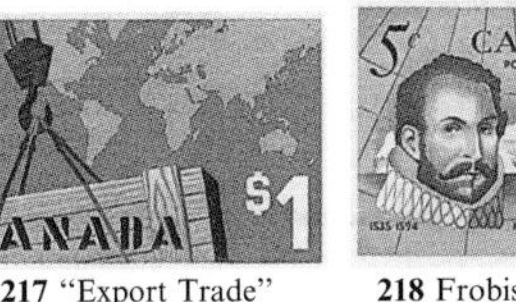

217 "Export Trade" — **218** Frobisher and barque "Gabriel"

1963.
536 **217** $1 red . . . . 4·75 2·00

1963. Sir Martin Frobisher Commemoration.
537 **218** 5c. blue 20 10

219 Horseman and Map

1963. Bicent of Quebec–Trois-Rivieres–Montreal Postal Service.
538 **219** 5c. brown and green . . . 15 10

220 Canada Geese — **221** Douglas DC-9 Airliner and Uplands Airport, Ottawa

1963.
540 **221** 7c. blue 35 70
540a 8c. blue 50 50
539 **220** 15c. blue . . . . 1·00 10

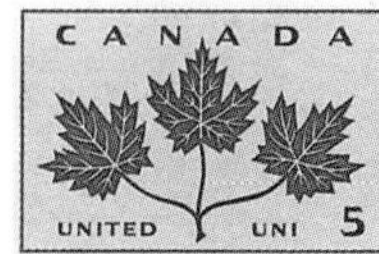

222 "Peace on Earth" — **223** Maple Leaves

1964. "Peace".
541 **222** 5c. ochre, blue & turq . . 15 10

1964. "Canadian Unity".
542 **223** 5c. lake and blue 10 10

224 White Trillium and Arms of Ontario

1964. Provincial Badges.
543 **224** 5c. green, brown and orange 40 20
544 – 5c. green, brown and yellow 40 20
545 – 5c. red, green and violet 30 20
546 – 5c. blue, red and green . . 30 20
547 – 5c. purple, green and brown 30 20
548 – 5c. brown, green and mauve 30 20
549 – 5c. lilac, green and purple 50 20
550 – 5c. green, yellow and red 30 20
551 – 5c. sepia, orange and green 30 20
552 – 5c. black, red and green 30 20
553 – 5c. drab, green and yellow 30 20
554 – 5c. blue, green and red . . 30 20
555 – 5c. red and blue 30 20
FLOWERS AND ARMS OF: No. 544, Madonna Lily, Quebec; 545, Purple Violet, New Brunswick; 546, Mayflower, Nova Scotia; 547, Dogwood, British Columbia; 548, Prairie Crocus, Manitoba; 549, Lady's Slipper, Prince Edward Island; 550, Wild Rose, Alberta; 551, Prairie Lily, Saskatchewan; 552, Pitcher Plant, Newfoundland; 553, Mountain Avens, Northwest Territories; 554, Fireweed, Yukon Territory; 555, Maple Leaf, Canada.

1964. Surch **8**.
556 **221** 8c. on 7c. blue 15 15

238 Fathers of the Confederation Memorial, Charlottetown

1964. Centenary of Charlottetown Conference.
557 **238** 5c. black 10 10

239 Maple Leaf and Hand with Quill Pen

1964. Centenary of Quebec Conference.
558 **239** 5c. red and brown 15 10

240 Queen Elizabeth II **241** "Canadian Family"

1964. Royal Visit.
559 **240** 5c. purple 15 10

1964. Christmas.
560 **241** 3c. red 10 10
561 5c. blue 10 10

242 "Co-operation"

1965. International Co-operation Year.
562 **242** 5c. green 35 10

243 Sir W. Grenfell

1965. Birth Centenary of Sir Wilfred Grenfell (missionary).
563 **243** 5c. green 20 10

244 National Flag

1965. Inauguration of National Flag.
564 **244** 5c. red and blue 15 10

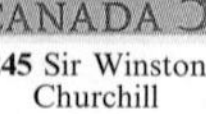

245 Sir Winston Churchill **246** Peace Tower, Parliament Buildings, Ottawa

1965. Churchill Commemoration.
565 **245** 5c. brown 15 10

1965. Inter-Parliamentary Union Conference, Ottawa.
566 **246** 5c. green 10 10

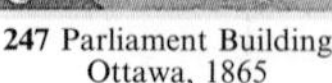

247 Parliament Buildings, Ottawa, 1865 **248** "Gold, Frankincense and Myrrh"

1965. Centenary of Proclamation of Ottawa as Capital.
567 **247** 5c. brown 10 10

1965. Christmas.
568 **248** 3c. green 10 10
569 5c. blue 10 10

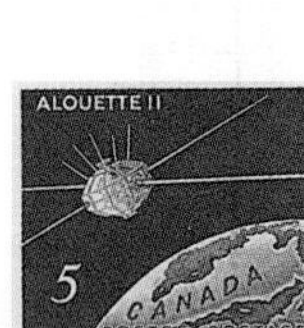

249 "Alouette 2" over Canada **250** La Salle

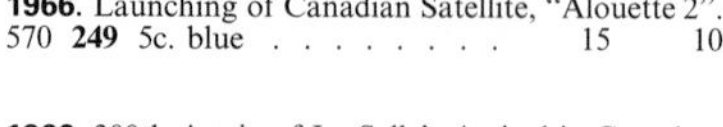

1966. Launching of Canadian Satellite, "Alouette 2".
570 **249** 5c. blue 15 10

1966. 300th Anniv of La Salle's Arrival in Canada.
571 **250** 5c. green 15 10

251 Road Signs **252** Canadian Delegation and Houses of Parliament

1966. Highway Safety.
572 **251** 5c. yellow, blue and black 15 10

1966. Centenary of London Conference.
573 **252** 5c. brown 10 10

253 Douglas Point Nuclear Power Station **254** Parliamentary Library, Ottawa

1966. Peaceful Uses of Atomic Energy.
574 **253** 5c. blue 10 10

1966. Commonwealth Parliamentary Association Conference, Ottawa.
575 **254** 5c. purple 10 10

255 "Praying Hands", after Durer **256** Flags and Canada on Globe

1966. Christmas.
576 **255** 3c. red 10 10
577 5c. orange 10 10

1967. Canadian Centennial.
578 **256** 5c. red and blue 10 10

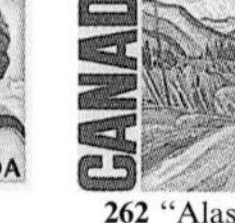

257 Queen Elizabeth, Northern Lights and Dog-team **262** "Alaska Highway" (A. Y. Jackson)

1967.

579 **257** 1c. brown 10 10
580 – 2c. green 10 10
581 – 3c. purple 30 10
582 – 4c. red 20 10
583 – 5c. blue 20 10
601 – 6c. red 45 10
607 – 6c. black 30 10
609 – 7c. green 30 10
584 **262** 8c. purple 25 30
610 – 8c. black 30 10
585 – 10c. olive 25 10
586 – 15c. purple 30 10
587 – 20c. blue . . . . 1·00 10
588 – 25c. green 75 10
589 – 50c. brown . . . . . . 1·25 10
590 – $1 red . . . . 1·75 65

DESIGNS—As Type **257**: 2c. Totem pole; 3c. Combine-harvester and oil derrick; 4c. Ship in lock; 5c., Harbour scene; 6c., 7c. "Transport"; 8c. (No. 610), Library of Parliament. As Type **262**: 10c. "The Jack Pine" (T. Thomson); 15c. "Bylot Island" (L. Harris); 20c. "Quebec Ferry" (J. W. Morrice); 25c. "The Solemn Land" (J. E. H. MacDonald); 50c. "Summer's Stores" (Grain elevators, J. Ensor); $1 "Oilfield" (near Edmonton, H. G. Glyde).

269 Canadian Pavilion **270** Allegory of "Womanhood" on Ballot-box

1967. World Fair, Montreal.
611 **269** 5c. blue and red 10 10

1967. 50th Anniv of Women's Franchise.
612 **270** 5c. purple and black . . . 10 10

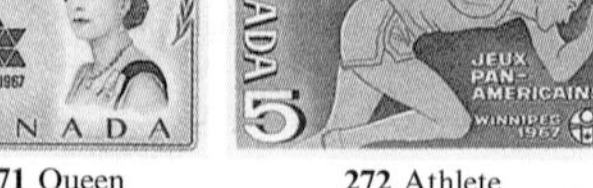

271 Queen Elizabeth II and Centennial Emblem **272** Athlete

1967. Royal Visit.
613 **271** 5c. plum and brown . . . 15 10

1967. Pan-American Games, Winnipeg.
614 **272** 5c. red 10 10

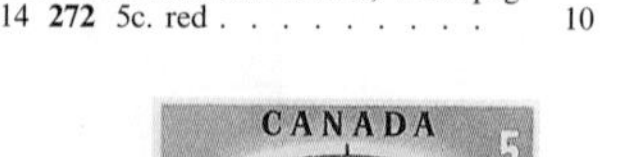

273 "World News"

1967. 50th Anniv of Canadian Press.
615 **273** 5c. blue 10 10

274 Governor-General Vanier

1967. Vanier Commemoration.
616 **274** 5c. black 10 10

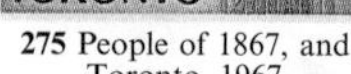

275 People of 1867, and Toronto, 1967 **276** Carol Singers

1967. Cent of Toronto as Capital City of Ontario.
617 **275** 5c. green and red 10 10

1967. Christmas.
618 **276** 3c. red 10 10
619 5c. green 10 10

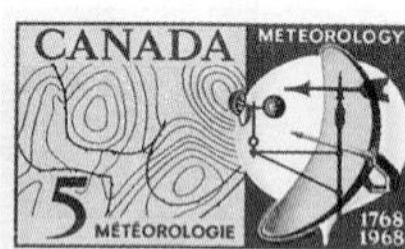

277 Grey Jays **278** Weather Map and Instruments

1968. Wild Life.
620 **277** 5c. multicoloured 30 10
See also Nos. 638/40.

1968. 20th Anniv of First Meteorological Readings.
621 **278** 5c. multicoloured 15 10

279 Narwhal

1968. Wild Life.
622 **279** 5c. multicoloured 15 10

280 Globe, Maple Leaf and Rain Gauge

1968. International Hydrological Decade.
623 **280** 5c. multicoloured 15 10

281 The "Nonsuch"

1968. 300th Anniv of Voyage of the "Nonsuch".
624 **281** 5c. multicoloured 20 10

282 Lacrosse Players **283** Front Page of "The Globe", George Brown and Legislative Building

1968. Lacrosse.
625 **282** 5c. multicoloured 15 10

1968. 150th Birth Anniv of George Brown (politician and journalist).
626 **283** 5c. multicoloured 10 10

284 H. Bourassa (politician and journalist) **286** Armistice Monument, Vimy

285 John McCrae, Battlefield and First Lines of "In Flanders Fields"

1968. Birth Centenary of Henri Bourassa.
627 **284** 5c. black, red and cream 10 10

1968. 50th Death Anniv of John McCrae (soldier and poet).
628 **285** 5c. multicoloured 10 10

1968. 50th Anniv of 1918 Armistice.
629 **286** 15c. black 30 40

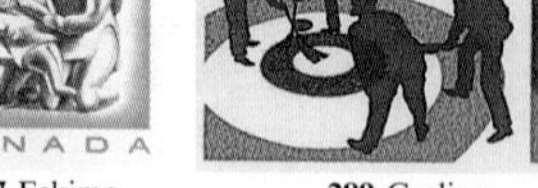

287 Eskimo Family (carving) **289** Curling

1968. Christmas.
630 **287** 5c. black and blue 10 10
631 – 6c. black and ochre . . . 10 10
DESIGN: 6c. "Mother and Child" (carving).

1969. Curling.
632 **289** 6c. black, blue and red . . 15 10

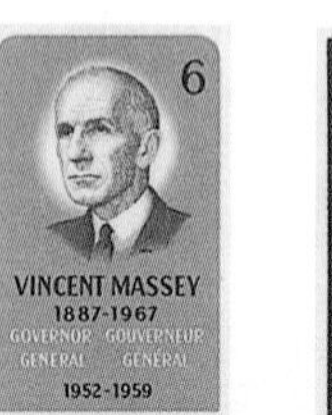

290 Vincent Massey **292** Globe and Tools

291 "Return from the Harvest Field" (Suzor-Cote)

1969. Vincent Massey, First Canadian-born Governor-General.
633 **290** 6c. sepia and ochre . . . 10 10

1969. Birth Centenary of Marc Aurele de Foy Suzor-Cote (painter).
634 **291** 50c. multicoloured . . . . 70 2·00

1969. 50th Anniv of I.L.O.
635 **292** 6c. green 10 10

293 Vickers Vimy Aircraft over Atlantic Ocean

1969. 50th Anniv of 1st Non-stop Transatlantic Flight.
636 **293** 15c. brown, green and blue 40 55

294 "Sir William Osler" (J. S. Sargent)

295 White-throated Sparrow

1969. 50th Death Anniv of Sir William Osler (physician).
637 **294** 6c. blue and brown . . . 20 10

1969. Birds. Multicoloured.
638 6c. Type **295** 25 10
639 10c. Savannah sparrow ("Ipswich Sparrow") (horiz) . . . . 35 1·10
640 25c. Hermit thrush (horiz) . . 1·10 3·50

298 Flags of Winter and Summer Games

300 Sir Isaac Brock and Memorial Column

299 Outline of Prince Edward Island showing Charlottetown

1969. Canadian Games.
641 **298** 6c. green, red and blue . . 10 10

1969. Bicentenary of Charlottetown as Capital of Prince Edward Island.
642 **299** 6c. brown, black and blue 20 10

1969. Birth Bicentenary of Sir Isaac Brock.
643 **300** 6c. orange, bistre and brown 10 10

301 Children of the World in Prayer

302 Stephen Butler Leacock, Mask and "Mariposa"

1969. Christmas.
644 **301** 5c. multicoloured 10 10
645 6c. multicoloured 10 10

1969. Birth Centenary of Stephen Butler Leacock (humorist).
646 **302** 6c. multicoloured 10 10

303 Symbolic Cross-roads

1970. Centenary of Manitoba.
647 **303** 6c. blue, yellow and red 15 10

304 "Enchanted Owl" (Kenojuak)

1970. Centenary of Northwest Territories.
648 **304** 6c. red and black 10 10

305 Microscopic View of Inside of Leaf

1970. International Biological Programme.
649 **305** 6c. green, yellow and blue 15 10

306 Expo 67 Emblem and stylized Cherry Blossom

1970. World Fair, Osaka. Multicoloured.
650 25c. Type **306** (red) . . . . . 1·50 2·25
651 25c. Dogwood (violet) . . . 1·50 2·25
652 25c. White trillium (green) . . 1·50 2·25
653 25c. White garden lily (blue) 1·50 2·25
NOTE: Each stamp shows a stylized cherry blossom, in a different colour, given above in brackets.

310 Henry Kelsey

1970. 300th Birth Anniv of Henry Kelsey (explorer).
654 **310** 6c. multicoloured 10 10

311 "Towards Unification"

1970. 25th Anniv of U.N.O.
655 **311** 10c. blue 50 50
656 15c. mauve and lilac . . . 50 50

312 Louis Riel (Metis leader)

313 Mackenzie's Inscription, Dean Channel

1970. Louis Riel Commemoration.
657 **312** 6c. blue and red 10 10

1970. Sir Alexander Mackenzie (explorer).
658 **313** 6c. brown 15 10

314 Sir Oliver Mowat (statesman)

1970. Sir Oliver Mowat Commemoration.
659 **314** 6c. red and black 10 10

315 "Isles of Spruce" (A. Lismer)

1970. 50th Anniv of "Group of Seven" (artists).
660 **315** 6c. multicoloured 10 10

316 "Horse-drawn Sleigh" (D. Niskala)

328 Sir Donald A. Smith

1970. Christmas. Children's Drawings. Mult.
661 5c. Type **316** 50 20
662 5c. "Stable and Star of Bethlehem" (L. Wilson) . . 50 20
663 5c. "Snowmen" (M. Lecompte) 50 20
664 5c. "Skiing" (D. Durham) . . 50 20
665 5c. "Santa Claus" (A. Martin) 50 20
666 6c. "Santa Claus" (E. Bhattacharya) 50 20
667 6c. "Christ in Manger" (J. McKinney) 50 20
668 6c. "Toy Shop" (N. Whateley) 50 20
669 6c. "Christmas Tree" (J. Pomperleau) 50 20
670 6c. "Church" (J. McMillan) 50 20
671 10c. "Christ in Manger" (C. Fortier) (37 × 20 mm) 30 30
672 15c. "Trees and Sledge" (J. Dojcak) (37 × 20 mm) 45 60

1970. 150th Birth Anniv of Sir Donald Alexander Smith.
673 **328** 6c. yellow, brown and green 15 10

329 "Big Raven" (E. Carr)

1971. Birth Centenary of Emily Carr (painter).
674 **329** 6c. multicoloured 20 30

330 Laboratory Equipment

332 Maple "Keys"

331 "The Atom"

1971. 50th Anniv of Discovery of Insulin.
675 **330** 6c. multicoloured 30 30

1971. Birth Centenary of Lord Rutherford (scientist).
676 **331** 6c. yellow, red and brown 20 20

1971. "The Maple Leaf in Four Seasons". Mult.
677 6c. Type **332** (spring) 20 20
678 6c. Green leaves (summer) . . 20 20
679 7c. Autumn leaves 20 20
680 7c. Withered leaves and snow (winter) 20 20

333 Louis Papineau

334 Chart of Coppermine River

1971. Death Centenary of Louis-Joseph Papineau (politician).
681 **333** 6c. multicoloured 15 20

1971. Bicentenary of Samuel Hearne's Expedition to the Coppermine River.
682 **334** 6c. red, brown and buff 40 40

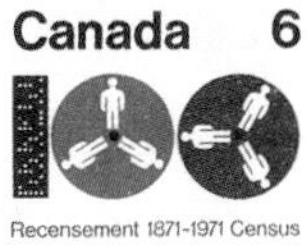

335 "People" and Computer Tapes

1971. Centenary of 1st Canadian Census.
683 **335** 6c. blue, red and black . . 30 20

336 Maple Leaves

1971. Radio Canada International.
684 **336** 15c. red, yellow and black 50 1·50

337 "B. C."

1971. Centenary of British Columbia's Entry into the Confederation.
685 **337** 7c. multicoloured 15 10

338 "Indian Encampment on Lake Huron" (Kane)

339 "Snowflake"

1971. Death Centenary of Paul Kane (painter).
686 **338** 7c. multicoloured 20 10

1971. Christmas.
687 **339** 6c. blue 10 10
688 7c. green 15 10
689 – 10c. silver and red . . . . 50 1·25
690 – 15c. silver, purple and lavender . . . . 65 2·00
DESIGN: 10c., 15c. "Snowflake" design similar to Type **339** but square (26 × 26 mm).

340 Pierre Laporte (Quebec Cabinet Minister)

341 Skaters

1971. 1st Anniv of Assassination of Pierre Laporte.
691 **340** 7c. black on buff 15 10

1972. World Figure Skating Championships, Calgary.
692 **341** 8c. purple 15 10

342 J. A. MacDonald
343 Forest, Central Canada

344 Vancouver

1972.
693 **342** 1c. orange 10 20
694 – 2c. green 10 10
695 – 3c. brown 10 40
696 – 4c. black 10 40
697 – 5c. mauve 10 10
698 – 6c. red 10 30
699 – 7c. brown 40 40
700 – 8c. blue 15 10
701 – 10c. red 75 10
702a **343** 10c. green, turquoise and orange 40 15
703b – 15c. blue and brown . . 1·00 10
704a – 20c. orange, violet and blue 65 10
705b – 25c. ultram and blue . . 1·00 10
706 – 50c. green, blue and brown 80 30
709a **344** $1 multicoloured 85 70
708 – $2 multicoloured . . . . 1·50 2·00
DESIGNS—As Type **342** (1 to 7c. show Canadian Prime Ministers): 2c. W. Laurier; 3c. R. Borden; 4c. W. L. Mackenzie King; 5c. R. B. Bennett; 6c. L. B. Pearson; 7c. Louis St. Laurent; 8, 10c. Queen Elizabeth II. As Type **343**: 15c. American bighorn; 20c. Prairie landscape from the air; 25c. Polar bears; 50c. Seashore, Eastern Canada. As Type **344**: $2 Quebec.

345 Heart

1972. World Health Day.
719 **345** 8c. red 30 10

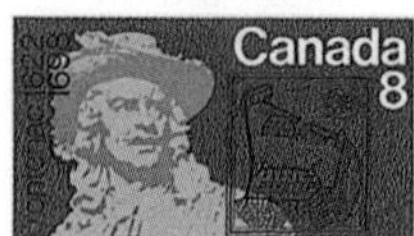

346 Frontenac and Fort Saint-Louis, Quebec

1972. 300th Anniv of Governor Frontenac's Appointment to New France.
720 **346** 8c. red, brown and blue 15 15

347 Plains Indians' Artefacts

347a Buffalo Chase

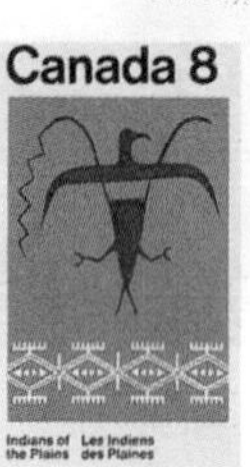

348 Thunderbird and Tribal Pattern
348a Dancer in Ceremonial Costume

1972. Canadian Indians. (a) Horiz designs showing Artefacts as T **347** or Scenes from Indian Life as T **347a**.
721 **347** 8c. multicoloured 40 10
722 **347a** 8c. brown, yellow & blk 40 10
723 – 8c. multicoloured 40 10
724 – 8c. multicoloured 40 10
725 – 8c. multicoloured 40 10
726 – 8c. brown, yellow & blk 40 10
727 – 8c. multicoloured 40 10
728 – 8c. multicoloured 40 10
729 – 10c. multicoloured . . . 40 20
730 – 10c. red, brown and black 40 20
TRIBES: Nos. 721/2, Plains Indians; Nos. 723/4, Algonkians; Nos. 725/6, Pacific Coast Indians; Nos. 727/8, Subarctic Indians; Nos. 729/30, Iroquoians.

(b) Vert designs showing Thunderbird and pattern as T **348** or Costumes as T **348a**.
731 **348** 8c. orange, red and black 40 15
732 **348a** 8c. multicoloured 40 15
733 – 8c. red, violet and black 40 10
734 – 8c. green, brown and black 40 10
735 – 8c. red and black 40 10
736 – 8c. multicoloured 40 10
737 – 8c. green, brown and black 40 10
738 – 8c. multicoloured 40 10
739 – 10c. brown, orange & blk 40 20
740 – 10c. multicoloured . . . 40 20
TRIBES: Nos. 731/2, Plains Indians; Nos. 733/4, Algonkians; Nos. 735/6, Pacific Coast Indians; Nos. 737/8, Subarctic Indians; Nos. 739/40, Iroquoians.

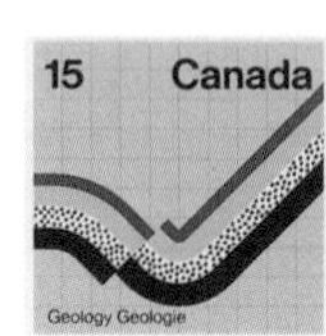

349 Earth's Crust
350 Candles

1972. Earth Sciences.
741 – 15c. multicoloured . . . . 1·10 1·90
742 – 15c. grey, blue and black 1·10 1·90
743 **349** 15c. multicoloured . . . . 1·10 1·90
744 – 15c. green, orange and black . . . . 1·10 1·90
DESIGNS AND EVENTS: No. 741 Photogrammetric surveying (12th Congress of International Society of Photogrammetry); No. 742 "Siegfried" lines (6th Conference of Int Cartographic Association); No. 743 (24th International Geological Congress); No. 744 Diagram of village at road-intersection (22nd Int Geographical Congress).

1972. Christmas. Multicoloured.
745 6c. Type **350** 15 10
746 8c. Type **350** 15 10
747 10c. Candles with fruits and pine boughs (horiz) . . . . 50 1·00
748 15c. Candles with prayer-book, caskets and vase (horiz) . . . . 60 1·40
Nos. 747/8 are size 36 × 20 mm.

351 "The Blacksmith's Shop" (Krieghoff)
352 F. de Montmorency-Laval

1972. Death Centenary of Cornelius Krieghoff (painter).
749 **351** 8c. multicoloured 30 15

1973. 350th Birth Anniv of Monsignor de Laval (1st Bishop of Quebec).
750 **352** 8c. blue, gold and silver 20 40

353 Commissioner French and Route of the March West

1973. Centenary of Royal Canadian Mounted Police.
751 **353** 8c. brown, orange and red 35 20
752 – 10c. multicoloured . . . . 1·00 1·25
753 – 15c. multicoloured . . . . 1·75 2·00
DESIGNS: 10c. Spectrograph; 15c. Mounted policeman.

354 Jeanne Mance

1973. 300th Death Anniv of Jeanne Mance (nurse).
754 **354** 8c. multicoloured 20 40

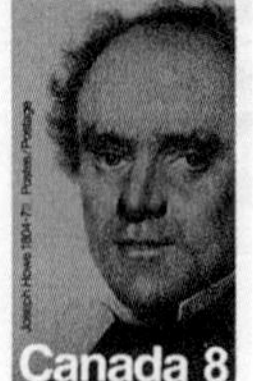

355 Joseph Howe
356 "Mist Fantasy" (MacDonald)

1973. Death Centenary of Joseph Howe (Nova Scotian politician).
755 **355** 8c. gold and black 20 40

1973. Birth Cent of J. E. H. MacDonald (artist).
756 **356** 15c. multicoloured 30 55

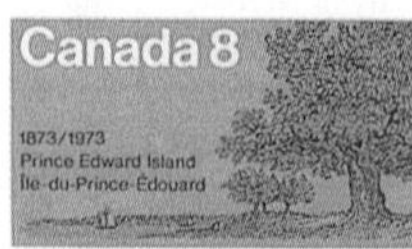

357 Oaks and Harbour

1973. Centenary of Prince Edward Island's Entry into the Confederation.
757 **357** 8c. orange and red . . . 20 30

358 Scottish Settlers

1973. Bicentenary of Arrival of Scottish Settlers at Pictou, Nova Scotia.
758 **358** 8c. multicoloured 25 20

359 Queen Elizabeth II

1973. Royal Visit and Commonwealth Heads of Government Meeting, Ottawa.
759 **359** 8c. multicoloured 25 20
760 15c. multicoloured . . . . 80 1·50

360 Nellie McClung
361 Emblem of 1976 Olympics

1973. Birth Centenary of Nellie McClung (feminist).
761 **360** 8c. multicoloured 20 50

1973. 1976 Olympic Games, Montreal (1st issue).
762 **361** 8c. multicoloured 25 15
763 15c. multicoloured . . . . 45 1·25
See also Nos. 768/71, 772/4, 786/9, 798/802, 809/11, 814/16, 829/32, 833/7 and 842/4.

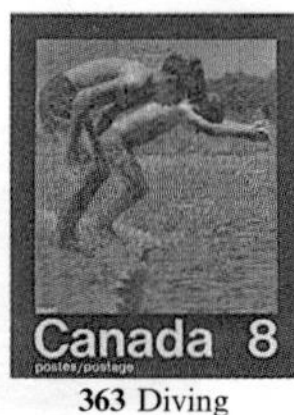

362 Ice-skate
363 Diving

1973. Christmas. Multicoloured.
764 6c. Type **362** 15 10
765 8c. Bird decoration 20 10
766 10c. Santa Claus (20 × 36 mm) . . . . . . 70 1·40
767 15c. Shepherd (20 × 36 mm) 80 1·75

1974. 1976 Olympic Games, Montreal. (2nd issue). "Summer Activities". Each blue.
768 8c. Type **363** 30 50
769 8c. "Jogging" 30 50
770 8c. Cycling 30 50
771 8c. Hiking 30 50

1974. 1976 Olympic Games, Montreal. (3rd issue). As T **361** but smaller (20 × 36½ mm).
772 **361** 8c.+2c. multicoloured . . 25 45
773 10c.+5c. multicoloured . . 40 1·00
774 15c.+5c. multicoloured . . 45 1·40

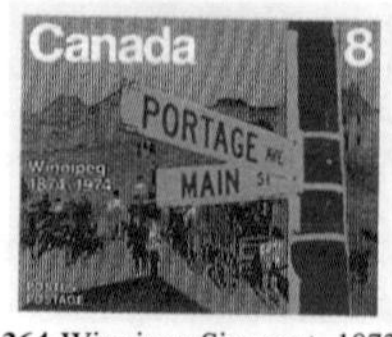

364 Winnipeg Signpost, 1872

1974. Winnipeg Centennial.
775 **364** 8c. multicoloured 20 15

365 Postmaster and Customer
366 "Canada's Contribution to Agriculture"

1974. Centenary of Canadian Letter Carrier Delivery Service. Multicoloured.
776 8c. Type **365** 50 80
777 8c. Postman collecting mail 50 80
778 8c. Mail handler 50 80
779 8c. Mail sorters 50 80
780 8c. Postman making delivery 50 80
781 8c. Rural delivery by car . . 50 80

1974. Centenary of "Agricultural Education". Ontario Agricultural College.
782 **366** 8c. multicoloured 20 20

367 Telephone Development

1974. Centenary of Invention of Telephone by Alexander Graham Bell.
783 **367** 8c. multicoloured 20 20

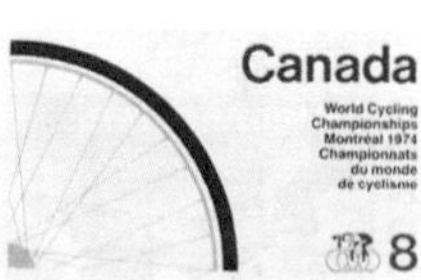

368 Bicycle Wheel

1974. World Cycling Championships, Montreal.
784 **368** 8c. black, red and silver 20 30

369 Mennonite Settlers

1974. Centenary of Arrival of Mennonites in Manitoba.
785 **369** 8c. multicoloured 20 20

1974. 1976 Olympic Games, Montreal (4th issue). "Winter Activities". As T **363**. Each red.
786 8c. Snow-shoeing 55 60
787 8c. Skiing 55 60
788 8c. Skating 55 60
789 8c. Curling 55 60

370 Mercury, Winged Horses and U.P.U. Emblem

1974. Centenary of U.P.U.
790 **370** 8c. violet, red and blue . . 15 15
791 15c. red, violet and blue 50 1·50

371 "The Nativity" (J. P. Lemieux)

1974. Christmas. Multicoloured.
792 6c. Type **371** 10 10
793 8c. "Skaters in Hull" (H. Masson) (34 × 31 mm) 10 10
794 10c. "The Ice Cone, Montmorency Falls" (R. C. Todd) 30 75
795 15c. "Village in the Laurentian Mountains" (C. A. Gagnon) . . . . . 35 1·10

372 Marconi and St. John's Harbour, Newfoundland

1974. Birth Centenary of Guglielmo Marconi (radio pioneer).
796 **372** 8c. multicoloured 20 20

373 Merritt and Welland Canal

1974. William Merritt Commemoration.
797 **373** 8c. multicoloured 20 30

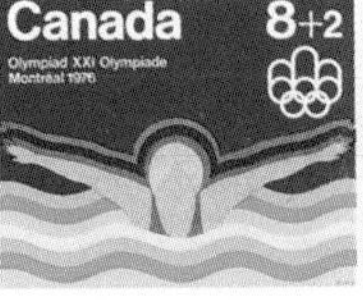

374 Swimming

376 "Anne of Green Gables" (Lucy Maud Montgomery)

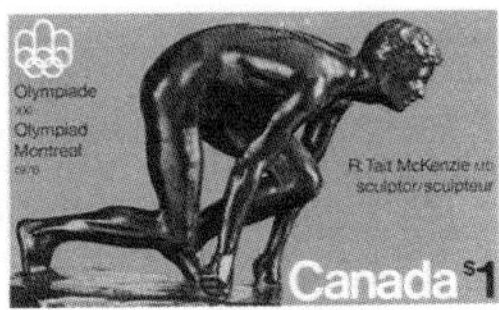

375 "The Sprinter"

1975. 1976 Olympic Games, Montreal (5th issue). Multicoloured.
798 8c.+2c. Type **374** 35 60
799 10c.+5c. Rowing . . . . . . 50 1·10
800 15c.+5c. Sailing . . . . . . 55 1·25

1975. 1976 Olympic Games, Montreal (6th issue). Multicoloured.
801 $1 Type **375** . . . . 1·50 2·25
802 $2 "The Diver" (vert) . . . . 2·25 4·25

1975. Canadian Writers (1st series). Multicoloured.
803 8c. Type **376** 30 10
804 8c. "Maria Chapdelaine" (Louis Hemon) 30 10
See also Nos. 846/7, 940/1 and 1085/6.

377 Marguerite Bourgeoys (founder of the Order of Notre Dame)

378 S. D. Chown (founder of United Church of Canada)

1975. Canadian Celebrities.
805 **377** 8c. multicoloured 60 40
806 – 8c. multicoloured 60 40
807 **378** 8c. multicoloured 30 75
808 – 8c. multicoloured 30 75

DESIGNS—As Type **377**: No. 806, Alphonse Desjardins (leader of Credit Union movement). As Type **378**: No. 808, Dr. J. Cook (first moderator of Presbyterian Church in Canada).

379 Pole-vaulting

380 "Untamed" (photo by Walt Petrigo)

1975. 1976 Olympics (7th issue). Multicoloured.
809 20c. Type **379** 40 50
810 25c. Marathon-running . . . 55 80
811 50c. Hurdling . . . . 70 1·25

1975. Centenary of Calgary.
812 **380** 8c. multicoloured 30 30

381 I. W. Y. Symbol

382 Fencing

1975. International Women's Year.
813 **381** 8c. grey, brown and black 30 30

1975. Olympic Games, Montreal (1976) (8th issue). Multicoloured.
814 8c.+2c. Type **382** 35 55
815 10c.+5c. Boxing . . . . . . 45 1·25
816 15c.+5c. Judo . . . . 55 1·50

383 "Justice-Justitia" (statue by W. S. Allward)

385 "Santa Claus" (G. Kelly)

384 "William D. Lawrence" (full-rigged ship)

1975. Centenary of Canadian Supreme Court.
817 **383** 8c. multicoloured 20 30

1975. Canadian Ships (1st series). Coastal Vessels.
818 **384** 8c. brown and black . . . 70 75
819 – 8c. green and black . . . 70 75
820 – 8c. green and black . . . 70 75
821 – 8c. brown and black . . . 70 75

DESIGNS: No. 819, "Neptune" (steamer); 820, "Beaver" (paddle-steamer); 821, "Quadra" (steamer).
See also Nos. 851/4, 902/5 and 931/4.

1975. Christmas. Multicoloured.
822 6c. Type **385** 15 10
823 6c. "Skater" (B. Cawsey) . . 15 10
824 8c. "Child" (D. Hebert) . . . 15 10
825 8c. "Family" (L. Caldwell) 15 10
826 10c. "Gift" (D. Lovely) . . . 30 50
827 15c. "Trees" (R. Kowalski) (horiz) 40 75

386 Text, Badge and Bugle

387 Basketball

1975. 50th Anniv of Royal Canadian Legion.
828 **386** 8c. multicoloured 20 20

1976. Olympic Games, Montreal (9th issue). Mult.
829 8c.+2c. Type **387** . . . . . . 1·25 85
830 10c.+5c. Gymnastics . . . . 50 1·25
831 20c.+5c. Soccer . . . . . . 70 1·50

388 Games Symbol and Snow Crystal

389 "Communications Arts"

1976. 12th Winter Olympic Games, Innsbruck.
832 **388** 20c. multicoloured 20 40

1976. Olympic Games, Montreal (10th issue). Multicoloured.
833 20c. Type **389** 40 25
834 25c. Handicrafts 65 75
835 50c. Performing Arts . . . . 95 1·60

390 Place Ville Marie and Notre-Dame Church

1976. Olympic Games, Montreal (11th issue). Multicoloured.
836 $1 Type **390** . . . . 2·25 4·50
837 $2 Olympic stadium and flags 2·75 5·50

391 Flower and Urban Sprawl

1976. HABITAT. U.N. Conference on Human Settlements, Vancouver.
838 **391** 20c. multicoloured 20 30

392 Benjamin Franklin and Map

1976. Bicentenary of American Revolution.
839 **392** 10c. multicoloured 20 35

393 Wing Parade before Mackenzie Building

394 Transfer of Olympic Flame by Satellite

1976. Centenary of Royal Military College. Mult.
840 8c. Colour party and Memorial Arch 15 20
841 8c. Type **393** 15 20

1976. Olympic Games, Montreal (12th issue). Multicoloured.
842 8c. Type **394** 20 10
843 20c. Carrying the Olympic flag 45 60
844 25c. Athletes with medals . . 45 85

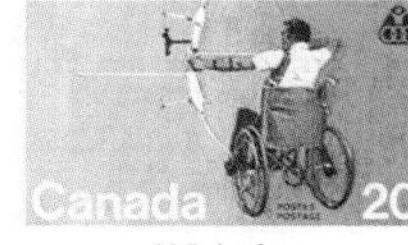

395 Archer

1976. Disabled Olympics.
845 **395** 20c. multicoloured 20 30

396 "Sam McGee" (Robert W. Service)

397 "Nativity" (F. Mayer)

1976. Canadian Writers (2nd series). Mult.
846 8c. Type **396** 15 40
847 8c. "Le Survenant" (Germaine Guevremont) 15 40

1976. Christmas. Stained-glass Windows. Multi.
848 8c. Type **397** 10 10
849 10c. "Nativity" (G. Maile & Son) 10 10
850 20c. "Nativity" (Yvonne Williams) 20 60

398 "Northcote" (paddle-steamer)

1976. Canadian Ships (2nd series). Inland Vessels.
851 **398** 10c. lt brown, brn & blk 45 60
852 – 10c. blue and black . . . 45 60
853 – 10c. blue and black . . . 45 60
854 – 10c. lt green, green & blk 45 60

DESIGNS: No. 852, "Passport" (paddle-steamer); 853, "Chicora" (paddle-steamer); 854, "Athabasca" (steamer).

399 Queen Elizabeth II

1977. Silver Jubilee.
855 **399** 25c. multicoloured 30 50

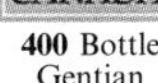

400 Bottle Gentian

401 Queen Elizabeth II (bas-relief by J. Huta)

402 Houses of Parliament

403 Trembling Aspen

404 Prairie Town Main Street

405 Fundy National Park

1977.

No.	Type	Description	Unused	Used
856	**400**	1c. multicoloured . . .	10	10
870	**402**	1c. blue	1·25	2·50
857	–	2c. multicoloured . . .	10	10
858	–	3c. multicoloured . . .	10	10
859	–	4c. multicoloured . . .	10	10
860	–	5c. multicoloured . . .	10	10
871	**402**	5c. lilac	65	1·00
861	–	10c. multicoloured . . .	15	10
867	**401**	12c. blue, grey and black	15	10
872	**402**	12c. blue	50	20
866	–	12c. multicoloured . . .	15	50
868	**401**	14c. red, grey and black	20	10
873	**402**	14c. red	15	10
875	**403**	15c. multicoloured . . .	15	10
866a	–	15c. multicoloured . . .	15	15
869	**401**	17c. black, grey and green	50	10
874	**402**	17c. green	30	10
876	–	20c. multicoloured . . .	15	10
877	–	25c. multicoloured . . .	15	10
878	–	30c. multicoloured . . .	20	10
869b	**401**	30c. dp pur, grey & pur	70	70

869c 32c. black, grey and blue . . . 50 60
879 – 35c. multicoloured . . . 25 10
883 **404** 50c. multicoloured . . . 85 60
883a – 60c. multicoloured . . . 65 50
881 – 75c. multicoloured . . . 85 1·00
882 – 80c. multicoloured . . . 85 90
884 **405** $1 multicoloured 90 50
884b – $1 multicoloured 85 45
884c – $1.50 multicoloured . . 2·00 2·50
885 – $2 multicoloured . . . . 1·25 45
885c – $2 multicoloured . . . . 3·75 1·50
885d – $5 multicoloured . . . . 4·00 2·50
885e – $5 multicoloured . . . . 7·00 4·00

DESIGN—As Type **400**: 2c. Red columbine; 3c. Canada lily; 4c. Hepatica; 5c. Shooting star; 10c. Franklin's lady's slipper orchid. 12c. Jewel-weed; 15c. (No. 866a) Canada violet. As Type **403**: 20c. Douglas fir; 25c. Sugar maple; 30c. Red oak; 35c. White pine. As Type **404**: 60c. Ontario City street; 75c. Eastern City street; 80c. Maritimes street. As Type **405**: $1 Glacier; $1.50, Waterton Lakes; $2 (No. 885) Kluane; $2 (No. 885c) Banff; $5 (No. 885d) Point Pelee; $5 (No. 885e) La Maurice.

406 Puma

407 "April in Algonquin Park"

1977. Endangered Wildlife (1st series).
886 **406** 12c. multicoloured 20 20
See also Nos. 906, 936/7, 976/7 and 1006/7.

1977. Birth Centenary of Tom Thomson (painter). Multicoloured.
887 12c. Type **407** 15 20
888 12c. "Autumn Birches" . . . 15 20

408 Crown and Lion

1977. Anniversaries. Multicoloured.
889 12c. Type **408** 15 20
890 12c. Order of Canada 15 20
EVENTS: No. 889, 25th anniv of First Canadian-born Governor-General; No. 890, 10th anniv of Order of Canada.

409 Peace Bridge, Niagara River

1977. 50th Anniv of Opening of Peace Bridge.
891 **409** 12c. multicoloured 15 15

410 Sir Sandford Fleming (engineer)

1977. Famous Canadians.
892 **410** 12c. blue 30 20
893 – 12c. brown 30 20
DESIGN: No. 893, Joseph E. Bernier (explorer) and "Arctic" (survey ship).

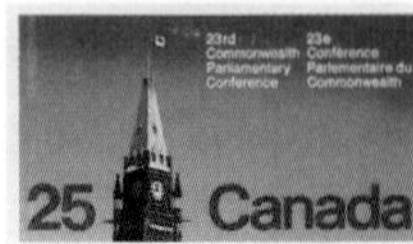

411 Peace Tower, Parliament Buildings, Ottawa

1977. 23rd Commonwealth Parliamentary Conference
894 **411** 25c. multicoloured 20 30

412 Hunter Braves following Star

1977. Christmas. Canada's first carol "Jesous Ahatonhia". Multicoloured.
895 10c. Type **412** 10 10
896 12c. Angelic choir 10 10
897 25c. Christ Child and "Chiefs from afar" 20 45

413 Seal Hunter (soapstone sculpture)

1977. Canadian Eskimos ("Inuits") (1st series). Hunting. Multicoloured.
898 12c. Type **413** 35 35
899 12c. Fishing with spear . . . 35 35
900 12c. Disguised archer 35 35
901 12c. Walrus hunting 35 35
See also Nos. 924/7, 958/61 and 989/92.

414 Pinky (fishing boat)

1977. Canadian Ships (3rd series). Sailing Craft. Multicoloured.
902 12c. Type **414** 20 35
903 12c. "Malahat" (schooner) 20 35
904 12c. Tern schooner 20 35
905 12c. Mackinaw boat 20 35

415 Peregrine Falcon

1978. Endangered Wildlife (2nd series).
906 **415** 12c. multicoloured 30 20

416 Pair of 1851 12d. Black Stamps

1978. "CAPEX '78" International Philatelic Exhibition, Toronto.
907 **416** 12c. black and sepia . . . 10 10
914 – 14c. blue, lt grey & grey 15 10
915 – 30c. red, lt grey and grey 25 40
916 – $1.25 violet, lt grey & grey . . . . 70 1·50
MS917 101 × 96 mm. Nos. 914/16 1·25 2·50
DESIGNS: 14c. Pair of 1855 10d. Cartier stamps; 30c. Pair of 1857 ½d. red stamps; $1.25, Pair of 1851 6d. Prince Albert stamps.

417 Games Emblem

1978. 11th Commonwealth Games, Edmonton (1st issue). Multicoloured.
908 14c. Type **417** 10 10
909 30c. Badminton 20 60
See also Nos. 918/21.

418 "Captain Cook" (Nathaniel Dance)

419 Hardrock Silver Mine, Cobalt, Ontario

1978. Bicentenary of Cook's 3rd Voyage. Mult.
910 14c. Type **418** 20 20
911 14c. "Nootka Sound" (J. Webber) 20 20

1978. Resources Development. Multicoloured.
912 14c. Type **419** 15 20
913 14c. Giant excavators, Athabasca Tar Sands . . . 15 20

1978. 11th Commonwealth Games, Edmonton (2nd issue). As T **417**. Multicoloured.
918 14c. Games stadium 20 20
919 14c. Running 20 20
920 30c. Alberta legislature building 50 50
921 30c. Bowls 50 50

420 Princes' Gate (Exhibition entrance)

421 Marguerite d'Youville

1978. Centenary of National Exhibition.
922 **420** 14c. multicoloured 15 30

1978. Marguerite d'Youville (founder of Grey Nuns) Commemoration.
923 **421** 14c. multicoloured 15 30

1978. Canadian Eskimos ("Inuits") (2nd series). Travel. As T **413**. Multicoloured.
924 14c. Woman on foot (painting by Pitseolak) . . 30 30
925 14c. "Migration" (soapstone sculpture of sailing umiak by Joe Talurinili) 30 30
926 14c. Aeroplane (stonecut and stencil print by Pudlo) . . 30 30
927 14c. Dogteam and dogsled (ivory sculpture by Abraham Kingmeatook) 30 30

422 "Madonna of the Flowering Pea" (Cologne School)

423 "Chief Justice Robinson" (paddle-steamer)

1978. Christmas. Paintings. Multicoloured.
928 12c. Type **422** 10 10
929 14c. "The Virgin and Child with St. Anthony and Donor" (detail, Hans Memling) 10 10
930 30c. "The Virgin and Child" (Jacopo di Cione) 25 90

1978. Canadian Ships (4th series). Ice Vessels. Multicoloured.
931 14c. Type **423** 45 65
932 14c. "St. Roch" (steamer) . . 45 65
933 14c. "Northern Light" (steamer) 45 65
934 14c. "Labrador" (steamer) . . 45 65

424 Carnival Revellers

425 Eastern Spiny Soft-shelled Turtle

1978. Quebec Carnival.
935 **424** 14c. multicoloured 20 20

1979. Endangered Wildlife (3rd series). Multicoloured.
936 17c. Type **425** 20 10
937 35c. Bowhead whale 90 90

426 Knotted Ribbon round Woman's Finger

427 Scene from "Fruits of the Earth" by Frederick Philip Grove

1979. Postal Code Publicity. Multicoloured.
938 17c. Type **426** 20 15
939 17c. Knotted string around man's finger 20 15

1979. Canadian Writers (3rd series). Multicoloured.
940 17c. Type **427** 15 15
941 17c. Scene from "Le Vaisseau d'Or" by Emile Nelligan 15 15

428 Charles-Michel de Salaberry (military hero)

429 Ontario

1979. Famous Canadians. Multicoloured.
942 17c. Type **428** 25 15
943 17c. John By (engineer) . . . 25 15

1979. Canada Day. Flags. Sheet 128 × 140 mm containing T **429** and similar horiz designs. Multicoloured.
MS944 17c. × 12; Type **429**; Quebec; Nova Scotia; New Brunswick; Manitoba; British Columbia; Prince Edward Island; Saskatchewan; Alberta; Newfoundland; Northwest Territories; Yukon Territory 2·75 4·50

430 Paddling Kayak

1979. Canoe-Kayak Championships.
956 **430** 17c. multicoloured 15 30

431 Hockey Players

1979. Women's Field Hockey Championships, Vancouver.
957 **431** 17c. black, yellow and green 15 30

1979. Canadian Eskimos (3rd series). Shelter and the Community. As T **413**. Multicoloured.
958 17c. "Summer Tent" (print by Kiakshuk" 15 20
959 17c. "Five Eskimos building an Igloo" (soapstone sculpture by Abraham) . . 15 20
960 17c. "The Dance" (print by Kalvak) 15 20
961 17c. "Inuit drum dance" (soapstone sculptures by Madeleine Isserkut and Jean Mapsalak) 15 20

432 Toy Train

1979. Christmas. Multicoloured.
962 15c. Type **432** 10 10
963 17c. Hobby-horse 10 10
964 35c. Rag doll (vert) 25 80

433 Child watering Tree of Life (painting by Marie-Annick Viatour)

1979. International Year of the Child.
965 **433** 17c. multicoloured 15 30

434 Canadair CL-215

1979. Canadian Aircraft (1st series). Flying Boats. Multicoloured.
966 17c. Type **434** 25 20
967 17c. Curtiss HS-2L 25 20
968 35c. Vickers Vedette 65 65
969 35c. Consolidated Canso . . 65 65
See also Nos. 996/9, 1026/9 and 1050/3.

435 Map of Arctic Islands

1980. Centenary of Arctic Islands Acquisition.
970 **435** 17c. multicoloured 15 30

436 Skier

1980. Winter Olympic Games, Lake Placid.
971 **436** 35c. multicoloured 55 85

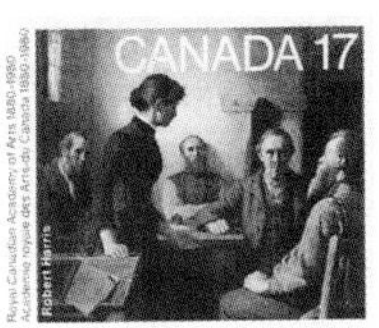
437 "A Meeting of the School Trustees" (Robert Harris)

1980. Centenary of Royal Canadian Academy of Arts. Multicoloured.
972 17c. Type **437** 25 20
973 17c. "Inspiration" (Philippe Hebert) 25 20
974 35c. "Sunrise on the Saguenay" (Lucius O'Brien) 50 55
975 35c. Thomas Fuller's design sketch for the original Parliament Buildings . . . 50 55

438 Canadian Whitefish

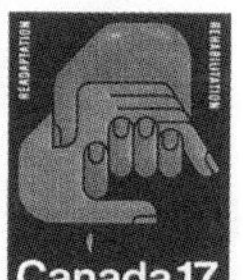

439 Garden Flowers

1980. Endangered Wildlife (4th series). Multicoloured.
976 17c. Type **438** 30 15
977 17c. Prairie chicken 30 15

1980. International Flower Show, Montreal.
978 **439** 17c. multicoloured 15 20

440 "Helping Hand"

441 Opening Bars of "O Canada"

1980. Rehabilitation.
979 **440** 17c. gold and blue 15 20

1980. Centenary of "O Canada" (national song). Multicoloured.
980 17c. Type **441** 15 15
981 17c. Calixa Lavallee (composer), Adolphe-Basile Routhier (original writer) and Robert Stanley Weir (writer of English version) 15 15

442 John G. Diefenbaker (statesman)

443 Emma Albani (singer)

1980. John G. Diefenbaker Commemoration.
982 **442** 17c. blue 15 20

1980. Famous Canadians. Multicoloured.
983 17c. Type **443** 15 25
984 17c. Healey Willan (composer) 15 25
985 17c. Ned Hanlan (oarsman) (horiz) 15 15

444 Alberta

1980. 75th Anniv of Alberta and Saskatchewan Provinces. Multicoloured.
986 17c. Type **444** 15 15
987 17c. Saskatchewan 15 15

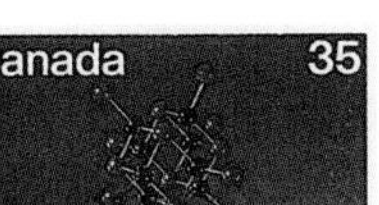
445 Uraninite Molecular Structure

446 "Christmas Morning" (J. S. Hallam)

1980. Uranium Resources.
988 **445** 35c. multicoloured 30 30

1980. Canadian Eskimos ("Inuits") (4th series). Spirits. As T **413**. Multicoloured.
989 17c. "Return of the Sun" (print, Kenojouak) 20 15
990 17c. "Sedna" (sculpture, Ashoona Kiawak) 20 15
991 35c. "Shaman" (print, Simon Tookoome) 35 55
992 35c. "Bird Spirit" (sculpture, Doris Hagiolok) 35 55

1980. Christmas. Multicoloured.
993 15c. Type **446** 10 10
994 17c. "Sleigh Ride" (Frank Hennessy) 15 10
995 35c. "McGill Cab Stand" (Kathleen Morris) . . . . 30 1·40

447 Avro (Canada) CF-100 Canuck Mk 5

1980. Canadian Aircraft (2nd series). Multicoloured.
996 17c. Type **447** 30 20
997 17c. Avro Type 683 Lancaster 30 20
998 35c. Curtiss JN-4 Canuck biplane 50 65
999 35c. Hawker Hurricane Mk I 50 65

448 Emmanuel-Persillier Lachapelle

449 Mandora (18th century)

1980. Dr. E.-P. Lachapelle (founder, Notre-Dame Hospital, Montreal) Commemoration.
1000 **448** 17c. brown, deep brown and blue 15 15

1981. "The Look of Music" Exhibition, Vancouver.
1001 **449** 17c. multicoloured . . . 15 15

450 Henrietta Edwards

1981. Feminists. Multicoloured.
1002 17c. Type **450** 30 30
1003 17c. Louise McKinney . . . 30 30
1004 17c. Idola Saint-Jean . . . 30 30
1005 17c. Emily Stowe 30 30

451 Vancouver Marmot

1981. Endangered Wildlife (5th series). Multicoloured.
1006 17c. Type **451** 15 10
1007 35c. American bison 35 30

452 Kateri Tekakwitha

453 "Self Portrait" (Frederick H. Varley)

1981. 17th-century Canadian Women. Statues by Emile Brunet.
1008 **452** 17c. brown and green . . 15 20
1009 – 17c. deep blue and blue 15 20
DESIGN: No. 1009, Marie de l'Incarnation

1981. Canadian Paintings. Multicoloured.
1010 17c. Type **453** 20 10
1011 17c. "At Baie Saint-Paul" (Marc-Aurele Fortin) (horiz) 20 10
1012 35c. "Untitled No 6" (Paul-Emile Borduas) 40 45

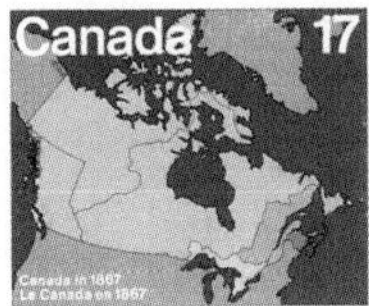
454 Canada in 1867

1981. Canada Day. Maps showing evolution of Canada from Confederation to present day. Multicoloured.
1013 17c. Type **454** 15 20
1014 17c. Canada in 1873 . . . . 15 20
1015 17c. Canada in 1905 . . . . 15 20
1016 17c. Canada since 1949 . . 15 20

455 Frere Marie-Victorin

456 The Montreal Rose

1981. Canadian Botanists. Multicoloured.
1017 17c. Type **455** 20 25
1018 17c. John Macoun 20 25

1981. Montreal Flower Show.
1019 **456** 17c. multicoloured . . . 15 20

457 Drawing of Niagara-on-the-Lake

458 Acadian Community

1981. Bicentenary of Niagara-on-the-Lake (town).
1020 **457** 17c. multicoloured . . . 15 20

1981. Centenary of First Acadia (community) Convention.
1021 **458** 17c. multicoloured . . . 15 20

459 Aaron R. Mosher

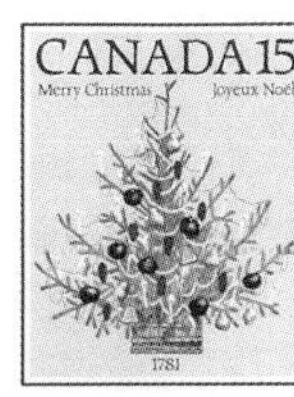
460 Christmas Tree, 1781

1981. Birth Centenary of Aaron R. Mosher (founder of Canadian Labour Congress).
1022 **459** 17c. multicoloured . . . 15 20

1981. Christmas. Bicentenary of First Illuminated Christmas Tree in Canada.
1023 15c. Type **460** 20 15
1024 15c. Christmas Tree, 1881 20 15
1025 15c. Christmas Tree, 1981 20 15

461 De Havilland Tiger Moth

462 Canadian Maple Leaf Emblem

1981. Canadian Aircraft (3rd series). Multicoloured.
1026 17c. Type **461** 20 15
1027 17c. Canadair CL-41 Tutor jet trainer 20 15
1028 35c. Avro (Canada) CF-102 jet airliner 35 40
1029 35c. De Havilland D.H.C.7 Dash 7 . . . . 35 40

1981.
1030a **462** A (30c.) red 20 25
No. 1030a was printed before a new first class domestic letter rate had been agreed, "A" representing the face value of the stamp, later decided to be 30c.

1982. As T **462** but including face values.
1033 **462** 5c. purple 10 20
1033d 8c. blue . . . . 1·50 2·25
1034 10c. green . . . . . . 1·25 2·00
1036 30c. red 35 30
1032 30c. red, grey and blue 30 40
1036b 32c. red . . . . 1·50 2·00
1032b 32c. red, brown and stone 45 45

463 1851 3d. Stamp

1982. "Canada 82" International Philatelic Youth Exhibition, Toronto. Stamps on Stamps. Mult.
1037 30c. Type **463** 30 30
1038 30c. 1908 Centenary of Quebec 15c. commemorative 30 30
1039 35c. 1935 10c. R.C.M.P . . 30 50
1040 35c. 1928 10c. 30 50
1041 60c. 1929 50c. . . . . . . 60 1·00
MS1042 159 × 108 mm. Nos. 1037/41 2·25 3·50

464 Jules Leger

465 Stylized drawing of Terry Fox

1982. Jules Leger (politician) Commemoration.
1043 **464** 30c. multicoloured . . . 20 20

1982. Cancer victim Terry Fox's "Marathon of Hope" (Trans-Canada fund-raising run) Commemoration.
1044 **465** 30c. multicoloured . . . 20 20

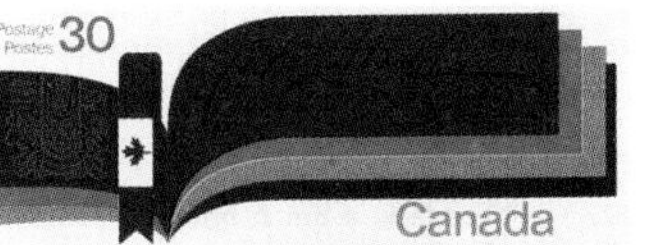
466 Stylized Open Book

1982. Patriation of Constitution.

1045 **466** 30c. multicoloured . . . 20 20

467 Male and Female Salvationists with Street Scene

1982. Centenary of Salvation Army in Canada.

1046 **467** 30c. multicoloured . . . 20 20

468 "The Highway near Kluane Lake" (Yukon Territory) (Jackson)

1982. Canada Day. Paintings of Canadian Landscapes. Sheet 139 × 139 mm, containing T **468** and similar horiz designs. Multicoloured.

MS1047 30c. × 12, Type **468**; "Street Scene, Montreal" (Quebec) (Hébert); "Breakwater" (Newfoundland) (Pratt); "Along Great Slave Lake" (Northwest Territories) (Richard); "Till Hill" (Prince Edward Island) (Lamb); "Family and Rainstorm" (Nova Scotia) (Colville); "Brown Shadows" (Saskatchewan) (Knowles); "The Red Brick House" (Ontario) (Milne); "Campus Gates" (New Brunswick) (Bobak); "Prairie Town—Early Morning" (Alberta) (Kerr); "Totems at Ninstints" (British Columbia) (Plaskett); "Doc Snider's House" (Manitoba) (FitzGerald) 4·75 6·00

469 Regina Legislative Building

1982. Centenary of Regina.

1048 **469** 30c. multicoloured . . . 20 20

470 Finish of Race

1982. Centenary of Royal Canadian Henley Regatta.

1049 **470** 30c. multicoloured . . . 20 25

471 Fairchild FC-2W1

1982. Canadian Aircraft (4th series). Bush Aircraft. Multicoloured.

1050 30c. Type **471** 35 20

1051 30c. De Havilland D.H.C.2 Beaver 35 20

1052 60c. Fokker Super Universal 65 85

1053 60c. Noorduyn Norseman 65 85

472 Decoy

475 Mary, Joseph and Baby Jesus

1982. Heritage Artefacts.

1054 **472** 1c. black, lt brn and brn 10 10

1055 – 2c. black, blue and green 10 10

1056 – 3c. black and deep blue 10 10

1057 – 5c. black, pink and brown 10 10

1058 – 10c. black, blue & turq 10 10

1059 – 20c. black, lt brn & brn 20 10

1060 – 25c. multicoloured . . . 35 10

1061 – 37c. black, grn & dp grn 60 40

1062 – 39c. black, grey and violet . . . . 1·75 1·25

1063 – 42c. multicoloured . . . 1·00 15

1064 – 48c. dp brn, brn & pink 70 40

1065 – 50c. black, lt blue & blue 1·75 20

1066 – 55c. multicoloured . . . 1·00 30

1067 – 64c. dp grey, blk & grey 80 35

1068 – 68c. black, lt brn & brn 1·75 50

1069 – 72c. multicoloured . . . 85 35

DESIGNS—VERT: 2c. Fishing spear; 3c. Stable lantern; 5c. Bucket; 10c. Weathercock; 20c. Skates; 25c. Butter stamp. HORIZ: 37c. Plough; 39c. Settle-bed; 42c. Linen chest; 48c. Cradle; 50c. Sleigh; 55c. Iron kettle; 64c. Kitchen stove; 68c. Spinning wheel; 72c. Hand-drawn cart.

1982. Christmas. Nativity Scenes.

1080 30c. Type **475** 20 10

1081 35c. The Shepherds 25 60

1082 60c. The Three Wise Men 45 1·50

476 Globes forming Symbolic Designs

478 Scene from Novel "Angeline de Montbrun" by "Laure Conan" (Felicite Angers)

477 Map of World showing Canada

1983. World Communications Year.

1083 **476** 32c. multicoloured . . . 30 30

1983. Commonwealth Day.

1084 **477** $2 multicoloured . . . . 2·00 3·25

1983. Canadian Writers (4th series).

1085 32c. Type **478** 40 90

1086 32c. Woodcut illustrating "Sea-gulls" (poem by E. J. Pratt) 40 90

479 St. John Ambulance Badge and "100"

480 Victory Pictogram

1983. Centenary of St. John Ambulance in Canada.

1087 **479** 32c. red, yellow and brown 30 30

1983. "Universiade 83" World University Games, Edmonton.

1088 **480** 32c. multicoloured . . . 25 15

1089 64c. multicoloured . . . 50 70

481 Fort William, Ontario

1983. Canada Day. Forts (1st series). Multicoloured.

1090 32c. Fort Henry, Ontario (44 × 22 mm) 65 80

1091 32c. Type **481** 65 80

1092 32c. Fort Rodd Hill, British Columbia 55 75

1093 32c. Fort Wellington, Ontario (28 × 22 mm) . . 55 75

1094 32c. Fort Prince of Wales, Manitoba (28 × 22 mm) 55 75

1095 32c. Halifax Citadel, Nova Scotia (44 × 22 mm) . . . 55 75

1096 32c. Fort Chambly, Quebec 55 75

1097 32c. Fort No. 1, Point Levis, Quebec 55 75

1098 32c. Coteau-du-Lac Fort, Quebec (28 × 22 mm) . . 55 75

1099 32c. Fort Beausejour, New Brunswick (28 × 22 mm) 65 80

See also Nos. 1163/72.

482 Scouting Poster by Marc Fournier (aged 21)

483 Cross Symbol

1983. Scouting in Canada (75th Anniv) and 15th World Scout Jamboree, Alberta.

1100 **482** 32c. multicoloured . . . 30 30

1983. 6th Assembly of the World Council of Churches, Vancouver.

1101 **483** 32c. green and lilac . . . 30 20

484 Sir Humphrey Gilbert (founder)

485 "NICKEL" Deposits

1983. 400th Anniv of Newfoundland.

1102 **484** 32c. multicoloured . . . 30 30

1983. Cent of Discovery of Sudbury Nickel Deposits.

1103 **485** 32c. multicoloured . . . 30 30

486 Josiah Henson and Escaping Slaves

1983. 19th-century Social Reformers. Multicoloured.

1104 32c. Type **486** 35 35

1105 32c. Father Antoine Labelle and rural village (32 × 26 mm) 35 35

487 Robert Stephenson's Locomotive "Dorchester", 1836

1983. Railway Locomotives (1st series). Mult.

1106 32c. Type **487** . . . . . . 90 1·00

1107 32c. Locomotive "Toronto", 1853 . . . . 90 1·00

1108 37c. Timothy Hackworth's locomotive "Samson", 1838 . . . . 90 1·00

1109 64c. Western Canadian Railway locomotive "Adam Brown", 1855 . . 1·40 2·25

See also Nos. 1132/5, 1185/8 and 1223/6.

488 School Coat of Arms

1983. Centenary of Dalhousie Law School.

1110 **488** 32c. multicoloured . . . 30 40

489 City Church

1983. Christmas. Churches. Multicoloured.

1111 32c. Type **489** 30 10

1112 37c. Family walking to church 40 90

1113 64c. Country chapel . . . . 1·00 2·00

490 Royal Canadian Regiment and British Columbia Regiment

491 Gold Mine in Prospecting Pan

1983. Canadian Army Regiments. Multicoloured.

1114 32c. Type **490** . . . . . . 75 1·25

1115 32c. Royal Winnipeg Rifles and Royal Canadian Dragoons . . . . 75 1·25

1984. 50th Anniv of Yellowknife.

1116 **491** 32c. multicoloured . . . 30 30

492 Montreal Symphony Orchestra

1983. 50th Anniv of Montreal Symphony Orchestra.

1117 **492** 32c. multicoloured . . . 35 30

493 Jacques Cartier

494 U.S.C.S. "Eagle"

1984. 450th Anniv of Jacques Cartier's Voyage to Canada.

1118 **493** 32c. multicoloured . . . 40 30

1984. Tall Ships Visit.

1119 **494** 32c. multicoloured . . . 35 30

495 Service Medal

496 Oared Galleys

1984. 75th Anniv of Canadian Red Cross Society.

1120 **495** 32c. multicoloured . . . 35 40

1984. Bicentenary of New Brunswick.

1121 **496** 32c. multicoloured . . . 35 30

497 St. Lawrence Seaway

1984. 25th Anniv of St. Lawrence Seaway.

1122 **497** 32c. multicoloured . . . 45 30

498 New Brunswick

1984. Canada Day. Paintings by Jean Paul Lemieux. Sheet 138 × 122 mm, containing T **498** and similar multicoloured designs.

MS1123 32c. × 12, Type **498**; British Columbia; Northwest Territories; Quebec; Manitoba; Alberta; Prince Edward Island; Saskatchewan; Nova Scotia (vert); Yukon Territory, Newfoundland; Ontario (vert) 6·50 7·00

The captions on the Northwest Territories and Yukon Territory paintings were transposed at the design stage.

499 Loyalists of 1784

1984. Bicentenary of Arrival of United Empire Loyalists.
1124 **499** 32c. multicoloured . . . 30 30

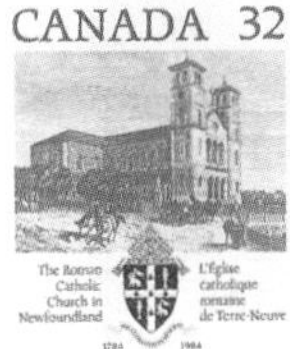

500 St. John's Basilica **501** Coat of Arms of Pope John Paul II

1984. Bicentenary of Roman Catholic Church in Newfoundland.
1125 **500** 32c. multicoloured . . . 30 25

1984. Papal Visit.
1126 **501** 32c. multicoloured . . . 40 20
1127 64c. multicoloured . . . 85 1·10

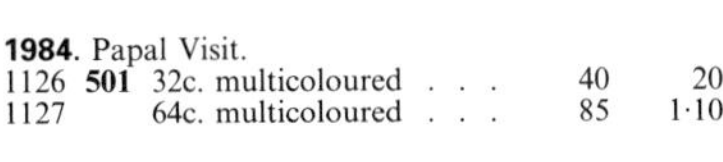

502 Louisbourg Lighthouse, 1734

1984. Canadian Lighthouse (1st series). Mult.
1128 32c. Type **502** . . . . . . 1·50 1·50
1129 32c. Fisgard Lighthouse, 1860 . . . . 1·50 1·50
1130 32c. Ile Verte Lighthouse, 1809 . . . . 1·50 1·50
1131 32c. Gibraltar Point Lighthouse, 1808 . . . . 1·50 1·50
See also Nos. 1176/9.

503 Great Western Railway Locomotive "Scotia", 1860

1984. Railway Locomotives (2nd series). Mult.
1132 32c. Type **503** . . . . . . 1·25 1·25
1133 32c. Northern Pacific Railroad locomotive "Countess of Dufferin", 1872 . . . . 1·25 1·25
1134 37c. Grand Trunk Railway Class E3 locomotive, 1886 1·25 1·50
1135 64c. Canadian Pacific Class D10a steam locomotive 1·75 2·50
MS1136 153 × 104 mm. As Nos. 1132/5, but with background colour changed from green to blue 5·00 6·50
No. MS1136 commemorates "CANADA '84" National Stamp Exhibition, Montreal.
See also Nos. 1185/8 and 1223/6.

504 "The Annunciation" (Jean Dallaire) **505** Pilots of 1914–18, 1939–45 and 1984

1984. Christmas. Religious Paintings. Multicoloured.
1137 32c. Type **504** 40 10
1138 37c. "The Three Kings" (Simone Bouchard) . . . 70 1·00
1139 64c. "Snow in Bethlehem" (David Milne) . . . . . 90 1·75

1984. 60th Anniv of Royal Canadian Air Force.
1140 **505** 32c. multicoloured . . . 35 30

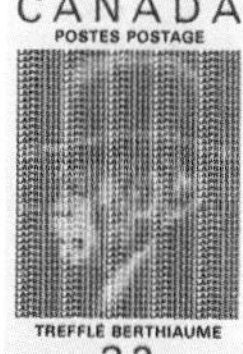

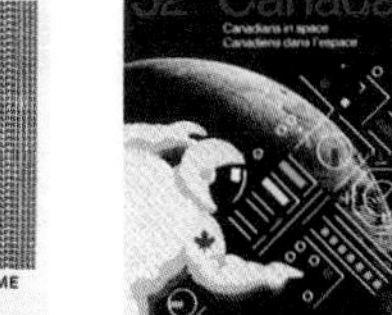

506 Treffle Berthiaume (editor) **508** Astronaut in Space, and Planet Earth

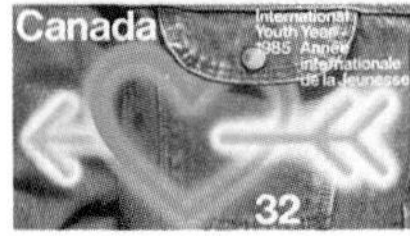

507 Heart and Arrow

1984. Centenary of "La Presse" (newspaper).
1141 **506** 32c. brown, red & lt brn 35 30

1985. International Youth Year.
1142 **507** 32c. multicoloured . . . 30 30

1985. Canadian Space Programme.
1143 **508** 32c. multicoloured . . . 40 30

509 Emily Murphy

1985. Women's Rights Activists. Multicoloured.
1144 32c. Type **509** 40 90
1145 32c. Therese Casgrain . . . 40 90

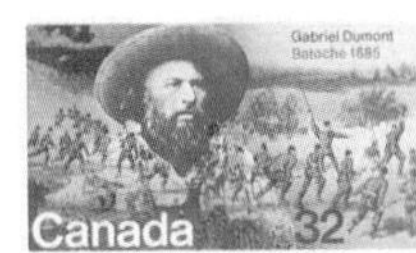

510 Gabriel Dumont (Metis leader) and Battle of Batoche, 1885

1985. Centenary of the North-West Rebellion.
1146 **510** 32c. blue, red and grey 30 30

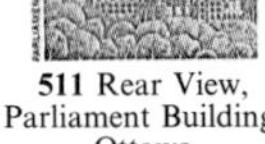

511 Rear View, Parliament Building, Ottawa **512** Queen Elizabeth II

512a Queen Elizabeth II in 1984 (from photo by Karsh)

1985.
1147b – 1c. green 70 80
1148 – 2c. green 20 75
1149 – 5c. brown 40 85
1150a – 6c. brown 50 30
1150b – 6c. purple . . . . . . 1·50 1·00
1151 **511** 34c. black . . . . . . 1·50 1·75
1155 34c. multicoloured . . 60 10
1158 34c. brown . . . . . . 2·25 2·75
1161 **512** 34c. black and blue . . 60 30
1152 **511** 36c. purple . . . . . 3·25 3·50
1156b 36c. multicoloured . . 30 45
1159 36c. red . . . . 1·25 55
1162 **512** 36c. purple . . . . . 2·75 1·10
1153 **511** 37c. blue . . . . . . 1·25 30
1157 – 37c. multicoloured . . 85 10
1162a **512a** 37c. multicoloured . . 2·25 10
1154 **511** 38c. blue . . . . . . 2·00 1·25
1157c – 38c. multicoloured . . 50 10
1160b **511** 38c. green 50 30
1162b **512a** 38c. multicoloured . . 55 20
1162c 39c. multicoloured . . 1·00 20
1162d 40c. multicoloured . . 95 20
1162e 42c. multicoloured . . 1·00 40
1162f 43c. multicoloured . . 1·25 65
1162g 45c. multicoloured . . 1·00 80
1162h 46c. multicoloured . . 50 45
1162i 47c. multicoloured . . 50 45
DESIGNS: 1, 5, 6c. (1150b) East Block, Parliament Building; 2, 6c. (1150a) West Block, Parliament Building; 37c. (1157) Front view, Parliament Building; 38c. (1157c) Side view, Parliament Building.

1985. Canada Day. Forts (2nd series). As T **481**. Multicoloured.
1163 34c. Lower Fort Garry, Manitoba 50 60
1164 34c. Fort Anne, Nova Scotia 50 60
1165 34c. Fort York, Ontario . . 50 60
1166 34c. Castle Hill, Newfoundland 50 60
1167 34c. Fort Whoop Up, Alberta 50 60
1168 34c. Fort Erie, Ontario . . 50 60
1169 34c. Fort Walsh, Saskatchewan 50 60
1170 34c. Fort Lennox, Quebec 50 60
1171 34c. York Redoubt, Nova Scotia 50 60
1172 34c. Fort Frederick, Ontario 50 60
Nos. 1163 and 1168 measure 44 × 22 mm and Nos. 1166/7 and 1171/2 28 × 22 mm.

513 Louis Hebert (apothecary) **514** Parliament Buildings and Map of World

1985. 45th International Pharmaceutical Sciences Congress of Pharmaceutical Federation, Montreal.
1173 **513** 34c. multicoloured . . . 45 35

1985. 74th Conference of Inter-Parliamentary Union, Ottawa.
1174 **514** 34c. multicoloured . . . 45 35

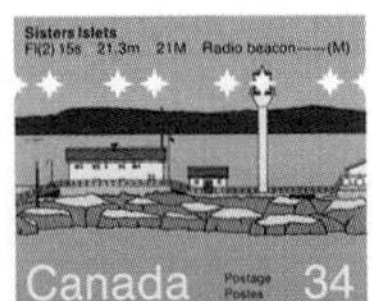

515 Guide and Brownie Saluting **516** Sisters Islets Lighthouse

1985. 75th Anniv of Girl Guide Movement.
1175 **515** 34c. multicoloured . . . 45 35

1985. Canadian Lighthouses (2nd series). Multicoloured.
1176 34c. Type **516** . . . . . . 1·75 1·75
1177 34c. Pelee Passage Lighthouse . . . . 1·75 1·75
1178 34c. Haut-fond Prince Lighthouse . . . . 1·75 1·75
1179 34c. Rose Blanche Lighthouse, Cains Island 1·75 1·75
MS1180 190 × 90 mm. Nos. 1176/9 6·50 7·00
No. **MS**1180 publicises "Capex 87" International Stamp Exhibition, Toronto.

517 Santa Claus in Reindeer-drawn Sleigh **518** Naval Personnel of 1910, 1939–45 and 1985

1985. Christmas. Santa Claus Parade. Multicoloured.
1181 32c. Canada Post's parade float . . . . 70 1·00
1182 34c. Type **517** 60 20
1183 39c. Acrobats and horse-drawn carriage . . . . . 70 1·25
1184 68c. Christmas tree, pudding and goose on float . . . 1·50 2·00

1985. Steam Railway Locomotives (3rd series). As T **503**. Multicoloured.
1185 34c. Grand Trunk Railway Class K2 . . . . 1·00 1·25
1186 34c. Canadian Pacific Class P2a . . . . 1·00 1·25
1187 39c. Canadian Northern Class O10a . . . . 1·25 1·50
1188 68c. Canadian Govt Railway Class H4D . . . 2·00 2·25

1985. 75th Anniv of Royal Canadian Navy.
1189 **518** 34c. multicoloured . . . 65 65

519 "The Old Holton House, Montreal" (James Wilson Morrice)

1985. 125th Anniv of Montreal Museum of Fine Arts.
1190 **519** 34c. multicoloured . . . 40 50

520 Map of Alberta showing Olympic Sites

1986. Winter Olympic Games, Calgary (1988) (1st issue).
1191 **520** 34c. multicoloured . . . 40 50
See also Nos. 1216/17, 1236/7, 1258/9 and 1281/4.

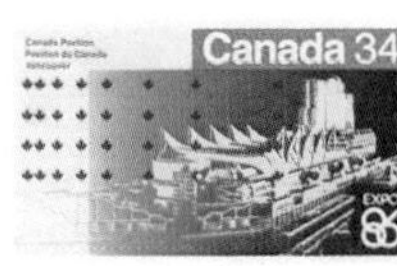

521 Canada Pavilion

1986. "Expo '86" World Fair, Vancouver (1st issue). Multicoloured.
1192 34p. Type **521** . . . . . . 1·00 50
1193 39p. Early telephone, dish aerial and satellite . . . . 1·75 2·50
See also Nos. 1196/7.

522 Molly Brant **523** Aubert de Gaspe and Scene from "Les Anciens Canadiens"

1986. 250th Birth Anniv of Molly Brant (Iroquois leader)
1194 **522** 34c. multicoloured . . . 40 50

1986. Birth Bicentenary of Philippe Aubert de Gaspe (author).
1195 **523** 34c. multicoloured . . . 40 50

1986. "Expo '86" World Fair, Vancouver (2nd issue). As T **521**. Multicoloured.
1196 34c. Expo Centre, Vancouver (vert) 70 50
1197 68c. Early and modern trains . . . . 1·40 2·75

524 Canadian Field Post Office and Cancellation, 1944

1986. 75th Anniv of Canadian Forces Postal Service.
1198 **524** 34c. multicoloured . . . 85 50

525 Great Blue Heron **526** Railway Rotary Snowplough

1986. Birds of Canada. Multicoloured.
1199 34c. Type **525** . . . . . . 1·50 1·75
1200 34c. Snow goose . . . . . 1·50 1·75

1201 34c. Great horned owl . . . 1·50 1·75
1202 34c. Spruce grouse . . . . 1·50 1·75

1986. Canada Day. Science and Technology. Canadian Inventions (1st series). Multicoloured.
1203 34c. Type **526** . . . . . . 1·10 1·50
1204 34c. Space shuttle "Challenger" launching satellite with Canadarm 1·10 1·50
1205 34c. Pilot wearing anti-gravity flight suit and Supermarine Spitfire . . . 1·10 1·50
1206 34c. Variable-pitch propeller and Avro 504 airplane . . 1·10 1·50
See also Nos. 1241/4 and 1292/5.

527 C.B.C. Logos over Map of Canada

1986. 50th Anniv of Canadian Broadcasting Corporation.
1207 **527** 34c. multicoloured . . . 40 50

528 Ice Age Artefacts, Tools and Settlement

1986. Exploration of Canada (1st series). Discoverers. Multicoloured.
1208 34c. Type **528** . . . . . . 1·00 1·50
1209 34c. Viking ships . . . . . 1·00 1·50
1210 34c. John Cabot's "Matthew", 1497, compass and Arctic char (fish) . . . . 1·00 1·50
1211 34c. Henry Hudson cast adrift, 1611 . . . . 1·00 1·50
MS1212 119 × 84 mm. Nos. 1208/11 4·50 5·50
No. **MS**1212 publicises "Capex '87" International Stamp Exhibition, Toronto.
See also Nos. 1232/5, 1285/8 and 1319/22.

529 Crowfoot (Blackfoot Chief) and Indian Village

1986. Founders of the Canadian West. Multicoloured.
1213 34c. Type **529** 60 85
1214 34c. James Macleod of the North West Mounted Police and Fort Macleod 60 85

530 Peace Dove and Globe

1986. International Peace Year.
1215 **530** 34c. multicoloured . . . 50 50

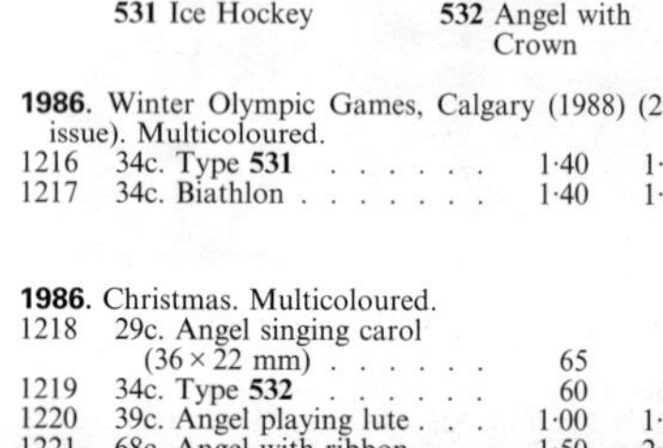

531 Ice Hockey **532** Angel with Crown

1986. Winter Olympic Games, Calgary (1988) (2nd issue). Multicoloured.
1216 34c. Type **531** . . . . . . 1·40 1·40
1217 34c. Biathlon . . . . 1·40 1·40

1986. Christmas. Multicoloured.
1218 29c. Angel singing carol (36 × 22 mm) 65 30
1219 34c. Type **532** 60 25
1220 39c. Angel playing lute . . . 1·00 1·50
1221 68c. Angel with ribbon . . . 1·50 2·50

533 John Molson with Theatre Royal, Montreal, "Accomodation" (paddle-steamer) and Railway Train

1986. 150th Death Anniv of John Molson (businessman).
1222 **533** 34c. multicoloured . . . 60 50

1986. Railway Locomotives (4th series). As T **503** but size 60 × 22 mm. Multicoloured.
1223 34c. Canadian National Class V-1-a diesel locomotive No. 9000 . . 1·50 1·50
1224 34c. Canadian Pacific Class T1a steam locomotive No. 9000 . . . . 1·50 1·50
1225 39c. Canadian National Class U-2-a steam locomotive . . . . 1·50 1·00
1226 68c. Canadian Pacific Class H1c steam locomotive No. 2850 . . . . 2·25 3·00

534 Toronto's First Post Office

1987. "Capex '87" International Stamp Exhibition, Toronto. Post Offices.
1227 34c. Type **534** 60 20
1228 36c. Nelson-Miramichi, New Brunswick 65 45
1229 42c. Saint-Ours, Quebec . . 70 65
1230 72c. Battleford, Saskatchewan . . . . . . 1·00 1·25
MS1231 155 × 92 mm. 36c. As No. 1227 and Nos. 1228/30, but main inscr in green 3·00 2·50

535 Etienne Brule exploring Lake Superior

1987. Exploration of Canada (2nd series). Pioneers of New France. Multicoloured.
1232 34c. Type **535** . . . . . . 1·00 1·25
1233 34c. Radisson and Des Groseilliers with British and French flags . . . . 1·00 1·25
1234 34c. Jolliet and Father Marquette on the Mississippi . . . . 1·00 1·25
1235 34c. Jesuit missionary preaching to Indians . . . 1·00 1·25

1987. Winter Olympic Games, Calgary (1988) (3rd issue). As T **531**. Multicoloured.
1236 36c. Speed skating 50 40
1237 42c. Bobsleighing 75 60

536 Volunteer Activities

1987. National Volunteer Week.
1238 **536** 36c. multicoloured . . . 30 35

537 Canadian Coat of Arms

539 R. A. Fessenden (AM Radio)

538 Steel Girder, Gear Wheel and Microchip

1987. 5th Anniv of Canadian Charter of Rights and Freedoms.
1239 **537** 36c. multicoloured . . . 50 35

1987. Centenary of Engineering Institute of Canada.
1240 **538** 36c. multicoloured . . . 50 40

1987. Canada Day. Science and Technology. Canadian Inventors (2nd series). Multicoloured.
1241 36c. Type **539** . . . . . . 95 1·25
1242 36c. C. Fenerty (newsprint pulp) . . . . 95 1·25
1243 36c. G.-E. Desbarats and W. Leggo (half-tone engraving) . . . . 95 1·25
1244 36c. F. N. Gisborne (first North American undersea telegraph) . . . . 95 1·25

540 "Segwun"

1987. Canadian Steamships. Multicoloured.
1245 36c. Type **540** . . . . . . 1·50 2·25
1246 36c. "Princess Marguerite" (52 × 22 mm) . . . . . . 1·50 2·25

541 Figurehead from "Hamilton", 1813

1987. Historic Shipwrecks. Multicoloured.
1247 36c. Type **541** . . . . . . 70 1·00
1248 36c. Hull of "San Juan", 1565 . . . . 70 1·00
1249 36c. Wheel from "Breadalbane", 1853 . . . 70 1·00
1250 36c. Bell from "Ericsson", 1892 . . . . 70 1·00

542 Air Canada Boeing 767-200 and Globe **543** Summit Symbol

1987. 50th Anniv of Air Canada.
1251 **542** 36c. multicoloured . . . 75 35

1987. 2nd Int Francophone Summit, Quebec.
1252 **543** 36c. multicoloured . . . 30 35

544 Commonwealth Symbol **545** Poinsettia

1987. Commonwealth Heads of Government Meeting, Vancouver.
1253 **544** 36c. multicoloured . . . 35 40

1987. Christmas. Christmas Plants. Multicoloured.
1254 31c. Decorated Christmas tree and presents (36 × 20 mm) 50 35
1255 36c. Type **545** 40 40
1256 42c. Holly wreath 75 50
1257 72c. Mistletoe and decorated tree 90 80

1987. Winter Olympic Games, Calgary (1988) (4th issue). As T **531**. Multicoloured.
1258 36c. Cross-country skiing . . 65 50
1259 36c. Ski-jumping 65 50

546 Football, Grey Cup and Spectators **547** Flying Squirrel

548a Runnymede Library, Toronto

1987. 75th Grey Cup Final (Canadian football championship), Vancouver.
1260 **546** 36c. multicoloured . . . 35 40

1988. Canadian Mammals and Architecture. Multicoloured. (a) As T **547**.
1261 1c. Type **547** 10 10
1262 2c. Porcupine 10 10
1263 3c. Muskrat 10 10
1264 5c. Varying hare 10 10
1265 6c. Red fox 10 10
1266 10c. Striped skunk 10 10
1267 25c. American beaver . . . 30 15
1268 43c. Lynx (26 × 20 mm) . . 1·40 30
1269 44c. Walrus (27 × 21 mm) 1·00 20
1270 45c. Pronghorn (27 × 21 mm) 40 40
1270c 46c. Wolverine (27 × 21 mm) 80 50
1271 57c. Killer whale (26 × 20 mm) . . . . . 2·00 55
1272 59c. Musk ox (27 × 21 mm) 2·25 1·00
1273 61c. Wolf (27 × 21 mm) . . 60 1·00
1273b 63c. Harbour porpoise (27 × 21 mm) . . . . . 1·00 1·25
1274 74c. Wapiti (26 × 20 mm) 1·60 50
1275 76c. Brown bear (27 × 21 mm) . . . . . 1·00 50
1276 78c. White whale (27 × 21 mm) 90 55
1276c 80c. Peary caribou (27 × 21 mm) . . . . . 1·00 60

(b) As T **548a**.
1277 $1 Type **548a** . . . . 1·25 30
1278 $2 McAdam Railway Station, New Brunswick 2·00 50
1279 $5 Bonsecours Market, Montreal . . . . 4·75 4·00

1988. Winter Olympic Games, Calgary (5th issue). As T **531**. Multicoloured.
1281 37c. Slalom skiing 75 50
1282 37c. Curling 75 50
1283 43c. Figure skating 75 45
1284 74c. Luge . . . . 1·25 80

549 Trade Goods, Blackfoot Encampment and Page from Anthony Henday's Journal

1988. Exploration of Canada (3rd series). Explorers of the West. Multicoloured.
1285 37c. Type **549** 85 60
1286 37c. Discovery and map of George Vancouver's voyage 85 60
1287 37c. Simon Fraser's expedition portaging canoes 85 60
1288 37c. John Palliser's surveying equipment and view of prairie 85 60

550 "The Young Reader" (Ozias Leduc)

1988. Canadian Art (1st series).
1289 **550** 50c. multicoloured . . . 70 70
See also Nos. 1327, 1384, 1421, 1504, 1539, 1589, 1629, 1681, 1721, 1825, 1912, 2011, 2097 and 2133.

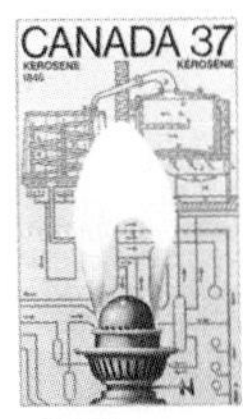

551 Mallard landing on Marsh

552 Kerosene Lamp and Diagram of Distillation Plant

1988. Wildlife and Habitat Conservation. Mult.

1290 37c. Type **551** 90 50
1291 37c. Moose feeding in marsh 90 50

1988. Canada Day. Science and Technology. Canadian Inventions (3rd series). Multicoloured.

1292 37c. Type **552** . . . . . . 75 1·00
1293 37c. Ears of Marquis wheat 75 1·00
1294 37c. Electron microscope and magnified image . . . 75 1·00
1295 37c. Patient under "Cobalt 60" cancer therapy . . . 75 1·00

553 "Papilio brevicauda"

1988. Canadian Butterflies. Multicoloured.

1296 37c. Type **553** 80 80
1297 37c. "Lycaeides idas" . . . 80 80
1298 37c. "Oeneis macounii" . . 80 80
1299 37c. "Papilio glaucus" . . . 80 80

554 St. John's Harbour Entrance and Skyline

1988. Centenary of Incorporation of St. John's, Newfoundland.

1300 **554** 37c. multicoloured . . . 35 40

555 Club Members working on Forestry Project and Rural Scene

1988. 75th Anniv of 4-H Clubs.

1301 **555** 37c. multicoloured . . . 35 40

556 Saint-Maurice Ironworks

557 Tahltan Bear Dog

1988. 250th Anniv of Saint-Maurice Ironworks, Quebec.

1302 **556** 37c. black, orange & brn 40 40

1988. Canadian Dogs. Multicoloured.

1303 37c. Type **557** . . . . . . 1·00 1·25
1304 37c. Nova Scotia duck tolling retriever . . . . . 1·00 1·25
1305 37c. Canadian eskimo dog 1·00 1·25
1306 37c. Newfoundland . . . . 1·00 1·25

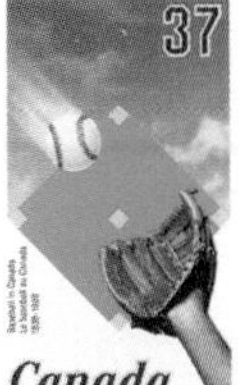

558 Baseball, Glove and Pitch

559 Virgin with Inset of Holy Child

1988. 150th Anniv of Baseball in Canada. Multicoloured.

1307 **558** 37c. multicoloured . . . 35 40

1988. Christmas. Icons. Multicoloured.

1308 32c. Holy Family (36 × 21 mm) 35 35
1309 37c. Type **559** 35 40
1310 43c. Virgin and Child . . . 40 45
1311 74c. Virgin and Child (different) 70 75

On No. 1308 the left-hand third of the design area is taken up by the bar code.

No. 1309 also commemorates the millennium of Ukrainian Christianity.

560 Bishop Inglis and Nova Scotia Church

1988. Bicentenary of Consecration of Charles Inglis (first Canadian Anglican bishop) (1987).

1312 **560** 37c. multicoloured . . . 35 40

561 Frances Ann Hopkins and "Canoe manned by Voyageurs"

1988. 150th Birth Anniv of Frances Anne Hopkins (artist).

1313 **561** 37c. multicoloured . . . 35 40

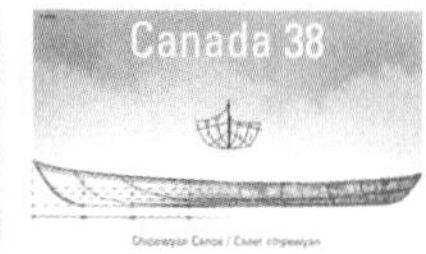

562 Angus Walters and "Bluenose" (yacht)

563 Chipewyan Canoe

1988. 20th Death Anniv of Angus Walters (yachtsman).

1314 **562** 37c. multicoloured . . . 40 40

1989. Small Craft of Canada (1st series). Native Canoes. Multicoloured.

1315 38c. Type **563** 85 70
1316 38c. Haida canoe 85 70
1317 38c. Inuit kayak 85 70
1318 38c. Micmac canoe 85 70

See also Nos. 1377/80 and 1428/31.

564 Matonabbee and Hearne's Expedition

1989. Exploration of Canada (4th issue). Explorers of the North. Multicoloured.

1319 38c. Type **564** . . . . . . 1·00 70
1320 38c. Relics of Franklin's expedition and White Ensign . . . . 1·00 70
1321 38c. Joseph Tyrell's compass, hammer and fossil . . . . 1·00 70
1322 38c. Vilhjalmur Stefansson, camera on tripod and sledge dog team . . . . . 1·00 70

565 Construction of Victoria Bridge, Montreal and William Notman

1989. Canada Day. "150 Years of Canadian Photography". Designs showing early photographs and photographers. Multicoloured.

1323 38c. Type **565** 60 60
1324 38c. Plains Indian village and W. Hanson Boorne 60 60
1325 38c. Horse-drawn sleigh and Alexander Henderson . . 60 60
1326 38c. Quebec street scene and Jules-Ernest Livernois . . 60 60

566 Tsimshian Ceremonial Frontlet, c. 1900

1989. Canadian Art (2nd series).

1327 **566** 50c. multicoloured . . . 55 60

567 Canadian Flag and Forest

1989. Self-adhesive. Multicoloured.

1328 38c. Type **567** . . . . . . 1·25 1·75
1328b 39c. Canadian flag and prairie . . . . 1·25 2·00
1328c 40c. Canadian flag and sea 1·25 1·25
1328d 42c. Canadian flag over mountains . . . . . . 1·50 2·00
1328e 43c. Canadian flag over lake . . . . 1·40 1·50

568 Archibald Lampman

569 "Clavulinopsis fusiformis"

1989. Canadian Poets. Multicoloured.

1329 38c. Type **568** 50 50
1330 38c. Louis-Honore Frechette 50 50

1989. Mushrooms. Multicoloured.

1331 38c. Type **569** 70 80
1332 38c. "Boletus mirabilis" . . 70 80
1333 38c. "Cantharellus cinnabarinus" 70 80
1334 38c. "Morchella esculenta" 70 80

570 Night Patrol, Korea

1989. 75th Anniv of Canadian Regiments. Mult.

1335 38c. Type **570** (Princess Patricia's Canadian Light Infantry) . . . . 1·25 1·40
1336 38c. Trench raid, France, 1914–18 (Royal 22e Regiment) . . . . 1·25 1·40

571 Globe in Box

572 Film Director

1989. Canada Export Trade Month.

1337 **571** 38c. multicoloured . . . 40 45

1989. Arts and Entertainment.

1338 **572** 38c. brown, dp brn & vio 65 55
1339 – 38c. brown, dp brn & grn 65 55
1340 – 38c. brown, dp brn & mve 65 55
1341 – 38c. brown, dp brn & bl 65 55

DESIGNS: No. 1339, Actors; No. 1340, Dancers; No. 1341, Musicians.

573 "Snow II" (Lawren S. Harris)

1989. Christmas. Paintings of Winter Landscapes. Multicoloured.

1342 33c. "Champ-de-Mars, Winter" (William Brymner) (35 × 21 mm) 90 55
1343 38c. "Bend in the Gosselin River" (Marc-Aurele Suzor-Cote) (21 × 35 mm) 40 35
1344 44c. Type **573** 60 50
1345 76c. "Ste. Agnes" (A. H. Robinson) . . . . 1·10 85

On No. 1342 the left-hand third of the design area is taken up by a bar code.

574 Canadians listening to Declaration of War, 1939

1989. 50th Anniv of Outbreak of Second World War (1st issue).

1346 **574** 38c. black, silver & pur 1·00 65
1347 – 38c. black, silver and grey . . . . 1·00 65
1348 – 38c. black, silver and green . . . . 1·00 65
1349 – 38c. black, silver and blue . . . . 1·00 65

DESIGNS: No. 1347, Army mobilization; No. 1348, British Commonwealth air crew training; No. 1349, North Atlantic convoy.

See also Nos. 1409/12, 1456/9, 1521/4, 1576/9, 1621/4, and 1625/8.

575 Canadian Flag

576

1989.

1350 **575** 1c. multicoloured . . . 20 1·00
1351 – 5c. multicoloured . . . 20 30
1352 – 39c. multicoloured . . 1·75 2·25
1354 **576** 39c. multicoloured . . 70 10
1360 – 39c. purple 60 75
1353 – 40c. multicoloured . . 2·00 2·50
1355 – 40c. multicoloured . . 80 10
1361 – 40c. blue 40 50
1356 – 42c. multicoloured . . 90 15
1362 – 42c. red 40 50
1357 – 43c. multicoloured . . 80 80
1363 – 43c. green . . . . . . 1·00 1·50
1358d – 45c. multicoloured . . 50 65
1364 – 45c. green 65 65
1359 – 46c. multicoloured . . 70 45
1365 – 46c. red 40 50
1367 – 46c. multicoloured . . 50 55
1368 – 48c. multicoloured . . 40 45

DESIGNS: Nos. 1351/3, 1360/5, As T **575** but different folds in flag. As T **576**: No. 1355, Flag over forest; 1356, Flag over mountains; 1357, Flag over prairie; 1358d, Flag and skyscraper; 1359, Flag and iceberg; 1367, Flag and inukshuk (Inuit cairn); 1368 Flag in front of Canada Post Headquarters, Ottawa.

No. 1359 comes with ordinary or self-adhesive gum and 1367/8 are self-adhesive.

577 Norman Bethune in 1937 and performing Operation, Montreal

1990. Birth Centenary of Dr. Norman Bethune (surgeon). Multicoloured.

1375 39c. Type **577** . . . . . . 1·00 1·25
1376 39c. Bethune in 1939, and treating wounded Chinese soldiers . . . . 1·00 1·25

1990. Small Craft of Canada (2nd series). Early Work Boats. As T **563**. Multicoloured.

1377 39c. Fishing dory . . . . . 90 1·10
1378 39c. Logging pointer . . . . 90 1·10
1379 39c. York boat . . . . . . 90 1·10
1380 39c. North canoe . . . . . 90 1·10

578 Maple Leaf Mosaic

1990. Multiculturalism.
1381 **578** 39c. multicoloured . . . 35 40

579 Mail Van (facing left)
580 Amerindian and Inuit Dolls

1990. "Moving the Mail". Multicoloured.
1382 39c. Type **579** 45 55
1383 39c. Mail van (facing right) 45 55

1990. Canadian Art (3rd series). As T **550**. Multicoloured.
1384 50c. "The West Wind" (Tom Thomson) 55 65

1990. Dolls. Multicoloured.
1385 39c. Type **580** . . . . . . 90 1·00
1386 39c. 19th-century settlers' dolls . . . . 90 1·00
1387 39c. Commerical dolls, 1917–36 . . . . 90 1·00
1388 39c. Commercial dolls, 1940–60 . . . . 90 1·00

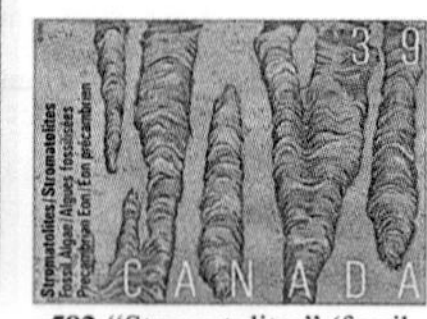

581 Canadian Flag and Fireworks
582 "Stromatolites" (fossil algae)

1990. Canada Day.
1389 **581** 39c. multicoloured . . . 50 50

1990. Prehistoric Canada (1st series). Primitive Life. Multicoloured.
1390 39c. Type **582** 90 75
1391 39c. "Opabinia regalis" (soft invertebrate) 90 75
1392 39c. "Paradoxides davidis" (trilobite) 90 75
1393 39c. "Eurypterus remipes" (sea scorpion) 90 75
See also Nos. 1417/20, 1568/71 and 1613/16.

583 Acadian Forest

1990. Canadian Forests. Multicoloured.
1394 39c. Type **583** 60 70
1395 39c. Great Lakes–St. Lawrence forest . . . 60 70
1396 39c. Pacific Coast forest . . 60 70
1397 39c. Boreal forest 60 70

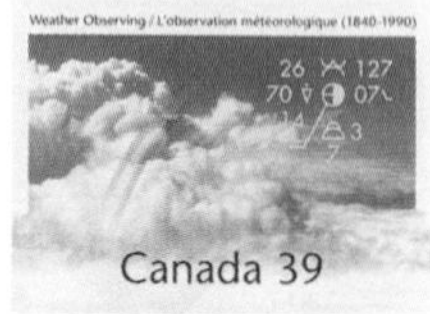

584 Clouds and Rainbow

1990. 150th Anniv of Weather Observing in Canada.
1398 **584** 39c. multicoloured . . . 40 50

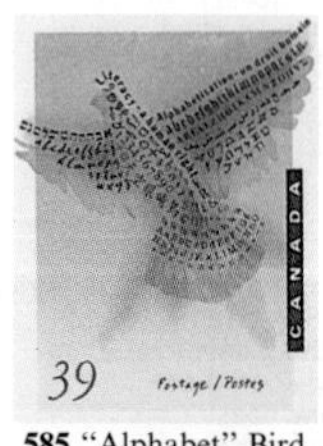

585 "Alphabet" Bird

1990. International Literacy Year.
1399 **585** 39c. multicoloured . . . 40 50

586 Sasquatch

1990. Legendary Creatures. Multicoloured.
1400 39c. Type **586** . . . . . . 1·00 1·10
1401 39c. Kraken . . . . 1·00 1·10
1402 39c. Werewolf . . . . . . 1·00 1·10
1403 39c. Ogopogo . . . . . . 1·00 1·10

587 Agnes Macphail
588 "Virgin Mary with Christ Child and St. John the Baptist" (Norval Morrisseau)

1990. Birth Centenary of Agnes Macphail (first woman elected to Parliament).
1404 **587** 39c. multicoloured . . . 40 50

1990. Christmas. Native Art.
1405 – 34c. multicoloured . . . 50 35
1406 **588** 39c. multicoloured . . . 40 40
1407 – 45c. multicoloured . . . 40 45
1408 – 78c. black, red and grey 70 75
DESIGNS—35 × 21 mm: 34c. "Rebirth" (Jackson Beardy). As T **588**: 45c. "Mother and Child" (Inuit sculpture, Cape Dorset); 78c. "Children of the Raven" (Bill Reid).
No. 1405 includes a bar code in the design.

1990. 50th Anniv of Second World War (2nd issue). As T **574**.
1409 39c. black, silver and green 1·40 1·40
1410 39c. black, silver and brown 1·40 1·40
1411 39c. black, silver and brown 1·40 1·40
1412 39c. black, silver and mauve 1·40 1·40
DESIGNS: No. 1409, Canadian family at home, 1940; 1410, Packing parcels for the troops; 1411, Harvesting; 1412, Testing anti-gravity flying suit.

589 Jennie Trout (first woman physician) and Women's Medical College, Kingston
590 Blue Poppies and Butchart Gardens, Victoria

1991. Medical Pioneers. Multicoloured.
1413 40c. Type **589** 90 90
1414 40c. Wilder Penfield (neurosurgeon) and Montreal Neurological Institute 90 90
1415 40c. Frederick Banting (discoverer of insulin) and University of Toronto medical faculty 90 90
1416 40c. Harold Griffith (anesthesiologist) and Queen Elizabeth Hospital, Montreal 90 90

1991. Prehistoric Canada (2nd series). Primitive Vertebrates. As T **582**. Multicoloured.
1417 40c. Foord's crossopt ("Eusthenopteron foordi") (fish fossil) . . . . 1·25 1·40
1418 40c. "Hylonomus lyelli" (land reptile) . . . . . . 1·25 1·40
1419 40c. Fossil conodonts (fossil teeth) . . . . 1·25 1·40
1420 40c. "Archaeopteris halliana" (early tree) . . . 1·25 1·40

1991. Canadian Art (4th series). As T **550**. Multicoloured.
1421 50c. "Forest, British Columbia" (Emily Carr) 1·00 1·25

1991. Public Gardens. Multicoloured.
1422 40c. Type **590** 55 55
1423 40c. Marigolds and International Peace Garden, Boissevain . . . 55 55
1424 40c. Lilac and Royal Botanical Gardens, Hamilton 55 55
1425 40c. Roses and Montreal Botanical Gardens . . . 55 55
1426 40c. Rhododendrons and Halifax Public Gardens 55 55

591 Maple Leaf
592 South Nahanni River

1991. Canada Day.
1427 **591** 40c. multicoloured . . . 50 60

1991. Small Craft of Canada (3rd series). As T **563**. Multicoloured.
1428 40c. Verchere rowboat . . . 1·25 1·25
1429 40c. Touring kayak . . . . 1·25 1·25
1430 40c. Sailing dinghy . . . . 1·25 1·25
1431 40c. Cedar strip canoe . . . 1·25 1·25

1991. Canadian Rivers (1st series). Multicoloured.
1432 40c. Type **592** . . . . . . 1·00 1·40
1433 40c. Athabasca River . . . 1·00 1·40
1434 40c. Boundary Waters, Voyageur Waterway . . . 1·00 1·40
1435 40c. Jacques-Cartier River 1·00 1·40
1436 40c. Main River . . . . . 1·00 1·40
See also Nos. 1492/6, 1558/62 and 1584/8.

593 "Leaving Europe"
594 Ski Patrol rescuing Climber

1991. Centenary of Ukrainian Immigration. Panels from "The Ukrainian Pioneer" by William Kurelek. Multicoloured.
1437 40c. Type **593** 80 85
1438 40c. "Canadian Winter" . . 80 85
1439 40c. "Clearing the Land" . . 80 85
1440 40c. "Harvest" 80 85

1991. Emergency Services. Multicoloured.
1441 40c. Type **594** . . . . . . 1·50 1·50
1442 40c. Police at road traffic accident . . . . 1·50 1·50
1443 40c. Firemen on extending ladder . . . . 1·50 1·50
1444 40c. Boeing-Vertol Chinook rescue helicopter and "Spindrift" (lifeboat) . . 1·50 1·50

595 "The Witched Canoe"
596 Grant Hall Tower

1991. Canadian Folktales. Multicoloured.
1445 40c. Type **595** 95 95
1446 40c. "The Orphan Boy" . . 95 95
1447 40c. "Chinook" 95 95
1448 40c. "Buried Treasure" . . 95 95

1991. 150th Anniv of Queen's University, Kingston.
1449 **596** 40c. multicoloured . . . 80 1·00

597 North American Santa Claus
598 Players jumping for Ball

1991. Christmas. Multicoloured.
1450 35c. British Father Christmas (35 × 21 mm) 80 40
1451 40c. Type **597** 90 20
1452 46c. French Bonhomme Noel . . . . 85 1·25
1453 80c. Dutch Sinterklaas . . . 1·60 2·75

1991. Basketball Centenary. Multicoloured.
1454 40c. Type **598** . . . . . . 1·25 75
MS1455 155 × 90 mm. 40c. Type **598**, but with shorter inscr below face value; 46c. Player taking shot; 80c. Player challenging opponent 6·00 5·50

1991. 50th Anniv of Second World War (3rd issue). As T **574**.
1456 40c. black, silver and blue 1·25 1·25
1457 40c. black, silver and brown 1·25 1·25
1458 40c. black, silver and lilac 1·25 1·25
1459 40c. black, silver and brown 1·25 1·25
DESIGNS: No. 1456, Women's services, 1941; 1457, Armament factory; 1458, Cadets and veterans, 1459, Defence of Hong Kong.

599 Blueberry
600 McIntosh Apple

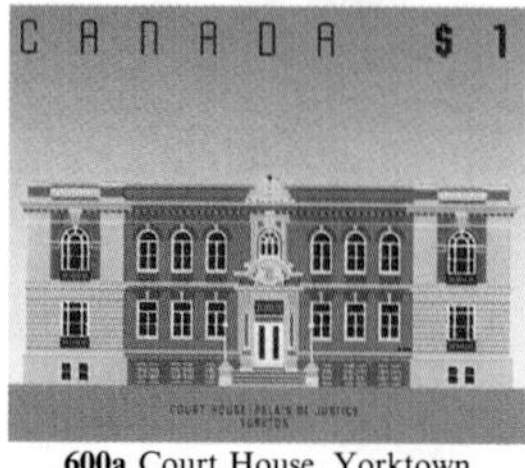

600a Court House, Yorktown

1991. Multicoloured. (a) Edible Berries. As T **599**.
1460 1c. Type **599** 10 10
1461 2c. Wild strawberry 10 10
1462 3c. Black crowberry 30 10
1463 5c. Rose hip 10 10
1464 6c. Black raspberry 10 10
1465 10c. Kinnikinnick 10 10
1466 25c. Saskatoon berry . . . 25 25

(b) Fruit and Nut Trees. As T **600**
1467 48c. Type **600** 50 35
1468 49c. Delicious apple . . . . 1·50 1·00
1469 50c. Snow apple . . . . . 1·00 1·00
1470 52c. Grauenstein apple . . . 1·10 50
1471 65c. Black walnut 70 50
1472 67c. Beaked hazelnut . . . 1·00 1·25
1473 69c. Shagbark hickory . . . 1·25 1·25
1474 71c. American chestnut . . 1·50 1·00
1475 84c. Stanley plum . . . . . 1·00 75
1476 86c. Bartlett pear . . . . . 1·00 1·00
1477 88c. Westcot apricot . . . . 1·75 1·60
1478 90c. Elberta peach . . . . . 1·00 1·00

(c) Architecture. As T **600a**
1479 $1 Type **600a** . . . . . . 2·00 1·00
1480a $2 Provincial Normal School, Truro . . . . . 2·75 1·60
1481 $5 Public Library, Victoria 4·50 4·75

601 Ski Jumping

1992. Winter Olympic Games, Albertville. Mult.
1482 42c. Type **601** 90 90
1483 42c. Figure skating 90 90
1484 42c. Ice hockey 90 90
1485 42c. Bobsleighing 90 90
1486 42c. Alpine skiing 90 90

602 Ville-Marie in 17th Century

1992. "CANADA 92" International Youth Stamp Exhibition, Montreal. Multicoloured.
1487 42c. Type **602** . . . . . . 1·00 1·25
1488 42c. Modern Montreal . . . 1·00 1·25
1489 48c. Compass rose, snow shoe and crow's nest of Cartier's ship "Grande Hermine" . . . . 1·50 1·00
1490 84c. Atlantic map, Aztec "calendar stone" and navigational instrument 2·25 2·50
MS1491 181 × 120 mm. Nos. 1487/90 6·00 6·00

1992. Canadian Rivers (2nd series). As T **592** but horiz. Multicoloured.
1492 42c. Margaree River . . . . 95 1·00
1493 42c. West (Eliot) River . . . 95 1·00
1494 42c. Ottawa River . . . . . 95 1·00

1495 42c. Niagara River . . . . 95 1·00
1496 42c. South Saskatchewan River . . . . 95 1·00

603 Road Bed Construction and Route Map

605 Jerry Potts (scout)

604 "Quebec, Patrimoine Mondial" (A. Dumas)

1992. 50th Anniv of Alaska Highway.
1497 **603** 42c. multicoloured . . . 85 70

1992. Olympic Games, Barcelona. As T **601**. Multicoloured.
1498 42c. Gymnastics . . . . . 1·00 1·10
1499 42c. Athletics . . . . 1·00 1·10
1500 42c. Diving . . . . 1·00 1·10
1501 42c. Cycling . . . . 1·00 1·10
1502 42c. Swimming . . . . . . 1·00 1·10

1992. Canada Day. Paintings. Sheet 190 × 256 mm, containing T **604** and similar diamond-shaped designs. Multicoloured.
MS1503 42c. Type **604**; 42c. "Christie Passage, Hurst Island, British Columbia" (E. J. Hughes); 42c. "Toronto, Landmarks of Time" (Ontario) (V. Mcindoe); 42c. "Near the Forks" (Manitoba) (S. Gouthro); 42c. "Off Cape St. Francis" (Newfoundland) (R. Shepherd); 42c. "Crowd at City Hall" (New Brunswick) (Molly Bobak); 42c. "Across the Tracks to Shop" (Alberta) (Janet Mitchell); 42c. "Cove Scene" (Nova Scotia) (J. Norris); 42c. "Untitled" (Saskatchewan) (D. Thauberger); 42c. "Town Life" (Yukon) (T. Harrison); 42c. "Country Scene" (Prince Edward Island) (Erica Rutherford); 42c. "Playing on an Igloo" (Northwest Territories) (Agnes Nanogak) 14·00 15·00

1992. Canadian Art (5th series). As T **550**. Multicoloured.
1504 50c. "Red Nasturtiums" (David Milne) . . . . . 1·40 1·10

1992. Folk Heroes. Multicoloured.
1505 42c. Type **605** . . . . . . 90 1·10
1506 42c. Capt. William Jackman and wreck of "Sea Clipper", 1867 . . . . . 90 1·10
1507 42c. Laura Secord (messenger) . . . . 90 1·10
1508 42c. Jos Montferrand (lumberjack) . . . . . . 90 1·10

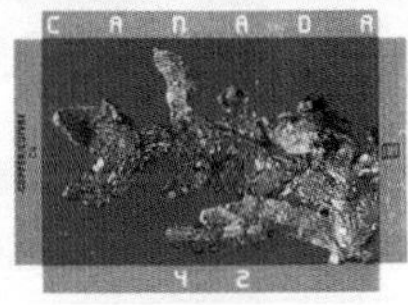

606 Copper

1992. 150th Anniv of Geological Survey of Canada. Minerals. Multicoloured.
1509 42c. Type **606** . . . . . . 1·25 1·50
1510 42c. Sodalite . . . . 1·25 1·50
1511 42c. Gold . . . . 1·25 1·50
1512 42c. Galena . . . . 1·25 1·50
1513 42c. Grossular . . . . . . 1·25 1·50

607 Satellite and Photographs from Space

1992. Canadian Space Programme. Multicoloured.
1514 42c. Type **607** . . . . . . 1·25 1·50
1515 42c. Space shuttle over Canada (hologram) (32 × 26 mm) . . . . . . 1·25 1·50

608 Babe Siebert, Skates and Stick

609 Companion of the Order of Canada Insignia

1992. 75th Anniv of National Ice Hockey League. Multicoloured.
1516 42c. Type **608** . . . . . . 1·25 1·50
1517 42c. Claude Provost, Terry Sawchuck and team badges . . . . 1·25 1·50
1518 42c. Hockey mask, gloves and modern player . . . 1·25 1·50

1992. 25th Anniv of the Order of Canada and Daniel Roland Michener (former Governor-General) Commermoration. Multicoloured.
1519 42c. Type **609** . . . . . . 1·25 1·50
1520 42c. Daniel Roland Michener . . . . 1·25 1·50

1992. 50th Anniv of Second World War (4th issue). As T **574**.
1521 42c. black, silver & brown 1·40 1·50
1522 42c. black, silver & green . . 1·40 1·50
1523 42c. black, silver & brown 1·40 1·50
1524 42c. black, silver and blue 1·40 1·50
DESIGNS: No. 1521, Reporters and soldier, 1942; 1522, Consolidated Liberator bombers over Newfoundland; 1523 Dieppe raid; 1524, U-boat sinking merchant ship.

610 Estonian Jouluvana

611 Adelaide Hoodless (women's movement pioneer)

1992. Christmas. Multicoloured.
1525 37c. North American Santa Claus (35 × 21 mm) . . . 85 80
1526 42c. Type **610** 40 20
1527 48c. Italian La Befana . . . 1·25 1·50
1528 84c. German Weihnachtsmann . . . . 1·75 2·50

1993. Prominent Canadian Women. Multicoloured.
1529 43c. Type **611** . . . . . . 85 1·10
1530 43c. Marie-Josephine Gerin-Lajoie (social reformer) 85 1·10
1531 43c. Pitseolak Ashoona (Inuit artist) . . . . . . 85 1·10
1532 43c. Helen Kinnear (lawyer) 85 1·10

612 Ice Hockey Players with Cup

613 Coverlet, New Brunswick

1993. Centenary of Stanley Cup.
1533 **612** 43c. multicoloured . . . 75 60

1993. Hand-crafted Textiles. Multicoloured.
1534 43c. Type **613** . . . . . . 1·00 1·25
1535 43c. Pieced quilt, Ontario 1·00 1·25
1536 43c. Doukhobor bedcover, Saskatchewan . . . . . . 1·00 1·25
1537 43c. Ceremonial robe, Kwakwaka'wakw . . . . 1·00 1·25
1538 43c. Boutonne coverlet, Quebec . . . . 1·00 1·25

1993. Canadian Art (6th series). As T **550**. Multicoloured.
1539 86c. "The Owl" (Kenojuak Ashevak) . . . . 2·00 2·50

614 Empress Hotel, Victoria

1993. Historic Hotels. Multicoloured.
1540 43c. Type **614** . . . . . . 70 1·00
1541 43c. Banff Springs Hotel . . 70 1·00
1542 43c. Royal York Hotel, Toronto . . . . 70 1·00
1543 43c. Le Chateau Frontenac, Quebec . . . . 70 1·00
1544 43c. Algonquin Hotel, St. Andrews . . . . . . 70 1·00

615 Algonquin Park, Ontario

616 Toronto Skyscrapers

1993. Canada Day. Provincial and Territorial Parks. Multicoloured.
1545 43c. Type **615** 70 80
1546 43c. De La Gaspesie Park, Quebec 70 80
1547 43c. Cedar Dunes Park, Prince Edward Island . . 70 80
1548 43c. Cape St. Mary's Seabird Reserve, Newfoundland 70 80
1549 43c. Mount Robson Park, British Columbia 70 80
1550 43c. Writing-on-Stone Park, Alberta 70 80
1551 43c. Spruce Woods Park, Manitoba 70 80
1552 43c. Herschel Island Park, Yukon 70 80
1553 43c. Cypress Hills Park, Saskatchewan 70 80
1554 43c. The Rocks Park, New Brunswick 70 80
1555 43c. Blomidon Park, Nova Scotia 70 80
1556 43c. Katannilik Park, Northwest Territories . . 70 80

1993. Bicentenary of Toronto.
1557 **616** 43c. multicoloured . . . 80 60

1993. Canadian Rivers (3rd series). As T **592**. Multicoloured.
1558 43c. Fraser River 70 90
1559 43c. Yukon River 70 90
1560 43c. Red River 70 90
1561 43c. St. Lawrence River . . 70 90
1562 43c. St. John River 70 90

617 Taylor's Steam Buggy, 1867

1993. Historic Automobiles (1st issue). Sheet 177 × 125 mm, containing T **617** and similar horiz designs. Multicoloured.
MS1563 43c. Type **617**; 43c. Russel "Model L" touring car, 1908; 49c. Ford "Model T" touring car, 1914 (43 × 22 mm); 49c. Studebaker "Champion Deluxe Starlight" coupe, 1950 (43 × 22 mm); 86c. McLaughlin-Buick "28–496 special", 1928 (43 × 22 mm); 86c. Gray-Dort "25 SM" luxury sedan, 1923 (43 × 22 mm) 7·50 8·00
See also Nos. **MS**1611, **MS**1636 and **MS**1683/4.

618 "The Alberta Homesteader"

1993. Folk Songs. Multicoloured.
1564 43c. Type **618** 70 90
1565 43c. "Les Raftmans" (Quebec) 70 90
1566 43c. "I'se the B'y that Builds the Boat" (Newfoundland) 70 90
1567 43c. "Onkwa:ri Tenhanonniahkwe" (Mohawk Indian) 70 90

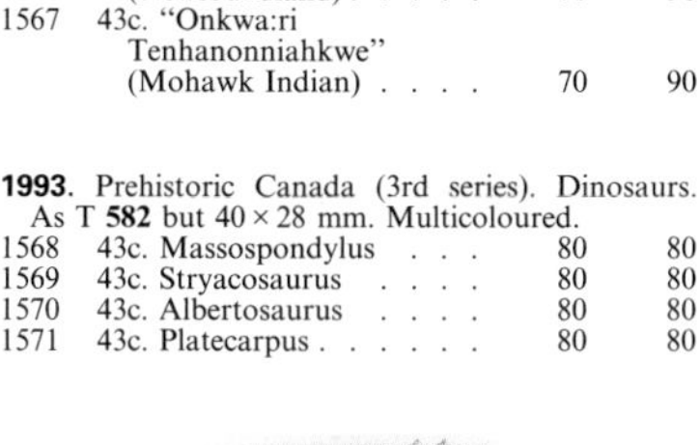

1993. Prehistoric Canada (3rd series). Dinosaurs. As T **582** but 40 × 28 mm. Multicoloured.
1568 43c. Massospondylus . . . 80 80
1569 43c. Stryacosaurus 80 80
1570 43c. Albertosaurus 80 80
1571 43c. Platecarpus 80 80

619 Polish Swiety Mikolaj

1993. Christmas. Multicoloured.
1572 38c. North American Santa Claus (35 × 22 mm) . . . 80 80
1573 43c. Type **619** 50 20
1574 49c. Russian Ded Moroz . . 1·00 1·25
1575 86c. Australian Father Christmas . . . . 1·75 2·50

1993. 50th Anniv of Second World War (5th issue). As T **574**.
1576 43c. black, silver and green 1·25 1·50
1577 43c. black, silver and blue 1·25 1·50
1578 43c. black, silver and blue 1·25 1·50
1579 43c. black, silver and brown 1·25 1·50
DESIGNS: No. 1576, Loading munitions for Russia, 1943; No. 1577, Loading bombs on Avro Lancaster; No. 1578, Escorts attacking U-boat; No. 1579, Infantry advancing, Italy.

620 (face value at right)

1994. Self-adhesive Greetings stamps. Mult.
1580 43c. Type **620** 70 90
1581 43c. As Type **620** but face value at left 70 90
It was intended that the sender should insert an appropriate greetings label into the circular space on each stamp before use.
For 45c. values in this design see Nos. 1654/5.

621 Jeanne Sauve

1994. Jeanne Sauve (former Governor-General) Commemoration.
1582 **621** 43c. multicoloured . . . 60 60

622 Timothy Eaton, Toronto Store of 1869 and Merchandise

1994. 125th Anniv of T. Eaton Company Ltd (department store group).
1583 **622** 43c. multicoloured . . . 55 75

1994. Canadian Rivers (4th series). As T **592**, but horiz. Multicoloured.
1584 43c. Saguenay River 60 75
1585 43c. French River 60 75
1586 43c. Mackenzie River . . . 60 75
1587 43c. Churchill River 60 75
1588 43c. Columbia River 60 75

1994. Canadian Art (7th series). As T **550**. Multicoloured.
1589 88c. "Vera" (detail) (Frederick Varley) . . . . 1·50 2·00

623 Lawn Bowls

1994. 15th Commonwealth Games, Victoria. Multicoloured.
1590 43c. Type **623** 40 50
1591 43c. Lacrosse 40 50
1592 43c. Wheelchair race 40 50
1593 43c. High jumping 40 50
1594 50c. Diving 45 65
1595 88c. Cycling . . . . 80 1·25

624 Mother and Baby

1994. International Year of the Family. Sheet 178 × 134 mm, containing T **624** and similar vert designs. Multicoloured.
MS1596 43c. Type **624**; 43c. Family outing; 43c. Grandmother and granddaughter; 43c. Computer class; 43c. Play group, nurse with patient and female lawyer 3·00 3·50

625 Big Leaf Maple Tree

1994. Canada Day. Maple Trees. Multicoloured.
1597 43c. Type **625** 70 80
1598 43c. Sugar maple 70 80
1599 43c. Silver maple 70 80
1600 43c. Striped maple 70 80
1601 43c. Norway maple 70 80
1602 43c. Manitoba maple . . . 70 80
1603 43c. Black maple 70 80
1604 43c. Douglas maple 70 80
1605 43c. Mountain maple . . . 70 80
1606 43c. Vine maple 70 80
1607 43c. Hedge maple 70 80
1608 43c. Red maple 70 80

626 Billy Bishop (fighter ace) and Nieuport 17
627 Symbolic Aircraft, Radar Screen and Clouds

1994. Birth Centenaries. Multicoloured.
1609 43c. Type **626** . . . . . . 75 1·00
1610 43c. Mary Travers ("La Bolduc") (singer) and musicians . . . . 75 1·00

1994. Historic Automobiles (2nd issue). Sheet 177 × 125 mm, containing horiz designs as T **617**. Multicoloured.
MS1611 43c. Ford "Model F60L-AMB" military ambulance, 1942–43; 43c. Winnipeg police wagon, 1925; 50c. Sicard snowblower, 1927 (43 × 22 mm); 50c. Bickle "Chieftain" fire engine, 1936 (43 × 22 mm); 88c. St. John Railway Company tramcar No. 40, 1894 (51 × 22 mm), 88c. Motor Coach Industries "Courier 50 Skyview" coach, 1950 (51 × 22 mm) 8·50 9·00
No. **MS**1611 was sold in a protective pack.

1994. 50th Anniv of I.C.A.O.
1612 **627** 43c. multicoloured . . . 60 60

1994. Prehistoric Canada (4th series). Mammals. As T **582**, but 40 × 28 mm. Multicoloured.
1613 43c. Coryphodon . . . . . 1·40 1·50
1614 43c. Megacerops . . . . . 1·40 1·50
1615 43c. Arctodus simus (bear) 1·40 1·50
1616 43c. Mammuthus primigenius (mammoth) 1·40 1·50

628 Carol Singing around Christmas Tree
629 Flag and Lake

1994. Christmas. Multicoloured.
1617 (–)c. Carol singer (35 × 21 mm) 70 80
1618 43c. Type **628** 45 20
1619 50c. Choir (vert) . . . . . 85 1·25
1620 88c. Couple carol singing in snow (vert) . . . . . . 2·00 2·75
No. 1617 is without face value, but was intended for use as a 38c. on internal greetings cards posted before 31 January 1995. The design shows a barcode at left.

1994. 50th Anniv of Second World War (6th issue). As T **574**.
1621 43c. black, silver and green 1·40 1·50
1622 43c. black, silver and red . . 1·40 1·50
1623 43c. black, silver and blue 1·40 1·50
1624 43c. black, silver and grey 1·40 1·50
DESIGNS: No. 1621, D-Day landings, Normandy; No. 1622, Canadian artillery, Normandy; No. 1623, Hawker Typhoons on patrol; No. 1624, Canadian infantry and disabled German self-propelled gun, Walcheren.

1995. 50th Anniv of Second World War (7th issue). As T **574**.
1625 43c. black, silver and purple 1·40 1·50
1626 43c. black, silver and brown 1·40 1·50
1627 43c. black, silver and green 1·40 1·50
1628 43c. black, silver and blue 1·40 1·50
DESIGNS: No. 1625, Returning troop ship; 1626, Canadian P.O.W.s celebrating freedom; 1627, Canadian tank liberating Dutch town; 1628, Parachute drop in support of Rhine Crossing.

1995. Canadian Art (8th series). As T **550**. Multicoloured
1629 88c. "Floraison" (Alfred Pellan) . . . . 1·25 1·75

1995. 30th Anniv of National Flag. No face value.
1630 **629** (43c.) multicoloured . . 50 50

630 Louisbourg Harbour

1995. 275th Anniv of Fortress of Louisbourg. Multicoloured.
1631 (43c.) Type **630** 50 60
1632 (43c.) Barracks (32 × 29 mm) 50 60
1633 (43c.) King's Bastion (40 × 29 mm) 50 60
1634 (43c.) Site of King's Garden, convent and hospital (56 × 29 mm) 50 60
1635 (43c.) Site of coastal fortifications 50 60

1995. Historic Automobiles (3rd issue). Sheet 177 × 125 mm, containing horiz designs as T **617**. Multicoloured.
MS1636 43c. Cockshutt "30" farm tractor, 1950; 43c. Bombadier "Ski-Doo Olympique 335" snowmobile, 1970; 50c. Bombadier "B-12 CS" multi-passenger snowmobile, 1948 (43 × 22 mm); 50c. Gotfredson "Model 20" farm truck, 1924 (43 × 22 mm); 88c. Robin-Nodwell "RN 110" tracked carrier, 1962 (43 × 22 mm); 88c. Massey-Harris "No. 21" self-propelled combine-harvester, 1942 (43 × 22 mm) 7·00 7·50
No. **MS**1636 was sold in a protective pack.

631 Banff Springs Golf Club, Alberta

1995. Centenaries of Canadian Amateur Golf Championship and of the Royal Canadian Golf Association. Multicoloured.
1637 43c. Type **631** 60 60
1638 43c. Riverside Country Club, New Brunswick . . 60 60
1639 43c. Glen Abbey Golf Club, Ontario 60 60
1640 43c. Victoria Golf Club, British Columbia 60 60
1641 43c. Royal Montreal Golf Club, Quebec 60 60

632 "October Gold" (Franklin Carmichael)

1995. Canada Day. 75th Anniv of "Group of Seven" (artists). Three sheets, each 180 × 80 mm, containing T **632** and similar square designs. Multicoloured.
MS1642 (a) 43c. Type **632**; 43c. "From the North Shore, Lake Superior" (Lawren Harris); 43c. "Evening, Les Eboulements, Quebec" (A. Jackson). (b) 43c. "Serenity, Lake of the Woods" (Frank Johnston); 43c. "A September Gale, Georgian Bay" (Arthur Lismer); 43c. "Falls, Montreal River" (J. E. H. MacDonald); 43c. "Open Window" (Frederick Varley). (c) 43c. "Mill Houses" (Alfred Casson); 43c. "Pembina Valley" (Lionel FitzGerald); 43c. "The Lumberjack" (Edwin Holgate)
Set of 3 sheets 9·00 10·00
The three sheets of No. **MS**1642 were sold together in an envelope which also includes a small descriptive booklet.

633 Academy Building and Ship Plan
634 Aspects of Manitoba

1995. Centenary of Lunenburg Academy.
1643 **633** 43c. multicoloured . . . 50 45

1995. 125th Anniv of Manitoba as Canadian Province.
1644 **634** 43c. multicoloured . . . 50 45

635 Monarch Butterfly

1995. Migratory Wildlife. Multicoloured.
1645 45c. Type **635** . . . . . . 90 1·25
1646 45c. Belted kingfisher* . . . 90 1·25
1647 45c. Belted kingfisher* . . . 90 1·25
1648 45c. Pintail . . . . 90 1·25
1649 45c. Hoary bat . . . . . . 90 1·25
*No. 1646: Inscr "aune migratrice" in error. No. 1647: Inscr corrected to "faune migratrice".

636 Quebec Railway Bridge

1995. 20th World Road Congress, Montreal. Bridges. Multicoloured.
1650 45c. Type **636** . . . . . . 1·25 1·40
1651 45c. 401-403-410 Interchange, Mississauga 1·25 1·40
1652 45c. Hartland Bridge, New Brunswick . . . . 1·25 1·40
1653 45c. Alex Fraser Bridge, British Columbia . . . . 1·25 1·40

1995. Self-adhesive Greetings stamps. As T **620**. Multicoloured. Imperf.
1654 45c. Face value at right . . 60 75
1655 45c. Face value at left . . . 60 75
It is intended the sender should insert an appropriate greetings label into the circular space on each stamp before use.

637 Mountain, Baffin Island, Polar Bear and Caribou

1995. 50th Anniv of Arctic Institute of North America. Multicoloured.
1656 45c. Type **637** . . . . . . 1·00 1·25
1657 45c. Arctic poppy, Auyuittuq National Park and cargo canoe . . . . 1·00 1·25
1658 45c. Inuk man and igloo . . 1·00 1·25
1659 45c. Ogilvie Mountains, dog team and ski-equipped airplane . . . . 1·00 1·25
1660 45c. Inuit children . . . . . 1·00 1·25

638 Superman
640 "The Nativity"

639 Prime Minister MacKenzie King signing U.N. Charter, 1945

1995. Comic Book Superheroes. Multicoloured.
1661 45c. Type **638** 75 85
1662 45c. Johnny Canuck 75 85
1663 45c. Nelvana 75 85
1664 45c. Captain Canuck . . . 75 85
1665 45c. Fleur de Lys 75 85

1995. 50th Anniv of United Nations.
1666 **639** 45c. multicoloured . . . 60 50

1995. Christmas. Sculptured Capitals from Ste.-Anne-de-Beaupre Basilica designed by Emile Brunet (Nos. 1668/70). Multicoloured.
1667 40c. Sprig of holly (35 × 22 mm) 65 65
1668 45c. Type **640** 50 20
1669 52c. "The Annunciation" . . 1·00 1·25
1670 90c. "The Flight to Egypt" 1·75 2·25

641 World Map and Emblem

1995. 25th Anniv of La Francophonie and The Agency for Cultural and Technical Co-operation.
1671 **641** 45c. multicoloured . . . 50 50

642 Concentration Camp Victims, Uniform and Identity Card

1995. 50th Anniv of the End of The Holocaust.
1672 **642** 45c. multicoloured . . . 50 50

643 American Kestrel

1996. Birds (1st series). Multicoloured.
1673 45c. Type **643** . . . . . . 1·10 1·10
1674 45c. Atlantic puffin . . . . 1·10 1·10
1675 45c. Pileated woodpecker . . 1·10 1·10
1676 45c. Ruby-throated hummingbird . . . . . . 1·10 1·10
See also Nos. 1717/20, 1779/82, 1865/8, 1974/7 and 2058/61.

644 "Louis R. Desmarais" (tanker), Three-dimensional Map and Radar Screen

1996. High Technology Industries. Multicoloured.
1677 45c. Type **644** 75 90
1678 45c. Canadair Challenger 601-3R, jet engine and navigational aid 75 90
1679 45c. Map of North America and eye 75 90
1680 45c. Genetic engineering experiment and Canola (plant) 75 90

1996. Canadian Art (9th series). As T **550**. Multicoloured.
1681 90c. "The Spirit of Haida Gwaii" (sculpture) (Bill Reid) . . . . 1·40 2·00

645 "One World, One Hope" (Joe Average)

1996. 11th International Conference on AIDS, Vancouver.
1682 **645** 45c. multicoloured . . . 70 70

1996. Historic Automobiles (4th issue). Sheet 177 × 125 mm, containing horiz designs as T **617**. Multicoloured.
MS1683 45c. Still Motor Co electric van, 1899; 45c. Waterous Engine Works steam roller, 1914; 52c. International "D.35" delivery truck, 1938; 52c. Champion road grader, 1936; 90c. White "Model WA 122" articulated lorry, 1947 (51 × 22 mm); 90c. Hayes "HDX 45-115" logging truck, 1975 (51 × 22 mm) 7·50 8·00
No. **MS**1683 also includes the "CAPEX '96" International Stamp Exhibition logo on the sheet margin and was sold in a protective pack.

1996. "CAPEX '96" International Stamp Exhibitiion, Toronto. Sheet 368 × 182 mm, containing horiz designs as Nos. **MS**1563, **MS**1611, **MS**1636 and **MS**1683, but with different face values, and one new design (45c.).
MS1684 5c. Bombadier "Ski–Doo Olympique 335" snowmobile, 1970; 5c. Cockshutt "30" farm tractor, 1950; 5c. Type **617**; 5c. Ford "Model F160L-AMB" military ambulance, 1942; 5c. Still Motor Co electric van, 1895; 5c. International "D.35" delivery truck, 1936; 5c. Russel "Model L" touring car, 1908; 5c. Winnipeg police wagon, 1925; 5c. Waterous Engine Works steam roller, 1914; 5c. Champion road grader, 1936; 10c. White "Model WA 122" articulated lorry, 1947 (51 × 22 mm); 10c. St. John Railway Company tramcar, 1894 (51 × 22 mm); 10c. Hayes "HDX 45-115" logging truck, 1975 (51 × 22 mm); 10c. Motor Couch Industries "Courier 50 Skyview" coach, 1950 (51 × 22 mm); 20c. Ford "Model T" touring car, 1914 (43 × 22 mm); 20c. McLaughlin-Buick "28-496 special", 1928 (43 × 22 mm); 20c. Bombadier "B-12 CS" multi-passenger snowmobile, 1948 (43 × 22 mm); 20c. Robin-Nodwell "RN 110" tracked carrier, 1962 (43 × 22 mm); 20c. Studebaker "Champion Deluxe Starlight" coupe, 1950 (43 × 22 mm); 20c. Gray-Dort "25 SM" luxury sedan, 1923 (43 × 22 mm); 20c. Gotfredson "Model 20" farm truck, 1924 (43 × 22 mm); 20c. Massey-Harris "No. 21" self-propelled combine-harvester, 1942 (43 × 22 mm); 20c. Bickle "Chieftain" fire engine, 1936 (43 × 22 mm); 20c. Sicard snowblower, 1927 (43 × 22 mm); 45c. Bricklin "SV-1" sports car, 1975 (51 × 22 mm) 8·00 9·00
The price quoted for No. **MS**1684 is for a folded example.

646 Skookum Jim Mason and Bonanza Creek

1996. Centenary of Yukon Gold Rush. Multicoloured.
1685 45c. Type **646** . . . . . . 80 1·00
1686 45c. Prospector and boats on Lake Laberge . . . . 80 1·00
1687 45c. Superintendent Sam Steele (N.W.M.P.) and U.S.A.–Canada border . . 80 1·00
1688 45c. Dawson saloon . . . . 80 1·00
1689 45c. Miner with rocker box and sluice . . . . 80 1·00

647 Patchwork Quilt Maple Leaf **648** Ethel Catherwood (high jump), 1928

1996. Canada Day. Self-adhesive. Imperf.
1690 **647** 45c. multicoloured . . . 50 50

1996. Canadian Olympic Gold Medal Winners. Multicoloured.
1691 45c. Type **648** 85 85
1692 45c. Etienne Desmarteau (56lb weight throw), 1904 85 85
1693 45c. Fanny Rosenfeld (400 m relay), 1928 . . . 85 85
1694 45c. Gerald Ouellette (small bore rifle, prone), 1956 . . 85 85
1695 45c. Percy Williams (100 and 200 m), 1928 . . . . 85 85

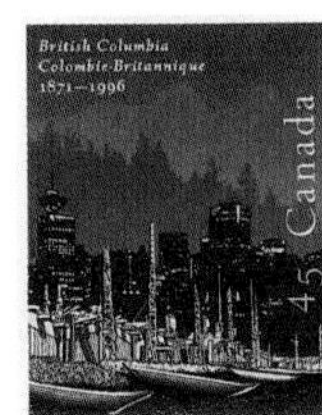

649 Indian Totems, City Skyline, Forest and Mountains **650** Canadian Heraldic Symbols

1996. 125th Anniv of British Columbia.
1696 **649** 45c. multicoloured . . . 50 50

1996. 22nd International Congress of Genealogical and Heraldic Sciences, Ottawa.
1697 **650** 45c. multicoloured . . . 50 50

651 "L'Arivee d'un Train en Gare" (1896)

1996. Centenary of Cinema. Two sheets, each 180 × 100 mm, containing T **651** and similar vert designs. Multicoloured. Self-adhesive.
MS1698 (a) 45c. Type **651**; 45c. "Back to God's Country" (1919); 45c. "Hen Hop!" (1942); "Pour la Suite du Monde" (1963); 45c. "Goin' Down the Road" (1970). (b) 45c. "Mon Oncle Antione" (1971); 45c. "The Apprenticeship of Duddy Kravitz" (1974); 45c. "Les Ordres" (1974); 45c. "Les Bons Debarras" (1980); 45c. "The Grey Fox" (1982) 8·50 9·50
The two sheets of No. **MS**1698 were sold together in an envelope with a descriptive booklet.

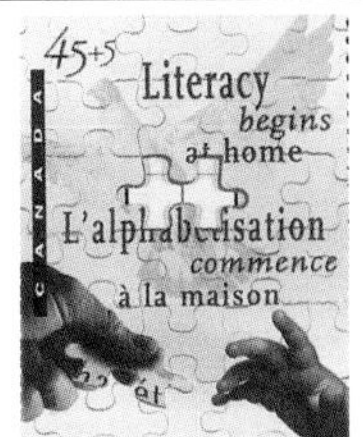

652 Interlocking Jigsaw Pieces and Hands

1996. Literacy Campaign.
1699 **652** 45c.+5c. mult 85 85

653 Edouard Montpetit and Montreal University

1996. Edouard Montpetit (academic) Commem.
1700 **653** 45c. multicoloured . . . 50 50

654 Winnie and Lt. Colebourn, 1914

1996. Stamp Collecting Month. Winnie the Pooh. Multicoloured.
1701 45c. Type **654** . . . . . . 90 1·10
1702 45c. Christopher Robin Milne and teddy bear, 1925 . . . . 90 1·10
1703 45c. Illustration from "Winnie the Pooh", 1926 90 1·10
1704 45c. Winnie the Pooh at Walt Disney World, 1996 90 1·10
MS1705 152 × 112 mm. Nos 1701/4 3·25 3·75

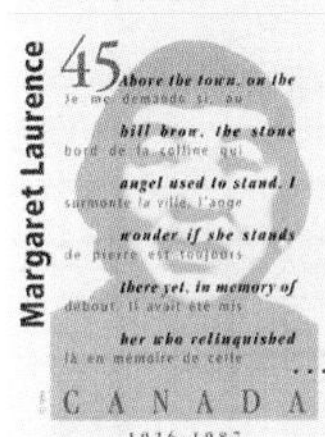

655 Margaret Laurence **656** Children tobogganing

1996. Canadian Authors.
1706 **655** 45c. multicoloured . . . 1·00 1·25
1707 – 45c. black, grey and red 1·00 1·25
1708 – 45c. multicoloured . . . 1·00 1·25
1709 – 45c. multicoloured . . . 1·00 1·25
1710 – 45c. multicoloured . . . 1·00 1·25
DESIGNS: No. 1707, Donald G. Creighton; 1708, Gabrielle Roy; 1709, Felix-Antoine Savard; 1710, Thomas C. Haliburton.

1996. Christmas. 50th Anniv of U.N.I.C.E.F. Multicoloured.
1711 45c. Type **656** 50 20
1712 52c. Father Christmas skiing . . . . 80 1·00
1713a 90c. Couple ice-skating . . 1·25 1·75

657 Head of Ox **659** Abbe Charles-Emile Gadbois

658 Man and Boy with Bike, and A. J. and J. W. Billes (company founders)

1997. Chinese New Year ("Year of the Ox").
1714 **657** 45c. multicoloured . . . 85 90
MS1715 155 × 75 mm. Nos. 1714 × 2 2·00 2·50
No. **MS**1715 is an extended fan shape with overall measurements as quoted.

1997. "HONG KONG '97" International Stamp Exhibition. As No. **MS**1715, but with exhibition logo added to the sheet margin in gold.
MS1716 155 × 75 mm. No. 1714 × 2 5·50 6·00

1997. Birds (2nd series). As T **643**. Multicoloured.
1717 45c. Mountain bluebird . . 80 85
1718 45c. Western grebe 80 85
1719 45c. Northern gannet . . . 80 85
1720 45c. Scarlet tanager 80 85

1997. Canadian Art (10th series). As T **550**. Multicoloured.
1721 90c. "York Boat on Lake Winnipeg, 1930" (Walter Phillips) . . . . 1·50 2·00

1997. 75th Anniv of the Canadian Tire Corporation.
1722 **658** 45c. multicoloured . . . 80 50

1997. Abbe Charles-Emile Gadbois (musicologist) Commemoration.
1723 **659** 45c. multicoloured . . . 50 50

660 Blue Poppy **662** Osgoode Hall and Seal of Law School

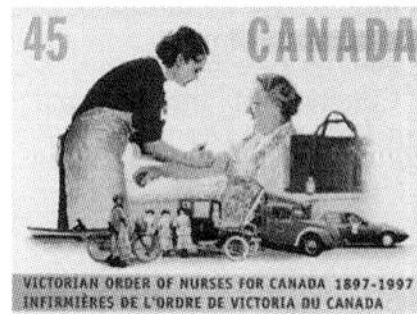

661 Nurse attending Patient

1997. "Quebec in Bloom" International Floral Festival.
1724 **660** 45c. multicoloured . . . 60 55

1997. Centenary of Victorian Order of Nurses.
1725 **661** 45c. multicoloured . . . 60 50

1997. Bicentenary of Law Society of Upper Canada.
1726 **662** 45c. multicoloured . . . 60 50

663 Great White Shark

1997. Ocean Fishes. Multicoloured.
1727 45c. Type **663** . . . . . . 1·00 1·25
1728 45c. Pacific halibut . . . . 1·00 1·25
1729 45c. Common sturgeon . . 1·00 1·25
1730 45c. Blue-finned tuna . . . 1·00 1·25

664 Lighthouse and Confederation Bridge

1997. Opening of Confederation Bridge, Northumberland Strait. Multicoloured.
1731 45c. Type **664** 90 90
1732 45c. Confederation Bridge and great blue heron . . 90 90

665 Gilles Villeneuve in Ferrari T-3

1997. 15th Death Anniv of Gilles Villeneuve (racing car driver). Multicoloured.
1733 45c. Type **665** . . . . . . 1·00 60
1734 90c. Villeneuve in Ferrari T-4 . . . . 1·75 2·00
MS1735 203 × 115 mm. Nos. 1733/4 each × 4 8·00 8·00

666 Globe and the "Matthew"

1997. 500th Anniv of John Cabot's Discovery of North America.
1736 **666** 45c. multicoloured . . . 75 55

667 Sea to Sky Highway, British Columbia, and Skier

1997. Scenic Highways (1st series). Multicoloured.
1737 45c. Type **667** . . . . . . 1·00 1·10
1738 45c. Cabot Trail, Nova Scotia, and rug-making 1·00 1·10
1739 45c. Wine route, Ontario, and glasses of wine . . . 1·00 1·10
1740 45c. Highway 34, Saskatchewan, and cowboy . . . . 1·00 1·10
See also Nos. 1810/13 and 1876/9.

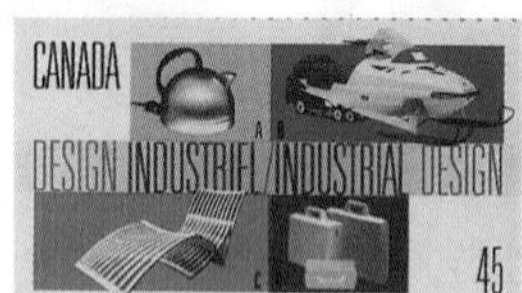

668 Kettle, Ski-bike, Lounger and Plastic Cases

1997. 20th Congress of International Council of Societies for Industrial Design.
1741 **668** 45c. multicoloured . . . 60 50

669 Caber Thrower, Bagpiper, Drummer and Highland Dancer

1997. 50th Anniv of Glengarry Highland Games, Ontario.
1742 **669** 45c. multicoloured . . . 75 50

670 Knights of Columbus Emblem

1997. Centenary of Knights of Columbus (welfare charity) in Canada.
1743 **670** 45c. multicoloured . . . 50 50

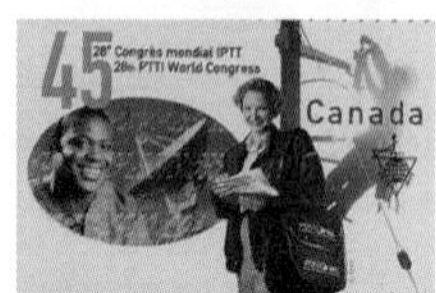

671 Postal and Telephone Workers with P.T.T.I. Emblem

1997. 28th World Congress of Postal, Telegraph and Telephone International Staff Federation, Montreal.
1744 **671** 45c. multicoloured . . . 50 50

672 C.Y.A.P. Logo

1997. Canada's Year of Asia Pacific.
1745 **672** 45c. multicoloured . . . 70 50

673 Paul Henderson celebrating Goal

1997. 25th Anniv of Canada–U.S.S.R. Ice Hockey Series. Multicoloured.
1746 45c. Type **673** 70 75
1747 45c. Canadian team celebrating 70 75

674 Martha Black

1997. Federal Politicians. Multicoloured.
1748 45c. Type **674** 70 90
1749 45c. Lionel Chevrier 70 90
1750 45c. Judy LaMarsh 70 90
1751 45c. Real Caouette 70 90

675 Vampire and Bat

1997. The Supernatural. Centenary of Publication of Bram Stoker's "Dracula". Multicoloured.
1752 45c. Type **675** 60 75
1753 45c. Werewolf 60 75
1754 45c. Ghost 60 75
1755 45c. Goblin 60 75

676 Grizzly Bear

1997. Mammals. Multicoloured.
1756 $1 Great northern diver ("Loon") (47 × 39 mm) . . 90 95
1757 $2 Polar bear (47 × 39 mm) 1·75 1·90
1758 $8 Type **676** . . . . 7·50 8·00

677 "Our Lady of the Rosary" (detail, Holy Rosary Cathedral, Vancouver)

1997. Christmas. Stained Glass Windows. Multicoloured.
1763a 45c. Type **677** 40 45
1764 52c. "Nativity" (detail, Leith United Church, Ontario) 55 55
1765 90c. "Life of the Blessed Virgin" (detail, St. Stephen's Ukrainian Catholic Church, Calgary) . . . . 90 1·25

678 Livestock and Produce

1997. 75th Anniv of Royal Agricultural Winter Fair, Toronto.
1766 **678** 45c. multicoloured . . . 75 55

679 Tiger

1998. Chinese New Year ("Year of the Tiger").
1767 **679** 45c. multicoloured . . . 60 50
MS1768 130 × 110 mm. As No. 1767 × 2 1·25 1·50
No. **MS**1768 is diamond-shaped with overall measurements as quoted.

680 John Robarts (Ontario, 1961–71)

681 Maple Leaf

1998. Canadian Provincial Premiers. Multicoloured.
1769 45c. Type **680** 60 60
1770 45c. Jean Lesage (Quebec, 1960–66) 60 60
1771 45c. John McNair (New Brunswick, 1940–52) . . . 60 60
1772 45c. Tommy Douglas (Saskatchewan, 1944–61) 60 60
1773 45c. Joseph Smallwood (Newfoundland, 1949–72) 60 60
1774 45c. Angus MacDonald (Nova Scotia, 1933–40, 1945–54) 60 60
1775 45c. W. A. C. Bennett (British Columbia, 1960–66) 60 60
1776 45c. Ernest Manning (Alberta, 1943–68) 60 60
1777 45c. John Bracken (Manitoba, 1922–43) . . . 60 60
1778 45c. J. Walter Jones (Prince Edward Island, 1943–53) 60 60

1998. Birds (3rd series). As T **643**. Multicoloured.
1779 45c. Hairy woodpecker . . 80 85
1780 45c. Great crested flycatcher 80 85
1781 45c. Eastern screech owl . . 80 85
1782 45c. Rosy finch ("Gray-crowned Rosy-finch") . . 80 85

1998. Self-adhesive Automatic Cash Machine Stamps. Imperf.
1783 **681** 45c. multicoloured . . . 45 40
For stamps in this design, but without "POSTAGE POSTES" at top left see Nos. 1836/40.

682 Coquihalla Orange Fly

1998. Fishing Flies. Multicoloured.
1784 45c. Type **682** 90 90
1785 45c. Steelhead Bee 90 90
1786 45c. Dark Montreal 90 90
1787 45c. Lady Amherst 90 90
1788 45c. Coho Blue 90 90
1789 45c. Cosseboom Special . . 90 90

683 Mineral Excavation, Oil Rig and Pickaxe

684 1898 2c. Imperial Penny Postage Stamp and Postmaster General Sir William Mulock

1998. Centenary of Canadian Institute of Mining, Metallurgy and Petroleum.
1790 **683** 45c. multicoloured . . . 60 50

1998. Centenary of Imperial Penny Postage.
1791 **684** 45c. multicoloured . . . 75 55

685 Two Sumo Wrestlers

1998. 1st Canadian Sumo Basho (tournament), Vancouver. Multicoloured.
1792 45c. Type **685** 65 75
1793 45c. Sumo wrestler in ceremonial ritual 65 75
MS1794 84 × 152 mm. Nos. 1792/3 1·00 1·25

686 St. Peters Canal, Nova Scotia

687 Staff of Aesculapius and Cross

1998. Canadian Canals. Multicoloured.
1795 45c. Type **686** . . . . . . 1·25 1·25
1796 45c. St. Ours Canal, Quebec 1·25 1·25
1797 45c. Port Carling Lock, Ontario . . . . 1·25 1·25
1798 45c. Lock on Rideau Canal, Ontario . . . . 1·25 1·25
1799 45c. Towers and platform of Peterborough Lift Lock, Trent–Severn Waterway, Ontario . . . . 1·25 1·25
1800 45c. Chambly Canal, Quebec . . . . 1·25 1·25
1801 45c. Lachine Canal, Quebec 1·25 1·25
1802 45c. Rideau Canal in winter, Ontario . . . . 1·25 1·25
1803 45c. Boat on Big Chute incline railway, Trent–Severn Waterway, Ontario 1·25 1·25
1804 45c. Sault Ste. Marie Canal, Ontario . . . . 1·25 1·25

1998. Canadian Health Professionals.
1805 **687** 45c. multicoloured . . . 75 55

688 Policeman of 1873 and Visit to Indian Village

1998. 125th Anniv of Royal Canadian Mounted Police. Multicoloured.
1806 45c. Type **688** 60 75
1807 45c. Policewoman of 1998 and aspects of modern law enforcement 60 75
MS1808 160 × 102 mm. Nos. 1806/7 1·00 1·40

689 William J. Roue (designer) and "Bluenose" (schooner)

1998. William James Roue (naval architect) Commemoration.
1809 **689** 45c. multicoloured . . . 50 50

1998. Scenic Highways (2nd series). As T **667**. Multicoloured.
1810 45c. Dempster Highway, Yukon, and caribou . . . 55 65
1811 45c. Dinosaur Trail, Alberta, and skeleton . . 55 65
1812 45c. River Valley Drive, New Brunswick, and fern 55 65
1813 45c. Blue Heron Route, Prince Edward Island, and lobster 55 65

Peinture
690 "Painting" (Jean-Paul Riopelle)

1998. 50th Anniv of "Refus Global" (manifesto of The Automatistes group of artists). Multicoloured. Self-adhesive. Imperf.
1814 45c. Type **690** . . . . . . 1·00 1·00
1815 45c. "La derniere campagne de Napoleon" (Fernand Leduc) (37 × 31½ mm) . . 1·00 1·00

1816 45c. "Jet fuligineux sur noir torture" (Jean-Paul Mousseau) . . . . 1·00 1·00
1817 45c. "Le fond du garde-robe" (Pierre Gauvreau) (29½ × 42 mm) . . . . . 1·00 1·00
1818 45c. "Joie lacustre" (Paul-Emile Borduas) . . . . . 1·00 1·00
1819 45c. "Seafarers Union" (Marcelle Ferron) (36 × 34 mm) . . . . . . 1·00 1·00
1820 45c. "Le tumulte a la machoire crispee" (Marcel Barbeau) (36 × 34 mm) . . 1·00 1·00

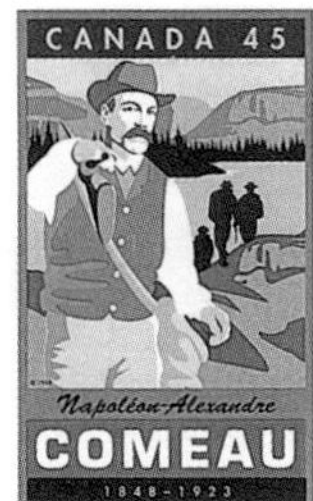

691 Napoleon-Alexandre Comeau (naturalist)

1998. Legendary Canadians. Multicoloured.
1821 45c. Type **691** 55 65
1822 45c. Phyllis Munday (mountaineer) 55 65
1823 45c. Bill Mason (film-maker) 55 65
1824 45c. Harry Red Foster (sports commentator) . . 55 65

1998. Canadian Art (11th series). As T **550**. Multicoloured.
1825 90c. "The Farmer's Family" (Bruno Bobak) . . . . . 80 1·10

692 Indian Wigwam

1998. Canadian Houses. Multicoloured.
1826 45c. Type **692** 50 60
1827 45c. Settler sod hut 50 60
1828 45c. Maison Saint-Gabriel (17th-century farmhouse), Quebec 50 60
1829 45c. Queen Anne style brick house, Ontario 50 60
1830 45c. Terrace of town houses 50 60
1831 45c. Prefabricated house . . 50 60
1832 45c. Veterans' houses . . . 50 60
1833 45c. Modern bungalow . . 50 60
1834 45c. Healthy House, Toronto 50 60

693 University of Ottawa

1998. 150th Anniv of University of Ottawa.
1835 **693** 45c. multicoloured . . . 50 50

1998. As T **681**, but without "POSTAGE POSTES" at top left. Self-adhesive gum, imperf (46c.) or ordinary gum, perf (others).
1839 **681** 45c. multicoloured . . . 65 75
1840 46c. multicoloured . . . 70 80
1836 55c. multicoloured . . . 80 80
1837 73c. multicoloured . . . 65 70
1838 95c. multicoloured . . . 1·25 1·40

694 Performing Animals

1998. Canadian Circus. Multicoloured.
1851 45c. Type **694** 90 90
1852 45c. Flying trapeze and acrobat on horseback . . 90 90
1853 45c. Lion tamer 90 90
1854 45c. Acrobats and trapeze artists 90 90
MS1855 133 × 133 mm. Nos. 1851/4 3·25 3·75

695 John Peters Humphrey (author of original Declaration draft)

1998. 50th Anniv of Universal Declaration of Human Rights.
1856 **695** 45c. multicoloured . . . 50 50

696 H.M.C.S. "Sackville" (corvette)

1998. 75th Anniv of Canadian Naval Reserve. Multicoloured.
1857 45c. Type **696** 50 65
1858 45c. H.M.C.S. "Shawinigan" (coastal defence vessel) . . 50 65

697 Angel blowing Trumpet — 698 Rabbit

1998. Christmas. Statues of Angels. Multicoloured.
1859 45c. Type **697** 60 20
1860b 52c. Adoring Angel . . . 70 55
1861b 90c. Angel at prayer . . . 1·40 1·75

1999. Chinese New Year ("Year of the Rabbit").
1862 **698** 46c. multicoloured . . . 50 50
MS1863 Circular 100 mm diam. **698** 95c. mult (40 × 40 mm) 1·75 1·50

No. **MS**1863 also exists with the "CHINA '99" World Stamp Exhibition, Beijing, logo overprinted in gold on the top of the margin.

699 Stylized Mask and Curtain — 701 "Marco Polo" (full-rigged ship)

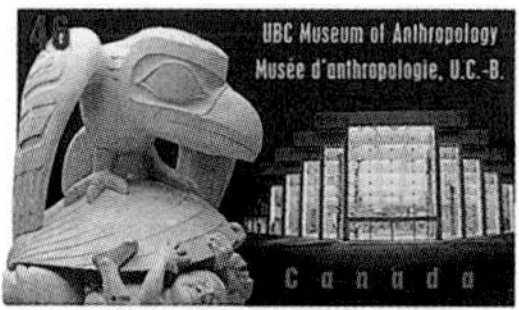

700 "The Raven and the First Men" (B. Reid) and The Great Hall

1999. 50th Anniv of Le Theatre du Rideau Vert.
1864 **699** 46c. multicoloured . . . 50 50

1999. Birds (4th series). As T **643**. Multicoloured. Ordinary or self-adhesive gum.
1865 46c. Northern goshawk . . 60 70
1866 46c. Red-winged blackbird 60 70
1867 46c. American goldfinch . . 60 70
1868 46c. Sandhill crane 60 70

1999. 50th Anniv of University of British Columbia Museum of Anthropology.
1873 **700** 46c. multicoloured . . . 50 50

1999. Canada–Australia Joint Issue. "Marco Polo" (emigrant ship).
1874 **701** 46c. multicoloured . . . 50 50
MS1875 160 × 95 mm. 85c. As No. 1728 of Australia. 46c. Type **701**. (No. **MS**1875 was sold at $1.25 in Canada) 1·75 1·75

No. **MS**1875 includes the "Australia '99" emblem on the sheet margin and was postally valid in Canada to the value of 46c.

The same miniature sheet was also available in Australia.

1999. Scenic Highways (3rd series). As T **667**. Multicoloured.
1876 46c. Route 132, Quebec, and hang-glider 55 60
1877 46c. Yellowhead Highway, Manitoba, and bison . . 55 60
1878 46c. Dempster Highway, Northwest Territories, and Indian village elder . . . 55 60
1879 46c. The Discovery Trail, Newfoundland, and whale's tailfin 55 60

702 Inuit Children and Landscape

1999. Creation of Nunavut Territory.
1880 **702** 46c. multicoloured . . . 50 50

703 Elderly Couple on Country Path

1999. International Year of Older Persons.
1881 **703** 46c. multicoloured . . . 50 50

704 Khanda (Sikh symbol) — 705 "Arethusa bulbosa" (orchid)

1999. Centenary of Sikhs in Canada.
1882 **704** 46c. multicoloured . . . 50 50

1999. 16th World Orchid Conference, Vancouver. Multicoloured.
1883 46c. Type **705** 60 60
1884 46c. "Amerorchis rotundifolia" 60 60
1885 46c. "Cypripedium pubescens" 60 60
1886 46c. "Platanthera psycodes" 60 60

706 Bookbinding — 707 "Northern Dancer" (racehorse)

1999. Traditional Trades. Multicoloured.

(a) Ordinary gum.
1887 1c. Type **706** 10 10
1888 2c. Decorative ironwork . . 10 10
1889 3c. Glass-blowing 10 10
1890 4c. Oyster farming 10 10
1891 5c. Weaving 10 10
1892 9c. Quilting 10 10
1893 10c. Wood carving 10 15
1894 25c. Leatherworking 20 25

(b) Self-adhesive.
1895 65c. Jewellery making (horiz) 60 65
1896 77c. Basket weaving (horiz) 70 75
1897 $1.25 Wood-carving (horiz) 1·10 1·25

1999. Canadian Horses. Multicoloured. Ordinary or self-adhesive gum.
1903 46c. Type **707** 60 70
1904 46c. "Kingsway Skoal" (rodeo horse) 60 70
1905 46c. "Big Ben" (show jumper) 60 70
1906 46c. "Armbro Flight" (trotter) 60 70

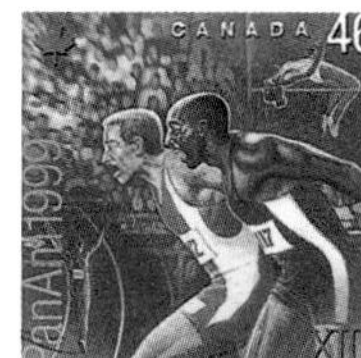

708 Logo engraved on Limestone — 709 Athletics

1999. 150th Anniv of Barreau du Quebec (Quebec lawyers' association).
1911 **708** 46c. multicoloured . . . 50 50

1999. Canadian Art (12th series). As T **550**. Mult.
1912 95c. "Coq licorne" (Jean Dallaire) . . . . 1·00 1·25

1999. 13th Pan-American Games, Winnipeg. Mult.
1913 46c. Type **709** 60 70
1914 46c. Cycling 60 70
1915 46c. Swimming 60 70
1916 46c. Football 60 70

1999. "China '99" International Stamp Exhibition, Beijing. Sheet 78 × 133 mm, containing Nos. 1883/6. Multicoloured.
MS1917 46c. Type **705**; 46c. Amerorchis rotundifolia; 46c. Cypripedium pubescens; 46c. Platanthera psycodes 2·25 2·75

710 Female Rower

1999. 23rd World Rowing Championships, St. Catharines.
1918 **710** 46c. multicoloured . . . 50 50

711 U.P.U. Emblem and World Map

1999. 125th Anniv of Universal Postal Union.
1919 **711** 46c. multicoloured . . . 50 50

712 De Havilland Mosquito F.B. VI

1999. 75th Anniv of Canadian Air Force. Mult.
1920 46c. Type **712** 50 55
1921 46c. Sopwith F.1 Camel . . 50 55
1922 46c. De Havilland Canada DHC-3 Otter 50 55
1923 46c. De Havilland Canada CC-108 Caribou 50 55
1924 46c. Canadair CL-28 Argus Mk 2 . . . . 50 55
1925 46c. Canadair (North American) F-86 Sabre 6 50 55
1926 46c. McDonnell Douglas CF-18 . . . . 50 55
1927 46c. Sopwith 5.F.1 Dolphin 50 55
1928 46c. Armstrong Whitworth Siskin IIIA 50 55
1929 46c. Canadian Vickers (Northrop) Delta II . . . 50 55
1930 46c. Sikorsky CH-124A Sea King helicopter 50 55
1931 46c. Vickers-Armstrong Wellington Mk II 50 55
1932 46c. Avro Anson Mk I . . 50 55
1933 46c. Canadair (Lockheed) CF-104G Starfighter . . . 50 55
1934 46c. Burgess-Dunne 50 55
1935 46c. Avro 504K 50 55

713 Fokker DR-1

1999. 50th Anniv of Canadian International Air Show. Multicoloured.
1936 46c. Type **713** 60 70
1937 46c. H101 Salto glider . . . 60 70
1938 46c. De Havilland DH100 Vampire Mk III 60 70
1939 46c. Wing walker on Stearman A-75 . . . . . 60 70

Nos. 1936/9 were printed together, se-tenant, forming a composite design which includes a nine-plane Snowbird formation of Canadair CT114 Tutor in the background.

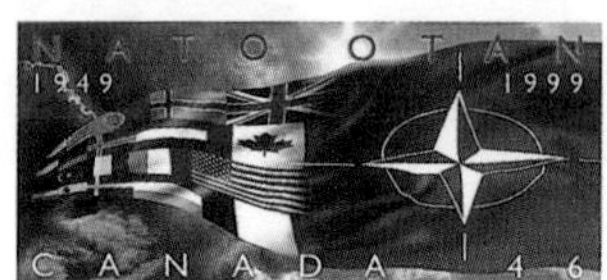

714 N.A.T.O. Emblem and National Flags

1999. 50th Anniv of North Atlantic Treaty Organization.
1940 **714** 46c. multicoloured . . . 50 50

715 Man ploughing on Book

1999. Centenary of Frontier College (workers' education organization).
1941 **715** 46c. multicoloured . . . 50 50

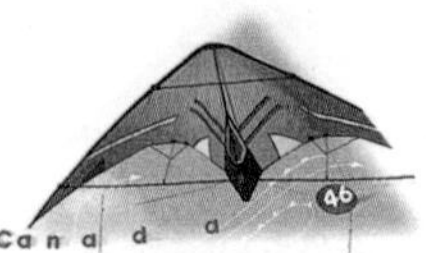
716 Master Control Sports Kite

1999. Stamp Collecting Month. Kites. Mult.
1942 46c. Type **716** 50 55
1943 46c. Indian Garden Flying Carpet (irregular rectangle, 35½ × 32 mm) 50 55
1944 46c. Gibson Girl box kite (horiz, 38½ × 25 mm) . . . 50 55
1945 46c. Dragon Centipede (oval, 39 × 29 mm) . . . 50 55

717 Boy holding Dove

1999. New Millennium. Three sheets, each 108 × 108 mm, containing T **717** and similar square designs in blocks of 4. Self-adhesive.
MS1946 – 46c. × 4 multicoloured 2·00 2·50
MS1947 **717** 55c. × 4 multicoloured 3·25 3·50
MS1948 – 95c. × 4 brown 3·75 4·50
DESIGNS: 46c. Holographic image of dove in flight; 95c. Dove with olive branch.

718 Angel playing Drum

1999. Christmas. Victorian Angels. Multicoloured.
1949 46c. Type **718** 60 20
1950 55c. Angel with toys 70 50
1951 95c. Angel with star . . . . 1·40 1·75

719 Portia White (singer)

1999. Millennium Collection (1st series). Entertainment and Arts. Miniature sheets, each 108 × 112 mm, containing T **719** and similar vert designs. Multicoloured.
MS1952 46c. Type **719**; 46c. Glenn Gould (pianist); 46c. Guy Lombardo (conductor of "Royal Canadians"); 46c. Félix Leclerc (musician, playwright and actor) 2·00 2·50
MS1953 46c. Artists looking at painting (Royal Canadian Academy of Arts); 46c. Cloud, stave and pencil marks (The Canada Council); 46c. Man with video camera (National Film Board of Canada); 46c. Newsreader (Canadian Broadcasting Corporation) 2·00 2·50
MS1954 46c. Calgary Stampede; 46c. Circus performers; 46c. Ice hockey (Hockey Night); 46c. Goalkeeper (Ice hockey live from The Forum) 2·00 2·50
MS1955 46c. IMAX cinema; 46c. Computer image (Softimage); 46c. Ted Rogers Sr ("Plugging in the Radio"); 46c. Sir William Stephenson (inventor of radio facsimile system) 2·00 2·50
MS1952/5 Set of 4 sheets 7·25 9·00
See also Nos. **MS**1959/62, **MS**1969/73 and **MS**1982/5.

720 Millennium Partnership Programme Logo

2000. Canada Millennium Partnership Programme.
1956 **720** 46c. red, green and blue 50 50

721 Chinese Dragon

2000. Chinese New Year ("Year of the Dragon").
1957 **721** 46c. multicoloured . . . 50 50
MS1958 150 × 85 mm. **721** 90c. multicoloured 1·00 1·25

2000. Millennium Collection (2nd series). Charities, Medical Pioneers, Peacekeepers and Social Reforms. Miniature sheets, each 108 × 112 mm, containing vert designs as T **719**. Multicoloured.
MS1959 46c. Providing equipment (Canadian International Development Agency); 46c. Dr. Lucille Teasdale (medical missionary); 46c. Terry Fox (Marathon of Hope); 46c. Delivering meal (Meals on Wheels) 1·60 2·00
MS1960 46c. Sir Frederick Banting (discovery of insulin); 46c. Armand Frappier (developer of BCG vaccine); 46c. Dr. Hans Selye (research into stress); 46c. "Dr. Maude Abbott" (pathologist) (M. Bell Eastlake) 1·60 2·00
MS1961 46c. Senator Raoul Dandurand (diplomat); 46c. Pauline Vanier and Elizabeth Smellie (nursing pioneers); 46c. Lester B. Pearson (diplomat); 46c. One-legged man (Ottawa Convention on Banning Landmines) 1·60 2·00
MS1962 46c. Nun and surgeon (medical care); 46c. "Women are persons" (sculpture by Barbara Paterson) (Appointment of women senators); 46c. Alphonse and Dorimène Desjardins (People's bank movement); 46c. Father Moses Coady (Adult education pioneer) 1·60 2·00
MS1959/62 Set of 4 sheets 5·75 7·25

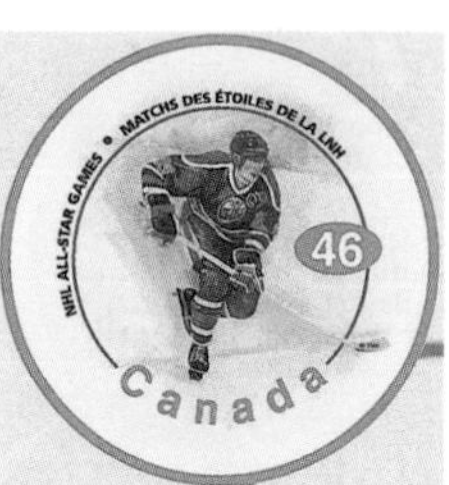

722 Wayne Gretzky (ice-hockey player)

2000. 50th National Hockey League All-Star Game. Multicoloured.
1963 46c. Type **722** 55 60
1964 46c. Gordie Howe (No. 9 in white jersey) 55 60
1965 46c. Maurice Richard (No. 9 in blue and red jersey) . . 55 60
1966 46c. Doug Harvey (No. 2) 55 60
1967 46c. Bobby Orr (No. 4) . . 55 60
1968 46c. Jacques Plante (No. 1) 55 60
See also Nos. 2052/7, 2118/23 and 2178/3.

2000. Millennium Collection (3rd series). First Inhabitants, Great Thinkers, Culture and Literary Legends, and Charitable Foundations. Miniature sheets, each 108 × 112 mm, containing vert designs as T **719**. Multicoloured.
MS1969 46c. Pontiac (Ottawa chief); 46c. Tom Longboat (long-distance runner); 46c. "Inuit Shaman" (sculpture by Paul Toolooktook); 46c. Shaman and patient (Indian medicine) 1·60 2·00
MS1970 46c. Prof. Marshall McLuhan (media philosopher); 46c. Northrop Frye (literary critic); 46c. Roger Lemelin (novelist); 46c. Prof. Hilda Marion Neatby (educator) 1·60 2·00
MS1971 46c. Bow of Viking longship (L'Anse aux Meadows World Heritage Site); 46c. Immigrant family (Pier 21 monument); 46c. Neptune mask (Neptune Theatre, Halifax); 46c. Auditorium and actor (The Stratford Festival) 1·60 2·00
MS1972 46c. W. O. Mitchell (writer); 46c. Gratien Gélinas (actor, producer and playwright); 46c. Text and fountain pen (Cercle du Livre de France); 46c. Harlequin and roses (Harlequin Books) 1·60 2·00
MS1973 46c. Hart Massey (Massey Foundation); 46c. Izaak Walton Killam and Dorothy Killam; 46f. Eric Lafferty Harvie (Glenbow Foundation); 46c. Macdonald Stewart Foundation 1·60 2·00
MS1969/73 Set of 5 sheets 7·25 9·00

2000. Birds (5th series). As T **643**. Multicoloured. Ordinary or self-adhesive gum.
1974 46c. Canadian warbler . . . 55 60
1975 46c. Osprey 55 60
1976 46c. Pacific diver ("Pacific Loon") 55 60
1977 46c. Blue jay 55 60

2000. Millennium Collection (4th series). Canadian Agriculture, Commerce and Technology. Miniature sheets, each 108 × 112 mm, containing vert designs as T **719**. Multicoloured.
MS1982 46c. Sir Charles Saunders (developer of Marquis wheat); 46c. Baby (Pablum baby food); 46c. Dr. Archibald Gowanlock Huntsman (frozen fish pioneer); 46c. Oven chips and field of potatoes (McCain Frozen Foods) 1·60 2·00
MS1983 46c. Early trader and Indian (Hudson's Bay Company); 46c. Satellite over earth (Bell Canada Enterprises); 46c. Jos. Louis biscuits and Vachon family (Vachon Family Bakery); 46c. Bread and eggs (George Weston Limited) 1·60 2·00
MS1984 46c. George Klein and cog wheels (inventor of electric wheelchair and micro-surgical staple gun); 46c. Abraham Gesner (developer of kerosene); 46c. Alexander Graham Bell (inventor of telephone); 46c. Joseph-Armand Bombadier (inventor of snowmobile) 1·60 2·00
MS1985 46c. Workers and steam locomotive (Rogers Pass rail tunnel); 46c. Manic 5 dam (Manicouagan River hydro-electric project); 46c. Mobile Servicing System for International Space Station (Canadian Space Program); 46c. CN Tower (World's tallest building) 1·60 2·00
MS1982/5 Set of 4 sheets 5·75 7·25

723 Judges and Supreme Court Building

2000. 125th Anniv of Supreme Court of Canada.
1986 **723** 46c. multicoloured . . . 50 50

724 Lethbridge Bridge, Synthetic Rubber Plant, X-ray of Heart Pacemaker and Microwave Radio System

2000. 75th Anniv of Ceremony for Calling of an Engineer.
1987 **724** 46c. multicoloured . . . 50 50
Each vertical pair completes the engineer's ring as shown on Type **274**.

725

2000. "Picture Postage" Greetings Stamps. Self-adhesive.
1988 **725** 46c. multicoloured . . . 50 50
No. 1988 was issued to include appropriate greetings labels which could be inserted into the rectangular space on each stamp.
See also Nos. 2045 and 2099.

726 Coastal-style Mailboxes in Autumn

2000. Traditional Rural Mailboxes. Multicoloured.
1989 46c. Type **726** 50 55
1990 46c. House and cow-shaped mailboxes in springtime 50 55
1991 46c. Tractor-shaped mailbox in summertime 50 55
1992 46c. Barn and duck-shaped mailboxes in winter . . . 50 55

727 Gorge and Fir Tree

2000. Canadian Rivers and Lakes. Multicoloured. Self-adhesive.
1993 55c. Type **727** 60 65
1994 55c. Lake and water lilies 60 65
1995 55c. Glacier and reflected mountains 60 65
1996 55c. Estuary and aerial view 60 65
1997 55c. Waterfall and forest edge 60 65
1998 95c. Iceberg and mountain river . . . . 95 1·10
1999 95c. Rapids and waterfall 95 1·10
2000 95c. Moraine and river . . . 95 1·10
2001 95c. Shallows and waves on lake . . . . 95 1·10
2002 95c. Forest sloping to waters edge and tree . . . . . . 95 1·10

728 Queen Elizabeth the Queen Mother with Roses

729 Teenager with Two Children

2000. Queen Elizabeth the Queen Mother's 100th Birthday.
2003 **728** 95c. multicoloured . . . 1·10 1·25

2000. Centenary of Boys and Girls Clubs of Canada.
2004 **729** 46c. multicoloured . . . 50 50

730 Clouds over Rockies and Symbol

2000. 57th General Conference Session of Seventh-day Adventist Church, Toronto.
2005 **730** 46c. multicoloured . . . 50 50

731 "Space Travellers and Canadian Flag" (Rosalie Anne Nardelli)

2000. "Stampin' the Future" (children's stamp design competition). Multicoloured.
2006 46c. Type **731** 60 60
2007 46c. "Travelling to the Moon" (Sarah Lutgen) . . 60 60

2008 46c. "Astronauts in shuttle" (Andrew Wright) 60 60
2009 46c. "Children completing Canada as jigsaw" (Christine Weera) 60 60
MS2010 114 × 90 mm. Nos. 2006/9 1·60 1·75

2000. Canadian Art (13th series). As T **550**. Mult.
2011 95c. "The Artist at Niagara, 1858" (Cornelius Krieghoff) . . . . 1·10 1·25

732 Tall Ships, Halifax Harbour

2000. Tall Ships Race. Multicoloured. Self-adhesive.
2012 46c. Type **732** 55 65
2013 46c. Tall ships, Halifax Harbour (face value top right) 55 65
Nos. 2012/13 are arranged as five se-tenant pairs on a background photograph of Halifax Harbour.

733 Workers, Factory and Transport

2000. Centenary of Department of Labour.
2014 **733** 46c. multicoloured . . . 50 50

734 Petro-Canada Sign, Oil Rig and Consumers

2000. 25th Anniv of Petro-Canada (oil company). Self-adhesive.
2015 **734** 46c. multicoloured . . . 50 50

735 Narwhal

2000. Whales. Multicoloured.
2016 46c. Type **735** 60 60
2017 46c. Blue whale (*Balaenoptera musculus*) 60 60
2018 46c. Bowhead whale (*Balaena mysticetus*) . . . 60 60
2019 46c. White whales (*Delphinapterus leucas*) . . 60 60
Nos. 2016/19 were printed together, se-tenant, with the backgrounds forming an overall composite design.

736

2000. "Picture Postage" Christmas Greetings. Self-adhesive.
2020 **736** 46c. multicoloured . . . 50 50
See also Nos. 2045/9 and 2099/103.

737 "The Nativity" (Susie Matthias)

738 Lieut.-Col. Sam Steele, Lord Strathcona's Horse

2000. Christmas. Religious Paintings by Mouth and Foot Artists. Multicoloured.
2021 46c. Type **737** 50 20
2022 55c. "The Nativity and Christmas Star" (Michael Guillemette) 65 60
2023 95c. "Mary and Joseph journeying to Bethlehem" (David Allan Carter) . . 1·25 1·50

2000. Canadian Regiments. Multicoloured.
2024 46c. Type **738** 55 60
2025 46c. Drummer, Voltigeurs de Quebec 55 60

739 Red Fox

740 Maple Leaves

2000. Wildlife. Multicoloured.
2026 60c. Type **739** 65 70
2027 75c. Grey wolf 80 95
2028 $1.05 White-tailed deer . . . 1·10 1·25

2000. Self-adhesive coil stamp.
2029 **740** 47c. multicoloured . . . 55 60
2030 48c. multicoloured . . . 40 45

2000. "Picture Postage" Greetings Stamps. As T **725** and **736**. Multicoloured. Self-adhesive.
2045 47c. Type **725** 50 50
2046 47c. Type **736** 50 50
2047 47c. Roses frame 50 50
2048 47c. Mahogany frame . . . 50 50
2049 47c. Silver frame 50 50

741 Green Jade Snake

2001. Chinese New Year. ("Year of the Snake").
2050 **741** 47c. multicoloured . . . 50 50
MS2051 112 × 75 mm. $1.05, Brown jade snake 1·10 1·40

2001. National Hockey League. All-Star Game Players (1st series). As T **722**. Multicoloured.
2052 47c. Jean Beliveau (wearing No. 4) 55 55
2053 47c. Terry Sawchuk (on one knee) 55 55
2054 47c. Eddie Shore (wearing No. 2) 55 55
2055 47c. Denis Potvin (wearing No. 5) 55 55
2056 47c. Bobby Hull (wearing No. 9) 55 55
2057 47c. Syl Apps (in Toronto jersey) 55 55
See also Nos. 2118/23 and 2178/83.

2001. Birds (6th series). As T **643**. Multicoloured. Ordinary or self-adhesive gum.
2058 47c. Golden eagle 55 55
2059 47c. Arctic tern 55 55
2060 47c. Rock ptarmigan . . . 55 55
2061 47c. Lapland bunting ("Lapland Longspur") . . 55 55

742 Highjumping

2001. 4th Francophonie Games. Multicoloured.
2066 47c. Type **742** 55 55
2067 47c. Folk dancing 55 55

743 Ice Dancing

2001. World Figure Skating Championships, Vancouver. Multicoloured.
2068 47c. Type **743** 55 55
2069 47c. Pairs 55 55
2070 47c. Men's singles 55 55
2071 47c. Women's singles . . . 55 55

744 3d. Beaver Stamp of 1851

2001. 150th Anniv of the Canadian Postal Service.
2072 **744** 47c. multicoloured . . . 50 50

745 Toronto Blue Jay Emblem, Maple Leaf and Baseball

2001. 25th Season of the Toronto Blue Jays (baseball team). Self-adhesive.
2073 **745** 47c. multicoloured . . . 50 50

746 North and South America on Globe

748 Christ on Palm Sunday and Khachkar (stone cross)

747 Butchart Gardens, British Columbia

2001. Summit of the Americas, Quebec.
2074 **746** 47c. multicoloured . . . 50 50

2001. Tourist Attractions (1st series). Multicoloured. Self-adhesive.
2075 60c. Type **747** 60 65
2076 60c. Apple Blossom Festival, Nova Scotia 60 65
2077 60c. White Pass and Yukon Route 60 65
2078 60c. Sugar Bushes, Quebec 60 65
2079 60c. Court House, Niagra-on-the-Lake, Ontario . . 60 65
2080 $1.05 The Forks, Winnipeg, Manitoba . . . . 1·10 1·25
2081 $1.05 Barkerville, British Columbia . . . . 1·10 1·25
2082 $1.05 Canadian Tulip Festival, Ontario . . . . 1·10 1·25
2083 $1.05 Auyuittuq National Park, Nunavut . . . . . 1·10 1·25
2084 $1.05 Signal Hill, St. John's, Newfoundland . . . . . 1·10 1·25
See also Nos. 2143/52.

2001. 1700th Anniv of Armenian Church.
2085 **748** 47c. multicoloured . . . 40 45

749 Cadets, Mackenzie Building and Military Equipment

2001. 125th Anniv of Royal Military College of Canada.
2086 **749** 47c. multicoloured . . . 40 45

750 Pole-vaulting

751 "Pierre Trudeau" (Myfanwy Pavelic)

2001. 8th International Amateur Athletic Federation World Championships, Edmonton. Multicoloured.
2087 47c. Type **750** 40 45
2088 47c. Sprinting 40 45

2001. Pierre Trudeau (former Prime Minister) Commemoration.
2089 **751** 47c. multicoloured . . . 40 45
MS2090 128 × 155 mm. No. 2090 × 4 1·60 1·75

752 "Morden Centennial" Rose (⅔-size illustration)

2001. Canadian Roses. Multicoloured. Self-adhesive.
2091 47c. Type **752** 40 45
2092 47c. "Agnes" 40 45
2093 47c. "Champlain" 40 45
2094 47c. "Canadian White Star" 40 45
MS2095 145 × 90 mm. Nos. 2091/4 1·60 1·75

753 Ottawa Chief Hassaki addressing Peace Delegates

2001. 300th Anniv of Great Peace Treaty of Montreal between American Indians and New France.
2096 **753** 47c. multicoloured . . . 40 45

2001. Canadian Art (14th series). As T **550**. Multicoloured.
2097 $1.05 "The Space Between Columns 21 (Italian)" (Jack Shadbolt) . . . . . 95 1·00

754 Clown juggling with Crutches and Handicapped Boy

2001. The Shriners (charitable organization) Commemoration.
2098 **754** 47c. multicoloured . . .

755 Toys and Flowers

2001. "Picture Postage" Greetings Stamps. Frames as Nos. 2045/7 and 2049, but each inscr "Domestic Lettermail Postes-lettres du regime interieur". Multicoloured. Self-adhesive.
2099 – As Type **725** 40 45
2100 – As Type **736** 40 45
2101 – Type **755** 40 45
2102 – Roses frame 40 45
2103 – Silver frame 40 45

756 Jean Gascon and Jean-Louis Roux (founders of Theatre du Nouveau Monde, Montreal)

2001. Theatre Anniversaries. Multicoloured.
2104 47c. Type **756** (50th anniv) 40 45
2105 47c. Ambrose Small (founder of Grand Theatre, London, Ontario) (centenary) . . . 40 45

757 Hot Air Balloons

2001. Stamp Collecting Month. Hot Air Balloons. Multicoloured, background colours given below. Self-adhesive.
2106 47c. Type **757** (green background) 40 45
2107 47c. Balloons with lavender background 40 45
2108 47c. Balloons with mauve background 40 45
2109 47c. Balloons with bistre background 40 45

758 Horse-drawn Sleigh and Christmas Lights

2001. Christmas. Festive Lights. Multicoloured.
2110 47c. Type **758** 40 45
2111 60c. Ice skaters and Christmas lights 55 60
2112 $1.05 Children with snowman and Christmas lights . . . . 95 1·00

759 Pattern of Ys Logo

2001. 150th Anniv of Y.M.C.A. in Canada.
2113 **759** 47c. multicoloured . . . 40 45

760 Statues from Canadian War Memorial, Ottawa and Badge

2001. 75th Anniv of Royal Canadian Legion.
2114 **760** 47c. multicoloured . . . 40 45

761 Queen Elizabeth II and Maple Leaf

2002. Golden Jubilee.
2115 **761** 48c. multicoloured . . . 40 45

762 Horse and Bamboo Leaves **763** Speed Skating

2002. Chinese New Year ("Year of the Horse"). Multicoloured.
2116 **762** 48c. multicoloured . . . 40 45
MS2117 102 × 102 mm. $1.25, Horse and peach blossom 1·10 1·25

2002. National Hockey League. All-Star Game Players (2nd series). As T **722**. Multicoloured.
2118 48c. Tim Horton (wearing Maple Leaf No. 7 jersey) 40 45
2119 48c. Guy Lafleur (wearing Canadiens No. 10 jersey) 40 45
2120 48c. Howie Morenz (wearing Canadiens jersey and brown gloves) 40 45
2121 48c. Glenn Hall (wearing Chicago Blackhawks jersey) 40 45
2122 48c. Red Kelly (wearing Maple Leaf No. 4 jersey) 40 45
2123 48c. Phil Esposito (wearing Boston Bruins No. 7 jersey) 40 45

2002. Winter Olympic Games, Salt Lake City. Multicoloured.
2124 48c. Type **763** 40 45
2125 48c. Curling 40 45
2126 48c. Aerial skiing 40 45
2127 48c. Women's ice hockey . . 40 45

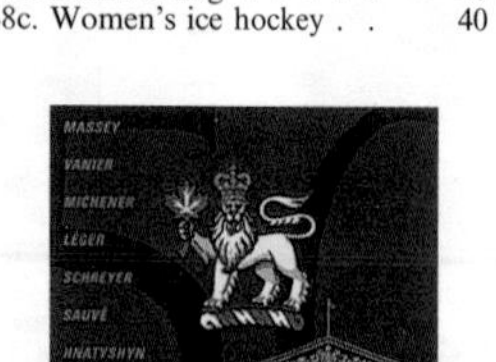

764 Lion Symbol of Governor General and Rideau Hall, Ottawa

2002. 50th Anniv of First Canadian Governor-General.
2128 **764** 48c. multicoloured . . . 40 45

765 University of Manitoba (125th Anniv)

2002. Canadian Universities' Anniversaries. Mult.
2129 48c. Type **765** 40 45
2130 48c. Universite Laval, Quebec (150th anniv of charter) 40 45
2131 48c. Trinity College, Toronto (150th anniv of foundation) 40 45
2132 48c. Saint Mary's University, Halifax (bicent) 40 45
See also Nos. 2190/1.

2002. Canadian Art (15th series). As T **550**. Multicoloured.
2133 $1.25 "Church and Horse" (Alex Colville) . . . . . 1·10 1·25

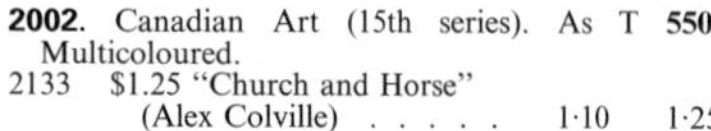

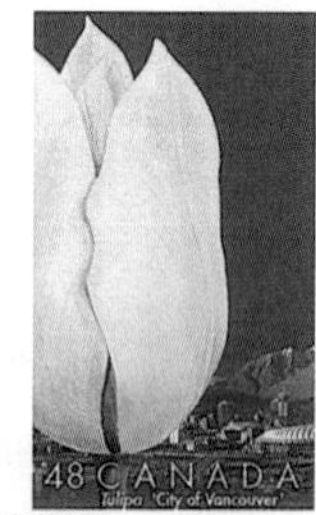

766 "City of Vancouver" Tulip and Vancouver Skyline

2002. 50th Canadian Tulip Festival, Ottawa. Tulips. Multicoloured. Self-adhesive.
2134 48c. Type **766** 40 45
2135 48c. "Monte Carlo" and Dows Lake tulip beds . . 40 45
2136 48c. "Ottawa" and National War Memorial 40 45
2137 48c. "The Bishop" and Ottawa Hospital 40 45

767 *Dendronepthea gigantea* and *Dendronepthea* (coral)

2002. Canada–Hong Kong Joint Issue. Corals. Multicoloured.
2138 48c. Type **767** 40 45
2139 48c. *Tubastrea, Echinogorgia* and island 40 45
2140 48c. North Atlantic pink tree coral, Pacific orange cup and North Pacific horn coral 40 45
2141 48c. North Atlantic giant orange tree coral and black coral 40 45
MS2142 161 × 87 mm. Nos. 2138/41 1·60 1·75

2002. Tourist Attractions (2nd series). As T **747**. Multicoloured. Self-adhesive.
2143 65c. Yukon Quest Sled Dog Race 60 65
2144 65c. Icefields Parkway, Alberta 60 65
2145 65c. Train in Agawa Canyon, Northern Ontario 60 65
2146 65c. Old Port, Montreal . . 60 65
2147 65c. Saw mill, Kings Landing, New Brunswick 60 65
2148 $1.25 Northern Lights, Northwest Territories . . 1·10 1·25
2149 $1.25 Stanley Park, British Columbia . . . . . . 1·10 1·25
2150 $1.25 Head-Smashed-In Buffalo Jump, Alberta . . 1·10 1·25
2151 $1.25 Saguenay Fjord, Quebec . . . . 1·10 1·25
2152 $1.25 Lighthouse, Peggy's Cove, Nova Scotia . . . 1·10 1·25

768 "Embacle" (Charles Daudelin)

2002. Sculptures. Multicoloured.
2153 48c. Type **768** 40 45
2154 48c. "Lumberjacks" (Leo Mol) 40 45

769 1899 Queen Victoria 2c. Stamp, Stonewall Post Office and Postmark

2002. Centenary of Canadian Postmasters and Assistants Association.
2155 **769** 48c. multicoloured . . . 40 45

770 World Youth Day Logo

2002. 17th World Youth Day, Toronto. Self-adhesive.
2156 **770** 48c. multicoloured . . . 40 45

2002. "Amphilex 2002" International Stamp Exhibition, Amsterdam. Ordinary gum.
MS2157 160 × 97 mm. As Nos. 2134/7 1·60 1·75

771 Hands gripping Rope and P.S.I. Logo

2002. Public Services International World Congress, Ottawa.
2158 **771** 48c. multicoloured . . . 40 45

772 Tree in Four Seasons

2002. 75th Anniv of Public Pensions.
2159 **772** 48c. multicoloured . . . 40 45

773 Mount Elbrus, Russia

2002. International Year of Mountains. Multicoloured. Self-adhesive.
2160 48c. Type **773** 40 45
2161 48c. Puncak Jaya, Indonesia 40 45
2162 48c. Mount Everest, Nepal 40 45
2163 48c. Mount Kilimanjaro, Tanzania 40 45
2164 48c. Vinson Massif, Antarctica 40 45
2165 48c. Mount Aconcagua, Argentina 40 45
2166 48c. Mount McKinley, U.S.A. 40 45
2167 48c. Mount Logan, Canada 40 45

774 Teacher writing on Board

2002. World Teachers' Day.
2168 **774** 48c. multicoloured . . . 40 45

775 Frieze from Toronto Stock Exchange and Globe

2002. 150th Anniv of Toronto Stock Exchange.
2169 **775** 48c. multicoloured . . . 40 45

776 Sir Sandford Fleming, Map of Canada and *Iris* (cable ship)

2002. Communications Centenaries. Multicoloured.
2170 48c. Type **776** (opening of Pacific Cable) 40 45
2171 48c. Guglielmo Marconi, Map of Canada and wireless equipment (first Transatlantic radio message) 40 45

777 "Genesis" (painting by Daphne Odjig)

2002. Christmas. Aboriginal Art. Multicoloured.
2172 48c. Type **777** 40 45
2173 65c. "Winter Travel" (painting by Cecil Youngfox) 60 65
2174 $1.25 "Mary and Child" (sculpture by Irene Katak Angutitaq) . . . . 1·10 1·25

778 Conductor's Hands and Original Orchestra

2002. Centenary of Quebec Symphony Orchestra.
2175 **778** 48c. multicoloured 40 45

779 Sculpture of Ram's Head

2003. Chinese New Year ("Year of the Ram"). Multicoloured.
2176 48c. Type **779** 40 45
MS2177 125 × 103 mm. $1.25 Sculpture of goat's head (33 × 57 mm) 1·00 1·25

2003. National Hockey League. All-Star Game Players (3rd series). As T **722**. Multicoloured. Ordinary or self-adhesive.
2178 48c. Frank Mahovlich (wearing Maple Leaf No. 27 jersey) 40 45
2179 48c. Raymond Bourque (wearing Boston Bruins No. 77 jersey) 40 45
2180 48c. Serge Savard (wearing Canadiens No.18 jersey) 40 45
2181 48c. Stan Mikita (wearing Chicago Blackhawks No. 21 jersey) 40 45
2182 48c. Mike Bossy (wearing New York Islanders No. 22 jersey) 40 45
2183 48c. Bill Durnan (wearing Canadiens jersey and brown gloves) 40 45

2003. Canadian Universities' Anniversaries. As T **765** but vert. Multicoloured.
2190 48c. Bishop's University, Quebec (150th anniv of university status) 40 45
2191 48c. University of Western Ontario, London (125th anniv) 40 45

780 Leach's Storm Petrel

2003. Bird Paintings by John Audubon. Multicoloured. Ordinary gum.
2195 48c. Type **780** 40 45
2196 48c. Brent goose ("Brant") 40 45
2197 48c. Great cormorant 40 45
2198 48c. Common murre 40 45

(b) Self-adhesive.
2199 65c. Gyrfalcon (vert) 55 60

781 Ranger looking through Binoculars

2003. 60th Anniv of Canadian Rangers.
2200 **781** 48c. multicoloured 40 45

782 Greek Figure with Dove

2003. 75th Anniv of American Hellenic Educational Progressive Association in Canada.
2201 **782** 48c. multicoloured 40 45

OFFICIAL STAMPS

1949. Optd **O.H.M.S.**
O162 **111** 1c. green (postage) 2·00 2·50
O163 **112** 2c. brown 12·00 12·00
O164 – 3c. purple (No. 378) 1·25 1·75
O165 **112** 4c. red 2·25 1·75
O166 – 10c. green (No. 402) 4·00 15
O167 – 14c. brown (No. 403) 4·50 2·50
O168 – 20c. grey (No. 404) 12·00 60
O169 – 50c. green (No. 405) £160 £120
O170 – $1 purple (No. 406) 45·00 48·00
O171 – 7c. blue (No. 407) (air) 24·00 7·00

1949. Optd **O.H.M.S.**
O172 **135** 1c. green 1·50 1·00
O173 – 2c. brown (No. 415) 2·50 1·50
O174 – 3c. purple (No. 416) 1·75 1·00
O175 – 4c. red (No. 417) 2·00 15
O176 – 5c. blue (No. 418) 3·50 2·00
O177 **141** 50c. green 32·00 28·00

1950. Optd **G.**
O178 **135** 1c. green (postage) 1·00 10
O179 – 2c. brown (No. 415) 2·00 2·25
O180 – 2c. green (No. 415a) 1·75 10
O181 – 3c. purple (No. 416) 2·00 10
O183 – 4c. red (No. 417) 2·00 20
O184 – 5c. blue (No. 418) 2·75 80
O193 **153** 7c. blue 1·75 2·00
O185 – 10c. green (No. 402) 3·00 10
O191 **142** 10c. purple 2·75 10
O186 – 14c. brown (No. 403) 13·00 4·00
O187 – 20c. grey (No. 404) 23·00 30
O194 – 20c. grey (No. 441) 2·00 10
O188 **141** 50c. green 12·00 12·00
O189 – $1 purple (No. 406) 65·00 65·00
O192 – $1 blue (No. 433) 60·00 65·00
O190 – 7c. blue (No. 407) (air) 24·00 13·00

1953. First Queen Elizabeth II stamps optd **G.**
O196 **158** 1c. brown 15 10
O197 2c. green 20 10
O198 3c. red 20 10
O199 4c. violet 30 10
O200 5c. blue 30 10

1953. Pictorial stamps optd **G.**
O206 **165** 10c. brown 40 10
O207 – 20c. green (No. 488) 2·25 10
O201 **160** 50c. green 3·00 2·00
O195 **154** $1 black 10·00 11·00

1955. Second Queen Elizabeth II stamps optd **G.**
O202 **161** 1c. brown 40 20
O203 2c. green 15 10
O204 4c. violet 40 10
O205 5c. blue 15 10

1963. Third Queen Elizabeth II stamps optd **G.**
O208 **215** 1c. brown 40 3·75
O209 2c. green 40 3·50
O210 4c. red 40 2·00
O211 5c. blue 40 1·00

OFFICIAL SPECIAL DELIVERY STAMPS

1950. Optd **O.H.M.S.**
OS20 10c. green (No. S15) 17·00 23·00

1950. Optd **G.**
OS21 10c. green (No. S15) 26·00 28·00

POSTAGE DUE STAMPS

D 1 D 2

1906.
D1 **D 1** 1c. violet 8·50 2·75
D3 2c. violet 19·00 1·00
D5 4c. violet 45·00 50·00
D7 5c. violet 25·00 3·25
D8 10c. violet 32·00 18·00

1930.
D 9 **D 2** 1c. violet 8·50 10·00
D10 2c. violet 7·50 1·90
D11 4c. violet 15·00 6·50
D12 5c. violet 16·00 28·00
D13 10c. violet 65·00 65·00

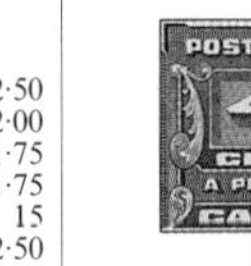

D 3 D 4

1933.
D14 **D 3** 1c. violet 9·50 14·00
D15 2c. violet 7·50 4·50
D16 4c. violet 12·00 14·00
D17 10c. violet 24·00 30·00

1935.
D18 **D 4** 1c. violet 80 10
D19 2c. violet 1·50 10
D20 3c. violet 4·50 5·00
D21 4c. violet 1·50 10
D22 5c. violet 3·50 1·75
D23 6c. violet 2·25 3·00
D24 10c. violet 70 10

D 5

1967. (a) Size 21 × 17½ mm.
D25 **D 5** 1c. red 1·75 4·00
D26 2c. red 1·00 1·00
D27 3c. red 1·00 4·25
D28 4c. red 2·75 1·25
D29 5c. red 4·25 4·50
D30 6c. red 1·60 3·75
D31 10c. red 2·00 2·50

(b) Size 19½ × 16 mm.
D32 **D 5** 1c. red 30 30
D33 2c. red 1·00 2·75
D34 3c. red 2·50 3·00
D35 4c. red 30 60
D36a 5c. red 30 1·75
D37 6c. red 2·75 3·75
D38 8c. red 30 45
D39 10c. red 30 45
D40 12c. red 30 50
D41 16c. red 1·75 3·25
D42 20c. red 30 1·25
D43 24c. red 30 1·75
D44 50c. red 40 2·25

REGISTRATION STAMPS

R 1

1875.
R1 **R 1** 2c. orange 60·00 1·00
R6 5c. green 80·00 1·25
R8 8c. blue £325 £225

SPECIAL DELIVERY STAMPS

S 1

1898.
S2 **S 1** 10c. green 45·00 65·00

S 2

1922.
S4 **S 2** 20c. red 35·00 6·50

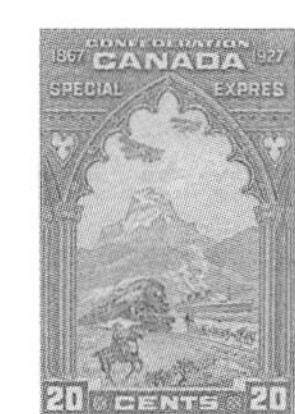
S 3 Mail-carrying, 1867 and 1927

1927. 60th Anniv of Confederation.
S5 **S 3** 20c. orange 11·00 10·00

S 4

1930.
S6 **S 4** 20c. red 42·00 7·00

1932. As Type **S 4**, but inscr "CENTS" instead of "TWENTY CENTS".
S7 20c. red 45·00 15·00

S 5 Allegory of Progress

1935.
S8 **S 5** 20c. red 3·50 2·75

S 6 Canadian Coat of Arms

1938.
S 9 **S 6** 10c. green 18·00 3·25
S10 20c. red 40·00 25·00

1939. Surch **10 10** and bars.
S11 **S 6** 10c. on 20c. red 10·00 9·00

S 8 Coat of Arms and Flags

S 9 Lockheed L.18 Lodestar

1942.
S12 **S 8** 10c. green (postage) 6·00 30
S13 **S 9** 16c. blue (air) 5·50 45
S14 17c. blue 4·25 55

1946.
S15 10c. green (postage) 3·00 30
S16 17c. blue (air) 4·50 4·50
DESIGNS: 10c. As Type **S 8** but with wreath of leaves; 17c. As Type **S 9** but with Canadair DC-4M North Star airplane.

CANAL ZONE Pt. 22

Territory adjacent to the Panama Canal leased by the U.S.A. from the Republic of Panama. The U.S. Canal Zone postal service closed on 30 September 1979.

1904. 100 centavos = 1 peso.
1906. 100 centesimos = 1 balboa.
1924. 100 cents = 1 dollar (U.S.).

1904. Stamps of Panama (with **PANAMA** optd twice) optd **CANAL ZONE** horiz in one line.
1 **5** 2c. red (No. 54) £375 £300
2 5c. blue (No. 55) £160 £120
3 10c. orange (No. 56) £275 £160

1904. Stamps of the United States of 1902 optd **CANAL ZONE PANAMA.**
4 **103** 1c. green . . . . 22·00 16·00
5 **117** 2c. red . . . . 20·00 17·00
6 **107** 5c. blue . . . . 70·00 45·00
7 **109** 8c. violet . . . . £120 60·00
8 **110** 10c. brown . . . . £100 65·00

Stamps of Panama overprinted.

1904. 1905 stamps optd **CANAL ZONE** in two lines.
9 **38** 1c. green . . . . 1·90 1·60
10 2c. red . . . . 3·25 1·75

1904. Stamps with **PANAMA** optd twice, optd **CANAL ZONE** in two lines or surch also.
11 **5** 2c. red (No. 54) . . . . . . 5·00 3·50
12 5c. blue (No. 55) . . . . . . 5·50 2·50
14 8c. on 50c. brown (No. 65) 22·00 16·00
13 10c. orange (No. 56) . . . . 15·00 8·50

1906. 1892 stamps surch **PANAMA** on both sides and **CANAL ZONE** and new value in centre between bars.
21 **5** 1c. on 20c. violet (No. 64) . . 1·25 1·10
22 2c. on 1p. red (No. 66) . . . 1·90 1·90

1906. 1906 stamps optd **CANAL ZONE** vert.
26 **42** 1c. black and green . . . . 1·60 85
27 **43** 2c. black and red . . . . . 2·25 95
28 **45** 5c. black and blue . . . . . 4·50 1·50
29 **46** 8c. black and purple . . . . 15·00 5·50
30 **47** 10c. black and violet . . . . 14·00 5·50

1909. 1909 stamps optd **CANAL ZONE** vert.
35 **48** 1c. black and green . . . . 3·00 1·25
36 **49** 2c. black and red . . . . . 3·00 1·25
37 **51** 5c. black and blue . . . . . 11·50 3·00
38 **52** 8c. black and purple . . . . 8·50 4·00
43 **53** 10c. black and purple . . . 38·00 6·75

1911. Surch **CANAL ZONE 10 cts.**
53 **38** 10c. on 13c. grey . . . . . 4·50 1·75

1914. Optd **CANAL ZONE** vert.
54 **38** 10c. grey . . . . 42·00 9·75

1915. 1915 and 1918 stamps optd **CANAL ZONE** vert.
55 1c. black and green (No. 162) 6·75 5·00
56 2c. black and red (No. 163) . . 7·75 3·25
57 5c. black and blue (No. 166) 9·00 5·00
58 10c. black & orange (No. 167) 18·00 11·00
59 12c. black & violet (No. 178) 13·50 4·75
60 15c. black & blue (No. 179) 42·00 18·00
61 24c. black & brown (No. 180) 60·00 16·00
62 50c. black & orange (No. 181) £375 £190
63 1b. black & violet (No. 182) £160 65·00

1921. 1921 stamps optd **CANAL ZONE** vert.
64 **65** 1c. green . . . . 3·00 1·00
65 – 2c. red (No. 186) . . . . . 2·25 1·10
66 **68** 5c. blue . . . . 8·50 3·50
67 – 10c. violet (No. 191) . . . . 14·00 5·75
68 – 15c. blue (No. 192) . . . . 38·00 13·50
69 – 24c. sepia (No. 194) . . . . 55·00 17·00
70 – 50c. black (No. 195) . . . . £120 80·00

1924. 1924 stamps optd **CANAL ZONE** vert.
72 **72** 1c. green . . . . 8·50 3·50
73 2c. red . . . . 6·50 2·25

1924. Stamps of the United States of 1922 optd **CANAL ZONE** horiz.
74 ½c. sepia (No. 559) 95 60
75 1c. green (No. 602) . . . . . 1·10 45
76 1½c. brown (No. 603) . . . . 1·50 1·00
103 2c. red (No. 604) . . . . . . 2·00 75
87 3c. violet (No. 638a) . . . . 3·00 2·25
88 5c. blue (No. 640) . . . . . 3·00 1·75
106 10c. orange (No. 645) . . . . 14·00 5·00
90 12c. purple (No. 693) . . . . 18·00 11·50
141 14c. blue (No. 695) . . . . . 3·75 2·25
92 15c. grey (No. 696) . . . . . 5·50 3·50
93 17c. black (No. 697) . . . . 3·00 2·40
94 20c. red (No. 698) . . . . . 6·00 2·50
95 30c. sepia (No. 700) . . . . 4·00 3·00
84 50c. mauve (No. 701) . . . . 60·00 35·00
97 $1 brown (No. 579) . . . . £100 45·00

1926. Liberty Bell stamp of United States optd **CANAL ZONE.**
101 **177** 2c. red . . . . 3·50 3·00

22 Gen. Gorgas

24 Panama Canal under Construction

1928.
107 **22** 1c. green 10 10
108 – 2c. red 20 15
109 **24** 5c. blue . . . . 1·90 35
110 – 10c. orange 30 20
111 – 12c. purple 60 50
112 – 14c. blue 80 80
113 – 15c. grey 60 40
114 – 20c. brown 50 20
115 – 30c. black 80 80
116 – 50c. mauve . . . . 1·25 55
PORTRAITS: 2c. Gen. Goethals. 10c. H. F. Hodges. 12c. Col. Gaillard. 14c. Gen. Sibert. 15c. Jackson Smith. 20c. Admiral Rousseau. 30c. Col. S. B. Williamson. 50c. Governor Blackburn.

1929. Air. Stamps of 1928 surch **AIR MAIL** and value.
124 – 10c. on 50c. mauve . . . . 7·50 5·50
117 **22** 15c. on 1c. green . . . . . 7·50 4·50
125 – 20c. on 2c. red . . . . . . 4·50 1·50
119 – 25c. on 2c. red . . . . . . 3·00 1·75

36 Steamer, Panama Canal

1931. Air.
126 **36** 4c. purple 55 65
127 5c. green 45 30
128 6c. brown 60 35
129 10c. orange 70 30
130 15c. blue . . . . 1·00 25
131 20c. violet . . . . 2·00 25
132 30c. red . . . . 2·75 1·00
133 40c. yellow . . . . 2·50 1·00
134 $1 black . . . . 8·50 1·75

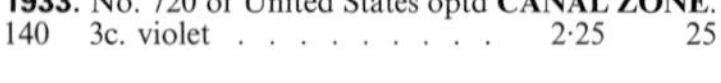

1933. No. 720 of United States optd **CANAL ZONE.**
140 3c. violet . . . . 2·25 25

38 Gen. Goethals

45 Balboa (before construction)

1934. 20th Anniv of Opening of Panama Canal.
142 **38** 3c. violet 15 10

1939. 25th Anniv of Opening of Panama Canal and 10th Anniv of Canal Zone Airmail Service. (a) Postage. As T **45**. Inscr "25TH ANNIVERSARY 1939 OPENING PANAMA CANAL 1914".
149 **45** 1c. green . . . . 1·25 75
150 – 2c. red 50 40
151 – 3c. violet . . . . 1·25 50
152 – 5c. blue . . . . 1·40 95
153 – 6c. orange . . . . 4·25 2·75
154 – 7c. black . . . . 2·75 1·40
155 – 8c. green . . . . 5·00 3·00
156 – 10c. blue . . . . 5·00 2·25
157 – 11c. green . . . . 14·00 10·00
158 – 12c. purple . . . . 7·00 5·50
159 – 14c. violet . . . . 16·00 10·00
160 – 15c. olive . . . . 22·00 11·00
161 – 18c. red . . . . 16·00 16·00
162 – 20c. brown . . . . 20·00 9·50
163 – 25c. orange . . . . 14·00 14·00
164 – 50c. purple . . . . 18·00 3·75
DESIGNS: 2c. Balboa (after construction); 3c., 5c. Gaillard Cut; 6c., 7c. Bas Obispo; 8c., 10c. Gatun Locks; 11c., 12c. Canal Channel; 14c., 15c. Gamboa; 18c., 20c. Pedro Miguel Locks; 25c.50c. Gatun Spillway.

(b) Air. Inscr "TENTH ANNIVERSARY AIR MAIL" and "25TH ANNIVERSARY OPENING PANAMA CANAL".
143 5c. black . . . . 3·25 3·00
144 10c. violet . . . . 3·25 2·25
145 15c. brown . . . . 3·25 1·10
146 25c. blue . . . . 16·00 11·00
147 30c. red . . . . 12·00 8·00
148 $1 green . . . . 30·00 30·00
DESIGNS—HORIZ: As Type **45**: 5c. Douglas DC-3 airplane over Sosa Hill; 10c. Douglas DC-3 airplane, Sikorsky S-42A flying boat and map of Central America; 15c. Sikorsky S-42A and Fort Amador; 25c. Sikorsky S-42A at Cristobal Harbour, Manzanillo Island; 30c. Sikorsky S-42A over Culebra Cut. $1 Sikorsky S-42A and palm trees.

1939. Stamps of United States (1938) optd **CANAL ZONE.**
165 **276** ½c. orange 15 10
166 – 1½c. brown (No. 801) . . 15 10

67 John F. Stevens

69 Northern Coati and Barro Colorado Island

1946. Portraits.
188 – ½c. red (Davis) 30 15
189 – 1½c. brown (Magoon) . . . 30 15
190 – 2c. red (Theodore Roosevelt) 15 10
191 **67** 5c. blue 30 10
192 – 25c. green (Wallace) . . . 1·10 60

1948. 25th Anniv of Establishment of Canal Zone Biological Area.
194 **69** 10c. black . . . . 1·40 80

70 "Arriving at Chagres on the Atlantic Side."

74 Western Hemisphere

1949. Centenary of the Gold Rush.
195 **70** 3c. blue 60 30
196 – 6c. violet 80 50
197 – 12c. green . . . . 1·40 1·00
198 – 18c. mauve . . . . 2·75 2·00
DESIGNS: 6c. "Up the Chagres River to Las Cruces"; 12c. "Las Cruces Trail to Panama"; 18c. "Leaving Panama for San Francisco".

1951. Air.
199 **74** 4c. purple 75 25
200 5c. green . . . . 1·00 60
201 6c. brown 50 15
202 7c. olive . . . . 1·00 35
210 8c. red 40 20
203 10c. orange . . . . 1·00 35
204 15c. purple . . . . 3·50 1·75
205 21c. blue . . . . 7·00 2·75
206 25c. yellow . . . . 9·50 2·25
207 31c. red . . . . 7·25 3·25
208 35c. blue . . . . 6·00 2·50
209 80c. black . . . . 4·50 90

75 Labourers in Gaillard Cut

76 Locomotive "Nueva Granada", 1852

1951. West Indian Panama Canal Labourers.
211 **75** 10c. red . . . . 6·75 2·75

1955. Centenary of Panama Railway.
212 **76** 3c. violet . . . . 2·75 90

77 Gorgas Hospital

1957. 75th Anniv of Gorgas Hospital.
213 **77** 3c. black on green 40 30

78 "Ancon II" (liner)

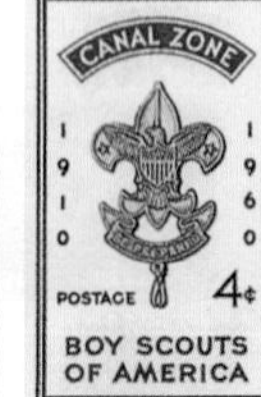

80 "First Class" Scout Badge

79 Roosevelt Medal and Map of Canal Zone

1958.
214 **78** 4c. turquoise 45 20

1958. Birth Centenary of Theodore Roosevelt.
215 **79** 4c. brown 40 25

1960. 50th Anniv of American Boy Scout Movement.
216 **80** 4c. ochre, red and blue . . 50 30

81 Administration Building, Balboa

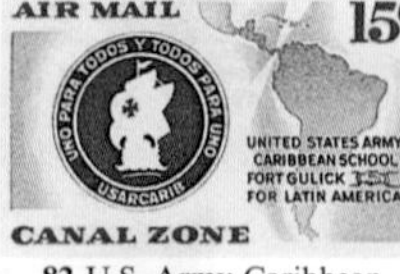

82 U.S. Army Caribbean School Crest

1960.
217 **81** 4c. purple 20 15

1961. Air.
221 **82** 15c. blue and red . . . . 1·40 60

83 Girl Scout Badge and Camp on Lake Gatun

1962. 50th Anniv of U.S. Girl Scout Movement.
222 **83** 4c. ochre, green and blue 40 25

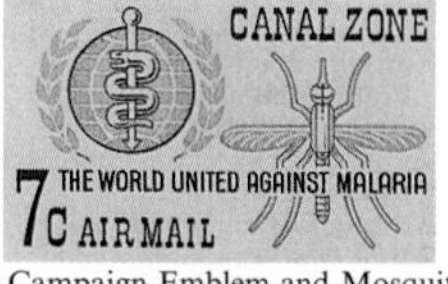

84 Campaign Emblem and Mosquito

1962. Air. Malaria Eradication.
223 **84** 7c. black on yellow 45 40

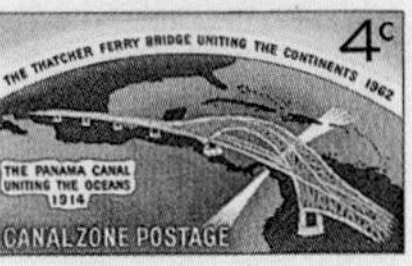

85 Thatcher Ferry Bridge

1962. Opening of Thatcher Ferry Bridge.
224 **85** 4c. black and silver 30 20

86 Torch of Progress

1963. Air. "Alliance for Progress".
225 **86** 15c. blue, green and black 1·10 75

87 Cristobal

1964. Air. 50th Anniv of Panama Canal.
226 **87** 6c. black and green 45 30
227 – 8c. black and red . . . . 1·75 75
228 – 15c. black and blue . . . . 1·25 45
229 – 20c. black and purple . . 2·00 85
230 – 30c. black and brown . . . 5·75 2·25
231 – 80c. black and bistre . . . 5·00 2·50
DESIGNS: 8c. Gatun Locks; 15c. Madden Dam; 20c. Gaillard Cut; 30c. Miraflores Locks; 80c. Balboa.

93 Seal and Jetliner

1965. Air.
232 **93** 6c. black and green 35 20
233 8c. black and red 30 10
234 10c. black and orange . . 30 10
235 11c. black and green . . . 40 15
236 13c. black and green . . . 95 20
237 15c. black and blue 50 15
238 20c. black and violet . . . 55 25
239 22c. black and violet . . . 75 55
240 25c. black and green . . . 60 40
241 30c. black and brown . . . 80 30

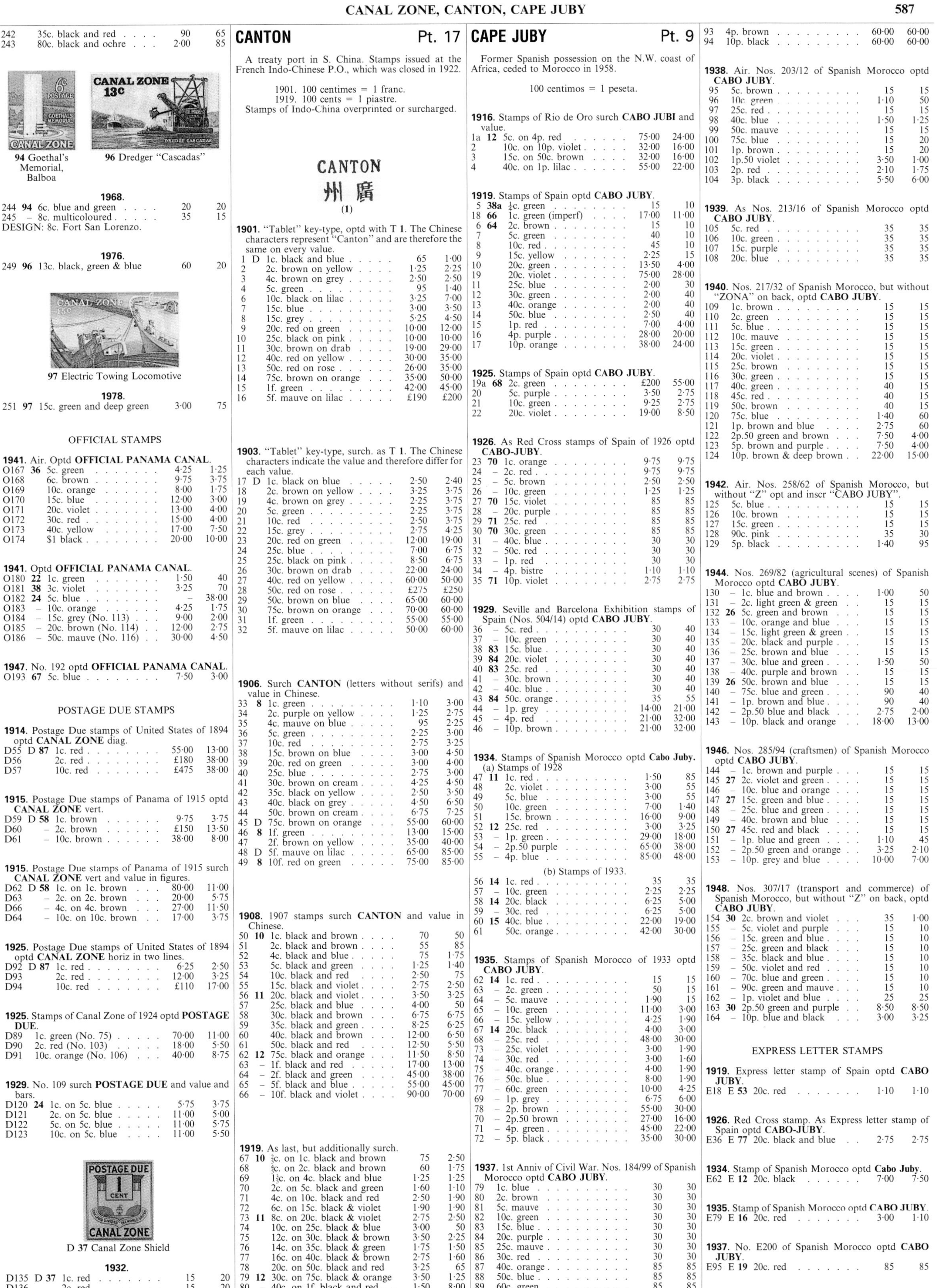

242 35c. black and red 90 65
243 80c. black and ochre . . . 2·00 85

94 Goethal's Memorial, Balboa

96 Dredger "Cascadas"

1968.
244 **94** 6c. blue and green 20 20
245 – 8c. multicoloured 35 15
DESIGN: 8c. Fort San Lorenzo.

1976.
249 **96** 13c. black, green & blue 60 20

97 Electric Towing Locomotive

1978.
251 **97** 15c. green and deep green 3·00 75

OFFICIAL STAMPS

1941. Air. Optd **OFFICIAL PANAMA CANAL.**
O167 **36** 5c. green . . . . 4·25 1·25
O168 6c. brown . . . . 9·75 3·75
O169 10c. orange . . . . . . 8·00 1·75
O170 15c. blue . . . . 12·00 3·00
O171 20c. violet . . . . 13·00 4·00
O172 30c. red . . . . 15·00 4·00
O173 40c. yellow . . . . . . 17·00 7·50
O174 $1 black . . . . 20·00 10·00

1941. Optd **OFFICIAL PANAMA CANAL.**
O180 **22** 1c. green . . . . 1·50 40
O181 **38** 3c. violet . . . . 3·25 70
O182 **24** 5c. blue . . . . – 38·00
O183 – 10c. orange . . . . . . 4·25 1·75
O184 – 15c. grey (No. 113) . . . 9·00 2·00
O185 – 20c. brown (No. 114) . . 12·00 2·75
O186 – 50c. mauve (No. 116) . . 30·00 4·50

1947. No. 192 optd **OFFICIAL PANAMA CANAL.**
O193 **67** 5c. blue . . . . 7·50 3·00

POSTAGE DUE STAMPS

1914. Postage Due stamps of United States of 1894 optd **CANAL ZONE** diag.
D55 D **87** 1c. red . . . . 55·00 13·00
D56 2c. red . . . . £180 38·00
D57 10c. red . . . . £475 38·00

1915. Postage Due stamps of Panama of 1915 optd **CANAL ZONE** vert.
D59 D **58** 1c. brown . . . . . . 9·75 3·75
D60 – 2c. brown . . . . . . £150 13·50
D61 – 10c. brown . . . . . . 38·00 8·00

1915. Postage Due stamps of Panama of 1915 surch **CANAL ZONE** vert and value in figures.
D62 D **58** 1c. on 1c. brown . . . 80·00 11·00
D63 – 2c. on 2c. brown . . . 20·00 5·75
D66 – 4c. on 4c. brown . . . 27·00 11·50
D64 – 10c. on 10c. brown . . 17·00 3·75

1925. Postage Due stamps of United States of 1894 optd **CANAL ZONE** horiz in two lines.
D92 D **87** 1c. red . . . . 6·25 2·50
D93 2c. red . . . . 12·00 3·25
D94 10c. red . . . . £110 17·00

1925. Stamps of Canal Zone of 1924 optd **POSTAGE DUE.**
D89 1c. green (No. 75) . . . . . 70·00 11·00
D90 2c. red (No. 103) . . . . . 18·00 5·50
D91 10c. orange (No. 106) . . . 40·00 8·75

1929. No. 109 surch **POSTAGE DUE** and value and bars.
D120 **24** 1c. on 5c. blue . . . . . 5·75 3·75
D121 2c. on 5c. blue . . . . . 11·00 5·00
D122 5c. on 5c. blue . . . . . 11·00 5·75
D123 10c. on 5c. blue . . . . 11·00 5·50

D 37 Canal Zone Shield

1932.
D135 D **37** 1c. red 15 20
D136 2c. red 15 20
D137 5c. red 40 25
D138 10c. red . . . . 1·60 1·50
D139 15c. red . . . . 1·25 1·10

CANTON Pt. 17

A treaty port in S. China. Stamps issued at the French Indo-Chinese P.O., which was closed in 1922.

1901. 100 centimes = 1 franc.
1919. 100 cents = 1 piastre.
Stamps of Indo-China overprinted or surcharged.

(1)

1901. "Tablet" key-type, optd with T **1**. The Chinese characters represent "Canton" and are therefore the same on every value.
1 D 1c. black and blue . . . . . 65 1·00
2 2c. brown on yellow . . . . 1·25 2·25
3 4c. brown on grey . . . . . 2·50 2·50
4 5c. green . . . . 95 1·40
6 10c. black on lilac . . . . . 3·25 7·00
7 15c. blue . . . . 3·00 3·50
8 15c. grey . . . . 5·25 4·50
9 20c. red on green . . . . . 10·00 12·00
10 25c. black on pink . . . . . 10·00 10·00
11 30c. brown on drab . . . . 19·00 29·00
12 40c. red on yellow . . . . . 30·00 35·00
13 50c. red on rose . . . . . . 26·00 35·00
14 75c. brown on orange . . . 35·00 50·00
15 1f. green . . . . 42·00 45·00
16 5f. mauve on lilac £190 £200

1903. "Tablet" key-type, surch. as T **1**. The Chinese characters indicate the value and therefore differ for each value.
17 D 1c. black on blue . . . . . 2·50 2·40
18 2c. brown on yellow . . . . 3·25 3·75
19 4c. brown on grey . . . . . 2·25 3·75
20 5c. green . . . . 2·25 3·75
21 10c. red . . . . 2·50 3·75
22 15c. grey . . . . 2·75 4·25
23 20c. red on green . . . . . 12·00 19·00
24 25c. blue . . . . 7·00 6·75
25 25c. black on pink . . . . . 8·50 6·75
26 30c. brown on drab . . . . 22·00 24·00
27 40c. red on yellow . . . . . 60·00 50·00
28 50c. red on rose £275 £250
29 50c. brown on blue . . . . 65·00 60·00
30 75c. brown on orange . . . 70·00 60·00
31 1f. green . . . . 55·00 55·00
32 5f. mauve on lilac . . . . . 50·00 60·00

1906. Surch **CANTON** (letters without serifs) and value in Chinese.
33 **8** 1c. green . . . . 1·10 3·00
34 2c. purple on yellow . . . . 1·25 2·75
35 4c. mauve on blue . . . . . 95 2·25
36 5c. green . . . . 2·25 3·00
37 10c. red . . . . 2·75 3·25
38 15c. brown on blue . . . . 3·00 4·50
39 20c. red on green . . . . . 3·00 4·00
40 25c. blue . . . . 2·75 3·00
41 30c. brown on cream . . . . 4·25 4·50
42 35c. black on yellow . . . . 2·50 3·50
43 40c. black on grey . . . . . 4·50 6·50
44 50c. brown on cream . . . . 6·75 7·25
45 D 75c. brown on orange . . . 55·00 60·00
46 **8** 1f. green . . . . 13·00 15·00
47 2f. brown on yellow . . . . 35·00 40·00
48 D 5f. mauve on lilac . . . . . 65·00 85·00
49 **8** 10f. red on green . . . . . 75·00 85·00

1908. 1907 stamps surch **CANTON** and value in Chinese.
50 **10** 1c. black and brown 70 50
51 2c. black and brown 55 85
52 4c. black and blue . . . . . 75 1·75
53 5c. black and green . . . . 1·25 1·40
54 10c. black and red . . . . 2·50 75
55 15c. black and violet . . . . 2·75 2·50
56 **11** 20c. black and violet . . . . 3·50 3·25
57 25c. black and blue . . . . 4·00 50
58 30c. black and brown . . . 6·75 6·75
59 35c. black and green . . . . 8·25 6·25
60 40c. black and brown . . . 12·00 6·50
61 50c. black and red . . . . 12·50 5·50
62 **12** 75c. black and orange . . . 11·50 8·50
63 – 1f. black and red . . . . . 17·00 13·00
64 – 2f. black and green . . . . 45·00 38·00
65 – 5f. black and blue . . . . . 55·00 45·00
66 – 10f. black and violet . . . . 90·00 70·00

1919. As last, but additionally surch.
67 **10** ⅖c. on 1c. black and brown 75 2·50
68 ⅘c. on 2c. black and brown 60 1·75
69 1⅗c. on 4c. black and blue 1·25 1·25
70 2c. on 5c. black and green 1·60 1·10
71 4c. on 10c. black and red 2·50 1·90
72 6c. on 15c. black & violet 1·90 1·90
73 **11** 8c. on 20c. black & violet 2·75 2·50
74 10c. on 25c. black & blue 3·00 50
75 12c. on 30c. black & brown 3·50 2·25
76 14c. on 35c. black & green 1·75 1·50
77 16c. on 40c. black & brown 2·75 1·60
78 20c. on 50c. black and red 3·25 65
79 **12** 30c. on 75c. black & orange 3·50 1·25
80 – 40c. on 1f. black and red . . 1·50 8·00
81 – 80c. on 2f. black and green 13·50 12·50
82 – 2p. on 5f. black and blue . . 14·00 16·00
83 – 4p. on 10f. black & violet 15·00 19·00

CAPE JUBY Pt. 9

Former Spanish possession on the N.W. coast of Africa, ceded to Morocco in 1958.

100 centimos = 1 peseta.

1916. Stamps of Rio de Oro surch **CABO JUBI** and value.
1a **12** 5c. on 4p. red . . . . . . 75·00 24·00
2 10c. on 10p. violet . . . . 32·00 16·00
3 15c. on 50c. brown . . . . 32·00 16·00
4 40c. on 1p. lilac . . . . . . 55·00 22·00

1919. Stamps of Spain optd **CABO JUBY.**
5 **38a** ¼c. green 15 10
18 **66** 1c. green (imperf) . . . . 17·00 11·00
6 **64** 2c. brown 15 10
7 5c. green 40 10
8 10c. red 45 10
9 15c. yellow . . . . 2·25 15
10 20c. green . . . . 13·50 4·00
19 20c. violet . . . . 75·00 28·00
11 25c. blue . . . . 2·00 30
12 30c. green . . . . 2·00 40
13 40c. orange . . . . 2·00 40
14 50c. blue . . . . 2·50 40
15 1p. red . . . . 7·00 4·00
16 4p. purple . . . . 28·00 20·00
17 10p. orange . . . . 38·00 24·00

1925. Stamps of Spain optd **CABO JUBY.**
19a **68** 2c. green . . . . £200 55·00
20 5c. purple . . . . 3·50 2·75
21 10c. green . . . . 9·25 2·75
22 20c. violet . . . . 19·00 8·50

1926. As Red Cross stamps of Spain of 1926 optd **CABO-JUBY.**
23 **70** 1c. orange . . . . 9·75 9·75
24 – 2c. red . . . . 9·75 9·75
25 – 5c. brown . . . . 2·50 2·50
26 – 10c. green . . . . 1·25 1·25
27 **70** 15c. violet 85 85
28 – 20c. purple 85 85
29 **71** 25c. red 85 85
30 **70** 30c. green 85 85
31 – 40c. blue 30 30
32 – 50c. red 30 30
33 – 1p. red 30 30
34 – 4p. bistre . . . . 1·10 1·10
35 **71** 10p. violet . . . . 2·75 2·75

1929. Seville and Barcelona Exhibition stamps of Spain (Nos. 504/14) optd **CABO JUBY.**
36 – 5c. red 30 40
37 – 10c. green 30 40
38 **83** 15c. blue 30 40
39 **84** 20c. violet 30 40
40 **83** 25c. red 30 40
41 – 30c. brown 30 40
42 – 40c. blue 30 40
43 **84** 50c. orange 35 55
44 – 1p. grey . . . . 14·00 21·00
45 – 4p. red . . . . 21·00 32·00
46 – 10p. brown . . . . 21·00 32·00

1934. Stamps of Spanish Morocco optd **Cabo Juby.**
(a) Stamps of 1928
47 **11** 1c. red . . . . 1·50 85
48 2c. violet . . . . 3·00 55
49 5c. blue . . . . 3·00 55
50 10c. green . . . . 7·00 1·40
51 15c. brown . . . . 16·00 9·00
52 **12** 25c. red . . . . 3·00 3·25
53 – 1p. green . . . . 29·00 18·00
54 – 2p.50 purple . . . . 65·00 38·00
55 – 4p. blue . . . . 85·00 48·00

(b) Stamps of 1933.
56 **14** 1c. red 35 35
57 – 10c. green . . . . 2·25 2·25
58 **14** 20c. black . . . . 6·25 5·00
59 – 30c. red . . . . 6·25 5·00
60 **15** 40c. blue . . . . 22·00 19·00
61 50c. orange . . . . 42·00 30·00

1935. Stamps of Spanish Morocco of 1933 optd **CABO JUBY.**
62 **14** 1c. red 15 15
63 – 2c. green 50 15
64 – 5c. mauve . . . . 1·90 15
65 – 10c. green . . . . 11·00 3·00
66 – 15c. yellow . . . . 4·25 1·90
67 **14** 20c. black . . . . 4·00 3·00
68 – 25c. red . . . . 48·00 30·00
73 – 25c. violet . . . . 3·00 1·90
74 – 30c. red . . . . 3·00 1·60
75 – 40c. orange . . . . 4·00 1·90
76 – 50c. blue . . . . 8·00 1·90
77 – 60c. green . . . . 10·00 4·25
69 – 1p. grey . . . . 6·75 6·00
78 – 2p. brown . . . . 55·00 30·00
70 – 2p.50 brown . . . . 27·00 16·00
71 – 4p. green . . . . 45·00 22·00
72 – 5p. black . . . . 35·00 30·00

1937. 1st Anniv of Civil War. Nos. 184/99 of Spanish Morocco optd **CABO JUBY.**
79 1c. blue 30 30
80 2c. brown 30 30
81 5c. mauve 30 30
82 10c. green 30 30
83 15c. blue 30 30
84 20c. purple 30 30
85 25c. mauve 30 30
86 30c. red 30 30
87 40c. orange 85 85
88 50c. blue 85 85
89 60c. green 85 85
90 1p. violet 85 85
91 2p. blue . . . . 60·00 60·00
92 2p.50 black . . . . 60·00 60·00
93 4p. brown . . . . 60·00 60·00
94 10p. black . . . . 60·00 60·00

1938. Air. Nos. 203/12 of Spanish Morocco optd **CABO JUBY.**
95 5c. brown 15 15
96 10c. green . . . . 1·10 50
97 25c. red 15 15
98 40c. blue . . . . 1·50 1·25
99 50c. mauve 15 15
100 75c. blue 15 20
101 1p. brown 15 20
102 1p.50 violet . . . . 3·50 1·00
103 2p. red . . . . 2·10 1·75
104 3p. black . . . . 5·50 6·00

1939. As Nos. 213/16 of Spanish Morocco optd **CABO JUBY.**
105 5c. red 35 35
106 10c. green 35 35
107 15c. purple 35 35
108 20c. blue 35 35

1940. Nos. 217/32 of Spanish Morocco, but without "ZONA" on back, optd **CABO JUBY.**
109 1c. brown 15 15
110 2c. green 15 15
111 5c. blue 15 15
112 10c. mauve 15 15
113 15c. green 15 15
114 20c. violet 15 15
115 25c. brown 15 15
116 30c. green 15 15
117 40c. green 40 15
118 45c. red 40 15
119 50c. brown 40 15
120 75c. blue . . . . 1·40 60
121 1p. brown and blue . . . . 2·75 60
122 2p.50 green and brown . . . 7·50 4·00
123 5p. brown and purple . . . . 7·50 4·00
124 10p. brown & deep brown . . 22·00 15·00

1942. Air. Nos. 258/62 of Spanish Morocco, but without "Z" opt and inscr "CABO JUBY".
125 5c. blue 15 15
126 10c. brown 15 15
127 15c. green 15 15
128 90c. pink 35 30
129 5p. black . . . . 1·40 95

1944. Nos. 269/82 (agricultural scenes) of Spanish Morocco optd **CABO JUBY.**
130 – 1c. blue and brown . . . . 1·00 50
131 – 2c. light green & green . . 15 15
132 **26** 5c. green and brown . . . 15 15
133 – 10c. orange and blue . . . 15 15
134 – 15c. light green & green . . 15 15
135 – 20c. black and purple . . . 15 15
136 – 25c. brown and blue . . . 15 15
137 – 30c. blue and green . . . . 1·50 50
138 – 40c. purple and brown . . 15 15
139 **26** 50c. brown and blue . . . 15 15
140 – 75c. blue and green 90 40
141 – 1p. brown and blue 90 40
142 – 2p.50 blue and black . . . 2·75 2·00
143 – 10p. black and orange . . 18·00 13·00

1946. Nos. 285/94 (craftsmen) of Spanish Morocco optd **CABO JUBY.**
144 – 1c. brown and purple . . . 15 15
145 **27** 2c. violet and green 15 15
146 – 10c. blue and orange . . . 15 15
147 **27** 15c. green and blue 15 15
148 – 25c. blue and green 15 15
149 – 40c. brown and blue . . . 15 15
150 **27** 45c. red and black 15 15
151 – 1p. blue and green . . . . 1·10 45
152 – 2p.50 green and orange . . 3·25 2·10
153 – 10p. grey and blue . . . . 10·00 7·00

1948. Nos. 307/17 (transport and commerce) of Spanish Morocco, but without "Z" on back, optd **CABO JUBY.**
154 **30** 2c. brown and violet . . . 35 1·00
155 – 5c. violet and purple . . . 15 10
156 – 15c. green and blue . . . 15 10
157 – 25c. green and black . . . 15 10
158 – 35c. black and blue . . . 15 10
159 – 50c. violet and red 15 10
160 – 70c. blue and green 15 10
161 – 90c. green and mauve . . . 15 10
162 – 1p. violet and blue 25 25
163 **30** 2p.50 green and purple . . 8·50 8·50
164 – 10p. blue and black . . . 3·00 3·25

EXPRESS LETTER STAMPS

1919. Express letter stamp of Spain optd **CABO JUBY.**
E18 E **53** 20c. red . . . . 1·10 1·10

1926. Red Cross stamp. As Express letter stamp of Spain optd **CABO-JUBY.**
E36 E **77** 20c. black and blue . . 2·75 2·75

1934. Stamp of Spanish Morocco optd **Cabo Juby.**
E62 E **12** 20c. black . . . . . . 7·00 7·50

1935. Stamp of Spanish Morocco optd **CABO JUBY.**
E79 E **16** 20c. red . . . . 3·00 1·10

1937. No. E200 of Spanish Morocco optd **CABO JUBY.**
E95 E **19** 20c. red 85 85

1940. No. E233 of Spanish Morocco optd **CABO JUBY.**
E125 E **21** 25c. red 30 30

CAPE OF GOOD HOPE Pt. 1

Formerly a British Colony, later the southern-most province of the Union of South Africa.

12 pence = 1 shilling;
20 shillings = 1 pound.

1 "Hope"

1853. Imperf.

18 1	1d. red	£130	£225
19	4d. blue	£130	50·00
20	6d. lilac	£170	£450
8b	1s. green	£225	£500

3

1861. Imperf.

13 3	1d. red	£14000	£2250
14	4d. blue	£10000	£1600

4 "Hope" seated, with vine and ram (with outer frame-line)

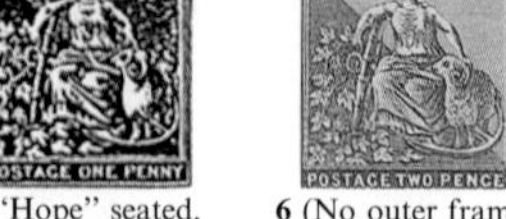

6 (No outer frame-line)

1864. With outer frame line. Perf.

23a 4	1d. red	80·00	21·00
24	4d. blue	£100	2·50
52a	6d. purple	8·00	20
53a	1s. green	75·00	40

1868. Surch.

32 4	1d. on 6d. violet	£470	90·00
33	1d. on 1s. green	65·00	42·00
34 6	3d. on 4d. blue	95·00	1·75
27 4	4d. on 6d. violet	£225	16·00

1880. No outer frame line.

48 6	½d. black	3·50	10
49	1d. red	3·50	10
36	3d. pink	£180	22·00
43	3d. purple	6·50	90
51	4d. blue	9·00	50
54	5s. orange	80·00	4·75

1880. Surch **THREEPENCE**.

35 6	3d. on 4d. pink	65·00	1·75

1880. Surch **3**.

37 6	"3" on 3d. pink	70·00	1·50

1882. Surch **One Half-penny**.

47 6	½d. on 3d. purple	24·00	3·00

1882.

61 6	½d. green	1·50	50
62	2d. brown	2·00	30
56	2½d. olive	7·00	10
63a	2½d. blue	3·75	10
64	3d. mauve	6·00	85
65	4d. olive	4·00	1·50
66	1s. green	60·00	3·50
67	1s. yellow	7·50	1·00

On the 2½d. stamps the value is in a white square at upper right-hand corner as well as at foot.

1891. Surch **2½d.**

55a 6	2½d. on 3d. mauve	3·00	20

1893. Surch **ONE PENNY**.

57a 6	1d. on 2d. brown	2·25	50

17 "Hope" standing. Table Bay in background

18 Table Mountain and Bay and Arms of the Colony

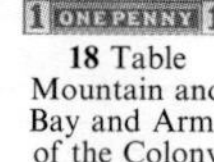

19

1893.

58 17	½d. green	1·75	10
59a	1d. red	1·25	10
60	3d. mauve	4·00	1·50

1900.

69 18	1d. red	2·25	10

1902. Various frames.

70 19	½d. green	2·00	10
71	1d. red	2·00	10
72	2d. brown	9·00	80
73	2½d. blue	2·75	6·50
74	3d. purple	7·00	75
75	4d. green	8·00	65
76	6d. mauve	15·00	30
77	1s. yellow	12·00	80
78	5s. orange	70·00	12·00

CAPE VERDE ISLANDS Pt. 9; Pt. 12

Islands in the Atlantic. Formerly Portuguese; became independent on 5 July 1975.

1877. 1000 reis = 1 milreis.
1913. 100 centavos = 1 escudo.

1877. "Crown" key-type inscr "CABO VERDE".

1 P	5r. black	1·25	95
2a	10r. yellow	6·75	4·00
18	10r. green	1·00	80
3	20r. bistre	90	75
19	20r. red	1·90	1·40
4	25r. pink	90	60
20	25r. lilac	1·60	1·10
5	40r. blue	30·00	20·00
21	40r. yellow	90	85
15	50r. green	30·00	20·00
22	50r. blue	2·50	1·90
7b	100r. lilac	3·00	1·40
8	200r. orange	1·60	1·10
9b	300r. brown	2·10	1·90

1886. "Embossed" key-type inscr "PROVINCIA DE CABO-VERDE".

33 Q	5r. black	1·50	1·00
34	10r. green	1·50	1·00
35	20r. red	2·75	1·90
26	25r. mauve	2·10	1·40
27	40r. brown	2·50	1·50
28	50r. blue	2·50	1·50
29	100r. brown	2·75	1·60
30	200r. lilac	6·00	3·75
31	300r. orange	6·50	4·25

1894. "Figures" key-type inscr "CABO-VERDE".

37 R	5r. orange	55	45
38	10r. mauve	60	50
39	15r. brown	1·50	1·00
40	20r. lilac	1·50	1·00
41	25r. green	1·10	85
42	50r. blue	1·10	85
51	75r. red	3·75	2·50
43	80r. green	4·00	3·50
44	100r. brown on buff	3·25	1·25
58	150r. red on rose	5·25	4·00
59	200r. blue on blue	5·25	3·00
46	300r. blue on buff	8·50	4·75

1898. "King Carlos" key-type inscr "CABO VERDE".

60 S	2½r. grey	20	15
61	5r. orange	20	15
62	10r. green	20	15
63	15r. brown	1·75	80
111	15r. green	55	40
64	20r. lilac	50	30
65	25r. green	1·10	50
112	25r. red	40	20
66	50r. blue	1·25	50
113	50r. brown	1·10	80
114	65r. blue	5·75	3·75
67	75r. red	2·10	1·10
115	75r. purple	95	75
68	80r. mauve	2·50	1·40
69	100r. blue on blue	1·10	65
116	115r. brown on pink	3·75	3·00
117	130r. brown on yellow	3·75	3·00
70	150r. brown on yellow	2·75	1·50
71	200r. purple on pink	1·25	90
72	300r. blue on pink	3·25	1·75
118	400r. blue on yellow	3·75	3·00
73	500r. black on blue	3·25	1·75
74	700r. mauve on yellow	8·50	7·00

1902. Key-types of Cape Verde Is. surch.

119 S	50r. on 65r. blue	1·10	1·00
75 Q	65r. on 5r. black	2·00	1·60
78 R	65r. on 10r. mauve	2·50	1·50
79	65r. on 20r. lilac	2·50	1·50
80	65r. on 100r. brn on buff	2·50	1·50
76 Q	65r. on 200r. lilac	2·00	1·60
77	65r. on 300r. orange	2·00	1·60
85 R	115r. on 5r. orange	1·50	1·25
82 Q	115r. on 10r. green	2·00	1·60
83	115r. on 20r. red	2·10	1·60
87 R	115r. on 25r. green	1·50	1·10
88	115r. on 150r. red on rose	2·75	2·40
90 Q	130r. on 50r. blue	2·00	1·60
93 R	130r. on 75r. red	1·00	1·00
96	130r. on 80r. green	1·10	95
92 Q	130r. on 100r. brown	2·00	1·60
97 R	130r. on 200r. blue on blue	1·25	1·25
106 V	400r. on 2½r. brown	55	45
98 Q	400r. on 25r. mauve	1·10	95
99	400r. on 40r. brown	1·50	1·40
101 R	400r. on 50r. blue	1·75	1·60
103	400r. on 300r. blue on buff	1·00	75

1902. "King Carlos" key-type of Cape Verde Is. optd **PROVISORIO**.

107 S	15r. brown	75	55
108	25r. green	75	55
109	50r. blue	75	55
110	75r. red	1·25	85

1911. "King Carlos" key-type of Cape Verde Is. optd **REPUBLICA**.

120 S	2½r. grey	15	15
121	5r. orange	15	15
122	10r. green	40	30
123	15r. green	25	15
124	20r. lilac	40	30
125	25r. red	30	20
126	50r. brown	3·00	2·25
127	75r. purple	45	30
128	100r. blue on blue	45	30
129	115r. brown on pink	40	35
130	130r. brown on yellow	40	35
131	200r. purple on pink	2·25	1·40
132	400r. blue on yellow	1·10	40
133	500r. black on blue	1·10	40
134	700r. mauve on yellow	1·10	65

1912. "King Manoel" key-type inscr "CABO VERDE" and optd **REPUBLICA**.

135 T	2½r. lilac	10	10
136	5r. black	10	10
137	10r. green	10	10
138	20r. red	90	60
139	25r. brown	25	10
140	50r. blue	1·40	1·25
141	75r. brown	40	35
142	100r. brown on green	40	35
143	200r. green on pink	60	35
144	300r. black on blue	60	35
145	400r. blue and black	1·25	1·10
146	500r. brown and olive	1·25	1·10

1913. Surch. **REPUBLICA CABO VERDE** and new value on "Vasco da Gama" issues of (a) Portuguese Colonies.

147	¼c. on 2½r. green	50	30
148	½c. on 5r. red	50	30
149	1c. on 10r. purple	35	30
150	2½c. on 25r. green	35	30
151	5c. on 50r. blue	70	60
152	7½c. on 75r. brown	85	75
153	10c. on 100r. brown	70	70
154	15c. on 150r. bistre	90	75

(b) Macao.

155	¼c. on ½a. green	50	40
156	½c. on 1a. red	50	40
157	1c. on 2a. purple	45	40
158	2½c. on 4a. green	45	40
159	5c. on 8a. blue	2·50	1·90
160	7½c. on 12a. brown	1·60	90
161	10c. on 16a. brown	80	70
162	15c. on 24a. bistre	1·75	1·25

(c) Timor.

163	¼c. on ½a. green	50	40
164	½c. on 1a. red	50	40
165	1c. on 2a. purple	45	40
166	2½c. on 4a. green	45	40
167	5c. on 8a. blue	2·50	1·90
168	7½c. on 12a. brown	2·00	1·40
169	10c. on 16a. brown	80	70
170	15c. on 24a. bistre	1·00	80

1913. Stamps of 1902 optd **REPUBLICA**.

171 S	75r. red (No. 110)	1·50	1·40
192 R	115r. on 5r. (No. 85)	30	20
193 Q	115r. on 10r. (No. 82)	50	40
195	115r. on 20r. (No. 83)	60	50
198 R	115r. on 25r. (No. 87)	40	30
200	115r. on 150r. (No. 88)	25	20
201 Q	130r. on 50r. (No. 90)	50	50
202 R	130r. on 75r. (No. 93)	40	30
204	130r. on 80r. (No. 96)	40	30
206 Q	130r. on 100r. (No. 92)	40	30
208 R	130r. on 200r. (No. 97)	40	30

1914. "Ceres" key-type inscr "CABO VERDE". Name and value in black.

219 U	¼c. green	10	10
220	½c. black	10	10
221	1c. green	10	10
222	1½c. brown	10	10
223	2c. red	10	10
224	2c. grey	15	15
180	2½c. violet	25	20
214	2½c. mauve	10	10
215	3c. orange	10	10
216	4c. red	10	15
228	4½c. grey	15	15
229	5c. blue	15	15
230	6c. mauve	15	15
231	7c. blue	15	15
232	7½c. brown	10	10
233	8c. grey	20	15
234	10c. red	10	10
235	12c. green	20	20
236	15c. pink	10	10
237	20c. green	15	10
238	24c. blue	40	35
239	25c. brown	40	35
188	30c. brown on green	1·50	1·25
240	30c. green	15	15
189	40c. brown on pink	90	80
241	40c. turquoise	15	15
190	50c. orange on orange	1·10	85
242	50c. mauve	30	20
243	60c. blue	40	30
244	60c. red	40	30
245	80c. red	1·50	55
191	1e. green on blue	1·10	85
246	1e. pink	1·90	1·00
247	1e. blue	1·75	1·10
248	2e. purple	1·90	1·10
249	5e. brown	4·00	3·50
250	10e. pink	7·00	6·25
251	20e. green	17·00	16·00

1921. Nos. 153/4 surch.

252	2c. on 15c. on 150r. brown	60	55
253	4c. on 10c. on 100r. brown	80	80

1921. No. 69 surch **6 c. REPUBLICA**.

254 S	6c. on 100r. blue on blue	80	80

1921. Charity Tax stamp of Portuguese Colonies (General issues) optd **CABO VERDE CORREIOS** or surch also.

255	¼ on 1c. green	15	15
256	½c. on 1c. green	15	15
257	1c. green	20	15

1922. Provisionals of 1913 surch **$04**.

260 R	4c. on 130r. on 75r. red (No. 202)	35	30
262	4c. on 130r. on 80r. green (No. 204)	45	40
265	4c. on 130r. on 200r. blue (No. 208)	35	30

1925. Provisional stamps of 1902 surch **Republica 40 C.**

267 V	40c. on 400r. on 2½r. brown (No. 106)	20	20
268 R	40c. on 400r. on 300r. blue on buff (No. 103)	30	30

1931. No. 245 surch **70 C.**

269 U	70c. on 80c. red	1·40	1·10

1934. As T 17 of Angola (new "Ceres" type).

270 17	1c. brown	10	10
271	5c. sepia	10	10
272	10c. mauve	10	10
273	15c. black	10	10
274	20c. grey	10	10
275	30c. green	10	10
276	40c. red	10	10
277	45c. blue	40	25
278	50c. brown	30	15
279	60c. olive	30	15
280	70c. brown	30	15
281	80c. green	30	15
282	85c. red	1·40	85
283	1e. red	95	15
284	1e.40 blue	1·00	75
285	2e. mauve	1·60	75
286	5e. green	7·00	1·75
287	10e. brown	12·50	6·25
288	20e. orange	25·00	11·00

1938. As Nos. 383/409 of Angola.

289	1c. olive (postage)	10	10
290	5c. brown	10	10
291	10c. red	10	10
292	15c. purple	35	25
293	20c. slate	20	15
294	30c. purple	20	15
295	35c. green	20	15
296	40c. brown	20	15
297	50c. mauve	20	15
298	60c. black	20	15
299	70c. violet	20	15
300	80c. orange	20	15
301	1e. red	25	15
302	1e.75 blue	60	40

303 2e. green 1·10 65
304 5e. olive 3·00 85
305 10e. blue 5·25 1·00
306 20e. brown 13·00 2·00
307 10c. red (air) 30 20
308 20c. violet 30 20
309 50c. orange 30 20
310 1e. blue 35 20
311 2e. red 65 30
312 3e. green 90 45
313 5e. brown 2·00 70
314 9e. red 4·75 1·50
315 10e. mauve 6·00 1·75

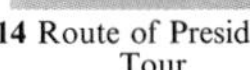

14 Route of President's Tour **16** Machado Point, Sao Vicente

17 Ribeira Brava, Sao Nicolau

1939. Pres. Carmona's 2nd Colonial Tour.
316 **14** 80c. violet on mauve 4·00 3·75
317 1e.75 blue on blue 26·00 22·00
318 20e. brown on cream 70·00 22·00

1948. Nos. 276 and 294 surch.
319 10c. on 30c. purple 50 40
320 25c. on 40c. red 65 40

1948.
321 **16** 5c. purple and bistre 50 30
322 – 10c. green and light green 50 30
323 **17** 50c. purple and lilac 95 30
324 – 1e. purple 3·50 1·00
325 – 1e.75 blue and green 4·00 1·40
326 – 2e. brown and ochre 9·50 1·60
327 – 5e. green and yellow 19·00 2·50
328 – 10e. red and orange 30·00 12·50
329 – 20e. violet and buff 75·00 21·00
DESIGNS—VERT: 10c. Ribeira Grande. HORIZ: 1e. Porto Grande, Sao Vicente; 1e.75, 5e. Mindelo, Sao Vicente; 2e. Joao de Evora beach, Sao Vicente; 10e. Volcano, Fogo; 20e. Paul.

1948. Honouring the Statue of Our Lady of Fatima. As T **33** of Angola.
330 50c. blue 6·75 3·25

1949. 75th Anniv of U.P.U. As T **39** of Angola.
331 1e. mauve 4·75 2·75

1950. Holy Year. As T **41/2** of Angola.
332 1e. brown 55 40
333 2e. blue 2·50 1·25

1951. Surch with figures and bars over old value.
334 10c. on 35c. (No. 295) 40 40
335 20c. on 70c. (No. 299) 55 50
336 40c. on 70c. (No. 299) 60 50
337 50c. on 80c. (No. 300) 60 50
338 1e. on 1e.75 (No. 302) 60 50
339 2e. on 10e. (No. 305) 3·50 1·25

1951. Termination of Holy Year. As T **44** of Angola.
340 2e. violet and mauve 1·00 70

1952. No. 302 surch with figures and cross over old values.
341 10c. on 1e.75 blue 85 85
342 20c. on 1e.75 blue 85 85
343 50c. on 1e.75 blue 3·75 3·50
344 1e. on 1e.75 blue 45 15
345 1e.50 on 1e.75 blue 45 15

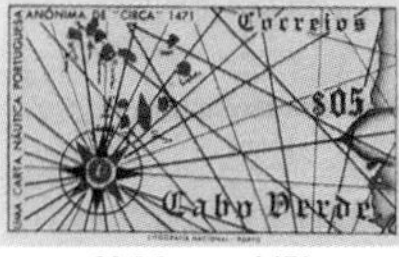

20 Map, c. 1471

21 V. Dias and G. de Cintra

1962. Portuguese Navigators as T **20/21**. Mult.
346 5c. Type **20** 10 10
347 10c. Type **21** 10 10
348 30c. D. Afonso and A. Fernandes 10 10
349 50c. Lancarote and S. da Costa 10 10
350 1e. D. Gomes and A. da Nola 15 10
351 2e. Princes Fernando and Henry the Navigator 55 10
352 3e. A. Goncalves and D. Dias 5·50 80
353 5e. A. Goncalves Baldaia and J. Fernandes 1·75 40
354 10e. D. Fanes da Gra and A. de Freitas 3·75 1·10
355 20e. Map, 1502 6·50 1·25

22 Doctor giving Injection **23** Facade of Monastery

1952. 1st Tropical Medicine Congress, Lisbon.
356 **22** 20c. black and green 35 30

1953. Missionary Art Exhibition.
357 **23** 10c. brown and olive 10 10
358 50c. violet and salmon 35 25
359 1e. green and orange 1·00 55

1953. Portuguese Stamp Centenary. As T **48** of Angola.
360 50c. multicoloured 1·00 55

1954. 4th Cent of Sao Paulo. As T **49** of Angola.
361 1e. black, green and buff 30 25

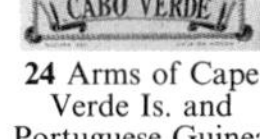

24 Arms of Cape Verde Is. and Portuguese Guinea **26** Prince Henry the Navigator

25 Arms of Praia

1955. Presidential Visit.
362 **24** 1e. multicoloured 30 25
363 1e.60c. multicoloured 50 40

1958. Centenary of City of Praia. Multicoloured.
364 **25** 1e. on yellow 30 20
365 2e.50 on salmon 45 50

1958. Brussels International Exn. As T **55** of Angola.
366 2e. multicoloured 40 20

1958. 6th International Congress of Tropical Medicine. As T **56** of Angola. Multicoloured.
367 3c. "Aloe vera" (plant) 2·75 1·25

1960. 500th Death Anniv of Prince Henry the Navigator.
368 **26** 2e. multicoloured 20 15

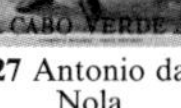

27 Antonio da Nola **28** "Education"

1960. 500th Anniv of Colonization of Cape Verde Islands. Multicoloured.
369 1e. Type **27** 30 25
370 2e.50 Diogo Gomes 80 60

1960. 10th Anniv of African Technical Co-operation Commission.
371 **28** 2e.50 multicoloured 55 30

29 Arms of Praia **30** Militia Regiment Drummer, 1806

1961. Urban Arms. As T **29**. Arms multicoloured; inscriptions in red and green; background colours given.
372 5c. buff 15 15
373 15c. blue 15 15
374 20c. yellow 15 15
375 30c. lilac 15 15
376 1e. green 35 15
377 2e. lemon 35 15
378 2e.50 pink 50 15
379 3e. brown 75 25
380 5e. blue 75 25
381 7e.50 olive 85 40
382 15e. mauve 1·40 60
383 30e. yellow 2·75 1·60
ARMS: 15c. Nova Sintra. 20c. Ribeira Brava. 30c. Assomada. 1e. Maio. 2e. Mindelo. 2e.50 Santa Maria. 3e. Pombas. 5e. Sal-Rei. 7e.50, Tarrafal. 15e. Maria Pia. 30e. San Felipe.

1962. Sports. As T **62** of Angola. Multicoloured.
384 50c. Throwing the javelin 15 15
385 1e. Discus thrower 50 15
386 1e.50 Batsman (cricket) 1·25 30
387 2e.50 Boxing 50 25
388 4e.50 Hurdler 80 55
389 12e.50 Golfers 1·60 1·00

1962. Malaria Eradication. Mosquito design as T **63** of Angola. Multicoloured.
390 2e.50 "Anopheles pretoriensis" 75 55

1963. 10th Anniv of T.A.P. Airline. As T **69** of Angola.
391 2e.50 multicoloured 45 30

1964. Centenary of National Overseas Bank. As T **71** of Angola but portrait of J. da S. M. Leal.
392 1e.50 multicoloured 50 40

1965. Centenary of I.T.U. As T **73** of Angola.
393 2e.50 multicoloured 1·00 80

1965. Portuguese Military Uniforms. Mult.
394 50c. Type **30** 15 15
395 1e. Militiaman, 1806 25 15
396 1e.50 Infantry Grenadiers officers, 1833 40 25
397 2e.50 Infantry grenadier, 1833 70 20
398 3e. Cavalry officer, 1834 1·00 30
399 4e. Infantry grenadier, 1835 70 40
400 5e. Artillery officer, 1848 70 40
401 10e. Infantry drum-major, 1856 1·40 1·10

1966. 40th Anniv of National Revolution. As T **77** of Angola, but showing different building. Multicoloured.
402 1e. Dr A. Moreira's Academy and Public Assistance Building 30 20

1967. Centenary of Military Naval Association. As T **79** of Angola. Multicoloured.
403 1e. F. da Costa and gunboat "Mandovy" 55 25
404 1e. 50 C. Araujo and minesweeper "Augusto Castilho" 85 40

1967. 50th Anniv of Fatima Apparitions. As T **80** of Angola. Multicoloured.
405 1e. Image of Virgin Mary 15 15

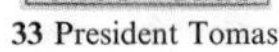

33 President Tomas **34** Port of Sao Vicente

1968. Visit of President Tomas of Portugal.
406 **33** 1e. multicoloured 15 15

1968. 500th Birth Anniv of Pedro Cabral (explorer). As T **84** of Angola. Multicoloured.
407 1e. Cantino's map, 1502 40 25
408 1e.50 Pedro Alvares Cabral (vert) 60 40

1968. "Produce of Cape Verde Islands". Mult.
409 50c. Type **34** 30 15
410 1e. "Purgueira" (Tatrophus curcus) (vert) 20 15
411 1e.50 Groundnuts (vert) 20 15
412 2e.50 Castor-oil plant (vert) 20 15
413 3e.50 "Inhame" (Dioscorea alata) (vert) 25 15
414 4e. Date palm (vert) 25 15
415 4e.50 "Goiabeira" (Psidium guajava) (vert) 35 20
416 5e. Tamarind (vert) 50 20
417 10e. Manioc (vert) 65 40
418 30e. Girl of Cape Verde (vert) 1·60 1·25

1969. Birth Centenary of Admiral Gago Coutinho. As T **86** of Angola. Multicoloured.
419 30c. Fairey IIID seaplane "Lusitania" and map of Lisbon-Rio flight (vert) 15 15

1969. 500th Birth Anniv of Vasco da Gama (explorer). Multicoloured. As T **87** of Angola.
420 1e.50 Vasco da Gama (vert) 15 15

1969. Centenary of Overseas Administrative Reforms. As T **88** of Angola.
421 2e. multicoloured 15 15

1969. 500th Birth Anniv of King Manoel I. As T **89** of Angola. Multicoloured.
422 3e. Manoel I 20 15

1970. Birth Centenary of Marshal Carmona. As T **91** of Angola. Multicoloured.
423 2e.50 Half-length portrait 25 20

35 Desalination Installation **37** Cabral, Flag and People

1971. Inauguration of Desalination Plant, Mindelo.
424 **35** 4e. multicoloured 55 45

1972. 400th Anniv of Camoens' "Lusiad" (epic poem). As T **96** of Angola. Multicoloured.
425 5e. Galleons at Cape Verde 75 20

1972. Olympic Games, Munich. As T **97** of Angola. Multicoloured.
426 4e. Basketball and boxing 30 20

1972. 50th Anniv of 1st Flight Lisbon–Rio de Janeiro. As T **98** of Angola. Multicoloured.
427 3e.50 Fairey IIID seaplane "Lusitania" near Sao Vicente 30 20

1973. Centenary of I.M.O./W.M.O. As Type **99** of Angola.
428 2e.50 multicoloured 30 20

1975. Independence. No. 407 optd **INDEPENDENCIA 5-Julho-75.**
430 1e. multicoloured 15 10

1975. 3rd Anniv of Amilcar Cabral's Assassination.
431 **37** 5e. multicoloured 20 15

38 Islanders with Broken Shackles

1976. 1st Anniv of Independence.
432 **38** 50c. multicoloured 10 10
433 3e. multicoloured 15 10
434 15e. multicoloured 40 20
435 50e. multicoloured 1·25 65

1976. Nos. 428, 424 and 415 optd **REPUBLICA DE.**
437 2e.50 multicoloured (No. 428) 15 10
438 4e. multicoloured (No. 424) 11·00 1·75
439 4e.50 multicoloured (No. 415) 1·00 1·00

40 Cabral and Map **41** Map of Islands

1976. 20th Anniv of PAIGC (Revolutionary Party).
440 **40** 1e. multicoloured 10 10

1977. Red Cross.
441 **41** 50c. multicoloured 10 10

42 Printed Circuit

43 Ashtray on Stand

1977. International Telecommunications Day.
442 **42** 5e.50 orange, brown & blk 15 10

1977. Craftsmanship in Coconut. Multicoloured.
443 20c. Type **43** 10 10
444 30c. Ornamental bell 10 10
445 50c. Lamp 10 10
446 1e. Nativity 10 10
447 1e.50 Desk lamp 10 10
448 5e. Storage jar 15 10
449 10e. Container with hinged lid 35 15
450 20e. Tobacco jar 65 20
451 30e. Stringed instrument . . 1·10 35

44 5r. Stamp, 1877

45 Congress Emblem

1977. Centenary of First Cape Verde Stamps.
452 **44** 4e. multicoloured 15 10
453 8e. multicoloured 25 10

1977. 3rd PAIGC Congress, Bissau.
454 **45** 3e.50 multicoloured 15 10

1978. No. 419 surch **3$00**.
455 3e. on 30c. multicoloured . . 15 10

47 Microwave Antenna

1978. 10th World Telecommunications Day.
456 **47** 3e.50 multicoloured 15 10

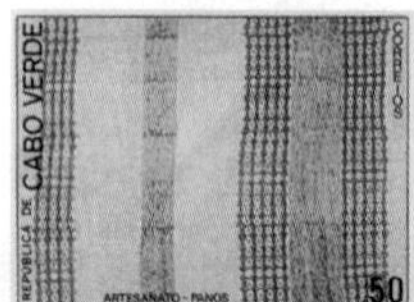

48 Textile Pattern

1978. Handicrafts. Multicoloured.
457 50c. Type **48** 10 10
458 1e.50 Carpet runner and map of Islands 10 10
459 2e. Woven ribbon and map of Islands 10 10
460 3e. Shoulder bag and map of Islands 10 10
461 10e. Woven Cushions (vert) 30 20

49 Map of Africa

51 Human Rights Emblem

50 Freighter "Cabo Verde"

1978. International Anti-Apartheid Year.
462 **49** 4e.50 multicoloured 15 10

1978. 1st Cape Verde Merchant Ship.
463 **50** 1e. multicoloured 50 10

1978. 30th Anniv of Declaration of Human Rights.
464 **51** 1e.50 multicoloured 10 10
465 2e. multicoloured 10 10

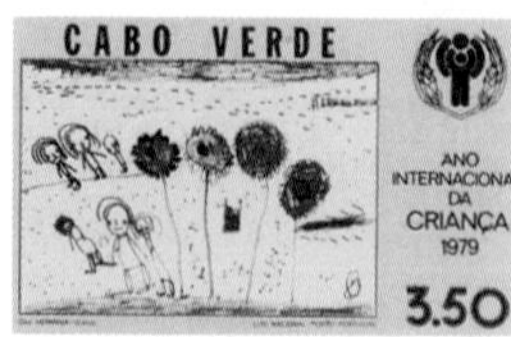

52 Children with Flowers

1979. International Year of the Child. Mult.
466 1e.50 Children with balloons and flags 10 10
467 3e.50 Type **52** 10 10

53 Monument

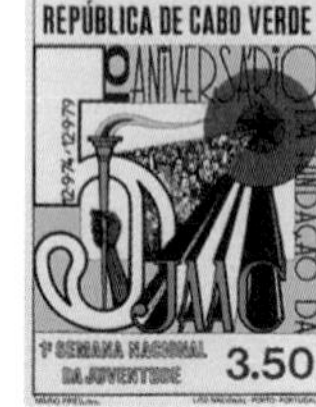

54 Poster

1979. 20th Anniv of Pindjiguiti Massacre.
468 **53** 4e.50 multicoloured 15 10

1979. 1st National Youth Week.
469 **54** 3e.50 multicoloured 15 10

55 Mindelo

1980. Centenary of Mindelo City.
470 **55** 4e. multicoloured 55 15

56 Family, Graph and Map

57 National Flag

1980. 1st Population and Housing Census.
471 **56** 3e.50 multicoloured 10 10
472 4e.50 multicoloured 15 10

1980. 5th Anniv of Independence (1st issue).
473 **57** 4e. multicoloured 10 10
See also Nos. 481/3.

58 Running

59 Stylized Bird

1980. Olympic Games, Moscow. Multicoloured.
474 1e. Type **58** 10 10
475 2e.50 Boxing 10 10
476 3e. Basketball 10 10
477 4e. Volleyball 10 10
478 20e. Swimming 55 25
479 50e. Tennis . . . . 1·25 50

1980. 5th Anniv of Independence (2nd issue).
481 **59** 4e. multicoloured 10 10
482 7e. multicoloured 15 10
483 11e. multicoloured 25 15

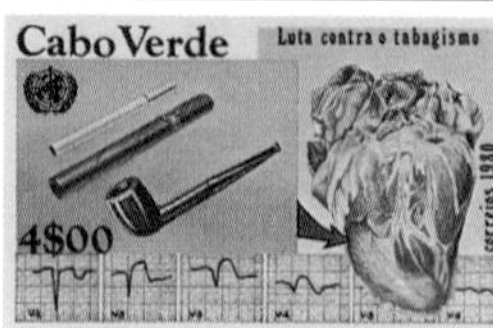

60 Cigarette, Cigar, Pipe and Diseased Heart

1980. World Health Day. Anti-smoking Campaign. Multicoloured.
484 4e. Type **60** 10 10
485 7e. Healthy lungs plus smoking equals diseased lungs 20 10

61 Albacore

1980. Marine Life. Multicoloured.
486 50c. Type **61** 10 10
487 4e.50 Atlantic horse-mackerel 15 10
488 8e. Mediterranean moray . . 40 15
489 10e. Brown meagre 40 15
490 12e. Skipjack tuna 50 20
491 50e. Blue shark . . . . . . 1·50 70

62 "Area Verdel"

1980. Freighters. Multicoloured.
492 3e. Type **62** 25 15
493 5e.50 "Ilha do Maio" 30 20
494 7e.50 "Ilha de Komo" . . . 65 25
495 9e. "Boa Vista" 65 25
496 12e. "Santo Antao" 75 35
497 30e. "Santiago" . . . . . . 1·75 75

63 "Lochnera rosea"

1980. Flowers. Multicoloured.
498 50c. Type **63** 10 10
499 4e.50 "Poinciana regia Bojer" 10 10
500 8e. "Mirabilis jalapa" . . . 25 10
501 10e. "Nerium oleander" . . . 25 10
502 12e. "Bougainvillea litoralis" 30 10
503 30e. "Hibiscus rosa sinenis" 70 30

64 Desert Scene and Hands holding plant

1981. Desert Erosion Prevention. Multicoloured.
504 4e.50 Type **64** 15 10
505 10e.50 Hands caring for plant and river scene 25 15

65 Map, Flag, and "Official Bulletin" announcing Constitution

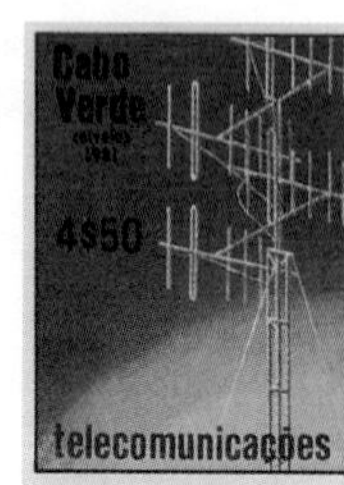

67 Antenna

1981. 6th Anniv of Constitution.
506 **65** 4e.50 multicoloured 15 10

1981. Telecommunications. Multicoloured.
508 4e.50 Type **67** 10 10
509 8e. Dish antenna 25 10
510 20e. Dish antenna and satellite 50 30

68 Disabled Person in Wheelchair and I.Y.D.P. Emblem

1981. International Year of Disabled Persons.
511 **68** 4e.50 multicoloured 15 10

69 Moorhens

1981. Birds. Multicoloured.
512 1e. Little egret (vert) 25 10
513 4e.50 Barn owl (vert) 40 20
514 8e. Grey-headed kingfisher (vert) 90 30
515 10e. Type **69** . . . . 1·90 40
516 12e. Helmet guineafowls . . 2·60 40

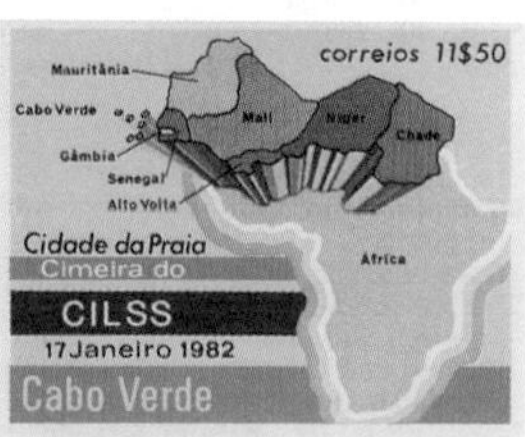

70 Map showing Member States

1982. CILSS Congress, Praia.
518 **70** 11e.50 multicoloured . . . 30 10

71 Tackle

1982. "Amilcar Cabral" Football Cup Competition. Multicoloured.
519 4e.50 Type **71** 15 10
520 7e.50 Running with ball . . . 20 10
521 11e.50 Goalmouth scene . . 30 10

72 Militiawomen

1982. 1st Anniv of Cape Verde Women's Organization. Multicoloured.
522 4e.50 Type **72** 15 10
523 8e. Women farmers 20 10
524 12e. Nursery teacher 30 10

73 Footballers

1982. World Cup Football Championship, Spain.
525 **73** 1e.50 multicoloured 10 10
526 – 4e.50 multicoloured 15 10
527 – 8e. multicoloured 20 10

528 – 10e.50 multicoloured . . . 25 10
529 – 12e. multicoloured 30 10
530 – 20e. multicoloured 50 30
DESIGNS: 4e.50 to 20e. Various football scenes.

74 "Morrissey-Ernestina"

1982. Return of Schooner "Morrissey-Ernestina".
532 **74** 12e. multicoloured . . . . 1·50 45

75 San Vicente Shipyard

1982. 7th Anniv of Independence.
533 **75** 10e.50 multicoloured . . . 1·25 45

76 "Hypolimnas misippus"

1982. Butterflies. Multicoloured.
534 2e. Type **76** 15 10
535 4e.50 "Melanitis lede" . . . 25 15
536 8e. "Catopsilia florella" . . . 40 20
537 10e.50 "Colias electo" . . . 55 20
538 11e.50 "Danaus chrysippus" 65 20
539 12e. "Papilio demodecus" . . 65 20

77 Amilcar Cabral

1983. Amilcar Cabral Symposium.
540 **77** 7e. multicoloured 15 10
541 10e.50 multicoloured . . . 20 10

78 Francisco Xavier de Cruz (composer)

1983. Composers and Poets. Multicoloured.
543 7e. Type **78** 15 10
544 14e. Eugenio Tavares (poet) 30 10

79 "World Communications Network" 80 Cape Verde Cone

1983. World Communications Year.
545 **79** 13e. multicoloured 20 10

1983. Shells. Multicoloured.
546 50c. Type **80** 10 10
547 1e. "Conus decoratus" . . . 10 10
548 3e. "Conus salreiensis" . . . 15 10
549 10e. "Conus verdensis" . . . 30 20
550 50e. "Conus cuneolus" . . . 1·40 90

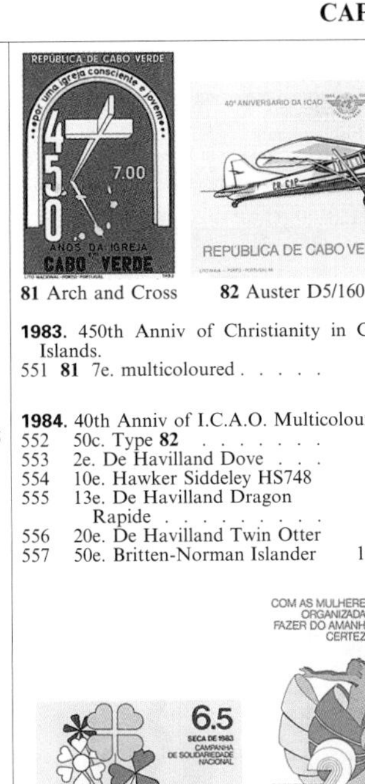

81 Arch and Cross 82 Auster D5/160 Husky

1983. 450th Anniv of Christianity in Cape Verde Islands.
551 **81** 7e. multicoloured 15 10

1984. 40th Anniv of I.C.A.O. Multicoloured.
552 50c. Type **82** 10 10
553 2e. De Havilland Dove . . . 10 10
554 10e. Hawker Siddeley HS748 25 15
555 13e. De Havilland Dragon Rapide 25 15
556 20e. De Havilland Twin Otter 50 30
557 50e. Britten-Norman Islander 1·10 65

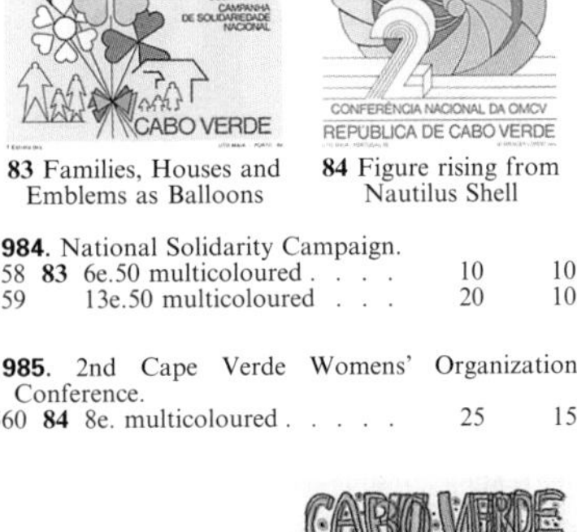

83 Families, Houses and Emblems as Balloons 84 Figure rising from Nautilus Shell

1984. National Solidarity Campaign.
558 **83** 6e.50 multicoloured 10 10
559 13e.50 multicoloured . . . 20 10

1985. 2nd Cape Verde Womens' Organization Conference.
560 **84** 8e. multicoloured 25 15

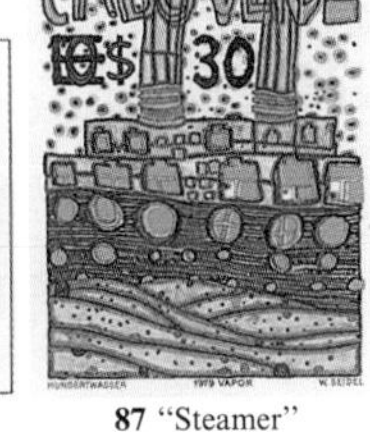

85 Emblem 87 "Steamer"

1985. 10th Anniv of Independence.
561 **85** 8e. multicoloured 15 10
562 12e. multicoloured 20 10

1985.
564 **87** 30e. on 10c. multicoloured 40 40

88 "Mabuya vaillanti" 89 Food in Pot over Fire

1986. Endangered Reptiles. Multicoloured.
566 8e. Type **88** 30 10
567 10e. "Tarentola gigas brancoensis" 35 10
568 15e. "Tarentola gigas gigas" 45 10
569 30e. "Hemidactylus bouvieri" 90 20

1986. World Food Day. Multicoloured.
571 8e. Type **89** 15 10
572 12e. Women pounding food in mortar 15 10
573 15e. Woman rolling flat bread with stone 20 10

90 Dove and Olive Branch

1986. International Peace Year.
574 **90** 12e. multicoloured 15 10
575 30e. multicoloured 40 20

91 Family Planning and Child Health Centre, Praia, and Woman breast-feeding Baby

1987. Child Survival Campaign. Multicoloured.
576 8e. Type **91** 15 10
577 10e. Assomada SOS children's village 15 10
578 12e. Family planning clinic, Mindelo, and nurse with child 15 10
579 16e. Children's home, Mindelo, and nurse with baby 25 10
580 100e. Calouste Gulbenkian kindergarten, Praia, and child writing . . . . 1·40 1·25

92 Mindelo City

1987. Tourism. Multicoloured.
581 1e. Type **92** 10 10
582 2e.50 Santo Antao island . . 10 10
583 5e. Fogo island 10 10
584 8e. Pillory, Velha City . . . 15 10
585 10e. Boa Entrada valley, Santiago island 15 10
586 12e. Fishing boats, Santiago 50 15
587 100e. Furna harbour, Brava island . . . . 1·40 65

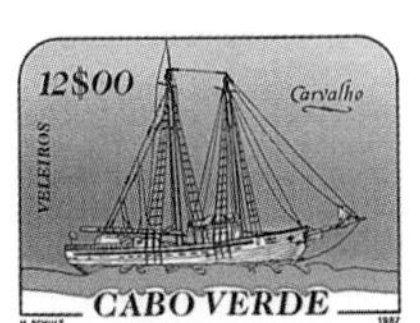

93 "Carvalho" (schooner)

1987. Sailing Ships. Multicoloured.
588 **93** 12e. black, mauve & blue 45 20
589 – 16e. black, blue & mauve 45 20
590 – 50e. black, blue & dp blue 1·90 70
DESIGNS: 16e. "Nauta" (cutter); 50e. "Maria Sony" (schooner).

94 Emblem

1987. 2nd National Development Plan.
592 **94** 8e. multicoloured 15 10

95 Moths on Stem

1988. Crop Protection. Multicoloured.
593 50c. Type **95** 10 10
594 2e. Caterpillars on plant treated with bio-insecticides 10 10
595 9e. Use of imported predators 20 10
596 13e. Use of imported predatorial insects 30 15
597 16e. Locust on stem 35 15
598 19e. Damaged wood 45 20

96 17th-century Dutch Map

1988. Antique Maps of Cape Verde Islands. Multicoloured.
600 1e.50 Type **96** 10 10
601 2e.50 18th-cent Belgian map 10 10
602 4e.50 18th-cent French map 10 10
603 9e.50 18th-cent English map 15 10
604 19e.50 19th-cent English map 30 15
605 20e. 18th-cent French map (vert) 30 15

97 Church of the Abbot of the Holy Shelter, Tarrafal, Santiago

1988. Churches. Multicoloured.
606 5e. Type **97** 10 10
607 8e. Church of Our Lady of Light, Maio 15 10
608 10e. Church of the Nazarene, Praia, Santiago 15 10
609 12e. Church of Our Lady of the Rosary, Sao Nicolau 20 10
610 15e. Church of the Nazarene, Mindelo, Sao Vicente . . . 25 15
611 20e. Church of Our Lady of Grace, Praia, Santiago . . 30 15

98 Boy filling Tin with Water

1988. Water Economy Campaign.
612 **98** 12e. multicoloured 20 10

99 Red Cross Workers

1988. 125th Anniv of Red Cross Movement.
613 **99** 7e. multicoloured 10 10

100 Group of Youths and Pres. Pereira

1988. 3rd Congress of African Party for the Independence of Cape Verde. Multicoloured.
614 7e. Type **100** 10 10
615 10e.50 Pres. Pereira and Perez de Cuellar (U.N. Secretary-General) 15 10
616 30e. Emblem and Pres. Pereira 50 25

101 Handball

1988. Olympic Games, Seoul. Multicoloured.
618 12e. Type **101** 20 10
619 15e. Tennis 25 15
620 20e. Football 30 15
621 30e. Boxing 50 25

102 Hot-air Balloon "Pro Juventute"

1989. 2nd Pro Juventute Congress.
623 **102** 30e. multicoloured 45 25

103 Silva

1989. Death Centenary of Roberto Duarte Silva (chemist).

624 **103** 12e.50 multicoloured 20 10

104 "Liberty guiding the People" (Eugene Delacroix)

1989. Bicentenary of French Revolution.

625 **104** 20e. multicoloured 30 15
626 24e. multicoloured 35 20
627 25e. multicoloured 40 20

105 Anniversary Emblem

1989. Centenary of Interparliamentary Union. Mult.

629 2e. Type **105** 10 10
630 4e. Dove 10 10
631 13e. National Assembly building 20 10

106 Fonte Lima Women firing Pots

1989. Traditional Pottery. Multicoloured.

632 13e. Type **106** 20 10
633 20e. Terra di Monti women and children arranging pots to bake in sun (vert) 30 15
634 24e. Terra di Monti woman shaping pot 35 20
635 25e. Fonte Lima women kneading clay (vert) 40 20

107 Boy and Truck

108 Pope John Paul II

1989. Christmas. Home-made Toys. Mult.

636 1e. Type **107** 10 10
637 6e. Boy with car on waste ground 10 10
638 8e. Boy with truck on pavement 15 10
639 11e.50 Boys with various vehicles 15 10
640 18e. Boys and sit-on scooter 30 15
641 100e. Boy with boat 1·50 75

1990. Papal Visit.

642 **108** 13e. multicoloured 20 10
643 20e. multicoloured 30 15

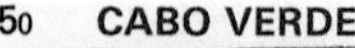
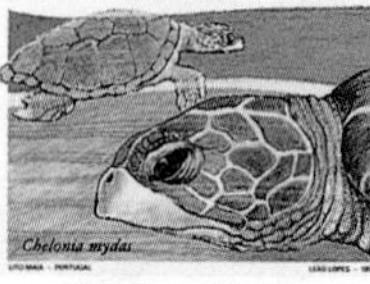
109 Green Turtles

1990. Turtles. Multicoloured.

645 50c. Type **109** 10 10
646 1e. Leatherback turtles 10 10
647 5e. Olive ridley turtles 10 10
648 10e. Loggerhead turtles 15 10
649 42e. Hawksbill turtles 65 35

110 Footballers

1990. World Cup Football Championship, Italy.

650 **110** 4e. multicoloured 10 10
651 – 7e.50 multicoloured 15 10
652 – 8e. multicoloured 15 10
653 – 100e. multicoloured 1·60 80

DESIGNS: 7e.50 to 100e. Different footballing scenes.

111 Face

1990. 1st Congress of Cape Verde Women's Movement.

655 **111** 9e. multicoloured 15 10

112 Teacher helping Boy to Read

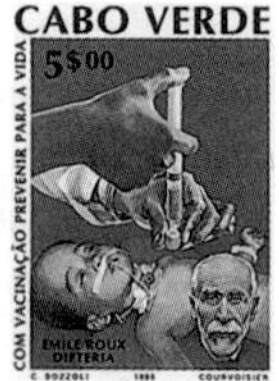
113 Diphtheria Treatment and Emile Roux (pioneer of antitoxic method)

1990. International Literacy Year. Multicoloured.

656 2e. Type **112** 10 10
657 3e. Teacher with adult class 10 10
658 15e. Teacher with flash-card 25 15
659 19e. Adult student pointing to letters on blackboard 30 15

1990. Vaccination Campaign. Multicoloured.

660 5e. Type **113** 10 10
661 13e. Tuberculosis vaccination and Robert Koch (discoverer of tubercle bacillus) 20 10
662 20e. Tetanus vaccination and Gaston Ramon 30 15
663 24e. Poliomyelitis oral vaccination and Jonas Edward Salk (discoverer of vaccine) 40 20

114 Musician on Bull's Back

1990. Traditional Stories. Multicoloured.

664 50c. Type **114** 10 10
665 2e.50 Fisherman and mermaid ("Joao Piquinote") 10 10
666 12e. Girl and snake 20 10
667 25e. Couple and eggs ("Ti Lobo, Ti Lobo") 40 20

115 World Map and Beam destroying AIDS Virus

1991. Anti-AIDS Campaign. Multicoloured.

668 13e. Type **115** 20 10
669 24e. Beam, AIDS virus and "SIDA" 40 20

116 Fishing Boat at Sea and Fishermen on Shore

1991. Fishing Industry. Multicoloured.

670 10e. Type **116** 20 15
671 24e. Fisherman removing hook from fish 70 30
672 25e. Fishing boats 55 30
673 50e. Fishermen taking in lines 1·10 65

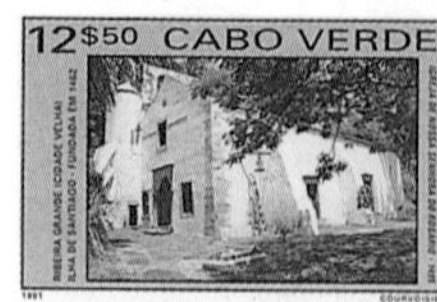
117 Our Lady of the Rosary Church

1991. Tourism. Ruins of Ribeira Grande, Santiago Island. Multicoloured.

674 12e.50 Type **117** 20 10
675 15e. Se Cathedral 25 15
676 20e. Sao Filipe fortress 30 15
677 30e. St. Francis's Convent 45 20

118 "Lavandula rotundifolia"

119 Guitar

1991. Medicinal Plants. Multicoloured.

679 10e. Type **118** 15 10
680 15e. "Micromeria forbesii" 25 15
681 21e. "Sarcostemma daltonii" 30 15
682 24e. "Periploca chevalieri" 40 20
683 30e. "Echium hypertropicum" 45 20
684 35e. "Erysimum caboverdeanum" 55 25

1991. Musical Instruments. Multicoloured.

685 10e. Type **119** 25 15
686 20e. Violin 50 35
687 29e. Guitar with five double strings 80 40
688 47e. Cimboa 1·25 75

120 Crib (Tito Livio Goncalves)

1991. Christmas. Multicoloured.

690 31e. Type **120** 50 25
691 50e. Fonte-Lima crib 80 40

121 Rose Apples

1992. Tropical Fruits. Multicoloured.

692 16e. Type **121** 35 15
693 25e. Mangoes 50 25
694 31e. Cashews 65 30
695 32e. Avocados 70 35

122 Ships anchored in Bay

1992. 500th Anniv of Discovery of America by Columbus. Columbus's Landings in Cape Verde Islands. Multicoloured.

696 40e. Type **122** 1·10 70
697 40e. Caravel 1·10 70

124 Throwing the Javelin

1992. Olympic Games, Barcelona. Multicoloured.

700 16e. Type **124** 35 15
701 20e. Weightlifting 40 20
702 32e. Pole vaulting 70 35
703 40e. Putting the shot 85 40

125 Oxen and Sugar Cane

1992. Production of Molasses. Multicoloured.

705 19e. Type **125** 35 15
706 20e. Crushing cane 35 15
707 37e. Feeding cane into mill 70 35
708 38e. Cooking molasses 70 35

126 Cat

1992. Domestic Animals. Multicoloured.

709 16e. Type **126** 30 15
710 31e. Chickens 55 25
711 32e. Dog (vert) 60 30
712 50e. Horse 90 45

127 "Tubastrea aurea"

1993. Corals. Multicoloured.

713 5e. Type **127** 10 10
714 31e. "Corallium rubrum" 55 25
715 37e. "Porites porites" 65 30
716 50e. "Millepora alcicornis" 90 45

129 King Ferdinand and Queen Isabella of Spain and Pope Alexander VI

130 "Palinurus charlestoni"

1993. 500th Annivs of Pope Alexander VI's Bulls (on Portuguese and Spanish spheres of influence) and of Treaty of Tordesillas. Multicoloured.

718 37e. Type **129** 65 30
719 37e. King Joao II of Portugal and Pope Julius II 65 30
720 38e. Astrolabe, quill and left-half of globe 70 35
721 38e. Map of Iberian Peninsula and right-half of globe with Cape Verde Islands highlighted 70 35

Stamps of the same value were issued together in se-tenant pairs, each pair forming a composite design.

1993. Lobsters. Multicoloured.

722 2e. Type **130** 10 10
723 10e. Brown lobster 20 10
724 17e. Royal lobster 30 15
725 38e. Stone lobster 70 35

131 Cory's Shearwater

1993. Nature Reserves. Multicoloured.

727 10e. Type **131** (Branco and Raso Islets) 25 15
728 30e. Brown booby (De Cima and Raso Islets) 80 25
729 40e. Magnificent frigate bird (Curral Velho and Baluarte Islets) 1·50 35
730 41e. Red-billed tropic bird (Raso and De Cima Islets) 1·90 40

132 Rose

1993. Flowers. Multicoloured.
731 5e. Type **132** 10 10
732 30e. Bird of Paradise flower 55 25
733 37e. Sweet William 65 30
734 50e. Cactus dahlia 90 45

133 Map and Prince Henry (½-size illustration)

1994. 600th Birth Anniv of Prince Henry the Navigator.
736 **133** 37e. multicoloured 55 25

134 Players and Giants Stadium, New York

1994. World Cup Football Championship, U.S.A. Multicoloured.
737 1e. Type **134** 10 10
738 20e. Referee showing red card and Rose Bowl, Los Angeles 30 15
739 37e. Scoring goal and Foxboro Stadium, Boston 55 25
740 38e. Linesman raising flag and Silverdome, Detroit . . 55 25

135 Sand Tiger

136 "Prata" Bananas

1994. Sharks. Multicoloured.
742 21e. Type **135** 45 15
743 27e. Black-tipped shark . . . 60 25
744 37e. Whale shark . . . . . . 1·00 50
745 38e. Velvet belly . . . . . . 1·00 50

1994. Bananas. Multicoloured.
746 12e. Type **136** 20 10
747 16e. "Pao" bananas (horiz) 25 10
748 30e. "Ana roberta" bananas 45 20
749 40e. "Roxa" bananas 60 30

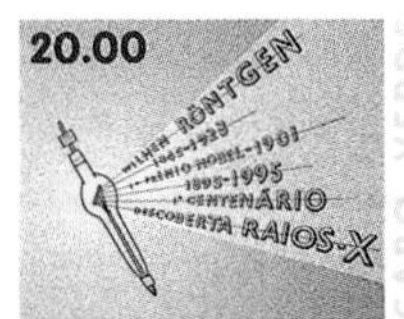

137 Fontes Pereira de Melo

1994. Lighthouses. Multicoloured.
751 2e. Type **137** 10 10
752 37e. Morro Negro 60 30
753 38e. D. Amelia (vert) 60 30
754 50e. D. Maria Pia (vert) . . . 80 40

138 X-Ray Tube and Dates

1995. Centenary of Discovery of X-Rays by Wilhelm Röntgen.
755 **138** 20e. multicoloured 30 15
756 37e. multicoloured 60 30

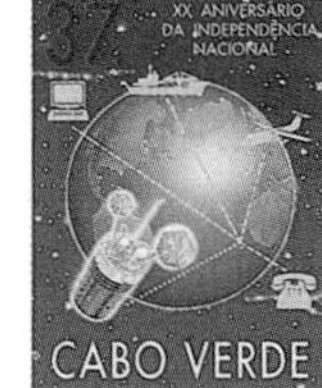

139 Child with Tuna

141 Communications

140 Wire-haired Fox Terrier and "Two Foxhounds and Fox Terrier" (John Emms)

1995. 50th Anniv of F.A.O. Multicoloured.
758 37e. Type **139** 70 30
759 38e. Globe and wheat ear . . 60 30

1995. Dogs. Heads of dogs and paintings. Mult.
760 1e. Type **140** 10 10
761 10e. Cavalier King Charles and "Shooting Over Dogs" (Richard Ansdell) 15 10
762 40e. German shepherd and rough collies 65 30
763 50e. Bearded collie and "Hounds at Full Cry" (Thomas Blinks) 80 40

1995. 20th Anniv of Independence.
764 **141** 37e. multicoloured . . . . 1·00 40

143 Horse Race

1995. St. Philip's Flag Festival, Fogo. Mult.
766 2e. Type **143** 10 10
767 10e. Preparing for horse race 15 10
768 37e. Preparing food and clapping to music 55 25
769 40e. Crowd watching final horse race 60 30

144 Grasshopper playing Guitar

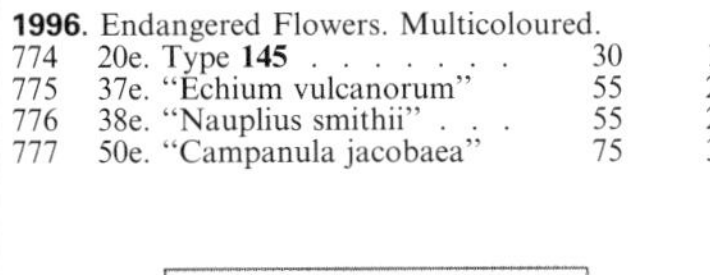

145 "Sonchus daltonii"

1995. Childrens' Stories. 300th Death Anniv of Jean de La Fontaine (writer). Scenes from "The Ant and the Grasshopper". Multicoloured.
770 10e. Type **144** 15 10
771 25e. Grasshopper in snowstorm looking through ants' window 40 20
772 38e. Ant laying-in supplies for winter 55 25
773 45e. Ants welcoming grasshopper into their home 70 35

1996. Endangered Flowers. Multicoloured.
774 20e. Type **145** 30 15
775 37e. "Echium vulcanorum" 55 25
776 38e. "Nauplius smithii" . . . 55 25
777 50e. "Campanula jacobaea" 75 35

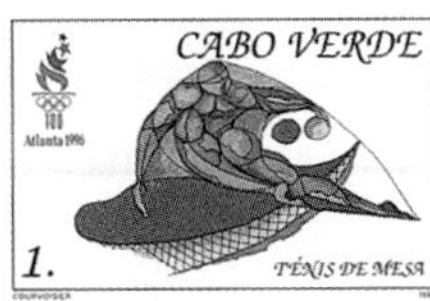

146 Table Tennis

1996. Olympic Games, Atlanta. Multicoloured.
778 1e. Type **146** 10 10
779 37e. Gymnastics 55 25
780 100e. Athletics . . . . 1·50 75

147 Student (Education of Girls)

148 Deep Sea Fishing

1996. 50th Anniv of U.N.I.C.E.F. Multicoloured.
781 20e. Type **147** 25 10
782 40e. Mother kissing child (Right to Love) 50 25

1996. Water Sports. Multicoloured.
783 2e.50 Type **148** 10 10
784 10e. Sailboard 20 10
785 22e.50 Jet skiing 30 15
786 100e. Surfing (horiz) . . . . 1·25 60

1997. Nos. 582 and 650/1 surch.
788 3e. on 2e.50 multicoloured . . 10 10
789 37e. on 4e. multicoloured . . 50 25
790 38e. on 7e.50 multicoloured 55 25

150 State Arms

1997. National Symbols. Multicoloured.
791 25e. Type **150** 30 15
792 37e. National anthem 40 20
793 50e. State flag 60 30

151 Small-toothed Sawfish

1997. The Small-toothed Sawfish. Multicoloured.
794 15e. Type **151** 20 10
795 15e. Underside of sawfish . . 20 10
796 15e. Sawfish and school of fishes 20 10
797 15e. Two sawfishes 20 10

152 Fish and Dolphins

1997. Oceans. Multicoloured.
798 45e. Type **152** 55 25
799 45e. Mermaid and merman 55 25
800 45e. Fishes, eel, coral and sunken gate 55 25

Nos. 798/800 were issued together, se-tenant, forming a composite design.

153 Yellow-finned Tuna

1997. Tuna. Multicoloured.
801 13e. Type **153** 15 10
802 21e. Big-eyed tuna 25 10
803 41e. Little tuna 50 25
804 45e. Skipjack tuna 55 25

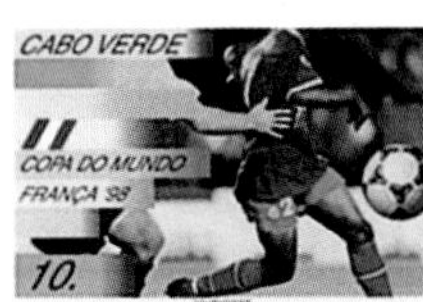

154 Players chasing Ball

1998. World Cup Football Championship, France. Multicoloured.
805 10e. Type **154** 10 10
806 30e. Ball in net (vert) 45 20
807 45e. Player with ball (vert) 55 25
808 50e. Globe, football and trophy 60 30

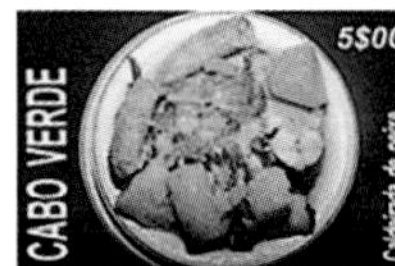

155 Fish Dish

1998. Local Cuisine.
809 **155** 5e. multicoloured 10 10
810 – 25e. multicoloured 30 15
811 – 35e. multicoloured 40 20
812 – 40e. multicoloured 45 20

DESIGNS: 25e. to 40e. Different food dishes.

156 Navigators reading Books and Banana Tree

1998. 500th Anniv (1997) of Vasco da Gama's Expedition to India. Multicoloured.
813 50e. Type **156** 60 30
814 50e. Seaman with sword and couple 60 30
815 50e. Compass rose and Portuguese galleon in harbour . . . . 1·00 40

Nos. 813/15 were issued together, se-tenant, forming a composite design.

157 Brava Island Costume

158 "Byblia ilithyia"

1998. Local Women's Costumes. Multicoloured.
816 10e. Type **157** 10 10
817 18e. Fogo Island 20 10
818 30e. Boa Vista Island 35 15
819 50e. Santiago Island 60 30

1999. Butterflies and Moths. Multicoloured.
820 5e. Type **158** 10 10
821 10e. "Aganais speciosa" . . . 10 10
822 20e. Crimson-speckled moth 25 10
823 30e. Painted lady 35 15
824 50e. Cabbage looper 60 30
825 100e. "Grammodes congenita" . . . . 1·25 60

159 Concorde in Flight

1999. 30th Anniv of Concorde (supersonic airplane). Multicoloured.
827 30e. Type **159** 35 15
828 50e. Concorde on airport apron 60 30

160 Alain Gerbault (solo yachtsman) and Mindelo Harbour

1999. "Philexfrance 99" International Stamp Exhibition, Paris, France. Multicoloured.
829 30e. Type **160** 40 20
830 50e. Roberto Duarte Silva (chemist) and Eiffel Tower, Paris 60 30

161 Globe in Envelope and U.P.U. Emblem

1999. 125th Anniv of Universal Postal Union. Mult.

832 30e. Type **161** 40 20
833 50e. Paper airplanes 60 30

Nos. 832/3 are not inscribed with the country name.

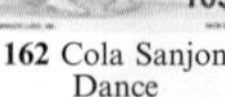

162 Cola Sanjon Dance — **163** Globe, Open Book and Hourglass

1999. Local Dances. Multicoloured.

834 10e. Type **162** 10 10
835 30e. Contradanca 30 15
836 50e. Desfile de Tabanca (horiz) 50 25
837 100e. Batuque (horiz) . . . . 1·00 50

2000. New Millennium. Multicoloured.

838 40e. Type **163** 40 20
839 50e. "2000" (horiz) 50 25

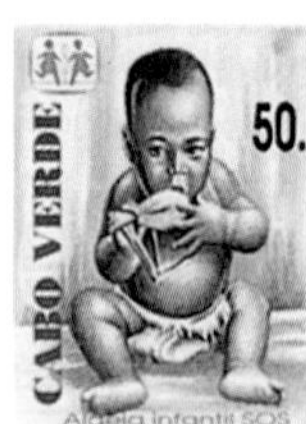

164 Baby

2000. 50th Anniv (1999) of S.O.S. Children's Villages. Multicoloured.

840 50e. Type **164** 50 25
841 100e. Child and emblem (horiz) . . . . 1·00 50

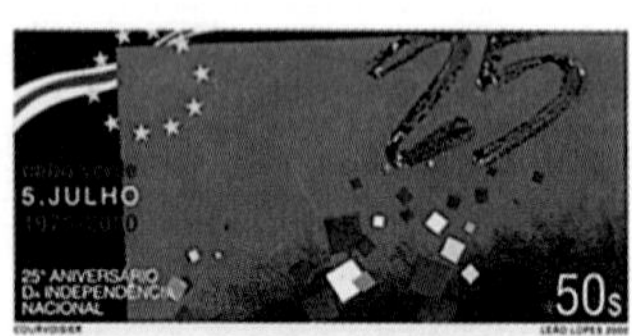

165 "25" and Emblem

2000. 25th Anniv of Independence.

842 **165** 50e. multicoloured 50 25

166 Gymnastics

2000. Olympic Games, Sydney. Multicoloured.

843 10e. Type **166** 10 10
844 40e. Taekwondo 40 20
845 50e. Athletics 50 25

167 Dragon Tree — **168** Students (left-hand detail)

2000. Dragon Tree.

847 **167** 5e. green 10 10
848 40e. red 50 25
849 60e. brown 70 35

2000. 134th Anniv of the Liceu de Sao Nicolau Seminary. Multicoloured.

850 60e. Type **168** 70 35
851 60e. Students (right-hand detail) 70 35
852 60e. Jose Alves Feio, Jose Julio Dias (co-founders) and Antonio Jose de Oliveira Boucas (Principal) (56 × 26 mm) 70 35

Nos. 850/2 were issued together, se-tenant, forming a composite design.

CHARITY TAX STAMPS

Used on certain days of the year as an additional postal tax on internal letters. Other values in some of the types were for use on telegrams only. The proceeds were devoted to public charities. If one was not affixed in addition to the ordinary postage, postage due stamps were used to collect the deficiency and the fine.

1925. As Marquis de Pombal issue of Portugal but inscr "CABO VERDE".

C266 C **73** 15c. violet 25 25
C267 – 15c. violet 25 25
C268 C **75** 15c. violet 25 25

C **16** St. Isabel — C **31** — C **32**

1948.

C321 C **16** 50c. green . . . . . . 1·25 85
C322 1e. red . . . . 2·50 1·00

1959. Surch.

C368 C **16** 50c. on 1e. red 50 30

1959. Colours changed.

C369 C **16** 50c. mauve . . . . . 1·10 65
C370 1e. blue . . . . 1·10 65

1967.

C406 C **31** 30c. multicoloured . . 15 15
C407 50c. mult (purple panel) 30 30
C408 50c. mult (red panel) 15 15
C409 1e. mult (brown panel) 45 45
C410 1e. mult (purple panel) 45 45

1968. Pharmaceutical Tax stamps surch as in Type C **32**.

C411a C **32** 50c. on 1c. black, orange and green 80 60
C412c 50c. on 2c. black, orange and green 40 25
C413 50c. on 3c. black, orange and green 55 40
C414 50c. on 5c. black, orange and green 55 40
C415 50c. on 10c. black, orange and green 65 55
C416 1e. on 1c. black, orange and green 1·50 1·00
C417a 1e. on 2c. black, orange and green 1·00 85

NEWSPAPER STAMP

1893. "Newspaper" key-type inscr "CABO VERDE".

N37 V 2½r. brown 55 35

POSTAGE DUE STAMPS

1904. "Due" key-type inscr "CABO VERDE".

D119 W 5r. green 15 15
D120 10r. grey 15 15
D121 20r. brown 15 15
D122 30r. orange 40 20
D123 50r. brown 20 15
D124 60r. brown . . . . . . 3·00 1·75
D125 100r. mauve 80 50
D126 130r. blue 80 50
D127 200r. red 85 75
D128 500r. lilac . . . . 2·10 1·50

1911. Nos. D119/28 optd **REPUBLICA**.

D135 W 5r. green 10 10
D136 10r. grey 10 10
D137 20r. brown 15 10
D138 30r. orange 15 10
D139 50r. brown 15 10
D140 60r. brown 30 20
D141 100r. mauve 30 20
D142 130r. blue 35 25
D143 200r. red 75 60
D144 500r. lilac 90 75

1921. "Due" key-type inscr "CABO VERDE" with currency in centavos.

D252 W ½c. green 10 10
D253 1c. slate 10 10
D254 2c. brown 10 10
D255 3c. orange 10 10
D256 5c. brown 10 10
D257 6c. brown 10 10
D258 10c. mauve 15 15
D259 13c. blue 30 25
D260 20c. red 30 25
D261 50c. grey 60 45

1925. As Nos. C266/8, optd **MULTA**.

D266 C **73** 30c. violet 25 25
D267 – 30c. violet 25 25
D268 C **75** 30c. violet 25 25

1952. As Type D **45** of Angola, but inscr "CABO VERDE". Numerals in red; name in black.

D356 10c. brown and grey . . . 10 10
D357 30c. black, blue & mauve 10 10
D358 50c. blue, green & yellow 10 10
D359 1e. blue and pale blue . . . 10 10
D360 2e. brown and orange . . . 20 20
D361 5e. green and grey 45 45

CAROLINE ISLANDS — Pt. 7

A group of islands in the Pacific Ocean, formerly a German protectorate; under Japanese mandate after 1918. Now under United States trusteeship.

100 pfennig = 1 mark.

1899. Stamps of Germany optd **Karolinen**.

7 **8** 3pf. brown . . . . 9·50 10·50
8 5pf. green . . . . 10·50 11·00
9 **9** 10pf. red . . . . 17·00 13·00
10 20pf. blue . . . . 17·00 19·00
11 25pf. orange . . . . 38·00 48·00
12 50pf. brown . . . . 42·00 42·00

1901. "Yacht" key-types inscr "KAROLINEN".

13 N 3pf. brown . . . . 65 1·40
14 5pf. green . . . . 65 1·40
15 10pf. red . . . . 80 3·50
16 20pf. blue . . . . 95 5·00
17 25f. black & red on yellow 1·25 10·00
18 30pf. black & orge on buff 1·25 10·00
19 40pf. black and red . . . . 1·10 11·00
20 50pf. black & pur on buff 1·40 14·00
21 80pf. black & red on rose . . 2·10 17·00
22 O 1m. red . . . . 3·50 42·00
23 2m. blue . . . . 6·00 60·00
24 3m. black . . . . 10·00 £110
25 5m. red and black £140 £425

1910. No. 13 surch **5 Pf**.

26 N 5pf. on 3pf. brown . . . . . — £4250

CASTELROSSO — Pt. 3

One of the Aegean Is. Occupied by the French Navy on 27 December 1915. The French withdrew in August 1921 and, after a period of Italian Naval administration, the island was included in the Dodecanese territory.

A. FRENCH OCCUPATION

100 centimes = 1 franc = 4 piastres.

1920. Stamps of 1902–20 of French Post Offices in Turkish Empire optd **B. N. F. CASTELLORIZO**.

F 1 A 1c. grey . . . . 30·00 30·00
F 2 2c. purple . . . . 30·00 30·00
F 3 3c. red . . . . 30·00 30·00
F 4 5c. green . . . . 38·00 38·00
F 5 B 10c. red . . . . 38·00 38·00
F 6 15c. red . . . . 55·00 55·00
F 7 20c. brown . . . . 60·00 60·00
F 8 1pi. on 20c. blue . . . . . 60·00 60·00
F 9 30c. lilac . . . . 65·00 65·00
F10 C 40c. red and blue £120 £120
F11 2pi. on 50c. brown & lilac £130 £130
F12 4pi. on 1f. red & green . . £170 £170
F13 20pi. on 5f. blue & brown £450 £450

1920. Optd **O. N. F. Castellorizo**. (a) On stamps of 1902–20 of French Post Offices in Turkish Empire.

F14 A 1c. grey . . . . 19·00 19·00
F15 2c. purple . . . . 19·00 19·00
F16 3c. red . . . . 19·00 19·00
F17 5c. green . . . . 19·00 19·00
F18 B 10c. red . . . . 21·00 21·00
F19 15c. red . . . . 26·00 26·00
F20 20c. brown . . . . 45·00 45·00
F21 1pi. on 25c. blue . . . . . 45·00 45·00
F22 30c. lilac . . . . 40·00 40·00
F23 C 40c. red and blue . . . . . 40·00 40·00
F24 2pi. on 50c. brown & lilac 40·00 40·00
F25 4pi. on 1f. red and green 55·00 55·00
F26 20pi. on 5f. blue & brown £250 £250

(b) On Nos. 334 and 341 of France.

F27 **18** 10c. red . . . . 26·00 16·00
F28 25c. blue . . . . 26·00 16·00

1920. Stamps of France optd **O F CASTELLORISO**.

F29 **18** 5c. green £120 £120
F30 10c. red £120 £120
F31 20c. red £120 £120
F32 25c. blue £120 £120
F33 **13** 50c. brown and lilac . . . £700 £700
F34 1f. red and green £700 £700

B. ITALIAN OCCUPATION

100 centesimi = 1 lira.

1922. Stamps of Italy optd **CASTELROSSO**.

15 **37** 5c. green . . . . 90 15·00
16 10c. red . . . . 90 15·00
17 15c. grey . . . . 90 18·00
18 **41** 20c. orange . . . . 90 18·00
19 **39** 25c. blue . . . . 90 15·00
20 40c. brown . . . . 90 15·00
21 50c. violet . . . . 90 17·00
22 60c. red . . . . 90 21·00
23 85c. brown . . . . 90 26·00
24 **34** 1l. brown and green . . . . 90 26·00

2

1923.

10 **2** 5c. green . . . . 1·90 11·00
11 10c. red . . . . 1·90 11·00
12 25c. blue . . . . 1·90 11·00
13 50c. purple . . . . 1·90 11·00
14 1l. brown . . . . 1·90 11·00

1930. Ferrucci stamps of Italy optd **CASTELROSSO**.

25 **114** 20c. violet . . . . 4·25 3·25
26 – 25c. green (No. 283) . . . 4·25 6·00
27 – 50c. black (as No. 284) . . 4·25 3·25
28 – 1l.25 blue (No. 285) . . . 4·25 8·00
29 – 5l.+2l. red (as No. 286) . . 15·00 35·00

1932. Garibaldi stamps of Italy optd **CASTELROSSO**.

30 – 10c. brown . . . . 15·00 25·00
31 **128** 20c. brown . . . . 15·00 25·00
32 – 25c. green . . . . 15·00 25·00
33 **128** 30c. blue . . . . 15·00 25·00
34 – 50c. purple . . . . 15·00 25·00
35 – 75c. red . . . . 15·00 25·00
36 – 1l.25 blue . . . . 15·00 25·00
37 – 1l.75+25c. brown . . . . . 15·00 25·00
38 – 2l.55+50c. red . . . . . . 15·00 25·00
39 – 5l.+1l. violet . . . . 15·00 25·00

CAUCA — Pt. 20

A State of Colombia, reduced to a Department in 1886, now uses Colombian stamps.

100 centavos = 1 peso.

2

1902. Imperf.

2 **2** 10c. black on red . . . . . . 1·00 1·00
3 20c. black on orange 85 85

CAVALLA (KAVALLA) — Pt. 16

French P.O. in a former Turkish port, now closed.

100 centimes = 1 franc.
40 paras = 1 piastre.

1893. Stamps of France optd **Cavalle** or surch also in figures and words.

41 **10** 5c. green . . . . 10·50 8·25
43 10c. black on lilac . . . . 14·50 10·50
45 15c. blue . . . . 22·00 13·00
46 1pi. on 25c. black on pink 17·00 12·50
47 2pi. on 50c. red . . . . . 55·00 38·00
48a 4pi. on 1f. green . . . . . 55·00 48·00
49 8pi. on 2f. brown on blue 70·00 65·00

1902. "Blanc", "Mouchon" and "Merson" key-types inscr "CAVALLE". The four higher values surch also.

50 A 5c. green . . . . 1·10 90
51 B 10c. red . . . . 1·10 95
52 15c. red . . . . 6·00 6·00
53 15c. orange . . . . 1·50 1·10
54 1pi. on 25c. blue . . . . . . 2·25 1·50
55 C 2pi. on 50c. brown & lilac 6·00 4·00
56 4pi. on 1f. red and green . . 8·00 6·00
57 8pi. on 2f. lilac and brown 10·00 9·00

CAYES OF BELIZE — Pt. 1

A chain of several hundred islands, coral atolls, reefs and sandbanks stretching along the eastern seaboard of Belize.

The following issues for the Cayes of Belize fall outside the criteria for full listing as detailed on page viii.

100 cents = 1 dollar.

APPENDIX

1984.

Marine Life, Map and Views, 1, 2, 5, 10, 15, 25, 75c., $3, $5.

250th Anniv of "Lloyd's List" (newspaper). 25, 75c., $1, $2.

Olympic Games, Los Angeles. 10, 15, 75c., $2.

90th Anniv of "Caye Service" Local Stamps. 10, 15, 75c., $2.

1985.

Birth Bicent of John J. Audubon (ornithologist). 25, 75c., $1, $3.

Shipwrecks. $1 × 4.

CAYMAN ISLANDS Pt. 1

A group of islands in the British West Indies. A dependency of Jamaica until August 1962, when it became a Crown Colony.

1900. 12 pence = 1 shilling;
20 shillings = 1 pound.
1969. 100 cents = 1 Jamaican dollar.

1

2

1900.

1a	1	½d. green	4·50	15·00
2		1d. red	4·00	2·25

1902.

8	2	½d. green	7·00	8·00
4		1d. red	10·00	9·00
10		2½d. blue	6·50	3·25
13		4d. brown and blue	32·00	60·00
11		6d. brown	16·00	38·00
14		6d. olive and red	32·00	70·00
12		1s. orange	32·00	48·00
15		1s. violet and green	55·00	80·00
16		5s. orange and green	£170	£300

1907. Surch **One Halfpenny.**

17	2	½d. on 1d. red	42·00	70·00

1907. Surch.

18	2	½d. on 5s. orange and green	£250	£350
19		1d. on 5s. orange and green	£250	£325
35		2½d. on 4d. brown and blue	£1500	£2250

11

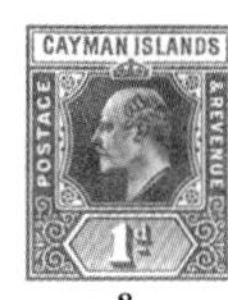

8

1907.

38	11	¼d. brown	2·00	50
25	8	½d. green	2·50	4·00
26		1d. red	1·50	75
27		2½d. blue	3·50	3·50
28		3d. purple on yellow	3·25	6·50
29		4d. black and red on yellow	50·00	70·00
30		6d. purple	9·50	35·00
31		1s. black on green	7·50	22·00
32		5s. green and red on yellow	38·00	60·00
34		10s. green and red on green	£160	£225

12

19

1912.

40	12	¼d. brown	1·00	40
41		½d. green	2·75	5·00
42		1d. red	3·25	2·50
43		2d. grey	1·00	10·00
44		2½d. blue	7·00	11·00
45a		3d. purple on yellow	3·50	8·00
46		4d. black and red on yellow	1·00	10·00
47		6d. purple	3·75	7·50
48b		1s. black on green	3·50	3·50
49		2s. purple and blue on blue	12·00	48·00
50		3s. green and violet	19·00	65·00
51		5s. green and red on yellow	75·00	£160
52b		10s. green and red on green	80·00	£140

1917. Surch **1½d** with **WAR STAMP.** in two lines.

54	12	1½d. on 2½d. blue	1·75	6·00

1917. Optd or surch as last, but with **WAR STAMP** in one line and without full point.

57	12	½d. green	60	2·50
58		1½d. on 2d. grey	1·50	7·00
56		1½d. on 2½d. blue	30	60
59		1½d. on 2½d. orange	80	1·25

1921.

69	19	¼d. brown	50	1·50
70		½d. green	50	30
71		1d. red	1·40	85
72		1½d. brown	1·75	30
73		2d. grey	1·75	4·00
74		2½d. blue	50	50
75		3d. purple on yellow	75	4·00
62		4d. red on yellow	1·00	4·00
76		4½d. green	2·25	3·00
77		6d. red	5·50	32·00
63		1s. black on green	1·25	9·50
80		2s. violet on blue	14·00	24·00
81		3s. violet	23·00	16·00
82		5s. green on yellow	24·00	45·00
83		10s. red on green	60·00	85·00

20 Kings William IV and George V

1932. Centenary of "Assembly of Justices and Vestry".

84	20	¼d. brown	1·50	1·00
85		½d. green	2·75	8·00
86		1d. red	2·75	7·50
87		1½d. orange	2·75	2·75
88		2d. grey	2·75	3·50
89		2½d. blue	2·75	1·50
90		3d. green	3·25	5·00
91		6d. purple	9·50	23·00
92		1s. black and brown	17·00	32·00
93		2s. black and blue	45·00	75·00
94		5s. black and green	80·00	£120
95		10s. black and red	£250	£350

21 Cayman Islands

1935.

96	21	¼d. black and brown	50	1·00
97	–	½d. blue and green	1·00	1·00
98	–	1d. blue and red	4·00	2·25
99	–	1½d. black and orange	1·50	1·75
100	–	2d. blue and purple	3·75	1·10
101	–	2½d. blue and black	3·25	1·25
102	21	3d. black and green	2·50	3·00
103	–	6d. purple and black	8·50	4·00
104	–	1s. blue and orange	6·00	6·50
105	–	2s. blue and black	45·00	35·00
106	–	5s. green and black	50·00	50·00
107	–	10s. black and red	70·00	90·00

DESIGNS—HORIZ: ½, 2d., 1s. Cat boat; 1d., 2s. Red-footed boobys ("Booby-birds"); 2½, 6d., 5s. Hawksbill turtles. VERT: 1½d., 10s. Queen or pink conch shells and coconut palms.

1935. Silver Jubilee. As T **13** of Antigua.

108	½d. black and green	15	1·00
109	2½d. brown and blue	1·00	1·00
110	6d. blue and olive	1·00	3·50
111	1s. grey and purple	7·00	7·00

1937. Coronation. As T **2** of Aden.

112	½d. green	30	1·40
113	1d. red	50	20
114	2½d. blue	95	40

26 Beach View

30 Hawksbill Turtles

1938.

115a	26	¼d. orange	10	65
116	–	½d. green	90	55
117	–	1d. red	30	75
118	26	1½d. black	30	10
119a	30	2d. violet	60	30
120	–	2½d. blue	40	20
120a	–	2½d. orange	2·50	50
121	–	3d. orange	40	15
121a	–	3d. blue	2·50	30
122a	30	6d. olive	2·50	1·25
123a	–	1s. brown	4·50	2·00
124a	26	2s. green	25·00	9·00
125	–	5s. red	32·00	15·00
126a	30	10s. brown	22·00	9·00

DESIGNS—HORIZ: ½d., 1s. Caribbean dolphin; 1d., 3d. Map of Islands; 2½d., 5s. "Rembro" (schooner).

1946. Victory. As T **9** of Aden.

127	1½d. black	20	10
128	3d. yellow	20	10

1948. Silver Wedding. As T **10/11** of Aden.

129	½d. green	10	10
130	10s. blue	14·00	14·00

1949. U.P.U. As T **20/25** of Antigua.

131	2½d. orange	30	60
132	3d. blue	1·50	1·90
133	6d. olive	60	1·90
134	1s. brown	60	30

31 Cat Boat

44 South Sound Lighthouse, Grand Cayman

1950.

135	31	¼d. blue and red	15	60
136	–	½d. violet and green	15	1·25
137	–	1d. olive and blue	60	75
138	–	1½d. green and brown	30	75
139	–	2d. violet and red	1·25	1·50
140	–	2½d. blue and black	1·25	60
141	–	3d. green and blue	1·40	1·50
142	–	6d. brown and blue	2·00	1·25
143	–	9d. red and green	6·00	2·00
144	–	1s. brown and orange	3·25	2·75
145	–	2s. violet and purple	8·50	9·50
146	–	5s. olive and violet	13·00	7·00
147	–	10s. black and red	17·00	14·00

DESIGNS: ½d. Coconut grove, Cayman Brac; 1d. Green turtle; 1½d. Making thatch rope; 2d. Cayman seamen; 2½d. Map; 3d. Parrotfish; 6d. Bluff, Cayman Brac; 9d. Georgetown Harbour. 1s. Turtle in "crawl"; 2s. "Ziroma" (schooner); 5s. Boat-building; 10s. Government offices, Grand Cayman.

1953. As 1950 issue but with portrait of Queen Elizabeth II as in T **44**.

148	¼d. blue and red	1·00	50
149	½d. violet and green	75	50
150	1d. olive and blue	70	40
151	1½d. green and brown	50	20
152	2d. violet and red	3·00	85
153	2½d. blue and black	3·50	80
154	3d. green and blue	4·00	60
155	4d. black and blue	2·00	40
156	6d. brown and blue	1·75	30
157	9d. red and green	6·00	30
158	1s. brown and orange	3·25	20
159	2s. violet and purple	13·00	8·00
160	5s. olive and violet	15·00	7·00
161	10s. black and red	15·00	7·50
161a	£1 blue	32·00	10·00

Portrait faces right on ¼d., 2d., 2½d., 4d., 1s. and 10s. values and left on others. The £1 shows a larger portrait of the Queen (vert).

1953. Coronation. As T **13** of Aden.

162	1d. black and green	30	1·75

46 Arms of the Cayman Islands

1959. New Constitution.

163	46	2½d. black and blue	45	2·25
164		1s. black and orange	55	50

48 Cat Boat

1962. Portraits as in T **48**.

165	–	¼d. green and red	55	1·00
166	48	1d. black and olive	80	20
167	–	1½d. yellow and purple	2·75	80
168	–	2d. blue and brown	1·00	30
169	–	2½d. violet and turquoise	85	1·00
170	–	3d. blue and red	30	10
171	–	4d. green and purple	1·25	60
172	–	6d. turquoise and sepia	3·25	30
173	48	9d. blue and purple	2·75	40
174	–	1s. sepia and red	80	10
175	–	1s.3d. turquoise and brown	3·75	2·00
176	–	1s.9d. turquoise and violet	16·00	1·25
177	–	5s. plum and green	9·50	7·00
178	–	10s. olive and blue	18·00	8·00
179	–	£1 red and black	19·00	17·00

DESIGNS—VERT: ¼d. Cuban amazon ("Cayman Parrot"); 9d. Angler with king mackerel; 10s. Arms; £1 Queen Elizabeth II. HORIZ: 1½d. "Schomburgkia thomsoniana" (orchid); 2d. Cayman Islands map; 2½d. Fisherman casting net; 3d. West Bay Beach; 4d. Green turtle; 6d. "Lydia E. Wilson" (schooner), 1s Iguana; 1s.3d. Swimming pool, Cayman Brac; 1s.9d. Water sports; 5s. Fort George.

1963. Freedom from Hunger. As T **28** of Aden.

180	1s.9d. red	30	15

1963. Centenary of Red Cross. As T **33** of Antigua.

181	1d. red and black	30	75
182	1s.9d. red and blue	70	1·75

1964. 400th Birth Anniv of Shakespeare. As T **34** of Antigua.

183	6d. purple	20	10

1965. Centenary of I.T.U. As T **36** of Antigua.

184	1d. blue and purple	15	10
185	1s.3d. purple and green	55	45

1965. I.C.Y. As T **37** of Antigua.

186	1d. purple and turquoise	15	10
187	1s. green and lavender	50	25

1966. Churchill Commemoration. As T **38** of Antigua.

188	¼d. blue	10	1·50
189	1d. green	40	10
190	1s. brown	1·10	10
191	1s.9d. violet	1·25	75

1966. Royal Visit. As T **39** of Antigua.

192	1d. black and blue	60	30
193	1s.9d. black and mauve	2·25	1·25

1966. World Cup Football Championship. As T **40** of Antigua.

194	1½d. multicoloured	15	10
195	1s.9d. multicoloured	50	25

1966. Inauguration of W.H.O. Headquarters, Geneva. As T **41** of Antigua.

196	2d. black, green and blue	60	15
197	1s.3d. black, purple and ochre	1·40	60

62 Telephone and Map

1966. International Telephone Links.

198	62	4d. multicoloured	20	20
199		9d. multicoloured	20	30

1966. 20th Anniv of U.N.E.S.C.O. As T **54/6** of Antigua.

200	1d. multicoloured	15	10
201	1s.9d. yellow, violet and olive	60	10
202	5s. black, purple and orange	1·50	70

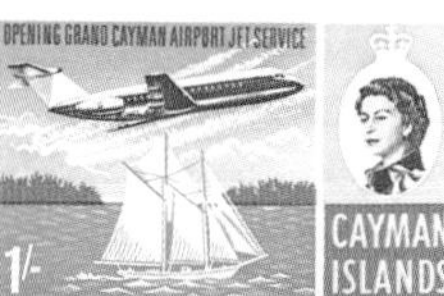

63 B.A.C One Eleven 200/400 Airliner over "Ziroma" (Cayman schooner)

1966. Opening of Cayman Jet Service.

203	63	1s. black, blue and green	35	30
204		1s.9d. purple, blue and green	40	35

64 Water-skiing

1967. International Tourist Year. Multicoloured.

205	4d. Type **64**	35	10
206	6d. Skin diving	35	30
207	1s. Sport fishing	35	30
208	1s.9d. Sailing	40	75

68 Former Slaves and Emblem

1968. Human Rights Year.

209	68	3d. green, black and gold	10	10
210		9d. brown, gold and green	10	10
211		5s. ultram, gold and green	30	90

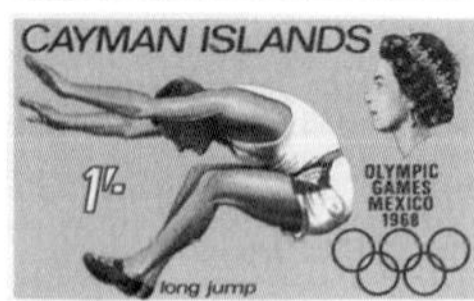

69 Long-jumping

1968. Olympic Games, Mexico. Multicoloured.
212 1s. Type **69** 15 10
213 1s.3d. High-jumping 20 25
214 2s. Pole-vaulting 20 75

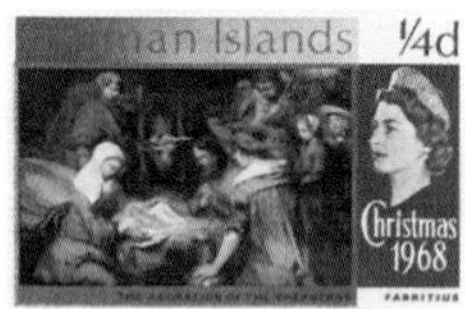

72 "The Adoration of the Shepherds" (Fabritius)

1968. Christmas. Multicoloured.
215 ¼d. Type **72*** 10 20
221 ¼d. Type **72*** 10 20
216 1d. "The Adoration of the Shepherds" (Rembrandt) 10 10
217 6d. Type **72** 15 10
218 8d. As 1d. 15 15
219 1s.3d. Type **72** 20 25
220 2s. As 1d. 25 35
*No. 215 has a brown background and No. 221 a bright purple one.

74 Grand Cayman Thrush ("Cayman Thrush")

1969. Multicoloured.
222 ¼d. Type **74** 10 75
223 1d. Brahmin cattle 10 10
224 2d. Blowholes on the coast 10 10
225 2½d. Map of Grand Cayman 15 10
226 3d. Georgetown scene . . . 10 10
227 4d. Royal "Poinciana" . . . 15 10
228 6d. Cayman Brac and Little Cayman on chart 20 10
229 8d. Motor vessels at berth . . 25 10
230 1s. Basket-making 15 10
231 1s.3d. Beach scene . . . . . 35 1·00
232 1s.6d. Straw-rope making . . 35 1·00
233 2s. Great barracuda . . . . 1·25 80
234 4s. Government House . . . 35 80
235 10s. Arms of the Cayman Islands (vert) . . . . . . 1·00 1·50
236 £1 black, ochre and red (Queen Elizabeth II) (vert) 1·25 2·00

1969. Decimal Currency. Nos. 222/36 surch **C-DAY 8th September 1969**. Multicoloured.
238 **74** ¼c. on ¼d. 10 75
239 – 1c. on 1d. 10 10
240 – 2c. on 2d. 10 10
241 – 3c. on 4d. 10 10
242 – 4c. on 2½d. 10 10
243 – 5c. on 6d. 10 10
244 – 7c. on 8d. 10 10
245 – 8c. on 3d. 15 10
246 – 10c. on 1s. 25 10
247 – 12c. on 1s.3d. . . . . . . 35 1·75
248 – 15c. on 1s.6d. . . . . . . 45 1·50
249 – 20c. on 2s. . . . . 1·25 1·75
250 – 40c. on 4s. 45 85
251 – $1 on 10s. . . . . 1·00 2·50
252 – $2 on £1 . . . . 1·50 3·25

90 "Madonna and Child" (Vivarini) **92** "Noli me tangere" (Titian)

1969. Christmas. Multicoloured. Background colours given.
253 **90** ¼c. red 10 10
254 ¼c. mauve 10 10
255 ¼c. green 10 10
256 ¼c. blue 10 10
257 – 1c. blue 10 10
258 **90** 5c. red 10 10
259 – 7c. green 10 10
260 **90** 12c. green 15 15
261 – 20c. purple 20 25
DESIGNS: 1c., 7c., 20c. "The Adoration of the Kings" (Gossaert).

1970. Easter. Multicoloured; frame colours given.
262 **92** ¼c. red 10 10
263 ¼c. green 10 10
264 ¼c. brown 10 10
265 ¼c. violet 10 10
266 10c. blue 35 10
267 12c. brown 40 10
268 40c. plum 55 60

93 Barnaby ("Barnaby Rudge")

1970. Death Centenary of Charles Dickens.
269 **93** 1c. black, green and yellow 10 10
270 – 12c. black, brown and red 25 10
271 – 20c. black, brown and gold 30 10
272 – 40c. black, ultram & blue 35 25
DESIGNS: 12c. Sairey Gamp ("Martin Chuzzlewit"); 20c. Mr. Micawber and David ("David Copperfield"); 40c. The "Marchioness" ("The Old Curiosity Shop").

97 Grand Cayman Thrush ("Cayman Thrush")

1970. Decimal Currency. Designs as Nos. 222/36, but with values inscribed in decimal currency as in T **97**.
273 ¼c. multicoloured 65 30
274 1c. multicoloured 10 10
275 2c. multicoloured 10 10
276 3c. multicoloured 20 10
277 4c. multicoloured 20 10
278 5c. multicoloured 35 10
279 7c. multicoloured 30 10
280 8c. multicoloured 30 10
281 10c. multicoloured 30 10
282 12c. multicoloured 90 75
283 15c. multicoloured . . . . . 1·25 3·50
284 20c. multicoloured . . . . . 3·25 1·25
285 40c. multicoloured 85 75
286 $1 multicoloured . . . . . . 1·25 4·75
287 $2 black, ochre and red . . . 2·00 4·75

98 The Three Wise Men

1970. Christmas.
288 **98** ¼c. green, grey and emerald 10 10
289 – 1c. black, yellow and green 10 10
290 **98** 5c. grey, orange and red 10 10
291 – 10c. black, yellow and red 10 10
292 **98** 12c. grey, green and blue 15 10
293 – 20c. black, yellow and green 20 15
DESIGN: 1, 10, 20c. Nativity scene and Globe.

100 Grand Cayman Terrapin

1971. Turtles. Multicoloured.
294 5c. Type **100** 30 25
295 7c. Green turtle 35 25
296 12c. Hawksbill turtle 55 30
297 20c. Turtle farm . . . . . . 1·00 1·40

101 "Dendrophylax fawcettii" **102** "Adoration of the Kings" (French 15th century)

1971. Orchids. Multicoloured.
298 ¼c. Type **101** . . . . 10 1·25
299 2c. "Schomburgkia thomsoniana" 60 90
300 10c. "Vanilla claviculata" . . 2·00 50
301 40c. "Oncidium variegatum" 4·00 3·50

1971. Christmas. Multicoloured.
302 ¼c. Type **102** 10 10
303 1c. "The Nativity" (Parisian, 14th century) 10 10
304 5c. "Adoration of the Magi" (Burgundian, 15th century) 10 10
305 12c. Type **102** 20 15
306 15c. As 1c. 20 25
307 20c. As 5c. 25 35
MS308 113 × 115 mm. Nos. 302/7 1·25 2·25

103 Turtle and Telephone Cable

1972. Co-axial Telephone Cable.
309 **103** 2c. multicoloured 10 10
310 10c. multicoloured 15 10
311 40c. multicoloured 30 40

104 Court House Building

1972. New Government Buildings. Multicoloured.
312 5c. Type **104** 10 10
313 15c. Legislative Assembly Building 10 10
314 25c. Type **104** 15 15
315 40c. As 15c. 20 30
MS316 121 × 108 mm. Nos. 312/15 50 2·00

1972. Royal Silver Wedding. As T **52** of Ascension but with Hawksbill Turtle and Queen or Pink Conch in background.
317 12c. violet 15 10
318 30c. green 15 20

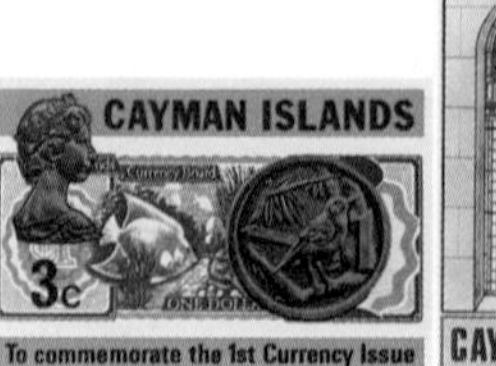

106 $1 Coin and Note **107** "The Way of Sorrow"

1972. First Issue of Currency. Multicoloured.
319 3c. Type **106** 20 10
320 6c. $5 Coin and note 20 70
321 15c. $10 Coin and note . . . 60 30
322 25c. $25 Coin and note . . . 80 45
MS323 128 × 107 mm. Nos. 319/22 3·50 3·25

1973. Easter. Stained-glass Windows. Multicoloured.
324 10c. Type **107** 15 10
325 12c. "Christ Resurrected" . . 20 10
326 20c. "The Last Supper" (horiz) 25 15
327 30c. "Christ on the Cross" (horiz) 30 25
MS328 122 × 105 mm. Nos. 324/7 (imperf) 1·00 1·60

108 "The Nativity" (Sforza Book of Hours) **109** White-winged Dove

1973. Christmas.
329 **108** 3c. multicoloured 10 10
330 – 5c. multicoloured 10 10
331 **108** 9c. multicoloured 15 10
332 – 12c. multicoloured 15 10
333 **108** 15c. multicoloured 15 15
334 – 25c. multicoloured 20 25
DESIGN: 5, 12, 25c. "The Adoration of the Magi" (Breviary of Queen Isabella).

1973. Royal Wedding. As T **47** of Anguilla. Background colour given. Multicoloured.
335 10c. green 10 10
336 30c. mauve 15 10

1974. Birds (1st series). Multicoloured.
337 3c. Type **109** . . . . 2·00 30
338 10c. Vitelline warbler . . . . 2·75 30
339 12c. Antillean grackle ("Greater Antillean Grackle") . . . . 2·75 30
340 20c. Great red-bellied woodpecker ("West Indian Red-bellied Woodpecker") 4·25 80
341 30c. Stripe-headed tanager . . 5·50 1·50
342 50c. Yucatan vireo . . . . . 7·00 5·50
See also Nos. 383/8.

110 Old School Building

1974. 25th Anniv of University of West Indies. Multicoloured.
343 12c. Type **110** 10 15
344 20c. New Comprehensive School 15 20
345 30c. Creative Arts Centre, Mona 15 60

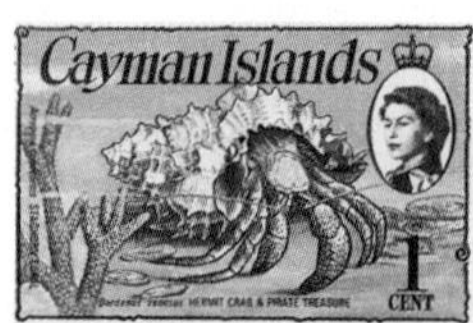

111 Hermit Crab and Staghorn Coral

1974. Size 41½ × 27 mm or 27 × 41½ mm. Mult.
346 1c. Type **111** . . . . 3·50 1·25
347 3c. Treasure-chest and lion's paw . . . . 3·50 75
348 4c. Treasure and spotted scorpionfish 50 70
349 5c. Flintlock pistol and brain coral . . . . 3·00 75
350 6c. Blackbeard and green turtle . . . . 35 2·25
366 8c. As 9c. . . . . 2·50 8·50
351 9c. Jewelled pomander and porkfish . . . . 4·00 10·00
352 10c. Spiny lobster and treasure . . . . 4·50 80
353 12c. Jewelled sword and dagger and sea-fan . . . 35 1·60
354 15c. Cabrit's murex and treasure . . . . 45 1·25
417 20c. Queen or pink conch and treasure . . . . . . 3·50 3·00
356 25c. Hogfish and treasure . . 45 70
357 40c. Gold chalice and seawhip . . . . 4·00 1·25
358 $1 Coat of arms (vert) . . . 2·75 3·25
419 $2 Queen Elizabeth II (vert) 7·50 6·50
For smaller designs see Nos. 445/52.

112 Sea Captain and Ship (Shipbuilding)

1974. Local Industries. Multicoloured.
360 8c. Type **112** 30 10
361 12c. Thatcher and cottage . . 25 10
362 20c. Farmer and plantation . . 25 20
MS363 92 × 132 mm. Nos. 360/2 1·50 3·25

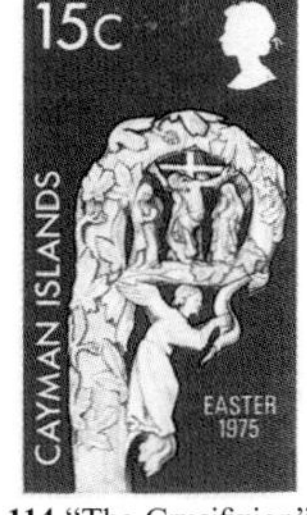

113 Arms of Cinque Ports and Lord Warden's Flag **114** "The Crucifixion"

1974. Birth Centenary of Sir Winston Churchill. Multicoloured.
380 12c. Type **113** 15 10
381 50c. Churchill's coat of arms 45 70
MS382 98 × 86 mm. Nos. 380/1 60 1·60

1975. Birds (2nd series). As T **109**. Multicoloured.
383 3c. Common flicker ("Yellow-shafted Flicker") 70 50
384 10c. Black-billed whistling duck ("West Indian Tree Duck") . . . . 1·25 50
385 12c. Yellow warbler . . . . 1·40 65
386 20c. White-bellied dove . . . 2·00 2·00
387 30c. Magnificent frigate bird 3·25 4·25
388 50c. Cuban amazon ("Cayman Amazon") . . . 3·75 12·00

1975. Easter. French Pastoral Staffs.
389 **114** 15c. multicoloured 10 20
390 – 35c. multicoloured 20 45
MS391 128 × 98 mm. Nos, 389/90 65 2·50
DESIGN: 35c. Pastoral staff similar to Type **114**.

115 Israel Hands

1975. Pirates. Multicoloured.
392 10c. Type **115** 30 15
393 12c. John Fenn 30 30
394 20c. Thomas Anstis 50 50
395 30c. Edward Low . . . . . 60 1·50

1975. Christmas. "Virgin and Child with Angels". As T **114**.
396 12c. multicoloured 10 10
397 50c. multicoloured 30 30
MS398 113 × 85 mm. Nos. 396/7 1·00 2·75

116 Registered Cover, Government House and Sub-Post Office

1975. 75th Anniv of First Cayman Islands Postage Stamp. Multicoloured.
399 10c. Type **116** 15 10
400 20c. ½d. stamp and 1890–94 postmark 20 15
401 30c. 1d. stamp and 1908 surcharge 30 25
402 50c. ½d. and 1d. stamps . . . 45 65
MS403 117 × 147 mm. Nos. 399/402 2·50 3·00

117 Seals of Georgia, Delaware and New Hampshire

1976. Bicentenary of American Revolution. Mult.
404 10c. Type **117** 40 15
405 15c. Carolina, New Jersey and Maryland seals 55 20
406 20c. Virginia, Rhode Island and Massachusetts seals . . 65 25
407 25c. New York, Connecticut and North Carolina seals 65 35
408 30c. Pennsylvania seal, Liberty Bell and U.S. Great Seal 70 40
MS409 166 × 124 mm. Nos. 404/8 4·00 8·00

118 "470" Dinghies **119** Queen Elizabeth II and Westminster Abbey

1976. Olympic Games, Montreal. Multicoloured.
410 20c. Type **118** 40 10
411 50c. Racing dinghy 70 50

1977. Silver Jubilee. Multicoloured.
427 8c. The Prince of Wales' visit, 1973 . . . . 10 20
428 30c. Type **119** 15 40
429 50c. Preparation for the Anointing (horiz) 30 75

120 Scuba Diving

1977. Tourism. Multicoloured.
430 5c. Type **120** 10 10
431 10c. Exploring a wreck . . . 15 10
432 20c. Royal gramma ("Fairy basslet") (fish) 45 20
433 25c. Sergeant major (fish) . . 55 35
MS434 146 × 89 mm. Nos. 430/3 2·00 4·00

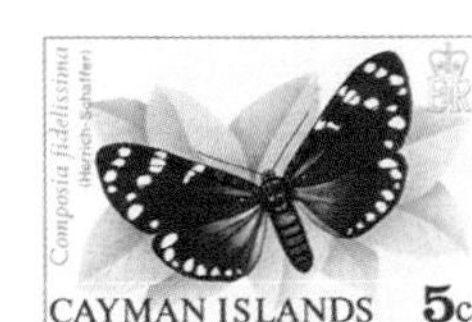

121 "Composia fidelissima" (moth)

1977. Butterflies and Moth. Multicoloured.
435 5c. Type **121** 75 20
436 8c. "Heliconius charithonia" 85 20
437 10c. "Danaus gilippus" . . . 85 20
438 15c. "Agraulis vanillae" . . . 1·25 45
439 20c. "Junonia evarete" . . . 1·25 45
440 30c. "Anartia jatrophae" . . 1·50 70

122 Cruise Liner "Southward" **123** "The Crucifixion" (Durer)

1978. New Harbour and Cruise Ships. Multicoloured.
441 3c. Type **122** 30 10
442 5c. Cruise liner "Renaissance" 30 10
443 30c. New harbour (vert) . . . 80 25
444 50c. Cruise liner "Daphne" (vert) . . . . 1·10 65

1978. As Nos. 346/7, 349, 352, 417, 357/8 and 419, but designs smaller, 40 × 26 mm or 26 × 40 mm.
445 1c. Type **111** . . . . 1·00 1·25
446 3c. Treasure chest and lion's paw 80 50
447 5c. Flintlock pistol and brain coral . . . . 1·50 2·00
448 10c. Spiny lobster and treasure . . . . 1·25 60
449 20c. Queen or pink conch and treasure . . . . 2·25 1·00
450 40c. Gold chalice and seawhip . . . . 13·00 15·00
451 $1 Coat of arms (vert) . . . 18·00 5·50
452 $2 Queen Elizabeth II (vert) 4·00 18·00

1978. Easter and 450th Death Anniv of Durer.
459 **123** 10c. mauve and black . . 30 10
460 – 15c. yellow and black . . 40 15
461 – 20c. turquoise and black 50 20
462 – 30c. lilac and black . . . 60 35
MS463 120 × 108 mm. Nos. 459/62 3·75 5·00
DESIGNS: 15c. "Christ at Emmaus"; 20c. "The Entry into Jerusalem"; 30c. "Christ washing Peter's Feet".

124 "Explorers" Singing Game **125** Yale of Beaufort

1978. 3rd International Council Meeting of Girls' Brigade. Multicoloured.
464 3c. Type **124** 20 10
465 10c. Colour party 25 10
466 20c. Girls and Duke of Edinburgh Award interests 40 20
467 50c. Girls using domestic skills 70 80

1978. 25th Anniv of Coronation.
468 **125** 30c. green, mauve and silver 20 25
469 – 30c. multicoloured 20 25
470 – 30c. green, mauve and silver 20 25
DESIGNS: No. 469, Queen Elizabeth II; 470, Barn owl.

126 Four-eyed Butterflyfish

1978. Fish (1st series). Multicoloured.
471 3c. Type **126** 25 10
472 5c. Grey angelfish 30 10
473 10c. Squirrelfish 45 10
474 15c. Queen parrotfish 60 30
475 20c. Spanish hogfish 70 35
476 30c. Queen angelfish 80 50

127 Lockheed L.18 Lodestar

1979. 25th Anniv of Owen Roberts Airfield. Mult.
477 3c. Type **127** 30 15
478 5c. Consolidated PBY-5A Catalina amphibian . . . 30 15
479 10c. Vickers Viking 1B . . . 35 15
480 15c. B.A.C. One Eleven 455 on tarmac 65 25
481 20c. Piper PA-31 Cheyenne II, Bell 47G Trooper helicopter and Hawker Siddeley H.S.125 . . . . . 75 35
482 30c. B.A.C. One Eleven 475 over airfield . . . . 1·00 50

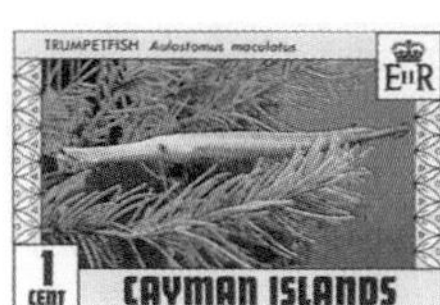

128 Trumpetfish

1979. Fishes (2nd series). Multicoloured.
483 1c. Type **128** 10 10
484 3c. Nassau grouper 25 10
485 5c. French angelfish 25 10
486 10c. Schoolmaster snapper . . 35 10
487 20c. Banded butterflyfish . . 55 25
488 50c. Black-barred soldierfish 1·00 70

129 1900 1d. Stamp

1979. Death Centenary of Sir Rowland Hill.
489 **129** 5c. black, carmine and blue 10 10
490 – 10c. multicoloured 15 10
491 – 20c. multicoloured 20 25
MS492 138 × 90 mm. 50c. mult 55 65
DESIGNS: 10c. Great Britain 1902 3d. purple on lemon; 20c. 1955 £1 blue.

130 The Holy Family and Angels

1979. Christmas. Multicoloured.
493 10c. Type **130** 15 10
494 20c. Angels appearing to Shepherds 25 10
495 30c. Nativity 30 20
496 40c. The Magi 40 30

131 Local Rotary Project

1980. 75th Anniv of Rotary International.
497 **131** 20c. blue, black and yellow 20 15
498 – 30c. blue, black and yellow 25 20
499 – 50c. blue, yellow and black 35 30
DESIGNS—VERT: 30c. Paul P. Harris (founder); 50c. Rotary anniversary emblem.

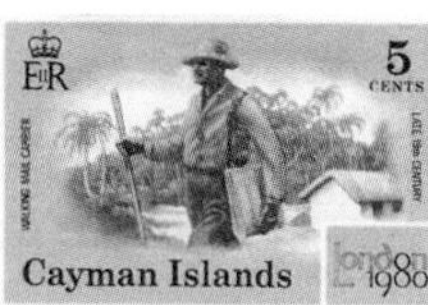

132 Walking Mail Carrier

1980. "London 1980" International Stamp Exhibition. Multicoloured.
500 5c. Type **132** 10 10
501 10c. Delivering mail by cat boat 15 10
502 15c. Mounted mail carrier . . 20 10
503 30c. Horse-drawn wagonette 25 15
504 40c. Postman on bicycle . . . 35 15
505 $1 Motor transport 45 55

133 Queen Elizabeth the Queen Mother at the Derby, 1976

1980. 80th Birthday of the Queen Mother.
506 **133** 20c. multicoloured 20 25

134 American Thorny Oyster

1980. Shells (1st series). Multicoloured.
507 5c. Type **134** 40 10
508 10c. West Indian murex . . . 40 10
509 30c. Angular triton 80 40
510 50c. Caribbean vase 90 80
See also Nos. 565/8 and 582/5.

135 Lantana

1980. Flowers (1st series). Multicoloured.
511 5c. Type **135** 15 10
512 15c. "Bauhinia" 20 10
513 30c. "Hibiscus Rosa" 30 10
514 $1 "Milk and Wine Lily" . . 70 90
See also Nos. 541/4.

136 Juvenile Tarpon and Fire Sponge

137 Eucharist

1980. Multicoloured.
515A 3c. Type **136** . . . . 1·00 1·50
516B 5c. Flat tree or mangrove-root oyster . . . . . . 1·25 80
517A 10c. Mangrove crab . . . . 50 1·00
518A 15c. Lizard and "Phyciodes phaon" (butterfly) . . . 1·00 1·50
519A 20c. Louisiana heron ("Tricoloured Heron") 1·50 2·00
520A 30c. Red mangrove flower 70 1·00
521A 40c. Red mangrove seeds 75 1·00
522A 50c. Waterhouse's leaf-nosed bat . . . . 1·25 1·50
523A $1 Black-crowned night heron . . . . 5·50 5·00
524A $2 Coat of arms . . . . . 1·50 3·75
525A $4 Queen Elizabeth II . . . 2·25 4·75

1981. Easter. Multicoloured.
526 3c. Type **137** 10 10
527 10c. Crown of thorns 10 10
528 20c. Crucifix 15 10
529 $1 Lord Jesus Christ 50 60

138 Wood Slave

1981. Reptiles and Amphibians. Multicoloured.
530 20c. Type **138** 25 20
531 30c. Cayman iguana 30 35
532 40c. Lion lizard 40 45
533 50c. Terrapin ("Hickatee") 45 55

139 Prince Charles

1981. Royal Wedding. Multicoloured.
534 20c. Wedding bouquet from Cayman Islands 15 10
535 30c. Type **139** 20 10
536 $1 Prince Charles and Lady Diana Spencer 50 75

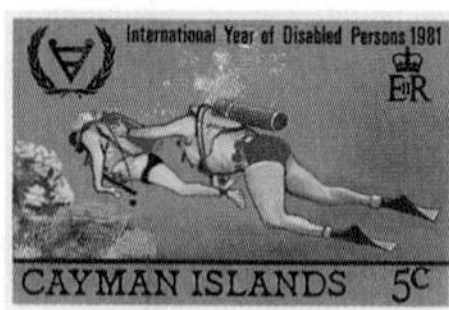

140 Disabled Scuba Divers

1981. Int Year for Disabled Persons. Mult.
537 5c. Type **140** 10 10
538 15c. Old school for the handicapped 25 20
539 20c. New school for the handicapped 30 25
540 $1 Disabled people in wheelchairs by the sea . . 1·25 85

1981. Flowers (2nd series). As T **135**. Multicoloured.
541 3c. Bougainvillea 10 10
542 10c. Morning Glory 15 10
543 20c. Wild amaryllis 25 25
544 $1 Cordia . . . . 70 1·75

141 Dr. Robert Koch and Microscope

1982. Centenary of Robert Koch's Discovery of Tubercle Bacillus. Multicoloured.
545 15c. Type **141** 25 25
546 30c. Koch looking through microscope (vert) 45 45
547 40c. Microscope (vert) . . . 70 70
548 50c. Dr. Robert Koch (vert) 80 80

142 Bride and Groom walking down Aisle

144 "Madonna and Child with the Infant Baptist"

143 Pitching Tent

1982. 21st Birthday of Princess of Wales. Mult.
549 20c. Cayman Islands coat of arms 30 35
550 30c. Lady Diana Spencer in London, June, 1981 . . . 70 45
551 40c. Type **142** 70 65
552 50c. Formal portrait . . . . 2·50 90

1982. 75th Anniv of Boy Scout Movement. Mult.
553 3c. Type **143** 15 10
554 20c. Scouts camping 40 40
555 30c. Cub Scouts and Leaders 60 55
556 50c. Boating skills 80 85

1982. Christmas. Raphael Paintings. Multicoloured.
557 3c. Type **144** 10 10
558 10c. "Madonna of the Tower" 20 20
559 20c. "Ansidei Madonna" . . 35 35
560 30c. "Madonna and Child" 50 50

145 Mace

1982. 150th Anniv of Representative Government. Multicoloured.
561 3c. Type **145** 10 30
562 10c. Old Courthouse 20 30
563 20c. Commonwealth Parliamentary Association coat of arms 35 50
564 30c. Legislative Assembly building 50 90

1983. Shells (2nd series). As T **134**. Multicoloured.
565 5c. Colourful Atlantic moon 15 30
566 10c. King helmet 25 30
567 20c. Rooster-tail conch . . . 30 40
568 $1 Reticulated cowrie-helmet 1·00 4·00

146 Legislative Building, Cayman Brac

1983. Royal Visit. Multicoloured.
569 20c. Type **146** 45 35
570 30c. Legislative Building, Grand Cayman 60 50
571 50c. Duke of Edinburgh (vert) . . . . 1·25 90
572 $1 Queen Elizabeth II (vert) 2·00 2·00
MS573 113 × 94 mm. Nos. 569/72 4·50 4·25

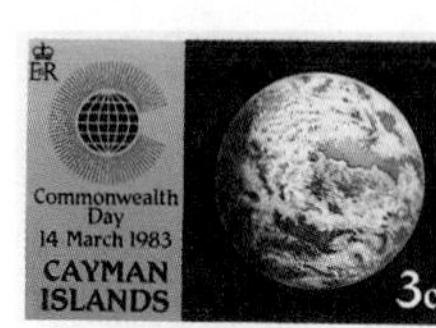

147 Satellite View of Earth

1983. Commonwealth Day. Multicoloured
574 3c. Type **147** 15 10
575 15c. Cayman Islands and Commonwealth flags . . . 35 30
576 20c. Fishing 40 35
577 40c. Portrait of Queen Elizabeth II 65 65

148 MRCU Cessna Ag Wagon

1983. Bicentenary of Manned Flight. Multicoloured.
578 3c. Type **148** 60 50
579 10c. Consolidated PBY-5A Catalina amphibian . . . 65 50
580 20c. Boeing 727-200 . . . . 1·25 1·50
581 40c. Hawker Siddeley H.S.748 . . . . 1·75 3·75

1984. Shells (3rd series). As T **134**. Multicoloured.
582 3c. Florida moon 70 40
583 10c. Austin's cone 80 40
584 30c. Leaning dwarf triton . . 2·25 2·75
585 50c. Filose or threaded turban . . . . 2·50 4·75

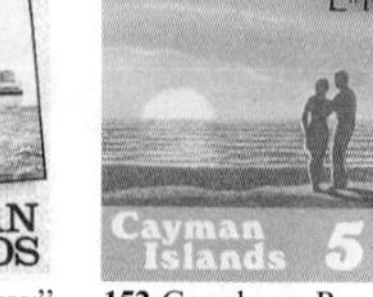

149 "Song of Norway" (cruise liner)

152 Couple on Beach at Sunset

151 Snowy Egret

1984. 250th Anniv of "Lloyd's List" (newspaper). Multicoloured.
586 5c. Type **149** 45 20
587 10c. View of old harbour . . 50 25
588 25c. Wreck of "Ridgefield" (freighter) . . . . 1·00 1·00
589 50c. "Goldfield" (schooner) 2·00 2·25
MS590 105 × 75 mm. $1 "Goldfield" (schooner) (different) 2·10 2·25

1984. Universal Postal Union Congress, Hamburg. No. 589 optd **U.P.U. CONGRESS HAMBURG 1984.**
591 50c. Schooner "Goldfield" . . 1·00 1·75

1984. Birds of the Cayman Islands (1st series). Multicoloured.
592 5c. Type **151** . . . . 1·00 75
593 10c. Bananaquit . . . . . . 1·00 75
594 35c. Belted kingfisher ("Kingfisher") . . . . . . 3·25 2·50
595 $1 Brown booby . . . . . . 6·00 11·00
See also Nos. 627/30.

1984. Christmas. Local Festivities. Multicoloured.
596 5c. Type **152** . . . . 70 1·25
597 5c. Family and schooner . . 70 1·25
598 5c. Carol singers . . . . . . 70 1·25
599 5c. East End bonfire . . . . 70 1·25
600 25c. Yachts . . . . 90 1·25
601 25c. Father Christmas in power-boat . . . . 90 1·25
602 25c. Children on beach . . . 90 1·25
603 25c. Beach party . . . . . . 90 1·25
MS604 59 × 79 mm. $1 As No. 599, but larger 27 × 41 mm 3·00 3·00
Nos. 596/9 and 600/3 were each printed together, se-tenant, the four designs of each value forming a composite picture of a beach scene at night (5c.) or in the daytime (25c.).

153 "Schomburgkia thomsoniana" (var. minor)

154 Freighter Aground

1985. Orchids. Multicoloured.
605 5c. Type **153** . . . . 1·00 30
606 10c. "Schomburgkia thomsoniana" . . . . . . 1·00 30
607 25c. "Encyclia plicata" . . . 2·50 1·00
608 50c. "Dendrophylax fawcettii" . . . . 3·75 3·00

1985. Shipwrecks. Multicoloured.
609 5c. Type **154** 90 50
610 25c. Submerged sailing ship 2·75 1·25
611 35c. Wrecked trawler . . . . 3·00 2·50
612 40c. Submerged wreck on its side . . . . 3·25 3·50

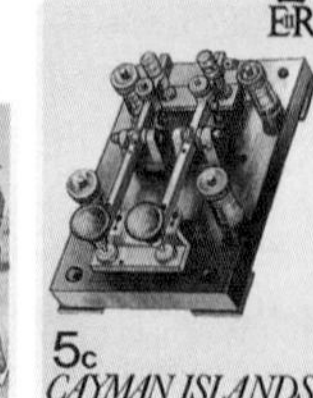

155 Athletics

156 Morse Key (1935)

1985. International Youth Year. Multicoloured.
613 5c. Type **155** 20 20
614 15c. Students in library . . . 35 30
615 25c. Football (vert) 65 55
616 50c. Netball (vert) . . . . . 1·25 2·00

1985. 50th Anniv of Telecommunications System. Multicoloured.
617 5c. Type **156** 40 50
618 10c. Hand cranked telephone 45 50
619 25c. Tropospheric scatter dish (1966) . . . . 1·25 80
620 50c. Earth station dish aerial (1979) . . . . 2·00 4·00

1986. 60th Birthday of Queen Elizabeth II. As T **110** of Ascension. Multicoloured.
621 5c. Princess Elizabeth at wedding of Lady May Cambridge, 1931 . . . . . 10 20
622 10c. In Norway, 1955 . . . . 15 20
623 25c. Queen inspecting Royal Cayman Islands Police, 1983 . . . . 1·50 75
624 50c. During Gulf tour, 1979 75 2·00
625 $1 At Crown Agents Head Office, London, 1983 . . . 1·10 2·50

157 Magnificent Frigate Bird

1986. Birds of the Cayman Islands (2nd series). Multicoloured.
627 10c. Type **157** . . . . 1·50 75
628 25c. Black-billed whistling duck ("West Indian Whistling Duck") (vert) . . 2·00 1·40
629 35c. La Sagra's flycatcher (vert) . . . . 2·25 2·50
630 40c. Yellow-faced grassquit 2·50 4·50

1986. Royal Wedding. As T **112** of Ascension. Multicoloured.
633 5c. Prince Andrew and Miss Sarah Ferguson 25 15
634 50c. Prince Andrew aboard H.M.S. "Brazen" . . . . 1·25 1·75

158 Red Coral Shrimp

159 Golf

1986. Marine Life. Multicoloured.
635 5c. Type **158** 40 75
636 10c. Yellow crinoid 40 50
637 15c. Hermit crab 35 60
638 20c. Tube dwelling anemone 35 1·25
639 25c. Christmas tree worm . . 45 2·50
640 35c. Porcupinefish . . . . . 70 2·75
641 50c. Orangeball anenome . . 80 4·25
642 60c. Basket starfish . . . . . 3·50 8·50
643 75c. Flamingo tongue . . . . 10·00 11·00
644 $1 Sea anenome . . . . . . 1·10 2·50
645 $2 Diamond blenny . . . . 1·25 4·25
646 $4 Rough file shell . . . . . 2·00 6·50

1987. Tourism. Multicoloured.
647 10c. Type **159** . . . . 2·25 1·25
648 15c. Sailing . . . . 2·25 1·25
649 25c. Snorkelling . . . . . . 2·25 1·50
650 35c. Paragliding . . . . . . 2·50 2·00
651 $1 Game fishing . . . . . . 5·00 10·00

160 Ackee

162 Poinsettia

161 Lion Lizard

1987. Cayman Islands Fruits. Multicoloured.
652 5c. Type **160** 65 65
653 25c. Breadfruit . . . . 1·50 55
654 35c. Pawpaw . . . . 1·50 70
655 $1 Soursop . . . . 3·50 6·50

1987. Lizards. Multicoloured.
656 10c. Type **161** . . . . 1·50 65
657 50c. Iguana . . . . 3·00 2·50
658 $1 Anole . . . . 4·25 4·50

1987. Flowers. Multicoloured.
659 5c. Type **162** 90 70
660 25c. Periwinkle . . . . . . 2·25 75
661 35c. Yellow allamanda . . . 2·25 1·10
662 75c. Blood lily . . . . 4·00 6·50

163 "Hemiargus ammon" and "Strymon martialis"   164 Green-backed Heron

1988. Butterflies. Multicoloured.
663 5c. Type **163** . . . . 1·25 65
664 25c. "Phocides pigmalion" . . 2·50 85
665 50c. "Anaea troglodyta" . . 4·00 3·75
666 $1 "Papilio andraemon" . . 5·00 5·00

1988. Herons. Multicoloured.
667 5c. Type **164** . . . . 1·25 65
668 25c. Louisiana heron . . . . 2·25 85
669 50c. Yellow-crowned night heron . . . . 3·00 3·00
670 $1 Little blue heron . . . . 3·50 4·25

165 Cycling   166 Princess Alexandra

1988. Olympic Games, Seoul. Multicoloured.
671 10c. Type **165** . . . . 2·00 85
672 50c. Cayman Airways Boeing 727 airliner and national team . . . . 3·00 2·75
673 $1 "470" dinghy . . . . . . 3·25 3·75
MS674 53 × 60 mm. $1 Tennis 4·00 3·00

1988. Visit of Princess Alexandra. Multicoloured.
675 5c. Type **166** . . . . 1·50 75
676 $1 Princess Alexandra in evening dress . . . . . . 5·50 5·00

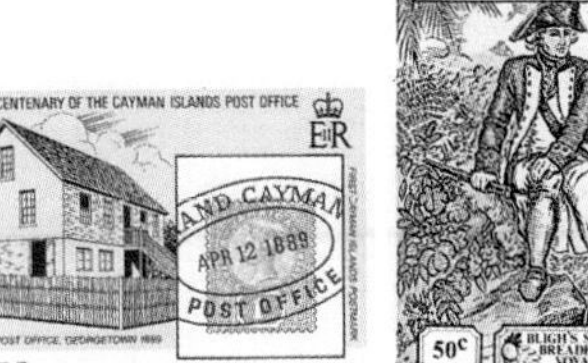

167 George Town Post Office, and Cayman Postmark on Jamaica 1d., 1889   168 Captain Bligh ashore in West Indies

1989. Centenary of Cayman Islands Postal Service. Multicoloured.
677 **167** 5c. multicoloured . . . . 85 1·00
678 – 25c. green, black and blue 2·00 1·00
679 – 35c. multicoloured . . . . 2·00 1·25
680 – $1 multicoloured . . . . 8·00 8·50
DESIGNS: 25c. "Orinoco" (mail steamer) and 1900 ½d. stamp; 35c. G.P.O., Grand Cayman and "London 1980" $1 stamp; $1 Cayman Airways B.A.C. One Eleven 200/400 airplane and 1966 1s. Jet Service stamp.

1989. Captain Bligh's Second Breadfruit Voyage, 1791–93. Multicoloured.
681 50c. Type **168** . . . . 3·50 4·00
682 50c. H.M.S. "Providence" (sloop) at anchor . . . . . 3·50 4·00
683 50c. Breadfruit in tubs and H.M.S. "Assistant" (transport) . . . . 3·50 4·00
684 50c. Sailors moving tubs of breadfruit . . . . 3·50 4·00
685 50c. Midshipman and stores 3·50 4·00
Nos. 681/5 were printed together, se-tenant, forming a composite design.

169 Panton House

170 Map of Grand Cayman, 1773, and Surveying Instruments

1989. Architecture. Designs showing George Town buildings. Multicoloured.
686 5c. Type **169** 60 60
687 10c. Town hall and clock tower 60 60
688 25c. Old Court House . . . 1·25 55
689 35c. Elmslie Memorial Church . . . . 1·40 75
690 $1 Post Office . . . . 3·00 5·00

1989. Island Maps and Survey Ships. Multicoloured.
691 5c. Type **170** . . . . 1·50 1·25
692 25c. Map of Cayman Islands, 1956, and surveying instruments . . . . 3·25 1·25
693 50c. H.M.S. "Mutine", 1914 4·50 4·25
694 $1 H.M.S. "Vidal", 1956 . . 7·50 9·00

171 French Angelfish

1990. Angelfishes. Multicoloured.
707 10c. Type **171** . . . . 1·25 70
708 25c. Grey angelfish . . . . . 2·25 90
709 50c. Queen angelfish . . . . 3·50 4·25
710 $1 Rock beauty . . . . . . 5·50 8·00

1990. 90th Birthday of Queen Elizabeth the Queen Mother. As T **134** of Ascension.
711 50c. multicoloured . . . . . 1·25 2·25
712 $1 black and blue . . . . . 2·75 4·00
DESIGNS—21 × 36 mm: 50c. Silver Wedding photograph, 1948. 29 × 37 mm: $1 King George VI and Queen Elizabeth with Winston Churchill, 1940.

172 "Danaus eresimus"

1990. "Expo 90" International Garden and Greenery Exhibition, Osaka. Butterflies. Multicoloured.
713 5c. Type **172** 65 60
714 25c. "Brephidium exilis" . . 1·50 1·10
715 35c. "Phyciodes phaon" . . . 1·75 1·25
716 $1 "Agraulis vanillae" . . . 4·00 6·50

173 Goes Weather Satellite

1991. International Decade for Natural Disaster Reduction. Multicoloured.
717 5c. Type **173** 80 60
718 30c. Meteorologist tracking hurricane . . . . 2·00 1·10
719 40c. Damaged buildings . . . 2·25 1·25
720 $1 U.S. Dept of Commerce weather reconnaisance Lockheed WP-3D Orion 5·00 7·50

174 Angels and "Datura candida"

1991. Christmas. Multicoloured.
721 5c. Type **174** 60 60
722 30c. Mary and Joseph going to Bethlehem and "Allamanda cathartica" . . 1·60 60
723 40c. Adoration of the Kings and "Euphorbia pulcherrima" . . . . . . 1·75 1·10
724 60c. Holy Family and "Guaiacum officinale" . . 2·50 4·25

175 Coconut Palm

177 Woman and Donkey with Panniers

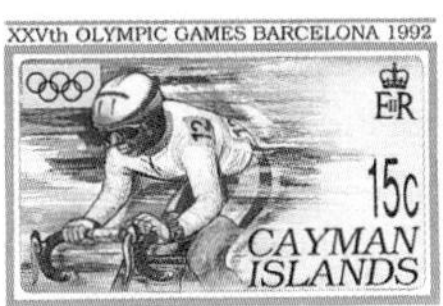

176 Single Cyclist

1991. Island Scenes. Multicoloured.
725 5c. Type **175** 50 30
726 15c. Beach scene (horiz) . . . 1·25 30
727 20c. Poincianas in bloom (horiz) 70 35
728 30c. Blowholes (horiz) . . . 1·25 50
729 40c. Police band (horiz) . . . 2·50 1·40
730 50c. "Song of Norway" (liner) at George Town . . 2·00 1·40
731 60c. The Bluff, Cayman Brac (horiz) . . . . 1·75 2·00
732 80c. Coat of arms . . . . . 1·50 2·25
733 90c. View of Hell (horiz) . . 1·60 2·25
734 $1 Game fishing (horiz) . . . 3·25 2·25
735 $2 "Nieuw Amsterdam" (1983) and "Holiday" (liners) in harbour . . . . 8·00 6·00
736 $8 Queen Elizabeth II . . . 16·00 17·00

1992. 40th Anniv of Queen Elizabeth II's Accession. As T **143** of Ascension. Multicoloured.
737 5c. Caymans' house 30 30
738 20c. Sunset over islands . . . 1·00 50
739 30c. Beach . . . . 1·10 65
740 40c. Three portraits of Queen Elizabeth . . . . 1·10 1·00
741 $1 Queen Elizabeth II . . . 2·00 3·50

1992. Olympic Games, Barcelona. Cycling. Mult.
742 15c. Type **176** . . . . 1·75 65
743 40c. Two cyclists . . . . . . 2·50 1·50
744 60c. Cyclist's legs . . . . . 3·00 3·25
745 $1 Two pursuit cyclists . . . 3·75 4·50

1992. Island Heritage. Multicoloured.
746 5c. Type **177** 50 50
747 30c. Fisherman weaving net 1·25 85
748 40c. Maypole dancing . . . 1·50 1·10
749 60c. Basket making . . . . . 2·50 3·50
750 $1 Cooking on caboose . . . 3·00 4·50

178 Yellow Stingray

1993. Rays. Multicoloured.
751 5c. Type **178** 70 60
752 30c. Southern stingray . . . 1·75 1·25
753 40c. Spotted eagle-ray . . . 2·00 1·50
754 $1 Manta . . . . 4·25 5·50

179 Turtle and Sailing Dinghies

180 Cuban Amazon with Wings spread

1993. Tourism. Multicoloured.
755 15c. Type **179** . . . . 1·25 1·50
756 15c. Tourist boat, fishing launch and scuba diver . . 1·25 1·50
757 15c. Golf . . . . 1·25 1·50
758 15c. Tennis . . . . 1·25 1·50
759 15c. Pirates and ship . . . . 1·25 1·50
760 30c. Liner, tourist launch and yacht . . . . 1·40 1·60
761 30c. George Town street . . 1·40 1·60
762 30c. Tourist submarine . . . 1·40 1·60
763 30c. Motor scooter riders and cyclist . . . . 1·40 1·60
764 30c. Cayman Airways Boeing 737 airliners . . . . 1·40 1·60

1993. Endangered Species. Cuban Amazon ("Grand Cayman Parrot"). Multicoloured.
765 5c. Type **180** . . . . 85 1·50
766 5c. On branch with wings folded . . . . 85 1·50
767 30c. Head of parrot . . . . 2·25 2·50
768 30c. Pair of parrots . . . . . 2·25 2·50

181 "Ionopsis utricularioides" and Manger

1993. Christmas. Orchids. Multicoloured.
769 5c. Type **181** 90 65
770 40c. "Encyclia cochleata" and shepherd . . . . 2·25 85
771 60c. "Vanilla pompona" and wise men . . . . 3·00 3·50
772 $1 "Oncidium caymanense" and Virgin Mary . . . . . 4·00 6·00

182 Queen Angelfish

1994. "Hong Kong '94" International Stamp Exhibition. Reef Life. Sheet 121 × 85 mm, containing T **182** and similar vert designs. Multicoloured.
MS773 60c. Type **182**; 60c. Diver with porkfish and short-finned hogfish; 60c. Rock beauty and Royal gramma; 60c. French angelfish and Banded butterflyfish 9·50 12·00

183 Flags of Great Britain and Cayman Islands

184 Black-billed Whistling Duck

1994. Royal Visit. Multicoloured.
774 5c. Type **183** . . . . 1·00 65
775 15c. Royal Yacht "Britannia" 2·00 1·00
776 30c. Queen Elizabeth II . . . 2·00 1·10
777 $2 Queen Elizabeth and Prince Philip disembarking 6·00 8·00

1994. Black-billed Whistling Duck ("West Indian Whistling Duck"). Multicoloured.
778 5c. Type **184** 90 70
779 15c. Duck landing on water (horiz) . . . . 1·60 75
780 20c. Duck preening (horiz) 1·60 80
781 80c. Duck flapping wings . . 3·50 4·50
782 $1 Adult and duckling . . . 4·00 5·00
MS783 71 × 45 mm. $1 As No. 782, but including Cayman Islands National Trust symbol 7·00 8·00

185 "Electrostrymon angelia"

186 H.M.S. "Convert" (frigate)

1994. Butterflies. Multicoloured.
784 10c. Type **185** . . . . 1·00 1·50
785 10c. "Eumaeus atala" . . . . 1·00 1·50

786 $1 "Eurema daira" 4·75 5·00
787 $1 "Urbanus dorantes" 4·75 5·00

1994. Bicentenary of Wreck of Ten Sail off Grand Cayman. Multicoloured.
788 10c. Type **186** 55 55
789 10c. Merchant brig and full-rigged ship 55 55
790 15c. Full-rigged ship near rock 75 50
791 20c. Long boat leaving full-rigged ship 85 55
792 $2 Merchant brig 4·50 7·50

187 Young Green Turtles

1995. Sea Turtles. Multicoloured.
793 10c. Type **187** 55 45
794 20c. Kemp's ridley turtle 80 55
795 25c. Hawksbill turtle 90 60
796 30c. Leatherback turtle 95 70
797 $1.30 Loggerhead turtle 3·50 4·75
798 $2 Pacific ridley turtles 4·50 6·00
MS799 167 × 94 mm. Nos. 793/8 10·00 11·00

188 Running

1995. C.A.R.I.F.T.A. and I.A.A.F. Games, George Town. Multicoloured.
800 10c. Type **188** 60 40
801 20c. High jumping 90 70
802 30c. Javelin throwing 1·25 80
803 $1.30 Yachting 4·25 6·00
MS804 100 × 70 mm. $2 Athletes with medals 5·00 6·50

1995. 50th Anniv of End of Second World War. As T **161** of Ascension. Multicoloured.
805 10c. Members of Cayman Home Guard 70 55
806 25c. "Comayagua" (freighter) 1·75 85
807 40c. U-boat "U125" 2·00 1·50
808 $1 U.S. Navy L-3 airship 3·75 5·50
MS809 75 × 85 mm. $1.30, Reverse of 1939–45 War Medal (vert) 2·50 3·00

189 Queen Elizabeth the Queen Mother

1995. 95th Birthday of Queen Elizabeth the Queen Mother. Sheet 70 × 90 mm.
MS810 **189** $4 multicoloured 8·50 9·50

190 Ox and Christ Child **191** Sea Grape

1995. Christmas. Nativity Animals. Multicoloured.
811 10c. Type **190** 70 30
812 20c. Sheep and lamb 1·25 45
813 30c. Donkey 1·75 60
814 $2 Camels 7·00 9·50
MS815 160 × 75 mm. Nos. 811/14 8·75 9·00

1996. Wild Fruit. Multicoloured.
816 10c. Type **191** 40 30
817 25c. Guava 85 50
818 40c. West Indian cherry 1·25 80
819 $1 Tamarind 2·50 3·25

192 "Laser" Dinghy **193** Guitar and Score of National Song

1996. Centenary of Modern Olympic Games. Multicoloured.
820 10c. Type **192** 40 30
821 20c. Sailboarding 70 60
822 30c. "Finn" dinghy 90 80
823 $2 Running 4·00 6·50

1996. National Identity. Multicoloured.
824 10c. Type **193** 35 30
825 20c. Cayman Airways Boeing 737-200 70 55
826 25c. Queen Elizabeth opening Legislative Assembly 75 50
827 30c. Seven Mile Beach 75 55
828 40c. Scuba diver and stingrays 1·00 75
829 60c. Children at turtle farm 1·50 1·10
830 80c. Cuban amazon ("Cayman Parrot") (national bird) 2·50 2·00
831 90c. Silver thatch palm (national tree) 1·75 2·00
832 $1 Cayman Islands flag 2·75 2·25
833 $2 Wild Banana Orchid (national flower) 4·75 5·50
834 $4 Cayman Islands coat of arms 9·00 12·00
835 $6 Cayman Islands currency 11·00 14·00

194 "Christmas Time on North Church Street" (Joanne Sibley)

1996. Christmas. Paintings. Multicoloured.
836 10c. Type **194** 40 30
837 25c. "Gone Fishing" (Lois Brezinsky) 70 50
838 30c. "Claus Encounters" (John Doak) 80 70
839 $2 "A Caymanian Christmas" (Debbie van der Bol) 4·00 6·50

1997. "HONG KONG '97" International Stamp Exhibition. Sheet 130 × 90 mm, containing design as No. 830 with "1997" imprint date. Multicoloured.
MS840 80c. Cuban amazon ("Cayman Parrot") 1·50 2·00

1997. Golden Wedding of Queen Elizabeth and Prince Philip. As T **173** of Ascension. Multicoloured.
841 10c. Queen Elizabeth 80 1·00
842 10c. Prince Philip and Prince Charles at Trooping the Colour 80 1·00
843 30c. Prince William horse riding, 1989 1·40 1·60
844 30c. Queen Elizabeth and Prince Philip at Royal Ascot 1·40 1·60
845 40c. Prince Philip at the Brighton Driving Trials 1·50 1·60
846 40c. Queen Elizabeth at Windsor Horse Show, 1993 1·50 1·60
MS847 110 × 70 mm. $1 Queen Elizabeth and Prince Philip in landau (horiz) 3·25 3·50

195 Children accessing Internet **196** Santa in Hammock

1997. Telecommunications. Multicoloured.
848 10c. Type **195** 35 25
849 25c. Cable & Wireless cable ship 70 45
850 30c. New area code "345" on children's T-shirts 75 60
851 60c. Satellite dish 1·50 2·25

1997. Christmas. Multicoloured.
852 10c. Type **196** 35 25
853 30c. Santa with children on the Bluff 65 45
854 40c. Santa playing golf 1·50 80
855 $1 Santa scuba diving 2·00 3·25

1998. Diana, Princess of Wales Commemoration. As T **91** of Kiribati. Multicoloured.
856 10c. Wearing gold earrings, 1997 40 40
857 20c. Wearing black hat 70 70
MS858 145 × 70 mm. 10c. As No. 856; 20c. As No. 857; 40c. With bouquet, 1995; $1 Wearing black and white blouse, 1983 (sold at $1.70 + 30c. charity premium) 3·50 4·00

1998. 80th Anniv of the Royal Air Force. As T **178** of Ascension. Multicoloured.
859 10c. Hawker Horsley 50 50
860 20c. Fairey Hendon 65 65
861 25c. Hawker Siddeley Gnat 75 75
862 30c. Hawker Siddeley Dominie 85 85
MS863 110 × 77 mm. 40c. Airco D.H.9; 60c. Spad 13 Scout; 80c. Airspeed Oxford; $1 Martin Baltimore 5·00 6·50

197 Black-billed Whistling Duck ("West Indian Whistling Duck") **198** Santa at the Blowholes

1998. Birds. Multicoloured.
864 10c. Type **197** 65 50
865 20c. Magnificent frigate bird ("Magnificent Frigatbird") 1·00 50
866 60c. Red-footed booby 2·00 2·00
867 $1 Cuban amazon ("Grand Cayman Parrot") 2·25 3·00

1998. Christmas. Multicoloured.
868 10c. Type **198** 30 25
869 30c. Santa diving on wreck of "Capt. Keith Tibbetts" 75 60
870 40c. Santa at Pedro Castle 90 75
871 60c. Santa arriving on Little Cayman 1·75 2·00

199 "They Rolled the Stone Away" (Miss Lassie)

1999. Easter. Paintings by Miss Lassie (Gladwyn Bush). Multicoloured.
884 10c. Type **199** 25 25
885 20c. "Ascension" (vert) 50 50
886 30c. "The World Praying for Peace" 65 65
887 40c. "Calvary" (vert) 85 85

200 "Cayman House" (Jessica Cranston)

1999. Vision 2008 Project. Children's Paintings. Multicoloured.
888 10c. Type **200** 40 20
889 30c. "Coral Reef" (Sarah Hetley) 1·00 55
890 40c. "Fisherman on North Sound" (Sarah Cuff) 1·10 70
891 $2 "Three Fish and a Turtle" (Ryan Martinez) 4·25 5·50

1999. Royal Wedding. As T **185** of Ascension. Multicoloured.
892 10c. Photographs of Prince Edward and Miss Sophie Rhys-Jones 50 30
893 $2 Engagement photograph 3·75 4·75

1999. 30th Anniv of First Manned Landing on Moon. As T **186** of Ascension. Multicoloured.
894 10c. Coastguard cutter on patrol during launch 35 25
895 25c. Firing of third stage rockets 70 60
896 30c. Buzz Aldrin descending to Moon's surface 75 65
897 60c. Jettisoning of lunar module 1·25 1·75
MS898 90 × 80 mm. $1.50, Earth as seen from Moon (circular, 40 mm diam) 2·75 3·50

1999. "Queen Elizabeth the Queen Mother's Century". As T **187** of Ascension. Multicoloured.
899 10c. Visiting anti-aircraft battery, London, 1940 45 30
900 20c. With children on her 94th birthday, 1994 65 55
901 30c. With Prince Charles and Prince William, 1997 80 80
902 40c. Reviewing Chelsea Pensioners, 1986 90 90
MS903 145 × 70 mm. $1.50, Duchess of York with Princess Elizabeth, 1926, and Royal Wedding, 1923 2·75 3·25

201 1969 Christmas ¼c. Stamp

1999. Christmas. Designs showing previous Christmas stamps. Multicoloured.
904 10c. Type **201** 40 25
905 30c. 1984 Christmas 5c. 70 50
906 40c. 1997 Christmas 10c. 85 65
907 $1 1979 Christmas 20c. (horiz) 1·90 2·75
MS908 111 × 100 mm. Nos. 904/7 2·75 3·50

2000. "Stamp Show 2000" International Stamp Exhibition, London. Kings and Queens of England. As T **223** of British Virgin Islands. Multicoloured.
909 10c. King Henry VII 35 50
910 40c. King Henry VIII 90 1·25
911 40c. Queen Mary I 90 1·25
912 40c. King Charles II 90 1·25
913 40c. Queen Anne 90 1·25
914 40c. King George IV 90 1·25
915 40c. King George V 90 1·25

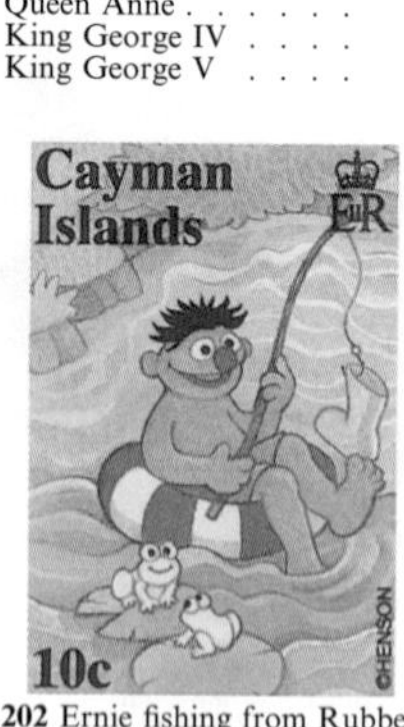

202 Ernie fishing from Rubber Ring

2000. "Sesame Street" (children's T.V. programme). Multicoloured.
916 10c. Type **202** 25 25
917 20c. Grover flying 40 50
918 20c. Zoe in airplane 40 50
919 20c. Oscar the Grouch in balloon 40 50
920 20c. The Count on motorbike 40 50
921 20c. Big Bird rollerskating 40 50
922 20c. Cookie Monster heading for Cookie Factory 40 50
923 20c. Type **202** 40 50
924 20c. Bert in rowing boat 40 50
925 20c. Elmo snorkeling 40 50
926 30c. As No. 920 55 55
MS927 139 × 86 mm. 20c. Elmo with stamps 60 80

Nos. 917/25 were printed together, se-tenant, with the backgrounds forming a composite design.

2000. 18th Birthday of Prince William. As T **191** of Ascension. Multicoloured.
928 10c. Prince William in 1999 (horiz) 30 25
929 20c. In evening dress, 1997 (horiz) 55 45

930 30c. At Muick Falls, 1997 . . 70 70
931 40c. In uniform of Parachute Regiment, 1986 . . . . . 90 95
MS932 175×95 mm. $1 As baby with toy mouse (horiz) and Nos. 928/31 5·50 5·50

203 Green Turtle

2000. Marine Life. Multicoloured.
933 10c. Type **203** 30 25
934 20c. Queen angel fish . . . 55 45
935 30c. Sleeping parrotfish . . . 75 65
936 $1 Green moray eel . . . . 2·75 3·00

204 Boy thinking about Drugs and Fitness

2000. National Drugs Council. Multicoloured.
937 10c. Type **204** 45 25
938 15c. Rainbow, sun, clouds and "ez2B Drug Free" . . 60 35
939 30c. Musicians dancing . . . 1·00 65
940 $2 Hammock between two palm trees . . . . 4·50 6·00

205 Children on Beach ("Backing Sand") 206 Woman on Beach

2000. Christmas. Traditional Customs. Mult.
941 10c. Type **205** 55 35
942 30c. Christmas dinner . . . . 1·25 70
943 40c. Yard dance . . . . . . 1·40 85
944 60c. Conch shell borders . . 2·00 2·25

2001. United Nations Women's Human Rights Campaign.
945 **206** 10c. multicoloured 35 35

207 Red Mangrove Cay

2001. Cayman Brac Tourism Project. Mult.
946 15c. Type **207** 50 40
947 20c. Peter's Cave (vert) . . . 60 50
948 25c. Bight Road steps (vert) 70 60
949 30c. Westerly Ponds 80 75
950 40c. Aerial view of Spot Bay 95 95
951 60c. The Marshes . . . . . 1·50 2·00

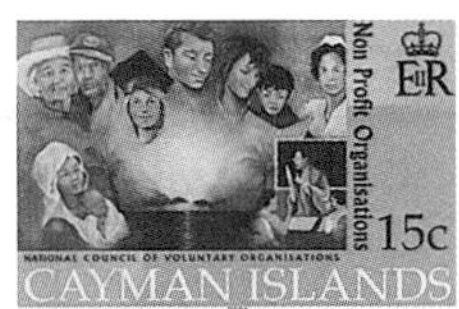

208 Work of National Council of Voluntary Organizations

2001. Non-Profit Organizations. Multicoloured.
952 15c. Type **208** 35 35
953 20c. Pet welfare (Cayman Humane Society) 50 50
954 25c. Stick figures (Red Cross and Red Crescent) 60 60
955 30c. Pink flowers (Cayman Islands Cancer Society) (vert) 70 70
956 40c. Women's silhouettes and insignia (Lions Club Breast Cancer Awareness Campaign) (vert) 85 85
MS957 145×95 mm. Nos. 952/6 (sold at $1.80) 3·00 3·50
No. **MS**957 was sold at $1.80 which included a 50c. donation to the featured organisations.

209 Children walking Home

2001. Transportation. Multicoloured.
958 15c. Type **209** 25 30
959 15c. Boy on donkey 25 30
960 20c. Bananas by canoe . . . 30 35
961 25c. Horse and buggy 40 45
962 30c. Catboats fishing 45 50
963 40c. Schooner 60 65
964 60c. Police cyclist (vert) . . 95 1·00
965 80c. Lady drivers . . . . . 1·25 1·40
966 90c. Launching *Cimboco* (motor coaster) (vert) . . 1·40 1·50
967 $1 Amphibian aircraft . . . 1·50 1·60
968 $4 Container ship . . . . . 6·25 6·50
969 $10 Boeing 767 airliner . . . 15·00 16·00

210 Father Christmas on Scooter with Children, Cayman Brac

2001. Christmas. Multicoloured.
970 15c. Type **210** 35 30
971 30c. Father Christmas on eagle ray, Little Cayman 65 55
972 40c. Father Christmas in catboat, Grand Cayman 80 80
973 60c. Father Christmas parasailing over Grand Cayman . . . . 1·25 1·40

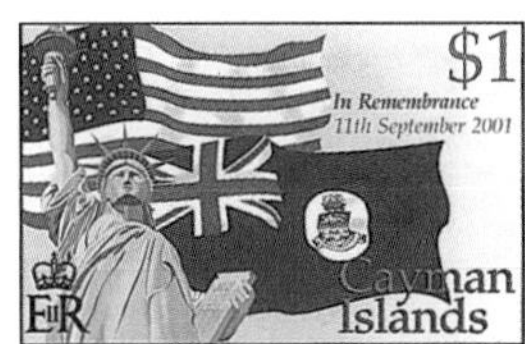

211 Statue of Liberty, U.S. and Cayman Flags

2002. In Remembrance. Victims of Terrorist Attacks on U.S.A. (11 September 2001).
974 **211** $1 multicoloured . . . . 2·00 2·50

2002. Golden Jubilee. As T **200** of Ascension.
975 15c. grey, blue and gold . . . 40 30
976 20c. multicoloured 55 40
977 30c. black, blue and gold . . 70 60
978 80c. multicoloured . . . . . 1·75 2·00
MS979 162×95 mm. Nos. 975/8 and $1 multicoloured 5·00 5·50
DESIGNS—HORIZ: 15c. Princess Elizabeth as young child; 20c. Queen Elizabeth in evening dress, 1976; 30c. Princess Elizabeth and Princess Margaret as Girl Guides, 1942; 80c. Queen Elizabeth at Newbury, 1996. VERT (38×51 mm)—$1 Queen Elizabeth after Annigoni.
Designs as Nos. 975/8 in No. **MS**979 omit the gold frame around each stamp and the "Golden Jubilee 1952–2002" inscription.

212 Snoopy painting Woodstock at Cayman Brac Bluff

2002. "A Cayman Vacation". Peanuts (cartoon characters by Charles Schulz). Multicoloured.
980 15c. Type **212** 35 30
981 20c. Charlie Brown and Sally at Hell Post Office, Grand Cayman 45 40
982 25c. Peppermint Patty and Marcie on beach, Little Cayman 55 50
983 30c. Snoopy as Red Baron and Boeing 737-200 over Grand Cayman 65 65
984 40c. Linus and Snoopy at Point of Sand, Little Cayman 85 85
985 60c. Charlie Brown playing golf at The Links, Grand Cayman . . . . 1·25 1·40
MS986 230×160 mm. Nos. 980/5 3·50 4·00
No. **MS**986 is die-cut in the shape of a suitcase.

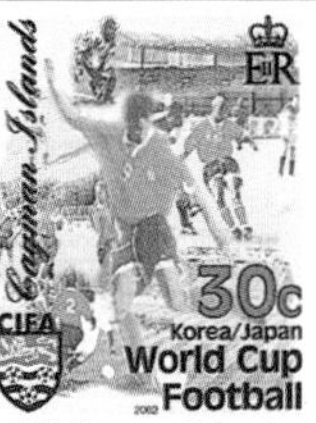

213 Cayman Islands Footballers

2002. World Cup Football Championship, Japan and Korea and 35th Anniv of Cayman Islands Football Association.
987 **213** 30c. multicoloured 35 40
988 40c. multicoloured 60 65

2002. Queen Elizabeth the Queen Mother Commemoration. As T **202** of Ascension.
989 15c. black, gold and purple 25 20
990 30c. multicoloured 35 40
991 40c. black, gold and purple 60 65
992 $1 multicoloured . . . . . . 1·50 1·60
MS993 145×70 mm. Nos. 991/2 2·10 2·25
DESIGNS: 15c. Queen Elizabeth at Red Corss and St. John's summer fair, London, 1943; 30c. Queen Mother at Royal Caledonian School, Bushey; 40c. Duchess of York in 1936; $1 Queen Mother at film premiere in 1989.
Designs in No. **MS**993 omit the "1900–2002" inscription and the coloured frame.

214 Angel Gabriel appearing to Virgin Mary

2002. Christmas. Multicoloured.
994 15c. Type **214** 25 30
995 20c. Mary and Joseph travelling to Bethlehem . . 30 35
996 30c. The Holy Family . . . 45 50
997 40c. Angel appearing to shepherds 60 65
998 60c. Three Wise Men . . . . 95 1·00
MS999 234×195 mm. Nos. 994/8 2·50 2·75

215 Catalina Flying Boat, North Sound, Grand Cayman

2002. 50th Anniv of Cayman Islands. Aviation. Multicoloured.
1000 15c. Type **215** 25 30
1001 20c. Grand Cayman Airport, 1952 . . . . . . 30 35
1002 25c. Cayman Brac Airways AC 50 . . . . 40 45
1003 30c. Cayman Airways Boeing 737 . . . . 45 50
1004 40c. British Airways Concorde at Grand Cayman, 1984 . . . . . 60 65
1005 $1.30 Island Air DHC 6 Twin Otter on Little Cayman . . . . 2·00 2·10

CENTRAL AFRICAN EMPIRE

Pt. 12

Central African Republic was renamed Central African Empire on 4 December 1976, when Pres. Bokassa became Emperor.

The country reverted to Central African Republic on his overthrow in 1979.

100 centimes = 1 franc.

1977. Various stamps of Central African Republic optd **EMPIRE CENTRAFRICAIN**.
439 **150** 3f. mult (postage) 40 35
444 **167** 10f. multicoloured 25 25
457 – 10f. red and blue (386) . . 25 25
459 **172** 10f. multicoloured 35 35
460 – 15f. multicoloured (391) 45 45
465 – 15f. brown, grn & bl (397) 25 25
445 – 20f. multicoloured (366) 25 25
461 – 20f. multicoloured (392) 40 40
446 – 25f. multicoloured (367) 25 25
451 – 25f. multicoloured (376) 25 25
449 **168** 30f. multicoloured 40 40
452 – 30f. multicoloured (377) 40 40
462 – 30f. multicoloured (393) 45 45
447 – 40f. multicoloured (370) 40 40
450 – 40f. multicoloured (373) 45 45
453 – 40f. multicoloured (378) 40 40
454 – 40f. multicoloured (380) 45 45
455 **170** 40f. multicoloured 40 40
456 – 40f. multicoloured (384) 40 40
458 – 40f. multicoloured (389) 40 35
482 – 40f. multicoloured (423) 65 55
466 – 50f. blue, brn & grn (398) 55 55
440 **163** 100f. multicoloured . . . 13·00 13·00
441 **164** 100f. grn, red & brn . . 1·25 1·25
442 **165** 100f. brn, grn & blue . . 1·60 1·60
468 **179** 100f. black and yellow . . 1·25 1·25
469 **180** 100f. purple, blue & grn 1·25 1·25
491 **185** 100f. multicoloured . . . 1·25 1·25
483 – 50f. mult (424) (air) . . . 45 30
448 – 100f. multicoloured (371) 85 85
463 **173** 100f. red and blue 90 90
467 **178** 100f. multicoloured . . . 85 85
484 – 100f. multicoloured (425) 85 85
464 **174** 200f. multicoloured . . . 1·90 1·90
443 **166** 500f. red, green & brown 6·25 6·25

1977. "Apollo–Soyuz" Space Link. Nos. 410/14 of Central African Republic optd **EMPIRE CENTRAFRICAIN**.
470 **181** 40f. mult (postage) . . . 50 50
471 – 50f. multicoloured 60 60
472 – 100f. multicoloured (air) 85 85
473 – 200f. multicoloured . . . 1·90 1·90
474 – 300f. multicoloured . . . 2·50 2·50

1977. Air. Bicentenary of American Revolution. Nos. 416/20 of Central African Republic optd **EMPIRE CENTRAFRICAIN**.
476 **182** 100f. multicoloured . . . 75 45
477 – 125f. multicoloured . . . 95 60
478 – 150f. multicoloured . . . 1·25 70
479 – 200f. multicoloured . . . 1·60 95
480 – 250f. multicoloured . . . 1·90 1·25

1977. Winners of Winter Olympic Games, Innsbruck. Nos. 426/30 of Central African Republic optd **EMPIRE CENTRAFRICAIN**.
485 – 40f. mult (postage) . . . 40 35
486 – 60f. multicoloured 50 35
487 **184** 100f. multicoloured (air) 65 45
488 – 200f. multicoloured . . . 1·50 85
489 – 300f. multicoloured . . . 2·25 1·25

1977. "Viking" Space Mission. Nos. 433/7 of Central African Republic optd **EMPIRE CENTRAFRICAIN**.
492 **186** 40f. mult (postage) . . . 40 30
493 – 60f. multicoloured 50 35
494 – 100f. multicoloured (air) 65 45
495 – 200f. multicoloured . . . 1·50 85
496 – 300f. multicoloured . . . 2·25 1·25

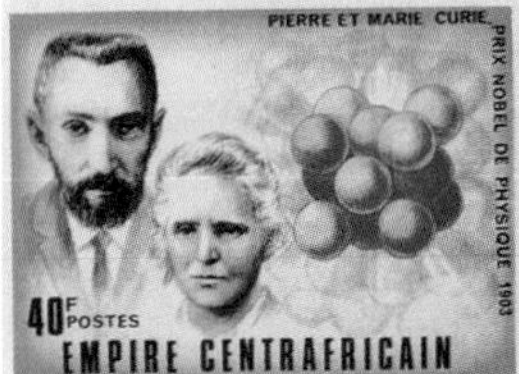

189 Pierre and Marie Curie (Physics, 1903)

1977. Nobel Prize-winners. Multicoloured.
503 40f. Type **189** (postage) . . . 60 25
504 60f. W. C. Rontgen (Physics, 1901) 60 35
505 100f. Rudyard Kipling (Literature, 1907) (air) . . 75 35
506 200f. Ernest Hemingway (Literature, 1954) . . . . 1·50 65
507 300f. L. Pirandello (Literature, 1934) . . . . 2·25 75

190 Roman Temple and Italy 1933 3l. stamp

1977. "Graf Zeppelin" Flights. Multicoloured.
509 40f. Type **190** (postage) . . . 60 25
510 60f. St. Basil's Cathedral, Moscow, and Russia 1930 40k. stamp 70 40
511 100f. North Pole and Germany 1931 "Polarfahrt" stamp (air) 1·10 45
512 200f. Museum of Science and Industry, Chicago, and Germany 1933 "Chicagofahrt" stamp . . 2·10 65
513 300f. Brandenburg Gate, Berlin, and German 1931 stamp . . . . 3·25 95

191 Charles Lindbergh and "Spirit of St. Louis"

1977. History of Aviation. Multicoloured.
515 50f. Type **191** 45 20
516 60f. Alberto Santos-Dumont and "14 bis" biplane 55 25
517 100f. Louis Bleriot and Bleriot XI 95 40
518 200f. Roald Amundsen and Dornier Wal flying boat 1·60 60
519 300f. Concorde 3·00 1·25

192 Lily **193** Group of Africans and Rotary Emblem

1977. Flowers. Multicoloured.
521 5f. Type **192** 50 35
522 10f. Hibiscus 1·00 60

1977. 20th Anniv of Bangui Rotary Club.
523 **193** 60f. multicoloured 1·90 1·25

194 Africans queueing beside Bible **195** Printed Circuit

1977. Bible Week.
524 **194** 40f. multicoloured 1·50 95

1977. World Telecommunications Day.
525 **195** 100f. orange, brown & blk 2·25 1·90

196 Doctor inoculating Child

1977. Air. World Health Day.
526 **196** 150f. multicoloured 1·00 70

197 Goalkeeper

1977. World Cup Football Championship (1978). Multicoloured.
527 50f. Type **197** 40 20
528 60f. Goalmouth melee 45 25
529 100f. Mid-field play 75 30
530 200f. World Cup poster 1·60 50
531 300f. Mario Jorge Lobo Zagalo (Argentine trainer) and Buenos Aires stadium 2·50 90

198 Emperor Bokassa I

1977. Coronation of Emperor Bokassa.
533 **198** 40f. mult (postage) 25 20
534 60f. multicoloured 40 25
535 100f. multicoloured 75 45
536 150f. multicoloured 1·25 70
537 200f. mult (air) 1·50 75
538 300f. multicoloured 2·25 1·25

199 Bangui Telephone Exchange

1978. Opening of Automatic Telephone Exchange, Bangui. Multicoloured.
541 40f. Type **199** 40 25
542 60f. Bangui Telephone Exchange (different) 50 35

200 Bokassa Sports Palace

1978. Bokassa Sports Palace. Multicoloured.
543 40f. Type **200** 40 25
544 60f. Sports Palace (different) 50 35

201 "The Holy Family"

1978. 400th Birth Anniv of Rubens. Mult.
545 60f. Type **201** 50 20
546 150f. "Marie de Medici" 1·10 40
547 200f. "The Artist's Sons" 1·60 60
548 300f. "Neptune" (horiz) 2·50 75

202 Black Rhinoceros

1978. Endangered Animals. Multicoloured.
550 40f. Type **202** 50 15
551 50f. Crocodile 65 20
552 60f. Leopard (vert) 75 25
553 100f. Giraffe (vert) 1·25 40
554 200f. African elephant 3·25 60
555 300f. Gorilla (vert) 3·75 1·00

203 Mail Coach and Satellite

1978. 100 Years of Progress in Posts and Telecommunications. Multicoloured.
556 40f. Type **203** (postage) 35 20
557 50f. Steam locomotive and space communications 5·50 2·75
558 60f. Paddle-steamer and ship-to-shore communications 45 25
559 80f. Renault car and "Pioneer" satellite 65 25
560 100f. Mail balloon and "Apollo"–"Soyuz" link-up (air) 75 40
561 200f. Seaplane "Comte da la Vaulx" and Concorde 1·50 65

205 H.M.S. "Endeavour" under Repair (after W. Byrne)

1978. 250th Birth Anniv of Captain Cook. Mult.
578 60f. Type **205** 1·00 35
579 80f. Cook on board "Endeavour" (vert) 75 25
580 200f. Landing party in New Hebrides 1·90 65
581 350f. Masked paddlers in canoe (after Webber) 3·75 1·25

206 Ife Bronze Head

1978. 2nd World Festival of Negro Arts, Lagos.
582 **206** 20f. black and yellow 25 20
583 – 30f. black and blue 25 20
584 – 60f. multicoloured 65 40
585 – 100f. multicoloured 1·10 65
DESIGNS—VERT: 30f. Carved mask. HORIZ: 60f. Dancers; 100f. Dancers with musical instruments.

207 Clement Ader and "Avion III"

1978. Air. Aviation Pioneers. Multicoloured.
586 40f. Type **207** 40 20
587 50f. Wright Brothers and glider No. III 40 20
588 60f. Alcock, Brown and Vickers Vimy 45 30
589 100f. Sir Alan Cobham and De Havilland D.H.50 90 45
590 150f. Dr. Claude Dornier and Dornier Gs1 flying boat 1·40 65

208 "Self-portrait"

1978. 450th Death Anniv of Albrecht Durer (artist). Multicoloured.
592 60f. Type **208** 50 20
593 80f. "The Four Apostles" 75 25
594 200f. "The Virgin and Child" 1·90 80
595 350f. "The Emperor Maxillian I" 3·25 1·25

1978. Air. "Philexafrique" Stamp Exhibition, Gabon (1st issue) and International Stamp Fair, Essen. As T **237** of Benin. Multicoloured.
596 100f. Red crossbills and Mecklenberg-Schwerin 1856 ¼s. stamp 1·50 1·25
597 100f. Crocodile and Central African Republic 1960 500f. stamp 1·50 1·25
See also Nos. 647/8.

209 Third Mummiform Coffin

1978. Treasures of Tutankhamun. Mult.
598 40f. Type **209** 35 20
599 60f. Tutankhamun and Ankhesenamun (back of gilt throne) 45 25
600 80f. Ecclesiastical throne 65 35
601 100f. Head of Tutankhamun (wooden statuette) 75 35
602 120f. Lion's head (funerary bedhead) 95 40
603 150f. Life-size statue of Tutankhamun 1·25 45
604 180f. Gilt throne 1·50 55
605 250f. Canopic coffin 1·90 75

210 Lenin speaking at the Smolny Institute **211** Catherine Bokassa

1978. 60th Anniv of Russian Revolution.
606 **210** 40f. multicoloured 40 25
607 – 60f. multicoloured 50 35
608 – 100f. black, grey and gold 90 40
609 – 150f. red, black and gold 1·40 65
610 – 200f. multicoloured 1·90 95
611 – 300f. multicoloured 2·50 1·25
DESIGNS—VERT: 60f. Lenin addressing crowd in Red Square; 200f. Lenin at Smolny Institute; 300f. Lenin and banner. HORIZ: 100f. Lenin, Krupskaya and family; 150f. Lenin, Cruiser "Aurora" and revolutionaries.

1978. 1st Anniv of Emperor Bokassa's Coronation. Multicoloured.
613 40f. Type **211** (postage) 40 20
614 60f. Emperor Bokassa 50 35
615 150f. The Emperor and Empress (horiz) (air) 1·25 70

212 Rowland Hill, Letter-weighing Scale and Penny Black

1978. Death Centenary of Sir Rowland Hill (1st issue). Multicoloured.
617 40f. Type **212** (postage) 35 20
618 50f. Postman on bicycle and U.S. 5c. stamp, 1847 40 25
619 60f. Danish postman and Austrian newspaper stamp, 1856 45 30
620 80f. Postilion, mail coach and Geneva 5+5c. stamp, 1843 65 25
621 100f. Postman, mail train and Tuscan 3l. stamp, 1860 (air) 3·25 1·60
622 200f. Mail balloon and French 10c. stamp, 1850 1·50 65
See also Nos. 671/4.

1978. Argentina's Victory in World Cup Football Championship. Nos. 527/31 optd **VAINQUEUR ARGENTINE**.
625 50f. Type **197** 40 25
626 60f. Goalmouth melee 45 35
627 100f. Mid-field play 75 45
628 200f. World Cup poster 1·50 95
629 300f. Mario Jorge Lobo Zagalo and Buenos Aires Stadium 2·25 1·25

214 Children painting and Dutch Master

1979. International Year of the Child (1st issue). Multicoloured.
631 40f. Type **214** (postage) 40 15
632 50f. Eskimo children and skier 50 20
633 60f. Benz automobile and children with toy car 65 20
634 80f. Satellite and children launching rocket 90 25
635 100f. Dornier Do-X flying boat and Chinese child flying kite (air) 95 40
636 200f. Hurdler and children playing leap-frog 1·90 45
See also Nos. 666/70.

215 High Jump

1979. Pre-Olympic Year (1st issue). Mult.
639 40f. Type **215** (postage) 35 15
640 50f. Cycling 40 20
641 60f. Weightlifting 45 20
642 80f. Judo 65 30

643 100f. Hurdles (air) 75 35
644 200f. Long jump 1·50 50
See also Nos. 676/70 and 705.

216 Co-operation Monument, "Aurivillius arata" and Hibiscus

1979. "Philexafrique" Exhibition (2nd issue). Mult.
647 60f. Type **216** 1·60 1·10
648 150f. Envelopes, van, canoeist and U.P.U. emblem 3·25 2·10

217 School Teacher

1979. 50th Anniv of International Bureau of Education.
649 **217** 70f. multicoloured 65 40

219 Chicken

1979. National Association of Farmers. Mult.
651 10f. Type **219** (postage) 1·25 90
652 20f. Bullock 1·25 90
653 40f. Sheep 2·50 1·75

654 60f. Horse (air) 3·50 1·60

OFFICIAL STAMPS

1977. Official stamps of Central African Republic optd **EMPIRE CENTRAFRICAIN**.
O498 **O 109** 5f. multicoloured 25 20
O499 40f. multicoloured 40 20
O500 100f. multicoloured 1·00 45
O501 140f. multicoloured 1·25 70
O502 200f. multicoloured 2·25 1·00

O 204 Coat of Arms

1978.
O564 **O 204** 1f. multicoloured 20 15
O565 2f. multicoloured 15 15
O566 5f. multicoloured 15 15
O567 10f. multicoloured 20 15
O568 15f. multicoloured 20 15
O569 20f. multicoloured 25 20
O570 30f. multicoloured 35 25
O571 40f. multicoloured 40 30
O572 50f. multicoloured 50 35
O673 60f. multicoloured 65 45
O574 100f. multicoloured 75 60
O575 130f. multicoloured 1·25 90
O576 140f. multicoloured 1·25 90
O577 200f. multicoloured 2·50 1·25

CENTRAL AFRICAN REPUBLIC

Pt. 12

Formerly Ubangi-Shari. An independent republic within the french Community.

100 centimes = 1 franc.

1 President Boganda

3 "Dactyloceras widenmanni"

4 Abyssinian Roller

1959. Republic. 1st Anniv. Centres multicoloured. Frame colours given.
1 **1** 15f. blue 35 25
2 – 25f. red 45 25
DESIGN—HORIZ: 25f. As Type **1** but flag behind portrait.

1960. 10th Anniv of African Technical Co-operation Commission. As T **62** of Cameroun.
3 50f. blue and green 1·25 75

1960.
4 – 50c. brn, red & turq (postage) 10 10
5 – 1f. myrtle, brown & violet 10 10
6 – 2f. myrtle, brown and green 15 15
7 – 3f. brown, red and olive 25 20
8 **3** 5f. brown and green 35 25
9 – 10f. blue, black and green 70 45
10 – 20f. red, black and green 1·50 65
11 – 85f. red, black and green 5·75 1·60

12 – 50f. turq, red & green (air) 4·25 1·40
13 **4** 100f. violet, brown & green 7·00 2·00
14 – 200f. multicoloured 12·00 4·75
15 – 250f. multicoloured 12·50 5·00
16 – 500f. brown, blue and green 42·00 8·50
BUTTERFLIES—As Type **3**: 50c., 3f. "Cymothoe sangaris"; 1f., 2f. "Charaxe mobilis"; 10f. "Charaxes ameliae"; 20f. "Charaxes zingha"; 85f. "Drurya antimachus". BIRDS—As Type **4**: 50f. Great blue turaco; 200f. Green turaco; 250f. Red-faced lovebirds; 500f. African fish eagle.
See also Nos. 42/5.

1960. National Festival. No. 2 optd **FETE NATIONALE 1-12-1960.**
17 25f. multicoloured 1·25 1·25

1960. Air. Olympic Games. No. 276 of French Equatorial Africa optd with Olympic rings, **XVIIe OLYMPIADE 1960 REPUBLIQUE CENTRAFRICAINE** and surch **250F** and bars.
18 250f. on 500f. blue, blk & grn 7·75 7·50

7 Pasteur Institute, Bangui

1961. Opening of Pasteur Institute, Bangui.
19 **7** 20f. multicoloured 75 65

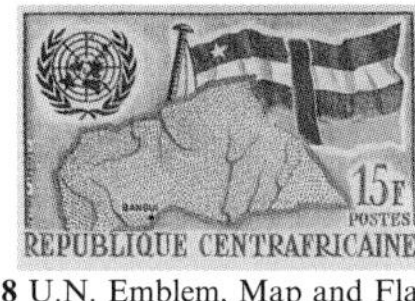

8 U.N. Emblem, Map and Flag

1961. Admission into U.N.O.
20 **8** 15f. multicoloured 40 35
21 25f. multicoloured 45 35
22 85f. multicoloured 1·40 95

1961. National Festival. Optd with star and **FETE NATIONALE 1-12-01.**
23 **8** 25f. multicoloured 1·75 1·75

1962. Air. "Air Afrique" Airline. As T **69** of Cameroun.
24 50f. violet, brown and green 95 60

1962. Union of African States and Madagascar Conference, Bangui. Surch **U.A.M. CONFERENCE DE BANGUI 25-27 MARS 1962 50F.**
25 **8** 50f. on 85f. multicoloured 1·25 1·25

1962. Malaria Eradication. As T **70** of Cameroun.
26 25f.+5f. slate 85 85

12 Hurdling

13 Pres. Dacko

1962. Sports.
27 **12** 20f. sep, yell & grn (postage) 45 35
28 – 50f. sepia, yellow and green 1·10 65

29 – 100f. sep, yell & grn (air) 2·10 1·40
DESIGNS—As Type **12**: 50f. Cycling. VERT: (26 × 47 mm): 100f. Pole-vaulting.

1962.
30 **13** 20f. multicoloured 35 20
31 25f. multicoloured 45 20

1962. 1st Anniv of Union of African and Malagasy States. As T **72** of Cameroun.
32 30f. green 65 45

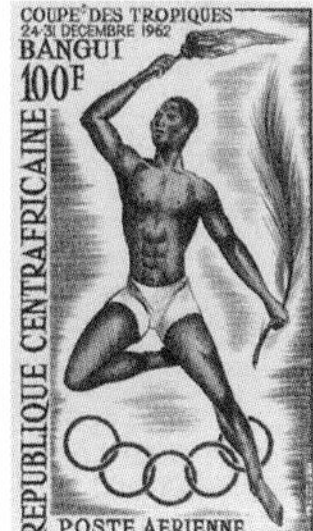

15 Athlete

18 "Posts and Telecommunications"

17 "National Army"

19 "Telecommunications"

1962. Air. "Coupe des Tropiques" Games, Bangui.
33 **15** 100f. brown, turquoise & red 2·25 1·40

1963. Freedom from Hunger. As T **76** of Cameroun.
34 25f.+5f. turquoise, brn & bis 75 75

1963. 3rd Anniv of Proclamation of Republic.
35 **17** 20f. multicoloured 60 40

1963. Air. African and Malagasy Posts and Telecommunications Union.
36 **18** 85f. multicoloured 1·60 80

1963. Space Telecommunications.
37 **19** 25f. green and purple 65 50
38 – 100f. green, orange & blue 1·60 1·40
DESIGN: 100f. Radio waves and globe.

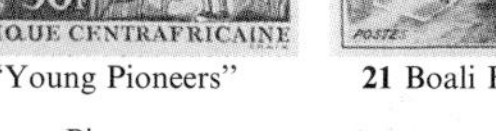
20 "Young Pioneers" 21 Boali Falls

1963. Young Pioneers.
39 **20** 30f. brown, blue & turquoise 65 45

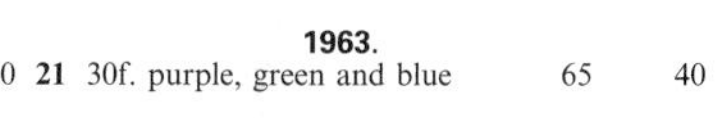
1963.
40 **21** 30f. purple, green and blue 65 40

22 Map of Africa and Sun

1963. Air. "African Unity".
41 **22** 25f. ultramarine, yellow & bl 55 35

23 "Colotis evippe"

24 "Europafrique"

1963. Butterflies. Multicoloured.
42 1f. Type **23** 20 15
43 3f. "Papilio dardanus" 30 25
44 4f. "Papilio lormieri" 50 30
45 60f. "Papilio zalmoxis" 3·50 2·25

1963. Air. European–African Economic Convention.
46 **24** 50f. multicoloured 2·25 1·75

25 ABJ-6 Diesel Railcar

26 U.N.E.S.C.O. Emblem, Scales of Justice and Tree

1963. Air. Bangui–Douala Railway Project.
47 – 20f. green, purple & brown 75 80
48 **25** 25f. chocolate, blue & brn 90 1·00
49 – 50f. violet, purple & brown 3·00 3·25
50 – 100f. purple, turquoise and brown 3·75 3·75
DESIGNS: (Diesel rolling stock)—HORIZ: 20f. ABJ-6 railcar; 100f. Diesel locomotive. VERT: 50f. Series BB500 diesel shunter.

1963. 15th Anniv of Declaration of Human Rights.
51 **26** 25f. bistre, green and brown 70 50

27 Bangui Cathedral

1964. Air.
52 **27** 100f. brown, green & blue 1·50 85

28 Cleopatra, Temple of Kalabsha **30** "Tree" and Sun Emblem

29 Radar Scanner

1964. Air. Nubian Monuments Preservation.
53 **28** 25f.+10f. mauve, bl & grn . . . 1·10 1·10
54 50f.+10f. brn, grn & turq . . 1·90 1·90
55 100f.+10f. pur, vio & grn . . 3·00 3·00

1964. Air. World Meteorological Day.
56 **29** 50f. violet, brown and blue . . 95 95

1964. International Quiet Sun Years.
57 **30** 25f. orange, ochre & turq . . 1·00 75

31 Map and African Heads of State **33** Pres. Kennedy

32 Throwing the Javelin

1964. Air. 5th Anniv of Equatorial African Heads of State Conference.
58 **31** 100f. multicoloured . . . . 1·60 85

1964. Air. Olympic Games, Tokyo.
59 **32** 25f. brown, green and blue . . 40 30
60 – 50f. red, black and green . . 85 40
61 – 100f. brown, blue and green . 1·90 85
62 – 250f. black, green and red . . 5·00 2·50
DESIGNS: 50f. Basketball; 100f. Running; 250f. Diving and swimming.

1964. Air. Pres. Kennedy Memorial Issue.
63 **33** 100f. brown, black & violet . 1·90 1·40

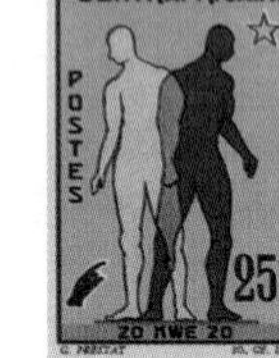

34 African Child **35** Silhouettes of European and African

1964. Child Welfare. Different portraits of children. As T **34**.
64 **34** 20f. brown, green & purple . . 35 25
65 – 25f. brown, blue and red . . 40 35
66 – 40f. brown, purple & green . 60 45
67 – 50f. brown, green and red . . 70 50

1964. French, African and Malagasy Co-operation. As T **88** of Cameroun.
68 25f. brown, red and green . . 60 40

1964. National Unity.
69 **35** 25f. multicoloured 65 40

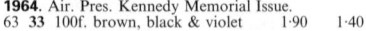

36 "Economic Co-operation"

1964. Air. "Europafrique".
70 **36** 50f. green, red and yellow . . 95 65

37 Handclasp

1965. Air. International Co-operation Year.
71 **37** 100f. multicoloured . . . . 1·60 85

38 Weather Satellite

1965. Air. World Meteorological Day.
72 **38** 100f. blue and brown . . . 1·60 85

39 Abraham Lincoln

1965. Air. Death Centenary of Abraham Lincoln.
73 **39** 100f. flesh, blue & green . . 1·60 85

40 Team of Oxen

1965. Harnessed Animals in Agriculture.
74 **40** 25f. red, brown and green . . 50 35
75 – 50f. purple, green and blue . 85 45
76 – 85f. brown, green and blue . 1·25 70
77 – 100f. multicoloured . . . . 1·60 90
DESIGNS: 50f. Ploughing with bullock; 85f. Ploughing with oxen; 100f. Oxen with hay cart.

41 Pouget-Maisonneuve Telegraph Instrument

1965. Centenary of I.T.U.
78 **41** 25f. blue, red & grn (post) . 50 40
79 – 30f. lake and green 60 45
80 – 50f. red and violet 90 65
81 – 85f. blue and purple . . . . 1·60 95
82 – 100f. brown, blue & green (48½ × 27 mm) (air) . . . 1·90 1·10
DESIGNS—VERT: 30f. Chappe's telegraph instrument; 50f. Doignon regulator for Hughes telegraph. HORIZ: 85f. Pouillet's telegraph apparatus; 100f. "Relay" satellite and I.T.U. emblem.

42 Women and Loom ("To Clothe") **43** Coffee Plant, Hammer Grubs and "Epicampoptera strandi"

1965. "M.E.S.A.N." Welfare Campaign. Designs depicting "Five Aims".
83 **42** 25f. green, brown and blue (postage) 45 35
84 – 50f. brown, blue and green . 75 45
85 – 60f. brown, blue and green . 85 60
86 – 85f. multicoloured . . . 1·25 65
87 – 100f. blue, brown and green (48 × 27 mm) (air) . . . . 1·25 70
DESIGNS: 50f. Doctor examining child, and hospital ("To care for"); 60f. Student and school ("To instruct"); 85f. Women and child, and harvesting scene ("To nourish"); 100f. Village houses ("To house"). "M.E.S.A.N.—Mouvement Evolution Social Afrique Noire".

1965. Plant Protection.
88 **43** 2f. purple, red and green . . 10 10
89 – 3f. red, green and black . . 25 15
90 – 30f. purple, green and red . 1·50 65
DESIGNS—HORIZ: 3f. Coffee plant, caterpillar and hawk-moth. VERT: 30f. Cotton plant caterpillar and rose-moth.

1965. Surch.
91 – 2f. on 3f. (No. 43) . . . . . 2·50 2·50
92 **1** 5f. on 15f. . . . . 2·50 2·50
93 – 5f. on 85f. (No. 76) 35 35
94 **13** 10f. on 20f. . . . . 3·25 3·25
95 – 10f. on 100f. (No. 77) . . . 45 45

45 Camp Fire **47** "Industry and Agriculture"

46 U.N. and Campaign Emblems

1965. Scouting.
96 **45** 25f. red, purple and blue . . 75 25
97 – 50f. brown and blue (Boy Scout) . . . . 1·00 60

1965. Freedom from Hunger.
98 **46** 50f. brown, blue and green . . 90 65

1965. Air. "Europafrique".
99 **47** 50f. multicoloured 80 50

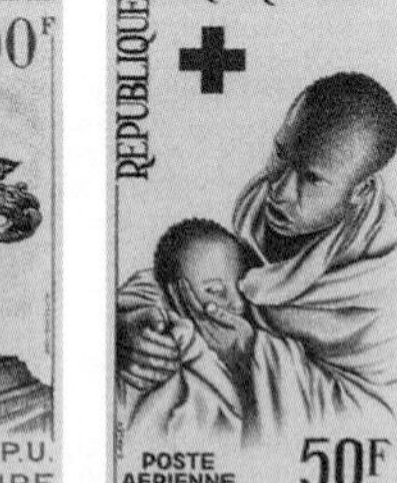

48 Mercury (statue after Coysevox) **49** Father and Child

1965. Air. 5th Anniv of Admission to U.P.U..
100 **48** 100f. black, blue & red . . 1·90 1·10

1965. Air. Red Cross.
101 **49** 50f. black, blue and red . . 1·00 50
102 – 100f. brown, green and red (Mother and Child) . . 2·10 1·00

50 Grading Diamonds **51** Mbaka Porter

1966. National Diamond Industry.
103 **50** 25f. brown, violet and red . . 75 40

1966. World Festival of Negro Arts, Dakar.
104 **51** 25f. multicoloured 65 40

52 W.H.O. Building **53** "Eulophia cucullata"

1966. W.H.O. Headquarters, Geneva. Inaug.
105 **52** 25f. violet, blue & yellow . . 65 40

1966. Flowers. Multicoloured.
106 2f. Type **53** 10 10
107 5f. "Lissochilus horsfalii" . . 20 10
108 10f. "Tridactyle bicaudata" . . 25 20
109 15f. "Polystachya" 50 25
110 20f. "Eulophia alta" 75 40
111 25f. "Microcelia macrorrhynchium" . . . . 1·00 50

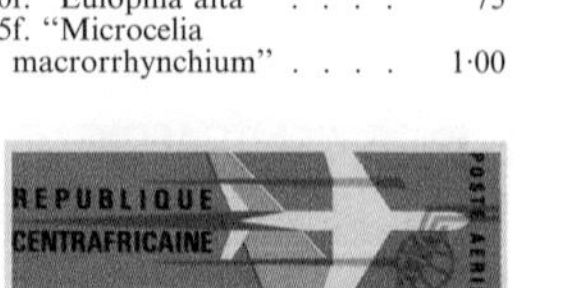

54 Douglas DC-8F Aircraft and "Air Afrique" Emblem

1966. Air. Inaug of "DC-8" Air Services.
112 **54** 25f. multicoloured 60 30

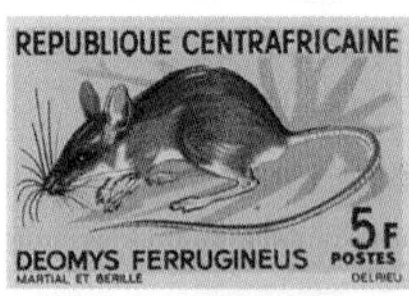

55 Congo Forest Mouse

1966. Rodents. Multicoloured.
113 5f. Type **55** 50 25
114 10f. Black-striped mouse . . 85 40
115 20f. Dollman's tree mouse . . 1·75 70

56 "Luna 9"

1966. Air. "Conquest of the Moon". Mult.
116 130f. Type **56** . . . . . . 1·60 95
117 130f. "Surveyor" . . . . . . 1·60 95
118 200f. "From the Earth to the Moon" (Jules Verne) . . . 2·75 1·60

57 Cernan **59** U.N.E.S.C.O. Emblem

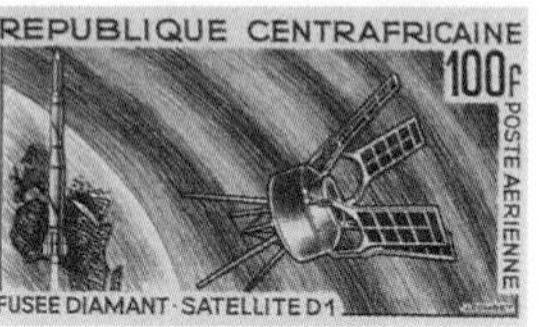

58 Satellite "D 1" and Rocket "Diamant"

1966. Air. Astronauts. Multicoloured.
120 50f. Type **57** 85 50
121 50f. Popovich 85 50

1966. Air. Launching of Satellite "D 1".
122 **58** 100f. purple and brown . . 1·60 80

1966. 20th Anniv of U.N.E.S.C.O.
123 **59** 30f. multicoloured 65 40

60 Symbols of Industry and Agriculture

61 Pres. Bokassa

1966. Air. Europafrique.
124 **60** 50f. multicoloured . . . . 1·10 75

1967.
125 **61** 30f. black, ochre & green 60 35

1967. Provisional Stamps. (a) Postage. No. 111 surch XX and value.
126 10f. on 25f. multicoloured . . 45 20

(b) Air. No. 112 with face value altered by obliteration of figure "2" in "25".
127 **54** 5f. multicoloured 25 20

63 Douglas DC-8 over Bangui M'Poko Airport

1967. Air.
128 **63** 100f. blue, green & brown 2·10 1·00

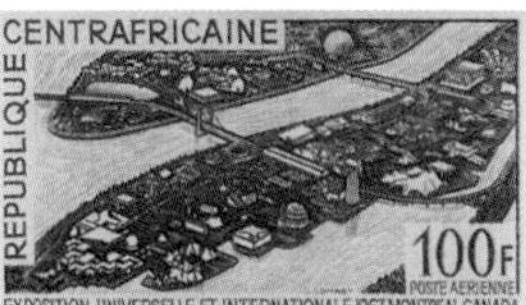

64 Aerial View of Fair

1967. Air. World Fair, Montreal.
129 **64** 100f. brown, ultram & bl 2·75 1·25

65 Central Market, Bangui

1967. Multicoloured.
130 30f. Type **65** 65 35
131 30f. Safari Hotel, Bangui . . 65 35

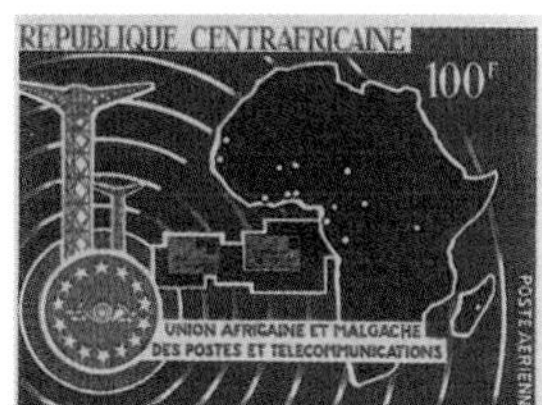

66 Map, Letters and Pylons

1967. Air. 5th Anniv of African and Malagasy Posts and Telecommunications Union (U.A.M.P.T.).
132 **66** 100f. purple, grn & red . . 1·50 70

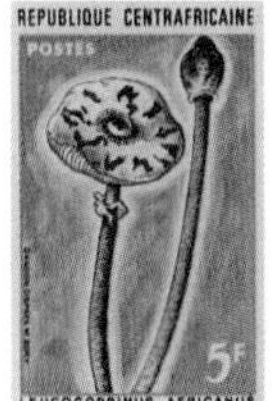

67 "Leucocoprinus africanus"

68 Projector, Africans and Map

1967. Mushrooms. Multicoloured.
133 5f. Type **67** 95 30
134 10f. "Synpodia arborescens" 1·25 60
135 15f. "Phlebopus sudanicus" 1·40 90
136 30f. "Termitomyces schimperi" . . . . 4·75 1·50
137 50f. "Psalliota sebedulis" . . 7·25 2·75

1967. "Radiovision" Service.
138 **68** 30f. blue, green and brown 65 40

69 Coiffure

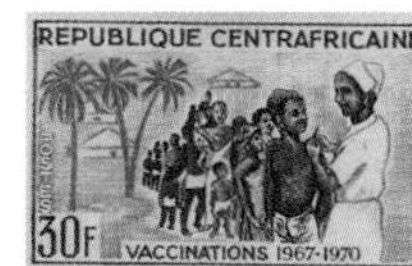

70 Inoculation Session

1967. Female Coiffures. Showing different hairstyles.
139 **69** 5f. brown and blue 25 20
140 – 10f. brown, choc & red . . 40 25
141 – 15f. brown, choc & grn . . 65 45
142 – 20f. brown, choc & orge 75 45
143 – 30f. brown, choc & purple 1·25 60

1967. Vaccination Programme, 1967–70.
144 **70** 30f. brown, green & red . . 65 45

71 Douglas DC-3

1967. Aircraft.
145 **71** 1f. grey, grn & brn (post) 20 10
146 – 2f. black, blue and purple 20 10
147 – 5f. black, green and blue 25 15
148 – 100f. brown, grn & bl (air) 1·75 80
149 – 200f. blue, brown and green . . . . 3·75 1·75
150 – 500f. slate, red and blue . . 11·00 4·50
DESIGNS—As T **71**: 2f. Beechcraft Baron; 5f. Douglas DC-4. 48 × 27 mm: 100f. Potez 25-TOE; 200f. Junkers 52/3m; 500f. Sud Aviation Caravelle.

72 Presidents Boganda and Bokassa

1967. Air. 9th Anniv of Republic.
151 **72** 130f. multicoloured . . . . 1·60 1·10

73 Primitive Shelter, Toulou

1967. 6th Pan-African Prehistory Congress, Dakar.
152 **73** 30f. blue, purple and red 65 25
153 – 50f. bistre, ochre & green 1·25 65
154 – 100f. purple, brown & blue 2·50 95
155 – 130f. red, green & brown 2·50 95
DESIGNS—VERT: 50f. Kwe perforated stone; 100f. Megaliths, Bouar. HORIZ: 130f. Rock drawings, Toulou.

74 Pres. Bokassa

1968. Air.
156 **74** 30f. multicoloured 60 35

75 Human Rights Emblem, Human Figures and Globe

1968. Air. Human Rights Year.
157 **75** 200f. red, green and violet 3·25 1·50

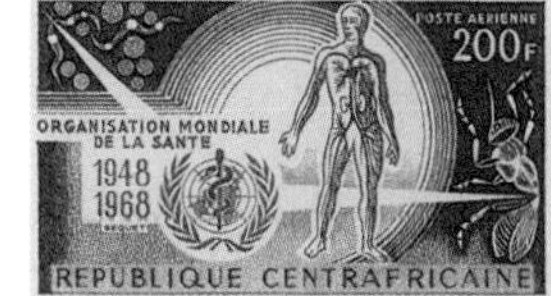

76 Human Figure and W.H.O. Emblem

1968. Air. 20th Anniv of W.H.O.
158 **76** 200f. red, blue & brown . . 3·50 1·90

77 Alpine Skiing

78 Parachute-landing on Venus

1968. Air. Olympic Games, Grenoble and Mexico.
159 **77** 200f. brown, blue and red 4·25 2·50
160 – 200f. brown, blue and red 4·25 2·50
DESIGN: No. 160, Throwing the javelin.

1968. Air. "Venus 4". Exploration of planet Venus.
161 **78** 100f. blue, turquoise & grn 1·60 80

79 Marie Curie and impaled Crab (of Cancer)

1968. Air. Marie Curie Commem.
162 **79** 100f. brown, violet & blue 1·90 1·00

80 Refinery and Tanker

1968. Inauguration of Petroleum Refinery, Port Gentil, Gabon.
163 **80** 30f. multicoloured 90 30

1968. Air. Surch. Nos. 165/6 are obliterated with digit.
164 **56** 5f. on 130f. (No. 116) . . . 15 10
165 – 10f. (100f. No. 148) . . . 20 15
166 – 20f. (200f. No. 149) . . . 35 25
167 – 50f. on 130f. (No. 117) . . 75 50

82 "CD-8" Bulldozer

1968. Bokassa Project.
168 **82** 5f. brown, black & green 25 15
169 – 10f. black, brown & green 40 25
170 – 20f. green, yellow & brown 65 25
171 – 30f. blue, drab and brown 95 45
172 – 30f. red, blue and green . . 95 50
DESIGNS: 10f. Baoule cattle; 20f. Spinning-machine; 30f. (No. 171), Automatic looms; 30f. (No. 172), "D4-C" bulldozer.

83 Bangui Mosque

1968. 2nd Anniv of Bangui Mosque.
173 **83** 30f. flesh, green and blue 70 40

84 Za Throwing-knife

1968. Hunting Weapons.
174 **84** 10f. blue and bistre 45 25
175 – 20f. green, brown & blue 60 35
176 – 30f. green, orange & blue 65 45
DESIGNS: 20f. Kpinga-Gbengue throwing-knife; 30f. Mbano cross-bow.

85 "Ville de Bangui" (1958)

1968. River Craft.
177 **85** 10f. blue, green and purple (postage) 50 40
178 – 30f. brown, blue & green 90 50
179 – 50f. black, brown & grn . . 1·40 65
180 – 100f. brown, grn & bl (air) 2·10 95
181 – 130f. blue, green & purple 2·10 1·25
DESIGNS: 30f. "J. B. Gouandjia" (1968); 50f. "Lamblin" (1944). LARGER (48 × 27 mm): 100f. "Pie X" (Bangui, 1894); 130f. "Ballay" (Bangui, 1891).

86 "Madame de Sevigne" (French School, 17th century)

1968. Air. "Philexafrique" Stamp Exhibition, Abidjan, Ivory Coast (1969) (1st issue).
182 **86** 100f. multicoloured . . . . 2·25 2·00

87 President Bokassa, Cotton Plantation, and Ubangui Chari stamp of 1930

1969. Air. "Philexafrique" Stamp Exhibition, Abidjan, Ivory Coast (2nd issue).
183 **87** 50f. black, green & brown 1·75 1·75

88 "Holocerina angulata"

1969. Air. Butterflies. Multicoloured.
184 10f. Type **88** 50 25
185 20f. "Nudaurelia dione" . . 75 35
186 30f. "Eustera troglophylla" (vert) . . . . 1·90 60
187 50f. "Aurivillius aratus" . . . 3·00 1·60
188 100f. "Epiphora albida" . . . 5·00 2·50

89 Throwing the Javelin

90 Miner and Emblems

1969. Sports. Multicoloured.
189 5f. Type **89** (postage) 20 10
190 10f. Start of race 25 15
191 15f. Football 40 20

192 50f. Boxing (air) 80 30
193 100f. Basketball . . . . . . 1·75 65
Nos. 192/3 are 48 × 28 mm.

1969. 50th Anniv of I.L.O.
194 **90** 30f. multicoloured 50 25
195 50f. multicoloured 75 40

91 "Apollo 8" over Moon's Surface

1969. Air. Flight of "Apollo 8" Around Moon.
196 **91** 200f. multicoloured . . . . 3·00 1·60

92 Nuremberg Spire and Toys

1969. Air. International Toy Fair, Nuremberg.
197 **92** 100f. black, purple & grn 3·25 1·75

1969. Air. Birth Bicentenary of Napoleon Bonaparte. As T **144** of Cameroun. Multicoloured.
198 100f. "Napoleon as First Consul" (Girodet-Trioson) (vert) . . . . 1·90 1·25
199 130f. "Meeting of Napoleon and Francis II of Austria" (Gros) . . . . 2·50 1·40
200 200f. "Marriage of Napoleon and Marie-Louise" (Rouget) . . . . 3·75 2·50

93 President Bokassa in Military Uniform

94 Pres. Bokassa, Flag and Map

1969.
201 **93** 30f. multicoloured 50 25

1969. 10th Anniv of A.S.E.C.N.A. As T **151** of Cameroun.
202 100f. blue . . . . 1·75 75

1970. Air. Die-stamped on gold foil.
203 **94** 2000f. gold . . . . 32·00 32·00

95 Garayah

97 F. D. Roosevelt (25th Death Anniv)

96 Flour Storage Depot

1970. Musical Instruments.
204 **95** 10f. brown, sepia & green 40 15
205 – 15f. brown and green . . . 45 20
206 – 30f. brown, lake & yellow 70 35
207 – 50f. blue and red . . . . . 1·00 40
208 – 130f. brown, olive & blue 3·25 1·00
DESIGNS—VERT: 130f. Gatta and Babylon. HORIZ: 15f. Ngombi; 30f. Xylophone; 50f. Nadla.

1970. Societie Industrielle Centrafricaine des Produits Alimentaires et Derives (S.I.C.P.A.D.) Project. Multicoloured.
209 25f. Type **96** 45 25
210 50f. Mill machinery 90 70
211 100f. View of flour mill . . . 1·40 1·00

1970. Air. World Leaders. Multicoloured.
212 100f. Lenin (birth centenary) 2·50 1·10
213 100f. Type **97** . . . . 1·50 85

1970. New U.P.U. Headquarters Building, Berne. As T **156** of Cameroun.
214 100f. vermilion, red and blue 1·40 65

1970. Air. Moon Landing of "Apollo 12". No. 196 optd **ATTERRISSAGE d'APOLLO 12 19 novembre 1969**.
215 **91** 200f. multicoloured . . . . 12·50 9·25

99 Pres. Bokassa

101 Silkworm

100 Cheese Factory, Sarki

1970.
216 **99** 30f. multicoloured . . . . 5·00 3·75
217 40f. multicoloured . . . . 6·25 4·50

1970. "Operation Bokassa" Development Projects. Multicoloured.
218 5f. Type **100** (postage) . . . 35 20
219 10f. M'Bali Ranch . . . . . 4·75 3·75
220 20f. Zebu bull and herdsman (vert) 65 45
221 40f. Type **101** . . . . 1·90 65
222 140f. Type **101** (air) . . . . 3·00 1·25

102 African Dancer

1970. Air. "Knokphila 70" Stamp Exhibition, Knokke, Belgium. Multicoloured.
223 100f. Type **102** . . . . 1·50 50
224 100f. African produce . . . . 1·50 50

103 Footballer

1970. Air. World Cup Football Championship, Mexico.
225 **103** 200f. multicoloured . . . 3·00 1·60

104 Central African Republic's Pavilion

1970. Air. "EXPO 70", Osaka, Japan.
226 **104** 200f. multicoloured . . . 3·50 1·75

105 Dove and Cogwheel

1970. Air. 25th Anniv of U.N.O.
227 **105** 200f. black, yellow & bl 3·00 1·50

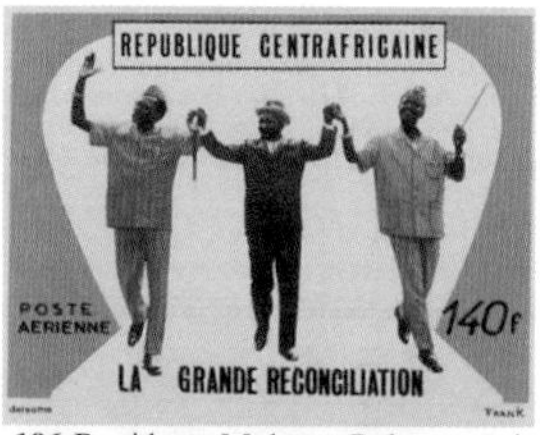

106 Presidents Mobutu, Bokassa and Tombalbaye

1970. Air. Reconciliation with Chad and Zaire.
228 **106** 140f. multicoloured . . . 1·90 80

107 Scaly Francolin and Helmeted Guineafowl

1971. Wildlife. Multicoloured.
229 5f.+5f. Type **107** . . . . . . 4·00 2·25
230 10f.+5f. Common duiker and true achatina (snail) . . . 4·75 2·75
231 20f.+5f. Hippopotamus, African elephant and tortoise in tug-of-war . . . 5·75 3·00
232 30f.+10f. Tortoise and Senegal coucal . . . . . 8·50 7·50
233 50f.+20f. Monkey and leopard . . . . 12·50 10·50

108 Lengue Dancer

1971. Traditional Dances. Multicoloured.
234 20f.+5f. Type **108** 50 25
235 40f.+10f. Lengue (diff) . . . 75 40
236 100f.+40f. Teke . . . . . . 2·25 1·25
237 140f.+40f. Englabolo . . . . 3·00 1·40

110 Monteir's Mormyrid

1971. Fishes. Multicoloured.
244 10f. Type **110** 40 30
245 20f. Trunk-nosed mormyrid 75 40
246 30f. Wilverth's mormyrid . . 1·10 70
247 40f. Elephant-nosed mormyrid . . . . 2·25 80
248 50f. Curve-nosed mormyrid 2·75 1·40

111 Satellite and Globe

1971. Air. World Telecommunications Day.
249 **111** 100f. multicoloured . . . 1·50 75

112 Berberati Cathedral

113 Gen. De Gaulle

1971. Consecration of Roman Catholic Cathedral, Berberati.
250 **112** 5f. multicoloured 25 15

1971. 1st Death Anniv of De Gaulle.
251 **113** 100f. multicoloured . . . 3·25 1·90

114 Lesser Bushbaby

1971. Animals: Primates. Multicoloured.
252 30f. Type **114** 65 60
253 40f. Western needle-clawed bushbaby 95 65
254 100f. Angwantibo (horiz) . . 2·25 1·40
255 150f. Potto (horiz) . . . . . 3·75 2·40
256 200f. Red colobus (horiz) . . 5·00 3·25

1971. Air. 10th Anniv of African and Malagasy Posts and Telecommunications Union. Similar to T **184** of Cameroun. Multicoloured.
257 100f. Headquarters and carved head . . . . 1·50 75

115 Shepard in Capsule

1971. Space Achievements. Multicoloured.
258 40f. Type **115** 45 30
259 40f. Gagarin in helmet . . . 45 30
260 100f. Aldrin in Space . . . . 1·10 45
261 100f. Leonov in Space . . . . 1·10 45
262 200f. Armstrong on Moon 2·25 1·00
263 200f. "Lunokhod 1" on Moon . . . . 2·25 1·00

116 Crab Emblem   **117** "Operation Bokassa"

1971. Air. Anti-cancer Campaign.
264 **116** 100f. multicoloured . . . 1·90 95

1971. 12th Year of Independence.
265 **117** 40f. multicoloured 65 40

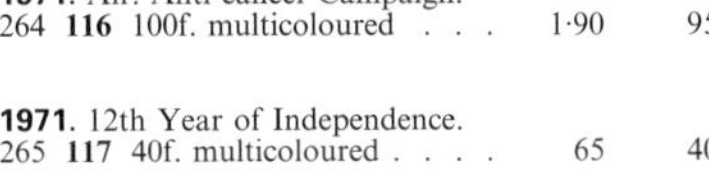

118 Racial Equality Year Emblem

1971. Racial Equality Year.
266 **118** 50f. multicoloured 65 40

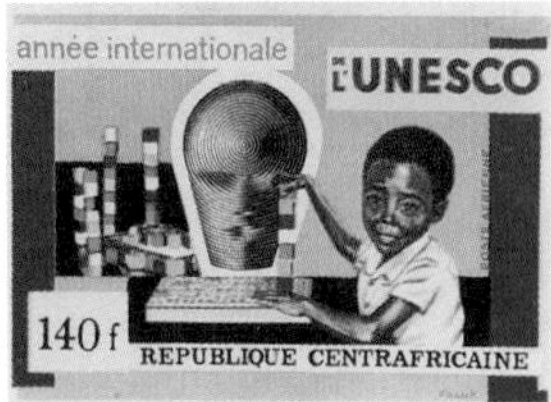

119 I.E.Y. Emblem and Child with Toy Bricks

1971. Air. 25th Anniv of U.N.E.S.C.O.
267 **119** 140f. multicoloured . . . 1·50 70

120 African Children

1971. Air. 25th Anniv of U.N.I.C.E.F.
268 **120** 140f.+50f. mult . . . . . 2·50 1·60

121 Arms and Parade   **122** Pres. G. Nasser

1972. Bokassa Military School.
269 **121** 30f. multicoloured 65 45

1972. Air. Nasser Commemoration.
270 **122** 100f. ochre, brown & red 1·60 80

123 Book Year Emblem   **124** Heart Emblem

1972. International Book Year.
271 **123** 100f. gold, yellow & brn 1·60 95

1972. World Heart Month.
272 **124** 100f. red, black & yellow 1·40 80

125 First-Aid Post   **126** Global Emblem

1972. Red Cross Day.
273 **125** 150f. multicoloured . . . 2·25 1·25

1972. World Telecommunications Day.
274 **126** 50f. black, yellow & red 75 50

127 Boxing

1972. Air. Olympic Games, Munich.
275 **127** 100f. bistre and brown . . 1·60 95
276 – 100f. violet and green . . 1·60 1·10
DESIGN—VERT: No. 276, Long-jumping.

128 Pres. Bokassa and Family

1972. Mothers' Day.
278 **128** 30f. multicoloured 75 40

129 Pres. Bokassa planting Cotton Bush   **130** Savings Bank Building

1972. "Operation Bokassa" Cotton Development.
279 **129** 40f. multicoloured 55 35

1972. Opening of New Postal Cheques and Savings Bank Building.
280 **130** 30f. multicoloured 50 35

131 "Le Pacifique" Hotel

1972. "Operation Bokassa" Completion of "Le Pacifique" Hotel.
281 **131** 30f. blue, red and green 35 25

132 Giraffe and Monkeys   **133** Postal Runner

134 Tiling's Postal Rocket, 1931

1972. Clock-faces from Central African HORCEN Factory. Multicoloured.
282 5f. Rhinoceros chasing African 20 20
283 10f. Camp fire and Native warriors 25 20
284 20f. Fishermen 60 30
285 30f. Type **132** 65 45
286 40f. Warriors fighting 90 65

1972. "CENTRAPHILEX" Stamp Exhibition, Bangui.
287 **133** 10f. mult (postage) . . . 25 20
288 – 20f. multicoloured 40 30
289 **134** 40f. orange, blue and slate (air) 55 45
290 – 50f. blue, slate & orange 70 50
291 – 150f. grey, orange & brn 1·90 1·25
292 – 200f. blue, orange & brn 2·75 1·90
DESIGNS—AS Type **133**: HORIZ: Protestant Youth Centre. As Type **134**: VERT: 50f. Douglas DC-3 and camel postman; 150f. "Sirio" satellite and rocket. HORIZ: 200f. "Intelsat 4" satellite and rocket.

135 University Buildings

1972. Inauguration of Bokassa University.
294 **135** 40f. grey, blue and red . . 55 35

136 Mail Van

1972. World U.P.U. Day.
295 **136** 100f. multicoloured . . . 1·75 85

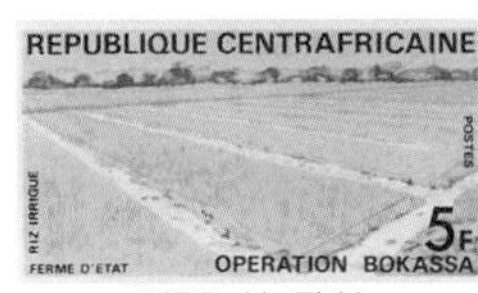

137 Paddy Field

1972. Bokassa Plan. State Farms. Multicoloured.
296 5f. Type **137** 20 15
297 25f. Rice cultivation 35 20

138 Four Linked Arrows   **140** Hotel Swimming Pool

1972. Air. "Europafrique".
298 **138** 100f. multicoloured . . . 1·25 75

1972. Air. Munich Olympic Gold Medal Winners. Nos. 275/6 optd as listed below.
299 **127** 100f. bistre and brown . . 1·25 80
300 – 100f. violet and green . . 1·25 80
OVERPRINTS: No. 299, **POIDS-MOYEN LEMECHEV MEDAILLE D'OR**. No. 300, **LONGUEUR WILLIAMS MEDAILLE D'OR**.

1972. Opening of Hotel St. Sylvestre.
302 **140** 30f. brown, turq & grn 40 30
303 – 40f. purple, green & blue 40 30
DESIGN: 40f. Facade of Hotel.

141 Landing Module and Lunar Rover on Moon

1972. Air. Moon Flight of "Apollo 16".
304 **141** 100f. green, blue & grey 1·25 60

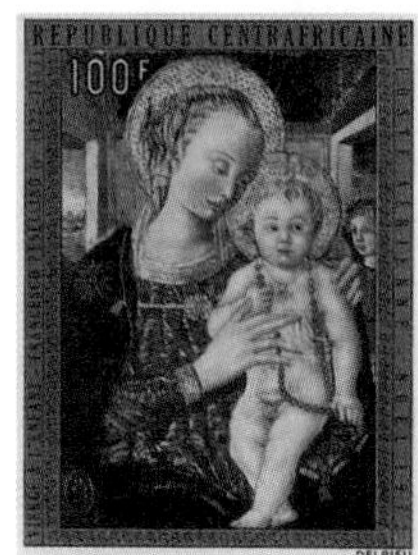

142 "Virgin and Child" (F. Pesellino)

1972. Air. Christmas. Multicoloured.
305 100f. Type **142** . . . . 1·60 95
306 150f. "Adoration of the Child" (F. Lippi) . . . . . 2·25 1·25

143 Learning to Write

1972. "Central African Mothers". Multicoloured.
307 5f. Type **143** 15 10
308 10f. Baby-care 25 20
309 15f. Dressing hair 25 20
310 20f. Learning to read 40 25
311 180f. Suckling baby . . . . 2·40 1·25
312 190f. Learning to walk . . . 2·40 1·25

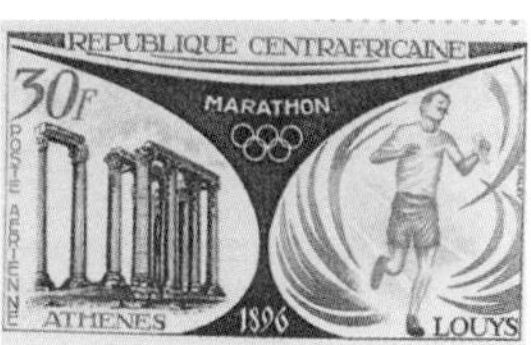

144 Louys (marathon), Athens, 1896

1972. Air. 75th Anniv of Revival of Olympic Games.
313 **144** 30f. purple, brown & grn 30 25
314 – 40f. green, blue & brown 35 25
315 – 50f. violet, blue and red 50 40
316 – 100f. purple, brn & grey 1·00 50
317 – 150f. black, blue & purple 1·60 1·10
DESIGNS: 40f. Barrelet (sculling), Paris, 1900; 50f. Prinstein (triple-jump), St. Louis, U.S.A., 1904; 100f. Taylor (400 m freestyle swimming), London, 1908; 150f. Johansson (Greco-Roman wrestling), Stockholm, 1912.

145 W.H.O. Emblem, Doctor and Nurse

1973. Air. 25th Anniv of W.H.O.
318 **145** 100f. multicoloured . . . 1·25 70

146 "Telecommunications"

1973. World Telecommunications Day.
319 **146** 200f. orange, blue & black 1·90 1·00

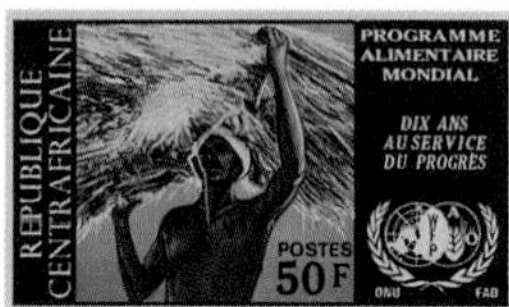

147 Harvesting

1973. 10th Anniv of World Food Programme.

320	**147**	50f. multicoloured	65	40

148 "Garcinia punctata"

1973. "Flora". Multicoloured.

321	10f. Type **148**	25	15
322	20f. "Bertiera racemosa"	35	20
323	30f. "Coryanthe pachyceras"	50	30
324	40f. "Combretodendron africanum"	70	30
325	50f. "Xylopia villosa"	85	45

149 Pygmy Chameleon

1973.

326	**149**	15f. multicoloured	60	25

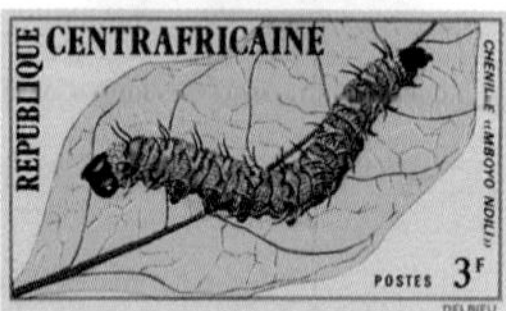

150 "Mboyo Ndili"

1973. Caterpillars. Multicoloured.

327	3f. Type **150**	25	20
328	5f. "Piwili"	40	25
329	25f. "Loulia Konga"	90	40

1973. African Solidarity "Drought Relief". No. 321 surch **SECHERESSE SOLIDARITE AFRICAINE** and value.

330	**148**	100f. on 10f. mult	1·25	95

1973. U.A.M.P.T. As Type **216** of Cameroun.

331	100f. red, brown and olive	1·10	70

1973. Air. African Fortnight, Brussels. As T **217** of Cameroun.

332	100f. brown and violet	1·00	60

152 African and Symbolic Map

1973. Air. Europafrique.

333	**152**	100f. red, green & brown	1·25	75

153 Bird with Letter

1973. Air. World U.P.U. Day.

334	**153**	200f. multicoloured	2·25	1·40

154 Weather Map

1973. Air. Centenary of I.M.O./W.M.O.

335	**154**	150f. multicoloured	1·90	85

155 Copernicus

1973. Air. 500th Birth Anniv of Copernicus.

336	**155**	100f. multicoloured	2·25	1·50

156 Pres. Bokassa 158 Launch

1973.

337	**156**	1f. mult (postage)	10	10
338		2f. multicoloured	10	10
339		3f. multicoloured	15	10
340		5f. multicoloured	15	10
341		10f. multicoloured	25	15
342		15f. multicoloured	25	20
343		20f. multicoloured	35	20
344		30f. multicoloured	35	25
345		40f. multicoloured	45	35
346	–	50f. multicoloured (air)	50	35
347	–	100f. multicoloured	1·00	50

DESIGNS—SQUARE (35×35 mm): 50f. Pres. Bokassa facing left. VERT (26×47 mm): 100f. Pres. Bokassa in military uniform.

1973. Air. Moon Flight of "Apollo 17".

348	**158**	50f. red, green & brown	50	30
349	–	65f. green, red & purple	60	35
350	–	100f. blue, brown & red	1·00	50
351	–	150f. green, brown & red	1·50	70
352	–	200f. green, red and blue	2·00	1·10

DESIGNS—HORIZ: 65f. Surveying lunar surfaces; 100f. Descent on Moon. VERT: 150f. Astronauts on Moon's surface; 200f. Splashdown.

159 Interpol Emblem within "Eye"

1973. 50th Anniv of Interpol.

353	**159**	50f. multicoloured	70	50

160 St. Theresa

1973. Air. Birth Centenary of St. Theresa of Lisieux.

354	**160**	500f. blue and light blue	5·00	3·50

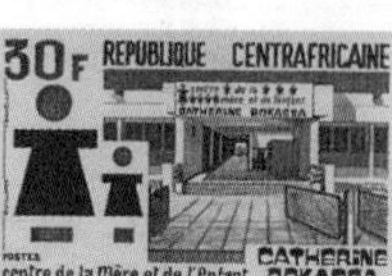

161 Main Entrance

1974. Opening of "Catherine Bokassa" Mother-and-Child Centre.

355	**161**	30f. brown, red and blue	35	25
356	–	40f. brown, blue and red	45	35

DESIGN: 40f. General view of Centre.

162 Cigarette-packing Machine

1974. "Centra" Cigarette Factory.

357	**162**	5f. purple, green & red	10	10
358	–	10f. blue, green & brown	25	15
359	–	30f. blue, green and red	30	20

DESIGNS: 10f. Administration block and factory building; 30f. Tobacco warehouse.

163 "Telecommunications" 165 Mother and Baby

164 "Peoples of the World"

1974. World Telecommunications Day.

360	**163**	100f. multicoloured	6·50	4·00

1974. World Population Year.

361	**164**	100f. green, red & brown	1·10	65

1974. 26th Anniv of W.H.O.

362	**165**	100f. brown, blue & grn	1·25	65

166 Letter and U.P.U. Emblem 168 Modern Building

167 Battle Scene

1974. Centenary of U.P.U.

363	**166**	500f. red, green & brown	4·00	3·00

1974. "Activities of Forces' Veterans". Mult.

364	10f. Type **167**	15	10
365	15f. "Today" (Peace-time activities)	20	15
366	20f. Planting rice	20	15
367	25f. Cattle-shed	25	20
368	30f. Workers hoeing	25	20
369	40f. Veterans' houses	40	20

1974. 10th Anniv of Central African Customs and Economics Union. As Nos. 734/5 of Cameroun.

370	40f. multicoloured (postage)	50	35
371	100f. multicoloured (air)	1·00	65

1975. "OCAM City" Project.

372	**168**	30f. multicoloured	25	20
373	–	40f. multicoloured	35	25
374	–	50f. multicoloured	40	30
375	–	100f. multicoloured	75	50

DESIGNS: Nos. 373/5, Various views similar to Type **150**.

1975. "J. B. Bokassa Pilot Village Project". As T **168**, but inscr "VILLAGE PILOTE J. B. BOKASSA".

376	25f. multicoloured	20	15
377	30f. multicoloured	30	20
378	40f. multicoloured	35	25

DESIGNS: Nos. 376/8, Various views similar to Type **168**.

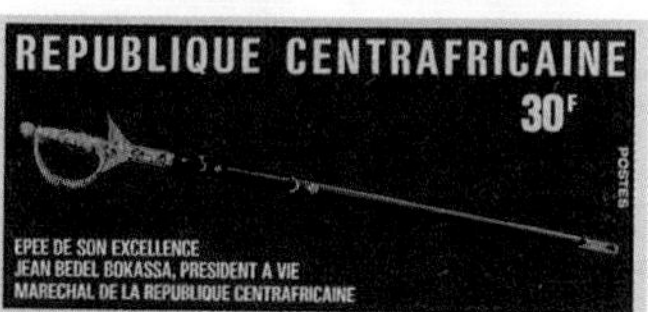

169 President Bokassa's Sword

1975. "Homage to President Bokassa". Mult.

379	30f. Type **169** (postage)	45	25
380	40f. President Bokassa's baton	45	30
381	50f. Pres. Bokassa in uniform (vert, 36×49 mm) (air)	50	35
382	100f. Pres. Bokassa in cap and cape (vert, 36×49 mm)	1·00	45

170 Foreign Minister and Ministry

1975. Government Buildings. Multicoloured.

383	40f. Type **170**	50	35
384	40f. Television Centre (36×23 mm)	50	35

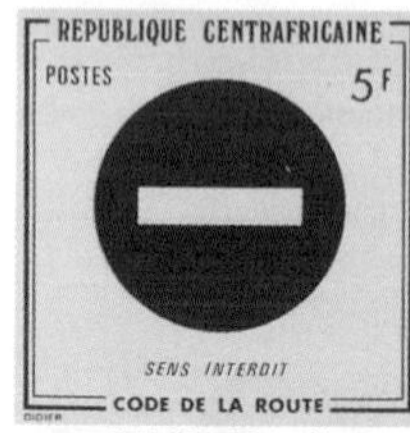

171 "No Entry"

1975. Road Signs.

385	**171**	5f. red and blue	10	10
386	–	10f. red and blue	15	10
387	–	20f. red and blue	20	15
388	–	30f. multicoloured	35	20
389	–	40f. multicoloured	50	25

SIGNS: 10f. "Stop"; 20f. "No stopping"; 30f. "School"; 40f. "Crossroads".

172 Kob 173 Carved Wooden Mask

1975. Wild Animals. Multicoloured.

390	10f. Type **172**	25	20
391	15f. Warthog	50	20
392	20f. Waterbuck	75	25
393	30f. Lion	75	35

1975. Air. "Arphila" International Stamp Exhibition, Paris.

394	**173**	100f. red, rose and blue	1·00	60

174 Dr. Schweitzer and Dug-out Canoe 175 Forest Scene

1975. Air. Birth Centenary of Dr. Albert Schweitzer.

395	**174**	200f. black, blue & brown	2·50	1·60

1975. Central African Woods.

396	**175**	10f. brown, green & red	20	15
397	–	15f. brown, green & blue	25	15
398	–	50f. blue, brown & green	45	20
399	–	100f. brown, blue & grn	95	55
400	–	150f. blue, brown & grn	1·25	95
401	–	200f. brown, red & green	1·75	1·25

DESIGNS—VERT: 15f. Cutting sapeles. HORIZ: 50f. Mobile crane; 100f. Log stack; 150f. Floating logs; 200f. Timber-sorting yard.

176 Women's Heads and Women Working

1975. International Women's Year.

402	**176**	40f. multicoloured	45	25
403		100f. multicoloured	1·25	65

177 River Vessel "Jean Bedel Bokassa"

1976. Air. Multicoloured.

404	30f. Type **177**	50	25
405	40f. Frontal view of "Jean Bedel Bokassa"	60	40

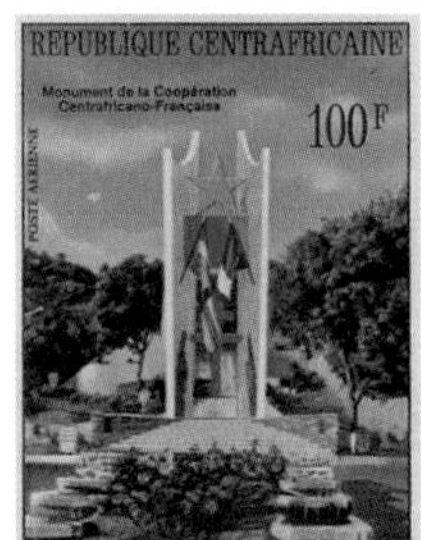

178 Co-operation Monument

1976. Air. Central African–French Co-operation and Visit of President Giscard d'Estaing. Mult.

406	100f. Type **178**	1·00	75
407	200f. Flags and Presidents Giscard d'Estaing and Bokassa	2·10	1·25

179 Alexander Graham Bell

1976. Telephone Centenary.

408	**179**	100f. black and yellow	1·25	75

180 Telecommunications Satellite

1976. World Telecommunications Day.

409	**180**	100f. purple, blue & grn	1·40	95

181 Rocket on Launch-pad

1976. Apollo–Soyuz Space Link. Multicoloured.

410	40f. Type **181** (postage)	45	25
411	50f. Blast-off	55	25
412	100f. "Soyuz" in flight (air)	75	25
413	200f. "Apollo" in flight	1·50	50
414	300f. Crew meeting in space	2·25	85

182 French Hussar

1976. Air. American Revolution Bicent. Mult.

416	100f. Type **182**	75	30
417	125f. Black Watch soldier	95	45
418	150f. German Dragoons' officer	1·10	50
419	200f. British Grenadiers' officer	1·90	55
420	250f. American Ranger	2·25	75

183 "Drurya antimachus"

1976. Butterflies. Multicoloured.

422	30f. Type **183** (postage)	1·25	75
423	40f. "Argema mittrei" (vert)	1·90	75
424	50f. "Acherontia atropos" and "Saturnia pyri" (air)	1·25	75
425	100f. "Papilio nireus" and "Heniocha marnois"	2·50	1·10

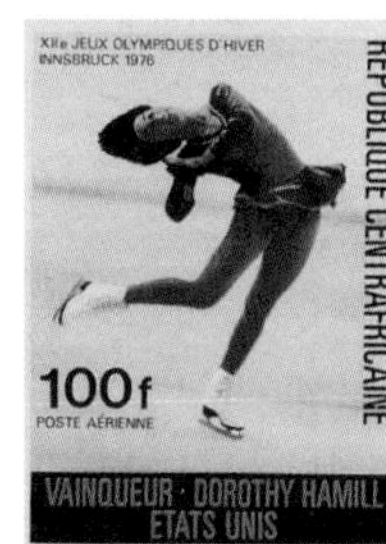

184 Dorothy Hamill of U.S.A. (figure skating)

1976. Medal Winners, Winter Olympic Games, Innsbruck. Multicoloured.

426	40f. Piero Gros of Italy (slalom) (horiz) (postage)	45	25
427	60f. Karl Schnabl and Toni Innauer of Austria (ski-jumping) (horiz)	55	35
428	100f. Type **184** (air)	70	35
429	200f. Alexandre Gorshkov and Ludmilla Pakhomova (figure-skating, pairs) (horiz)	1·25	60
430	300f. John Curry of Great Britain (figure-skating)	2·25	95

185 U.P.U. Emblem, Letters, and Types of Mail Transport

1976. World U.P.U. Day.

432	**185**	100f. multicoloured	1·60	95

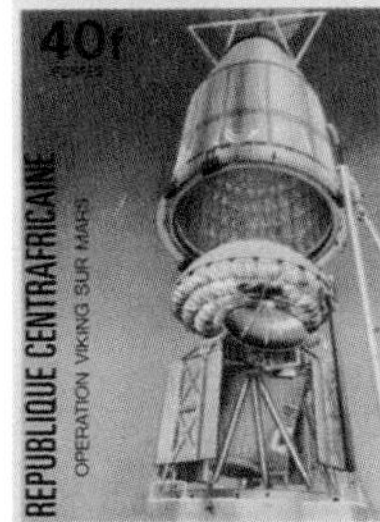

186 Assembly of "Viking"

1976. "Viking" Space Mission to Mars. Multicoloured.

433	40f. Type **186** (postage)	45	25
434	60f. Launch of "Viking"	55	35
435	100f. Parachute descent on Mars (air)	70	35
436	200f. "Viking" on Mars (horiz)	1·25	60
437	300f. "Viking" operating gravel scoop	2·25	75

Issues between 1977 and 1979 are listed under **CENTRAL AFRICAN EMPIRE**.

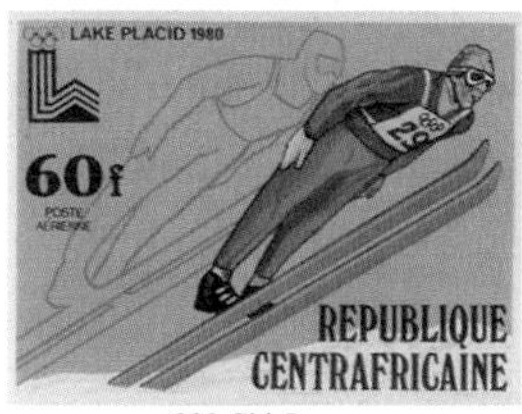

220 Ski Jump

1979. Air. Winter Olympic Games, Lake Placid (1980). Multicoloured.

655	60f. Type **220**	45	20
656	100f. Downhill skiing	75	35
657	200f. Ice hockey	1·60	80
658	300f. Skiing (slalom)	2·25	1·10

1979. "Apollo 11" Moon Landing. 10th Anniv. Nos. 433/7 optd **ALUNISSAGE APOLLO XI JUILLET 1969** and lunar module.

660	**186**	40f. mult (postage)	40	35
661	–	60f. multicoloured	45	40
662	–	100f. multicoloured (air)	75	50
663	–	200f. multicoloured	1·25	85
664	–	300f. multicoloured	2·25	1·10

222 Thumbellina (Andersen) **224** Basketball

223 Steam Locomotive, U.S.A. Stamp and Hill

1979. International Year of the Child (2nd issue). Multicoloured.

666	30f. Type **222**	25	15
667	40f. Sleeping Beauty (horiz)	35	20
668	60f. Hansel and Gretel	50	25
669	200f. The Match Girl (horiz)	1·25	60
670	250f. The Little Mermaid	1·90	70

1979. Death Centenary of Sir Rowland Hill (2nd issue). Multicoloured.

671	60f. Type **223**	90	20
672	100f. Locomotive "Champion" (1882, U.S.A.), French stamp and Hill	1·25	35
673	150f. Steam locomotive, German stamp and Hill	1·75	45
674	250f. Steam locomotive, British stamp and Hill	3·25	95

1979. Olympic Games, Moscow (2nd issue). Basketball.

676	**224**	50f. multicoloured	40	20
677	–	125f. multicoloured	90	35
678	–	200f. multicoloured	1·50	60
679	–	300f. multicoloured	2·25	85
680	–	500f. multicoloured	3·75	1·25

DESIGNS: 125f. to 500f. Views of different basketball matches.

1980. Various stamps, including one unissued, of Central African Empire optd **REPUBLIQUE CENTRAFRICAINE**.

681	**192**	5f. multicoloured	10	10
682	–	10f. mult (No. 522)	10	10
683	–	20f. multicoloured (Balambo (stand))	15	10
684	**206**	20f. black and yellow	15	10
685	–	30f. black and blue (No. 583)	25	15

226 "Viking"

1980. Space Exploration. Multicoloured.

686	40f. Type **226** (postage)	35	15
687	50f. "Apollo"–"Soyuz" link	40	20
688	60f. "Voyager"	45	20
689	100f. European Space Agency	75	25
690	150f. Early satellites (air)	1·25	30
691	200f. Space shuttle	1·60	45

1980. Air. Winter Olympic Medal Winners. Nos. 655/8 optd as listed below.

693	**220**	60f. multicoloured	45	20
694	–	100f. multicoloured	75	35
695	–	200f. multicoloured	1·60	80
696	–	300f. multicoloured	2·25	1·10

OVERPRINTS: 60f. **VAINQUEUR INNAVER AUTRICHE**; 100f. **VAINQUEUR MOSER-PROELL AUTRICHE**; 200f. **VAINQUEUR ETATS-UNIS**; 300f. **VAINQUEUR STENMARK SUEDE**.

228 Telephone and Sun

1980. World Telecommunications Day. Mult.

698	100f. Type **228**	90	50
699	150f. Telephone and sun (different)	1·25	65

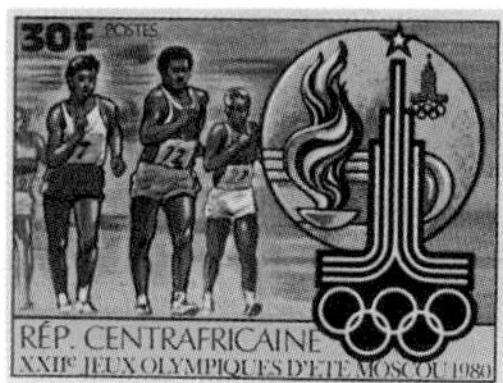

229 Walking

1980. Olympic Games, Moscow (3rd issue). Mult.

700	30f. Type **229** (postage)	35	15
701	40f. Women's relay	40	20
702	70f. Running	60	20
703	80f. Women's high jump	65	30
704	100f. Boxing (air)	75	25
705	150f. Hurdles	1·10	30

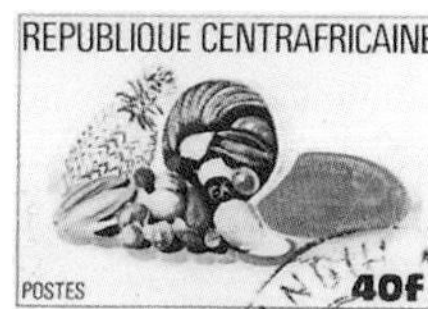

229a Fruit

1980.

706a	**229a**	40f. multicoloured		

230 Agriculture **232** "Foligne Madonna" (detail)

1980. European-African Co-operation. Mult.

707	30f. Type **230** (postage)	25	15
708	40f. Industry	40	15
709	70f. Communications	65	20
710	100f. Building construction and rocket	95	45
711	150f. Meteorological satellite (air)	1·25	30
712	200f. Space shuttle	1·50	45

1980. Olympic Medal Winners. Nos. 676/80 optd.

717	50f. **MEDAILLE OR YOUGOSLAVIE**	40	20
718	125f. **MEDAILLE OR URSS**	90	45

719 200f. **MEDAILLE OR URSS** 1·50 65
720 300f. **MEDAILLE ARGEN TITALIE** 2·25 1·00
721 500f. **MEDAILLE BRONZE URSS** 3·75 1·50

1980. Christmas. Multicoloured.
722 60f. Type **232** 50 20
723 150f. "Virgin and Saints" 1·25 50
724 250f. "Conestabile Madonna" 2·00 85

1980. 5th Anniv of African Posts and Telecommunications Union. As T **269** of Benin.
725 70f. multicoloured 65 40

233 Peruvian Football Team

1981. World Cup Football Championship, Spain (1982). Multicoloured.
726 10f. Type **233** (postage) 15 10
727 15f. Scottish team 20 15
728 20f. Mexican team 25 15
729 25f. Swedish team 25 15
730 30f. Austrian team 30 15
731 40f. Polish team 35 20
732 50f. French team 50 20
733 60f. Italian team 55 25
734 70f. West German team 75 30
735 80f. Brazilian team 75 30
736 100f. Dutch team (air) 75 25
737 200f. Spanish team 1·25 35

234 "Fight between Jacob and the Angel"

236 I.T.U. and W.H.O. Emblems and Ribbons forming Caduceus

1981. Air. 375th Birth Anniv of Rembrandt. Multicoloured.
739 60f. Type **234** 50 20
740 90f. "Christ in the Tempest" 75 25
741 150f. "Jeremiah mourning the Destruction of Jerusalem" 1·25 50
742 250f. "Anna accused by Tobit of Theft of a Goat" 2·25 60

1981. Olympic Games Winners. Nos. 701/5 optd with events and names of winners.
744 30f. Type **229** (postage) 25 15
745 40f. Women's relay 30 20
746 70f. Running 50 30
747 80f. Women's high jump 55 35
748 100f. Boxing (air) 45 30
749 150f. Hurdles 70 45

OPTS—30f. **50 KM. MARCHE HARTWIG GAUDER – G.D.R.**; 40f. **4 × 400 M. DAMES – U.R.S.S.**; 70f. **100 M. COURSE HOMMES ALAN WELLS – G.B.R.**; 80f. **SAUT EN HAUTEUR DAMES SARA SIMEONI – ITALIE**; 100f. **BOXE 71 KG ARMANDO MARTINEZ – CUBA**; 150f. **110 M. HAIES HOMMES THOMAS MUNKELT – G.D.R.**

1981. World Telecommunications Day.
751 **236** 150f. multicoloured 1·10 65

237 Boeing 747 carrying Space Shuttle "Enterprise"

1981. Conquest of Space. Multicoloured.
752 100f. "Apollo 15" and jeep on the Moon 75 30
753 150f. Type **237** 1·10 50
754 200f. Space Shuttle launch 1·60 55
755 300f. Space Shuttle performing experiment in space 2·50 90

238 "Family of Acrobats with a Monkey"

1981. Birth Bicentenary of Pablo Picasso. Mult.
757 40f. Type **238** (postage) 35 15
758 50f. "The Balcony" 50 20
759 80f. "The Artist's Son as Pierrot" 90 25
760 100f. "The Three Dancers" 1·10 35
761 150f. "Woman and Mirror with Self-portrait" (air) 1·75 40
762 200f. "Sleeping Woman, the Dream" 1·90 45

239 Tractor and Plough breaking Chain

1981. 1st Anniv of Zimbabwe's Independence.
764 **239** 100f. multicoloured 75 45
765 150f. multicoloured 1·10 50
766 200f. multicoloured 1·60 65

240 Prince Charles

1981. Royal Wedding (1st issue). Multicoloured.
767 75f. Type **240** 55 20
768 100f. Lady Diana Spencer 70 30
769 150f. St. Paul's Cathedral 1·10 45
770 175f. Couple and Prince's personal Standard 1·40 55

See also Nos. 772/7.

241 Lady Diana Spencer with Children

1981. Royal Wedding (2nd issue). Multicoloured.
772 40f. Type **241** (postage) 30 15
773 50f. Investiture of the Prince of Wales 35 20
774 80f. Lady Diana Spencer at Althorp House 60 25
775 100f. Prince Charles in naval uniform 75 30
776 150f. Prince of Wales's feathers (air) 1·10 35
777 200f. Highgrove House 1·40 45

242 C. V. Rietschoten

1981. Navigators. Multicoloured.
779 40f. Type **242** (postage) 35 25
780 50f. M. Pajot 45 40
781 60f. L. Jaworski 55 50
782 80f. M. Birch 75 55
783 100f. O. Kersauson (air) 80 65
784 200f. Sir Francis Chichester 1·75 1·25

243 Renault, 1906

1981. 75th Anniv of French Grand Prix Motor Race. Multicoloured.
786 20f. Type **243** 25 10
787 40f. Mercedes-Benz, 1937 45 15
788 50f. Matra-Ford, 1969 50 25
789 110f. Tazio Nuvolari 1·10 45
790 150f. Jackie Stewart 1·25 65

244 Emperor's Crown pierced by Dayonet

1981. Overthrow of the Empire. Multicoloured.
792 5f. Type **244** 10 10
793 10f. Type **244** 15 10
794 25f. Axe splitting crown, and angel holding map 20 15
795 60f. As 25f. 45 25
796 90f. Emperor Bokassa's statue being toppled and map of Republic 70 30
797 500f. As 90f. 3·75 1·60

245 F.A.O. Emblem

1981. World Food Day.
798 **245** 90f. green, brown & yell 75 25
799 110f. green, brown & bl 90 30

246 Lizard

247 Plumed Guineafowl ("Komba")

1981. Air. Reptiles. Multicoloured.
800 30f. Type **246** 50 15
801 60f. Snake 55 20
802 110f. Crocodile 1·10 30

1981. Birds. Multicoloured.
803 50f. Type **247** 90 50
804 90f. Schlegel's francolin ("Dodoro") 1·40 60
805 140f. Black-headed bunting and ortolan bunting ("Kaya") 2·40 1·10

248 Bank Building

1981. Central African States' Bank.
806 **248** 90f. multicoloured 75 25
807 110f. multicoloured 90 30

249 "Madonna and Child" (Fra Angelico)

1981. Christmas. Various paintings showing Virgin and Child by named artists. Multicoloured.
808 50f. Type **249** (postage) 35 20
809 60f. Cosme-Tura 45 25
810 90f. Bramantino 65 30
811 110f. Memling 80 45
812 140f. Correge (air) 95 30
813 200f. Gentileschi 1·60 45

250 Scouts with Packs

1982. 75th Anniv of Boy Scout Movement. Mult.
815 100f. Type **250** 75 35
816 150f. Three scouts (horiz) 1·10 55
817 200f. Scouts admiring mountain view (horiz) 1·25 75
818 300f. Scouts taking oath 2·25 1·10

251 African Elephant

1982. Animals. Multicoloured.
820 60f. Type **251** (postage) 50 35
821 90f. Giraffe 70 40
822 100f. Addax 75 45
823 110f. Okapi 85 50
824 300f. Mandrill (air) 2·25 1·25
825 500f. Lion 3·75 2·10

252 "Grandfather Snowman"

1982. Norman Rockwell Illustrations. Mult.
827 30f. Type **252** 25 15
828 60f. "Croquet Players" 55 25
829 110f. "Women talking" 1·00 35
830 150f. "Searching" 1·25 50

253 Vickers Valentia biplane, 1928

1982. Transport. Multicoloured.
831 5f. Astra Torres AT-16 airship, 1919 (postage) 15 15
832 10f. Beyer-Garrat 1 locomotive 2·50 1·60

833 20f. Bugatti "Royale" car, 1926 . . . . 20 15
834 110f. Type **253** 80 40
835 300f. Nuclear-powered freighter "Savannah" (air) 3·50 1·75
836 500f. Space shuttle . . . . . 4·25 1·25

254 George Washington

1982. Anniversaries. Multicoloured.
838 200f. "Le Jardin de Bellevue" (E. Manet) (150th birth anniv) (horiz) . . . . . . 2·25 60
839 300f. Type **254** (250th birth anniv) . . . . 2·25 85
840 400f. Goethe (150th death anniv) . . . . 3·00 1·25
841 500f. Princess of Wales (21st Birthday) . . . . 3·75 1·90

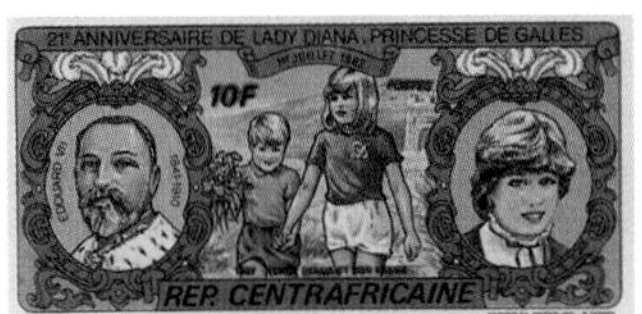

255 Edward VII and Lady Diana Spencer with her Brother

1982. 21st Birthday of Princess of Wales. Mult.
843 5f. George II and portrait of Lady Diana as child (postage) 10 10
844 10f. Type **255** 15 10
845 20f. Charles I and Lady Diana with guinea pig . . 20 15
846 110f. George V and Lady Diana as student in Switzerland 80 25
847 300f. Charles II and Lady Diana in skiing clothes (air) . . . . 2·25 65
848 500f. George IV and Lady Diana as nursery teacher 3·75 1·25

256 Football

1982. Olympic Games, Los Angeles. (1984). Multicoloured.
850 5f. Type **256** (postage) . . . 10 10
851 10f. Boxing 15 10
852 20f. Running 20 15
853 110f. Hurdling 80 25
854 300f. Diving (air) . . . . . . 2·25 65
855 500f. Show jumping . . . . 3·75 1·25

257 Weather Satellite **259** Pestle and Mortar, Chopping Board and Dish

1982. Space Resources. Multicoloured.
857 5f. Space shuttle and scientist (Food resources) (postage) 10 10
858 10f. Type **257** 15 10
859 20f. Space laboratory (Industrial use) 20 15
860 110f. Astronaut on Moon (Lunar resources) 80 25
861 300f. Satellite and energy map (Planetary energy) (air) . . . . 2·25 65
862 500f. Satellite and solar panels (Solar energy) . . . 3·75 1·25

1982. Birth of Prince William of Wales. Nos. 767/70 optd **NAISSANCE ROYALE 1982**.
864 **240** 75f. multicoloured 50 25
865 – 100f. multicoloured . . . 60 35
866 – 150f. multicoloured . . . 1·10 50
867 – 175f. multicoloured . . . 1·50 75

1982. Utensils. Multicoloured.
869 5f. Basket of vegetables (horiz) 10 10
870 10f. As No. 869 . . . . . . 15 10
871 25f. Flagon made from decorated gourd 20 15
872 60f. As No. 871 . . . . . . 40 20
873 120f. Clay jars (horiz) . . . . 1·00 35
874 175f. Decorated bowls (horiz) 1·25 50
875 300f. Type **259** . . . . 2·50 1·10

260 Footballers

1982. World Cup Football Championship Results. Unissued stamps optd as T **260**. Multicoloured.
876 60f. **ITALIE 1er ALLEMAGNE 2e (R.F.A.)** 50 25
877 150f. **POLOGNE 3e** . . . . 1·10 50
878 300f. **FRANCE 4e** . . . . . 2·50 1·10

261 Jean Tubind **262** Globe and U.P.U. Emblem

1982. Painters. Multicoloured.
880 40f. Type **261** 35 15
881 70f. Pierre Ndarata and 10f. stamp 55 25
882 90f. As No. 881 . . . . . . 75 30
883 140f. Type **261** . . . . 1·10 45

1982. U.P.U. Day.
884 **262** 60f. violet, blue and red 50 25
885 120f. violet, yellow & red 1·00 45

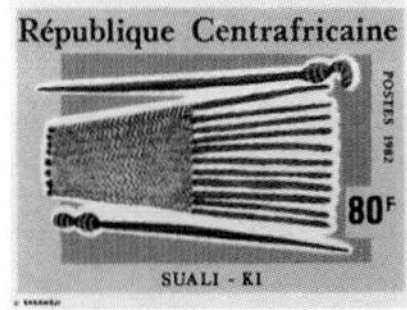

263 Hairpins and Comb

1983. Hair Accessories.
886 **263** 20f. multicoloured 10 10
887 30f. multicoloured 25 15
888 70f. multicoloured 50 25
889 80f. multicoloured 70 30
890 120f. multicoloured . . . 95 35

264 Koch and Microscope

1982. Centenary of Discovery of Tubercle Bacillus by Dr. Robert Koch.
891 **264** 100f. mauve and black . . 85 30
892 120f. red and black . . . 1·00 45
893 175f. blue and black . . . 1·60 60

265 Emblem

1982. 10th Anniv of United Nations Environment Programme.
894 **265** 120f. blue, orange & blk 1·00 35
895 150f. blue, yellow & blk 1·10 50
896 300f. blue, green & black 2·25 1·00

266 Granary

1982.
897 **266** 60f. multicoloured 50 25
898 80f. multicoloured 75 35
899 120f. multicoloured . . . 1·00 50
900 200f. multicoloured . . . 1·75 85

267 "The Beautiful Gardener" **268** Stylized Transmitter

1982. Air. Christmas. Paintings by Raphael. Multicoloured.
901 150f. Type **267** . . . . 1·60 35
902 500f. "The Holy Family" . . 4·00 1·25

1983. I.T.U. Delegates' Conference, Nairobi (1982).
903 **268** 100f. multicoloured . . . 75 30
904 120f. multicoloured . . . 1·00 45

269 Steinitz

1983. Chess Masters. Multicoloured.
905 5f. Type **269** (postage) . . . 10 10
906 10f. Aaron Niemsovich . . . 10 10
907 20f. Aleksandr Alekhine . . . 15 10
908 110f. Botvinnik . . . . . . 1·10 30
909 300f. Boris Spassky (air) . . 2·50 75
910 500f. Bobby Fischer . . . . 4·00 1·40

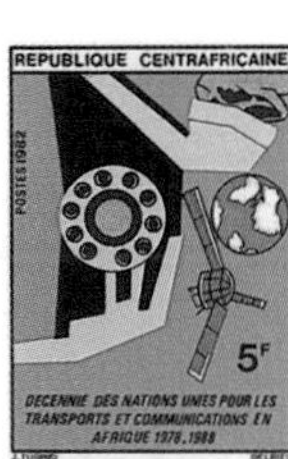

270 George Washington **271** Telephone, Satellite and Globe

1983. Celebrities. Multicoloured.
912 20f. Type **270** (postage) . . . 15 10
913 110f. Pres. Tito of Yugoslavia 90 25
914 500f. Princess of Wales with Prince William (air) . . . 3·75 1·00

1983. U.N. Decade for African Transport and Communications. Multicoloured.
916 5f. Type **271** 15 15
917 60f. Type **271** 50 20
918 120f. Radar screen and map of Africa 95 40
919 175f. As No. 918 . . . . . . 1·25 60

272 Billy Hamilton and Bruno Pezzey

1983. World Cup Football Championship, Spain. Multicoloured.
920 5f. Type **272** (postage) . . . 10 10
921 10f. Sergeij Borovski and Zbigniew Boniek 10 10
922 20f. Pierre Littbarski and Jesus Maria Zamora . . . 15 10
923 110f. Zico and Alberto Pajsarella 85 25
924 300f. Paolo Rossi and Smolarek (air) . . . . . . 2·25 60
925 500f. Rummenigge and Alain Giresse . . . . 3·75 95

273 "Entombment"

1983. Easter. Paintings by Rembrandt. Mult.
927 100f. Type **273** 75 35
928 300f. "Christ on the Cross" 2·25 1·10
929 400f. "Descent from the Cross" . . . . 3·00 1·50

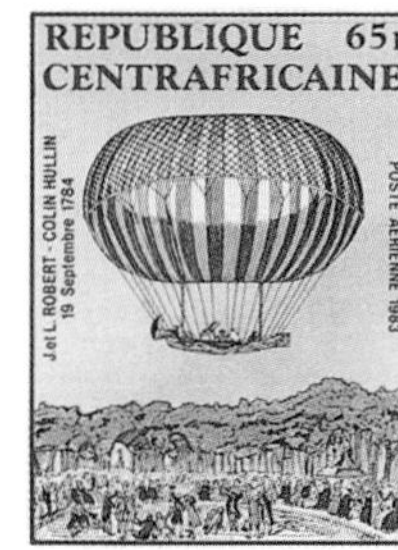

274 J. and L. Robert and Colin Hullin's Balloon, 1784

1983. Air. Bicentenary of Manned Flight. Mult.
930 65f. Type **274** 60 30
931 130f. John Wise and "Atlantic", 1859 . . . . . 1·10 55
932 350f. "Ville d'Orleans", Paris, 1870 . . . . 3·00 1·50
933 400f. Modern advertising balloon . . . . 3·50 1·60

275 Emile Levassor, Rene Panhard and Panhard-Levassor Car, 1895 **276** I.M.O. Emblem

1983. Car Manufacturers. Multicoloured.
935 10f. Type **275** (postage) . . . 10 10
936 20f. Henry Ford and first Ford car, 1896 . . . . . . 15 10
937 30f. Louis Renault and first Renault car, 1899 . . . . 20 15
938 80f. Ettore Bugatti and Bugatti "Type 37", 1925 70 25
939 400f. Enzo Ferrari and Ferrari "815 Sport", 1940 (air) . . . . 3·25 85
940 500f. Ferdinand Porsche and Porsche "356 Coupe", 1951 3·75 1·00

1983. 25th Anniv of Int Maritime Organization.
942 **276** 40f. blue, lt blue & turq 35 15
943 100f. multicoloured . . . 85 35

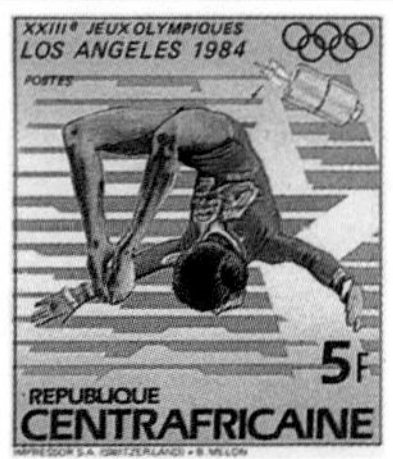

277 Gymnastics

1983. Olympic Games, Los Angeles. Mult.
944 5f. Type **277** (postage) 15 15
945 40f. Javelin 25 15
946 60f. High jump 45 20
947 120f. Fencing 95 25
948 200f. Cycling (air) 1·50 35
949 300f. Sailing 2·25 60

278 W.C.Y. Emblem and Satellite

1983. World Communications Year. Mult.
951 50f. Type **278** 40 20
952 130f. W.C.Y. emblem and satellite (different) 1·00 45

279 Horse Jumping

1983. Air. Pre-Olympic Year. Multicoloured.
953 100f. Type **279** 80 40
954 200f. Dressage 80 65
955 300f. Jumping double jump 2·50 75
956 400f. Trotting 3·00 1·00

280 Andre Kolingba **281** Antenna, Bangui M'Poko Earth Station

1983. 2nd Anniv of Military Committee for National Recovery.
958 **280** 65f. multicoloured 55 20
959 130f. multicoloured 1·10 40

1983. Bangui M'Poko Earth Station.
960 **281** 130f. multicoloured 1·10 50

282 Flower and Broken Chain on Map of Africa

1983. Namibia Day.
961 **282** 100f. green, lt grn & red 75 35
962 200f. multicoloured 1·50 75

283 J. Montgolfier and Balloon

1983. Bicentenary of Manned Flight. Mult.
963 50f. Type **283** (postage) 35 15
964 100f. J. Blanchard and Channel crossing, 1785 75 35
965 200f. Joseph Gay-Lussac and ascent to 4000 m, 1804 1·60 65
966 300f. Henri Giffard and steam-powered dirigible airship, 1852 2·25 1·00
967 400f. Santos-Dumont and airship "Ballon No. 6", Paris, 1901 (air) 3·00 1·25
968 500f. A. Laquot and captive observation balloon, 1914 3·75 1·50

284 "Global Communications"

1983. World Communications Year. U.P.U. Day.
970 **284** 205f. multicoloured 1·75 90

285 Black Rhinoceros

1983. Endangered Animals. Multicoloured.
971 10f. Type **285** (postage) 10 10
972 40f. Two rhinoceros 65 20
973 70f. Black rhinoceros (different) 75 20
974 180f. Black rhinoceros and young 3·50 1·25
975 400f. Rangers attending sick rhinoceros (air) 6·50 3·25
976 500f. Wild animals and flag 7·50 3·75

286 Handicapped Person and Old Man

1983. National Day of the Handicapped and Old.
978 **286** 65f. orange and mauve 50 25
979 130f. orange and blue 1·00 50
980 250f. orange and green 1·50 75

287 Fish Pond

1983. Fishery Resources. Multicoloured.
981 25f. Type **287** 15 10
982 65f. Net fishing 70 25
983 100f. Traditional fishing 80 35
984 130f. Butter catfish, eel and cichlids on plate 1·60 70
985 205f. Weir basket 1·60 70

288 "The Annunciation" (Leonardo da Vinci)

1984. Air. Christmas. Multicoloured.
986 130f. Type **288** 95 25
987 205f. "The Virgin of the Rocks" (Leonardo da Vinci) 1·60 45
988 350f. "Adoration of the Shepherds" (Rubens) 2·50 80
989 500f. "A. Goubeau before the Virgin" (Rubens) 3·75 1·00

289 Bush Fire

1984. Nature Protection. Multicoloured.
990 30f. Type **289** 75 25
991 130f. Soldiers protecting wildlife from hunters 1·10 70

290 Goethe and Scene from "Faust"

1984. Celebrities. Multicoloured.
992 50f. Type **290** (postage) 40 15
993 100f. Henri Dunant and battle scene 75 35
994 200f. Alfred Nobel 1·60 55
995 300f. Lord Baden-Powell and scout camp 2·25 90
996 400f. President Kennedy and first foot-print on Moon (air) 3·00 90
997 500f. Prince and Princess of Wales 3·75 1·00

291 Fixed Bar

1984. Air. Olympic Games, Los Angeles. Gymnastics. Multicoloured.
999 65f. Type **291** 50 20
1000 100f. Parallel bars 85 25
1001 130f. Ribbon (horiz) 1·10 30
1002 205f. Cord 1·90 45
1003 350f. Hoop 3·00 85

292 "Madonna and Child" (Raphael)

1984. Paintings. Multicoloured.
1005 50f. Type **292** (postage) 35 15
1006 100f. "The Madonna of the Pear" (Durer) 75 20
1007 200f. "Aldobrandini Madonna" (Raphael) 1·60 35
1008 300f. "Madonna of the Pink" (Durer) 2·25 70
1009 400f. "Virgin and Child" (Correggio) (air) 3·00 1·50
1010 500f. "The Bohemian" (Modigliani) 3·75 2·10

293 "Le Pericles" (mail ship)

1984. Transport. Multicoloured. (a) Ships.
1012 65f. Type **293** 50 25
1013 120f. "Pereire" (steamer) 90 50
1014 250f. "Admella" (passenger steamer) 1·75 85
1015 400f. "Royal William" (paddle-steamer) 3·00 1·50
1016 500f. "Great Britain" (steam/sail) 3·75 2·10

(b) Locomotives.
1017 110f. CC-1500 ch 85 20
1018 240f. Series 210, 1968 1·90 40
1019 350f. 231-726, 1937 2·75 60
1020 440f. Pacific Series S3/6, 1908 3·50 75
1021 500f. Henschel 151 Series 45, 1937 4·00 85

Nos. 1017/21 each include an inset portrait of George Stephenson in the design.

294 Forest **295** Weighing Baby and Emblem

1984. Forest Resources. Multicoloured.
1022 70f. Type **294** 65 25
1023 130f. Log cabin and timber 1·25 50

1984. Infant Survival Campaign. Multicoloured.
1024 10f. Type **295** 15 10
1025 30f. Vaccinating baby 30 25
1026 65f. Feeding dehydrated baby 50 30
1027 100f. Mother, healthy baby and foodstuffs 95 50

296 Bangui-Kette Conical Trap

1984. Fish Traps. Multicoloured.
1028 50f. Type **296** 60 30
1029 80f. Mbres fish trap 85 50
1030 150f. Bangui-Kette round fish trap 1·60 50

297 Galileo and "Ariane" Rocket **298** "Leptoporus lignosus"

1984. Space Technology. Multicoloured.
1031 20f. Type **297** (postage) 15 10
1032 70f. Auguste Piccard and stratosphere balloon "F.N.R.S." 50 20
1033 150f. Hermann Oberth and satellite 1·10 45
1034 205f. Albert Einstein and "Giotto" satellite 1·50 55
1035 300f. Marie Curie and "Viking I" and "II" (air) 2·50 65
1036 500f. Dr. U. Merbold and "Navette" space laboratory 3·75 95

1984. Fungi. Multicoloured.
1038 5f. Type **298** (postage) 10 10
1039 10f. "Phlebopus sudanicus" 20 10
1040 40f. "Termitomyces letestui" 45 20
1041 130f. "Lepiota esculenta" 1·25 60
1042 300f. "Termitomyces aurantiacus" (air) 3·25 1·40
1043 500f. "Termitomyces robustus" 5·75 2·25

299 Hibiscus **300** G. Boucher (speed skating)

1984. Flowers. Multicoloured.
1045 65f. Type **299** 60 35
1046 130f. Canna . . . . 1·10 50
1047 205f. Water Hyacinth . . . 1·75 85

1984. Winter Olympic Gold Medallists. Mult.
1048 30f. Type **300** (postage) . . 20 15
1049 90f. W. Hoppe, R. Wetzig, D. Schauerhammer and A. Kirchner (bobsleigh) 70 25
1050 140f. P. Magoni (ladies' slalom) . . . . 1·10 35
1051 200f. J. Torvill and C. Dean (ice skating) . . . . . . 1·50 50
1052 400f. M. Nykanen (90 m ski jump) (air) . . . . 3·00 90
1053 400f. Russia (ice hockey) . . 3·75 1·00

301 Workers sowing Cotton Seeds

1984. Economic Campaign. Multicoloured.
1055 25f. Type **301** 25 20
1056 40f. Selling cotton 45 30
1057 130f. Cotton market . . . . 1·25 50

302 Woman picking corn

1984. World Food Day.
1058 **302** 205f. multicoloured . . . 1·75 85

303 Abraham Lincoln

1984. Celebrities. Multicoloured.
1059 50f. Type **303** (postage) . . 45 15
1060 90f. Auguste Piccard (undersea explorer) . . . 80 30
1061 120f. Gottlieb Daimler (automobile designer) . . 1·25 35
1062 200f. Louis Bleriot (pilot) 1·90 55
1063 350f. A. Karpov (chess champion) (air) . . . . . . 3·00 75
1064 400f. Henri Dunant (founder of Red Cross) . . . . . 3·00 85

304 Profile, Water and Emblem

1984. Bangui Rotary Club and Water.
1066 **304** 130f. multicoloured . . . 1·25 35
1067 205f. multicoloured . . . 1·90 60

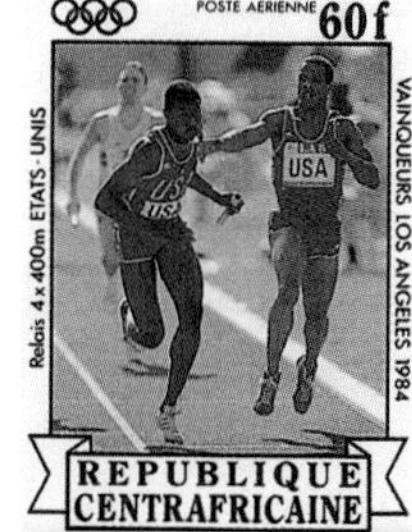

305 United States (4 × 400 m relay)

1985. Air Olympic Games Gold Medallists. Multicoloured.
1068 60f. Type **305** 45 20
1069 140f. E. Moses (400 m hurdles) . . . . . 1·10 30
1070 300f. S. Aouita (5000 m) . . 2·50 75
1071 440f. D. Thompson (decathlon) . . . . 3·50 1·00

306 "Virgin and Infant Jesus" (Titian)

1985. Air. Christmas (1984). Multicoloured.
1073 130f. Type **306** 95 45
1074 350f. "Virgin with Rabbit" (Titian) . . . . 2·50 1·10
1075 400f. "Virgin and Child" (Titian) . . . . 3·00 1·25

307 Eastern Screech Owls

1985. Air. Birth Bicentenary of John J. Audubon (ornithologist) (1st issue). Multicoloured.
1076 60f. Type **307** . . . . . . 1·25 70
1077 110f. Mangrove cuckoo (vert) . . . . 1·90 1·10
1078 200f. Mourning doves (vert) 3·25 1·75
1079 500f. Wood ducks . . . . . 8·00 4·50
See also Nos. 1099/1104.

1985. International Exhibitions. Nos. 1014/15 and 1019/20 overprinted as listed below.
1083 250f. multicoloured . . . . 1·90 95
1084 350f. multicoloured . . . . 2·50 1·10
1085 400f. multicoloured . . . . 3·75 1·90
1086 440f. multicoloured . . . . 3·00 1·40
OVERPRINTS: 250f. **ARGENTINA '85 BUENOS AIRES** and emblem; 350f. **TSUKUBA EXPO '85**; 400f. **Italia '85 ROME** and emblem; 440f. **MOPHILA '85 HAMBOURG**.

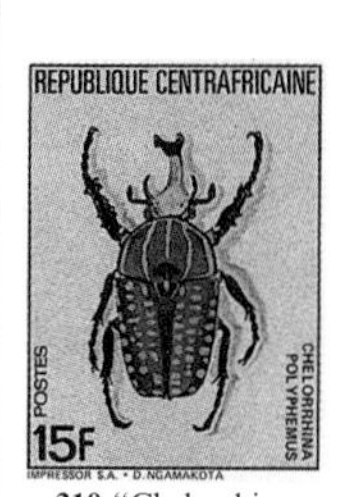

310 "Chelorrhina polyphemus"

312 Blue Jay

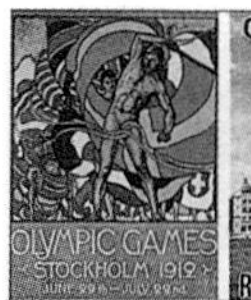
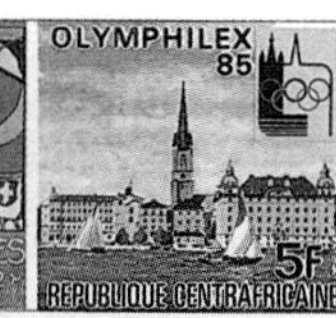

311 Olympic Games Poster and Stockholm

1985. Beetles. Multicoloured.
1088 15f. Type **310** 20 15
1089 20f. "Fornasinius russus" 25 15
1090 25f. "Goliathus giganteus" 30 15
1091 65f. "Goliathus meleagris" 80 50

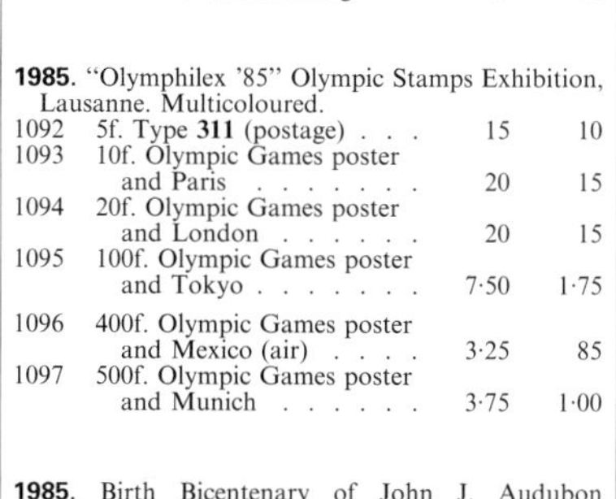

1985. "Olymphilex '85" Olympic Stamps Exhibition, Lausanne. Multicoloured.
1092 5f. Type **311** (postage) . . . 15 10
1093 10f. Olympic Games poster and Paris 20 15
1094 20f. Olympic Games poster and London 20 15
1095 100f. Olympic Games poster and Tokyo . . . . 7·50 1·75
1096 400f. Olympic Games poster and Mexico (air) . . . . 3·25 85
1097 500f. Olympic Games poster and Munich . . . . . . 3·75 1·00

1985. Birth Bicentenary of John J. Audubon (ornithologist) (2nd issue). Multicoloured.
1099 40f. Type **312** (postage) . . 45 25
1100 80f. Chuck Will's widow . . 85 55
1101 130f. Ivory-billed woodpecker . . . . . . 1·10 80
1102 250f. Collie's magpie-jay . . 2·50 1·75
1103 300f. Mangrove cuckoo (horiz) (air) . . . . 2·75 1·90
1104 500f. Barn swallow (horiz) 5·50 3·75

313 Delivering Post by Van

1985. "Philexafrique" Stamp Exhibition, Lome, Togo (1st issue). Multicoloured.
1106 200f. Type **313** . . . . . . 1·90 1·00
1107 200f. Scouts and flag . . . 1·90 1·00
See also Nos. 1154/5.

314 Tiger and Rudyard Kipling

1985. Int Youth Year (1st issue). Multicoloured.
1108 100f. Type **314** . . . . . . 1·00 30
1109 200f. Men on horseback and Joseph Kessel . . . . . . 1·90 55
1110 300f. Submarine gripped by octopus and Jules Verne 2·25 1·10
1111 400f. Mississippi stern-wheeler, Huckleberry Finn and Mark Twain . . . . 3·00 1·75
See also Nos. 1163/68.

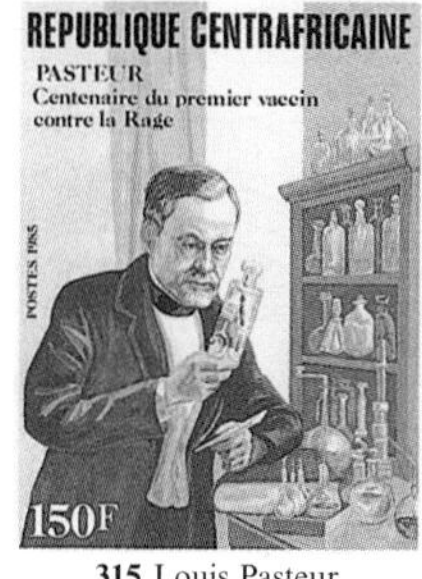

315 Louis Pasteur

1985. Anniversaries. Multicoloured.
1112 150f. Type **315** (centenary of discovery of anti-rabies vaccine) (postage) . . . . 1·75 40
1113 200f. Henri Dunant (founder of Red Cross) and 125th anniv of Battle of Solferino (horiz) . . . . 1·90 50
1114 300f. Girl guides (75th anniv of Girl Guide Movement) (air) . . . . 1·90 75
1115 450f. Queen Elizabeth the Queen Mother (85th birthday) . . . . 3·25 1·25
1116 500f. Statue of Liberty (cent) 3·75 1·50

316 Pele and Footballers

1985. World Cup Football Championship, Mexico. Multicoloured.
1117 5f. Type **316** (postage) . . . 10 10
1118 10f. Harald "Tony" Schumacher 15 10
1119 20f. Paolo Rossi 15 15
1120 350f. Kevin Keegan (wrongly inscr "Kervin") 2·75 90
1121 400f. Michel Platini (air) . . 3·00 90
1122 500f. Karl Heinz Rummenigge . . . . . . 3·75 1·00

317 La Kotto Waterfalls

318 Pope with Hand raised in Blessing

1985.
1124 **317** 65f. multicoloured . . . 60 25
1125 90f. multicoloured . . . 75 30
1126 130f. multicoloured . . . 1·10 50

1985. Papal Visit. Multicoloured.
1127 65f. Type **318** 55 25
1128 130f. Pope John Paul II in Communion robes . . . 1·10 50

319 Soldier using Ox-drawn Plough

1985. Economic Campaign. Multicoloured.
1129 5f. Type **319** 15 10
1130 60f. Soldier sowing cotton 35 20
1131 130f. Soldier sowing cotton (different) . . . . 1·00 35

320 As Young Girl with her Brother

1985. 85th Birthday of Queen Elizabeth the Queen Mother. Multicoloured.
1132 100f. Type **320** (postage) . . 60 20
1133 200f. Queen Mary with Duke and Duchess of York . . . . 1·50 35
1134 300f. Duchess of York inspecting Irish Guards 2·25 70
1135 350f. Duke and Duchess of York with the young Princesses . . . . . . 2·50 80
1136 400f. In the Golden State Coach at Coronation of King George VI (air) . . 3·00 90
1137 500f. At the service for her Silver Wedding . . . . . 3·75 1·00

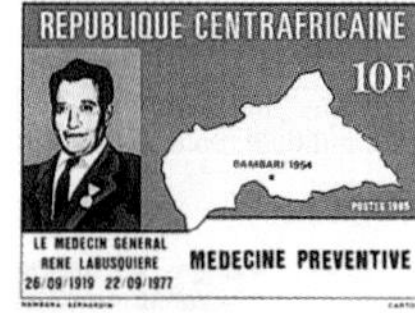

321 Dr. Labusquiere and Map of Republic

1985. 8th Death Anniv of General Doctor Labusquiere. Multicoloured.
1139 **321** 10f. multicoloured . . . 15 10
1140 45f. multicoloured . . . 35 20
1141 110f. multicoloured . . . 1·00 35

322 Mail Van delivering Parcels to Local Post Office

1985. Postal Service. Multicoloured.
1142 15f. Type **322** 15 10
1143 60f. Van collecting mail from local post office . . 45 20
1144 150f. Vans at main post office . . . . 1·10 50

323 Gagarin, Korolev and Space Station Complex

1985. Space Research. Multicoloured.
1145 40f. Type **323** (postage) . . 20 10
1146 110f. Copernicus and "Cassini" space probe . . 75 25
1147 240f. Galileo and "Viking" orbiter . . . . 1·75 50
1148 300f. T. von Karman and astronaut recovering satellite . . . . 2·25 70
1149 450f. Percival Lowell and "Viking" space probe (air) 3·50 90
1150 500f. Dr. U. Merbold and "Columbus" space station 3·75 1·00

324 Damara Solar Energy Plant

1985.
1152 **324** 65f. multicoloured . . . 55 25
1153 130f. multicoloured . . . 1·10 50

325 Ouaka Sugar Refinery

1985. "Philexafrique" Stamp Exhibition, Lome, Togo (2nd issue). Multicoloured.
1154 250f. Nature studies . . . . 3·25 1·60
1155 250f. Type **325** . . . . . . 2·10 1·40

326 Pres. Mitterrand, Gen. Kolingba and Flags

1985. Visit of President Mitterrand of France.
1156 **326** 65f. multicoloured . . . 50 20
1157 130f. multicoloured . . . 1·00 45
1158 160f. multicoloured . . . 1·40 60

327 Map and U.N. Emblem

328 "Virgin and Angels" (Master of Burgo de Osma)

1985. 40th Anniv of U.N.O. and 25th Anniv of Central African Republic Membership.
1159 **327** 140f. multicoloured . . . 1·10 50

1985. Air. Christmas. Multicoloured.
1160 100f. Type **328** 80 25
1161 200f. "Nativity" (Louis Le Nain) . . . . 1·75 1·00
1162 400f. "Virgin and Child with Dove" (Piero di Cosimo) 3·25 1·00

329 Leonardo da Vinci and "Madonna of the Eyelet"

1985. Int Youth Year (2nd issue). Multicoloured.
1163 40f. Type **329** (postage) . . 30 15
1164 80f. Johann Sebastian Bach 75 20
1165 100f. Diego Velasquez and "St. John of Patmos" . . 1·00 20
1166 250f. Franz Schubert and illustration of "King of Aulnes" . . . . 2·00 50
1167 400f. Francisco Goya and "Vicente Osario de Moscoso" (air) . . . . . 3·50 90
1168 500f. Wolfgang Amadeus Mozart . . . . 4·00 1·00

330 Halley and "Comet"

1985. Appearance of Halley's Comet (1st issue). Multicoloured.
1170 100f. Type **330** (postage) . . 60 20
1171 200f. Newton's telescope . . 1·50 35
1172 300f. Halley and Newton observing comet . . . . 2·25 45
1173 350f. American space probe and comet . . . . 2·50 80
1174 400f. Sun, Russian space probe and diagram of comet trajectory (air) . . 3·00 90
1175 500f. Infra-red picture of comet . . . . 3·75 1·00
See also Nos. 1184/8.

331 Columbus with Globe

1986. 480th Death Anniv of Christopher Columbus (explorer). Multicoloured.
1177 90f. Type **331** (postage) . . 70 20
1178 110f. Receiving blessing . . 85 25
1179 240f. Crew going ashore in rowing boat . . . . . . 2·00 1·25
1180 300f. Columbus with American Indians . . . . 2·50 60
1181 400f. Ships at sea in storm (air) . . . . 3·50 2·00
1182 500f. Sun breaking through clouds over fleet . . . . 4·00 2·25

332 Halley and Comet

1986. Air. Appearance of Halley's Comet (2nd issue). Multicoloured.
1184 110f. Type **332** 80 25
1185 130f. "Giotto" space probe 1·00 25
1186 200f. Comet and globe . . . 1·50 45
1187 300f. "Vega" space probe 2·25 60
1188 400f. Space shuttle . . . 3·25 95

1986. Nos. 874/5 surch.
1188a – 30f. on 175f. mult . . .
1188b **259** 65f. on 300f. mult . . .

333 Spiky Hair Style

334 Communications

1986. Traditional Hair Styles. Multicoloured.
1189 20f. Type **333** 20 10
1190 30f. Braids around head . . 25 15
1191 65f. Plaits 30 25
1192 160f. Braids from front to back of head . . . . . . 1·50 50

1986. Franco-Central African Week. Mult.
1193 40f. Type **334** 30 15
1194 60f. Youth 50 20
1195 100f. Basket weaver (craft) 75 30
1196 130f. Cyclists (sport) . . . . 1·25 50

335 "Allamanda neriifolia"

1986. Flora and Fauna. Multicoloured.
1197 25f. Type **335** (postage) . . 20 15
1198 65f. Bongo (horiz) 50 20
1199 160f. "Plumieria acuminata" 1·10 40
1200 300f. Cheetah (horiz) . . . 2·25 1·00
1201 400f. "Eulophia erthoplata" (air) . . . . 2·75 90
1202 500f. Leopard (horiz) . . . 3·75 1·75

336 Palm Tree and Bossongo Oil Refinery

1986. Centrapalm. Multicoloured.
1204 25f. Type **336** 20 15
1205 65f. Type **336** 50 30
1206 120f. Palm tree and Bossongo agro-industrial complex 85 60
1207 160f. As No. 1206 . . . . . 1·25 50

337 Pointer

1986. Dogs and Cats. Multicoloured.
1208 10f. Type **337** (postage) . . 15 10
1209 20f. Egyptian mau 25 15
1210 200f. Newfoundland . . . . 1·75 50
1211 300f. Borzoi (air) . . . . . 2·50 60
1212 400f. Persian red . . . . . 3·50 80

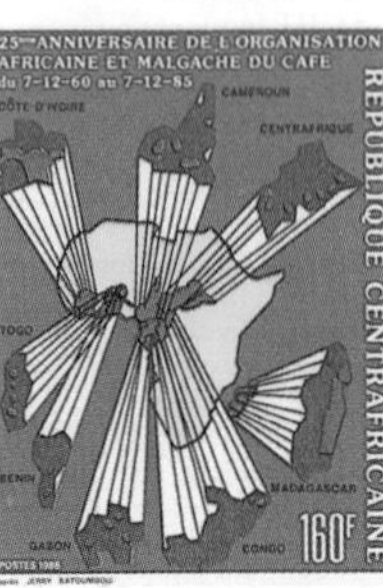

338 Map of Africa showing Member Countries

1986. 25th Anniv of African and Malagasy Coffee Producers Organization.
1214 **338** 160f. multicoloured . . . 1·40 60

339 Trophy, Brazilian flag, L.-A. Muller and Socrates

1986. World Cup Football Championship, Mexico. Multicoloured.
1215 30f. Type **339** (postage) . . 20 15
1216 110f. Trophy, Belgian flag, V. Scifo and F. Ceulemans 70 20
1217 160f. Trophy, French flag. Y. Stopyra and M. Platini 1·00 25
1218 350f. Trophy, West German flag, A. Brehme and H. Schumacher . . . . . 2·50 70
1219 450f. Trophy, Argentinian flag and Diego Maradona (air) . . . . 3·00 1·00

340 Judith Resnik and Astronaut

341 People around Globe within Emblem

1986. Anniversaries and "Challenger" Astronauts Commemoration. Multicoloured.
1221 15f. Type **340** (postage) . . 15 10
1222 25f. Frederic Bartholdi and torch (centenary of Statue of Liberty) 25 15
1223 70f. Elvis Presley (9th death anniv) 95 20
1224 300f. Ronald MacNair and man watching astronaut on screen . . . . 2·10 65
1225 485f. on 70f. No. 1223 . . . 5·25 1·00
1226 450f. Christa McAulife and Shuttle lifting off (air) . . 3·25 1·10

1986. International Peace Year.
1228 **341** 160f. multicoloured . . . 1·40 65

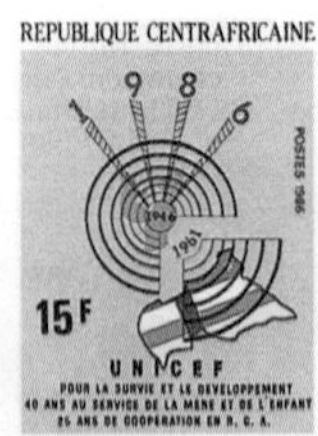

342 Globe, Douglas DC-10 and "25"

343 Emblem and Flag as Map

1986. 25th Anniv of Air Afrique.
1229 **342** 200f. multicoloured . . . 1·50 85

1986. U.N.I.C.E.F. Child Survival Campaign. Multicoloured.
1230 15f. Type **343** 15 10
1231 130f. Doctor vaccinating child . . . . 1·10 50
1232 160f. Basket of fruit and boy holding fish on map 2·25 1·00

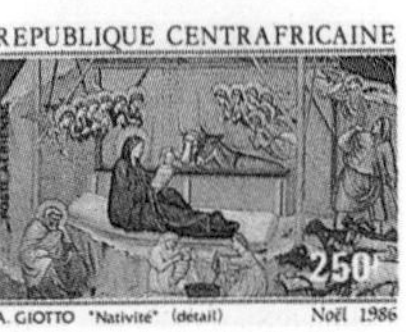

344 "Nativity" (detail, Giotto)

1986. Air. Christmas. Multicoloured.
1233 250f. Type **344** . . . . . . 1·90 60
1234 440f. "Adoration of the Magi" (detail, Sandro Botticelli) (vert) . . . . . 3·25 1·10
1235 500f. "Nativity" (detail, Giotto) (different) . . . . 4·00 1·10

345 Transmission Mast, People with Radios and Baskets of Produce

1986. African Telecommunications Day. Telecommunications and Agriculture. Mult.
1236 170f. Type **345** (Rural Radio Agriculture Project) . . . 1·40 75
1237 265f. Lorry, satellite, men using telephones and sacks of produce . . . . 2·10 1·10

346 Steam Locomotive Class "DH 2 Green Elephant" and Alfred de Glehn

1986. 150th Anniv of German Railways. Mult.
1238 40f. Type **346** (postage) . . 50 10
1239 70f. Rudolf Diesel (engineer) and steam locomotive No. 1829 Rheingold . . . 80 15
1240 160f. Electric locomotive Type 103 Rapide and Carl Golsdorf . . . . . 2·00 40
1241 300f. Wilhelm Schmidt and Beyer-Garratt type steam locomotive . . . . 3·50 95
1242 400f. De Bousquet and compound locomotive Class 3500 (air) . . . . . 4·75 1·10

347 Player returning Ball

1986. Air. Olympic Games, Seoul (1988) (1st issue). Tennis. Multicoloured.
1244 150f. Type **347** . . . . . . 1·25 45
1245 250f. Player serving (vert) 2·25 60
1246 440f. Right-handed player returning to left-handed player (vert) . . . . . . 3·00 1·10
1247 600f. Left-handed player returning to right-handed player . . . . 4·50 1·25
See also Nos. 1261/4, 1310/13 and 1315/18.

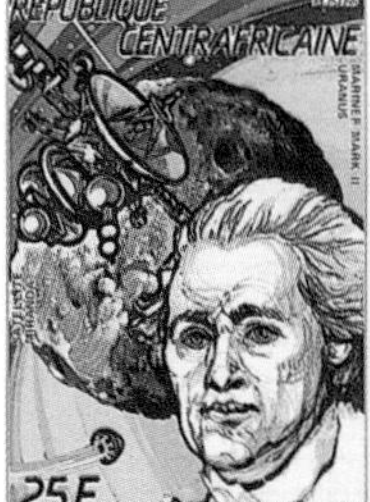

348 "Miranda" Satellite, Uranus, "Mariner II" and William Herschel (astronomer)

349 Footballer and "Woman with Umbrella" Fountain

1987. Space Research. Multicoloured.
1248 25f. Type **348** (postage) . . 20 15
1249 65f. Mars Rover vehicle and Werner von Braun (rocket pioneer) 45 20
1250 160f. "Mariner II", Titan and Rudolf Hanel . . . . 1·25 35
1251 300f. Space ship "Hermes", space platform "Eureka" and Patrick Baudry . . . 2·25 70
1252 400f. Halley's Comet, "Giotto" space probe and Dr. U. Keller (air) . . . . 2·75 85
1253 500f. European space station "Columbus", Wubbo Ockels and Ulf Merbold 3·25 1·00

1987. Olympic Games, Barcelona (1992). Mult.
1255 30f. Type **349** (postage) . . 25 15
1256 150f. Judo competitors and Barcelona Cathedral . . . 1·00 40
1257 265f. Cyclist and Church of the Holy Family . . . . 1·90 65
1258 350f. Diver and Christopher Columbus's tomb (air) . . 2·50 85
1259 495f. Runner and human tower . . . . 3·75 1·10

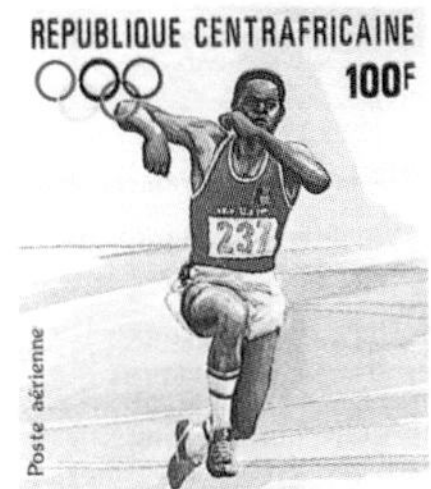

350 Triple Jumping

1987. Air. Olympic Games, Seoul (1988) (2nd issue). Multicoloured.
1261 100f. Type **350** 75 25
1262 200f. High jumping (horiz) 1·50 50
1263 300f. Long jumping (horiz) 2·25 75
1264 400f. Pole vaulting . . . . 3·00 1·00

351 Two-man Luge

352 Peace Medal

1987. Winter Olympic Games, Calgary (1988) (1st issue). Multicoloured.
1266 20f. Type **351** (postage) . . 20 15
1267 140f. Cross-country skiing 1·10 40
1268 250f. Figure skating . . . . 1·90 65
1269 300f. Ice hockey (air) . . . 2·25 75
1270 400f. Slalom . . . . 2·75 1·00
See also Nos. 1320/3.

1987. International Peace Year (1986).
1272 **352** 50f. brown, blue & blk 35 25
1273 160f. brown, grn & blk 1·25 65

1987. 10th Death Anniv of Elvis Presley (singer). Nos. 1223 and 1225 optd **Elvis Presley 1977–1987**.
1274 70f. multicoloured 75 50
1275 485f. on 70f. multicoloured 5·00 1·75

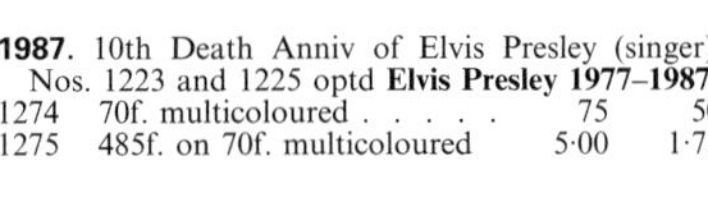
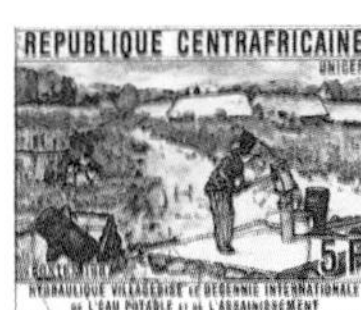

354 Woman at Village Pump

1987. International Decade of Drinkable Water. Multicoloured.
1276 5f. Type **354** . . . .
1277 10f. Woman at village pump (different) . . . .
1278 200f. Three women at village pump . . . . . .

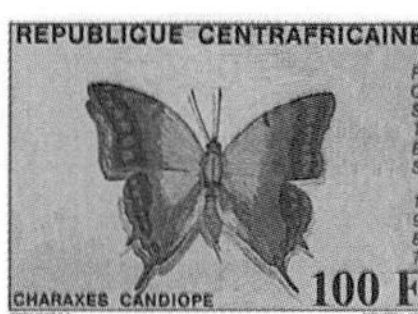

355 "Charaxes candiope"

1987. Butterflies. Multicoloured.
1279 100f. Type **355** 75 55
1280 120f. "Graphium leonidas" 95 60
1281 130f. "Charaxes brutus" . . 1·10 60
1282 160f. "Salamis aetiops" . . 1·25 70

356 Nola Football Team

1987. Campaign for Integration of Pygmies.
1283 **356** 90f. multicoloured . . . 1·10 75
1284 160f. multicoloured . . . 1·75 1·10

357 James Madison (U.S. President, 1809–17)

1987. Anniversaries and Celebrities. Mult.
1285 40f. Type **357** (bicent of U.S. constitution) (postage) 30 15
1286 160f. Queen Elizabeth II and Prince Philip (40th wedding anniv) . . . . . 1·25 25
1287 200f. Steffi Graf (tennis player) . . . . 1·60 45
1288 300f. Gary Kasparov (chess champion) and "The Chess Players" (after Honore Daumier) (air) . . 2·50 75
1289 400f. Boris Becker (tennis player) . . . . 3·00 1·00

358 Brontosaurus

1988. Prehistoric Animals. Multicoloured.
1291 50f. Type **358** 35 15
1292 65f. Triceratops 50 15
1293 100f. Ankylosaurus 75 25
1294 160f. Stegosaurus . . . . . 1·25 45
1295 200f. Tyrannosaurus rex (vert) . . . . 1·50 50
1296 240f. Corythosaurus (vert) 1·90 65
1297 300f. Allosaurus (vert) . . . 2·25 75
1298 350f. Brachiosaurus (vert) 2·75 95

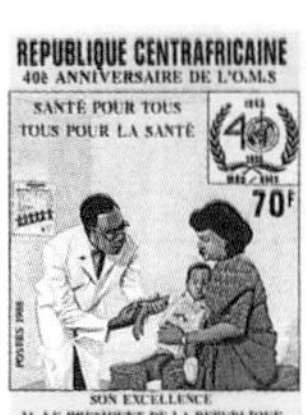

359 Pres. Kolingba vaccinating Baby

360 Carmine Bee Eater

1988. 40th Anniv of W.H.O.
1299 **359** 70f. multicoloured . . . 60 40
1300 120f. multicoloured . . . 1·60 45

1988. Scouts and Birds. Multicoloured.
1301 25f. Type **360** (postage) . . 15 10
1302 170f. Red-crowned bishop 1·10 80
1303 300f. Lesser pied kingfisher 3·25 2·25
1304 400f. Red-cheeked cordon-bleu (air) . . . . 2·75 2·40
1305 450f. Lizard buzzard . . . . 3·50 2·75

361 Schools replanting Campaign

1988. National Tree Day. Multicoloured.
1307 50f. Type **361** 35 25
1308 100f. Type **361** 75 50
1309 130f. Felling tree and planting saplings . . . . 1·10 60

362 1972 100f. Stamp and Beam Exercise

1988. Air. Olympic Games, Seoul (3rd issue). Gymnastics. Multicoloured.
1310 90f. Type **362** 75 25
1311 200f. 1964 50f. stamp and beam exercise (horiz) . . 1·50 35
1312 300f. 1964 100f. stamp and vault exercise (horiz) . . . 2·25 75
1313 400f. 1964 250f. stamp and parallel bars exercise (horiz) . . . . 3·00 1·10

363 Running

364 Cross-country Skiing

1988. Olympic Games, Seoul (4th issue). Mult.
1315 150f. Type **363** (postage) . . 1·10 25
1316 300f. Judo . . . . 2·25 60
1317 400f. Football (air) . . . . 2·75 85
1318 450f. Tennis . . . . 3·00 1·00

1988. Winter Olympic Games, Calgary (2nd issue). Multicoloured.
1320 170f. Type **364** (postage) . . 1·25 30
1321 350f. Ice hockey . . . . . 2·25 60
1322 400f. Downhill skiing (air) 2·75 85
1323 450f. Slalom . . . . 3·00 1·00

1988. Nos. 1302/5 surch.
1325 30f. on 170f. mult (postage) 40 20
1326 70f. on 300f. mult . . . . . 1·50 85
1327 160f. on 400f. mult (air) . . 2·50 1·40
1328 200f. on 450f. mult . . . . 3·00 1·90

366 Hospital and Grounds

1988. 1st Anniv of L'Amitie Hospital. Mult.
1329 5f. Type **366** 15 10
1330 60f. Aerial view of hospital complex 50 35
1331 160f. Hospital entrance . . 1·25 75

367 Buildings Complex

1988. 30th Anniv of Republic. Multicoloured.
1332 65f. Family on map, flags and dove . . . .
1334 240f. Type **367** . . . . . .

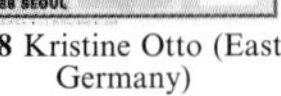

368 Kristine Otto (East Germany)

369 Hebmuller and Volkswagen Cabriolet, 1953

1989. Olympic Games, Seoul, Gold Medal Winners. Multicoloured.

1335 150f. Type **368** (100 m butterfly and 100 m backstroke) (postage) . . . . 1·00 35
1336 240f. Matt Biondi (100 m freestyle) . . . . 1·50 50
1337 300f. Florence Griffith-Joyner (U.S.A.) (100 and 200 m sprints) . . . . . 1·90 75
1338 450f. Pierre Durand (France) (show jumping) (air) . . . . 3·00 1·10

1989. Transport. Multicoloured.

1340 20f. Type **369** (postage) . . 20 15
1341 205f. Werner von Siemens and his first electric locomotive, 1879 . . . . 2·25 75
1342 300f. Dennis Conner and "Stars and Stripes" (winner of Americas Cup yacht races) . . . . . . 2·25 65
1343 400f. Andre Citroen and "16 Six" car, 1955 . . . . . 3·00 1·00
1344 450f. Mare Seguin and Decauville Mallet locomotive, 1895 (air) . . 3·75 75

370 Allegory in Honour of Liberty

1989. Bicentenary of French Revolution and "Philexfrance 89" International Stamp Exhibition, Paris (1st issue). Multicoloured.

1346 200f. Type **370** . . . . . . 1·75 60
1347 300f. Declaration of Rights of Man . . . . 2·50 1·25

See also Nos. 1366/9.

371 Statue of Liberty at Night

1989. Centenary of Statue of Liberty. Mult.

1349 150f. Type **371** . . . . . . 1·10 60
1350 150f. Maintenance worker 1·10 60
1351 150f. Close-up of face . . . 1·10 60
1352 200f. Maintenance worker (different) . . . . 1·40 95
1353 200f. Colour party in front of statue . . . . 1·40 95
1354 200f. Close-up of head at night . . . . 1·40 95

373 "Apollo 11" Astronaut on Moon

1989. Air. 20th Anniv of First Manned Landing on Moon. Multicoloured.

1355 40f. Type **373** 30 20
1356 80f. "Apollo 15" astronaut and moon buggy 55 25
1357 130f. "Apollo 16" module landing in sea . . . . . 1·00 50
1358 1000f. "Apollo 17" astronaut on Moon . . . 7·50 2·25

374 Champagnat, Map and "Madonna and Child"

1989. Birth Bicentenary of Marcelino Champagnat (founder of Marist Brothers). Multicoloured.

1359 15f. Type **374** 15 15
1360 50f. Champagnat, cross, globe and emblem 35 25
1361 160f. Champagnat and flags (horiz) . . . . 1·40 1·00

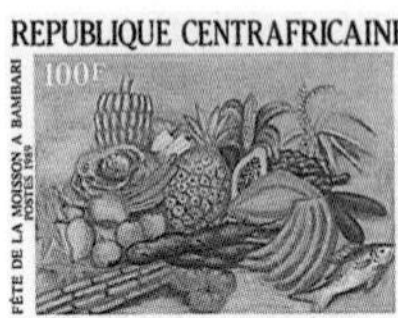

375 Food Products

1989. Bambari Harvest Festival. Multicoloured.

1362 100f. Type **375** . . . . . . 1·25 65
1363 160f. Ploughing with oxen 1·25 60

376 Raising of Livestock

1989. World Food Day. Multicoloured.

1364 60f. Type **376** 50 35
1365 240f. Soldiers catching poachers . . . . 2·00 1·10

377 Gen. Kellermann and Battle of Valmy

1989. Bicentenary of French Revolution and "Philexfrance 89" International Stamp Exhibition, Paris (2nd issue). Multicoloured.

1366 160f. Type **377** (postage) . . 1·25 35
1367 200f. Gen. Dumouriez and Battle of Jemappes (wrongly inscr "JEMMAPES") . . . . 1·60 50
1368 500f. Gen. Pichegru and capture of Dutch fleet (air) . . . . 4·50 1·25
1369 600f. Gen. Hoche and Royalist landing at Quiberon . . . . 4·25 1·00

378 Players and Trophy

1989. Victory in 1987 African Basketball Championships, Tunis (1st issue). Multicoloured.

1371 160f. Type **378** . . . . . . 1·25 60
1372 240f. National team with medals and trophy (horiz) 1·60 80
1373 500f. Type **378** . . . . . . 4·00 1·75

See also Nos. 1383/4.

379 Governor's Palace, 1906

1989. Centenary of Bangui. Multicoloured.

1374 100f. Type **379** 75 35
1375 160f. Bangui post office . . 1·10 90
1376 200f. A. Dosilie (founder of Bangui post office) (vert) 1·50 85
1377 1000f. Michel Dolisie and Chief Gbembo agreeing peace pact (vert) . . . . 7·25 3·75

380 Footballer and Palermo Cathedral Belltower

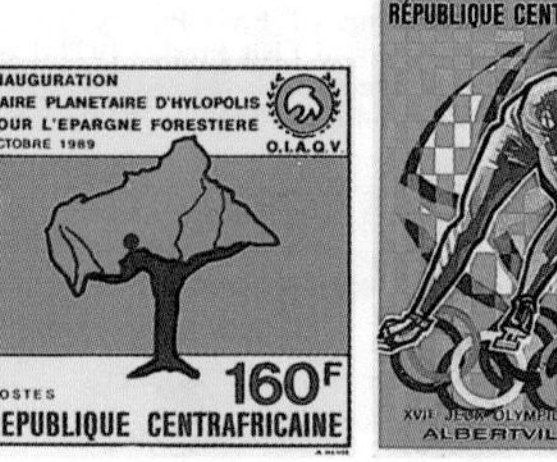

381 Trophy and Map of Africa

1989. World Cup Football Championship, Italy (1990) (1st issue). Multicoloured.

1378 20f. Type **380** (postage) . . 20 15
1379 160f. Footballer and St. Francis's church, Bologna . . . . 1·10 35
1380 200f. Footballer and Old Palace, Florence . . . . 1·50 50
1381 120f. Footballer and Church of Trinita dei Monti, Rome (air) 90 35

See also Nos. 1405/8.

1990. Victory in 1987 African Basketball Championships, Tunis (2nd issue).

1383 **381** 100f. multicoloured . . . 80 35
1384 130f. multicoloured . . . 1·10 60

382 Tree with Map as Foliage

383 Speed Skating

1990. Inauguration (1989) of Forest Conservation Organization.

1385 **382** 160f. multicoloured . . . 1·40 65

1990. Winter Olympic Games, Albertville (1992). Multicoloured.

1386 10f. Type **383** (postage) . . 15 15
1387 60f. Cross-country skiing . . 45 25
1388 500f. Slalom skiing (air) . . 3·75 95
1389 750f. Ice dancing . . . . . 5·50 1·25

384 "Euphaera eusemoides"

1990. Scouts and Butterflies. Multicoloured.

1391 25f. Type **384** 20 15
1392 65f. Becker's glider 45 15
1393 160f. "Pseudacraea clarki" 1·10 25
1394 250f. Giant charaxes . . . . 1·75 50
1395 300f. "Euphaedra gausape" 2·25 60
1396 500f. Red swallowtail . . . 3·75 85

385 Throwing the Javelin

1990. Olympic Games, Barcelona (1992). Mult.

1398 10f. Type **385** (postage) . . 15 15
1399 40f. Running 35 15
1400 130f. Tennis 95 25
1401 240f. Hurdling (horiz) . . . 1·75 50
1402 400f. Yachting (horiz) (air) 3·00 85
1403 500f. Football (horiz) . . . 3·75 1·00

386 Footballers and Globe

1990. Air. World Cup Football Championship, Italy (2nd issue).

1405 **386** 5f. multicoloured 10 10
1406 – 30f. multicoloured 20 15
1407 – 500f. multicoloured . . . 3·25 1·00
1408 – 1000f. multicoloured . . 7·50 1·60

DESIGNS: 30 to 1000f. Various footballing scenes.

387 Pres. Gorbachev of U.S.S.R., Map of Malta and Pres. Bush of U.S.A.

1990. Anniversaries and Events. Multicoloured.

1409 120f. Type **387** (summit conference, Malta) (postage) 85 20
1410 130f. Sir Rowland Hill and Penny Black (150th anniv of first postage stamps) 85 20
1411 160f. Galileo space probe and planet Jupiter . . . . 1·10 25
1412 200f. Pres. Gorbachev meeting Pope John Paul II, statue of Saturn and dove . . . . 1·50 35
1413 240f. Neil Armstrong and eagle (21st anniv of first manned landing on Moon) . . . . 1·90 45
1414 250f. Concorde, German experimental Maglev train and Rotary International emblem . . . . 3·75 50
1415 300f. Don Mattingly (baseball player) and New York Yankees club badge (air) . . . . 2·25 60
1416 500f. Charles de Gaulle (French statesman, birth centenary) . . . . 3·75 85

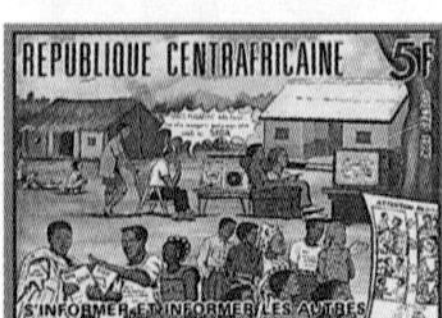

388 AIDS Information on Radio, Television and Leaflets

1991. Anti-AIDS Campaign. Multicoloured.

1418 5f. Type **388** 15 10
1419 70f. Type **388** 55 35
1420 120f. Lecture on AIDS (vert) 85 50

389 Demonstrators

1991. Protection of Animals. Multicoloured.

1421	15f. Type **389**	15	10
1422	60f. Type **389**	50	25
1423	100f. Decrease in elephant population, 1945–2045 (vert)	75	35

390 Butter Catfish

1991. Fishes. Multicoloured.

1424	50f. Type **390**	50	35
1425	160f. Type **390**	2·10	1·00
1426	240f. Distichodus	3·50	1·90

391 President Kolingba

1992. 10th Anniv (1991) of Assumption of Power by Military Committee under Andre Kolingba.

1427	**391**	160f. multicoloured	1·25	50

392 Count Ferdinand von Zeppelin (airship pioneer)

1992. Celebrities, Anniversaries and Events. Multicoloured.

1428	80f. Type **392** (75th death anniv) (postage)	40	10
1429	140f. Henri Dunant (founder of Red Cross)	95	15
1430	160f. Michael Schumacher (racing driver)	1·10	25
1431	350f. Brandenburg Gate (bicent) and Konrad Adenauer (German Federal Republic Chancellor) signing 1949 constitution	2·50	75
1432	500f. Pope John Paul II (tour of West Africa) (air)	3·50	90
1433	600f. Wolfgang Amadeus Mozart (composer, death bicent (1991))	4·50	1·00

393 Dam **395** Breastfeeding

394 Compass Rose and Organization Emblem

1993. River M'Bali Dam. Multicoloured.

1435	160f. Type **393**	80	15
1436	200f. People fishing near dam (self-sufficiency in food)	1·00	25

1993. International Customs Day and 40th Anniv of Customs Co-operation Council.

1437	**394**	240f. multicoloured	1·10	25

1993. International Nutrition Conference, Rome (1992). Multicoloured.

1438	90f. Type **395**	40	10
1439	140f. Foodstuffs	70	15

396 Bangui University

1993.

1440	**396**	100f. multicoloured	50	15

397 Masako Owada as Baby

1993. Wedding of Crown Prince Naruhito of Japan and Masako Owada. Multicoloured.

1441	50f. Type **397** (postage)	10	10
1442	65f. Prince Naruhito as child with parents	25	10
1443	160f. Masako Owada at Harvard University, U.S.A.	70	15
1444	450f. Prince Naruhito at Oxford University (air)	1·75	50

398 Presley singing "Heartbreak Hotel" (1956)

1993. 16th Death Anniv of Elvis Presley (entertainer). Multicoloured.

1446	200f. Type **398**	1·00	15
1447	300f. "Love Me Tender", 1957	1·50	25
1448	400f. "Jailhouse Rock", 1957	1·75	30
1449	600f. "Harum Scarum", 1965 (air)	2·50	50

399 First World Cup Final, 1928, and Uruguay v. Argentina, 1930

1993. World Cup Football Championship, U.S.A. (1994). History of the World Cup. Multicoloured.

1451	40f. Type **399**	10	10
1452	50f. Italy v. Czechoslovakia, 1934, and Italy v. Hungary, 1938	10	10
1453	60f. Uruguay v. Brazil, 1950, and Germany v. Hungary, 1954	15	10
1454	80f. Brazil v. Sweden, 1958, and Brazil v. Czechoslovakia, 1962	20	10
1455	160f. England v. West Germany, 1966, and Brazil v. Italy, 1970	40	15
1456	200f. West Germany v. The Netherlands, 1974, and Argentina v. The Netherlands, 1978	55	20
1457	400f. Italy v. West Germany, 1982, and Argentina v. West Germany, 1986	1·00	35
1458	500f. West Germany v. Argentina, 1990, and 1994 Championship emblem and player	1·40	45

400 Baron Pierre de Coubertin (founder of modern games)

1993. Centenary (1996) of Modern Olympic Games. Multicoloured.

1460	90f. Ancient Greek athlete	25	10
1461	90f. Type **400**	25	10
1462	90f. Charles Bennett (running), Paris, 1900	25	10
1463	90f. Etienne Desmarteau (stone throwing), St. Louis, 1904	25	10
1464	90f. Harry Porter (high jump), London, 1908	25	10
1465	90f. Patrick MacDonald (putting the shot), Stockholm, 1912	25	10
1466	90f. Coloured and black Olympic rings (1916)	25	10
1467	90f. Frank Loomis (400 m hurdles), Antwerp, 1920	25	10
1468	90f. Albert White (diving), Paris, 1924	25	10
1469	100f. El Ouafi (marathon), Amsterdam, 1928	25	10
1470	100f. Eddie Tolan (100 m), Los Angeles, 1932	25	10
1471	100f. Jesse Owens (100 m, long jump and 200 m hurdles), Berlin, 1936	25	10
1472	100f. Coloured and black Olympic rings (1940)	25	10
1473	100f. Coloured and black Olympic rings (1944)	25	10
1474	100f. Tapio Rautavaara (throwing the javelin), London, 1948	25	10
1475	100f. Jean Boiteux (400 m freestyle swimming), Helsinki, 1952	25	10
1476	100f. Petrus Kasterman (three-day equestrian event), Melbourne, 1956	25	10
1477	100f. Sante Gaiardoni (cycling), Rome, 1960	25	10
1478	160f. Anton Geesink (judo), Tokyo, 1964	40	15
1479	160f. Bob Beamon (long jump), Mexico, 1968	40	15
1480	160f. Mark Spitz (swimming), Munich, 1972	40	15
1481	160f. Nadia Comaneci (gymnastics (beam)), Montreal, 1976	40	15
1482	160f. Aleksandre Ditjatin (gymnastics (rings) and dressage), Moscow, 1980	40	15
1483	160f. J. F. Lamour (sabre), Los Angeles, 1984	40	15
1484	160f. Pierre Durand (show jumping), Seoul, 1988	40	15
1485	160f. Michael Jordan (basketball), Barcelona, 1992	40	15
1486	160f. Footballer and Games emblem, Atlanta, 1996	40	15

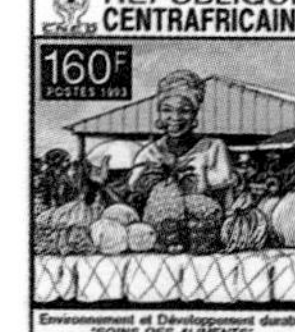

401 Man planting Sapling, and Animals **402** Woman selling Foodstuffs

1993. Biodiversity. Multicoloured.

1487	100f. Type **401**	25	10
1488	130f. Man amongst flora and fauna (vert)	35	15

1993. The Environment and Sustainable Development. Multicoloured.

1489	160f. Type **402**	40	15
1490	240f. Woman tending cooking pot	60	20

403 Saltoposuchus

1993. Prehistoric Animals. Multicoloured.

1491	25f. Type **403**	10	10
1492	25f. Rhamphorhynchus	10	10
1493	25f. Dimorphodon	10	10
1494	25f. Archaeopteryx	10	10
1495	30f. "Compsognathos longipes"	10	10
1496	30f. "Cryptocleidus oxoniensis"	10	10
1497	30f. Stegosaurus	10	10
1498	30f. Cetiosaurus	10	10
1499	50f. Brontosaurus	10	10
1500	50f. "Corythosaurus casuarius"	10	10
1501	50f. Styracosaurus	10	10
1502	50f. Gorgosaurus	10	10
1503	500f. Scolosaurus	1·40	45
1504	500f. Trachodon	1·40	45
1505	500f. Struthiomimus	1·40	45
1506	500f. "Tarbosaurus bataar"	1·40	45

Nos. 1491/1506 were issued together, se-tenant, forming a composite design of a volcanic landscape.

404 Th. Haug (combined skiing, Chamonix, 1924)

1994. Winter Olympic Games, Lillehammer, Norway. Previous Medal Winners. Multicoloured.

1508	100f. Type **404**	25	10
1509	100f. J. Heaton (luge, St. Moritz, 1928)	25	10
1510	100f. B. Ruud (ski jumping, Lake Placid, 1932)	25	10
1511	100f. I. Ballangrud (speed skating, Garmisch-Partenkirchen, 1936)	25	10
1512	100f. G. Fraser (slalom, St. Moritz, 1948)	25	10
1513	100f. West German 4-man bobsleigh team (Oslo, 1952)	25	10
1514	100f. U.S.S.R. ice hockey team (Cortina d'Ampezzo, 1956)	25	10
1515	100f. J. Vuarnet (downhill skiing, Squaw Valley, 1960)	25	10
1516	200f. M. Goitschel (giant slalom, Innsbruck, 1964)	50	15
1517	200f. Jean-Claud Killy (special slalom, Grenoble, 1968)	50	15
1518	200f. U. Wehling (cross-country skiing, Sapporo, 1972)	50	15
1519	200f. Irina Rodnina and Aleksandr Zaitsev (figure skating, Innsbruck, 1976)	50	15
1520	200f. E. Heiden (speed skating, Lake Placid, 1980)	50	15
1521	200f. Katarina Witt (figure skating, Sarajevo, 1984)	50	15
1522	200f. J. Mueller (single luge, Calgary, 1988)	50	15
1523	200f. E. Grospiron (acrobatic skiing, Albertville, 1992)	50	15
1524	200f. Speed skiing, Lillehammer, 1994	50	15

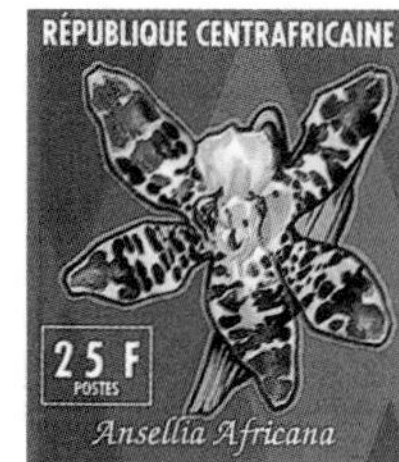

405 "Ansellia africa"

1994. Flowers, Vegetables, Fruit and Fungi. Multicoloured.

1525	25f. Type **405**	10	10
1526	30f. Yams	10	10
1527	40f. Oranges	10	10
1528	50f. Termite mushroom	10	10
1529	60f. "Polystachia bella" (flower)	15	10
1530	65f. Manioc	15	10
1531	70f. Banana	15	10
1532	80f. "Synpodia arborescens" (wrongly inscr "Sympodia") (fungi)	20	10
1533	90f. "Aerangis rhodosticta" (flower)	20	10
1534	100f. Maize	25	10
1535	160f. Mango	40	15
1536	200f. "Phlebopus sudanicus" (fungi)	50	15
1537	300f. Coffee beans	75	25
1538	400f. Sweet potato	95	30
1539	500f. "Angraecum eburneum" (flower)	1·25	40

1540 600f. "Leucocoprinus africanus" (fungi) . . . . 1·50 50

Nos. 1525/40 were issued together, se-tenant, the backgrounds forming a composite design.

MILITARY FRANK STAMPS

1963. Optd **FM**. No. M1 also has the value obliterated with two bars. Centre multicoloured; frame colour given.

M35 **1** (–) on 15f. blue . . . . . 4·50
M36 15f. blue . . . . 3·00

OFFICIAL STAMPS

O **41** Arms O **109** Arms

1965.

O78 O **41** 1f. multicoloured . . . 15 10
O79 2f. multicoloured . . . 10 10
O80 5f. multicoloured . . . 10 10
O81 10f. multicoloured . . . 25 10
O82 20f. multicoloured . . . 35 30
O83 30f. multicoloured . . . 70 50
O84 50f. multicoloured . . . 80 70
O85 100f. multicoloured . . 2·10 1·00
O86 130f. multicoloured . . 3·00 1·90
O87 200f. multicoloured . . 4·75 2·25

1971.

O238 O **109** 5f. multicoloured . . 10 10
O239 30f. multicoloured . . 30 20
O240 40f. multicoloured . . 50 25
O241 100f. multicoloured 1·25 55
O242 140f. multicoloured 2·25 75
O243 200f. multicoloured 2·75 1·25

POSTAGE DUE STAMPS

D **15** "Sternotomis gama" (Beetle)

1962. Beetles.

D33 50c. brown and turquoise . . 10 10
D34 50c. turquoise and brown . . 10 10
D35 1f. brown and green 10 10
D36 1f. green and brown 10 10
D37 2f. pink and black 10 10
D38 2f. green, black and pink . . 10 10
D39 5f. green and brown 25 25
D40 5f. green and brown 25 25
D41 10f. green, black and drab 50 50
D42 10f. drab, black and green 50 50
D43 25f. brown, black and green 1·40 1·40
D44 25f. brown, green and black 1·40 1·40

DESIGNS: No. D33, Type D **15**; D34, "Sternotomis virescens"; D35, "Augosoma centaurus"; D36, "Phosphorus virescens" and "Ceroplesis carabarica"; D37, "Ceroplesis S.P."; D38, "Cetoine scaraboidae"; D39, "Cetoine scaraboidae"; D40, "Macrorhina S.P."; D41, "Taurina longiceps"; D42, "Phryneta leprosa"; D43, "Monohamus griseoplagiatus"; D44, "Jambonus trifasciatus".

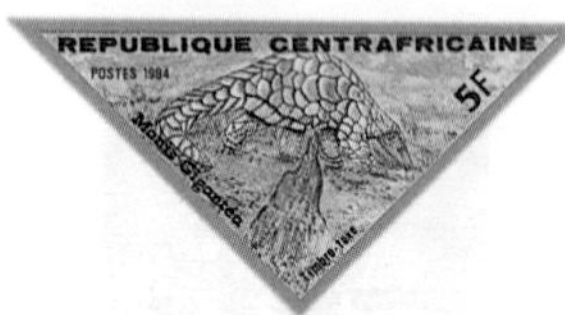

D **308** Giant Pangolin ("Manis gigantea")

1985.

D1080 D **308** 5f. multicoloured . . 10 10
D1081 20f. multicoloured 20 20
D1082 30f. multicoloured 25 25

APPENDIX

The following stamps have either been issued in excess of postal needs or have not been availble to the public in reasonable quantities at face value. Such stamps may later be given full listing if there is evidence of regular postal use.

All the stamps listed below are embossed on gold foil.

1977.

Coronation of Emperor Bokassa. Air 2500f.

1978.

100 Years of Progress in Posts and Telecommunications. Air 1500f.

Death Centenary of Sir Rowland Hill. Air 1500f.

1979.

International Year of the Child. Air 1500f.

Olympic Games, Moscow. Air 1500f. ("The Discus-thrower")

Space Exploration. Air 1500f.

1980.

Olympic Games, Moscow. Air 1500f. (Relay)

European-African Co-operation. Air 1500f.

World Cup Football Championship, Spain. Air 1500f.

1981.

Olympic Games Medal Winners. 1980 Olympic Games issue optd. Air 1500f.

Birth Centenary of Pablo Picasso. Air 1500f.

Wedding of Prince of Wales. Air 1500f.

Navigators. Air 1500f.

Christmas. Air 1500f.

1982.

Animals and Rotary International. Air 1500f.

Transport. Air 1500f.

21st Birthday of Princess of Wales. Air 1500f.

Olympic Games, Los Angeles.Air 1500f. (horiz)

Space Resources. Air 1500f.

1983.

Chess Masters. Air 1500f.

World Cup Football Championship, Spain. Air 1500f.

Car Manufacturers. Air 1500f.

Olympic Games, Los Angeles. Air 1500f. (vert)

Bicentenary of manned flight. Air 1500f.

1984.

Winter Olympic Gold Medalists. Air 1500f.

Celebrities. Air 1500f.

1985.

85th Birthday of Queen Elizabeth the Queen Mother. Air 1500f.

Appearence of Halley's Comet. Air 1500f.

480th Death Anniv of Christopher Columbus. Air 1500f.

1988.

Olympic Games, Seoul. Air 1500f.

Scouts and Birds. Air 1500f.

1989.

Olympic Games, Seoul, Gold Medal Winner. Air 1500f.

Bicentenary of French Revolution. Air 1500f.

World Cup Football Championship, Italy. Air 1500f.

1990.

Winter Olympic Games, Albertville (1992). Air 1500f.

Scouts and Butterflies. Air 1500f.

Birth Centenary of Charles de Gaulle. Air 1500f.

1993.

Wedding of Crown Prince Naruhito of Japan and Masako Owada. Air 1500f.

16th Death Anniv of Elvis Presley. Air 1500f.

World Cup Football Championship, U.S.A. (1994). Air 1500f.

Visit of Pope John Paul II to Africa. Air 1500f.

1994.

Winter Olympic Games, Lillehammer. Air 1500f.

CENTRAL LITHUANIA Pt. 10

Became temporarily independent in 1918 and was subsequently absorbed by Poland.

100 fenigi = 1 mark.

1 3 Girl

1920. Imperf or perf.

1 **1** 25f. red 10 10
20 25f. green 20 30
2 1m. blue 10 10
21 1m. brown 20 30
3 2m. violet 15 15
22 2m. yellow 20 30

1920. Stamps of Lithuania of 1919 surch **SRODKOWA LITWA POCZTA**, new value and Arms of Poland and Lithuania. Perf.

4 **5** 2m. on 15s. violet . . . . . 6·50 8·00
5 4m. on 10s. red . . . . . . 4·00 5·00
6 4m. on 20s. blue . . . . . . 6·00 8·00
7 4m. on 30s. orange . . . . . 5·00 6·00
8 **6** 6m. on 50s. green . . . . . 6·00 7·00
9 6m. on 60s. red and violet . . 6·00 7·00
10 6m. on 75s. red & yellow . . 6·00 8·00
11 **7** 10m. on 1a. red & grey . . . 12·00 14·00
12 10m. on 3a. red & brown . . £450 £550
13 10m. on 5a. red and green . . £450 £550

1920. Imperf or perf. Inscr "LITWA SRODKOWA".

14 **3** 25f. grey 15 15
15 – 1m. orange 20 15
16 – 2m. red 40 50
17 – 4m. olive and yellow 60 75
18 – 6m. grey and red . . . . . 1·00 1·25
19 – 10m. yellow and brown . . . 1·50 2·00

DESIGNS: 1m. Warrior; 2m. Ostrabrama Gate, Vilnius; 4m. St. Stanislaus Cathedral and Tower, Vilnius; 6m. Rector's insignia; 10m. Gen. Zeligowski.

1921. Fund for Polish Participation in Plebiscite for Upper Silesia. Surch **NA SLASK** and new value. Imperf or perf.

23 **1** 25f.+2m. red 50 60
24 25f.+2m. green 50 60
25 1m.+2m. blue 60 80
26 1m.+2m. brown 60 80
27 2m.+2m. violet . . . . . . 70 1·10
28 2m.+2m. yellow . . . . . . 70 1·10

1921. Red Cross Fund. Nos. 16/17 surch with cross and value. Imperf or perf.

29 2m.+1m. red 50 65
30 4m.+1m. green and yellow . . 50 65

1921. White Cross Fund. As Nos. 16, 17 and 19, but with cross and value in white added. Imperf or perf.

31 2m.+1m. purple 30 30
32 4m.+1m. green and buff . . . 30 30
33 10m.+2m. yellow and brown 30 30

13 St. Nicholas Cathedral **14** St. Stanislaus Cathedral

1921. Imperf or perf.

34 **13** 1m. yellow and slate 30 40
35 **14** 2m. green and red 30 40
36 – 3m. green 40 50
37 – 4m. brown 40 60
38 – 5m. brown 40 60
39 – 6m. buff and green 40 60
40 – 10m. buff and purple . . . 60 80
41 – 20m. buff and brown . . . 60 90

DESIGNS—HORIZ: 4m. Queen Jadwiga and King Wladislaw Jagiello; 6m. Poczobut Observatory, Vilnius University; 10m. Union of Lithuania and Poland, 1569; 20m. Kosciuszko and Mickiewicz. VERT: 3m. Arms (Eagle); 5m. Arms (Shield).

21 Entry into Vilnius **22** General Zeligowski

1921. Ist Anniv of Entry of Gen. Zeligowski into Vilnius. Imperf or perf.

42 **21** 100m. blue and bistre . . . 1·75 1·75
43 **22** 150m. green and brown . . 2·25 2·25

24 Arms

1922. Opening of National Parliament. Inscr "SEJM—WILNIE". Imperf or perf.

44 – 10m. brown . . . . 1·50 1·75
45 **24** 25m. red and buff . . . . . 1·75 1·90
46 – 50m. blue . . . . 2·75 3·00
47 – 75m. lilac . . . . 4·00 4·50

DESIGNS—HORIZ: 50m. National Assembly, Vilnius. VERT: 10m. Agriculture; 75m. Industry.

POSTAGE DUE STAMPS

D **9** Government Offices

1921. Inscr "DOPLATA". Imperf or perf.

D23 D **9** 50f. red 50 60
D24 – 1m. green 50 60
D25 – 2m. purple 50 60
D26 – 3m. purple 75 90
D27 – 5m. purple 75 90
D28 – 20m. red . . . . 1·00 1·25

DESIGNS—HORIZ: 2m. Castle on Troki Island. VERT: 1m. Castle Hill, Vilnius; 3m. Ostrabrama Gate, Vilnius; 5m. St. Stanislaus Cathedral; 20m. (larger) St. Nicholas Cathedral.

CEYLON Pt. 1

An island to the south of India formerly under British administration, then a self-governing Dominion. The island became a Republic within the Commonwealth on 22 May 1972 and was renamed Sri Lanka (q.v.).

1857. 12 pence = 1 shilling;
20 shillings = 1 pound.
1872. 100 cents = 1 rupee.

1

2

4

8

1857. Imperf.

17 **4** ½d. lilac £170 £180
2 **1** 1d. blue . . . . £650 28·00
3 2d. green . . . . £150 55·00
4 **2** 4d. red £50000 £4500
5 **1** 5d. brown £1500 £150
6 6d. brown £1800 £140
7 **2** 8d. brown £22000 £1500
8 9d. brown £32000 £900
9 **1** 10d. orange £800 £300
10 1s. violet £4500 £200
11 **2** 1s.9d. green £750 £800
12 2s. blue £5500 £1200

The prices of these imperf stamps vary greatly according to condition. The above prices are for fine copies with four margins. Poor to medium specimens are worth much less.

1861. Perf.

48c **4** ½d. lilac . . . . 27·00 28·00
49 **1** 1d. blue . . . . £100 4·50
50 2d. green . . . . 65·00 9·50
64b 2d. yellow . . . . 48·00 7·00
65b **2** 4d. red . . . . 50·00 13·00
22 **1** 5d. brown . . . . 80·00 8·00
66c 5d. green . . . . 30·00 45·00
67b 6d. brown . . . . 30·00 32·00
56 **2** 8d. brown . . . . 85·00 42·00
69b 9d. brown . . . . 42·00 6·00
70b **1** 10d. orange . . . . 45·00 11·00
71b 1s. violet . . . . 85·00 6·50
72b **2** 2s. blue . . . . £110 12·00

1866. The 3d. has portrait in circle.

61 **8** 1d. blue . . . . 20·00 8·00
62 – 3d. red . . . . 65·00 38·00

9

10

30

1872. Various frames.

256 **9** 2c. brown . . . . 2·50 30
147 2c. green . . . . 2·50 15
122 **10** 4c. grey . . . . 32·00 1·50
148 4c. purple . . . . 3·00 30
149 4c. red . . . . 3·75 11·00
258 4c. yellow . . . . 3·00 2·75
150a – 8c. yellow . . . . 3·50 7·00
126 – 16c. violet . . . . 80·00 2·75
127 – 24c. green . . . . 50·00 2·00
128 – 32c. grey . . . . £150 15·00
129 – 36c. blue . . . . £150 17·00
130 – 48c. red . . . . 70·00 5·00
131 – 64c. brown . . . . £250 60·00
132 – 90c. grey . . . . £190 26·00
201 **30** 1r.12 red . . . . 22·00 20·00

138 2r.50 red £450 £300
249 2r.50 purple on red 28·00 48·00

1882. Nos. 127 and 131 surch in words and figures.
142 16c. on 24c. green 23·00 6·50
143 20c. on 64c. brown 9·00 5·00

1885. As Nos. 148/132 surch **Postage & Revenue** and value in words.
178 5c. on 4c. red 19·00 3·50
179 5c. on 8c. yellow 60·00 7·00
180 5c. on 16c. violet 90·00 11·00
154 5c. on 24c. green £2500 £100
182 5c. on 24c. purple — £500
155 5c. on 32c. grey 55·00 15·00
156 5c. on 36c. blue £250 9·00
157 5c. on 48c. red £1000 55·00
158 5c. on 64c. brown 90·00 5·50
159 5c. on 96c. grey £425 65·00

1885. As Nos. 126/249 surch with new value in words.
184 10c. on 16c. violet £4750 £1000
162 10c. on 24c. green £450 £110
185 10c. on 24c. purple 13·00 6·00
163 10c. on 36c. blue £375 £170
174 10c. on 64c. brown 60·00 95·00
186 15c. on 16c. violet 10·00 7·00
165 20c. on 24c. green 55·00 18·00
166a 20c. on 32c. grey 60·00 45·00
167 25c. on 32c. grey 14·00 4·50
168 28c. on 48c. red 38·00 6·00
169x 30c. on 36c. blue 11·00 8·50
170 56c. on 96c. grey 23·00 18·00
176 1r.12 on 2r.50 red 90·00 42·00

1885. Surch **REVENUE AND POSTAGE 5 CENTS**.
187 5c. on 8c. lilac (as No. 150a) 15·00 1·40

1885. As Nos. 126/32 surch in words and figures.
188 10c. on 24c. purple 9·00 6·50
189 15c. on 16c. yellow 55·00 8·50
190 28c. on 32c. grey 22·00 2·50
191 30c. on 36c. olive 28·00 14·00
192 56c. on 96c. grey 48·00 14·00

1885. Surch **1 R. 12 C.**
193 **30** 1r.12 on 2r.50 red 38·00 80·00

39 **28**

43

1886.
245 **39** 3c. brown and green 3·25 45
257 3c. green 2·50 55
195 **28** 5c. purple 2·25 10
259 **39** 6c. red and black 1·50 45
260 12c. olive and red 4·00 7·00
196 15c. olive 4·75 1·25
261 15c. blue 5·50 1·25
198 25c. brown 3·75 1·00
199 28c. grey 17·00 1·40
247 30c. mauve and brown 4·25 2·00
262 75c. black and brown 4·75 6·00
263 **43** 1r.50 red 19·00 35·00
264 2r.25 blue 30·00 35·00

1887. Nos. 148/9 surch. A. Surch **TWO CENTS**.
202 **10** 2c. on 4c. purple 1·40 80
203 2c. on 4c. red 2·25 30

B. Surch **TWO**.
204 **10** 2c. on 4c. purple 75 30
205 2c. on 4c. red 4·75 20

C. Surch **2 Cents** and bar.
206 **10** 2c. on 4c. purple 60·00 28·00
207 2c. on 4c. red 2·25 75

D. Surch **Two Cents** and bar.
208 **10** 2c. on 4c. purple 45·00 18·00
209 2c. on 4c. red 2·50 1·10

E. Surch **2 Cents** without bar.
210 **10** 2c. on 4c. purple 45·00 26·00
211 2c. on 4c. red 10·00 1·00

1890. Surch **POSTAGE Five Cents REVENUE**.
233 **39** 5c. on 15c. olive 3·25 1·90

1891. Surch **FIFTEEN CENTS**.
239 **39** 15c. on 25c. brown 10·00 11·00
240 15c. on 28c. grey 14·00 8·50

1892. Surch **3 Cents** and bar.
241 **10** 3c. on 4c. purple 1·00 3·25
242 3c. on 4c. red 3·50 6·50
243 **39** 3c. on 28c. grey 3·75 3·25

1898. Surch **Six Cents**.
250 **39** 6c. on 15c. green 70 75

1898. Surch with new value.
254 **30** 1r.50 on 2r.50 grey 20·00 45·00
255 2r.25 on 2r.50 yellow 35·00 80·00

44 **45**

1903. Various frames.
277 **44** 2c. brown 1·50 10
278 **45** 3c. green (A) 1·50 15
293 3c. green (B) 1·00 75
279 4c. orange and blue 1·75 1·50
268 – 5c. purple 1·50 60
289 – 5c. purple 2·50 10
281 – 6c. red 1·25 15
291 – 6c. red 1·25 10
294 **45** 10c. olive and red 2·00 2·25
282 12c. olive and red 1·50 1·75
283 15c. blue 1·50 60
284 25c. brown 6·00 3·75
295 25c. grey 2·50 1·50
285 30c. violet and green 2·50 3·00
296 50c. brown 4·00 7·50
286 75c. blue and orange 5·25 8·00
297 1r. purple on yellow 7·50 10·00
287 1r.50 grey 24·00 10·00
298 2r. red on yellow 15·00 27·00
288 2r.25 brown and green 22·00 29·00
299 5r. black on green 38·00 65·00
300 10r. black on red 80·00 £170

(A) has value in shaded tablet; (B) in white tablet as in Type **45**.

Nos. 268 and 281 have the value in words; Nos. 289 and 291 in figures.

52 **57**

1912.
301 **52** 1c. brown 1·00 10
307a 2c. orange 30 20
339 3c. green 2·75 75
340 3c. grey 75 20
341 5c. purple 50 15
342 6c. red 2·00 75
343 6c. violet 1·00 15
345 9c. red on yellow 80 30
346 10c. olive 1·40 40
347a 12c. red 1·00 2·25
311a 15c. blue 1·75 1·25
349a 15c. green on yellow 1·50 1·00
350b 20c. blue 3·50 45
351 25c. yellow and blue 1·60 1·90
352a 30c. green and violet 2·75 1·25
353 50c. black and red 1·60 80
315 1r. purple on yellow 3·00 3·50
355 2r. black and red on yellow 7·00 7·50
317 5r. black on green 17·00 28·00
318 10r. purple & blk on red 60·00 80·00
319 20r. black and red on blue £110 £120

Large type, As Bermuda T **15**.
358 50r. purple £375
359 100r. black £1400
360 100r. purple and blue £1300

1918. Optd **WAR STAMP**, No. 335 surch **ONE CENT** and bar also.
335 **52** 1c. on 5c. purple 50 40
330 2c. orange 20 40
332 3c. green 20 50
333 5c. purple 50 30

1918. Surch **ONE CENT** and bar.
337 **52** 1c. on 5c. purple 15 25

1926. Surch with new value and bar.
361 **52** 2c. on 3c. grey 80 1·00
362 5c. on 6c. violet 50 40

1927.
363 **57** 1r. purple 2·50 1·25
364 2r. green and red 3·75 2·75
365 5r. green and purple 14·00 20·00
366 10r. green and orange 32·00 80·00
367 20r. purple and blue 95·00 £180

60 Adam's Peak

1935. King George V.
368 – 2c. black and red 30 40
369 **60** 3c. black and green 35 40
370 – 6c. black and blue 30 30
371 – 9c. green and orange 1·00 65
372 – 10c. black and purple 1·25 2·25
373 – 15c. brown and green 1·00 50
374 – 20c. black and blue 1·75 2·50
375 – 25c. blue and brown 1·40 1·25
376 – 30c. red and green 3·00 2·75
377 – 50c. black and violet 8·50 1·75
378 – 1r. violet and brown 17·00 16·00

DESIGNS—VERT: 2c. Tapping rubber; 6c. Colombo Harbour; 9c. Plucking tea; 20c. Coconut palms. HORIZ: 10c. Hill paddy (rice); 15c. River scene; 25c. Temple of the Tooth, Kandy; 30c. Ancient irrigation tank; 50c. Indian elephants; 1r. Trincomalee.

1935. Silver Jubilee. As T **13** of Antigua.
379 6c. blue and grey 65 30
380 9c. green and blue 70 1·25
381 20c. brown and blue 4·25 2·75
382 50c. grey and purple 5·25 9·00

1937. Coronation. As T **2** of Aden.
383 6c. red 65 15
384 9c. green 2·50 3·25
385 20c. blue 3·50 3·00

70 Sigiriya (Lion Rock)

1938. As 1935 issue but with portrait of King George VI, and "POSTAGE & REVENUE" omitted.
386b – 2c. black and red 2·00 10
387d **60** 3c. black and green 80 10
387f – 5c. green and orange 30 10
388 – 6c. black and blue 30 10
389 **70** 10c. black and blue 2·25 10
390 – 15c. green and brown 2·00 10
391 – 20c. black and blue 3·25 10
392a – 25c. blue and brown 4·25 10
393 – 30c. red and green 11·00 1·75
394e – 50c. black and violet 3·75 20
395 – 1r. blue and brown 16·00 1·25
396 – 2r. black and red 13·00 2·50
396b – 2r. black and violet 2·00 1·60

DESIGNS—VERT: 5c. Coconut palms; 20c. Plucking tea; 2r. Ancient guard-stone, Anuradhapura. Others, same as for corresponding values of 1935 issue.

1938. As T **57**, but head of King George VI to right.
397a 5r. green and purple 14·00 3·00

1940. Surch with new value and bars.
398 3c. on 6c. blk & bl (No. 388) 25 10
399 3c. on 20c. blk & bl (No. 391) 2·25 1·50

1946. Victory. As T **9** of Aden.
400 6c. blue 10 15
401 15c. brown 10 50

75 Parliament Building

1947. New Constitution.
402 **75** 6c. black and blue 10 15
403 – 10c. black, orange and red 15 20
404 – 15c. green and purple 15 80
405 – 25c. yellow and green 15 20

DESIGNS—VERT: 10c. Adam's Peak; 25c. Anuradhapura. HORIZ: 15c. Temple of the Tooth.

79 Lion Flag of Dominion

80 D. S. Senanayake

1949. 1st Anniv of Independence.
406 **79** 4c. red, yellow and brown 15 20
407 **80** 5c. brown and green 10 10
408 **79** 15c. red, yellow and orange 30 15
409 **80** 25c. brown and blue 15 65

No. 408 is larger, 28 × 22 mm.

82 Globe and Forms of Transport

1949. 75th Anniv of U.P.U. Inscr as in T **82**. Designs showing globe.
410 **82** 5c. brown and green 75 10
411 – 15c. black and red (horiz) 1·10 2·00
412 – 25c. black and blue (vert) 1·10 1·10

85 Kandyan Dancer

88 Sigiriya (Lion Rock)

90 Ruins at Madirigiriya

1950.
413 **85** 4c. purple and red 10 10
414 – 5c. green 10 10
415 – 15c. green and violet 1·50 30
416 **88** 30c. red and yellow 30 40
417 – 75c. blue and orange 4·00 10
418 **90** 1r. blue and brown 1·75 30

DESIGNS—VERT (As Types **85** and **88**): 5c. Kiri Vehera, Polonnaruwa; 15c. Vesak orchid. (As Type **90**): 75c. Octagon Library, Temple of the Tooth.

94 Coconut Trees

99 Tea Plantation

1951.
419 – 2c. brown and turquoise 10 1·00
420 – 3c. black and violet 10 1·00
421 – 6c. sepia and green 10 30
422 **94** 10c. green and grey 75 65
423 – 25c. orange and blue 10 20
424 – 35c. red and green 1·50 1·50
425 – 40c. brown 4·50 90
426 – 50c. slate 30 10
427 **99** 85c. black and turquoise 60 20
428 – 2r. blue and brown 6·50 1·25
429 – 5r. brown and orange 4·75 1·40
430 – 10r. brown and buff 35·00 9·50

DESIGNS—VERT (As Type **94**): 2c. Sambars, Ruhuna National Park; 3c. Ancient guardstone, Anuradhapura; 6c. Harvesting rice; 25c. Sigiriya fresco; 35c. Star orchid. (As Type **99**): 5r. Bas-relief, Anuradhapura; 10r. Harvesting rice. HORIZ (As Type **94**): 40c. Rubber plantation; 50c. Outrigger canoe. (As Type **99**): 2r. River Gal Dam.

103 Ceylon, Mace and Symbols of Progress

104 Queen Elizabeth II

1952. Colombo Plan Exhibition.
431 **103** 5c. green 10 10
432 15c. blue 30 60

1953. Coronation.
433 **104** 5c. green 1·25 10

105 Ceremonial Procession

106 King Coconuts

1954. Royal Visit.
434 **105** 10c. blue 50 10

1954.
435 **106** 10c. orange, brown and buff 10 10

107 Farm Produce

1955. Royal Agricultural and Food Exhibition.
436 **107** 10c. brown and orange 10 10

108 Sir John Kotelawala and House of Representatives

1956. Prime Minister's 25 Years of Public Service.
437 **108** 10c. green 10 10

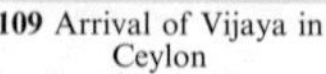

109 Arrival of Vijaya in Ceylon

110 Lampstand and Dharmachakra

1956. Buddha Jayanti. Inscr "2500".
438 **109** 3c. blue and grey 15 15
439 **110** 4c.+2c. yellow and blue 20 75
440 – 10c.+5c. red, yell & grey 20 75
441 – 15c. blue 25 10
DESIGNS—VERT: 10c. Hand of Peace and Dharmachakra. HORIZ: 15c. Dharmachakra encircling the globe.

113 Mail Transport

114 Stamp of 1857

1957. Stamp Centenary.
442 **113** 4c. red and turquoise . . 75 40
443 10c. red and blue 75 10
444 **114** 35c. brown, yellow and blue 30 50
445 85c. brown, yellow & grn 80 1·60

1958. Nos. 439/40 with premium obliterated with bars.
446 **110** 4c. yellow and blue . . . 10 10
447 – 10c. red, yellow and grey 10 10

117 Kandyan Dancwer

118 "Human Rights"

1958. As Nos. 413 and 419 etc, and 435, but with inscriptions changed as in T **117**.
448 2c. brown and turquoise . . 10 50
449 3c. black and violet 10 70
450 4c. purple and red 10 10
451 5c. green . . . . 10 1·60
452 6c. sepia and green 10 65
453 10c. orange, brown and buff 10 10
454 15c. green and violet . . . . 3·50 80
455 25c. orange and blue . . . 10 10
456 30c. red and yellow . . . . 15 1·40
457 35c. red and green . . . . 6·50 30
459 50c. slate 30 10
460a 75c. blue and orange . . . 9·00 2·25
461 85c. black and turquoise . . 3·75 4·75
462 1r. blue and brown 60 10
463 2r. blue and brown . . . . 1·00 30
464 5r. brown and orange . . . 4·50 30
465 10r. brown and buff . . . . 10·00 1·00

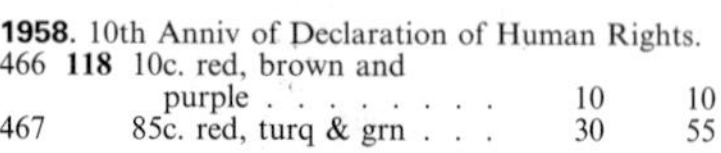

1958. 10th Anniv of Declaration of Human Rights.
466 **118** 10c. red, brown and purple 10 10
467 85c. red, turq & grn . . . 30 55

119 Portraits of Founders and University Buildings

1959. Institution of Pirivena Universities.
468 **119** 10c. orange and blue . . 10 10

120 "Uprooted Tree"

121 S. W. R. D. Bandaranaike

1960. World Refugee Year.
469 **120** 4c. brown and gold . . . 10 60
470 25c. violet and gold . . . 10 15

1961. Prime Minister Bandaranaike Commemoration.
471 **121** 10c. blue and turquoise 10 10
See also Nos. 479 and 481.

122 Ceylon Scout Badge

123 Campaign Emblem

1962. Golden Jubilee of Ceylon Boy Scouts Association
472 **122** 35.c buff and blue 15 10

1962. Malaria Eradication.
473 **123** 25c. red and drab 10 10

124 De Havilland Leopard Moth and Hawker Siddeley Comet 4

1963. 25th Anniv of Airmail Services.
474 **124** 50c. black and blue . . . 50 50

125 "Produce" and Campaign Emblem

2

(126)

1963. Freedom from Hunger.
475 **125** 5c. red and blue . . . . 30 2·00
476 25c. brown and olive . . 1·75 30

1963. No. 450 surch with T **126**.
477 2c. on 4c. purple and red . . 10 10

127 "Rural Life"

131 Anagarika Dharmapala (Buddhist missionary)

129 Terrain, Indian Elephant and Tree

1963. Golden Jubilee of Ceylon Co-operative Movement (1962).
478 **127** 60c. red and black 90 60

1963. Design as T **121**, but smaller (21 × 26 mm) and with inscription rearranged at top.
479 10c. blue 10 10
481 10c. violet and grey 10 10
No. 481 has a decorative pattern at foot instead of the inscription.

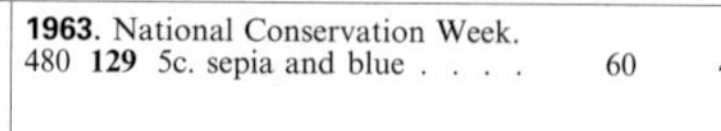

1963. National Conservation Week.
480 **129** 5c. sepia and blue 60 40

1964. Birth Centenary of A. Dharmapala (founder of Maha Bodhi Society)
482 **131** 25c. sepia and yellow . . 10 10

135 D. S. Senanayake

143 Ceylon Jungle Fowl

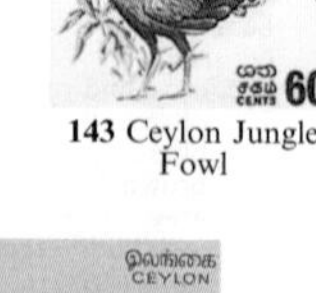

138 Ruins at Madirigiriya

1964.
485 – 5c. multicoloured . . . . 2·00 1·50
486 **135** 10c. green 80 10
487 – 10c. green 10 10
488 – 15c. multicoloured . . . . 3·00 30
489 **138** 20c. purple and buff . . . 20 25
494 **143** 60c. multicoloured . . . . 4·00 1·25
495 – 75c. multicoloured . . . . 2·75 70
497 – 1r. brown and green . . . 1·00 30
499 – 5r. multicoloured . . . . 5·00 4·50
500 – 10r. multicoloured . . . . 19·00 3·50
MS500a 148 × 174 mm. As Nos. 485, 488, 494 and 495 (imperf) 7·00 12·00
DESIGNS—HORIZ (As Type **143**): 5c. Southern grackle ("Grackle"); 15c. Common peafowl ("Peacock"); 75c. Asian black-headed oriole ("Oriole"). (As Type **138**): 5r. Girls transplanting rice. VERT (As Type **135**): 10c. (No. 487) Similar portrait, but large head and smaller inscriptions. (21 × 35 mm): 1r. Tea plantation. (23 × 36 mm): 10r. Map of Ceylon.

150 Exhibition Buildings and Cogwheels

1964. Industrial Exhibition.
501 – 5c. multicoloured 10 75
502 **150** 5c. multicoloured 10 75
No. 501 is inscribed "INDUSTRIAL EXHIBITION" in Sinhala and Tamil, No. 502 in Sinhala and English.

151 Trains of 1864 and 1964

1964. Centenary of Ceylon Railways.
503 – 60c. blue, purple and green . . . . 2·75 40
504 **151** 60c. blue, purple and green . . . . 2·75 40
No. 503 is inscribed "RAILWAY CENTENARY" in Sinhala and Tamil, No. 504 in Sinhala and English.

152 I.T.U. Emblem and Symbols

1965. Centenary of I.T.U.
505 **152** 2c. blue and red . . . . 1·00 1·10
506 30c. brown and red . . . 3·00 45

153 I.C.Y. Emblem

1965. International Co-operation Year.
507 **153** 3c. blue and red . . . . 1·25 1·00
508 50c. black, red and gold 3·25 50

154 Town Hall, Colombo

1965. Centenary of Colombo Municipal Council.
509 **154** 25c. green and sepia . . . 20 20

1965. No. 481 surch **5**.
510 5c. on 10c. violet and grey . . 10 40

157 Kandy and Council Crest

1966. Centenary of Kandy Municipal Council.
512 **157** 25c. multicoloured 20 20

158 W.H.O. Building

159 Rice Paddy and Map of Ceylon

1966. Inauguration of W.H.O. Headquarters, Geneva.
513 **158** 4c. multicoloured . . . . 1·75 3·00
514 1r. multicoloured . . . . 6·75 1·50

1966. International Rice Year. Multicoloured.
515 6c. Type **159** 20 75
516 30c. Rice paddy and globe 30 15

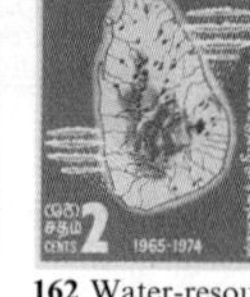

161 U.N.E.S.C.O. Emblem

162 Water-resources Map

1966. 20th Anniv of U.N.E.S.C.O.
517 **161** 3c. multicoloured . . . . 2·00 2·75
518 50c. multicoloured . . . . 5·50 30

1966. International Hydrological Decade.
519 **162** 2c. brown, yellow and blue 30 85
520 2r. multicoloured . . . . 1·50 2·25

163 Devotees at Buddhist Temple

1967. Poya Holiday System. Multicoloured.
521 5c. Type **163** 15 60
522 20c. Mihintale 15 10
523 35c. Sacred Bo-tree, Anuradhapura 15 15
524 60c. Adam's Peak 15 10

167 Galle Fort and Clock Tower

1967. Centenary of Galle Municipal Council.
525 **167** 25c. multicoloured 70 20

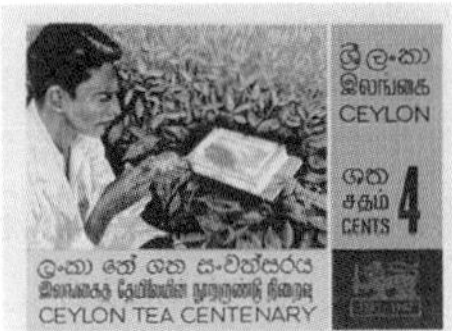

168 Field Research

1967. Centenary of Ceylon Tea Industry. Mult.
526 4c. Type **168** 60 80
527 40c. Tea-tasting equipment 1·75 1·50
528 50c. Leaves and bud . . . . 1·75 20
529 1r. Shipping tea . . . . . . 1·75 10

172 Elephant Ride

1967. International Tourist Year.
530 **172** 45c. multicoloured . . . . 2·25 80

1967. 1st National Stamp Exhibition. No. **MS**500a optd "**FIRST NATIONAL STAMP EXHIBITION 1967**".
MS531 148 × 174 mm. Nos. 485, 488, 494/5. Imperf 5·50 6·00

173 Ranger, Jubilee Emblem and Flag

1967. Golden Jubilee of Ceylon Girl Guides' Association.
532 **173** 3c. multicoloured 50 20
533 25c. multicoloured 75 10

174 Colonel Olcott and Buddhist Flag

1967. 60th Death Anniv of Colonel Olcott (theosophist).
534 **174** 15c. multicoloured 30 20

175 Independence Hall **177** Sir D. B. Jayatilleke

1968. 20th Anniv of Independence. Multicoloured.
535 5c. Type **175** 10 55
536 1r. Lion flag and sceptre . . 50 10

1968. Birth Centenary of Sir Baron Jayatilleke (scholar and statesman).
537 **177** 25c. brown 10 10

178 Institute of Hygiene

1968. 20th Anniv of World Health Organization.
538 **178** 50c. multicoloured 10 10

179 Vickers Super VC-10 over Terminal Building

1968. Opening of Colombo Airport.
539 **179** 60c. multicoloured 60 10

181 Open Koran and "1400"

1968. 1400th Anniv of Koran.
541 **181** 25c. multicoloured 10 10

182 Human Rights Emblem

1968. Human Rights Year.
542 **182** 2c. multicoloured 10 15
543 20c. multicoloured 10 10
544 40c. multicoloured 10 10
545 2r. multicoloured . . . . 70 3·25

183 All-Ceylon Buddhist Congress Headquarters

1968. Golden Jubilee of All-Ceylon Buddhist Congress.
546 **183** 5c. multicoloured 10 50

184 E. W. Perera (patriot) **185** Symbols of Strength in Savings

1969. Perera Commemoration.
547 **184** 60c. brown 10 30

1969. Silver Jubilee of National Savings Movement.
548 **185** 3c. multicoloured 10 10

186 Seat of Enlightenment under Sacred Bodhi Tree **188** A. E. Goonesinghe

1969. Vesak Day. Inscr "Wesak".
549 **186** 4c. multicoloured 10 50
550 – 6c. multicoloured 10 50
551 **186** 35c. multicoloured 10 10
DESIGN: 6c. Buduresmala (six-fold Buddha-rays).

1969. Goonesinghe Commemoration.
552 **188** 15c. multicoloured 10 10

189 I.L.O. Emblem

1969. 50th Anniv of I.L.O.
553 **189** 5c. black and blue 10 10
554 25c. black and red 10 10

190 Convocation Hall, University of Ceylon **194** Ath Pana (Elephant Lamp)

1969. Educational Centenary. Multicoloured.
555 4c. Type **190** 10 80
556 35c. Lamp of learning, globe and flags (horiz) 20 10
557 50c. Uranium atom 20 10
558 60c. Symbols of scientific education 30 10

1969. Archaeological Centenary. Multicoloured.
559 6c. Type **194** . . . . 25 1·50
560 1r. Rock fortress of Sigiriya 25 10

196 Leopard

1970. Wild Life Conservation. Multicoloured.
561 5c. Water buffalo . . . . . 50 1·25
562 15c. Slender loris . . . . . . 1·00 30
563 50c. Spotted deer . . . . . . 1·00 1·25
564 1r. Type **196** . . . . 1·00 1·75

197 Emblem and Symbols

1970. Asian Productivity Year.
565 **197** 60c. multicoloured 10 10

198 New U.P.U. H.Q. Building **199** Oil Lamp and Caduceus

1970. New U.P.U. Headquarters Building.
566 **198** 50c. orange, black and blue 20 10
567 1r.10 red, black and blue 3·00 30

1970. Centenary of Colombo Medical School.
568 **199** 5c. multicoloured 40 80
569 45c. multicoloured 40 60

200 Victory March and S. W. R. D. Bandaranaike

1970. Establishment of United Front Government.
570 **200** 10c. multicoloured 10 10

201 U.N. Emblem and Dove of Peace **202** Keppetipola Dissawa

1970. 25th Anniv of United Nations.
571 **201** 2r. multicoloured . . . . 2·00 3·25

1970. 152nd Death Anniv of Keppetipola Dissawa (Kandyan patriot).
572 **202** 25c. multicoloured 10 10

203 Ola Leaf Manuscript

1970. International Education Year.
573 **203** 15c. multicoloured . . . . 2·00 1·25

204 C. H. de Soysa **205** D. E. H. Pedris (patriot)

1971. 135th Birth Anniv of C. H. de Soysa (philanthropist)
574 **204** 20c. multicoloured 15 50

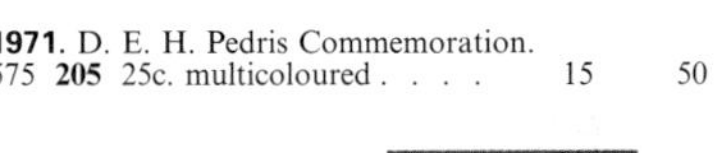

1971. D. E. H. Pedris Commemoration.
575 **205** 25c. multicoloured 15 50

206 Lenin **207** Ananda Rajakaruna

1971. Lenin Commemoration.
576 **206** 40c. multicoloured 15 50

1971. Poets and Philosophers.
577 **207** 5c. blue 10 15
578 – 5c. brown 10 15
579 – 5c. orange 10 15
580 – 5c. blue 10 15
581 – 5c. brown 10 15
PORTRAITS: No. 578, Arumuga Navalar; 579, Rev. S. Mahinda; 580, Ananda Coomaraswamy; 581, Cumaratunga Munidasa.

1971. Surch in figures.
582 **186** 5c. on 4c. multicoloured 6·00 1·75
583 **190** 5c. on 4c. multicoloured 10 1·25
584 **200** 15c. on 10c. multicoloured 10 30
585 – 25c. on 6c. mult (No. 550) 30 60
586 **194** 25c. on 6c. multicoloured 30 1·75

209 Colombo Plan Emblem and Ceylon

1971. 20th Anniv of Colombo Plan.
587 **209** 20c. multicoloured 15 30

210 Globe and C.A.R.E. Package

1971. 20th Anniv of Co-operative for American Relief Everywhere.
588 **210** 50c. blue, violet and lilac 35 30

211 W.H.O. Emblem and Heart

1972. World Health Day.
589 **211** 25c. multicoloured . . . . 2·25 60

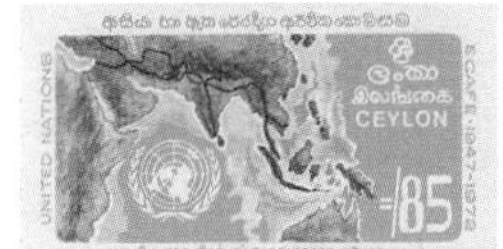

212 Map of Asia and U.N. Emblem

1972. 25th Anniv of E.C.A.F.E.
590 **212** 85c. multicoloured . . . . 4·50 2·75

OFFICIAL STAMPS

1895. Stamps of Queen Victoria optd **On Service.**
O 1 **9** 2c. green . . . . 8·00 45
O 8 2c. brown . . . . 7·00 60
O 2 **39** 3c. brown and green . . . 10·00 80
O 9 3c. green . . . . 8·00 2·00
O 3 **28** 5c. purple . . . . 3·25 30
O 4 **39** 15c. olive . . . . 12·00 50
O10 15c. blue . . . . 16·00 60
O 5 25c. brown . . . . 10·00 1·75
O 6 30c. mauve and brown . . 13·00 60
O11 75c. black and brown . . 5·50 6·50
O 7 **30** 1r.12 red . . . . 75·00 55·00

1903. Stamps of King Edward VII optd **On Service.**
O12 **44** 2c. brown . . . . 12·00 1·00
O13 **45** 3c. green . . . . 7·00 2·00
O14 – 5c. purple (No. 268) . . . 18·00 1·50
O15 **45** 15c. blue . . . . 27·00 2·50
O16 25c. brown . . . . 21·00 18·00
O17 30c. violet and green . . . 11·00 1·50

For later issues see **SRI LANKA**.

CHAD Pt. 6; Pt. 12

Formerly a dependency of Ubangi-Shari. Became one of the separate colonies of Fr. Equatorial Africa in 1937. In 1958 became a republic within the French Community.

100 centimes = 1 franc.

1922. Stamps of Middle Congo, colours changed, optd **TCHAD**.
1 **1** 1c. pink and violet . . . . . 50 2·75
2 2c. brown and pink . . . . 90 2·75
3 4c. blue and violet . . . . . 1·75 3·00
4 5c. brown and green . . . . 1·90 3·25
5 10c. green and turquoise . . 3·25 3·75
6 15c. violet and pink . . . . 3·25 4·00
7 20c. green and violet . . . . 5·75 7·50
8 **2** 25c. brown and chocolate . . 10·00 13·50
9 30c. red . . . . 2·50 3·25
10 35c. blue and pink . . . . . 3·25 4·25
11 40c. brown and green . . . . 3·50 4·50
12 45c. violet and green . . . . 3·75 4·50
13 50c. blue and light blue . . . 2·50 4·50
14 60 on 75c. violet on pink . . 4·75 6·50
15 75c. pink and violet . . . . 3·75 4·25
16 **3** 1f. blue and pink . . . . . . 13·50 16·00
17 2f. blue and violet . . . . . 19·00 24·00
18 5f. blue and brown . . . . . 16·00 22·00

1924. Stamps of 1922 and similar stamps further optd **AFRIQUE EQUATORIALE FRANCAISE**.
19 **1** 1c. pink and violet . . . . . 25 2·50
20 2c. brown and pink . . . . 15 2·25
21 4c. blue and violet . . . . . 15 2·25
22 5c. brown and green . . . . 50 2·50
23 10c. green and turquoise . . 2·00 2·75
24 10c. red and grey . . . . . 80 2·50
25 15c. violet and red . . . . . 60 2·25
26 20c. green and violet . . . . 1·75 2·50
27 **2** 25c. brown and chocolate . . 1·60 2·50
28 30c. red . . . . 85 2·50
29 30c. grey and blue . . . . . 65 2·25
30 30c. olive and green . . . . 2·00 3·00
31 35c. blue and pink . . . . . 75 2·50
32 40c. brown and green . . . . 2·00 2·50
33 45c. violet and green . . . . 1·60 2·75
34 50c. blue and light blue . . . 85 2·75
35 50c. green and purple . . . . 2·50 1·75
36 60 on 75c. violet on pink . . 40 2·75
37 65c. brown and blue . . . . 3·50 4·25
38 75c. pink and violet . . . . 1·00 2·75
39 75c. blue and light blue . . . 2·00 2·50
40 75c. purple and brown . . . 3·25 4·00
41 90c. carmine and red . . . . 5·00 10·00
42 **3** 1f. blue and pink . . . . . . 2·50 2·50
43 1f.10 green and blue . . . . 3·00 4·25
44 1f.25 brown and blue . . . . 7·75 11·50
45 1f.50 ultramarine and blue 4·75 11·50
46 1f.75 brown and mauve . . . 50·00 60·00
47 2f. blue and violet . . . . . 3·25 3·75
48 3f. mauve on pink . . . . . 7·50 15·00
49 5f. blue and brown . . . . . 3·75 4·25

1925. Stamps of Middle Congo optd **TCHAD** and **AFRIQUE EQUATORIALE FRANCAISE** and surch also.
50 **3** 65 on 1f. brown and green 2·25 3·50
51 85 on 1f. brown and green 2·50 3·50
52 **2** 90 on 75c. red and pink . . 2·75 3·50
53 **3** 1f.25 on 1f. blue & ultram 1·50 3·00
54 1f.50 on 1f. blue & ultram 2·75 3·50
55 3f. on 5f. brown and red . . 3·75 6·00
56 10f. on 5f. green and red . . 12·00 14·50
57a 20f. on 5f. violet & orange 19·00 19·00

1931. "Colonial Exhibition" key-types inscr "TCHAD".
58 E 40c. green . . . . 4·00 7·00
59 F 50c. mauve . . . . 4·50 7·00
60 G 90c. red . . . . 3·50 5·50
61 H 1f.50 blue . . . . 4·50 6·50

2 "Birth of the Republic"

3 Flag, Map and U.N. Emblem

1959. 1st Anniv of Republic.
62 **2** 15f. multicoloured . . . . . 3·00 1·10
63 – 25f. lake and myrtle 80 75
DESIGN: 25f. Map and birds.

1960. 10th African Technical Co-operation Commission. As T **62** of Cameroun.
64 50f. violet and purple . . . . 1·60 1·75

1960. Air. Olympic Games. No. 276 of French Equatorial Africa surch with Olympic rings and **XVIIe OLYMPIADE 1960 REPUBLIQUE DU TCHAD 250F**.
65 250f. on 500f. blue, black & grn . . . . 9·50 9·50

1961. Admission into U.N.
66 **3** 15f. multicoloured 45 20
67 25f. multicoloured 50 25
68 85f. multicoloured . . . . . 1·60 80

4 Shari Bridge and Hippopotamus

1961.
69 – 50c. green and black 10 10
70 – 1f. green and black 10 10
71 – 2f. brown and black 10 10
72 – 3f. orange and green 10 10
73 – 4f. red and black 10 10
74 **4** 5f. lemon and black 20 15
75 – 10f. pink and black 20 20
76 – 15f. violet and black 45 20
77 – 20f. red and black 55 30
78 – 25f. blue and black 60 30
79 – 30f. blue and black 70 45
80 – 60f. yellow and black . . . . 1·40 65
81 – 85f. orange and black . . . . 1·60 95
DESIGNS (with animal silhouettes)—VERT: 50c. Biltine and Dorcas gazelle; 1f. Logone and elephant; 2f. Batha and lion; 3f. Salamat and buffalo; 4f. Ouaddai and greater kudu; 10f. Abtouyour and bullock; 15f. Bessada and Derby's eland; 20f. Tibesti and moufflon; 25f. Tikem Rocks and hartebeest; 30f. Kanem and cheetah; 60f. Borkou and oryx; 85f. Guelta D'Archei and addax.

5 Red Bishops

1961. Air.
82 **5** 50f. black, red and green . . 3·00 1·10
83 – 100f. multicoloured . . . . . 6·75 2·00
84 – 200f. multicoloured . . . . . 12·00 3·75
85 – 250f. blue, orange and green 15·00 5·25
86 – 500f. multicoloured . . . . . 30·00 11·00
BIRDS: 100f. Scarlet-chested sunbird; 200f. African paradise flycatcher; 250f. Malachite kingfisher; 500f. Carmine bee eater.

1962. Air. "Air Afrique" Airline. As T **69** of Cameroun.
87 25f. blue, brown and black . . 60 25

1962. Malaria Eradication. As T **70** of Cameroun.
88 25f.+5f. orange 75 75

1962. Sports. As T **12** of Central African Republic. Multicoloured.
89 20f. Relay-racing (horiz) (postage) 45 30
90 50f. High-jumping (horiz) . . 1·10 55
91 100f. Throwing the discus (air) 2·50 1·25
The 100f. is 26 × 47 mm.

1962. 1st Anniv of Union of African and Malagasy States. As No. 328 of Cameroun.
92 **72** 30f. blue 70 40

1963. Freedom from Hunger. As T **76** of Cameroun.
93 25f.+5f. blue, brown & green 80 80

6 Pres. Tombalbaye

7 Carved Thread-weight

1963.
94 **6** 20f. multicoloured 45 20
95 85f. multicoloured . . . . . 1·10 55

1963. Air. African and Malagasy Posts and Telecommunications Union. As T **11** of Central African Republic.
96 85f. multicoloured . . . . . . 1·25 55

1963. Space Telecommunications, As Nos. 37/8 of Central African Republic.
97 25f. violet, emerald and green 50 35
98 100f. blue and pink . . . . . 2·00 1·25

1963. Air. 1st Anniv of "Air Afrique" and Inauguration of "DC-8" Service. As T **11** of Congo Republic.
99 50f. multicoloured . . . . . . 1·50 75

1963. Air. European–African Economic Convention. As T **24** of Central African Republic.
100 50f. multicoloured . . . . . 1·00 60

1963. Sao Art.
101 **7** 5f. orange and turquoise . . 10 10
102 – 15f. purple, slate and red . . 30 25
103 – 25f. brown and blue 60 35
104 – 60f. bronze and brown . . . 1·40 60
105 – 80f. bronze and brown . . . 1·60 80
DESIGNS: 15f. Ancestral mask; 25f. Ancestral statuette; 60f. Gazelle's-head pendant; 80f. Pectoral.

1963. 15th Anniv of Declaration of Human Rights. As Central African Republic T **26**.
106 25f. purple and green 65 35

8 Broussard Monoplane

1963. Air.
107 **8** 100f. blue, green & brown 2·25 1·25

9 Pottery

1964. Sao Handicrafts.
108 **9** 10f. black, orange & blue 30 20
109 – 30f. red, black and yellow 55 30
110 – 50f. black, red and green . . 1·00 45
111 – 85f. black, yellow & purple 1·25 65
DESIGNS: 30f. Canoe-building; 50f. Carpet-weaving; 85f. Blacksmith working iron.

10 Rameses II in War Chariot, Abu Simbel

1964. Air. Nubian Monuments Preservation Fund.
112 **10** 10f.+5f. violet, grn & red 60 35
113 25f.+5f. purple, grn & red 95 50
114 50f.+5f. turq, grn & red . . 1·90 1·40

1964. World Meteorological Day. As T **14** of Congo Republic.
115 50f. violet, blue and purple 1·00 50

11 Cotton

1964. Multicoloured.
116 20f. Type **11** 95 50
117 25f. Flamboyant tree . . . . 1·10 55

1964. Air. 5th Anniv of Equatorial African Heads of State Conf. As T **31** of Central African Republic.
118 100f. multicoloured . . . . . 1·50 75

12 Globe, Chimneys and Ears of Wheat

1964. Air. Europafrique.
119 **12** 50f. orange, purple & brn 1·00 55

13 Football

1964. Air. Olympic Games. Tokyo.
120 **13** 25f. green, lt green & brn 75 45
121 – 50f. brown, indigo & blue 1·00 55
122 – 100f. black, green and red 2·00 1·10
123 – 200f. black, bistre and red 4·25 2·10
DESIGNS—VERT: 50f. Throwing the javelin; 100f. High-jumping. HORIZ: 200f. Running.

1964. Air. Pan-African and Malagasy Post and Telecommunications Congress, Cairo. As T **23** of Congo Republic.
124 25f. sepia, red and mauve . . 60 25

1964. French, African and Malagasy Co-operation. As T **88** of Cameroun.
125 25f. brown, blue and red . . 60 30

14 Pres. Kennedy

15 National Guard

1964. Air. Pres. Kennedy Commem.
126 **14** 100f. multicoloured . . . . 1·75 1·10

1964. Chad Army. Multicoloured.
127 20f. Type **15** 50 20
128 25f. Standard-bearer and troops of Land Forces . . 55 25

16 Barbary Sheep

1964. Fauna. Protection. Multicoloured.
129 5f. Type **16** 25 15
130 10f. Addax 35 20
131 20f. Scimitar oryx 65 30
132 25f. Giant eland (vert) 95 35
133 30f. Giraffe, African buffalo and lion (Zakouma Park)(vert) . . . . 1·25 50
134 85f. Greater kudu (vert) . . . 3·00 1·10

17 Perforator of Olsen's Telegraph Apparatus

1965. I.T.U. Centenary.
135 **17** 30f. brown, red and green 55 25
136 – 60f. green, red and brown 1·00 45
137 – 100f. green, brown & red 1·90 80
DESIGNS—VERT: 60f. Milde's telephone. HORIZ: 100f. Distributor of Baudot's telegraph apparatus.

18 Badge and Mobile Gendarmes

1965. National Gendarmerie.
138 **18** 25f. multicoloured 60 35

19 I.C.Y. Emblem

1965. Air. International Co-operation Year.
139 **19** 100f. multicoloured . . . . 1·25 70

20 Abraham Lincoln

1965. Air. Death Centenary of Abraham Lincoln.
140 **20** 100f. multicoloured . . . . 1·75 75

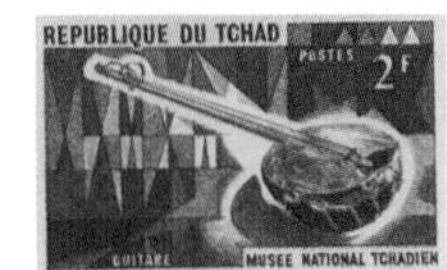

21 Guitar

1965. Native Musical Instruments.
141 – 1f. brown & grn (postage) 10 10
142 **21** 2f. brown, purple and red 10 10
143 – 3f. lake, black and brown 20 15
144 – 15f. green, orange and red 50 25
145 – 60f. green and lake . . . . 1·60 80

146 – 100f. ultram, brn & bl (48½ × 27 mm) (air) . . . 1·90 1·25
DESIGNS—VERT: 1f. Drum and seat; 3f. Shoulder drum; 60f. Harp. HORIZ: 15f. Viol; 100f. Xylophone.

22 Sir Winston Churchill

1965. Air. Churchill Commemoration.
147 **22** 50f. black and green . . . 1·00 50

23 Dr. Albert Schweitzer (philosopher and missionary) and "Appealing Hands"

1966. Air. Schweitzer Commemoration.
148 **23** 100f. multicoloured . . . . 1·90 95

24 Mask in Mortar **26** W.H.O. Building

1966. World Festival of Negro Arts, Dakar.
149 **24** 15f. purple, bistre & blue 35 20
150 – 20f. brown, red and green 50 25
151 – 60f. purple, blue and red 1·40 55
152 – 80f. green, brown & violet 2·10 85

DESIGNS—Sao Art: 20f. Mask; 60f. Mask (different) (All from J. Courtin's excavations at Bouta Kebira); 80f. Armband (from I.N.T.S.H. excavations, Gawi).

1966. No. 94 surch.
153 **6** 25f. on 20f. multicoloured 60 30

1966. Inaug of W.H.O. Headquarters, Geneva.
154 **26** 25f. blue, yellow and red 45 20
155 32f. blue, yellow & green 50 25

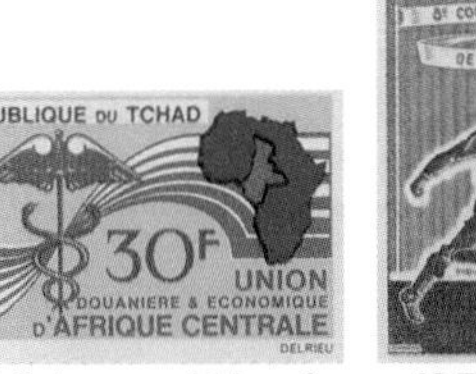

27 Caduceus and Map of Africa **28** Footballer

1966. Central African Customs and Economic Union.
156 **27** 30f. multicoloured 60 30

1966. World Cup Football Championship.
157 **28** 30f. red, green and emerald 50 25
158 – 60f. red, black and blue . . 1·25 50
DESIGN—VERT: 60f. Footballer (different).

29 Youths, Flag and Arms

1966. Youth Movement.
159 **29** 25f. multicoloured 60 30

30 Columns **31** Skull of Lake Chad Man ("Tchadanthropus uxoris")

1966. 20th Anniv of U.N.E.S.C.O.
160 **30** 32f. blue, violet and red . . 65 50

1966. Air. Inauguration of "DC-8" Air Services. As T **54** of Central African Republic.
161 30f. grey, black and green . . 60 25

1966. Archaeological Excavation.
162 **31** 30f. slate, yellow and red 1·60 75

32 White-throated Bee Eater

1966. Air. Birds. Multicoloured.
163 50f. Greater blue-eared glossy starling . . . . 3·50 1·40
164 100f. Type **32** . . . . 4·50 2·40
165 200f. African pigmy kingfisher . . . . 8·50 2·50
166 250f. Red-throated bee eater 12·50 3·25
167 500f. Little green bee eater 18·00 7·00

33 Battle-axe **35** Sportsmen and Dais on Map

34 Congress Palace

1966. Prehistoric Implements.
168 **33** 25f. brown, blue and red 35 25
169 – 30f. black, brown & blue 45 25
170 – 85f. brown, red and blue 1·50 60
171 – 100f. brown, turq & sepia 1·75 85
DESIGNS: 30f. Arrowhead; 85f. Harpoon; 100f. Sandstone grindstone and pounder. From Tchad National Museum.

1967. Air.
173 **34** 25f. multicoloured 55 25

1967. Sports Day.
174 **35** 25f. multicoloured 60 35

36 "Colotis protomedia klug"

1967. Butterflies. Multicoloured.
175 5f. Type **36** 20 15
176 10f. "Charaxes jasius epijasius L" 35 20
177 20f. "Junonia cebrene trim" 1·00 50
178 130f. "Danaida petiverana H.D." . . . . 3·25 1·40

37 Lions Emblem **39** H.Q. Building

38 Dagnaux's Breguet "19" Aircraft

1967. Air. 50th Anniv of Lions International.
179 **37** 50f.+10f. multicoloured . . 1·25 65

1967. Air. 1st Anniv of Air Chad Airline.
180 **38** 25f. green, blue & brown 55 40
181 – 30f. indigo, green and blue 75 40
182 – 50f. brown, green & blue 1·25 75
183 – 100f. red, blue and green 2·50 1·10
DESIGNS: 30f. Latecoere "631" flying-boat; 50f. Douglas "DC-3"; 100f. Piper Cherokee "6".

1967. Air. 5th Anniv of U.A.M.P.T. As T **66** of Central African Republic.
184 100f. brown, bistre & mve . . 1·25 75

1967. Opening of W.H.O. Regional Headquarters, Brazzaville.
185 **39** 30f. multicoloured 60 30

40 Scouts and Jamboree Emblem

1967. World Scout Jamboree, Idaho. Multicoloured.
186 25f. Type **40** 45 20
187 32f. Scout and Jamboree emblem 65 25

41 Flour Mills

1967. Economic Development.
188 **41** 25f. slate, brown and blue 45 20
189 – 30f. blue, brown & green 55 30
DESIGN: 30f. Land reclamation, Lake Bol.

42 Woman and Harpist **43** Emblem of Rotary International

1967. Bailloud Mission in the Ennedi. Rock paintings.
190 – 2f. choc, brn & red (post) 20 15
191 – 10f. red, brown and violet 45 25
192 **42** 15f. lake, brown and blue 55 25
193 – 20f. red, brown and green 1·25 50
194 – 25f. red, brown and blue 1·60 60
195 – 30f. lake, brown and blue 1·00 50
196 – 50f. lake, brown and green 1·90 80

197 – 100f. red, brn & grn (air) 3·00 1·40
198 – 125f. lake, brown & blue 4·25 2·10
DESIGNS: 2f. Archers; 10f. Male and female costumes; 20f. Funeral vigil; 25f. "Dispute"; 30f. Giraffes; 50f. Cameleer pursuing ostrich. (48 × 27 mm): 100f. Masked dancers; 125f. Hunters and hare.

1968. 10th Anniv of Rotary Club, Fort Lamy.
199 **43** 50f. multicoloured 95 45

44 Downhill Skiing

1968. Air. Winter Olympic Games, Grenoble.
200 **44** 30f. brown, green & purple 95 35
201 – 100f. blue, green & turq . . 2·50 1·10
DESIGN—VERT: 100f. Ski-jumping.

45 Chancellor Adenauer **46** "Health Services"

1968. Air. Adenauer Commemoration.
202 **45** 52f. brown, lilac and green 1·00 50

1968. Air. Anniv of W.H.O.
204 **46** 25f. multicoloured 45 20
205 32f. multicoloured 55 25

47 Allegory of Irrigation

1968. International Hydrological Decade.
206 **47** 50f. blue, brown & green 75 30

48 "The Snake-charmer"

1968. Air. Paintings by Henri Rousseau. Mult.
207 100f. Type **48** . . . . 2·50 1·60
208 130f. "The War" (49 × 35 mm) . . . . . . 3·75 2·25

49 College Building, Student and Emblem

1968. National College of Administration.

209 **49** 25f. purple, blue and red 45 25

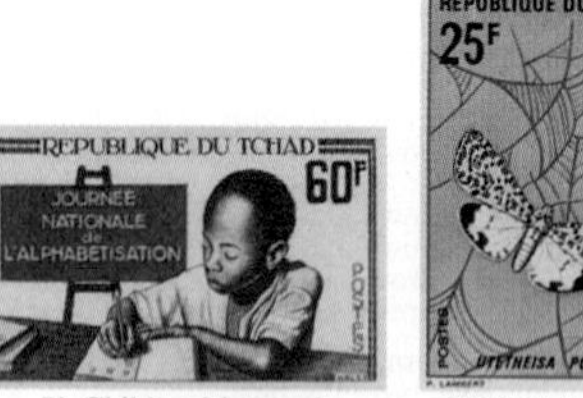

50 Child writing and Blackboard

52 "Utetheisa pulchella"

51 Harvesting Cotton

1968. Literacy Day.

210 **50** 60f. black, blue & brown 80 35

1968. Cotton Industry.

211 **51** 25f. purple, green & blue 50 20

212 – 30f. brown, blue & green 50 20

DESIGN—VERT: 30f. Loom, Fort Archambault Mill.

1968. Butterflies and Moths. Multicoloured.

213 25f. Type **52** 1·10 35

214 30f. "Ophideres materna" 1·40 35

215 50f. "Gynanisa maja" 2·75 70

216 100f. "Epiphora bauhiniae" 3·75 1·25

53 Hurdling

1968. Air. Olympic Games, Mexico.

217 **53** 32f. chocolate, grn & brn 80 50

218 – 80f. purple, blue and red 1·75 75

DESIGN: 80f. Relay-racing.

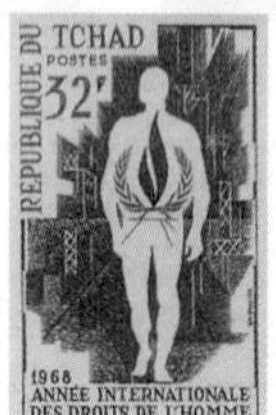

54 Human Rights Emblem within Man

1968. Human Rights Year.

219 **54** 32f. red, green and blue 60 25

1969. Air. "Philexafrique" Stamp Exn, Abidjan, Ivory Coast (1st issue). As T **137** of Cameroun. Multicoloured.

220 100f. "The actor Wolf, called Bernard" (J. L. David) 2·75 2·75

1969. Air. "Philexafrique" Stamp Exn, Abidjan, Ivory Coast (2nd issue). As T **138** of Cameroun. Multicoloured.

221 50f. Moundangs dancers and Chad postage due stamp of 1930 1·90 1·90

55 G. Nachtigal and Tibesti landscape, 1869

1969. Air. Chad Explorers.

222 – 100f. violet, green & blue 1·75 75

223 **55** 100f. purple, blue & brown 1·75 75

DESIGN: No. 222, H. Barth (portrait) and aboard canoe, Lake Region, 1851.

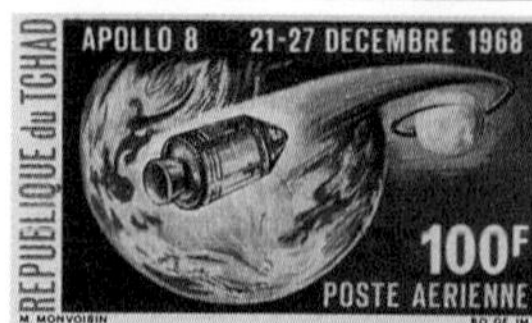

56 "Apollo 8" circling Moon

1969. Air. Flight of "Apollo 8" around the Moon.

224 **56** 100f. black, blue & orange 1·75 75

57 St. Bartholomew

1969. Jubilee Year of Catholic Church. Mult.

225 50c. St. Paul 10 10

226 1f. St. Peter 10 10

227 2f. St. Thomas 10 10

228 5f. St. John the Evangelist 10 10

229 10f. Type **57** 10 10

230 20f. St. Matthew 25 15

231 25f. St. James the Less 25 15

232 30f. St. Andrew 30 20

233 40f. St. Jude 35 20

234 50f. St. James the Greater 45 25

235 85f. St. Philip 70 45

236 100f. St. Simon 80 55

58 Mahatma Gandhi

59 Motor Vehicles and I.L.O. Emblem

1969. Air. "Apostles of Peace".

237 **58** 50f. brown and green 95 45

238 – 50f. sepia and agate 95 45

239 – 50f. brown and pink 95 45

240 – 50f. brown and blue 95 45

DESIGNS: No. 238, President Kennedy; No. 239, Martin Luther King; No. 240, Robert F. Kennedy.

1969. 50th Anniv of I.L.O.

242 **59** 32f. blue, purple & green 60 30

60 Cipolla, Baran and Sambo (pair with cox)

61 "African Woman" (Bezombes)

1969. "World Solidarity". Multicoloured. (a) Gold Medal Winners, Mexico Olympics.

243 1f. Type **60** 25 25

244 1f. R. Beamon (long-jump) 25 25

245 1f. I. Becker (women's pentathlon) 25 25

246 1f. C. Besson (women's 400 m) 25 25

247 1f. W. Davenport (110 m hurdles) 25 25

248 1f. K. Dibiasi (diving) 25 25

249 1f. R. Fosbury (high-jump) 25 25

250 1f. M. Gamoudi (5000 m) 25 25

251 1f. Great Britain (sailing) 25 25

252 1f. J. Guyon (cross-country riding) 25 25

253 1f. D. Hemery (200 m hurdles) 25 25

254 1f. S. Kato (gymnastics) 25 25

255 1f. B. Klinger (small bore rifle shooting) 25 25

256 1f. R. Matson (shot put) 25 25

257 1f. R. Matthes (100 m backstroke) 25 25

258 1f. D. Meyer (women's 200 m freestyle) 25 25

259 1f. Morelon and Trentin (tandem cycle) 25 25

260 1f. D. Rebillard (4000 m cycle pursuit) 25 25

261 1f. T. Smith (200 m) 25 25

262 1f. P. Trentin (1000 m cycle) 25 25

263 1f. F. Vianelli (196 km cycle race) 25 25

264 1f. West Germany (dressage) 25 25

265 1f. M. Wolke (welterweight boxing) 25 25

266 1f. Zimmermann and Esser (women's kayak pair) 25 25

(b) Paintings.

267 1f. Type **61** 25 25

268 1f. "Mother and Child" (Gauguin) 25 25

269 1f. "Holy Family" (Murillo) (horiz) 25 25

270 1f. "Adoration of the Kings" (Rubens) 25 25

271 1f. "Three Negroes" (Rubens) 25 25

272 1f. "Woman with Flowers" (Veneto) 25 25

62 Presidents Tombalbaye and Mobutu

1969. Air. 1st Anniv of Central African States Union.

273 **62** 1000f. gold, red and blue 20·00 20·00

This stamp is embossed in gold foil; colours of flags enamelled.

63 "Cochlospermum tinctorium"

1969. Flowers. Multicoloured.

274 1f. Type **63** 10 10

275 4f. "Parkia biglobosa" 20 15

276 10f. "Pancratium trianthum" 30 20

277 15f. "Ipomoea aquatica" 45 20

1969. Air. Birth Bicentenary of Napoleon Bonaparte. Multicoloured. As T **144** of Cameroun.

278 30f. "Napoleon visiting the Hotel des Invalides" (Veron-Bellecourt) 95 50

279 85f. "The Battle of Wagram" (H. Vernet) 1·90 1·00

280 130f. "The Battle of Austerlitz" (Gerard) 3·50 1·90

64 Frozen Carcases

1969. Frozen Meat Industry.

281 **64** 25f. red, green and orange 35 20

282 – 30f. brown, slate & green 50 25

DESIGN: 30f. Cattle and refrigerated abattoir, Farcha.

1969. 5th Anniv of African Development Bank. As T **146** of Cameroun.

283 30f. brown, green and red 45 25

66 Astronaut and Lunar Module

1969. Air. 1st Man on the Moon. Embossed on gold foil.

289 **66** 1000f. gold 22·00 22·00

67 Nile Mouthbrooder

68 President Tombalbaye

1969. Fishes.

290 **67** 2f. purple, grey and green 20 10

291 – 3f. grey, red and blue 30 25

292 – 5f. blue, yellow and ochre 55 25

293 – 20f. blue, green and red 1·75 60

FISHES: 3f. Deep-sided citharinid; 5f. Nile pufferfish; 20f. Lesser tigerfish.

1969. 10th Anniv of A.S.E.C.N.A. As T **150** of Cameroun.

294 30f. orange 55 30

1970. President Tombalbaye.

295 **68** 25f. multicoloured 45 20

69 "Village Life" (G. Narcisse)

1970. Air. African Paintings. Multicoloured.

296 100f. Type **69** 2·10 1·00

297 250f. "Market Woman" (I. N'Diaye) 4·00 1·60

298 250f. "Flower-seller" (I. N'Diaye) (vert) 4·00 1·60

70 Lenin

72 Osaka Print

71 Class and Torchbearers

1970. Birth Centenary of Lenin.

299 **70** 150f. black, cream & gold 2·50 1·25

1970. New U.P.U. Headquarters Building, Berne. As T **156** of Cameroun.

300 30f. brown, violet and red 55 30

1970. International Education Year.

301 **71** 100f. multicoloured 1·50 80

1970. Air. World Fair "EXPO 70", Osaka, Japan.

302 **72** 50f. green, blue and red 45 30

303 – 100f. blue, green and red 75 45

304 – 125f. slate. brown & red 1·00 55

DESIGNS: 100f. Tower of the Sun; 125f. Osaka print (different).

1970. Air. "Apollo" Moon Flights. Nos. 164/6 surch with new value, and optd with various inscriptions and diagrams concerning space flights.

305 **32** 50f. on 100f. mult ("Apollo 11") 1·50 1·00

306 – 100f. on 200f. mult ("Apollo 12") 2·75 1·40

307 – 125f. on 250f. mult ("Apollo 13") 4·25 2·25

74 Meteorological Equipment and "Agriculture"

76 Ahmed Mangue (Minister of Education)

75 "DC-8-63" over Airport

1970. World Meteorological Day.
308 **74** 50f. grey, green & orange 75 30

1970. Air. "Air Afrique" DC-8 "Fort Lamy".
309 **75** 30f. multicoloured 75 35

1970. Ahmed Mangue (air crash victim) Commem.
310 **76** 100f. black, red and gold 1·10 50

77 Tanning

1970. Trades and Handicrafts.
311 **77** 1f. bistre, brown and blue 10 10
312 – 2f. brown, blue and green 15 10
313 – 3f. violet, brown & mauve 20 15
314 – 4f. brown, bistre & green 25 15
315 – 5f. brown, green and red 35 35
DESIGNS—VERT: 2f. Dyeing; 4f. Water-carrying. HORIZ: 3f. Milling palm-nuts for oil; 5f. Copper-founding.

78 U.N. Emblem and Dove **79** "The Visitation" (Venetian School, 15th cent)

1970. 25th Anniv of United Nations.
316 **78** 32f. multicoloured 60 35

1970. Air. Christmas. Multicoloured.
317 20f. Type **79** 50 30
318 25f. "The Nativity" (Venetian School, 15th cent) 75 35
319 30f. "Virgin and Child" (Veneziano) 95 45

80 Map and O.C.A.M. Building

1971. O.C.A.M. (Organization Commune Africane et Malgache) Conference, Fort Lamy.
320 **80** 30f. multicoloured 60 30

81 Maritius "Post Office" 2d. of 1847

1971. Air. "PHILEXOCAM" Stamp Exhibition, Fort-Lamy.
321 **81** 10f. slate, brown & turq . . 30 20
322 – 20f. brown, black & turq 45 20
323 – 30f. brown, black and red 55 30
324 – 60f. black, brown & purple 80 50
325 – 80f. slate, brown and blue 1·25 70
326 – 100f. brown, slate & blue 1·60 95
DESIGNS—20f. Tuscany 3 lire of 1860; 30f. France 1f. of 1849; 30f., 60f. U.S.A. 10c. of 1847; 80f. Japan 5 sen of 1872; 100f. Saxony 3pf. of 1850.

82 Pres. Nasser **83** "Racial Harmony" Tree

1971. Air. 1st Death Anniv of Gamal Abdel Nasser (Egypt).
328 **82** 75f. multicoloured 80 35

1971. Racial Equality Year.
329 **83** 40f. red, green and blue . . 75 30

1971. Air. Reconciliation with Central African Republic and Zaire. As T **106** of Central African Republic.
330 100f. multicoloured . . . . . 1·50 75

84 Map and Dish Aerial

1971. World Telecommunications Day.
331 **84** 5f. orge, red & bl (postage) 20 15
332 – 40f. green, brown & pur 55 25
333 – 50f. black, brown & red . . 75 30
334 – 125f. red, green & blue (air) . . . . 1·90 85
DESIGNS: 40f. Map and communications tower; 50f. Map and satellite. (48 × 27 mm): 125f. Map and telecommunications symbols.

85 Scouts by Camp-fire

1971. Air. World Scout Jamboree, Asagiri, Japan.
335 **85** 250f. multicoloured . . . . 3·75 1·90

86 Great Egret

1971. Air.
336 **86** 1000f. multicoloured . . . 29·00 16·00

87 Ancient Marathon Race

1971. Air. 75th Anniv of Modern Olympic Games. Multicoloured.
337 40f. Type **87** 55 30
338 45f. Ancient stadium, Olympia 80 35
339 75f. Ancient wrestling . . . . 1·00 50
340 130f. Athens Stadium, 1896 Games . . . . 1·75 85

88 Sidney Bechet **89** Gen. de Gaulle

1971. Air. Famous American Black Musicians. Multicoloured.
341 50f. Type **88** . . . . 1·25 50
342 75f. Duke Ellington . . . . 1·60 75
343 100f. Louis Armstrong . . . 2·50 1·25

1971. Air. 1st Death Anniv of De Gaulle.
344 – 200f. gold, blue and light blue . . . . 6·25 6·25
345 **89** 200f. gold, green & yellow 6·25 6·25
DESIGN: No. 344, Governor-General Felix Eboue.

1971. Air. 10th Anniv of African and Malagasy Posts and Telecommunications Union. As T **184** of Cameroun. Multicoloured.
347 100f. Headquarters building and Sao carved animal head . . . . 1·25 60

90 Children's Heads

1971. 25th Anniv of U.N.I.C.E.F.
348 **90** 50f. blue, green & purple 85 35
On the above stamp, "24e" has been obliterated and "25e" inserted in the commemorative inscription.

91 Gorane Nangara Dancers

1971. Chad Dancers. Multicoloured.
349 10f. Type **91** 30 20
350 15f. Yondo initiates 45 25
351 30f. M'Boum (vert) 80 35
352 40f. Sara Kaba (vert) . . . . 1·25 55

93 Presidents Pompidou and Tombalbaye

1972. Visit of French President.
354 **93** 40f. multicoloured . . . . 1·25 60

94 Bobsleighing

1972. Air. Winter Olympic Games, Sapporo, Japan.
355 **94** 50f. red and blue 70 40
356 – 100f. green and purple . . 1·50 60
DESIGN: 100f. Slalom.

95 Human Heart **96** "Gorrizia dubiosa"

1972. World Heart Month.
357 **95** 100f. red, blue and violet 1·50 75

1972. Insects, Multicoloured.
358 1f. Type **96** 10 10
359 2f. "Argiope sector" 20 15
360 3f. "Nephila senegalense" . . 25 15
361 4f. "Oryctes boas" 35 25
362 5f. "Hemistigma albipunctata" 45 25
363 25f. "Dinothrombium tinctorium" 45 30
364 30f. "Bupreste sternocera H." 50 30
365 40f. "Hyperechia bomboides" 60 35
366 50f. "Chrysis" (Hymenoptere) 95 50
367 100f. "Tithoes confinis" (Longicore) . . . . 2·50 85
368 130f. "Galeodes araba" (Solifuge) . . . . 3·75 1·40

1972. Air. U.N.E.S.C.O. "Save Venice" Campaign. As T **191** of Cameroun. Multicoloured.
369 40f. "Harbour Panorama" (detail, Caffi) 95 50
370 45f. "Venice Panorama" (detail, Caffi) (horiz) . . . 1·25 60
371 140f. "Grand Canal" (detail, Caffi) . . . . 3·00 1·40

97 Hurdling

1972. Olympic Games, Munich. Multicoloured.
372 50f. Type **97** 75 35
373 130f. Gymnastics . . . . . . 1·50 75
374 150f. Swimming . . . . . . 1·90 85

98 Alphonse Daudet and Scene from "Tartarin de Tarascon"

1972. Air. International Book Year.
376 **98** 100f. brown, red & purple 1·50 75

99 Dromedary

1972. Domestic Animals.
377 **99** 25f. brown and violet . . . 45 20
378 – 30f. blue and mauve . . . 50 25
379 – 40f. brown and green . . . 70 30
380 – 45f. brown and blue . . . 85 35
DESIGNS: 30f. Horse; 40f. Saluki hound; 45f. Goat.

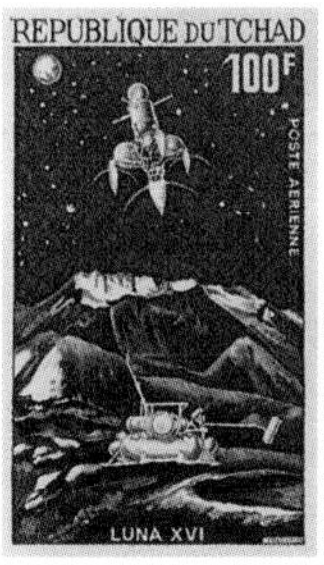

100 "Luna 16" and Moon Probe **101** Tobacco Production

1972. Air. Russian Moon Exploration.
381 **100** 100f. violet, brown & blue 1·40 70
382 – 150f. brown, blue & purple . . . . 2·10 80
DESIGN—HORIZ: 150f. "Lunokhod 1" Moon vehicle.

1972. Economic Development.
383 **101** 40f. green, red & brown 50 25
384 – 50f. brown, green & blue 75 35
DESIGN: 50f. Ploughing with oxen.

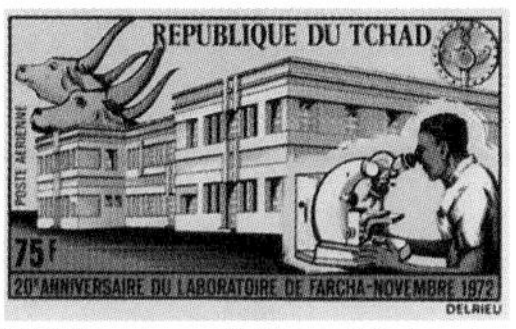

102 Microscope, Cattle and Laboratory

1972. Air. 20th Anniv of Farcha Veterinary Laboratory.
385 **102** 75f. multicoloured 80 35

103 Massa Warrior

1972. Chad Warriors. Multicoloured.
386 15f. Type **103** 55 25
387 20f. Moudang archer 70 35

104 King Faisal and Pres. Tombalbaye

1972. Visit of King Faisal of Saudi Arabia. Multicoloured.
388 100f. Type **104** (postage) . . 1·90 95
389 75f. King Faisal and Ka'aba, Mecca (air) . . . . 1·00 50

105 Gen. Gowon, Pres. Tombalbaye and Map

1972. Visit of Gen. Gowon, Nigerian Head-of-State.
390 **105** 70f. multicoloured 75 30

106 "Madonna and Child" (G. Bellini)

1972. Air. Christmas. Paintings. Multicoloured.
391 40f. Type **106** 45 25
392 75f. "Virgin and Child" (bas-relief, Da Santivo, Dall' Occhio) 80 45
393 80f. "Nativity" (B. Angelico) (horiz) . . . . 1·25 65
394 90f. "Adoration of the Magi" (P. Perugino) . . . . . . 1·60 80

107 Commemorative Scroll

1972. 50th Anniv of U.S.S.R.
395 **107** 150f. multicoloured . . . 1·50 55

108 High-jumping

1973. 2nd African Games, Lagos. Multicoloured.
396 50f. Type **108** 75 35
397 125f. Running . . . . 1·40 60
398 200f. Putting the shot . . . . 2·00 1·00

109 Copernicus and Planetary System Diagram

1973. Air. 500th Birth Anniv of Nicholas Copernicus.
400 **109** 250f. grey, brown & mve 4·00 1·90

1973. African Solidarity. "Drought Relief". No. 377 surch **SECHERESSE SOLIDARITE AFRICAINE 100F**.
401 **99** 100f. on 25f. brown & vio 1·60 90

1973. U.A.M.P.T. As Type **216** of Cameroun.
402 100f. green, red & brown . . 1·50 75

111 "Skylab" over Globe

1974. Air. "Skylab" Exploits.
403 **111** 100f. brown, red & blue 1·25 55
404 – 150f. turquoise, blue & brn . . . . 1·90 80
DESIGN: 150f. Close-up of "Skylab".

112 Chad Mother and Children

1974. 1st Anniv of Chad Red Cross.
405 **112** 30f.+10f. multicoloured 60 60

113 Football Players

1974. Air. World Cup Football Championship, West Germany.
406 **113** 50f. brown and red . . . 50 30
407 – 125f. green and red (vert) 1·40 60
408 – 150f. red and green . . . 1·90 95
DESIGNS: Nos. 407/8, Footballers in action similar to Type **113**.

114 Chad Family **116** Rotary Emblem

115 U.P.C. Emblem and Mail Canoe

1974. Air. World Population Year.
409 **114** 250f. brown, green & bl 3·00 1·60

1974. Air. Centenary of U.P.U.
410 **115** 30f. brown, red & green 50 25
411 – 40f. black and blue . . . 2·75 1·50
412 – 100f. blue, brown & blk 1·60 70
413 – 150f. violet, green & turq 2·25 75
DESIGNS—U.P.U. Emblem and: 40f. Electric train; 100f. Jet airliner; 150f. Satellite.

1975. 70th Anniv of Rotary International.
414 **116** 50f. multicoloured 75 35

117 Heads of Women of Four Races

1975. Air. International Women's Year.
415 **117** 250f. multicoloured . . . 3·75 1·90

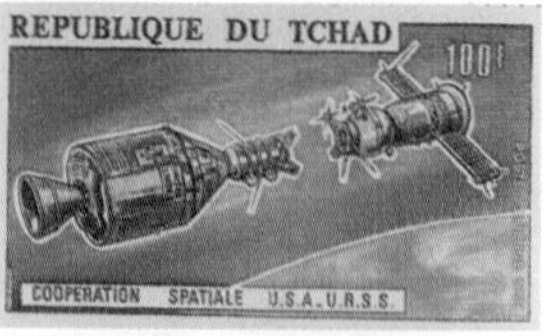

118 "Apollo" and "Soyuz" Spacecraft about to dock

1975. Air. "Apollo–Soyuz" Test Project.
416 **118** 100f. brown, blue & green 1·10 50
417 – 130f. brown, blue & green 1·40 75
DESIGN: 130f. "Apollo" and "Soyuz" spacecraft docked.

119 "Craterostigma plantagineum"

1975. Flowers. Multicoloured.
418 5f. Type **119** 10 10
419 10f. "Tapinanthus globiferus" 20 15
420 15f. "Commelina forsalaei" (vert) 30 15
421 20f. "Adenium obasum" . . 35 15
422 25f. "Hibiscus esulenus" . . 60 20
423 30f. "Hibiscus sabdariffa" . . 75 25
424 40f. "Kigelia africana" . . . 1·10 30

120 Football

1975. Air. Olympic Games, Montreal (1976).
425 **120** 75f. green and red 80 30
426 – 100f. brown, blue & red 1·25 55
427 – 125f. blue and brown . . 1·40 80
DESIGNS: 100f. Throwing the discus; 125f. Running.

1975. Air. Successful Rendezvous of "Apollo–Soyuz" Mission. Optd **JONCTION 17 JUILLET 1975**.
428 **118** 100f. brown, blue & grn 1·10 70
429 – 130f. brown, blue & grn 1·40 90

122 Stylized British and American Flags

1975. Air. Bicentenary of American Revolution.
430 **122** 150f. blue, red & brown 1·90 95

123 "Adoration of the Shepherds" (Murillo)

1975. Air. Christmas. Religious Paintings. Mult.
431 40f. Type **123** 55 35
432 75f. "Adoration of the Shepherds" (G. de la Tour) 1·00 55
433 80f. "Virgin of the Bible" (R. van der Weyden) (vert) . . 1·25 60
434 100f. "Holy Family with the Lamb" (attrib. Raphael) (vert) . . . . 1·90 95

124 Alexander Graham Bell and Satellite

1976. Telephone Centenary.
435 **124** 100f. multicoloured . . . 1·00 50
436 125f. multicoloured . . . 1·50 75

125 U.S.S.R. (ice hockey)

1976. Winter Olympics. Medal-winners, Innsbruck. Multicoloured.
437 60f. Type **125** (postage) . . . 75 35
438 90f. Ski-jumping (K. Schnabl, Austria) 95 40
439 250f. Bobsleighing (West Germany) (air) . . . . . 2·25 75
440 300f. Speed-skating (J. E. Storholt, Norway) . . . . 2·75 1·10
These stamps were not issued without overprints.

126 Paul Revere (after Copley) and his Night Ride

1976. Air. Bicentenary of American Revolution.
442 100f. Type **126** 80 25
443 125f. Washington (after Stuart) and "Washington crossing the Delaware" (detail, Leutze) 95 35
444 150f. Lafayette offering his services to America . . . . 1·25 45
445 200f. Rochambeau and detail "Siege of Yorktown" (Couder) . . . . 1·60 70
446 250f. Franklin (after Duplessis) and "Declaration of Independence" (detail, Trumball) . . . . 2·25 80

127 Hurdles

1976. Olympic Games, Montreal. Multicoloured.
448 45f. Type **127** (postage) . . . 60 25
449 100f. Boxing (air) 95 35
450 200f. Pole vaulting . . . . . 1·90 55
451 300f. Putting the shot . . . . 2·75 95

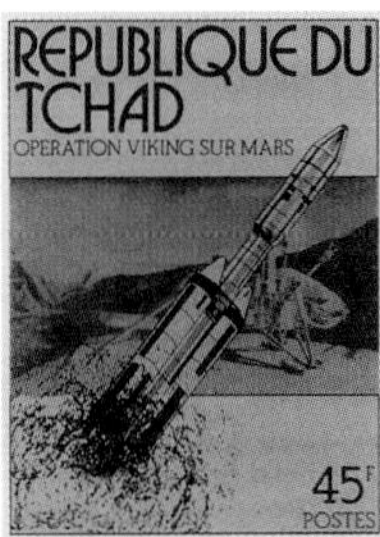

128 Launch of "Viking"

1976. "Viking" landing on Mars. Mult.
453 45f. Type **128** (postage) . . . 45 20
454 90f. Trajectory of flight . . . 80 30
455 100f. Descent to Mars (air) 85 35
456 200f. "Viking" in flight . . . 1·60 50
457 250f. "Viking" on landing approach . . . . 1·90 75

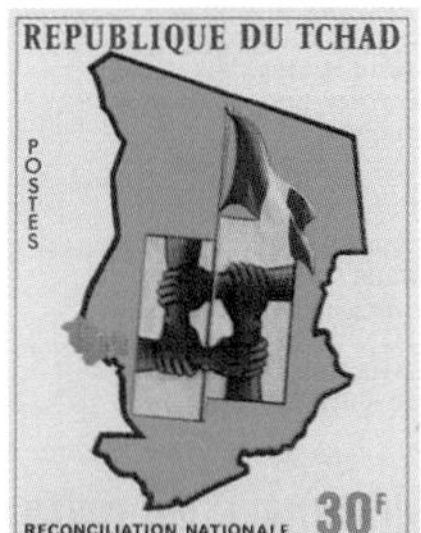

129 Flag and Clasped Hands on Map of Chad

1976. National Reconciliation. Mult.
459 30f. Type **129** 35 25
460 60f. Type **129** 85 30
461 120f. Map, people and various occupations . . . 1·60 70

130 Release of Political Prisoners

1976. 1st Anniv of April 1st Revolution. Mult.
462 30f. Type **130** 25 20
463 60f. Officer-cadets on parade 50 30
464 120f. Type **130** . . . . 1·10 55

131 Concorde

1976. Air. Concorde's First Commercial Flight.
465 **131** 250f. blue, red & black . . 4·25 2·75

132 Gourd and Ladle

1976. Pyrograved Gourds.
466 **132** 30f. multicoloured 30 20
467 – 60f. multicoloured 60 25
468 – 120f. multicoloured . . . . 1·25 60
DESIGNS: 60f., 120f. Gourds with different decorations.

1976. Nobel Prizewinners. As T **189** of Central African Empire. Multicoloured.
469 45f. Robert Koch (Medicine, 1905) 95 35
470 90f. Anatole France (Literature, 1921) . . . . 1·25 60
471 100f. Albert Einstein (Physics, 1921) (air) . . . . 1·25 30
472 200f. Dag Hammarskjold (Peace, 1961) . . . . . . 1·90 50
473 300f. Dr. S. Tomonaga (Physics, 1965) . . . . . . 2·75 75

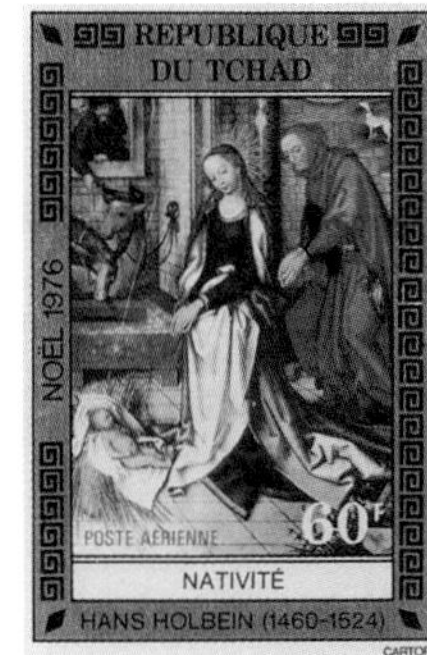

133 "The Nativity" (Hans Holbein)

1976. Air. Christmas. Multicoloured.
475 30f. "The Nativity" (Altdorfer) 30 20
476 60f. Type **133** 55 30
477 120f. "Adoration of the Shepherds" (Honthorst) (horiz) . . . . 1·00 60
478 150f. "Adoration of the Magi" (David) (horiz) . . 1·60 95

134 "Lesdiguieres Bridge"

1976. Air. Centenary of Impressionism. Paintings by Johan Bathold Jongkind. Multicoloured.
479 100f. Type **134** . . . . 1·40 70
480 120f. "Warship" . . . . . . 3·00 1·10

1977. Zeppelin Flights. As T **190** of Central African Empire. Multicoloured.
481 100f. Friedrichshafen and German 50pf. stamp, 1936 (postage) . . . . 1·25 50
482 125f. Polar scene and German 1m. stamp, 1931 (air) . . . . 1·10 30
483 150f. Chicago store and German 4m. stamp, 1933 2·00 45
484 175f. New York, London and German 2m. stamp, 1928 4·00 75
485 200f. New York and U.S. $2.60 stamp, 1930 . . . . 2·75 85

1977. Air. 10th Anniv of International French Language Council. As T **204** of Benin.
487 100f. multicoloured 85 50

135 Simon Bolivar

1977. Great Personalities. Multicoloured.
488 150f. Type **135** . . . . 1·25 50
489 175f. Joseph J. Roberts . . . 1·50 50
490 200f. Queen Wilhelmina . . . 1·75 60
491 200f. General de Gaulle . . . 2·50 85
493 250f. Coronation of Queen Elizabeth II (horiz) . . . . 2·50 90
492 325f. King Baudouin and Queen Fabiola . . . . . . 2·75 95

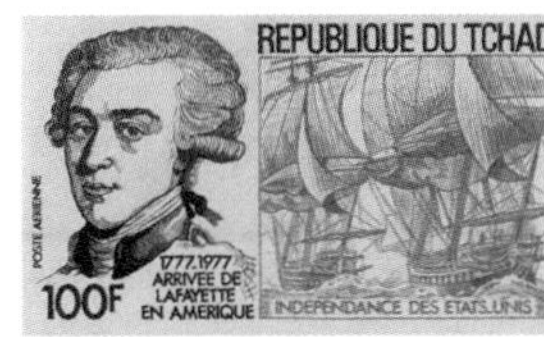

137 Lafayette and Arrival in America

1977. Air. Bicentenary of American Independence. Multicoloured.
495 100f. Type **137** . . . . 1·10 50
496 120f. Abraham Lincoln . . . 1·25 60
497 150f. F. J. Madison . . . . 1·75 75

138 Radio Aerial, Sound Waves and Map

1977. Posts and Telecommunications Emblems.
498 – 30f. black and yellow . . 35 20
499 **138** 60f. multicoloured 70 25
500 – 120f. multicoloured . . . 1·25 60
DESIGNS—HORIZ (47 × 26 mm): 30f. Posthorn and initials "ONPT". VERT (26 × 36 mm): 120f. Telecommunications skyline and initials "TIT".

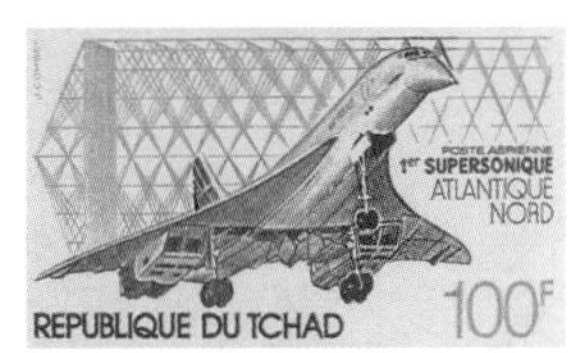

139 Concorde

1977. Air. "North Atlantic"—Concorde and Lindbergh Commemorations.
501 **139** 100f. blue, red & lt blue 75 45
502 – 120f. brown, blue & grn 85 50
503 – 150f. violet, red & green 1·10 65
504 – 200f. orange, pur & brn 1·60 85
505 – 300f. blue, purple & blk 2·50 1·25
DESIGNS: 120f. to 300f. Various portraits of Lindbergh with "Spirit of St. Louis" against different backgrounds.

140 "Mariner 10"

1977. Air. Space Research.
506 **140** 100f. blue, olive & green 80 50
507 – 200f. brown, green & red 1·75 1·00
508 – 300f. brown, grn & bistre 2·50 1·25
DESIGNS: 200f. "Luna 21"; 300f. "Viking".

141 Running **142** "Back Pain"

1977. Air. Sports.
509 **141** 30f. brown, red & blue . . 30 20
510 – 60f. brown, blue & orge 55 30
511 – 120f. multicoloured . . . 1·00 50
512 – 125f. mauve, violet & grn 1·25 60
DESIGNS: 60f. Volleyball; 120f. Football; 125f. Basketball.

1977. World Rheumatism Year.
513 **142** 30f. red, green and violet 35 20
514 – 60f. red, violet and green 55 25
515 – 120f. blue, red & lt blue 1·25 60
DESIGNS—HORIZ: 60f. "Neck pain". VERT: 120f. "Knee pain".

1977. Air. 1st Commercial Paris–New York Flight of Concorde. Optd **PARIS NEW-YORK 22.11.77.**
516 **139** 100f. blue, red & lt blue 2·25 1·25

144 Saving a Goal

1977. World Football Cup Championship. Mult.
517 40f. Type **144** 35 15
518 60f. Heading the ball 55 20
519 100f. Referee 95 30
520 200f. Foot kicking ball . . . 1·90 60
521 300f. Pele (Brazilian player) 3·00 95

145 "Christ in the Manger" (detail)

1977. Air. Christmas. Paintings by Rubens. Mult.
523 30f. Type **145** 45 25
524 60f. "Virgin and Child with Two Donors" 75 35
525 100f. "The Adoration of the Shepherds" . . . . 1·25 60
526 125f. "The Adoration of the Magi" (detail) . . . . . . 1·60 80

1978. Coronation of Queen Elizabeth II. No. 493 optd **ANNIVERSAIRE DU COURONNEMENT 1953–1978.**
527 250f. multicoloured . . . . . 2·50 1·50

147 Antoine de Saint-Exupery

1978. Air. History of Aviation. Multicoloured.
529 40f. Type **147** 50 20
530 50f. Wright Brothers and aircraft in flight 60 25
531 80f. Hugo Junkers 85 45
532 100f. Italo Balbo . . . . . . 1·10 55
533 120f. "Concorde" . . . . . 1·25 75

1978. Air. "Philexafrique" Stamp Exhibition, Gabon (1st issue), and International Stamp Fair, Essen. As T **237** of Benin. Multicoloured.
535 100f. Grey heron and Mecklenburg-Strelitz, ⅓sgr. stamp, 1864 . . . . 2·75 1·90
536 100f. Black rhinoceros and Chad 500f. stamp, 1961 . . 2·75 1·90

148 "Portrait"

150 Head and Unhealthy and Healthy Villages

149 "Helene Fourment"

1978. 450th Death Anniv of Albrecht Durer (artist). Multicoloured.
537 60f. Type **148** 50 15
538 150f. "Jacob Muffel" . . . . 1·40 30
539 250f. "Young Girl" . . . . 2·25 60
540 350f. "Oswolt Krel" . . . . 3·50 80

1978. 400th Birth Anniv of Peter Paul Rubens (artist). Multicoloured.
541 60f. "Abraham and Melchisedek" (horiz) . . . 60 15
542 120f. Type **149** . . . . 1·10 25

543 200f. "David and the Elders of Israel" (horiz) . . . . . 1·90 60
544 300f. "Anne of Austria" . . 3·25 85

1978. National Health Day.
546 **150** 60f. multicoloured 60 35

1978. World Cup Football Championship Finalists. Nos. 517/21 optd with teams and scores of past finals.
547 **144** 40f. multicoloured 35 20
548 – 60f. multicoloured 50 30
549 – 100f. multicoloured . . . 85 50
550 – 200f. multicoloured . . . 1·90 95
551 – 300f. multicoloured . . . 3·00 1·50
OPTS: 40f. **1962 BRESIL-TCHECOSLOVAQUIE 3-1**; 60f. **1966 GRAND BRETAGNE-ALLEMAGNE (RFA) 4-2**; 100f. **1970 BRESIL-ITALIE 4-1**; 200f. **1974 ALLEMAGNE (RFA)-PAYS BAS 2-1**; 300f. **1978 ARGENTINE-PAYS BAS 3-1**.

152 Camel Riders, Satellites and U.P.U. Emblem

1978. "Philexafrique 2" Exhibition, Libreville, Gabon (2nd issue).
553 **152** 60f. red, mauve & blue . . 1·60 95
554 – 150f. multicoloured . . . 3·00 2·25
DESIGN: 150f. Mother and child, native village and hibiscus.

153 Sand Gazelle

1979. Endangered Animals. Multicoloured.
555 40f. Type **153** 45 15
556 50f. Addax 50 15
557 60f. Scimitar oryx 60 20
558 100f. Cheetah . . . . 1·00 40
559 150f. African ass . . . . . . 1·60 50
560 300f. Black rhinoceros . . . 3·25 90

154 African Boy and Wall Painting

1979. International Year of the Child. Mult.
561 65f. Type **154** 50 20
562 75f. Asian girl 55 25
563 100f. European child and doves 80 30
564 150f. African boys and drawing of boats . . . . . 1·25 50

1979. 10th Anniv of "Apollo 11" Moon Landing. Nos. 453/7 optd with lunar module and **ALUNISSAGE APOLLO XI JUILLET 1969**.
567 45f. Type **128** (postage) . . . 35 25
568 90f. Trajectory of flight . . . 80 35
569 100f. Descent on Mars (air) 75 50
570 200f. "Viking" in flight . . . 1·50 85
571 250f. "Viking" on landing approach . . . . 1·90 1·10

157 Hurdles

1979. Air. Olympic Games, Moscow 1980. Mult.
573 15f. Type **157** 20 15
574 30f. Hockey 30 20
575 250f. Swimming . . . . . . 1·90 70
576 350f. Running . . . . . . 2·50 90

158 Reed Canoe and Austrian 10k. stamp, 1910

1979. Air. Death Centenary of Sir Rowland Hill. Multicoloured.
578 65f. Type **158** 50 15
579 100f. Sailing canoe and U.S. $1 stamp of 1894 . . . . . 85 30
580 200f. "Curacao" (paddle-steamer) and French 1f. stamp of 1853 . . . . . . 1·75 60
581 300f. "Calypso" (liner) and Holstein 1¼s. stamp of 1864 . . . . 2·25 1·10

159 Slalom
160 "Concorde" and Map of Africa

1979. Winter Olympic Games, Lake Placid (1980). Multicoloured.
583 20f. Type **159** 20 15
584 40f. Biathlon 35 15
585 60f. Ski jump (horiz) 40 15
586 150f. Women's giant slalom 1·10 35
587 350f. Cross-country skiing (horiz) . . . . 2·50 80
588 500f. Downhill skiing (horiz) 3·75 1·25

1980. 20th Anniv of African Air Safety Organization (ASECNA).
589 **160** 15f. multicoloured 30 10
590 30f. multicoloured 45 25
591 60f. multicoloured 90 50

1981. Various stamps optd **POSTES 1981** or surch also.
592 **157** 30f. on 15f. multicoloured 75 60
593 – 30f. mult (No. 574) . . . 75 60
594 **158** 60f. on 65f. multicoloured 1·50 1·00
595 – 60f. on 100f. mult (No. 579) . . . . . . 1·50 1·00

162 Footballer

1982. World Cup Football Championship, Spain. Multicoloured.
596 30f. Hungary (postage) . . . 25 15
597 40f. Type **162** 30 15
598 50f. Algeria 35 20
599 60f. Argentina 45 20
600 80f. Brazil (air) 55 20
601 300f. West Germany . . . . 2·25 70
DESIGNS: As T **162** but each value showing different team's footballer.

163 Lady Diana and her Brother (1967)

1982. 21st Birthday of Princess of Wales. Mult.
603 30f. Lady Diana in christening robe (1961) (postage) 30 15
604 40f. Portrait of Lady Diana (1965) 35 15
605 50f. Type **163** 45 20
606 60f. Lady Diana and her pony (1975) 55 20
607 80f. Lady Diana in Switzerland (1977) (air) . . 60 20
608 300f. Lady Diana as nursery teacher (1980) . . . . . . 2·50 70

164 West German Scouts

1982. 75th Anniv of Scout Movement. Mult.
610 30f. Type **164** (postage) . . . 35 15
611 40f. Upper Volta scouts . . . 35 15
612 50f. Mali scouts and African dancers 50 20
613 60f. Scottish scout, piper and dancer 60 20
614 80f. Kuwait scouts (air) . . . 55 20
615 300f. Chad cub scout . . . . 2·25 70

165 Judo

1982. Olympic Games, Los Angeles (1984) (1st issue). Multicoloured.
617 30f. Gymnastics (horse exercise) (postage) 30 15
618 40f. Show jumping 30 15
619 50f. Type **165** 35 20
620 60f. High jumping 60 20
621 80f. Hurdling (air) 55 20
622 300f. Gymnastics (floor exercise) . . . . 2·25 70
See also Nos. 678/83 and 735/8.

1982. Birth of Prince William of Wales. Nos. 603/8 optd **21 JUIN 1982 WILLIAM ARTHUR PHILIP LOUIS PRINCE DE GALLES**.
624 30f. Type **163** (postage) . . . 30 15
625 40f. Portrait of Lady Diana as a young girl 35 15
626 50f. Lady Diana and her brother 45 20
627 60f. Lady Diana with her pony 50 20
628 80f. Lady Diana in Switzerland (air) 60 20
629 300f. Lady Diana with children . . . . 2·50 70

167 Marco Tardelli (Italy) and Passarella (Argentine)

1983. World Cup Football Championship Results. Multicoloured.
631 30f. Type **167** (postage) . . . 25 10
632 40f. Paolo Rossi (Italy) and Zico (Brazil) 30 15
633 50f. Pierre Littbarski (West Germany) and Platini (France) 35 20
634 60f. Gabriele Oriali (Italy) and Smolarek (Poland) . . 45 20
635 70f. Boniek (Poland) and Alain Giresse (France) (air) 55 20
636 300f. Bruno Conti (Italy) and Paul Breitner (West Germany) . . . . 2·25 70

168 Philidor and 19th-century European Rook

1982. Chess Grand Masters. Multicoloured.
638 30f. Type **168** (postage) . . . 35 15
639 40f. Paul Morphy and 19th-century Chinese knight 50 15
640 50f. Howard Staunton and Lewis knight 60 25
641 60f. Jean-Paul Capablanca and African knight 75 25
642 80f. Boris Spassky and Staunton knight (air) . . . 1·25 25
643 300f. Anatoly Karpov and 19th-century Chinese knight . . . . 3·00 1·00

169 K. E. Tsiolkovski and "Soyuz"

1983. Exploitation of Space. Multicoloured.
645 30f. Type **169** (postage) . . . 25 10
646 40f. R. H. Goddard and space telescope 30 15
647 50f. Korolev and ultra-violet telescope 35 20
648 60f. Von Braun and Space Shuttle 45 20
649 80f. Esnault Pelterie and "Ariane" rocket and "Symphonie" satellite (air) 55 25
650 300f. H. Oberth and construction of orbiting space station . . . . . . 2·25 70

170 Charles and Robert Balloon, 1783

1983. Air. Balloons. Multicoloured.
652 100f. Type **170** 95 50
653 200f. Blanchard balloon, Berlin, 1788 . . . . 1·90 95
654 300f. Charles Green balloon, London, 1837 (horiz) . . . 2·50 1·75
655 400f. Modern advertising airship (horiz) . . . . . . 3·25 1·75

171 Bobsleigh

1983. Winter Olympic Games, Sarajevo. Mult.
657 30f. Type **171** (postage) . . . 25 10
658 40f. Speed skating 30 15
659 50f. Cross-country skiing . . 30 20
660 60f. Ice hockey 35 20
661 80f. Ski jump (air) 55 20
662 300f. Downhill skiing . . . . 2·25 70

172 Montgolfier Brothers and "Le Martial" Balloon, 1783

1983. Bicentenary of Manned Flight. Multicoloured.
664 25f. Type **172** (postage) . . . 20 15
665 45f. Pilatre de Rozier and first manned flight, 1783 35 20
666 50f. Jacques Garnerin and balloon (first parachute descent, 1797) 35 20
667 60f. J. P. Blanchard and balloon at Chelsea, 1784 45 30
668 80f. H. Giffard and steam-powered dirigible, 1852 (air) 75 40
669 250f. Zeppelin and airship "L 21", 1900 . . . . 2·10 1·25

173 Gottlieb Daimler, Karl Benz and Mercedes "Type S," 1927

1983. Car Manufacturers. Multicoloured.
671 25f. Type **173** (postage) . . . 30 10
672 35f. Friedrich von Martini and Torpedo, Martini "Type GC 32", 1913 . . . 45 15
673 50f. Walter P. Chrysler and Chrysler "70", 1926 . . . 70 20
674 60f. Nicola Romeo and Alfa Romeo "6 C 1750 Grand Sport", 1929 . . . . . . 75 20
675 80f. Stewart Rolls, Henry Royce and "Phantom II Continental", 1934 (air) . . 95 20
676 250f. Lord Shrewsbury and Talbot-Lago "Record", 1948 . . . . 2·50 70

174 Kayak

1983. Olympic Games, Los Angeles (2nd issue). Multicoloured.
678 25f. Type **174** (postage) . . . 20 10
679 45f. Long jumping 30 15
680 50f. Boxing 35 15
681 60f. Discus-throwing 45 20
682 80f. Relay race (air) 60 20
683 350f. Horse jumping . . . . 2·50 70

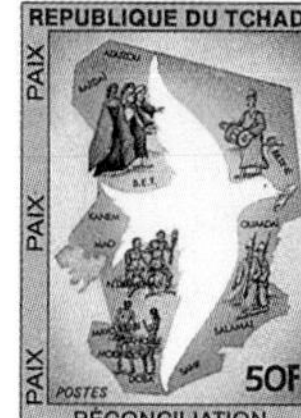

175 Dove on Map

1983. Peace and Reconciliation. Multicoloured.
685 50f. Type **175** (postage) . . . 35 15
686 50f. Foodstuffs on map . . . 45 20
687 50f. President Habre 35 15
688 60f. As No. 687 . . . . . . 45 15
689 80f. Type **175** 65 25
690 80f. As No. 686 . . . . . . 80 30
691 80f. As No. 687 . . . . . . 65 25
692 100f. As No. 687 . . . . . . 75 25
693 150f. Type **175** (air) . . . . 1·00 30
694 150f. As No. 686 . . . . . . 1·40 50
695 200f. Type **175** . . . . . . 1·25 45
696 200f. As No. 686 . . . . . . 1·75 65

1983. 15th World Scout Jamboree, Canada. Nos. 610/15 optd **XV WORLD JAMBOREE MONDIAL ALBERTA CANADA 1983**.
697 30f. multicoloured (postage) 25 15
698 40f. multicoloured 30 15
699 50f. multicoloured 35 20
700 60f. multicoloured 45 20
701 80f. multicoloured (air) . . . 55 20
702 300f. multicoloured . . . . . 2·25 70

1983. 60th Anniv of Int Chess Federation. Nos. 638/43 optd **60e ANNIVERSAIRE FEDERATION MONDIAL D'ECHECS 1924–1984**.
704 30f. multicoloured (postage) 50 20
705 40f. multicoloured 60 20
706 50f. multicoloured 60 25
707 60f. multicoloured 75 25
708 80f. multicoloured (air) . . . 1·25 45
709 300f. multicoloured . . . . . 3·75 1·25

178 Chad Martyrs

1984. Celebrities. Multicoloured.
711 50f. Type **178**(postage) . . . 35 15
712 200f. P. Harris and Rotary Headquarters, U.S.A. . . . 1·50 35
713 300f. Alfred Nobel and will 2·50 60
714 350f. Raphael and "Virgin with the Infant and St. John the Baptist" . . . 3·75 75
715 400f. Rembrandt and "The Holy Family" (air) . . . . 3·75 85
716 500f. Goethe and Scenes from "Faust" . . . . 4·25 1·00

179 Martyrs Memorial

1984. Martyrs Memorial.
718 **179** 50f. mult (postage) . . . 35 15
719 80f. multicoloured 60 25
720 120f. multicoloured . . . 85 25
721 200f. multicoloured (air) 1·60 50
722 250f. multicoloured . . . 2·25 75

180 Durer and Painting

1984. Celebrities and Events. Multicoloured.
723 50f. Type **180** (postage) . . . 75 15
724 200f. Henri Dunant and battle scene . . . . 1·75 35
725 300f. Early telephone and satellite receiving station, Goonhilly Downs . . . . 2·25 60
726 350f. President Kennedy and first foot-print on Moon 2·75 75
727 400f. Infra-red satellite picture (Europe–Africa co-operation) (air) . . . . . 2·50 75
728 500f. Prince and Princess of Wales . . . . 3·75 1·00

181 "Communications"

1984. World Communications Year.
730 **181** 50f. mult (postage) . . . 45 15
731 60f. multicoloured 50 35
732 70f. multicoloured 50 35
733 125f. multicoloured (air) 1·00 55
734 250f. multicoloured . . . 1·90 1·10

182 Two-man Kayak

1984. Air. Olympic Games, Los Angeles (3rd issue). Multicoloured.
735 100f. Type **182** 75 25
736 200f. Kayaks (close-up) . . . 1·50 50
737 300f. One-man kayak . . . . 2·25 75
738 400f. Coxed fours . . . . . 3·00 1·00

183 Class 13 Kitson Steam Locomotive

1984. Historic Transport. Multicoloured.
740 50f. Type **183** (postage) . . . 1·50 1·00
741 200f. Sailing boat on Lake Chad . . . . 1·75 65
742 300f. Graf Zeppelin (airship) 3·00 1·25
743 350f. Six-wheel Renault automobile, 1930 . . . . . 2·75 1·25
744 400f. Bloch "120" airplane (air) . . . . 2·50 1·50
745 500f. Douglas "DC-8" airplane . . . . . . 3·75 2·00

184 African with broken Manacles
185 Pres. Hissein Habre

1984. 2nd Anniv of Entrance of Government Forces in N'Djamena.
747 **184** 50f. multicoloured 50 25

1984.
748 **185** 125f. black, blue & yellow 1·25 50

186 British East Indiaman

1984. Transport. Multicoloured. (a) Ships.
749 90f. Type **186** 95 45
750 125f. "Vera Cruz" (steamer) 1·25 55
751 200f. "Carlisle Castle" (sail merchantman) . . . . . . 2·25 75
752 300f. "Britannia" (steamer) 2·75 1·25

(b) Locomotives.
753 100f. Series 701, 1885, France 1·25 15
754 150f. "Columbia", 1888, Belgium . . . . 1·90 25
755 250f. Mediterranean locomotive, 1900, Italy . . 3·00 40
756 350f. MAV 114 . . . . . . 4·50 55

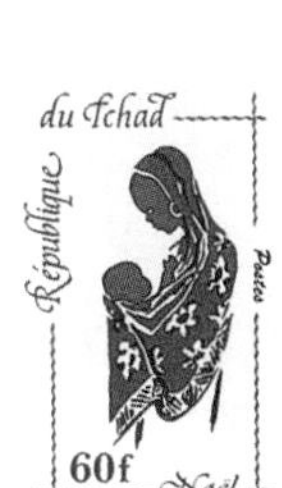

187 Virgin and Child
188 Guitars

1984. Christmas.
757 **187** 50f. brown and blue . . . 45 15
758 60f. brown and orange . . 50 20
759 80f. brown and green . . 65 25
760 85f. brown and purple . . 70 25
761 100f. brown and orange 85 30
762 135f. brown and blue . . 1·25 45

1985. European Music Year. Multicoloured.
763 20f. Type **188** 20 10
764 25f. Harps 25 15
765 30f. Xylophones 30 15
766 50f. Drums 45 20
767 70f. As No. 766 . . . . . . 55 20
768 80f. As No. 764 . . . . . . 75 30
769 100f. Type **188** 90 45
770 250f. As No. 765 . . . . . . 2·25 85

189 "Chlorophyllum molybdites"

1985. Fungi. Multicoloured.
771 25f. Type **189** 55 30
772 30f. "Tulostoma volvulatum" 70 35
773 50f. "Lentinus tuberregium" 1·00 45
774 70f. As No. 773 . . . . . . 1·40 60
775 80f. "Podaxis pistillaris" . . 1·75 65
776 100f. Type **189** . . . . . . 2·50 1·00

190 Stylized Tree and Scout

1985. Air. "Philexafrique" Stamp Exhibition, Lome, Togo (1st issue). Multicoloured.
777 200f. Type **190** . . . . 1·90 1·50
778 200f. Fokker "27" airplane 1·90 1·50
See also Nos. 808/9.

191 Abraham Lincoln

1985. Celebrities. Multicoloured.
779 25f. Type **191** (postage) . . . 20 10
780 45f. Henri Dunant (founder of Red Cross) 45 15
781 50f. Gottlieb Daimler (automobile designer) . . . 60 15
782 60f. Louis Bleriot (pilot) (air) 55 30
783 80f. Paul Harris (founder of Rotary International) . . . 55 20
784 350f. Auguste Piccard (undersea explorer) . . . . 3·75 1·60

192 Figures within Geometric Pattern
193 Sun and Hands breaking through Darkness

1985. International Youth Year. Multicoloured.
786 70f. Type **192** 50 25
787 200f. Figures on ribbon around globe . . . . . . 1·50 75

1985. 3rd Anniv of Entrance of Government Forces in N'DJamena. Multicoloured.
788 70f. Type **193** 55 25
789 70f. Claw attacking hand . . 55 25
790 70f. Pres. Hissein Habre (36 × 48 mm) 25 20
791 110f. Type **193** 80 35
792 110f. As No. 789 . . . . . . 80 35
793 110f. As No. 790 . . . . . . 1·10 35

194 Saddle-bill Stork ("Jabiru")
196 Sitatunga

195 Fokker Friendship, Farman M.F.11 and Emblem

1985. Birth Bicentenary of John J. Audubon (ornithologist).
794 **194** 70f. black, blue & brown 1·40 85
795 – 110f. olive, green & brown . . . . 2·00 1·25

796 – 150f. blue, red and olive 3·00 1·90
797 – 200f. dp blue, mauve & bl 3·50 2·10
DESIGNS: 110f. Ostrich ("Autruche"); 150f. Marabou stork ("Marabout"); 200f. Secretary bird ("Messager Serpentaire").

1985. Air. 25th Anniv of ASECNA (navigation agency). Multicoloured.
799 70f. Type **195** 50 30
800 110f. Fokker "F.27" "Friendship" and "Spirit of St. Louis" 75 50
801 250f. Fokker "F.27" "Friendship" and Vickers Vimy 1·90 1·25

1985. Mammals.
802 **196** 50f. brown, bl & dp brn 55 35
803 – 70f. brown, green and red 70 50
804 – 250f. multicoloured 2·50 1·60
DESIGNS—HORIZ: 70f. Greater kudus. VERT: 250f. Bearded mouflons.

197 U.N. Emblem on Peace Dove and Girl with Flowers

1985. 40th Anniv of U.N.O. and 25th Anniv of U.N. Membership.
806 **197** 200f. blue, red & brown 1·50 1·00
807 – 300f. blue, red & yellow 2·25 1·50
DESIGN: 300f. U.N. emblem as flower with peace doves forming stalk.

198 Girl with Posy, Youth Ceremony and I.Y.Y. Emblem

1985. Air. "Philexafrique" Stamp Exhibition, Lome, Togo (2nd issue). Multicoloured.
808 250f. Type **198** (International Youth Year) 2·25 1·90
809 250f. Computer terminal, liner, airplane, diesel freight train, rocket and U.P.U. emblem 4·25 1·00

199 Hugo

1985. Air. Death Centenary of Victor Hugo (writer).
810 **199** 70f. blue, sepia and brown 50 35
811 110f. brown, green & red 75 50
812 250f. black, red & orange 1·90 1·00
813 300f. purple, blue and red 2·25 1·25

200 Nativity **201** Pictures of Visit on Map

1985. Air. Christmas.
814 **200** 250f. multicoloured 1·90 75

1986. Visit of President to Interior.
815 **201** 100f. yellow, black & grn 95 50
816 170f. yellow, black & pink 1·90 75
817 200f. yellow, black & grn 2·25 1·25

1987. Various stamps surch.
818 – 170f. on 300f. mult (725) (postage) 70 60
819 – 230f. on 300f. blue, red and yellow (807) 1·00 85
820 – 240f. on 300f. mult (742) 1·00 85
822 **175** 100f. on 200f. mult (air) 70 55
823 – 100f. on 200f. mult (696) 60 60
824 – 100f. on 250f. mult (669) 70 55
825 – 100f. on 300f. mult (643) 40 30
826 – 100f. on 300f. mult (662) 40 30
827 **179** 170f. on 200f. mult 70 60
828 **181** 170f. on 250f. mult 1·10 90
829 – 170f. on 300f. mult (601) 70 60
830 – 170f. on 300f. mult (622) 70 60
831 – 240f. on 300f. mult (636) 1·00 90

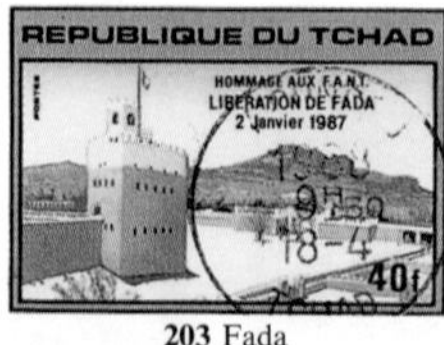

203 Fada

1987. Liberation of Fada.
832 **203** 40f. multicoloured

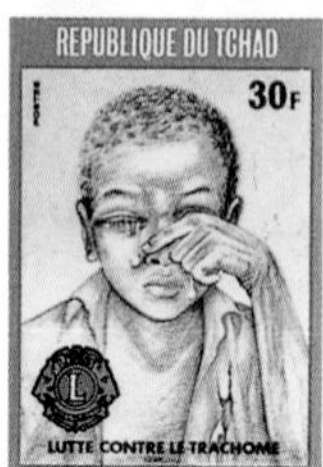

204 Boy suffering from Trachoma

1987. Lions Club Anti-trachoma Campaign. Mult.
835 30f. Type **204**
837 100f. Type **204**
838 120f. Healthy boy and afflicted boys (horiz)
840 200f. Doctor examining boy (horiz)

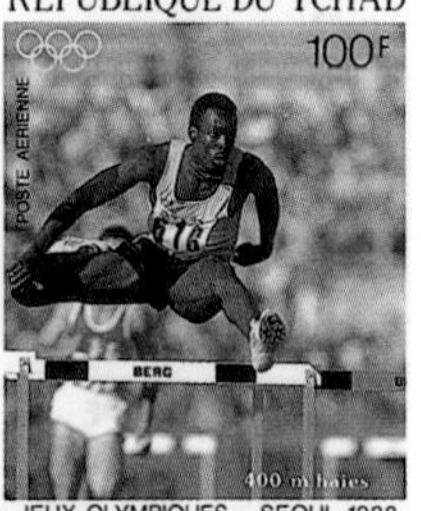

205 400 m Hurdles

1988. Air. Olympic Games, Seoul. Multicoloured.
841 100f. Type **205** 75 25
842 170f. 5000 m (horiz) 1·25 35
843 200f. Long jump (horiz) 1·50 50
844 600f. Triple jump 4·50 1·40

206 Barbary Sheep

1988. Endangered Animals. Barbary Sheep. Mult.
846 25f. Type **206** 25 20
847 45f. Mother and lamb 50 25
848 70f. Two sheep 75 30
849 100f. Two adults with lamb 1·00 50

207 President and Crowd on Map **208** Boy posting Letter

1989. "Liberation".
850 **207** 20f. multicoloured 25 15
851 25f. multicoloured 25 15
852 40f. multicoloured 35 20
853 100f. multicoloured 1·00 30
854 170f. multicoloured 1·60 50

1989. World Post Day.
855 **208** 100f. multicoloured
856 120f. multicoloured
857 170f. multicoloured
858 250f. multicoloured

209 N'Djamena Cathedral and Pope with Crucifix

1990. Visit of Pope John Paul II. Multicoloured.
859 20f. Type **209** 25 10
860 80f. Cathedral and Pope (different) 70 35
861 100f. Type **209** 95 60
862 170f. As No. 860 1·60 1·10

210 Traditional Hairstyle

1990.
863 **210** 100f. multicoloured 45 25
864 120f. multicoloured 55 30
865 170f. multicoloured 80 45
866 250f. multicoloured 1·10 65

215 Queues and Nurse vaccinating Child **216** Torch, Hands with Broken Manacles and Ballot Box

1991. "Child Vaccination—Assured Future".
880 **215** 30f. multicoloured 25 20
881 100f. multicoloured 75 45
882 170f. multicoloured 1·25 75
883 180f. multicoloured 1·25 75
884 200f. multicoloured 1·50 1·00

1991. Day of Freedom and Democracy.
885 **216** 10f. multicoloured 10 10
886 20f. multicoloured 20 15
887 40f. multicoloured 30 20
888 70f. multicoloured 50 30
889 130f. multicoloured 95 60
890 200f. multicoloured 1·50 80

217 Mother and Child **219** Mother and Child, Globe and Cereals

218 Class

1992. 20th Anniv of Medecins sans Frontieres (medical relief organization).
891 **217** 20f. multicoloured 20 10
892 45f. multicoloured 30 20
893 85f. multicoloured 70 35
894 170f. multicoloured 1·25 70
895 300f. multicoloured 2·25 1·10

1992. Literacy Campaign.
896 **218** 25f. multicoloured 20 10
897 40f. multicoloured 30 20
898 70f. multicoloured 50 25
899 100f. multicoloured 75 35
900 180f. multicoloured 1·25 60
901 200f. multicoloured 1·50 95

1992. International Nutrition Conference, Rome.
902 **219** 10f. multicoloured 15 10
903 60f. multicoloured 45 25
904 120f. multicoloured 95 55
905 500f. multicoloured 3·50 1·60

MILITARY FRANK STAMPS

1965. No. 77 optd **F.M.**
M148 20f. red and black £250 £250

M 24 Soldier with Standard **M 92** Shoulder Flash of 1st Regiment

1966. No value indicated.
M149 **M 24** (–) multicoloured 1·50 1·00

1972. No value indicated.
M353 **M 92** (–) multicoloured 75 35

OFFICIAL STAMPS

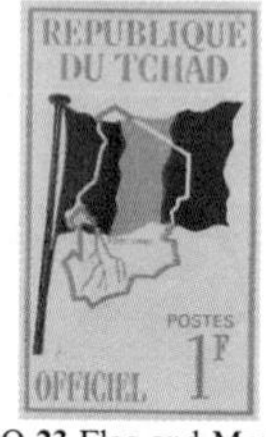

O 23 Flag and Map

1966. Flag in blue, yellow and red.
O148 **O 23** 1f. blue 10 10
O149 2f. grey 10 10
O150 5f. black 15 10
O151 10f. blue 25 10
O152 25f. orange 25 15
O153 30f. turquoise 40 20
O154 40f. red 45 20
O155 50f. purple 55 25
O156 85f. green 85 45
O157 100f. brown 1·40 50
O158 200f. red 2·50 95

POSTAGE DUE STAMPS

1928. Postage Due type of France optd **TCHAD A. E. F.**
D58 **D 11** 5c. blue 10 2·50
D59 10c. brown 35 2·50
D60 20c. olive 35 2·50
D61 25c. red 40 2·75
D62 30c. red 50 2·75
D63 45c. green 55 3·00
D64 50c. purple 40 3·25
D65 60c. brown on cream 90 4·00
D66 1f. red on cream 90 4·00
D67 2f. red 1·60 7·00
D68 3f. violet 90 4·25

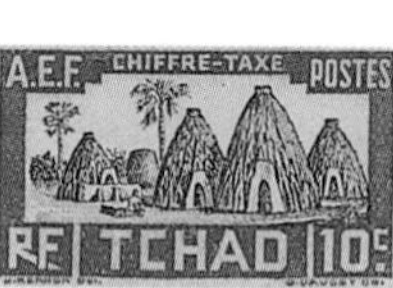

D 3 Village of Straw Huts **D 4** Pirogue on Lake Chad

1930.
D69 **D 3** 5c. olive and blue 25 2·75
D70 10c. brown and red 50 3·00
D71 20c. brown and green 1·75 3·00
D72 25c. brown and blue 1·90 3·25
D73 30c. green and brown 1·75 3·25
D74 45c. olive and green 2·25 3·50
D75 50c. brown & mauve 2·50 4·00
D76 60c. black and lilac 3·25 5·00
D77 **D 4** 1f. black and brown 4·00 5·25
D78 2f. brown and mauve 4·00 8·50
D79 3f. brown and red 20·00 55·00

D 6 Gonoa Hippopotamus

1962.
D 89 50c. bistre 10 10
D 90 50c. brown 10 10
D 91 1f. blue 10 10
D 92 1f. green 10 10
D 93 2f. red 15 15
D 94 2f. red 15 15
D 95 5f. myrtle 30 30
D 96 5f. violet 30 30
D 97 10f. brown 75 75
D 98 10f. brown 75 75

D 99	25f. purple	1·75	1·75
D100	25f. violet	1·75	1·75

DESIGNS (rock-paintings): No. D89, Type D **6**; D90, Gonoa kudu; D91, Two Gonoa antelopes; D92, Three Gonoa antelopes; D93, Gonoa antelope; D94, Tibestiram; D95, Tibestiox; D96, Oudingueur boar; D97, Gonoa elephant; D98, Gira-Gira rhinoceros; D99, Bardai warrior; D100, Gonoa masked archer. The two designs in each value are arranged in tete-beche pairs throughout the sheet.

D **65** Kanem Puppet

1969. Native Puppets.

D284	D **65**	1f. brown, red & grn	10	10
D285	–	2f. brown, grn & red	10	10
D286	–	5f. green and brown	10	10
D287	–	10f. brown, pur & grn	20	20
D288	–	25f. brown, pur & grn	45	25

DESIGNS: 2f. Kotoko doll; 5f. Copper doll; 10f. Kotoko (diff); 25f. Guera doll.

APPENDIX

The following stamps have either been issued in excess of postal needs or have not been available to the public in reasonable quantities at face value. Such stamps may later be given full listing if there is evidence of regular postal use.

1970.

"Apollo programme". Postage 40f.; Air 15, 25f.

Birth Bicent of Napoleon. Air. 10, 25, 32f.

World Cup Football Championship, Mexico. Air 5f.

World Cup. Previous Winners. 1, 4f., 5f. × 2.

"Expo 70" World Fair, Osaka, Japan. Japanese Paintings. 50c., 1, 2f.

Christmas. Paintings. Postage 3, 25f.; Air 32f.

Past Olympic Venues. Postage 3, 8, 20f.; Air 10, 35f.

1971.

Space Exploration. 8, 10, 35f.

Winter Olympic Games, Sapporo, Japan. Japanese Paintings. 50c., 1, 2f.

Kings and Queens of France. Postage 25f. × 2, 30, 32, 35f., 40f. × 2, 50f. × 4, 60f.; Air 40, 50, 60, 70, 75, 80f., 100f. × 5, 150f., 200f. × 4.

150th Death Anniv of Napoleon. Air. 10f.

Famous Paintings. 1, 4, 5f.

Past Olympic Venues. Postage 15, 20f.; Air 25, 50f.

Winter Olympic Games, Sapporo, Japan. Optd on 1970 "Expo 70" issue 50c., 1, 2f.

Olympic Games Munich. World Cup Previous Winners issue (1970) optd **1f.**

1972.

Moon Flight of "Apollo 15". Air 40, 80, 150, 250, 300, 500f.

"Soyuz 11" Disaster. Air 30, 50, 100, 200, 300, 400f.

Pres. Tombalbaye. Postage 30, 40f.; Air 70, 80f.

Winter Olympic Games, Sapporo, Japan. Postage 25, 75, 150f.; Air 130, 200f.

13th World Scout Jamboree, Asagiri, Japan (1971). Postage 30, 70, 80f.; Air 100, 200f.

Medal Winners, Sapporo Winter Olympics. Postage 25, 75, 100, 130f.; Air 150, 200f.

Olympic Games, Munich. Postage 20, 40, 60f.; Air 100, 120, 150f.

African Animals. Air 20, 30, 100, 130, 150f.

Medal Winners, Munich Olympics (1st series). Postage 10, 20, 40, 60f.; Air 150, 250f.

Medal Winners, Munich Olympics (2nd series). Gold frames, Postage 20, 30, 50f.; Air 150, 250f.

1973.

Locomotives. 10, 40, 50, 150, 200f.

Domestic Animals (2nd issue). Postage 20, 30f.; Air 100, 130, 150f.

Horses. 20, 60, 100, 120f.

Airplanes. Air 5, 25, 70, 150, 200f.

Christmas. Postage 30, 40, 55f.; Air 60, 250f.

Other issues exist which were prepared by various agencies, but it is uncertain whether these were placed on sale in Chad. They include further values in the "Kings and Queens of France" series.

All the stamps below are on gold foil.

1982.

World Cup Football Championship, Spain. Air 1500f.

21st Birthday of Princess of Wales. Air 1500f.

75th Anniv of Scout Movement. Air 1500f.

Olympic Games, Los Angeles. Air 1500f.

Birth of Prince William of Wales. 21st Birthday of Princess of Wales stamp optd. Air 1500f.

1983.

World Cup Football Championship Results. Air 1500f.

Chess Grand Masters. Air 1500f.

Exploitation of Space. Air 1500f.

Winter Olympic Games, Sarajevo. Air 1500f.

Bicentary of Manned Flight. Air 1500f.

Olympic Games, Los Angeles. Air 1500f.

CHAMBA Pt. 1

An Indian "convention" state of the Punjab.

Stamps of India overprinted.

12 pies = 1 anna; 16 annas = 1 rupee.

1886. Queen Victoria. Optd **CHAMBA STATE** in two lines.

1	23	½a. turquoise	25	45
2	–	1a. purple	1·00	1·25
4	–	1a.6p. brown	1·10	9·50
6	–	2a. blue	1·10	1·25
7	–	2a.6p. green	29·00	80·00
9	–	3a. orange	1·25	4·00
11	–	4a. green (No. 96)	4·50	5·00
12	–	6a. brown (No. 80)	3·00	14·00
14	–	8a. mauve	6·00	7·50
16	–	12a. purple on red	4·75	11·00
17	–	1r. grey (No. 101)	35·00	£100
18	37	1r. green and red	6·00	12·00
19	38	2r. red and brown	80·00	£270
20		3r. brown and green	85·00	£225
21		5r. blue and violet	95·00	£400

1900. Queen Victoria. Optd **CHAMBA STATE** in two lines.

22	40	3p. red	20	50
23		3p. grey	20	1·60
25	23	½a. green	30	80
26	–	1a. red	20	30
27	–	2a. lilac	7·00	23·00

1903. King Edward VII. Optd **CHAMBA STATE** in two lines.

28	41	3p. grey	15	85
30	–	½a. green (No. 122)	25	20
31	–	1a. red (No. 123)	1·00	35
33	–	2a. lilac	1·00	2·25
34	–	3a. orange	2·50	3·50
35	–	4a. olive	3·75	14·00
36	–	6a. bistre	3·00	17·00
37	–	8a. mauve	3·75	16·00
39	–	12a. purple on red	5·50	22·00
40	–	1r. green and red	6·00	19·00

1907. King Edward VII. Optd **CHAMBA STATE** in two lines.

41	–	½a. green (No. 149)	75	2·75
42	–	1a. red (No. 150)	1·00	3·00

1913. King George V. Optd **CHAMBA STATE** in two lines.

43	55	3p. grey	10	55
44	56	½a. green	30	60
45a	57	1a. red	70	2·50
55		1a. brown	1·60	3·50
56	58	1½a. brown (No. 163)	22·00	£100
57		1½a. brown (No. 165)	1·25	4·50
58		1½a. red	75	16·00
47	59	2a. purple	2·25	7·50
59	61	2a.6p. blue	60	3·00
60		2a.6p. orange	1·40	14·00
48	62	3a. orange	2·50	6·00
61		3a. blue	2·50	17·00
49	63	4a. olive	2·00	3·25
50	64	6a. bistre	2·25	4·25
51a	65	8a. mauve	3·75	9·00
52	66	12a. red	3·00	10·00
53	67	1r. brown and green	12·00	22·00

1921. No. 192 of India optd **CHAMBA**.

54	57	9p. on 1a. red	1·00	17·00

1927. Stamps of India (King George V) optd **CHAMBA STATE** in one line.

62	55	3p. grey	10	1·10
63	56	½a. green	20	1·50
76	79	½a. green	1·00	7·50
64	80	9p. green	2·25	12·00
65	57	1a. brown	1·60	60
77	81	1a. brown	1·25	60
66	82	1a.3p. mauve	1·10	4·50
67w	58	1½a. red	4·50	5·00
68	70	2a. lilac	1·25	2·00
78	59	2a. red	85	20·00
69	61	2a.6p. orange	1·40	13·00
70	62	3a. blue	1·00	15·00
80		3a. red	2·00	8·50
71	71	4a. green	80	4·00
81	63	4a. olive	2·75	12·00
72	64	6a. bistre	26·00	£150
73	65	8a. mauve	1·40	8·50
74	66	12a. red	1·40	10·00
75	67	1r. brown and green	5·00	21·00

1938. Stamps of India (King George VI Nos. 247/64) optd **CHAMBA STATE**.

82	91	3p. slate	6·00	10·00
83		½a. brown	1·00	6·00
84		9p. green	6·50	25·00
85		1a. red	1·00	2·00
86	92	2a. red	4·25	8·50
87	–	2a.6p. violet	5·00	20·00
88	–	3a. green	5·50	19·00
89	–	3a.6p. blue	5·50	22·00
90	–	4a. brown	17·00	17·00
91	–	6a. green	16·00	48·00
92	–	8a. violet	17·00	42·00
93	–	12a. red	11·00	45·00
94	93	1r. slate and brown	25·00	50·00
95		2r. purple and brown	48·00	£250
96		5r. green and blue	80·00	£375
97		10r. purple and red	£130	£500
98		15r. brown and green	£160	£800
99		25r. slate and purple	£225	£850

1942. Stamps of India (King George VI) optd **CHAMBA**. (a) On issue of 1938

100	91	½a. brown	30·00	22·00
101		1a. red	40·00	28·00
102	93	1r. slate and brown	18·00	15·00
103		2r. purple and brown	24·00	£200
104		5r. green and blue	45·00	£225
105		10r. purple and red	65·00	£425
106		15r. brown and green	£140	£650
107		25r. slate and purple	£140	£650

(b) On issue of 1940.

108	100a	3p. slate	70	3·75
109		½a. mauve	70	3·75
110		9p. green	1·00	12·00
111		1a. red	1·00	3·25
112	101	1½a. violet	1·00	8·00
113		2a. red	4·00	8·50
114		3a. violet	14·00	28·00
115		3½a. blue	7·00	30·00
116	102	4a. brown	9·00	9·00
117		6a. green	12·00	35·00
118		8a. violet	12·00	42·00
119		12a. purple	18·00	55·00
120	–	14a. purple (No. 277)	10·00	3·00

OFFICIAL STAMPS

Stamps of India overprinted.

1886. Queen Victoria. Optd **SERVICE CHAMBA STATE**.

O 1	23	½a. turquoise	20	10
O 3	–	1a. purple	1·00	10
O 5	–	2a. blue	1·25	1·40
O 7	–	3a. orange	2·00	9·00
O 8	–	4a. green (No. 96)	2·25	4·00
O10	–	6a. brown (No. 80)	4·25	9·00
O13	–	8a. mauve	1·50	1·75
O14	–	12a. purple on red	7·50	35·00
O15	–	1r. grey (No. 101)	13·00	£100
O16	37	1r. green and red	6·00	30·00

1902. Queen Victoria. Optd **SERVICE CHAMBA STATE**.

O17	40	3p. grey	30	50
O18	23	½a. green	30	2·75
O20	–	1a. red	60	40
O21	–	2a. lilac	9·00	26·00

1903. King Edward VII. Optd **SERVICE CHAMBA STATE**.

O22	41	3p. grey	25	15
O24		½a. green (No. 122)	25	10
O25		1a. red (No. 123)	75	30
O27	–	2a. lilac	1·00	60
O28	–	4a. olive	3·50	15·00
O29	–	8a. mauve	4·50	14·00
O31	–	1r. green and red	1·75	9·00

1907. King Edward VII. Optd **SERVICE CHAMBA STATE**.

O32	–	½a. green (No. 149)	40	75
O33	–	1a. red (No. 150)	2·25	1·50

1913. King George V Official stamps optd **CHAMBA STATE**.

O34	55	3p. grey	20	40
O36	56	½a. green	10	10
O38	57	1a. red	10	10
O47		1a. brown	2·25	50
O40	59	2a. lilac (No. O83)	1·10	11·00
O41	63	4a. olive (No. O86)	1·10	14·00
O42	65	8a. mauve	1·75	15·00
O43	67	1r. brown and green	4·00	24·00

1914. King George V Postage stamps optd **SERVICE CHAMBA STATE**.

O44	59	2a. lilac (No. 166)	14·00	
O45	63	4a. olive (No. 210)	11·00	

1921. No O97 of India optd **CHAMBA**.

O46	57	9p. on 1a. red	15	6·00

1927. King George V Postage stamps optd **CHAMBA STATE SERVICE**.

O48	55	3p. grey	50	30
O49	56	½a. green	35	15
O61	79	½a. green	3·00	50
O50	80	9p. green	2·25	8·00
O51	57	1a. brown	20	10
O62	81	1a. brown	2·50	45
O52	82	1¼a. mauve	5·00	60
O53	70	2a. lilac	1·25	60
O63	59	2a. red	3·50	1·00
O54	71	4a. olive	1·10	1·50
O65	63	4a. green	5·50	4·50
O55	65	8a. mauve	3·75	7·00
O56	66	12a. red	2·50	18·00
O57	67	1r. brown and green	11·00	32·00
O58		2r. red and orange	21·00	£180
O59		5r. blue and violet	40·00	£250
O60		1r. green and red	60·00	£250

1938. King George VI Postage stamps of India optd **CHAMBA STATE SERVICE**.

O66	91	9p. green	11·00	45·00
O67		1a. red	11·00	2·50
O68	93	1r. slate and brown	£350	£800
O69		2r. purple and brown	38·00	£300
O70		5r. green and blue	60·00	£375
O71		10r. purple and red	90·00	£650

1940. Official stamps of India optd **CHAMBA**.

O72	O 20	3p. grey	70	70
O73		½a. brown	14·00	2·00
O74		½a. purple	70	2·25
O75		9p. green	4·50	7·50
O76		1a. red	70	1·75
O77		1a.3p. brown	48·00	15·00
O78		1½a. violet	4·75	6·00
O79		2a. orange	4·75	5·50
O80		2½a. violet	2·25	18·00
O81		4a. brown	4·50	9·00
O82w		8a. violet	11·00	48·00

1942. King George VI Postage stamps of India optd **CHAMBA SERVICE**.

O83	93	1r. slate and brown	20·00	£170
O84		2r. purple and brown	35·00	£225
O85		5r. green and blue	65·00	£350
O86		10r. purple and red	80·00	£600

CHARKHARI Pt. 1

A state of Central India. Now uses Indian stamps.

12 pies = 1 anna; 16 annas = 1 rupee.

1

2

1894. Imperf. No gum.

10	1	¼a. purple	1·75	2·50
6a		½a. purple	2·50	3·00
7a		1a. green	4·00	4·50
8a		2a. green	7·00	8·00
9a		4a. green	6·00	9·50

1909. Perf or imperf.

15a	2	1p. brown	3·50	38·00
16		1p. blue	60	45
33		1p. violet	16·00	£120
32		1p. green	50·00	£170
25		½a. red	1·50	1·50
34		½a. olive	1·25	14·00
35		½a. brown	5·00	22·00
36		½a. black	55·00	£150
18a		1a. green	1·75	1·60
40		1a. brown	8·00	22·00
41		1a. red	90·00	55·00
19		2a. blue	3·00	3·25
43		2a. grey	45·00	55·00
20		4a. green	3·50	4·75
44		4a. red	3·00	19·00
21		8a. red	7·50	16·00
22		1r. brown	13·00	32·00

4

7 Imlia Palace

5

1912. Imperf.

28	4	1p. violet	7·00	5·00

1922. Imperf.

29	5	1a. violet	70·00	80·00

1931. Perf.

45	–	½a. green	1·25	10
46	7	1a. sepia	1·40	10
47	–	2a. violet	1·00	10
48	–	4a. olive	1·10	15
49	–	8a. mauve	1·40	10
50	–	1r. green and red	2·00	20
51	–	2r. red and brown	3·50	25
52	–	3r. brown and green	10·00	40
53	–	5r. blue and lilac	8·50	50

DESIGNS—HORIZ: ½a. The Lake; 2a. Industrial school; 4a. Bird's-eye view of city; 8a. Fort; 1r. Guest House; 2r. Palace Gate; 3r. Temples at Rainpur; 5r. Goverdhan Temple.

1940. Nos. 21/2 surch.

54	2	½a. on 8a. red	27·00	£110
55		1a. on 1r. brown	85·00	£350
56		"1 ANNA" on 1r. brown	£600	£650

CHILE Pt. 20

A republic on the W. coast of S. America.

1853. 100 centavos = 1 peso.
1960. 10 milesimos = 1 centesimo; 100 centesimos = 1 escudo.
1975. 100 centavos = 1 peso.

1 Columbus

9

10

1853. Imperf.

29	1	1c. yellow	18·00	20·00
17		5c. brown	£100	11·00
37		5c. red	23·00	6·50
32		10c. blue	32·00	5·00
33		20c. green	35·00	28·00

1867. Perf.

41	9	1c. orange	12·50	1·25
43		2c. black	17·00	2·75
45		5c. red	13·00	90
46		10c. blue	13·00	1·10
48		20c. green	22·00	2·00

1877. Roul.

49	10	1c. slate	2·00	75
50		2c. orange	9·00	1·50
51		5c. lake	11·50	50
52		10c. blue	10·00	1·60
53		20c. green	13·00	2·50

12

15

1878. Roul.

55	12	1c. green	1·00	15
57		2c. red	1·00	15
58		5c. red	5·00	25
59a		5c. blue	1·50	50
60a		10c. orange	2·25	10
61		15c. green	2·50	15
62		20c. grey	2·50	35
63		25c. brown	2·50	15
64		30c. red	5·00	2·00
65a		50c. violet	2·50	1·00
66	15	1p. black and brown	13·50	2·00

16

18

1900. Roul.

82	16	1c. green	75	10
83		2c. red	75	10
84a		5c. blue	3·50	25
85		10c. lilac	4·00	35
79		20c. grey	4·00	1·25
80		30c. brown	4·50	1·25
81		50c. brown	5·50	1·50

1900. Surch **5**.

86	12	5c. on 30c. red	1·00	20

1901. Perf.

87	18	1c. green	25	15
88		2c. red	35	15
89		5c. blue	1·10	15
90		10c. black and red	2·10	25
91		30c. black and violet	6·75	65
92		50c. black and red	6·50	1·75

1903. Surch **Diez CENTAVOS**.

93	16	10c. on 30c. brown	1·60	95

20 Huemul (mountain deer)

24 Pedro Valdivia

1904. Animal supporting shield at left without mane and tail. Optd **CORREOS** in frame.

94	20	2c. brown	25	15
95		5c. red	40	15
96		10c. olive	1·40	40

1904. As T **20**, but animal with mane and tail optd **CORREOS** in frame and the 1p. also surch **CENTAVOS 3 3**.

97	20	2c. brown	5·00	
98		3c. on 1p. brown	35	20
99		5c. red	6·00	
100		10c. green	12·00	

1904. Surch **CORREOS** in frame and new value.

101	24	1c. on 20c. blue	25	15
102		3c. on 5c. red	40·00	40·00
103		12c. on 5c. red	85	35

26 Christopher Columbus

28 Christopher Columbus

27 Christopher Columbus

1905.

104	26	1c. green	25	15
105		2c. red	25	15
106		3c. brown	60	25
107		5c. blue	60	15
108	27	10c. black and grey	1·25	15
109		12c. black and lake	5·25	2·00
110		15c. black and lilac	1·25	15
111		20c. black and brown	2·50	15
112		30c. black and green	3·50	25
113		50c. black and blue	3·50	25
114	28	1p. grey and green	12·50	8·50

1910. Optd **ISLAS DE JUAN FERNANDEZ** or surch also.

115	27	5c. on 12c. black & red	40	30
116	28	10c. on 1p. grey & green	1·10	65
117		20c. on 1p. grey & green	1·75	1·00
118		1p. grey and green	3·50	2·40

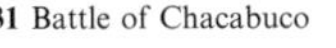

31 Battle of Chacabuco **33** San Martin Monument

1910. Centenary of Independence. Centres in black.

119	–	1c. green	25	15
120	31	2c. lake	25	15
121	–	3c. brown	1·00	65
122	–	5c. blue	35	10
123	–	10c. brown	1·50	25
124	–	12c. red	3·00	90
125	–	15c. slate	1·60	65
126	–	20c. orange	2·50	1·00
127	–	25c. blue	3·50	2·40
128	–	30c. mauve	3·25	1·40
129	–	50c. olive	6·75	1·50
130	33	1p. yellow	13·50	4·50
131	–	2p. red	13·50	3·75
132	–	5p. green	35·00	17·00
133	–	10p. purple	30·00	13·50

DESIGNS—HORIZ: 1c. Oath of Independence; 3c. Battle of Roble; 5c. Battle of Maipu; 10c. Fight between frigates "Lautaro" and "Esmeralda"; 12c. Capture of the "Maria Isabella"; 15c. First sortie of the liberating forces; 20c. Abdication of O'Higgins; 25c. First Chilean Congress. VERT: 30c. O'Higgins Monument; 50c. Carrera Monument; 2p. General Blanco; 5p. General Zenteno; 10p. Admiral Cochrane.

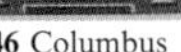

46 Columbus **47** Valdivia **49** O'Higgins

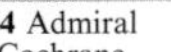

64 Admiral Cochrane **50** Freire **52** Prieto

65 M. Rengifo **57** A. Pinto

1911. Inscr "CHILE CORREOS".

135	46	1c. green	15	10
136	47	2c. red	15	10
150	46	2c. red	15	10
137	–	3c. sepia	50	35
151	–	4c. sepia	20	10
138	49	5c. blue	15	10
161	64	5c. blue	35	15
152	–	8c. grey	70	30
139	50	10c. black and grey	50	30
153	49	10c. black and blue	70	30
140	–	12c. black and red	85	30
154	–	14c. black and red	70	10
141	52	15c. black and purple	70	30
142	–	20c. black and orange	1·40	15
167	–	25c. black and blue	50	15
168	–	30c. black and brown	1·50	15
155	52	40c. black and purple	4·50	65
186	65	40c. black and violet	40	15
170	–	50c. black and green	1·50	15
156	–	60c. black and blue	8·50	1·60
171	–	80c. black and sepia	1·90	55
188	57	1p. black and green	70	10
189	–	2p. black and red	3·25	30
190	–	5p. black and olive	8·00	70
190a	–	10p. black and orange	8·00	1·00

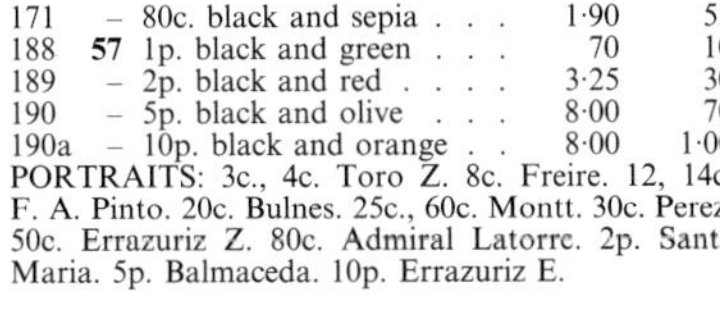

PORTRAITS: 3c., 4c. Toro Z. 8c. Freire. 12, 14c. F. A. Pinto. 20c. Bulnes. 25c., 60c. Montt. 30c. Perez. 50c. Errazuriz Z. 80c. Admiral Latorre. 2p. Santa Maria. 5p. Balmaceda. 10p. Errazuriz E.

61 Columbus **62** Valdivia **63** Columbus

1915. Larger Stars.

157	61	1c. green	20	10
158	62	2c. red	20	10
160	61	4c. brown (small head)	30	10
159	63	4c. brown (large head)	25	10

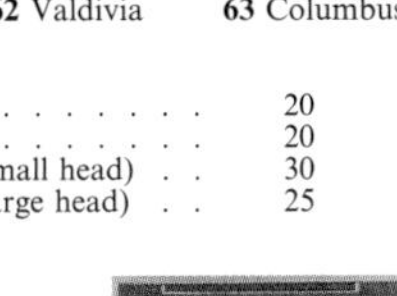

67 Chilean Congress Building **67a** O'Higgins

1923. Pan-American Conference.

176	67	2c. red	15	10
177		4c. brown	15	10
178		10c. black and blue	15	10
179		20c. black and orange	40	15
180		40c. black and mauve	70	20
181		1p. black and green	85	35
182		2p. black and red	3·00	40
183		5p. black and green	10·00	2·25

1927. Air. Unissued stamp surch **Correo Aereo** and value.

184	67a	40c. on 10c. blue & brn	£200	30·00
184a		80c. on 10c. blue & brn	£200	42·00
184b		1p.20 on 10c. bl & brn	£200	50·00
184c		1p.60 on 10c. bl & brn	£200	50·00
184d		2p. on 10c. blue & brn	£200	50·00

1928. Air. Optd **CORREO AEREO** and bird or surch also.

191	–	20c. blk & orge (No. 141)	35	15
199	65	40c. black and violet	40	20
200	57	1p. black and green	1·10	35
194	–	2p. black & red (No. 189)	1·60	25
201	64	3p. on 5c. blue	40·00	30·00
195	–	5p. black & ol (No. 190)	2·75	70
196	49	6p. on 10c. black & blue	50·00	30·00
198	–	10p. blk & orge (No. 190a)	9·00	2·75

1928. As Types of 1911, but inscr "CORREOS DE CHILE".

205	64	5c. blue	50	10
206		5c. green	50	10
204	49	10c. black and blue	75	25
208	52	15c. black and purple	1·75	10
209	–	20c. black and orange (As No. 142)	4·00	15
210	–	25c. black and blue (As No. 167)	75	10
211	–	30c. black and brown (As No. 168)	55	20
212	–	50c. black and green (As No. 170)	50	10

1929. Air. Nos. 209/12 optd **CORREO AEREO** and bird.

213a		20c. black and orange	25	15
214		25c. black and blue	40	15
215		30c. black and brown	25	15
216		50c. black and green	35	15

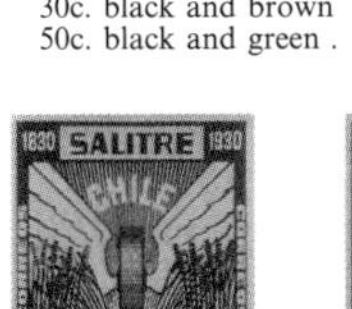

71 Winged Wheel **72** Sower

1930. Centenary of Nitrate Industry.

217	71	5c. green	35	15
218		10c. brown	35	15
219		15c. violet	35	15
220	–	25c. slate (Girl harvester)	1·40	15
221	72	70c. blue	3·25	1·00
222		1p. green (24½ × 30 mm)	2·50	50

73 Andean Condor and Fokker Super Universal Airplane **75** Ford 4AT Trimotor over Los Cerrillos Airport

1931. Air. Inscr "LINEA AEREA NACIONAL".

223	73	5c. green	40	25
224		10c. brown	40	25
225		20c. red	40	10
226a	–	50c. sepia	40	25
227	75	50c. blue	1·75	85
228	–	1p. violet	55	30
229	–	2p. slate	1·50	25
230	75	5p. red	3·50	60

DESIGN: 50c. (No. 226a), 1p., 2p. Fokker Super Universal airplane.

76 O'Higgins **79** Mariano Egana

1931.

231	76	10c. blue	1·00	10
232	–	20c. brown (Bulnes)	85	10
233	–	30c. mauve (Perez)	1·40	10

1934. Centenary of Constitution of 1833.

234	79	30c. mauve	50	25
235	–	1p.20 blue	90	25

PORTRAIT: 1p.20, Joaquin Tocornal (24½ × 29 mm).

83 Fokker Super Universal Aircraft over Globe **87** Diego de Almagro

1934. Air. As T **83**.

236		10c. green	15	10
237		15c. green	25	20
238		20c. blue	20	15
239		30c. black	20	15
239a		40c. blue	20	15
240		50c. brown	20	15
241		60c. black	20	15
356a		70c. blue	30	20
243		80c. green	20	15
244		1p. grey	20	15
245		2p. blue	20	15
360		3p. brown	25	15
361		4p. brown	25	15
248		5p. red	20	10
249		6p. brown	35	15
250		8p. green	30	10
251		10p. purple	35	15
252		20p. olive	35	15
253		30p. grey	35	10
254		40p. violet	70	40
255a		50p. purple	85	40

DESIGNS—21 × 25 mm: 10, 15, 20c. Fokker Super Universal over Santiago; 30, 40, 50c. Junkers G.24 over landscape; 60c. Condor in flight; 70c. Airplane and star; 80c. Condor and statue of Caupolican; 25 × 29 mm: 1, 2p. Type **83**; 3, 4, 5p. Stinson Faucett F.19 seaplane in flight; 6, 8, 10p. Northrop Alpha monoplane and rainbow; 20, 30p. Stylized Dornier Wal flying boat and compass; 40, 50p. Airplane riding a storm.

1936. 400th Anniv of Discovery of Chile.

256	–	5c. red	35	15
257	–	10c. violet	15	10
258	–	20c. mauve	20	10
259	–	25c. blue	2·00	55
260	–	30c. green	20	10
261	–	40c. black	2·00	50
262	–	50c. blue	1·10	20
263	–	1p. green	1·50	35
264	–	1p.20 blue	1·25	45
265	87	2p. brown	1·25	55
266	–	5p. red	3·50	1·40
267	–	10p. purple	9·00	7·00

DESIGNS: 5c. Atacama desert; 10c. Fishing boats; 20c. Coquito palms; 25c. Sheep. 30c. Coal mines; 40c. Lonquimay forests; 50c. Lota coal port; 1p. "Orduna" (liner), Valparaiso; 1p.20. Mt. Puntiaguda; 5p. Cattle; 10p. Shovelling nitrate.

88 Laja Waterfall **90** "Calbuco" (fishing boat)

1938.

268	88	5c. purple	15	10
269	–	10c. red	15	10
269a	–	15c. red	15	10
270	–	20c. blue	45	10
271	–	30c. pink	15	10
272	–	40c. green	15	10
273	–	50c. violet	15	10
274	90	1p. orange	15	10
275	–	1p.80 blue	85	20
338h	–	2p. red	50	10
278	–	5p. green	35	10
338j	–	10p. purple	1·10	10

DESIGNS—As Type **88**: 10c. Rural landscape; 15c. Boldo tree; 20c. Nitrate works; 30c. Mineral spas; 40c. Copper mine; 50c. Petroleum tanks. As Type **90**: 1p.80, Osorno Volcano; 2p. "Conte de Biancamano" (freighter) and "Ponderoso" (tug); 5p. Lake Villarrica; 10p. Steam locomotive No. 908.

92 "Abtao" (armed steamer) and Policarpo Toro

1940. 50th Anniv of Occupation of Easter Island and Local Hospital Fund.

279	92	80c.+2p.20 red & green	2·00	1·40
280	–	3p.60+6p.40 green and red	2·00	1·40

DESIGN: 3p.60, "Abtao" and E. Eyraud.

93 Western Hemisphere

1940. 50th Anniv of Pan-American Union.

281	93	40c. green	20	10

1940. Air. Surch with winged device above new values.

282	73	80c. on 20c. red	45	25
283	75	1p.60 on 5p. red	3·25	85
284	–	5p.10 on 2p. slate (No. 229)	2·50	1·00

96 Fray Camilo Henriquez **97** Founding of Santiago

1941. 400th Anniv of Santiago.

285	96	10c. red	30	15
286	–	40c. green	40	10
287	–	1p.10 red	1·00	85
288	97	1p.80 blue	1·00	50
289	–	3p.60 blue	3·25	1·60

PORTRAITS—As Type **96**: 40c. P. Valdivia. 1p.10, B. V. MacKenna. 3p.60, D. B. Arana.

98 Potez 56 and Globe **99** Sikorsky S-43 Amphibian and Galleon

1941. Air. No. 304 is dated "1541–1941" and commemorates the 4th Centenary of Santiago.

290	–	10c. olive	30	10
291	–	10c. mauve	30	10
316	–	10c. blue	20	10
292	98	20c. red	30	10
318		20c. green	20	10
294		20c. brown	20	10
295	–	30c. violet	30	10
295a	–	30c. olive	20	10
296	–	40c. brown	30	10
297	–	40c. blue	20	10
324	–	50c. red	30	10
325	–	50c. orange	30	10
299a	–	60c. green	20	15
326	–	60c. orange	30	10
300	–	70c. red	60	20
301	–	80c. blue	3·00	35
302	–	80c. olive	20	15
303a	–	90c. brown	30	10
304	99	1p. blue	60	20
304a		1p. green and blue	30	10
305	–	1p.60 violet	30	15
306	–	1p.80 violet	30	10
307	–	2p. lake	85	25
308	–	2p. brown	60	10
309	–	3p. green	1·25	45
310a	–	3p. violet and yellow	2·50	25
334	–	3p. violet and orange	85	15
311	–	4p. violet and brown	2·00	55
335	–	4p. green	85	30
336a	–	5p. brown	35	20
336	–	5p. red	35	25
314	–	10p. green and blue	9·50	4·00
337	–	10p. blue	85	25

DESIGNS: (each incorporating a different type of airplane): 10c. Steeple; 20c. Flag; 40c. Stars; 50c. Mountains; 60c. Tree; 70c. Estuary; 80c. Shore; 90c. Sun rays; 1p.60, 1p.80, Wireless mast; 2p. Compass; 3p. Telegraph wires; 4p. Rainbow; 5p. Factory; 10p. Snow-capped mountain.

See also Nos. 395 etc.

101 V. Letelier

102 University of Chile

103 Coat of arms and Aeroplane

1942. Centenary of Santiago de Chile University.
339 **101** 30c. red (postage) 20 10
340 – 40c. green 20 10
341 – 90c. violet . . . . 1·50 70
342 **102** 1p. brown . . . . 1·00 40
343 – 1p.80 blue . . . . 2·50 1·40

344 **103** 100p. red (air) . . . . . 30·00 20·00
DESIGNS—As Type **101**: 40c. A. Bello; 90c. M. Bulnes; 1p.80, M. Montt.

104 Manuel Bulnes

105 Straits of Magellan

1944. Centenary of Occupation of Magellan Straits.
345 **104** 15c. black 15 10
346 – 30c. red 15 10
347 – 40c. green 15 10
348 – 1p. brown 85 25
349 **105** 1p.80 blue . . . . 1·25 70
PORTRAITS: 30c. J. W. Wilson. 40c. D. D. Almeida. 1p. Jose de los Santos Mardones.

106 "Lamp of Life"

1944. International Red Cross.
350 **106** 40c. black, red and green 50 10
351 – 1p.80 red and blue . . . 1·00 50
DESIGN: 1p.80, Serpent and chalice symbol of Hygiene.

107 O'Higgins (after J. G. de Castro)

108 Battle of Rancagua (after Subercaseaux)

1944. Death Centenary of Bernardo O'Higgins.
367 **107** 15c. black and red 15 10
368 – 30c. black and brown . . . 25 10
369 – 40c. black and green . . . 25 10
370 **108** 1p.80 black and blue . . 1·25 80
DESIGNS—As Type **108**: 30c. Battle of the Maipu; 40c. Abdication of O'Higgins.

109 Columbus Lighthouse, Dominican Republic

110 Andres Bello

1945. 450th Anniv of Discovery of America by Columbus.
371 **109** 40c. green 30 15

1946. 80th Death Anniv of Andres Bello (educationist).
372 **110** 40c. green 15 10
373 1p.80 blue 15 10

111 Antarctic Territory

113 Miguel de Cervantes

112 Eusebio Lillo and Ramon Carnicer

1947.
374 **111** 40c. red 40 15
375 2p.50 blue . . . . 1·25 30

1947. Centenary of National Anthem.
376 **112** 40c. green 15 10

1947. 400th Birth Anniv of Cervantes.
377 **113** 40c. red 15 10

114 Arturo Prat and "Esmeralda" (sail corvette)

1948. Birth Centenary of Arturo Prat.
378 **114** 40c. blue 35 10

115 O'Higgins

119 "Chiasognathus granti"

1948.
379 **115** 60c. black 10 10

1948. No. 272 surch **VEINTE CTS.** and bar.
380 20c. on 40c. green 10 10

1948. Centenary of Publication on Chilean Flora and Fauna. Botanical and zoological designs, as T **119** inscr "CENTENARIO DEL LIBRO DE GAY 1844–1944".
381a/y 60c. blue (postage) 80 35
382a/y 2p.60 green . . . . 1·50 90

383a/y 3p. red (air) . . . . 1·60 1·10
Each value in 25 different designs. Prices are for individual stamps.

120 Airline Badge

121 B. V. Mackenna

1949. Air. 20th Anniv of National Airline.
384 **120** 2p. blue 15 25

1949. Vicuna Mackenna Museum.
385 **121** 60c. blue (postage) . . . 10 10

386 3p. red (air) 15 10

122 Wheel and Lamp

1949. Cent of School of Arts and Crafts, Santiago.
387 **122** 60c. mauve (postage) . . 15 10
388 – 2p.60 blue 30 20

389 – 5p. green (air) 45 30
390 – 10p. brown 75 40
DESIGNS: 2p.60, Shield and book; 5p. Shield, book and factory; 10p. Wheel and column.

123 Heinrich von Stephan

124 Douglas DC-6B and Globe

1950. 75th Anniv of U.P.U.
391 **123** 60c. red (postage) 10 10
392 2p.50 blue 45 20

393 **124** 5p. green (air) 30 20
394 10p. brown 60 35

1950. Air. As T **98/99**.
395 20c. brown 15 10
396 40c. violet 15 10
404c 60c. blue 25 10
398 1p. green 15 10
399 2p. brown 15 10
404f 3p. blue 15 10
401 4p. orange 30 10
402 5p. violet 15 10
403 10p. green 20 10
480 20p. brown 30 10
481 50p. green 35 10
482 100p. red 75 10
483 200p. blue 80 10
DESIGNS (each including an aeroplane): 20c. Mountains; 40c. Coastline; 60c. Fishing vessel; 1p. Araucanian pine tree; 2p. Chilean flag; 3p. Dock crane; 4p. River; 5p. Industrial plant; 10p. Landscape; 20p. Aerial railway; 50p. Mountainous coastline; 100p. Antarctic map; 200p. Rock "bridge" in sea.

126 Crossing the Andes (after Y. Prades)

1951. Death Centenary of Gen. San Martin.
405 – 60c. blue (postage) . . . 10 10

406 **126** 5p. purple (air) 50 15
PORTRAIT (25 × 29 mm): 60c. San Martin.

1951. Air. No. 303a surch **UN PESO**.
407 1p. on 90c. brown 15 10

128 Issabella the Catholic

1952. 500th Birth Anniv of Issabella the Catholic.
408 **128** 60c. blue (postage) . . . 10 10

409 10p. red (air) 40 20

1952. Surch **40 Ctvs.**
410 **115** 40c. on 60c. black 10 10

1952. Air. No. 302 surch **40 Centavos**.
411 40c. on 80c. olive 15 10

116 M. de Toro y Zambrano

131 Arms of Valdivia

132 Old Spanish Watch-tower

1952.
379b **116** 80c. green 15 10
379c – 1p. turquoise (O'Higgins) 10 10
446 – 2p. lilac (Carrera) . . . 10 10
447 – 3p. blue (R. Freire) . . . 10 10
448 – 5p. sepia (M. Bulnes) . . 10 10
449 – 10p. violet (F. A. Pinto) 10 10
450 – 50p. red (M. Montt) . . 35 10

1953. 400th Anniv of Valdivia.
414 **131** 1p. blue (postage) 15 10
415 – 2p. violet 15 10
416 – 3p. green 35 10
417 – 5p. brown 45 10

418 **132** 10p. red (air) . . . . . . 1·25 20
DESIGNS—As Type **132**: 2p. Ancient cannons, Corral Fort; 3p. Valdivia from the river; 5p. Street scene (after old engraving).

133 J. Toribio Medina

134 Stamp of 1853

1953. Birth Centenary of Toribio Medina.
419 **133** 1p. brown 15 10
420 2p.50 blue 25 10

1953. Chilean Stamp Centenary.
421 **134** 1p. brown (postage) . . . 15 10

422 100p. turquoise (air) . . . 3·00 1·75

135 Map and Graph

136 Aircraft of 1929 and 1954

1953. 12th National Census.
423 **135** 1p. green 10 10
424 2p.50 blue 15 10
425 3p. brown 25 15
426 4p. red 35 15

1954. Air. 25th Anniv of National Air Line.
427 **136** 3p. blue 10 10

137 Arms of Angol

138 I. Domeyko

1954. 400th Anniv of Angol City.
428 **137** 2p. red 10 15

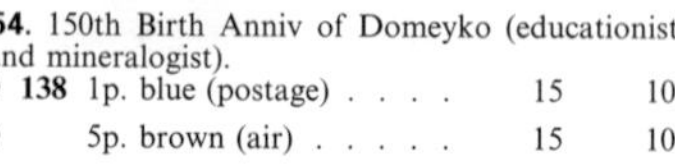

1954. 150th Birth Anniv of Domeyko (educationist and mineralogist).
429 **138** 1p. blue (postage) 15 10

430 5p. brown (air) 15 10

139 Locomotive "Tiger", 1856

1954. Centenary of Chilean Railways.
431 **139** 1p. red (postage) 20 25

432 10p. purple (air) . . . . 90 1·25

140 Arturo Prat **141** Arms of Vina del Mar

1954. 75th Anniv of Naval Battle of Iquique.
433 **140** 2p. violet 15 10

1955. Int Philatelic Exhibition, Valparaiso.
434 **141** 1p. blue 15 10
435 – 2p. red 15 10
DESIGN: 2p. Arms of Valparaiso.

142 Dr. A. del Rio **143** Christ of the Andes

1955. 14th Pan-American Sanitary Conference.
436 **142** 2p. blue 10 10

1955. Exchange of Visits between Argentine and Chilean Presidents.
437 **143** 1p. blue (postage) 15 10
438 100p. red (air) . . . . . 1·90 75

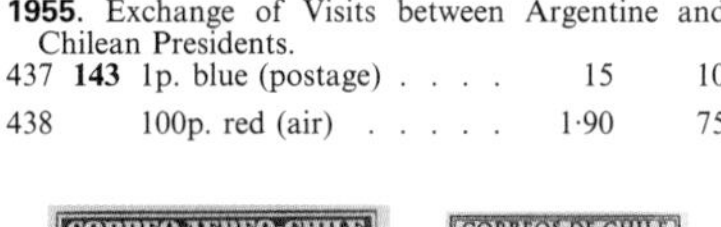

144 De Havilland Comet 1 **145** M. Rengifo

1955. Air.
441a **144** 100p. green 75 15
441b – 200p. blue . . . . . . 4·50 75
441c – 500p. red . . . . 6·00 75
AIRCRAFT: 200p. Morane Saulnier Paris I. 500p. Douglas DC-6B.

1955. Death Centenary of Joaquin Prieto (President, 1833–41).
442 **145** 3p. blue 10 10
443 – 5p. red (Egana) 10 10
444 – 50p. purple (Portales) . . 1·40 25
For 15p. in similar design see under Compulsory Tax Stamps.

147 Bell Trooper Helicopter and Bridge **148** F. Santa Maria

149 Atomic Symbol and Cogwheels

1956. Air.
451 – 1p. red 20 10
452 **147** 2p. sepia 20 10
455 – 5p. violet 20 10
456 – 10p. green 15 10
456a – 20p. blue 15 10
456b – 50p. red 20 10
DESIGNS: 1p. De Havilland Venom FB.4; 5p. Diesel locomotive and Douglas DC-6B; 10p. Oil derricks and Douglas DC-6B; 20p. De Havilland Venom FB.4 and Easter Island monolith; 50p. Douglas DC-2 and control tower.
See also Nos. 524/7.

1956. 25th Anniv of Santa Maria Technical University, Valparaiso.
457 **148** 5p. brown (postage) . . . 15 10
458 **149** 20p. green (air) 25 15
459 – 100p. violet 70 40
DESIGN—As Type **149**: 100p. Aerial view of University.

150 Gabriela Mistral **151** Arms of Osorno

1958. Gabriela Mistral (poetess, Nobel Prize Winner).
460 **150** 10p. brown (postage) . . 15 10
461 100p. green (air) 30 10

1958. 400th Anniv of Osorno.
462 **151** 10p. red (postage) 15 10
463 – 50p. green 35 10
464 – 100p. blue (air) 65 25
PORTRAITS: 50p. G. H. de Mendoza. 100p. O'Higgins.

152 "La Araucana" (poem) and Antarctic Map **153** Arms of Santiago de Chile

1958. Antarctic issue.
465 **152** 10p. blue (postage) . . . 20 10
466 – 200p. purple . . . . . . 3·25 1·25
467 **152** 20p. violet (air) 45 10
468 – 500p. blue . . . . 5·50 1·75
DESIGN: 200p., 500p. Chilean map of 1588.

1958. National Philatelic Exhibition, Santiago.
469 **153** 10p. purple (postage) . . 15 10
470 50p. green (air) 25 10

154 **155** Antarctic Territory

1958. Cent of Chilean Civil Servants' Savings Bank.
471 **154** 10p. blue (postage) . . . 10 10
472 50p. brown (air) 25 10

1958. I.G.Y.
473 **155** 40p. red (postage) 40 10
474 50p. green (air) 50 15

156 Religious Emblems **157** Bridge, Valdivia

1959. Air. Human Rights Day.
475 **156** 50p. red . . . . 65 1·00

1959. Centenary of German School, Valdivia and Philatelic Exhibition.
476 **157** 40p. green (postage) . . . 20 10
477 – 20p. red (air) 15 15
DESIGN—VERT: 20p. A. C. Anwandter (founder).

158 Expedition Map **159** D. Barros-Arana

1959. 400th Anniv of Juan Ladrillero's Expedition of 1557.
484 **158** 10p. violet (postage) . . . 25 10
485 50p. green (air) 35 10

1959. 50th Death Anniv of D. Barros-Arana (historian).
486 **159** 40p. blue (postage) . . . 15 10
487 100p. lilac (air) 40 20

160 J. H. Dunant (founder)

1959. Red Cross Commemoration.
488 **160** 20p. lake & red (postage) 20 10
489 50p. black & red (air) . . 25 10

161 F. A. Pinto **162** Choshuenco Volcano

1960. (a) Portraits as T **161**.
490 – 5m. turquoise 10 10
491 **161** 1c. red 10 10
493 – 5c. blue 10 10

(b) Views as T **162**.
492 **162** 2c. blue 10 10
492a 2c. blue ($23\frac{1}{2} \times 18$ mm) 10 10
494 – 10c. green 20 10
495 – 20c. blue 35 10
496 – 1E. turquoise 40 15
DESIGNS—As Type **161**: 5m. M. Bulnes; 5c. M. Montt. As Type **162**: 10c. R. Maule Valley; 20c., 1E. Inca Lake.

163 Martin 4-0-4 Airplane and Dock Crane **164** Refugee Family

1960. Air (Inland).
497 – 1m. orange 10 10
498 – 2m. green 10 10
499 **163** 3m. violet 10 10
500 – 4m. olive 10 10
501 – 5m. turquoise 10 10
502 – 1c. blue 10 10
503 – 2c. brown 25 10
504 – 5c. green . . . . 1·90 15
505 – 10c. red 45 10
506 – 20c. blue 60 10
DESIGNS: Airplane over—1m. Araucanian pine; 2m. Chilean flag; 4m. River; 5m. Industrial plant; 1c. Landscape; 2c. Aerial railway; 5c. Mountainous coastline; 10c. Antarctic map; 20c. Rock "bridge" in sea.

1960. World Refugee Year.
507 **164** 1c. green (postage) . . . 35 10
508 10c. violet (air) 60 10

165 Arms of Chile

1960. 150th Anniv of 1st National Government (1st issue).
509 **165** 1c. brn & red (postage) 15 10
510 10c. chestnut & brn (air) 20 10
See also Nos. 512/23.

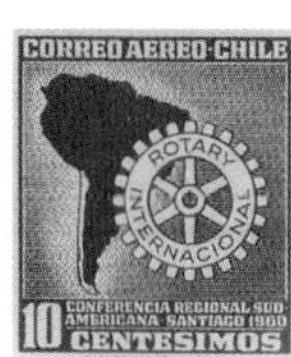

166 Rotary Emblem and Map

1960. Air. Rotary International S. American Regional Conference, Santiago.
511 **166** 10c. blue 25 10

167 J. M. Carrera **168** "Population"

1960. 150th Anniv of 1st National Government (2nd issue). (a) Postage.
512 – 1c. red and brown 15 10
513 – 5c. turquoise & green . . 15 10
514 – 10c. purple and brown . . 15 10
515 – 20c. green and blue . . . 15 10
516 – 50c. red and brown . . . 50 10
517 **167** 1E. brown and green . . 1·40 40
DESIGNS—HORIZ: 1c. Palace of Justice; 10c. M. de Toro y Zambrano and M. de Rozas; 20c. M. de Salas and Juan Egana; 50c. M. Rodriguez and J. Mackenna. VERT: 5c. Temple of the National Vow.

(b) Air.
518 – 2c. violet and red 10 10
519 – 5c. purple and blue 15 10
520 – 10c. bistre and brown . . . 15 10
521 – 20c. violet and blue 25 10
522 – 50c. blue and green 45 20
523 – 1E. brown and red . . . . 1·40 40
DESIGNS—HORIZ: 2c. Palace of Justice; 10c. J. G. Martin and J. G. Argomedo; 20c. J. A. Eyzaguirre and J. M. Infante; 50c. Bishop J. I. Cienfuegos and Fray C. Henriquez. VERT: 5c. Temple of the National Vow. 1E. O'Higgins.

1961. Air (Foreign). As T **147** or **144** (10c. and 50c.), but values in new currency.
524 5m. brown 15 10
525 1c. blue 10 10
526 2c. blue 10 10
527 5c. red 10 10
528 10c. blue 10 10
529 20c. red 10 10
530 50c. turquoise 10 10
DESIGNS: 5m. Diesel locomotive and Douglas DC-6B; 1c. Oil derricks and Douglas DC-6B; 2c. De Havilland Venom FB.4 and monolith; 5c. Douglas DC-2 and control tower; 10c. De Havilland Comet 1; 20c. Morane Saulnier Paris I; 50c. Douglas DC-6B.

1961. National Census. 13th Population Census (5c.); 2nd Housing Census (10c.).
531 **168** 5c. green 40 10
532 – 10c. violet (buildings) . . 40 10

169 Pedro de Valdivia **170** Congress Building

1961. Earthquake Relief Fund. Inscr "ESPANA A CHILE".
533 **169** 5c.+5c. green and pink (postage) . . . . 1·00 15
534 – 10c.+10c. violet & buff . . 1·00 15
535 – 10c.+10c. brown and orange (air) . . . . . 1·00 20
536 – 20c.+20c. red and blue . . 1·00 20
PORTRAITS: No. 534, J. T. Medina. No. 535, A. de Ercilla. No. 536, Gabriela Mistral.

1961. 150th Anniv of 1st National Congress.
537 **170** 2c. brown (postage) . . . 40 10
538 10c. green (air) . . . . . 1·10 70

171 Footballers and Globe

1962. World Football Championships, Chile.
539 **171** 2c. blue (postage) 10 10
540 – 5c. green 15 10
541 – 5c. purple (air) 15 10
542 **171** 10c. lake 25 10
DESIGN—HORIZ: Nos. 540/1, Goalkeeper and stadium.

172 Mother and Child

1963. Freedom from Hunger.
543 **172** 3c. purple (postage) . . . 10 10
544 – 20c. green (air) 15 10
DESIGN—HORIZ: 20c. Mother holding out food bowl.

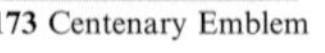

173 Centenary Emblem **174** Fire Brigade Monument

1963. Red Cross Centenary.
545 **173** 3c. red & grey (postage) 10 10
546 – 20c. red and grey (air) . . 15 10
DESIGN—HORIZ: 20c. Centenary emblem and silhouette of aircraft.

1963. Centenary of Santiago Fire Brigade.
547 **174** 3c. violet (postage) . . . 10 10
548 – 30c. red (air) 30 15
DESIGN—HORIZ: (39 × 30 mm): 30c. Fire engine of 1863.

175 Band encircling Globe **176** Enrique Molina

1964. Air. "Alliance for Progress" and Pres. Kennedy Commemoration
549 **175** 4c. blue 10 10

1964. Molina Commemoration (founder of Concepcion University).
550 **176** 4c. bistre (postage) . . . 10 10
551 60c. violet (air) 10 10

1965. Casanueva Commemoration. As T **176** but portrait of Mons. Carlos Casanueva, Rector of Catholic University.
552 4c. purple (postage) 10 10
553 60c. green (air) 10 10

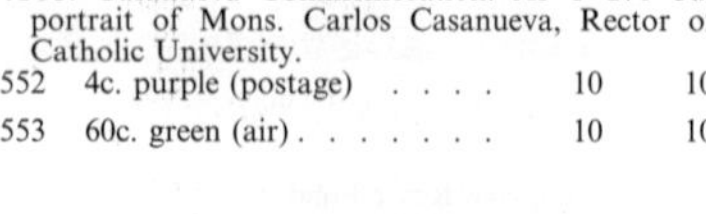

177 Battle Scene (after Subercaseaux)

1965. Air. 150th Anniv of Battle of Rancagua.
554 **177** 5c. brown and green . . . 10 10

178 Monolith **179** I.T.U. Emblem and Symbols

1965. Easter Island Discoveries.
555 **178** 6c. purple 10 10
556 10c. mauve 15 10

1965. Air. Centenary of I.T.U.
557 **179** 40c. purple and red . . . 15 10

180 Crusoe on Juan Fernandez **181** Skier descending slope

1965. Robinson Crusoe Commemoration.
558 **180** 30c. red 15 10

1965. World Skiing Championships.
559 **181** 4c. green (postage) . . . 15 10
560 – 20c. blue (air) 10 10
DESIGN—HORIZ: 20c. Skier crossing slope.

182 Angelmo Harbour **183** Aviators, Monument

1965. Air.
561 **182** 40c. brown 30 10
562 **183** 1E. red 20 10

184 Copihue (National Flower) **185** A. Bello

1965.
563 **184** 15c. red and green . . . 15 10
563a 20c. red and green . . . 15 10

1965. Air. Death Centenary of Andres Bello (poet).
564 **185** 10c. red 10 10

186 Dr. L. Sazie **187** Skiers

1966. Death Centenary of Dr. L. Sazie.
565 **186** 1E. green . . . . 1·25 10

1966. Air. World Skiing Championships.
566 – 75c. red and lilac 20 10
567 – 3E. ultramarine and blue 40 10
568 **187** 4E. brown and blue . . . 85 25
DESIGN—HORIZ: (38 × 25 mm): 75c., 3E. Skier in slalom race.

188 Ball and Basket **189** J. Montt

1966. Air. World Basketball Championships.
569 **188** 13c. red 15 10

1966.
570 **189** 30c. violet 10 10
571 – 50c. brown (G. Riesco) 10 10

190 W. Wheelwright and Paddle-steamers "Chile" and "Peru"

1966. 125th Anniv (1965) of Arrival of Paddle-steamers "Chile" and "Peru".
572 **190** 10c. ultram & bl (postage) 40 10
573 70c. blue and green (air) 60 10

191 "Learning" **193** Chilean Flag and Ships

192 I.C.Y. Emblem

1966. Education Campaign.
574 **191** 10c. purple 10 10

1966. International Co-operation Year (1965).
575 **192** 1E. brn & green (postage) 1·75 10
576 3E. red and blue (air) . . 60 20

1966. Air. Antofagasta Centenary.
577 **193** 13c. purple 10 10

194 Capt. Pardo and "Yelcho" (coastguard vessel)

1967. 50th Anniv of Pardo's Rescue of Shackleton Expedition.
578 **194** 20c. turquoise (postage) 1·40 10
579 – 40c. blue (air) 30 15
DESIGN: 40c. Capt. Pardo and Antarctic sectoral map.

195 Chilean Family **197** Pine Forest

196 R. Dario (poet)

1967. 8th International Family Planning Congress.
580 **195** 10c. black and purple (postage) 10 10
581 80c. black and blue (air) 20 10

1967. Air. Birth Centenary of Ruben Dario (Nicaraguan poet).
582 **196** 10c. blue 15 10

1967. National Afforestation Campaign.
583 **197** 10c. green & bl (postage) 10 10
584 75c. green & brown (air) 20 10

198 Lions Emblem

1967. 50th Anniv of Lions International.
585 **198** 20c. blue & brn (postage) 15 10
586 1E. violet & yellow (air) 15 10
587 5E. blue and yellow . . . 1·40 50

199 Chilean Flag

1967. 150th Anniv of National Flag.
588 **199** 80c. red & blue (post) . . 20 10
589 50c. red and blue (air) . . 15 10

200 I.T.Y. Emblem

1967. Air. International Tourist Year.
590 **200** 30c. black and blue . . . 10 10

201 Cardinal Caro **203** Farmer and Wife

202 San Martin and O'Higgins

1967. Birth Centenary of Cardinal Caro.
591 **201** 20c. lake (postage) . . . 35 20
592 40c. violet (air) 75 15

1968. 150th Anniv of Battles of Chacabuco and Maipu.
593 **202** 3E. blue (postage) 10 10
594 2E. violet (air) 10 10

1968. Agrarian Reform.
595 **203** 20c. black, green and orange (postage) . . . 15 10
596 50c. black, green and orange (air) 15 10

204 Juan I. Molina (scientist) and "Lamp of Learning" **205** Hand supporting Cogwheel

1968. Molina Commemoration.
597 **204** 2E. purple (postage) . . . 10 10
598 – 1E. green (air) 10 10
DESIGN: 1E. Molina and books.

1968. 4th Manufacturing Census.
599 **205** 30c. red 15 10

206 Map, "San Sebastian" (galleon) and "Alonso de Erckla" (ferry)

1968. "Five Towns" Centenaries.
600 **206** 30c. blue (postage) . . . 50 10
601 – 1E. purple (air) 15 10
DESIGN—VERT: 1E. Map of Chiloe Province.

207 Club Emblem

1968. 40th Anniv of Chilean Automobile Club.

602	**207**	1E. red (postage)	20	10
603		5E. blue (air)	15	15

208 Chilean Arms

1968. Air. State Visit of Queen Elizabeth II.

604	**208**	50c. brown and green	15	10
605	–	3E. brown and blue	15	10
606	–	5E. purple and plum	25	15

DESIGN—HORIZ: 3E. Royal arms of Great Britain. VERT: 5E. St. Edward's Crown on map of South America.

209 Don Francisco Garcia Huidobro (founder)

1968. 225th Anniv of Chilean Mint.

608	**209**	2E. blue & red (postage)	10	10
609	–	5E. brown and green	20	10
610	–	50c. purple & yell (air)	10	10
611	–	1E. red and blue	15	15

DESIGNS: 50c. First Chilean coin and press; 1E. First Chilean stamp printed by the mint (1915); 5E. Philip V of Spain.

210 Satellite and Dish Aerial

1969. Inauguration of "ENTEL-CHILE" Satellite Communications Ground Station, Longovilo (1st issue).

613	**210**	30c. blue (postage)	10	10
614		2E. purple (air)	20	10

See also Nos. 668/9.

211 Red Cross Symbols

1969. 50th Anniv of League of Red Cross Societies.

615	**211**	2E. red & violet (postage)	15	10
616		5E. red and black (air)	15	10

212 Rapel Dam

1969. Rapel Hydro-electric Project.

617	**212**	40c. green (postage)	10	10
618		3E. blue (air)	15	10

213 Rodriguez Memorial

1969. 150th Death Anniv of Col. Manuel Rodriguez.

619	**213**	2E. red (postage)	10	10
620		30c. brown (air)	10	10

214 Open Bible

1969. 400th Anniv of Spanish Translation of Bible.

621	**214**	40c. brown (postage)	10	10
622		1E. green (air)	15	10

215 Hemispheres and I.L.O. Emblem

1969. 50th Anniv of I.L.O.

623	**215**	1E. grn & blk (postage)	10	10
624		2E. purple & black (air)	10	10

216 Human Rights Emblem

217 "EXPO" Emblem

1969. Human Rights Year (1968).

625	**216**	4E. red and blue (postage)	35	25
626		4E. red and brown (air)	45	25

1969. World Fair "EXPO 70", Osaka, Japan.

628	**217**	3E. blue (postage)	10	10
629		5E. red (air)	15	10

218 Mint, Santiago (18th cent)

1970. Spanish Colonization of Chile.

630	**218**	2E. purple	20	10
631	–	3E. red	15	10
632	–	4E. blue	15	10
633	–	5E. brown	15	10
634	–	10E. green	15	10

DESIGNS—HORIZ: 5E. Cal y Canto Bridge. VERT: 3E. Pedro de Valdivia; 4E. Santo Domingo Church, Santiago; 10E. Ambrosio O'Higgins.

219 Policarpo Toro and Map

1970. 80th Anniv of Seizure of Easter Island.

636	**219**	5E. violet (postage)	25	10
637		50c. turquoise (air)	35	10

221 Chilean Schooner and Arms

1970. 150th Anniv of Capture of Valdivia by Lord Cochrane.

640	**221**	40c. lake (postage)	45	10
641		2E. blue (air)	90	10

222 Paul Harris

223 Mahatma Gandhi

1970. Birth Centenary of Paul Harris (founder of Rotary International).

642	**222**	10E. blue (postage)	90	20
643		1E. red (air)	30	15

1970. Birth Centenary of Gandhi.

644	**223**	40c. green (postage)	2·50	20
645		1E. brown (air)	30	15

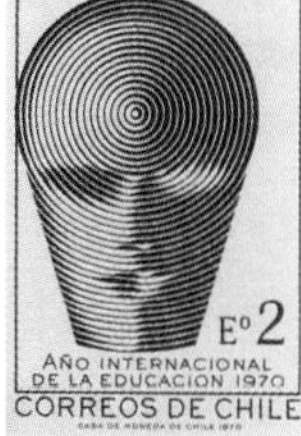

225 Education Year Emblem

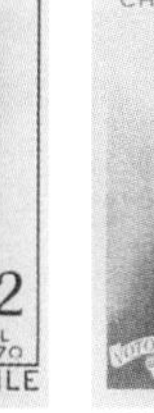

226 "Virgin and Child"

1970. International Education Year.

648	**225**	2E. red (postage)	10	10
649		4E. brown (air)	15	10

1970. O'Higgins National Shrine, Maipu.

650	**226**	40c. green (postage)	10	10
651		1E. blue (air)	15	15

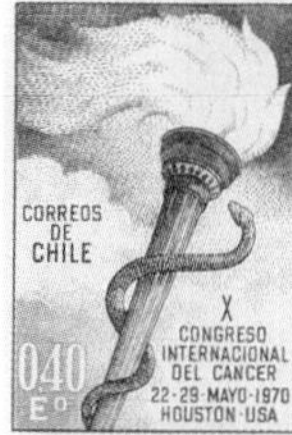

227 Snake and Torch Emblem

228 Chilean Arms and Copper Symbol

1970. 10th Int Cancer Congress, Houston, U.S.A.

652	**227**	40c. purple & bl (postage)	80	10
653		2E. brown and green (air)	50	10

1970. Copper Mines Nationalization.

654	**228**	40c. red & brn (postage)	15	10
655		3E. green & brown (air)	25	10

229 Globe, Dove and Cogwheel

1970. 25th Anniv of United Nations.

656	**229**	3E. vio & red (postage)	10	10
657		5E. green and red (air)	20	10

1970. Nos. 613/14 surch.

658	**210**	52c. on 30c. blue (postage)	30	10
659		52c. on 2E. purple (air)	50	15

231 Freighter "Lago Maihue" and Ship's Wheel

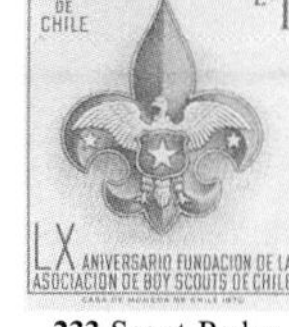

233 Scout Badge

232 Bernardo O'Higgins and Fleet

1971. State Maritime Corporation.

660	**231**	52c. red (postage)	30	10
661		5E. brown (air)	50	10

1971. 150th Anniv of Peruvian Liberation Expedition.

662	**232**	5E. grn & blue (postage)	35	10
663		1E. purple & blue (air)	50	10

1971. 60th Anniv of Chilean Scouting Association.

664	**233**	1E. brn & grn (postage)	20	10
665		5c. green & lake (air)	20	10

234 Young People and U.N. Emblem

1971. 1st Latin-American Meeting of U.N.I.C.E.F. Executive Council, Santiago (1969).

666	**234**	52c. brn & blue (postage)	10	10
667		2E. green & blue (air)	15	10

1971. Longovilo Satellite Communications Ground Station (2nd issue). As T **210**, but with "LONGOVILO" added to centre inscr and wording at foot of design changed to "PRIMERA ESTACION LATINOAMERICANA".

668	40c. green (postage)	30	10
669	2E. brown (air)	50	15

235 Diver with Harpoon Gun

1971. 10th World Underwater Fishing Championships, Iquique.

670	**235**	1E.15 myrtle and green	65	10
671		2E.35 ultramarine & blue	15	10

239 Magellan and Caravel

1971. 450th Anniv of Discovery of Magellan Straits.

676	**239**	35c. plum and blue	30	10

240 Dagoberto Godoy and Bristol Monoplane over Andes

1971. 1st Trans-Andes Flight (1918) Commem.

677	**240**	1E.15 green and blue	20	10

241 Statue of the Virgin, San Cristobal

1971. 10th Postal Union of the Americas and Spain Congress, Santiago.

678	**241**	1E.15 blue	75	10
679	–	2E.35 blue and red	45	10
680	–	4E.35 red	45	10

681 – 9E.35 lilac 45 10
682 – 18E.35 mauve 60 10
DESIGNS—VERT: 4E.35, St. Francis's Church, Santiago. HORIZ: 2E.35, U.P.A.E. emblem; 9E.35, Central Post Office, Santiago; 18E.35, Corregidor Inn.

242 Cerro el Tololo Observatory

1972. Inauguration of Astronomical Observatory, Cerro el Tololo.
683 **242** 1E.95 blue & dp blue . . 20 10

243 Boeing 707 over Tahiti

1972. 1st Air Service Santiago–Easter Island–Tahiti.
684 **243** 2E.35 purple and ochre 30 10

244 Alonso de Ercilla y Zuniga

246 Human Heart

245 Antarctic Map and Dog-sledge

1972. 400th Anniv (1969) of "La Araucana" (epic poem by de Ercilla y Zungia).
685 **244** 1E. brown (postage) . . . 15 10
686 2E. blue (air) 20 15

1972. 10th Anniv of Antarctic Treaty.
687 **245** 1E.15 black and blue . . 80 15
688 3E.50 blue and green . . 55 10

1972. World Heart Month.
689 **246** 1E.15 red and black . . . 20 10

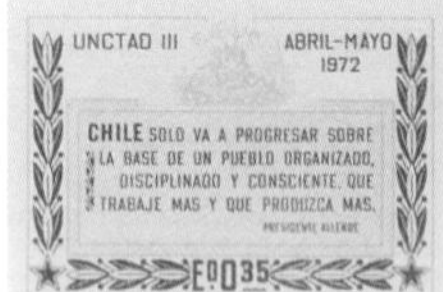

247 Text of Speech by Pres. Allende

1972. 3rd United Nations Conference on Trade and Development, Santiago.
690 **247** 35c. green and brown . . 25 15
691 – 1E.15 violet and blue . . 10 10
692 **247** 4E. violet and pink . . . 50 25
693 – 6E. blue and orange . . . 20 10
DESIGNS: 1E.15, 6E. Conference Hall Santiago.
Nos. 690 and 692 each include a se-tenant label showing Chilean workers and inscr "CORREOS DE CHILE". The stamp was only valid for postage with the label attached.

248 Soldier and Crest

1972. 150th Anniv of O'Higgins Military Academy.
694 **248** 1E.15 yellow and blue . . 15 10

249 Copper Miner

250 Barquentine "Esmeralda"

1972. Copper Mines Nationalization Law (1971).
695 **249** 1E.15 blue and red . . . 15 10
696 5E. black, blue and red 30 10

1972. 150th Anniv of Arturo Prat Naval College.
697 **250** 1E.15 purple . . . . . . 1·00 20

251 Observatory and Telescope

1972. Inauguration of Cerro Calan Observatory.
698 **251** 50c. blue 20 10

252 Dove with Letter

1972. International Correspondence Week.
699 **252** 1E.15 violet & mauve . . 15 10

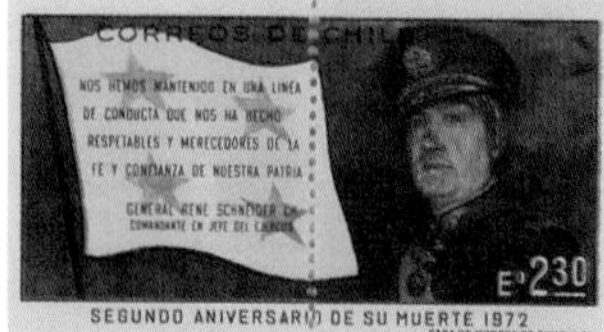

253 Gen. Schneider, Flag and Quotation

1972. 2nd Death Anniv of General Rene Schneider.
700 **253** 2E.30 multicoloured . . . 30 20

254 Book and Students

1972. International Book Year.
701 **254** 50c. black and red 15 10

255 Folklore and Handicrafts

1972. Tourist Year of the Americas.
702 **255** 1E.15 black and red . . . 15 10
703 – 2E.65 purple and blue . . 40 10
704 – 3E.50 brown and red . . 15 10
DESIGNS—HORIZ: 2E.65, Natural produce. VERT: 3E.50, Stove and rug.

256 Carrera in Prison

257 Antarctic Map

1973. 150th Death Anniv of General J. M. Carrera.
705 **256** 2E.30 blue 20 10

1973. 25th Anniv of General Bernardo O'Higgins Antarctic Base.
706 **257** 10E. red and blue 35 15

258 "Latorre" (cruiser) and Emblem

259 Telescope

1973. 50 Years of Chilean Naval Aviation.
707 **258** 20E. blue and brown . . 55 10

1973. Inaug of La Silla Astronomical Observatory.
708 **259** 2E.30 black and blue . . 20 10

260 Interpol Emblem

261 Bunch of Grapes

1973. 50th Anniv of Interpol.
709 **260** 30E. blue, black & brown 1·40 20
710 – 50E. black and red . . . 1·40 25
DESIGN: 50E. Fingerprint superimposed on globe.

1973. Chilean Wine Exports. Multicoloured.
711 20E. Type **261** 50 10
712 100E. Inscribed globe . . . . 1·00 20

1974. Centenary of World Meteorological Organization. No. 668 surch **"Centenario de la Organizacion Meteorologica Mundial IMO-W-MO 1973"** and value.
713 27E.+3E. on 40c. green . . . 15 10

263 U.P.U. Headquarters Building, Berne

1974. Centenary of U.P.U. Unissued stamp surch.
714 **263** 500E. on 45c. green . . . 85 20

264 Bernardo O'Higgins and Emblems

1974. Chilean Armed Forces.
715 **264** 30E. yellow and red . . . 20 10
716 – 30E. lake and red 20 10
717 – 30E. blue and light blue 20 10
718 – 30E. blue and lilac . . . 20 10
719 – 30E. emerald and green 20 10
DESIGNS: No. 716, Soldiers with mortar; No. 717, Naval gunners; No. 718, Air Force pilot; No. 719, Mounted policeman.

1974. 500th Birth Anniv (1973) of Copernicus. No. 683 surch **"V Centenario del Nacimiento de Copernico 1473 - 1973"** and value.
720 **242** 27E.+3E. on 1E.95 blue and deep blue 30 10

1974. Centenary of Vina del Mar. No. 496 surch **"Centenario de la ciudad de Vina del Mar 1874 - 1974"** and value.
721 27E.+3E. on 1E. turquoise 15 10

267 Football and Globe

269 Police and Gloved Hand

1974. World Cup Football Championships, West Germany.
722 **267** 500E. orange and red . . 20 10
723 – 1000E. blue & dp blue . . 1·00 15
DESIGN—HORIZ: 1000E. Football on stylized stadium.

1974. Various stamps surch.
724 **212** 47E.+3E. on 40c. green 15 10
725 **228** 67E.+3E. on 40c. red and brown 15 10
726 **214** 97E.+3E. on 40c. brown 15 10
727 **223** 100E. on 40c. green . . . 20 10
728 – 300E. on 50c. brown (No. 571) 20 10

1974. Campaign for Prevention of Traffic Accidents.
729 **269** 30E. brown and green . . 25 10

270 Manutara and Part of Globe

271 Core of Globe

1974. Inaugural LAN Flight to Tahiti, Fiji and Australia. Each green and brown.
730 200E. Type **270** 40 15
731 200E. Tahitian dancer and part of Globe 40 15
732 200E. Map of Fiji and part of Globe 40 15
733 200E. Eastern grey kangaroo and part of Globe 40 15

1974. International Symposium of Volcanology, Santiago de Chile.
734 **271** 500E. orange & brown . . 60 10

1974. Inauguration of Votive Temple. No. 650 surch **24 OCTUBRE 1974 INAUGURACION TEMPLO VOTIVO** and value.
735 **226** 100E. on 40c. green . . . 15 10

273 Map of Robinson Crusoe Island

275 F. Vidal Gormaz and Seal

274 O'Higgins and Bolivar

1974. 400th Anniv of Discovery of Juan Fernandez Archipelago. Each brown and blue.
736 200E. Type **273** 85 20
737 200E. Chontas (hardwood palm-trees) 40 20

738 200E. Mountain goat 40 20
739 200E. Spiny lobster 40 20

1974. 150th Anniv of Battles of Junin and Ayacucho.
740 **274** 100E. brown and buff . . 20 10

1975. Centenary of Naval Hydrographic Institute.
741 **275** 100E. blue and mauve . . 20 10

1975. Surch **Revalorizada 1975** and value.
742 **228** 70c. on 40c. red & brown 15 10

277 Dr. Schweitzer **278** Lighthouse

1975. Birth Centenary of Dr. Albert Schweitzer (missionary).
743 **277** 500E. brown and yellow 35 10

1975. 50th Anniv of Valparaiso Lifeboat Service. Each blue and green.
744 150E. Type **278** 55 20
745 150E. Wreck of "Teotopoulis" 75 25
746 150E. "Cap Christiansen" (lifeboat) 75 25
747 150E. Survivor in water . . . 55 20

279 Sail/steam Corvette "Baquedano"

1975. 30th Anniv of Shipwreck of Sail Frigate "Lautaro".
749 **279** 500E. black and green . . 75 20
750 – 500E. black and green . . 75 20
751 – 500E. black and green . . 75 20
752 – 500E. black and green . . 75 20
753 **279** 800E. black and brown 1·00 25
754 – 800E. black and brown 1·00 25
755 – 800E. black and brown 1·00 25
756 – 800E. black and brown 1·00 25
757 **279** 1000E. black and blue . . 1·25 25
758 – 1000E. black and blue . . 1·25 25
759 – 1000E. black and blue . . 1·25 25
760 – 1000E. black and blue . . 1·25 25
DESIGNS: Nos. 750, 754, 758, Sail frigate "Lautaro"; Nos. 751, 755, 759, Cruiser "Chacabuco"; Nos. 752, 756, 760, Cadet barquentine "Esmeralda".

280 "The Happy Mother" (A. Valenzuela) **281** Diego Portales (politician)

1975. International Women's Year. Chilean Paintings. Multicoloured.
761 50c. Type **280** 65 15
762 50c. "Girl" (F. J. Mandiola) 65 15
763 50c. "Lucia Guzman" (P. L. Rencoret) 65 15
764 50c. "Unknown Woman" (Magdalena M. Mena) . . 65 15

1975. Inscr "D. PORTALES".
765 **281** 10c. green 20 10
765a 20c. lilac 10 10
765b 30c. orange 10 10
766 50c. brown 15 10
767 1p. blue 15 10
767a 1p.50 brown 15 10
767b 2p. black 15 10
767c 2p.50 brown 15 10
767d 3p.50 red 15 10
768 5p. mauve 15 15
For this design inscr "DIEGO PORTALES", see Nos. 901 etc.

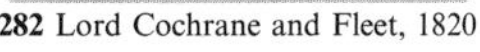

282 Lord Cochrane and Fleet, 1820

1975. Birth Bicentenary of Lord Thomas Cochrane. Multicoloured.
769 1p. Type **282** 80 25
770 1p. Cochrane's capture of Valdivia, 1820 . . . . . . 80 25
771 1p. Capture of "Esmeralda", 1820 . . . . 80 25
772 1p. Cruiser "Cochrane", 1874 80 25
773 1p. Destroyer "Cochrane", 1962 . . . . 80 25

283 Flags of Chile and Bolivia

1976. 150th Anniv of Bolivia's Independence.
774 **283** 1p.50 multicoloured . . . 1·75 10

284 Lake of the Incas

1976. 6th General Assembly of Organization of American States.
775 **284** 1p.50 multicoloured . . . 1·40 10

285 George Washington

1976. Bicentenary of American Revolution.
776 **285** 5p. multicoloured . . . . 1·50 15

286 Minerva and Academy Emblem

1976. 50th Anniv of Polytechnic Military Academy.
777 **286** 2p.50 multicoloured . . . 1·00 10

287 Indian Warrior

1976. 3rd Anniv of Military Junta. Multicoloured.
778 1p. Type **287** 25 15
779 2p. Andean condor with broken chain . . . . . . 2·50 1·00
780 3p. Winged woman ("Rebirth of the Country") 25 15

288 Chilean Base, Antarctica

1977. Presidential Visit to Antarctica.
781 **288** 2p. multicoloured . . . . 5·25 25

289 College Emblem and Cultivated Field **290** Statue of Justice

1977. Cent of Advanced Agricultural Education.
782 **289** 2p. multicoloured . . . . 1·40 15

1977. 150th Anniv of Supreme Court.
783 **290** 2p. brown and grey . . . 1·40 10

291 Globe within "Eye"

1977. 11th Pan-American Ophthalmological Congress.
784 **291** 2p. multicoloured . . . . 2·00 10

292 Police Emblem and Activities

1977. 50th Anniv of Chilean Police Force. Multicoloured.
785 2p. Type **292** 60 10
786 2p. Mounted carabinero (vert) 25 10
787 2p. Policewoman with children (vert) 25 10
788 2p. Torres del Paine and Osorno Volcano (vert) . . 25 10

293 "Intelsat" Satellite and Globe

1977. World Telecommunications Day.
789 **293** 2p. multicoloured 25 10

294 Front Page, Press and Schooner

1977. 150th Anniv of Newspaper "El Mercurio de Valparaiso".
790 **294** 2p. multicoloured 20 15

295 St. Francis of Assisi **296** "Science and Technology"

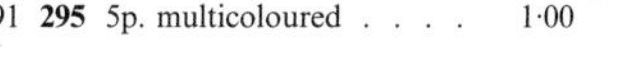
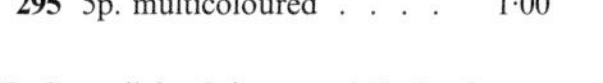

1977. 750th Death Anniv of St. Francis of Assisi.
791 **295** 5p. multicoloured . . . . 1·00 15

1977. Council for Science and Technology.
792 **296** 4p. multicoloured 40 15

297 Weaving (Mothers' Centres) **298** Diego de Almagro (discoverer of Chile)

1977. 4th Anniv of Government Junta. Welfare Facilities. Multicoloured.
793 5p. Type **297** 55 10
794 5p. Nurse with cripple (Care of the Disabled) 55 10
795 10p. Children dancing (Protection of Minors) (horiz) . . . . 1·00 15
796 10p. Elderly man (Care for the Aged) (horiz) . . . . . 1·00 15

1977. Columbus Day.
797 **298** 5p. brown 45 10

299 Boy, Christmas Bell and Post Box

1977. Christmas.
798 **299** 2p.50 multicoloured . . . 15 15

300 Freighter loading Timber

1978. Timber Export. Multicoloured.
799 10p. Type **300** . . . . 1·00 25
800 20p. As T **300** but inscr "CORREOS" and with ship flying Chilean flag . . 1·50 35

301 Papal Arms and Globe

1978. World Peace Day.
801 **301** 10p. multicoloured . . . 80 15

302 University

1978. 50th Anniv of Catholic University, Valparaiso.
802 **302** 25p. multicoloured . . . 2·50 60

303 "Bernardo O'Higgins" (Gil de Castro)

1978. Birth Bicentenary of Bernardo O'Higgins (1st issue).
803 **303** 10p. multicoloured . . . 1·00 15
See also Nos. 804, 806/8 and 816.

304 Chacabuco Victory Monument

1978. Birth Bicentenary of Bernardo O'Higgins (2nd issue), and 5th Anniv of Military Junta.
804 **304** 10p. multicoloured . . . 1·00 15

305 Teacher writing on Blackboard

1978. 10th Anniv and 9th Meeting of Inter-American Council for Education, Science and Culture.
805 **305** 15p. multicoloured . . . 60 15

306 "The Last Moments at Rancagua" (Pedro Subercaseaux)

1978. Birth Bicentenary of Bernardo O'Higgins (3rd issue).
806 **306** 30p. multicoloured . . . 2·00 65

307 "First National Naval Squadron" (Thomas Somerscales)

1978. Birth Bicentenary of Bernardo O'Higgins (4th issue).
807 **307** 20p. multicoloured . . . 1·75 80

308 Medallion

1978. Birth Bicentenaries of O'Higgins (5th issue) and San Martin.
808 **308** 7p. multicoloured 30 10

309 Council Emblem **310** Three Kings

1978. 30th Anniv of International Council of Military Sports.
809 **309** 50p. multicoloured . . . 3·50 1·00

1978. Christmas. Multicoloured.
810 3p. Type **310** 65 15
811 11p. Virgin and Child . . . . 1·25 20

311 Bernardo and Rodulfo Philippi

1978. The Philippi Brothers (scientists and travellers).
812 **311** 3p.50 multicoloured . . . 20 10

1979. No. 765 surch **$ 3.50.**
813 **281** 3p.50 on 10c. green . . . 15 10

313 Flowers and Flags of Chile and Salvation Army

1979. 70th Anniv of Salvation Army in Chile.
814 **313** 10p. multicoloured . . . 55 25

314 Pope Paul VI

1979. Pope Paul VI Commemoration.
815 **314** 11p. multicoloured . . . 80 25

315 Battle of Maipu Monument

1979. Birth Bicentenary of Bernardo O'Higgins (6th issue).
816 **315** 8p.50 multicoloured . . . 55 20

316 "Battle of Iquique" (Thomas Somerscales)

1979. Naval Battle Centenaries. Multicoloured.
817 3p.50 Type **316** 75 25
818 3p.50 "Battle of Punta Gruesa" (Alvaro Casanova Zenteno) 75 25
819 3p.50 "Battle of Angamos" (Alvaro Casanova Zenteno) 75 25

317 Diego Portales **319** Monument at Puntas Arenas (Miodrag Zivkovic)

318 Horse-drawn Ambulance

1979.
820 **317** 1p.50 brown 15 10
821 2p. grey 10 10
822 3p.50 red 10 10
823 4p.50 blue 20 10
824 5p. red 20 10
825 6p. green 20 10
826 7p. yellow 20 10
827 10p. blue 25 10
828 12p. orange 10 10

The 1p.50, 3p.50, 5p. and 6p. are inscribed "D. PORTALES" and have the imprint "CAMONEDA CHILE". The 2p., 4p.50, 7p. and 10p. are inscribed "DIEGO PORTALES" and have the imprint "CASA DE MONEDA DE CHILE".

1979. 75th Anniv of Chilean Red Cross.
831 **318** 25p. multicoloured . . . 2·75 60

1979. Centenary of Yugoslav Immigration.
832 **319** 10p. multicoloured . . . 45 15

320 Children in Playground (Kiochi Kayano Gomez)

1979. International Year of the Child. Mult.
833 9p.50 Type **320** 45 30
834 11p. Running girl (Carmed Pizarro Toto) (vert) . . . 55 35
835 12p. Children dancing in circle (Ana Pizarro Munizaga) . . . . 1·00 50

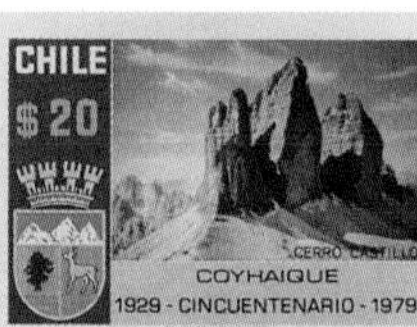

321 Laveredo and Arms of Coyhaique

1979. 50th Anniv of Coyhaique.
836 **321** 20p. multicoloured . . . 80 40

322 Exhibition Emblem and Posthorn

1979. 3rd World Telecommunications Exhibition, Geneva.
837 **322** 15p. grey, blue & orange 70 30

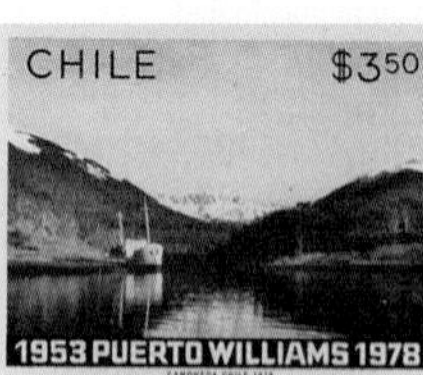

323 Canal

1979. 25th Anniv of Puerto Williams, Navirino Island.
838 **323** 3p.50 multicoloured . . . 70 15

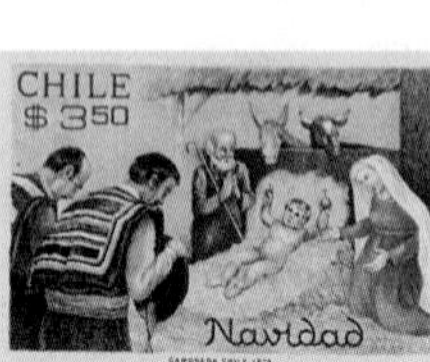

324 Chileans adoring Child Jesus **325** Rafael Sotomayor (Minister of War)

1979. Christmas.
839 **324** 3p.50 multicoloured . . . 1·10 20

1979. Military Heroes. Each ochre and brown.
840 3p.50 Type **325** 50 10
841 3p.50 General Erasmo Escala (Commander in Chief of Army) 50 10
842 3p.50 Colonel (later General) Emilio Sotomayor (Commander of troops at Battle of Dolores) 50 10
843 3p.50 Colonel Eleuterio Ramirez (Commander of 2nd Line Regiment) . . . 50 10

326 Bell Model 205 Iroquois Rescue Helicopter at Tinguiririca Volcano

1980. 50th Anniv of Chilean Air Force. Mult.
844 3p.50 Type **326** 40 15
845 3p.50 Consolidated Catalina Skua amphibian in Antarctic 40 15
846 3p.50 Northrop Tiger II jet fighter in Andes 40 15

327 Rotary Emblem and Globe

1980. 75th Anniv of Rotary International.
847 **327** 10p. multicoloured . . . 80 25

328 "The Death of Bueras" (Pedro Leon Carmona) **329** "Gen. Manuel Gaquedano" (after Pedro Subercaseaux)

1980. Cavalry Charge led by Colonel Santiago Bueras at Battle of Maipu, 1818.
848 **328** 12p. multicoloured . . . 65 30

1980. Centenary of Battle of Arica Head. Mult.
849 3p.50 Type **329** 25 10
850 3p.50 Gen. Pedro Largos (43 × 26 mm) 25 10
851 3p.50 Col. Juan Jose San Martin (43 × 26 mm) . . . 25 10

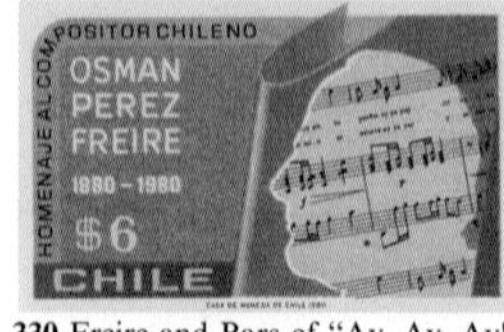

330 Freire and Bars of "Ay, Ay, Ay!"

1980. Birth Centenary of Osman Perez Freire (composer).
852 **330** 6p. multicoloured 35 15

331 Mt. Gasherbrum II, Chilean flag and Ice-pick

1980. Chilean Himalayan Expedition (1979).
853 **331** 15p. multicoloured . . . 1·00 35

332 "St Vincent de Paul" (stained glass window, former Mother House)
334 Mummy of Inca Child

333 Andean Condor

1980. 125th Anniv of Sisters of Charity in Chile.
854 **332** 10p. multicoloured . . . 50 25

1980. 7th Anniv of Military Government.
855 **333** 3p.50 multicoloured . . . 40 20

1980. 150th Anniv of National History Museum. Multicoloured.
856 5p. Type **334** 55 15
857 5p. Claudio Gay (founder) (after Alejandro Laemlein) 55 15

335 "Pablo Burchard" (Pedro Lira)
336 Emblem and Buildings

1980. Centenary of National Museum of Fine Arts.
858 **335** 3p.50 multicoloured . . . 20 10

1980. "Fisa '80" International Fair, Santiago.
859 **336** 3p.50 multicoloured . . . 20 10

337 "Family and Angels" (Sara Hinojosa Orellana)
338 Infantryman

1980. Christmas. Multicoloured.
860 3p.50 Type **337** 85 10
861 10p.50 "The Holy Family" (Catalina Imboden Fernandez) . . . . 1·10 20

1980. Army Uniforms of 1879 (1st series). Multicoloured.
862 3p.50 Type **338** 55 15
863 3p.50 Cavalry officer (parade uniform) 55 15
864 3p.50 Artillery officer 55 15
865 3p.50 Colonel of Engineers (parade uniform) 55 15
See also Nos. 887/90.

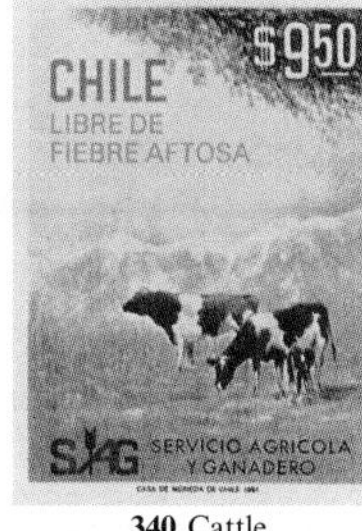

339 Congress Emblem

340 Cattle

1980. 23rd International Congress of Military Medicine and Pharmacy, Santiago.
866 **339** 11p.50 multicoloured . . 55 30

1981. Eradication of Foot and Mouth Disease from Chile.
867 **340** 9p.50 multicoloured . . . 45 20

341 Robinson Crusoe Island

1981. Tourism. Multicoloured.
868 3p.50 Type **341** 25 15
869 3p.50 Easter Island monoliths 60 15
870 10p.50 Gentoo penguins, Antarctica . . . . 1·75 50

342 "Javiera Carrera" (after D. M. Pizarro) and Flag

1981. Birth Bicentenary of Javiera Carrera (creator of first national flag).
871 **342** 3p.50 multicoloured . . . 20 10

343 U.P.U. Emblem

1981. Centenary of U.P.U. Membership.
872 **343** 3p. multicoloured 25 15

344 Unloading Cargo from Lockheed Hercules

1981. 1st Anniv of Lieutenant Marsh Antarctic Air Force Base.
873 **344** 3p.50 multicoloured . . . 50 15

345 I.T.U. and W.H.O. Emblems and Ribbons forming Caduceus

1981. World Telecommunications Day.
874 **345** 3p.50 multicoloured . . . 20 15

346 Arturo Prat Antarctic Naval Base

1981. 20th Anniv of Antarctic Treaty.
875 **346** 3p.50 multicoloured . . . 1·00 20

347 Capt. Jose Luis Araneda

1981. Centenary of Battle of Sangrar.
876 **347** 3p.50 multicoloured . . . 25 15

348 Philatelic Society Yearbook and Medal

1981. 92nd Anniv of Philatelic Society of Chile.
877 **348** 4p.50 multicoloured . . . 25 15

349 "Exchange of Speeches between Minister Recabarren and Indian Chief Conuepan at the Nielol Hill" (Hector Robles Acuna)

1981. Centenary of Temuco City.
878 **349** 4p.50 multicoloured . . . 25 15

350 Exports (embroidery by J.L. Gutierrez)

1981. Exports.
879 **350** 14p. multicoloured . . . 65 20

351 Moneda Palace (seat of Government)

1981. 8th Anniv of Military Government.
880 **351** 4p.50 multicoloured . . . 25 15

352 St. Vincent de Paul

1981. 400th Birth Anniv of St. Vincent de Paul (founder of Sisters of Charity).
881 **352** 4p.50 multicoloured . . . 25 15

353 Medallion by Rene Thenot, Quill and Law Code

1981. Birth Bicentenary of Andres Bello (statesman, lawyer, and founder of Chile University). Multicoloured.
882 4p.50 Type **353** 25 15
883 9p.50 Profile of Bello and three of his books 40 20
884 11p.50 University of Chile arms and Nicanor Plaza's statue of Bello 45 20

354 Flag on Map of South America and Police Badge

1981. 2nd South American Uniformed Police Congress, Santiago.
885 **354** 4p.50 multicoloured . . . 30 15

355 F.A.O. and U.N. Emblems

1981. World Food Day.
886 **355** 5p.50 multicoloured . . . 30 15

1981. Army Uniforms of 1879 (2nd series). As T **338**. Multicoloured.
887 5p.50 Infantryman 55 20
888 5p.50 Military School cadet 55 20
889 5p.50 Cavalryman 55 20
890 5p.50 Artilleryman 55 20

356 Mother and Child

1981. International Year of Disabled Persons.
891 **356** 5p.50 multicoloured . . . 30 15

357 "Nativity" (Ruth Tatiana Aguero Eguiliz)

1981. Christmas. Multicoloured.
892 5p.50 Type **357** 75 10
893 11p.50 "The Three Kings" (Ignacio Jorge Manriquez Gonzalez) 95 20

358 Dario Salas

1981. Birth Cent of Dario Salas (educationist).
894 **358** 5p.50 multicoloured . . . 25 15

359 Main Buildings of University

1981. 50th Anniv of Federico Santa Maria Technical University, Valparaiso.
895 **359** 5p.50 multicoloured . . . 25 15

360 Fair Emblem

1982. "Fida '82" International Air Fair.
896 **360** 4p.50 multicoloured . . . 30 15

361 Cardinal Caro and Chilean Family

1982. 1st Anniv of New Constitution. Mult.
897 4p.50 Type **361** 25 15
898 11p. Diego Portales and national arms 45 20
899 30p. Bernardo O'Higgins and national arms 65 40

362 Globe on Chilean Flag

363 Pedro Montt (President, 1906–10)

1982. 12th Panamerican Institute of Geography and History General Assembly.
900 **362** 4p.50 multicoloured . . . 25 15

1982. As T **281** but inscr "DIEGO PORTALES" and designs as T **363**.
901 **281** 1p. blue 60 10
902 – 1p. blue 10 10
903 **281** 1p.50 orange 10 10
904 2p. grey 10 10
905 – 2p. lilac 10 10
906 **281** 2p.50 yellow 10 10
907 **363** 4p.50 mauve 30 10
908 – 5p. red 10 10
909 **281** 5p. mauve 60 10
910 – 7p. blue 25 10
911 – 10p. black 15 10
DESIGNS: Nos. 902, 905, 908, 910, 911, Ramon Barros Luco (President, 1911–15).

364 Dassault Mirage IIIC Airplane and Chilean Air Force and American Air Forces Co-operation System Badges

1982. American Air Forces Co-operation System.
916 **364** 4p.50 multicoloured . . . 50 15

365 Trawler and Map

367 Capt. Ignacio Carrera Pinto

366 Scout Emblems and Brownsea Island

1982. Fisheries Exports.
917 **365** 20p. multicoloured . . . 2·00 80

1982. 75th Anniv of Boy Scout Movement and 125th Birth Anniv of Lord Baden-Powell (founder). Multicoloured.
918 4p.50 Type **366** 75 15
919 4p.50 Lord Baden-Powell and Brownsea Island 75 15
Nos. 918/19 were printed together, se-tenant, forming a composite design.

1982. Centenary of Battle of Concepcion. Mult.
920 4p.50 Type **367** 25 20
921 4p.50 Sub-lieutenant Arturo Perez Canto 25 20
922 4p.50 Sub-lieutenant Julio Montt Salamanca 25 20
923 4p.50 Sub-lieutenant Luis Cruz Martinez 25 20

368 Old Man at Window

1982. World Assembly on Ageing, Vienna.
924 **368** 4p.50 multicoloured . . . 25 15

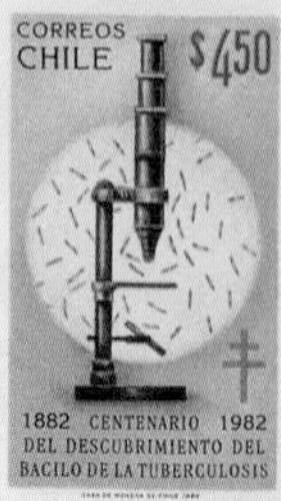

369 Microscope and Bacillus

1982. Centenary of Discovery of Tubercle Bacillus.
925 **369** 4p.50 multicoloured . . . 30 15

370 National Flag and Flame of Freedom

1982. 9th Anniv of Military Government.
926 **370** 4p.50 multicoloured . . . 25 15

1982. Nos. 688/9 surch.
927 **245** 1p. on 3E.50 blue & grn 30 10
928 **246** 2p. on 1E.15 red & black 35 10

372 "Nativity" (Mariela Espinoza Fuetes)

1982. Christmas. Multicoloured.
929 10p. Type **372** 25 10
930 25p. "Adoration of the Shepherds" (Jared Jeria Abarca) (vert) . . . . . . 1·25 40

373 "Virgin Mary and Marcellus" (stained-glass window, Sacred Heart of Jesus Church, Barcelona)

374 "El Sur", Quill and Printing Press

1982. 9th World Union of Former Marist Alumni Congress.
931 **373** 7p. multicoloured . . . . 1·60 40

1982. Cent of Concepcion's Newspaper "El Sur".
932 **374** 7p. multicoloured 25 15

375 "Steamship Copiapo" (W. Yorke)

1982. 110th Anniv of South American Steamship Company.
933 **375** 7p. multicoloured . . . . 1·50 30

376 Club Badge, Radio Aerial, Dove and Globe

1982. 60th Anniv of Radio Club of Chile.
934 **376** 7p. multicoloured 25 10

377 Arms of Sovereign Miltary Order

1983. Postal Agreement with Sovereign Military Order of Malta. Multicoloured.
935 25p. Type **377** 65 40
936 50p. Arms of Chile . . . . . 1·00 55

378 Badge

380 Child watching Railway

379 Cardinal Samore

1983. 50th Anniv of Criminal Investigation Bureau.
937 **378** 20p. multicoloured . . . 65 20

1983. Cardinal Antonio Samore Commem.
938 **379** 30p. multicoloured . . . 80 25

1983. Centenary of Valparaiso Incline Railway.
939 **380** 40p. multicoloured . . . 1·25 65

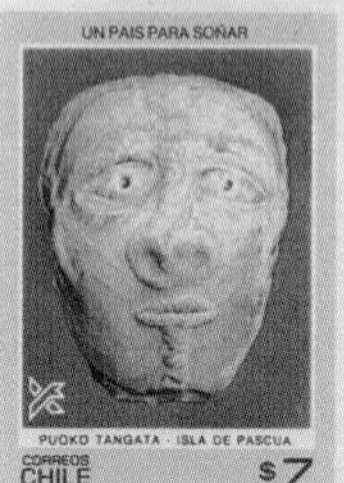

381 Puoko Tangata (carved head from Easter Island)

383 General Francisco Morazan

382 Winged Girl with Broken Chains

1983. Tourism. Multicoloured.
940 7p. Type **381** 25 15
941 7p. Ruins of Pucar de Quitor, San Pedro de Atacama . . 25 15
942 7p. Rock painting, Rio Ibanez, Aisen 25 15
943 7p. Diaguita pot 25 15

1983. 10th Anniv of Military Government. Mult.
944 7p. Type **382** 50 15
945 7p. Young couple with flag 50 15
946 10p. Family with torch . . . 55 15
947 40p. National arms . . . . . 1·10 40

1983. Famous Hondurans. Multicoloured.
948 7p. Type **383** 20 10
949 7p. Sabio Jose Cecilio del Valle 20 10

384 Central Post Office, Santiago

385 "Holy Family" (Lucrecia Cardenas Gomez)

1983. World Communications Year. Mult.
950 7p. Type **384** 55 10
951 7p. Space Shuttle "Challenger" 55 10
Nos. 950/1 were printed together in se-tenant pairs within the sheet forming a composite design.

1983. Christmas. Children's Paintings. Mult.
952 10p. "Nativity" (Hanny Chacon Scheel) 25 10
953 30p. Type **385** 90 25

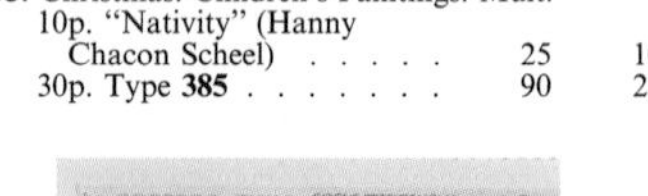

386 Presidential Coach, 1911

1984. Railway Centenary. Multicoloured.
954 9p. Type **386** . . . . . . 1·40 60
955 9p. Service car and tender . . 1·40 60
956 9p. Class 80 steam locomotive, 1929 . . . . . 1·40 60
Nos. 954/6 were printed together, se-tenant, forming a composite design.

387 Juan Luis Sanfuentes

1984. (a) Inscr "CORREOS CHILE".
989 **387** 5p. red 10 10
958 9p. green 15 10
959 10p. grey 15 10
960 15p. blue 15 10
(b) Inscr "D.S. No. 20 CHILE".
961 **387** 9p. brown 15 10
962 15p. blue 15 10
963 20p. yellow 20 10

388 Piper Pillan Trainer and Flags

1984. 3rd International Aeronautical Fair.
966 **388** 9p. multicoloured 85 10

389 Agriculture, Industry and Science

1984. 20th Anniv of Chilean Nuclear Energy Commission.
967 **389** 9p. multicoloured 25 10

1984. Nos. 944/5 surch.
968 9p. on 7p. Type **382** 65 10
969 9p. on 7p. Young couple with flag 65 10

391 Chilean Women's Antarctic Expedition

1984. Chile's Antarctic Territories. Mult.
970 15p. Type **391** 90 50
971 15p. Villa Las Estrellas Antarctic settlement . . . 75 30
972 15p. Scouts visiting Antarctic, 1983 . . . . 75 30

392 Parinacota Church (Tarapaca Region)

1984. 10th Anniv of Regionalization. Mult.
973 9p. Type **392** 50 20
974 9p. El Tatio geyser (Antofagasta Region) . . . 50 20
975 9p. Copper miners (Atacama Region) 50 20
976 9p. El Tololo observatory (Coquimbo Region) . . . 50 20
977 9p. Valparaiso harbour (Valparaiso Region) . . . 75 20
978 9p. Stone images (Easter Island Province) 50 20
979 9p. St. Francis's Church (Santiago Metropolitan Region) 50 20
980 9p. El Huique Hacienda (Libertador General Bernardo O'Higgins Region) 50 20
981 9p. Hydro-electric dam and reservoir, Machicura (Maule Region) 50 20
982 9p. Sta. Juana de Gaudalcazar Fort (Bio Bio Region) 50 20
983 9p. Araucana woman (Araucania Region) 50 20
984 9p. Church, Guar Island (Los Lagos Region) 50 20
985 9p. South Highway (Aisen del General Carlos Ibanez del Campo Region) 50 20
986 9p. Shepherd (Magallanes Region) 50 20
987 9p. Villa Las Estrellas (Chile Antarctic Territories) . . . 75 30

393 Pedro Sarmiento de Gamboa and Map

1984. 400th Anniv of Spanish Settlements on Straits of Magellan.
988 **393** 100p. multicoloured . . . 2·25 80

394 Antonio Varas de la Barra (founder) and Coin

1984. Centenary of State Savings Bank.
990 **394** 35p. multicoloured . . . 50 20

395 Flame and Bernardo O'Higgins Monument

1984. 11th Anniv of Military Government.
991 **395** 20p. multicoloured . . . 30 15

396 Clown

1984. Centenary of Circus in Chile.
992 **396** 45p. multicoloured . . . 80 25

397 Blue Whale

1984. Endangered Animals. Multicoloured.
993 9p. Type **397** 70 20
994 9p. Juan Fernandez fur seal 70 20
995 9p. Chilean guemal 70 20
996 9p. Long-tailed chinchilla . . 70 20

398 "Shepherds following Star" (Ruth M. Flores Rival)

1984. Christmas. Multicoloured.
997 9p. Type **398** 15 10
998 40p. "Bethlehem" (Vianka Pastrian Navea) 95 30

399 Satellite and Planetarium

1984. Inaug of Santiago University Planetarium.
999 **399** 10p. multicoloured . . . 30 15

400 Andean Hog-nosed Skunk

401 Flags and Emblem

1985. Flora and Fauna. Multicoloured.
1000 10p. Type **400** 60 25
1001 10p. "Leucocoryne purpurea" 60 25
1002 10p. Black-winged stilt . . . 90 30
1003 10p. Marine otter 60 25
1004 10p. "Balbisia peduncularis" 60 25
1005 10p. Patagonian conure . . 90 30
1006 10p. Southern pudu 60 25
1007 10p. "Fuchsia magellanica" 60 25
1008 10p. Common diuca finch 90 30
1009 10p. Argentine grey fox . . 60 25
1010 10p. "Alstroemeria sierrae" 60 25
1011 10p. Austral pygmy owl . . 90 30

1985. 25th Anniv (1986) of American Air forces Co-operation System.
1012 **401** 45p. multicoloured . . . 1·50 1·00

402 Chile and Argentina Flags and Papal Arms

1985. Chilean–Argentinian Peace Treaty.
1013 **402** 20p. multicoloured . . . 45 25

403 Kentenich and Schoenstatt Sanctuary, La Florida

1985. Birth Centenary of Father Jose Kentenich (founder of Schoenstatt Movement).
1014 **403** 40p. multicoloured . . . 75 40

404 Landscape and Shrimp

1985. Antarctic Territories and 25th Anniv of Antarctic Treaty. Multicoloured.
1015 15p. Type **404** 50 30
1016 20p. Seismological Station, O'Higgins Base 65 40
1017 35p. Earth receiving station, Anvers Island . . . . . . 1·10 70

405 "Canis fulvipes"

1985. Endangered Animals. Multicoloured.
1018 20p. Type **405** 70 30
1019 20p. James's flamingo . . . 1·90 40
1020 20p. Giant coot . . . . . . 1·90 40
1021 20p. Huidobria otter 70 30

406 Doves and "J"

1985. International Youth Year (1022) and 40th Anniv of U.N.O. (1023). Multicoloured.
1022 15p. Type **406** 20 15
1023 15p. U.N. emblem 20 15

407 Farmer with Haycart

1985. Occupations. Each in brown.
1024 10p. Type **407** 10 15
1025 10p. Photographer with plate camera 10 15
1026 10p. Street entertainer . . . 10 15
1027 10p. Basket maker 10 15

408 Carrera and Statue

1985. Birth Bicentenary of Gen. Jose Miguel Carrera (Independence leader and first President).
1028 **408** 40p. multicoloured . . . 75 30

409 "Holy Family"

411 Escort of Light Infantry, 1818

410 "Nativity" (Jennifer Gomez)

1985. Chilean Art.
1029 **409** 10p. brown and ochre 10 15

1985. Christmas. Multicoloured.
1030 15p. Type **410** 20 10
1031 100p. Man with donkey (Esteban Morales Medina) (vert) . . . . 2·00 90

1985. 16th American Armies Conference. Mult.
1032 20p. Type **411** 35 20
1033 35p. Officer of the Hussars of the Grand Guard, 1813 75 30

412 Moon, Earth and Comet

1985. Appearance of Halley's Comet.
1034 **412** 45p. multicoloured . . . 35 20

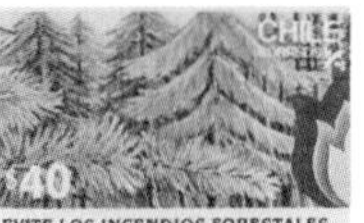

413 Living Trees and Flame **414** Saltpetre

1985. Forest Fires Prevention. Multicoloured.
1036 40p. Type **413** 65 20
1037 40p. Burnt trees and flame 70 20

1986. Exports. Each brown and blue.
1038 12p. Type **414** 15 10
1039 12p. Iron 15 10
1040 12p. Copper 15 10
1041 12p. Molybdenum 15 10

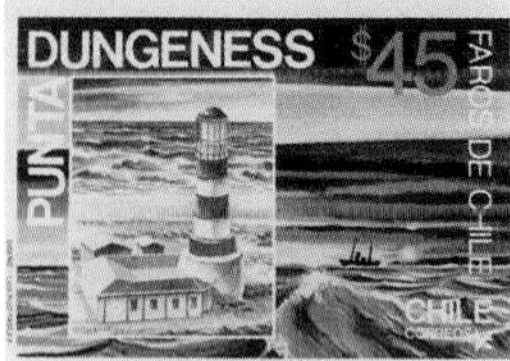

415 Dungeness Point Lighthouse

1986. Chilean Lighthouses. Multicoloured.
1042 45p. Type **415** 45 25
1043 45p. Evangelistas lighthouse in storm 45 25

416 St. Lucia Hill, Santiago

1986. Death Centenary of Benjamin Vicuna Mackenna (Municipal Superintendent).
1044 **416** 30p. multicoloured . . . 30 20

417 Diego Portales

1986 Unissued stamp surch.
1045 **417** 12p. on 3p.50 mult . . . 70 10

418 National Stadium, Chile, 1962

1986. World Cup Football Championship, Mexico. Multicoloured.
1046 15p. Type **418** 15 10
1047 20p. Azteca Stadium, Mexico, 1970 . . . . . . 20 15
1048 35p. Maracana Stadium, Brazil, 1950 . . . . . . 35 25
1049 50p. Wembley Stadium, England, 1966 . . . . . 50 40

419 Birds flying above City

1986. Environmental Protection. Mult.
1050 20p. Type **419** 20 10
1051 20p. Fish 30 10
1052 20p. Full litter bin in forest 20 10

420 "Santiaguillo" (caravel) and flags

421 Emblem

1986. 450th Anniv of Valparaiso.
1053 **420** 40p. multicoloured . . . 85 30

1986. 25th Anniv of Inter-American Development Bank.
1054 **421** 45p. multicoloured . . . 40 20

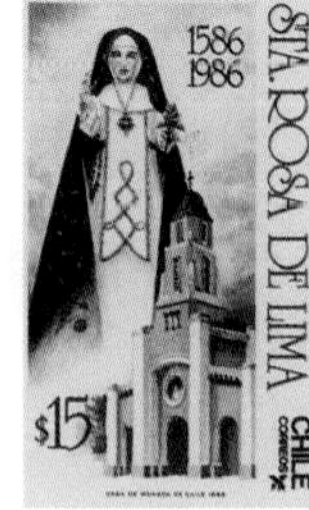

422 St. Rosa and Pelequen Sanctuary

1986. 400th Birth Anniv of St. Rosa of Lima.
1055 **422** 15p. multicoloured . . . 15 10

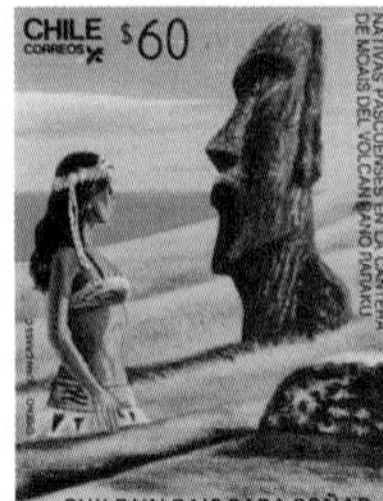

423 Stone Head on Raraku Volcano

1986. Easter Island. Multicoloured.
1056 60p. Type **423** . . . . . . 1·00 25
1057 100p. Tongariki ruins . . . 1·60 45

424 Flags, Stamps in Album, Magnifying Glass and Tweezers

1986. "Ameripex '86" International Stamp Exhibition, Chicago.
1059 **424** 100p. multicoloured . . 1·40 50

425 Schooner "Ancud"

1986. Naval Traditions. Multicoloured.
1060 35p. Type **425** 80 45
1061 35p. Brigantine "Aguila" . . 80 45
1062 35p. Sail corvette "Esmeralda" 80 45
1063 35p. Sail frigate "O'Higgins" 80 45

426 "Gate of Serenity"

1986. Paintings by Juan F. Gonzalez. Mult.
1064 30p. "Rushes and Chrysanthemums" 25 15
1065 30p. Type **426** 25 15

427 Antarctic Terns

1986. Antarctic Fauna. Sea Birds. Mult.
1066 40p. Type **427** . . . . . . 1·40 55
1067 40p. Blue-eyed cormorants 1·40 55
1068 40p. Emperor penguins . . 1·40 55
1069 40p. Antarctic skuas . . . . 1·40 55

428 Pedro de Ona (poet)

1986. Chilean Literature. Multicoloured.
1070 20p. Type **428** 15 15
1071 20p. Vicente Huidobro . . . 15 15

429 Major-General, 1878

1986. Centenary of Military Academy. Mult.
1072 45p. Type **429** 65 20
1073 45p. Major, 1950 . . . . . 65 20

430 Diaguita Art

1986. Indian Art. Multicoloured.
1074 30p. Type **430** 20 15
1075 30p. Mapuche art 20 15

431 "Nativity" (Begona Andrea Orrego Castro)

1986. Christmas. Multicoloured.
1076 15p. Type **431** 15 10
1077 105p. "Shrine and Mountains" (Andrea Maribel Riquelme Labarde) . . . . 1·60 80

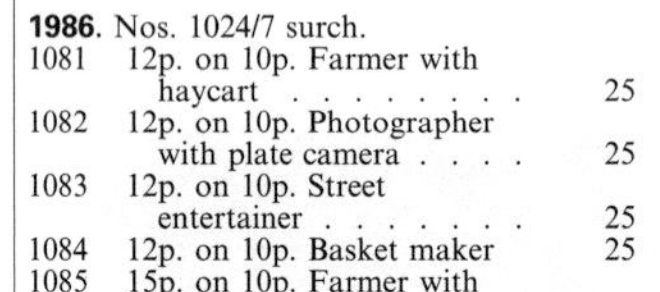

432 Shepherds looking at Hill Town

433 Emblem and Globe

1986. Christmas.
1078 **432** 12p. multicoloured . . . 20 10

1986. International Peace Year.
1079 **433** 85p. multicoloured . . . 1·00 50

1986. No. 1029 surch.
1080 **409** 12p. on 10p. brown and ochre 15 10

1986. Nos. 1024/7 surch.
1081 12p. on 10p. Farmer with haycart 25 10
1082 12p. on 10p. Photographer with plate camera 25 10
1083 12p. on 10p. Street entertainer 25 10
1084 12p. on 10p. Basket maker 25 10
1085 15p. on 10p. Farmer with haycart 25 10
1086 15p. on 10p. Photographer with plate camera 25 10
1087 15p. on 10p. Street entertainer 25 10
1088 15p. on 10p. Basket maker 25 10

436 Profiles and Flag

1986. Women's Voluntary Organization.
1089 **436** 15p. multicoloured . . . 15 10

437 Virgin of Carmelites

439 "The Guitarist of Quinchamali"

438 Kitson Meyer Steam Locomotive No. 59

1986. 60th Anniv of Coronation of Virgin of the Carmelites.
1090 **437** 25p. multicoloured . . . 40 15

1987. Railways.
1091 **438** 95p. multicoloured . . . 1·75 80

1987. Folk Tales. (a) As T **439**.
1092 **439** 15p. green 20 10
1093 – 15p. blue 40 10
1094 – 15p. brown 20 10
1095 – 15p. mauve 20 10

(b) Discount stamps. Inscr "D/S No 20" in colour of stamp in right-hand margin and dated "1992".
1092C 15p. As Type **439** 10 10
1093C 15p. As No. 1093 . . . . 10 10
1094C 15p. As No. 1094 . . . . 10 10
1095C 15p. As No. 1095 . . . . 10 10

DESIGNS: No. 1093, "El Caleuche"; 1094, "El Pihuychen"; 1095, "La Lola".

440 Rowing Boat and Storage Tanks

1987. 40th Anniv of Capt. Arturo Prat Antarctic Naval Base. Multicoloured.
1096 100p. Type **440** . . . . . . 2·50 1·10
1097 100p. Buildings and rowing boat at jetty . . . . . . 2·50 1·10

Nos. 1096/7 were printed together, se-tenant, forming a composite design.

441 Pope and "Christ the Redeemer" Statue

1987. Visit of Pope John Paul II. Mult.
1098 20p. Type **441** 10 10
1099 25p. Votive Temple, Maipu 35 10
1100 90p. "Cross of the Seas", Magellan Straits . . . . 1·10 50
1101 115p. "Virgin of the Hill" statue, Santiago . . . . . 1·60 80

442 Horse-riding Display

443 Players and Ball

1987. 60th Anniv of Carabineers. Mult.
1103 50p. Type **442** 65 15
1104 50p. Sea rescue by Air Police 65 15

1987. World Youth Football Cup. Mult.
1105 45p. Type **443** 50 15
1106 45p. Player and Concepcion stadium 50 15
1107 45p. Player and Antofagasta stadium 50 15
1108 45p. Player and Valparaiso stadium 50 15

444 Battleship "Almirante Latorre"

1987. Naval Tradition. Multicoloured.
1110 60p. Type **444** 95 45
1111 60p. Cruiser "O'Higgins" . . 95 45

445 Portales and "El Vigia" Newspaper

1987. 150th Death Anniv of Diego Portales (statesman).
1112 **445** 30p. multicoloured . . . 40 10

446 Works Projects

1987. Centenary of Ministry of Public Works.
1113 **446** 25p. multicoloured . . . 1·00 30

447 School Entrance

1987. Centenary of Infantry School. Mult.
1114 50p. Type **447** 25 10
1115 100p. Soldiers and national flag 80 40

448 "Chiasognathus granti"

449 Family

1987. Flora and Fauna. Multicoloured.
1116 25p. Type **448** 40 25
1117 25p. Sanderling 50 30
1118 25p. Peruvian guemal . . . 40 25
1119 25p. Chilean palm 40 25
1120 25p. "Colias vauthieri" (butterfly) 50 25
1121 25p. Osprey 50 30
1122 25p. Commerson's dolphin 50 25
1123 25p. Mountain cypress . . . 40 25
1124 25p. San Fernandez Island spiny lobster 40 25
1125 25p. Fernandez firecrown 50 30
1126 25p. Vicuna 50 25
1127 25p. Arboreal fern 40 25
1128 25p. Spider-crab 45 25
1129 25p. Lesser rhea 50 30
1130 25p. Mountain viscacha . . 50 25
1131 25p. Giant cactus 40 25

1987. International Year of Shelter for the Homeless.
1132 **449** 40p. multicoloured . . . 45 10

450 Emblem

452 "Holy Family" (Ximena Soledad Rosales Opazo)

451 Condell, Battle of Iquique and Statue

1987. "fisa'87", 25th International Santiago Fair.
1133 **450** 20p. multicoloured . . . 10 15

1987. Death Centenary of Admiral Carlos Condell.
1134 **451** 50p. multicoloured . . . 1·00 60

1987. Christmas. Multicoloured.
1135 30p. Type **452** 35 10
1136 100p. "Star over Bethlehem" (Marcelo Bordones Meneses) . . . . 1·00 60

453 Casting

454 "Nativity"

1987. "Cobre '87" International Copper Conference, Vina del Mar.
1137 **453** 40p. multicoloured . . . 20 10

1987. Christmas. (a) Non-discount.
1139 **454** 15p. blue and orange . . 20 10

(b) Discount stamps. Additionally inscr "D.S. No. 20".
1140 **454** 15p. blue and orange . . 20 10

455 Non-smokers inhaling Smoke

457 Freire

456 "Capitan Luis Alcazar" (supply ship) and Antarctic Landscape

1987. Anti-smoking Campaign.
1141 **455** 15p. blue and orange . . 20 10

1987. 25th Anniv of National Antarctic Research Commission.
1142 **456** 45p. multicoloured . . . 1·25 40

1987. Birth Bicentenary of General Ramon Freire Serrano (Director, 1823–27).
1143 **457** 20p. red and purple . . 25 20

458 Violin and Frutillar Church and Lake

1988. 20th Music Weeks, Frutillar.
1144 **458** 30p. multicoloured . . . 15 10

459 St. John with Boy (after C. Di Girolamo)

460 Bird, Da Vinci's Glider, Wright's Flyer 1, Junkers Ju 52/3m, De Havilland Vampire and Grumman Tomcat

1988. Death Centenary of St. John Bosco (founder of Salesian Brothers).
1145 **459** 40p. multicoloured . . . 45 10

1988. "Fida'88" 5th International Air Fair.
1146 **460** 60p. blue and deep blue 75 25

461 Shot Putting, Pole Vaulting and Javelin Throwing

1988. Olympic Games, Seoul. Multicoloured.
1147 50p. Type **461** 60 45
1148 100p. Swimming, cycling and running . . . . . . 1·25 1·00

1988. Discount stamp. No. 958 surch **$20 D.S.No 20**.
1150 **387** 20p. on 9p. green . . . 10 20

463 Kava-Kava Head

1988. Easter Island. (a) Inscr "CORREOS" only.
1151 **463** 20p. black and pink . . 25 15
1152 – 20p. black and pink . . 25 15

(b) Discount stamps. As T **463** but additionally inscr "D.S.No 20".
1153 **463** 20p. black and yellow . . 25 15
1154 – 20p. black and yellow . . 25 15

DESIGN: Nos. 1152, 1154, Tangata Manu bird-man (petroglyph).

464 Medal, Scientist, Bull and Farm Workers

1988. 150th Anniv of National Agricultural Society.
1155 **464** 45p. multicoloured . . . 25 15

465 Tending Accident Victim

1988. 125th Anniv of Red Cross.
1156 **465** 150p. multicoloured . . 2·25 2·00

466 Gipsy Moth, Boeing 767, Mirage 50 and Merino

1988. Birth Centenary of Commodore Arturo Merino Benitez (air pioneer).
1157 **466** 35p. multicoloured . . . 45 10

467 Cadet Barquentine "Esmeralda"

1988. Naval Tradition. Multicoloured.
1158 50p. Type **467** 75 45
1159 50p. "Capt. Arturo Prat" (stained glass window, Valparaiso Naval Museum) 75 45

468 Vatican City and University Arms

1988. Centenary of Pontifical Catholic University of Chile.
1160 **468** 40p. multicoloured . . . 45 10

469 Esslingen Locomotive No. 3331

1988. Railway Anniversaries. Multicoloured.
1161 60p. Type **469** (75th anniv of Arica–La Paz railway) 2·40 1·25
1162 60p. North British locomotive No. 45 (cent of Antofagasta–Bolivia railway) 35 25

470 Chemistry Student

1988. 175th Anniv of Jose Miguel Carrera National Institute.
1164 **470** 45p. multicoloured . . . 25 15

471 "Chloraea chrysantha"

1988. Flowers. Multicoloured.
1165 30p. Type **471** 45 10
1166 30p. "Lapogeria rosea" . . 45 10
1167 30p. "Nolana paradoxa" . . 45 10
1168 30p. "Rhodophiala advena" 45 10
1169 30p. "Schizanthus hookeri" 45 10
1170 30p. "Acacia caven" 45 10
1171 30p. "Cordia decanda" . . 45 10
1172 30p. "Leontochir ovallei" 45 10
1173 30p. "Alstroemeria pelegrina" 45 10
1174 30p. "Copiapoa cinerea" . . 45 10
1175 30p. "Salpiglossis sinuata" 45 10
1176 30p. "Leucocoryne coquimbensis" 45 10
1177 30p. "Eucryphia glutinosa" 45 10
1178 30p. "Calandrinia longiscapa" 45 10
1179 30p. "Desfontainia spinosa" 45 10
1180 30p. "Sophora macrocarpa" 45 10

472 Commander Policarpo Toro and "Angamos"

1988. Centenary of Incorporation of Easter Island into Chile. Multicoloured.
1181 50p. Type **472** 75 20
1182 50p. Map of Easter Island and globe 55 20
1183 100p. Dancers 90 50
1184 100p. Petroglyphs of bird-men 90 50

473 Bleriot XI over Town

1988. 70th Anniv of First National Airmail Service.
1186 **473** 150p. multicoloured . . 90 60

474 Pottery

1988. 15th Anniv of Centre for Education of Women. Traditional Crafts. Multicoloured.
1187 25p. Type **474** 10 10
1188 25p. Embroidery 10 10

475 Policeman and Brigade Members

1988. Schools' Security Brigade.
1189 **475** 45p. multicoloured . . . 20 10

476 "Nativity" (Paulette Thiers)

477 Cancelled 1881 2c. Stamp

1988. Christmas. Multicoloured.
1190 35p. Type **476** 15 10
1191 100p. "Family going to church" (Jose M. Lamas) 70 35

1988. Centenary of Chile Philatelic Society.
1192 **477** 40p. multicoloured . . . 45 10

478 Child in Manger

479 Manuel Bulnes and Battle of Yungay, 1839

1988. Christmas. (a) Non-discount.
1193 **478** 20p. purple and yellow 10 10

(b) Discount stamps. As T **478** but additionally inscr "D.S. No. 20".
1194 **478** 20p. purple and yellow 10 10

1989. Historic Heroes. Multicoloured.
1195 50p. Type **479** 20 10
1196 50p. Soldier and battle scene 20 10
1197 100p. Roberto Simpson and Battle of Casma, 1839 . . 1·25 55
1198 100p. Sailor and battle scene 1·25 55

480 St. Ambrose's Church, Vallenar (bicentenary)

483 Sister Teresa of the Andes

1989. Town Anniversaries. Multicoloured.
1199 30p. Type **480** 10 10
1200 35p. Craftsman, Combarbala (bicent) . . . 15 10
1201 45p. Laja Falls, Los Angeles (250th anniv) 20 10
See also No. 1306.

1989. Various stamps surch. (a) Surch **$25** only.
1202 25p. on 15p. green (1092) 10 10
1203 25p. on 15p. blue (1093) . . 30 10
1204 25p. on 15p. brown (1094) 10 10
1205 25p. on 15p. mauve (1095) 10 10
1206 25p. on 20p. black and pink (1151) 10 10
1207 25p. on 20p. black and pink (1152) 10 10
1208 25p. on 20p. black and yellow (1153) 10 10
1209 25p. on 20p. black and yellow (1154) 10 10

(b) Surch **D.S. No 20 $25**.
1210 25p. on 20p. black and pink (1151) 10 10
1211 25p. on 20p. black and pink (1152) 10 10

1989. Beatifications. Multicoloured.
1212 40p. Type **483** 20 10
1213 40p. Laura Vicuna 20 10

484 Christopher Columbus

1989. "Exfina '89" Stamp Exhibition, Santiago. Multicoloured.
1214 100p. Type **484** 70 35
1215 100p. "Nina", "Santa Maria" and "Pinta" . . . 95 40

485 Container Ship and Trawler

1989. 50th Anniv of Energy Production Corporation. Multicoloured.
1217 60p. Type **485** 90 20
1218 60p. Tree trunks on trailer and factory 25 15
1219 60p. Telephone tower and pylon 25 15
1220 60p. Coal wagons and colliery 25 15

486 Town and Sketch

1989. Birth Centenary of Gabriela Mistral (writer). Multicoloured.
1221 30p. Type **486** 15 10
1222 30p. Mistral with children 15 10
1223 30p. Mistral writing 15 10
1224 30p. Mistral receiving Nobel Prize 15 10

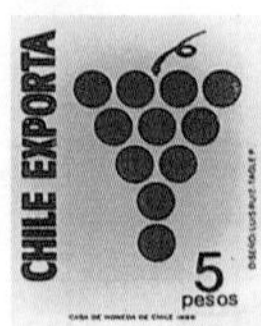

487 Grapes

1989. Exports. (a) Inscr as T **487**.
1225 **487** 5p. blue 15 10
1226 – 5p. red and blue 15 10
1227 **487** 10p. deep blue & blue 15 10
1228 – 10p. red and blue . . . 15 10
1229 **487** 25p. blue and green . . 10 10
1230 – 25p. red and green . . 10 10
1350 **487** 45p. blue and mauve . . 15 10
1351 – 45p. red and mauve . . 15 10

(b) Discount stamps. As T **487** but additionally inscr "D.S. No. 20".
1231 **487** 25p. blue and yellow . . 10 10
1232 – 25p. red and yellow . . 10 10
1352 **487** 45p. blue and yellow . . 15 15
1353 – 45p. red and yellow . . 15 15
DESIGNS: Nos. 1226, 1228, 1230, 1232, 1351, 1353, Apple.

488 Battle Scene, Soldiers and "Justice"

1989. 150th Anniv of Army Court of Justice.
1233 **488** 50p. multicoloured . . . 20 10

489 Monument

490 Victoria, Vina del Mar

1989. Frontier Guards' Martyrs' Monument.
1234 **489** 35p. multicoloured . . . 15 10

1989. Transport.
1235 **490** 30p. black and orange 15 10
1236 – 35p. black and blue . . 35 10
1237 – 40p. black and green . . 20 10
1238 – 45p. black and green . . 55 10
1239 – 50p. black and red . . . 55 10
1240 – 60p. black and bistre . . 45 15
1241 – 100p. black and green 65 35
DESIGNS—VERT: 35p. Scow, Chiloe Archipelago. HORIZ: 40p. Ox-cart, Cautin; 45p. Raft ferry, Rio Palena; 50p. Lighters, Gen. Carrera Lake; 60p. Valparaiso incline railway; 100p. Santiago funicular.
See also Nos. 1346 and 1458.

491 Scientist and Bearded Penguins

1989. 25th Anniv of Chilean Antarctic Institute.
1245 **491** 150p. multicoloured . . 2·10 1·00

492 Present Naval Engineers School and "Chacabuco" (first school)

1989. Centenary of Naval Engineering. Mult.
1246 45p. Type **492** 40 10
1247 45p. Sailors in engine room 40 10
1248 45p. Destroyer, Aerospatiale Dauphin 2 helicopter and submarine 40 10
1249 45p. Launch of "Aquiles" (patrol boat) 40 10

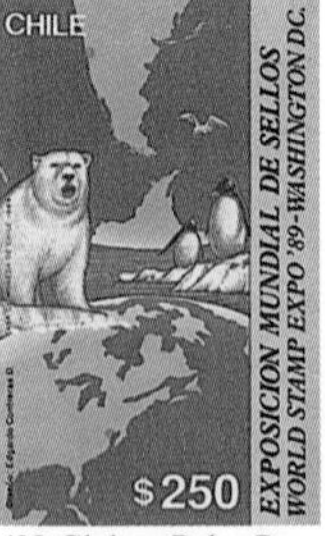

493 Globes, Polar Bear and Gentoo Penguins

494 Atacamena Culture

1989. "World Stamp Expo '89" International Stamp Exhibition, Washington D.C.
1250 **493** 250p. multicoloured . . 3·00 1·75

1989. America. Pre-Columbian Cultures. Mult.
1252 30p. Type **494** 40 10
1253 150p. Selk'nam and Onas cultures . . . . 1·25 60

495 Balls

497 Vicuna, Lauca

496 "Rowing to Church" (Cristina Lopez)

1989. Christmas. (a) As T **495**.
1254 **495** 25p. yellow and green . . 10 10
1255 – 25p. yellow and green . . 10 10

(b) Discount stamps. Additionally inscr "D.S. No 20".
1256 **495** 25p. red and green . . . 10 10
1257 – 25p. red and green . . . 10 10
DESIGN: Nos. 1255, 1257, Bells.

1989. Christmas.
1258 **496** 100p. multicoloured . . 80 40

1990. National Parks. Multicoloured.
1259 35p. Type **497** 30 10
1260 35p. Chilian flamingo, Salar de Surire 50 20
1261 35p. Cactus, La Chimba . . 30 10
1262 35p. Guanaco, Pan de Azucar 30 10
1263 35p. Long-tailed meadowlark, Fray Jorge 50 20
1264 35p. Sooty tern, Rapa Nui 50 20
1265 35p. Lesser grison, La Campana 30 10
1266 35p. Torrent duck, Rio Clarillo 50 20
1267 35p. Mountain cypress, Rio de los Cipreses 30 10
1268 35p. Black-necked swan, Laguna de Torca 50 20
1269 35p. Puma, Laguna del Laja 40 20
1270 35p. Araucaria, Villarrica 30 10
1271 35p. "Philesia magellanica", Vicente Perez Rosales . . 30 10
1272 35p. "Nothofagus pumilio", Dos Lagunas 30 10
1273 35p. Leopard seal, Laguna San Rafael 40 20
1274 35p. Lesser rhea, Torres del Paine 50 20

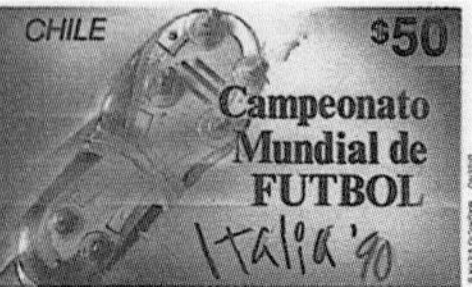

498 Boot

1990. World Cup Football Championship, Italy. Multicoloured.
1275 50p. Type **498** 20 10
1276 50p. Hand 20 10
1277 50p. Ball in net 20 10
1278 50p. Player 20 10

499 Vickers Wibault I Biplane, 1927–37

1990. Chilean Airforce Airplanes. Multicoloured.

1279 40p. Type **499** 25 10
1280 40p. Curtiss O1E Falcon, 1928–40 . . . . 25 10
1281 40p. Pitts S-2A (Falcons aerobatic team, 1981–90) 25 10
1282 40p. Extra 33 (Falcons aerobatic team, 1990) . . 25 10

No. 1282 is inscribed "EXTRA 300".

500 Inca

1990. 500th Anniv of Discovery of America by Columbus. Multicoloured.

1284 60p. Type **500** 20 10
1285 60p. Spanish officer 20 10

501 Valparaiso

1990. Ports. Multicoloured.

1286 40p. Type **501** 15 10
1287 40p. San Vicente 15 10

502 "Piloto Pardo" (Antarctic supply ship)

1990. Naval Tradition. Multicoloured.

1288 50p. Type **502** 70 30
1289 50p. "Yelcho" (survey ship) 70 30

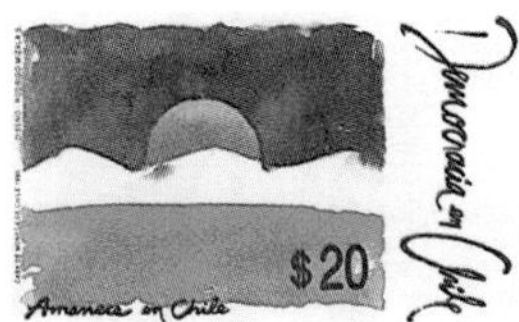

503 "Sunrise in Chile"

1990. "Democracy in Chile". Multicoloured.

1290 20p. Type **503** 10 10
1291 30p. Dove ("Peace in Chile") 10 10
1292 60p. "ChiLe" ("Rejoicing in Chile") 45 10
1293 100p. Star ("Thus Chile pleases me") 70 25

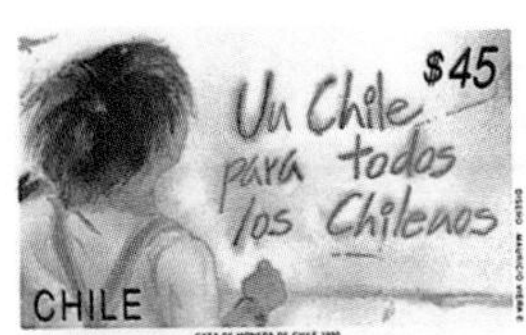

504 Child and Slogan

1990. "One Chile for All Chileans".

1295 **504** 45p. multicoloured . . . 15 10

505 Sir Rowland Hill

506 Flags

1990. 150th Anniv of the Penny Black.

1297 **505** 250p. multicoloured . . 1·50 75

1990. Centenary of Organization of American States.

1299 **506** 150p. multicoloured . . 95 40

507 Purplish Scallop and Diver with Net

1990. Fishing. Multicoloured.

1300 40p. Type **507** 25 15
1301 40p. Giant wedge clam and man with net 25 15
1302 40p. Swordfish ("Albacora") and harpooner on "San Antonio" (fishing boat) 40 15
1303 40p. Marine spider crab and fishing boat raising catch 40 15
1304 40p. Chilean hake ("Merluza") and trawler 40 15
1305 40p. Women baiting hooks 40 15

1990. Town Anniversaries. 250th Anniv of San Felipe. As T **480**. Multicoloured.

1306 50p. Curimon Convent . . . 20 10

508 Aerosol

509 Salvador Allende

1990. Environmental Protection. Each red and black.

(a) As T **508**.

1307 35p. Type **508** 15 10
1308 35p. Tree and tree stumps 15 10
1309 35p. Factory chimneys emitting smoke 15 10
1310 35p. Oil tanker polluting wildlife and sea 40 10
1311 35p. Deer escaping from burning forest 15 10

(b) Discount stamps. Additionally inscr "D.S. No 20".

1312 35p. Type **508** 15 10
1313 35p. As No. 1308 . . . . . 15 10
1314 35p. As No. 1309 . . . . . 15 10
1315 35p. As No. 1310 . . . . . 40 10
1316 35p. As No. 1311 . . . . . 15 10

See also Nos. 1421/30.

1990. Presidents.

1317 **509** 35p. black and blue . . 15 10
1318 – 35p. black and blue . . 15 10
1319 – 40p. black and green . . 15 10
1320 – 45p. black and green . . 15 10
1321 – 50p. black and red . . 20 10
1322 – 60p. black and red . . . 20 10
1323 – 70p. black and blue . . 25 15
1324 – 80p. black and blue . . 30 20
1325 – 90p. black and brown . . 30 20
1326 – 100p. black & brown . . 35 25

DESIGNS: No. 1318, Eduardo Frei; 1319, Jorge Alessandri; 1320, Gabriel Gonzalez; 1321, Juan Antonio Rios: 1322, Pedro Aguirre Cerda; 1323, Juan E. Montero; 1324, Carlos Ibanez; 1325, Emiliano Figueroa; 1326, Arturo Alessandri.

510 Opening Ceremony

1990. Rodeo. Multicoloured.

1327 45p. Type **510** 15 10
1328 45p. Riders saluting crowd 15 10
1329 45p. Rider reining in . . . 15 10
1330 45p. Two riders cornering steer 15 10

511 Chilean Flamingoes

1990. America. The Natural World. Mult.

1331 30p. Type **511** 85 20
1332 150p. South American fur seals . . . . 1·40 40

512 Chilean State Arms and Spanish Royal Arms

1990. State Visit by King Juan Carlos and Queen Sofia of Spain. Multicoloured.

1333 100p. Type **512** 70 25
1334 100p. Spanish and Chilean (at right) State Arms . . 70 25

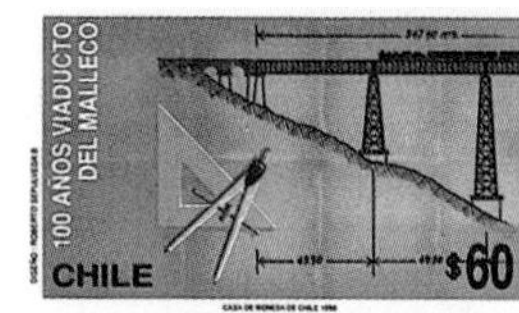

513 Construction Diagram of Viaduct

1990. Centenary of Malleco Viaduct. Mult.

1335 60p. Type **513** 55 20
1336 60p. Boy waving to steam train on completed viaduct 55 20

Nos. 1335/6 were printed together, se-tenant, forming a composite design.

514 Antarctic Skua, Whale and Supply Ship

1990. 50th Anniv of Chilean Antarctic Territory. Multicoloured.

1337 250p. Type **514** . . . . . . 1·25 85
1338 250p. Adelie penguins, Bell Model 206 jet helicopters and tents . . . . 2·00 80

515 Children decorating Tree

1990. Christmas. (a) As T **515**.

1340 **515** 35p. green & emerald . . 10 10

(b) Discount stamps. Additionally inscr "D.S. No 20".

1341 **515** 35p. green and orange 10 10

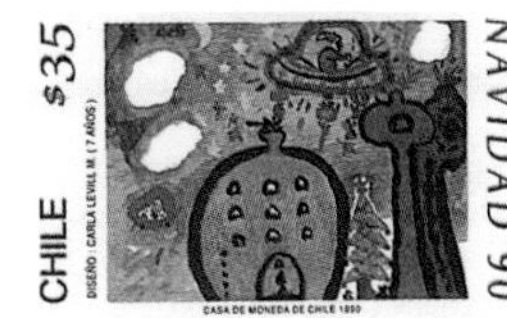

516 Santa Claus in Space (Carla Levill)

1990. Christmas. Children's drawings. Mult.

1342 35p. Type **516** 10 10
1343 150p. Television on sea bed (Jose M. Lamas) 70 35

517 Assembly Hall

1990. National Congress. Multicoloured.

1344 100p. Type **517** 75 25
1345 100p. Painting above dais 75 25

1991. Discount stamp. As No. 1238 but colour changed and additionally inscr "D.S. No 20".

1346 45p. black and yellow . . . 40 10

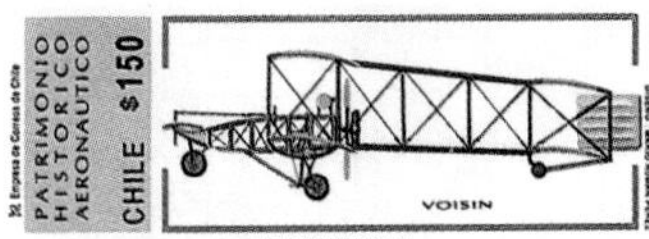

518 Casa Colorada

1991. 450th Anniv of Santiago. Multicoloured.

1347 100p. Type **518** 75 25
1348 100p. City landmarks . . . 75 25

519 Voisin "Boxkite"

1991. Aviation History. Multicoloured.

1354 150p. Type **519** 90 45
1355 150p. Royal Aircraft Factory S.E.5A 90 45
1356 150p. Morane Saulnier MS 35 . . . . 90 45
1357 150p. Consolidated PBY-5A/OA-10 Catalina amphibian 90 45

520 Map, Player and Left Half of Ball

1991. America Cup Football Championship. Mult.

1358 100p. Type **520** 75 25
1359 100p. Right half of ball and goalkeeper 75 25

Nos. 1358/9 were printed together, se-tenant, forming a composite design.

521 Drill and Miner

1991. Coal Mining. Multicoloured.

1360 200p. Type **521** . . . . . . 1·60 45
1361 200p. Miners emptying truck 1·90 45

522 Youths and Emblem

525 Santiago Cathedral

523 Dish and Hanging Ornaments

1991. Centenary of Scientific Society.

1362 **522** 45p. black and green . . 15 10

1991. Traditional Crafts. Multicoloured.

1363 90p. Type **523** 55 25
1364 90p. Carvings and ceramics 55 25

1991. Various stamps surch.

1365 **463** 45p. on 20p. black and yellow 15 10
1366 – 45p. on 20p. black and yellow (1154) 15 10

1367 **487** 45p. on 25p. blue & yell 15 10
1368 – 45p. on 25p. red and yellow (1232) 15 10

1991. National Monuments.
1369 **525** 300p. black, pink & brn 1·90 70

526 Dish Aerial and Transmission Masts

1991. World Telecommunications Day.
1370 **526** 90p. multicoloured . . . 65 25

527 Pope Leo XIII and Factory Line

528 Capt. L. Pardo and Sir Ernest Shackleton

1991. Centenary of "Rerum Novarum" (papal encyclical on workers' rights).
1371 **527** 100p. multicoloured . . 65 25

1991. Naval Tradition. 75th Anniv of Pardo's Rescue of Shackleton Expedition. Multicoloured.
1372 50p. Type **528** 40 10
1373 50p. "Yelcho" (coast-guard vessel) 75 25
1374 50p. Chilean sailor sighting stranded men on Elephant Island 40 10
1375 50p. "Endurance" 75 25

529 Flags and Globe

531 "Maipo" (container ship)

530 Building and Police Officers

1991. 21st General Assembly of Organization of American States, Santiago.
1377 **529** 70p. multicoloured . . . 80 15

1991. Opening of New Police School.
1378 **530** 50p. Multicoloured . . . 15 10

1991. National Merchant Navy Day.
1379 **531** 45p. black and red . . . 45 10

532 Opening Ceremony

1991. 11th Pan-American Games, Havana. Mult.
1380 100p. Type **532** 60 25
1381 100p. Cycling, running and basketball competitors . . 60 25

533 Carriage and Building

1991. Bicentenary of Los Andes.
1382 **533** 100p. multicoloured . . 60 25

534 Common Octopus

536 "Woman in Red" (Pedro Reszka)

535 Nitrate Processing and Jose Balmaceda (President, 1886–91)

1991. Marine Life. Multicoloured.
1383 50p. Type **534** 30 15
1384 50p. "Durvillaea antarctica" 30 15
1385 50p. Lenguado 45 15
1386 50p. "Austromegabalanus psittacus" 30 15
1387 50p. Barnacle rock shell ("Concholepas concholepas") 30 15
1388 50p. Crab ("Cancer setosus") 30 15
1389 50p. "Lessonia nigrescens" 30 15
1390 50p. Sea-urchin 30 15
1391 50p. Crab ("Homalaspis plana") 30 15
1392 50p. "Porphyra columbina" 30 15
1393 50p. Loro knife-jaw . . . 45 15
1394 50p. "Chorus giganteus" . . 30 15
1395 50p. Rock shrimp 30 15
1396 50p. Peruvian anchovy . . . 45 15
1397 50p. "Gracilaria sp." . . . 30 15
1398 50p. "Pyura chilensis" . . . 30 15

1991. Centenary of 1891 Revolution. Pre-Revolution Events. Multicoloured.
1399 100p. Type **535** 90 25
1400 100p. Education and Balmaceda 60 25

1991. Paintings. Multicoloured.
1401 50p. Type **536** 40 10
1402 70p. "The Traveller" (Camilo Mori) . . . . . 1·25 30
1403 200p. "Head of Child" (Benito Rebolledo) . . . 90 45
1404 300p. "Child in Fez" (A. Valenzuela Puelma) 2·00 70

537 Map of South American Interests in Antartica

1991. 30th Anniv of Antarctica Treaty. Mult.
1405 80p. Type **537** 70 20
1406 80p. Wildlife 90 45

538 Glove in Envelope (Guillermo Suarez)

1991. International Letter Writing Week. Children's drawings. Multicoloured.
1407 45p. Type **538** 45 10
1408 70p. Human figures in envelope (Jorge Vargas) 60 15

539 Amerindians watching Columbus's Fleet

1991. America. Voyages of Discovery. Mult.
1409 50p. Type **539** 30 15
1410 150p. Columbus's fleet and navigator . . . . 1·40 65

540 Line Drawing of Neruda

541 Boy and Stars

1991. 20th Anniv of Award of Nobel Prize for Literature to Pablo Neruda. Multicoloured, colour of cap given.
1411 **540** 45p. blue 15 10
1412 45p. red 15 10
Nos. 1411/12 were issued together, se-tenant, the backgrounds of the stamps forming a composite design of one of Neruda's manuscripts.

1991. Christmas. Multicoloured.
1414 45p. Type **541** 15 10
1415 100p. Girl and stars 30 25

542 Postman making Delivery

544 Houses and Figures

1991. Christmas. (a) As T **542**.
1416 **542** 45p. mauve and violet 15 10
1417 – 45p. mauve and violet 30 10

(b) Discount stamps. Additionally inscr "D.S. No 20" in left-hand margin.
1418 **542** 45p. mauve and violet 15 10
1419 – 45p. mauve and violet 30 20
DESIGN: Nos. 1417, 1419, Starlit town.

1992. No. 1238 surch **$60.**
1420 60p. on 45p. black & green 40 15

1992. Environmental Protection. As Nos. 1307/16 but values and colours changed. (a) As T **508**, each yellow and green.
1421 60p. Type **508** 20 15
1422 60p. As No. 1308 . . . . . 20 15
1423 60p. As No. 1309 . . . . . 20 15
1424 60p. As No. 1310 . . . . . 40 15
1425 60p. As No. 1311 . . . . . 20 15

(b) Discount stamps. Additionally inscr "D.S. No 20". Each orange and green.
1426 60p. Type **508** 20 15
1427 60p. As No. 1308 . . . . . 20 15
1428 60p. As No. 1309 . . . . . 20 15
1429 60p. As No. 1310 . . . . . 40 15
1430 60p. As No. 1311 . . . . . 20 15

1992. 16th Population and Housing Census.
1431 **544** 60p. blue, orange & blk 20 15

545 Score and Mozart

1992. Death Bicentenary of Wolfgang Amadeus Mozart (composer). Multicoloured.
1432 60p. Type **545** 50 15
1433 200p. Mozart playing harpsichord . . . . . . 1·10 50

546 Stylized Jet Fighter

1992. "Fidae '92" International Air and Space Fair.
1435 **546** 60p. multicoloured . . . 20 15

547 Arms and Church, San Jose de Maipo

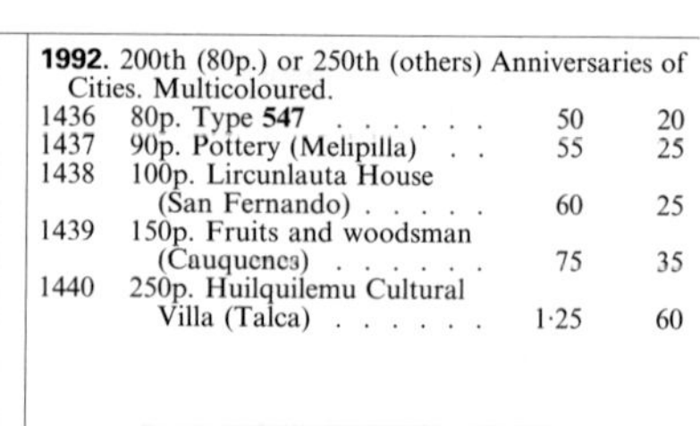

1992. 200th (80p.) or 250th (others) Anniversaries of Cities. Multicoloured.
1436 80p. Type **547** 50 20
1437 90p. Pottery (Melipilla) . . 55 25
1438 100p. Lircunlauta House (San Fernando) 60 25
1439 150p. Fruits and woodsman (Cauquenes) 75 35
1440 250p. Huilquilemu Cultural Villa (Talca) . . . . . . 1·25 60

548 Chilean Pavilion

1992. "Expo '92" World's Fair, Seville. Mult.
1441 150p. Type **548** 90 35
1442 200p. Iceberg . . . . 1·10 50

549 "Morula praecipua", Maculated Conch and Dragon's-head Cowrie

1992. Marine Flora and Fauna of Easter Island. Multicoloured.
1444 60p. Type **549** 35 20
1445 60p. "Codium pocockiae" 35 20
1446 60p. Easter Island swordfish ("Myripristis tiki") . . . 50 20
1447 60p. Seaweed 35 20
1448 60p. Fuentes' wrasse ("Pseudolabrus fuentesi") 50 20
1449 60p. Coral 35 20
1450 60p. Spiny lobster 35 20
1451 60p. Sea urchin 35 20

550 Statues, Liner and Launch

1992. Easter Island Tourism. Multicoloured.
1452 200p. Type **550** 85 50
1453 200p. Airplane, dancers and hill-carving 85 50
Nos. 1452/3 were issued together, se-tenant, forming a composite design.

551 Sun shining through Doorway and Handicapped People

552 Flags and Emblem

1992. National Council for the Handicapped.
1454 **551** 60p. multicoloured . . . 20 15

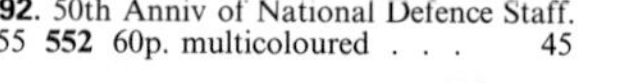

1992. 50th Anniv of National Defence Staff.
1455 **552** 60p. multicoloured . . . 45 15

553 "Simpson" (submarine)

1992. 75th Anniv of Chilean Submarine Fleet. Multicoloured.
1456 150p. Type **553** 90 35
1457 250p. Officer using periscope 1·40 60

1992. Discount stamp. As No. 1240 but additionally inscr "D/S No 20".
1458 60p. black and bistre . . . 1·10 30

1992. Nos. 1350/3 surch **$60**.
1459 **487** 60p. on 45p. blue & mve 20 15
1460 – 60p. on 45p. red & mve 20 15
1461 **487** 60p. on 45p. blue & yell 20 15
1462 – 60p. on 45p. red & yell 20 15

1992. Nos. 1416/19 surch **$60**.
1463 **542** 60p. on 45p. mauve and violet (1416) 20 15
1464 – 60p. on 45p. mauve and violet (1417) 35 15
1465 **542** 60p. on 45p. mauve and violet (1418) 20 15
1466 – 60p. on 45p. mauve and violet (1419) 35 15

556 Emperor Penguin

1992. The Emperor Penguin. Multicoloured.
1467 200p. Type **556** . . . . . . 1·40 50
1468 250p. Adult and chick . . . 1·75 60

557 Santiago Central Post Office

1992. National Monuments.
1470 **557** 200p. multicoloured . . 1·25 50

558 Columbus and Navigation Instruments

1992. America. 500th Anniv of Discovery of America by Columbus. Multicoloured.
1471 200p. Type **558** . . . . . . 1·25 50
1472 250p. Church, map of Americas and "Santa Maria" . . . . 1·10 70

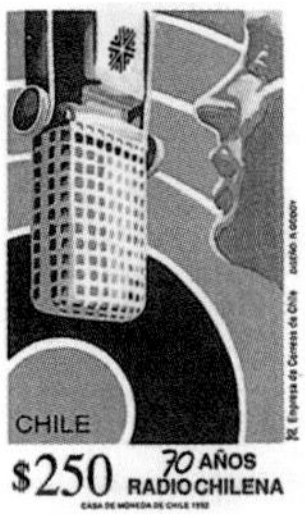

559 Presenter at Microphone

560 O'Higgins, Flag and Monument

1992. 70th Anniv of Chilean Radio.
1473 **559** 250p. multicoloured . . 1·40 60

1992. 150th Death Anniv of Bernardo O'Higgins.
1474 **560** 60p. multicoloured . . . 20 15

561 Arrau as a Child

1992. Claudio Arrau (pianist). Multicoloured
1475 150p. Type **561** 80 35
1476 200p. Arrau playing piano 1·10 50

562 Statue

563 Nativity

1992. 150th Anniv of University of Chile. Mult.
1478 200p. Type **562** . . . . . . 1·00 50
1479 200p. Coat of arms, statues and clock . . . . 1·00 50
Nos. 1478/9 were issued together, se-tenant, forming a composite design.

1992. Christmas. (a) As T **563**.
1480 **563** 60p. brown and stone . . 20 15
1481 – 60p. brown and stone . . 20 15

(b) Discount stamps. Additionally inscr "DS/20" in right-hand margin.
1482 **563** 60p. red and stone . . . 20 15
1483 – 60p. red and stone . . . 20 15
DESIGN: Nos. 1481, 1483, Nativity (different).

564 Dam

1992. 23rd Ministerial Meeting of Latin-American Energy Organization.
1484 **564** 70p. black and yellow . . 25 20

565 Hands and Stars

1992. National Human Rights Day.
1485 **565** 100p. multicoloured . . 55 25

566 Achao Church

567 St. Ignatius de Loyola (founder)

1993. Churches. (a) As T **566**.
1487 **566** 70p. black and pink . . 25 20
1488 – 70p. black and pink . . 25 20

(b) Discount stamps. Additionally inscr "DS/20" in left-hand margin.
1489 **566** 70p. black and yellow . . 25 20
1490 – 70p. black and yellow . . 25 20
DESIGN: Nos. 1488, 1490, Castro church.
See also Nos. 1507/15.

1993. 400th Anniv of Jesuits' Arrival in Chile.
1491 **567** 200p. multicoloured . . 1·25 75

568 St. Teresa

569 Finger-Puppets

1993. Canonization of St. Teresa of the Andes.
1493 **568** 300p. multicoloured . . 1·50 70

1993. International Theatre Festival.
1494 **569** 250p. multicoloured . . 1·10 60

570 Satellite in Orbit

1993. 2nd Pan-American Space Conference.
1495 **570** 150p. multicoloured . . 80 35

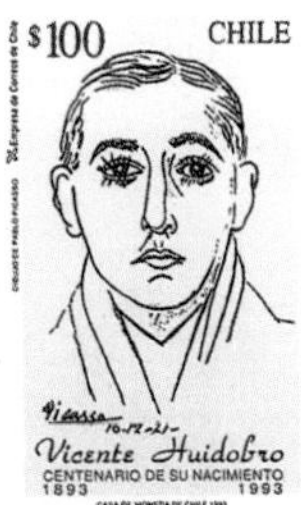

571 Clotario Blest (Trade Union leader)

572 Drawing of Huidobro by Picasso

1993. Labour Day.
1497 **571** 70p. multicoloured . . . 50 20

1993. Birth Centenary of Vicente Huidobro (poet). Each black, stone and red.
1498 100p. Type **572** 30 25
1499 100p. Drawing of Huidobro by Juan Gris 30 25

573 Watterous, 1902

1993. Fire Engines (1st series). Multicoloured.
1500 100p. Type **573** 60 25
1501 100p. Merryweather, 1872 60 25
See also Nos. 1568/71.

574 Douglas B-26 Invader

1993. Aviation and Space. Multicoloured.
1503 100p. Type **574** 60 25
1504 100p. Mirage M 50 Pantera 60 25
1505 100p. Sanchez Besa biplane 60 25
1506 100p. Bell-47 Dl helicopter 60 25

1993. Churches. (a) As T **566**.
1507 10p. black and green . . . 10 10
1508 20p. black and brown . . . 10 10
1509 30p. black and orange . . . 10 10
1510 40p. black and blue . . . 10 10
1511 50p. black and green . . . 15 10
1512 80p. black and buff . . . 25 20
1513 90p. black and green . . . 25 20
1514 100p. black and grey . . . 30 25

(b) Discount stamp. Additionally inscr "DS/20" at left.
1515 80p. black and lilac 25 20
1516 90p. black and red 25 20
1517 100p. black and yellow . . . 30 25
CHURCHES: 10p. Chonchi; 20p. Vilupulli; 30p. Llau-Llao; 40p. Dalcahue; 50p. Tenaun; 80p. Quinchao; 90p. Quehui; 100p. Nercon.

575 Nortina

577 Early Coin Production

576 "Late Dawn" (Mario Carreno)

1993. Regional Variations of La Cueca (national dance). Multicoloured.
1525 70p. Type **575** 45 15
1526 70p. Central 45 15
1527 70p. Chilota 45 15

1993. Santiago, Iberian-American City of Culture 1993. Paintings. Multicoloured.
1528 80p. Type **576** 50 20
1529 90p. "Summer" (Gracia Barrios) 50 20
1530 150p. "Protection" (Roser Bru) (vert) 70 35
1531 200p. "Tango, Valparaiso" (Nemesio Antunez) . . . 1·00 45

1993. 250th Anniv of Chilean Mint.
1532 **577** 250p. multicoloured . . 1·25 55

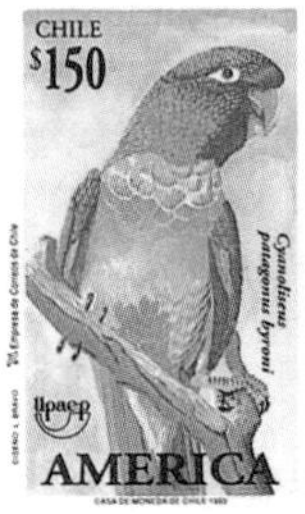

578 Patagonian Conure

579 Underground Train

1993. America. Endangered Animals. Mult.
1534 150p. Type **578** 90 35
1535 200p. Chilean guemal . . . 1·40 45

1993. 25th Anniv of Chilean Metro.
1536 **579** 80p. multicoloured . . . 45 20

580 "Ancud" (schooner) off Santa Ana Point

1993. 150th Anniv of Chilean Possession of Strait of Magellan.
1537 **580** 100p. multicoloured . . 40 25

581 Marines in Inflatable Assault Boats

1993. Naval Tradition. Multicoloured.
1538 80p. Type **581** (175th anniv of Marines) 25 20
1539 80p. Sailors making fast patrol boat (125th anniv of Alejandro Navarette Training School) 25 20
1540 80p. "Esmeralda" (cadet barquentine) and cadets in traditional "unloading the cannon" exercise (175th anniv of Arturo Prat Naval College) 25 20
1541 80p. "Sailing of First Squadron" (175th anniv) (painting, Alvaro Casanova Zenteno) . . . 25 20

582 Carved Figures

1993. International Year of Indigenous Peoples.
1542 **582** 100p. multicoloured . . 60 25

583 Holy Family **584** Adelie Penguins

1993. Christmas. (a) Sold at face value.
1543 **583** 70p. lilac and stone . . . 20 15

(b) Discount stamp. Additionally inscribed "DS/20" in right-hand margin.
1544 **583** 70p. blue and green . . 20 15

1993. Chilean Antarctic Territory. Mult.
1545 200p. Type **584** . . . . . . 1·40 45
1546 250p. Adelie penguin with young . . . . 1·60 55

585 Plaza de Armas, Ancud

1993. City Anniversaries. Multicoloured.
1548 80p. Type **585** (225th) . . . 35 20
1549 80p. Matriz church, Curico (250th) 35 20
1550 80p. Corner Pillar House, Rancagua (250th) 35 20

586 Hands

1994. International Year of the Family.
1551 **586** 100p. multicoloured . . 55 25

587 Violin

1994. 26th Music Weeks, Frutillar. Mult.
1552 150p. Type **587** 90 35
1553 150p. Cello 90 35
Nos. 1552/3 were issued together, se-tenant, forming a composite design.

588 Sukhoi Su-30 Flanker

1994. "Fidae '94" International Air and Space Fair. Multicoloured.
1554 300p. Type **588** . . . . . . 1·60 65
1555 300p. Vought Sikorsky OS2U3 Kingfisher seaplane . . . . 1·60 65
1556 300p. Lockheed F-117A Stealth . . . . 1·60 65
1557 300p. Northrop F-5E Tiger III . . . . 1·60 65

589 Ears of Grain

1994. 50th Anniv of Chile Agronomical Engineers' College.
1558 **589** 220p. multicoloured . . 1·50 45

1994. Nos. 1092/5 surch **$80**.
1559 80p. on 15p. green 25 20
1560 80p. on 15p. blue 35 20
1561 80p. on 15p. brown 25 20
1562 80p. on 15p. mauve 25 20

591 Skeletons buried under Cactus

1994. 75th Anniv of Concepcion University. Details of "Latin American Presence" (mural by Jorge Gonzalez Camarena). Multicoloured.
1563 250p. Type **591** . . . . . . 1·50 55
1564 250p. Faces . . . . 1·50 55
1565 250p. Building pyramid from spare parts . . . . 1·50 55
1566 250p. Cablework in building 1·50 55
Nos. 1563/6 were issued together, se-tenant, forming a composite design.

592 Gentoo Penguins and Harbour

1994. 30th Anniv of Chilean Antarctic Institute. Multicoloured.
1567 300p. Type **592** . . . . . . 1·90 65
1568 300p. Antarctic base . . . . 1·90 65
Nos. 1567/8 were issued together, se-tenant, forming a composite design.

593 "Vanessa terpsichore"

1994. Butterflies. Multicoloured.
1569 100p. Type **593** 60 25
1570 100p. "Hypsochila wagenknechti" 60 25
1571 100p. Polydamas swallowtail ("Battus polydamas") . . 60 25
1572 100p. "Polythysana apollina" 60 25
1573 100p. "Satyridae" 60 25
1574 100p. "Tetraphloebia stellygera" 60 25
1575 100p. "Eroessa chilensis" . . 60 25
1576 100p. Cloudless sulphur ("Phoebis sennae") . . . 60 25

594 Merryweather Steam Fire Engine, 1869

1994. Fire Engines (2nd series). Mult.
1577 150p. Type **594** 80 35
1578 150p. Poniente steam fire engine, 1863 . . . . . 80 35
1579 150p. Mieusset steam fire engine, 1905 . . . . . 80 35
1580 150p. Merryweather motor fire engine, 1903 . . . . 80 35

595 Bust and Banner

1994. Centenary of Javiera Carrera School for Girls, Santiago.
1581 **595** 200p. multicoloured . . 85 45

596 Door Panels, Porvenir (centenary)

1994. Town Anniversaries. Multicoloured.
1582 90p. Type **596** 50 20
1583 100p. Railway station, Villa Alemana (cent) . . . . . 1·00 25
1584 150p. Church, Constitucion (bicentenary) 70 35
1585 200p. Fountain and church, Linares (bicent) 90 45
1586 250p. Steam locomotive and statue, Copiapo (250th) 2·25 55
1587 300p. La Serena (450th) . . 1·60 65

597 Painting by Carlos Maturana **600** Fr. Hurtado

599 First Chilean Mail Van

1994. 20th International Very Large Data Bases Conference, Santiago.
1588 **597** 100p. multicoloured . . 30 25

1994. Nos. 1487/8 and 1544 surch **$80**.
1589 **566** 80p. on 70p. blk & pink 25 20
1590 – 80p. on 70p. blk & pink 25 20
1591 **583** 80p. on 70p. blue & grn 25 20

1994. America. Postal Transport. Mult.
1592 80p. Type **599** 50 20
1593 220p. De Havilland D.H.60G Gipsy Moth (first Chilean mail plane) 1·10 50

1994. Beatification of Fr. Alberto Hurtado.
1594 **600** 300p. blue, green & blk 1·40 70

601 Madonna and Child **603** "Almirante Williams" (destroyer)

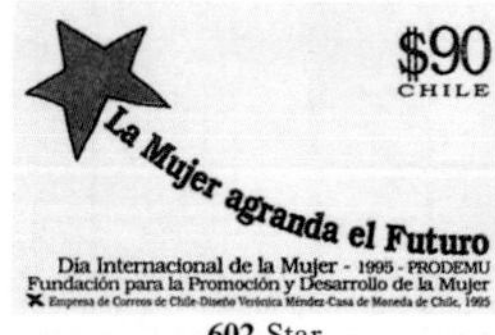

602 Star

1994. Christmas. (a) Sold at face value.
1595 **601** 80p. multicoloured . . . 25 20

(b) Discount stamp. Additionally inscribed "DS/20" at foot.
1596 **601** 80p. multicoloured . . . 25 20

1995. International Women's Day. Mult.
1597 90p. Type **602** 55 25
1598 90p. Moon and sun 55 25
1599 90p. Dove 55 25
1600 90p. Earth 55 25

1995. Naval Tradition.
1601 **603** 100p. multicoloured . . 30 25

604 Emblem **605** Arms

1995. United Nations World Summit for Social Development, Copenhagen.
1602 **604** 150p. multicoloured . . 75 35

1995. 150th Anniv of Conciliar Seminary of Ancud.
1603 **605** 200p. multicoloured . . 90 45

606 Stained Glass Window, Santiago Cathedral

1995. 400th Anniv of Augustinian Order in Chile.
1604 **606** 250p. multicoloured . . 1·10 60

607 Religious Mask, Limari

1995. Rock Paintings. Multicoloured.
1605 150p. Type **607** 75 35
1606 150p. Herdsmen and llamas, Taira 75 35
1607 150p. Whale, Tal-tal 75 35
1608 150p. Masks, Encanto Valley 75 35

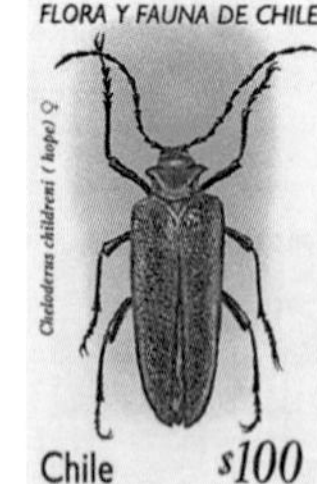

608 Camera and Director's Chair **610** "Cheloderus childreni"

609 Arms and Express Steam Train

1995. Centenary of Motion Pictures. Mult.
1609 100p. Type **608** 55 25
1610 100p. Advertising poster for "The Kid" 55 25
1611 100p. Early cinema advertising poster 55 25
1612 100p. Advertising poster for "Valparaiso Mi Amor" 55 25

1995. Bicentenary of Parral.
1613 **609** 200p. multicoloured . . 1·00 50

1995. Flora and Fauna. Multicoloured.
1614 100p. Type **610** 55 25
1615 100p. "Eulychnia acida" (cactus) 55 25

1616 100p. "Chiasognathus grantii" (stag beetle) . . . 55 25
1617 100p. "Browningia candelaris" (cactus) . . . 55 25
1618 100p. "Capiapoa dealbata" (cactus) 55 25
1619 100p. "Acanthinodera cummingi" (beetle) . . . 55 25
1620 100p. "Neoporteria subgibbosa" (cactus) . . . 55 25
1621 100p. "Semiotus luteipennis" (beetle) 55 25

611 Congress Emblem

1995. 2nd World Police Congress, Santiago.
1622 **611** 200p. multicoloured . . 90 45

612 "Tower of Babel V" (Mario Toral)

1995. 30th Anniv of Ministry of Housing and Town-planning.
1623 **612** 200p. multicoloured . . 90 45

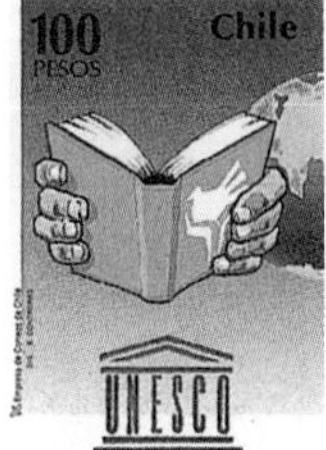

613 Bello 614 Open Book and Emblem

1995. 25th Anniv of Andres Bello Agreement (South American co-operation in education. science and culture).
1624 **613** 250p. purple and black 1·10 60

1995. 50th Anniversaries. Multicoloured.
1625 100p. Type **614** (U.N.E.S.C.O.) 30 25
1626 100p. Globes and handshake (U.N.O.) 30 25
1627 100p. Seedling in hand (F.A.O.) 30 25
Nos. 1625/7 were issued together, se-tenant, forming a composite design.

51° CONGRESO MUNDIAL DE CAPITANES DEL CABO DE HORNOS

615 Farming (M. Cruces) 616 Sailing Ship and Cape Horn

1995. America. Environmental Protection. Children's Paintings. Multicoloured.
1628 100p. Type **615** 55 25
1629 250p. Forestry (E. Munoz) (horiz) . . . . 1·00 55

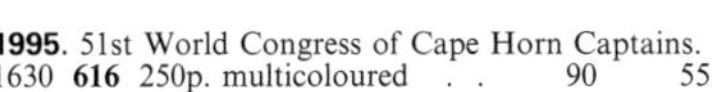
1995. 51st World Congress of Cape Horn Captains.
1630 **616** 250p. multicoloured . . 90 55

617 Crib and Inhabitants of North Chile 618 Carlos Dittborn (trainer) and Arica Stadium

1995. Christmas. (a) Sold at face value.
1631 **617** 90p. blue and violet . . 25 20
1632 – 90p. blue and violet . . 25 20

(b) Discount stamps. Additionally inscr "DS/20".
1633 **617** 90p. green and purple . . 25 20
1634 – 90p. green and purple . . 25 20
DESIGNS: Nos. 1632, 1634, Crib and people of South Chile.

1995. Centenary of Chile Football Federation. Mult.
1635 100p. Type **618** 55 25
1636 100p. Hugo Lepe (player) 55 25
1637 100p. Eladio Rojas (player) 55 25
1638 100p. Honorino Landa (player) 55 25

619 Mistral

1995. 50th Anniv of Award of Nobel Prize for Literature to Gabriela Mistral.
1639 **619** 300p. blue and black . . 1·25 65

620 Penguins

1995. Chilean Antarctic Territory. The Macaroni Penguin. Multicoloured.
1640 100p. Type **620** 60 25
1641 250p. Penguins (different) 1·50 55

621 Kiwi Fruit and Container Ship

1995. 60th Anniv of Chilean Exports Association. Fruit. Multicoloured.
1643 100p. Type **621** 40 25
1644 100p. Grapes and container ship 40 25
1645 100p. Peaches and container ship 40 25
1646 100p. Apples and container ship 40 25
1647 100p. Soft fruit and airplane 40 25

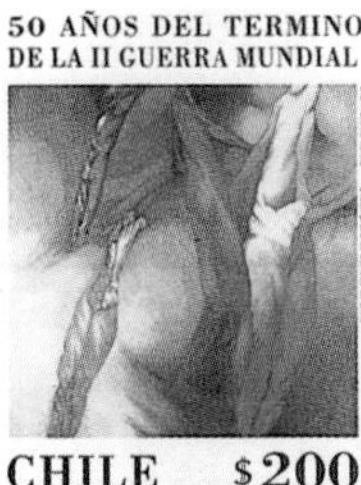

622 "Reunion" (Mario Toral) 623 Oil Rig

1995. 50th Anniv of End of Second World War.
1648 **622** 200p. multicoloured . . 90 45

1995. 50th Anniv of Discovery of Oil in Chile. Multicoloured.
1649 100p. Type **623** 40 25
1650 100p. Concon Refinery (grass in foreground) . . 40 25
1651 100p. Concepcion Refinery 40 25
1652 100p. Rig (different) 40 25

624 Embraer EMB-145

1996. "FIDAE '96" International Air and Space Fair, Santiago. Aircraft. Multicoloured.
1653 400p. Type **624** . . . . . . 2·50 90
1654 400p. Mirage M5M Elkan 2·50 90
1655 400p. De Havilland D.H.C. 6 Twin Otter . . . . . . 2·50 90
1656 400p. Saab JAS-39 Gripen 2·50 90

625 School

1996. 175th Anniv of Serena Boys' School.
1657 **625** 100p. multicoloured . . 75 25

626 Old Cordoba Rail Station, Seville

1996. "Espamer" and "Aviation and Space" Spanish and Latin American Stamp Exhibitions, Seville, Spain. Multicoloured.
1658 200p. Type **626** . . . . . . 1·10 25
1659 200p. Lope de Vega Theatre, Seville 85 45

ESCULTORES CHILENOS
$150
CHILE

627 Extinguish Matches Properly 629 "Weather Rose" (Ricardo Mesa)

628 "Esmeralda" (cadet barquentine) in Dry-dock

1996. Safety Precautions. Multicoloured.
(a) Accidents in the Home.
1660 50p. Type **627** 15 10
1661 50p. Do not leave boiling water unattended 15 10
1662 50p. Keep sharp objects away from children . . . 15 10
1663 50p. Protect electrical sockets 15 10
1664 50p. Do not improvise electrical connections . . 15 10
1665 50p. Do not play the television or radio too loud 15 10
1666 50p. Check gas connections regularly 15 10
1667 50p. Do not overload electrical circuits 15 10
1668 50p. Keep inflammable materials away from fire 15 10
1669 50p. Do not leave toys lying around on the floor . . . 15 10

(b) Road Safety.
1670 50p. Use crossings 15 10
1671 50p. Obey the instructions of the traffic police . . . 15 10
1672 50p. Only cross on the green light 15 10
1673 50p. Wait on the pavement for buses 15 10
1674 50p. Do not cross the road between vehicles 15 10
1675 50p. Do not travel on the step of buses 15 10
1676 50p. Walk on the side of the road facing on-coming traffic 15 10
1677 50p. Look out for drains . . 15 10
1678 50p. Do not play ball in the road 15 10
1679 50p. Bicyclists should obey the Highway Code . . . 15 10

(c) Safety at School.
1680 50p. Do not panic in emergencies 15 10
1681 50p. Do not run around corners 15 10
1682 50p. Do not play practical jokes 15 10
1683 50p. Do not sit on banisters or railings 15 10
1684 50p. Do not run on the stairs 15 10
1685 50p. Do not drink while walking 15 10
1686 50p. Do not swing on your chair 15 10
1687 50p. Do not play with pointed or sharp objects 15 10
1688 50p. Do not open doors sharply 15 10
1689 50p. Go straight home after school and do not stop to talk to strangers 15 10

(d) Safety in the Workplace.
1690 50p. Wear protective clothing 15 10
1691 50p. Do not work with tools in bad condition 15 10
1692 50p. Keep your attention on your work (man at lathe) 15 10
1693 50p. Always use the proper tools 15 10
1694 50p. Work carefully (man at filing cabinet) 15 10
1695 50p. Do not leave objects on the stairs 15 10
1696 50p. Do not carry so much that you cannot see where you are going 15 10
1697 50p. Check ladders are safe 15 10
1698 50p. Always keep the workplace clean and tidy 15 10
1699 50p. Remove old nails first 15 10

(e) Enjoy Leisure Safely.
1700 50p. Only swim in the permitted areas 15 10
1701 50p. Do not put any part of the body out of the window of a moving vehicle 15 10
1702 50p. Avoid excessive exposure to the sun . . . 15 10
1703 50p. Do not contaminate swimming water with detergents 15 10
1704 50p. Do not throw litter . . 15 10
1705 50p. Always put out fires before leaving them . . . 15 10
1706 50p. Do not play pranks in water 15 10
1707 50p. Check safety precautions 15 10
1708 50p. Do not fly kites near overhead electrical lines 15 10
1709 50p. Do not run by the side of swimming pools . . . 15 10

(f) Alcohol and Drugs Awareness.
1710 50p. Do not drink and drive 15 10
1711 50p. Do not drink if you are pregnant 15 10
1712 50p. Do not give in to peer pressure 15 10
1713 50p. Being under the influence of alcohol is irresponsible in the workplace 15 10
1714 50p. Do not destroy your family through alcohol . . 15 10
1715 50p. You do not need drugs to have a good time . . . 15 10
1716 50p. You do not need drugs to succeed 15 10
1717 50p. You do not need drugs to entertain 15 10
1718 50p. Do not abandon your friends and family for drugs 15 10
1719 50p. Without drugs you are free and safe 15 10

1996. Centenary of Dry-dock No. 1, Talcahuano.
1720 **628** 200p. multicoloured . . 70 45

1996. Modern Sculpture. Multicoloured.
1721 150p. Type **629** 70 35
1722 150p. "Friendship" (Francisca Cerda) 70 35
1723 200p. "Memory" (Fernando Undurraga) (horiz) . . . 70 35
1724 200p. "Andean Airs" (Benito Rojo) (horiz) . . 70 35

630 Addict and Syringe full of Pills

1996. International Day against Drug Abuse.
1725 **630** 250p. multicoloured . . 75 55

631 Boxing Glove

1996. Centenary of National Olympic Committee and Modern Olympic Games. Olympic Games, Atlanta. Multicoloured.
1726 450p. Type **631** . . . . . . 2·25 1·00
1727 450p. Running shoe . . . . 2·25 1·00
1728 450p. Rollerblade . . . . . 2·25 1·00
1729 450p. Ball . . . . 2·25 1·00

632 School

1996. 150th Anniv of San Fernando School.
1730 **632** 200p. multicoloured . . 85 45

633 Polluted Forest

1996. 4th International Congress on Earth Sciences. Multicoloured.
1731 200p. Type **633** 95 45
1732 200p. Industrial pollution 95 45
1733 200p. Deforestation 95 45
1734 200p. Map, camera and cracked earth 95 45
Nos. 1731/4 were issued together, se-tenant, forming a composite design.

634 Crookesite and Open-cast Mine

1996. Mining. Multicoloured.
1735 150p. Type **634** 70 35
1736 150p. Lapis lazuli and pendant 70 35
1737 150p. Bornite and calcium and crates 70 35
1738 150p. Azurite and atacamite 70 35

635 St. John Leonardi (founder)

1996. 50th Anniv of Order of Mother of God in Chile.
1739 **635** 200p. multicoloured . . 90 45

636 German-style Wooden house and Mt. Osorno

1996. 150th Anniv of German Immigration. Multicoloured.
1740 250p. Type **636** . . . . . . 1·00 50
1741 300p. "German Fountain" (monument) . . . . . . 1·10 60

637 King Penguins

1996. Chilean Antarctic Territory. Mult.
1742 250p. Type **637** . . . . . . 1·40 50
1743 300p. Adult and young king penguins . . . . 1·75 60

638 Lancia Fire Engine, 1937

1996. Centenary of Castro Fire Service. Mult.
1745 200p. Type **638** 90 40
1746 200p. Ford V8 fire engine, 1940 . . . . 90 40
1747 200p. Gorlitz G. A. Fischer 4-speed motor pump, 1930s 90 40
1748 200p. Lever-action pump, 1907 . . . . 90 40

639 Rafting, Vicente Perez Rosales National Park

1996. National Parks. Multicoloured.
1749 100p. Type **639** 55 25
1750 100p. Horse riding, Torres del Paine National Park 55 25
1751 100p. Cross-country skiing, Puyehue National Park 55 25
1752 100p. Walking, Pan de Azucar National Park . . 55 25

640 Latorre and "Almirante Latorre" (destroyer)

641 Women with Child

1996. 150th Birth Anniv of Admiral Juan Jose Latorre.
1753 **640** 200p. multicoloured . . 70 40

1996. America. Costumes. Multicoloured.
1754 100p. Type **641** 55 25
1755 100p. Men with horse . . . 55 25
1756 250p. Men on horseback . . 95 50

642 "Visual History of a Nation" (Mario Toral) (left-hand detail)

644 The Three Kings

643 Beach, Arms and Cathedral, Arica

1996. 6th Ibero-Latin American Heads of State Summit, Santiago. Multicoloured.
1757 110p. Type **642** 55 25
1758 110p. Right-hand detail of painting 55 25
Nos. 1757/8 were issued together, se-tenant, forming a composite design.

1996. Cities. 1st Anniv of Arica Law. Multicoloured.
1759 100p. Type **643** 55 25
1760 150p. Llamas and Chilean flamingoes, Parinacota Province 65 30

1996. Christmas. (a) Face value in black.
1761 **644** 100p. multicoloured . . 30 25

(b) Discount stamp. Additionally inscribed "DS/20" at foot and with face value in orange.
1762 **644** 100p. multicoloured . . 30 25

645 Pablo Neruda (poet), Gabriela Mistral (writer) and Nobel Prize Medal

1996. Visit of King and Queen of Sweden.
1763 **645** 300p. multicoloured . . 1·40 60

646 Children, Star and Globe

1996. 50th Anniv of U.N.I.C.E.F.
1764 **646** 200p. multicoloured . . 80 40

647 Church

1997. Centenary of Frontera Region. Mult.
1765 110p. Type **647** (centenary of Christian and Missionary Church Alliance) 60 25
1766 110p. Mountain valley (cent of Lonquimay Municipality) 60 25

648 Base Camp

649 La Pincoya

1997. 50th Anniv of Arturo Prat Antarctic Naval Base.
1767 250p. Type **648** . . . . . . 1·00 50
1768 300p. Monument and flags (horiz) . . . . 1·25 60

1997. Mythology. (a) As T **649**.
1769 40p. black and blue 10 10
1770 110p. black and orange . . 30 25

(b) Discount stamp. Additionally inscr "DS/20".
1778 110p. black and green . . . 30 25
DESIGN: Nos. 1770, 1778, La Fiura.

650 "Justice" and National Flag

1997. 70th Anniv of Controller General.
1781 **650** 110p. multicoloured . . 55 25

651 Underground Train in Station

1997. Inauguration of Metro Line No. 5.
1782 **651** 200p. multicoloured . . 1·25 60

652 Masonic Symbols and Flags

1997. 50th Anniv of Interamerican Masonic Confederation and 17th Grand General Assembly, Santiago.
1783 **652** 250p. multicoloured . . 1·00 50

653 Von Stephan

1997. Death Centenary of Heinrich von Stephan (founder of Universal Postal Union).
1785 **653** 250p. multicoloured . . 1·00 50

654 Books

1997. World Books and Copyright Day.
1786 **654** 110p. multicoloured . . 55 25

655 "Death to the Invader, Chile"

1997. Birth Centenary of David Alfaro Siqueiros (painter). Designs showing details of his murals in the Mexican School, Chillan, Chile. Multicoloured.

1787 150p. Type **655** 70 30
1788 200p. "Death to the Invader, Mexico" 95 40

656 Arms and Town Hall

1997. Centenary of Providencia.

1790 **656** 250p. multicoloured . . 1·10 50

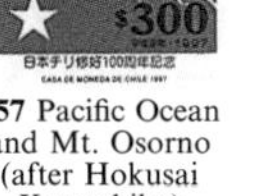

657 Pacific Ocean and Mt. Osorno (after Hokusai Katsushika)

658 Award, National Flag and "Thumbs-up" Sign

1997. Centenary of Chile–Japan Relations.

1791 **657** 300p. multicoloured . . 1·10 60

1997. National Centre for Productivity and Quality.

1792 **658** 110p. multicoloured . . 75 25

659 Transmission from University of Chile to "El Mercurio" (newspaper) Offices

1997. 75th Anniv of First Radio Broadcast in Chile.

1793 **659** 110p. multicoloured . . 80 25

660 Postman on Bicycle, 1997

1997. America. The Postman. Multicoloured.

1794 110p. Type **660** 55 25
1795 250p. Late 19th-century mounted postman 95 50

661 Carlo Morelli in "Rigoletto"

662 Jack-in-a-Box and Baubles on Tree

1997. Opera Singers. Multicoloured.

1796 120p. Type **661** 35 25
1797 200p. Pedro Navia in "La Boheme" 55 40
1798 250p. Renato Zanelli in "Faust" 70 50
1799 300p. Rayen Quitral in "The Magic Flute" . . . . . . 1·10 60
1800 500p. Ramon Vinay in "Othello" . . . . 1·60 70

1997. Christmas. (a) "NAVIDAD '97" in blue.

1801 **662** 110p. multicoloured . . 30 25

(b) Discount stamp. "NAVIDAD '97" in orange and additionally inscr "D/S 20" below face value.

1802 **662** 110p. multicoloured . . 30 25

663 Cancelling Letters

664 Great Dane

1997. 250th Anniv of Postal Service in Chile. Multicoloured.

1803 120p. Type **663** 85 25
1804 300p. Man posting letter . . 1·60 60

1998. Dogs. Multicoloured. (a) As T **664**.

1805 120p. Type **664** 25 20
1806 120p. Dalmatian 25 20

(b) Discount stamps. Additionally inscr "DS/20".

1807 120p. Type **664** 25 20
1808 120p. As No. 1806 . . . . 25 20

665 Prat and "Esmeralda" (sail corvette)

666 Summit Emblem

1998. 150th Birth Anniv of Captain Arturo Prat Chacon.

1809 **665** 120p. multicoloured . . 40 25

1998. 2nd Summit of the Americas, Santiago.

1810 **666** 150p. multicoloured . . 35 25

667 Vets treating Horse

1998. Centenary of Army Veterinary Service. Mult.

1812 250p. Type **667** 55 40
1813 350p. Vet using stethoscope on horse 80 55

668 "Los Zambos de Calama" (Mauricio Moran)

1998. Paintings. Multicoloured.

1814 350p. Type **668** 80 55
1815 400p. "Soaking Watermelon" (Roser Bru) 90 65

669 Monk writing in Book

1998. 150th Anniv of Capuchin Order in Chile. Multicoloured.

1816 150p. Type **669** 35 25
1817 250p. Monk treating man's leg 55 40

670 Players

1998. World Cup Football Championship, France. Multicoloured.

1818 250p. Type **670** 55 40
1819 350p. Players and trophy . . 80 55
1820 500p. Players and map of France . . . . 1·10 75
1821 700p. Attacker and goalkeeper . . . . 1·50 1·10

671 Bearded Penguin and Emblem

1998. 25th Meeting of Scientific Committee on Antarctic Research (1823) and 10th Meeting of Council of Managers of National Antarctic Programmes (1824), Concepcion. Multicoloured.

1823 250p. Type **671** 55 40
1824 350p. Two gentoo penguins on map of Antarctica and emblem 80 55

672 Lighthouse

1998. International Year of the Ocean (1st issue). 150th Anniv of General Office for Territorial Waters and the Merchant Navy.

1825 **672** 500p. multicoloured . . 1·10 85

673 Iceberg and Ocean

1998. International Year of the Ocean (2nd issue).

1826 **673** 400p. blue, violet and black 90 60
1827 – 400p. blue, violet and black 90 60
1828 – 500p. multicoloured . . 1·10 75

DESIGNS: No. 1827, Compass rose, map of South Chile and ocean; 1828, Easter Island monolith and ocean.

674 Clara Solovera

1998. Composers and Folk Singers. Multicoloured.

1829 200p. Type **674** 45 30
1830 250p. Francisco Flores del Campo 55 40
1831 300p. Victor Jara 65 45
1832 350p. Violeta Parra 80 55

675 Delivery to Letter Box and Dog

1998. World Stamp Day.

1833 **675** 250p. multicoloured . . 55 40

676 Bilbao

1998. 175th Birth Anniv of Francisco Bilbao (writer).

1834 **676** 250p. purple, blue and orange 55 40

677 Amanda Labarca (educationist)

1998. America. Famous Women.

1835 **677** 120p. mauve, blue and black 25 20
1836 – 250p. yellow, mauve and black 55 40

DESIGN: 250 p, Marta Brunet (writer).

678 "Self-portrait" (Augusto Eguiluz)

1998. Paintings. Multicoloured.

1837 300p. Type **678** 65 45
1838 450p. "Solitary Tree" (Agustin Abarca) (horiz) 1·00 70

679 Arms and University

680 Rufous-collared Sparrow

1998. 70th Anniv of Valparaiso Catholic University.

1840 **679** 130p. multicoloured . . 30 20

1998. Birds. Multicoloured.

1841 10p. Type **680** 10 10
1842 20p. Austral blackbird . . . 10 10
1845 50p Magellanic woodpecker (vert) 10 10
1849 100p Peregrine falcon (vert) 25 20

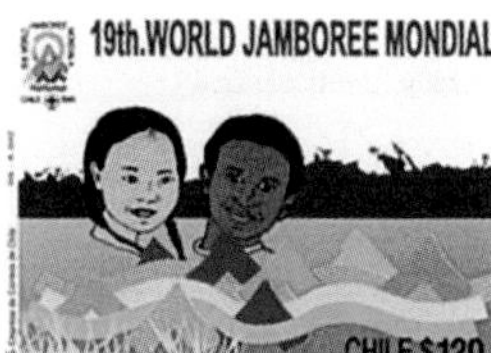

681 Children and Tents

1998. 19th World Scout Jamboree, Picarquin. Mult.

1856 120p. Type **681** 25 20
1857 200p. Lord Baden-Powell (founder of Scout movement) 40 30
1858 250p. Tents and doves . . . 55 40
1859 300p. Scout, tents and globe 65 45
1860 1000p. Emblem and singsong (vert) . . . . . 2·25 1·50

682 Capt. Alberto Larraguibel and Horse

1999. 50th Anniv of World Equestrian High Jump Record.
1862 **682** 200p. multicoloured . . 45 35

683 Fire Engine, 1990

1999. Centenary of Temuco Fire Department. Mult.
1863 140p. Type **683** 35 25
1864 200p. Ford fire engine, 1929 45 35
1865 300p. Ford K 1800 fire engine, 1955 . . . . . . 70 50
1866 350p. Mercedes Benz fire engine, 1967 . . . . . . 75 55

684 Chamber

1999. 1000th Session of Chilean Chamber of Deputies.
1868 **684** 140p. multicoloured . . 35 25

685 Facade

1999. 150th Anniv of Sagrados College.
1869 **685** 250p. multicoloured . . 60 45

686 Pedro Aguirre Cerda (Chilean President, 1938–41)

689 Weddell Seal and Blue-eyed Cormorants

687 Man with Sphere on Shoulder

1999. 60th Anniv of Economic Development Corporation.
1870 **686** 140p. multicoloured . . 35 25

1999. Centenary of Chilean Insurance Association.
1871 **687** 140p. multicoloured . . 35 25

1999. Antarctica. Multicoloured.
1873 360p. Type **689** 85 60
1874 450p. Bearded penguin . . . 1·10 80

690 Easter Island, Dancers, Ship and Figures

1999. Easter Island.
1876 **690** 360p. multicoloured . . 85 60

691 Business and Arts School

1999. 150th Anniv of Santiago University. Mult.
1877 140p. Type **691** 35 25
1878 250p. State Technical University 60 45
1879 300p. Woman using microscope, computer and building 70 50

692 J. L. Molina (naturalist), Statue of Humboldt, Mountains and Llamas

1999. Bicentenary of Alexander von Humboldt's Exploration of South America. Multicoloured.
1880 300p. Type **692** 70 50
1881 360p. Rodulfo A. Philippi (medical doctor and naturalist), statue of Humboldt and humboldt penguins 85 60

693 Cardinal Silva and Crucifix

1999. Cardinal Raul Silva Henrique Commemoration. Multicoloured.
1882 140p. Type **693** 35 25
1883 200p. Silva and image of Christ 45 35

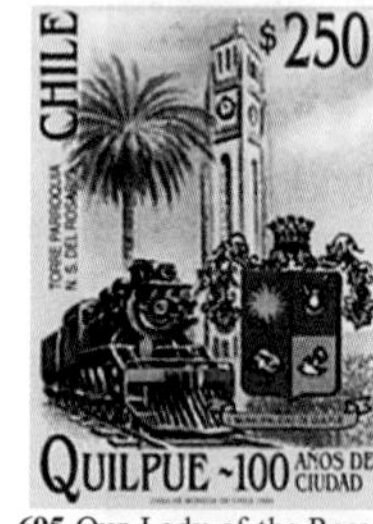
694 Chinese and Chilean Flags with Pagoda

1999. "China 1999" International Stamp Exhibition, Peking. Multicoloured.
1884 140p. Type **694** 35 25
1885 450p. Chinese and Chilean Flags with junk . . . . . 1·10 80

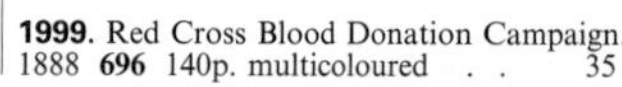
695 Our Lady of the Rosary Church Tower, Train and Arms

696 Nurse and Donor

1999. Centenary of Quilpue City.
1887 **695** 250p. multicoloured . . 60 45

1999. Red Cross Blood Donation Campaign.
1888 **696** 140p. multicoloured . . 35 25

697 People in Glass Ball

1999. 75th Anniv of Employment Legislation.
1889 **697** 320p. multicoloured . . 75 55

698 Emblem

1999. 42nd International Congress of Confederation of Authors' and Composers' Societies, Santiago.
1890 **698** 170p. multicoloured . . 40 30

699 Elderly Couple watching Children

1999. International Year of Elderly Persons.
1891 **699** 250p. multicoloured . . 60 45

700 Post Box, 1854

1999. 125th Anniv of Universal Postal Union. Multicoloured.
1892 300p. Type **700** 70 50
1893 360p. Gold coloured post box, 1900 . . . . 85 60

701 Bomb releasing Doves

1999. America. A New Millennium without Arms. Multicoloured.
1894 140p. Type **701** 35 25
1895 320p. Broken bomb 75 55

702 Felipe Herrera Lane (first President, 1960–71) and Projects

1999. 40th Anniv of Inter-American Development Bank.
1896 **702** 360p. multicoloured . . 85 60

703 Globe and Chilean Flag

1999. Holy Year 2000.
1897 **703** 450p. multicoloured . . 1·10 80

704 Clock Face, "2000" and Fireworks (½-size illustration)

1999. New Millennium. Multicoloured. (a) As T **704**.
1898 170p. Type **704** 40 30

(b) Discount stamps. Additionally inscr "D.S. 20".
1899 170p. Type **704** 40 30

Nos. 1898/9 each include the prize draw coupons shown in T **704**.

705 Recabarren and Blest

1999. Trade Union Leaders. Multicoloured.
1900 200p. Type **705** 45 35
1901 200p. Jimenez and Bustos 45 35

Nos. 1900/1 were issued together, se-tenant, forming a composite design.

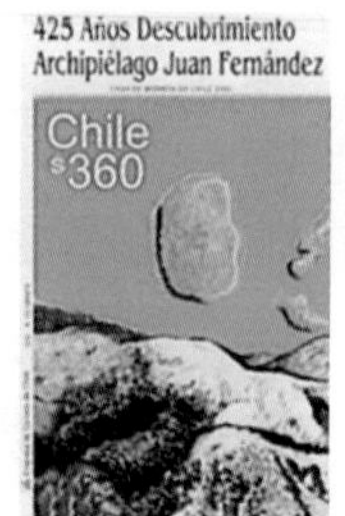
706 Mountains and Map of Islands

2000. Discovery of Juan Fernandez Archipelago. Multicoloured.
1902 360p. Type **706** 85 60
1903 360p. Mountains and map of islands (different) . . . 85 60
1904 360p. Fernandez firecrown and mountains 85 60
1905 360p. *Rhaphythamnus venustus* (plant) 85 60
1906 360p. Lobster 85 60
1907 360p. Antennae of lobster and anchored boat . . . 85 60
1908 360p. Plant and boat . . . 85 60
1909 360p. *Gavilea insularis* (orchid) 85 60

Nos. 1902/9 were issued together, se-tenant, forming a composite design.

707 Condorito celebrating

2000. 50th Anniv (1999) of Condorito (cartoon character) by Rene Rios. Multicoloured.
1910 150p. Type **707** 35 25
1911 260p. Playing football . . . 60 45
1912 480p. As a fireman . . . . 1·10 80
1913 980p. On horseback . . . . 2·40 1·75

708 Dancer and Local Crafts

2000. Easter Island. Multicoloured.
1915 200p. Type **708** 50 45
1916 260p. Statue and rock carving 60 45
1917 340p. Statue and man wearing headdress 80 60
1918 480p. Dancer and text . . . 1·10 80

709 Steam Locomotive and Pot

2000. Centenary of Carahue. Multicoloured.
1919 220p. Type **709** 55 40
1920 220p. Potato tubers and plant 55 40
Nos. 1919/20 were issued together, se-tenant, forming a composite design.

710 Iguanodon

2000. Discount stamps. Prehistoric Animals. Mult.
1921 150p. Type **710** 35 25
1922 150p. Plesiosaur 35 25
1923 150p. Titanosaurus 35 25
1924 150p. Milodon 35 25

711 Emblem, Printing Press and Office

2000. Centenary of *El Mercurio* (newspaper).
1925 **711** 370p. multicoloured . . 90 65

712 Emblems

2000. 4th National Masonic Lodge Congress.
1926 **712** 460p. multicoloured . . 1·10 80

713 *Quillaja saponaria*

2000. Medicinal Plants. Multicoloured.
1927 200p. Type **713** 40 25
1928 360p. *Fabiana imbricata* . . 70 45

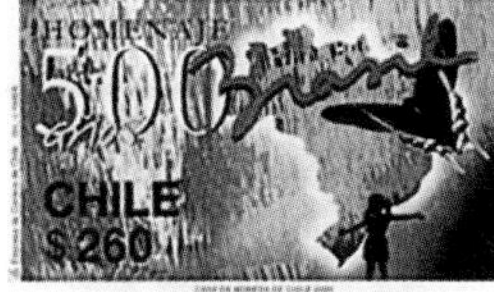

714 Map and Butterfly

2000. 500th Anniv of Discovery of Brazil.
1929 **714** 260p. multicoloured . . 50 30

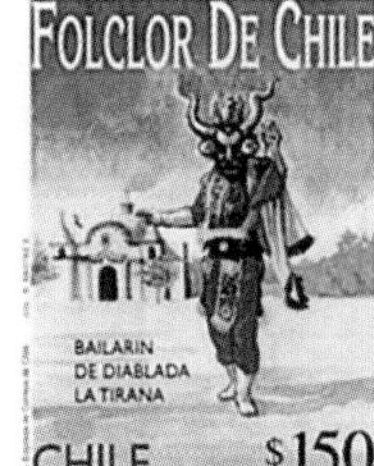

715 Man wearing Costume (Bailarin de Diablada Festival, La Tirana)

2000. Religious Festivals. Multicoloured.
1931 150p. Type **715** 30 20
1932 200p. Girl wearing costume (San Pedro de Atacama fiesta) 40 25
1933 370p. Men dancing (La Candelaria Copiapo fiesta) 75 45
1934 460p. Drummer (Chinese Dance of Andacollo) . . 90 55

716 San Martin

2000. 150th Death Anniv of General Jose de San Martin.
1935 **716** 320p. multicoloured . . 65 40

717 Emblem, Globe and Weather Symbols **718** Magellanic Penguin (*Spheniscus magellanicus*)

2000. 50th Anniv of World Meteorological Organization.
1936 **717** 320p. multicoloured . . 65 40

2000. Antarctica. Multicoloured.
1937 450p. Type **718** 90 55
1938 650p. Humpback whales (*Megaptera novaeangliae*) (horiz) . . . . 1·25 1·40
1939 940p. Killer whale (*Orcinus orca*) (horiz) . . . . . 1·90 2·00
No. 1937 is inscribed "Sphenis" in error.

719 Tennis, Football, Athletics and Sydney Opera House

2000. Olympic Games, Sydney. Multicoloured.
1941 290p. Type **719** 60 40
1942 290p. Archery, high jumping, cycling and Australian flag 60 40
Nos. 1941/2 were issued together, se-tenant, forming a composite design.

720 Native Chileans with Axe and Bow

2000. 450th Anniv of City of Concepcion. Depicting paintings by G. de la Fuente Riojas. Multicoloured.
1943 250p. Type **720** 50 30
1944 250p. Chileans and Spanish Conquistadors 50 30
1945 250p. Hand and scenes of destruction 50 30
1946 250p. Seated woman with shield 50 30
1947 250p. Horse, locomotive and coal truck 50 30
1948 250p. Modern Chileans and child 50 30
Nos. 1943/8 were issued together, se-tenant, forming a composite design.

721 Child's Hand holding Adult's Hand

2000. America. A.I.D.S. Awareness Campaign. Multicoloured.
1949 150p. Type **721** 30 20
1950 220p. Joined hands showing bones 45 30

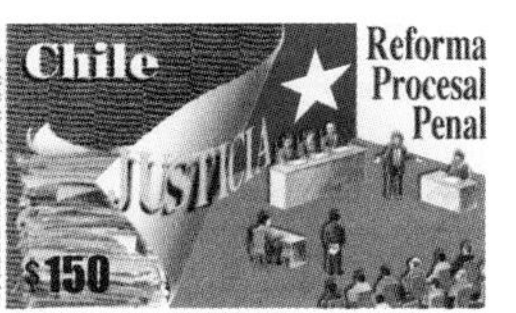

722 Documents and Courtroom

2000. Penal Reform.
1951 **722** 150p. multicoloured . . 30 20

723 Star

2000. Christmas. Multicoloured. (a) As T **723**.
1953 150p. Type **723** 30 20
1954 150p. Silhouette of sleigh and reindeer above church 30 20
1955 150p. The Three Wise Men 30 20
1956 150p. Star on Christmas tree 30 20
1957 150p. Boy posting letter . . 30 20
1958 150p. Boy asleep 30 20
1959 150p. Man with bowl of fish and hindquarters of oxen 30 20
1960 150p. Jesus in manger . . . 30 20
1961 150p. Mary and Joseph . . . 30 20
1962 150p. Girl decorating tree 30 20

(b) Discount stamps. As Nos. 1953/62 additionally inscr "D S/20" above (Nos. 1963/7) or below (Nos. 1968/72) face value.
1963 150p. As No. 1953 . . . . 30 20
1964 150p. As No. 1954 . . . . 30 20
1965 150p. As No. 1955 . . . . 30 20
1966 150p. As No. 1956 . . . . 30 20
1967 150p. As No. 1957 . . . . 30 20
1968 150p. As No. 1958 . . . . 30 20
1969 150p. As No. 1959 . . . . 30 20
1970 150p. As No. 1960 . . . . 30 20
1971 150p. As No. 1961 . . . . 30 20
1972 150p. As No. 1962 . . . . 30 20
Nos. 1953/62 and Nos. 1963/72 respectively were issued together, se-tenant, forming a composite design.

724 Wild Cat, Gibbon and Ostrich

2001. 75th Anniv of Santiago National Zoo. Multicoloured.
1973 160p. Type **724** 30 20
1974 160p. Lion, elephant and bird 30 20
1975 160p. Polar bears 30 20
1976 160p. Hippopotamus, chameleon and fox . . . 30 20
Nos. 1973/6 were issued together, se-tenant, forming a composite design.

725 Antiguo de Yumbel Church and Statue

2001. San Sebastian de Yumbel Festival.
1977 **725** 210p. multicoloured . . 35 20

726 Hurtado sweeping and Car **727** Slender-billed Conure (*Enicognathus leptorhynchus*)

2001. Birth Centenary of Fr. Alberto Hurtado. Multicoloured.
1978 160p. Type **726** 30 20
1979 340p. Hurtado and children 30 20

2001. Discount Stamps. Birds. Multicoloured. Inscr "D/S No. 20".
1980 160p. Type **727** 30 20
1981 160p. Moustached turaka (*Pteroptochos megapodius*) 30 20
1982 160p. Chilean mockingbird (*Mimus thenca*) 30 20
1983 160p. Fernandez firecrown (*Sephanoides fernandensis*) 30 20

728 Flag, Globe and Industries

2001. 42nd Annual Reunion of the Governors of Inter-American Development Bank and Inter-American Investments Corporation.
1984 **728** 230p. multicoloured . . 80 50

729 Lockheed C-130 Hercules (transport)

2001. Chilean Airforce Anniversaries. Mult.
1985 260p. Type **729** (50th anniv of Chilean Air Force in Antarctica) 45 30
1986 260p. Flugzeugbau Extra-300 (20th anniv of High Acrobactics Squadron) 45 30
1987 260p. North American AT-6 Texan (75th anniv of No. 1 Aviation Group) 45 30
1988 260p. Consolidated PBY-5A/OA-10 Catalina (amphibian) (50th Anniv of first flight to Easter Island) 45 30

730 Mine, Products and Molten Copper

2001. 30th Anniv of Nationalization of Copper Industry. Multicoloured.
1989 **730** 400p. multicoloured . . 70 40
MS1990 118 × 97 mm. 2000p. Miner and digger 3·50 3·50

731 Ambulance, Organs and Medical Staff

2001. Organ Donation Campaign.
1991 **731** 160p. multicoloured . . 30 20

732 Pampas Cat (*Lynchailurus colocolo*)

2001. Endangered Species.

1992	**732**	100p. multicoloured	10	10

ACKNOWLEDGEMENT OF RECEIPT STAMP

1894. Portrait of Columbus. Inscr "A.R.". Perf or Imperf.

AR77		5c. brown	1·40	1·40

COMPULSORY TAX STAMPS

T **100** Arms of Talca

T **224** Chilean Arms

1942. Talca Bicentenary.

T338	**T 100**	10c. blue	10	10

1955. Death Centenary of Pres. Prieto. As T **145**.

T445		15p. green	15	10

PORTRAIT: 15p. Pres. Prieto.

1970. Postal Tax. No. 492a and 555 surch **E° O,10 Art. 77 LEY 17272.**

T638	**162**	10c. on 2c. blue	10	10
T639	**178**	10c. on 6c. purple	10	10

1971. Postal Modernization.

T646	**T 224**	10c. blue	15	10
T647		15c. red	15	10

1971. Postal Modernization. Nos. T646/7 surch.

T673	**T 224**	15c. on 10c. blue	10	10
T674		20c. on 15c. red	10	10
T675		50c. on 15c. red	10	10

OFFICIAL STAMPS

1928. Stamps of 1911 inscr "CHILE CORREOS" optd **Servicio del ESTADO.**

O190	**49**	10c. black and blue	3·75	1·00
O191	–	20c. (No. 142)	1·60	50
O192	–	25c. (No. 167)	4·25	50
O193	–	50c. (No. 170)	1·75	50
O194	**57**	1p. black and green	2·75	70

1930. Stamps inscr "CORREOS DE CHILE" optd **Servicio del ESTADO.**

O217	**49**	10c. (No. 204)	2·00	70
O234	**76**	10c. blue	1·60	35
O219	–	20c. (No. 209)	90	25
O235	–	20c. brown (No. 232)	1·10	25
O220	–	25c. (No. 210)	90	25
O221	–	50c. (No. 212)	1·10	35

1934. Stamps inscr "CORREOS DE CHILE" optd **OFICIAL.**

O236	**64**	5c. green (No. 206)	70	35
O237	**76**	10c. blue	70	35
O238	–	20c. brown (No. 232)	4·50	35

1939. Optd **Servicio del ESTADO.**

O279	–	50c. violet (No. 273)	4·50	2·00
O280	**90**	1p. orange	3·75	2·50

1941. Nos. 269/338j optd **OFICIAL.**

O281	–	10c. red	1·75	1·00
O282	–	15c. red	95	25
O283	–	20c. blue	4·50	2·75
O284	–	30c. red	45	25
O285	–	40c. green	45	25
O286	–	50c. violet	3·00	50
O339	**90**	1p. orange	2·00	80
O288	–	1p.80 blue	8·00	4·75
O442	–	2p. red	1·60	1·00
O383	–	5p. green	3·00	1·25
O443	–	10p. purple	10·00	5·00

1953. No. 379c optd **OFICIAL.**

O386		1p. turquoise	85	35

1956. Nos. 446/450 optd **OFICIAL.**

O451		2p. lilac	2·40	50
O452		3p. blue	8·00	4·00
O453		5p. sepia	1·50	40
O454a		10p. violet	1·25	40
O455		50p. red	5·00	1·40

1958. Optd **OFICIAL.**

O469	**152**	10p. blue	£140	35·00

1960. No. 493 optd **OFICIAL.**

O507		5c. blue	3·75	1·25

POSTAGE DUE STAMPS

D 18 D 19 D 68

1895.

D 98	**D 18**	1c. red on yellow	1·25	40
D 99		2c. red on yellow	1·25	40
D100		4c. red on yellow	1·25	40
D101		6c. red on yellow	1·25	40
D102		8c. red on yellow	1·25	40
D103		10c. red on yellow	1·25	40
D104		20c. red on yellow	1·25	40
D 93		40c. red on yellow	3·00	90
D 94		50c. red on yellow	4·00	1·00
D 95		60c. red on yellow	6·00	1·50
D 96		80c. red on yellow	7·00	3·00
D109		100c. red on yellow	20·00	11·50
D 97		1p. red on yellow	12·00	6·00

1898.

D110	**D 19**	1c. red	60	50
D111		2c. red	75	60
D112		4c. red	1·75	1·25
D113		10c. red	60	60
D114		20c. red	60	60

1924.

D184	**D 68**	2c. red and blue	1·25	1·00
D185		4c. red and blue	1·25	1·00
D186		8c. red and blue	1·25	1·00
D187		10c. red and blue	1·25	1·00
D188		20c. red and blue	1·25	1·00
D189		40c. red and blue	1·25	1·00
D190		60c. red and blue	1·25	1·00
D191		80c. red and blue	1·25	1·00
D192		1p. red and blue	1·40	2·50
D193		2p. red and blue	2·00	4·00
D194		5p. red and blue	2·50	4·00

CHINA Pt. 17

People's Republic in Eastern Asia, formerly an Empire.

CHINESE CHARACTERS

Simple	Formal	
半	半	= ½
一	壹	= 1
二	貳	= 2
三	叁	= 3
四	肆	= 4
五	伍	= 5
六	陸	= 6
七	柒	= 7
八	捌	= 8
九	玖	= 9
十	拾	= 10
百	佰	= 100
千	仟	= 1,000
萬	萬	= 10,000
	分	= cent
	圓	= dollar

Examples:

十五	= 15
五十	= 50
叁佰圓	= 300 dollars
伍仟圓	= 5,000 dollars

CHINESE EMPIRE

1878. 100 candarins = 1 tael.
1897. 100 cents = 1 dollar.

1 Dragon

2

1878.

7	**1**	1ca. green	£120	90·00
2		3ca. red	£180	60·00
3		5ca. orange	£300	70·00

1885.

13	**2**	1ca. green	8·00	7·50
14		3ca. mauve	40·00	5·00
15		5ca. yellow	50·00	7·50

4

10

1894. Dowager Empress's 60th Birthday.

16	**4**	1ca. orange	12·00	7·50
17	–	2ca. green	12·00	10·00
18	–	3ca. yellow	12·00	3·50
19	–	4ca. pink	30·00	18·00
20	**4**	5ca. orange	65·00	45·00
21	–	6ca. brown	18·00	8·00
22	**10**	9ca. green	35·00	10·00
23		12ca. orange	85·00	40·00
24	–	24ca. red	£100	50·00

DESIGNS—VERT: (as Type **4**): 2ca. to 4ca. and 6ca. Dragon. HORIZ: (as Type **10**): 24ca. Junks.

1897. Surch in English and Chinese characters.

78	–	½c. on 3ca. yellow (No. 18)	5·00	4·00
34	**2**	1c. on 1ca. green	25·00	16·00
79	**4**	1c. on 1ca. orange	7·00	5·00
80	–	2c. on 2ca. green (No. 17)	8·00	2·50
35	**2**	2c. on 3ca. mauve	65·00	45·00
40	–	4c. on 4ca. pink (No. 19)	10·00	5·00
36	**2**	5c. on 5ca. yellow	60·00	25·00
41	–	5c. on 5ca. orange (No. 20)	12·00	5·00
42	–	8c. on 6ca. brown (No. 21)	14·00	5·00
43	–	10c. on 6ca. brown (No. 21)	60·00	60·00
63	**10**	10c. on 9ca. green	48·00	30·00
64		10c. on 12ca. orange	75·00	60·00
46	–	30c. on 24ca. red (No. 24)	80·00	40·00

17

24

30 Carp

31 Bean Goose

1897. Surch in English and Chinese characters.

88	**17**	1c. on 3c. red	45·00	30·00
89		2c. on 3c. red	55·00	30·00
90		4c. on 3c. red	£200	80·00
91		$1 on 3c. red	£900	£600
92		$5 on 3c. red	£5000	£3250

1897. Inscr "IMPERIAL CHINESE POST".

96	**24**	½c. purple	1·75	3·00
97		1c. yellow	2·50	1·00
98		2c. orange	2·50	50
99		4c. brown	3·00	75
100		5c. red	5·00	2·00
101		10c. green	8·50	1·75
102	**30**	20c. lake	20·00	6·50
103		30c. red	35·00	15·00
104		50c. green	40·00	24·00
105	**31**	$1 red	£170	£130
106		$2 orange and yellow	£900	£950
107		$5 green and red	£500	£650

32 Dragon

33 Carp

34 Bean Goose

1898. Inscr "CHINESE IMPERIAL POST".

121	**32**	½c. brown	1·00	10
122		1c. buff	1·00	10
123		2c. red	1·50	15
151		2c. green	2·00	20
152		3c. green	2·00	25
124		4c. brown	3·00	55
153a		4c. red	4·00	90
112		5c. pink	8·00	1·50
126		5c. orange	15·00	5·00
154		5c. mauve	4·00	15
155		7c. red	5·00	3·50
127		10c. green	6·00	15
156		10c. blue	7·00	20
157	**33**	16c. green	15·00	5·75
128		20c. purple	8·00	80
115		30c. red	11·00	4·00
130		50c. green	18·00	2·75
131	**34**	$1 red and orange	£160	12·00
132		$2 purple and yellow	£270	48·00
119		$5 green and orange	£475	£150

36 Temple of Heaven

1909. 1st Year of Reign of Emperor Hsuan T'ung.
165 **36** 2c. green and orange . . . 1·25 80
166 3c. blue and orange . . . 1·50 90
167 7c. purple and orange . . . 1·25 1·50

POSTAGE DUE STAMPS

1904. Stamps of 1898 optd **POSTAGE DUE** in English and Chinese characters.
D137 **32** ½c. brown . . . . . . 3·00 4·00
D138 1c. buff . . . . . . 3·00 2·00
D139a 2c. red . . . . . . 5·50 2·75
D140 4c. brown . . . . . . 5·50 3·75
D141 5c. red . . . . . . 11·00 5·00
D142 10c. green . . . . . . 20·00 4·00

D 37

1904.
D143 **D 37** ½c. blue . . . . . . 2·00 85
D144 1c. blue . . . . . . 5·00 75
D168 1c. brown . . . . . . 4·00 3·00
D145 2c. blue . . . . . . 5·00 75
D169 2c. brown . . . . . . 9·00 12·00
D146 4c. blue . . . . . . 5·25 85
D170 4c. brown £2000
D147 5c. blue . . . . . . 5·75 1·25
D171 5c. brown £900 £750
D148 10c. blue . . . . . . 6·00 1·75
D149 20c. blue . . . . . . 14·00 3·50
D150 30c. blue . . . . . . 18·00 5·25

CHINESE REPUBLIC

1912. 100 cents = 1 dollar.
1948. 100 cents = 1 gold yuan.
1949. 100 cents = 1 silver yuan.

1912. Optd vert with four Chinese characters signifying "Republic of China".
192 **32** ½c. brown 50 25
193 1c. buff 65 20
194 2c. green . . . . 1·25 25
221 3c. green . . . . 1·25 20
196 4c. red . . . . 2·50 40
197 5c. mauve . . . . 4·00 20
198 7c. lake . . . . 5·00 2·50
225 10c. blue . . . . 4·00 15·00
200 **33** 16c. olive . . . . 10·00 4·50
227 20c. red . . . . 10·00 1·00
202 30c. red . . . . 13·00 2·50
203 50c. green . . . . 18·00 2·50
204 **34** $1 red and salmon . . . . £160 12·50
205 $2 red and yellow . . . . £130 35·00
232 $5 green and salmon . . . £350 £325

41 Dr. Sun Yat-sen

1912. Revolution Commemoration.
242 **41** 1c. orange . . . . 1·25 1·00
243 2c. green . . . . 1·25 1·00
244 3c. blue . . . . 1·25 40
245 5c. mauve . . . . 1·25 85
246 8c. sepia . . . . 1·75 1·75
247 10c. blue . . . . 1·75 1·00
248 16c. olive . . . . 7·50 8·00
249 20c. lake . . . . 6·50 5·00
250 50c. green . . . . 30·00 14·00
251 $1 red . . . . 75·00 25·00
252 $2 brown £250 £180
253 $5 slate . . . . 75·00 £110

1912. As T **41** but portrait of Pres. Yuan Shih-kai, inscr "Commemoration of the Republic".
254 1c. orange . . . . 1·25 1·00
255 2c. green . . . . 1·25 1·00
256 3c. blue . . . . 1·25 30
257 5c. mauve . . . . 1·25 1·00
258 8c. sepia . . . . 3·50 4·00
259 10c. blue . . . . 2·75 1·00
260 16c. olive . . . . 6·00 5·00
261 20c. lake . . . . 5·75 2·75
262 50c. green . . . . 18·00 10·00
263 $1 red . . . . 42·00 18·00
264 $2 brown . . . . 45·00 14·00
265 $5 slate £140 £110

43 Junk
44 Reaper
45 Entrance Hall of Classics, Peking

1913.
287 **43** ½c. sepia 20 10
269 1c. orange 35 10
289a 1½c. purple 85 75
270 2c. green . . . . 1·00 10
271 3c. green . . . . 1·40 10
292 4c. red . . . . 1·75 10
314 4c. grey . . . . 11·00 40
315 4c. olive . . . . 2·00 20
293 5c. mauve . . . . 1·50 10
294 6c. grey . . . . 2·25 45
317 6c. red . . . . 2·75 25
318 6c. brown . . . . 25·00 4·00
295 7c. violet . . . . 5·00 2·00
296 8c. orange . . . . 4·00 20
297 10c. blue . . . . 4·00 10
298 **44** 13c. brown . . . . 3·75 65
278 15c. brown . . . . 9·00 4·00
323 15c. blue . . . . 5·00 30
324 16c. olive . . . . 5·00 30
325 20c. lake . . . . 5·00 30
326 30c. purple . . . . 5·00 30
282 50c. green . . . . 10·00 1·50
304 **45** $1 black and yellow . . . 30·00 65
328 $1 sepia and brown . . . 16·00 65
305 $2 black and blue . . . 48·00 1·75
329 $2 brown and blue . . . 32·00 1·25
306 $5 black and red . . . £150 24·00
330 $5 green and red . . . 70·00 7·00
307 $10 black and green . . . £475 £140
331 $10 mauve and green . . £200 30·00
308 $20 black and orange . . £2000 £1800
332 $20 blue and purple . . . £325 60·00

1920. Flood Relief Fund. Surch with new value in English and Chinese characters.
349 **43** 1c. on 2c. green . . . . . 5·00 2·00
361 2c. on 3c. green . . . . . 4·00 20
350 3c. on 4c. red . . . . . 7·50 1·75
351 5c. on 6c. grey . . . . . 10·00 6·00

47 Curtiss JN-4 "Jenny" over Great Wall of China

I II

1921. Air. Tail fin of aeroplane as Type I.
352 **47** 15c. black and green . . . 16·00 14·00
353 30c. black and red . . . . 16·00 14·00
354 45c. black and purple . . . 18·00 18·00
355 60c. black and blue . . . . 20·00 18·00
356 90c. black and olive . . . 28·00 24·00
For similar stamps in this type but with tail fin as Type II, see Nos. 384a/8.

48 Yen Kung-cho, Pres. Hsu Shih-chang and Chin Yung-peng
53 Temple of Heaven

1921. 25th Anniv of Chinese National Postal Service.
357 **48** 1c. orange . . . . 3·50 1·00
358 3c. turquoise . . . . . . 3·50 40
359 6c. grey . . . . 5·00 3·50
360 10c. blue . . . . 5·75 2·75

1923. Adoption of the Constitution.
362 **53** 1c. orange . . . . 2·00 60
363 3c. turquoise . . . . . . 2·00 50
364 4c. red . . . . 4·00 1·75
365 10c. blue . . . . 7·50 1·50

1925. Surch in English and Chinese characters.
366 **43** 1c. on 2c. green . . . . . 1·00 10
367 1c. on 3c. green 30 10
369 1c. on 4c. olive . . . . . 1·25 10
370 3c. on 4c. grey . . . . . 3·00 10
The figures in this surcharge are at the top and are smaller than for the 1920 provisionals.

55 Marshal Chang Tso-lin
56 General Chiang Kai-shek

1928. Assumption of Title of Marshal of the Army and Navy by Chang Tso-lin.
372 **55** 1c. orange . . . . 1·00 1·00
373 4c. olive . . . . 1·00 1·00
374 10c. blue . . . . 5·00 4·00
375 $1 red . . . . 38·00 45·00

1929. Unification of China under Gen. Chiang Kai-shek.
376 **56** 1c. orange . . . . 3·00 40
377 4c. olive . . . . 4·50 45
378 10c. blue . . . . 10·00 1·50
379 $1 red . . . . 95·00 40·00

57 Mausoleum at Nanking
58 Dr. Sun Yat-sen

1929. State Burial of Dr. Sun Yat-sen.
380 **57** 1c. orange . . . . 1·00 50
381 4c. olive . . . . 1·00 50
382 10c. blue . . . . 5·00 1·00
383 $1 red . . . . 42·00 22·00

1929. Air. As T **47**, but tail fin of airplane as Type II.
384a **47** 15c. black and green . . . 4·00 20
385 30c. black and red . . . . 4·50 35
386 45c. black and purple . . 5·00 5·00
387 60c. black and blue . . . 7·00 5·00
388 90c. black and olive . . . 11·00 10·00

1931.
389 **58** 1c. orange 40 20
396 2c. olive 30 10
391 4c. green 85 10
398 5c. green 40 10
399 15c. green 65 40
400 15c. red 60 10
401 20c. blue 90 15
402 25c. blue . . . . 1·00 10
403a $1 sepia and brown . . . 3·75 15
735 $1 violet . . . . 30 2·00
404a $2 brown and blue . . . 6·50 50
736 $2 olive . . . . 30 4·00
405a $5 black and red . . . . 12·00 2·00
737 $20 green . . . . 1·50 75
738 $30 brown 30 65
739 $50 orange 60 65

59 "Nomads of the Desert"
60 General Teng K'eng

1932. North-West China Scientific Expedition.
406 **59** 1c. orange . . . . 25·00 30·00
407 4c. olive . . . . 25·00 30·00
408 5c. red . . . . 25·00 30·00
409 10c. blue . . . . 25·00 30·00

1932. Martyrs of the Revolution.
410 **60** ½c. brown 15 10
508 – 1c. orange 10 10
509 – 2c. blue 10 15
412 **60** 2½c. purple 30 15
511 – 3c. brown 10 15
512 **60** 4c. lilac 10 20
513 – 5c. orange 10 50
514 – 8c. orange 10 10
515 – 10c. purple 10 15
516 – 13c. green 10 50
517 – 15c. purple 30 45
417 – 17c. green 60 10
418 – 20c. red 60 10
519 – 20c. blue 25 10
520 – 21c. brown 40 30
521 – 25c. purple 25 40
541 – 28c. green 30 75
542 – 30c. purple 20 25
543 – 40c. orange 20 25
544 – 50c. green 20 10
DESIGNS: 1, 25, 50c. Ch'en Ying-shih; 2, 10, 17, 28c. Shung Chiao-jen; 3, 5, 15, 30c. Liao Chung-k'ai; 8, 13, 21c. Chu Chih-hsin; 20, 40c. Gen. Huang Hsing.

61 Junkers F-13 over Great Wall

1932. Air.
422 **61** 15c. green 30 15
556 25c. orange 20 60
557 30c. red 20 60
558 45c. purple . . . . 30 1·00
559 50c. brown 20 60
560 60c. blue 20 95
561 90c. green . . . . 20 1·00
562 $1 green 30 60
563 $2 brown 25 60
564 $5 red 30 50

62 Tan Yen-kai
63

1933. Tan Yen-kai Memorial.
440 **62** 2c. olive . . . . 1·50 85
441 5c. green . . . . 2·50 15
442 25c. blue . . . . 6·00 60
443 $1 red . . . . 42·00 20·00

1936. "New Life" Movement. Symbolic designs as T **63**.
444 **63** 2c. olive . . . . 1·25 25
445 5c. green . . . . 1·40 15
446 – 20c. blue (various emblems) 3·75 40
447 – $1 red (Lighthouse) . . . . 24·00 7·00

66 "Postal Communications."
72 Dr. Sun Yat-sen

1936. 40th Anniv of Chinese National Postal Service.
448 **66** 2c. orange . . . . 2·25 60
449 – 5c. green . . . . 1·25 15
450 – 25c. blue . . . . 3·00 25
451 – 100c. red . . . . 18·00 6·50
DESIGNS: 5c. The Bund, Shanghai; 25c. G.P.O., Shanghai; 100c. Ministry of Communications, Nanking.

1936. Surch in figures and Chinese characters.
452 **44** 5c. on 15c. blue . . . . . 1·50 20
453 5c. on 16c. olive . . . . . 2·50 35

1937. Surch in figures and Chinese characters.
454 **58** 1 on 4c. green 50 20
455 – 8 on 40c. orange (No. 543) 65 40
456 **58** 10 on 25c. blue 50 10

1938.
462 **72** 2c. green 10 10
464 3c. red 10 10
489 5c. green 10 10
492 8c. green 10 10
469 10c. green 10 10
470 15c. red . . . . 85 1·25
471 16c. brown 40 50
472 25c. blue 75 75
494 30c. red 50 25
495 50c. blue 75 20
496 $1 sepia and brown . . . 3·00 40
497 $2 brown and blue . . . . 2·25 40
498 $5 green and red . . . . 3·00 50
499 $10 violet and green . . . 5·00 2·50
500 $20 blue and purple . . . 10·00 4·25
For dollar values in single colours, see Nos. 666 etc.
For 15c. brown see Japanese Occupation of China: IV Shanghai and Nanking No. 12.

74 Chinese and U.S. Flags and Map of China

1939. 150th Anniv of U.S. Constitution. Flags in red and blue.
501 **74** 5c. green 70 30
502 25c. blue . . . . 1·00 85
503 50c. brown . . . . 2·00 2·00
504 $1 red . . . . 3·50 3·50

肆 暫
分 4 作
(76)

1940. Surch as T **76**.
577 **72** 3c. on 5c. green . . . . . 1·00 2·00
582 4c. on 5c. green 75 20
619 7c. on 8c. green . . . . . 1·25 1·25

77 Dr. Sun Yat-sen
78 Industry

1941.
583 **77** ½c. brown 15 15
584 1c. orange 20 10
585 2c. blue 20 15
586 5c. green 20 15
587 8c. orange . . . . 60 1·00
588 8c. green 40 20
589 10c. green 15 10
590 17c. green . . . . 4·00 5·00
591 25c. purple 30 30
592 30c. red 30 25
593 50c. blue 40 15
594 $1 black and brown . . . 50 10
595 $2 black and blue 65 20
596 $5 black and red . . . . 1·00 40

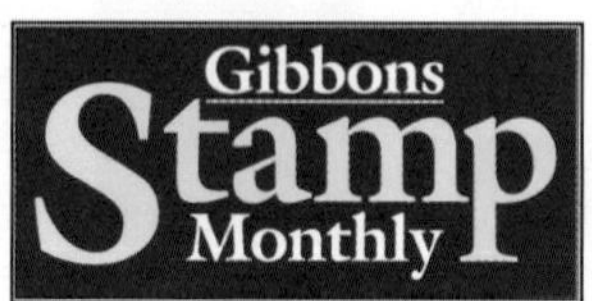
Gibbons
Stamp
Monthly

597 $10 black and green 2·75 2·25
598 $20 black and purple 3·00 2·50

1941. Thrift Movement.
599 **78** 8c. green 40 65
600 21c. brown 50 80
601 28c. olive 65 90
602 33c. red 90 1·00
603 50c. blue 1·00 1·10
604 $1 purple 1·25 1·40

(**79**) (**81**) **82** Dr. Sun Yat-sen

1941. 30th Anniv of Republic. Optd with T **79**.
606 – 1c. orange (No. 508) 1·25 1·50
607 **72** 2c. green 1·25 1·50
608 **60** 4c. lilac 1·25 1·50
609 **72** 8c. green 1·25 1·50
610 10c. green 1·25 1·50
611 16c. brown 1·25 1·50
612 – 21c. brown (No. 520) 1·25 1·50
613 – 28c. green (No. 541) 1·25 1·50
614 **72** 30c. red 1·25 1·50
615 $1 sepia and brown 1·50 1·50

1942. Provincial surcharges. Surch as T **81**.
622 **60** 1c. on ½c. brown 75 1·50
624 **77** 1c. on ½c. brown 80 2·00
690g – 20c. on 13c. green (516) 1·00 5·00
691i **72** 20c. on 16c. brown 1·00 5·00
693e – 20c. on 17c. green (417) 1·50 5·50
694f – 20c. on 21c. brown (520) 50 6·50
695e – 20c. on 28c. green (541) 75 7·50
625 **72** 40c. on 50c. blue 2·75 4·25
627 **77** 40c. on 50c. blue 4·00 6·00
626 – 40c. on 50c. green (544) 5·00 6·00
689a 50c. on 16c. brown 2·25 1·40

1942.
628 **82** 10c. green 10 1·25
629 16c. olive 15·00 24·00
630 20c. olive 10 1·25
631 25c. purple 10 1·75
632 30c. red 10 95
642 30c. brown 20 9·00
633 40c. brown 10 1·25
634 50c. green 10 10
635 $1 red 75 10
636 $1 olive 10 20
637 $1.50 blue 10 40
638 $2 green 10 10
645 $2 blue 4·75 7·50
646 $2 purple 10 15
639 $3 yellow 20 20
640 $4 brown 30 30
641 $5 red 20 20
650 $6 violet 60 60
651 $10 brown 15 10
652 $20 blue 15 10
653 $50 green 4·50 15
654 $70 violet 5·50 35
655 $100 brown 60 45

1942. As T **72** but emblem at top redrawn with solid background. Perf, imperf or roul.
666 **72** $4 blue 60 1·00
667 $5 grey 1·40 1·25
656 $10 brown 1·40 1·00
657 $20 green 1·40 75
658 $20 red 12·50 6·75
659 $30 purple 1·00 45
660 $40 red 1·25 50
661 $50 blue 1·50 1·00
662 $100 brown 6·00 4·00

(**83**) (**83a**)

(T **83** Trans. "Surcharge for Domestic Postage Paid")

1942. Surch as T **83**.
688e **82** 16c. olive 30·00 30·00

1943. No 688e surch as T **83a**.
701e **82** 50c. on 16c. olive 4·00 4·00

89 Dr. Sun Yat-sen **91** Savings Bank and Money Box

90 War Refugees

1944.
702 **89** 40c. red 30 5·50
703 $2 brown 30 10
704 $3 red 15 10
705 $3 brown 75 45
706 $6 grey 15 25
707 $10 red 10 10
708 $20 pink 10 10
709 $50 brown 4·25 20
710 $70 violet 35 20

1944. War Refugees' Relief Fund. Various frames.
724 **90** $2+$2 on 50c.+50c. blue 1·00 3·00
725 $4+$4 on 8c.+8c. green 1·00 3·00
726 $5+$5 on 21c.+21c. brn 1·50 3·00
727 $6+$6 on 28c.+28c. olive 2·50 3·00
728 $10+$10 on 33c.+33c. red 3·00 3·00
729 $20+$20 on $1+$1 violet 4·00 4·00

1944.
731 **91** $40 slate 30 80
732 $50 green 30 30
733 $100 brown 30 25
734 $200 green 30 25

92 Dr. Sun Yat-sen **93** Dr. Sun Yat-sen

1944. 50th Anniv of Kuomintang.
740 **92** $2 green 1·50 2·50
741 $5 brown 1·75 2·75
742 $6 purple 2·50 5·00
743 $10 blue 3·25 5·50
744 $20 red 3·75 7·50

1945. 20th Death Anniv of Dr. Sun Yat-sen.
746 **93** $2 green 75 1·50
747 $5 brown 75 1·50
748 $6 blue 1·00 2·00
749 $10 blue 1·50 1·40
750 $20 red 2·00 3·50
751 $30 buff 2·50 4·50

94 Dr. Sun Yat-sen **96** Pres. Lin Sen

95 Gen. Chiang Kai-shek

1945.
758 **94** $2 green 25 60
759 $5 green 20 35
760 $10 blue 10 10
761 $20 red 10 10

1945. Equal Treaties with Great Britain and U.S.A., abolishing Foreign Concessions. Flags in national colours.
762 **95** $1 blue 75 1·50
763 $2 green 75 1·50
764 $5 olive 75 1·50
765 $6 brown 75 1·50
766 $10 red 3·25 6·00
767 $20 red 4·00 7·00

1945. In Memory of President Lin Sen.
768 **96** $1 black and blue 1·00 2·00
769 $2 black and green 1·00 2·00
770 $5 black and red 1·00 2·00
771 $6 black and violet 1·25 2·00
772 $10 black and brown 2·50 4·00
773 $20 black and olive 3·50 6·00

(**97**) (**98**) (**99**)

1945. Chinese National Currency (C.N.C.). Various issues surch as T **97** (for Japanese controlled Government at Shanghai and Nanking) and further surch as T **98**.
774 **72** 10c. on $20 on 3c. red 10 1·50
775 – 15c. on $30 on 2c. blue (509) 10 1·50
776 **77** 25c. on $50 on 1c. orange 10 1·25
777 **72** 50c. on $100 on 3c. red 10 50
778 **60** $1 on $200 on 1c. orange (508) 10 15
779 **72** $2 on $400 on 3c. red 10 35
780 **77** $5 on $1000 on 1c. orange 10 10

1945. Kaifeng provisionals. C.N.C. surcharges. Stamps of Japanese Occupation of North China surch as T **99**.
781 **60** $10 on 20c. lake (No. 166) 10·00 12·00
782 $20 on 40c. orge (No. 168) 11·00 15·00
783 $50 on 30c. red (No. 167) 10·00 14·00

100 Pres. Chiang Kai-shek **101** Pres. Chiang Kai-shek

1945. Inauguration of Pres. Chiang Kai-shek. Flag in blue and red.
784 **100** $2 green 45 1·00
785 $4 blue 75 1·00
786 $5 olive 75 1·25
787 $6 brown 1·50 2·00
788 $10 grey 4·00 6·50
789 $20 red 4·50 6·50

1945. Victory. Flag in red.
790 **101** $20 green and blue 10 15
791 $50 brown and blue 60 60
792 $100 blue 20 25
793 $300 red and blue 30 15

(**102**) **103** Dr. Sun Yat-sen

1945. C.N.C. surcharges. Nos. 410, 412, 514, 516/17, 519/20 and 541 surch as T **102** (value tablet at top).
794 $3 on 2½c. purple 14·00 16·00
795 $10 on 15c. purple 10 15
796 $20 on 8c. orange 10 10
797 $20 on 20c. blue 30 10
798 $30 on ½c. brown 10 1·00
799 $50 on 21c. brown 15 10
806 $70 on 13c. green 10 10
802 $100 on 28c. green 15 10

1945. No gum.
808 **103** $20 red 10 10
809 $30 blue 10 15
810 $40 orange 60 1·00
811 $50 green 1·00 25
812 $100 brown 15 10
813 $200 brown 15 10

(**104**) (**108**)

1946. Air. C.N.C. surcharges. Surch as T **104**.
820 **61** $23 on 30c. red 10 1·00
821 $53 on 15c. green 10 90
822 $73 on 25c. orange 10 1·25
823 $100 on $2 brown 10 35
824 $200 on $5 red 10 15

1946. C.N.C. surcharges. Surch as T **108** (octagonal value tablet at bottom).
898 – $10 on 1c. orange (508) 10 65
903 **77** $10 on 1c. orange 30 1·50
896 **72** $20 on 2c. green 10 1·25
904 **77** $20 on 2c. blue 10 1·00
899 – $20 on 3c. brown (511) 10 1·00
897 **72** $20 on 3c. red 10 1·00
879 – $20 on 8c. orange (514) 10 1·40
869 **72** $20 on 8c. green 1·50 1·50
882 **77** $20 on 8c. orange 80 4·00
883 **77** $20 on 8c. green 10 80
900 **60** $30 on 4c. lilac 10 50
880 – $50 on 5c. orange (513) 10 25
876 **72** $50 on 5c. green 20 10
884 **77** $50 on 5c. green 80 10

(**105**)

107 Dr. Sun Yat-sen

1946. C.N.C. surcharges. Surch as T **105** (rectangular value tablet at bottom). (a) Box with chequered pattern.
831 **72** $20 on 3c. red 10 1·40
846 – $20 on 8c. orange (514) 10 1·00
832 **72** $50 on 3c. red 10 50
833 $50 on 5c. green 15 60
847 – $50 on 5c. orange (513) 10 30
851 **77** $50 on 5c. green 65 1·25
854 **82** $50 on $1 green 10 25
848 – $100 on 1c. orange (508) 10 10
834 **72** $100 on 3c. red 10 10
842 $100 on 8c. green 25 15
852 **77** $100 on 8c. green 50 30
860 **58** $100 on $1 purple 50 10
868 **107** $100 on $20 red 50 10
837 **72** $200 on 10c. green 10 10
861 **58** $200 on $4 blue 30 10
855 **82** $250 on $1.50 blue 50 2·00
862 **58** $250 on $2 green 30 30
863 $250 on $5 red 40 10
838 **72** $300 on 10c. green 10 15
853 **77** $300 on 10c. green 10 95
839 **72** $500 on 3c. red 20 15
864 **58** $500 on $20 green 15 10
865 $800 on $30 brown 10 3·00
830 $1000 on 2c. green 1·00 10
856 **82** $1000 on $2 green 50 25
857 $1000 on $2 blue 25 2·00
858 $1000 on $2 brown 30 25
866 **94** $1000 on $2 green 10 2·50
859 **82** $2000 on $5 red 50 60
867 **94** $2000 on $5 green 15 45

(b) Box with diamond pattern.
978 **58** $500 on $20 green 10 10
979 **107** $1250 on $70 orange 10 4·50
980 **118** $1800 on $350 buff 10 5·00
974 **82** $2000 on $3 yellow 50 40
976 **89** $2000 on $3 red 10 15
975 **82** $3000 on $3 yellow 15 25
977 **89** $3000 on $3 brown 15 95

1946.
885 **107** $20 red 7·50 20
886 $30 blue 30 20
887 $50 violet 25 15
888 $70 orange 12·00 2·00
889 $100 red 10 10
890 $200 green 10 10
891 $500 green 30 15
892 $700 brown 15 1·50
893 $10000 purple 25 15
894 $3000 blue 30 10
895 $5000 red and green 75 10

109 Douglas DC-4 over Mausoleum of Dr. Sun Yat-sen

110 Pres. Chiang Kai-shek

1946. Air. No gum.
905 **109** $27 blue 10 75

1946. President's 60th Birthday.
906 **110** $20 red 30 50
907 $30 green 30 70
908 $50 orange 30 60
909 $100 green 50 90
910 $200 yellow 75 80
911 $300 red 75 50

For stamps of this type, but additionally inscribed with four characters around head, see Taiwan Nos. 30/5, or North Eastern Provinces, Nos. 48/53.

111 National Assembly House, Nanking

112 Entrance to Dr. Sun Yat-sen Mausoleum

1946. Opening of National Assembly, Nanking. No gum.
912 **111** $20 green 10 30
913 $30 blue 20 40
914 $50 brown 30 40
915 $100 red 30 30

1947. 1st Anniv of Return of Government to Nanking.
942 **112** $100 green 20 40
943 $200 blue 30 40
944 $250 red 30 75
945 $350 brown 30 75
946 $400 purple 50 55

For stamps of this type but additionally inscribed with four characters above numeral of value, see Taiwan, Nos. 36/40, or North Eastern Provinces, Nos. 65/70.

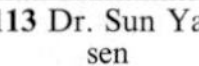

113 Dr. Sun Yat-sen

114 Confucius

115 Confucius's Lecture School

116 Tomb of Confucius

118 Dr. Sun Yat-sen and Plum Blossoms

1947.

947 **113** $500 olive 30 20
948 $1,000 red and green . . 40 20
949 $2,000 lake and blue . . . 45 20
950 $5,000 black and orange 50 20

1947. Confucius Commem. No gum.

951 **114** $500 red 50 60
952 **115** $800 brown 40 80
953 **116** $1,250 green . . . . . . 40 1·10
954 $1,800 blue . . . . 40 1·50

DESIGN—HORIZ: $1,800, Confucian Temple.

1947. (a) With noughts for cents. No gum.

955 **118** $150 blue . . . . 20 15·00
956 $250 violet . . . . 20 4·50
957 $500 green 20 10
958 $1,000 red 20 10
959 $2,000 orange 20 10
960 $3,000 blue 20 10
961 $4,000 grey 20 20
962 $5,000 brown 20 10
963 $6,000 purple 20 20
964 $7,000 brown 20 20
965 $10,000 red and blue . . 40 10
966 $20,000 green and red . . 1·00 10
967 $50,000 blue and green . . 1·10 10
968 $100,000 green & orange 4·00 15
969 $200,000 blue and purple 4·00 15
970 $300,000 orange & brown 5·00 40
971 $500,000 brown & green 5·50 40

(b) Without noughts for cents.

1032 **118** $20,000 red 40 30
1033 $30,000 brown 10 10
1034 $40,000 green 10 15
1035 $50,000 blue 10 10
1036 $100,000 olive 10 10
1037 $200,000 purple 20 10
1038 $300,000 green . . . . . 2·25 90
1039 $500,000 mauve 20 10
1040 $1,000,000 red 10 10
1041 $2,000,000 orange . . . 10 10
1042 $3,000,000 bistre 10 50
1043 $5,000,000 blue . . . . 5·00 75

119 Map of Taiwan and Chinese Flag

122 Postal Kiosk

1947. Restoration of Taiwan (Formosa) (1st issue).

972 **119** $500 red . . . . 25 1·00
973 $1,250 green . . . . . . 25 1·00

See also Nos. 1003/4.

1947. Progress of the Postal Service.

981 – $500 red 30 50
982 **122** $1,000 violet 30 50
983 $1,250 green 30 75
984 – $1,800 blue . . . . 30 1·00

DESIGN: $500, $1,800, Mobile Post Office.

123 Air, Sea and Rail Transport

124 Postboy and Motor Van

1947. 50th Anniv of Directorate General of Posts.

985 **123** $100 violet 30 90
986 **124** $200 green 30 90
987 $300 lake 30 90
988 – $400 red 30 90
989 – $500 blue 30 90

DESIGN—As T **123**: $400, $500, Junk and airplane.

126 Book of the Constitution and National Assembly Building

1947. Adoption of the Constitution.

990 **126** $2,000 red 50 60
991 $3,000 blue 50 60
992 $5,000 green 50 60

127 Reproductions of 1947 and 1912 Stamps

1948. Perf or imperf. (a) Nanking Philatelic Exn.

1001 **127** $5,000 red . . . . 75 3·00

(b) Shanghai Philatelic Exhibition.

1002 **127** $5,000 green . . . . . . 75 3·00

128 Sun Yat-sen Memorial Hall

1948. Restoration of Taiwan (Formosa) to Chinese Rule (2nd issue).

1003 **128** $5,000 lilac . . . . . . 50 1·00
1004 $10,000 red . . . . . . 50 1·00

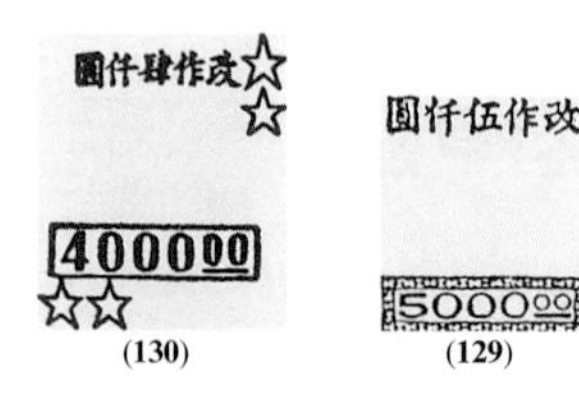

(130) (129)

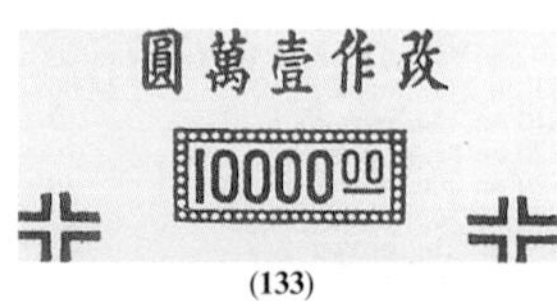

(133)

1948. "Re-valuation" surcharges. (a) Surch as T **130**.

1012 **118** $4,000 on $100 red . . . 20 20·00
1013 $5,000 on $100 red . . . 15 10
1014 $8,000 on $800 brown 30 1·00

(b) Surch as T **129**.

1005 **82** $5,000 on $1 green . . . 10 15
1007 $5,000 on $2 green . . . 15 10
1008 **103** $10,000 on $20 red . . . 20 10
1018 **82** $15,000 on 10c. green . . 20 50
1015 $15,000 on 50c. green . . 20 75
1019 $15,000 on $4 purple . . 20 50
1020 $15,000 on $6 blue . . . 30 50
1009 $20,000 on 10c. green . . 10 15
1010 $20,000 on 50c. green . . 10 35
1011 $30,000 on 30c. red . . . 10 40
1016 $40,000 on 20c. olive . . 20 75
1017 $60,000 on $4 brown . . 25 30

(c) Air. Surch as T **133**.

1022 **61** $10,000 on 30c. red . . . 10 75
1028 **109** $10,000 on $27 blue . . 10 1·50
1023 **61** $20,000 on 25c. orange 10 75
1024 $30 on 90c. olive . . . . 10 1·00
1025 $50,000 on 60c. blue . . 10 1·00
1026 $50,000 on $1 green . . 10 90

On No. 1028 the Chinese characters read vertically.

135 Great Wall of China

137 "Hai Tien" (freighter) and "Eton" (steamer) of 1872

138 "Kiang Ya" (freighter) (138a)

1948. Tuberculosis Relief Fund. Cross in red. Perf or imperf. No gum.

1029 **135** $5,000+$2,000 violet . . 15 2·50
1030 $10,000+$2,000 brown 15 2·50
1031 $15,000+$2,000 grey . . 15 2·50

1948. 75th Anniv of China Merchants' Steam Navigation Company. No gum.

1044 **137** $20,000 blue . . . . . . 50 2·00
1045 $30,000 mauve . . . . . 50 2·00
1046 **138** $40,000 brown . . . . . 50 2·75
1047 $60,000 red . . . . . . 50 2·75

1948. C.N.C. surcharge. Surch with T **138a**.

1048 **107** $5,000 on $100 claret . . 9·00 40·00

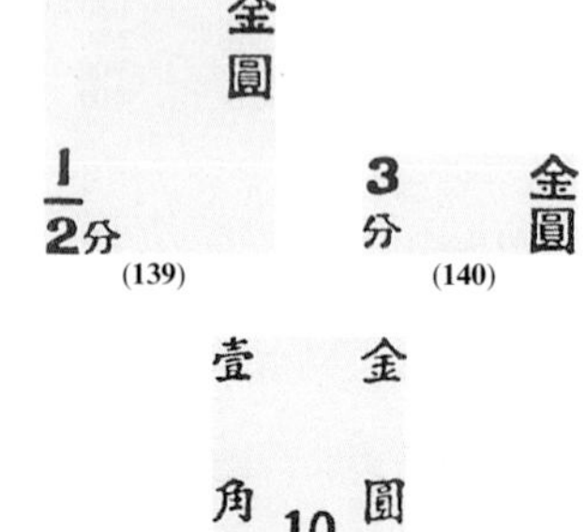

(139) (140)

(141)

1948. Gold Yuan surcharges. (a) Surch as T **139** or **140**.

1049 **82** ½c. on 30c. brown . . . 10 4·00
1050 **118** ½c. on $500 green . . . 10 25
1051 **107** 1c. on $20 red . . . . . 10 2·00
1052 **82** 2c. on $1.50 blue . . . . 25 3·00
1053 3c. on $5 red . . . . . 10 3·00
1054 4c. on $1 red . . . . . 10 3·00
1055 5c. on 50c. green 10 40

(b) Surch as T **141**.

1056 **89** 5c. on $20 red . . . . 10 1·00
1057 **103** 5c. on $30 blue . . . . 10 1·25
1058 **72** 10c. on 2c. green . . . 20 1·50
1059 **60** 10c. on 2½c. purple . . 25 1·00
1061 **82** 10c. on 25c. brown . . 10 1·10
1062 **89** 10c. on 40c. red . . . 10 1·25
1063 **82** 10c. on $1 green . . . 10 15
1065 **89** 10c. on $2 brown . . . 10 20
1066 **82** 10c. on $20 blue . . . 10 20
1067 **89** 10c. on $20 red . . . £250 £180
1068 **94** 10c. on $20 red . . . 10 60
1069 **107** 10c. on $20 red . . . 75 3·00
1070 **103** 10c. on $30 blue . . . 10 1·50
1071 **89** 10c. on $70 violet . . 10 35
1072 **118** 10c. on $7,000 brown 2·00 1·25
1073 10c. on $20,000 red . . 15 4·00
1074 **89** 20c. on $6 purple . . . 10 35
1075 **58** 20c. on $30 brown . . 15 4·00
1076 **107** 20c. on $30 blue . . . 60 3·25
1077 20c. on $100 red . . . 15 3·25
1079 **60** 50c. on ½c. brown . . 10 60
1081 **82** 50c. on 20c. green . . 15 50
1082 50c. on 30c. red . . . 10 1·25
1083 50c. on 40c. brown . . 10 80
1084 **89** 50c. on 40c. red . . . 10 1·00
1085a **82** 50c. on $4 purple . . . 25 1·90
1086 50c. on $20 blue . . . 10 20
1087 **94** 50c. on $20 red . . . 50 1·50
1088 **107** 50c. on $20 red . . . 10 1·25
1089 **82** 50c. on $70 lilac . . . 30 30
1090a **118** 50c. on $6,000 purple 15 1·25
1091 **82** $1 on 30c. brown . . . 10 20
1092 $1 on 40c. brown . . . 10 10
1093 $1 on $1 red . . . . . 50 1·75
1094 $1 on $5 red 60 35
1095 **89** $2 on $2 brown 10 25
1096 **102** $2 on $20 red 10 20
1097 **107** $2 on $100 red 15 20
1098 – $5 on 17c. green (417) 75 75
1099 **89** $5 on $2 brown 20 25
1100 **118** $5 on $30,000 blue . . 10 1·25
1101 – $8 on 20c. blue (519) 50 50
1102 **118** $8 on $30,000 brown 10 2·00
1103 – $10 on 40c. orange (543) . . . . 1·25 1·00
1104 **89** $10 on $2 brown . . . 20 15
1105 $20 on $2 brown . . . 25 15
1106 **107** $20 on $20 red . . . . 5·00 3·00
1107 **82** $50 on 30c. red . . . 20 30
1108 **89** $50 on $2 brown . . . 30 15
1109 **107** $80 on $20 red . . . . 10 1·00
1110 **82** $100 on $1 green . . . 25 1·00
1111 **89** $100 on $2 brown . . . 35 30
1112 **118** $20,000 on $40,000 green . . . . 5·00 6·00
1113 $50,000 on $20,000 red 1·25 25
1114 $50,000 on $30,000 brown . . . . 10·00 5·00
1115 $100,000 on $20,000 red 5·00 4·00
1116 $100,000 on $30,000 brown . . . . 1·75 10
1117 $200,000 on $40,000 green . . . . 5·00 6·50
1118 $200,000 on $50,000 blue . . . . 5·00 8·00

(142)

(144)

143 Liner, Train and Airplane

145 Dr. Sun Yat-sen

1949. Gold Yuan surcharges. Parcels Post stamps surch as T **142**.

1119 P **104** $200 on $3,000 orange 1·00 60
1120 $500 on $5,000 blue 1·25 40
1121 $1,000 on $10,000 vio 2·00 55

1949. Gold Yuan surcharges. Revenue stamps surch. (a) As T **144**.

1136 **143** 50c. on $20 brown . . . 10 60
1137 $1 on $15 orange . . . 10 5·50
1127 $2 on $50 blue . . . . 10 1·25
1144 $3 on $50 blue 10 50
1138 $5 on $500 brown . . . 10 35
1129 $10 on $30 mauve . . . 10 55
1140 $15 on $20 brown . . . 10 45
1141 $25 on $20 brown . . . 10 20
1145 $50 on $50 blue 10 40
1147 $50 on $300 green . . . 25 60
1130 $80 on $50 blue . . . . 20 1·25
1146 $100 on $50 blue . . . 35 50
1124 $200 on $50 blue . . . 80 1·00
1142 $200 on $500 brown . . 50 65
1125 $300 on $50 blue . . . 1·10 1·25
1143 $500 on $15 orange . . 1·40 4·00
1134 $500 on $30 mauve . . 65 3·00
1135 $1,000 on $50 blue . . 8·00 8·00
1148 $1,000 on $100 olive . . 2·75 5·00
1126 $1,500 on $50 blue . . 65 1·75
1151 $2,000 on $300 green . . 35 30

(b) As T **144** but with key pattern inverted at top and bottom.

1183 **143** $50 on $10 green . . . 8·00 10·00
1184 $100 on $10 green . . 1·50 4·50
1185 $500 on $10 green . . 75 4·00
1186 $1,000 on $10 green . . 75 4·50
1187 $5,000 on $20 brown . . 20·00 12·00
1188 $10,000 on $20 brown 8·00 4·50
1189 $50,000 on $20 brown 12·00 6·00
1190 $100,000 on $20 brown 12·00 6·00
1191 $500,000 on $20 brown £275 £110
1192 $2,000,000 on $20 brn £500 £300
1193 $5,000,000 on $20 brn £600 £375

1949.

1152 **145** $1 orange 30 40
1153 $10 green 30 30
1154 $20 purple 10 40
1155 $50 green 10 30
1156 $100 brown 10 10
1157 $200 red 10 10
1158 $500 mauve 10 15
1159 $800 red . . . . 10 2·75
1160 $1,000 blue 15 10
1168 $2,000 violet . . . . . 10 1·50
1169 $5,000 blue 10 20
1177 $5,000 red 40 50
1170 $10,000 brown 10 10
1171 $20,000 green . . . . . 10 1·50
1179 $20,000 orange 40 75
1172 $50,000 pink 10 40
1180 $50,000 blue . . . . . 1·25 2·00
1173 $80,000 brown . . . . . 10 4·00
1174 $100,000 green 40 20
1181 $200,000 blue . . . . . 1·75 2·00
1182 $500,000 purple . . . . 1·75 1·75

For stamps of Type **145** in Silver Yuan currency see Nos. 1348/56.

146 Steam Locomotive

147 Douglas DC-4

148 Postman on Motor Cycle

149 Mountains

1949. No value indicated. Perf or roul.

1211 **146** Orange (Ord. postage) 4·00 1·50
1212 **147** Green (Air Mail) . . . . 6·00 6·00
1213 **148** Mauve (Express) . . . . 6·50 7·00
1214 **149** Red (Registration) . . . 7·00 7·00

Owing to the collapse of the Gold Yuan the above were sold at the rate for the day for the service indicated.

(154) (159)

1949. Gold Yuan currency. Revenue stamps optd as T **154**. No gum.

1232 **143** $10 green (B) . . . . . 25·00 24·00
1233 $30 mauve (A) . . . . . £100 50·00
1234 $50 blue (C) . . . . . 24·00 24·00
1235 $100 olive (D) . . . . . 45·00 40·00
1236 $200 purple (A) . . . . . 10·00 8·00
1237 $500 green (A) . . . . . 10·00 8·00

Opt. translation: (A) Domestic Letter Fee. (B) Express Letter Fee. (C) Registered Letter Fee. (D) Air Mail Fee.

1949. Silver Yuan surcharges. Revenue stamps surch as T **159**. No gum.

1312 **143** 1c. on $20 brown . . . 40·00 45·00
1284 1c. on $5,000 brown . . 6·00 4·75
1285 4c. on $100 olive . . . 5·00 3·25
1286 4c. on $3,000 orange . . 5·00 1·10
1313 10c. on $20 brown . . . 40·00 45·00
1287 10c. on $50 blue . . . 6·75 2·50
1288 10c. on $1,000 red . . . 7·00 3·00
1289 20c. on $1,000 red . . . 7·00 4·50
1290 50c. on $30 mauve . . . 7·50 4·75
1291 50c. on $50 blue . . . 18·00 2·00
1292 $1 on $50 blue . . . . 13·00 5·25

On Nos. 1312 and 1313 the key pattern is inverted at top and bottom.

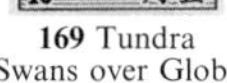

169 Tundra Swans over Globe **170** Globe and Doves

1949. No gum.

1344 **169** $1 orange . . . . 10·00 10·50
1345 $2 blue . . . . 24·00 14·50
1346 $5 red . . . . 40·00 21·00
1347 $10 green . . . . 50·00 26·00

1949. Silver Yuan currency.

1348 **145** 1c. green . . . . 15·00 10·00
1349 2c. orange . . . . 4·00 15·00
1350 4c. green 10 50
1351 10c. lilac 10 20
1352 16c. red . . . . 10 15·00
1353 20c. blue . . . . 10 5·00
1354 50c. brown . . . . 50 30·00
1355 100c. blue £175 £225
1356 500c. red £275 £250

1949. 75th Anniv of U.P.U. Value optd in black. Imperf. No gum.

1357 **170** $1 orange . . . . 5·00 9·00

171 Buddha's Tower, Peking **172** Bronze Bull

1949. Value optd. Roul.

1358 **171** 15c. green and brown . . 6·50 8·00
1359 **172** 40c. red and green . . . 7·50 8·00

(173) (174)

1949. Silver Yuan surcharges. (a) Chungking issue. Surch as T **173**.

1360 **145** 2½c. on $50 green . . . 2·25 3·25
1361 2½c. on $50,000 blue . . 4·00 3·25
1362 5c. on $1,000 blue . . 4·00 3·00
1363 5c. on $20,000 orange . . 75 1·25
1364 5c. on $200,000 blue . . 4·50 3·00
1365 5c. on $500,000 purple . . 4·50 3·00
1366 10c. on $5,000 red . . . 4·50 3·25
1367 10c. on $10,000 brown . . 4·75 3·25
1368 15c. on $200 red . . . . 5·00 14·00
1369 25c. on $100 brown . . . 9·50 20·00

(b) Canton issue. Surch as T **174**.

1371 **145** 1c. on $100 brown . . . 4·00 6·50
1372 2½c. on $500 mauve . . . 6·50 7·50
1374 15c. on $10 green . . . . 9·00 10·00
1375 15c. on $20 purple . . . 15·00 11·00

EXPRESS DELIVERY STAMP

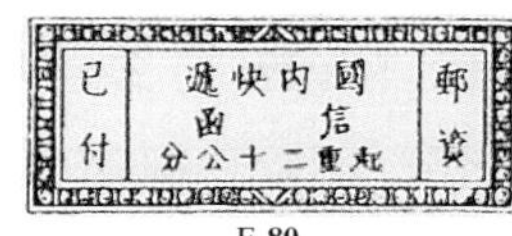

E **80**

1941. Perf. No gum.

E617 E **80** (No value) red & yellow . . . . 25·00 18·00

This stamp was sold at $2, which included ordinary postage.

MILITARY POST STAMPS

(M **85**) M **93** Entrenched Soldiers

1942. Optd variously as Type M **85**.

M682 **72** 8c. olive . . . . 6·50 9·00
M684 **77** 8c. green . . . . 6·00 11·00
M676 8c. orange £425
M683 **72** 16c. olive . . . . 20·00 24·00
M677 **82** 16c. olive . . . . 6·50 12·00
M678 50c. green . . . . 6·50 10·00
M679 $1 red . . . . 5·25 9·00
M680 $1 olive . . . . 5·50 9·00
M681 $2 green . . . . 5·75 11·00
M687 $2 purple . . . . 30·00 38·00

1945.

M745 M **93** (No value) red . . . 1·00 12·00

PARCELS POST STAMPS

P **90** P **104** P **112**

1944.

P711 P **90** $500 green . . . . . — 50
P712 $1,000 blue . . . . . — 60
P713 $3,000 red . . . . . — 70
P714 $5,000 brown . . . . . — 16·00
P715 $10,000 purple . . . . . — 30·00

1946.

P814 P **104** $3,000 orange . . . . — 50
P815 $5,000 blue . . . . — 50
P816 $10,000 violet . . . . — 2·25
P817 $20,000 red . . . . — 4·25

1947. Type P **112** and similar design.

P925 $1,000 yellow . . . . — 40
P926 $3,000 green . . . . — 40
P927 $5,000 red . . . . — 40
P928 $7,000 blue . . . . — 40
P929 $10,000 red . . . . — 40
P930 $30,000 olive . . . . — 1·50
P931 $50,000 black . . . . — 1·50
P932 $70,000 brown . . . . — 1·75
P933 $100,000 purple . . . . — 1·75
P934 $200,000 green . . . . — 1·90
P935 $300,000 pink . . . . — 2·00
P936 $500,000 plum . . . . — 2·00
P937 $3,000,000 blue . . . . — 2·50
P938 $5,000,000 lilac . . . . — 3·75
P939 $6,000,000 grey . . . . — 4·00
P940 $8,000,000 red . . . . — 4·50
P941 $10,000,000 olive . . . . — 5·00

圓拾伍圓金
50
圓拾伍圓金

(P **146**)

1949. Gold Yuan surcharges. 1947 issue surch as Type P **146**.

P1194 $10 on $3,000 green . . . — 2·00
P1195 $20 on $5,000 red . . . — 2·00
P1196 $50 on $10,000 red . . . — 2·00
P1197 $100 on $3,000,000 blue . . — 2·50
P1198 $200 on $5,000,000 lilac . . — 2·50
P1199 $500 on $1,000 yellow . . — 3·00
P1200 $1,000 on $7,000 blue . . — 3·00

Parcels post stamps were not on sale in unused condition; those now on the market were probably stocks seized by the Communists.

POSTAGE DUE STAMPS

1912. Chinese Empire Postage Due Stamps optd with vertical row of Chinese characters.

D207 D **37** ½c. blue . . . . 1·00 55
D208 1c. brown . . . . 1·25 50
D209 2c. brown . . . . 2·00 70
D210 4c. blue . . . . 4·00 1·75
D211 5c. blue £110 £110
D212 5c. brown . . . . 6·00 2·25
D213 10c. blue . . . . 8·50 3·50
D214 20c. blue . . . . 9·00 9·00
D215 30c. blue . . . . 16·00 16·00

(D **41**) D **46** D **62**

1912. Optd with Type D **41**.

D233 D **37** ½c. blue . . . . 8·00 5·00
D234 ½c. brown . . . . 1·75 70
D235 1c. brown . . . . 1·75 60
D236 2c. brown . . . . 2·00 1·00
D237 4c. blue . . . . 6·00 1·50
D238 5c. brown . . . . 9·50 4·00
D239 10c. blue . . . . 16·00 8·00
D240 20c. brown . . . . 19·00 30·00
D241 30c. blue . . . . 22·00 40·00

1913.

D341 D **46** ½c. blue 50 20
D342 1c. blue 70 20
D343 2c. blue 85 20
D344 4c. blue . . . . 1·00 40
D345 5c. blue . . . . 1·75 40
D346 10c. blue . . . . 4·25 75
D347 20c. blue . . . . 6·25 2·75
D340 30c. blue . . . . 11·00 10·00

1932.

D432 D **62** ½c. orange 25 10
D433 1c. orange 25 10
D434 2c. orange 35 15
D435 4c. orange 45 25
D569 5c. orange 15 40
D570 10c. orange 15 30
D571 20c. orange 20 30
D572 30c. orange 25 35
D573 50c. orange 25 30
D574 $1 orange 35 40
D575 $2 orange 60 50

欠 暫
資 作

(D **75**) ("Temporary-use Postage Due")

1940. Optd with Type D **75**.

D545 **72** $1 brown and red . . . 4·00 10·00
D546 $2 brown and blue . . . 5·00 10·00

D **90** D **94** D **112**

1944. No gum.

D717 D **90** 10c. green . . . . . . 10 2·00
D718 20c. blue . . . . . . 10 2·00
D719 40c. red . . . . . . 10 2·00
D720 50c. green . . . . . . 10 2·00
D721 60c. blue . . . . . . 15 4·00
D722 $1 red . . . . . . 10 2·00
D723 $2 purple . . . . . . 10 2·00

1945.

D752 D **94** $2 red . . . . . . 10 1·25
D753 $6 red . . . . . . 10 1·25
D754 $8 red . . . . . . 10 1·60
D755 $10 red . . . . . . 10 1·25
D756 $20 red . . . . . . 10 1·00
D757 $30 red 10 60

1947.

D916 D **112** $50 purple . . . . . 10 2·00
D917 $80 purple . . . . . 10 2·00
D918 $100 purple . . . . . 10 2·00
D919 $160 purple . . . . . 10 2·00
D920 $200 purple . . . . . 10 2·00
D921 $400 purple . . . . . 10 2·00
D922 $500 purple . . . . . 10 2·00
D923 $800 purple . . . . . 10 2·00
D924 $2,000 purple . . . . 10 2·00

(D **127**) (D **146**)

1948. Surch as Type D **127**.

D 993 D **94** $1,000 on $20 purple 10 3·00
D 994 $2,000 on $30 purple 10 2·00
D 995 $3,000 on $50 purple 10 2·00
D 996 $4,000 on $100 pur 10 3·00
D 997 $5,000 on $200 pur 10 1·75
D 998 $10,000 on $300 pur 10 80
D 999 $20,000 on $500 pur 10 80
D1000 $30,000 on $1,000 pur 10 50

1949. Gold Yuan surcharges. Surch as Type D **146**.

D1201 **102** 1c. on $40 orange . . 30 10·00
D1202 2c. on $40 orange . . 30 10·00
D1203 5c. on $40 orange . . 30 10·00
D1204 10c. on $40 orange . . 30 10·00
D1205 20c. on $40 orange . . 30 10·00
D1206 50c. on $40 orange . . 30 10·00
D1207 $1 on $40 orange . . . 30 8·00
D1208 $2 on $40 orange . . . 30 8·00
D1209 $5 on $40 orange . . . 40 8·00
D1210 $10 on $40 orange . . 50 5·00

REGISTRATION STAMP

1941. Roul. No gum.

R617 E **80** (No value) grn & buff 25·00 18·00

This stamp was sold at $1.50 which included ordinary postage.

CHINESE PROVINCES

Manchuria

A. KIRIN AND HEILUNGKIANG

用貼黑吉限

(1) (2)

Stamps of China optd

1927. Stamps of 1913 optd with T **1**.

1 **43** ½c. sepia 45 25
2 1c. orange 60 10
3 1½c. purple . . . . 1·75 1·50
4 2c. green . . . . 1·75 45
5 3c. green . . . . 1·50 75
6 4c. olive . . . . 1·50 10
7 5c. mauve . . . . 2·00 30
8 6c. red . . . . 1·75 90
9 7c. violet . . . . 3·00 2·25
10 8c. orange . . . . 3·50 1·75
11 10c. blue . . . . 3·00 10
12 **44** 13c. brown . . . . 4·25 3·50
13 15c. blue . . . . 4·00 1·50
14 16c. olive . . . . 4·75 3·25
15 20c. lake . . . . 5·00 2·25
16 30c. purple . . . . 7·00 2·75
17 50c. green . . . . 12·00 3·25
18 **45** $1 sepia and brown . . . . 30·00 5·00
19 $2 brown and blue . . . . 50·00 10·00
20 $5 green and red £160 £140

1928. Chang Tso-lin stamps optd with T **2**.

21 **55** 1c. orange . . . . 1·25 1·50
22 4c. olive . . . . 1·75 1·75
23 10c. blue . . . . 4·00 4·50
24 $1 red . . . . 32·00 32·00

1929. Unification stamps optd as T **2**.

25 **56** 1c. orange . . . . 1·25 1·40
26 4c. olive . . . . 2·00 2·00
27 10c. blue . . . . 11·00 5·00
28 $1 red . . . . 60·00 65·00

1929. Sun Yat-sen Memorial stamps optd as T **2**.

29 **57** 1c. orange . . . . 1·00 1·00
30 4c. olive . . . . 1·00 1·00
31 10c. blue . . . . 7·00 3·00
32 $1 red . . . . 38·00 38·00

B. NORTH-EASTERN PROVINCES

Issues made by the Chinese Nationalist Government of Chiang Kai-shek.

1 Dr. Sun Yat-sen (2)

1946. Surch as T **2**.

1 **1** 50c. on $5 red . . . . . . 20 3·00
2 50c. on $10 green . . . . . 20 3·00
3 $1 on $10 green . . . . . . 20 2·00
4 $2 on $20 purple . . . . . 20 1·50
5 $4 on $50 brown . . . . . . 20 1·25

(3) (4)

1946. Stamps of China optd with T **3** (= "Limited for use in North East").

6 – 1c. orange (508) . . . . . . 10 4·00
7 – 3c. brown (511) . . . . . . 25 3·50
8 – 5c. orange (513) . . . . . . 10 2·50
9 **72** 10c. green . . . . 25 3·25
11 20c. blue . . . . 20 3·50

1946. Stamps of China surch as T **4** but larger.

14 – $5 on $50 on 21c. brown (No. 799) . . . . 50·00 55·00
15 – $10 on $100 on 28c. green (No. 802) . . . . 60·00 70·00
16 **91** $20 on $200 green . . . . . . 50·00 55·00

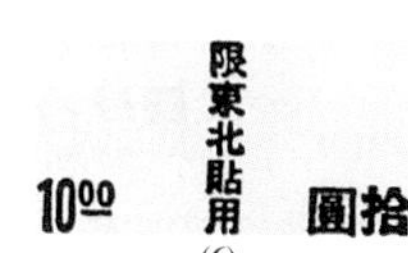

5 Dr. Sun Yat-sen (6)

1946.

17	5	5c. lake	10	2·50
18		10c. orange	10	2·50
19		20c. green	15	2·50
20		25c. brown	10	2·75
21		50c. orange	10	2·25
22		$1 blue	15	1·75
23		$2 purple	15	2·00
24		$2.50 blue	10	2·75
25		$3 brown	15	2·25
26		$4 brown	15	2·75
27		$5 green	10	2·25
28		$10 red	10	1·25
29		$20 olive	10	1·00
34		$22 black	60·00	65·00
35		$44 red	12·00	20·00
36		$50 violet	10	50
37		$65 green	60·00	75·00
38		$100 green	10	50
39		$109 green	65·00	75·00
40		$200 brown	10	1·00
41		$300 green	10	2·00
42		$500 red	10	50
43		$1,000 orange	10	20

1946. Nanking National Assembly stamps of China surch as T **6**.

44	111	$2 on $20 green	40	2·50
45		$3 on $30 blue	40	2·50
46		$5 on $50 brown	40	2·50
47		$10 on $100 red	40	2·50

7 Pres. Chiang Kai-shek (note characters to right of head)

(8)

1947. President's 60th Birthday.

54	7	$2 red	50	3·00
55		$3 green	80	3·00
56		$5 red	80	3·00
57		$10 green	80	3·00
58		$20 orange	1·00	3·00
59		$30 red	1·00	3·00

For other stamps as Types **7** and **9** but with different Chinese characters, see China–Taiwan Types **4** and **5.**

1947. Stamps of China surch as T **8**.

60	107	$100 on $1,000 purple	80	3·25
61		$300 on $3,000 blue	80	3·25
62	58	$500 on $30 brown	45	3·75
63	107	$500 on $5,000 red & green	75	3·25

9 Entrance to Dr. Sun Yat-sen Mausoleum (note characters above face value)

(10)

1947. 1st Anniv of Return of Govt. to Nanking.

64	9	$2 green	50	1·50
65		$4 blue	50	1·50
66		$6 red	50	1·50
67		$10 brown	50	1·50
68		$20 purple	50	1·50

1948. Surch as T **10**.

70	5	$1,500 on 20c. green	15	3·50
71		$3,000 on $1 blue	15	3·75
72		$4,000 on 25c. brown	15	3·00
73		$8,000 on 50c. orange	10	2·50
74		$10,000 on 10c. orange	10	2·50
75		$50,000 on $109 green	25	2·75
76		$100,000 on $65 green	35	2·50
77		$500,000 on $22 black	50	2·75

No. 70 has five characters on the left side of the surcharge and No. 77 four characters.

MILITARY POST STAMPS

1946. Military Post stamp of China optd as T **3** but larger.

M13	M 93	(No value) red	2·00	14·00

(M 10)

1947. Surch with Type M **10**.

M69	5	$44 on 50c. orange	8·00	32·00

PARCELS POST STAMPS

P 11 (P 12)

1948.

P78	P 11	$500 red	30·00
P79		$1,000 red	60·00
P80		$3,000 olive	75·00
P81		$5,000 blue	£120
P82		$10,000 green	£150
P83		$20,000 blue	£150

1948. Parcels Post stamp of China surch with Type P **12**.

P84		$500,000 on $5,000,000 lilac (No. P938)	–	£140

Parcels Post stamps were not on sale unused.

POSTAGE DUE STAMPS

D 7 (D 13)

1947.

D48	D 7	10c. blue	40	6·00
D49		20c. blue	40	6·00
D50		50c. blue	40	4·50
D51		$1 blue	10	3·25
D52		$2 blue	10	4·25
D53		$5 blue	10	4·25

1948. Surch as Type D **13**.

D85	D 7	$10 on 10c. blue	10	7·00
D86		$20 on 20c. blue	10	7·00
D87		$50 on 50c. blue	10	7·00

Sinkiang

(Chinese Turkestan)

A province between Tibet and Mongolia. Issued distinguishing stamps because of its debased currency. The following are all optd on stamps of China.

(1) (3)

1915. 1913 issue optd with T **1**.

17	43	½c. sepia	30	25
2		1c. orange	75	10
49		1½c. purple	1·50	2·00
3		2c. green	1·25	50
4		3c. green	1·25	10
5		4c. red	1·40	60
52		4c. grey	7·50	3·50
53		4c. olive	4·50	1·50
6		5c. mauve	1·25	40
7		6c. grey	1·40	70
55		6c. red	3·50	1·00
56		6c. brown	15·00	14·00
8		7c. violet	2·00	2·00
9		8c. orange	2·75	1·40
10		10c. blue	3·00	25
60	44	13c. brown	5·50	4·50
11		15c. brown	3·50	2·50
61		15c. blue	6·00	2·50
12		16c. olive	4·00	2·75
63		20c. lake	6·00	1·50
14		30c. purple	6·50	2·50
65		50c. green	10·00	3·50
34	45	$1 black and yellow	20·00	3·75
66		$1 sepia and brown	22·00	3·50
35		$2 black and blue	35·00	12·00
67		$2 brown and blue	26·00	8·50
36		$5 black and red	75·00	22·00
68		$5 green and red	50·00	17·00
37		$10 black and green	£225	£150
69		$10 mauve and green	£140	£120
38		$20 black and yellow	£550	£425
70		$20 blue and purple	£160	£140

1921. 25th Anniv of Chinese National Postal Service stamps optd with T **3**.

39	48	1c. orange	1·25	1·50
40		3c. turquoise	1·25	1·50
41		6c. grey	2·75	2·50
42		10c. blue	32·00	32·00

(4)

1923. Adoption of the Constitution stamps optd with T **4**.

43	53	1c. orange	3·25	3·25
44		3c. turquoise	3·25	3·25
45		4c. red	3·25	3·25
46		10c. blue	4·75	4·25

(5) (6)

1928. Assumption of Title of Marshal of the Army and Navy by Chang Tso-lin. Optd with T **5**.

71	55	1c. orange	1·40	1·25
72		4c. olive	2·25	2·25
73		10c. blue	5·50	5·00
74		$1 red	35·00	38·00

1929. Unification of China. Optd as T **5**.

75	56	1c. orange	3·00	2·50
76		4c. olive	3·00	2·75
77		10c. blue	8·50	3·50
78		$1 red	60·00	50·00

1929. Sun Yat-sen State Burial. Optd as T **5**.

79	57	1c. orange	1·50	1·25
80		4c. olive	2·50	2·25
81		10c. blue	6·00	3·25
82		$1 red	35·00	28·00

1932. Air. Handstamped on Sinkiang issues as T **6** ("By Air Mail").

83	43	5c. mauve (No. 6)	£300	£225
84		10c. blue (No. 10)	£300	£170
85	44	15c. blue (No. 61)	£2000	£600
86		30c. purple (No. 14)	£900	£750

1932. Dr. Sun Yat-sen stamps optd as T **3**.

87	58	1c. orange	1·25	2·25
95		2c. olive	1·25	1·25
103		4c. green	1·00	2·25
104		5c. green	1·25	1·50
105		15c. green	1·75	3·50
114		15c. red	2·50	2·50
115		20c. blue	2·00	75
107		25c. blue	2·00	75
108		$1 sepia and brown	6·50	5·50
100		$2 brown and blue	18·00	13·00
101		$5 black and red	24·00	25·00

1933. Tan Yen-kai Memorial. Optd as T **5**.

117	62	2c. olive	2·25	2·25
118		5c. green	2·75	1·25
119		25c. blue	7·00	3·50
120		$1 red	45·00	42·00

1933. Martyrs' issue optd as T **3**.

121	60	½c. sepia	10	1·00
122	–	1c. orange	10	85
167	–	2c. blue	30	2·25
123	60	2½c. mauve	20	1·75
124	–	3c. brown	20	2·00
169	60	4c. lilac	40	2·50
125	–	8c. orange	20	2·00
126	–	10c. purple	20	2·00
171	–	13c. green	60	3·25
172	–	15c. purple	60	3·25
173	–	17c. olive	75	3·25
137	–	20c. lake	20	4·25
174	–	20c. blue	75	3·00
175	–	21c. sepia	60	3·50
185	–	25c. purple	1·00	5·00
176	–	28c. olive	75	3·25
130	–	30c. red	25	3·25
131	–	40c. orange	25	3·50
132	–	50c. green	25	3·25

1940. Dr. Sun Yat-sen stamps optd as T **3**.

139	72	2c. olive	30	1·50
140		3c. red	30	2·25
141		5c. green	30	1·25
143		8c. olive	40	1·10
144		10c. green	40	1·25
145		15c. red	1·00	3·25
146		16c. olive	1·00	3·50
147		25c. blue	1·40	3·25
156		30c. red	1·00	2·75
158		50c. blue	1·50	3·00
160		$1 brown and red	1·75	5·00
161		$2 brown and blue	1·75	6·00
162		$5 green and red	1·75	7·50
163		$10 violet and green	2·00	7·50
164		$20 blue and red	3·00	11·00

(8) (9)

1942. Air. Air stamps optd with T **8** or larger.

187	61	15c. green	4·00	7·00
197		25c. orange	5·00	10·00
198		30c. red	5·00	10·00
190		45c. purple	6·00	10·00
199		50c. brown	6·00	12·00
192		60c. blue	6·00	12·00
193		90c. olive	25·00	27·00
194		$1 green	7·50	13·00
200		$2 brown	25·00	24·00
201		$5 red	32·00	24·00

1942. Thrift stamps optd as T **8**.

221	78	8c. green	5·00	10·00
215		21c. brown	5·00	10·00
216		28c. olive	5·00	10·00
223		33c. red	6·50	10·00
218		50c. blue	7·50	10·00
225		$1 purple	10·00	15·00

1943. Dr. Sun Yat-sen stamps optd as T **3**.

227	82	10c. green	15	6·00
228		20c. olive	15	5·50
229		25c. purple	30	10·00
230		30c. red	15	6·50
231		40c. brown	15	6·00
232		50c. green	15	6·00
233		$1 red	35	5·50
234		$1 olive	25	5·00
235		$1.50 blue	25	8·00
236		$2 green	75	6·50
237		$3 yellow	35	6·50
238		$5 red	45	6·50

1943. Stamps optd with T **9**.

239	72	10c. green	7·50	15·00
240	–	20c. blue (No. 519)	7·50	14·00
241	72	50c. blue	7·50	12·00

1944. Dr. Sun Yat-sen stamps optd as T **3**.

248	77	$4 blue	1·50	10·00
249		$5 grey	2·75	10·00
250		$10 brown	2·75	10·00
251		$20 green	1·40	11·00
243		$20 red	5·00	13·00
253		$30 purple	3·00	13·00
245		$40 red	3·75	13·00
255		$50 blue	3·50	14·00
247		$100 brown	11·00	17·00

(10)

1944. Nos. 227 and 229 of Sinkiang surch as T **10**.

257	82	12c. on 10c. green	7·00	20·00
258		24c. on 25c. purple	7·00	20·00

1945. Stamps optd as T **3**.

259	89	40c. red	35	16·00
260		$3 red	35	14·00

(11)

1949. Silver Yuan surcharges. Sun Yat-sen issues of China surch as T **11**.

261	107	1c. on $100 red (No. 889)	6·00	11·00
262		3c. on $200 green (No. 890)	6·00	14·00
263		5c. on $500 green (No. 891)	6·00	10·00
264	136	10c. on $20,000 red (No. 1032)	9·00	10·00
265		50c. on $4,000 grey (No. 961)	26·00	20·00
266		$1 on $6,000 purple (No. 963)	30·00	25·00

Szechwan

A province of China. Issued distinguishing stamps because of its debased currency.

(1)

Stamps of China optd with T **1**.

1933. Issue of 1913.

1	43	1c. orange	3·00	75
2		5c. mauve	6·00	20
3	44	50c. green	20·00	50

1933. Dr. Sun Yat-sen issue.

4	58	2c. olive	1·50	50
5		5c. green	1·50	10
6		15c. green	3·50	2·75
7		15c. red	7·00	7·50
8		25c. blue	6·00	40
9		$1 sepia and brown	18·00	2·75
10		$2 brown and blue	40·00	3·75
11		$5 black and red	80·00	12·00

1933. Martyrs issue (Nos. 410 etc).

12	60	½c. sepia	30	20
13	–	1c. orange	40	10
14	60	2½c. mauve	95	50
15	–	3c. brown	1·25	55
16	–	8c. orange	1·40	75
17	–	10c. purple	1·90	15
18	–	13c. green	2·75	60
19	–	17c. olive	2·25	1·10
20	–	20c. lake	3·00	50
21	–	30c. red	3·50	45
22	–	40c. orange	14·00	85
23	–	50c. green	16·00	1·10

Yunnan

A province of China which issued distinguishing stamps because of its debased currency.

(1) (2) (3)

Stamps of China optd.

1926. Issue of 1913, optd with T **1**.

1	43	½c. sepia	30	45
2		1c. orange	1·25	10
3		1½c. purple	1·25	1·25
4		2c. green	2·00	55
5		3c. green	1·75	40
6		4c. olive	1·75	10
7		5c. mauve	3·00	35
8		6c. red	3·75	1·25
9		7c. violet	4·75	2·50
10		8c. orange	5·50	2·00

11 10c. blue 3·75 20
12 44 13c. brown 5·50 4·25
13 15c. blue 5·00 1·50
14 16c. olive 6·00 3·25
15 20c. lake 5·50 1·75
16 30c. purple 16·00 11·00
17 50c. green 8·50 5·00
18 45 $1 sepia and brown 22·00 8·50
19 $2 brown and blue 45·00 14·00
20 $5 green and red £140 £150

1929. Unification of China. Optd with T **2**.
21 56 1c. orange 1·75 1·50
22 4c. olive 2·50 1·25
23 10c. blue 9·00 2·00
24 $1 red 70·00 55·00

1929. Sun Yat-sen State Burial. Optd as T **2**.
25 57 1c. orange 1·75 1·50
26 4c. olive 1·75 1·00
27 10c. blue 7·00 1·50
28 $1 red 45·00 40·00

1932. Dr. Sun Yat-sen stamps optd with T **3**.
29 58 1c. orange 80 75
30 2c. olive 95 1·10
44 4c. green 1·75 1·50
45 5c. green 2·00 75
46 15c. green 4·50 4·75
47 15c. red 5·00 7·00
32 20c. blue 3·00 85
48 25c. blue 7·50 3·50
33 $1 sepia and brown 20·00 16·00
34 $2 brown and blue 45·00 30·00
35 $5 black and red £100 85·00

1933. Tan Yen-kai Memorial. Optd with T **2**.
52 62 2c. olive 1·75 2·25
53 5c. green 2·00 1·00
54 25c. blue 5·75 2·25
55 $1 red 48·00 48·00

1933. Martyrs issue optd as T **3**.
56 60 ½c. sepia 65 1·00
57 – 1c. orange 1·25 20
58 60 2½c. mauve 1·50 2·50
59 – 3c. brown 3·25 3·25
60 – 8c. orange 8·50 8·00
61 – 10c. purple 3·75 3·50
62 – 13c. green 3·75 3·75
63 – 17c. olive 3·75 3·75
64 – 20c. lake 4·00 2·00
65 – 30c. red 8·50 7·00
66 – 40c. orange 14·00 15·00
67 – 50c. green 16·00 7·50

COMMUNIST CHINA

Issues were made by various Communist administrations from 1930 onwards. These had limited local availability and are outside the scope of this catalogue. For details of such issues see Part 17.

In 1946 (North East China) and 1949 these local issues were consolidated into Regional People's Post stamps for those local administrations listed below.

A. East China People's Post

EC 105 Methods of Transport

1949. 7th Anniv of Shandong Communist Postal Administration.
EC322 EC 105 $1 green 60 1·25
EC323 $2 green 20 85
EC324 $3 red 20 45
EC325 $5 brown 20 35
EC326 $10 blue 35 1·00
EC327 $13 violet 20 80
EC328 $18 blue 20 80
EC329 $21 red 30 1·00
EC330 $30 green 20 65
EC331 $50 red 70 80
EC332 $100 green 12·00 11·00
The $5 has an overprinted character obliterating a Japanese flag on the tower.

EC 106 Steam Train and Postal Runner

EC 107 Victorious Troops and Map of Battle

1949. Dated "1949.2.7".
EC333 EC 106 $1 green 20 85
EC334 $2 green 30 65
EC335 $3 red 20 65
EC336 $5 brown 20 55
EC337 $10 blue 75 1·10
EC338 $13 violet 25 90
EC339 $18 blue 20 1·10
EC340 $21 red 20 1·75
EC341 $30 green 2·50 1·90
EC342 $50 red 35 2·75
EC343 $100 green 1·00 55
For stamps as Type EC **106**, but dated "1949", see Nos. EC364/71.

1949. Victory in Huaihai Campaign.
EC344 EC 107 $1 green 20 80
EC345 $2 green 35 70
EC346 $3 red 20 70
EC347 $5 brown 20 40
EC348 $10 blue 60 60
EC349 $13 violet 20 80
EC350 $18 blue 20 80
EC351 $21 red 20 90
EC352 $30 green 1·00 75
EC353 $50 red 50 1·00
EC354 $100 green 4·00 2·00

EC 108 Maps of Shanghai and Nanjing

1949. Liberation of Nanjing and Shanghai.
EC355 EC 108 $1 red 20 1·25
EC356 $2 green 20 1·00
EC357 $3 violet 20 75
EC358 $5 brown 20 50
EC359 $10 blue 20 75
EC360 $30 green 40 1·00
EC361 $50 red 85 75
EC362 $100 green 1·25 15
EC363 $500 orange 3·50 75

1949. As Type EC **106** but dated "1949".
EC364 $10 blue 20 25
EC365a $15 red 20 25
EC366 $30 green 20 10
EC367 $50 red 20 10
EC368 $60 green 20 1·60
EC369 $100 green 6·00 80
EC370 $1,600 violet 2·00 4·25
EC371 $2,000 purple 2·00 3·75

EC 111 Zhu De, Mao Tse-tung and Troops

EC 112 Mao Tse-tung

1949. 22nd Anniv of Chinese People's Liberation Army.
EC378 EC 111 $70 orange 20 10
EC379 $270 red 20 15
EC380 $370 green 20 40
EC381 $470 purple 35 60
EC382 $570 blue 30 45
For other values in this design with only three characters in bottom panel, see South West China Nos. SW9/19.

1949.
EC383 EC 112 $10 blue 3·00 3·25
EC384 $15 red 3·00 3·50
EC385 $70 brown 20 35
EC386 $100 purple 20 20
EC387 $150 orange 20 30
EC388 $200 green 20 10
EC389 $500 blue 20 10
EC390 $1,000 red 20 15
EC391 $2,000 green 20 3·50

(EC 113) ("Chinese People's Postal Service East China Region")

1949. Stamps of Nationalist China surch as Type EC **113**.
EC392 145 $400 on $200 red 18·00 30
EC393 $1,000 on $50 green 60 25
EC394 $1,200 on $100 green 25 1·75
EC395 $1,600 on $20,000 grn 25 2·25
EC396 $2,000 on $1,000 blue 25 15

PARCELS POST STAMPS
Stamps of Nationalist China surch.

$200 $500 $1,000
政郵東華
$2,000 $5,000 $10,000
(ECP 110)

1949. No. 1347 surch as Type ECP **110**.
ECP372 169 $200 on $10 green 16·00 8·00
ECP373 $500 on $10 green 16·00 3·75
ECP374 $1,000 on $10 green 18·00 7·00
ECP375 $2,000 on $10 green 26·00 13·00
ECP376 $5,000 on $10 green 40·00 21·00
ECP377 $10,000 on $10 green 75·00 29·00

(ECP 114) (ECP 115)

1949. Nos. 1344/6 and unissued 10c. surch as Type ECP **114**.
ECP397 169 $5,000 on 10c. blue 30·00 19·00
ECP398 $10,000 on $1 orange 48·00 30·00
ECP399 $20,000 on $2 blue 90·00 65·00
ECP400 $50,000 on $5 red £300 85·00

1949. Nos. P711/2 and P926/7 surch as Type ECP **115**.
ECP401 P 90 $5,000 on $500 green 20 10·00
ECP402 $10,000 on $1 blue 80·00 40·00
ECP403 P 112 $20,000 on $3 green £120 75·00
ECP404 $50,000 on $5 red 2·00 50·00

B. North China People's Post

(NC 68) (NC 69)

(NC 70)

1949. Surch "North China People's Postal Administration". (a) Surch as Type NC **68**.
NC258 $5 on $500 orange 20·00 15·00
NC259 $6 on $500 orange 24·00 20·00
NC260 $12 on $200 red 4·00 5·00

(b) Surch as Type NC **69**.
NC261 $3 on 2 (20c.) brown £200 £120
NC262 $3 on 5 (50c.) blue 15·00 10·00
NC263 $5 on 2 (20c.) brown 15·00 10·00
NC264 $5 on 5 (50c.) blue £250 £150

(c) Surch as Type NC **70**.
NC265 $1 on $60 red 18·00 16·00
NC266 $5 on $80 purple 14·00 12·00
NC267 $6 on $2 brown 65·00 15·00
NC268 $6 on $40 brown 15·00 10·00
NC269 $6 on $80 purple £325 £250

NC 71 Infantry

NC 72 Industry

1948. Imperf.
NC270 NC 71 50c. purple 60 80
NC271 $1 blue 7·50 7·00
NC272 $2 green 1·00 1·50
NC273 $3 violet 30 1·10
NC274 $5 brown 90 1·25
NC275 NC 72 $6 purple 50 1·00
NC276 NC 71 $10 green 1·00 1·75
NC277 $12 red 2·00 1·50
The 50c. and $6 have value in Chinese characters only.

(NC 73) "People's Postal Service North China" (NC 74)

1949. Surch as Type NC **73**. (a) On stamp of Nationalist China.
NC278 $100* on $100 red 14·00 50

(b) On stamps of North Eastern Provinces.
NC279 5 50c. on 5c. red 60 3·50
NC280 $1 on 10c. orange 75 1·00
NC281 $2 on 20c. green 30·00 2·50
NC282 $3 on 50c. orange 30 3·00
NC283 $4 on $5 green 4·00 2·75
NC284 $6 on $10 red 60 1·00
NC285 $10 on $300 green 2·75 2·50
NC286 $12 on $1 blue 1·40 1·50
NC287 $18 on $3 brown 1·75 1·00
NC288 $20* on 50c. orange 1·25 75
NC290 $20 on $20 green 1·50 80
NC291 $30 on $2.50 blue 1·75 1·50
NC292 $40 on 25c. brown 2·00 1·50
NC293 $50 on $109 green 4·00 1·50
NC294 $80* on $1 blue 7·00 1·00
NC295 $100 on $65 green 8·00 1·75

1949. Surch as Type NC **74**. (a) On stamps of Nationalist China.
NC296 107 $100* on $100 red 25·00 7·50
NC297 $300* on $700 brown 8·00 2·50
NC298 118 $500* on $500 green 7·50 1·00
NC299 $3,000* on $3,000 blue 8·50 2·00

(b) On stamps of North Eastern Provinces.
NC300a 5 $1* on 25c. brown 25 1·00
NC301 $2 on 20c. green 1·75 1·25
NC302 $3 on 50c. orange 25 1·00
NC303 $4 on $5 green 1·90 1·75
NC305 $6 on $10 red 2·00 1·00
NC306 $10* on $300 green 9·00 2·25
NC307 $12 on $1 blue 95 70
NC308 $20* on 50c. orange 10·00 1·90
NC309 $20* on $20 green 5·00 60
NC310 $40* on 25c. brown 6·75 90
NC311 $50* on $109 green 10·00 1·00
NC312 $80* on $1 blue 7·50 1·00
*On these stamps the bottom character in the left-hand column of overprints is square in shape.

NC 75

1949. Labour Day. Perf or imperf.
NC313 NC 75 $20 red 2·00 1·75
NC314 $40 blue 2·00 1·75
NC315 $60 brown 2·00 2·25
NC316 $80 green 2·75 2·25
NC317 $100 violet 3·50 2·25

NC 79 Mao Tse-tung

NC 80

1949. 28th Anniv of Chinese Communist Party. Perf or imperf.
NC327A NC 79 $10 red 1·00 1·00
NC328A NC 80 $20 blue 50 75
NC329A NC 79 $50 orange 2·00 1·50
NC330A NC 80 $80 green 50 75
NC331A NC 79 $100 violet 2·50 1·50
NC332A NC 80 $120 green 50 1·00
NC333A NC 79 $140 purple 3·50 1·75

政郵民人
暫 拾 華
用 圓 北
(NC **81**) ("People's Postal Service North China")

1949. Surch as Type NC **81**. (a) On stamp of Nationalist China.
NC334 118 $10 on $7,000 brown 15·00 7·50

(b) On stamps of North Eastern Provinces.
NC336 5 $10 on $10 red 5·00 1·25
NC337 $30 on 20c. green 4·00 1·50
NC338 $50 on $44 red 3·75 25
NC339 $100 on $3 brown 8·00 1·50
NC341 $200 on $4 brown 20·00 7·00

NC 83 Gate of Heavenly Peace, Peking

NC 84 Field Workers and Factory

1949.
NC349 NC 83 $50 orange 2·50 6·50
NC350 $100 red 20 30
NC351 $200 green 1·00 35
NC352 $300 purple 5·00 70
NC353 $400 blue 5·00 70
NC354 $500 brown 7·00 60
NC355 $700 violet 3·00 2·50

1949.
NC356 NC 84 $1,000 orange 4·00 60
NC357 $3,000 blue 20 90
NC358 $5,000 red 20 10
NC359 $10,000 brown 30 1·75

PARCELS POST STAMPS
Stamps of Nationalist China surch.

政郵民人
元百捌
北 華
(NCP **76**)

1949. Surch as Type NCP **76**.
NCP318 P 112 $300 on $6,000,000 grey – 32·00
NCP319 $400 on $8,000,000 red – 32·00

NCP320	$500 on $10,000,000 green	–	35·00
NCP321	$800 on $5,000,000 lilac	–	35·00
NCP322	$1 on $3,000,000 blue	–	40·00

NC 77 Pagoda (NCP 78)

1949. Money Order stamps. Type NC 77 surch as Type NCP 78. No gum.

NCP323	$6 on $5 red	6·00	2·25
NCP324	$6 on $50 grey	6·00	2·25
NCP325	$50 on $20 purple	7·00	2·00
NCP326	$100 on $10 green	10·00	4·25

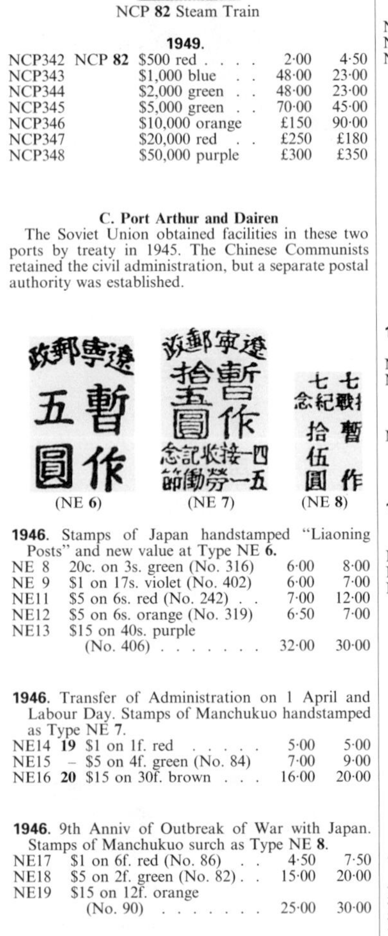

NCP 82 Steam Train

1949.

NCP342	NCP 82	$500 red	2·00	4·50
NCP343		$1,000 blue	48·00	23·00
NCP344		$2,000 green	48·00	23·00
NCP345		$5,000 green	70·00	45·00
NCP346		$10,000 orange	£150	90·00
NCP347		$20,000 red	£250	£180
NCP348		$50,000 purple	£300	£350

C. Port Arthur and Dairen

The Soviet Union obtained facilities in these two ports by treaty in 1945. The Chinese Communists retained the civil administration, but a separate postal authority was established.

(NE 6) (NE 7) (NE 8)

1946. Stamps of Japan handstamped "Liaoning Posts" and new value at Type NE 6.

NE 8	20c. on 3s. green (No. 316)	6·00	8·00
NE 9	$1 on 17s. violet (No. 402)	6·00	7·00
NE11	$5 on 6s. red (No. 242)	7·00	12·00
NE12	$5 on 6s. orange (No. 319)	6·50	7·00
NE13	$15 on 40s. purple (No. 406)	32·00	30·00

1946. Transfer of Administration on 1 April and Labour Day. Stamps of Manchukuo handstamped as Type NE 7.

NE14	19	$1 on 1f. red	5·00	5·00
NE15	–	$5 on 4f. green (No. 84)	7·00	9·00
NE16	20	$15 on 30f. brown	16·00	20·00

1946. 9th Anniv of Outbreak of War with Japan. Stamps of Manchukuo surch as Type NE 8.

NE17	$1 on 6f. red (No. 86)	4·50	7·50
NE18	$5 on 2f. green (No. 82)	15·00	20·00
NE19	$15 on 12f. orange (No. 90)	25·00	30·00

(NE 9) (NE 10)

1946. 1st Anniv of Japanese Surrender. Stamps of Manchukuo surch as Type NE 9.

NE20	–	$1 on 12f. orange (No. 90)	8·00	9·00
NE21	19	$5 on 1f. red	16·00	18·00
NE22	13	$15 on 5f. black	32·00	30·00

1946. 35th Anniv of Chinese Revolution. Stamps of Manchukuo surch as Type NE 10.

NE23	$1 on 6f. red (No. 86)	7·00	8·00
NE24	$5 on 12f. orange (No. 90)	16·00	16·00
NE25	$15 on 2f. green (No. 82)	32·00	32·00

(NE 11) (NE 12)

1946. 10th Death Anniv of Lu Xun (author). Stamps of Manchukuo surch as Type NE 11.

NE26	19	$1 on 1f. red	18·00	15·00
NE27	–	$5 on 6f. red (No. 86)	25·00	30·00
NE28	–	$15 on 12f. orange (No. 90)	40·00	45·00

1947. 29th Anniv of Red Army. Stamps of Manchukuo surch as Type NE 12.

NE29	–	$1 on 2f. green (No. 82)	20·00	20·00
NE30	–	$5 on 6f. red (No. 86)	35·00	35·00
NE31	13	$15 on 13f. brown	£110	£130

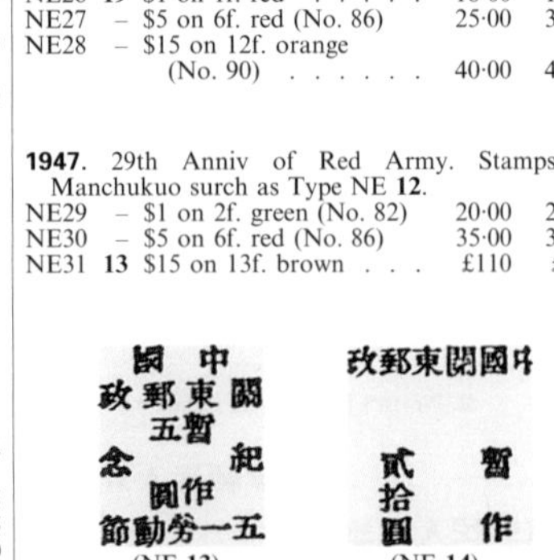

(NE 13) (NE 14)

1947. Labour Day. Stamps of Manchukuo surch as Type NE 13.

NE32	–	$1 on 2f. green (No. 82)	8·00	8·00
NE33	–	$5 on 6f. red (No. 86)	20·00	20·00
NE34	20	$15 on 30f. brown	40·00	45·00

1947. Stamps of Manchukuo surch. "Guangdong Postal Service, China" and new value as Type NE 14.

NE35	–	$5 on 2f. green (No. 82)	20·00	20·00
NE36	–	$15 on 4f. green (No. 84)	30·00	20·00
NE37	20	$20 on 30f. brown	38·00	38·00

NE 15 (NE 16)

1948. 30th Anniv of Red Army. Surch as on Type NE 15. (a) On stamps of Manchukuo.

NE39	$10 on 2f. green (No. 82)	70·00	50·00
NE40	$20 on 6f. red (No. 86)	90·00	75·00

(b) On label (Type NE 15) commemorating 2,600th Anniv of Japanese Empire.

NE41	$100 on (no value) blue and brown	£400	£350

1948. Stamps of Manchukuo surch "Guangdong Postal Administration" and new value as Type NE 16.

NE42	$20 on 2f. green (No. 82)	£100	£100
NE43	$50 on 4f. green (No. 84)	£200	£180
NE44	$100 on 20f. brown (No. 152)	£275	£225

(NE 17) (NE 18)

1948. 31st Anniv of Russian October Revolution. Stamps of Manchukuo surch as Type NE 17.

NE45	19	$10 on 1f. red	£120	£120
NE46	–	$50 on 2f. green (No. 82)	£225	£225
NE47	–	$100 on 4f. green (No. 84)	£325	£325

1948. Guangdong Agricultural and Industrial Exhibition Stamps of Manchukuo surch as Type NE 18.

NE48	$10 on 2f. green (No. 82)	£180	£150
NE49	$50 on 20f. brown (No. 95)	£750	£550

(NE 19) (NE 20)

1948. Stamps of Japan and Manchukuo surch "Chinese Postal Administration: Guangdong Posts and Telegraphs" and new values. (a) No. 316 of Japan surch with Type NE 19.

NE50	$5 on 3s. green	32·00	20·00

(b) Stamps of Manchukuo surch as Type NE 19.

NE51	$10 on 1f. red (No. 80)	75·00	50·00
NE52	$50 on 2f. green (No. 82)	£200	£130
NE53	$100 on 4f. green (No. 84)	£300	£225

(c) Stamps of Manchukuo surch as Type NE 20.

NE54	$10 on 2f. green (No. 82)	85·00	50·00
NE55	$50 on 1f. red (No. 80)	£100	70·00

NE 21 Peasant and Artisan

NE 23 Dalian Port

1949.

NE56	NE 21	$5 green	2·00	8·00
NE57	–	$10 orange	25·00	25·00
NE58	NE 23	$50 red	14·00	12·00

DESIGN—VERT: $10, "Transport".

For designs as Type NE 23 but with different character in bottom panel, see No. NE62.

NE 24 "Labour"

NE 25 Mao Tse-tung

1949. Labour Day.

NE59	NE 24	$10 red	15·00	18·00

1949. 28th Anniv of Chinese Communist Party.

NE61	NE 25	$50 red	25·00	22·00

1949. Bottom panel inscr "Lushuan and Dalian Post and Telegraphic Administration".

NE62	NE 23	$50 red	24·00	18·00

NE 27 Heroes' Monument, Dalian

1949. 4th Anniv of Victory over Japan and Opening of Dalian Industrial Fair.

NE63	NE 27	$10 red, blue & lt bl	32·00	35·00
NE64		$10 red, blue & green	10·00	12·00

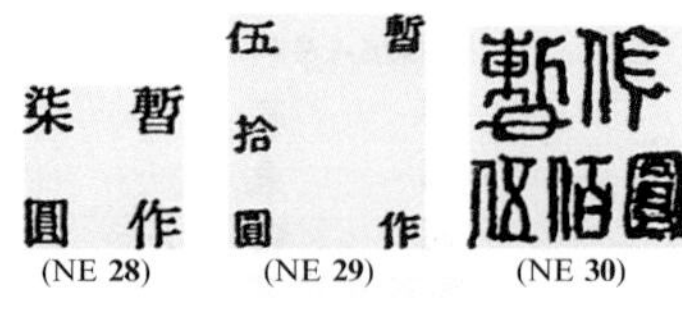

(NE 28) (NE 29) (NE 30)

1949. Nos. NE56/7 surch as Types NE 28/30.

NE65	NE 28	$7 on $5 green	13·00	10·00
NE66	NE 29	$50 on $5 green	38·00	35·00
NE67		$100 on $10 orange	£250	£250
NE68	NE 30	$500 on $5 green	£500	
NE69	NE 29	$500 on $10 orge	£1000	£1100
NE70	NE 30	$500 on $10 orge	£450	£425

NE 31 Acclamation of Mao Tse-tung

1949. Founding of Chinese People's Republic.

NE71	NE 31	$35 red, yellow & bl	14·00	14·00

NE 32 Stalin and Lenin

1949. 32nd Anniv of Russian October Revolution.

NE72	NE 32	$10 green	9·00	9·00

NE 33 Josef Stalin

NE 34 Gate of Heavenly Peace, Peking

1949. Stalin's 70th Birthday.

NE73	NE 33	$20 purple	16·00	18·00
NE74		$35 red	16·00	18·00

1950.

NE75	NE 34	$10 blue	6·50	4·50
NE76		$20 green	30·00	14·00
NE77		$35 red	1·25	3·50
NE78		$50 lilac	2·00	3·50
NE79		$100 mauve	1·25	9·50

All Soviet forces were withdrawn by 26 May 1955 and the stamps of the Chinese People's Republic are now in use.

D. North-East China People's Post

NE 48 Mao Tse-tung

NE 49 Mao Tse-tung

1946.

NE133	NE 48	$1 violet	5·00	6·00
NE134	NE 49	$2 red	1·75	2·75
NE135		$5 orange	2·25	2·75
NE136		$10 blue	1·75	2·75

NE 50 Map of China with Communist Lion, Japanese Wolf and Chiang Kai-shek

NE 51 Railwaymen

1946. 10th Anniv of Seizure of Chiang Kai-shek at Xi'an.

NE137	NE 50	$1 violet	50	3·50
NE138		$2 orange	50	3·50
NE139		$5 brown	3·50	5·50
NE140		$10 green	10·00	8·00

1947. 24th Anniv of Massacre of Strikers at Zhengzhou Station.

NE141	NE 51	$1 red	1·25	3·25
NE142		$2 green	1·50	3·25
NE143		$5 red	1·50	3·25
NE144		$10 green	4·50	6·75

NE 52 Women Cheering

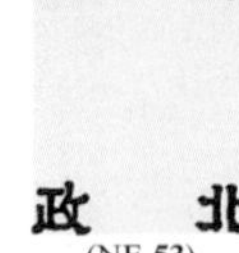

(NE 53)

1947. International Women's Day.

NE145	NE 52	$5 red	50	3·50
NE146		$10 brown	50	3·50

1947. Optd with Type NE 53 ("North East Postal Service").

NE147	NE 53	$5 red	5·00	4·50
NE148		$10 brown	5·00	4·50

NE 54 Children's Troop-comforts Unit

NE 55 Peasant and Workman

1947. Children's Day.

NE149	NE 54	$5 red	3·00	3·50
NE150		$10 green	3·00	3·75
NE151		$30 orange	4·00	4·75

1947. Labour Day.

NE152	NE 55	$10 red	1·00	2·50
NE153		$30 blue	2·00	2·50
NE154		$50 green	2·75	2·50

NE 56 "Freedom" (NE 57)

1947. 28th Anniv of Students' Rebellion, Peking University.

NE155	NE 56	$10 green	3·00	3·25
NE156		$30 brown	3·00	3·25
NE157		$50 violet	3·00	3·25

1947. Surch as Type NE 57.

NE158	NE 48	$50 on $1 violet	15·00	14·00
NE159	NE 49	$50 on $2 red	15·00	14·00
NE160b	NE 48	$100 on $1 violet	15·00	15·00
NE161	NE 49	$100 on $2 red	15·00	15·00

NE 58 Youths with Banner

1947. 22nd Anniv of Nanjing Road Incident, Shanghai.

NE162	NE 58	$2 red and mauve	1·50	2·50
NE163		$5 red and green	1·50	2·50
NE164		$10 red & yellow	2·00	2·50
NE165		$20 red & violet	2·00	2·50
NE166		$30 red & brown	3·00	3·00
NE167		$50 red and blue	5·00	3·50
NE168		$100 red & brown	7·50	5·00

NE 59 Mao Tse-tung

1947. 26th Anniv of Chinese Communist Party.

NE170	NE 59	$10 red	5·00	6·50
NE171		$30 mauve	5·00	6·75
NE172		$50 purple	8·00	7·00
NE173		$100 red	12·00	9·00

NE 60 Hand grasping rifle

NE 61 Mountains and River

1947. 10th Anniv of Outbreak of War with Japan.

NE174	NE 60	$10 orange	5·00	5·50
NE175		$30 green	5·00	5·50
NE176		$50 blue	6·00	5·50
NE177		$100 brown	7·50	5·50

1947. 2nd Anniv of Japanese Surrender.

NE179	NE 61	$10 brown	7·50	8·00
NE180		$30 green	7·50	8·00
NE181		$50 green	5·00	8·00
NE182		$100 brown	12·00	8·00

(NE 62)

NE 63 Map of Manchuria

1947. Surch as Type NE 62.

NE183	NE 48	$5 on $1 violet	20·00	20·00
NE184	NE 49	$10 on $2 red	20·00	20·00

1947. 16th Anniv of Japanese Attack on Manchuria.

NE185	NE 63	$10 green	6·00	7·50
NE186		$20 mauve	4·00	7·50
NE187		$30 brown	2·00	7·50
NE188		$50 red	10·00	7·50

NE 64 Mao Tse-tung

NE 65 Offices of N.E. Political Council

1947.

NE189	NE 64	$1 purple	2·50	6·00
NE190		$5 green	3·00	6·00
NE191		$10 green	10·00	12·00
NE192		$15 violet	5·00	10·00
NE193		$20 red	40	3·50
NE194		$30 green	20	3·50
NE195		$50 brown	15·00	13·00
NE213		$50 green	1·00	3·00
NE196		$90 blue	75	10·00
NE197		$100 red	30	5·00
NE215		$150 red	2·00	4·50
NE214		$250 lilac	75	4·25
NE228		$300 green	32·00	32·00
NE198		$500 orange	10·00	6·50
NE229		$1,000 yellow	60	2·50

For stamps as Type NE 64 but with "YUAN" in top right tablet, see Nos. NE236/40.

1947. 35th Anniv of Chinese Republic.

NE199	NE 65	$10 yellow	15·00	22·00
NE200		$20 red	15·00	22·00
NE201		$100 brown	50·00	35·00

NE 66

NE 67 Tomb of Gen. Li Zhaolin

1947. 11th Anniv of Seizure of Chiang Kai-shek at Xi'an.

NE202	NE 66	$30 red	5·00	10·00
NE203		$90 blue	6·50	12·00
NE204		$150 green	8·50	12·00

1948. 2nd Death Anniv of Gen. Li Zhaolin.

NE205	NE 67	$30 green	10·00	12·00
NE206		$150 lilac	10·00	12·00

NE 68 Flag and Globe

NE 69 Youth with Torch

1948. Labour Day.

NE207	NE 68	$50 red	4·00	10·00
NE208		$150 green	2·00	12·00
NE209		$250 violet	1·00	20·00

1948. Youth Day.

NE210	NE 69	$50 green	10·00	10·00
NE211		$150 brown	10·00	10·00
NE212		$250 red	15·00	13·00

(NE 70)

NE 71 Crane Operator

1948. Surch as Type NE 70.

NE217a	NE 64	$100 on $1 purple	18·00	18·00
NE218		$100 on $15 violet	15·00	15·00
NE219		$300 on $5 green	20·00	20·00
NE220		$300 on $30 green	7·50	12·00
NE221		$300 on $90 blue	7·50	12·00
NE230	NE 49	$500 on $2 red	6·00	7·50
NE222	NE 64	$500 on $50 green	8·50	13·00
NE231	NE 49	$1,500 on $5 orge	6·00	7·50
NE223	NE 64	$1,500 on $150 red	7·50	15·00
NE232	NE 49	$2,500 on $10 blue	6·00	7·50
NE224	NE 64	$2,500 on $300 grn	7·50	15·00

1948. All-China Labour Conference.

NE225	NE 71	$100 red & pink	50	2·50
NE226		$300 brown & yell	3·00	4·50
NE227		$500 blue & green	1·25	2·50

NE 72 Workman, Soldier and Peasant

NE 74 "Production in Field and Industry"

1948. Liberation of the North East.

NE233	NE 72	$500 red	5·00	5·50
NE234		$1,500 green	7·00	7·50
NE235		$2,500 brown	11·00	10·00

1949. As Type NE 64 but "YUAN" at top right.

NE236	$300 green	1·50	3·50
NE237	$500 orange	2·00	2·50
NE238	$1,500 green	20	2·50
NE239	$4,500 brown	20	2·75
NE240	$6,500 blue	20	3·25

1949.

NE241	NE 74	$5,000 blue	3·75	5·50
NE242		$10,000 orange	20	4·25
NE243		$50,000 green	20	5·00
NE244		$100,000 violet	20	11·00

NE 75 Workers and Banners

NE 76 Workers' Procession

1949. Labour Day.

NE245	NE 75	$1,000 red and blue	30	1·50
NE246		$1,500 red and blue	30	1·50
NE247		$4,500 red & brown	30	1·50
NE248		$6,500 brown & grn	30	1·50
NE249		$10,000 purple & bl	1·00	1·50

1949. 28th Anniv of Chinese Communist Party.

NE250	NE 76	$1,500 red, vio & bl	30	1·50
NE251		$4,500 red, brn & bl	40	1·50
NE252		$6,500 red, pink & bl	1·25	1·50

NE 77 North-East Heroes, Monument

NE 78 Factory

1949. 4th Anniv of Japanese Surrender.

NE253	NE 77	$1,500 red	20	1·50
NE254		$4,500 green	75	1·50
NE255		$6,500 blue	85	1·50

REPRINTS. The note above No. 1401 of China also refers here to Nos. NE257/60, 261/3, 271/4, 286/89 and 312/4.

1949.

NE256	NE 78	$1,500 red	35	1·75

1949. 1st Session of Chinese People's Political Conference. As T **181** of People's Republic but with additional inscr.

NE257	$1,000 blue	5·00	7·50
NE258	$1,500 red	5·00	7·50
NE259	$3,000 green	5·00	7·50
NE260	$4,500 purple	5·00	8·50

1949. World Federation of Trade Unions, Asiatic and Australasian Conference, Peking. As T **182** of People's Republic but with additional inscr.

NE261	$5,000 red	60·00	40·00
NE262	$20,000 green	60·00	40·00
NE263	$35,000 blue	£100	50·00

(NE 79)

1949. Surch as T NE 79.

NE264	NE 64	$2,000 on $300 green	5·00	6·50
NE265		$2,000 on $4,500 brown	32·00	28·00
NE266		$2,500 on $1,500 green	30	5·00
NE267		$2,500 on $6,500 blue	16·00	15·00
NE268	NE 78	$5,000 on $1,500 red	75	2·50
NE269	NE 64	$20,000 on $4,500 brown	20	3·50
NE270		$35,000 on $300 green	20	3·50

1950. Chinese People's Political Conference. As T **183/4** of People's Republic but with additional inscr.

NE271	$1,000 red	7·50	8·00
NE272	$1,500 blue	7·50	8·00
NE273	$5,000 purple	8·50	8·00
NE274	$20,000 green	10·00	8·00

1950. As T **185** of People's Republic but with additional four-character inscr.

NE303	185	$250 brown	10	5·00
NE275		$500 green	10	2·00
NE276		$1,000 orange	10	1·25
NE277		$1,000 mauve	10	2·00
NE306		$2,000 green	10	2·00
NE307		$2,500 yellow	20	2·00
NE300		$5,000 orange	1·50	1·25
NE309		$10,000 brown	30	2·00
NE310		$12,500 purple	50	6·00
NE283		$20,000 purple	40	2·00
NE301		$30,000 red	2·50	4·50
NE284		$35,000 blue	60	4·50
NE285		$50,000 green	2·50	4·50
NE302		$100,000 violet	1·00	4·50

1950. Foundation of People's Republic. Additional inscr at left.

NE286	188	$5,000 red, yell & grn	40·00	40·00
NE287		$10,000 red, yell & brn	40·00	40·00
NE288		$20,000 red, yell & pur	50·00	40·00
NE289		$30,000 red, yell & bl	60·00	55·00

1950. Peace Campaign. Additional characters below olive branch.

NE290	191	$2,500 brown	10·00	10·00
NE291		$5,000 green	10·00	10·00
NE292		$20,000 blue	12·00	12·00

1950. 1st Anniv of People's Republic. Additional characters at left. Flag in red, yellow and brown.

NE293	193	$1,000 violet	26·00	30·00
NE294		$2,500 brown	28·00	30·00
NE295		$5,000 green (44×53 mm)	40·00	30·00
NE296		$10,000 green	50·00	35·00
NE297		$20,000 blue	60·00	40·00

1950. 1st All-China Postal Conference. Additional characters at left.

NE298	194	$2,500 brown & green	5·00	5·00
NE299		$5,000 green and red	5·00	5·00

1950. Sino–Soviet Treaty. Additional characters in top right-hand coner.

NE312	195	$2,500 red	8·00	8·00
NE313		$5,000 green	8·00	8·00
NE314		$20,000 blue	12·00	12·00

PARCELS POST STAMPS

NEP 82

1951.

NEP315	NEP 82	$1,000,000 violet	40·00
NEP316		$300,000 purple	£100
NEP317		$500,000 green	£170
NEP318		$1,000,000 red	£300

E. North-West China People's Post

NW 25 Mao Tse-tung

NW 26 Great Wall

1949. Imperf.

NW 97	NW 25	$50 pink	2·50	3·25
NW 98	NW 26	$100 blue	20	50
NW 99	NW 25	$200 orange	4·00	3·75
NW100	NW 26	$400 brown	3·00	2·00

F. South-West China People's Post

SW 3 Zhu De, Mao Tse-tung and Troops

SW 4 Map of China with Flag in S.W.

1949.

SW 9	SW 3	$10 blue	5·00	3·50
SW10		$20 purple	20	2·25
SW11		$30 orange	20	1·00
SW12		$50 green	50	75
SW13		$100 red	25	60
SW14		$200 blue	1·75	75
SW15		$300 violet	5·00	1·25
SW16		$500 grey	7·50	3·25
SW17		$1,000 purple	10·00	6·00
SW18		$2,000 green	18·00	15·00
SW19		$5,000 orange	20·00	20·00

For other values in this design see East China, Nos. EC378/82.

1950. Liberation of the South West.
SW20 SW 4 $20 blue . . . . . . 25 1·00
SW21 $30 green . . . . . 1·60 2·25
SW22 $50 red . . . . . . 35 1·25
SW23 $100 brown . . . . 75 1·25

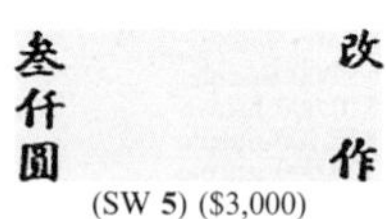
(SW 5) ($3,000)

伍仟圓 ($5,000) 壹萬圓 ($10,000) 貳萬圓 ($20,000) 伍萬圓 ($50,000)

1950. Surch as Type SW **5** (characters in left-hand column of surcharge differ as indicated in illustrations and footnote).
SW24 SW 4 $60 on $30 green . . 15·00 12·00
SW25 $150 on $30 green . . 14·00 10·00
SW26 $300 on $20 blue . . 1·25 2·25
SW27 $300 on $100 brown 15·00 6·00
SW28 $1,500 on $100 brown . . . . . . 15·00 10·00
SW29 $3,000 on $50 red . . 8·50 7·00
SW30 $5,000 on $50 red . . 4·00 5·50
SW31 $10,000 on $50 red 40·00 20·00
SW32 $20,000 on $50 red 5·00 20·00
SW33 $50,000 on $50 red 4·00 40·00
Nos. SW24 and SW26/7 have three characters in left-hand column; Nos. SW25 and SW28 have five.

G. Chinese People's Republic

1949. Yuans.
1955. 100 fen = 1 yuan.

GUM or NO GUM. Nos. 1401/1891 were issued without gum (except Nos. 1843/5 and 1850/7). From No. 1892 onwards all postage stamps were issued with gum, unless otherwise stated. From 1965 some issues seem to have no gum, though in fact they bear an adhesive substance.

SERIAL MARKINGS. Issues other than definitive issues are divided into two categories: "commemorative" and "special". Figures below the design of each stamp of such issues indicate: (a) serial number of the issue; (b) number of stamps in the issue; (c) number of stamps within the issue; and (d) year of issue (from No. 1557 on). Neither chronological order of issue nor sequence of value is always strictly followed. From No. 2343 these serial markings were omitted until No. 2433.

REPRINTS were later made in replacementof exhausted stocks by the Chinese Postal Administration for sale to stamp collectors and were not available for postal purposes. Nos. 1401/11, 1432/5, 1456/8, 1464/73, 1507/9, 1524/37 and 1543/52. Our prices are for originals. For notes describing the distinguishing features of the reprints, see Stanley Gibbons Part 17 (China) Catalogue.

For other values in the following types see North East China.

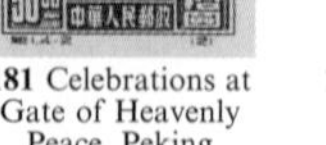
181 Celebrations at Gate of Heavenly Peace, Peking

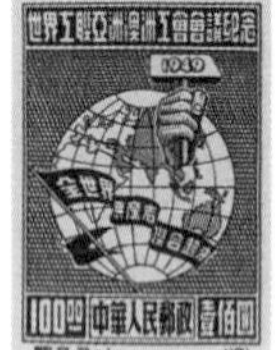
182 Globe, Fist and Banner

1949. Celebration of First Session of Chinese People's Political Conference.
1401 **181** $30 blue . . . . 1·75 1·50
1402 $50 red . . . . 1·90 1·50
1403 $100 green . . . . . . 1·90 1·50
1404 $200 purple . . . . . . 2·00 1·50

1949. World Federation of Trade Unions. Asiatic and Australasian Congress, Peking.
1405 **182** $100 red . . . . 4·50 3·50
1406 $300 green . . . . . . 4·50 2·50
1407 $500 blue . . . . 4·50 3·50

183 Conference Hall

184 Mao Tse-tung

1950. Chinese People's Political Conference.
1408 **183** $50 red . . . . 3·50 2·50
1409 $100 blue . . . . 3·50 2·50
1410 **184** $300 purple . . . . . . 3·50 2·50
1411 $500 green . . . . . . 3·50 2·50

185 Gate of Heavenly Peace, Peking

1950.
1412 **185** $200 green . . . . . . 8·00 50
1413 $300 lake 20 80
1414 $500 red 20 20
1415 $800 orange . . . . . 60·00 30
1420a $1,000 lilac . . . . . . 1·00 20
1417 $2,000 olive . . . . . 7·00 15
1420b $3,000 brown . . . . . 1·00 40
1418 $5,000 pink 10 60
1419 $8,000 blue . . . . . 10 12·00
1420c $10,000 brown . . . . . 1·00 30
See also Nos. 1481a/7 and 1493/8.

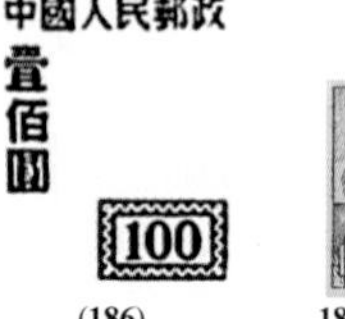
(186)

187 Harvesters and Ox

1950. Surch as T **186**. Perf or roul.
1427 **148** $100 on (–) mauve . . . 40 1·25
1428 **149** $200 on (–) red . . . . 1·75 1·00
1429 **147** $300 on (–) green . . . 15 1·50
1424 **146** $500 on (–) orange . . . 30 15
1430 $800 on (–) orange . . . 3·25 30
1426 $1,000 on (–) orange . . 20 20

1950. Unissued stamp of East China surch.
1431 **187** $20,000 on $10,000 red £400 32·00

188 Mao Tse-tung, Flag and Parade

1950. Foundation of People's Republic on 1 October 1949.
1432 **188** $800 red, yellow & green 25·00 7·75
1433 $1,000 red, yellow & brn 25·00 7·75
1434 $2,000 red, yellow & pur 30·00 7·25
1435 $3,000 red, yellow & blue . . . . 30·00 9·25

中國人民郵政 伍拾圓 ☆ 50
(189)

中國人民郵政 壹佰圓 ★★ 100
(190)

1950. Stamps of North Eastern Provinces surch as T **189**.
1436 **5** $50 on 20c. green . . . . 4·00 5·00
1437 $50 on 25c. brown . . . . 2·25 3·00
1438 $50 on 50c. orange 50 50
1439 $100 on $2.50 blue 50 50
1440 $100 on $3 brown . . . . 3·25 3·00
1441 $100 on $4 brown . . . . 3·25 5·00
1442 $100 on $5 green . . . . 3·25 2·75
1443 $100 on $10 red . . . . 11·50 7·50
1444 $400 on $20 green . . . . 70·00 32·00
1445 $400 on $44 red . . . . 2·00 3·00
1446 $400 on $65 green . . . . £110 60·00
1447 $400 on $100 green . . . . 30·00 7·50
1448 $400 on $200 brown . . . . 60·00 14·00
1449 $400 on $300 green . . . . 60·00 15·00

1950. Nos. 1344/7 and unissued values of Nationalist China (Whistling Swans) surch as T **190**.
1450 **169** $50 on 10c. blue 10 50
1451 $100 on 16c. green . . 10 35
1452 $100 on 50c. green . . 20 20
1453 $200 on $1 orange . . 20 20
1453a $200 on $2 blue . . . . 6·00 50
1454 $400 on $5 red 20 30
1455 $400 on $10 green . . . 40 65
1455a $400 on $20 purple . . 50 95
Nos. 1451/2 are imperf.

191 "Peace" (after Picasso)

192 Gate of Heavenly Peace, Peking

1950. Peace Campaign (1st issue).
1456 **191** $400 brown . . . . . . 12·00 4·50
1457 $800 green . . . . . . 12·00 4·50
1458 $2,000 blue . . . . . . 12·00 5·00
See also Nos. 1510/12 and 1590/2.

1950. Clouds redrawn.
1481a **192** $100 blue 20 20
1482 $200 green . . . . . . 7·50 1·25
1483 $300 lake 20 80
1483a $400 green . . . . . . 7·50 20
1484 $500 red 30 20
1462 $800 orange . . . . . 12·00 10
1485a $1,000 violet 30 25
1463 $2,000 olive . . . . . 4·00 30
1486a $3,000 brown . . . . . 40 1·00
1487 $5,000 pink . . . . . 40 1·25

193 Flag of People's Republic

194 "Communications"

1950. 1st Anniv of People's Republic. Flag in red, yellow and brown.
1464 **193** $100 violet . . . . . . 15·00 4·00
1465 $400 brown . . . . . . 15·00 4·00
1466 $800 green (44 × 53 mm) 15·00 4·00
1467 $1,000 olive . . . . . . 20·00 8·00
1468 $2,000 blue . . . . . . 35·00 10·00

1950. 1st All-China Postal Conference.
1469 **194** $400 brown and green 7·25 3·50
1470 $800 green and red . . . 7·25 1·75

195 Stalin greets Mao Tse-tung

1950. Sino-Soviet Treaty.
1471 **195** $400 red . . . . 8·00 6·00
1472 $800 green . . . . . . 10·00 2·75
1473 $2,000 blue . . . . . . 14·00 5·00

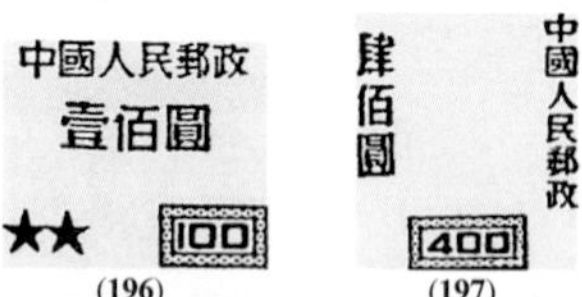
(196) (197)

1950. Nos. EC364/5a, EC367 and EC370/1 of East China People's Post surch as T **196**.
1474 $50 on $10 blue 15 40
1475 $100 on $15 red 10 25
1476 $300 on $50 red 10 25
1477 $400 on $1,600 purple . . . 2·75 1·25
1478 $400 on $2,000 lilac . . . . 1·00 70

1950. Stamps of East China surch as T **197**.
1479 EC **112** $50 on $10 blue . . 10 45
1480 $400 on $15 red . . 10 35
1481 $400 on $2,000 green 2·50 50

198 Temple of Heaven and Ilyushin Il-18

1951. Air.
1488 **198** $1,000 red . . . . 35 1·00
1489 $3,000 green 40 75
1490 $5,000 orange 80 75
1491 $10,000 green and purple 1·60 1·40
1492 $30,000 brn and blue . . 3·50 3·50

1951. Pink network background.
1493 **185** $10,000 brown . . . . . 75 5·00
1494 $20,000 olive . . . . . 1·40 2·25
1495 $30,000 green . . . . . 60·00 35·00
1496 $50,000 violet . . . . . 60·00 22·00
1497 $100,000 red £3000 £120
1498 $200,000 blue £2500 £200

(200)

201 Mao Tse-tung

1951. Surch as T **200**. Perf or roul.
1503 **148** $5 on (–) mauve . . . . 3·25 1·00
1500 **147** $10 on (–) green 25 75
1501 **149** $15 on (–) red 20 75
1506 **146** $25 on (–) orange . . . 70 75

1951. 30th Anniv of Chinese Communist Party.
1507 **201** $400 brown . . . . . . 3·75 2·50
1508 $500 green . . . . . . 4·25 2·50
1509 $800 red . . . . 5·00 1·50

202 Dove of Peace, after Picasso

1951. Peace Campaign (2nd issue).
1510 **202** $400 brown . . . . . . 10·00 4·00
1511 $800 green . . . . . . 10·00 2·50
1512 $1,000 violet . . . . . . 10·00 2·75

(203)

204 National Emblem

1951. Money Order stamps as North China, Type NC **77**, surch with T **203**. Perf or roul.
1513 $50 on $2 green . . . . . . 75 2·00
1515 $50 on $5 orange 30 70
1517 $50 on $50 grey 20 15

1951. National Emblem Issue. Yellow network background.
1519 **204** $100 blue . . . . 4·00 2·25
1520 $200 brown . . . . . . 4·00 2·40
1521 $400 orange . . . . . . 5·00 1·60
1522 $500 green . . . . . . 5·25 1·60
1523 $800 red . . . . 5·25 1·60

205 Lu Hsun

1951. 15th Death Anniv of Lu Hsun (author).
1524 **205** $400 violet . . . . . . 3·50 2·00
1525 $800 green . . . . . . 5·50 1·00

206 Rebels at Chintien

1951. Centenary of Taiping Rebellion.
1526 **206** $400 green . . . . . . 5·50 3·25
1527 $800 red . . . . 5·50 2·50
1528 – $800 orange . . . . . . 5·50 2·50
1529 – $1,000 blue . . . . . . 5·50 2·75
DESIGN: Nos. 1528/9, Coin and Documents of Taiping "Heavenly Kingdom of Great Peace".

207 Peasants and Tractor

1952. Agrarian Reform.

1530	**207**	$100 red	4·00	2·25
1531		$200 blue	4·00	2·25
1532		$400 brown	4·50	2·00
1533		$800 green	4·50	1·25

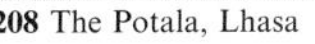

208 The Potala, Lhasa 209 "Child Protection"

1952. Liberation of Tibet.

1534	**208**	$400 red	5·50	1·60
1535	–	$800 green	5·50	1·60
1536	**208**	$800 red	5·50	1·60
1537	–	$1,000 violet	5·50	1·60

DESIGN: Nos. 1535, 1537 Tibetan ploughing with yaks.

1952. Int Child Protection Conference, Vienna.

1538	**209**	$400 green	60	10
1539		$800 blue	60	10

210 Hammer and Sickle 211 Gymnast

1952. Labour Day. Dated "1952".

1540	**210**	$800 red	20	10
1541	–	$800 green	20	10
1542	–	$800 brown	20	10

DESIGNS: No. 1541, Hand and dove; No. 1542, Hammer, dove and ear of corn.

1952. Gymnastics by Radio. As T **211**.

1543	$400 red (14–17)	3·00	1·00
1544	$400 deep blue (18–21)	3·00	1·00
1545	$400 purple (22–25)	3·00	1·00
1546	$400 green (26–29)	3·00	1·00
1547	$400 red (30–33)	3·00	1·00
1548	$400 blue (34–37)	3·00	1·00
1549	$400 orange (38–41)	3·00	1·00
1550	$400 violet (42–45)	3·00	1·00
1551	$400 bistre (46–49)	3·00	1·00
1552	$400 pale blue (50–53)	3·00	1·00

DESIGNS: Various gymnastic exercises, the stamps in each colour being arranged in blocks of four throughout the sheet, each block showing four stages of the exercise depicted. Where two stages are the same, the stamps differ only in the serial number in brackets, in the right-hand corner of the bottom margin of the stamp. The serial numbers are shown above after the colours of the stamps.

Prices are for single stamps.

212 "A Winter Hunt" (A.D. 386–580)

1952. "Glorious Mother Country" (1st issue). Tun Huang Mural Paintings.

1553	**212**	$800 sepia	50	30
1554	–	$800 brown	50	30
1555	–	$800 slate	50	30
1556	–	$800 purple	50	30

PAINTINGS: No. 1554, "Benefactor" (A.D. 581–617). No. 1555, "Celestial Flight" (A.D. 618–906). No. 1556, "Tiger" (A.D. 618–906).

See also Nos. 1565/8, 1593/96, 1601/4 and 1628/31.

213 Marco Polo Bridge, Lukouchiao

1952. 15th Anniv of War with Japan.

1557	**213**	$800 blue	75	30
1558	–	$800 green	75	30
1559	–	$800 plum	75	30
1560	–	$800 red	75	30

DESIGNS (dated "1937–1952"): No. 1558, Victory at Pinghsingkwan; No. 1559, Departure of New Fourth Army from Central China; No. 1560, Mao Tse-tung and Chu The.

214 Airman, Sailor and Soldier 217 Dove of Peace over Pacific Ocean

216 Huai River Barrage

1952. 25th Anniv of People's Liberation Army.

1561	**214**	$800 red	30	25
1562	–	$800 green	30	25
1563	–	$800 violet	50	30
1564	–	$800 brown	50	30

DESIGNS—HORIZ: No. 1562, Soldier, tanks and guns; 1563, Sailor and destroyers; 1564, Pilot, Ilyushin Il-4 DB-3 bomber and Mikoyan Gurevich MiG-15 jet fighters.

1952. "Glorious Mother Country" (2nd issue).

1565	**216**	$800 violet	25	10
1566	–	$800 red	25	10
1567	–	$800 purple	30	10
1568	–	$800 green	30	10

DESIGNS: No. 1566, Chungking–Chengtu railway viaduct; 1567, Oil refinery; 1568, Tractor, disc harrows and combine drill.

1952. Asia and Pacific Ocean Peace Conference.

1569	**217**	$400 purple	50	25
1570	–	$800 orange	50	25
1571	**217**	$800 red	60	30
1572	–	$2,500 green	60	30

DESIGNS—HORIZ: Nos. 1570 and 1572, Doves and globe.

218 Peasants collecting food for the Front

1952. 2nd Anniv of Chinese Volunteer Force in Korea.

1573	–	$800 blue	50	25
1574	**218**	$800 red	50	25
1575	–	$800 violet	50	30
1576	–	$800 brown	60	30

DESIGNS (dated "1950–1952"): HORIZ: No. 1573, Marching troops. No. 1575, Infantry attack. No. 1576, Meeting of Chinese and North Korean soldiers.

220 Textile Worker

1953. International Women's Day.

1578	**220**	$800 red	30	25
1579	–	$800 green	30	25

DESIGN: No. 1579, Woman harvesting grain.

221 Shepherdess 222 Karl Marx

1953.

1580	–	$50 purple	70	15
1581	**221**	$200 green	1·40	35
1582	–	$250 blue	5·00	2·00
1583	–	$800 turquoise	75	10
1584	–	$1,600 grey	70	25
1585	–	$2,000 orange	2·25	10

DESIGNS: $50, Mill girl; $250, Carved lion; $800, Lathe-operator; $1,600, Miners; $2, Old Palace, Peking.

1953. 135th Birth Anniv of Karl Marx.

1586	**222**	$400 brown	70	25
1587		$800 green	70	25

223 Workers and Flags 224 Dove of Peace

1953. 7th National Labour Union Conference.

1588	**223**	$400 blue	25	20
1589		$800 red	25	20

1953. Peace Campaign (3rd issue).

1590	**224**	$250 green	50	30
1591		$400 brown	50	30
1592		$800 violet	60	30

225 Horseman and Steed (A.D. 386–580)

1953. "Glorious Mother Country" (3rd issue).

1593	**225**	$800 green	50	10
1594	–	$800 orange	50	10
1595	–	$800 blue	50	10
1596	–	$800 red	50	10

PAINTINGS: No. 1594, Court players (A.D. 386–580). No. 1595, Battle scene (A.D. 581–617). No. 1596, Ox-drawn palanquin (A.D. 618–906).

226 Mao Tse-tung and Stalin at Kremlin

1953. 35th Anniv of Russian Revolution.

1597	**226**	$800 green	25	10
1598	–	$800 red	25	10
1599	–	$800 blue	75	10
1600	–	$800 brown	75	10

DESIGNS—HORIZ: No. 1598, Lenin addressing revolutionaries. VERT: No. 1599, Statue of Stalin; No. 1600, Stalin making speech.

227 Compass (300 B.C.) 228 Rabelais (writer)

1953. "Glorious Mother Country" (4th issue). Scientific instruments.

1601	**227**	$800 black	25	10
1602	–	$800 green	25	10
1603	–	$800 slate	30	10
1604	–	$800 brown	30	10

DESIGNS: No. 1602, Seismoscope (A.D. 132); 1603, Drum cart for measuring distances (A.D. 300); 1604, Armillary sphere (A.D. 1437).

1953. Famous Men.

1605	**228**	$250 green	40	25
1606	–	$400 purple	40	25
1607	–	$800 blue	40	30
1608	–	$2,200 brown	40	30

PORTRAITS: $400, Jose Marti (Cuban revolutionary). $800, Chu Yuan (poet). $2,200, Copernicus (astronomer).

229 Flax Mill, Harbin

1954. Industrial Development.

1609	**229**	$100 brown	25	15
1610	–	$200 green	30	15
1611	–	$250 violet	25	15
1612	–	$400 sepia	25	15
1613	–	$800 purple	25	15
1614	–	$800 blue	25	15
1615	–	$2,000 red	25	15
1616	–	$3,200 brown	25	15

DESIGNS: No. 1610, Tangku Harbour; 1611, Tienshui–Lanchow Railway; 1612, Heavy machine works; 1613, Blast furnace; 1614, Open-cast mines, Fuhsin; 1615, North-East Electric power station; 1616, Geological survey team.

230 Gate of Heavenly Peace, Peking 231 Statue of Lenin and Stalin at Gorki

232 Lenin Speaking 233 Painted Pottery (c. 2000 B.C.)

1954.

1617	**230**	$50 red	10	10
1618		$100 blue	10	10
1619		$200 green	10	10
1620		$250 blue	2·25	50
1621		$400 green	45	10
1622		$800 orange	10	10
1623		$1,600 grey	10	10
1624		$2,000 olive	10	10

1954. 30th Death Anniv of Lenin.

1625	**231**	$400 green	90	45
1626	–	$800 brown	1·75	40
1627	**232**	$2,000 red	90	30

DESIGN: (25 × 37 mm) $800, Lenin (full-face portrait).

1954. "Glorious Mother Country" (5th issue).

1628	**233**	$800 brown	25	20
1629	–	$800 black	25	20
1630	–	$800 turquoise	30	20
1631	–	$800 lake	30	20

DESIGNS—As Type **233**: No. 1629, Musical stone (1200 B.C.); 1630, Bronze basin (816 B.C.); 1631, Lacquered wine cup and cosmetic tray (403–221 B.C.).

234 Heavy Rolling Mill 235 Statue of Stalin

1954. Anshan Steel Works.

1632	–	$400 turquoise	55	25
1633	**234**	$800 purple	55	25

DESIGN: $400, Seamless steel-tubing mill.

1954. 1st Death Anniv of Stalin.

1634	**235**	$400 black	1·60	30
1635	–	$800 sepia	75	30
1636	–	$2,000 red	1·10	45

DESIGNS—VERT: $800, Full-face portrait of Stalin (26 × 37 mm). HORIZ: $2, Stalin and hydro-electric station (42½ × 25 mm).

236 Exhibition Building

1954. Russian Economic and Cultural Exn, Peking.

1637	**236**	$800 brown on yellow	8·50	2·00

237 The Universal Fixture **238** Woman Worker

239 Rejoicing Crowds

1954. Workers' Inventions.
1638 **237** $400 green 50 40
1639 – $800 red 50 30
DESIGN: $800, The reverse repeater.

1954. 1st Session of National Congress.
1640 **238** $400 purple 30 20
1641 **239** $800 red 30 20

240 "New Constitution"

1954. Constitution Commemoration.
1642 **240** $400 brown on buff . . 20 15
1643 $800 red on yellow . . . 20 15

241 Pylons **242** Nurse and Red Cross Worker

1955. Development of Overhead Transmission of Electricity.
1644 **241** $800 blue . . . . 1·50 50

1955. 50th Anniv of Chinese Red Cross.
1645 **242** 8f. red and green . . . . 8·50 1·40

243 Miner **244** Gate of Heavenly Peace, Peking

1955.
1646 **243** ½f. brown 85 10
1647 – 1f. purple 85 10
1648 – 2f. green . . . . 3·00 10
1648a – 2½f. blue . . . . . . 1·75 10
1649 – 4f. green . . . . 2·40 10
1650 – 8f. red . . . . 6·00 10
1650b – 10f. red . . . . . . 11·00 35
1651 – 20f. blue . . . . . . 11·00 40
1652 – 50f. grey . . . . 9·75 55
1653 **244** 1y. red . . . . 1·25 10
1654 2y. brown . . . . . . 1·40 10
1655 5y. grey . . . . 2·75 35
1656 10y. red . . . . 4·75 1·50
1657 20y. violet . . . . . . 10·00 4·50
DESIGNS—As Type **243**: 1f. Lathe operator; 2f. Airman; 2½ f. Nurse; 4f. Soldier; 8f. Foundry worker; 10f. Chemist; 20f. Farm girl; 50f. Sailor.

246 Workmen and Industrial Plant **247** Chang-Heng (A.D. 78–139, astronomer)

1955. 5th Anniv of Sino–Russian Treaty.
1658 – 8f. brown . . . . 5·00 1·00
1659 **246** 20f. olive . . . . 7·00 1·00
DESIGN—HORIZ: (37 × 32 mm): 8f. Stalin and Mao Tse-tung.

1955. Scientists of Ancient China.
1660 **247** 8f. sepia on buff . . . . 2·25 25
1661 – 8f. blue on buff . . . . 2·25 25
1662 – 8f. black on buff . . . . 2·25 25
1663 – 8f. purple on buff . . . 2·25 25
PORTRAITS: No. 1661, Tsu Chung-chi (429–500, mathematician). No. 1662, Chang-Sui (683–727, astronomer). No. 1663, Li-Shih-chen (1518–1593, pharmacologist).

248 Foundry

1955. Five Year Plan. Frames in black.
1664 **248** 8f. red and orange . . . 40 10
1665 – 8f. brown and yellow . . 40 10
1666 – 8f. yellow and black . . 40 10
1667 – 8f. violet and blue . . . 40 10
1668 – 8f. yellow and brown . . 40 10
1669 – 8f. yellow and red . . . 40 10
1670 – 8f. grey and blue 40 10
1671 – 8f. orange and black . . 40 10
1672 – 8f. yellow and brown . . 40 10
1673 – 8f. red and orange . . . 40 10
1674 – 8f. yellow and green . . 40 10
1675 – 8f. red and yellow . . . 40 10
1676 – 8f. yellow and grey . . . 40 15
1677 – 8f. yellow and blue . . . 40 10
1678 – 8f. orange and blue . . . 40 10
1679 – 8f. yellow and brown . . 40 10
1680 – 8f. red and brown . . . 40 10
1681 – 8f. yellow and brown . . 40 10
DESIGNS—No. 1665, Electricity pylons; No. 1666, Mining machinery; No. 1667, Oil tankers and derricks; No. 1668, Heavy machinery workshop; No. 1669, Factory guard and industrial plant; No. 1670, Textile machinery; No. 1671, Factory workers; No. 1672, Combine-harvester; No. 1673, Dairy herd and farm girl; No. 1674, Dam; No. 1675, Artists decorating pottery; No. 1676, Lorry; No. 1677, Freighter and wharf; No. 1678, Surveyors; No. 1679, Students; No. 1680, Man, woman and child; No. 1681, Workers' rest home.

249 Lenin

1955. 85th Birth Anniv of Lenin.
1682 **249** 8f. blue . . . . 7·50 25
1683 20f. lake . . . . 7·50 1·40

250 Engels

1955. 60th Death Anniv of Engels.
1684 **250** 8f. red . . . . 7·00 25
1685 20f. sepia . . . . 7·00 1·25

251 Capture of Lu Ting Bridge

1955. 20th Anniv of Long March by Communist Army.
1686 **251** 8f. red . . . . 5·00 60
1687 – 8f. blue . . . . 8·00 1·25
DESIGN—VERT: (28 × 46 mm): No. 1687, Crossing the Ta Hsueh Mountains.

252 Convoy of Lorries

1956. Opening of Sikang–Tibet and Tsinghai–Tibet Highways.
1688 **252** 4f. blue 50 35
1689 – 8f. brown 50 20
1690 – 8f. red 50 20
DESIGNS—VERT: (21 × 42 mm): No. 1689, Suspension bridge: Tatu River. HORIZ: As T **252**: No. 1690, Opening ceremony, Lhasa.

254 Gate of Heavenly Peace

1956. Views of Peking.
1691 – 4f. red . . . . 3·00 10
1692 – 4f. green . . . . 3·00 10
1693 **254** 8f. red . . . . 3·00 10
1694 – 8f. blue . . . . 3·00 10
1695 – 8f. brown . . . . 3·00 10
VIEWS: No. 1691, Summer Palace; 1692, Peihai Park; 1694, Temple of Heaven; 1695, Great Throne Hall, Tai Ho Palace.

255 Salt Production

1956. Archaeological Discoveries at Chengtu.
1696 **255** 4f. green 40 10
1697 – 4f. black 40 10
1698 – 8f. sepia 50 10
1699 – 8f. sepia 40 10
DESIGNS—HORIZ: (Brick carvings of Tung Han Dynasty, A.D. 25–200): No. 1697, Residence; No. 1698, Hunting and farming; No. 1699, Carriage crossing bridge.

256 **257** Gate of Heavenly Peace, Peking

1956. National Savings.
1700 **256** 4f. buff . . . . 4·50 30
1701 8f. red . . . . 5·50 25

1956. 8th National Communist Party Congress.
1702 **257** 4f. green . . . . 3·00 30
1703 8f. red . . . . 4·50 30
1704 16f. red . . . . 5·50 65

258 Dr. Sun Yat-sen **259** Putting the Shot

1956. 90th Birth Anniv of Dr. Sun Yat-sen.
1705 **258** 4f. brown . . . . 7·00 25
1706 8f. blue . . . . 6·00 1·40

1955. 1st Chinese Workers' Athletic Meeting, 1955. Inscr "1955". Flower in red and green; inscr in brown.
1707 **259** 4f. lake . . . . 1·10 10
1708 – 4f. purple (Weightlifting) 1·10 35
1709 – 8f. green (Sprinting) . . 1·50 10
1710 – 8f. blue (Football) . . . 2·00 40
1711 – 8f. brown (Cycling) . . . 1·50 10

260 Assembly Line

1957. Lorry Production.
1712 – 4f. brown 25 10
1713 **260** 8f. blue 40 10
DESIGN: 4f. Changchun motor plant.

261 Nanchang Revolutionaries

1957. 30th Anniv of People's Liberation Army.
1714 **261** 4f. violet . . . . 7·75 60
1715 – 4f. green . . . . 7·75 60
1716 – 8f. brown . . . . 7·75 50
1717 – 8f. blue . . . . 7·75 50
DESIGNS: No. 1715, Meeting of Red Armies at Chinkangshan; No. 1716, Liberation Army crossing the Yellow River; No. 1717, Liberation of Nanking.

262 Congress Emblem **263** Yangtse River Bridge

1957. 4th W.F.T.U. Congress, Leipzig.
1718 **262** 8f. brown . . . . 4·00 50
1719 22f. blue . . . . 3·00 50

1957. Opening of Yangtse River Bridge, Wuhan.
1720 **263** 8f. red 50 10
1721 – 20f. blue . . . . 1·00 15
DESIGN: 20f. Aerial view of bridge.

264 Fireworks over Kremlin **265** Airport Scene

1957. 40th Anniv of Russian Revolution.
1722 **264** 4f. red . . . . 4·25 20
1723 – 8f. sepia . . . . 4·25 20
1724 – 20f. green . . . . . . 5·50 30
1725 – 22f. brown . . . . . . 5·50 50
1726 – 32f. blue . . . . 9·25 1·25
DESIGNS: 8f. Soviet emblem, globe and broken chains; 20f. Dove of Peace and plant; 22f. Hands supporting book bearing portraits of Marx and Lenin; 32f. Electricity power pylon.

1957. Air.
1727 **265** 16f. blue . . . . 4·50 30
1728 – 28f. olive . . . . 10·00 2·00
1729 – 35f. black . . . . 13·00 1·75
1730 – 52f. blue . . . . 15·00 75
DESIGNS—Lisunov Li-2 over: 28f. mountain highway; 35f. railway tracks; 52f. collier at station.

266 Yellow River Dam and Power Station

1957. Harnessing of the Yellow River.
1731 – 4f. orange . . . . 7·75 30
1732 **266** 4f. blue . . . . 7·75 1·00
1733 – 8f. lake . . . . 7·75 70
1734 – 8f. green . . . . 7·75 30
DESIGNS: No. 1731, Map of Yellow River; No. 1733, Yellow River ferry; No. 1734, Aerial view of irrigation on Yellow River.

267 Ploughing

1957. Co-operative Agriculture. Multicoloured.
1735 8f. Farmer enrolling for farm 50 10
1736 8f. Type **267** 50 10
1737 8f. Tree-planting 50 10
1738 8f. Harvesting 50 10

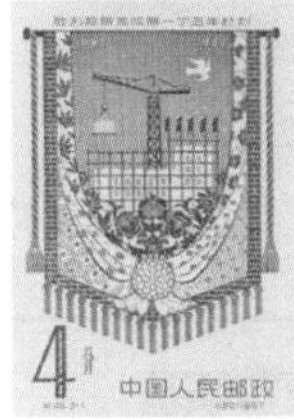

268 "Peaceful Construction" **269** High Peak Pagoda, Tenfeng

1958. Completion of First Five Year Plan.
1739 **268** 4f. green and cream . . 50 10
1740 – 8f. red and cream . . . 50 10
1741 – 16f. blue and cream . . 50 10
DESIGNS: 8f. "Industry and Agriculture" (grapple and wheat-sheaves); 16f. "Communications and Transport" (steam train on viaduct and ship).

1958. Ancient Chinese Pagodas.
1742 **269** 8f. brown . . . . 1·40 25
1743 – 8f. blue . . . . 1·40 10
1744 – 8f. brown . . . . 1·40 15
1745 – 8f. green . . . . 1·40 10
DESIGNS: No. 1743, One Thousand League Pagoda, Tali; No. 1744, Buddha Pagoda, Yinghsien; No. 1745, Flying Rainbow Pagoda, Hungchao.

270 Trilobite of Hao Li Shan **271**

1958. Chinese Fossils.
1746 **270** 4f. blue 85 10
1747 – 8f. sepia 85 10
1748 – 16f. green 85 35
DESIGNS: 8f. Dinosaur of Lufeng; 16f. "Sinomegaceros pachyospeus" (deer).

1958. Unveiling of People's Heroes Monument, Peking.
1749 **271** 8f. red . . . . 12·00 1·40

272 Karl Marx (after Zhukov) **273** Cogwheels of Industry

1958. 140th Birth Anniv of Karl Marx.
1750 **272** 8f. brown . . . . 7·50 1·40
1751 – 22f. myrtle . . . . . . 7·50 1·00
DESIGN: 22f. Marx addressing German workers' Educational Association, London.

1958. 8th All-China Trade Union Congress, Peking.
1752 **273** 4f. blue . . . . 6·50 1·75
1753 8f. purple . . . . 6·50 50

274 Federation Emblem **275** Mother and Child

1958. 4th International Democratic Women's Federation Congress, Vienna.
1754 **274** 8f. blue . . . . 8·50 40
1755 20f. green . . . . 8·50 2·00

1958. Chinese Children. Multicoloured.
1756 8f. Type **275** . . . . 9·75 1·10
1757 8f. Watering sunflowers . . 9·75 1·10
1758 8f. "Hide and seek" . . . . 9·75 1·10
1759 8f. Children sailing boat . . 9·75 1·10

276 Kuan Han-ching (playwright) **277** Peking Planetarium

1958. 700th Anniv of Works of Kuan Han-ching.
1760 – 4f. green on cream . . . 6·00 2·50
1761 **276** 8f. purple on cream . . 8·00 1·00
1762 – 20f. black on cream . . 12·00 1·25
DESIGNS: Scenes from Han-ching's comedies: 4f. "The Butterfly Dream"; 20f. "The Riverside Pavilion".

1958. Peking Planetarium.
1763 **277** 8f. green . . . . 3·50 80
1764 – 20f. blue . . . . 5·00 40
DESIGN: 20f. Planetarium in operation.

278 Marx and Engels **279** Tundra Swan and Radio Pylon

1958. 110th Anniv of "Communist Manifesto".
1765 **278** 4f. purple . . . . 6·00 1·75
1766 – 8f. blue . . . . 6·00 40
DESIGN: 8f. Front cover of first German "Communist Manifesto".

1958. Organization of Socialist Countries' Postal Administrations Conference, Moscow.
1767 **279** 4f. blue . . . . 7·50 1·00
1768 8f. green . . . . 7·50 75

280 Peony and Doves **281** Chang Heng's Weather-cock

1958. International Disarmament Conf, Stockholm.
1769 **280** 4f. red . . . . 10·00 2·00
1770 – 8f. green . . . . 10·00 2·00
1771 – 22f. brown . . . . . . 7·50 1·75
DESIGNS: 8f. Olive branch; 22f. Atomic symbol and factory plant.

1958. Chinese Meteorology.
1772 **281** 8f. black on yellow . . . 80 10
1773 – 8f. black on blue 80 10
1774 – 8f. black on green . . . 80 10
DESIGNS: No. 1773. Meteorological balloon; No. 1774, Typhoon signal-tower.

282 Union Emblem within figure "5" **283** Chrysanthemum

1958. 5th International Students' Union Congress, Peking.
1775 **282** 8f. purple . . . . 7·50 50
1776 22f. green . . . . 5·50 1·00

1958. Flowers.
1777 – 1½f. mauve (Peony) . . . 4·00 35
1778 – 3f. green (Lotus) . . . . 14·00 1·40
1779 **283** 5f. orange . . . . 2·00 35

284 Telegraph Building, Peking

1958. Opening of Peking Telegraph Building.
1780 **284** 4f. olive . . . . 1·50 30
1781 8f. red . . . . 2·75 20

285 Exhibition Emblem and Symbols

1958. National Exhibition of Industry and Communications.
1782 **285** 8f. green . . . . 6·75 80
1783 – 8f. red . . . . 6·75 80
1784 – 8f. brown . . . . 6·75 80
DESIGNS: No. 1783, Chinese dragon riding the waves; No. 1784, Horses in the sky.

286 Labourer on Reservoir Site **287** Sputnik and ancient Theodolite

1958. Inauguration of Ming Tombs Reservoir.
1785 **286** 4f. brown 50 10
1786 – 8f. blue 50 10
DESIGN: 8f. Ming Tombs Reservoir.

1958. Russian Sputnik Commemoration.
1787 **287** 4f. red . . . . 3·25 20
1788 – 8f. violet . . . . 3·25 20
1789 – 10f. green . . . . 3·50 1·10
DESIGNS: 8f. Third Russian sputnik encircling globe; 10f. Three Russian sputniks encircling globe.

288 Chinese and Korean Soldiers

1958. Return of Chinese People's Volunteers from Korea.
1790 **288** 8f. purple . . . . 1·10 10
1791 – 8f. brown . . . . 1·10 10
1792 – 8f. red . . . . 1·10 10
DESIGNS: No. 1791, Chinese soldier embracing Korean woman; No. 1792, Girl presenting bouquet to Chinese soldier.

289 Forest Landscape

1958. Afforestation Campaign.
1793 **289** 8f. green . . . . 3·00 75
1794 – 8f. slate . . . . 3·00 20
1795 – 8f. violet . . . . 3·00 20
1796 – 8f. blue . . . . 3·00 20
DESIGNS—VERT: No. 1794, Forest patrol. HORIZ: No. 1795, Tree-felling by power-saw. No. 1796, Tree planting.

290 Atomic Reactor

1958. Inauguration of China's First Atomic Reactor.
1797 **290** 8f. blue . . . . 4·50 40
1798 – 20f. brown . . . . 7·50 2·00
DESIGN: 20f. Cyclotron in action.

291 Children with Model Aircraft **292** Rooster

1958. Aviation Sports.
1799 **291** 4f. red 60 10
1800 – 8f. myrtle 60 10
1801 – 10f. sepia 60 10
1802 – 20f. slate . . . . 1·75 15
DESIGNS: 8f. Gliders. 10f. Parachutists; 20f. Yakovlev Yak-18U trainers.

1959. Chinese Folk Paper-cuts.
1803 – 8f. black on violet . . . 7·00 50
1804 – 8f. black on green . . . 7·00 50
1805 **292** 8f. black on red . . . . 7·00 50
1806 – 8f. black on blue . . . . 7·00 50
DESIGNS: No. 1803, Camel. 1804, Pomegranate; 1806, Actress on stage.

293 Mao Tse-tung and Steel Workers **294** Chinese Women

1959. Steel Production Progress. Inscr "1958".
1807 **293** 4f. red . . . . 3·50 1·00
1808 – 8f. purple . . . . 4·50 80
1809 – 10f. red . . . . 6·00 1·00
DESIGNS: 8f. Battery of steel furnaces; 10f. Steel "blowers" and workers.

1959. International Women's Day.
1810 **294** 8f. green on cream . . . 1·00 35
1811 – 22f. mauve on cream . . 1·50 10
DESIGN: 22f. Russian and Chinese women.

295 Natural History Museum, Peking **296** Barley

1959. Opening of Natural History Museum, Peking.
1812 **295** 4f. turquoise 80 10
1813 8f. sepia 80 10

1959. Successful Harvest, 1958.
1814 8f. red (Type **296**) . . . . . 1·90 10
1815 8f. red (Rice) . . . . 1·90 10
1816 8f. red (Cotton) . . . . . . 1·90 10
1817 8f. red (Soya beans, groundnuts and rape) . . 1·90 10

297 Workers with Marx–Lenin Banner **298** Airport Building

1959. Labour Day. Inscr "1889–1959".
1818 **297** 4f. blue . . . . 4·00 80
1819 – 8f. red . . . . 6·00 70
1820 – 22f. green . . . . 5·00 30
DESIGNS: 8f. Hands clasping Red Flag; 22f. "5.1" and workers.

1959. Inauguration of Peking Airport.
1821 **298** 8f. black on lilac . . . . 6·50 95
1822 – 10f. black on green . . . 9·00 30
DESIGN: 10f. Ilyushin Il-14P at airport.

299 Students with Banners **300** F. Joliot-Curie (first President)

1959. 40th Anniv of "May 4th" Students' Rising.
1823 **299** 4f. red, brown and olive 12·00 7·00
1824 – 8f. red, brown & bistre 22·00 2·25
DESIGN: 8f. Workers with banners.

1959. 10th Anniv of World Peace Council.
1825 **300** 8f. purple 4·50 2·00
1826 – 22f. violet 7·50 50
DESIGN: 22f. Silhouettes of European, Chinese and Negro.

301 Stamp Printing Works, Peking

1959. Sino-Czech Co-operation in Postage Stamp Production.
1827 **301** 8f. myrtle 8·50 1·50

302

1959. World Table Tennis Championships, Dortmund.
1828 **302** 4f. blue and black 2·50 30
1829 8f. red and black 4·00 70

303 Moon Rocket **304** "Prologue"

1959. Launching of First Lunar Rocket.
1830 **303** 8f. red, blue & black 13·00 1·75

1959. 1st Anniv of People's Communes.
1831 **304** 8f. red 70 20
1832 – 8f. dull purple 70 20
1833 – 8f. orange 70 20
1834 – 8f. green 70 20
1835 – 8f. blue 70 20
1836 – 8f. olive 70 20
1837 – 8f. blue 70 20
1838 – 8f. mauve 70 20
1839 – 8f. black 70 20
1840 – 8f. green 70 20
1841 – 8f. violet 70 20
1842 – 8f. red 70 20
DESIGNS: No. 1832, Steel worker ("Rural Industries"); No. 1833, Farm girl ("Agriculture"); No. 1834, Salesgirl ("Trade"); No. 1835, Peasant ("Study"); No. 1836, Militiaman ("Militia"); No. 1837, Cook with tray of food ("Community Meals"); No. 1838, Child watering flowers ("Nursery"); No. 1839, Old man with pipe ("Old People's Homes"); No. 1840, Health worker ("Public Health"); No. 1841, Young flautist ("Recreation and Entertainment"); No. 1842, Star-shaped flower ("Epilogue").

305 Mao Tse-tung and Gate of Heavenly Peace, Peking **306** Republican Emblem

1959. 10th Anniv of People's Republic. (a) 1st issue. Inscr "1949–1959". With gum.
1843 **305** 8f. red and brown 10·00 1·75
1844 – 8f. red and blue 7·00 1·75
1845 – 22f. red and green 7·00 1·50
DESIGNS: No. 1844, Marx, Lenin and Kremlin; No. 1845, Dove of peace and globe.

(b) 2nd issue. Emblem in red and yellow; inscriptions in yellow; background colours given.
1846 **306** 4f. turquoise 4·50 2·75
1847 8f. lilac 4·50 40
1848 10f. blue 5·50 50
1849 20f. buff 8·00 1·75

307 Steel Plant

(c) 3rd issue. Inscr "1949–1959". Frames in purple; centre colours given. With gum.
1850 **307** 8f. red 1·25 20
1851 – 8f. drab 1·25 50
1852 – 8f. bistre 1·25 30
1853 – 8f. blue 1·25 30
1854 – 8f. salmon 1·25 30
1855 – 8f. green 1·25 40
1856 – 8f. turquoise 1·25 30
1857 – 8f. lilac 1·25 30
DESIGNS: No. 1851, Coal-mine. No. 1852, Steelmill; No. 1853, Double-decked bridge; No. 1854, Combine-harvester; No. 1855, Dam construction; No. 1856, Textile mill; No. 1857, Chemical works.

308 Rejoicing Populace

(d) 4th Issue. Multicoloured.
1858 8f. Type **308** 2·50 1·00
1859 10f. Rejoicing people and industrial plant (vert) 5·00 40
1860 20f. Tree, banners and people carrying wheat and flowers (vert) 5·00 1·00

309 Mao Tse-tung proclaiming Republic

(e) 5th issue.
1861 **309** 20f. lake 22·00 7·25

310 Boy Bugler ("Summer Camps") **311** Exhibition Emblem and Symbols of Communication

1959. 10th Anniv of Chinese Youth Pioneers.
1862 – 4f. yellow, red & black 3·50 10
1863 **310** 4f. red and blue 3·50 10
1864 – 8f. red and brown 3·50 10
1865 – 8f. red and blue 3·50 10
1866 – 8f. red and green 4·50 10
1867 – 8f. red and purple 4·50 75
DESIGNS: No. 1862, Pioneers' emblem; No. 1864, Schoolgirl with flowers and satchel ("Study"); No. 1865, Girl with rain gauge ("Science"); No. 1866, Boy with sapling ("Forestry"); No. 1867, Girl skater ("Athletic Sports").

1959. National Exhibition of Industry and Communications, Peking. Inscr "1949–1959".
1868 **311** 4f. blue 45 15
1869 – 8f. red 30 15
DESIGN: 8f. Exn emblem and symbols of industry.

312 Cultural Palace of the Nationalities **313** "Statue of Sport"

1959. Inauguration of Cultural Palace of the Nationalities. Peking.
1870 **312** 4f. black and red 4·25 50
1871 8f. black and green 4·25 50

1959. 1st National Games, Peking. Multicoloured.
1872 8f. Type **313** 1·40 30
1873 8f. Parachuting 1·40 30
1874 8f. Pistol-shooting 1·40 30
1875 8f. Diving 1·40 30
1876 8f. Table tennis 1·40 30
1877 8f. Weightlifting 1·40 30
1878 8f. High jumping 1·40 30
1879 8f. Rowing 1·40 30
1880 8f. Running 1·40 30
1881 8f. Basketball 1·40 30
1882 8f. Fencing 1·40 30
1883 8f. Motor cycling 1·40 30
1884 8f. Gymnastics 1·40 30
1885 8f. Cycling 1·40 30
1886 8f. Horse-racing 1·40 30
1887 8f. Football 3·50 1·40

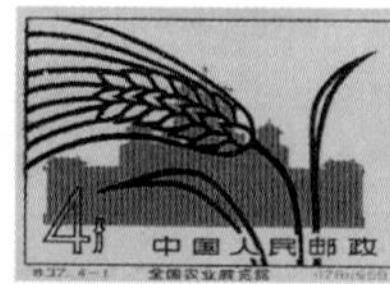
314 Wheat (Main Pavilion)

1960. Opening of National Agricultural Exhibition Hall, Peking.
1888 **314** 4f. black, red & orange 40 20
1889 – 8f. black and blue 40 20
1890 – 10f. black and brown 50 30
1891 – 20f. black and turquoise 1·50 30
DESIGNS: 8f. Meteorological symbols (Meteorological Pavilion); 10f. Cattle (Animal Husbandry Pavilion); 20f. Fishes (Aquatic Products Pavilion).

315 Crossing the Chinsha River

1960. 25th Anniv of Conference during the Long March, Tsunyi, Kweichow.
1892 – 4f. blue 9·00 1·50
1893 – 8f. turquoise 9·00 3·50
1894 **315** 10f. green 18·00 1·50
DESIGNS: 4f. Conference Hall, Tsunyi; 8f. Mao Tse-tung and flags.

316 Clara Zetkin (founder) **317** Chinese and Soviet Workers

1960. 50th Anniv of International Women's Day. Frame and inscriptions black. Centre colours given.
1895 **316** 4f. blue, black & flesh 1·50 40
1896 – 8f. multicoloured 1·50 10
1897 – 10f. multicoloured 1·50 20
1898 – 22f. multicoloured 5·00 40
DESIGNS: 8f. Mother, child and dove; 10f. Woman tractor-driver; 22f. Women of three races.

1960. 10th Anniv of Sino-Soviet Treaty.
1899 **317** 4f. brown 7·00 1·00
1900 – 8f. black, yellow & red 7·00 1·00
1901 – 10f. blue 8·00 3·00
DESIGNS: 8f. Flowers and Sino-Soviet emblems; 10f. Chinese and Soviet soldiers.

318 Flags of Hungary and China **319** Lenin Speaking

1960. 15th Anniv of Hungarian Liberation.
1902 **318** 8f. multicoloured 9·50 1·75
1903 – 8f. red, black and blue 9·50 3·25
DESIGN: No. 1903, Parliament Building, Budapest.

1960. 90th Birth Anniv of Lenin.
1904 **319** 4f. lilac 4·50 75
1905 – 8f. black and red 5·50 2·25
1906 – 20f. brown 11·00 2·00
DESIGNS: 8f. Lenin (portrait); 20f. Lenin talking with Red Guards (after Vasilyev).

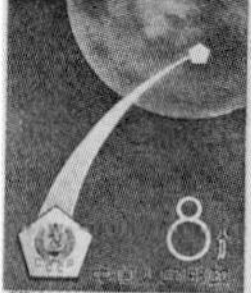
320 "Lunik 2" **321** View of Prague

1960. Lunar Rocket Flights.
1907 **320** 8f. red 4·25 75
1908 – 10f. green ("Lunik 3") 4·25 75

1960. 15th Anniv of Liberation of Czechoslovakia.
1909 – 8f. multicoloured 8·50 1·50
1910 **321** 8f. green 8·50 2·50
DESIGN—VERT: No. 1909, Child pioneers and flags of China and Czechoslovakia.

SERIAL NUMBERS. In this and many later multicoloured sets containing several stamps of the same denomination, the serial number is quoted in brackets to assist identification. This is the last figure in the bottom left corner of the stamp.

322 Narial Bouquet Goldfish

1960. Chinese Goldfish. Multicoloured.
1911 4f. (1) Type **322** 23·00 4·00
1912 4f. (2) Black-backed telescopic-eyed goldfish 27·00 4·00
1913 4f. (3) Bubble-eyed goldfish 27·00 5·00
1914 4f. (4) Ranchu goldfish 8·00 3·00
1915 8f. (5) Pearl-scaled goldfish 40·00 6·00
1916 8f. (6) Black moor goldfish 40·00 6·00
1917 8f. (7) Celestial goldfish 8·00 2·50
1918 8f. (8) Oranda goldfish 8·00 2·50
1919 8f. (9) Purple oranda goldfish 8·00 2·50
1920 8f. (10) Red-capped goldfish 8·00 2·50
1921 8f. (11) Red-capped oranda goldfish 27·00 6·00
1922 8f. (12) Red veil-tailed goldfish 27·00 6·00

323 Sow with Litter

1960. Pig-breeding.
1923 **323** 8f. black and red 15·00 1·50
1924 – 8f. black and green 15·00 1·50
1925 – 8f. black and mauve 15·00 5·00
1926 – 8f. black and olive 19·00 1·50
1927 – 8f. black and orange 19·00 5·00
DESIGNS: No. 1924, Pig being inoculated; No. 1925, Group of pigs; No. 1926, Pig and feeding pens; No. 1927, Pig and crop-bales.

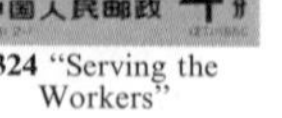

324 "Serving the Workers" **325** N. Korean and Chinese Flags, and Flowers

1960. 3rd National Literary and Art Workers' Congress, Peking. Inscr "1960".
1928 **324** 4f. red, sepia and green 7·00 1·50
1929 – 8f. red, bistre & turq 10·00 2·00
DESIGN: 8f. Inscribed stone seal.

1960. 15th Anniv of Liberation of Korea.
1930 **325** 8f. red, yellow and green 13·00 3·00
1931 – 8f. red, indigo and blue 13·00 3·00
DESIGN: No. 1931, "Flying Horse" of Korea.

326 Peking Railway Station

1960. Opening of New Peking Railway Station.

1932	326	8f. multicoloured	11·00	3·50
1933	–	10f. blue, cream & turq	16·00	4·25

DESIGN: 10f. Steam train arriving at station.

327 Chinese and N. Vietnamese Flags, and Children

328 Worker and Spray Fan

1960. 15th Anniv of N. Vietnam Republic.

1934	327	8f. red, yellow & black	5·50	1·00
1935	–	8f. multicoloured	5·50	2·00

DESIGN—VERT: No. 1935, "Lake of the Returning Sword", Hanoi.

1960. Public Health Campaign.

1936	328	8f. black and orange	2·10	10
1937	–	8f. green and blue	2·10	10
1938	–	8f. brown and blue	2·10	20
1939	–	8f. lake and brown	2·10	20
1940	–	8f. blue and turquoise	2·10	65

DESIGNS: No. 1937, Spraying insecticide; No. 1938, Cleaning windows; No. 1939, Medical examination of child; No. 1940, "Tai Chi Chuan" (Chinese physical drill).

329 Facade of Great Hall

1960. Completion of "Great Hall of the People". Multicoloured.

1941	8f. Type **329**	10·00	2·50
1942	10f. Interior of Great Hall	16·00	4·00

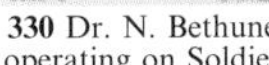

330 Dr. N. Bethune operating on Soldier

331 Friedrich Engels

1960. 70th Birth Anniv of Dr. Norman Bethune (Canadian surgeon with 8th Route Army).

1943	330	8f. grey, black and red	4·25	1·00
1944	–	8f. brown	4·25	30

PORTRAIT. No. 1943 Dr. N. Bethune.

1960. 140th Birth Anniv of Engels.

1945	–	8f. brown	7·00	1·75
1946	331	10f. orange and blue	10·00	2·25

DESIGN: 8f. Engels addressing congress at The Hague.

332 Big "Ju-I"

333 "Yue Jin"

1960. Chrysanthemums. Background colours given. Multicoloured.

1947	–	4f. blue	10·50	1·10
1948	–	4f. pink	21·00	1·10
1949	–	8f. grey	10·50	1·10
1950	332	8f. blue	10·50	1·10
1951	–	8f. green	10·50	1·10
1952	–	8f. violet	10·50	1·10
1953	–	8f. olive	10·50	1·10
1954	–	8f. turquoise	35·00	1·10
1955	–	10f. grey	10·50	1·10
1956	–	10f. brown	10·50	1·10
1957	–	20f. blue	10·50	1·10
1958	–	20f. red	28·00	3·50
1959	–	22f. brown	17·00	7·75
1960	–	22f. red	35·00	12·00
1961	–	30f. green	10·50	5·50
1962	–	30f. mauve	10·50	5·50
1963	–	35f. green	13·00	5·50
1964	–	52f. purple	13·00	9·25

CHRYSANTHEMUMS: No. 1947, "Hwang Shih Pa". No. 1948, "Green Peony". No. 1949, "Er Chiao". No. 1951, "Ju-I" with Golden Hooks. No. 1952, "Golden Peony". No. 1953, "Generalissimo's Banner". No. 1954, "Willow Thread". No. 1955, "Cassia on Salver of Hibiscus". No. 1956, "Pearls on Jade Salver". No. 1957, "Red Gold Lion". No. 1958, "Milky White Jade". No. 1959, "Purple Jade with Fragrant Beads". No. 1960, "Cassia on Ice Salver". No. 1961, "Inky Black Lotus". No. 1962, "Jade Bamboo Shoot of Superior Class". No. 1963, "Smiling Face". No. 1964, "Swan Ballet".

1960. 1st Chinese-built Freighter. Launching. No gum.

1965	333	8f. blue	3·75	1·00

334 Pantheon, Paris

336 Chan Tien-yu

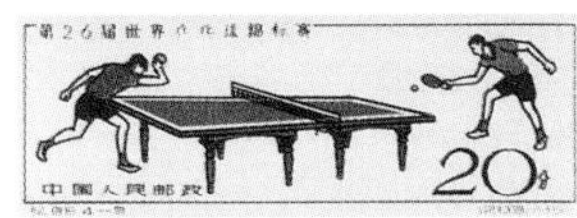

335 Table Tennis Match

1961. 90th Anniv of Paris Commune.

1966	334	8f. black and red	9·50	1·25
1967	–	8f. sepia and red	9·50	1·25

DESIGN: No. 1967, Proclamation of Commune.

1961. 26th World Table Tennis Championships, Peking. Multicoloured.

1968	8f. Championship emblem and jasmine	2·25	20
1969	10f. Table tennis bat and ball and Temple of Heaven	2·50	55
1970	20f. Type **335**	2·75	55
1971	22f. Peking Workers Gymnasium	3·00	30

1961. Birth Centenary of Chan Tien-yu (railway construction engineer).

1972	336	8f. black and sage	3·50	30
1973	–	10f. brown and sepia	6·50	1·10

DESIGN: 10f. Steam train on Peking-Changchow Railway.

337 Congress Building, Shanghai

1961. 40th Anniv of Chinese Communist Party. Flags, red; frames, gold.

1974	337	4f. purple	11·00	55
1975	–	8f. green	11·00	1·50
1976	–	10f. brown	11·00	5·25
1977	–	20f. blue	16·00	1·25
1978	–	30f. red	22·00	2·00

DESIGNS: 8f. "August 1" Building, Nanchang; 10f. Provisional Central Govt. Building, Juichin; 20f. Pagoda Hill, Yenan; 30f. Gate of Heavenly Peace, Peking.

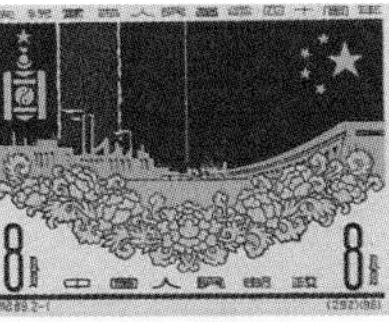

338 Flags of China and Mongolia

339 "August 1" Building, Nanchang

1961. 40th Anniv of Mongolian People's Revolution.

1979	338	8f. red, blue & yellow	10·00	1·40
1980	–	10f. orange, yellow & grn	17·00	6·50

DESIGN: 10f. Mongolian Government Building.

1961. Size 24 × $16\frac{1}{2}$ mm. No gum.

1981	339	1f. blue	8·25	35
1982		$1\frac{1}{2}$f. red	14·00	35
1983		2f. green	8·75	1·40
1984	A	3f. violet	28·00	1·75
1985		4f. green	2·25	10
1986		5f. green	1·75	10
1987	B	8f. green	1·50	10
1988		10f. purple	3·50	10
1989		20f. blue	1·00	10
1990	C	22f. brown	1·00	10
1991		30f. blue	1·00	10
1992		50f. red	1·40	10

DESIGNS: A, Tree and Sha Chow Pa Building, Juichin; B, Yenan Pagoda; C, Gate of Heavenly Peace, Peking.

For redrawn, smaller, designs see Nos. 2010/21.

340 Military Museum

1961. People's Revolutionary Military Museum.

1993	340	8f. brown, green & blue	17·00	1·50
1994		10f. black, green & brn	17·00	1·50

341 Uprising at Wuhan

1961. 50th Anniv of Revolution of 1911.

1995	341	8f. black and grey	10·00	2·25
1996	–	10f. black and brown	15·00	1·00

DESIGN—VERT: 10f. Dr. Sun Yat-sen.

342 Donkey

343 Tibetans Rejoicing

1961. Tang Dynasty Pottery (618–907 A.D.). Centres multicoloured. Background colours given.

1997	342	4f. blue	8·25	50
1998	–	8f. green	8·50	50
1999	–	8f. purple	8·50	50
2000	–	10f. blue	10·00	75
2001	–	20f. olive	10·50	2·50
2002	–	22f. turquoise	11·50	4·00
2003	–	30f. red	13·00	10·00
2004	–	50f. slate	13·00	5·00

DESIGNS: No. 1998, Donkey; Nos. 1999/2002, Various horses; Nos. 2003/4, Various camels.

1961. "Rebirth of the Tibetan People".

2005	343	4f. brown and buff	5·50	55
2006	–	8f. brown and turquoise	6·50	75
2007	–	10f. brown and yellow	9·50	1·25
2008	–	20f. brown and pink	19·00	2·25
2009	–	30f. brown and blue	32·00	3·50

DESIGNS: 8f. Sower; 10f. Tibetan celebrating "bumper crop"; 20f. "Responsible Citizens"; 30f. Tibetan children.

343a "August l" Building, Nanchang

344 Lu Hsun (after Hsieh Chia-seng)

1962. Size $20\frac{1}{2} \times 16\frac{1}{2}$ mm. No gum.

2010	343a	1f. blue	50	10
2011		2f. green	50	10
2013	A	3f. violet	50	10
2014	343a	3f. brown	1·75	75
2015	A	4f. green	50	10
2016	B	4f. red	2·00	75
2017	C	8f. green	80	10
2018		10f. purple	1·00	10
2019		20f. blue	1·00	10
2020	B	30f. blue	1·75	10
2021		52f. red	1·90	1·00

DESIGNS: A, Tree and Sha Chow Pa Building, Juichin; B, Gate of Heavenly Peace, Peking; C, Yenan Pagoda.

1962. 80th Birth Anniv of Lu Hsun (writer).

2022	344	8f. black and red	1·75	50

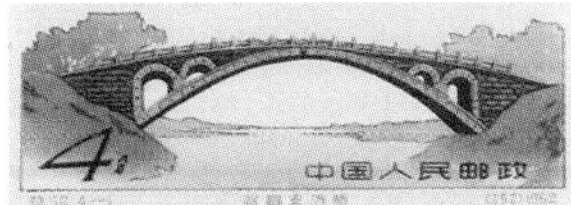

345 Anchi Bridge, Chaohsien

1962. Ancient Chinese Bridges.

2023	345	4f. violet and lavender	1·75	30
2024	–	8f. slate and green	1·75	30
2025	–	10f. sepia and bistre	2·50	65
2026	–	20f. blue and turquoise	3·50	1·25

BRIDGES: 8f. Paotai, Soochow. 10f. Chupu, Kuanhsien. 20f. Chenyang, Sankiang.

346 Tu Fu

347 Manchurian Cranes and Trees

1962. 1250th Birth Anniv of Tu Fu (poet).

2027	–	4f. black and bistre	11·00	70
2028	346	8f. black and turquoise	11·00	1·50

DESIGN: 4f. Tu Fu's Memorial, Chengtu.

1962. "The Sacred Crane". Paintings by Chen Chi-fo. Multicoloured.

2029	8f. Type **347**	20·00	3·25
2030	10f. Two cranes in flight	20·00	3·75
2031	20f. Crane on rock	20·00	4·75

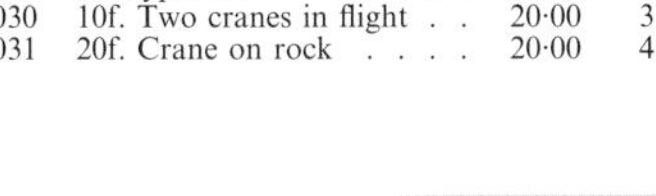

348 Cuban Soldier

349 Torch and Map

1962. "Support for Cuba".

2032	348	8f. black and lake	23·00	7·00
2033	–	10f. black and green	23·00	2·50
2034	–	22f. black and blue	50·00	17·00

DESIGNS: 10f. Sugar-cane planter; 22f. Militiaman and woman.

1961. "Support for Algeria".

2035	349	8f. orange and brown	75	15
2036	–	22f. brown and ochre	75	20

DESIGN: 22f. Algerian patriots.

350 Mei Lan-fang (actor)

351 Han "Flower Drum" Dance

1962. "Stage Art of Mei Lan-fang". Multicoloured. Each showing Lan-fang in stage costume with items given below.

2037	4f. Type **350**	70·00	10·00
2038	8f. Drum	20·00	3·00
2039	8f. Fan	20·00	2·50
2040	10f. Swords	20·00	3·00
2041	20f. Bag	20·00	4·00
2042	22f. Ribbons (horiz)	40·00	8·00
2043	30f. Loom (horiz)	80·00	25·00
2044	50f. Long sleeves (horiz)	65·00	20·00

1962. Chinese Folk Dances (1st issue). Multicoloured. No gum.

2045	4f. Type **351**	85	35
2046	8f. Mongolian "Ordos"	85	35
2047	10f. Chuang "Catching shrimp"	1·00	35
2048	20f. Tibetan "Fiddle"	1·25	35
2049	30f. Yi "Friend"	2·00	75
2050	50f. Uighur "Tambourine"	5·25	1·40

See also Nos. 2104/15.

352 Soldiers storming the Winter Palace, Petrograd

1962. 45th Anniv of Russian Revolution.

2051	–	8f. brown and red	18·00	1·00
2052	352	20f. bronze and red	25·00	2·00

DESIGN—VERT: 8f. Lenin leading soldiers.

353 Revolutionary Statue and Map

354 Tsai Lun (A.D. ?–121, inventor of paper making process)

1962. 50th Anniv of Albanian Independence.
2053 **353** 8f. sepia and blue . . . 1·75 40
2054 – 10f. multicoloured . . . 2·50 60
DESIGN: 10f. Albanian flag and girl pioneer.

1962. Scientists of Ancient China. Multicoloured.
2055 4f. Type **354** . . . . 6·25 30
2056 4f. Paper-making . . . . . 3·25 30
2057 8f. Sun Szu-miao (581–682, physician) . . . . 3·25 30
2058 8f. Preparing medical treatise . . . . 3·25 30
2059 10f. Shen Ko (1031–1095, geologist) . . . . 3·25 40
2060 10f. Making field notes . . 4·00 50
2061 20f. Ku Shou-chin (1231–1316, astronomer) . . . . 7·75 2·75
2062 20f. Astronomical equipment 7·75 2·75

355 Tank Monument, Havana

1963. 4th Anniv of Cuban Revolution.
2063 **355** 4f. sepia and red . . . . 24·00 1·50
2064 – 4f. black and green . . . 17·00 1·50
2065 – 8f. lake and brown . . . 17·00 1·50
2066 – 8f. lake and brown . . . 55·00 4·50
2067 – 10f. black and buff . . . 55·00 6·00
2068 – 10f. sepia, red and blue 55·00 16·00
DESIGNS—As Type **355**: No. 2064, Cuban revolutionaries; No. 2067, Cuban soldier; No. 2068, Castro and Cuban flag. LARGER (48½ × 27 mm) No. 2065, Crowd in Havana (value on left); No. 2066, Crowd in Peking (value on right).

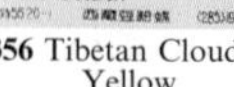
356 Tibetan Clouded Yellow

357 Marx and Engels

1963. Butterflies. Multicoloured. No gum.
2069 4f. (1) Type **356** . . . . . . 6·25 50
2070 4f. (2) Tritailed glory . . . 6·25 50
2071 4f. (3) Neumogeni jungle queen . . . . 6·25 50
2072 4f. (4) Washan swordtail . . 6·25 50
2073 4f. (5) Striped ringlet . . . 6·25 50
2074 8f. (6) Green dragontail . . 12·50 50
2075 8f. (7) Dilunuleted peacock 12·50 50
2076 8f. (8) Yamfly . . . . . . 12·50 50
2077 8f. (9) Golden kaiser-i-hind 12·50 50
2078 8f. (10) Mushaell hair-streak 12·50 50
2079 10f. (11) Yellow orange-tip 12·50 75
2080 10f. (12) Great jay . . . . 12·50 75
2081 10f. (13) Striped punch . . 12·50 75
2082 10f. (14) Beck butterfly . . . 12·50 75
2083 10f. (15) Omei skipper . . . 12·50 75
2084 20f. (16) Philippine birdwing 7·50 1·50
2085 20f. (17) Keeled apollo . . 7·50 1·50
2086 22f. (18) Blue-banded king crow . . . . 7·50 4·00
2087 30f. (19) Solskyi copper . . 7·50 7·50
2088 50f. (20) Clipper . . . . . 15·00 15·00

1983. 145th Birth Anniv of Karl Marx. No gum.
2089 – 8f. black, pink & gold 5·50 1·50
2090 – 8f. red and gold . . . 5·50 1·50
2091 **357** 8f. brown and gold . . . 5·50 1·50
DESIGNS: No. 2089, Marx; No. 2090, Slogan "Workers of the World Unite" over cover of 1st edition of "Communist Manifesto".

358 Child with Top

359 Giant Panda eating Apples

1963. Children. Multicoloured, background colours given. No gum.
2092 **358** 4f. turquoise 70 10
2093 – 4f. brown 70 10
2094 – 8f. grey 70 10
2095 – 8f. blue 70 10
2096 – 8f. beige 70 10
2097 – 8f. slate 70 10
2098 – 8f. green 70 10
2099 – 8f. grey 70 10
2100 – 10f. green . . . . 1·60 80
2101 – 10f. violet . . . . 1·60 80
2102 – 20f. drab . . . . 5·00 1·50
2103 – 20f. green . . . . 5·00 1·50
DESIGNS (each shows a child): No. 2093, Eating candied hawberries; No. 2094, As "traffic policeman"; No. 2095, With toy windmill; No. 2096, Listening to caged cricket; No. 2097, With toy sword; No 2098, Embroidering; No. 2099, With umbrella; No. 2100, Playing with sand; No. 2101, Playing table tennis; No. 2102, Doing sums; No. 2103, Flying kite.

1963. Chinese Folk Dances (2nd issue). As T **351** but inscr "(261) 1962" to "(266) 1962" in bottom right corner. Multicoloured. No gum.
2104 4f. Puyi "Weaving Cloth" 1·00 10
2105 8f. Kazakh . . . . 1·00 10
2106 10f. Olunchun . . . . . . 1·00 10
2107 20f. Kaochan "Labour" . . 1·00 35
2108 30f. Miao "Reed-pipe" . . . 1·75 60
2109 50f. Korean "Fan" . . . . 5·25 85

1963. Chinese Folk Dances (3rd issue). As T **351** but inscr "(279) 1963" to "(284) 1963" in bottom right corner. Multicoloured. No gum.
2110 4f. Yu "Wedding Ceremony" . . . . 1·40 20
2111 8f. Pai "Encircling Mountain Forest" . . . . 1·40 20
2112 10f. Yao "Long Drum" . . 1·60 20
2113 20f. Li "Third Day of Third Month" . . . . 1·60 40
2114 30f. Kava "Knife" . . . . 2·75 50
2115 50f. Tai "Peacock" . . . . 4·25 85

1963. Giant Panda. Perf or imperf.
2116 **359** 8f. black and blue . . . . 25·00 2·00
2117 – 8f. black and green . . . 25·00 5·00
2118 – 10f. black and drab . . 25·00 3·00
DESIGNS—As Type **278**. No. 2117, Giant panda eating bamboo shoots. HORIZ: (52 × 31 mm): No. 2118, Two giant pandas.

360 Table Tennis Player

361 Snub-nosed Monkey

1963. 27th World Table-Tennis Championships.
2119 **360** 8f. grey . . . . 11·00 1·00
2120 – 8f. brown . . . . 11·00 1·50
DESIGN: No. 2120, Trophies won by Chinese team.

1963. Snub-nosed Monkeys. Multicoloured.
2121 8f. Type **361** . . . . 8·00 1·50
2122 10f. Two monkeys . . . . . 8·00 1·50
2123 22f. Two monkeys on branch of tree . . . . . . 12·00 5·00

362 Old Pines of Hwangshan

1963. Hwangshan Landscapes. Multicoloured.
2124 4f. (1) Mount of The Green Jade Screen (vert) . . . . 11·50 1·00
2125 4f. (2) The Guest-welcoming Pines (vert) . . . . 11·50 1·00
2126 4f. (3) Pines and rocks behind the lake (vert) . . 11·50 1·00
2127 4f. (4) Terrace of Keeping Cool (vert) . . . . 11·50 1·00
2128 8f. (5) Mount of the Heavenly Capital (vert) 16·00 1·00
2129 8f. (6) Mount of Scissors (vert) . . . . 16·00 1·00
2130 8f. (7) Forest of Ten Thousand Pines (vert) . . 16·00 1·00
2131 8f. (8) The Flowering Bush in a Dream (vert) . . . . 16·00 1·00
2132 10f. (9) Mount of the Lotus Flower . . . . 21·00 1·00
2133 10f. (10) Cumulus Flood Wave of the Eastern Lake 21·00 1·00
2134 10f. (11) Type **362** . . . . . 21·00 1·00
2135 10f. (12) Cumulus on the Eastern Lake . . . . . . 21·00 1·00
2136 20f. (13) The Stalagmite Mountain Range . . . . 28·00 7·50
2137 22f. (14) The Apes of the Stone watch the lake below . . . . 38·00 10·00
2138 30f. (15) The Forest of Lions . . . . £100 40·00
2139 50f. (16) The Fairy Isles of Peng Lai . . . . 85·00 20·00

363 Football

364 Clay Rooster and Goat

1963. "GANEFO" Athletic Games, Jakarta, Indonesia.
2140 **363** 8f. red & black on lav 11·00 75
2141 – 8f. blue & black on buff 11·00 75
2142 – 8f. brown & blk on blue 11·00 75
2143 – 8f. purple & blk on mve 11·00 75
2144 – 10f. multicoloured . . . 16·00 2·50
DESIGNS—As Type **282**: No. 2141, Throwing the discus; No. 2142, Diving; No. 2143, Gymnastics. HORIZ: (48½ × 27½ mm). No. 2144, Athletes on parade.

1963. Chinese Folk Toys. Multicoloured. No gum.
2145 4f. (1) Type **364** 85 20
2146 4f. (4) Cloth camel 85 20
2147 4f. (7) Cloth tigers 85 20
2148 8f. (2) Clay ox and rider . . 85 20
2149 8f. (5) Cloth rabbit, wooden figure and clay cock . . . 85 20
2150 8f. (8) Straw cock 85 20
2151 10f. (3) Cloth donkey and clay bird 85 20
2152 10f. (6) Clay lion 85 20
2153 10f. (9) Clay-paper tumbler and cloth tiger 85 20

365 Vietnamese Family

366 Cuban and Chinese Flags

1963. "Liberation of South Vietnam". Mult.
2154 8f. Type **365** . . . . 4·50 1·00
2155 8f. Vietnamese with flag . . 4·50 1·00

1964. 5th Anniv of Cuban Revolution. Mult.
2156 8f. Type **366** . . . . 8·00 1·00
2157 8f. Boy waving flag . . . . 14·00 4·00

367 Woman driving Tractor

368 "Sino-African Friendship"

1964. "Women of the People's Commune". Multicoloured.
2158 8f. (1) Type **367** . . . . . 1·10 20
2159 8f. (2) Harvesting . . . . . 1·10 20
2160 8f. (3) Picking cotton . . . 1·10 20
2161 8f. (4) Picking fruit . . . . 1·10 20
2162 8f. (5) Reading book . . . 1·10 30
2163 8f. (6) Holding rifle . . . . 1·10 40

1964. African Freedom Day.
2164 **368** 8f. multicoloured 75 25
2165 – 8f. brown and black . . 75 25
DESIGN: No. 2165, African beating drum.

369 Marx, Engels, Lenin and Stalin

1964. Labour Day.
2166 **369** 8f. black, red & gold . . 16·00 3·50
2167 – 8f. black, red & gold . . 9·00 2·00
DESIGN: No. 2167, Workers and banners.

370 History Museum

1964. No gum.
2168 **370** 1f. brown 10 10
2169 A 1½f. purple 10 10
2170 B 2f. green 10 10
2171 C 3f. green 15 10
2172 **370** 4f. blue 15 10
2172a A 5f. purple 50 10
2173 B 8f. red 50 10
2174 C 10f. drab 75 10
2175 **370** 20f. violet 75 10
2176 A 22f. orange . . . . . 1·40 10
2177 B 30f. green . . . . . . 2·10 40
2177a C 50f. blue . . . . . . 5·00 2·00
DESIGNS: A, Gate of Heavenly Peace; B, Great Hall of the People; C, Military Museum.

371 Date Orchard, Yenan

372 Map of Vietnam and Flag

1964. "Yenan-Shrine of the Chinese Revolution". Yenan buildings. Multicoloured.
2178 8f. (1) Type **371** . . . . . . 15·00 45
2179 8f. (2) Central Auditorium, Yang Chia Ling . . . . 3·75 25
2180 8f. (3) Mao Tse-tung's Office and Residence at Date Orchard, Yenan . . . . . 3·75 25
2181 8f. (4) Auditorium, Wang Chia Ping . . . . 3·75 30
2182 8f. (5) Border Region Assembly Hall . . . . . 22·00 75
2183 52f. (6) Pagoda Hill . . . . 12·50 5·00

1964. South Vietnam Victory Campaign.
2184 **372** 8f. multicoloured . . . . 12·50 2·50

373 "The Alchemist's Glowing Crucible" (peony)

374 "Chueh" (wine cup)

1964. Chinese Peonies. Multicoloured.
2185 4f. (1) Type **373** . . . . . . 5·75 1·00
2186 4f. (2) Night-shining Jade 5·75 1·00
2187 8f. (3) Purple Kuo's Cap . . 9·50 1·00
2188 8f. (4) Chao Pinks . . . . . 9·50 1·00
2189 8f. (5) Yao Yellows . . . . 9·50 1·00
2190 8f. (6) Twin Beauties . . . 9·50 1·00
2191 8f. (7) Ice-veiled Rubies . . 9·50 1·00
2192 10f. (8) Gold-sprinkled Chinese Ink . . . . . . 12·00 1·00
2193 10f. (9) Cinnabar Jar . . . 12·00 1·00
2194 10f. (10) Lantien Jade . . . 13·50 1·00
2195 10f. (11) Imperial Robe Yellow . . . . 14·50 2·00
2196 10f. (12) Hu Reds . . . . . 14·50 2·00
2197 20f. (13) Pea Green . . . . 29·00 5·00
2198 43f. (14) Wei Purples . . . 35·00 20·00
2199 52f. (15) Intoxicated Celestial Peach . . . . . 60·00 15·00

1964. Bronze Vessels of the Yin Dynasty (before 1050 B.C.).
2200 **374** 4f. (1) black, grn & yell 6·00 20
2201 – 4f. (2) black, grn & yell 6·00 20
2202 – 8f. (3) black, grn & yell 7·50 30

2203 – 8f. (4) black, blue & grn 7·50 30
2204 – 10f. (5) black and drab 9·00 40
2205 – 10f. (6) black, grn & yell 9·00 40
2206 – 20f. (7) black and grey 11·00 3·50
2207 – 20f. (8) black, bl & yell 11·00 3·50
DESIGNS: No. 2201, "Ku" (beaker); 2202, "Kuang" (wine urn); 2203, "Chia" (wine cup); 2204, "Tsun" (wine vessel); 2205, "Yu" (wine urn); 2206, "Tsun" (wine vessel); 2207, "Ting" (ceremonial cauldron).

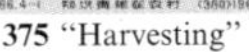
375 "Harvesting"

376 Marx, Engels and Trafalgar Square, London (vicinity of old St. Martin's Hall)

1964. Agricultural Students. Multicoloured.
2208 8f. (1) Type **375** . . . . . . 1·60 30
2209 8f. (2) "Sapling planting" . . 1·60 30
2210 8f. (3) "Study" . . . . . . 1·60 30
2211 8f. (4) "Scientific experiment" . . . . . . 1·60 30

1964. Centenary of "First International".
2212 **376** 8f. red, brown and gold 35·00 7·50

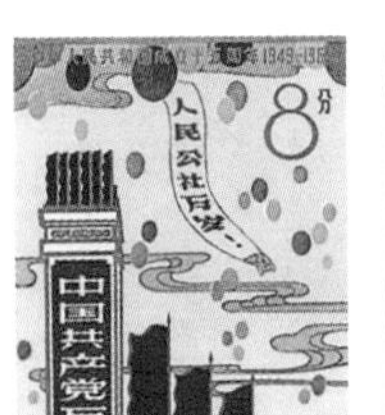
377 Rejoicing People

378 Oil Derrick

1964. 15th Anniv of People's Republic. Mult.
2213 8f. (1) Type **377** . . . . . . 14·00 1·75
2214 8f. (2) Chinese flag . . . . . 14·00 1·75
2215 8f. (3) As T **377** in reverse 14·00 1·75
Nos. 2213/5 were issued in the form of a triptych, in sheets.

1964. Petroleum Industry. Multicoloured.
2216 4f. Geological surveyors and van (horiz) . . . . 48·00 3·00
2217 8f. Type **378** . . . . 22·00 1·00
2218 8f. Oil-extraction equipment 22·00 1·00
2219 10f. Refinery . . . . 38·00 1·00
2220 20f. Railway petroleum trucks (horiz) . . . . . . 90·00 8·00

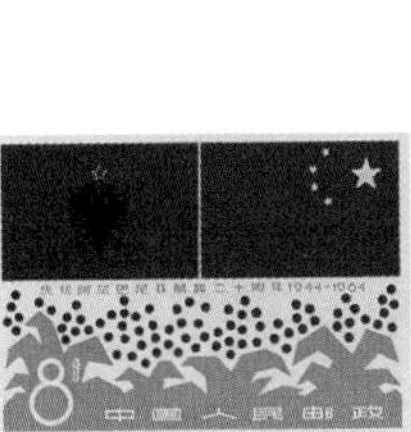

379 Albanian and Chinese Flags and Plants

380 Dam under Construction

1964. 20th Anniv of Liberation of Albania.
2221 **379** 8f. multicoloured . . . . 10·00 1·25
2222 – 10f. black, red & yellow 12·00 5·75
DESIGN: 10f. Enver Hoxha and Albanian arms.

1964. Hsinankiang Hydro-electric Power Station. Multicoloured.
2223 4f. Type **380** . . . . 60·00 2·25
2224 8f. Installation of turbo-generator rotor . . . . . 14·50 1·00
2225 8f. Main dam . . . . 45·00 1·40
2226 20f. Pylon . . . . 70·00 7·50

381 Fertilisers

1964. Chemical Industry. Main design and inscr in black; background colours given.
2227 **381** 8f. (1) red . . . . 2·00 20
2228 – 8f. (2) green . . . . . . 2·00 20
2229 – 8f. (3) brown . . . . . 2·00 20
2230 – 8f. (4) mauve . . . . . 2·00 20
2231 – 8f. (5) blue . . . . . . 2·00 20
2232 8f. (6) orange . . . . . 2·00 20
2233 – 8f. (7) violet . . . . . 2·00 20
2234 – 8f. (8) turquoise . . . . 2·00 20
DESIGNS: (2), Plastics; (3), Medicinal drugs; (4), Rubber; (5), Insecticides; (6), Acids; (7), Alkalis; (8), Synthetic fibres.

382 Mao Tse-tung standing in Room

1965. 30th Anniv of Tsunyi Conference. Mult.
2235 8f. (1) Type **382** . . . . . . 30·00 7·50
2236 8f. (2) Mao Tse-tung (vert) (26½ × 36 mm) . . . . . 15·00 10·00
2237 8f. (3) "Victory at Loushan Pass" . . . . 25·00 14·00

383 Conference Hall

384 Lenin

1965. 10th Anniv of Bandung Conference. Mult.
2238 8f. Type **383** . . . . 1·00 30
2239 8f. Rejoicing Africans and Asians . . . . 1·00 30

1965. 95th Birth Anniv of Lenin.
2240 **384** 8f. multicoloured . . . . 10·50 4·00

385 Table Tennis Player

386 All China T.U. Federation Team scaling Mt. Minya Konka

1965. World Table Tennis Championships, Peking.
2241 **385** 8f. (1) multicoloured . . 20 10
2242 – 8f. (2) multicoloured . . 20 10
2243 – 8f. (3) multicoloured . . 20 10
2244 – 8f. (4) multicoloured . . 20 10
DESIGNS: Nos. 2242/4 each show different views of table tennis players.

1965. Chinese Mountaineering Achievements. Each black, yellow and blue.
2245 8f. (1) Type **386** . . . . . . 4·00 50
2246 8f. (2) Men and women's mixed team on slopes of Muztagh Ata . . . . . . 5·00 50
2247 8f. (3) Climbers on Mt. Jolmo Lungma . . . . . 5·00 50
2248 8f. (4) Women's team camping on Kongur Tiubie Tagh . . . . . . 5·00 50
2249 8f. (5) Climbers on Shishma Pangma . . . . 6·00 2·00

387 Marx and Lenin

388 Tseping

1965. Organization of Socialist Countries' Postal Administrations Conference, Peking.
2250 **387** 8f. multicoloured . . . . 12·00 4·00

1965. "Chingkang Mountains – Cradle of the Chinese Revolution". Multicoloured.
2251 4f. (1) Type **388** . . . . . . 7·00 40
2252 8f. (2) Sanwantsun . . . . 7·00 40
2253 8f. (3) Octagonal Building, Maoping . . . . 28·00 40
2254 8f. (4) River and bridge at Lungshih . . . . 21·00 75
2255 8f. (5) Tachingtsun . . . . 14·00 75
2256 10f. (6) Bridge at Lungyuankou . . . . . 14·00 40
2257 10f. (7) Hwangyangchieh . . 10·00 75
2258 52f. (8) Chingkang peaks . . 10·00 6·00

389 Soldiers with Texts

1965. People's Liberation Army. Mult.
2259 8f. (1) Type **389** . . . . . . 18·00 3·25
2260 8f. (2) Soldiers reading book 18·00 3·25
2261 8f. (3) Soldier with grenade-thrower . . . . 18·00 1·50
2262 8f. (4) Giving tuition in firing rifle . . . . 18·00 1·50
2263 8f. (5) Soldiers at rest (vert) 9·50 1·50
2264 8f. (6) Bayonet charge (vert) 9·50 1·50
2265 8f. (7) Soldier with banners (vert) . . . . 9·50 4·00
2266 8f. (8) Military band (vert) 9·50 2·25

390 "Welcome to Peking"

391 Soldier firing Weapon

1965. Chinese–Japanese. Youth Meeting, Peking. Multicoloured.
2267 4f. (1) Type **390** 60 30
2268 8f. (2) Chinese and Japanese youths with linked arms 60 30
2269 8f. (3) Chinese and Japanese girls 60 30
2270 10f. (4) Musical entertainment . . . . . . 1·00 30
2271 22f. (5) Emblem of Meeting 3·00 1·00

1965. "Vietnamese People's Struggle".
2272 **391** 8f. (1) brown and red . . 1·90 50
2273 – 8f. (2) olive and red . . 1·90 50
2274 – 8f. (3) purple and red . . 1·90 50
2275 – 8f. (4) black and red . . 1·90 50
DESIGNS—VERT: (2) Soldier with captured weapons; (3) Soldier giving victory salute. HORIZ: (48½ × 26 mm): (4) "Peoples of the world".

392 "Victory"

393 Football

1965. 20th Anniv of Victory over Japanese.
2276 – 8f. (1) multicoloured . . 15·00 5·00
2277 – 8f. (2) green and red . . 8·00 80
2278 **392** 8f. (3) sepia and red . . 8·00 80
2279 – 8f. (4) green and red . . 8·00 80
DESIGNS—HORIZ: (50½ × 36 mm): (1) Mao Tse-tung writing. As Type **392**—HORIZ: (2) Soldiers crossing Yellow River. (4) Recruits in cart.

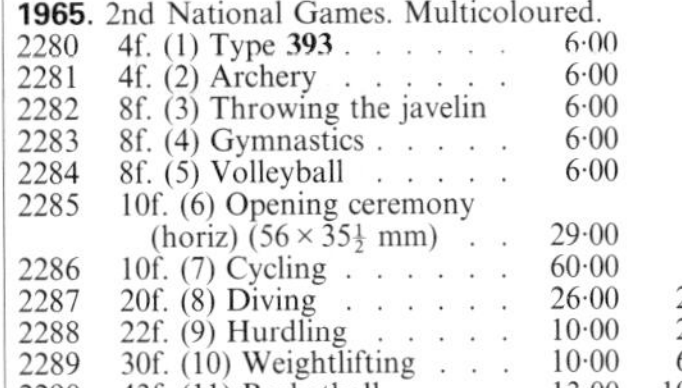

1965. 2nd National Games. Multicoloured.
2280 4f. (1) Type **393** . . . . . . 6·00 30
2281 4f. (2) Archery . . . . . . 6·00 30
2282 8f. (3) Throwing the javelin 6·00 30
2283 8f. (4) Gymnastics . . . . . 6·00 30
2284 8f. (5) Volleyball . . . . . 6·00 30
2285 10f. (6) Opening ceremony (horiz) (56 × 35½ mm) . . 29·00 30
2286 10f. (7) Cycling . . . . . . 60·00 30
2287 20f. (8) Diving . . . . . . 26·00 2·50
2288 22f. (9) Hurdling . . . . . 10·00 2·75
2289 30f. (10) Weightlifting . . . 10·00 6·00
2290 43f. (11) Basketball . . . . 13·00 10·00

394 Textile Workers

1965. Women in Industry. Multicoloured.
2291 8f. (1) Type **394** . . . . . . 6·50 40
2292 8f. (2) Machine building . . 6·50 40
2293 8f. (3) Building construction 6·50 40
2294 8f. (4) Studying . . . . . . 6·50 60
2295 8f. (5) Militia guard . . . . 6·50 3·00

395 Children playing with Ball

1966. Children's Games. Multicoloured.
2296 4f. (1) Type **395** 50 30
2297 4f. (2) Racing 50 30
2298 8f. (3) Tobogganing 50 30
2299 8f. (4) Exercising 50 30
2300 8f. (5) Swimming 50 30
2301 8f. (6) Shooting 50 30
2302 10f. (7) Jumping with rope 80 30
2303 52f. (8) Playing table tennis 1·25 50

396 Mobile Transformer

1966. New Industrial Machines.
2304 **396** 4f. (1) black and yellow 6·25 50
2305 – 8f. (2) black and blue . . 9·50 30
2306 – 8f. (3) black and pink . . 9·50 30
2307 – 8f. (4) black and olive 9·50 30
2308 – 8f. (5) black and purple 9·50 30
2309 – 10f. (6) black and grey 12·50 30
2310 – 10f. (7) black & turq . . 12·50 2·00
2311 – 22f. (8) black and lilac 25·00 5·00
DESIGNS—VERT: (2), Electron microscope; (4), Vertical boring and turning machine; (6), Hydraulic press; (8), Electron accelerator. HORIZ: (3), Lathe; (5), Gear-grinding machine; (7), Milling machine.

397 Women of Military and Other Services

1966. Women in Public Service. Mult.
2312 8f. (1) Type **397** 70 25
2313 8f. (2) Train conductress . . 70 25
2314 8f. (3) Red Cross worker . . 70 25
2315 8f. (4) Kindergarten teacher 70 25
2316 8f. (5) Roadsweeper 70 25
2317 8f. (6) Hairdresser 70 25
2318 8f. (7) Bus conductress . . . 70 25
2319 8f. (8) Travelling saleswoman 70 25
2320 8f. (9) Canteen worker . . . 70 25
2321 8f. (10) Rural postwoman 70 25

398 "Thunderstorm" (sculpture)

399 Dr. Sun Yat-sen

1966. Afro-Asian Writers' Meeting.
2322 **398** 8f. black and red . . . . 2·00 50
2323 – 22f. gold, yellow & red 4·00 1·60
DESIGN: 22f. Meeting emblem.

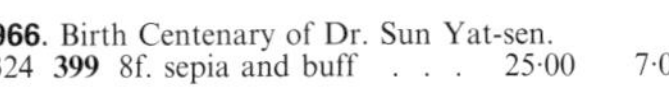

1966. Birth Centenary of Dr. Sun Yat-sen.
2324 **399** 8f. sepia and buff . . . 25·00 7·00

400 Athletes with Mao Tse-tung's Portrait

1966. "Cultural Revolution" Games. Multicoloured.
2325 8f. (1) Type **400** . . . . . . 21·00 6·00
2326 8f. (2) Athletes with linked arms hold Mao texts . . 21·00 6·00
2327 8f. (3) Two women athletes with Mao texts . . . . . 21·00 5·00
2328 8f. (4) Athletes reading Mao texts . . . . 21·00 5·00
SIZES: No. 2326, As Type **400**, but vert; Nos. 2327/8, 36½ × 25 mm.

401 Mao's Appreciation of Lu Hsun (patriot and writer)

402 "Be Resolute ..." (Mao Tse-tung)

1966. 30th Death Anniv of Lu Hsun.
2329 **401** 8f. (1) black & orange 40·00 15·00
2330 – 8f. (2) black, flesh & red 40·00 15·00
2331 – 8f. (3) black & orange 40·00 15·00
DESIGNS: (2) Lu Hsun; (3) Lu Hsun's manuscript.

1967. Heroic Oilwell Firefighters.
2332 **402** 8f. (1) gold, red & black 22·00 12·00
2333 – 8f. (2) black and red . . 25·00 9·00
2334 – 8f. (3) black and red . . 25·00 9·00
DESIGNS—HORIZ: (48 × 27 mm): (2) Drilling Team No. 32111 fighting flames. VERT: (3) Smothering flames with tarpaulins.

403 Liu Ying-chun (military hero)

1967. Liu Ying-chun Commem. Multicoloured.
2335 8f. (1) Type **403** . . . . . . 22·00 6·50
2336 8f. (2) Liu Ying-chun holding book of Mao texts . . . . 22·00 6·50
2337 8f. (3) Liu Ying-chun holding horse's bridle . . 22·00 6·50
2338 8f. (4) Liu Ying-chun looking at film slide . . . 22·00 6·50
2339 8f. (5) Liu Ying-chun lecturing . . . . 22·00 6·50
2340 8f. (6) Liu Ying-chun making fatal attempt to stop bolting horse . . . . 22·00 6·50

404 Soldier, Nurse, Workers and Banners

1967. 3rd Five-Year Plan. Multicoloured.
2341 8f. (1) Type **404** . . . . . 30·00 7·50
2342 8f. (2) Armed woman, peasants and banners . . 30·00 7·50

405 Mao Tse-tung

406 Mao Text (39 characters)

1967. "Thoughts of Mao Tse-tung" (1st issue). Similar designs showing Mao texts each gold and red. To assist identification of Nos. 2344/53 the total number of Chinese characters within the frames are given. (a) Type **405**.
2343 8f. multicoloured . . . . . 85·00 15·00

(b) As Type **406**. Red outer frames.
2344 8f. Type **406** . . . . 75·00 12·00
2345 8f. (50 characters) . . . . . 75·00 12·00
2346 8f. (39–in six lines) . . . . 75·00 12·00
2347 8f. (53) . . . . 75·00 12·00
2348 8f. (46) . . . . 75·00 12·00

(c) As Type **406**. Gold outer frames.
2349 8f. (41) . . . . 75·00 12·00
2350 8f. (49) . . . . 75·00 12·00
2351 8f. (35) . . . . 75·00 12·00
2352 8f. (22) . . . . 75·00 12·00
2353 8f. (29) . . . . 75·00 12·00
See also No. 2405.

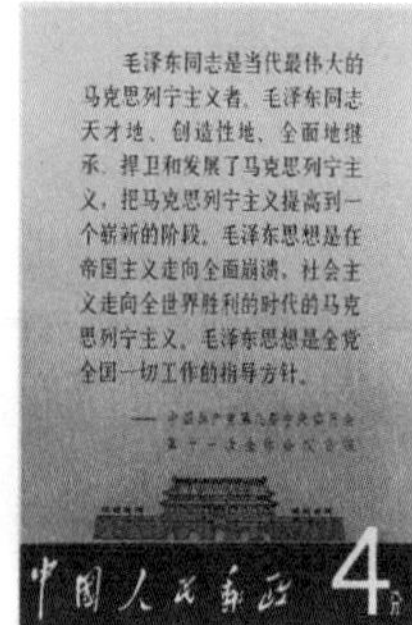

407 Text praising Mao

1967. Labour Day.
2354 **407** 4f. multicoloured . . . . 50·00 14·00
2355 – 8f. multicoloured . . . . 40·00 14·00
2356 – 8f. multicoloured . . . . 50·00 14·00
2357 – 8f. multicoloured . . . . 40·00 14·00
2358 – 8f. multicoloured . . . . 40·00 14·00
DESIGNS (Mao Tse-tung and): No. 2355, Poem; No. 2356, Multi-racial crowd with texts; No. 2357, Red Guards. (36 × 50½ mm): Mao with hand raised in greeting.
For stamps similar to No. 2358, see Nos. 2367/9.

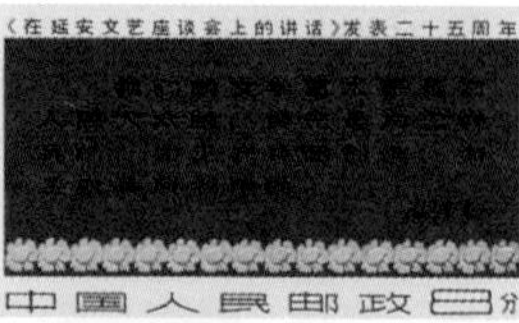

408 Mao Text

1967. 25th Anniv of Mao Tse-tung's "Talks on Literature and Art".
2359 **408** 8f. black, red & yellow £130 25·00
2360 – 8f. black, red & yellow £150 30·00
2361 – 8f. multicoloured . . . . £150 30·00
DESIGNS: No. 2360, As Type **408** but different text. (50 × 36½ mm): No. 2361, Mao supporters in procession.

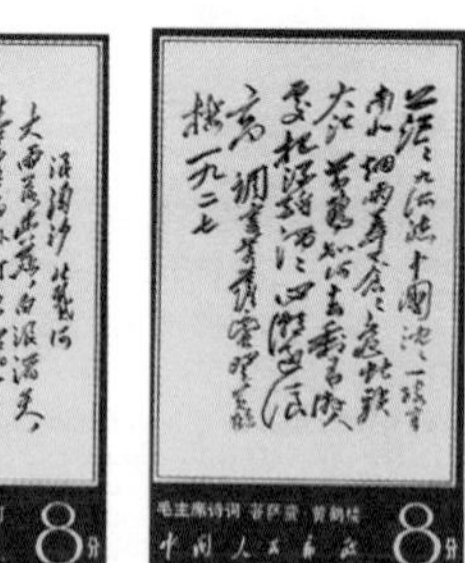

409 Mao Tse-tung

410 Mao Tse-tung and Lin Piao

1967. 46th Anniv of Chinese Communist Party.
2362 **409** 4f. red . . . . 12·00 7·50
2363 8f. red . . . . 50·00 7·50
2364 35f. brown . . . . . . 35·00 25·00
2365 43f. red . . . . 40·00 25·00
2366 52f. red . . . . 75·00 20·00

1967. "Our Great Teacher". Multicoloured.
2367 8f. Type **410** . . . . £120 30·00
2368 8f. Mao Tse-tung (horiz) . . 50·00 18·00
2369 10f. Mao Tse-tung conferring with Lin Piao (horiz) . . . . £150 30·00
For 8f. stamp showing Mao with hand raised in greeting, see No. 2358.

411 Mao Tse-tung as "Sun"

1967. 18th Anniv of People's Republic. Mult.
2370 8f. Type **411** . . . . . . 48·00 8·50
2371 8f. Mao Tse-tung with representatives of Communist countries . . 29·00 8·50

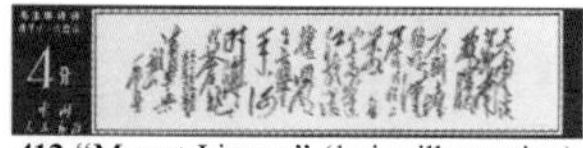

412 "Mount Liupan" (½-size illustration)

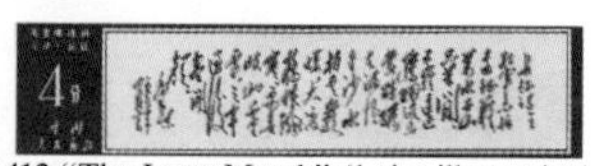

413 "The Long March" (½-size illustration)

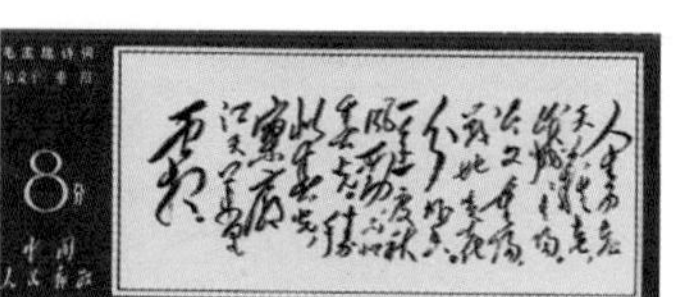

414 "Double Ninth"

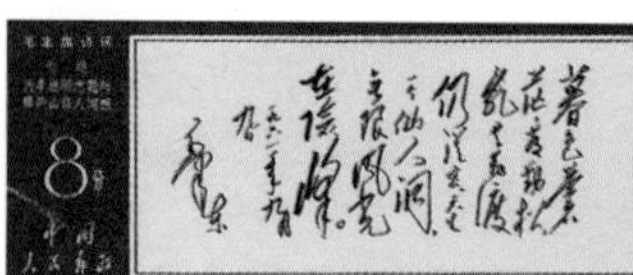

415 "Fairy Cave"

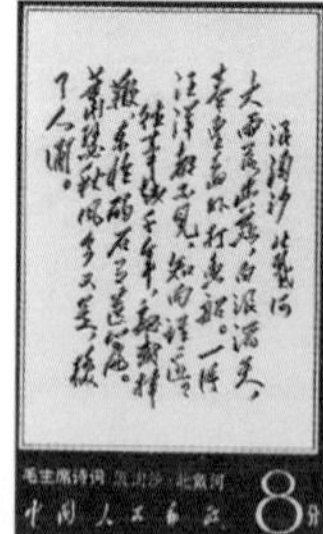

416 "Huichang"

417 "Yellow Crane Pavilion"

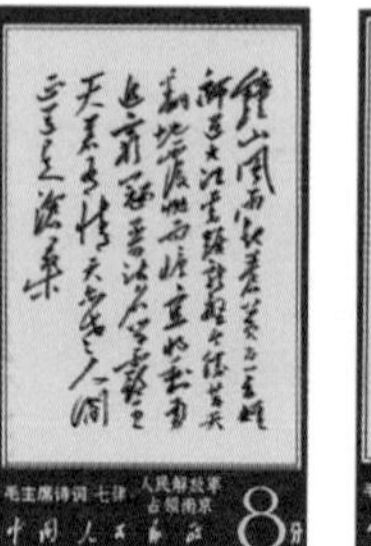
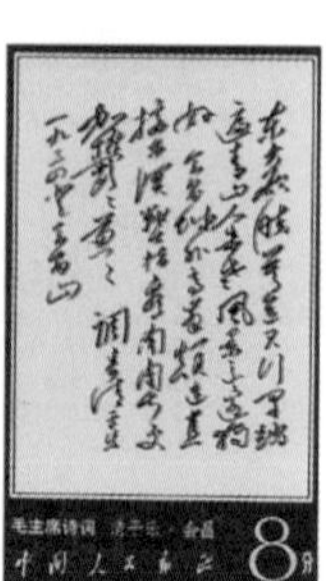

418 "Beidahe"

419 "Swimming"

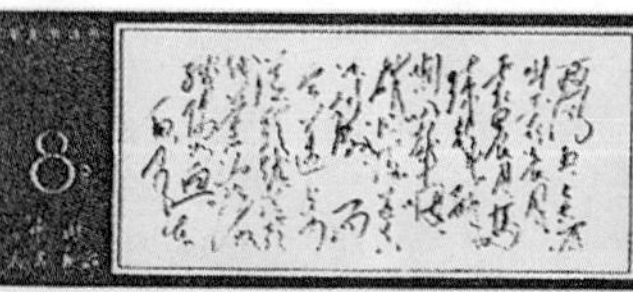

420 "Loushanguan Pass"

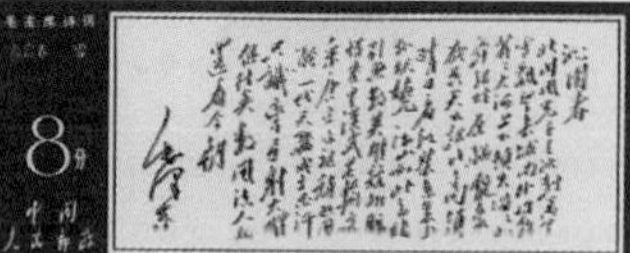

421 "Snow"

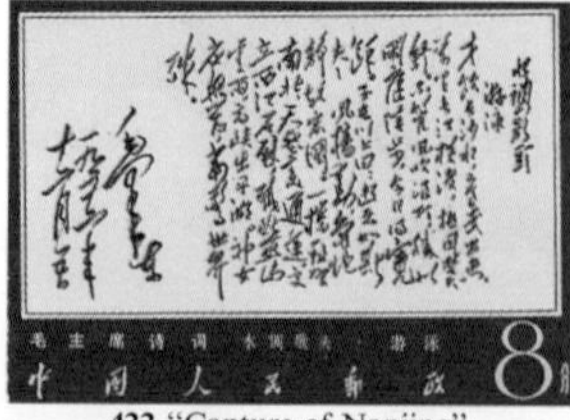

422 "Capture of Nanjing"

423 Mao Writing Poems at Desk

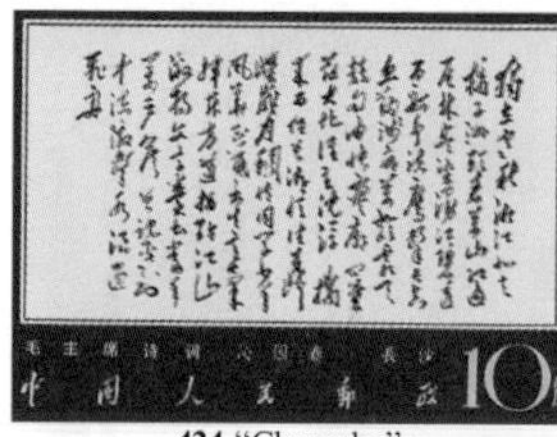

424 "Changsha"

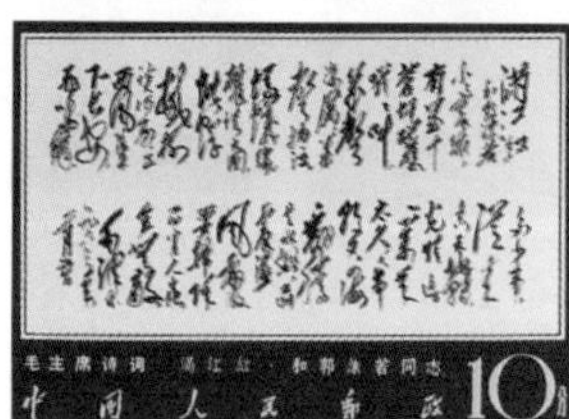

425 "Reply to Guo Moro"

1967. Poems of Mao Tse-tung.
2372 **412** 4f. black, yellow & red 50·00 14·00
2373 **413** 4f. black, yellow & red 65·00 14·00
2374 **414** 8f. black, yellow & red 65·00 12·00
2375 **415** 8f. black, yellow & red 70·00 12·00
2376 **416** 8f. black, yellow & red £190 12·00
2377 **417** 8f. black, yellow & red £120 20·00
2378 **418** 8f. black, yellow & red £225 20·00
2379 **419** 8f. black, yellow & red 80·00 20·00
2380 **420** 8f. black, yellow & red 80·00 20·00
2381 **421** 8f. black, yellow & red 80·00 20·00
2382 **422** 8f. black, yellow & red 80·00 12·00
2383 **423** 10f. multicoloured . . . 32·00 12·00
2384 **424** 10f. black, yellow & red 32·00 12·00
2385 **425** 10f. black, yellow & red 32·00 12·00

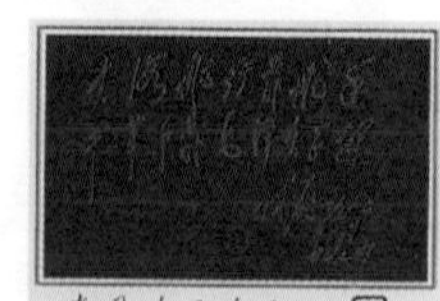

426 Epigram on Chairman Mao by Lin Piao

1967. Fleet Expansionists' Congress.
2386 **426** 8f. gold and red . . . . 26·00 8·50

427 Mao Tse-tung and Procession

1968. "Revolutionary Literature and Art" (1st issue). Multicoloured designs showing scenes from People's Operas.
2387 8f. Type **427** . . . . 50·00 9·00
2388 8f. "Raid on the White Tiger Regiment" . . . . 40·00 9·00
2389 8f. "Taking Tiger Mountain" . . . . 50·00 8·00
2390 8f. "On the Docks" . . . . 35·00 8·00

2391 8f. "Shachiapang" . . . . . 40·00 8·00
2392 8f. "The Red Lantern" (vert) . . . . 35·00 8·00

428 "Red Detachment of Women" (ballet)

1968. "Revolutionary Literature and Art" (2nd issue). Multicoloured.
2393 8f. Type **428** . . . . 40·00 9·00
2394 8f. "The White-haired Girl" (ballet) . . . . 40·00 9·00
2395 8f. Mao Tse-tung, Symphony Orchestra and Chorus (50 × 36 mm) . . 80·00 11·00

429 Mao Tse-tung ("Unite still more closely")

1968. Mao's Anti-American Declaration.
2396 **429** 8f. brown, gold and red 45·00 12·00

430 **431**

432 **433**

434

1968. "Directives of Mao Tse-tung".
2397 **430** 8f. brown, red & yellow £190 40·00
2398 **431** 8f. brown, red & yellow £190 40·00
2399 **432** 8f. brown, red & yellow £190 40·00
2400 **433** 8f. brown, red & yellow £190 40·00
2401 **434** 8f. brown, red & yellow £190 40·00

435 Inscription by Lin Piao. 26 July, 1965

1968. 41st Anniv of People's Liberation Army.
2402 **435** 8f. black, gold and red 12·00 5·00

436 "Chairman Mao goes to Anyuan" (Liu Chunhua)

1968. Mao's Youth.
2403 **436** 8f. multicoloured . . . . 26·00 8·00

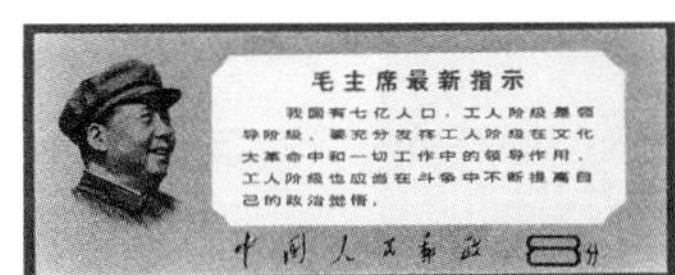

438 Mao Tse-tung and Text

1968. "Thoughts of Mao Tse-tung" (2nd issue).
2405 **438** 8f. brown and red . . . 48·00 14·00

439 Displaying "The Words of Mao Tse-tung"

1968. "The Words of Mao Tse-tung". No gum.
2406 **439** 8f. multicoloured . . . . 15·00 3·00

440 Yangtse Bridge

1968. Completion of Yangtse Bridge, Nanking. Multicoloured. No gum.
2407 4f. Type **440** . . . . 3·75 90
2408 8f. Buses on bridge . . . . 9·75 4·00
2409 8f. View of end portals . . . 7·25 2·50
2410 10f. Aerial view . . . . . . 2·50 1·25
Nos. 2408/9 are larger, size 49 × 27 mm.

441 Li Yu-ho singing "I am filled with Courage and Strength"

1969. Songs from "The Red Lantern" Opera. Multicoloured. No gum.
2411 8f. Type **441** . . . . 15·00 7·50
2412 8f. Li Ti-mei singing "Hatred in my Heart" . . 30·00 7·50

442 Communist Party Building, Shanghai

1969. No gum.
2413 **442** 1½f. red, brown & lilac 60 50
2414 – 8f. brown, grn & cream 2·00 75
2415 – 8f. red and purple . . . 60 15
2416 – 8f. brown and blue . . . 1·50 40
2417 – 20f. blue, purple & red 2·10 1·00
2418 – 50f. brown and green . . 1·75 40
DESIGNS: "Historic Sites of the Revolution"; Size 27 × 22 mm—No. 2414, Pagoda Hill, Yenan; No. 2415, Gate of Heavenly Peace, Peking; No. 2418. Mao Tse-tung's house, Yenan. Size as T **442**—No. 2416, People's Heroes Monument, Peking; No. 2417, Conference Hall, Tsunyi.
See also Nos. 2455/65.

443 Rice Harvesters

1969. Agricultural Workers. Mult. No gum.
2419 4f. Type **443** . . . . 4·00 2·00
2420 8f. Grain harvest . . . . . 9·00 1·75
2421 8f. Study Group with "Thoughts of Mao" . . . 55·00 7·50
2422 10f. Red Cross worker with mother and child . . . . 4·00 1·50

444 Snow Patrol **445** Farm Worker

1969. Defence of Chen Pao Tao in the Ussur River. Multicoloured. No gum.
2423 8f. Type **444** . . . . 6·00 2·50
2424 8f. Guards by river (horiz) 5·00 2·50
2425 8f. Servicemen and Militia (horiz) . . . . 20·00 3·00
2426 35f. As No. 2424 . . . . . 5·00 2·75
2427 43f. Type **444** . . . . 6·00 2·75

1969. "The Chinese People" (woodcuts). No gum.
2428 **445** 4f. purple and orange . . 20 20
2429 – 8f. purple and orange . . 60 25
2430 – 10f. green and orange . . 90 60
DESIGNS: 8f. Foundryman. 10f. Soldier.

446 Chin Hsun-hua in Water **447** Tractor-driver

1970. Heroic Death of Chin Hsun-hua in Kirin Border Floods. No gum.
2431 **446** 8f. black and red . . . . 17·00 5·00

1970. No gum.
2432 **447** 5f. black, red & orange 60 40
2433 – 1y. black and red . . . 4·00 1·10
DESIGN—HORIZ: 1y. Foundryman.

448 Cavalry Patrol **449** "Yang Tse-jung, Army Scout"

1970. 43rd Anniv of People's Liberation Army. No gum.
2434 **448** 8f. multicoloured . . . . 6·75 3·25

1970. "Taking Tiger Mountain" (Revolutionary opera). Multicoloured. No gum.
2435 8f. (1) Type **449** . . . . . 15·00 2·50
2436 8f. (2) "The patrol sets out" (horiz) . . . . 15·00 2·50
2437 8f. (3) "Leaping through the forest" . . . . 15·00 2·50
2438 8f. (4) "Li Yung-chi's farewell" (27 × 48 mm) . . 15·00 2·50
2439 8f. (5) "Yang Tse-jung in disguise" (27 × 48 mm) . . 15·00 2·50
2440 8f. (6) "Congratulating Yang Tse-jung" (horiz) 40·00 2·50

450 Soldiers in Snow

1970. 2nd Anniv of Defence of Chen Pao Tao. No gum.
2441 **450** 4f. multicoloured . . . . 1·75 1·00

451 Communard Standard **453** Workers and Great Hall of the People, Peking

452 Communist Party Building, Shanghai

1971. Cent of Paris Commune. Mult. No gum.
2442 **451** 4f. multicoloured . . . . 40·00 10·00
2443 – 8f. brown, pink and red 80·00 20·00
2444 – 10f. red, brn and pink 40·00 10·00
2445 – 22f. brown, red & pink 40·00 10·00
DESIGNS—HORIZ: 8f. Fighting in Paris, March 1871; 22f. Communards in Place Vendome. VERT: 10f. Commune proclaimed at the Hotel de Ville.

1971. 50th Anniv of Chinese Communist Party. Multicoloured. No gum.
2446 4f. (12) Type **452** . . . . . 9·00 1·25
2447 4f. (13) National Peasant Movement Inst., Canton 9·00 1·25
2448 8f. (14) Chingkang Mountains . . . . 7·50 1·25
2449 8f. (15) Conference Building, Tsunyi . . . . 7·50 1·25
2450 8f. (16) Pagoda Hill, Yenan 7·50 1·25
2452 8f. (18) Workers and Industry . . . . 16·00 3·00
2453 8f. (19) Type **453** . . . . . 16·00 3·00
2454 8f. (20) Workers and Agriculture . . . . 16·00 3·00
2451 22f. (17) Gate of Heavenly Peace, Peking . . . . . . 6·00 1·25
SIZES: As Type **452**. Nos. 2447/2450 and 2451. As Type **453**. Nos. 2452/4.

454 National Peasant Movement Institute, Canton **455** Welcoming Bouquets

1971. Revolutionary Sites. Multicoloured. No gum.
2455 1f. Communist Party Building, Shanghai (vert) 10 10
2456 2f. Type **454** 10 10
2457 3f. Site of 1929 Congress, Kutien 10 10
2458 4f. Mao Tse-tung's house, Yenan 15 10
2459 8f. Gate of Heavenly Peace, Peking 15 10
2460 10f. Monument, Chingkang Mountains 25 10
2461 20f. River bridge, Yenan . . 40 15
2462 22f. Mao's birthplace, Shaoshan 70 20
2463 35f. Conference Building, Tsunyi . . . . 1·00 20
2464 43f. Start of the Long March, Chingkang Mountains . . . . 1·40 35
2465 52f. People's Palace, Peking 1·75 55

1971. "Afro-Asian Friendship" Table Tennis Tournament, Peking. Multicoloured. No gum.
2466 8f. (22) Type **455** . . . . . 4·00 1·00
2467 8f. (23) Group of players . . 4·00 1·00
2468 8f. (24) Asian and African players . . . . 4·00 1·00
2469 43f. (21) Tournament badge 14·50 2·50

456 Enver Hoxha making speech
457 Conference Hall, Yenan

1971. 30th Anniv of Albanian Worker's Party. Multicoloured. No gum.
2470 8f. (25) Type **456** . . . . . 7·25 4·00
2471 8f. (26) Party Headquarters 6·00 1·50
2472 8f. (27) Albanian flag, rifle and pick . . . . 6·00 1·50
2473 52f. (28) Soldier and Worker's Militia (horiz) 6·50 4·00

1972. 30th Anniv of Publication of "Yenan Forum's Discussions on Literature and Art". Multicoloured. No gum.
2474 8f. (33) Type **457** . . . . . 5·50 1·60
2475 8f. (34) Army choir . . . . 5·50 1·60
2476 8f. (35) "Brother and Sister" 7·00 1·60
2477 8f. (36) "Open-air Theatre" 7·00 1·60
2478 8f. (37) "The Red Lantern" (opera) . . . . 7·00 1·60
2479 8f. (38) "Red Detachment of Women" (ballet) . . . . 7·00 1·60

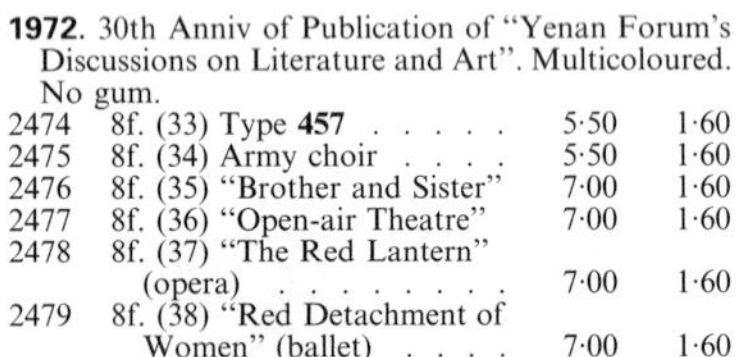
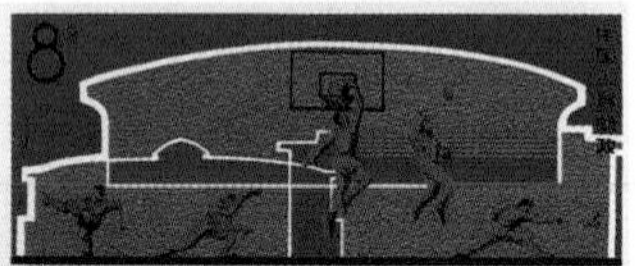

458 Ball Games

1972. 10th Anniv of Mao Tse-tungs's Edict on Physical Culture. Multicoloured. No gum.
2480 8f. (39) Type **458** . . . . . 7·00 1·50
2481 8f. (40) Gymnastics . . . . 7·00 1·50
2482 8f. (41) Tug-of-War . . . . 7·00 1·50
2483 8f. (42) Rock-climbing . . . 7·00 1·50
2484 8f. (43) High-diving . . . . 7·00 1·50
Nos. 2481/4 are size 26 × 36 mm.

460 Freighter "Fenglei"

1972. Chinese Merchant Shipping. Multicoloured. No gum.
2485 8f. (29) Type **460** . . . . . 8·00 1·75
2486 8f. (30) Tanker "Taching No. 30" . . . . 8·00 1·75
2487 8f. (31) Cargo-liner "Chang Seng" . . . . 8·00 1·75
2488 8f. (32) Dredger "Hsienfeng" . . . . . . 8·00 1·75

461 Championship Badge
462 Wang Chin-hsi, the "Iron Man"

1972. 1st Asian Table Tennis Championships, Peking. Multicoloured. No gum.
2489 8f. (45) Type **461** . . . . . 4·00 75
2490 8f. (46) Welcoming crowd (horiz) . . . . 4·00 75
2491 8f. (47) Game in progress (horiz) . . . . 4·00 75
2492 22f. (48) Players from three countries . . . . 2·50 1·50

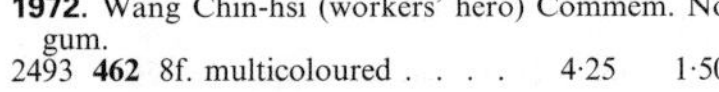

1972. Wang Chin-hsi (workers' hero) Commem. No gum.
2493 **462** 8f. multicoloured . . . . 4·25 1·50

463 Cliff-edge Construction
464 Giant Panda eating Bamboo Shoots

1972. Construction of Red Flag Canal. Mult.
2494 8f. (49) Type **463** . . . . . 2·10 80
2495 8f. (50) "Youth" tunnel . . 2·10 80
2496 8f. (51) "Taoguan bridge" 2·10 80
2497 8f. (52) Cliff-edge canal . . 2·10 80

1973. China's Giant Pandas.
2498 **464** 4f. (61) multicoloured . . 2·00 3·50
2499 – 8f. (59) mult (horiz) . . 2·00 3·50
2500 – 8f. (60) mult (horiz) . . 2·00 3·50
2501 – 10f. (58) multicoloured £100 15·00
2502 – 20f. (57) multicoloured 85·00 15·00
2503 – 43f. (62) multicoloured 9·00 6·00
DESIGNS: 8f. to 43f. Different brush and ink drawings of pandas.

465 "New Power in the Mines" (Yang Shi-guang)
466 Girl dancing

1973. International Working Women's Day. Mult.
2504 8f. (63) Type **465** . . . . . 3·00 1·50
2505 8f. (64) "Woman Committee Member" (Tang Hsiaoming) . . . . 3·00 1·50
2506 8f. (65) "I am a Sea-gull" (Army telegraph line woman) (Pan Jiajun) . . 3·00 1·50

1973. Children's Day. Multicoloured.
2507 8f. (86) Type **466** . . . . . 1·90 50
2508 8f. (87) Boy musician . . . 1·90 50
2509 8f. (88) Boy with scarf . . . 1·90 50
2510 8f. (89) Boy with tambourine . . . . 1·90 50
2511 8f. (90) Girl with drum . . 1·90 50

467 Badge of Championships
468 "Hsi-erh"

1973. Asian. African and Latin-American Table Tennis Invitation Championships. Multicoloured.
2512 8f. (91) Type **467** . . . . . 2·50 50
2513 8f. (92) Visitors . . . . . . 2·50 50
2514 8f. (93) Player . . . . . . 2·50 50
2515 22f. (94) Guest players . . . 1·50 50

1973. Revolutionary Ballet "Hsi-erh" ("The White-haired Girl"). Multicoloured.
2516 8f. (53) Type **468** . . . . . 4·75 1·10
2517 8f. (54) Hsi-erh escapes from Huang (horiz) . . . . . 4·75 1·10
2518 8f. (55) Hsi-erh meets Tachun (horiz) . . . . . 4·75 1·10
2519 8f. (56) Hsi-erh becomes a soldier . . . . 4·75 1·10

469 Fair Building

1973. Chinese Exports Fair, Canton.
2520 **469** 8f. multicoloured . . . . 3·50 1·25

470 Mao's Birthplace, Shaoshan
471 Steam and Diesel Trains

1973. No gum.
2521 **470** 1f. green & light green 35 10
2522 – 1½f. red and yellow . . . 35 20
2523 – 2f. blue and green . . . 35 10
2524 – 3f. green and yellow . . 35 10
2525 – 4f. red and yellow . . . 35 10
2526 – 5f. brown and yellow . . 35 10
2527 – 8f. purple and flesh . . . 35 10
2528 – 10f. blue and flesh . . . 35 10
2529 – 20f. red and buff 65 10
2530 – 22f. violet and yellow . . 90 10
2531 – 35f. purple and yellow 1·25 15
2532 – 43f. brown and buff . . 1·60 25
2533 – 50f. blue and mauve . . 2·10 70
2534 – 52f. brown and yellow 2·75 90
2535 **471** 1y. multicoloured . . . 2·00 25
2536 – 2y. multicoloured . . . 1·60 40
DESIGNS—As Type **470**: 1½ f. National Peasant Movement Institute, Shanghai. 2f. National Institute, Kwangchow. 3f. Headquarters Building, Nanching uprising. 4f. Great Hall of the People, Peking, 5f. Wen Chia Shih. 8f. Gate of Heavenly Peace, Peking. 10f. Chingkang Mountains. 20f. Kutien Congress building. 22f. Tsunyi Congress building. 35f. Bridge, Yenan. 43f. Hsi Pai Po. 50f. "Fairy Gate", Lushan. 52f. People's Heroes Monument, Peking. As Type **471**: 2y. Trucks on mountain road.

472 "Phoenix" Pot
473 Dance Routine

1973. Archaeological Treasures. Multicoloured.
2537 4f. (66) Type **472** . . . . . 1·75 20
2538 4f. (67) Silver pot . . . . . 1·75 20
2539 8f. (68) Porcelain horse and groom . . . . 1·40 10
2540 8f. (69) Figure of woman . . 1·40 10
2541 8f. (70) Carved pedestals . . 90 10
2542 8f. (71) Bronze horse . . . 90 10
2543 8f. (72) Gilded "frog" . . . 90 10
2544 8f. (73) Lamp-holder figurine 90 10
2545 10f. (74) Tripod jar 45 50
2546 10f. (75) Bronze vessel . . . 45 50
2547 20f. (76) Bronze wine vessel 2·00 75
2548 52f. (77) Tray with tripod 2·00 1·50

1974. Popular Gymnastics. Multicoloured.
2549 8f. (1) Type **473** . . . . . . 7·00 2·75
2550 8f. (2) Rings exercise . . . 7·00 2·75
2551 8f. (3) Dancing on beam . . 7·00 2·75
2552 8f. (4) Handstand on parallel bars . . . . . . 7·00 2·75
2553 8f. (5) Trapeze exercise . . . 8·00 2·75
2554 8f. (6) Vaulting over horse 8·00 2·75

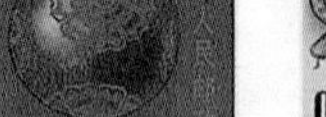

474 Lion Dance
475 Man reading Book

1974. Acrobatics. Multicoloured.
2555 8f. (1) Type **474** . . . . . . 6·00 2·25
2556 8f. (2) Handstand on chairs 6·00 2·25
2557 8f. (3) Diabolo team (horiz) 6·00 2·25
2558 8f. Revolving jar (horiz) . . 7·00 2·25
2559 8f. (5) Spinning plates . . . 7·00 2·25
2560 8f. (6) Foot-juggling with parasol . . . . 7·00 2·25

1974. Huhsien Paintings. Multicoloured.
2561 8f. (1) Type **475** . . . . . . 2·25 1·00
2562 8f. (2) Mineshaft (23 × 57 mm) . . . . . . 2·25 1·00
2563 8f. (3) Workers hoeing field (horiz) . . . . 2·25 1·00
2564 8f. (4) Workers eating (horiz) . . . . 2·25 1·00
2565 8f. (5) Wheatfield landscape (57 × 23 mm) . . . . . . 2·25 1·00
2566 8f. (6) Harvesting (horiz) . . 2·25 1·00

476 Postman

1974. Centenary of U.P.U. Multicoloured.
2567 8f. (1) Type **476** . . . . . . 6·00 2·50
2568 8f. (2) People of five races 6·00 2·50
2569 8f. (3) Great Wall of China 6·00 2·50

477 Inoculating Children

1974. Country Doctors. Multicoloured.
2570 8f. (1) Type **477** . . . . . . 1·75 90
2571 8f. (2) On country visit (vert) . . . . 1·75 90
2572 8f. (3) Gathering herbs (vert) 1·75 90
2573 8f. (4) Giving acupuncture 1·75 90

478 Wang Chin-hsi, "The Iron Man"

1974. Chairman Mao's Directives on Industrial and Agricultural Teaching. Multicoloured. (a) "Learning Industry from Taching".
2574 8f. (1) Type **478** . . . . . . 2·00 90
2575 8f. (2) Pupils studying Mao's works . . . . 2·00 90
2576 8f. (3) Oil-workers sinking well . . . . 2·00 90
2577 8f. (4) Consultation with management . . . . . . 2·00 90
2578 8f. (5) Taching oilfield as development site . . . . 2·00 90

(b) "Learning Agriculture from Tachai".
2579 8f. (1) Tachai workers looking to future . . . . 2·25 90
2580 8f. (2) Construction workers 1·40 90
2581 8f. (3) Agricultural workers making field tests . . . . 2·25 90
2582 8f. (4) Trucks delivering grain to State granaries 1·40 90
2583 8f. (5) Workers going to fields . . . . 1·40 90

479 National Day Celebrations

480 Steel Worker, Taching

1974. 25th Anniv of Chinese People's Republic. Multicoloured. (a) National Day.
2584 8f. Type **479** . . . . 5·50 2·50

(b) Chairman Mao's Directives.
2585 8f. (1) Type **480** . . . . . . 1·50 80
2586 8f. (2) Agricultural worker, Tachai . . . . 1·50 80
2587 8f. (3) Coastal guard . . . . 1·50 80

481 Fair Building

1974. Chinese Exports Fair, Canton.
2588 **481** 8f. multicoloured . . . . 3·25 1·25

482 Revolutionary Monument, Permet
483 Capital Stadium

1974. 30th Anniv of Albania's Liberation. Mult.

2589	8f. Type **482**	2·75	1·25
2590	8f. Albanian patriots	2·75	1·25

1974. Peking Buildings. No gum.

2591	**483** 4f. black and green	15	15
2592	– 8f. black and blue	15	10

DESIGN: 8f. Hotel Peking.

484 Water-cooled Turbine Generator

1974. Industrial Production. Multicoloured.

2593	8f. (78) Type **484**	19·00	4·00
2594	8f. (79) Mechanical rice sprouts transplanter	20·00	4·00
2595	8f. (80) Universal cylindrical grinding machine	19·00	4·00
2596	8f. (81) Mobile rock drill (vert)	19·00	4·00

485 Congress Delegates

1975. 4th National People's Congress, Peking. Multicoloured.

2597	8f. (1) Type **485**	4·00	1·50
2598	8f. (2) Flower-decked rostrum	4·00	1·50
2599	8f. (3) Farmer, worker, soldier and steel mill	4·00	1·50

486 Teacher Studying

1975. Country Women Teachers. Multicoloured.

2600	8f. (1) Type **486**	9·75	2·00
2601	8f. (2) Teacher on rounds	9·75	2·00
2602	8f. (3) Open-air class	9·75	2·00
2603	8f. (4) Primary class aboard boat	9·75	2·00

487 Broadsword

1975. "Wushu" (popular sport). Multicoloured.

2604	8f. (1) Type **487**	4·25	1·75
2605	8f. (2) Sword exercises	4·25	1·75
2606	8f. (3) "Boxing"	4·25	1·75
2607	8f. (4) Leaping with spear	4·25	1·75
2608	8f. (5) Cudgel exercise	4·25	1·75
2609	43f. (6) Cudgel versus spears (60 × 30 mm)	5·00	3·50

488 "Mass Revolutionary Criticism"

489 Parade of Athletes

1975. Criticism of Confucius and Liu Piao. Multicoloured.

2610	8f. (1) Type **488**	6·00	1·50
2611	8f. (2) "Leaders of the production brigade"	6·00	1·50
2612	8f. (3) "The battle continues" (horiz)	6·00	1·50
2613	8f. (4) "Liberated slave – pioneer critic" (horiz)	6·00	1·50

1975. 3rd National Games, Peking. Mult.

2614	8f. (1) Type **489**	1·50	30
2615	8f. (2) Athletes studying (horiz)	1·50	30
2616	8f. (3) Volleyball players (horiz)	1·50	30
2617	8f. (4) Athlete, soldier, farmer and worker	1·50	30
2618	8f. (5) Various sports (horiz)	1·50	30
2619	8f. (6) Ethnic types and horse racing (horiz)	1·50	30
2620	35f. (7) Children and divers	4·00	2·00

490 Members of Expedition

492 Children sticking Posters

491 "Studying Together"

1975. Chinese Ascent of Mount Everest. Mult.

2621	8f. (2) Type **490**	80	25
2622	8f. (3) Mountaineers with flag (horiz)	80	25
2623	43f. (1) View of Mount Everest (horiz)	1·50	50

1975. National Conference "Learning Agriculture from Tachai". Multicoloured.

2624	8f. (1) Type **491**	3·00	1·00
2625	8f. (2) "Promote Hard Work"	3·00	1·00
2626	8f. (3) Chinese combine-harvester	3·00	1·00

1975. "Children's Progress". Multicoloured.

2627	8f. (1) Girl and young boy	1·25	50
2628	8f. (2) Type **492**	1·25	50
2629	8f. (3) Studying	1·25	50
2630	8f. (4) Harvesting	1·25	50
2631	52f. (5) Tug-of-war	6·75	2·25

493 Ploughing Paddy Field

1975. Mechanised Farming. Multicoloured.

2632	8f. (1) Type **493**	2·40	90
2633	8f. (2) Mechanical rice seedlings transplanter	2·40	90
2634	8f. (3) Irrigation pump	2·40	90
2635	8f. (4) Spraying cotton field	2·40	90
2636	8f. (5) Combine harvester	2·40	90

494 Bridge over Canal

1976. Completion of 4th Five-year Plan. Mult.

2637	8f. (1) Harvest scene	3·00	80
2638	8f. (2) Type **494**	3·00	80
2639	8f. (3) Fertilizer plant	3·00	80
2640	8f. (4) Textile factory	3·00	80
2641	8f. (5) Iron foundry	3·00	80
2642	8f. (6) Steam coal train	3·00	1·00
2643	8f. (7) Hydro-electric power station	3·00	80
2644	8f. (8) Shipbuilding	3·00	80
2645	8f. (9) Oil industry	3·00	80
2646	8f. (10) Pipe-line and harbour	3·00	80
2647	8f. (11) Diesel train on viaduct	5·00	1·00
2648	8f. (12) Crystal formation (scientific research)	5·00	80
2649	8f. (13) Classroom (rural education)	5·00	80
2650	8f. (14) Workers' health centre	5·00	80
2651	8f. (15) Workers' flats	5·00	80
2652	8f. (16) Department store	5·00	80

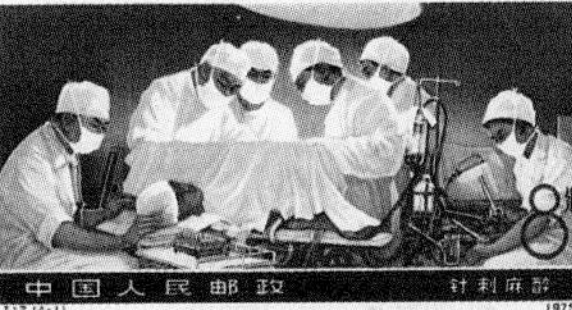

495 Heart Surgery

1976. Medical Services' Achievements. Mult.

2653	8f. (1) Type **495**	3·00	80
2654	8f. (2) Restoration of tractor-driver's severed arm	3·00	80
2655	8f. (3) Exercise of fractured arm	3·00	80
2656	8f. (4) Cataract operation – patient threading needle	3·00	80

496 Students studying at "May 7" School

1976. 10th Anniv of Mao's "May 7 Directive". Multicoloured.

2657	8f. (1) Type **496**	2·50	80
2658	8f. (2) Students in agriculture	2·50	80
2659	8f. (3) Students in production team	2·50	80

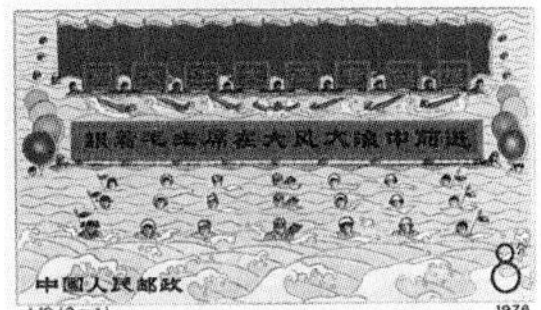

497 Formation of Swimmers

1976. 10th Anniv of Chairman Mao's Swim in Yangtse River. Multicoloured.

2660	8f. (1) Type **497**	2·50	80
2661	8f. (2) Swimmers crossing Yangtse	2·50	90
2662	8f. (3) Swimmers in surf	2·50	80

Nos. 2661/2 are smaller, 35 × 27 mm.

498 Students with Rosettes

1976. "Going to College". Multicoloured.

2663	8f. (1) Type **498**	2·40	70
2664	8f. (2) Study group	2·40	70
2665	8f. (3) On-site instructions	2·40	70
2666	8f. (4) Students operating computer	2·40	70
2667	8f. (5) Return of graduates from college	2·40	70

499 Electricity Lineswoman

501 Peasant arranging Student's Headband

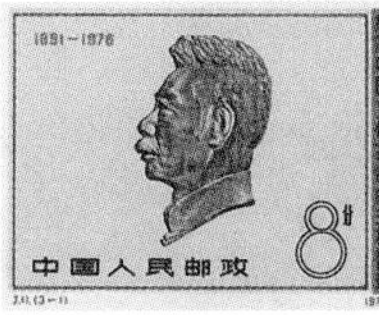

500 Lu Hsun

1976. Maintenance of Electric Power Lines. Multicoloured.

2668	8f. (1) Type **499**	2·50	70
2669	8f. (2) Linesman replacing insulator	2·50	70
2670	8f. (3) Linesman using hydraulic lift	2·50	70
2671	8f. (4) Technician inspecting transformer	2·50	70

1976. 95th Birth Anniv of Lu Hsun (revolutionary leader). Multicoloured.

2672	8f. (1) Type **500**	4·25	1·40
2673	8f. (2) Lu Hsun sick, writing in bed	4·25	1·40
2674	8f. (3) Lu Hsun, workers and soldiers	4·25	1·40

1976. Students and Country Life. Multicoloured.

2675	4f. (1) Type **501**	1·25	30
2676	8f. (2) Student teaching farm woman (horiz)	1·25	30
2677	8f. (3) Irrigation survey	1·25	30
2678	8f. (4) Agricultural student testing wheat (horiz)	1·25	30
2679	10f. (5) Student feeding lamb	2·00	1·00
2680	20f. (6) Frontier guards (horiz)	4·00	1·50

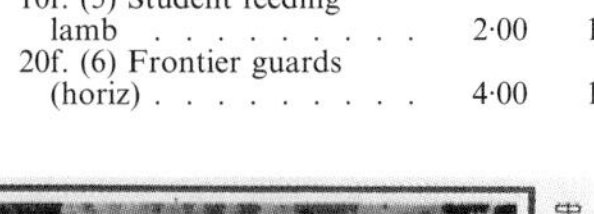

502 Mao Tse-tung's Birthplace

1976. Shaoshan Revolutionary Sites. Mult.

2681	4f. (1) Type **502**	1·40	60
2682	8f. (2) School building	1·40	50
2683	8f. (3) Peasants' Association building	1·40	50
2684	10f. (4) Railway station	1·40	60

503 Chou En-lai

504 Statue of Lui Hu-lan

1977. 1st Death Anniv of Chou En-lai. Mult.

2685	8f. (1) Type **503**	2·00	80
2686	8f. (2) Chou En-lai making report	2·00	80
2687	8f. (3) Chou meeting "Iron Man" Wang Chin-hsi (horiz)	2·00	80
2688	8f. (4) Chou with provincial representatives (horiz)	2·00	80

1977. 30th Death Anniv of Lin Hu-lan (heroine and martyr). Multicoloured.

2689	8f. (1) Type **504**	6·00	1·25
2690	8f. (2) Text by Mao Tse-tung	2·50	1·25
2691	8f. (3) Lin Hu-lan and people	2·50	1·25

505 Revolutionaries and Text

1977. 30th Anniv of 1947 Taiwan Rising. Mult.

2692	8f. Type **505**	1·50	75
2693	10f. Three Taiwanese with banner	2·50	1·00

506 Weapon Maintenance

1977. Chinese Militiawomen. Multicoloured.

2694	8f. (1) Type **506**	4·00	1·25
2695	8f. (2) On horseback	4·00	1·25
2696	8f. (3) Directing traffic in tunnel	4·00	1·25

507 Sheep Rearing

508 Cadre Members

1977. Multicoloured.

2697	1f. Coal mining	20	10
2698	1½f. Type **507**	10	20
2699	2f. Exports	20	10
2700	3f. Forest and diesel-train	20	10
2701	4f. Hydro-electric power	10	10
2702	5f. Fishing	50	10
2703	8f. Agriculture	10	10
2704	10f. Radio tower and mail-vans	15	10
2705	20f. Steel production	20	10
2706	30f. Road transport	20	10
2707	40f. Textile manufacture	25	15
2708	50f. Tractor assembly	40	10

2709 60f. Oil-rigs and setting sun . . . 45 15
2710 70f. Railway viaduct, Yangtse Gorge 85 35

1977. Promoting Tachai-type Developments. Mult.
2711 8f. (1) Type **508** . . . . . . 1·25 75
2712 8f. (2) Modern cultivation . . 1·25 75
2713 8f. (3) Reading wall newspaper . . . . 1·25 75
2714 8f. (4) Reclaiming land for agriculture . . . . 1·25 75

509 Party Leader addressing Workers

1977. "Taching-type" Industrial Conference. Mult.
2715 8f. (1) Type **509** . . . . . . 1·75 85
2716 8f. (2) Drilling for oil in snowstorm . . . . 1·75 85
2717 8f. (3) Man with banner over mass formation of workers . . . . 1·75 85
2718 8f. (4) Smiling workers and industrial scene . . . . . 1·75 85

510 Mongolians Rejoicing

511 Rumanian Flag

1977. 30th Anniv of Inner Mongolian Autonomous Region. Multicoloured.
2719 8f. Type **510** 50 30
2720 10f. Mongolian industrial scene and iron ore train . . 85 40
2721 20f. Mongolian pasture . . 1·50 75

1977. Centenary of Rumanian Independence. Mult.
2722 8f. Type **511** . . . . 1·00 25
2723 10f. "The Battle of Smirdan" (Grigorescu) . . 1·50 75
2724 20f. Mihai Viteazu Memorial . . . . 2·00 75

512 Yenan and Floral Border

1977. 35th Anniv of Yenan Forum on Literature and Art. Multicoloured.
2725 8f. (1) Type **512** 75 35
2726 8f. (2) Hammer, sickle and gun 75 35

513 Chu Teh, National People's Congress Chairman

514 Soldier, Sailor and Airman under Banner of Mao Tse-tung

1977. 1st Death Anniv of Chu Teh.
2727 **513** 8f. (1) multicoloured . . 75 30
2728 – 8f. (2) multicoloured . . 75 30
2729 – 8f. (3) black, bl & gold 75 30
2730 – 8f. (4) black, bl & gold 75 30
DESIGNS—VERT: No. 2728, Chu Teh during his last session of Congress. HORIZ: No. 2729, Chu Teh at his desk. No. 2730, Chu Teh on horseback as Commander of People's Liberation Army.

1977. People's Liberation Army Day. Mult.
2731 8f. (1) Type **514** . . . . . . 1·60 60
2732 8f. (2) Soldiers in Ching-kang Mountains . . . . 1·60 60
2733 8f. (3) Guerrilla fighters returning to base . . . . 1·60 60
2734 8f. (4) Chinese forces crossing Yangtse River . . 1·60 60
2735 8f. (5) "The Steel Wall" (National Defence Forces) 1·60 60

515 Red Flags and Crowd

1977. 11th National Communist Party Congress. Multicoloured.
2736 8f. (1) Type **515** . . . . . . 4·00 1·00
2737 8f. (2) Mao banner and procession . . . . 4·00 1·00
2738 8f. (3) Hammer and sickle banner and procession . . 4·00 1·00

516 Mao Tse-tung

1977. 1st Death Anniv of Mao Tse-tung. Mult.
2739 8f. (1) Type **516** . . . . . . 1·00 45
2740 8f. (2) Mao as young man 1·00 45
2741 8f. (3) Making speech . . . 1·00 45
2742 8f. (4) Mao broadcasting . . 1·00 45
2743 8f. (5) Mao with Chou En-lai and Chu Teh (horiz) 1·25 45
2744 8f. (6) Reviewing the army 1·25 45

517 Mao Memorial Hall

1977. Completion of Mao Memorial Hall, Peking. Multicoloured.
2745 8f. (1) Type **517** . . . . . . 2·50 1·10
2746 8f. (2) Commemoration text 2·50 1·10

518 Tractors transporting Oil-rig

1978. Development of Petroleum Industry. Mult.
2747 8f. (1) Type **518** 50 10
2748 8f. (2) Clearing wax from oil well 50 10
2749 8f. (3) Laying pipe-line . . . 50 10
2750 8f. (4) Tung Fang Hung oil refinery, Peking 65 20
2751 8f. (5) Loading a tanker, Taching 75 20
2752 20f. (6) Oil-rig and drilling ship "Exploration" . . . 2·75 80

519 Rifle Shooting from Sampan

1978. "Army and People are One Family". Multicoloured.
2753 8f. (1) Type **519** . . . . . . 1·25 75
2754 8f. (2) Helping with rice harvest . . . . 1·25 75

520 Great Banner of Chairman Mao

521 "Learn from Comrade Lei Feng" (Inscription by Mao Tse-tung)

1978. 5th National People's Congress. Mult.
2755 8f. (1) Type **520** 80 40
2756 8f. (2) Constitution 80 40
2757 8f. (3) Emblems of modernization 80 40

1978. Lei Feng (Communist fighter) Commem.
2758 **521** 8f. (1) gold and red . . . 1·50 50
2759 – 8f. (2) gold and red . . . 1·50 50
2760 – 8f. (3) multicoloured . . 1·50 50
DESIGNS: No. 2759, Inscription by Chairman Hua; No. 2760, Lei Feng reading Mao's works.

522 Hsiang Ching-yu (Women's Movement Pioneer)

523 Conference Emblem and Tien on Men Gate, Peking

1978. International Working Women's Day.
2761 **522** 8f. (1) black, red & gold 75 35
2762 – 8f. (2) black, red & gold 75 35
DESIGN: No. 2762, Yang Kai-hui (communist fighter).

1978. National Science Conference. Mult.
2763 8f. (1) Type **523** 75 40
2764 8f. (2) Flags 75 40
2765 8f. (3) Emblem, flag and globe 75 40

524 Launching a Radio-sonde

525 Galloping Horse

1978. Meteorological Services. Multicoloured.
2766 8f. (1) Type **524** 60 20
2767 8f. (2) Radar station 60 20
2768 8f. (3) Weather forecasting with computers 60 20
2769 8f. (4) Commune group observing sky 60 20
2770 8f. (5) Cloud-dispersing rockets 60 20

1978. Galloping Horses.
2771 **525** 4f. (1) multicoloured . . 1·00 50
2772 – 8f. (2) multicoloured . . 1·00 50
2773 – 8f. (3) multicoloured . . 1·00 55
2774 – 10f. (4) multicoloured . . 1·00 55
2775 – 20f. (5) multicoloured . . 4·00 65
2776 – 30f. (6) multicoloured . . 3·00 75
2777 – 40f. (7) mult (horiz) . . 3·00 1·00
2778 – 50f. (8) mult (horiz) . . 4·00 1·00
2779 – 60f. (9) mult (horiz) . . 3·00 2·00
2780 – 70f. (10) mult (horiz) . . 4·00 3·00
DESIGNS: No. 2772/80, various paintings of horses by Hsu Pei-hung.

526 Football

527 Material Feeder

1978. "Building up Strength for the Revolution". Multicoloured.
2782 8f. (2) Type **526** 40 10
2783 8f. (3) Swimming 40 10
2784 8f. (4) Gymnastics 40 10
2785 8f. (5) Running 40 10
2786 20f. (1) Group exercises . . 1·10 20
The 20f. is larger, 48 × 27 mm.

1978. Chemical Industry Development. Fabric Production. Multicoloured.
2787 8f. (1) Type **527** 80 20
2788 8f. (2) Drawing-out threads 80 20
2789 8f. (3) Weaving 80 20
2790 8f. (4) Dyeing and printing 80 20
2791 8f. (5) Finished products . . 80 20

528 Conference Emblem

529 Grassland Improvement, Mongolia

1978. National Finance and Trade Conference. Multicoloured.
2792 8f. (1) Type **528** 75 20
2793 8f. (2) Inscription by Mao Tse-tung 75 20

1978. Progress in Animal Husbandry. Mult.
2794 8f. (1) Type **529** . . . . . . 1·00 25
2795 8f. (2) Sheep rearing by the Kazakhs . . . . 1·00 25
2796 8f. (3) Shearing sheep, Tibet 1·00 25

530 Automated loading of Burning Coke

1978. Iron and Steel Industry. Mult.
2797 8f. (1) Type **530** . . . . . . 1·00 25
2798 8f. (2) Checking molten iron 50 25
2799 8f. (3) Pouring molten steel 50 25
2800 8f. (4) Steel-rolling mill . . 50 25
2801 8f. (5) Loading steel train 1·00 25

531 Soldier

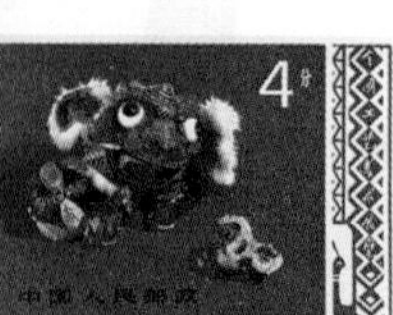
532 Cloth Toy Lion

1978. Army Modernization. Multicoloured.
2802 8f. (1) Type **531** 85 30
2803 8f. (2) Soldier firing missile 85 30
2804 8f. (3) Amphibious landing 85 30

1978. Arts and Crafts. Multicoloured.
2805 4f. (1) Type **532** 45 15
2806 8f. (2) Three-legged pot (vert) 45 10
2807 8f. (3) Lacquerware rhinoceros 55 10
2808 10f. (4) Embroidered kitten (vert) 55 15
2809 20f. (5) Basketware 65 20
2810 30f. (6) Cloissone pot (vert) 70 30
2811 40f. (7) Lacquerware plate and swan 85 40
2812 50f. (8) Boxwood carving (vert) . . . . 1·00 50
2813 60f. (9) Jade carving . . . . 1·25 40
2814 70f. (10) Ivory carving (vert) 1·40 70

533 Worker, Peasant and Intellectual

534 "Panax ginseng"

1978. 4th National Women's Congress.
2816 **533** 8f. multicoloured . . . . 1·50 50

1978. Medicinal Plants. Multicoloured.
2817 8f. (1) Type **534** 60 15
2818 8f. (2) "Datura metel" . . . 60 15
2819 8f. (3) "Belamcanda chinensis" 60 15
2820 8f. (4) "Platycodon grandiflorum" 60 15
2821 55f. (5) "Rhododendron dauricum" . . . . 2·40 75

535 Cogwheel, Grain, Rocket and Flag **536** Emblem, Open Book and Flowers

1978. 9th National Trades Union Congress.
2822 **535** 8f. multicoloured . . . . 2·10 75

1978. 10th National Congress of Communist Youth League.
2823 **536** 8f. multicoloured . . . . 2·10 75

537 Chinese and Japanese Children exchanging Gifts **538** Hui, Han and Mongolian

1978. Signing of Chinese–Japanese Treaty of Peace and Friendship. Multicoloured.
2824 8f. Type **537** 30 15
2825 55f. Great Wall of China and Mt. Fuji . . . . . . 1·75 65

1978. 20th Anniv of Ningsia Hui Autonomous Region. Multicoloured.
2826 8f. (1) Type **538** 85 30
2827 8f. (2) Coal loading machine, Holan colliery 85 30
2828 10f. (3) Irrigation and Chingtunghsia power station 85 30

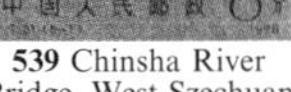

539 Chinsha River Bridge, West Szechuan **540** Transplanting Rice Seedlings by Machine

1978. Highway Bridges. Multicoloured.
2829 8f. (1) Type **539** 70 30
2830 8f. (2) Hsinghong Bridge, Wuhsi 70 30
2831 8f. (3) Chiuhsikou Bridge, Fengdu 70 30
2832 8f. (4) Chinsha Bridge . . . 70 30
2833 60f. (5) Shangyeh Bridge, Sanmen . . . . 1·90 90

1978. Water Country Modernization. Mult.
2835 8f. (1) Type **540** . . . . . 2·25 1·00
2836 8f. (2) Crop spraying . . . 2·25 1·00
2837 8f. (3) Selecting seeds . . . 2·25 1·00
2838 8f. (4) Canal-side village . . 2·25 1·00
2839 8f. (5) Delivering and storing grain . . . . . . 2·25 1·00

Nos. 2835/9 were issued together, se-tenant, forming a composite design.

541 Festivities

1978. 20th Anniv of Kwangsi Chuang Autonomous Region. Multicoloured.
2840 8f. (1) Type **541** . . . . . 2·25 40
2841 8f. (2) Industrial complexes (vert) . . . . 2·25 40
2842 10f. (3) River scene (vert) 1·50 1·00

542 Tibetan Peasant reporting Mineralogical Discovery **543** Pair of Golden Pheasants on Rock

1978. Mining Development. Multicoloured.
2843 4f. Type **542** 50 25
2844 8f. Miners with pneumatic drill 50 15
2845 10f. Open-cast mining . . . 1·25 25
2846 20f. Electric mine train . . . 1·50 40

1979. Golden Pheasants. Multicoloured.
2847 4f. Type **543** . . . . 1·25 70
2848 8f. Pheasant in flight . . . . 3·75 1·25
2849 45f. Pheasant looking for food . . . . 3·00 3·00

544 Einstein **545** Woman, Monster and Phoenix

1979. Birth Centenary of Albert Einstein (physicist).
2850 **544** 8f. brown, gold & slate 1·40 40

1979. Silk Paintings from a Tomb of the Warring States Period (475–221 B.C.). Multicoloured.
2851 8f. Type **545** . . . . 2·10 20
2852 60f. Man riding dragon . . 1·40 1·25

546 Jing Shan **547** Hammer and Sickle

1979. Peking Scenes. Multicoloured.
2853 1y. Type **546** 75 10
2854 2y. Summer Palace . . . . 1·50 40
2855 5y. Beihai Park . . . . . . 4·00 85

1979. 90th Anniv of International Labour Day.
2856 **547** 8f. multicoloured . . . . 1·25 50

548 Memorial Frieze

1979. 60th Anniv of May 4th Movement. Mult.
2857 8f. (1) Type **548** 70 20
2858 8f. (2) Girl and symbols of progress 70 20

549 Children of Different Races

1979. International Year of the Child. Mult.
2859 8f. I.Y.C. emblem and children with balloons . . 1·50 50
2860 60f. Type **549** . . . . 8·75 3·00

550 Spring over Great Wall

1979. The Great Wall. Multicoloured.
2861 8f. (1) Type **550** . . . . . . 1·50 75
2862 8f. (2) Summer over Great Wall . . . . 1·50 75
2863 8f. (3) Autumn over Great Wall . . . . 1·50 75
2864 60f. (4) Winter over Great Wall . . . . 11·00 5·00

551 Roaring Tiger

1979. Manchurian Tiger. Paintings by Liu Jiyou. Multicoloured.
2866 4f. Type **551** . . . . 1·00 50
2867 8f. Two young tigers . . . . 1·00 50
2868 60f. Tiger at rest . . . . . 3·25 1·10

552 Mechanical Harvester

1979. Trades of the People's Communes. Mult.
2869 4f. (1) Type **552** (Agriculture) 75 30
2870 8f. (2) Planting a sapling (Forestry) . . . . 1·00 30
2871 8f. (3) Herding ducks (Stock raising) . . . . 1·00 30
2872 8f. (4) Basket weaving . . . 1·00 30
2873 10f. (5) Fishermen with handcarts of fish (Fishing) 2·00 50

554 Games' Emblem, Running, Volleyball and Weightlifting

1979. 4th National Games.
2875 **554** 8f. (1) multicoloured . . 30 30
2876 – 8f. (2) multicoloured . . 30 30
2877 – 8f. (3) black, grn & red 30 30
2878 – 8f. (4) black, red & grn 30 30

DESIGNS: No. 2876, Football, badminton, high jumping and ice skating. No. 2877, Fencing, skiing, gymnastics and diving. No. 2878, Motor cycling, table tennis, basketball and archery.

555 National Flag and Mountains

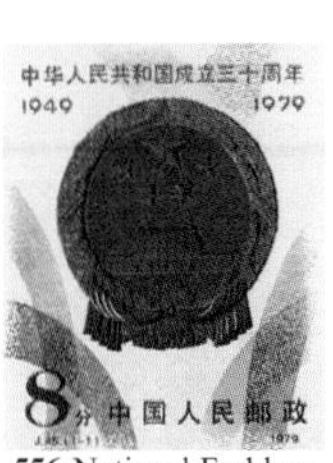

556 National Emblem

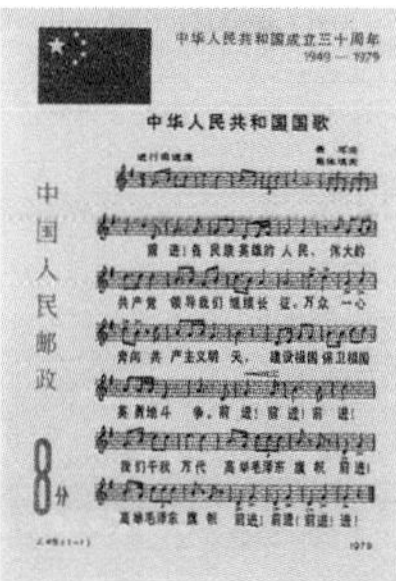

557 National Anthem

558 Dancers and Drummer **559** Tractor and Crop-spraying Antonov An-2

1979. 30th Anniv of People's Republic of China. Multicoloured.
2880 8f. (1) National flag and rainbow . . . . 1·90 70
2881 8f. (2) Type **555** . . . . . . 1·90 70
2882 8f. Type **556** . . . . 1·25 25
2884 8f. Type **557** . . . . 3·00 1·00
2885 8f. (1) Type **558** 75 15
2886 8f. (2) Dancers and tambourine player 75 15
2887 8f. (3) Dancers and banjo player 75 15
2888 8f. (4) Dancers and drummer 75 15
2889 8f. (1) Type **559** 85 15
2890 8f. (2) Computer and cogwheels 85 15
2891 8f. (3) Rocket, jet fighter and submarine 85 15
2892 8f. (4) Atomic symbols . . . 85 15

560 Exhibition Emblem **561** Children with Model Aircraft

1979. National Exhibition of Juniors' Scientific and Technological Works.
2893 **560** 8f. multicoloured . . . . 1·25 50

1979. Study of Science from Childhood. Mult.
2894 8f. (1) Type **561** 65 20
2895 8f. (2) Girls with microscope and test tube 65 20
2896 8f. (3) Children with telescope 65 20
2897 8f. (4) Boy catching butterflies 65 20
2898 8f. (5) Girl noting weather readings 65 20
2899 60f. (6) Boys with model boat . . . . 2·50 75

562 Yu Shan

1979. Taiwan Views. Multicoloured.
2901 8f. (1) Type **562** 85 45
2902 8f. (2) Sun Moon Lake . . 85 45
2903 8f. (3) Chikan Tower . . . 85 45
2904 8f. (4) Suao-Hualien highway 85 45
2905 55f. (5) Tian Xiang Falls . . 2·50 1·00
2906 60f. (6) Moonlight over Banping Mountain . . . 3·50 1·60

563 Symbols of Literature and Art

1979. 4th National Congress of Literary and Art Workers. Multicoloured.
2907 4f. Type **563** 50 30
2908 8f. Seals, hammer, sickle, rifle, atomic symbol and flowers . . . . 1·10 30

564 "Shaoshan" Type Electric Locomotive

1979. Railway Construction. Multicoloured.
2909 8f. (1) Type **564** . . . . . . 1·50 40
2910 8f. (2) Modern railway viaduct . . . . 1·50 40
2911 8f. (3) Goods train crossing bridge . . . . 1·50 40

565 "Chrysanthemum Petal"

1979. Camellias of Yunnan. Multicoloured.
2912 4f. (1) Type **565** 70 30
2913 8f. (2) "Lion Head" 70 30
2914 8f. (3) Camellia "Chrysantha (Hu) Tuyama" 70 30
2915 10f. (4) "Small Osmanthus Leaf" 70 30
2916 20f. (5) "Baby Face" . . . 1·75 55
2917 30f. (6) "Cornelian" . . . . 3·25 65
2918 40f. (7) Peony Camellia . . 2·50 65
2919 50f. (8) "Purple Gown" . . 2·50 75
2920 60f. (9) "Dwarf Rose" . . . 1·90 75
2921 70f. (10) "Willow Leaf Spinel Pink" . . . . . . 1·90 75

567 Dr. Bethune attending Wounded Soldier

568 Central Archives Hall

1979. 40th Death Anniv of Dr. Norman Bethune. Multicoloured.
2924 8f. Type **567** 55 10
2925 70f. Bethune Memorial, Mausoleum of Martyrs, Shijiazhuang . . . . . . 2·75 75

1979. International Archives Weeks. Mult.
2926 8f. (1) Type **568** 85 20
2927 8f. (2) Gold cabinet containing documents of Ming and Ching dynasties (vert) 85 20
2928 60f. (3) Imperial Archives Main Hall . . . . 7·75 1·75

569 Waterfall Cave, Home of Monkey King

570 Stalin

1979. Scenes from "Pilgrimage to the West" (Chinese classical novel). Multicoloured.
2929 8f. (1) Type **569** . . . . . . 1·50 75
2930 8f. (2) Necha, son of Li, fighting Monkey . . . . 1·50 75
2931 8f. (3) Monkey in Mother Queen's peach orchard . . 1·50 75
2932 8f. (4) Monkey in alchemy furnace . . . . 1·50 75
2933 10f. (5) Monkey fighting White Bone Demon . . . 4·25 75
2934 20f. (6) Monkey extinguishing fire with palm-leaf fan . . . . . . 4·25 75
2935 60f. (7) Monkey fighting Spider Demon in Cobweb Cave . . . . 3·25 3·00
2936 70f. (8) Monkey on scripture-seeking route to India . . . . 7·25 3·00

1979. Birth Centenary of Stalin.
2937 **570** 8f. (1) brown . . . . . 1·25 40
2938 – 8f. (2) black . . . . . . 1·25 40
DESIGN: No. 2038, Stalin appealing for unity against Germany.

571 Peony

572 Meng Liang, "Hongyang Cave"

1980. Paintings of Qi Baishi.
2939 **571** 4f. (1) multicoloured . . 75 15
2940 – 4f. (2) multicoloured . . 75 15
2941 – 8f. (3) multicoloured . . 75 10
2942 – 8f. (4) black, blue & red 75 10
2943 – 8f. (5) multicoloured . . 75 10
2944 – 8f. (6) black, grey & red 75 10
2945 – 8f. (7) multicoloured . . 75 10
2946 – 8f. (8) multicoloured . . 75 50
2947 – 10f. (9) blk, yell and red 1·50 15
2948 – 20f. (10) grey, brn & blk 1·50 20
2949 – 30f. (11) multicoloured 1·50 30
2950 – 40f. (12) multicoloured 1·50 50
2951 – 50f. (13) blk, grey & red 3·00 75
2952 – 55f. (14) multicoloured 3·75 75
2953 – 60f. (15) blk, grey & red 5·00 1·50
2954 – 70f. (16) multicoloured 6·25 2·25
DESIGNS: No. 2940, Squirrels and grapes; 2941, Crabs and wine; 2942, Tadpoles in mountain spring; 2943, Chicks; 2944, Lotus; 2945, Red plum; 2946, River kingfisher; 2947, Bottle gourds; 2948, "The Voice of Autumn"; 2949, Wisteria; 2950, Chrysanthemums; 2951, Shrimps; 2952, Litchi; 2953, Cabbages and mushrooms; 2954, Peaches.

1980. Facial Make-up in Peking Operas. Mult.
2956 4f. (1) Type **572** . . . . . . 1·25 40
2957 4f. (2) Li Kui, "Black Whirlwind" . . . . . . 1·25 40
2958 8f. (3) Huang Gai, "Meeting of Heroes" . . . . 1·75 60
2959 8f. (4) Monkey King, "Havoc in Heaven" . . . 1·75 60
2960 10f. (5) Lu Zhishen, "Wild Boar Forest" . . . . . . 2·25 80
2961 20f. (6) Lian Po, "Reconciliation between the General and the Minister" . . . . 4·50 1·50
2962 60f. (7) Zhang Fei, "Reed Marsh" . . . . 8·25 3·00
2963 70f. (8) Dou Erdun, "Stealing the Emperor's Horse" . . . . 9·00 3·25

573 Chinese Olympic Committee Emblem

574 Bear Macaque

1980. Winter Olympic Games, Lake Placid. Multicoloured.
2964 8f. (1) Type **573** 50 35
2965 8f. (2) Speed skating 50 35
2966 8f. (3) Figure skating . . . 50 35
2967 60f. (4) Skiing . . . . . . 3·50 1·25

1980. New Year. Year of the Monkey.
2968 **574** 8f. red, black and gold £170 50·00

575 Klara Zetkin (journalist and politician)

1980. 70th Anniv of International Working Women's Day.
2969 **575** 8f. black, yellow & brn 1·25 65

576 Orchard

1980. Afforestation. Multicoloured.
2970 4f. Type **576** 70 15
2971 8f. Highway lined with trees 70 20
2972 10f. Aerial sowing by Antonov An-2 biplane . . 1·40 25
2973 20f. Factory amongst trees 1·40 60

577 Apsaras (celestial beings)

1980. 2nd National Conference of Chinese Scientific and Technical Association.
2974 **577** 8f. multicoloured . . . . 1·25 55

578 Freighter

1980. Mail Transport. Multicoloured.
2975 2f. Type **578** . . . . 1·00 75
2976 4f. Mail bus . . . . 1·25 75
2977 8f. Travelling post office coach . . . . 2·50 1·00
2978 10f. Tupolev Tu-154 airplane . . . . 3·00 1·40

579 Cigarette damaging Heart and Lungs

1980. Anti-smoking Campaign. Multicoloured.
2979 8f. Type **579** . . . . 1·75 40
2980 60f. Face smoking and face holding flower in mouth, symbolising choice of smoking or health . . . . 5·00 2·25

580 Jian Zhen Memorial Hall, Yangzhou

1980. Return of High Monk Jian Zhen's Statue. Multicoloured.
2981 8f. (1) Type **580** . . . . . . 2·50 50
2982 8f. (2) Statue of Jian Zhen (vert) . . . . 2·50 50
2983 60f. (3) Junk in which Jian Zhen travelled to Japan 16·00 5·75

581 Lenin

582 "Swallow Chick" Kite

1980. 110th Birth Anniv of Lenin.
2984 **581** 8f. brown, pink & green 1·60 65

1980. Kites. Multicoloured.
2985 8f. (1) Type **582** . . . . . . 1·50 45
2986 8f. (2) "Slender swallow" kite . . . . 1·50 45
2987 8f. (3) "Semi-slender swallow" kite . . . . . . 1·50 45
2988 70f. (4) "Dual swallows" kite . . . . 12·00 4·50

583 Hare running in Fright

1980. Scenes from "Gu Dong" (Chinese fairy tale). Multicoloured.
2989 8f. (1) Type **583** . . . . . . 1·00 55
2990 8f. (2) Hare tells other animals "Gu Dong is coming" . . . . 1·00 55
2991 8f. (3) Lion asks "What is Gu Dong?" . . . . . . 1·00 55
2992 8f. (4) Animals discover sound of "Gu Dong" is made by falling papaya 1·00 55

584 Silhouette of Ilyushin Il-86 Jetliner and Plan of Terminal Building

585 Stag

1980. Peking International Airport. Multicoloured.
2993 8f. Type **584** . . . . 1·00 30
2994 10f. Airplane and runway lights . . . . 1·50 50

1980. Sika Deer. Multicoloured.
2995 4f. Type **585** 80 65
2996 8f. Doe and fawn 80 65
2997 60f. Herd . . . . 5·25 2·10

586 "White Lotus"

1980. Lotus Paintings by Yu Zhizhen. Mult.
2998 8f. (1) Type **586** . . . . . . 2·00 90
2999 8f. (2) "Rose-tipped Snow" 2·00 90
3000 8f. (3) "Buddha's Seat" . . 2·00 90
3001 70f. (4) "Variable Charming Face" . . . . 17·00 6·00

587 Returned Pearl Cave and Sword-cut Stone

1980. Guilin Landscapes. Multicoloured.
3003 8f. (1) Type **587** . . . . . . 1·50 45
3004 8f. (2) Distant view of three mountains . . . . . . 1·50 45
3005 8f. (3) Nine-horse Fresco Hill . . . . 1·50 45
3006 8f. (4) Egrets around the aged banyan . . . . . . 1·50 45
3007 8f. (5) Western Hills at sunset (vert) . . . . . . 1·50 45
3008 8f. (6) Moonlight on the Lijiang River (vert) . . . 1·50 45
3009 60f. (7) Springhead and ferry (vert) . . . . . . 9·50 3·00
3010 70f. (8) Scenic path at Yangshuo (vert) . . . . . 10·50 3·00

588 Exhibition Gateway

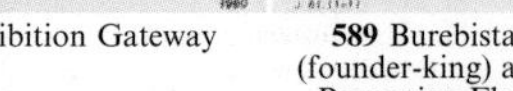

589 Burebista (founder-king) and Rumanian Flag

1980. China Exhibition in United States. Mult.
3011 8f. Type **588** 75 40
3012 70f. Great Wall and emblems of San Francisco, Chicago and New York . . . . 4·25 2·25

1980. 2050th Anniv of Dacian State.
3013 **589** 8f. multicoloured . . . . 1·60 65

590 "Sea of Clouds" (Liu Haisu)

1980. U.N.E.S.C.O. Exhibition of Chinese Paintings and Drawings. Multicoloured.
3014 8f. (1) Type **590** . . . . . . 1·10 40
3015 8f. (2) "Black-naped Oriole and Magnolia" (Yu Feian) (vert) . . . . . . 1·50 70
3016 8f. (3) "Tending Bactrian Camels" (Wu Zuoren) . . 1·10 40

591 Quzi Tower in Spring

1980. Liu Yuan (Tarrying Garden), Suzhou. Mult.
3017 8f. (1) Type **591** . . . . . . 5·75 2·10
3018 8f. (2) Yuancui Pavilion in Summer . . . . 5·75 2·10
3019 10f. (3) Hanbi Shanfang in Autumn . . . . 5·75 2·40
3020 60f. (4) Guanyun Peak in Winter . . . . 32·00 10·00

592 Xu Guangqi

593 Pistol-shooting

1980. Scientists of Ancient China. Multicoloured.
3021 8f. (1) Type **592** (agriculturalist and astronomer) . . . . . . 2·25 65
3022 8f. (2) Li Bing (hydraulic engineer) . . . . 2·25 65
3023 8f. (3) Jia Sixie (agronomist) 2·25 65
3024 60f. (4) Huang Daopo (textile expert) . . . . . 10·00 3·00

1980. 1st Anniv of Return to International Olympic Committee. Multicoloured.
3025 **593** 4f. (1) brown, yell & mve 50 10
3026 – 8f. (2) brown, yell & grn 75 15
3027 – 8f. (3) brown, yell & blue 75 15
3028 – 10f. (4) brown, yell & orge . . . . 1·10 35
3029 – 60f. (5) multicoloured . . 3·75 1·00
DESIGNS: No. 3026, Gymnastics; No. 3027, Diving; No. 3028, Volleyball; No. 3029, Archery.

594 White Flag Dolphin

595 Cock

1980. White Flag Dolphin. Multicoloured.
3030 8f. Type **594** . . . . 1·25 25
3031 60f. Two dolphins . . . . . 6·00 1·00

1981. New Year. Year of the Cock.
3032 **595** 8f. multicoloured . . . . 8·50 2·00

596 Early Morning

1981. Scenes of Xishuang Banna. Multicoloured.
3033 4f. (1) Type **596** 60 20
3034 4f. (2) Mountain village of Dai nationality 60 20
3035 8f. (3) Rainbow over Lanchang River . . . . . 1·25 25
3036 8f. (4) Ancient Temple (vert) 1·25 25
3037 8f. (5) Moonlit night (vert) 1·25 25
3038 60f. (6) Phoenix tree in bloom (vert) . . . . . . 7·00 2·50

597 Flower Basket Lantern

1981. Palace Lanterns. Multicoloured.
3039 4f. (1) Type **597** 95 45
3040 8f. (2) Dragons playing with a pearl . . . . 1·50 40
3041 8f. (3) Dragon and phoenix 1·50 40
3042 8f. (4) Treasure bowl . . . 1·50 40
3043 20f. (5) Flower and birds . . 4·25 1·00
3044 60f. (6) Peony lantern painted with fishes . . . 11·50 4·00

598 Crossing the River

1981. Marking the Gunwale (Chinese fable). Multicoloured.
3045 8f. (1) Chinese text of story 70 35
3046 8f. (2) Type **598** 70 35
3047 8f. (3) The sword drops in the water 70 35
3048 8f. (4) Making mark on gunwale 70 35
3049 8f. (5) Diving into river to recover sword 70 35

599 Chinese Elm

600 Vase with Two Tigers (Song Dynasty)

1981. Miniature Landscapes (dwarf trees). Mult.
3050 4f. (1) Type **599** 45 35
3051 8f. (2) Juniper 70 30
3052 8f. (3) Maidenhair tree . . . 70 30
3053 10f. (4) Chinese Juniper (horiz) . . . . 1·10 30
3054 20f. (5) Wild Kaki persimmon (horiz) . . . . 2·00 1·00
3055 60f. (6) Single-seed juniper (horiz) . . . . 6·25 1·40

1981. Ceramics from Cizhou Kilns. Multicoloured.
3056 4f. (1) Type **600** 35 30
3057 8f. (2) Carved black glazed vase (Jin dynasty) (horiz) 55 25
3058 8f. (3) Amphora with apricot blossoms (modern) 55 25
3059 8f. (4) Jar with two phoenixes (Yuan dynasty) (horiz) 55 25
3060 10f. (5) Flat flask with dragon and phoenix (Yuan dynasty) (horiz) . . 1·25 30
3061 60f. (6) Vessel with tiger-shaped handles (modern) (horiz) . . . . 4·00 1·40

601 Giant Panda "Stamp"

1981. People's Republic of China Stamp Exhibition, Japan. Multicoloured.
3062 8f. Type **601** 75 15
3063 60f. Cockerel and junk "stamps" . . . . 1·90 85

602 Qinchuan Bull

603 Inscription by Chou En-lai

1981. Cattle. Multicoloured.
3064 4f. (1) Type **602** 50 15
3065 8f. (2) Binhu buffalo 50 10
3066 8f. (3) Yak 50 10
3067 8f. (4) Black and white dairy cattle 50 10
3068 10f. (5) Red pasture bull . . 75 25
3069 55f. (6) Simmental crossbreed bull . . . . . 5·00 1·25

1981. "To Deliver Mail for Ten Thousand Li, Has Bearing on Arteries and Veins of the Country".
3070 **603** 8f. multicoloured 50 15

604 I.T.U. and W.H.O. Emblems and Ribbons forming Caduceus

605 Safety in Building Construction

1981. World Telecommunications Day.
3071 **604** 8f. multicoloured 50 15

1981. National Safety Month. Multicoloured.
3072 8f. (1) Type **605** 40 15
3073 8f. (2) Mining safety 40 15
3074 8f. (3) Road safety 40 15
3075 8f. (4) Farming and forestry safety 40 15

606 Trunk Call Building

607 St. Bride Vase (Men's singles)

1981.
3076 **606** 8f. brown . . . . 1·60 40

1981. Chinese Team's Victories at World Table Tennis Championships. Multicoloured.
3077 8f. (3) Type **607** 25 15
3078 8f. (4) Iran Cup (Men's doubles) 25 15
3079 8f. (5) G. Geist Prize (Women's singles) 25 15
3080 8f. (6) W. J. Pope Trophy (Women's doubles) . . . 25 15
3081 8f. (7) Heydusek Prize (Mixed doubles) 25 15
3082 20f. (1) Swathling Cup (Men's team) 80 15
3083 20f. (2) Marcel Corbillon Cup (Women's team) . . 80 15

608 Hammer and Sickle

609 Five Veterans Peak

1981. 60th Anniv of Chinese Communist Party.
3084 **608** 8f. multicoloured 75 25

1981. Lushan Mountains. Multicoloured.
3085 8f. (1) Type **609** 70 20
3086 8f. (2) Hanpo Pass (horiz) 70 20
3087 8f. (3) Yellow Dragon Pool and Waterfall 70 20
3088 8f. (4) Sunlit Peak (horiz) 70 20
3089 8f. (5) Three-layer Spring . . 70 20
3090 8f. (6) Stone and pines (horiz) 70 20
3091 60f. (7) Dragon Head Cliff 7·50 2·50

610 Silver Ear ("Tremella fuciformis")

1981. Edible Mushrooms. Multicoloured.
3092 4f. (1) Type **610** 60 15
3093 8f. (2) Veiled stinkhorn ("Dictyophora indusiata") 80 15
3094 8f. (3) "Hericium erinaceus" 80 15
3095 8f. (4) "Russula rubra" . . 80 15
3096 10f. (5) Shii-take mushroom ("Lentinus edodes") . . . 1·25 20
3097 70f. (6) White button mushroom ("Agaricus bisporus") . . . . 3·00 75

611 Medal

612 Huangguoshu Waterfall

1981. Quality Month.
3098 **611** 8f. (1) silver, black and red 75 20
3099 8f. (2) gold, brown and red 75 20

1981.
3100 – 1f. green 10 10
3101 – 1½f. red 10 10
3102 – 2f. green 10 10
3103 **612** 3f. brown 10 10
3118 – 3f. dp brn, brn & lt brn 10 10
3104 – 4f. violet 10 10
3119 – 4f. mauve and lilac . . . 10 10
3105 – 5f. brown 10 10
3106 – 8f. blue 10 10
3107 – 10f. purple 10 10
3121 – 10f. brown 20 10
3108 – 20f. green 55 10
3122 – 20f. blue 25 10
3109 – 30f. brown 25 10
3110 – 40f. black 35 10
3111 – 50f. mauve 35 10
3112 – 70f. black 55 10
3113 – 80f. red 55 10
3114 – 1y. lilac 65 10
3115 – 2y. green 85 15
3116 – 5y. blue . . . . 1·75 25
DESIGNS—VERT: 1f. Xishuang Banna. 1½f. Huashan Mountain. 2f. Taishan Mountain. 4f. Palm trees, Hainan. 5f. Pagoda, Huqiu Hill, Suzhou. 8f. Great Wall. 10f. North-east Forest. HORIZ: 20f. Herding sheep on Tianshan Mountain. 30f. Sheep on grassland, Inner Mongolia. 40f. Stone Forest. 50f. Pagodas, Ban Pingshan Mountain, Taiwan. 70f. Mt. Zhumulangma. 80f. Seven Star Grotto, Guangdong. 1y. Gorge, Yangtze River. 2y. Guilin. 5y. Mt. Huangshan.

613 Stone Forest in Autumn

1981. Stone Forest. Multicoloured.
3125 8f. (1) Stone Forest in a mist 45 15
3126 8f. (2) Type **613** 45 15
3127 8f. (3) Pool in Stone Forest 45 15
3128 10f. (4) Dawn over Stone Forest (vert) 60 15
3129 70f. (5) Stone Forest by starlight (vert) . . . . . 5·50 1·50

614 Lu Xun as Youth

1981. Birth Centenary of Lu Xun (writer).
3130 **614** 8f. black, green & yell 50 15
3131 – 20f. blk, brn & dp brn 1·00 50
DESIGN: 20f. Lu Xun in later life.

615 Dr. Sun Yat-sen

616 "Tree" symbolizing Co-ordination

1981. 70th Anniv of 1911 Revolution.

3132 **615** 8f. (1) multicoloured . . 40 15
3133 – 8f. (2) black, grn & yell 40 15
3134 – 8f. (3) black, pk & yell 40 15

DESIGNS: No. 3133, Grave of 72 Martyrs, Huang Hua Gate; No. 3134, Headquarters of Military Government of Hubei Province.

1981. Asian Conference of Parliamentarians on Population and Development. Multicoloured.

3135 8f. Type **616** 15 10
3136 70f. Design symbolizing Enlightenment 90 35

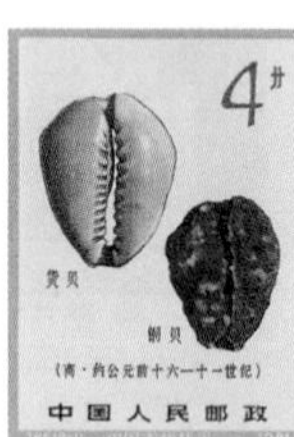

617 Money Cowrie and Cowrie-shaped Bronze Coin

618 Hands and Globe with I.Y.D.P. Emblem

1981. Ancient Chinese Coins (1st series). Minted before 221 B.C. Multicoloured.

3137 4f. (1) Type **617** 40 15
3138 4f. (2) Shovel coin 40 15
3139 8f. (3) Shovel coin inscribed "Li" 50 10
3140 8f. (4) Shovel coin inscribed "An Yi Er Jin" 50 10
3141 8f. (5) Knife coin inscribed "Qi Fa Ha" 50 10
3142 8f. (6) Knife coin inscribed "Jie Mo Zhi Fa Hua" . . 50 10
3143 60f. (7) Knife coin inscribed "Cheng Bai" . . . . . . 3·00 70
3144 70f. (8) Circular coin with hole inscribed "Gong" . . 4·25 1·40

See also Nos. 3162/69.

1981. International Year of Disabled Persons.

3145 **618** 8f. multicoloured 25 15

619 Daiyu

620 Volleyball Player

1981. The Twelve Beauties of Jinling from "A Dream of Red Mansions" by Cao Xueqin. Multicoloured. Designs showing paintings by Liu Danzhai.

3146 4f. (1) Type **619** 80 15
3147 4f. (2) Baochai chases butterfly 80 15
3148 8f. (3) Yuanchun visits parents 95 20
3149 8f. (4) Yingchun reading Buddhist sutras 95 20
3150 8f. (5) Tanchun forms poetry society 95 20
3151 8f. (6) Xichun painting . . . 95 20
3152 8f. (7) Xiangyun picking up necklace 95 20
3153 10f. (8) Liwan lectures her son . . . . 1·40 25
3154 20f. (9) Xifeng hatches plot 1·60 65
3155 30f. (10) Sister Qiao escapes 1·90 80
3156 40f. (11) Keqing relaxing . . 2·10 2·25
3157 80f. (12) Miaoyu serves tea 8·00 2·50

1981. Victory of Chinese Women's Team in World Cup Volleyball Championships. Multicoloured.

3159 8f. Type **620** 15 10
3160 20f. Player holding Cup . . 65 30

621 Dog

622 Nie Er and Score of "March of the Volunteers"

1982. New Year. Year of the Dog.

3161 **621** 8f. multicoloured . . . . 3·00 75

1982. Ancient Chinese Coins (2nd series). As T **617**. Multicoloured.

3162 4f. (1) Guilian ("Monster Mask") 15 15
3163 4f. (2) Shu shovel coin . . . 15 15
3164 8f. (3) Xia Zhuan shovel coin 20 10
3165 8f. (4) Han Dan shovel coin 20 10
3166 8f. (5) Pointed-head knife coin 20 10
3167 8f. (6) Ming knife coin . . . 20 10
3168 70f. (7) Jin Hua knife coin 2·00 50
3169 80f. (8) Yi Liu Hua circular coin . . . . 2·40 70

1982. 70th Anniv of Nie Er (composer).

3170 **622** 8f. multicoloured 30 15

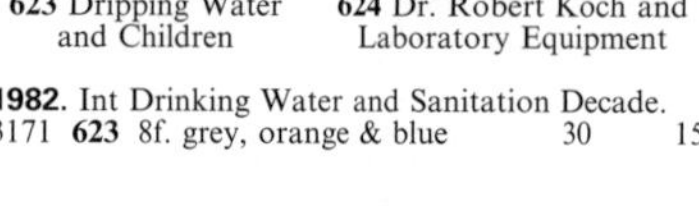

623 Dripping Water and Children

624 Dr. Robert Koch and Laboratory Equipment

1982. Int Drinking Water and Sanitation Decade.

3171 **623** 8f. grey, orange & blue 30 15

1982. Centenary of Discovery of Tubercle Bacillus.

3172 **624** 8f. multicoloured 30 15

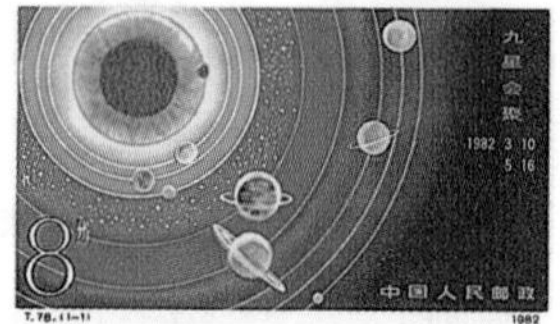

625 Building on Fire, Hoses and Fire Engine

627 "Hemerocallis flava" and "H. fulva"

626 Solar System

1982. Fire Control. Multicoloured.

3173 8f. (1) Type **625** 60 15
3174 8f. (2) Chemical fire extinguisher 60 15

1982. "Cluster of Nine Planets" (planetary conjunction).

3175 **626** 8f. multicoloured 45 20

1982. Medicinal Plants. Multicoloured.

3176 4f. (1) Type **627** 20 10
3177 8f. (2) "Fritillaria unibracteata" 40 10
3178 8f. (3) "Aconitum carmichaeli" 40 10
3179 10f. (4) "Lilium brownii" . . 45 20
3180 20f. (5) "Arisaema consanguineum" . . . . 1·10 25
3181 70f. (6) "Paeonia lactiflora" 1·60 80

628 Soong Ching Ling addressing First Plenary Session

1982. 1st Death Anniv of Soong Ching Ling (former Head of State). Multicoloured.

3183 8f. Type **628** 30 15
3184 20f. Portrait of Soong Ching Ling 65 30

629 Sable

1982. The Sable. Multicoloured.

3185 8f. Type **629** 70 20
3186 80f. Sable running . . . . . 3·50 1·75

630 Census Emblem

631 Text, Emblem and Globe

1982. National Census.

3187 **630** 8f. multicoloured 25 10

1982. Second U.N. Conference on the Exploration and Peaceful Uses of Outer Space, Vienna.

3188 **631** 8f. multicoloured 25 10

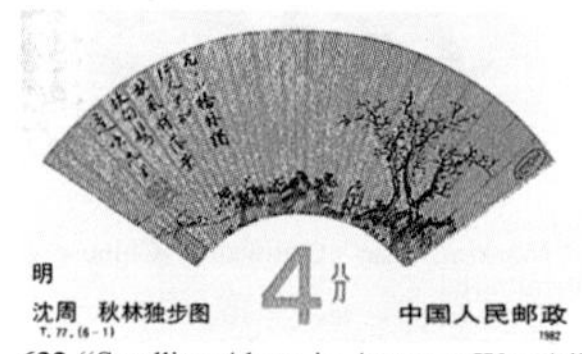

632 "Strolling Alone in Autumn Woods" (Shen Zhou)

1982. Fan Paintings of the Ming and Qing Dynasties. Multicoloured.

3189 4f. (1) Type **632** 35 10
3190 8f. (2) "Jackdaw on withered Tree" (Tang Yin) 75 30
3191 8f. (3) "Bamboos and Sparrows" (Zhou Zhimian) 75 30
3192 10f. (4) "Writing Poem under Pine" (Chen Hongshou and Bai Han) 1·00 15
3193 20f. (5) "Chrysanthemums" (Yun Shouping) . . . . . 1·25 30
3194 70f. (6) "Masked Hawfinch, Grape Myrtle and Chinese Parasol" (Wang Wu) . . 4·25 2·25

634 Society Emblem

635 Orpiment

1982. 60th Anniv of Chinese Geological Society.

3196 **634** 8f. gold, stone & black 25 10

1982. Minerals. Multicoloured.

3197 4f. Type **635** 15 10
3198 8f. Stibnite 20 10
3199 10f. Cinnabar 25 10
3200 20f. Wolframite 40 20

636 "12", Hammer and Sickle and Great Hall of the People

637 Hoopoe

1982. 12th National Communist Party Congress.

3201 **636** 8f. multicoloured 60 10

1982. Birds. Multicoloured.

3202 8f. (1) Type **637** 75 60
3203 8f. (2) Barn swallow 75 60
3204 8f. (3) Black-naped oriole 75 60
3205 20f. (4) Great tit . . . . . 1·75 1·25
3206 70f. (5) Great spotted woodpecker . . . . . . 3·50 3·00

638 "Plum Blossom" (Guan Shanyue)

1982. 10th Anniv of Normalization of Diplomatic Relations with Japan. Multicoloured.

3208 8f. Type **638** 25 10
3209 70f. "Hibiscus" (Xiao Shufang) . . . . 1·50 35

639 Globe, Profiles and Ear of Wheat

640 Guo Moruo

1982. World Food Day.

3210 **639** 8f. multicoloured 45 10

1982. 90th Birth Anniv of Guo Moruo (writer). Multicoloured.

3211 8f. Type **640** 15 10
3212 20f. Guo Moruo writing . . 30 10

641 Head of Bodhisattva

642 Dr. D. S. Kotnis

1982. Sculptures of Liao Dynasty. Mult.

3213 8f. (1) Type **641** 60 10
3214 8f. (2) Bust of Bodhisattva 60 10
3215 8f. (3) Boy on lotus flower 60 10
3216 70f. (4) Bodhisattva . . . . 3·00 1·10

1982. 40th Death Anniv of Dr. D. S. Kotnis.

3218 **642** 8f. green and black . . . 40 10
3219 – 70f. lilac and black . . . 1·60 70

DESIGN: Dr. Kotnis in army uniform.

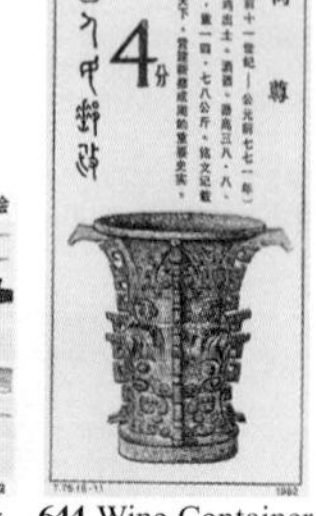

643 Couple holding Flaming Torch

644 Wine Container

1982. 11th National Communist Youth League Congress.

3220 **643** 8f. multicoloured 25 10

1982. Bronzes of Western Zhou Dynasty. Mult.

3221 4f. (1) Type **644** 50 20
3222 4f. (2) Cooking vessel . . . 50 20
3223 8f. (3) Food container . . . 60 20

3224 8f. (4) Cooking vessel with ox head and dragon design 60 20
3225 8f. (5) Ram-shaped wine container 60 20
3226 10f. (6) Wine jar . . . . . 1·00 25
3227 20f. (7) Food bowl . . . . 2·50 35
3228 70f. (8) Wine container . . . 7·25 1·75

645 "Pig" (Han Meilin) **646** Harp

1983. New Year. Year of the Pig.
3229 **645** 8f. multicoloured . . . . 3·00 80

1983. Stringed Musical Instruments.
3230 **646** 4f. (1) green and brown 1·00 20
3231 – 8f. (2) purple, grn & brn 1·75 40
3232 – 8f. (3) multicoloured . . 1·75 40
3233 – 10f. (4) multicoloured . . 2·50 70
3234 – 70f. (5) multicoloured . . 12·00 3·00
DESIGNS—VERT: 8f. (3231), Four string guitar; 10f. Four string lute; 70f. Three string lute. HORIZ: 8f. (3232), Qin.

647 "February 7" Monument, Jiangan **648** Zhang Gong attracted by Yingying's Beauty

1983. 60th Anniv of Peking–Hankow Railway Workers' Strike.
3235 **647** 8f. (1) yellow, blk & grey 50 15
3236 – 8f. (2) stone, brown and lilac 50 15
DESIGN: No. 3236, "February 7" Memorial tower, Zhengzhou.

1983. Scenes from "The Western Chamber" (musical drama by Wang Shifu). Multicoloured.
3237 8f. (1) Type **648** . . . . . . 1·75 50
3238 8f. (2) Zhang Gong and Yingying listening to music . . . . 1·75 50
3239 10f. (3) Zhang Gong and Yingying's wedding . . . 2·75 1·40
3240 80f. (4) Zhang Gong and Yingying parting at Chanting Pavilion . . . . 12·50 4·00

649 Karl Marx **650** Tomb, Mt. Qiaoshan, Huangling

1983. Death Centenary of Karl Marx.
3242 **649** 8f. grey and black . . . 15 10
3243 – 20f. lilac and black . . . 70 15
DESIGN: 20f. "Marx making Speech" (Wen Guozhang).

1983. Tomb of the Yellow Emperor. Mult.
3244 8f. Type **650** 50 30
3245 10f. Hall of Founder of Chinese Culture (horiz) 1·25 30
3246 20f. Xuanyuan cypress . . . 2·25 80

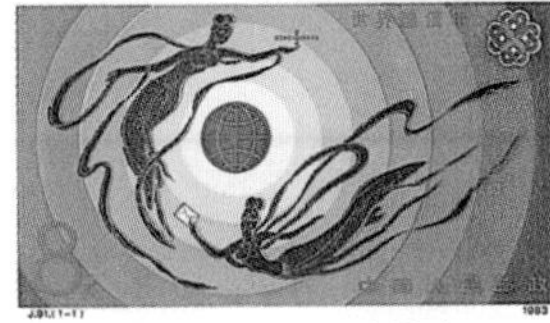

651 Messengers and Globe

1983. World Communications Year.
3247 **651** 8f. multicoloured 30 15

652 Chinese Alligator

1983. Chinese Alligator. Multicoloured.
3248 8f. Type **652** 50 10
3249 20f. Alligator and hatching eggs . . . . 2·10 30

653 "Scratching" (Wang Yani)

1983. Children's Paintings. Multicoloured.
3250 8f. (1) Type **653** 25 10
3251 8f. (2) "I Love the Great Wall" (Liu Zhong) . . . 25 10
3252 8f. (3) "Kitten" (Tang Axi) 25 10
3253 8f. (4) "The Sun, Birds, Flowers and Me" (Bu Hua) 25 10

654 Congress Hall

1983. 6th National People's Congress. Mult.
3254 8f. Type **654** 25 10
3255 20f. Score of National Anthem 40 15

655 Terracotta Soldiers **656** Sun Yujiao

1983. Terracotta Figures from Qin Shi Huang's Tomb. Multicoloured.
3256 8f. (1) Type **655** 40 20
3257 8f. (2) Heads figures 40 20
3258 10f. (3) Soldiers and horses 75 30
3259 70f. (4) Aerial view of excavation . . . . 4·25 1·25

1983. Female Roles in Peking Opera. Mult.
3261 4f. (1) Type **656** 40 10
3262 8f. (2) Chen Miaochang . . 60 15
3263 8f. (3) Bai Suzhen 60 15
3264 8f. (4) Sister Thirteen . . . 60 15
3265 10f. (5) Qin Xianglian . . . 80 20
3266 20f. (6) Yang Yuhuan . . . 1·50 25
3267 50f. (7) Cui Yingying . . . 4·50 55
3268 80f. (8) Mu Guiying . . . . 8·75 95

657 Li Bai (poet) **659** Games Emblem

658 Woman and Women working

1983. Poets and Philosophers of Ancient China. Paintings by Liu Lingcang. Multicoloured.
3269 8f. (1) Type **657** 55 20
3270 8f. (2) Du Fu (poet) 55 20
3271 8f. (3) Han Yu (philosopher) 55 20
3272 70f. (4) Liu Zongyuan (philosopher) . . . . . . 6·00 2·00

1983. 5th National Women's Congress.
3273 **658** 8f. multicoloured 20 10

1983. 5th National Games. Multicoloured.
3274 4f. (1) Type **659** 35 10
3275 8f. (2) Gymnastics 40 20
3276 8f. (3) Badminton 40 20
3277 8f. (4) Diving 40 20
3278 20f. (5) High jump 80 40
3279 70f. (6) Windsurfing . . . . 2·10 1·00

660 "One Child per Couple"

1983. Family Planning. Multicoloured.
3280 8f. (1) Type **660** 15 10
3281 8f. (2) "Population, cultivated fields and grain" 15 10

661 Hammer and Cogwheel as "10"

1983. 10th National Trade Union Congress.
3282 **661** 8f. multicoloured 30 10

662 Mute Swan

1983. Swans. Multicoloured.
3283 8f. (1) Type **662** 30 30
3284 8f. (2) Mute swans 30 30
3285 10f. Tundra swans . . . . 75 1·00
3286 80f. (4) Whooper swans in flight . . . . 2·25 2·00

663 Liu Shaoqi

1983. 85th Birth Anniv of Liu Shaoqi (former Head of State).
3287 **663** 8f. (1) multicoloured . . 55 10
3288 – 8f. (2) multicoloured . . 55 10
3289 – 8f. (3) brown, bl & gold 55 10
3290 – 8f. (4) brown, bl & gold 55 10
DESIGNS: No. 3288, Liu reading a speech; 3289, Liu making a speech; 3290, Liu meeting model worker Shi Chuanxiang.

664 $100 National Emblem Stamp, 1951 **665** Mao Tse-tung in 1925

1983. National Stamp Exhibition, Peking. Mult.
3291 8f. Type **664** 20 10
3292 20f. North West China $1 Yanan Pagoda stamp, 1946 . . . . 80 40

1983. 90th Birth Anniv of Mao Tse-tung.
3293 **665** 8f. (1) multicoloured . . 20 10
3294 – 8f. (2) stone, brn & gold 20 10
3295 – 10f. (3) grey, brn & gold 50 15
3296 – 20f. (4) multicoloured . . 1·25 20
DESIGNS: No. 3294, Mao Tse-tung in Yanan, 1945. 3295, Mao Tse-tung inspecting Yellow River, 1952. 3296, Mao Tse-tung in library, 1961.

666 "Rat" (Zhan Tong) **667** Young Girl with Ball

1984. New Year. Year of the Rat.
3297 **666** 8f. black, yellow & red 2·50 70

1984. Child Welfare. Multicoloured.
3298 8f.+2f. Type **667** 20 15
3299 8f.+2f. Young boy with toy panda 20 15

668 Women with Dog

1984. Tang Dynasty Painting "Beauties wearing Flowers" by Zhou Fang. Details of scroll. Mult.
3300 8f. Type **668** . . . . 1·00 20
3301 10f. Women and Manchurian crane . . . . 1·00 50
3302 70f. Women, dog and Manchurian crane . . . . 6·25 3·00

669 "The Spring of Shanghai" **670** Ren Bishi

1984. Chinese Roses. Multicoloured.
3304 4f. (1) Type **669** 25 10
3305 8f. (2) "Rosy Dawn of the Pujiang River" 30 10
3306 8f. (3) "Pearl" 30 10
3307 10f. (4) "Black Whirlwind" 65 10
3308 20f. (5) "Yellow Flower in the Battlefield" 90 20
3309 70f. (6) "Blue Phoenix" . . 2·25 50

1984. 80th Birth Anniv of Ren Bishi (member of Communist Party Secretariat) (1st issue).
3310 **670** 8f. brown, black & pur 20 10
See also Nos. 3361/3.

671 Japanese Crested Ibis

1984. Japanese Crested Ibis. Multicoloured.
3311 8f. (1) Type **671** 35 25
3312 8f. (2) Ibis wading 35 25
3313 80f. (3) Ibis perching . . . 2·40 1·75

672 Red Cross Activities

1984. 80th Anniv of Chinese Red Cross Society.
3314 **672** 8f. multicoloured 35 15

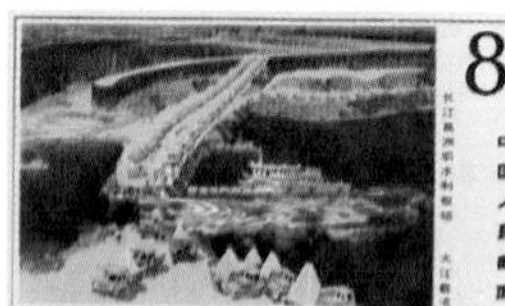

673 Building Dam

1984. Gezhou Dam Project. Multicoloured.
3315 8f. Type **673** 10 10
3316 10f. View of dam and lock gates (vert) 40 10
3317 20f. Freighter in lock . . . 70 15

674 Inverted Image Tower and Yilang Pavilion

1984. Zhuo Zheng Garden, Suzhou. Mult.
3318 8f. (1) Type **674** 20 10
3319 8f. (2) Loquat Garden . . . 20 10
3320 10f. (3) Water court of Xiao Cang Lang 25 15
3321 70f. (4) Yuanxiang Hall and Yiyu Study . . . . 2·10 60

675 Pistol Shooting

1984. Olympic Games, Los Angeles. Multicoloured.
3322 4f. Type **675** 10 10
3323 8f. High jumping 10 10
3324 8f. Weightlifting 10 10
3325 10f. Gymnastics 10 10
3326 20f. Volley ball 25 15
3327 80f. Diving 85 50

676 Calligraphy

677 Tianjin

1984. Art Works by Wu Changshuo. Mult.
3329 4f. (1) Type **676** 10 10
3330 4f. (2) "Pair of Peaches" . . 10 10
3331 8f. (3) "Lotus" 45 15
3332 8f. (4) "Wisteria" 45 15
3333 8f. (5) "Peony" 45 15
3334 10f. (6) "Autumn Chrysanthemum" 55 15
3335 20f. (7) "Plum Blossom" . . 1·25 25
3336 70f. (8) Seal and impression 3·25 65

1984. Luanhe River–Tianjin Water Diversion Project. Multicoloured.
3337 8f. Type **677** 10 10
3338 10f. Locks and canal (horiz) 10 10
3339 20f. Tunnel and sculpture 50 15

678 Chinese and Japanese Pagodas

1984. Chinese–Japanese Youth Friendship Festival. Multicoloured.
3340 8f. Type **678** 10 10
3341 20f. Girls watering shrub . . 25 15
3342 80f. Young people dancing 85 80

679 Factory Worker

1984. 35th Anniv of People's Republic. Mult.
3343 8f. (1) Type **679** 10 10
3344 8f. (2) Girl and rainbow . . 10 10
3345 8f. (4) Girl and symbols of science 10 10
3346 8f. (5) Soldier 10 10
3347 20f. (3) Flag and Manchurian cranes (36 × 50 mm) 40 25

680 Chen Jiageng

1984. 110th Birth Anniv of Chen Jiageng (educationist and patriot). Multicoloured.
3348 8f. Type **680** 15 10
3349 80f. Jimei School 65 30

681 The Maiden's Study

1984. Scenes from "Peony Pavilion" (drama) by Tang Xianzu. Paintings by Dai Dunbang. Multicoloured.
3350 8f. (1) Type **681** 50 15
3351 8f. (2) Du Liniang dreaming 50 15
3352 20f. (3) Du Liniang drawing self-portrait . . . . . . 1·10 25
3353 70f. (4) Du Liniang and Liu Mengmei married . . . . 3·50 1·10

682 Baoguo Temple

1984. Landscapes of Mt. Emei Shan. Mult.
3355 4f. (1) Type **682** 45 10
3356 8f. (2) Leiyin Temple . . . 55 10
3357 8f. (3) Hongchun Lawn . . 55 10
3358 10f. (4) Elephant Bath Pool 70 15
3359 20f. (5) Woyun Temple . . 1·25 25
3360 80f. (6) Shining Cloud Sea, Jinding . . . . 3·25 1·10

683 Ren Bishi

684 Flowers in Chinese Vase

1984. 80th Birth Anniv of Ren Bishi (2nd issue).
3361 **683** 8f. brown and purple . . 10 10
3362 – 10f. black and lilac . . . 15 10
3363 – 20f. black and brown . . 40 20
DESIGNS: 10f. Ren Bishi reading speech at Communist Party Congress; 20f. Ren Bishi saluting.

1984. Chinese Insurance Industry.
3364 **684** 8f. multicoloured 15 10

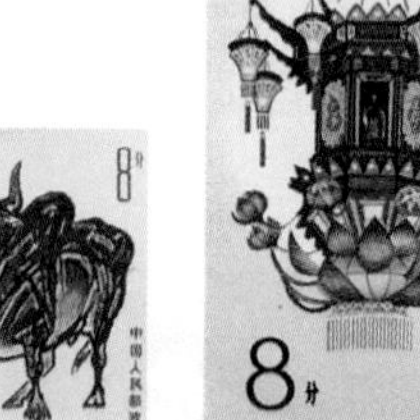

685 "Ox" (Yao Zhonghua)

687 Lotus of Good Luck

686 "Zunyi Meeting" (Liu Xiangping)

1985. New Year. Year of the Ox.
3365 **685** 8f. multicoloured 30 15

1985. 50th Anniv of Zunyi Meeting. Mult.
3366 8f. Type **686** 10 10
3367 20f. "Arrival of the Red Army in Northern Shaanxi" (Zhao Yu) . . . 60 15

1985. Festival Lanterns. Multicoloured.
3368 8f. (1) Type **687** 50 15
3369 8f. (2) Auspicious dragon and phoenix 50 15
3370 8f. (3) A hundred flowers blossoming 50 15
3371 70f. (4) Prosperity and affluence . . . . 1·75 60

688 Stylized Dove and Women's Open Hands

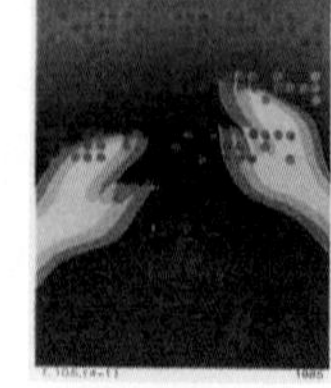

689 Hands reading Braille

1985. United Nations Decade for Women.
3372 **688** 20f. multicoloured . . . 25 10

1985. Welfare Fund for the Handicapped. Multicoloured.
3373 8f.+2f. (1) Type **689** 40 15
3374 8f.+2f. (2) Lips and sign language 40 15
3375 8f.+2f. (3) Learning to use artificial limb 40 15
3376 8f.+2f. (4) Stylized figure in wheelchair 40 15

690 "Green Calyx" Mei

691 Headquarters

1985. Mei Flowers. Multicoloured.
3377 8f. (1) Type **690** 15 10
3378 8f. (2) "Pendant" mei . . . 15 10
3379 8f. (3) "Contorted dragon" mei 15 10
3380 10f. (4) "Cinnabar" mei . . 20 10
3381 20f. (5) "Versicolor" mei . . 75 15
3382 80f. (6) "Apricot" mei . . . 2·50 65

1985. 60th Anniv of All-China Trade Unions Federation.
3384 **691** 8f. multicoloured 20 10

692 Bird and Children

1985. International Youth Year.
3385 **692** 20f. multicoloured . . . 30 15

693 Giant Panda

694 Xian Xinghai (bust, Cao Chongen)

1985. Giant Panda. Multicoloured.
3386 8f. Type **693** 10 10
3387 20f. Giant panda (different) (horiz) 40 15
3388 50f. Giant panda (different) 60 30
3389 80f. Two giant pandas (horiz) 85 40

1985. 80th Birth Anniv of Xian Xianghai (composer).
3391 **694** 8f. multicoloured 25 10

695 Agnes Smedley

696 Zheng He (navigator)

1985. American Journalists in China.
3392 **695** 8f. brown, stone and ochre 10 10
3393 – 20f. olive, grey and stone 15 10
3394 – 80f. purple, lilac and cream 50 20
DESIGNS: 20f. Anna Louise Strong; 80f. Edgar Snow.

1985. 580th Anniv of Zheng He's First Voyage to Western Seas. Multicoloured.
3395 8f. (1) Type **696** 10 10
3396 8f. (2) Zheng He on elephant 10 10
3397 20f. (3) Exchanging goods 20 10
3398 80f. (4) Bidding farewell . . 75 45

697 "Self-portrait"

1985. 90th Birth Anniv of Xu Beihong (artist). Multicoloured.

3399		8f. Type **697**	10	10
3400		20f. Xu Beihong at work	20	15

698 Lin Zexu **699** "Prosperity"

1985. Birth Bicentenary of Lin Zexu (statesman).

3401	**698**	8f. multicoloured	15	10
3402	–	80f. brown and black	55	25

DESIGN—55 × 23 mm. 80f. "Burning opium at Humen" (relief).

1985. 20th Anniv of Tibet Autonomous Region. Multicoloured.

3403		8f. Type **699**	10	10
3404		10f. "Celebration"	15	10
3405		20f. "Harvest"	35	10

700 Chinese Army at Lugouqiao

1985. 40th Anniv of Victory over Japan.

3406	**700**	8f. black, brown & red	10	10
3407	–	80f. black, brown & red	75	40

DESIGN: 80f. Defending the Great Wall.

701 Cycling

1985. 2nd National Workers' Games, Peking. Multicoloured.

3408		8f. Type **701**	10	10
3409		20f. Hurdling	25	15

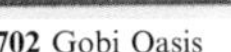
702 Gobi Oasis **703** Athletes and Silhouette of Woman

1985. 30th Anniv of Xinjiang Uygur Autonomous Region. Multicoloured.

3410		8f. Type **702**	10	10
3411		10f. Oilfield and Lake Tianchi (54 × 26 mm)	15	10
3412		20f. Tianshan pasture	35	15

1985. 1st National Youth Games, Zhengzhou.

3413	**703**	8f. multicoloured	10	10
3414	–	20f. red, blue and black	25	10

DESIGN: 20f. Basketball players and silhouette of man.

704 Forbidden City (½-size illustration)

1985. 60th Anniv of Imperial Palace Museum.

3415	**704**	8f. (1) multicoloured	10	10
3416	–	8f. (2) multicoloured	10	10
3417	–	20f. (3) multicoloured	20	10
3418	–	80f. (4) multicoloured	70	30

DESIGNS: Nos. 3416/18, Different parts of Forbidden City.

705 Zou Taofen **706** Memorial Pavilion

1985. 90th Anniv of Zou Taofen (journalist).

3419	**705**	8f. black, brown & silver	10	10
3420	–	20f. black, green & silver	30	10

DESIGN: 20f. Premier Chou En-lai's inscription in memory of Zou Taofen.

1985. 50th Anniv of December 9th Movement.

3421	**706**	8f. multicoloured	15	10

707 "Tiger" **708** First Experimental Satellite

1986. New Year. Year of the Tiger.

3422	**707**	8f. multicoloured	45	15

1986. Space Research. Multicoloured.

3423		4f. (1) Type **708**	10	10
3424		8f. (2) Mil-Mi8 helicopters recovering satellites	10	10
3425		8f. (3) Underwater launched rocket	10	10
3426		10f. (4) Rocket launched from land	15	10
3427		20f. (5) Dish aerial	30	15
3428		70f. (6) Satellite and diagram of orbit	60	45

709 Dong Biwu **710** Lin Boqu

1986. Birth Centenary of Dong Biwu (founder of Chinese Communist Party).

3429	**709**	8f. black and brown	10	10
3430	–	20f. black and brown	20	10

DESIGN: 20f. At meeting for ratification of U.N. Charter, Los Angeles, 1945.

1986. Birth Centenary of Lin Boqu (politician).

3431	**710**	8f. brown and black	10	10
3432	–	20f. brown and black	20	10

DESIGN: 20f. At Yanan.

711 He Long

1986. 90th Birth Anniv of He Long (politician).

3433	**711**	8f. black and brown	10	10
3434	–	20f. black and brown	20	10

DESIGN: 20f. On horse.

712 Skin Tents, Inner Mongolia **713** Comet and Earth

1986. Traditional Houses.

3435	**712**	1f. green, brown & grey	10	10
3436	–	1½f. brown, red & blue	10	10
3437	–	2f. brown and bistre	10	10
3438	–	3f. black and brown	10	10
3439	–	4f. red and black	10	10
3439a	–	5f. black, grey & green	10	10
3440	–	8f. grey, red and black	10	10
3441	–	10f. black and orange	15	10
3441b	–	15f. black, grey & grn	15	10
3442	–	20f. grey, green & blk	65	10
3442b	–	25f. black, grey & pink	25	15
3443	–	30f. lilac, blue & brown	15	10
3444	–	40f. brn, pur & stone	30	15
3445	–	50f. blue, mve & dp bl	15	15
3445b	–	80f. black, grey & blue	70	25
3446	–	90f. black and red	70	25
3447	–	1y. brown and grey	35	20
3448	–	1y.10 blue, blk & brn	40	25
3448a	–	1y.30 blk, grey & red	40	20
3448b	–	1y.60 blue & black	40	25
3448c	–	2y. black, grey & brown	60	25

DESIGNS: 1½f. Tibet. 2f. North-East China. 3f. Hunan. 4f. Jiangsu. 5f. Shandong. 8f. Peking. 10f. Yunnan. 15f. Guangxi. 20f. Shanghai. 25f. Ningxia. 30f. Anhui. 40f. North Shaanxi. 50f. Sichuan. 80f. Shanxi. 90f. Taiwan. 1y. Fujian. 1y.10, Zhejiang, 1y.30, Qinghai. 1y.60, Guizhou. 2y. Jiangxi.

1988. Appearance of Halley's Comet.

3449	**713**	20f. grey and blue	20	10

714 Cranes

1986. Great White Crane. Multicoloured.

3450		8f. Type **714**	10	10
3451		10f. Crane flying (vert)	25	20
3452		70f. Four cranes (vert)	75	45

715 Li Weihan

1986. 90th Birth Anniv of Li Weihan (politician). Each green and black.

3454		8f. Type **715**	10	10
3455		20f. Li Weihan at work	20	10

716 Stylized People on Dove

1986. International Peace Year.

3456	**716**	8f. multicoloured	20	10

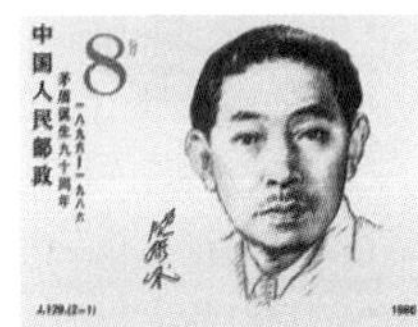
717 Mao Dun

1986. 90th Birth Anniv of Mao Dun (writer). Each grey, black and brown.

3457		8f. Type **717**	10	10
3458		20f. Mao Dun and manuscript	20	10

718 Wang Jiaxiang

1986. 80th Birth Anniv of Wang Jiaxiang (first People's Republic ambassador to U.S.S.R.). Multicoloured.

3459		8f. Type **718**	10	10
3460		20f. Wang Jiaxiang at Yan'an	20	10

719 Flowers on Desk

1986. Teachers' Day.

3461	**719**	8f. multicoloured	15	10

720 "Magnolia sinensis"

1986. Magnolias. Multicoloured.

3462		8f. (1) Type **720**	40	10
3463		8f. (2) "Manglietia patungensis"	40	10
3464		70f. (3) "Alcimandra cathcartii"	2·50	70

721 Sun Yat-sen (120th birth anniv) **724** Zhu De

1986. 75th Anniv of 1911 Revolution. Leaders. Multicoloured.

3466		8f. Type **721**	10	10
3467		10f. Huang Xing (70th death anniv)	40	10
3468		40f. Zhang Taiyan (50th death anniv)	90	15

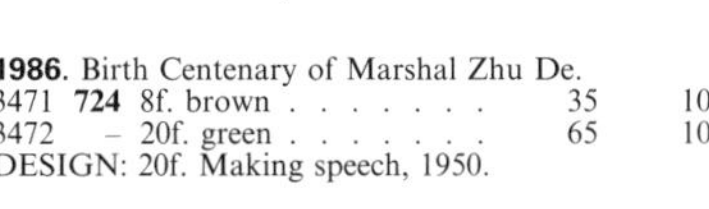
1986. Birth Centenary of Marshal Zhu De.

3471	**724**	8f. brown	35	10
3472	–	20f. green	65	10

DESIGN: 20f. Making speech, 1950.

725 Archery **726** "Rabbit"

1986. Sport in Ancient China. Each grey, black and red.

3473		8f. (1) Type **725**	90	10
3474		8f. (2) Weiqi (horiz)	90	10
3475		10f. (3) Golf (horiz)	1·25	40
3476		50f. (4) Football	3·50	85

1987. New Year. Year of the Rabbit.

3477	**726**	8f. multicoloured	50	15

727 Xu Xiake **728** Steller's Sea Eagle

1987. 400th Birth Anniv of Xu Xiake (explorer). Multicoloured.

3478		8f. Type **727**	1·00	20
3479		20f. Recording observations in cave	2·25	60
3480		40f. Climbing mountain	4·50	1·25

1987. Birds of Prey. Multicoloured.

3481		8f. (1) Black kite (horiz)	70	25
3482		8f. (2) Type **728**	70	30
3483		10f. (3) Himalayan griffon	1·40	30
3484		90f. (4) Upland buzzard (horiz)	5·00	1·75

729 Hawk Kite

1987. Kites. Multicoloured.
3485 8f. (1) Type **729** 20 10
3486 8f. (2) Centipede 20 10
3487 30f. (3) The Eight Diagrams 1·00 15
3488 30f. (4) Phoenix 1·00 15

730 Liao Zhongkai **731** "Eventful Years"

1987. 110th Birth Anniv of Liao Zhongkai (politician). Multicoloured.
3489 8f. Type **730** 10 10
3490 20f. Liao Zhongkai with wife 15 10

1987. 90th Birth Anniv of Ye Jianying (revolutionary and co-founder of People's Army). Portraits. Multicoloured.
3491 8f. Type **731** 45 10
3492 10f. "Founder of the State" 55 10
3493 30f. "Everywhere Green Hills" 1·50 15

732 Worshipping Bodhisattvas (Northern Liang Dynasty)

1987. Dunhuang Cave Murals (1st series). Mult.
3494 8f. Type **732** 50 10
3495 10f. Deer King Jataka (Northern Wei dynasty) 60 15
3496 20f. Heavenly musicians (Northern Wei dynasty) 2·00 50
3497 40f. Flying Devata (Northern Wei dynasty) 3·00 1·25
See also Nos. 3553/6, 3682/5, 3811/14, 3910/13 and 4131/4.

733 "Happy Holiday" (Yan Qinghu) **734** Town

1987. Children's Day. Childrens' drawings. Mult.
3499 8f. (1) Type **733** 10 10
3500 8f. (2) Children with doves and balloons (Liu Yuan) 10 10

1987. Improvements in Rural Areas. Multicoloured.
3501 8f. (1) Type **734** 40 10
3502 8f. (2) Fresh foods (horiz) 40 10
3503 10f. (3) Feeding cattle (horiz) 60 10
3504 20f. (4) Outdoor cinema 90 20

735 Emblem **736** Globe

1987. Postal Savings.
3505 **735** 8f. turquoise, yell & red 15 10

1987. Centenary of Esperanto (invented language).
3506 **736** 8f. blue, black & green 15 10

737 Flag over Great Wall

1987. 60th Anniv of People's Liberation Army. Multicoloured.
3507 8f. (1) Type **737** 35 10
3508 8f. (2) Soldier and rocket launcher 35 10
3509 10f. (3) Sailor and submarine 1·00 15
3510 30f. (4) Pilot and jet fighters 1·00 15

738 Dove above Houses

1987. Int Year of Shelter for the Homeless.
3511 **738** 8f. multicoloured 15 10

739 Chinese Character **740** Pan Gu inventing the Universe

1987. China Art Festival, Peking.
3512 **739** 8f. black, red and gold 15 10

1987. Folk Tales. Multicoloured.
3513 4f. (1) Type **740** 35 10
3514 8f. (2) Nu Wa creating human being 50 10
3515 8f. (3) Yi shooting nine suns 50 10
3516 10f. (4) Chang'e flying to the moon 60 10
3517 20f. (5) Kua Fu chasing the sun 90 15
3518 90f. (6) Jing Wei filling the sea 2·75 95

741 Sun rising behind Party Flag

1987. 13th National Communist Party Congress.
3519 **741** 8f. multicoloured 10 10

742 Yellow Crane Tower, Wuhan

1987. Ancient Buildings. Multicoloured.
3520 8f. (1) Type **742** 40 10
3521 8f. (2) Yue Yang Tower 40 10
3522 10f. (3) Teng Wang Pavilion 70 10
3523 90f. (4) Peng Lai Pavilion 3·25 1·40

743 Pole Vaulting

1987. 6th National Games, Guangdong Province. Multicoloured.
3525 8f. (1) Type **743** 40 10
3526 8f. (2) Women's softball 40 10
3527 30f. (3) Weightlifting 70 15
3528 50f. (4) Diving 1·25 20

745 Shi Jin practising Martial Arts

1987. Literature. "Outlaws of the Marsh" (1st series). Multicoloured.
3530 8f. Type **745** 30 10
3531 10f. Sagacious Lu uprooting willow tree 50 10
3532 30f. Lin Chon sheltering in temple of mountain spirit 1·50 50
3533 50f. Song Jian helping Chao Gai to escape 3·25 1·10
See also Nos. 3614/17, 3778/81, 3854/7 and 4248/51.

746 Dragon **747** Cai Yuanpri

1988. New Year. Year of the Dragon.
3535 **746** 8f. multicoloured 25 15

1988. 120th Birth Anniv of Cai Yuanpei (educationist). Multicoloured.
3536 8f. Type **747** 10 10
3537 20f. Cai Yuanpei seated in chair 15 10

748 Tao Zhu

1988. 80th Birth Anniv of Tao Zhu (Communist Party official). Multicoloured.
3538 8f. Type **748** 10 10
3539 20f. Tao Zhu (half-length portrait) 15 10

749 Harvest Festival

1988. Flourishing Rural Areas of China. Mult.
3540 8f. Type **749** 45 10
3541 10f. Couple with fish, flowers and chickens 55 10
3542 20f. Couple making scientific study 75 40
3543 30f. Happy family 1·00 65

750 Flag and Rainbow **751** Wuzhi Mountain

1988. 7th National People's Congress.
3544 **750** 8f. multicoloured 15 10

1988. Establishment of Hainan Province. Mult.
3545 8f. Type **751** 10 10
3546 10f. Wanquan River 10 10
3547 30f. Beach 20 10
3548 1y.10 Bay and deer 60 30

752 Li Siguang (geologist)

1988. Scientists (1st series). Multicoloured.
3549 8f. Type **752** 10 10
3550 10f. Zhu Kezhen (meteorologist) 10 10
3551 20f. Wu Youxun (physicist) 15 10
3552 30f. Hua Luogeng (mathematician) 20 10
See also Nos. 3702/5 and 3821/4.

1988. Dunhuang Cave Murals (2nd series). As T **732**. Multicoloured.
3553 8f. (1) Hunting (Western Wei dynasty) 35 10
3554 8f. (2) Fighting (Western Wei dynasty) 35 10
3555 10f. (3) Farming (Northern Zhou dynasty) 50 35
3556 90f. (4) Building pagoda (Northern Zhou dynasty) 1·60 80

753 Healthy Trees and Hand holding back polluted Soil

1988. Environmental Protection. Multicoloured.
3557 8f. (1) Type **753** 10 10
3558 8f. (2) Doves in clean air and hand holding back polluted air 10 10
3559 8f. (3) Fishes in clean water and hand holding back polluted water 25 10
3560 8f. (4) Peaceful landscape and hand holding back noise waves 10 10

755 Games Emblem

1988. 11th Asian Games, Peking (1990) (1st issue). Multicoloured.
3562 8f. Type **755** 10 10
3563 30f. Games mascot 15 10
See also Nos. 3653/6 and 3695/3700.

756 Warrior, Longmen Grotto, Henan **757** Peony

1988. Art of Chinese Grottoes.
3564 – 2y. brown & light brown 40 10
3565 **756** 5y. black and brown 75 15
3566 – 10y. brown and stone 1·50 35
3567 – 20y. black and brown 3·00 1·50
DESIGNS: 2y. Buddha, Yungang Grotto, Shanxi. 10y. Bodhisattva, Maijishan Grotto, Gansu. 20y. Woman with chickens, Dazu Grotto, Sichuan.

1988. 10th Anniv of Chinese–Japanese Treaty of Peace and Friendship. Multicoloured.
3568 8f. Type **757** 10 10
3569 1y.60 Cherry blossom 60 30

758 Coal Wharf, Quinghuangdao

1988. Achievements of Socialist Construction (1st series). Multicoloured.
3570 8f. Type **758** 30 15
3571 10f. Ethylene works, Shangdong 10 10
3572 20f. Baoshan steel works, Shanghai 10 10
3573 30f. Television centre, Peking 15 10
See also Nos. 3691/22, 3678/81 and 3759/62.

759 Taishan Temple

1988. Mount Taishan Views. Multicoloured.
3574 8f. Type **759** 40 10
3575 10f. Ladder to Heaven 45 10
3576 20f. Daguang Park 60 10
3577 90f. Sun Watching Peak 2·75 1·25

760 Liao Chengzhi **761** Cycling

1988. 80th Birth Anniv of Liao Chengzhi (Communist Party leader). Multicoloured.
3578 8f. Type **760** 10 10
3579 20f. Liao Chengzhi at work 15 10

1988. 1st National Peasant Games. Multicoloured.
3580 8f. Type **761** 10 10
3581 20f. Wushu 15 10

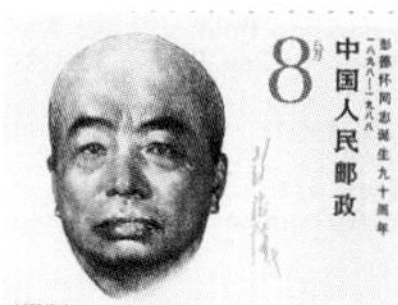
762 Peng Dehuai

1988. 90th Birth Anniv of General Peng Dehuai. Multicoloured.
3582 8f. Type **762** 10 10
3583 20f. In uniform 15 10

763 Battle against Lu Bu

1988. Literature. "Romance of the Three Kingdoms" by Luo Guanzhong (1st series). Multicoloured.
3584 8f. (1) Heroes become sworn brothers (horiz) 45 10
3585 8f. (2) Type **763** 45 10
3586 30f. (3) Fengyi Pavilion (horiz) . . . . 1·25 55
3587 50f. (4) Discussing heroes over wine . . . . 2·00 95
See also Nos. 3711/14, 3807/10, 3944/7 and 4315/18.

764 People in Heart **765** Stag's Head

1988. International Volunteers' Day.
3589 **764** 20f. multicoloured . . . 15 10

1988. Pere David's Deer. Multicoloured.
3590 8f. Type **765** 45 10
3591 40f. Herd 85 15

766 Da Yi Pin

1988. Orchids. Multicoloured.
3592 8f. Type **766** 50 10
3593 10f. Dragon 50 10
3594 20f. Large phoenix tail . . . 1·10 45
3595 50f. Silver-edged black orchid . . . . 2·10 70

767 Snake **768** Qu Quibai

1989. New Year. Year of the Snake.
3597 **767** 8f. multicoloured 25 15

1989. 90th Birth Anniv of Qu Qiubai (writer). Multicoloured.
3598 8f. Type **768** 10 10
3599 20f. Qu Qiubai (half-length portrait) 15 10

769 Pheasant

1989. Brown Eared-pheasant. Multicoloured.
3600 8f. Type **769** 10 10
3601 50f. Two pheasants 30 20

770 "Heaven" (top section)

1989. Silk Painting from Han Tomb, Mawangdui, Changsha. Multicoloured.
3602 8f. Type **770** 25 10
3603 20f. "Earth" (central section) 25 10
3604 30f. "Underworld" (bottom section) 25 10

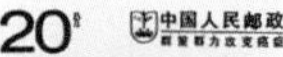
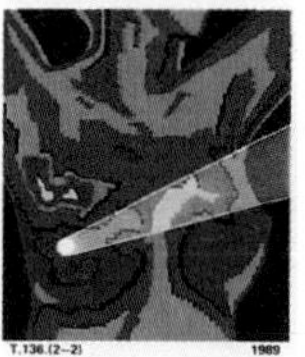

771 Diagnosis by Thermography **773** Children

772 Memorial Frieze

1989. Anti-cancer Campaign.
3606 **771** 8f. grey, red & black . . 10 10
3607 – 20f. multicoloured . . . 10 10
DESIGN: 8f. Crab and red crosses.

1989. 70th Anniv of May 4th Movement.
3608 **772** 8f. multicoloured 15 10

1989. 40th International Children's Day. Children's paintings. Multicoloured.
3609 8f.+4f. (1) Type **773** 10 10
3610 8f.+4f. (2) Child and penguins 10 10
3611 8f.+4f. (3) Child flying on bird 10 10
3612 8f.+4f. (4) Boy and girl playing ball 10 10

774 Globe, Doves and Lectern

1989. Cent of Interparliamentary Union.
3613 **774** 20f. multicoloured . . . 15 10

1989. Literature. "Outlaws of the Marsh" (2nd series). As T **745**. Multicoloured.
3614 8f. Wu Song killing tiger on Jingyang Ridge 10 10
3615 10f. Qin Ming riding through hail of arrows . . 15 10
3616 20f. Hua Rong shooting wild goose 50 10
3617 1y.30 Li Kui fighting Zhang Shun on sampan . . . . 1·60 60

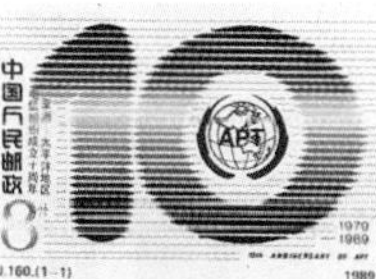
775 Anniversary Emblem

1989. 10th Anniv of Asia–Pacific Telecommunity.
3618 **775** 8f. multicoloured 10 10

1989. Achievements of Socialist Construction (2nd series). As T **758**. Multicoloured.
3619 8f. International telecommunications building, Peking (vert) . . 10 10
3620 10f. Xi Qu coal mine, Gu Jiao 10 10
3621 20f. Long Yang Gorge hydro-electric power station, Qinghai 15 10
3622 30f. Da Yao Shan tunnel on Guangzhou–Heng Yang railway 35 20

776 Five Peaks of Mt. Huashan

1989. Mount Huashan. Multicoloured.
3623 8f. Type **776** 10 10
3624 10f. View from top of Mt. Huashan 15 10
3625 20f. Thousand Foot Precipice 20 15
3626 90f. Blue Dragon Ridge . . 65 35

777 "Fable of the White Snake" (stage design, Ye Qianyu)

1989. Contemporary Art. Multicoloured.
3627 8f. Type **777** 10 10
3628 20f. "Lijiang River in Fine Rain" (Li Keran) 20 10
3629 50f. "Marching Together" (oxen) (Wu Zuoren) . . . 90 40

778 Doves and 1949 $50 Stamp **780** Ribbons and Gate of Heavenly Peace, Peking

779 Lecturing in Temple of Apricot, Qufu

1989. 40th Anniv of Chinese People's Political Conference.
3630 **778** 8f. red, blue and black 15 10

1989. 2540th Birth Anniv of Confucius (philosopher). Multicoloured.
3631 8f. Type **779** 10 10
3632 1y.60 Confucius in ox-drawn cart 50 25

1989. 40th Anniv of People's Republic. Mult.
3634 8f. Type **780** 10 10
3635 10f. Flowers and ribbons . . 10 10
3636 20f. Stars and ribbons . . . 10 10
3637 40f. Buildings and ribbons 25 15

781 Woman using Camera

1989. 150th Anniv of Photography.
3640 **781** 8f. multicoloured 15 10

782 Li Dazhao

1989. Birth Centenary of Li Dazhao (co-founder of Chinese Communist Party). Multicoloured.
3641 8f. Type **782** 10 10
3642 20f. Li Dazhao and script 15 10

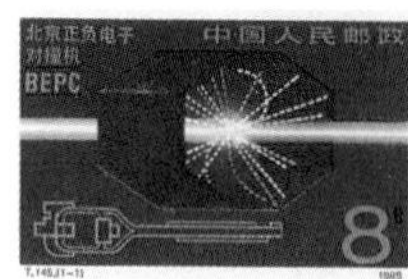
783 Diagram of Collider in Action

1989. Peking Electron-Positron Collider.
3643 **783** 8f. multicoloured 10 10

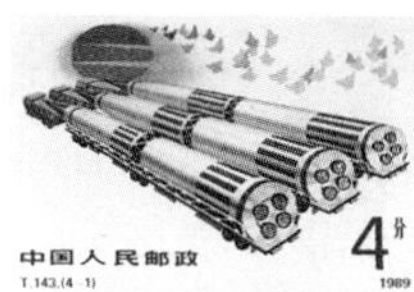
784 Rockets

1989. National Defence. Multicoloured.
3644 4f. Type **784** 10 10
3645 8f. Rocket on transporter 10 10
3646 10f. Rocket launch (vert) . . 15 10
3647 20f. Jettison of fuel tank . . 25 10

785 Spring Morning, Su Causeway

1989. West Lake, Hangzhou. Multicoloured.
3648 8f. Type **785** 10 10
3649 10f. Crooked Courtyard . . 10 10
3650 30f. Moon over Three Pools 45 20
3651 40f. Snow on Broken Bridge 90 25

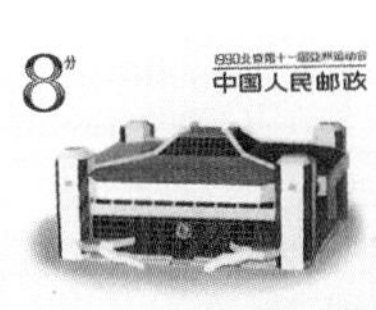

786 Peking College Gymnasium **787** Horse

1989. 11th Asian Games, Peking (1990) (2nd issue). Multicoloured.
3653 8f. Type **786** 10 10
3654 10f. Northern Suburbs swimming pool 10 10
3655 30f. Workers' Stadium . . . 10 10
3656 1y.60 Chaoyang Gymnasium 50 25

1990. New Year. Year of the Horse.
3657 **787** 8f. multicoloured 25 15

788 Narcissi **789** Bethune and Medical Team in Canada

1990. Narcissi. Multicoloured.
3658 8f. Type **788** 10 10
3659 20f. Natural group of narcissi 10 10

3660 30f. Arrangement of narcissi . . . 20 10
3661 1y.60 Arrangement (different) 75 35

1990. Birth Centenary of Norman Bethune (surgeon). Multicoloured.
3662 8f. Type **789** 10 10
3663 1y.60 Bethune and medical team in China 50 20

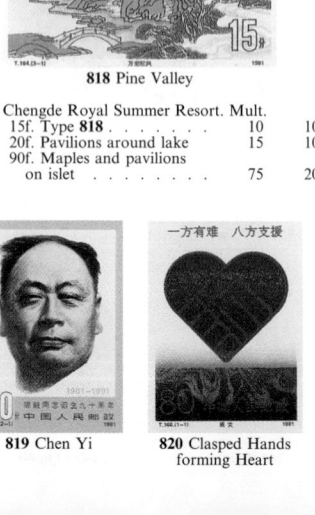

790 Emblem **791** Birds flying above Trees

1990. 80th International Women's Day.
3664 **790** 20f. red, green and black 15 10

1990. Tree Planting Day. Multicoloured.
3665 8f. Type **791** 10 10
3666 10f. Trees in city 10 10
3667 20f. Great Wall and trees 15 10
3668 30f. Forest and field of wheat 25 15

792 Ban Po Plate **793** Li Fuchun

1990. Pottery. Multicoloured.
3669 8f. Type **792** 10 10
3670 20f. Miao Di Gou dish . . 10 10
3671 30f. Ma Jia Yao jar 20 10
3672 50f. Ma Chang jar 30 20

1990. 90th Birth Anniv of Li Fuchun (politician). Multicoloured.
3673 8f. Type **793** 10 10
3674 20f. Li Fuchun (different) 40 10

794 Charioteer **795** Snow Leopard

1990. 10th Anniv of Discovery of Bronze Chariots in Emperor Qin Shi Huang's Tomb. Multicoloured.
3675 8f. Type **794** 15 10
3676 50f. Horse's head 35 15

1990. Achievements of Socialist Construction (3rd series). As T **758**. Multicoloured.
3678 8f. Second automobile factory 10 10
3679 10f. Yizheng chemical and fibre company 10 10
3680 20f. Shengli oil field 15 10
3681 30f. Qinshan nuclear power station 20 15

1990. Dunhuang Cave Murals (3rd series). Sui Dynasty. As T **732**. Multicoloured.
3682 8f. Flying Devatas 10 10
3683 10f. Worshipping Bodhisattva (vert) 10 10
3684 30f. Saviour Avalokitesvara (vert) 50 15
3685 50f. Indra 70 20

1990. The Snow Leopard. Multicoloured.
3686 8f. Type **795** 10 10
3687 50f. Leopard stalking . . . 25 10

796 West Fujian Communications Bureau (Red Posts) 4p. Stamp

1990. 60th Anniv of Communist China Stamp Issues. Multicoloured.
3688 8f. Type **796** 10 10
3689 20f. Chinese Soviet Republic 1c. stamp 15 10

797 Zhang Wentian **798** Emblem

1990. 90th Birth Anniv of Zhang Wentian (revolutionary).
3690 8f. Type **797** 10 10
3691 20f. Zhang Wentian and Zunyi Meeting venue . . 15 10

1990. International Literacy Year.
3692 **798** 20f. multicoloured . . . 10 10

799 Great Wall, Film and Screen **801** Athletics

1990. 85th Anniv of Chinese Films.
3693 **799** 20f. multicoloured . . . 10 10

1990. 11th Asian Games, Peking (3rd issue). Multicoloured.
3695 4f. Type **801** 10 10
3696 8f. Gymnastics 10 10
3697 10f. Martial arts 10 10
3698 20f. Volleyball 10 10
3699 30f. Swimming 45 10
3700 1y.60 Shooting . . . . . . 1·00 50

802 Zhang Yuzhe (astronomer)

1990. Scientists (2nd series). Multicoloured.
3702 8f. Lin Qiaozhi (gynaecologist) 10 10
3703 10f. Type **802** 10 10
3704 20f. Hou Debang (chemist) 15 10
3705 30f. Ding Ying (agronomist) 20 15

803 Towering Temple

1990. Mount Hengshan, Hunan Province. Mult.
3706 8f. Type **803** 10 10
3707 10f. Aerial view of mountain 15 10
3708 20f. Trees and buildings on slopes 30 20
3709 50f. Zhurong Peak 85 20

1990. Literature. "Romance of the Three Kingdoms" by Luo Guanzhong (2nd series). As T **763**. Multicoloured.
3711 20f. (1) Cao Cao leading night attack on Wuchao (horiz) 15 10
3712 20f. (2) Liu Bei calling at Zhuge Liang's thatched cottage 15 10
3713 30f. (3) General Zhao rescuing A Dou single-handedly (horiz) 60 15
3714 50f. (4) Zhang Fei repulsing attackers at Changban Bridge 75 25

805 Revellers listening to Music

1990. Painting "Han Xizai's Night Revels" by Gu Hongzhong. Multicoloured.
3715 50f. (1) Type **805** 60 20
3716 50f. (2) Drummer and dancers 60 20
3717 50f. (3) Women attending man with fan and man and women in alcove . . 60 20
3718 50f. (4) Women playing flutes and couple by painted screen 60 20
3719 50f. (5) Young couple and women attending seated man 60 20

Nos. 3715/19 were printed together, se-tenant, forming a composite design.

806 Sheep **808** Wreath on Wall and Last Verse of the "Internationale"

807 Yuzui (dam at Dujiang)

1991. New Year. Year of the Sheep.
3720 **806** 20f. multicoloured . . . 25 15

1991. Dujiangyan Irrigation Project. Mult.
3721 20f. Type **807** 10 10
3722 50f. Feishayan (weir) . . . 15 10
3723 80f. Baopingkou (diversion of part of River Minjiang through new opening in Yulei Mountain) 70 20

1991. 120th Anniv of Paris Commune.
3724 **808** 20f. multicoloured . . . 10 10

809 Apple **810** Saiga

1991. Family Planning. Multicoloured.
3725 20f. Type **809** 10 10
3726 50f. Child's and adult's hands within heart . . . 25 10

1991. Horned Ruminants. Multicoloured.
3727 20f. Type **810** 15 20
3728 20f. Takin 15 10
3729 50f. Argali 25 10
3730 2y. Ibex 70 35

811 Dancers **812** Map and Emperor Penguins

1991. 40th Anniv of Chinese Administration of Tibet. Multicoloured.
3731 25f. Type **811** 10 10
3732 50f. Rainbows over mountain road 15 10

1991. 30th Anniv of Implementation of Antarctic Treaty.
3734 **812** 20f. multicoloured . . . 20 10

813 "Rhododendron delavayi"

1991. Rhododendrons. Multicoloured.
3735 10f. Type **813** 10 10
3736 15f. "Rhododendron molle" 10 10
3737 20f. "Rhododendron simsii" 35 10
3738 20f. "Rhododendron fictolacteum" 35 10
3739 50f. "Rhododendron agglutinatum" (vert) . . . 50 10
3740 80f. "Rhododendron fortunei" (vert) 65 15
3741 90f. "Rhododendron giganteum" (vert) 70 20
3742 1y.60 "Rhododendron rex" (vert) . . . . 1·10 40

814 Pleasure Boat on Lake Nanhu (venue of first Party congress)

1991. 70th Anniv of Chinese Communist Party. Multicoloured.
3744 20f. Type **814** 30 15
3745 50f. Party emblem 15 10

815 Statue, Xuxian

1991. 2200th Anniv of Peasant Uprising led by Chen Sheng and Wu Guang.
3746 **815** 20f. black, brown and deep brown 15 10

816 Hanging Temple

1991. Mount Hengshan, Shanxi Province. Mult.
3747 20f. Type **816** 15 10
3748 20f. Snow-covered peak . . 15 10
3749 55f. "Shrine of Hengshan" carved in rock face . . . 35 20
3750 80f. Temples in Flying Stone Grotto 75 30

817 Mammoths and Man

1991. 13th International Union for Quaternary Research Conference, Peking.
3751 **817** 20f. multicoloured . . . 15 10

818 Pine Valley

1991. Chengde Royal Summer Resort. Mult.
3752 15f. Type **818** 10 10
3753 20f. Pavilions around lake 15 10
3754 90f. Maples and pavilions on islet 75 20

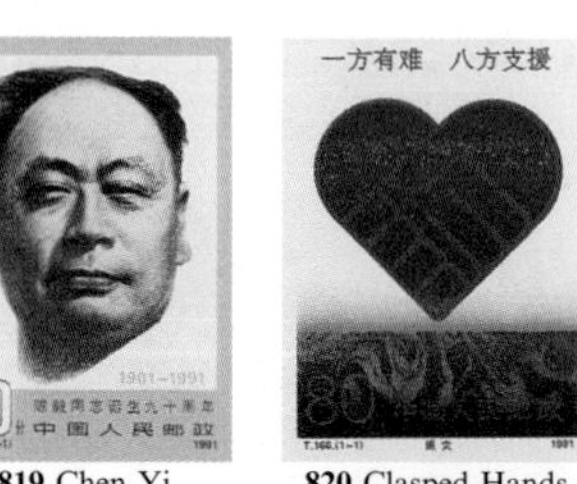

819 Chen Yi **820** Clasped Hands forming Heart

1991. 90th Birth Anniv of Chen Yi (co-founder of People's Army).
3756 20f. Type **819** 10 10
3757 50f. Verse "The Green Pine" written by Chen Yi . . . 15 10

1991. Flood Disaster Relief.
3758 **820** 80f. multicoloured . . . 25 10

The proceeds from the sale of No. 3758 were donated to the International Decade for Natural Disaster Reduction National Committee.

1991. Achievements of Socialist Construction (4th series). As T **758**. Multicoloured.
3759 20f. Luoyang glassworks . . 10 10
3760 25f. Urumchi chemical fertilizer works 10 10
3761 55f. Shenyang–Dalian expressway 20 10
3762 80f. Xichang satellite launching centre 50 15

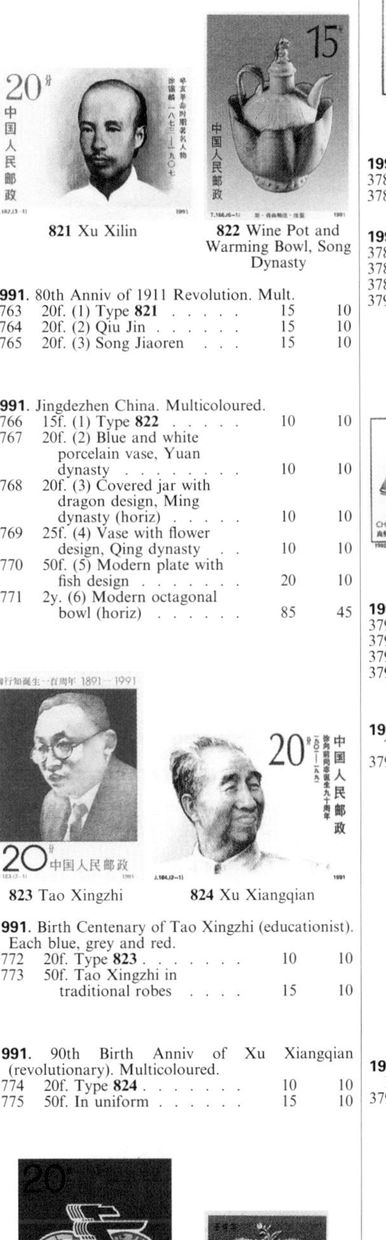

821 Xu Xilin

822 Wine Pot and Warming Bowl, Song Dynasty

1991. 80th Anniv of 1911 Revolution. Mult.
3763 20f. (1) Type **821** 15 10
3764 20f. (2) Qiu Jin 15 10
3765 20f. (3) Song Jiaoren . . . 15 10

1991. Jingdezhen China. Multicoloured.
3766 15f. (1) Type **822** 10 10
3767 20f. (2) Blue and white porcelain vase, Yuan dynasty 10 10
3768 20f. (3) Covered jar with dragon design, Ming dynasty (horiz) 10 10
3769 25f. (4) Vase with flower design, Qing dynasty . . 10 10
3770 50f. (5) Modern plate with fish design 20 10
3771 2y. (6) Modern octagonal bowl (horiz) 85 45

823 Tao Xingzhi

824 Xu Xiangqian

1991. Birth Centenary of Tao Xingzhi (educationist). Each blue, grey and red.
3772 20f. Type **823** 10 10
3773 50f. Tao Xingzhi in traditional robes 15 10

1991. 90th Birth Anniv of Xu Xiangqian (revolutionary). Multicoloured.
3774 20f. Type **824** 10 10
3775 50f. In uniform 15 10

825 Emblem

826 Monkey

1991. 1st Women's World Football Championship, Guangdong Province. Multicoloured.
3776 20f. Type **825** 10 10
3777 50f. Player 15 10

1991. Literature. "Outlaws of the Marsh" (3rd series). As T **745**. Multicoloured.
3778 20f. (1) Dai Zong delivers forged letter from Liangshan Marsh 10 10
3779 25f. (2) Yi Zhangqing captures Stumpy Tiger Wang 40 10
3780 25f. (3) Mistress Gu rescues Xie brothers from Dengzhou jail 40 10
3781 90f. (4) Sun Li gains entrance to Zhu family manor in guise of military magistrate 70 30

1992. New Year. Year of the Monkey. Paper-cut designs.
3783 **826** 20f. multicoloured . . . 10 10
3784 – 50f. black and red . . . 20 20

DESIGN: 50f. Magpies and plum blossom around Chinese character for monkey.

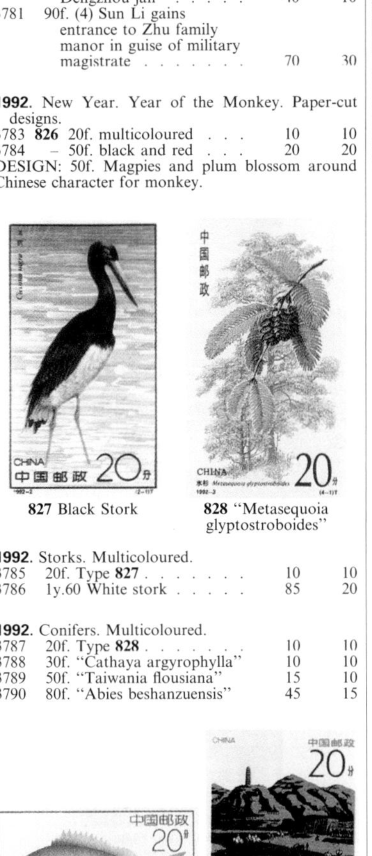

827 Black Stork

828 "Metasequoia glyptostroboides"

1992. Storks. Multicoloured.
3785 20f. Type **827** 10 10
3786 1y.60 White stork 85 20

1992. Conifers. Multicoloured.
3787 20f. Type **828** 10 10
3788 30f. "Cathaya argyrophylla" 10 10
3789 50f. "Taiwania flousiana" 15 10
3790 80f. "Abies beshanzuensis" 45 15

829 Madai Seabream

830 River Crossing at Yanan

1992. Offshore Breeding Projects. Multicoloured.
3791 20f. Type **829** 30 10
3792 25f. Prawn 10 10
3793 50f. Farrer's scallops . . . 20 15
3794 80f. "Laminaria japonica" (seaweed) 40 20

1992. 50th Anniv of Publication of Mao Tse-tung's Talks at the Yanan Forum on Literature and Art.
3795 **830** 20f. black, orange & red 10 10

831 Flower and Landscape on Globe

1992. World Environment Day. 20th Anniv of U. N. Environment Conference, Stockholm.
3796 **831** 20f. multicoloured . . . 10 10

832 Seven-spotted Ladybird

833 Basketball

1992. 19th International Entomology Congress, Peking. Insects. Multicoloured.
3797 20f. Type **832** 10 10
3798 30f. "Sympetrum croceolum" (dragonfly) 10 10
3799 50f. "Chrysopa septempunctata" (lacewing) 15 10
3800 2y. Praying mantis 90 40

1992. Olympic Games, Barcelona. Mult.
3801 20f. Type **833** 10 10
3802 25f. Gymnastics (horiz) . . 10 10
3803 50f. Diving (horiz) 15 10
3804 80f. Weightlifting 30 15

834 Emblem

835 Manchurian Cranes over Great Wall

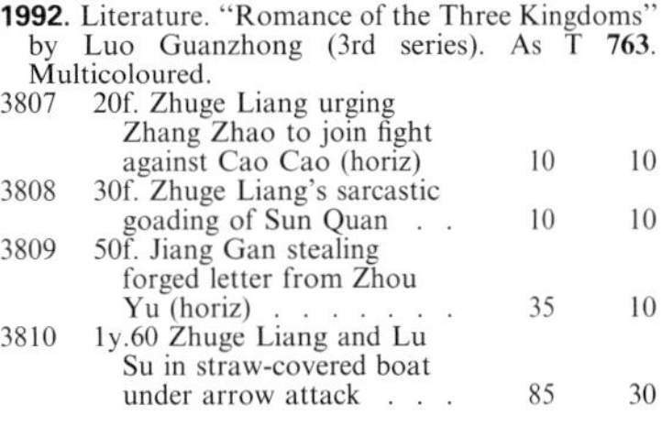

1992. International Space Year.
3806 **834** 20f. multicoloured . . . 10 10

1992. Literature. "Romance of the Three Kingdoms" by Luo Guanzhong (3rd series). As T **763**. Multicoloured.
3807 20f. Zhuge Liang urging Zhang Zhao to join fight against Cao Cao (horiz) 10 10
3808 30f. Zhuge Liang's sarcastic goading of Sun Quan . . 10 10
3809 50f. Jiang Gan stealing forged letter from Zhou Yu (horiz) 35 10
3810 1y.60 Zhuge Liang and Lu Su in straw-covered boat under arrow attack . . . 85 30

1992. Dunhuang Cave Murals (4th series). Tang Dynasty. As T **732**. Multicoloured.
3811 20f. Bodhisattva (vert) . . . 10 10
3812 25f. Musical performance (vert) 10 10
3813 55f. Flight on a dragon . . 20 10
3814 80f. Emperor Wudi dispatching his envoy Zhang Qian to the western regions 55 15

1992. 20th Anniv of Normalization of Diplomatic Relations with Japan. Multicoloured.
3816 20f. Type **835** 20 20
3817 2y. Japanese and Chinese girls and dove 45 25

836 Statue of Mazu, Meizhou Islet

837 Party Emblem

1992. Mazu, Sea Goddess.
3818 **836** 20f. brown and blue . . 10 10

1992. 14th National Communist Party Congress.
3819 **837** 20f. multicoloured . . . 10 10

838 Jiao Yulu

839 Xiong Qinglai (mathematician) and Formula

1992. 70th Birth Anniv of Jiao Yulu (Party worker).
3820 **838** 20f. multicoloured . . . 10 10

1992. Scientists (3rd series). Multicoloured.
3821 20f. Type **839** 10 10
3822 30f. Tang Feifan (microbiologist) and medal 10 10
3823 50f. Zhang Xiaoqian (doctor) and hospital scene 15 10
3824 1y. Liang Sicheng (architect) and plan 25 30

840 Luo Ronghuan in Officer's Uniform

841 State Arms

1992. 90th Birth Anniv of Luo Ronghuan (army leader). Multicoloured.
3825 20f. Type **840** 10 10
3826 50f. Luo Ronghuan as young man 10 10

1992. 10th Anniv of Constitution.
3827 **841** 20f. multicoloured . . . 10 10

842 Liu Bocheng in Officer's Uniform

843 "Spring" (Zhou Baiqi)

1992. Birth Centenary of Liu Bocheng (army leader).
3828 **842** 20f. multicoloured . . . 10 10
3829 – 50f. deep green & green 10 10

DESIGN—VERT: 50f. Liu Bocheng as young man.

1992. Qingtian Stone Carvings. Multicoloured.
3830 10f. Type **843** 10 10
3831 20f. "Chinese Sorghum" (Lin Rukui) 10 10
3832 40f. "Harvest" (Zhang Aiting) 15 10
3833 2y. "Blooming Flowers and Full Moon" (Ni Dongfang) 65 40

844 Cock

845 Song Qing-ling

1993. New Year. Year of the Cock. Paper-cut designs by Cai Lanying.
3834 **844** 20f. red and black . . . 15 10
3835 – 50f. white, red & black 50 10

DESIGN: 50f. Flowers around Chinese character for rooster.

1993. Birth Centenary of Song Qing-ling (Sun Yat-sen's wife). Multicoloured.
3836 20f. Type **845** 10 10
3837 1y. Song Qing-ling with children 20 10

846 Bactrian Camel

1993. Bactrian Camel. Multicoloured.
3838 20f. Type **846** 15 10
3839 1y.60 Adult with young . . 40 15

847 Flag, Basket of Flowers and Streamers

1993. 8th National People's Congress, Peking.
3840 **847** 20f. multicoloured . . . 10 10

848 Players

849 Sportswomen

1993. Go.
3841 **848** 20f. multicoloured . . . 10 10
3842 – 1y.60 red, black & gold 30 15

DESIGN: 1y.60, "China Vogue" (black) and "linked stars" (white) formations on board.

1993. 1st East Asian Games, Shanghai. Mult.
3843 50f. Type **849** 10 10
3844 50f. Dong dong (mascot) . . 10 10

Nos. 3843/4 were printed together, se-tenant, forming a composite design of Shanghai Stadium.

850 Li Jishen

1993. Revolutionaries (1st series). Each brown and black.

3845	20f. Type **850**	10	10
3846	30f. Zhang Lan (vert)	10	10
3847	50f. Shan Junru (vert)	15	10
3848	1y. Huang Yanpei	35	20

See also Nos. 3888/91.

851 "Phyllostachys nigra"

1993. Bamboo. Multicoloured.

3849	20f. Type **851**	10	10
3850	30f. "Phyllostachys aureosulcata spectabilis"	10	10
3851	40f. "Bambusa ventricosa"	15	10
3852	1y. "Pseudosasa amabilis"	35	25

1993. Literature. "Outlaws of the Marsh" (4th series). As T **745**. Multicoloured.

3854	20f. Yin Tianxi and gang capturing Chai Jin	10	10
3855	30f. Shi Qian stealing Xu Ning's armour	10	10
3856	50f. Xu Ning teaching use of barbed lance	40	10
3857	2y. Shi Xiu saving Lu Junyi from execution	95	35

852 Crater Lake in Winter

1993. Changbai Mountains. Multicoloured.

3858	20f. Type **852**	10	10
3859	30f. Mountain tundra in autumn	10	10
3860	50f. Waterfall in summer	20	10
3861	1y. Forest in spring	40	20

853 Games Emblem and Temple of Heaven **854** "Losana", Temple of Ancestors

1993. 7th National Games, Peking.

3862	**853** 20f. multicoloured	10	10

1993. 1500th Anniv of Longmen Grottoes, Luoyang. Multicoloured.

3863	20f. Type **854**	10	10
3864	30f. "Sakyamuni", Middle Binyang Cave	10	10
3865	50f. "King of Northern Heavens" standing on Yaksha	20	10
3866	1y. "Bodhisattva", Guyang Cave	35	20

855 Queen Bee and Workers on Comb

1993. The Honey Bee. Multicoloured.

3868	10f. Type **855**	10	10
3869	15f. Bee extracting nectar	10	10
3870	20f. Two bees on blossom	10	10
3871	2y. Two bees among flowers	85	35

856 Bowl, New Stone Age

1993. Lacquer Work. Multicoloured.

3872	20f. Type **856**	10	10
3873	30f. Duck-shaped container (from Marquis Yi's tomb), Warring States Period	10	10
3874	50f. Plate decorated with foliage (Zhang Cheng), Yuan Dynasty	15	10
3875	1y. Chrysanthemum-shaped container, Qing Dynasty	35	20

857 Mao Tse-tung in North Shaanxi

1993. Birth Centenary of Mao Tse-tung. Mult.

3876	20f. Type **857**	10	10
3877	1y. Mao in library	20	10

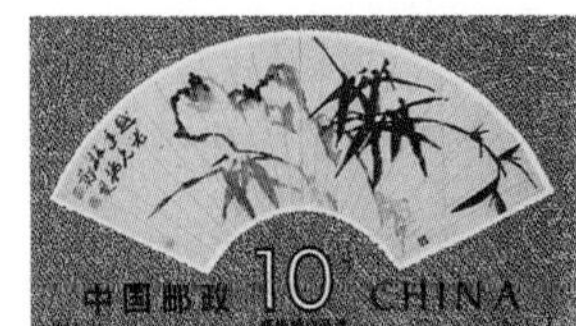

858 Fan Painting of Bamboo and Rock

1993. 300th Birth Anniv of Zheng Banqiao (artist). Multicoloured.

3879	10f. Type **858**	10	10
3880	20f. Orchids	10	10
3881	20f. Orchids, bamboo and rock (scroll) (vert)	10	10
3882	30f. Bamboo (scroll) (vert)	35	10
3883	50f. Chrysanthemum in vase	45	10
3884	1y.60 Calligraphy on fan	1·25	25

859 Yang Hucheng **860** Dog (folk toy, Hebei)

1993. Birth Centenary of General Yang Hucheng.

3885	**859** 20f. multicoloured	10	10

1994. New Year. Year of The Dog.

3886	**860** 20f. multicoloured	15	10
3887	– 50f. black, red & yellow	50	10

DESIGN: 50f. Dogs and flowers around Chinese character for dog.

861 Ma Xulun

1994. Revolutionaries (2nd series). Each brown and black.

3888	20f. Chen Qiyou (horiz)	10	10
3889	20f. Chen Shutong	10	10
3890	50f. Type **861**	20	10
3891	50f. Xu Deheng (horiz)	20	10

862 Great Siberian Sturgeon

1994. Sturgeons. Multicoloured.

3892	20f. Type **862**	10	10
3893	40f. Chinese sturgeon	20	10
3894	50f. Chinese paddlefish	25	10
3895	1y. Yangtze sturgeon	55	25

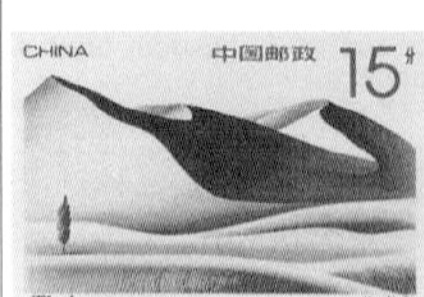

863 Tree in Dunes **864** Ming Dynasty Three-legged Round Teapot

1994. "Making the Desert Green". Multicoloured.

3896	15f. Type **863**	10	10
3897	20f. Flower-covered dune	10	10
3898	40f. Forest of poplars	40	10
3899	50f. Oasis	50	10

1994. Yixing Unglazed Teapots. Multicoloured.

3900	20f. Type **864**	10	10
3901	30f. Qing dynasty four-legged square teapot	10	10
3902	50f. Qing dynasty patterned teapot	15	10
3903	1y. Modern teapot	55	20

865 Entrance Gate

1994. 70th Anniv of Huang-pu Military Academy.

3904	**865** 20f. multicoloured	10	10

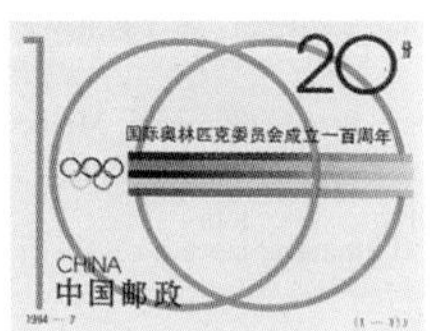

866 "100" and Olympic Rings

1994. Centenary of Int Olympic Committee.

3905	**866** 20f. multicoloured	10	10

867 Tao Yuanming (poet)

1994. Writers. Each black, brown and red.

3906	20f. Type **867**	10	10
3907	30f. Cao Zhi (poet)	10	10
3908	50f. Sima Qian (historian)	20	15
3909	1y. Qu Yuan (poet)	35	25

1994. Dunhuang Cave Murals (5th series). Tang Dynasty Frescoes in Mogao Caves. As T **732**. Multicoloured.

3910	10f. Flying Devata	10	10
3911	20f. Vimalakirti on dais	10	10
3912	50f. Zhang Yichao's forces	40	10
3913	1y.60 Sorceresses	75	35

868 Zhaojun

1994. Marriage of Zhaojun (from Han court) and Monarch of Xiongnu. Multicoloured.

3914	20f. Type **868**	10	10
3915	50f. Journey to Xiongnu	40	10

869 Emblem **870** Heaven's South Gate

1994. 6th Far East and South Pacific Games for the Disabled, Peking.

3917	**869** 20f. multicoloured	10	10

1994. U.N.E.S.C.O. World Heritage Site. Wulingyuan. Multicoloured.

3918	20f. Type **870**		
3919	30f. Shentangwan	10	10
3920	50f. No. One Bridge (horiz)	15	15
3921	1y. Writing Brush Peak (horiz)	55	25

871 Jade Maiden Peak

1994. Mt. Wuyi. Multicoloured.

3923	50f. (1) Type **871**	35	10
3924	50f. (2) Nine Turns Brook	35	10
3925	50f. (3) Hanging Block	35	10
3926	50f. (4) Elevated Meadow	35	10

Nos. 3923/6 were issued together, se-tenant, forming a composite design.

872 Examining Scroll **873** Whooping Crane

1994. Paintings by Fu Baoshi. Multicoloured.

3927	10f. Waterfall and river	10	10
3928	20f. Type **872**	10	10
3929	20f. Tree	10	10
3930	40f. Musicians	20	15
3931	50f. Wooded landscape	25	15
3932	1y. Scholars	45	30

1994. Cranes. Multicoloured.

3933	20f. Type **873**	20	10
3934	2y. Black-necked crane	65	30

875 White Emperor's City

1994. Gorges of Yangtse River. Mult.

3936	10f. (1) Type **875**	10	10
3937	20f. (2) River steamer in Qutang Gorge	10	10
3938	20f. (3) Small boat in Wuxia Gorge	10	10
3939	30f. (4) Goddess Peak	10	10
3940	50f. (5) Boats in Xiling Gorge	25	15
3941	1y. (6) Qu Yuan Memorial Hall	40	30

1994. Literature. "Romance of the Three Kingdoms" by Luo Guanzhong (4th series). As T **763**. Multicoloured.

3944	20f. Cao Cao composing poem with lance in hand (horiz)	10	10
3945	30f. Liu Bei's wedding to sister of Sun Quan	10	10
3946	50f. Ambush at Xiaoyaojin (horiz)	20	10
3947	1y. Lu Xun's forces destroying Liu Bei's camps	35	20

877 Shenzhen

1994. Special Economic Zones. Multicoloured.

3949	50f. (1) Type **877**	15	10
3950	50f. (2) Zhuhai	15	10
3951	50f. (3) Shantou	15	10
3952	50f. (4) Xiamen	15	10
3953	50f. (5) Hainan	15	10

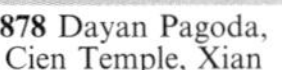

878 Dayan Pagoda, Cien Temple, Xian

879 Pig

1994. Pagodas. Each black, lightt brown and brown.

3954	20f. (1) Type **878**	10	10
3955	20f. (2) Zhenguo Pagoda, Kaiyuan Temple, Quanzhou	10	10
3956	50f. (3) Liuhe Pagoda, Kaihua Temple, Hangzhou	15	10
3957	2y. (4) Youguo Temple, Kaifeng	60	30

1995. New Year. Year of the Pig.

3959	**879**	20f. multicoloured	15	10
3960	–	50f. black and red	15	10

DESIGN: 50f. Chinese character ("pig") and pigs.

880 Willows beside River Songhua

1995. Winter in Jilin. Multicoloured.

3961	20f. Type **880**	15	10
3962	50f. Jade tree on hillside (vert)	15	10

881 Relief Map and Tropic of Cancer

1995. Mt. Dinghu. Multicoloured.

3963	15f. (1) Type **881**	10	10
3964	20f. (2) Ravine	10	10
3965	20f. (3) Monastery on hillside and forest-covered slopes	10	10
3966	2y.30 (4) Pair of silver pheasants in forest	65	35

882 Summit Emblem

1995. United Nations World Summit for Social Development, Copenhagen.

3967	**882**	20f. multicoloured	10	10

883 Snowy Owl

1995. Owls. Multicoloured.

3968	10f. Eagle owl	15	10
3969	20f. Long-eared owl	20	10
3970	50f. Type **883**	30	10
3971	1y. Eastern grass owls	60	20

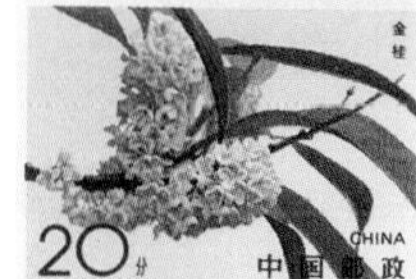

884 "Osmanthus fragrans thunbergii"

1995. Sweet Osmanthus. Multicoloured.

3972	20f. (1) Type **884**	10	10
3973	20f. (2) "Osmanthus fragrans latifolius"	10	10
3974	50f. (3) "Osmanthus fragrans aurantiacus"	25	10
3975	1y. (4) "Osmanthus fragrans semperflorens"	45	20

885 Player

1995. World Table Tennis Championships, Tianjin. Multicoloured.

3976	20f. Type **885**	10	10
3977	50f. Stadium	10	10

886 Ladies and Courtiers

1995. "Spring Outing" by Zhang Xuan. Details of the painting. Multicoloured.

3979	50f. (1) Type **886**	50	10
3980	50f. (2) Courtiers on horseback	50	10

Nos. 3979/80 were issued together, se-tenant, forming a composite design.

887 Donglu Play, Shanxi

1995. Shadow Play. Regional characters. Mult.

3981	20f. (1) Type **887**	10	10
3982	40f. (2) Luanxain play, Hebei	10	10
3983	50f. (3) Xiaoyi play, Shanxi	15	10
3984	50f. (4) Dayi play, Sichuan	15	10

888 Siyuan

1995. Motorway Interchanges, Peking. Mult.

3985	20f. Type **888**	10	10
3986	30f. Tianningsi	10	10
3987	50f. Yuting	10	10
3988	1y. Anhui	25	15

890 Asian Elephants at River

1995. 20th Anniv of China–Thailand Diplomatic Relations. Multicoloured.

3990	1y. (1) Type **890**	25	10
3991	1y. (2) Asian elephants at river (face value at left)	25	10

Nos. 3990/1 were issued together, se-tenant, forming a composite design.

891 East and West Dongting Hills

1995. Lake Taihu. Multicoloured.

3992	20f. (1) Type **891**	10	10
3993	20f. (2) Tortoise Islet in spring	10	10
3994	50f. (3) Li Garden in summer	15	10
3995	50f. (4) Jichang Garden in autumn	15	10
3996	230f. (5) Plum Garden in winter	90	35

893 Yucheng Post, Jiangsu

1995. "China'96" International Stamp Exhibition, Peking. Ancient Chinese Post Offices. Mult.

3999	20f. Type **893**	10	10
4000	50f. Jimingshan Post, Hebei	15	10

894 Hill Gate

1995. 1500th Anniv of Shaolin Temple, Henan. Multicoloured.

4001	20f. Type **894**	10	10
4002	20f. Pagoda Forest	10	10
4003	50f. Martial arts practice (detail of fresco, White Robe Hall)	15	10
4004	100f. Thirteen monks rescue the Prince of Qin (detail of fresco)	30	15

895 New Stone Age Jar

1995. Tibetan Culture. Multicoloured.

4005	20f. Type **895**	10	10
4006	30f. Helmet (7th century)	10	10
4007	50f. Celestial chart	15	10
4008	100f. Pearl and coral mandala	30	15

896 Koalas in Eucalyptus Tree

1995. Endangered Animals. Multicoloured.

4009	20f. Type **896**	10	10
4010	2y.90 Giant pandas amongst bamboo	90	25

897 Japanese Attack in North China, 7 July 1937

1995. 50th Anniv of End of Second World War and of War against Japan. Multicoloured.

4011	10f. (1) Type **897**	10	10
4012	20f. (2) Battle of Taier Village	10	10
4013	20f. (3) Battle at Great Wall	10	10
4014	50f. (4) Guerrillas	15	10
4015	50f. (5) Forces at Mangyo, Burma	15	10
4016	60f. (6) Airplane donated by overseas Chinese	15	10
4017	100f. (7) Liberation of Taiwan, October 1945	25	15
4018	100f. (8) Crew on deck of battleship	25	15

898 Woman's Profile and Flags (equality)

899 Great Wall at Jinshanling Hill

1995. 4th World Conference on Women, Peking. Multicoloured.

4019	15f. Type **898**	10	10
4020	20f. Woman's profile and wheel of colours (development)	10	10
4021	50f. Woman's profile and dove (peace)	15	10
4022	60f. Dove and flower (friendship)	20	15

1995. The Great Wall of China.

4024	–	5f. turquoise, bl & blk	10	10
4024a	–	10f. black and green	10	10
4024b	–	20f. black and lavender	10	10
4025	–	30f. black and yellow	10	10
4025a	–	40f. black and pink	10	10
4026	–	50f. black, brn & yell	10	10
4027	**899**	60f. black and brown	15	10
4027a	–	60f. black and yellow	15	10
4027b	–	80f. multicoloured	15	10
4028	–	100f. black and red	15	10
4029	–	150f. black and green	20	10
4031	–	200f. black and pink	30	15
4032	–	230f. black and green	45	30
4032a	–	270f. mauve, blk & grn	50	35
4035	–	290f. black and blue	50	35
4036	–	300f. black and green	40	25
4036a	–	320f. mve, blk & lav	45	25
4037	–	420f. black and orange	60	35
4037a	–	440f. light brown, black and brown	60	35
4038	–	500f. black, brn & bl	70	40
4038a	–	540f. black and blue	80	45
4038b	–	10y. multicoloured	1·75	80
4038c	–	20y. multicoloured	3·25	1·60
4038d	–	50y. grey, blk & grn	8·75	4·25

DESIGNS: 5f. Hushan section of wall; 10f. Wall at Jiumenkou Pass; 20f. Wall at Shanhaiguan; 30f. Wall at Huangya Pass; 40f. Jinshanling section of wall; 50f. Wall seen from Gubeikou; 60f. (4027a), Huanghua Tower and wall; 80f. Mutianyu section of wall; 100f. Wall seen from Badaling; 150f. Wall at Jurong Pass; 200f. Wall at Zijing Pass; 230f. Wall at Shanhaiguan Pass; 270f. Wall at Pingxingguan Pass; 290f. Laolongtou (end of wall); 300f. Wall at Niangziguan Pass; 320f. Wall at Desheng Pass; 420f. Wall at Pianguan Pass; 440f. Wall at Yanmen Pass; 500f. Bianjing Tower; 540f. Zhenbei Tower; 10y. Huama section; 20y. Wall at Sanguankou Pass; 50y. Wall at Jiayuguan Pass.

900 Dawn on Heavenly Terrace Peak

1995. The Jiuhua Mountains, Anhui. Mult.

4039	10f. (1) Type **900**	10	10
4040	20f. (2) Hall of Meditation (vert)	10	10
4041	20f. (3) Hall of the Mortal Body	10	10
4042	50f. (4) Sunset at Zhiyuan Temple	20	10
4043	50f. (5) Roc listening to Scriptures (rock formation) (vert)	20	10
4044	290f. (6) Phoenix pine	70	40

901 Black and White Film

1995. Centenary of Motion Pictures. Mult.

4045	20f. Type **901**	10	10
4046	50f. Colour film	10	10

902 Flag and New York Headquarters

1995. 50th Anniv of U.N.O. Multicoloured.
4047 20f. Type **902** 10 10
4048 50f. Anniversary emblem and "flags" 10 10

903 Blessing Spot

1995. Sanqing Mountain. Multicoloured.
4049 20f. Type **903** 10 10
4050 20f. Spring Goddess 10 10
4051 50f. Music charm (vert) 15 10
4052 100f. Supernatural python (rock formation) (vert) 60 20

904 Central Mountain Temple and Huang Gai Peak

1995. Mount Song. Multicoloured.
4053 20f. Type **904** 10 10
4054 50f. Moonrise over Fawang Temple 15 10
4055 60f. Shaolin Temple in snow 15 10
4056 1y. Mountain ridge 55 20

905 Victoria Harbour

1995. Hong Kong. Multicoloured.
4057 20f. Type **905** 10 10
4058 50f. Central Plaza 15 10
4059 60f. Hong Kong Cultural Centre 15 10
4060 290f. Repulse Bay 1·10 35

906 Sun Zi **907** Rat

1995. "Art of War" (book) by Sun Zi. Mult.
4061 20f. Type **906** 10 10
4062 20f. Elaborating strategies 10 10
4063 30f. Capturing Ying 10 10
4064 50f. Battle at Ailing 15 10
4065 100f. Conference at Huangchi 55 20

1996. New Year. Year of the Rat. Mult.
4066 20f. Type **907** 40 10
4067 50f. Pattern and Chinese character 40 10

908 Speed Skating

1996. 3rd Asian Winter Games, Harbin. Mult.
4068 50f. Type **908** 15 10
4069 50f. Ice hockey 15 10
4070 50f. Figure skating 15 10
4071 50f. Skiing 15 10
Nos. 4068/71 were issued together, se-tenant, forming a composite design.

909 Cable Route

1996. Inaug of Korea–China Submarine Cable.
4072 **909** 20f. multicoloured 10 10

910 Palace Complex

1996. Shenyang Imperial Palace. Multicoloured.
4073 50f. Type **910** 45 10
4074 50f. Pagoda and buildings 45 10
Nos. 4073/4 were issued together, se-tenant, forming a composite design.

911 Tianjin Posts Bureau

1996. Cent of Chinese State Postal Service. Mult.
4075 10f. Type **911** 10 10
4076 20f. Former Directorate General of North China Posts building, Peking 10 10
4077 50f. Postal headquarters of Chinese Soviet Republic, Zhongshi, Jiangxi 20 10
4078 100f. Present Peking postal complex 35 20

912 Calligraphy

1996. Paintings by Huang Binhong. Mult.
4080 20f. (1) Type **912** 10 10
4081 20f. (2) Mountain landscape 10 10
4082 40f. (3) Mount Qingcheng in rain 40 10
4083 50f. (4) View from Xiling 50 10
4084 50f. (5) Landscape 50 10
4085 230f. (6) Flowers 1·10 45

913 Shenyang F-8 Jet Fighter

1996. Chinese Aircraft. Multicoloured.
4086 20f. (1) Type **913** 10 10
4087 50f. (2) Nanchang A-5 jet fighter 15 10
4088 50f. (3) Xian Y-7 transport 15 10
4089 100f. (4) Harbin Y-12 utility plane 60 15

914 Green Scenery of Lijing River

1996. Bonsai Landscapes. Multicoloured.
4090 20f. (1) Type **914** 10 10
4091 20f. (2) Glistening Divine Peak 10 10
4092 50f. (3) Melting snow fills the river 15 10
4093 50f. (4) Eagle Beak Rock 15 10
4094 100f. (5) Memorable Years 60 15
4095 100f. (6) Peaks rising in Rosy Clouds 60 15

915 Sago Cycad ("Cycas revoluta")

1996. Cycads. Multicoloured.
4096 20f. Type **915** 10 10
4097 20f. Panzhihua cycad ("Cycas panzhihuaensis") 10 10
4098 50f. Nepal cycad 15 10
4099 230f. Polytomous cycad 55 30

916 Great Wall of China at Jinshan Ridge

1996. 25th Anniv of China–San Marino Diplomatic Relations. Multicoloured.
4100 100f. Type **916** 40 10
4101 100f. Walled rampart, San Marino 40 10
Nos. 4100/1 were issued together, se-tenant, forming a composite design.

919 Paddy Agricultural Tool

1996. Hemudu Archaeological Site, Yuyao, Zhejiang. Multicoloured.
4104 20f. Type **919** 10 10
4105 50f. Building supports 10 10
4106 100f. Paddles 45 10
4107 230f. Dish engraved with two birds and sun 70 25

921 Children rejoicing **922** "The Discus Thrower" (Miron)

1996. Children. Multicoloured.
4109 20f. Type **921** 10 10
4110 30f. Girls pushing child in wheelchair in rain 10 10
4111 50f. Expedition to Antarctica 10 10
4112 100f. Planting sapling 50 10

1996. Centenary of Modern Olympic Games.
4113 **922** 20f. multicoloured 10 10

923 "Land"

1996. Preserve Land. Designs showing Chinese characters. Multicoloured.
4114 20f. Type **923** 10 10
4115 50f. "Cultivation" 10 10

924 Jinglue Terrace

1996. Jinglue Terrace, Guangxi Zhuang. Mult.
4116 20f. Type **924** 10 10
4117 50f. Structure of Zhenwu Pavilion 10 10

925 Red Flag Car

1996. Motor Vehicles. Multicoloured.
4118 20f. Type **925** 10 10
4119 20f. Dongfeng two-door truck 10 10
4120 50f. Jiefang four-door truck 10 10
4121 100f. Peking four-wheel drive 50 15

926 Banbidian Village, Kaiping District

1996. 20th Anniv of Tangshan Earthquake. Development of New City. Multicoloured.
4122 20f. (1) Type **926** 10 10
4123 50f. (2) East Hebei Cement Works 20 10
4124 50f. (3) Earthquake memorials, Xinhua Road 10 10
4125 100f. (4) Bulk carrier in Jingtang Harbour 45 15

927 Emblem, Globe and "30"

1996. 30th Int Geological Conference, Peking.
4126 **927** 20f. multicoloured 10 10

928 Tianchi Lake

1996. Tianshan Mountains, Xinjiang.
4127 **928** 20f. (1) multicoloured 10 10
4128 – 50f. (2) multicoloured 10 10
4129 – 50f. (3) blue, mve & blk 10 10
4130 – 100f. (4) multicoloured 50 15
DESIGNS—VERT: No. 4128, Waterfalls; 4129, Snow-capped mountain peaks. HORIZ: No. 4130, Mountains and landscape.

1996. Dunhuang Cave Murals (6th series). As T **732**. Multicoloured.
4131 10f. Mount Wutai (Five Dynasties) (vert) 10 10
4132 20f. Li Shengtian, King of Khotan (Five Dynasties) (vert) 10 10
4133 50f. Guanyin, Goddess of Mercy, saves boat (Northern Song period) 10 10
4134 100f. Worshipping Bodhisattvas (Western Xia) 50 15

929 Tombs

1996. Emperors' Tombs of Western Xia Dynasty, Yinchuan, Ningxia Hui. Multicoloured.

4136 20f. Type **929** 10 10
4137 20f. Divine Gate ornament 10 10
4138 50f. Stone base from Stele Pavilion 10 10
4139 100f. Piece of stele from Shouling Tomb 50 10

930 Datong–Qinhuangdao Line

1996. Railways. Multicoloured.

4140 15f. Type **930** 10 10
4141 20f. Lanzhou–Xinjiang line 10 10
4142 50f. Peking–Kowloon line 25 20
4143 100f. Peking West railway station 45 35

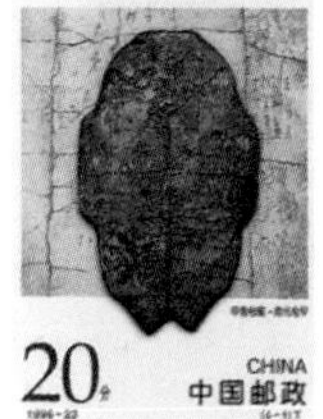

931 Shang Dynasty Tortoise Shell **932** Ye Ting

1996. Ancient Archives. Multicoloured.

4144 20f. Type **931** 10 10
4145 20f. Han Dynasty wood slip inscribed with divinations on a marriage 10 10
4146 50f. Ming dynasty iron scroll conferring merit on General Li Wen 10 10
4147 100f. Qing dynasty diplomatic credentials (1905) 25 15

1996. Birth Cent of Ye Ting (revolutionary). Mult.

4148 20f. Type **932** 10 10
4149 50f. Ye Ting in uniform 10 10

933 Emblem

1996. 96th Interparliamentary Union Conference, Peking.

4150 **933** 20f. multicoloured 10 10

934 Transport and Telecommunications

1996. Pudong Area of Shanghai. Mult.

4151 10f. (1) Type **934** 10 10
4152 20f. (2) People's Bank of China branch, Lujiazui finance and business area 10 10
4153 20f. (3) Jinqiao export centre 10 10
4154 50f. (4) Garden of Advance Science and Technology, Zhangjiang 40 10
4155 60f. (5) Customs House, Waigaoqiao bonded area 40 10
4156 100f. (6) Apartment blocks 50 15

935 Chinese Rocket "Long March"

1996. 47th Congress of International Astronautical Federation. Multicoloured.

4158 20f. Type **935** 10 10
4159 100f. Communications satellite 20 10

936 Singapore

1996. City Scenes. Multicoloured.

4160 20f. Type **936** 10 10
4161 290f. Panmen Gate, Suzhou 90 15

937 Red Army in Marshland

1996. 60th Anniv of Long March by Communist Army. Multicoloured.

4162 20f. Type **937** 35 10
4163 50f. Reunion of three armies 50 10

938 Two Gods

1996. Tianjin Clay Statuettes. Multicoloured.

4164 20f. (1) Type **938** 10 10
4165 50f. (2) Seated man blowing sugar figure 10 10
4166 50f. (3) Woman and child returning from fishing 10 10
4167 100f. (4) Women painting at table 50 15

939 Bank of China

1996. Economic Growth in Hong Kong. Mult.

4168 20f. Type **939** 10 10
4169 40f. Container terminal 10 10
4170 60f. Airplane taking off from Kai Tak Airport 40 10
4171 290f. Stock exchange 95 25

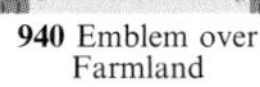

940 Emblem over Farmland **941** "Horse treading on Flying Swallow" (bronze) and Great Wall of China

1997. 1st National Agricultural Census.

4172 **940** 50f. multicoloured 10 10

1997. Tourist Year.

4173 **941** 50f. multicoloured 10 10

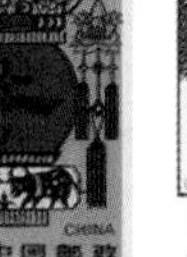

942 Chinese Lantern **943** "Pine on Mount Huangshan"

1997. New Year. Year of the Ox. Mult.

4174 50f. Type **942** 35 10
4175 150f. Ox 65 15

1997. Birth Centenary of Pan Tianshou (artist). Multicoloured.

4176 50f. (1) Type **943** 40 10
4177 50f. (2) "Rosy Clouds of Dawn" 40 10
4178 100f. (3) "Clearing Up after Mould Rains" 80 35
4179 100f. (4) "Chrysanthemum and Bamboo" 80 35
4180 150f. (5) "Sleeping Cat" 1·60 70
4181 150f. (6) "Corner of Lingyan Brook" 1·60 70

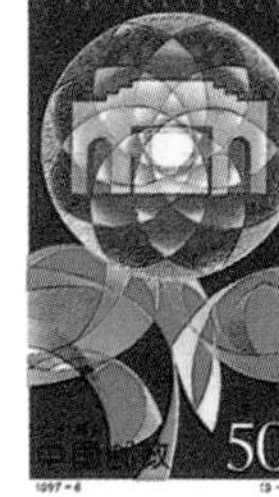

944 Tea Tree at Lancang, Yunnan **945** Celebration

1997. Tea. Multicoloured.

4182 50f. (1) Type **944** 10 10
4183 50f. (2) Statue of Lu Yu (author of "Classic of Tea") 10 10
4184 150f. (3) Tea grinder (Tang dynasty) (horiz) 60 15
4185 150f. (4) "Tea Party at Huishan" (Wen Zhenming) (horiz) 60 15

1997. 50th Anniv of Autonomous Region of Inner Mongolia. Multicoloured.

4186 50f. (1) Type **945** 10 10
4187 50f. (2) People of different cultures ("Unity") (horiz) 10 10
4188 200f. (3) Galloping horses ("Advance") (horiz) 80 15

946 Lady Amherst's Pheasant

1997. Rare Pheasants. Multicoloured.

4189 50f. Type **946** 10 10
4190 540f. Common pheasant 1·25 40

947 Zengchong Drum Tower **948** Buddha and Attendant Bodhisattva (Northern Wei dynasty)

1997. Dong Architecture. Multicoloured.

4191 50f. (1) Type **947** 10 10
4192 50f. (2) Baier drum tower 10 10
4193 150f. (3) Wind and rain bridge over River Nanjiang (horiz) 60 10
4194 150f. (4) Wind and rain shelter in field (horiz) 60 10

1997. Maiji Grottoes, Gansu Province. Mult.

4195 50f. (1) Type **948** 10 10
4196 50f. (2) Attendant Bodhisattva and disciple (Northern Wei dynasty) 10 10
4197 100f. (3) Maid servant (Western Wei dynasty) 15 10
4198 150f. (4) Buddha (Western Wei dynasty) 50 10
4199 150f. (5) Attendant Bodhisattva (Northern Zhou dynasty) 50 10
4200 200f. (6) Provider (Song dynasty) 55 15

949 Sino-British Joint Declaration and Red Roses

1997. Return of Hong Kong to China. Mult.

4201 50f. Type **949** 35 10
4202 150f. Basic Law and mixed roses 50 10

950 Taihuai Temple

1997. Ancient Temples, Wutai Mountain. Mult.

4205 40f. (1) Type **950** 10 10
4206 50f. (2) Great Hall, Nanchan Temple 10 10
4207 50f. (3) Eastern Hall, Foguang ("Buddhist Light") Temple 10 10
4208 150f. (4) Bronze Hall, Xiantong ("Revelation") Temple 60 10
4209 150f. (5) Bodhisattva Summit 60 10
4210 200f. (6) Zhenhai Temple 85 15

951 Tanks

1997. 70th Anniv of People's Liberation Army. Multicoloured.

4211 50f. (1) Type **951** 10 10
4212 50f. (2) Frigate flotilla 10 10
4213 50f. (3) Jet fighter 10 10
4214 50f. (4) Ballistic missile 10 10
4215 200f. (5) Tank, destroyer and jet fighters 90 15

952 Scene from "A Dream of Red Mansions" (carved by Jiang Yilin) **954** "Rosa rugosa"

953 Emblem

1997. Shoushan Stone Carvings. Mult.

4216 50f. (1) Type **952** 10 10
4217 50f. (2) "Rhinoceros basking in Sunshine" (Zhou Jinting) 10 10
4218 150f. (3) "Fragrance and Jade" 60 10
4219 150f. (4) "Li the Cripple, Han Zhongli and Lu Dongbin in drunken Joy" (Lin Fada) 60 10

1997. 15th National Communist Party Congress.

4221 **953** 50f. multicoloured 10 10

1997. Roses. Multicoloured.

4222 150f. Type **954** 50 10
4223 150f. "Aotearoa" of New Zealand 50 10

Nos. 4222/3 were issued together, se-tenant, forming a composite design.

955 Putting the Shot and Athletes

1997. 8th National Games, Shanghai. Mult.
4224 50f. Type **955** 35 10
4225 150f. Mascot and stadium 45 10

956 Hall of Prayer for Good Harvests

1997. Temple of Heaven, Peking. Mult.
4227 50f. (1) Type **956** 10 10
4228 50f. (2) Imperial Vault of Heaven 10 10
4229 150f. (3) Circular mound altar 60 10
4230 150f. (4) Hall of Abstinence 60 10

958 Archers' Tower, Jar and Gate Tower

1997. Xi'an City Walls. Multicoloured.
4232 50f. (1) Type **958** 10 10
4233 50f. (2) Archers' Tower . . 10 10
4234 150f. (3) Watchtower . . . 45 10
4235 150f. (4) South-west corner tower 45 10

959 Diversion Canal

1997. Three Gorges Project (damming of Yangtse River). Multicoloured.
4236 50f. Type **959** 10 10
4237 50f. Dam under construction 10 10
Nos. 4236/7 were issued together, se-tenant, forming a composite design.

960 Temple of the Heavenly Queen

1997. Macao. Multicoloured.
4238 50f. Type **960** 10 10
4239 100f. Lianfeng (Lotus Peak) Temple 35 10
4240 150f. Great Sanba Archway (former facade of St. Paul's Church) 55 10
4241 200f. Songshan (Pine Hill) Lighthouse 70 10

961 Metallurgy in Ancient China

1997. Achievement in 1996 of Production of over 100,000,000 Tons of Steel a Year. Multicoloured.
4242 50f. Type **961** 10 10
4243 150f. Modern steel works 55 10

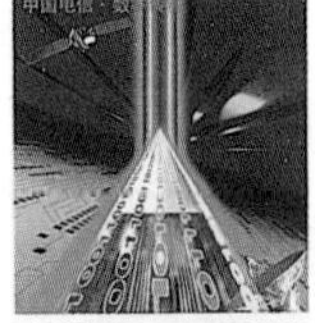

962 Digital Transmission

963 Cloth Tiger (Guo Qiuying)

1997. Telecommunications. Multicoloured.
4244 50f. (1) Type **962** 10 10
4245 50f. (2) Program-controlled switch and computer . . . 10 10
4246 150f. (3) Digital communication 60 10
4247 150f. (4) Mobile communication 60 10

1997. Literature. "Outlaws of the Marsh" (5th series). As T **745**. Multicoloured.
4248 40f. (1) Hu Yanzhuo tricks Guan Sheng 10 10
4249 50f. (2) Lu Junyi captures Shi Wengong 10 10
4250 50f. (3) Yan Qing wrestles with Qing Tianzhu . . . 10 10
4251 150f. (4) Hong Tianlei defeats government troops 80 10

1998. New Year. Year of the Tiger. Mult.
4253 50f. Type **963** 10 10
4254 150f. Chinese character . . 60 10

964 Keyuan Garden

1998. Villas and Gardens in Guangdong. Mult.
4255 50f. Type **964** 10 10
4256 50f. Liangyuan Garden . . 10 10
4257 100f. Qinghiu Garden . . . 40 10
4258 200f. Yuyin Villa 45 10

965 Deng Xiaoping

1998. 1st Death Anniv of Deng Xiaoping. Mult.
4259 50f. (1) Type **965** 10 10
4260 50f. (2) During Liberation War 10 10
4261 50f. (3) With Mao Tse-tung 10 10
4262 100f. (4) As Chairman of Military Commission . . 15 10
4263 150f. (5) Making speech . . 45 10
4264 200f. (6) In south China . . 55 20

966 Officers and Badge

1998. People's Police. Multicoloured.
4265 40f. (1) Type **966** 10 10
4266 50f. (2) Officers using computer and patrol officers using radio . . . 10 10
4267 50f. (3) Officer and elderly woman 10 10
4268 100f. (4) Officer on traffic control duty 15 10
4269 150f. (5) Officers on fire duty 45 10
4270 200f. (6) Border guards . . 55 15

967 State Arms

968 Chou En-lai on Horseback

1998. 9th National People's Congress, Peking.
4271 **967** 50f. multicoloured . . . 10 10

1998. Birth Centenary of Chou En-lai.
4272 **968** 50f. black, cream & red 10 10
4273 – 50f. black, cream & red 10 10
4274 – 150f. black, cream & red 45 10
4275 – 150f. multicoloured . . . 45 10
DESIGNS: No. 4273, Walking; 4274, Wearing floral decoration; 4275, Clapping.

969 Fangcao Lake

1997. World Heritage Site. Jiuzhaigou (nine-village valley). Multicoloured.
4276 50f. (1) Type **969** 10 10
4277 50f. (2) Wuhua Lake . . . 10 10
4278 150f. (3) Shuzheng Falls . . 45 10
4279 150f. (4) Nuorilang Falls . . 45 10

970 House on Stilts

1998. Dai Architecture, Xishuangbanna. Mult.
4281 50f. (1) Type **970** 10 10
4282 50f. (2) Ornamental well . . 10 10
4283 150f. (3) Pavilion and streamers 60 10
4284 150f. (4) Pagoda 60 10

971 Haikou

1998. Hainan Special Economic Zone. Mult.
4285 50f. (1) Type **971** 10 10
4286 50f. (2) Yangpu 10 10
4287 150f. (3) Sanya Phoenix International Airport . . 60 10
4288 150f. (4) Monument, Yalongwan 60 10

972 Yingtian Academy

1998. Ancient Academies. Multicoloured.
4289 50f. (1) Type **972** 10 10
4290 50f. (2) Songyang Academy 10 10
4291 150f. (3) Yuelu Academy . . 60 10
4292 150f. (4) Bailu Academy . . 60 10

973 University Buildings

1998. Centenary of Peking University.
4293 **973** 50f. multicoloured . . . 10 10

974 Congress Emblem

1998. 22nd U.P.U. Congress, Peking (1999). Mult.
4294 50f. Type **974** 10 10
4295 540f. Emblem (vert) . . . . 1·10 45

975 Mountain Peaks

1998. Shennongjia (primitive forest). Mult.
4296 50f. (1) Type **975** 10 10
4297 50f. (2) River gorge 10 10
4298 150f. (3) Forest 45 10
4299 150f. (4) Grasslands 45 10

976 Great Hall of the People of Chongqing

1998. Chongqing. Multicoloured.
4300 50f. Type **976** 10 10
4301 150f. Chongqing port . . . 20 10

977 "Tiger"

1998. Paintings by He Xiangning. Mult.
4302 50f. Type **977** 10 10
4303 100f. "Lion" (vert) 15 10
4304 150f. "Plum Blossom" (vert) 45 15

978 Grasslands

1998. Xilingguole Grasslands, Inner Mongolia. Multicoloured.
4305 50f. (1) Type **978** 10 10
4306 50f. (2) Meadow steppe . . . 10 10
4307 150f. (3) Forest of poplars and birches 60 10

979 Baishilazi

1998. Jingpo Lake, Heilonjiang. Multicoloured.
4309 50f. (1) Type **979** 10 10
4310 50f. (2) Pearl Gate 10 10
4311 50f. (3) Mt. Xiaogushan . . 10 10
4312 50f. (4) Diaoshuilou waterfall 10 10
Nos. 4309/12 were issued together, se-tenant, forming a composite design.

980 Wurzburg Palace, Germany

1998. World Heritage Sites. Multicoloured.
4313 50f. Type **980** 35 10
4314 540f. Puning Temple, Chengde 1·25 45

1998. Literature. "The Romance of the Three Kingdoms" by Luo Guanzhong (5th series). As T **763**. Multicoloured.
4315 50f. (1) Liu Bei appoints a Guardian for his Heir at Baidi City (horiz) 10 10
4316 50f. (2) Zhuge Liang leads his army home 10 10
4317 100f. (3) Funeral of Zhuge Liang (horiz) 15 10
4318 150f. (4) Three Kingdoms united under the reign of Jin 45 10

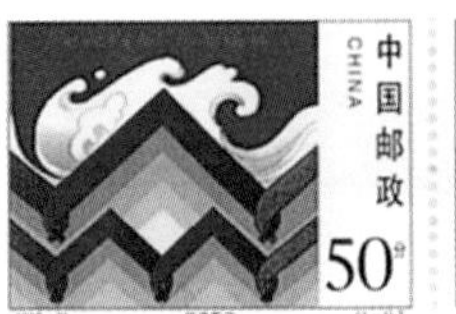
981 Wave and Houses

1998. Flood Relief Fund.
4320 **981** 50f. (+50f.) mult 15 10

No. 4320 includes the se-tenant premium-carrying tab shown in Type **981**. The premium was used to help the victims of floods in the Yangtse and Songhuajiang River areas.

982 Louvre Palace, Paris

1998. Ancient Palaces. Multicoloured.
4321 50f. Type **982** 10 10
4322 200f. Imperial Palace, Peking 55 15

983 Face

1998. Rock Paintings, Helan Mountains. Mult.
4323 50f. Type **983** 10 10
4324 100f. Hunting 15 10
4325 150f. Ox 55 10

984 Vase with Five Spouts (Northern Song Dynasty)

1998. Longquan Pottery. Multicoloured.
4326 50f. (1) Type **984** 10 10
4327 50f. (2) Vase with phoenix ears (Southern Song dynasty) 10 10
4328 50f. (3) Double gourd vase (Yuan dynasty) 10 10
4329 150f. (4) Ewer decorated with three fruits (Ming dynasty) 50 10

985 Meridian Gate

1998. Mausoleum of King Yandi, Yanling County, Hunan. Multicoloured.
4330 50f. Type **985** 10 10
4331 100f. Saluting Pavilion 15 10
4332 150f. Tomb 55 10

986 Men discussing Campaign (Yi Rongsheng)

1998. 50th Anniv of Liberation War. Multicoloured.
4334 50f. (1) Type **986** 10 10
4335 50f. (2) Conquering Jinzhou (Ren Mengzhang, Zhang Hongzan, Li Shuji and Guang Tingbo) 10 10
4336 50f. (3) Battle of Huaihai (Chen Qi, Zhao Guangtao, Chen Jian and Wei Chuyu) 10 10
4337 50f. (4) Liberating Peking (Zhang Ruwei, Deng Jiaju, Wu Changjiang and Shen Yaoyi) 10 10
4338 150f. (5) Supporting the Front (Cui Kaixi) 60 10

987 Liu Shaoqi

1998. Birth Centenary of Liu Shaoqi (Chairman of the Republic, 1959–68).
4339 **987** 50f. (1) multicoloured 10 10
4340 – 50f. (2) black, buff and red 10 10
4341 – 50f. (3) multicoloured 10 10
4342 – 150f. (4) multicoloured 50 10

DESIGNS—VERT: No. 4340, Shaoqi at Seventh National Communist Party Congress. HORIZ: No. 4341, Presented with necklace of flowers while on diplomatic mission; 4342, Working at desk.

988 Chillon Castle, Lake Geneva, Switzerland

1998. Lakes. Multicoloured.
4343 50f. Type **988** 35 10
4344 540f. Bridge 24, Slender West Lake, Yangzhou 1·25 45

989 Canal Fork

1998. Lingqu Canal. Multicoloured.
4345 50f. Type **989** 10 10
4346 50f. Bridge over canal (vert) 10 10
4347 150f. Lock (vert) 45 10

990 Road into Macao

1998. Macao. Multicoloured.
4348 50f. Type **990** 10 10
4349 100f. Bridge and buildings 15 10
4350 150f. Macao Stadium 50 10
4351 200f. Airport 65 15

991 Deng Xiaoping at Third Plenary Session

1998. 20th Anniv of Third Plenary Session of 11th Central Committee of Chinese Communist Party. Multicoloured.
4352 50f. Type **991** 10 10
4353 150f. Deng Xiaoping Theory and buildings 45 10

993 Ceramic Rabbit (Zhang Chang)

1999. New Year. Year of the Rabbit. Multicoloured.
4355 50f. Type **993** 10 10
4356 150f. Chinese character ("Good Luck") 45 10

994 Ploughing

1999. Stone Carvings of Han Dynasty.
4357 **994** 50f. (1) green, cream and black 10 10
4358 – 50f. (2) brown, cream and black 10 10
4359 – 50f. (3) blue, cream and black 10 10
4360 – 50f. (4) brown, cream and black 10 10
4361 – 150f. (5) green, cream and black 50 10
4362 – 150f. (6) lilac, cream and black 50 10

DESIGNS: No. 4358, Weaving; 4359, Dancing; 4360, Carriage and outriders; 4361, Jing Ke's attempted assassination of Emperor Qinshihuang; 4362, Goddess Chang'e flying to moon.

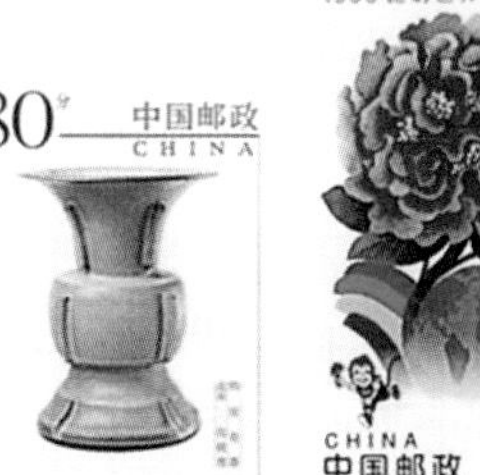
995 Wine Vessel, Northern Song Dynasty **996** Peony and Globe

1999. Ceramics from the Jun Kiln, Henan. Multicoloured.
4363 80f. Type **995** 10 10
4364 100f. Wine vessel, Northern Song Dynasty (different) 15 10
4365 150f. Double-handled stove, Yuan Dynasty 55 10
4366 200f. Double-handled vase, Yuan Dynasty 65 15

1999. World Horticulture Fair, Kunming. Mult.
4367 80f. Type **996** 10 10
4368 200f. Exhibition halls and tree 30 15

997 Stag

1999. Red Deer. Multicoloured.
4369 80f. (1) Type **997** 10 10
4370 80f. (2) Doe and fawns 10 10

998 Puji Temple

1999. Putuo Mountain, Lianhuayang. Mult.
4371 30f. Type **998** 10 10
4372 60f. Nantian Gate (vert) 10 10
4373 60f. Step beach 10 10
4374 80f. Pantuo Rock 10 10
4375 80f. Fanyin Cave (vert) 10 10
4376 280f. Fayu Temple 40 20

1000 Fang Zhimin (sculpture)

1999. Birth Centenary of Fang Zhimin (revolutionary). Multicoloured.
4378 80y. Type **1000** 10 10
4379 80y. Full-length portrait of Fang Zhimin 10 10

1001 First Congress Building, Berne, Switzerland (1874)

1999. 22nd Universal Postal Union Congress, Peking. Multicoloured.
4380 80f. Type **1001** 10 10
4381 540f. 22nd Congress building, Peking 1·10 45

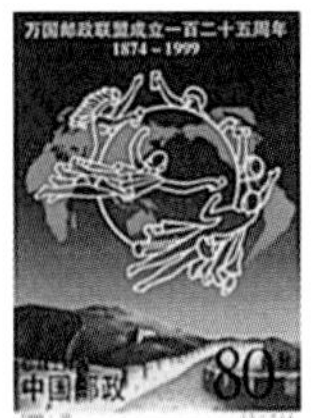
1002 U.P.U. Emblem and Great Wall **1003** Emblem

1999. 125th Anniv of Universal Postal Union.
4383 **1002** 80f. multicoloured 10 10

1999. International Year of the Elderly.
4384 **1003** 80f. multicoloured 10 10

1004 Conference Hall

1999. 50th Anniv of Chinese People's Political Conference. Multicoloured.
4385 60f. Type **1004** 10 10
4386 80f. Mao Tse-tung and emblem (vert) 10 10

1005 Han Couple

1999. 50th Anniv of People's Republic. Ethnic Groups. Couples from different ethnic groups. Multicoloured.
4387 80f. (1) Type **1005** 10 10
4388 80f. (2) Mongolian 10 10
4389 80f. (3) Hui 10 10
4390 80f. (4) Tibetan 10 10
4391 80f. (5) Uygur 10 10
4392 80f. (6) Miao 10 10
4393 80f. (7) Yi 10 10
4394 80f. (8) Zhuang 10 10
4395 80f. (9) Bouyei 10 10

4396 80f. (10) Korean 10 10
4397 80f. (11) Manchu 10 10
4398 80f. (12) Dong 10 10
4399 80f. (13) Yao 10 10
4400 80f. (14) Bai 10 10
4401 80f. (15) Tujia 10 10
4402 80f. (16) Hani 10 10
4403 80f. (17) Kazak 10 10
4404 80f. (18) Dai 10 10
4405 80f. (19) Li 10 10
4406 80f. (20) Lisu 10 10
4407 80f. (21) Va 10 10
4408 80f. (22) She 10 10
4409 80f. (23) Gaoshan 10 10
4410 80f. (24) Lahu 10 10
4411 80f. (25) Sui 10 10
4412 80f. (26) Dongxiang 10 10
4413 80f. (27) Naxi 10 10
4414 80f. (28) Jingpo 10 10
4415 80f. (29) Kirgiz 10 10
4416 80f. (30) Tu 10 10
4417 80f. (31) Daur 10 10
4418 80f. (32) Mulam 10 10
4419 80f. (33) Qiang 10 10
4420 80f. (34) Blang 10 10
4421 80f. (35) Salar 10 10
4422 80f. (36) Maonan 10 10
4423 80f. (37) Gelao 10 10
4424 80f. (38) Xibe 10 10
4425 80f. (39) Achang 10 10
4426 80f. (40) Primi 10 10
4427 80f. (41) Tajik 10 10
4428 80f. (42) Nu 10 10
4429 80f. (43) Uzbek 10 10
4430 80f. (44) Russian 10 10
4431 80f. (45) Ewenki 10 10
4432 80f. (46) De'ang 10 10
4433 80f. (47) Bonan 10 10
4434 80f. (48) Yugur 10 10
4435 80f. (49) Gin 10 10
4436 80f. (50) Tatar 10 10
4437 80f. (51) Derung 10 10
4438 80f. (52) Oroqen 10 10
4439 80f. (53) Hezhen 10 10
4440 80f. (54) Monba 10 10
4441 80f. (55) Lhoba 10 10
4442 80f. (56) Jino 10 10

1006 Mt. Kumgang, North Korea

1999. 50th Anniv of China–North Korea Diplomatic Relations. Multicoloured.
4443 80f. (1) Type **1006** 10 10
4444 80f. (2) Mt. Lushan, China 10 10

1007 Children reading

1008 Early Cambrian Chengjiang Biota Fossil

1999. 10th Anniv of Project Hope (promotion of rural education).
4445 **1007** 80f. multicoloured . . . 10 10

1999. 50th Anniv of Chinese Academy of Sciences. Multicoloured.
4446 80f. (1) Type **1008** 10 10
4447 80f. (2) Underwater robot 10 10
4448 80f. (3) Head and mathematical equation (vert) 10 10
4449 80f. (4) Astronomical telescope (vert) 10 10

1009 Li Lisan

1011 Rongzhen in Uniform

1010 Sino-Portuguese Joint Declaration

1999. Birth Centenary of Li Lisan (trade unionist). Multicoloured.
4450 80f. Type **1009** 10 10
4451 80f. Li Lisan (different) . . 10 10

1999. Return of Macao to China. Multicoloured.
4452 80f. Type **1010** 10 10
4453 150f. Basic Law of Macao Special Region and Great Wall of China . . . 20 10

1999. Birth Centenary of Nie Rongzhen (revolutionary). Multicoloured.
4456 80f. Type **1011** 10 10
4457 80f. Rongzhen in chair . . . 10 10

1012 1961 8f. 1911 Revolution Stamp and Dr. Sun Yat-sen

1999. The Twentieth Century. Multicoloured.
4458 60f. (1) Type **1012** 10 10
4459 60f. (2) 1989 8f. May 4th Movement stamp 10 10
4460 80f. (3) 1991 20f. Chinese Communist Party stamp 10 10
4461 80f. (4) 1995 20f. (No. 4013) End of Second World War and of War against Japan stamp 10 10
4462 80f. (5) 1959 20f. People's Republic anniversary stamp and Mao Tse-tung 10 10
4463 200f. (6) 1989 20f. National Defence stamp 35 15
4464 260f. (7) 1996 500f. Pudong Area of Shanghai stamp 35 20
4465 280f. (8) Deng Xiaoping and fireworks (based on 1997 800f. Return of Hong Kong to China stamp) . . 40 25

1013 Chinese Dragon

1014 Welcoming the Spring Festival

2000. New Year. Year of the Dragon. Each black, gold and red.
4466 80f. Type **1013** 10 10
4467 2y.80 "The Sun Rising in the Eastern Sky" and Chinese character for dragon 40 25

2000. Spring Festival. Multicoloured.
4468 80f. Type **1014** 10 10
4469 80f. Bidding farewell to the outgoing year 10 10
4470 2y.80 Offering sacrifices to the God of Land 40 25

1016 Neolithic Jade Dragon

2000. Chinese Dragon Artefacts. Multicoloured.
4473 60f. (1) Type **1016** 10 10
4474 80f. (2) Dragon-shaped brooch, Warring States 15 10
4475 80f. (3) Eaves tile with carved dragon, Han Dynasty 15 10
4476 80f. (4) Coiled dragon on copper mirror, Tang Dynasty 15 10
4477 80f. (5) Bronze dragon, Jin Dynasty 15 10
4478 2y.80 (6) Dragon decoration from Qing Dynasty Red Sandalwood Throne . . . 45 25

1017 Wanxian Bridge

2000. Road Bridges over the Yangtze River. Mult.
4479 80f. (1) Type **1017** 15 10
4480 80f. (2) Huangshi 15 10
4481 80f. (3) Tongling 15 10
4482 2y.80 (4) Jiangyin 45 25

1018 Cangshan Mountain and Erhai Lake

2000. Landscapes of Dali, Yunnan Province. Mult.
4483 80f. (1) Type **1018** 15 10
4484 80f. (2) Three Pagodas, Chongsheng Temple . . . 15 10
4485 80f. (3) Jizu Mountain . . . 15 10
4486 2y.80 (4) Shibao Mountain 45 25

1019 Mulan weaving Cloth

2000. Literature. *Mulan* (folk tale). Multicoloured.
4487 80f. (1) Type **1019** 15 10
4488 80f. (2) Mulan dressed as male soldier 15 10
4489 80f. (3) Mulan on horseback 15 10
4490 80f. (4) Mulan resuming her female identity 15 10

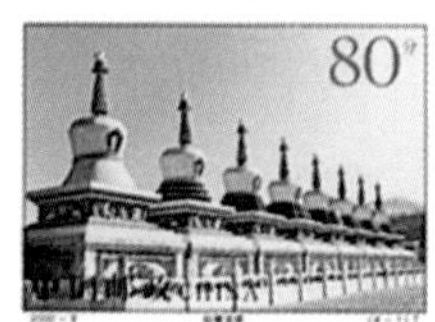
1020 Good Luck Treasure Pagoda

2000. Taer Lamasery, Qinghai Province. Mult.
4491 80f. (1) Type **1020** 15 10
4492 80f. (2) Big Golden Tile Palace 15 10
4493 80f. (3) Big Scripture Hall 15 10
4494 2y.80 (4) Banqen Residence 45 25

1021 Li Fuchan and Cai Chang

2000. Birth Centenaries of Li Fuchan and Cai Chang (revolutionary couple).
4495 **1021** 80f. black, buff and brown 15 10

1022 "Entering a New Century" (Ling Lifei)

2000. New Millennium. Winning Entries in National Children's "Prospects in the New Century" Stamp Design Competition. Mult.
4496 30f. (1) Type **1022** 10 10
4497 60f. (2) "I Build a Bridge to Connect the Mainland with Taiwan" (Wang Yumeng) 10 10
4498 60f. (3) "Palace in a Tree" (Li Zhao) 10 10
4499 80f. (4) "Protecting the Earth" (Chen Zhuo) . . . 15 10
4500 80f. (5) "Communications in the New Century" (Qin Tian) 15 10
4501 80f. (6) "Space Travel" (Wang Yiru) 15 10
4502 2y.60 (7) "The Earth gets Younger" (Tian Yuan) . . 40 15
4503 2y.80 (8) "World Peace" (Song Zhili) 45 25

1023 Chen Yun

2000. 95th Birth Anniv of Chen Yun (revolutionary). Multicoloured.
4504 80f. (1) Type **1023** 15 10
4505 80f. (2) Chen Yun wearing white jacket and hat (vert) 15 10
4506 80f. (3) Chen Yun wearing black jacket (vert) 15 10
4507 2y.80 (4) Chen Yun 45 25

1024 He-Pot (Chinese wine vessel)

2000. Pots. Multicoloured.
4508 80f. (1) Type **1024** 15 10
4509 80f. (2) Horse milk pot, Kazakhstan 15 10

1025 Great Peak

2000. Laoshan Mountain. Multicoloured.
4510 80f. (1) Type **1025** 15 10
4511 80f. (2) Yangkou Bay . . . 15 10
4512 80f. (3) Beijiu Lake 15 10
4513 2y.80 (4) Taiqing Palace . . 45 25

1027 Grandma Carp telling a Story

2000. *Small Carp Leap Through Dragon Gate* (children's story). Multicoloured.
4516 80f. (1) Type **1027** 15 10
4517 80f. (2) Searching for Dragon Gate 15 10
4518 80f. (3) Uncle Crab helping Carp 15 10
4519 80f. (4) Carp leaping through Dragon Gate . . 15 10
4520 80f. (5) Aunt Swallow delivering a letter 15 10

1028 Financial Central District

2000. Shenzhen Special Economic Zone. Mult.
4526 80f. (1) Type **1028** 15 10
4527 80f. (2) China International New and Hi-Tech Achievement Fair Exhibition Centre 15 10
4528 80f. (3) Yantian Harbour . . 15 10
4529 80f. (4) Shenzhen Bay . . . 15 10
4530 2y.80 (5) Shekou Industrial District 15 10

1030 Coconut Forest Bay, Hainan

2000. Beaches. Multicoloured.
4532 80f. (1) Type **1030** 15 10
4533 80f. (2) Paradero seashore, Matanzas, Cuba 15 10

1031 Puppets

2000. Masks and Puppets. Multicoloured.
4534 80f. (1) Type **1031** 15 10
4535 80f. (2) Carnival masks . . 15 10

1032 "Eternal Fidelity" Palace Lamp **1033** Confucius

2000. Relics from Tomb of Liu Sheng. Multicoloured.
4536 80f. (1) Type **1032** 15 10
4537 80f. (2) Bronze pot with dragon design 15 10
4538 80f. (3) Boshan incense burner with gold inlay . . 15 10
4539 2y.80 (4) Rosefinch-shaped cup 15 10

2000. Ancient Thinkers. Each black, red and brown.
4540 60f. (1) Type **1033** 15 10
4541 80f. (2) Mencius 15 10
4542 80f. (3) Lao Zi 15 10
4543 80f. (4) Zhuang Zi 15 10
4544 80f. (5) Mo Zi 15 10
4545 2y.80 (6) Xun Zi 15 10

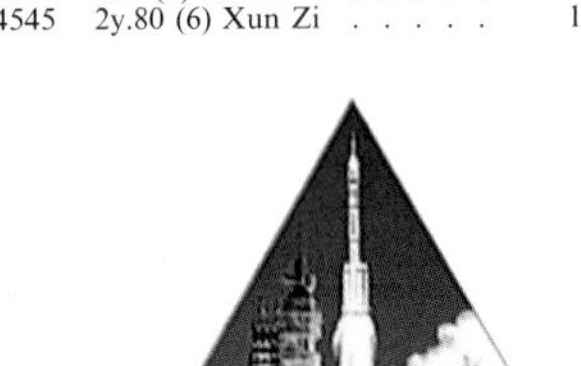

1034 Launch of *Shenzhou*

2000. Test Flight of *Shenzhou* (spacecraft). Mult.
4546 80f. Type **1034** 15 10
4547 80f. Orbiting Earth 15 10

1035 Meteorological Satellite

2000. 50th Anniv of World Meteorological Organization. Multicoloured.
4548 80f. (1) Type **1035** 15 10
4549 80f. (2) Meteorological equipment and Qinghai–Tibet plateau 15 10
4550 80f. (3) Computers and numbers 15 10
4551 2y.80 (4) Airplane and wind flow diagram 15 10

1036 Scarlet Kaffir Lily **1037** Jingshu Bell, Western Zhou Dynasty

2000. Flowers. Multicoloured.
4552 80f. (1) Type **1036** 15 10
4553 80f. (2) Noble clivia 15 10
4554 80f. (3) Golden striat kaffir lily 15 10
4555 2y.80 (4) White kaffir lily . . 15 10

2000. Ancient Bells. Multicoloured.
4557 80f. (1) Type **1037** 15 10
4558 80f. (2) Su chime bell, Spring and Autumn Period 15 10
4559 80f. (3) Jingyun bell, Tang Dynasty 15 10
4560 2y.80 (4) Qianlong bell, Qing Dynasty 15 10

1038 Sun, Moon and Observatory **1039** Snake

2001. New Millennium. Multicoloured.
4561 60f. (1) Type **1038** 10 10
4562 80f. (2) Globe and white dove 15 10
4563 80f. (3) Child's hands, leaf and World map (horiz) 15 10
4564 80f. (4) Silhouette of head and circuit board (horiz) 15 10
4565 2y.80 (5) Sun, stars and sundial 50 30

2001. New Year. Year of the Snake. Multicoloured.
4566 80f. Type **1039** 15 10
4567 2y.80 "Fortune Illuminates all Things" and Chinese character for snake . . . 50 30

1040 Tang Qin

2001. Chou (Clown) Roles in Peking Opera. Multicoloured.
4568 80f. (1) Type **1040** 15 10
4569 80f. (2) Liu Lihua 15 10
4570 80f. (3) Gao Lishi 15 10
4571 80f. (4) Jiang Gan 15 10
4572 80f. (5) Yang Xiangwu . . . 15 10
4573 2y.80 (6) Shi Qian 50 30

1042 Zhouzhuang, Kunshan

2001. Ancient Towns, Taihu Lake Valley. Multicoloured.
4575 80f. (1) Type **1042** 15 10
4576 80f. (2) Tongli, Wujiang . . 15 10
4577 80f. (3) Wuzhen, Tongziang 15 10
4578 80f. (4) Nanxun, Huzhou . . 15 10
4579 80f. (5) Luzhi, Wuxian . . . 15 10
4580 2y.80 (6) Xitang, Jiashan . . 50 30

1043 "Ying Ning"

2001. Classical Literature. *Strange Stories from a Chinese Studio* by Pu Songling. Multicoloured.
4581 60f. (1) Type **1043** 15 10
4582 80f. (2) "A Bao" 15 10
4583 80f. (3) "Mask of Evildoer" 15 10
4584 2y.80 (4) "Stealing Peach" 50 30

1044 Queen Mother (detail)

2001. Yongle Temple Murals, Shanxi. "Portrait of Paying Homage to Xianyuan Emperor". Multicoloured.
4586 60f. (1) Type **1044** 15 10
4587 80f. (2) Jade Lady presenting treasure . . . 15 10
4588 80. (3) Celestial Worthy of the East 15 10
4589 2y.80 (4) Venus and Mercury 50 30

1045 Nanyan Hall in Autumn **1046** Pottery Vase

2001. Mount Wudang, Hubei Province. Multicoloured.
4590 60f. (1) Type **1045** 10 10
4591 80f. (2) Zixiao Temple in winter 15 10
4592 80f. (3) Taizi slope in summer 15 10

2001. Chinese Pottery. Multicoloured.
4594 80f. (1) Type **1046** 15 10
4595 80f. (2) Teapot 15 10

1047 Dragon Boat Race

2001. Duanwu Dragon Boat Festival. Multicoloured.
4596 80f. (1) Type **1047** 15 10
4597 80f. (2) Vase, mobile and flowers 15 10
4598 2y.80 (3) Dragon's head and expulsion of five poisons 50 30

1048 Wang Jinmei

2001. Leaders of the Chinese Communist Party. Multicoloured.
4599 80f. (1) Type **1048** 15 10
4600 80f. (2) Zhao Shiyan 15 10
4601 80f. (3) Deng Enming . . . 15 10
4602 80f. (4) Cai Hesen 15 10
4603 80f. (5) He Shuheng 15 10

1049 Party Flag

2001. 80th Anniv of Chinese Communist Party.
4604 **1049** 80f. red, yellow and black 15 10

1050 Emblem

2001. Choice of Beijing as 2008 Olympic Host City.
4605 **1050** 80f. multicoloured . . . 15 10

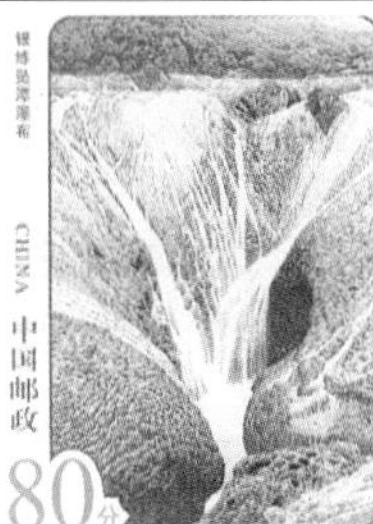

1051 Yinlianzhuitan Waterfall

2001. Waterfalls. Multicoloured.
4606 80f. (1) Type **1051** 15 10
4607 80f. (2) Doupotang Waterfall (horiz) 15 10
4608 80f. (3) Dishuitan Waterfall 15 10

1052 Pigeon Nest

2001. Beidaihe Summer Resort. Multicoloured.
4610 60f. (1) Type **1052** 10 10
4611 80f. (2) Umbrellas, Zhonghai Beach 15 10
4612 80f. (3) Sailing dinghies, Lianfeng Hill 15 10
4613 2y.80 Windsurfers, Tiger Stone 50 30

1053 "2001" and Emblem

2001. 21st World University Games, Beijing. Multicoloured.
4614 60f. Type **1053** 10 10
4615 80f. "2001" and sports pictograms 15 10
4616 2y.80 "2001" and globes . . 50 30

1054 Water Diversion Canal

2001. Datong River Diversion Project. Mult.
4617 80f. (1) Type **1054** 15 10
4618 80f. (2) Overland pipes, Xianming Gorge 15 10
4619 80f. (3) Canal tunnel 15 10
4620 2y.80 (4) Aqueduct, Zhuanglang River 50 30

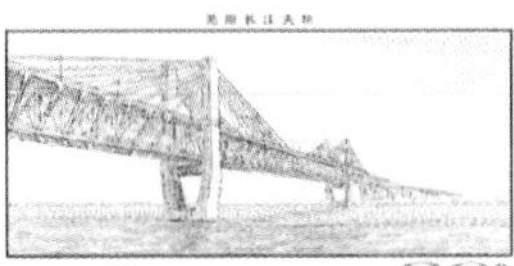

1055 Wuhu Bridge over Yangtze River

2001. Wuhu Bridge. Multicoloured.
4621 80f. Type **1055** 15 10
4622 2y.80 Road section of Wuhu Bridge 50 30

1056 *Paphiopedilum malipoense*

2001. Orchids. Multicoloured.
4623 80f. (1) Type **1056** 15 10
4624 80f. (2) *Paphiopedilum dianthum* 15 10
4625 80f. (3) *Paphiopedilum markianum* 15 10
4626 2y.80 (4) *Paphiopedilum appletonianum* 50 30

1057 Mask of San Xing Dui

2001. Golden Masks. Multicoloured.
4628 80f. Type **1057** 15 10
4629 80f. Mask of Tutankhamun 15 10
Stamps in similar designs were also issued by Egypt.

1058 Emblem

2001. 9th Asia Pacific Economic Co-operation Conference, Shanghai.
4630 **1058** 80f. multicoloured . . . 15 10

1059 Ertan Hydroelectric Power Station (½-size illustration)

2001. Sheet 150 × 85 mm.
MS4631 **1059** 8y. multicoloured 1·25 1·25

1060 Horse galloping

2001. Six Steeds (relief sculptures), Zhaoling Mausoleum. Multicoloured.
4632 60f. (1) Type **1060** 10 10
4633 80f. (2) Galloping 15 10
4634 80f. (3) Trotting 10 10
4635 80f. (4) With rider 15 10
4636 80f. (5) Trotting 15 10
4637 2y.80 (6) Galloping 40 20

1061 Chinese Junk

2001. Ancient Sailing Craft. Multicoloured.
4638 80f. Type **1061** 15 10
4639 80f. Portuguese caravel . . . 15 10
Stamps in the same design were issued by Portugal.

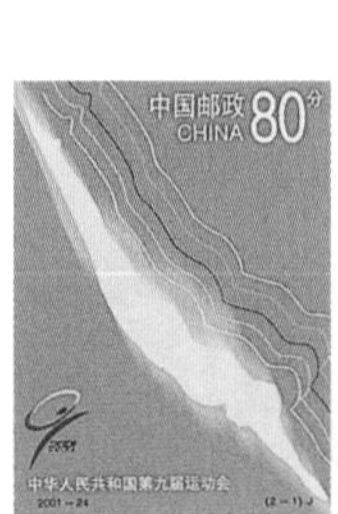

1062 Diving **1063** Liupanshan Mountains

2001. 9th National Games, Guangzhou. Mult.
4640 80f. Type **1062** 15 10
4641 2y.80 Volleyball 40 20
MS4642 140 × 90 mm. Nos. 4640/1 55 55

2001. Liupanshan Mountains. Multicoloured.
4643 80f. (1) Type **1063** 15 10
4644 80f. (2) Forest, Liangdianxia Gorge 15 10
4645 80f. (3) Old Dragon Pool, Jinghe River 15 10
4646 2y.80 (4) Wild Lotus Valley, West Gorge 40 20

1064 Lending an Umbrella by the Lake **1065** Emblem

2001. Tale of Xu Xian and the White Snake. Multicoloured.
4647 80f. (1) Type **1064** 15 10
4648 80f. (2) Stealing the Immortal Grass 15 10
4649 80f. (3) Flooding the Jinshan Hill 15 10
4650 2y.80 (4) Meeting at the Broken Bridge 40 20

2001. China's Membership of World Trade Organization.
4651 **1065** 80f. multicoloured . . . 15 10

1066 Zheng's advancing Fleet

2001. 340th Anniv of Zheng Chenggong's Seizure of Formosa (Taiwan) from Dutch Colonists. Each drab, black and red.
4652 80f. (1) Type **1066** 15 10
4653 80f. (2) Populace offering troops food and water . . 15 10
4654 2y.80 Zheng viewing island 40 20

1067 Engineers and Route of Railway (½-size illustration)

2001. Construction of the Qinghai--Tibet Railway. Sheet 135 × 114 mm.
MS4655 **1067** 8y. multicoloured 1·25 1·25

1068 Horse **1069** "A Couple of Eagles"

2002. New Year. Year of the Horse. Multicoloured.
4656 80f. Type **1068** 15 10
4657 2y.80 Chinese character for horse 40 20

2002. Paintings by Badashanren. Multicoloured.
4658 60f. (1) Type **1069** 10 10
4659 80f. (2) "A Single Pine Tree" 15 10
4660 80f. (3) "Lotus Flowers" . . 15 10
4661 80f. (4) "Chrysanthemum in a Vase" 15 10
4662 2y.60 (5) "A Couple of Magpies on a Rock" . . 40 20
4663 2y.80 (6) "Landscape after Dong Yuan's Style" . . . 40 20

1070 Forest Protection **1071** Yellow-bellied Tragopan

2002. Environmental Protection. Multicoloured.
4664 5f. Maintaining low birth rate 10 10
4665 10f. Type **1070** 10 10
4666 30f. Mineral resources protection 10 10
4668 60f. Air pollution prevention 10 10
4670 80f. Water resources protection 15 10
4673 1y.50 Ocean protection . . . 20 10

2002. Birds. Multicoloured.
4675 80f. Type **1071** 15 10
4676 1y. Biddulph's ground jay 15 10
4677 2y. Taiwan blue magpie . . 30 15
4680 4y.20 Przewalski's redstart 60 30
4683 5y.40 Koslow's bunting . . 70 35

1072 Golden Camellia (*Camellia nitidissima*) **1073** Yaqin

2002. Flowers. Multicoloured.
4690 80f. Type **1072** 15 10
4691 80f. Cannonball tree flower (*Couroupita guianensis*) . . 15 10
Stamps showing similar subjects were issued by Malaysia.

2002. Stringed Musical Instruments. Multicoloured.
4692 60f. (1) Type **1073** 10 10
4693 80f. (2) Erhu 15 10
4694 80f. (3) Banhu 15 10
4695 80f. (4) Satar 15 10
4696 2y.80 (5) Matouqin 40 20

1074 "The Royal Carriage" (Yan Liben) (½ size-illustration)

2002. Sheet 160 × 82 mm.
MS4697 **1074** 8y. multicoloured 1·25 1·25

1075 Wine Vessel

2002. Northern Song Dynasty Ceramics. Mult.
4698 60f. (1) Type **1075** 10 10
4699 80f. (2) Three-legged basin 15 10
4700 80f. (3) Bowl 15 10
4701 2y.80 (4) Dish 40 20

2001. Classical Literature. Strange Stories from a Chinese Studio by Pu Songling (2nd series). Vert designs as T **1043**. Multicoloured.
4702 60f. (1) "Xi Fangping" . . . 10 10
4703 80f. (2) "Pianpian" . . . 15 10
4704 80f. (3) "Tian Qilang" . . . 15 10
4705 2y.80 (4) "Bai Qiulian" . . 40 20

1076 Wuliang Taoist Temple **1078** Ruyi (good luck symbol)

1077 Sifang Street

2002. Qianshan Mountain. Views of the mountain. Multicoloured.
4706 80f. (1) Type **1076** 15 10
4707 80f. (2) Maitreya peak . . . 15 10
4708 80f. (3) Longquan temple 15 10
4709 2y.80 (4) "Terrace of the Immortals" (peak) 40 20
Nos. 4706/9 were issued together, se-tenant, forming a composite design.

2002. Lijiang City.
4710 **1077** 80f. red 15 10
4711 – 80f. green (vert) 15 10
4712 – 2y.80 blue 40 20
MS4713 145 × 101 mm Nos. 4710/12 70 70
DESIGNS: 80f. Bridges over city river; 2y.80, Traditional Naxi house.

2002. Greetings Stamp.
4714 **1078** 80f. multicoloured . . . 15 10

1079 Footballer

2002. World Cup Football Championship, Japan and South Korea. Multicoloured.
4715 80f. Type **1079** 15 10
4716 2y. Players tackling 30 15

1080 Maota Pagoda Lighthouse **1082** "Avalokitesvara of the Sun and Moon"

1081 Lijia Gorge Hydro-electric Power Station

2002. Lighthouses.
4717 **1080** 80f. (1) black and green 15 10
4718 – 80f. (2) black and ochre 15 10
4719 – 80f. (3) black and grey 15 10
4720 – 80f. (4) black, brown and orange 15 10
4721 – 80f. (5) black and red 15 10
DESIGNS: 80f. (2) Jianxin pagoda lighthouse; 80f. (3) Huaniaoshan; 80f. (4) Laotieshan; 80f. (5)Lin'gao.

2002. Hydro-electric Power Generation and Water Control on the Yellow River. Multicoloured.
4722 80f. (1) Type **1081** 15 10
4723 80f. (2) Liujia Gorge Hydro-electric Power Station . . 15 10
4724 80f. (3) Qingtong Gorge dam 15 10
4725 80f. (4) Sanmen Gorge dam 15 10
MS4726 115 × 96 mm 8y. Xiaolangdi dam (39 × 59 mm) 1·25 1·25

2002. Stone Carvings, Dazu County, Sichuan Province. Multicoloured.
4727 80f. (1) Type **1082** 15 10
4728 80f. (2) Samantabhadra riding elephant, North Mountain 15 10
4729 80f. (3) Three Avatamsaka Sages, Holy Summit Mountain 15 10
4730 80f. (4) Man wearing headdress (statue), Cave of the Three Emperors, Stone Gate Mountain . . 15 10
MS4731 130 × 96 mm 8y. "Avalokitesvara of a Thousand Hands" (39 × 59 mm) 1·25 1·25

1083 *Ammopiptanthus mongolicus*

2002. Desert Plants. Multicoloured.
4732 80f. (1) Type **1083** 15 10
4733 80f. (2) *Calligonum rubicundum* 15 10
4734 80f. (3) *Hedysarum scoparium* 15 10
4735 2y. (4) *Tamarix leptostachys* 30 15

MILITARY POST STAMPS

M 225

M 892 Armed Forces

1953.
M1593 **M 225** $800 yellow, red and orange . . . 85·00 40·00
M1594 $800 yellow, red and purple . . . £500
M1595 $800 yellow, red and blue . . £28000

Nos. M1593/5 were issued for the use of the Army, Air Force and Navy respectively.

1995. No gum.
M3998 **M 892** 20f. multicoloured 10 10

POSTAGE DUE STAMPS

D 192

D 233

1950.
D1459 **D 192** $100 blue 10 85
D1460 $200 blue 10 85
D1461 $500 blue . . . . . 10 1·00
D4462 $800 blue . . . . . 11·00 30
D1463 $1,000 blue 10 50
D1464 $2,000 blue 10 75
D1465 $5,000 blue 10 80
D1466 $8,000 blue . . . . 15 1·50
D1467 $10,000 blue . . . . 15 2·50

1954.
D1628 **D 233** $100 red 80 25
D1629 $200 red 50 25
D1630 $500 red 40 25
D1631 $800 red 25 25
D1632 $1,600 red 25 25

CHINA—TAIWAN (FORMOSA)

A. CHINESE PROVINCE

The island of Taiwan was ceded by China to Japan in 1895 and was returned to China in 1945 after the defeat of Japan. From 1949 Taiwan was controlled by the remnants of the Nationalist Government under Chiang Kai-shek.

1945. 100 sen = 1 yen.
1947. 100 cents = 1 yuan (C.N.C.).

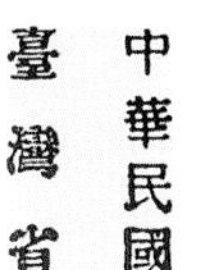
(1) "Taiwan Province, Chinese Republic"

1945. Optd as Type **1**. (a) On stamps as Nos. J1/3 of Japanese Taiwan. Imperf.
1 **J 1** 3s. red . . . . 1·00 4·50
2 5s. green . . . . 1·00 75
3 10s. blue . . . . 1·00 75
4 30s. blue . . . . 5·00 4·50
5 40s. purple . . . . 5·00 3·25
6 50s. grey . . . . 4·00 2·25
7 1y. green . . . . 5·00 2·25

(b) On stamps of Japan. Imperf.
8 **87** 5y. olive (No. 424) . . . 9·00 7·50
9 **88** 10y. purple (No. 334) . . . . 15·00 12·00

(2) (3)

1946. Stamps of China surch as T **2** with two to four characters in lower line denoting value.
10 – 2s. on 2c. blue (No. 509) 10 1·25
11 – 5s. on 5c. orange (No. 513) 10 50
12 **60** 10s. on 4c. lilac 10 60
13 – 30s. on 15c. pur (No. 517) 10 75
19 **107** 50s. on $20 red . . . . 10 1·00
16 **58** 65s. on $20 green . . . . 30 1·00
15 – $1 on 20c. blue (No. 519) 15 1·00
17 **58** $1 on $30 brown 30 85
65 **60** $2 on 2½c. red 40 75
18 **58** $2 on $50 orange 50 80
20 **107** $3 on $100 red 10 75
77 **103** $5 on $40 orange 30 90
78 **107** $5 on $50 violet 40 45
79 $5 on $70 orange . . . . 10 1·00
80 $5 on $100 red 40 25
21 $5 on $200 green 10 60
67 **82** $10 on $3 yellow . . . . 2·00 1·50
82 **118** $10 on $150 blue 50 65
22 **107** $10 on $500 green 10 40
66 **72** $20 on 2c. green 40 75
71 **89** $20 on $3 red . . . . . 1·50 1·00
83 **118** $20 on $250 violet 25 50
23 **107** $20 on $700 brown 20 50
68 **82** $50 on 50c. green . . . . 1·25 85
24 **107** $50 on $1,000 red 85 60
72 **89** $100 on $20 pink 40 25
73 **94** $100 on $20 red £500
25 **107** $100 on $3,000 blue . . . 1·00 70
74 **94** $200 on $10 blue . . . . 2·10 75
70 **72** $500 on $30 purple . . . . 8·00 2·25
81 **107** $600 on $100 red . . . . 7·50 1·25
69 **82** $800 on $4 brown . . . . 6·00 2·50
85 **118** $1,000 on $20,000 red . . . 3·25 1·50
75 **94** $5,000 on $10 blue . . . . 5·25 2·25
76 $10,000 on $20 red . . . . 5·25 1·75
84 **118** $200,000 on $3,000 blue . . £425 14·00

1946. Opening of National Assembly, Nanking. Issue of China surch as Type **3**.
26 **111** 70s. on $20 green . . . . 1·50 2·25
27 $1 on $30 blue . . . . . 1·50 2·25
28 $2 on $50 brown . . . . 1·50 2·25
29 $3 on $100 red . . . . . 1·50 2·25

4 President Chiang Kai-shek (note characters to right of head)

5 Entrance to Dr. Sun Yat-sen Mausoleum (note characters above face value)

1947. President's 60th Birthday.
30 **4** 70s. red . . . . 1·50 2·00
31 $1 green . . . . 1·50 2·00
32 $2 red . . . . 1·50 2·00
33 $3 green . . . . 1·50 2·00
34 $7 orange . . . . 1·50 2·00
35 $10 red . . . . 1·50 2·00

1947. 1st Anniv of Return of Government to Nanking.
36 **5** 50s. green . . . . 2·00 2·75
37 $3 blue . . . . 2·00 2·75
38 $7.50 red . . . . 2·00 2·75
39 $10 brown . . . . 2·00 2·75
40 $20 purple . . . . 2·00 2·75

For other stamps as Types **4** and **5**, but with different Chinese characters, see N.E. Provinces Types **7** and **9**.

1947. No gum.
41 **169** $1 brown . . . . 30 1·50
42 $2 brown . . . . 40 1·25
43 $3 green 40 75
44 $5 orange 40 60
45 $9 blue . . . . 1·50 2·50
46 $10 red 30 75
47 $20 green 30 50
59 $25 green 50 35
48 $50 purple 40 35
49 $100 blue 40 35
50 $200 brown 40 35
60 $5,000 orange . . . . 5·50 85
61 $10,000 green . . . . 5·50 2·25
62 $20,000 brown . . . . 5·50 2·25
63 $30,000 blue . . . . 5·50 1·00
64 $40,000 brown . . . . 4·50 80

6 Sun Yat-sen and Palms

(7)

1948. "Re-valuation" surcharges. Surch as T **7**.
51 **6** $25 on $100 blue . . . . . 1·00 1·75
52 $300 on $3 green 75 45
53 $500 on $7.50 orange . . . 2·75 1·50
54 $1,000 on 30c. grey . . . . 7·00 3·75
55 $1,000 on $3 green . . . . 1·25 35
56 $2,000 on $3 green 90 45
57 $3,000 on $3 green . . . . 7·00 1·75
58 $3,000 on $7.50 orange . . . 65·00 3·00

1949. No value indicated. Stamps of China optd with five Chinese characters, similar to top line of T **2**.
86 **146** (–) Orange (Ord. postage) 3·50 75
87 **147** (–) Green (Air Mail) . . 4·00 95
88 **148** (–) Mauve (Express) . . . 4·00 1·10
89 **149** (–) Red (Registration) . . . 4·00 1·10

PARCELS POST STAMPS

1948. As Type P **112** of China, with six Chinese characters in the sky above the lorry.
P65 $100 green . . . . – 50
P66 $300 red . . . . – 50
P67 $500 olive . . . . – 50
P68 $1,000 black . . . . – 50
P69 $3,000 purple . . . . – 50

Parcels Post stamps were not on sale in unused condition.

POSTAGE DUE STAMPS

D 7

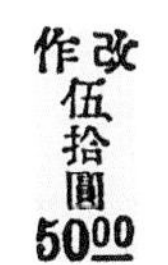
(D 8)

(D 9)

1948.
D51 **D 7** $1 blue . . . . 2·10 3·00
D52 $3 blue . . . . 2·10 3·25
D53 $5 blue . . . . 2·10 3·00
D54 $10 blue . . . . 2·10 3·25
D55 $20 blue . . . . 2·10 3·00

1949. "Re-valuation" surcharges. Surch as Type D **8**.
D65 **D 7** $50 on $1 blue . . . . . 5·00 3·50
D66 $100 on $3 blue . . . . 5·00 2·50
D67 $300 on $5 blue . . . . 5·00 2·00
D68 $500 on $10 blue . . . . 5·00 2·00

1949. Handstamped with Type D **9**.
D86 **6** $1,000 on $3 green (No. 55) 42·00 8·00
D87 $3,000 on $3 green (No. 57) 27·00 17·00
D88 $5,000 orange (No. 60) . . 45·00 22·00

B. CHINESE NATIONALIST REPUBLIC

1949. 100 cents = 1 silver yuan (or New Taiwan Yuan).

Silver Yuan Surcharges.

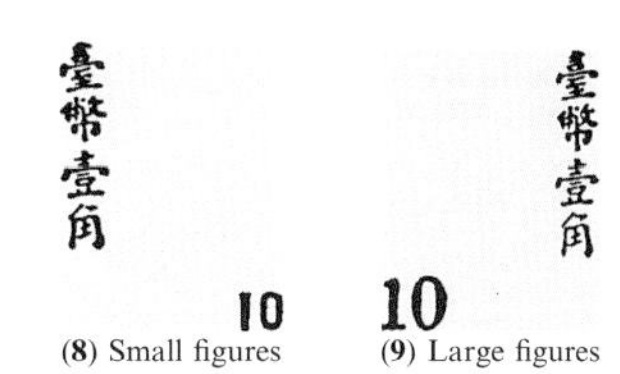
(**8**) Small figures (**9**) Large figures

1949. Stamps of Taiwan Province surch. (a) With T **8**.
90 **6** 10c. on $50 purple . . . . . 32·00 4·50

(b) As T **9** (figures at right).
91 **6** 2c. on $30,000 blue . . . . 32·00 11·00
92 10c. on $40,000 brown . . . 70·00 11·00

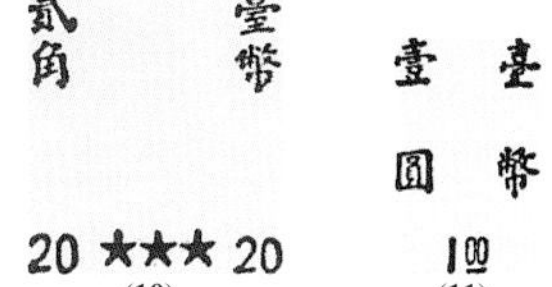
(**10**) (**11**)

1949. Stamps of North Eastern Provinces (Manchuria), surch as T **10**.
93 **5** 2c. on $44 red . . . . . . £100 9·00
95 5c. on $44 red . . . . . . £100 3·00
96 10c. on $44 red . . . . . £120 1·90
97 20c. on $44 red £160 20
98 30c. on $44 red . . . . . £200 7·50
99 50c. on $44 red . . . . . £240 5·00

1950. Surch as T **11** on stamp of China but with no indication of value.
100 **169** $1 on (–) green . . . . . £160 14·00
101 $2 on (–) green . . . . . £160 13·00
102 $5 on (–) green . . . . . £1200 55·00
103 $10 on (–) green . . . . £1500 50·00
104 $20 on (–) green £3250 £400

1950. Stamps of China surch. (a) As T **8** (figure "5" at left).
105 **118** 5c. on $200,000 purple . . 4·50 2·25

(b) As T **9** (figures at left).
106 **118** 3c. on $30,000 brown . . 3·75 4·00
107 3c. on $40,000 green . . 3·75 3·75
108 3c. on $50,000 blue . . 4·50 4·50
108a 10c. on $4,000 grey . . . 8·00 6·00
109 10c. on $6,000 purple . . 13·50 6·75
110 10c. on $20,000 red . . 13·50 6·75
110a 10c. on $2,000,000 orge 13·50 6·75
110b 20c. on $500,000 mauve 32·00 10·00
110c 20c. on $1,000,000 red 42·00 7·00
110d 30c. on $3,000,000 bistre 50·00 10·00
110e 50c. on $5,000,000 blue 95·00 10·50

GUM. All the following stamps to No. 616 were issued without gum except where otherwise stated.

12 Koxinga

1950. Rouletted. (a) Postage.
111 **12** 3c. grey . . . . 2·00 1·00
112 10c. brown . . . . 2·00 10
113 15c. yellow . . . . 18·00 2·50
114 20c. green . . . . 2·00 10
115 30c. red . . . . 40·00 9·00
116 40c. orange . . . . 4·75 10
117 50c. brown . . . . 9·50 10
118 80c. red . . . . 4·75 3·00
119 $1 violet . . . . 16·00 20
120 $1.50 green . . . . 65·00 8·00
121 $1.60 blue . . . . 80·00 75
122 $2 mauve . . . . 19·00 75
123 $5 turquoise . . . . 95·00 4·00

(b) Air. With character at each side of head.
124 **12** 60c. blue . . . . 12·00 7·50

13 Peasant and Ballot Box

15 Peasant and Scroll

1951. Division of Country into Self-governing Districts. Perf or imperf.
125 **13** 40c. red . . . . 22·00 10
126 $1 blue . . . . 38·00 90
127 $1.60 purple . . . . . . 50·00 75
128 $2 brown . . . . £100 8·50

1951. Silver Yuan surcharges. As T **169** of China but without value, surch as T **14**.
129 $5 on (–) green . . . . . 42·00 7·00
130 $10 on (–) green . . . . . £180 5·00
131 $20 on (–) green . . . . . £400 25·00
132 $50 on (–) green . . . . . £500 75·00

1952. Land Tax Reduction. Perf or imperf.
133 **15** 20c. orange . . . . 35·00 50
134 40c. green . . . . 48·00 30
135 $1 brown . . . . 75·00 4·00
136 $1.40 blue . . . . £150 2·00
137 $2 grey . . . . £225 38·00
138 $5 red . . . . £375 5·00

16 President and Rejoicing crowds

(**17**)

1952. 2nd Anniv of Re-election of Pres. Chiang Kai-shek. Flag in red and blue. Eight characters in scroll. Perf or imperf.
139 **16** 40c. red . . . . 9·50 30
140 $1 green . . . . 29·00 2·00
141 $1.60 orange . . . . 50·00 1·50
142 $2 blue . . . . £110 38·00
143 $5 purple . . . . £140 2·00

See also Nos. 151/6.

1952. Stamps of China surch. with T **17**.
144 **145** 3c. on 4c. grn (No. 1350) 4·00 2·50
145 3c. on 10c. lilac (No. 1351) . . . . . . 7·50 3·75
146 3c. on 20c. bl (No. 1353) 4·00 2·00
147 3c. on 50c. brown (No. 1354) . . . . . . 12·00 7·50

(**18**) (**19**)

1953. T **169** of China, but without value, surch as T **18**.
148 $10 on (–) green . . . . . . £140 12·00
149 $20 on (–) green . . . . . . £425 24·00
150 $50 on (–) green £1400 £600

1953. 3rd Anniv of Re-election of Pres. Chiang Kai-shek. As T **16** but eleven characters in scroll. Flag in red and blue. Perf or imperf.
151 10c. orange . . . . 22·00 2·00
152 20c. green . . . . 22·00 2·00
153 40c. red . . . . 22·00 1·00
154 $1.40 blue . . . . 45·00 4·00
155 $2 sepia . . . . £100 6·00
156 $5 purple . . . . £170 15·00

1953. Surch as T **19**.
157 **12** 3c. on $1 violet . . . . . 85 1·00
158 10c. on 15c. yellow . . . . 10·00 1·00
159 10c. on 30c. red . . . . . 2·75 50
160 20c. on $1.60 blue . . . . 2·75 30

20 Doctor, Nurses and Patients

21 Pres. Chiang Kai-shek

1953. Establishment of Anti-tuberculosis Assn. Cross of Lorraine in red. On paper with coloured network.

161 **20** 40c. brown on stone . . . 4·25 20
162 $1.60 blue on turquoise . . 20·00 1·00
163 $2 green on yellow . . . . 32·00 85
164 $5 red on flesh . . . . . . 80·00 13·50

1953.

165 **21** 10c. brown . . . . 1·60 10
166 20c. purple . . . . 1·50 10
167 40c. green . . . . 1·50 10
168 50c. purple . . . . 4·00 10
169 80c. brown . . . . 11·00 4·00
170 $1 green . . . . 6·00 10
171 $1.40 blue . . . . 8·00 60
172 $1.60 red . . . . 8·00 10
173 $1.70 green . . . . 14·00 7·50
174 $2 brown . . . . 8·00 10
175 $3 blue . . . . £140 14·00
176 $4 turquoise . . . . 12·00 1·50
177 $5 red . . . . 8·00 50
178 $10 green . . . . 14·00 4·00
179 $20 purple . . . . 48·00 6·00

22 Silo Bridge over River Cho-Shui-Chi

23 Sapling, Tree and Plantation

1954. Completion of Silo Bridge. Various frames.

180 **22** 40c. red . . . . 7·00 30
181 – $1.60 blue £100 65
182 **22** $3.60 black . . . . 32·00 3·00
183 – $5 mauve . . . . £110 8·00

DESIGN: $1.60, $5, Silo Bridge.

1954. Afforestation Day.

184 **23** 40c. green . . . . 12·50 40
185 – $10 violet . . . . £100 9·00
186 – $20 red . . . . 42·00 1·60
187 – $50 blue . . . . 65·00 5·00

DESIGNS: $10, Tree plantation and houses; $20, Planting seedling; $50, Map of Taiwan and tree.

24 Runner

25 Douglas DC-6 over City Gate, Taipeh

1954. Youth Day.

188 **24** 40c. blue . . . . 14·00 60
189 $5 red . . . . 50·00 7·50

1954. Air. 15th Anniv of Air Force Day.

190 **25** $1 brown . . . . 20·00 60
191 – $1.60 black . . . . 10·00 10
192 – $5 blue . . . . 20·00 60

DESIGNS: $1.60, Republic F-84G Thunderjets over Chung Shang Bridge, Taipeh. $5, Doves over Chi Kan Lee (Fort Zeelandia) in Tainan City.

26 Refugees crossing Pontoon Bridge

27 Junk and Bridge

1954. Relief Fund for Chinese Refugees from North Vietnam.

193 **26** 40c.+10c. blue . . . . . . 14·50 1·50
194 $1.60+40c. purple . . . . 45·00 20·00
195 $5+$1 red £100 £100

1954. 2nd Anniv of Overseas Chinese League.

196 **27** 40c. orange . . . . 20·00 10
197 $5 blue . . . . 10·00 1·75

28 "Chainbreaker"

分 叁

(29)

1955. Freedom Day.

198 **28** 40c. green . . . . 4·00 10
199 – $1 olive . . . . 15·00 3·00
200 – $1.60 red . . . . 11·00 1·50

DESIGNS: $1, Soldier with torch and flag; $1.60, Torch and figures "1.23".

1955. Surch. as T **29**.

201 **12** 3c. on $1 violet . . . . . 4·50 1·25
202 20c. on 40c. orange . . . . 4·50 15

31 Pres. Chiang Kai-shek and Sun Yat-sen Memorial Building

1955. 1st Anniv of President Chiang Kai-shek's Second Re-election.

203 **31** 20c. olive . . . . 3·25 10
204 40c. green . . . . 3·25 10
205 $2 red . . . . 8·50 40
206 $7 blue . . . . 14·50 65

角 壹

0.10

(32)

33 Air Force Badge

1955. Nos. 116/18, 120 and 124 surch as T **32**. Nos. 212/14 have additional floral ornament below two characters at top.

207 **12** 10c. on 80c. red . . . . . 4·50 40
208 10c. on $1.50 green . . . . 4·50 75
212 20c. on 40c. orange . . . . 5·00 10
213 20c. on 50c. brown . . . . 5·50 10
214 20c. on 60c. blue . . . . . 7·50 1·75

1955. Armed Forces' Day.

209 **33** 40c. blue . . . . 5·00 10
210 $2 red . . . . 19·00 1·00
211 $7 green . . . . 16·00 70

35 Flags of U.N. and Taiwan

36 Pres. Chiang Kai-shek

1955. 10th Anniv of U.N.O.

215 **35** 40c. blue . . . . 3·00 10
216 $2 red . . . . 7·50 75
217 $7 green . . . . 7·50 1·75

1955. President's 69th Birthday. With gum.

218 **36** 40c. brown, blue and red 6·00 30
219 $2 blue, green and red . . 11·00 1·25
220 $7 green, brown and red 22·00 3·25

37 Sun Yat-sen's Birthplace

角 貳

0.20

(38)

1955. 90th Birth Anniv (1956) of Dr. Sun Yat-sen.

221 **37** 40c. blue . . . . 4·00 30
222 $2 brown . . . . 8·00 1·00
223 $7 red . . . . 10·50 1·75

1956. Nos. 1213 and 1211 of China surch as T **38**.

232 **148** 3c. on (–) mauve 75 40
224 **146** 20c. on (–) orange I . . . 2·25 10
304 20c. on (–) orange II . . . 1·75 10

On No. 232 the characters are smaller and there are leaves on either side of the "3".

(I) Surch with Type **38**. (II) The characters are below the figures.

39 Old and Modern Postal Transport

40 Children at Play

1956. 60th Anniv of Postal Service.

225 **39** 40c. red . . . . 2·00 15
226 $1 blue . . . . 4·00 1·60
227 $1.60 brown . . . . 6·00 1·10
228 $2 green . . . . 10·00 2·00

1956. Children's Day.

229 **40** 40c. green . . . . 1·25 20
230 $1.60 blue . . . . 2·75 40
231 $2 red . . . . 6·00 1·00

42 Earliest and Latest Steam Locomotives

43 Pres. Chiang Kai-shek

1956. 75th Anniv of Chinese Railways.

233 **42** 40c. red . . . . 5·00 25
234 $2 blue . . . . 6·50 55
235 $8 green . . . . 10·00 2·00

1956. 70th Birthday of President Chiang Kai-shek. Various portraits of President. With gum.

236 **43** 20c. orange . . . . 3·00 10
237 – 40c. red . . . . 3·00 10
238 – $1 blue . . . . 8·00 20
239 – $1.60 purple . . . . 10·00 10
240 – $2 brown . . . . 18·00 20
241 – $8 turquoise . . . . 42·00 50

SIZES—21½ × 30 mm: 20c., 40c.; 26½ × 26½ mm: $1, $1.60; 30 × 21½ mm: $2, $8.

分 叁

3

(44)

角 壹

0.10

(45)

46 Telecommunications Symbols

1956. No. 1212 of China surch with T **44**.

242 **147** 3c. on (–) green 75 15

1956. No. 1214 of China surch with T **45**.

243 **149** 10c. on (–) red 75 15

1956. 75th Anniv of Chinese Telegraph Service.

244 **46** 40c. blue . . . . 1·00 10
245 $1.40 red . . . . 2·00 10
246 $1.60 green . . . . 3·00 10
247 $2 brown . . . . 7·00 20

47 Map of China

48 Mencius with his Mother

1957. (a) Printed in one colour.

248 **47** 3c. blue 20 10
249 10c. violet . . . . 1·50 15
250 20c. orange . . . . 1·50 10
251 40c. red . . . . 1·50 10
252 $1 brown . . . . 3·00 10
253 $1.60 green . . . . 6·00 15

(b) With frames in blue.

268 **47** 3c. blue 10 10
269 10c. violet 50 10
270 20c. orange 60 10
271 40c. red . . . . 2·00 10
272 $1 brown . . . . 3·75 20
273 $1.60 green . . . . 4·50 10

1957. Mothers' Teaching.

254 **48** 40c. green . . . . 3·00 10
255 – $3 brown . . . . 4·00 50

DESIGN: $3, Marshal Yueh Fei with his mother.

49 Chinese Scout Badges and Rosettes

1957. 50th Anniv of Boy Scout Movement, Jubilee Jamboree and Birth Centenary of Lord Baden-Powell (Founder).

256 **49** 40c. violet 50 10
257 $1 green . . . . 1·75 15
258 $1.60 blue . . . . 2·00 10

50 Globe, Radio Mast and Microphone

51 Highway Map of Taiwan

1957. 30th Anniv of Chinese Broadcasting Service.

259 **50** 40c. salmon 30 10
260 50c. mauve 75 15
261 $3.50 blue . . . . 1·75 30

1957. 1st Anniv of Taiwan Cross-Island Highway Project.

262 **51** 40c. green . . . . 2·50 10
263 $1.40 blue . . . . 6·25 50
264 $2 sepia . . . . 7·25 50

52 Freighter "Hai Min" and River Vessel "Kiang Foo"

53 "Batocera lineolata" (longhorn beetle)

1957. 85th Anniv of China Merchants' Steam Navigation Co.

265 **52** 40c. blue 80 10
266 80c. purple . . . . 2·00 25
267 $2.80 red . . . . 3·00 40

1958. Insects. Multicoloured. With gum.

274 10c. Type **53** 80 25
275 40c. "Papilio maraho" (butterfly) . . . . 1·00 10
276 $1 Atlas moth . . . . 1·75 20
277 $1.40 "Erasmia pulchella" (moth) . . . . 4·00 40
278 $1.60 "Cheirotonus macleayi" (beetle) . . . . 5·00 20
279 $2 Great mormon (butterfly) 6·00 60

54 "Phalaenopsis amabilis"

1958. Taiwan Orchids. Orchids in natural colours; backgrounds in colours given. With gum.

280 **54** 20c. brown . . . . 1·75 10
281 – 40c. violet . . . . 1·75 10
282 – $1.40 purple . . . . . . 3·75 20
283 – $3 blue . . . . 6·00 25

ORCHIDS—VERT: 40c. "Laeliacattleya"; $1.40, "Cycnoches chlorochilon klotzsch". HORIZ: $3, "Dendrobium phalaenopsis".

55 W.H.O. Emblem

56 Presidential Mansion, Taipeh

1958. 10th Anniv of W.H.O.

284 **55** 40c. blue 20 10
285 $1.60 red 70 15
286 $2 purple . . . . 1·10 20

1958.

290a **56** $5 green . . . . 8·00 10
290b $5.60 violet . . . . 8·00 30
290c $6 orange . . . . 8·00 10
290d $10 green . . . . 7·50 10
290e $20 red . . . . 13·50 10
289 $50 brown . . . . 60·00 8·00
290 $100 blue . . . . £120 10·00

58 Ploughman

1958. 10th Anniv of Joint Commission on Chinese Rural Reconstruction.

291 **58** 20c. green 60 10
292 40c. black 75 10
293 $1.40 purple . . . . 2·25 10
294 $3 blue . . . . 3·75 30

59 President Chiang Kai-shek Reviewing Troops

1958. 72nd Birthday of President Chiang Kai-shek and National Day Review. With gum.
295 **59** 40c. multicoloured . . . . 1·25 10

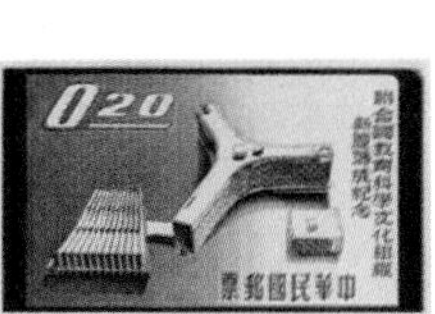

60 U.N.E.S.C.O. Headquarters, Paris

61 Flame of Freedom encircling Globe

1958. Inaug of U.N.E.S.C.O. Headquarters.
296 **60** 20c. blue 30 10
297 40c. green 80 10
298 $1.40 red 80 10
299 $3 purple . . . . 1·25 25

1958. 10th Anniv of Declaration of Human Rights.
300 **61** 40c. green 35 10
301 60c. sepia 35 10
302 $1 red 80 10
303 $3 blue . . . . 1·10 25

1958. No. 192 surch **350**.
305 $3.50 on $5 blue . . . . . . 7·00 2·00

64 The Constitution

65 Chu Kwang Tower, Quemoy

1958. 10th Anniv of Constitution.
306 **64** 40c. green . . . . 1·10 10
307 50c. purple . . . . 1·25 10
308 $1.40 red . . . . 4·00 10
309 $3.50 blue . . . . 4·00 30

1959.
310 **65** 3c. orange 10 10
311 5c. olive 50 10
312 10c. lilac 10 10
313 20c. blue 10 10
314 40c. brown 10 10
315 50c. turquoise 80 10
316 $1 red 80 10
317 $1.40 green . . . . 3·00 10
318 $2 myrtle . . . . 3·00 10
319 $2.80 mauve . . . . 9·00 60
320 $3 slate . . . . 5·00 10
See also Nos. 367/82f.

66 Slaty-backed Gull

67 I.L.O. Emblem and Headquarters, Geneva

1959. Air. With gum.
321 **66** $8 black, blue and green 5·50 50

1959. 40th Anniv of I.L.O.
322 **67** 40c. blue 60 10
323 $1.60 brown 65 10
324 $3 green 75 10
325 $5 red 80 25

68 Scout Bugler

1959. 10th World Scout Jamboree, Manila.
326 **68** 40c. red 65 10
327 50c. blue . . . . 1·50 30
328 $5 green . . . . 3·00 75

69 Inscribed Rock on Mt. Tai-wu, Quemoy

1959. Defence of Quemoy (Kinmen) and Matsu Islands, 1958.
329 **69** 40c. brown 40 10
330 – $1.40 blue . . . . 1·00 15
331 – $2 green . . . . 2·00 50
332 **69** $3 blue . . . . 3·00 50
DESIGN—(41 × 23½ mm): $1.40, $2, Map of Taiwan, Quemoy and Matsu Islands.

70

1959. International Correspondence Week.
333 **70** 40c. blue 85 10
334 $1 red 85 15
335 $2 sepia 85 10
336 $3.50 red . . . . 1·25 30

71 National Science Hall

72 Confederation Emblem

1959. Inauguration of Taiwan National Science Hall. With gum.
337 **71** 40c. multicoloured . . . . 1·50 10
338 – $3 mult (different view) . . 2·75 35

1959. 10th Anniv of International Confederation of Free Trade Unions.
339 **72** 40c. green . . . . 1·10 10
340 $1.60 purple . . . . 1·25 10
341 $3 orange . . . . 1·50 20

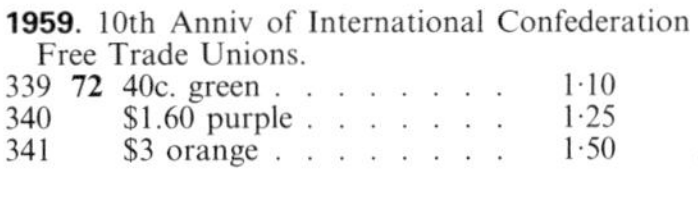

73 Sun Yat-sen and Abraham Lincoln

74 "Bomb Burst" by Thunder Tiger Aerobatic Squadron

1959. 150th Birth Anniv of Lincoln. With gum.
342 **73** 40c. multicoloured 30 10
343 $3 multicoloured 50 25

1960. Air. Chinese Air Force Commem. With gum.
344 **74** $1 multicoloured . . . . . 7·00 75
345 – $2 multicoloured . . . . . 6·00 30
346 – $5 multicoloured . . . . . 8·00 1·10
DESIGNS—HORIZ: (Various aerobatics): $2, Loop; $5, Diamond formation flying over jet fighter.

75 Night Delivery

76 "Uprooted Tree"

1960. Introduction of "Prompt Delivery" and "Postal Launch" Services.
347 **75** $1.40 purple . . . . 1·75 30
348 $1.60 blue "Yu-Khi" (postal launch) . . . . . 1·75 50

1960. World Refugee Year. With gum.
349 **76** 40c. green, brown & black 30 10
350 $3 green, orange & black 40 25

77 Cross-Island Highway

79 Winged Tape-reel

1960. Inaug of Taiwan Cross-Island Highway.
351 **77** 40c. green 60 10
352 – $1 blue . . . . 3·00 20
353 – $2 purple . . . . 1·75 15
354 **77** $3 brown . . . . 3·00 25
DESIGN—VERT: $1, $2, Tunnels on the Highway.

1960. Visit of Pres. Eisenhower. Nos. 331/2 optd **WELCOME U.S. PRESIDENT DWIGHT D. EISENHOWER 1960** in English and Chinese.
355 – $2 green . . . . 1·75 1·00
356 **69** $3 blue . . . . 2·00 1·00

1960. Phonopost (tape-recordings) Service.
357 **79** $2 red . . . . 1·75 20

80 "Flowers and Red-billed Blue Magpies" (after Hsiao Yung)

81 Youth Corps Flag and Summer Activities

1960. Ancient Chinese Paintings from Palace Museum Collection (1st series). With gum.
358 – $1 multicoloured . . . . . 5·50 40
359 – $1.40 multicoloured . . . 9·50 75
360 **80** $1.60 multicoloured . . . 13·00 1·90
361 – $2 multicoloured . . . . . 17·00 2·10
PAINTINGS—HORIZ: $1, "Two Riders" (after Wei Yen). $1.40, "Two Horses and Groom" (after Han Kan). $2, "A Pair of Green-winged Teals in a Rivulet" (after Monk Hui Ch'ung).
See also Nos. 451/4, 577/80 and 716/19.

1960. Youth Summer Activities.
362 **81** 50c. green . . . . 1·10 10
363 – $3 brown . . . . 1·40 30
DESIGN—HORIZ: $3, Youth Corps Flag and other summer activities.

82 "Forest Cultivation"

83 Chu Kwang Tower, Quemoy

1960. 5th World Forestry Congress, Seattle. Multicoloured. With gum.
364 $1 Type **82** . . . . 2·50 10
365 $2 "Forest Protection" (trees and sika deer) . . . . . 3·75 65
366 $3 "Lumber Production" (cable railway) . . . . . . 4·50 30

1960. As T **65** but redrawn.
367 **83** 3c. brown 10 10
382 10c. green . . . . 1·25 15
368 40c. violet 10 10
369 50c. orange 25 10
370 60c. purple 15 10
371 80c. green 10 10
372 $1 green . . . . 2·00 10
373 $1.20 green . . . . 1·00 10
374 $1.50 blue . . . . 1·25 10
375 $2 red 90 10
376 $2.50 blue 90 15
377 $3 green . . . . 1·50 10
378 $3.20 brown . . . . 5·00 10
379 $3.60 blue . . . . 4·00 20
382f $4 green . . . . 6·00 15
380 $4.50 red . . . . 5·00 30

84 Diving

85 Bronze Wine Vase (Shang Dynasty)

1960. Sports. With gum.
383 **84** 50c. brown, yellow & blue 60 10
384 – 80c. violet, yellow & purple 60 10
385 – $2 multicoloured . . . . . 1·40 10
386 – $2.50 black and orange . . 1·60 25
387 – $3 multicoloured . . . . . 2·50 35
388 – $3.20 multicoloured . . . . 3·75 40
DESIGNS: 80c. Discus-throwing; $2, Basketball; $2.50, Football; $3, Hurdling; $3.20, Sprinting.

1961. Ancient Chinese Art Treasures (1st series). With gum.
389 **85** 80c. multicoloured . . . . 1·75 10
390 – $1 indigo, blue and red . . 3·50 20
391 – $1.20 blue, brown & yellow 3·50 25
392 – $1.50 brown, blue & mauve 4·00 70
393 – $2 brown, violet and green 4·00 40
394 – $2.50 black, lilac and blue 5·00 60
DESIGNS: $1, Bronze cauldron (Chou); $1.20, Porcelain vase (Sung); $1.50, Jade perforated tube (Chou); $2, Porcelain jug (Ming); $2.50, Jade flower vase (Ming).
See also Nos. 408/13 and 429/34.

86 Farmer and Mechanical Plough

87 Mme. Chiang Kai-shek

1961. Agricultural Census.
395 **86** 80c. purple 60 10
396 $2 green . . . . 3·00 75
397 $3.20 red . . . . 4·50 50

1961. 10th Anniv (1960) of Chinese Women's Anti-Aggression League. With gum.
398 **87** 80c. black, red & turquoise 1·00 10
399 $1 black, red and green . . 2·75 15
400 $2 black, red and brown 2·75 15
401 $3.20 black, red and purple 4·50 1·10

88 Taiwan Lobster

89 Jeme Tien-yao and Locomotive

1961. Mail Order Service.
402 **88** $3 myrtle . . . . 5·50 75

1961. Birth Centenary of Jeme Tien-yao (railway engineer).
403 – 80c. violet . . . . 2·00 15
404 **89** $2 black . . . . 5·00 60
DESIGN: 80c. As Type **89** but locomotive heading right.

90 Pres. Chiang Kai-shek

91 Convair 880 Jetliner ("The Mandarin Jet"), Biplane and Flag

1961. 1st Anniv of Chiang Kai-shek's Third Term Inauguration. With gum.
405 – 80c. multicoloured . . . . 1·25 10
406 **90** $2 multicoloured . . . . . 5·75 1·00

DESIGN—HORIZ: 80c. Map of China inscr (in Chinese) "Recovery of the Mainland".

1961. 40th Anniv of Chinese Civil Air Service. With gum.
407 **91** $10 multicoloured . . . . 5·50 30

1961. Ancient Chinese Art Treasures (2nd issue). As T **85**. With gum.
408 80c. multicoloured . . . . . 2·00 10
409 $1 blue, brown and bistre . . 4·00 20
410 $1.50 blue and salmon . . . 6·25 75
411 $2 red, black and blue . . . 9·25 25
412 $4 blue, sepia and red . . . 11·00 45
413 $4.50 brown, sepia and blue 11·00 1·75
DESIGNS—VERT: 80c. Palace perfumer (Ching); $1, Corn vase (Warring States); $2, Jade tankard (Sung). HORIZ: $1.50, Bronze bowl (Chou); $4, Porcelain bowl (Southern Sung); $4.50, Jade chimera (Han).

92 Sun Yat-sen and Chiang Kai-shek **93** Lotus Lake

1961. 50th National Day. With gum.
414 **92** 80c. brown, blue and grey 1·50 10
415 – $5 multicoloured . . . . . 4·50 1·00
DESIGN—HORIZ: $5, Map and flag.

1961. Taiwan Scenery. Multicoloured. With gum.
416 80c. Pitan (Green Lake) (vert) 6·75 10
417 $1 Type **93** . . . . 11·00 50
418 $2 Sun-Moon Lake . . . . . 13·00 30
419 $3.20 Wulai Waterfall (vert) 17·00 75

94 Steel Furnace **95** Atomic Reactor, National Tsing Hwa University

1961. Taiwan Industries. With gum.
420 – 80c. indigo, brown & blue 1·75 10
421 **94** $1.50 multicoloured . . . 3·00 60
422 – $2.50 multicoloured . . . 4·75 55
423 – $3.20 indigo, brown & blue 7·00 50
DESIGNS—VERT: 80c. Oil refinery. $2.50, Aluminium manufacture. HORIZ: $3.20, Fertilizer plant.

1961. 1st Taiwan Atomic Reactor Inauguration. Multicoloured. With gum.
424 80c. Type **95** . . . . 1·10 10
425 $2 Interior of reactor . . . . 4·00 1·00
426 $3.20 Reactor building (horiz) 4·50 75

96 Telegraph Wires and Microwave Reflector Pylons **97** Postal Segregating, Facing and Cancelling Machine

1961. 80th Anniv of Chinese Telecommunications. Multicoloured. With gum.
427 80c. Type **96** . . . . 1·00 10
428 $3.20 Microwave parabolic antenna (horiz) . . . . . 2·75 70

1962. Ancient Chinese Art Treasures (3rd issue). As T **85**. With gum.
429 80c. brown, violet and red . . 7·00 10
430 $1 purple, brown and blue 9·50 15
431 $2.40 blue, brown and red . . 24·00 40
432 $3 multicoloured . . . . . . 60·00 1·50
433 $3.20 red, green and blue . . 65·00 15
434 $3.60 multicoloured . . . . 60·00 1·50
DESIGNS—VERT: 80c. Jade topaz twin wine vessel (Chiang). $1, Bronze pouring vase (Warring States). $2.40, Porcelain vase (Ming). $3, Tsun bronze wine vase (Shang). $3.20, Porcelain jar (Ching). $3.60, Jade perforated disc (Han).

1962.
435 **97** 80c. purple . . . . 1·60 10

98 Mt. Yu Weather Station **99** Distribution of Milk and U.N. Emblem

1962. World Meteorological Day.
436 **98** 80c. brown 75 10
437 – $1 blue . . . . 1·50 40
438 – $2 green . . . . 1·75 75
DESIGNS—HORIZ: $1, Route-map of Typhoon Pamela. VERT: $2, Weather balloon passing globe.

1962. 15th Anniv of U.N.I.C.E.F.
439 **99** 80c. red 40 10
440 $3.20 green . . . . 1·75 60

100 Campaign Emblem **101** Yu Yu-jen (journalist)

1962. Malaria Eradication. With gum.
441 **100** 80c. red, green and blue 1·10 10
442 $3.60 brown, grn & dp brn . . . . 1·60 25

1962. "Elder Reporter" Yu Yu-jen Commemoration. With gum.
443 **101** 80c. sepia and pink . . . 1·60 25

102 Koxinga **103** Co-operative Emblem

1962. Tercentenary of Koxinga's Recovery of Taiwan. With gum.
444 **102** 80c. purple . . . . 3·25 10
445 $2 green . . . . 6·00 35

1962. 40th International Co-operative Day.
446 **103** 80c. brown 75 10
447 – $2 lilac . . . . 2·00 35
DESIGN: $2, Global handclasp.

104 U.N.E.S.C.O. Symbols **105** Emperor T'ai Tsu (Ming Dynasty)

1962. U.N.E.S.C.O. Activities Commem.
448 **104** 80c. mauve 50 10
449 – $2 lake . . . . 1·50 35
450 – $3.20 green . . . . . . 1·50 25
DESIGNS—HORIZ: $2, U.N.E.S.C.O. emblem on open book. $3.20, Emblem linking hemispheres.

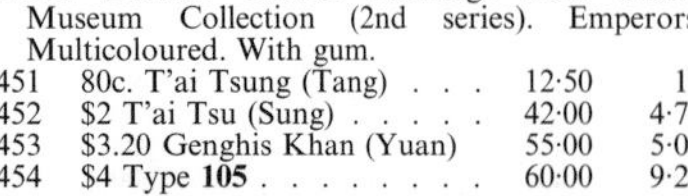

1962. Ancient Chinese Paintings from Palace Museum Collection (2nd series). Emperors. Multicoloured. With gum.
451 80c. T'ai Tsung (Tang) . . . 12·50 10
452 $2 T'ai Tsu (Sung) . . . . . 42·00 4·75
453 $3.20 Genghis Khan (Yuan) 55·00 5·00
454 $4 Type **105** . . . . 60·00 9·25

106 "Lions" Emblem and Activities **107** Pole Vaulting

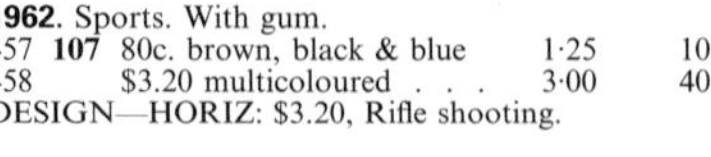

1962. 45th Anniv of Lions International With gum.
455 **106** 80c. multicoloured . . . . 1·50 10
456 $3.60 multicoloured . . . 2·50 60

1962. Sports. With gum.
457 **107** 80c. brown, black & blue 1·25 10
458 $3.20 multicoloured . . . 3·00 40
DESIGN—HORIZ: $3.20, Rifle shooting.

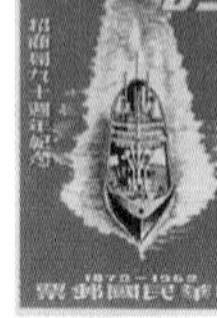

108 Young Farmers **109** Liner

1962. 10th Anniv of Chinese 4-H Clubs.
459 **108** 80c. red . . . . 1·00 10
460 – $3.20 green . . . . 1·75 30
DESIGN: $3.20, 4-H Clubs emblem.

1962. 90th Anniv of China Merchants' Steam Navigation Co. Multicoloured. With gum.
461 80c. Type **109** . . . . 1·75 10
462 $3.60 Freighter "Hai Min" and Pacific route-map (horiz) . . . . 4·50 70

110 Harvesting **111** Youth, Girl, Torch and Martyrs Monument, Huang Hua Kang

1963. Freedom from Hunger. With gum.
463 **110** $10 multicoloured . . . . 4·50 1·00

1963. 20th Youth Day.
464 **111** 80c. purple 75 10
465 $3.20 green . . . . 2·00 60

112 Barn Swallows and Pagoda **113** Refugee in Tears

1963. 1st Anniv of Asian-Oceanic Postal Union. With gum. Multicoloured.
466 80c. Type **112** . . . . 5·00 30
467 $2 Northern gannet . . . . 6·00 1·00
468 $6 Manchurian crane and pine tree (vert) . . . . . . 14·00 3·75

1963. Refugees' Flight from Mainland.
469 **113** 80c. black . . . . 1·50 10
470 – $3.20 red . . . . 3·00 40
DESIGN—HORIZ: $3.20, Refugees on march.

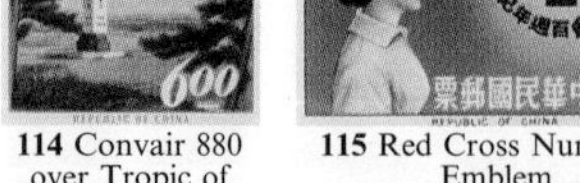

114 Convair 880 over Tropic of Cancer Monument, Kiai **115** Red Cross Nurse and Emblem

1963. Air. Multicoloured. With gum.
471 $2.50 Suspension Bridge, Pitan (horiz) . . . . 6·00 30
472 $6 Type **114** . . . . 10·00 1·00
473 $10 Lion-head Mountain, Sinchu . . . . 14·00 2·00

1963. Red Cross Centenary. With gum.
474 **115** 80c. red and black . . . . 3·50 30
475 – $10 red, green and blue 12·00 2·50
DESIGN: $10, Globe and scroll.

116 Basketball **117** Freedom Torch

1963. 2nd Asian Basketball Championships, Taipeh.
476 **116** 80c. mauve . . . . 1·00 10
477 – $2 violet . . . . 2·00 60
DESIGN: $2, Hands reaching for inscribed ball.

1963. 15th Anniv of Declaration of Human Rights.
478 **117** 80c. green 60 10
479 – $3.20 red . . . . 1·25 20
DESIGN—HORIZ: $3.20, Human figures and scales of justice.

118 Country Scene **119** Dr. Sun Yat-sen and his Book "Three Principles of the People"

1963. "Good-People, Good-Deeds" Campaign. Multicoloured. With gum.
480 40c. Type **118** . . . . 3·00 10
481 $4.50 Lighting candle . . . . 7·00 1·00

1983. 10th Anniv of Land-to-Tillers Programme. With gum.
482 **119** $5 multicoloured . . . . 12·00 1·00

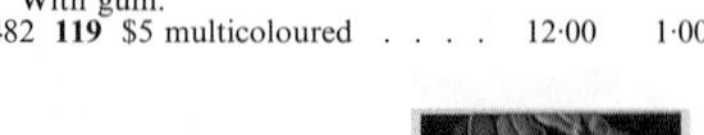

120 Torch of Liberty **121** Broadleaf Cactus

1964. 10th Anniv of Liberty Day.
483 **120** 80c. orange 50 10
484 – $3.20 blue . . . . 2·00 50
DESIGN—VERT: $3.20, Hands with broken manacles.

1964. Taiwan Cacti. Multicoloured. With gum.
485 80c. Type **121** . . . . 1·25 10
486 $1 Crab cactus . . . . 7·00 60
487 $3.20 Nopalxochia . . . . . 5·00 30
488 $5 Grizzly-Bear cactus . . . 12·00 1·00

122 Wu Chih-hwei (politician) **123** Chu Kwang Tower, Quemoy

1964. 99th Birth Anniv of Wu Chih-hwei (politician).
489 **122** 80c. brown . . . . 1·75 10

1964.
490 **123** 3c. purple 10 10
491 5c. green 10 10
492 10c. green 40 10
493 20c. green 15 10
494 40c. red 15 10
495 50c. purple 40 10
496 80c. orange 60 10
497 $1 violet 30 10
498 $1.50 purple . . . . . . 10·00 50
499 $2 purple . . . . 1·25 10
500 $2.50 blue . . . . 1·40 10
501 $3 grey . . . . 2·00 10
502 $3.20 blue . . . . 2·00 10
504 $4 green . . . . 3·00 10

124 Nurse and Florence Nightingale
125 Weir

1964. Nurses Day.
506 – 80c. violet . . . . 1·60 10
507 **124** $4 red . . . . 4·25 40
DESIGN—HORIZ: 80c. Nurses holding candlelight ceremony.

1964. Inaug of Shihmen Reservoir. With gum. Mult.
508 80c. Type **125** . . . . 3·00 10
509 $1 Irrigation channel . . . . 4·00 10
510 $3.20 Dam and powerhouse 8·50 10
511 $5 Main spillway . . . . . . 12·50 3·00

126 Ancient Ship and Modern Freighter
127 Bananas

1964. Navigation Day.
512 **126** $2 orange . . . . 1·00 10
513 $3.60 green . . . . 3·00 50

1964. Taiwan Fruits. Multicoloured. With gum.
514 80c. Type **127** . . . . 7·00 20
515 $1 Oranges . . . . 14·00 1·50
516 $3.20 Pineapples . . . . . 23·00 70
517 $4 Water-melons . . . . . . 35·00 2·00

128 Lockheed Starfighters, "Tai Ho", "Tai Choa" and "Tai Tsung" (destroyers) and Artillery
129 Globe and Flags of Formosa and U.S.A.

1964. Armed Forces Day.
518 **128** 80c. blue . . . . 1·00 10
519 $6 purple . . . . 3·50 75

1964. New York World's Fair (1st issue). With gum.
520 **129** 80c. multicoloured . . . . . . 5·00 30
521 – $5 multicoloured . . . . 7·00 75
DESIGN—HORIZ: $5, Taiwan Pavilion at Fair.
See also Nos. 550/1.

130 Cowman holding Calf
131 Cycling

1964. Animal Protection.
522 **130** $2 purple . . . . 1·00 60
523 $4 blue . . . . 5·25 1·25

1964. Olympic Games, Tokyo.
524 **131** 80c. blue 75 10
525 – $1 red . . . . 1·75 10
526 – $3.20 green . . . . 2·50 10
527 – $10 violet . . . . 3·75 1·25
DESIGNS: $1, Runner breasting tape; $3.20, Gymnastics; $10, High jumping.

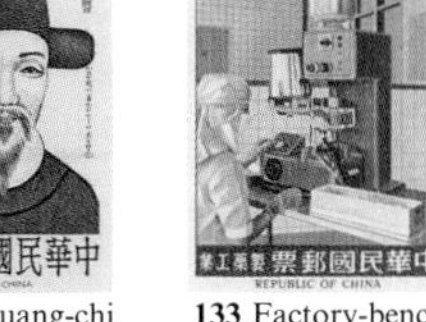

132 Hsu Kuang-chi (statesman)
133 Factory-bench ("Pharmaceutics")

1964. Famous Chinese.
528 **132** 80c. blue . . . . 2·50 10
See also Nos. 558/9, 586/7, 599, 606/9, 610, 738/40, 960 and 1072/7.

1964. Taiwan Industries. Multicoloured. With gum.
529 40c. Type **133** . . . . 2·50 20
530 $1.50 Loom ("Textiles") (horiz) . . . . 4·50 1·75
531 $2 Refinery ("Chemicals") . . 7·00 20
532 $3.60 Cement-mixer ("Cement") (horiz) . . . . 9·50 1·25

134 Dr. Sun Yat-sen (founder)
135 Mrs. Eleanor Roosevelt and "Human Rights" Emblem

1964. 70th Anniv of Kuomintang.
533 **134** 80c. green . . . . 2·50 10
534 $3.60 purple . . . . . . 5·50 60

1964. 16th Anniv of Declaration of Human Rights.
535 **135** $10 brown and violet . . 2·25 45

136 Law Code and Scales of Justice
137 Rotary Emblem and Mainspring

1965. 20th Judicial Day.
536 **136** 80c. red . . . . 1·00 10
537 $3.20 green . . . . 2·00 20

1965. 60th Anniv of Rotary International.
538 **137** $1.50 red 60 10
539 $2 green 60 10
540 $2.50 blue . . . . 2·00 25

138 "Double Carp"
139 Mme. Chiang Kai-shek

1965.
541 **138** $5 violet . . . . 4·00 10
542 $5.60 blue . . . . 5·50 70
543 $6 brown . . . . 5·50 10
544 $10 mauve . . . . 27·00 10
545 $20 red . . . . 38·00 1·50
546 $50 green . . . . 38·00 1·50
547 $100 red . . . . 55·00 2·40
See also Nos. 695/698ab.

1965. 15th Anniv of Chinese Women's Anti-Aggression League. With gum.
548 **139** $2 multicoloured . . . . 15·00 70
549 $6 multicoloured . . . . 26·00 6·00

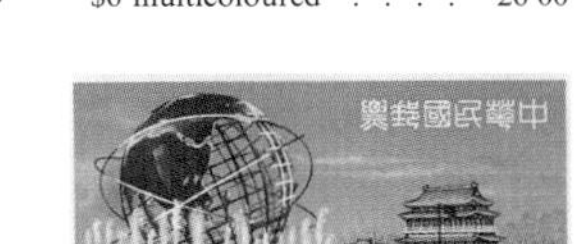

140 Unisphere and Taiwan Pavilion, N.Y. Fair

1965. New York World's Fair (2nd issue). Multicoloured. With gum.
550 $2 Type **140** . . . . 8·00 40
551 $10 Peacock and various birds ("100 birds paying tribute to Queen Phoenix") 32·00 3·00

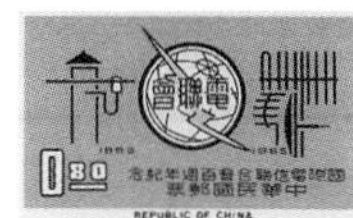

141 I.T.U. Emblem and Symbols

1965. Centenary of I.T.U. Multicoloured. With gum.
552 80c. Type **141** . . . . 1·10 10
553 $5 I.T.U. emblem and symbols (vert) . . . . . . 2·75 50

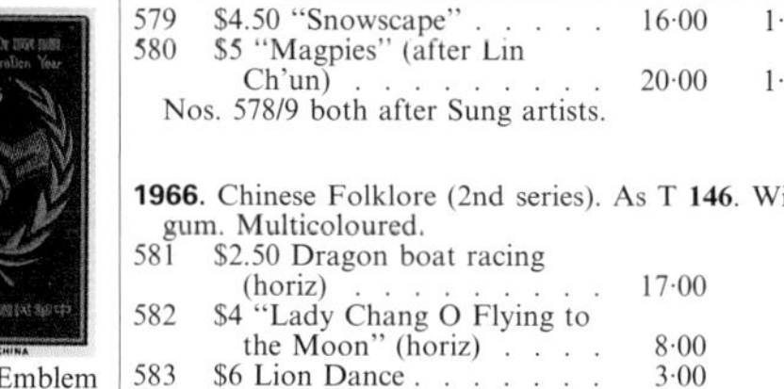

142 Madai Seabream
143 I.C.Y. Emblem

1965. Taiwan Fishes. Mult. With gum.
554 40c. Type **142** . . . . 3·00 30
555 80c. Silver pomfret . . . . . 5·00 30
556 $2 Skipjack tuna (vert) . . . 7·50 75
557 $4 Moonfish . . . . 12·50 1·00

1965. Famous Chinese. Portraits as T **132**.
558 $1 red (Confucius) . . . . . 4·75 10
559 $3.60 blue (Mencius) . . . . 6·00 50

1965. Int Co-operation Year. Mult. With gum.
560 $2 Type **143** . . . . 3·00 10
561 $6 I.C.Y. emblem (horiz) . . 3·00 80

144 Road Crossing
145 Dr. Sun Yat-sen

1965. Road Safety.
562 **144** $1 purple . . . . 1·40 10
563 $4 red . . . . 2·50 50

1965. Birth Centenary of Dr. Sun Yat-sen. Multicoloured. With gum.
564 $1 Type **145** . . . . 4·00 15
565 $4 As T **145** but with portrait, etc., on right . . . 8·00 40
566 $5 Dr. Sun Yat-sen and flags (horiz) . . . . 14·00 1·00

146 Children with Firework
147 Lien Po, "Marshal and Prime Minister Reconciled"

1965. Chinese Folklore (1st Series). Multicoloured. With gum.
567 $1 Type **146** . . . . 7·50 70
568 $4.50 Dragon dance . . . . 7·50 2·40
See also Nos. 581/3 and 617.

1966. Painted Faces of Chinese Opera. Multicoloured. With gum.
569 $1 Type **147** . . . . 16·00 40
570 $3 Kuan Yu, "Reunion at Ku City" . . . . 16·00 75
571 $4 Chang Fei, "Long Board Slope" . . . . 16·00 90
572 $6 Buddha, "The Flower-scattering Angel" . . . . . 32·00 3·00

148 Pigeon holding Postal Emblem
149 "Fishing on a Snowy Day" (After artist of the "Five Dynasties")

1966. 70th Anniv of Chinese Postal Services. Multicoloured. With gum.
573 $1 Type **148** . . . . 2·50 10
574 $2 Postman by Chu memorial stone (horiz) . . . . 3·50 10
575 $3 Postal Museum (horiz) . . 3·50 45
576 $4 "Postman climbing" . . . 7·00 1·50

1966. Ancient Chinese Paintings from Palace Museum Collection (3rd series). With gum. Multicoloured.
577 $2.50 Type **149** . . . . . . 7·00 70
578 $3.50 "Calves on the Plain" 10·50 70
579 $4.50 "Snowscape" . . . . . 16·00 1·75
580 $5 "Magpies" (after Lin Ch'un) . . . . 20·00 1·75
Nos. 578/9 both after Sung artists.

1966. Chinese Folklore (2nd series). As T **146**. With gum. Multicoloured.
581 $2.50 Dragon boat racing (horiz) . . . . 17·00 70
582 $4 "Lady Chang O Flying to the Moon" (horiz) . . . . 8·00 10
583 $6 Lion Dance . . . . 3·00 15

150 Flags of Argentine and Chinese Republics
151 Lin Sen

1966. 150th Anniv of Argentine Republic's Independence. With gum.
584 **150** $10 multicoloured . . . . 3·00 50

1966. Birth Centenary of Lin Sen (statesman).
585 **151** $1 sepia . . . . 2·10 10

1966. Famous Chinese. Portraits as T **132**.
586 $2.50 sepia . . . . 4·50 10
587 $3.50 red . . . . 5·50 15
PORTRAITS: $2.50, General Yueh Fei. $3.50, Wen Tien-hsiang (statesman).

153 Bean Geese
154 Pres. Chiang Kai-shek

1966.
588 **153** $3.50 brown . . . . . . 1·25 25
589 $4 red 75 10
590 $4.50 green . . . . 2·00 15
591 $5 purple 75 10
592 $5.50 green . . . . 1·25 20
593 $6 blue . . . . 6·00 1·75
594 $6.50 violet . . . . 1·75 30
595 $7 black . . . . 1·25 10
596 $8 red . . . . 1·75 10

1966. President Chiang Kai-shek's re-election for 4th Term. With gum. Multicoloured.
597 $1 Type **154** . . . . 2·10 10
598 $5 President in Uniform . . . 4·50 50

1966. Famous Chinese. Portrait as T **132**.
599 $1 blue (Tsai Yuan-Pei, scholar) . . . . 2·50 10

155 Various means of Transport
156 Boeing 727-100 over Chilin Pavilion, Grand Hotel, Taipeh

1967. Development of Taiwan Communications. Multicoloured. With gum.
600 $1 Mobile postman and microwave station (vert) . . 1·25 10
601 $5 Type **155** . . . . 2·50 30

1967. Air. Multicoloured. With gum.
602 $5 Type **156** . . . . 5·00 10
603 $8 Boeing 727-100 over Palace Museum, Taipeh . . 5·00 50

157 Pres. Chiang Kai-shek
158 "God of Happiness" (wood carving)

1967. Chiang Kai-shek's 4th Presidential Term. With gum.
604 **157** $1 multicoloured . . . . 2·00 10
605 $4 multicoloured . . . . 2·00 50

1967. Famous Chinese. Poets. Portraits. As T **132**.
606 $1 black (Chu Yuan) . . . . 2·75 20
607 $2 brown (Li Po) . . . . . 4·25 50
608 $2.50 brown (Tu Fu) . . . . 5·50 50
609 $3 green (Po Chu-i) . . . . 6·00 50

1967. Famous Chinese. Portrait as T **132**.
610 $1 black (Chiu Ching, female revolutionary) . . . . . . 4·00 10

1967. Chinese Handicrafts. Multicoloured. With gum.
611 $1 Type **158** . . . . 3·25 10
612 $2.50 Vase and dish . . . . 4·25 15
613 $3 Chinese dolls . . . . . . 5·50 30
614 $5 Palace lanterns . . . . . 9·00 75

159 "WACL" on World Map
160 Muller's Barbet

1967. 1st World Anti-Communist League Conference, Taipei.
615 **159** $1 red 40 10
616 $5 blue 75 15

GUM. From No. 617 all stamps were issued with gum unless otherwise stated.

1967. Chinese Folklore (3rd series). Stilts Pastime. As T **146**.
617 $4.50 multicoloured . . . . 1·75 15
DESIGN: "The Fisherman and the Wood-cutter" (Chinese play on stilts).

1967. Taiwan Birds. Multicoloured.
618 $1 Type **160** . . . . 3·50 15
619 $2 Maroon oriole (horiz) . . 8·50 35
620 $2.50 Japanese green pigeon (horiz) . . . . 11·00 60
621 $3 Formosan blue magpie (horiz) . . . . 11·00 60
622 $5 Crested serpent eagle . . . 13·00 1·00
623 $8 Mikado pheasant (horiz) 13·00 1·00

161 Chung Hsing Pagoda
162 Flags and China Park, Manila

1967. International Tourist Year. Multicoloured.
624 $1 Type **161** . . . . 1·75 10
625 $2.50 Yeh Liu National Park (coastal scene) (horiz) . . . 5·00 40
626 $4 Statue of Buddha (horiz) 5·50 40
627 $5 National Palace Museum, Taipei (horiz) . . . . . . 7·00 50

1967. China–Philippines Friendship.
628 **162** $1 multicoloured 50 10
629 $5 multicoloured . . . . 1·50 40

163 Chungshan Building, Yangmingshan
164 Taroko Gorge

1968.
630 **163** 5c. brown 10 10
631 10c. green 15 15
632 50c. purple 10 10
633 $1 red 15 10
634 $1.50 green . . . . 4·50 20
635 $2 purple . . . . 1·40 10
636 $2.50 blue . . . . 1·40 10
637 $3 blue . . . . 1·50 10
For redrawn design see Nos. 791/8.

1968. 17th Pacific Area Travel Association Conference, Taipei. Multicoloured.
638 $5 Type **164** . . . . 3·50 60
689 $8 Chungshan Building, Yangmingshan . . . . . . 2·75 60

165 Harvesting Sugar-cane
166 Vice-Pres. Cheng

1968. Sugar-cane Technologists Congress, Taiwan.
640 **165** $1 multicoloured . . . . 1·60 10
641 $4 multicoloured . . . . 3·25 50

1968. 3rd Death Anniv of Vice-Pres. Chen Cheng.
642 **166** $1 multicoloured . . . . 1·00 10

167 Bean Geese
168 Jade Cabbage (Ching Dynasty)

1968. 90th Anniv of Chinese Postage Stamps.
643 **167** $1 red . . . . 1·00 25

1968. Chinese Art Treasures, National Palace Museum (1st series). Multicoloured.
645 $1 Type **168** . . . . 1·50 10
646 $1.50 Jade battle-axe (Warring States period) . . 3·50 35
647 $2 Lung-ch'uan porcelain flower bowl (Sung dynasty) (horiz) . . . . 3·50 10
648 $2.50 Yung Cheng enamelled vase (Ching dynasty) . . . 4·00 50
649 $4 Agate "fingered" flower-holder (Ching dynasty) (horiz) . . . . 4·50 50
650 $5 Sacrificial vessel (Western Chou) . . . . 5·00 75
See also Nos. 682/7 and 732/7.

169 W.H.O. Emblem on "20"
170 Sun, Planets and "Rainfall"

1968. 20th Anniv of W.H.O.
651 **169** $1 green 30 10
652 $5 red 85 30

1968. International Hydrological Decade.
653 **170** $1 green and orange . . . 30 10
654 $4 blue and orange . . . 85 10

171 "A City of Cathay" (Section of hand-scroll painting)

1968. "A City of Cathay" (Scroll, Palace Museum) (1st series).
655 **171** $1 (1) multicoloured . . . 2·00 10
656 – $1 (2) multicoloured . . . 2·00 10
657 – $1 (3) multicoloured . . . 2·00 10
658 – $1 (4) multicoloured . . . 2·00 10
659 – $1 (5) multicoloured . . . 2·00 10
660 – $5 multicoloured . . . . 15·00 2·50
661 – $8 multicoloured . . . . 17·00 2·50
DESIGNS—As Type **171**: Nos. 655/9 together show panorama of the city ending with the palace. LARGER (61 × 32 mm). $5, City wall and gate; $8, Great bridge.

The five $1 stamps were issued together se-tenant in horiz strips, representing the last 11 feet of the 37 foot scroll, which is viewed from right to left as it is unrolled.
The stamps may be identified by the numbers given in brackets, which correspond to the numbers in the bottom right-hand corners of the stamps.
See also Nos. 699/703.

172 Map and Radio "Waves"
173 Human Rights Emblem

1968. 40th Anniv of Chinese Broadcasting Service.
662 **172** $1 grey, ultram & blue . . 40 10
663 – $4 red and blue . . . . . 1·00 10
DESIGN—VERT: $4, Stereo broadcast "waves".

1968. Human Rights Year.
664 **173** $1 multicoloured 40 10
665 $5 multicoloured . . . . 1·00 10

174 Harvesting Rice
175 Throwing the Javelin

1968. Rural Reconstruction.
666 **174** $1 brown, ochre & yellow 40 10
667 $5 bronze, green & yellow 1·00 30

1968. Olympic Games, Mexico. Multicoloured.
668 $1 Type **175** 50 10
669 $2.50 Weightlifting 75 10
670 $5 Pole-vaulting (horiz) . . . 1·00 20
671 $8 Hurdling (horiz) . . . . . 1·50 40

176 President Chiang Kai-shek and Main Gate, Whampoa Military Academy

1968. "President Chiang Kai-shek's Meritorious Services". Multicoloured.
672 $1 Type **176** 50 10
673 $2 Reviewing Northern Expedition Forces . . . . 1·25 20
674 $2.50 Suppression of bandits 4·00 60
675 $3.50 Marco Polo Bridge and Victory Parade, Nanking, 1945 . . . . 1·50 25
676 $4 Chinese Constitution . . . 1·75 25
677 $5 National flag . . . . . . 2·25 30
Each stamp bears the portrait of President Chiang Kai-shek as in Type **176**.

177 Cockerel
178 National Flag

1968. New Year Greetings. "Year of the Cock".
678 **177** $1 multicoloured . . . . 20·00 10
679 $4.50 multicoloured . . . 26·00 5·00

1968. 20th Anniv of Chinese Constitution.
680 **178** $1 multicoloured 75 10
681 $5 multicoloured . . . . 1·00 15

1969. Chinese Art Treasures, National Palace Museum (2nd series). Multicoloured as T **168**.
682 $1 Jade buckle (Ching dynasty) (horiz) 75 10
683 $1.50 Jade vase (Sung dynasty) . . . . 1·75 25
684 $2 Cloisonne enamel teapot (Ching dynasty) (horiz) . . 1·00 10
685 $2.50 Bronze sacrificial vessel (Kuei) (horiz) . . . . . . 1·75 40
686 $4 Hsuan-te "heavenly ball" vase (Ming dynasty) . . 2·75 60
687 $5 "Gourd" vase (Ching dynasty) . . . . 4·00 60

179 Servicemen and Savings Emblem
180 Ti (flute)

1969. 10th Anniv of Forces' Savings Services.
688 **179** $1 brown 40 10
689 $4 blue . . . . 1·00 15

1969. Chinese Musical Instruments. Mult.
690 $1 Type **180** . . . . 1·00 10
691 $2.50 Sheng (pipes) . . . . . 1·50 15
692 $4 P'i-p'a (lute) . . . . . . 2·00 30
693 $5 Cheng (zither) . . . . . . 2·00 15

181 Chungshan Building, Yangmingshan
182 "Double Carp"

1969. 10th Kuomintang Congress.
694 **181** $1 multicoloured 55 10

1969.
695ab **182** $10 blue . . . . 2·50 10
695c $14 red . . . . 2·50 10
696ab $20 brown . . . . . . 2·50 10
697ab $50 green . . . . . . 5·00 15
698ab $100 red . . . . 6·50 35
Type **182** is a redrawn version of Type **138**.

1969. "A City of Cathay" (scroll) (2nd series). As T **171**. Multicoloured.
699 $1 "Musicians" . . . . . . 1·00 10
700 $1 "Bridal chair" . . . . . 1·00 10
701 $2.50 Emigrants with ox-cart 1·00 60
702 $5 "Scroll gallery" . . . . . 5·25 45
703 $8 "Roadside cafe" . . . . . 8·50 60
Nos. 699/70 form a composite picture of a bridal procession.

184 I.L.O. Emblem
185 "Food and Clothing"

1969. 50th Anniv of I.L.O.
704 **184** $1 blue 50 10
705 $8 red . . . . 1·00 20

1969. "Model Citizen's Life" Movement.
706 **185** $1 red 20 10
707 – $2.50 blue 70 15
708 – $4 green 70 15
DESIGNS: $2.50, "Housekeeping and Road Safety"; $4, "Schooling and Recreation".

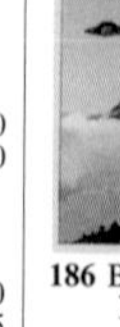
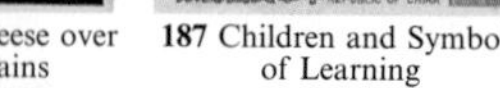

186 Bean Geese over Mountains
187 Children and Symbols of Learning

1969. Air. Multicoloured.
709 $2.50 Type **186** . . . . . . 4·25 75
710 $5 Bean geese over sea . . . 4·25 50
711 $8 Bean geese over land (horiz) . . . . 4·25 50

1969. 1st Anniv of Nine-year Free Education System.
712 **187** $1 red 30 10
713 – $2.50 green 50 15
714 – $4 blue . . . . 1·00 15
715 **187** $5 brown . . . . 1·25 20
DESIGNS—VERT: $2.50 and $4, Children and school.

188 "Flowers and Ring-necked Pheasants", Ming dynasty (Lu Chih)
189 "Charles Mallerin" Rose

1969. Ancient Chinese Paintings from Palace Museum Collection (4th series). "Birds and Flowers". Multicoloured.

716 $1 Type **188** . . . . 1·75 20
717 $2.50 "Bamboos and Ring-necked Pheasants" (Sung dynasty) . . . . 3·75 30
718 $5 "Flowers and Birds" (Sung dynasty) . . . . . . 9·25 60
719 $8 "Twin Manchurian Cranes and Flowers" (G. Castiglione, Ching dynasty) . . . . 9·25 1·00

1969. Roses. Multicoloured.

720 $1 Type **189** . . . . 1·60 10
721 $2.50 "Golden Sceptre" . . . 2·50 20
722 $5 "Peace" . . . . 3·25 30
723 $8 "Josephine Bruce" . . . . 5·25 25

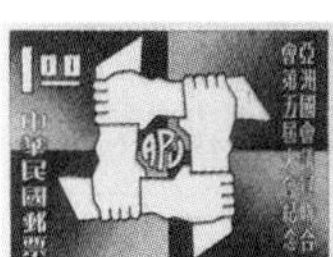

190 Launching Missile
191 A.P.U. Emblem

1969. 30th Air Defence Day.

724 **190** $1 purple 80 10

1969. 5th Asian Parliamentarians' Union General Assembly. Taipeh.

725 **191** $1 red 40 10
726 $5 green 75 15

192 Pekingese Dogs
193 Satellite and Earth Station

1969. New Year Greetings. "Year of the Dog".

727 **192** 50c. multicoloured . . . . 2·00 10
728 $4.50 multicoloured . . . 5·00 1·00

1969. Inauguration of Satellite Earth Station, Yangmingshan.

729 **193** $1 multicoloured 90 10
730 $5 multicoloured . . . . 1·90 30
731 $8 multicoloured . . . . 2·60 50

1970. Chinese Art Treasures, National Palace Museum (3rd series). As T **168**. Multicoloured.

732 $1 Lacquer vase (Ching dynasty) . . . . 1·00 10
733 $1.50 Agate grinding-stone (Ching dynasty) (horiz) . . 1·75 15
734 $2 Jade carving (Ching dynasty) (horiz) . . . . . 1·75 10
735 $2.50 "Shepherd and Ram" jade carving (Han dynasty) (horiz) . . . . 2·00 30
736 $4 Porcelain jar (Ching dynasty) . . . . 2·00 30
737 $5 "Bull" porcelain urn (Northern Sung dynasty) 4·25 60

1970. Famous Chinese. Portraits as T **132**.

738 $1 red . . . . 2·00 10
739 $2.50 green . . . . 1·90 15
740 $4 blue . . . . 2·00 35

PORTRAITS: $1, Hsuan Chuang (traveller). $2.50, Hua To (physician). $4, Chu Hsi (philosopher).

194 Taiwan Pavilion and EXPO Emblem
195 Chungshan Building, Yangmingshan

1970. World Fair "EXPO 70", Osaka, Japan. Multicoloured.

741 $5 Type **194** 40 15
742 $8 Pavilion encircled by national flags 90 40

1970.

743 **195** $1 red 50 20

For redrawn design see No. 1039.

196 Rain-cloud, Palm and Recording Apparatus
197 Martyrs' Shrine

1970. World Meteorological Day. Mult.

744 $1 Type **196** 50 10
745 $8 "Nimbus 3" satellite (horiz) . . . . 1·00 35

1970. Revolutionary Martyrs' Shrine. Mult.

746 $1 Type **197** 75 10
747 $8 Shrine gateway . . . . . 1·25 40

198 General Yueh Fei ("Loyalty")

1970. Chinese Opera. "The Virtues". Opera characters. Multicoloured.

748 $1 Type **198** 75 20
749 $2.50 Emperor Shun tortured by stepmother ("Filial Piety") . . . . 2·50 35
750 $5 Chin Liang-yu "The Lady General" ("Chastity") . . 4·00 35
751 $8 Kuan Yu and groom ("Fidelity") . . . . 5·00 50

199 Three Horses at Play

1970. "One Hundred Horses" (handscroll by Lang Shih-ning (G. Castiglione)). Multicoloured.

752 $1 (1) Horses on plain . . . 50 10
753 $1 (2) Horses on plain (different) 50 10
754 $1 (3) Horses playing 50 10
755 $1 (4) Horses on river bank 50 10
756 $1 (5) Horses crossing river 50 10
757 $5 Type **199** . . . . 5·00 75
758 $8 Groom roping horses . . 6·50 50

SERIAL NUMBERS. are indicated to aid identification of the above and certain other sets. For key to Chinese numerals see table at the beginning of CHINA.

200 Old Lai-tsu dropping Buckets
201 Chiang Kai-shek's Moon Message

1970. Chinese Folk-tales (1st series). Mult.

759 10c. Type **200** 20 10
760 10c. Yien-tsu disguised as a deer 20 10
761 10c. Hwang Hsiang with fan 20 10
762 10c. Wang Shiang fishing . . 25 10
763 10c. Chu Hsiu-chang reunited with mother 20 10
764 50c. Emperor Wen tasting mother's medicine 40 10
765 $1 Lu Chi dropping oranges 60 15
766 $1 Yang Hsiang fighting tiger 60 15

See also Nos. 817/24, 1000/7, 1064/7, 1210/13 and 1312/15.

1970. 1st Man on the Moon. Multicoloured.

767 $1 Type **201** 60 10
768 $5 "Apollo 11" astronauts (horiz) . . . . 1·00 30
769 $8 "First step on the Moon" 2·00 50

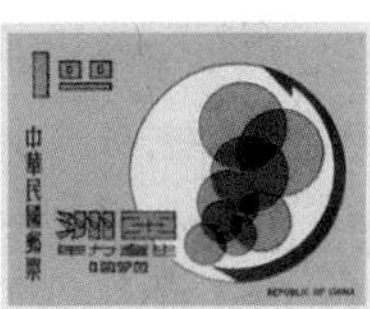

202 Productivity Symbol
203 Flags of Taiwan and United Nations

1970. Asian Productivity Year.

770 **202** $1 multicoloured 50 10
771 $5 multicoloured . . . . 1·00 35

1970. 25th Anniv of United Nations.

772 **203** $5 multicoloured . . . . 1·25 40

204 Postal Zone Map
205 "Cultural Activities" (10th month)

1970. Postal Zone Numbers Campaign. Mult.

773 $1 Type **204** 90 10
774 $2.50 Postal Zone emblem (horiz) . . . . 1·00 35

1970. "Occupations of the Twelve Months" Hanging Scrolls. Multicoloured. (a) "Winter".

775 $1 Type **205** . . . . 2·40 10
776 $2.50 "School Buildings" (11th month) . . . . . . 6·00 1·00
777 $5 "Games in the Snow" (12th month) . . . . . . 8·50 75

(b) "Spring".

778 $1 "Lantern Festival" (1st month) . . . . 2·75 10
779 $2.50 "Apricots in Blossom" (2nd month) . . . . 3·50 1·00
780 $5 "Purification Ceremony" (3rd month) . . . . . . 4·25 60

(c) "Summer".

781 $1 "Summer Shower" (4th month) . . . . 2·75 10
782 $2.50 "Dragon boat Festival" (5th month) . . . . 4·00 1·00
783 $5 "Lotus Pond" (6th month) 4·00 50

(d) "Autumn".

784 $1 "Weaver Festival" (7th month) . . . . 3·00 10
785 $2.50 "Moon Festival" (8th month) . . . . 4·25 1·00
786 $5 "Chrysanthemum Blossom" (9th month) . . 6·25 35

The month numbers are given by the Chinese characters in brackets, which follow the face value on the stamps.

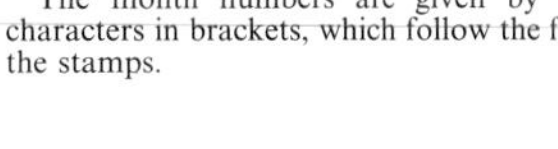
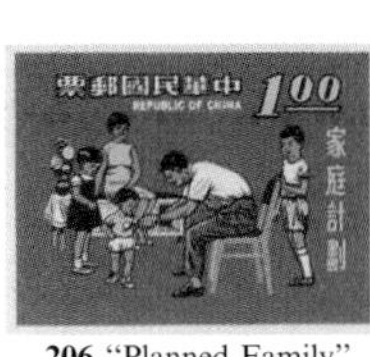

206 "Planned Family"
207 Toy Pig

1970. Family Planning. Multicoloured.

787 $1 Type **206** 60 10
788 $4 "Family excursion" (vert) 1·25 35

1970. New Year Greetings. "Year of the Boar".

789 **207** 50c. multicoloured . . . . 2·25 30
790 $4.50 multicoloured . . . 3·00 1·00

208 Chungshan Building, Yangmingshan
209 Shin-bone Tibia

1971.

791 **208** 5c. brown 15 10
792 10c. green 15 10
793 50c. red 25 10
794 $1 red 25 10
795 $1.50 blue . . . . 1·10 10
796 $2 purple . . . . 3·00 10
797 $2.50 green . . . . 4·25 10
798 $3 blue . . . . 4·25 10

Type **208** is a redrawn version of Type **163**.

1971. Taiwan Shells. Multicoloured.

799 $1 Type **209** 90 10
800 $2.50 Kuroda's lyria . . . . 1·10 30
801 $5 "Conus stupa kuroda" . . 1·75 50
802 $8 Rumphius's slit shell . . . 3·00 25

210 Savings Book and Certificate
211 Chinese greeting African Farmer

1971. National Savings Campaign. Mult.

803 $1 Type **210** 45 10
804 $4 Hand dropping coin in savings bank . . . . . . 1·00 20

1971. 10th Anniv of Sino-African Technical Co-operation Committee. Multicoloured.

805 $1 Type **211** 40 10
806 $8 Rice-growing (horiz) . . . 80 35

212 Red and White Flying Squirrel
213 Pitcher delivering ball

1971. Taiwan Animals. Multicoloured.

807 $1 Taiwan macaque (vert) . . 70 10
808 $2 Type **212** . . . . 1·50 50
809 $3 Chinese pangolin . . . . 2·00 65
810 $5 Sika deer . . . . 2·50 75

1971. World Little League Baseball Championships, Taiwan. Multicoloured.

811 $1 Type **213** 30 10
812 $2.50 Players at base (horiz) 40 15
813 $4 Striker and catcher . . . 75 15

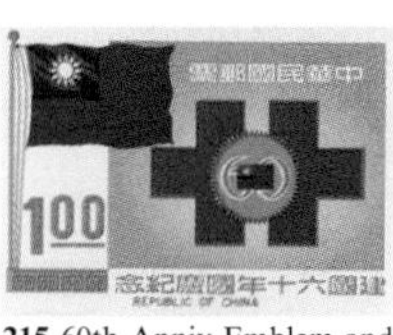

(**214**)
215 60th Anniv Emblem and flag

1971. Victory of "Tainan Giants" in World Little League Baseball Championships, Williamsport (U.S.A.). Optd with T **214**.

814 **163** $1 red 60 10
815 $2.50 blue . . . . 1·25 20
816 $3 blue . . . . 1·25 20

1971. Chinese Folk-tales (2nd series). As T **200**. Multicoloured.

817 10c. Yu Hsun and elephant 15 10
818 10c. Tsai Hsun with mulberries 15 10
819 10c. Tseng Sun with firewood 15 10
820 10c. Kiang Keh and bandits 15 10
821 10c. Tsu Lu with sack of rice 15 10
822 50c. Meng Chung gathering bamboo shoots 40 10
823 $1 Tung Yung and wife . . . 1·25 35
824 $1 Tzu Chien shivering with cold . . . . 1·25 35

1971. 60th National Day. Multicoloured.

825 $1 Type **215** 45 10
826 $2.50 National anthem, map and flag 60 10

827 $5 Pres. Chiang Kai-shek, constitution and flag . . . 75 35
828 $8 Dr. Sun Yat-sen, "Three Principles" and flag . . . 1·00 40

216 A.O.P.U. Emblem

1971. Asian-Oceanic Postal Union Executive Committee Session, Taipeh.
829 **216** $2.50 multicoloured . . . 50 30
830 $5 multicoloured 60 15

217 "White Frost Hawk"

1971. "Ten Prized Dogs" (paintings on silk by Lang Shih-ning (G. Castiglione)). Multicoloured.
831 $1 Type **217** . . . . 1·10 10
832 $1 "Black Dog with Snow-white Claws" . . . . . . 3·25 10
833 $2 "Star-glancing Wolf" . . 3·50 10
834 $2 "Yellow Leopard" . . . . 4·50 10
835 $2.50 "Golden-winged Face" 3·00 85
836 $2.50 "Flying Magpie" . . . 10·50 85
837 $5 "Young Black Dragon" 4·25 75
838 $5 "Heavenly Lion" . . . . 10·50 75
839 $8 "Young Grey Dragon" . . 4·25 65
840 $8 "Mottle-coated Tiger" . . 12·00 65

218/221 Squirrels

1971. New Year Greetings. "Year of the Rat".
841 **218** 50c. multicoloured 80 10
842 **219** 50c. multicoloured 80 10
843 **220** 50c. multicoloured 80 10
844 **221** 50c. multicoloured 80 10
845 **218** $4.50 multicoloured . . . 4·00 40
846 **219** $4.50 multicoloured . . . 4·00 40
847 **220** $4.50 multicoloured . . . 4·00 40
848 **221** $4.50 multicoloured . . . 4·00 40
The four designs in each value were issued together, se-tenant, forming a composite design.

222 Flags of Taiwan and Jordan

1971. 50th Anniv of Hashemite Kingdom of Jordan.
849 **222** $5 multicoloured . . . . 1·00 30

223 Freighter "Hai King"

1971. Centenary of China Merchants Steam Navigation Company. Multicoloured.
850 **223** $4 blue, red and green . . 75 40
851 – $7 multicoloured . . . . 1·25 25
DESIGN—VERT: $7. Liner on Pacific.

224 Downhill Skiing

1972. Winter Olympic Games, Sapporo, Japan.
852 **224** $1 black, yellow and blue 25 10
853 – $5 black, orange & green 65 20
854 – $8 black, red and grey . . 75 30
DESIGNS: $5, Cross-country skiing; $8, Giant slalom.

225 Yung Cheng Vase 226 Doves

1972. Chinese Porcelain. (1st series). Ch'ing Dynasty. Multicoloured.
855 $1 Type **225** 75 10
856 $2 Kang Hsi jar . . . . . . 1·25 30
857 $2.50 Yung Cheng jug . . . 1·50 40
858 $5 Chien Lung vase . . . . 1·75 20
859 $8 Chien Lung jar . . . . . 3·25 40
See also Nos. 914/18, 927/31 and 977/81.

1972. 10th Anniv of Asian-Oceanic Postal Union.
860 **226** $1 black and blue 80 10
861 $5 black and violet . . . 1·25 40

227 "Dignity with Self-Reliance" (Pres. Chiang Kai-shek) 229 First Day Covers

228 Mounted Messengers

1972.
862 **227** 5c. brown and yellow . . 15 10
863 10c. blue and orange . . 10 10
863b 20c. purple and green . . 20 10
864 50c. lilac and purple . . 20 15
865 $1 red and blue 10 10
866 $1.50 yellow and blue . . 20 10
867 $2 violet, purple & orge 30 10
868 $2.50 green and red . . 75 10
869 $3 red and green 50 10

1972. "The Emperor's Procession" (Ming dynasty handscrolls). Multicoloured. (a) First issue.
870 $1 (1) Pagoda and crowds . . 40 10
871 $1 (2) Seven carriages 40 10
872 $1 (3) Emperor's coach . . . 40 10
873 $1 (4) Horsemen with flags 40 10
874 $1 (5) Horsemen and Emperor 40 10
875 $2.50 Type **228** . . . . . . 5·00 25
876 $5 Guards . . . . 5·00 25
877 $8 Imperial sedan chair . . . 5·00 20

(b) Second issue.
878 $1 (1) Three ceremonial barges 40 10
879 $1 (2) Sedan chairs 40 10
880 $1 (3) Two ceremonial barges 40 10
881 $1 (4) Horsemen and mounted orchestra 40 10
882 $1 (5) Two carriages 40 10
883 $2.50 City gate . . . . . . 5·00 25
884 $5 Mounted orchestra . . . 5·00 25
885 $8 Ceremonial barge . . . . 7·00 30
Nos. 870/4 are numbered from right to left and Nos. 878/82 are numbered from left to right. They were each issued together, se-tenant, forming composite designs showing the departure of the procession from the palace and its return.
Nos. 875/7 and 883/5 show enlarged details from the scrolls.
See also Nos. 937/50 and 1040/7.

1972. Philately Day.
886 **229** $1 blue 25 10
887 $2.50 green 25 15
888 $8 red . . . . 1·25 15
DESIGNS—VERT: $2.50, Magnifying glass and stamps. HORIZ: $8, Magnifying glass, perforation-gauge and tweezers.

(230) 231 Emperor Yao

1972. Taiwan's Victories in Senior and Little World Baseball Leagues. Nos. 865/7 and 869 optd with T **230**.
889 **227** $1 red and blue 25 10
890 $1.50 yellow and blue . . 40 20
891 $2 violet, purple & orange 40 15
892 $3 red and green 40 20

1972. Chinese Cultural Heroes.
893 **231** $3.50 blue 50 30
894 – $4 red 50 10
895 – $4.50 violet 60 20
896 – $5 green 60 10
897 – $5.50 purple . . . . . . 1·40 35
898 – $6 orange . . . . 1·40 30
899 – $7 brown . . . . 2·00 10
900 – $8 blue . . . . 2·25 15
DESIGNS: $4, Emperor Shun; $4.50, Yu the Great; $5, King T'ang; $5.50, King Weng; $6, King Wu; $7, Chou Kung; $8, Confucius.

232 Mountaineering 233 Microwave Systems and Electronic Sorting Machine

1972. 20th Anniv of China Youth Corps. Multicoloured.
902 $1 Type **232** 35 10
903 $2.50 Winter sport 50 10
904 $4 Diving 65 15
905 $8 Parachuting . . . . . . 1·00 45

1972. Improvement of Communications.
906 **233** $1 red 30 10
907 – $2.50 blue 50 20
908 – $5 purple 90 30
DESIGNS—HORIZ: $2.50, Boeing 721-100 airliner and "Hai Mou" (container ship); $5, Diesel railcar and motorway.

234 "Eyes" and J.C.I. Emblem 235 Cow and Calf

1972. 27th World Congress of Junior Chamber International, Taipeh.
909 **234** $1 multicoloured 30 10
910 $5 multicoloured 60 20
911 $8 multicoloured 60 30

1972. New Year Greetings. "Year of the Ox".
912 **235** 50c. black and red . . . . 1·40 25
913 $4.50 brown, red & yellow 2·00 75

1973. Chinese Porcelain (2nd series). Ming Dynasty. As T **225**. Multicoloured.
914 $1 Fu vase . . . . 1·00 10
915 $2 Floral vase . . . . 1·50 10
916 $2.50 Ku vase . . . . 1·75 20
917 $5 Hu flask . . . . 2·50 30
918 $8 Garlic-head vase . . . . 3·75 30

236 "Kicking the Shuttlecock" 237 Bamboo Sampan

1973. Chinese Folklore (1st series). Mult.
919 $1 Type **236** 40 10
920 $4 "The Fisherman and the Oyster-fairy" (horiz) . . . 90 15
921 $5 "Lady in a Boat" (horiz) 90 15
922 $8 "The Old Man and the Lady" . . . . 1·25 35
See also Nos. 982/3 and 1037/8.

1973. Taiwan Handicrafts (1st series). Mult.
923 $1 Type **237** 60 10
924 $2.50 Marble vase (vert) . . 75 10
925 $5 Glass plate 85 15
926 $8 Aborigine Doll (vert) . . . 90 25
See also Nos. 988/91.

1973. Chinese Porcelain (3rd series). Ming Dynasty. Horiz. designs as T **225**. Multicoloured.
927 $1 Dragon stem-bowl 60 10
928 $2 Dragon pot 85 10
929 $2.50 Covered jar with lotus decor . . . . 1·50 10
930 $5 Covered jar showing horses . . . . 1·50 15
931 $8 "Immortals" bowl . . . . 2·25 15

238 Contractors' Equipment 239 Pres. Chiang Kai-shek and Flag

1973. 12th Convention of International Federation of Asian and Western Pacific Contractors' Association.
932 **238** $1 multicoloured 30 10
933 – $5 blue and black 50 15
DESIGN—HORIZ: $5, Bulldozer.

1973. Inauguration of Pres. Chiang Kai-shek's 5th Term of Office.
934 **239** $1 multicoloured 50 10
935 $4 multicoloured 80 15

240 Lin Tse-hsu (statesman)

1973. Lin Tse-hsu Commemoration.
936 **240** $1 purple 35 10

1973. "Spring Morning in the Han Palace" (Ming dynasty handscroll). As T **228**. Mult. (a) First issue.
937 $1 (1) Palace gate 20 10
938 $1 (2) Feeding green peafowl 40 10
939 $1 (3) Emperor's wife 20 10
940 $1 (4) Ladies and pear tree 20 10
941 $1 (5) Music pavilion 20 10
942 $5 Giant rock (vert) . . . . 4·75 50
943 $8 Lady musicians (vert) . . 6·00 20

(b) Second issue.
944 $1 (6) Game with flowers . . 20 10
945 $1 (7) Leisure room 20 10
946 $1 (8) Ladies with teapots . . 20 10
947 $1 (9) Artist at work 20 10
948 $1 (10) Palace wall and guards 20 10
949 $5 Playing game at table (vert) . . . . 4·75 50
950 $8 Swatting insect (vert) . . . 6·00 20
Nos. 937/41 and 944/8 are numbered from right to left and were each issued together, se-tenant. When the two strips are placed side by side, they form a composite design showing the complete handscroll.
Nos. 942/3 and 949/50 show enlarged details from the scroll.

241 "Bamboo" (Hsiang Te-hsin)

1973. Ancient Chinese Fan Paintings (1st series). Multicoloured.
951 $1 Type **241** 80 10
952 $2.50 "Flowers" (Sun K'O-hung) . . . . 2·00 10
953 $5 "Landscape" (Ch'iu Ying) 3·25 20
954 $8 "Seated Figure and Tree" (Shen Chou) . . . . 3·00 20
See also Nos. 1052/5.

243 Emblem of World Series **245** Interpol Emblem

1973. Little League World Baseball Series. Taiwan Victory in Twin Championships.
955 **243** $1 blue, red and yellow 45 10
956 $4 blue, green & yellow 75 15

1973. 50th Anniv of International Criminal Police Organization (Interpol).
957 **245** $1 blue and orange 30 10
958 $5 green and orange 60 15
959 $8 purple and orange 80 25

1973. Famous Chinese. Portrait as T **132**.
960 $1 violet (Ch'iu Feng-chia (poet)) 55 10

246 Dam and Power Station

1973. Opening of Tsengwen Reservoir. Mult.
961 $1 Upper section of reservoir 10 10
962 $1 Middle section of reservoir 10 10
963 $1 Lower section of reservoir 10 10
964 $5 Type **246** (30 × 22 mm) 1·50 25
965 $8 Spillway (50 × 22 mm) 1·90 15
The $1 values together show complete map of reservoir (each 38 × 26 mm).

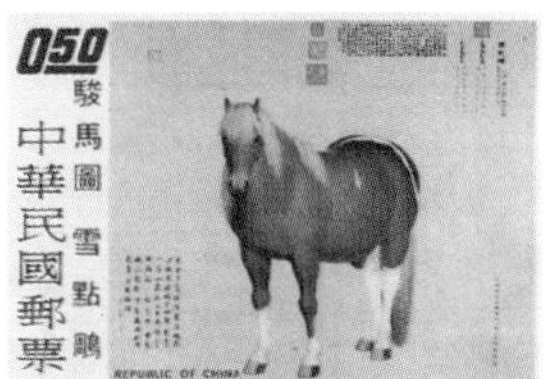

247 "Snow-dotted Eagle"

1973. Paintings of Horses. Multicoloured.
966 50c. Type **247** 10 10
967 $1 "Comfortable Ride" 20 10
968 $1 "Red Flower Eagle" 20 10
969 $1 "Cloud-running Steed" 20 10
970 $1 "Sky-running Steed" 20 10
971 $2.50 "Red Jade Steed" 4·50 25
972 $5 "Thunder-clap Steed" 6·50 25
973 $8 "Arabian Champion" 9·00 20

248 Tiger **249** Road Tunnel Taroko Gorge

1973. New Year Greetings. "Year of the Tiger".
975 **248** 50c. multicoloured 60 10
976 $4.50 multicoloured 1·00 30

1974. Chinese Porcelain (4th series). Sung Dynasty. As T **225**. Multicoloured.
977 $1 Ko vase 75 10
978 $2 Kuan vase (horiz) 75 10
979 $2.50 Ju bowl (horiz) 1·00 20
980 $5 Kuan incense burner (horiz) 1·10 20
981 $8 Chun incense burner (horiz) 1·40 20

1974. Chinese Folklore (2nd series). As T **236**. Multicoloured.
982 $1 Balancing pot 50 10
983 $8 Magicians (horiz) 1·00 20

1974. Taiwan Scenery (1st series). Mult.
984 $1 Type **249** 60 10
985 $2.50 Luce Chapel, Tungai University 70 10
986 $5 Tzu En Pagoda, Sun Moon Lake 1·25 15
987 $8 Goddess of Mercy Statue, Keelung 1·50 15
See also Nos. 992/5.

1974. Taiwan Handicrafts (2nd series). As T **237**. Multicoloured.
988 $1 "Fighting Cocks" (brass) 40 10
989 $2.50 "Fruits" (jade) 50 15
990 $5 "Fisherman" (wood-carving) (vert) 70 15
991 $8 "Bouquet of Flowers" (plastic) (vert) 1·00 15

1974. Taiwan Scenery (2nd series). As T **249** but all horiz. Multicoloured.
992 $1 Dr. Sun Yat-Sen Memorial Hall, Taipeh 40 10
993 $2.50 Reaching-Moon Tower, Cheng Ching Lake 55 10
994 $5 Seashore, Lanyu 1·00 15
995 $8 Inter-island bridge, Penghu 1·40 15

250 Pres. Chiang Kai-shek **251** Long-distance Runner

1974. 50th Anniv of Chinese Military Academy.
996 **250** $1 mauve 40 10
997 – $14 blue 85 30
DESIGN—VERT: $14, Cadets on parade.

1974. 80th Anniv of International Olympic Committee.
998 **251** $1 blue, black & red 20 10
999 – $8 multicoloured 60 15
DESIGN: $8, Female relay runner.

1974. Chinese Folk tales (3rd series). As T **200**. Multicoloured.
1000 50c. Wen Yen-po retrieving ball 45 10
1001 50c. T'i Ying pleading for mercy 45 10
1002 50c. Wang Ch'i in battle 45 10
1003 50c. Wang Hua returning gold 45 10
1004 $1 Pu Shih offering sheep to the emperor 50 10
1005 $1 Szu Ma Kuang saving playmate from water-jar 50 10
1006 $1 Tung Yu at study 50 10
1007 $1 K'ung Yung selecting the smallest pear 50 10

252 "Crape Myrtle" (Wei Sheng)

1974. Ancient Chinese Moon-shaped Fan-paintings (1st series). Multicoloured.
1008 $1 Type **252** 85 10
1009 $2.50 "White Cabbage and Insects" (Hsu Ti) 1·00 20
1010 $5 "Hibiscus and Rock" (Li Ti) 1·50 20
1011 $8 "Pomegranates and Narcissus Fly-catcher" (Wu Ping) 2·25 40
See also Nos. 1068/71 and 1115/1118.

253 "The Battle of Marco Polo Bridge" **254** Chrysanthemum

1974. Armed Forces' Day.
1012 **253** $1 multicoloured 35 10

1974. Chrysanthemums.
1014 **254** $1 multicoloured 40 10
1015 – $2.50 multicoloured 85 20
1016 – $5 multicoloured 1·25 20
1017 – $8 multicoloured 1·75 15
DESIGNS: Nos. 1015/17, various chrysanthemums.

255 Chinese Pavilion **256** Steel Mill, Kaohsiung

1974. "Expo 74" World Fair, Spokane, Washington. Multicoloured.
1018 $1 Type **255** 20 10
1019 $8 Fairground map 50 15

1974. Major Construction Projects (1st series). Chinese inscr in single-line characters, figures of value solid.* Multicoloured.
1020 50c. Type **256** 10 10
1021 $1 Taiwan North link railway 30 10
1022 $2 Petrochemical works, Kaohsiung 15 10
1023 $2.50 TRA trunk line electrification 50 10
1024 $3 Taichung harbour (horiz) 30 10
1025 $3.50 Taoyuan international airport (horiz) 30 10
1026 $4 Taiwan North–south motorway (horiz) 30 10
1027 $4.50 Giant shipyard, Kaohsiung (horiz) 50 25
1028 $5 Su-ao port (horiz) 50 10
*The first series can also be distinguished by the Chinese and English inscr at the foot being in different colours; in the second and third series only one colour is used.
See also Nos. 1122a/1122i and 1145/1153.

257 White Button Mushrooms **258** Baseball Strikers

1974. Edible Fungi. Multicoloured.
1029 $1 Type **257** 55 10
1030 $2.50 Oyster fungus 90 20
1031 $5 Veiled stinkhorn 1·40 25
1032 $8 Golden mushrooms 1·40 30

1974. Taiwan Triple Championship Victories in World Little League Baseball Series, U.S.A. Multicoloured.
1033 $1 Type **258** 25 10
1034 $8 Player and banners 50 15

259 Chinese Hare

1974. New Year Greetings. "Year of the Hare".
1035 **259** 50c. multicoloured 35 10
1036 $4.50 multicoloured 1·25 25

1975. Chinese Folklore (3rd series). As T **236**. Multicoloured.
1037 $4 Acrobat 50 15
1038 $5 Jugglers with diabolo 1·00 20

260 Chungshan Building, Yangmingshan **261** Sun Yat-sen Memorial Hall, Taipeh

1975.
1039 **260** $1 red 25 15
Type **260** is a redrawn version of Type **195**.

1975. "New Year Festivals" (handscroll by Ting Kuan-p'eng). As T **228**. Multicoloured.
1040 $1 (1) Greetings 20 10
1041 $1 (2) Entertainer 20 10
1042 $1 (3) Crowd and musicians 20 10
1043 $1 (4) Picnic 20 10
1044 $1 (5) Puppet show 20 10
1045 $2.50 New Year greetings 2·50 30
1046 $5 Children buying fireworks 4·25 30
1047 $8 Entertainer with monkey and dog 5·25 45
Nos. 1040/4 were issued together, se-tenant, forming a composite design.

1975. 50th Death Anniv of Dr. Sun Yat-sen.
1048 $1 Type **261** 25 10
1049 $4 Sun Yat-sen's handwriting 40 15
1050 $5 Bronze statue of Sun Yat-sen (vert) 50 15
1051 $8 Sun Yat-sen Memorial Hall, St. John's University, U.S.A 75 15

1975. Ancient Chinese Fan Paintings (2nd series). As T **241**. Multicoloured.
1052 $1 "Landscape" (Li Liu-fang) 75 10
1053 $2.50 "Landscape" (Wen Cheng-ming) 75 20
1054 $5 "Landscape" (Chou Ch'en) 1·60 20
1055 $8 "Landscape" (T'ang Yin) 2·00 15

262 "Yuan-chin" Coin (Chou dynasty) **263** "Lohan, the Cloth-bag Monk" (Chang Hung)

1975. Ancient Chinese Coins (1st series). Mult.
1056 $1 Type **262** 50 10
1057 $4 "Pan-liang" coin (Chin dynasty) 85 15
1058 $5 "Five chu" coin (Han dynasty) 1·00 15
1059 $8 "Five chu" coin (Liang dynasty) 1·25 10
See also Nos. 1111/14 and 1184/7.

1975. Ancient Chinese Figure Paintings. Mult.
1060 $2 Type **263** 75 10
1061 $4 "Lao-tzu on buffalo" (Chao Pu-chih) 1·75 15
1062 $5 "Shih-te" (Wang-wen) 3·00 15
1063 $8 "Splashed-ink Immortal" (Liang K'ai) 3·00 15

1975. Chinese Folk-tales (4th series). As T **200**. Multicoloured.
1064 $1 Chu-Yin reading by light of fireflies 20 10
1065 $2 Hua Mu-lan going to battle disguised as a man 35 10
1066 $2 Ling Kou Chien living a humble life 40 10
1067 $5 Chou Ch'u defeating the tiger 1·00 25

1975. Ancient Chinese Moon-shaped Fan Paintings (2nd series). As T **252**. Multicoloured.
1068 $1 "Cherry-apple blossoms" (Lin Ch'un) 75 10
1069 $2 "Spring blossoms and a colourful butterfly" (Ma K'uei) 90 10
1070 $5 "Monkeys and deer" (I Yuan-chi) 1·10 20
1071 $8 "Tree sparrows among bamboo" (anon.) 2·40 40

1975. Famous Chinese. Martyrs of War against Japan. Portraits as T **132**.
1072 $2 red (Gen. Chang Tzu-chung) 25 10
1073 $2 brown (Maj.-Gen. Kao Chih-hang) 25 10
1074 $2 green (Capt. Sha Shih-chiun) 25 10
1075 $5 brown (Maj-Gen. Hsieh Chin-yuan) 40 15
1076 $5 blue (Lt. Yen Hai-wen) 40 15
1077 $5 blue (Lt.-Gen. Tai An-lan) 40 15

264 "Lotus Pond with Willows"

1975. Madame Chiang Kai-shek's Landscape Paintings (1st series). Multicoloured.
1078 $2 Type **264** 1·00 10
1079 $5 "Sun breaks through Mountain Clouds" 1·50 30
1080 $8 "A Pair of Pine Trees" 3·75 40
1081 $10 "Fishing and Farming" 4·75 55
See also Nos. 1139/1142 and 1727/30.

265 Rectangular Cauldron

266 Dragon, Nine-Dragon Wall, Peihai

1975. Ancient Bronzes (1st series). Mult.
1082 $2 Type **265** 50 10
1083 $5 Cauldron with "Phoenix" handles (horiz) 75 15
1084 $8 Flat jar (horiz) . . . . . 1·50 25
1085 $10 Wine vessel . . . . . . 2·00 30
See also Nos. 1119/22.

1975. New Year Greetings. "Year of the Dragon".
1086 **266** $1 multicoloured 50 10
1087 $5 multicoloured . . . . 1·00 20

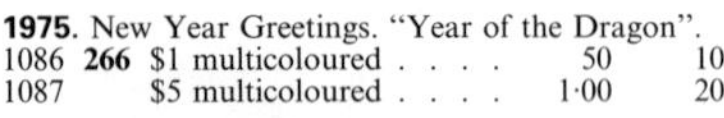

267 Techi Dam

268 Biathlon

1975. Completion of Techi Reservoir. Mult.
1088 $2 Type **267** 25 10
1089 $10 Dam and reservoir . . . 50 30

1976. Winter Olympic Games, Innsbruck. Mult.
1090 $2 Type **268** 30 10
1091 $5 Luge 40 15
1092 $8 Skiing 60 15

269 "Chin"

1976. Chinese Musical Instruments (1st series). Multicoloured.
1093 $2 Type **269** 40 10
1094 $5 "Se" (string instrument) 60 10
1095 $8 "Standing Kong-ho" (harp) 70 15
1096 $10 "Sleeping Kong-ho" (harp) 85 20
See also Nos. 1156/9.

270 Postman collecting Mail

1976. 80th Anniv of Chinese Postal Service. Multicoloured.
1097 $2 Type **270** 20 10
1098 $5 Mail-sorting systems (vert) 30 15
1099 $8 Mail transport (vert) . . . 1·00 15
1100 $10 Traditional and modern post deliveries 70 20

271 Pres. Chiang Kai-shek

1976. 1st Death Anniv of President Chiang Kai-shek. Multicoloured.
1102 $2 Type **271** 30 10
1103 $2 People paying homage (horiz) 30 10
1104 $2 Lying-in-state (horiz) . . 30 10
1105 $2 Start of funeral procession (horiz) 30 10
1106 $5 Roadside obeisance (horiz) 40 15
1107 $8 Altar, Tzuhu Guest-house (horiz) 50 20
1108 $10 Tzuhu Guest-house (horiz) 75 25

272 Chinese and U.S. Flags

273 "Kung Shou Pu" Coin (Shang/ Chou Dynasties)

1976. Bicentenary of American Revolution.
1109 **272** $2 multicoloured 20 10
1110 $10 multicoloured . . . 50 25

1976. Ancient Chinese Coins (2nd series). Mult.
1111 $2 Type **273** 50 10
1112 $5 "Chien Tsu Pu" coin (Chao Kingdom) 75 15
1113 $8 "Yuan Tsu Pu" coin (Tsin Kingdom) 90 20
1114 $10 "Fang Tsu Pu" coin (Chin/Han Dynasties) . . 1·25 25

1976. Ancient Chinese Moon-shaped Fan-paintings (3rd series) As T **252**. Multicoloured.
1115 $2 "Hibiscus" (Li Tung) . . 50 10
1116 $5 "Lilies" (Lin Chun) . . . 1·25 15
1117 $8 "Two Sika Deer, Mushrooms and Pine" (Mou Chung-fu) . . . . 1·75 30
1118 $10 "Wild Flowers and Japanese Quail" (Li An-chung) . . . . 4·75 45

1976. Ancient Bronzes (2nd series). As T **265**. Multicoloured.
1119 $2 Square cauldron 50 10
1120 $5 Round cauldron 80 10
1121 $8 Wine vessel . . . . . . 1·00 15
1122 $10 Wine vessel with legs . . 1·25 20
No. 1119 is similar to Type **265**, but has four characters at left only.

1976. Major Construction Projects (2nd series). Designs as Nos. 1020/8, but Chinese inscr in double-lined characters. Figures of value solid. Multicoloured.
1122a $1 As No. 1021 . . . . . 50 10
1122b $2 As No. 1023 . . . . . 50 10
1122c $3 As No. 1024 . . . . . 30 10
1122d $4 As No. 1026 . . . . . 30 10
1122e $5 As Type **256** 30 10
1122f $6 As No. 1025 . . . . . 40 10
1122g $7 As No. 1027 . . . . . 45 10
1122h $8 As No. 1022 . . . . . 50 15
1122i $9 As No. 1028 . . . . . 50 20
See also Nos. 1145/53.

274 Chiang Kai-shek and Mother

1976. 90th Birth Anniv of President Chiang Kai-shek. Multicoloured.
1123 $2 Type **274** 30 10
1124 $5 Chiang Kai-shek 30 15
1125 $10 Chiang Kai-shek and Dr. Sun Yat-sen in railway carriage (horiz) 85 50

275 Chinese and KMT Flags

1976. 11th Kuomintang National Congress. Mult.
1126 $2 Type **275** 20 10
1127 $10 President Chiang Kai-shek and Dr. Sun Yat-sen 40 25

276 Brazen Serpent

277 "Bird and Plum Blossom" (Ch'en Hung-shou)

1976. New Year Greetings. "Year of the Snake".
1129 **276** $1 multicoloured 60 10
1130 $5 multicoloured . . . . 1·10 10

1977. Ancient Chinese Paintings. "Three Friends of Winter".
1131 $2 Type **277** . . . . 1·00 10
1132 $8 "Wintry Days" (Yang Wei-chen) . . . . 2·25 25
1133 $10 "Rock and Bamboo" (Hsia Ch'ang) . . . . . 2·50 20

278 Black-naped Orioles

1977. Taiwan Birds. Multicoloured.
1134 $2 Type **278** . . . . 1·00 10
1135 $8 River kingfisher . . . . 1·25 50
1136 $10 Pheasant-tailed jacana 2·00 50

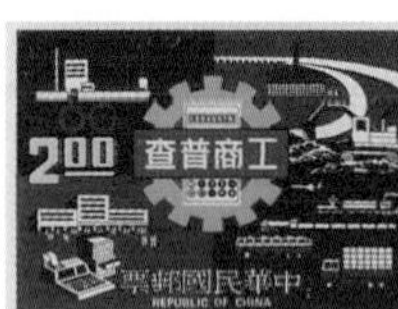
279 Emblems of Industry and Commerce

1977. Industry and Commerce Census.
1137 **279** $2 multicoloured 35 15
1138 $10 multicoloured . . . 90 35

280 "Green Mountains rising into Clouds"

1977. Madame Chiang Kai-shek's Landscape Paintings (2nd series). Multicoloured.
1139 $2 Type **280** 80 10
1140 $5 "Boat amidst Spring's Beauty" . . . . 1·00 20
1141 $8 "Scholar beside the Rivulet" . . . . 2·25 15
1142 $10 "Green Water rising to meet the Bridge" . . . . 3·00 30

281 W.A.C.L. Emblem

282 Steel Mill, Kaohsiung

1977. 10th World Anti-Communist League Conf.
1143 **281** $2 multicoloured 20 10
1144 $10 multicoloured . . . 50 15

1977. Major Construction Projects (3rd series). Designs as Nos. 1122a/i, but redrawn with double lined figures of value as in T **282**. Multicoloured.
1145 $1 Taiwan North link railway 50 10
1146 $2 TRA trunk line electrification 50 10
1147 $3 Taichung harbour (horiz) 30 10
1148 $4 Taiwan North–south highway (horiz) 25 10
1149 $5 Type **282** 35 10
1150 $6 Taoyuan international airport (horiz) 35 10
1151 $7 Giant shipyard, Kaohsiung (horiz) 40 10
1152 $8 Petrochemical works, Kaohsiung 50 10
1153 $9 Su-ao port (horiz) . . . 60 10

283 "Blood Donation"

1977. Blood Donation Movement.
1154 **283** $2 red, black and yellow 20 10
1155 – $10 red and black . . . 50 15
DESIGN—VERT: $10, "Blood Transfusion".

284 San-hsien

285 "Idea leuconoe"

1977. Chinese Musical Instruments (2nd series). Multicoloured.
1156 $2 Type **284** 40 10
1157 $5 Tung-hsiao (wind instrument) 70 10
1158 $8 Yang-chin (xylophone) 80 12
1159 $10 Pai-hsiao (pipes) 90 15

1977. Taiwan Butterflies. Multicoloured.
1160 $2 Type **285** 60 10
1161 $4 Great orange-tip 80 20
1162 $6 "Stichophthalma howqua" . . . . 1·00 25
1163 $10 "Atrophaneura horishanus" . . . . . . 1·75 15

286 "National Palace Museum"

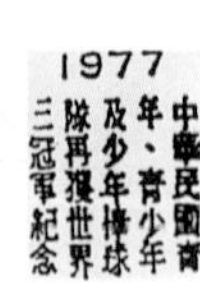
(287)

1977. Children's Drawings. Multicoloured.
1164 $1 Type **286** 15 10
1165 $2 "Festival of Sea Goddess" 25 10
1166 $4 "Boats on Lan-yu" . . . 35 10
1167 $5 "Temple" (vert) 45 10

1977. Triple Championships of the 1977 Little League World Baseball Series. Nos. 1146 and 1152 optd with Type **287**.
1168 $2 multicoloured 50 15
1169 $8 multicoloured 50 15

288 Plate

289 Lions Club Emblem

1977. Ancient Chinese Carved Lacquer Ware (1st series). Multicoloured.
1170 $2 Type **288** 60 10
1171 $5 Bowl 85 10
1172 $8 Box 85 10
1173 $10 Three-tiered box . . . . 1·00 15
See also Nos. 1206/1209.

1977. 60th Anniv of Lions International.
1174 **289** $2 multicoloured 20 10
1175 $10 multicoloured . . . 50 15

290 "Cheng" Government Standard Mark

291 Human Figure and Diagram of Heart

1977. Standardization Movement.
1176 **290** $2 multicoloured 35 10
1177 $10 multicoloured . . . 90 15

1977. Prevention of Heart Disease Campaign.
1178 **291** $2 multicoloured 20 10
1179 $10 multicoloured . . . 50 15

292 White Horse

293 First Page of Constitution

1977. New Year Greetings. "Year of the Horse". Details from "One Hundred Horses" by Lang Shih-ning (Giuseppe Castiglione). Multicoloured.
1180 $1 Type **292** 35 10
1181 $5 Two Horses (horiz) . . . 90 15

1977. 30th Anniv of Constitution. Mult.
1182 $2 Type **293** 20 10
1183 $10 President Chiang accepting constitution . . 50 20

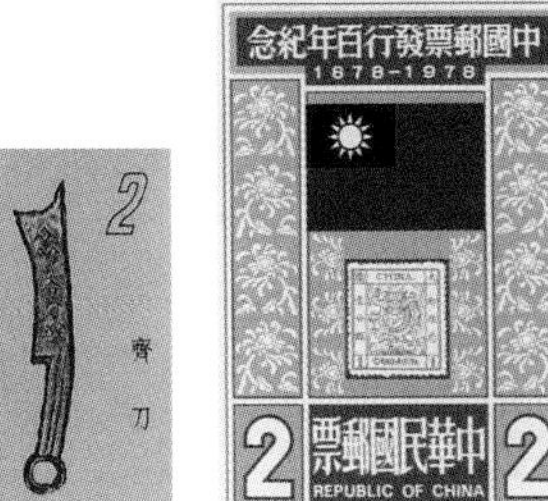
294 "Three-character" Knife (Chi State)
295 "Dragon" Stamp, 1878

1978. Ancient Chinese Coins (3rd series). Mult.
1184 $2 Type **294** 50 10
1185 $5 Longer sharp-headed knife (Yen State) 90 10
1186 $8 Sharp-headed knife (Yet State) . . . . 1·00 15
1187 $10 Chao or Ming knife . . 1·25 20

1978. Cent of Chinese Postage Stamp. Mult.
1188 $2 Type **295** 40 10
1189 $5 "Dr. Sun Yat-sen" stamp, 1941 . . . . . . 50 10
1190 $10 "Chiang Kai-shek" stamp, 1958 . . . . . . 75 20

296 Dr. Sun Yat-sen Memorial Hall

1978. "Rocpex" Taipeh 1978 Philatelic Exhibition. Multicoloured.
1192 $2 Type **296** 20 10
1193 $10 "Dragon" and 1977 "New Year" stamps . . . 75 20

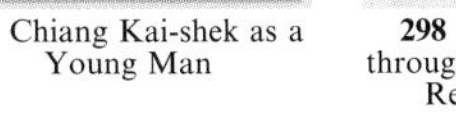

297 Chiang Kai-shek as a Young Man
298 Section through Nuclear Reactor

1978. 3rd Death Anniv of Pres. Chiang Kai-shek. Multicoloured.
1194 $2 Type **297** 25 10
1195 $5 Chiang on horseback (horiz) 40 10
1196 $8 Chiang making speech (horiz) 60 15
1197 $10 Reviewing armed forces 80 20

1978. Nuclear Power Plant.
1198 **298** $10 multicoloured . . . 60 15

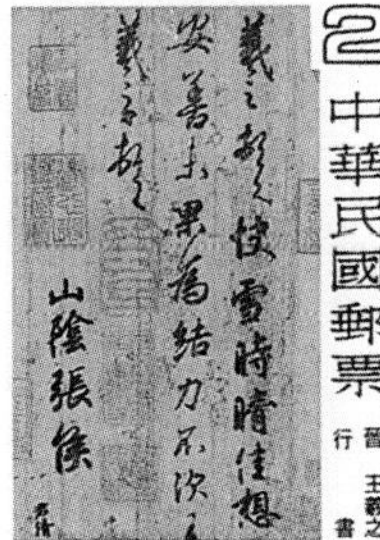
299 Letter by Wang Hsi-chih

300 Human Figure in Polluted Environment

1978. Chinese Calligraphy. Multicoloured.
1199 $2 Type **299** 60 10
1200 $4 Eulogy of Ni K'uan by Chu Sui-liang . . . . . . 1·50 15
1201 $6 Inscription on poem "Lake Tai" by Wen Cheng-ming . . . . 1·75 25
1202 $8 Autobiography by Huai-su . . . . 3·00 30
1203 $10 Poem by Ch'ang Piao 5·25 40

1978. Cancer Prevention.
1204 **300** $2 green, yellow & red 15 10
1205 $10 blue, green & dp blue 35 15

1978. Ancient Chinese Carved Lacquer Ware (2nd series). As T **288**. Multicoloured.
1206 $2 Square box 30 10
1207 $5 Box on legs 40 10
1208 $8 Round box 60 15
1209 $10 Vase (vert) 90 20

1978. Chinese Folk-tales (5th series). As T **200**. Multicoloured.
1210 $1 Tsu Ti brandishing sword 20 10
1211 $2 Pan Ch'ao throwing down pen 50 10
1212 $2 Tien Tan's "Fire Bull Battle" 75 10
1213 $5 Liang Hung-yu as army drummer . . . . 1·10 10

1978. Triple Championships of the Little League World Baseball Series. Nos. 1148 and 1150 optd as T **287**, but with four lines of characters and dated 1978.
1214 $4 Taiwan North–south highway 20 15
1215 $6 Taoyuan international airport 40 25

302 Yellow Orange-tip

1978. Taiwan Butterflies. Multicoloured.
1216 $2 Type **302** 30 10
1217 $4 Two-brand crow 70 10
1218 $6 Common map butterfly 1·10 15
1219 $10 "Atrophaneura polyeuctes" . . . . 1·10 25

303 Jamboree Badge, Camp and Scout Salute

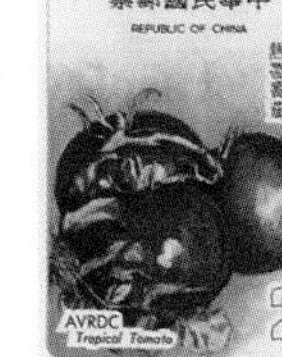
304 Tropical Tomatoes

1978. Taiwanese Boy Scouts' 5th Jamboree.
1220 **303** $2 multicoloured 40 10
1221 $10 multicoloured . . . 60 20

1978. Asian Vegetable Research and Development Centre. Multicoloured.
1222 $2 Type **304** 40 10
1223 $10 Tropical tomatoes (different) 85 25

305 Aerial View of Bridge

306 National Flag

1978. Opening of the Sino-Saudi Bridge. Mult.
1224 $2 Type **305** 50 10
1225 $6 Close-up of bridge . . . 90 15

1978.
1226 **306** $1 red and blue 15 10
1377 $1 red and blue 20 10
1378 $1.50 red, blue & yellow 45 10
1227 $2 red and blue 15 10
1379 $2 red, blue and yellow 20 10
1297 $3 red, blue and green 35 10
1380 $3 red and blue 30 10
1298 $4 red, blue and brown 30 15
1381 $4 red, blue and light blue 30 10
1228 $5 red, blue and green 30 10
1382 $5 red, blue and brown 30 10
1229 $6 red, blue and orange 40 10
1300 $7 red, blue and brown 40 10
1384 $7 red, blue and green 50 10
1230 $8 red, blue and green 45 10
1385 $8 red, blue & deep red 45 10
1386 $9 red, blue and green 60 10
1231 $10 red, blue and lt blue 75 15
1387 $10 red, blue and violet 55 10
1302 $12 red, blue and mauve 60 25
1389 $14 red, blue and green 1·25 10

The $1 values differ in the face value, which is printed in colour on No. 1226, whilst on No. 1377 it is white.

Nos. 1377/8, 1379, 1380, 1381, 1382 and the $6 to $14 values are as Type **306** but have solid background panel to face value and inscr.

307 "Imitation of the Three Sheep by Emperor Hsuan-tsung of the Ming Dynasty" (Emperor Kao-tsung)

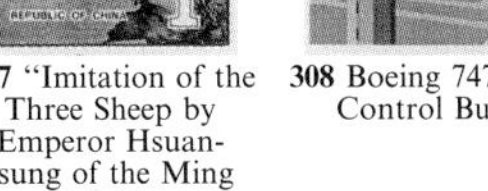
308 Boeing 747-100 and Control Building

1978. New Year Greetings. "Year of the Sheep".
1232 **307** $1 multicoloured 50 10
1233 $5 multicoloured 80 15

1978. Completion of Taoyuan International Airport. Multicoloured.
1234 $2 Type **308** 35 10
1235 $10 Passenger terminal building (horiz) 60 25

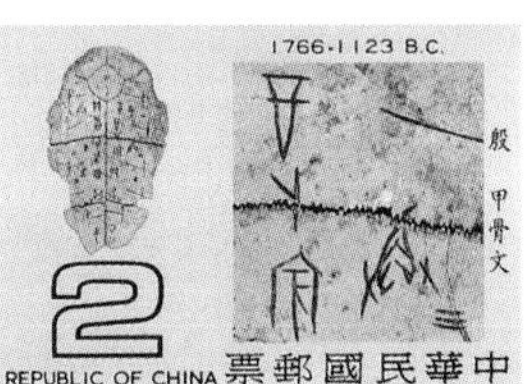
309 Oracle Bones and Inscription (Yin Dynasty)

1979. Origin and Development of Chinese Characters. Multicoloured.
1236 $2 Type **309** 60 10
1237 $5 "Leh-chi" cauldron and inscription (Spring and Autumn period) . . . . . 1·00 15
1238 $8 Engraved seal and seal-style characters (Western Han dynasty) . . . . . . 1·40 25
1239 $10 Square plain-style characters inscribed on stone (Eastern Han dynasty) . . . . 2·50 45

310 Chihkan Tower, Tainan

1979. Tourism. Multicoloured.
1240 $2 Type **310** 35 10
1241 $5 Confucius Temple, Tainan 35 15
1242 $8 Koxinga Shrine, Tainan 35 25
1243 $10 Eternal Castle, Tainan 1·50 30

311/314 "Children Playing Games on a Winter Day" (⅔-size illustration)

1979. Sung Dynasty Painting.
1244 **311** $5 multicoloured . . . . 2·25 65
1245 **312** $5 multicoloured . . . . 2·25 65
1246 **313** $5 multicoloured . . . . 2·25 65
1247 **314** $5 multicoloured . . . . 2·25 65

Nos. 1244/7 were printed together, se-tenant, forming the composite design illustrated.

315 Lu Hao-tung (revolutionary)

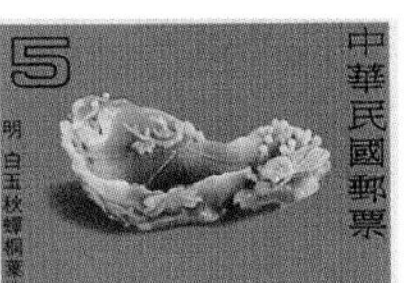
316 White Jade Brush Washer (Ming dynasty)

1979. Famous Chinese.
1249 **315** $2 blue 40 10

1979. Ancient Chinese Jade (1st series). Multicoloured.
1250 $2 Yellow jade brush holder embossed with clouds and dragons (Sung dynasty) (vert) 35 10
1251 $5 Type **316** 80 15
1252 $8 Dark green jade brush washer carved with clouds and dragons (Ch'ing dynasty) 95 20
1253 $10 Bluish jade washer in shape of lotus (Ch'ing dynasty) . . . . 1·40 25

See also Nos. 1291/4.

317 Plum Blossom

318 Houses

1979.
1254a **317** $10 blue 40 10
1255a $20 brown 80 10
1255ba $40 red . . . . 1·60 10
1256a $50 green . . . . . . 2·00 10
1257 $100 red . . . . . . 3·50 10
1257b $300 red and violet . . 14·00 2·00
1257c $500 red and brown 23·00 4·75

The $300 and $500 are size 25 × 33 mm.

1979. Environmental Protection. Mult.
1258 $2 Type **318** 15 10
1259 $10 Rural scene (horiz) . . 55 25

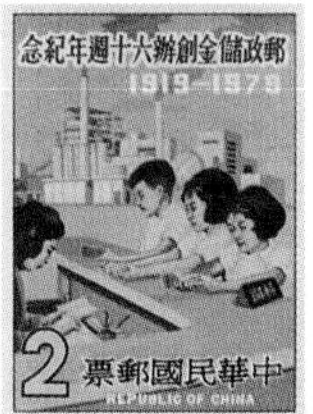
319 Savings Bank Counter

1979. 60th Anniv of Postal Savings Bank. Multicoloured.
1260 $2 Type **319** 20 10
1261 $5 Savings bank queue . . . 30 15
1262 $8 Computer and savings book (horiz) 45 20
1263 $10 Money box and "tree" emblem (horiz) 60 25

320 Steere's Liocichla

1979. Birds. Multicoloured.
1264 $2 Swinhoe's pheasant . . . 50 10
1265 $8 Type **320** . . . . 1·25 40
1266 $10 Formosan yuhina . . . 2·00 60

321 Sir Rowland Hill **322** Jar with Rope Pattern

1979. Death Centenary of Sir Rowland Hill.
1267 **321** $10 multicoloured . . . 75 25

1979. Ancient Chinese Pottery. Multicoloured.
1268 $2 Type **322** (Shang dynasty) 30 10
1269 $5 Two handled jar (Shang dynasty) 65 15
1270 $8 Red jar with "ears" (Han dynasty) . . . . 1·00 20
1271 $10 Green glazed jar (Han dynasty) . . . . 1·50 25

323 Children and I.Y.C. Emblem **324** "Trees on a Winter Plain" (Li Ch'eng)

1979. International Year of the Child.
1272 **323** $2 multicoloured 25 10
1273 $10 multicoloured . . . 50 25

1979. Ancient Chinese Paintings. Mult.
1274 $2 Type **324** (Sung dynasty) 60 10
1275 $5 "Bamboo" (Wen T'ung, Sung dynasty) . . . . . 1·60 15
1276 $8 "Old Tree, Bamboo and Rock" (Chao Mengfu, Yuan dynasty) . . . . . 2·40 20
1277 $10 "Twin Pines" (Li K'an, Yuan dynasty) . . . . . 3·50 25

325 Taiwan Macaque **326** Competition Emblem and Symbols of Ten Trades

1979. New Year Greetings. "Year of the Monkey".
1278 **325** $1 multicoloured 75 10
1279 $6 multicoloured . . . . 1·00 25

1979. 10th National Vocational Training Competition, Taichung.
1280 **326** $2 multicoloured 20 10
1281 $10 multicoloured . . . 50 25

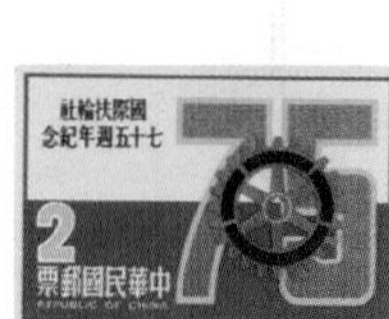
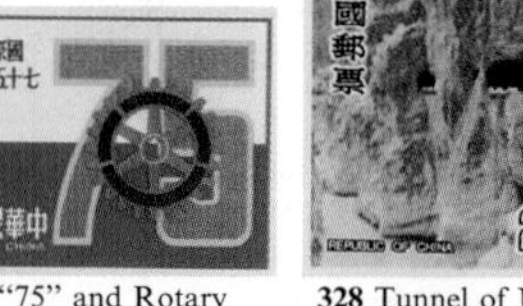
327 "75" and Rotary Emblem **328** Tunnel of Nine Turns

1980. 75th Anniv of Rotary International. Mult.
1282 $2 Type **327** 25 10
1283 $12 Anniversary emblem and symbols of Rotary's services (vert) 50 25

1980. Tourism. Scenic Spots on the East–West Cross-Island Highway. Multicoloured.
1284 $2 Type **328** 25 10
1285 $8 Mt. Hohuan (horiz) . . . 50 15
1286 $12 Bridge, Tien Hsiang . . 1·00 30

329 Shih Chien-ju (hero of revolution) **330** Chung-cheng Memorial Hall

1980. Famous Chinese.
1287 **329** $2 brown 25 10

1980. 5th Death Anniv of Chiang Kai-shek. Multicoloured.
1288 $2 Type **330** 20 10
1289 $8 Quotation of Chiang Kai-shek 40 15
1290 $12 Bronze statue of Chiang Kai-shek 50 30

1980. Ancient Chinese Jade (2nd series). As T **316**. Multicoloured.
1291 $2 Kuang (cup) decorated with dragons (Sung dynasty) (vert) 50 10
1292 $5 Dark green jade melon-shaped brush washer (Ming dynasty) 90 15
1293 $8 Bluish jade Po Monk's alms bowl (Ch'ing dynasty) . . . . 1·10 20
1294 $10 Yellow jade brush washer (Ch'ing dynasty) 1·40 25

331 Tzu-Ch'iang Squadron over Presidential Mansion

1980. Air. Multicoloured.
1303 $5 Type **331** 35 10
1304 $7 Boeing 747-100 airliner and insignia of CAL (state airline) 75 20
1305 $12 National Flag and Boeing 747-100 . . . . . 90 30

332 "Wasted Resources" **333** Military Official

1980. Energy Conservation.
1306 **332** $2 multicoloured 20 10
1307 $12 multicoloured . . . 50 30

1980. T'ang Dynasty Tri-coloured Pottery. Multicoloured.
1308 $2 Type **333** 70 10
1309 $5 Chickens . . . . 1·25 10
1310 $8 Horse . . . . 1·60 20
1311 $10 Camel . . . . 1·50 25

1980. Chinese Folk-tales (6th series). As T **200**. Multicoloured.
1312 $1 Grinding mortar into a needle 20 10
1313 $2 Returning lost articles . . 30 10
1314 $2 Wen Tien-hsiang in prison 55 10
1315 $5 Sending coal to poor during snow 75 15

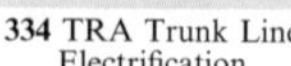
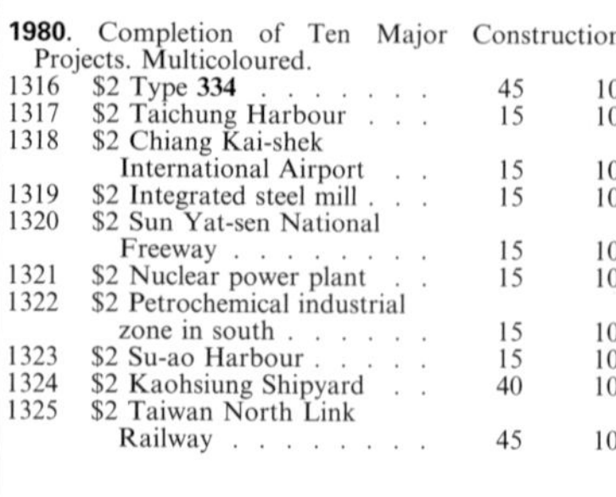
334 TRA Trunk Line Electrification **335** Money Boxes within Ancient Chinese Coin

1980. Completion of Ten Major Construction Projects. Multicoloured.
1316 $2 Type **334** 45 10
1317 $2 Taichung Harbour . . . 15 10
1318 $2 Chiang Kai-shek International Airport . . 15 10
1319 $2 Integrated steel mill . . . 15 10
1320 $2 Sun Yat-sen National Freeway 15 10
1321 $2 Nuclear power plant . . 15 10
1322 $2 Petrochemical industrial zone in south 15 10
1323 $2 Su-ao Harbour 15 10
1324 $2 Kaohsiung Shipyard . . 40 10
1325 $2 Taiwan North Link Railway 45 10

1980. 10th National Savings Day. Mult.
1327 $2 Type **335** 20 10
1328 $12 Hand placing coin in money box 45 25

336/339 Landscape (⅗-size illustration)

1980. Painting by Ch'iu Ying.
1329 **336** $5 multicoloured . . . . 2·25 20
1330 **337** $5 multicoloured . . . . 2·25 20
1331 **338** $5 multicoloured . . . . 2·25 20
1332 **339** $5 multicoloured . . . . 2·25 20
Nos. 1329/32 were printed together, se-tenant, forming the composite design illustrated.

340 Cock **341** Heads, Flag and Census Form

1980. New Year Greetings. "Year of the Cock".
1334 **340** $1 multicoloured 75 10
1335 $6 multicoloured . . . . 2·00 25
See also No. 2047.

1980. Population and Housing Census. Mult.
1337 $2 Type **341** 20 10
1338 $12 Flag and buildings (horiz) 50 30

342 Central Weather Bureau

1981. Completion of Meteorological Satellite Ground Station, Taipei. Multicoloured.
1339 $2 "TIROS-N" weather satellite (vert) 20 10
1340 $10 Type **342** 50 30

343 "Happiness"

344 "Wealth"

345 "Longevity"

346 "Joy"

1981. New Year Calligraphy.
1341 **343** $5 gold, red and black 90 25
1342 **344** $5 gold, red and black 90 25
1343 **345** $5 gold, red and black 90 25
1344 **346** $5 gold, red and black 90 25

347 Candle and Siamese Twins

1981. International Year for Disabled Persons.
1345 **347** $2 multicoloured 20 10
1346 $10 multicoloured . . . 50 30

348 Mt. Ali

1981. Tourism. Multicoloured.
1347 $2 Type **348** 30 10
1348 $7 Oluanpi 55 15
1349 $12 Sun Moon Lake . . . . 1·00 25

349 "Children on River Bank"

1981. Children's Day. Children's Drawings. Mult.
1350 $1 Type **349** 15 10
1351 $2 "Cable-cars" 20 10
1352 $5 "Lobsters" 30 10
1353 $7 "Village" 40 15

350 Main Gate Chiang Kai-shek Memorial Hall

1981. 6th Death Anniv of Chiang Kai-shek.
1712 **350** 10c. red 10 10
1354 20c. violet 10 10
1714 30c. green 10 10
1355 40c. red 10 10
1356 50c. brown 10 10
1717 60c. blue 10 10

351 Brush Washer (Hsuan-te ware)

352 Electric and First Steam Locomotives

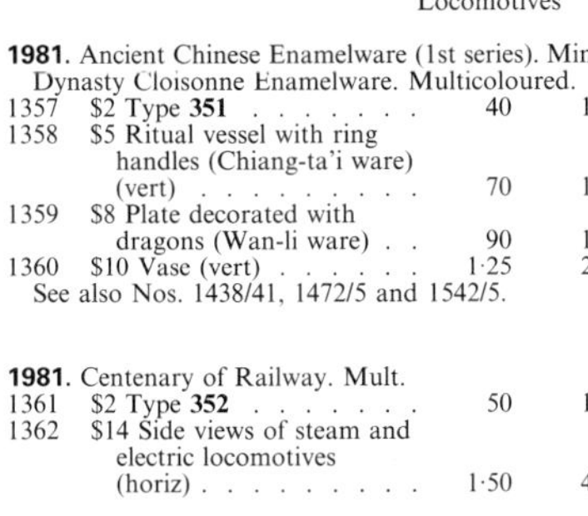

1981. Ancient Chinese Enamelware (1st series). Ming Dynasty Cloisonne Enamelware. Multicoloured.
1357 $2 Type **351** 40 10
1358 $5 Ritual vessel with ring handles (Chiang-ta'i ware) (vert) 70 10
1359 $8 Plate decorated with dragons (Wan-li ware) . . 90 10
1360 $10 Vase (vert) . . . . . . 1·25 25
See also Nos. 1438/41, 1472/5 and 1542/5.

1981. Centenary of Railway. Mult.
1361 $2 Type **352** 50 10
1362 $14 Side views of steam and electric locomotives (horiz) . . . . 1·50 40

353 "Liagore rubromaculata"

1981. Crabs. Multicoloured.
1363 $2 Type **353** 20 10
1364 $5 "Ranina ranina" (vert) 40 10
1365 $8 "Platymaia wyvillethomsoni" 55 15
1366 $14 "Lambrus nummifera" (vert) . . . . 1·00 35

354 Bureau Emblem

355 The Cowherd

1981. 40th Anniv of Central Weather Bureau.
1367 **354** $2 multicoloured 20 10
1368 $14 multicoloured . . . 75 35

1981. Fairy Tales. "The Cowherd and the Weaving Maid". Multicoloured.
1369 $2 Type **355** 50 10
1370 $4 The cowherd watching the weaving maid through rushes 60 10
1371 $8 The cowherd and the weaving maid on opposite sides of Heavenly River 1·00 15
1372 $14 The cowherd and the weaving maid meeting on bridge of magpies . . . . 2·10 35

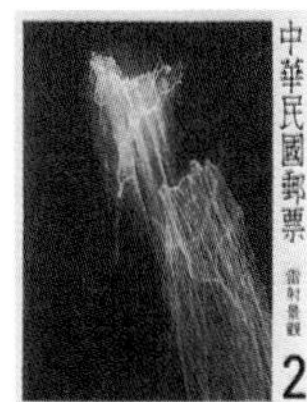

356 Laser Display

1981. Lasography Exhibition. Designs showing different laser displays.
1373 **356** $2 multicoloured 20 10
1374 – $5 multicoloured 30 10
1375 – $8 multicoloured 40 15
1376 – $14 multicoloured . . . 90 40

357 Goalkeeper catching Ball

359 Chinese Republic Anniv Emblem and "Stamps"

358 Officers watching Battle from Mound

1981. Athletics Day. Multicoloured.
1390 $5 Women soccer players 20 10
1391 $5 Type **357** 20 10

1981. 70th Anniv of Founding of Chinese Republic. Multicoloured.
1392 $2 Type **358** 15 10
1393 $2 Officer clenching fist and soldiers awaiting battle . . 15 10
1394 $2 Officer on horseback saluting 15 10
1395 $2 Attacking buildings . . . 15 10
1396 $3 Attacking fortifications 35 10
1397 $3 Dockside scene 60 20
1398 $8 Chiang Kai-shek 60 10
1399 $14 Sun Yat-sen 90 15

1981. "Rocpex Taipei '81" International Stamp Exhibition.
1401 **359** $2 multicoloured 15 10
1402 $14 multicoloured . . . 50 35

360 Detail of Scroll

1981. Sung Dynasty painting "One Hundred Young Boys". Designs showing details of Scroll.
1403 **360** $2 (1) multicoloured . . 1·90 25
1404 – $2 (2) multicoloured . . 1·90 25
1405 – $2 (3) multicoloured . . 1·90 25
1406 – $2 (4) multicoloured . . 1·90 25
1407 – $2 (5) multicoloured . . 1·90 25
1408 – $2 (6) multicoloured . . 1·90 25
1409 – $2 (7) multicoloured . . 1·90 25
1410 – $2 (8) multicoloured . . 1·90 25
1411 – $2 (9) multicoloured . . 1·90 25
1412 – $2 (10) multicoloured . . 1·90 25
See note below No. 661 on identification of designs.
Nos. 1403/12 were printed together in se-tenant blocks of ten (5 × 2) within the sheet, each strip of five forming a composite design.

361 Dog

362 Information-using Services and Emblem

1981. New Year Greetings. "Year of the Dog".
1413 **361** $1 multicoloured . . . . 1·00 10
1414 $10 multicoloured . . . 1·75 25
See also No. 2048.

1981. Information Week.
1416 **362** $2 multicoloured 25 10

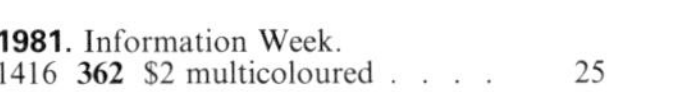

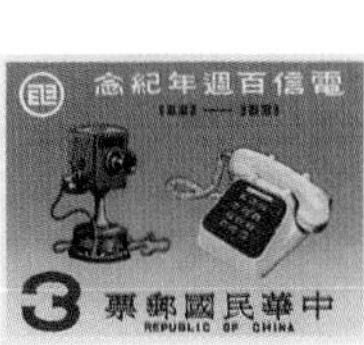

363 Telephones of 1881 and 1981

364 Arrangement in Basket

1981. Centenary of Chinese Telecommunications Service. Multicoloured.
1417 $2 Map and hand holding telephone handset (vert) 20 10
1418 $3 Type **363** 30 10
1419 $8 Submarine cable map . . 45 10
1420 $18 Computer and telecommunication units (vert) 65 20

1982. Chinese Flower Arrangements. Mult.
1421 $2 Type **364** 25 10
1422 $3 Arrangement in jug . . . 40 10
1423 $8 Arrangement in vase . . 75 10
1424 $18 Arrangement in holder 1·25 20

365 Kuan Yu leaves for Cheng City

1982. Scenes from "The Ku Cheng Reunion" (opera). Multicoloured.
1425 $2 Type **365** 55 10
1426 $3 Chang Fei refuses to open city gates 70 10
1427 $4 Chang Fei apologises to Kuan Yu 90 10
1428 $18 Liu Pei, Kuan Yu and Chang Fei are reunited 1·75 30

366 Dr. Robert Koch and Tubercle Bacillus

367 Chang Shih-liang (revolutionary)

1982. Centenary of Discovery of Tubercle Bacillus.
1429 **366** $2 multicoloured 15 10

1982. Famous Chinese.
1430 **367** $2 red 15 10

368 "Martyrs' Shrine"

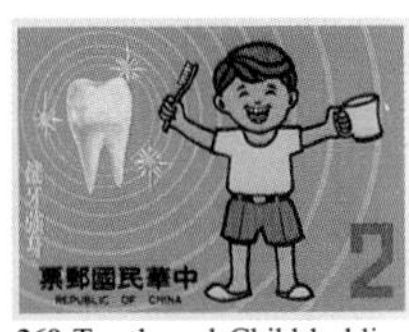

369 Tooth and Child holding Toothbrush and Mug

1982. Children's Day. Children's paintings.
1431 $2 Type **368** 30 10
1432 $3 "House Yard" 45 10
1433 $5 "Cattle Herd" 60 10
1434 $8 "A Sacrificial Ceremony for a Plentiful Year" . . . 90 10

1982. Dental Health. Multicoloured.
1435 $2 Type **369** 25 10
1436 $3 Methods of cleaning teeth 45 10
1437 $10 Dental check-up 85 10

1982. Ancient Chinese Enamelware (2nd series). As T **351**. Multicoloured.
1438 $2 Champleve cup and plate (Ch'ien-lung ware) 45 10
1439 $5 Cloisonne duck container (Ch'ien-lung ware) (vert) 60 10
1440 $8 Painted incense burner (K'ang-hsi period) . . . . 1·10 10
1441 $12 Cloisonne Tibetan lama milk-tea pot (Ch'ien-lung ware) (vert) . . . . . . 1·75 15

370 "Spring Dawn" (Meng Hao-jan)

1982. Chinese Classical Poetry (1st series). Tang Dynasty Poems. Multicoloured.
1442 $2 Type **370** . . . . 1·50 10
1443 $3 "On Looking for a Hermit and not Finding Him" (Chia Tao) . . . . 3·25 10
1444 $5 "Summer Dying" (Liu Yu-hsi) . . . . 6·75 10
1445 $18 "Looking at the Snow Drifts on South Mountains" (Tsu Yung) 7·50 55
See also Nos. 1476/9, 1524/7, 1594/7, 1866/9, 1910/13 and 2074/7.

371 Softball

1982. 5th World Women's Softball Championship, Taipeh.
1446 **371** $2 multicoloured 40 10
1447 $18 multicoloured . . . 85 20

372 Scouts on Rope Bridge, and Lord Baden-Powell

1982. 75th Anniv of Boy Scout Movement and 125th Birth Anniv of Lord Baden-Powell. Multicoloured.
1448 $2 Type **372** 25 10
1449 $18 Emblem, scouts making frame and camp 80 15

373 Tweezers holding Stamp

374 Carved Lion

1982. Philately Day. Multicoloured.
1450 $2 Type **373** 40 10
1451 $18 Examining stamp album with magnifying glass . . 80 20

1982. Tsu Shih Temple, Sanhsia. Multicoloured.
1452 $2 Type **374** 40 10
1453 $3 Lion brackets (horiz) . . 50 10
1454 $5 Carved sub-lintels in passageway 75 10
1455 $18 Temple roofs (horiz) . . 1·75 20

1982. Chinese Folk-tales (7th series). Stories from "36 Examples of Filial Piety" by Wu Yen-huan, As T **200**. Multicoloured.
1456 $1 Shao K'ang supporting his mother 25 10
1457 $2 Hsun Kuan leading soldier reinforcements to her father 45 10
1458 $3 Ku Yen-wu refusing to serve Ch'ing dynasty . . . 60 10
1459 $5 Ting Ch'un-liang caring for his paralysed father 1·00 10

375 Riding Horses

1982. 30th Anniv of China Youth Corps. Multicoloured.
1460 $2 Type **375** 10 10
1461 $3 Flag and water sport (vert) 15 10
1462 $18 Mountaineering 50 20

376 Lohan with Boy Attendant and Monkey

378 Pig

1982. Lohan (Buddhist Saint) Scroll Paintings by Liu Sung-nien. Multicoloured.
1463 $2 Type **376** . . . . 1·50 10
1464 $3 Monk presenting seated Lohan with scroll . . . . 2·00 10
1465 $18 Tribal king paying homage to seated Lohan 5·00 40

1982. New Year. "Year of the Pig".
1468 **378** $1 multicoloured . . . . 1·25 10
1469 $10 multicoloured . . . 2·25 25
See also No. 2049.

1983. Ancient Chinese Enamelware (3rd series). Ch'ing Dynasty Enamelware. As T **351**. Multicoloured.
1472 $2 Square basin with rounded corners 25 10
1473 $3 Vase decorated with landscape panels (vert) . . 75 10

1474 $4 Blue teapot with flower pattern . . . . 1·25 10
1475 $18 Cloisonne elephant with vase on back (vert) . . . 1·40 20

379 "Wan-hsi-sha" (Yen Shu)

380 Hsin-hsien Concealed Fall, Wawa Valley

1983. Chinese Classical Poetry (2nd series). Sung Dynasty Lyrical Poems. Multicoloured.
1476 $2 Type **379** . . . . 2·50 10
1477 $3 "Ch'ing-yu-an" (Ho Chu) 3·75 10
1478 $5 "Su-mu-che" (Fan Chung-yen) . . . . . . 4·50 10
1479 $11 "Hsing-hsiang-tzu" (Ch'ao Pu-chih) . . . . . 7·00 25

1983. Landscapes. Multicoloured.
1480 $2 Type **380** 75 10
1481 $3 University Pond, Chitou Forest 90 10
1482 $18 Mount Jade (horiz) . . 1·10 20

381 Matteo Ricci and Astrolabe

1983. 400th Anniv of Matteo Ricci's (missionary) Arrival in China. Multicoloured.
1483 $2 Type **381** 35 10
1484 $18 Matteo Ricci and Great Wall 70 20

382 Wu Ching-heng (Chairman of development committee)

383 Hsu Hsien meets Pai Su-chen

1983. 70th Anniv of Mandarin Phonetic Symbols. Multicoloured.
1485 $2 Type **382** 35 10
1486 $18 Children studying symbols 70 25

1983. Fairy Tales. "Lady White Snake". Multicoloured.
1487 $2 Type **383** 40 10
1488 $3 Pai Su-chen steals Tree of Life 50 10
1489 $3 Confrontation with Fahai at Chin Shan Temple . . 1·00 10
1490 $18 Pai Su-chen is imprisoned beneath Thunder Peak Pagoda . . 2·25 30

384 Pot with Cord Pattern

385 Communication Emblems circling Globe

1983. Ancient Chinese Bamboo Carvings. Multicoloured.
1491 $2 Type **384** 40 10
1492 $3 Vase with Tao-t'ien motif 75 10
1493 $4 Carved mountain scene with figures 75 10
1494 $18 Brush-holder with relief showing ladies . . . . . 1·50 20

1983. World Communications Year. Mult.
1495 $2 Type **385** 75 10
1496 $18 W.C.Y. emblem 90 20

386 Grouper

387 T.V. Screen, Antenna and Radio Waves

1983. Protection of Fishery Resources. Mult.
1497 $2 Type **386** 40 10
1498 $18 Lizardfish . . . . . . 1·00 25

1983. Journalists' Day.
1499 **387** $2 multicoloured 15 10

388 Yurt

389 Brown Shrike

1983. Mongolian and Tibetan Scenes.
1500 $2 Type **388** 40 10
1501 $3 Potala Palace 65 10
1502 $5 Sheep on prairie 80 10
1503 $11 Camel caravan . . . . 1·10 20

1983. 2nd East Asian Bird Protection Conference. Multicoloured.
1504 $2 Type **389** 75 10
1505 $18 Grey-faced buzzard-eagle . . . . 1·00 40

390 Pink Plum Blossom

391 Congress Emblem

1983. Plum Blossom. Multicoloured.
1506 $2 Type **390** 15 10
1507 $3 Red plum blossom . . . 20 10
1508 $5 Plum blossom and pagoda 45 15
1509 $11 White plum blossom . . 1·00 15

1983. 38th Jaycees International World Congress. Multicoloured.
1510 $2 Type **391** 25 10
1511 $18 Emblems and globe . . 80 20

392 World Map as Heart

393 Rat

1983. 8th Asian-Pacific Cardiology Congress. Mult.
1512 $2 Type **392** 25 10
1513 $18 Heart and electrocardiogram 80 20

1983. New Year. "Year of the Rat".
1514 **393** $1 multicoloured 85 10
1515 $10 multicoloured . . . 2·00 20
See also No. 2038.

394 Mother and Child reading and Chin Ting Prize

1983. National Reading Week. Mult.
1517 $2 Type **394** 20 10
1518 $18 Chin Ting prize (for outstanding publications) books and father and son reading (vert) 80 20

395 Boeing 737 over Chiang Kai-shek Airport

396 Soldiers with Flags

1984. Air. 37th Anniv of Civil Aeronautics Administration. Multicoloured.
1519 $7 Type **395** 35 15
1520 $11 Boeing 747 over Chung-cheng Memorial Hall (horiz) 50 15
1521 $18 Boeing 737 over Sun Yat-sen Memorial Hall (horiz) 65 20

1984. World Freedom Day. Multicoloured.
1522 $2 Type **396** 20 10
1523 $18 Globe and people of the world 80 20

397 "Hsiao-liang-chou" (Kuan Yun-shih)

1984. Chinese Classical Poetry (3rd series). Yuan Dynasty Lyric Poems. Multicoloured.
1524 $2 Type **397** . . . . 3·00 20
1525 $3 "A Lady holds a fine fan of silk", "Tien-ching-sha" (Po P'u) . . . . 4·50 25
1526 $5 "Picnic under banana leaves "Ch'ing-chiang-yin" (Chang Ko-chin) . . . . 5·00 25
1527 $18 "Plum blossoms in the snowbound wilderness "Tien-ching-sha" (Shang Cheng-shu) . . . . 12·50 1·40

398 Forest Scene

400 Lin Chueh-min (revolutionary)

1984. Forest Resources. Multicoloured.
1528 $2 Type **398** 35 10
1529 $2 Reservoir and dam . . . 35 10
1530 $2 Camp in forest 35 10
1531 $2 Wooded slopes 35 10
Nos. 1528/31 were printed together se-tenant, forming a composite design.

1984. Famous Chinese.
1536 **400** $2 green 15 10

401 Agency Emblem and Broadcasting Equipment

402 "Five Auspicious Tokens"

1984. 60th Anniv of Central News Agency. Mult.
1537 $2 Type **401** 15 10
1538 $10 Agency emblem and satellite communications 45 15

1984. 85th Birth Anniv of Chang Ta-chien (artist). Multicoloured.
1539 $2 Type **402** . . . . 1·75 10
1540 $5 "The God of Longevity" 2·25 15
1541 $18 "Lotus Blossoms in Ink Splash" . . . . 5·00 40

1984. Ancient Chinese Enamelware (4th series). Ch'ing Dynasty Enamelware. As T **351**. Mult.
1542 $2 Lidded cup and teapot on tray 20 10
1543 $3 Cloisonne wine vessel on phoenix (vert) 50 10
1544 $4 Yellow teapot with pink and blue chrysanthemum decoration 75 15
1545 $18 Cloisonne candle-holder on bird . . . . 1·50 40

403 Boeing 747-200 circling Globe

1984. Inauguration of China Airlines Global Service. Multicoloured.
1546 $2 Type **403** 20 10
1547 $7 Globe and Boeing 747-200 . . . . 60 20
1548 $11 Boeing 747-200 over New York 85 30
1549 $18 Boeing 747-200 over Netherlands . . . . . . 1·50 55

404 Judo

1984. Olympic Games, Los Angeles. Mult.
1550 $2 Type **404** 15 10
1551 $5 Archery (vert) 35 15
1552 $18 Swimming . . . . . . 1·00 60

405 Container Ship "Ming Comfort"

406 "Gentiana arisanensis"

1984. 30th Navigation Day. Multicoloured.
1553 $2 Type **405** 45 10
1554 $18 "Prosperity" (tanker) 1·00 65

1984. Alpine Plants. Multicoloured.
1555 $2 Type **406** 35 10
1556 $3 "Epilobium nankotaiza nense" 55 10
1557 $5 "Adenophora uehatae" 80 15
1558 $18 "Aconitum fukutomei" 2·25 25

407 Scholars listening to Music

408 Volleyball Players

1984. Sung Dynasty Painting "The Eighteen Scholars". Multicoloured.
1559 $2 Type **407** . . . . 1·25 10
1560 $3 Scholars playing chess . . 2·75 10
1561 $5 Scholars writing . . . . 1·50 15
1562 $18 Scholars painting . . . 6·00 65

1984. Athletics Day. Multicoloured.
1563 $5 Type **408** 25 15
1564 $5 Volleyball player 25 15
Nos. 1563/4 were printed together, se-tenant, forming a composite design.

409 Union Emblem

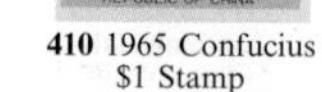
410 1965 Confucius $1 Stamp

1984. 20th Anniv of Asian-Pacific Parliamentarians' Union.
1565 **409** $10 multicoloured 50 25

1984. New Postal Museum Building, Taipeh. Multicoloured.
1566 $2 Type **410** 10 10
1567 $5 1933 Sun Yat-sen 5c. stamp 25 15
1568 $18 New Postal Museum building 1·40 65

411 Flag and Emblem

412 Commission Services

1984. Grand Alliance for China's Reunification Convention.
1570 **411** $2 multicoloured 30 10

1984. 30th Anniv of Vocational Assistance Commission for Retired Servicemen.
1571 **412** $2 multicoloured 30 10

413 Pine Tree

414 Ox

1984. Pine, Bamboo and Plum (1st series). Multicoloured.
1572 $2 Type **413** 20 10
1573 $8 Bamboo 60 20
1574 $10 Plum blossom 60 20
See also Nos. 1633/5, 1783/5 and 1845/7.

1984. New Year Greetings. "Year of the Ox".
1575 **414** $1 multicoloured 1·00 10
1576 $10 multicoloured 2·00 20
See also No. 2039.

415 Legal Code Book and Scales

416 Ku-kang Lake and Pagoda, Quemoy

1985. Judicial Day.
1578 **415** $5 multicoloured 50 15

1985. Scenery of Quemoy and Matsu. Mult.
1579 $2 Type **416** 15 10
1580 $5 Kuang-hai stone, Quemoy 45 15
1581 $8 Sheng-li reservoir, Matsu 1·50 20
1582 $10 Tung-chu lighthouse, Matsu 1·50 20

417 Sir Robert Hart and 1878 3c. Stamp

418 Lo Fu-hsing

1985. 150th Anniv of Sir Robert Hart (founder of Chinese Postal Service).
1583 **417** $2 multicoloured 30 10

1985. Birth Centenary of Lo Fu-hsing (patriot).
1584 **418** $2 multicoloured 30 10

419 Tsou Jung

421 Lily

420 Main Gate, Chung-cheng Memorial Hall

1985. 80th Death Anniv of Tsou Jung (revolutionary).
1585 **419** $3 green 35 10

1985. 10th Death Anniv of President Chiang Kai-shek. Multicoloured.
1586 $2 Type **420** 15 10
1587 $8 Tzuhu, President Chiang's temporary resting place 60 20
1588 $10 President Chiang Kai-shek (vert) 80 20

1985. Mothers' Day. Multicoloured.
1589 $2 Type **421** 25 10
1590 $2 Carnation 25 10

422 View of Tunnel

423 Girl Guide saluting

1985. 1st Anniv of Kaohsiung Cross-harbour Tunnel.
1591 **422** $5 multicoloured 60 15

1985. 75th Anniv of Girl Guide Movement.
1592 **423** $2 multicoloured 10 10
1593 $18 multicoloured 80 25

424 "Buxom is the Peach Tree..."

1985. Chinese Classical Poetry (4th series). Poems from "Book of Odes", edited by Confucius. Multicoloured.
1594 $2 Type **424** 75 10
1595 $5 "Thick grows that tarragon ..." 1·50 15
1596 $8 "Thick grow the rush leaves ..." 2·25 20
1597 $10 "... The snowflakes fly" 3·25 20

425 Wax Jambo

1985. Fruit. Multicoloured.
1598 $2 Type **425** 50 10
1599 $3 Guavas 75 10
1600 $5 Carambolas 90 15
1601 $8 Lychees 1·50 20

426 Dragon Boat

427 Lady of Rank, T'ang Dynasty

1985. Ch'ing Dynasty Ivory Carvings. Mult.
1602 $2 Type **426** 65 10
1603 $3 Carved landscape 75 10
1604 $5 Melon-shaped water container 1·25 15
1605 $18 Brush-holder (vert) 1·50 35

1985. 4th Asian Costume Conference. Chinese Costumes (1st series). Multicoloured.
1606 $2 Type **427** 85 10
1607 $5 Palace woman, Sung dynasty 90 10
1608 $8 Lady of rank, Yuan dynasty 1·60 20
1609 $11 Lady of rank, Ming dynasty 1·90 25
See also Nos. 1687/90, 1767/70, 1833/6, 1906/9 and 1973/6.

428 Bird feeding Chicks

1985. Social Welfare.
1610 **428** $2 multicoloured 25 10

429 North Gate, Taipeh

430 Oak Tree

1985. Historic Buildings (1st series). Mult.
1611 $2 Type **429** 20 10
1612 $5 San Domingo fort, Tamsui 45 15
1613 $8 Lung Shan Temple, Lukang 60 20
1614 $10 Confucius Temple, Changhua 1·00 20
See also Nos. 1700/3.

1985. Bonsai. Multicoloured.
1615 $2 Type **430** 20 10
1616 $5 Five-leaf pine 45 15
1617 $8 Lohan pine 60 20
1618 $18 Banyan 1·50 25

431 World Trade Centre and Sports Goods Logo

432 Flag, Map and Scenes of Peace

1985. Trade Shows. Multicoloured.
1619 $2 Type **431** 20 10
1620 $2 Toys and gifts logo (blue and red) 20 10
1621 $2 Electronics logo (blue) 20 10
1622 $2 Machinery logo (black and orange) 20 10
Nos. 1619/22 were printed together, se-tenant, forming a composite design depicting Taipeh World Trade Centre.

1985. 40th Anniv of Return of Taiwan to China. Multicoloured.
1623 $2 Type **432** 30 10
1624 $18 Chiang Kai-shek and triumphal arch 65 25

433 Emblem

434 Sun Yat-sen

1985. 7th Asian Federation for the Mentally Retarded Conference, Taipeh.
1625 **433** $2 multicoloured 25 10
1626 $11 multicoloured 60 25

1985. 120th Birth Anniv of Sun Yat-sen.
1627 **434** $2 multicoloured 25 10
1628 $18 multicoloured 1·25 25

435 Tiger

436 Emblem

1985. New Year Greetings. "Year of the Tiger".
1629 **435** $1 multicoloured 50 10
1630 $10 multicoloured 2·40 20
See also No. 2040.

1985. 50th Anniv of Postal Simple Life Insurance.
1632 **436** $2 multicoloured 20 10

437 Pine Tree

1986. Pine, Bamboo and Plum (2nd series). Multicoloured.
1633 $1 Type **437** 25 10
1634 $11 Bamboo 65 20
1635 $18 Plum blossom 1·10 25

438 Detail of Scroll

1986. Painting "Hermit Anglers on a Mountain Stream" by T'ang Yin. Designs showing details of the scroll. Multicoloured.
1636 $2 (1) Type **438** 90 10
1637 $2 (2) Pavilions on bank 90 10
1638 $2 (3) Anglers in boats near waterfall 90 10
1639 $2 (4) Pavilions on stilts 90 10
1640 $2 (5) Anglers in boat near island 90 10
Nos. 1636/40 were printed together, forming a composite design.
See note below No. 661 on identification of designs in se-tenant strips.

439 Gladioli in Vase

440 Loading and unloading Boeing 747 Mail Plane

1986. Flower Arrangements (1st series). Mult.
1641 $2 Type **439** 10 10
1642 $5 Roses in double wicker holders 35 10
1643 $8 Roses and fern in pot on stand 65 10
1644 $10 Various flowers in large and small pots 80 10
See also Nos. 1741/4.

1986. 90th Anniv of Post Office. Mult.
1645 $2 Type **440** 15 10
1646 $5 Postman on motorcycle (vert) 30 10

1647 $8 Customer at cash dispenser and clerk at savings bank computer terminal (vert) 45 10
1648 $10 Electronic sorting machine and envelopes circling globe 65 15

441 Chen Tien-hva (revolutionary writer)

442 Mountain shrouded in Mist

1986. Famous Chinese.
1650 **441** $2 violet 10 10

1986. Yushan National Park. Multicoloured.
1651 $2 Type **442** 35 10
1652 $5 People on mountain top 80 10
1653 $8 Snow covered mountain peak . . . . 1·10 10
1654 $10 Forest on mountain side 1·50 15

443 Hydro-electric Power Station

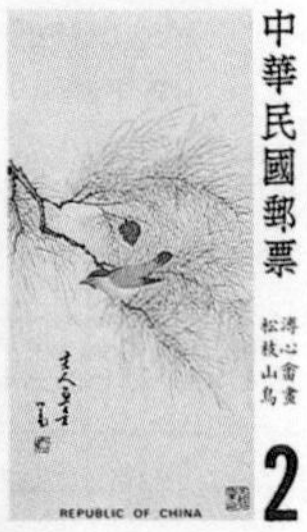

444 Taiwan Firecrest in Tree

1986. Power Stations. Multicoloured.
1655 $2 Type **443** 35 10
1656 $8 Thermo-electric power station 60 10
1657 $10 Nuclear power station 75 15

1986. Paintings by P'u Hsin-yu. Mult.
1658 $2 Type **444** . . . . 1·50 20
1659 $8 Landscape . . . . 2·25 10
1660 $10 Woman in garden . . . 2·75 15

445 Emblems

446 Green-winged Macaw

1986. 25th Anniv of Asian Productivity Organization and 30th Anniv of China Productivity Centre.
1661 **445** $2 multicoloured 15 10
1662 $11 multicoloured . . . 75 20

1986. Protection of Intellectual Property.
1663 **446** $2 multicoloured 90 20

447 Starck's Damselfish ("Chrysiptera starcki")

(448)

1986. Coral Reef Fishes, Multicoloured.
1664 $2 Type **447** 30 10
1665 $2 Copper-banded butterflyfish ("Chelmon rostratus") 30 10
1666 $2 Pearl-scaled butterflyfish ("Chaetodon xanthurus") 30 10
1667 $2 Four-spotted butterflyfish ("Chaetodon quadrimaculatus") 30 10
1668 $2 Meyer's butterflyfish ("Chaetodon meyeri") . . 30 10
1669 $2 Japanese swallow ("Genicanthus semifasciatus") (female) 30 10
1670 $2 Japanese swallow ("Genicanthus semifasciatus") (male) . . 30 10
1671 $2 Blue-ringed angelfish ("Pomacanthus annularis") 30 10
1672 $2 Harlequin tuskfish ("Lienardella fasciata") 30 10
1673 $2 Undulate triggerfish ("Balistapus undulatus") 30 10

1986. 60th Anniv of Chiang Kai-shek's Northward Expedition. Nos. 1229 and 1386 surch as T **448**.
1674 **306** $2 on $6 red, bl & orge 15 15
1675 $8 on $9 red, bl & grn 35 25

449 Tzu Mu Bridge

450 Yingtai and Shanpo going to School

1986. Road Bridges. Multicoloured.
1676 $2 Type **449** 45 10
1677 $5 Chang Hung bridge over Hsiu-ku-luan-chi 70 10
1678 $8 Kuan Fu bridge over Hsintien River . . . . . 1·10 10
1679 $10 Kuan Tu bridge over Tanshui River . . . . . 1·50 15

1986. Folk Tales. "Love between Liang Shanpo and Chu Yingtai". Multicoloured.
1680 $5 Type **450** 50 10
1681 $5 Classmates 50 10
1682 $5 Yingtai and Shanpo by lake 50 10
1683 $5 Yingtai telling Shanpo she is to be married . . . 50 10
1684 $5 Ascending to heaven as butterflies 50 10

451 Children playing by Lake and Rainbow

452 Lady of Warring States Period

1986. Cleanliness and Courtesy. Mult.
1685 $2 Type **451** 30 10
1686 $8 Children helping others in street 50 10

1986. Chinese Costumes (2nd series). Mult.
1687 $2 Lady of rank, Shang dynasty 70 10
1688 $5 Type **452** . . . . 1·25 10
1689 $8 Empress's assembly dress, later Han dynasty . . . . 2·00 10
1690 $10 Beribboned dress of lady of rank, Wei and Tsin dynasties . . . . . 3·00 25

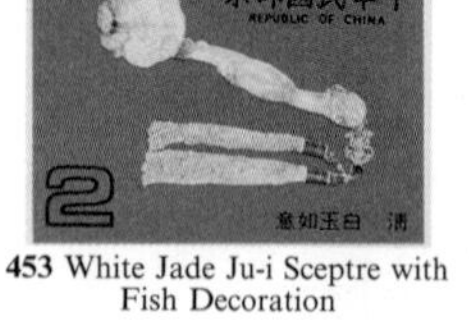

453 White Jade Ju-i Sceptre with Fish Decoration

1986. Ch'ing Dynasty Ju-i (1st series). Mult.
1691 $2 Type **453** 40 10
1692 $3 Coral ju-i sceptre with fungus motif 60 10
1693 $4 Redwood ju-i sceptre inlaid with precious stones 75 10
1694 $18 Gold-painted ju-i sceptre with three abundances (fruit) . . . . 1·50 25
See also Nos 1735/8.

454 Chiang Kai-shek and Books

1986. Birth Cent of Chiang Kai-shek. Mult.
1695 $2 Type **454** 55 10
1696 $5 Chiang Kai-shek, flag, map and crowd 45 10
1697 $8 Chiang Kai-shek, emblem and youths 70 10
1698 $10 Chiang Kai-shek, flags on globe and clasped hands 80 15

455 Erh-sha-wan Gun Emplacement, Keelung

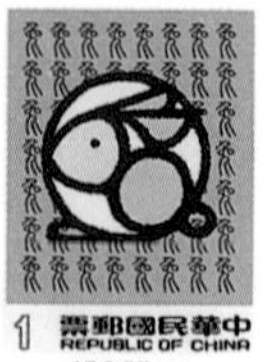

456 Hare

1986. Historic Buildings (2nd series). Mult.
1700 $2 Chin-kuang-fu House, Pei-pu 30 10
1701 $5 Type **455** 75 10
1702 $8 Hsi T'ai fort 80 10
1703 $10 Matsu Temple, Peng-hu 1·00 15

1986. New Year Greetings. "Year of the Hare".
1704 **456** $1 multicoloured 45 10
1705 $10 multicoloured . . . 1·90 15
See also No. 2041.

457 Shrubs on Rock Formation

458 Glove Puppet

1987. Kenting National Park. Multicoloured.
1707 $2 Type **457** 30 10
1708 $5 Rocky outcrop 70 10
1709 $8 Sandy bay . . . . 1·00 10
1710 $10 Rocky bays . . . . . . 1·50 15

1987. Puppets. Multicoloured.
1721 $2 Type **458** 30 10
1722 $5 String puppet 85 10
1723 $18 Shadow show puppet 1·25 25

459 Envelope, Parcel and Globe

460 Wu Yueh (revolutionary)

1987. Speedpost Service.
1724 **459** $2 multicoloured 30 10
1725 $18 multicoloured . . . 1·00 25

1987. Famous Chinese.
1726 **460** $2 red 30 10

461 "Singing Creek with Bamboo Orchestra"

1987. Madame Chiang Kai-shek's Landscape Paintings (3rd series). Each black, stone and red.
1727 $2 Type **461** 50 10
1728 $5 "Mountains draped in Clouds" . . . . 1·40 10
1729 $5 "Vista of Tranquility" . . 1·75 10
1730 $10 "Mountains after a Snowfall" . . . . 2·10 15

462 Bodhisattva Head, Northern Wei Dynasty

463 View of Dam

1987. Ancient Chinese Stone Carvings. Mult.
1731 $5 Type **462** 70 10
1732 $5 Standing Buddha, Northern Ch'i dynasty . . 70 10
1733 $5 Bodhisattva head, T'ang dynasty 70 10
1734 $5 Seated Buddha, T'ang dynasty 70 10

1987. Ch'ing Dynasty Ju-i (2nd series). As T **453**. Multicoloured.
1735 $2 Silver ju-i sceptre with fungus decoration of pearls and precious stones 30 10
1736 $3 Gold ju-i sceptre with Eight Treasures decoration of pearls and precious stones 35 10
1737 $4 Gilt ju-i sceptre inlaid with precious stones and kingfisher feather 50 10
1738 $18 Gilt ju-i sceptre with wirework and inlaid with malachite . . . . 2·00 25

1987. Feitsui Reservoir Inauguration. Multicoloured.
1739 $2 Type **463** 25 10
1740 $18 View of reservoir . . . 80 25

1987. Flower Arrangements (2nd series). As T **439**. Multicoloured.
1741 $2 Roses and pine twig in holder 25 10
1742 $5 Flowers in pot 45 10
1743 $8 Tasselled pendant hanging from bamboo in vase 80 10
1744 $10 Pine in flask . . . . . 1·00 15

464 Emblem

465 Soldiers firing from behind Barricades

1987. 70th Lions Clubs International Convention, Taipeh.
1745 **464** $2 multicoloured 25 10
1746 $18 multicoloured . . . 1·00 25

1987. 50th Anniv of Start of Sino-Japanese War. Multicoloured.
1747 $1 Type **465** 15 10
1748 $2 Chiang Kai-shek making speech from balcony . . . 25 10
1749 $5 Crowd throwing money onto flag 40 10
1750 $6 Columns of soldiers and tanks on mountain road 50 10
1751 $8 General giving written message to Chiang Kai-shek 75 10
1752 $18 Pres. and Madame Chiang Kai-shek at front of crowd . . . . 1·10 25

466 Airplane flying to Left

467 Wang Yun-wu

1987. Air. Multicoloured.
1753 $9 Type **466** 50 15
1754 $14 Airplane 75 20
1755 $18 Airplane flying to right 1·00 25

1987. Birth Centenary (1988) of Wang Yun-wu (lexicographer).
1756 **467** $2 black 25 10

468 Trees on Islands and Fisherman

1987. Painting "After Chao Po-su's 'Red Cliff'" by Wen Cheng-ming. Designs showing details of the scroll. Multicoloured.
1757 $3 (1) Type **468** 65 10
1758 $3 (2) Tree and three figures on island 65 10
1759 $3 (3) House in walled enclosure on island . . . 65 10
1760 $3 (4) Figures in doorway of building and horse in stable 65 10
1761 $3 (5) Cliffs and sea 65 10
1762 $3 (6) Islets, trees and figures on shore 65 10

1763 $3 (7) Trees among cliffs . . 65 10
1764 $3 (8) People in sampan . . 65 10
1765 $3 (9) Building surrounded by trees and cliffs 65 10
1766 $3 (10) Cliffs, trees and waterfall 65 10

Nos. 1757/66 were printed together, se-tenant, forming a composite design.
See note below No. 661 on identification of designs in se-tenant strips.

469 Han Lady of Rank, Early Ch'ing Dynasty
470 Ta Chen Tian, Confucius Temple, Taichung

1987. Chinese Costumes (3rd series). Mult.
1767 $1.50 Type **469** 50 10
1768 $3 Manchu bannerman's wife, Ch'ing dynasty . . . 60 10
1769 $7.50 Woman's Manchu-style Ch'i-p'ao, early Republic period . . . . . 1·40 10
1770 $18 Jacket and skirt, early Republic period . . . . . 2·75 35

1987. International Confucianism and the Modern World Symposium, Taipeh. Multicoloured.
1771 $3 Type **470** 20 10
1772 $18 Confucius and fresco . . 80 25

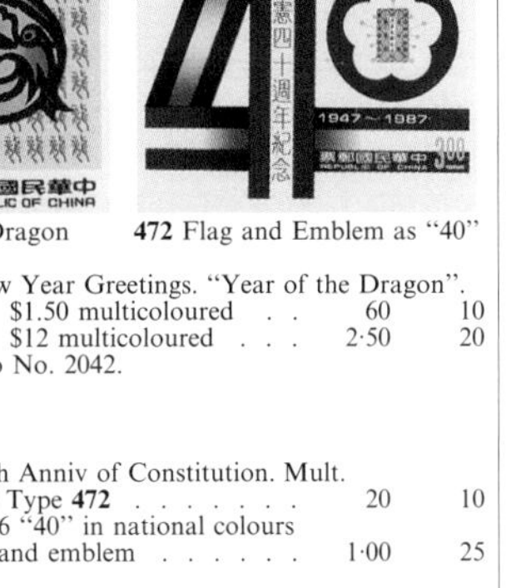

471 Dragon
472 Flag and Emblem as "40"

1987. New Year Greetings. "Year of the Dragon".
1773 **471** $1.50 multicoloured . . 60 10
1774 $12 multicoloured . . . 2·50 20
See also No. 2042.

1987. 40th Anniv of Constitution. Mult.
1776 $3 Type **472** 20 10
1777 $16 "40" in national colours and emblem . . . . . . 1·00 25

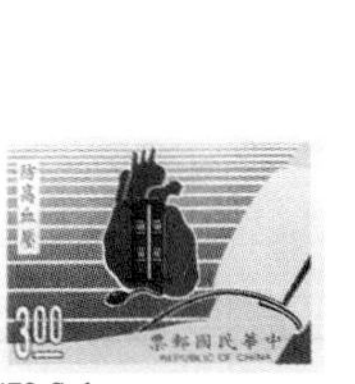
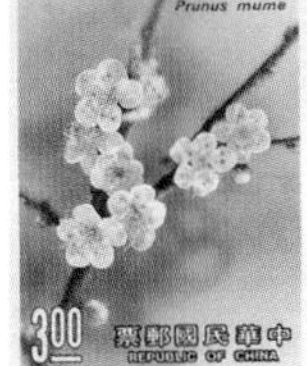

473 Sphygmomanometer
474 Plum

1988. Nat Health. Prevent Hypertension Campaign.
1778 **473** $3 multicoloured 25 10

1988. Flowers (1st series). Multicoloured.
1779 $3 Type **474** 50 10
1780 $7.50 Apricot . . . . 1·10 10
1781 $12 Peach . . . . 1·50 20
See also Nos. 1798/1800, 1809/11 and 1829/31.

475 Pine Tree
476 Modelled Dough Figurines

1988. Pine, Bamboo and Plum (3rd series). Multicoloured.
1783 $1.50 Type **475** 25 10
1784 $7.50 Bamboo 45 10
1785 $16 Plum blossom 85 25

1988. Traditional Handicrafts. Multicoloured.
1786 $3 Type **476** 50 10
1787 $7.50 Blown sugar fish . . . 90 10
1788 $16 Sugar painting . . . . 1·25 25

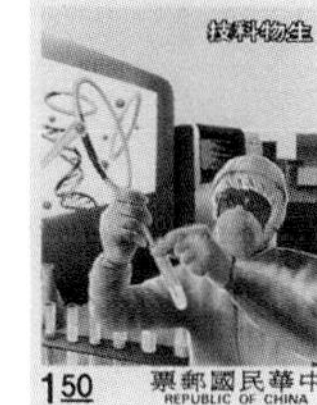

477 Hsu Hsi-lin (revolutionary)
478 Bio-technology

1988. Famous Chinese.
1789 **477** $3 brown 25 10

1988. Science and Technology. Multicoloured.
1790 $1.50 Type **478** 15 10
1791 $3 Surveyors at oil field (energy) 20 10
1792 $7 Syringe piercing letter "B" (hepatitis control) . . 25 10
1793 $7.50 Mechanised production line (automation) 30 10
1794 $10 Satellite and computer terminal (information) . . 40 15
1795 $12 Laser (electro-optics) . . 50 20
1796 $16 Laboratory worker (materials) 65 25
1797 $16.50 Tin of fruit and technician (food technology) 65 25

1988. Flowers (2nd series). As T **474**. Mult.
1798 $3 Tree peony 50 10
1799 $7.50 Pomegranate . . . . 1·10 10
1800 $12 East Indian lotus . . . 1·50 20

479 Policemen on Point Duty and Motor Cycle

1988. Police Day. Multicoloured.
1802 $3 Type **479** 40 10
1803 $12 Communications operator and fire-fighters 75 20

480 Butler's Pigmy Frog

1988. Amphibians. Multicoloured.
1804 $1.50 Type **480** 30 10
1805 $3 Taipeh striped slender frog 40 10
1806 $7.50 "Microhyla inornata" 1·25 10
1807 $16 Tree frog . . . . 2·50 35

481 "60" on Map

1988. 60th Anniv of Broadcasting Corporation of China.
1808 **481** $3 multicoloured 25 10

1988. Flowers (3rd series). As T **474**. Mult.
1809 $3 Garden balsam 50 10
1810 $7.50 Sweet osmanthus . . 90 10
1811 $12 Chrysanthemum . . . . 1·25 20

482 Chiang Kai-shek and Soldiers

1988. 30th Anniv of Kinmen Bombardment. Multicoloured.
1813 $1.50 Type **482** 25 10
1814 $3 Chiang Kai-shek and soldier reporters 25 10
1815 $7.50 Soldiers firing howitzer 65 10
1816 $12 Tank battle 75 20

483 Basketball Player

1988. Sports Day. Multicoloured.
1817 $5 Type **483** 20 10
1818 $5 Two basketball players 20 10
1819 $5 Baseball hitter 20 10
1820 $5 Baseball catcher 20 10

484 Crater

1988. Yangmingshan National Park. Mult.
1821 $1.50 Type **484** 50 10
1822 $3 Lake 75 10
1823 $7.50 Mountains . . . . . 1·25 10
1824 $16 Lake and mountains . . 1·75 25

485-88 "Lofty Mount Lu"

1988. Painting by Shen Chou.
1825 **485** $5 multicoloured . . . . 1·10 10
1826 **486** $5 multicoloured . . . . 1·10 10
1827 **487** $5 multicoloured . . . . 1·10 10
1828 **488** $5 multicoloured . . . . 1·10 10
Nos. 1825/8 were printed together, se-tenant, forming the composite design illustrated.

1988. Flowers (4th series). As T **474**. Mult.
1829 $3 Cotton rose hibiscus . . 65 10
1830 $7.50 Camellia 90 10
1831 $12 Narcissus . . . . 1·25 20

1988. Chinese Costumes (4th series). As T **469**. Multicoloured.
1833 $2 Nobleman with tall hat, Shang dynasty 75 10
1834 $3 Ruler with topknot, Warring States period . . 85 10
1835 $7.50 Male official with writing brush in hair, Wei-chin dynasty . . . . 1·10 10
1836 $12 Male court official with hanging brush on hat, late Northern dynasties . . . 2·00 20

489 Snake
490 Tai Ch'uan-hsien

1988. New Year Greetings. "Year of the Snake".
1837 **489** $2 multicoloured . . . . 1·25 10
1838 $13 multicoloured . . . 1·75 20
See also No. 2043.

1989. Birth Centenary (1990) of Tai Ch'uan-hsien (Civil Service reformer).
1840 **490** $3 black 35 10

491 Pres. Chiang Ching-kuo

1989. 1st Death Anniv of President Chiang Ching-Kuo. Multicoloured.
1841 $3 Type **491** 15 10
1842 $6 Chiang Ching-kuo, political rally and voters 40 10
1843 $7.50 Chiang Ching-kuo at docks 85 15
1844 $16 Chiang Ching-kuo with children . . . . 1·00 25

492 Pine Tree

1989. Pine, Bamboo and Plum (4th series). Multicoloured.
1845 $3 Type **492** 10 10
1846 $16.50 Bamboo 65 25
1847 $21 Plum blossom 80 30

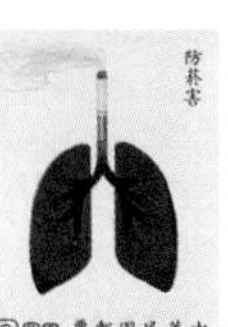

493 Ni Ying-tien
494 Lungs smoking

1989. 79th Death Anniv of Ni Ying-tien (revolutionary).
1848 **493** $3 black 30 10

1989. Anti-smoking Campaign.
1849 **494** $3 multicoloured 30 10

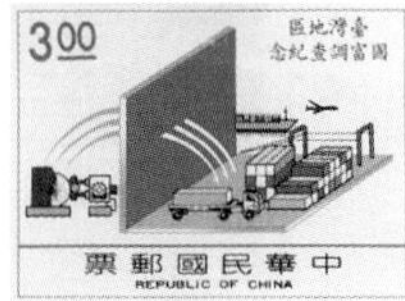

495 Mu Tou Yu Lighthouse
496 Distribution of Industrial Goods

1989. Lighthouses. White panel at foot. Mult.
1850 75c. Type **495** 10 10
1851 $2 Lu Tao lighthouse . . . 10 10
1852 $2.25 Pen Chia Yu lighthouse 15 10
1853 $3 Pitou Chiao lighthouse 15 10
1854 $4.50 Tungyin Tao lighthouse 25 10
1855 $6 Chilai Pi lighthouse . . . 35 25
1856 $7 Fukwei Chiao lighthouse 45 30
1857 $7.50 Hua Yu lighthouse . . 50 30
1858 $9 Oluan Pi lighthouse . . . 60 25
1859 $10 Kaohsiung lighthouse 75 40
1860 $10.50 Yuweng Tao lighthouse 75 30
1861 $12 Tungchu Tao lighthouse 80 50
1862 $13 Yeh Liu lighthouse . . 90 35
1863 $15 Tungchi Yu lighthouse 1·10 70
1864 $16.50 Chimei Yu lighthouse 1·25 65
For designs with blue panel at foot, see Nos. 2003/15.

1989. National Wealth Survey.
1865 **496** $3 multicoloured 40 10

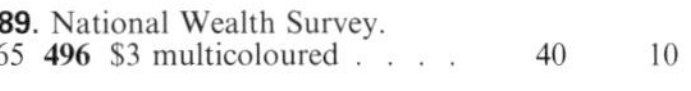

497 "I once tended nine Fields of Orchids"

1989. Chinese Classical Poetry (5th series). Poems from "Ch'u Ts'u". Multicoloured.
1866 $3 Type **497** 30 10
1867 $7.50 "No grief is greater than parting" 80 10

1868 $12 "...living remote and neglected" . . . . 1·50 20
1869 $16 "The horse will not gallop into servitude" . . 2·00 25

498 Underground Train

1989. Completion of Taipeh Underground Section of Western Railway Line. Multicoloured.
1870 $3 Type **498** 50 10
1871 $16 Train in cutting . . . . 1·25 25

499 Blue Triangle

1989. Butterflies (1st series). Multicoloured.
1872 $2 Type **499** 50 15
1873 $3 Great mormon 85 15
1874 $7.50 Chequered swallowtail 1·40 20
1875 $9 Common rose . . . . . 2·00 20
See also Nos. 1902/5.

500 Pumpkin Teapot
501 Fan Chung-yen

1989. Teapots (1st series). Multicoloured.
1876 $2 Type **500** 60 10
1877 $3 Clay teapot 90 10
1878 $12 "Chopped wood" teapot 1·50 25
1879 $16 Clay pear teapot . . . 2·00 30
See also Nos. 1946/50.

1989. Birth Millenary of Fan Chung-yen (civil service reformer).
1880 **501** $12 multicoloured . . . 65 25

502 Trees and Right Side of Mountain

1989. Painting "Autumn Colours on the Ch'iao and Hua Mountains" by Ch'iao Mengfu. Designs showing details of the scroll. Multicoloured.
1881 $7.50 (1) Type **502** 75 15
1882 $7.50 (2) Left side of mountain and trees . . . 75 15
1883 $7.50 (3) Trees and house 75 15
1884 $7.50 (4) Mountain, trees and house 75 15
Nos. 1872/5 were printed together, se-tenant, forming a composite design.

503 Insured Groups and Family
504 Liwu River Gorge

1989. Social Welfare.
1885 **503** $3 multicoloured 30 10

1989. Taroko National Park. Multicoloured.
1886 $2 Type **504** 20 10
1887 $3 North Peak of Chilai, Taroko Mountain 40 10
1888 $12 Waterfalls 80 25
1889 $16 Chingshui Cliff . . . . 1·10 30

505 Horse
506 Yu Lu

1989. New Year Greetings. "Year of the Horse".
1890 **505** $2 multicoloured 40 10
1891 $13 multicoloured . . . 1·25 25
See also No. 2044.

1990. Door Gods. Multicoloured.
1893 $3 Type **506** 50 20
1894 $3 Shen Shu 50 20
1895 $7.50 Wei-ch'ih Ching-te (facing right) . . . . . . 1·00 40
1896 $7.50 Ch'in Shu-pao (facing left) . . . . 1·00 40

507 Lishan
508 Crystal containing Emblem and Industrial Symbols

1990. Tourism. Multicoloured.
1897 $2 Type **507** 25 10
1898 $18 Fir tree at Tayuling (vert) . . . . 1·00 25

1990. 40th Anniv of National Insurance.
1899 **508** $3 multicoloured 50 10

509 Harbour and Tanks

1990. Yung-An Hsiang Liquefied Natural Gas Terminal. Multicoloured.
1900 $3 Type **509** 35 10
1901 $16 Gas tanker and map showing pipeline route (vert) . . . . 1·00 25

510 African Monarch
511 Court Official, Northern Wei Period to T'ang Dynasty

1990. Butterflies (2nd series). Multicoloured.
1902 $2 Orange tiger 30 10
1903 $3 Type **510** 35 10
1904 $7.50 "Pieris canidia" . . . 75 20
1905 $9 Peacock . . . . 1·10 25

1990. Chinese Costumes (5th series). Mult.
1906 $2 Type **511** 40 10
1907 $3 Civil official in winged hat and green robe, Three Kingdoms period to Ming dynasty 50 10
1908 $7.50 Royal guard in bamboo hat, Yuan dynasty 70 15
1909 $12 Highest grade civil official in robe decorated with crane bird, Ming dynasty 90 40

512 "Spring Song at Midnight"

1990. Chinese Classical Poetry (6th series). Multicoloured.
1910 $3 Type **512** 50 10
1911 $7.50 Couple on river bank ("Summer Song at Midnight") 70 15
1912 $12 Girl washing clothes in river ("Autumn Song at Midnight") . . . . 1·00 20
1913 $16 Snow-bound river scene ("Winter Song at Midnight") . . . . 1·25 25

513 Japanese Black Pine
514 Bamboo-shaped Glass Snuff Bottle

1990. Bonsai. Multicoloured.
1914 $3 Type **513** 40 10
1915 $6.50 "Ehretia microphylla" 60 10
1916 $12 "Buxus harlandii" . . . 90 20
1917 $16 "Celtis sinensis" . . . . 1·25 25

1990. Snuff Bottles. Multicoloured.
1918 $3 Type **514** 30 10
1919 $6 Glass bottle with peony design 60 10
1920 $9 Melon-shaped amber bottle 90 15
1921 $16 White jade bottle . . . 1·10 25

515 Taiwan Firecrest
516 Running

1990. Birds. Multicoloured.
1922 $2 Type **515** 50 25
1923 $3 Formosan barwing . . . 60 25
1924 $7.50 White-eared sibia . . 80 30
1925 $16 Formosan yellow tit . . 1·10 80

1990. Sports. Multicoloured.
1926 $2 Type **516** 20 10
1927 $3 Long jumping 35 10
1928 $7 Pole vaulting 70 10
1929 $16 Hurdling . . . . 1·00 25

517 Curtiss Tomahawk II Fighters and Air Crews

1990. 50th Anniv of Arrival of "Flying Tigers" American Volunteer Group.
1930 **517** $3 multicoloured 40 10

518 Cats

1990. Children's Drawings. Multicoloured.
1931 $2 Type **518** 30 10
1932 $3 Common peafowl . . . 40 20
1933 $7.50 Chickens 80 15
1934 $12 Cattle market . . . . . 1·25 20

519 National Theatre
520 Cowrie Shells

1990. Cultural Buildings in Chiang Kai-shek Memorial Park, Taipeh.
1935 **519** $3 orange, dp blue & bl 30 10
1936 – $12 mauve, violet & lilac 90 20
DESIGN: $12 National Concert Hall.

1990. Ancient Coins. "Shell" Money. Mult.
1937 $2 Type **520** 20 10
1938 $3 Oyster shell 35 10
1939 $6.50 Bone 60 15
1940 $7.50 Bronze 70 15
1941 $9 Jade . . . . 1·00 20

521 Sheep
522 Hu Shih

1990. New Year Greetings. "Year of the Sheep".
1942 **521** $2 multicoloured 50 10
1943 $13 multicoloured . . . 1·00 20
See also No. 2045.

1990. Birth Centenary of Hu Shih (written Chinese reformer).
1945 **522** $3 violet 30 10

523 Teapot with Dragon Spout and Handle
524 Happiness

1991. Teapots (2nd series). Multicoloured.
1946 $2 Blue and white teapot with phoenix design . . . 25 10
1947 $3 Type **523** 40 10
1948 $9 Teapot with floral design on lid and landscape on body 70 15
1949 $12 Rectangular teapot with passion flower design . . 90 20
1950 $16 Brown rectangular teapot with floral decoration . . . . 1·10 25

1991. Greetings Stamps. Gods of Prosperity. Multicoloured.
1951 $3 Type **524** 40 10
1952 $3 Wealth 40 10
1953 $7.50 Longevity (with white beard) 60 15
1954 $7.50 Joy 60 15

525 "Petasites formosanus"
526 Hsiung Cheng-chi (revolutionary)

1991. Plants (1st series). Multicoloured.
1955 $2 Type **525** 25 10
1956 $3 "Heloniopsis acutifolia" 35 10
1957 $7.50 "Disporum shimadai" 60 15
1958 $9 "Viola nagasawai" . . . 70 15
See also Nos. 1969/72, 1995/8 and 2026/9.

1991. Famous Chinese.
1959 **526** $3 blue 35 10

527 Agriculture

528 Bamboo Hobby-horse

1991. 80th Anniv (1992) of Founding of Chinese Republic. Multicoloured.
1960 $3 Type **527** 35 10
1961 $7.50 Industry 75 10
1962 $12 Dancer and leisure equipment . . . . 1·25 20
1963 $16 Transport and communications . . . . . 1·50 30

1991. Children's Games (1st series). Mult.
1964 $3 Type **528** 25 10
1965 $3 Woven-grass grasshoppers 25 10
1966 $3 Spinning tops 25 10
1967 $3 Windmills 25 10
See also Nos. 2056/9, 2120/3 and 2184/7.

1991. Plants (2nd series). As T **525**. Mult.
1969 $2 "Gaultheria itoana" . . 30 10
1970 $3 "Lysionotus montanus" . 40 10
1971 $7.50 "Leontopodium microphyllum" 75 15
1972 $9 "Gentiana flavo-maculata" . . . . 1·00 15

529 Male Official's Summer Court Dress

530 Heart, Pedestrian Crossing and Hand

1991. Chinese Costumes (6th series). Ch'ing Dynasty. Multicoloured.
1973 $2 Male official's winter court dress with dragon design 40 10
1974 $3 Type **529** 50 10
1975 $7.50 Male official's winter overcoat 95 15
1976 $12 Everyday skull-cap, jacket and travelling robe 1·75 20

1991. Road Safety. Multicoloured.
1977 $3 Type **530** 35 10
1978 $7.50 Hand, road and broken bottle ("Don't Drink and Drive") . . . 75 15

531 Ch'ing Dynasty Cloisonne Lion

532 Strawberries

1991. No value expressed. Multicoloured.
1979 (–) Type **531** 20 15
1980 (–) Cloisonne lioness 80 25
Nos. 1979/80 were sold at the prevailing rates for domestic ordinary and domestic prompt delivery letters.

1991. Fruits. Multicoloured.
1981 $3 Type **532** 50 10
1982 $7.50 Grapes 55 15
1983 $9 Mango 70 20
1984 $16 Sugar apple . . . . . . 1·10 25

533 Formosan Whistling Thrush

1991. River Birds. Multicoloured.
1985 $5 Type **533** 50 20
1986 $5 Brown dipper 50 20
1987 $5 Mandarins 50 20
1988 $5 Black-crowned night herons 50 20
1989 $5 Little egrets 50 20
1990 $5 Plumbeous redstarts . . 50 20
1991 $5 Little forktail 50 20
1992 $5 Grey wagtail 50 20
1993 $5 River kingfishers 50 20
1994 $5 Pied wagtails 50 20
Nos. 1985/94 were printed together, se-tenant, forming a composite design.

1991. Plants (3rd series). As T **525**. Mult.
1995 $3.50 "Rosa transmorrisonensis" . . . 45 10
1996 $5 "Impatiens devolii" . . . 75 10
1997 $9 "Impatiens uniflora" . . 1·00 20
1998 $12 "Impatiens taye-monii" 1·25 20

534 Rock Climbing

1991. International Camping and Caravanning Federation Rally, Fulung Beach. Multicoloured.
1999 $2 Type **534** 25 10
2000 $3 Fishing 35 10
2001 $7.50 Bird-watching 50 15
2002 $10 Boys with pail wading in water 75 20

1991. Lighthouses. As Nos. 1851/3 and 1855/64 but with blue panel at foot.
2003 50c. As No. 1863 . . . . . 10 10
2004 $1 As No. 1851 . . . . . 10 10
2005 $3.50 As No. 1855 . . . . 25 10
2006 $5 As No. 1856 . . . . . 35 10
2007 $7 As No. 1853 . . . . . 45 10
2008 $9 As No. 1858 . . . . . 60 15
2009 $10 As No. 1859 . . . . . 70 10
2010 $12 As No. 1861 . . . . . 75 15
2011 $13 As No. 1852 . . . . . 80 15
2012 $19 As No. 1857 . . . . . 1·10 20
2013 $20 As No. 1862 . . . . . 1·25 20
2014 $26 As No. 1860 . . . . . 1·40 25
2015 $28 As No. 1864 . . . . . 1·75 30

535 Peacock

536 Monkey

1991. "Peacocks" by Giuseppe Castiglione. Designs showing details of painting. Multicoloured.
2020 $5 Type **535** 50 25
2021 $20 Peacock displaying tail 1·90 1·00

1991. New Year Greetings. "Year of the Monkey".
2023 **536** $3.50 multicoloured . . 50 10
2024 $13 multicoloured . . . 1·10 25
See also No. 2046.

1991. Plants (4th series). As T **525**. Mult.
2026 $3.50 "Kalanchoe garambiensis" 40 10
2027 $5 "Pieris taiwanensis" . . . 75 10
2028 $9 "Pleione formosana" . . 1·00 20
2029 $12 "Elaeagnus oldhamii" 1·25 20

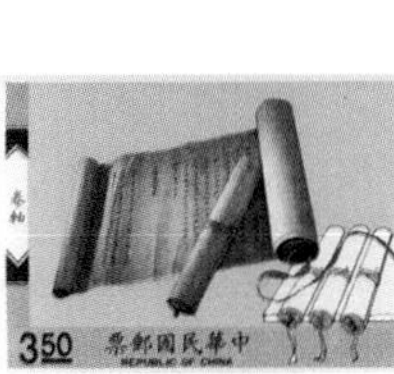

537 Scrolls

538 Peace in the Wake of Firecrackers

1992. International Book Fair, Taipeh. Mult.
2030 $3.50 Type **537** 30 10
2031 $5 Folded-leaves book . . . 40 10
2032 $9 Butterfly-bound books 75 15
2033 $15 Sewn books . . . . . 1·10 25

1992. Greetings Stamps. Nienhwas (paintings conveying wishes for the coming year). Mult.
2034 $5 Type **538** 50 10
2035 $5 Elephant with riders (Good fortune and satisfaction) 50 10
2036 $12 Children and five "birds" (Five blessings upon the house) 70 20
2037 $12 Children angling for large fish (Abundance for every year) 70 20

1992. Signs of Chinese Zodiac. As previous designs but with additional symbol in top left-hand corner.
2038 **393** $5 multicoloured 50 10
2039 **414** $5 multicoloured 50 10
2040 **435** $5 multicoloured 50 10
2041 **456** $5 multicoloured 50 10
2042 **471** $5 multicoloured 50 10
2043 **489** $5 multicoloured 50 10
2044 **505** $5 multicoloured 50 10
2045 **521** $5 multicoloured 50 10
2046 **536** $5 multicoloured 50 10
2047 **340** $5 multicoloured 50 10
2048 **361** $5 multicoloured 50 10
2049 **378** $5 multicoloured 50 10
Nos. 2038/49 were issued together in se-tenant blocks of 12 stamps within the sheet. The stamps are listed in order from right to left of the block.

539 Taiwan Red Cypress ("Chamaecyparis formosensis")

540 Mother and son (Spring)

1992. Forest Resources. Conifers. Mult.
2051 $5 Type **539** 55 10
2052 $5 Taiwan cypress ("Chamaecyparis taiwanensis") 55 10
2053 $5 Taiwan incense cedar ("Calocedrus formosana") 55 10
2054 $5 Ranta fir ("Cunninghamia konishii") 55 10
2055 $5 Taiwania ("Taiwania cryptomerioides") 55 10
Nos. 2051/5 were printed together, se-tenant, forming a composite design.

1992. Children's Games (2nd series). As T **528**. Multicoloured.
2056 $5 Walking on tin cans . . 40 10
2057 $5 Chopstick guns 40 10
2058 $5 Rolling hoops 40 10
2059 $5 Grass fighting 40 10

1992. Parent–Child Relationships. Mult.
2061 $3.50 Type **540** 40 10
2062 $5 Mother carrying child on back (summer) 50 10
2063 $9 Mother and child pushing toy rabbits (autumn) 75 15
2064 $10 Mother feeding child (winter) 90 15

542 Vase decorated with Bats and Longevity Characters

543 Lion and Stone Pavilion

1992. Glassware decorated with Enamel. Mult.
2066 $3.50 Type **542** 30 10
2067 $5 Gourd-shaped vase decorated with landscape and children at play . . . 40 10
2068 $7 Vase with peony decoration 50 15
2069 $17 Vase showing mother teaching child to read . . 1·10 25

1992. Stone Lions from Lugouqiao Bridge.
2070 **543** $5 blue and brown . . . 40 10
2071 – $5 green and violet . . . 40 10
2072 – $12 orange and green . . 70 20
2073 – $12 violet and black . . 70 20
DESIGNS: No. 2071, Bridge and lioness with cub; 2070, Bridge parapet and lion; 2073, Bridge parapet and lioness with two cubs.

544 "People make Friends and are tied to Each Other as Roots to a Plant"

1992. Chinese Classical Poetry (7th series). Multicoloured.
2074 $3.50 Type **544** 30 10
2075 $5 Couple at window ("Conjugal love will last forever") 40 10
2076 $9 Couple in garden ("Man takes pains to uphold virtue/Till one's hair turns forever grey") 80 15
2077 $15 "Tartar horses lean toward the north wind" 1·25 25

545 Drummer and Crowd

546 "Two Birds perched on a Red Camellia Branch"

1992. Temple Fair. Multicoloured.
2078 $5 Type **545** 45 10
2079 $5 Man with basket dancing 45 10
2080 $5 Musicians 45 10
2081 $5 Man pushing cart . . . 45 10
2082 $5 Women and children . . 45 10
Nos. 2078/82 were printed together, se-tenant, forming a composite design.

1992. Ming Dynasty Silk Tapestries. Mult.
2083 $5 Type **546** 50 10
2084 $12 "Two Birds playing on a Peach Branch" . . . . 1·00 20

547 Cart in "The General and the Premier"

548 Steam Locomotive and Train

1992. Chinese Opera Props. Multicoloured.
2086 $3.50 Type **547** 50 10
2087 $5 Ship in "The Lucky Pearl" 60 10
2088 $9 Horse in "Chao-chun serves as an Envoy" . . . 80 15
2089 $12 Sedan chair in "Escort to the Wedding" 90 15

1992. Alishan Mountain Railway. Mult.
2090 $5 Type **548** 30 15
2091 $15 Diesel locomotive and train . . . . 1·10 35

549 Chinese River Otter

550 Cock

1992. Mammals. Multicoloured.
2092 $5 Type **549** 25 10
2093 $5 Formosan flying fox . . 25 10
2094 $5 Formosan clouded leopard 25 10
2095 $5 Formosan black bear . . 25 10

1992. New Year Greetings. "Year of the Cock". Multicoloured.
2096 $3.50 Type **550** 20 10
2097 $13 Cock (facing left) . . . 75 15

552 Schall and Astronomical Instruments

1992. 400th Birth Anniv of Johann Adam Schall von Bell (missionary astronomer).
2100 **552** $5 multicoloured 40 10

553 Satisfaction for Every Year

1993. Greetings Stamps. Nienhwas (paintings conveying wishes for the coming year). Multicoloured.
2101 $5 Type **553** 50 10
2102 $5 Birds and flowers (Joy) 50 10
2103 $12 Butterfly and flowers (Happiness and longevity) 1·10 15
2104 $12 Flowers in vase (Wealth and peace) . . . . 1·10 15

554 Applying Enamel and Glass Decoration to Temple Roof

1992. International Traditional Crafts Exhibition, Taipeh, Multicoloured.
2105 $3.50 Type **554** 30 10
2106 $5 Ceremonial lantern . . . 40 10
2107 $9 Pottery jars 65 10
2108 $15 Oil-paper umbrella . . . 1·00 20

555 Pan Gu creating Universe

1993. The Creation. Multicoloured.
2109 $3.50 Type **555** 30 10
2110 $5 Pan Gu creating animals (horiz) 35 10
2111 $9 Nu Wa creating human beings (horiz) 70 10
2112 $19 Nu Wa mending the sky with smelted stone . . . . 1·25 20

556 Mandarins **557** Water Lily

1993. Lucky Animals (1st series).
2113 **556** $3.50 multicoloured . . 30 10
2114 – $5 multicoloured 35 10
2115 – $10 red and black . . . 75 15
2116 – $15 multicoloured . . . 1·00 20
DESIGNS: $5, Chinese unicorn; $10, Deer; $15, Crane.
See also Nos. 2151/4.

1993. Water Plants, Multicoloured.
2117 $5 Type **557** 40 10
2118 $9 Taiwan cow lily 75 10
2119 $12 Water hyacinth 85 15

1993. Children's Games (3rd series). As T **528**. Multicoloured.
2120 $5 Tossing sandbags 40 10
2121 $5 Bamboo dragonflies . . . 40 10
2122 $5 Skipping 40 10
2123 $5 Duel of strength with rope passed round waists 40 10

560 Ching-Kang-Chang Plateau (source)

1993. Yangtze River. Multicoloured.
2127 $3.50 Type **560** 35 10
2128 $3.50 Turn in river (Chinsha River) 35 10
2129 $5 Roaring Tiger Gorge (white water in narrow ravine) 40 10
2130 $5 Chutang Gorge (calm water in wide gorge) . . . 40 10
2131 $9 Dragon Gate, Pawu and Titsui Gorges 80 10

561 Noise Pollution and Music

1993. Environmental Protection. Children's Drawings. Multicoloured.
2132 $5 Type **561** 35 10
2133 $17 Family looking out over green fields (vert) . . . . 1·10 20

562 Cup with Tou-Ts'ai Figures

1993. Ch'eng-hua Porcelain Cups of Ming Dynasty. Multicoloured.
2134 $3.50 Type **562** 30 10
2135 $5 Chicken decoration . . . 35 10
2136 $7 Flowers and fruits of four seasons decoration 55 10
2137 $9 Dragon decoration . . . 75 10

563 Graphic Design **564** Child on Father's Shoulders

1993. 32nd International Vocational Training Competition, Taipeh. Multicoloured.
2138 $3.50 Type **563** 30 10
2139 $5 Computer technology . . 35 10
2140 $9 Carpentry 65 10
2141 $12 Welding 80 15

1993. Parent–Child Relationships. Mult.
2142 $3.50 Type **564** 30 10
2143 $5 Father playing flute to child 40 10
2144 $9 Child reading to father 75 10
2145 $10 Father pointing at bird 75 15

566 Persimmons **567** Gymnastics

1993. Fruits. Multicoloured.
2147 $5 Type **566** 40 10
2148 $5 Peaches 40 10
2149 $12 Loquats 60 15
2150 $12 Papayas 60 15

1993. Lucky Animals (2nd series). As T **556**. Mult.
2151 $1 Blue dragon (representing Spring, wood and the East) 20 10
2152 $2.50 White tiger (Autumn, metal and the West) . . . 30 10
2153 $9 Linnet (Summer, fire and the South) 60 15
2154 $19 Black tortoise (Winter, water and the North) . . 1·10 20

1993. Taiwan Area Games, Taoyuan. Mult.
2155 $5 Type **567** 25 10
2156 $5 Taekwondo 25 10

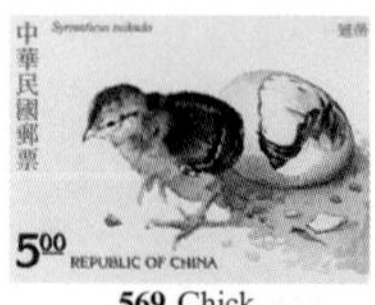

568 Stone Lion, New Park, Taipeh **569** Chick

1993. Stone Lions. Multicoloured.
2157 $3.50 Type **568** 30 10
2158 $5 Hsinchu City Council building 40 10
2159 $9 Temple, Hsinchu City . . 70 10
2160 $12 Fort Providentia, Tainan 95 15

1993. Mikado Pheasant. Multicoloured.
2161 $5 Type **569** 55 20
2162 $5 Mother and chicks . . . 55 20
2163 $5 Immature male and female 55 20
2164 $5 Adults 55 20
Nos. 2161/4 were issued together, se-tenant, forming a composite design.

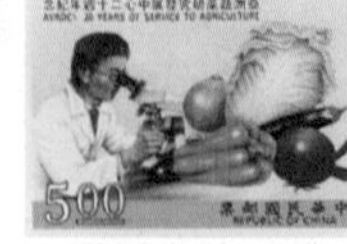

570 Dog **571** Scientist and Vegetables

1993. New Year Greetings. "Year of the Dog". Multicoloured.
2165 $3.50 Type **570** 15 10
2166 $13 Dog (facing left) 65 15

1993. 20th Anniv of Asian Vegetable Research and Development Centre. Multicoloured.
2168 $5 Type **571** 30 10
2169 $13 Scientists and fields of crops 75 15

573 Courtroom **574** Cutting Bamboo

1994. Inauguration of Taiwan Constitutional Court.
2171 **573** $5 multicoloured 30 10

1994. Traditional Paper Making. Multicoloured.
2172 $3.50 Type **574** 25 10
2173 $3.50 Cooking bamboo . . 25 10
2174 $5 Moulding bamboo pulp in wooden panels 40 10
2175 $5 Stacking wet paper for pressing 40 10
2176 $12 Drying paper 80 15

575 "Clivia miniata" **576** Wind Lion Lord

1994. Flowers. Multicoloured.
2177 $5 Type **575** 40 10
2178 $12 "Cymbidium sinense" 80 15
2179 $19 "Primula malacoides" 1·25 20

1994. Kinmen Wind Lion Lords.
2180 **576** $5 multicoloured 45 10
2181 – $9 multicoloured 80 10
2182 – $12 multicoloured . . . 1·00 15
2183 – $17 multicoloured . . . 1·25 20
DESIGNS: $9 to $17 Different Lion Lord statues.

577 Sailing Paper Boats **578** Playing Chess

1994. Children's Games (4th series). Mult.
2184 $5 Type **577** 40 10
2185 $5 Fighting with water-guns 40 10
2186 $5 Throwing paper plane . . 40 10
2187 $5 Human train 40 10

1994. Rural Pastimes. Multicoloured.
2189 $5 Type **578** 35 10
2190 $10 Playing the flute 60 10
2191 $12 Telling stories 85 15
2192 $19 Drinking tea . . . . . 1·25 20

579 Malaysian Night Heron and Chicks **580** Book with Hand on Cover

1994. Parent–Child Relationships. Birds with their Young. Multicoloured.
2193 $5 Type **579** 30 25
2194 $7 Little tern (horiz) 50 45
2195 $10 Common noddy (horiz) 75 60
2196 $12 Muller's barbet 85 90

1994. Protection of Intellectual Property Rights. Multicoloured.
2197 $5 Type **580** 30 10
2198 $15 Head with locked computer disk as brain . . 70 15

581 Caring for the Young **582** Anniversary Emblem and Olympic Rings

1994. International Rotary Clubs Convention, Taipeh. "Towards an Harmonious Society". Multicoloured.
2199 $5 Type **581** 30 10
2200 $17 Caring for the aged . . 70 20

1994. Centenary of International Olympic Committee. Multicoloured.
2201 $5 Type **582** 30 10
2202 $15 Running, high jumping and weight-lifting 70 15

583 Summit of Dah-pa Mountain **584** Chien Mu

1994. Shei-pa National Park. Multicoloured.
2203 $5 Type **583** 40 10
2204 $7 Shei-san Valley 50 10
2205 $10 Holy Ridge 70 10
2206 $17 Shiah-tsuei Pool . . . . 1·00 20

1994. Birth Centenary of Chien Mu (academic).
2207 **584** $5 multicoloured 35 10

585 Window

1994. International Year of the Family. Mult.
2208 $5 Type **585** 40 10
2209 $15 Globe and house . . . 70 25

586 Sueirenjy making Flame **587** Lin Yutang

1994. Invention Myths. Multicoloured.
2210 $5 Type **586** 40 10
2211 $10 Fushijy drawing Pa-kua characters 75 10
2212 $12 Shennungjy making pitchfork 80 20
2213 $15 Tsangjier inventing pictorial characters . . . 1·00 25

1994. Birth Centenary of Dr. Lin Yutang (essayist and lexicographer).
2214 **587** $5 multicoloured 25 10

588 Cheng Ho's Junk

589 Dr. Sun Yat-sen (founder)

1994. World Trade Week. Multicoloured.
2215 $5 Type **588** 30 10
2216 $17 Cheng Ho and route map around South Asia 70 15

1994. Centenary of Kuomintang Party. Mult.
2217 $5 Type **589** 30 10
2218 $19 Modern developments and voter placing slip in ballot box 80 15

590 Pig

591 Yen Chia-kan

1994. New Year Greetings. "Year of the Pig". Multicoloured.
2219 $3.50 Type **590** 15 10
2220 $13 Pig (facing left) 60 15

1994. 1st Death Anniv of Yen Chia-kan (President, 1974–78). Multicoloured.
2222 $5 Type **591** 25 10
2223 $15 Visiting farmers 70 15

592 Horse's Back

593 Begonia

1995. Traditional Architecture. Roof Styles. Mult.
2224 $5 Type **592** 35 10
2225 $5 Swallow's tail 35 10
2226 $12 Talisman (stove and bowl) 55 15
2227 $19 Cylinder-shaped brick 90 20

1995. Chinese Engravings. Flowers. Mult.
2228 $3.50 Type **593** 20 10
2229 $5 Rose 25 10
2230 $19 Flower 75 15
2231 $26 Climbing rose . . . . . 1·00 15
For these designs, but with the characters for the country name in a different order, see Nos. 2480/3.

594 Rotating Wheel of Pipes

595 Courtiers

1995. Irrigation Techniques from "Tian Gong Kai Wu" (encyclopaedia) by Sung Yin-shing. Multicoloured.
2232 $3.50 Type **594** 20 10
2233 $3.50 Donkey turning wheel to raise water 20 10
2234 $5 Pedal-driven device to raise water 35 10
2235 $12 Man turning wheel to raise water 85 15
2236 $13 Well . . . . 1·00 15

1995. "Beauties on an Outing" by Lee Gong-lin. Details of the painting. Multicoloured.
2237 $9 Type **595** 45 10
2238 $9 Courtier and beauty with child 45 10
2239 $9 Courtier with two beauties 45 10
2240 $9 Courtier 45 10
Nos. 2237/40 were issued together, se-tenant, forming a composite design.

596 Emblem and Landscape

597 Chinese Showy Lily

1995. Inaug of National Health Insurance Plan.
2242 **596** $12 multicoloured . . . 55 15

1995. Bulbous Flowers. Multicoloured.
2243 $5 Type **597** 35 10
2244 $12 Blood lily 45 15
2245 $19 Hyacinth 70 20

598 Opening Lines

1995. Chinese Calligraphy. "Cold Food Observance" (poem) by Su Shih.
2246 **598** $5 (1) multicoloured . . 65 10
2247 – $5 (2) multicoloured . . 65 10
2248 – $5 (3) multicoloured . . 65 10
2249 – $5 (4) multicoloured . . 65 10
Nos. 2246/9 were issued together, se-tenant, forming a composite design; the stamps are numbered in Chinese numerals to the right of the face value, from right to left.

599 Red Peony

600 Hand, Birds and Cracked Symbol

1995. Peonies. Paintings by Tsou I-kuei. Self-adhesive. Imperf.
2250 $5 Type **599** . . . . 2·00 10
2251 $5 Pink peony . . . . . . 2·00 10

1995. Anti-drugs Campaign. Multicoloured.
2252 $5 Type **600** 30 10
2253 $15 Arm and syringe forming cross 65 15

601 Old Hospital Building

1995. Centenary of National Taiwan University Hospital, Taipeh. Multicoloured.
2254 $5 Type **601** 25 10
2255 $19 New building 70 20

602 Chichi Bay

1995. Tourism. East Coast National Scenic Area. Multicoloured.
2256 $5 Type **602** 30 10
2257 $5 Shihyuesan (rocky promontory) 30 10
2258 $12 Hsiaoyehlieu (eroded rocks) 50 15
2259 $15 Changhong Bridge . . . 80 15

603 Mating

604 Bird feeding on Branch

1995. The Cherry Salmon. Multicoloured.
2260 $5 Type **603** 30 10
2261 $7 Female digging redd . . 45 10
2262 $10 Fry hatching 65 10
2263 $17 Fry swimming 80 20

1995. Chinese Engravings. Birds. Mult.
2264 $2.50 Type **604** 10 10
2265 $7 Bird on branch of peach tree 30 10
2266 $13 Bird preening 50 10
2267 $28 Yellow bird 80 20
For these designs with different face values and the order of the characters in the country name changed, see Nos. 2532/7.

605 "Tubastraea aurea"

606 Pasteur

1995. Marine Life. Multicoloured.
2268 $3.50 Type **605** 20 10
2269 $3.50 "Chromodoris elizabethina" 20 10
2270 $5 "Spirobranchus giganteus corniculatus" 40 10
2271 $17 "Himerometra magnipinna" 70 20

1995. Death Cent of Louis Pasteur (chemist).
2272 **606** $17 multicoloured . . . 90 20

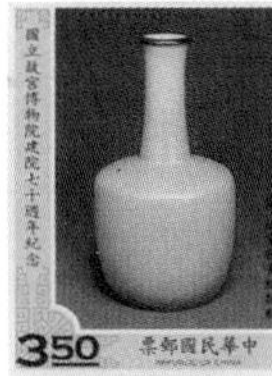

607 Porcelain Vase

608 Soldiers

1995. 70th Anniv of National Palace Museum. Multicoloured.
2273 $3.50 "Strange Peaks and Myriad Trees" (painting) (horiz) 20 10
2274 $3.50 Type **607** 20 10
2275 $5 X Fu-K'uei Ting bronze three-fronted vessel . . . 45 10
2276 $26 "The Fragrance of Flowers" (quatrain) (horiz) . . . . 1·00 25

1995. 50th Anniv of End of Sino-Japanese War. Multicoloured.
2277 $5 Type **608** 25 10
2278 $19 Taiwan flag, map and city 90 20

609 Common Green Turtle ("Chelonia mydas")

610 Scientists in Crop Field

1995. Year of the Sea Turtle. Multicoloured.
2280 $5 Type **609** 35 10
2281 $5 Loggerhead turtle ("Caretta caretta") . . . 35 10
2282 $5 Olive ridley turtle ("Lepidochelys olivacea") 35 10
2283 $5 Hawksbill turtle ("Eretmochelys imbricata") 35 10

1995. Centenary of Taiwan Agricultural Research Institute. Multicoloured.
2284 $5 Type **610** 25 10
2285 $28 Scientists in greenhouse growing anthuriums . . . 1·10 30

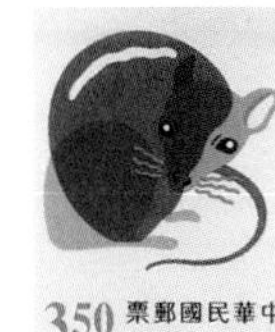

611 Rat

612 Escorting Bride to Ceremony

1995. New Year Greetings. "Year of the Rat". Multicoloured.
2286 $3.50 Type **611** 15 10
2287 $13 Rat (different) 85 15

1996. Traditional Wedding Ceremonies. Mult.
2289 $5 Type **612** 30 10
2290 $12 Honouring Heaven, Earth and ancestors . . . 65 10
2291 $19 Nuptial chamber . . . 90 15

613 Sharon Fruit

618 "Bougainvillea spectabilis"

614-17 "Scenic Dwelling at Chu-Ch'u"

1996. Chinese Engravings of Fruit by Hu Chen-yan.
2292 **613** $9 multicoloured 35 10
2293 – $12 multicoloured . . . 45 10
2294 – $15 multicoloured . . . 55 10
2295 – $17 multicoloured . . . 65 10
DESIGNS: $12 to $17, Different fruits.
For other values with the order of the characters in the country name reversed see Nos. 2580/2.

1996. Painting by Wang Meng.
2296 **614** $5 multicoloured 25 10
2297 **615** $5 multicoloured 25 10
2298 **616** $5 multicoloured 25 10
2299 **617** $5 multicoloured 25 10
Nos. 2296/9 were issued together, se-tenant, forming the composite design illustrated.

1996. Flowering Vines. Multicoloured.
2300 $5 Type **618** 30 10
2301 $12 Wisteria 65 10
2302 $19 Wood rose 90 15

619 Postboxes

620 Lecture and University

1996. Centenary of Chinese State Postal Service. Multicoloured.
2303 $5 Type **619** 30 10
2304 $9 Weighing equipment . . 55 10
2305 $12 Postal transport 65 10
2306 $13 Modern technology . . 70 10

1996. Centenary of National Chiao Tung University.
2308 **620** $19 multicoloured . . . 90 15

621 Chimei Giant Lion

1996. Tourism. Penghu National Scenic Area. Multicoloured.
2309 $5 Type **621** 30 10
2310 $5 Chipei beach (sand-spit) 30 10
2311 $12 Tungpan Yu 65 15
2312 $17 Tingkou Yu 85 15

622 Hand holding Family (charity)

1996. 30th Anniv of Tzu-Chi Foundation (Buddhist relief organization). Multicoloured.
2313 $5 Type **622** 30 10
2314 $19 Hospital patient in tulip petal (medicine) 70 20

623 With National Flag

1996. Inauguration of First Directly-elected President. Designs showing President Lee Teng-Hui and Vice-President Lien Chan. Multicoloured.

2315 $3.50 Type **623** 20 10
2316 $5 Outside Presidential Office building 35 10
2317 $13 Asia-Pacific Operations Hub Project 70 10
2318 $15 Meeting public at celebrations 75 15

624 Monument

1996. South China Sea Archipelago. Pratas and Itu Aba Islands. Multicoloured.

2320 $5 Type **624** 30 10
2321 $12 Monument (different) 65 10

625 Modern Gymnast and Cyclist
626 Feeding Silkworms

1996. Centenary of Modern Olympic Games. Multicoloured.

2323 $5 Type **625** 30 10
2324 $15 Ancient Greek athletes 75 15

1996. Silk Production Techniques from "Tian Gong Kai Wu" (encyclopaedia) by Sung Yin-shing. Multicoloured.

2325 $5 Type **626** 30 10
2326 $5 Picking out cocoons . . 30 10
2327 $7 Degumming raw silk . . 45 10
2328 $10 Reeling raw silk 60 10
2329 $13 Weaving silk 70 15

627 Bamboo
628 Tou-kung Bracket

1996. Chinese Engravings. Plants. Mult.

2330 $1 Type **627** 10 10
2331 $10 Orchid 35 10
2332 $20 Plum tree 75 15

1996. Traditional Architecture. Roof Supports. Multicoloured.

2333 $5 Type **628** 30 10
2334 $5 Chiue-ti bracket 30 10
2335 $10 Bu-tong beam 50 10
2336 $19 Dye-tou structure . . . 85 15

629 "Princess Iron Fan" (1941)

1996. Chinese Film Production. Mult.

2337 $3.50 Type **629** 25 10
2338 $3.50 "Chin Shan Bi Xie" (1957) 25 10
2339 $5 "Oyster Girl" (1964) . . 40 10
2340 $19 "City of Sadness" (1989) 85 20

630 Children dancing
631 "Autumn Scene with Wild Geese"

1996. Winning Entries in Children's Stamp Design Competition. Multicoloured.

2341 $5 Type **630** 35 10
2342 $5 Children playing in park 35 10
2343 $5 Black and white spotted cat 35 10
2344 $5 Container ship 35 10
2345 $5 Children showering . . . 35 10
2346 $5 Chinese gods and crowd 35 10
2347 $5 Pair of peacocks 35 10
2348 $5 Flying horse and rainbow 35 10
2349 $5 Elephant 35 10
2350 $5 Man and striped animals 35 10
2351 $5 Painting paper lampshades 35 10
2352 $5 Flock of geese 35 10
2353 $5 Children joining hands in garden 35 10
2354 $5 Archer 35 10
2355 $5 Children on ostrich's back 35 10
2356 $5 New Year celebrations 35 10
2357 $5 Butterflies on bamboo plant 35 10
2358 $5 Goatherd 35 10
2359 $5 Water-lilies on pond . . 35 10
2360 $5 Cats eating fish 35 10

1996. 10th Asian International Stamp Exhibition, Taipeh. Ancient Paintings from National Palace Museum. Multicoloured.

2361 $5 Type **631** 30 10
2362 $7 "Reeds and Wild Geese" 40 10
2363 $13 "Wild Geese gathering on Shore of Reeds" . . . 65 10
2364 $15 "Wild Geese on Bank in Autumn" 70 15

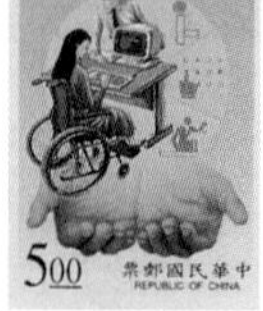
632 Bar Code and Graph
633 Disabled Worker and Open Hands

1996. 50th Anniv of Merchants' Day. Mult.

2366 $5 Type **632** 30 10
2367 $26 Line graph and globe 1·10 20

1996. Caring for the Handicapped. Mult.

2368 $5 Type **633** 30 10
2369 $19 Disabled boy painting, emblems within honeycomb and hands forming heart (employment) 85 15

634 Ox
636 Early Porcelain Production

1996. New Year Greetings. "Year of the Ox". Multicoloured.

2370 $3.50 Type **634** 20 10
2371 $13 Ox (different) 65 10

1997. Porcelain Production Techniques from "Tian Gong Kai Wu" (encyclopaedia) by Sung Yin-shing. Multicoloured.

2374 $5 Type **636** 30 10
2375 $5 Improved shaping . . . 30 10
2376 $7 Painting 35 10
2377 $10 Glazing 45 10
2378 $13 Firing 60 10

637 Dragons and Carp (from window, Longsan Temple, Lukang)
638 Peace Doves and Memorial

1997. (a) T **637**.

2379 **637** $50 red . . . . 1·90 30
2380 $60 blue . . . . 2·25 35
2381 $70 red . . . . 2·50 40
2382 $100 green . . . . . . 3·75 55

(b) As T **637** but with outer decorated frame. Size 25 × 33 mm.

2386 **637** $300 violet and blue . . 13·00 1·60
2387 $500 red and carmine . . 20·00 2·75

For $50 and $100 values in different colours and with the characters in the country name in reverse order see Nos. 2573/4.

1997. 50th Anniv of 228 Incident (civilian demonstration against government).

2390 **638** $19 multicoloured . . . 80 15

639 "Rhododendron x mucronatum"
640 River, Trees and Wildlife

1997. Shrubs. Multicoloured.

2391 $5 Type **639** 30 10
2392 $12 "Hibiscus rosa-sinensis" 55 10
2393 $19 "Hydrangea macrophylla" 80 15

1997. Protection of Water Resources. Mult.

2394 $5 Type **640** 30 10
2395 $19 Rivers and trees 80 15

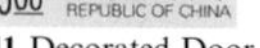

641 Decorated Door
642 "Dorcus formosanus"

1997. Traditional Architecture. Mult.

2396 $5 Type **641** 30 10
2397 $5 Gable wall 30 10
2398 $10 Brick wall-carving . . . 45 10
2399 $19 Verandah 80 15

1997. Insects. Multicoloured.

2400 $5 Type **642** 30 10
2401 $7 Giant katydid 35 10
2402 $10 Philippine birdwing . . 45 10
2403 $17 Big-headed stick insect 75 15

643 Alunite

1997. Minerals. Multicoloured.

2404 $5 Type **643** 30 10
2405 $5 Aragonite 30 10
2406 $12 Enargite 55 10
2407 $19 Hokutolite 80 15

644 Nanyashan Coastline
645 Train and Chingshuei Cliffs (northern loop)

1997. Tourism. North-east Coast National Scenic Area. Multicoloured.

2408 $5 Type **644** 30 10
2409 $5 Pitou Coastline (rocky shore) 30 10
2410 $12 Stone pillar, Nanya . . 55 10
2411 $19 Tsaoling historic trail 80 15

1997. Completion of Round-island Railway System. Multicoloured.

2412 $5 Type **645** 30 10
2413 $28 Train leaving tunnel (southern loop) . . . . . 1·25 20

646 Integrated Circuit and Communications Equipment

1997. Electronic Industry. Multicoloured.

2414 $5 Type **646** 25 10
2415 $26 Circuit board, portable computer, mobile phone and synthesized keyboard 1·00 15

647 Shaolinquan

1997. Martial Arts. Multicoloured.

2416 $5 Type **647** 25 10
2417 $5 Form and will boxing (vert) 25 10
2418 $9 Taijiquan 40 10
2419 $19 Eight diagrams boxing (vert) 75 15

648 "Hsi Hsiang Chi" (Wang Shih-fu)
649 Bitan Bridge over River Shindian

1997. Chinese Classical Opera. Multicoloured.

2420 $5 Type **648** 25 10
2421 $5 "Dan Daw Huei" (Kuan Han-chin) 25 10
2422 $12 "Han Guong Chiou" (Ma Jyi-yuan) 50 10
2423 $15 "Wu Tong Yu" (Bai Pu) 60 10

1997. Inauguration of Second Northern Freeway. Multicoloured.

2424 $5 Type **649** 25 10
2425 $19 Hsinchu Interchange . . 75 15

650 Badminton
651 Palm of Buddha

1997. Sports. Multicoloured.

2426 $5 Type **650** 25 10
2427 $12 Bowling 50 10
2428 $19 Lawn tennis 75 15

1997. Classical Literature. "Journey to the West" (Ming dynasty novel). Multicoloured.

2429 $3.50 Type **651** 20 10
2430 $3.50 Pilgrimage of T'ang Monk 20 10
2431 $5 The Flaming Mountain 25 10
2432 $20 The Cobweb Cave . . . 80 15

652 Purple-crowned Lory

1997. Birds. Illustrations from the Ching dynasty "Bird Manual". Multicoloured.

2433 $5 Type **652** 25 10
2434 $5 Green magpie (on branch with small orange flowers) 25 10
2435 $5 Blue-crowned hanging parrot (green bird with red throat and rump) . . 25 10
2436 $5 Niltavas sp. (two birds with orange breasts) . . . 25 10
2437 $5 Red-billed blue magpie (with long blue tail) . . . 25 10
2438 $5 David's laughing thrush (on branch with red flowers) 25 10
2439 $5 Przewalski's rosefinch (on branch with orange-centred white flowers) 25 10
2440 $5 Common rosefinch (on branch with yellow flowers) 25 10
2441 $5 Mongolian trumpeter finch (on branch with white flowers and red hips) 25 10
2442 $5 Long-tailed minivets (two black and red birds) . . . 25 10
2443 $5 Black-naped oriole (on branch with weeping leaves) 25 10
2444 $5 Yellow-headed buntings (two birds on branch with thorns and small pink flowers) 25 10

2445 $5 Bohemian waxwing (on branch with large blue flowers) 25 10
2446 $5 Mongolian trumpeter finches (two birds on branch with large pink flowers) 25 10
2447 $5 Chinese jungle mynah (with "bristles" above beak) 25 10
2448 $5 Java sparrow (with white patch on neck) 25 10
2449 $5 Long-tailed parakeet (on branch with small blue flowers) 25 10
2450 $5 Black-winged starling (by stream) 25 10
2451 $5 Cloven-feathered dove (two green and white birds) 25 10
2452 $5 Wryneck (on ground) . . 25 10

653 Tiger

654 Pres. Chiang

1997. New Year Greetings. "Year of the Tiger".
2453 **653** $3.50 multicoloured . . 20 10
2454 $13 multicoloured . . . 55 10

1998. 10th Death Anniv of Chiang Ching-kuo (President 1978–88).
2456 **654** $5 brown 20 10
2457 – $19 red 70 15
DESIGN—HORIZ: $19 Chiang and applauding crowd.

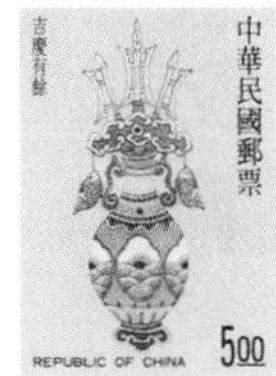

655 "Abundance"

656 "Gaillardia pulchella var. picta"

1998. Wishes for the Coming Year. Mult.
2458 $5 Type **655** 20 10
2459 $5 Flowers springing from lidded bowl ("Harmony") 20 10
2460 $12 Peonies in containers ("Honour and Wealth") 45 10
2461 $12 Flowers in vase and oranges in bowl ("Luck") 45 10

1998. Herbaceous Flowers. Multicoloured.
2462 $5 Type **656** 20 10
2463 $12 "Kalanchoe blossfeldiana" 45 10
2464 $19 "Portulaca oleracea var. granatus" 70 15

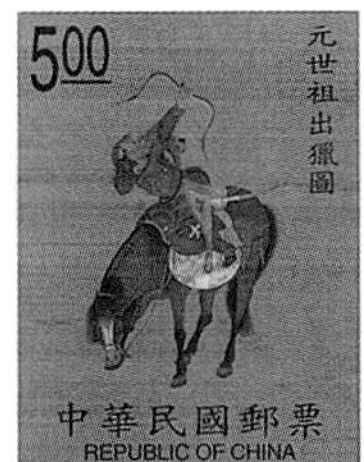

657 Horseman drawing Bow

1998. Painting by Liu Kuan-tao. Mult.
2465 $5 Type **657** 20 10
2466 $19 Kublai Khan and entourage on hunting expedition (63 × 40 mm) 70 15

658 "A Frog has only One Mouth"

1998. Children's Nursery Rhymes. Mult.
2468 $5 Type **658** 20 10
2469 $5 Mouse and cat ("A Little Mouse climbs an Oil Lamp") 20 10
2470 $12 Children and fireflies ("Fireflies") 45 10
2471 $19 Girl and egret carrying baskets ("Egrets") 70 15

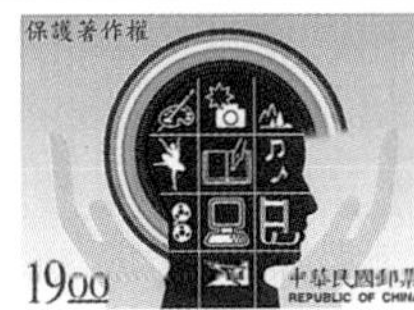

659 Cultural Symbols within Human Head

1998. 70th Anniv of Copyright Law.
2472 **659** $19 multicoloured . . . 70 15

660 "Chung K'uei Moving" (Kung Kai)

661 Emblem and Cherry Blossom

1998. Ancient Paintings of Chung K'uei (mythological figure). Multicoloured.
2473 $5 Type **660** 20 10
2474 $20 Chung K'uei dancing ("An Auspicious Occasion") 75 15

1998. 125th Anniv of International Law Association and 68th Conference, Taipeh.
2475 **661** $15 multicoloured . . . 55 10

662 Grain Barge

663 Begonia

1998. Ships and Vehicles from "Tian Gong Kai Wu" (encyclopaedia) by Sung Yin-shing. Multicoloured.
2476 $5 Type **662** 20 10
2477 $7 Six-oared ferry boat . . 25 10
2478 $10 One-wheel horse-drawn carriage 35 10
2479 $13 Man pushing one-wheel cart 50 10

1998. Chinese Engravings. Flowers. Designs as Nos. 2228/31 but with values changed and Chinese characters for the country name in reverse order as in T **663**. Multicoloured.
2480 $7 Type **663** 25 10
2481 $19 As No. 2229 . . . . 70 10
2482 $20 As No. 2230 . . . . 75 10
2483 $26 As No. 2231 . . . . 1·00 15

664 Pao-yu visits Garden

1998. Classical Literature. "Red Chamber Dream" (novel) by Tsao Hsueh-Chin. Multicoloured.
2484 $3.50 Type **664** 15 10
2485 $3.50 Tai-yu burying flowers 15 10
2486 $5 Pao-chai playing with butterflies 50 10
2487 $5 Hsiang-yun in drunken sleep 50 10

665 Scout Badge (⅔-size illustration)

1998. 20th Asia-Pacific and Eighth China National Scout Jamboree, Pingtung University. Multicoloured.
2488 $5 Type **665** 20 10
2489 $5 Tents 20 10

666 Carved Base of Pillar

667 Table Tennis

1998. Traditional Architecture. Multicoloured.
2490 $5 Type **666** 20 10
2491 $5 Carved stone ramp ("spirit way") between staircases 20 10
2492 $10 Carved base (with fishes) of column 35 10
2493 $19 Carved stone drainage spout 70 10

1998. Sports. Multicoloured.
2494 $5 Type **667** 20 10
2495 $5 Table tennis player serving 20 10
2496 $7 Rugby player with ball 25 10
2497 $7 Rugby players 25 10
Stamps of the same value were issued together, se-tenant, forming a composite design.

668 "The Fox borrows the Tiger's Ferocity"

1998. Chinese Fables. Multicoloured.
2498 $5 Type **668** 20 10
2499 $5 "A Frog in a Well" . . . 20 10
2500 $12 "Adding Legs to a Drawing of a Snake" . . 45 10
2501 $19 "The Snipe and the Clam at a Deadlock" . . 70 10

670 Taiwushan

1998. Kinmen National Park. Multicoloured.
2508 $5 Type **670** 20 10
2509 $5 Kuningtou Cliff 20 10
2510 $12 Teyueh Tower and Huang Hui-huang's House, Shuitou 45 10
2511 $19 Putou beach, Leihyu . . 70 10

671 Hodgson's Hawk Eagle ("Spizaetus nipalensis")

672 Mountain and Pavilions

1998. Birds. Multicoloured.
2512 $5 Type **671** 20 10
2513 $5 Hodgson's hawk eagle in flight 20 10
2514 $5 Crested serpent eagle ("Spilornis cheela") on branch 20 10
2515 $5 Crested serpent eagle carrying snake 20 10
2516 $10 Black kite ("Milvus migrans") on rock 35 10
2517 $10 Black kite in flight . . . 35 10
2518 $10 Indian black eagle ("Ictinaetus malayensis") on branch 35 10
2519 $10 Indian black eagle in flight 35 10
Nos. 2512/13, 2514/15, 2516/17 and 2518/19 respectively were issued together, se-tenant, each pair forming a composite design.

1998. Ching Dynasty Jade Mountain Carvings. Mult.
2520 $5 Type **672** 20 10
2521 $5 Men working in jade mine (horiz) 20 10
2522 $7 Men washing elephant (horiz) 25 10
2523 $26 Five men on a mountain . . . . 1·00 15

673 Rabbit

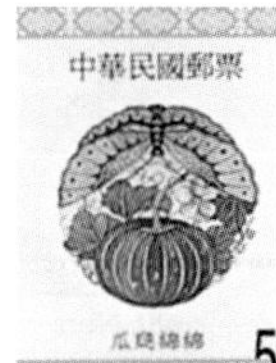

674 Butterfly and Pumpkin ("Many Descendants")

1998. New Year Greetings. "Year of the Rabbit". Multicoloured.
2525 $3.50 Type **673** 15 10
2526 $13 Rabbit (different) . . . 50 10

1999. Wishes for the Coming Year. Multicoloured.
2528 $5 Type **674** 20 10
2529 $5 Mandarins (ducks) and lotus flowers ("Good marriage that brings sons") 20 10
2530 $12 Egret ("Prosperity") . . 45 10
2531 $12 Goldfish and flowers ("Abundance") 45 10

1999. Chinese Engravings. Birds and Plants. Designs as Nos. 2264/7 and 2330/1 but with values and Chinese characters for the country name in reverse order as in T **663**. Multicoloured.
2532 $1 Type **604** 10 10
2533 $3.50 As No. 2265 . . . . . 15 10
2534 $5 As No. 2266 . . . . . 20 10
2535 $10 As No. 2267 . . . . . 35 10
2536 $12 Type **627** 45 10
2536a $20 As No. 2482 . . . . . 80 35
2537 $28 As No. 2331 . . . . . 1·10 20
2537a $34 As No. 2649 . . . . . 1·40 60

676 "Gloxinia"

677 Boy towing Toy Elephant

1999. Indoor Flowers. Multicoloured.
2539 $5 Type **676** 20 10
2540 $12 African violet 45 10
2541 $19 Flamingo flower 70 10

1999. Illustrations from "Joy in Peacetime" (Ching Dynasty book). Lantern Festival. Multicoloured.
2542 $5 Type **677** 20 10
2543 $5 Women, children and crane 20 10
2544 $7 Children playing with toy animals 25 10
2545 $26 Children playing . . . 1·00 15

678 Hanging Cylinder

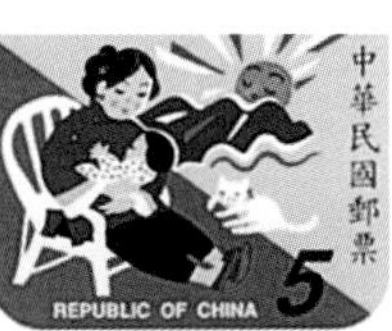

679 "Baby Sleeps"

1999. Traditional Architecture. Decorative Features. Multicoloured.
2547 $5 Type **678** 20 10
2548 $5 Taishi screen 20 10
2549 $10 Xuanyu (gable decoration) 35 10
2550 $19 Wood carving 70 10

1999. Nursery Rhymes. Multicoloured.
2551 $5 Type **679** 20 10
2552 $5 Mother comforting baby frightened by storm ("Be Brave") 20 10
2553 $12 Mother and baby rocking ("Rock, Rock, Rock") 45 10
2554 $19 Mother, baby, cat and flies ("Buggie Flies") . . . 70 10

680 Atayal Ancestor Festival

682 "Washing Cotton Yarn" (Liang Chenyu)

681 Nurses treating Patients

1999. Taiwan's Aboriginal Culture. Multicoloured.
2555 $5 Type **680** 20 10
2556 $5 Dancers with hip bells (Saisat Festival of the Dwarfs) 20 10
2557 $5 Circle of singers (Bunun Millet Harvest Song) . . 20 10
2558 $5 Line of singers in red coats (Tsou Victory Festival) 20 10
2559 $5 Dancers and millet biscuits mounted on board (Rukai Harvest Festival) 20 10
2560 $5 Men with bamboo poles (Paiwan Bamboo Festival) 20 10
2561 $5 Procession of men carrying yellow scarves (Puyuma Harvest Ceremony) 20 10
2562 $5 Line of women dancers with white headdresses (Ami Harvest Ceremony) 20 10
2563 $5 Launch of new fishing boat (Yami Boat Ceremony) 20 10

1999. Centenary of International Council of Nurses. Multicoloured.
2564 $5 Type **681** 60 10
2565 $17 Globe and nurse carrying tray . . . . . . 1·40 10

1999. Chinese Classical Opera (Legends of the Ming Dynasty). Multicoloured.
2566 $5 Type **682** 20 10
2567 $5 "The Story of a Pipa" (Kaoming) 20 10
2568 $12 "The Story of Hung Fu" (Chang Fengyi) . . . 45 10
2569 $15 "Paiyueh Pavilion" (Shi Hui) 55 10

683 Coins

1999. 50th Anniv of Introduction of the Silver Yuan. Multicoloured.
2571 $5 Type **683** 20 10
2572 $25 Banknotes 95 15

684 Dragons and Carp (from window, Longsan Temple, Lukang)

685 Childern giving Present

1999. (a) As Nos. 2379, 2382, 2386 and 2387 but with Chinese characters for the country name in reverse order, as in T **684**, and colours changed.
2573 **684** $50 green . . . . 1·90 30
2574 $100 brown . . . . 4·00 60

(b) as T **684** but with outer decorated frame. Size 25 × 33 mm.
2578 $300 red and blue . . . . 11·00 4·50
2579 $500 red and brown . . . . 17·00 7·00

1999. Chinese Engravings of Fruit by Hu Chen-yan. Designs as Nos. 2292/4 but with Chinese characters for the country name in reverse order, and values changed. Multicoloured.
2580 50c. As Type **613** 10 10
2581 $6 As $12 . . . . 20 10
2582 $25 As $15 . . . . 95 15

1999. Fathers' Day. Multicoloured.
2584 $5 Type **685** 20 10
2585 $25 Father teaching boy to ride bike 95 10

686 Peony Lobster (Taiwanese Cuisine)

1999. Chinese Regional Dishes. Multicoloured.
2586 $5 Type **686** 10 10
2587 $5 Buddha jumps the wall (Fukien) (plate, teapot, jar and cups) 10 10
2588 $5 Flower hors d'oeuvres (Cantonese) 10 10
2589 $5 Dongpo pork (Kiangsu and Chekiang) (plate, bowl and double handled jar) 10 10
2590 $5 Stewed fish jaws (Shanghai) (plate decorated with strawberries) 10 10
2591 $5 Beggar's chicken (Hunan) (with folded napkin) . . . 10 10
2592 $5 Carp jumping over dragon's gate (Szechwan) (on silver platter) 10 10
2593 $5 Peking duck (Peking) (in silver dish) 10 10

687 Scuba Diving

1999. Outdoor Activities. Multicoloured.
2594 $5 Type **687** 10 10
2595 $6 Canoeing 20 10
2596 $10 Surfing 35 10
2597 $25 Windsurfing 95 15

688 Stage and Audience

1999. Taiwanese Opera. Multicoloured.
2598 $5 Type **688** 10 10
2599 $6 Preparation in the dressing room 20 10
2600 $10 Two actresses 35 10
2601 $25 Actress as clown . . . 95 15

690 Yellow-headed Amazon

691 Dragon

1999. Birds (1st series). Illustrations from the Ching Dynasty Bird Manual. Multicoloured.
2603 $5 Type **690** 20 10
2604 $5 Golden-winged parakeet 20 10
2605 $12 Grey parrot 50 10
2606 $25 Chattering lory . . . . 1·10 20
See also Nos. 2671/4 and 2740/3.

1999. New Year Greetings. "Year of the Dragon". Multicoloured.
2607 $3.50 Type **691** 15 10
2608 $13 Dragon (different) . . . 55 10

692 ST-1 Communication Satellite over Earth

1999. Year 2000. Multicoloured.
2610 $5 Type **692** (information) 20 10
2611 $5 Deer and river (environmental protection) 20 10
2612 $12 Modern buildings and high-speed train (industry and economy) 50 10
2613 $15 Dove and St. Peter's Basilica,Vatican City (peace) 65 10

693 Emperor Chia-Ching's "Coloured Cloud Dragon" Writing Brushes (Ming Dynasty)

2000. Traditional Chinese Writing Equipment. Mult.
2616 $5 Type **693** 20 10
2617 $5 Emperor Lung Ching's "Imperial Dragon Fragrance" ink stick (Ming Dynasty) (vert) . . 20 10
2618 $7 "Clear Heart House" (calligraphy, Tsai Hsiang) (Sung Dynasty) (vert) . . 30 10
2619 $26 "Celadon Toad Inkstone" (Sung Dynasty) 1·10 20

694 Kaoping River Bridge Pylon

2000. Inauguration of Second Southern Freeway. Multicoloured.
2620 $5 Type **694** 20 10
2621 $12 Main junction, Tainan 50 10

695 Branch, Fields and Houses

2000. Seasonal Periods (1st series). Designs depicting the six seasonal periods of Spring. Multicoloured.
2623 $5 Type **695** ("Commencement of Spring") 20 10
2624 $5 Man ploughing fields in the rain ("Rain Water") 20 10
2625 $5 Forks of lightning, little egret and cattle egret("Waking of Insects") 20 10
2626 $5 Men transplanting rice seedlings (Spring Equinox) 20 10
2627 $5 Basket of fruit and houses ("Pure Brightness") 20 10
2628 $5 Rain, farmer and river ("Grain Rain") 20 10
See also Nos. 2636/41, 2652/7 and 2675/80.

696 Shuanghsi River and School Gates, Waishuanghsi Campus

697 Three Heroes at Altar

2000. Centenary of Soochow University. Mult.
2629 $5 Type **696** 20 10
2630 $25 Justice statue, Soochow Law School, Taipeh campus and Ansu Hall, Waishuanghsi campus . . 1·10 20

2000. Classical Literature. *Romance of the Three Kingdoms* by Luo Guanzhong (1st series). Mult.
2631 $3.50 Type **697** 15 10
2632 $3.50 Guan Yu reading at night 15 10
2633 $5 Couple in cottage receiving guest 20 10
2634 $20 Arrows raining down on sampans 85 10

698 Crops and Mountains

2000. Seasonal Periods (2nd series). Designs depicting the six seasonal periods of Summer. Multicoloured.
2636 $5 Type **698** ("Commencement of Summer") 20 10
2637 $5 Water wheel and houses in rain ("Little Fullness") 20 10
2638 $5 Ears of grain and houses ("Husks of Grain") . . . 20 10
2639 $5 Insect on plant and houses (Summer Solstice) 20 10
2640 $5 Palm leaf fan and fields ("Lesser Heat") 20 10
2641 $5 Watermelons ("Great Heat") 20 10
Nos. 2636/41 were issued together, se-tenant, forming a composite design.

699 Chen Shui-bian and Lu Hsiu-lien

2000. Inauguration of Chen Shui-bian as 10th President and Lu Hsiu-lien as Vice-President. Mult.
2642 $5 Type **699** 20 10
2643 $5 Presidential Office building 20 10

700 Hsialiao

701 Taiwan Giant Sacred Tree

2000. Monuments Marking the Tropic of Cancer. Multicoloured.
2645 $5 Type **700** 20 10
2646 $12 Wuho 55 10
2647 $25 Chingpu . . . . 1·10 20

2000. Chinese Engravings of Fruit by Hu Chen-yan. As No. 2295 but with Chinese characters for the country name in reverse order, as in T **683**, and with value (2648) or new design changed.
2648 $32 multicoloured . . . . . 1·40 25
2649 $34 multicoloured . . . . . 1·50 25

2000. Sacred Trees. Multicoloured.
2650 $5 Type **701** 20 10
2651 $39 Sacred Sleeping Moon Tree . . . . 1·60 25

702 Grain drying

2000. Seasonal Periods (3rd series). Depicting the six seasonal periods of Autumn. Multicoloured.
2652 $5 Type **702** ("Commencement of Autumn") 20 10
2653 $5 Rick and village ("Bounds of Heat") . . . 20 10
2654 $5 Dew covered leaves ("White Dew") 20 10
2655 $5 Red leaves ("Autumn Equinox") 20 10
2656 $5 Bare tree ("Cold Dew") 20 10
2657 $5 Frost on plant ("Descent of Hoar Frost") 20 10
Nos. 2652/57 were issued together, se-tenant. forming a composite design.

2000. No. 1784 surch **350**.
2658 $3.50 on $7.50 multicoloured 15 10

704 Red Spider Lily

705 Seismograph and map of Taiwan

2000. Poisonous Plants. Multicoloured.
2659 $5 Type **704** 20 10
2660 $5 Odollam erberus-tree (*Cerbera manghas*) 20 10
2661 $12 Rosary pea 55 10
2662 $20 Oleander 85 10

2000. Earthquakes. Multicoloured.
2663 $5 Type **705** 20 10
2664 $12 Rescue workers 55 10
2665 $25 Earthquake drills . . . 1·10 20

706 *Anotogaster sieboldii*

2000. Dragonflies. Multicoloured.
2666 $5 Type **706** 20 10
2667 $5 *Lamelligomphus formosanus* (horiz) 20 10
2668 $12 *Neurothemis ramburii* (horiz) 50 20
2669 $12 *Trithemis festiva* 50 20

707 White's Thrush

2000. Birds (2nd series). Illustrations from the Ching Dynasty Bird Manual. Multicoloured.
2671 $5 Type **707** 20 10
2672 $5 Brambling 20 10
2673 $12 Rothschild's mynah . . 50 20
2674 $25 Southern grackle . . . 1·00 40

708 Lake, Mountains and Bowl

2000. Seasonal Periods (4th series). Designs depicting the six seasonal periods of Winter. Multicoloured.
2675 $5 Type **708** ("Commencement of Winter") 20 10
2676 $5 Trees covered in snow ("Lesser Snow") 20 10
2677 $5 Mountains covered in snow ("Great Snow") . . 20 10
2678 $5 Rice balls in bowl ("Winter Solstice") . . . 20 10
2679 $5 Houses and tree branch covered in snow ("Lesser Cold") 20 10
2680 $5 Log cabin covered in snow ("Great Cold") . . 20 10
Nos. 2675/80 were issued together, se-tenant, forming a composite design.

709 Palace Lamp Boulevard and Classrooms

2000. 50th Anniv of Tamkang University. Mult.
2681 $5 Type **709** 20 10
2682 $25 Maritime Museum and "Scroll Plaza" (sculpture) 1·00 40

710 Snake **712** Cruise Ship and Buildings

2000. New Year Greetings. "Year of the Snake". Multicoloured.
2683 $3.50 Type **710** 15 10
2684 $13 Snake (different) . . . 55 25

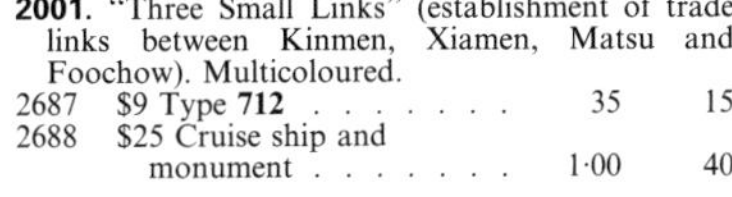

2001. "Three Small Links" (establishment of trade links between Kinmen, Xiamen, Matsu and Foochow). Multicoloured.
2687 $9 Type **712** 35 15
2688 $25 Cruise ship and monument . . . . 1·00 40

713 Lotus Blossoms ("Marital Bliss") **715** Apples

714 Aquarius

2001. Wishes for the Coming Year. Multicoloured.
2689 $5 Type **713** 20 10
2690 $5 Loganberries, lichees and walnuts ("Success in one's career") 20 10
2691 $12 Pomegranates ("Producing many offspring") 50 20
2692 $12 Peonies and pair of Chinese bulbuls ("Growing old together with wealth and high position") 50 20

2001. Signs of the Western Zodiac (1st series). Air Signs. Multicoloured.
2693 $5 Type **714** 20 10
2694 $12 Gemini 50 20
2695 $25 Libra . . . . 1·00 40
See also Nos. 2708/10, 2726/8 and 2755/7.

2001. Fruits (1st series). Multicoloured.
2696 $5 Type **715** 20 10
2697 $7 Guavas 30 15
2698 $12 Pears 50 20
2699 $25 Melons . . . . 1·00 40
See also Nos. 2732/5 and 2785/8.

716 Main Peak

2001. Mount Jade. Views of Mount Jade. Mult.
2700 $5 Type **716** 20 10
2701 $5 Western peak 20 10
2702 $12 Northern peak 50 20
2703 $25 Eastern peak . . . . . 1·00 40

717 Girls playing with Ball ("Little Ball")

2001. Children's Playtime Rhymes. Multicoloured.
2704 $5 Type **717** 20 10
2705 $5 Children sitting in a circle ("Point to the Water Vat") 20 10
2706 $12 Boys dancing ("Pangolin") 50 20
2707 $25 Children playing ("Shake and Stamp") . . 1·00 40

2001. Signs of the Western Zodiac (2nd series). Earth Signs. As T **714**. Multicoloured.
2708 $5 Capricorn 20 10
2709 $12 Taurus 50 20
2710 $25 Virgo . . . . 1·00 40

718 Sakyamuni Buddha, Northern Wei Dynasty

2001. Ancient Statues of Buddha. Multicoloured.
2711 $5 Type **718** 20 15
2712 $9 Seated Buddha, Tang Dynasty 35 15
2713 $12 Mahavairocana Buddha, Sung Dynasty 50 20

719 Thresher

2001. Early Agricultural Implements. Multicoloured.
2715 $5 Type **719** 20 10
2716 $7 Ox plough 30 15
2717 $10 Bamboo baskets and yoke 45 20
2718 $25 Coir raincoat and hat 1·00 80

720 Mackay **721** Girl dancing, Globe and Emblem

2001. Death Centenary of George Leslie Mackay (missionary and educator).
2719 **720** $25 multicoloured . . . 1·00 80

2001. Kiwanis International (community organization) Convention, Taipeh. Multicoloured.
2720 $5 Type **721** 20 10
2721 $25 Mother and child within heart . . . . 1·00 80

722 Dragon

2001. Kites. Multicoloured.
2722 $5 Type **722** 20 10
2723 $5 Phoenix 20 10
2724 $5 Tiger 20 10
2725 $5 Fish 20 10

2001. Signs of the Western Zodiac (3rd series). Fire Signs. As T **714**. Multicoloured.
2726 $5 Aries 20 10
2727 $12 Leo 50 20
2728 $25 Sagittarius . . . . . . 1·00 80

723 Medium-Capacity Car

2001. Rapid Transit System, Taipeh. Multicoloured.
2729 $5 Type **723** 20 10
2730 $12 Passengers and tickets 45 20
MS2731 125 × 60 mm. $25 Chientan Station, Tamshui Line (84 × 42 mm) 90 90

2001. Fruits (2nd series). As T **715**. Multicoloured.
2732 $1 Plums 10 10
2733 $3.50 Tangerines 15 10
2734 $20 Longans 70 30
2735 $40 Grapefruit . . . . . . 1·40 60

724 Keeper and Monkeys ("Now Three, Now Four")

2001. Chinese Fables. Multicoloured.
2736 $5 Type **724** 20 10
2737 $5 Man selling weapons ("Selling the All Penetrating Sword and Unyielding Shield") . . . 20 10
2738 $12 Farmer sitting under tree ("Waiting by the Tree for the Rabbit") . . . 45 20
2739 $25 Old man and children ("An Old Fool Moves Mountains") 90 40

725 Japanese Waxwing

2001. Birds (3rd series). Showing illustrations from the Ching Dynasty Bird Manual. Multicoloured.
2740 $5 Type **725** 20 10
2741 $5 Siberian rubythroat . . . 20 10
2742 $12 White-rumped munia 45 20
2743 $25 Great barbet 90 40

726 Second Terminal, Chiang Kai-shek International Airport

2001. 90th Anniv of Republic of China. Multicoloured.
2744 $5 Type **726** 20 10
2745 $5 Computer screens, lap top computer, mobile phone and Globe 20 10
2746 $12 Dance, National Theatre 45 20
2747 $15 Dolphins 55 25

727 Flame, Karate, Javelin and Table Tennis

2001. National Games, Kaohsiung and Pingtung. Multicoloured.
2748 $5 Type **727** 20 10
2749 $25 Swimming, athletics, weightlifting and map . . 90 40

728 Pitcher

2001. 34th World Baseball Championship and 21st Asia Baseball Tournament. Multicoloured.
2750 $5 Type **728** 20 10
2751 $5 Batter 20 10
2752 $12 Catcher 45 20
2753 $20 Base runner 70 30
MS2754 120 × 85 mm. Nos. 2750/3 1·40 1·40

2001. Signs of the Western Zodiac (4th series). Water Signs. As T **714**. Multicoloured.
2755 $5 Pisces 20 10
2756 $12 Cancer 45 20
2757 $25 Scorpio 90 40

729 Mozhaonu holding Fan ("Thunder Storm")

2001. Taiwanese Puppet Theatre. Showing puppets. Multicoloured.
2758 $5 Type **729** 20 10
2759 $6 Taiyangau ("Rising Winds, Surging Clouds") 20 10
2760 $10 Kuangdao ("Thunder Crazy Sword") 35 15
2761 $25 Chin Chia-chien ("Thunder Golden Light") 90 40

730 Old School Building, Shuiyan Road, Taipeh **731** Horse

2001. Centenary of National Defence Medical Centre. Multicoloured.
2762 $5 Type **730** 20 10
2763 $25 New school building and medical staff 90 40

2001. New Year Greetings. "Year of the Horse". Multicoloured.
2764 $3.50 Type **731** 15 10
2765 $13 Horse (different) 45 20
MS2766 78 × 102 mm. Nos. 2764/5, each × 2 1·25 1·25

732 Yu Pin

2001. Birth Centenary of Yu Pin (religious leader).
2767 **732** $25 multicoloured . . . 90 40
MS2768 80 × 60 mm. $25 As No. 2767 90 40

733 Carnations

2001. Greetings Stamps. Multicoloured.
2769 $5 Type **733** 20 10
2770 $5 White lilies 20 10
2771 $5 Pink violas 20 10
2772 $5 Orange flowers with yellow centres 20 10
2773 $5 Pink flowers with five petals 20 10
2774 $5 Pink roses 20 10
2775 $5 Christmas tree decorations 20 10
2776 $5 Poinsettia 20 10
2777 $5 Purple ball-shaped flowers 20 10
2778 $5 Sunflowers 20 10

734 Students with Flags

2002. 50th Anniv of Fu Hsing Kang College (military university). Multicoloured.
2779 $5 Type **734** 20 10
2780 $25 University buildings and statue 90 40

735 Vase containing Lotus Flower and Sweet Osmanthus ("Producing many offspring")

2002. Wishes for the Coming Year. Multicoloured.
2781 $5 Type **735** 20 10
2782 $5 Orchid and osmanthus plants ("Person of high morality") 20 10
2783 $12 Vase containing peonies and flowering crabapple ("Hall full of the rich and famous") 45 20
2784 $12 Vase containing roses ("Safe and peaceful in all four seasons") 45 20

2002. Fruits (3rd series). As T **715**. Multicoloured.
2785 $6 Avocados 20 10
2786 $10 Lychees 40 20
2787 $17 Dates 60 25
2788 $32 Passionfruit . . . . . . 1·10 45

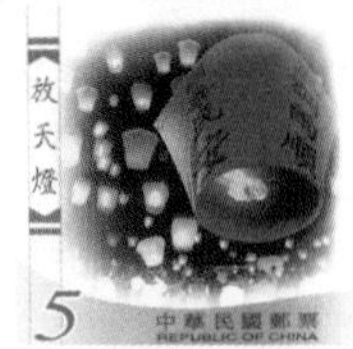

736 Lantern Festival (Pinghsi and Shihfen)

2002. Traditional Folk Festivals (1st series). Multicoloured.
2789 $5 Type **736** 20 10
2790 $5 Fireworks display (Yanshui) 20 10
2791 $10 Matsu (sea goddess) procession (Peikang) . . . 40 20
2792 $20 Dragon boat race . . . 75 30

737 Mountain in Winter

2001. Mount Hsueh. Views of Mount Hsueh. Multicoloured.
2793 $5 Type **737** 20 10
2794 $5 North ridge 20 10
2795 $12 Slopes in autumn . . . 45 20
2796 $25 Glacial cirques (bowl-shaped depressions) . . . 90 40

POSTAGE DUE STAMPS

(D 12) (D 15)

1950. Surch as Type D **12**.
D105 **6** 4c. on $100 blue . . . . 11·50 9·00
D106 10c. on $100 blue . . . . 22·00 5·50
D107 20c. on $100 blue . . . . 11·50 10·00
D108 40c. on $100 blue . . . . 30·00 22·00
D109 $1 on $100 blue . . . . . 30·00 40·00

1951. No. 524 of China surch as Type D **15**.
D133 40c. on 40c. orange . . . . 19·00 13·00
D134 80c. on 40c. orange . . . . 19·00 12·00

(D 19) D 43

1953. Revenue stamps as T **143** of China surch as Type D **19**.
D151 10c. on $50 blue . . . . . 16·00 5·00
D152 20c. on $100 olive . . . . 16·00 5·00
D153 40c. on $20 brown . . . . 19·00 1·50
D154 80c. on $500 green . . . . 35·00 2·50
D155 100c. on $30 mauve . . . . 35·00 8·50

1956.
D236 D **43** 20c. red and blue . . . 2·50 50
D237 40c. green and buff . . 2·50 50
D238 80c. brown and grey . 3·75 75
D239 $1 blue and mauve . . 6·00 75

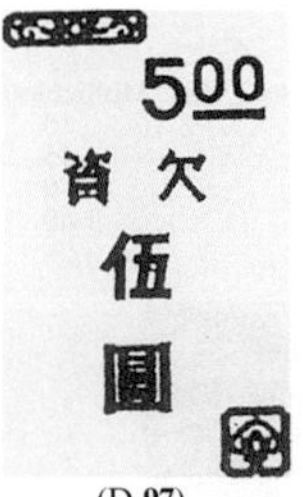

(D 97) D 152

1961. Surch with Type D **97**.
D429 **56** $5 on $20 red . . . . . 6·50 3·00

1964. Surch as Type D **97**.
D490 **83** 10c. on 80c. green . . . 50 30
D491 20c. on $3.60 blue . . . 50 40
D492 40c. on $4.50 red . . . 75 35

1966.
D588 D **152** 10c. brown and lilac 10 25
D589 20c. blue and yellow 15 25
D590 50c. ultram & blue 3·00 40
D591 $1 violet and flesh 55 15
D592 $2 green and blue 55 15
D593 $5 red and buff . . 75 20
D594a $10 purple & mauve 11·50 1·00

D 399

1984.
D1532a D **399** $1 red and blue . . 40 10
D1533a $2 yellow and blue 40 10
D1534 $3 green & mauve 40 10
D1535a $5 blue and yellow 50 15
D1536 $5.50 mauve & bl 50 15
D1537 $7.50 yellow & vio 60 25
D1538b $10 yellow and red 60 20
D1539 $20 blue and green 1·10 65

CHINA EXPEDITIONARY FORCE Pt. 1

Stamps used by Indian military forces in China.

12 pies = 1 anna; 16 annas = 1 rupee.

Stamps of India optd **C.E.F.**

1900. Queen Victoria.
C 1 **40** 3p. red . . . . 40 1·25
C 2 **23** ½a. green 75 30
C 3 – 1a. purple . . . . 4·00 1·50
C11 – 1a. red . . . . 28·00 8·00
C 4 – 2a. blue . . . . 3·00 9·00
C 5 – 2a.6p. green . . . . . . 2·75 13·00
C 6 – 3a. orange . . . . 2·75 16·00
C 7 – 4a. green (No. 96) . . . . 2·75 7·50
C 8 – 8a. mauve . . . . 2·75 18·00
C 9 – 12a. purple on red . . . . 16·00 16·00
C10 **37** 1r. green and red . . . . 21·00 21·00

1904. King Edward VII.
C12c **41** 3p. grey . . . . 4·50 6·50
C13 – 1a. red (No. 123) . . . . 7·50 70
C14 – 2a. lilac . . . . 14·00 2·50
C15 – 2a.6p. blue . . . . 3·25 5·00
C16 – 3a. orange . . . . 3·75 4·00
C17 – 4a. olive . . . . 8·50 12·00
C18 – 8a. mauve . . . . 8·00 7·50
C19 – 12a. purple on red . . . . 11·00 19·00
C20 – 1r. green and red . . . . 13·00 28·00

1909. King Edward VII.
C21 ½a. green (No. 149) . . . . 1·75 1·50
C22 1a. red (No. 150) . . . . . 2·25 30

1913. King George V.
C23 **55** 3p. grey . . . . 4·50 26·00
C24 **56** ½a. green . . . . 3·50 6·00
C25 **57** 1a. red . . . . 4·00 4·00
C26 **58** 1½a. brown (No. 163) . . 23·00 75·00
C27 **59** 2a. lilac . . . . 17·00 60·00
C28 **61** 2a.6p. blue . . . . 11·00 25·00
C29 **62** 3a. orange . . . . 25·00 £190
C30 **63** 4a. olive . . . . 22·00 £150
C32 **65** 8a. mauve . . . . 25·00 £325
C33 **66** 12a. red . . . . 22·00 £110
C34 **67** 1r. brown and green . . . 60·00 £275

BRITISH RAILWAY ADMINISTRATION

1901. No. 121 of China surch **B.R.A. 5 Five Cents**.
BR133b **32** 5c. on ½c. brown . . . £325 £100

CHRISTMAS ISLAND Pt. 1

Situated in the Indian Ocean about 600 miles south of Singapore. Formerly part of the Straits Settlements and then of the Crown Colony of Singapore, Christmas Island was occupied by the Japanese from 31 March 1942 until September 1945. It reverted to Singapore after liberation but subsequently became an Australian territory on 15 October 1958.

1958. 100 cents = 1 Malayan dollar.
1968. 100 cents = 1 Australian dollar.

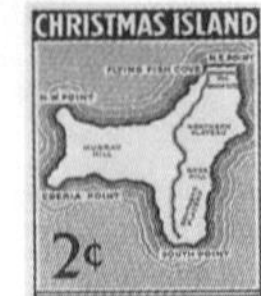

1 Queen Elizabeth II 2 Map

1958. Type of Australia with opt and value in black.
1 **1** 2c. orange 55 80
2 4c. brown 60 30
3 5c. mauve 60 50
4 6c. blue . . . . 1·00 30
5 8c. sepia . . . . 1·75 50
6 10c. violet . . . . 1·00 30
7 12c. red . . . . 1·75 1·75
8 20c. blue . . . . 1·00 1·75
9 50c. green . . . . 1·75 1·75
10 $1 turquoise . . . . 1·75 1·75

1963.
11 **2** 2c. orange 90 35
12 – 4c. brown 50 15
13 – 5c. purple 50 20
14 – 6c. blue 40 35
15 – 8c. black . . . . 2·25 35
16 – 10c. violet 40 15
17 – 12c. red 40 25
18 – 20c. blue . . . . 1·00 20
19 – 50c. green . . . . 1·00 20
20 – $1 yellow . . . . 1·75 35

DESIGNS—VERT: 4c. Moonflower; 5c. Robber crab; 8c. Phosphate train; 10c. Raising phosphate. HORIZ: 6c. Island scene; 12c. Flying Fish cove; 20c. Loading cantilever; 50c. Christmas Island frigate bird. LARGER (35 × 21 mm): $1 White-tailed tropic bird.

1965. 50th Anniv of Gallipoli Landing. As T **184** of Australia, but slightly larger (22 × 34½ mm).
21 10c. brown, black and green 30 1·00

12 Golden-striped Grouper

1968. Fishes. Multicoloured.
22 1c. Type **12** 45 45
23 2c. Moorish idol 60 20
24 3c. Long-nosed butterflyfish 60 30
25 4c. Pink-tailed triggerfish . . 60 20
26 5c. Regal angelfish 60 20
27 9c. White-cheeked surgeonfish 60 40
28 10c. Lionfish 60 20
28a 15c. Saddle butterflyfish . . . 7·00 2·50
29 20c. Ornate butterflyfish . . . 1·50 55
29a 30c. Giant ghost pipefish . . 7·00 2·50
30 50c. Clown surgeonfish . . . 1·75 1·50
31 $1 Meyer's butterflyfish . . . 1·75 2·00

13 "Angel" (mosaic) 14 "The Ansidei Madonna" (Raphael)

1969. Christmas.
32 **13** 5c. multicoloured 20 30

1970. Christmas. Paintings. Multicoloured.
33 3c. Type **14** 20 15
34 5c. "The Virgin and Child, St. John the Baptist and an Angel" (Morando) 20 15

15 "The Adoration of the Shepherds" (attr to the School of Seville) 16 H.M.S. "Flying Fish" (survey ship), 1887

1971. Christmas. Multicoloured.
35 6c. Type **15** 30 50
36 20c. "The Adoration of the Shepherds" (Reni) . . . . . 70 1·00

1972. Ships. Multicoloured.
37 1c. "Eagle" (merchant sailing ship), 1714 . . . . 25 60
38 2c. H.M.S. "Redpole" (gunboat), 1890 . . . . . 30 70
39 3c. "Hoi Houw" (freighter), 1959 . . . . 30 70
40 4c. "Pigot" (sailing ship), 1771 40 75
41 5c. "Valetta" (cargo-liner), 1968 . . . . 40 75
42 6c. Type **16** 40 75
43 7c. "Asia" (sail merchantman), 1805 . . . . 40 75
44 8c. "Islander" (freighter), 1929–60 . . . . 45 80
45 9c. H.M.S. "Imperieuse" (armoured cruiser), 1888 . . 65 70
46 10c. H.M.S. "Hecate" (coast defence turret ship), 1871 . . 50 80
47 20c. "Thomas" (galleon), 1615 50 1·00
48 25c. Royal Navy sail sloop, 1864 . . . . 50 1·75
49 30c. "Cygnet" (flute), 1688 . . 50 1·00
50 35c. "Triadic" (freighter), 1958 50 1·00
51 50c. H.M.S. "Amethyst" (frigate), 1857 . . . . . . 50 1·50
52 $1 "Royal Mary" (warship), 1643 . . . . 70 1·75

No. 45 is inscribed "H.M.S. Imperious", No. 46 "H.M.S. Egeria" and No. 48 "H.M.S. Gordon", all in error.

17 Angel of Peace

19 Mary and Holy Child within Christmas Star

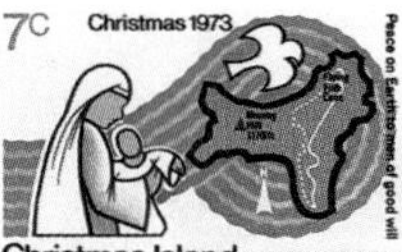
18 Virgin and Child, and Map

1972. Christmas. Multicoloured.
53 3c. Type **17** 15 40
54 3c. Angel of Joy 15 40
55 7c. Type **17** 20 50
56 7c. As No. 54 . . . . 20 50

1973. Christmas.
57 **18** 7c. multicoloured 25 35
58 25c. multicoloured . . . . . 75 1·00

1974. Christmas.
59 **19** 7c. mauve and grey 25 60
60 30c. orange, yellow and grey 75 2·50

20 "The Flight into Egypt"

21 Dove of Peace and Star of Bethlehem

1975. Christmas.
61 **20** 10c. yellow, brown and gold 25 35
62 35c. pink, blue and gold . . 50 1·75

1976. Christmas.
63 **21** 10c. red, yellow and mauve 15 45
64 – 10c. red, yellow and mauve 15 45
65 **21** 35c. violet, blue and green 20 55
66 – 35c. violet, blue and green 20 55
DESIGNS: Nos. 64 and 66 are "mirror-images" of Type **21**.

22 William Dampier (explorer)

1977. Famous Visitors. Multicoloured.
67 1c. Type **22** 15 80
68 2c. Captain de Vlamingh (explorer) 20 80
69 3c. Vice-Admiral MacLear . . 30 80
70 4c. Sir John Murray (oceanographer) 30 90
71 5c. Admiral Aldrich 30 40
72 6c. Andrew Clunies Ross (first settler) 30 60
73 7c. J. J. Lister (naturalist) . . 30 40
74 8c. Admiral of the Fleet Sir William May 35 70
75 9c. Henry Ridley (botanist) . . 40 1·60
76 10c. George Clunies Ross (phosphate miner) 55 55
77 20c. Captain Joshua Slocum (yachtsman) 50 75
78 45c. Charles Andrews (naturalist) 60 45
79 50c. Richard Hanitsch (biologist) . . . . 70 1·60
80 75c. Victor Purcell (scholar) 60 1·25
81 $1 Fam Choo Beng (educator) 60 1·25
82 $2 Sir Harold Spencer-Jones (astronomer) . . . . 65 2·00

23 Australian Coat of Arms on Map of Christmas Island

1977. Silver Jubilee.
83 **23** 45c. multicoloured 45 55

24 "A Partridge in a Pear Tree"

25 Abbott's Booby

1977. Christmas. "The Twelve Days of Christmas". Multicoloured.
84A 10c. Type **24** 10 20
85A 10c. "Two turtle doves" . . 10 20
86A 10c. "Three French hens" . . 10 20
87A 10c. "Four calling birds" . . 10 20
88A 10c. "Five gold rings" . . . 10 20
89A 10c. "Six geese a-laying" . . 10 20
90A 10c. "Seven swans a-swimming" 10 20
91A 10c. "Eight maids a-milking" 10 20
92A 10c. "Nine ladies dancing" 10 20
93A 10c. "Ten lords a-leaping" 10 20
94A 10c. "Eleven pipers piping" 10 20
95A 10c. "Twelve drummers drumming" 10 20

1978. 25th Anniv of Coronation.
96 – 45c. black and blue 45 75
97 – 45c. multicoloured 45 75
98 **25** 45c. black and blue 45 75
DESIGNS: No. 96, White Swan of Bohun; No. 97, Queen Elizabeth II.

26 "Christ Child"

27 Chinese Children

1978. Christmas Scenes from "The Song of Christmas". Multicoloured.
99 10c. Type **26** 15 20
100 10c. "Herald Angels" 15 20
101 10c. "Redeemer" 15 20
102 10c. "Israel" 15 20
103 10c. "Star" 15 20
104 10c. "Three Wise Men" . . . 15 20
105 10c. "Manger" 15 20
106 10c. "All He Stands For" . . 15 20
107 10c. "Shepherds Come" . . . 15 20

1979. International Year of the Child. Children of different races. Multicoloured, colours of inscr given.
108 20c. green (Type **27**) 30 45
109 20c. turquoise (Malay children) 30 45
110 20c. lilac (Indian children) . . 30 45
111 20c. red (European children) 30 45
112 20c. yellow ("Oranges and Lemons") 30 45

28 1958 2c. Definitive

1979. Death Centenary of Sir Rowland Hill. Multicoloured.
113 20c. Type **28** 20 40
114 20c. 1963 2c. map definitive 20 40
115 20c. 1965 50th Anniv of Gallipoli Landing 10c. commemorative 20 40
116 20c. 1964 4c. Pink-tailed triggerfish definitive 20 40
117 20c. 1969 Christmas 5c. . . 20 40

29 Wise Men following Star

1979. Christmas. Multicoloured.
118 20c. Type **29** 20 30
119 55c. Virgin and Child 45 70

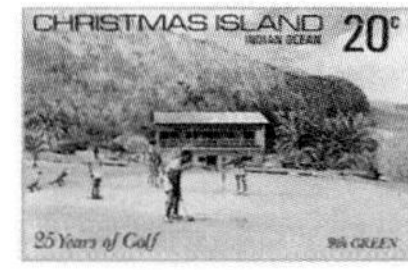
30 9th Green

1980. 25th Anniv of Christmas Island Golf Club. Multicoloured.
120 20c. Type **30** 35 50
121 55c. Clubhouse . . . . . . 40 1·00

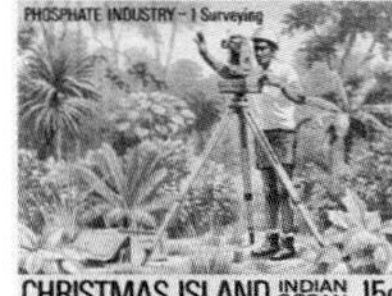
31 Surveying

1980. Phosphate Industry (1st series). Multicoloured.
122 15c. Type **31** 15 25
123 22c. Drilling for samples . . 15 30
124 40c. Sample analysis 20 45
125 55c. Mine planning 25 55
See also Nos. 126/9, 136/9 and 140/3.

1980. Phosphate Industry (2nd series). As T **31**. Multicoloured.
126 15c. Jungle clearing 15 15
127 22c. Overburden removal . . 15 20
128 40c. Open cut mining 20 25
129 55c. Restoration 20 30

32 Angel with Harp

33 "Cryptoblepharus egeriae"

1980. Christmas. Multicoloured.
130 15c. Type **32** 10 25
131 15c. Angel with wounded soldier 10 25
132 22c. Virgin and Child 15 30
133 22c. Kneeling couple 15 30
134 60c. Angel with harp (different) 20 20
135 60c. Angel with children . . 20 30

1981. Phosphate Industry (3rd series). As T **31**. Multicoloured.
136 22c. Screening and Stockpiling 15 15
137 28c. Train loading 20 20
138 40c. Railing 25 25
139 60c. Drying 25 25

1981. Phosphate Industry (4th series). As T **31**. Multicoloured.
140 22c. Crushing 15 20
141 28c. Conveying 20 25
142 40c. Bulk storage 30 40
143 60c. "Consolidated Venture" (bulk carrier) loading . . . 35 55

1981. Reptiles. Multicoloured.
144 24c. Type **33** 20 20
145 30c. "Emoia nativitata" . . . 25 25
146 40c. "Lepidodactylus listeri" 30 30
147 60c. "Cyrtodactylus sp. nov." 35 35

34 Scene from Carol "Away in a Manger"

1981. Christmas.
148 **34** 18c. silver, dp blue & bl . . 30 50
149 – 24c. multicoloured 30 55
150 – 40c. multicoloured 35 65
151 – 60c. multicoloured 40 75
DESIGNS: 24c. to 60c. show various scenes from carol "Away in a Manger".

35 Reef Heron

1982. Birds. Multicoloured.
152 1c. Type **35** 70 30
153 2c. Common noddy ("Noddy") 70 30
154 3c. White-bellied swiftlet ("Glossy Swiftlet") 70 70
155 4c. Christmas Island imperial pigeon ("Imperial Pigeon") 70 70
156 5c. Christmas Island white-eye ("Silvereye") 80 70
157 10c. Island thrush ("Thrush") 70 70
158 25c. Red-tailed tropic bird ("Silver Bosunbird") . . . 1·25 60
159 30c. Emerald dove 80 70
160 40c. Brown booby 80 55
161 50c. Red-footed booby . . . 80 55
162 65c. Christmas Island frigate bird ("Frigatebird") . . . 80 55
163 75c. White-tailed tropic bird ("Golden Bosunbird") . . 90 65
164 80c. Australian kestrel ("Nankeen Kestrel") (vert) 1·25 2·00
165 $1 Moluccan hawk owl ("Hawk-owl") (vert) . . . 2·50 2·50
166 $2 Australian goshawk ("Goshawk") . . . . . . 1·75 4·00
167 $4 Abbott's booby (vert) . . 3·00 3·25

36 Joseph

37 "Mirror" Dinghy and Club House

1982. Christmas. Origami Paper Sculptures. Mult.
168 27c. Type **36** 30 30
169 50c. Angel 45 45
170 75c. Mary and baby Jesus . . 65 65

1983. 25th Anniv of Christmas Island Boat Club. Multicoloured.
171 27c. Type **37** 20 30
172 35c. Ocean-going yachts . . . 20 35
173 50c. Fishing launch and cargo ship (horiz) 25 40
174 75c. Dinghy-racing and cantilever (horiz) 25 60

38 Maps of Christmas Island and Australia, Eastern Grey Kangaroo and White-tailed Tropic Bird

1983. 25th Anniv of Australian Territory. Mult.
175 24c. Type **38** 50 30
176 30c. Christmas Island and Australian flag 60 50
177 85c. Maps of Christmas Island and Australia, and Boeing 727 . . . . 1·40 1·60

39 Candle and Holly

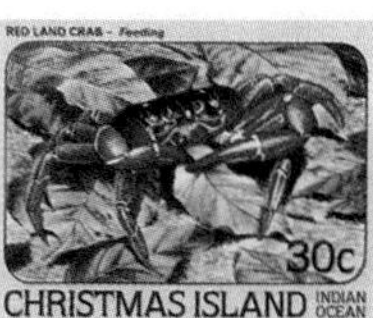
40 Feeding on Leaf

1983. Christmas. Candles. Multicoloured.
178 24c. Type **39** 20 20
179 30c. Six gold candles 30 40
180 85c. Candles . . . . 70 1·25

1984. Red Land Crab. Multicoloured.
181 30c. Type **40** 25 30
182 40c. Migration 30 40
183 55c. Development stages . . 30 50
184 85c. Adult females and young 45 70

41 "Leucocoprinus fragilissimus"

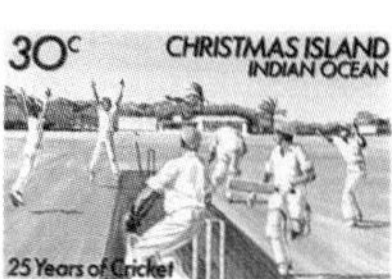
42 Run-out

1984. Fungi. Multicoloured.
185 30c. Type **41** 25 55
186 40c. "Microporus xanthopus" 30 70
187 45c. "Hydropus anthidepes" ("Trogia anthidepas") . . 35 80

188 55c. "Haddowia longipes" . . 35 90
189 85c. "Phillipsia domingensis" 45 1·25

1984. 25th Anniv of Cricket on Christmas Island. Multicoloured.
190 30c. Type **42** 30 85
191 40c. Bowled-out . . . . . . 30 1·10
192 50c. Batsman in action . . . 35 1·50
193 85c. Fielder diving for catch 55 1·75

43 Arrival of Father Christmas

1984. Christmas and "Ausipex" International Stamp Exhibition, Melbourne. Sheet 100 × 100 mm containing T **43** and similar horiz designs. Multicoloured.
MS194 30c. Type **43**; 55c. Distribution of presents; 85c. Departure of Father Christmas 2·25 2·50

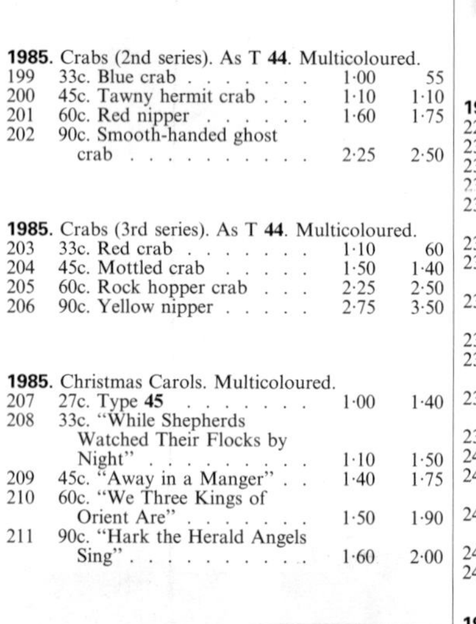

44 Robber Crab **45** "Once in Royal David's City"

1985. Crabs (1st series). Multicoloured.
195 30c. Type **44** . . . . 1·00 70
196 40c. Horn-eyed ghost crab . . 1·10 1·10
197 55c. Purple hermit crab . . . 1·50 1·60
198 85c. Little nipper . . . . . . 2·25 2·50

1985. Crabs (2nd series). As T **44**. Multicoloured.
199 33c. Blue crab . . . . 1·00 55
200 45c. Tawny hermit crab . . . 1·10 1·10
201 60c. Red nipper . . . . . . 1·60 1·75
202 90c. Smooth-handed ghost crab . . . . 2·25 2·50

1985. Crabs (3rd series). As T **44**. Multicoloured.
203 33c. Red crab . . . . 1·10 60
204 45c. Mottled crab . . . . . 1·50 1·40
205 60c. Rock hopper crab . . . 2·25 2·50
206 90c. Yellow nipper . . . . . 2·75 3·50

1985. Christmas Carols. Multicoloured.
207 27c. Type **45** . . . . 1·00 1·40
208 33c. "While Shepherds Watched Their Flocks by Night" . . . . 1·10 1·50
209 45c. "Away in a Manger" . . 1·40 1·75
210 60c. "We Three Kings of Orient Are" . . . . 1·50 1·90
211 90c. "Hark the Herald Angels Sing" . . . . 1·60 2·00

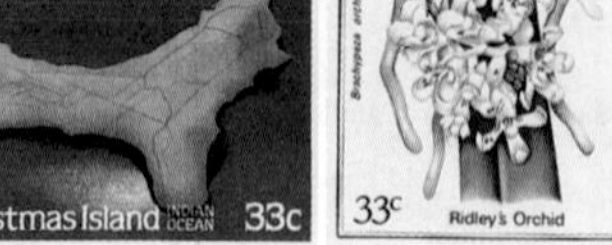

46 Halley's Comet over Christmas Island **47** Ridley's Orchid

1986. Appearance of Halley's Comet. Multicoloured.
212 33c. Type **46** 45 80
213 45c. Edmond Halley . . . . 55 1·10
214 60c. Comet and "Consolidated Venture" (bulk carrier) loading phosphate . . . . 70 2·25
215 90c. Comet over Flying Fish Cove . . . . 80 2·50

1986. Native Flowers. Multicoloured.
216 33c. Type **47** 50 55
217 45c. Hanging flower 30 85
218 60c. Hoya . . . . 30 1·50
219 90c. Sea hibiscus . . . . . 35 2·00

1986. Royal Wedding. As T **112** of Ascension. Multicoloured.
220 33c. Prince Andrew and Miss Sarah Ferguson 45 50
221 90c. Prince Andrew piloting helicopter, Digby, Canada, 1985 . . . . 95 1·75

48 Father Christmas and Reindeer in Speed Boat

1986. Christmas. Multicoloured.
222 30c. Type **48** 85 60
223 36c. Father Christmas and reindeer on beach . . . . 1·00 60
224 55c. Father Christmas fishing 1·50 1·50
225 70c. Playing golf . . . . . . 2·75 3·50
226 $1 Sleeping in hammock . . 2·75 4·00

49 H.M.S. "Flying Fish" and Outline Map of Christmas Island

1987. Centenary of Visits by H.M.S. "Flying Fish" and H.M.S. "Egeria". Multicoloured.
227 36c. Type **49** 40 75
228 90c. H.M.S. "Egeria" and outline map . . . . 70 2·50

50 Blind Snake **51** Children watching Father Christmas in Sleigh

1987. Wildlife. Multicoloured.
229 1c. Type **50** 40 90
230 2c. Blue-tailed skink 40 90
231 3c. Insectivorous bat 90 90
232 5c. Grasshopper 90 90
233 10c. Christmas Island fruit bat 90 90
234 25c. Gecko . . . . 1·00 1·00
235 30c. "Mantis religiosa" (mantid) . . . . 1·25 1·25
236 36c. Moluccan hawk owl ("Hawk-owl") . . . . . 3·00 1·75
237 40c. Bull-mouth helmet . . 1·75 1·75
237a 41c. Nudibranch ("Phidiana" sp.) . . . . 1·25 70
238 50c. Textile or cloth of gold cone . . . . 1·75 1·75
239 65c. Brittle stars . . . . . 1·40 1·25
240 75c. Regal angelfish . . . . 1·40 1·75
241 90c. "Appias paulina" (butterfly) . . . . 3·75 3·25
242 $1 "Hypolimnas misippus" (butterfly) . . . . 3·75 3·25
243 $2 Shrew . . . . 3·75 7·00
244 $5 Green turtle . . . . . . 4·50 7·00

1987. Christmas. Sheet 165 × 65 mm, containing T **51** and similar multicoloured designs.
MS245 30c. Type **51**; 37c. Father Christmas distributing gifts (48 × 22 mm); 90c. Children with presents (48 × 22 mm); $1 Singing carols 4·00 4·00
The stamps within No. **MS**245 form a composite design of a beach scene.

1988. Bicentenary of Australian Settlement. Arrival of First Fleet. As Nos. 1105/9 of Australia, but each inscribed "CHRISTMAS ISLAND Indian Ocean" and "AUSTRALIA BICENTENARY".
246 37c. Aborigines watching arrival of Fleet, Botany Bay . . . . 1·50 1·75
247 37c. Aboriginal family and anchored ships . . . . . 1·50 1·75
248 37c. Fleet arriving at Sydney Cove . . . . 1·50 1·75
249 37c. Ship's boat . . . . . . 1·50 1·75
250 37c. Raising the flag, Sydney Cove, 26 January 1788 . . 1·50 1·75
Nos. 246/50 were printed together, se-tenant, forming a composite design.

52 Captain William May **53** Pony and Trap, 1910

1988. Cent of British Annexation. Mult.
251 37c. Type **52** 35 40
252 53c. Annexation ceremony . . 50 55
253 95c. H.M.S. "Imperieuse" (armoured cruiser) firing salute 90 95
254 $1.50 Building commemorative cairn . . . 1·40 1·50

1988. Cent of Permanent Settlement. Mult.
255 37c. Type **53** 60 40
256 55c. Phosphate mining, 1910 85 55
257 70c. Steam locomotive, 1914 1·25 85
258 $1 Arrival of first aircraft, 1957 . . . . 1·50 1·25

54 Beach Toys **55** Food on Table ("Good Harvesting")

1988. Christmas. Toys and Gifts. Multicoloured.
259 32c. Type **54** 40 35
260 39c. Flippers, snorkel and mask 50 40
261 90c. Model soldier, doll and soft toys . . . . 1·10 1·10
262 $1 Models of racing car, lorry and jet aircraft . . . 1·25 1·25

1989. Chinese New Year. Multicoloured.
263 39c. Type **55** 45 40
264 70c. Decorations ("Prosperity") 80 70
265 90c. Chinese girls ("Good Fortune") . . . . 1·10 90
266 $1 Lion dance ("Progress Every Year") . . . . . . 1·25 1·00

56 Sir John Murray

1989. 75th Death Anniv of Sir John Murray (oceanographer). Multicoloured.
267 39c. Type **56** 50 50
268 80c. Map of Christmas Island showing Murray Hill . . . 1·25 95
269 $1 Oceanographic equipment 1·50 1·25
270 $1.10 H.M.S. "Challenger" (survey ship), 1872 . . . . 1·75 1·50

57 Four Children **58** "Huperzia phlegmaria"

1989. Malay Hari Raya Festival. Multicoloured.
271 39c. Type **57** 55 50
272 55c. Man playing tambourine 80 70
273 80c. Girl in festival costume 1·25 1·00
274 $1.10 Christmas Island Mosque . . . . 1·60 1·40

1989. Ferns. Multicoloured.
275 41c. Type **58** 75 60
276 65c. "Asplenium polydon" . . 1·10 85
277 80c. Common bracken . . . 1·40 1·00
278 $1.10 Birds-nest fern . . . . 1·60 1·40

59 Virgin Mary and Star **61** First Sighting, 1615

1989. Christmas. Multicoloured.
279 36c. Type **59** 60 40
280 41c. Christ Child in manger 60 45
281 80c. Shepherds and star . . . 1·50 80
282 $1.10 Three Wise Men following star . . . . . . 1·60 1·10

1989. "Melbourne Stampshow '89". Nos. 237a and 242 optd with Stampshow logo.
283 41c. Nudibranch ("Phidiana sp.") . . . . 1·00 45
284 $1 "Hypolimnas misippus" (butterfly) . . . . 2·50 1·00

1990. 375th Anniv of Discovery of Christmas Island. Multicoloured.
285 41c. Type **61** . . . . 1·00 50
286 $1.10 Second sighting and naming, 1643 . . . . . . 1·25 1·40

62 Miniature Tractor pulling Phosphate **63** Male Abbott's Booby

1990. Christmas Island Transport. Multicoloured.
287 1c. Type **62** 15 20
288 2c. Phosphate train 40 40
289 3c. Diesel railcar No. 8802 (vert) 20 20
290 5c. Loading road train . . . 40 40
291 10c. Trishaw (vert) 30 30
292 15c. Terex truck 65 65
293 25c. Articulated bus 30 30
294 30c. Cable passenger carriage (vert) 30 35
295 40c. Passenger barge (vert) 35 40
296 50c. Kolek (outrigger canoe) 55 55
297 65c. Flying Doctor aircraft and ambulance . . . . . 3·75 1·50
298 75c. Commercial van . . . . 1·50 1·50
299 90c. Vintage lorry . . . . . 1·50 1·75
300 $1 Water tanker . . . . . . 1·50 1·75
301 $2 Traction engine . . . . . 2·50 3·25
302 $5 Steam locomotive No. 1 3·25 4·75

1990. Abbott's Booby. Multicoloured.
303 10c. Type **63** 85 30
304 20c. Juvenile male . . . . . 1·40 50
305 29c. Female with egg . . . . 1·60 55
306 41c. Pair with chick . . . . 2·25 70
MS307 122 × 68 mm. 41c. Male with wings spread; 41c. Male on branch; 41c. Female with fledgling 5·00 3·00
The three stamps within No. **MS**307 form a composite design and are without the W.W.F. logo.

64 1977 Famous Visitors 9c. Stamp

1990. Centenary of Henry Ridley's Visit.
308 41c. Type **64** 55 65
309 75c. Ridley (botanist) in rainforest . . . . 85 1·75

1990. "New Zealand 1990" International Stamp Exhibition, Auckland. No. **MS**307 optd "**NZ 1990 WORLD STAMP EXHIBITION AUCKLAND, NEW ZEALAND, 24 AUGUST – 2 SEPTEMBER 1990**" in purple on the sheet margins.
MS310 122 × 68 mm. 41c. Male with wings spread; 41c. Male on branch; 41c. Female with fledgling 6·50 7·50

65 "Corymborkus veratrifolia" **66** "Islander" (freighter), 1898

1990. Christmas. Flowers. Multicoloured.
311 38c. Type **65** . . . . 1·10 70
312 43c. "Hoya aldrichii" . . . . 1·25 75
313 80c. "Quisqualis indica" . . . 2·25 2·75
314 $1.20 "Barringtonia racemosa" . . . . 2·75 3·50

1991. Centenary of First Phosphate Mining Lease. Multicoloured.
316 43c. Type **66** . . . . 1·00 90
317 43c. Miners loading tipper wagons, 1908 . . . . . . 1·00 90
318 85c. Shay steam locomotive No. 4, 1925 . . . . . . 1·40 1·25

319 $1.20 Extracting phosphate, 1951 . . . . 1·75 1·60
320 $1.70 Land reclamation, 1990 2·00 1·90
Nos. 316/20 were printed together, se-tenant, forming a composite forest design.

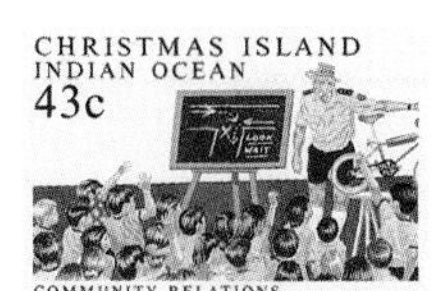

67 Teaching Children Road Safety

1991. Christmas Island Police Force. Multicoloured.
321 43c. Type **67** . . . . 1·50 1·00
322 43c. Traffic control . . . . . 1·50 1·00
323 90c. Airport customs . . . . 2·25 3·25
324 $1.20 Police launch "Fregata Andrews" towing rescued boat . . . . 3·00 3·00
MS325 135 × 88 mm. Nos. 321/4 8·50 6·00

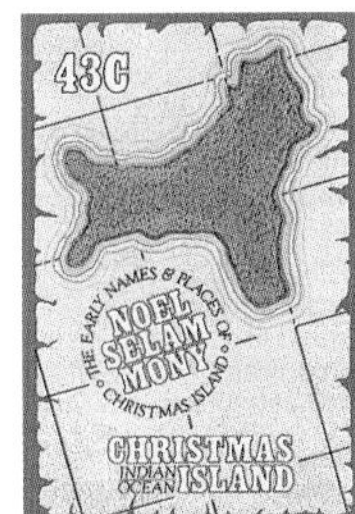

68 Map of Christmas Island, 1991

1991. Maps of Christmas Island. Multicoloured.
326 43c. Type **68** . . . . 1·00 65
327 75c. Goos Atlas, 1666 . . . 1·75 1·10
328 $1.10 De Manevillette, 1745 2·25 1·60
329 $1.20 Comberford, 1667 . . . 2·25 1·90

69 "Bruguiera gymnorrhiza"

1991. Local Trees. Multicoloured.
330 43c. Type **69** . . . . 1·00 65
331 70c. "Syzgium operculatum" 1·50 1·00
332 85c. "Ficus microcarpa" . . 1·75 1·25
333 $1.20 "Arenga listeri" . . . . 2·00 1·60

70 "Family round Christmas Tree" (S'ng Yen Luiw)

1991. Christmas. Children's Paintings. Mult.
334 38c. Type **70** 75 75
335 38c. "Opening Presents" (Liew Ann Nee) 75 75
336 38c. "Beach Party" (Foo Pang Chuan) 75 75
337 38c. "Christmas Walk" (Too Lai Peng) 75 75
338 38c. "Santa Claus and Christmas Tree" (Jesamine Wheeler) 75 75
339 43c. "Santa Claus fishing" (Ho Puay Ha) 75 60
340 $1 "Santa Claus in Boat" (Ng Hooi Hua) . . . . . 1·50 1·50
341 $1.20 "Santa Claus surfing" (Yani Kawi) . . . . 1·75 1·75

71 Discussing Evacuation, 1942 **72** Snake's-head Cowrie

1992. 50th Anniv of Partial Evacuation. Mult.
342 45c. Type **71** . . . . 1·00 1·00
343 45c. Families waiting to embark . . . . 1·00 1·00
344 $1.05 Ferrying evacuees to "Islander" . . . . 2·50 2·50
345 $1.20 Departure of "Islander" (freighter) . . . 2·75 2·75

1992. Shells. Multicoloured.
346 5c. Tiger cowrie 50 70
347 10c. Type **72** 70 70
348 15c. Scorpion conch . . . . 1·00 70
349 20c. Royal oak scallop . . . 1·00 70
350 25c. Striped engina . . . . . 1·00 70
351 30c. Prickly Pacific drupe . . 1·00 70
352 40c. Reticulate distorsio . . . 1·00 75
353 45c. Tapestry turban . . . . 1·25 75
354 50c. Beautiful goblet . . . . 1·25 75
355 60c. Captain cone . . . . . 1·50 80
356 70c. Layonkaire's turban . . 1·50 90
357 80c. Chirage spider conch . . 1·75 1·00
358 90c. Common delphinia . . . 1·75 1·25
359 $1 Ceramic vase . . . . . . 1·75 1·50
360 $2 Partridge tun . . . . . . 1·40 1·75
361 $5 Strawberry drupe . . . . 3·50 3·75

73 Torpedoing of "Eidsvold"

1992. 50th Anniv of Sinkings of "Eidsvold" and "Nissa Maru". Multicoloured.
362 45c. Type **73** . . . . 1·25 75
363 80c. "Eidsvold" sinking . . . 2·00 2·00
364 $1.05 "Nissa Maru" under attack . . . . 2·50 3·25
365 $1.20 "Nissa Maru" beached 2·50 3·50

1992. "Kuala Lumpur '92" International Philatelic Exhibition. No. 361 optd with exhibition symbol.
366 $5 Strawberry drupe . . . . 9·00 7·00

75 Jungle **76** Abbott's Booby

1992. Christmas. Multicoloured.
367 40c. Type **75** . . . . 90 1·25
368 40c. Red-tailed tropic bird and brown booby over rock . . . . 90 1·25
369 45c. Brown boobies on headland . . . . 90 1·25
370 $1.05 Red-tailed tropic bird, brown booby and cliffs . . 1·60 1·75
371 $1.20 Cliffs . . . . 1·60 1·75
Nos. 367/71 were printed together, se-tenant, forming a composite coastal design.

1993. Seabirds. Multicoloured.
372 45c. Type **76** 60 85
373 45c. Christmas Island frigate bird 60 85
374 45c. Common noddy 60 85
375 45c. White-tailed ("Golden Bosunbird") tropic bird 60 85
376 45c. Brown booby 60 85
MS377 140 × 70 mm. Nos. 372/6 2·75 3·50
Nos. 372/6 were printed together, se-tenant, forming a composite design.

77 Dolly Beach

1993. Scenic Views of Christmas Island. Mult.
378 85c. Type **77** . . . . 1·25 1·50
379 95c. Blow Holes . . . . . . 1·50 2·00
380 $1.05 Merrial Beach . . . . 1·60 2·25
381 $1.20 Rainforest . . . . . . 1·75 2·25

78 Turtle on Beach

1993. Christmas. Multicoloured.
382 40c. Type **78** . . . . 1·00 70
383 45c. Crabs and wave . . . . 1·00 70
384 $1 Christmas Island frigate bird and rainforest . . . . 2·25 3·25

79 Map of Christmas Island

1993. 350th Anniv of Naming of Christmas Island.
385 **79** $2 multicoloured . . . . . 3·00 3·50

80 Pekingese

1994. Chinese New Year ("Year of the Dog"). Multicoloured.
386 45c. Type **80** . . . . 1·00 1·40
387 45c. Mickey (Christmas Island dog) . . . . 1·00 1·40
MS388 106 × 70 mm. Nos. 386/7 2·50 3·25

81 Shay Locomotive No. 4

1994. Steam Locomotives. Multicoloured.
389 85c. Type **81** . . . . 1·75 1·75
390 95c. Locomotive No. 9 . . . 1·75 2·00
391 $1.20 Locomotive No. 1 . . 2·00 2·25

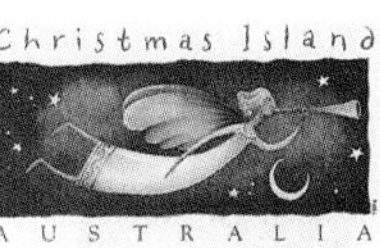

82 "Brachypeza archytas" **83** Angel blowing Trumpet

1994. Orchids. Multicoloured.
392 45c. Type **82** . . . . 1·10 1·40
393 45c. "Thelasis capitata" . . . 1·10 1·40
394 45c. "Corymborkis veratrifolia" . . . . 1·10 1·40
395 45c. "Flickingeria nativitatis" 1·10 1·40
396 45c. "Dendrobium crumenatum" . . . . . . 1·10 1·40

1994. Christmas. Multicoloured.
397 40c. Type **83** 80 60
398 45c. Wise Man holding gift 80 60
399 80c. Star over Bethlehem . . 1·75 2·50

84 Pig

1995. Chinese New Year ("Year of the Pig").
400 **84** 45c. multicoloured 75 60
401 – 85c. multicoloured . . . . 1·25 1·75
MS402 106 × 71 mm. Nos. 400/1 2·00 2·50
DESIGN: 85c. Pig (different).

85 Golfer playing Shot

1995. 40th Anniv of Christmas Island Golf Course.
403 **85** $2.50 multicoloured . . . 4·25 4·25

86 Father Christmas with Map on Christmas Island Frigate Bird

1995. Christmas Multicoloured
404 40c. Type **86** 80 60
405 45c. Father Christmas distributing presents . . . 80 60
406 80c. Father Christmas waving goodbye . . . . 1·75 2·50

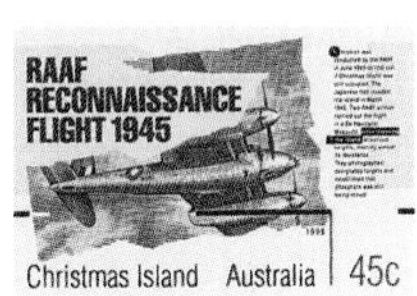

87 De Havilland D.H.98 Mosquito on Reconnaissance Mission

1995. 50th Anniv of End of Second World War. Each black, stone and red.
407 45c. Type **87** 95 95
408 45c. H.M.S. "Rother" (frigate) 95 95

88 Lemon-peel Angelfish

1995. Marine Life. Multicoloured.
412 20c. Pink-tailed triggerfish . . 15 20
413 30c. Japanese inflator-filefish ("Longnose filefish") . . . 20 25
414 45c. Princess anthias 30 35
415 75c. Type **88** 55 60
416 85c. Moon wrasse 60 65
417 90c. Spotted boxfish 65 70
418 95c. Moorish idol 70 75
419 $1 Emperor angelfish 70 75
420 $1.20 Glass-eyed snapper ("Glass bigeye") 85 90

89 Rat with Drum

1996. Chinese New Year ("Year of the Rat"). Multicoloured.
425 45c. Type **89** . . . . 1·00 1·25
426 45c. Rat with tambourine . . 1·00 1·25
MS427 106 × 70 mm. Nos. 425/6 2·25 2·50

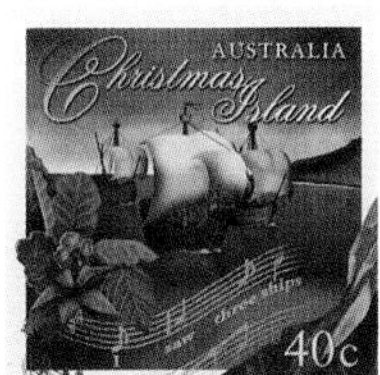

90 Christmas Island White-Eye ("White-eye") **91** Three Ships approaching Island

1996. Christmas Island Land Birds. Multicoloured.
428 45c. Type **90** 75 50
429 85c. Moluccan hawk owl ("Hawk-owl") . . . . . . 1·75 2·00

1996. Christmas. "I saw Three Ships" (carol). Multicoloured.
430 40c. Type **91** 75 60
431 45c. Madonna and Child with ships at anchor . . . 75 60
432 80c. Ships leaving . . . . . 1·60 2·10

1996. 300th Anniv of Willem de Vlamingh's Discovery of Christmas Island. As No. 1667 of Australia.
433 45c. multicoloured 75 75

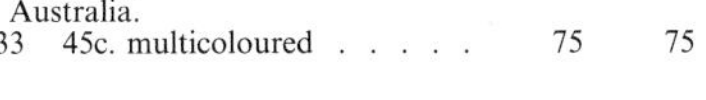

92 Ox facing Right

1997. Chinese New Year ("Year of the Ox"). Multicoloured.
434 45c. Type **92** 90 90
435 45c. Ox facing left 90 90
MS436 106 × 70 mm. Nos. 434/5 1·75 2·25

93 Father Christmas reading Letter

1997. Christmas. Multicoloured.
437 40c. Type **93** 55 50
438 45c. Father Christmas carving wooden boat 55 50
439 80c. Father Christmas in sleigh . . . . 1·10 1·50

94 Tiger

1998. Chinese New Year ("Year of the Tiger"). Multicoloured.
440 45c. Type **94** 90 90
441 45c. Tiger with head facing left 90 90
MS442 106 × 70 mm. Nos. 440/1 2·00 2·25

95 Christmas Island Frigate Bird

1998. Marine Life. Multicoloured.
443 5c. Type **95** 20 30
444 5c. Four ambon chromis . . 20 30
445 5c. Three ambon chromis . . 20 30
446 5c. One pink anemonefish . . 20 30
447 5c. Three pink anemonefish 20 30
448 10c. Reef heron ("Eastern Reef Egret") 25 30
449 10c. Whitelined cod 25 30
450 10c. Pyramid butterflyfish . . 25 30
451 10c. Dusky parrotfish 25 30
452 10c. Spotted garden eel . . . 25 30
453 25c. Sooty tern 30 35
454 25c. Stripe-tailed damselfish ("Scissortail sergeant") . . 30 35
455 25c. Thicklip wrasse 30 35
456 25c. Blackaxil chromis . . . 30 35
457 25c. Orange anthias 30 35
458 45c. Brown booby 35 40
459 45c. Green turtle 35 40
460 45c. Pink anemonefish . . . 35 40
461 45c. Blue sea star 35 40
462 45c. Kunie's chromodoris . . 35 40
Nos. 443/62 were printed together, se-tenant, with the backgrounds forming a composie design.

96 Orchid Tree

1998. Christmas. Flowering Trees. Multicoloured.
463 40c. Type **96** 60 50
464 80c. Flame tree . . . . . . 1·25 1·40
465 95c. Sea hibiscus . . . . . . 1·40 1·75

97 Leaping Rabbit

1999. Chinese New Year ("Year of the Rabbit"). Multicoloured.
466 45c. Type **97** 70 80
467 45c. Rabbit with pestle and mortar 70 80
MS468 106 × 70 mm. Nos. 466/7 1·40 1·60

98 Carnival Dragon (Fong Jason) (Community Arts Festival)

1999. Festivals. Children's Paintings. Mult.
469 45c. Type **98** 60 60
470 45c. Red crab holding Easter egg (Community Arts Festival, Siti Zanariah Zainal) 60 60
471 85c. Ghost and child (Tan Diana) (Hungry Ghost Festival) (vert) . . . . . . 95 1·10
472 $1.20 Walls of Mecca (Anwar Ramlan) (Hari Raya Haji Festival) (vert) . . . . . . 1·25 1·40

99 Santa Claus in Hammock

1999. Christmas. Multicoloured.
473 40c. Type **99** 60 60
474 45c. Santa Claus with Christmas pudding 60 60
475 95c. Santa Claus in sleigh pulled by Abbott's boobies 1·40 1·75

100 Chinese Dragon

2000. Chinese New Year ("Year of the Dragon"). Multicoloured.
476 45c. Type **100** 65 75
477 45c. Chinese dragon facing left 65 75
MS478 106 × 70 mm. Nos. 476/7 1·25 1·50

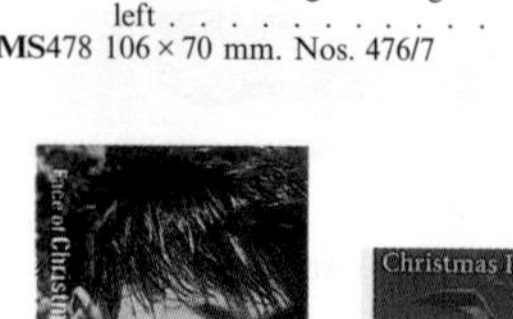
101 Yeow Jian Min

102 The Three Kings

2000. New Millennium. "Face of Christmas Island". Multicoloured.
479 45c. Type **101** 50 60
480 45c. Ida Chin (schoolgirl) . . 50 60
481 45c. Ho Tak Wah (elderly man) 50 60
482 45c. Thomas Faul and James Neill (young boys) 50 60
483 45c. Siti Sanniah Kawi (mother of three) 50 60

2000. Christmas. "We Three Kings" (carol). Mult.
484 40c. Type **102** 50 55
485 40c. Birds with Three Gifts 50 55
486 45c. Crabs with Three Gifts 50 55

103 Green Snake

2001. Chinese New Year ("Year of the Snake"). Mult.
487 45c. Type **103** 60 50
488 $1.35 Silver snake . . . . . 1·50 1·75
MS489 106 × 70 mm. Nos. 487/8 2·25 2·50

104 *Chaetocalathus semisupinus*

2001. International Stamps. Fungi. Multicoloured.
490 $1 Type **104** 90 90
491 $1.50 *Pycnoporus sanguineus* 1·25 1·50

105 Rat

106 Imperial Pigeon

2002. Chinese New Year ("Year of the Horse"). Multicoloured.
492 5c. Type **105** 15 15
493 5c. Ox 15 15
494 5c. Tiger 15 15
495 5c. Rabbit 15 15
496 15c. Dragon 20 20
497 15c. Snake 20 20
498 15c. Horse (gold) 20 20
499 15c. Goat 20 20
500 25c. Monkey 30 30
501 25c. Cock 30 30
502 25c. Dog 30 30
503 25c. Pig 30 30
504 45c. Horse (purple) 50 50
505 $1.35 Horse (gold) . . . . . 1·25 1·50
MS506 106 × 70 mm. Nos. 504/5 1·75 2·00

2002. Endangered Species. Christmas Island Birds. Multicoloured.
507 45c. Type **106** 50 50
508 45c. Christmas Island hawk owl 50 50
509 $1 Goshawk . . . . 1·00 1·00
510 $1.50 Thrush . . . . 1·40 1·60

107 Yellow Goat

2003. Chinese New Year ("Year of the Goat"). As T **107** plus designs as Nos. 492/503 with backgrounds in mauve and some values changed. Multicoloured.
511 10c. Type **105** 10 10
512 10c. Ox 10 10
513 10c. Tiger 10 10
514 10c. Rabbit 10 10
515 15c. Dragon 10 15
516 15c. Snake 10 15
517 15c. Horse 10 15
518 15c. Goat (animal in gold) . . 10 15
519 25c. Monkey 20 25
520 25c. Cock 20 25
521 25c. Dog 20 25
522 25c. Pig 20 25
523 50c. Type **107** 35 40
524 $1.50 Blue goat . . . . . . 1·10 1·25
MS525 105 × 70 mm. Nos. 523/4 1·40 1·50
Nos. 492/503 have red backgrounds.

CILICIA Pt. 16

A district in Asia Minor, occupied and temporarily controlled by the French between 1919 and 20 October 1921. The territory was then returned to Turkey.

40 paras = 1 piastre.

1919. Various issues of Turkey optd **CILICIE**. A. On No. 726 (surch Printed Matter stamp optd with Star and Crescent).
1 **15** 5pa. on 10pa. green . . . . 1·25 1·50

B. On 1901 issue optd with Star and Crescent.
2 **21** 1pi. blue (No. 543) . . . . 70 1·10
32 1pi. blue (No. 631) . . . . 1·25 1·50

C. On 1909 issue optd with Star and Crescent (No. 7 also optd as T **24**).
4 **28** 20pa. red (No. 572) . . . . 1·25 1·25
35 20pa. red (No. 643) . . . . 1·25 1·25
7 1pi. blue (No. 649) £1300 £700
8 1pi. blue (No. 645) . . . . 5·50 4·50

D. On 1913 issue.
36 **30** 20pa. pink . . . . 1·00 1·25

E. On Pictorial issue of 1914.
37 **32** 2pa. purple . . . . 55 1·00
11 – 4pa. brown (No. 500) . . . 1·00 1·60
12 – 6pa. blue (No. 502) . . . . 6·00 4·50
13 – 1¼pi. brown and grey (No. 507) . . . . 1·60 2·10

F. On Postal Anniv issue of 1916.
14 **60** 5pa. green 70 40
15 20pa. blue . . . . 1·25 1·50
40 1pi. black and violet 95 95
17 5pi. black and brown . . . 1·25 2·25

G. On Pictorial issues of 1916 and 1917.
18 **73** 10pa. green . . . . 1·40 1·60
19 **76** 50pa. blue . . . . 4·25 2·10
41 **69** 5pi. on 2pa. blue (No. 914) 1·40 1·60
21 **63** 25pi. red on buff . . . . . 1·60 2·10
22 **64** 50pi. red . . . . 1·50 1·50
23 50pi. blue . . . . 12·50 15·00

H. On Armistice issue of 1919 optd with T **81** of Turkey.
24 **76** 50pa. blue . . . . 5·00 3·00
25 **77** 2pi. blue and brown . . . . 1·40 1·60
26 **78** 5pi. brown and blue . . . . 7·25 2·75

1919. Various issues of Turkey optd **Cilicie**. A. On No. 726 (surch Printed Matter stamp optd with Star and Crescent).
46 **15** 5pa. on 10pa. green . . . . 1·25 1·60

B. On 1901 issue optd with Star and Crescent.
47 **21** 1pi. blue (No. 543) . . . . 1·25 1·50
48 1pi. blue (No. 631) . . . . 1·25 1·60
49 1pi. blue (No. 669) . . . . 55·00 35·00

C. On 1908 issue optd with T **24** and Star and Crescent.
50 **25** 20pa. red . . . . 6·50 3·50

D. On 1909 issue optd with Star and Crescent (No. 52 also optd as T **24**).
52a **28** 20pa. red (No. 643) . . . . 1·40 1·50
52 20pa. red (No. 647) . . . . 1·25 1·25

E. On 1913 issue.
53 **30** 5pa. bistre . . . . 2·10 2·10
54 20pa. pink . . . . 90 1·60

F. On Pictorial issue of 1914.
55 **32** 2pa. purple . . . . 70 1·40
56 – 4pa. brown (No. 500) . . . 70 1·25

G. On Postal Anniv issue of 1916.
57 **60** 20pa. blue . . . . 85 1·25
58 1pi. black and violet . . . . 85 1·00
59 5pi. black and brown . . . 1·10 1·50

H. On Pictorial issues of 1916 and 1917.
60 **72** 5pa. orange . . . . 1·75 2·40
61 **75** 1pi. blue . . . . 1·25 1·75
62 **69** 5pi. on 2pa. blue (No. 914) 5·00 5·00
63 **64** 50pi. green on yellow . . . 27·00 18·00

1919. Various issues of Turkey optd **T.E.O. Cilicie**. A. On No. 726 (surch Printed Matter stamp optd with Star and Crescent).
69 **15** 5pa. on 10pa. green . . . . 90 1·10

B. On 1892 issue optd with Star and Crescent and Arabic surch.
70 **15** 10pa. on 20pa. red (No. 630) 40 98

C. On 1909 issue optd with Star and Crescent.
71 **28** 20pa. red (No. 572) . . . . 1·50 1·50
72 20pa. red (No. 643) . . . . 1·10 1·40

D. On 1909 issue optd with Tougra and surch in Turkish.
73 **28** 5pa. on 2pa. green (No. 938) 70 40

E. On Pictorial stamp of 1914.
74 – 1pi. blue (No. 505) 70 85

F. On Postal Anniv issue of 1916.
75 **60** 5pa. green . . . . £120 60·00
76 20pa. blue . . . . 70 1·00
77 1pi. black and violet . . . . 90 2·25

G. On Postal Anniv issue of 1916 optd with Star and Crescent.
78 **60** 10pa. red (No. 654) 45 45

H. On Pictorial issues of 1916 and 1917.
79 **72** 5pa. orange 35 70
80 **73** 10pa. green . . . . 60 1·10
81 **74** 20pa. red 55 60
82 **77** 2pi. blue and brown . . . . 1·00 75
83 **78** 5pi. brown and blue . . . . 85 1·00
84 **69** 5pi. on 2pa. blue . . . . . 4·00 4·50
85 **63** 25pi. red on buff . . . . . 4·00 4·50
86 **64** 50pi. green on yellow . . . 55 40

I. On Charity stamp of 1917.
87 **65** 10pa. purple . . . . 1·00 1·10

1920. "Mouchon" key-type of French Levant surch **T.E.O. 20 PARAS**.
88 B 20pa. on 10c. red . . . . . 1·00 1·10

7

1920. Surch **OCCUPATION MILITAIRE Francaise CILICIE** and value.
89 **7** 70pa. on 5pa. red . . . . . 85 1·40
90 3½pi. on 5pa. red . . . . . 85 1·40

1920. Stamps of France surch **O.M.F. Cilicie** and new value.
100 **11** 5pa. on 2c. red 25 90
101 **18** 10pa. on 5c. green 25 55
102 20pa. on 10c. red . . . . 25·00 80
103 1pi. on 25c. blue 35 65
104 **15** 2pi. on 15c. green 40 83
105 **13** 5pi. on 40c. red and blue 45 1·25
106 10pi. on 50c. brown & lav 83 1·40
107 50pi. on 1f. red and green 1·20 1·75
108 100pi. on 5f. blue & yellow 13·88 14·00

1920. Stamps of France surch **O.M.F. Cilicie SAND. EST** and new value.
109 **11** 5pa. on 2c. red . . . . . 3·00
110 **18** 10pa. on 5c. green . . . . 3·00
111 20pa. on 10c. red . . . . 2·10
112 1pi. on 25c. blue . . . . . 1·90
113 **15** 2pi. on 15c. green . . . . 6·25

114 **13** 5pi. on 40c. red and blue 40·00
115 20pi. on 1f. red and green 60·00

1921. Air. Nos. 104/5 optd **POSTE PAR AVION** in frame.
116 **15** 2pi. on 15c. green £6500
117 **13** 5pi. on 40c. red and blue £6500

POSTAGE DUE STAMPS

1919. Postage Due stamps of Turkey optd **CILICIE**.
D27 **D 49** 5pa. brown 1·50 2·10
D28 **D 50** 20pa. red 1·60 2·10
D29 **D 51** 1pi. blue 4·00 4·00
D45 **D 52** 2pi. blue 2·75 3·00

1919. Postage Due stamps of Turkey optd **Cilicie**.
D64 **D 49** 5pa. brown 1·50 2·10
D65 **D 50** 20pa. red 1·40 2·10
D66 **D 51** 1pi. blue 4·00 4·00
D67 **D 52** 2pi. blue 3·50 3·75

1921. Postage Due Stamps of France surch **O.M.F. Cilicie** and value.
D118 **D 11** 1pi. on 10c. brown 4·00 4·50
D119 2pi. on 20c. olive 3·50 4·50
D120 3pi. on 30c. red 3·75 4·50
D121 4pi. on 50c. purple 3·75 4·50

CISKEI Pt. 1

The Republic of Ciskei was established on 4 December 1981, being constructed from tribal areas formerly part of the Republic of South Africa.

This independence did not receive international political recognition. We are satisfied, however, that the stamps had "de facto" acceptance for the carriage of mail outside Ciskei.

Ciskei was formally re-incorporated into South Africa on 27 April 1994.

100 cents = 1 rand.

1 Dr. Lennox Sebe, Chief Minister

2 Green Turaco

1981. Independence. Multicoloured.
1 5c. Type **1** 10 10
2 15c. Coat of arms 20 15
3 20c. Flag 30 30
4 25c. Mace 35 25

1981. Birds. Multicoloured.
5 1c. Type **2** 20 15
6 2c. Cape wagtail 20 15
7 3c. White-browed coucal 50 15
8 4c. Yellow-tufted malachite sunbird 20 15
9 5c. Stanley crane 20 15
10 6c. African red-winged starling 20 15
11 7c. Giant kingfisher 20 15
12 8c. Hadada ibis 30 15
13 9c. Black cuckoo 30 15
14 10c. Black-collared barbet 30 15
14a 11c. African black-headed oriole 55 30
14b 12c. Malachite kingfisher 70 30
14c 14c. Hoopoe 1·00 30
15 15c. African fish eagle 30 30
15a 16c. Cape puff-back flycatcher 65 30
15b 18c. Long-tailed whydah 1·00 30
16 20c. Cape longclaw 40 30
16a 21c. Lemon dove 1·50 60
17 25c. Cape dikkop 30 30
18 30c. African green pigeon 40 40
19 50c. Brown-necked parrot 60 60
20 1r. Narina's trogon 90 1·25
21 2r. Cape eagle owl 1·75 2·50

3 Cecilia Makiwane (first Xhosa nurse)

4 Boom Sprayer

1982. Nursing. Multicoloured.
22 8c. Type **3** 15 10
23 15c. Operating theatre 30 30
24 20c. Matron lighting nurse's lamp (horiz) 40 40
25 25c. Nurses and patient (horiz) 50 50

1982. Pineapple Industry. Multicoloured.
26 8c. Type **4** 10 10
27 15c. Harvesting 20 25
28 20c. Despatch to cannery 25 30
29 30c. Packing for local market 30 35

5 Brown Hare

1982. Small Mammals. Multicoloured.
30 8c. Type **5** 15 15
31 15c. Cape fox 25 25
32 20c. Cape ground squirrel 30 30
33 25c. Caracal 40 40

6 Assegai

7 Dusky Shark

1983. Trees (1st series). Multicoloured.
34 8c. Cabbage tree 15 10
35 20c. Type **6** 30 30
36 25c. Cape chestnut 35 35
37 40c. Outeniqua yellowwood 50 55
See also Nos. 52/5.

1983. Sharks. Multicoloured.
38 8c. Type **7** 15 15
39 20c. Sand tiger ("Ragged-tooth shark") 30 30
40 25c. Tiger shark (57 × 21 mm) 35 35
41 30c. Scalloped hammerhead (57 × 21 mm) 40 40
42 40c. Great white shark (57 × 21 mm) 50 50

8 Lovedale

9 White Drill Uniform

1983. Educational Institutions.
43 **8** 10c. lt brown, brown & black 10 10
44 – 20c. lt brown, brown & black 20 20
45 – 25c. brown, red and black 25 25
46 – 40c. lt brown, brown & black 40 45
DESIGNS: 20c. Fort Hare; 25c. Healdtown; 40c. Lennox Sebe.

1983. British Military Uniforms (1st series). 6th Warwickshire Regiment of Foot, 1821–27. Multicoloured.
47 20c. Type **9** 40 40
48 20c. Light Company privates 40 40
49 20c. Grenadier Company sergeants 40 40
50 20c. Undress blue frock coats 40 40
51 20c. Officer and field officer in parade order 40 40
See also Nos. 64/8 and 95/8.

1984. Trees (2nd series). As T **6**. Multicoloured.
52 10c. "Rhus chirindensis" 15 15
53 20c. "Phoenix reclinata" 25 35
54 25c. "Ptaeroxyon obliquum" 30 40
55 40c. "Apodytes dimidiata" 40 55

10 Sandprawn

1984. Fish-bait. Multicoloured.
56 11c. Type **10** 20 15
57 20c. Coral worm 30 30
58 25c. Bloodworm 35 35
59 30c. Red-bait 40 40

11 Banded Martin ("Banded Sand Martin")

1984. Migratory Birds. Multicoloured.
60 11c. Type **11** 25 20
61 25c. House martin 50 50
62 30c. Greater striped swallow 60 60
63 45c. Barn swallow ("European Swallow") 80 85

1984. British Military Uniforms (2nd series). Cape Mounted Rifles. As T **9**. Multicoloured.
64 25c. (1) Trooper in field and sergeant in undress uniforms, 1830 45 45
65 25c. (2) Trooper and sergeant in full dress, 1835 45 45
66 25c. (3) Officers in undress, 1830 45 45
67 25c. (4) Officers in full dress, 1827–34 45 45
68 25c. (5) Officers in full dress, 1834 45 45
The stamps are numbered as indicated in brackets.

12 White Steenbras

1985. Coastal Angling. Multicoloured.
69 11c. Type **12** 20 15
70 25c. Bronze seabream 30 30
71 30c. Kob 40 45
72 50c. Spotted grunt 70 80

13 Brownies holding Handmade Doll

1985. International Youth Year. 75th Anniv of Girl Guide Movement. Multicoloured.
73 12c. Type **13** 15 15
74 25c. Rangers planting trees 25 25
75 30c. Guides with flag 30 30
76 50c. Guides building fire 60 65

14 Furniture making

1985. Small Businesses. Multicoloured.
77 12c. Type **14** 15 10
78 25c. Dressmaking 30 30
79 30c. Welding 30 30
80 50c. Basketry 60 65

15 "Antelope"

16 Earth showing Africa

1985. Sail Troopships. Multicoloured.
81 12c. Type **15** 20 15
82 25c. "Pilot" 45 45
83 30c. "Salisbury" 45 45
84 50c. "Olive Branch" 80 85

1986. Appearance of Halley's Comet. Mult.
85 12c. (1) Earth showing South America 70 70
86 12c. (2) Type **16** 70 70
87 12c. (3) Stars and Moon 70 70
88 12c. (4) Moon and Milky Way 70 70
89 12c. (5) Milky Way and stars 70 70
90 12c. (6) Earth showing Australia 70 70
91 12c. (7) Earth and meteor 70 70
92 12c. (8) Meteor, Moon and comet tail 70 70
93 12c. (9) Comet head and Moon 70 70
94 12c. (10) Sun 70 70

Nos. 85/94 were issued in sheetlets of 10 stamps forming a composite design of the southern skies in April. Each stamp is inscribed with a number from "A1-10" to "A10-10". The first number is given in brackets in the listing to aid identification.

17 Fifer in Winter Dress

18 Welding Bicycle Frame

1986. British Military Uniforms (3rd series). 98th Regiment of Foot. Multicoloured.
95 14c. Type **17** 20 15
96 20c. Private in summer dress 30 30
97 25c. Grenadier in full summer dress 35 35
98 30c. Sergeant-major in full winter dress 50 50

1986. Bicycle Factory, Dimbaza. Multicoloured.
99 14c. Type **18** 20 15
100 20c. Spray-painting frame 30 30
101 25c. Installing wheelspokes 35 35
102 30c. Final assembly 50 50

19 President Dr. Lennox Sebe

20 "Boletus edulis"

1986. 5th Anniv of Independence. Multicoloured.
103 14c. Type **19** 15 15
104 20c. National Shrine, Ntaba kaNdoda 20 30
105 25c. Legislative Assembly, Bisho 20 35
106 30c. Automatic telephone exchange, Bisho 25 50

1987. Edible Mushrooms. Multicoloured.
107 14c. Type **20** 25 15
108 20c. "Macrolepiota zeyheri" 40 40
109 25c. "Termitomyces spp" 50 50
110 30c. "Russula capensis" 60 60

21 Nkone Cow and Calf

22 Wire Windmill

1987. Nkone Cattle. Multicoloured.
111 16c. Type **21** 20 15
112 20c. Nkone cow 25 30
113 25c. Nkone bull 30 35
114 30c. Herd of Nkone 40 55

1987. Homemade Toys. Multicoloured.
115 16c. Type **22** 20 15
116 20c. Rag doll 25 30
117 25c. Clay horse (horiz) 30 35
118 30c. Wire car (horiz) 40 55

23 Seven Birds

24 Bush Lily

1987. Folklore (1st series). Sikulume. Mult.
119 16c. Type **23** 20 15
120 20c. Cannibals chasing Sikulume 25 30

121 25c. Sikulume attacking the inabulele 30 35
122 30c. Chief Mangangezulu chasing Sikulume and his bride 40 55
See also Nos. 127/36, 153/6 and 161/4

1988. Protected Flowers. Multicoloured.
123 16c. Type **24** 20 15
124 30c. Harebell 35 35
125 40c. Butterfly iris 40 40
126 50c. Vlei lily 60 65

25 Numbakatali crying and Second Wife feeding Black Crows

1988. Folklore (2nd series). Mbulukazi. Mult.
127 16c. Type **25** 30 35
128 16c. Numbakatali telling speckled pigeons of her childlessness 30 35
129 16c. Numbakatali finding children in earthenware jars 30 35
130 16c. Broad Breast sees Mbulukazi and brother at river 30 35
131 16c. Broad Breast asking to marry Mbulukazi 30 35
132 16c. Broad Breast and his two wives, Mbulukazi and her half-sister Mahlunguluza 30 35
133 16c. Mahlunguluza pushing Mbulukazi from precipice to her death 30 35
134 16c. Mbulukazi's ox tearing down Mahlunguluza's hut 30 35
135 16c. Ox licking Mbulukazi back to life 30 35
136 16c. Mahlunguluza being sent back to her father in disgrace 30 35

26 Oranges and Grafted Rootstocks in Nursery

1988. Citrus Farming. Multicoloured.
137 16c. Type **26** 20 15
138 30c. Lemons and inarching rootstock onto mature tree 40 40
139 40c. Tangerines and fruit being hand-picked 50 50
140 50c. Oranges and fruit being graded 60 65

27 "Amanita phalloides" **28** Kat River Dam

1988. Poisonous Fungi. Multicoloured.
141 16c. Type **27** 75 30
142 30c. "Chlorophyllum molybdites" . . . . 1·10 75
143 40c. "Amanita muscaria" . . 1·40 1·10
144 50c. "Amanita pantherina" 1·60 1·25

1989. Dams. Multicoloured.
145 16c. Type **28** 35 25
146 30c. Cata dam 55 50
147 40c. Binfield Park dam . . . 65 65
148 50c. Sandile dam 70 80

29 Taking Eggs from Rainbow Trout

1989. Trout Hatcheries. Multicoloured.
149 18c. Type **29** 25 15
150 30c. Fertilized eyed trout ova and alevins 45 45
151 40c. Five-week-old fingerlings 55 55
152 50c. Adult male 60 65

30 Lion and Little Jackal killing Eland **31** Cape Horse-cart

1989. Folklore (3rd series). Little Jackal and the Lion. Multicoloured.
153 18c. Type **30** 20 15
154 30c. Little Jackal's children carrying meat to clifftop home 35 35
155 40c. Little Jackal pretending to be trapped 40 40
156 50c. Lion falling down cliff face 45 50

1989. Animal-drawn Transport. Multicoloured.
157 18c. Type **31** 20 15
158 30c. Jubilee spider 35 35
159 40c. Ballantine half-tent ox-drawn wagon 40 40
160 50c. Voortrekker wagon . . . 45 50

32 Mpunzikazi offering Food to Five Heads **33** Handweaving on Loom

1990. Folklore (4th series). The Story of Makanda Mahlanu (Five Heads). Multicoloured.
161 18c. Type **32** 20 15
162 30c. Five Heads killing Mpunzikazi with his tail 35 35
163 40c. Mpunzanyana offering food to Five Heads 40 40
164 50c. Five Heads transformed into a man 45 50

1990. Handmade Carpets. Multicoloured.
165 21c. Type **33** 30 20
166 35c. Spinning 50 50
167 40c. Dyeing yarn 70 70
168 50c. Knotting carpet 70 70

34 Wooden Beam Plough, 1855

1980. Ploughs. Multicoloured.
169 21c. Type **34** 25 20
170 35c. Triple disc plough, 1895 40 40
171 40c. Reversible disc plough, 1895 . . . . 50 50
172 50c. "Het Volk" double furrow plough, 1910 . . . 60 65

35 Prickly Pear Vendor

1990. Prickly Pear. Multicoloured.
173 21c. Type **35** 30 20
174 35c. Prickly pear bushes . . 50 50
175 40c. Whole and opened fruits 60 60
176 50c. Bushes in bloom 70 80

36 African Marsh Owl ("Marsh Owl") **37** Sao Bras (now Mossel Bay) on Map, 1500

1991. Owls. Multicoloured.
177 21c. Type **36** 95 40
178 35c. African scops owl ("Scops") . . . . 1·25 80
179 40c. Barn owl . . . . 1·60 1·00
180 50c. African wood owl ("Wood") . . . . 1·75 1·40

1991. Stamp Day. D'Ataide's Letter of 1501. Multicoloured.
181 25c. Type **37** 70 70
182 25c. Bartolomeo Dias's ship foundering off Cabo Tormentoso (now Cape of Good Hope) during voyage to India, 1500 . . . . . 70 70
183 25c. Captain Pedro d'Ataide landing at Sao Bras, 1601 70 70
184 25c. D'Ataide leaving letter relating death of Dias on tree 70 70
185 25c. Captain Joao da Nova finding letter, 1501 . . . . 70 70
The inscriptions at the foot of Nos. 181 and 182 are transposed.

38 Comet Nucleus

1991. The Solar System. Multicoloured.
186 1c. Type **38** 20 15
187 2c. Trojan asteroids 20 15
188 5c. Meteoroids 20 15
189 7c. Pluto 30 15
190 10c. Neptune 30 15
191 20c. Uranus 50 20
192 25c. Saturn 60 20
193 30c. Jupiter 65 30
194 35c. Planetoids in asteroid belt 65 40
195 40c. Mars 80 50
196 50c. The Moon 80 70
197 60c. Earth 80 80
198 1r. Venus . . . . 1·00 1·25
199 2r. Mercury . . . . 1·60 2·00
200 5r. The Sun . . . . 2·25 3·25
MS201 197 × 93 mm. Nos. 186/200 10·00 10·00

39 Fort Armstrong and Xhosa Warrior

1991. 19th-century Frontier Forts. Multicoloured.
202 27c. Type **39** 30 30
203 45c. Keiskamma Hoek Post and Sir George Grey (governor of Cape Colony, 1854–58) 45 55
204 65c. Fort Hare and Xhosa Chief Sandile 55 70
205 85c. Peddie Cavalry Barracks and cavalryman . . . . . 75 1·25

40 Cumulonimbus

1992. Cloud Formations. Multicoloured.
206 27c. Type **40** 40 25
207 45c. Altocumulus 55 65
208 65c. Cirrus 65 80
209 85c. Cumulus . . . . 75 1·10

41 "Intelsat VI" Communications Satellite

1992. International Space Year. Satellites over Southern Africa. Multicoloured.
210 35c. Type **41** 40 25
211 70c. "G P S Navstar" (navigation) 80 80
212 90c. "Meteosat" (meteorology) . . . . . . 1·10 1·10
213 1r.05 "Landsat VI" (Earth resources survey) . . . . . 1·25 1·40

42 Universal Disc-harrow, 1914

1992. Agricultural Tools. Multicoloured.
214 35c. Type **42** 40 25
215 70c. Clod crusher and pulveriser, 1914 . . . . . 80 70
216 90c. Self-dump hay rake, 1910 . . . . 1·10 95
217 1r.05 McCormick hay tedder, 1900 . . . . 1·10 1·10

43 Mpekweni Sun Marine Resort

1992. Hotels. Multicoloured.
218 35c. Type **43** 40 25
219 70c. Katberg Protea Hotel . . 80 80
220 90c. Fish River Sun Hotel . . 1·10 1·10
221 1r.05 Amatola Sun Hotel, Amatole Mountains . . . 1·10 1·25

44 Vasco da Gama, "Sao Gabriel" and Voyage round Cape of Good Hope, 1497 **45** Island Canary

1993. Navigators. Multicoloured.
222 45c. Type **44** 65 30
223 65c. James Cook, H.M.S. "Endeavour" and first voyage, 1768–71 . . . . . 1·10 75
224 85c. Ferdinand Magellan, "Vitoria" and circumnavigation, 1519 . . 1·25 90
225 90c. Sir Francis Drake, "Golden Hind" and circumnavigation, 1577–80 1·25 95
226 1r.05 Abel Tasman, "Heemskerk" and discovery of Tasmania, 1642 . . . . 1·40 1·25
The ship on No. 222 is wrongly inscribed "San Gabriel", that on No. 224 "Victoria" and that on No. 226 "Heemskerck".

1993. Cage Birds. Multicoloured.
227 45c. Type **45** 45 30
228 65c. Budgerigar 70 60
229 85c. Peach-faced lovebirds . . 90 80
230 90c. Cockatiel 95 85
231 1r.05 Gouldian finch . . . . 1·00 1·10

46 Goshen Church (Moravian Mission), Whittlesea

1993. Churches and Missions.
232 **46** 45c. stone, black and red 35 20
233 – 65c. blue, black and red . . 60 60
234 – 85c. brown, black and red 80 80
235 – 1r.05 yellow, black and red 90 1·00
DESIGNS: 65c. Kamastone Mission Church; 85c. Richie Thompson Memorial Church (Hertzog Mission), near Seymour; 1r.05, Bryce Ross Memorial Church (Pirie Mission), near Dimbaza.

47 Jointed Cactus **48** "Losna" (steamer) (near Fish River), 1921

1993. Invader Plants. Multicoloured.
236 45c. Type **47** 40 30
237 65c. Thorn apple 70 60

238 85c. Coffee weed 90 80
239 1r.05 Poisonous wild tobacco 1·00 1·00
MS240 98 × 125 mm. Nos. 236/9 2·75 2·75

1994. Shipwrecks. Multicoloured.
241 45c. Type **48** 65 30
242 65c. "Catherine" (barque) (Waterloo Bay), 1846 . . . 1·10 60
243 85c. "Bennebroek" (East Indiaman) (near Mtana River), 1713 . . . . . . 1·25 90
244 1r.05 "Sao Joao Baptista" (galleon) (between Fish and Kei Rivers), 1622 . . . . 1·40 1·25

49 "Herman Steyn"

1994. Hybrid Roses. Multicoloured.
245 45c. Type **49** 35 30
246 70c. "Esther Geldenhuys" . . 60 60
247 95c. "Margaret Wasserfall" 80 80
248 1r.15 "Professor Fred Ziady" 1·00 1·00
MS249 149 × 114 mm. Nos. 245/8 2·50 2·75

COCHIN Pt. 1

A state of South West India. Now uses Indian stamps.

6 puttans = 5 annas.
12 pies = 1 anna; 16 annas = 1 rupee.

1 Emblems of State

1892. Value in "puttans".
5a **1** ½put. orange . . . . 1·60 1·50
2 1put. purple . . . . 2·75 2·00
3 2put. violet . . . . 2·00 2·25

3 **5**

1903. Value in "pies" or "puttans". With or without gum.
16 **3** 3pies. blue 70 10
17 ½put. green (smaller) . . . . 1·10 40
18 **5** 1put. red . . . . 1·75 10
19 **3** 2put. violet . . . . 2·50 50

1909. Surch **2**. No gum.
22 **3** 2 on 3 pies. mauve 15 50

8 Raja Rama Varma I **10** Raja Rama Varma II

1911. Value in "pies" or "annas".
26 **8** 2p. brown 30 10
27 3p. blue 75 10
28 4p. green . . . . 1·50 10
29 9p. red . . . . 1·10 10
30 1a. orange . . . . 2·75 10
31 1½a. purple . . . . 5·50 45
32 2a. grey . . . . 7·50 40
33 3a. red . . . . 35·00 35·00

1916. Various frames.
35b **10** 2p. brown . . . . 1·60 10
36 4p. green . . . . 1·00 10
37 6p. brown . . . . 2·50 10
38 8p. brown . . . . 1·50 10
39 9p. red . . . . 16·00 25
40 10p. blue . . . . 3·00 10
41a 1a. orange . . . . 8·50 30
42 1½a. purple . . . . 2·25 20
43 2a. grey . . . . 4·25 10
44 2¼a. green . . . . 4·25 3·25
45 3a. red . . . . 11·00 35

1922. Surch with figure and words.
46 **8** 2p. on 3p. blue 40 30

1928. Surch **ONE ANNA ANCHAL & REVENUE** and value in native characters.
50 **10** 1a. on 2¼a. green . . . . . 5·00 12·00

1932. Surch in figures and words both in English and in native characters.
51 **10** 3p. on 4p. green . . . . . 1·10 90
52 3p. on 8p. brown . . . . . 1·25 2·50
53 9p. on 10p. blue . . . . . 1·50 3·00

18 Maharaja Rama Varma III **26** Maharaja Kerala Varma II

1933.
54 **18** 2p. brown 60 30
55 4p. green 60 10
56 6p. red 70 10
57 1a. orange 70 10
58 1a.8p. red . . . . 3·00 4·50
59 2a. grey . . . . 4·50 90
60 2¼a. green . . . . 1·50 15
61 3a. orange . . . . 5·00 1·60
62 3a.4p. violet . . . . 1·50 1·40
63 6a.8p. sepia . . . . 1·75 10·00
64 10a. blue . . . . 3·00 12·00

1934. Surch with figure and words.
65 **10** 6p. on 8p. brown 75 60
66 6p. on 10p. blue . . . . . 1·75 2·00

1939. Optd **ANCHAL**.
74 **18** 1a. orange . . . . 75 1·60

1939. Surch in words only.
75 **18** 3p. on 1a.8p. red . . . . . £160 75·00
77 6p. on 1a.8p. red . . . . . 3·00 19·00

1943. Surch **SURCHARGED** and value in words.
79 **18** 3p. on 4p. green . . . . . 6·00 4·00
76 3p. on 1a.8p. red . . . . . 3·50 8·00
78 1a.3p. on 1a.8p. red . . . . 1·00 30

1943. Surch **ANCHAL SURCHARGED NINE PIES.**
84 **18** 9p. on 1a. orange . . . . . 17·00 5·50

1943. Surch **ANCHAL** and value in words.
81a **18** 6p. on 1a. orange . . . . £100 60·00
82 9p. on 1a. orange £110 £120

1943.
85 **26** 2p. brown . . . . 1·60 2·50
87a 4p. green . . . . 3·00 3·75
88 6p. brown . . . . 1·50 10
89 9p. blue . . . . 28·00 1·00
90a 1a. orange . . . . 21·00 42·00
91 2¼a. green . . . . 21·00 2·25

1944. Surch with value in words only.
93 **26** 2p. on 6p. brown . . . . . 75 3·00
94 3p. on 4p. green . . . . . 3·00 10
96 3p. on 6p. brown 85 20
97 4p. on 6p. brown . . . . . 3·50 9·50

1944. Surch **SURCHARGED** and value in words.
95 **26** 3p. on 4p. green . . . . . 4·00 10
92c 1a.3p. on 1a. orange . . . – £2750

1944. Surch **ANCHAL NINE PIES.**
92a **26** 9p. on 1a. orange . . . . 4·75 2·50

1944. Surch **ANCHAL SURCHARGED NINE PIES.**
92b **26** 9p. on 1a. orange . . . . 5·00 2·50

28 Maharaja Ravi Varma **29** Maharaja Ravi Varma

1944.
98 **28** 9p. blue . . . . 12·00 2·25
99 1a.3p. mauve . . . . 5·00 8·50
100 1a.9p. blue . . . . 8·00 13·00

1946. No gum.
101 **29** 2p. brown . . . . 1·75 10
102 3p. red 50 15
103 4p. green . . . . £1700 80·00
104 6p. brown . . . . 20·00 3·75
105 9p. blue 50 10
106 1a. orange . . . . 6·50 26·00
107 2a. black . . . . 90·00 8·00
108 3a. red . . . . 60·00 6·00

For No. 106, optd "U.S.T.C." or "T.-C." with or without surch, see Travancore-Cochin.

30 Maharaja Kerala Varma III **31** Chinese Nets

1948.
109 **30** 2p. brown . . . . 1·75 15
110 3p. red 75 15
111 4p. green . . . . 12·00 2·00
112 6p. brown . . . . 14·00 20
113 9p. blue . . . . 2·50 20
114 2a. black . . . . 48·00 1·00
115 3a. orange . . . . 55·00 75
116 3a.4p. violet . . . . 70·00 £350

1949.
117 **31** 2a. black . . . . 3·75 6·00
118 – 2¼a. green (Dutch palace) 2·75 6·00

SIX PIES

ആറു പൈ

(33)

1949. Surch as T **33**.
121 **29** 3p. on 9p. blue . . . . . 8·50 18·00
124a **30** 3p. on 9p. blue . . . . . 2·50 50
126 6p. on 9p. blue . . . . . 1·25 40
119 **28** 6p. on 1a.3p. mauve . . . 3·75 3·75
122 **29** 6p. on 1a.3p. mauve . . . 13·00 13·00
120 1a. on 1a.9p. blue . . . . 1·00 1·25
123 1a. on 1a.9p. blue . . . . 3·00 2·00

1949. Surch **SIX PIES** or **NINE PIES** only.
127 **29** 6p. on 1a. orange . . . . 55·00 £120
128 9p. on 1a. orange . . . . 75·00 £120

OFFICIAL STAMPS

1913. Optd **ON C G S.**
O1 **8** 3p. blue £120 10
O2 4p. green . . . . 8·50 10
O3a 9p. red . . . . 15·00 10
O4 1½a. purple . . . . 38·00 10
O5 2a. grey . . . . 13·00 10
O6 3a. red . . . . 48·00 35
O7 6a. violet . . . . 42·00 2·00
O8 12a. blue . . . . 38·00 6·50
O9 1½r. green . . . . 32·00 60·00

1919. Optd **ON C G S.**
O10 **10** 4p. green . . . . 3·75 10
O11 6p. brown . . . . 7·50 10
O26 8p. brown . . . . 7·00 10
O13 9p. red . . . . 50·00 10
O27 10p. blue . . . . 6·00 10
O15 1½a. purple . . . . . . 5·50 10
O28 2a. grey . . . . 28·00 15
O17 2¼a. green . . . . 12·00 10
O29 3a. red . . . . 8·00 15
O19 6a. violet . . . . 32·00 50
O19a 12a. blue . . . . 15·00 3·50
O19b 1½r. green . . . . 23·00 £100

1923. Official stamps surch in figures and words.
O32 **10** 6p. on 8p. brown . . . . 2·25 10
O33 6p. on 10p. blue . . . . 4·00 10
O20b **8** 8p. on 9p. red £130 20
O21 **10** 8p. on 9p. red . . . . . 70·00 10
O23 **8** 10p. on 9p. red . . . . . £800 10·00
O22 **10** 10p. on 9p. red . . . . . 65·00 70

1933. Optd **ON C G S.**
O34 **18** 4p. green . . . . 2·50 10
O35 6p. red . . . . 2·50 10
O52 1a. orange . . . . 1·00 10
O37 1a.8p. red . . . . 1·50 30
O38 2a. grey . . . . 12·00 10
O39 2¼a. green . . . . 4·00 10
O53 3a. orange . . . . 3·00 1·00
O41 3a.4p. violet . . . . . . 1·50 15
O42 6a.8p. sepia . . . . . . 1·50 20
O43 10a. blue . . . . 1·50 70

1943. Official stamp surch **NINE PIES.**
O57 **10** 9p. on 1½a. purple . . . . £400 22·00

1943. Official stamps surch **SURCHARGED** and value in words.
O63 **18** 3p. on 4p. green . . . . £100 45·00
O58 3p. on 1a.8p. red . . . . 5·50 1·40
O66 1a.3p. on 1a. orange . . . £275 90·00
O61 1a.9p. on 1a.8p. red . . . 80 30

1943. Official stamps surch in words.
O62 **18** 3p. on 4p. green . . . . 21·00 7·00
O64 3p. on 1a. orange . . . . 2·00 3·00
O65 9p. on 1a. orange . . . . £200 45·00
O59 9p. on 1a.8p. red . . . . £100 26·00
O60 1a.9p. on 1a.8p. red . . . 2·50 1·75

1944. Optd **ON C G S.**
O68 **26** 4p. green . . . . 25·00 4·00
O69b 6p. brown 70 10
O70 1a. orange . . . . £1900 45·00
O71 2a. black . . . . 4·25 55
O72 2¼a. green . . . . 2·75 85
O73a 3a. red . . . . 7·00 40

1944. Official stamps surch **SURCHARGED** and value in words.
O75 **26** 3p. on 4p. green . . . . 4·50 30
O78 9p. on 6p. brown . . . . 3·50 30
O80 1a.3p. on 1a. orange . . . 3·25 10

1944. Official stamps surch in words.
O74 **26** 3p. on 4p. green . . . . 2·75 10
O76 3p. on 1a. orange . . . . 18·00 4·25
O77 9p. on 6p. brown . . . . 7·50 2·25
O79 1a.3p. on 1a. orange . . . 7·00 1·40

1946. Optd **ON C G S.**
O81 **28** 9p. blue . . . . 2·75 10
O82 1a.3p. mauve . . . . . . 1·60 20
O83 1a.9p. blue 40 90

1948. Optd **ON C G S.**
O84 **29** 3p. red . . . . 1·00 10
O85 4p. green . . . . 27·00 8·00
O86 6p. brown . . . . 7·00 8·00
O87 9p. blue 75 10
O88 1a.3p. mauve . . . . . . 2·75 60
O89 1a.9p. blue . . . . 2·75 40
O90 2a. black . . . . 13·00 3·00
O91 2¼a. green . . . . 20·00 3·00

1949. Optd **ON C G S.**
O92 **30** 3p. red . . . . 1·25 15
O93 4p. green . . . . 1·10 30
O94 6p. brown . . . . 2·50 10
O95 9p. blue . . . . 2·50 10
O96 2a. black . . . . 1·50 15
O97 2¼a. green . . . . 2·75 5·00
O98 3a. orange . . . . 1·10 50
O99 3a.4p. violet . . . . . . 35·00 32·00

1949. Official stamps surch as T **33**.
O103 **30** 6p. on 3p. red . . . . . 1·00 60
O104 9p. on 4p. green . . . . 75 2·00
O100 **28** 1a. on 1a.9p. blue . . . 60 60
O101 **29** 1a. on 1a.9p. blue . . . 20·00 14·00

1949. Optd **SERVICE**.
O105 **30** 3p. on 9p. (No. 125) . . 60 65

For later issues see **TRAVANCORE-COCHIN**.

COCHIN-CHINA Pt. 6

A former French colony in the extreme S. of Indo-China, subsequently incorporated into French Indo-China.

100 centimes = 1 franc.

1886. Stamps of French Colonies surch.
1 **J** 5 on 25c. brown on yellow . . £160 £110
2 5 on 2c. brown on yellow . . 14·50 16·00
3 5 on 25c. brown on yellow . . 20·00 19·00
4 5 on 25c. black on red . . . . 40·00 34·00

Nos. 1 and 4 are surcharged with numeral only; Nos. 2 and 3 are additionally optd **C. CH.**

COCOS (KEELING) ISLANDS Pt.1

Islands in the Indian Ocean formerly administered by Singapore and transferred to Australian administration on 23 November 1955.

1963. 12 pence = 1 shilling;
20 shillings = 1 pound.
1966. 100 cents = 1 dollar (Australian).

5 Jukong (sailboat) **6** White Tern

1963.
1 – 3d. brown . . . . 1·00 1·50
2 – 5d. blue . . . . 1·50 80
3 – 8d. red . . . . 1·00 1·75
4 – 1s. green . . . . 1·00 75
5 **5** 2s. purple . . . . 11·00 2·75
6 **6** 2s.3d. green . . . . 14·00 2·75

DESIGNS—HORIZ (As Type **5**): 3d. Copra industry; 1s. Palms. (As Type **6**): 5d. Lockheed Super Constellation airliner. VERT (As Type **5**): 8d. Map of islands.

1965. 50th Anniv of Gallipoli Landing. As T **184** of Australia, but slightly larger (22 × 34½ mm).
7 5d. brown, black and green . . 60 45

With the introduction of decimal currency on 14 February 1966, Australian stamps were used in Cocos Islands until the 1969 issue.

7 Reef Clam

9 "Dragon", 1609

1969. Decimal Currency. Multicoloured.
8 1c. Lajonkaines turbo shell (vert) . . . 30 60
9 2c. Elongate or small giant clam (vert) . . . 75 80
10 3c. Type **7** . . . 40 20
11 4c. Floral blenny (fish) . . . 30 50
12 5c. "Porites cocosensis" (coral) 35 30
13 6c. Atrisignis flyingfish . . . 75 75
14 10c. Buff-banded rail . . . 75 70
15 15c. Java sparrow . . . 75 30
16 20c. Red-tailed tropic bird . . 75 30
17 30c. Sooty tern . . . 75 30
18 50c. Reef heron (vert) . . . 75 30
19 $1 Great frigate bird (vert) . . 1·50 75

1976. Ships. Multicoloured.
20 1c. Type **9** . . . 30 40
21 2c. H.M.S. "Juno", 1857 (horiz) . . . 30 40
22 5c. H.M.S. "Beagle", 1836 (horiz) . . . 30 40
23 10c. H.M.A.S. "Sydney", 1914 (horiz) . . . 35 40
24 15c. S.M.S. "Emden", 1914 (horiz) . . . 60 55
25 20c. "Ayesha", 1907 (horiz) 60 65
26 25c. T.S.S. "Islander", 1927 60 75
27 30c. M.V. "Cheshire", 1951 60 75
28 35c. Jukong (sailboat) (horiz) 60 75
29 40c. C.S. "Scotia", 1900 (horiz) . . . 60 75
30 50c. R.M.S. "Orontes", 1929 60 75
31 $1 Royal Yacht "Gothic", 1954 . . . 75 1·00

10 Map of Cocos (Keeling) Islands, Union Flag, Stars and Trees

1979. Inauguration of Independent Postal Service and First Statutory Council. Multicoloured.
32 20c. Type **10** . . . 25 40
33 50c. Council seat and jukong (sailboat) . . . 35 85

11 Forceps Fish

12 "Peace on Earth"

1979. Fishes. Multicoloured.
34 1c. Type **11** . . . 30 1·00
35 2c. Ornate butterflyfish . . . 30 30
36 5c. Barbier . . . 50 1·10
37 10c. Meyer's butterflyfish . . 30 1·00
38 15c. Pink wrasse . . . 30 30
39 20c. Clark's anemonefish . . 45 30
39a 22c. Undulate triggerfish . . 45 30
40 25c. Red-breasted wrasse . . 45 1·00
40a 28c. Guineafowl wrasse . . 35 35
41 30c. Madagascar butterflyfish 50 45
42 35c. Cocos-Keeling angelfish 50 1·60
43 40c. Coral hogfish . . . 55 90
44 50c. Clown wrasse . . . 85 75
45 55c. Yellow-tailed tamarin . . 60 1·25
45a 60c. Greasy grouper . . . 60 75
46 $1 Palette surgeonfish . . . 75 3·50
47 $2 Melon butterflyfish . . . 1·00 3·50

1979. Christmas. Multicoloured.
48 25c. Type **12** . . . 25 40
49 55c. Atoll seascape ("Goodwill") . . . 40 70

13 Star, Map of Cocos (Keeling) Islands and Island Landscape

1980. Christmas. Multicoloured.
50 15c. Type **13** . . . 10 10
51 28c. The Three Kings . . . 15 15
52 60c. Adoration . . . 40 40

14 "Administered by the British Government, 1857"

15 "Eye of the Wind" and Map of Cocos (Keeling) Islands

1980. 25th Anniv of Territorial Status under Australian Administration. Multicoloured.
53 22c. Type **14** . . . 15 15
54 22c. Arms of Ceylon . . . 15 15
55 22c. Arms of Straits Settlements . . . 15 15
56 22c. Arms of Singapore . . . 15 15
57 22c. Arms and flag of Australia . . . 15 15

1980. "Operation Drake" (round the world expedition) and 400th Anniv of Sir Francis Drake's Circumnavigation of the World. Multicoloured.
58 22c. Type **15** . . . 25 15
59 28c. Routes map (horiz) . . . 25 15
60 35c. Sir Francis Drake and "Golden Hind" . . . 25 15
61 60c. Prince Charles (patron) and "Eye of the Wind" (brigantine) . . . 45 30

16 Aerial View of Animal Quarantine Station

1981. Opening of Animal Quarantine Station. Multicoloured.
62 22c. Type **16** . . . 15 15
63 45c. Unloading livestock . . . 20 30
64 60c. Livestock in pen . . . 20 35

17 Consolidated Catalina Flying Boat "Guba"

1981. Aircraft. Multicoloured.
65 22c. Type **17** . . . 25 25
66 22c. Consolidated Liberator and Avro Lancastrian . . . 25 25
67 22c. Douglas DC-4 and Lockheed Constellation . . 25 25
68 22c. Lockheed Electra . . . 25 25
69 22c. Boeing 727-100 airliners 25 25

18 Prince Charles and Lady Diana Spencer

1981. Royal Wedding.
70 **18** 24c. multicoloured . . . 30 20
71 60c. multicoloured . . . 50 60

19 "Angels we have heard on High"

1981. Christmas. Scenes and Lines from Carol "Angels we have heard on High". Multicoloured.
72 18c. Type **19** . . . 10 10
73 30c. "Shepherds why this Jubilee?" . . . 20 20
74 60c. "Come to Bethlehem and see Him" . . . 35 35

20 "Pachyseris speciosa" and "Heliofungia actiniformis" (corals)

1981. 150th Anniv of Charles Darwin's Voyage. Multicoloured.
75 24c. Type **20** . . . 25 15
76 45c. Charles Darwin in 1853 and "Pavona cactus" (coral) 40 30
77 60c. H.M.S. "Beagle", 1832, and "Lobophyllia hemprichii" (coral) . . . 45 35
MS78 130 × 95 mm. 24c. Cross-section of West Island; 24c. Cross-section of Home Island 75 85

21 Queen Victoria

1982. 125th Anniv of Annexation of Cocos (Keeling) Islands to British Empire. Multicoloured.
79 24c. Type **21** . . . 15 15
80 45c. Union flag . . . 25 25
81 60c. Captain S. Fremantle (annexation visit, 1857) . . 30 35

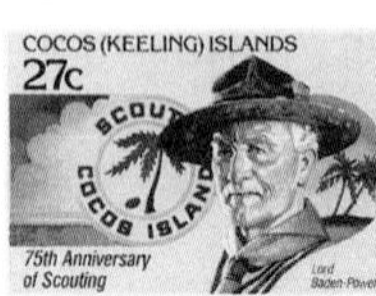

22 Lord Baden-Powell

1982. 75th Anniv of Boy Scout Movement. Multicoloured.
82 27c. Type **22** . . . 25 25
83 75c. "75" and map of Cocos (Keeling) Islands (vert) . . . 60 1·50

23 "Precis villida"

24 "Call His Name Immanuel"

1982. Butterflies and Moths. Multicoloured.
84 1c. Type **23** . . . 1·00 60
85 2c. "Cephonodes picus" (horiz) . . . 40 40
86 5c. "Macroglossom corythus" (horiz) . . . 1·50 70
87 10c. "Chasmina candida" . . 40 40
88 20c. "Nagia linteola" (horiz) 40 65
89 25c. "Eublemma rivula" . . . 40 75
90 30c. "Eurrhyparodes tricoloralis" . . . 40 65
91 35c. "Hippotion boerhaviae" (horiz) . . . 1·50 75
92 40c. "Euploea core" . . . 40 80
93 45c. "Psara hipponalis" (horiz) 50 80
94 50c. "Danaus chrysippus" (horiz) . . . 60 1·25
95 55c. "Hypolimnas misippus" 60 70
96 60c. "Spodoptera litura" . . . 65 1·75
97 $1 "Achaea janata" . . . 2·75 2·75
98 $2 "Panacra velox" (horiz) . . 2·00 2·75
99 $3 "Utetheisa pulchelloides" (horiz) . . . 2·75 2·75

1982. Christmas. Multicoloured.
100 21c. Type **24** . . . 25 30
101 35c. "I bring you good tidings" . . . 40 40
102 75c. "Arise and flee into Egypt" . . . 1·00 1·25

25 "God will look after us" (Matt. 1:20)

26 Hari Raya Celebration

1983. Christmas. Extracts from New Testament. Multicoloured.
103 24c. Type **25** . . . 30 45
104 24c. "Our baby King, Jesus" (Matthew. 2:2) . . . 30 45
105 24c. "Your Saviour is born" (Luke. 2:11) . . . 30 45
106 24c. "Wise men followed the Star" (Matthew. 2:9–10) . . 30 45
107 24c. "And worship the Lord" (Matthew. 2:11) . . . 30 45

1984. Cocos-Malay Culture (1st series). Mult.
108 45c. Type **26** . . . 45 25
109 75c. Melenggok dancing . . . 65 50
110 85c. Cocos-Malay wedding 75 55
See also Nos. 128/31.

27 Unpacking Barrel

1984. 75th Anniv of Cocos Barrel Mail. Multicoloured.
111 35c. Type **27** . . . 40 25
112 55c. Jukong awaiting mail ship . . . 75 50
113 70c. P & O mail ship "Morea" . . . 85 55
MS114 125 × 95 mm. $1 Retrieving barrel 1·00 1·25

28 Captain William Keeling

29 Malay Settlement, Home Island

1984. 375th Anniv of Discovery of Cocos (Keeling) Islands. Multicoloured.
115 30c. Type **28** . . . 60 40
116 65c. "Hector" . . . 1·25 90
117 95c. Mariner's astrolabe . . . 1·50 1·25
118 $1.10 Map circa 1666 . . . 1·60 1·50

1984. "Ausipex" International Stamp Exhibition, Melbourne. Multicoloured.
119 45c. Type **29** . . . 75 50
120 55c. Airstrip, West Island . . 85 60
MS121 130 × 95 mm. $2 Jukongs (native craft) racing 2·75 2·50

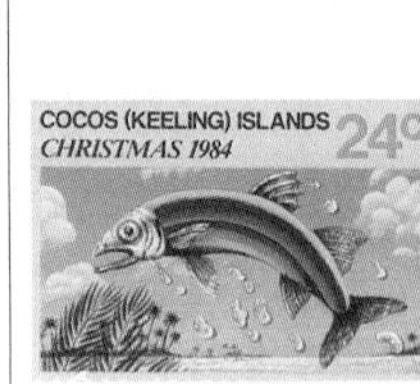

30 "Rainbow" Fish

32 Jukong-building

31 Cocos Islanders

1984. Christmas. Multicoloured.
122 24c. Type **30** . . . 50 60
123 35c. "Rainbow" butterfly . . 1·10 1·40
124 55c. "Rainbow" bird . . . 1·25 2·00

1984. Integration of Cocos (Keeling) Islands with Australia. Sheet 90 × 52 mm, containing T **31** and similar horiz design. Multicoloured.
MS125 30c. Type **31**; 30c. Australian flag on island 1·50 1·25

1985. Cocos-Malay Culture (2nd series). Handicrafts. Multicoloured.
126 30c. Type **32** . . . 75 35
127 45c. Blacksmithing . . . 1·00 55
128 55c. Woodcarving . . . 1·25 65

33 C.S. "Scotia"

1985. Cable-laying Ships. Multicoloured.
129 33c. Type **33** . . . 1·50 40
130 65c. C.S. "Anglia" . . . 2·25 1·60
131 80c. C.S. "Patrol" . . . 2·25 2·25

34 Red-footed Booby

35 Mantled Top

1985. Birds of Cocos (Keeling) Islands. Mult.
132 33c. Type **34** . . . . 1·75 2·00
133 60c. Nankeen night heron (juvenile) (horiz) . . . . . 2·00 2·50
134 $1 Buff-banded rail (horiz) 2·25 2·50
Nos. 132/4 were issued together, se-tenant, forming a composite design.

1985. Shells and Molluscs. Multicoloured.
135 1c. Type **35** . . . . 60 1·25
136 2c. Rang's nerite . . . . . . 60 1·25
137 3c. Jewel box . . . . 60 1·25
138 4c. Money cowrie . . . . . 1·00 1·25
139 5c. Purple Pacific drupe . . . 60 1·25
140 10c. Soldier cone . . . . . . 70 1·50
141 15c. Merlin-spike auger . . . 2·00 1·25
142 20c. Pacific strawberry cockle 2·00 1·50
143 30c. Lajonkaire's turban . . 2·00 1·50
144 33c. Reticulate mitre . . . . 2·25 1·50
145 40c. Common spider conch 2·25 1·50
146 50c. Fluted giant clam or scaled tridacna . . . . . . 2·25 1·75
147 60c. Minstrel cowrie . . . . 2·25 2·00
148 $1 Varicose nudibranch . . . 3·25 3·00
149 $2 Tesselated nudibranch . . 3·50 4·00
150 $3 Hamincea cymballum . . 4·25 4·75

36 Night Sky and Palm Trees

1985. Christmas. Sheet 121 × 88 mm, containing T **36** and similar horiz designs.
MS151 27c. × 4 multicoloured 2·00 2·75
The stamps within No. **MS**151 show a composite design of the night sky seen through a grove of palm trees. The position of the face value on the four stamps varies. Type **36** shows the top left design. The top right stamp shows the face value at bottom right, the bottom left at top left and the bottom right at top right.

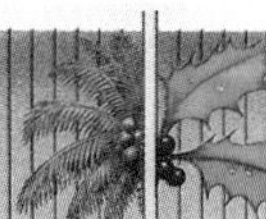

37 Charles Darwin, c. 1840

38 Coconut Palm and Holly Sprigs

1986. 150th Anniv of Charles Darwin's Visit. Multicoloured.
152 33c. Type **37** 70 60
153 60c. Map of H.M.S. "Beagle's" route, Australia to Cocos Islands . . . . . 1·25 2·25
154 $1 H.M.S. "Beagle" . . . . 1·75 2·75

1986. Christmas. Multicoloured.
155 30c. Type **38** 60 60
156 90c. Nautilus shell and Christmas tree bauble . . . 2·00 2·75
157 $1 Tropical fish and bell . . 2·00 2·75

39 Jukong

1987. Sailing Craft. Multicoloured.
158 36c. Type **39** . . . . 1·10 1·50
159 36c. Ocean racing yachts . . 1·10 1·50
160 36c. "Sarimanok" (replica of early dhow) . . . . 1·10 1·50
161 36c. "Ayesha" (schooner) . . 1·10 1·50
Nos. 158/61 were printed together, se-tenant, each strip forming a composite background design.

40 Beach, Direction Island

1987. Cocos Islands Scenes. Multicoloured.
162 70c. Type **40** . . . . 1·40 1·40
163 90c. Palm forest, West Island 1·75 2·00
164 $1 Golf course . . . . 2·75 3·00

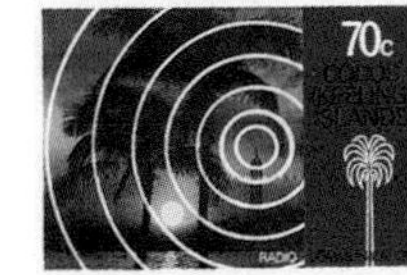

41 Radio Transmitter and Palm Trees at Sunset

1987. Communications. Multicoloured.
165 70c. Type **41** . . . . 1·25 1·50
166 75c. Boeing 727-100 airliner at terminal . . . . 1·50 1·75
167 90c. "Intelsat 5" satellite . . 1·75 2·25
168 $1 Airmail letter and globe 2·00 2·25

42 Batik Printing

1987. Cocos (Keeling) Islands Malay Industries. Multicoloured.
169 45c. Type **42** . . . . 1·25 1·50
170 65c. Jukong building . . . . 1·75 2·00
171 75c. Copra production . . . 2·00 2·25

43 Hands releasing Peace Dove and Map of Islands

44 Coconut Flower

1987. Christmas. Multicoloured.
172 30c. Type **43** 40 40
173 90c. Local children at Christmas party . . . . . 1·25 1·90
174 $1 Island family and Christmas star . . . . . . 1·50 1·90

1988. Bicentenary of Australian Settlement. Arrival of First Fleet. As Nos. 1105/9 of Australia but each inscr "COCOS (KEELING) ISLANDS" and "AUSTRALIA BICENTENARY".
175 37c. Aborigines watching arrival of Fleet, Botany Bay . . . . 1·90 2·00
176 37c. Aboriginal family and anchored ships . . . . . . 1·90 2·00
177 37c. Fleet arriving at Sydney Cove . . . . 1·90 2·00
178 37c. Ship's boat . . . . . . 1·90 2·00
179 37c. Raising the flag, Sydney Cove, 26 January 1788 . . 1·90 2·00
Nos. 175/9 were printed together, se-tenant, forming a composite design.

1988. Life Cycle of the Coconut. Multicoloured.
180 37c. Type **44** 50 40
181 65c. Immature nuts . . . . . 75 1·00
182 90c. Coconut palm and mature nuts . . . . 1·10 1·75
183 $1 Seedlings . . . . 1·25 1·75
MS184 102 × 91 mm. Nos. 180/3 4·00 4·50

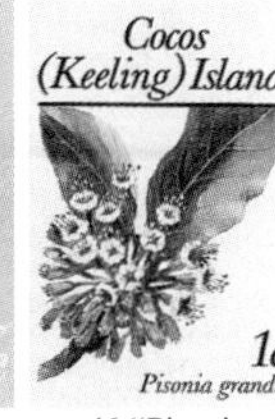

45 Copra 3d. Stamp of 1963

46 "Pisonia grandis"

1988. 25th Anniv of First Cocos (Keeling) Islands Stamps. Each showing stamp from 1963 definitive set.
185 **45** 37c. green, black and blue 1·25 1·00
186 – 55c. green, black and brown . . . . 1·75 1·50
187 – 65c. blue, black and lilac 1·90 2·25
188 – 70c. red, black and grey . . 1·90 2·50
189 – 90c. purple, black and grey 2·25 2·75
190 – $1 green, black and brown 2·25 2·75
DESIGNS: 55c. Palms 1s.; 65c. Lockheed Super Constellation airplane 5d.; 70c. Map 8d.; 90c. "Jukong" (sailboat) 2s.; $1 White tern 2s.3d.

1988. Flora. Multicoloured.
191 1c. Type **46** 50 80
192 2c. "Cocos nucifera" 50 80
193 5c. "Morinda citrifolia" . . . 1·00 90
194 10c. "Cordia subcordata" . . 70 90
195 30c. "Argusia argentea" . . . 1·00 1·25
196 37c. "Calophyllum inophyllum" . . . . 1·50 1·00
197 40c. "Barringtonia asiatica" 1·00 1·25
198 50c. "Caesalpinia bonduc" 1·25 3·00
199 90c. "Terminalia catappa" . . 1·75 4·00
200 $1 "Pemphis acidula" . . . . 1·75 2·50
201 $2 "Scaevola sericea" . . . . 2·50 2·50
202 $3 "Hibiscus tiliaceus" . . . 3·50 3·75

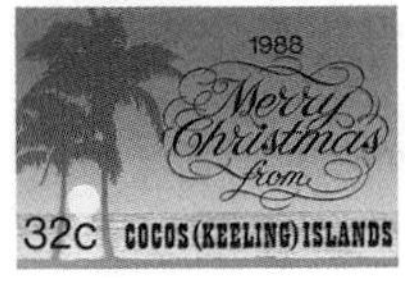

47 Beach at Sunset

1988. Christmas
204 **47** 32c. multicoloured 80 50
205 90c. multicoloured . . . . 1·75 2·50
206 $1 multicoloured . . . . . 2·00 2·50

48 Captain P. G. Taylor

49 Jukong and Star

1989. 50th Anniv of First Indian Ocean Aerial Survey.
207 **48** 40c. multicoloured 80 65
208 – 70c. multicoloured . . . . 1·75 2·50
209 – $1 multicoloured . . . . . 2·00 2·50
210 – $1.10 blue, lilac and black 2·25 2·75
DESIGNS: 70c. Consolidated Catalina flying boat "Guba" and crew; $1 "Guba" over Direction Islands; $1.10, Unissued Australia 5s. stamp commemorating flight.

1989. Christmas.
211 **49** 35c. multicoloured 85 60
212 80c. multicoloured . . . . 2·50 3·00
213 $1.10 multicoloured . . . 2·50 3·00

50 H.M.A.S. "Sydney" (cruiser)

1989. 75th Anniv of Destruction of German Cruiser "Emden". Multicoloured.
214 40c. Type **50** . . . . 1·75 1·75
215 70c. "Emden" . . . . 2·00 2·00
216 $1 "Emden's" steam launch 2·25 2·25
217 $1.10 H.M.A.S. "Sydney" (1914) and crest . . . . . 2·25 2·25

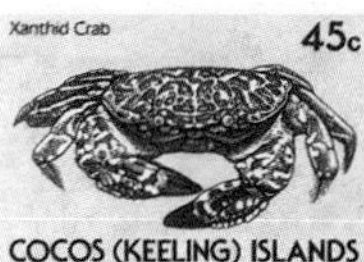

51 Xanthid Crab

1990. Cocos Islands Crabs. Multicoloured.
219 45c. Type **51** . . . . . . 1·75 75
220 75c. Ghost crab . . . . . . 2·25 2·00
221 $1 Red-backed mud crab . . 2·50 2·25
222 $1.30 Coconut crab (vert) . . 2·75 3·00

52 Captain Keeling and "Hector", 1609

1990. Navigators of the Pacific.
223 **52** 45c. mauve . . . . 2·75 1·25
224 – 75c. mauve and blue . . . 3·00 3·25
225 – $1 mauve and stone . . . 3·50 3·75
226 – $1.30 mauve and buff . . . 4·25 5·00
DESIGNS: 75c. Captain Fitzroy and H.M.S. "Beagle", 1836; $1 Captain Belcher and H.M.S. "Samarang", 1846, $1.30, Captain Fremantle and H.M.S. "Juno", 1857.

1990. "New Zealand 1990" International Stamp Exhibition, Auckland. No. 188 optd with logo and **NEW ZEALAND 1990 24 AUG 2 SEP AUCKLAND**.
228 70c. red, black and grey . . . 3·25 3·50
MS229 127 × 90 mm. As Nos. 194, 199 and 201, but self-adhesive 7·00 7·00

1990. No. 187 surch **$5**.
230 $5 on 65c. blue, black and lilac . . . . 18·00 18·00

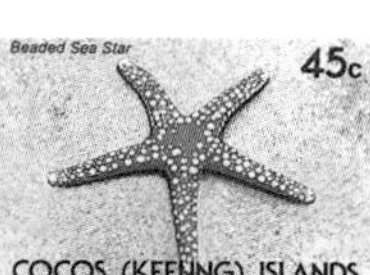

55 Cocos Atoll from West and Star

58 Beaded Sea Star

1990. Christmas. Multicoloured.
231 40c. Type **55** . . . . 70 1·00
232 70c. Cocos atoll from south 1·50 2·50
233 $1.30 Cocos atoll from east 2·75 3·00

1990. Nos. 140/1, 143 and 146/7 surch **POSTAGE PAID** plus additional words as indicated.
236 (1c.) on 30c. Lajonkaire's turban (**LOCAL**) . . . . . 1·75 2·50
235 (43c.) on 10c. Soldier cone (**MAINLAND**) . . . . . . 1·40 1·75
237 70c. on 60c. Minstrel cowrie (**ZONE 1**) . . . . 1·50 2·50
238 80c. on 50c. Fluted giant clam or scaled tridacna (**ZONE 2**) . . . . 1·75 3·25
239 $1.20 on 15c. Marlin-spike auger (**ZONE 5**) . . . . . 2·00 3·50

1991. Starfish and Sea Urchins. Multicoloured.
240 45c. Type **58** . . . . 1·25 75
241 75c. Feather star . . . . . . 2·00 2·25
242 $1 Slate pencil urchin . . . . 2·00 2·25
243 $1.30 Globose sea urchin . . . 2·75 3·25

59 Cocos Islands

1991. Malay Hari Raya Festival. Multicoloured.
244 45c. Type **59** . . . . 1·00 65
245 75c. Island house . . . . . 1·75 2·25
246 $1.30 Islands scene . . . . . 2·50 3·25

60 Child praying

1991. Christmas. Multicoloured.
247 38c. Type **60** . . . . 1·00 70
248 43c. Child dreaming of Christmas Day . . . . . . 1·00 70
249 $1 Child singing . . . . . . 2·25 2·25
250 $1.20 Child fascinated by decorations . . . . 2·75 3·50
MS251 118 × 74 mm. 38c., 43c., $1, $1.20, Local children's choir 7·00 7·50
The four values in No. **MS**251 form a composite design.

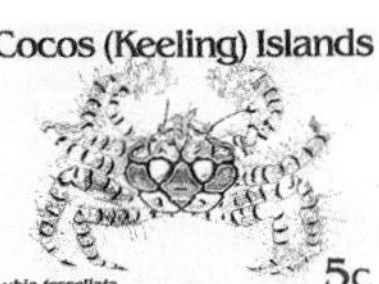

61 "Lybia tessellata"

1992. Crustaceans. Multicoloured.
252 5c. Type **61** . . . . 80 1·00
253 10c. "Pilodius areolatus" . . 1·25 1·25
254 20c. "Trizopagurus strigatus" 1·50 1·50
255 30c. "Lophozozymus pulchellus" . . . . 1·75 1·75
256 40c. "Thalamitoides quadridens" . . . . 1·75 1·75
257 45c. "Calcinus elegans" (vert) 1·75 1·75
258 50c. "Clibarius humilis" . . . 2·00 2·00

259 60c. "Trapezia rufopunctata" (vert) . . . . 2·25 2·25
260 80c. "Pylopaguropsis magnimanus" (vert) . . . 2·50 2·75
261 $1 "Trapezia ferruginea" (vert) . . . . 2·50 2·75
262 $2 "Trapezia guttata" (vert) 3·50 4·25
263 $3 "Trapezia cymodoce" (vert) . . . . 4·00 4·25

62 "Santa Maria"

64 R.A.F. Supermarine Spitfires on Island Airstrip

63 Buff-banded Rail searching for Food

1992. 500th Anniv of Discovery of America by Columbus.
264 **62** $1.05 multicoloured . . . 2·50 2·75

1992. Endangered Species. Buff-banded Rail. Mult.
265 10c. Type **63** 70 85
266 15c. Banded rail with chick 90 1·10
267 30c. Two rails drinking . . . 1·25 1·40
268 45c. Rail and nest . . . . . 1·50 1·60
MS269 165 × 78 mm. 45c. Two rails by pool; 85c. Chick hatching; $1.20, Head of rail 7·00 7·00

1992. 50th Anniv of Second World War. Mult.
270 45c. Type **64** . . . . 2·00 1·25
271 85c. Mitsubishi A6M Zero-Sen aircraft bombing Kampong . . . . 2·75 3·50
272 $1.20 R.A.F. Short Sunderland flying boat . . 3·25 4·25

65 Waves breaking on Reef

66 "Lobophyllia hemprichii"

1992. Christmas. Multicoloured.
273 40c. Type **65** . . . . 1·25 70
274 80c. Direction Island . . . . 2·50 3·00
275 $1 Moorish idols (fish) and coral . . . . 2·50 3·00

1993. Corals. Multicoloured.
276 45c. Type **66** 75 55
277 85c. "Pocillopora eydouxi" 1·25 1·75
278 $1.05 "Fungia scutaria" . . . 1·75 2·00
279 $1.20 "Sarcophyton sp" . . . 1·75 2·25

67 Plastic 5r. Token

68 Primary School Pupil

1993. Early Cocos (Keeling) Islands Currency. Multicoloured.
280 45c. Type **67** . . . . 1·50 80
281 85c. 1968 1r. plastic token . . 2·00 2·50
282 $1.05 1977 150r. commemorative gold coin 2·50 2·75
283 $1.20 1910 plastic token . . . 2·50 3·00

1993. Education. Multicoloured.
284 5c. Type **68** 50 85
285 45c. Secondary school pupil 1·00 60
286 85c. Learning traditional crafts . . . . 2·00 2·25
287 $1.05 Learning office skills 2·50 3·00
288 $1.20 Seaman training . . . 3·00 3·25

69 Lifeboat and Crippled Yacht

1993. Air-Sea Rescue. Multicoloured.
289 45c. Type **69** . . . . 2·25 1·25
290 85c. Israeli Aircraft Industry Westwind Seascan (aircraft) 3·25 3·50
291 $1.05 "R.J. Hawke" (ferry) 3·50 4·75
MS292 135 × 61 mm. Nos. 289/91 8·00 8·50

70 Peace Doves

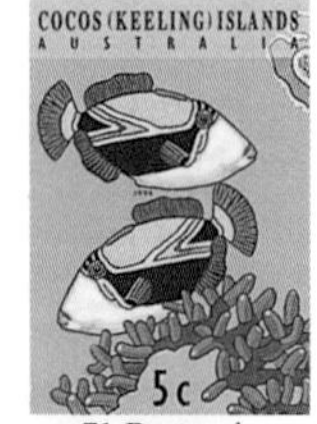

71 Rectangle Triggerfish and Coral

1993. Christmas.
293 **70** 40c. multicoloured . . . . 1·50 80
294 80c. multicoloured . . . . 2·75 3·25
295 $1 multicoloured . . . . . 2·75 3·25

1994. Transfer of Postal Service to Australia Post. Multicoloured.
296 5c. Type **71** 35 45
297 5c. Three rectangle triggerfish and map section 35 45
298 5c. Two rectangle triggerfish and map section 35 45
299 5c. Two rectangle triggerfish, map section and red coral 35 45
300 5c. Rectangle triggerfish with red and brown corals . . . 35 45
301 10c. Green turtles on beach 35 45
302 10c. Two green turtles . . . 35 45
303 10c. Crowd of young green turtles 35 45
304 10c. Green turtle and map section 35 45
305 10c. Green turtle, pyramid butterflyfish and map section 35 45
306 20c. Three pyramid butterflyfish and map section 55 65
307 20c. Pyramid butterflyfish with brown coral 55 65
308 20c. Two pyramid butterflyfish and coral . . 55 65
309 20c. Three pyramid butterflyfish and coral . . 55 65
310 20c. Coral, pyramid butterflyfish and map section 55 65
311 45c. Jukongs with map of airport 60 70
312 45c. Two jukongs with red or blue sails and map section 60 70
313 45c. Jukong in shallows . . . 60 70
314 45c. Two jukongs with red or yellow sails and map section 60 70
315 45c. Two jukongs, one with blue jib, and map section 60 70

Nos. 296/315 were printed together, se-tenant, with the backgrounds forming a composite map.

72 Prabu Abjasa Puppet

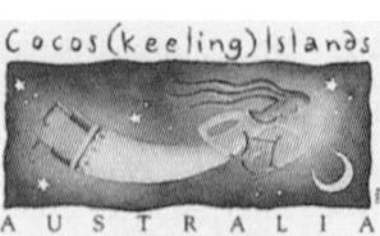

73 Angel playing Harp

1994. Shadow Puppets. Multicoloured.
316 45c. Type **72** 65 50
317 90c. Prabu Pandu . . . . . 1·25 1·50
318 $1 Judistra . . . . 1·40 1·50
319 $1.35 Abimanju . . . . . . 1·50 2·00

1994. Seasonal Festivals. Multicoloured.
320 40c. Type **73** 50 50
321 45c. Wise Man holding gift 55 50
322 80c. Mosque at night . . . . 1·00 1·75

74 White-tailed Tropic Bird and Blue-faced Booby ("Masked Booby")

1995. Sea-birds of North Keeling Island. Multicoloured.
323 45c. Type **74** 75 50
324 85c. Great frigate bird and white tern . . . . 1·00 1·50
MS325 106 × 70 mm. Nos. 323/4 1·75 2·25

75 Yellow Crazy Ant

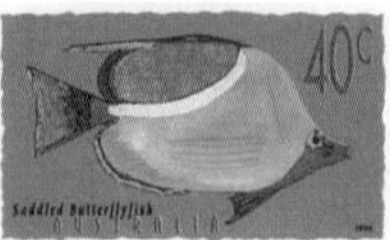

76 Saddle Butterflyfish

1995. Insects. Multicoloured.
326 45c. Type **75** . . . . 1·00 1·25
327 45c. Aedes mosquito . . . . 1·00 1·25
328 45c. Hawk moth . . . . . . 1·00 1·25
329 45c. Scarab beetle . . . . . 1·00 1·25
330 45c. Lauxaniid fly . . . . . 1·00 1·25
331 $1.20 Common eggfly (butterfly) . . . . 1·50 1·75

Nos. 326/30 were printed together, se-tenant, forming a composite design.

1995. Marine Life. Multicoloured.
332 5c. Redspot wrasse 10 10
333 30c. Blue-throated triggerfish ("Gilded triggerfish") 20 25
334 40c. Type **76** 30 35
335 45c. Arc-eyed hawkfish . . 60 60
335a 45c. Wideband fusilier . . . 30 35
335b 45c. Striped surgeonfish . . 30 35
335c 45c. Orangeband surgeonfish 30 35
335d 45c. Indo-Pacific sergeant 30 35
335e 70c. Crowned squirrelfish 50 55
336 75c. Orange-pine unicornfish 55 60
337 80c. Blue tang 60 65
338 85c. Juvenile twin-spotted wrasse ("Humpback wrasse") 60 65
339 90c. Threadfin butterflyfish 65 70
339a 95c. Sixstripe wrasse 70 75
340 $1 Bluestripe snapper . . . 70 75
341 $1.05 Longnosed butterflyfish 75 80
342 $1.20 Freckled hawkfish . . 85 90
343 $2 Powder-blue surgeonfish 1·40 1·50
343a $5 Goldback anthias . . . 3·50 3·75

77 Members of Malay Community

78 Black Rhinoceros with Calf

1996. Hari Raya Puasa Festival. Multicoloured.
344 45c. Type **77** 65 60
345 75c. Beating drums . . . . . 1·25 1·50
346 85c. Preparing festival meal 1·25 1·75

1996. Cocos Quarantine Station. Multicoloured.
347 45c. Type **78** . . . . 1·00 1·00
348 50c. Alpacas . . . . 1·00 1·50
349 $1.05 Boran cattle . . . . . 1·50 2·25
350 $1.20 Ostrich with chicks . . 1·75 2·25

79 Dancers and Tambourine

80 "Wrapped Present" (Lazina Brian)

1997. Hari Raya Puasa Festival. Multicoloured.
351 45c. Type **79** 65 60
352 75c. Girl clapping and sailing dinghies . . . . 1·00 1·60
353 85c. Dancers on beach and food . . . . 1·25 1·60

1998. Hari Raya Puasa Festival. Paintings by children. Multicoloured.
354 45c. Type **80** 70 75
355 45c. "Mosque" (Azran Jim) 70 75
356 45c. "Cocos Malay Woman" (Kate Gossage) 70 75
357 45c. "Yacht" (Matt Harber) 70 75
358 45c. "People dancing" (Rakin Chongkin) 70 75

81 Preparing Food on Beach

1999. Hari Raya Puasa Festival. Multicoloured.
359 45c. Type **81** 65 75
360 45c. Woman with child and jukongs on beach 65 75
361 45c. Jukongs and palm fronds 65 75
362 45c. Two men watching jukongs 65 75
363 45c. Jukong and white flowers 65 75

82 Jukong (Cocos sailing boat)

1999. Island Wildlife. Multicoloured.
364 5c. Type **82** 35 40
365 5c. Bennett's and ornate butterflyfish 35 40
366 5c. Green and hawksbill turtles 35 40
367 5c. Yellow-tailed anemonefish and various butterflyfish 35 40
368 5c. Hump-headed wrasse . . 35 40
369 10c. Yacht, Direction Island 35 40
370 10c. Black-backed butterflyfish 35 40
371 10c. Moorish idols 35 40
372 10c. "Pseudoanthias cooperi" (fish) 35 40
373 10c. Red-tailed tropic birds 35 40
374 25c. Blue-faced booby . . . 50 60
375 25c. Lesser wanderer (butterfly) 50 60
376 25c. Lesser and greater frigate birds 50 60
377 25c. "Hippotion velox" (moth) 50 60
378 25c. Common eggfly (butterfly) 50 60
379 45c. White tern 65 75
380 45c. Red-tailed tropic bird and great frigate bird . . . 65 75
381 45c. Chinese rose 65 75
382 45c. Meadow argus (butterfly) 65 75
383 45c. Sea hibiscus 65 75

Nos. 364/83 were printed together, se-tenant, with the backgrounds forming a composite design.

83 Ratma Anthoney

2000. New Millennium. "Face of Cocos (Keeling) Islands". Multicoloured.
384 45c. Type **83** 55 65
385 45c. Nakia Haji Dolman (schoolgirl) 55 65
386 45c. Muller Eymin (elderly man) 55 65
387 45c. Courtney Press (toddler) 55 65
388 45c. Mhd Abu-Yazid (school boy) 55 65

84 Little Nipper (crab)

2000. Endangered Species. Crabs of Cocos (Keeling) Islands. Multicoloured.
389 5c. Type **84** 25 35
390 5c. Purple crab 25 35
391 45c. Smooth-handed ghost crab 55 65
392 45c. Horn-eyed ghost crab . . 55 65

85 Loggerhead Turtle

2002. Turtles. Multicoloured.
393 45c. Type **85** 30 35
394 45c. Hawksbill turtle 30 35
395 45c. Leatherback turtle . . . 30 35
396 45c. Green turtle 30 35

OFFICIAL STAMPS

1991. No. 182 surch **OFFICIAL PAID MAINLAND**.

O1		(43c.) on 90c. Coconut palm and mature nuts	†	90·00

No. O1 was not sold to the public in unused condition.

COLOMBIA Pt. 20

A republic in the N.W. of South America. Formerly part of the Spanish Empire, Colombia became independent in 1819. The constituent states became the Granadine Confederation in 1858. The name was changed to the United States of New Granada in 1861, and the name Colombia was adopted later the same year.

100 centavos = 1 peso.

Prices. For the early issues prices in the used column are for postmarked copies, pen-cancellations are generally worth less.

1

3

1859. Imperf.

1	1	2½c. green	70·00	80·00
2		5c. blue	70·00	70·00
8		5c. slate	55·00	45·00
9		10c. yellow	45·00	40·00
5		20c. blue	70·00	48·00
6		1p. red	48·00	80·00

1861. Imperf.

11	3	2½c. black	£1000	£400
12		5c. yellow	£160	£120
13		10c. blue	£650	£120
14		20c. red	£350	£150
15		1p. red	£800	£250

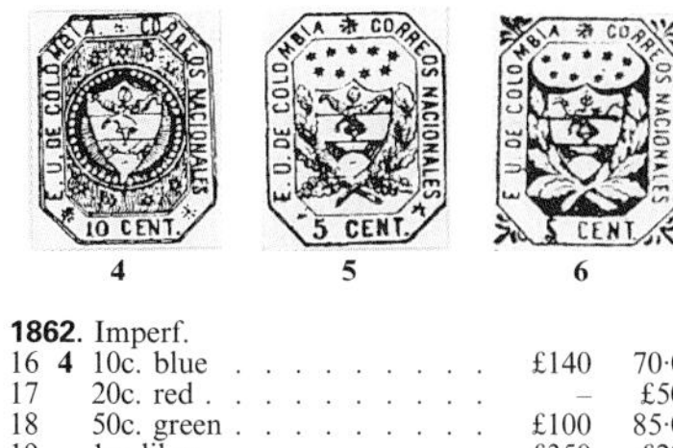
4 5 6

1862. Imperf.

16	4	10c. blue	£140	70·00
17		20c. red	–	£500
18		50c. green	£100	85·00
19		1p. lilac	£350	£225

1862. Imperf.

21	5	5c. orange	55·00	42·00
24		10c. blue	90·00	13·50
23		20c. red	£130	35·00
25		50c. green	£150	£110

1863. Imperf.

26	6	5c. orange	42·00	32·00
27		10c. blue	32·00	13·50
28		20c. red	65·00	32·00
29		50c. green	55·00	32·00
30		1p. mauve	£275	£110

7 8 9

1865. Imperf.

31	7	1c. red	8·00	8·00
32	8	2½c. black on lilac	20·00	13·50
33	9	5c. orange	35·00	17·00
34		10c. violet	40·00	6·00
35		20c. blue	45·00	13·50
37		50c. green	60·00	32·00
38		1p. red	70·00	13·50

10 12 19

1865. Imperf.

39	10	25c. black on blue	45·00	35·00
40		50c. black on yellow	35·00	40·00
41		1p. black on red	£110	£100

1866. Imperf. Various Arms Designs.

44	12	5c. orange	42·00	25·00
45	–	10c. lilac	13·00	6·00
46	–	20c. blue	27·00	15·00
47	–	50c. green	10·50	10·50
48	–	1p. red	60·00	20·00
49	–	5p. black on green	–	£130
50	–	10p. black on red	£275	£120

1868. Arms (various frames) inscr "ESTADOS UNIDOS DE COLOMBIA". Imperf.

51	19	5c. yellow	60·00	42·00
52		10c. lilac	1·25	70
54		20c. blue	1·25	45
55		50c. green	1·25	85
57		1p. red	3·00	1·25

24 25

26 27

28 30

1869. Imperf.

58	24	2½c. black on violet	3·50	1·40

1870. Imperf.

59a	25	1c. green	3·00	2·10
60		1c. red	2·10	2·10
61	26	2c. brown	45	45
62	27	5c. orange	55	35
65a	28	10c. mauve	55	25
67		25c. black on blue	6·50	6·00
87		25c. green	15·00	15·00

1870. Different frames. Imperf.

69	30	5p. black on green	5·00	4·25
71		10p. black on red	5·50	3·25

See also Nos. 118/19.

32 Andean Condor 33 35

1876. Imperf.

84	32	5c. violet	5·75	1·90
85	33	10c. brown	90	25
86	–	20c. blue	1·10	35

DESIGN: 20c. As Type 33 but with different frame.

1881. Imperf.

93	35	1c. green	2·75	1·75
99		2c. red	80	65
100		5c. blue	1·75	45
101		10c. purple	1·25	85
97		20c. black	1·40	55

39 40

1881. Imperf.

102	39	1c. black on green	1·25	1·25
103		2c. black on rose	1·25	1·25
104		5c. black on lilac	1·75	75

1883. Inscr "CORREOS NACIONALES DE LOS E.E. U.U. DE COLOMBIA".

106a	40	1c. yellow on green	35	35
107		2c. red on pink	45	45
109		5c. blue on blue	45	25
111		10c. orange on yellow	25	25
112		20c. mauve on lilac	35	35
113		50c. brown on buff	90	90
114		1p. red on blue	3·00	55
115		5p. brown on yellow	2·50	2·25
116		10p. black on red	5·50	6·50

1886. Perf.

118	30	5p. brown	1·25	1·00
119		10p. black on lilac	1·25	1·00

42

43 Gen. Sucre

44 Bolivar

46 Gen. Nerino

1886.

120	42	1c. green	1·75	60
121	43	2c. red on pink	75	75
124	44	5c. blue on blue	2·10	15
125	–	10c. orange (Pres. Nunez)	1·40	25
126	46	20c. violet on lilac ("REPULICA")	90	35
137		20c. violet on lilac ("REPUBLICA")	1·10	50
130	42	50c. brown on buff	40	45
132		1p. mauve	2·10	1·00
133		5p. brown	8·50	5·00
134		5p. black	10·00	7·50
135		10p. black on pink	16·00	4·25

See also Nos. 162/4a.

48

51 50

1890.

143	48	1c. green on green	2·50	85
144	51	2c. red on pink	70	50
145	50	5c. blue on blue	55	20
147	51	10c. brown on yellow	55	20
148		20c. violet	1·60	1·60

See also Nos. 149, etc.

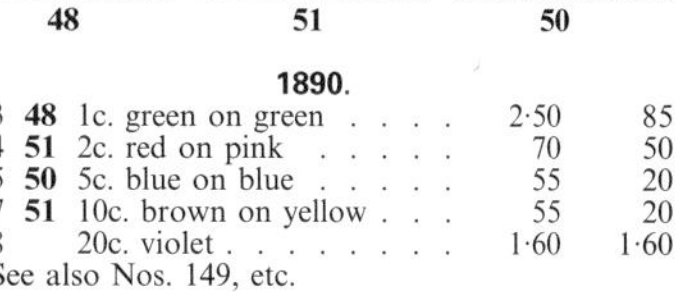

53

54

55

58

61

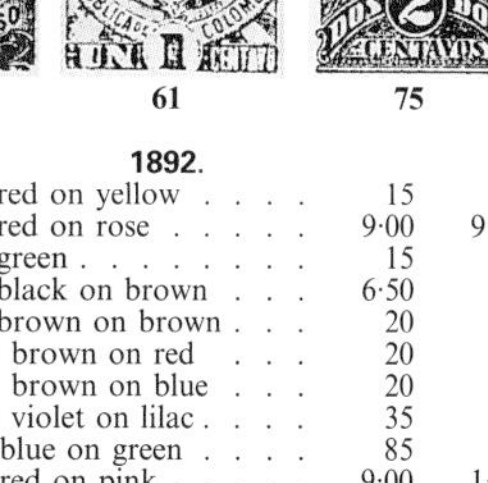
75

1892.

149b	48	1c. red on yellow	15	10
150	53	2c. red on rose	9·00	9·00
151a		2c. green	15	10
152a	50	5c. black on brown	6·50	20
153	54	5c. brown on brown	20	20
155	51	10c. brown on red	20	20
156	55	20c. brown on blue	20	20
159	42	50c. violet on lilac	35	20
161	58	1p. blue on green	85	20
162	42	5p. red on pink	9·00	1·25
164		10p. blue	7·50	1·25

1898.

171	61	1c. red on yellow	25	25
172		5c. brown on brown	25	25
173		10c. brown on red	3·25	1·25
174		50c. blue on lilac	1·00	75

For stamps showing map of Panama and inscr "COLOMBIA" see Panama Nos. 5/18.

For provisionals issued at Cartagena during the Civil War, 1899–1902, see list in Stanley Gibbons Stamp Catalogue Part 20 (South America).

1902. Arms in various frames. Imperf or perf.

259	75	½c. brown	85	85
260		1c. green	2·50	2·10
192		2c. black on red	15	15
261		2c. blue	60	35
193		4c. red on green	15	15
194		4c. blue on green	20	20
195		5c. green on green	15	15
196		5c. blue on blue	10	10
262		5c. red	60	60
197		10c. black on pink	15	15
263		10c. mauve	85	25
198		20c. brown on brown	15	15
199		20c. blue on brown	20	20
200		50c. green on red	45	45
201		50c. blue on red	1·50	1·50
202		1p. purple on brown	25	25

82

85 River Magdalena

1903. Imperf or perf.

203	82	5p. green on blue	9·00	4·25
204		10p. green on green	9·00	9·00
205		50p. orange on red	45·00	42·00
206		100p. blue on red	38·00	35·00

Nos. 205/6 are larger (31 × 38 mm).

1902. Imperf or perf.

212	85	2c. green	80	80
213		2c. blue	80	80
214		2c. red	10·00	10·00
215	–	10c. red	50	50
216	–	10c. pink	50	50
219	–	10c. orange	8·00	8·00
242	–	10c. blue on brown	1·75	1·75
243	–	10c. blue on green	5·00	4·25
247	–	10c. blue on red	2·50	2·50
245	–	10c. blue on lilac	13·00	13·00
220	–	20c. violet	40	40
221	–	20c. blue	3·25	3·25
224	–	20c. red	12·00	12·00

DESIGNS: 10c. Iron Quay, Savanilla, with eagle above; 20c. Hill of La Popa.

88 Gunboat "Cartagena"

89 Bolivar

90 General Pinzon

91

92

1903. Imperf or perf.

225	88	5c. blue	2·10	2·10
226		5c. brown	3·25	3·25
227	89	50c. green	5·00	5·00
228		50c. brown	4·25	4·25
230		50c. orange	4·25	4·25
231		50c. red	3·25	3·25
233	90	1p. brown	90	65
234		1p. red	90	90
235		1p. blue	3·50	3·25
237	91	5p. brown	6·00	6·00
238		5p. purple	3·75	3·75
239		5p. green	6·00	6·00
240	92	10p. green	6·50	6·00
241		10p. purple	14·00	14·00

93

96

97

98 President Marroquin

1902.

248	93	1c. green on yellow	20	20
249		2c. red on pink	20	20
250		5c. blue	20	20
251		10c. brown on yellow	20	20
252		20c. mauve on pink	20	10
253		50c. red on green	1·00	1·25
254		1p. black on yellow	3·25	2·50
255		5p. blue on blue	20·00	15·00
256		10p. brown on pink	14·00	11·00

1904.

270	96	½c. yellow	55	10
274		1c. green	40	10
278		2c. red	40	10
281		5c. blue	1·00	10
283		10c. violet	45	20
284		20c. black	75	15
286	97	1p. brown	13·00	1·60
287	98	5p. black and red	38·00	30·00
288		10p. black and blue	42·00	32·00

102 Camilo Torres

104 Narino demanding Liberation of Slaves

1910. Centenary of Independence.
345 **102** ½c. black and purple 35 20
346 – 1c. green 35 10
347 – 2c. red 35 10
348 – 5c. blue 1·00 25
349 – 10c. purple 6·50 5·00
350 – 20c. brown 12·00 7·50
351 **104** 1p. purple 75·00 22·00
352 – 10p. lake £300 £200
DESIGNS—As Type **102**: 1c. P. Salavarrieta; 2c. Narino; 5c. Bolivar; 10c. Caldas; 20c. Santander. As Type **104**: 10p. Bolivar resigning.

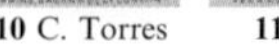
110 C. Torres

113 Arms

111 Boyaca Monument

123 La Sabana Station

112 Cartagena

1917. Portraits as T **110**.
357 **110** ½c. yellow (Caldas) 10 15
358 1c. green (Torres) 10 10
393 **113** 1½c. brown 45 45
359 **110** 2c. red (Narino) 10 10
380 **113** 3c. red on yellow 20 10
394 3c. blue 20 15
360 **110** 4c. purple (Santander) 45 10
395 4c. blue (Santander) 20 10
361 5c. blue (Bolivar) 2·50 20
396 5c. red (Bolivar) 2·50 15
397 **113** 8c. blue 20 15
362 **110** 10c. grey (Cordoba) 2·50 20
398 10c. blue (Cordoba) 6·50 35
363 **110** 20c. red 1·40 25
399 **113** 30c. bistre (Caldas) 7·00 25
400 **123** 40c. brown 14·00 4·50
364 **112** 50c. red 1·60 25
606 50c. red (San Pedro Alejandrino) 8·25 3·75
365a **110** 1p. blue (Sucre) 10·00 40
366 2p. orange (Cuervo) 12·00 25
367 5p. grey (Ricaurte) 35·00 10·00
401 5p. violet (Ricaurte) 3·50 35
368 **113** 10p. brown 35·00 8·50
402 10p. green 5·00 90
For similar 40c. see No. 541.

1918. Surch **Especie Provisional** and value.
374 **96** 0.00½c. on 20c. black 70 10
376 0.03c. on 10c. violet 1·40 35

115

124

1918.
378 **115** 3c. red 75 10

1918. Air. No. 359 optd **1er Servicio Postal Aereo 6-18-19**.
379 2c. red £2500 £1600

1920. As T **75**, **96** and **113** but with "PROVISIONAL" added in label across design.
381 **96** ½c. yellow 1·10 20
382 1c. green 55 10
383 2c. red 55 20
384 **113** 3c. green 40 20
385 **96** 5c. blue 90 25
386 10c. violet 5·00 1·25
387 10c. blue 8·50 4·00
388 20c. green 6·00 3·25
389 **75** 50c. red 7·50 2·50

1921. No. 360 surch **PROVICIONAL $003**.
390 $0.03 on 4c. purple 65 20

1921. No. 360 surch **PROVISIONAL $0.03**.
392 $0.03 on 4c. purple 2·75 75

1924.
403 **124** 1c. red 75 25
404 3c. blue 65 25

1925. Large fiscal stamps surch **CORREOS 1 CENTAVO** or optd **CORREOS PROVISIONAL**.
405 1c. on 3c. brown 55 10
406 4c. purple 55 25

127

129 Death of Bolivar (after P. A. Quijano)

1926.
410 **127** 1c. green 40 10
411 4c. blue 40 10

1930. Death Centenary of Bolivar.
412 **129** 4c. black and blue 25 10

132

133 Galleon

1932. Air. Optd **CORREO AEREO**.
413 **132** 5c. yellow 3·25 3·25
414 10c. purple 80 25
415 15c. green 1·40 1·40
416 20c. red 80 45
417 30c. blue 80 25
418 40c. lilac 1·60 55
419 50c. olive 3·50 2·50
420 60c. brown 3·50 2·50
421 80c. green 10·00 8·50
422 **133** 1p. blue 8·50 5·00
423 2p. red 26·00 19·00
424 3p. mauve 55·00 50·00
425 5p. olive 75·00 65·00
These and similar stamps without the "CORREO AEREO" overprint were issues of a private air company and are not listed in this catalogue.

1932. Nos. 395 and 399 surch.
427 1c. on 4c. blue 20 10
428 20c. on 30c. bistre 7·00 20

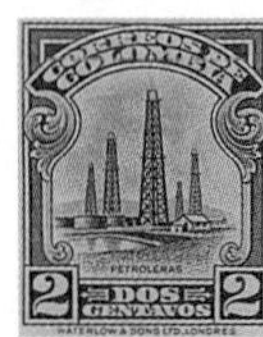
137 Oil Wells

138 Coffee Plantation

140 Gold Mining

141 Columbus

1932. 1c. is vert, 8c. is horiz.
429 – 1c. green (Emeralds) 85 10
430 **137** 2c. red (Oil) 85 10
431 **138** 5c. brown (Coffee) 85 10
432 – 8c. blue (Platinum) 7·50 25
485 **140** 10c. yellow (Gold) 6·50 10
486 **141** 20c. blue 21·00 60

142 Coffee

143 Gold

1932. Air.
435 **142** 5c. brown and orange 45 20
436 – 10c. black and red 85 20
437 – 15c. violet and green 40 15
438 – 15c. violet and red 5·00 15
439 – 20c. green and red 85 10
440 – 20c. olive and green 4·00 25
441 **142** 30c. brown and blue 3·25 10
442 – 40c. bistre and violet 1·60 10
443 – 50c. brown and green 13·00 1·25
444 – 60c. violet and brown 2·50 25
445 **142** 80c. brown and green 15·00 65
446 **143** 1p. bistre and blue 13·00 70
447 2p. bistre and red 14·00 1·90
448 – 3p. green and violet 21·00 7·00
449 – 5p. green and olive 50·00 19·00
DESIGNS—As Type **142**: 10c., 50c. Cattle; 15c., 60c. Oil Wells; 20c., 40c. Bananas. As Type **143**: 3p., 5p. Emeralds.

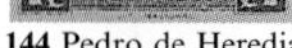
144 Pedro de Heredia

148 Coffee Plantation

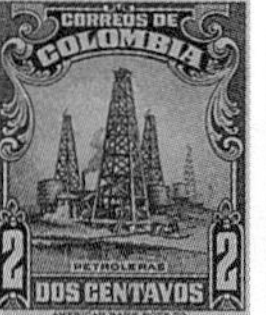
147 Oil Wells

151 Allegory of 1935 Olympiad

1934. 400th Anniv of Cartagena.
451 **144** 1c. green 1·50 55
452 5c. brown 2·50 55
453 8c. blue 1·50 55

1934. Air. 4th Centenary of Cartagena. Surch **CARTAGENA 1533 1933** and value.
454 – 10c. on 50c. brown and green (No. 443) 3·50 3·50
455 **142** 15c. on 80c. brn & grn 3·50 3·50
456 **143** 20c. on 1p. bis & bl 5·50 6·00
457 30c. on 2p. bistre and red 6·00 6·00

1934.
458 **147** 2c. red 10 10
459 **148** 5c. brown 3·50 10
460 – 10c. orange 17·00 10
DESIGN: 10c. Gold miner facing left.

1935. 3rd National Olympiad. Inscr "III OLIMPIADA BARRANQUILLA 1935".
461 – 2c. orange and green 75 25
462 – 4c. green 75 25
463 **151** 5c. yellow and brown 75 20
464 – 7c. red 1·75 1·50
465 – 8c. mauve and black 1·75 1·50
466 – 10c. blue and brown 1·75 1·10
467 – 12c. blue 1·75 1·90
468 – 15c. red and blue 4·25 3·00
469 – 18c. yellow and purple 5·00 5·00
470 – 20c. green and violet 5·00 3·25
471 – 24c. blue and green 6·00 4·25
472 – 50c. orange and blue 6·00 3·75
473 – 1p. blue and olive 60·00 38·00
474 – 2p. blue and green £100 70·00
475 – 5p. blue and violet £300 £250
476 – 10p. blue and black £650 £500
DESIGNS—VERT: 2c. Footballers; 4c. Discus thrower; 1p. G.P.O.; 2p. "Flag of the Race" Monument; 5p. Arms; 10p. Andean condor. HORIZ: 7c. Runners; 8c. Tennis player; 10c. Hurdler; 12c. Pier; 15c. Athlete; 18c. Baseball; 20c. Seashore; 24c. Swimmer; 50c. Aerial view of Barranquilla.

152 Nurse and Patients

1935. Obligatory Tax. Red Cross.
477 **152** 5c. red and green 1·75 45

1935. Surch **12 CENTAVOS**.
478 12c. on 1p. blue (No. 365a) 4·25 1·25

154 Simon Bolivar

155 Tequendama Falls

1937.
487 **154** 1c. green 10 10
488 **155** 10c. red 10 10
489 12c. blue 3·75 1·25

156 Footballer

157 Discus Thrower

1937. 4th National Olympiad.
490 **156** 3c. green 80 55
491 **157** 10c. red 3·25 1·60
492 – 1p. black 30·00 24·00
DESIGN: 1p. Runner (20½ × 27 mm).

159 Exhibition Palace

161 Mother and Child

1937. Barranquilla Industrial Exhibition.
493 **159** 5c. purple 1·60 25
494 – 15c. blue 6·00 3·25
495 – 50c. brown 17·00 6·00
DESIGNS—HORIZ: 15c. Stadium. VERT: 50c. "Flag of the Race" Monument.

1937. Obligatory Tax. Red Cross.
509 **161** 5c. red 1·40 55

1937. Surch in figures and words.
510 **156** 1c. on 3c. green 60 55
511 **155** 2c. on 12c. blue 30 30
512 – 5c. on 8c. blue (No. 432) 35 25
513 – 5c. on 8c. blue (No. 397) 35 25
514 **155** 10c. on 12c. blue 4·25 85

164 Entrance to Church of the Rosary

166 "Bochica" (Indian god)

1938. 400th Anniv of Bogota.
515 – 1c. green 15 15
516 **164** 2c. red 15 10
517 – 5c. black 20 10
518 – 10c. brown 40 25
519 **166** 15c. blue 3·25 90
520 – 20c. mauve 3·25 90
521 – 1p. brown 30·00 25·00
DESIGNS—VERT: 1c. "Calle del Arco" ("Street of the Arch") Old Bogota; 5c. Bogota Arms; 10c. G. J. de Quesada. HORIZ (larger): 20c. Convent of S. Domingo; 1p. First Mass on Site of Bogota.

168 Proposed P.O., Bogota

1939. Obligatory Tax. P.O. Rebuilding Fund.
522 **168** ¼c. blue 10 10
564 ¼c. purple 10 10
523 ½c. red 10 10
524 1c. violet 10 10
567 1c. orange 10 10
525 2c. green 25 10
526 20c. brown 3·25 30

1939. Air. Surch **5 cts** or **15 cts** and bar.
527 5c. on 20c. (No. 439) 25 20
528 5c. on 40c. (No. 442) 25 20
530 15c. on 30c. (No. 441) 60 15
531 15c. on 40c. (No. 442) 1·10 25

171 Bolivar

172 Coffee Plantation

173 Arms of Colombia

174 Columbus 175 Caldas 176 La Sabana Station

1939.
533 **171** 1c. green 10 10
535 **172** 5c. brown 10 10
536 5c. blue 10 10
538 **173** 15c. blue 1·40 10
539 **174** 20c. black 17·00 30

540 **175** 30c. olive . . . . 5·50 40
541 **176** 40c. brown . . . . 28·00 14·00
For similar 40c. see No. 400.

178 Proposed New P.O., Bogota

1940. Obligatory Tax. P.O. Rebuilding Fund.
542 **178** ½c. blue 10 10
543 ½c. red 10 10
544 1c. violet 10 10
545 2c. green 15 10
546 20c. brown . . . . 1·60 25

179 "Arms and the Law" **180** Bridge at Boyaca

1940. Death Centenary of Gen. Santander.
547 – 1c. olive 20 20
548 **179** 2c. red 25 15
549 – 5c. brown 25 20
550 – 8c. red 90 40
551 – 10c. yellow 45 40
552 – 15c. blue . . . . 1·10 55
553 – 20c. green . . . . 1·40 60
554 **180** 50c. violet . . . . 2·50 2·10
555 – 1p. red . . . . 11·00 10·00
556 – 2p. orange . . . . 35·00 32·00
DESIGNS—VERT: 1c. Gen. Santander; 5c. Medallion of Santander by David; 8c. Santander's statue, Cucuta; 15c. Church at Rosario. HORIZ: 10c. Santander's birthplace, Rosario; 20c. Battlefield at Paya; 1p. Death of Santander; 2p. Victorious Army at Zamora.

181 Tobacco Plant **182** Santander **183** Garcia Rovira

184 General Sucre **185** "Protection"

1940.
557 **181** 8c. green and red 45 30
558 **182** 15c. blue 80 25
559 **183** 20c. grey . . . . 4·00 25
560 – 40c. brown (Galan) . . . 2·50 40
561 **184** 1p. black . . . . 11·00 1·25
562 1p. violet . . . . 2·50 70

1940. Obligatory Tax. Red Cross Fund.
563 **185** 5c. red 25 15

186 Pre-Colombian Monument **187** Proclamation of Independence

1941. Air.
568 **186** 5c. grey 25 10
691 5c. yellow 20 10
742 5c. blue 35 15
747 5c. red 35 15
569 – 10c. orange 25 10
692 – 10c. red 20 10
743 – 10c. blue 35 20
570 – 15c. red 25 10
693 – 15c. blue 20 10
571 – 20c. green 40 10
694 – 20c. violet 20 10
745 – 20c. blue 45 25
749 – 20c. red 45 25
572 **186** 30c. blue 40 10
695 30c. green 35 10
750 30c. red 75 10
573 – 40c. purple . . . . 1·60 10
696 – 40c. grey 55 10
574 – 50c. green . . . . 1·60 10
697 – 50c. red 65 10
575 – 60c. purple . . . . 1·60 10
698 – 60c. olive 85 10
576 **186** 80c. olive . . . . 4·00 35
699 80c. brown . . . . 1·25 10
577 **187** 1p. black and blue . . . 4·00 20
700 1p. brown and olive . . . 3·00 35
578 – 2p. black and red . . . . 8·00 1·25
701 – 2p. blue and green . . . 3·75 55
579 **187** 3p. black and violet . . . 14·00 4·00
702 3p. black and red . . . . 7·00 3·50
580 – 5p. black and green . . . 35·00 17·00
703 – 5p. green and sepia . . . 20·00 8·50
DESIGNS: As Type **186**: 10c., 40c. "El Dorado" Monument; 15c., 50c. Spanish Fort, Cartagena; 20c., 60c. Street in Old Bogota. As Type **187**. 2p., 5p. National Library, Bogota.

188 Arms of Palmira **189** Home of Jorge Isaacs (author)

1942. 8th National Agricultural Exn, Palmira.
581 **188** 30c. red . . . . 5·00 70

1942. Honouring J. Isaacs.
582 **189** 50c. green . . . . 3·25 35

190 Peace Conference Delegates

1942. 40th Anniv of Wisconsin Peace Treaty ending Civil War.
583 **190** 10c. orange . . . . 3·25 45

1943. Surch **$ 0.0½ MEDIO CENTAVO**.
584 **168** ½c. on 1c. violet 10 10
585 ½c. on 2c. green 10 10
586 ½c. on 20c. brown 20 20

1944. Surch **5 Centavos**.
587 5c. on 10c. orge (No. 460) . . 20 15

193 National Shrine **194** San Pedro, Alejandrino

1944.
592 **193** 30c. olive . . . . 2·10 1·25
593 **194** 50c. red . . . . 2·10 1·25

1944. Surch with new values in figures and words.
594 **172** 1c. on 5c. brn (No. 535) 15 15
595 2c. on 5c. brn (No. 535) 15 15

195 Banner **199** Manuel Murillo Toro

196 Viceroy Solis Building

1944. 75th Anniv of General Benefit Institution of Cundinamarca.
596 **195** 2c. blue and yellow . . . 10 10
597 – 5c. blue and yellow . . . 10 10
598 – 20c. black and green . . . 95 75
599 – 40c. black and red . . . 4·25 3·25
600 **196** 1p. black and red . . . . 8·50 6·50
DESIGNS: As T **195**: 5c. Arms of the Institution; 20c. Manuel Murillo Toro. As T **196**: 40c. St. Juan de Dios Maternity Hospital.

1944.
602 **199** 5c. olive 35 20

201 Proposed P.O., Bogota (**202** Stalin, Roosevelt and Churchill)

1945. Obligatory Tax. P.O. Rebuilding Fund.
609 **201** ½c. blue 10 10
610 ½c. brown 10 10
611 ½c. red 10 10
612 ½c. mauve 10 10
613 1c. violet 10 10
614 1c. orange 10 10
615 1c. green 10 10
616 2c. green 10 10
617a 20c. brown 80 10

1945. Victory. Optd with T **202**.
618 **172** 5c. brown 25 15

203 Clock Tower, Cartagena **204** Fort San Sebastian Cartagena

1945.
621 **203** 50c. green . . . . 2·50 80

1945. Air.
622 **204** 5c. grey 20 10
623 – 10c. orange 20 10
624 – 15c. red 20 10
625 **204** 20c. green 25 10
626 – 30c. blue 35 10
627 – 40c. red 55 10
628 **204** 50c. green 70 15
629 – 60c. purple . . . . 3·25 80
630 – 80c. grey . . . . 5·00 55
631 – 1p. blue . . . . 5·00 55
632 – 2p. red . . . . 7·50 2·40
DESIGNS—As Type **204**: 10c., 30c., 60c. Tequendama Falls; 15c., 40c., 80c. Santa Marta. HORIZ (larger): 1p., 2p. Capitol, Bogota.

207 Sierra Nevada of Santa Maria

1945. 25th Anniv of 1st Air Mail Service in America.
633 **207** 20c. green . . . . 1·25 60
634 – 30c. blue . . . . 1·25 60
635 – 50c. red . . . . 1·25 60
DESIGNS: 30c. Junkers F-13 seaplane "Tolima"; 50c. San Sebastian Fortress, Cartagena.

1946. Surch **1** above **UN CENTAVO**.
636 **138** 1c. on 5c. brown 15 15

209 Gen. Sucre **211** Map of South America **212** Bogota Observatory

1946.
638 **209** 1c. blue and brown . . . 20 10
639 2c. red and violet 20 10
640 5c. blue and olive 20 10
641 9c. red and green 45 35
642 10c. orange and blue . . 35 25
643 20c. orange and black . . 45 25
644 30c. green and red 45 25
645 40c. red and green 45 25
646 50c. violet and purple . . 45 25
The 5c. to 50c. are larger (23½ × 32 mm).

1946. Obligatory Tax. Red Cross Fund. Optd with red cross.
647 **172** 5c. brown (No. 535) . . . 25 20

1946.
648 **211** 15c. blue 25 10

1946.
649 **212** 5c. brown 10 10
650 5c. blue 10 10

213 Andres Bello **214** Joaquin de Cayzedo y Cuero

1946. 80th Death Anniv of Andres Bello (poet and teacher).
651 **213** 3c. brown (postage) . . . 25 15
652 10c. orange 40 10
653 15c. black 55 10
654 5c. blue (air) 25 15

1946.
655 **214** 2p. turquoise . . . . . . 5·00 45
656 2p. green 65 20

215 Proposed New P.O., Bogota **217** Coffee Plant

1946. Obligatory Tax. P.O. Rebuilding Fund.
657 **215** 3c. blue 15 10

1946. 5th Central American and Caribbean Games, Barranquilla. As No. 621 optd **V JUEGOS C. A. Y DEL C. 1946**.
658 50c. red . . . . 2·50 1·60

1947.
659 **217** 5c. multicoloured 35 10

218 "Masdevallia Nicterina" **220** Antonio Narino

1947. Colombian Orchids. Multicoloured.
660 1c. Type **218** 10 10
661 2c. "Miltonia vexillaria" . . 10 10
662 5c. "Cattleya dowiana aurea" 45 20
663 5c. "Cattleya chocoensis" . . 45 20
664 5c. "Odontoglossum crispum" 45 20
665 10c. "Cattleya labiata trianae" 65 15

1947. Obligatory Tax. Optd **SOBRETASA** in fancy letters.
666 **183** 20c. grey (No. 559) . . . 4·25 1·75
676 **141** 20c. blue (No. 486) . . . 25·00 17·00

1947. 4th Pan-American Press Conf, Bogota.
667 **220** 5c. blue on blue (post) . . 25 15
668 – 10c. brown on blue . . . 35 15
669 – 5c. blue on blue (air) . . 20 10
670 – 10c. red on blue 35 20
PORTRAITS: No. 668, A. Urdaneta y Urdaneta; 669, F. J. de Caldas; 670, M. del Socorro Rodriguez.

222 Arms of Colombia and Cross **223** J. C. Mutis and J. J. Triana

224 M. A. Caro and R. J. Cuervo

1947. Obligatory Tax. Red Cross Fund.
671 **222** 5c. lake 20 10
704 5c. red 20 10

1947.
673 **223** 25c. green 35 15
675 **224** 3p. purple 45 10

225 Bogota Cathedral

1948. 9th Pan-American Congress, Bogota. Inscr as in T **225**.
677 **225** 5c. brown (postage) . . . 15 10
678 – 10c. orange 25 20
679 – 15c. blue 25 20

680 – 5c. brown (air) 15 10
681 – 15c. blue 35 25
DESIGNS—No. 678, National Capitol; 679, Foreign Office; 680, Chancellery; 681, Raphael Court, Capitol.

1948. Obligatory Tax. Savings Bank stamps surch **COLOMBIA SOBRETASA 1 CENTAVO**. Various designs.
682 1c. on 5c. brown 10 10
683 1c. on 10c. violet 10 10
684 1c. on 25c. red 10 10
685 1c. on 50c. blue 10 10

1948. Optd **C** (= "CORREOS"). No gum.
686 **168** 1c. orange 10 10

1948. Optd **CORREOS**.
687 **201** 1c. olive 10 10
688 2c. green 10 10
689 20c. brown 20 10

232 Simon Bolivar **234** Carlos Martinez Silva

233 Proposed New P.O., Bogota

1948.
690 **232** 15c. green 35 15

1948. Obligatory Tax. P.O. Rebuilding Fund.
705 **233** 1c. red 10 10
706 2c. green 10 10
707 3c. blue 10 10
708 5c. grey 10 10
709 10c. violet 20 10
See also Nos. 756 and 758/62.

1949.
710 **234** 40c. red 35 10

235 Julio Garavito Armero **236** Dr. Juan de Dios Carrasquilla

1949. J. G. Armero (mathematician).
711 **235** 4c. green 25 15

1949. 75th Anniv of National Agricultural Society.
712 **236** 5c. bistre 20 10

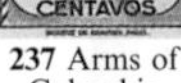

237 Arms of Colombia **238** Allegory of Justice

1949. New Constitution.
713 **237** 15c. blue (postage) 20 10
714 **238** 5c. green (air) 15 10
715 – 10c. orange 15 10
DESIGN: 10c. Allegory of Constitution.

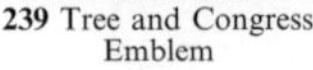

239 Tree and Congress Emblem

240 F. J. Cisneros

1949. 1st Forestry Congress, Bogota.
716 **239** 5c. olive 20 10

1949. 50th Death Anniv of Francisco Javier Cisneros (engineer).
717 **240** 50c. blue and brown 1·00 50
718 50c. violet and green 1·00 50
719 50c. yellow and purple 1·00 50

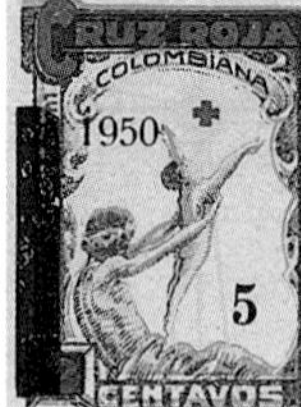

241 Mother and Child

1950. Red Cross Fund. Surch with new value and date as in T **241**.
720 **241** 5 on 2c. multicoloured 80 35

1950. Obligatory Tax. Optd **SOBRETASA**.
721 **172** 5c. blue 15 10

243 "Masdevallia Chimaera" **244** Santo Domingo Post Office

1950. 75th Anniv of U.P.U.
722 **243** 1c. brown 30 10
723 – 2c. violet 30 10
724 – 3c. mauve 10 10
725 – 4c. green 20 10
726 – 5c. orange 35 10
727 – 11c. red 1·60 75
728 **244** 18c. blue 80 40
DESIGNS—VERT: 3c. "Cattleya labiata trianae"; 4c. "Masdevallia nicterina"; 5c. "Cattleya dowiana aurea". HORIZ: 2c. "Odontoglossum crispum"; 11c. "Miltonia vexillaria".

245 Antonio Baraya (patriot) **246** Farm

1950.
729 **245** 2c. red 10 10

1950.
730 **246** 5c. red and buff 30 15
731 5c. green and turquoise 30 15
732 5c. blue and light blue 30 15

247 Arms of Bogota **248** Map and Badge

1950.
733 **247** 5p. green 1·60 10
734 – 10p. orange (Arms of Colombia) 2·40 15

1951. 60th Anniv of Colombian Society of Engineers.
735 **248** 20c. red, yellow and blue 35 15

249 Arms of Colombia and Cross **250** Fray Bartolome de Las Casas

1951. Obligatory Tax. Red Cross Fund.
736 **249** 5c. red 20 15
737 **250** 5c. red 20 15
738 5c. green and red 20 10

251 D. G. Valencia **254** Dr. Nicolas Osorio

1951. 8th Death Anniv of D. G. Valencia (poet and orator).
739 **251** 25c. black 40 10

1951. Surch **1 centavo**.
740 **233** 1c. on 3c. blue 10 10

1951. Nationalization of Barranca Oilfields. Optd **REVERSION CONCESION MARES 25 Agosto 1951.**
741 **147** 2c. red 10 10

1952. Colombian Doctors.
751 **254** 1c. blue 10 10
752 – 1c. blue (P. Martinez) 10 10
753 – 1c. bl (E. Uriocoechea) 10 10
754 – 1c. blue (Jose M. Lombana) 10 10

255 Proposed New P.O., Bogota **256** Manizales Cathedral

1952.
755 **255** 5c. blue 15 10
756 **233** 20c. brown 8·00 10
757 **201** 25c. grey 12·00 1·60
758 **233** 25c. green 20 10
759 – 50c. orange 25·00 14·00
760 – 1p. red 55 25
761 – 2p. purple 27·00 2·50
762 – 2p. violet 65 10
DESIGN: 50c. to 2p. Similar to T **233** but larger, 24½ × 19 mm.
Owing to a shortage of postage stamps the above obligatory tax types were issued for ordinary postal use.

1952. Obligatory Tax. No. 759 surch.
763 8c. on 50c. orange 15 10

1952. Centenary of Manizales.
764 **256** 23c. black and blue 25 15

1952. 1st Latin-American Congress of Iron Specialists. Surch **1952 1' CONFERENCIA SIDERURGICA LATINO-AMERICANA.** and new value
765 **223** 15c. on 25c. green (postage) 30 20
766 **186** 70c. on 80c. red (air) 75 25

258 Queen Isabella and Columbus Monument

1953. 500th Birth Anniv of Isabella the Catholic.
767 **258** 23c. black and blue 35 35

1953. Air. Optd **CORREO AEREO** or surch also.
768 **233** 5c. on 8c. blue 15 10
769 15c. on 20c. brown 25 10
770 15c. on 25c. green 65 10
771 25c. green 30 10

1953. Air. Optd **AEREO**.
772 **155** 10c. red 15 10

EXTRA RAPIDO. Stamps bearing this overprint or inscription were used to prepay the additional cost of air carriage of inland mail handled by the National Postal Service from 1953 to 1964. Subsequently remaining stocks of these stamps were used for other classes of correspondence. Since the 1920s regular air service for inland and foreign mail has been provided by the Air Postal Service, a separate undertaking which is administered by the Avianca airline and for which the regular air stamps are used.

1953. Air. No. 727 surch **CORREO EXTRA RAPIDO 5 5**.
773 5c. on 11c. red 20 10

262

1953. Air. Fiscal stamps optd as in T **262** or surch also.
774 **262** 1c. on 2c. green 10 10
775 50c. red 10 10

263

1953. Air. Real Estate Tax stamps optd as in T **263**.
776 **263** 5c. red 15 10
777 20c. brown 20 10

1953. Surch.
778 – 40c. on 1p. red (No. 760) 45 10
779 **214** 50c. on 2p. green 45 10

266 Don M. Ancizar **267** Map of South America

1953. Colombian Chorographical Commission Centenary. Portraits inscr as in T **266**.
780 **266** 14c. red and black 40 30
781 – 23c. blue and black 35 20
782 – 30c. sepia and black 35 15
783 – 1p. green and black 15 10
PORTRAITS: 23c. J. J. Triana; 30c. M. Ponce de Leon; 1p. A. Codazzi.

1953. 2nd National Philatelic Exhibition, Bogota. Real Estate Tax stamps surch as in T **267**.
784 **267** 5c. on 5p. mult (post) 35 15
785 – 15c. on 10p. multicoloured (air) 40 25
DESIGN: 15c. Map of Colombia.

1953. Air. Optd **CORREO EXTRA-RAPIDO** or surch also.
786 **233** 2c. on 8c. blue 10 10
787 10c. violet 15 10

269 Fountain, Tunja **271** Map of Colombia

270 Pastelillo Fort, Cartagena

1954. Air.
788 – 5c. purple 30 10
789 – 10c. black 20 10
790 – 15c. red 20 10
791 – 15c. vermilion 20 10
792 – 20c. brown 30 10
793 – 25c. blue 30 10
794 – 25c. purple 30 10
795 – 30c. brown 15 10
796 – 40c. blue 25 10
797 – 50c. purple 25 10
798 **269** 60c. sepia 35 10
799 – 80c. lake 25 20
800 – 1p. black and blue 1·40 20
801 **270** 2p. black and green 3·75 25
802 – 3p. black and red 5·00 55
803 – 5p. green and brown 7·00 1·40
804 **271** 10p. olive and red 8·50 3·50

DESIGNS. As Type **269**—VERT: 5c., 30c. Galeras volcano, Pasto; 15c. red, 50c. Bolivar Monument, Boyaca; 15c. vermilion, 25c. (2) Sanctuary of the Rocks, Narino; 20c., 80c. Nevado del Ruiz Mts., Manizales; 40c. J. Isaacs Monument, Cali. HORIZ: 10c. San Diego Monastery, Bogota. As Type **270**—HORIZ: 1p. Girardot Stadium, Medellin; 3p. Santo Domingo Gateway and University, Popayan. As Type **271**—HORIZ: 5p. Sanctuary of the Rocks, Narino.

1954. Surch.
805 **266** 5c. on 14c. red & black . . . 30 15
806 **256** 5c. on 23c. black & blue . . . 30 15

272 Andean Condor carrying Shield   **273**

1954. Air.
807 **272** 5c. purple 50 20

1954. 400th Anniv of Franciscan Community in Colombia.
808 **273** 5c. brown, green & sepia . . . 25 15

1954. Obligatory Tax. Red Cross Fund. No. 807 optd with cross and bar in red.
809 **272** 5c. purple . . . . 1·60 40

275 Soldier, Flag and Arms of Republic

1954. National Army Commemoration.
810 **275** 5c. blue (postage) 20 10
811 15c. red (air) 30 10

276

1954. 7th National Athletic Games, Cali. Inscr "VII JUEGOS ATLETICOS", etc.
812 – 5c. blue (postage) 15 10
813 **276** 10c. red 25 10
814 – 15c. brown (air) 25 15
815 **276** 20c. green 60 35
DESIGN: 5c., 15c. Badge of the Games.

277   **278** Saint's Convent and Cell, Cartagena

1954. 50th Anniv of Colombian Academy of History.
816 **277** 5c. green and blue 20 10

1954. Death Tercentenary of San Pedro Claver.
817 **278** 5c. green (postage) . . . 15 10
819 – 15c. brown (air) 30 10
DESIGN: 15c. San Pedro Claver Church, Cartagena.

279 Mercury   **280** Archbishop Mosquera

1954. 1st International Fair, Bogota.
821 **279** 5c. orange (postage) . . . 25 10
822 15c. blue (air) 25 10
823 50c. red ("EXTRA RAPIDO") 30 10

1954. Air. Death Cent of Archbishop Mosquera.
824 **280** 2c. green 10 10

281 Virgin of Chiquinquira

1954. Air.
825 **281** 5c. mult (brown frame) . . . 10 10
826 5c. mult (violet frame) . . 10 10

282 Tapestry presented by Queen Margaret of Austria

1954. Tercentenary of Senior College of Our Lady of the Rosary, Bogota.
827 **282** 5c. black & orge (postage) . . 25 15
828 – 10c. blue 25 15
829 – 15c. brown 35 15
830 – 20c. brown and black . . . 60 25
832 **282** 15c. black & red (air) . . 35 15
833 – 20c. blue 55 15
834 – 25c. brown 55 15
835 – 50c. red and black 85 30
DESIGNS—VERT: Nos. 828, 833, Friar Cristobal de Torres (founder). HORIZ: Nos. 829, 834, Cloisters and statue; 830, 835, Chapel and coat of arms.

283 Paz de Rio Steel Works   **284** J. Marti

1954. Inauguration of Paz del Rio Steel Plant.
837 **283** 5c. black & bl (postage) . . 15 10
838 20c. black & green (air) . . 70 45

1955. Birth Cent of Marti (Cuban revolutionary).
839 **284** 5c. red (postage) 15 10
840 – 15c. green (air) 25 10

285 Badge, Flags and Korean Landscape

1955. Colombian Forces in Korea.
841 **285** 10c. purple (postage) . . 25 10
842 20c. green (air) 25 15

286 Merchant Marine Emblem   **287** M. Fidel Suarez

1955. Greater Colombia Merchant Marine Commemoration. Inscr as in T **286**.
843 **286** 15c. green (postage) . . . 20 10
844 – 20c. violet 85 15
846 **286** 25c. black (air) 35 10
847 – 50c. green . . . . 1·40 15
DESIGN—HORIZ: 20, 50c. "City of Manizales" (freighter) and skyscrapers.

1955. Air. Birth Centenary of Marco Fidel Suarez (President, 1918–21).
849 **287** 10c. blue 15 10

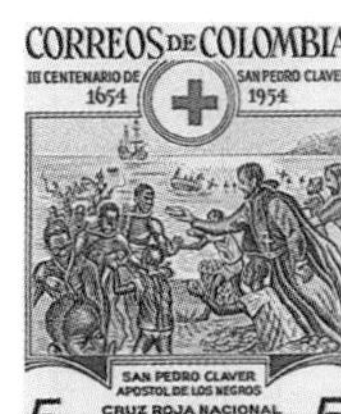

288 San Pedro Claver feeding Slaves

1955. Obligatory Tax. Red Cross Fund and 300th Anniv of San Pedro Claver.
850 **288** 5c. purple and red 25 10

289 Hotel Tequendama and San Diego Church

1955.
851 **289** 5c. blue and light blue (postage) 15 10
852 15c. lake and pink (air) . . 25 10

290 Bolivar's Country House

1955. 50th Anniv of Rotary International.
853 **290** 5c. blue (postage) 15 10
854 15c. red (air) 25 10

291 Belalcazar, De Quesada and Balboa

1955. 7th Postal Union Congress of the Americas and Spain. Inscr as in T **291**.
855 **291** 2c. brn & grn (postage) . . 10 10
856 – 5c. brown and blue . . . 15 10
857 – 23c. black and blue . . . 2·25 50
859 – 15c. black and red (air) . . 15 10
860 – 20c. black and brown . . 25 10
862 – 2c. black and brown ("EXTRA RAPIDO") . . 10 10
863 – 5c. sepia and yellow . . . 15 10
864 – 1p. brown and slate . . . 12·00 5·50
865 – 2p. black and violet . . . 7·50 6·50
DESIGNS—HORIZ: 2c. (No. 855), Type **291**; 2c. (No. 862), Atahualpa, Tisquesuza, Montezuma; 5c. (No. 856), San Martin, Bolivar and Washington; 5c. (No. 863), King Ferdinand, Queen Isabella and coat of arms; 15c. O'Higgins, Santander and Sucre; 20c. Marti, Hidalgo and Petion; 23c. Colombus, "Santa Maria", "Pinta" and "Nina"; 1p. Artigas, Lopez and Murillo; 2p. Calderon, Baron de Rio Branco and De La Mar.

292 J. E. Caro   **293** Salamanca University

1955. Death Cent of Jose Eusebio Caro (poet).
866 **292** 5c. brown (postage) . . . 10 10
867 15c. green (air) 25 10

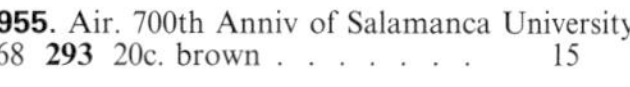
1955. Air. 700th Anniv of Salamanca University.
868 **293** 20c. brown 15 10

294 Gold Mining, Narino

1956. Regional Industries. Inscr "DEPARTAMENTO", "PROVIDENCIA" (No. 874), "INTENDENCIA" (2p. to 5p.) or "COMISARIA" (10p.).
869 – 2c. green and red 10 10
870 – 3c. black and purple . . . 10 10
871 – 3c. brown and blue . . . 10 10
872 – 3c. violet and green . . . 10 10
873 – 4c. black and green . . . 30 10
874 – 5c. black and blue 20 10
875 – 5c. slate and red 30 10
876 – 5c. olive and brown . . . 30 10
877 – 5c. brown and olive . . . 25 10
878 – 5c. brown and blue . . . 30 10
879 – 10c. black and yellow . . 25 10
880 – 10c. brown and green . . 20 10
881 – 10c. brown and blue . . . 20 10
882 – 15c. black and blue . . . 25 10
883 – 20c. blue and brown . . . 30 10
884 – 23c. red and blue 35 15
885 – 25c. black and olive . . . 35 15
886 **294** 30c. brown and blue . . . 30 10
887 – 40c. brown and purple . . 10 10
888 – 50c. black and green . . . 30 10
889 – 60c. green and sepia . . . 25 10
890 – 1p. slate and purple . . . 90 10
891 – 2p. brown and green . . . 1·90 25
892 – 3p. black and red . . . . 1·75 35
893 – 5p. blue and brown . . . 4·00 25
894 – 10p. green and brown . . 9·50 3·00
DESIGNS—As Type **294**. HORIZ: 2c. Barranquilla naval workshops, Atlantico; 4c. Fishing, Cartagena Port, Bolivar; 5c. (No. 875) View of Port, San Andres; 5c. (No. 876) Cocoa, Cauca; 5c. (No. 877) Prize cattle, Cordoba; 23c. Rice harvesting, Huila; 25c. Bananas, Magdalena; 40c. Tobacco, Santander; 50c. Oil wells of Catatumbo, Norte de Santander; 60c. Cotton harvesting, Tolima. VERT: 3c. (3), Allegory of Industry, Antioquia; 5c. (No. 874) Map of San Andres Archipelago; 5c. (No. 878) Steel plant, Boyaca; 10c. (3), Coffee, Caldas; 15c. Cathedral at Sal Salinas de Zipaquira, Cundinamarca; 20c. Platinum and map, Choco. LARGER (37½ × 27 mm)—HORIZ: 1p. Sugar factory, Valle del Cauca; 2p. Cattle fording river, Meta; 3p. Statue and River Amazon, Leticia; 5p. Landscape, La Guajira. VERT: 10p. Rubber tapping, Vaupes.

295 Henri Dunant and S. Samper Brush

1956. Obligatory Tax. Red Cross Fund.
895 **295** 5c. brown 20 10

1956. Air. No. 783 optd **EXTRA-RAPIDO**.
896 1p. green and black 25 10

297 Columbus and Lighthouse

1956. Columbus Memorial Lighthouse.
897 **297** 3c. black (postage) . . . 15 10
898 15c. blue (air) 20 10
899 3c. green ("EXTRA RAPIDO") 15 10

298 Altar of St. Elisabeth and Sarcophagus of Jimenez de Quesada, Primada Basilica, Bogota   **299** St. Ignatius of Loyola

1956. 700th Anniv of St. Elisabeth of Hungary.
900 **298** 5c. purple (postage) . . . 15 10
901 15c. brown (air) 30 15

1956. 400th Death Anniv of St. Ignatius of Loyola.
902 **299** 5c. blue (postage) 15 10
903 5c. brown (air) 20 10

300 Javier Pereira **302** Dairy Farm

1956. Pereira Commemoration.
904 **300** 5c. blue (postage) 10 10
905 20c. red (air) 10 10

1957. Air. No. 874 optd **EXTRA-RAPIDO**.
906 5c. black and blue 20 10

1957. Air. As No. 580 (colours changed) optd **EXTRA-RAPIDO**.
907 5p. black and buff . . . . . 6·00 3·75

1957. 25th Anniv of Agricultural Credit Bank.
908 **302** 1c. olive (postage) 10 10
909 – 2c. brown 10 10
910 – 5c. blue 15 10
911 **302** 5c. orange (air) 15 10
912 – 10c. green 25 20
913 – 15c. black 25 10
914 – 20c. red 40 30
915 – 5c. brown ("EXTRA RAPIDO") 15 10
DESIGNS: 2c., 10c. Farm tractor; 5c. (No. 910), 15c. Emblem of agricultural prosperity; 5c. (No. 915), Livestock; 20c. Livestock.

303 Racing Cyclist

1957. Air. 7th Round Colombia Cycle Race.
916 **303** 2c. brown 15 15
917 5c. blue 25 25

304 Arms and Gen. Rayes (founder) **305** Father J. M. Delgado

1957. 50th Anniv of Military Cadet School.
918 **304** 5c. blue (postage) 15 10
919 – 10c. orange 20 10
921 **304** 15c. red (air) 20 10
922 – 20c. brown 30 10
DESIGN: 10c., 20c. Arms and Military Cadet School.

1957. Father Delgado Commemoration.
923 **305** 2c. lake (postage) 10 10
924 10c. blue (air) 15 10

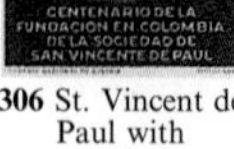

306 St. Vincent de Paul with Children **308** Fencer

307 Signatories to Bogota Postal Convention of 1838, and U.P.U. Monument, Berne

1957. Centenary of Colombian Order of St. Vincent de Paul.
925 **306** 1c. green (postage) . . . 10 10
926 5c. red (air) 15 10

1957. 14th U.P.U. Congress, Ottawa and International Correspondence Week.
927 **307** 5c. green (postage) . . . 15 10
928 10c. grey 15 10
929 15c. brown (air) 20 10
930 25c. blue 20 10

1957. 3rd S. American Fencing Championships.
931 **308** 4c. purple (postage) . . . 20 10
932 20c. brown (air) 35 10

309 Discovery of Hypsometry by F. J. de Caldas **310** Nurses with Patient, and Ambulance

1958. International Geophysical Year.
933 **309** 10c. black (postage) . . . 30 10
934 25c. green (air) 45 10
935 1p. violet ("EXTRA RAPIDO") 15 10

1958. Obligatory Tax. Red Cross Fund.
936 **310** 5c. red and black 15 10

1958. Nos. 882 and 884 surch.
937 5c. on 15c. black and blue . . 10 10
938 5c. on 23c. red and blue . . 25 20

1958. Air. No. 888 optd **AEREO**.
939 50c. black and green 20 10

313 Father R. Almanza and San Diego Church, Bogota

1958. Father Almanza Commemoration.
940 **313** 10c. lilac (postage) . . . 10 10
941 25c. grey (air) 30 10
942 10c. green ("EXTRA RAPIDO") 10 10

1958. Nos. 780/2 surch **CINCO** (5c.) or **VEINTE** (20c.).
943 **266** 5c. on 14c. red & black 15 10
944 – 5c. on 30c. sepia & black 10 10
945 – 20c. on 23c. blue & blk 25 15

315 Msr. Carrasquilla and Rosario College, Bogota

1959. Birth Centenary of Msr. R. M. Carrasquilla.
946 **315** 10c. brown (postage) . . 15 10
947 25c. red (air) 20 10
948 1p. blue 60 20

1959. Surch **20c.** and ornament.
949 **258** 20c. on 23c. black & bl 25 15

1959. As No. 826 but with "CORREO EXTRA RAPIDO" obliterated.
950 **281** 5c. multicoloured 10 10

1959. No. 794 surch.
951 10c. on 25c. purple 15 10

318 Luz Marina Zuluaga ("Miss Universe 1959") **320** J. E. Gaitan (political leader)

1959. "Miss Universe 1959" Commemoration.
952 **318** 10c. mult (postage) . . . 10 10
953 1p.20 mult (air) 65 45
954 5p. mult ("EXTRA RAPIDO") . . . . . . 25·00 24·00

1959. No. 873 surch.
955 2c. on 4c. black and green . . 30 10

1959. J. E. Gaitan Commem. Nos. 956 and 958 are surch on T **320**.
956 **320** 10c. on 3c. grey 15 10
957 30c. purple 25 15
958 2p. on 1p. black ("EXTRA RAPIDO") 60 25

1959. Air. Surch.
960 **269** 50c. on 60c. sepia . . . . 5·00 30

323 Capitol, Bogota **324** Santander

1959.
961 **323** 2c. brn & blue (postage) 10 10
962 3c. violet and black . . . 10 10
963 **324** 5c. brown and yellow . . 15 10
964 – 5c. ultramarine & blue . . 15 10
965 – 10c. black and red 15 10
966 **324** 10c. black and green . . . 15 10
967 – 35c. black and grey (air) 1·75 10
PORTRAIT (as Type **324**): Nos. 964/5, 967, Bolivar.

1959. Air. Unification of Airmail Rates. Optd **UNIFICADO** within outline of aeroplane.
968 **299** 5c. brown 15 10
969 **302** 5c. orange 35 35
970 **306** 5c. red 20 20
971 **155** 10c. red (No. 772) 10 10
972 – 10c. black (No. 789) . . . 20 10
973 **304** 15c. red 30 10
974 – 20c. brown (No. 792) . . 20 10
975 – 20c. brown (No. 922) . . 10 10
976 **308** 20c. brown 25 15
977 – 25c. blue (No. 793) . . . 25 10
978 – 25c. purple (No. 794) . . 25 10
979 **313** 25c. grey 25 10
980 **315** 25c. red 30 10
981 – 30c. brown (No. 795) . . 20 10
982 **269** 50c. on 60c. sepia (No. 960) 15 10
983 **315** 1p. blue 35 10
984 **318** 1p.20 multicoloured . . . 45 35
985 **270** 2p. black and green . . . 2·10 20
986 – 3p. black & red (No. 802) 7·00 45
987 – 5p. grn & brn (No. 803) 7·50 45
988 **271** 10p. olive and red . . . . 9·50 1·60

326 Colombian 2½c. stamp of 1859 and Postman with Mule **328** 2c. Air Stamp of 1918, Junkers F-13 "Colombia" and Lockheed Constellation

1959. Colombian Stamp Cent. Inscr "1859 1959".
989 **326** 5c. grn & orge (postage) 20 15
990 – 10c. blue and lake 40 15
991 **326** 15c. green and red 35 10
992 – 25c. brown and blue . . . 2·25 1·25
993 – 25c. red and brown (air) 40 20
994 – 50c. blue and red 55 20
995 – 1p.20 brown and green . . 2·10 1·25
996 – 10c. lilac and bistre "EXTRA-RAPIDO") 20 10
DESIGNS—VERT: Colombian stamps of 1859 (except No. 993): No. 990, 5c. and river steamer; 992, 10c. and steam locomotive "Cordoba"; 993, Postal decree of 1859 and Pres. M. Ospina; 996, 10c. and map of Colombia. HORIZ: No. 994, 20c. and Junkers F-13 seaplane "Colombia"; 995, 1p. and Lockheed Constellation airliner over valley.

1959. Air. 40th Anniv of Colombian "AVIANCA" Air Mail Services.
998 **328** 35c. red, black and blue 15 10
999 – 60c. black and green . . . 25 15
DESIGN: 60c. As Type **328** but without Colombian 2c. stamp.

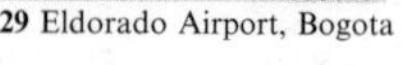

329 Eldorado Airport, Bogota **331** A. von Humboldt (after J. K. Stieler)

1960. Air.
1002 **329** 35c. orange and black 45 20
1003 60c. red and grey . . . 35 35
1004 1p. blue and grey ("EXTRA RAPIDO") 1·00 45

1960. Death Centenary of Alexander von Humboldt (naturalist). Animals.
1005 – 5c. brn & turq (postage) 10 10
1006 **331** 10c. sepia and red . . . 10 10
1007 – 20c. purple and yellow 20 10
1008 – 35c. brown (air) 45 10
1009 – 1p.30 brown and red . . 1·25 90
1010 – 1p.45 lemon and blue . . 1·00 45
DESIGNS—VERT: 5c. Two-toed sloth; 20c. Long-haired spider monkey. HORIZ: 35c. Giant anteater; 1p.30, Nine-banded armadillo; 1p.45, "Blue" parrotfish.

332 "Anthurium andreanum" **333** Refugee Family

1960. Colombian Flowers.
1011 **332** 5c. mult (postage) . . . 20 10
1012 A 20c. yellow, green & sep 10 10
1013 B 5c. multicoloured (air) 10 10
1014 5c. multicoloured 10 10
1015 A 10c. yellow, green & bl 10 10
1016 C 20c. multicoloured . . . 10 10
1017 D 25c. multicoloured . . . 35 10
1018 C 35c. multicoloured . . . 25 10
1019 B 60c. multicoloured . . . 35 20
1020 **332** 60c. multicoloured . . . 35 10
1021 1p.45 multicoloured . . 90 35
1022 C 5c. multicoloured ("EXTRA RAPIDO") 10 10
1023 D 10c. multicoloured . . . 10 10
1024 **332** 1p. multicoloured . . . 90 55
1025 A 1p. yellow, green & sepia 90 55
1026 B 1p. multicoloured . . . 90 55
1027 C 1p. multicoloured . . . 90 55
1028 D 1p. multicoloured . . . 90 55
1029 C 2p. multicoloured . . . 1·60 80
FLOWERS: A, "Espelitia grandiflora"; B, "Passiflora mollissima"; C, Odontoglossum luteo purpureum"; D, "Stanhopea tigrina".

1960. Air. World Refugee Year.
1030a **333** 60c. grey and green . . 15 15

334 Lincoln Statue, Washington **335** "House of the Flower Vase"

1960. 150th Birth Anniv of Abraham Lincoln.
1032 **334** 20c. blk & mve (postage) 15 10
1033 40c. black & brown (air) 45 25
1034 60c. black and red . . . 25 10

1960. 150th Anniv of Independence.
1035 – 5c. brn & grn (postage) 10 10
1036 **335** 20c. purple and brown 15 10
1037 – 20c. yellow, blue & mve 10 15
1038 – 5c. multicoloured (air) 15 10
1039 – 5c. sepia and violet . . . 15 10
1040 – 35c. multicoloured . . . 20 10
1041 – 60c. green and brown . . 40 10
1042 – 1p. green and red . . . 35 20
1043 – 1p.20 indigo and blue . . 35 20
1044 – 1p.30 black and orange 35 20
1045 – 1p.45 multicoloured . . 65 55
1046 – 1p.65 brown and green 45 35
DESIGNS—VERT: No. 1035, Cartagena coins of 1811–13; 1038, Arms of Cartagena; 1037, Arms of Mompos; 1043, Statue of A. Galan. HORIZ: No. 1039, J. Camacho, J. T. Lozano and J. M. Pey; 1040, 1045, Colombian Flag; 1041, A. Rosillo, A. Villavicencio and J. Caicedo; 1042, B. Alvares and J. Gutierrez; 1044, Front page of "La Bagatela" (newspaper); 1046, A. Santos, J. A. Gomez and L. Mejia.

336 St. Luisa de Marillac and Sanctuary **337** St. Isidro Labrador (after G. Vasquez)

1960. Obligatory Tax. Red Cross Fund.
1048 **336** 5c. red and brown . . . 20 10
1049 – 5c. red and blue 20 10
DESIGN: No. 1049, H. Dunant and battle scene.

1960. St. Isidro Labrador Commem (1st issue).
1050 **337** 10c. mult (postage) . . . 10 10
1051 – 20c. multicoloured . . . 15 10
1052 **337** 35c. multicoloured (air) 20 10
DESIGN: 20c. "The Nativity" (after Vasquez).
See also Nos. 1126/8.

338 U.N. Headquarters, New York

339 Highway Map of Northern Colombia

1960. U.N. Day.
1054 **338** 20c. red and black . . . 15 10

1961. 8th Pan-American Highway Congress.
1056 **339** 20c. brn & bl (postage) 30 25
1057 10c. purple & green (air) 30 25
1058 20c. red and blue 30 25
1059 30c. black and green . . 30 25
1060 10c. blue and green ("EXTRA RAPIDO") 30 25

340 Alfonso Lopez (statesman)

341 Text from Resolution of Confederated Cities

1961. 75th Birth Anniv of Alfonso Lopez (President, 1934–38 and 1941–45).
1061 **340** 10c. brn & red (postage) 15 10
1062 20c. brown and violet . . 15 10
1063 35c. brown & blue (air) 35 10
1064 10c. brown and green ("EXTRA RAPIDO") 15 10

1961. 50th Anniv of Valle del Cauca.
1066 – 10c. mult (postage) . . . 10 10
1067 **341** 20c. brown and black . . 15 10
1068 – 35c. brown & olive (air) 30 10
1069 – 35c. brown and green . . 30 10
1070 – 1p.30 sepia and purple 35 15
1071 – 1p.45 green and brown 35 15
1072 – 10c. brown and olive ("EXTRA RAPIDO") 15 10
DESIGNS—HORIZ: 10c. (No. 1066), La Ermita Church, bridge and arms of Cali; 35c. (No. 1068), St. Francis' Church, Cali; 1p.30, Conservatoire; 1p.45, Agricultural College, Palmira. VERT: 10c. (No. 1072), Aerial view of Cali; 35c. (No. 1069), University emblem.

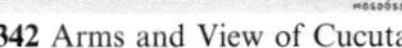

342 Arms and View of Cucuta

345 Arms of Barranquilla

1961. 50th Anniv of North Santander.
1073 – 20c. mult (postage) . . . 15 10
1074 **342** 20c. multicoloured . . . 15 10
1075 – 35c. green & bistre (air) 45 10
1076 – 10c. purple & green ("EXTRA RAPIDO") 15 10
DESIGNS—HORIZ: No. 1073, Arms of Ocana and Pamplona; 1075, Panoramic view of Cucuta. VERT: No. 1076, Villa del Rosario, Cucuta.

1961. Air. Optd **Aereo** (1077) or **AEREO** (others) and airplane or surch also.
1077 **332** 5c. multicoloured 10 10
1078 – 5c. brown & turquoise (No. 1005) 10 10
1079 – 10c. on 20c. purple and yellow (No. 1007) . . 10 10

1961. Atlantico Tourist Issue.
1080 – 10c. mult (postage) . . . 10 10
1081 **345** 20c. red, blue and yellow 15 10
1082 – 20c. multicoloured . . . 15 10
1083 – 35c. sepia and red (air) 45 10
1084 – 35c. red, yellow & green 35 10
1085 – 35c. blue and gold . . . 65 10
1086 – 1p.45 brown and green 45 20
1088 – 10c. yellow and brown ("EXTRA RAPIDO") 15 10
DESIGNS—VERT: No. 1080, Arms of Popayan; 1082, Arms of Bucaramanga; 1083, Courtyard of Tourist Hotel; 1087, Holy Week procession, Popayan. HORIZ: No. 1084, View of San Gill; 1085, Barranquilla Port; 1086, View of Velez.

346 Nurse M. de la Cruz

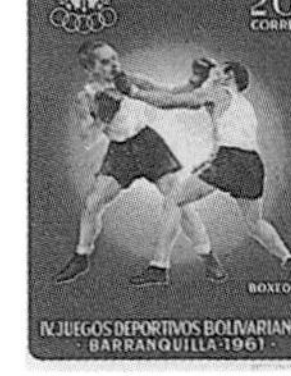

347 Boxing

1961. Red Cross Fund. Cross in red.
1090 **346** 5c. brown 15 10
1091 5c. purple 15 10

1961. 4th Bolivarian Games. Inscr as in T **347**. Multicoloured.
1092 20c. Type **347** (postage) . . 20 10
1093 20c. Basketball 10 10
1094 20c. Running 10 10
1095 25c. Football 20 10
1096 35c. Diving (air) 25 10
1097 35c. Tennis 25 10
1098 1p.45 Baseball 35 15
1099 10c. Statue and flags ("EXTRA RAPIDO") . . 10 10
1100 10c. Runner with Olympic torch ("EXTRA RAPIDO") 10 10

348 "S.E.M." Emblem and Mosquito

349 Society Emblem

1962. Malaria Eradication.
1102 **348** 20c. red & ochre (post) 15 15
1103 – 50c. blue and ochre . . . 15 15
1104 **348** 40c. red & yellow (air) 15 15
1105 – 1p.45 blue and grey . . 40 40
1106 – 1p. blue and green ("EXTRA RAPIDO") 2·75 2·75
DESIGN: 50c., 1p., 1p.45, Campaign emblem and mosquito.

1962. 6th National Engineers' Congress, 1961 and 75th Anniv of Colombian Society of Engineers.
1107 **349** 10c. mult (postage) . . . 20 20
1108 – 5c. red and blue (air) . . 10 10
1109 – 10c. brown and green . . 30 15
1110 – 15c. brown and purple 25 15
1111 **349** 2p. multicoloured ("EXTRA RAPIDO") 1·60 90
DESIGNS: No. 1108, A. Ramos and Engineering Faculty, Cauca University, Popayan; 1109, M. Triana, A. Arroyo and Monserrate cable and funicular railway; 1110, D. Sanchez and first Society H.Q., Bogota.

350 O.E.A. Emblem

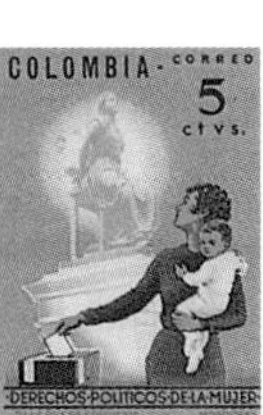

351 Mother Voting and Statue of Policarpa Salavarrieta

1962. 70th Anniv of Organization of American States (O.E.A.). Flags multicoloured; background colours given.
1112 **350** 25c. red & blk (postage) 15 10
1114 35c. blue & black (air) 15 10

1962. Women's Franchise.
1115 **351** 5c. black, grey and brown (postage) . . . 10 10
1116 10c. black, grey and blue 15 10
1117 5c. blk, grey & pink (air) 10 10
1118 35c. black, grey & buff 25 10
1119 45c. black, grey & green 25 10
1120 45c. black, grey & mauve 25 10

353 Scouts in Camp

354 St. Isidro Labrador (after G. Vasquez)

1962. 30th Anniv of Colombian Boy Scouts and 25th Anniv of Colombian Girl Scouts. As T **353** but without "EXTRA RAPIDO".
1121 **353** 10c. brn & turq (postage) 10 10
1122 15c. brown & red (air) 25 10
1123 – 40c. lake and red 15 10
1124 – 1p. blue and Salmon . . 30 15
1125 **353** 1p. violet & yellow ("EXTRA RAPIDO") 3·50 3·25
DESIGN: 40c., 1p. Girl Scouts.

1962. St. Isidro Labrador Commem (2nd issue).
1126 **354** 10c. multicoloured . . . 10 10
1127 – 10c. mult (air—"EXTRA RAPIDO") 10 10
1128 **354** 2p. multicoloured . . . 2·50 1·50
DESIGN: 10c. (No. 1127), "The Nativity" (after G. Vasquez).

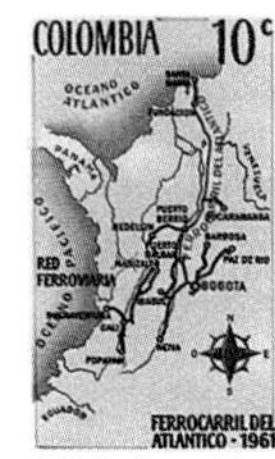

355 Railway Map

356 Posthorn

1962. Completion of Colombia Atlantic Railway.
1129 **355** 10c. red, green and olive (postage) 30 20
1130 – 5c. myrtle & sepia (air) 30 10
1131 **355** 10c. red, turq & bistre 30 20
1132 – 1p. brown and purple . . 4·50 45
1133 – 5p. brown, blue & grn ("EXTRA RAPIDO") 10·00 4·50
DESIGNS—HORIZ: 5c. 1854 steam and 1961 diesel locomotives; 1, 5p. Pres. A. Parra and R. Magdalena railway bridge.

1962. 50th Anniv of Postal Union of the Americas and Spain.
1134 **356** 20c. gold & bl (postage) 15 10
1135 – 50c. gold & green (air) 30 10
1136 **356** 60c. gold and purple . . 20 10
DESIGN: 50c. Posthorn, dove and map.

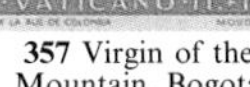

357 Virgin of the Mountain, Bogota

358 Centenary Emblem

1963. Ecumenical Council, Vatican City.
1137 **357** 60c. mult (postage) . . . 20 10
1138 – 60c. red, yell & gold (air) 10 10
DESIGN: No. 1138, Pope John XXIII.

1963. Obligatory Tax. Red Cross Centenary.
1139 **358** 5c. red and bistre . . . 10 10

359 Hurdling and Flags

1963. Air. South American Athletic Championships, Cali.
1140 **359** 20c. multicoloured . . . 15 10
1141 80c. multicoloured . . . 15 10

360 Bolivar Monument

361 Tennis Player

1963. Air. Centenary of Pereira.
1142 **360** 1p.90 brown and blue . . 10 10

1963. Air. 30th South American Tennis Championships, Medellin.
1143 **361** 55c. multicoloured . . . 25 10

362 Pres. Kennedy and Alliance Emblem

363 Veracruz Church

1963. Air. "Alliance for Progress".
1144 **362** 10c. multicoloured . . . 10 10

1964. Air. National Pantheon, Veracruz Church. Multicoloured.
1145 1p. Type **363** 25 10
1146 2p. "The Crucifixion" . . . 35 20

364 Cartagena

1964. Air. Cartagena Commemoration.
1147 **364** 3p. multicoloured . . . 80 55

365 Eleanor Roosevelt

1964. Air. 15th Anniv of Declaration of Human Rights.
1148 **365** 20c. brown and olive . . 10 10

366 A. Castilla (composer and founder) and Music

1964. Air. Tolima Conservatoire Commem.
1149 **366** 30c. turquoise & bistre 20 10

367 Manuel Mejia and Coffee Growers' Flag Emblem

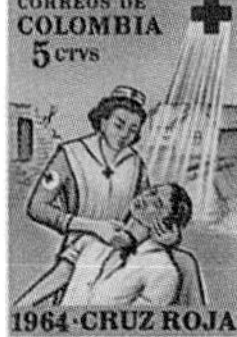

368 Nurse with Patient

1965. Manuel Mejia Commemoration.
1150 **367** 25c. brn & red (postage) 10 10
1151 – 45c. sepia & brown (air) 15 10
1152 – 5p. black and green . . 1·60 30
1153 – 10p. black and blue . . 2·10 25
DESIGNS: 45c. Gathering coffee-beans; 5p. Mule transport; 10p. Freighter "Manuel Mejia" at Buenaventura Port. Each design includes a portrait of M. Mejia, director of the National Coffee Growers' Association.

1965. Obligatory Tax. Red Cross Fund.
1154 **368** 5c. blue and red 10 10

369 I.T.U. Emblem and "Waves" **370** Orchid ("Cattleya trianae")

1965. Air. Centenary of I.T.U.
1155 **369** 80c. indigo, red and blue . . . 15 10

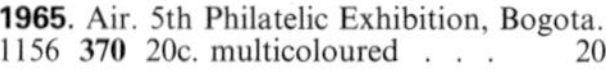

1965. Air. 5th Philatelic Exhibition, Bogota.
1156 **370** 20c. multicoloured . . . 20 10

371 Satellites, Telegraph Pole and Map

1965. Air. Cent of Colombian Telegraphs. Mult.
1157 60c. Type **371** 15 10
1158 60c. Statue of Pres. Murrillo Toro, Bogota (vert) . . . 15 10

372 Junkers F-13 Seaplane "Colombia" (1920)

1965. Air. "History of Colombian Aviation". Multicoloured.
1159 5c. Type **372** 10 10
1160 10c. Dornier Wal Do-J (1924) 10 10
1161 20c. Dornier Do-B Merkur seaplane (1926) 20 10
1162 50c. Ford 5-AT Trimotor (1932) 20 10
1163 60c. De Havilland Gipsy Moth (1930) 30 10
1164 1p. Douglas DC-4 (1947) . . 35 10
1165 1p.40 Douglas DC-3 (1944) 20 15
1166 2p.80 Lockheed Constellation (1951) . . . 45 30
1167 3p. Boeing 720B jet liner (1961) 65 55

See also No. E1168.

373 Badge, and Car on Mountain Road

1966. Air. 25th Anniv (1965) of Colombian Automobile Club.
1168 **373** 20c. multicoloured . . . 10 10

374 J. Arboleda (writer)

375 Red Cross and Children as Nurse and Patient

1966. Julio Arboleda Commemoration.
1169 **374** 5c. multicoloured 10 10

1966. Obligatory Tax. Red Cross Fund.
1170 **375** 5c.+5c. mult 10 10

376 16th-century Galleon

1966. History of Maritime Mail. Multicoloured.
1171 5c. Type **376** 20 10
1172 15c. Riohacha brigantine (1850) 35 15
1173 20c. Uraba schooner 35 15
1174 40c. Steamer and barge, Magdalena, 1900 . . . . 65 15
1175 50c. Modern freighter . . . 1·90 1·00

377 Hogfish

1966. Fishes. Multicoloured.
1176 80c. Type **377** (postage) . . 30 10
1177 10p. Spotted electric ray . . 4·75 3·25
1178 2p. Pacific flyingfish (air) . . 15 20
1179 2p.80 Blue angelfish 50 30
1180 20p. King mackerel . . . . 8·75 5·75

378 Arms of Colombia, Venezuela and Chile **379** C. Torres (patriot)

1966. Visits of Chilean and Venezuelan Presidents.
1181 **378** 40c. mult (postage) . . . 10 10
1182 1p. multicoloured (air) 25 10
1183 1p.40 multicoloured . . 25 10

1967. Famous Colombians.
1184 **379** 25c. vio & yell (postage) 10 10
1185 – 60c. purple and yellow 10 10
1186 – 1p. green and yellow . . 35 10
1187 – 80c. blue & yellow (air) 15 10
1188 – 1p.70 black and yellow 30 10

PORTRAITS: 60c. J. T. Lozano (naturalist); 80c. Father F. R. Mejia (scholar); 1p. F. A. Zea (writer); 1p.70, J. J. Casas (diplomat).

380 Map of Signatory Countries

1967. "Declaration of Bogota".
1189 **380** 40c. mult (postage) . . . 15 10
1190 60c. multicoloured . . . 15 10
1191 3p. multicoloured (air) 30 15

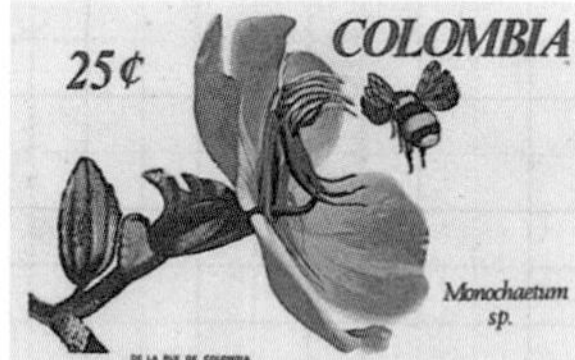

381 "Monochaetum" and Bee

1967. National Orchid Congress and Tropical Flora and Fauna Exhibition, Medellin. Multicoloured.
1192 25c. Type **381** (postage) . . 10 10
1193 2p. "Passiflora vitifolia" and butterfly 45 35
1194 1p. "Cattleya dowiana" (vert) (air) 15 10
1195 1p.20 "Masdevallia coccinea" (vert) 10 10
1196 5p. "Catasetum macrocarpum" and bee 55 10

382 Nurse's Cap

383 Lions Emblem

1967. Obligatory Tax. Red Cross Fund.
1198 **382** 5c. red and blue 10 10

1967. 50th Anniv of Lions International.
1199 **383** 10p. mult (postage) . . . 1·40 35
1200 25c. multicoloured (air) 15 10

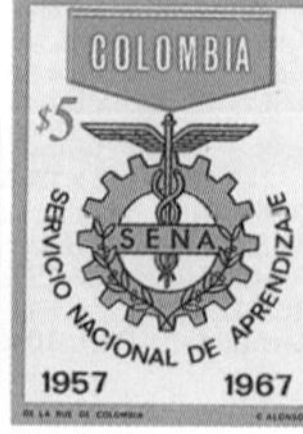

384 "Caesarean Operation, 1844" (from painting by Grau) **385** S.E.N.A. Emblem

1967. Air. 6th Colombian Surgeons' Congress, Bogota and Centenary of National University.
1201 **384** 80c. multicoloured . . . 15 10

1967. 10th Anniv of National Apprenticeship Service.
1202 **385** 5p. black, gold and green (postage) . . . . . . 1·25 20
1203 2p. black, gold and red (air) 20 10

386 Calima Diadem **387** Radio Antenna

1967. Administrative Council of U.P.U. Consultative Commission of Postal Studies. Main design and lower inscr in brown and gold.
1204 **386** 1p.60 pur (postage) . . . 15 10
1205 – 3p. blue 35 10
1206 – 30c. red (air) 20 10
1207 – 5p. red 90 20
1208 – 20p. violet . . . . . . 7·00 4·25

DESIGNS (Colombian archaeological treasures) VERT: 30c. Chief's head-dress; 5p. Cauca breastplate; 20p. Quimbaya jug. HORIZ: 3p. Tolima anthropomorphic figure and postal "pigeon on globe" emblem.

1968. "21 Years of National Telecommunications Services". Inscr "1947–1968".
1210 **387** 50c. mult (postage) . . . 15 10
1211 – 1p. multicoloured . . . 30 10
1212 – 50c. mult (air) 15 10
1213 – 1p. yellow, grey & blue 30 10

DESIGNS: No. 1211, Communications network; 1212, Diagram; 1213, Satellite.

388 The Eucharist **389** "St. Augustine" (Vasquez)

1968. 39th International Eucharistic Congress, Bogota (1st issue).
1214 **388** 60c. mult (postage) . . . 15 10
1215 80c. multicoloured (air) 15 10
1216 3p. multicoloured . . . 35 10

1968. 39th International Eucharistic Congress, Bogota (2nd Issue). Multicoloured.
1217 25c. Type **389** (postage) . . 10 10
1218 60c. "Gathering Manna" (Vasquez) 10 10
1219 1p. "Betrothal of the Virgin and St. Joseph" (B. de Figueroa) 10 10
1220 5p. "La Lechuga" (Jesuit Statuette) 25 20
1221 10p. "Pope Paul VI" (painting by Franciscan Missionary Mothers) . . 55 10
1222 80c. "The Last Supper" (Vasquez) (horiz) (air) . . 15 10
1223 1p. "St. Francis Xavier's Sermon" (Vasquez) . . . 25 10
1224 2p. "Elijah's Dream" (Vasquez) 10 10
1225 3p. As No. 1220 . . . . . 25 10
1226 20p. As No. 1221 . . . . . 3·25 90

390 Pope Paul VI

391 University Arms

1968. Pope Paul's Visit to Colombia. Multicoloured.
1228 25c. Type **390** (postage) . . 15 10
1229 80c. Reception podium (horiz) (air) 15 10
1230 1p.20 Pope Paul giving Blessing 10 10
1231 1p.80 Cathedral, Bogota . . 10 15

1968. Centenary of National University.
1232 **391** 80c. mult (postage) . . . 10 10
1233 – 20c. red, green and yellow (air) 10 10

DESIGN: 20c. Mathematical symbols.

392 Antioquia 2½c. Stamp of 1858 **393** Institute Emblem and Split Leaf

1968. Centenary of First Antioquia Stamps.
1234 **392** 30c. blue and green . . . 10 10

1969. 25th Anniv (1967) of Inter-American Agricultural Sciences Institute.
1236 **393** 20c. mult (postage) . . . 10 10
1237 1p. multicoloured (air) 15 10

394 Pen and Microscope

1969. Air. 20th Anniv of University of the Andes.
1238 **394** 5p. multicoloured . . . 45 10

395 Von Humboldt and Andes (Quindio Region)

1969. Air. Birth Bicentenary of Alexander von Humboldt (naturalist).
1239 **395** 1p. green and brown . . 15 10

396 Junkers F-13 Seaplane and Map **397** Red Cross

1969. Air. 50th Anniv of 1st Colombian Airmail Flight. Multicoloured.
1240 1p. Type **396** 25 15
1241 1p.50 Boeing 720B and globe 30 10

See also Nos. 1249/50.

1969. Obligatory Tax. Colombian Red Cross.
1243 **397** 5c. red and violet . . . 10 10

398 "The Battle of Boyaca" (J. M. Espinosa)

1969. 150th Anniv of Independence. Mult.
1244 20c. Type **398** (postage) . . 15 10
1245 30c. "Liberation Army crossing Pisba Pass" (F. A. Caro) 15 10
1246 2p.30 "Entry into Santa Fe" (I. Castillo-Cervantes) (air) 20 20

399 Institute Emblem **400** Cranial Diagram

1969. Air. 20th Anniv of Colombian Social Security Institute.
1247 **399** 20c. green and black . . 10 10

1969. Air. 13th Latin-American Neurological Congress, Bogota.
1248 **400** 70c. multicoloured . . . 20 10

401 Junkers F-13 Seaplane and Puerto Colombia **402** Child posting Christmas Card

1969. Air. 50th Anniv of "Avianca" Airline. Multicoloured.
1249 2p. Type **401** 40 10
1250 3p.50 Boeing 720B and globe 35 25

1969. Air. Christmas. Multicoloured.
1252 60c. Type **402** 15 10
1253 1p. Type **402** 15 10
1254 1p.50 Child with Christmas presents 45 10

403 "Poverty" **405** National Sports Institute Emblem

404 Dish Aerial and Ancient Head

1970. Colombian Social Welfare Institute and 10th Anniv of Children's Rights Law.
1255 **403** 30c. multicoloured . . . 10 10

1970. Air. Opening of Satellite Earth Station, Choconta.
1256 **404** 1p. black, red & green 40 10

1970. Air. 9th National Games, Ibague (1st issue).
1257 **405** 1p.50 black, yell & grn 25 15
1258 – 2p.30 multicoloured . . 15 20
DESIGN: 2p.30, Dove and rings (Games emblem).
See also No. 1265.

406 Exhibition Emblem

1970. Air. 2nd Fine Arts Biennial, Medellin
1259 **406** 30c. multicoloured . . . 10 10

407 Dr. E. Santos (founder) and Buildings

1970. Air. 30th Anniv (1969) of Territorial Credit Institute.
1260 **407** 1p. black, yellow & grn 15 10

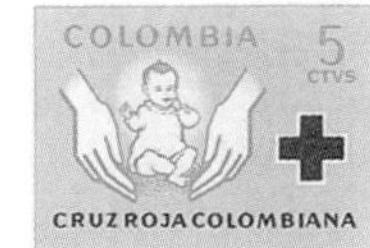

408 U.N. Emblem, Scales and Dove **409** Hands protecting Child

1970. Air. 25th Anniv of United Nations.
1261 **408** 1p.50 yellow, bl & ultram 20 10

1970. Obligatory Tax. Colombian Red Cross.
1262 **409** 5c. red and blue 10 10

410 Theatrical Mask

1970. Latin-American University Theatre Festival. Manizales.
1263 **410** 30c. brown, orange & blk 10 10

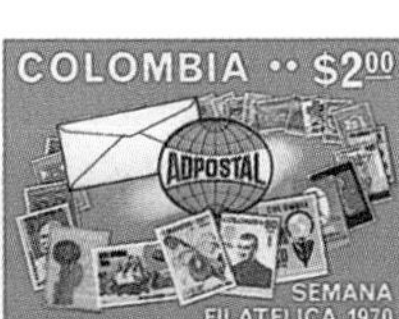

411 Postal Emblem, Letter and Stamps

1970. Philatelic Week.
1264 **411** 2p. multicoloured . . . 30 10

412 Discus-thrower and Ibague Arms

1970. 9th National Games, Ibague (2nd issue).
1265 **412** 80c. brown, green & yell 20 10

413 "St. Teresa" (B. de Figueroa) **414** Int Philatelic Federation Emblem

1970. St. Teresa of Avila's Elevation to Doctor of the Universal Church. No. 1267 optd **AEREO**.
1266 **413** 2p. mult (postage) . . . 10 10
1267 2p. mult (air) 30 10

1970. Air. "EXFILCA 70" Stamp Exhibition, Caracas, Venezuela.
1268 **414** 10p. multicoloured . . . 1·50 20

415 Chicha Maya Dance **416** Stylized Athlete

1970. Folklore Dances and Costumes. Mult.
1269 1p. Type **415** (postage) . . . 35 10
1270 1p.10 Currulao dance . . . 35 10
1271 60c. Napanga costume (air) 20 15
1272 1p. Joropo dance 20 10
1273 1p.30 Guabina dance . . . 30 10
1274 1p.30 Bambuco dance . . . 20 10
1275 1p.30 Cumbia dance 20 10

1971. Air. 6th Pan-American Games, Cali (1st issue).
1277 **416** 1p.50 multicoloured . . 35 45
1278 – 2p. orange, green & blk 35 40
DESIGN: 2p. Games emblem.

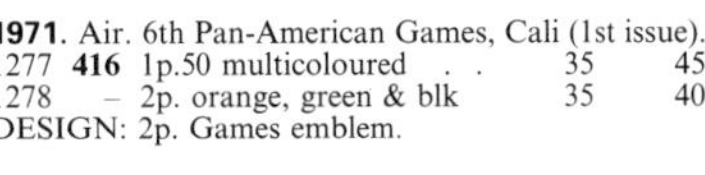

417 G. Alzate Avendano

1971. Air. 10th Anniv of Gilberto Alzate Avendano (politician).
1279 **417** 1p. multicoloured . . . 15 25

418 Priest's House, Guacari

1971. 400th Anniv of Guacari (town).
1280 **418** 1p. multicoloured . . . 25 10

419 Commemorative Medal

1971. Air. Centenary of Bank of Bogota.
1281 **419** 1p. gold, brown & green 40 20

420 Sports Centre **421** Weightlifting

1971. Air. 6th Pan-American Games (2nd issue) and "EXFICALI 71" Stamp Exhibition, Cali. Mult.
1282 1p.30 Type **420** (yellow emblem) 40 30
1283 1p.30 Football 40 30
1284 1p.30 Wrestling 40 30
1285 1p.30 Cycling 40 30
1286 1p.30 Volleyball 40 30
1287 1p.30 Diving 40 30
1288 1p.30 Fencing 40 30
1289 1p.30 Type **420** (green emblem) 40 30
1290 1p.30 Sailing 40 30
1291 1p.30 Show-jumping 40 30
1292 1p.30 Athletics 40 30
1293 1p.30 Rowing 40 30
1294 1p.30 Cali emblem 40 30
1295 1p.30 Netball 40 30
1296 1p.30 Type **420** (blue emblem) 40 30
1297 1p.30 Stadium 40 30
1298 1p.30 Baseball 40 30
1299 1p.30 Hockey 40 30
1300 1p.30 Type **421** 40 30
1301 1p.30 Medals 40 30
1302 1p.30 Boxing 40 30
1303 1p.30 Gymnastics 40 30
1304 1p.30 Rifle-shooting 40 30
1305 1p.30 Type **420** (red emblem) 40 30

422 "Bolivar at Congress" (after S. Martinez-Delgado)

1971. 150th Anniv of Great Colombia Constituent Assembly, Rosario del Cucuta.
1306 **422** 80c. multicoloured . . . 15 10

423 "Battle of Carabobo" (M. Tovar y Tovar)

1971. Air. 150th Anniv of Battle of Carabobo.
1307 **423** 1p.50 multicoloured . . 15 15

424 C.I.M.E. Emblem

1972. 20th Anniv of Inter-Governmental Committee on European Migration.
1308 **424** 60c. black and grey . . . 25 10

425 I.C.E.T.E.X. Symbol

1972. 20th Anniv of Institute of Educational Credit and Technical Training Abroad.
1309 **425** 1p.10 brown and green 20 10

426 Rev. Mother Francisca del Castillo

1972. 300th Birth Anniv of Reverend Mother Francisca J. del Castillo.
1310 **426** 1p.20 multicoloured . . 20 10

427 Soldier and Frigate "Almirante Padilla"

1972. 20th Anniv of Colombian Troops' Participation in Korean War.
1311 **427** 1p.20 multicoloured . . 1·25 15

428 Hat and Ceramics 429 "Maxillaria triloris" (orchid)

1972. Colombian Crafts and Products. Mult.
1312 1p.10 Type **428** (postage) . . 30 10
1313 50c. Woman in shawl (air) 30 10
1314 1p. Male doll 20 10
1315 3p. Female doll 20 25

1972. 10th National Stamp Exhibition and 7th World Orchid-growers' Congress, Medellin. Mult.
1316 20p. Type **429** (postage) . . 5·00 25
1317 1p.30 "Mormodes rolfeanum" (orchid) (horiz) (air) 15 10

430 Uncut Emeralds and Pendant 432 Congo Dance

431 Pres. Narino's House

1972. Colombian Emeralds.
1318 **430** 1p.10 multicoloured . . 30 10

1972. 400th Anniv of Leyva (town).
1319 **431** 1p.10 multicoloured . . 30 10

1972. Air. Barranquilla International Carnival.
1320 **432** 1p.30 multicoloured . . 10 10

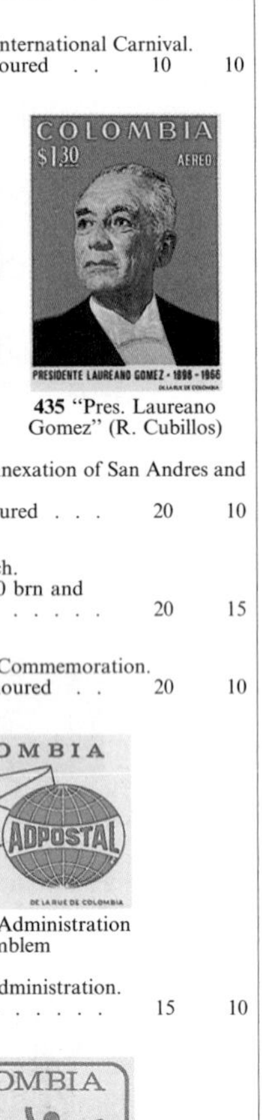

433 Island Scene 435 "Pres. Laureano Gomez" (R. Cubillos)

1972. 150th Anniv of Annexation of San Andres and Providencia Islands.
1321 **433** 60c. multicoloured . . . 20 10

1972. Air. No. 1142 surch.
1322 **360** 1p.30 on 1p.90 brn and bl 20 15

1972. Air. Pres. Gomez Commemoration.
1323 **435** 1p.30 multicoloured . . 20 10

436 Postal Administration Emblem

1972. National Postal Administration.
1324 **436** 1p.10 green 15 10

437 Colombian Family

1972. "Social Front for the People" Campaign.
1325 **437** 60c. orange 10 10

438 Pres. Guillermo Valencia 439 Benito Juarez

1972. Air. Pres. Valencia Commemoration.
1326 **438** 1p.30 multicoloured . . 25 10

1972. Air. Death Centenary of Benito Juarez (Mexican statesman).
1327 **439** 1p.50 multicoloured . . 20 10

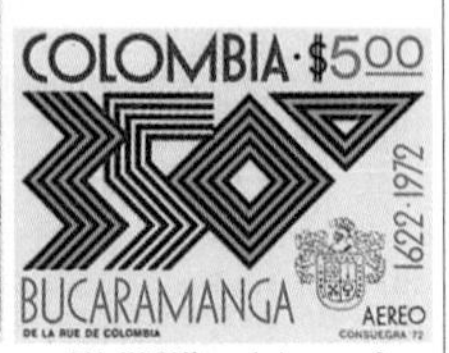

440 "La Rebeca" Monument 441 "350" and Arms of Bucaramanga

1972. Air. "La Rebeca" Monument, Centenary Park, Bogota.
1328 **440** 80c. multicoloured . . . 25 30
1329 1p. multicoloured . . . 20 10

1972. Air. 350th Anniv of Bucaramanga (city).
1330 **441** 5p. multicoloured . . . 30 10

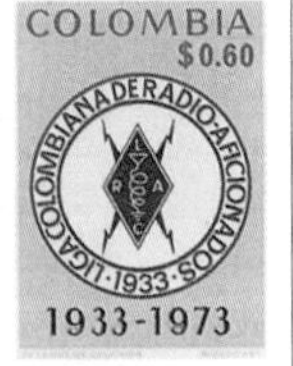

442 University Buildings 443 League Emblems

1973. Air. 350th Anniv of Javeriana University.
1331 **442** 1p.30 brown and green 25 10
1332 1p.50 brown and blue . . 25 10

1973. 40th Anniv of Colombian Radio Amateurs League.
1333 **443** 60c. red, dp blue & blue 15 10

444 Tamalameque Vessel 445 "Battle of Maracaibo" (M. F. Rincon)

1973. Inauguration of Museum of Pre-Colombian Antiques, Bogota. Multicoloured.
1334 60c. Type **444** (postage) . . 25 10
1335 1p. Tairona axe-head . . . 45 10
1336 1p.10 Muisca jug 30 10
1337 1p. As No. 1335 (air) . . . 40 35
1338 1p.30 Sinu vessel 20 10
1339 1p.70 Quimbaya vessel . . . 25 20
1340 3p.50 Tumaco figurine . . . 50 30

1973. Air. 150th Anniv of Naval Battle of Maracaibo.
1341 **445** 10p. multicoloured . . . 3·25 30

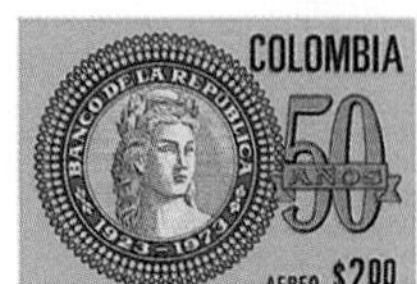

446 Banknote Emblem

1973. Air. 50th Anniv of Republican Bank.
1342 **446** 2p. multicoloured . . . 25 10

1973. Air. No. 1306 optd **AEREO**.
1343 **422** 80c. multicoloured . . . 15 10

448 "Pres. Ospina" (after C. Leudo) 449 Arms of Toro

1973. Air. 50th Anniv of Ministry of Communications.
1344 **448** 1p.50 multicoloured . . 20 10

1973. Air. 400th Anniv of Toro.
1345 **449** 1p. multicoloured . . . 15 10

450 Bolivar at Bombona

1973. Air. 150th Anniv of Battle of Bombona.
1346 **450** 1p.30 multicoloured . . 20 10

451 "General Narino" (after J. M. Espinosa) 452 Young Child

1973. 150th Death Anniv of General Antonio Narino.
1347 **451** 60c. multicoloured . . . 15 10

1973. Child Welfare Campaign.
1348 **452** 1p.10 multicoloured . . 20 10

453 Fiscal Emblem

1974. 50th Anniv of Republic's General Comptrollership.
1349 **453** 80c. black, brown & bl 15 10

454 Copernicus 455 Andes Communications and Map

1974. Air. 500th Birth Anniv of Copernicus.
1350 **454** 2p. multicoloured . . . 20 15

1974. Air. Meeting of Communications Ministers, Andean Group, Cali.
1351 **455** 2p. multicoloured . . . 10 15

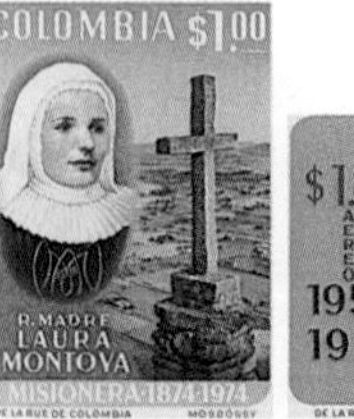

456 Laura Montoya and Cross 457 Television Set with Inravision Emblem

1974. Birth Centenary of Revd. Mother Laura Montoya (missionary).
1352 **456** 1p. multicoloured . . . 15 10

1974. Air. 20th Anniv of Inravision (National Institute of Radio and Television).
1353 **457** 1p.30 black, brn & orge 20 10

458 Athlete

1974. 10th National Games, Pereira.
1354 **458** 2p. brown, red & yellow 20 10

459 Rivera and Statue

1974. 50th Anniv of Novel "La Voragine".
1355 **459** 10p. multicoloured . . . 35 15

460 Aquatic Emblem

1974. Air. 2nd World Swimming Championships, Cali (1975).
1356 **460** 4p.50 blue, turq & blk 30 15

461 Condor Emblem

1974. Air. Centenary of Bank of Colombia.
1357 **461** 1p.50 multicoloured . . 20 10

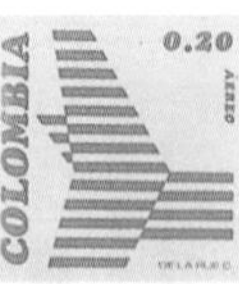

462 Tailplane

1974. Air.
1358 **462** 20c. brown 10 10

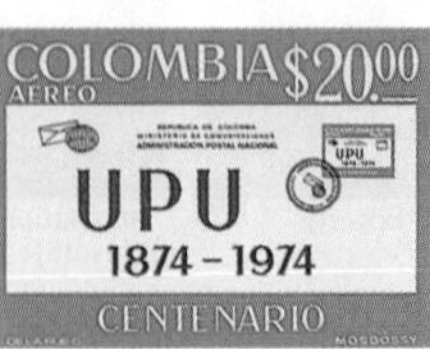

463 U.P.U. "Letter"

1974. Air. Centenary of Universal Postal Union (1st issue).
1359 **463** 20p. red, blue & black 1·10 30
See also Nos. 1363/6.

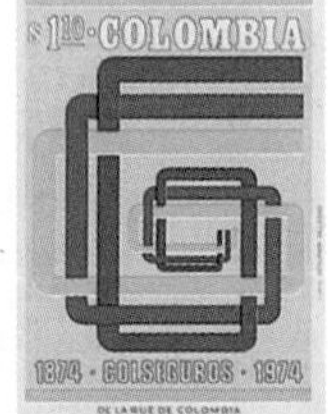

464 General Jose Maria Cordoba 465 "Progress and Expansion"

1974. Air. 150th Anniv of Battles of Junin and Ayacucho.
1360 **464** 1p.30 multicoloured . . 20 10

1974. Centenary of Colombian Insurance Company.
1361 **465** 1p.10 mult (postage) . . 20 10
1362 3p. mult (air) 35 10

466 White-tailed Trogon and U.P.U. "Letter"

467 La Quiebra Tunnel

1974. Air. Centenary of U.P.U. (2nd issue). Colombian Birds. Multicoloured.
1363 1p. Type **466** 75 40
1364 1p.30 Red-billed toucan (horiz) 75 50
1365 2p. Andean cock of the rock (horiz) . . . . 1·50 50
1366 2p.50 Scarlet macaw . . . . 1·50 60
Nos. 1364/6 also depict the U.P.U. "letter".

1974. Centenary of Antioquia Railway.
1367 **467** 1p.10 multicoloured . . 90 35

468 Boy with Ball

1974. Christmas. Multicoloured.
1368 80c. Type **468** 10 10
1369 1p. Girl with racquet . . . 10 15

469 "Protect the Trees"

1975. Air. Colombian Ecology. Multicoloured.
1370 1p. Type **469** 20 10
1371 6p. "Protect the Amazon" 20 15

470 "Wood No. 1" (R. Roncancio)

1975. Air. Colombian Art. Multicoloured.
1372 2p. Type **470** . . . . 1·00 30
1373 3p. "The Market" (M. Diaz Vargas) (vert) . . . . . . 1·75 30
1374 4p. "Child with Thorn" (G. Vazquez) (vert) . . . 15 10
1375 5p. "The Annunciation" (Santaferena School) (vert) 45 30

471 Gold Cat

1975. Pre-Colombian Archaeological Discoveries. Sinu Culture. Multicoloured.
1376 80c. Type **471** (postage) . . 20 10
1377 1p.10 Gold necklace 20 10
1378 2p. Nose pendant (air) . . . 40 10
1379 10p. "Alligator" staff ornament . . . . 2·10 35

472 Marconi and "Elettra" (steam yacht)

473 Santa Marta Cathedral

1975. Birth Centenary of Guglielmo Marconi (radio pioneer).
1380 **472** 3p. multicoloured . . . 75 10

1975. 450th Anniv of Santa Marta. Multicoloured.
1381 80c. Type **473** (postage) . . 10 10
1382 2p. "El Rodadero" (sea-front), Santa Marta (horiz) (air) 20 10

474 Maria de J. Paramo (educationalist)

475 Pres. Nunez

1975. International Women's Year.
1383 **474** 4p. multicoloured . . . 25 10

1975. 150th Birth Anniv of President Rafael Nunez.
1384 **475** 1p.10 multicoloured . . 15 10

476 Arms of Medellin

479 Sugar Cane

1975. 300th Anniv of Medellin.
1385 **476** 1p. multicoloured . . . 25 10
See also Nos. 1386, 1388, 1394, 1404, 1419, 1434, 1481/3, 1672/4, 1678/9, 1752, 1758, 1859 and 1876.

1976. Centenary of Reconstruction of Cucuta City. As T **476**.
1386 1p.50 multicoloured 30 10

1976. Surch.
1387 **471** 1p.20 on 80c. mult . . . 15 10

1976. Arms of Cartagena. As T **476**.
1388 1p.50 multicoloured 20 10

1976. 4th Cane Sugar Export and Production Congress, Cali.
1389 **479** 5p. green and black . . 45 10

480 Bogota

1976. Air. Habitat. U.N. Conference on Human Settlements. Multicoloured.
1390 10p. Type **480** . . . . . . 1·10 35
1391 10p. Barranquilla . . . . . 1·10 35
1392 10p. Cali . . . . 1·10 35
1393 10p. Medellin . . . . 1·10 35

1976. Arms of Ibague. As T **476**.
1394 1p.20 multicoloured 15 10

481 University Emblem and "90"

482 M. Samper

1976. Air. 90th Anniv of Colombia University.
1395 **481** 5p. multicoloured . . . 20 10

1976. Air. 150th Birth Anniv of Miguel Samper (statesman and writer).
1396 **482** 2p. multicoloured . . . 20 10

483 Early Telephone

484 "Callicore sp."

1976. Air. Telephone Centenary.
1397 **483** 3p. multicoloured . . . 20 10

1976. Colombian Fauna and Flora. Multicoloured.
1398 3p. Type **484** 75 10
1399 5p. "Morpho sp." (butterfly) 1·25 20
1400 20p. Black anthurium (plant) . . . . 1·10 25

485 Purace Indians, Cauca

486 Rotary Emblem

1976.
1401 **485** 1p.50 multicoloured . . 10 10

1976. 50th Anniv of Colombian Rotary Club.
1402 **486** 1p. multicoloured . . . 10 10

487 Boeing 747 Jumbo Jet

1976. Air. Inaug of Avianca Jumbo Jet Service.
1403 **487** 2p. multicoloured . . . 15 10

1976. 535th Anniv of Tunja City Arms. As T **476**.
1404 1p.20 multicoloured 15 10

488 "The Signing of Declaration of Independence" (left-hand detail of painting, Trumbull)

489 Police Handler and Dog

1976. Bicentenary of American Revolution.
1405 **488** 30p. multicoloured . . . 1·75 1·10
1406 – 30p. multicoloured . . . 1·75 1·10
1407 – 30p. multicoloured . . . 1·75 1·10
DESIGNS: Nos. 1406/7 show different portions of the painting.

1976. National Police.
1408 **489** 1p.50 multicoloured . . 25 10

490 Franciscan Convent

1976. Air. 150th Anniv of Panama Congress.
1409 **490** 6p. multicoloured . . . 20 20

1977. Surch.
1411 **475** 2p. on 1p.10 mult (postage) 25 10
1412 – 2p. on 1p.20 mult (No. 1404) 20 10
1413 **489** 2p. on 1p.50 mult . . . 20 10
1414 **487** 3p. on 2p. mult (air) . . 15 10

494 Coffee Plant and Beans

495 Coffee Grower with mule

1977. Air. Coffee Production.
1416 **494** 3p. multicoloured . . . 15 10
1416a 3p.50 multicoloured . . 20 10

1977. Air. 50th Anniv of National Federation of Coffee Growers.
1417 **495** 10p. multicoloured . . . 20 15

496 Beethoven and Score of Ninth Symphony

1977. Air. 150th Anniv of Beethoven.
1418 **496** 8p. multicoloured . . . 25 15

1977. Arms of Popayan. As T **476**.
1419 5p. multicoloured 30 15

497 Mother feeding Baby

498 Wattled Jacana and "Eichhornia crassipes"

1977. Nutrition Campaign.
1420 **497** 2p. multicoloured . . . 15 10
1420a 2p.50 multicoloured . . 80 10

1977. Colombian Birds and Plants. Multicoloured.
1421 10p. Type **498** (postage) . . 2·25 50
1422 20p. Plum-throated cotinga and "Pyrostegia venusta" 2·50 60
1423 5p. Crimson-mantled woodpecker and "Meriania" (air) . . . . 1·50 50
1424 5p. American purple gallinule and "Nymphaea" . . . . . . 1·50 50
1425 10p. Pampadour cotinga and "Cochlospermum orinocense" . . . . . . 2·75 60
1426 10p. Northern royal flycatcher and "Jacaranda copaia" . . . . 2·75 60

499 Games Emblem

500 "La Cayetana" (E. Grau)

1977. Air. 13th Central American and Caribbean Games, Medellin (1978).
1427 **499** 6p. multicoloured . . . 25 10

1977. Air. 20th Anniv of Female Suffrage. Multicoloured.
1428 8p. Type **500** 20 20
1429 8p. "Nayade" (Beatriz Gonzalez) 20 20

501 "Judge Francisco Antonio Moreno y Escandon" (J. Gutierrez)

502 "Fidel Cano" (Francisco Cano)

1977. Air. Bicentenary of National Library. Mult.
1430 20p. Type **501** 55 10
1431 25p. "Viceroy Manuel de Guiror" (unknown artist) 55 20

1977. 90th Anniv of "El Espectador" Magazine by Fidel Cano.
1432 **502** 4p. multicoloured . . . 20 10

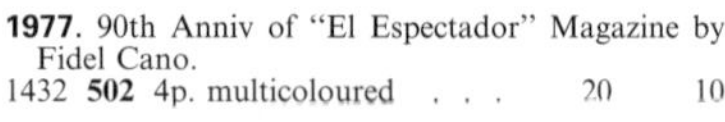

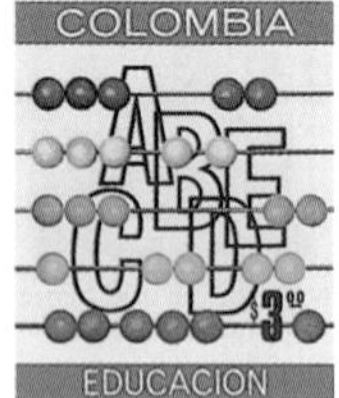

503 Abacus and Alphabet

1977. Popular Education.
1433 **503** 3p. multicoloured . . . 15 10

1977. Arms of Barranquilla. As T **476**.
1434 5p. multicoloured 30 15

504 Dr. F. L. Acosta

505 Cauca University Arms

1977. Air. Birth Centenary of Dr. Federico Lleras Acosta (veterinary surgeon).
1435 **504** 5p. multicoloured . . . 30 10

1977. Air. 150th Anniv of Cauca University.
1436 **505** 5p. multicoloured . . . 25 10

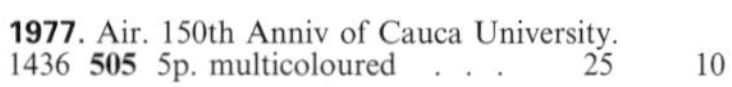

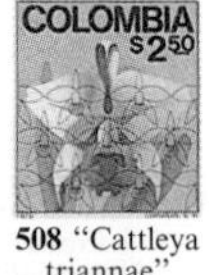

506 "Cudecom" Building, Bogota

508 "Cattleya triannae"

1977. Air. 90th Anniv of Society of Colombian Engineers.
1437 **506** 1p.50 multicoloured . . 10 10

1977. Air. No. 1364 surch **$2.00**.
1438 2p. on 1p.30 multicoloured 90 25

1978.
1439 **508** 2p.50 multicoloured . . 25 10
1439a 3p. multicoloured . . . 25 10

509 Tayronan Lost City

510 "Creator of Energy" (A. Betancourt)

1978. Air.
1440 **509** 3p.50 multicoloured . . 35 10

1978. Air. 150th Anniv of Antioquia University Law School.
1441 **510** 4p. multicoloured . . . 20 10

511 Column of the Slaves

512 "Catalina"

1978. Air. 150th Anniv of Ocana Convention.
1442 **511** 2p.50 multicoloured . . 15 10

1978. Air. 150th Anniv of Cartagena University.
1443 **512** 4p. multicoloured . . . 20 10

513 Running

1978. 13th Central American and Caribbean Games, Medellin. Multicoloured.
1444 10p. Type **513** 35 25
1445 10p. Basketball 35 25
1446 10p. Baseball 35 25
1447 10p. Boxing 35 25
1448 10p. Cycling 35 25
1449 10p. Fencing 35 25
1450 10p. Football 35 25
1451 10p. Gymnastics 35 25
1452 10p. Judo 35 25
1453 10p. Weightlifting 35 25
1454 10p. Wrestling 35 25
1455 10p. Swimming 35 25
1456 10p. Tennis 35 25
1457 10p. Shooting 35 25
1458 10p. Volleyball 35 25
1459 10p. Water polo 35 25

514 "Sigma 2" (A. Herran)

515 Human Figure from Gold Pendant

1978. Centenary of Bogota Chamber of Commerce.
1460 **514** 8p. multicoloured . . . 20 20

1978. Air. Tolima Culture.
1461 **515** 3p.50 multicoloured . . 20 20

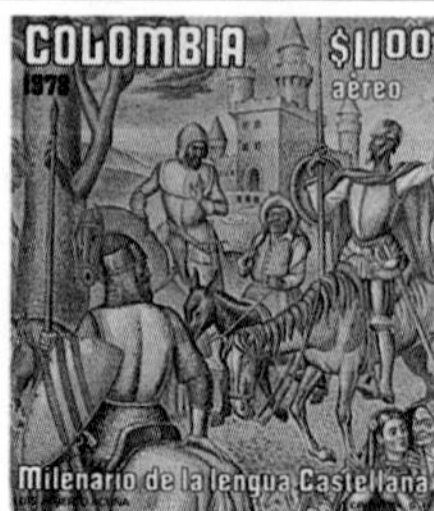

516 "Apotheosis of the Spanish Language" (Left-hand detail of mural, L. A. Acuna)

1978. Air. Millenary of Castilian Language. Multicoloured.
1462 11p. Type **516** 55 50
1463 11p. Central detail 55 50
1464 11p. Right-hand detail . . . 55 50
Nos. 1462/4 were issued together, se-tenant, forming a composite design.

517 Presidential Guard

1978. Air. 50th Anniv of Presidential Guard Battalion.
1465 **517** 9p. multicoloured . . . 25 25

518 Human Figure

519 General Tomas Cipriano de Mosquera

1978. Air. Muisca Culture.
1466 **518** 3p.50 multicoloured . . 20 10

1978. Death Centenary of General Tomas Cipriano de Mosquera (statesman).
1467 **519** 6p. multicoloured . . . 20 20

520 El Camarin de Carmen, Bogota

521 Gold Owl Ornament

1978. Air. "Espamer '78" Stamp Exhibition, Bogota.
1468 **520** 30p. multicoloured . . . 1·75 20

1978. Air. Calima Culture.
1470 **521** 3p.50 multicoloured . . 20 10
1470a 4p. multicoloured . . . 25 10

522 "Virgin and Child" (Gregorio Vasquez)

523 Church and Bullring

1978. Air. Christmas.
1471 **522** 2p.50 multicoloured . . 10 10

1978. Air. Manizales Fair.
1472 **523** 7p. multicoloured . . . 25 15

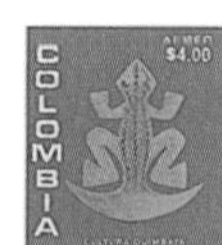

524 Frog in beaten Gold

525 Children playing Hopscotch

1979. Air. Quimbaya Culture.
1473 **524** 4p. multicoloured . . . 15 10

1979. Air. International Year of the Child. Multicoloured.
1474 8p. Type **525** 30 10
1475 12p. Child in sou'wester and oilskins 20 20
1476 12p. Child at blackboard (horiz) 20 20

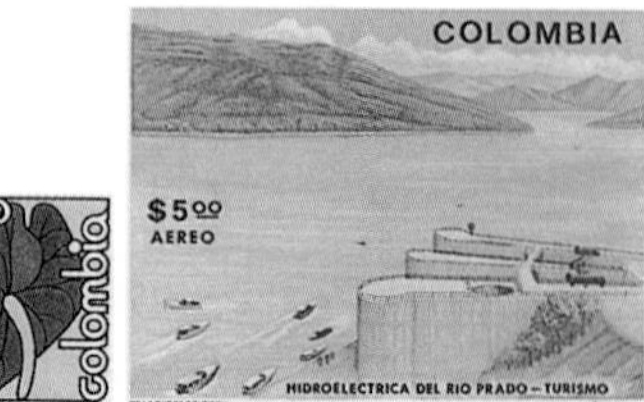

526 Anthurium

527 Rio Prado Hydro-electric Barrage

1979. Anthurium Flowers from Narino. Multicoloured, background colours given.
1477 **526** 3p. light green 25 10
1478 3p. red 25 10
1479 3p. green 25 10
1480 3p. blue 25 10

1979. Arms. As T **476**. Multicoloured.
1481 4p. Sogamoso 45 10
1482 10p. Socorro 20 15
1483 10p. Santa Cruz y San Gil de la Nueva Baeza . . . 20 15

1979. Air. Tourism. Multicoloured.
1484 5p. Type **527** 35 10
1485 7p. River Amazon 60 30
1486 8p. Tomb, San Agustin Archaeological Park . . . 25 20
1487 14p. San Fernando Fort, Cartagena 45 35

528 "Jimenez de Quesada" (after C. Leudo)

1979. Air. 400th Death Anniv of Gonzalo Jimenez de Quesada (conquistador).
1488 **528** 20p. multicoloured . . . 1·60 65

529 Hill and First Stamps of Great Britain and Colombia

1979. Air. Death Centenary of Sir Rowland Hill.
1489 **529** 15p. multicoloured . . . 25 25

530 "Uribe" (after Acevedo Bernal)

1979. 65th Death Anniv of General Rafael Uribe Uribe (statesman).
1490 **530** 8p. multicoloured . . . 30 15

531 "Village" (Leonor Alarcon)

1979. 20th Anniv of Community Works Boards.
1491 **531** 15p. multicoloured . . . 85 30

532 Three Kings and Soldiers

1979. Air. Christmas. Multicoloured.
1492 3p. Type **532** 75 40
1493 3p. Nativity 75 40
1494 3p. Shepherds 75 40

533 River Magdalena Bridge and Avianca Emblem

534 Gold Nose Pendant

1979. Air. 350th Anniv of Barranquilla and 60th Anniv of Avianca National Airline.
1495 **533** 15p. multicoloured . . . 25 15

1980. Air. Tairona Culture.
1496 **534** 3p. multicoloured . . . 25 10

535 "Boy playing Flute" (Judith Leyster)

536 Antonio Jose de Sucre

1980. Air. 2nd International Music Competition, Ibague.
1497 **535** 6p. multicoloured . . . 30 10

1980. Air. 150th Death Anniv of General Antonio Jose de Sucre.
1498 **536** 12p. multicoloured . . . 20 15

537 "The Watchman" (Edgar Negret)

1980. Air. Modern Sculpture.
1499 **537** 25p. multicoloured . . . 1·40 1·25

538 Television Screen

1980. Inaug of Colour Television in Colombia.
1500 **538** 5p. multicoloured . . . 25 10

539 Bullfighting Poster (H. Courttin)

540 "Learn to Write"

1980. Tourism. Festival of Cali.
1501 **539** 5p. multicoloured . . . 35 15

1980. The Alphabet.
1502 **540** 4p. black, brown & grn 25 10
1503 – 4p. multicoloured . . . 25 10
1504 – 4p. brown, blk & lt brn 25 10
1505 – 4p. multicoloured . . . 40 15
1506 – 4p. brown, black & grn 25 10
1507 – 4p. black and turquoise 25 10
1508 – 4p. black and green . . 25 10
1509 – 4p. mauve, black & grn 40 15
1510 – 4p. black and blue . . . 25 10
1511 – 4p. black and green . . 25 10
1512 – 4p. green, black & brown 25 10
1513 – 4p. multicoloured . . . 25 10
1514 – 4p. brown, black & grn 25 10
1515 – 4p. multicoloured . . . 25 10
1516 – 4p. yellow, black & grn 25 10
1517 – 4p. black, brown & yell 25 10
1518 – 4p. brown, black & turq 25 10
1519 – 4p. brown, black & grn 25 10
1520 – 4p. brown, black & grn 25 10
1521 – 4p. yellow, black & turq 25 10
1522 – 4p. green, black & blue 40 15
1523 – 4p. brown, black & grn 25 10
1524 – 4p. green, black & lt grn 25 10
1525 – 4p. multicoloured . . . 25 10
1526 – 4p. multicoloured . . . 25 10
1527 – 4p. brown, black & grn 25 10
1528 – 4p. multicoloured . . . 40 15
1529 – 4p. multicoloured . . . 25 10
1530 – 4p. brown, black & grn 25 10
1531 – 4p. brown and black . . 25 10

DESIGNS: No. 1503, "a" Eagle; 1504, "b" Buffalo; 1505, "c" Andean Condor; 1506, "ch" Chimpanzee; 1507, "d" Dolphin; 1508, "e" Elephant; 1509, "f" Greater Flamingo; 1510, "g" Seagull; 1511, "h" Hippopotamus; 1512, "i" Iguana; 1513, "j" Giraffe; 1514, "k" Koala; 1515, "l" Lion; 1516, "ll" Llama; 1517, "m" Blackbird; 1518, "n" Otter; 1519, Gnu; 1520, "o" Bear; 1521, "p" Pelican; 1522, "q" Resplendent Quetzal; 1523, "r" Rhinoceros; 1524, "s" Grasshopper; 1525, "t" Tortoise; 1526, "u" Magpie; 1527, "v" Viper; 1528, "w" Wagon with animals; 1529, "x" Fox playing xylophone; 1530, "y" Yak; 1531, "z" Fox.

541 "Miraculous Virgin" (statue, Real del Sarte)

1980. Air. 150th Anniv of Apparition of Holy Virgin to Sister Catalina Labouri Gontard in Paris.
1532 **541** 12p. multicoloured . . . 45 15

542 "Country Scene, San Gil" (painting, Luis Roncancio)

1980. Air. Agriculture.
1533 **542** 12p. multicoloured . . . 1·00 30

543 Villavicencio Song Festival

1980. Tourism. Festivals. Multicoloured.
1534 5p. Type **543** 30 15
1535 9p. Vallenato festival . . . 15 15

544 Gustavo Uribe Ramirez and "Samanea saman"

1980. 12th Death Anniv of Gustavo Uribe Ramirez (ecologist).
1536 **544** 10p. multicoloured . . . 35 15

545 Narino Palace

1980. Narino Palace (Presidential residence).
1537 **545** 5p. multicoloured . . . 30 10

546 Monument to First Pioneers, Armenia

1980. City of Armenia.
1538 **546** 5p. multicoloured . . . 30 10

547 Olaya Herrera (after Miguel Diaz Varges)

549 Athlete with Torch

548 "Simple Simon"

1980. Air. Birth Centenary of Dr. Enrique Olaya Herrera (President, 1930–34).
1539 **547** 20p. multicoloured . . . 45 25

1980. Air. Christmas. Illustrations to stories by Rafael Pombo. Multicoloured.
1540 4p. Type **548** 25 15
1541 4p. "The Cat's Seven Lives" 25 15
1542 4p. "The Walking Tadpole" 25 15

1980. 11th National Games, Neiva.
1543 **549** 5p. multicoloured . . . 20 10

550 Golfers

551 Crab pierced by Sword

1980. Air. 28th World Golf Cup, Cajica.
1544 **550** 30p. multicoloured . . . 2·10 1·50

1980. 20th Anniv of Colombian Anti-cancer League.
1545 **551** 10p. multicoloured . . . 35 20

552 "Justice" and University Emblem

1980. 50th Anniv of Refounding of Pontifical Xavier University Law Faculty.
1546 **552** 20p. multicoloured . . . 25 30

553 "Bolivar's Last Moments" (Marcos Leon Marino)

1980. 150th Death Anniv of Simon Bolivar. Multicoloured.
1547 25p. Type **553** (postage) . . 45 35
1548 6p. Bolivar and his last proclamation (air) 25 25

554 St. Pedro Claver

555 Statue of Bird, San Agustin

1981. Air. 400th Birth Anniv of St. Pedro Claver.
1549 **554** 15p. multicoloured . . . 20 30

1981. Air. Archaeological Discoveries. Mult.
1550 7p. Type **555** 30 15
1551 7p. Hypogeum (funeral chamber), Tierradentro 30 15
1552 7p. Hypogeum, Tierradentro (different) 30 15
1553 7p. Statue of man, San Agustin 30 15

556 "Square Abstract" (Omar Rayo)

1981. Air. 4th Biennial Arts Exhibition, Medellin. Multicoloured.
1554 20p. Type **556** 30 20
1555 25p. "Flowers" (Alejandro Obregon) 40 30
1556 50p. "Child with Hobby Horse" (Fernando Botero) 1·50 1·25

557 Diver

1981. Air. 8th South American Swimming Championships, Medellin.
1557 **557** 15p. multicoloured . . . 25 30

558 Santamaria Bull Ring

1981. Air. 50th Anniv of Santamaria Bull Ring, Bogota.
1558 **558** 30p. multicoloured . . . 1·50 80

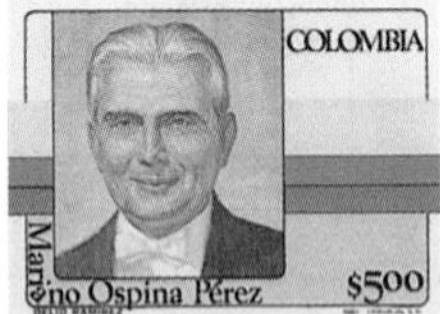

559 Mariano Ospina Perez (after Delio Ramirez)

1981. Presidents of Colombia (1st series). Multicoloured.
1559 5p. Type **559** 25 10
1560 5p. Eduardo Santos (after Ines Acevedo) 25 10
1561 5p. Miguel Abadia Mendez (after Gomez Compuzano) 25 10
1562 5p. Jose Vicente Concha (after Acevedo Bernal) . . 25 10
1563 5p. Carlos E. Restrepo . . . 25 10
1564 5p. Rafael Reyes (after Acevedo Bernal) 25 10
1565 5p. Santiago Perez 25 10
1566 5p. Manuel Murillo Toro (after Moreno Otero) . . . 25 10
1567 5p. Jose Hilario Lopez . . . 25 10
1568 5p. Jose Maria Obando . . 25 10
See also Nos. 1569/78, 1579/88, 1599/1608, 1615/24 and 1634/43.

1981. Presidents of Colombia (2nd series). Multicoloured.
1569 7p. Type **559** . . . . 2·75 35
1570 7p. As No. 1560 . . . . . 2·75 35
1571 7p. As No. 1561 . . . . . 2·75 35
1572 7p. As No. 1562 . . . . . 2·75 35
1573 7p. As No. 1563 . . . . . 2·75 35
1574 7p. As No. 1564 . . . . . 2·75 35
1575 7p. As No. 1565 . . . . . 2·75 35
1576 7p. As No. 1566 . . . . . 2·75 35
1577 7p. As No. 1567 . . . . . 2·75 35
1578 7p. As No. 1568 . . . . . 2·75 35

1981. Presidents of Colombia (3rd series). As T **559**. Multicoloured.
1579 7p. Pedro Alcantara Herran 2·10 20
1580 7p. Mariano Ospina Rodriguez (after Coriolando Leudo) . . . 2·10 20
1581 7p. Tomas Cipriano de Mosquera . . . . 2·10 20
1582 7p. Santos Gutierrez . . . . 2·10 20
1583 7p. Aquileo Parra (after Constancio Franco) . . . 2·10 20
1584 7p. Rafael Nunez . . . . . 2·10 20
1585 7p. Marco Fidel Suarez (after Jesus Maria Duque) 2·10 20
1586 7p. Pedro Nel Ospina (after Coriolano Leudo) . . . 2·10 20
1587 7p. Enrique Olaya Herrera (after M. Diaz Vargas) . . 2·10 20
1588 7p. Alfonso Lopez Pumarejo (after Luis F. Uscategui) 2·10 20

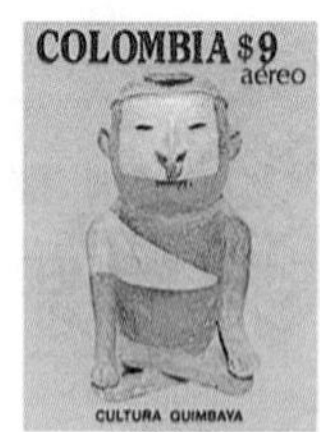

560 Crossed-legged Figure

1981. Air. Quimbaya Culture. Multicoloured.
1589 9p. Type **560** 40 15
1590 9p. Seated figure 40 15
1591 9p. Printing block and print 40 15
1592 9p. Clay pot 40 15

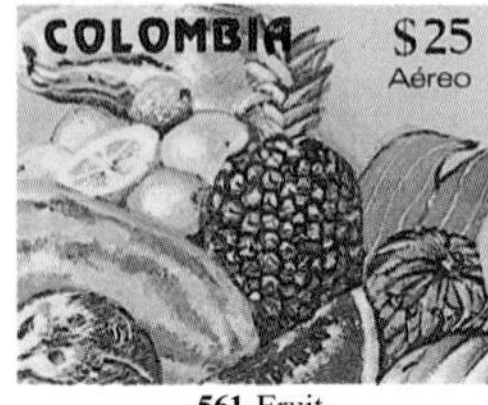

561 Fruit

1981. Air. Fruit. Designs showing fruit.
1593 **561** 25p. multicoloured . . . 2·10 1·40
1594 – 25p. multicoloured . . . 2·10 1·40
1595 – 25p. multicoloured . . . 2·10 1·40
1596 – 25p. multicoloured . . . 2·10 1·40
1597 – 25p. multicoloured . . . 2·10 1·40
1598 – 25p. multicoloured . . . 2·10 1·40
Nos. 1593/8 were issued together in se-tenant blocks of six forming a composite design.

1981. Presidents of Colombia (4th series). As T **559**. Multicoloured.
1599 7p. Manuel Maria Mallarino 1·00 15
1600 7p. Santos Acosta . . . . . 1·00 15
1601 7p. Eustorgio Salgar . . . . 1·00 15
1602 7p. Julian Trujillo . . . . . 1·00 15
1603 7p. Francisco Javier Zaldua (after Francisco Valles) 1·00 15
1604 7p. Jose Eusebio Otalora (after Ricardo Moros) . . 1·00 15
1605 7p. Miguel Antonio Caro 1·00 15
1606 7p. Manuel A. Sanclemente (after Epifanio Garay) . . 1·00 15
1607 7p. Laureano Gomez (after Jose Bascones) . . . . . 1·00 15
1608 7p. Guillermo Leon Valencia (after Luis Angel Rengifo) . . . . 1·00 15

562 "Comunero tearing down Edict" (Manuela Beltran)

1981. Air. Bicentenary of Comuneros Uprising.
1609 **562** 20p. multicoloured . . . 25 30

563 Jose Maria Villa and West Bridge **564** Restrepo (after R. Acevedo Bernal)

1981. West Bridge, Santa Fe de Antioquia.
1610 **563** 60p. multicoloured . . . 65 10

1981. Air. Birth Centenary of Jose Manuel Restrepo (historian).
1611 **564** 35p. multicoloured . . . 35 15

565 Anniversary Emblem **566** Los Nevados National Park

1981. 50th Anniv of Caja Agraria (peasants' bank).
1612 **565** 15p. multicoloured . . . 15 10

1981. Los Nevados National Park.
1613 **566** 20p. multicoloured . . . 20 10

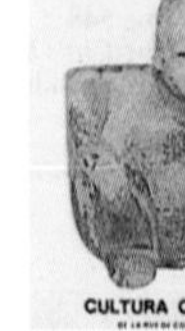

567 Andres Bello **568** Squatting Figure

1981. Birth Centenary of Andres Bello (poet).
1614 **567** 18p. multicoloured . . . 20 15

1981. Presidents of Colombia (5th series). As T **559**. Multicoloured.
1615 7p. Bartolome Calvo (after Miguel Diaz Vargas) . . 60 15
1616 7p. Sergio Camargo 60 15
1617 7p. Jose Maria Rojas Garrido 60 15
1618 7p. J. M. Campo Serrano (after H. L. Brown) . . . 60 15
1619 7p. Eliseo Payan (after R. Moros Urbina) 60 15
1620 7p. Carlos Holguin (after Coriolano Leudo) 60 15
1621 7p. Jose Manuel Marroquin (after Rafael Tavera) . . 60 15
1622 7p. Ramon Gonzalez Valencia (after Jose Maria Vidal) 60 15
1623 7p. Jorge Holguin (after M. Salas Yepes) 60 15
1624 7p. Ruben Piedrahita Arango 60 15

1981. Air. Calima Culture. Multicoloured.
1625 9p. Type **568** 80 15
1626 9p. Vessel with two spouts 80 15
1627 9p. Human-shaped vessel with two spouts 80 15
1628 9p. Pot 80 15

569 1c. Stamp of 1881

1981. Air. Centenary of Admission to U.P.U.
1629 **569** 30p. green and pink . . 30 20

570 Girl with Water Jug

1981. Colombian Solidarity.
1631 **570** 30p. brown, blk & orge 70 30
1632 – 30p. brown, blk & orge 70 30
1633 – 30p. brown, blk & orge 70 30
DESIGNS: No. 1632, Baby with basket; 1633, Boy sitting on wheelbarrow.

1982. Presidents of Colombia (6th series). As T **559**. Multicoloured.
1634 7p. Simon Bolivar 50 15
1635 7p. Francisco de Paula Santander 50 15
1636 7p. Joaquin Mosquera (after C. Franco) 50 15
1637 7p. Domingo Caicedo . . . 50 15
1638 7p. Jose Ignacio de Marquez (after C. Franco) 50 15
1639 7p. Juan de Dios Aranzazu 50 15
1640 7p. Jose de Obaldia (after Jesus M. Duque) 50 15
1641 7p. Guillermo Quintero Calderon (after Silvano Cuellar) 50 15
1642 7p. Carlos Lozano y Lozano (after Helio Ramirez) . . 50 15
1643 7p. Roberto Urdaneta Arbelaez (after Jose Bascones Agneto) 50 15

571 Solano Bay, Choco

1982. Air. Tourism. Multicoloured.
1644 20p. Type **571** 25 30
1645 20p. Tota Lake, Boyaca . . 25 30
1646 20p. Corrales, Boyaca . . . 25 30

573 Gun Club Emblem

1982. Air. Centenary of Bogota Gun Club.
1648 **573** 20p. multicoloured . . . 25 15

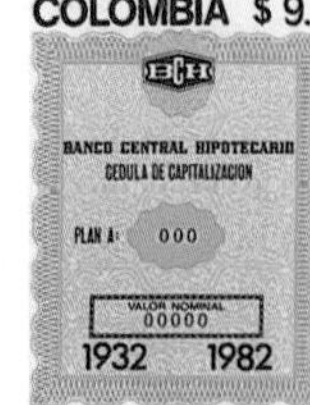

574 Flower Arrangement in Basket **576** Capitalization Certificate

575 Zoomorphic Figure (crocodile)

1982. Country Flowers. Designs showing flower arrangements. Multicoloured.
1649 7p. Type **574** 75 15
1650 7p. Pink arrangement in basket 75 15
1651 7p. Red roses in pot 75 15
1652 7p. Lilac and white arrangement in basket . . 75 15
1653 7p. Orange and yellow arrangement in basket . . 75 15
1654 7p. Mixed arrangement in vase 75 15
1655 7p. Pink roses in vase . . . 75 15
1656 7p. Daisies in pot 75 15
1657 7p. Bouquet of yellow roses 75 15
1658 7p. Pink and yellow arrangement 75 15

1982. Air. Tairona Culture.
1659 **575** 25p. gold, black & brown 90 35
1660 – 25p. gold, black & mve 90 35
1661 – 25p. gold, black & green 90 35
1662 – 25p. gold, black & mve 90 35
1663 – 25p. gold, black & blue 90 35
1664 – 25p. gold, black & red 90 35
DESIGNS—VERT: No. 1660, Anthropomorphic figure with crest; 1661, Anthropomorphic figure with two crests; 1662, Anthropozoomorphic figure; 1663, Anthropozoomorphic figure with elaborate headdress; 1664, Pectoral.

1982. 50th Anniv of Central Mortgage Bank.
1665 **576** 9p. green and black . . 35 20

577 State Governor's Palace, Pereira

1982. Air. Pereira City.
1666 **577** 35p. multicoloured . . . 35 20

578 Biplane and Badge

1982. Air. American Air Forces Co-operation.
1667 **578** 18p. multicoloured . . . 25 15

579 St. Thomas Aquinas **580** St. Theresa of Avila (after Zurbaran)

1982. St. Thomas Aquinas Commemoration.
1668 **579** 5p. multicoloured . . . 15 10

1982. 400th Death Anniv of St. Theresa of Avila.
1669 **580** 5p. multicoloured . . . 15 10

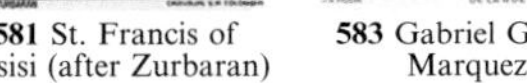

581 St. Francis of Assisi (after Zurbaran) — 583 Gabriel Garcia Marquez

582 Magdalena River

1982. 800th Birth Anniv of St. Francis of Assisi.
1670 **581** 5p. multicoloured . . . 15 10

1982. Air. Tourism.
1671 **582** 30p. multicoloured . . . 2·25 70

1982. Town Arms. As T **476**. Multicoloured.
1672 10p. Buga 25 10
1673 16p. Rionegro 45 15
1674 23p. Honda 25 20

1982. Award of Nobel Prize for Literature to Gabriel Garcia Marquez.
1675 **583** 7p. grey & grn (postage) 25 15
1676 25p. grey & blue (air) . . 20 10
1677 30p. grey and brown . . 25 10

1983. Town Arms. As T **476**. Multicoloured.
1678 10p. San Juan de Pasto . . 30 15
1679 20p. Santa Fe de Bogota . . 25 10

584 "Liberty Fort" (drawing in National Archives)

1983. Air. San Andres Archipelago.
1680 **584** 25p. multicoloured . . . 25 10

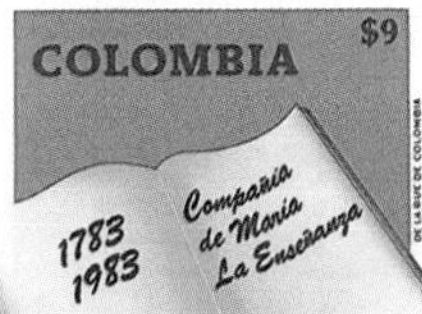

585 Open Book

1983. Bicentenary of First Girls' School, Santa Fe de Bogota.
1681 **585** 9p. grey, black & gold 25 15

586 Sunset

1983. Air. Las Gaviotas Ecological Centre.
1682 **586** 12p. multicoloured . . . 15 10

587 Self-portrait — 588 Radio Bands

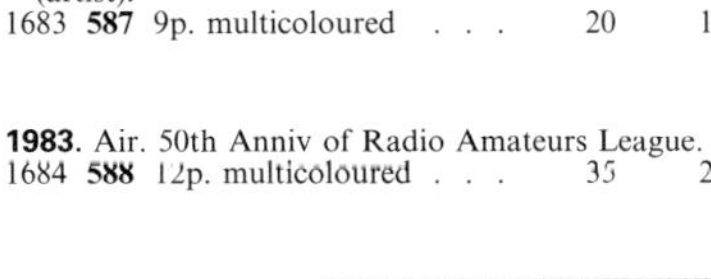

1983. Death Centenary of Jose Maria Espinosa (artist).
1683 **587** 9p. multicoloured . . . 20 10

1983. Air. 50th Anniv of Radio Amateurs League.
1684 **588** 12p. multicoloured . . . 35 20

589 "Dona Rangel de Cuellas donating Territory" (Marcos L. Marino) — 590 Bolivar

1983. 250th Anniv of Cucuta.
1685 **589** 9p. multicoloured . . . 30 15

1983. Birth Bicentenary of Simon Bolivar.
1686 **590** 9p. mult (postage) . . . 25 10
1687 – 30p. yell, bl & red (air) 35 25
1688 – 100p. multicoloured . . 1·25 85

DESIGNS—HORIZ: 30p. Bolivar as national flag. VERT: 100p. Bolivar and flag.

591 Porfirio Barba Jacob (after Frank Linas) — 592 "Passiflora laurifolia"

1983. Birth Centenary of Porfirio Barba Jacob.
1689 **591** 9p. brown and black . . 20 10

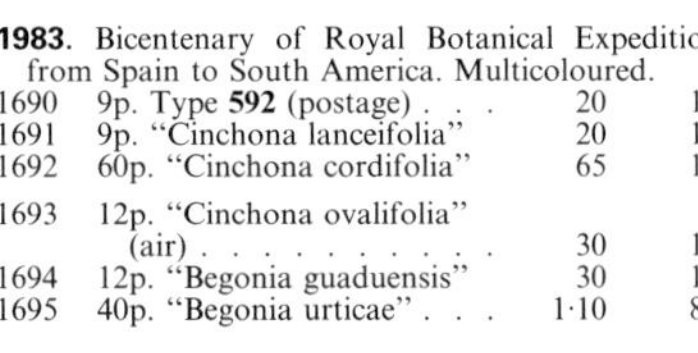

1983. Bicentenary of Royal Botanical Expedition from Spain to South America. Multicoloured.
1690 9p. Type **592** (postage) . . . 20 10
1691 9p. "Cinchona lanceifolia" 20 10
1692 60p. "Cinchona cordifolia" 65 15
1693 12p. "Cinchona ovalifolia" (air) 30 15
1694 12p. "Begonia guaduensis" 30 15
1695 40p. "Begonia urticae" . . . 1·10 80

593 Plaza de la Aduana

1983. Air. 450th Anniv of Cartagena. Mult.
1696 12p. Type **593** 30 15
1697 35p. Cartagena buildings and monuments 80 20

594 "Dawn in the Andes" (Alejandro Obregon) — 595 Scout Badge

1983.
1698 **594** 20p. mult (postage) . . . 75 25
1699 30p. mult (air) . . . . . 1·25 35

1983. Air. 75th Anniv of Boy Scout Movement.
1700 **595** 12p. multicoloured . . . 20 15

596 Santander — 597 Coffee

1984. Francisco de Paula Santander (President of New Granada, 1832–37).
1701 **596** 12p. green 25 15
1702 12p. blue 25 15
1703 12p. red 25 15

1984. Air. Exports.
1704 **597** 14p. purple & green . . 10 10

598 Admiral Jose Prudencio Padilla

1984. Anniversaries. Multicoloured.
1705 10p. Type **598** (birth bicentenary) 75 20
1706 18p. Luis A. Calvo (composer, birth cent) . . 35 15
1707 20p. Diego Fallon (writer, 150th birth anniv) 35 15
1708 20p. Candelario Obeso (writer, death cent) . . . 1·00 30
1709 22p. Luis Eduardo Lopez de Mesa (writer, birth centenary) 45 15

599 Rainbow over Countryside — 600 Stylized Globe on Stand

1984. Marandua, City of the Future.
1710 **599** 15p. mult (postage) . . . 30 15
1711 30p. mult (air) 20 20

1984. Air. 45th Congress of Americanists, Bogota.
1712 **600** 45p. multicoloured . . . 30 30

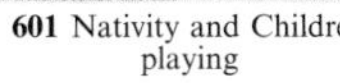

601 Nativity and Children playing — 602 Maria Concepcion Loperena

1984. Christmas.
1713 **601** 12p. mult (postage) . . . 25 10
1714 14p. mult (air) 30 10

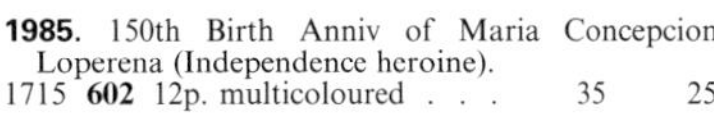

1985. 150th Birth Anniv of Maria Concepcion Loperena (Independence heroine).
1715 **602** 12p. multicoloured . . . 35 25

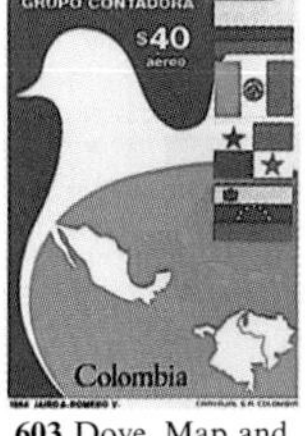

603 Dove, Map and Members' Flags — 604 Mejia and Farman F.40 Type Biplane

1985. Air. Contadora Group.
1716 **603** 40p. multicoloured . . . 40 25

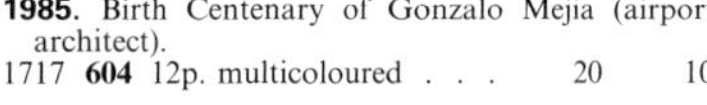

1985. Birth Centenary of Gonzalo Mejia (airport architect).
1717 **604** 12p. multicoloured . . . 20 10

605 "Married Couple" (Pedro nel Gomez)

1985.
1718 **605** 37p. mult (postage) . . . 25 10
1719 40p. mult (air) 40 25

606 Capybara — 607 Straight-billed Woodcreepers

1985. Fauna. Multicoloured. (a) Mammals.
1720 12p. Type **606** (postage) . . 15 10
1721 15p. Ocelot 35 25
1722 15p. Spectacled bear 35 25
1723 20p. Mountain tapir 35 25

(b) Birds.
1724 14p. Lineated woodpeckers (air) 60 40
1725 20p. Type **607** 60 25
1726 50p. Coppery-bellied pufflegs . . . . 1·40 70
1727 55p. Blue-crowned motmots 1·60 80

608 Scenery and Gardel — 609 "Gloria" (cadet ship), "Caldas" (frigate) and Naval Officer

1985. 50th Death Anniv of Carlos Gardel (singer).
1728 **608** 15p. multicoloured . . . 20 10

1985. Air. 50th Anniv of Almirante Padilla Naval College.
1729 **609** 20p. multicoloured . . . 1·25 45

610 Group of Colombians — 611 Alphabet Tree

1985. Air. National Census.
1730 **610** 20p. multicoloured . . . 35 25

1985. National Education Year.
1731 **611** 15p. multicoloured . . . 30 15

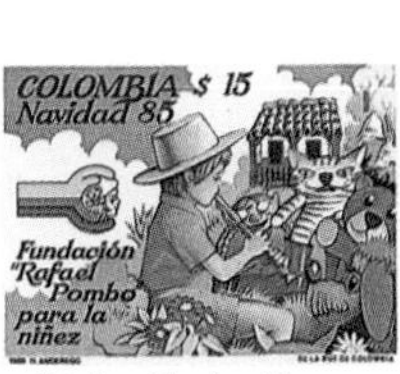

612 Boy Playing Flute to Toys — 613 Pumarejo

1985. Christmas. Multicoloured.
1732 15p. Type **612** (postage) . . 25 15
1733 20p. Girl looking at dressed tree (air) 30 20

1986. Air. Birth Centenary of Alfonso Lopez Pumarejo (President, 1934–38 and 1942–45).
1734 **613** 24p. multicoloured . . . 30 15

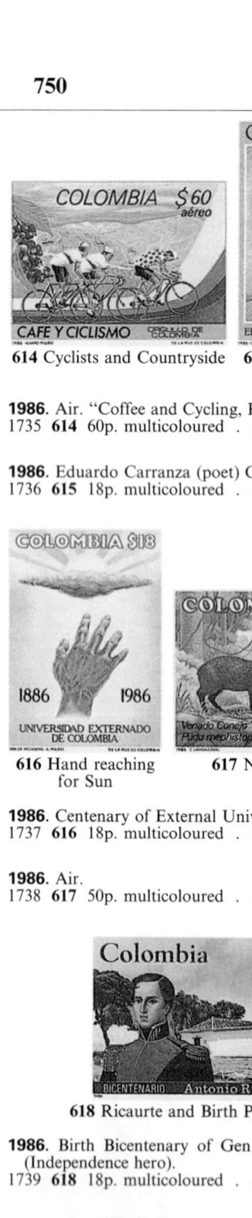

614 Cyclists and Countryside

615 Carranza (after Carlos Dupuy)

1986. Air. "Coffee and Cycling, Pride of Colombia".
1735 **614** 60p. multicoloured . . . 45 25

1986. Eduardo Carranza (poet) Commemoration.
1736 **615** 18p. multicoloured . . . 20 15

616 Hand reaching for Sun

617 Northern Pudu

1986. Centenary of External University.
1737 **616** 18p. multicoloured . . . 30 20

1986. Air.
1738 **617** 50p. multicoloured . . . 60 35

618 Ricaurte and Birth Place, Leiva

1986. Birth Bicentenary of Gen. Antonio Ricaurte (Independence hero).
1739 **618** 18p. multicoloured . . . 20 15

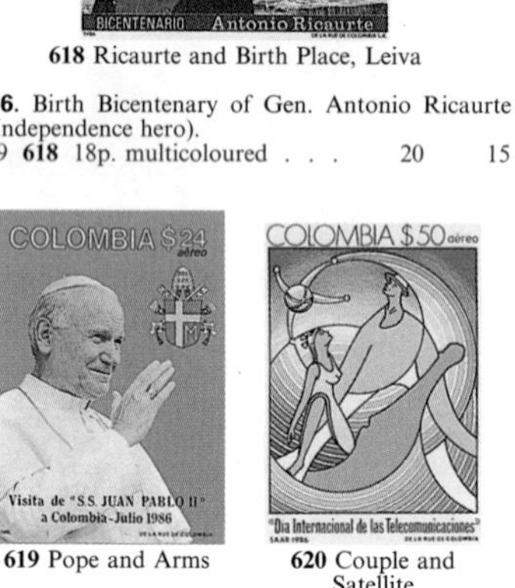

619 Pope and Arms

620 Couple and Satellite

1986. Air. Visit of Pope John Paul II (1st issue).
1740 **619** 24p. multicoloured . . . 35 20
See also Nos. 1745/6.

1986. Air. World Communications Day.
1741 **620** 50p. multicoloured . . . 60 35

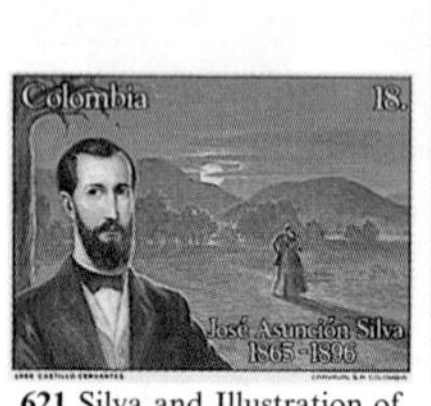

621 Silva and Illustration of "Nocturne"

622 Girl and Doves

1986. 90th Death Anniv of Jose Asuncion Silva (poet).
1742 **621** 18p. multicoloured . . . 20 15

1986. Air. International Peace Year.
1743 **622** 55p. multicoloured . . . 65 40

623 Martinez

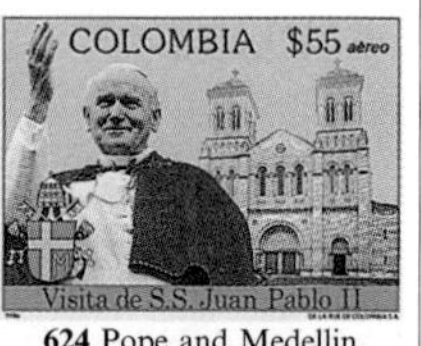

624 Pope and Medellin Cathedral

1986. 10th Death Anniv of Fernando Gomez Martinez (politician and founder of "El Colombiano" newspaper).
1744 **623** 24p. multicoloured . . . 30 20

1986. Air. Visit of Pope John Paul II (2nd issue). Multicoloured.
1745 55p. Type **624** 50 45
1746 60p. Pope giving blessing in Bogota 50 45

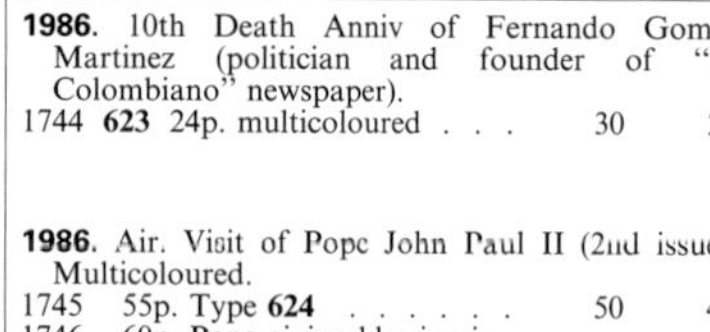

625 Montejo

626 Computer Portrait of Bach

1986. Air. Birth Centenary of Enrique Santos Montejo (journalist and editor of "El Tiempo").
1748 **625** 25p. multicoloured . . . 30 20

1986. Air. Composers' Birth Anniversaries (1985). Multicoloured.
1749 70p. Type **626** (300th anniv) 65 60
1750 100p. "The Permanency of Baroque" (300th annivs of Handel and Bach and 400th anniv of H. Schutz) 75 55

627 De La Salle (founder) and National Colours

1986. Air. Centenary of Brothers of Christian Schools in Colombia.
1751 **627** 25p. multicoloured . . . 30 15

628 Convent of Mercy

1986. 450th Anniv of Santiago de Cali.
1752 20p. Arms (as T **476**) . . . 15 10
1753 25p. Type **628** 15 10

629 Piece of Coal and National Colours

630 Castro Silva

1986. Air. Completion of El Cerrejon Coal Complex.
1754 **629** 55p. multicoloured . . . 40 40

1986. Birth Centenary (1985) of Jose Vincente Castro Silva (Principal of Senior College of the Rosary).
1755 **630** 20p. multicoloured . . . 25 15

631 "The Five Signatories" (detail, R. Vasquez)

1986. Air. Centenary of Constitution.
1756 **631** 25p. multicoloured . . . 30 20

1986. Arms of Antioquia. As T **476**.
1758 55p. multicoloured 20 10

632 Garcia Lorca

1986. Air. 50th Death Anniv of Federico Garcia Lorca (poet).
1759 **632** 60p. multicoloured . . . 35 25

633 Symbolic Prism

634 Maya

1986. Centenary of Fine Art Faculty and 50th Anniv of Architecture Faculty at National University.
1760 **633** 40p. multicoloured . . . 20 30

1986. 6th Death Anniv of Rafael Maya (poet and critic).
1761 **634** 25p. multicoloured . . . 30 20

635 Andean Condor

636 "Thanks! Friends of the World"

1986.
1762 **635** 20p. blue 35 20
1763 25p. blue 35 20

1986. Air. Thanks for Help after Devastation of Armero by Volcanic Eruption, 1985.
1767 **636** 50p. multicoloured . . . 60 35

637 Mestiza Virgin (from crib at Pasto)

638 Left-hand Side of Mural

1986. Air. Christmas.
1768 **637** 25p. multicoloured . . . 30 15

1987. Air. 450th Anniv of Popayan City. "The Apotheosis of Popayan" by Ephram Martinez Zambrano. Multicoloured.
1769 100p. Type **638** . . . . . . 1·40 75
1770 100p. Right-hand side of mural . . . . 1·40 75
Nos. 1769/70 were printed together, se-tenant, forming a composite design.

639 Uribe Mejia

640 "Conversion of St. Augustine of Hippo"

1987. Birth Centenary (1986) of Pedro Uribe Mejia (coffee industry pioneer).
1771 **639** 25p. multicoloured . . . 30 15

1987. Air. 1600th Anniv of Conversion of St. Augustine.
1772 **640** 30p. multicoloured . . . 10 10

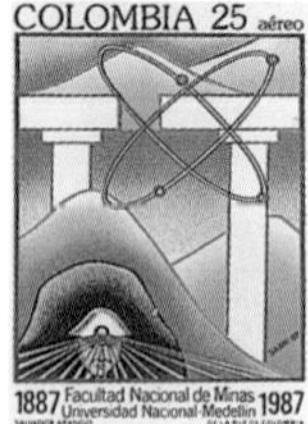

641 Atomic Diagram, Pit Props and Miner in Shaft

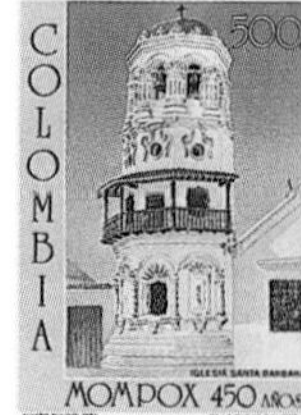

642 St. Barbara's Church

1987. Air. Centenary of National Mines Faculty of National University, Medellin.
1773 **641** 25p. multicoloured . . . 10 10

1987. 450th Anniv of Mompox City.
1774 **642** 500p. multicoloured . . 2·50 2·50

643 Hawk-headed Parrot

644 White Horse

1987. Fauna.
1775 **643** 30p. green (postage) . . 90 25
1776 – 30p. purple 45 20
1777 – 30p. red (air) 90 25
1778 – 35p. brown 15 20
DESIGNS—HORIZ: No. 1776, Boutu; 1778, South American red-lined turtle. VERT: No. 1777, Greater flamingo.
See also Nos. 1807/9, 1815/17, 1823/6 and 1855/8.

1987. Air. Pure-bred Horses. Multicoloured.
1779 60p. Type **644** 45 35
1780 70p. Black horse 45 35

645 Mastheads, Fidel Cano (founder), Luis Cano, Luis Gabriel Cano Isaza and Alfonso Cano Isaza (editors)

1987. Air. Cent of "El Espectador" (newspaper).
1781 **645** 60p. multicoloured . . . 25 15

646 Isaacs and Scene from "Maria"

1987. 150th Birth Anniv of Jorge Isaacs (writer).
1782 **646** 70p. multicoloured . . . 25 10

648 Mutis and Illustration of "Condor"

1987. 33rd Death Anniv of Aurelio Martinez Mutis (poet).
1785 **648** 90p. multicoloured . . . 1·25 55

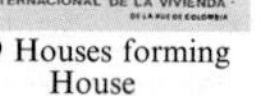

649 Houses forming House

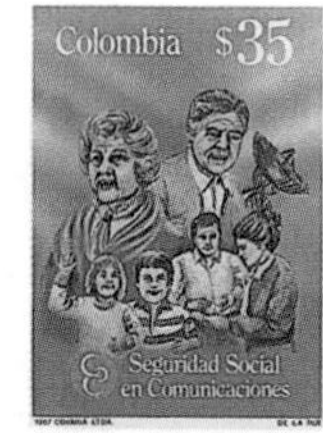

650 Family and Dish Aerial

1987. Air. International Year of Shelter for the Homeless.
1786 **649** 60p. multicoloured . . . 65 35

1987. Social Security and Communications.
1787 **650** 35p. multicoloured . . . 30 20

651 Flags

652 Nativity Scene in Globe

1987. Air. 1st Meeting of Eight Latin-American Presidents of Contadora and Lima Groups, Acapulco, Mexico.
1788 **651** 80p. multicoloured . . . 55 55

1987. Air. Christmas.
1789 **652** 30p. multicoloured . . . 30 15

653 Houses, Telephone Wires and Dials

1987. Air. Rural Telephone Network.
1790 **653** 70p. multicoloured . . . 35 10

654 Mountain Sanctuaries

655 Flower (Life)

1988. Air. 450th Anniv of Bogota (1st issue).
1791 **654** 70p. multicoloured . . . 25 70
See also Nos. 1803/4.

1988. 40th Anniv of Declaration of Human Rights (1st issue).
1792 **655** 30p. green 10 10
1793 – 35p. red 10 10
1794 – 40p. lilac 15 10
1795 – 40p. blue 10 10
DESIGNS—VERT: No. 1793, Road (Freedom of choice). HORIZ: 1794, Circle of children (Freedom of association); 1795, Couple on bench (Communication).
See also Nos. 1840/1.

657 Mask

1988. Air. Gold Museum, Bogota. Multicoloured.
1796 70p. Type **657** 30 30
1797 80p. Votive figure 60 30
1798 90p. Human figure 85 65

658 Pasto Cathedral

659 Waterfall

1988. 450th Anniv of Pasto.
1799 **658** 60p. multicoloured . . . 40 20

1988. Centenary of Bogota Water Supply and Sewerage Organization.
1800 **659** 100p. multicoloured . . 35 10

660 Score and Composers

661 M. Currea de Aya

1988. Centenary (1987) of National Anthem by Rafael Nunez and Oreste Sindici.
1801 **660** 70p. multicoloured . . . 25 25

1988. Birth Centenary of Maria Currea de Aya (women's rights pioneer).
1802 **661** 80p. multicoloured . . . 25 10

662 Modern Bogota

664 College

1988. Air. 450th Anniv of Bogota (2nd issue). Multicoloured.
1803 80p. Type **662** 55 30
1804 90p. Street in old Bogota (horiz) 60 30

1988. Fauna. As T **643**.
1807 35p. brown 25 15
1808 35p. green 25 15
1809 40p. orange 25 15
DESIGNS—HORIZ: No. 1807, Crab-eating racoon; 1808, Caribbean monk seal; 1809, Giant otter.

1988. Centenary of Return of Society of Jesus to St. Bartholomew's Senior College.
1810 **664** 120p. multicoloured . . 35 20

665 Eduardo Santos

666 Mother and Children

1988. Personalities. Multicoloured.
1811 80p. Type **665** (birth centenary) (postage) . . . 45 25
1812 90p. Jorge Alvarez Lleras (astronomer) 45 25
1813 80p. Zipa Tisquesusa (16th-century Indian chief) (air) 45 25

1988. Air. Christmas.
1814 **666** 40p. multicoloured . . . 15 10

1988. Fauna. As T **643**.
1815 40p. grey (postage) 15 10
1816 45p. violet 75 25
1817 45p. blue (air) 75 25
DESIGNS—HORIZ: No. 1815, American manatee; 1816, Masked trogon. VERT: No. 1817, Blue-bellied curassow.

667 Andres Bello College

1988.
1818 **667** 115p. multicoloured . . 35 20

668 Building and Nieto Caballero

669 Gomez

1989. Air. Birth Centenary of Agustin Nieto Caballero (educationalist).
1819 **668** 100p. multicoloured . . 30 15

1989. Air. Birth Centenary of Laureano Gomez (President, 1950–53).
1820 **669** 45p. multicoloured . . . 15 10

670 Map

1989. Air. International Coffee Organization.
1821 **670** 110p. multicoloured . . 30 15

671 Modern Flats, Recreation Area and Hands holding Brick

1989. Air. 12th Habitat U.N. Conference on Human Settlements, Cartagena.
1822 **671** 100p. multicoloured . . 20 10

1989. Fauna. As T **643**.
1823 40p. brown (postage) . . . 10 10
1824 45p. black 75 25
1825 55p. brown 15 10
1826 45p. blue (air) 10 10
DESIGNS—HORIZ: No. 1823, White-tailed deer; 1824, Harpy eagle; 1826, Blue discus. VERT: No. 1825, False anole.

672 Emblem

1989. 25th Anniv of Adpostal (postal administration).
1827 **672** 45p. multicoloured . . . 10 10

673 Hands

675 "Simon Bolivar" (Pedro Jose Figueroa)

1989. Air. Bicentenary of French Revolution.
1828 **673** 100p. multicoloured . . 20 10

1989. 170th Anniv of Liberation Campaign. Multicoloured.
1830 40p. Type **675** 10 10
1831 40p. "Santander" (Figueroa) 10 10
1832 45p. "Bolivar and Santander during the Campaign for the Plains" (J. M. Zamora) (46 × 37 mm) . . 10 10
1833 45p. "From Boyaca to Santa Fe" (left-hand detail) (Francisco de P. Alvarez) (29 × 36 mm) 10 10
1834 45p. Right-hand detail (29 × 36 mm) 10 10
1835 45p. Mounted officer and foot soldiers (left-hand detail) (31 × 51 mm) . . . 35 10
1836 45p. Mounted officer (centre detail) (33 × 51 mm) . . . 35 10
1837 45p. Mounted soldiers with flag (right-hand detail) (31 × 51 mm) 35 35
Nos. 1833/4 and 1835/7 (showing details of triptych by A. de Santa Maria) were issued together, se-tenant, each forming a composite design.

676 Founder's House

1989. 450th Anniv of Tunja.
1839 **676** 45p. multicoloured . . . 10 10

1989. Human Rights (2nd issue). As T **655**.
1840 45p. brown (postage) . . . 10 10
1841 55p. green (air) 15 10
DESIGNS—HORIZ: 45p. Musicians (Culture). VERT: 55p. Family.

677 Healthy Children and Shadowy Figures

678 Gold Ornaments of Quimbaya, Calima and Tolima

1989. Air. Anti-drugs Campaign.
1842 **677** 115p. multicoloured . . 25 15

1989. Air. America. Pre-Columbian Crafts. Multicoloured.
1843 115p. Type **678** 25 15
1844 130p. Indian making pot and Sinu ceramic figure (horiz) 25 15

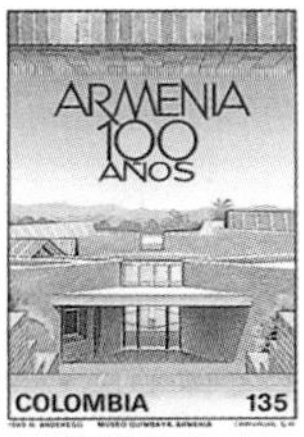

679 Quimbaya Museum

680 Mantilla

1989. Centenary of Armenia City.
1815 **679** 135p. multicoloured . . 25 15

1989. Air. 45th Death Anniv of Joaquin Quijano Mantilla (chronicler).
1846 **680** 170p. multicoloured . . 75 20

681 Boeing 767 and Globe

682 "The Fathers of the Fatherland leaving Congress" (R. Acevedo Bernal)

1989. Air.
1847 **681** 130p. multicoloured . . 45 15

1989. Air. 170th Anniv of Creation of First Republic of Colombia (1851) and 168th Anniv of its Constitution (others). Multicoloured.
1848 130p. Type **682** 55 15
1849 130p. "Church of the Rosary, Cucuta" (Carmelo Fernandez) . . 55 15
1850 130p. Republic's arms . . . 55 15
1851 130p. "Bolivar at Congress of Angostura" (46 × 36 mm) (Tito Salas) 55 15

683 Nativity (Barro-Raquira clay figures)

684 "Plaza de la Aduana" (H. Lemaitre)

1989. Air. Christmas.
1852 **683** 55p. multicoloured . . . 40 10

1990. Air. Presidential Summit, Cartagena.
1853 **684** 130p. multicoloured . . 60 40

685 Headphones on Marble Head

687 "Espeletia hartwegiana"

686 Cuervo Borda and National Museum

1990. Air. 50th Anniv of Colombia National Radio.
1854 **685** 150p. multicoloured . . 30 15

1990. Fauna. As T **643**.
1855 50p. grey 10 10
1856 50p. purple 10 10
1857 60p. brown 15 10
1858 60p. brown 60 20
DESIGNS: No. 1855, Grey fox; 1856, Common poison-arrow frog; 1857, Pygmy marmoset; 1858, Sun-bittern.

1990. Air. Velez City Arms. As T **476**.
1859 60p. multicoloured 15 10

1990. Air. Birth Centenary (1989) of Teresa Cuervo Borda (artist).
1860 **686** 60p. multicoloured . . . 15 10

1990. Multicoloured.
1861 60p. Type **687** 15 10
1862 60p. "Ceiba pentandra" (horiz) 15 10
1863 70p. "Ceroxylon quindiuense" 15 10
1864 70p. "Tibouchina lepidota" 15 10

688 Theatrical Masks

689 Statue, Bogota

1990. Air. 2nd Iberian-American Theatre Festival, Bogota.
1865 **688** 150p. gold, brown & orge 60 15

1990. 150th Death Anniv of Francisco de Paula Santander (President of New Granada, 1832–37). Multicoloured.
1866 50p. Type **689** (postage) . . 40 10
1867 60p. Gateway of National Pantheon (air) 40 10
1868 60p. "General Santander with the Constitution" (Jose Maria Espinosa) . . 40 10
1869 70p. Santander, organizer of public education (after F. S. Guitierrez) 40 10
1870 70p. "The Postal Carrier" (Jose Maria del Castillo) (horiz) 40 10

690 Postmen

1990. Air. 150th Anniv of the Penny Black.
1872 **690** 150p. multicoloured . . 30 15

691 Cadet, Arms and School

693 Graph

692 Cable

1990. 50th Anniv of General Santander Police Cadets School.
1873 **691** 60p. multicoloured . . . 15 10

1990. Air. Trans-Caribbean Submarine Fibre Optic Cable.
1874 **692** 150p. multicoloured . . 60 15

1990. Air. 50th Anniv of I.F.I.
1875 **693** 60p. multicoloured . . . 15 10

1990. Arms of Cartago. As T **476**.
1876 50p. multicoloured 35 10

695 Map

696 Women on Beach

1990. Air. 10th Anniv of Organization of American States.
1878 **695** 130p. multicoloured . . 55 15

1990. La Guajira.
1879 **696** 60p. multicoloured . . . 15 10

697 Indian wearing Gold Ornaments

698 St. John Bosco (founder) and Boys

1990. Air. 50th Anniv of Gold Museum, Bogota.
1880 **697** 170p. multicoloured . . 35 20

1990. Centenary of Salesian Brothers in Colombia.
1881 **698** 60p. multicoloured . . . 15 10

699 Brown Pelican, Roseate Spoonbills and Dolphins

1990. Air. America. Natural World. Multicoloured.
1882 150p. Type **699** . . . . . . 1·00 30
1883 170p. Land animals and Salvin's curassows . . . . 1·00 30

700 Christ Child

701 Monastery

1990. Air. Christmas.
1884 **700** 70p. multicoloured . . . 15 10

1990. Air. Monastery of Nostra Senhora de las Lajas, Ipiales.
1885 **701** 70p. multicoloured . . . 15 10

702 Titles and Abstract

703 Christ of the Miracles, Buga Church

1991. Air. Bicentenary of "La Prensa".
1886 **702** 170p. multicoloured . . 30 15

1991.
1887 **703** 70p. multicoloured . . . 15 10

704 "Anaea syene"

705 Humpback Whale leaping from Water

1991. Butterflies. Multicoloured.
1888 70p. Type **704** (postage) . . 15 10
1889 70p. "Callithea philotima" (horiz) 15 10
1890 80p. "Thecla coronata" 15 10
1891 80p. "Agrias amydon" (horiz) (air) 15 10
1892 170p. "Morpho rhetenor" (horiz) 30 15
1893 190p. "Heliconius longarenus ernestus" (horiz) 35 20

1991. Air. Marine Mammals. Multicoloured.
1894 80p. Type **705** 15 10
1895 170p. Humpback whale diving 60 15
1896 190p. Amazon dolphins (horiz) 65 20

706 National Colours

1991. New Constitution.
1897 **706** 70p. multicoloured . . . 15 10
See also No. 1914.

707 Dario Echandia Olaya (after Delio Ramirez)

708 Girardot (after Jose Maria Espinosa)

1991. 2nd Death Anniv of Dario Echandia Olaya.
1898 **707** 80p. multicoloured . . . 15 10

1991. Birth Bicent of Colonel Atanasio Girardot.
1899 **708** 70p. multicoloured . . . 15 10

709 Galan

710 Stone Statue of God, San Agustin

1991. 2nd Death Anniv of Luis Carlos Galan Sarmiento (politician).
1900 **709** 80p. multicoloured . . . 15 10

1991. Pre-Columbian Art. Multicoloured.
1901 80p. Type **710** (postage) . . 15 10
1902 90p. Burial vessel, Tierradentro 15 10
1903 90p. Statue, San Agustin (air) 15 10
1904 210p. Gold flyingfish, San Agustin (horiz) 50 20

711 Sailfish

1991.
1905 **711** 830p. multicoloured . . 2·50 1·00

712 Cloisters of St. Augustine's, Tunja

1991. Architecture. Multicoloured.
1906 80p. Type **712** (postage) . . 15 10
1907 90p. Bridge, Chia 15 10
1908 90p. Roadside chapel, Pamplona (vert) (air) . . 15 10
1909 190p. Church of the Conception, Santa Fe de Bogota (vert) 60 20

713 "Santa Maria"

714 Lleras Camargo (after Rafael Salas)

1991. Air. America. Voyages of Discovery. Mult.
1910 90p. Type **713** 35 20
1911 190p. Amerindians and approaching ship 85 30

1991. 1st Death Anniv of Alberto Lleras Camargo (President, 1945–46 and 1958–62).
1912 **714** 80p. multicoloured . . . 15 10

715 Police Officers, Transport, Emblem and Flag

1991. Centenary of Police.
1913 **715** 80p. multicoloured . . . 30 10

1991. Air. New Constitution (2nd issue). As No. 1897 but new value and additionally inscr "SANTAFE DE BOGOTA. D.C. Julio 4 de 1991".
1914 90p. multicoloured 15 10

716 Member Nations' Flags

717 First Government Building, Sogamoso

1991. Air. 5th Group of Rio Presidential Summit, Cartagena.
1915 **716** 190p. multicoloured . . 30 15

1991.
1916 **717** 80p. multicoloured . . . 10 10

718 "Adoration of the Kings" (Baltazar de Figueroa)

719 D. Turbay Quintero

1991. Air. Christmas.
1917 **718** 90p. multicoloured . . . 15 10

1992. Diana Turbay Quintero (journalist) Commemoration.
1918 **719** 80p. multicoloured . . . 10 10

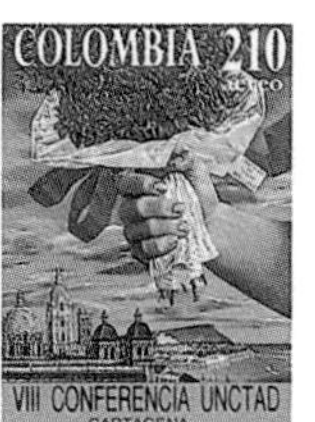

720 Hand holding Posy of Flowers

721 Cut Flowers

1992. Air. 8th U.N. Conference on Trade and Development Session, Cartagena.
1919 **720** 210p. multicoloured . . 35 20

1992. Air. Exports.
1920 90p. Type **721** 15 10
1921 210p. Fruits and nuts (horiz) 35 20

722 Statue of General Santander, Barranquilla (R. Verlet)

723 Music, Book and Paint Brush

1992. Birth Bicentenary of General Francisco de Paula Santander. Multicoloured.
1922 80p. Type **722** (postage) . . 10 10
1923 190p. Francisco de Paula Santander (after Sergio Trujillo Magnenat) (air) 30 15

1992. Air. Copyright Protection.
1925 **723** 190p. multicoloured . . 30 15

725 Lievano Aguirre

726 Enrique Low Murtra (1st anniv)

1992. 10th Death Anniv of Indalecio Lievano Aguirre (ambassador to United Nations).
1928 **725** 80p. multicoloured . . . 10 10

1992. Death Anniversaries of Justice Ministers. Multicoloured.
1929 100p. Type **726** 15 10
1930 110p. Rodrigo Lara Bonilla (8th anniv) 20 10

727 Town Arms and Rings

1992. 14th National Games, Barranquilla.
1931 **727** 110p. multicoloured . . 20 10

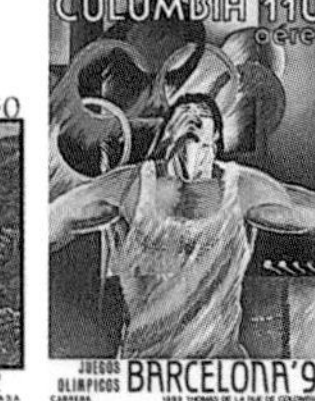

728 Landscape

729 Athlete and Olympic Rings

1992. Air. 2nd U.N. Conference on Environment and Development, Rio de Janeiro. Paintings by Roberto Palomino. Multicoloured.
1932 230p. Type **728** 35 20
1933 230p. Birds in trees 35 20

1992. Air. Olympic Games, Barcelona.
1934 **729** 110p. multicoloured . . 20 10

730 "Discovery of America by C. Columbus" (Dali)

1992. Air. America. Multicoloured.
1935 230p. Type **730** 80 30
1936 260p. "America Magic, Myth and Legend" (Al. Vivero) . . . . 1·00 75

731 American Crocodile

1992. Endangered Animals. Multicoloured.
1937 100p. Type **731** 15 10
1938 100p. Andean condor (vert) 45 30

732 Maria Lopez de Escobar (founder)

734 Map of the Americas

733 Avianca Colombia McDonnell Douglas MD-83

1992. 50th Anniv of House of Mother and Child.
1939 **732** 100p. mult (postage) . . 15 10
1940 110p. mult (air) 20 10

1992. Air.
1941 **733** 110p. multicoloured . . 20 10

1992. Meeting of First Ladies of the Americas and the Caribbean, Cartagena.
1942 **734** 100p. multicoloured . . 15 10

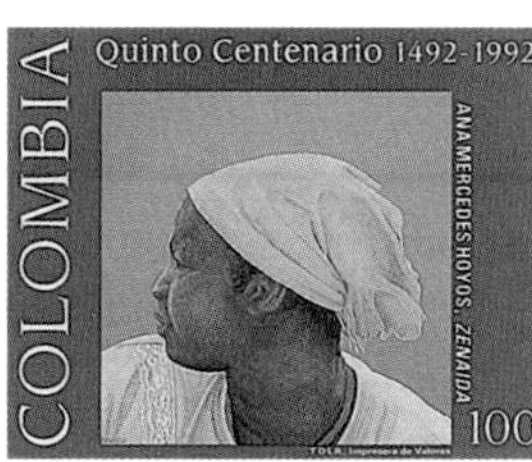

735 "Zenaida" (Ana Mercedes Hoyos)

1992. 500th Anniv of Discovery of America by Columbus. Paintings.
1943 **735** 100p. mult (postage) . . 15 10
1944 – 110p. multicoloured . . 20 10
1946 – 110p. mult (air) 20 10
1947 – 230p. multicoloured . . 35 20
1948 – 260p. green and violet 40 20

DESIGNS: 110p. (1944), "Study for 1/500" (Beatriz Gonzalez); 110p. (1946), "Blue Eagle" (Alejandro Obregon); 230p. "Cantileo" (Luis Luna); 260p. "Maize" (Antonio Caro).

736 Recycling

1992.
1949 **736** 100p. multicoloured . . 15 10

737 Front Curtain

1992. Air. Columbus Theatre.
1950 **737** 230p. multicoloured . . 35 20

739 "Nativity" (Carlos Alfonso Mendez)

1992. Christmas. Children's Drawings. Mult.
1952 100p. Type **739** (postage) . . 15 10
1953 110p. Kings approaching stable (Catalina del Valle) (air) 20 10

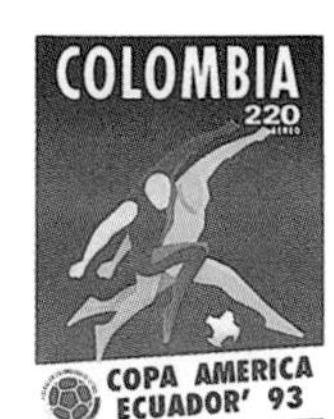

740 G. Lara

748 Footballers

742 Campaign Emblem

1992. Air. 10th Death Anniv of Gloria Lara (ambassador to the United Nations).
1954 **740** 230p. multicoloured . . 40 20

1993. Lions Club International Amblyopia Prevention Campaign.
1956 **742** 100p. multicoloured . . 15 10

1993. Air. America Cup Football Championship, Ecuador.
1962 **748** 220p. multicoloured . . 35 20

749 Prisoners

1993. Bicentenary of French Declaration of Human Rights. Multicoloured.
1963 150p. Type **749** (postage) . . 25 15
1964 150p. The elderly 25 15
1965 200p. The infirm 35 20
1966 200p. Children 35 20
1968 220p. Women (air) 35 20
1969 220p. The poor 35 20
1970 460p. Environmental protection . . . . 1·00 40
1971 520p. Immigrants . . . . . 1·10 45

750 Amerindian (Jose Luis Correal)

752 Green-winged Macaw ("Papagayo")

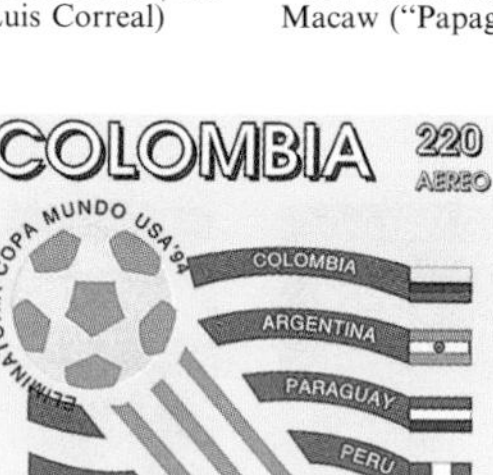

751 Emblem and Flags

1993. Air. International Year of Indigenous Peoples.
1972 **750** 460p. multicoloured . . 70 35

1993. Air. World Cup Football Championship, U.S.A. (1994) (1st issue).
1973 **751** 220p. multicoloured . . 35 20
See also Nos. 2006/9.

1993. The Amazon. Multicoloured.
1974 150p. Type **752** (postage) . . 60 40
1975 150p. Anaconda 20 10
1976 220p. Water-lilies (air) . . . 35 20
1977 220p. Ipecacuanha flower 35 20

753 Cotton-headed Tamarin

755 Nativity

754 Alberto Pumarejo (politician)

1993. Air. America. Endangered Animals. Mult.
1979 220p. Type **753** 35 20
1980 220p. American purple gallinule 60 30
1981 460p. Andean cock of the rock 90 40
1982 520p. American manatee . . 80 40

1993. Famous Colombians. Multicoloured.
1983 150p. Type **754** 20 10
1984 150p. Lorencita Villegas de Santos (First Lady, 1938–42) 20 10
1985 150p. Meliton Rodriguez (photographer) 20 10
1986 150p. Tomas Carrasquilla (writer) 20 10

1993. Christmas. Multicoloured.
1987 200p. Type **755** (postage) . . 30 15
1988 220p. Shepherd (air) 35 20

756 San Andres y Providencia

1993. Tourism. Multicoloured.

1989	220p. Type **756**	35	20
1990	220p. Cocuy National Park	35	20
1991	220p. La Cocha Lake	35	20
1992	220p. Waterfall, La Macarena mountains	35	20
1993	460p. Chicamocha (vert)	70	35
1994	460p. Sierra Nevada de Santa Marta (vert)	70	35
1995	520p. Embalse de Penol (vert)	80	40

See also No. E1996.

757 Museum Entrance

759 Yellow-eared Conure

1993. 170th Anniv of National Museum.

1997	**757** 150p. multicoloured	20	10

1994. Birds. Multicoloured.

1999	180p. Type **759** (postage)	70	45
2000	240p. Bogota rail	90	60
2001	270p. Toucan barbets (horiz) (air)	1·10	70
2002	560p. Cinnamon teals (horiz)	2·10	1·40

760 Emblem

1994. Air. International Decade for Natural Disaster Reduction. National Disaster Prevention System.

2003	**760** 630p. blue, yellow & red	95	50

762 Escriva de Balaguer

1994. Air. Beatification of Josemaria Escriva de Balaguer (founder of Opus Dei).

2005	**762** 560p. multicoloured	85	45

763 Trophy and Player and Emblem on Flag

1994. World Cup Football Championship, U.S.A. (2nd issue). Multicoloured.

2006	180p. Type **763** (postage)	25	15
2008	270p. Match scene, trophy and emblem (air)	40	20
2009	560p. Trophy, emblem, ball and national colours (vert)	85	45

764 Flagpoles **765** "Self-portrait"

1994. Air. 4th Latin American Presidential Summit, Cartagena.

2011	**764** 630p. multicoloured	95	50

See also No. E2010.

1994. Birth Centenary of Ricardo Rendon (painter).

2012	**765** 240p. black	30	15

766 Biplane and William Knox Martin

1994. Air. 75th Anniv of First Airmail Flight.

2013	**766** 270p. multicoloured	35	20

767 Emblem

1994. 40th Anniv of Radio and Television Network.

2014	**767** 180p. multicoloured	25	15

768 Numbers, Graphs and Pie Chart **770** Horse and Bicycle

1994. 1993 Census.

2015	**768** 240p. multicoloured	30	15

1994. Air. America. Postal Transport. Mult.

2017	**770** 270p. multicoloured	35	20

See also No. E2018.

771 Founders and Pi Symbol

1994. Centenary of Colombian Society of Engineers.

2019	**771** 180p. multicoloured	25	15

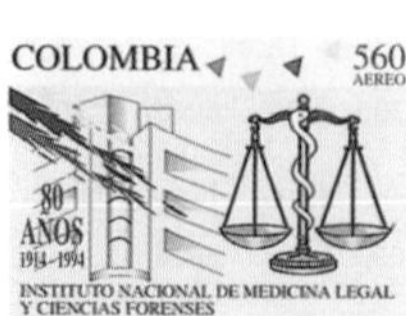

772 Building and Scales

1994. Air. 80th Anniv of National Institute of Legal Medicine and Forensic Sciences.

2020	**772** 560p. multicoloured	75	40

773 Three Wise Men

1994. Air. Christmas.

2021	**773** 270p. multicoloured	35	20

See also No. E2022.

774 1921 SCADTA 30c. Stamp

775 Common Iguana

1995. Air. 75th Anniv (1994) of Sociedad Colombo-Alemana de Transportes Aereos (SCADTA) (private air company contracted to carry mail).

2023	**774** 330p. pink, brown & blk	60	25

1995. Air. Flora and Fauna. Multicoloured.

2024	650p. Type **775**	85	45
2025	650p. Iguana facing left	85	45
2026	750p. Forest (left detail)	1·00	50
2027	750p. Forest (right detail)	1·00	50

Stamps of the same value were issued together in se-tenant pairs, each pair forming a composite design.

776 1920 10c. Stamp

1995. Air. 75th Anniv of Compania Colombiana de Navagacion Aerea (private air company contracted to carry mail).

2028	**776** 330p. multicoloured	45	25

778 Jose Miguel Pey

1995. Colombian Patriots. Multicoloured.

2030	270p. Type **778** (revolutionary)	35	20
2031	270p. Jorge Tadeo Lozana (zoologist and revolutionary)	35	20
2032	270p. Antonio Narino (journalist and politician)	35	20
2033	270p. Camilo Torres (lawyer and revolutionary)	35	20
2034	270p. Jose Fernandez Madrid (doctor and revolutionary)	35	20
2035	270p. Jose Maria del Castillo y Rada (lawyer)	35	20
2036	270p. Custodio Garcia Rovira (revolutionary)	35	20
2037	270p. Antonio Villavicencio (revolutionary)	35	20
2038	270p. Liborio Mejia (lawyer and historian)	35	20
2039	270p. Rafael Urdaneta (diplomat)	35	20
2040	270p. Juan Garcia del Rio (writer and politician)	35	20
2041	270p. Gen. Jose Maria Melo	35	20
2042	270p. Gen. Tomas Herrera	35	20
2043	270p. Froilan Largacha (acting President, Feb–June 1863)	35	20
2044	270p. Salvader Camacho Roldan (writer)	35	20
2045	270p. Gen. Ezequiel Hurtado (acting President, Apr–Aug 1884)	35	20
2046	270p. Dario Echandia Olaya (lawyer)	35	20
2047	270p. Alberto Lleras Camargo (President, 1945–46)	35	20
2048	270p. Gen. Gustavo Rojas Pinilla (President, 1953–57)	35	20
2049	270p. Carlos Lleras Restrepo (President, 1966–70)	35	20

779 Farmers on Hillside

1995. Air. 50th Anniv of F.A.O.

2050	**779** 750p. multicoloured	1·00	50

780 Bello

781 Fireman

1995. Air. 25th Anniv of Andres Bello (scholar and writer). Agreement on Intellectual Co-operation.

2051	**780** 650p. multicoloured	85	45

1995. Air. Centenary of Fire Brigade of Bogota.

2052	**781** 330p. multicoloured	45	25

782 Emblem

783 Anniversary Emblem

1995. Air. 50th Anniv of National Chamber of Commerce.

2053	**782** 330p. multicoloured	45	25

1995. Air. 50th Anniv of U.N.O.

2054	**783** 750p. multicoloured	45	25

784 Emblem **786** Obando (after Efrain Martinez)

1995. Air. 1st Pacific Ocean Games, Cali.

2055	**784** 750p. multicoloured	1·00	50

1995. Birth Bicentenary of General Jose Maria Obando.

2057	**786** 220p. multicoloured	25	15

787 San Filipe de Barajas Castle

1995. Air. 11th Non-aligned Countries' Conference, Cartagena de Indias.

2058	**787** 650p. multicoloured	80	40

788 Estela Lopez Pomareda in "Maria", Charlie Chaplin and Jackie Coogan

1995. Air. Centenary of Motion Pictures.

2059	**788** 330p. black and brown	40	20

789 Harvesting Poppies for Opium **790** Anniversary Emblem

1995. Air. World Campaign against Drug Trafficking. Multicoloured.
2060 330p. Type **789** 40 20
2061 330p. Manacled hands (horiz) 40 20

1995. Air. 25th Anniv of Andean Development Corporation.
2062 **790** 650p. multicoloured . . 80 40

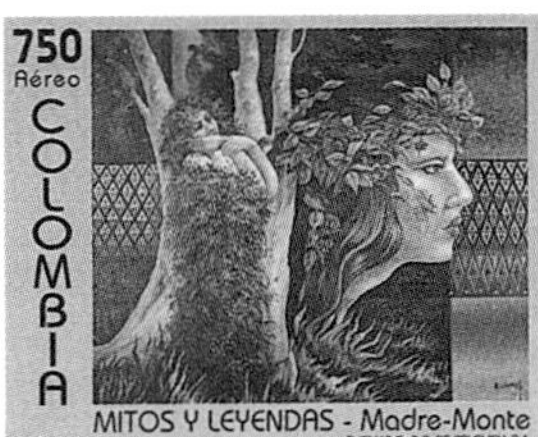

792 Madre-Monte

1995. Air. Myths and Legends (1st issue). Multicoloured.
2065 750p. Type **792** 90 45
2066 750p. La Llorana 90 45
2067 750p. El Mohan (river spirit) 90 45
2068 750p. Alligator man 90 45
Nos. 2065/8 were issued together, se-tenant, in sheetlets in which the background colour gradually changes down the sheet; each design therefore occurs in four slightly different colours.
See also Nos. 2085/8.

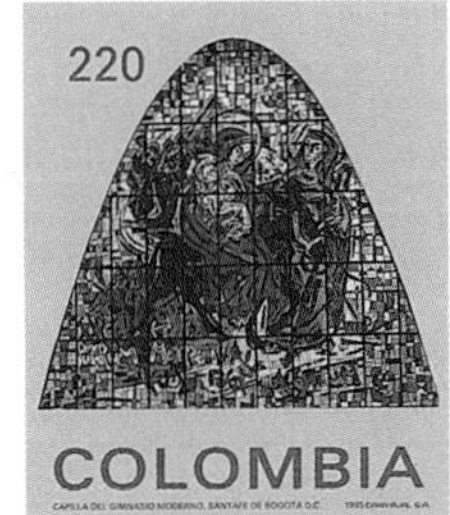

793 Holy Family

1995. Christmas. Stained Glass Windows from Chapel of the Apostles, Bogota School. Mult.
2069 220p. Type **793** (postage) . . 25 15
2070 330p. Nativity (air) 40 20

794 Asuncion Silva

1996. Air. Death Centenary of Jose Asuncion Silva (poet).
2071 **794** 400p. multicoloured . . 50 25

795 Painting by Luz Maria Tobon Mesa

COLOMBIA 900 AEREO
POLICARPA SALAVARRIETA
796 Salavarrieta (after Jose Maria Espinosa)

1996. Air. Providence Island.
2072 **795** 800p. multicoloured . . 1·00 50

1996. Air. Birth Bicentenary of Policarpa Salavarrieta.
2073 **796** 900p. multicoloured . . 1·10 55

COLOMBIA 400
Poeta - León De Greiff
1895 - 1995
797 De Greiff (Ricardo Rendon)

799 Santa Maria la Antigua del Darien

1996. 1st Death Anniv of Leon De Greiff (poet).
2074 **797** 400p. black 50 25

1996. Town Arms. Multicoloured.
2076 400p. Type **799** 50 25
2077 400p. San Sebastian de Mariquita 50 25
2078 400p. Marinilla 50 25
2079 400p. Santa Cruz de Mompox 50 25

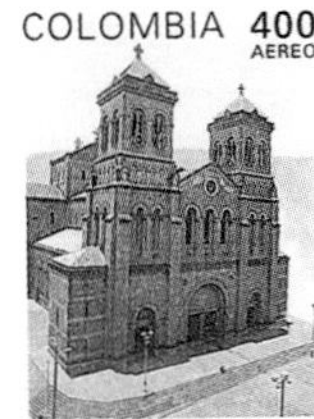

801 Medellin Cathedral

1996. Air.
2081 **801** 400p. multicoloured . . 50 25

803 Mosquera Courtyard

1996. 150th Anniv of National Capitol, Bogota.
2083 **803** 400p. multicoloured . . 50 25

804 National Archive, Bogota

1996. Air.
2084 **804** 400p. multicoloured . . 50 25

1996. Air. Myths and Legends (2nd issue). Multicoloured.
2085 900p. The Creation of Koguin . . . . 1·10 55
2086 900p. Yonna Wayu . . . . 1·10 55
2087 900p. Jaguar-man . . . . . 1·10 55
2088 900p. Lord of the Animals 1·10 55

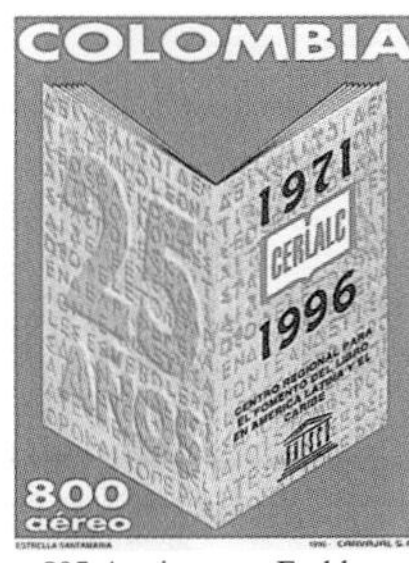

805 Anniversary Emblem

1996. Air. 25th Anniv of Regional Centre for the Development of Books in Latin America and Caribbean.
2089 **805** 800p. brn, blk & dp brn 95 50

806 Guitar and Notes

808 Golf Course

807 Jorge Isaacs and Pump

1996. 50th Anniv of Society of Colombian Authors and Composers.
2090 **806** 400p. multicoloured . . 50 25

1996. Air. Pioneers of Petroleum Industry. Multicoloured.
2091 800p. Type **807** 95 50
2092 800p. Francisco Burgos Rubio and refinery (at night) 95 50
2093 800p. Diego Martinez Camargo and drilling tower 95 50
2094 800p. Prisciliano Cabrales Lora and drilling platform 1·25 60
2095 800p. Manuel Maria Palacio and firefighting tug . . . 1·25 90
2096 800p. Roberto de Mares and refinery 95 50
2097 800p. General Virgilio Barco Maldonado and workmen 95 50
2098 800p. Workmen and Ecopetrol (state petroleum industry) emblem 95 50

1996. Air. 50th Anniv of Colombian Golf Federation.
2099 **808** 400p. multicoloured . . 50 25

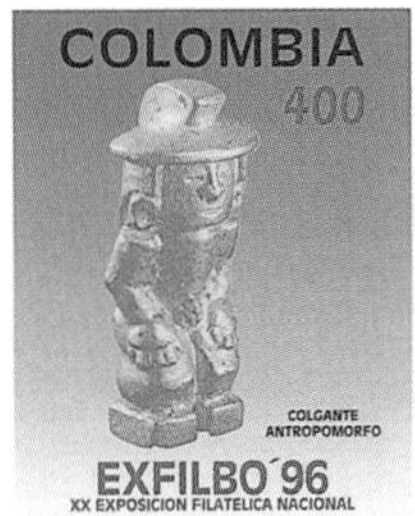

809 Pre-Columban Pendant, Malagana Treasure

1996. "Exfilbo '96" National Stamp Exn, Bogota.
2100 **809** 400p. multicoloured . . 50 25

811 Postman delivering Letter

1996. Christmas. The Annunciation. Mult.
2102 400p. Type **811** (postage) . . 50 25
2103 400p. Woman reading letter and postman (air) 50 25

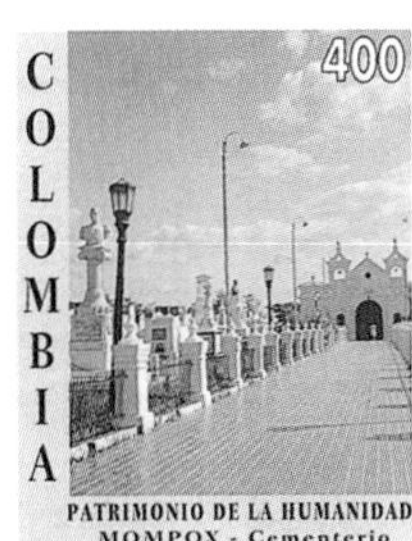

813 Cemetary, Mompox

1996. U.N.E.S.C.O. World Heritage Sites. Mult.
2106 400p. Type **813** 50 25
2107 400p. San Agustin Archaeological Park . . . 50 25
2108 400p. Palace of the Inquisition, Cartagena . . 50 25
2109 400p. Underground tomb, Tierradentro Archaeological Park . . . 50 25

814 Children holding Hands

815 Hurtado

1997. Air. Children's Rights.
2110 **814** 400p. multicoloured . . 45 25

1997. 2nd Death Anniv of Alvaro Gomez Hurtado (lawyer and politician).
2111 **815** 400p. black and blue . . 45 25

816 Film Reels and Harbour Tower

COLOMBIA 400 AEREO
SEGURO SOCIAL
Para Siempre
SALUD · PENSIONES
PROTECCION LABORAL
817 Emblem

1997. Air. Centenary of Colombian Cinema and 53rd International Union of Film Archives Congress, Cartagena de Indias.
2112 **816** 800p. multicoloured . . 90 45

1997. Air. 50th Anniv (1996) of State Social Security.
2113 **817** 400p. multicoloured . . 45 25

818 Hand holding Mobile Phone

1997. Air. Centenary (1996) of Ericsson Company in Colombia.
2114 **818** 900p. multicoloured . . 90 45

819 Cattle

1997. Air. Cordoba Cattle Fair.
2115 **819** 400p. multicoloured . . 30 15

820 "Maria Varilla in the Clouds" (William Vive)

1997. Porro National Festival, San Pelayo.
2116 **820** 400p. multicoloured . . 30 15

821 Typewriter

1997. 50th Anniv of Bogota Journalists' Association.
2117 **821** 400p. multicoloured . . 30 15

822 Museum Buildings

1997. Air. 1st Anniv of Numismatic Museum at State Mint, Bogota.
2118 **822** 800p. multicoloured . . 65 35

823 Palm

1997. Air. Vegetable Ivory Palm Production Project.
2119 **823** 900p. multicoloured . . 70 35

824 Barco

1997. Virgilio Barco (President, 1986–90) Commem.
2120 **824** 500p. multicoloured . . 40 20

825 Straightening Contorted Tree and Healthy Couple

1997. Air. 50th Anniv of Colombian Society of Orthopaedic Surgery and Traumatology.
2121 **825** 1000p. multicoloured . . 80 40

826 Luis Carlos Lopez (poet)

1997. Air. Personalities. Multicoloured.
2122 500p. Type **826** 40 20
2123 500p. Aurelio Arturo (poet) 40 20
2124 500p. Enrique Perez Arbelaez (botanist and historian) 40 20
2125 500p. Jose Maria Gonzalez Benito (mathematician and astronomer) 40 20
2126 500p. Jose Manuel Rivas Sacconi (philologist and diplomat) 40 20
2127 500p. Eduardo Lemaitre Roman (historian and journalist) 40 20
2128 500p. Diojenes Arrieta (journalist and politician) 40 20
2129 500p. Gabriel Turbay Abunader (politician and diplomat) 40 20
2130 500p. Guillermo Echavarria Misas (aviation pioneer) 40 20
2131 500p. Juan Friede Alter (historian) 40 20
2132 500p. Fabio Lozano Torrijos (diplomat) . . . 40 20
2133 500p. Lino de Pombo (engineer and diplomat) 40 20
2134 500p. Cacica Gaitana (Indian resistance leader) 40 20
2135 500p. Josefa Acevedo de Gomez (writer) 40 20
2136 500p. Domingo Bioho (Black leader) 40 20
2137 500p. Soledad Acosta de Samper (historian) 40 20
2138 500p. Maria Cano Marquez (workers' leader) 55 30
2139 500p. Manuel Quintin Lame (native leader) 40 20
2140 500p. Ezequiel Uricoechea (linguist and naturalist) 40 20
2141 500p. Juan Rodriguez Freyle (chronicler) 40 20
2142 500p. Gerardo Reichel-Dolmatoff (archaeologist) 40 20
2143 500p. Ramon de Zubiria (educationist) 40 20
2144 500p. Esteban Jaramillo (economist) 40 20
2145 500p. Pedro Fermin de Vargas (economist) . . . 40 20

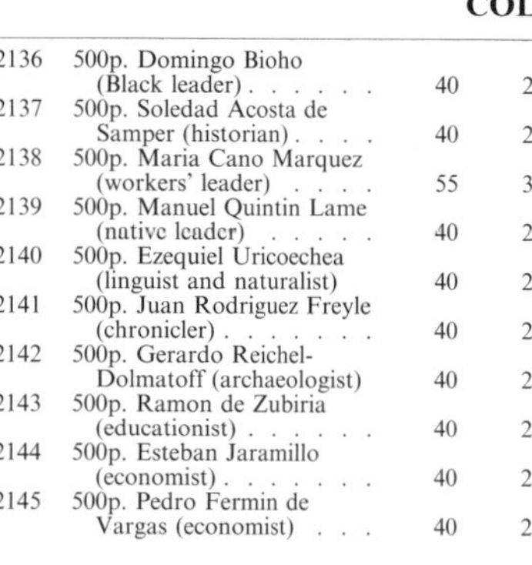

827 National Flag, Dove and Children playing

1997. Peace. Multicoloured.
2146 500p. Type **827** (postage) . . 40 20
2147 1100p. Children holding hands in ring (air) 85 45

828 Postman on Moped

1997. America. The Postman. Multicoloured.
2148 500p. Type **828** (postage) . . 40 20
2149 1100p. Postman raising envelope to night sky (air) 85 45

829 Pregnant Women

830 Dove Emblem

1998. Air. 50th Anniv of W.H.O. Safe Motherhood.
2150 **829** 1100p. multicoloured . . 65 35

1998. Air. 4th Bolivarian Stamp Exhibition, Santafe de Bogota.
2151 **830** 1000p. orange and blue 60 30

831 Gaitan

832 Colombian Flag and Map of the Americas

1998. 50th Death Anniv of Jorge Eliecer Gaitan.
2152 **831** 500p. multicoloured . . 30 15

1998. Air. 50th Anniv of Organization of American States.
2153 **832** 1000p. multicoloured . . 60 30

833 Cogs

1998. 50th Anniv of Santander Industrial University.
2154 **833** 500p. multicoloured . . 30 15

834 "Gloria" (cadet ship) and Dolphins

1998. Air. International Year of the Ocean.
2155 **834** 1100p. multicoloured . . 65 35

835 Football Boot

1998. Air. World Cup Football Championship, France. Multicoloured.
2156 1100p. Type **835** 65 35
2157 1100p. Ball 65 35
2158 1100p. Goalkeeper's glove 65 35
Nos. 2156/8 were issued together, se-tenant, forming a composite design.

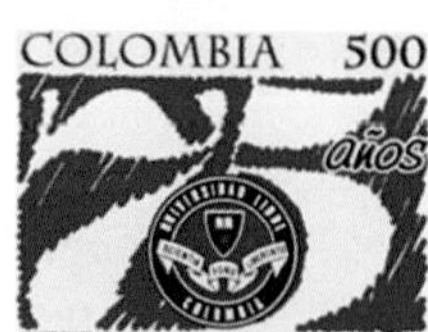

836 University Arms

1998. 75th Anniv of Colombia Free University.
2159 **836** 500p. black and red . . 30 15

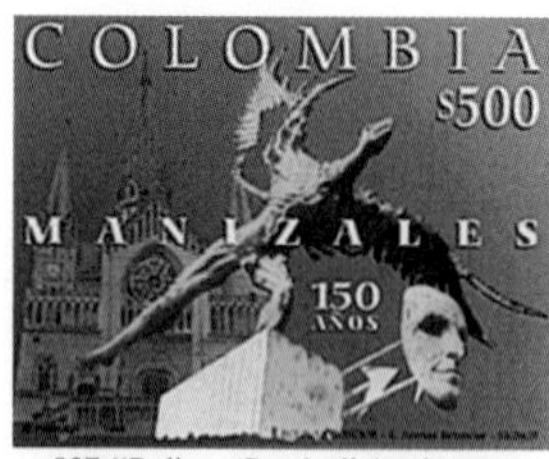

837 "Bolivar Condor" (sculpture, R. Arenas Betancur) and Cathedral

1998. 150th Anniv of Manizales.
2160 **837** 500p. multicoloured . . 30 15

838 Gold Coin, Tairona Culture

839 Borrero

1998. 75th Anniversaries. Multicoloured.
2161 500p. Type **838** (National Bank) 30 15
2162 500p. Gold sheaf of corn, Malagana Culture (Comptroller-General's Office) 30 15
2163 500p. Gold mask, Quimbaya Culture (Banking Superintendent's Office) 30 15

1998. 1st Death Anniv of Misael Pastrana Borrero (President, 1970–74).
2164 **839** 500p. multicoloured . . 30 15

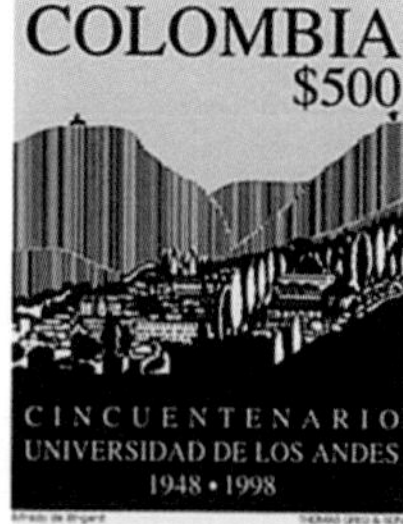

840 The Andes and University Campus

1998. 50th Anniv of University of the Andes, Bogota.
2165 **840** 500p. black and yellow 30 15

841 Woman panning for Gold, and Cherubs

843 Academy of Languages Arms

842 Bochica

1998. Christmas. Multicoloured.
2166 500p. Type **841** (postage) . . 30 15
2167 1000p. Three kings, camel and star (air) 60 30
2168 1000p. Nativity 60 30
Nos. 2167/8 were issued together, se-tenant, forming a composite design.

1998. Air. Muisca Mythology. Multicoloured.
2169 1000p. Type **842** 60 30
2170 1000p. Chiminigua 60 30
2171 1000p. Bachue and Huitica 60 30
Nos. 2169/71 were issued together, se-tenant, forming a composite design.

1998. Arms of Colombian Academies. Mult.
2172 500p. Type **843** 30 15
2173 500p. Medicine 30 15
2174 500p. Law 30 15
2175 500p. History 30 15
2176 500p. Physical and Natural Sciences 30 15
2177 500p. Economics 30 15
2178 500p. Ecclesiastical History 30 15

844 Soledad Roman de Nunez (First Lady, 1880–82 and 1884–94)

845 Lopez (after G. Ricci)

1999. America (1998). Famous Women. Mult.
2179 600p. Type **844** (postage) . . 35 20
2180 1200p. Bertha Hernandez de Ospina (politician) (air) 70 35

1999. Birth Bicentenary of Jose Hilario Lopez (President, 1849–53).
2181 **845** 1000p. multicoloured . . 60 30

846 Green Turtle

1999. Turtles. Multicoloured.
2182 1300p. Type **846** 80 49
2183 1300p. Leatherback turtle ("Dermochelys coriacea") 80 40
2184 1300p. Hawksbill turtle ("Eretmochelys imbricata") 80 40
Nos. 2182/4 were issued together, se-tenant, forming a composite design.

847 Colombian and Japanese Suns across the Pacific

1999. 70 Years of Japanese Emigration to Colombia.
2185 **847** 1300p. multicoloured (yellow sun at left) 80 40
2186 1300p. multicoloured (red sun at left) 80 40
Nos. 2185/6 were issued together, se-tenant, forming a composite design.

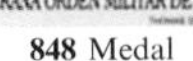

848 Medal **850** Zuleta Angel

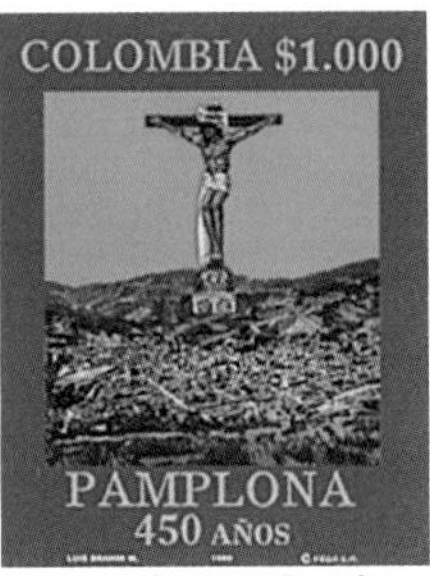

849 Crucifix above Pamplona

1999. 900th Anniv of Sovereign Military Order of Malta.
2187 **848** 1200p. multicoloured 70 35

1999. 450th Anniv of Pamplona.
2188 **849** 1000p. multicoloured 60 30

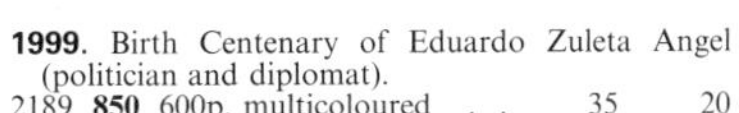

1999. Birth Centenary of Eduardo Zuleta Angel (politician and diplomat).
2189 **850** 600p. multicoloured 35 20

851 Colombian Olympic Committee Emblem

1999. 13th Pan-American Games, Winnipeg. Mult.
2190 1200p. Type **851** 70 35
2191 1200p. Running (facing right) 70 35
2192 1200p. Weightlifting (facing left) 70 35
2193 1200p. Cycling (facing right) 70 35
2194 1200p. Shooting (facing left) 70 35
2195 1200p. Roller blading (facing right) 70 35
2196 1200p. Running (facing left) 70 35
2197 1200p. Weightlifting (facing right) 70 35
2198 1200p. Cycling (facing left) 70 35
2199 1200p. Shooting (facing right) 70 35
2200 1200p. Roller blading (facing left) 70 35

852 Robles **854** Flowers leaving Hands

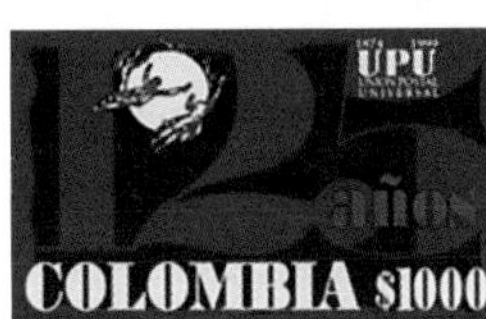

853 "125" and Emblem

1999. 150th Birth Anniv of Luis A. Robles.
2201 **852** 600p. multicoloured 35 20

1999. 125th Anniv of Universal Postal Union. Each lilac, violet and gold.
2202 1000p. Type **853** 60 30
2203 1300p. Emblem 85 45

1999. America. A New Millennium without Arms. Multicoloured.
2204 1200p. Type **854** 75 40
2205 1200p. Flowers moving towards hands 75 40
Nos. 2204/5 were issued together, se-tenant, forming a composite design.

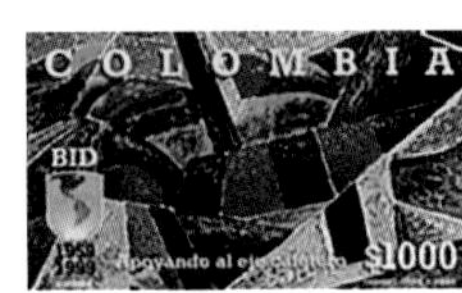

855 Landscape

1999. 40th Anniv of International Development Bank. Multicoloured.
2206 1000p. Type **855** 60 30
2207 1000p. Landscape, sunbeams and red fruits 60 30
Nos. 2206/7 were issued together, se-tenant, forming a composite design.

856 Nativity

1999. Christmas. Multicoloured.
2208 600p. Type **856** 35 20
2209 600p. Angel and Three Wise Men 35 20
Nos. 2208/9 were issued together, se-tenant, forming a composite design.

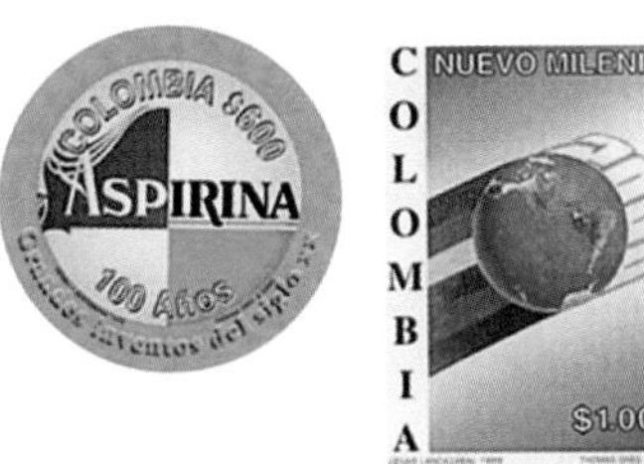

857 Emblem **858** Rainbow, Globe and "2000"

1999. Centenary of Invention of Aspirin (drug).
2210 **857** 600p. multicoloured 35 20

2000. New Millennium. Multicoloured.
2211 1000p. Type **858** 60 30
2212 1000p. Man with Colombian flag and dove 60 30

859 University Arms

2000. 50th Anniv of Medellin University.
2213 **859** 1000p. multicoloured 60 30

860 Faria Bermudez

2000. 20th Death Anniv (1999) of Father Jose Rafael Faria Bermudez.
2214 **860** 1300p. brown and black 85 45

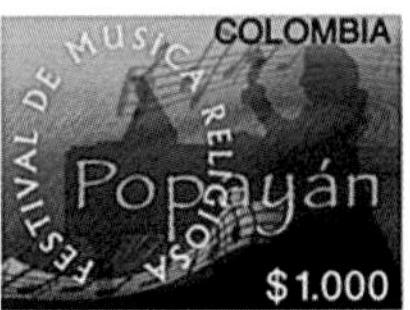

861 Pianist and Score

2000. Religious Music Festival, Popayan.
2215 **861** 1000p. multicoloured 60 40

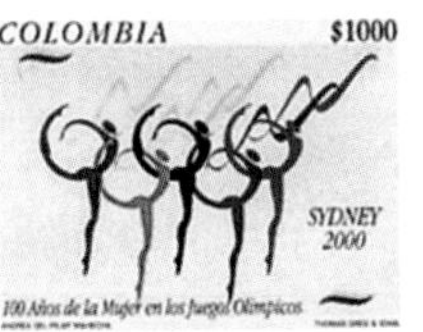

862 Stylized Figures forming Olympic Rings

2000. Olympic Games, Sydney.
2216 **862** 1000p. multicoloured 60 40

863 Male and Female Symbols under Umbrella

2000. A.I.D.S. Awareness Campaign.
2217 **863** 1000p. multicoloured 60 40

864 Weather Vane

2000. 50th Anniv of World Meteorological Society.
2218 **864** 1000p. multicoloured 60 40

865 Footprints

2000. National Birth Register
2219 **865** 1000p. multicoloured 60 40

866 "Archangel" (Fernando Botero)

2001. Botero Foundation, Bogota. Multicoloured.
2220 650p. Type **866** 40 25
2221 650p. "Gypsy with Tamborine" (Jean Baptiste Camille Corot) 40 25
2222 650p. "Vera Sergine Renoir" (Pierre-Auguste Renoir) 40 25
2223 650p. "Man on Horse" (Botero) 40 25
2224 650p. "Mother Superior" (Botero) 40 25
2225 650p. "Town" (Botero) 40 25
2226 650p. "Flowers" (Botero) 40 25
2227 650p. "Cezanne" (Botero) 40 25
2228 650p. "The Patio" (Botero) 40 25
2229 650p. "Absinthe Drinker at Grenelle" (Henri Toulouse-Lautrec) 40 25
2230 650p. "The Pequeno Valley" (Jean Baptiste Camille Corot) 40 25
2231 650p. "The Studio" (Botero) 40 25

PRIVATE AIR COMPANIES

The "LANSA" and Avianca Companies operated inland and foreign air mail services on behalf of the Government and issued the following stamps. Later only the Avianca Company performed this service and the regular air stamps were used on the mail without overprints.

Similar issues were also made by Compania Colombiana de Navegacion Aerea during 1920. These are very rare and will be found listed in the Stanley Gibbons Stamp Catalogue, Part 20 (South America).

A. "LANSA" (Lineas Aereas Nacionales Sociedad Anonima).

1 Wing

1950. Air.
1 **1** 5c. yellow 15 10
2 10c. red 25 15
3 15c. blue 25 10
4 20c. green 40 25
5 30c. purple 1·25 1·25
6 60c. brown 1·50 1·75

With background network colours in brackets.
7 **1** 1p. grey (buff) 6·00 7·50
8 2p. blue (green) 8·50 9·50
9 5p. red (red) 29·00 29·00
The 1p. was also issued without the network.

1950. Air. Nos. 691/7 and 700/3 optd **L**.
10 5c. yellow 15 10
11 10c. red 15 10
12 15c. blue 15 10
13 20c. violet 15 10
14 30c. green 15 15
15 40c. grey 3·50 15
16 50c. red 55 15
17 1p. purple and green 4·25 1·75
18 2p. blue and green 8·50 3·25
19 3p. black and red 8·50 9·50
20 5p. turquoise and sepia 28·00 28·00

1951. As Nos. 696/703 but colours changed and optd **L**.
21 40c. orange 90 55
22 50c. blue 90 55
23 60c. grey 90 45
24 80c. red 75 45
25 1p. red and vermilion 3·75 3·75
26 2p. blue and red 4·50 4·50
27 3p. green and brown 8·25 7·25
28 5p. grey and yellow 21·00 23·00

B. Avianca Company.

1950. Air. Nos. 691/703 optd **A**.
1 5c. yellow 10 10
2 10c. red 15 10
3 15c. blue 10 10
4 20c. violet 20 10
5 30c. green 15 10
6 40c. grey 45 10
7 50c. red 25 10
8 60c. olive 75 15
9 80c. brown 1·40 15
10 1p. purple and green 1·60 15
11 2p. blue and green 5·00 1·60

12 3p. black and red . . . . . . 8·50 7·50
13 5p. turquoise and sepia . . . 25·00 22·00

1951. Air. As Nos. 696/703 but colours changed and optd **A**.
14 40c. orange . . . . 4·50 25
15 50c. blue . . . . 6·25 25
16 60c. grey . . . . 1·75 15
17 80c. red 60 15
18 1p. red and vermilion . . . . 2·10 15
19 1p. brown and green . . . . 2·25 35
20 2p. blue and red . . . . . 2·10 35
21 3p. green and brown . . . . 4·50 90
22 5p. grey and yellow . . . . . 8·25 90
The 60c. also comes with the **A** in the centre.
All values except the 2p. and 3p. exist without the overprint.

ACKNOWLEDGEMENT OF RECEIPT STAMPS

AR **60** AR **100**

1894.
AR169 AR **60** 5c. red . . . . . . 2·50 2·10

1902. Similar to Type AR **60**. Imperf or perf.
AR265 5c. blue . . . . 12·00 12·00
AR211 10c. blue on blue 90 90

1903. No. 197 optd **Habilitado Medellin A R**.
AR258 **75** 10c. black on pink . . 13·00

1904. No. 262 optd **A R**.
AR266 **75** 5c. red . . . . 21·00 21·00

1904.
AR290 AR **100** 5c. blue . . . . . 7·50 3·50

AR **106** A. Gomez AR **117** Map of Colombia

1910.
AR354 AR **106** 5c. green & orge 6·00 15·00

1917. Inscr "AR".
AR371 **123** 4c. brown . . . . 12·50 11·00
AR372 AR **117** 5c. brown . . . . 5·00 4·00

OFFICIAL STAMPS

1937. Optd **OFICIAL**.
O496 – 1c. green (No. 429) . . 10 10
O497 **137** 2c. red (No. 430) . . . 20 20
O498 – 5c. brown (No. 431) . . 10 10
O499 – 10c. orge (No. 485) . . 25 20
O500 **156** 12c. blue 90 25
O501 **141** 20c. blue . . . . . . 1·40 65
O502 **110** 30c. bistre . . . . . . 2·10 65
O503 **123** 40c. brown . . . . . . 22·00 14·00
O504 **112** 50c. red . . . . . . 1·75 80
O505 **110** 1p. blue . . . . . . 14·00 6·00
O506 2p. orange . . . . . . 15·00 6·00
O507 5p. grey . . . . . . 50·00 50·00
O508 **57** 10p. brown £110 £110

REGISTRATION STAMPS

R **12** R **32**

1865. Imperf.
R42 R **12** 5c. black . . . . 90·00 45·00

1865. Type similar to R **12**, but letter "R" in star. Imperf.
R43 5c. black . . . . £100 50·00

1870. Imperf.
R73 R **32** 5c. black . . . . 2·50 2·50

1870. Type similar to R **32** but with "R" in centre and inscr "REJISTRO". Imperf.
R74 5c. black . . . . 1·10 90

1881. Eagle and arms in oval frame, inscr "RECOMENDADA" at foot. Imperf or pin-perf.
R105 10c. lilac . . . . 30·00 30·00

R **42** R **48**

1883. Perf.
R117 R **42** 10c. red on orange . . 80 1·00

1899.
R141 R **48** 10c. red . . . . 5·00 3·50
R166 10c. brown . . . . . 1·40 75

R **85**

1902. Imperf or perf.
R264 R **85** 10c. purple . . . . . 4·00 4·00
R207 20c. red on blue . . . 80 80
R208 20c. blue on blue . . . 1·25 1·25

R **94**

1902. Perf.
R257 R **94** 10c. purple . . . . . 19·00 19·00

R **99**

1904.
R289 R **99** 10c. purple . . . . . 13·00 35

R **105** Execution of 24 February, 1810

1910.
R353 R **105** 10c. black and red . . 20·00 50·00

R **114** Puerto Colombia

1917.
R369 R **114** 4c. blue and green . . 35 3·25
R370 – 10c. blue . . . . . . 7·50 25
DESIGN: 10c. Tequendama Falls.

R **127**

1925.
R409 R **127** (10c.) blue . . . . . 9·50 1·75

1932. Air. Air stamps of 1932 optd **R**.
R426 **132** 20c. red . . . . 6·00 4·25
R450 – 20c. green & red (439) 6·00 75

SPECIAL DELIVERY STAMPS

E **118** Express Messenger

1917.
E373 E **118** 5c. green . . . . . . 5·00 4·25

E **310**

1958. Air.
E936 E **310** 25c. red and blue . . 25 15

1959. Air. Unification of Air Mail Rates. Optd **UNIFICADO** within outline of airplane.
E989 E **310** 25c. red and blue . . 45 10

E **361** Boeing 720B on Back of "Express" Letter

1963. Air.
E1143 E **361** 50c. black & red . . 20 10

1966. Air. "History of Colombian Aviation". As T **372**. Inscr "EXPRESO". Multicoloured.
E1168 80c. Boeing 727 jetliner (1966) 10 15

E **647** Numeral

1987.
E1783 E **647** 25p. green and red 25 15
E1784 30p. green and red 25 15

E **663** Sailfish "Istiaphorus amaricanus"

1988. No Value expressed.
E1805 E **663** (A) blue . . . . . . 2·25 1·10
E1806 (B) blue 75 15

E **724** Black & Chestnut Eagle E **738** Postman climbing out of Envelope

1992. No value expressed. Multicoloured.
E1926 B (200p.) Type E **724** . . 1·00 50
E1927 A (950p.) Spectacled bear 2·50 75

1992. World Post Day. No value expressed.
E1951 E **738** B (200p.) mult . . . 35 20

E **741** "Three Musicians"

1993. Fernando Botero (painter) Commemoration. No value expressed.
E1955 E **741** B multicoloured . . 35 20

E **743** Parading "Virgin of the Sorrows"

1993. Popayan Holy Week. No value expressed.
E1957 E **743** B multicoloured . . 35 20

E **744** Mother and Child E **745** Mother House, Pasto

1993. 90th Anniv of Pan-American Health Organization. No value expressed.
E1958 E **744** B multicoloured . . 35 20

1993. Centenary of Franciscan Convent of Mary Immaculate. No value expressed.
E1959 E **745** B multicoloured . . 35 20

E **746** Stamps, Magnifying Glass and Tweezers E **747** Cano

1993. 18th National Stamp Exhibition. No value expressed.
E1960 E **746** B multicoloured . . 35 20

1993. 7th Death Anniv of Guillermo Cano (newspaper editor).
E1961 E **747** 250p. multicoloured 40 20

1993. Tourism. As T **756**. Multicoloured.
E1996 250p. Otun Lake (vert) . . 35 20

E **758** Marie Poussepin (founder) E **761** Biplane

1994. Order of Sisters of the Presentation.
E1998 E **758** 300p. multicoloured 45 25

1994. 75th Anniv of Air Force.
E2004 E **761** 300p. multicoloured 45 25

1994. 4th Latin American Presidential Summit, Cartagena. As T **764**. Multicoloured.
E2010 300p. Setting sun over harbour walls 45 25

E **769** Emblem

1994. International Year of The Family.
E2016 E **769** 300p. multicoloured 40 20

1994. American Postal Transport. As T **770**. Multicoloured.
E2018 300p. Men carrying "stamps" depicting van, ship and aircraft 40 20

1994. Christmas. As T **773**. Multicoloured.
E2022 300p. Nativity 40 20

E **777** Championship Advertising Poster and Gold Ornament

1995. B.M.X. World Championship, Melgar.
E2029 E **777** 400p. multicoloured 55 30

E **785** Bicycle

1995. World Cycling Championships, Bogota and Boyaca.
E2056 E **785** 400p. multicoloured 50 25

E **791** Hands protecting Lake and Marine Angelfish

E **798** Emblem on Cross

1995. America. Environmental Protection. Multicoloured.
E2063 400p. Type E **791** 50 25
E2064 400p. Hands protecting tree 50 25

1996. 400th Anniv of Order of St. John of God in Colombia.
E2075 E **798** 500p. multicoloured 60 30

E **800** Trains

1996. Inauguration (1995) of Medellin Underground Railway.
E2080 E **800** 500p. multicoloured 1·50 75

E **802** Runners

1996. Olympic Games, Atlanta. Centenary of Modern Olympic Games.
E2082 E **802** 500p. multicoloured 60 30

E **812** Fruit Seller

1996. America. Traditional Costumes.
E2104 500p. Type E **812** 60 30
E2105 500p. Fisherman 60 30

TOO LATE STAMPS

L **47** L **59**

1888. Perf.
L136 L **47** 2½c. black on lilac . . 4·00 1·50

1892. Perf.
L167 L **59** 2½c. blue on red . . . 4·00 3·25

L **86** L **107**

1902. Imperf or perf.
L209 L **86** 5c. violet on red . . . 45 45

1914. Perf.
L355 L **107** 2c. brown . . . . . . 8·50 6·00
L356 5c. green . . . . . . 8·50 6·00

COMORO ISLANDS Pt. 6; Pt. 12

An archipelago N.W. of Madagascar comprising Anjouan, Great Comoro, Mayotte and Moheli. A French colony from 1891, Mayotte became an Overseas Department of France in December 1974, the remaining islands forming the Independent State of Comoro.

100 centimes = 1 franc.

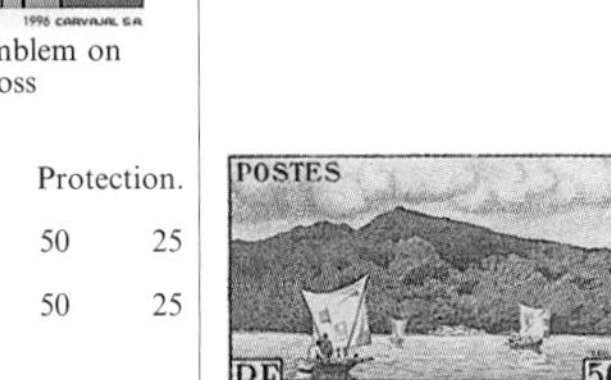

1 Anjouan Bay

2 Native Woman

6 Mutsamudu Village

1950.
1 **1** 10c. blue (postage) . . . . . 15 1·00
2 50c. green 15 25
3 1f. brown 25 15
4 **2** 2f. green 35 20
5 – 5f. violet 50 90
6 6f. purple . . . . 45 1·00
7 – 7f. red 80 65
8 – 10f. green 90 60
9 – 11f. blue . . . . 80 1·60
10 – 15f. brown 75 70
11 – 20f. red 85 80
12 – 40f. indigo and blue . . . 22·00 13·00
13 **6** 50f. red and green (air) . . . 2·50 3·00
14 – 100f. brown and red . . . . 3·25 4·25
15 – 200f. red, green and violet . . 19·00 15·00
DESIGNS (as Type **1**)—HORIZ: 7f., 10f., 11f. Mosque at Moroni; 40f. Coelacanth. VERT: 15f., 20f. Ouani Mosque, Anjouan. (As Type **6**)—HORIZ: 100f. Natives and Mosque de Vendredi; 200f. Ouani Mosque, Anjouan (different).

1952. Military Medal Cent. As T **48** of Cameroun.
16 15f. blue, yellow and green . . 22·00 35·00

1954. Air. 10th Anniv of Liberation. As T **52** of Cameroun.
17 15f. red and brown . . . . . 21·00 28·00

9 Village Pump

1956. Economic and Social Development Fund.
18 **9** 9f. violet . . . . 75 3·00

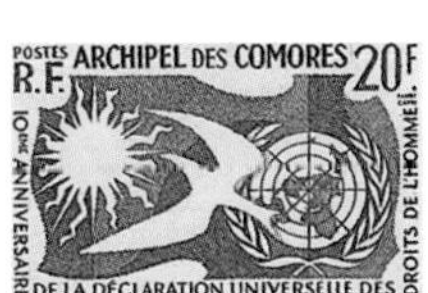

10 "Human Rights"

1958. 10th Anniv of Declaration of Human Rights.
19 **10** 20f. green and blue . . . . 5·00 10·00

1959. Tropical Flora. As T **58** of Cameroun. Mult.
20 10f. "Colvillea" (horiz) . . . . 1·75 3·00

11 Radio Station, Dzaoudzi

1960. Inaug of Comoro Broadcasting Service.
21 **11** 20f. green, violet and red . . 75 1·75
22 – 25f. green, brown and blue 90 1·60
DESIGN: 25f. Radio mast and map.

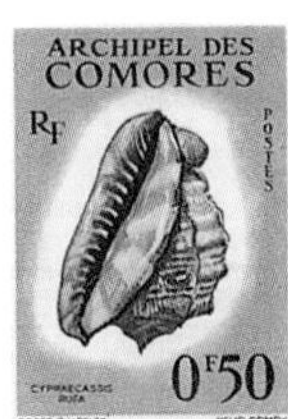

12 Bull-mouth Helmet

12a Giant Clam

1962. Multicoloured. (a) Postage. Sea Shells.
23 50c. Type **12** . . . . 70 2·00
24 1f. Common harp . . . . . . 1·00 1·75
25 2f. Ramose murex . . . . . . 1·75 3·00
26 5f. Giant green turban . . . . 2·75 3·75
27 20f. Scorpion conch . . . . . 8·50 12·50
28 25f. Trumpet triton . . . . . 12·00 14·50
(b) Air. Marine Plants.
29 100f. Type **12a** . . . . 8·50 13·50
30 500f. Stoney coral . . . . . . 21·00 32·00

1962. Malaria Eradication. As T **70** of Cameroun.
31 25f.+5f. red . . . . 1·50 4·75

1962. Air. 1st Trans-Atlantic T.V. Satellite Link. As Type F **23** of Andorra.
32 25f. mauve, purple and violet 2·50 1·40

14 Emblem in Hands and Globe

14a Centenary Emblem

1963. Freedom from Hunger.
33 **14** 20f. green and brown . . . 2·50 5·75

1963. Red Cross Centenary.
34 **14a** 50f. red, grey and green . . 5·75 8·00

15 Globe and Scales of Justice

16 Tobacco Pouch

1963. 15th Anniv of Declaration of Human Rights.
35 **15** 15f. green and red . . . . . 5·25 9·50

1963. Handicrafts. (a) Postage. As T **17**.
36 **16** 3f. ochre, red and green . . 1·00 2·25
37 – 4f. myrtle, purple & orange 1·00 2·50
38 – 10f. brown, green & chest 85 3·00
(b) Air. Size 27 × 48 mm.
39 – 65f. red, brown and green . . 2·75 4·25
40 – 200f. pink, red & turq . . . 6·25 7·00
DESIGNS: 4f. Perfume-burner; 10f. Lamp bracket; 65f. Baskets; 200f. Filigree pendant.

16a "Philately"

17 Pirogue

1964. "PHILATEC 1964" International Stamp Exhibition, Paris.
41 **16a** 50f. red, green and blue . . 2·00 5·25

1964. Native Craft. Multicoloured.
42 15f. Type **17** (postage) . . . . 2·50 3·50
43 30f. Boutre felucca . . . . . 4·50 6·50
44 50f. Mayotte pirogue (air) . . 3·50 3·50
45 85f. Schooner . . . . 5·25 4·25
Nos. 44/5 are larger, 27 × 48½ mm.

18 Boxing (Ancient bronze plaque)

19 Medal

1964. Air. Olympic Games, Tokyo.
46 **18** 100f. green, brown & choc 6·50 10·50

1964. Air. Star of Grand Comoro.
47 **19** 500f. multicoloured . . . . 16·00 20·00

20 "Syncom" Communications Satellite, Telegraph Poles and Morse Key

21 Great Hammerhead

1965. Air. Centenary of I.T.U.
48 **20** 50f. blue, green and grey . . 9·00 23·00

1965. Marine Life.
49 – 1f. green, orange and violet 1·60 2·00
50 **21** 12f. black, blue and red . . 2·00 2·50
51 – 20f. red and green . . . . . 2·50 3·00
52 – 25f. brown, red and green 5·00 3·75
DESIGNS—VERT: 1f. Spiny lobster; 25f. Spotted grouper. HORIZ: 20f. Scaly turtle.

1966. Air. Launching of 1st French Satellite. As Nos. 1696/7 of France.
53 25f. lilac, blue and violet . . . 3·50 5·75
54 30f. lilac, violet and blue . . . 4·50 5·75

21a Satellite "D1"

1966. Air. Launching of Satellite "D1".
55 **21a** 30f. purple, green & orange 1·90 2·25

22 Lake Sale

1966. Comoro Views. Multicoloured.
56 15f. Type **22** (postage) . . . . 75 2·00
57 25f. Itsandra Hotel, Moroni 1·25 1·50
58 50f. The Battery, Dzaoudzi (air) . . . . 2·50 4·00
59 200f. Ksar Fort, Mutsamudu (vert) . . . . 5·50 6·50

Nos. 58/9 are larger, 48 × 27 mm and 27 × 48 mm respectively.

23 Anjouan Sunbird

1967. Birds. Multicoloured.

No.		Description	Unused	Used
60		2f. Type **23** (postage)	3·75	3·00
61		10f. Madagascar malachite kingfisher	4·25	4·25
62		15f. Mascarene fody	7·75	6·25
63		30f. Courol	17·00	13·50
64		75f. Madagascar paradise flycatcher (vert) (27 × 48 mm) (air)	9·25	9·75
65		100f. Blue-cheeked bee eater (vert) (27 × 48 mm)	12·00	13·50

24 Nurse tending Child

25 Slalom Skiing

1967. Comoro Red Cross.

No.	Type	Description	Unused	Used
66	**24**	25f.+5f. purple, red & grn	2·25	3·50

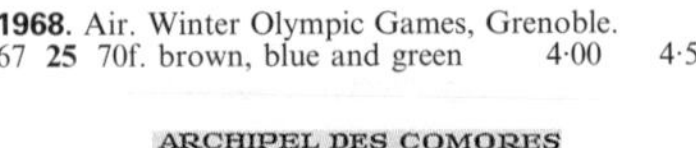

1968. Air. Winter Olympic Games, Grenoble.

No.	Type	Description	Unused	Used
67	**25**	70f. brown, blue and green	4·00	4·50

26 Bouquet, Sun and W.H.O. Emblem

1968. 20th Anniv of W.H.O.

No.	Type	Description	Unused	Used
68	**26**	40f. red, violet and green	85	1·25

27 Powder-blue Surgeonfish

28 Human Rights Emblem

1968. Fishes.

No.	Type	Description	Unused	Used
69	**27**	20f. bl, yell & red (postage)	2·75	4·25
70	–	25f. blue, orange & turq	3·50	5·25
71	–	50f. ochre, blue & pur (air)	5·75	4·75
72	–	90f. ochre, green & emer	8·25	6·50

DESIGNS—As T **27**: 25f. Emperor angelfish. 48 × 27 mm: 50f. Moorish idol; 90f. Oriental sweetlips.

1968. Human Rights Year.

No.	Type	Description	Unused	Used
73	**28**	60f. green, brown & orange	2·75	4·75

29 Swimming

1968. Air. Olympic Games, Mexico.

No.	Type	Description	Unused	Used
74	**29**	65f. multicoloured	3·00	4·00

30 Prayer Mat and Worshipper

1969. Msoila Prayer Mats.

No.	Type	Description	Unused	Used
75	**30**	20f. red, green and violet	95	2·25
76	–	30f. green, violet and red	1·25	2·50
77	–	45f. violet, red and green	2·50	3·25

DESIGNS: As Type **30**, but worshipper stooping (30f.) or kneeling upright (45f.).

31 Vanilla Flower

1969. Flowers, Multicoloured.

No.	Type	Description	Unused	Used
78		10f. Type **31** (postage)	1·60	2·50
79		15f. Ylang-ylang blossom	1·60	2·50
80		50f. "Heliconia" (vert) (air)	4·25	4·00
81		85f. Tuberose (vert)	5·50	4·75
82		200f. Orchid (vert)	10·00	8·00

32 Concorde in Flight

1969. Air. 1st Flight of Concorde.

No.	Type	Description	Unused	Used
83	**32**	100f. purple and brown	11·50	18·00

33 I.L.O. Building, Geneva

1969. 50th Anniv of I.L.O.

No.	Type	Description	Unused	Used
84	**33**	5f. grey, green and orange	1·50	2·25

34 Poinsettia

35 "EXPO" Panorama

1970. Flowers.

No.	Type	Description	Unused	Used
85	**34**	25f. multicoloured	3·00	2·75

1970. New U.P.U. Headquarters Building, Berne. As T **156** of Cameroun.

No.	Type	Description	Unused	Used
86		65f. brown, green and violet	3·75	4·00

1970. Air. World Fair "EXPO 70", Osaka, Japan. Multicoloured.

No.	Type	Description	Unused	Used
87		60f. Type **35**	4·25	3·25
88		90f. Geisha and map of Japan	5·25	3·25

36 Chiromani Costume, Anjouan

37 Mosque de Vendredi, Moroni

1970. Comoro Costumes. Multicoloured.

No.	Type	Description	Unused	Used
89		20f. Type **36**	2·50	2·50
90		25f. Bouiboui, Great Comoro	3·00	2·50

1970.

No.	Type	Description	Unused	Used
91	**37**	5f. turquoise, green and red	2·00	2·25
92		10f. violet, green & purple	2·25	2·50
93		40f. brown, green and red	3·00	2·75

38 Great Egret

1971. Birds, Multicoloured.

No.	Type	Description	Unused	Used
94		5f. Type **38**	1·90	2·25
95		10f. Comoro olive pigeon	1·90	2·25
96		15f. Green-backed heron	2·25	2·50
97		25f. Comoro blue pigeon	2·75	2·75
98		35f. Humblot's flycatcher	4·00	3·75
99		40f. Allen's gallinule	6·25	4·25

39 Sunset, Moutsamoudou (Anjouan)

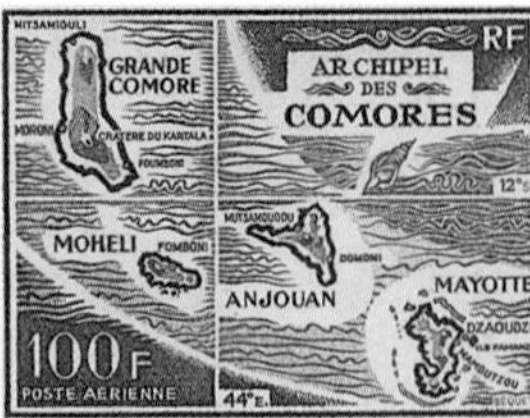

40 Map of Comoro Archipelago

1971. Air. Comoro Landscapes. Multicoloured.

No.	Type	Description	Unused	Used
100	**39**	15f. multicoloured	1·60	1·90
101	–	20f. multicoloured	1·75	2·25
102	–	65f. multicoloured	3·00	2·75
103	–	85f. multicoloured	3·75	3·25
104	**40**	100f. brown, green & bl	8·00	6·50

DESIGNS—(As Type **39**): 20f. Sada village (Mayotte); 65f. Ruined palace, Iconi (Great Comoro); 85f. Offshore islands; Moumatchoua (Moheli).

See also Nos. 124/8, 132/6, 157/60 and 168/71.

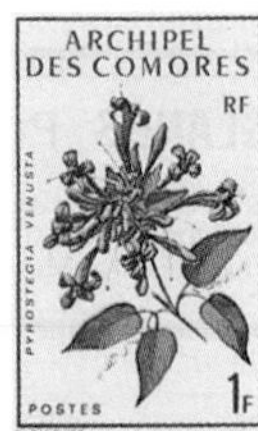

41 "Pyrostegia venusta"

1971. Tropical Plants. Multicoloured.

No.	Type	Description	Unused	Used
105		1f. Type **41** (postage)	1·75	2·25
106		3f. "Allamanda cathartica" (horiz)	1·75	2·25
107		20f. "Plumeria rubra"	3·50	3·25
108		60f. "Hibiscus schizopetalous" (air)	3·25	3·75
109		85f. "Acalypha sanderii"	7·50	5·25

The 60 and 85f. are 27 × 48 mm.

42 Lithograph Cone

1971. Sea Shells. Multicoloured.

No.	Type	Description	Unused	Used
110		5f. Type **42**	1·75	2·25
111		10f. Lettered cone	2·00	2·25
112		20f. Princely cone	2·50	2·75
113		35f. Polished nerite	3·75	2·75
114		60f. Serpent's-head cowrie	6·00	3·25

1971. 1st Death Anniv of Charles de Gaulle. Designs as Nos. 1937 and 1940 of France.

No.	Type	Description	Unused	Used
115		20f. black and purple	3·00	3·25
116		35f. black and purple	3·50	3·75

44 Mural, Airport Lounge

1972. Air. Inauguration of New Airport, Moroni.

No.	Type	Description	Unused	Used
117	**44**	65f. multicoloured	1·75	2·25
118	–	85f. multicoloured	2·25	2·25
119	–	100f. green, brown & blue	3·50	3·25

DESIGNS: 85f. Mural similar to T **44**; 100f. Airport Buildings.

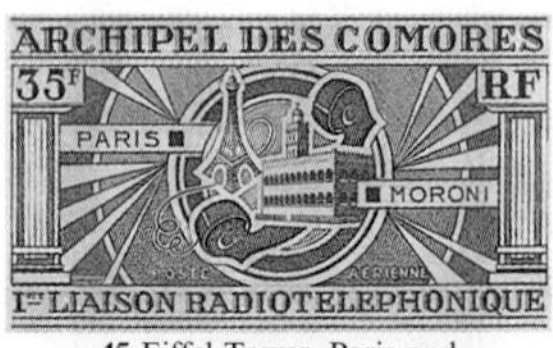

45 Eiffel Tower, Paris and Telecommunications Centre, Moroni

1972. Air. Inauguration of Paris–Moroni Radio-Telephone Link.

No.	Type	Description	Unused	Used
120	**45**	35f. red, purple & blue	2·50	2·25
121	–	75f. red, violet and blue	2·50	2·25

DESIGN: 75f. Telephone conversation.

46 Underwater Spear-fishing

1972. Air. Aquatic Sports.

No.	Type	Description	Unused	Used
122	**46**	70f. red, green and blue	7·25	5·25

47 Pasteur, Crucibles and Microscope

1972. 150th Birth Anniv of Louis Pasteur.

No.	Type	Description	Unused	Used
123	**47**	65f. blue, brown & orange	4·75	4·00

1972. Air. Anjouan Landscapes. (a) As T **39**. Multicoloured.

No.	Type	Description	Unused	Used
124		20f. Fortress wall, Cape Sima	1·60	1·90
125		35f. Bambao Palace	1·75	2·25
126		40f. Palace, Domoni	1·75	2·25
127		60f. Gomajou Island	2·75	2·75

(b) As T **40**.

No.	Type	Description	Unused	Used
128	–	100f. green, blue & brown	5·75	5·25

DESIGN: 100f. Map of Anjouan.

48 Pres. Said Mohamed Cheikh

50 Bank

1973. Air. Said Mohamed Cheikh, President of Comoro Council, Commemoration.

No.	Type	Description	Unused	Used
129	**48**	20f. multicoloured	1·90	2·25
130		35f. multicoloured	2·25	2·50

1973. Air. International Coelacanth Study Expedition. No. 72 surch **Mission Internationale pour l'etude du Coelacanthe** and value.

No.	Type	Description	Unused	Used
131		120f. on 90f. brn, grn & emer	10·50	7·00

1973. Great Comoro Landscapes. (a) Postage. As T **39**. Multicoloured.

No.	Type	Description	Unused	Used
132		10f. Goulaivoini	2·25	1·90
133		20f. Mitsamiouli	2·50	2·25
134		35f. Foumbouni	3·00	2·75
135		50f. Moroni	3·75	3·25

(b) Air. As Type **40**.

No.	Type	Description	Unused	Used
136	–	135f. purple, green & violet	10·50	6·25

DESIGN—VERT: 135f. Map of Great Comoro.

1973. Moroni Buildings. Multicoloured.

No.	Type	Description	Unused	Used
137		5f. Type **50**	2·00	2·25
138		15f. Post Office	2·25	2·50
139		20f. Prefecture	2·50	2·75

51 Volcanic Eruption

1973. Air. Karthala Volcanic Eruption (Sept 1972).

No.	Type	Description	Unused	Used
140	**51**	120f. multicoloured	9·50	6·50

52 Dr. G. A. Hansen

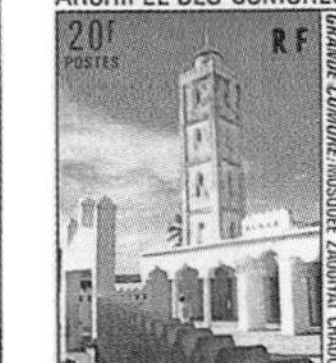

54 Zaouiyat Chaduli Mosque

53 Pablo Picasso (artist)

1973. Air Centenary of Hansen's Identification of Leprosy Bacillus.
141 **52** 100f. green, purple & blue . . 4·75 3·75

1973. Air. 500th Birth Anniv of Nicolas Copernicus. As T **52**.
142 150f. purple, blue & ultram . . 6·25 5·25
DESIGN: 150f. Copernicus and solar system.

1973. Air. Picasso Commemoration.
143 **53** 200f. multicoloured . . . . 12·00 8·00

1973. Mosques. Multicoloured.
145 20f. Type **54** . . . . 2·00 2·75
146 35f. Salimata Hamissi Mosque (horiz) . . . . . 2·75 2·75

55 Star and Ribbon

56 Said Omar Ben Soumeth (Grand Mufti of the Comoros)

1974. Air. Order of the Star of Anjouan.
147 **55** 500f. gold, blue & brown . . 16·00 13·00

1974. Air. Multicoloured.
148 135f. Type **56** . . . . 4·00 2·75
149 200f. Ben Soumeth seated (vert) . . . . 5·50 4·50

57 Doorway of Mausoleum

58 Wooden Combs

1974. Mausoleum of Shaikh Said Mohamed.
150 **57** 35f. brown, black & green . . 2·75 2·75
151 – 50f. brown, black & green . . 3·75 2·75
DESIGN: 50f. Mausoleum.

1974. Comoro Handicrafts (1st series). Mult.
152 15f. Type **58** . . . . 1·90 2·25
153 20f. Three-legged table . . . 2·25 2·25
154 35f. Koran lectern (horiz) . . 3·00 2·75
155 75f. Sugar-cane press (horiz) . . 5·25 3·50
See also Nos. 164/7.

59 Mother and Child

1974. Comoros Red Cross Fund.
156 **59** 35f.+10f. brown & red . . 2·00 2·75

1974. Air. Mayotte Landscapes. (a) As T **39**. Multicoloured.
157 20f. Moya beach . . . . . . 1·75 1·90
158 35f. Chiconi . . . . 1·90 1·90
159 90f. Mamutzu harbour . . . 4·00 3·25

(b) As T **40**.
160 120f. green and blue . . . . 7·25 4·75
DESIGN—VERT: 120f. Map of Mayotte.

60 U.P.U. Emblem and Globe

1974. Centenary of Universal Postal Union.
161 **60** 30f. red, brown and green . . 2·75 3·00

61 Boeing 707 taking off

1975. Inauguration of Direct Moroni–Hahaya–Paris Air Service.
162 **61** 135f. blue, green and red . . 7·25 6·25

62 Rotary Emblem, Moroni Clubhouse and Map

1975. Air. 70th Anniv of Rotary International and 10th Anniv of Moroni Rotary Club.
163 **62** 250f. multicoloured . . . . 9·50 8·75

63 Bracelet

1975. Comoro Handicrafts (2nd series).
164 **63** 20f. brown and purple . . 2·50 2·25
165 – 35f. brown and green . . . 2·50 2·50
166 – 120f. brown and blue . . . 6·00 4·50
167 – 135f. brown and red . . . 8·75 5·25
DESIGNS: 35f. Diadem; 120f. Sabre; 125f. Dagger.

1975. Moheli Landscapes. (a) Postage. As T **39**. Multicoloured.
168 30f. Mohani Village . . . . 2·75 2·50
169 50f. Djoezi Village . . . . . 3·25 2·75
170 55f. Chirazian tombs . . . . 4·25 3·25

(b) Air. As T **40**.
171 230f. green, blue and brown . . 12·00 8·00
DESIGN: 230f. Map of Moheli.

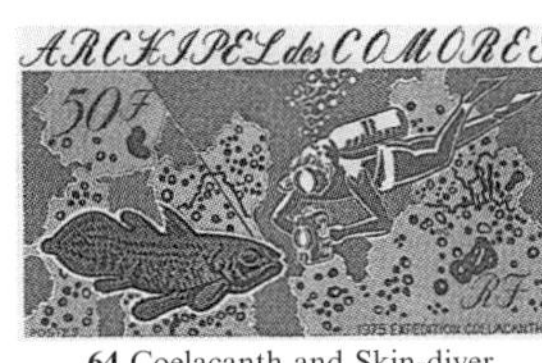

64 Coelacanth and Skin-diver

1975. Coelacanth Expedition.
172 **64** 50f. bistre, blue & brown . . 6·50 4·50

65 Tambourine-player

1975. Folklore Dances. Multicoloured.
173 100f. Type **65** . . . . 60·00 60·00
174 150f. Dancers with tambourines . . . . 60·00 60·00

66 Athlete and Athens, 1896 Motifs

1976. Olympic Games, Munich (1972) and Montreal (1976). Multicoloured.
175 20f. Type **66** (postage) . . . 15 10
176 25f. Running 15 10
177 40f. Athlete and Paris, 1900 motif 25 15
178 75f. High-jumping 45 20
179 100f. Exercises and World's Fair, St. Louis, 1904 motif (air) 55 35
180 500f. Gymnast on bars . . . 3·75 1·40

67 Government House, Flag and Map

1976. 1st Anniv of Independence. Multicoloured.
182 **67** 30f. multicoloured 25 15
183 50f. multicoloured 35 20

68 Agricultural Scene and U.N. Stamp

1976. 25th Anniv of U.N. Postal Services. Multicoloured.
184 15f. Type **68** (postage) . . . 10 10
185 30f. Surgery scene and U.N.W.H.O. stamp 20 10
186 50f. Village scene and U.N.I.C.E.F. stamp . . . 3·75 50
187 75f. Telecommunications satellite and U.N. I.T.U. stamp 45 20
188 200f. Concorde, airship "Graf Zeppelin" and U.N. I.C.A.O. stamp (air) . . . 2·50 85
189 400f. Lufthansa jet airliner and U.N. U.P.U. stamp . . 3·00 1·40

69 Copernicus, and Rocket on Launch-pad

1976. "Success of Operation Viking", and Bicentenary of American Revolution. Multicoloured.
191 5f. Type **69** (postage) 10 10
192 10f. Einstein, Sagan and Young (horiz) 10 10
193 25f. "Viking" orbiting Mars . . 15 10
194 35f. Vikings' discovery of America (horiz) 50 20
195 100f. U.S. flag and Mars landing 65 30
196 500f. First colour photograph of Martian terrain (horiz) (air) . . . . 4·00 1·25

70 U.N. Headquarters, New York and Flags

1976. 1st Anniv of Comoro Islands Admission to United Nations.
198 **70** 40f. multicoloured 30 20
199 50f. multicoloured 40 25

71 President Lincoln and Bombardment of Fort Sumter

1976. Bicentenary of American Revolution. Showing various battle scenes of American Civil War. Multicoloured.
200 10f. Type **71** (postage) . . . 10 10
201 30f. General Beauregard and Bull Run (vert) 20 10
202 50f. General Johnston and Antietam 30 15
203 100f. General Meade and Gettysburg (air) 55 30
204 200f. General Sherman and Chattanooga (vert) . . . . 1·40 45
205 400f. General Pickett and Appomattox . . . . 2·75 90

72 Andean Condor

74 Giffard's Dirigible, 1851 and French Locomotive, 1837

73 Wolf

1976. "Endangered Animals" (1st series). Multicoloured.
207 15f. Type **72** (postage) . . . 1·75 55
208 20f. Tiger cat (horiz) 50 15
209 35f. Leopard 65 15
210 40f. White rhinoceros (horiz) . . 90 40
211 75f. Mountain nyala . . . . 1·60 45
212 400f. Orang-utan (horiz) (air) . . 4·50 1·25

1977. "Endangered Animals" (2nd series). Mult.
214 10f. Type **73** (postage) . . . 10 10
215 30f. Aye-aye 20 10
216 40f. Banded duiker 65 15
217 50f. Giant tortoise 80 15
218 200f. Ocelot (air) . . . . . . 1·90 55
219 400f. Galapagos penguin ("Manchot des Galapagos") . . . . . . 7·00 3·00

1977. History of Communications. Airships and Railways. Multicoloured.
221 20f. Type **74** (postage) . . . 30 10
222 25f. Santos-Dumont's airship "Ballon No. 6" (1906) and Brazilian steam locomotive (19th century) 65 15
223 50f. Russian airship "Astra" (1914) and "Trans-Siberian Express" (1905) 90 20
224 75f. British airship R-34 (1919) and "Southern Belle" pullman express (1910–25) . . . . 1·10 30
225 200f. U.S. Navy airship "Los Angeles" (1930) and Pacific locomotive (1930) (air) . . 4·25 50
226 500f. German airship "Hindenburg", 1933, and "Rheingold" express, 1933 . . 7·75 1·50

75 Koch, Morgan, Fleming, Muller and Waksman (medicine)

1977. Nobel Prize Winners. Multicoloured.
228 30f. Type **75** (postage) . . . 20 10
229 40f. Michelson, Bragg, Raman and Zernike (physics) 20 15
230 50f. Tagore, Yeats, Russell and Hemingway (literature) 30 15
231 100f. Rontgen, Becquerel, Planck, Lawrence and Einstein (physics) 80 25
232 200f. Ramsey and Marie Curie (chemistry), Banting and Hench (medicine) and Perrin (physics) (air) . . . 1·40 45
233 400f. Dunant, Briand, Schweitzer and Martin Luther King (peace) . . . 3·25 90

The 200f. wrongly attributes the chemistry prize to all those depicted and gives the date 1913 instead of 1911 for Marie Curie. On the 50 and 100f. names are wrongly spelt.

76 "Clara, Ruben's Daughter"

1977. 400th Birth Anniv of Peter Paul Rubens (1st issue). Multicoloured.
235 20f. Type **76** (postage) . . . 10 10
236 25f. "Suzanne Fourment" . . 15 10
237 50f. "Venus in front of Mirror" 55 15
238 75f. "Ceres" 70 25
239 200f. "Young Girl with Blond Hair" (air) . . . . 1·40 95
240 500f. "Helene Fourment in Wedding Dress" . . . . . 4·50 1·25

See also Nos. 407/10.

77 Queen Elizabeth II, Westminster Abbey and Guards

1977. Air. Silver Jubilee of Queen Elizabeth II.
242 **77** 500f. multicoloured . . . . 3·25 1·40

79 Swordfish

1977. Fishes. Multicoloured.
256 30f. Type **79** (postage) . . . 20 10
257 40f. Oriental sweetlips . . . 55 15
258 50f. Lionfish 80 15
259 100f. Racoon butterflyfish . . 1·60 25
260 200f. Clown anemonefish (air) 2·00 65
261 400f. Black-spotted puffer . . 3·50 1·75

80 Jupiter Lander

1977. Space Research. Multicoloured.
263 30f. Type **80** (postage) . . . 20 10
264 50f. Uranus probe (vert) . . 35 15
265 75f. Venus probe 45 20
266 100f. Space shuttle (vert) . . 55 25
267 200f. "Viking 3" (air) . . . . 1·25 45
268 400f. "Apollo–Soyuz" link (vert) . . . . 2·40 90

1977. Air. First Paris–New York Commercial Flight of Concorde. No. 188 optd **Paris-New-York - 22 nov. 1977**.
270 200f. multicoloured . . . . . 2·75 2·00

82 Allen's Gallinule

1978. Birds. Multicoloured.
271 15f. Type **82** (postage) . . . 50 25
272 20f. Blue-cheeked bee eater 70 35
273 35f. Madagascar malachite kingfisher 85 45
274 40f. Madagascar paradise flycatcher 95 55
275 75f. Anjouan sunbird . . . . 1·60 80
276 400f. Great egret (air) . . . . 6·25 3·75

83 Greek Ball Game and Modern Match

1978. World Cup Football Championship, Argentina. Multicoloured.
278 30f. Type **83** (postage) . . . 20 10
279 50f. Breton football 25 15
280 75f. 14th-century London game 45 25
281 100f. 18th-century Italian game 55 25
282 200f. 19th-century English game (air) . . . . 1·10 45
283 400f. English cup-tie, 1891 . . 2·50 85

84 "Oswolt Krel"

1978. 450th Death Anniv of Albrecht Durer (artist) (1st issue). Multicoloured.
286 20f. Type **84** (postage) . . . 10 10
287 25f. "Elspeth Tucher" . . . 15 10
288 50f. "Hieronymus Holzshuher" 35 15
289 75f. "Young Girl" 50 25
290 200f. "Emperor Maximilian I" (air) . . . . 1·10 45
291 500f. "Young Girl" (detail) 3·25 1·10

See also Nos. 411/15.

85 Bach

1978. Composers. Multicoloured.
293 30f. Type **85** (postage) . . . 20 10
294 40f. Mozart 25 15
295 50f. Berlioz 35 15
296 100f. Verdi 90 25
297 200f. Tchaikovsky (air) . . . 1·60 45
298 400f. Gershwin . . . . . . 3·25 85

Following a revolution on 13 May 1978, it was announced that sets showing Butterflies or commemorating the 25th Anniversary of the Coronation of Queen Elizabeth II, 10th World Telecommunications Day and Aviation History had not been placed on sale in the islands and were not valid for postage there.

86 Rowland Hill, Locomotive "Adler" and Saxony 3pf. Stamp, 1860

1978. Death Centenary of Sir Rowland Hill. Multicoloured.
300 20f. Type **86** (postage) . . . 1·75 50
301 30f. Penny-farthing and Netherlands 5c. stamp, 1852 . . . . 20 10
302 40f. Early letter-box and 2d. blue 25 15
303 75f. Pony Express and U.S. stamp, 1847 . . . . . . 45 20
304 200f. Airship and French 20c. stamp, 1863 (air) . . . . . 1·50 65
305 400f. Postman and Basel 2½r. stamp, 1845 . . . . 2·50 85

87 Interpreting Meteorological Satellite Photographs

1978. European Space Agency. Multicoloured.
307 10f. Type **87** (postage) . . . 10 10
308 25f. Writing weather forecast 15 10
309 35f. Aiding wrecked ship . . 70 20
310 50f. Telecommunications as teaching aid 35 15
311 100f. Boeing 727 landing (air) 75 40
312 500f. Space shuttle . . . . . 3·25 1·10

1978. Argentina's Victory in World Cup Football Championship. Nos. 278/284 optd **REP. FED. ISLAMIQUE DES COMORES 1 ARGENTINE 2 HOLLANDE 3 BRESIL**.
314 **83** 30f. mult (postage) 20 10
315 – 50f. multicoloured 35 15
316 – 75f. multicoloured 45 20
317 – 100f. multicoloured 50 25
318 – 200f. multicoloured (air) 1·40 45
319 – 400f. multicoloured . . . . 2·50 85

89 Philidor, Anderssen and Steinitz

1979. Chess Grand Masters. Multicoloured.
321 40f. Type **89** (postage) . . . 20 10
322 100f. Venetian players and pieces 80 20
323 500f. Alekhine, Spassky and Fischer (air) . . . . 4·00 1·10

90 Galileo and "Voyager 1"

1979. Exploration of the Solar System. Mult.
324 20f. Type **90** (postage) . . . 10 10
325 30f. Kepler and "Voyager 2" 15 10
326 40f. Copernicus and "Voyager 1" 20 10
327 100f. Huygens and "Voyager 2" 45 20
328 200f. Herschel and "Voyager 2" (air) . . . . 1·40 35
329 400f. Leverrier and "Voyager 2" . . . . 2·50 80

91 Kayak

1979. Olympic Games, Moscow (1980). Mult.
330 10f. Type **91** (postage) . . . 10 10
331 25f. Swimming 15 10
332 35f. Archery 20 10
333 50f. Pole vault 25 15
334 75f. Long jump 35 20
335 500f. High jump (air) . . . . 3·25 1·00

92 "Charaxes defulvata"

1979. Fauna. Multicoloured.
336 30f. Type **92** 50 15
337 50f. Courol . . . . 1·25 60
338 75f. Blue-cheeked bee eater 1·75 90

1979. Optd or surch **REPUBLIQUE FEDERALE ISLAMIQUE DES COMORES**. (a) Birds, Nos. 271/275.
339 15f. Type **82** 40 40
340 30f. on 35f. Madagascar malachite kingfisher . . . 70 70
341 50f. on 20f. Blue-cheeked bee eater . . . . 1·10 1·10
342 50f. on 40f. Madagascar paradise flycatcher . . . . 1·25 1·25
343 200f. on 75f. Anjouan sunbird . . . . 3·25 3·25

(b) World Cup, Nos. 278/282.
344 1f. on 100f. Italian game (postage) 10 10
345 2f. on 75f. London game . . 10 10
346 3f. on 30f. Type **83** 10 10
347 50f. Breton football 35 35
348 200f. English game (air) . . . 1·40 1·40

1979. Nos. 293/7 surch or optd **Republique Federale Islamique des Comores**.
349 – 5f. on 100f. Verdi (post) . . 10 10
350 **85** 30f. J. S. Bach 25 25
351 – 40f. Mozart 25 25
352 – 50f. Berlioz 40 40
353 – 50f. on 200f. Tchaikovsky (air) 65 65

94 State Coach

1979. 25th Anniv of Coronation of Queen Elizabeth II. Multicoloured.
354 5f. on 25f. Type **94** (postage) 10 10
355 10f. Drum Major 15 15
356 50f. on 40f. Queen carrying orb and sceptre 40 40
357 100f. St. Edward's Crown . . 80 80
358 50f. on 200f. Herald reading Proclamation (air) 65 65

Nos. 354/8 were only valid for postage overprinted as in Type **94**.

95 "Papilio dardanus-cenea stoll"

1979. Butterflies. Multicoloured.
359 5f. on 20f. Type **95** 10 10
360 15f. "Papilio dardanus–brown" 15 15
361 30f. "Chrysiridia croesus" . . 40 30
362 50f. "Precis octavia" 80 70
363 75f. "Bunaea alcinoe" . . . 1·25 1·00
Nos. 359/63 were only valid for postage overprinted as in Type **95**.

96 Otto Lilienthal and Glider

1979. History of Aviation. Multicoloured.
364 30f. Type **96** (postage) . . . 30 30
365 50f. Wright Brothers 50 50
366 50f. on 75f. Louis Bleriot . . 50 50
367 100f. Claude Dornier . . . . 1·00 1·00
368 200f. Charles Lindbergh (air) 1·25 1·25
Nos. 364/8 were only valid for postage overprinted as in Type **96**.

97 Tobogganing **98** Lychees

1979. International Year of the Child (1st issue). Multicoloured.
369 20f. Astronauts (postage) . . 10 10
370 30f. Type **97** 15 10
371 40f. Painting 20 10
372 100f. Locomotive "Rocket", 1829, and toy train . . . . 4·00 60
373 200f. Football (air) . . . . . 1·40 35
374 400f. Canoeing . . . . . . 2·50 80
See also Nos. 389/90.

1979. Fruit. Multicoloured.
375 60f. Type **98** 40 15
376 70f. Papaws 45 20
377 100f. Avocado pears 80 30
378 125f. Bananas . . . . 1·00 35

101 Rotary Emblem and Village Scene

1979. Air. Rotary International.
388 **101** 400f. multicoloured . . . 4·50 2·50

102 Mother and Child on Boat **103** Basketball

1979. Air. International Year of the Child (2nd issue). Multicoloured.
389 200f.+30f. Type **102** . . . . 2·50 2·25
390 250f. Mother and baby . . . 2·50 1·60

1979. Indian Ocean Olympic Games.
391 **103** 200f. multicoloured . . . 1·50 90

1979. Various stamps optd **REPUBLIQUE FEDERALE ISLAMIQUE DES COMORES.**
(a) Air. Apollo–Soyuz Space Test Project (Appendix).
392 100f. Presidents Brezhnev and Ford with astronauts . . . 80 80
393 200f. Space link-up . . . . . 1·40 1·40
(b) Bicentenary of American Revolution (Appendix).
394 25f. Fremont, Kit Carson and dancing Indian 15 15
395 35f. D. Boone, Buffalo Bill and wagon train 20 20
396 75f. H. Wells, W. Fargo and stagecoach ambush 40 40
(c) Winter Olympic Games, Innsbruck (Appendix).
397 35f. Speed skating 20 20
(d) Telephone Centenary (Appendix).
398 75f. Philip Reis 40 40
(e) Air. Olympic Games, Munich and Montreal.
399 100f. multicoloured (No. 179) 80 80
(f) U.N. Postal Services.
400 75f. mult (No. 187) 40 40
(g) Endangered Animals.
401 35f. mult (No. 209) 30 20
402 40f. mult (No. 210) 40 25
(h) Nobel Prize Winners.
403 100f. mult (No. 231) 80 80
(i) Rubens.
404 25f. mult (No. 236) 15 15
(j) Durer.
405 25f. mult (No. 287) 15 15
406 75f. mult (No. 289) 40 40

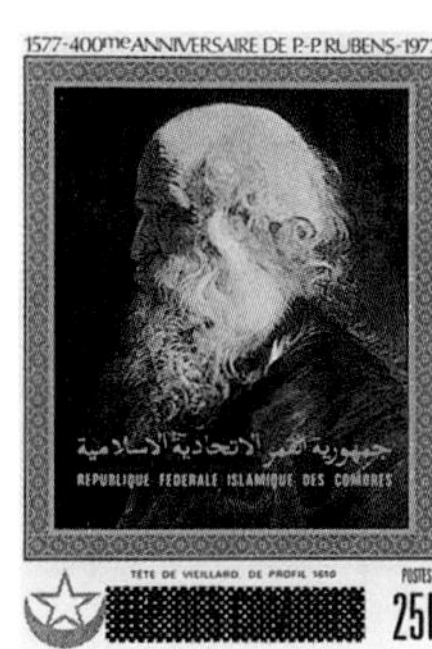

105 "Profile Head of Old Man"

1979. 400th Birth Anniv of Peter Paul Rubens (artist) (2nd issue). Multicoloured.
407 25f. Type **105** 15 15
408 35f. "Young Girl with Flag" 20 20
409 50f. "Isabelle d'Este, Margave of Mantua" . . . 35 35
410 75f. "Philip IV, King of Spain" 40 40

106 "Portrait of Young Girl"

1979. 450th Death Anniv of Albrecht Durer (artist) (2nd issue). Multicoloured.
411 20f. "Self-portrait" (postage) 15 15
412 30f. "Young Man" 20 20
413 40f. Type **106** 25 25
414 100f. "Jerome" (air) 80 80
415 200f. "Jacob Muffel" . . . . 1·40 1·40

107 Satellite and Receiving Station

1979. 10th World Telecommunications Day. Multicoloured.
416 75f. Satellites 40 40
417 100f. Two satellites 45 45
418 200f. Type **107** . . . . . . 1·40 90

108 Pirogue

1980. Handicrafts. Multicoloured.
419 60f. Type **108** 65 20
420 100f. Anjouan puppet 80 25

109 Sultan Said Ali

1980. Sultans. Multicoloured.
421 40f. Type **109** 20 15
422 60f. Sultan Ahmed 30 15

110 Dimadjou Dispensary

1980. Air. 75th Anniv of Rotary International and 15th Anniv of Moroni Rotary Club (100f.).
423 100f. Type **110** 80 35
424 260f. Concorde airplane . . . 2·25 1·10

111 Sherlock Holmes and Sir Arthur Conan Doyle

1980. 50th Death Anniv of Sir Arthur Conan Doyle (writer).
425 **111** 200f. multicoloured . . . 1·50 95

112 Grand Mosque and Holy Ka'aba, Mecca

1980. 1350th Anniv of Occupation of Mecca by Mohammed.
426 **112** 75f. multicoloured 60 25

113 Dome of the Rock

1980. Year of the Holy City, Jerusalem.
427 **113** 60f. multicoloured 55 20

114 Kepler, Copernicus

1980. 50th Anniv of Discovery of Pluto.
428 **114** 400f. violet, red & mauve 3·25 2·00

115 Avicenna

1980. Birth Millenary of Avicenna (physician and philosopher).
429 **115** 60f. multicoloured 65 25

116 Mermoz, Dabry, Gimie and Seaplane "Comte da la Vaulx"

1980. 50th Anniv of First South Atlantic Flight.
430 **116** 200f. multicoloured . . . 2·25 1·40

1981. Various stamps surch.
431 15f. on 200f. multicoloured (No. 425) (postage) 10 10
432 20f. on 75f. mult (No. 426) 15 15
433 40f. on 125f. mult (No. 378) 25 25
434 60f. on 75f. mult (No. 338) 1·50 75
435 30f. on 200f. multicoloured (No. 430) (air) 30 30

118 Team posing with Shield

1981. World Cup Football Championship, Spain (1982). Multicoloured.
436 60f. Footballers coming on Field (vert) 30 15
437 75f. Type **118** 35 20
438 90f. Captains shaking hands 40 20
439 100f. Tackle 45 25
440 150f. Players hugging after goal (vert) . . . . 1·10 30

119 "Bowls and Pot"

1981. Birth Centenary of Pablo Picasso. Mult.
442 40f. "Dove and Rainbow" . . 20 10
443 70f. "Still-life on Chest of Drawers" 55 15
444 150f. "Studio with Plaster Head" . . . . 1·10 35
445 250f. Type **119** . . . . 1·90 55
446 500f. "Red Tablecloth" . . . 4·00 1·40

120 "Apollo" Launch

1981. Conquest of Space. Multicoloured.

No.	Description	Unused	Used
447	50f. Type **120**	25	15
448	75f. Space Shuttle launch	35	20
449	100f. Space Shuttle releasing fuel tank	45	30
450	450f. Space Shuttle in orbit	3·00	1·10

121 Buckingham Palace

1981. British Royal Wedding. Multicoloured.

No.	Description	Unused	Used
452	125f. Type **121**	90	25
453	200f. Highgrove House	1·40	45
454	450f. Caernarvon Castle	2·75	1·00

1981. Design as Type O **99** but inscr "POSTES 1981".

No.	Description	Unused	Used
456	5f. green, black & brn	10	10
457	15f. green, black & yell	10	10
458	25f. green, black & red	15	10
459	35f. green, black & lt grn	20	10
460	75f. green, black & blue	35	20

1981. Various stamps surch.

No.	Type	Description	Unused	Used
461	**114**	5f. on 400f. violet, red and mauve (postage)	10	10
462	–	20f. on 90f. mult (No. 438)	10	10
463	–	45f. on 100f. mult (No. 377)	20	10
464	–	45f. on 100f. mult (No. 420)	20	10
465	–	10f. on 70f. mult (No. 443) (air)	10	10
466	**110**	10f. on 100f. mult	10	10
467	**102**	50f. on 200f.+30f. mult	25	15
468	–	50f. on 260f. mult (No. 424)	60	30

123 Mercedes, 1914

1981. 75th Anniv of French Grand Prix Motor Race. Multicoloured.

No.	Description	Unused	Used
469	20f. Type **123**	10	10
470	50f. Delage, 1925	50	15
471	75f. Rudi Caracciola	65	20
472	90f. Stirling Moss	80	20
473	150f. Maserati, 1957	1·25	30

124 Scouts preparing to Sail

1981. 75th Anniv of Boy Scout Movement. Multicoloured.

No.	Description	Unused	Used
475	50f. Type **124**	25	15
476	75f. Paddling pirogue	75	20
477	250f. Sailing felucca	1·75	80
478	350f. Scouts looking out to sea from boat	2·50	85

125 Goethe

1982. 150th Death Anniv of Goethe (poet).

No.	Type	Description	Unused	Used
480	**125**	75f. multicoloured	35	20
481		350f. multicoloured	2·40	85

126 Princess of Wales

1982. 21st Birthday of Princess of Wales.

No.	Type	Description	Unused	Used
482	**126**	200f. multicoloured	1·40	45
483	–	300f. multicoloured	2·00	70

DESIGN: 300f. Different portrait of Princess.

1982. Birth of Prince William of Wales. Nos. 452/4 optd **NAISSANCE ROYALE 1982**.

No.	Description	Unused	Used
485	125f. Type **121**	90	25
486	200f. Highgrove House	1·40	45
487	450f. Caernarvon Castle	2·75	1·60

1982. World Cup Football Championship Winners. Nos. 436/40 optd.

No.	Description	Unused	Used
489	60f. Type **117**	30	15
490	75f. Team posing with shield (horiz)	35	20
491	90f. Captains shaking hands (horiz)	40	20
492	100f. Tackle (horiz)	45	25
493	150f. Players hugging after goal	1·10	55

OVERPRINTS: 60f., 150f. **ITALIE - ALLEMAGNE (R.F.A.) 3 - 1.**; 75f., 90f., 100f. **ITALIE 3 ALLEMAGNE (R.F.A.) 1.**

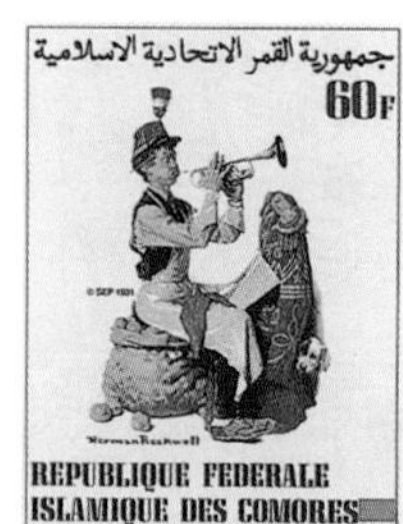

129 Boy playing Trumpet

1982. Norman Rockwell Paintings. Multicoloured.

No.	Description	Unused	Used
495	60f. Type **129**	30	15
496	75f. Sleeping porter	2·75	75
497	100f. Couple listening to early radio	80	25
498	150f. Children playing leapfrog	1·10	30
499	200f. Tramp cooking sausages	1·50	45
500	300f. Boy talking to clown	2·25	70

130 Sultan Said Mohamed Sidi

1982. Sultans. Multicoloured.

No.	Description	Unused	Used
501	30f. Type **130**	15	10
502	60f. Sultan Ahmed Abdallah	30	15
503	75f. Sultan Salim (horiz)	35	20
504	300f. Sultans Said Mohamed Sidi and Ahmed Abdallah (horiz)	2·10	95

131 Montgolfier Brothers' Balloon, 1783

1983. Air. Bicentenary of Manned Flight. Mult.

No.	Description	Unused	Used
505	100f. Type **131**	80	35
506	200f. Vincenzo Lunardi's balloon over London, 1784	1·40	65
507	300f. Blanchard and Jeffries crossing the Channel, 1785	2·25	1·00
508	400f. Henri Giffard's steam-powered dirigible airship, 1852 (horiz)	3·00	1·25

132 Type "470" Dinghy

1983. Air. Pre-Olympic Year. Multicoloured.

No.	Description	Unused	Used
510	150f. Type **132**	1·40	65
511	200f. "Flying Dutchman"	1·60	80
512	300f. Type "470" (different)	2·40	1·25
513	400f. "Finn" class dinghies	3·50	1·75

133 Lake Ziani

1983. Landscapes. Multicoloured.

No.	Description	Unused	Used
515	60f. Type **133**	50	20
516	100f. Sunset	65	35
517	175f. Chiromani (vert)	1·10	60
518	360f. Itsandra beach	2·25	1·00
519	400f. Anjouan	2·75	1·25

134 Moheli

1983. Portraits. Multicoloured.

No.	Description	Unused	Used
520	30f. Type **134**	15	10
521	35f. "Mask of Beauty"	45	15
522	50f. Mayotte	45	15

135 Pure-bred Arab

1983. Horses. Multicoloured.

No.	Description	Unused	Used
523	75f. Type **135**	55	25
524	100f. Anglo-Arab	65	35
525	125f. Lipizzan	90	40
526	150f. Tennessee	1·10	50
527	200f. Appaloosa	1·40	65
528	300f. Pure-bred English	2·25	1·00
529	400f. Clydesdale	2·75	1·00
530	500f. Andalusian	3·50	1·25

136 "Double Portrait" 137 Symbols of Development

1983. 500th Birth Anniv of Raphael. Mult.

No.	Description	Unused	Used
531	100f. Type **136**	65	35
532	200f. Fresco detail	1·40	65
533	300f. "St. George and the Dragon"	2·00	75
534	400f. "Balthazar Castiglione"	2·75	1·00

1984. Air. International Conference on Development of Comoros.

No.	Type	Description	Unused	Used
535	**137**	475f. multicoloured	3·25	1·75

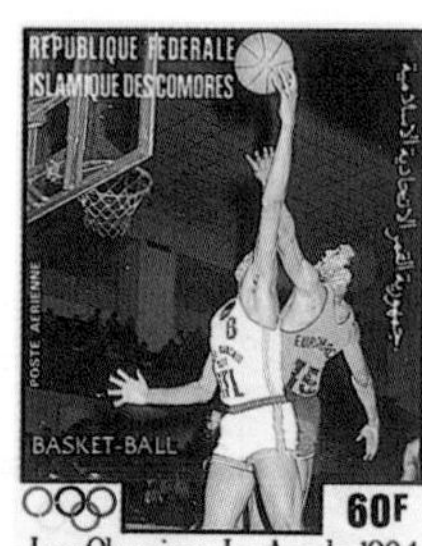

138 Basketball

1984. Air. Olympic Games, Los Angeles. Mult.

No.	Description	Unused	Used
536	60f. Type **138**	25	20
537	100f. Basketball (different)	70	35
538	165f. Basketball (different)	1·00	55
539	175f. Baseball (horiz)	1·10	55
540	200f. Baseball (different) (horiz)	1·40	55

139 "William Fawcett"

1984. Transport. Multicoloured. (a) Ships.

No.	Description	Unused	Used
542	100f. Type **139**	80	70
543	150f. "Lightning"	1·50	80
544	200f. "Rapido"	1·75	90
545	350f. "Sindia"	3·25	2·40

(b) Automobiles.

No.	Description	Unused	Used
546	100f. De Dion Bouton and Trepardoux, 1885	1·10	35
547	150f. Benz "Victoria", 1893	1·50	45
548	200f. Colombia electric, 1901	2·00	55
549	350f. Fiat, 1902	3·00	80

140 Barn Swallows

1985. Air. Birth Bicentenary of John J. Audubon (ornithologist). Multicoloured.

No.	Description	Unused	Used
550	100f. Type **140**	1·50	90
551	125f. Northern oriole	1·60	1·10
552	150f. Red-shouldered hawk (horiz)	1·90	1·25
553	500f. Red-breasted sapsucker (horiz)	6·25	4·50

142 Harbours

1985. Air. "Philexafrique" Stamp Exhibition, Lome, Togo (1st issue). Multicoloured.
555 200f. Type **142** . . . . 2·00 1·00
556 200f. Scouts walking along road . . . . 1·50 85
See also Nos. 576/7.

143 Victor Hugo (novelist, death centenary)

1985. Anniversaries. Multicoloured.
557 100f. Type **143** . . . . 1·00 30
558 200f. Jules Verne (novelist) (80th death anniv) . . . . 1·40 60
559 300f. Mark Twain (150th birth anniv) . . . . 2·25 1·00
560 450f. Queen Elizabeth, the Queen Mother (85th birth anniv) (vert) . . . . 2·75 1·00
561 500f. Statue of Liberty (centenary) (vert) . . . . . 3·25 1·25
The 200f. and 300f. also commemorate International Youth Year.

144 Map and Flag on Sun

1985. Air. 10th Anniv of Independence.
562 **144** 10f. multicoloured 10 10
563 15f. multicoloured 10 10
564 125f. multicoloured . . . 1·10 40
565 300f. multicoloured . . . 2·50 1·10

145 Arthritic Spider Conch

1985. Shells. Multicoloured.
566 75f. Type **145** 70 35
567 125f. Silver conch . . . . . 1·00 45
568 200f. Costate tun . . . . . . 1·60 60
569 300f. Elephant's snout . . . 2·50 75
570 450f. Orange spider conch . . 3·75 1·00

146 U.N. Emblem and Map of Islands

1985. 10th Anniv of Membership of U.N.O.
571 **146** 5f. multicoloured 10 10
572 30f. multicoloured 15 10
573 75f. multicoloured 35 30
574 125f. multicoloured 90 40
575 400f. multicoloured . . . 2·50 1·50

147 Runners ("Youth")

1985. Air. "Philexafrique" Stamp Exhibition, Lome, Togo (2nd issue). Multicoloured.
576 250f. Type **147** . . . . 1·60 90
577 250f. Earth mover and road construction ("Development") . . . . . 1·60 90

148 Globe, Galleon, Wright Type A Biplane and Rocket Capsule

1985. 20th Anniv of Moroni Rotary Club.
578 **148** 25f. multicoloured 25 15
579 75f. multicoloured 75 30
580 125f. multicoloured . . . 1·40 45
581 500f. multicoloured . . . 4·25 1·40

149 "Astraeus hygrometricus"

1985. Fungi. Multicoloured.
582 75f. "Boletus edulis" 80 45
583 125f. "Sarcoscypha coccinea" 1·00 60
584 200f. "Hypholoma fasciculare" . . . . 1·60 60
585 350f. Type **149** . . . . . . 3·00 90
586 500f. "Armillariella mellea" 4·00 1·40

150 Sikorsky S-43 Amphibian

1985. Air. 50th Anniv of Union des Transports Aeriennes. Multicoloured.
587 25f. Type **150** 10 10
588 75f. Douglas DC-9 airplane and camel 45 30
589 100f. Douglas DC-4, DC-6, Nord 2501 Noratlas and De Havilland Heron 2 aircraft 55 35
590 125f. Maintenance 90 40
591 1000f. Emblem and Latecoere 28, Sikorsky S-43, Douglas DC-10 and Boeing 747-200 aircraft (35 × 47 mm) . . . 7·75 4·25

151 Edmond Halley, Comet and "Giotto" Space Probe

1986. Air. Appearance of Halley's Comet. Multicoloured.
593 125f. Type **151** 90 40
594 150f. Giacobini-Zinner comet, 1959 . . . . 1·10 55
595 225f. J. F. Encke and Encke comet, 1961 . . . . 1·60 75
596 300f. Computer enhanced picture of Bradfield comet, 1980 . . . . 2·10 1·10
597 450f. Halley's comet and "Planet A" space probe . . 3·00 1·50

152 Footballers

1986. Air. World Cup Football Championship, Mexico. Designs showing footballers.
598 **152** 125f. multicoloured . . . 90 40
599 – 210f. multicoloured . . . 1·40 70
600 – 500f. multicoloured . . . 3·25 1·50
601 – 600f. multicoloured . . . 4·00 1·75

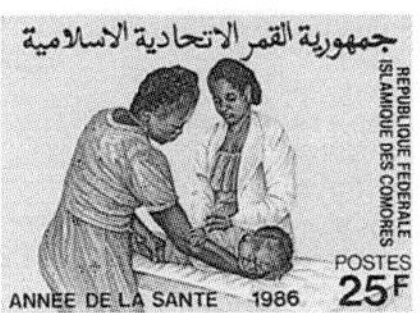

153 Doctor examining Child

1986. World Health Year. Multicoloured.
602 25f. Type **153** 10 10
603 100f. Doctor weighing child 70 35
604 200f. Nurse innoculating baby . . . . 1·40 70

154 Ndzoumara (wind instrument)
155 Server

1986. Musical Instruments. Multicoloured.
605 75f. Type **154** 55 25
606 125f. Ndzedze (string instrument) 80 40
607 210f. Gaboussi (string instrument) . . . . 1·40 70
608 500f. Ngoma (drums) . . . . 3·25 1·50

1987. Air. Tennis as 1988 Olympic Games Discipline. Multicoloured.
609 150f. Type **155** . . . . 1·10 50
610 250f. Player preparing shot 2·00 75
611 500f. Player being lobbed . . 3·50 1·25
612 600f. Players each side of net 4·00 1·50

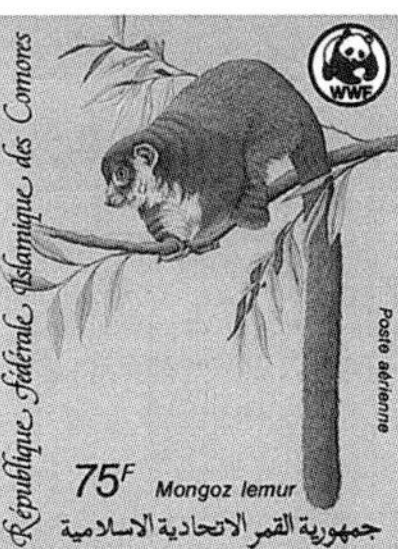

156 On Tree Branch

1987. Air. Endangered Animals. Mongoose-Lemur. Multicoloured.
613 75f. Type **156** 65 25
614 100f. Head of mongoose-lemur with ruff 90 30
615 125f. Mongoose-lemur on rock . . . . 1·40 40
616 150f. Head of mongoose-lemur without ruff . . . . 1·50 50

157 Women working in Field

1987. Woman and Development. Multicoloured.
617 75f. Type **157** 55 25
618 125f. Woman picking musk seeds (vert) . . . . 1·10 40
619 1000f. Woman making basket 6·75 2·25

158 Men's Downhill

1987. Air. Winter Olympic Games, Calgary (1988). Multicoloured.
620 150f. Type **158** 90 50
621 225f. Ski jumping . . . . . . 1·40 80
622 500f. Women's slalom . . . 3·25 1·50
623 600f. Men's luge . . . . . . 4·00 1·75

159 Didier Daurat, Raymond Vanier and "Air Bleu"

1987. Air. Aviation. Multicoloured.
624 200f. Type **159** . . . . 1·40 45
625 300f. Letord 4 Lorraine and route map (1st regular airmail service, Paris–Le Mans–St. Nazaire, 1918) 2·00 70
626 500f. Morane Saulnier Type H and route map (1st airmail flight, Villacoublay–Pauillac, 1913) . . . . . . 3·25 1·25
627 1000f. Henri Pequet flying Humber-Sommer biplane (1st aerophilately exn, Allahabad) (36 × 49 mm) 6·75 1·75

160 Ice Skating

1988. Multicoloured. (a) Winter Olympic Games, Calgary.
628 75f. Type **160** (postage) . . . 30 25
629 125f. Speed skating 50 40
630 350f. Two-man bobsleigh . . 2·25 75
631 400f. Biathlon (air) . . . . . 2·75 1·00

(b) Olympic Games, Seoul.
633 100f. Relay (postage) 65 30
634 150f. Showjumping . . . . . 1·00 50
635 500f. Pole-vaulting . . . . . 3·25 1·25
636 600f. Football (air) . . . . . 4·00 1·25

161 Kiwanis International Emblem and Hand supporting Figures

1988. Child Health Campaigns. Multicoloured.
638 75f. Type **161** 30 25
639 125f. Kiwanis emblem, wheelchair and crutch . . 80 40
640 210f. Kiwanis emblem and man with children (country inscr in black) . . . . . . 1·25 70
641 210f. As No. 640 but country inscr in white . . . . . 1·25 70
642 425f. As No. 639 . . . . . . 2·50 1·40
643 425f. As No. 639 but with Lions International emblem 2·50 1·40
644 500f. Type **161** . . . . 3·25 1·50
645 500f. As Type **161** but with Rotary emblem . . . . . 3·25 1·50

162 Throwing the Discus

163 Columbus and "Santa Maria"

1988. Olympic Games, Barcelona (1992) (1st issue). Multicoloured.
646 75f. Type **162** (postage) . . . 30 25
647 100f. Rowing (horiz) 65 30
648 125f. Cycling (horiz) 90 40
649 150f. Wrestling (horiz) . . . 1·00 50
650 375f. Basketball (air) . . . . 2·75 90
651 600f. Tennis . . . . 4·00 1·10
See also Nos. 709/14.

1988. 500th Anniv (1992) of Discovery of America by Columbus. Multicoloured.
653 75f. Type **163** (postage) . . . 75 30
654 125f. Martin Alonzo Pinzon and "Pinta" . . . . 1·00 50
655 150f. Vicente Yanez Pinzon and "Nina" . . . . 1·25 60
656 250f. Search for gold . . . . 1·60 85
657 375f. Wreck of "Santa Maria" (air) . . . . 2·50 1·00
658 450f. Preparation for fourth voyage . . . . 3·50 1·25

1988. Nos. 641, 643 and 645 (125 and 400f. with colours changed) surch.
660 75f. on 210f. multicoloured 55 25
661 125f. on 425f. multicoloured 80 40
662 200f. on 425f. multicoloured 1·40 65
663 300f. on 500f. multicoloured 1·90 1·00
664 400f. on 500f. multicoloured 2·75 1·25

1988. Olympic Games Medal Winners for Tennis. Nos. 609/12 optd.
665 150f. Optd **Medalle d'or Seoul Miloslav Mecir (Tchec.)** . . 1·00 50
666 250f. Optd **Medaille d'argent Seoul Tim Mayotte (U.S.A)** 1·60 1·10
667 500f. Optd **Medaille d'or Seoul Steffi Graf (R.F.A.)** 3·25 2·50
668 600f. Optd **Medaille d'argent Seoul Gabriela Sabatini (Argentine)** . . . . 4·00 2·75

166 Alberto Santos-Dumont and "14 bis"

1988. Air. Aviation Pioneers.
669 **166** 100f. purple 80 30
670 – 150f. mauve . . . . . . 1·10 50
671 – 200f. black . . . . . . 1·40 65
672 – 300f. brown . . . . . . 2·00 1·00
673 – 500f. blue . . . . . . 3·25 1·75
674 – 800f. green . . . . . . 5·25 2·25
DESIGNS: 150f. Wright Type A and Orville and Wilbur Wright; 200f. Louis Bleriot and Bleriot XI; 300f. Farman Voisin No. 1 bis and Henri Farman; 500f. Gabriel and Charles Voisin and Voisin "Boxkite"; 800f. Roland Garros and Morane Saulnier Type I.

167 Galileo Galilei

168 Yuri Gagarin (cosmonaut) and Daughters

1988. Appearance of Halley's Comet. Mult.
675 200f.+10f. Type **167** . . . . 1·40 40
676 200f.+10f. Nicolas Copernicus . . . . 1·40 40
677 200f.+10f. Johannes Kepler 1·40 40
678 200f.+10f. Edmond Halley . . 1·40 40
679 200f.+10f. Japanese "Planet A" space probe . . . . . 1·40 40
680 200f.+10f. American "Ice" space probe . . . . . . 1·40 40
681 200f.+10f. "Planet A" space probe (different) . . . . . 1·40 40
682 200f.+10f. Russian "Vega" space probe . . . . 1·40 40

1988. Personalities. Multicoloured.
684 150f. Type **168** (20th death anniv) (postage) . . . . . 1·00 50
685 300f. Henri Dunant (founder of Red Cross) (125th anniv of Red Cross Movement) 2·00 75
686 400f. Roger Clemens (baseball player) . . . . . 2·50 1·25
687 500f. Gary Kasparov (chess player) (air) . . . . . . 4·00 1·75
688 600f. Paul Harris (founder of Rotary International) (birth centenary) . . . . 4·00 1·25

169 Alain Prost (racing driver) and Formula 1 Racing Car

1988. Cars, Trains and Yachts. Multicoloured.
690 75f. Type **169** (postage) . . . 1·10 25
691 125f. George Stephenson (railway engineer), "Rocket" and Borsig Class 05 steam locomotive, 1935, Germany . . . . 1·25 40
692 500f. Ettore Bugatti (motor manufacturer) and Aravis "Type 57" . . . . 3·25 1·00
693 600f. Rudolph Diesel (engineer) and German Class V200 diesel locomotive . . . . 4·00 1·50
694 750f. Dennis Conner and "Stars and Stripes" (America's Cup contender) (air) . . . . 5·00 1·50
695 1000f. Michael Fay and "New Zealand" (America's Cup contender) . . . . . 6·75 1·75

170 "Papilio nireus aristophontes" (female)

1989. Scouts, Butterflies and Birds. Multicoloured.
697 50f. Type **170** (postage) . . . 20 10
698 75f. "Papilio nireus aristophontes" (male) . . . 55 15
699 150f. "Charaxes fulvescens separanus" . . . . 1·10 40
700 375f. Bronze mannikin . . . 2·75 75
701 450f. "Charaxes castor comoranus" (air) . . . . . 3·00 80
702 500f. Madagascar white-eye 3·75 1·00

171 Aussat "K3" and N. Uphoff (individual dressage)

1989. Satellites and Olympic Games Medal Winners for Equestrian Events. Multicoloured.
704 75f. Type **171** (postage) . . . 30 15
705 150f. "Brasil sat" and P. Durand (individual show jumping) . . . . 1·00 40
706 375f. "ECS 4" and J. Martinek (modern pentathlon) . . . . 2·50 60
707 600f. "Olympus 1" and M. Todd (cross-country) (air) . . . . 4·00 1·25

172 Running

1989. Olympic Games, Barcelona (1992) (2nd issue). Multicoloured.
709 75f. Type **172** (postage) . . . 55 15
710 150f. Football . . . . 1·00 40
711 300f. Tennis . . . . 2·00 50
712 375f. Baseball . . . . 2·50 65
713 500f. Gymnastics (air) . . . 3·25 85
714 600f. Table tennis . . . . . 4·00 1·10

173 Dr. Joseph-Ignace Guillotin and Guillotine

1989. Bicentenary of French Revolution. Mult.
716 75f. Type **173** (postage) . . . 55 15
717 150f. Soldiers with cannon (Battle of Valmy) and Gen. Kellermann . . . . 1·00 40
718 375f. Jean Cottereau (Chouan) and Vendeens . . 2·25 60
719 600f. Invasion of Les Tuileries (air) . . . . . . 4·00 1·00

1989. Various stamps surch.
721 25f. on 250f. mult (No. 656) (postage) 35 10
722 150f. on 200f. mult (No. 532) 1·00 40
723 150f. on 200f. mult (No. 558) 1·00 40
724 150f. on 200f. mult (No. 604) 1·00 40
725 5f. on 250f. multicoloured (No. 390) (air) 10 10
726 25f. on 250f. mult (No. 610) 10 10
727 50f. on 250f. mult (No. 576) 20 10
728 50f. on 250f. mult (No. 577) 20 10
729 150f. on 200f. mult (No. 511) 1·00 50
730 150f. on 200f. mult (No. 555) 1·00 50
731 150f. on 200f. mult (No. 556) 1·00 40
732 150f. on 200f. black (No. 671) . . . . 1·00 60

175 Airport Pavilion

1990.
733 **175** 5f. orange, brown & red 10 10
734 10f. orange, brown & bl 10 10
735 25f. orange, brown & grn 10 10
736 – 50f. black and red 20 10
737 – 75f. black and blue . . . 35 10
738 – 150f. black and green . . 1·00 35
DESIGNS: 50 to 150f. Federal Assembly.

176 Player challenging Goalkeeper

1990. Air. World Cup Football Championship, Italy (1st issue). Multicoloured.
739 75f. Type **176** 65 10
740 150f. Player heading ball . . 1·00 35
741 500f. Overhead kick . . . . 3·25 1·25
742 1000f. Player evading tackle 6·75 1·75
See also Nos. 743/8.

177 Brazilian Player

1990. World Cup Football Championship, Italy (2nd issue). Multicoloured.
743 50f. Type **177** (postage) . . . 20 10
744 75f. English player 35 10
745 100f. West German player . . 50 25
746 150f. Belgian player . . . . 1·00 35
747 375f. Italian player (air) . . . 2·50 85
748 600f. Argentinian player . . . 4·00 85

178 U.S. Space Telescope

1990. Multicoloured.
750 75f. Type **178** (postage) . . . 60 10
751 150f. Pope John Paul II and Mikhail Gorbachev, 1989 1·00 35
752 200f. Kevin Mitchell (San Francisco Giants baseball player) . . . . 1·40 50
753 250f. De Gaulle and Adenauer, 1962 . . . . . 1·60 50
754 300f. "Titan 2002" space probe . . . . 2·00 70
755 375f. French TGV Atlantique express train and Concorde airplane . . . . 3·25 1·00
756 450f. Gary Kasparov (World chess champion) and Anderssen v Steinitz chess match (air) . . . . 3·25 1·00
757 500f. Paul Harris (founder of Rotary International) and symbols of health, hunger and humanity . . . . . . 3·25 75

179 Edi Reinalter (skiing, 1948)

180 Dish Aerial, Moroni Volo-volo

1990. Winter Olympics, Albertville (1992). Medal Winners at previous Games. Multicoloured.
759 75f. Type **179** (postage) . . . 35 10
760 100f. Canada (ice hockey, 1924) 50 25
761 375f. Baroness Gratia Schimmelpenninck van der Oye (skiing, 1936) (air) . . 2·50 85
762 600f. Hasu Haikki (ski jumping, 1948) . . . . . . 4·00 85

1991.
764 **180** 75f. multicoloured 60 10
765 150f. multicoloured . . . 1·00 35
766 225f. multicoloured . . . 1·40 55
767 300f. multicoloured . . . 2·00 70
768 500f. multicoloured . . . 3·25 1·25

181 Emblem and Leaves

1991. Indian Ocean Commission Conference.
769 **181** 75f. multicoloured 60 10
770 150f. multicoloured . . . 1·00 60
771 225f. multicoloured . . . 1·40 90

182 De Gaulle and Battle of Koufra, 1941

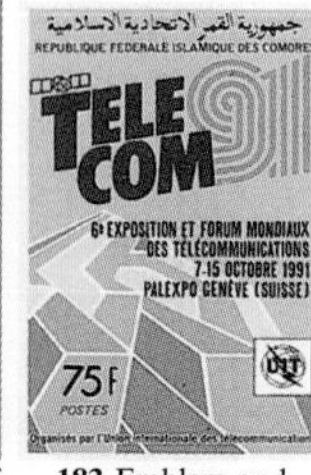
183 Emblem and Stylized View of Exhibition

1991. 50th Anniv of World War II. Multicoloured.
772 125f. Type **182** (postage) . . 90 30
773 150f. Errol Flynn in "Adventures in Burma" . . 1·00 35
774 300f. Henry Fonda in "The Longest Day" . . . . . . 2·00 70
775 375f. De Gaulle and Battle of Britain, 1940 . . . . . . 2·25 70

776 450f. Humphrey Bogart in "Sahara" (air) . . . . . . 3·00 75
777 500f. De Gaulle and Battle of Monte Cassino, 1944 . . . 3·25 75

1991. "Telecom '91" Int Telecommunications Exhibition, Geneva. Multicoloured.
779 75f. Type **183** 60 35
780 150f. Emblem (horiz) . . . . 1·00 80

184 Weather Space Station "Columbus"

1991. Anniversaries and Events. Multicoloured.
781 100f. Type **184** (postage) . . 70 15
782 150f. Gandhi (43rd death anniv) . . . . 1·00 25
783 250f. Henri Dunant (founder of Red Cross) (90th anniv of award of Nobel Peace Prize) . . . . 1·60 40
784 300f. Wolfgang Amadeus Mozart (composer, death bicentenary) . . . . 2·00 55
785 375f. Brandenburg Gate (bicent and second anniv of fall of Berlin Wall) . . . . 2·50 70
786 400f. Konrad Adenauer (German Chancellor) signing new constitution (25th death anniv) . . . . 2·50 70
787 450f. Elvis Presley (entertainer, 14th death anniv) (air) . . . . 3·25 80
788 500f. Ferdinand von Zeppelin (airship pioneer, 75th death anniv) . . . . 3·25 80

185 Cep

1992. Fungi and Shells. Multicoloured.
789 75f. Type **185** (postage) . . . 60 15
790 125f. Textile cone 80 35
791 150f. Puff-ball . . . . 1·50 55
792 150f. Bull-mouth helmet (shell) . . . . 1·00 40
793 500f. Map cowrie (air) . . . 3·25 1·00
794 600f. Scarlet elf cups . . . . 6·50 1·25

186 Ham (chimpanzee) on "Mercury" flight, 1960

1992. Space Research. Multicoloured.
796 75f. Type **186** (postage) . . . 60 10
797 125f. "Mars Observer" space probe 90 20
798 150f. Felix (cat) and "Veronique" rocket, 1963 1·10 50
799 150f. "Mars Rover" and "Marsokod" space vehicles 1·00 50
800 500f. "Phobos" project (air) 3·25 90
801 600f. Laika (dog) and "Sputnik 2" flight, 1957 . . 4·00 1·10

187 "Endeavour" (space shuttle), Capt. James Cook and H.M.S. "Endeavour"

1992. Space and Nautical Exploration. Mult.
803 75f. Type **187** (postage) . . . 70 15
804 100f. "Cariane" space microphone, Sir Francis Drake and "Golden Hind" 90 20
805 150f. Infra-red astronomical observation device, John Smith and "Susan Constant" . . . . 1·40 30
806 225f. Space probe "B", Robert F. Scott and "Discovery" . . . . 1·75 45
807 375f. "Magellan" (Venus space probe), Ferdinand Magellan and ship (air) . . 3·25 80
808 500f. "Newton" (satellite), Vasco da Gama and "Sao Gabriel" . . . . 3·75 1·10

188 Map **189** Footballers

1993. 30th Anniv of Organization of African Unity.
810 **188** 25f. multicoloured 10 10
811 50f. multicoloured 20 10
812 75f. multicoloured 60 35
813 150f. multicoloured . . . 1·00 80

1993. World Cup Football Championship, U.S.A. (1994).
814 **189** 25f. multicoloured 10 10
815 75f. multicoloured 35 10
816 100f. multicoloured . . . 70 15
817 150f. multicoloured . . . 95 25

190 I.T.U. Emblem

1993. World Telecommunications Day. "Telecommunications and Human Development".
818 **190** 50f. multicoloured 20 10
819 75f. multicoloured 35 10
820 100f. multicoloured . . . 70 15
821 150f. multicoloured . . . 1·00 55

191 Edaphosaurus

1994. Prehistoric Animals. Multicoloured.
822 75f. Type **191** 25 10
823 75f. Moschops 25 10
824 75f. Kentrosaurus 25 10
825 75f. Compsognathus 25 10
826 75f. Sauroctonus 25 10
827 75f. Ornitholestes 25 10
828 75f. Styracosaurus 25 10
829 75f. Acanthopholis 25 10
830 150f. Edmontonia 50 20
831 150f. Struthiomimus 50 20
832 150f. Diatryma 50 20
833 150f. Uintatherium 50 20
834 450f. Dromiceiomimus . . . 2·10 60
835 450f. Iguanodon . . . . . . 2·10 60
836 525f. Synthetoceras . . . . . 2·50 75
837 525f. Euryapteryx . . . . . 2·50 75

192 "Hibiscus syriacus"

1994. Plants. Multicoloured.
839 75f. Type **192** 25 10
840 75f. Cashew nut 25 10
841 75f. Butter mushroom . . . 40 15
842 150f. "Pyrostegia venusta" (flower) 50 20
843 150f. Manioc (root) 50 20
844 150f. "Lycogala epidendron" (fungus) 80 35
845 525f. "Allamanda cathartica" (flower) . . . . 2·25 75
846 525f. Cacao (nut) . . . . . 2·25 75
847 525f. "Clathrus ruber" (fungus) . . . . 3·00 1·00

193 Purple-tip ("Colotis zoe")

1994. Insects. Multicoloured.
848 75f. Type **193** 25 10
849 75f. "Charaxes comoranus" (butterfly) 25 10
850 75f. "Hypurgus ova" (beetle) 25 10
851 150f. Death's-head hawk moth ("Acherontia atropos") 50 20
852 150f. "Verdant hawk moth ("Euchloron megaera") . . 50 20
853 150f. "Onthophagus catta" (beetle) 50 20
854 450f. African monarch ("Danaus chrysippus") (butterfly) . . . . 2·25 60
855 450f. "Papilio phorbanta" (butterfly) . . . . 2·25 60
856 450f. "Echinosoma bolivari" (beetle) . . . . 2·25 60

OFFICIAL STAMPS

O **99** Comoro Flag

1979.
O379 O **99** 5f. grn, blk & azure 10 10
O380 10f. grn, blk & grey 10 10
O381 20f. grn, blk & stone 10 10
O382 30f. green, blk & bl 20 10
O383 40f. grn, blk & yell 25 15
O384 60f. grn, blk & lt grn 30 25
O384a 75f. grn, blk & lt grn 25 15
O385 100f. grn, blk & yell 80 35
O386 – 100f. mult 70 35
O386a – 125f. mult 90 55
O387 – 400f. mult . . . . . 2·75 1·50
DESIGNS: Nos. O386, O386a, O387, Pres. Cheikh.

POSTAGE DUE STAMPS

D **9** Mosque in Anjouan   D **10** Coelacanth

1950.
D16 D **9** 50c. green . . . . 15 3·25
D17 1f. brown . . . . 15 3·25

1954.
D18 D **10** 5f. sepia and green . . 25 3·50
D19 10f. violet and brown 2·50 3·50
D20 20f. indigo and blue . . 70 4·00

D **78** Pineapple

1977. Multicoloured.
D244 1f. Hibiscus (horiz) 10 10
D245 2f. Type D **78** 10 10
D246 5f. White butterfly (horiz) 10 10
D247 10f. Chameleon (horiz) . . 10 10
D248 15f. Banana flower (horiz) 10 10
D249 20f. Orchid (horiz) 10 10
D250 30f. "Allamanda cathartica" (horiz) . . . 20 10
D251 40f. Cashew nuts 25 15
D252 50f. Custard apple 25 15
D253 100f. Breadfruit (horiz) . . 70 25
D254 200f. Vanilla (horiz) . . . . 1·60 45
D255 500f. Ylang-ylang flower (horiz) . . . . 4·00 1·10

APPENDIX

The following stamps have either been issued in excess of postal needs or have not been available to the public in reasonable quantities at face value. Such stamps may later be given full listing if there is evidence of regular postal use.

1975.

Various stamps optd **ETAT COMORIEN** or surch also.

Birds issue (No. 60). 10f. on 2f.

Fishes issue (No. 71). Air 50f.

Birds issue (No. 99). 40f.

Comoro Landscapes issue (Nos. 102/4). Air 75f. on 65f., 100f. on 85f., 100f.

Tropical Plants issue (Nos. 105/9). Postage 5f. on 1f., 5f. on 3f.; Air 75f. on 60f., 100f. on 85f.

Seashells issue (No. 114). 75f. on 60f.

Aquatic Sports issue (No. 122). Air 75f. on 70f.

Anjouan Landscapes issue (Nos. 126/8). Air 40f., 75f. on 60f., 100f.

Said Mohamed Cheikh issue (Nos. 129/30). Air 20f., 35f.

Great Comoro Landscapes issue (Nos. 134 and 136). Postage 35f.; Air 200f. on 135f.

Moroni Buildings issue (No. 139). 20f.

Karthala Volcano issue (No. 140). Air 200f. on 120f.

Hansen issue (No. 141). Air 100f.

Copernicus issue (No. 142). Air 400f. on 150f.

Picasso issue (No. 143). Air 200f.

Mosques issue (Nos. 145/6). 15f. on 20f., 25f. on 35f.

Star of Anjouan issue (No. 147). 500f.

Said Omar Ben Soumeth issue (Nos. 148/9). Air 100f. on 135f., 200f.

Shaikh Said Mohamed issue (No. 150). 30f. on 35f.

Handicrafts issue (Nos. 153/5). 20f., 30f. on 35f., 75f.

Mayotte Landscapes issue (Nos. 157/60). Air 10f. on 20f., 30f. on 35f., 100f. on 90f., 200f. on 120f.

U.P.U. Centenary issue (No. 161). 500f. on 30f.

Air Service issue (No. 162). Air 100f. on 135f.

Rotary issue (No. 163). Air 400f. on 250f.

Handicrafts issue (Nos. 164/7). 15f. on 20f., 30f. on 35f., 100f. on 120f., 200f. on 135f.

Moheli Landscapes issue (Nos. 168/71). Postage 30f., 50f., 50f. on 55f.; Air 200f. on 230f.

Coelacanth issue (No. 172). 50f.

Folk-dances issue (Nos. 173/4). 100f., 100f. on 150f.

Apollo–Soyuz Space Test Project. Postage 10, 30, 50f.; Air 100, 200, 400f. Embossed on gold foil. Air 1500f.

1976.

Bicent of American Revolution. Postage 15, 25, 35, 40, 75f.; Air 500f. Embossed on gold foil: Air 1000f.

Winter Olympic Games, Innsbruck. Postage 5, 30, 35, 50f.; Air 200, 400f. Embossed on gold foil. Air 1000f.

Children's Stories. Postage 15, 30, 35, 40, 50f.; Air 400f.

Telephone Centenary. Postage 10, 25, 75f.; Air 100, 200, 500f.

Bicentenary of American Revolution (Early Settler and Viking Space Rocket). Embossed on gold foil. Air 1500f.

Bicent of American Revolution (J. F. Kennedy and Apollo). Embossed on gold foil. Air 1500f.

1978.

World Cup Football Championship, Argentina. Embossed on gold foil. Air 1000f.

Death Centenary of Sir Rowland Hill. Embossed on gold foil. Air 1500f.

Argentina's World Cup Victory. Optd on World Cup issue. Air 1000f.

1979.

International Year of the Child. Embossed on gold foil. Air 1500f.

1988.

Rotary International. Embossed on gold foil. Air 1500f.

1989.

Scouts, Butterflies and Birds. Embossed on gold foil. Air 1500f.

Satellites and Olympic Winners. Embossed on gold foil. Air 1500f.

Bicentenary of French Revolution. Embossed on gold foil. Air 1500f.

1990.

World Cup Football Championship. Embossed on gold foil. Air 1500f.

Winter Olympic Games, Albertville (1992). Embossed on gold foil. Air 1500f.

1991.

Birth Centenary of Charles De Gaulle (1990). Embossed on gold foil. Air 1500f.

1992.

Olympic Games, Barcelona. Boxing. Embossed on gold foil. Air 1500f.

CONFEDERATE STATES OF AMERICA Pt. 22

Stamps issued by the seceding states in the American Civil War.

1 Jefferson Davis

2 T. Jefferson

1861. Imperf.
1 **1** 5c. green . . . . £100 70·00
3 **2** 10c. blue . . . . £130 95·00

3 Jackson

4 Jefferson Davis

1862. Imperf.
4 **3** 2c. green £350 £400
5 **1** 5c. blue . . . . 60·00 55·00
6 **2** 10c. red £600 £300

1862. Imperf.
7 **4** 5c. blue . . . . 6·00 11·00

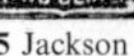

5 Jackson

6 Jefferson Davis

9 Washington

1863. Imperf or perf (10c.).
9 **5** 2c. red . . . . 30·00 £170
10 **6** 10c. blue (TEN CENTS) . . £475 £300
12 10c. blue (10 CENTS) . . . 5·00 9·00
14 **9** 20c. green . . . . 25·00 £200

CONGO (BRAZZAVILLE) Pt. 6; Pt. 12

Formerly Middle Congo. An independent republic within the French Community.

1 "Birth of the Republic"

1959. 1st Anniv of Republic.
1 **1** 25f. multicoloured 55 25

1960. 10th Anniv of African Technical Co-operation Commission. As T **62** of Cameroun.
2 50f. lake and green 65 60

1960. Air. Olympic Games. No. 276 of French Equatorial Africa optd with Olympic rings and **XVIIe OLYMPIADE 1960 REPUBLIQUE DU CONGO 250F.**
3 250f. on 500f. blue, black & grn 6·75 6·75

2 Pres. Youlou

3 U.N. Emblem, map and Flag

1960.
4 **2** 15f. green, red and turquoise 25 15
5 85f. blue and red . . . . . . 1·40 50

1961. Admission into U.N.O.
6 **3** 5f. multicoloured 15 10
7 20f. multicoloured 25 20
8 100f. multicoloured . . . . . 1·40 90

4 "Thesium tencio"

1961. Air.
9 – 100f. purple, yellow & green 2·25 1·40
10 – 200f. yellow, turq & brown 4·00 2·00
11 **4** 500f. yellow, myrtle & brown 11·00 5·00
FLOWERS: 100f. "Helicrysum mechowiam"; 200f. "Cogniauxia podolaena".

1961. Air. Foundation of "Air Afrique" Airline. As T **69** of Cameroun.
12 50f. purple, myrtle and green 1·10 45

6 Rainbow Runner

7 Brazzaville Market

1961. Tropical Fish.
13 **6** 50c. multicoloured 10 10
14 – 1f. brown and green 10 10
15 – 2f. brown and blue 10 10
15a – 2f. red, brown and green . . 45 10
16 **6** 3f. green, orange and blue 20 15
17 – 5f. sepia, brown and green 30 15
18 – 10f. brown and turquoise . . 1·00 25
18a – 15f. purple, green & violet 1·60 90
FISH: 1, 2f. (No. 15), Sloan's viperfish ("Chauliodus sloanei"); 2f. (No. 15a), Fishes pursued by squid; 5f. Giant marine hatchetfish; 10f. Long-toothed fangtooth; 15f. Johnson's deep sea angler.

1962.
19 **7** 20f. red, green and black . . 55 15

1962. Malaria Eradication. As T **70** of Cameroun.
20 25f.+5f. brown 80 80

8 "Yang-tse" (freighter) loading Timber, Pointe Noire

1962. Air. International Fair, Pointe Noire.
21 **8** 50f. multicoloured . . . . . 2·00 90

1962. Sports. As T **12** of Central African Republic.
22 20f. sepia, red & blk (postage) 30 25
23 50f. sepia, red and black . . . 65 50
24 100f. sepia, red and black (air) 2·00 1·00
DESIGNS—HORIZ: 20f. Boxing; 50f. Running. VERT: (26 × 47 mm): 100f. Basketball.

1962. Union of African and Malagasy States. 1st Anniv. As No. 328 of Cameroun.
25 **72** 30f. violet 90 50

1962. Freedom from Hunger. As T **76** of Cameroun.
26 25f.+5f. turquoise, brn & bl 80 80

9 Town Hall, Brazzaville and Pres. Youlou

1963. Air.
27 **9** 100f. multicoloured £120 £120

9a "Costus spectabilis" (K. Schum)

10 King Makoko's Gold Chain

1963. Air. Flowers. Multicoloured.
28 100f. Type **9a** . . . . 2·75 1·60
29 250f. "Acanthus montanus T. anders" . . . . 5·50 2·75

1963. Air. African and Malagasy Posts and Telecommunications Union. As T **18** of Central African Republic.
30 85f. red, buff and violet . . . 1·25 75

1963. Space Telecommunications. As Nos. 37/8 of Central African Republic.
31 25f. blue, orange and green . . 45 30
32 100f. violet, brown and blue 1·25 1·10

1963. Folklore and Tourism.
33 **10** 10f. bistre and black 25 30
34 – 15f. multicoloured 30 25
DESIGN: 15f. Kebekebe mask.
See also Nos. 45/6 and 62/4.

11 Airline Emblem

1963. Air. 1st Anniv of "Air Afrique", and Inaug of DC-8 Service.
35 **11** 50f. multicoloured 60 45

12 Liberty Square, Brazzaville

1963. Air.
36 **12** 25f. multicoloured 60 35
See also No. 56.

1963. Air. European-African Economic Convention. As T **24** of Central African Republic.
37 50f. multicoloured 70 50

1963. 15th Anniv of Declaration of Human Rights. As T **26** of Central African Republic.
38 25f. blue, turquoise & brown 45 30

13 Statue of Hathor, Abu Simbel

1964. Air. Nubian Monuments.
39 **13** 10f.+5f. violet & brown . . 35 20
40 25f.+5f. brown & turq . . . 45 40
41 50f.+5f. turquoise & brn . . 1·40 90

14 Barograph

1964. World Meteorological Day.
42 **14** 50f. brown, blue & green . . 70 65

15 Machinist

16 Emblem and Implements of Manual Labour

1964. "Technical Instruction".
43 **15** 20f. brown, mauve & turq 35 25

1964. Manual Labour Rehabilitation.
44 **16** 80f. green, red and sepia . . 1·10 45

17 Diaboua Ballet

19 Wood Carving

18 Tree-felling

1964. Folklore and Tourism. Multicoloured.
45 30f. Type **17** 90 30
46 60f. Kebekebe dance (vert) . . 1·40 65

1964. Air.
47 **18** 100f. brown, red and green 1·60 70

1964. Congo Sculpture.
48 **19** 50f. sepia and red . . . . . 1·00 45

20 Students in Classroom

1964. Development of Education.
49 **20** 25f. red, purple and blue . . 40 30

1964. Air. 5th Anniv of Equatorial African Heads of State Conference. As T **31** of Central African Republic.
50 100f. multicoloured . . . . . 1·25 65

21 Sun, Ears of Wheat, and Globe within Cogwheel

1964. Air. Europafrique.
51 **21** 50f. yellow, blue and red . . 70 50

22 Stadium, Olympic Flame and Throwing the Hammer

1964. Air. Olympic Games, Tokyo. Sport and flame orange.
52 **22** 25f. violet and brown . . . 35 25
53 – 50f. purple and olive 60 40
54 – 100f. green and brown . . . 1·50 85
55 – 200f. olive and red . . . . 2·75 1·75
DESIGNS—Stadium, Olympic Flame and: VERT: 50f. Weightlifting; 100f. Volleyball. HORIZ: 200f. High-jumping.

1964. 1st Anniv of Revolution and National Festival. As T **12** but inscr "1er ANNIVERSAIRE DE LA REVOLUTION FETE NATIONALE 15 AOUT 1964".
56 20f. multicoloured 65 20

23 Posthorns, Envelope and Radio Mast

1964. Air. Pan-African and Malagasy Posts and Telecommunications Congress, Cairo.
57 **23** 25f. sepia and red 35 25

1964. French, African and Malagasy Co-operation. As T **88** of Cameroun.
58 25f. brown, green and red . . 45 35

24 Dove, Envelope and Radio Mast

1965. Establishment of Posts and Telecommunications Office, Brazzaville.
59 **24** 25f. multicoloured 35 25

25 Town Hall, Brazzaville and Arms

1965. Air.
60 **25** 100f. multicoloured . . . . 1·10 55

26 "Europafrique"

1965. Air. Europafrique.
61 **26** 50f. multicoloured 60 40

27 African Elephant

29 Pres. Massamba-Debat

28 Cadran de Breguet's Telegraph and "Telstar"

1965. Folklore and Tourism.
62 – 15f. purple, green and blue 80 25
63 **27** 20f. black, blue and green 65 30
64 – 85f. multicoloured . . . . . 2·25 1·40
DESIGNS—VERT: 15f. Bushbuck; 85f. Dancer on stilts.

1965. Air. Centenary of I.T.U.
65 **28** 100f. brown and blue . . . 2·00 80

1965. Portrait in sepia.
66 **29** 20f. yellow, green & brown 25 15
66a 25f. green, turquoise & brn 35 20
66b 30f. orange, turq & brn . . 40 20

30 Sir Winston Churchill

31 Pope John XXIII

1965. Air. Famous Men.
67 – 25f. on 50f. sepia and red 45 45
68 **30** 50f. sepia and green 90 90
69 – 80f. sepia and blue . . . . 1·60 1·60
70 – 100f. sepia and yellow . . . . 2·25 2·25
PORTRAITS: 25f. Lumumba; 80f. Pres. Boganda; 100f. Pres. Kennedy.

1965. Air. Pope John Commemoration.
71 **31** 100f. multicoloured . . . . 1·50 90

32 Athletes and Map of Africa

33 Natives hauling Log

1965. 1st African Games, Brazzaville. Inscr "PREMIERS JEUX AFRICAINS". Mult.
72 25f. Type **32** 40 30
73 40f. Football (34½ × 34½ mm) 55 40
74 50f. Handball (34½ × 34½ mm) 60 40
75 85f. Running (34½ × 34½ mm) 1·00 65
76 100f. Cycling (34½ × 34½ mm) 1·40 85

1965. Air. National Unity.
77 **33** 50f. brown and green . . . 60 40

34 "World Co-operation"

1965. Air. International Co-operation Year.
78 **34** 50f. multicoloured 90 55

35 Arms of Congo

37 Trench-digging

36 Lincoln

1965.
79 **35** 20f. multicoloured 30 15

1965. Air. Death Centenary of Abraham Lincoln.
80 **36** 90f. multicoloured 90 50

1966. Village Co-operative.
81 **37** 25f. multicoloured 30 20

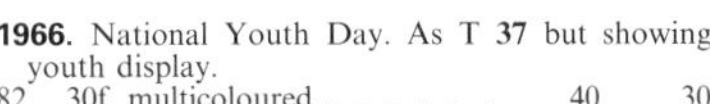

1966. National Youth Day. As T **37** but showing youth display.
82 30f. multicoloured 40 30

38 De Gaulle and Flaming Torch

1966. Air. 22nd Anniv of Brazzaville Conference.
83 **38** 500f. brown, red & green . . 24·00 19·00

39 Weaving

40 People and Clocks

1966. World Festival of Negro Arts, Dakar. Multicoloured.
84 30f. Type **39** 45 25
85 85f. Musical Instrument (horiz) 1·40 65
86 90f. Mask . . . . 1·40 85

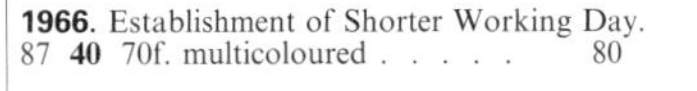

1966. Establishment of Shorter Working Day.
87 **40** 70f. multicoloured 80 40

41 W.H.O. Building

1966. Inaug of W.H.O. Headquarters, Geneva.
88 **41** 50f. violet, yellow and blue 65 40

42 Satellite "D1" and Brazzaville Tracking Station

1966. Air. Launching of Satellite "D1".
89 **42** 150f. black, red and green 2·25 1·10

43 St. Pierre Claver Church

44 Volleyball

1966.
90 **43** 70f. multicoloured 80 40

1966. Sports.
91 **44** 1f. brown, bistre and blue 10 10
92 – 2f. brown, green and blue 15 10
93 – 3f. brown, lake and green 15 15
94 – 5f. brown, blue and green 20 15
95 – 10f. violet, turquoise & grn 25 20
96 – 15f. brown, violet and lake 35 30
DESIGNS—VERT: 2f. Basketball; 5f. Sportsmen; 10f. Athlete; 15f. Football. HORIZ: 3f. Handball.

45 Jules Rimet Cup and Globe

46 Corn, Atomic Emblem and Map

1966. World Cup Football Championship, England.
97 **45** 30f. multicoloured 45 30

1966. Air. Europafrique.
98 **46** 50f. multicoloured 55 35

47 Pres. Massamba-Debat and Presidential Palace, Brazzaville

1966. Air. 3rd Anniv of Congolese Revolution. Multicoloured.
99 25f. Type **47** 30 15
100 30f. Robespierre and Bastille, Paris 35 20
101 50f. Lenin and Winter Palace, St. Petersburg 80 30

1966. Air. Inauguration of DC-8F Air Services. As T **54** of Central African Republic.
103 30f. yellow, black and violet 60 25

48 Dr. Albert Schweitzer

1966. Air. Schweitzer Commemoration.
104 **48** 100f. multicoloured . . . . 1·50 85

49 View of School

1966. Inaug of Savorgnan de Brazza High School.
105 **49** 30f. multicoloured 35 20

50 Pointe-Noire Railway Station

51 Silhouette of Congolese, and U.N.E.S.C.O. Emblem

1966.
106 **50** 60f. red, brown and green 1·75 75

1966. 20th Anniv of U.N.E.S.C.O.
107 **51** 90f. blue, brown & green 1·10 80

52 Balumbu Mask

53 Cancer "The Crab", Microscope and Pagoda

1966. Congolese Masks.
108 **52** 5f. sepia and red 20 15
109 – 10f. brown and blue . . . 25 15
110 – 15f. blue, sepia & brown 25 25
111 – 20f. multicoloured 65 25
MASKS: 10f. Kuyu; 15f. Bakwele; 20f. Bateke.

1966. Air. 9th Int Cancer Congress, Tokyo.
112 **53** 100f. multicoloured . . . . 1·25 80

54 Sociable Weaver

55 Medal, Ribbon and Map

1967. Air. Birds. Multicoloured.
113 50f. Type **54** . . . . 3·75 1·10
114 75f. European bee eater . . . 4·25 1·60
115 100f. Lilac-breasted roller . . 6·75 2·00
116 150f. Regal sunbird . . . . . 8·00 2·75
117 200f. South African crowned crane . . . . 9·00 3·00
118 250f. Secretary bird . . . . . 11·00 4·50
119 300f. Black-billed turaco . . 15·00 5·25

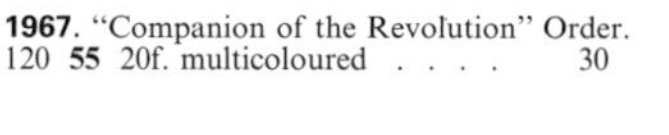

1967. "Companion of the Revolution" Order.
120 **55** 20f. multicoloured 30 25

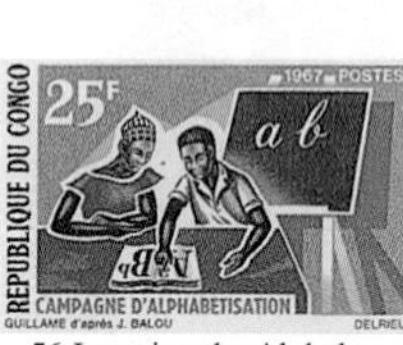

56 Learning the Alphabet (Educational Campaign)

57 Mahatma Gandhi

1967. Education and Sugar Production Campaigns. Multicoloured.
121 25f. Type **56** 35 30
122 45f. Cutting sugar-cane . . . 90 30

1967. Gandhi Commemoration.
123 **57** 90f. black and blue . . . . 1·25 55

58 Prisoner's Hands in Chains

59 Ndumba, Lady of Fashion

1967. Air. African Liberation Day.
124 **58** 500f. multicoloured . . . . 7·75 3·25

1967. Congolese Dolls. Multicoloured.
125 5f. Type **59** 15 15
126 10f. Fruit seller 25 20
127 25f. Girl pounding saka-saka 30 20
128 30f. Mother and child . . . 35 25

60 Congo Scenery

61 "Europafrique"

1967. International Tourist Year.
129 **60** 60f. red, orange and green 65 40

1967. Europafrique.
130 **61** 50f. multicoloured 55 30

62 "Sputnik 1" and "Explorer 6"

1967. Air. Space Exploration.
131 **62** 50f. blue, violet & brown 55 30
132 – 75f. lake and slate . . . . 1·00 40
133 – 100f. blue, red & turquoise 1·40 65
134 – 200f. red, blue and lake . . 2·50 1·50
DESIGNS: 75f. "Ranger 6" and "Lunik 2"; 100f. "Mars 1" and "Mariner 4"; 200f. "Gemini" and "Vostok".

63 Brazzaville Arms

1967. 4th Anniv of Congo Revolution.
135 **63** 30f. multicoloured 40 20

1967. Air. 5th Anniv of African and Malagasy Posts and Telecommunications Union. As T **66** of Central African Republic.
136 100f. green, red and brown 1·10 65

64 Jamboree Emblem, Scouts and Tents

1967. Air. World Scout Jamboree, Idaho.
137 **64** 50f. blue, brown & chestnut 55 30
138 – 70f. red, green and blue . . 80 40
DESIGN: 70f. Saluting hand, Jamboree camp and emblem.

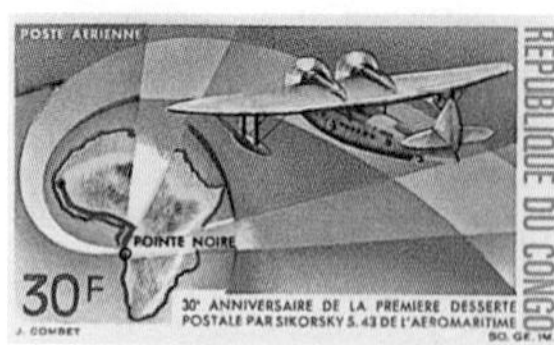

65 Sikorsky S-43 Amphibian and Map

1967. Air. 30th Anniv of Aeromaritime Airmail Link.
139 **65** 30f. multicoloured 40 25

66 Dove, Human Figures and U.N. Emblem

67 Young Congolese

1967. U.N. Day and Campaign in Support of U.N.
140 **66** 90f. multicoloured . . . . 1·25 65

1967. 21st Anniv of U.N.I.C.E.F.
141 **67** 90f. black, blue & brown 1·25 65

68 Albert Luthuli (winner of Nobel Peace Prize) and Dove

70 Arms of Pointe Noire

69 Global Dance

1968. Luthuli Commemoration.
142 **68** 30f. brown and green . . . 35 30

1968. Air. "Friendship of the Peoples".
143 **69** 70f. brown, green & blue 75 40

1968.
144 **70** 10f. multicoloured 35 30

71 "Old Man and His Grandson" (Ghirlandaio)

1968. Air. Paintings. Multicoloured.
145 30f. Type **71** 45 30
146 100f. "The Horatian Oath" (J.-L. David) (horiz) . . . 1·60 65
147 200f. "The Negress with Peonies" (Bazille) (horiz) 3·25 1·60
See also Nos. 209/13.

72 "Mother and Child"

73 Diesel Train crossing Mayombe Viaduct

1968. Mothers' Festival.
148 **72** 15f. black, blue and red . . 30 25

1968.
149 **73** 45f. lake, blue and green 2·25 40

74 Beribboned Rope

1968. Air. 5th Anniv of Europafrique.
150 **74** 50f. multicoloured 55 25

75 Daimler, 1889

1968. Veteran Motor Cars. Multicoloured.
151 5f. Type **75** (postage) 20 15
152 20f. Berliet, 1897 . . . . . . 35 20
153 60f. Peugeot, 1898 . . . . . 1·40 40
154 80f. Renault, 1900 . . . . . 2·00 90
155 85f. Fiat, 1902 . . . . 2·50 1·40
156 150f. Ford, 1915 (air) . . . . 2·50 1·40
157 200f. Citroen . . . . 3·50 1·50

1968. Inauguration of Petroleum Refinery, Port Gentil, Gabon. As T **80** of Central African Republic.
158 30f. multicoloured 60 25

76 Dr. Martin Luther King

78 Robert Kennedy

77 "The Barricade" (Delacroix)

1968. Air. Martin Luther King Commemoration.
159 **76** 50f. black, green & emerald 60 30

1968. Air. 5th Anniv of Revolution Paintings. Multicoloured.
160 25f. Type **77** . . . . 1·40 45
161 30f. "Destruction of the Bastille" (H. Robert) . . . 1·40 55

1968. Air. Robert Kennedy Commemoration.
162 **78** 50f. black, green and red 55 30

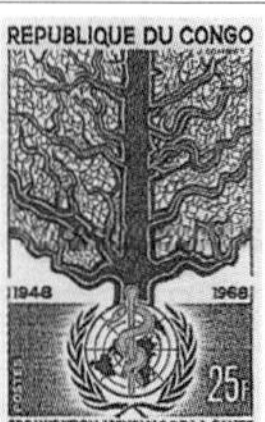

79 "Tree of Life" and W.H.O. Emblem

1968. 20th Anniv of W.H.O.
163 **79** 25f. red, purple and green 30 15

80 Start of Race

1968. Air. Olympic Games, Mexico.
164 **80** 5f. brown, blue and green 10 10
165 – 20f. green, brown & blue 30 15
166 – 60f. brown, green and red 60 35
167 – 85f. brown, red and slate 1·40 50
DESIGNS—VERT: 20f. Football; 60f. Boxing. HORIZ: 85f. High-jumping.

1968. Air. "Philexafrique" Stamp Exn, Abidjan (1969) (1st issue). As T **86** of Central African Republic.
168 100f. multicoloured . . . . . 2·25 1·60
DESIGN: 100f. "G. de Gueidan writing" (N. de Largilliere).

1969. Air. "Philexafrique" Stamp Exhibition, Abidjan, Ivory Coast (2nd issue). As T **138** of Cameroun.
169 50f. green, brown & mauve 2·50 1·00
DESIGN: 50f. Pointe-Noire harbour, lumbering and Middle Congo stamp of 1933.

1969. Air. Birth Bicentenary of Napoleon Bonaparte. As T **144** of Cameroun. Multicoloured.
170 25f. Battle of Rivoli (C. Vernet) 90 30
171 50f. "Battle of Marengo" (Pahou) . . . . 1·40 80
172 75f. "Battle of Friedland" (H. Vernet) . . . . 2·25 1·25
173 100f. "Battle of Jena" (Thevenin) . . . . 3·25 1·40

81 "Che" Guevara

1969. Air. Ernesto "Che" Guevara (Latin-American revolutionary) Commemoration.
174 **81** 90f. brown, orange & lake 80 40

82 Doll and Toys

1969. Air. International Toy Fair, Nuremberg.
175 **82** 100f. slate, mauve & orange . . . . 2·50 85

83 Beribboned Bar

1969. Air. Europafrique.
176 **83** 50f. violet, black & turq . . 45 25

1969. 5th Anniv of African Development Bank. As T **146** of Cameroun.
177 25f. brown, red and green . . 25 15
178 30f. brown, green and blue 30 15

85 Modern Bicycle

1969. Cycles and Motor-cycles.
180 **85** 50f. purple, orange & brn 80 30
181 – 75f. black, lake & orange 80 35
182 – 80f. green, blue & purple 85 45
183 – 85f. green, slate & brown 1·25 55
184 – 100f. multicoloured . . . . 1·40 65
185 – 150f. brown, red & black 2·00 80
186 – 200f. pur, dp grn & grn . . 3·25 1·40
187 – 300f. green, purple & blk 5·50 2·25
DESIGNS: 75f. "Hirondelle" cycle; 80f. Folding cycle; 85f. "Peugeot" cycle; 100f. "Excelsior Manxman" motor-cycle; 150f. "Norton" motor-cycle; 200f. "Brough Superior" motor-cycle; 300f. "Matchless and N.I.G.-J.A.P.S." motor-cycle

86 Series ZE Diesel-electric Train entering Mbamba Tunnel

1969. African International Tourist Year. Mult.
188 40f. Type **86** . . . . 2·50 40
189 60f. Series ZE diesel-electric train crossing the Mayombe (horiz) . . . . 3·25 50

87 Mortar Tanks

1969. Loutete Cement Works.
190 **87** 10f. slate, brown and lake 10 10
191 – 15f. violet, blue & brown 25 15
192 – 25f. blue, brown and red 30 25
193 – 30f. blue, violet & ultram 35 25
DESIGNS—VERT: 15f. Mixing tower; 25f. Cableway. HORIZ: 30f. General view of works.

1969. 10th Anniv of A.S.E.C.N.A. As T **150** of Cameroun.
195 100f. brown . . . . 2·00 75

88 Harvesting Pineapples

1969. 50th Anniv of I.L.O.
196 **88** 25f. brown, green & blue 30 20
197 – 30f. slate, purple and red 35 20
DESIGN: 30f. Operating lathe.

89 Textile Plant

1970. "SOTEXCO" Textile Plant, Kinsoundi.
198 **89** 15f. black, violet & green 20 15
199 – 20f. green, red and purple 25 15
200 – 25f. brown, blue & lt blue 30 15
201 – 30f. brown, red and slate 35 15
DESIGNS: 20f. Spinning machines; 25f. Printing textiles; 30f. Checking finished cloth.

90 Linzolo Church

91 Artist at work

1970. Buildings.
202 **90** 25f. green, brown & blue 35 15
203 – 90f. brown, green & blue 80 35
DESIGN: HORIZ: 90f. Cosmos Hotel, Brazzaville.

1970. Air. "Art and Culture".
204 **91** 100f. brown, plum & grn 1·40 50
205 – 150f. plum, lake & green 2·00 75
206 – 200f. brown, choc & ochre 2·75 1·50
DESIGNS: 150f. Lesson in wood-carving; 200f. Potter at wheel.

92 Diosso Gorges

1970. Tourism.
207 **92** 70f. purple, brown & grn 90 35
208 – 90f. purple, green & brown 1·40 45
DESIGN: 90f. Foulakari Falls.

1970. Air. Paintings. As T **71**. Multicoloured.
209 150f. "Child with Cherries" (J. Russell) . . . . 2·75 1·25
210 200f. "Erasmus" (Holbein the younger) . . . . 4·00 1·50
211 250f. "Silence" (Bernadino Luini) . . . . 4·00 1·90
212 300f. "Scenes from the Scio Massacre" (Delacroix) . . 5·50 2·75
213 500f. "Capture of Constantinople" (Delacroix) . . . . 8·00 3·75

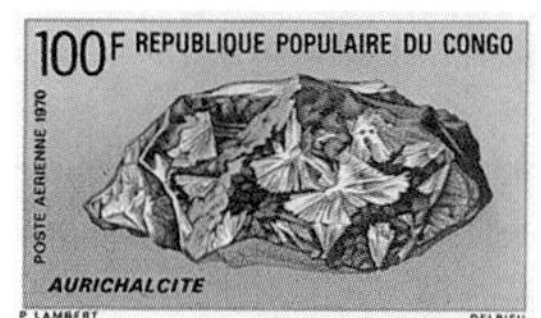

93 Aurichalcite

1970. Air. Minerals. Multicoloured.
214 100f. Type **93** . . . . 2·75 1·25
215 150f. Dioptase . . . . 3·25 1·50

94 "Volvaria esculenta"

1970. Mushrooms. Multicoloured.
216 5f. Type **94** 50 20
217 10f. "Termitomyces entolomoides" 55 25
218 15f. "Termitomyces microcarpus" 85 35
219 25f. "Termitomyces aurantiacus" . . . . 1·75 45
220 30f. "Termitomyces mammiformis" . . . . . . 3·00 55
221 50f. "Tremella fuciformis" . . 4·50 1·25

95 Laying Cable **96** Mother feeding Child

1970. Laying of Coaxial Cable, Brazzaville–Pointe Noire.
222 **95** 25f. buff, brown and blue 1·75 45
223 – 30f. brown and green . . . 2·00 55
DESIGN: 30f. Diesel locomotive and cable-laying gang.

1970. New U.P.U. Headquarters Building, Berne. As T **156** of Cameroun.
224 30f. purple, slate and plum 45 25

1970. Mothers' Day. Multicoloured.
225 85f. Type **96** 75 40
226 90f. Mother suckling baby . . 85 45

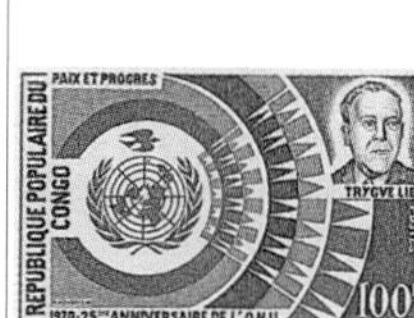

97 U.N. Emblem and Trygve Lie **98** Lenin in Cap

1970. 25th Anniv of United Nations.
227 **97** 100f. blue, indigo and lake 1·10 70
228 – 100f. lilac, red and lake . . 1·10 70
229 – 100f. green, turq & lake . . 1·10 70
DESIGNS—VERT: No. 228, as Type **97**, but with portrait of Dag Hammarskjold. HORIZ: No. 229, as Type **97**, but with portrait of U Thant and arrangement reversed.

1970. Air. Birth Centenary of Lenin.
231 **98** 45f. brown, yellow & grn 65 45
232 – 75f. brown, red and blue 1·10 65
DESIGN: 75f. Lenin seated (after Vassiliev).

99 "Brillantaisia vogeliana"

1970. "Flora and Fauna". Multicoloured.
(a) Flowers. Horiz designs.
233 1f. Type **99** 10 10
234 2f. "Plectranthus decurrens" 10 10
235 3f. "Myrianthemum mirabile" 10 10
236 5f. "Connarus griffonianus" 15 10
(b) Insects. Vert designs.
237 10f. "Sternotomis variabilis" 30 20
238 15f. "Chelorrhina polyphemus" 80 20
239 20f. "Metopodontus savagei" 90 30

100 Karl Marx

1970. Air. Founders of Communism.
240 **100** 50f. brown, green & red 50 30
241 – 50f. brown, blue and red 50 30
DESIGN: No. 241, Friedrich Engels.

101 Kentrosarus

1970. Prehistoric Creatures. Multicoloured.
242 15f. Type **101** 30 25
243 20f. Dinotherium (vert) . . . 1·10 55
244 60f. Brachiosaurus (vert) . . 2·25 80
245 80f. Arsinoitherium . . . . . 2·75 1·50

102 "Mikado 141" Steam Locomotive, 1932

1970. Locomotives of Congo Railways (1st series).
246 **102** 40f. black, green & purple 2·40 1·10
247 – 60f. black, green & blue 2·75 1·25
248 – 75f. black, red and blue 4·25 1·75
249 – 85f. red, green & orange 6·00 2·50
DESIGNS: 60f. Super-Golwe steam locomotive, 1947; 75f. Alsthom Series BB 1100 diesel locomotive, 1962; 85f. Diesel locomotive No. BB BB 302, 1969.
See also Nos. 371/4.

103 Lilienthal's Glider, 1891

1970. Air. History of Flight and Space Travel.

No.	Type	Description	Mint	Used
250	103	45f. brown, blue and red	60	25
251	–	50f. green and brown	60	25
252	–	70f. brown, red and blue	70	35
253	–	90f. brown, olive & blue	1·10	50

DESIGNS: 50f. Lindbergh's "Spirit of St. Louis", 1927; 70f. "Sputnik I"; 90f. First man on the Moon, 1969.

104 "Wise Man"

1970. Air. Christmas. Stained-glass Windows, Brazzaville Cathedral. Multicoloured.

No.	Description	Mint	Used
254	100f. Type **104**	90	45
255	150f. "Shepherd"	1·60	70
256	250f. "Angels"	2·75	1·40

105 "Cogniauxia padolaena"

106 Marilyn Monroe

1971. Tropical Flowers. Multicoloured.

No.	Description	Mint	Used
258	1f. Type **105**	10	10
259	2f. "Celosia cristata"	10	10
260	5f. "Plumeria acutifolia"	10	10
261	10f. "Bauhinia variegata"	45	15
262	15f. "Euphorbia pulcherrima"	65	25
263	20f. "Thunbergia grandiflora"	1·10	25

See also D264/9.

1971. Air. Great Names of the Cinema.

No.	Type	Description	Mint	Used
270	106	100f. brown, blue & grn	2·75	35
271	–	150f. mauve, blue & pur	2·75	50
272	–	200f. brown and blue	2·75	75
273	–	250f. plum, blue & green	2·75	90

PORTRAITS: 150f. Martine Carol; 200f. Eric K. von Stroheim; 250f. Sergei Eisenstein.

107 "Carrying the Cross" (Veronese)

1971. Air. Easter. Religious Paintings. Mult.

No.	Description	Mint	Used
274	100f. Type **107**	95	55
275	150f. "Christ on the Cross" (Burgundian School c. 1500) (vert)	1·60	65
276	200f. "Descent from the Cross" (Van der Weyden)	2·75	90
277	250f. "The Entombment" (Flemish School c. 1500) (vert)	3·25	1·40
278	500f. "The Resurrection" (Memling) (vert)	6·75	2·50

108 Telecommunications Map

1971. Air. Pan-African Telecommunications Network.

No.	Type	Description	Mint	Used
279	108	70f. multicoloured	60	30
280		85f. multicoloured	1·00	35
281		90f. multicoloured	1·40	45

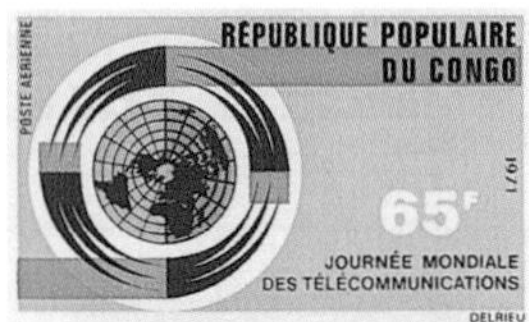

109 Global Emblem

1971. Air. World Telecommunications Day.

No.	Type	Description	Mint	Used
282	109	65f. multicoloured	55	25

110 Green Night Adder

111 Afro-Japanese Allegory

1971. Reptiles. Multicoloured.

No.	Description	Mint	Used
283	5f. Type **110**	15	10
284	10f. African egg-eating snake (horiz)	15	10
285	15f. Flap-necked chameleon	55	15
286	20f. Nile crocodile (horiz)	90	20
287	25f. Rock python (horiz)	1·10	30
288	30f. Gaboon viper	1·40	65
289	40f. Brown house snake (horiz)	1·60	80
290	45f. Jameson's mamba	2·25	90

1971. Air. "Philatokyo 1971" Stamp Exn, Tokyo.

No.	Type	Description	Mint	Used
291	111	75f. black, mauve & violet	90	35
292	–	150f. brown, red & purple	1·25	65

DESIGN: 150f. "Tree of Life", Japanese girl and African in mask.

112 "Pseudimbrasia deyrollei"

1971. Caterpillars. Multicoloured.

No.	Description	Mint	Used
293	10f. Type **112**	35	25
294	15f. "Bunaca alcinoe" (vert)	35	25
295	20f. "Epiphora vacuna ploetzi"	80	35
296	25f. "Imbrasia eblis"	1·40	45
297	30f. "Imbrasia dione" (vert)	2·25	1·00
298	40f. "Holocera angulata"	2·75	1·25

113 Japanese Scout

114 Olympic Torch

1971. World Scout Jamboree, Asagiri, Japan (1st issue). On foil.

No.	Type	Description	Mint	Used
299	113	90f. silver (postage)	2·00	1·40
300	–	90f. silver	2·00	1·40
301	–	90f. silver	2·00	1·40
302	–	90f. silver	2·00	1·40
303	–	1000f. gold (air)	10·00	

DESIGNS—VERT: No. 300, French Scout; 301, Congolese Scout; 302, Lord Baden-Powell. HORIZ: No. 303, Scouts and Lord Baden-Powell.

See also Nos. 306/9.

1971. Air. Olympic Games, Munich.

No.	Type	Description	Mint	Used
304	114	150f. red, green & purple	1·40	70
305	–	350f. violet, green & brn	4·00	2·00

DESIGN—HORIZ: 350f. Sporting cameos within Olympic rings.

115 Scout Badge, Dragon and Congolese Wood-carving

1971. Air. World Scout Jamboree, Asagiri, Japan (2nd issue).

No.	Type	Description	Mint	Used
306	115	85f. purple, brown & grn	65	30
307	–	90f. brown, violet & lake	70	35
308	–	100f. green, red & brown	90	45
309	–	250f. brown, red & green	2·25	95

DESIGNS—HORIZ: 250f. Congolese mask, geisha and scout badge. VERT: 90f. African and Japanese mask; 100f. Japanese woman and African.

116 Running

1971. Air. 75th Anniv of Modern Olympic Games.

No.	Type	Description	Mint	Used
310	116	75f. brown, blue and red	60	30
311	–	85f. brown, blue and red	65	30
312	–	90f. brown and violet	1·00	40
313	–	100f. brown and blue	1·10	45
314	–	150f. brown, red & green	2·00	75

DESIGNS: 85f. Hurdling; 90f. Various events; 100f. Wrestling; 150f. Boxing.

117 "Cymothae sangaris"

1971. Butterflies. Multicoloured.

No.	Description	Mint	Used
315	30f. Type **117**	65	35
316	40f. "Papilio dardanus" (vert)	1·25	55
317	75f. "Iolaus timon"	2·25	1·10
318	90f. "Papilio phorcas" (vert)	3·00	1·60
319	100f. "Euchloron megaera"	4·00	2·25

118 African and European Workers

1971. Racial Equality Year.

No.	Type	Description	Mint	Used
320	118	50f. multicoloured	55	30

119 De Gaulle and Congo 1966 Brazzaville Conference Stamp

1971. Air. 1st Death Anniv of General De Gaulle.

No.	Type	Description	Mint	Used
321	119	500f. brown, green & red	11·00	11·00
322	–	1000f. red & grn on gold	19·00	
323	–	1000f. red & grn on gold	19·00	

DESIGNS—VERT (29 × 38 mm): No. 322, Tribute by Pres. Ngouabi; 323, De Gaulle and Cross of Lorraine.

1971. Air. 10th Anniv of African and Malagasy Posts and Telecommunications Union. Similar to T **184** of Cameroun. Multicoloured.

No.	Description	Mint	Used
324	100f. U.A.M.P.T. H.Q. and Congolese woman	1·00	45

1971. Inauguration of Brazzaville–Pointe Noire Cable Link. Surch **REPUBLIQUE POPULAIRE DU CONGO INAUGURATION DE LA LIAISON COXIALE 18-11-71** and new value.

No.	Type	Description	Mint	Used
325	95	30f. on 25f. buff, brn & bl	1·60	30
326	–	40f. on 30f. brown and green (No. 223)	2·00	30

121 Congo Republic Flag and Allegory of Revolution

1971. Air. 8th Anniv of Revolution.

No.	Type	Description	Mint	Used
327	121	100f. multicoloured	1·40	40

122 Congolese with Flag

1971. Air. 2nd Anniv of Congolese Workers' Party, and Adoption of New National Flag. Multicoloured.

No.	Description	Mint	Used
328	30f. Type **122**	25	10
329	40f. National flag	35	20

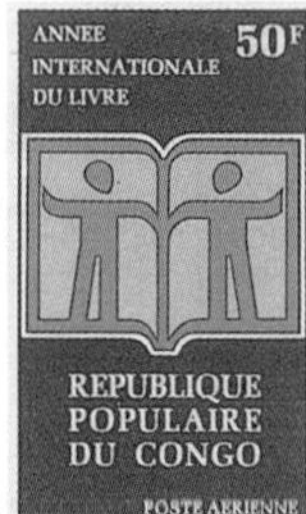

123 Map and Emblems

125 Book Year Emblem

124 Lion

1971. "Work–Democracy–Peace".

No.	Type	Description	Mint	Used
330	123	30f. multicoloured	25	20
331		40f. multicoloured	30	15
332		100f. multicoloured	75	40

1972. Wild Animals.

No.	Type	Description	Mint	Used
333	124	1f. brown, blue & green	10	10
334	–	2f. brown, green and red	10	10
335	–	3f. brown, orge and red	15	10
336	–	4f. brown, blue & violet	45	10
337	–	5f. brown, green and red	55	15
338	–	20f. brown, blue & orge	1·40	55
339	–	30f. green, emer & brn	2·00	80
340	–	40f. black, green and blue	2·75	1·00

DESIGNS—HORIZ: 2f. African elephants; 3f. Leopard; 4f. Hippopotamus; 20f. Potto; 30f. De Brazza's monkey. VERT: 5f. Gorilla; 40f. Pygmy chimpanzee.

1972. Air. International Book Year.

No.	Type	Description	Mint	Used
341	125	50f. green, yellow & red	65	25

126 Team Captain with Cup

127 Girl with Bird

1973. Air. Congolese Victory in Africa Football Cup. Multicoloured.

No.	Description	Mint	Used
342	100f. Type **126**	1·40	50
343	100f. Congolese team (horiz)	1·40	50

1973. Air. U.N. Environmental Conservation Conference, Stockholm.

No.	Type	Description	Mint	Used
344	127	85f. green, blue & orange	1·40	90

128 Miles Davis

1973. Air. Famous Negro Musicians.
345 **128** 125f. multicoloured . . . 1·60 65
346 – 140f. red, lilac & mauve 1·60 70
347 – 160f. green, emer & orge 1·90 1·00
348 – 175f. purple, red & blue 2·00 1·00
DESIGNS: 140f. Ella Fitzgerald; 160f. Count Basie; 175f. John Coltrane.

129 Hurdling

1973. Air. Olympic Games, Munich (1972).
349 **129** 100f. violet and mauve . . 90 50
350 – 150f. violet and green . . 1·40 65
351 – 250f. red and blue . . . . 2·75 1·40
DESIGNS—VERT: 150f. Pole-vaulting. HORIZ: 250f. Wrestling.

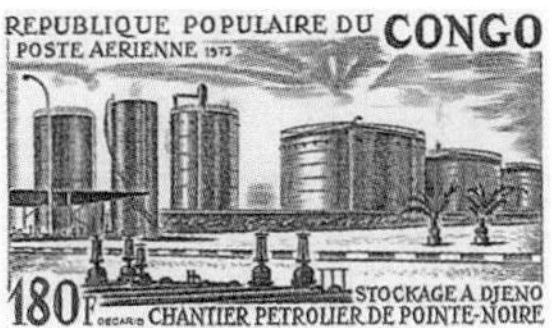

130 Oil Tanks, Djeno

1973. Air. Oil Installations, Pointe Noire.
352 **130** 180f. indigo, red & blue 2·25 1·40
353 – 230f. black, red and blue 2·75 1·40
354 – 240f. purple, blue & red 3·00 1·50
355 – 260f. black, red and blue 4·75 1·90
DESIGNS—VERT: 230f. Oil-well head; 240f. Drill in operation. HORIZ: 260f. Off-shore oil-rig.

131 Lunar Module and Astronaut on Moon

1973. Air. Moon Flight of "Apollo 17".
356 **131** 250f. multicoloured . . . 3·00 1·75

132 "Telecommunications"

1973. Air. World Telecommunications Day.
357 **132** 120f. multicoloured . . . 1·40 65

133 Copernicus and Solar System

1973. Air. 500th Birth Anniv of Copernicus (astronomer).
358 **133** 50f. green, blue & lt blue 45 35

134 Rocket and African Scenes

1973. Air. Centenary of World Meteorological Organization.
359 **134** 50f. multicoloured . . . . 1·00 35

135 W.H.O. Emblem **137** General View of Brewery

136 "Study of a White Horse"

1973. 25th Anniv of W.H.O. Multicoloured.
360 40f. Type **135** 35 20
361 50f. Design similar to T **135** (horiz) 45 25

1973. Air. Paintings by Delacroix. Multicoloured.
362 150f. Type **136** . . . . 1·40 1·25
363 250f. "Sleeping Lion" . . . . 3·25 2·00
364 300f. "Tiger and Lion" . . . 4·00 2·25
See also Nos. 384/6 and 437/40.

1973. Congo Brewers' Association. Views of Kronenbourg Brewery.
365 **137** 30f. blue, red & lt blue . . 25 20
366 – 40f. grey, orange & red 30 20
367 – 75f. blue, red and black 55 30
368 – 85f. multicoloured . . . . 1·00 40
369 – 100f. multicoloured . . . 1·25 55
370 – 250f. green, brown & red 2·25 1·40
DESIGNS: 40f. Laboratory; 75f. Regulating vats; 85f. Control console; 100f. Bottling plant; 250f. Capping bottles.

1973. Locomotives of Congo Railways (2nd series). As T **102**. Multicoloured.
371 30f. Golwe steam locomotive c. 1935 . . . . 2·10 85
372 40f. Diesel-electric locomotive, 1935 . . . . . 3·00 1·25
373 75f. Whitcomb diesel-electric locomotive, 1946 . . . . . 4·75 2·10
374 85f. Alsthom Series CC200 diesel-electric locomotive, 1973 . . . . 5·50 2·40

138 Stamp Map, Album, Dancer and Oil Rig **139** President Marien Ngouabi

1973. Air. International Stamp Exhibition, Brazzaville and 10th Anniv of Revolution.
375 **138** 30f. grey, lilac & brown 2·50 50
376 – 40f. red, brown & purple 30 25
377 **138** 100f. blue, brown & pur 4·75 1·25
378 – 100f. lilac, purple & red 1·10 60
DESIGNS: 40f., 100f. Map, album and Globes.

1973. Air.
379 **139** 30f. multicoloured 25 10
380 40f. multicoloured 30 15
381 75f. multicoloured 60 30

1973. Pan-African Drought Relief. No. 236 surch **100F SECHERESSE SOLIDARITE AFRICAINE**.
382 100f. on 5f. multicoloured . . 1·40 50

1973. 12th Anniv of African and Malagasy Posts and Telecommunications Union. As T **216** of Cameroun.
383 100f. violet, blue and purple 1·10 50

1973. Air. Europafrique. As T **136**. Multicoloured.
384 100f. "Wild Dog" . . . . . 2·25 1·10
385 100f. "Lion and Leopard" . . 2·25 1·10
386 100f. "Adam and Eve in Paradise" . . . . 2·25 1·10
Nos. 384/6 are details taken from J. Brueghel's "Earth and Paradise".

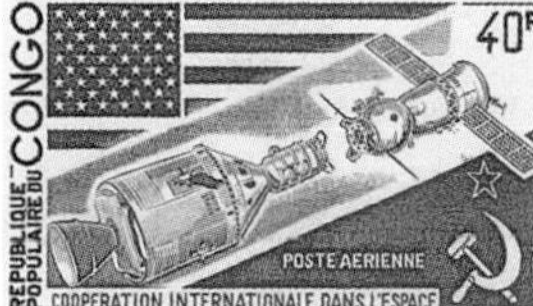

141 "Apollo" and "Soyuz" Spacecraft

1973. Air. International Co-operation in Space.
387 **141** 40f. brown, red & blue . . 30 25
388 – 80f. blue, red and green 80 40
DESIGN: 80f. Spacecraft docked.

142 U.P.U. Monument and Satellite

1973. Air. U.P.U. Day.
389 **142** 80f. blue & ultramarine 60 35

1973. Air. "Skylab" Space Laboratory. As T **141**.
390 30f. green, brown and blue 30 15
391 40f. green, red and orange . . 35 25
DESIGNS: 30f. Astronauts walking outside "Skylab"; 40f. "Skylab" and "Apollo" spacecraft docked.

143 Hive and Bees

1973. "Labour and Economy".
392 **143** 30f. green, blue and red 50 20
393 40f. green, blue & green 55 20

144 Congo Family and Emblems

1973. 10th Anniv of World Food Programme.
394 **144** 30f. brown and red . . . 25 15
395 – 40f. orange, green & blue 30 25
396 – 100f. brown, green & orge 75 45
DESIGNS—HORIZ: 40f. Ears of corn and emblems. VERT: 100f. Ear of corn, granary and emblems.

145 Goalkeeper **146** Runners

1973. Air. World Football Cup Championship, West Germany (1974). (1st issue).
397 **145** 40f. green, dp brn & brn 35 25
398 – 100f. green, red & violet 1·25 45
DESIGN: 100f. Forward.
See also Nos. 403 and 408.

1973. Air. 2nd African Games, Lagos, Nigeria.
399 **146** 40f. red, green & brown 35 25
400 100f. green, red & brown 1·25 45

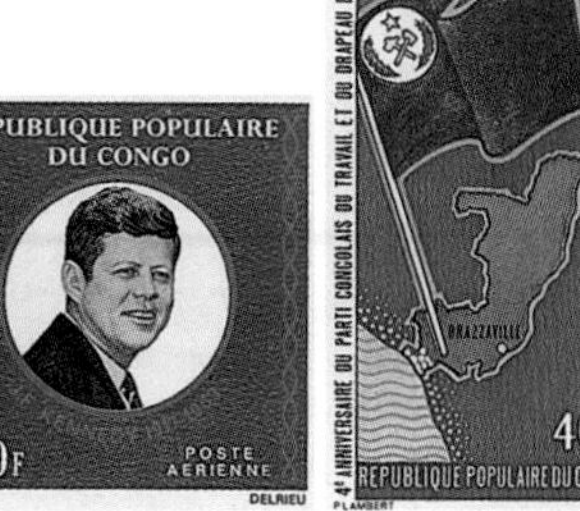

147 Pres. John F. Kennedy **148** Map and Flag

1973. Air. 10th Death Anniv of President Kennedy.
401 **147** 150f. black, gold & blue 1·40 70

1973. Air. 4th Anniv of Congo Workers' Party.
402 **148** 40f. multicoloured 30 20

149 Players seen through Goalkeeper's Legs

1974. Air. World Cup Football Championship, West Germany (2nd issue).
403 **149** 250f. green, red & brown 2·50 1·40

150 Globe, Flags and Names of Dead Astronauts

1974. Air. Conquest of Space.
404 **150** 30f. brown, blue & red . . 25 15
405 – 40f. multicoloured 35 25
406 – 100f. brown, blue & red 85 55
DESIGNS: 40f. Gagarin and Shepard; 100f. Leonov in space, and Armstrong on Moon.

151 A. Cabral **152** Spacecraft docking

1974. 1st Death Anniv of Cabral (Guinea-Bissau guerilla leader).
407 **151** 100f. purple, red & blue 70 45

1974. Air. West Germany's Victory in World Cup Football Championship. As T **149**.
408 250f. brown, pink and blue 2·75 1·40
DESIGN: Footballers within ball.

1974. Air. Soviet-American Space Co-operation.
409 **152** 200f. blue, violet and red 1·40 90
410 – 300f. blue, brown & red 2·50 1·25
DESIGN—HORIZ: 300f. Spacecraft on segments of globe.

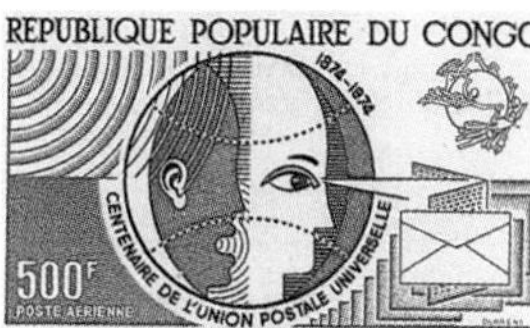

153 "Sound and Vision"

1974. Air. Centenary of U.P.U.
411 **153** 500f. black and red . . . 5·00 2·75

154 Felix Eboue and Cross of Lorraine

1974. 30th Death Anniv of Eboue ("Free French" Leader).
412 **154** 30f. multicoloured 50 35
413 40f. multicoloured 65 45

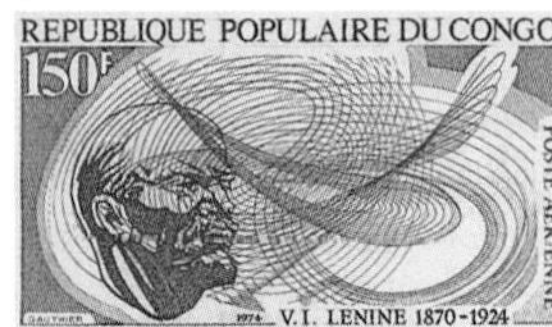

155 Lenin

1974. Air. 30th Death Anniv of Lenin.
414 **155** 150f. orange, red & green 1·40 90

1974. Birth Centenary of Churchill. As T **154**. Multicoloured.
415 200f. Churchill and Order of the Garter 1·75 1·00

1974. Birth Centenary of Guglielmo Marconi (radio pioneer). As T **154**. Multicoloured.
416 200f. Marconi and early apparatus 1·75 85

1974. Air. Centenary of Berne Convention. No. 411 surch **9 OCTOBRE 1974 300F**.
417 **153** 300f. on 500f. blk & red 2·75 1·40

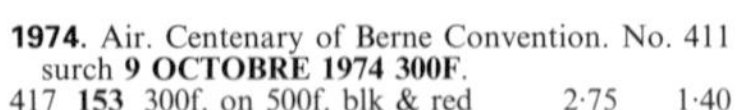

157 Pineapple

1974. Congolese Fruits. Multicoloured.
418 30f. Type **157** 35 25
419 30f. Bananas 35 25
420 30f. Safous 35 25
421 40f. Avocado pears 65 25
422 40f. Mangoes 65 25
423 40f. Papaya 65 25
424 40f. Oranges 65 25

158 Gen. Charles De Gaulle

1974. 30th Anniv of Brazzaville Conference.
425 **158** 100f. brown and green 2·25 1·40

1974. 10th Anniv of Central African Customs and Economic Union. As Nos. 734/5 of Cameroun.
426 40f. mult (postage) 35 20
427 100f. multicoloured (air) 90 45

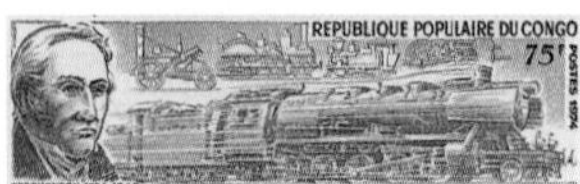

159 George Stephenson (railway pioneer) and Early and Modern Locomotives (½-size illustration)

1974. 150th Anniv (1975) of Public Railways.
428 **159** 75f. olive and green 1·60 60

160 Irish Setter

1974. Dogs. Multicoloured.
429 30f. Type **160** 55 25
430 40f. Borzoi 65 25
431 75f. Pointer 1·40 65
432 100f. Great Dane 1·90 70

1974. Cats. As T **160**. Multicoloured.
433 30f. Havana chestnut 55 25
434 40f. Red Persian 65 25
435 75f. British blue 1·40 65
436 100f. Serval 1·90 75

1974. Air. Impressionist Paintings. As T **136**. Mult.
437 30f. "The Argenteuil Regatta" (Monet) 80 50
438 40f. "Seated Dancer" (Degas) (vert) 90 55
439 50f. "Girl on Swing" (Renoir) (vert) 1·40 80
440 75f. "Girl in Straw Hat" (Renoir) (vert) 1·90 1·00

161 National Fair

1974. Air. National Fair, Brazzaville.
441 **161** 30f. multicoloured 55 25

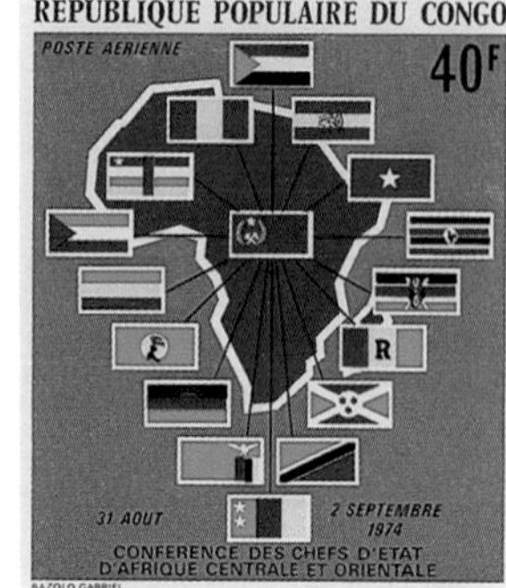

162 African Map and Flags

1974. Air. African Heads-of-State Conference, Brazzaville.
442 **162** 40f. multicoloured 60 25

163 Flags and Dove

1974. 5th Anniv of Congo Labour Party.
443 **163** 30f. red, yellow & green 25 15
444 – 40f. brown, red & yellow 80 25
DESIGN: 40f. Hands holding flowers and hammer.

164 U Thant and U.N. Headquarters Building

1975. 1st Death Anniv of U Thant (U.N. Secretary-General).
445 **164** 50f. multicoloured 40 25

1975. 1st Death Anniv of Paul G. Hoffman (U.N. Programme for Underdeveloped Countries administrator). As T **164**. Multicoloured.
446 50f. Hoffman and U.N. "Laurel Wreath" (vert) 35 25

166 Workers and Development

1975. National Economic Development.
447 **166** 40f. multicoloured 30 25

167 Mao Tse-tung and Map of China

1975. 25th Anniv (1974) of Chinese People's Republic.
448 **167** 75f. red, mauve & blue 1·60 80

168 Woman with Hoe

1975. 10th Anniv of Revolutionary Union of Congolese Women.
449 **168** 40f. multicoloured 30 20

169 Paris–Brussels Line, 1890 (½-size illustration)

1975. Air. Railway History. Multicoloured.
450 50f. Type **169** 1·10 50
451 75f. Santa Fe Line, 1880 2·40 60

170 "Five Weeks in a Balloon"

1975. Air. 70th Anniv of Jules Verne (novelist). Multicoloured.
452 40f. Type **170** 80 40
453 50f. "Around the World in 80 Days" 4·00 1·00

171 Line-up of Team

1975. Victory of Cara Football Team in Africa Cup. Multicoloured.
454 30f. Type **171** 30 25
455 40f. Receiving trophy (vert) 35 25

172 1935 Citroen and Notre Dame Cathedral, Paris

1975. Veteran Cars. Multicoloured.
456 30f. Type **172** 55 20
457 40f. 1911 Alfa Romeo and St. Peter's Rome 65 20
458 50f. 1926 Rolls Royce and Houses of Parliament, London 80 30
459 75f. 1893 C. F. Duryea and Manhattan skyline, New York 1·40 35

173 "Soyuz" Spacecraft

1975. Air. "Apollo–Soyuz" Space Test Project.
460 **173** 95f. black, red & brown 80 35
461 – 100f. black, violet & blue 90 40
DESIGN: 100f. "Apollo" Spacecraft.

174 Tipoye Carriage

1975. Traditional Congo Transport. Multicoloured.
462 30f. Type **174** 55 20
463 40f. Pirogue 65 30

175 "Raising the Flag"

1975. 2nd Anniv of Institutions of Popular Tasks.
464 **175** 30f. multicoloured 25 20

176 Conference Hall

1975. 3rd Anniv of Congolese National Conference.
465 **176** 40f. multicoloured 35 25

177 Fishing with Wooden Baskets

1975. Traditional Fishing. Multicoloured.
466 30f. Type **177** 30 20
467 40f. Fishing with line (vert) 90 30
468 60f. Fishing with spear (vert) 80 25
469 90f. Fishing with net 1·40 80

178 Chopping Firewood 179 "Esanga"

1975. Domestic Chores. Multicoloured.
470 30f. Type **178** 25 15
471 30f. Pounding meal 25 15
472 40f. Preparing manioc (horiz) 40 20

1975. Traditional Musical Instruments. Mult.
473 30f. Type **179** 55 20
474 40f. "Kalakwa" 65 25
475 60f. "Likembe" 1·00 30
476 75f. "Ngongui" 1·10 40

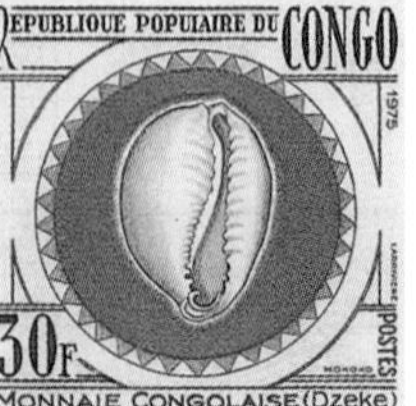

180 "Dzeke" Money Cowrie

1975. Ancient Congolese Money.
477 **180** 30f. ochre, brown & red 40 25
478 – 30f. ochre, violet & brn 30 20
478a **180** 35f. orange and brown 45 30
478b – 35f. red, bistre and violet 35 25
479 – 40f. brown and blue 45 25

480 – 50f. blue and brown . . 45 25
481 – 60f. brown and green . . 55 30
482 – 85f. green and red . . . 1·00 35
DESIGNS: 30, 35 (478b) f. "Okengo" iron money; 40f. Gallic coin (60 B.C.); 50f. Roman coin (37 B.C.); 60f. Danubian coin (2nd century B.C.); 85f. Greek coin (4th century B.C.).

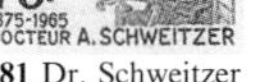

181 Dr. Schweitzer

183 Boxing

182 "Moschops"

1975. Birth Centenary of Dr. Albert Schweitzer.
483 **181** 75f. green, mauve & brn 1·10 40

1975. Prehistoric Animals. Multicoloured.
484 55f. Type **182** 70 25
485 75f. "Tyrannosaurus" . . . . 1·10 30
486 95f. "Cryptocleidus" . . . . 1·90 65
487 100f. "Stegosauras" . . . . 2·50 90

1975. Air. Olympic Games, Montreal (1976). Multicoloured.
488 40f. Type **183** 30 25
489 50f. Basketball 35 25
490 85f. Cycling (horiz) 80 35
491 95f. High jumping (horiz) . . 1·00 35
492 100f. Throwing the javelin (horiz) . . . . 1·25 40
493 150f. Running (horiz) . . . . 1·60 65

184 Alexander Fleming (biochemist) (20th Death Anniv)

1975. Celebrities.
494 **184** 60f. black, green and red 65 30
495 – 95f. black, blue and red 1·25 50
496 – 95f. green, red and lilac 1·10 40
DESIGNS: No. 495, Clement Ader (aviation pioneer) (50th death anniv); 496, Andre Marie Ampere (physicist) (birth bicent).

185 U.N. Emblem with Laurel Wreaths

1975. 30th Anniv of U.N.O.
497 **185** 95f. blue, red and green 80 40

186 Map of Africa and Sportsmen

1975. Air. 10th Anniv of 1st African Games, Brazzaville.
498 **186** 30f. multicoloured 30 25

187 Chained Women and Broken Link

1975. International Women's Year. Multicoloured.
499 35f. Type **187** 35 15
500 60f. Global handclasp . . . 45 30

188 Pres. Ngouabi and Crowd with Flags

1975. 6th Anniv of Congolese Workers' Party. Multicoloured.
501 30f. Type **188** (postage) . . . 25 20
502 35f. "Echo"–P.C.T. "man" with roll of newsprint and radio waves (36 × 27 mm) 30 20
503 60f. Party members with flag (26 × 38 mm) (air) 35 25

189 River Steamer "Alphonse Fondere"

1976. Air. Old-time Ships. Multicoloured.
504 5f. Type **189** 25 20
505 10f. Paddle-steamer "Hamburg", 1839 . . . . 35 20
506 15f. Paddle-steamer "Gomer", 1831 . . . . . 35 20
507 20f. Paddle-steamer "Great Eastern", 1858 . . . . . . 35 20
508 30f. Type **189** 55 20
509 40f. As 10f. 60 45
510 50f. As 15f. 65 45
511 60f. As 20f. 85 60
512 95f. River steamer "J.M. White II" 1878 . . . . . 1·40 90

190 "The Peasant Family" (L. le Nain)

1976. Air. Europafrique. Paintings. Multicoloured.
513 60f. Type **190** 80 15
514 80f. "Boy with spinning Top" (Chardin) . . . . 1·00 55
515 95f. "Venus and Aeneas" (Poussin) . . . . 1·10 55
516 100f. "The Sabines" (David) 1·50 80

191 Alexander Graham Bell and Early Telephone

1976. Telephone Centenary.
517 **191** 35f. brown, light brown and yellow (postage) . . 30 25
518 60f. red, mve & pink (air) 40 25

192 Fruit Market

1976. Market Scenes. Multicoloured.
519 35f. Type **192** 25 20
520 60f. Laying out produce . . . 90 25

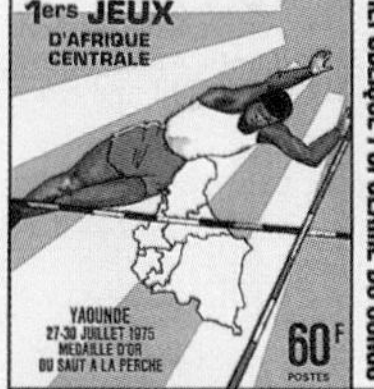

193 Congolese Woman

194 Pole-vaulting

1976. Congolese Women's Hair-styles.
521 **193** 35f. multicoloured 30 25
522 – 60f. multicoloured 45 25
523 – 95f. multicoloured 70 35
524 – 100f. multicoloured . . . 1·00 40
DESIGNS: 60f. to 100f. Various Congolese Women's hair-styles.

1976. 1st Central African Games, Yaounde. Multicoloured.
525 60f. Type **194** (postage) . . . 45 30
526 95f. Long-jumping 75 45
527 150f. Running (air) . . . . . 1·25 60
528 200f. Throwing the discus . . 1·90 90

195 Kob

196 Saddle-bill Storks ("Jabirus")

1976. Congolese Fauna. Multicoloured.
529 5f. Type **195** 10 10
530 10f. African buffaloes 15 10
531 15f. Hippopotami 15 15
532 20f. Warthog 65 25
533 25f. African elephants 80 30

1976. Birds. Multicoloured.
534 5f. Type **196** 35 30
535 10f. Shining-blue kingfisher ("Martin-Pecheur") (37 × 37 mm) . . . . . . 1·75 50
536 20f. Crowned cranes ("Grues Couronnees") (37 × 37 mm) 2·00 90

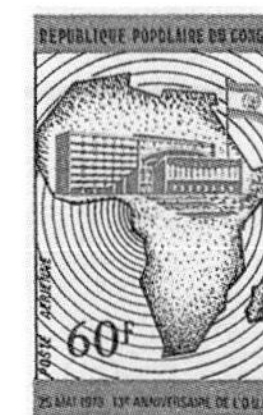

197 O.A.U. Building on Map

198 Cycling

1976. Air. 13th Anniv of O.A.U.
537 **197** 60f. multicoloured 35 25

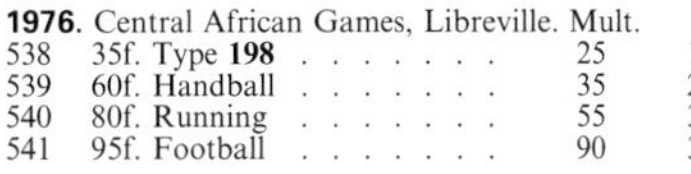

1976. Central African Games, Libreville. Mult.
538 35f. Type **198** 25 15
539 60f. Handball 35 25
540 80f. Running (air) 55 30
541 95f. Football 90 35

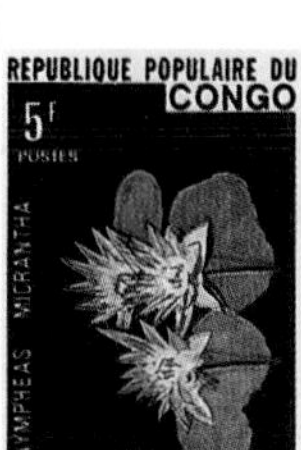

199 "Nymphaea micrantha"

200 Pioneers' Emblem

1976. Tropical Flowers. Multicoloured.
542 5f. Type **199** 10 10
543 10f. "Heliotrope" 10 10
544 15f. "Strelitzia reginae" . . . 20 10

1976. National Pioneers Movement.
545 **200** 35f. multicoloured 20 20

201 "Spirit of 76" (detail, A. M. Willard)

1976. Bicent of American Revolution. Mult.
546 100f. Type **201** 55 25
547 125f. Destruction of George III's statue 90 35
548 150f. Gunners-Battle of Princeton 90 40
549 175f. Wartime generals . . . 1·25 50
550 200f. Surrender of Gen. Burgoyne, Saratoga . . . 1·40 60

202 Pirogue Race

1977. Pirogue Racing. Multicoloured.
552 35f. Type **202** 60 30
553 60f. Race in progress 85 45

203 Butter Catfish

1977. Freshwater Fishes. Multicoloured.
554 10f. Type **203** 10 10
555 15f. Big-eyed catfish 10 10
556 25f. Citharinid 45 10
557 35f. Mbessi mormyrid . . . 65 15
558 60f. "Mongandza" . . . . . 1·25 55

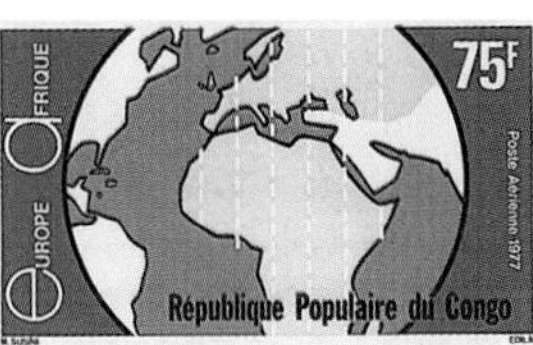

204 Map of Europe and Africa

1977. Air. Europafrique.
559 **204** 75f. multicoloured 45 35

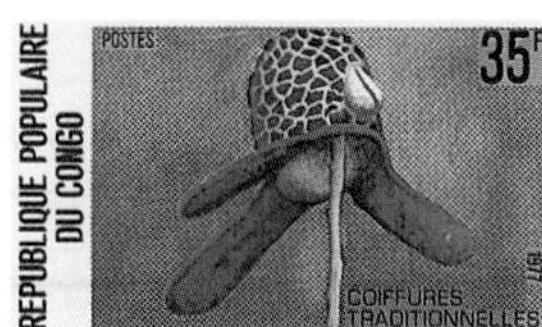

205 Headdress

1977. Traditional Headdresses. Multicoloured.
560 35f. Type **205** (postage) . . . 30 20
561 60f. Headdress with tail . . . 80 25
562 250f. Two headdresses (air) 2·25 1·40
563 300f. Headdresses with beads 2·50 1·60

206 Wrestling

1977. Bondjo Wrestling.
564 – 25f. multicoloured 20 10
565 **206** 40f. multicoloured 25 15
566 – 50f. multicoloured 35 25
DESIGNS—VERT: 25f., 50f. Different wrestling scenes.

207 "Schwaben", 1911

1977. History of the Zeppelin. Multicoloured.
567 40f. Type **207** 25 20
568 60f. "Viktoria Luise", 1913 35 30
569 100f. "Bodensee" 80 30
570 200f. "Graf Zeppelin" . . . 1·25 45
571 300f. "Graf Zeppelin II" . . 2·50 60

208 Rising Sun of "Revolution"

1977. 14th Anniv of Revolution.
573 **208** 40f. multicoloured 25 25

209 "Flow of Trade"

1977. Air. G.A.T.T. Trade Convention, Lome.
574 **209** 60f. black and red 45 25

210 Hugo and Scene from "Hunchback of Notre Dame"

1977. 175th Birth Anniv of Victor Hugo.
575 **210** 35f. brown, red and blue 25 15
576 – 60f. green, drab and blue 35 25
577 – 100f. brown, blue & red 70 45
DESIGNS: 60f. Scene from "Les Miserables"; 100f. Scene from "The Toilers of the Sea".

211 Newton and Constellations

1977. Air. 250th Death Anniv of Isaac Newton.
578 **211** 140f. mauve, green & brn 1·50 90

212 Mao Tse-tung

1977. 1st Death Anniv of Mao Tse-tung.
579 **212** 400f. gold and red . . . . 4·50 2·75

213 Rubens

1977. 400th Birth Anniv of Peter Paul Rubens.
580 **213** 600f. gold and blue . . . 6·75 5·50

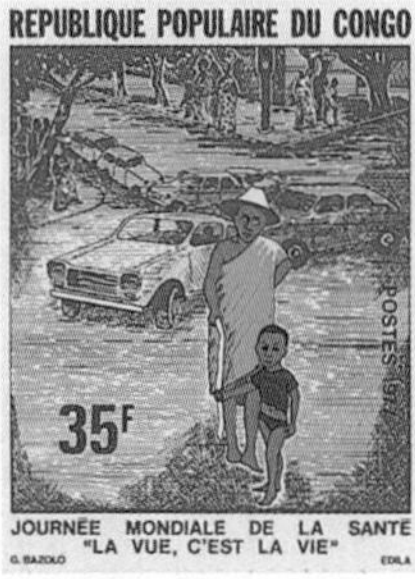

214 Child leading Blind Person

1977. Fight Against Blindness.
581 **214** 35f. multicoloured 30 25

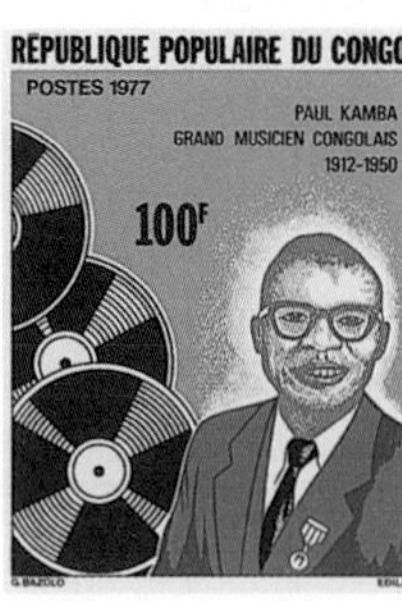

215 Paul Kamba and Records

1977. Paul Kamba (musician) Commemoration.
582 **215** 100f. multicoloured . . . 80 40

216 Trajan Vuia and his Vuia No. 1

1977. Aviation History. Multicoloured.
583 60f. Type **216** 35 20
584 75f. Bleriot and Bleriot XI over Channel 40 20
585 100f. Roland Garros and Morane Saulnier Type 1 80 30
586 200f. Lindbergh and "Spirit of St. Louis" . . . . . . 1·50 45
587 300f. Tupolev Tu-144 . . . . 2·00 65

217 General de Gaulle

1977. Historic Personalities, and Silver Jubilee of Queen Elizabeth II. Multicoloured.
589 200f. Type **217** . . . . 1·90 45
590 200f. King Baudouin of Belgium . . . . 1·50 45
591 250f. Queen and Prince Philip in open car . . . . 1·50 65
592 300f. Queen Elizabeth . . . . 2·00 70

218 Ambete Statue **219** "The Apostle Simon"

1978. Congolese Sculpture.
594 **218** 35f. lake, brown & green 30 25
595 – 85f. brown, green & lake 90 35
DESIGN: 85f. Babembe statue.

1978. 400th Birth Anniv of Peter Paul Rubens (2nd issue). Multicoloured.
596 60f. Type **219** 65 20
597 140f. "The Duke of Lerma" 1·10 35
598 200f. "Madonna and Saints" 1·50 50
599 300f. "The Artist and his Wife" . . . . 2·25 65

220 Pres. Ngouabi making Speech

1978. 1st Death Anniv of President Marien Ngouabi.
601 **220** 35f. black, yellow & red 15 15
602 – 60f. multicoloured 30 20
603 – 100f. black, yellow & red 45 35
DESIGNS—HORIZ: 60f. Pres. Ngouabi at his desk. VERT: 100f. Portrait of Pres. Ngouabi.

221 Ferenc Puskas (Hungary)

1978. World Cup Football Championship, Argentina. Famous Players. Multicoloured.
604 60f. Type **221** 35 20
605 75f. Giacinto Facchetti (Italy) 40 20
606 100f. Bobby Moore (England) 55 25
607 200f. Raymond Kopa (France) . . . . 1·60 50
608 300f. Pele (Brazil) . . . . . 2·25 65

222 Pearl S. Buck (Literature, 1938)

1978. Nobel Prize Winners. Multicoloured.
610 60f. Type **222** 40 25
611 75f. Fridtjof Nansen and camp scene (Peace) 40 20
612 100f. Henri Bergson and "Elan Vita" (Literature) . . 55 30
613 200f. Alexander Fleming and penicillin (Medicine) . . . 1·50 60
614 300f. Gerhart Hauptmann and hands with book (Literature) . . . . 2·00 65

223 Purple Heron **224** Okapi

1978. Air. Birds. Multicoloured.
616 65f. Mallard . . . . 2·00 95
617 75f. Type **223** . . . . 2·00 1·10
618 150f. Great reed warbler . . 4·00 1·50
619 240f. Hoopoe . . . . 5·25 2·40

1978. Endangered Animals. Multicoloured.
620 35f. Type **224** 25 20
621 60f. African buffalo (horiz) 45 30
622 85f. Black rhinoceros (horiz) 1·10 40
623 150f. Chimpanzee . . . . . 1·60 50
624 200f. Hippopotamus (horiz) 2·25 1·10
625 300f. Kob . . . . 4·00 1·40

225 Clenched Fist, Emblem and Crowd

1978. 11th World Youth and Students Festival, Havana, Cuba.
626 **225** 35f. multicoloured 30 25

226 Pyramids, Egypt

1978. The Seven Wonders of the Ancient World. Multicoloured.
627 35f. Type **226** 20 15
628 50f. Hanging Gardens of Babylon (vert) 25 20
629 60f. Statue of Zeus, Olympia (vert) 35 20
630 95f. Colossos of Rhodes (vert) 50 25
631 125f. Mausoleum, Halicarnassus (vert) . . . 90 30
632 150f. Temple of Artemis, Ephesus . . . . 1·10 40
633 200f. Pharos, Alexandria (vert) . . . . 2·00 65
634 300f. Map showing sites of the Seven Wonders . . . . 2·25 65

1978. 25th Anniv of Coronation of Queen Elizabeth II. Nos. 591/2 optd **ANNIVERSAIRE DU COURONNEMENT 1953 - 1978**.
635 250f. Queen Elizabeth and Prince Philip in open car 2·00 85
636 300f. Queen Elizabeth II . . 2·25 1·40

228 Kwame Nkrumah and Map of Africa

1978. Kwame Nkrumah (Ghanaian statesman) Commemoration.
638 **228** 60f. multicoloured 35 20

229 Hunting Wild Pigs

1978. Multicoloured.
639 35f. Type **229** 25 20
640 50f. Smoking fish 35 30
641 60f. Hunter with kill (vert) 35 20
642 140f. Woman hoeing (vert) 1·10 40

1978. Air. "Philexafrique" Stamp Exhibition, Libreville, Gabon (1st issue) and International Stamp Fair, Essen, West Germany. As T **237** of Benin. Multicoloured.
643 100f. Peregrine Falcon and Wurttemberg 1851 1k. stamp . . . . 1·50 1·10
644 100f. Leopard and Congo 1978 240f. stamp . . . . . 1·50 1·10
See also Nos. 668/9.

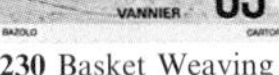

230 Basket Weaving

232 Satellites, Antennae and Map of Africa

231 "Kalchreut"

1978. Occupations. Multicoloured.
645 85f. Type **230** 50 25
646 90f. Wood sculpture 50 25

1978. 450th Death Anniv of Albrecht Durer (artist). Multicoloured.
647 65f. Type **231** 35 20
648 150f. "Elspeth Tucher" . . . 1·00 35
649 250f. "Grasses" . . . . . . 1·40 60
650 350f. "Self-portrait" . . . . 2·50 90

1978. Air. Pan African Telecommunications.
651 **232** 100f. red, green & orange 90 35

1978. World Cup Football Championship Winners. Nos. 604/8 optd with names of past winners.
652 **221** 60f. multicoloured 35 25
653 – 75f. multicoloured 40 30
654 – 100f. multicoloured . . . 55 35
655 – 200f. multicoloured . . . 1·60 60
656 – 300f. multicoloured . . . 2·25 1·00
OPTS: 60f. **1962 VAINQUEUR BRESIL**; 75f. **1966 VAINQUEUR GRANDE BRETAGNE**; 100f. **1970 VAINQUEUR BRESIL**; 200f. **1974 VAINQUEUR ALLEMAGNE (RFA)**; 300f. **1978 VAINQUEUR ARGENTINE**.

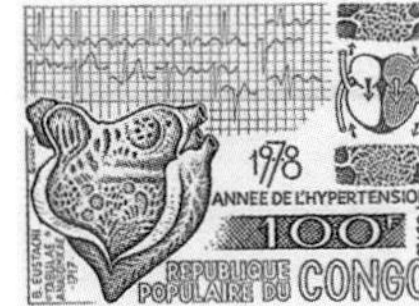

234 Diseased Heart, Blood Pressure Graph and Circulation Diagram

1978. World Hypertension Year.
658 **234** 100f. brown, red & turq 80 35

235 Road to the Sun

1978. 9th Anniv of Congolese Workers' Party.
659 **235** 60f. multicoloured 30 15

236 Captain Cook and Native Feast

1979. Death Bicentenary of Captain James Cook. Multicoloured.
660 65f. Type **236** 35 20
661 150f. Easter Island monuments . . . . 1·40 35
662 250f. Hawaiian canoes . . . 2·00 70
663 350f. H.M.S. "Resolution" and H.M.S. "Adventure" at anchor . . . . 2·75 1·10

237 Pres. Ngouabi

1979. 2nd Anniv of Assassination of President Ngouabi.
664 **237** 35f. multicoloured 20 15
665 60f. multicoloured 35 20

238 I.Y.C. Emblem and Child

1979. International Year of the Child.
666 **238** 45f. multicoloured 25 20
667 75f. multicoloured 30 15

239 "Solanum torvum" and Earthenware Jars

1979. "Philexafrique" Stamp Exhibition, Libreville, Gabon (2nd issue).
668 **239** 60f. multicoloured 90 45
669 – 150f. orange, brn & grn 2·50 1·40
DESIGN: 150f. U.P.U. emblem, Concorde airplane, postal runner and diesel locomotive.

240 Rowland Hill, Diesel Locomotive and German 5m., Stamp, 1900

1979. Death Centenary of Sir Rowland Hill. Multicoloured.
670 65f. Type **240** 60 10
671 100f. Steam locomotive and French "War Orphans" stamp of 1917 . . . . . 80 15
672 200f. Diesel locomotive and U.S. Columbus stamp of 1893 . . . . 1·75 30
673 300f. Steam locomotive and England–Australia "First Aerial Post" vignette . . . 3·00 90

241 Pres. Salvador Allende

1979. Salvador Allende (former President of Chile) Commemoration.
675 **241** 100f. multicoloured . . . 80 25

242 "The Teller of Legends"

1979. African Folk Tales as Part of Children's Education.
676 **242** 45f. multicoloured 55 20

243 Handball Players

244 Map of Africa filled with Heads

1979. Marien Ngouabi Handball Cup. Mult.
677 45f. Type **243** 30 20
678 75f. Handball players 40 25
679 250f. Cup on map of Africa, player and Marien Ngouabi (vert) (22 × 37 mm) . . . . . . 1·75 70

1979. Air. 5th Pan-African Youth Conference, Brazzaville.
680 **244** 45f. multicoloured 30 20
681 75f. multicoloured 45 30

246 Congo Map and Flag

1979. 16th Anniv of Revolution.
683 **246** 50f. multicoloured 25 15

247 Abala Peasant Woman

1979. Air.
684 **247** 150f. multicoloured . . . 1·40 60

249 Bach and Musical Instruments

1979. Personalities. Multicoloured.
686 200f. Type **249** . . . . 1·60 50
687 200f. Albert Einstein and astronauts on the Moon 1·60 50

250 Yoro

1979. Yoro Fishing Port. Multicoloured.
688 45f. Type **250** 30 20
689 75f. Yoro at night 40 25

251 Moukoukoulou Dam and Power Station

1979. Moukoukoulou Hydro-electric Power Station.
690 **251** 20f. multicoloured 15 10
691 45f. multicoloured 65 20

1979. Air. 10th Anniv of "Apollo 11" Moon Landing. Optd **ALUNISSAGE APOLLO XI JUILLET 1969**.
692 – 80f. blue, red and green (No. 388) 35 35
693 **173** 95f. blk, red & crimson 45 45
694 – 100f. brown, blue and red (No. 406) 45 45
695 – 100f. black, violet and blue (No. 461) 45 45
696 – 300f. blue, brown and red (No. 410) . . . . . . 1·90 1·90

253 Fencer

1979. Air. Pre-Olympic Year (1st issue) Multicoloured.
697 65f. Runner, map of Africa and Olympic rings (horiz) 30 20
698 100f. Boxer (horiz) 50 25
699 200f. Type **253** . . . . . . 1·40 40
700 300f. Footballer (horiz) . . . 2·00 65
701 500f. Olympic emblem . . . 3·25 1·40
See also Nos. 716/9.

254 ASECNA Emblem and Douglas DC-10

1979. 20th Anniv of ASECNA (African Air Safety Organization).
702 **254** 100f. multicoloured . . . 70 45

255 Party Emblem Workers and Flowers

256 Cross-country Skiing

1979. 10th Anniv of Congolese Workers' Party.
703 **255** 45f. multicoloured 25 15

1979. Air. Winter Olympic Games, Lake Placid (1980). Multicoloured.
704 40f. Type **256** 20 15
705 60f. Slalom 30 20
706 200f. Ski-jump . . . . 1·40 40
707 350f. Downhill skiing (horiz) 2·50 80
708 500f. Skier (vert, 31 × 46 mm) 3·25 1·10

257 Emblem and Globe **259** Long jump

1980. 15th Anniv of National Posts and Telecommunications Office.
709 **257** 45f. multicoloured 25 15
710 95f. multicoloured 45 25

1980. Air. Winter Olympic Games Medal Winners. Nos. 704/8 optd with names of winners.
711 40f. Cross-country skiing . . 20 15
712 60f. Slalom 30 20
713 200f. Ski jump . . . . 1·40 45
714 350f. Downhill skiing . . . . 2·50 1·00
715 500f. Skier . . . . 3·25 1·40
OVERPRINTS: 40f. **VAINQUEUR ZIMIATOV U.R.S.S.**; 60f. **VAINQUEUR MOSERPROELL Autriche**; 200f. **VAINQUEUR TOMANEN Finlande**; 350f. **VAINQUEUR STOCK AUTRICHE**; 500f. **VAINQUEURS STENMARK-WENZEL**.

1980. Air. Olympic Games, Moscow.
716 **259** 75f. multicoloured 55 10
717 – 150f. mult (horiz) . . . . 1·10 25
718 – 250f. multicoloured . . . 1·60 45
719 – 350f. multicoloured . . . 2·25 60
Nos. 717/19 show different views of the long jump.

260 Pope John Paul II

1980. Papal Visit.
721 **260** 100f. multicoloured . . . 1·10 30

261 Rotary Emblem

1980. 75th Anniv of Rotary International.
722 **261** 150f. multicoloured . . . 1·10 45

262 Glass Works

1980. Pointe Noire Glass Works. Multicoloured.
723 30f. Type **262** 15 10
724 35f. Glass works (different) 45 10

263 Claude Chappe and Semaphore Tower

1980. Claude Chappe Commemoration.
725 **263** 200f. multicoloured . . . 1·60 1·10

264 Real Madrid Stadium

1980. Air. World Cup Football Championship, Spain (1982). Multicoloured.
726 60f. Type **264** 30 15
727 75f. Real Zaragoza 35 15
728 100f. Atletico de Madrid . . 45 20
729 150f. Valencia C.F. . . . . . 1·00 30
730 175f. R.C.D. Espanol . . . . 1·40 35

265 Floating Quay

1980. Port of Mossaka. Multicoloured.
732 45f. Type **265** 25 15
733 90f. Aerial view of port . . . 40 20

266 "Crucifixion"

1980. Air. Paintings by Rembrandt. Multicoloured.
734 65f. "Adoration of the Shepherds" (detail) (horiz) 30 10
735 100f. "Entombment" (horiz) 45 25
736 200f. "Christ at Emmaus" (horiz) . . . . 1·40 40
737 300f. "Annunciation" . . . . 2·00 60
738 500f. Type **266** . . . . 4·00 1·10

267 Jacques Offenbach (composer)

1980. Air. Death Anniversaries. Multicoloured.
739 100f. Albert Camus (writer) (20th anniv) 80 35
740 150f. Type **267** (centenary) 1·40 90

268 "Papilio dardanus"

1980. Butterflies. Multicoloured.
741 5f. Type **268** 10 10
742 15f. "Kallima aethiops" . . . 10 10
743 20f. "Papilio demodocus" . . 15 10
744 60f. "Euphaedra" 55 40
745 90f. "Hypolimnas misippus" 1·10 50

269 Hospital

1980. "31 July" Hospital.
747 **269** 45f. multicoloured 25 20

270 Man presenting Human Rights Charter

1980. 32nd Anniv of Human Rights Convention. Multicoloured.
748 350f. Type **270** . . . . . . 2·25 1·10
749 500f. Man breaking chains 3·25 2·00

271 Raffia Dancing Skirts

1980. Air. Traditional Dancing Costumes. Mult.
750 250f. Type **271** . . . . 2·25 70
751 300f. Tam-tam dancers (vert) 2·50 1·40
752 350f. Masks . . . . 3·00 1·60

272 Clenched Fists, Flag and Dove **273** Coffee and Cocoa Trees on Map of Congo

1980. 17th Anniv of Revolution. Multicoloured.
753 75f. Citizens and State emblem (36 × 23 mm) . . . 35 25
754 95f. Type **272** 45 30
755 150f. Dove carrying state emblem (36 × 23 mm) . . . 1·00 45

1980. Coffee and Cocoa Day. Multicoloured.
756 45f. Type **273** 25 20
757 95f. Coffee and cocoa beans 80 35

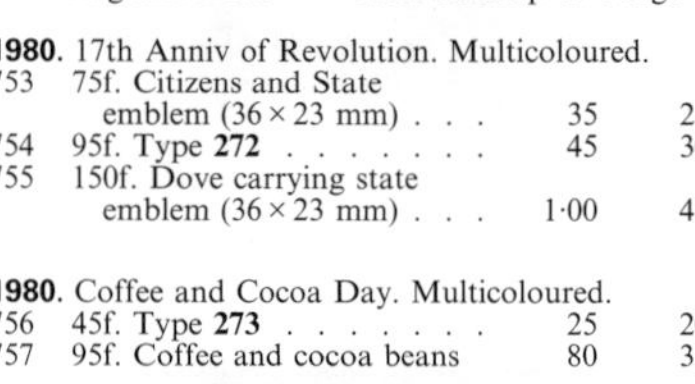

274 Cut Logs

1980. Forest Exploitation. Multicoloured.
758 70f. Type **274** 35 25
759 75f. Lorry with logs 35 25

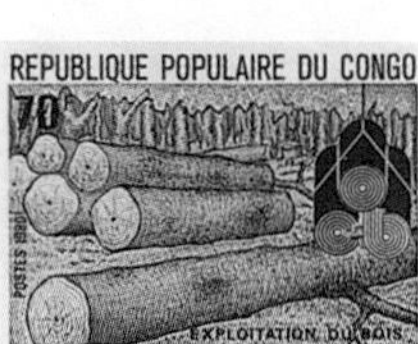

275 President Neto

1980. 1st Death Anniv of President Neto.
760 **275** 100f. multicoloured . . . 45 30

276 Olive-bellied Sunbird ("Souimanga Olivatre")

1980. Birds. Multicoloured.
761 45f. Type **276** . . . . 1·25 55
762 75f. Red-crowned bishop ("Travailleur a Tete Rouge") . . . . 1·75 60
763 90f. Moorhen ("Poule d'Eauafricaine") . . . . . 2·10 70
764 150f. African pied wagtail ("Alouette Canelle") . . . 3·25 1·50
765 200f. Yellow-mantled whydah (vert) . . . . 4·00 1·75
766 250f. "Geai-bleu" (vert) . . . 2·10 85

277 Conference Emblem

1980. World Tourism Conference, Manila.
768 **277** 100f. multicoloured . . . 80 45

278 Child Writing

1980. Return to School.
769 **278** 50f. multicoloured 25 15

279 The First House

1980. Brazzaville Centenary.
770 **279** 45f. ochre, grey & brown 25 15
771 – 65f. lt brown, brn & orge 55 20
772 – 75f. multicoloured 65 50
773 – 150f. multicoloured . . . 1·25 1·00
774 – 200f. multicoloured . . . 1·60 1·40
DESIGNS: 65f. First native village; 75f. The old Town Hall; 150f. Brazzaville from the Bacongo Promontory, 1912; 200f. Meeting between Savorgnan de Brazza (explorer) and Makoko (local chieftain).

280 Cataracts

1980. The River Congo. Multicoloured.
775 80f. Type **280** 65 50
776 150f. Bridge at Djoue . . . . 1·40 65

1980. Air. Olympic Medal Winners. Nos. 716/19 optd.
777 75f. **DOMBROWSKI (RDA)** 60 25
778 150f. **SANEIEV (URSS)** . . 1·00 45
779 250f. **SIMEONI (IT)** . . . . 1·50 80
780 350f. **THOMPSON (GB)** . . 2·25 1·40

282 Stadium and Sportsmen

1980. Revolutionary Stadium. Heroes of Congolese Sport.
782 **282** 60f. multicoloured 55 20

283 New Railway Bridge

1980. Realignment of Railway.
783 **283** 75f. multicoloured . . . . 1·00 25

284 Mangoes

1980. Loudima Fruit Station. Multicoloured.
784 10f. Type **284** 10 10
785 25f. Oranges 15 10
786 40f. Lemons 45 10
787 85f. Mandarins 65 20

1980. 5th Anniv of African Posts and Telecommunications Union. As T **269** of Benin.
788 100f. multicoloured 45 35

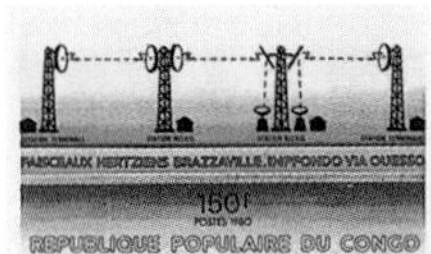

285 Microwave Communication

1980. Communications. Multicoloured.
789 75f. Moungouni Earth Station (36 × 36 mm) . . . 60 25
790 150f. Type **285** . . . . 1·00 45

286 Presentation of Marien Ngouabi Handball Cup

1981. African Handball Champions. Mult.
791 100f. Type **286** 90 30
792 150f. Team members . . . . 1·10 45

287 Pres. Sassou-Nguesso

1981. President Sassou-Nguesso.
793 **287** 45f. multicoloured 20 15
794 75f. multicoloured 40 25
795 100f. multicoloured . . . 45 30

288 Space Shuttle

1981. Conquest of Space. Multicoloured.
796 100f. "Luna 17" 45 25
797 150f. Type **288** . . . . . . 1·00 35
798 200f. Satellite and space shuttle . . . . 1·40 45
799 300f. Space shuttle approaching landing strip 2·00 70

289 Head and Dove

290 Twin Palm Tree

1981. Anti-Apartheid Campaign.
801 **289** 100f. blue 45 30

1981. The Twin Palm Tree of Louingui.
802 **290** 75f. multicoloured 65 25

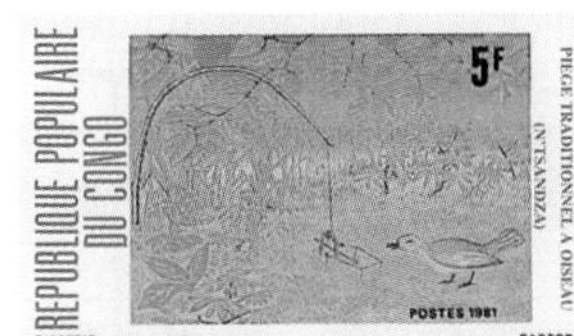

291 Bird approaching Snare

1981. Traditional Snares and Traps. Mult.
803 5f. Type **291** 10 10
804 10f. Bird in snare (vert) . . . 10 10
805 15f. Rodent approaching snare 10 10
806 20f. Rodent in snare 10 10
807 30f. Sprung trap 15 10
808 35f. Deer approaching trap 20 10

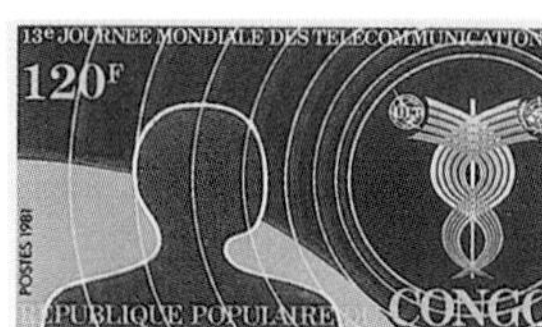

292 Human Figure and Caduceus

1981. World Telecommunications Day.
809 **292** 120f. multicoloured . . . 90 35

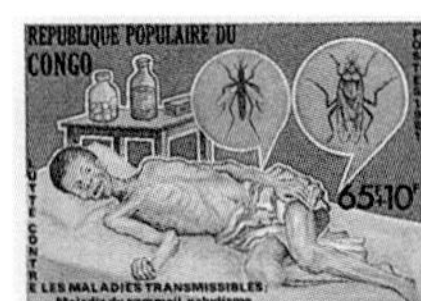

293 Sleeping Sickness and Malaria Victim

1981. Campaign against Transmissible Diseases. Multicoloured.
810 40f.+5f. Doctor, nurse, patients and mosquito . . 25 20
811 65f.+10f. Type **293** 45 20

294 Collecting Rubber

1981. Rubber Extraction. Multicoloured.
812 50f. Tapping rubber tree . . 20 15
813 70f. Type **294** 40 30

295 Helping a Disabled Person

1981. International Year of Disabled People.
814 **295** 45f. blue, purple & red . . 20 15
815 – 75f.+5f. multicoloured . . 65 30
DESIGN: 75f. Disabled people superimposed on globe.

296 "The Studio"

1981. Air. Birth Centenary of Pablo Picasso. Multicoloured.
816 100f. Type **296** 90 30
817 150f. "Landscape Land and Sea" . . . . 1·40 40
818 200f. "The Studio at Cannes" 1·60 50
819 300f. "Still-life with Water Melon" . . . . 2·75 85
820 500f. "Large Still-life" . . . 4·50 1·40

297 King Maloango and Mausoleum

1981. Mausoleum of King Maloango. Mult.
821 75f. Mausoleum 60 20
822 150f. Type **297** . . . . 1·10 45

298 Prince Charles, Lady Diana Spencer and Coach

1981. Wedding of Prince of Wales. Mult.
823 100f. Type **298** 85 30
824 200f. Couple and Landau . . 1·40 25
825 300f. Couple and horses . . . 2·25 85

299 Preparing Food

1981. World Food Day.
827 **299** 150f. multicoloured . . . 1·25 45

300 Bird carrying Letter

1981. Universal Postal Union Day.
828 **300** 90f. blue, red and grey . . 65 25

301 Guardsman

1981. Royal Guard.
829 **301** 45f. multicoloured 25 15

302 Spraying Cassava

1981. Campaign for the Control of Cassava Beetle.
830 **302** 75f. multicoloured 90 20

303 Bandaging a Patient

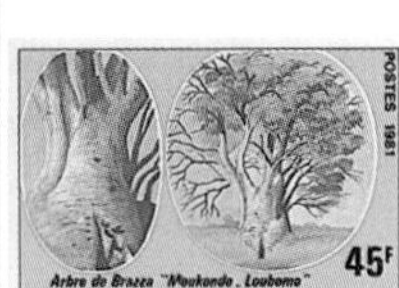

304 Brazza's Tree

1981. Red Cross. Multicoloured.
831 10f. Type **303** 10 10
832 35f. Inoculating a young girl 20 10
833 60f. Nurse and villagers . . . 30 15

1981. Tree of Brazza.
834 **304** 45f. multicoloured 25 15
835 75f. multicoloured 35 20

305 Fetish

306 Bangou Caves

1981. Fetishes.
836 **305** 15f. multicoloured 10 10
837 – 25f. multicoloured 15 10
838 – 45f. multicoloured 20 15
839 – 50f. multicoloured 50 15
840 – 60f. multicoloured 55 20
DESIGNS: 25f. to 60f. Different fetishes.

1981. Bangou Caves.
841 **306** 20f. multicoloured 10 10
842 25f. multicoloured 15 10

307 "Congolese Coiffure"

1982. Ivory Sculptures by R. Engongodzo. Multicoloured.
843 25f. Type **307** 15 10
844 35f. "Congo Coiffure" (different) 20 10
845 100f. "King Makoko, his Queen and Counsellor" (horiz) 45 25

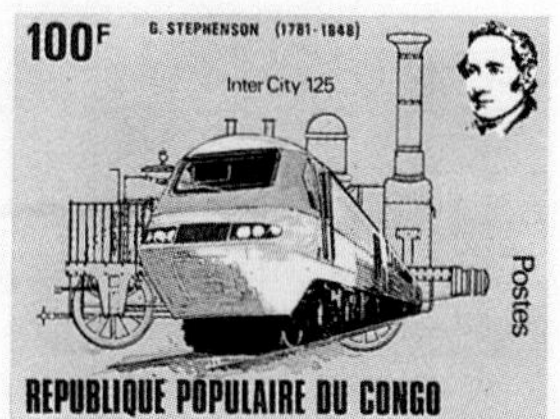

308 "Patentee" and Inter-City 125 Express Train, Great Britain

1982. Birth Bicentenary (1981) of George Stephenson (railway engineer). Multicoloured.

846 100f. Type **308** 60 30
847 150f. "Hikari" express train, Japan 95 45
848 200f. Advanced Passenger Train (APT), Great Britain 1·40 60
849 300f. TGV 001 locomotive, France . . . . 2·25 90

309 Scout with Binoculars

1982. 75th Anniv of Boy Scout Movement. Multicoloured.

850 100f. Type **309** 45 25
851 150f. Scout reading map . . 1·00 35
852 200f. Scout talking to village woman . . . . 1·40 45
853 300f. Scouts on rope bridge 2·00 70

310 Franklin D. Roosevelt

1982. Anniversaries. Multicoloured.

855 150f. Type **310** (birth cent) 1·10 35
856 250f. George Washington on horseback (250th birth anniv) . . . . 1·90 60
857 350f. Johann von Goethe (writer) (150th death anniv) 2·50 80

311 Princess of Wales and Candles

1982. 21st Birthday of Princess of Wales. Mult.

858 200f. Type **311** . . . . 1·40 45
859 300f. Princess and "21" . . . 2·00 70

312 Road Building

1982. Five Year Plan. Multicoloured.

861 60f. Type **312** 65 20
862 100f. Telecommunications . . 90 25
863 125f. Operating theatre equipment . . . . 1·10 30
864 150f. Hydro-electric project 1·50 55

313 Dish Antenna

1982. I.T.U. Delegates' Conference, Nairobi.

865 **313** 300f. multicoloured . . . 2·25 1·10

314 Mosque, Medina

1982. Air. 1350th Death Anniv of Mohammed.

866 **314** 400f. multicoloured . . . 3·00 1·40

315 W.H.O. Regional Office

1982. World Health Organization Regional Office, Brazzaville.

867 **315** 125f. multicoloured . . . 90 30

316 Mother feeding Baby

1982. Health Campaign.

868 **316** 100f. multicoloured . . . 80 25

1982. Birth of Prince William of Wales. Nos. 823/25 optd **NAISSANCE ROYALE 1982**.

869 100f. multicoloured 45 25
870 200f. multicoloured . . . . . 1·40 80
871 300f. multicoloured . . . . . 2·00 1·10

318 Dr. Robert Koch and Bacillus

1982. Centenary of Discovery of Tubercle Bacillus.

873 **318** 250f. multicoloured . . . 2·25 1·10

1982. World Cup Football Championship Results. Nos. 724/28 optd.

874 60f. **EQUIPE QUATRIEME FRANCE** 25 20
875 75f. **EQUIPE TROISIEME POLOGNE** 35 20
876 100f. **EQUIPE SECONDE ALLEMAGNE (RFA)** . . 45 25
877 150f. **EQUIPE VAINQUEUR/ITALIE** . . 1·00 35
878 175f. **ITALIE–ALLEMAGNE (RFA) 3 1** . . . . 1·40 65

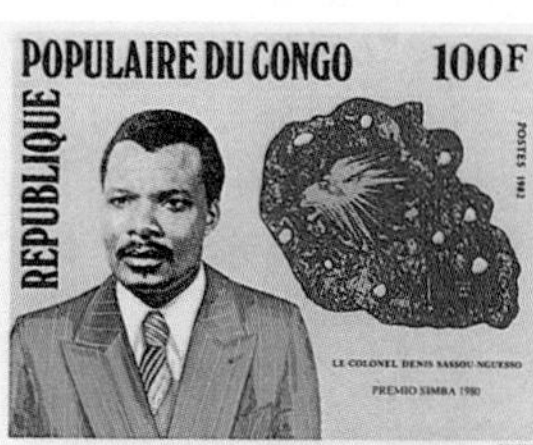

320 Pres. Sassou-Ngeusso and Prize

1982. Award of 1980 Simba Prize to Pres. Sassou-Nguesso.

880 **320** 100f. multicoloured . . . 45 25

321 Turtle

1982. Turtles.

881 **321** 30f. multicoloured 15 10
882 – 45f. multicoloured 55 15
883 – 55f. multicoloured 80 55

DESIGNS: 45, 55f. Different turtles.

322 Amelia Earhart and "Friendship"

1982. 50th Anniv of Amelia Earhart's Transatlantic Flight.

884 **322** 150f. lt brown, grn & brn 1·25 80

323 "La Malafoutier"

324 Grey Parrots nesting in Hole in Tree

1982.

885 **323** 100f. multicoloured . . . 80 25

1982. Birds' Nests. Multicoloured.

886 40f. Type **324** 90 20
887 75f. Palm tree and nest . . . 1·50 20
888 100f. Nest hanging from branch . . . . 1·75 25

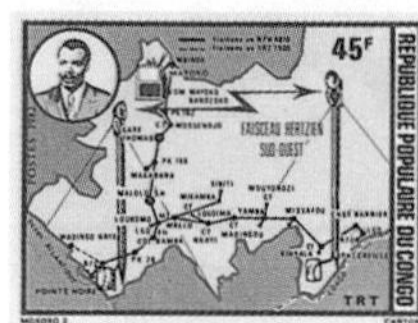

325 Map of Network

1982. Hertzian Wave Network.

889 **325** 45f. multicoloured 20 15
890 60f. multicoloured 25 20
891 95f. multicoloured 45 25

326 Council Headquarters, Brussels

1983. 30th Anniv of Customs Co-operation Council.

892 **326** 100f. multicoloured . . . 45 25

327 Marien N'Gouabi Mausoleum

1983.

893 **327** 60f. multicoloured 25 20
894 80f. multicoloured 35 20

328 Raffia Weaving

1983.

895 **328** 150f. multicoloured . . . 1·10 35

329 Chess Pieces

1983. Chess Pieces Carved by R. Engongonzo. Multicoloured.

896 40f. Type **329** 20 10
897 60f. Close-up of white pawn, king, queen and bishop . . 55 20
898 95f. Close-up of black rook, bishop, queen and king . . 1·00 55

330 Blacksmiths

1983.

899 **330** 45f. multicoloured 45 15

331 Study for "The Transfiguration"

1983. Easter. 500th Birth Anniv of Raphael. Multicoloured.

900 200f. Type **331** . . . . 1·60 45
901 300f. "Deposition from the Cross" (horiz) . . . . . . 2·25 70
902 400f. "Christ in his Glory" 2·75 90

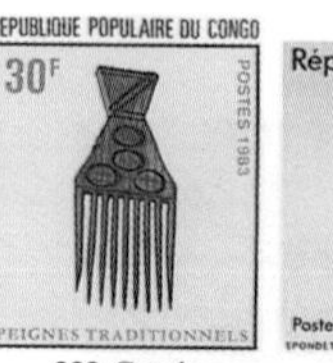

332 Comb

333 "Pila ovata"

1983. Traditional Combs. Multicoloured.

903 30f. Type **332** 15 10
904 70f. Comb (different) 55 25
905 85f. Three combs 65 30

1983. Shells. Multicoloured.

906 35f. Type **333** 25 20
907 65f. True achatina 50 35

334 Windsurfing

1983. Air. Pre-Olympic Year.

908	**334**	100f. multicoloured	80	40
909	–	200f. mult (horiz)	1·10	50
910	–	300f. multicoloured	1·40	75
911	–	400f. multicoloured	3·25	1·00

DESIGNS: 200 to 400f. Various windsurfing scenes.

335 Montgolfier Balloon, 1783 **336** Hands holding Gun and Pick

1983. Air. Bicentenary of Manned Flight. Mult.

913	100f. Type **335**	1·10	40
914	200f. Montgolfier balloon "Le Flesselles", 1784	1·60	50
915	300f. Auguste Piccard's stratosphere balloon "F.N.R.S.", 1931	2·25	75
916	400f. Modern hot-air balloon	3·25	1·00

1983. 20th Anniv of Revolution.

918	**336**	60f. multicoloured	25	20
919		100f. multicoloured	65	35

337 Mgr. A. Carrie and Church of the Sacred Heart, Loango

1983. Centenary of Evangelism. Multicoloured.

920	150f. Type **337**	1·10	50
921	250f. Mgr. Augouard and St. Joseph's Church, Linzolo	1·75	80

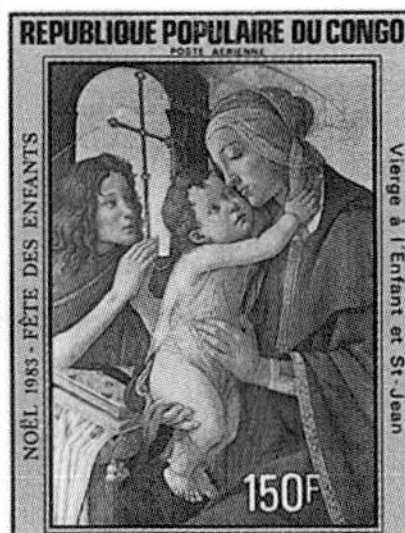

338 Thunbergia **339** "Virgin and Child with St. John"

1984. Flowers. Multicoloured.

922	5f. Type **338**	10	10
923	15f. Bougainvillaea (horiz)	10	10
924	20f. Anthurium	15	10
925	45f. Allamanda (horiz)	30	25
926	75f. Hibiscus	45	40

1984. Air. Christmas. Paintings by Botticelli. Multicoloured.

927	150f. Type **339**	1·10	30
928	350f. "Virgin and Child" (St. Barnabas)	2·50	1·00
929	500f. "Virgin and Child"	3·50	1·25

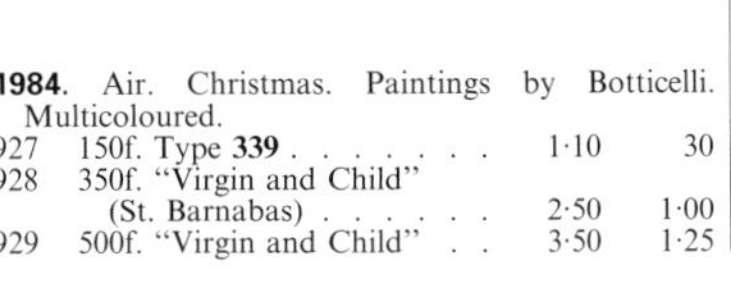

340 "Vase of Flowers" (Manet)

1984. Air. Paintings. Multicoloured.

930	100f. Type **340**	55	50
931	200f. "The Small Holy Family" (Raphael)	1·40	50
932	300f. "La Belle Jardiniere" (detail) (Raphael)	2·00	70
933	400f. "The Virgin of Lorette" (Raphael)	2·75	1·00
934	500f. "Richard Wagner" (Giuseppe Tivoli)	3·25	1·25

341 Peace Dove

1984. 34th Anniv of World Peace Council.

935	**341**	50f. multicoloured	30	25
936		100f. multicoloured	55	50

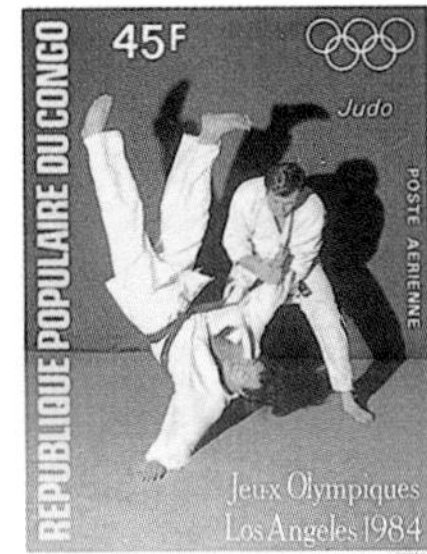

342 Judo

1984. Air. Olympic Games, Los Angeles. Mult.

937	45f. Type **342**	30	25
938	75f. Judo (different) (horiz)	45	40
939	150f. Wrestling (horiz)	1·10	55
940	175f. Fencing (horiz)	1·10	60
941	350f. Fencing (different) (horiz)	2·50	1·00

343 Mushroom Cloud

1984. Campaign against Weapons of Mass Destruction.

943	**343**	200f. black, brown & orge	1·40	55

344 Rice

1984. Agriculture. Multicoloured.

944	10f. Type **344**	10	10
945	15f. Pineapples	10	10
946	60f. Manioc (vert)	35	30
947	100f. Palms (vert)	80	50

345 Congress Palace

1984. Chinese–Congolese Co-operation.

948	**345**	60f. multicoloured	35	30
949		100f. multicoloured	80	50

346 Loulombo Station

1984. 50th Anniv of Congo Railways. Mult.

950	10f. Type **346**	15	15
951	25f. Chinese workers' camp at Les Bandas	45	20
952	125f. "50" forming bridge and tunnel	2·40	65
953	200f. Headquarters building	3·50	95

347 Alsthom CC203 Diesel Locomotive

1984. Transport. Multicoloured. (a) Locomotives.

954	100f. Type **347**	85	15
955	150f. Alsthom BB 103 diesel	1·25	20
956	300f. Diesel locomotive No. BB BB 301	2·75	45
957	500f. BB420 diesel train "L'Eclair"	4·50	85

(b) Ships.

958	100f. Pusher tug	80	55
959	150f. Pusher tug (different)	1·25	65
960	300f. Buoying boat	2·50	90
961	500f. "Saint" (freighter)	3·75	1·10

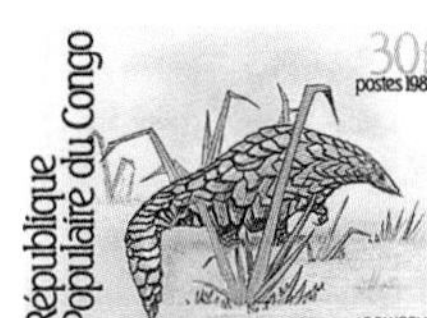

348 Giant Ground Pangolin

1984. Animals. Multicoloured.

962	30f. Type **348**	25	15
963	70f. Bat	50	35
964	85f. African civet	90	45

Nos. 962/4 are inscribed "1983".

349 Fish in Basket **350** Polio Victims and Hand

1984. World Fisheries Year. Multicoloured.

965	5f. Type **349**	15	10
966	20f. Casting nets	30	10
967	25f. Fishes	25	10
968	40f. Men pulling nets in	40	20
969	55f. Boat net and fishes	50	30

1984. Anti-polio Campaign. Multicoloured.

970	250f. Type **350**	2·00	1·10
971	300f. Polio victims within target	2·50	1·40

351 M'bamou Palace Hotel, Brazzaville **352** S. van den Berg, Windsurfing

1984.

972	**351**	60f. multicoloured	35	30
973		100f. multicoloured	80	50

1984. Air. Olympic Games Yachting Gold Medal Winners. Multicoloured.

974	100f. Type **352**	75	30
975	150f. U.S.A., "Soling" class (horiz)	1·10	40
976	200f. Spain, "470" dinghy (horiz)	1·50	60
977	500f. U.S.A., "Flying Dutchman" two-man dinghy	3·75	1·25

353 Floating Logs

1984. Floating Logs on River Congo. Mult.

978	60f. Type **353**	50	25
979	100f. Logs and boat on river	1·00	50

354 "The Holy Family" **355** "Zonocerus variegatus"

1985. Air. Christmas. Multicoloured.

980	100f. Type **354**	65	30
981	200f. "Virgin and Child" (G. Bellini) (horiz)	1·40	60
982	400f. "Virgin and Child with Angels" (Cimabue)	2·75	1·00

1985.

983	**355**	125f. multicoloured	1·10	40

357 Black-headed Grosbeaks

1985. Air. Birth Bicentenary of John J. Audubon (ornithologist). Multicoloured.

985	100f. Type **357**	1·50	50
986	150f. Scarlet ibis	1·40	60
987	200f. Red-tailed hawk (horiz)	3·75	75
988	350f. Labrador duck	6·25	1·00

358 Funeral Procession

1985. Burial of Teke Chief.

989	**358**	225f. multicoloured	1·60	70

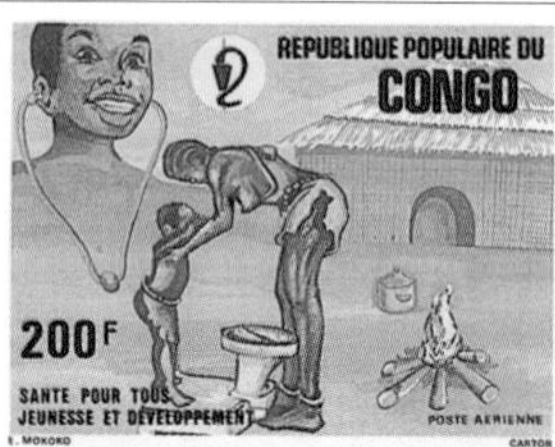

359 Mother weighing Child

1985. "Philexafrique" Stamp Exhibition, Lome, Togo (1st issue). Multicoloured.
990 200f. Type **359** . . . . 1·90 1·40
991 200f. Boy writing and man ploughing field . . . . . . 1·90 1·40
See also Nos. 1004/5.

360 "Trichoscypha acuminata"

361 Brazzaville Lions Club Pennant

1985. Fruits. Multicoloured.
992 5f. Type **360** 10 10
993 10f. "Aframomum africanum" 10 10
994 125f. "Gambeya lacuurtiana" 90 40
995 150f. "Landolphia jumelei" 1·10 65

1985. 30th Anniv of Lions Club.
996 **361** 250f. multicoloured . . . 1·90 75

362 Moscow Kremlin, Soldier and Battlefield

1985. 40th Anniv of End of World War II.
997 **362** 60f. multicoloured 45 15

363 Doves forming Heart

1985. Air. 25th Anniv of U.N. Membership.
998 **363** 190f. multicoloured . . . 1·40 60

365 Girl Guide with Yellow-bellied Wattle-eye (International Youth Year)

1985. Anniversaries and Events. Multicoloured.
999 150f. Type **365** . . . . . . 1·75 85
1000 250f. Jacob Grimm (folklorist) and scene from "Snow White and the Seven Dwarfs" (birth bicentenary) (International Youth Year) . . . . . . 1·60 75
1001 350f. Johann Sebastian Bach (composer) and organ (300th birth anniv) (European Music Year) 2·25 80
1002 450f. Queen Elizabeth, the Queen Mother (85th birthday) (vert) . . . . . 2·75 90
1003 500f. Statue of Liberty (centenary) (vert) . . . . 3·25 1·10

366 Construction Equipment within Heads and Building

1985. "Philexafrique" Stamp Exhibition, Lome, Togo (2nd issue). Multicoloured.
1004 250f. Type **366** . . . . . . 2·00 1·40
1005 250f. Loading mail at airport . . . . 2·00 1·40

367 Emblem and Rainbow

368 "Coprinus"

1985. Air. 40th Anniv of U.N.O.
1006 **367** 180f. multicoloured . . . 1·25 55

1985. Fungi. Multicoloured.
1007 100f. Type **368** . . . . . . 1·10 40
1008 150f. "Cortinarius" . . . . 1·60 55
1009 200f. "Armillariella mellea" 2·00 60
1010 300f. "Dictyophora" . . . . 2·50 75
1011 400f. "Crucibulum vulgare" 3·75 1·00

369 "Virgin and Child" (Gerard David)

1985. Air. Christmas. Multicoloured.
1012 100f. Type **369** 65 30
1013 200f. "Adoration of the Magi" (Hieronymus Bosch) . . . . 1·40 60
1014 400f. "Virgin and Child" (Anthony Van Dyck) (horiz) . . . . 2·75 1·10

370 Edmond Halley and Computer Picture of Comet

1986. Air. Appearance of Halley's Comet. Multicoloured.
1015 125f. Type **370** 80 40
1016 150f. West's Comet, 1976 (vert) . . . . 1·00 55
1017 225f. Ikeya-Seki Comet, 1965 (vert) . . . . 1·50 60
1018 300f. "Giotto" space probe and comet trajectory . . . 2·00 70
1019 350f. Comet and "Vega" space probe . . . . . . 2·50 80

371 President planting Sapling

372 Boys and Hoops with Handles

1986. National Tree Day. Multicoloured.
1020 60f. Type **371** 25 20
1021 200f. Map, tree and production of oxygen and carbon dioxide . . . . . 1·40 75

1986. Children's Hoop Races. Multicoloured.
1022 5f. Type **372** 10 10
1023 10f. Boy with hoop on string 10 10
1024 60f. Boys racing with hoops (horiz) 25 20

373 Cosmos-Frantel Hotel

1986. Air.
1026 **373** 250f. multicoloured . . . 1·60 95

375 Emptying Rubbish into Dustbin

376 Woman carrying Basket on Head

1986. World Environment Day. Multicoloured.
1030 60f. Type **375** 50 20
1031 125f. Woman dumping rubbish in street 90 35

1986. Traditional Methods of Carrying Goods. Multicoloured.
1032 5f. Type **376** 10 10
1033 10f. Woman carrying basket at back held by rope from head 10 10
1034 60f. Man carrying wood on shoulder 50 20

377 Footballers

1986. Air. World Cup Football Championship, Mexico.
1035 **377** 150f. multicoloured . . . 1·00 55
1036 – 250f. multicoloured . . . 1·75 65
1037 – 440f. multicoloured . . . 3·00 90
1038 – 600f. multicoloured . . . 4·25 1·40
DESIGNS: 250f. to 600f. Various football scenes.

378 Sisters tending Patients

379 Programme Emblem

1986. Centenary of Sisters of St. Joseph of Cluny Mission.
1039 **378** 230f. multicoloured . . . 1·60 90

1986. International Communications Development Programme.
1040 **379** 40f. multicoloured . . . 15 10
1041 60f. multicoloured . . . 25 20
1042 100f. multicoloured . . . 45 35

380 Emblem

381 Foodstuffs

1986. International Peace Year.
1043 **380** 100f. blue, grn & lt grn 45 35

1986. World Food Day. Multicoloured.
1044 75f. Type **381** 60 20
1045 120f. Woman spoon-feeding child 90 40

382 Woman holding Child and Windmill with Medical Symbols

383 Douglas DC-10 and "25" on Map

1986. U.N.I.C.E.F. Child Survival Campaign. Multicoloured.
1046 15f. Type **382** 10 10
1047 30f. Children (horiz) 15 10
1048 70f. Woman and child . . . 55 20

1986. Air. 25th Anniv of Air Afrique.
1049 **383** 200f. multicoloured . . . 1·40 65

384 Lenin

386 "Virgin and Child"

385 Men's Slalom

1986. 27th U.S.S.R. Communist Party Congress.
1050 **384** 100f. multicoloured . . . 90 30

1986. Air. Winter Olympic Games, Calgary (1988). Multicoloured.
1051 150f. Type **385** . . . . . . 1·00 55
1052 250f. Four-man bobsleigh (vert) . . . . 1·75 70
1053 440f. Ladies cross-country skiing (vert) . . . . . . 3·00 1·00
1054 600f. Ski-jumping . . . . . 4·25 1·50

1986. Air. Christmas. Paintings by Rogier van der Weyden. Multicoloured.
1055 250f. Type **386** . . . . . . 1·60 60
1056 440f. "Nativity" . . . . . . 3·00 90
1057 500f. "Virgin of the Pink" 3·25 1·10

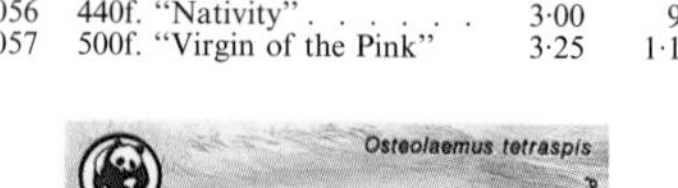

387 "Osteolaemus tetraspis"

1987. Air. Crocodiles. Multicoloured.
1058 75f. Type **387** 90 20
1059 100f. "Crocodylus cataphractus" . . . . . . 1·00 30
1060 125f. "Osteolaemus tetraspis" (different) . . . 1·10 40
1061 150f. "Crocodylus cataphractus" (different) 1·40 50

388 Pres. Sassou-Nguesso and Map **389** Traditional Marriage Ceremony

1987. Election of Pres. Sassou-Nguesso as Chairman of Organization of African Unity.
1062 **388** 30f. multicoloured . . . 15 10
1063 45f. multicoloured . . . 20 15
1064 75f. multicoloured . . . 55 20
1065 120f. multicoloured . . . 90 40

1987.
1066 **389** 5f. multicoloured 10 10
1067 15f. multicoloured . . . 10 10
1068 20f. multicoloured . . . 10 10

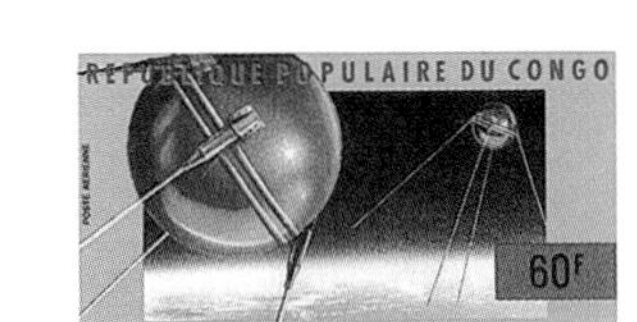

390 "Sputnik"

1987. Air. 30th Anniv of First Artificial Space Satellite.
1069 **390** 60f. multicoloured . . . 50 15
1070 240f. multicoloured . . . 1·75 1·25

391 Starting Back-stroke Race

1987. Air. Olympic Games, Seoul (1988) (1st issue). Swimming. Multicoloured.
1071 100f. Type **391** 65 30
1072 200f. Freestyle . . . . . . 1·40 45
1073 300f. Breast-stroke . . . . 2·00 65
1074 400f. Butterfly . . . . . . 2·75 90
See also Nos. 1121/4.

392 Blue Lake, National Route 2

1987.
1076 **392** 5f. multicoloured 10 10
1077 15f. multicoloured . . . 10 10
1078 75f. multicoloured . . . 80 20
1079 120f. multicoloured . . . 1·00 40

393 Flags and Pres. Ngouabi **395** Emblem

394 "Precis almanta"

1987. 10th Death Anniv of President Marien Ngouabi.
1080 **393** 75f. multicoloured . . . 55 20
1081 120f. multicoloured . . . 90 40

1987. Butterflies. Multicoloured.
1082 75f. "Precis epiclelia" 65 25
1083 120f. "Deilephila nerii" . . 1·00 45
1084 450f. "Euryphene senegalensis" . . . . . . 3·25 1·00
1085 550f. Type **394** . . . . . . 3·75 1·50

1987. African Men of Science Congress.
1086 **395** 15f. multicoloured . . . 10 10
1087 90f. multicoloured . . . 40 30
1088 230f. multicoloured . . . 1·50 85

396 Fist and Broken Manacle **397** Hands putting Money into Pot within Map

1987. Anti-Apartheid Campaign. Multicoloured.
1089 60f. Type **396** 25 15
1090 240f. Chain forming outline of map, Nelson Mandela and bars (26 × 38 mm) . . 1·75 90

1987. African Fund.
1091 **397** 25f. multicoloured . . . 10 10
1092 50f. multicoloured . . . 20 15
1093 70f. multicoloured . . . 55 20

398 Babies being Vaccinated

1987. National Vaccination Campaign. Mult.
1094 30f. Type **398** (postage) . . 15 10
1095 45f. Doctor vaccinating child (vert) 45 15
1096 500f. Queue waiting for vaccination (air) . . . . 4·00 2·75

399 Handball Player, Map and Runner

1987. 4th African Games, Nairobi.
1097 **399** 75f. multicoloured . . . 55 20
1098 120f. multicoloured . . . 90 40

400 Follereau

1987. 10th Death Anniv of Raoul Follereau (leprosy pioneer).
1099 **400** 120f. multicoloured . . . 1·00 40

401 Coubertin and Greece 1896 1d. Stamp

1987. Air. 50th Death Anniv of Pierre de Coubertin (founder of modern Olympic games). Multicoloured.
1100 75f. Type **401** 55 20
1101 120f. Runners and France 1924 10c. stamp 90 40
1102 350f. Congo 1964 100f. stamp and hurdler . . . . 2·50 90
1103 600f. High jumper and Congo 1968 85f. stamp 4·00 1·40

402 Basket of Produce and Hands holding Ears of Wheat

1987. 40th Anniv of F.A.O.
1104 **402** 300f. multicoloured . . . 2·00 1·00

403 Hillside Farming and Produce within "2000"

1987. "Food Self-sufficiency by Year 2000".
1105 **403** 20f. multicoloured . . . 10 10
1106 55f. multicoloured . . . 50 20
1107 100f. multicoloured . . . 80 30

404 Simon Kimbangu **406** Writer crossing through "Apartheid"

405 Lenin inspecting Parade in Red Square

1987. Birth Centenary of Simon Kimbangu (founder of Church of Jesus Christ on Earth). Multicoloured.
1108 75f. Type **404** 55 20
1109 120f. Kimbangu feeding grey parrot . . . . 1·50 80
1110 240f. Kimbanguiste Temple, Nkamba (horiz) . . . . . 1·90 90

1988. 70th Anniv of Russian Revolution.
1112 **405** 75f. multicoloured . . . 90 55
1113 120f. multicoloured . . . 1·40 80

1988. African Anti-Apartheid Writers.
1114 **406** 15f. multicoloured . . . 10 10
1115 60f. multicoloured . . . 25 15
1116 75f. multicoloured . . . 55 20

407 Schweitzer and Hospital

1988. Air. 75th Anniv of Arrival at Lambarene of Dr. Albert Schweitzer (missionary).
1117 **407** 240f. multicoloured . . . 1·90 90

408 Samuel Morse **409** Banknote and Field within "10"

1988. 150th Anniv of Morse Telegraph. Mult.
1118 90f. Type **408** 65 25
1119 120f. Morse and telegraph equipment 90 35

1988. 10th Anniv of International Agricultural Development Fund.
1120 **409** 240f. multicoloured . . . 1·50 80

1988. Air. Olympic Games, Seoul (2nd issue). Modern Pentathlon. As T **391**. Multicoloured.
1121 75f. Swimming 55 20
1122 170f. Cross-country running (vert) . . . . 1·25 55
1123 200f. Shooting . . . . . . 1·40 65
1124 600f. Horse-riding . . . . . 4·00 1·25

411 Eucalyptus Plantation, Brazzaville **412** Hands holding Gun and Pick

1988. Anti-desertification Campaign. Mult.
1126 5f. Type **411** 10 10
1127 10f. Stop sign and man chopping down tree . . . 10 10

1988. 25th Anniv of Revolution. Multicoloured.
1128 75f. Type **412** 55 20
1129 75f. People tending crops . . 55 20
1130 120f. Pres. Sassou-Nguesso holding aubergine 80 35

413 Yoro Fishing Village

1988.
1131 35f. Type **413** 20 10
1132 40f. Place de la Liberte . . 20 10

414 People on Map and Jet Fighters attacking Virus

1988. 1st International Day against A.I.D.S.
1133 **414** 60f. multicoloured . . . 30 10
1134 – 75f. multicoloured . . . 55 20
1135 – 180f. black, red & blue 1·25 85
DESIGNS: 75f. Virus consisting of healthy and infected people; 180f. Globe and laurel branches.

415 Pres. Sassou-Nguesso addressing Crowd

1989. 10th Anniv of 5 February Movement. Multicoloured.
1136 75f. Type **415** 55 20
1137 120f. Pres. Sassou-Nguesso and symbols of progress 2·25 75

416 Emblems

1989. 40th Anniv of Declaration of Human Rights.
1138 **416** 120f. multicoloured . . . 80 35
1139 350f. multicoloured . . . 2·00 1·10

417 Bari

1989. Air. World Cup Football Championship, Italy (1990) (1st issue). Multicoloured.
1140 75f. Type **417** 55 20
1141 120f. Rome 90 35
1142 500f. Florence . . . . . . 3·50 80
1143 550f. Naples . . . . 4·00 1·10
See also Nos. 1174/7.

418 "Storming of the Bastille" (detail, J. P. Houel)

1989. Air. "Philexfrance 89" International Stamp Exhibition. Multicoloured.
1144 300f. Type **418** (bicent of French revolution) . . . 2·25 1·00
1145 400f. "Eiffel Tower" (G. Seurat) (centenary of Eiffel Tower (1986)) . . . 2·75 1·25

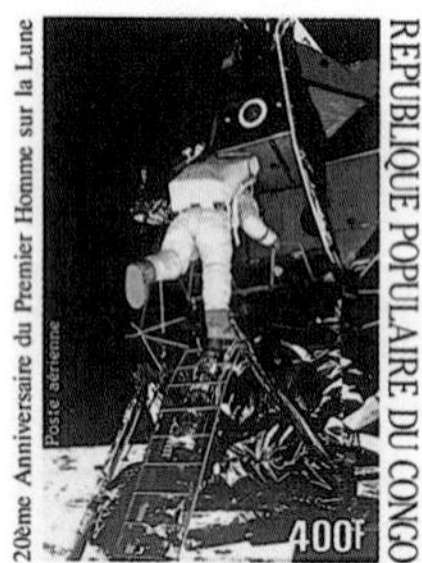

419 Astronaut and Landing Module

1989. Air. 20th Anniv of First Manned Landing on Moon. Multicoloured.
1146 400f. Type **419** . . . . . . 2·75 1·25
1147 400f. Astronaut on lunar surface . . . . 2·75 1·25

420 Marien Ngouabi

1989. 50th Birth Anniv (1988) of Marien Ngouabi (President, 1969–77).
1148 **420** 240f. black, yell & mve 1·60 65

421 Henri Dunant (founder), Volunteer with Child and Anniversary Emblem

422 Emblem on Dove

1989. 125th Anniv (1988) of Red Cross.
1149 75f. Type **421** (postage) . . 55 20
1150 120f. Emblem, Dunant and Congolese Red Cross station (air) 90 35

1989. 25th Anniv of Organization of African Unity.
1151 **422** 120f. multicoloured . . . 90 35

423 "Opuntia phaeacantha"

1989. Cacti. Multicoloured.
1152 35f. Type **423** 15 10
1153 40f. "Opuntia ficus-indica" 15 10
1154 60f. "Opuntia erinacea" (horiz) 50 15
1155 75f. "Opuntia rufida" . . . 55 20
1156 120f. "Opuntia leptocaulis" (horiz) 90 40

424 Banknote, Coins and Woman

1989. 25th Anniv of African Development Bank.
1158 **424** 75f. multicoloured . . . 55 20
1159 120f. multicoloured . . . 90 40

425 Ice Dancing

1989. Winter Olympic Games, Albertville (1992) (1st issue). Multicoloured.
1160 75f. Type **425** 30 20
1161 80f. Cross-country skiing . . 30 20
1162 100f. Speed skating 65 30
1163 120f. Luge 80 40
1164 200f. Slalom . . . . 1·40 45
1165 240f. Ice hockey . . . . . . 1·40 50
1166 400f. Ski jumping . . . . . 2·75 70
See also Nos. 1245/6.

426 Doctor examining Patient

427 Emblem and People with raised Fists

1989. 40th Anniv of W.H.O. Multicoloured.
1168 60f. Type **426** 55 15
1169 75f. Blood donation (vert) 65 55

1989. 20th Anniv of Congolese Workers' Party.
1170 **427** 75f. multicoloured . . . 55 20
1171 120f. multicoloured . . . 90 40

1990. Local Health Campaigns. Nos. 1168/9 optd **NOTRE PLANETE, NOTRE SANTE PENSER GLOBALEMENT AGIR LOCALEMENT.**
1172 60f. multicoloured 55 45
1173 75f. multicoloured 65 55

429 Footballers

430 Family supporting Open Book

1990. Air. World Cup Football Championship, Italy (2nd issue). Designs showing footballers.
1174 **429** 120f. multicoloured . . . 90 40
1175 – 240f. multicoloured . . . 1·75 60
1176 – 500f. multicoloured . . . 3·25 1·00
1177 – 600f. multicoloured . . . 4·00 1·25

1990. International Literacy Year.
1178 **430** 75f. black, yellow & blue 55 20

431 Ramblas, Barcelona

1990. Olympic Games, Barcelona (1992) (1st issue). Multicoloured.
1179 100f. Type **431** (postage) . . 65 30
1180 150f. Yachting (horiz) . . . 1·10 35
1181 200f. Yachting (different) (horiz) . . . . 1·40 45
1182 240f. Market stalls, Barcelona (horiz) . . . . 1·40 65
1183 350f. Harbour, Barcelona (horiz) (air) . . . . 2·50 75
1184 500f. Monument, Barcelona 3·25 1·00
See also Nos. 1322/7.

432 Turtle Dove ("Tourterelle des boris")

1990. Birds. Multicoloured.
1186 25f. Type **432** 35 30
1187 50f. Dartford warbler ("Fauvette Pitchou") (vert) 70 40
1188 70f. Common kestrel ("Faucon Crecerelle") (vert) . . . . 1·25 70
1189 150f. Grey parrot ("Perroquet Gris") (vert) 2·25 1·60

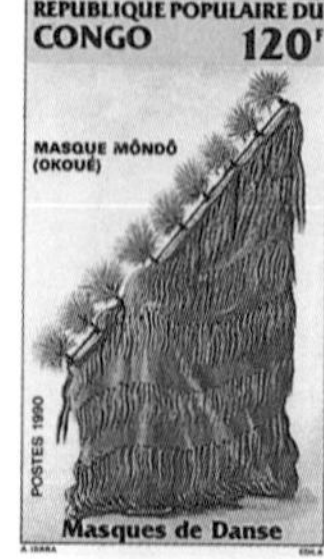

433 Mondo Mask

435 Sunflower

434 Necklace

1990. Dance Masks. Multicoloured.
1190 120f. Type **433** 90 40
1191 360f. Bapunu mask . . . . 2·50 1·25
1192 400f. Kwele mask . . . . . 2·75 1·40

1990. Traditional Royal Necklaces. Multicoloured.
1193 75f. Type **434** 55 20
1194 100f. Money cowrie necklace 55 35

1990. Flowers. Multicoloured.
1195 30f. Type **435** 15 10
1196 45f. "Cassia alata" (horiz) 20 10
1197 75f. Opium poppy 55 20
1198 90f. "Acalypha sanderil" . . 65 25

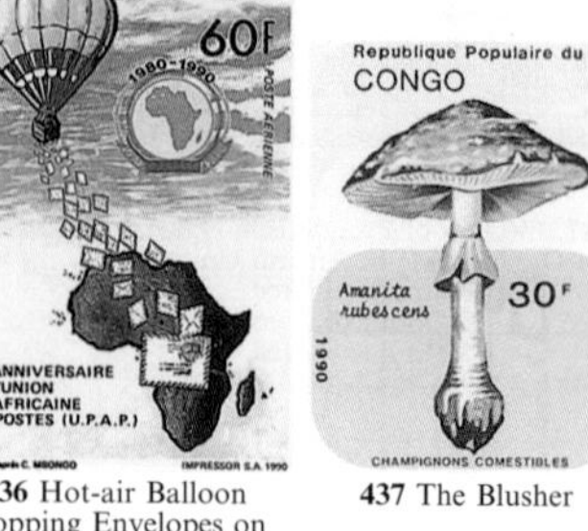

436 Hot-air Balloon dropping Envelopes on Africa

437 The Blusher

1991. Air. 10th Anniv of Pan-African Postal Union. Multicoloured.
1199 60f. Type **436** 40 20
1200 120f. Envelopes on map of Africa 90 55

1991. Fungi. Multicoloured.
1201 30f. Type **437** 25 10
1202 45f. "Catathelasma imperiale" 35 15
1203 75f. Caesar's mushroom . . 55 25
1204 90f. Royal boletus 65 30
1205 120f. Deer mushroom . . . 1·00 45
1206 150f. "Boletus chrysenteron" 1·10 50
1207 200f. Horse mushroom . . . 1·60 70

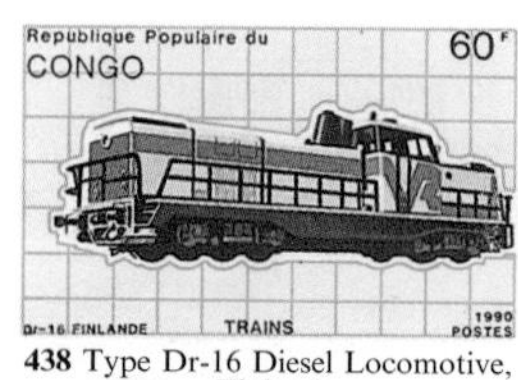

438 Type Dr-16 Diesel Locomotive, Finland

1991. Trains. Multicoloured.
1209 60f. Type **438** 90 15
1210 75f. TGV express, France 1·10 20
1211 120f. Suburban S-350 electric railcar, Italy . . . 1·75 30
1212 200f. Type DE 24000 diesel locomotive, Turkey . . . 3·25 55
1213 250f. DE 1024 diesel-electric locomotive, Germany . . 4·00 70

439 Canoe, Palm Tree and Setting Sun

440 Congolese Woman

1991. International African Tourism Year. Multicoloured.
1215 75f. Type **439** 55 20
1216 120f. Zebra and map of Africa 90 55

1991.
1217 **440** 15f. blue 10 10
1218 30f. green 15 10
1219 60f. yellow 30 15
1220 75f. mauve 35 20
1221 120f. brown 60 30

441 Christopher Columbus (after Sebastian del Pombo)

442 "Kalanchoe pinnata"

1991. 500th Anniv (1992) of Discovery of America by Columbus. Multicoloured.

1222 20f. Type **441** 10 10
1223 35f. Christopher Columbus 15 10
1224 40f. Christopher Columbus (different) 20 10
1225 55f. "Santa Maria" 60 20
1226 75f. "Nina" 80 30
1227 150f. "Pinta" . . . . 1·40 55
1228 200f. Arms and signature of Columbus . . . . 1·40 80

1991. Medicinal Plants. Multicoloured.

1229 15f. "Ocimum viride" (horiz) 10 10
1230 20f. Type **442** 10 10
1231 30f. "Euphorbia hirta" (horiz) 15 10
1232 60f. "Catharantheus roseus" 30 15
1233 75f. "Bidens pilosa" 60 20
1234 100f. "Brillantasia patula" 80 50
1235 120f. "Cassia occidentalis" 90 65

443 Route Map

1991. Centenary of Trans-Siberian Railway. Mult.

1236 120f. Type **443** . . . . . . 1·50 45
1237 240f. Russian Class N steam locomotive superimposed on map . . . . 2·25 80

444 Honey fungus

1991. Scouts, Butterflies and Fungi. Mult.

1238 35f. "Euphaedra eusemoides" (butterfly) (postage) 15 10
1239 40f. Type **444** 40 15
1240 75f. "Palla decius" (butterfly) 60 20
1241 80f. "Kallima ansorgei" (butterfly) 65 20
1242 500f. "Cortinarius speciocissimus" (fungus) (air) . . . . 3·75 1·40
1243 600f. "Graphium illyris" (butterfly) . . . . 4·00 1·40

445 Ice Hockey

1991. Air. Winter Olympic Games, Albertville (1992) (2nd issue). Multicoloured.

1245 120f. Type **445** 90 30
1246 300f. Speed skating . . . . 2·00 70

446 "Telecom 91"

1991. "Telecom 91" World Telecommunications Exhibition, Geneva. Multicoloured.

1248 75f. Type **446** 60 20
1249 120f. Stylized view of exhibition (vert) 90 55

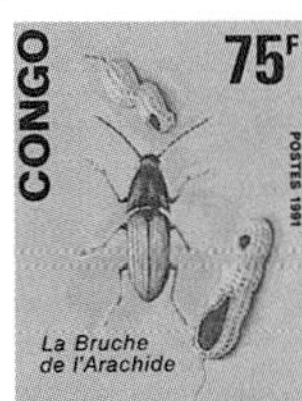

447 Beetle and Peanuts **448** Woman drinking at Waterfall

1991. Harmful Insects. Multicoloured.

1250 75f. Type **447** 60 20
1251 120f. Stag beetle (horiz) . . 90 30
1252 200f. Beetle and coffee . . . 1·40 50
1253 300f. Goliath beetle . . . . 2·25 70

1991. "Water is Life".

1254 **448** 75f. multicoloured . . . 60 20

449 Pintail **450** Breaking Chain and Hand holding Dove

1991. Wild Ducks. Multicoloured.

1255 75f. Type **449** 60 20
1256 120f. Eider (vert) 90 30
1257 200f. Common shoveler (vert) . . . . 1·40 90
1258 240f. Mallard . . . . 1·60 1·10

1991. 30th Anniv of Amnesty International. Multicoloured.

1259 40f. Candle, barbed wire and sun 20 10
1260 75f. Type **450** 35 20
1261 80f. Boy holding human rights banner and soldiers threatening boy (horiz) . . 65 45

451 1891 5c. on 1c. "Commerce" stamp

1991. Centenary of Congolese Stamps.

1262 **451** 75f. green and brown . . 60 45
1263 – 120f. dp brn, grn & brn 1·10 90
1264 – 240f. multicoloured . . . 2·00 1·40
1265 – 500f. multicoloured . . . 3·50 2·75

DESIGNS: 120f. 1900 1c. "Leopard in ambush" stamp; 240f. 1959 25f. "Birth of the Republic" stamp; 500f. "Commerce", "Leopard" and "Republic" stamps.

452 Ferrari "512 S"

1991. Cars and Space. Multicoloured.

1266 35f. Type **452** (postage) . . 15 10
1267 40f. Vincenzo Lancia and Lancia "Stratos" 20 10
1268 75f. Airship "Graf Zeppelin", Maybach "Type 12" car and Wilhelm Maybach 45 25
1269 80f. Mars space probe 40 20
1270 500f. "Magellan" space probe over Venus (air) . . 3·25 80
1271 600f. "Ulysses" space probe photographing sun spot 4·00 90

453 Small Blue

1991. Butterflies. Multicoloured.

1273 75f. Type **453** 35 20
1274 120f. Charaxes 80 30
1275 240f. Leaf butterfly (vert) . . 1·60 90
1276 300f. Butterfly on orange (vert) . . . . 2·00 1·40

454 General De Gaulle

1991. De Gaulle and Africa. Multicoloured.

1277 75f. Type **454** 65 20
1278 120f. De Gaulle, soldiers and Free French flag (vert) 90 30
1279 240f. De Gaulle making speech, Brazzaville, 1940 1·75 1·10

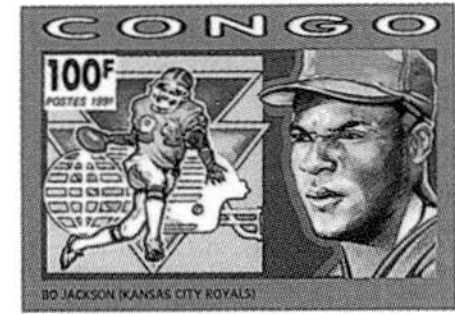

455 Bo Jackson (American footballer)

1991. Celebrities and International Organizations. Multicoloured.

1280 100f. Type **455** 50 25
1281 150f. Nick Faldo (golfer) . . 1·00 35
1282 200f. Rickey Henderson and Barry Bonds (baseball players) . . . . 1·40 50
1283 240f. Gary Kasparov (World chess champion) 1·75 55
1284 300f. Starving child and Lions International and Rotary International emblems . . . . 2·00 70
1285 350f. Wolfgang Amadeus Mozart (composer) . . . 2·75 80
1286 400f. De Gaulle and Churchill visiting the Eastern Front, 1944 . . . 2·75 95
1287 500f. Henry Dunant (founder of Red Cross) 3·25 1·00

456 Painting

1991. Paintings. Multicoloured.

1289 75f. Type **456** 60 20
1290 120f. Couple in silhouette (vert) 90 30

457 Diana Monkey

1991. Primates. Multicoloured.

1291 30f. Type **457** 15 10
1292 45f. Chimpanzee 20 10
1293 60f. Gelada (vert) 55 15
1294 75f. Hamadryas baboon (vert) 80 20
1295 90f. Pigtail macaque (vert) 90 20
1296 120f. Gorilla (vert) . . . . 1·10 30
1297 240f. Mandrill (vert) . . . . 2·25 55

458 "Sputnik 2" and Laika (space dog)

1992. Celebrities, Anniversaries and Events. Mult.

1299 50f. Type **458** (35th anniv of space flight) (postage) . . 45 10
1300 75f. Martin Luther King (Nobel Peace Prize winner, 1964) and Gandhi 60 20
1301 120f. Meteosat "MOP-2" and "ERS-1" satellites, globe and stern trawler ("Europe-Africa") . . . . 1·25 40
1302 300f. Konrad Adenauer (German statesman, 25th death anniv) and crowd before Brandenburg Gate (3rd anniv of opening of Berlin Wall) . . . . . . 2·00 70
1303 240f. "Graf Zeppelin", Ferdinand von Zeppelin (75th death anniv) and Maybach Zeppelin motor car (air) . . . . 1·40 70
1304 500f. Pope and globe (Papal visit to Africa) . . . . . 3·25 1·00

459 Juan de la Cosa and Map **460** Secretary Bird

1992. "Genova 92" International Thematic Stamp Exhibition. Multicoloured.

1306 75f. Type **459** 80 20
1307 95f. Martin Alonso Pinzon and astrolabe . . . . . . 1·00 25
1308 120f. Alonso de Ojeda and hourglass . . . . 1·40 30
1309 200f. Vicente Yanez Pinzon and sun clock . . . . . 2·00 45
1310 250f. Bartholomew Columbus and quadrant 2·25 55

1992. Birds. Multicoloured.

1312 60f. Type **460** 65 15
1313 75f. Saddle-bill stork . . . 80 20
1314 120f. Wattled crane . . . . 1·10 30
1315 200f. Black-headed heron . . 1·90 45
1316 250f. Greater flamingo . . . 2·75 55

461 Lion **462** "Madonna of the Grand Duke" (Raphael)

1992. Big Cats. Multicoloured.

1318 45f. Type **461** 50 25
1319 60f. Tiger 70 35
1320 75f. Lynx 85 40
1321 95f. Caracal . . . . 1·10 55
1322 250f. Ocelot . . . . 2·75 1·40

1992. Christmas. Multicoloured.

1324 95f. Type **462** 70 25
1325 200f. "Madonna of the Book" (Sandro Botticelli) 1·40 50
1326 250f. "Carondelet Madonna" (Fra Bartolommeo) . . . . . 1·75 1·10

No. 1325 is wrongly inscribed "Boticelli" and No. 1326 "Bartolomeo".

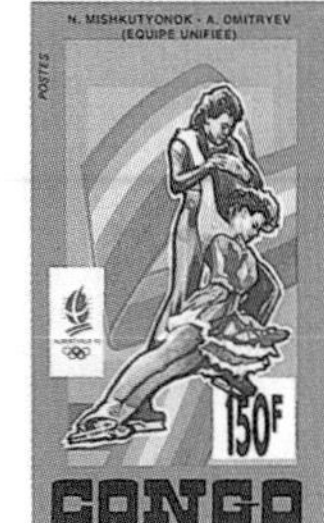

463 Baseball and Towers of Church of the Holy Family **464** N. Mishkutienok and A. Dmitriev (Unified Team)

1992. Olympic Games, Barcelona (2nd issue). Multicoloured.

1328 75f. Type **463** (postage) . . 35 20
1329 100f. Running and "The Muses" (Eusebio Arnau) 50 25
1330 150f. Hurdling and painted dome (Miguel Barcelo) of Market Theatre . . . . . 1·00 35
1331 200f. High jumping and Sant Pau hospital . . . . 1·40 50

1332 400f. Putting the shot and "Miss Barcelona" (Joan Miro) (air) . . . . 2·75 85
1333 500f. Table tennis and "Don Juan of Austria" (galley) 3·25 1·00

1992. Winter Olympic Games Gold Medal Winners. Multicoloured.
1335 150f. Type **464** (pairs figure skating) (postage) . . . . 1·00 35
1336 200f. Austrian team (four-man bobsleighing) . . . . 1·40 50
1337 500f. Gunda Niemann (Germany, women's speed skating) (air) . . . . . . 3·25 90
1338 600f. Bjorn Daehlie (Norway, 50 km cross-country skiing) . . . . . 4·00 1·00

No. 1338 is wrongly inscribed "Blorn Daehlle".

465 African Red-tailed Buzzard ("Charognard")

467 Topi

466 Overhead Volley

1993. Birds of Prey. Multicoloured.
1340 45f. Type **465** 20 10
1341 75f. Ruppell's griffon ("Vautour") 60 20
1342 120f. Verreaux's eagle ("Aigle") 80 55

1993. World Cup Football Championship, U.S.A. (1994).
1343 **466** 75f. multicoloured . . . 80 20
1344 – 95f. multicoloured . . . 1·00 25
1345 – 120f. multicoloured . . . 1·40 30
1346 – 200f. multicoloured . . . 2·00 50
1347 – 250f. multicoloured . . . 2·75 65

DESIGNS: 95f. to 250f. Different footballing scenes.

1993. Animals. Multicoloured.
1349 60f. Type **467** 60 15
1350 75f. Grant's gazelle 80 20
1351 95f. Quagga . . . . 1·00 25
1352 120f. Leopard . . . . . . 1·25 25
1353 200f. African buffalo . . . 2·00 25
1354 250f. Hippopotamus . . . . 2·50 30
1355 300f. Hooded vulture . . . 3·00 35
1356 350f. Lioness and cub . . . 3·25 55

Nos. 1349/56 were issued together, se-tenant, forming a composite design.

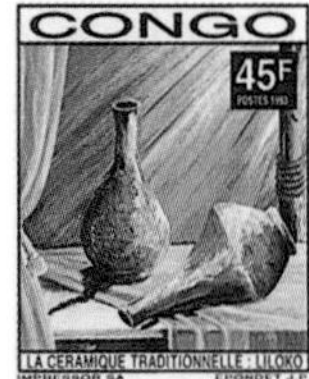

468 Jars from Liloko

1993. Traditional Pottery. Multicoloured.
1357 45f. Type **468** 20 10
1358 75f. Jug from Mbeya . . . 35 20
1359 120f. Jar from Mbeya . . . 60 30

470 Show Jumping

1993. Summer Olympic Games, Atlanta (1996) and Winter Olympic Games, Lillehammer, Norway (1994). Multicoloured.
1366 50f. Type **470** (postage) . . 25 15
1367 75f. Cycling 35 20
1368 120f. Two-man dinghy . . . 60 30
1369 240f. Fencing . . . . 1·40 55
1370 300f. Hurdling (air) . . . . 2·25 70
1371 400f. Figure skating . . . . 2·75 95
1372 500f. Basketball . . . . . . 3·25 90
1373 600f. Ice hockey . . . . . 4·00 1·25

471 "Hibiscus schizopetalus"

1993. Wild Flowers. Multicoloured.
1375 75f. Type **471** 35 20
1376 95f. "Pentas lanceolata" . . 45 25
1377 120f. "Ricinus communis" 90 30
1378 200f. "Delonix regia" . . . 1·50 50
1379 250f. "Stapelia gigantea" . . 1·90 90

OFFICIAL STAMPS

O 68 Arms

1968.
O142 **O 68** 1f. multicoloured . . . 10 10
O143 2f. multicoloured . . . 10 10
O144 5f. multicoloured . . . 10 10
O145 10f. multicoloured . . 20 15
O146 25f. multicoloured . . 20 10
O147 30f. multicoloured . . 45 20
O148 50f. multicoloured . . 60 30
O149 85f. multicoloured . . 1·50 65
O150 100f. multicoloured . . 1·75 1·10
O151 200f. multicoloured . . 2·50 1·60

POSTAGE DUE STAMPS

D 7 Letter-carrier

1961. Transport designs.
D19 **D 7** 50c. bistre, red & blue 10 10
D20 – 50c. bistre, purple & bl 10 10
D21 – 1f. brown, red & green 10 10
D22 – 1f. green, red and lake 10 10
D23 – 2f. brown, green & bl . . 10 15
D24 – 2f. brown, green & bl . . 10 15
D25 – 5f. sepia and violet . . . 15 15
D26 – 5f. sepia and violet . . . 15 15
D27 – 10f. brown, blue & grn 1·00 40
D28 – 10f. brown and green . . 1·00 40
D29 – 25f. brown, blue & turq 1·10 1·10
D30 – 25f. black and blue . . . 1·10 1·10

DESIGNS: D20, Holste Broussard monoplane; D21, Hammock-bearers; D22, "Land Rover" car; D23, Pirogue; D24, River steamer of 1932; D25, Cyclist; D26, Motor lorry; D27, Steam locomotive, 1932; D28, Diesel locomotive; D29, Seaplane of 1935; D30, Boeing 707 airliner.

1971. Tropical Flowers. Similar to T **105**, but inscr "Timbre-Taxe". Multicoloured.
D264 1f. Stylized bouquet 10 10
D265 2f. "Phaeomeria magnifica" 10 10
D266 5f. "Millettia laurentii" . . 10 10
D267 10f. "Polianthes tuberosa" 15 15
D268 15f. "Pyrostegia venusta" 20 20
D269 20f. "Hibiscus rosa sinensis" 25 25

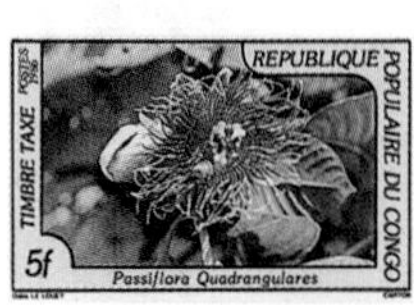

D 374 Passion Flower

1986. Flowers and Fruit. Multicoloured.
D1027 5f. Type **D 374** 10 10
D1028 10f. Canna lily 10 10
D1029 15f. Pineapple 10 10

APPENDIX

The following stamps have either been issued in excess of postal needs or have not been available to the public in reasonable quantities at face value. Such stamps may later be given full listing if there is evidence of regular postal use.

All embossed on gold foil

1991.

Scout and Butterfly. Air 1500f.

Winter Olympic Games, Albertville (1992). Air 1500f.

1992.

Olympic Games, Barcelona. Air 1500f.

CONGO DEMOCRATIC REPUBLIC (EX ZAIRE) Pt. 14

In May 1997 Zaire changed its name to the Democratic Republic of Congo after President Mobutu and his Government was overthrown by a rebellion led by Laurent Kabila.

New Currency

July 1998. 100 cents = 1 congolise franc.

273 Mother Teresa

274 Diana Princess of Wales

1998. 1st Death Anniv of Mother Teresa (founder of Missionaries of Charity).
1494 **273** 50000z. multicoloured . . 1·25 80

1998. 1st Death Anniv of Diana, Princess of Wales. Multicoloured.
1496 50000z. Type **274** . . . . . 1·10 80
1497 50000z. Wearing white jacket with blue collar . . 1·10 80
1498 50000z. Wearing large hat 1·10 80
1499 50000z. Wearing white top with blue dots . . . . . . 1·10 80
1500 50000z. Wearing neck scarf 1·10 80
1501 50000z. Wearing pearl necklace . . . . 1·10 80
1502 100000z. Wearing tiara . . . 2·10 1·60
1503 100000z. Wearing black top 2·10 1·60
1504 100000z. Resting head on hands . . . . 2·10 1·60
1505 100000z. Wearing cream top 2·10 1·60
1506 125000z. Wearing red and black dress . . . . . . 2·50 2·00
1507 125000z. Wearing cream jacket . . . . 2·50 2·00
1508 125000z. Profile . . . . . . 2·50 2·00
1509 125000z. Wearing tiara . . . 2·50 2·00

275 Building

1999. Independence. Multicoloured.
1511 25c. Type **275** 50 50
1512 50c. Coat of Arms 95 95
1513 75c. Making speech . . . . 1·40 1·40
1514 1f.25 Procession . . . . . . 2·40 2·40
1515 3f. Crowd and man breaking chains . . . . . 5·50 5·50

No. 1511 also exists imperforate.

276 Men fighting in Boat

1999. *Outlaws of the Marsh* (Chinese literature). Multicoloured.
1517 1f.45 Type **276** . . . . . . 1·10 1·10
1518 1f.45 Men fighting in blacksmith's shop . . . . 1·10 1·10
1519 1f.45 Men gathered around tree . . . . 1·10 1·10
1520 1f.45 Men writing . . . . . 1·10 1·10
1521 1f.50 Crowds fighting . . . 1·10 1·25
1522 1f.50 Man pulling tree from ground . . . . 1·10 1·25
1523 1f.50 Man threatening other man with sword . . . . . 1·10 1·25
1524 1f.50 Man climbing over balcony . . . . 1·10 1·25
1525 1f.60 Men outside fort . . . 1·25 1·25
1526 1f.60 Man in snow storm . . 1·25 1·25
1527 1f.60 Man killing tiger . . . 1·25 1·25
1528 1f.60 Man reading writing on wall . . . . 1·25 1·25
1529 1f.70 Crowds fighting . . . 1·25 1·40
1530 1f.70 Man drawing sword 1·25 1·40
1531 1f.70 Man jumping from balcony . . . . 1·25 1·40
1532 1f.70 Man lifting other man 1·25 1·40
1533 1f.80 Archer on horseback 1·40 1·40
1534 1f.80 Men sitting round table eating . . . . . . 1·40 1·40
1535 1f.80 Joust . . . . 1·40 1·40
1536 1f.80 Man tearing scroll . . 1·40 1·40

277 Rat

1999. Chinese Horoscope. Multicoloured.
1538 78c. Type **277** 85 40
1539 78c. Ox 85 40
1540 78c. Tiger 85 40
1541 78c. Rabbit 85 40
1542 78c. Dragon 85 40
1543 78c. Snake 85 40
1544 78c. Horse 85 40
1545 78c. Goat 85 40
1546 78c. Monkey 85 40
1547 78c. Cockerel 85 40
1548 78c. Dog 85 40
1549 78c. Pig 85 40

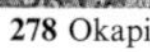
278 Okapi

279 Four-coloured Bush Shrike (*Telophorus quadricolor*)

2000. Flora and Fauna. Multicoloured.
1550 1f. Type **278** 55 55
1551 1f. Common kestrel 55 55
1552 1f. Giraffe and rainbow . . 55 55
1553 1f. Giraffe 55 55
1554 1f. Mandrill 55 55
1555 1f. Savannah baboon . . . 55 55
1556 1f. Leopard 55 55
1557 1f. Birdwing butterflies . . . 55 55
1558 1f. Hippopotamus 55 55
1559 1f. Hadada ibis 55 55
1560 1f. Water lilies 55 55
1561 1f. Steenbok 55 55
1562 7f.80 Lion (47 × 34 mm) . . 3·75 2·75

Nos. 1550/61 were issued together, se-tenant, forming a composite design.

2000. Flora and Fauna of Africa. Multicoloured.
1564 1f. Type **279** 45 35
1565 1f.50 Leopard (*Panthera pardus*) 70 55
1566 1f.50 Sun 80 80
1567 1f.50 *Pieris citrina* (butterfly) 80 80
1568 1f.50 European bee eater (*Merops apiaster*) 80 80
1569 1f.50 Red-backed shrike (*Lanius collurio*) 80 80
1570 1f.50 Village weaver (*Ploceus cucullatus*) 80 80
1571 1f.50 *Charaxes pelias* . . . 80 80
1572 1f.50 Green charaxes (*Charaxes eupale*) 80 80
1573 1f.50 Giraffe (*Giraffa camelopardalis*) 80 80
1574 1f.50 Bushbaby (*Galago moholi*) 80 80
1575 1f.50 *Strelitzia reginae* (flower) 80 80
1576 1f.50 Thomson's gazelle (*Gazella thomsoni*) 80 80
1577 1f.50 Hoopoe (*Upupa epops*) 80 80
1578 2f. Puku (*Kobus vardoni*) . . 95 95
1579 2f. Protomedia (*Colotis protomedia*) 95 95
1580 3f. Ground pangolin (*Smutsia temminckii*) . . . 1·40 1·40
1581 3f. *Cararina abyssinica* (flower) . . . . 1·40 1·40

Nos. 1566/1577 were issued together, se-tenant, forming a composite design.

280 Leopard Cat (*Felis bengalensis*)

2000. Wild Cats and Dogs. Multicoloured.
1583 1f.50 Type **280** 80 80
1584 1f.50 African golden cat (*Felis aurata*) 80 80
1585 1f.50 Caracal (*Felis caracal*) 80 80
1586 1f.50 Puma (*Felis concolor*) 80 80
1587 1f.50 Black-footed cat (*Felis nigripes*) 80 80
1588 1f.50 Lion (*Panthera leo*) . . 80 80
1589 1f.50 Clouded leopard (*Neofelis nebulosa*) 80 80
1590 1f.50 Margay (*Felis wiedii*) 80 80
1591 1f.50 Cheetah (*Acinonyx jubatus*) 80 80
1592 1f.50 Spainsh lynx (*Felis pardina*) 80 80
1593 1f.50 Jaguarundi (*Felis yagouarundi*) 80 80
1594 1f.50 Serval (*Felis serval*) . . 80 80
1595 2f. Black-backed jackal (*Canis mesomelas*) . . . . 1·00 1·00
1596 2f. Bat-eared fox (*Otocyon megalotis*) . . . . 1·00 1·00
1597 2f. Bush dog (*Speothos venaticus*) . . . . 1·00 1·00
1598 2f. Coyote (*Canis latrans*) 1·00 1·00
1599 2f. Dhole (*Cuon alpinus*) . . 1·00 1·00
1600 2f. Fennec fox (*Fennecus zerda*) . . . . 1·00 1·00
1601 2f. Grey fox (*Urocyon cinereoargenteus*) . . . . 1·00 1·00
1602 2f. Wolf (*Canis lupus*) . . . 1·00 1·00
1603 2f. Kit fox (*Vulpes macrotis*) 1·00 1·00
1604 2f. Maned wolf (*Chrysocyon brachyurus*) . . . . 1·00 1·00
1605 2f. Racoon-dog (*Nyctereutes procyonoides*) . . . . . . 1·00 1·00
1606 2f. Red fox (*Vulpes vulpes*) 1·00 1·00

281 "2000" and Mountains

2000. New Millennium.
1608 **281** 4f.50 multicoloured . . . 1·00 1·00
1609 9f. multicoloured . . . . 1·90 1·90
1610 15f. multicoloured . . . 3·25 3·25

CONGO (KINSHASA) Pt. 14

This Belgian colony in Central Africa became independent in 1960. There were separate issues for the province of Katanga (q.v.).

In 1971 the country was renamed ZAIRE and later issues will be found under that heading.

1967. 100 sengi = 1 (li)kuta;
100 (ma)kuta = 1 zaire.

1960. Various stamps of Belgian Congo optd **CONGO** or surch also. (a) Flowers issue of 1952. Multicoloured.
360 10c. "Dissotis" 20 10
361 10c. on 15c. "Protea" 20 10
362 20c. "Vellozia" 20 10
363 40c. "Ipomoea" 20 10
364 50c. on 60c. "Euphorbia" . . 20 10
365 50c. on 75c. "Ochna" 20 10
366 1f. "Hibiscus" 20 10
367 1f.50 "Schizoglossum" . . . 20 10
368 2f. "Ansellia" 20 10
369 3f. "Costus" 40 10
370 4f. "Nymphaea" 40 20
371 5f. "Thunbergia" 40 10
372 6f.50 "Thonningia" 60 10
373 8f. "Gloriosa" 80 20
374 10f. "Silene" . . . . . . 1·25 20
375 20f. "Aristolochia" . . . . . 2·50 55
376 50f. "Eulophia" . . . . . . 14·00 3·75
377 100f. "Cryptosepalum" . . . 24·00 6·25

(b) Wild Animals issue of 1959.
378 10c. brown, sepia and blue 15 10
379 20c. blue and red 15 10
380 40c. brown and blue 15 10
381 50c. multicoloured 15 10
382 1f. black, green & brown . . 15 10
383 1f.50 black and yellow . . . 20 10
384 2f. black, brown and red . . 30 10
385 3f.50 on 3f. blk, pur & slate 35 10
386 5f. brown, green and sepia 50 15
387 6f.50 brown, yellow and blue 65 15
388 8f. bistre, violet and brown 80 30
389 10f. multicoloured . . . . . 1·00 35

(c) Madonna.
390 **102** 50c. brown, ochre & chest 50 50

(d) African Technical Co-operation Commission. Inscr in French or Flemish.
391 **103** 3f.50 on 3f. sal & slate . . 40 40

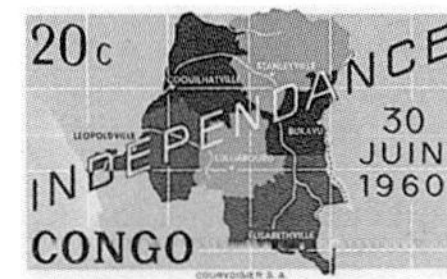

106 Congo Map

1960. Independence Commemoration.
392 **106** 20c. bistre 10 10
393 50c. red 10 10
394 1f. green 10 10
395 1f.50 brown 10 10
396 2f. mauve 10 10
397 3f.50 violet 10 10
398 5f. blue 15 10
399 6f.50 black 20 10
400 10f. orange 30 20
401 20f. blue 50 30

107 Congo Flag and People breaking Chain

109 Pres. Kasavubu

1961. 2nd Anniv of Congo Independence Agreement. Flag in yellow and blue.
402 **107** 2f. violet 10 10
403 3f.50 red 10 10
404 6f.50 brown 20 10
405 10f. green 25 15
406 20f. mauve 45 30

1961. Coquilhatville Conf. Optd **CONFERENCE COQUILHATVILLE AVRIL-MAI-1961**.
407 **106** 20c. bistre 60 60
408 50c. red 60 60
409 1f. green 60 60
410 1f.50 brown 60 60
411 2f. mauve 60 60
412 3f.50 violet 60 60
413 5f. blue 60 60
414 6f.50 black 60 60
415 10f. orange 60 60
416 20f. blue 60 60

1961. 1st Anniv of Independence. Inscr as in T **109**. Portraits and inscriptions in sepia.
417 **109** 10c. yellow 10 10
418 20c. red 10 10
419 40c. turquoise 10 10
420 50c. salmon 10 10
421 1f. lilac 10 10
422 1f.50 brown 10 10
423 2f. green 10 10
424 – 3f.50 mauve 15 10
425 – 5f. grey . . . . 1·75 15
426 – 6f.50 blue 30 10
427 – 8f. olive 35 10
428 – 10f. blue 75 10
429 – 20f. orange 75 15
430 – 50f. blue . . . . 1·40 30
431 – 100f. green . . . . 2·50 50

DESIGNS—HORIZ: 3f.50 to 8f. Pres. Kasavubu and map of Congo Republic. VERT: 10f. to 100f. Pres. Kasavubu in full uniform and outline map.

1961. Re-opening of Parliament. Optd **REOUVERTURE du PARLEMENT JUILLET 1961**.
432 **109** 10c. yellow 10 10
433 20c. red 10 10
434 40c. turquoise 10 10
435 50c. salmon 30 20
436 1f. lilac 30 20
437 1f.50 brown 80 70
438 2f. green 80 70
439 – 5f. grey (No. 425) 80 70
440 – 10f. violet (No. 428) . . . 80 85

111 Dag Hammarskjold

112 Campaign Emblem

1962. Dag Hammarskjold Commemoration.
441 **111** 10c. brown and grey . . . 10 10
442 20c. blue and grey 10 10
443 30c. bistre and grey . . . 10 10
444 40c. blue and grey 10 10
445 50c. red and grey 10 10
446 3f. olive and grey . . . . 2·50 1·60
447 6f.50 violet and grey . . . 70 50
448 8f. brown and grey . . . 80 60

1962. Malaria Eradication.
449 **112** 1f.50 brown, black & yell 10 10
450 2f. turq, brown & green 30 15
451 6f.50 lake, black & blue 15 10

1962. Reorganization of Aboula Ministry. Optd **"Paix, Travail, Austerite..., C. ADOULA 11 juillet 1962.**
452 **111** 10c. brown and grey . . . 10 10
453 20c. blue and grey 10 10
454 30c. bistre and grey . . . 10 10
455 40c. blue and grey 10 10
456 50c. red and grey . . . . 1·25 50
457 3f. olive and grey 15 10
458 6f.50 violet and grey . . . 20 10
459 8f. brown and grey . . . 30 15

114

1963. 1st Participation in U.P.U. Congress.
460 **114** 2f. violet . . . . 1·40 1·00
461 4f. red 10 10
462 7f. blue 20 10
463 20f. green 30 15

115 Emblem, Bears and Tractor

116 Whale-headed Stork

1963. Freedom from Hunger.
464 **115** 5f.+2f. violet & mauve . . 15 10
465 9f.+4f. green & yellow . . 30 20
466 12f.+6f. violet & blue . . 35 25
467 20f.+10f. green & red . . 1·75 1·60

1963. Protected Birds.
468 – 10c. multicoloured 15 10
469 – 20c. blue, black and red 15 10
470 – 30c. black, brown & grn 15 10
471 – 40c. black, orange & grey 15 10
472 **116** 1f. black, green & brown 30 15
473 – 2f. blue, brown and red 7·00 1·25
474 – 3f. black, pink and green 55 20
475 – 4f. blue, green and red . 55 20
476 – 5f. black, red and blue . . 85 20
477 – 6f. black, bistre & violet 7·00 1·25
478 – 7f. indigo, blue & turq . . 1·25 20
479 – 8f. blue, yellow & orange 1·40 20
480 – 10f. black, red and blue 1·40 20
481 – 20f. black, red & yellow 2·50 30

BIRDS—VERT: 10c. Eastern white pelicans ("Pelicans"); 30c. African open-bill stork ("Bec-Duvert"); 2f. Marabou stork ("Marabout"); 4f. Congo peafowl ("Paon Congolais"); 6f. Secretary bird ("Serpentaire"); 8f. Sacred ibis ("Ibis Sacre"). HORIZ: 20c. Crested guineafowl ("Pintables de Schouteden"); 40c. Abdim's stork ("Cigoon a Ventre Blanc"); 3f. Greater flamingos ("Flamants Roses"); 5f. Hartlaub's duck ("Canards de Hartlaub"); 7f. Black-casqued hornbill ("Calaos"); 10f. South African crowned cranes ("Grue Cauronnse"); 20f. Saddle-bill stork ("Jabiru d'Afrique").

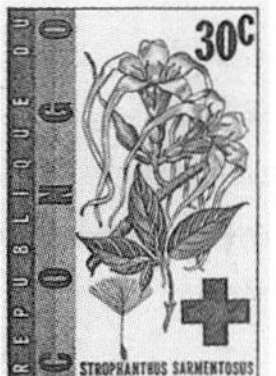

117 Strophanthus ("S. sarmentosus")

118 "Reconciliation"

1963. Red Cross Centenary. Cross in red.
482 **117** 10c. green and violet . . . 10 10
483 A 20c. blue and red 10 10
484 **117** 30c. red and green 10 10
485 A 40c. violet and blue . . . 10 10
486 **117** 5f. lake and olive 10 10
487 A 7f. purple and orange . . 10 10
488 B 9f. olive 20 10
489 20f. violet . . . . 1·60 70

DESIGNS—VERT: A, "Cinchona ledgeriana". HORIZ: B, Red Cross nurse.

1963. "National Reconciliation".
490 **118** 4f. multicoloured 90 30
491 5f. multicoloured 10 10
492 9f. multicoloured 15 10
493 12f. multicoloured 20 10

119 Kabambare Sewer, Leopoldville

1963. European Economic Community Aid.
494 **119** 20c. multicoloured 10 10
495 A 30c. multicoloured 10 10
496 B 50c. multicoloured 10 10
497 **119** 3f. multicoloured 90 35
498 A 5f. multicoloured 10 10
499 B 9f. multicoloured 15 10
500 A 12f. multicoloured 15 10

DESIGNS: A, Tractor and bridge on plan; B, Construction of Ituri Road.

120 N'Djili Airport, Leopoldville

1963. "Air Congo" Commemoration.
501 **120** 2f. multicoloured 10 10
502 – 5f. multicoloured 10 10
503 **120** 6f. multicoloured 90 40
504 – 7f. multicoloured 10 10
505 **120** 30f. multicoloured 25 15
506 – 50f. multicoloured 40 25

DESIGN: 5f., 7f., 50f. Mailplane and control tower.

1963. 15th Anniv of Declaration of Human Rights. Optd **10 DECEMBRE 1948 10 DECEMBRE 1963 15e anniversaire DROITS DE L'HOMME**.
507 **114** 2f. violet 10 10
508 4f. red 10 10
509 7f. blue 20 20
510 20f. green 20 20

122 Student in Laboratory

1964. 10th Anniv of Lovanium University. Mult.
511 50c. Type **122** 10 10
512 1f.50 University buildings . . 10 10
513 8f. Atomic and nuclear reactor symbols . . . . . 1·75 1·60
514 25f. University arms and buildings 20 15
515 30f. Type **122** 20 20
516 60f. As 1f.50 . . . . 40 30
517 75f. As 8f. 50 50
518 100f. As 25f. 70 60

1964. Various stamps surch over coloured metallic panels. (a) Stamps of Belgian Congo surch **REPUBLIQUE DU CONGO** and value.
519 – 1f. on 20c. (No. 340) . . . 10 10
520 – 2f. on 1f.50 (No. 306) . . . 6·25 2·25
521 – 5f. on 6f.50 (No. 348) . . . 15 15
522 – 8f. on 6f.50 (No. 311) . . . 60 25

(b) Stamps of Congo (Kinshasa) surch.
523 – 1f. on 20c. (No. 379) . . 10 10
524 – 1f. on 6f.50 (No. 372) . . 10 10
525 – 2f. on 1f.50 (No. 367) . . 10 10
530 **109** 3f. on 20c. 25 20
531 4f. on 40c. 25 20
526 – 5f. on 6f.50 (No. 387) . . 45 20
528 **106** 6f. on 6f.50 . . . . . . 30 20
529 7f. on 20c. 40 25

125 Pole-vaulting

1964. Olympic Games, Tokyo.
532 **125** 5f. sepia, grey and red . . 10 10
533 – 7f. violet, red and green 80 40
534 – 8f. brown, yellow & blue 10 10
535 **125** 10f. purple, blue & purple 10 10
536 – 20f. brown, green & orge 20 10
537 – 100f. brown, mauve & grn 80 20

DESIGNS—VERT: 7f., 20f. Throwing the javelin. HORIZ: 8f., 100f. Hurdling.

OCCUPATION OF STANLEYVILLE. During the occupation of Stanleyville from 5 August to 24 November, 1964, stocks of a number of contemporary issues were overprinted **REPUBLIQUE POPULAIRE** and issued by the rebel authorities.

126 National Palace

1964. National Palace, Leopoldville.
538 **126** 50c. mauve and blue . . . 10 10
539 1f. blue and purple . . . 10 10
540 2f. brown and violet . . . 10 10
541 3f. green and brown . . . 10 10
542 4f. orange and blue . . . 10 10
543 5f. violet and green . . . 10 10
544 6f. brown and orange . . 10 10
545 7f. olive and brown . . . 10 10
546 8f. red and blue . . . . . 2·00 35
547 9f. violet and red 10 10
548 10f. brown and green . . 10 10
549 20f. blue and brown . . . 10 10
550 30f. red and green 15 10
551 40f. blue and purple . . . 25 10
552 50f. brown and green . . 35 10
553 100f. black and orange . . 65 15

127 Pres. Kennedy **128** Rocket and Unisphere

1964. Pres. Kennedy Commemoration.
554 **127** 5f. blue and black 10 10
555 6f. purple and black . . . 10 10
556 9f. brown and black . . . 10 10
557 30f. violet and black . . . 30 10
558 40f. green and black . . . 2·00 60
559 60f. brown and black . . 50 25

1965. New York World's Fair.
560 **128** 50c. purple and black . . 10 10
561 1f.50 blue and violet . . . 10 10
562 2f. brown and green . . . 10 10
563 10f. green and red 70 40
564 18f. blue and brown . . . 10 10
565 27f. red and green 25 10
566 40f. grey and red 40 15

129 Football

1965. 1st African Games, Leopoldville.
567 – 5f. black, brown & blue 10 10
568 **129** 6f. red, black and blue . . 10 10
569 – 15f. black, green & orange 10 10
570 – 24f. black, green & mve 20 10
571 **129** 40f. blue, black & turq . . 1·25 45
572 – 60f. purple, black & blue 45 15
SPORTS—VERT: 5f., 24f. Basketball; 15f., 60f. Volleyball.

130 Telecommunications Satellites

1965. Centenary of I.T.U. Multicoloured.
573 6f. Type **130** 10 10
574 9f. Telecommunications satellites (different view) . . 10 10
575 12f. Type **130** 10 10
576 15f. As 9f. 10 10
577 18f. Type **130** . . . . . . 1·00 30
578 20f. As 9f. 15 10
579 30f. Type **130** 25 10
580 40f. As 9f. 30 10

131 Parachutist and troops landing

1965. 5th Anniv of Independence.
581 **131** 5f. brown and blue . . . 10 10
582 6f. brown and orange . . 10 10
583 7f. brown and green . . . 45 20
584 9f. brown and mauve . . 10 10
585 18f. brown and yellow . . 15 10

132 Matadi Port

1965. International Co-operation Year.
586 **132** 6f. blue, black & yellow 10 10
587 – 8f. brown, black & blue 10 10
588 – 9f. turq, black & brown 10 10
589 **132** 12f. mauve, black & grey 80 30
590 – 25f. olive, black and red 20 10
591 – 60f. grey, black & yellow 40 10
DESIGNS: 8f., 25f. Katanga mines; 9f., 60f. Tshopo Barrage, Stanleyville.

133 Medical Care

1965. Congolese Army.
592 **133** 2f. blue and red 10 10
593 5f. brown, red and pink 10 10
594 – 6f. brown and blue . . . 10 10
595 – 7f. green and yellow . . . 10 10
596 – 9f. brown and green . . . 10 10
597 – 10f. brown and green . . 40 40
598 – 18f. violet and red 15 10
599 – 19f. brown & turquoise 60 40
600 – 20f. brown and blue . . . 15 10
601 – 24f. multicoloured 20 15
602 – 30f. multicoloured 25 10
DESIGNS—HORIZ: 6f., 9f. Feeding child; 7, 18f. Bridge-building. VERT: 10f., 20f. Building construction; 19f. Telegraph line maintenance; 24f., 30f. Soldier and flag.

1966. World Meteorological Day. Nos. 590/1 optd **6e Journee Meteorologique Mondiale / 23.3.66** (on coloured metallic panel) and W.M.O. Emblem.
603 25f. olive, black and red . . 75 45
604 60f. grey, black and yellow 75 50

135 Carved Stool and Head

1966. World Festival of Negro Arts, Dakar.
605 **135** 10f. black, red and grey 10 10
606 – 12f. black, green & blue 10 10
607 – 15f. black, blue & purple 15 15
608 – 53f. black, red and blue 1·10 90
DESIGNS—VERT: 12f. Statuettes; 53f. Statuettes of women. HORIZ: 15f. Woman's head and carved goat.

136 Pres. Mobutu and Fish Workers

1966. Pres. Mobutu Commemoration.
609 **136** 2f. brown and blue . . . 10 10
610 – 4f. brown and red . . . 10 10
611 – 6f. brown and olive . . . 65 60
612 – 8f. brown and turquoise 10 10
613 – 10f. brown and lake . . . 10 10
614 – 12f. brown and violet . . 10 10
615 – 15f. brown and green . . 10 10
616 – 24f. brown and mauve . . 20 15
DESIGNS (Pres. Mobutu and): 4f. Harvesting pyrethrum; 6f. Building construction; 8f. Winnowing maize; 10f. Cotton-picking; 12f. Harvesting fruit; 15f. Picking coffee-beans; 24f. Harvesting pineapples.

1966. Inaug of W.H.O. Headquarters, Geneva. Nos. 550/3 optd **O.M.S. Geneve 1966** and W.H.O. Emblem.
618 **126** 30f. red and green 70 70
619 40f. blue and purple . . . 70 70
620 50f. brown and green . . 75 75
621 100f. black and orange . . 75 75

139 Footballer

1966. World Cup Football Championship.
622 **139** 10f. green, violet & brown 10 10
623 – 30f. green, violet & purple 25 20
624 – 50f. brown, blue & green 85 80
625 – 60f. gold, sepia & green 45 40
DESIGNS: 30f. Two footballers; 50f. Three footballers; 60f. Jules Rimet Cup and football.

1966. World Cup Football Championship Final. Nos. 622/5 optd **FINALE ANGLETERRE - ALLEMAGNE 4 - 2**.
626 **139** 10f. green, violet & brown 25 45
627 – 30f. green, violet & purple 80 1·40
628 – 50f. brown, blue & green 1·25 1·75
629 – 60f. gold, sepia and green 1·40 2·25

1967. 4th African Unity Organization (O.U.A.) Conf, Kinshasa. Nos. 538/43 surch **4e Sommet OUA KINSHASA du 11 au 14 - 9 - 67** and value.
631 **126** 1k. on 2f. 10 10
632 3k. on 5f. 10 10
633 5k. on 4f. 20 15
634 6k.60 on 1f. 25 20
635 9k.60 on 50c. 40 25
636 9k.80 on 3f. 50 40

1967. New Constitution. Nos. 609/10 and 592 surch **1967 NOUVELLE CONSTITUTION** with coloured metallic panel obliterating old value.
639 **136** 4k. on 2f. 20 15
640 **133** 5k. on 2f. 20 15
641 – 21k. on 4f. 90 70

1967. 1st Congolese Games, Kinshasa. Nos. 567 and 569 surch **1ers Jeux Congolais 25/6 au 2/7/67 Kinshasa** and value.
642 1k. on 5f. 10 10
643 9.6k. on 15f. 50 50

1967. 1st Flight by Air Congo BAC "One-Eleven". No. 504 surch **1er VOL BAC ONE ELEVEN 14/5/67** and value.
644 9.6k. on 7f. 70 20

1968. World Children's Day (8.10.67). Nos. 586 and 588 surch **JOURNEE MONDIALE DE L'ENFANCE 8 - 10 - 67** and new value.
645 **132** 1k. on 6f. 10 10
646 9k. on 9f. 50 50

1968. International Tourist Year (1967). Nos. 538, 541 and 544 surch **Annee Internationale du Tourisme 24-10-67** and new value.
647 **126** 5k. on 50c. 20 20
648 10k. on 6f. 40 40
649 15k. on 3f. 60 60

1968. (a) No. 540 surch.
650 **126** 1k. on 2f. 10 10

(b) Surch (coloured panel obliterating old value, and new value surch on panel. Panel colour given first, followed by colour of new value). (i) Nos. 538 and 542.
651 **126** 2k. on 50c. (bronze and black) 10 10
652 2k. on 50c. (blue and white) 10 10
653 9.6k. on 4f. (black and white) 50 45

(ii) No. 609.
654 **136** 10k. on 2f. (black and white) 55 10

152 Leaping Leopard

1968.
655 **152** 2k. black on green . . . 15 10
656 9.6k. black on red 65 15

1968. As Nos. 609, etc, but with colours changed and surch in new value.
657 **136** 15s. on 2f. brown & blue 10 10
658 – 1k. on 6f. brown & chest 10 10
659 – 3k. on 10f. brown & grn 10 10
660 – 5k. on 12f. brown & orge 20 15
661 – 20k. on 15f. brown & grn 70 50
662 – 50k. on 24f. brown & pur 1·90 1·25

154 Human Rights Emblem

1968. Human Rights Year.
663 **154** 2k. green and blue . . . 10 10
664 9.6k. red and green . . . 40 25
665 10k. brown and lilac . . . 40 25
666 40k. violet and brown . . 1·50 1·10

1969. 4th O.C.A.M. (Organization Commune Africaine et Malgache) Summit Meeting, Kinshasa. Nos. 663/6 with colours changed optd **4EME SOMMET OCAM 27-1-1969 KINSHASA** and emblem.
667 **154** 2k. brown and green . . . 10 10
668 9.60k. green and pink . . 40 25
669 10k. blue and grey . . . 40 25
670 40k. violet and blue . . . 1·50 1·10

156 Map of Africa and "Cotton"

1969. International Fair, Kinshasa (1st Issue).
671 **156** 2k. multicoloured 10 10
672 – 6k. multicoloured 30 30
673 – 9.6k. multicoloured . . . 40 20
674 – 9.8k. multicoloured . . . 40 35
675 – 11.6k. multicoloured . . . 50 50
DESIGNS: Map of Africa and: 6k. "Copper"; 9.6k. "Coffee"; 9.8k. "Diamonds"; 11.6k. "Palm-oil".

157 Fair Entrance

1969. Inaug of Int Fair, Kinshasa (2nd issue).
676 **157** 2k. purple and gold . . . 10 10
677 – 3k. blue and gold 10 10
678 – 10k. green and gold . . . 40 40
679 – 25k. red and gold . . . . 1·00 85
DESIGNS: 3k. "Gecomin" (mining company) pavilion; 10k. Administration building; 25k. African Unity Organization pavilion.

158 Congo Arms **159** Pres. Mobutu

1969.
680 **158** 10s. red and black 10 10
681 15s. blue and black . . . 10 10
682 30s. green and black . . . 10 10
683 60s. purple and black . . 10 10
684 90s. bistre and black . . 10 10
685 **159** 1k. multicoloured 10 10
686 2k. multicoloured 10 10
687 3k. multicoloured 15 10
688 5k. multicoloured 15 15
689 6k. multicoloured 20 15
690 9.6k. multicoloured . . . 30 25
691 10k. multicoloured . . . 40 30
692 20k. multicoloured . . . 80 60
693 50k. multicoloured . . . 2·00 1·75
694 100k. multicoloured . . . 4·00 3·50

160 "The Well-sinker" (O. Bonnevalle)

1969. 50th Anniv of International Labour Organization. Paintings. Multicoloured.
695 3k. Type **160** 15 15
696 4k. "Cocoa Production" (J. van Noten) 20 15
697 8k. "The Harbour" (C. Meunier) (vert) 70 25

698 10k. "The Poulterer" (H. Evenepoel) 45 35
699 15k. "Industry" (C. Meunier) 85 50

162 Pres. Mobutu, Map and Flag

1970. 10th Anniv of Independence.

701 **162** 10s. multicoloured 10 10
702 90s. multicoloured 10 10
703 1k. multicoloured 10 10
704 2k. multicoloured 10 10
705 7k. multicoloured 25 15
706 10k. multicoloured . . . 40 25
707 20k. multicoloured . . . 80 50

1970. Surch. (a) National Palace series.

708 **126** 10s. on 1f. 10 10
709 20s. on 2f. 10 10
710 30s. on 3f. 10 10
711 40s. on 4f. 10 10
712 60s. on 7f. 80 75
713 90s. on 9f. 80 75
714 1k. on 6f. 15 10
715 3k. on 30f. 80 75
716 4k. on 40f. 15 10
717 5k. on 50f. . . . . . . 2·00 1·90
718 10k. on 100f. 90 75

(b) Congolese Army series.

719 90s. on 9f. (No. 596) 15 10
720 1k. on 7f. (No. 595) 15 10
721 2k. on 24f. (No. 601) 15 10

(c) Pres. Mobutu series.

722 **136** 20s. on 2f. 15 10
723 – 40s. on 4f. (No. 610) . . 15 10
724 – 1k. on 12f. (No. 614) . . 80 70
725 – 2k. on 24f. (No. 616) . . 15 10

164 I.T.U. Headquarters, Geneva

1970. United Nations Commemorations.

726 **164** 1k. olive, green and pink 10 10
727 – 2k. grey, green and orange 10 10
728 – 6k.60 red, pink and blue 25 25
729 **164** 9k.60 multicoloured . . . 30 30
730 – 9k.80 sepia, brown and bl 35 35
731 – 10k. sepia, brown and lilac 35 35
732 – 11k. sepia, brown and pink 40 40

DESIGNS AND EVENTS: 1k., 9k.60, (I.T.U. World Day); 2k., 6k.60, New U.P.U. Headquarters, Berne (Inauguration); 9k.80, 10k., 11k. U.N. Headquarters, New York (25th anniversary).

165 Pres. Mobutu and Independence Arch

1970. 5th Anniv of "New Regime".

733 **165** 2k. multicoloured 10 10
734 10k. multicoloured . . . 45 35
735 20k. multicoloured . . . 85 80

166 "Apollo 11"

1970. Visit of "Apollo 11" Astronauts to Kinshasa.

736 **166** 1k. blue, black and red 10 10
737 – 2k. violet, black and red 10 10
738 – 7k. black, orange and red 25 25
739 – 10k. black, pink and red 35 35
740 – 30k. black, green and red 1·00 1·00

DESIGNS: 2k. Astronauts on Moon; 7k. Pres. Mobutu decorating wives; 10k. Pres. Mobutu with astronauts; 30k. Astronauts after splashdown.

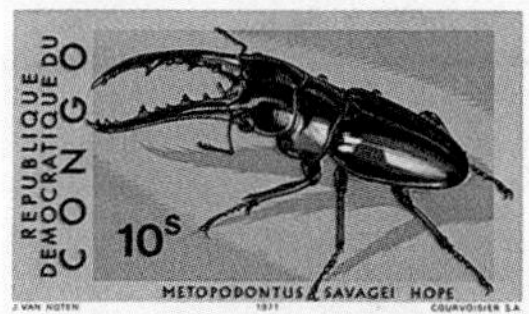

167 "Metopodontus savagei"

1971. Insects. Multicoloured.

741 10s. Type **167** 25 15
742 50s. "Cicindela regalis" . . . 25 15
743 90s. "Magacephala catenulata" 25 15
744 1k. "Stephanorrhina guttata" 25 15
745 2k. "Pupuricenus congoanus" 25 15
746 3k. "Sagra tristis" 50 25
747 5k. "Steraspis subcalida" . . 1·75 80
748 10k. "Mecosaspis explanata" 2·40 1·25
749 30k. "Goliathus meleagris" 5·75 3·25
750 40k. "Sternotomis virescens" 8·25 4·75

168 "Colotis protomedia"

1971. Butterflies and Moths. Multicoloured.

751 10s. Type **168** 25 15
752 20s. "Rhodophitus simplex" 25 15
753 70s. "Euphaedra overlaeti" 25 15
754 1k. "Argema bouvieri" . . . 25 15
755 3k. "Cymothoe reginae-elisabethae" 50 25
756 5k. "Miniodes maculifera" 1·40 60
757 10k. "Salamis temora" . . . 1·90 90
758 15k. "Eronia leda" . . . . . 3·75 1·60
759 25k. "Cymothoe sangaris" . . 5·00 2·50
760 40k. "Euchloron megaera" 8·00 4·50

169 "Four Races" around Globe

170 Pres. Mobutu and Obelisk

1971. Racial Equality Year.

761 **169** 1k. multicoloured 10 10
762 4k. multicoloured 15 15
763 5k. multicoloured 20 20
764 10k. multicoloured . . . 40 40

1971. 4th Anniv of Popular Revolutionary Movement (M.P.R.).

765 **170** 4k. multicoloured 15 15

171 "Hypericum bequaertii"

1971. Tropical Plants. Multicoloured.

766 1k. Type **171** 35 15
767 4k. "Dissotis brazzae" . . . 70 30
768 20k. "Begonia wollast" . . . 3·50 1·50
769 25k. "Cassia alata" . . . . . 4·50 1·90

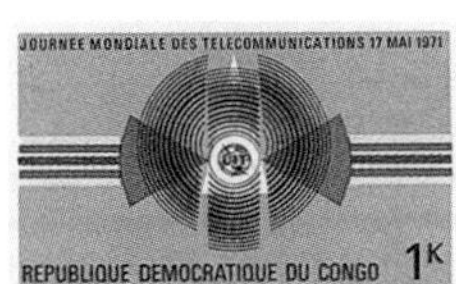

172 I.T.U. Emblem (International Telecommunications Day)

1971. "Telecommunications and Space". Mult.

770 1k. Type **172** 10 10
771 3k. Dish aerial (Satellite Earth Station, Kinshasa) 15 15
772 6k. Map of Pan-African telecommunications network 30 30

173 Savanna Monkey

1971. Congo Monkeys. Multicoloured.

773 10s. Type **173** 30 15
774 20s. Moustached monkey (vert) 30 15
775 70s. De Brazza's monkey . . 45 15
776 1k. Yellow baboon 45 25
777 3k. Pygmy chimpanzee (vert) 75 50
778 5k. Black mangabey (vert) . . 1·75 1·25
779 10k. Owl-faced monkey . . . 3·25 2·40
780 15k. Diana monkey . . . . 5·25 3·50
781 25k. Western black-and-white colobus (vert) . . . . . . 9·00 6·00
782 40k. L'Hoest's monkey (vert) 12·00 8·50

174 Hotel Inter-Continental

1971. Opening of Hotel Inter-Continental, Kinshasa.

783 **174** 2k. multicoloured 10 10
784 12k. multicoloured . . . 50 50

175 "Reader"

1971. Literacy Campaign. Multicoloured.

785 50s. Type **175** 10 10
786 2k.50 Open book and abacus 20 10
787 7k. Symbolic alphabet . . . 45 35

For later issues see **ZAIRE**.

COOK ISLANDS Pt. 1

A group of islands in the South Pacific under New Zealand control, including Aitutaki, Niue, Penrhyn and Rarotonga. Granted self-government in 1965.

See also issues for Aitutaki and Penrhyn Island.

1892. 12 pence = 1 shilling; 20 shillings = 1 pound.
1967. 100 cents = 1 dollar.

1

1892.

1 1 1d. black 27·00 26·00
2 1½d. mauve 40·00 38·00
3 2½d. blue 40·00 38·00
4 10d. red £140 £130

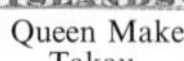

2 Queen Makea Takau — 3 White Tern or Torea

1893.

11ba 3 ½d. blue 4·25 5·25
28 ½d. green 2·75 3·25
13 2 1d. brown 15·00 15·00
12 1d. blue 5·00 4·50
29 1d. red 4·00 3·00
43 1½d. mauve 8·00 4·00
15a 3 2d. brown 8·50 6·50
16a 2 2½d. red 15·00 9·00
32 2½d. blue 3·75 7·00
9 5d. black 16·00 13·00
18a 3 6d. purple 19·00 22·00
19 2 10d. green 18·00 48·00
46 3 1s. red 27·00 85·00

1899. Surch **ONE HALF PENNY.**
21 2 ½d. on 1d. blue 32·00 42·00

1901. Optd with crown.
22 2 1d. brown £180 £140

1919. New Zealand stamps (King George V) surch **RAROTONGA** and value in native language in words.
56 62 ½d. green 40 1·00
47 53 1d. red 1·00 3·00
57 62 1½d. brown 50 75
58 2d. yellow 1·50 1·75
48a 2½d. blue 2·00 2·25
49a 3d. brown 2·25 2·00
50c 4d. violet 1·75 4·25
51a 4½d. green 1·75 8·00
52a 6d. red 1·75 5·50
53 7½d. brown 1·50 5·50
54a 9d. green 2·00 15·00
55a 1s. red 2·75 18·00

9 Captain Cook landing — 17 Harbour, Rarotonga and Mt. Ikurangi

1920. Inscr "RAROTONGA".
81 9 ½d. black and green 4·50 8·50
82 – 1d. black and red 6·00 2·25
72 – 1½d. black and blue 8·50 8·50
83 – 2½d. brown and blue 5·00 24·00
73 – 3d. black and brown 2·25 5·50
84 17 4d. green and violet 8·00 16·00
74 – 6d. brown and orange 3·00 8·50
75 – 1s. black and violet 5·00 17·00

DESIGNS—VERT: 1d. Wharf at Avarua; 1½d. Captain Cook (Dance); 2½d. Te Po, Rarotongan chief; 3d. Palm tree. HORIZ: 6d. Huts at Arorangi; 1s. Avarua Harbour.

1921. New Zealand stamps optd **RAROTONGA.**
76 F 4 2s. blue 27·00 55·00
77 2s.6d. brown 19·00 50·00
78 5s. green 27·00 65·00
79 10s. red 60·00 £100
89 £1 red 95·00 £170

1926. "Admiral" type of New Zealand optd **RAROTONGA.**
90 71 2s. blue 10·00 40·00
92 3s. mauve 16·00 42·00

1931. No. 77 surch **TWO PENCE.**
93 2d. on 1½d. black and blue 9·50 2·75

1931. Arms type of New Zealand optd **RAROTONGA.**
95 F 6 2s.6d. brown 10·00 22·00
96 5s. green 17·00 50·00
97 10s. red 35·00 90·00
98 £1 pink 85·00 £140

20 Captain Cook landing — 22 Double Maori Canoe

1932. Inscribed "COOK ISLANDS".
106 20 ½d. black and green 1·00 4·50
107 – 1d. black and red 1·25 2·00
108 22 2d. black and brown 1·50 50
140 – 2½d. black and blue 65 1·75
110 – 4d. black and blue 1·50 50
142 – 6d. black and orange 2·50 2·00
105 – 1s. black and violet 8·50 22·00

DESIGNS—VERT: 1d. Captain Cook. HORIZ: 2½d. Natives working cargo; 4d. Port of Avarua; 6d. R.M.S. "Monowai"; 1s. King George V.

1935. Jubilee. As 1932 optd **SILVER JUBILEE OF KING GEORGE V. 1910-1935.**
113 1d. red 60 1·40
114 2½d. blue 1·00 2·50
115 6d. green and orange 3·50 6·00

1936. Stamps of New Zealand optd **COOK ISLANDS.**
116 71 2s. blue 13·00 45·00
131w F 6 2s.6d. brown 18·00 23·00
117 71 3s. mauve 13·00 70·00
132 F 6 5s. green 9·50 22·00
133w 10s. red 48·00 70·00
134 £1 pink 50·00 80·00
135w £3 green 55·00 £160
98b £5 blue £170 £325

1937. Coronation. T **106** of New Zealand optd **COOK IS'DS.**
124 106 1d. red 40 50
125 2½d. blue 80 50
126 6d. orange 80 35

29 King George VI — 30 Native Village

1938.
143 29 1s. black and violet 1·50 2·25
128 30 2s. black and orange 18·00 13·00
145 – 3s. blue and green 30·00 30·00

DESIGN—HORIZ: 3s. Native canoe.

32 Tropical Landscape — 34 Ngatangiia Channel, Rarotonga

1940.
130 32 3d. on 1½d. black & purple 50 50

1946. Peace. Peace stamps of New Zealand of 1946 optd **COOK ISLANDS.**
146 132 1d. green 40 10
147 – 2d. purple 40 50
148 – 6d. brown and red 50 50
149 139 8d. black and red 50 50

1949.
150 34 ½d. violet and brown 10 1·00
151 – 1d. brown and green 3·50 2·00
152 – 2d. brown and red 2·00 2·00
153 – 3d. green and blue 1·75 2·00
154 – 5d. green and violet 5·50 1·50
155 – 6d. black and red 5·50 2·75
156 – 8d. olive and orange 55 3·75
157 – 1s. blue and brown 4·25 3·75
158 – 2s. brown and red 3·00 13·00
159 – 3s. blue and green 9·50 24·00

DESIGNS—HORIZ: 1d. Captain Cook and map of Hervey Is; 2d. Rarotonga and Rev. John Williams; 3d. Aitutaki and palm trees; 5d. Rarotonga Airfield; 6d. Penrhyn village; 8d. Native hut. VERT: 1s. Map and statue of Capt. Cook; 2s. Native hut and palms; 3s. "Matua" (inter-island freighter).

1953. Coronation. As Types of New Zealand but inscr "COOK ISLANDS".
160 164 3d. brown 1·00 85
161 166 6d. grey 1·25 1·50

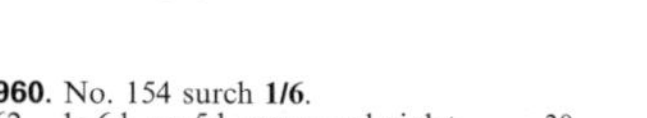

1960. No. 154 surch **1/6.**
162 1s.6d. on 5d. green and violet 30 30

45 Tiare Maori — 52 Queen Elizabeth II

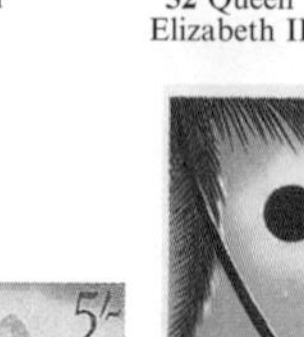

55 Rarotonga — 56 Eclipse and Palm

1963.
163 45 1d. green and yellow 45 50
164 – 2d. red and yellow 20 50
165 – 3d. yellow, green and violet 70 50
166 – 5d. blue and black 8·00 1·50
167 – 6d. red, yellow and green 1·00 50
168 – 8d. black and blue 4·25 1·50
169 – 1s. yellow and green 40 50
170 52 1s.6d. violet 2·75 2·00
171 – 2s. brown and blue 1·00 75
172 – 3s. black and green 1·25 1·00
173 55 5s. brown and blue 11·00 3·75

DESIGNS—VERT (As Type **45**): 2d. Fishing god; 8d. Long-tailed tuna. HORIZ (As Type **45**): 3d. Frangipani (plant); 5d. White tern ("Love Tern"); 6d. Hibiscus; 1s. Oranges. (As Type **55**): 2s. Island scene; 3s. Administration Centre, Mangaia.

1965. Solar Eclipse Observation, Manuae Island.
174 56 6d. black, yellow and blue 20 10

57 N.Z. Ensign and Map

1965. Internal Self-government.
175 57 4d. red and blue 20 10
176 – 10d. multicoloured 20 15
177 – 1s. multicoloured 20 15
178 – 1s.9d. multicoloured 50 1·25

DESIGNS: 10d. London Missionary Society Church; 1s. Proclamation of Cession, 1900; 1s.9d. Nikao School.

1966. Churchill Commemoration. Nos. 171/3 and 175/7 optd **In Memoriam SIR WINSTON CHURCHILL 1874 – 1965.**
179 57 4d. red and blue 75 30
180 – 10d. multicoloured 1·50 45
181 – 1s. multicoloured 1·50 65
182 – 2s. brown and blue 1·50 1·25
183 – 3s. black and green 1·50 1·25
184 55 5s. brown and blue 2·00 1·75

1966. Air. Various stamps optd **Airmail** and Douglas DC-3 airplane or surch in addition.
185 – 6d. red, yell & grn (No. 167) 1·25 20
186 – 7d. on 8d. blk & bl (No. 168) 2·00 25
187 – 10d. on 3d. green and violet (No. 165) 1·00 15
188 – 1s. yellow and green (No. 169) 1·00 15
189 52 1s.6d. violet 1·50 1·25
190 – 2s.3d. on 3s. black and green (No. 172) 1·00 65
191 55 5s. brown and blue 1·75 1·50
192 – 10s. on 2s. brown and blue (No. 171) 1·75 12·00
193 – £1 pink (No. 143) 12·00 17·00

63 "Adoration of the Magi" (Fra Angelico)

1966. Christmas. Multicoloured.
194a 1d. Type **63** 10 10
195a 2d. "The Nativity" (Memling) 20 10
196a 4d. "Adoration of the Wise Men" (Velazquez) 30 15
197a 10d. "Adoration of the Wise Men" (H. Bosch) 30 20
198a 1s.6d. "Adoration of the Shepherds" (J. de Ribera) 40 35

68 Tennis and Queen Elizabeth II

1967. 2nd South Pacific Games, Noumea. Mult.
199 ½d. Type **68** (postage) 10 10
200 1d. Basketball and Games emblem 10 10
201 4d. Boxing and Cook Islands Team badge 10 10
202 7d. Football and Queen Elizabeth II 20 15
203 10d. Running and Games Emblem (air) 20 15
204 2s.3d. Running and Cook Islands' Team badge 25 65

1967. Decimal currency. Various stamps surch.
205 45 1c. on 1d. 45 1·50
206 – 2c. on 2d. (No. 164) 10 10
207 – 2½c. on 3d. (No. 165) 20 10
209 57 3c. on 4d. 15 10
210 – 4c. on 5d. (No. 166) 7·50 30
211 – 5c. on 6d. (No. 167) 15 10
212 56 5c. on 6d. 5·00 40
213 – 7c. on 8d. (No. 168) 30 10
214 – 10c. on 1s. (No. 169) 15 10
215 52 15c. on 1s.6d. 2·00 1·00
216 – 30c. on 3s. (No. 172) 19·00 3·75
217 55 50c. on 5s. 4·00 1·25
218 – $1 and 10s. on 10d. (No. 176) 16·00 5·50
219 – $2 on £1 (No. 134) 50·00 70·00
220 – $6 on £3 (No. 135) 95·00 £120
221 – $10 on £5 (No. 136) £150 £180

75 Village Scene, Cook Islands 1d. Stamp of 1892 and Queen Victoria

1967. 75th Anniv of First Cook Islands Stamps. Multicoloured.
222 1c. (1d.) Type **75** 10 10
223 3c. (4d.) Post Office, Avarua, Rarotonga and Queen Elizabeth II 15 10
224 8c. (10d.) Avarua, Rarotonga and Cook Islands 10d. stamp of 1892 30 15
225 18c. (1s.9d.) "Moana Roa", (inter-island ship), Douglas DC-3 aircraft, map and Captain Cook 1·40 30
MS226 134 × 109 mm. Nos. 222/5 1·75 2·75

The face values are expressed in decimal currency and in the Sterling equivalent.

79 Hibiscus

81 Queen Elizabeth and Flowers

1967. Flowers. Multicoloured.
227A ½c. Type **79** 10 10
228A 1c. "Hibiscus syriacus" 10 10
229A 2c. Frangipani 10 10
230A 2½c. "Clitoria ternatea" 20 10
231B 3c. "Suva Queen" 40 10
232A 4c. Water lily (wrongly inscribed "Walter Lily") 70 1·00
233B 4c. Water lily 2·50 10
234B 5c. "Bauhinia bipinnata rosea" 30 10
235B 6c. Yellow hibiscus 30 10
236B 8c. "Allamanda cathartica" 30 10
237B 9c. Stephanotis 30 10
238B 10c. "Poinciana regia flamboyant" 30 10
239A 15c. Frangipani 40 10
240B 20c. Thunbergia 3·50 1·25
241A 25c. Canna lily 80 30
242A 30c. "Euphorbia pulcherrima poinsettia" 65 50
243A 50c. "Gardinia taitensis" 1·00 55

244B $1 Queen Elizabeth II . . 1·25 80
245B $2 Queen Elizabeth II . . 2·25 1·50
246A $4 Type **81** . . . . . . 1·75 4·00
247A $6 Type **81** . . . . . . 2·00 5·50
247cA $8 Type **81** . . . . . . 6·00 15·00
248A $10 Type **81** . . . . . . 3·75 12·00

97 "Ia Orana Maria"

1967. Gauguin's Polynesian Paintings.
249 **97** 1c. multicoloured 10 10
250 – 3c. multicoloured 15 10
251 – 5c. multicoloured 20 10
252 – 8c. multicoloured 25 10
253 – 15c. multicoloured 50 15
254 – 22c. multicoloured 65 20
MS255 156 × 132 mm. Nos. 249/54 1·75 1·25
DESIGNS: 3c. "Riders on the Beach"; 5c. "Still Life with Flowers" and inset portrait of Queen Elizabeth; 8c. "Whispered Words"; 15c. "Maternity"; 22c. "Why are you angry?".

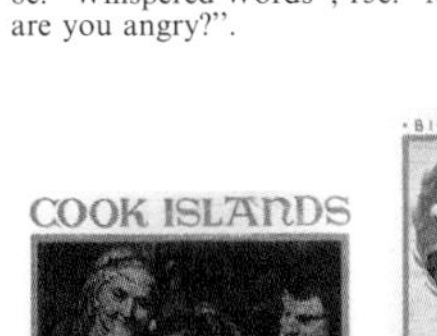
98 "The Holy Family" (Rubens)

100 "Matavai Bay, Tahiti" (J. Barralet)

1967. Christmas. Renaissance Paintings.
256 **98** 1c. multicoloured 10 10
257 – 3c. multicoloured 10 10
258 – 4c. multicoloured 10 10
259 – 8c. multicoloured 20 15
260 – 15c. multicoloured 35 15
261 – 25c. multicoloured 40 15
DESIGNS: 3c. "The Epiphany" (Durer); 4c. "The Lucca Madonna" (J. van Eyck); 8c. "The Adora-tion of the Shepherds" (J. da Bassano); 15c. "The Nativity" (El Greco); 25c. "The Madonna and Child" (Correggio).

1968. Hurricane Relief. Nos. 231, 233, 251, 238, 241 and 243/4 optd **HURRICANE RELIEF PLUS** and premium.
262 3c.+1c. multicoloured 15 15
263 4c.+1c. multicoloured 15 15
264 5c.+2c. multicoloured 15 15
265 10c.+2c. multicoloured . . . 15 15
266 25c.+5c. multicoloured . . . 20 20
267 50c.+10c. multicoloured . . . 25 30
268 $1+10c. multicoloured . . . 35 50
On No. 264 silver blocking obliterates the design area around the lettering.

1968. Bicentenary of Captain Cook's First Voyage of Discovery.
269 **100** ½c. mult (postage) 10 10
270 – 1c. multicoloured 15 10
271 – 2c. multicoloured 35 20
272 – 4c. multicoloured 50 20
273 – 6c. multicoloured (air) . . 60 35
274 – 10c. multicoloured 60 35
275 – 15c. multicoloured 70 50
276 – 25c. multicoloured 80 75
DESIGNS—VERT: 1c. "Island of Huaheine" (John Cleveley); 2c. "Town of St. Peter and St. Paul, Kamchatka" (J. Webber); 4c. "The Ice Islands" (Antarctica: W. Hodges). HORIZ: 6c. "Resolution" and "Discovery" (J. Webber); 10c. "The Island of Tahiti" (W. Hodges); 15c. "Karakakooa, Hawaii" (J. Webber); 25c. "The Landing at Middleburg" (J. Sherwin).

102 Dinghy-sailing

1968. Olympic Games, Mexico. Multicoloured.
277 1c. Type **102** 10 10
278 5c. Gymnastics 10 10
279 15c. High-jumping 25 10
280 20c. High-diving 25 10
281 30c. Cycling 60 20
282 50c. Hurdling 50 25

103 "Madonna and Child" (Titian)

1968. Christmas. Multicoloured.
283 1c. Type **103** 10 10
284 4c. "The Holy Family of the Lamb" (Raphael) 15 10
285 10c. "The Madonna of the Rosary" (Murillo) 25 10
286 20c. "Adoration of the Magi" (Memling) 40 10
287 30c. "Adoration of the Magi" (Ghirlandaio) 45 10
MS288 114 × 177 mm. Nos. 283/7 1·25 1·60

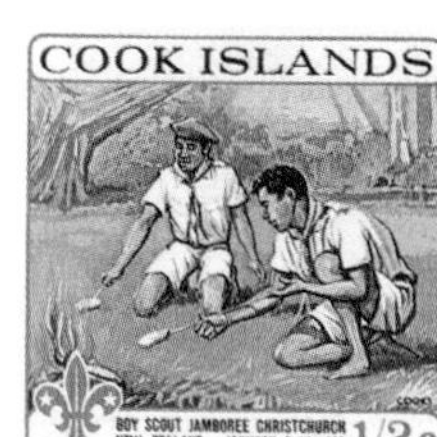
104 Campfire Cooking

1969. Diamond Jubilee of New Zealand Scout Movement and 5th National (New Zealand) Jamboree. Multicoloured.
289 ½c. Type **104** 10 10
290 1c. Descent by rope 10 10
291 5c. Semaphore 15 10
292 10c. Tree-planting 20 10
293 20c. Constructing a shelter 25 15
294 30c. Lord Baden-Powell and island scene 45 25

105 High Jumping

1969. 3rd South Pacific Games, Port Moresby. Multicoloured.
295 ½c. Type **105** 10 30
296 ½c. Footballer 10 30
297 1c. Basketball 50 40
298 1c. Weightlifter 50 40
299 4c. Tennis-player 50 50
300 4c. Hurdler 50 50
301 10c. Javelin-thrower 55 50
302 10c. Runner 55 50
303 15c. Golfer . . . . 1·75 1·50
304 15c. Boxer . . . . 1·75 1·50
MS305 174 × 129 mm. Nos. 295/304 7·00 6·00

106 Flowers, Map and Captain Cook (½-size illustration)

1969. South Pacific Conference, Noumea. Mult.
306 5c. Premier Albert Henry . . 30 20
307 10c. Type **106** . . . . 1·00 60
308 25c. Flowers, map and arms of New Zealand 40 60
309 30c. Queen Elizabeth II, map and flowers 40 70

107 "Virgin and Child with Saints Jerome and Dominic" (Lippi)

1969. Christmas. Multicoloured.
310 1c. Type **107** 10 10
311 4c. "The Holy Family" (Fra Bartolomeo) 10 10
312 10c. "The Adoration of the Shepherds" (A. Mengs) . . 15 10
313 20c. "Madonna and Child with Saints" (Robert Campin) 25 20
314 30c. "The Madonna of the Basket" (Correggio) . . . 25 30
MS315 132 × 97 mm. Nos. 310/14 1·00 1·50

108 "The Resurrection of Christ" (Raphael)

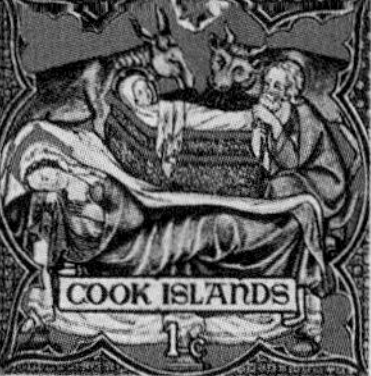
115 Mary, Joseph, and Christ in Manger

110 The Royal Family

1970. Easter.
316 **108** 4c. multicoloured 10 10
317 – 8c. multicoloured 10 10
318 – 20c. multicoloured 15 10
319 – 25c. multicoloured 20 10
MS320 132 × 162 mm. Nos. 316/19 1·25 1·25
DESIGNS: "The Resurrection of Christ" by Dirk Bouts (8c.), Altdorfer (20c.), Murillo (25c.).

1970. "Apollo 13". Nos. 233, 236, 239/40, 242 and 245/6 optd **KIA ORANA APOLLO 13 ASTRONAUTS Te Atua to Tatou Irinakianga**.
321 4c. multicoloured 10 10
322 8c. multicoloured 10 10
323 15c. multicoloured 10 10
324 20c. multicoloured 40 15
325 30c. multicoloured 20 20
326 $2 multicoloured 60 90
327a $4 multicoloured . . . . . 1·00 2·75

1970. Royal Visit to New Zealand. Multicoloured.
328 5c. Type **110** 50 30
329 30c. Captain Cook and H.M.S. "Endeavour" . . . 2·00 1·75
330 $1 Royal Visit commemorative coin . . . . 3·00 3·00
MS331 145 × 97 mm. Nos. 328/30 9·00 9·50

1970. 5th Anniv of Self-Government. Nos. 328/30 optd **FIFTH ANNIVERSARY SELF-GOVERNMENT AUGUST 1970**.
332 **110** 5c. multicoloured 40 15
333 – 30c. multicoloured 80 35
334 – $1 multicoloured . . . . 1·00 90
On No. 332, the opt is arranged in one line around the frame of the stamp.

1970. Surch **FOUR DOLLARS $4.00**.
335a **81** $4 on $8 multicoloured 1·50 2·00
336a $4 on $10 multicoloured 1·50 1·75

1970. Christmas. Multicoloured.
337 1c. Type **115** 10 10
338 4c. Shepherds and Apparition of the Angel 10 10
339 10c. Mary showing Child to Joseph 15 10
340 20c. The Wise Men bearing Gifts 20 20
341 30c. Parents wrapping Child in swaddling clothes . . . 25 35
MS342 100 × 139 mm. Nos. 337/41 1·00 1·50

1971. Surch **PLUS 20c UNITED KINGDOM SPECIAL MAIL SERVICE**.
343 30c.+20c. (No. 242) 30 50
344 50c.+20c. (No. 243) . . . . 1·00 1·75
The premium of 20c. was to prepay a private delivery service fee in Great Britain during the postal strike. The mail was sent by air to a forwarding address in the Netherlands. No. 343 was intended for ordinary airmail ½ oz. letters, and No. 344 included registration fee.

117 Wedding of Princess Elizabeth and Prince Philip

1971. Royal Visit of Duke of Edinburgh. Multicoloured.
345 1c. Type **117** 20 50
346 4c. Queen Elizabeth, Prince Philip, Prince Charles and Princess Anne at Windsor 60 1·10
347 10c. Prince Philip sailing . . 1·00 1·25
348 15c. Prince Philip in polo gear . . . . 1·00 1·25
349 25c. Prince Philip in naval uniform, and Royal Yacht, "Britannia" . . . . 1·25 2·00
MS350 168 × 122 mm. Nos. 345/9 5·00 8·00

1971. 4th South Pacific Games, Tahiti. Nos. 238, 241 and 242 optd **Fourth South Pacific Games Papeete** and emblem or surch also.
351 10c. multicoloured 10 10
352 10c.+1c. multicoloured . . . 10 10
353 10c.+3c. multicoloured . . . 10 10
354 25c. multicoloured 15 10
355 25c.+1c. multicoloured . . . 15 10
356 25c.+3c. multicoloured . . . 15 10
357 30c. multicoloured 15 10
358 30c.+1c. multicoloured . . . 15 10
359 30c.+3c. multicoloured . . . 15 10
The stamps additionally surch 1c. or 3c. helped to finance the Cook Islands' team at the games.

1971. Nos. 230, 233, 236/7 and 239 surch **10c**.
360 10c. on 2½c. multicoloured . . 15 25
361 10c. on 4c. multicoloured . . 15 25
362 10c. on 8c. multicoloured . . 15 25
363 10c. on 9c. multicoloured . . 15 25
364 10c. on 15c. multicoloured . . 15 25

121 "Virgin and Child" (Bellini)

123 St. John

1971. Christmas.
365 **121** 1c. multicoloured 10 10
366 – 4c. multicoloured 10 10
367 – 10c. multicoloured 25 10
368 – 20c. multicoloured 50 20
369 – 30c. multicoloured 50 35
MS370 135 × 147 mm. Nos. 365/9 1·75 2·75
MS371 92 × 98 mm. 50c. + 5c. "The Holy Family in a Garland of Flowers" (Jan Brueghel and Pieter van Avont) (41 × 41 mm) 75 1·40
DESIGNS: Various paintings of the "Virgin and Child" by Bellini. Similar to Type **121**.

1972. 25th Anniv of South Pacific Commission. No. 244 optd **SOUTH PACIFIC COMMISSION FEB. 1947 – 1972**.
372 $1 multicoloured 40 75

1972. Easter. Multicoloured.
373 5c. Type **123** 10 10
374 10c. Christ on the Cross . . 10 10
375 30c. Mary, Mother of Jesus 25 40
MS376 79 × 112 mm. Nos. 373/5 forming triptych of "The Crucifixion" 1·00 2·25

1972. Hurricane Relief. (a) Nos. 239, 241 and 243 optd **HURRICANE RELIEF PLUS** and premium.
379 15c.+5c. multicoloured . . . 20 20
380 25c.+5c. multicoloured . . . 20 20
382 50c.+10c. multicoloured . . . 25 25

(b) Nos. 373/5 optd **Hurricane Relief Plus** and premium.
377 5c.+2c. multicoloured 15 15
378 10c.+2c. multicoloured . . . 15 15
381 30c.+5c. multicoloured . . . 20 20

126/7 Rocket heading for Moon

1972. Apollo Moon Exploration Flights. Mult.
383 5c. Type **126** 20 15
384 5c. Type **127** 20 15
385 10c. Lunar module and astronaut 20 15
386 10c. Astronaut and experiment 20 15
387 25c. Command capsule and Earth 25 20
388 25c. Lunar Rover 25 20
389 30c. Sikorsky Sea King helicopter 75 40
390 30c. Splashdown 75 40
MS391 83 × 205 mm. Nos. 383/90 4·00 5·00
These were issued in horizontal se-tenant pairs of each value, forming one composite design.

1972. Hurricane Relief. Nos. 383/390 surch **HURRICANE RELIEF Plus** and premium.
392 5c.+2c. multicoloured 10 10
393 5c.+2c. multicoloured 10 10
394 10c.+2c. multicoloured . . . 10 10
395 10c.+2c. multicoloured . . . 10 10
396 25c.+2c. multicoloured . . . 15 15
397 25c.+2c. multicoloured . . . 15 15
398 30c.+2c. multicoloured . . . 25 15
399 30c.+2c. multicoloured . . . 25 15
MS400 83 × 205 mm. No. **MS**391 surch 3c. on each stamp 2·50 3·50

129 High-jumping

130 "The Rest on the Flight into Egypt" (Caravaggio)

1972. Olympic Games, Munich. Multicoloured.
401 10c. Type **129** 20 10
402 25c. Running 40 15
403 30c. Boxing 40 20
MS404 88 × 78 mm. 50c. + 5c. Pierre de Coubertin 1·00 2·00
MS405 84 × 133 mm. Nos. 401/3 1·25 2·00

1972. Christmas. Multicoloured.
406 1c. Type **130** 10 10
407 5c. "Madonna of the Swallow" (Guercino) . . . 25 10
408 10c. "Madonna of the Green Cushion" (Solario) 35 10
409 20c. "Madonna and Child" (di Credi) 55 20
410 30c. "Madonna and Child" (Bellini) 85 30
MS411 141 × 152 mm. Nos. 406/10 3·00 3·50
MS412 101 × 82 mm. 50c. + 5c. "The Holy Night" (Correggio) (31 × 43 mm) 75 1·50

131 Marriage Ceremony

133 "Noli me Tangere" (Titian)

132 Taro Leaf

1972. Royal Silver Wedding. Each black and silver.
413 5c. Type **131** 25 15
414 10c. Leaving Westminster Abbey 35 25
415 15c. Bride and bridegroom (40 × 41 mm) 45 50
416 30c. Family group (67 × 40 mm) 55 75

1973. Silver Wedding Coinage.
417 **132** 1c. gold, mauve and black 10 10
418 – 2c. gold, blue and black 10 10
419 – 5c. silver, green and black 10 10
420 – 10c. silver, blue and black 20 10
421 – 20c. silver, green and black 30 10
422 – 50c. silver, mauve and black 50 15
423 – $1 silver, blue and black 75 30
DESIGNS—HORIZ (37 × 24 mm): 2c. Pineapple; 5c. Hibiscus. (46 × 30 mm): 10c. Oranges; 20c. White tern; 50c. Striped bonito. VERT: (32 × 55 mm): $1 Tangaroa.

1973. Easter. Multicoloured.
424 5c. Type **133** 15 10
425 10c. "The Descent from the Cross" (Rubens) 20 10
426 30c. "The Lamentation of Christ" (Durer) 25 10
MS427 132 × 67 mm. Nos. 424/6 55 1·25

1973. Easter. Children's Charity. Designs as Nos. 424/6 in separate miniature sheets 67 × 87 mm, each with a face value of 50c. + 5c.
MS428 As Nos. 424/6 Set of 3 sheets 1·00 1·75

134 Queen Elizabeth II in Coronation Regalia

137 The Annunciation

136 Tipairua

1973. 20th Anniv of Queen Elizabeth's Coronation.
429 **134** 10c. multicoloured 50 90
MS430 64 × 89 mm. 50c. as 10c. 2·50 2·25

1973. 10th Anniv of Treaty Banning Nuclear Testing. Nos. 234, 236, 238 and 240/2 optd **TENTH ANNIVERSARY CESSATION OF NUCLEAR TESTING TREATY**.
431 5c. multicoloured 10 10
432 8c. multicoloured 10 10
433 10c. multicoloured 10 10
434 20c. multicoloured 15 15
435 25c. multicoloured 20 15
436 30c. multicoloured 20 15

1973. Maori Exploration of the Pacific. Sailing Craft. Multicoloured.
437 ½c. Type **136** 10 10
438 1c. Wa'a Kaulua 10 10
439 1½c. Tainui 15 10
440 5c. War canoe 40 15
441 10c. Pahi 50 15
442 15c. Amatasi 75 65
443 25c. Vaka 90 80

1973. Christmas. Scene from a 15th-century Flemish "Book of Hours". Multicoloured.
444 1c. Type **137** 10 10
445 5c. The Visitation 10 10
446 10c. Annunciation to the Shepherds 10 10
447 20c. Epiphany 15 10
448 30c. The Slaughter of the Innocents 20 15
MS449 121 × 128 mm. Nos. 444/8 55 1·40
See also No. **MS**454.

138 Princess Anne

140 "Jesus carrying the Cross" (Raphael)

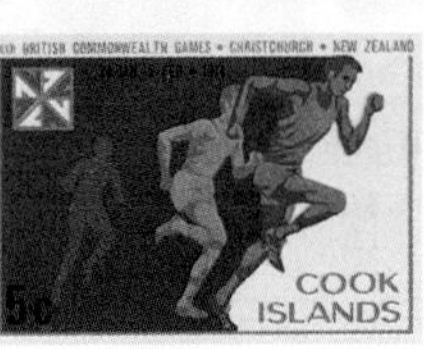
139 Running

1973. Royal Wedding. Multicoloured.
450 25c. Type **138** 20 10
451 30c. Captain Mark Phillips 25 10
452 50c. Princess Anne and Captain Phillips 30 15
MS453 119 × 100 mm. Nos. 450/2 55 35

1973. Christmas. Children's Charity. Designs as Nos. 444/8 in separate miniature sheets 50 × 70 mm, each with a face value of 50c. + 5c.
MS454 As Nos. 444/8 Set of 5 sheets 75 80

1974. British Commonwealth Games, Christchurch. Multicoloured.
455 1c. Diving (vert) 10 10
456 3c. Boxing (vert) 10 10
457 5c. Type 139 . . . . 10 10
458 10c. Weightlifting 10 10
459 30c. Cycling 40 25
MS460 115 × 90 mm. 50c. Discobolus 40 55

1974. Easter. Multicoloured.
461 5c. Type **140** 10 10
462 10c. "The Holy Trinity" (El Greco) 15 10
463 30c. "The Deposition of Christ" (Caravaggio) . . . 25 20
MS464 130 × 70 mm. Nos. 461/3 1·50 50

1974. Easter. Children's Charity. Designs as Nos. 461/3 in separate miniature sheets 59 × 87 mm, each with a face value of 50c. + 5c.
MS465 As Nos. 461/3 Set of 3 sheets 70 1·40

141 Grey Bonnet

142 Queen Elizabeth II

1974. Sea Shells. Multicoloured.
466 ½c. Type **141** 30 10
467 1c. Common Pacific vase . . 30 10
468 1½c. True heart cockle . . . 30 10
469 2c. Terebellum conch 30 10
470 3c. Bat volute 45 10
471 4c. Gibbose conch 50 10
472 5c. Common hairy triton . . 50 10
473 6c. Serpent's head cowrie . . 50 1·75
474 8c. Granulate frog shell . . . 60 10
475 10c. Fly-spotted auger . . . 60 10
476 15c. Episcopan mitre 70 20
477 20c. Butterfly moon . . . . 1·00 20
478 25c. Royal oak scallop . . . 1·00 1·75
479 30c. Soldier cone . . . . . . 1·00 30
480 50c. Textile or cloth of gold cone . . . . 8·50 4·50
481 60c. Red-mouth olive . . . . 8·50 4·50
482 $1 Type **142** . . . . 3·00 4·50
483 $2 Type **142** . . . . 1·75 2·25
484 $4 Queen Elizabeth II and sea shells (60 × 39 mm) . . 2·50 6·50
485 $6 As $4 (60 × 39 mm) . . . 15·00 7·00
486 $8 As $4 (60 × 39 mm) . . . 18·00 8·50
487 $10 As $4 (60 × 39 mm) . . . 21·00 9·00

143 Footballer and Australasian Map

1974. World Cup Football Championship, West Germany. Multicoloured.
488 25c. Type **143** 20 10
489 50c. Map and Munich Stadium 35 25
490 $1 Footballer, stadium and World Cup 55 45
MS491 89 × 100 mm. Nos. 488/90 1·00 2·75

144 Obverse and Reverse of Commemorative $2.50 Silver Coin

146 "Madonna of the Goldfinch" (Raphael)

145 Early Stamps of Cook Islands

1974. Bicentenary of Captain Cook's Second Voyage of Discovery.
492 **144** $2.50 silver, black and violet . . . . 12·00 7·00
493 – $7.50 silver, black and green . . . . 20·00 13·00
MS494 73 × 73 mm. Nos. 492/3 35·00 48·00
DESIGN: $7.50, As Type **144** but showing $7.50 coin.

1974. Centenary of U.P.U. Multicoloured.
495 10c. Type **145** 20 15
496 25c. Old landing strip, Rarotonga, and stamp of 1898 . . . . 30 40
497 30c. Post Office, Rarotonga, and stamp of 1920 . . . . 30 40
498 50c. U.P.U. emblem and stamps 30 65
MS499 118 × 79 mm. Nos. 495/8 1·00 1·75

1974. Christmas. Multicoloured.
500 1c. Type **146** 10 10
501 5c. "The Sacred Family" (Andrea del Sarto) 20 10
502 10c. "The Virgin adoring the Child" (Correggio) 25 10
503 20c. "The Holy Family" (Rembrandt) 40 20
504 30c. "The Virgin and Child" (Rogier van der Weyden) 50 30
MS505 114 × 133 mm. Nos. 500/4 1·40 2·00

147 Churchill and Blenheim Palace

1974. Birth Centenary of Sir Winston Churchill. Multicoloured.
506 5c. Type **147** 15 10
507 10c. Churchill and Houses of Parliament 15 10
508 25c. Churchill and Chartwell 25 20
509 30c. Churchill and Buckingham Palace 25 25
510 50c. Churchill and St. Paul's Cathedral 30 50
MS511 108 × 114 mm. Nos. 506/10 1·25 1·00

1974. Christmas. Children's Charity. Designs as Nos. 500/504 in separate miniature sheets 53 × 69 mm, each with a face value of 50c. + 5c.
MS512 As Nos. 500/4 Set of 5 sheets 1·00 1·00

148 Vasco Nunez de Balboa and Discovery of Pacific Ocean (1513)

1975. Pacific Explorers. Multicoloured.
513 1c. Type **148** 15 10
514 5c. Fernando de Magellanes and map (1520) 65 20
515 10c. Juan Sebastian del Cano and "Vitoria" (1520) . . . 1·25 20
516 25c. Friar Andres de Urdaneta and ship (1564–67) . . . . 2·25 75
517 30c. Miguel Lopez de Legazpi and ship (1564–67) . . . . 2·25 80

149 "Apollo" Capsule

1975. "Apollo–Soyuz" Space Project. Mult.
518 25c. Type **149** 35 15
519 25c. "Soyuz" capsule 35 15
520 30c. "Soyuz" crew 40 15
521 30c. "Apollo" crew 40 15
522 50c. Cosmonaut within "Soyuz" 45 25
523 50c. Astronauts within "Apollo" 45 25
MS524 119 × 119 mm. Nos. 518/23 1·50 1·00
These were issued in horizontal se-tenant pairs of each value, forming one composite design.

150 $100 Commemorative Gold Coin

1975. Bicentenary of Captain Cook's 2nd Voyage.
525 **150** $2 brown, gold and violet 2·50 1·75

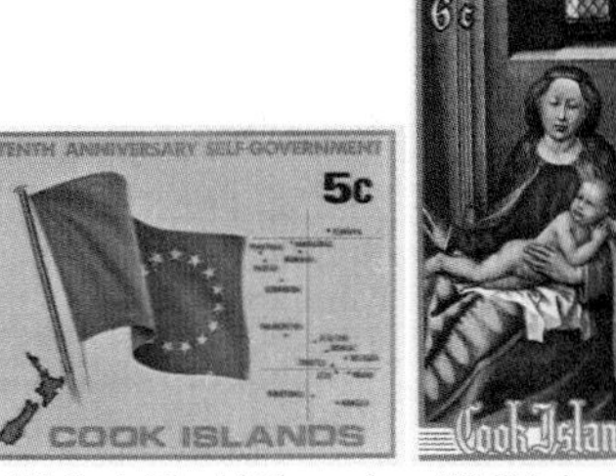

151 Cook Islands' Flag and Map

152 "Madonna by the Fireside" (R. Campin)

1975. 10th Anniv of Self-government.
526 5c. Type **151** 40 10
527 10c. Premier Sir Albert Henry and flag (vert) 45 10
528 25c. Rarotonga and flag 80 30

1975. Christmas. Multicoloured.
529 6c. Type **152** 15 10
530 10c. "Madonna in the Meadow" (Raphael) 15 10
531 15c. "Madonna of the Oak" (att. Raphael) 25 10
532 20c. "Adoration of the Shepherds" (J. B. Maino) 25 15
533 35c. "The Annunciation" (Murillo) 40 20
MS534 110 × 124 mm. Nos. 529/33 1·10 90

1975. Christmas. Children's Charity. Designs as Nos. 529/33 in separate miniature sheets 53 × 71 mm, each with a face value of 75c. + 5c.
MS535 As Nos. 529/33 Set of 5 sheets 1·10 1·25

153 "Entombment of Christ" (Raphael)

1976. Easter. Multicoloured.
536 7c. Type **153** 30 10
537 15c. "Pieta" (Veronese) 50 15
538 35c. "Pieta" (El Greco) 75 25
MS539 144 × 55 mm. Nos. 536/8 1·50 85

1976. Easter. Children's Charity. Designs as Nos. 536/8 in separate miniature sheets 69 × 69 mm, each with a face value of 60c. + 5c.
MS540 As Nos. 536/8 Set of 3 sheets 1·10 1·40

154 Benjamin Franklin and H.M.S. "Resolution"

1976. Bicent of American Revolution. Mult.
541 $1 Type **154** 6·00 1·50
542 $2 Captain Cook and H.M.S. "Resolution" 8·00 2·50
MS543 118 × 58 mm. $3 Cook, Franklin and H.M.S. "Resolution" (74 × 31 mm) 13·00 6·50

1976. Visit of Queen Elizabeth to U.S.A. Nos. 541/2 optd **Royal Visit July 1976**.
544 **154** $1 multicoloured 4·00 1·50
545 – $2 multicoloured 6·00 2·50
MS546 $3 Cook, Franklin and H.M.S. "Resolution" 7·00 5·50

156 Hurdling

157 "The Visitation"

1976. Olympic Games, Montreal. Multicoloured.
547 7c. Type **156** 20 10
548 7c. Hurdling (value on left) 20 10
549 15c. Hockey (value on right) 40 15
550 15c. Hockey (value on left) 40 15
551 30c. Fencing (value on right) 40 15
552 30c. Fencing (value on left) 40 15
553 35c. Football (value on right) 40 20
554 35c. Football (value on left) 40 20
MS555 104 × 146 mm. Nos. 547/54 3·50 2·00

1976. Christmas. Renaissance Sculptures. Mult.
556 6c. Type **157** 10 10
557 10c. "Adoration of the Shepherds" 10 10
558 15c. "Adoration of the Shepherds" (different) 15 10
559 20c. "The Epiphany" 20 20
560 35c. "The Holy Family" 25 25
MS561 116 × 110 mm. Nos. 556/60 1·00 1·75

1976. Christmas. Children's Charity. Designs as Nos. 556/60 in separate miniature sheets 66 × 80 mm, each with a face value of 75c. + 5c.
MS562 As Nos. 556/60 Set of 5 sheets 1·10 1·10

158 Obverse and Reverse of $5 Mangaia Kingfisher Coin

1976. National Wildlife and Conservation Day.
563 **158** $1 multicoloured 1·00 1·00

159 Imperial State Crown

1977. Silver Jubilee. Multicoloured.
564 25c. Type **159** 40 50
565 25c. The Queen with regalia 40 50
566 50c. Westminster Abbey 50 65
567 50c. Coronation coach 50 65
568 $1 The Queen and Prince Philip 80 90
569 $1 Royal Visit, 1974 80 90
MS570 130 × 136 mm. As Nos. 564/9 (borders and "COOK ISLANDS" in a different colour) 2·25 2·00

160 "Christ on the Cross"

161 "Virgin and Child" (Memling)

1977. Easter. 400th Birth Anniv of Rubens. Multicoloured.
571 7c. Type **160** 35 10
572 15c. "Christ on the Cross" 55 15
573 35c. "The Deposition of Christ" 1·10 30
MS574 118 × 65 mm. Nos. 571/3 1·40 1·60

1977. Easter. Children's Charity. Designs as Nos. 571/3 in separate miniature sheets 60 × 79 mm, each with a face value of 60c. + 5c.
MS575 As Nos. 571/3 Set of 3 sheets 1·00 1·00

1977. Christmas. Multicoloured.
576 6c. Type **161** 25 10
577 10c. "Madonna and Child with Saints and Donors" (Memling) 25 10
578 15c. "Adoration of the Kings" (Geertgen) 35 10
579 20c. "Virgin and Child with Saints" (Crivelli) 45 15
580 35c. "Adoration of the Magi" (16th century Flemish school) 60 20
MS581 118 × 111 mm. Nos. 576/80 1·40 1·75

1977. Christmas. Children's Charity. Designs as Nos. 576/80 in separate miniature sheets 69 × 69 mm, each with a face value of 75c. + 5c.
MS582 As Nos. 576/80 Set of 5 sheets 1·00 1·25

162 Obverse and Reverse of $5 Cook Islands Swiftlet Coin

1977. National Wildlife and Conservation Day.
583 **162** $1 multicoloured 1·00 65

163 Captain Cook and H.M.S. "Resolution" (from paintings by N. Dance and H. Roberts)

1978. Bicent of Discovery of Hawaii. Mult.
584 50c. Type **163** 1·00 60
585 $1 Earl of Sandwich and Cook landing at Owhyhee (from paintings by Thomas Gainsborough and J. Cleveley) 1·45 75
586 $2 Obverse and reverse of $200 coin and Cook monument, Hawaii 1·60 1·25
MS587 118 × 95 mm. Nos. 584/6 5·00 7·50

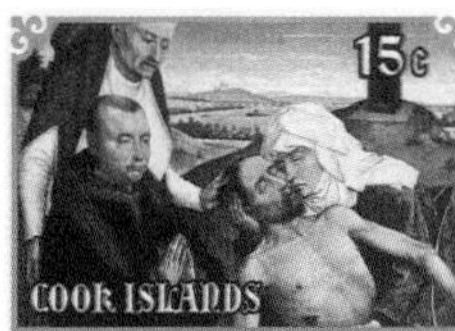

164 "Pieta" (Van der Weyden)

1978. Easter. Paintings from the National Gallery, London. Multicoloured.
588 15c. Type **164** 40 25
589 35c. "The Entombment" (Michelangelo) 50 40
590 75c. "The Supper at Emmaus" (Caravaggio) 75 65
MS591 114 × 96 mm. Nos. 588/90 1·50 2·00

1978. Easter. Children's Charity. Designs as Nos. 588/90 in separate miniature sheets, 85 × 72 mm, each with a face value of 60c. + 5c.
MS592 As Nos. 588/90 Set of 3 sheets 1·10 1·10

165 Queen Elizabeth II

169 "The Virgin and Child" (Van Der Weyden)

168 Obverse and Reverse of Cook Islands Warblers $5 Coin

1978. 25th Anniv of Coronation. Multicoloured.
593 50c. Type **165** 25 30
594 50c. The Lion of England 25 30
595 50c. Imperial State Crown 25 30
596 50c. Statue of Tangaroa (god) 25 30
597 70c. Type **165** 25 30
598 70c. Sceptre with Cross 25 30
599 70c. St. Edward's Crown 25 30
600 70c. Rarotongan staff god 25 30
MS601 103 × 142 mm. Nos. 593/600* 1·00 1·50
*In No. **MS**601 the designs of Nos. 595 and 599 are transposed.

1978. Nos. 466, 468, 473/4 and 478/82 surch.
602 5c. on 1½c. True heart cockle 60 10
603 7c. on ½c. Type **141** 65 15
604 10c. on 6c. Serpent's-head cowrie 70 15
605 10c. on 8c. Granulate frog shell 70 15
606 15c. on ½c. Type **141** 70 20
607 15c. on 25c. Royal oak scallop 70 20
608 15c. on 30c. Soldier cone 70 20
609 15c. on 50c. Textile or cloth of gold cone 70 20
610 15c. on 60c. Red-mouth olive 70 20
611 17c. on ½c. Type **141** 90 25
612 17c. on 50c. Textile or cloth of gold cone 90 25

1978. 250th Birth Anniv of Captain James Cook. Nos. 584/6 optd **1728 250th ANNIVERSARY OF COOK'S BIRTH 1978**.
613 50c. Type **163** 2·00 75
614 $1 Earl of Sandwich and Cook landing at Owhyhee 2·25 1·00
615 $2 $200 commemorative coin and Cook monument, Hawaii 2·50 2·00
MS616 Nos. 613/15 14·00 17·00

1978. National Wildlife and Conservation Day.
617 **168** $1 multicoloured 1·00 1·00

1978. Christmas. Paintings. Multicoloured.
618 15c. Type **169** 45 15
619 17c. "The Virgin and Child" (Crivelli) 45 20
620 35c. "The Virgin and Child" (Murillo) 80 35
MS621 107 × 70 mm. Nos. 618/20 1·50 1·50

1979. Christmas. Children's Charity. Designs as Nos. 618/20 in separate miniature sheets 57 × 87 mm, each with a face value of 75c. +5c.
MS622 As Nos. 618/20 Set of 3 sheets 1·00 1·00

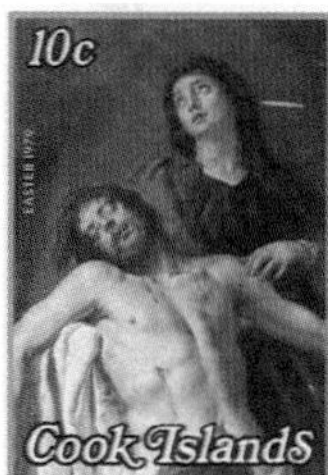

170 Virgin with Body of Christ

171 "Captain Cook" (James Weber)

1979. Easter. Details of Painting "Descent" by Gaspar de Crayar. Multicoloured.
623 10c. Type **170** 25 10
624 12c. St. John 30 20
625 15c. Mary Magdalene 35 25
626 20c. Weeping angels 45 30
MS627 83 × 100 mm. As Nos. 623/6, but each with a charity premium of 2c. 65 75
Stamps from No. **MS**627 are slightly smaller, 32 × 40 mm, and are without borders.

1979. Death Bicentenary of Captain Cook. Mult.
628 20c. Type **171** 40 20
629 30c. H.M.S. "Resolution" 50 35
630 35c. H.M.S. "Royal George" (ship of the line) 50 45
631 50c. "Death of Captain Cook" (George Carter) 55 60
MS632 78 × 112 mm. Nos. 628/31 1·75 1·25
Stamps from No. **MS**632 have black borders.

172 Post-Rider

174 Brother and Sister

1979. Death Centenary of Sir Rowland Hill. Mult.
633 30c. Type **172** 20 20
634 30c. Mail coach 20 20
635 30c. Automobile 20 20
636 30c. Diesel train 20 20
637 35c. "Cap-Hornier" (full-rigged ship) 20 20
638 35c. River steamer 20 20
639 35c. "Deutschland" (liner) 20 20
640 35c. "United States" (liner) 20 20
641 50c. Balloon "Le Neptune" 30 25
642 50c. Junkers F13 airplane 30 25

643 50c. Airship "Graf Zeppelin" 30 25
644 50c. Concorde 30 25
MS645 132 × 104 mm. Nos. 633/44 3·75 4·00

1979. Nos. 466, 468 and 481 surch.
646 6c. on ½c. Type **141** 20 30
647 10c. on 1½c. Cockle shell 25 20
648 15c. on 60c. Olive shell 40 40

1979. International Year of the Child. Mult.
649 30c. Type **174** 25 25
650 50c. Boy with tree drum 40 40
651 65c. Children dancing 50 50
MS652 102 × 75 mm. As Nos. 649/51, but each with a charity premium of 5c. 1·00 1·50
Designs for stamps from No. **MS**652 are as Nos. 649/51 but have I.Y.C. emblem in red.

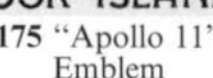

175 "Apollo 11" Emblem

177 Glass Christmas Tree Ornaments

176 Obverse and Reverse of $5 Rarotongan Fruit Dove Coin

1979. 10th Anniv of "Apollo 11" Moon Landing. Multicoloured.
653 30c. Type **175** 40 55
654 50c. "Apollo 11" crew 50 75
655 60c. Neil Armstrong on the Moon 65 80
656 65c. Splashdown recovery 70 90
MS657 119 × 105 mm. Nos. 653/6 2·75 2·50

1979. National Wildlife and Conservation Day.
658 **176** $1 multicoloured 1·60 2·50

1979. Christmas. Multicoloured.
659 6c. Type **177** (postage) 10 10
660 10c. Hibiscus and star 10 10
661 12c. Poinsettia, bells and candle 15 10
662 15c. Poinsettia leaves and Tiki (god) 15 15
663 20c. Type **177** (air) 20 15
664 25c. As No. 660 25 20
665 30c. As No. 661 30 25
666 35c. As No. 662 35 30

1980. Christmas. As Nos. 659/66 but with charity premium.
667 6c.+2c. Type **177** (postage) 10 10
668 10c.+2c. Hibiscus and star 15 15
669 12c.+2c. Poinsettia, bells and candle 15 20
670 15c.+2c. Poinsettia leaves and Tiki (god) 15 20
671 20c.+4c. Type **177** (air) 15 25
672 25c.+4c. As No. 660 15 25
673 30c.+4c. As No. 661 20 30
674 35c.+4c. As No. 662 25 35

178 "Flagellation"

181 Queen Elizabeth the Queen Mother

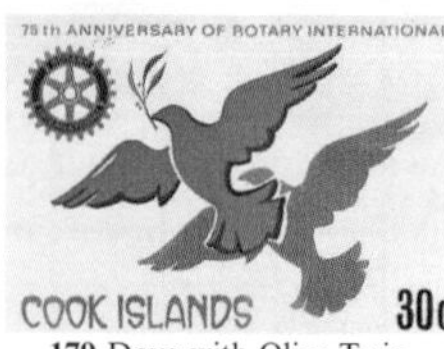

179 Dove with Olive Twig

1980. Easter. Illustrations by Gustav Dore. Each gold and brown.
675 20c. Type **178** 25 20
676 20c. "Crown of Thorns" 25 20
677 30c. "Jesus Insulted" 35 30
678 30c. "Jesus Falls" 35 30
679 35c. "The Crucifixion" 40 30
680 35c. "The Descent from the Cross" 40 30
MS681 120 × 110 mm. As Nos. 675/80, but each with a charity premium of 2c. 1·10 1·50

1980. Easter. Children's Charity. Designs as Nos. 675/80 in separate miniature sheets 60 × 71 mm, each with a face value of 75c. + 5c.
MS682 As Nos. 675/80 Set of 6 sheets 1·00 1·50

1980. 75th Anniv of Rotary International. Mult.
683 30c. Type **179** 35 35
684 35c. Hibiscus flower 40 40
685 50c. Ribbons 50 50
MS686 72 × 113 mm. Nos. 683/5, but each with a charity premium of 3c. 1·10 1·50

1980. "Zeapex 80" International Stamp Exhibition, Auckland. Nos. 633/44 optd **ZEAPEX STAMP EXHIBITION—AUCKLAND 1980** and New Zealand 1865 1s. Stamp.
687 30c. Type **172** 35 25
688 30c. Mail coach 35 25
689 30c. Automobile 35 25
690 30c. Diesel train 35 25
691 35c. "Cap-Hornier" (full-rigged ship) 40 30
692 35c. River steamer 40 30
693 35c. "Deutschland" (liner) 40 30
694 35c. "United States" (liner) 40 30
695 50c. Balloon "Le Neptune" 60 35
696 50c. Junkers "F13" airplane 60 35
697 50c. Airship"Graf Zeppelin" 60 35
698 50c. Concorde 60 35
MS699 132 × 104 mm. Nos. 687/98 6·00 6·00

1980. 80th Birthday of the Queen Mother.
701 **181** 50c. multicoloured 1·00 1·00
MS702 64 × 78 mm. **181** $2 multicoloured 1·25 1·75

182 Satellites orbiting Moon

1980. 350th Death Anniv of Johannes Kepler (astronomer). Multicoloured.
703 12c. Type **182** 50 35
704 12c. Space-craft orbiting Moon 50 35
705 50c. Space-craft orbiting Moon (different) 1·00 80
706 50c. Astronaut and Moon vehicle 1·00 80
MS707 122 × 122 mm. Nos. 703/6 2·75 2·75

183 Scene from novel "From the Earth to the Moon"

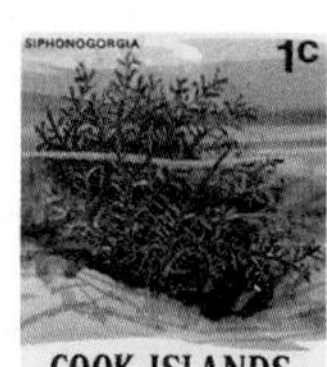

184 "Siphonogorgia"

1980. 75th Death Anniv of Jules Verne (author).
708 **183** 20c. multicoloured 45 35
709 – 20c. multicoloured 45 35
710 – 30c. multicoloured (mauve background) 55 45
711 – 30c. multicoloured (blue background) 55 45
MS712 121 × 122 mm. Nos. 708/11 2·75 2·25
DESIGNS: Showing scenes from the novel "From the Earth to the Moon".

1980. Corals (1st series). Multicoloured.
713 1c. Type **184** 30 30
714 1c. "Pavona praetorta" 30 30
715 1c. "Stylaster echinatus" 30 30
716 1c. "Tubastraea" 30 30
717 3c. "Millepora alcicornis" 30 30
718 3c. "Junceella gemmacea" 30 30
719 3c. "Fungia fungites" 30 30
720 3c. "Heliofungia actiniformis" 30 30
721 4c. "Distichopora violacea" 30 30
722 4c. "Stylaster" 30 30
723 4c. "Gonipora" 30 30
724 4c. "Caulastraea echinulata" 30 30
725 5c. "Ptilosarcus gurneyi" 30 30
726 5c. "Stylophora pistillata" 30 30
727 5c. "Melithaea squamata" 30 30
728 5c. "Porites andrewsi" 30 30
729 6c. "Lobophyllia bemprichii" 30 30
730 6c. "Palauastrea ramosa" 30 30
731 6c. "Bellonella indica" 30 30
732 6c. "Pectinia alcicornis" 30 30
733 8c. "Sarcophyton digitatum" 30 30
734 8c. "Melithaea albitincta" 30 30
735 8c. "Plerogyra sinuosa" 30 30
736 8c. "Dendropyllia gracilis" 30 30
737 10c. As Type **184** 30 30
738 10c. As No. 714 30 30
739 10c. As No. 715 30 30
740 10c. As No. 716 30 30
741 12c. As No. 717 30 30
742 12c. As No. 718 30 30
743 12c. As No. 719 30 30
744 12c. As No. 720 30 30
745 15c. As No. 721 30 30
746 15c. As No. 722 30 30
747 15c. As No. 723 30 30
748 15c. As No. 724 30 30
749 20c. As No. 725 35 30
750 20c. As No. 726 35 30
751 20c. As No. 727 35 30
752 20c. As No. 728 35 30
753 25c. As No. 729 35 30
754 25c. As No. 730 35 30
755 25c. As No. 731 35 30
756 25c. As No. 732 35 30
757 30c. As No. 733 40 30
758 30c. As No. 734 40 30
759 30c. As No. 735 40 30
760 30c. As No. 736 40 30
761 35c. Type **184** 45 35
762 35c. As No. 714 45 35
763 35c. As No. 715 45 35
764 35c. As No. 716 45 35
765 50c. As No. 717 65 75
766 50c. As No. 718 65 75
767 50c. As No. 719 65 75
768 50c. As No. 720 65 75
769 60c. As No. 721 75 75
770 60c. As No. 722 75 75
771 60c. As No. 723 75 75
772 60c. As No. 724 75 75
773 70c. As No. 725 2·50 75
774 70c. As No. 726 2·50 75
775 70c. As No. 727 2·50 75
776 70c. As No. 728 2·50 75
777 80c. As No. 729 2·50 80
778 80c. As No. 730 2·50 80
779 80c. As No. 731 2·50 80
780 80c. As No. 732 2·50 80
781 $1 As No. 733 3·75 1·00
782 $1 As No. 734 3·75 1·00
783 $1 As No. 735 3·75 1·00
784 $1 As No. 736 3·75 1·00
785 $2 As No. 723 12·00 2·25
786 $3 As No. 720 12·00 2·25
787 $4 As No. 726 4·50 13·00
788 $6 As No. 715 6·00 16·00
789 $10 As No. 734 27·00 35·00
Nos. 761/74 are 30 × 40 mm, and Nos. 785/9, which include a portrait of Queen Elizabeth II in each design, are 55 × 35 mm.
See also Nos. 966/94.

185 Annunciation

187 Prince Charles

186 "The Crucifixion" (from book of Saint-Amand)

1980. Christmas. Scenes from 13th-century French Prayer Books. Multicoloured.
801 15c. Type **185** 25 15
802 30c. The Visitation 35 25
803 40c. The Nativity 45 30
804 50c. The Epiphany 60 40
MS805 89 × 114 mm. Nos. 801/4 1·50 1·50

1981. Christmas. Children's Charity. Designs as Nos. 801/4 in separate miniature sheets 55 × 68 mm, each with a face value of 75c +5c. Imperf.
MS806 As Nos. 801/4 Set of 4 sheets 1·50 1·50

1981. Easter. Illustrations from 12th-century French Prayer Books. Multicoloured.
807 15c. Type **186** 30 30
808 25c. "Placing in Tomb" (from book of Ingeburge) 35 35
809 40c. "Mourning at the Sepulchre" (from book of Ingeburge) 45 45
MS810 72 × 116 mm. As Nos. 807/9, but each with a charity premium of 2c. 1·00 1·00

1981. Easter. Children's Charity. Designs as Nos. 807/9 in separate miniature sheets 64 × 53 mm, each with a face value of 75c. + 5c. Imperf.
MS811 As Nos. 807/9 Set of 3 sheets 1·10 1·10

1981. Royal Wedding. Multicoloured.
812 $1 Type **187** 50 1·10
813 $2 Prince Charles and Lady Diana Spencer 60 1·40
MS814 106 × 59 mm. Nos. 812/13 1·10 2·50

188 Footballers

1981. World Cup Football Championship, Spain (1982). Designs showing footballers. Mult.
815 20c. Type **188** 40 20
816 20c. Figures to right of stamp 40 20
817 30c. Figures to left 50 30
818 30c. Figures to right 50 30
819 35c. Figures to left 50 35
820 35c. Figures to right 50 35
821 50c. Figures to left 65 45
822 50c. Figures to right 65 45
MS823 180 × 94 mm. As Nos. 815/22, but each with a charity premium of 3c. 5·50 7·00
The two designs of each value were printed together, se-tenant, in horizontal pairs throughout the sheet, forming composite designs.

1981. International Year for Disabled Persons. Nos. 812/13 surch **+5c.**
824 $1+5c. Type **187** 75 1·75
825 $2+5c. Prince Charles and Lady Diana Spencer 1·00 2·50
MS826 106 × 59 mm. $1 + 10c, $2 + 10c. As Nos. 824/5 1·25 4·00

190 "Holy Virgin with Child"

1982. Christmas. Details of Paintings by Rubens. Multicoloured.
827 8c. Type **190** 55 20
828 15c. "Coronation of St. Catherine" 65 35
829 40c. "Adoration of the Shepherds" 90 80
830 50c. "Adoration of the Magi" 1·00 1·00
MS831 86 × 110 mm. As Nos. 827/30, but each with a charity premium of 3c. 3·50 4·00

1982. Christmas. Children's Charity. Designs as Nos. 827/30 in separate miniature sheets 62 × 78 mm, each with a face value of 75c. +5c.
MS832 As Nos. 827/30 Set of 4 sheets 3·50 4·00

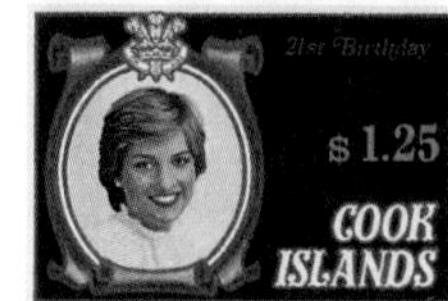

191 Princess of Wales (inscr "21st Birthday")

1982. 21st Birthday of Princess of Wales. Multicoloured.
833 $1.25 Type **191** 2·25 1·50
834 $1.25 As Type **191**, but inscr "1 July 1982" 2·25 1·50
835 $2.50 Princess (inscr "21st Birthday") (different) 3·00 2·25
836 $2.50 As No. 835, but inscr "1 July 1982" 3·00 2·25
MS837 92 × 72 mm. $1.25, Type **191**; $2.50, As No. 835. Both inscribed "21st Birthday 1 July 1982" 7·00 4·50

1982. Birth of Prince William of Wales (1st issue). Nos. 812/13 optd.
838 $1 Type **187** 1·50 1·25
839 $1 Type **187** 1·50 1·25
840 $2 Prince Charles and Lady Diana Spencer 2·50 2·00
841 $2 Prince Charles and Lady Diana Spencer 2·50 2·00
MS842 106 × 59 mm. Nos. 812/13 optd **21 JUNE 1982. ROYAL BIRTH** 4·00 4·00
OPTS: Nos. 838 and 840, **ROYAL BIRTH 21 JUNE 1982**; 839 and 841, **PRINCE WILLIAM OF WALES**.

1982. Birth of Prince William of Wales (2nd issue). As Nos. 833/6 but with changed inscriptions. Multicoloured.
843 $1.25 As Type **191**, inscribed "Royal Birth" 2·25 1·00
844 $1.25 As Type **191**, inscribed "21 June 1982" 2·25 1·00
845 $2.50 As No. 835, inscribed "Royal Birth" 2·75 1·50
846 $2.50 As No. 835, inscribed "21 June 1982" 2·75 1·50
MS847 92 × 73 mm. $1.25, As Type **191**; $2.50, As No. 835. Both inscribed "Royal Birth 21 June 1982". 6·00 2·75

193 "The Accordionist" (inscr "Serenade")

194 Franklin D. Roosevelt

1982. Norman Rockwell (painter) Commemoration. Multicoloured.

848 5c. Type **193** 15 10
849 10c. "Spring" (inscr "The Hikers") 20 15
850 20c. "The Doctor and the Doll" 25 25
851 30c. "Home from Camp" . . 25 30

1982. Air. American Anniversaries. Multicoloured.

852 60c. Type **194** . . . . 1·50 80
853 80c. Benjamin Franklin . . . 1·75 1·00
854 $1.40 George Washington . . 2·00 2·25
MS855 116 × 60 mm. Nos. 852/4 4·75 3·00

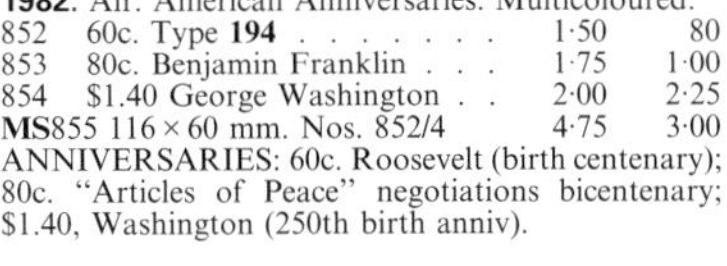

ANNIVERSARIES: 60c. Roosevelt (birth centenary); 80c. "Articles of Peace" negotiations bicentenary; $1.40, Washington (250th birth anniv).

195 "Virgin with Garlands" (detail, Rubens) and Princess Diana with Prince William

1982. Christmas.

856 **195** 35c. multicoloured . . . . 1·50 70
857 – 48c. multicoloured . . . . 2·00 1·50
858 – 60c. multicoloured . . . . 2·25 2·00
859 – $1.70 multicoloured . . . 3·25 4·25
MS860 104 × 83 mm. 60c. × 4. Designs, each 27 × 32 mm, forming complete painting "Virgin with Garlands" 6·50 7·50

DESIGNS: 48c. to $1.70, Different details from Ruben's painting "Virgin with Garlands".

196 Princess Diana and Prince William

1982. Christmas. Birth of Prince William of Wales. Children's Charity. Sheet 73 × 59 mm.

MS861 **196** 75c. + 5c. multicoloured 2·75 3·50

No. **MS**861 comes with 4 different background designs showing details from painting "Virgin with Garlands" (Rubens).

197 Statue of Tangaroa

198 Scouts using Map and Compass

1983. Commonwealth Day. Multicoloured.

862 60c. Type **197** 60 50
863 60c. Rarotonga oranges . . . 60 50
864 60c. Rarotonga Airport . . . 60 50
865 60c. Prime Minister Sir Thomas Davis 60 50

1983. 75th Anniv of Boy Scout Movement and 125th Anniv of Lord Baden-Powell (founder). Multicoloured.

866 12c. Type **198** 55 20
867 12c. Hiking 55 20
868 36c. Campfire cooking . . . 80 40
869 36c. Erecting tent 80 40
870 48c. Hauling on rope . . . . 1·00 55
871 48c. Using bos'n's chair . . . 1·00 55
872 60c. Digging hole for sapling 1·00 70
873 60c. Planting sapling . . . . 1·00 70
MS874 161 × 132 mm. As Nos. 866/73, but each with a premium of 2c. 3·00 3·50

1983. 15th World Scout Jamboree, Alberta, Canada. Nos. 866/73 optd **XV WORLD JAMBOREE** (Nos. 875, 877, 879, 881) or **ALBERTA, CANADA 1983** (others).

875 12c. Type **198** 60 20
876 12c. Hiking 60 20
877 36c. Campfire cooking . . . 90 40
878 36c. Erecting tent 90 40
879 48c. Hauling on rope . . . . 1·10 55
880 48c. Using bos'n's chair . . . 1·10 55
881 60c. Digging hole for sapling 1·25 70
882 60c. Planting sapling . . . . 1·25 70
MS883 161 × 132 mm. As Nos. 875/82, but each with a premium of 2c. 2·75 3·25

1983. Various stamps surch.

884 – 18c. on 8c. mult (No. 733) 75 50
885 – 18c. on 8c. mult (No. 734) 75 50
886 – 18c. on 8c. mult (No. 735) 75 50
887 – 18c. on 8c. mult (No. 736) 75 50
888 – 36c. on 15c. mult (No. 745) . . . . . . 1·25 85
889 – 36c. on 15c. mult (No. 746) . . . . . . 1·25 85
890 – 36c. on 15c. mult (No. 747) . . . . . . 1·25 85
891 – 36c. on 15c. mult (No. 748) . . . . . . 1·25 85
892 – 36c. on 30c. mult (No. 757) . . . . . . 1·25 85
893 – 36c. on 30c. mult (No. 758) . . . . . . 1·25 85
894 – 36c. on 30c. mult (No. 759) . . . . . . 1·25 85
895 – 36c. on 30c. mult (No. 760) . . . . . . 1·25 85
896 **184** 36c. on 35c. mult . . . . 1·25 85
897 – 36c. on 35c. mult (No. 762) . . . . . . 1·25 85
898 – 36c. on 35c. mult (No. 763) . . . . . . 1·25 85
899 – 36c. on 35c. mult (No. 764) . . . . . . 1·25 85
900 – 48c. on 25c. mult (No. 753) . . . . . . 1·50 1·25
901 – 48c. on 25c. mult (No. 754) . . . . . . 1·50 1·25
902 – 48c. on 25c. mult (No. 755) . . . . . . 1·50 1·25
903 – 48c. on 25c. mult (No. 756) . . . . . . 1·50 1·25
904 – 72c. on 70c. mult (No. 773) . . . . . . 2·50 1·75
905 – 72c. on 70c. mult (No. 774) . . . . . . 2·50 1·75
906 – 72c. on 70c. mult (No. 775) . . . . . . 2·50 1·75
907 – 72c. on 70c. mult (No. 776) . . . . . . 2·50 1·75
908 – 96c. on $1.40 multicoloured (No. 854) 2·00 2·00
909 – 96c. on $2 mult (No. 813) 8·50 5·50
910 – 96c. on $2.50 mult (No. 835) . . . . . . 3·00 3·00
911 – 96c. on $2.50 mult (No. 836) . . . . . . 3·00 3·00
912 – $5.60 on $6 mult (No. 788) . . . . . . 23·00 18·00
913 – $5.60 on $10 mult (No. 789) . . . . . . 23·00 18·00

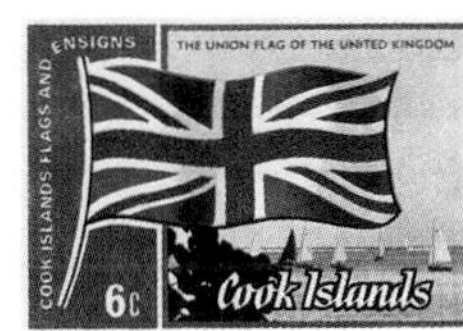

202 Union Flag

1983. Cook Islands Flags and Ensigns. Multicoloured.

914 6c. Type **202** (postage) . . . 65 60
915 6c. Group Federal flag . . . 65 60
916 12c. Rarotonga ensign . . . 80 65
917 12c. Flag of New Zealand . . 80 65
918 15c. Cook Islands' flag (1973–79) 80 65
919 15c. Cook Islands' National flag 80 65
920 20c. Type **202** (air) 80 70
921 20c. Group Federal flag . . . 80 70
922 30c. Rarotonga ensign . . . 90 75
923 30c. Flag of New Zealand . . 90 75
924 35c. Cook Islands' flag (1973–1979) 95 75
925 35c. Cook Islands' National flag 95 75
MS926 Two sheets, each 132 × 120 mm. (a) Nos. 914/19. (b) Nos. 920/5. P 13 2·75 4·25

203 Dish Aerial, Satellite Earth Station

204 "La Belle Jardiniere"

1983. World Communications Year.

927 – 36c. multicoloured 70 80
928 – 48c. multicoloured 85 95
929 **203** 60c. multicoloured . . . . 1·10 1·50
930 – 96c. multicoloured . . . . 1·75 2·75
MS931 90 × 65 mm. $2 multicoloured 2·25 2·50

DESIGNS: 36, 48, 96c. Various satellites.

1983. Christmas. 500th Birth Anniv of Raphael. Multicoloured.

932 12c. Type **204** 70 40
933 18c. "Madonna and Child with five Saints" 95 60
934 36c. "Madonna and Child with St. John" . . . . . . 1·60 1·60
935 48c. "Madonna of the Fish" 2·00 2·00
936 60c. "Madonna of the Baldacchino" . . . . . . 2·50 3·50
MS937 139 × 113 mm. As Nos. 932/6, but each with a premium of 3c. 2·00 2·50

1983. Christmas. 500th Birth Anniv of Raphael. Children's Charity. Designs as Nos. 932/6 in separate miniature sheets 66 × 82 mm., each with a face value of 85c. + 5c.

MS938 As Nos. 932/6 Set of 5 sheets 4·50 3·75

205 Montgolfier Balloon, 1783

1984. Bicentenary (1983) of Manned Flight. Mult.

939 36c. Type **205** 50 50
940 48c. Ascent of Adorne, Strasbourg, 1784 . . . . 60 60
941 60c. Balloon driven by sails, 1785 . . . . 75 90
942 72c. Ascent of man on horse, 1798 . . . . 90 1·10
943 96c. Godard's aerial acrobatics, 1850 . . . . . 1·00 1·40
MS944 104 × 85 mm. $2.50, Blanchard and Jeffries crossing Channel, 1785 1·50 2·25
MS945 122 × 132 mm. As Nos. 939/43, but each with a premium of 5c. 1·50 2·25

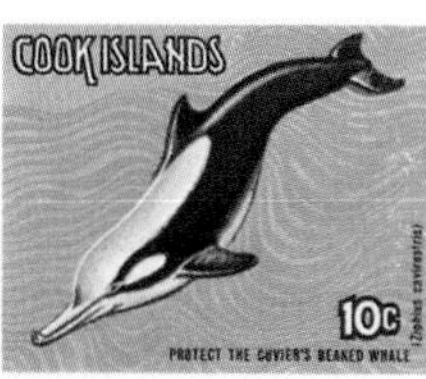

206 Cuvier's Beaked Whale

1984. Save the Whale. Multicoloured.

946 10c. Type **206** 50 50
947 18c. Risso's dolphin 75 75
948 20c. True's beaked whale . . 75 75
949 24c. Long-finned pilot whale 80 80
950 30c. Narwhal 90 90
951 36c. White whale . . . . . . 1·10 1·10
952 42c. Common dolphin . . . 1·40 1·40
953 48c. Commerson's dolphin 1·60 1·60
954 60c. Bottle-nosed dolphin . . 1·90 1·90
955 72c. Sowerby's beaked whale 2·00 2·00
956 96c. Common porpoise . . . 2·50 2·50
957 $2 Boutu . . . . 3·25 3·25

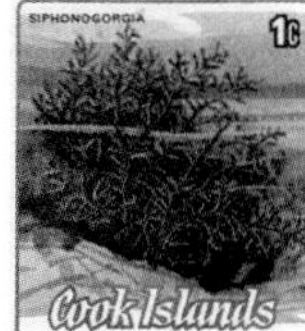

207 Athens, 1896

208 "Siphonogorgia"

1984. Olympic Games, Los Angeles. Multicoloured.

958 18c. Type **207** 50 40
959 24c. Paris, 1900 . . . . . . 55 45
960 36c. St. Louis, 1904 . . . . 65 55
961 48c. London, 1948 . . . . . 75 65
962 60c. Tokyo, 1964 . . . . . . 85 75
963 72c. Berlin, 1936 . . . . . . 1·00 90
964 96c. Rome, 1960 . . . . . . 1·10 1·00
965 $1.20 Los Angeles, 1930 . . . 1·25 1·25

1984. Corals (2nd series). New designs and Nos. 785/9 surch. Multicoloured.

966 1c. Type **208** 30 10
967 2c. "Millepora alcicornis" . . 30 10
968 3c. "Distichopora violacea" 40 10
969 5c. "Ptilosarcus gurneyi" . . 45 10
970 10c. "Lobophyllia bemprichii" 50 10
971 12c. "Sarcophyton digitatum" 60 15
972 14c. "Pavona praetorta" . . 60 15
973 18c. "Junceella gemmacea" 70 20
974 20c. "Stylaster" 70 20
975 24c. "Stylophora pistillata" 70 20
976 30c. "Palauastrea ramosa" 1·00 25
977 36c. "Melithaea albitincta" 1·25 30
978 40c. "Stylaster echinatus" . . 1·25 30
979 42c. "Fungia fungites" . . . 1·25 35
980 48c. "Gonipora" . . . . . . 1·25 35
981 50c. "Melithaea squamata" 1·75 45
982 52c. "Bellonella indica" . . . 1·75 60
983 55c. "Plerogyra sinuosa" . . 1·75 65
984 60c. "Tubastraea" . . . . . 1·90 70
985 70c. "Heliofungia actiniformis" . . . . . . 2·00 85
986 85c. "Caulastraea echinulata" 2·25 1·00
987 96c. "Porites andrewsi" . . . 2·50 1·10
988 $1.10 "Pectinia alcicornis" . . 2·50 1·40
989 $1.20 "Dendrophyllia gracilis" . . . . 2·50 1·50
990 $3.60 on $2 "Gonipora" (55 × 35 mm) . . . . . . 5·50 4·00
991 $4.20 on $3 "Heliofungia actiniformis" (55 × 35 mm) 6·00 5·00
992 $5 on $4 "Stylophora pistillata" (55 × 35 mm) . . 6·50 5·50
993 $7.20 on $6 "Stylaster echinatus" (55 × 35 mm) . . 8·50 8·50
994 $9.60 on $10 "Melithaea albitincta" (55 × 35 mm) . . 10·00 10·00

1984. Olympic Gold Medal Winners. Nos. 963/5 optd.

995 72c. Berlin, 1936 (optd **Equestrian Team Dressage Germany**) 60 65
996 96c. Rome, 1960 (optd **Decathlon Daley Thompson Great Britain**) 80 85
997 $1.20 Los Angeles, 1930 (optd **Four Gold Medals Carl Lewis U.S.A.**) . . . . 1·00 1·10

211 Captain Cook's Cottage, Melbourne

1984. "Ausipex" International Stamp Exhibition, Melbourne. Multicoloured.

998 36c. Type **211** . . . . . . 2·00 1·50
999 48c. H.M.S. "Endeavour" careened for Repairs" (Sydney Parkinson) . . . 3·25 2·50
1000 60c. "Cook's landing at Botany Bay" (E. Phillips Fox) . . . . 3·50 3·25
1001 $2 "Captain James Cook" (John Webber) . . . . . 4·25 4·25
MS1002 140 × 100 mm. As Nos. 998/1001, but each with a face value of 90c. 7·50 7·50

1984. Birth of Prince Henry. Nos. 812 and 833/6 variously optd or surch also (No. 1007).

1003 $1.25 Optd **Commemorating- 15 Sept. 1984** (No. 833) 1·75 1·25
1004 $1.25 Optd **Birth H.R.H. Prince Henry** (No. 834) 1·75 1·25
1005 $2.50 Optd **Commemorating- 15 Sept. 1984** (No. 835) 2·50 2·25
1006 $2.50 Optd **Birth H.R.H. Prince Henry** (No. 836) 2·50 2·25
1007 $3 on $1 Optd **Royal Birth Prince Henry 15 Sept. 1984** (No. 812) . . . . . 4·50 4·50

213 "Virgin on Throne with Child" (Giovanni Bellini)

214 Downy Woodpecker

1984. Christmas. Multicoloured.
1008 36c. Type **213** . . . . . . 1·50 40
1009 48c. "Virgin and Child" (anonymous, 15th century) . . . . 1·60 60
1010 60c. "Virgin and Child with Saints" (Alvise Vivarini) 1·75 80
1011 96c. "Virgin and Child with Angels" (H. Memling) . . 2·00 1·60
1012 $1.20 "Adoration of Magi" (G. Tiepolo) . . . . . . 2·25 2·00
MS1013 120 × 113 mm. As Nos. 1008/12, but each with a premium of 5c. 4·25 3·25

1984. Christmas. Designs as Nos. 1008/12 in separate miniature sheets 62 × 76 mm, each with a face value of 95c. + 5c.
MS1014 As Nos. 1008/12 Set of 5 sheets 5·00 5·50

1985. Birth Bicentenary of John J. Audubon (ornithologist). Designs showing original paintings. Multicoloured.
1015 30c. Type **214** . . . . . . 2·50 1·25
1016 55c. Black-throated blue warbler . . . . 2·75 1·75
1017 65c. Yellow-throated warbler . . . . 3·00 2·25
1018 75c. Chestnut-sided warbler 3·25 2·75
1019 95c. Dickcissel . . . . . . 3·25 3·00
1020 $1.15 White-crowned sparrow . . . . 3·25 3·50
MS1021 Three sheets, each 76 × 75 mm. (a) $1.30, Red-cockaded woodpecker. (b) $2.80, Seaside sparrow. (c) $5.30, Zenaida dove Set of 3 sheets 13·00 8·50

215 "The Kingston Flyer" (New Zealand)

1985. Famous Trains. Multicoloured.
1022 20c. Type **215** 40 50
1023 55c. Class 625 locomotive (Italy) 55 85
1024 65c. Gotthard electric locomotive (Switzerland) 60 90
1025 75c. Union Pacific diesel locomotive No. 6900 (U.S.A.) . . . . 75 1·10
1026 95c. Canadian National "Super Continental" type diesel locomotive (Canada) . . . . 75 1·25
1027 $1.15 TGV express train (France) . . . . 80 1·50
1028 $2.20 "The Flying Scotsman" (Great Britain) 85 2·50
1029 $3.40 "Orient Express" . . 90 3·75
No. 1023 is inscribed "640" in error.

216 "Helena Fourment" (Peter Paul Rubens)

217 "Lady Elizabeth 1908" (Mabel Hankey)

1985. International Youth Year. Multicoloured.
1030 55c. Type **216** . . . . . . 3·25 2·75
1031 65c. "Vigee-Lebrun and Daughter" (E. Vigee-Lebrun) . . . . 3·50 3·25
1032 75c. "On the Terrace" (Renoir) . . . . 3·75 3·50
1033 $1.30 "Young Mother Sewing" (M. Cassatt) . . 4·75 6·50
MS1034 103 × 106 mm. As Nos. 1030/3, but each with a premium of 10c. 8·00 5·50

1985. Life and Times of Queen Elizabeth the Queen Mother. Designs showing paintings. Multicoloured.
1035 65c. Type **217** 40 50
1036 75c. "Duchess of York, 1923" (Savely Sorine) . . 45 60
1037 $1.15 "Duchess of York, 1925" (Philip de Laszlo) 55 85
1038 $2.80 "Queen Elizabeth, 1938" (Sir Gerald Kelly) 1·40 2·25
MS1039 69 × 81 mm. $5.30, As $2.80 2·50 3·50
For these designs in a miniature sheet, each with a face value of 95c., see No. **MS**1079.

218 Albert Henry (Prime Minister, 1965–78)

219 Golf

1985. 20th Anniv of Self-government. Mult.
1040 30c. Type **218** 80 60
1041 50c. Sir Thomas Davis (Prime Minister, 1978–April 1983 and from November 1983) . . . . 1·25 1·25
1042 65c. Geoffrey Henry (Prime Minister, April–November 1983) . . . . 1·50 1·75
MS1043 134 × 70 mm. As Nos. 1040/2, but each with a face value of 55c. 1·75 2·00

1985. South Pacific Mini Games, Rarotonga. Multicoloured.
1044 55c. Type **219** . . . . . . 4·00 3·50
1045 65c. Rugby . . . . 4·00 4·00
1046 75c. Tennis . . . . 5·50 6·00
MS1047 126 × 70 mm. Nos. 1044/6, but each with a premium of 10c. 11·00 13·00

220 Sea Horse, Gearwheel and Leaves

221 "Madonna of the Magnificat"

1985. Pacific Conference, Rarotonga.
1048 **220** 55c. black, gold and red 1·10 65
1049 – 65c. black, gold and violet . . . . 1·25 80
1050 – 75c. black, gold and green . . . . 1·40 1·10
MS1051 126 × 81 mm. As Nos. 1048/50, but each with a face value of 50c. 1·60 2·00
No. 1048 shows the South Pacific Bureau for Economic Co-operation logo and is inscribed "S.P.E.C. Meeting, 30 July–1 August 1985, Rarotonga". No. 1049 also shows the S.P.E.C. logo, but is inscribed "South Pacific Forum, 4–6 August 1985, Rarotonga". No. 1050 shows the Pacific Islands Conference logo and the inscription "Pacific Islands Conference, 7–10 August 1985, Rarotonga".

1985. Christmas. Virgin and Child Paintings by Botticelli. Multicoloured.
1052 55c. Type **221** . . . . . . 2·25 1·25
1053 65c. "Madonna with Pomegranate" . . . . . 2·50 1·25
1054 75c. "Madonna and Child with Six Angels" . . . . 2·75 1·60
1055 95c. "Madonna and Child with St. John" . . . . . 3·00 2·00
MS1056 90 × 104 mm. As Nos. 1052/5, but each with a face value of 50c. 5·00 3·75

1985. Christmas. Virgin and Child Paintings by Botticelli. Square designs (46 × 46 mm) as Nos. 1052/5 in separate miniature sheets, 50 × 51 mm, with face values of $1.20, $1.45, $2.20 and $2.75. Imperf.
MS1057 As Nos. 1052/5 Set of 4 sheets 9·00 11·00

222 "The Eve of the Deluge" (John Martin)

223 Queen Elizabeth II

1986. Appearance of Halley's Comet. Paintings. Multicoloured.
1058 55c. Type **222** . . . . . . 1·25 1·25
1059 65c. "Lot and his Daughters" (Lucas van Leyden) . . . . 1·40 1·40
1060 75c. "Auspicious Comet" (from treatise c. 1857) . . 1·50 1·50
1061 $1.25 "Events following Charles I" (Herman Saftleven) . . . . 2·25 2·25
1062 $2 "Ossian receiving Napoleonic Officers" (Anne Louis Girodet-Trioson) . . . . 3·00 3·00
MS1063 130 × 100 mm. As Nos. 1058/62, but each with a face value of 70c. 4·75 6·00
MS1064 84 × 63 mm. $4 "Halley's Comet of 1759 over the Thames" (Samuel Scott) 7·50 8·50

1986. 60th Birthday of Queen Elizabeth II. Designs showing formal portraits.
1065 **223** 95c. multicoloured . . . 1·40 1·50
1066 – $1.25 multicoloured . . 1·60 1·75
1067 – $1.50 multicoloured . . 1·75 2·00
MS1068 Three sheets, each 44 × 75 mm. As Nos. 1065/7, but with face values of $1.10, $1.95 and $2.45 Set of 3 sheets 10·00 11·00

224 U.S.A. 1847 Franklin 5c. Stamp and H.M.S. "Resolution" at Rarotonga

1986. "Ameripex '86" International Exhibition, Chicago. Multicoloured.
1069 $1 Type **224** . . . . 5·00 3·75
1070 $1.50 Chicago . . . . . . 3·50 4·25
1071 $2 1975 definitive $2, Benjamin Franklin and H.M.S. "Resolution" . . 6·00 5·50

225 Head of Statue of Liberty

226 Miss Sarah Ferguson

1986. Centenary of Statue of Liberty. Multicoloured.
1072 $1 Type **225** 75 85
1073 $1.25 Hand and torch of Statue . . . . 90 1·10
1074 $2.75 Statue of Liberty . . . 2·00 2·50

1986. Royal Wedding. Multicoloured.
1075 $1 Type **226** . . . . 1·25 1·25
1076 $2 Prince Andrew . . . . . 2·00 2·50
1077 $3 Prince Andrew and Miss Sarah Ferguson (57 × 31 mm) . . . . . . 2·50 3·50

1986. "Stampex '86" Stamp Exhibition, Adelaide. No. **MS**1002 optd **Stampex 86 Adelaide**.
MS1078 90c. × 4 multicoloured 7·00 6·50
The "Stampex '86" exhibition emblem is also overprinted on the sheet margin.

1986. 86th Birthday of Queen Elizabeth the Queen Mother. Designs as Nos. 1035/8 in miniature sheet, 91 × 116 mm, each with a face value of 55c. Multicoloured.
MS1079 55c. × 4. As Nos. 1035/8 8·00 7·50

228 "Holy Family with St. John the Baptist and St. Elizabeth"

1986. Christmas. Paintings by Rubens. Mult.
1080 55c. Type **228** . . . . . . 1·75 1·00
1081 $1.30 "Virgin with the Garland" . . . . 2·75 2·75
1082 $2.75 "Adoration of the Magi" (detail) . . . . . 5·50 6·00
MS1083 140 × 100 mm. As Nos. 1080/2, but each size 36 × 46 mm with a face value of $2.40 12·00 13·00
MS1084 80 × 70 mm. $6.40, As No. 1081 but size 32 × 50 mm 12·00 13·00

1986. Visit of Pope John Paul II to South Pacific. Nos. 1080/2 surch **FIRST PAPAL VISIT TO SOUTH PACIFIC POPE JOHN PAUL II NOV 21-24 1986**.
1085 55c.+10c. Type **228** . . . . 2·75 2·00
1086 $1.30+10c. "Virgin with the Garland" . . . . 3·50 2·50
1087 $2.75+10c. "Adoration of the Magi" (detail) . . . . 6·00 3·75
MS1088 140 × 100 mm. As Nos. 1085/7, but each size 36 × 46 mm with a face value of $2.40 + 10c. 12·00 13·00
MS1089 80 × 70 mm. $6.40 + 50c. As No. 1086 but size 32 × 50 mm 12·00 13·00

1987. Various stamps surch. (a) On Nos. 741/56, 761/76 and 787/8.
1090 10c. on 15c. "Distichopora violacea" 20 20
1091 10c. on 15c. "Stylaster" . . 20 20
1092 10c. on 15c. "Gonipora" . . 20 20
1093 10c. on 15c. "Caulastraea echinulata" 20 20
1094 10c. on 25c. "Lobophyllia bemprichii" 20 20
1095 10c. on 25c. "Palauastrea ramosa" 20 20
1096 10c. on 25c. "Bellonella indica" 20 20
1097 10c. on 25c. "Pectinia alcicornis" 20 20
1098 18c. on 12c. "Millepora alcicornis" 25 25
1099 18c. on 12c. "Junceella gemmacea" 25 25
1100 18c. on 12c. "Fungia fungites" 25 25
1101 18c. on 12c. "Heliofungia actiniformis" 25 25
1102 18c. on 20c. "Ptilosarcus gurneyi" 25 25
1103 18c. on 20c. "Stylophora pistillata" 25 25
1104 18c. on 20c. "Melithaea squamata" 25 25
1105 18c. on 20c. "Porites andrewsi" 25 25
1106 55c. on 35c. Type **184** . . . 40 45
1107 55c. on 35c. "Pavona praetorta" 40 45
1108 55c. on 35c. "Stylaster echinatus" 40 45
1109 55c. on 35c. "Tubastraea" . . 40 45
1110 65c. on 50c. As No. 1098 45 50
1111 65c. on 50c. As No. 1099 45 50
1112 65c. on 50c. As No. 1100 45 50
1113 65c. on 50c. As No. 1101 45 50
1114 65c. on 60c. As No. 1090 45 50
1115 65c. on 60c. As No. 1091 45 50
1116 65c. on 60c. As No. 1092 45 50
1117 65c. on 60c. As No. 1093 45 50
1118 75c. on 70c. As No. 1102 55 60
1119 75c. on 70c. As No. 1103 55 60
1120 75c. on 70c. As No. 1104 55 60
1121 75c. on 70c. As No. 1105 55 60
1122 $6.40 on $4 "Stylophora pistillata" . . . . 4·50 4·75
1123 $7.20 on $6 "Stylaster echinatus" . . . . 5·00 5·25

(b) On Nos. 812/13.
1124 $9.40 on $1 Type **187** . . . 15·00 16·00
1125 $9.40 on $2 Prince Charles and Lady Diana Spencer 15·00 16·00

(c) On Nos. 835/6.
1126 $9.40 on $2.50 Princess of Wales (inscribed "21st Birthday") . . . . . . 15·00 16·00
1127 $9.40 on $2.50 As No. 1126, but inscribed "1 July 1982" . . . . 15·00 16·00

(d) On Nos. 966/8, 971/2, 975, 979/80, 982 and 987/9.
1128 5c. on 1c. Type **208** 20 20
1129 5c. on 2c. "Millepora alcicornis" 20 20
1130 5c. on 3c. "Distichopora violacea" 20 20
1131 5c. on 12c. "Sarcophyton digitatum" 20 20
1132 5c. on 14c. "Pavona praetorta" 20 20
1133 18c. on 24c. "Stylophora pistillata" 25 25

1134 55c. on 52c. "Bellonella indica" 40 45
1135 65c. on 42c. "Fungia fungites" 45 50
1136 75c. on 48c. "Gonipora" 55 60
1137 95c. on 96c. "Porites andrewsi" 70 75
1138 95c. on $1.10 "Pectinia alcicornis" 70 75
1139 95c. on $1.20 "Dendrophyllia gracilis" 70 75

(e) On Nos. 998/1001.

1140 $1.30 on 36c. Type **211** 2·00 2·00
1141 $1.30 on 48c. "The "Endeavour" careened for Repairs" (Sydney Parkinson) 2·00 2·00
1142 $1.30 on 60c. "Cook's landing at Botany Bay" (E. Phillips Fox) 2·00 2·00
1143 $1.30 on $2 "Captain James Cook" (John Webber) 2·00 2·00

(f) On Nos. 1065/7.

1144 **223** $2.30 on 95c. mult 7·00 8·00
1145 – $2.80 on $1.25 mult 7·00 8·00
1146 – $2.80 on $1.50 mult 7·00 8·00

(g) On Nos. 1075/7.

1147 $2.80 on $1 Type **226** 6·00 6·50
1148 $2.80 on $2 Prince Andrew 6·00 6·50
1149 $2.80 on $3 Prince Andrew and Miss Sarah Ferguson (57 × 31 mm) 6·00 6·50

1987. Various stamps surch.

1150 $2.80 on $2 "Gonipora" (No. 785) 3·00 3·25
1151 $5 on $3 "Heliofungia actiniformis" (No. 786) 5·00 5·50
1152 $9.40 on $10 "Melithaea albitincta" (No. 789) 8·00 9·00
1153 $9.40 on $1 Type **187** (No. 838) 8·00 9·00
1154 $9.40 on $1 Type **187** (No. 839) 8·00 9·00
1155 $9.40 on $2 Prince Charles and Lady Diana Spencer (No. 840) 8·00 9·00
1156 $9.40 on $2 Prince Charles and Lady Diana Spencer (No. 841) 8·00 9·00
MS1157 106 × 59 mm. $9.20 on $1 Type **187**; $9.20 on $2 Prince Charles and Lady Diana Spencer 12·00 15·00

1987. Hurricane Relief. Various stamps surch **HURRICANE RELIEF** and premium. (a) On Nos. 1035/8.

1158 65c.+50c. Type **217** 1·00 1·00
1159 75c.+50c. "Duchess of York, 1923" (Savely Sorine) 1·10 1·10
1160 $1.15+50c. "Duchess of York, 1925" (Philip de Laszlo) 1·40 1·50
1161 $2.80+50c. "Queen Elizabeth, 1938" (Sir Gerald Kelly) 2·50 3·25
MS1162 69 × 81 mm. $5.30 + 50c. As $2.80 + 50c. 5·00 6·50

(b) On Nos. 1058/62.

1163 55c.+50c. Type **222** 85 85
1164 65c.+50c. "Lot and his Daughters" (Lucas van Leyden) 90 90
1165 75c.+50c. "Auspicious Comet" (from treatise c. 1587) 1·10 1·10
1166 $1.50+50c. "Events following Charles I" (Herman Saftleven) 1·40 1·50
1167 $2+50c. "Ossian receiving Napoleonic Officers" (Anne Louis Girodet-Trioson) 2·00 2·50

(c) On Nos. 1065/7.

1168 **223** 95c.+50c. mult 1·25 1·25
1169 – $1.25+50c. mult 1·50 1·50
1170 – $1.50+50c. mult 1·60 1·60
MS1171 Three sheets, each 44 × 75 mm. As Nos. 1168/70, but with face values of $1.10 + 50c., $1.95 + 50c., $2.45 + 50c. Set of 3 sheets 10·00 11·00

(d) On Nos. 1069/71.

1172 $1+50c. Type **224** 4·00 4·00
1173 $1.50+50c. Chicago 2·25 2·75
1174 $2+50c. 1975 definitive $2, Benjamin Franklin and H.M.S. "Resolution" 4·25 4·25

(e) On Nos. 1072/4.

1175 $1+50c. Type **225** 1·00 1·25
1176 $1.25+50c. Hand and torch of Statue 1·25 1·50
1177 $2.75+50c. Statue of Liberty 2·25 3·00

(f) On Nos. 1075/7.

1178 $1+50c. Type **226** 1·25 1·25
1179 $2+50c. Prince Andrew 2·00 2·25
1180 $3+50c. Prince Andrew and Miss Sarah Ferguson (57 × 31 mm) 2·75 3·25

(g) On Nos. 1080/2.

1181 55c.+50c. Type **228** 85 85
1182 $1.30+50c. "Virgin with the Garland" 1·50 1·75
1183 $2.75+50c. "The Adoration of the Magi" (detail) 2·50 3·00
MS1184 140 × 100 mm. As Nos. 1181/3, but each size 36 × 46 mm with a face value of $2.40 + 50c. 12·00 13·00
MS1185 80 × 70 mm. $6.40 + 50c. As No. 1182, but size 32 × 50 mm 7·00 8·00

(h) On Nos. 1122, 1134/7 and 1150/1.

1186 55c.+25c. on 52c. "Bellonella indica" 80 80
1187 65c.+25c. on 42c. "Fungia fungites" 90 90
1188 75c.+25c. on 48c. "Gonipora" 1·00 1·00
1189 95c.+25c. on 96c. "Porites andrewsi" 1·25 1·25
1190 $2.80+50c. on $2 "Gonipora" 3·50 3·50
1191 $5+50c. on $3 "Heliofungia actiniformis" 5·50 6·00
1192 $6.40+50c. on $4 "Stylophora pistillata" 7·00 8·00

1987. Royal Ruby Wedding. Nos. 484 and 787 optd **ROYAL WEDDING FORTIETH ANNIVERSARY**.

1193 $4 Queen Elizabeth II and sea shells 5·50 5·50
1194 $4 Queen Elizabeth II and "Stylophora pistillata" 5·50 5·50

233 "The Holy Family" (Rembrandt)

1987. Christmas. Different paintings of the Holy Family by Rembrandt.

1195 **233** $1.25 multicoloured 2·50 2·25
1196 – $1.50 multicoloured 3·00 2·50
1197 – $1.95 multicoloured 4·50 4·50

234 Olympic Commemorative $50 Coin

1988. Olympic Games, Seoul. Multicoloured.

1200 $1.50 Type **234** 4·00 2·50
1201 $1.50 Olympic torch and Seoul Olympic Park 4·00 2·50
1202 $1.50 Steffi Graf playing tennis and Olympic medal 4·00 2·50
MS1203 131 × 81 mm. $10 Combined design as Nos. 1200/2, but measuring 114 × 47 mm. 11·00 12·00

Nos. 1200/2 were printed together, se-tenant, forming a composite design.

1988. Olympic Tennis Medal Winners, Seoul. Nos. 1200/2 optd.

1204 $1.50 Type **234** (optd **MILOSLAV MECIR CZECHOSLOVAKIA GOLD MEDAL WINNER MEN'S TENNIS**) 3·25 2·25
1205 $1.50 Olympic torch and Seoul Olympic Park (optd **TIM MAYOTTE UNITED STATES GABRIELA SABATINI ARGENTINA SILVER MEDAL WINNERS**) 3·25 2·25
1206 $1.50 Steffi Graf playing tennis and Olympic medal (optd **GOLD MEDAL WINNER STEFFI GRAF WEST GERMANY**) 3·25 2·25
MS1207 131 × 81 mm. $10 Combined design as Nos. 1200/2, but measuring 114 × 47 mm (optd **GOLD MEDAL WINNER SEOUL OLYMPIC GAMES STEFFI GRAF – WEST GERMANY**) 12·00 11·00

236 "Virgin and Child"

1988. Christmas.

1208 **236** 70c. multicoloured 2·75 2·00
1209 – 85c. multicoloured 3·00 2·25
1210 – 95c. multicoloured 3·25 2·50
1211 – $1.25 multicoloured 4·00 3·25
MS1212 80 × 100 mm. $6.40, multicoloured (45 × 60 mm) 7·50 9·50

DESIGNS: 85c., 95c., $1.25, Various versions of the "Virgin and Child" by Durer.

237 "Apollo 11" leaving Earth

1989. 20th Anniv of First Manned Landing on Moon. Multicoloured.

1213 40c. Type **237** 1·75 1·75
1214 40c. Lunar module over Moon 1·75 1·75
1215 55c. Aldrin stepping onto Moon 2·00 2·00
1216 55c. Astronaut on Moon 2·00 2·00
1217 65c. Working on lunar surface 2·25 2·25
1218 65c. Conducting experiment 2·25 2·25
1219 75c. "Apollo 11" leaving Moon 2·25 2·25
1220 75c. Splashdown in South Pacific 2·25 2·25
MS1221 108 × 91 mm. $4.20, Astronauts on Moon 5·00 6·00

238 Rarotonga Flycatcher

1989. Endangered Birds of the Cook Islands. Multicoloured.

1222 15c. Type **238**(postage) 2·00 2·00
1223 20c. Pair of Rarotonga flycatchers 2·00 2·00
1224 65c. Pair of Rarotonga fruit doves 2·75 2·75
1225 70c. Rarotonga fruit dove 2·75 2·75
MS1226 Four sheets, each 70 × 53 mm. As Nos. 1222/5, but with face values of $1, $1.25, $1.50, $1.75 and each size 50 × 32 mm (air) Set of 4 sheets 9·00 10·00

239 Villagers

1989. Christmas. Details from "Adoration of the Magi" by Rubens. Multicoloured.

1227 70c. Type **239** 1·40 1·40
1228 85c. Virgin Mary 1·60 1·60
1229 95c. Christ Child 1·75 2·00
1230 $1.50 Boy with gift 2·00 3·00
MS1231 85 × 120 mm. $6.40, "Adoration of the Magi" (45 × 60 mm) 11·00 13·00

240 Reverend John Williams and L.M.S. Church

1990. Christianity in the Cook Islands. Multicoloured.

1232 70c. Type **240** 85 85
1233 85c. Mgr. Bernardine Castanie and Roman Catholic Church 1·00 1·10
1234 95c. Elder Osborne Widstoe and Mormon Church 1·10 1·40
1235 $1.60 Dr. J. E. Caldwell and Seventh Day Adventist Church 1·90 2·25
MS1236 90 × 90 mm. As Nos. 1232/5, but with a face value of 90c. 4·75 6·00

241 "Woman writing a Letter" (Terborch)

243 Queen Elizabeth the Queen Mother

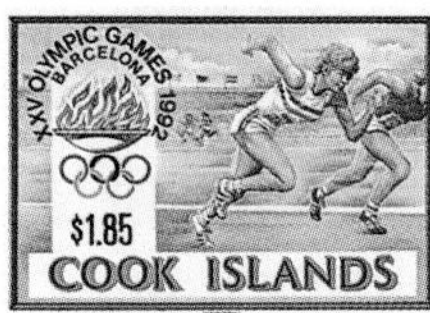

242 Sprinting

1990. 150th Anniv of the Penny Black. Designs showing paintings. Multicoloured.

1237 85c. Type **241** 1·10 1·25
1238 $1.15 "George Gisze" (Holbein the Younger) 1·50 1·75
1239 $1.55 "Mrs. John Douglas" (Gainsborough) 1·90 2·25
1240 $1.85 "Portrait of a Gentleman" (Durer) 2·25 2·50
MS1241 82 × 150 mm. As Nos. 1237/40, but each with a face value of $1.05 8·50 9·50

1990. Olympic Games, Barcelona, and Winter Olympic Games, Albertville (1992) (1st issue). Multicoloured.

1242 $1.85 Type **242** 5·00 5·00
1243 $1.85 Cook Islands $50 commemorative coin 5·00 5·00
1244 $1.85 Skiing 5·00 5·00
MS1245 109 × 52 mm. $6.40, As Nos. 1242/4, but size 80 × 26 mm. 13·00 14·00

See also Nos. 1304/10.

1990. 90th Birthday of Queen Elizabeth the Queen Mother.

1246 **243** $1.85 multicoloured 5·00 4·75
MS1247 66 × 101 mm. **243** $6.40, multicoloured 11·00 13·00

244 "Adoration of the Magi" (Memling)

1990. Christmas. Religious Paintings. Mult.

1248 70c. Type **244** 1·75 1·60
1249 85c. "Holy Family" (Lotto) 1·90 1·75
1250 95c. "Madonna and Child with Saints John and Catherine" (Titian) 2·25 2·00
1251 $1.50 "Holy Family" (Titian) 3·75 5·00
MS1252 98 × 110 mm. $6.40, "Madonna and Child enthroned, surrounded by Saints" (Vivarini) (vert) 11·00 12·00

1990. "Birdpex '90" Stamp Exhibition, Christchurch, New Zealand. No. **MS**1226 optd **Birdpex '90**.

MS1253 Four sheets, each 70 × 53 mm. As Nos. 1222/5, but with face values of $1, $1.25, $1.50, $1.75 and each size 50 × 32 mm Set of 4 sheets 14·00 15·00

246 Columbus (engraving by Theodoro de Bry)

249 Red-breasted Wrasse

248 "Adoration of the Child" (G. delle Notti)

1991. 500th Anniv (1992) of Discovery of America by Columbus (1st issue).

1254	**246** $1 multicoloured	2·75	2·75

See also No. 1302.

1991. 65th Birthday of Queen Elizabeth II. No. 789 optd **65TH BIRTHDAY**.

1255	$10 "Melithaea albitincta"	14·00	15·00

1991. Christmas. Religious Paintings. Mult.

1256	70c. Type **248**	2·25	1·75
1257	85c. "The Birth of the Virgin" (B. Murillo)	2·50	2·00
1258	$1.15 "Adoration of the Shepherds" (Rembrandt)	3·00	3·00
1259	$1.50 "Adoration of the Shepherds" (L. le Nain)	4·50	6·00
MS1260	79 × 103 mm. $6.40, "Madonna and Child" (Lippi) (vert)	11·00	12·00

1992. Reef Life (1st series). Multicoloured with white borders.

1261	5c. Type **249**	70	70
1262	10c. Blue sea star	70	70
1263	15c. Bicoloured angelfish ("Black and gold angelfish")	75	75
1264	20c. Spotted pebble crab	85	85
1265	25c. Black-tipped grouper ("Black-tipped cod")	85	85
1266	30c. Spanish dancer	85	85
1267	50c. Regal angelfish	1·25	1·25
1268	80c. Big-scaled soldierfish ("Squirrel fish")	1·50	1·50
1269	85c. Red pencil sea urchin	3·25	2·75
1270	90c. Red-spotted rainbowfish	4·00	2·75
1271	$1 Cheek-lined wrasse	4·00	2·75
1272	$2 Long-nosed butterflyfish	4·00	3·50
1273	$3 Red-spotted rainbowfish	3·25	4·00
1274	$5 Blue sea-star	4·25	6·50
1275	$7 "Pygoplites diacanthus"	9·00	13·00
1276	$10 Spotted pebble crab	11·00	14·00
1277	$15 Red pencil sea urchin	18·00	19·00

The 25, 50c., $1 and $2 include a silhouette of the Queen's head.

For designs in a larger size, 40 × 30 mm, and with brown borders, see Nos. 1342/52.

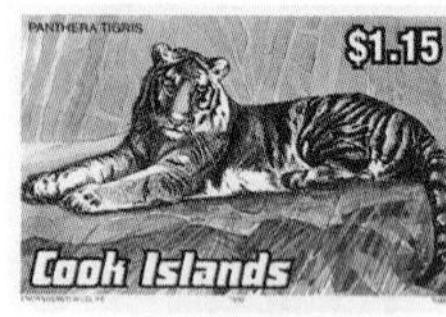

250 Tiger

1992. Endangered Wildlife. Multicoloured.

1279	$1.15 Type **250**	1·25	1·25
1280	$1.15 Indian elephant	1·25	1·25
1281	$1.15 Brown bear	1·25	1·25
1282	$1.15 Black rhinoceros	1·25	1·25
1283	$1.15 Chimpanzee	1·25	1·25
1284	$1.15 Argali	1·25	1·25
1285	$1.15 Heaviside's dolphin	1·25	1·25
1286	$1.15 Eagle owl	1·75	1·25
1287	$1.15 Bee hummingbird	1·75	1·25
1288	$1.15 Puma	1·25	1·25
1289	$1.15 European otter	1·25	1·25
1290	$1.15 Red kangaroo	1·25	1·25
1291	$1.15 Jackass penguin	1·75	1·25
1292	$1.15 Asian lion	1·25	1·25
1293	$1.15 Peregrine falcon	1·75	1·25
1294	$1.15 Persian fallow deer	1·25	1·25
1295	$1.15 Key deer	1·25	1·25
1296	$1.15 Alpine ibex	1·25	1·25
1297	$1.15 Mandrill	1·25	1·25
1298	$1.15 Gorilla	1·25	1·25
1299	$1.15 "Vanessa atalanta" (butterfly)	1·25	1·25
1300	$1.15 Takin	1·25	1·25
1301	$1.15 Ring-tailed lemur	1·25	1·25

251 Columbus and Landing in New World

1992. 500th Anniv of Discovery of America by Columbus (2nd issue).

1302	**251** $6 multicoloured	7·50	8·00
MS1303	128 × 84 mm. $10 As T **251**, but detail of landing party only (40 × 29 mm)	7·00	8·50

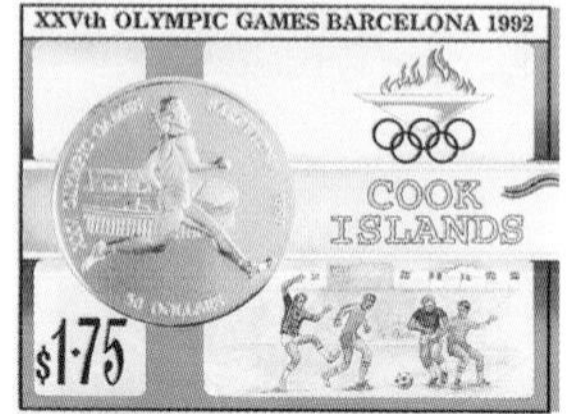

252 Football and $50 Commemorative Coin

1992. Olympic Games, Barcelona (2nd issue). Multicoloured.

1304	$1.75 Type **252**	2·50	2·50
1305	$1.75 Olympic gold medal	2·50	2·50
1306	$1.75 Basketball and $10 coin	2·50	2·50
1307	$2.25 Running	3·50	3·50
1308	$2.25 $10 and $50 coins	3·50	3·50
1309	$2.25 Cycling	3·50	3·50
MS1310	155 × 91 mm. $6.40, Javelin throwing	12·00	13·00

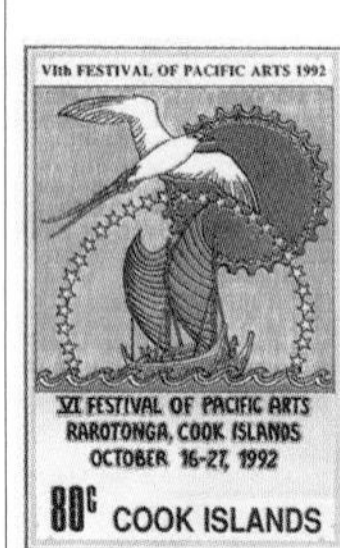

253 Festival Poster

255 "Worship of Shepherds" (Parmigianino)

1992. 6th Festival of Pacific Arts, Rarotonga. Multicoloured.

1311	80c. Type **253**	1·50	1·50
1312	85c. Seated Tangaroa carving	1·50	1·50
1313	$1 Seated Tangaroa carving (different)	1·60	1·60
1314	$1.75 Standing Tangaroa carving	2·50	3·25

1992. Royal Visit by Prince Edward. Nos. 1311/14 optd **ROYAL VISIT**.

1315	80c. Type **253**	2·00	2·00
1316	85c. Seated Tangaroa carving	2·00	2·00
1317	$1 Seated Tangaroa carving (different)	2·25	2·25
1318	$1.75 Standing Tangaroa carving	3·75	4·25

1992. Christmas. Religious Paintings by Parmigianino. Multicoloured.

1319	70c. Type **255**	1·00	1·00
1320	85c. "Virgin with Long Neck"	1·25	1·25
1321	$1.15 "Virgin with Rose"	1·50	1·75
1322	$1.90 "St. Margaret's Virgin"	2·75	3·75
MS1323	86 × 102 mm. $6.40, As 85c. but larger (36 × 46 mm)	9·00	10·00

256 Queen in Garter Robes

258 "Virgin with Child" (Filippo Lippi)

257 Coronation Ceremony

1992. 40th Anniv of Queen Elizabeth II's Accession. Multicoloured.

1324	80c. Type **256**	1·75	1·50
1325	$1.15 Queen at Trooping the Colour	2·00	2·00
1326	$1.50 Queen in evening dress	2·75	3·00
1327	$1.95 Queen with bouquet	3·00	3·50

1993. 40th Anniv of Coronation. Multicoloured.

1328	$1 Type **257**	2·75	1·75
1329	$2 Coronation photograph by Cecil Beaton	4·00	3·75
1330	$3 Royal family on balcony	6·50	5·50

1993. Christmas. Religious Paintings. Mult.

1331	70c. Type **258**	80	80
1332	85c. "Bargellini Madonna" (Lodovico Carracci)	95	95
1333	$1.15 "Virgin of the Curtain" (Rafael Sanzio)	1·40	1·60
1334	$2.50 "Holy Family" (Agnolo Bronzino)	3·25	3·75
1335	$4 "Saint Zachary Virgin" (Parmigianino) (32 × 47 mm)	4·00	5·00

259 Skiing, Flags and Ice Skating (½-size illustration)

1994. Winter Olympic Games, Lillehammer.

1336	**259** $5 multicoloured	8·00	8·50

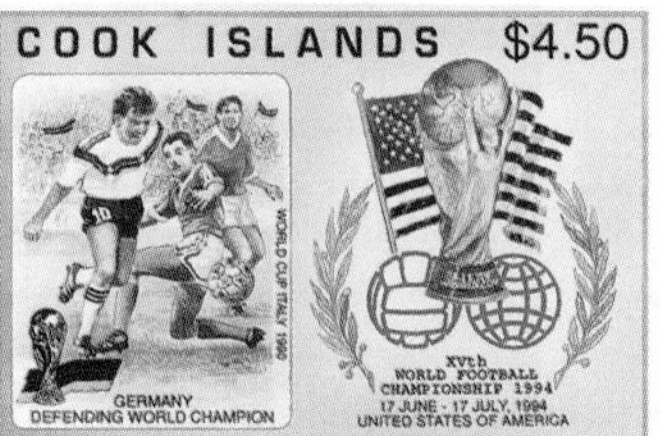

260 Cup on Logo with German and Argentinian Players

1994. World Cup Football Championship, U.S.A.

1337	**260** $4.50 multicoloured	6·00	7·00

261 Neil Armstrong taking First Step on Moon

1994. 25th Anniv of First Manned Moon Landing. Multicoloured.

1338	$2.25 Type **261**	3·75	3·75
1339	$2.25 Astronaut on Moon and view of Earth	3·75	3·75
1340	$2.25 Astronaut and flag	3·75	3·75
1341	$2.25 Astronaut with reflection in helmet visor	3·75	3·75

1994. Reef Life (2nd series). As Nos. 1261 and 1263/71, but each 40 × 30 mm and with brown borders.

1342	5c. Type **249**	50	50
1344	15c. Bicoloured angelfish	60	60
1345	20c. Spotted pebble crab	65	65
1346	25c. Black-tipped grouper	70	70
1347	30c. Spanish dancer	70	70
1348	50c. Regal angelfish	85	85
1349	80c. Big-scaled soldierfish	1·10	1·10
1350	85c. Red pencil sea urchin	1·10	1·10
1351	90c. Red-spotted rainbowfish	1·25	1·25
1352	$1 Cheek-lined wrasse	1·40	1·40

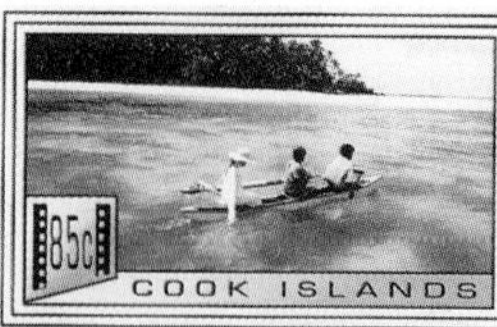

262 Actors in Outrigger Canoe

1994. Release of "The Return of Tommy Tricker" (film shot in Cook Islands). Scenes from film. Multicoloured.

1359	85c. Type **262**	1·10	1·25
1360	85c. Male and female dancers	1·10	1·25
1361	85c. European couple on beach	1·10	1·25
1362	85c. Aerial view of island	1·10	1·25
1363	85c. Two female dancers	1·10	1·25
1364	85c. Cook Islands couple on beach	1·10	1·25
1364a	90c. Type **262**	65	80
1364b	90c. As No. 1360	65	80
1364c	90c. As No. 1361	65	80
1364d	90c. As No. 1362	65	80
1364e	90c. As No. 1363	65	80
1364f	90c. As No. 1364	65	80

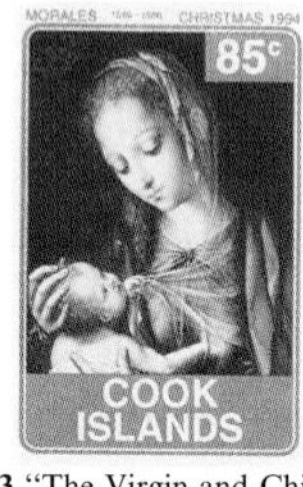

263 "The Virgin and Child" (Morales)

1994. Christmas. Religious Paintings. Mult.

1365	85c. Type **263**	1·75	1·75
1366	85c. "Adoration of the Kings" (Gerard David)	1·75	1·75
1367	85c. "Adoration of the Kings" (Foppa)	1·75	1·75
1368	85c. "The Madonna and Child with St. Joseph and Infant Baptist" (Baroccio)	1·75	1·75
1369	$1 "Madonna with Iris" (Durer)	1·75	1·75
1370	$1 "Adoration of the Shepherds" (Le Nain)	1·75	1·75
1371	$1 "The Virgin and Child" (school of Leonardo)	1·75	1·75
1372	$1 "The Mystic Nativity" (Botticelli)	1·75	1·75

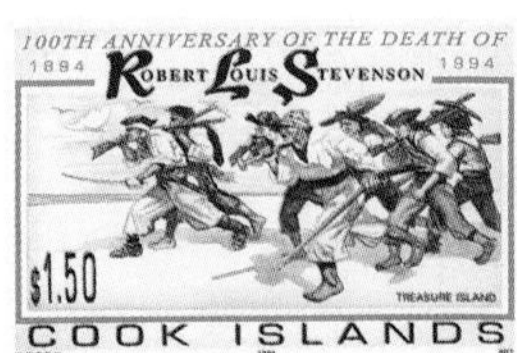

264 Pirates ("Treasure Island")

1994. Death Centenary of Robert Louis Stevenson (author). Multicoloured.

1373	$1.50 Type **264**	2·50	2·50
1374	$1.50 Duel ("David Balfour")	2·50	2·50
1375	$1.50 Mr. Hyde, ("Dr. Jekyll and Mr. Hyde")	2·50	2·50
1376	$1.50 Rowing boat and sailing ship ("Kidnapped")	2·50	2·50

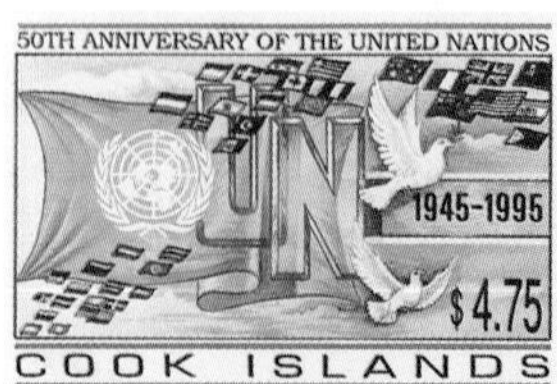

265 U.N. and National Flags with Peace Doves

1995. 50th Anniv of United Nations.

1377	**265** $4.75 multicoloured	4·75	6·50

266 Queen Elizabeth the Queen Mother and Coat of Arms

1995. 95th Birthday of Queen Elizabeth the Queen Mother.
1378 **266** $5 multicoloured . . . . 9·50 8·50

267 German Delegation signing Unconditional Surrender at Rheims

1995. 50th Anniv of End of Second World War. Multicoloured.
1379 $3.50 Type **267** . . . . . . 7·50 7·50
1380 $3.50 Japanese delegation on U.S.S. "Missouri", Tokyo Bay . . . . . . 7·50 7·50

1995. 50th Anniv of F.A.O. As T **265**. Mult.
1381 $4.50 F.A.O. and U.N. emblems . . . . 4·75 6·50

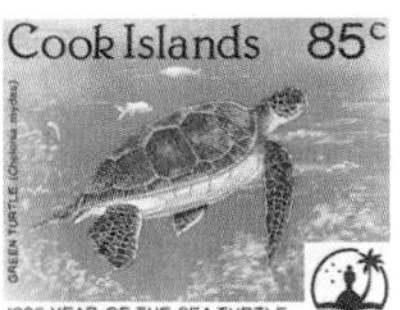

268 Green Turtle

1995. Year of the Sea Turtle. Multicoloured.
1382 85c. Type **268** . . . . . . 1·75 1·60
1383 $1 Hawksbill turtle . . . . 2·00 1·75
1384 $1.75 Green turtle on beach 3·00 3·25
1385 $2.25 Young hawksbill turtles hatching . . . . . 3·75 4·00

269 Emblem and Throwing the Discus

1996. Olympic Games, Atlanta. Multicoloured.
1386 85c. Type **269** . . . . . . 1·50 1·50
1387 $1 Athlete with Olympic Torch . . . . 1·75 1·75
1388 $1.50 Running . . . . . . 2·50 2·50
1389 $1.85 Gymnastics . . . . . 2·75 2·75
1390 $2.10 Ancient archery . . . 3·00 3·00
1391 $2.50 Throwing the javelin 3·00 3·00

270 Queen Elizabeth II

1996. 70th Birthday of Queen Elizabeth II. Multicoloured.
1392 $1.90 Type **270** . . . . . . 2·75 2·75
1393 $2.25 Wearing tiara . . . . 3·25 3·25
1394 $2.75 In Garter robes . . . 3·50 3·50
MS1395 103 × 152 mm. Designs as Nos. 1392/4, but each with a face value of $2.50 13·00 13·00

1997. 28th South Pacific Forum. Nos. 1364a/f optd **28th South Pacific Forum** (Nos. 1396, 1399/1400) or **12–22 September 1997** (Nos. 1397/8 and 1401). Multicoloured.
1396 90c. Type **262** . . . . . . 1·00 1·25
1397 90c. As No. 1360 . . . . . 1·00 1·25
1398 90c. As No. 1361 . . . . . 1·00 1·25
1399 90c. As No. 1362 . . . . . 1·00 1·25
1400 90c. As No. 1363 . . . . . 1·00 1·25
1401 90c. As No. 1364 . . . . . 1·00 1·25

272 "Lampides boeticus" (female)

1997. Butterflies. Multicoloured.
1402 5c. Type **272** 10 10
1403 10c. "Vanessa atalanta" . . 10 10
1404 15c. "Lampides boeticus" (male) 10 15
1405 20c. "Papilio godeffroyi" . . 15 20
1406 25c. "Danaus hamata" . . . 15 20
1407 30c. "Xois sesara" 20 25
1408 50c. "Vagrans egista" . . . 30 35
1409 70c. "Parthenos sylvia" . . 45 50
1410 80c. "Hyblaea sanguinea" 50 55
1411 85c. "Melanitis leda" . . . 55 60
1412 90c. "Ascalapha odorata" 60 65
1413 $1 "Precis villida" 65 70
1414 $1.50 "Parthenos sylvia" . . 95 1·00
1415 $2 "Lampides boeticus" (female) . . . . 1·25 1·40
1416 $3 "Precis villida" . . . . . 1·90 2·00
1417 $4 "Melanitis leda" . . . . 2·50 2·75
1418 $5 "Vagrans egista" . . . . 3·25 3·50
1419 $7 "Hyblaea sanguinea" . . 4·50 4·75
1420 $10 "Vanessa atalanta" . . 7·00 7·25
1421 $15 "Papilio godeffroyi" . . 10·00 10·50
The $1 includes an outline portrait of Queen Elizabeth II. Nos. 1414/21 are larger, 41 × 25 mm, with the Queen's portrait included on the $4 to $15.

273 Queen Elizabeth and Prince Philip

1997. Golden Wedding of Queen Elizabeth and Prince Philip.
1424 **273** $2 multicoloured . . . . 2·25 2·50
MS1425 76 × 102 mm. **273** $5 multicoloured 7·00 7·00

274 Diana, Princess of Wales

277 Lady Elizabeth Bowes-Lyon

1998. Diana, Princess of Wales Commemoration.
1426 **274** $1.15 multicoloured . . 1·25 1·25
MS1427 70 × 100 mm. $3.50, Princess Diana and guard of honour 4·50 4·50

1998. Children's Charities. No. **MS**1427 surch **+$1 CHILDREN'S CHARITIES**.
MS1428 70 × 100 mm. $3.50 + $1 Princess Diana and guard of honour 3·50 4·25

1999. New Millennium. Nos. 1311/14 optd **KIA ORANA THIRD MILLENNIUM**.
1429 80c. Type **253** 65 65
1430 85c. Seated Tangaroa carving 70 70
1431 $1 Seated Tangaroa carving (different) 80 80
1432 $1.75 Standing Tangaroa carving . . . . . 1·40 1·75

2000. Queen Elizabeth the Queen Mother's 100th Birthday.
1433 **277** $4.50 brown and blue . . 3·75 3·75
1434 – $4.50 brown and blue . . 3·75 3·75
1435 – $4.50 multicoloured . . 3·75 3·75
1436 – $4.50 multicoloured . . 3·75 3·75
MS1437 73 × 100 mm. $6 multicoloured 4·25 4·50
DESIGNS: 1434, Lady Elizabeth Bowes-Lyon as young woman; 1435, Queen Mother wearing green outfit; 1436, Queen Mother wearing pearl earrings and necklace; **MS**1437, Queen Mother in blue hat and plum jacket.

278 Ancient Greek Runner on Urn

2000. Olympic Games, Sydney. Multicoloured.
1438 $1.75 Type **278** . . . . . . 1·75 1·90
1439 $1.75 Modern runner . . . 1·75 1·90
1440 $1.75 Ancient Greek archer 1·75 1·90
1441 $1.75 Modern archer . . . 1·75 1·90
MS1442 99 × 90 mm. $3.90, Olympic torch in Cook Islands 2·50 2·75

2001. Suwarrow Wildlife Sanctuary. Nos. 1279/90 surch **80c SUWARROW SANCTUARY**.
1443 80c. on $1.15 Heavisides's dolphin 85 95
1444 80c. on $1.15 Eagle owl . . 85 95
1445 80c. on $1.15 Bee hummingbird 85 95
1446 80c. on $1.15 Puma 85 95
1447 80c. on $1.15 European otter 85 95
1448 80c. on $1.15 Red kangaroo 85 95
1449 90c. on $1.15 Type **250** . . 85 95
1450 90c. on $1.15 Indian elephant 85 95
1451 90c. on $1.15 Brown bear 85 95
1452 90c. on $1.15 Black rhinoceros 85 95
1453 90c. on $1.15 Chimpanzee 85 95
1454 90c. on $1.15 Argali 85 95

2002. Christmas. Nos. 1248/51 and 1256/9 optd **CHRISTMAS 2002** or surch.
1455 20c. on 70c. Type **244** . . . 15 20
1456 20c. on 70c. Type **248** . . . 15 20
1457 80c. on $1.15 "Adoration of the Shepherds" (Rembrandt) 50 55
1458 85c. "Holy Family" (Lotto) 55 60
1459 85c. "The Birth of the Virgin" (B. Murillo) . . . 55 60
1460 90c. on $1.50 "Adoration of the Shepherds" (L. le Nain) 60 65
1461 95c. "Madonna and Child with Saints John and Catherine" (Titian) . . . 60 65
1462 $1 on $1.50 "The Holy Family" (Titian) . . . . 95 1·00

OFFICIAL STAMPS

1975. Nos. 228, etc, optd **O.H.M.S.** or surch also.
O 1 1c. multicoloured . . . . .
O 2 2c. multicoloured . . . . .
O 3 3c. multicoloured . . . . .
O 4 4c. multicoloured . . . . .
O 5 5c. on 2½c. multicoloured
O 6 8c. multicoloured . . . . .
O 7 10c. on 6c. multicoloured
O 8 18c. on 20c. multicoloured
O 9 25c. on 9c. multicoloured
O 10 30c. on 15c. multicoloured
O 11 50c. multicoloured . . . .
O 12 $1 multicoloured . . . . .
O 13 $2 multicoloured . . . . .
O 14 $4 multicoloured . . . . .
O 15 $6 multicoloured . . . . .
O1/15 Set of 15 . . . . † 8·00
These stamps were only sold to the public cancelled-to-order and not in unused condition.

1978. Nos. 466/7, 474, 478/81, 484/5, 542 and 568/9 optd **O.H.M.S.** or surch also.
O16 – 1c. mult (No. 467) . . . 60 10
O17 **141** 2c. on ½c. multicoloured 60 10
O18 – 5c. on ½c. multicoloured 60 10
O19 – 10c. on 8c. mult (No. 474) 65 10
O20 – 15c. on 50c. mult (No. 480) 90 10
O21 – 18c. on 60c. mult (No. 481) 90 15
O22 – 25c. mult (No. 478) . . . 1·00 20
O23 – 30c. mult (No. 479) . . . 1·00 25
O24 – 35c. on 60c. mult (No. 481) . . . . . . 1·25 30
O25 – 50c. mult (No. 480) . . . 1·75 35
O26 – 60c. mult (No. 481) . . . 2·00 45
O27 – $1 mult (No. 568) . . . 4·50 65
O28 – $1 mult (No. 569) . . . 4·50 65
O29 – $2 mult (No. 542) . . . 7·00 2·25
O30 – $4 mult (No. 484) . . . 13·00 2·25
O31 – $6 mult (No. 485) . . . 13·00 3·50

1985. Nos. 786/8, 862/5, 969/74, 976, 978, 981, 984/6 and 988/9 optd **O.H.M.S.** or surch also.
O32 5c. "Ptilosarcus gurneyi" . . 50 50
O33 10c. "Lobophyllia bemprichii" 50 50
O34 12c. "Sarcophyton digitatum" . . . . . . 3·50 60
O35 14c. "Pavona praetorta" . . 3·50 60
O36 18c. "Junceella gemmacea" 3·50 60
O37 20c. "Stylaster" 60 50
O38 30c. "Palauastrea ramosa" 60 50
O39 40c. "Stylaster echinatus" . 60 50
O40 50c. "Melithaea squamata" 4·50 70
O41 55c. on 85c. "Caulastraea echinulata" 70 50
O42 60c. "Tubastraea" 70 60
O43 70c. "Heliofungia actiniformis" . . . . . . 5·00 85
O46 75c. on 60c. Type **197** . . 3·00 1·00
O47 75c. on 60c. Rarotonga oranges . . . . 3·00 1·00
O48 75c. on 60c. Rarotonga Airport . . . . 3·00 1·00
O49 75c. on 60c. Prime Minister Sir Thomas Davis . . . . 3·00 1·00
O44 $1.10 "Pectinia alcicornis" 1·10 90
O45 $2 on $1.20 "Dendrophyllia gracilis" . . . . 2·00 1·75
O50 $5 on $3 "Heliofungia actiniformis" . . . . . . 13·00 4·75
O51 $9 on $4 "Stylophora pistillata" . . . . 8·00 9·00
O52 $14 on $6 "Stylaster echinatus" . . . . . . 12·50 14·00
O53 $18 on $10 "Melithaea albitincta" . . . . 18·00 18·00

1995. Nos. 1261/6 optd **O.H.M.S.**
O54 5c. Type **249** 40 50
O55 10c. Blue sea star 40 50
O56 15c. Bicoloured angelfish . . 50 50
O57 20c. Spotted pebble crab . . 55 55
O58 25c. Black-tipped grouper . . 60 60
O59 30c. Spanish dancer 60 60
O60 50c. Regal angelfish 80 80
O61 80c. Big-scaled soldierfish . . 1·25 1·25
O62 85c. Red pencil sea urchin 1·25 1·25
O63 90c. Red-spotted rainbowfish 1·25 1·25
O64 $1 Cheek-lined wrasse . . . 1·25 1·25
O65 $2 Long-nosed butterflyfish 2·25 2·25
O66 $3 Red-spotted rainbowfish 3·00 3·00
O67 $5 Blue sea star . . . . . 4·00 4·25
O68 $7 "Pygoplites diacanthus" 5·50 6·00
O69 $10 Spotted pebble crab . . 7·50 8·50

COSTA RICA Pt. 15

A republic of Central America. Independent since 1821.

1863. 8 reales = 1 peso.
1881. 100 centavos = 1 peso.
1901. 100 centimos = 1 colon.

1

8 General P. Fernandez

14 Pres. Soto

1863.
1 **1** ½r. blue 50 35
3 2r. red 55 85
4 4r. green . . . . 6·00 6·00
5 1p. orange . . . . 12·00 12·00

1881. Surch.
6 **1** 1c. on ½r. blue . . . . 1·10 4·50
8 2c. on ½r. blue . . . . 90 2·10
9 5c. on ½r. blue . . . . 2·75 7·25

1882. Surch **U.P.U.** and value.
10 **1** 5c. on ½r. blue . . . . 30·00 30·00
11 10c. on 2r. red . . . . 30·00 30·00
12 20c. on 4r. green . . . . . . 90·00 90·00

1883.
13 **8** 1c. green 40 25
14 2c. red 40 30
15 5c. violet . . . . 7·25 25
16 10c. orange . . . . 21·00 2·75
17 40c. blue 45 55

1887.
18 **14** 5c. violet . . . . 3·25 25
19 10c. orange 90 50

1887. Fiscal stamps similar to T **8** and **14** optd **CORREOS**.
20 1c. red . . . . 1·50 65
21 5c. brown . . . . 1·50 45

17 Pres. Soto

19

1889. Various frames.
22 **17** 1c. brown 25 25
23 2c. green 20 20
24 5c. orange 40 25
25 10c. lake 20 20
26 20c. green 20 20
27 50c. red 45 80
28 1p. blue . . . . 65 1·25
29 2p. violet . . . . 6·00 7·00
30 5p. olive . . . . 15·00 18·00
31 10p. black . . . . 38·00 35·00

1892. Various frames.
32 **19** 1c. blue 20 20
33 2c. orange 20 20
34a 5c. mauve 20 20
35 10c. green 50 25
36 20c. red . . . . 6·00 25
37 50c. blue . . . . 3·00 2·00
38 1p. green on yellow . . . 55 80
39 2p. red on grey . . . . . 1·50 50
40 5p. blue on blue . . . . 1·25 50
41a 10p. brown on buff . . . . 4·25 2·40

29 Juan Santamaria

31 Puerto Limon

1901. Various designs dated "1900".
42 **29** 1c. black and green 40 10
43 – 2c. black and red 25 15
52 – 4c. black and purple . . . 1·90 75
44 **31** 5c. black and blue 35 15
53 – 6c. black and olive . . . 4·50 2·40
45 – 10c. black and brown . . . 1·00 15
46 – 20c. black and lake . . . 2·75 15
54 – 25c. brown and lilac . . . 8·75 20
47 – 50c. blue and red . . . . 2·40 70
48 – 1col. black and olive . . . 38·00 7·50
49 – 2col. black and red . . . 6·50 1·75

50 – 5col. black and brown . . . 17·00 1·75
51 – 10col. red and green . . . . 13·50 1·40
DESIGNS—VERT: 2c. Juan Mora F; 4c. Jose M. Canas; 6c. Julian Volio; 10c. Braulio (wrongly inscr "BRANLIO") Carrillo; 25c. Eusebio Figueroa; 50c. Jose M. Castro; 1col. Puente de Birris; 2col. Juan Rafael Mora; 5col. Jesus Jimenez. HORIZ: 20c. National Theatre; 10col. Arms.

1905. No. 46 surch **UN CENTIMO** in ornamental frame.
55 1c. on 20c. black and lake . . 50 50

43 Juan Santamaria

44 Juan Mora

1907. Dated "1907".
57 **43** 1c. blue and brown 50 20
58 **44** 2c. black and green 45 20
69 – 4c. blue and red . . . . . 3·00 65
60 – 5c. blue and orange 35 20
71 – 10c. black and blue . . . . 4·25 10
72 – 20c. black and olive . . . . 4·75 2·40
63 – 25c. slate and lavender . . . 1·10 35
74 – 50c. blue and red . . . . . 17·00 4·25
75 – 1col. black and brown . . . 8·25 4·25
76 – 2col. green and red . . . . 42·00 16·00
PORTRAITS: 4c. Jose M. Canas. 5c. Mauro Fernandez. 10c. Braulio Carrillo. 20c. Julian Volio. 25c. Eusebio Figueroa. 50c. Jose M. Castro. 1col. Jesus Jimenez. 2col. Juan Rafael Mora.

53 Juan Santamaria

54 Julian Volio

1910. Various frames.
77 **53** 1c. brown 10 10
78 – 2c. green (Juan Mora F.) . . 20 10
79 – 4c. red (Jose M. Canas) . . 20 10
80 – 5c. orange (Mauro Fernandez) 20 10
81 – 10c. blue (B. Carrillo) . . . 10 10
82 **54** 20c. olive 20 10
83 – 25c. purple (Eusebio Figueroa) . . . . 4·25 50
84 – 1col. brown (Jesus Jimenez) 40 25

1911. Optd **1911** between stars.
85 **29** 1c. black and green 50 35
86 **43** 1c. blue and brown 35 35
88 **44** 2c. black and green 35 35

1911. Optd **Habilitado 1911**.
93 4c. black and purple (No. 52) 1·00 10
90 5c. blue and orange (No. 60) 1·00 10
91 10c. black and blue (No. 71) 3·00 2·75

59 Liner "Antilles"

62

1911. Surch **Correos Un centimo** or **Correos S 5 centimos**.
94 **59** 1c. on 10c. blue 30 15
96 1c. on 25c. violet 30 15
97 1c. on 50c. brown 55 45
98 1c. on 1c. brown 55 45
99 1c. on 5c. red 90 65
100 1c. on 10c. brown . . . . 1·10 95
101 5c. on 5c. orange 55 20

1912. Surch **Correos Dos centimos 2**.
102 **62** 2c. on 5c. brown . . . . . 8·75 2·40
109 2c. on 10c. blue . . . . . £140 60·00
104 2c. on 50c. red . . . . . . 5·00 5·00
105 2c. on 1c. brown . . . . . 22·00 3·00
112 2c. on 2c. red . . . . . . 2·50 90
107 2c. on 5c. green . . . . . 8·75 2·40
108 2c. on 10col. purple . . . 11·00 3·25

67 Plantation and Administration Building

1921. Centenary of Coffee Cultivation.
115 **67** 5c. black and blue . . . . 1·00 85

68 Simon Bolivar

69

1921.
116 **68** 15c. violet 25 15

1921. Cent of Independence of Central America.
117 **69** 5c. violet 25 35

70 Juan Mora and Julio Acosta

1921. Centenary of Independence.
118 **70** 2c. black and orange . . . 50 50
119 3c. black and green 50 50
120 6c. black and red 65 55
121 15c. black and blue . . . . 1·75 1·75
122 30c. black and brown . . . 2·75 2·75

1922. Coffee Publicity. Nos. 77/81 and 116 optd with sack inscr "CAFE DE COSTA RICA".
123 **53** 1c. brown 10 10
124 – 2c. green 15 10
125 – 4c. red 15 15
126 – 5c. orange 15 15
127 – 10c. blue 30 25
128 **68** 15c. violet 75 70

1922. Optd **CORREOS 1922**.
129 **69** 5c. violet 40 25

1922. Surch with red cross and **5c.**
130 5c.+5c. orange (No. 80) . . . 50 25

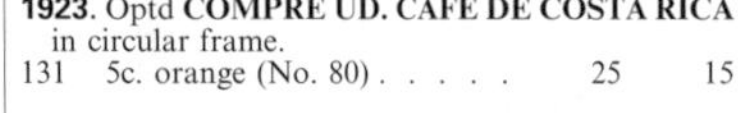

1923. Optd **COMPRE UD. CAFE DE COSTA RICA** in circular frame.
131 5c. orange (No. 80) 25 15

77 Jesus Jimenez (statesman)

81 Coffee-growing

80 National Monument

1923. Birth Centenary of J. Jimenez.
132 **77** 2c. brown 15 15
133 4c. green 15 15
134 5c. blue 35 15
135 20c. red 20 20
136 1col. violet 35 35

1923.
137 **80** 1c. purple 10 10
138 **81** 2c. yellow 20 15
139 – 4c. green 40 35
140 – 5c. blue 70 10
141 – 5c. green 20 10
142 – 10c. brown 85 15
143 – 10c. red 25 10
144 – 12c. red . . . . 7·00 1·75
145 – 20c. blue . . . . 3·00 60
146 – 40c. orange . . . . 2·75 90
147 – 1col. olive 75 40

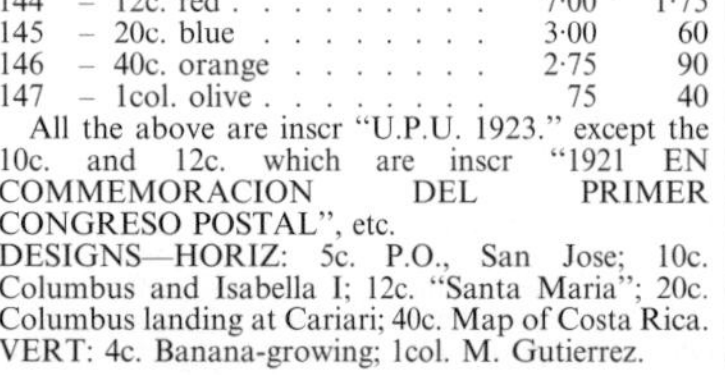

All the above are inscr "U.P.U. 1923." except the 10c. and 12c. which are inscr "1921 EN COMMEMORACION DEL PRIMER CONGRESO POSTAL", etc.
DESIGNS—HORIZ: 5c. P.O., San Jose; 10c. Columbus and Isabella I; 12c. "Santa Maria"; 20c. Columbus landing at Cariari; 40c. Map of Costa Rica. VERT: 4c. Banana-growing; 1col. M. Gutierrez.

85 Don R. A. Maldonado y Velasco

86 Map of Guanacaste

1924.
148 **85** 2c. green 15 10
For 3c. green see No. 211 and for other portraits as T **85** see Nos. 308/12.

1924. Cent of Province of Nicoya (Guanacaste).
149 **86** 1c. red 35 20
150 2c. purple 35 20
151 5c. green 35 20
152 10c. orange . . . . 1·25 50
153 – 15c. blue 40 45
154 – 20c. grey 65 45
155 – 25c. brown 90 75
DESIGN: 15c., 20c., 25c. Church at Nicoya.

88 Discus Thrower

93 Arms and Curtiss "Jenny"

1925. Inscr "JUEGOS OLIMPICOS". Imperf or perf.
156 **88** 5c. green . . . . 2·00 2·40
157 – 10c. red . . . . 2·00 2·40
158 – 20c. blue . . . . 4·00 3·50
DESIGNS—VERT: 10c. Trophy. HORIZ: 20c. Parthenon.

1926. Surch with values in ornamental designs.
159 3c. on 5c. (No. 140) 20 15
160 6c. on 10c. (No. 142) 35 25
161 30c. on 40c. (No. 146) . . . 50 40
162 45c. on 1col. (No. 147) . . . 55 50

1926. Surch with value between bars.
163 10c. on 12c. red (No. 144) . . 2·25 45

1926. Air.
164 **93** 20c. blue . . . . 1·25 40

94 Heredia Normal School

1926. Dated "1926".
165 – 3c. blue 15 15
166 – 6c. brown 25 20
167 **94** 30c. orange 35 25
168 – 45c. violet 90 50
DESIGNS: 3c. St. Louis College, Cartago; 6c. Chapui Asylum, San Jose; 45c. Ruins of Ujarras.

1928. Lindbergh Good Will Tour of Central America. Surch with aeroplane, **LINDBERGH ENERO 1928** and new value.
169 10c. on 12c. red (No. 144) . . 13·00 8·50

1928. Surch **5 5**.
170 **68** 5c. on 15c. violet 15 10

1929. Surch **CORREOS** and value.
171 **62** 5c. on 2col. red . . . . . 1·00 35
173 13c. on 40c. green . . . . 1·25 40

98 Post Office

103 Juan Rafael Mora

1930. Types of 1923 reduced in size and dated "1929" as T **98**.
174 – 1c. purple (as No. 137) . . 10 10
175 **98** 5c. green 10 10
176 – 10c. red (as No. 143) . . . 35 10

1930. Air. No. O178 surch **CORREO 1930 AEREO**, Bleriot XI airplane and new value.
177 **O 95** 8c. on 1col. 50 40
178 20c. on 1col. 70 50
179 40c. on 1col. . . . . . 1·40 1·00
180 1col. on 1col. . . . . . 2·00 1·40

1930. Air. Optd **CORREO AEREO** (No. 181) or **Correo Aereo** (others) or surch also.
182 **62** 5c. on 10c. brown 90 25
181 – 10c. red (No. 143) 45 15
183 **62** 20c. on 50c. blue . . . . . 1·25 25
184 40c. on 50c. blue . . . . . 1·25 50
185 1col. orange . . . . 2·75 80

1931.
186 **103** 13c. red 25 15

1931. Air. Fiscal stamps (Arms design) inscr "TIMBRE 1929" (or "1930", 3col.), surch **Habilitado 1931 Correo Aereo** and new value.
190 2col. on 2col. green . . . . . 16·00 16·00
191 3col. on 5col. brown . . . . 16·00 16·00
192 5col. on 10col. black . . . . 16·00 16·00

1932. Air. Telegraph stamp optd with wings inscr **CORREO CR AEREO**.
193 **62** 40c. green . . . . 3·50 80

106

1932. 1st National Philatelic Exhibition.
194 **106** 3c. orange 15 15
195 5c. green 25 25
196 10c. red 25 25
197 20c. blue 35 35
See also Nos. 231/4.

107 Ryan Brougham over La Sabana Airport, San Jose

1934. Air.
198 **107** 5c. green 15 10
507 5c. deep blue 10 10
508 5c. pale blue 10 10
199 10c. red 15 10
509 10c. green 10 10
510 10c. turquoise 10 10
200 15c. brown 30 10
511 15c. red 10 10
201 20c. blue 45 10
202 25c. orange 55 15
512 35c. violet 35 10
203 40c. brown 55 10
204 50c. black 40 15
205 60c. yellow 75 25
206 75c. violet . . . . 1·10 40
207 – 1col. red 85 10
208 – 2col. blue 90 35
209 – 5col. black . . . . 2·40 2·40
210 – 10col. brown . . . . . . 4·00 4·00
DESIGN: 1, 2, 5, 10col. Allegory of the Air Mail.

1934.
211 **85** 3c. green 10 10

109 Nurse at Altar

111 Our Lady of the Angels

1935. Costa Rican Red Cross Jubilee.
212 **109** 10c. red 35 15

1935. 300th Anniv of Apparition of Our Lady of the Angels.
213 – 5c. green 15 10
214 **111** 10c. red 35 15
215 – 30c. orange 50 25
216 – 45c. violet 65 40
217 **111** 50c. black . . . . 1·10 45
DESIGNS: 5c., 30c. Aerial view of Cartago; 45c. Allegory of the Apparition.

112 Cocos Island

1936.
218 **112** 4c. brown 25 10
219 8c. violet 30 15
220 25c. orange 35 15
221 35c. brown 50 15
222 40c. brown 40 25
223 50c. yellow 40 35
224 2col. green . . . . 4·75 3·75
225 5col. green . . . . 12·00 7·25

113 Cocos Island and Fleet of Columbus

1936.
226 **113** 5c. green 85 20
227 10c. red 1·10 20

114 Airplane over Mt. Poas

1937. Air. 1st Annual Fair.
228 **114** 1c. black 10 10
229 2c. brown 10 10
230 3c. violet 10 10

1937. 2nd National Philatelic Exhibition. As T **106**, but inscr "DICIEMBRE 1937".
231 **106** 2c. purple 15 15
232 3c. black 15 15
233 5c. green 15 15
234 10c. orange 15 15

115 Tunny

116 Native and Donkey carrying Bananas

117 Puntarenas

1937. National Exhibition, San Jose (1st Issue).
235 **115** 2c. black (postage) 20 15
236 **116** 5c. green 25 15
237 – 10c. red 35 20
238 **117** 2c. black (air) 10 10
239 5c. green 10 10
240 20c. blue 30 25
241 1col.40 brown 1·75 1·75
DESIGN—As Type **116**: 10c. Coffee gathering.

118 Purple Guaria Orchid "Carrleya skinneri"

119 National Bank

1938. National Exhibition, San Jose (2nd Issue).
242 **118** 1c. violet & grn (postage) 15 10
243 3c. brown 15 10
244 **119** 1c. violet (air) 10 10
245 3c. red 10 10
246 10c. red 15 10
247 75c. brown 90 90
DESIGN—As Type **118**: 3c. Cocoa-bean.

1938. No. 145 optd **1938**.
248 20c. blue 35 15

121 La Sabana Airport

1940. Air. Opening of San Jose Airport.
249 **121** 5c. green 10 10
250 10c. red 15 10
251 25c. blue 15 15
252 35c. brown 30 30
253 60c. orange 45 45
254 85c. violet 60 50
255 2col.35 green 3·25 3·25

1940. No. 168 variously surch **15 CENTIMOS** in ornamental frame.
256 15c. on 45c. violet 25 20
There are five distinct varieties of this surcharge.

1940. Pan-American Health Day. Unissued stamps prepared for the 8th Pan-American Child Welfare Congress optd **DIA PANAMERICANO DE LA SALUD 2. DICIEMBRE 1940**. (a) Postage. Allegorical design.
261 5c. green 20 10
262 10c. red 25 15
263 20c. blue 50 20
264 40c. brown 85 70
265 55c. orange 1·40 60

(b) Air. View of Duran Sanatorium.
266 10c. red 15 10
267 15c. violet 15 15
268 25c. blue 30 25
269 35c. brown 45 45
270 60c. green 35 35
271 75c. olive 75 85
272 1col.35 orange 3·25 3·25
273 5col. brown 14·00 14·00
274 10col. mauve 27·00 27·00

1940. Air. Pan-American Aviation Day. Surch **AERO Aviacion Panamericana Dic. 17 1940** and value.
275 15c. on 50c. yellow 50 50
276 30c. on 50c. yellow 50 50

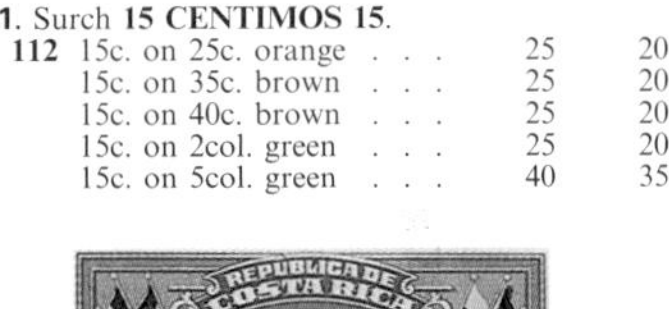

1941. Surch **15 CENTIMOS 15**.
277 **112** 15c. on 25c. orange 25 20
278 15c. on 35c. brown 25 20
279 15c. on 40c. brown 25 20
280 15c. on 2col. green 25 20
281 15c. on 5col. green 40 35

131 Stadium and Flag

132 Football Match

1941. Central American and Caribbean Football Championship.
282 **131** 5c. green (postage) 45 25
283 10c. orange 40 25
284 15c. red 55 25
285 25c. blue 60 25
286 40c. brown 1·90 75
287 50c. violet 2·40 90
288 75c. orange 4·75 1·90
289 1col. red 7·75 3·75
290 **132** 15c. red (air) 45 15
291 30c. blue 50 25
292 40c. brown 50 40
293 50c. violet 65 45
294 60c. green 85 50
295 75c. yellow 1·40 75
296 1col. mauve 2·40 2·40
297 1col.40 red 5·00 5·00
298 2col. green 9·50 9·50
299 5col. black 21·00 21·00

1941. Air. Costa Rica–Panama Boundary Treaty. Optd **Mayo 1941 Tratado Limitrofe Costa Rica – Panama** or surch also.
300 **107** 5c. on 20c. blue 20 15
301 15c. on 20c. blue 25 20
302 40c. on 75c. violet 40 25
303 – 65c. on 1col. red (No. 207) 40 30
304 – 1col.40 on 2col. blue (No. 208) 1·90 1·90
305 – 5col. black (No. 209) 6·50 6·50
306 – 10col. brown (No. 210) 7·50 7·50

1941. As Type **85** but with new portraits.
308 – 3c. orange 10 10
309 – 3c. purple 10 10
310 – 3c. red 10 10
310a – 3c. blue 10 10
311 – 5c. violet 10 10
312 – 5c. black 10 10
PORTRAITS: 3c. (Nos. 308/10) C. G. Viquez. 3c. (No. 310a) Mgr. B. A. Thiel. 5c. J. J. Rodriguez.

136 New Decree and Restored University

1941. Restoration of National University.
313 – 5c. green (postage) 25 10
314 **136** 10c. orange 30 10
315 – 15c. red 40 10
316 **136** 25c. blue 60 25
317 – 50c. brown 1·50 75
318 **136** 15c. red (air) 25 15
319 – 30c. blue 40 15
320 **136** 40c. orange 45 35
321 – 60c. blue 55 50
322 **136** 1col. violet 2·00 1·60
323 – 2col. black 5·00 3·75
324 **136** 5col. purple 16·00 13·00
DESIGN—(Nos. 313, 315, 317, 319, 321 and 323): The original Decree and University.

1941. Surch.
325 5c. on 6c. brn (No. 166) 15 15
326 15c. on 20c. blue (No. 248) 25 15

139 "V", Torch and Flags

140 Francisco Morazan

1942. War Effort.
327 **139** 5c. red 20 10
328 5c. orange 20 10
329 5c. green 20 10
330 5c. blue 20 10
331 5c. violet 20 10

1942. Portraits and dates.
332 A 1c. lilac (postage) 10 10
333 B 2c. black 10 10
334 C 3c. blue 10 10
335 D 5c. turquoise 10 10
336 5c. green 10 10
337 **140** 15c. red 10 10
338 E 25c. blue 20 15
339 F 50c. violet 1·25 50
340 G 1col. black 2·00 1·00
341 H 2col. orange 2·40 1·25
341a I 5c. brown (air) 10 10
342 A 10c. red 10 10
342a 10c. olive 10 10
342b J 15c. violet 10 10
343 K 25c. blue 15 10
344 L 30c. brown 15 10
345 D 40c. blue 25 10
346 40c. red 25 15
347 **140** 45c. purple 35 25
348 M 45c. black 20 15
349 E 50c. green 90 20
350 50c. orange 20 20
351 N 55c. purple 25 20
352 F 60c. blue 45 15
353 60c. green 20 15
354 G 65c. red 45 25
355 65c. blue 25 20
356 O 75c. green 40 25
357 H 85c. orange 55 35
358 85c. violet 65 45
359 P 1col. black 65 30
360 1col. red 50 20
361 Q 1col.05 sepia 60 40
362 R 1col.15 brown 90 85
363 1col.15 green 1·25 85
364 B 1col.40 violet 1·40 1·25
365 1col.40 yellow 85 75
366 C 2col. black 2·10 85
367 2col. olive 65 35
PORTRAITS: A, J. Mora Fernandez. B, B. Carranza. C, T. Guardia. D, M. Aguilar. E, J. M. Alfaro. F, F. M. Oreamuno. G, J. M. Castro. H, J. R. Mora. I, S. Lara. J, C. Duran. K, A. Esquivel. L, V. Herrera. M, J. R. de Gallegos. N, P. Fernandez. O, B. Soto. P, J. M. Montealegre. Q, B. Carrillo. R, J. Jimenez.

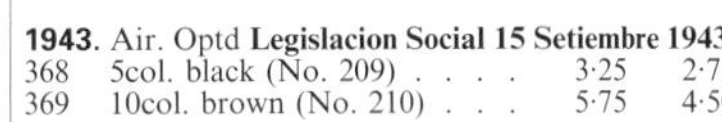

1943. Air. Optd **Legislacion Social 15 Setiembre 1943**.
368 5col. black (No. 209) 3·25 2·75
369 10col. brown (No. 210) 5·75 4·50

142 San Ramon

143 Allegory of Flight

1944. Centenary of San Ramon.
370 **142** 5c. green (postage) 10 10
371 10c. orange 15 10
372 15c. red 20 10
373 40c. grey 55 50
374 50c. blue 90 45
375 **143** 10c. orange (air) 15 10
376 15c. red 20 15
377 40c. blue 35 25
378 45c. red 40 35
379 60c. green 30 25
380 1col. brown 65 50
381 1col.40 grey 3·75 3·00
382 5col. violet 9·50 9·00
383 10col. black 27·00 24·00

1944. Ratification of Costa Rica and Panama Boundary Treaty. Optd **La entrevista ... 1944**.
384 **139** 5c. orange 10 10
385 5c. green 10 10
386 5c. blue 10 10
387 5c. violet 10 10

1944. Air. No. 207 optd **1944**.
388 1col. red 45 40

1945. Air. Official Air stamps of 1934 optd **1945** in oblong network frame.
389 **107** 5c. green 40 35
390 10c. red 40 35
391 15c. brown 40 35
392 20c. blue 40 40
393 25c. orange 40 40
394 40c. brown 40 40
395 50c. black 40 40
396 60c. yellow 55 40
397 75c. violet 45 40
398 – 1col. red (No. O220) 45 40
399 – 2col. blue (No. O221) 3·00 2·75
400 – 5col. black (No. O222) 3·75 3·25
401 – 10col. brown (No. O223) 5·50 5·00

1945. Air stamps. Telegraph stamps as Type **62** optd **CORREO AEREO 1945** and bar.
402 **62** 40c. green 80 45
403 50c. blue 1·00 45
404 1col. orange 2·40 75

148 Mauro Fernandez

149 Coffee Gathering

1945. Birth Centenary of Fernandez.
405 **148** 20c. green 15 10

1945.
406 **149** 5c. black and green 10 10
407 10c. black and orange 15 10
408 20c. black and red 20 15

150 Florence Nightingale and Nurse Cavell

1945. Air. 60th Anniv of National Red Cross Society.
409 **150** 1col. black 50 35

1946. Air. Central American and Caribbean Football Championship. As Type **132**, but inscribed "FEBRERO 1946".
410 **132** 25c. green 45 40
411 30c. orange 45 40
412 55c. blue 55 40

1946. Surch **15 15**.
413 **148** 15c. on 20c. green 15 10

152 San Juan de Dios Hospital
153 Ascension Esquivel

1946. Air. Centenary of San Juan de Dios Hospital.
414 **152** 5c. black and green . . . 10 10
415 10c. black and brown . . 10 10
416 15c. black and red . . . 10 10
417 25c. black and blue . . . 15 15
418 30c. black and orange . . 25 20
419 40c. black and olive . . . 15 15
420 50c. black and violet . . . 25 25
421 60c. black and green . . . 50 45
422 75c. black and brown . . 40 35
423 1col. black and blue . . . 50 25
424 2col. black and brown . . 55 60
425 3col. black and purple . . 1·40 1·40
426 5col. black and yellow . . 1·75 1·75

1947. Air. Former Presidents.
427 – 2col. black and blue . . . 65 50
428 **153** 3col. black and red . . . 1·00 65
429 – 5col. black and green . . 1·50 1·00
430 – 10col. black and orange 3·00 1·90
PORTRAITS: 2col. Rafael Iglesias. 5col. Cleto Gonzalez Viquez. 10col. Ricardo Jimenez.

1947. No. O228 optd **CORREOS 1947**.
431 **57** 5c. green 50 10

1947. Air. Nos. 410/2 surch **Habilitado para C 0.15 Decreto No. 16 de 28 abril de 1947**.
432 **132** 15c. on 25c. green 55 45
433 15c. on 30c. orange . . . 55 45
434 15c. on 55c. blue 55 45

156 Columbus at Cariari
158 Franklin D. Roosevelt

1947. Air.
435 **156** 25c. black and green . . . 65 15
436 30c. black and blue . . . 65 15
437 40c. black and orange . . 85 20
438 45c. black and violet . . . 1·10 35
439 50c. black and red . . . . 1·25 35
440 65c. black and brown . . 3·00 90

1947. Air. Stamps of 1942 surch **C0.15**.
441 E 15c. on 50c. orange 15 15
442 F 15c. on 60c. green 15 15
443 O 15c. on 75c. green 15 15
444 P 15c. on 1col. red 20 20
445 Q 15c. on 1col.5 sepia 15 15

1947.
446 **158** 5c. green (postage) . . . 10 10
447 10c. red 10 10
448 15c. blue 15 15
449 25c. orange 15 15
450 30c. red 35 25
451 15c. green (air) 10 10
452 30c. red 15 10
453 45c. brown 25 25
454 65c. orange 25 25
455 75c. blue 35 25
456 1col. green 50 45
457 2col. black 75 60
458 5col. red . . . . 1·50 1·50

159 Miguel de Cervantes Saavedra

1947. 400th Birth Anniv of Cervantes.
459 **159** 30c. blue 20 10
460 55c. red 35 25

160 Steam Locomotive "Maria Cecilia"

1947. Air. 50th Anniv of Pacific Electric Railway.
461 **160** 35c. black and green . . . 4·75 1·50

161 National Theatre
162 Rafael Iglesias

1948. Air. 50th Anniv of National Theatre.
462 **161** 15c. black and blue . . . 15 10
463 20c. black and red 15 15
464 **162** 35c. black and green . . . 25 20
465 **161** 45c. black and violet . . . 35 25
466 50c. black and red 35 25
467 75c. black and purple . . 45 45
468 1col. black and green . . 85 65
469 2col. black and lake . . . 1·25 90
470 **162** 5col. black and yellow . . 2·10 2·00
471 10col. black and blue . . 4·75 3·00

1948. Air. Surch **HABILITADO PARA C 0.35**.
472 **156** 35c. on 40c. blk & orge 60 30

1949. Air. 125th Anniv of Annexation of Guanacaste. Nos. 361, 409, 363 and 365 variously surch **1824-1949 125 Aniversario de la Anexion Guanacaste** and value.
473 Q 35c. on 1col. 5 sepia . . . 15 15
474 **150** 50c. on 1col. black . . . 25 15
475 R 55c. on 1col.15 green . . 45 35
476 B 55c. on 1col.40 yellow . . 45 35

165 Globe and Dove

1950. Air. 75th Anniv of U.P.U.
477 **165** 15c. red 15 10
478 25c. blue 15 10
479 1col. green 35 15

166 Battle of El Tejar, Cartago

167 Capture of Limon

1950. Air. Inscr "GUERRA DE LIBERACION NACIONAL 1948".
480 **166** 15c. black and red 15 10
481 **167** 20c. black and green . . . 20 15
482 – 25c. black and blue . . . 25 15
483 – 35c. black and brown . . 25 15
484 – 55c. black and violet . . . 55 25
485 – 75c. black and orange . . 55 35
486 – 80c. black and grey . . . 55 50
487 – 1col. black and orange . . 75 55
DESIGNS—VERT: 80c., 1col. Dr. C. L. Valverde. HORIZ: 25c. La Lucha Ranch; 35c. Trench of San Isidro Battalion; 55c., 75c. Observation post.

169 Bull
170 Queen Isabella and Caravels

1950. Air. National Agriculture and Industries Fair. Centres in black.
488 **169** 1c. green 10 10
489 A 2c. blue 10 10
490 B 3c. brown 10 10
491 C 5c. blue 10 10
492 **169** 10c. green 10 10
493 A 30c. violet 30 10
494 D 45c. orange 25 15
495 C 50c. grey 35 10
496 B 65c. blue 45 25
497 D 80c. red 45 30
498 **169** 2col. orange . . . . . . 1·25 1·00
499 A 3col. blue . . . . 3·75 2·40
500 C 5col. red . . . . 4·00 3·75
501 D 10col. red . . . . 4·00 3·75
DESIGNS—VERT: A, Fishing; B, Pineapple; C, Bananas; D, Coffee.

1952. Air. 500th Anniv of Isabella the Catholic.
502 **170** 15c. red 30 10
503 20c. orange 35 20
504 25c. blue 60 10
505 55c. green . . . . 1·25 50
506 2col. violet . . . . 3·00 1·00

1953. Air. Surch **15 15** within ornaments.
513 **158** 15c. on 30c. red 15 10
514 15c. on 45c. brown . . . 15 10
515 15c. on 65c. orange . . . 15 10

1953. Air. Surch **HABILITADO PARA CINCO CENTIMOS 1953**.
515a **155** 5c. on 30c. blk & blue 1·60 1·25
516 5c. on 40c. blk & orge 20 15
517 5c. on 45c. blk & vio . . 20 15
518 5c. on 65c. blk & brn . . 50 35

173

1953. Fiscal stamps surch as in T **173**.
519 **173** 5c. on 10c. green 10 10

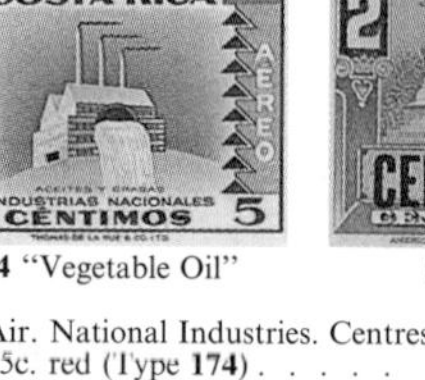

174 "Vegetable Oil"
(175)

1954. Air. National Industries. Centres in black.
520 5c. red (Type **174**) 10 10
520a 5c. blue (Type **174**) 15 10
521 10c. indigo (Pottery) 10 10
521a 10c. blue (Pottery) 15 10
522 15c. green (Sugar) 10 10
522a 15c. yellow (Sugar) 15 10
523 20c. violet (Soap) 10 10
524 25c. lake (Timber) 10 10
525 30c. lilac (Matches) 30 20
526 35c. purple (Textiles) . . . 15 10
527 40c. black (Leather) 25 15
528 45c. green (Tobacco) . . . 50 25
529 50c. purple (Confectionery) 35 10
530 55c. yellow (Canning) . . . 25 10
531 60c. brown (General industries) 60 35
532 65c. red (Metals) 45 50
533 75c. violet (Pharmaceutics) 65 45
533a 75c. red (as No. 533) . . . 25 15
533b 80c. violet (as No. 533) . . 45 40
534 1col. turq (Paper) 35 20
535 2col. mauve (Rubber) . . . 55 55
536 3col. green (Aircraft) . . . 90 55
537 5col. black (Marble) . . . . 1·40 45
538 10col. yellow (Beer) . . . . 4·00 3·00

1955. Fiscal stamps optd for postal use as in T **175**.
539 **175** 5c. on 2c. green 10 10
540 15c. on 2c. green 15 10

176 Rotary Emblem over Central America
177 Map of Costa Rica

1956. Air. 50th Anniv Rotary International.
542 **176** 10c. green 10 10
543 – 25c. blue 15 10
544 – 40c. brown 35 25
545 – 45c. red 25 20
546 – 60c. purple 25 20
547 – 2col. orange 45 45
DESIGNS: 25c. Emblem, hand and boy; 40c., 2col. Emblem and hospital; 45c. Emblem, leaves and Central America; 60c. Emblem and lighthouse.

1957. Air. Centenary of War of 1856–67.
548 **177** 5c. blue 25 10
549 – 10c. green 10 10
550 – 15c. orange 10 10
551 – 20c. brown 15 10
552 – 25c. blue 15 10
553 – 30c. violet 20 15
554 – 35c. red 20 15
555 – 40c. black 20 15
556 – 45c. red 25 15
557 – 50c. blue 25 15
558 – 55c. ochre 40 15
559 – 60c. red 30 25
560 – 65c. red 35 25
561 – 70c. yellow 45 30
562 – 75c. green 40 25
563 – 80c. sepia 45 35
564 – 1col. black 50 35
DESIGNS: 10c. Map of Guanacaste; 15c. Wartime inn; 20c. Santa Rosa house; 25c. Gen. D. J. M. Quiros; 30c. Old Presidential Palace; 35c. Minister D. J. B. Calvo; 40c. Dr. Luis Molina; 45c. Gen. D. J. J. Mora; 50c. Gen. D. J. M. Canas; 55c. Juan Santamaria Monument; 60c. National Monument; 65c. A. Vallerriestra; 70c. Pres. R. Castilla Marquesado of Peru; 75c. San Carlos Fortress; 80c. Vice-President D. F. M. Oreamuno of Costa Rica; 1col. Pres. D. J. R. Mora of Costa Rica.

1958. Obligatory Tax. Christmas. Nos. 489 and 521a surch **SELLO DE NAVIDAD PRO - CIUDAD DE LOS NINOS 5 5**.
565 A 5c. on 2c. black & blue . . 10 10
566 – 5c. on 10c. black & blue . . 25 10

179 Pres. Gonzalez Viquez
180 Pres. R. J. Oreamuno and Electric Locomotive No. 31

1959. Air. Birth Centenaries of Presidents Gonzalez (1958) and Oreamuno (1959).
567 **179** 5c. blue and pink 10 10
568 – 10c. slate and red 10 10
569 – 15c. black and slate . . . 10 10
570 – 20c. brown and red . . . 1·00 25
571 – 35c. blue and purple . . . 15 15
572 – 55c. violet and brown . . 25 20
573 – 80c. blue 40 35
574 **180** 1col. lake and orange . . 3·50 45
575 – 2col. lake and black . . . 60 45
DESIGNS—As Type **179**: 10c. Pres. Oreamuno. As Type **180**: Pres. Gonzalez and: 15c. Highway bridge; 55c. Water pipe-line; 80c. National Library. Pres. Oreamuno and: 20c. Puntarenas Quay; 35c. Post Office, San Jose. 2col. Both presidents and open book inscr "PROBIDAD" ("Honesty").

181 Father Flanagan
182 Goal Attack

1959. Obligatory Tax. Christmas. Inscr "SELLO DE NAVIDAD".
576 **181** 5c. green 20 10
577 – 5c. mauve 20 10
578 – 5c. olive 20 10
579 – 5c. black 20 10
PAINTINGS: No. 577, "Girl with braids" (after Modigliani). No. 578, "Boy with a clubfoot" (after Ribera). No. 579, "The boy blowing on charcoal" (after "El Greco").

1960. Air. 3rd Pan-American Football Games.
580 **182** 10c. blue 10 10
581 – 25c. blue 15 10
582 – 35c. red 15 15
583 – 50c. brown 20 15
584 – 85c. turquoise 40 50
585 – 5col. purple . . . . . . 1·25 1·25
DESIGNS: 25c. Player heading ball; 35c. Defender tackling forward; 50c. Referee bouncing ball; 85c. Goalkeeper seizing ball; 5col. Player kicking high ball.

183 "Uprooted Tree"
184 Prof. J. A. Facio

1960. Air. World Refugee Year.
586 **183** 35c. blue and yellow . . . 20 15
587 85c. black and pink . . . 40 35

1960. Birth Centenary of Professor Justo A. Facio.
588 **184** 10c. red 10 10

185 "OEA" and Banner

1960. Air. 6th and 7th Chancellors' Reunion Conference, Organization of American States, San Jose. Multicoloured.
589 25c. Type **185** 15 10
590 35c. "OEA" within oval chains 35 30
591 55c. Clasped hands and chains 50 40
592 5col. Flags in form of flying bird . . . . 1·90 1·75
593 10col. "OEA" on map of Costa Rica, and flags . . . 3·00 2·40

186 St. Louise de Marillac, Sister of Charity and Children

1960. Air. 300th Death Anniv of St. Vincent de Paul.
594 **186** 10c. green 10 10
595 – 25c. lake 10 10
596 – 50c. blue 25 15
597 – 1col. bistre 40 35
598 – 5col. sepia . . . . 1·25 95
DESIGNS—HORIZ: St. Vincent de Paul, and: 25c. Two-storey building; 1col. Modern building; 50c. As Type **186**, but scene shows Sister at bedside. VERT: 5col. Stained-glass window picturing St. Vincent de Paul with children.

187 Father Peralta

1960. Obligatory Tax. Christmas. Inscr "SELLO DE NAVIDAD".
599 **187** 5c. brown 35 10
600 – 5c. orange 35 10
601 – 5c. red 35 10
602 – 5c. blue 35 10
DESIGNS: No. 600, "Girl" (after Renoir); No. 601, "The Drinkers" (after Velasquez); No. 602, "Children Singing" (sculpture, after Zuniga).

188 Running

1960. Air. Olympics Game, Rome. Centres and inscriptions in black.
603 1c. yellow (T **188**) 10 10
604 2c. blue (Diving) 10 10
605 3c. red (Cycling) 10 10
606 4c. yellow (Weightlifting) . . 10 10
607 5c. green (Tennis) 10 10
608 10c. red (Boxing) 10 10
609 25c. turquoise (Football) . . 10 10
610 85c. mauve (Basketball) . . . 55 45
611 1col. grey (Baseball) 65 55
612 10col. lavender (Pistol-shooting) . . . . 5·50 4·50

1961. Air. 15th World Amateur Baseball Championships. No. 533a optd **XV Campeonato Mundial de Beisbol de Aficionados** or surch also.
613 25c. on 75c. black and red 20 10
614 75c. black and red 55 25

190 M. Aguilar

191 Prof. M. Obregon

1961. Air. 1st Continental Lawyers' Conference.
615 **190** 10c. blue 10 10
616 – 10c. purple 10 10
617 – 25c. violet 15 10
618 – 25c. sepia 15 10
PORTRAITS: No. 616, A. Brenes. No. 617, A. Gutierrez. No. 618, V. Herrera.
See also Nos. 628/31.

1961. Air. Birth Centenary of Obregon.
619 **191** 10c. turquoise 10 10

192 Granary (F.A.O.)

1961. Air. United Nations Commemoration.
620 **192** 10c. green 10 10
621 – 20c. orange 15 15
622 – 25c. slate 20 15
623 – 30c. blue 20 15
624 – 35c. red 50 25
625 – 45c. violet 35 20
626 – 85c. blue 40 30
627 – 10col. black . . . . . . 3·00 2·40
DESIGNS: 20c. "Medical Care" (W.H.O.); 25c. Globe and workers (I.L.O.); 30c. Globe and communications satellite "Correo 1B" (I.T.U.); 35c. Compass and rocket (W.M.O.); 45c. "The Thinker" (statue) and open book (U.N.E.S.C.O.); 85c. Douglas DC-6 airliner and globe (I.C.A.O.); 10col. "Spiderman" on girder (International Bank).

1961. Air. 9th Central American Medical Congress. As T **190** but inscr "NOVENO CONGRESO MEDICO", etc.
628 10c. violet 10 10
629 10c. turquoise 10 10
630 25c. sepia 15 10
631 25c. purple 15 10
PORTRAITS: No. 628, Dr. E. J. Roman. No. 629, Dr. J. M. S. Alfaro. No. 630, Dr. A. S. Llorente. No. 631, Dr. J. J. U. Giralt.

1961. Air. Children's City Christmas issue. No. 522 surch **SELLO DE NAVIDAD PRO-CIUDAD DE LOS NINOS 5 5**.
632 5c. on 10c. black and green 15 10

1962. Air. Surch in figures.
633 10c. on 15c. black and green (No. 522) 10 10
634 25c. on 15c. black and green (No. 522) 10 10
635 35c. on 50c. black and purple (No. 529) 70 15
636 85c. on 80c. blue (No. 573) 55 45

1962. Air. 2nd Central American Philatelic Convention. Optd **II CONVENCION FILATELICA CENTROAMERICANA SETIEMBRE 1962**.
637 30c. blue (No. 623) 45 35
638 2col. red and black (No. 575) 85 65

1962. Air. No. 522 surch **C 0.10**.
639 10c. on 15c. black & green 10 10

1962. Air. Fiscal stamps as T **175** optd **CORREO AEREO** and surch with new value for postal use.
640 25c. on 2c. green 10 10
641 35c. on 2c. green 15 10
642 45c. on 2c. green 25 20
643 85c. on 2c. green 45 35

198 "Virgin and Child" (after Bellini)

199 Jaguar

1962. Obligatory Tax. Christmas.
644 **198** 5c. sepia 40 10
645 A 5c. green 40 10
646 B 5c. blue 40 10
647 C 5c. red 40 10
DESIGNS: A, "Angel with Violin" (after Mellozo); B, Mgr. Ruben Odio; C, "Child's Head" (after Rubens).
See also Nos. 674/7.

1963. Air.
648 – 5c. brown and olive . . . 10 10
649 – 10c. blue and orange . . . 10 10
650 **199** 25c. yellow and blue . . 20 10
651 – 30c. brown and green . . 35 30
652 – 35c. brown and bistre . . 65 30
653 – 40c. blue and green . . . 70 45
654 – 85c. black and green . . . 1·10 70
655 – 5col. brown and green . . 5·75 4·75
ANIMALS (As Type **199**): 5c. Paca. 10c. Bairds tapir. 30c. Ocelot. 35c. White-tailed deer. 40c. American manatee. 85c. White-throated capuchin. 5col. White-lipped peccary.

200 Arms and Campaign Emblem

202 Anglo-Costa Rican Bank

1963. Air. Malaria Eradication.
656 **200** 25c. red 10 10
657 35c. brown 15 15
658 45c. blue 25 20
659 85c. green 45 35
660 1col. blue 55 45

1963. Obligatory Tax Fund for Children's Village. Nos. 644/7 surch **1963 10 CENTIMOS**.
661 **198** 10c. on 5c. sepia 15 15
662 A 10c. on 5c. green 15 15
663 B 10c. on 5c. blue 15 15
664 C 10c. on 5c. red 15 15

1963. Anglo-Costa Rican Bank Centenary.
665 **202** 10c. blue 10 10

203 ½ real Stamp of 1863 and Sail Merchantman "William le Lacheur"

1963. Air. Stamp Centenary.
666 **203** 25c. blue and purple . . . 50 15
667 – 2col. orange and grey . . 1·25 85
668 – 3col. green and ochre . . 2·00 1·50
669 – 10col. brown and green 9·00 4·00
DESIGNS: 2col. 2 reales stamp of 1863 and Postmaster-General R. B. Carrillo; 3col. 4 reales stamp of 1863 and mounted postman and pack-mule of 1839; 10col. 1 peso stamp of 1863 and mule-drawn mail van.

1963. Unissued animal designs as T **199**. Surch.
670 10c. on 1c. brown and green 15 10
671 25c. on 2c. sepia and brown 20 10
672 35c. on 3c. brown and green 25 15
673 85c. on 4c. brown and green 55 25
ANIMALS: 1c. Tamandua. 2c. Grey fox. 3c. Nine-banded armadillo. 4c. Giant anteater.

1963. Obligatory Tax. Christmas. As Nos. 644/7 but inscr "1963" and new colours.
674 **198** 5c. blue 20 10
675 A 5c. red 20 10
676 B 5c. black 20 10
677 C 5c. sepia 20 10

205 Pres. Orlich (Costa Rica)

206 Puma (clay statuette)

1963. Air. Presidential Reunion, San Jose. Portraits in sepia.
678 **205** 25c. purple 10 10
679 – 30c. mauve 15 10
680 – 35c. ochre 15 15
681 – 85c. blue 40 25
682 – 1col. brown 40 30
683 – 3col. green . . . . 1·00 65
684 – 5col. slate . . . . 1·40 1·00
PRESIDENTS: 30c. Rivera (Salvador). 35c. Ydigoras (Guatemala). 85c. Villeda (Honduras). 1col. Somoza (Nicaragua). 3col. Chiari (Panama). 5col. Kennedy (U.S.A.).

1963. Air. Archaeological Discoveries.
685 **206** 5c. turquoise and green 10 10
686 – 10c. turquoise and yellow 10 10
687 – 25c. sepia and red 10 10
688 – 30c. turquoise and buff 10 10
689 – 35c. green and salmon . . 15 10
690 – 45c. brown and blue . . . 15 10
691 – 50c. brown and blue . . . 15 10
692 – 55c. brown and green . . 20 10
693 – 75c. brown and buff . . . 20 15
694 – 85c. brown and yellow . . 55 35
695 – 90c. brown and yellow . . 45 35
696 – 1col. brown and blue . . 40 25
697 – 2col. turquoise & yellow 70 45
698 – 3col. brown and green . . 1·25 80
699 – 5col. brown & yellow . . 1·25 75
700 – 10col. green and mauve 2·00 1·90
DESIGNS—HORIZ: 10c. Ceremonial stool; 1col. Twin beakers; 2col. Alligator. VERT: 25c. Man (statuette); 30c. Dancer; 35c. Vase; 45c. Deity; 50c. Frog; 55c. "Eagle" bell; 75c. Multi-limbed deity; 85c. Kneeling effigy; 90c. "Bird" jug; 3col. Twin-tailed lizard; 5col. Child; 10col. Stone effigy of woman.

207 Flags

210 Mgr. R. Odio and Children

1964. Air. "Centro America".
701 **207** 30c. multicoloured 35 25

1964. Air. Surch.
702 – 5c. on 30c. (No. 688) . . 10 10
703 **207** 15c. on 30c. 10 10
704 – 15c. on 85c. (No. 694) . . 10 10
See Nos. 745/9.

1964. Paris Postal Conf. No. 695 surch **C 0.15 CONFERENCIA POSTAL DE PARIS - 1864**.
705 15c. on 90c. brn & yellow . . 10 10

1964. Obligatory Tax. Christmas. Inscr "SELLO DE NAVIDAD", etc.
706 **210** 5c. brown 15 10
707 A 5c. blue 15 10
708 B 5c. purple 15 10
709 C 5c. green 15 10
DESIGNS: A, Teacher and child; B, Children at play; C, Children in class.

211 A. Gonzalez F.

213 Handfuls of Grain

1965. Air. 50th Anniv of National Bank.
710 **211** 35c. green 10 10

1965. Air. 75th Anniv of Chapui Hospital. No. 697 surch **75 ANIVERSARIO ASILO CHAPUI 1890–1965**.
711 2col. turquoise and yellow . . 60 45

1965. Air. Freedom from Hunger.
712 – 15c. black, grey & brown 10 10
713 **213** 35c. black and buff . . . 15 10
714 – 50c. green and blue . . . 20 15
715 – 1col. silver, black & green 35 20
DESIGNS—HORIZ: 15c. Map and grain silo; 1col. Douglas DC-8 airliner over map. VERT: 50c. Children and population graph.

214 National Children's Hospital

215 L. Briceno B.

1965. Christmas Charity. Obligatory Tax. Inscr "SELLO DE NAVIDAD", etc.
716 **214** 5c. green 15 10
717 A 5c. brown 15 10
718 B 5c. red 15 10
719 C 5c. blue 15 10
DESIGNS—As Type **214**: A, Father Casiano; B, Poinsettia. DIAMOND: C, Father Christmas with children.

1965. Air. Incorporation of Nicoya District.
720 **215** 5c. slate, black & brown 10 10
721 – 10c. slate and blue . . . 10 10
722 – 15c. slate and bistre . . 10 10
723 – 35c. slate and blue . . . 10 10
724 – 50c. violet and grey . . . 15 10
725 – 1col. slate and ochre . . . 40 25
DESIGNS: 10c. Nicoya Church; 15c. Incorporation scroll; 35c. Map of Guanacaste Province; 50c. Provincial dance; 1col. Guanacaste map and produce.

216 Running

217 Pres. John F. Kennedy and "Mercury" Space Capsule encircling Globe

1965. Air. Olympic Games (1964). Mult.
726 5c. Type **216** 10 10
727 10c. Cycling 10 10
728 40c. Judo 15 10
729 65c. Handball 25 15
730 80c. Football 35 20
731 1col. Olympic torches 45 25

1965. Air. 2nd Death Anniv of Pres. Kennedy. Multicoloured.
732 45c. Type **217** 15 15
733 55c. Kennedy in San Jose Cathedral (vert) 25 15
734 85c. President with son (vert) 35 25
735 1col. Facade of White House, Washington (vert) 35 30

218 Fire Engine 219 Angel

1966. Air. Centenary of Fire Brigade.
736 **218** 5c. red and black 10 10
737 – 10c. red and yellow . . . 10 10
738 – 15c. black and red 10 10
739 – 35c. yellow and black . . 40 10
740 – 50c. red and blue 75 10
DESIGNS—VERT: 10c. Fire engine of 1866; 15c. Firemen with hoses; 35c. Brigade badge; 50c. Emblem of Central American Fire Brigades Confederation.

1966. Obligatory Tax. Christmas. Inscr "SELLO DE NAVIDAD", etc.
741 **219** 5c. blue 15 10
742 – 5c. red (Trinkets) 15 10
743 – 5c. green (Church) . . . 15 10
744 – 5c. brown (Reindeer) . . 15 10

1966. Air. (a) Surch with new value.
745 – 15c. on 30c. (No. 688) . . . 10 10
746 – 15c. on 45c. (No. 690) . . . 10 10
747 – 35c. on 75c. (No. 693) . . . 15 10
748 – 35c. on 55c. (No. 733) . . . 15 10
749 – 50c. on 85c. (No. 734) . . . 25 15

(b) Revenue stamps (as T **175**) surch **CORREOS DE COSTA RICA AEREO** and value.
750 15c. on 5c. blue 10 10
751 35c. on 10c. red 15 10
752 50c. on 20c. red 25 15

221 Central Bank, San Jose 222 Telecommunications Building, San Pedro

1967. Obligatory Tax. Social Plan for Postal Workers.
753 10c. blue 10 10
DESIGN—as Type **221** (34 × 26 mm.): 10c. Post Office, San Jose.

1967. Air. 50th Anniv of Central Bank.
754 **221** 5c. green 10 10
755 15c. brown 10 10
756 35c. red 15 10

1967. Air. Costa Rican Electrical Industry
757 – 5c. black 10 10
758 **222** 10c. mauve 10 10
759 – 15c. orange 10 10
760 – 25c. blue 10 10
761 – 35c. green 15 10
762 – 50c. brown 25 15
DESIGNS—VERT: 5c. Electric pylons; 15c. Central Telephone Exchange, San Jose. HORIZ: 25c. La Garita Dam; 35c. Rio Macho Reservoir; 50c. Cachi Dam.

223 "Chondrorhyncha aromatica" 224 O.E.A. Emblem and Split Leaf

1967. Air. University Library. Orchids. Mult.
763 5c. Type **223** 10 10
764 10c. "Miltonia endresii" . . . 10 10
765 15c. "Stanhopea cirrhata" . . 10 10
766 25c. "Trichopilia suavis" . . 15 10
767 35c. "Odontoglossum schlieperianum" 20 15
768 50c. "Cattleya skinneri" . . . 25 15
769 1col. "Cattleya dowiana" . . 45 35
770 2col. "Odontoglossum chiriquense" . . . . 1·00 40

1967. Air. 25th Anniv of Inter-American Institute of Agricultural Science.
771 **224** 50c. ultramarine & blue 15 10

225 Madonna and Child 226 LACSA Emblem

1967. Obligatory Tax. Christmas.
772 **225** 5c. green 10 10
773 5c. mauve 10 10
774 5c. blue 10 10
775 5c. turquoise 10 10

1967. Air. 20th Anniv (1966) of LACSA (Costa Rican Airlines). Multicoloured.
776 40c. Type **226** 10 10
777 45c. LACSA emblem and jetliner (horiz) 15 10
778 50c. Wheel and emblem . . . 15 15

227 Church of Solitude 228 Scouts in Camp

1967. Air. Churches and Cathedrals (1st series).
779 **227** 5c. green 10 10
780 – 10c. blue 10 10
781 – 15c. purple 10 10
782 – 25c. ochre 10 10
783 – 30c. brown 10 10
784 – 35c. blue 10 10
785 – 40c. orange 10 10
786 – 45c. green 10 10
787 – 50c. olive 15 10
788 – 55c. brown 15 10
789 – 65c. mauve 15 15
790 – 75c. sepia 20 15
791 – 80c. yellow 25 20
792 – 85c. purple . . . . 1·10 20
793 – 90c. green . . . . 1·10 25
794 – 1col. slate 25 25
795 – 2col. green 75 90
796 – 3col. orange . . . . . . 2·10 1·25
797 – 5col. blue . . . . 2·00 1·50
798 – 10col. red . . . . 2·50 2·00
DESIGNS: 10c. Santo Domingo Basilica, Heredia; 15c. Tilaran Cathedral; 25c. Alajuela Cathedral; 30c. Church of Mercy; 35c. Our Lady of the Angels Basilica; 40c. San Rafael Church, Heredia; 45c. Ruins, Ujarras; 50c. Ruins of Parish Church, Cartago; 55c. San Jose Cathedral; 65c. Parish Church, Puntarenas; 75c. Orosi Church; 80c. Cathedral of San Isidro the General; 85c. San Ramon Church; 90c. Church of the Forsaken; 1col. Coronado Church; 2col. Church of St. Teresita; 3col. Parish Church, Heredia; 5col. Carmelite Church; 10col. Limon Cathedral.
See also Nos. 918/33.

1968. Air. Golden Jubilee (1966) of Scout Movement in Costa Rica. Multicoloured.
799 15c. Scout on traffic control (vert) 10 10
800 25c. Scouts tending campfire (vert) 15 10
801 35c. Scout badge and flags (vert) 20 15
802 50c. Type **228** 25 15
803 65c. First scout troop on parade (1916) 35 20

229 "Madonna and Child" 230 Running

1968. Christmas Charity. Obligatory Tax.
805 **229** 5c. black 10 10
806 5c. purple 10 10
807 5c. brown 10 10
808 5c. red 10 10

1969. Air. Olympic Games, Mexico. Mult.
809 30c. Type **230** 10 10
810 40c. Woman breasting tape . . 15 10
811 55c. Boxing 25 15
812 65c. Cycling 30 15
813 75c. Weightlifting 30 15
814 1col. High-diving 35 25
815 3col. Rifle-shooting 90 55

231 Exhibition Emblem 232 Arms of San Jose

1969. Air. "Costa Rica 69" Philatelic Exn.
816 **231** 35c. multicoloured 10 10
817 40c. multicoloured 15 10
818 50c. multicoloured 15 10
819 2col. multicoloured . . . 1·10 40

1969. Coats of Arms. Multicoloured.
820 15c. Type **232** 10 10
821 35c. Cartago 10 10
822 50c. Heredia 15 10
823 55c. Alajuela 15 15
824 65c. Guanacaste 25 15
825 1col. Puntarenas 60 15
826 2col. Limon 70 35

233 I.L.O. Emblem 234 Map on Football

1969. Air. 50th Anniv of I.L.O.
827 **233** 35c. turquoise and black 15 10
828 50c. red and black 20 10

1969. Air. 4th CONCACAF Football Championships. Multicoloured.
829 65c. Type **234** 20 15
830 75c. Goalmouth melee . . . 20 15
831 85c. Players with ball 25 15
832 1col. Two players with ball 30 20

235 Madonna and Child 236 Stylized Crab

1969. Christmas. Charity. Obligatory Tax.
833 **235** 5c. turquoise 10 10
834 5c. lake 10 10
835 5c. blue 10 10
836 5c. orange 10 10

1970. Air. 10th Inter-American Cancer Congress, San Jose.
837 **236** 10c. black and mauve . . 10 10
838 15c. black and yellow . . 10 10
839 50c. black and orange . . 15 10
840 1col.10 black and green 30 15

238 Costa Rican stamps and Magnifier 239 Japanese Vase and Flowers

1970. Air. "Costa Rica 70" Philatelic Exhibition.
843 **238** 1col. red and blue 55 20
844 2col. mauve and blue . . 1·10 45

1970. Air. Expo 70. Multicoloured.
845 10c. Type **239** 10 10
846 15c. Ornamental cart (horiz) 10 10
847 35c. Sun tower (horiz) . . . 15 10
848 40c. Tea-ceremony (horiz) . . 15 10
849 45c. Coffee-picking 15 10
850 55c. View of Earth from Moon 15 10

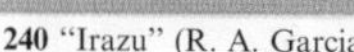

240 "Irazu" (R. A. Garcia) 241 "Holy Child"

1970. Air. Costa Rican Paintings. Mult.
851 25c. Type **240** 30 10
852 45c. "Escazu Valley" (M. Bertheau) 30 10
853 80c. "Estuary Landscape" (T. Quiros) 65 15
854 1col. "The Other Face" (C. Valverde) 45 15
855 2col.50 "Madonna" (L. Daell) (vert) . . . . . 1·25 60

1970. Christmas Charity. Obligatory Tax.
856 **241** 5c. mauve 10 10
857 5c. brown 10 10
858 5c. olive 10 10
859 5c. violet 10 10

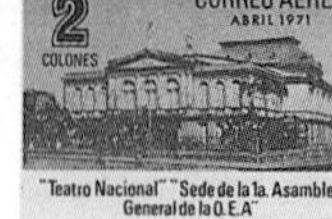

242 Costa Rican Arms of 21 October 1964 243 National Theatre, San Jose

1971. Air. Various Costa Rican Coats of Arms (with dates). Multicoloured.
860 5c. Type **242** 10 10
861 10c. 27 November 1906 . . . 10 10
862 15c. 29 September 1848 . . . 10 10
863 25c. 21 April 1840 . . . . . 10 10
864 35c. 22 November 1824 . . . 10 10
865 50c. 2 November 1824 . . . 10 10
866 1col. 6 March 1824 . . . . . 15 10
867 2col. 10 May 1823 . . . . . 60 20

1971. Air. O.E.A. General Assembly. San Jose.
868 **243** 2col. purple 35 25

244 J. M. Delgado and M. J. Arce (Salvador)

1971. Air. 150th Anniv of Central American Independence. Multicoloured.
869 5c. Type **244** 10 10
870 10c. M. Larreinaga and M. A. de la Cerda (Nicaragua) 10 10
871 15c. J. C. del Valle and D. de Herrera (Honduras) . . . 10 10
872 35c. P. Alvarado and F. del Castillo (Costa Rica) . . . 10 10
873 50c. A. Larrazabal and P. Molina (Guatemala) . . 10 10
874 1col. O.D.E.C.A. flag (vert) 15 10
875 2col. O.D.E.C.A. emblem (vert) 35 25
O.D.E.C.A. = Organization of Central American States.

245 Cradle on "PAX" 246 Federation Emblem

1971. Christmas Charity. Obligatory Tax.
876 **245** 10c. orange 10 10
877 10c. brown 10 10
878 10c. green 10 10
879 10c. blue 10 10

1971. Air. 50th Anniv of Costa Rican Football Federation.
880 **246** 50c. multicoloured 10 10
881 60c. multicoloured 10 10

247 "Children of the World" 248 Guanacaste Tree

1972. Air. 25th Anniv of U.N.I.C.E.F.
882 **247** 50c. multicoloured 10 10
883 1col.10 multicoloured . . 20 15

1972. Air. Bicentenary of Liberia City. Mult.
884 20c. Type **248** 10 10
885 40c. Hermitage, Liberia . . . 10 10
886 55c. Mayan petroglyphs . . . 10 10
887 60c. Clay head (vert) 15 10

250 Farmer's Family and Farm

251 Inter-American Stamp Exhibitions

1972. Air. 30th Anniv of O.E.A. Institute of Agricultural Sciences (IICA).
892 **250** 20c. multicoloured 10 10
893 – 45c. multicoloured 10 10
894 – 50c. yellow, green & blk 10 10
895 – 10col. multicoloured 1·10 60
DESIGNS—HORIZ: 45c. Cattle. VERT: 50c. Tree-planting; 10col. Agricultural worker and map.

1972. Air. "Exfilbra 72" Stamp Exhibition.
896 **251** 50c. brown and orange 10 10
897 2col. violet and blue 35 25

252 Madonna and Child

253 First Book printed in Costa Rica

1972. Christmas Charity. Obligatory Tax.
898 **252** 10c. red 10 10
899 10c. lilac 10 10
900 10c. blue 10 10
901 10c. green 10 10

1972. Air. International Book Year. Mult.
902 20c. Type **253** 10 10
903 50c. National Library, San Jose (horiz) 10 10
904 75c. Type **253** 15 10
905 5col. As 50c. 60 45

254 View near Irazu

255 Madonna and Child

1972. Air. American Tourist Year. Mult.
906 5c. Type **254** 10 10
907 15c. Entrance to Culebra Bay 10 10
908 20c. Type **254** 10 10
909 25c. As 15c. 10 10
910 40c. Manuel Antonio Beach 10 10
911 45c. Costa Rican Tourist Institute emblem 10 10
912 50c. Lindora Lake 10 10
913 60c. Post Office Building, San Jose (vert) 15 10
914 80c. As 40c. 15 15
915 90c. As 45c. 15 15
916 1col. As 50c. 15 15
917 2col. As 60c. 35 25

1973. Air. Churches and Cathedrals (2nd series). As Nos. 779/94 but colours changed.
918 **227** 5c. grey 10 10
919 – 10c. green 10 10
920 – 15c. orange 10 10
921 – 25c. brown 10 10
922 – 30c. purple 10 10
923 – 35c. violet 15 10
924 – 40c. green 15 10
925 – 45c. brown 15 10
926 – 50c. red 10 10
927 – 55c. blue 10 10
928 – 65c. black 15 10
929 – 75c. red 15 10
930 – 80c. green 15 10
931 – 85c. lilac 15 15
932 – 90c. red 15 15
933 – 1col. blue 15 15

1973. Obligatory Tax. Christmas Charity.
934 **255** 10c. red 10 10
935 10c. purple 10 10
936 10c. black 10 10
937 10c. brown 10 10

256 Flame Emblem

257 O.E.A. Emblem

1973. Air. 25th Anniv of Declaration of Human Rights.
938 **256** 50c. red and blue 10 10

1973. Air. 25th Anniv of Organization of American States.
939 **257** 20c. red and blue 10 10

258 J. Vargas Calvo

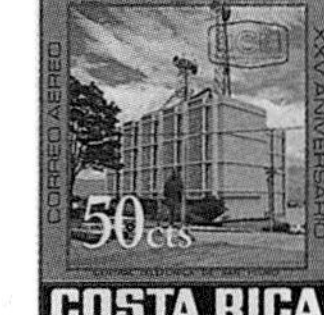

260 Telephone Centre, San Pedro

1974. Air. Costa Rican Composers. Mult.
940 20c. Type **258** 10 10
941 20c. Alejandro Monestel 10 10
942 20c. Julio Mata 10 10
943 60c. Julio Fonseca 15 10
944 2col. Rafael Chaves 35 25
945 5col. Manuel Gutierrez 85 70

1974. Air. Fiscal stamps as Type **175** (but without surcharge) optd **HABILITADO PARA CORREO AEREO**.
946 50c. brown 10 10
947 1col. violet 15 10
948 2col. orange 35 20
949 5col. green 85 70

1974. Air. 25th Anniv of Costa Rican Electrical Institute. Multicoloured.
950 50c. Type **260** 10 10
951 65c. Control Room, Rio Macho (horiz) 15 10
952 85c. Power house, Rio Macho 15 15
953 1col.25 Cachi Dam, Rio Macho (horiz) 20 15
954 2col. Institute H.Q. building 35 20

261 "Exfilmex" Emblem

262 Couple on Map

1974. Air. "Exfilmex" Stamp Exhibition, Mexico City.
955 **261** 65c. green 15 10
956 3col. pink 50 35

1974. Air. 25th Anniv of 4-S Clubs.
957 **262** 20c. emerald and green 10 10
958 – 50c. multicoloured 10 10
DESIGN. 50c. Young agricultural workers.

263 Brenes Mesen

264 Child's and Adult's Hands

1974. Air. Birth Centenary of Roberto Brenes Mesen (educator).
959 **263** 20c. black and brown 10 10
960 – 85c. black and red 15 15
961 – 5col. brown and black 85 70
DESIGNS—VERT: 85c. Brenes Mesen's "Poems of Love and Death". HORIZ: 5col. Brenes Mesen's hands.

1974. Air. 50th Anniv of Costa Rican Insurance Institute.
962 – 20c. multicoloured 10 10
963 – 50c. multicoloured 10 10
964 **264** 65c. multicoloured 10 15
965 – 85c. multicoloured 15 15
966 – 1col.25 black and gold 20 15
967 – 2col. multicoloured 35 20
968 – 2col.50 multicoloured 45 35
969 – 20col. multicoloured 2·50 2·40
DESIGNS—HORIZ: 20c. R. Jimenez Oreamuno and T. Soley Guell (founders); 50c. Spade ("Harvest Insurance"). VERT: 85c. Paper boat within hand ("Marine Insurance"); 1col.25, Institute emblem; 2col. Arm in brace ("Workers' Rehabilitation"); 2col.50, Hand holding spanner ("Risks at Work"); 20col. House in protective hands ("Fire Insurance").

265 W.P.Y. Emblem

266 "Boys eating Cakes" (Murillo)

1974. Air. World Population Year.
970 **265** 2col. red and blue 35 20

1974. Obligatory Tax. Christmas.
971 **266** 10c. red 10 10
972 – 10c. purple 10 10
973 – 10c. black 10 10
974 – 10c. blue 10 10
DESIGNS: No. 972, "The Beautiful Gardener" (Raphael); No. 973, "Maternity" (J. R. Bonilla); No. 974, "The Prayer" (J. Reynolds).

267 Oscar J. Pinto (football pioneer)

268 "Mormodes buccinator"

1974. Air. 1st Central American Olympic Games, Guatemala (1973). Each grey and blue.
975 20c. Type **267** 10 10
976 50c. D. A. Montes de Oca (shooting champion) 10 10
977 1col. Eduardo Garnier (promoter of athletics) 15 10

1975. Air. 1st Central American Orchids Exhibition. Multicoloured.
978 25c. Type **268** 10 10
979 25c. "Gongora claviodora" 10 10
980 25c. "Masdevallia ephippium" 10 10
981 25c. "Encyclia spondiadum" 10 10
982 65c. "Lycaste skinneri alba" 40 10
983 65c. "Peristeria elata" 40 10
984 65c. "Miltonia roezelii" 40 10
985 65c. "Brassavola digbyana" 40 10
986 80c. "Epidendrum mirabile" 50 15
987 80c. "Barkeria lindleyana" 50 15
988 80c. "Cattleya skinneri" 50 15
989 80c. "Sobralia macrantha splendens" 50 15
990 1col.40 "Lycaste cruenta" 65 15
991 1col.40 "Oncidium obryzatum" 65 15
992 1col.40 "Gongora armeniaca" 65 15
993 1col.40 "Sievekingia suavis" 65 15
994 1col.75 "Hexisea imbricata" 65 20
995 2col.15 "Warcewiczella discolor" 65 20
996 2col.50 "Oncidium kramerianum" 90 35
997 3col.25 "Cattleya dowiana" 1·25 40

269 Emblem of Costa Rica Radio Club

1975. Air. 16th Convention of Radio Amateurs Federation of Central America and Panama, San Jose.
998 **269** 1col. purple and black 15 10
999 – 1col.10 red and blue 20 15
1000 – 2col. blue and black 35 20
DESIGNS—VERT: 1col.10, Federation emblem within "V" of Flags. HORIZ: 2col. Federation emblem.

270 Nicoyan Beach

1975. Air. 150th Anniv of Annexation of Nicoya. Multicoloured.
1001 25c. Type **270** 10 10
1002 75c. Cattle-drive 15 15
1003 1col. Colonial church 15 15
1004 3col. Savannah riders (vert) 50 40

271 3c. Philatelic Exhibition Stamp of 1932

1975. Air. 6th National Philatelic Exhibition, San Jose.
1005 **271** 2col.20 orange & black 40 35
1006 – 2col.20 green and black 40 35
1007 – 2col.20 red and black 40 35
1008 – 2col.20 blue and black 40 35
DESIGNS: Stamps of 1932. No. 1006, 5c. stamp; No. 1007, 10c. stamp; No. 1008, 20c. stamp.

272 I.W.Y. Emblem

273 U.N. Emblem

1975. Air. International Women's Year.
1009 **272** 40c. red and blue 10 10
1010 1col.25 blue and black 20 15

1975. Air. 30th Anniv of United Nations.
1011 **273** 10c. blue and black 10 10
1012 – 60c. multicoloured 10 10
1013 – 1col.20 multicoloured 20 15
DESIGNS—HORIZ: 60c. General Assembly. VERT: 1col.20, U.N. Headquarters, New York.

274 "The Visitation"

275 "Children with Tortoise" (F. Amighetti)

1975. Air. "The Christmas Tradition". Paintings by Jorge Gallardo. Multicoloured.
1014 50c. Type **274** 10 10
1015 1col. "The Nativity and the Comet" 15 10
1016 5col. "St. Joseph in his workshop" 60 45

1975. Obligatory Tax. Christmas. Children's Village. Multicoloured.
1017 **275** 10c. brown 10 10
1018 – 10c. purple 10 10
1019 – 10c. grey 10 10
1020 – 10c. blue 10 10
DESIGNS: No. 1018, "The Virgin of the Carnation" (Da Vinci); No. 1019, "Happy Dreams" (child in bed—Sonia Romero); No. 1020, "Child with Pigeon" (Picasso).

276 Schoolboy and Flags

277 Prof. A. M. Brenes Mora

1976. Air. 20th Anniv of "20–30" Youth Clubs in Costa Rica.
1021 **276** 1col. multicoloured 15 10

1976. Birth Centenary (1970) of Professor A. M. Brenes Mora (botanist).
1022 **277** 1col. violet (postage) 15 15
1023 – 5c. multicoloured (air) 10 10
1024 – 30c. multicoloured 10 10
1025 – 55c. multicoloured 10 10
1026 – 2col. multicoloured 35 20
1027 – 10col. multicoloured 1·10 85
DESIGNS: 5c. "Quercus brenesii"; 30c. "Maxillaria albertii"; 55c. "Calathea brenesii"; 2col. "Brenesia costaricensis"; 10col. "Philodendron brenesii".
No. 1023 is wrongly inscribed "brenessi".

278 Open Book as "Flower"

281 Early and Modern Telephones

280 Mounted Postman with Pack Mule

1976. Air. Costa Rican Literature. Mult.
1028 15c. Type **278** 10 10
1029 1col.10 Reader with "T.V. eye" 15 15
1030 5col. Book and flag (horiz) 55 45

1976. Centenary (1974) of U.P.U.
1032 **280** 20c. black and yellow . . 10 10
1033 – 50c. multicoloured . . . 10 10
1034 – 65c. multicoloured . . . 15 10
1035 – 85c. multicoloured . . . 15 15
1036 – 2col. black and blue . . 35 25
DESIGNS—HORIZ: 50c., 5c. U.P.U. stamp of 1882; 65c., 10c. U.P.U. stamp of 1882; 85c., 20c. U.P.U. stamp of 1882. VERT: 2col. U.P.U. Monument, Berne.

1976. Telephone Centenary.
1037 **281** 1col.60 black and blue 25 20
1038 – 2col. black, brown & grn 35 20
1039 – 5col. black and yellow 55 45
DESIGNS: 2col. Costa Rica's first telephone; 5col. Alexander Graham Bell.

282 Emblems and Costa Rica 2c. Stamp of 1901 with Centre Inverted

1976. Air. 7th National Philatelic Exhibition.
1040 **282** 50c. multicoloured . . . 10 10
1041 1col. multicoloured . . . 15 10
1042 2col. multicoloured . . . 35 20

283 Emblem of Comptroller General

284 "Girl in Wide-brimmed Hat" (Renoir)

1976. Air. 25th Anniv of Comptroller General.
1044 **283** 35c. blue and black . . . 10 10
1045 – 2col. black, brown & bl 35 20
DESIGN—VERT: 2col. Amadeo Quiros Blanco (1st Comptroller).

1976. Obligatory Tax. Christmas.
1046 **284** 10c. lake 10 10
1047 – 10c. purple 10 10
1048 – 10c. slate 10 10
1049 – 10c. blue 10 10
DESIGNS: No 1047, "Virgin and Child" (Hans Memling); No. 1048, "Meditation" (Floria Pinto de Herrero); No. 1049, "Gaston de Mezerville" (Lolita Zeller de Peralta).

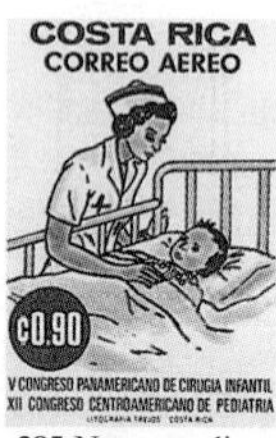

285 Nurse tending Child

286 "L.A.C.S.A." encircling Globe

1976. Air. 5th Pan-American Children's Surgery Congress. Multicoloured.
1050 90c. Type **285** 15 15
1051 1col.10 National Children's Hospital (horiz) 20 15

1976. Air. 30th Anniv of LACSA Airline. Mult.
1052 1col. Type **286** 20 10
1053 1col.20 Route-map of LACSA services 25 15
1054 3col. LACSA emblem and Costa Rican flag 65 45

287 Boston Tea Party

1976. Air. Bicent of American Revolution. Mult.
1055 2col.20 Type **287** 70 25
1056 5col. Declaration of Independence 55 45
1057 10col. Ringing the Independence Bell (vert) 1·10 85

288 Boruca Textile

289 Tree of Guanacaste

1977. Air. National Handicrafts Project. Mult.
1058 75c. Type **288** 15 10
1059 1col.50 Decorative handicraft in wood . . . 25 15

1977. Air. 50th Anniv of Rotary Club, San Jose.
1060 **289** 40c. green, blue and yellow 10 10
1061 – 50c. black, blue and yellow 10 10
1062 – 60c. black, blue and yellow 10 10
1063 – 3col. multicoloured . . . 50 40
1064 – 10col. black, blue and yellow . . . . . . 1·25 85
DESIGNS—VERT: 50c. Felipe J. Alvarado (founder); 10col. Paul Harris, founder of Rotary International. HORIZ: 60c. Dr. Blanco Cervantes Hospital; 3col. Map of Costa Rica.

290 Juana Pereira

291 Alonso de Anguciana de Gamboa

1977. Air. 50th Anniv of Coronation of Our Lady of the Angels (Patron Saint of Costa Rica).
1065 50c. Type **290** 10 10
1066 1col. First church of Our Lady of the Angels (horiz) 15 10
1067 1col.10 Our Lady of the Angels 20 15
1068 1col.25 Our Lady's crown 25 15

1977. Air. 400th Anniv of Foundation of Esparza.
1069 **291** 35c. purple, mve & blk 10 10
1070 – 75c. brown, red & black 15 10
1071 – 1col. dp bl, bl & blk . . 15 10
1072 – 2col. green and black . . 35 25
DESIGNS: 75c. Church of Esparza; 1col. Our Lady of Candelaria, Patron Saint of Esparza; 2col. Diego de Artieda y Chirino.

292 Child

293 Institute Emblem

1977. Air. 20 Years of "CARE" in Costa Rica. Multicoloured.
1073 80c. Type **292** 15 10
1074 1col. Soya beans (horiz) . . 15 10

1977. Air. 25th Anniv of Hispanic Cultural Institute of Costa Rica. Multicoloured.
1075 50c. Type **293** 10 10
1076 1col.40 First map of the Americas, 1540 (40 × 30 mm) 25 20

294 "Our Lady of Mercy Church" (R. Ulloa)

295 Health Ministry on Map

1977. Air. Mystical Paintings. Multicoloured.
1077 50c. Type **294** 10 10
1078 1col. "Christ" (F. Pinto de Herrero) 15 10
1079 5col. "St. Francis and the Birds" (L. Gonzalez de Saenz) 55 45

1977. Air. 50th Anniv of Health Ministry.
1080 **295** 1col.40 multicoloured . . 25 20

296 "Child's Head" (Rubens)

297 Weaving

1977. Obligatory Tax. Christmas.
1081 **296** 10c. red 10 10
1082 – 10c. blue 10 10
1083 – 10c. green 10 10
1084 – 10c. purple 10 10
DESIGNS: No. 1082, "Tenderness" (Cristina Fournier); No. 1083, "Abstraction" (Amparo Cruz); No. 1084, "Mariano Goya" (Francisco de Goya).

1978. Air. 21st Congress of Confederation of Latin American Tourist Organizations. Multicoloured.
1085 50c. Type **297** 10 10
1086 1col. Picnic 15 15
1087 2col. Beach scene 35 20
1088 5col. Fruit market 55 45
1089 10col. Lake scene . . . . . 1·25 85

298 Reader with Book

299 Jose de San Martin

1978. National Literacy Campaign.
1090 **298** 50c. blue, black & orge 10 10

1978. Air. Birth Bicent of Jose de San Martin.
1091 **299** 5col. multicoloured . . . 60 40

300 Globe

301 "XXV"

1978. Air. 50th Anniv of Pan-American Institute of Geography and History.
1092 **300** 5col. blue, gold & lt blue 50 60

1978. Air. 30th Anniv of Central American University Confederation.
1093 **301** 80c. blue 15 10

302 Emblems

1978. Air. 6th Inter-American Philatelic Exn, Buenos Aires.
1094 **302** 2col. turq, gold & blk . . 35 25

1978. Air. 50th Anniv of 1st PanAm Flight in Costa Rica. Nos. 994/6 optd **"50 Aniversario del primer vuelo de PAN AM en Costa Rica 1928 – 1978"**.
1095 1col.75 "Hexisea imbricata" 25 20
1096 2col.15 "Warcewiczella discolor" 35 25
1097 2col.50 "Oncidium kramerianum" 40 30

1978. Air. 50th Anniv of Lindbergh's Visit to Costa Rica. Nos. 994/6 optd **"50 Aniversario de la visita de Lindbergh a Costa Rica 1928 – 1978"**.
1098 1col.75 "Hexisea imbricata" 30 20
1099 2col.15 "Warcewiczella discolor" 35 25
1100 2col.50 "Oncidium kramerianum" 40 30

1978. Air. Carlos Maria Ulloa Hospital Centenary. Nos. 964 and 968 surch **"Centenario del Asilo Carlos Maria Ulloa 1878 – 1978"** and new value.
1101 50c. on 65c. multicoloured 10 10
1102 2col. on 2col.50 mult . . . 35 25

306 Star over Map of Costa Rica

308 "Christmas Winds" (L. F. Chacon)

1978. Air. Christmas.
1103 **306** 50c. blue and black . . . 10 10
1104 1col. mauve and black 15 15
1105 5col. red and black . . . 55 55

1978. Air. Nos. 982/5 and 995/6 surch.
1106 50c. on 65c. "Lycaste skinneri alba" 10 10
1107 50c. on 65c. "Peristeria elata" 10 10
1108 50c. on 65c. "Miltonia roezelii" 10 10
1109 50c. on 65c. "Brassavola digbyana" 10 10
1110 1col.20 on 2col.15 "Warcewiczella discolor" 20 15
1111 2col. on 2col.50 "Oncidium kramerianum" 35 25

1978. Obligatory Tax. Christmas. Children's Village.
1112 **308** 10c. slate 10 10
1113 10c. red 10 10
1114 – 10c. mauve 10 10
1115 – 10c. blue 10 10
DESIGN: Nos. 1114/15, "Girl playing with Kite" (sculpture by Nester Zeledon).

309 "The Flying Men", Chorotega Ritual

310 Domingo Rivas

1978. Air. 500th Anniv of Gonzalo Fernandez de Oviedo (first chronicler of Spanish Indies).
1116 **309** 85c. multicoloured . . . 15 10
1117 – 1col.20 blue and black 20 15
1118 – 10col. multicoloured . . 1·25 75
DESIGNS—HORIZ: 1col.20, Oviedo giving his "History of Indies" to Duke of Calabria. VERT: 10col. Lord of Oviedo's coat of arms.

1978. Air. Centenary of San Jose Cathedral.
1119 **310** 1col. blue and black . . 15 15
1120 – 20col. multicoloured . . 2·10 2·00
DESIGN: 20c. San Jose Cathedral.

311 Cocos Island

1979. Air. Presidential Visit to Cocos Island. Mult.
1121 90c. Type **311** 15 10
1122 2col.10 Cocos Island (different) 35 25
1123 3col. Cocos Island (different) 50 35
1124 5col. Moon over Cocos Island (vert) 55 60
1125 10col. Commemorative plaque and people with flag (vert) . . . . 1·00 75

312 Shrimp

1979. Air. Conservation of Marine Fauna. Multicoloured.
1127 60c. Type **312** 10 10
1128 85c. Mahogany snapper . . 15 10
1129 1col.80 Yellow corvina . . . 40 20
1130 3col. Lobster 50 35
1131 10col. Frigate mackerel . . 1·50 75

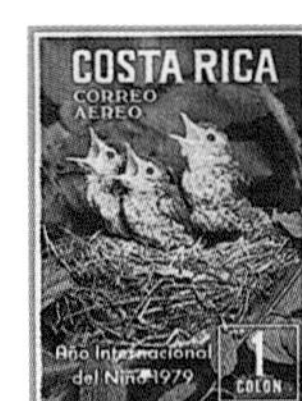

313 Hungry Nestlings (Song Thrushes)

1979. Air. International Year of the Child.
1132 **313** 1col. multicoloured . . . 75 45
1133 2col. multicoloured . . . 2·10 90
1134 20col. multicoloured . . 10·50 4·75

315 Microwave Transmitters

1979. Air. 30th Anniv of Costa Rican Electricity Institute. Multicoloured.
1136 1col. Arenal Dam 20 15
1137 5col. Type **315** 60 65

316 Sir Rowland Hill and Penny Black

1979. Air. Death Centenary of Sir Rowland Hill.
1138 – 5col. mauve and blue . . 55 45
1139 **316** 10col. blue and black . . 90 65
DESIGN: 5col. Sir Rowland Hill and first Costa Rican stamp.

317 "Waiting" (Hernan Gonzalez)

318 "Danaus plexippus"

1979. Air. National Sculpture Competition. Multicoloured.
1140 60c. Type **317** 10 10
1141 1col. "The Heroes of Misery" (Juan Ramon Bonilla) 20 15
1142 2col.10 "Bullocks" (Victor M. Bermudez) (horiz) . . 30 25
1143 5col. "Chlorite Head" (Juan Rafael Chacon) 65 65
1144 20col. "Motherhood" (Francisco Zuniga) . . . 2·50 2·10

1979. Air. Butterflies. Multicoloured.
1145 60c. Type **318** 15 10
1146 1col. "Phoebis philea" . . . 35 15
1147 1col.80 "Rothschildia sp." 45 35
1148 2col.10 "Prepona omphale" 50 35
1149 2col.60 "Marpesia marcella" 70 55
1150 4col.05 "Morpho cypris" . . 95 75

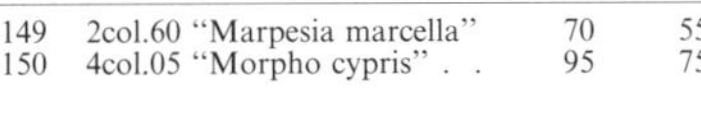

319 "Green House" (M. Murillo)

320 Jose Joaquin Rodriguez Zeledon

1979. Air. 30th Anniv of S.O.S. Children's Villages. Children's Paintings. Multicoloured.
1151 2col.50 Type **319** 45 30
1152 5col. "Four houses" (L. Varela) 60 65
1153 5col.50 "Blue house" (M. Perez) 65 70

1979. Air. Costa Rican Presidents (1st series).
1154 **320** 10c. blue 10 10
1155 – 60c. purple 10 10
1156 – 85c. red 15 10
1157 – 1col. orange 20 10
1158 – 2col. brown 35 25
DESIGNS: 60c. Rafael Iglesias Castro; 85c. Ascension Esquivel Ibarra; 1col. Cleto Gonzalez Viquez; 2col. Ricardo Jimenez Oreamuno.
See also Nos. 1180/4 and 1256/60.

321 Holy Family

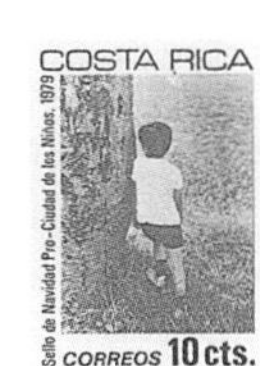

322 Boy leaning on Tree

1979. Air. Christmas.
1159 **321** 1col. multicoloured . . . 20 15
1160 1col.60 multicoloured . . 30 20

1979. Obligatory Tax. Christmas. Children's Village.
1161 **322** 10c. blue 10 10
1162 10c. orange 10 10
1163 10c. mauve 10 10
1164 10c. green 10 10

323 Tree

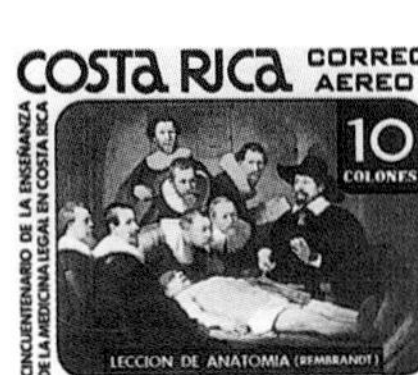

324 "Anatomy Lesson" (Rembrandt)

1980. Air. Reafforestation.
1165 **323** 1col. brown, blue & grn 20 15
1166 3col.40 brown, ol & grn 35 45

1980. Air. 50th Anniv of Legal Medical Teaching in Costa Rica.
1167 **324** 10col. multicoloured . . 90 90

325 Rotary Anniversary Emblem

326 Puerto Limon

1980. Air. 75th Anniv of Rotary International.
1168 **325** 2col.10 green, yellow and black 35 25
1169 5col. multicoloured . . . 50 40

1980. Air. 14th International Symposium on Remote Sensing of the Environment. Multicoloured.
1170 2col.10 Type **326** 35 25
1171 5col. Gulf of Nicoya, Guanacaste 50 40

327 Football

328 Poas Volcano

1980. Air. Olympic Games, Moscow. Mult.
1172 1col. Type **327** 20 15
1173 3col. Cycling 30 40
1174 4col.05 Baseball 40 30
1175 20col. Swimming . . . . . 1·50 2·00

1980. Air. 10th Anniv of National Parks Service.
1176 1col. Type **328** 20 15
1177 2col.50 Beach at Cahuita . . 45 30

329 Jose Maria Zeledon Brenes (lyric writer)

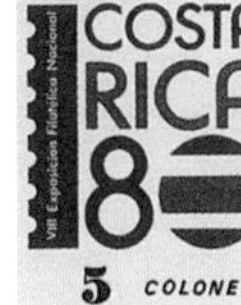

330 Exhibition Emblem

1980. Air. National Anthem. Multicoloured.
1178 1col. Type **329** 20 15
1179 10col. Manuel Maria Gutierrez (composer) . . 90 90

1980. Air. Costa Rican Presidents (2nd series). As T **320**.
1180 1col. red 20 15
1181 1col.60 turquoise 30 20
1182 1col.80 brown 30 20
1183 2col.10 green 35 25
1184 3col. lilac 55 40
DESIGNS: 1col. Alfredo Gonzalez; 1col.60, Federico Tinoco; 1col.80, Francisco Aguilar; 2col.10, Julio Acosta; 3col. Leon Cortes.

1980. Air. 8th National Stamp Exhibition.
1185 **330** 5col. multicoloured . . . 90 65
1186 20col. multicoloured . . 2·40 2·00

331 Fruit

332 "Giant Poro" (Jorge Carvajal)

1980. Air. Costa Rican Produce. Mult.
1187 10c. Type **331** 10 10
1188 60c. Chocolate 10 10
1189 1col. Coffee 20 15
1190 2col.10 Bananas 35 25
1191 3col.40 Flowers 35 45
1192 5col. Cane sugar 60 15

1980. Air. Paintings. Multicoloured.
1193 1col. Type **332** 20 15
1194 2col.10 "Secret Look" (Rolando Cubero) 35 25
1195 2col.45 "Consuelo" (Fernando Carballo) (31 × 32 mm) 45 30
1196 3col. "Volcano" (Lola Fernandez) 30 40
1197 4col.05 "Hearing Mass" (Francisco Amighetti) . . 40 30

333 "Madonna and Child" (Raphael)

334 Boy on Swing

1980. Air. Christmas. Multicoloured.
1198 1col. Type **333** 20 15
1199 10col. "Madonna, Jesus and St. John" (Raphael) . . . 90 90

1980. Obligatory Tax. Christmas. Children's Village.
1200 **334** 10c. red 10 10
1201 10c. yellow 10 10
1202 10c. blue 10 10
1203 10c. green 10 10

335 New Harbour, Caldera

336 Harpy Eagle

1980. Air. "Paying your Taxes Means Progress". Multicoloured.
1204 1col. Type **335** 20 15
1205 1col.30 Juan Santamaria International Airport (32 × 25 mm) 30 15
1206 2col.10 River Frio railway bridge . . . . 5·75 1·25
1207 2col.60 Highway to Colon City (25 × 32 mm) 45 35
1208 5col. Regional postal centre, Huetar 50 40

1980. Air. Fauna. Multicoloured.
1209 2col.10 Type **336** . . . . . 1·90 55
1210 2col.50 Scarlet macaw . . . 2·50 60
1211 3col. Puma 55 40
1212 5col.50 Black-handed spider monkey . . . . 1·00 1·75

337 Monge and Magazine "Repertorio Americano"

1980. Air. Birth Centenary of Joaquin Garcia Monge.
1213 **337** 1col.60 blue, yell & red 30 20
1214 3col. blue, lt bl & red . . 30 40

338 Arms of Aserri

339 Rodrigo Facio Brenes (rector)

1981. Air. Cornea Bank.
1215 **338** 1col. multicoloured . . . 20 15
1216 1col.80 multicoloured . . 30 25
1217 5col. blue 50 40
DESIGNS: 1col.80, Eye; 5col. Abelardo Rojas (founder).

1981. Air. 40th Anniv of University of Costa Rica and 20th Anniv of Medical School.
1218 – 5c. multicoloured 10 10
1219 – 10c. multicoloured . . . 10 10
1220 – 50c. multicoloured . . . 10 10
1221 – 1col.30 multicoloured . . 10 10
1222 – 3col.40 multicoloured . . 25 20
1223 **339** 4col.05 grn, bl & dp bl 30 20
DESIGNS: HORIZ: 5c. Medical-surgical clinic; 10c. Physiology lesson; 50c. Medical School and Dr. Antonia Pena Chavarria (first Dean); 1col.30, School of Music and Fine Arts; 3col.40, Carlos Monge Alfaro Library.

340 Ass-drawn Mail Van, 1857

1981. Air. 150th Birth Anniv of Heinrich von Stephan (founder of U.P.U.).
1224 – 1col. lt blue, grn & bl . . 20 15
1225 **340** 2col.10 yell, red & brn 4·75 2·50
1226 – 10col. grey, mve & grn 1·75 1·25
DESIGNS: 1col. Mail carried by mule, 1839; 10col. Carrying mail to Sarapiqui, 1858.

341 I.T.U. and W.H.O. Emblems and Ribbons forming Caduceus

342 Sts. Peter and Paul

1981. Air. World Telecommunications Day.
1227 **341** 5col. blue and black 50 40
1228 25col. multicoloured 2·40 1·75

1981. Air. Centenary of Consecration of Bernardo August Thiel as Bishop of San Jose. Mult.
1229 1col. Type **342** 10 10
1230 1col. St. Vincent de Paul 10 10
1231 1col. Death of St. Joseph 10 10
1232 1col. Archangel St. Michael 10 10
1233 1col. Holy Family 10 10
1234 2col. Bishop Thiel 15 10

343 Juan Santamaria (national hero)
344 Potter

1981. Air. Homage to the Province of Alajuela. Multicoloured.
1235 1col. Type **343** (150th birth anniv) 10 10
1236 2col.45 Alajuela Cathedral 20 15

1981. Air. Banco Popular and the Development of the Community. Multicoloured.
1237 15c. Type **344** 10 10
1238 1col.60 Building construction 15 10
1239 1col.80 Farming 15 10
1240 2col.50 Fishermen 30 15
1241 3col. Nurse and patient 25 15
1242 5col. Rural guard 45 30

345 Leon Fernandez Bonilla (founder)
346 Disabled Person in Wheelchair holding Scales of Justice

1981. Air. National Archives. Multicoloured.
1243 1col.40 Type **345** 15 10
1244 2col. Arms of National Archives 15 15
1245 3col. University of Santo Tomas (horiz) 25 15
1246 3col.50 Model of new archives' building (horiz) 30 25

1981. Air. International Year of Disabled Persons.
1247 – 1col. multicoloured 10 10
1248 **346** 2col.60 deep orange, orange and black 25 25
1249 – 10col. multicoloured 60 40
DESIGNS—VERT: 1col. Steps and disabled person in wheelchair. HORIZ: 10col. Healthy person helping disabled towards the sun.

347 F.A.O. Emblem

348 Boy in Pedal-car

1981. Air. World Food Day.
1250 **347** 5col. multicoloured 45 30
1251 10col. multicoloured 60 55

1981. Obligatory Tax. Christmas. Children's Village.
1252 **348** 10c. red 10 10
1253 10c. orange 10 10
1254 10c. blue 10 10
1255 10c. green 10 10

1981. Air. Costa Rican Presidents (3rd series) As T **320**.
1256 1col. red 10 10
1257 2col. orange 15 15
1258 3col. green 25 15
1259 5col. blue 20 30
1260 10col. blue 45 55
DESIGNS: 1c. Rafael Angel Calderon Guardia; 2col. Teodoro Picado Milchalski; 3col. Jose Figueres Ferrer; 5col. Otilio Ulate Blanco; 10col. Mario Echandi Jimenez.

349 Arms of Bar Association

1982. Air. Centenary of Bar Association.
1261 **349** 1col. blue and black 10 10
1262 – 2col. multicoloured 15 10
1263 – 20col. green and black 90 45
DESIGNS—VERT: 2col. Eusebio Figueroa (first president of Association). HORIZ: 20col. Bar Association building.

350 Housing

1982. Air. Costa-Rican Progress. Mult.
1264 95col. Type **350** 10 10
1265 1col.15 Farmers' fairs 10 10
1266 1col.45 Grade and high schools 15 10
1267 1col.65 National plan for drinking water 15 10
1268 1col.80 Rural health 15 10
1269 2col.10 Playgrounds 20 10
1270 2col.35 National Theatre Square 20 10
1271 2col.60 Dish aerial (International and national telephone system) 20 15
1272 3col. Electric railway to Atlantic coast 3·25 1·00
1273 4col.05 Irrigation at Guanacaste 35 15

351 Fountain, Central Park

352 Saint's Stone

1982. Air. Bicentenary of Alajuela. Mult.
1274 5col. Type **351** 20 20
1275 10col. Juan Santamaria Historical and Cultural Museum (horiz) 40 10
1276 15col. Christ of Esquipulas Church 60 20
1277 20col. Mgr. Estevan Lorenzo de Tristan 80 45
1278 25col. Padre Juan Manuel Lopez del Corral 1·00 60

1982. Air. 50th Anniv of Perez Zeledon County. Multicoloured.
1279 10c. Type **352** 10 10
1280 50c. Monument to Mothers 10 10
1281 1col. Pedro Perez Zeledon 10 10
1282 1col.25 San Isidro Labrador Church 10 10
1283 3col.50 Municipal building (horiz) 30 15
1284 4col.25 County arms 35 15

1982. Air. Nos. 1070 and 1207 surch.
1285 3col. on 75c. red and black 25 15
1286 5col. on 2col.60 mult 45 20

1982. Air. 9th National Stamp Exhibition. Nos. 1005/8 surch **IX EXPOSICION FILATELICA - 1982** and new value.
1287 **271** 8col.40 on 2col.20 orange and black 35 35
1288 – 8col.40 on 2col.20 green and black 35 35
1289 – 8col.40 on 2col.20 red and black 35 35
1290 – 8col.40 on 2col.20 blue and black 35 35
1291 **271** 9col.70 on 2col.20 orange and black 45 45
1292 – 9col.70 on 2col.20 green and black 45 45
1293 – 9col.70 on 2col.20 red and black 45 45
1294 – 9col.70 on 2col.20 blue and black 45 45

355 Dr Robert Koch and Cross of Lorraine

356 Student at Lathe

1982. Air. Centenary of Discovery of Tubercle Bacillus.
1295 – 1col.50 red and black 15 10
1296 **355** 3col. grey and black 25 15
1297 – 3col.30 multicoloured 30 15
DESIGNS: 1col.50, Koch and anti-T.B. Campaign emblem; 3col.30, Koch and Ministry of Public Health Building, San Jose.

1982. Obligatory Tax. Christmas. Children's Village.
1298 **356** 10c. red 10 10
1299 10c. grey 10 10
1300 10c. violet 10 10
1301 10c. blue 10 10

357 Blood Donors Association Emblem

358 Migration Committee Emblem

1982. Air. 7th Pan-American Blood Donors Congress. Multicoloured.
1302 **357** 30col. multicoloured 90 75
1303 – 50col. red, blue & black 1·50 75
DESIGN: 50col. Congress emblem.

1982. Air. 30th Anniv of Intergovernmental Migration Committee.
1304 **358** 8col.40 lt blue, bl & blk 35 20
1305 – 9col.70 blue and black 45 20
1306 – 11col.70 mult 55 25
1307 – 13col.05 bl, blk & grey 55 30
DESIGNS—HORIZ: 11col.70, Emblem and handshake; 13col.05, Emblem within double-headed arrow. VERT: 9col.70, Emblem.

359 "St. Francis" (El Greco)

360 Pope John Paul II

1983. Air. 800th Birth Anniv (1982) of St. Francis of Assisi.
1308 **359** 4col.80 brown, blk & bl 20 10
1309 – 7col.40 brn, blk & grey 30 10
DESIGN: 7col.40, Portrait of Francis by unknown artist.

1983. Air. Papal Visit.
1310 **360** 5col. brown, yell & bl 25 10
1311 10col. brown, grn & bl 50 20
1312 15col. brown, mve & bl 1·00 30

361 W.C.Y. Emblem

362 Egg

1983. World Communications Year.
1313 **361** 10c. multicoloured 10 10
1314 50c. multicoloured 10 10
1315 10col. multicoloured 50 20

1983. 1st World Conference on Human Rights, Alajuela (1982).
1316 **362** 20col. grey and black 1·00 40

363 U.P.U. Monument, Berne, and 1883 2c. Stamp

1983. Centenary of U.P.U. Membership.
1317 **363** 3col. yellow, red & blk 45 10
1318 – 10col. yellow, bl & blk 90 20
DESIGN: 10col. Central Post Office, San Jose, and 1883 40c. stamp.

364 "Alliance Building, San Jose" (Cristina Fournier)

365 Bolivar (after Francisco Zuniga)

1983. Centenary of French Alliance (French language-teaching association).
1319 **364** 12col. multicoloured 55 25

1983. Air. Birth Bicentenary of Simon Bolivar.
1320 **365** 10col. multicoloured 50 20

1983. Nos. 1308/9 surch.
1321 10c. on 4col.80 brown, black and blue 10 10
1321a 50c. on 4col.80 brown, black and blue 10 10
1322 1col.50 on 7col.40 brown, black and grey 15 10
1323 3col. on 7col.40 brown, black and grey 20 10

367 Repairing Wheelchair

368 Three Kings

1988. Obligatory Tax. Christmas. Children's Village.
1324 **367** 10c. red 10 10
1325 10c. orange 10 10
1326 10c. blue 10 10
1327 10c. green 10 10

1983. Christmas. Multicoloured.
1328 1col.50 Type **368** 15 10
1329 1col.50 Holy Family and Shepherds 15 10
1330 1col.50 People bearing gifts 15 10
Nos. 1328/30 were printed together, se-tenant, forming a composite design.

369 Fisherman

370 Resplendent Quetzal ("Quetzal")

1983. Fisheries Development.
1331 **369** 8col.50 multicoloured 60 15

1984. Birds. Multicoloured.
1332 10c. Type **370** 45 25
1333 50c. Red-legged honey-creeper ("Mielero Patirrojo") (horiz) 45 25
1334 1col. Clay-coloured thrush ("Mirlo Pardo") (horiz) 50 25
1335 1col.50 Blue-crowned motmot ("Momotode Diadema Azul") 60 25
1336 3col. Green violetear ("Colibri orejivioloceo verde") 1·25 45
1337 10col. Blue and white swallow ("Golondirina Azul y Blanca") (horiz) 3·75 75

371 Jose Joaquin Mora

1984. 1856 Campaign Heroes. Multicoloured.
1339 50c. Type **371** 10 10
1340 1col.50 Pancha Carrasco . . 10 10
1341 3col. Juan Santamaria (horiz) 10 10
1342 8col.50 Juan Rafael Mora Porras 35 30

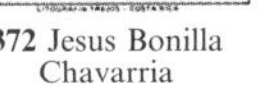

372 Jesus Bonilla Chavarria
373 Necklace Bead

1984. Musicians.
1343 **372** 3col. 50 violet and black 15 10
1344 – 5col. red and black . . . 20 15
1345 – 12col. green and black 15 10
1346 – 13col. yellow and black 20 10
DESIGNS: 5col. Benjamin Gutierrez; 12col. Pilar Jimenez; 13col. Jose Daniel Zuniga.

1984. Jade Museum Artifacts. Multicoloured.
1347 4col. Type **373** 15 10
1348 7col. Seated figure 25 20
1349 10col. Ceramic dish (horiz) 35 30

374 Basketball Players
375 Street Scene

1984. Olympic Games, Los Angeles. Mult.
1350 1col. Type **374** 10 10
1351 8col. Swimming 10 10
1352 11col. Cycling 15 10
1353 14col. Running 20 10
1354 20col. Boxing 25 10
1355 30col. Football 35 10

1984. Centenary of Public Street Lighting.
1356 **375** 6col. multicoloured . . . 20 15

376 Emblem and National Independence Monument

1984. 10th National Philatelic Exhibition. Mult.
1357 10col. Type **376** 35 30
1358 10col. Emblem and Juan Mora Fernandez statue 35 30

377 National Coat of Arms
378 Child on Tricycle

1984.
1360 **377** 100col. blue . . . . . . 2·40 1·90
1361 100col. yellow . . . . . 2·40 1·90

1984. Obligatory Tax. Christmas. Children's Village.
1362 **378** 10c. violet 10 10

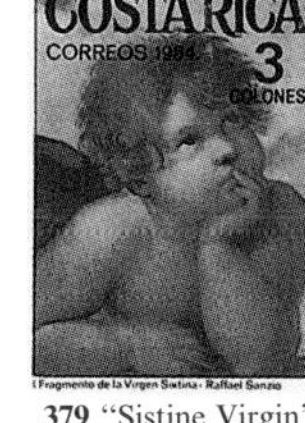

379 "Sistine Virgin" (detail, Raphael)
380 Cyclists

1984. Christmas. Multicoloured.
1363 3col. Type **379** 10 10
1364 3col. "Sistine Virgin" (detail) (different) 10 10

1984. 20th Costa Rica Cycle Race.
1365 **380** 6col. multicoloured . . . 15 15

381 Emblem and 1968 Scouting Jubilee Stamp

1985. International Youth Year.
1366 **381** 11col. multicoloured . . 25 20

382 Workers' Monument (Francisco Zuniga)
383 U.N. Emblem and 1935 Red Cross Jubilee Stamp

1985. "National Values".
1367 **382** 6col. mauve and black 15 15
1368 – 11col. yell, blk & bl . . 25 20
1369 – 13col. multicoloured . . 35 30
1370 – 30col. multicoloured . . 70 70
DESIGNS—As T **382**. 11col. First printing press (Freedom of speech); 13col. Dove, flag and globe (Neutrality); 65 × 35 mm—30col. Nos. 1367/9.

1985. Centenary of Costa Rican Red Cross.
1371 **383** 3col. red, brown & blk 10 10
1372 – 5col. black, red and grey 15 10
DESIGN: 5col. U.N. Emblem and 1946 Red Cross Society stamp.

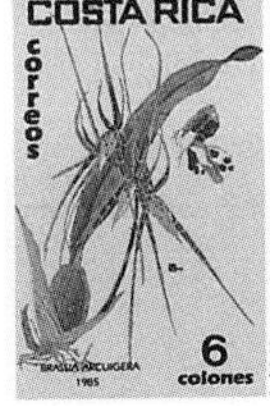

384 Hands holding "S"
385 "Brassia arcuigera"

1985. 50th Anniv of Saprissa Football Club.
1373 **384** 3col. mauve and green 10 10
1374 – 3col. black and mauve 10 10
1375 – 6col. mauve, brn & grn 15 15
DESIGNS: As T **384**—Hands holding football; 34 × 26 mm—6col. Ricardo Saprissa and Saprissa Stadium.

1985. Orchids. Multicoloured.
1376 6col. Type **385** 10 10
1377 6col. "Encyclia peraltensis" 10 10
1378 6col. "Maxillaria especie" 10 10
1379 13col. "Oncidium turialbae" 30 25
1380 13col. "Trichopilia marginata" 30 25
1381 13col. "Stanhopea ecornuta" 30 25

386 1940 25c. Stamp and Hand holding Tweezers
387 Hands reaching out to Child

1985. 11th National Stamp Exhibition.
1382 **386** 20col. bl, ultram & pink 50 45

1985. Obligatory Tax. Christmas. Children's Village.
1383 **387** 10c. brown 10 10

388 Children looking at Star

1985. Christmas.
1384 **388** 3col. multicoloured . . . 10 10

390 Costa Rica Lyceum
391 Land and Cattle College Project

1986. Centenary of Free Compulsory Education.
1390 **390** 3col. brown & lt brown 10 10
1391 30col. brown and pink 60 20
DESIGN: 30col. Mauro Fernandez Acuna (education Minister).

1986. 27th Annual Inter-American Development Bank Assembly, San Jose. Multicoloured.
1392 10col. Type **391** 20 15
1393 10col. Bank emblem 20 15
1394 10col. Cape Blanco fisherman 40 15

392 Francisco J. Orlich Bolmarcich
393 Pique (mascot)

1986. Former Presidents of Costa Rica.
1395 **392** 3col. green 10 10
1396 – 3col. green 10 10
1397 – 3col. green 10 10
1398 – 3col. green 10 10
1399 – 3col. green 10 10
1400 – 6col. brown 15 10
1401 – 6col. brown 15 10
1402 – 6col. brown 15 10
1403 – 6col. brown 15 10
1404 – 6col. brown 15 10
1405 – 10col. orange 20 15
1406 – 10col. orange 20 15
1407 – 10col. orange 20 15
1408 – 10col. orange 20 15
1409 – 10col. orange 20 15
1410 – 11col. grey 20 15
1411 – 11col. grey 20 15
1412 – 11col. grey 20 15
1413 – 11col. grey 20 15
1414 – 11col. grey 20 15
1415 – 13col. brown 25 20
1416 – 13col. brown 25 20
1417 – 13col. brown 25 20
1418 – 13col. brown 25 20
1419 – 13col. brown 25 20
DESIGNS: Nos. 1395, 1400, 1405, 1410, 1415, Type **392**; 1396, 1401, 1406, 1411, 1416, Jose Joaquin Trejos Fernandez; 1397, 1402, 1407, 1412, 1417, Daniel Oduber Quiros; 1398, 1403, 1408, 1413, 1418, Rodrigo Carazo Odio; 1399, 1404, 1409, 1414, 1419, Luis Alberto Monge Alvarez.

1986. World Cup Football Championship. Mexico.
1420 **393** 1col. multicoloured . . . 10 10
1421 – 1col. multicoloured . . . 10 10
1422 – 4col. multicoloured . . . 10 10
1423 – 6col. pur, brn & black 15 10
1424 – 11col. pur, red & blk . 20 15
DESIGNS:—VERT: No. 1420, 1422, Type **393**. HORIZ: No. 1421, 1423, Footballs and players; 1424, Footballs and players (different).

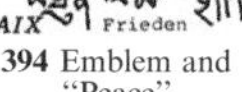
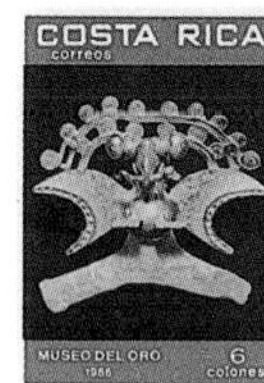

394 Emblem and "Peace"
395 Gold Artefact

1986. International Peace Year. Each bearing the Year emblem and "Peace" in various languages (first language given in brackets).
1425 **394** 5col. blue and brown (Hoa Binh) 10 10
1426 – 5col. blue and brown (Vrede) 10 10
1427 – 5col. blue and brown (Pace) 10 10

1986. Exhibits in Gold Museum. Mult.
1428 6col. Type **395** 15 10
1429 6col. Figure with three-lobed base 15 10
1430 6col. Frog 15 10
1431 6col. Centipede 15 10
1432 6col. Two monkeys in sun 15 10
1433 13col. Figure with dragon-head arms 25 10
1434 13col. Two monkeys 25 10
1435 13col. Animal-shaped figure 25 10
1436 13col. Sun with ball pendant 25 10
1437 13col. Figure within frame 25 10

396 Child
397 Fork-lift Truck and Airplane (Osvaldo Andres Gonzalez Vega)

1986. Obligatory Tax. Christmas. Children's Village.
1438 **396** 10c. brown 10 10

1986. Air. 40th Anniv of LACSA (national airline). Children's Drawings. Multicoloured.
1439 1col. Airplane flying over house and van (Adriana Elias Hidalgo) 10 10
1440 7col. Type **397** 15 15
1441 16col. Airplane, letters and photographs (David Valverde Rodiguez) . . . 30 25

398 Lattice-winged Bat
399 Extracting Snake's Venom (detail of mural, Francisco Amighetti)

1986. Flora and Fauna. Bats and Frogs. Multicoloured.
1442 2col. Type **398** 10 10
1443 3col. Common long-tongued bat 10 10
1444 4col. White bat 10 10
1445 5col. Group of white bats 10 10
1446 6col. "Agalychnis callidryas" (frog) 15 10
1447 10col. "Dendrobates pumilio" (frog) 20 15
1448 11col. "Hyla ebraccata" (frog) 20 15
1449 20col. "Phyllobates lugubris" (frog) 40 35

1987. National Science and Technology Day.
1451 **399** 8col. multicoloured . . . 20 15

400 Statuette
401 Arms of San Jose Province

1987. Centenary of National Museum. Pre-Colombian Art. Multicoloured.
1452 8col. Type **400** 20 15
1453 8col. Jug in form of human figure 20 15
1454 8col. Vase in form of human figure 20 15
1455 8col. Stone jar 20 15
1456 8col. Pot with human-type legs and arms 20 15
1457 15col. Bowl (horiz) 30 25
1458 15col. Carving of animal defeating human (horiz) 30 25
1459 15col. Flask (horiz) 30 25

1987. 250th Anniv of San Jose.
1460 **401** 20col. multicoloured . . 30 25
1461 – 20col. red, black & bl . . 30 25
1462 – 20col. red, black & bl . . 30 25
DESIGNS: Nos. 1461, Donkey cart in cobbled street; 1462, View down street.

402 16th-century Map of Audiencia, Guatemala

1987. Columbus Day.
1463 **402** 30col. brown and yellow 70 40

403 Map by Bartholomew Columbus, 1503
404 Cross and Doves

1987. 500th Anniv (1992) of Discovery of America by Columbus (1st issue). Each brown and yellow.
1464 4col. Type **403** 10 10
1465 4col. 16th-century map of Costa Rica 10 10
See also Nos. 1480, 1496, 1521 and 1538/40.

1987. Obligatory Tax. Christmas, Children's Village.
1466 **404** 10c. blue and brown . . 10 10

405 "Village Scene" (Fausto Pacheco)
406 Pres. Arias and National Flag

1987. International Year of Shelter for the Homeless.
1467 **405** 1col. multicoloured . . . 10 10

1987. Award of Nobel Peace Prize to Pres. Oscar Arias Sanchez.
1468 **406** 10col. multicoloured . . 15 15

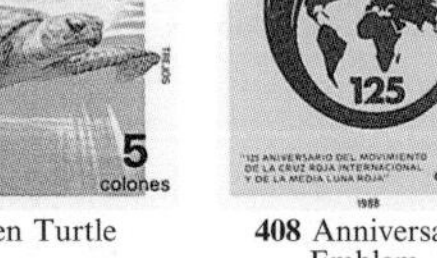

407 Green Turtle
408 Anniversary Emblem

1988. 17th Annual General Assembly of International Union for Nature Conservation. Multicoloured.
1469 5col. Type **407** 10 10
1470 5col. Golden toad on leaf 10 10
1471 5col. Emperor (butterfly) . . 15 10

1988. 125th Anniv of Red Cross.
1472 **408** 30col. red and blue . . . 45 40

409 Man with Pen and Radio (Adult Education)
410 Symbols of Bank Activities

1988. Costa Rica–Liechtenstein Cultural Co-operation.
1473 **409** 18col. red, brown & grn 30 25
1474 – 20col. multicoloured . . 30 25
DESIGN: 20col. Headphones on books (radio broadcasts).

1988. 125th Anniv of Anglo–Costa Rican Bank.
1475 **410** 3col. blue, red & yellow 10 10

411 Games Emblem
412 Roman Macava and Curtiss Robin

1988. Olympic Games, Seoul. Multicoloured.
1476 25col. Type **411** 40 35
1477 25col. Games mascot . . . 40 35

1988. Airmail Pioneers.
1478 **412** 10col. multicoloured . . 25 15

413 School Courtyard
414 Amerindian Necklace

1988. Centenary of Girls' High School.
1479 **413** 10col. brown & yellow 15 10

1988. 500th Anniv (1992) of Discovery of America by Columbus (2nd issue).
1480 **414** 4col. multicoloured . . . 10 10

415 Dengo and College
416 Former Observation Tower

1988. Birth Centenary of Omar Dengo (Director of Heredia Teachers' College).
1481 **415** 10col. brown, grey & bl 15 10

1988. Cent of National Meteorological Institute.
1482 **416** 2col. multicoloured . . . 10 10

417 "Eschweilera costarricensis"
418 Map of France and Costa Rican National Monument

1989. Flowers. Multicoloured.
1483 5col. Type **417** 10 10
1484 10col. "Heliconia wagneriana" 15 10
1485 15col. "Heliconia lophocarpa" 20 15
1486 20col. "Aechmea magdalenae" 30 25
1487 25col. "Psammisia ramiflora" 35 30
1488 30col. Passion flower . . . 45 40

1989. Bicentenary of French Revolution.
1489 **418** 30col. black, blue & red 45 40

419 Sugar Mill
420 Corn Grinder

1989. 151st Anniv of Grecia County.
1490 **419** 10col. multicoloured . . 15 10

1989. America. Pre-Columbian Artefacts. Mult.
1491 50col. Type **420** 75 20
1492 100col. Granite sphere, 1500 A.D. . . . . 1·50 40

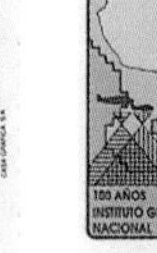

422 Orchid
423 Dr. Henri Pittier (first Director)

1989. "100 Years of Democracy" Presidents' Summit.
1493 **422** 10col. multicoloured . . 15 10

1989. Centenary of National Geographical Institute.
1494 **423** 18col. multicoloured . . 20 15

424 Teacher and Children
425 Pre-Columbian Gold Frog and Spanish Coin

1989. Obligatory Tax. Christmas. Children's Village.
1495 **424** 1col. blue, green & black 10 10

1989. 500th Anniv (1992) of Discovery of America by Columbus (3rd issue).
1496 **425** 4col. multicoloured . . . 10 10

426 "Exporting Coffee" (painting in theatre by Jose Villa)
427 Football in Cube

1990. Centenary of National Theatre.
1497 **426** 5col. multicoloured . . . 10 10

1990. World Cup Football Championship, Italy.
1498 **427** 5col. multicoloured . . . 10 10

428 "50 U"

1990. 50th Anniv of University of Costa Rica.
1499 **428** 18col. multicoloured . . 15 10

429 "Education Democracy Peace"
431 Painting by Juan Ramirez

1990. Patriotic Symbols.
1500 **429** 100col. blue and black 90 30
1501 – 200col. multicoloured . . 1·90 65
1502 – 500col. multicoloured . . 4·75 1·60
DESIGNS: 200col. Map of Costa Rica in national colours; 500col. State arms.

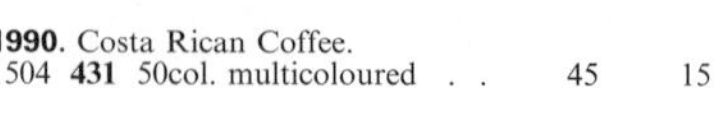

1991. Air. No. 1491 optd **LEY 7097 CORREO AEREO**.
1503 **420** 50col. multicoloured . . 45 15

1990. Costa Rican Coffee.
1504 **431** 50col. multicoloured . . 45 15

432 Penny Black
433 Heredia Hospital

1990. 150th Anniv of the Penny Black.
1505 **432** 50col. black and blue . . 45 15

1990. Hospital Centenaries.
1506 **433** 50col. blue, orge & grn 45 15
1507 – 100col. orange, bl & grn 90 30
DESIGN: 100col. National Psychiatric Hospital.

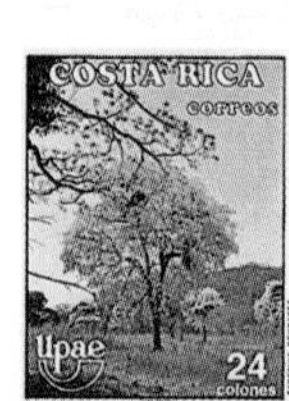

434 Yellow-bark Tree ("Tabebuia ochracea")
436 "Banana Picker" (Alleardo Villa, Ceiling of Grand Staircase)

1990. America. The Natural World. Mult.
1508 18col. Scarlet macaw ("Ara macao") 65 15
1509 18col. Buffon's macaw ("Ara ambigua") 65 15
1510 24col. Carao tree ("Cassia grandis") 20 10
1511 24col. Type **434** 20 10

1990. Obligatory Tax. Children's Village. No. 1490 optd **LEY 7157 PRO-CIUDAD DE LOS NINOS 1990**.
1512 **419** 10col. multicoloured . . 10 10

1991. Air. Paintings in National Theatre.
1516 **436** 30col. multicoloured . . 30 10

437 Costa Rica and Panama Flags and Seals
439 Route of First Voyage on Stone Globe

1991. 50th Anniv of Costa Rica–Panama Boundary Treaty.
1517 **437** 10col. multicoloured . . 10 10
1518 – 10col. black and blue . . 10 10
1519 – 10col. blue, brown & blk 10 10
DESIGNS: No. 1518. Presidents meeting: 1519, Map.

1991. Air. "Exfilcori '91" National Stamp Exhibition. No. 1501 optd **Aereo EXFILCORI '91**.
1520 200col. multicoloured . . . 1·75 60

1991. 500th Anniv (1992) of Discovery of America by Columbus (4th issue).
1521 **439** 4col. red, black and blue 10 10

1991. Air. Centenary of Basketball. No. 1474 optd **CENTENARIO DEL BALONCESTO CORREO AEREO**.
1522 20col. multicoloured 20 10

1991. Nos. 1482 and 1342 surch.
1523 **416** 1col. on 2col. mult . . . 10 10
1524 – 3col. on 8col.50 mult . . 10 10

443 Dr. Rafael Angel Calderon Guardia Hospital

444 Child praying

1991. Air. 50th Anniv of Social Security Administration.
1525 **443** 15col. multicoloured . . 15 10

1991. Obligatory Tax. Christmas. Children's Village.
1526 **444** 10col. blue 10 10

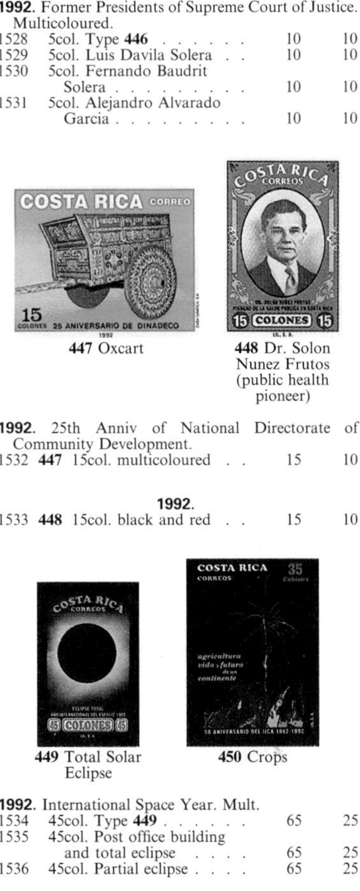

445 "La Poesia" (Vespaciano Bignami)

446 Benito Serrano Jimenez

1992. Air. Paintings in National Theatre.
1527 **445** 35col. multicoloured . . 30 10

1992. Former Presidents of Supreme Court of Justice. Multicoloured.
1528 5col. Type **446** 10 10
1529 5col. Luis Davila Solera . . 10 10
1530 5col. Fernando Baudrit Solera 10 10
1531 5col. Alejandro Alvarado Garcia 10 10

447 Oxcart

448 Dr. Solon Nunez Frutos (public health pioneer)

1992. 25th Anniv of National Directorate of Community Development.
1532 **447** 15col. multicoloured . . 15 10

1992.
1533 **448** 15col. black and red . . 15 10

449 Total Solar Eclipse

450 Crops

1992. International Space Year. Mult.
1534 45col. Type **449** 65 25
1535 45col. Post office building and total eclipse 65 25
1536 45col. Partial eclipse 65 25

1992. 50th Anniv of Inter-American Institute for Agricultural Co-operation.
1537 **450** 35col. multicoloured . . 30 10

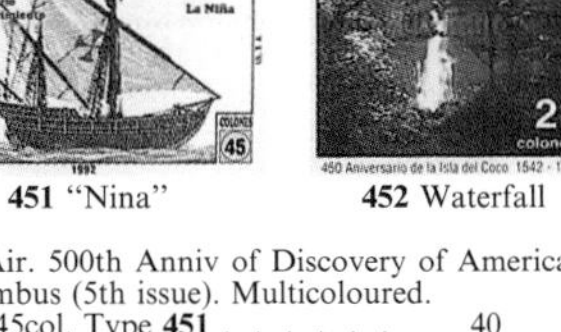

451 "Nina"

452 Waterfall

1992. Air. 500th Anniv of Discovery of America by Columbus (5th issue). Multicoloured.
1538 45col. Type **451** 40 15
1539 45col. "Santa Maria" . . . 40 15
1540 45col. "Pinta" 40 15

1992. 450th Anniv of Discovery of Coco Island. Multicoloured.
1541 2col. Type **452** 10 10
1542 15col. View of cliffs from sea 15 10

453 Drilling

454 American Chameleon

1992. Obligatory Tax. Christmas. Children's Village.
1543 **453** 10col. red 10 10

1992. America. Coco Island Fauna. Mult.
1544 15col. Type **454** 15 10
1545 35col. Cocos finch . . . . . 2·10 45

1992. Centenary of Limon. No. 1500 optd **CENTENARIO DE LIMON**.
1546 **429** 100col. blue and black 90 30

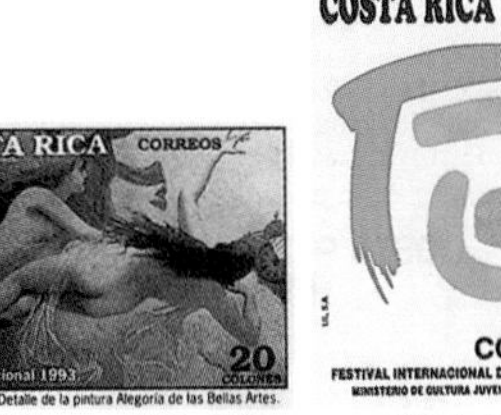

456 "Allegory of the Fine Arts" (detail, R. Fontana)

457 Emblem

1993. Paintings in National Theatre.
1547 **456** 20col. multicoloured . . 20 10

1993. Air. International Arts Festival.
1548 **457** 45col. multicoloured . . 40 15

1993. No. 1494 surch.
1549 **423** 5col. on 18col. mult . . 10 10

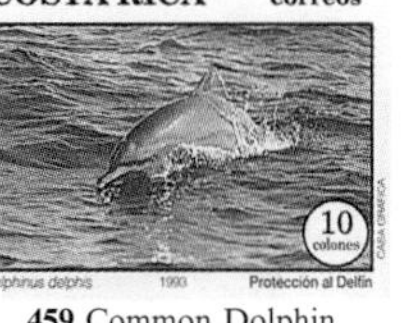

459 Common Dolphin

460 Emblem

1993. Dolphins. Multicoloured.
1550 10col. Type **459** 10 10
1551 20col. Striped dolphins . . . 20 10

1993. 40th Anniv of Civil Service Statute.
1552 **460** 5col. multicoloured . . . 10 10

461 Anniversary Emblem

462 Communication Zone

1993. 50th Anniv of Chamber of Industry.
1553 **461** 45col. multicoloured . . 35 15

1993. 25th Anniv of University of Costa Rica School of Communication and Sciences.
1554 **462** 20col. black, red & blue 15 10

463 "Passiflora vitifolia"

1993. Tropical Rainforest Flora. Mult.
1555 2col. Type **463** 10 10
1556 35col. "Gurania megistantha" 25 10

464 Campaigners

465 Association Emblem

1993. 50th Anniv of Guaranteed Social Rights.
1557 **464** 20col. multicoloured . . 15 10

1993. 15th International Customs Officers' Associations Congress.
1558 **465** 45col. multicoloured . . 35 15

466 Carpentry

467 Dish Aerial

1993. Obligatory Tax. Christmas. Children's Village.
1559 **466** 10col. multicoloured . . 10 10

1993. Air. 30th Anniv of Costa Rican Electrical Institute's Responsibility for Development of Telecommunications.
1560 **467** 45col. multicoloured . . 35 15

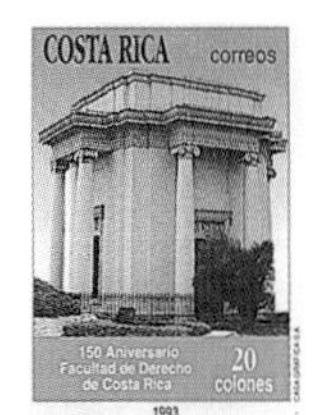

468 Prof. Castro

469 Assembly Hall

1993. Birth Centenary of Miguel Angel Castro Carazo (founder of Commercial School).
1561 **468** 20col. red and blue . . . 15 10

1993. 150th Anniv of Costa Rica University Faculty of Law.
1562 **469** 20col. multicoloured . . 15 10

470 "The Dancer" (Adriatico Froli)

471 Mural (Luis Feron)

1994. National Theatre.
1563 **470** 20col. multicoloured . . 15 10

1994. Air. 150th Anniv of Ministry of Government and Police.
1564 **471** 45col. multicoloured . . 35 15

472 Flamingo Tongue

473 Hands forming Shelter

1994. Marine Animals. Multicoloured.
1565 5col. Type **472** 10 10
1566 10col. "Ophioderma rubicundum" 10 10
1567 15col. Black-barred soldierfish 10 10
1568 20col. King angelfish . . . 15 10
1569 35col. Creole-fish 25 10
1570 45col. "Tubastraea coccinea" 35 15
1571 50col. "Acanthaster planci" 40 15
1572 55col. "Ocypode sp." . . . 45 15
1573 70col. Speckled balloon-fish 55 20

1994. Air. International Year of the Family.
1575 **473** 45col. multicoloured . . 35 15

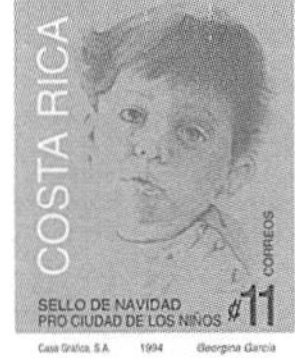

474 Child

1994. Obligatory Tax. Christmas. Children's Village.
1576 **474** 11col. green and lilac . . 10 10

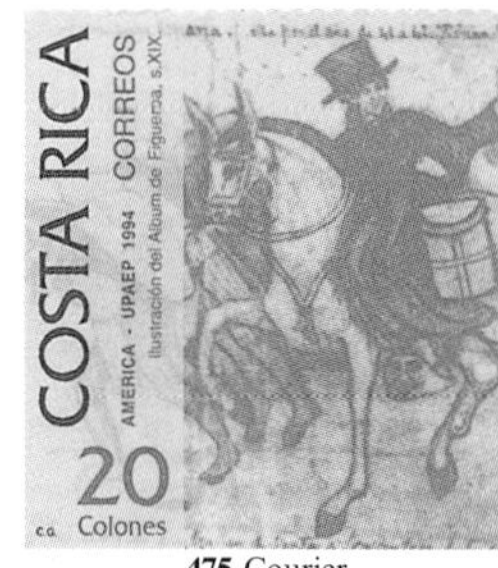

475 Courier

1994. America. Postal Transport. Details of an illustration from "Album de Figueroa". Each orange, light orange and blue.
1577 20col. Type **475** 15 10
1578 20col. Rear of pack ox . . . 15 10
Nos. 1577/8 were issued together in se-tenant pairs with intervening label, each strip forming a composite design.

476 "Federico" (Luis Delgado)

477 Antonio Jose de Sucre (President of Bolivia. 1826–28)

1995. 90th Anniv of Rotary International.
1579 **476** 20col. multicoloured . . 15 10

1995. Anniversaries. Multicoloured.
1580 10col. Type **477** (birth bicentenary) 15 10
1581 30col. Jose Marti (poet and Cuban revolutionary) (death centenary) 20 10

478 "Rider" (sculpture, Nestor Varela)

480 "The Boy and the Cloud" (Francisco Amighetti)

1995. 50th Anniv of Guanacaste Institute.
1582 **478** 50col. green, blk & gold 35 15

1995. No. 1561 surch **5**.
1583 **468** 5col. on 20col. red & bl 10 10

1995. 50th Anniv of U.N.O.
1584 **480** 5col. multicoloured . . . 10 10

481 Woman holding Baby

482 "January"

1995. Obligatory Tax. Christmas. Children's Village.
1585 **481** 12col. multicoloured . . 10 10

1995. 13th National Stamp Exn. Seasonal paintings by Lola Fernandez. Multicoloured.
1587 50col. Type **482** 35 15
1588 50col. "November" 35 15

483 Jabiru

1995. America. Environmental Protection. Multicoloured. Rouletted.
1589 30col. Type **483** 20 10
1590 40col. Coastline 25 10
1591 40col. Woodland and lake 25 10
1592 50col. Leaf cutting ant . . . 35 15

484 Steam Locomotive

1996. Postcards from Limon. Multicoloured.
1594 30col. Type **484** 30 15
1595 30col. Freighter at quay . . 50 15
1596 30col. View of Port Moin 15 10
1597 30col. "Fruitsellers" (Diego Villalobos) 15 10
1598 30col. "Calypso" (Jorge Esquivel) 15 10

485 Douglas DC-3

1996. Air. 50th Anniv of LACSA (national airline). Multicoloured.
1599 5col. Type **485** 10 10
1600 10col. Curtiss C-46 Commando 10 10
1601 20col. Beechcraft 10 10
1602 30col. Douglas DC-6B . . . 15 10
1603 35col. B.A.C. One Eleven 20 10
1604 40col. Convair CV 440 Metropolitan 25 10
1605 45col. Lockheed L.188 Electra 25 10
1606 50col. Boeing 727-200 . . . 30 10
1607 55col. Douglas DC-8 . . . . 30 10
1608 60col. Airbus Industrie A320 35 15

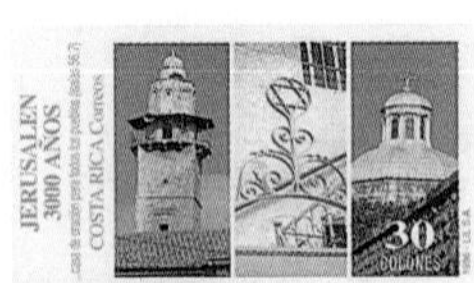

486 Mosque, Synagogue and Christian Church

1996. 3000th Anniv of Jerusalem.
1609 **486** 30col. multicoloured . . 15 10

487 Maria del Milagro Paris and Francisco Rivas

1996. Olympic Games, Atlanta. Costa Rican Swimmers. Multicoloured.
1610 5col. Type **487** 10 10
1611 5col. Sylvia Poll and Federico Yglesias 10 10
1612 5col. Claudia Poll and Alfredo Cruz 10 10

Nos. 1610/12 were issued together, se-tenant, forming a composite design of a swimming pool.

488 Juana del Castillo (wife of Jose Maria Castro)

489 Water Droplet and Leaves

1996. 175th Anniv of Independence. Mult.
1613 30col. Type **488** 15 10
1614 30col. Juan Mora (President, 1849–59) 15 10
1615 30col. Jose Maria Castro (President, 1847–49 and 1866–68) 15 10
1616 30col. Pacifica Fernandez (wife of Juan Mora) . . . 15 10

1996. "Water is Life". 35th Anniv of Aqueducts and Sewers.
1617 **489** 15col. multicoloured . . 10 10

490 "Christmas Carol" (J. M. Sanchez)

491 "Countrywomen" (Gonzalo Morales)

1996. Obligatory Tax. Christmas. Children's Village.
1618 **490** 14col. red and yellow . . 10 10

1996. America. Traditional Costumes. Mult.
1619 45col. Type **491** 20 10
1620 45col. "Lemon Black" (Manuel de la Cruz Gonzalez) (horiz) 20 10

492 Procession passing Palm-topped Wall

494 Child and Man listening to Radio

493 Class, 1930s

1997. Entrance of the Saints, San Ramon. Details of a painting by Jorge Carvajal. Multicoloured.
1621 30col. Type **492** 15 10
1622 30col. Church on hill behind procession 15 10
1623 30col. Procession passing beneath tree 15 10

Nos. 1621/3 were issued together, se-tenant, forming a composite design of the painting.

1997. Centenary of School of Fine Arts.
1624 **493** 50col. multicoloured . . 25 10

1997. 50th Anniv of Radio Nederland.
1625 **494** 45col. multicoloured . . 20 10

495 Postmen

1997. America. The Postman. 14th National Stamp Exhibition.
1626 **495** 30col. multicoloured . . 15 10

496 Church (Roberto Cambronero)

497 Antonio Obando Chan (bust, Olger Villegas)

1997. Bicentenary of Church of the Immaculate Conception, Heredia.
1627 **496** 50col. multicoloured . . 25 10

1997. Obligatory Tax. Christmas. Children's Village.
1628 **497** 15col. multicoloured . . 10 10

498 Arche de la Defense and Ball

1998. World Cup Football Championship, France.
1629 **498** 50col. black, blue & red 25 10

499 Figueres demolishing Fort Bellavista's Walls

1998. 50th Anniv of Second Republic. Mult.
1630 10col. Type **499** 10 10
1631 30col. Pres. Jose Figueres 15 10
1632 45col. Type **499** 20 10
1633 50col. Sledgehammer destroying wall 25 10

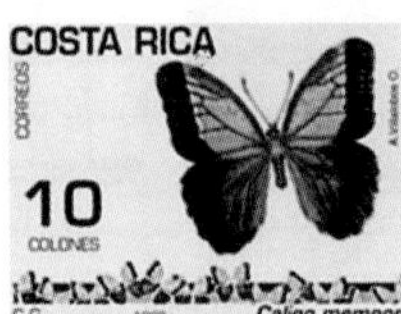

500 "Caligo memnon"

1998. Butterflies. Multicoloured.
1635 10col. Type **500** 10 10
1636 15col. Emperor 10 10
1637 20col. Orange swallowtail 10 10
1638 30col. Malachite 10 10
1639 35col. Great southern white 15 10
1640 40col. "Parides iphidamas" 15 10
1641 45col. "Smyrna blomfildia" 20 10
1642 50col. "Callicore pitheas" 20 10
1643 55col. Orion 20 10
1644 60col. Monarch 25 10

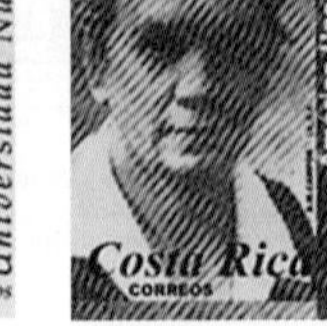

501 "Generation of Knowledge" (Julio Escamez)

502 Carmen Lyra (writer)

1998. 25th Anniv of National University, Heredia.
1645 **501** 50col. multicoloured . . 20 10

1998. America. Famous Women.
1646 **502** 50col. orange, brown and ochre 20 10

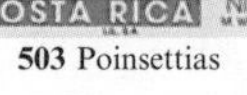

503 Poinsettias

504 Gandhi

1998. Obligatory Tax. Christmas. Children's Village. Multicoloured (except No. 1649).
1647 16col. Poinsetta (gold background) 10 10
1648 16col. Type **503** 10 10
1649 16col. Berries on branch (green, black and red) . . 10 10

1998. 50th Death Anniv of Mahatma Gandhi.
1650 **504** 50col. multicoloured . . 20 10

505 South American Red-lined Turtle

1998. 50th Anniv of International Nature Protection Union. Turtles. Multicoloured.
1651 60col. Type **505** 25 10
1652 70col. Mexican red turtle ("Rhinoclemmys pulcherrima") 30 10
1653 70col. Snapping turtle ("Chelydra serpentina") 30 10

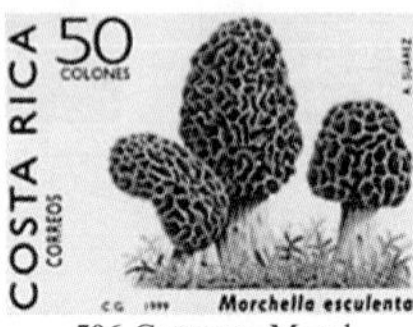

506 Common Morel

1999. Fungi. Multicoloured.
1654 50col. Type **506** 20 10
1655 50col. Cep (*Boletus edulis*) 20 10

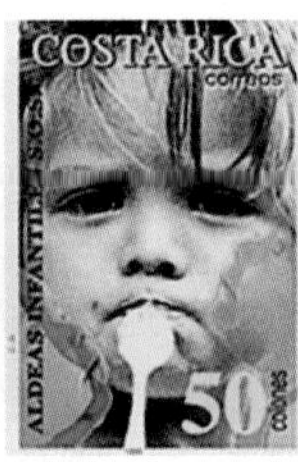

507 Boy

1999. 50th Anniv of S.O.S. Children's Villages.
1656 **507** 50col. multicoloured . . 50 10

508 Man minding Cart outside Telephone Box

509 Sanabria Martinez

1999. 50th Anniv of National Electricity Corporation.
1657 **508** 75col. multicoloured . . 35 15

1999. Birth Centenary of Victor Sanabria Martinez (Archbishop of San Jose).
1658 **509** 300col. violet . . . . . 1·40 50

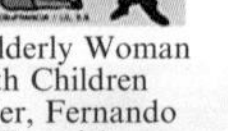

510 Elderly Woman with Children (poster, Fernando Francia)

512 Village and Children

511 Woman helping Children

1999. International Year of the Elderly.
1659 **510** 50col. multicoloured . . 20 10

1999. 50th Anniv of Supreme Elections Tribunal.
1660 **511** 70col. multicoloured . . 30 10

1999. Obligatory Tax. Christmas. Children's Village.
1661 **512** 17col. multicoloured . . 10 10

513 Granados

1999. Carmen Granados Death Commemoration.
1662 **513** 50col. multicoloured . . 20 10

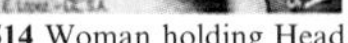
514 Woman holding Head 515 Globe

1999. America. A New Millennium without Arms. Multicoloured.
1663 50col. Type **514** 20 10
1664 70col. Man 30 10

1999. 125th Anniv of Universal Postal Union.
1665 **515** 75col. multicoloured . . 35 15

516 Orchid

1999. "Philexfrance 99" International Stamp Exhibition, Paris. Multicoloured.
1666 300col. Type **516** . . . . . 1·40 50
1667 300col. Orchid and Eiffel Tower . . . . 1·40 50

517 Jaguar

2000. 50th Anniv of Central Bank of Costa Rica. Multicoloured.
1668 60col. Type **517** 25 10
1669 60col. Scorpion 25 10
1670 60col. Bat 25 10
1671 60col. Crab 25 10
1672 60col. Dragon 25 10
1673 90col. Obverse and reverse of ½-escudo gold coin, 1825 . . . . 40 15
1674 90col. Obverse and reverse of ½-unze gold coin, 1850 40 15
1675 90col. Obverse and reverse of ¼-peso silver coin, 1850 40 15
1676 90col. Obverse and reverse of 20 pesos gold coin, 1873 . . . . 40 15
1677 90col. Obverse and reverse of 1-colon coin, 1900 . . 40 15

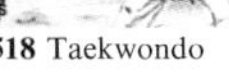

518 Taekwondo 519 Calderon Guardia

2000. Olympic Games, Sydney. Multicoloured.
1678 60col. Type **518** 30 20
1679 60col. Cycling 30 20
1680 60col. Swimming 30 20
1681 60col. Football 30 20
1682 70col. Running 30 20
1683 70col. Boxing 30 20
1684 70col. Gymnastics 30 20
1685 70col. Tennis 30 20

Stamps of the same value were issued together, se-tenant, in blocks of four stamps, each block forming the composite design of a map of Australia with the sport appearing within the outline of the map

2000. Birth Centenary of Rafael Angel Calderon Guardia (politician).
1686 **519** 100col. blue 35 25

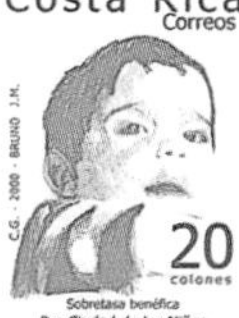
520 "Fisherman in Cojímar"

2000. Birth Centenary of Max Jiminez (artist). Multicoloured.
1687 50col. Type **520** 15 10
1688 50col. "Adamant" 15 10

521 Child's Face 522 Family

2000. Obligatory Tax. Christmas. Children's Village.
1689 **521** 20col. green 10 10
1690 20col. red 10 10
1691 20col. blue 10 10
1692 20col. brown 10 10

2000. A.I.D.S. Awareness. Multicoloured.
1693 60col. Type **522** 20 15
1694 90col. Man between blocks of colour 30 20

523 Nativity Scene

2000. Christmas
1695 **523** 100col. multicoloured . . 35 25

524 Cocos Cuckoo (*Coccyzus ferrugineus*)

2001. America. UNESCO. World Heritage Sites. Coco Island. Birds. Multicoloured.
1696 95col. Type **524** 40 25
1697 115col. Cocos finch (*Pinaroloxias inornata*) . . 50 30

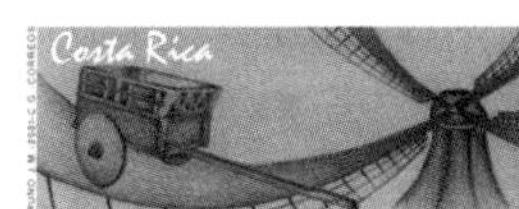
525 Cart and Windmill (½-size illustration)

2001. 150th Anniv of Costa Rica–Netherlands Co-operation Treaty.
1698 **525** 65col. multicoloured . . 25 15

2001. No. 1502 surch.
1699 65col. on 500col. multicoloured 25 15
1700 80col. on 500col. multicoloured 30 20
1701 95co. on 500col. multicoloured 40 25

2001. No. 1602 surch **C5.00**.
1702 5col. on 30col. multicoloured 10 10

528 Guaria Turrialba (*Cattleya dowiana*)

2001. Spain–Costa Ricen Stamp Exhibition, San Jose. Orchids. Multicoloured.
1703 65col. Type **528** 25 15
1704 65col. Trichophilia 25 15

529 Boy pushing Furniture on Barrow

2001. Child Labour Eradication Campaign.
1705 **529** 100col. multicoloured . . 40 25

530 Child holding Stamp and Magnifier

2001. Obligatory Tax. Christmas. Children's Village. Multicoloured, colour of right-hand title panel given.
1706 **530** 21col. violet 10 10
1707 21col. green 10 10
1708 21col. red 10 10
1709 21col. yellow 10 10

531 Steam Locomotive and Guardia

2001. Tomas Guardia (former President and railway pioneer) Commemoration.
1710 **531** 65col. multicoloured . . 25 15

EXPRESS DELIVERY STAMPS

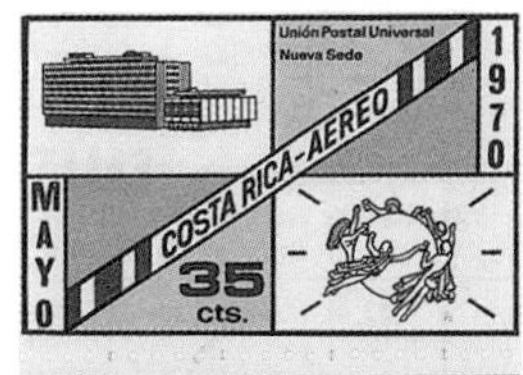

E 237 New U.P.U. Headquarters Building and Emblem

1970. Air. New U.P.U. Headquarters Building.
E841 E **237** 35c. multicoloured . . 15 10
E842 60c. multicoloured . . 20 10

In Type E **237** "ENTREGA INMEDIATA" is in the form of a perforated tab.

No. E842 has the same main design, but the tab is inscr "EXPRES".

E **249** Winged Letter

1972.
E888 E **249** 75c. brown & red . . 15 15
E889 75c. green & red . . . 15 15
E890 75c. mauve & red . . 15 15
E891 1col.50 blue & red . . 45 25

E **279** Concorde

1976.
E1031 E **279** 1col. multicoloured 25 15
E1135 – 2col. multicoloured 50 30
E1136 – 2col. multicoloured 50 30
E1137 – 4col. multicoloured 55 25

Nos. E1135/7 is as Type E **279**, but inscribed "EXPRESS".

OFFICIAL STAMPS

Various issues optd **OFICIAL** except where otherwise stated.

1883. Stamps of 1883.
O35 **8** 1c. green 45 45
O36 2c. red 40 40
O22 5c. violet . . . . 2·75 2·75
O37 10c. orange . . . . . . 3·50 3·50
O38 40c. blue . . . . 2·50 2·10

1887. Stamps of 1887.
O39 **14** 5c. violet . . . . 1·60 1·60
O40 10c. orange 40 40

1889. Stamps of 1889.
O41 **17** 1c. brown 25 20
O42 2c. blue 25 20
O43 5c. orange 25 20
O44 10c. lake 25 20
O45 20c. green 25 20
O46 50c. red 60 60

1892. Stamps of 1892.
O47 **19** 1c. blue 25 20
O48 2c. orange 25 20
O49 5c. mauve 25 20
O50 10c. green 60 60
O51 20c. red 25 20
O52 50c. blue 60 50

1901. Stamps of 1901 (Nos. 42/48).
O53 1c. black and green 35 35
O54 2c. black and red 35 35
O61 4c. black and purple . . . . 1·25 1·25
O55 5c. black and blue 35 35
O62 6c. black and olive . . . . . 1·25 1·25
O56 10c. black and brown . . . 60 60
O57 20c. black and lake 80 80
O63 25c. brown and lilac . . . . 5·25 3·25
O58 50c. blue and red . . . . . 1·75 1·75
O59 1col. black and olive . . . . 55·00 32·00

1903. Stamp of 1901 optd **PROVISORIO OFICIAL**.
O60 2c. black & red (No. 43) . . 2·00 2·00

1908. Stamps of 1907 (Nos. 57/76).
O77 1c. blue and brown 10 10
O78 2c. black and green 10 10
O79 4c. blue and red 10 10
O80 5c. blue and orange 15 15
O81 10c. black and blue 85 85
O82 25c. slate and lavender . . . 15 15
O83 50c. blue and red 25 25
O84 1col. black and brown . . . 45 45

1917. Stamps of 1910 optd **OFICIAL 15-VI-1917**.
O115 5c. orange (No. 80) 20 20
O116 10c. blue (No. 81) 15 15

1920. No. 82 surch **OFICIAL 15 CENTIMOS**.
O117 15c. on 20c. olive 35 35

1921. Official stamps of 1908 optd **1921–22** or surch also.
O123 4c. blue & red (No.O79) . . 30 30
O124 6c. on 1c. blue & brown (No. O77) 35 35
O125 20c. on 25c. slate and lavender (No. O82) . . . 35 35
O126 50c. blue & red (No. O83) 1·50 1·50
O127 1col. black & brn (No. O84) . . . . 3·00 3·00

1921. No. O115 surch **10 CTS**.
O128 10c. on 5c. orange 35 25

1923. Stamps of 1923.
O137 **77** 2c. brown 20 20
O138 4c. green 10 10
O139 5c. blue 20 20
O140 20c. red 15 15
O141 1col. violet 25 25

O 95

1926.
O169 O **95** 2c. black and blue . . 10 10
O231 2c. black and lilac . . 10 10
O170 3c. black and red . . . 10 10
O232 3c. black and brown 10 10
O171 4c. black and blue . . 10 10
O233 4c. black and red . . . 10 10
O172 5c. black and green . . 10 10
O173 6c. black and yellow 10 10
O235 8c. black and brown 10
O174 10c. black and red . . 10 10
O175 20c. black and green 10 10
O237 20c. black and blue . . 10 10
O176 30c. black and orange 10 10
O238 40c. black and orange 15 15
O177 45c. black and brown 15 15
O239 55c. black and lilac . . 25
O178 1col. black and lilac 20 20
O240 1col. black and brown 20 20
O241 2col. black and blue 40 40
O242 5col. black & yellow 1·50 1·50
O243 10col. blue and black 9·50 9·50

1934. Air. Air stamps of 1934.
O211 **107** 5c. green 25 25
O212 10c. red 25 25

O213 15c. brown 40 40
O214 20c. blue 60 60
O215 25c. orange 60 60
O216 40c. brown 70 70
O217 50c. black 70 70
O218 60c. yellow 80 80
O219 75c. violet 80 80
O220 – 1col. red . . . . 1·25 1·25
O221 – 2col. blue . . . . 3·50 3·50
O222 – 5col. black . . . . . . 6·50 6·50
O223 – 10col. brown . . . . . 7·50 7·50

1936. Stamps of 1936.
O228 **113** 5c. green 20 10
O229 10c. red 20 10

POSTAGE DUE STAMPS

D 42 D 64

1903.
D55 **D 42** 5c. blue . . . . 4·50 90
D56 10c. brown . . . . . . 4·50 70
D57 15c. green . . . . . . 1·90 1·60
D58 20c. red . . . . 2·10 1·60
D59 25c. blue . . . . 2·75 1·60
D60 30c. brown . . . . . . 4·25 2·50
D61 40c. olive . . . . . . 4·25 2·50
D62 50c. red . . . . 4·25 2·10

1915.
D115 **D 64** 2c. orange 10 10
D116 4c. blue 10 10
D117 8c. green 35 35
D118 10c. violet 15 15
D119 20c. brown 15 15

CRETE Pt. 3

Former Turkish island in the E. Mediterranean under the joint protection of Gt. Britain, France, Italy and Russia from 1898 to 1908, when the island was united to Greece. This was recognized by Turkey in 1913. Greek stamps now used.

100 lepta = 1 drachma.

1 Hermes

2 Hera

3 Prince George of Greece

4 Talos

1900.
1 **1** 1l. brown 65 20
12 1l. yellow 55 55
2 **2** 5l. green . . . . 1·25 20
3 **3** 10l. red . . . . 2·00 20
4 **2** 20l. red . . . . 7·75 1·25
13 20l. orange . . . . 4·00 70
15 **3** 25l. blue . . . . 8·00 65
14 **1** 50l. blue . . . . 11·00 11·50
16 50l. lilac . . . . 26·00 16·00
17 **4** 1d. violet . . . . 26·00 16·00
18 – 2d. brown . . . . 8·00 6·00
19 – 5d. black and green . . . . 8·00 7·00
DESIGNS (as Type **4**): 2d. Minos; 5d. St. George and Dragon.

ΠΡΟΣΩΡΙΝΟΝ
(7) ("Provisional")

1900. Optd as T **7**.
5 **3** 25l. blue . . . . 2·00 1·40
6 **1** 50l. lilac . . . . 1·40 80
7 **4** 1d. violet . . . . 9·50 4·00
8 – 2d. brown (No. 18) . . . . 26·00 16·00
9 – 5d. black & green (No. 19) . . 60·00 70·00

1904. Surch **5** twice.
20 **2** 5 on 20l. orange . . . . . . 3·25 75

10 Rhea

12 Prince George of Greece

16 Europa and Jupiter

1905.
21 **10** 2l. lilac . . . . 1·40 30
22 – 5l. green . . . . 4·00 30
23 **12** 10l. red . . . . 4·00 30
24 – 20l. green . . . . 4·00 75
25 – 25l. blue . . . . 5·00 70
26 – 50l. brown . . . . 3·75 3·50
27 **16** 1d. sepia and red . . . . . 65·00 50·00
28 – 3d. black and orange . . . 45·00 28·00
29 – 5d. black and olive . . . . 32·00 13·50
DESIGNS—As Type **10**: 5l. Europa; 20l. Miletus; 25l. Triton; 50l. Ariadne. As Type **16**: 3d. Minos ruins. 44 × 28½ mm: 5d. Mt. Ida.

19 High Commissioner A. T. A. Zaimis

1907. Various designs.
30 **19** 25l. black and blue . . . . 35·00 1·40
31 – 1d. black and green . . . . 9·00 6·25
DESIGN—HORIZ: (larger): 1d. Landing of Prince George of Greece at Suda.

21 Hermes

ΕΛΛΑΣ
(22) ("Greece")

1908. Optd as T **22** in various sizes and styles.
32 **1** 1l. brown 40 20
33 **10** 2l. lilac 40 20
34 – 5l. green (No. 22) 55 20
35 **3** 10l. red 80 40
36 **21** 10l. red . . . . 2·40 65
37 – 20l. green (No. 24) . . . 4·50 65
38 **19** 25l. black and blue . . . . 10·00 1·40
63 – 25l. blue (No. 25) . . . . 3·00 55
39 – 50l. brown (No. 26) . . . . 5·00 5·00
40 **16** 1d. sepia and red . . . . 65·00 55·00
52 – 1d. black & grn (No. 31) . . 11·00 11·00
41 – 2d. brown (No. 18) . . . 9·50 9·50
42 – 3d. black & orge (No. 28) 40·00 28·00
43 – 5d. black & olive (No. 29) 40·00 24·00

1909. Optd with T **7** and **22** or surch with new value also.
44 **1** 1l. yellow (No. 12) . . . . 1·10 1·10
45 **D 8** 1l. red (No. D10) . . . . 1·10 1·10
46 2 on 20l. red (No. D73) 1·10 1·10
47 2 on 20l. red (No. D13) 1·10 1·10
48 **2** 5 on 20l. red (No. 4) . . . 80·00 80·00
49 5 on 20l. orange (No. 13) 1·10 1·10

OFFICIAL STAMPS

O 21

1908.
O32 **O 21** 10l. red . . . . 15·00 1·40
O33 30l. blue . . . . 30·00 2·50
In the 30l. the central figures are in an oval frame.

1908. Optd with T **22**.
O44 **O 21** 10l. red . . . . 16·00 1·40
O45 30l. blue . . . . 30·00 1·40

POSTAGE DUE STAMPS

D 8

1901.
D10 **D 8** 1l. red 45 50
D11 5l. red . . . . 1·10 40
D12 10l. red . . . . 1·10 25
D13 20l. red . . . . 1·50 70
D14 40l. red . . . . 12·00 11·00
D15 50l. red . . . . 12·00 11·00
D16 1d. red . . . . 12·00 11·00
D17 2d. red . . . . 13·00 11·00

1901. Surch "1 drachma" in Greek characters.
D18 **D 8** 1d. on 1d. red . . . . . 8·75 8·00

1908. Optd with T **22**.
D70 **D 8** 1l. red 25 30
D45 5l. red . . . . 1·00 20
D72 10l. red 55 25
D47 20l. red . . . . 2·50 80
D74 40l. red . . . . 8·00 7·50
D75 50l. red . . . . 11·00 10·00
D76 1d. red . . . . 18·00 18·00
D51 1d. on 1d. red (No. D18) 9·50 9·50
D52 2d. red . . . . 18·00 18·00

REVOLUTIONARY ASSEMBLY, 1905

In March, a revolt in favour of union with Greece began, organized by Venizelos with headquarters at Theriso, South of Canea. The revolt collapsed in November 1905.

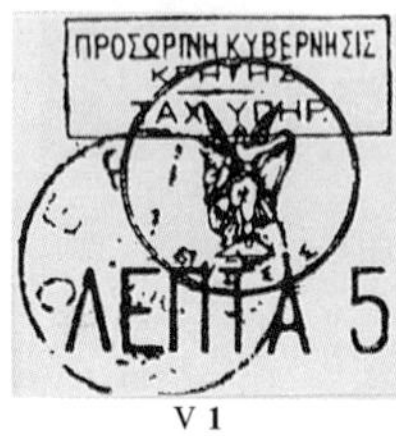
V 1

V 2 Crete enslaved

1905. Imperf.
V1 **V 1** 5l. red and green . . . . 13·50 7·00
V2 10l. green and red . . . . 13·50 7·00
V3 20l. blue and red . . . . 13·50 7·00
V4 50l. green and violet . . . 13·50 7·00
V5 1d. red and blue . . . . . 13·50 7·00

1905.
V 6 **V 2** 5l. orange . . . . 40 1·10
V 7 10l. grey . . . . 40 1·10
V 8 20l. mauve . . . . 1·05 2·10
V 9 50l. blue . . . . 2·75 4·25
V10 – 1d. violet and red . . . . 4·25 4·25
V11 – 2d. brown and green . . 4·25 5·00
DESIGN: 1, 2d. King George of Greece.

CROATIA Pt. 3

Part of Hungary until 1918 when it became part of Yugoslavia. In 1941 it was proclaimed an independent state but in 1945 it became a constituent republic of the Federal People's Republic of Yugoslavia.

In 1991 Croatia became independent.

April 1941. 100 paras = 1 dinar.
Sept 1941. 100 banicas = 1 kuna.
1991. 100 paras = 1 dinar.
1994. 100 lipa = 1 kuna.

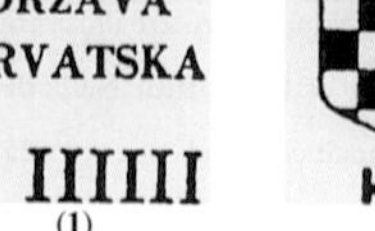

(1) (2)

1941. Stamps of Yugoslavia optd as T **1** ("Independent Croat State").
1 **99** 50p. orange . . . . 1·00 2·25
2 1d. green . . . . 1·00 2·25
3 1d.50 red . . . . 1·00 1·00
4 2d. mauve . . . . 1·00 1·75
5 3d. brown . . . . 2·50 4·50
6 4d. blue . . . . 2·50 5·00
7 5d. blue . . . . 2·50 5·00
8 5d.50 violet . . . . 2·50 5·50

1941. Stamps of Yugoslavia optd as T **2**.
9 **99** 25p. black 20 30
10 50p. orange 20 30
11 1d. green 20 30
12 1d.50 red 20 30
13 2d. pink 20 60
14 3d. brown 20 90
15 4d. blue . . . . 25 1·00
16 5d. blue . . . . 40 1·00
17 5d.50 violet . . . . . . 40 1·25
18 6d. blue . . . . 50 1·75
19 8d. brown . . . . 80 2·00
20 12d. violet . . . . 90 2·50
21 16d. purple . . . . 1·00 3·00
22 20d. blue . . . . 1·25 3·50
23 30d. pink . . . . 2·00 5·50

(3)

(4)

1941. Stamps of Yugoslavia surch as T **3**.
24 **99** 1d. on 3d. brown 15 40
25 2d. on 4d. blue 15 40

1941. Founding of Croatian Army. Nos. 414/26 of Yugoslavia optd with T **4**.
25a **99** 25p. black . . . .
25b 50p. orange . . . . . .
25c 1d. green . . . .
25d 1d.50 red . . . .
25e 2d. pink . . . .
25f 3d. brown . . . .
25g 4d. blue . . . .
25h 5d. blue . . . .
25i 5d.50 violet . . . . . .
25j 6d. blue . . . .
25k 8d. brown . . . .
25l 12d. violet . . . .
25m 16d. purple . . . . . .
25n 20d. blue . . . .
25o 30d. pink . . . .
Set of 15 . . . . £150 £375
Sold at double face value.

1941. Stamps of Yugoslavia optd as T **2** but without shield.
26 **109** 1d.50+1d.50 black . . . . 5·00 10·00
27 – 4d.+3d. brown (No. 457) 5·00 10·00

1941. Postage Due stamps of Yugoslavia optd **NEZAVISNA DRZAVA HRVATSKA FRANCO**.
28 **D 56** 50p. violet 20 30
29 2d. blue 30 60
30 5d. orange 30 60
31 10d. brown 35 90

7 Mt. Ozalj

8 Banja Luka

1941.
32 **7** 25b. red 25 25
33 – 50b. green 10 10
34 – 75b. olive 10 10
35 – 1k. green 10 10
36 – 1k.50 green 10 10
37 – 2k. red 10 10
38 – 3k. red 10 10
39 – 4k. blue 10 10
40 – 5k. black 75 75
41 – 5k. blue 10 10
42 – 6k. olive 10 10
43 – 7k. orange 10 10
44 – 8k. brown 10 10
45 – 10k. violet 40 30
46 – 12k. brown 50 50
47 – 20k. brown 40 30
48 – 30k. brown 55 50
49 – 50k. green . . . . 1·00 1·00
50 **8** 100k. violet . . . . 1·60 2·25
DESIGNS: 50b. Waterfall at Jajce; 75b. Varazdin; 1k. Mt. Velebit; 1k.50, Zelenjak; 2k. Zagreb Cathedral; 3k. Church at Osijek; 4k. River Drina; 5k. (No. 40), Konjic Bridge; 5k. (No. 41), Modern building at Zemun; 6k. Dubrovnik; 7k. R. Save in Slavonia; 8k. Mosque at Sarajevo; 10k. Lake Plitvice; 12k. Klis Fortress near Split; 20k. Hvar; 30k. Harvesting in Syrmia; 50k. Senj.

9 Croat (Sinj) Costume

10 Emblems of Germany, Croatia and Italy

1941. Red Cross.
51 **9** 1k.50+1k.50 blue 35 60
52 – 2k.+2k. brown 35 70
53 – 5k.+4k. red . . . . 85 1·75
COSTUMES: 2k. Travnik. 4k. Turopolje.

1941. Eastern Volunteer Fund.
54 **10** 4k.+2k. blue . . . . 1·00 2·75

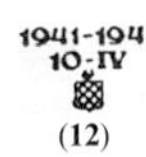

11 Glider (12)

1942. Aviation Fund. Glider in flight as T **11**.
55 **11** 2k.+2k. brown (vert) . . . 40 60
56 – 2k.50+2k.50 green . . . . 60 1·00
57 – 3 k+3k. red (vert) . . . . 75 1·25
58 – 4k.+4k. blue . . . . . . 85 1·90
DESIGNS—HORIZ: 2k.50, Glider (different); 4k. Seaplane glider. VERT: 3k. Boy with model glider.

1942. 1st Anniv of Croat Independence. Optd with T **12**.
59 2k. brown (as No. 37) 15 35
60 5k. red (as No. 40) 25 70
61 10k. green (as No. 45) . . . . 40 1·00

1942. Banja Luka Philatelic Exhibition. Inscr "F.I." in top right corner.
62 **8** 100k. violet . . . . 1·40 3·75

1942. Surch **0.25kn** and bar.
63 0.25k. on 2k. red (No. 37) . . 20 50

14 Trumpeters 15 Sestine (Croatia)

1942. National Relief Fund.
64 **14** 3k.+1k. red . . . . 40 1·00
65 – 4k.+2k. brown . . . . . . 60 1·10
66 – 5k.+5k. blue . . . . 80 1·90
DESIGNS—HORIZ: 4k. Procession beneath triumphal archways. VERT: 5k. Mother and child.

1942. Red Cross Fund. Peasant girls in provincial costumes.
67 **15** 1k.50+50b. brown . . . . . 60 1·25
68 – 3k.+1k. violet . . . . 60 1·25
69 – 4k.+2k. blue . . . . 80 1·75
70 – 10k.+5k. bistre . . . . . . 1·00 2·10
71 **15** 13k.+6k. red . . . . 2·00 4·50
COSTUMES: 3k. Slavonia. 4k. Bosnia. 10k. Dalmatia.

15a Red Cross Sister 16 M. Gubec

1942. Charity Tax. Red Cross Fund. Cross in red.
71a **15a** 1k. green 20 60

1942. Croat ("Ustascha") Youth Fund.
72 **16** 3k.+6k. red 25 70
73 – 4k.+7k. brown 25 70
PORTRAIT: 4k. A. Starcevic.

17 19 Arms of Zagreb

1943. Labour Front. Vert designs showing workers as T **17**.
74 **17** 2k.+1k. brown and olive . . 1·50 3·25
75 – 3k.+3k. brown & purple . . 1·50 3·25
76 – 7k.+4k. brown & grey . . . 1·50 3·25

1943. 7th Centenary of Foundation of Zagreb.
77 **19** 3k.50 (+ 6k.50) blue . . . . 1·10 3·75

1943. Pictorial designs as T **8**, but with views surrounded by frame line.
78 3k.50 brown 35 40
79 12k.50 black 35 70
DESIGNS: 3k.50, Trakoscan Castle; 12k.50, Veliki Tabor.

21 A. Pavelic 22 Krsto Frankopan

1943. Croat ("Ustascha") Youth Fund.
80 **21** 5k.+3k. red 15 65
81 7k.+5k. green 15 65

1943. Famous Croats.
82 – 1k. blue 15 30
83 **22** 2k. olive 15 30
84 – 3k.50 red 15 50
PORTRAITS: 1k. Katarina Zrinska. 3k.50, Peter Zrinski.

23 Croat Sailor and Motor Torpedo Boats

1943. Croat Legion Relief Fund.
85 **23** 1k.+50b. green 10 25
86 – 2k.+1k. red 10 25
87 – 3k.50+1k.50 blue 10 25
88 – 9k.+4k.50 brown 10 25
DESIGNS: 2k. Pilot and Heinkel bomber; 3k.50, Infantrymen; 9k. Mechanized column.

24 St. Mary's Church and Cistercian Monastery, 1650

1943. Philatelic Exhibition, Zagreb.
89 **24** 18k.+9k. blue . . . . 1·40 4·00

1943. Return of Sibenik to Croatia. Optd **HRVATSKO MORE 8, IX. 1943**.
90 **24** 18k.+9k. blue . . . . 3·25 9·00

26 Nurse and Patient 26a

1943. Red Cross Fund.
91 – 1k.+50b. blue 20 50
92 – 2k.+1k. red 20 50
93 – 3k.50+1k.50 blue 20 50
94 **26** 8k.+3k. brown 20 50
95 9k.+4k. green 20 50
96 – 10k.+5k. violet 30 75
97 **26** 12k.+6k. blue 30 90
98 – 12k.50+6k. brown . . . . 50 1·25
99 **26** 18k.+8k. orange . . . . . 75 1·90
100 32k.+12k. grey . . . . . . 1·25 2·75
DESIGN: 1k., 2k., 3k.50, 10k., 12k.50, Mother and children.

1943. Charity Tax. Red Cross Fund. Cross in red.
100a **26a** 2k. blue 20 50

27 A. Pavelic 28 Ruder Boskovic

1943.
101 **27** 25b. red 10 15
105 50b. blue 10 15
102 75b. green 10 15
106 1k. green 10 15
107 1k.50 violet 10 15
108 2k. red 10 15
109 3k. red 10 15
110 3k.50 blue 10 15
111 4k. purple 10 15
103 5k. blue 10 15
112 8k. brown 10 15
113 9k. red 10 15
114 10k. purple 10 15
115 12k. brown 10 15
116 12k.50 black 10 15
117 18k. brown 10 15
104 32k. brown 10 15
118 50k. green 10 15
119 70k. orange 30 60
120 100k. violet . . . . 70 1·40
The design of the 25b., 75b., 5k., and 32k. is $20\frac{1}{2} \times 26$ mm, the rest are 22×28 mm.

1943. Honouring Ruder Boskovic (astronomer).
121 **28** 3k.50 red 15 35
122 12k.50 purple 30 50

29 Posthorn 30 St. Sebastian

1944. Postal and Railway Employees' Relief Fund.
123 **29** 7k.+3k.50 brn, red & bis 20 40
124 – 16k.+8k. blue 20 50
125 – 24k.+12k. red 30 70
126 – 32k.+16k. black & red . . 65 1·10
DESIGNS—VERT: 16k. Dove, airplane and globe; 24k. Mercury. HORIZ: 32k. Winged wheel.

1944. War Invalids' Relief Fund.
127 **30** 7k.+3k.50 mauve & red . . 20 50
128 – 16k.+8k. green 25 70
129 – 24k.+12k. yell, brn & red 25 70
130 – 32k.+16k. blue . . . . . . 45 1·10
DESIGNS—HORIZ: 16k. Blind man and cripple; 32k. Death of Peter Svacic, 1094. VERT: 24k. Mediaeval statuette.

31 The Legion in Action 32 Jure-Ritter Francetic

1944. Croat Youth Fund. No. 134 perf, others imperf.
131 **31** 3k.50+1k.50 brown 10 15
132 – 12k.50+6k.50 blue 10 15
134 **32** 12k.50+287k.50 black . . . 3·50 11·50
133 18k.+9k. brown 10 15
DESIGN: No. 132, Sentries on the Drina.

33

1944. Labour Front. Inscr "D.R.S.".
135 **33** 3k.50+1k. red 10 20
136 – 12k.50+6k. brown 40 65
137 – 18k.+9k. blue 15 35
138 – 32k.+16k. green 15 35
DESIGNS: 12k.50, Digging; 18k. Instruction; 32k. "On Parade".

34 Bombed Home 35 War Victim

1944. Charity Tax. War Victims.
138b **34** 1k. green 10 15
138c **35** 2k. red 10 15
138d 5k. green 10 15
138e 10k. blue 15 35
138f 20k. brown 40 85

36 37 Storm Division Soldiers

1944. Red Cross. Cross in red.
139 **36** 2k.+1k. green 10 30
140 3k.50+1k.50 red 15 40
141 12k.50+6k. blue 20 50

1945. Creation of Croatian Storm Division on 9th October 1944.
142 **37** 50k.+50k. red and grey . . 42·00 £100
143 – 70k.+70k. sepia & grey . . 42·00 £100
144 – 100k.+100k. bl & grey . . 42·00 £100
DESIGNS: 70k. Storm Division soldiers in action; 100k. Divisional emblem.

38 39

1945. Postal Employees' Fund.
145 **38** 3k.50+1k.50 grey 10 20
146 – 12k.50+6k. purple 10 30
147 – 24k.+12k. green 15 35
148 – 50k.+25k. purple 20 60
DESIGNS: 12k.50, Telegraph linesman; 24k. Telephone switchboard; 50k. The postman calls.

1945. Labour Day.
149 **39** 3k.50 brown . . . . 20 1·25

40 Interior of Zagreb Cathedral 41 Statue of the Virgin and Shrine

1991. Obligatory Tax. Workers' Fund. Mass for Croatia. Perf or imperf.
150 **40** 1d.20 gold and black . . . 40 40

1991. Obligatory Tax. Workers' Fund. 700th Anniv of Shrine of the Virgin, Trsat. Perf or imperf.
151 **41** 1d.70 multicoloured . . . 50 50

42 State Arms 43 Members of Parliament

1991. Obligatory Tax. Workers' Fund. Rally in Ban Jelacic Square, Zagreb. Perf or imperf.
152 **42** 2d.20 multicoloured . . . 50 50
See also No. 170.

1991. Obligatory Tax. Workers' Fund. First Multiparty Session of Croatian Parliament, 30 May 1990. Perf or imperf.
153 **43** 2d.20 multicoloured . . . 50 50

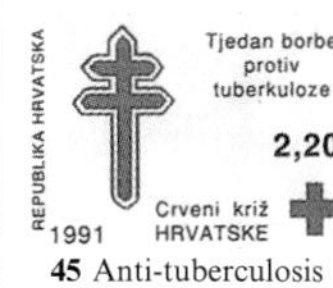

44 Sud Aviation Caravelle Jetliner over Zagreb Cathedral and Dubrovnik 45 Anti-tuberculosis Emblem

1991. Air.
154 **44** 1d. blue, black and red . . 30 30
155 – 2d. multicoloured 30 30
156 – 3d. multicoloured 30 30
DESIGNS: 2d. Bell tower and ruins of Diocletian's Palace, Split; 3d. Sud Aviation Caravelle jetliner over Zagreb Cathedral and Pula amphitheatre.

1991. Obligatory Tax. Anti-tuberculosis Week.
157 **45** 2d.20 red and blue 30 30

46 Ban Jelacic Statue

48 First Article of Constitution in Croatian

1991. Obligatory Tax. Workers' Fund. Re-erection of Ban Josip Jelacic Equestrian Statue, Zagreb. Perf or imperf.
158 **46** 2d.20 multicoloured . . . 50 50

1991. No. 150 surch **4**" **HPT** and posthorn.
159 **40** 4d. on 1d.20 gold & blk . . 35 35

1991. Obligatory Tax. Workers' Fund. 1st Anniv of New Constitution. Multicoloured. Perf or imperf.
160 2d.20 Type **48** 30 30
161 2d.20 Text in English 80 80
162 2d.20 Text in French 80 80
163 2d.20 Text in German . . . 80 80
164 2d.20 Text in Russian 80 80
165 2d.20 Text in Spanish 80 80

49 Book of Croatian Independence

50 17th-century Crib Figures, Kosljun Monastery, Krk

1991. Recognition of Independence.
166 **49** 30d. multicoloured . . . . 1·10 1·10

1991. Christmas.
167 **50** 4d. multicoloured 60 60

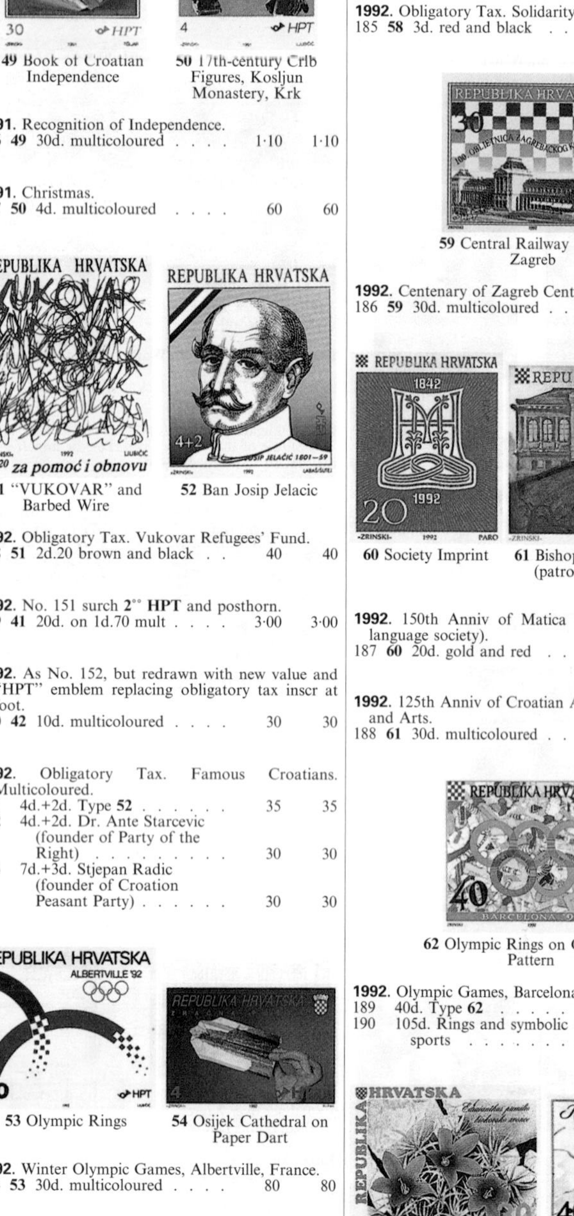

51 "VUKOVAR" and Barbed Wire

52 Ban Josip Jelacic

1992. Obligatory Tax. Vukovar Refugees' Fund.
168 **51** 2d.20 brown and black . . 40 40

1992. No. 151 surch **2**" **HPT** and posthorn.
169 **41** 20d. on 1d.70 mult . . . . 3·00 3·00

1992. As No. 152, but redrawn with new value and "HPT" emblem replacing obligatory tax inscr at foot.
170 **42** 10d. multicoloured 30 30

1992. Obligatory Tax. Famous Croatians. Multicoloured.
171 4d.+2d. Type **52** 35 35
172 4d.+2d. Dr. Ante Starcevic (founder of Party of the Right) 30 30
173 7d.+3d. Stjepan Radic (founder of Croation Peasant Party) 30 30

53 Olympic Rings

54 Osijek Cathedral on Paper Dart

1992. Winter Olympic Games, Albertville, France.
174 **53** 30d. multicoloured 80 80

1992. Air.
175 **54** 4d. multicoloured 25 20

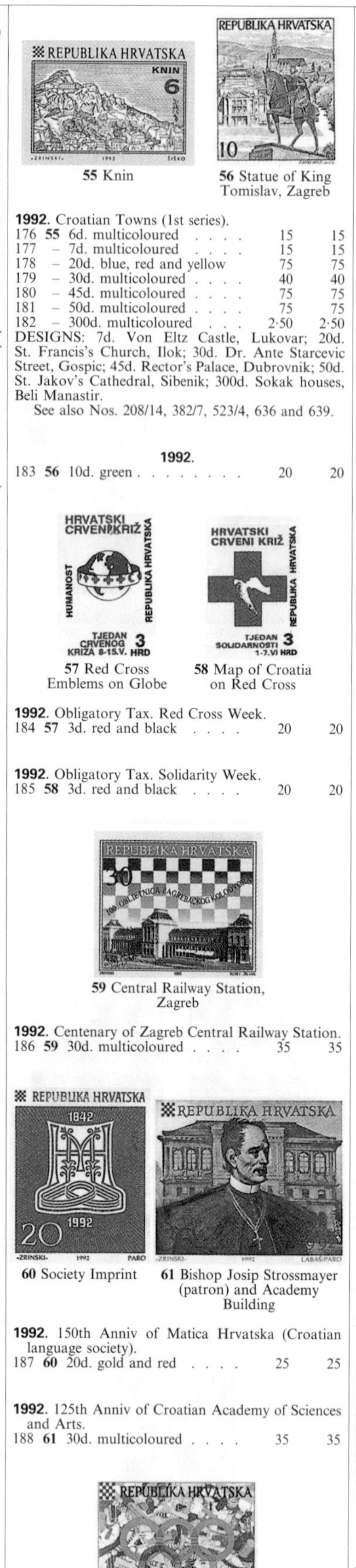

55 Knin

56 Statue of King Tomislav, Zagreb

1992. Croatian Towns (1st series).
176 **55** 6d. multicoloured 15 15
177 – 7d. multicoloured 15 15
178 – 20d. blue, red and yellow 75 75
179 – 30d. multicoloured 40 40
180 – 45d. multicoloured 75 75
181 – 50d. multicoloured 75 75
182 – 300d. multicoloured . . . 2·50 2·50
DESIGNS: 7d. Von Eltz Castle, Lukovar; 20d. St. Francis's Church, Ilok; 30d. Dr. Ante Starcevic Street, Gospic; 45d. Rector's Palace, Dubrovnik; 50d. St. Jakov's Cathedral, Sibenik; 300d. Sokak houses, Beli Manastir.
See also Nos. 208/14, 382/7, 523/4, 636 and 639.

1992.
183 **56** 10d. green 20 20

57 Red Cross Emblems on Globe

58 Map of Croatia on Red Cross

1992. Obligatory Tax. Red Cross Week.
184 **57** 3d. red and black 20 20

1992. Obligatory Tax. Solidarity Week.
185 **58** 3d. red and black 20 20

59 Central Railway Station, Zagreb

1992. Centenary of Zagreb Central Railway Station.
186 **59** 30d. multicoloured 35 35

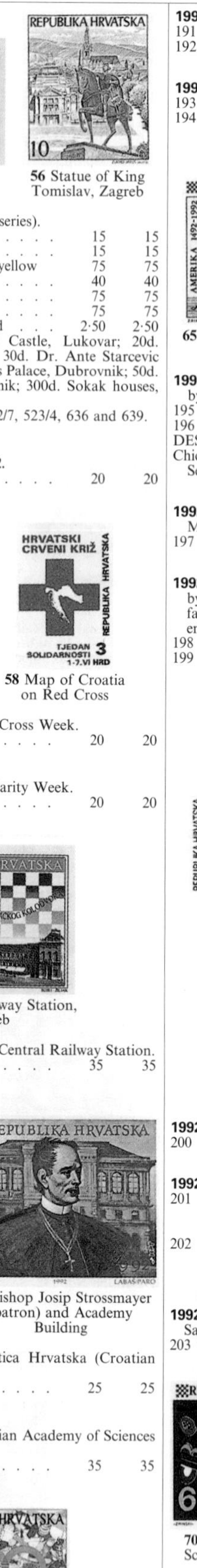

60 Society Imprint

61 Bishop Josip Strossmayer (patron) and Academy Building

1992. 150th Anniv of Matica Hrvatska (Croatian language society).
187 **60** 20d. gold and red 25 25

1992. 125th Anniv of Croatian Academy of Sciences and Arts.
188 **61** 30d. multicoloured 35 35

62 Olympic Rings on Computer Pattern

1992. Olympic Games, Barcelona. Mult.
189 40d. Type **62** 35 35
190 105d. Rings and symbolic sports 65 65

63 Bellflowers

64 Blue Rock Thrush

1992. Flowers. Multicoloured.
191 30d. Type **63** 25 25
192 85d. Degenia (vert) 50 50

1992. Environmental Protection. Mult.
193 40d. Type **64** 25 25
194 75d. Red-spot snake 50 50

65 15th-century Carrack, Dubrovnik

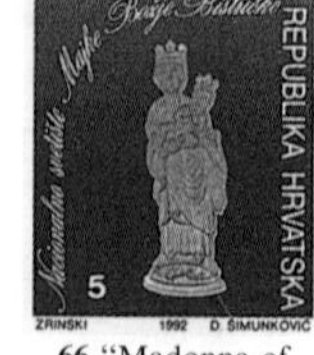

66 "Madonna of Bistrica"

1992. Europa. 500th Anniv of Discovery of America by Columbus (1st issue).
195 **65** 30d. multicoloured 30 30
196 – 75d. black and red 75 75
DESIGN: 75d. "Indian Horseman" (bronze statue in Chicago by Ivan Mestrovic).
See also Nos. 198/9.

1992. Obligatory Tax. Fund for National Shrine to Madonna of Bistrica.
197 **66** 5d. gold and blue 20 20

1992. Europa. 500th Anniv of Discovery of America by Columbus (2nd issue). As Nos. 195/6, but new face values and with additional C.E.P.T. posthorns emblem.
198 **65** 60d. multicoloured 50 50
199 – 130d. black, red and gold (as No. 196) . . . . . . 1·10 1·10

67 Red Cross

69 Dove and Coat of Arms

68 "25"

1992. Obligatory Tax. Anti-tuberculosis Week.
200 **67** 5d. red and black 20 20

1992. Croatian Language Anniversaries. Mult.
201 40d. Type **68** (25th anniv of Croatian Language Declaration) 25 25
202 130d. "100" (centenary of Croatian "Orthography" by Dr. I. Broz) 45 45

1992. 750th Anniv of Grant of Royal City Charter to Samobor.
203 **69** 90d. multicoloured 35 35

70 Remains of Altar Screen from Uzdolje Church

71 St. George and the Dragon

1992. 1100th Anniv of Duke Mucimir's Donation (judgement in ecclesiastical dispute).
204 **70** 60d. multicoloured 25 25

1992. Obligatory Tax. Croatian Anti-cancer League.
205 **71** 15d. multicoloured 20 20
See also No. 255.

72 Seal of King Bela IV

1992. 750th Anniv of Zagreb's Charter from King Bela IV.
206 **72** 180d. multicoloured . . . 50 50

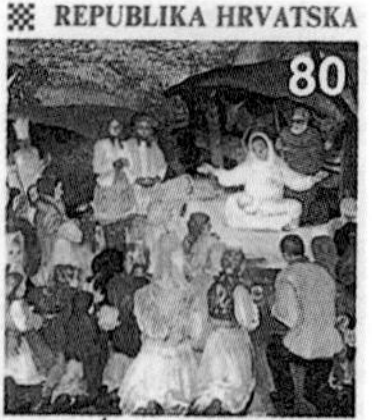

73 "Croatian Christmas" (Ljubo Babic)

1992. Christmas.
207 **73** 80d. multicoloured 25 25

74 Former Town Hall, Vinkovci

75 Lorkovic

1992. Croatian Towns (2nd series). Mult.
208 100d. Type **74** 25 20
209 200d. Castle, Pazin (vert) . . 35 30
210 500d. Jelacic Square, Slavonski Brod 80 75
211 1000d. Town Hall, Jelacic Square, Varazdin . . . . . 1·25 1·00
212 2000d. Zorin cultural centre, Karlovac . . . . 1·40 1·25
213 5000d. St. Donat's Church and St. Stosija's Cathedral belltower, Zadar (vert) . . 1·60 1·50
214 10000d. Pirovo peninsula and Franciscan monastery, Vis 3·00 2·75

1992. Death Centenary of Blaz Lorkovic (political economist).
218 **75** 250d. multicoloured . . . 50 50

76 Coiled National Colours

77 Bunic-Vucic

1992. 150th Anniv of "Kolo" (literary Magazine).
219 **76** 300d. multicoloured . . . 60 60

1992. 400th Birth Anniv of Ivan Bunic-Vucic (poet).
220 **77** 350d. multicoloured . . . 65 65

78 Ljudevit Gaj Square, Krapina

1993. 800th Anniv of Krapina.
221 **78** 300d. multicoloured . . . 60 60

79 Tesla

1993. 50th Death Anniv of Nikola Tesla (physicist).
222 **79** 250d. multicoloured . . . 50 50

80 Quinquerez ("self-portrait")

1993. Death Cent of Ferdo Quiquerez (painter).
223 **80** 100d. multicoloured . . . 25 25

81 Red Deer

1993. Animals of the Kapacki Rit Swamp. Multicoloured.
224 500d. Type **81** 70 70
225 550d. White-tailed sea eagle 80 80

82 Sulentic ("self-portrait")

1993. Birth Centenary of Zlatko Sulentic (painter).
226 **82** 350d. multicoloured . . . 45 45

83 Kursalon, Lipik

1993. Centenary of Lipik Spa.
227 **83** 400d. multicoloured . . . 45 45

84 Kovacic (statue, Vojin Bakic)

1993. 50th Death Anniv of Ivan Goran Kovacic (writer).
228 **84** 200d. multicoloured . . . 30 30

85 Minceta Fortress, Dubrovnik

1993. 59th P.E.N. Literary Congress, Dubrovnik.
229 **85** 800d. multicoloured . . . 1·00 1·00

86 Ivan Kakaljevic (writer)

87 Mask and Split Theatre

1993. 150th Anniv of First Speech in Croatian Language made to Croatian Parliament.
230 **86** 500d. multicoloured . . . 45 45

1993. Centenary of Split Theatre.
231 **87** 600d. multicoloured . . . 45 45

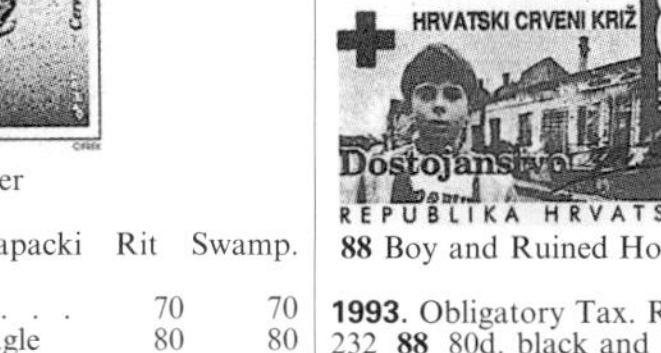

88 Boy and Ruined House

89 Pag in 16th Century

1993. Obligatory Tax. Red Cross Week.
232 **88** 80d. black and red 20 20

1993. 550th Anniv of Refoundation of Pag.
233 **89** 800d. multicoloured . . . 60 60

90 Dove

91 Girl at Window

1993. 1st Anniv of Croatia's Membership of U.N.
234 **90** 500d. multicoloured . . . 40 40

1993. Obligatory Tax. Solidarity Week.
235 **91** 100d. black and red . . . 20 20

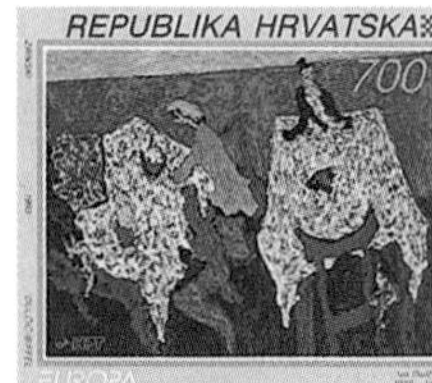

92 "In the Cafe" (Ivo Dulcic)

1993. Europa. Contemporary Art. Mult.
236 700d. Type **92** 40 40
237 1000d. "The Waiting Room" (Miljenko Stancic) 60 60
238 1100d. "Two Figures" (Lijubo Ivancic) 80 80

93 "Homodukt" (Milivoj Bijelic)

1993. 45th Art Biennial, Venice. Mult.
239 250d. Type **93** 25 25
240 600d. "Snails" (Ivo Dekovic) 45 45
241 1000d. "Esa carta de mi flor" (Zeljko Kipke) 70 70

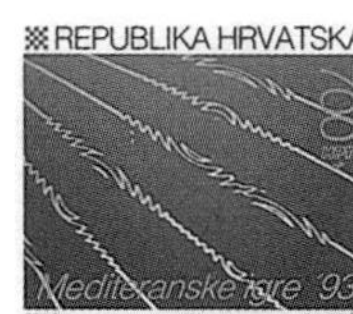

94 Symbolic Running Track

1993. 12th Mediterranean Games, Roussillon (Languedoc), France.
242 **94** 700d. multicoloured . . . 45 45

95 "Slavonian Oaks"

1993. 150th Birth Anniv of Adolf Waldinger (painter).
243 **95** 300d. multicoloured . . . 25 25

96 Battle of Krbava, 1493

1993. Anniversaries of Famous Battles. 16th-century engravings.
244 800d. Type **96** 50 50
245 1300d. Battle of Sisak, 1593 90 90

97 Krleza (after Marija Ujevic)

1993. Birth Centenary of Miroslav Krleza (writer).
246 **97** 400d. multicoloured . . . 30 30

98 Cardinal Stepinac

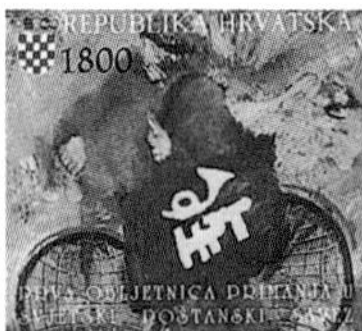

99 Croatian Postman

1993. Obligatory Tax. Cardinal Stepinac Foundation.
247 **98** 150d. black, mauve & gold 20 20

1993. 1st Anniv of Croatia's Membership of Universal Postal Union.
248 **99** 1800d. multicoloured . . . 85 85

100 Paljetak

1993. Birth Centenary of Vlaho Paljetak (singer-songwriter).
249 **100** 500d. multicoloured . . . 30 30

101 Peter Zrinski and Krsto Frankopan

1993. Obligatory Tax. Zrinski-Frankopan Foundation.
250 **101** 200d. blue and grey . . . 20 20

102 "Freedom of Croatia" (central motif of 1918 stamp)

1993. Stamp Day.
251 **102** 600d. multicoloured . . . 30 30

103 Red Cross

1993. Obligatory Tax. Anti-tuberculosis Week.
252 **103** 300d. green, black & red 20 20

104 Antonio Magini's Map of Istria, 1620

105 Smiciklas

1993. 50th Anniv of Incorporation of Istria, Rijeka and Zadar into Croatia.
253 **104** 2200d. multicoloured . . 80 80

1993. 150th Birth Anniv of Tadija Smiciklas (historian).
254 **105** 800d. black, gold and red 30 30

1993. Obligatory Tax. Croatian Anti-cancer League.
255 **71** 400d. multicoloured . . . 20 20

106 Allegory of Birth of Croatian History on Shores of the Adriatic

1993. Centenary of National Archaeological Museum, Split.
256 **106** 1000d. multicoloured . . 40 40

107 Girl In Heart

108 Croatian and French Flags and Soldiers

1993. Obligatory Tax. Save Croatian Children Fund.
257 **107** 400d. red, blue and black 20 20

1993. 50th Anniv of Uprising of 13th Pioneer Battalion, Villefranche-de-Rouergue, France.
258 **108** 3000d. multicoloured . . 95 95

109 Tomic

110 Astronomical Diagram

1993. 150th Birth Anniv of Josip Eugen Tomic (writer).
259 **109** 900d. brown, green & red 30 30

1993. 850th Anniv of Publication of "De Essentiis" by Herman Dalmatin.
260 **110** 1000d. multicoloured . . 30 30

111 Christmas on the Battlefield

112 Skiers

1993. Christmas. Multicoloured.
261 1000d. Type **111** 35 35
262 4000d. "Nativity" (fresco, St. Mary's Church, Dvigrad) . . . . 1·40 1·40

1993. Cent of Competitive Skiing in Croatia.
263 **112** 1000d. multicoloured . . 35 35

113 Decorations and Badge

1993. 125th Anniv of Croatian Militia.
264 **113** 1100d. multicoloured . . 35 35

114 Printing Press

1994. 500th Anniv of Printing of First Croatian Book (a Glagolitic missal), Senj.
265 **114** 2200d. brown and red . . 70 70

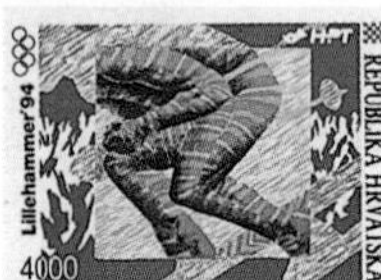

115 Skier

1994. Winter Olympic Games, Lillehammer, Norway.
266 **115** 4000d. multicoloured . . 1·10 1·10

116 Iguanodon **117** Masthead

1994. Croatian Dinosaur Fossils from West Istria. Multicoloured.
267 2400d. Type **116** 60 60
268 4000d. Iguanodon, skeleton and map . . . . 1·00 1·00
Nos. 267/8 were issued together, se-tenant, forming a composite design.

1994. 150th Anniv of "Zora Dalmatinska" (literary periodical).
269 **117** 800d. multicoloured . . . 30 30

118 University, Emperor Leopold I's Seal and Vice-chancellor's Chain **119** Wolf

1994. 325th Anniv of Croatian University, Zagreb.
270 **118** 2200d. multicoloured . . 70 70

1994. Planet Earth Day.
271 **119** 3800d. multicoloured . . 1·25 1·25

120 Safety Signs and Worker wearing Protective Clothing **121** Globe and Map

1994. 75th Anniv of I.L.O. and 50th Anniv of Philadelphia Declaration (social charter).
272 **120** 1000d. multicoloured . . 40 40

1994. Obligatory Tax. Red Cross Week.
273 **121** 500d. black, stone & red 20 20

122 Flying Man (17th-century idea by Faust Vrancic) **123** Red Cross

1994. Europa. Inventions. Multicoloured.
274 3800d. Type **122** . . . . . . 1·25 1·25
275 4000d. Quill and pencil writing surname (technical pencil by Slavoljub Penkala, 1906) (32 × 23 mm) . . . . . . 1·25 1·25

1994. Obligatory Tax. Solidarity Week.
276 **123** 50l. red, black and grey 20 20

124 Croatian Iris **125** Petrovic

1994. Flowers. Multicoloured.
277 2k.40 Type **124** 75 75
278 4k. Meadow saffron . . . . 1·25 1·25

1994. 1st Death Anniv of Drazen Petrovic (basketball player).
279 **125** 1k. multicoloured 35 35

126 Plitvice Lakes

1994. 150th Anniv of Tourism in Croatia. Multicoloured.
280 80l. Type **126** 20 20
281 1k. River Krka 25 25
282 1k.10 Kornati Islands 40 40
283 2k.20 Kopacki Trscak ornithological reserve . . . 70 70
284 2k.40 Opatija Riviera 80 80
285 3k.80 Brijuni Islands . . . . 1·25 1·25
286 4k. Trakoscan Castle, Zagorje . . . . 1·40 1·40

127 Baranovic at Keyboard **128** Monstrance

1994. Musical Anniversaries.
287 **127** 1k. multicoloured 35 35
288 – 2k.20 silver, black & red 65 65
289 – 2k.40 multicoloured . . . 80 80
DESIGNS—VERT: 1k. Type **127** (birth centenary of Kresimir Baranovic (composer and conductor/director of Croatian National Theatre Opera, Zagreb, 1915–40)); 2k.20, Vatroslav Lisinski (composer, 175th birth anniv). HORIZ: 2k.40, Score and harp player (350th anniv of Pauline song-book).

1994. Obligatory Tax. Ludbreg Shrine.
290 **128** 50l. multicoloured 20 20

129 Men dressed in Croatian and American Colours **130** Mother and Children

1994. Centenary of Croatian Brotherhood in U.S.A.
291 **129** 2k.20 multicoloured . . . 70 60

1994. Obligatory Tax. Save Croatian Children Fund.
292 **130** 50l. multicoloured 20 20

131 Family **132** St. George and the Dragon

1994. International Year of the Family.
293 **131** 80l. multicoloured 30 30

1994. Obligatory Tax. Croatian Anti-Cancer League.
294 **132** 50l. multicoloured 20 20

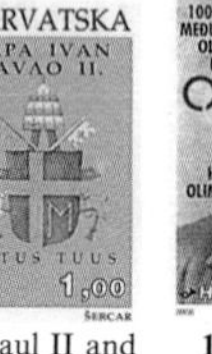

133 Pope John Paul II and his Arms **134** Franjo Bucar (Committee member, 1920–46)

1994. Papal Visit.
295 **133** 1k. multicoloured 35 35

1994. Cent of International Olympic Committee.
296 **134** 1k. multicoloured 40 40

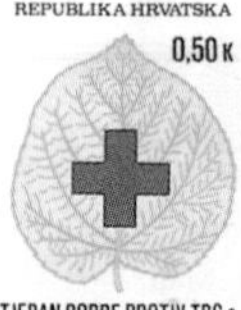

135 Red Cross on Leaf **136** The Little Prince (book character)

1994. Obligatory Tax. Anti-tuberculosis Week.
297 **135** 50l. red, green & black . . 20 20

1994. 50th Death Anniv of Antoine de Saint-Exupery (writer).
298 **136** 3k.80 multicoloured . . . 1·00 1·00

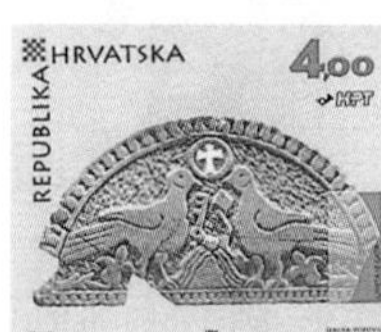

137 "Resurrection" (lunette, Gati, Omis)

1994. 13th International Convention on Christian Archaeology, Split and Porec.
299 **137** 4k. multicoloured . . . . 1·10 1·10

138 "Still Life with Fruits and Basket" (Marino Tartaglia)

1994. Paintings. Multicoloured.
300 2k.40 Type **138** 60 60
301 3k.80 "In the Park" (Milan Steiner) 95 95
302 4k. "Self-portrait" (Vilko Gecan) . . . . 1·25 1·25

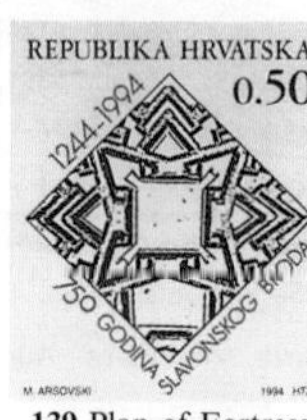

139 Plan of Fortress

1994. Obligatory Tax. 750th Anniv of Slavonski Brod.
303 **139** 50l. yellow, black & red 20 20

140 I.O.C. Centenary Emblem and Flame

1994. Obligatory Tax. National Olympic Committee. Designs incorporating either the National Olympic Committee emblem or the International Olympic Committee centenary emblem.
304 50l. Type **140** 20 20
305 50l. As T **140** but with National Olympic Committee emblem 20 20
306 50l. Tennis and national emblem (vert) 20 20
307 50l. Football and centenary emblem (vert) 20 20
308 50l. As No. 306 but with centenary emblem (vert) . . 20 20
309 50l. As No. 307 but with national emblem (vert) . . 20 20
310 50l. Basketball and centenary emblem (vert) 20 20
311 50l. Handball and national emblem (vert) 20 20
312 50l. As No. 310 but with national emblem (vert) . . 20 20
313 50l. As No. 311 but with centenary emblem (vert) . . 20 20
314 50l. Kayaks and national emblem (vert) 20 20
315 50l. Water polo and centenary emblem (vert) . . 20 20
316 50l. As No. 314 but with centenary emblem (vert) . . 20 20
317 50l. As No. 315 but with national emblem (vert) . . 20 20
318 50l. Running and centenary emblem (vert) 20 20
319 50l. Gymnastics and national emblem (vert) 20 20
320 50l. As No. 318 but with national emblem (vert) . . 20 20
321 50l. As No. 319 but with centenary emblem (vert) . . 20 20

141 Cover of "Gazophylacium" **142** St. Mark's Church and Gas Lamp

1994. 400th Birth Anniv of Ivan Belostenec (lexicographer).
322 **141** 2k.20 multicoloured . . . 70 70

1994. 900th Annivs of Zagreb (323/5) and Zagreb Bishopric (326). Multicoloured.
323 1k. Type **142** 30 30
324 1k. Street scene from early film, Maxi Cat (cartoon character) and left side of Zagreb Exchange 30 30
325 1k. Right side of Zagreb Exchange, S. Penkala's biplane and Cibona building 30 30
326 4k. 15th-century bishop's crosier and 17th-century view of Zagreb by Valvasor . . . . 1·00 1·00
Nos. 323/6 were issued together, se-tenant, forming a composite design.

143 "Epiphany" (relief, Vrhovac Church)

1994. Christmas.
328 **143** 1k. multicoloured 35 30

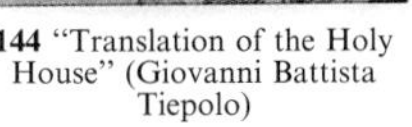

144 "Translation of the Holy House" (Giovanni Battista Tiepolo)

145 Modern Tie

1994. 700th Anniv of St. Mary's Sanctuary, Loreto.
329 **144** 4k. multicoloured . . . . 1·10 1·10

1995. Ties. Multicoloured.
330 1k.10 Type **145** 25 25
331 3k.80 English dandy, 1810 . . 80 80
332 4k. Croatian soldier, 1630 . . 85 85

146 St. Catherine's Church and Monastery, Zagreb, and Jesuit

1995. Monasteries. Multicoloured.
334 1k. Type **146** (350th anniv) 20 20
335 2k.40 St. Paul's Monastery, Visovac, and Franciscan monk (550th anniv) . . . 50 50

147 Istrian Short-haired Hunting Dog

1995. Dogs. Multicoloured.
336 2k.20 Type **147** 50 50
337 2k.40 Posavinian hunting dog 50 50
338 3k.80 Istrian wire-haired hunting dog . . . . 1·00 1·00

148 Rowing

1995. Obligatory Tax. National Olympic Committee. Multicoloured.
339 50l. Type **148** 15 15
340 50l. Petanque 15 15
341 50l. Monument to Drazen Petrovic, Olympic Park, Lausanne 15 15
342 50l. Tennis 15 15
343 50l. Basketball 15 15

149 Reconstruction of Emperor Diocletian's Palace

1995. 1700th Anniv of Split. Multicoloured.
344 1k. Type **149** 20 20
345 2k.20 "Split Harbour" (Emanuel Vidovic) 40 40
346 4k. View of city and bust of Marko Marulic (Ivan Mestrovic) 80 80

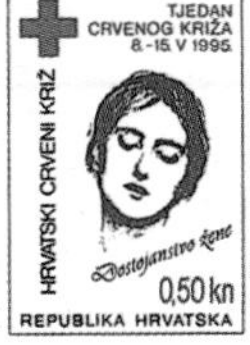

150 Player

151 Woman's Head

1995. World Handball Championship, Iceland.
348 **150** 4k. multicoloured 80 80

1995. Obligatory Tax. Red Cross Week.
349 **151** 50l. black and red 15 15

152 Storm Clouds and Clear Sky

1995. Europa. Peace and Freedom. Mult.
350 2k.40 Type **152** 50 50
351 4k. Angel (detail of sculpture, Francesco Robba) 80 80

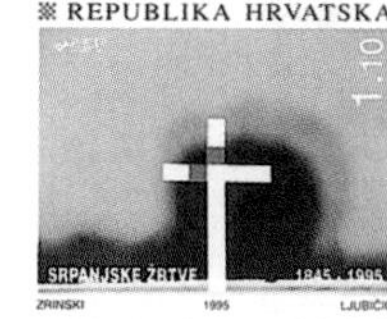

153 Shadow behind Cross

1995. 150th Anniv of July Riots (352) and 50th Anniv of Croatian Surrender at Bleiburg (353). Multicoloured.
352 1k.10 Type **153** 25 25
353 3k.80 Sunrise behind cross . . 80 80

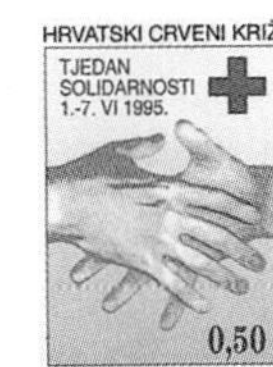

154 Arms and Hand holding Rose

155 Hands

1995. Independence Day.
354 **154** 1k.10 multicoloured . . . 25 25

1995. Obligatory Tax. Solidarity Week.
355 **155** 50l. multicoloured 15 15

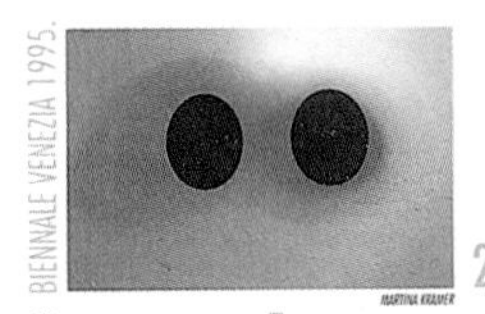

156 "Installation" (detail) (Martina Kramer)

1995. 46th Art Biennale, Venice. Work by Croatian artists. Multicoloured.
356 2k.20 Type **156** 45 45
357 2k.40 "Paracelsus Paraduchamps" (Mirk Zrinscak) (vert) 50 50
358 4k. "Shadows/136" (Goran Petercol) 80 80

157 "St. Antony" (detail of polyptych by Ljubo Babic, St. Antony's Sanctuary, Zagreb)

1995. 800th Birth Anniv of St. Antony of Padua.
359 **157** 1k. multicoloured 20 20

158 Loggerhead Turtle

1995. Animals. Multicoloured.
360 2k.40 Type **158** 60 60
361 4k. Bottle-nosed dolphin . . 90 90

159 Osijek Cathedral

160 "Croatian Pieta"

1995. Obligatory Tax. Restoration of Sts. Peter and Paul's Cathedral, Osijek.
362 **159** 65l. multicoloured 15 15

1995. Obligatory Tax. "Holy Mother of Freedom" War Memorial.
363 **160** 65l. on 50l. blk, red & bl 70 70
364 – 65l. black, red and blue 15 15
365 – 65l. blue and yellow . . . 15 15
DESIGN: 65l. Projected memorial church.
Nos. 364/5 were not issued without surcharge.

161 Town and Fortress

1995. Liberation of Knin.
366 **161** 1k.30 multicoloured . . . 30 30

162 Electric Power Plant

1995. Centenary of Jaruga Hydro-electric Power Station, River Krka.
367 **162** 3k.60 multicoloured . . . 75 75

163 Postman

1995. Stamp Day.
368 **163** 1k.30 multicoloured . . . 30 30

165 Suppe and Heroine of "The Fair Galatea" (operetta)

1995. Death Centenary of Franz von Suppe (composer).
370 **165** 6k.50 multicoloured . . . 1·40 1·40

166 Petrinja Fortress (after Valvasor) and Cavalrymen

167 Ivo Tijardovic

1995. 400th Anniv of Habsburg Capture of Petrinja.
371 **166** 2k.20 multicoloured . . . 45 45

1995. Composers' Anniversaries. Mult.
372 1k.20 Type **167** (birth centenary) 25 25
373 1k.40 Lovro von Matacic (10th death) 30 30
374 6k.50 Jakov Gotovac (birth centenary) . . . . 1·40 1·40

168 Herman Bolle (architect, 150th birth)

1995. Anniversaries. Multicoloured.
375 1k.30 Type **168** 30 30
376 2k.40 Izidor Krsnjavi (artist and art administrator, 150th birth) 50 50
377 3k.60 Gala curtain by Vlaho Bukovac (cent of National Theatre) 75 75

169 Children in Nest

170 Left-hand Detail of Curtain

1995. Obligatory Tax. Save Croatian Children Fund.
378 **169** 65l. multicoloured 15 15

1995. Obligatory Tax. Centenary of National Theatre, Zagreb. Details of gala curtain by Vlaho Bukovac. Multicoloured.
379 65l. Type **170** 15 15
380 65l. Central detail 15 15
381 65l. Right-hand detail 15 15
Nos. 379/81 were issued together, se-tenant, forming a composite design.

171 Zagrebacka Street, Bjelovar

1995. Croatian Towns (3rd series). Mult.
382 1k. Type **171** 20 20
383 1k.30 St. Peter and St. Paul's Cathedral, Osijek (vert) . . 30 30
384 1k.40 Castle, Cakovec (vert) 30 30
385 2k.20 Rovinj 45 45
386 2k.40 Korcula 50 50
387 3k.60 Town Hall, Zupanja 75 75

172 "50"

1996. 50th Anniversaries. Multicoloured.
395 3k.60 Type **172** (U.N.O.) . . 75 75
396 3k.60 "5" and "FAO" within biscuit forming "50" (F.A.O.) 75 75

173 Spiro Brusina (zoologist)

174 Birds flying through Sky

1995. Anniversaries. Multicoloured.
397 1k. Type **173** (150th birth) . . 20 20
398 2k.20 Bogoslav Sulek (philologist, death cent) . . 45 45
399 6k.50 Faust Vrancic's "Dictionary of Five European Languages" (400th anniv of publication) . . . . 1·40 1·40

1995. Obligatory Tax. Anti-drugs Campaign.
400 **174** 65l. multicoloured 15 15

175 Breast Screening

176 Hands reading Braille

1995. Obligatory Tax. Croatian Anti-cancer League. Breast Screening Campaign.
401 **175** 65l. multicoloured 15 15

1995. Centenary of Institute for Blind Children, Zagreb.
402 **176** 1k.20 red, yellow & black 25 25

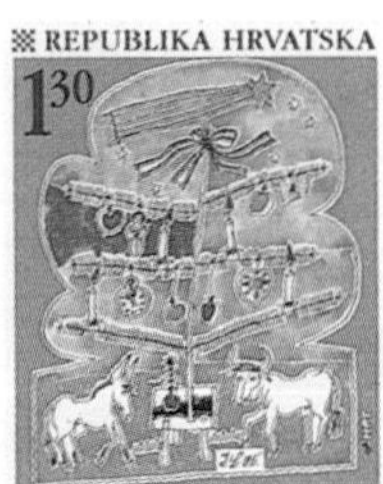

177 Animals under Christmas Tree

1995. Christmas.
403 **177** 1k.30 multicoloured . . . 30 30

178 Polo, Animals in Boat and Court of Kublai Khan

1995. 700th Anniv of Marco Polo's Return from China.
404 **178** 3k.60 multicoloured . . . 75 75

179 Hrvatska Kostajnica

180 Lectionary of Bernardin of Split, 1495 (first printed book using Cakavian dialect)

1995. Liberated Towns. Multicoloured.
405 20l. Type **179** 10 10
406 30l. Slunj 10 10
407 50l. Gracac 10 10
408 1k.20 Drnis (vert) 25 25
409 6k.50 Glina . . . . 1·40 1·40
410 10k. Obrovac (vert) . . . . . 2·00 2·00

1995. Incunabula. Multicoloured.
420 1k.40 Type **180** 30 30
421 3k.60 Callipers and last page of "Spovid Opcena" (manual for confessors), 1496 (first book printed in Croatia) 75 75

181 Crucifix

182 Breast Cancer Campaign

1996. Events and Anniversaries. Mult.
422 1k.30 St. Marko Krizevcanin (detail of mosaic (Ante Starcevic), St. Marko's Church, Zagreb) (canonization) 30 30
423 1k.30 Type **181** (700th anniv of veneration of miraculous crucifix, St. Guido's Church, Rijeka) 30 30
424 1k.30 Ivan Merz (teacher and Catholic youth worker, birth centenary) 30 30

1996. Obligatory Tax. 30th Anniv of Anti-cancer League.
425 **182** 65l. multicoloured 15 15

183 Eugen Kvaternik (125th anniv of Rakovica Uprising)

184 Madonna and Child and Church

1996. Anniversaries. Multicoloured.
426 1k.20 Type **183** 25 25
427 1k.40 Ante Starcevic (founder of Part of the Right, death centenary) (vert) 30 30
428 2k.20 Stjepan Radic (founder of Croatian Peasant Party) (125th birth anniv and 75th anniv of Peasant Republic constitution) (vert) 45 45
429 3k.60 Collage (75th anniv of Labin Republic) (vert) . . 75 75

1996. Obligatory Tax. St. Mary of Bistrica Sanctuary.
430 **184** 65l. multicoloured 15 15

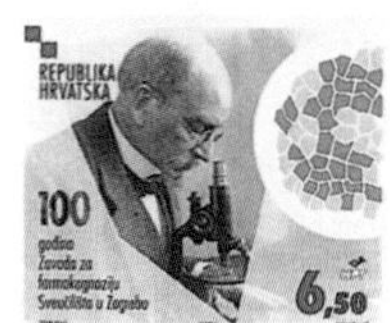

185 Julije Domac (founder) and Culture

1996. Centenary of Pharmacology Institute, University of Zagreb.
431 **185** 6k.50 multicoloured . . . 1·40 1·40

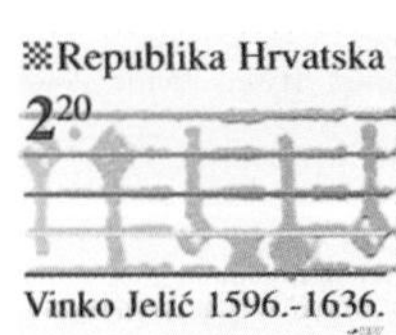

186 Score

187 Cvijeta Zuzoric (beauty)

1996. Music Anniversaries. Multicoloured.
432 2k.20 Type **186** (400th birth anniv of Vinko Jelic, composer) 45 45
433 2k.20 "O" over musical bars (150th anniv of "Love and Malice" (first Croatian opera) by Vatroslav Lisinski) 45 45
434 2k.20 Josip Slavenski (composer, birth cent) . . 45 45
435 2k.20 "Lijepa nasa domovino" (birth bicent of Antun Mihanovic and 175th birth anniv of Josip Runjanin (composers of National Anthem)) 45 45

1996. Europa. Famous Women. Mult.
436 2k.20 Type **187** 45 45
437 3k.60 Ivana Brlic-Mazuranic (writer) 75 75

188 Olympic Rings

189 Nikola Subic Zrinski of Sziget (Ban of Croatia)

1996. Obligatory Tax. National Olympic Committee.
438 **188** 65l. multicoloured 15 15

1996. 16th and 17th-century Members of Zrinski and Frankopan Families. Multicoloured.
439 1k.30 Type **189** 30 30
440 1k.40 Nikola Zrinski (Ban of Croatia) 30 30
441 2k.20 Petar Zrinski (Ban of Croatia) 45 45
442 2k.40 Katarina Zrinski (wife of Petar and sister of Fran Krsto Frankopan) 50 50
443 3k.60 Fran Krsto Frankopan (writer and revolutionary) 75 75

190 Child outside House

191 Soldier carrying Child

1996. Obligatory Tax. Red Cross Fund.
445 **190** 65l. black and red 15 15

1996. 5th Anniv of National Guard.
446 **191** 1k.30 multicoloured . . . 30 30

192 Istrian Bluebell

193 Child with Red Cross Parcel

1996. Flowers. Multicoloured.
447 2k.40 Type **192** 45 45
448 3k.60 Dubrovnik corn-flower 75 75

1996. Obligatory Tax. Solidarity Week.
449 **193** 65l. black and red 15 15

194 Football

1996. European Football Championship, England.
450 **194** 2k.20 black and red . . . 45 45

195 Konscak's Map of California

196 Children sitting outside House

1996. 250th Anniv of Father Ferdinand Konscak's Expedition to Lower California.
451 **195** 2k.40 multicoloured . . . 45 45

1996. Obligatory Tax. Save Croatian Children Fund.
452 **196** 65l. multicoloured 15 15

197 Anniversary Emblem

198 Man holding Dumb-bell and Falcon

1996. Obligatory Tax. 800th Anniv of Osijek.
453 **197** 65l. blue, orange & grey 15 15

1996. 150th Birth Anniv of Josip Fon (founder of Croatian Falcon gymnastics society).
454 **198** 1k.40 multicoloured . . . 30 30

199 Olympic Colours and Rings

200 Cathedral

1996. Olympic Games, Atlanta, and Centenary of Modern Olympics.
455 **199** 3k.60 multicoloured . . . 75 75

1996. Obligatory Tax. Restoration of Dakovo Cathedral.
456 **200** 65l. multicoloured 15 15

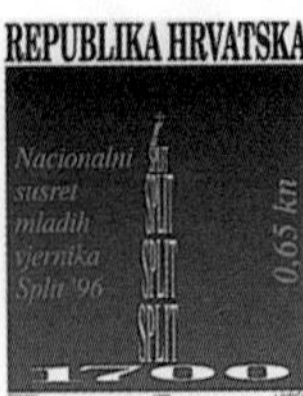

201 "Church Tower"

202 Crucifix

1996. Obligatory Tax. 1700th Anniv of Split.
457 **201** 65l. ultramarine and blue 15 15

1996. Obligatory Tax. Vukovar.
458 **202** 65l. multicoloured 15 15

203 Lighted Candle, Shell and Lilies

204 Tweezers holding Stamp

1996. Obligatory Tax. Anti-drugs Campaign.
459 **203** 65l. multicoloured 15 15

1996. Stamp Day. 5th Anniv of Issue of First Postage Stamp by Independent Croatia.
460 **204** 1k.30 multicoloured . . . 30 30

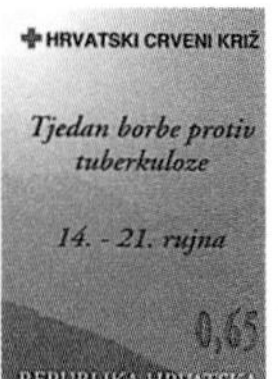

205 Mountains

206 St. Elias's Chapel, Zumberak

1996. Obligatory Tax. Anti-tuberculosis Week.
461 **205** 65l. multicoloured 15 15

1996. 700th Anniv of First Written Reference to Zumberak.
462 **206** 2k.20 multicoloured . . . 45 45

207 Illuminated Page

208 Fishes and Spear

1996. Early Middle Ages. Multicoloured.
463 1k.20 Type **207** (900th anniv of "Vekenega's Book of Gospels") 25 25
464 1k.40 Gottschalk (Benedictine abbot) (1150th anniv of Gottschalk's visit to Duke of Trpimir) 30 30

1996. Millenary of First Written Reference to Fishing in Croatia.
465 **208** 1k.30 multicoloured . . . 30 30

209 Gjuro Pilar (geologist, 150th anniv)

1996. Scientists' Birth Anniversaries. Mult.
466 2k.40 Type **209** 50 50
467 2k.40 Frane Bulic (archaeologist, 150th anniv) 50 50
468 2k.40 Ante Sercer (otolaryngologist, cent) . . 50 50

210 Sir Frederick Banting and Charles Best (discoverers)

1996. Obligatory Tax. Croatian Diabetic Council. 75th Anniv of Discovery of Insulin.
469 **210** 65l. gold, yellow & black . . . 15 15

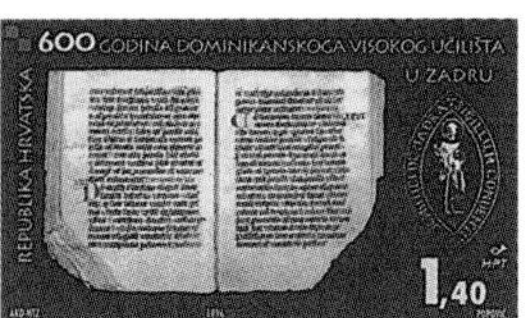

211 Laws of Dominican Nuns, Zadar

1996. 600th Anniv of Founding of Dominican General High School (university), Zadar.
470 **211** 1k.40 multicoloured . . . 30 30

212 "Rain" (Menci Crncic)

1996. 20th-century Paintings. Multicoloured.
471 1k.30 Type **212** 30 30
472 1k.40 "Peljesac-Korcula Channel" (Mato Medovic) 30 30
473 3k.60 "Pink Dream" (Vlaho Bukovac) 75 75

213 "Mother of God of Remete", Zagreb

214 Children of Different Races

1996. Obligatory Tax.
474 **213** 65l. multicoloured 15 15

1996. 50th Anniv of U.N.I.C.E.F.
475 **214** 3k.60 multicoloured . . . 75 75

215 Sts. Peter's and Paul's Cathedral

216 Nativity

1996. 800th Anniv of First Written Reference to Osijek. Multicoloured.
476 2k.20 Type **215** 45 45
477 2k.20 Riverbank and view down street 45 45

1996. Christmas.
478 **216** 1k.30 multicoloured . . . 30 30

217 Bond and Bank

218 Mihanovic

1996. Anniversaries. Multicoloured.
479 2k.40 Type **217** (150th anniv of founding of First Croatian Savings Bank, Zagreb) 50 50
480 3k.60 Frontispiece (bicent of publication of "The Principles of the Corn Trade" by Josip Sipus) . . 75 75

1997. Obligatory Tax. Birth Bicentenary (1996) of Antun Mihanovic.
481 **218** 65l. multicoloured 15 15

219 "Professor Baltazar" (Zagreb School of Animated Film)

1997. Centenary of Croatian Films. Mult.
482 1k.40 Oktavijan Miletic (cameraman and director) filming "Vatroslav Lisinski" (first Croatian sound film), 1944 . . . . . 30 30
483 1k.40 Type **219** 30 30
484 1k.40 Mirjana Bohanev-Vidovic and Relja Basic in "Who Sings Means No Harm", 1970 . . . . . . 30 30

220 Dr. Ante Starcevic's House

221 Don Quixote and Windmill

1997. Obligatory Tax.
485 **220** 65l. multicoloured 15 15

1997. Birth Anniversaries. Multicoloured.
486 2k.20 Type **221** (450th anniv of Miguel de Cervantes (author of "Don Quixote")) 45 45
487 3k.60 Metal type (600th anniv of Johannes Gutenberg (inventor of printing)) (horiz) 75 75

222 Woman

223 "Big Joseph" by Vladimir Nazor (illus. Sasa Santel)

1997. Obligatory Tax. Croatian Anti-cancer League.
488 **222** 65l. multicoloured 15 15

1997. Europa. Tales and Legends.
489 – 1k.30 multicoloured . . . 30 30
490 **223** 3k.60 red, black & gold 75 75
DESIGNS—HORIZ: 1k.30, Elves from "Stribor's Forest" by Ivana Brlic-Mazuranic (illus. Cvijeta Job).

224 Noble Pen Shell

225 Comforting Hand

1997. Molluscs and Insects. Multicoloured.
491 1k.40 Type **224** 30 30
492 2k.40 "Radziella styx" (cave beetle) 50 50
493 3k.60 Giant tun 75 75

1997. Obligatory Tax. Red Cross Week.
494 **225** 65l. multicoloured 15 15

226 Pres. Franjo Tudjman

1997. 5th Anniv of Croatia's Membership of United Nations.
495 **226** 6k.50 multicoloured . . . 1·40 1·40

227 Ludwig Zamenhof (inventor)

1997. Croatian Esperanto (invented language) Conference.
496 **227** 1k.20 multicoloured . . . 25 25

228 Congress Emblem

1997. 58th Congress of International Amateur Rugby Federation, Dubrovnik.
497 **228** 2k.20 multicoloured . . . 40 40

229 "Vukovar" (Zlatko Atac) (¾-size illustration)

1997. Rebuilding of Vukovar.
498 **229** 6k.50 multicoloured . . . 1·25 1·25

230 King Petar Svacic (1095–97)

1997. Kings of Croatia. Multicoloured.
499 1k.30 Type **230** (900th death anniv) 25 25
500 2k.40 King Stjepan Drzislav (996–97) 45 45

231 16th-century Dubrovnik Courier (after Nicole de Nicolai)

232 Tennis

1997. Stamp Day.
501 **231** 2k.30 multicoloured . . . 45 45

1997. Olympic Medal Winners. Mult.
502 1k. Type **232** (Goran Ivanisevic—bronze (singles and doubles), Barcelona 1992) 20 20
503 1k.20 Basketball (silver, Barcelona 1992) 25 25
504 1k.40 Water polo (silver, Atlanta 1996) (27 × 31 mm) 25 25
505 2k.20 Handball (gold, Atlanta 1996) (27 × 31 mm) 40 40

233 Turkish Attack on Sibenik, 1647

1997. Defence of Sibenik. Multicoloured.
506 1k.30 Type **233** (350th anniv of defence against the Turks) 25 25
507 1k.30 Air attack on Sibenik, 1991 . . . . 25 25

234 Frane Petric (philosopher)

235 Parliamentary Session (after Ivan Zasche) and Ivan Kukuljevic (politician)

1997. Anniversaries. Multicoloured.
508 1k.40 Type **234** (400th death anniv) 25 25
509 1k.40 "Madonna and Child" (detail from the polyptich of St. Michael in Franciscan Church, Cavtat) (500th anniv of first recorded work of Vicko Lovrin (artist)) 25 25
510 1k.40 Frano Krsinic (sculptor, birth cent) . . . 25 25
511 1k.40 Dubravko Dujsin (actor, 50th death anniv) 25 25

1997. Anniversaries. Multicoloured.
512 2k.20 Type **235** (150th anniv of promulgation of Croatian as official language) 40 40
513 3k.60 Zagreb and elevation of school (centenary of Croatian Grammar School, Zadar) 70 70

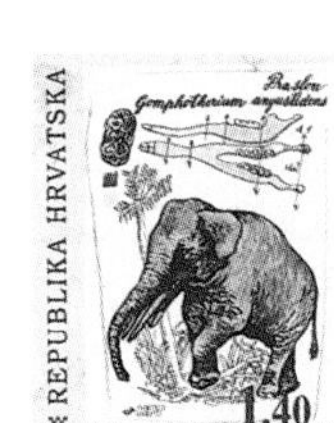

236 Primordial Elephant

1997. Palaeontological Finds. Multicoloured.
514 1k.40 Type **236** 25 25
515 2k.40 Fossil of "Viviparus novskaensis" (periwinkle) 45 45

237 "Painter in the Pond" (Nikola Masic)

1997. Paintings. Multicoloured.
516 1k.30 Type **237** 25 25
517 2k.20 "Angelus" (Emanuel Vidovic) 40 40
518 3k.60 "Tree in the Snow" (Slava Raskaj) 70 70

238 Child Jesus in the Stable

239 "Electra" by Sophocles

1997. Christmas. Multicoloured.
519 1k.30 Type **238** 25 25
520 3k.60 "Birth of Jesus" (Isidor Krsnjavi) (33 × 59 mm) . . 70 70

1997. Literary Anniversaries. Multicoloured.
521 1k. Type **239** (400th anniv of publication of collected translations by Dominko Zlataric) 20 20
522 1k.20 Closed book (300th birth anniv of Filip Grabovac and 250th anniv of publication of his "Best of Folk Speech and the Illyric or Croatian Language") 25 25

240 Ilok

241 Score and Varazdin (Baroque Evenings)

1998. Croatian Towns (4th series).
523 **240** 5k. violet, brown & red 95 95
524 – 10k. brown, violet & red 2·00 2·00
DESIGN: 10k. Dubrovnik.

1998. Europa. National Festivals. Mult.
531 1k.45 Type **241** 30 30
532 4k. Dubrovnik (Summer Festival) 75 75

242 Olympic Rings and Japanese Red Sun

1998. Winter Olympic Games, Nagano, Japan.
533 **242** 2k.45 multicoloured . . . 45 45

243 Jelacics Flag and Battle near Moor (lithograph)

1998. Historical Events of 1848. Mult.
534 1k.60 Type **243** 30 30
535 1k.60 "Croatian Assembly in Session" (Dragutin Weingartner) 30 30
536 4k. Ban Josip Jelacic (after Ivan Zasche) (21 × 31 mm) 75 75

244 Mimara

245 Caesar's Mushroom

1998. Birth Centenary of Ante Topic Mimara (art collector).
537 **244** 2k.65 multicoloured . . . 50 50

1998. Fungi. Multicoloured.
538 1k.30 Type **245** 25 25
539 1k.30 Saffron milk cup ("Lactarius deliciosus") . . 25 25
540 7k.20 "Morchella conica" . . 1·40 1·40

246 Stepinac

247 Magnifying Glass over Fingerprint and Dubrovnik

1998. Birth Centenary of Cardinal Alojzije Stepinac (Archbishop of Zagreb).
541 **246** 1k.50 multicoloured . . . 30 30

1998. 27th European Regional Conference of Interpol, Dubrovnik.
542 **247** 2k.45 multicoloured . . . 50 50

249 Football

1998. World Cup Football Championship, France.
544 **249** 4k. multicoloured 75 75

250 Title Page of "Slavonic Fairy"

1998. Writers' Anniversaries. Multicoloured.
545 1k.20 Type **250** (450th birth anniv of Juraj Barakovic (poet)) 25 25
546 1k.50 Milan Begovic (50th death anniv) 30 30
547 1k.60 Mate Balota (birth centenary) 30 30
548 2k.45 Antun Gustav Matos (125th birth anniv) 50 50
549 2k.65 Matija Antun Relkovic (death bicentenary) 50 50
550 4k. Antun Branko Simic (birth centenary) 75 75

251 Text on Water

1998. 19th Danube Countries Conference, Osijek.
551 **251** 1k.80 multicoloured . . . 35 35

252 Betlheim

1998. Birth Centenary of Dr. Stjepan Betlheim (psychoanalyst).
552 **252** 1k.50 multicoloured . . . 30 30

254 Liburnian Sewn Boat (1st century B.C.)

1998. Croatian Ships. Multicoloured.
554 1k.20 Type **254** 25 25
555 1k.50 Condura (11th–12th centuries) 30 30
556 1k.60 Ragusan (Dubrovnik) carrack (16th century) . . 30 30
557 1k.80 Istrian bracera 35 35
558 2k.45 River Neretva sailing barge 50 50
559 2k.65 Barque 50 50
560 4k. "Vila Velebita" (sail/steam cadet ship) 75 75
561 7k.20 "Amorela" (car ferry) 1·40 1·40
562 20k. "King Petar Kresimir IV" (missile corvette) . . . 3·75 3·75

255 Mail Coach and Posthorn

1998. Stamp Day. 150th Anniv of Creation of Croatian Supreme Postal Administration.
563 **255** 1k.50 multicoloured . . . 30 30

256 Font and Cathedral

1998. 700th Anniv of Sibenik Bishopric and Proclamation of Sibenik as a Free Borough.
564 **256** 4k. multicoloured 75 75

257 Pope John Paul II

1998. 2nd Papal Visit.
565 **257** 1k.50 multicoloured . . . 30 30

258 Horse Tram, Osijek

1998. Transport. Multicoloured.
566 1k.50 Type **258** 30 30
567 1k.50 First motor car in Zagreb, 1901 . . . . . . 30 30
568 1k.50 Electric train, Karlovac–Rijeka line (125th anniv) 30 30
569 1k.50 Aerial view of Ostrovica–Delnice section of Zagreb–Rijeka motorway 30 30
570 7k.20 Zagreb funicular railway (19 × 23 mm) . . . 1·40 1·40

259 "Adoration of the Shepherds" (detail, from breviary "Officinum Virginis" illus by Klovic)

1998. Christmas. 500th Birth Anniv of Julije Klovic (artist).
571 **259** 1k.50 multicoloured . . . 30 30

260 Ibrisimovic

1998. 300th Death Anniv of Father Luka Ibrisimovic (revolutionary).
572 **260** 1k.90 multicoloured . . . 35 35

261 Distorted Tree bound to Stake

262 "Cypress" (Frano Simunovic)

1998. 50th Anniv of Universal Declaration of Human Rights.
573 **261** 5k. multicoloured 95 95

1998. 20th-century Art. Multicoloured.
574 1k.90 "Paromlin Road" (Josip Vanista) (horiz) . . 35 35
575 2k.20 Type **262** 40 40
576 5k. "Coma" (interactive video installation, Dalibor Martinis) 95 95

263 Flags

264 Haulik

1999. Zagreb Fair.
577 **263** 1k.80 multicoloured . . . 35 35

1999. 130th Death Anniv of Cardinal Juraj Haulik (first Archbishop of Zagreb).
578 **264** 5k. multicoloured 95 95

265 Mljet Island National Park

1999. Europa. Parks and Gardens. Multicoloured.
579 1k.80 Type **265** 30 30
580 5k. River Lonja Basin Nature Park 85 85

266 Viper

1999. The Orsini's Viper. Multicoloured.
581 2k.20 Type **266** 35 35
582 2k.20 Viper on alert 35 35
583 2k.20 Two vipers 35 35
584 2k.20 Viper's head 35 35

267 Anniversary Emblem

268 Orlando's Pillar with Mask

1999. 50th Anniv of Council of Europe.
585 **267** 2k.80 multicoloured . . . 45 45

1999. 19th Foundation of European Carnival Cities Convention, Dubrovnik.
586 **268** 2k.30 multicoloured . . . 40 40

269 1 Kreutzer Coin, 1849

1999. 150th Anniv of Minting of Jelacic Kreutzer (587) and Fifth Anniv of Croatian Kuna (588). Multicoloured.
587 2k.30 Type **269** 40 40
588 5k. One kuna coin 85 85

270 Vladimir Nazor (writer)

1999. Anniversaries. Multicoloured.
589 1k.80 Type **270** (50th death anniv) 30 30
590 2k.30 Ferdo Livadic (composer, birth bicentenary) 40 40
591 2k.50 Ivan Rendic (sculptor, 150th birth anniv) 45 45
592 2k.80 Milan Lenuci (urban planner, 150th birth anniv) 45 45
593 3k.50 Vjekoslav Klaic (historian, 150th birth anniv) 60 60
594 4k. Emilij Laszowski (historian, 50th death anniv) 70 70
595 5k. Antun Kanizlic (religious writer and poet, 300th birth anniv) 85 85

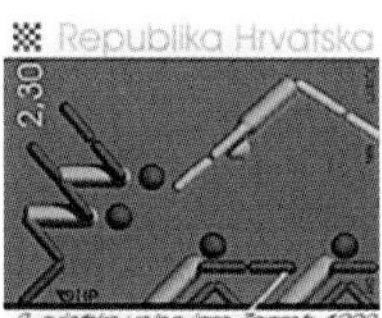

271 Basilica and Mosaics of Bishop Euphrasius, St. Maurus and Fish

1999. Euphrasian Basilica, Porec.
596 **271** 4k. multicoloured 70 70

272 Swimming, Diving and Rowing

1999. 2nd World Military Gamzes, Zagreb.
597 **272** 2k.30 multicoloured . . . 40 40

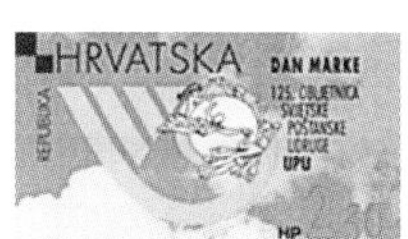

273 Reconstruction of Woman, Skull Fragments and Stone Tools

1999. Centenary of Discovery of Remains of Early Man in Krapina. Multicoloured.
598 1k.80 Type **273** 30 30
599 4k. Dragutin Gorjanovic-Kramberger (palaeontologist and discoverer of remains) and bone fragments 70 70
Nos. 598/9 were issued together, se-tenant, forming a composite design.

274 U.P.U. Emblem and Clouds

1999. World Post Day. 125th Anniv of Universal Postal Union.
600 **274** 2k.30 multicoloured . . . 40 40

275 Lace, "Jesus expelling the Merchants from the Temple" (detail of fresco, Ivan Ranger), and Angel, St. Mary's Church

1999. 600th Anniv of Founding of Paulist Monastery of the Blessed Virgin Mary in Lepoglava. Multicoloured.
601 5k. Type **275** 85 85
602 5k. Altar angel and facade of St. Mary's Church 85 85
603 5k. St. Elizabeth (statue), detail of choir gallery and lace 85 85

276 Josip Jelacic, Ban of Croatia (after C. Lanzelli)

1999. 150th Anniv of Composing of the Jelacic March by Johann Strauss, the Elder.
604 **276** 3k.50 multicoloured . . . 60 60

277 Cloud and Chemical Symbol for Ozone

1999. World Ozone Layer Protection Day.
605 **277** 5k. multicoloured 85 85

278 Pazin Grammar School

1999. School Anniversaries. Multicoloured.
606 2k.30 Type **278** (centenary) 40 40
607 3k.50 Pozega Grammar School (300th anniv) . . . 60 60

279 Hebrang
280 "Madonna of the Rose-garden" (Blaz Jurjev of Trogir)

1999. Birth Cent of Andrija Hebrang (politician).
608 **279** 1k.80 multicoloured . . . 30 10

1999. "Croats—Christianity, Culture, Art" Exhibition, Vatican City.
609 **280** 5k. multicoloured 85 85

281 "Nativity for my Children" (plaster relief, Mila Wood)

1999. Christmas.
610 **281** 2k.30 multicoloured . . . 35 35

282 "Winter Landscape" (Gabrijel Jurkic)

1999. Modern Art. Multicoloured.
611 2k.30 Type **282** 35 35
612 3k.50 "Klek" (Oton Postruznik) 55 55
613 5k. "Stone Table" (Ignjat Job) (vert) 75 75

283 Tudjman
284 Angel

1999. Death Commem of President Franjo Tudjman.
614 **283** 2k.30 black and red . . . 35 35
615 5k. blue, black and red 75 75

2000. Holy Year 2000.
616 **284** 2k.30 multicoloured . . . 35 35

285 Woman's Face
286 Latin Text, Building and Archbishop Stjepan Cosmi (founder)

2000. St. Valentines Day.
617 **285** 2k.30 multicoloured . . . 35 35

2000. 300th Anniv of Split Grammar School.
618 **286** 2k.80 multicoloured . . . 40 40

287 Typewriter
288 "The Lamentation" (Andrija Medulic)

2000. Centenary of Association of Croatian Writers.
619 **287** 2k.30 black and red . . . 35 35

2000. Anniversaries. Multicoloured.
620 1k.80 Type **288** (artist, 500th birth anniv) 30 30
621 2k.30 Matija Petar Katancic (poet, 250th birth anniv) 35 35
622 2k.80 Marija Ruzicka-Strozzi (actress, 150th birth anniv) 40 40
623 3k.50 Statue of Marko Marulic (writer, 550th birth anniv) 55 55
624 5k. "Madonna with the Child and Saints" (Blaz Jurjev Trogiranin) (artist, 550th death anniv) (47 × 25 mm) 75 75

289 Map of Croatia and European Union Stars

2000. Europa. 50th Anniv of Schuman Plan (proposal for pooling the coal and steel industries of France and West Germany). Multicoloured.
625 2k.30 Type **289** 35 35
626 5k. "Building Europe" (vert) 75 75

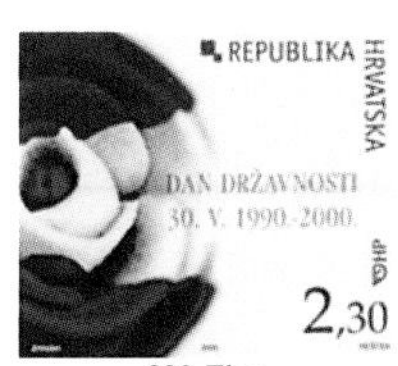

290 Flag

2000. 10th Anniv of Independence.
627 **290** 2k.30 multicoloured . . . 35 35

292 *Micromeria croatica*

2000. Flowers. Multicoloured.
629 3k.50 Type **292** 55 55
630 5k. *Geranium dalmaticum* . . 75 75

293 Statute and Postcard of Kastav

2000. 600th Anniv of the Kastav Statute.
631 **293** 1k.80 multicoloured . . . 30 30

294 Blanusa Gospel and "2000"

2000. World Mathematics Year.
632 **294** 3k.50 multicoloured . . . 55 55

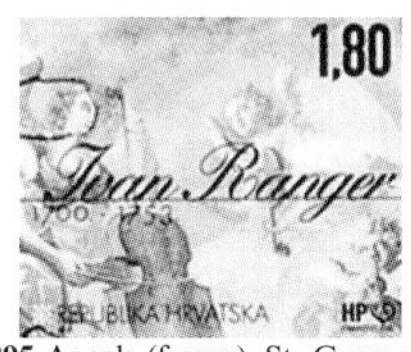

295 Angels (fresco), St. George's Church, Purga

2000. 300th Birth Anniv of Ivan Ranger (artist).
633 **295** 1k.80 multicoloured . . . 30 30

297 Latin Text

2000. 800th Birth Anniv of Toma, Archdeacon of Split.
635 **297** 3k.50 black, silver and blue 55 55

298 Vis

2000. Croatian Towns (5th series).
636 – 2k.30 multicoloured . . . 40 40
639 **298** 3k.50 multicoloured . . . 60 60
DESIGN: 2k.30, Makarska.

299 Austrian Empire 1850 9k. Stamp and Postmark

2000. World Post Day. Multicoloured.
641 2k.30 Type **299** (150th anniv of first stamp in territory of Croatia) 40 40
642 2k.30 Automatic sorting machine (introduction of automatic sorting system) 40 40

300 Basketball, Football, Handball, Water-polo and Tennis Balls

2000. Olympic Games, Sydney.
643 **300** 5k. multicoloured 85 85

301 "Nativity" (relief, Church of the Blessed Virgin Mary, Ogulin)

2000. Christmas.
644 **301** 2k.30 multicoloured . . . 40 40

302 "Korcula" (Vladimir Varlaj)

2000. Paintings (1st series). Multicoloured.
645 1k.80 Type **302** 30 30
646 2k.30 "Brusnik" (Duro Tiljak) 40 40
647 5k. "Boats" (Ante Kastelancic) 85 85
See also Nos. 675/7.

303 White Dove, Ship and Village

2001. New Millennium.
648 **303** 2k.30 multicoloured . . . 40 40

305 Scene from *Radmio and Ljubmir* (poem)

2001. 500th Death Anniv of Dzore Drzic (playwright).
650 **305** 2k.80 multicoloured . . . 45 45

306 Black Rider (comic strip character)

2001. Birth Centenary of Andrija Maurovic (comic strip illustrator).
651 **306** 5k. multicoloured 85 85

307 Goran Ivanisevic

2001. Croatian Sporting Victories. Multicoloured.
652 2k.50 Type **307** (Wimbledon Men's Champion) 40 40
653 2k.80 Janica Kostelic (Alpine Skiing World Cup Women's Champion) . . . 45 45

308 Olive Tree, Kastel Stafilic

2001.
654 **308** 1k.80 multicoloured . . . 30 30

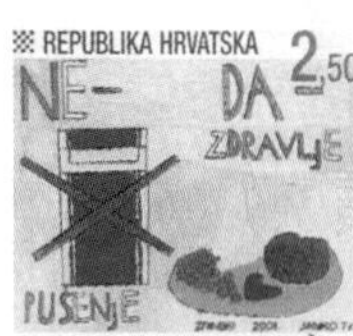

309 Water (green splash to left)

2001. Europa. Water Resources. Multicoloured.
655 3k.50 Type **309** 60 60
656 5k. Water (blue splash to right) 85 85
Nos. 655/6 were issued together, se-tenant, forming a composite design.

310 Poster (Mikele Janko)

2001. World No Smoking Day.
657 **310** 2k.50 multicoloured . . . 40 40

311 Apollo (*Parnassius apollo*)

2001. Butterflies. Multicoloured.
658 2k.50 Type **311** 40 40
659 2k.80 Scarce large blue (*Maculinea teleius*) 45 45
660 5k. False ringlet (*Coenonympha oedippus*) . . 85 85

312 Vukovar

2001.
661 **312** 2k.80 multicoloured . . . 45 45

314 Mouths

2001. World Esperanto Congress, Zagreb.
663 **314** 5k. multicoloured 85 85

315 Woman and Wall

2001. 50th Anniv of United Nations Commissioner for Refugees (No. 664) and I.O.M. International Organization for Migration (No. 665). Mult.
664 1k.80 Type **315** 30 30
665 5k. Refugees and 50IOM . . 85 85

316 Perforated Blocks of Colour

2001. Stamp Day.
666 **316** 2k.50 multicoloured . . . 40 40

317 Croatian Sheep Dog

2001. Dog Breeds. Multicoloured.
667 1k.80 Type **317** 35 35
668 5k. Dalmatian 90 90

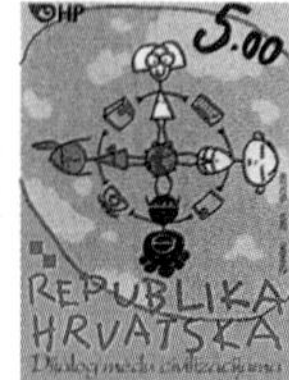

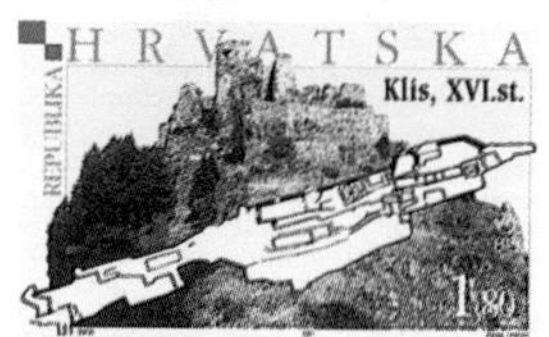

318 Head of "Our Lady of Konvale" (statue) **319** Children encircling Globe

2001. 10th Anniv of Republic of Croatia.
669 **318** 2k.30 multicoloured . . . 40 40

2001. U.N. Year of Dialogue among Civilizations.
670 **319** 5k. multicoloured 90 90

320 Klis (16th-century)

2001. Fortresses. Multicoloured.
671 1k.80 Type **320** 35 35
672 2k.50 Ston (14th-century) . . 45 45
673 3k.50 Sisak (16th-century) . . 60 60

321 Adoration of the Magi (altarpiece), The Visitation of Mary Church, Cucerje **323** Lavoslav Ruzicka, (Chemistry, 1939)

322 "Amphitheatre Ruins" (Vjekoslav Parac)

2001. Christmas
674 **321** 2k.30 multicoloured . . . 40 40

2001. Paintings (2nd series). Multicoloured.
675 2k.50 Type **322** 45 45
676 2k.50 "Maternite du Port-Royal" (Leo Junek) . . . 45 45
677 5k. "Nude with a Baroque Figure" (Slavko Sohaj) (vert) 90 90

2001. Nobel Prize Winners. Multicoloured.
678 2k.80 Type **323** 45 25
679 3k.50 Vladimir Prelog (Chemistry, 1975) 60 60
680 5k. Ivo Andric (Literature, 1961) 90 90

324 Ivan Gucetic

2002. Anniversaries. Multicoloured.
681 1k.80 Type **324** (writer, 500th death anniv) 35 35
682 2k.30 Dobrisa Cesaric (writer, birth centenary) 40 40
683 2k.50 Juraj Rattkay (historian, 350th anniv of publication of *Memoria Regum et Banorum Regnorum Dalmatia, Croatiae et Sclavoniae Ab Origine sua usque ad praesentem Annum 1652 deducta* (history of Croatia)) 45 45
684 2k.80 Franjo Vranjanin Laurana (sculptor, 500th death anniv) 50 50
685 3k.50 Augustin Kazotic (Bishop of Zagreb, 300th anniv of beatification) . . . 65 65
686 5k. Matko Laginja (politician and writer, 150th birth anniv) 95 95

325 Skier

2002. Winter Olympic Games, Salt Lake City, U.S.A.
687 **325** 5k. multicoloured 95 95

326 Barcode and "Reaper" (drawing, Robert Franges Mihanovic)

2002. 150th Anniv of Croatian Chamber of Economy.
688 **326** 2k.50 multicoloured . . . 45 45

327 9th-century Gable bearing Prince Trpimir's Name (detail, altar partition, Rizinice Church)

2002. 1150th Anniv of Prince Trpimir's Deed of Gift of Land to Archbishop of Salona. Sheet 116 × 59 mm.
MS689 multicoloured 2·75 2·75

328 Kuharic

2002. Cardinal Franjo Kuharic (Archbishop of Zagreb) Commemoration.
690 **328** 2k.30 multicoloured . . . 2·75 2·75

329 "Divan"

2002. 80th Death Anniv of Vlaho Bukovac (artist).
691 **329** 5k. multicoloured 95 95
A stamp in a similar design was issued by Czech Republic.

330 Arms

2002. 750th Anniv of Royal Borough of Krizevci.
692 **330** 1k.80 multicoloured . . . 35 35

331 Facade

2002. Centenary of Post Office Building, Varazdin.
693 **331** 2k.30 multicoloured . . . 40 40

OFFICIAL STAMPS

O 11

O 12

1942.
O55 O **11** 25b. red 10 10
O56 50b. grey 10 10
O57 75b. green 10 10
O58 1k. brown 10 10
O59 2k. blue 10 10
O60 3k. red 10 10
O61 3k.50 red 10 10
O62 4k. purple 10 10
O63 5k. blue 20 40
O64 6k. violet 10 10
O65 10k. green 10 10
O66 12k. red 15 30
O67 12k.50 orange 10 10
O68 20k. blue 20 40
O69 O **12** 30k. grey and brown . . 15 30
O70 40k. grey and violet . . 15 30
O71 50k. grey and red . . . 50 1·00
O72 100k. salmon & black 50 1·00

POSTAGE DUE STAMPS

1941. Nos. D259/63 of Yugoslavia optd **NEZAVISNA DRZAVA HRVATSKA** in three lines above a chequered shield.
D26 D **10** 50p. violet 20 40
D27 1d. red 20 40
D28 2d. blue . . . . 6·00 12·50
D29 5d. orange . . . . . . 65 1·25
D30 10d. brown . . . . . . 3·00 8·00

D 9

D 15

1941.
D51 D **9** 50b. red 15 45
D52 1k. red 15 45
D53 2k. red 20 60
D54 5k. red 35 90
D55 10k. red . . . . 50 1·25

1942.
D67 D **15** 50b. olive and blue . . 15 30
D68 1k. olive and blue . . . 15 35
D69 2k. olive and blue . . . 15 35
D76 4k. olive and blue . . . 10 20
D70 5k. olive and blue . . . 20 40
D78 6k. olive and blue . . . 10 55
D79 10k. blue and indigo . . 15 50
D80 15k. blue and indigo . . 15 50
D72 20k. blue and indigo . . 80 1·60

SERBIAN POSTS IN CROATIA

100 paras = 1 dinar.

REPUBLIC OF SRPSKA KRAJINA

Following Croatia's declaration of independence from Yugoslavia on 30 May 1991 fighting broke out between Serb inhabitants, backed by units of the Yugoslav Federal Army, and Croatian forces. By January 1992, when a ceasefire sponsored by the United Nations and the European Community became effective, the Croatian Serbs and their allies controlled 30% of the country organized into the districts of the Krajina, Western Slavonia and Eastern Slavonia. These were declared peace-keeping zones under United Nations supervision and the Yugoslav Army withdrew. In 1993 the Serbs proclaimed the Republic of Srpska Krajina, covering all three areas, and elections for a separate president and parliament were held in January 1994.

K 1 Stag, Kopacevo Marsh

K 3 Coat of Arms

1993.
K1 K **1** 200d. green and yellow . . 25 25
K2 – 500d. black and red . . . 65 65
K3 – 1000d. green and yellow 1·40 1·40
K4 – 1000d. green and yellow 1·40 1·40
K5 – 2000d. black and red . . 3·00 3·00
DESIGNS: No. K2, Krka Monastery; K3, Town walls, Knin; K4, Ruined house, Vukovar; K5, Coat of arms.
For 100000d. in same design as No. K2 see No. K12.

1993. Issued at Knin. Nos. 2594/5 of Yugoslavia surch.
K6 5000d. on 3d. black and red 65 65
K7 10000d. on 2d. blue and red 65 65

1993.
K8 K **3** A blue and red 45 45
No. K8 was sold at the internal letter rate.

K 4 Citadel, Knin

A
(K5)

K 6 Helmet and Swords

1993.
K 9 K **4** 5000d. green and red . . 10 10
K10 – 10000d. green and red 15 15
K11 – 50000d. blue and red . . 75 75
K12 – 100000d. blue and red 1·50 1·50
DESIGNS: 10000d. Heron, Kopacevo Marsh; 50000d. Icon and church, Vukovar; 100000d. Krka Monastery.

Currency Reform

1993. No. K8 surch with Type K **5** (Cyrillic letter "D").
K13 K **3** "D" on A blue and red 40 40
No. K13 was sold at the new internal letter rate.

1993. Nos. K9/12 surch with Type K **5** (Cyrillic letter "D").
K14 K **4** "D" on 5000d. grn & red 45 45
K15 – "D" on 10000d. green and red 85 85
K16 – "D" on 50000d. blue and red . . . . . . 2·50 2·50
K17 – "D" on 100000d. blue and red . . . . . . 8·50 8·50

1993.
K18 K **6** R blue . . . . 1·10 1·10
No. K18 was sold at the internal registered letter rate.

K 7 St. Simeon

1994. Serb Culture and Tradition. Mult.
K19 50p. Type K **7** 80 80
K20 80p. Krajina coat of arms (vert) . . . . 1·25 1·25
K21 1d. "The Vucedol Dove" (carving) (vert) . . . . . 1·75 1·75

K 8 Cup-and-saucer

K 9 Krka Monastery

1994. Climbing Plants. Multicoloured.
K22 30p. Type K **8** 60 60
K23 40p. "Dipladenia" 85 85
K24 60p. Black-eyed Susan . . . 1·25 1·25
K25 70p. Climbing rose . . . . 1·50 1·50

1994.
K26 K **9** 5p. red 10 10
K27 – 10p. brown 20 20
K28 – 20p. green 40 40
K29 – 50p. red 55 55
K30 – 60p. violet 70 70
K31 – 1d. blue . . . . 2·25 2·25
DESIGNS: 10p. Carin; 20p. Vukovar; 50p. Monument, Batina; 60p. Ilok; 1d. Lake, Plitvice.

K 10 "The Flower of Life" (memorial to Jasenovac Concentration Camp victims)

K 11 "A" over Mosaic

1995. 50th Anniv of End of Second World War.
K32 K **10** 60p. multicoloured . . 1·40 1·40

1995.
K33 K **11** A red 30 30
No. K33 was sold at the internal letter rate.

K 12 Krcic Waterfall, Knin

1995.
K34 K **12** 10p. blue 10 10
K35 – 20p. ochre 10 10
K36 – 40p. red 20 20
K37 – 2d. blue . . . . . . 1·10 1·10
K38 – 5d. brown . . . . . 2·75 2·75
DESIGNS: 20p. Benkovac; 40p. Citadel, Knin; 2d. Petrinja; 5d. Pakrac.

In May 1995 the Croatian army occupied Western Slavonia and in August 1995 the Krajina and these areas were reincorporated into the Republic of Croatia. The only surviving part of the Serbian territories, Eastern Slavonia, was, by agreement, placed under temporary United Nations administration in November 1995 and was subsequently called Sremsko Baranjska Oblast (Srem and Baranya Region).

SREMSKO BARANJSKA OBLAST

K 13 Common Cormorant ("Phalocrocorax carbo"), Kopacevo Marsh

1995. Protected Species. Multicoloured.
K39 80p. Type K **13** 90 90
K40 80p. Chamois, Lika 90 90

K 14 St. Dimitriev's Church, Dalj

K 15 Vukovar Marina, River Danube

1995. Churches (1st series).
K41 K **14** 5p. green 10 10
K42 – 10p. red 15 15
K43 – 30p. mauve 35 35
K44 – 50p. brown 80 80
K45 – 1d. blue . . . . 1·10 1·10
DESIGNS: 10p. St. Peter and St. Paul's Church, Bolman; 30p. St. Nicholas's Church, Mirkovci; 50p. St. Nicholas's Church, Tenja; 1d. St. Nicholas's Church, Vukovar.
See also Nos. K48/53.

1996. River Danube Co-operation.
K46 K **15** 1d. multicoloured . . . 1·50 1·50

K 16 The Worker's Hall, Vukovar

K 17 Archangel Church, Darda

1996.
K47 K **16** A red 30 30
No. K47 was sold at the internal letter rate.

1996. Churches (2nd series).
K48 K **17** 10p. brown 10 10
K49 – 50p. violet 10 10
K50 – 1d. green 15 15
K51 – 2d. green 45 45
K52 – 5d. blue . . . . 1·90 1·90
K53 – 10d. blue . . . . 3·75 3·75
DESIGNS: 50p. St. George's Church, Knezevo; 1 d St. Nicholas's Church, Jagodnjak; 2d. Archangel Gabriel's Church, Brsadin; 5d. St. Stephen's Church, Borovo Selo; 10d. St. Nicholas's Church, Pacetin.

K 18 Nikola Tesla

K 19 Milica Stojadinovic-Srpkinja (1830–78) (poetess)

1996. 140th Birth Anniv of Nikola Tesla (inventor).
K54 K **18** 1d.50 multicoloured . . 1·50 1·50

1996. Europa, Famous Women, Mult.
K55 1d.50 Type K **19** . . . . . 2·50 2·50
K56 1d.50 Mileva Marie-Einstein (1875–1948) (mathematician) . . . . . 2·50 2·50

K 20 Jasna Sekaric (Olympic gold medal winner)

K 21 Milutin Milankovic

1996. Centenary of Modern Olympic Games.
K57 K **20** 1d.50 multicoloured . . 1·25 1·25

1996. Milutin Milankovic (geophysicist) Commemoration (1879–1958).
K58 K **21** 1d.50 multicoloured . . 1·25 1·25

K 22 "Madonna and Child" (icon)

K 23 Pigeon

1996. Christmas.
K59 K **22** 1d.50 multicoloured . . 1·25 1·25

1997. Domestic Pets. Multicoloured.
K60 1d. Type K **23** 50 50
K61 1d. Budgerigar 50 50
K62 1d. Cat 50 50
K63 1d. Black labrador 50 50

1997. No. K18 surch or optd (No. K67) with crosses obliterating former name.
K64 K **6** 10p. on R blue 10 10
K65 20p. on R blue 10 10
K66 30p. on R blue 15 15
K67 R (90p.) blue 40 40
K68 1d. on R blue 30 30
K69 1d.50 on R blue 60 60
K70 2d. on R blue 80 80
K71 5d. on R blue . . . . 1·50 1·50
K72 10d. on R blue . . . . 3·75 3·75
K73 20d. on R blue . . . . 9·00 9·00

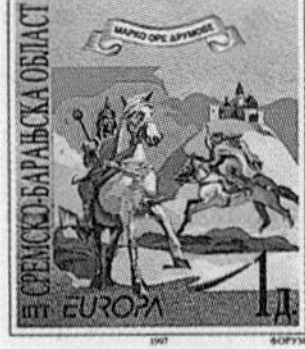

K 25 St. Peter and St. Paul's Cathedral, Orolik
K 26 Prince Marko and The Turks

1997. Restoration of Orthodox Church, Ilok.
K74 K 25 50p.+50p. blue 35 35
K75 – 60p.+50p. mauve . . . 35 35
K76 – 1d.20+50p. red 55 55
DESIGNS: 60p. St. George's Church, Tovarnik; 1d.20, Church, Negoslavci.

1997. Europa. Tales and Legends. Mult.
K77 1d. Type K 26 . . . . . 70 70
K78 1d. Emperor Trajan 70 70

The postal administration of the Srem and Baranya Region was reincorporated into that of the Republic of Croatia on 19 May 1997. Eastern Slavonia was returned to Croatian control on 15 January 1998.

CUBA Pt. 15

An island in the W. Indies, ceded by Spain to the United States in 1898. A republic under U.S. protection until 1901 when the island became independent. The issues to 1871, except Nos. 13, 14, 19, 20/7, 32, 44 and 48, were for Puerto Rico also.

1855. 8 reales plata fuerte (strong silver reales) = 1 peso.
1866. 100 centimos = 1 escudo.
1871. 100 centimos = 1 peseta.
1881. 100 milesimas = 100 centavos = 1 peso.
1898. 100 cents = 1 U.S. dollar.
1899. 100 centavos = 1 peso.

SPANISH COLONY

1 5

1855. Imperf.
6 1 ½r. green . . . . 5·00 50
9 ½r. blue . . . . 2·50 50
10 1r. green . . . . 2·40 50
11a 2r. red . . . . 9·25 2·75
Nos. 10/11 optd **HABILITADO POR LA NACION** were issues of Philippines (Nos. 44/5).

1855. No. 11a surch **Y** ¼.
12 1 Y¼ on 2r. red . . . . . . £160 55·00

1862. Imperf.
13 5 ¼r. black on buff . . . . . 9·50 11·50

6 7

1864. Imperf.
14 6 ¼r. black on buff . . . . . 11·50 16·00
15 ½r. green . . . . 3·00 50
16 ½r. green on pink . . . . . 9·00 1·50
17 1r. blue on brown . . . . 2·50 55
18b 2r. red . . . . 15·00 4·50

1866. Dated "1866". Imperf.
19 7 5c. mauve . . . . 21·00 27·00
20 10c. blue . . . . 2·75 60
21 20c. green . . . . 1·25 60
22 40c. pink . . . . 7·00 5·50

1866. No. 14 optd **66**. Imperf.
23 6 ¼r. black on buff . . . . . . 42·00 55·00

1867. Dated "1867". Perf.
24 7 5c. mauve . . . . 32·00 15·00
25 10c. blue . . . . 16·00 60
26 20c. green . . . . 11·00 60
27 40c. pink . . . . 11·00 12·00

9 11

1868. Dated "1868".
28 9 5c. lilac . . . . 11·00 9·00
29 10c. blue . . . . 2·50 1·00
30 20c. green . . . . 4·50 2·25
31 40c. pink . . . . 11·00 5·25

1868. Nos. 28/31 optd **HABILITADO POR LA NACION**.
36 9 5c. lilac . . . . 42·00 27·00
37 10c. blue . . . . 42·00 27·00
38 20c. green . . . . 42·00 27·00
39 40c. pink . . . . 42·00 27·00

1869. Dated "1869".
32 9 5c. pink . . . . 17·00 8·50
33 10c. brown . . . . 2·50 1·25
34 20c. orange . . . . 4·00 1·90
35 40c. lilac . . . . 24·00 8·00

1869. Nos. 32/5 optd **HABILITADO POR LA NACION**.
40 9 5c. pink . . . . 95·00 32·00
41 10c. brown . . . . 40·00 25·00
42 20c. orange . . . . 35·00 25·00
43 40c. lilac . . . . 50·00 25·00

1870.
44 11 5c. blue . . . . £120 55·00
45 10c. green . . . . 1·50 50
46 20c. brown . . . . 1·50 50
47 40c. pink . . . . £120 28·00

12 13

1871. Dated "1871".
48 12 12c. lilac . . . . 10·00 8·00
49 25c. blue . . . . 1·60 60
50 50c. green . . . . 1·60 60
51 1p. brown . . . . 23·00 5·50

1873.
52 13 12½c. green . . . . 16·00 9·00
53 25c. grey . . . . 1·50 50
54 50c. brown 85 50
55 1p. brown . . . . £200 28·00

1874. Dated "1874".
56 12 12½c. brown . . . . 6·50 6·00
57 25c. blue 45 40
58 50c. lilac 55 40
59 1p. red . . . . £100 50·00

14 15

1875.
60 14 12½c. mauve 60 85
61 25c. blue 30 15
62 50c. green 30 15
63 1p. brown . . . . 6·00 3·25

1876. Inscr "ULTRAMAR 1876".
64 15 12½c. green . . . . 1·40 1·50
65a 25c. lilac 45 25
66 50c. blue 45 25
67 1p. black . . . . 5·75 2·75

1877. Inscr "CUBA 1877".
68 15 10c. green . . . . 17·00
69 12½c. lilac . . . . 4·50 3·00
70 25c. green 30 10
71 50c. black 30 10
72 1p. brown . . . . 22·00 8·75

1878. Inscr "CUBA 1878".
73 15 5c. blue 25 20
74 10c. black . . . . 45·00
75a 12½c. bistre . . . . 2·40 1·75
76a 25c. green 15 10
77 50c. green 15 10
78 1p. red . . . . 6·00 3·75

1879. Inscr "CUBA 1879".
79 15 5c. black 35 25
80 10c. orange . . . . 70·00 30·00
81 12½c. pink 35 25
82 25c. blue 35 25
83 50c. grey 35 25
84 1p. bistre . . . . 11·00 7·25

1880. "Alfonso XII" key-type inscr "CUBA 1880".
85 X 5c. green 25 10
86 10c. red . . . . 50·00
87 12½c. lilac 25 10
88 25c. lilac 25 10
89 50c. brown 25 10
90 1p. brown . . . . 3·00 1·90

1881. "Alfonso XII" key-type inscr "CUBA 1881".
91 X 1c. green 25 10
92 2c. pink . . . . 26·00
93a 2½c. bistre 50 10
94 5c. lilac 25 10
95 10c. brown 25 10
96 20c. brown . . . . 3·25 3·25

1882. "Alfonso XII" key-type inscr "CUBA".
97 X 1c. green 35 15
98 2c. pink . . . . 1·40 15
118 2½c. brown 20 10
119 2½c. mauve 65 45
100 5c. lilac . . . . 1·40 20
123 5c. grey . . . . 1·75 25
101 10c. brown 30 10
126 10c. blue 85 55
121 20c. brown . . . . 11·00 1·90
122 20c. lilac . . . . 11·00 2·75

1883. 1882 issue optd or surch with fancy pattern.
103 X 5c. lilac . . . . 1·50 80
106 5 on 5c. lilac . . . . . . 1·00 65
104 10c. brown . . . . 4·00 3·75
107 10 on 10c. brown . . . . 1·60 1·00
105 20c. brown . . . . 65·00 29·00
111 20 on 20c. brown . . . . 16·00 11·50
The surcharges exist in four different patterns.

1890. "Baby" key-type inscr "ISLA DE CUBA".
135 Y 1c. brown . . . . 8·75 5·50
147 1c. grey . . . . 5·00 2·75
159 1c. blue . . . . 2·10 30
169 1c. purple 65 20
136 2c. blue . . . . 4·75 1·75
148 2c. brown 95 35
160 2c. pink . . . . 21·00 4·25
170 2c. red . . . . 5·50 15
137 2½c. green . . . . 6·50 3·50
149 2½c. orange . . . . 29·00 8·00
161 2½c. mauve . . . . 1·90 20
171 2½c. pink 40 15
138 5c. grey 50 55
150 5c. green 60 35
172 5c. blue 30 15
139 10c. brown . . . . 1·90 70
151 10c. pink . . . . 1·25 35
173 10c. green . . . . 1·50 15
140 20c. purple 50 45
152 20c. blue . . . . 6·50 6·50
162 20c. brown . . . . 16·00 8·50
174 20c. lilac . . . . 9·50 4·25
175 40c. brown . . . . 19·00 10·00
176 80c. brown . . . . 32·00 15·00

1898. "Curly Head" key-type inscr "CUBA 1898 Y 99".
183 Z 1m. brown 20 15
184 2m. brown 20 15
185 3m. brown 20 15
186 4m. brown . . . . 2·50 1·25
187 5m. brown 15 15
188 1c. purple 15 15
189 2c. green 15 15
190 3c. brown 15 15
191 4c. orange . . . . 6·00 2·00
192 5c. pink 55 15
193 6c. blue 20 15
194 8c. brown 50 20
195 10c. red 65 20
196 15c. grey . . . . 2·50 20
197 20c. purple 30 10
198 40c. mauve . . . . 1·60 15
199 60c. black . . . . 1·75 15
200 80c. brown . . . . 8·00 6·00
201 1p. green . . . . 8·00 6·00
202 2p. blue . . . . 16·00 6·00

OFFICIAL STAMPS

1860. As Nos. O50/3 of Spain but without full points after "OFICIAL" and "ONZAS" or "LIBRA". Imperf.
O12 ½o. black on yellow . . . . – 30·00
O13 1o. black on pink . . . . . – 30·00
O14 4o. black on green . . . . – £170
O15 1l. black on blue . . . . . – £350
The face values of Nos. O12/15 are expressed in onzas (ounces) or libra (pound), referring to the maximum weight for which each value could prepay postage.

PRINTED MATTER STAMPS

All Printed Matter stamps are key-types inscribed "CUBA IMPRESOS".

1888. "Alfonso XII".
P129 X ½m. black 15 10
P130 1m. black 15 10
P131 2m. black 15 10
P132 3m. black 70 40
P133 4m. black . . . . 1·10 70
P134 8m. black . . . . 5·50 2·40

1890. "Baby".
P141 Y ½m. brown 45 35
P142 1m. brown 45 35
P143 2m. brown 75 50
P144 3m. brown 75 50
P145 4m. brown . . . . 6·25 3·50
P146 8m. brown . . . . 6·25 3·50

1892. "Baby".
P153 Y ½m. lilac 10 10
P154 1m. lilac 10 10
P155 2m. lilac 20 10
P156 3m. lilac . . . . 1·50 50
P157 4m. lilac . . . . 3·50 3·00
P158 8m. lilac . . . . 6·00 4·25

1894. "Baby".
P163 Y ½m. pink 15 10
P164 1m. pink 40 10
P165 2m. pink 40 10
P166 3m. pink . . . . 1·40 60
P167 4m. pink . . . . 2·50 70
P168 8m. pink . . . . 5·25 3·00

1896. "Baby".
P177 Y ½m. green 15 10
P178 1m. green 15 10
P179 2m. green 15 10
P180 3m. green . . . . 1·50 50
P181 4m. green . . . . 3·50 3·00
P182 8m. green . . . . 6·00 4·25

UNITED STATES ADMINISTRATION

1899. Stamps of United States of 1894 surch **CUBA** and value.
246 1c. on 1c. green (No. 283) . . 4·00 35
247 2c. on 2c. red (No. 270) . . . 4·25 30
248 2½c. on 2c. red (No. 270) . . . 2·50 40
249 3c. on 3c. violet (No. 271) . . 7·50 1·40
250 5c. on 5c. blue (No. 286) . . 8·00 1·25
251 10c. on 10c. brown (No. 289) 15·00 5·00

29 Statue of Columbus

1899.
307 29 1c. green . . . . 1·10 10
308 – 2c. red . . . . 1·10 10
303 – 3c. purple . . . . 2·00 15
304 – 5c. blue . . . . 3·25 45
310 – 10c. brown . . . . 2·25 35
DESIGNS: 2c. Palms; 3c. Statue of "La India" (Woman); 5c. Liner "Umbria" (Commerce); 10c. Ploughing Sugar Plantation.

POSTAGE DUE STAMPS

1899. Postage Due stamps of United States of 1894 surch **CUBA** and value.
D253 D 87 1c. on 1c. red . . . . 35·00 4·00
D254 2c. on 2c. red . . . . 35·00 4·00
D255 5c. on 5c. red . . . . 35·00 4·00
D256 10c. on 10c. red . . . 21·00 1·90

SPECIAL DELIVERY STAMP

1899. No. E283 of United States surch **CUBA. 10 c. de PESO.**
E252 E 46 10c. on 10c. blue . . . £100 80·00

INDEPENDENT REPUBLIC

1902. Surch **UN CENTAVO HABILITADO OCTUBRE 1902** and figure **1**.
306 1c. on 3c. purple (No. 303) 1·75 40

36 Major-General Antonio Maceo
37 B. Maso

1907.
311 36 50c. black and slate . . . 1·10 40
318 50c. black and violet . . . 1·10 40

1910.
312 37 1c. violet and green 55 15
320 1c. green 85 10
313 – 2c. green and red . . . . 1·10 10
321 – 2c. red 85 10
314 – 3c. blue and violet 55 20
315 – 5c. green and blue . . . . 10·00 75
322 – 5c. blue . . . . 2·00 10
316 – 8c. violet and olive 55 20
323 – 8c. black and olive . . . . 2·00 35
317 – 10c. blue and sepia . . . . 4·50 25
319 – 1p. black and slate . . . . 6·50 3·00
324 – 1p. black . . . . 4·00 1·10
PORTRAITS: 2c. M. Gomez. 3c. J. Sanguily. 5c. I. Agramonte. 8c. C. Garcia. 10c. Mayia. 1p. C. Roloff.

40 Map of W. Indies
43 Gertrudis Gomez de Avellaneda

1914.
325 40 1c. green 40 15
326 2c. red 40 15
328 3c. violet . . . . 2·00 25
329 5c. blue . . . . 2·25 15
330 8c. olive . . . . 2·25 65
331 10c. brown . . . . 3·75 70
332 10c. olive . . . . 3·25 70
333 50c. orange . . . . 28·00 9·00
334 $1 slate . . . . 40·00 17·00

1914. Birth Centenary of Gertrudis Gomez de Avellaneda (poetess).
335 43 5c. blue . . . . 8·00 3·00

44 Jose Marti
47

1917.
336 44 1c. green 65 10
337 – 2c. red (Gomez) 65 10
338 – 3c. violet (La Luz) 65 10
339 – 5c. blue (Garcia) 65 10
349a – 8c. brown (Agramonte) 2·75 20
341 – 10c. brown (Palma) 1·60 10
342 – 20c. green (Saco) 5·00 45
343 – 50c. red (Maceo) 8·00 45
344 – 1p. black (Cespedes) 8·00 45

1927. 25th Anniv of Republic.
352 47 25c. violet 8·50 3·25

48 PN 9 Flying Boat over Havana Harbour

1927. Air.
353 48 5c. blue 3·25 1·40

49 T. Estrada Palma

1928. 6th Pan-American Conference.
354 49 1c. green 25 15
355 – 2c. red 25 15
356 – 5c. blue 55 25
357 – 8c. brown 3·75 1·50
358 – 10c. brown 55 45
359 – 13c. orange 1·10 50
360 – 20c. olive 1·40 60
361 – 30c. purple 4·50 1·25
362 – 50c. red 4·50 1·75
363 – 1p. black 9·00 5·00
DESIGNS: 2c. Gen. G. Machado; 5c. El Morro, Havana; 8c. Railway Station, Havana; 10c. President's Palace; 13c. Tobacco plantation; 20c. Treasury Secretariat; 30c. Sugar Mill; 50c. Havana Cathedral; 1p. Galician Immigrants' Centre, Havana.

1928. Air. Lindbergh Commemoration. Optd **LINDBERGH FEBRERO 1928**.
364 48 5c. red 4·00 1·60

51 The Capitol, Havana
52 Hurdler

1929. Inauguration of Capitol.
365 51 1c. green 25 20
366 2c. red 30 35
367 5c. blue 40 30
368 10c. brown 75 35
369 20c. purple 3·25 1·40

1930. 2nd Central American Games, Havana.
370 52 1c. green 55 35
371 2c. red 55 40
372 5c. blue 85 40
373 10c. brown 1·40 85
374 20c. purple 9·00 3·00

1930. Air. Surch **CORREO AEREO NACIONAL** and value.
375 47 10c. on 25c. violet 2·75 1·10

54 Fokker Super Trimotor over Beach

1931. Air.
376 54 5c. green 20 10
377 8c. red 2·25 60
378 10c. blue 25 10
379 15c. red 60 25
380 20c. brown 65 10
381 30c. purple 1·10 25
382 40c. orange 2·75 45
383 50c. green 3·00 50
384 1p. black 5·75 1·75

55 Ford "Tin Goose" over Forest

1931. Air.
385 55 5c. purple 20 10
386 10c. black 25 10
387 20c. red 1·25 35
388 20c. pink 2·25 70
389 50c. blue 3·75 1·00
390 50c. turquoise 2·75 90

56 Mangos of Baragua
57 Battle of Mal Tiempo

1933. 35th Anniv of War of Independence.
391 56 3c. brown 80 20
392 57 5c. blue 60 30
393 – 10c. green 1·60 30
394 – 13c. red 1·90 90
395 – 20c. black 4·00 3·25
DESIGNS—HORIZ: 10c. Battle of Coliseo; 13c. Maceo, Gomez and Zayas. VERT: 20c. Campaign Monument.

1933. Establishment of Revolutionary Govt. Stamps of 1917 optd **GOBIERNO REVOLUCIONARIO 4-9-1933** or surch also.
396 44 1c. green 85 30
397 – 2c. on 3c. vio (No. 338) 85 30

59 Dr. Carlos J. Finlay
61 Map of Caribbean

1934. 101st Birth Anniv of C. J. Finlay ("yellow-fever" researcher).
398 59 2c. red 1·10 35
399 5c. blue 2·00 45

1935. Air. Havana–Miami "Air Train". Surch **PRIMER TREN AEREO INTERNACIONAL. 1935 O'Meara y du Pont + 10 cts.** Imperf or perf.
400 54 10c.+10c. red 4·25 4·25

1936. Free Port of Matanzas. Inscr as in T **61**. Perf or imperf (same prices).
401 61 1c. green (postage) 20 15
402 – 2c. red 30 15
403 – 4c. purple 1·25 20
404 – 5c. blue 1·50 35
405 – 8c. brown 1·40 55
406 – 10c. green 1·40 55
407 – 20c. brown 2·75 2·25
408 – 50c. slate 7·00 3·25

409 – 5c. violet (air) 40 20
410 – 10c. orange 1·00 20
411 – 20c. green 2·75 80
412 – 50c. black 10·50 4·00
DESIGNS—POSTAGE: 2c. Matanzas Bay and Free Zone; 4c. "Rex" (liner) in Mantanzas Bay; 5c. Ships in the Free Zone; 8c. Bellamar Caves; 10c. Yumuri Valley; 20c. Yumuri River; 50c. Sailing ship and steamer. AIR: 5c. Aerial panorama; 10c. Airship "Macon" over Concord Bridge; 20c. Airplane "Cuatro Vientos" over Matanzas; 50c. San Severino Fortress.

63 President J. M. Gomez
64 Gen. J. M. Gomez Monument

1936. Inauguration of Gomez Monument.
413 63 1c. green 1·60 45
414 64 2c. red 2·10 65

65 "Peace and Labour"

66 Maximo Gomez Monument

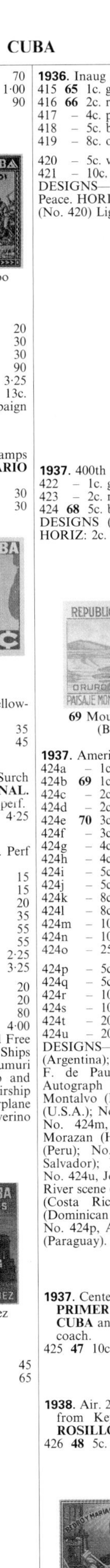

1936. Inaug of Maximo Gomez Monument.
415 65 1c. green (postage) 30 15
416 66 2c. red 30 15
417 – 4c. purple 55 15
418 – 5c. blue 2·75 70
419 – 8c. olive 4·00 1·10

420 – 5c. violet (air) 2·25 1·40
421 – 10c. brown 4·00 2·00
DESIGNS—VERT: 4c. Flaming torch; 8c. Dove of Peace. HORIZ: 5c. (No. 418) Army of Liberation; 5c. (No. 420) Lightning; 10c. "Flying Wing".

68 Caravel and Sugar Cane

1937. 400th Anniv of Cane Sugar Industry.
422 – 1c. green 1·10 45
423 – 2c. red 80 20
424 68 5c. blue 2·50 40
DESIGNS (each with caravel in upper triangle). HORIZ: 2c. Early sugar mill; 5c. Modern sugar mill.

69 Mountain View (Bolivia)
70 Camilo Henriquez (Chile)

1937. American Writers and Artists Assn.
424a – 1c. green (postage) 55 55
424b 69 1c. green 55 55
424c – 2c. red 55 55
424d – 2c. red 55 55
424e 70 3c. violet 85 85
424f – 3c. violet 85 85
424g – 4c. brown 85 85
424h – 4c. brown 1·75 1·75
424i – 5c. blue 1·10 1·10
424j – 5c. blue 1·10 1·10
424k – 8c. green 3·25 3·25
424l – 8c. green 1·40 1·40
424m – 10c. brown 1·75 1·75
424n – 10c. brown 1·75 1·75
424o – 25c. lilac 35·00 18·00

424p – 5c. red (air) 3·75 3·25
424q – 5c. red 3·75 3·25
424r – 10c. blue 3·75 3·25
424s – 10c. blue 3·75 3·25
424t – 20c. green 6·00 5·50
424u – 20c. green 6·00 5·50
DESIGNS—VERT: No. 424a, Arms of the Republic (Argentina); No. 424c, Arms (Brazil); No. 424f, Gen. F. de Paula Santander (Colombia); No. 424g, Autograph of Jose Marti (Cuba); No. 424j, Juan Montalvo (Ecuador); No. 424k, Abraham Lincoln (U.S.A.); No. 4241, Quetzal and scroll (Guatemala); No. 424m, Arms (Haiti); No. 424n, Francisco Morazan (Honduras); No. 424r, Inca gate, Cuzco (Peru); No. 424s, Atlacatl (Indian warrior) (El Salvador); No. 424t, Simon Bolivar (Venezuela); No. 424u, Jose Rodo (Uruguay). HORIZ: No. 424d, River scene (Canada); No. 424h, National Monument (Costa Rica); No. 424i, Columbus Lighthouse (Dominican Republic); No. 424o, Ships of Columbus; No. 424p, Arch (Panama); No. 424q, Carlos Lopez (Paraguay).

1937. Centenary of Cuban Railway. Surch **1837 1937 PRIMER CENTENARIO FERROCARRIL EN CUBA** and value either side of an early engine and coach.
425 47 10c. on 25c. violet 5·50 1·00

1938. Air. 25th Anniv of D. Rosillo's Overseas Flight from Key West to Havana. Optd **1913 1938 ROSILLO Key West-Habana**.
426 48 5c. orange 3·75 1·75

74 Pierre and Marie Curie
75 Allegory of Child Care

1938. International Anti-cancer Fund. 40th Anniv of Discovery of Radium.
427 74 2c.+1c. red 2·50 95
428 5c.+1c. blue 2·50 95

1938. Obligatory Tax. Anti-T.B. Fund.
429 75 1c. green 30 20

76 Native and Cigar

80 Calixto Garcia

1939. Havana Tobacco Industry.
430 76 1c. green 20 10
431 – 2c. red 45 10
432 – 5c. blue 1·00 15
DESIGNS: 2c. Cigar, globe and wreath of leaves; 5c. Tobacco plant and box of cigars.

1939. Air. Experimental Rocket Post. Optd **EXPERIMENTO DEL COHETE Postal ANO DE 1939.**
433 55 10c. green 35·00 5·50

1939. Birth Centenary of Gen. Calixto Garcia. Perf or imperf.
434 80 2c. red 55 20
435 – 5c. blue 1·10 45
DESIGN: 5c. Garcia on horseback.

82 Nurse and Child

83 Gonzalo de Quesada and Union Flags

84 Rotarian Symbol, Flag and Tobacco Plant

1939. Obligatory Tax. Anti-T.B.
436 82 1c. red 30 10

1940. 50th Anniv of Pan-American Union.
437 83 2c. red 1·10 55

1940. Rotary International Convention.
438 84 2c. red 1·75 80

85 Lions, Emblem, Flag and Palms

86 Dr. Gutierrez

1940. Lions International Convention, Havana.
439 85 2c. red 1·75 80

1940. Centenary of Publication of First Cuban Medical Review.
440 86 2c. red 85 55
441 5c. blue 1·40 55

87 Sir Rowland Hill and G.B. 1d. of 1840 and Cuba Issues of 1855 and 1899

1940. Air. Centenary of 1st Adhesive Postage Stamps.
443 87 10c. brown 4·50 2·50

88 "Health" protecting Children

89 Heredia and Niagara Falls

1940. Obligatory Tax. Children's Hospital and Anti-T.B. Funds.
445 88 1c. blue 20 10

1940. Air. Death Centenary of J. M. Heredia y Campuzaono (poet).
446 – 5c. green 2·25 1·10
447 89 10c. grey 2·75 1·40
DESIGN: 5c. Heredia and palms.

90 General Moncada and Sword **91** Moncada riding into Battle

1941. Birth Centenary of H. Moncada.
448 **90** 3c. brown . . . . 1·00 50
449 **91** 5c. blue . . . . 1·00 50

92 Mother and Child **95** "Labour, Wealth of America"

1941. Obligatory Tax. Anti-T.B.
450 **92** 1c. brown 20 10

1942. American Democracy. Imperf or perf.
451 – 1c. green 25 10
452 – 3c. brown 35 15
453 **95** 5c. blue 55 20
454 – 10c. mauve . . . . 1·40 65
455 – 13c. red . . . . 2·00 85
DESIGNS: 1c. Western Hemisphere; 3c. Cuban Arms and portraits of Maceo, Bolivar, Juarez and Lincoln; 10c. Tree of Fraternity, Havana; 13c. Statue of Liberty.

98 Gen. Ignacio Agramonte Loynaz **99** Rescue of Sanguily

1942. Birth Centenary of Gen. I. A. Loynaz.
456 **98** 3c. brown 75 40
457 **99** 5c. blue . . . . 1·50 55

100 "Victory" **102** "Unmask Fifth Columnists"

1942. Obligatory Tax. Red Cross Fund.
458 **100** ½c. orange 20 10
459 ½c. grey 20 10

1942. Obligatory Tax. Anti-T.B. Fund. Optd **1942.**
460 **92** 1c. red 30 10

1943. Anti-Fifth Column.
461 **102** 1c. green 25 15
462 – 3c. red 45 15
463 – 5c. blue 45 20
464 – 10c. brown . . . . 1·75 70
465 – 13c. purple . . . . 2·25 1·10
DESIGNS—HORIZ: (45 × 25 mm.) 5c. Woman in snake's coils ("The Fifth Column is like the Serpent — destroy it"); 10c. Men demolishing column with battering-ram ("Fulfil your patriotic duty by destroying the Fifth Column"). As Type **102**. 13c. Woman with monster "Don't be afraid of the Fifth Column. Attack it". VERT: Girl with finger to lips "Be Careful! The Fifth Column is spying on you".

105 Eloy Alfaro, Flags of Ecuador and Cuba and Scroll of Independence

1943. Birth Centenary of E. Alfaro (former President of Ecuador).
466 **105** 3c. green . . . . 1·25 55

106 "The Long Road to Retirement" **107** "Health" Protecting Child

1943. Postal Employees' Retirement Fund.
467 **106** 1c. green 65 35
470 3c. red 55 35
471 5c. blue 90 35

1943. Obligatory Tax. Anti-tuberculosis.
473 **107** 1c. brown 20 10

108 Columbus **109** Discovery of Tobacco

1944. 450th Anniv of Discovery of America.
474 **108** 1c. green (postage) . . . 20 15
475 – 3c. brown 30 15
476 – 5c. blue 40 20
477 **109** 10c. violet . . . . 2·25 65
478 – 13c. red . . . . 6·50 1·25
479 – 5c. olive (air) . . . . . . 1·50 35
480 – 10c. grey . . . . 1·75 65
DESIGNS—VERT: 3c. Bartolome de las Casas; 5c. (No. 476), Statue of Columbus. HORIZ: 5c. (No. 479) Mountains of Gibara; 10c. (No. 480), Columbus Lighthouse; 13c. Columbus at Pinar del Rio.

110 Carlos Roloff **111** American Continents and Brazilian "Bull's Eyes" stamps

1944. Birth Centenary of Major-Gen. Roloff.
481 **110** 3c. violet 95 30

1944. Cent of 1st American Postage stamps.
482 **111** 3c. brown . . . . 1·75 55

112 Society Seal **113** Governor Las Casas and Bishop Penalver

1945. 150th Anniv of Economic Society of Friends of Havana.
483 **112** 1c. green 35 15
484 **113** 2c. red 65 30

115 Old Age Pensioners

1945. Postal Employees' Retirement Fund.
485 **115** 1c. green 20 10
487 2c. red 40 15
489 5c. blue 75 30

116 Valdes

1946. Death Centenary of Gabriel de la Concepcion Valdes (poet).
491 **116** 2c. red 85 45

117 Manuel Marquez Sterling **118** Red Cross and Globe

1946. Founding of "Manuel Marquez Sterling" Professional School of Journalism.
492 **117** 2c. red 85 45

1946. 80th Anniv of International Red Cross.
493 **118** 2c. red 90 45

119 Prize Cattle and Dairymaid **120** Franklin D. Roosevelt

1947. National Cattle Show.
494 **119** 2c. red . . . . 1·10 35

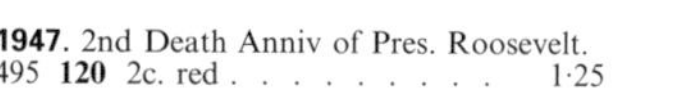

1947. 2nd Death Anniv of Pres. Roosevelt.
495 **120** 2c. red . . . . 1·25 35

121 Antonio Oms and Pensioners

1947. Postal Employees' Retirement Fund.
496 **121** 1c. green 15 15
497 2c. red 25 15
498 5c. blue 75 30

122 Marta Abreu

1947. Birth Centenary of M. Abreu (philanthropist).
499 **122** 1c. green 30 15
500 – 2c. red 45 20
501 – 5c. blue 65 30
502 – 10c. violet . . . . 1·40 65
DESIGNS: 2c. Allegory of Charity; 5c. Monument; 10c. Allegory of Patriotism.

123 Dr. G. A. Hansen and Isle of Pines

1948. Int Leprosy Relief Congress, Havana.
503 **123** 2c. red 90 40

124 Council of War

1948. Air. 50th Anniv of War of Independence.
504 **124** 8c. black and yellow . . . 1·90 85

125 Woman and Child **126** Death of Marti

1948. Postal Employees' Retirement Fund.
506 **125** 1c. green 30 15
507 2c. red 30 15
508 5c. blue 75 30

1948. 50th Death Anniv of Jose Marti.
509 **126** 2c. red 35 20
510 – 5c. blue . . . . 1·10 35
DESIGN: 5c. Marti disembarking at Playitas.

127 Gathering Tobacco **129** Antonio Maceo

1948. Havana Tobacco Industry.
511 **127** 1c. green 15 10
512 – 2c. red 20 10
513 – 5c. blue 35 15
DESIGNS: 2c. Girl with box of cigars and flag; 5c. Cigar and shield.

This set comes again redrawn with smaller designs of 21 × 25 mm.

1948. Birth Centenary of Gen. Maceo.
514 – 1c. green 10 10
515 **129** 2c. red 15 10
516 – 5c. blue 25 15
517 – 8c. brown and black . . . 35 30
518 – 10c. green and brown . . 45 20
519 – 20c. blue and red . . . . 1·75 75
520 – 50c. blue and red . . . . 3·00 2·00
521 – 1p. violet and black . . . 6·00 2·75
DESIGNS—VERT: 1c. Equestrian statue of Maceo; 5c. Mausoleum at El Cacahual. HORIZ: 8c. Maceo and raised swords; 10c. Maceo leading charge; 20c. Maceo at Peralejo; 50c. Declaration at Baragua; 1p. Death of Maceo at San Pedro.

131 Symbol of Medicine **132** Morro Castle and Lighthouse

1948. 1st Pan-American Pharmaceutical Congress.
522 **131** 2c. red 95 40

1949. Centenary of El Morro Lighthouse.
523 **132** 2c. red . . . . 1·25 50

133 Jagua Castle

1949. Centenary of Newspaper "Hoja Economica" and Bicentenary of Jagua Fortress.
524 **133** 1c. green 40 20
525 2c. red 65 35

134 M. Sanguily **135** Isle of Pines

1949. Birth Centenary of Manuel Sanguily y Garritte (poet).
526 **134** 2c. red 35 20
527 5c. blue 90 35

1949. 20th Anniv of Return of Isle of Pines to Cuba.
528 **135** 5c. blue 95 35

136 Ismael Cespedes **137** Woman and Child

1949. Postal Employees' Retirement Fund.
529 **136** 1c. green 25 15
530 2c. red 25 15
531 5c. blue 75 30

1949. Obligatory Tax. Anti-tuberculosis.
532 **137** 1c. blue 25 10
547 1c. red 25 10
No. 547 is dated "1950".

138 Enrique Collazo **139** E. J. Varona

1950. Birth Centenary of Gen. Collazo.
533 **138** 2c. red 30 15
534 5c. blue 90 35

1950. Birth Centenary of Varona (writer).
535 **139** 2c. red 35 20
536 5c. blue 90 35

1950. National Bank Opening. No. 512 optd **BANCO NACIONAL DE CUBA INAUGURACION 27 ABRIL 1950.**
540 2c. red 90 35

1950. 75th Anniv of U.P.U. Optd **U.P.U. 1874 1949.**
541 **127** 1c. green 35 15
542 – 2c. pink (As No. 512) . . 40 25
543 – 5c. blue (As No. 513) . . 95 35

142 Balanzategui, Pausa and Railway Crash **143** F. Figueredo

1950. Postal Employees' Retirement Fund.
544 **142** 1c. green . . . . 2·50 1·10
545 2c. red . . . . 2·50 1·10
546 5c. blue . . . . 7·00 2·25

1951. Postal Employees' Retirement Fund.
548 **143** 1c. green 55 20
549 2c. red 55 20
550 5c. blue 90 35

144 Foundation Stone **145** Narciso Lopez

1951. Obligatory Tax. P.O. Rebuilding Fund.
551 **144** 1c. violet 25 10

1951. Centenary of Cuban Flag.
552 – 1c. red, bl & grn (postage) 30 15
553 **145** 2c. black and red 50 25
554 – 5c. red and blue . . . . 1·10 50
555 – 10c. red, blue and violet 2·00 70
556 – 5c. red, blue & olive (air) 1·40 45
557 – 8c. red, blue and brown 1·75 65
558 – 25c. red, blue and black 2·25 1·10
DESIGNS—VERT: 1c. Miguel Teurbe Tolon; 5c. (No. 554) Emilia Teurbe Tolon; 8c. Raising the flag; 10c. Flag; 25c. Flag and El Morro lighthouse. HORIZ: 5c. (No. 556) Lopez landing at Cardenas.

147 Clara Maass, Newark Memorial and Las Animas, Havana, Hospitals

1951. 50th Death Anniv of Clara Maass (nurse).
559 **147** 2c. red . . . . 1·00 40

148 Capablanca (after E. Valderrama) **149** Chessboard showing end of Capablanca v. Lasker

1951. 30th Anniv of Jose Capablanca's Victory in World Chess Championship.
562 **148** 1c. orge & grn (postage) . . . . . . 1·75 45
563 – 2c. brown and red . . . 2·25 85
564 E **150** 5c. blue and black . . . 5·50 1·75
565 **149** 5c. yellow & green (air) 2·75 85
566 – 8c. purple and blue . . 4·00 1·10
567 **148** 25c. sepia & brown . . 7·00 1·90
DESIGN—VERT: 2c., 8c. Capablanca playing chess.

151 Dr. A. Guiteras Holmes **152** Morrillo Fortress

1951. 16th Death Anniv of Dr. A. Guiteras Holmes in skirmish at Morrillo.
568 **151** 1c. green (postage) . . . 45 15
569 – 2c. red 65 30
570 **152** 5c. blue . . . . 1·40 50
571 **151** 5c. mauve (air) . . . . . 1·60 1·10
572 – 8c. green . . . . 2·25 1·60
573 **152** 25c. black . . . . 4·00 2·75
DESIGN—HORIZ: 2c., 8c. Guiteras framing social laws.

153 Mother and Child **154** Christmas Emblems

1951. Obligatory Tax. Anti-tuberculosis.
575 **153** 1c. brown 20 10
576 1c. red 20 10
577 1c. green 20 10
578 1c. blue 20 10

1951. Christmas Greetings.
579 **154** 1c. red and green . . . . 2·00 55
580 2c. green and red . . . . 2·50 65

155 Jose Maceo **156** General Post Office **157** Isabella the Catholic

1952. Birth Centenary of Gen. Maceo.
581 **155** 2c. brown 50 15
582 5c. blue 90 35

1952. Obligatory Tax. P.O. Rebuilding Fund.
583 **156** 1c. blue 20 10
584 1c. red 55 15

1952. 5th Birth Centenary of Isabella the Catholic.
585 **157** 2c. red (postage) . . . . 3·00 75
586 25c. purple (air) . . . . . 5·25 1·25

1952. As No. 549 surch with new value. (a) Postage.
588 **143** 10c. on 2c. brown . . . . 1·25 40

(b) Air. Optd **AEREO** in addition.
589 **143** 5c. on 2c. brown 45 20
590 8c. on 2c. brown 65 20
591 10c. on 2c. brown . . . . 1·10 20
592 25c. on 2c. brown . . . . 1·10 45
593 50c. on 2c. brown . . . . 3·75 1·40
594 1p. on 2c. brown . . . . 5·50 2·75

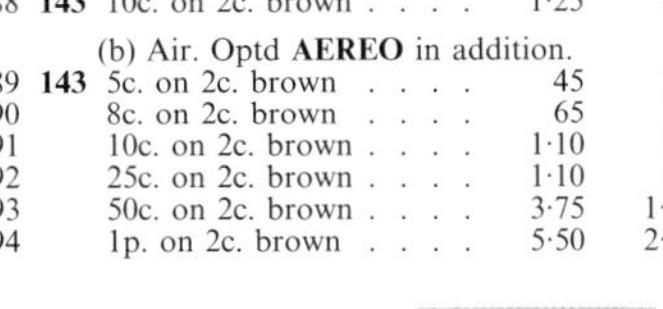

159 Proclamation of Republic **160** Statue, Havana University

1952. 50th Anniv of Republic.
595 **159** 1c. black & grn (postage) 20 15
596 – 2c. black and red 30 15
597 – 5c. black and blue 40 15
598 – 8c. black and brown . . . 55 15
599 – 20c. black and olive . . . 1·40 50
600 – 50c. black and orange . . 2·75 90
601 – 5c. green & violet (air) 55 25
602 **160** 8c. green and red 55 35
603 – 10c. green and blue . . . 1·40 55
604 – 25c. green and purple . . 1·75 85
DESIGNS—HORIZ:—POSTAGE: 2c. Estrada Palma and Estevez Romero; 5c. Barnet, Finlay, Guiteras and Nunez; 8c. The Capitol; 20c. Map showing central highway; 50c. Sugar factory. AIR: 5c. Rural school; 10c. Presidential Palace; 25c. Banknote.

162 Seaplane and Route of Flight **164** Coffee Beans

1952. Air. 39th Anniv of Florida–Cuba flight by A. Parla.
605 **162** 8c. black . . . . 1·25 30
606 – 25c. blue . . . . 2·75 85
DESIGN—HORIZ: 25c. Agustin Parla Orduna and Curtiss A-1 seaplane.

1952. Bicentenary of Coffee Cultivation.
608 **164** 1c. green 35 15
609 – 2c. red 55 30
610 – 5c. green and blue 95 35
DESIGNS: 2c. Plantation worker and map; 5c. Coffee plantation.

165 Col. C. Hernandez

1952. Postal Employees' Retirement Fund.
611 **165** 1c. green (postage) . . . 20 15
612 2c. red 40 15
613 5c. blue 40 15
614 8c. black . . . . 1·00 35
615 10c. red . . . . 1·10 40
616 20c. brown . . . . 4·00 2·75
617 5c. orange (air) 25 10
618 8c. green 45 10
619 10c. brown 50 15
620 15c. green 55 20
621 20c. turquoise 55 30
622 25c. red 85 40
623 30c. violet . . . . 1·75 40
624 45c. mauve . . . . 1·90 1·40
625 50c. blue . . . . 1·60 85
626 1p. yellow . . . . 5·00 2·50

166 A. A. De La Campa **167** Statue, Havana University

168 Dominguez, Estebanez and Capdevila (defence lawyers)

1952. 81st Anniv of Execution of Eight Rebel Medical Students.
627 **166** 1c. black & grn (postage) 15 10
628 – 2c. black and red 30 15
629 – 3c. black and violet . . . 35 15
630 – 5c. black and blue 35 15
631 – 8c. black and sepia . . . 65 35
632 – 10c. black and brown . . 75 30
633 – 13c. black and purple . . 1·90 45
634 – 20c. black and olive . . . 2·25 65
635 **167** 5c. blue and indigo (air) 85 35
636 **168** 25c. green and orange . . 2·25 80
PORTRAITS: 2c. C. A. de la Torre. 3c. A. Bermudez. 5c. E. G. Toledo. 8c. A. Laborde. 10c. J. De M. Medina. 13c. P. Rodriguez. 20c. C. Verdugo.

169 Child's Face **170** Christmas Tree

1952. Obligatory Tax. Anti- tuberculosis.
637 **169** 1c. orange 25 10
638 1c. red 25 10
639 1c. green 25 10
640 1c. blue 25 10

1952. Christmas.
641 **170** 1c. red and green . . . . 2·75 1·75
642 3c. green and violet . . . 2·75 1·75

171 Marti's Birthplace **172** Dr. Rafael Montoro

1953. Birth Centenary of Jose Marti.
643 **171** 1c. brn & grn (postage) 15 10
644 – 1c. brown and green . . . 15 10
645 – 3c. brown and violet . . . 25 15
646 – 3c. brown and violet . . . 25 15
647 – 5c. brown and blue . . . 35 15
648 – 5c. brown and blue . . . 35 15
649 – 10c. black and brown . . 90 30
650 – 10c. black and brown . . 75 30
651 – 13c. brown and green . . 1·60 55
652 – 13c. brown and green . . 1·60 55
653 – 5c. black & red (air) . . . 25 15
654 – 5c. black and red 25 15
655 – 8c. black and green . . . 30 15
656 – 8c. black and green . . . 30 15
657 – 10c. red and blue 40 15
658 – 10c. blue and red 40 15
659 – 15c. black and violet . . . 50 25
660 – 15c. black and violet . . . 50 25
661 – 25c. red and brown . . . 1·75 60
662 – 25c. red and brown . . . 1·75 60
663 – 50c. blue and yellow . . . 2·75 1·00
DESIGNS—HORIZ: No. 644, Marti before Council of War; No. 645, Prison wall; No. 647, "El Abra" ranch; No. 652, First edition of "Patria"; No. 656, House of Maximo Gomez, Montecristi; No. 658, Marti as an orator; No. 663, "Fragua Martiana" (modern building). VERT: No. 646, Marti in prison; No. 648, Allegory of Marti's poems; No. 649, Marti and Bolivar Statue, Caracas; No. 650, Marti writing; No. 651, Revolutionaries' meeting-place; No. 653, Marti in Kingston, Jamaica; No. 654, Marti in Ibor City; No. 655, Manifesto of Montecristi; No. 657, Marti's portrait; No. 659, Marti's first tomb; No. 660, Obelisk at Des Rios; No. 661, Monument in Havana; No. 662, Marti's present tomb.

1953. Birth Centenary of Montoro (statesman).
664 **172** 3c. purple . . . . 1·00 45

173 Dr. F. Carrera Justiz **174** Lockheed Constellation

1953.
665 **173** 3c. red . . . . 1·00 45

1953. Air.
666 **174** 8c. brown 55 25
667 15c. red . . . . 1·10 60
668 – 2p. brown and green . . . 11·00 4·50
670 – 2p. myrtle and blue . . . 11·00 4·50
669 – 5p. brown and blue . . . 22·00 7·50
671 – 5p. myrtle and red . . . 19·00 9·50
DESIGN: Nos. 668/71, Constellation facing right.

1953. No. 512 surch.
672 3c. on 2c. red 55 30

176 Congress Building **177**

1953. 1st Int Accountancy Congress, Havana.
673 **176** 3c. blue (postage) 70 35
674 – 8c. red (air) . . . . . . 1·60 55
675 – 25c. green . . . . 2·50 85
DESIGNS: 8c. Congress building and "Cuba"; 25c. Aerial view of building and airplane.

1953. Obligatory Tax. Anti-T.B.
676 **177** 1c. red 20 10

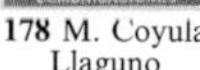

178 M. Coyula Llaguno　**179** Postal Employees' Retirement Association Flag

1954. Postal Employees' Retirement Fund. Inscr "1953".
677 **178** 1c. green (postage) 30 10
678 – 3c. red 30 10
679 **179** 5c. blue 55 15
680 – 8c. red 1·10 45
681 – 10c. sepia 2·25 65

682 – 5c. blue (air) 55 25
683 – 8c. purple 65 25
684 – 10c. orange 1·00 25
685 **179** 1p. grey 3·50 2·00
PORTRAITS—VERT: Nos. 678, 680, F.L.C. Hensell; Nos. 681, 683, A. G. Rojas; No. 684, G. H. Saez. HORIZ: No. 682, M. C. Llaguno.

180 Jose Marti　**181** Hauling Sugar

1954. Portraits. Roul. (No. 1180a/b) or perf. (others).
686 **180** 1c. green 15 10
990 1c. red 35 15
1680 1c. blue 10 10
687 – 2c. red (Gomez) 10 10
991 – 2c. olive (Gomez) 45 15
1681 – 2c. green (Gomez) 15 10
688 – 3c. violet (de la Luz Caballero) 10 10
1180a – 3c. orange (Caballero) 25 15
689 – 4c. mauve (Aldama) 10 10
690 – 5c. blue (Garcia) 15 10
691 – 8c. lake (Agramonte) 15 10
692 – 10c. sepia (Palma) 20 10
693 – 13c. red (Finlay) 30 10
1180b – 13c. brown (Finlay) 95 25
694 – 14c. grey (Sanchez) 55 15
695 – 20c. olive (Saco) 1·40 35
1682 – 20c. violet (Saco) 1·40 20
696 – 50c. ochre (Maceo) 2·00 40
697 – 1p. orange (Cespedes) 3·00 40

1954. Air. Sugar Industry.
698 – 5c. green 35 10
699 – 8c. brown 85 35
700 **181** 10c. green 85 35
701 – 15c. brown 1·75 50
702 – 20c. blue 80 10
703 – 25c. red 65 30
704a – 30c. purple 1·90 75
705 – 40c. blue 3·25 65
706 – 45c. violet 3·00 65
707 – 50c. blue 3·00 65
708 – 1p. blue 7·25 1·25
DESIGNS—VERT: 5c. Sugar cane; 1p. A. Reinoso. HORIZ: 8c. Sugar harvesting; 15c. Train load of sugar cane; 20c. Modern sugar factory; 25c. Evaporators; 30c. Stacking sugar in sacks; 40c. Loading sugar on ship; 45c. Oxen hauling cane; 50c. Primitive sugar factory.

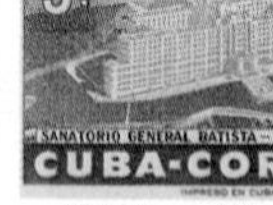

182 Jose M. Rodriguez　**183** View of Sanatorium

1954. Birth Centenary of Rodriguez.
709 **182** 2c. sepia and lake 45 25
710 – 5c. sepia and blue 90 45
DESIGN: 5c. Rodriguez on horseback.

1954. General Batista Sanatorium.
711 **183** 3c. blue (postage) 90 40
712 9c. green (air) 1·75 65

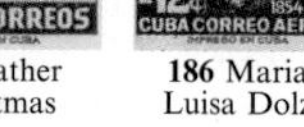

184　**185** Father Christmas　**186** Maria Luisa Dolz

1954. Obligatory Tax. Anti-T.B.
713 **184** 1c. red 20 10
714 1c. green 20 10
715 1c. blue 20 10
716 1c. violet 20 10

1954. Christmas Greetings.
717 **185** 2c. green and red 3·00 1·40
718 4c. red and green 3·00 1·40

1954. Birth Centenary of Maria Dolz (educationist).
719 **186** 4c. blue (postage) 95 35
720 12c. mauve (air) 1·75 75

187 Boy Scouts and Cuban Flag　**189** Major-Gen. F. Carrillo

188 P. P. Harris and Rotary Emblem

1954. 3rd National Scout Camp.
721 **187** 4c. green 95 40

1955. 50th Anniv of Rotary International.
722 **188** 4c. blue (postage) 95 55
723 12c. red (air) 1·75 65

1955. Birth Centenary of Carrillo.
724 **189** 2c. blue and red 45 20
725 – 5c. sepia and blue 75 35
DESIGN: 5c. Half-length portrait.

190 1855 Stamp and "La Volanta"

1955. Centenary of First Cuban Postage Stamps and 50th Anniv of First Republican Stamps.
726 – 2c. blue & pur (postage) 35 10
727 **190** 4c. green and buff 55 35
728 – 10c. red and blue 3·50 65
729 – 14c. orange and green 3·25 1·40

730 – 8c. green & blue (air) 55 20
731 – 12c. red and green 65 20
732 – 24c. blue and red 2·25 55
733 – 30c. brown & orange 1·75 85
DESIGNS (a) With 1855 stamp: 2c. Old Square and Convent of St. Francis; 10c. Havana in 19th century; 14c. Captain-General's residence and Plaza de Armas; (b) With 1855 and 1905 stamps: 8c. Palace of Fine Arts; 12c. Plaza de la Fraternidad; 24c. Aerial view of Havana; 30c. Plaza de la Republica.

191 Maj.-Gen. Menocal　**192** Mariel Bay

1955. Postal Employees' Retirement Fund.
734 **191** 2c. green (postage) 45 10
735 – 4c. mauve 55 25
736 – 10c. blue 95 35
737 – 14c. grey 2·25 85

738 **192** 8c. green and red (air) 55 25
739 – 12c. blue and brown 1·10 55
740 – 1p. ochre and green 3·00 1·75
DESIGNS—As Type **191**: HORIZ: 4c. Gen. E. Nunez; 14c. Dr. A. de Bustamante. VERT: 10c. J. Gomez. As Type **192**: HORIZ: 12c. Varadero Beach; 1p. Vinales Valley.

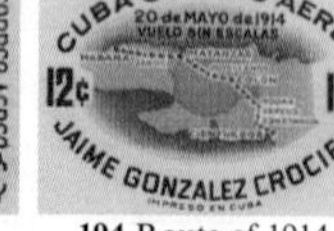

193 Cuban Academy　**194** Route of 1914 Flight

1955. Air. Centenary of Tampa, Florida.
741 **193** 12c. brown and red 1·60 65

1955. Air. 35th Death Anniv of Crocier (aviator).
742 **194** 12c. green and red 85 35
743 – 30c. mauve and green 1·60 65
DESIGN: 30c. Crocier in aircraft cockpit.

195　**196** Wright Flyer 1

1955. Obligatory Tax. Anti-T.B.
744 **195** 1c. orange 30 15
745 1c. yellow 30 15
746 1c. blue 30 15
747 1c. mauve 30 15

1955. Air. Int Philatelic Exhibition, Havana.
748 **196** 8c. black, red and blue 1·25 55
749 – 12c. black, green and red 1·40 55
750 – 24c. black, violet & red 1·60 85
751 – 30c. black, blue & orange 3·50 1·90
752 – 50c. black olive & orange 5·50 2·25
DESIGNS: 12c. Lindbergh's airplane "Spirit of St. Louis"; 24c. Airship "Graf Zeppelin"; 30c. Lockheed Super Constellation airplane; 50c. Convair Delta Dagger airplane.

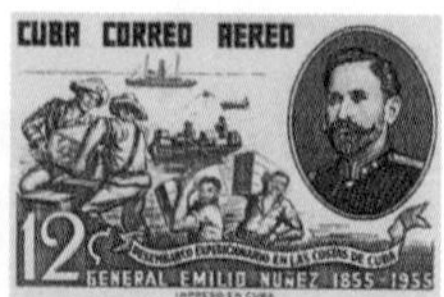

197 Wild Turkey　**198** Expedition Disembarking

1955. Christmas Greetings.
754 **197** 2c. green and red 3·00 1·40
755 4c. lake and green 3·00 1·40

1955. Birth Centenary of General Nunez.
756 – 4c. lake (postage) 90 35
757 – 8c. blue and red (air) 1·75 45
758 **198** 12c. green and brown 1·75 65
DESIGNS—VERT: ($22\frac{1}{2} \times 32\frac{1}{2}$ mm.): 4c. Portrait of Nunez. HORIZ: As Type **198**: 8c. "Three Friends" (tug).

199 Bishop P. A. Morell de Santa Cruz　**200** J. del Casal

1956. Bicentenary of Cuban Postal Service.
759 – 4c. blue & brn (postage) 90 40
760 **199** 12c. green & brown (air) 1·60 40
PORTRAIT: 4c. F. C. de la Vega.

1956. Postal Employees' Retirement Fund.
761 **200** 2c. black & grn (postage) 20 15
762 – 4c. black and mauve 55 20
763 – 10c. black and blue 90 35
764 – 14c. black and violet 1·90 75
765 – 8c. black & brown (air) 55 30
766 – 12c. black and ochre 85 35
767 – 30c. black and blue 1·60 55
PORTRAITS: 4c. Luisa Perez de Zambrana. 8c. Gen. J. Sanguily. 10c. J. Clemente Zenea. 12c. Gen. J. M. Aguirre. 14c. J. J. Palma. 30c. Col. E. Fonts Sterling.

201 Victor Munoz　**202** Mother and Baby

1956. Munoz Commemoration.
768 **201** 4c. brown and green 90 40

1956. Air. Mothers' Day.
769 **202** 12c. blue and red 1·75 40

203 Aerial View of Temple　**204** Gundlach's Hawk

1956. Masonic Grand Lodge of Cuba Temple, Havana.
770 – 4c. blue (postage) 95 40
771 **203** 12c. green (air) 1·75 45
DESIGN: 4c. Ground level view of Temple.

1956. Air. Birds.
772 – 8c. blue 1·40 25
773 – 12c. grey 9·00 25
783 – 12c. green 3·25 70
774 **204** 14c. olive 2·10 30
775 – 19c. brown 2·10 60
776 – 24c. mauve 2·10 70
777 – 29c. green 3·00 70
778 – 30c. brown 3·25 1·00
779 – 50c. slate 6·00 1·25
780 – 1p. red 13·00 2·75
784 – 1p. blue 6·50 5·25
781 – 2p. purple 22·00 5·00
785 – 2p. red 19·00 13·00
782 – 5p. red 55·00 9·50
786 – 5p. purple 42·00 32·00
DESIGNS—HORIZ: 8c. Wood duck; 12c. (2) Plain pigeon; 29c. Goosander; 30c. Northern bobwhite; 2p. (2) Northern jacana. VERT: 19c. Herring gull; 24c. American white pelican; 50c. Great blue heron; 1p. (2) Common caracara; 5p. (2) Ivory-billed woodpecker.

205 H. de Blanck　**207** Church of Our Lady of Charity

1956. Air. Birth Centenary of H. De Blanck (composer).
787 **205** 12c. blue 1·60 45

1956. Air. Inaug of Philatelic Club of Cuba Building. No. 776 but colour changed and surch **Inauguracion Edificio Club Filatelico de la Republica de Cuba Julio 13 de 1956** and value.
788 – 8c. on 24c. orange 1·75 80

1956. Inscr "NTRA. SRA. DE LA CARIDAD", etc.
789 – 4c. blue & yell (postage) 95 40
790 **207** 12c. green & red (air) 1·90 55
DESIGN: 4c. Our Lady of Charity over landscape.

208　**209**

1956. Air. 250th Birth Anniv of Benjamin Franklin.
792 **208** 12c. brown 1·75 40

1956. "Grito de Yara" (War of Independence). Commem.
793 **209** 4c. sepia and green 95 35

(210)　**211**

1956. Air. 12th Inter-American Press Assn. Meeting. As No. 781 but colour changed and surch with T **210**.
794 – 12c. on 2p. grey 1·75 80

1956. Obligatory Tax. Anti-T.B.
795 **211** 1c. red 20 10
796 1c. green 20 10
797 1c. blue 20 10
798 1c. brown 20 10

212　**213** Prof. R. G. Menocal

1956. Christmas Greetings.
799 **212** 2c. red and green 3·00 1·40
800 4c. green and red 3·00 1·40

1956. Birth Centenary of Prof. R. G. Menocal.
801 **213** 4c. brown 90 35

214a Martin M. Delgado

215 Scouts around Camp Fire

1957. Birth Centenary of Delgado (patriot).

802	**214a**	4c. green	90	40

1957. Birth Centenary of Lord Baden-Powell.

803	**215**	4c. green & red (postage)	1·10	45
804	–	12c. slate (air)	1·75	85

DESIGN—VERT: 12c. Lord Baden-Powell.

216 "The Art Critics" (Melero)

217 Hanabanilla Falls

1957. Postal Employees' Retirement Fund.

805	–	2c. green & brn (postage)	35	15
806	**216**	4c. red and brown	65	25
807	–	10c. olive and brown	95	35
808	–	14c. blue and brown	1·10	40
809	**217**	8c. blue and red (air)	40	15
810	–	12c. green and red	1·60	30
811	–	30c. olive and violet	1·75	50

DESIGNS—HORIZ: As Type **216** (Paintings): 2c. "The Blind" (Vega); 10c. "Carriage in the Storm" (Menocal); 14c. "The Convalescent" (Romanach); As Type **217**: 12c. Sierra de Cubitas; 30c. Puerto Boniato.

218 Posthorn Emblem of Cuban Philatelic Society

219 Juan F. Steegers

1957. Stamp Day. Cuban Philatelic Exn.

812	**218**	4c. bl, brn & red (postage)	90	35
813	–	12c. brn, yell & grn (air)	1·40	50

DESIGN: 12c. Philatelic Society Building, Havana.

1957. Birth Centenary of Steegers (fingerprint pioneer).

814	**219**	4c. blue (postage)	90	35
815	–	12c. brown (air)	1·40	45

DESIGN: 12c. Thumbprint.

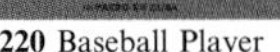
220 Baseball Player

221 Nurse Victoria Bru Sanchez

1957. Air. Youth Recreation. Centres in brown.

816	**220**	8c. green on green	85	30
817	–	12c. lilac on lavender	1·10	55
818	–	24c. blue on blue	1·75	85
819	–	30c. flesh on orange	2·25	1·40

DESIGNS—12c. Ballet dancer; 24c. Diver; 30c. Boxers.

1957. Nurse Victoria Bru Sanchez Commem.

820	**221**	4c. blue	90	35

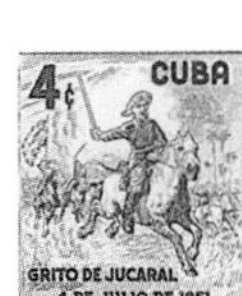
222 J. de Aguero leading Patriots

223 Youth with Dogs and Cat

1957. Joaquin de Aguero (patriot) Commem.

821	**222**	4c. green (postage)	90	35
822	–	12c. blue (portrait) (air)	1·40	50

1957. 50th Anniv of Band of Charity (for prevention of cruelty to animals).

823	**223**	4c. green (postage)	90	55
824	–	12c. brown (air)	1·40	40

DESIGN: 12c. Jeanette Ryder (founder).

224 Col. R. Manduley del Rio (patriot)

225 J. M. Heredia y Girard

1957. Col. R. Manduley del Rio. Commem.

825	**224**	4c. green	2·25	1·40

1957. Air. J. M. Heredia y Girard (poet). Commem.

826	**225**	8c. violet	95	35

226 Palace of Justice, Havana

1957. Inauguration of Palace of Justice.

827	**226**	4c. grey (postage)	90	35
828		12c. green (air)	1·40	40

227 Army Leaders of 1856

228 J. R. Gregg

1957. Centenary of Cuban Army of Liberation.

829	**227**	4c. brown and green	65	35
830		4c. brown and blue	65	35
831		4c. brown and pink	65	35
832		4c. brown and yellow	65	35
833		4c. brown and lilac	65	35

1957. Air. J. R. Gregg (shorthand pioneer) Commem.

834	**228**	12c. green	1·40	40

229 Cuba's First Publication, 1723

230 Jose Marti Public Library

1957. "Jose Marti" Public Library. Inscr "BIBLIOTECA NACIONAL".

835	**229**	4c. slate (postage)	90	35
836	–	8c. blue (air)	40	20
837	**230**	12c. sepia	1·25	40

DESIGN—VERT: As Type **230**: 8c. D. F. Caneda, first Director.

231 U.N. Emblem and Map of Cuba

1957. Air. U.N. Day.

838	**231**	8c. brown and green	65	30
839		12c. green and red	1·25	35
840		30c. mauve and blue	2·50	80

232 Fokker Trimotor "General New" and Map

1957. Air. 30th Anniv of Inaug of Air Mail Services between Havana and Key West, Florida.

841	**232**	12c. blue and purple	1·75	45

233

235 Courtyard

1957. Obligatory Tax. Anti-tuberculosis.

842	**233**	1c. red	30	10
843		1c. green	30	10
844		1c. blue	30	10
845		1c. grey	30	10

1957. Centenary of 1st Cuban Teachers' Training College.

846	**235**	4c. brn & grn (postage)	90	35
847	–	12c. buff and blue (air)	95	35
848	–	30c. sepia and red	1·60	45

DESIGNS—VERT: 12c. School facade. HORIZ: 30c. General view of school.

236 Street Scene, Trinidad

237 Christmas Crib

1957. Postal Employees' Retirement Fund.

849	**236**	2c. brown & bl (postage)	20	10
850	–	4c. green and brown	45	15
851	–	10c. sepia and red	70	30
852	–	14c. green and red	1·10	25
853	–	8c. black and red (air)	45	20
854	–	12c. black and brown	95	35
855	–	30c. brown and grey	1·75	45

DESIGNS—VERT: 4c. Sentry-box on old wall of Havana; 10c. Calle Padre Pico (street), Santiago de Cuba; 12c. Sancti Spiritus Church; 14c. Church and street scene, Camaguey. HORIZ: 8c. "El Viso" Fort, El Caney; 30c. Concordia Bridge, Matanzas.

1957. Christmas. Multicoloured centres.

856	**237**	2c. sepia	2·25	1·10
857		4c. black	2·25	1·10

239 Dayton Hedges and Textile Factories

240 Dr. F. D. Roldan

1958. Dayton Hedges (founder of Cuban Textile Industry) Commemoration.

858	**239**	4c. blue (postage)	1·40	65
859		8c. green (air)	1·40	65

1958. Dr. Francisco D. Roldan (physiotherapy pioneer) Commemoration.

861	**240**	4c. green	95	35

241 "Diario de la Marina" Building

1958. 125th Anniv of "Diario de la Marina" Newspaper.

862	–	4c. olive (postage)	95	35
863	**241**	29c. black (air)	1·75	85

PORTRAIT—VERT: 4c. J. I. Rivero y Alonso (journalist).

242 Map of Cuba showing Postal Routes of 1756

243 Gen. J. M. Gomez

1958. Stamp Day and National Philatelic Exhibition, Havana. Inscr as in T **242**.

864	**242**	4c. myrtle, buff and blue (postage)	95	40
865	–	29c. indigo, buff and blue (air)	1·90	85

DESIGN: 29c. Ocean map showing sea-post routes of 1765.

1958. Birth Centenary of Gen. J. M. Gomez.

866	**243**	4c. blue (postage)	90	35
867	–	12c. myrtle (air)	1·25	50

DESIGN: 12c. Gomez at Arroyo Blanco.

244 Dr. T. Romay Chacon

245 Dr. C. de la Torre

246 Painted Polymita

1958. Famous Cubans. Portraits as T **244**.

(a) Doctors. With emblem of medicine.

868	2c. brown and green	45	15
869	4c. black and green	45	15
870	10c. red and green	45	15
871	14c. blue and green	65	15

(b) Lawyers. With emblem of law.

872	2c. sepia and red	50	15
873	4c. black and red	50	15
874	10c. green and red	50	15
875	14c. blue and red	55	20

(c) Composers. With lyre emblem of music.

876	2c. brown and blue	40	15
877	4c. purple and blue	40	15
878	10c. green and blue	55	15
879	14c. red and blue	60	15

PORTRAITS—Doctors: 2c. Type **244**. 4c. A. A. Aballi. 10c. F. G. del Valle. 14c. V. A. de Castro. Lawyers: 2c. J. M. G. Montes. 4c. J. A. G. Lanuza. 10c. J. B. H. Barreiro. 14c. P. G. Llorente. Composers: 2c. N. R. Espadero. 4c. I. Cervantes. 10c. J. White. 14c. B. de Salas.

1958. Birth Cent of De la Torre (archaeologist).

880	**245**	4c. blue (postage)	95	35
881	**246**	8c. red, yellow & blk (air)	2·25	85
882	–	12c. sepia on green	3·25	1·40
883	–	30c. green on pink	5·00	2·00

DESIGNS—As Type **246**: 12c. "Megalocnus rodens"; 30c. "Perisphinctes spinatus" (ammonite).

247 Felipe Poey (naturalist)

248 "Papilio caiguanabus" (butterfly)

1958. Poey Commemoration. Designs as T **247/8** inscr "1799–FELIPE POEY–1891".

884	–	2c. blk & lav (postage)	40	15
885	**247**	4c. sepia	95	35
886	**248**	8c. multicoloured (air)	1·75	35
887	–	12c. orange, black & grn	2·00	45
888	–	14c. multicoloured	2·50	45
889	–	19c. multicoloured	3·25	55
890	–	24c. multicoloured	3·25	1·00
891	–	29c. blue, brown & black	5·50	2·25
892	–	30c. brown, green & blk	8·50	3·25

DESIGNS—VERT: 2c. Cover of Poey's book; 12c. "Teria gundlachia"; 14c. "Teria ebriola"; 19c. "Nathalis felicia" (all butterflies). HORIZ: 24c. Tobacco fish; 29c. Butter hamlet; 30c. Tattler sea bass (all fishes).

249 Theodore Roosevelt

250 National Tuberculosis Hospital

1958. Birth Centenary of Roosevelt.
893 **249** 4c. green (postage) . . . 95 35
894 – 12c. sepia (air) . . . . . 1·40 50
DESIGN—HORIZ: 12c. Roosevelt leading Rough Riders at San Juan 1898.

1958. Obligatory Tax. Anti-T.B.
895 **250** 1c. brown 20 10
896 1c. green 20 10
897 1c. red 20 10
898 1c. grey 20 10

251 U.N.E.S.C.O. Headquarters, Paris

252 "Cattleyopsis lindenii" (orchid)

1958. Air. Inaug of U.N.E.S.C.O. Headquarters.
899 **251** 12c. green . . . . 1·25 45
900 – 30c. blue . . . . 1·60 65
DESIGN: 30c. Facade composed of letters "UNESCO" and map of Cuba.

1958. Christmas. Orchids. Multicoloured.
901 2c. Type **252** . . . . 2·50 1·10
902 4c. "Oncidium guibertianum" 2·50 1·10

253 "The Revolutionary"

254 Gen. A. F. Crombet

1959. Liberation Day.
903 **253** 2c. black and red 65 25

1959. Gen. Crombet Commemoration.
904 **254** 4c. myrtle 90 35

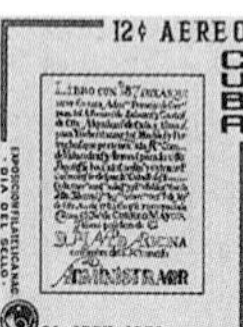

255 Postal Notice of 1765

256 Hand Supporting Sugar Factory

1959. Air. Stamp Day and National Philatelic Exhibition, Havana.
905 **255** 12c. sepia and blue . . . 1·10 35
906 – 30c. blue and sepia . . . 1·40 65
DESIGN: 30c. Administrative postal book of St. Cristobal, Havana, 1765.

1959. Agricultural Reform.
907 **256** 2c.+1c. blue and red (postage) 65 20
908 – 12c.+3c. green and red (air) . . . . 1·40 45
DESIGN (42 × 30 mm.): 12c. Farm workers and factory plant.

257 Red Cross Nurse

1959. "For Charity".
909 **257** 2c.+1c. red 35 25

1959. Air. American Society of Travel Agents Convention, Havana. No. 780 (colour changed) surch **CONVENCION ASTA OCTUBRE 17 1959 12c.** and bar.
910 12c. on 1p. green . . . . . . 1·90 1·00

259 Teresa Garcia Montes (founder)

260 Pres. C. M. de Cespedes

1959. Musical Arts Society Festival, Havana.
911 **259** 4c. brown (postage) . . . 90 35
912 – 12c. green (air) . . . . . 1·40 55
DESIGN—HORIZ: 12c. Society Headquarters, Havana.

1959. Cuban Presidents.
913 2c. slate (Type **260**) 35 15
914 2c. green (Betancourt) . . . 35 15
915 2c. violet (Calvar) 35 15
916 2c. brown (Maso) 35 15
917 4c. red (Spotorno) 65 20
918 4c. brown (Palma) 65 20
919 4c. black (F. J. de Cespedes) 65 20
920 4c. violet (Garcia) 65 20

261 Rebel Attack at Moncada Barracks

264 Pres. T. Estrada Palma Monument

1960. 1st Anniv of Cuban Revolution.
921 **261** 1c. grn, red & bl (postage) 15 10
922 – 2c. green, sepia and blue 1·25 15
923 – 10c. green, red and blue 1·40 55
924 – 12c. green, purple & blue 1·90 65
925 – 8c. green, red & bl (air) 2·50 50
926 – 12c. green, purple & brn 1·40 35
927 – 29c. red, black & green 1·75 70
DESIGNS: 2c. Rebels disembarking from "Granma"; 8c. Battle of Santa Clara; 10c. Battle of the Uvero; 12c. postage, "The Invasion" (Rebel and map of Cuba); 12c. air, Rebel Army entering Havana; 29c. Passing on propaganda ("Clandestine activities in the towns").

1960. Surch **HABILITADO PARA** and value (No. 932 without **PARA**).
928 **256** 2c. on 2c.+1c. blue and red (postage) 90 20
929 – 2c. on 4c. mve (No. 689) 65 35
930 – 2c. on 5c. blue (690) . . . 65 35
931 – 2c. on 13c. red (693) . . . 65 35
932 – 10c. on 20c. olive (342) 1·10 45
933 – 12c. on 12c.+3c. green and red (908) (air) . . . 1·40 55

1960. Surch in figures.
934 – 1c. on 4c. (No. 869) (postage) 40 15
935 – 1c. on 4c. (No. 873) . . . 40 15
936 – 1c. on 4c. (No. 877) . . . 40 15
937 **245** 1c. on 4c. blue 40 15
938 1c. on 4c. (No. 902) . . . 45 25
939 **254** 1c. on 4c. myrtle 40 15
940 **260** 1c. on 4c. brown 40 15
941 – 2c. on 14c. (No. 694) . . 80 15
942 **54** 12c. on 40c. orge (air) . . 1·40 50
943 – 12c. on 45c. (No. 706) . . 1·40 50

1960. Postal Employees' Retirement Fund.
944 **264** 1c. brn & blue (postage) 15 10
945 – 2c. green and red 35 10
946 – 10c. brown and red 65 25
947 – 12c. green and violet . . . 1·10 45
948 – 8c. grey and red (air) . . 55 15
949 – 12c. blue and red . . . . 1·40 35
950 – 30c. violet and red . . . 1·75 50
MONUMENTS—VERT: 2c. "Mambi Victorioso"; 8c. Marti; 10c. Marta Abreu; 12c. (No. 947) Agramonte; 12c. (No. 949) Heroes of Cacarajicara. HORIZ: 30c. Dr. C. de la Torriente.

(265)

266 Pistol-shooting

1960. Air. Stamp Day and National Philatelic Exn, Havana. Nos. 772/3 in new colours optd with T **265**.
951 8c. yellow 55 35
952 12c. red . . . . 1·50 50

1960. Olympic Games.
954 – 1c. vio (Sailing) (postage) 45 20
955 **266** 2c. orange . . . . 1·00 35
956 – 8c. blue (Boxing) (air) . . 85 30
957 – 12c. red (Running) . . . 1·40 55

267 C. Cienfuegos and View of Escolar

1960. 1st Death Anniv of Cienfuegos (revolutionary leader). Centre multicoloured.
959 **267** 2c. sepia . . . . 1·00 15

268 Air Stamp of 1930, Ford "Tin Goose" Airplane and "Sputnik"

1960. Air. 80th Anniv of National Airmail Service. Centre multicoloured.
960 **268** 8c. violet . . . . 3·25 1·40

270 Ipomoea

271 Tobacco Plant and Bars of "Christmas Hymn"

1960. Christmas. Inscr "NAVIDAD 1960–61". (a) T **270**.
961 1c. multicoloured 55 55
962 2c. multicoloured 75 75
963 10c. multicoloured . . . . . 1·50 1·50
(b) As T **271**.
964a/d 1c. multicoloured . . . . 1·75 1·40
965a/d 2c. multicoloured . . . . 2·75 2·50
966a/d 10c. multicoloured . . . . 5·00 4·75
DESIGNS: As T **271** (same for each value) a, T **271**. b, Mariposa. c, Lignum-vitae. d, Coffee plant.
Prices are for single stamps.

272

1960. Sub-industrialized Countries Conference.
967 **272** 1c. black, yellow and red (postage) 15 10
968 – 2c. multicoloured 15 10
969 – 6c. red, black and cream 1·10 40
970 – 8c. multicoloured (air) . . 40 15
971 – 12c. multicoloured . . . . 1·10 15
972 – 30c. red and grey . . . . 1·40 50
973 – 50c. multicoloured . . . . 1·75 60
DESIGNS—HORIZ: 2c. Graph and symbols; 6c. Cogwheels; 12c. Workers holding lever; 30c. Maps. VERT: 8c. Hand holding machete; 50c. Upraised hand.

273 J. Menendez

274 Jose Marti and "Declaration of Havana"

1961. Jesus Menendez Commemoration.
974 **273** 2c. sepia and green . . . 85 25

1961. Air. Declaration of Havana.
975 **274** 8c. red, black and yellow 75 65
976 12c. violet, black & buff 1·25 1·00
977 30c. brown, black & blue 3·00 2·75
The above were issued with part of background text of the declaration in English, French and Spanish. Prices the same for each language.

275 U.N. Emblem within Dove of Peace

1961. 15th Anniv of U.N.O.
979 **275** 2c. brn & grn (postage) 25 10
980 10c. green and purple . . 1·00 45
982 8c. red and yellow (air) 45 20
983 12c. blue and orange . . 1·10 40

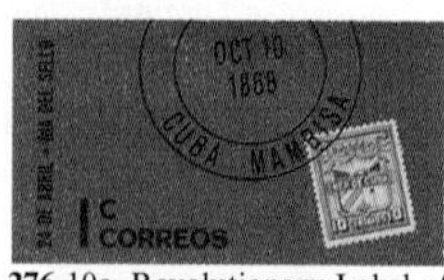

276 10c. Revolutionary Label of 1874 and "CUBA MAMBISA" "Postmark"

1961. Stamp Day. Inscr "24 DE ABRIL DIA DEL SELLO".
985 **276** 1c. red, green and black 15 10
986 – 2c. orange, slate & black 30 15
987 – 10c. turq, red & black . . 1·25 45
DESIGNS: 2c., 50c. stamp of 1907 and "CUBA REPUBLICANA" "postmark"; 10c., 2c. stamp of 1959 and "CUBA REVOLUCIONARIA" "postmark".

1961. May Day. Optd **PRIMERO DE MAYO 1961 ESTAMOS VENCIENDO**.
988 **273** 2c. sepia and green . . . 1·00 20

278

1961. "For Peace and Socialism".
989 **278** 2c. multicoloured . . . . 1·00 20
No. 989 is lightly printed on back with pattern of wavy lines and multiple inscr "CORREOS CUBA" in buff.

1961. Air. Surch **HABILITADO PARA 8 cts.**
992 **174** 8c. on 15c. red 50 30
993 **54** 8c. on 20c. brown 50 30

1961. 1st Official Philatelic Exhibition. No. 987 optd **primera exposicion filatelica oficial oct. 7-17, 1961.**
994 10c. turq, red and black . . . 1·00 35

281 Book and Lamp

1961. Education Year.
995 **281** 1c. red, black and green 10 10
996 2c. red, black and blue . . 15 10
997 10c. red, black and violet 60 20
998 12c. red, black & orange 1·10 45
The 2, 10 and 12c. show the letters "U", "B" and "A" on the book forming the word "CUBA".

282 "Polymita sulfurosa flammulata"

283 "Polymita picta fulminata"

1961. Christmas. Inscr "NAVIDAD 1961–62". Multicoloured. (a) Various designs as T **282**.
999 1c. Type **282** 30 15
1000 2c. Cuban grassquit (vert) 2·50 50
1001 10c. "Othreis toddi" (horiz) 1·75 70
(b) Various designs as T **283**.
1002a/d 1c. Snails (horiz) 30 15
1003a/d 2c. Birds (vert) . . . . . 2·50 50
1004a/d 10c. Butterflies (horiz) . . 1·75 70

DESIGNS: No. 1002a, Type **283**; 1002b, "Polymita p. nigrofasciata"; 1002c, "Polymita p. fuscolimbata"; 1002d, "Polymita p. roseolimbata"; 1003a, Cuban macaw; 1003b, Cuban trogon; 1003c, Bee hummingbird; 1003d, Ivory-billed woodpecker; 1004a, "Uranidia boisduvalii"; 1004b, "Phoebis avellaneda"; 1004c, "Phaloe cubana"; 1004d, "Papoilio gundlacchianus".
Prices are for single stamps.

284 Castro Emblem

285 Hand with Machete

1962. 3rd Anniv of Cuban Revolution. Emblem in yellow, red, grey and blue. Colours of background and inscriptions given.
1005 **284** 1c. grn & pink (postage) 45 25
1006 2c. black and orange . . 95 30
1007 8c. brown & blue (air) 45 20
1008 12c. ochre and green . . 1·10 35
1009 30c. violet and yellow . . 1·40 1·10

1962. Air. 1st Anniv of Socialist Republic's First Sugar Harvest.
1010 **285** 8c. sepia and red 50 15
1011 12c. black and lilac . . . 1·10 40

286 Armed Peasant and Tractor

1962. National Militia.
1012 **286** 1c. black and green . . . 20 10
1013 – 2c. black and blue . . . 35 20
1014 – 10c. black and orange 1·10 35
DESIGNS: 2c. Armed worker and welder; 10c. Armed woman and sewing-machinist.

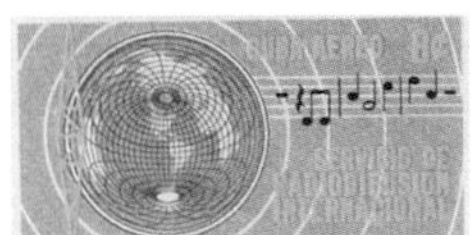

287 Globe and Music Emblem

1962. Air. International Radio Service. Inscr and aerial yellow; musical notation black; lines on globe brown, background colours given.
1015 **287** 8c. grey 55 20
1016 12c. blue . . . . 1·10 35
1017 30c. green . . . . 1·60 85
1018 1p. lilac . . . . 3·25 2·25

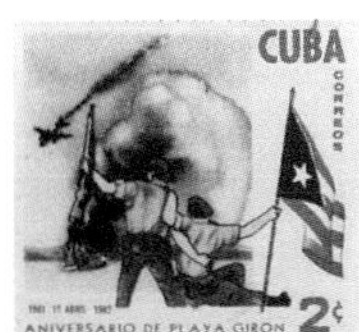

288 Soldiers, Aircraft and Burning Ship

1962. 1st Anniv of "Playa Giron" (Sea Invasion Attempt of Cuban Exiles).
1019 **288** 2c. multicoloured 40 10
1020 3c. multicoloured 40 10
1021 10c. multicoloured . . . 1·75 50

289 Arrival of First Mail from the Indies

1962. Stamp Day.
1022 **289** 10c. black and red on cream . . . . 3·00 60

290 Clenched Fist Salute

1962. Labour Day.
1023 **290** 2c. black on buff 20 10
1024 3c. black on red 35 20
1025 10c. black on blue . . . 1·10 45

291 Wrestling

1962. National Sports Institute (I.N.D.E.R.) Commemoration. As T **291**. On cream paper.
1026a/e 1c. brown and red . . . 20 10
1027a/e 2c. red and green 20 15
1028a/e 3c. blue and red . . . . 1·00 15
1029a/e 9c. purple and blue . . . 40 15
1030a/e 10c. orange and purple 45 20
1031a/e 13c. black and red . . . 50 30
DESIGNS: No. 1026a, Type **291**; 1026b, Weight-lifting; 1026c, Gymnastics; 1026d, Judo; 1026e, Throwing the discus; 1027a, Archery; 1027b, Roller skating; 1027c, Show jumping; 1027d, Ninepin bowling; 1027e, Cycling; 1028a, Rowing (coxed four); 1028b, Speed boat; 1028c, Swimming; 1028d, Kayak; 1028e, Yachting; 1029a, Football; 1029b, Tennis; 1029c, Baseball; 1029d, Basketball; 1029e, Volleyball; 1030a, Underwater fishing; 1030b, Shooting; 1030c, Model airplane flying; 1030d, Water polo; 1030e, Boxing; 1031a, Pelota; 1031b, Sports stadium; 1031c, Jai alai; 1031d, Chess; 1031e, Fencing.
Prices are for single stamps.

292 A. Santamaria and Soldiers

1962. 9th Anniv of "Rebel Day".
1032 **292** 2c. lake and blue 35 25
1033 – 3c. blue and lake 65 35
DESIGN: 3c. Santamaria and children.

293 Dove and Festival Emblem

1962. World Youth Festival, Helsinki.
1034 **293** 2c. multicoloured 45 20
1035 – 3c. multicoloured 65 30
DESIGN: 3c. As Type **293** but with "clasped hands" instead of dove.

294 Czech 5k. "Praga 1962" stamp of 1961

1962. Air. International Stamp Exn, Prague.
1037 **294** 31c. multicoloured . . . 2·50 1·00

295 Rings and Boxing Gloves

1962. 9th Central American and Caribbean Games, Jamaica.
1039 **295** 1c. ochre and red . . . 10 10
1040 – 2c. ochre and blue . . . 15 10
1041 – 3c. ochre and purple . . . 15 10
1042 – 13c. ochre and green . . 1·00 55
DESIGNS: Rings and: 2c. Tennis rackets; 3c. Baseball bats; 13c. Rapiers and mask.

296 "Cuban Women"

1962. 1st Cuban Women's Federation National Congress.
1043 **296** 9c. red, green and black 45 20
1044 – 13c. black, blue & green 1·25 50
DESIGN—VERT: 13c. Mother and child, and Globe.

297 Running

1962. 1st Latin-American University Games. Multicoloured.
1045 1c. Type **297** 20 10
1046 2c. Baseball 20 10
1047 3c. Netball 45 20
1048 13c. Globe . . . . 1·10 45

298 Microscope and Parasites

1962. Malaria Eradication. Mult.
1049 1c. Type **298** 30 20
1050 2c. Mosquito and pool . . . 30 20
1051 3c. Cinchona plant and formulae 95 30

299 "Epicrates angulifer B" (snake)

300 Cuban Night Lizard

1962. Christmas. Inscr "NAVIDAD 1962–63". Multicoloured. (a) Various designs as T **299**.
1052 2c. Type **299** 35 15
1053 3c. "Cubispa turquino" (vert) 50 45
1054 10c. Jamacian long-tongued bat . . . . 2·00 1·00

(b) Various designs as T **300**.
1055a/d 2c. Reptiles 35 15
1056a/d 3c. Insects (vert) 50 45
1057a/d 10c. Mammals . . . . . 2·00 1·00
DESIGNS: No. 1055a, Type **300**; 1055b, Knight anole; 1055c, Wright's ground boa; 1055d, Cuban ground iguana; 1056a, "Chrysis superba"; 1056b, "Essosthutha roberto"; 1056c, "Hortensia conciliata"; 1056d, "Lachnopus argus"; 1057a, Desmarest's hutia; 1057b, Prehensile-tailed hutia; 1057c, Cuban solenodon; 1057d, Desmarest's hutia (white race).
Prices are for single stamps.

301 Titov and "Vostok 2"

1963. Cosmic Flights (1st issue).
1058 – 1c. blue, red and yellow 20 10
1059 **301** 2c. green, purple & yell 35 20
1060 – 3c. violet, red & yellow 35 20
DESIGNS: 1c. Gagarin and "Vostok 1"; 3c. Nikolaev, Popovich and "Vostoks 3 and 4".
See also Nos. 1133/4.

302 Attackers

1963. 6th Anniv of Attack on Presidential Palace.
1061 **302** 9c. black and red 55 15
1062 – 13c. purple and blue . . 65 35
1063 – 30c. green and red . . . 1·60 65
DESIGNS: 13c. Rodriguez, C. Servia, Machado and Westbrook; 30c. J. Echeverria and M. Mora.

303 Baseball

1963. 4th Pan-American Games, Sao Paulo.
1064 **303** 1c. green 45 20
1065 – 13c. red (Boxing) . . . . 1·40 40

304 "Mask" Letter Box

1963. Stamp Day.
1066 **304** 3c. black and brown . . 45 20
1067 – 10c. black and violet . . 1·10 45
DESIGN: 10c. 19th-century Post Office, Cathedral Place, Havana.

305 Revolutionaries and Statue

1963. Labour Day. Multicoloured.
1068 3c. Type **305** 30 10
1069 13c. Celebrating Labour Day . . . . 1·00 45

306 Child

1963. Children's Week.
1070 **306** 3c. brown and blue . . . 30 15
1071 30c. red and blue . . . . 1·40 65

307 Ritual Effigy

308 "Breaking chains of old regime"

1963. 60th Anniv of Montane Anthropological Museum.
1072 **307** 2c. brown and salmon 45 15
1073 – 3c. purple and blue . . . 45 15
1074 – 9c. grey and red 75 40
DESIGNS—HORIZ: 3c. Carved chair; VERT: 9c. Statuette.

1963. 10th Anniv of "Rebel Day".
1075 **308** 1c. black and pink . . . 15 10
1076 – 2c. purple and lt blue . . 15 10
1077 – 3c. sepia and lilac . . . 15 10
1078 – 7c. purple and green . . 15 10
1079 – 9c. purple and yellow . . 40 20
1080 – 10c. green and ochre . . 1·00 35
1081 – 13c. blue and buff . . . 1·40 60
DESIGNS: 2c. Palace attack; 3c. "The Insurrection"; 7c. "Strike of April 9th" (defence of radio station); 9c. "Triumph of the Revolution" (upraised flag and weapons); 10c. "Agrarian Reform and Nationalization" (artisan and peasant); 13c. "Victory of Giron" (soldiers in battle).

309 Star Apple

310 "Roof and Window"

1963. Cuban Fruits. Multicoloured.
1082 1c. Type **309** 15 10
1083 2c. Chiromoya 15 10
1084 3c. Cashew nut 20 15

1085 10c. Custard apple 95 35
1086 13c. Mango . . . . 1·40 1·00

1963. 7th Int Architects Union Congress, Havana.
1087 3c. multicoloured 25 10
1088 3c. multicoloured 25 10
1089 3c. black, blue and bistre . . 25 10
1090 3c. multicoloured 25 10
1091 13c. multicoloured 90 45
1092 13c. multicoloured 90 45
1093 13c. red, olive and black . . 90 45
1094 13c. multicoloured 90 45
DESIGNS—VERT: No. 1087, Type **310**; Nos. 1090/2, Symbols of building construction as Type **310**. HORIZ: Nos. 1089/90 and 1093, Sketches of urban buildings; No. 1094, as Type **310** (girders and outline of house).

311 Hemingway and Scene from "The Old Man and the Sea"

1963. Ernest Hemingway Commemoration.
1095 **311** 3c. brown and blue . . . 20 10
1096 – 9c. turquoise and mauve 45 20
1097 – 13c. black and green . . 1·25 55
DESIGNS—Hemingway and: 9c. Scene from "For Whom the Bell Tolls"; 13c. Residence at San Francisco de Paula, near Havana.

312 "Zapateo" (dance) after V. P. de Landaluze

1964. 50th Anniv of National Museum.
1098 **312** 2c. multicoloured 20 10
1099 – 3c. multicoloured 50 15
1100 – 9c. multicoloured 75 40
1101 – 13c. black and violet . . 1·25 75
DESIGNS—VERT: (32 × 42½ mm.): 3c. "The Rape of the Mulattos" (after C. Enriquez); 9c. Greek amphora; 13c. "Dilecta Mea" (bust, after J. A. Houdon).

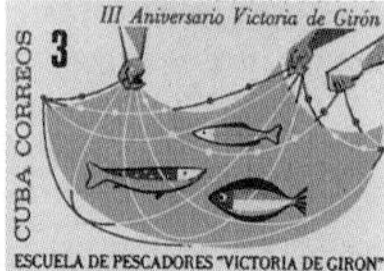

313 B. J. Borrell (revolutionary) **314** Fish in Net

1964. 5th Anniv of Revolution.
1102 **313** 2c. black, orange & grn 20 10
1103 – 3c. black, orange & red 30 15
1104 – 10c. black, orange & pur 55 25
1105 – 13c. black, orange & bl 1·10 50
PORTRAITS: 3c. M. Salado. 10c. O. Lucero. 13c. S. Gonzalez (revolutionaries).

1964. 3rd Anniv of Giron Victory.
1106 **314** 3c. multicoloured 20 10
1107 – 10c. black, grey & bistre 40 25
1108 – 13c. slate, black & orge 1·10 45
DESIGNS—HORIZ: 10c. Victory Monument. VERT: 13c. Fallen eagle.

315 V. M. Pera (1st Director of Military Posts, 1868–71)

1964. Stamp Day.
1109 **315** 3c. blue and brown . . . 35 15
1110 – 13c. green and lilac . . . 1·25 45
DESIGN: 13c. Cuba's first (10c.) military stamp.

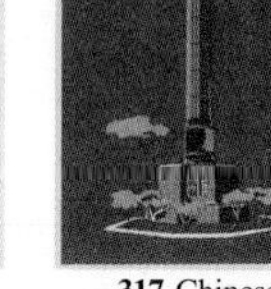

316 Symbolic "1" **317** Chinese Monument, Havana

1964. Labour Day.
1111 **316** 3c. multicoloured 20 15
1112 – 13c. multicoloured . . . 85 45
DESIGN: 13c. As Type **316** but different symbols within "1".

1964. Cuban–Chinese Friendship.
1113 **317** 1c. multicoloured 15 10
1114 – 2c. red, olive and black 25 10
1115 – 3c. multicoloured 40 15
DESIGNS—HORIZ: 2c. Cuban and Chinese. VERT: 3c. Flags of Cuba and China.

318 Globe

1964. U.P.U. Congress, Vienna.
1116 **318** 13c. brown, green & red 55 20
1117 – 30c. black, bistre & red 1·10 45
1118 – 50c. black, blue and red 2·25 75
DESIGNS: 30c. H. von Stephan (founder of U.P.U.); 50c. U.P.U. Monument, Berne.

319 Mutton Snapper

1964. Popular Savings Movement. Mult.
1119 1c. Type **319** 25 10
1120 2c. Cow 25 10
1121 13c. Poultry . . . . 1·25 45

320 "Rio Jibacoa"

1964. Cuban Merchant Fleet. Multicoloured.
1122 1c. Type **320** 25 10
1123 2c. "Camilo Cienfuegos" . . 35 10
1124 3c. "Sierra Maestra" 55 10
1125 9c. "Bahia de Siguanea" . . 1·40 40
1126 10c. "Oriente" . . . . . . 3·50 75

321 Vietnamese Fighter **322** Raul Gomez Garcia and Poem

1964. "Unification of Vietnam" Campaign. Mult.
1127 2c. Type **321** 15 10
1128 3c. Vietnamese shaking hands across map 20 15
1129 10c. Hand and mechanical ploughing 45 20
1130 13c. Vietnamese, Cuban and flags . . . . 1·10 45

1964. 11th Anniv of "Rebel Day".
1131 **322** 3c. black, red and ochre 20 10
1132 – 13c. multicoloured . . . 90 40
DESIGN: 13c. Inscr "LA HISTORIA ME ABSOLVERA" (Castro's book).

1964. Cosmic Flights (2nd issue). As T **301**.
1133 9c. yellow, violet and red . . 75 40
1134 13c. yellow, red and green 1·40 55
DESIGNS: 9c. "Vostok-5" and Bykovksy; 13c. "Vostok-6" and Tereshkova.

323 Start of Race

1964. Olympic Games, Tokyo.
1135 – 1c. yellow, blue and purple 20 10
1136 – 2c. multicoloured 20 10
1137 – 3c. brown, black & red 20 10
1138 **323** 7c. violet, blue and orange 40 15
1139 – 10c. yellow, purple & bl 85 40
1140 – 13c. multicoloured . . . 1·50 65
DESIGNS—VERT: 1c. Gymnastics; 2c. Rowing; 3c. Boxing. HORIZ: 10c. Fencing; 13c. Games symbols.

325 Satellite and Globe

326 Rocket and part of Globe

1964. Cuban Postal Rocket Experiment. 25th Anniv Various rockets and satellites. (a) Horiz. designs as T **325**.
1141 **325** 1c. multicoloured 15 10
1142 – 2c. multicoloured 35 15
1143 – 3c. multicoloured 45 25
1144 – 9c. multicoloured . . . . 1·25 45
1145 – 13c. multicoloured . . . 1·75 1·00

(b) Horiz. designs as T **326**.
1146 – 1c. multicoloured 15 10
1147 – 2c. multicoloured 35 15
1148 – 3c. multicoloured 45 25
1149 – 9c. multicoloured . . . . . 1·25 45
1150 – 13c. multicoloured . . . . 1·75 1·00

(c) Larger 44 × 28 mm.
1151 – 50c. green and black . . . 2·50 1·60
DESIGN: 50c. Cuban Rocket Post 10c. Stamp of 1939.

Nos. 1141 and 1146, 1142 and 1147, 1143 and 1148, 1144 and 1149, 1145 and 1150 were printed together in five sheets of 25, each comprising four stamps as Type **325** plus five se-tenant stamp-size labels inscribed overall "1939 COHETE POSTAL CUBANO 25 ANIVERSARIO 1964" forming a centre cross and four blocks of four different stamps as Type **326** in each corner. The four-stamp design incorporates different subjects, which together form a composite design around a globe.

Prices are for single stamps.

1964. 1st Three-Manned Space Flight. As No. 1151 but colours changed. Optd **VOSJOD-1 octubre 12 1964 PRIMERA TRIPULACION DEL ESPACIO** and large rocket.
1153 50c. green and brown . . . 2·75 1·10

328 Lenin addressing Meeting **329** Leopard

1964. 40th Death Anniv of Lenin.
1154 **328** 3c. black and orange . . 20 10
1155 – 13c. red and violet . . . 45 25
1156 – 30c. black and blue . . . 1·00 55
DESIGNS—HORIZ: 13c. Lenin mausoleum. VERT: 30c. Lenin and hammer and sickle emblem.

1964. Havana Zoo Animals. Multicoloured.
1157 1c. Type **329** 10 10
1158 2c. Indian elephant (vert) . . 10 10
1159 3c. Red deer (vert) 15 10
1160 4c. Eastern grey kangaroo 20 10
1161 5c. Lions 25 10
1162 6c. Eland 25 10
1163 7c. Common zebra 25 15
1164 8c. Striped hyena 45 15
1165 9c. Tiger 45 15
1166 10c. Guanaco 50 15
1167 13c. Chimpanzees 50 15
1168 20c. Collared Peccary . . . 70 20
1169 30c. Common racoon (vert) 1·00 50
1170 40c. Hippopotamus . . . . 2·10 85
1171 50c. Brazilian tapir . . . . 2·75 1·10
1172 60c. Dromedary (vert) . . . 3·00 1·50
1173 70c. American Bison . . . . 3·00 1·50
1174 80c. Asiatic black bear (vert) 3·75 1·90
1175 90c. Water buffalo . . . . 3·75 2·40
1176 1p. Roe deer at Zoo Entrance . . . . 4·75 2·40

330 Jose Marti

1964. "Liberators of Independence". Multicoloured. Each showing portraits and campaigning scenes.
1177 1c. Type **330** 15 10
1178 2c. A. Maceo 20 15
1179 3c. M. Gomez 45 25
1180 13c. C. Garcia . . . . . . 1·00 55

331 Dwarf Cup Coral

332 Small Flower Coral

1964. Christmas. Inscr "NAVIDAD 1964–65". Multicoloured. (a) As T **331**.
1181 2c. Type **331** 35 25
1182 3c. Sea anemone 65 35
1183 10c. Stone lily . . . . . . 1·00 65

(b) As T **332**.
1184a/d 2c. Coral 35 25
1185a/d 3c. Jellyfish 65 35
1186a/d 10c. Sea stars and urchins . . . . 1·00 65
DESIGNS: No. 1184a, Type **332**; 1184b, Elkhorn coral; 1184c, Dense moosehorn coral; 1184d, Yellow brain coral; 1185a, Portuguese man-of-war; 1185b, Moon jellyfish; 1185c, Thimble jellyfish; 1185d, Upside-down jellyfish; 1186a, Big-spined sea-urchin; 1186b, Edible sea urchin; 1186c, Caribbean brittle star; 1186d, Reticulated sea star.

Prices are for single stamps.

333 Dr. Tomas Romay **334** Map of Latin America and Part of Declaration

1964. Birth Bicentenary of Dr. Tomas Romay (scientist).
1187 **333** 1c. black and bistre . . . 20 10
1188 – 2c. sepia and brown . . 20 10
1189 – 3c. brown and bistre . . 30 15
1190 – 10c. black and bistre . . 1·00 40
DESIGNS—VERT: 2c. First vaccination against smallpox. HORIZ: 3c. Dr. Romay and extract from his treatise on the vaccine; 10c. Dr. Romay's statue.

1964. 2nd Declaration of Havana. Mult.
1191 3c. Type **334** 45 30
1192 13c. Map of Cuba and native receiving revolutionary message . . 1·75 90

The two stamps have the declaration superimposed in tiny print across each horiz. row of five stamps, thus requiring strips of five to show the complete declaration.

335 "Maritime Post" (diorama)

1965. Inauguration of Cuban Postal Museum. Mult.
1193 13c. Type **335** . . . . . . 2·75 65
1194 30c. "Insurgent Post" (diorama) . . . . 1·90 1·00

336 "Sondero" (schooner)

1965. Cuban Fishing Fleet. Multicoloured. Fishing crafts.
1196 1c. Type **336** 15 10
1197 2c. "Omicron" 25 10
1198 3c. "Victoria" 35 15
1199 9c. "Cardenas" 55 25
1200 10c. "Sigma" . . . . 2·10 50
1201 13c. "Lambda" . . . . . . 3·25 80

337 Lydia Doce

1965. International Women's Day. Multicoloured.
1202 3c. Type **337** 55 25
1203 13c. Clara Zetkin 85 45

338 Jose Antonio Echeverria University City

1965. "Technical Revolution". Inscr "REVOLUCION TECNICA".
1204 **338** 3c. black, brown and chestnut 25 15
1205 – 13c. multicoloured . . . 1·10 45
DESIGN: 13c. Scientific symbols.

339 Leonov

1965. "Voskhod 2", Space flight.
1206 **339** 30c. brown and blue . . 1·40 55
1207 – 50c. blue and magenta 2·75 1·10
DESIGN: 50c. Beliaiev, Leonov and "Voskhod 2".

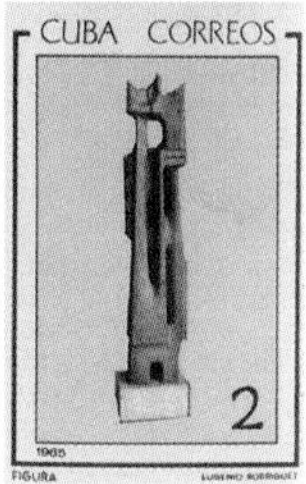

340 "Figure" (after E. Rodrigues) **341** Lincoln Statue, Washington

1965. National Museum Treasures. Mult.
1208 2c. Type **340** (27 × 42 mm) 30 10
1209 3c. "Landscape with sunflowers" (V. Manuel) (31 × 42 mm) 30 15
1210 10c. "Abstract" (W. Lam) (42 × 31 mm) 80 30
1211 13c. "Children" (E. Ponce) (39 × 33½ mm) . . . . . 1·40 55

1965. Death Centenary of Abraham Lincoln.
1212 – 1c. brown, grey and yellow 10 10
1213 – 2c. ultramarine & blue 25 10
1214 **341** 3c. black, red and blue 55 30
1215 – 13c. black, orange & bl 1·10 50
DESIGNS—HORIZ: 1c. Cabin at Hodgenville, Kentucky (Lincoln's birthplace); 2c. Lincoln Monument, Washington. VERT: 13c. Abraham Lincoln.

342 18th-century Mail Ship and Old Postmarks (bicent of Maritime Mail)

1965. Stamp Day.
1216 **342** 3c. bistre and red . . . 1·50 20
1217 – 13c. red, black and blue 1·40 45
DESIGN: 13c. Cuban; 10c. "Air Train" stamp of 1935 and glider train over Capitol, Havana.

343 Sun and Earth's Magnetic Pole

1965. International Quiet Sun Year. Multicoloured.
1218 1c. Type **343** 20 10
1219 2c. I.Q.S.Y. emblem (vert) 20 10
1220 3c. Earth's magnetic fields 35 10
1221 6c. Solar rays 40 15
1222 30c. Effect of solar rays on various atmospheric layers 1·40 40
1223 50c. Effect of solar rays on satellite orbits . . . . . . 1·90 95
Nos. 1221/3 are larger, 47 × 20 mm. or 20 × 47 mm. (30c.).

344 Telecommunications Station

1965. Centenary of I.T.U. Multicoloured.
1225 1c. Type **344** 15 10
1226 2c. Satellite (vert) 15 10
1227 3c. "Telstar" 20 10
1228 10c. "Telstar" and receiving station (vert) 65 20
1229 30c. I.T.U. emblem . . . . 1·75 65

345 Festival Emblem and Flags

1965. World Youth and Students Festival. Multicoloured.
1230 13c. Type **345** 75 35
1231 30c. Soldiers of three races and flags . . . . 1·60 45

346 M. Perez (pioneer balloonist), Balloon and Satellite

1965. Matias Perez Commemoration.
1232 **346** 3c. black and red . . . . 1·10 85
1233 – 13c. black and blue . . . 1·40 85
DESIGN: 13c. As Type **346**, but with rockets in place of satellite.

347 Rose (Europe)

1965. Flowers of the World. Multicoloured.
1234 1c. Type **347** 15 10
1235 2c. Chrysanthemum (Asia) 15 10
1236 3c. Strelitzia (Africa) 20 10
1237 4c. Dahlia (N. America) . . 20 10
1238 5c. Orchid (S. America) . . 55 15
1239 13c. "Grevillea banksii" (Oceania) . . . . 1·75 75
1240 30c. "Brunfelsia nitida" (Cuba) . . . . 2·25 1·40

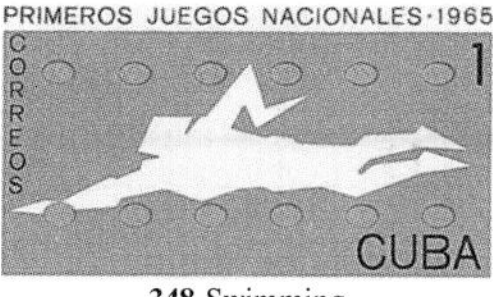

348 Swimming

1965. First National Games.
1241 **348** 1c. multicoloured 15 10
1242 – 2c. multicoloured 20 10
1243 – 3c. black, red and grey 45 20
1244 – 30c. black, red and grey 1·50 55
SPORTS: 2c. Basketball. 3c. Gymnastics. 30c. Hurdling.

349 Anti-tank gun

1965. Museum of the Revolution. Mult.
1245 1c. Type **349** 10 10
1246 2c. Tank 10 10
1247 3c. Bazooka 20 10
1248 10c. Rebel Uniform 55 20
1249 13c. Launch "Granma" and compass . . . . 1·60 40

350 C. J. Finlay **351** "Anetia numidia" (butterfly)

1965. 50th Death Anniv of Carlos J. Finlay (malaria researcher).
1250 – 1c. black, green & blue 10 10
1251 – 2c. brown, ochre and black 15 10
1252 **350** 3c. brown and black . . 15 10
1253 – 7c. black and lilac . . . 20 10
1254 – 9c. bronze and black . . 40 20
1255 – 10c. black and blue . . . 85 25
1256 – 13c. multicoloured . . . 1·25 55
DESIGNS—HORIZ: 1c. Finlay's signature. VERT: 2c. Yellow fever mosquito; 7c. Finlay's microscope; 9c. Dr. C. Delgado; 10c. Finlay's monument; 13c. Finlay demonstrating his theories, after painting by Valderrama.

1965. Cuban Butterflies. Multicoloured.
1257 2c. Type **351** 40 15
1258 2c. "Carathis gortynoides" 40 15
1259 2c. "Hymenitis cubana" . . 40 15
1260 2c. "Eubaphe heros" . . . 40 15
1261 2c. "Dismorphia cubana" 40 15
1262 3c. "Siderone nemesis" . . . 50 25
1263 3c. "Syntomidopsis variegata" 50 25
1264 3c. "Ctenuchidia virgo" . . 50 25
1265 3c. "Lycorea ceres" 50 25
1266 3c. "Eubaphe disparilis" . . 50 25
1267 13c. "Anetia cubana" . . . 2·00 75
1268 13c. "Prepona antimache" 2·00 75
1269 13c. "Sylepta regnalis" . . 2·00 75
1270 13c. "Chlosyne perezi" . . . 2·00 75
1271 13c. "Anaea clytemnestra" 2·00 75

352 20c. Coin of 1962

1965. 50th Anniv of Cuban Coinage. Mult.
1273 1c. Type **352** 10 10
1274 2c. 1p. coin of 1934 . . . . 10 10
1275 3c. 40c. coin of 1962 . . . . 15 15
1276 8c. 1p. coin of 1915 . . . . 30 15
1277 10c. 1p. coin of 1953 . . . 75 35
1278 13c. 20p. coin of 1915 . . . 1·10 40

353 Oranges

1965. Tropical Fruits. Multicoloured.
1279 1c. Type **353** 10 10
1280 2c. Custard-apples 10 10
1281 3c. Papayas 15 15
1282 4c. Bananas 20 10
1283 10c. Avocado pears 30 15
1284 13c. Pineapples 55 50
1285 20c. Guavas . . . . 1·40 50
1286 50c. Mameys . . . . 2·75 85

354 Northern Oriole **355** Painted Bunting

1965. Christmas. Vert. designs showing bird life.
(a) As T **354**. Multicoloured.
1287 3c. Type **354** . . . . 2·50 1·60
1288 5c. Scarlet tanager . . . . . 3·00 2·10
1289 13c. Indigo bunting . . . . 6·75 3·75

(b) As T **355**.
1290a/d 3c. multicoloured . . . . 2·50 1·60
1291a/d 5c. multicoloured . . . . 3·00 2·10
1292a/d 13c. multicoloured . . . 6·75 3·75
DESIGNS: No. 1290a, Type **355**; 1290b, American redstart; 1290c, Blackburnian warbler; 1290d, Rose-breasted grosbeak; 1291a, Yellow-throated warbler; 1291b, Blue-winged warbler; 1291c, Prothonotary warbler; 1291d, Hooded warbler; 1292a, Blue-winged teal; 1292b, Wood duck; 1292c, Common shoveler; 1292d, Black-crowned night heron.
Prices are for single stamps.

356 Hurdling

1965. 7th Anniv of International Athletics, Havana. Multicoloured.
1293 1c. Type **356** 15 10
1294 2c. Throwing the discus . . 15 10
1295 3c. Putting the shot 35 10
1296 7c. Throwing the javelin . . 35 20
1297 9c. High-jumping 45 25
1298 10c. Throwing the hammer 95 40
1299 13c. Running . . . . 1·25 60

357 Sharksucker

1965. National Aquarium. Multicoloured.
1300 1c. Type **357** 20 10
1301 2c. Skipjack/Bonito tuna . . 20 10
1302 3c. Sergeant major 40 10
1303 4c. Sailfish 45 10
1304 5c. Nassau grouper 45 10
1305 10c. Mutton snapper . . . 60 20
1306 13c. Yellow-tailed snapper 2·00 60
1307 30c. Squirrelfish . . . . . . 3·25 90

358 A. Voisin, Cuban and French Flags

1965. 1st Death Anniv of Prof. Andre Voisin (scientist).
1308 **358** 3c. multicoloured 40 20
1309 – 13c. multicoloured . . . 1·10 40
DESIGN: 13c. Similar to Type **358** but with microscope and plant in place of cattle.

359 Skoda Omnibus

1965. Cuban Transport. Multicoloured.
1310 1c. Type **359** 10 10
1311 2c. Ikarus omnibus 10 10
1312 3c. Leyland omnibus . . . 15 10
1313 4c. Russian-built Type TEM-4 diesel locomotive . . . . 2·25 45
1314 7c. French-built BB. 69,000 diesel locomotive . . . . 2·25 45
1315 10c. Tug "R.D.A." . . . . 1·00 25
1316 13c. Freighter "13 de Marzo" . . . . 1·60 45
1317 20c. Ilyushin IL-18 airliner 1·75 65

360 Infantry Column

1966. 7th Anniv of Revolution. Mult.
1318 1c. Type **360** 20 10
1319 2c. Soldier and tank 20 10
1320 3c. Sailor and torpedo-boat 45 10
1321 10c. MiG-21 jet fighter . . . 1·00 30
1322 13c. Rocket missile . . . . 1·25 25
SIZES—As Type **360**: 2c., 3c. HORIZ: ($38\frac{1}{2} \times 23\frac{1}{2}$ mm): 10c., 13c.

361 Conference Emblem

1966. Tricontinental Conference, Havana.
1323 **361** 2c. multicoloured 15 10
1324 – 3c. multicoloured 20 10
1325 – 13c. multicoloured . . . 95 40
DESIGNS: 3c., 13c. As Type **361** but re-arranged.

362 Guardalabarca Beach

1966. Tourism. Multicoloured.
1326 1c. Type **362** 10 10
1327 2c. La Gran Piedra (mountain resort) 15 10
1328 3c. Guama, Las Villas (country scene) 35 15
1329 13c. Waterfall, Soroa (vert) 1·40 40

363 Congress Emblem and "Treating Patient" (old engraving)

1966. Medical and Stomachal Congresses, Havana. Multicoloured.
1330 3c. Type **363** 25 10
1331 13c. Congress emblem and children receiving treatment . . . . 1·10 40

364 Afro-Cuban Doll

1966. Cuban Handicrafts. Multicoloured.
1332 1c. Type **364** 10 10
1333 2c. Sombreros 10 10
1334 3c. Vase 10 10
1335 7c. Gourd lampshades . . . 15 10
1336 9c. Rare-wood lampstand 35 15
1337 10c. "Horn" shark (horiz) 55 25
1338 13c. Painted polymita shell necklace and earrings (horiz) . . . . 1·10 45

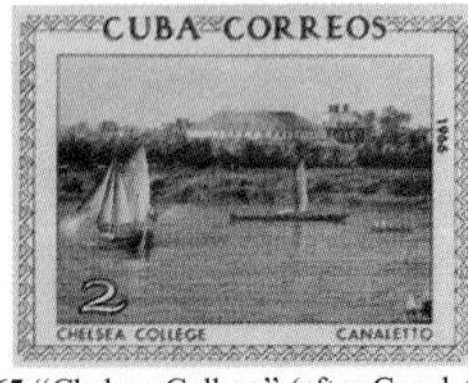

365 "Chelsea College" (after Canaletto)

1966. National Museum Exhibits. Inscr "1966". Multicoloured.
1339 1c. Ming Dynasty vase (vert) 10 10
1340 2c. Type **365** 40 10
1341 3c. "Portrait of a Young Girl" (after Goya) (vert) 35 20
1342 13c. Portrait of Fayum (vert) . . . . 1·40 45

366 Cosmonauts in Training **367** Tank in Battle

1966. 5th Anniv of 1st Manned Space Flight. Multicoloured.
1343 1c. Tsiolkovsky and diagram (horiz) 10 10
1344 2c. Type **366** 10 10
1345 3c. Gagarin, rocket and globe (horiz) 20 10
1346 7c. Nikolaev and Popovich 35 10
1347 9c. Tereshkova and Bykovsky (horiz) 45 20
1348 10c. Komarov, Feoktistov and Yegorov (horiz) . . . 55 25
1349 13c. Leonov in space (horiz) 1·10 45

1966. 5th Anniv of Giron Victory.
1350 **367** 2c. black, green and bistre 10 10
1351 – 3c. black, blue and red 40 10
1352 – 9c. black, brown & grey 20 10
1353 – 10c. black, blue and green 70 15
1354 – 13c. black, brown and blue . . . . 1·40 50
DESIGNS: 3c. "Houston" (freighter) sinking; 9c. Disabled tank and poster-hoarding; 10c. Young soldier; 13c. Operations map.

368 Interior of Postal Museum (1st Anniv)

1966. Stamp Day.
1355 **368** 3c. green and red 45 10
1356 – 13c. brown, black & red 1·40 45
DESIGN: 13c. Stamp collector and Cuban 2c. stamp of 1959.

369 Bouquet and Anvil **370** W.H.O. Building

1966. Labour Day. Multicoloured.
1357 2c. Type **369** 15 10
1358 3c. Bouquet and Machete 15 10
1359 10c. Bouquet and Hammer 45 20
1360 13c. Bouquet and parts of globe and cogwheel . . . 1·10 60

1966. Inaug of W.H.O. Headquarters, Geneva.
1361 **370** 2c. black, green & yell 15 10
1362 – 3c. black, blue and yellow 35 10
1363 13c. black, yellow and blue . . . . 1·10 45
DESIGNS (W.H.O. Building on): 3c. Flag; 13c. Emblem.

371 Athletics **372** Makarenko Pedagogical Institute

1966. 10th Central American and Caribbean Games.
1364 **371** 1c. sepia and green . . . 10 10
1365 – 2c. sepia and orange . . 10 10
1366 – 3c. brown and yellow . . 10 10
1367 – 7c. blue and mauve . . . 15 10
1368 – 9c. black and blue . . . 30 15
1369 – 10c. black and brown . . 55 15
1370 – 13c. blue and red . . . . 1·25 40
DESIGNS—HORIZ: 2c. Rifle-shooting. VERT: 3c. Baseball; 7c. Volleyball; 9c. Football; 10c. Boxing; 13c. Basketball.

1966. Educational Development.
1371 **372** 1c. black and green . . . 10 10
1372 – 2c. black, ochre & yellow 10 10
1373 – 3c. black, ultram & bl 15 10
1374 – 10c. black, brown & grn 35 20
1375 – 13c. multicoloured . . . 95 40
DESIGNS: 2c. Alphabetization Museum; 3c. Lamp (5th anniv of National Alphabetization Campaign); 10c. Open-air class; 13c. "Farmers' and Workers' Education".

373 "Agrarian Reform"

1966. Air. "Conquests of the Revolution". Multicoloured.
1376 1c. Type **373** 15 10
1377 2c. "Industrialisation" . . . 15 10
1378 3c. "Urban Reform" . . . 20 10
1379 7c. "Eradication of Unemployment" 20 10
1380 9c. "Education" 40 15
1381 10c. "Public Health" . . . 85 15
1382 13c. Paragraph from Castro's book, "La Historia me Absolvera" 1·10 30

374 Workers with Flag

1966. 12th Revolutionary Workers' Union Congress, Havana.
1383 **374** 3c. multicoloured 55 20

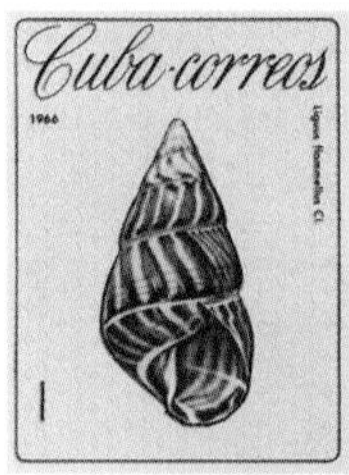

375 Flamed Cuban Liguus **377** Arms of Pinar del Rio

376 Pigeon and Breeding Pen

1966. Cuban Shells. Multicoloured.
1384 1c. Type **375** 20 10
1385 2c. Measled cowrie 25 15
1386 3c. West Indian fighting conch 35 15
1387 7c. Rough American scallops 40 20
1388 9c. Crenate liguus 50 20
1389 10c. Atlantic trumpet triton 80 30
1390 13c. Archer's Cuban liguus 1·90 55

1966. Pigeon-breeding. Multicoloured.
1391 1c. Type **376** 20 10
1392 2c. Pigeon and time-clock 20 10
1393 3c. Pigeon and pigeon-loft 20 15
1394 7c. Pigeon and breeder tending pigeon-loft . . . 35 20
1395 9c. Pigeon and pigeon-yard 35 25
1396 10c. Pigeon and breeder placing message in capsule 1·10 35
1397 13c. Pigeons in flight over map of Cuba ($44\frac{1}{2} \times 28$ mm) . . . . . . 1·75 60

1966. National and Provincial Arms. Mult.
1398 1c. Type **377** 10 10
1399 2c. Arms of Havana 10 10
1400 3c. Arms of Matanzas . . . 15 10
1401 4c. Arms of Las Villas . . . 20 10
1402 5c. Arms of Camaguey . . . 30 15
1403 9c. Arms of Oriente 45 30
1404 13c. National Arms (26×44 mm) . . . . . . 1·00 40

378 "Queen" and Simultaneous Games

1966. 17th Chess Olympiad, Havana.
1405 – 1c. black and green 10 10
1406 – 2c. black and blue . . . 10 10
1407 – 3c. black and red 20 10
1408 – 9c. black and ochre . . . 35 20
1409 **378** 10c. black and mauve . . 85 30
1410 – 13c. black, blue & turq 1·10 65
DESIGNS—VERT: 1c. "Pawn"; 2c. "Rook"; 3c. "Knight"; 9c. "Bishop". HORIZ: 13c. Olympiad Emblem and "King".

380 Lenin Hospital

1966. Cuban–Soviet Friendship. Mult.
1412 2c. Type **380** 15 10
1413 3c. World map and "Havana" (tanker) . . . 40 10
1414 10c. Cuban and Soviet technicians 60 20
1415 13c. Cuban fruit-pickers and Soviet tractor technicians 1·10 55

381 A. Roldan and Music of "Fiesta Negra"

1966. Song Festival.
1416 **381** 1c. brown, black & grn 10 10
1417 – 2c. brown, black & mve 10 10
1418 – 3c. brown, black & blue 25 10
1419 – 7c. brown, black & vio 40 10
1420 – 9c. brown, black & yell 40 20
1421 – 10c. brn, blk & orge . . 1·25 30
1422 – 13c. brown, black & bl 1·75 60
CUBAN COMPOSERS AND WORKS: 2c. E. S. de Fuentes and "Tu" (habanera, Cuban dance). 3c. M. Simons and "El Manisero". 7c. J. Anckermann and "El arroyo que murmura". 9c. A. G. Caturla and "Pastoral Lullaby". 10c. E. Grenet and "Ay Mama Ines". 13c. E. Lecuona and "La Comparsa" (dance).

382 Bacteriological Warfare **383** A. L. Fernandez ("Nico") and Beach Landing

1966. "Genocide in Viet-Nam". Mult.
1423 2c. Type **382** 10 10
1424 3c. Gas warfare 20 10
1425 13c. "Conventional" bombing . . . . 1·10 45

1966. 10th Anniv of 1956 Revolutionary Successes. Portrait in black and brown.
1426 **383** 1c. brown and green . . 10 10
1427 – 2c. brown and purple . . 10 10
1428 – 3c. brown and purple . . 15 10
1429 – 7c. brown and blue . . . 20 15
1430 – 9c. brown and turquoise 35 15
1431 – 10c. brown and olive . . 1·25 35
1432 – 13c. brown and orange 1·10 55
HEROES AND SCENES: 2c. C. Gonzalez and beach landing. 3c. J. Tey and street fighting. 7c. T. Aloma and street fighting. 9c. O. Parellada and street fighting. 10c. J. M. Marquez and beach landing. 13c. F. Pais and trial scene.

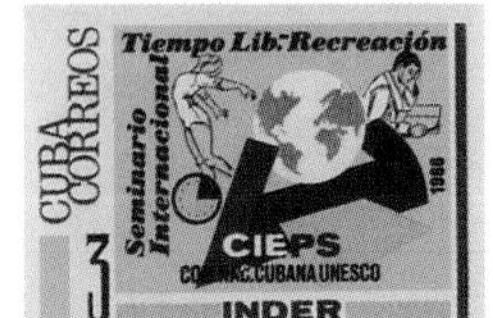

384 Globe and Recreational Activities

1966. International Leisure Time and Recreation Seminar. Multicoloured.
1433 3c. Type **384** 15 10
1434 9c. Clock, eye and world map 85 20
1435 13c. Seminar poster . . . . 1·10 45

385 Arrow and Telecommunications Symbols

1966. 1st National Telecommunications Forum. Multicoloured.
1436 3c. Type **385** 20 10
1437 10c. Target and satellites . . 85 20
1438 13c. Shell and satellites ($28\frac{1}{2}\times36$ mm) . . . . . 1·25 45

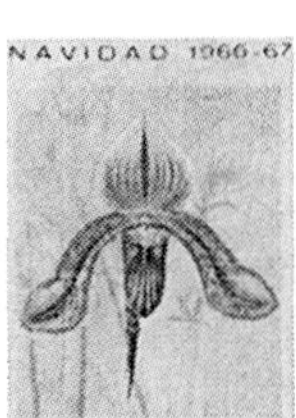

386 "Cypripedium eurilochus"
387 "Cattleya speciosissima"

1966. Christmas. Orchids. Multicoloured.
(a) As T **386**.
1440 1c. Type **386** 30 15
1441 3c. "Cypripedium hookerae volunteanum 45 25
1442 13c. "Cypripedium stonei" 1·75 95

(b) As T **387**.
1443a/d 1c. multicoloured 30 15
1444a/d 3c. multicoloured 45 25
1445a/d 13c. multicoloured . . . 1·75 95
DESIGNS: No. 1443a, Type **387**; 1443b, "Cattleya mendelli"; 1443c, "Cattleya trianae"; 1443d, "Cattleya labiata"; 1444a, "Cypripedium morganiae"; 1444b, "Cattleya" "Countess of Derby"; 1444c, "Cattleya gigas"; 1444d, "Cypripedium stonei"; 1445a, "Cattleya mendelli" "Countess of Montrose"; 1445b, "Oncidium macranthum"; 1445c, "Cattleya aurea"; 1445d, "Laelia anceps".
Prices are for single stamps.

388 Flag and Hands ("1959—Liberation")

1966. 8th Anniv of Revolution. Mult.
1446 3c. Type **388** 15 10
1447 3c. Clenched fist ("1960—Agrarian Reform") . . . 15 10
1448 3c. Hands holding pencil ("1961—Education") . . 15 10
1449 3c. Hand protecting plant ("1965—Agriculture") . . 15 10
1450 13c. Head of Rodin's statue, "The Thinker", and arrows ("1962—Planning") (vert) 90 35
1451 13c. Hands moving lever ("1963—Organization") (vert) 90 35
1452 13c. Hand holding plant within cogwheel ("1964—Economy") (vert) 90 35
1453 13c. Hand holding rifle-butt, and part of globe ("1966—Solidarity") (vert) 90 35

389 "Spring" (after J. Arche)

1967. National Museum Exhibits. Paintings (1st series). Multicoloured.
1454 1c. "Coffee-pot" (A. A. Leon) (vert) 30 10
1455 2c. "Peasants" (E. Abela) (vert) 40 10
1456 3c. Type **389** 60 15
1457 13c. "Still Life" (Amelia Pelaez) (vert) . . . . . . 1·50 75
1458 30c. "Landscape" (G. Escalante) . . . . . 3·75 1·40
See also Nos. 1648/54, 1785/91, 1871/7, 1900/6, 2005/11, 2048/54, 2104/9, 2180/5, 2260/5, 2346/51, 2430/5, 2530/5, 2620/5, 2685/90, 2816/21, 3218/23 and 3229/34.

390 Menelao Mora, Jose A. Echeverria and Attack on Presidential Palace

1967. National Events of 13 March 1957.
1459 **390** 3c. green and black . . . 15 10
1460 – 13c. brown and black . . 1·50 50
1461 – 30c. blue and black . . . 1·40 55
DESIGNS ($36\frac{1}{2}\times24\frac{1}{2}$ mm.): 13c. Calixto Sanchez and "Corynthia" landing; 30c. Dionisio San Roman and Cienfuegos revolt.

391 "Homo habilis"

1967. "Prehistoric Man". Multicoloured.
1462 1c. Type **391** 10 10
1463 2c. "Australopithecus" . . . 15 10
1464 3c. "Pithecanthropus erectus" 15 10
1465 4c. Peking man 20 15
1466 5c. Neanderthal man . . . 30 20
1467 13c. Cro-Magnon man carving ivory tusk . . . . 1·00 45
1468 20c. Cro-Magnon man painting on wall of cave 2·00 65

392 Victoria

1967. Stamp Day. Carriages. Multicoloured.
1469 3c. Type **392** 20 15
1470 9c. Volanta 95 30
1471 13c. Quitrin . . . . 1·40 55

393 Cuban Pavilion

1967. "Expo 67", Montreal.
1472 **393** 1c. multicoloured 20 10
1473 – 2c. multicoloured 20 10
1474 – 3c. multicoloured 25 10
1475 – 13c. multicoloured . . . 1·25 55
1476 – 20c. multicoloured . . . 1·50 60
DESIGNS: 2c. Bathysphere, satellite and met. balloon ("Man as Explorer"); 3c. Ancient rock-drawing and tablet ("Man as Creator"); 13c. Tractor, ear of wheat and electronic console ("Man as Producer"); 20c. Olympic athletes ("Man in the Community").

394 "Eugenia malaccencis"
395 "Giselle"

1967. 150th Anniv of Cuban Botanical Gardens. Multicoloured.
1477 1c. Type **394** 20 10
1478 2c. "Jacaranda filicifolia" . . 20 10
1479 3c. "Coroupita guianensis" 30 10
1480 4c. "Spathodea campanulata" 30 10
1481 5c. "Cassia fistula" 40 15
1482 13c. "Plumieria alba" . . . 1·25 65
1483 20c. "Erythrina poeppigiana" . . . . . . 2·00 75

1967. Int Ballet Festival, Havana. Mult.
1484 1c. Type **395** 30 10
1485 2c. "Swan Lake" 30 10
1486 3c. "Don Quixote" 35 10
1487 4c. "Calaucan" 75 15
1488 13c. "Swan Lake" (different) 1·60 60
1489 20c. "Nutcracker" . . . . . 2·25 1·00

396 Baseball

1967. 5th Pan-American Games, Winnipeg. Mult.
1490 1c. Type **396** 15 10
1491 2c. Swimming 15 10
1492 3c. Basketball (vert) 30 10
1493 4c. Gymnastics (vert) . . . 30 10
1494 5c. Water-polo (vert) . . . 40 15
1495 13c. Weight-lifting . . . . . 1·25 35
1496 20c. Hurling the javelin . . 2·25 65

397 L. A. Turcios Lima, Map and OLAS Emblem

1967. 1st Conference of Latin-American Solidarity Organization (OLAS), Havana.
1497 13c. black, red and blue . . 95 40
1498 13c. black, red and brown 95 40
1499 13c. black, red and lilac . . 95 40
1500 13c. black, red and green . . 95 40
DESIGNS: No. 1497, Type **397**; No. 1498, Fabricio Ojidia; No. 1499, L. de La Puente Uceda; No. 1500, Camilo Torres; Martyrs of Guatemala, Venezuela, Peru and Colombia respectively. Each with map and OLAS emblem.

398 "Portrait of Sonny Rollins" (Alan Davie)

1967. "Contemporary Art" (Havana Exn from the Paris "Salon de Mayo"). Various designs showing modern paintings. Sizes given in millimetres. Multicoloured.
1501 1c. Type **398** 20 20
1502 1c. "Twelve Selenites" (F. Labisse) (39×41) . . 20 20
1503 1c. "Night of the Drinker" (F. Hundertwasser) (53×41) 20 20
1504 1c. "Figure" (Mariano) (48×41) 20 20
1505 1c. "All-Souls" (W. Lam) (45×41) 20 20
1506 2c. "Darkness and Cracks" (A. Tapies) (37×54) . . . 30 20
1507 2c. "Bathers" (G. Singier) (37×54) 30 20
1508 2c. "Torso of a Muse" (J. Arp) (37×46) 30 20
1509 2c. "Figure" (M. W. Svanberg) (57×54) . . . 30 20
1510 2c. "Oppenheimer's Information" (Erro) (37×41) 30 20
1511 3c. "Where Cardinals are Born" (Max Ernst) (37×52) 50 30
1512 3c. "Havana Landscape" (Portocarrero) (37×41) 50 30
1513 3c. "EG 12" (V. Vasarely) (37×42) 50 30
1514 3c. "Frisco" (A. Calder) (37×50) 50 30
1515 3c. "The Man with the Pipe" (Picasso) (37×52) 50 30
1516 4c. "Abstract Composition" (S. Poliakoff) (36×50) . . 60 40
1517 4c. "Painting" (Bram van Velde) (36×68) 60 40
1518 4c. "Sower of Fires" (detail, Matta) (36×47) 60 40
1519 4c. "The Art of Living" (R. Magritte) (36×50) . . 60 40
1520 4c. "Poem" (J. Miro) (36×56) 60 40
1521 13c. "Young Tigers" (J. Messagier) (50×33) . . 1·25 60
1522 13c. "Painting" (Vieira da Silva) (50×36) . . . . . 1·25 60
1523 13c. "Live Cobra" (P. Alechinsky) (50×35) 1·25 60
1524 13c. "Stalingrad" (detail, A. Jorn) (50×46) . . . . 1·25 60
1525 30c. "Warriors" (E. Pignon) (55×32) . . . . 6·00 2·50

399 Common Octopus

1967. World Underwater Fishing Championships. Multicoloured.
1527 1c. Green moray 20 10
1528 2c. Type **399** 20 10
1529 3c. Great barracuda 20 10
1530 4c. Bull shark 40 10
1531 5c. Spotted Jewfish 75 30
1532 13c. Chupare stingray . . . 1·75 75
1533 20c. Green turtle . . . . . 2·75 85

400 "Sputnik 1"

1967. Soviet Space Achievements. Mult.
1534 1c. Type **400** 10 10
1535 2c. "Lunik 3" 10 10
1536 3c. "Venusik" 15 10
1537 4c. "Cosmos" 20 10
1538 5c. "Mars 1" 30 15
1539 9c. "Electron 1, 2" 40 20
1540 10c. "Luna 9" 55 35
1541 13c. "Luna 10" . . . . . . 1·25 50

401 "Storming the Winter Palace" (from painting by Sokolov, Skalia and Miasnikova)

1967. 50th Anniv of October Revolution. Paintings. Multicoloured.
1543 1c. Type **401** 20 10
1544 2c. "Lenin addressing 2nd Soviet Congress" (Serov) (48×36) 20 10
1545 3c. "Lenin in the year 1919" (Nalbandian) (35×37) . . 30 10
1546 4c. "Lenin explaining the GOELRO Map" (Schmatko) (48×36) . . . 30 15
1547 5c. "Dawn of the Five-Year Plan" construction work (Romas) (50×36) . . . . 1·75 50
1548 13c. "Kusnetzkroi steel Furnace No. 1" (Kotov) (36×51) . . . . 1·25 50
1549 30c. "Victory Jubilation" (Krivonogov) (50×36) . . 1·75 75

402 Royal Force Castle, Havana

1967. Historic Cuban Buildings. Multicoloured.
1550 1c. Type **402** 10 10
1551 2c. Iznaga Tower, Trinidad ($26\frac{1}{2}\times47\frac{1}{2}$) 15 10
1552 3c. Castle of Our Lady of the Angels, Cienfuegos ($41\frac{1}{2}\times29$) 20 10
1553 4c. Church of St. Francis of Paula, Havana ($41\frac{1}{2}\times29$) 20 10

1554 13c. Convent of St. Francis, Havana (39 × 13) . . . . 1·10 45
1555 30c. Morro Castle, Santiago de Cuba (43 × 26) . . . . 1·75 75

403 Ostrich

404 Golden Pheasant

1967. Christmas. Birds of Havana Zoo. Mult. (a) As T **403**.
1556 1c. Type **403** 65 70
1557 3c. Hyacinth macaw . . . . 1·25 1·10
1558 13c. Greater flamingoes . . 3·00 90

(b) As T **404**.
1559a/d 1c. multicoloured 65 70
1560a/d 3c. multicoloured . . . . 1·25 1·10
1561a/d 13c. multicoloured . . . 3·00 1·90
DESIGNS: No. 1559a, Type **404**; 1559b, White stork; 1559c, Crowned crane; 1559d, Emu; 1560a, Grey parrot; 1560b, Chattering lory; 1560c, Keel-billed toucan; 1560d, Sulphur-crested cockatoo; 1561a, American white pelican, 1561b, Egyptian goose; 1561c, Mandarin; 1561d, Black swan.
Prices are for single stamps.

405 "Che" Guevara

1968. Major Ernesto "Che" Guevara Commem.
1562 **405** 13c. black and red . . . 1·75 50

406 Man and Tree ("Problems of Artistic Creation, Scientific and Technical Work")

1968. Cultural Congress, Havana. Mult.
1563 3c. Chainbreaker cradling flame ("Culture and Independence") (vert) . . 10 10
1564 3c. Hand with spanner and rifle ("Integral Formation of Man") (vert) 10 10
1565 13c. Demographic emblems ("Intellectual Responsibility") (vert) . . 85 30
1566 13c. Hand with communications emblems ("Culture and Mass-Communications Media") (vert) 90 35
1567 30c. Type **406** . . . . . . 1·25 65

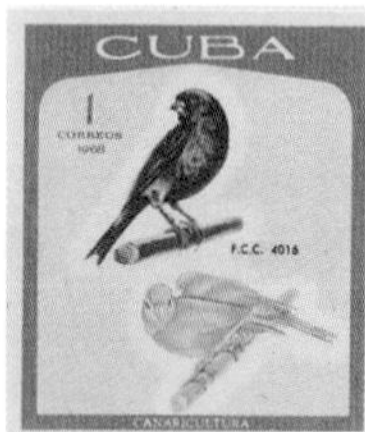

407 Canaries

1968. Canary-breeding.
1568 **407** 1c. multicoloured 10 10
1569 – 2c. multicoloured 10 10
1570 – 3c. multicoloured 10 10
1571 – 4c. multicoloured 15 10
1572 – 5c. multicoloured 30 15
1573 – 13c. multicoloured . . . 1·40 55
1574 – 20c. multicoloured . . . 1·60 65
DESIGNS: Canaries and breeding cycle—mating, eggs, incubation and rearing young.

408 "The Village Postman" (after J. Harris)

1968. Stamp Day. Multicoloured.
1575 13c. Type **408** . . . . . . 1·10 35
1576 30c. "The Philatelist" (after G. Sciltian) . . . . 1·60 50

409 Nurse tending Child ("Anti-Polio Campaign")

1968. 20th Anniv of W.H.O.
1577 **409** 13c. black, red and olive 1·10 40
1578 – 30c. black, blue & olive 1·40 55
DESIGN: 30c. Two doctors ("Hospital Services").

410 "Children"

1968. International Children's Day.
1579 **410** 3c. multicoloured 55 20

411 "Cuatro Vientos" and Route Map

1968. 35th Anniv of Seville–Camaguey Flight by Barberan and Collar. Multicoloured.
1580 13c. Type **411** . . . . . . 1·40 30
1581 30c. Captain M. Barberan and Lieut. J. Collar . . . 1·40 40

412 "Canned Fish"

1968. Cuban Food Products. Multicoloured.
1582 1c. Type **412** 10 10
1583 2c. "Milk Products" 15 10
1584 3c. "Poultry and Eggs" . . 25 20
1585 13c. "Cuban Rum" . . . . 1·40 35
1586 20c. "Canned Shell-fish" . . 1·60 50

413 Siboney Farmhouse

1968. 15th Anniv of Attack on Moncada Barracks. Multicoloured.
1587 3c. Type **413** 10 10
1588 13c. Map of Santiago de Cuba and assault route 1·00 40
1589 30c. Students and school buildings (on site of Moncada Barracks) . . . 1·60 55

414 Committee Members and Emblem

1968. 8th Anniv of Revolutionary Defence Committee.
1590 **414** 3c. multicoloured 55 15

415 Che Guevara and Rifleman

1968. Day of the Guerrillas.
1591 **415** 1c. black, green & gold 10 10
1592 – 3c. black, brown & gold 10 10
1593 – 9c. multicoloured 30 10
1594 – 10c. black, green and gold 60 15
1595 13c. black, pink & gold 1·10 45
DESIGNS—"Che" Guevara and: 3c. Machine-gunners; 9c. Riflemen; 10c. Soldiers cheering; 13c. Map of Caribbean and South America.

416 C. M. de Cespedes and Broken Wheel

1968. Centenary of Cuban War of Independence. Multicoloured.
1596 1c. Type **416** 10 10
1597 1c. E. Betances and horsemen 10 10
1598 1c. I. Agramonte and monument 10 10
1599 1c. A. Maceo and "The Protest" 10 10
1600 1c. J. Marti & patriots . . . 10 10
1601 3c. M. Gomez and "Invasion" 10 10
1602 3c. J. A. Mella and declaration 10 10
1603 3c. A. Guiteras and monument 10 10
1604 3c. A. Santamaria and riflemen 10 10
1605 3c. F. Pais & graffiti 10 10
1606 9c. J. Echeverria and students 50 15
1607 13c. C. Cienfuegos and rebels . . . . 1·25 45
1608 30c. "Che" Guevara and Castro addressing meeting 1·50 70

418 Parade of Athletes, Olympic Flag and Flame

1968. Olympic Games, Mexico. Multicoloured.
1610 1c. Type **418** 10 10
1611 2c. Basketball (vert) 10 10
1612 3c. Throwing the hammer (vert) 10 10
1613 4c. Boxing 15 10
1614 5c. Water-polo 20 10
1615 13c. Pistol-shooting . . . . 1·10 40
1616 30c. Calendar-stone ($32\frac{1}{2}$ × 50 mm) . . . . . 1·60 55

419 Crop-spraying

1968. Civil Activities of Cuban Armed Forces. Multicoloured.
1618 3c. Type **419** 10 10
1619 9c. "Che Guevara" Brigade 40 10
1620 10c. Road-building Brigade 60 20
1621 13c. Agricultural Brigade . . 1·25 50

420 "Manrique de Lara's Family" (J.-B. Vermay)

1968. 150th Anniv of San Alejandro Painting School. Multicoloured.
1622 1c. Type **420** 20 10
1623 2c. "Seascape" (L. Romanach) (48 × 37) 30 10
1624 3c. "Wild Cane" (A. Rodriguez) (40 × 48) 30 10
1625 4c. "Self-portrait" (M. Melero) (40 × 50) . . 30 15
1626 5c. "The Lottery List" (J. J. Tejada) (48 × 37) 60 30
1627 13c. "Portrait of Nina" (A. Menocal) (40 × 50) . . 1·40 50
1628 30c. "Landscape" (E. S. Chartrand) (54 × 37) . . . 2·25 75

421 Cuban Flag and Rifles

1969. 10th Anniv of "The Triumph of the Rebellion".
1630 **421** 13c. multicoloured . . . 1·10 40

422 Gutierrez and Sanchez

1969. Cent of Villaclarenos Patriots Rebellion.
1631 **422** 3c. multicoloured 55 20

423 Mariana Grajales, Rose and Statue

1969. Cuban Women's Day.
1632 **423** 3c. multicoloured 55 20

424 Cuban Pioneers

1969. Cuban Pioneers and Young Communist Unions. Multicoloured.
1633 3c. Type **424** 20 15
1634 13c. Young Communists . . 1·00 50

425 Guaimaro Assembly

1969. Centenary of Guaimaro Assembly.
1635 **425** 3c. brown and sepia . . 55 20

426 "The Postman" (J. C. Cazin)

1969. Cuban Stamp Day. Multicoloured.
1636 13c. Type **426** . . . . . . 1·10 45
1637 30c. "Portrait of a Young Man" (George Romney) (36 × 44 mm) . . . . . . 1·75 65

427 Agrarian Law, Headquarters, Eviction of Family, and Tractor

1969. 10th Anniv of Agrarian Reform.
1638 **427** 13c. multicoloured . . . 1·10 45

428 Hermit Crab in West Indian Chank

1969. Crustaceans. Multicoloured.
1639 1c. Type **428** 15 10
1640 2c. Spiny shrimp 15 10
1641 3c. Spiny lobster 15 10
1642 4c. Blue crab 15 15
1643 5c. Land crab 40 15
1644 13c. Freshwater prawn . . . 1·75 40
1645 30c. Pebble crab . . . . . 3·00 60

429 Factory and Peasants

1969. 50th Anniv of I.L.O. Mult.
1646 3c. Type **429** 20 15
1647 13c. Worker breaking chain 1·10 45

430 "Flowers" (R. Milian)

1969. National Museum Paintings (2nd series). Multicoloured.
1648 1c. Type **430** 10 10
1649 2c. "The Annunciation" (A. Eiriz) 10 10
1650 3c. "Factory" (M. Pogolotti) 75 15
1651 4c. "Territorial Waters" (L. M. Pedro) 40 10
1652 5c. "Miss Sarah Gale" (John Hoppner) 40 10
1653 13c. "Two Women wearing Mantillas" (I. Zuloaga) 1·25 45
1654 30c. "Virgin and Child" (F. Zurbaran) . . . . . 1·75 55
SIZES—HORIZ: 2c. As No. 1648. VERT: 3c. As No. 1648. 4c. 40 × 44 mm; 5c. and 30c. 40 × 46 mm; 13c. 38 × 42 mm.

431 Television Cameras and Emblem

1969. Cuban Radiodiffusion Institute. Mult.
1655 3c. Type **431** 20 15
1656 13c. Broadcasting tower and "Globe" . . . . 1·10 50
1657 1p. TV Reception diagram 2·50 1·10

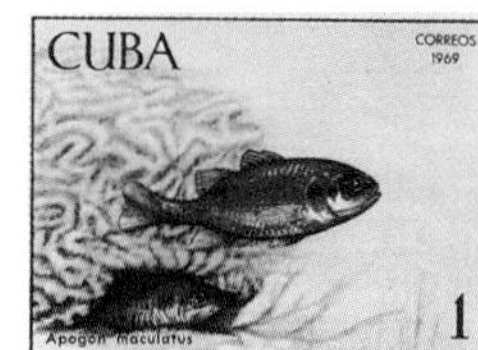

432 Flamefish

1969. Cuban Pisciculture. Multicoloured.
1658 1c. Type **432** 15 10
1659 2c. Spanish hogfish 15 10
1660 3c. Yellow-tailed damselfish 25 10
1661 4c. Royal gramma 25 10
1662 5c. Blue chromis 35 10
1663 13c. Black-barred soldierfish 2·10 40
1664 30c. Man-of-war fish (vert) 2·75 65

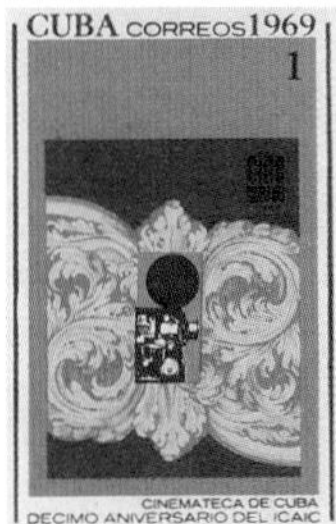

433 "Cuban Film Library"

1969. 10th Anniv of Cuban Cinema Industry. Multicoloured.
1665 1c. Type **433** 10 10
1666 3c. "Documentaries" . . . 15 10
1667 13c. "Cartoons" . . . . . 1·10 50
1668 30c. "Full-length Features" 1·75 60

434 "Napoleon in Milan". (A. Appiani (the Elder))

1969. Paintings in Napoleonic Museum, Havana. Multicoloured.
1669 1c. Type **434** 20 10
1670 2c. "Hortensia de Beauharnais" (F. Gerard) 25 10
1671 3c. "Napoleon-First Consul" (J. B. Regnault) 25 10
1672 4c. "Elisa Bonaparte" (R. Lefevre) 30 10
1673 5c. "Napoleon planning the Coronation" (J. G. Vibert) 50 25
1674 13c. "Corporal of Cuirassiers" (J. Meissonier) . . . . . 1·75 55
1675 30c. "Napoleon Bonaparte" (R. Lefevre) . . . . . 2·50 65
SIZES—VERT: 2c. 42½ × 55 mm; 3c. 46 × 56½ mm; 4c., 13c., 44 × 63 mm; 30c. 45½ × 60 mm. HORIZ: 5c. 64 × 47 mm.

435 Baseball Players

1969. Cuba's Victory in World Amateur Baseball Championships, Dominican Republic.
1676 **435** 13c. multicoloured . . . 1·25 50

436 Von Humboldt, Book and American Eel

1969. Birth Bicentenary of Alexander von Humboldt. Multicoloured.
1677 3c. Type **436** 25 10
1678 13c. Night monkey . . . . 1·75 75
1679 30c. Andean condors . . . 3·75 1·00

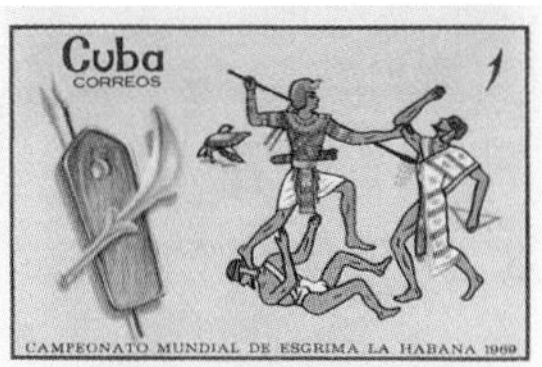

437 Ancient Egyptians in Combat

1969. World Fencing Championships, Havana. Multicoloured.
1683 1c. Type **437** 20 10
1684 2c. Roman Gladiators . . . 20 10
1685 3c. Norman and Viking . . 20 10
1686 4c. Medieval tournament . . 25 10
1687 5c. French musketeers . . . 30 10
1688 13c. Japanese samurai . . . 1·25 35
1689 30c. Mounted Cubans, War of Independence . . . . 1·75 60

438 Militiaman

1969. 10th Anniv of National Revolutionary Militias.
1691 **438** 3c. multicoloured 55 20

439 Major Cienfuegos and Wreath on Sea

1969. 10th Anniv of Disappearance of Major Camilo Cienfuego.
1692 **439** 13c. multicoloured . . . 1·10 50

440 Strawberries and Grapes

1969. Agriculture and Livestock Projects. Multicoloured.
1693 1c. Type **440** 10 10
1694 1c. Onion and asparagus . . 10 10
1695 1c. Rice 10 10
1696 1c. Bananas 10 10
1697 3c. Pineapple (vert) 20 10
1698 3c. Tobacco plant (vert) . . 20 10
1699 3c. Citrus fruits (vert) . . . 20 10
1700 3c. Coffee (vert) 20 10
1701 3c. Rabbits (vert) 20 10
1702 10c. Pigs (vert) 25 10
1703 13c. Sugar-cane . . . . . . 1·40 55
1704 30c. Bull . . . . 1·75 65

441 Stadium and Map of Cuba (2nd National Games)

1969. Sporting Events of 1969. Multicoloured.
1705 1c. Type **441** 10 10
1706 2c. Throwing the discus (9th Anniv Games) 10 10
1707 3c. Running (Barrientos commemoration) (vert) . . 10 10
1708 10c. Basketball (2nd Olympic Trial Games) (vert) 20 10
1709 13c. Cycling (6th Cycle Race) (vert) . . . . . 1·50 55
1710 30c. Chessmen and Globe (7th Capablanca Int. Chess Tournament, Havana) (vert) . . . . . 2·00 85

442 "Plumbago capensis"

443 "Petrea volubilis"

1969. Christmas. Flowers. (a) As T **442**. Mult.
1711 1c. Type **442** 25 10
1712 3c. "Turnera ulmifolia" . . 55 20
1713 13c. "Delonix regia" . . . . 1·25 75

(b) As T **443**.
1714a/d 1c. multicoloured 25 10
1715a/d 3c. multicoloured 55 20
1716a/d 13c. multicoloured . . . 1·25 75
DESIGNS: No. 1714a, Type **443**; 1714b, "Clitoria ternatea"; 1714c, "Duranta repens"; 1714d, "Ruellia tuberosa"; 1715a, "Thevetia peruviana"; 1715b, "Hibiscus elatus"; 1715c, "Allamanda cathartica"; 1715d, "Cosmos sulphureus"; 1716a, "Nerium oleander" (wrongly inscr "Neriun"); 1716b, "Cordia sebestena"; 1716c, "Lochnera rosea"; 1716d, "Jatropha integerrima".
Prices are for single stamps.

444 River Snake

1969. Swamp Fauna. Multicoloured.
1717 1c. Type **444** 10 10
1718 2c. Banana frog 10 10
1719 3c. Giant tropical gar (fish) 10 10
1720 4c. Dwarf hutia (vert) . . . 15 20
1721 5c. Alligator 15 10
1722 13c. Cuban Amazon (vert) 3·50 60
1723 30c. Red-winged blackbird (vert) . . . . 4·50 1·00

445 "Jibacoa Beach" (J. Hernandez)

446 Yamagua

1970. Tourism. Multicoloured.
1724 1c. Type **445** 10 10
1725 3c. "Trinidad City" 10 10
1726 13c. Santiago de Cuba . . . 1·25 55
1727 30c. Vinales Valley . . . . 1·75 65

1970. Medicinal Plants. Multicoloured.
1728 1c. Type **446** 10 10
1729 3c. Albahaca Morada . . . 10 10
1730 10c. Curbana 25 10
1731 13c. Romerillo . . . . . . 1·25 55
1732 30c. Marilope . . . . 1·60 65
1733 50c. Aguedita . . . . 2·25 80

447 Weightlifting

1970. 11th Central American and Caribbean Games. Multicoloured.
1734 1c. Type **447** 10 10
1735 3c. Boxing 10 10
1736 10c. Gymnastics 15 10
1737 13c. Athletics 1·10 40
1738 30c. Fencing 1·60 60

448 "Enjoyment of Life"

1970. "EXPO 70" World Fair, Osaka, Japan. Multicoloured.
1740 1c. Type **448** 10 10
1741 2c. "Uses of nature" (vert) 10 10
1742 3c. "Better Living Standards" 20 10
1743 13c. "International Co-operation" (vert) 1·25 35
1744 30c. Cuban Pavilion 1·75 55

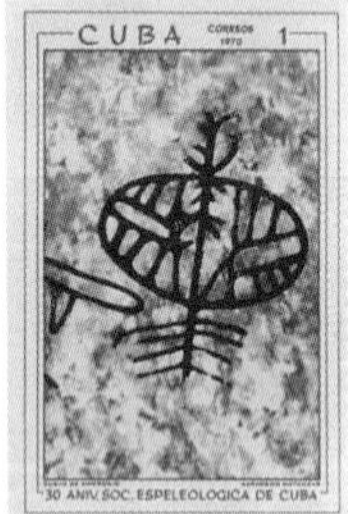

449 Oval Pictograph, Ambrosio Cave

1970. 30th Anniv of Cuban Speleological Society.
1745 **449** 1c. red and brown 10 10
1746 – 2c. black and brown 10 10
1747 – 3c. red and brown 10 10
1748 – 4c. black and brown 10 10
1749 – 5c. black, red and brown 15 10
1750 – 13c. black and brown 1·10 50
1751 – 30c. red and brown 2·25 55
DESIGNS—HORIZ: (42 × 32½ mm): 2c. Cave 1, Punta del Este, Isle of Pines; 5c. As 2c. (different); 30c. Stylized fish, Cave 2, Punta del Este. VERT: 3c. Stylized mask, Pichardo Cave, Sierra de Cubitas; 4c. Conical complex, Ambrosio Cave, Varadero; 13c. Human face, Garcia Robiou Cave, Catalina de Guines.

450 J. D. Blino, Balloon and Spacecraft

1970. Aviation Pioneers. Multicoloured.
1752 3c. Type **450** 50 10
1753 13c. A. Theodore, balloon and satellite 1·75 45

451 "Lenin in Kazan" (O. Vishniakov) (½-size illustration)

1970. Birth Centenary of Lenin. Paintings. Mult.
1754 1c. Type **451** 10 10
1755 2c. "Lenin's Youth" (Prager) 10 10
1756 3c. "The 2nd Socialist Party Congress" (Vinogradov) 10 10
1757 4c. "The First Manifesto" (Golubkov) 15 10
1758 5c. "The First Day of Soviet Power" (Babasiuk) 15 10
1759 13c. "Lenin in the Smolny Institute" (Sokolov) 1·25 45
1760 30c. "Autumn in Gorky" (Varlamov) 1·75 55
SIZES: 4, 5c. As Type **451**: 2, 3, 13, 30c. 70 × 34 mm.

452 "The Letter" (J. Archer)

1970. Cuban Stamp Day. Paintings. Mult.
1762 13c. Type **452** 1·10 45
1763 30c. "Portrait of a Cadet" (anonymous) (35 × 49 mm) 1·40 55

453 Da Vinci's Anatomical Drawing, Earth and Moon

1970. World Telecommunications Day.
1764 **453** 30c. multicoloured 1·40 55

454 Vietnamese Fisherman

1970. 80th Birthday of Ho Chi Minh (North Vietnamese leader). Multicoloured.
1765 1c. Type **454** 10 10
1766 3c. Cultivating rice-fields 20 10
1767 3c. Two Vietnamese children 20 10
1768 3c. Children entering air-raid shelter 20 10
1769 3c. Camouflaged machine-shop 25 10
1770 3c. Rice harvest 25 10
1771 13c. Pres. Ho Chi Minh 1·10 50
SIZES: Nos. 1766/7, 33 × 44½ mm, Nos. 1768, 1770, 33½ × 46 mm, No. 1769, 35 × 42 mm, No. 1771, 34½ × 39½ mm.

455 Tobacco Plantation and "Eden" Cigar band

1970. "Cuban Cigar Industry". Multicoloured.
1772 3c. Type **455** 10 10
1773 13c. 19 th century cigar factory and "El Mambi" band 95 50
1774 30c. Packing cigars (19th-century) and "Gran Pena" band 1·50 70

456 Cane crushing Machinery

1970. Cuban Sugar Harvest Target. "Over 10 million Tons". Multicoloured.
1775 1c. Type **456** 10 10
1776 2c. Sowing and crop-spraying 10 10
1777 3c. Cutting sugar-cane 10 10
1778 10c. Ox-cart and diesel-electric locomotive 3·00 30
1779 13c. Modern cane cutting machine 1·00 20
1780 30c. Cane-cutters and globe (vert) 1·40 50
1781 1p. Sugar warehouse 2·75 1·25

457 P. Figueredo and National Anthem (original version)

1970. Death Centenary of Pedro Figueredo (composer of National Anthem). Multicoloured.
1782 3c. Type **457** 20 10
1783 20c. 18 98 version of anthem 1·10 40

458 Cuban Girl, Flag and Federation Badge

1970. 10th Anniv of Cuban Women's Federation.
1784 **458** 3c. multicoloured 50 35

459 "Peasant Militia" (S. C. Moreno)

1970. National Museum Paintings (3rd series). Multicoloured.
1785 1c. Type **459** 10 10
1786 2c. "Washerwoman" (A. Fernandez) 10 10
1787 3c. "Puerta del Sol, Madrid" (L. P. Alcazar) 10 10
1788 4c. "Fishermen's Wives" (J. Sorolla) 10 10
1789 5c. "Portrait of a Lady" (T. de Keyser) 15 10
1790 13c. "Mrs. Edward Foster" (Lawrence) 1·25 45
1791 30c. "Tropical Gipsy" (V. M. Garcia) 1·75 65
SIZES—HORIZ: 2c., 3c. 46 × 42 mm. SQUARE. 4c. 41 × 41 mm. VERT: 5c., 13c., 30c. 39 × 46 mm.

460 Crowd in Jose Marti Square, Havana (½-size illustration)

1970. 10th Anniv of Havana Declaration.
1792 **460** 3c. blue, red & black 15 10

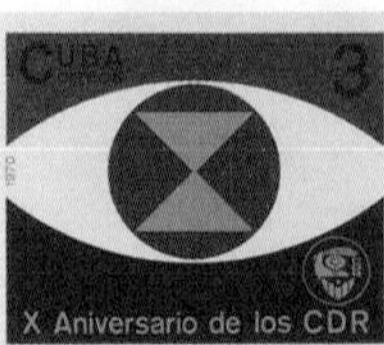

461 C. D. R. Emblem

1970. 10th Anniv of Revolution Defence Committees.
1793 **461** 3c. multicoloured 40 15

462 Laboratory, Emblem and Microscope

1970. 39th A.T.A.C. (Sugar Technicians Assn) Conference.
1794 **462** 30c. multicoloured 1·50 50

463 Helmeted Guineafowl

1970. Wildlife. Multicoloured.
1795 1c. Type **463** 90 30
1796 2c. Black-billed whistling duck 1·00 30
1797 3c. Common pheasant 1·25 30
1798 4c. Mourning dove 1·40 30
1799 5c. Northern bobwhite 1·50 40
1800 13c. Wild boar 1·50 70
1801 30c. White-tailed deer 2·50 1·00

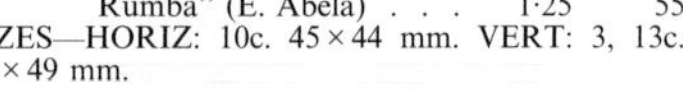

464 "Black Magic Parade" (M. Puente)

1970. Afro-Cuban Folklore Paintings. Mult.
1802 1c. Type **464** 10 10
1803 3c. "Zapateo Hat Dance" (V. L. Landaluze) 10 10
1804 10c. "Los Hoyos Conga Dance" (D. Ravenet) 50 40
1805 13c. "Climax of the Rumba" (E. Abela) 1·25 55
SIZES—HORIZ: 10c. 45 × 44 mm. VERT: 3, 13c. 37 × 49 mm.

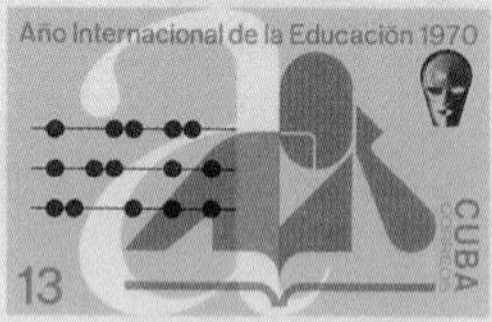

465 Common Zebra on Road Crossing

1970. Road Safety Week. Multicoloured.
1806 3c. Type **465** 35 15
1807 9c. Prudence the Bear on point duty 55 15

466 Letter "a" and Abacus

1970. International Education Year. Mult.
1808 13c. Type **466** 1·10 20
1809 30c. Microscope and cow 1·40 45

467 Cuban Blackbird

468 Cuban Pygmy Owl

1970. Christmas. Birds. Multicoloured. (a) As T **467**.
1810 1c. Type **467** 75 30
1811 3c. Oriente warbler 1·75 40
1812 13c. Zapata sparrow 3·25 1·00

(b) As T **468**.
1813a/d 1c. multicoloured 75 30
1814a/d 3c. multicoloured 1·75 40
1815a/d 13c. multicoloured 3·25 1·00
DESIGNS: No. 1813a, Type **468**; 1813b, Cuban tody; 1813c, Cuban green woodpecker; 1813d, Zapata wren; 1814a, Cuban solitaire; 1814b, Blue-grey gnatcatcher; 1814c, Cuban vireo; 1814d, Yellow-headed warbler; 1815a, Hook-billed kite; 1815b, Gundlach's hawk; 1815c, Blue-headed quail dove; 1815d, Cuban conure.
Prices are for single stamps.

469 School Badge and Cadet Colour-party

1970. "Camilo Cienfuegos" Military School.
1816 **469** 3c. multicoloured 40 20

470 "Reporter" with Pen

1971. 7th Journalists International Organization Congress, Havana.
1817 **470** 13c. multicoloured . . . 95 35

471 Lockheed 8A Sirius

1971. 35th Anniv of Camaguey–Seville Flight by Menendez Pelaez. Multicoloured.
1818 13c. Type **471** . . . . . . 1·40 20
1819 30c. Lieut. Menendez Pelaez and map . . . . 1·75 50

472 Meteorological Class **473** Games Emblem

1971. World Meteorological Day. Multicoloured.
1820 1c. Type **472** 10 10
1821 3c. Hurricane map (40 × 36 mm) 10 10
1822 8c. Meteorological equipment 55 20
1823 30c. Weather radar systems (horiz) . . . . 2·50 80

1971. 6th Pan-American Games, Cali, Colombia. Multicoloured.
1824 1c. Type **473** 10 10
1825 2c. Athletics 10 10
1826 3c. Rifle-shooting (horiz) . . 10 10
1827 4c. Gymnastics 10 10
1828 5c. Boxing 10 10
1829 13c. Water-polo (horiz) . . 1·10 25
1830 30c. Baseball (horiz) . . . . 1·50 40

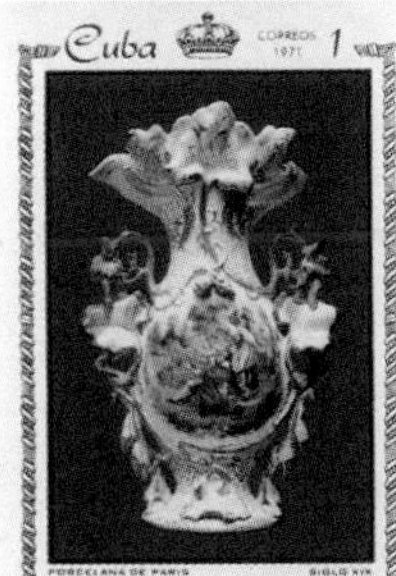

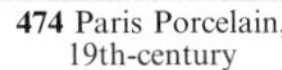

474 Paris Porcelain, 19th-century **475** Mother and Child

1971. Porcelain and Mosaics in Metropolitan Museum, Havana. Multicoloured.
1831 1c. Type **474** 10 10
1832 3c. Mexican pottery bowl, 17th-century 10 10
1833 10c. 19th-century Paris porcelain (similar to T **474**) 20 10
1834 13c. "Colosseum" Italian mosaic, 19th-century . . . 1·10 20
1835 20c. 17th-century Mexican pottery dish (similar to 3c.) . . . . 1·10 45
1836 30c. "St. Peter's Square" (Italian mosaic 19th-cent.) 1·40 50
SIZES—VERT: 3c. 46 × 54 mm. 10c. as Type **474**. 20c. 43 × 49 mm. HORIZ: 13c., 30c. 50 × 33 mm.

1971. 10th Anniv of Cuban Infant Centres.
1837 **475** 3c. multicoloured 35 10

476 Cosmonaut in Training

1971. 10th Anniv of First Manned Space Flight. Multicoloured.
1838 1c. Type **476** 10 10
1839 2c. Speedometer test 10 10
1840 3c. Medical examination . . 10 10
1841 4c. Acceleration tower . . . 10 10
1842 5c. Pressurisation test . . . 10 10
1843 13c. Cosmonaut in gravity chamber . . . . 1·00 25
1844 30c. Crew in flight simulator 1·25 55

477 Cuban and Burning Ship

1971. 10th Anniv of Giron Victory.
1846 **477** 13c. multicoloured . . . 1·50 40

478 Sailing Packet "Windsor Castle" attacked by French Privateer Brig "Jeune Richard" (1807)

1971. Stamp Day. Multicoloured.
1847 13c. Type **478** . . . . . . 1·75 60
1848 30c. Mail steamer "Orinoco", 1851 . . . . 2·50 80

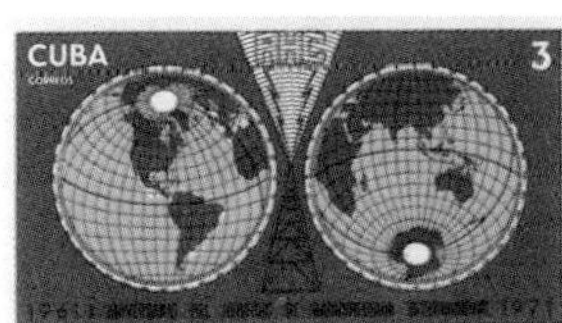

479 Transmitter and Hemispheres

1971. 10th Anniv of Cuban International Broadcasting Services.
1849 **479** 3c. multicoloured 20 10
1850 50c. multicoloured . . . 2·10 60

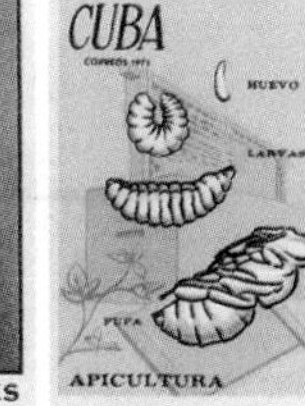
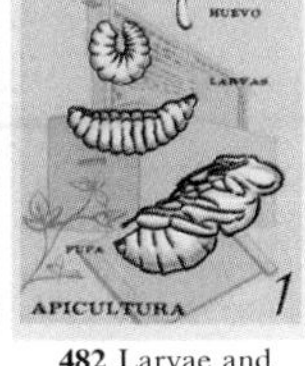

480 "Cattleya skinnerii" **482** Larvae and Pupae

481 Loynaz del Castillo and "Invasion Hymn"

1971. Tropical Orchids (1st series). Mult.
1851 1c. Type **480** 10 10
1852 2c. "Vanda hibrida" 10 10
1853 3c. "Cypripedium callossum" 15 10
1854 4c. "Cypripedium glaucophyllum" 20 10
1855 5c. "Vanda tricolor" 20 10
1856 13c. "Cypripedium mowgh" 1·50 30
1857 30c. "Cypripedium solum" 2·25 55
See also Nos. 1908/14 and 2012/18.

1971. Birth Centenary of Enrique Loynaz del Castillo (composer).
1858 **481** 3c. multicoloured 40 20

1971. Apiculture. Multicoloured.
1859 1c. Type **482** 15 10
1860 3c. Working bee 15 10
1861 9c. Drone 30 10
1862 13c. Defending the hive . . 1·60 25
1863 30c. Queen bee . . . . . . 2·25 55

483 "The Ship" (Lydia Rivera)

1971. Exhibition of Children's Drawings. Havana. Multicoloured.
1864 1c. Type **483** 10 10
1865 3c. "Little Train" (Yuri Ruiz) 45 15
1866 9c. "Sugar-cane Cutter" (Horacio Carracedo) . . . 10 10
1867 10c. "Return of Cuban Fisherman" (Angela Munoz and Lazaro Hernandez) 25 15
1868 13c. "The Zoo" (Victoria Castillo) 85 25
1869 20c. "House and Garden" (Elsa Garcia) . . . . . . 1·40 45
1870 30c. "Landscape" (Orestes Rodriguez) (vert) . . . . 1·60 65
SIZES: 9c., 13c. 45 × 35 mm, 10c. 45 × 38 mm, 20c. 47 × 42 mm, 30c. 39 × 49 mm.

1971. National Museum Paintings (4th series). As T **459**. Multicoloured.
1871 1c. "St. Catherine of Alexandria" (Zurbaran) 10 10
1872 2c. "The Cart" (F. Americo) (horiz) 10 10
1873 3c. "St. Christopher and the Child" (J. Bassano) . . . 10 10
1874 4c. "Little Devil" (R. Portocarrero) 10 10
1875 5c. "Portrait of a Lady" (N. Maes) 10 10
1876 13c. "Phoenix" (R. Martinez) . . . . . . 1·00 30
1877 30c. "Sir William Pitt" (Gainsborough) . . . . . 1·40 50
SIZES: 1, 3c. 30 × 56 mm, 2c. 48 × 37 mm, 4, 5c. 37 × 49 mm, 13, 30c. 39 × 49 mm.

485 Bonefish

1971. Sport Fishing. Multicoloured.
1878 1c. Type **485** 15 10
1879 2c. Great amberjack 15 10
1880 3c. Large-mouthed black bass 15 10
1881 4c. Dolphin (fish) 20 10
1882 5c. Atlantic tarpon 25 15
1883 13c. Wahoo . . . . 1·40 40
1884 30c. Blue marlin . . . . . 2·40 65

486 Ball within "C"

1971. World Amateur Baseball Championships. Multicoloured.
1885 3c. Type **486** 15 10
1886 1p. Hand holding globe within "C" . . . . 2·75 1·10

487 "Dr. F. Valdes Dominguez" (artist unknown)

1971. Centenary of Medical Students' Execution. Multicoloured.
1887 3c. Type **487** 20 10
1888 13c. "Students Execution" (M. Mesa) (62 × 47 mm) 90 30
1889 30c. "Captain Federico Capdevila" (unknown artist) . . . . 1·40 40

488 American Kestrel

1971. Death Centenary of Ramon de la Sagra (naturalist). Cuban Birds. Multicoloured.
1890 1c. Type **488** 55 25
1891 2c. Cuban pygmy owl . . . 55 25
1892 3c. Cuban trogon 75 25
1893 4c. Great lizard cuckoo . . 90 30
1894 5c. Fernandina's flicker . . 1·10 40
1895 13c. Stripe-headed tanager (horiz) . . . . 2·10 70
1896 30c. Red-legged thrush (horiz) . . . . 3·75 1·40
1897 50c. Cuban emerald and ruby-throated hummingbirds (56 × 30 mm) . . . . . . 7·00 2·10

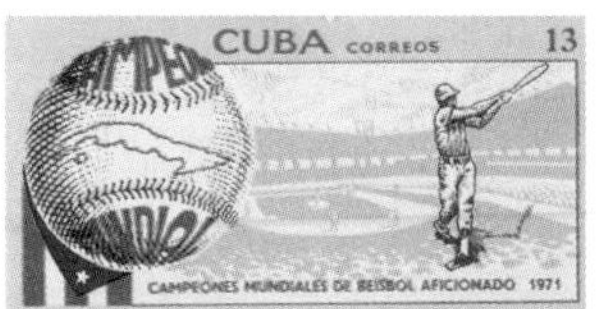

489 Baseball Player and Global Emblem

1971. Cuba's Victory in World Amateur Baseball.
1898 **489** 13c. multicoloured . . . 1·00 45

490 "Children of the World"

1971. 25th Anniv of U.N.I.C.E.F.
1899 **490** 13c. multicoloured . . . 1·10 45

1972. National Museum Paintings (5th series). As T **459**. Multicoloured.
1900 1c. "The Reception of Ambassadors" (V. Carpaccio) 10 10
1901 2c. "Senora Malpica" (G. Collazo) 10 10
1902 3c. "La Chorrera Fortress (E. Chartrand) 10 10
1903 4c. "Creole Landscape" (C. Enriquez) 10 10
1904 5c. "Sir William Lemon" (G. Romney) 10 10
1905 13c. "La Tajona Beach" (H. Cleenewek) . . . . . 1·25 30
1906 30c. "Valencia Beach" (J. Sorolla y Bastida) . . 2·25 70
SIZES: 1c., 3c. 51 × 33 mm, 2c. 28 × 53 mm, 4c., 5c. 36 × 44 mm, 13c., 30c. 43 × 34 mm.

492 "Capitol" Stamp of 1929 (now Natural History Museum)

1972. 10th Anniv of Academy of Sciences.
1907 **492** 13c. purple and yellow 95 40

1972. Tropical Orchids (2nd series). As T **480**. Multicoloured.
1908 1c. "Brasso Cattleya sindorossiana" 25 10
1909 2c. "Cypripedium doraeus" 25 10
1910 3c. "Cypripedium exul" . . 25 10
1911 4c. "Cypripedium rosydawn" 25 10
1912 5c. "Cypripedium champolliom" 25 10
1913 13c. "Cypripedium bucolique" . . . . 1·75 75
1914 30c. "Cypripedium sullanum" . . . . 2·50 90

493 "Eduardo Agramonte" (F. Martinez)

1972. Death Centenary of Dr. E. Agramonte (surgeon and patriot).
1915 **493** 3c. multicoloured 30 15

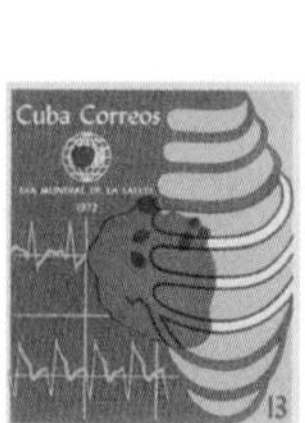

494 Human Heart and Thorax
496 "Vincente Mora Pera" (Postmaster General, War of Independence) (R. Loy)

495 "Sputnik 1"

1972. World Health Day.
1916 **494** 13c. multicoloured . . . 95 40

1972. "History of Space". Multicoloured.
1917 1c. Type **495** 10 10
1918 2c. "Vostok 1" 10 10
1919 3c. Valentina Tereshkova in capsule 20 10
1920 4c. A. Leonov in space . . . 25 10
1921 5c. "Lunokhod 1" moon Vehicle 25 10
1922 13c. Linking of "Soyuz" capsules . . . . 1·25 35
1923 30c. Dobrovolsky, Volkov and Pataiev, victims of "Soyuz 11" disaster . . . 1·50 45

1972. Stamp Day. Multicoloured.
1924 13c. Type **496** 85 40
1925 30c. Mambi Mailcover of 1897 (48 × 39 mm) . . . . 1·40 45

497 Cuban Workers
498 Jose Marti and Ho Chi Minh

1972. Labour Day.
1926 **497** 3c. multicoloured 40 20

1972. 3rd Symposium on Indo-China War. Multicoloured.
1927 3c. Type **498** 20 10
1928 13c. Bombed house (38 × 29 mm) 80 30
1929 30c. Symposium emblem . . 95 45

1972. Paintings from the Metropolitan Museum, Havana (6th series). As T **430**. Multicoloured.
1930 1c. "Salvador del Muro" (J. del Rio) 10 10
1931 2c. "Louis de las Casas" (J. del Rio) 10 10
1932 3c. "Christopher Columbus" (anonymous) 20 10
1933 4c. "Tomas Gamba" (V. Escobar) 25 10
1934 5c. "Maria Galarraga" (V. Escobar) 25 10
1935 13c. "Isabella II of Spain" (F. Madrazo) . . . . . 1·25 35
1936 30c. "Carlos III of Spain" (M. Melero) . . . . . . 1·50 50
SIZES—VERT: (35 × 44 mm) 1930/34, (34 × 52 mm) 1935/6.

500 Children in Boat

1972. Children's Song Competition.
1937 **500** 3c. multicoloured 50 20

501 Ilyushin Il-18, Map and Flags

1972. Air. 1st Anniv of Havana–Santiago de Chile Air Service.
1938 **501** 25c. multicoloured . . . 1·40 55

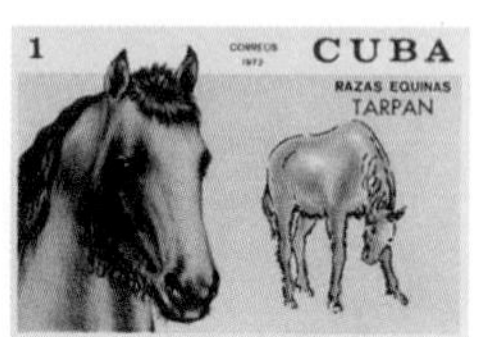

502 Tarpan

1972. Thoroughbred Horses. Multicoloured.
1939 1c. Type **502** 10 10
1940 2c. Kertag 10 10
1941 3c. Creole 10 10
1942 4c. Andalusian 10 10
1943 5c. Arab 10 10
1944 13c. Quarter-horse . . . . 2·00 50
1945 30c. Pursang . . . . 2·50 75

503 Frank Pais

1972. 15th Death Anniv of Frank Pais.
1946 **503** 13c. multicoloured . . . 85 40

504 Athlete and Emblem

1972. Olympic Games, Munich.
1947 **504** 1c. orange and brown . . 10 10
1948 – 2c. purple, blue & orge 10 10
1949 – 3c. green, yellow & blk 10 10
1950 – 4c. bl, yell & brn 10 10
1951 – 5c. red, black & yellow 10 10
1952 – 13c. lilac, green & blue 1·10 35
1953 – 30c. blue, red and green 1·40 50
DESIGNS—HORIZ: 2c. "M" and boxing; 3c. "U" and weightlifting; 4c. "N" and fencing; 5c. "I" and rifle-shooting; 13c. "C" and running; 30c. "H" and basketball.

505 "Landscape with Tree-trunks" (D. Ramos)

1972. International Hydrological Decade. Mult.
1955 1c. Type **505** 10 10
1956 3c. "Cyclone" (T. Lorenzo) 15 10
1957 8c. "Vineyards" (D. Ramos) 35 10
1958 30c. "Forest and Stream" (A. R. Morey) (vert) . . . 1·10 45

506 "Papilio thoas oviedo"

1972. Butterflies from the Gundlach Collection. Multicoloured.
1959 1c. Type **506** 10 10
1960 2c. "Papilio devilliers" . . . 15 10
1961 3c. "Papilio polixenes polixenes" 15 10
1962 4c. "Papilio androgeus epidaurus" 15 10
1963 5c. "Papilio cayguanabus' 25 10
1964 13c. "Papilio andraemon hernandezi" . . . . . 2·75 60
1965 30c. "Papilio celadon" . . . 3·50 80

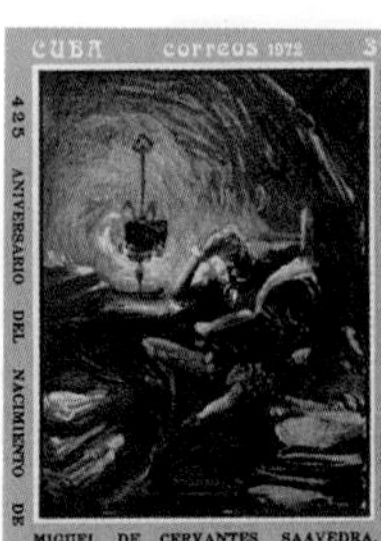

507 "In La Mancha" (A. Fernandez)

1972. 425th Birth Anniv of Cervantes. Paintings by A. Fernandez. Multicoloured.
1966 3c. Type **507** 10 10
1967 13c. "Battle with the Wine Skins" (horiz) . . . . . 1·25 35
1968 30c. "Don Quixote of La Mancha" . . . . 1·50 40

508 E. "Che" Guevara and Map of Bolivia

1972. 5th Anniv of Guerrillas' Day. Mult.
1970 3c. Type **508** 10 10
1971 13c. T. "Tania" Bunke and map of Bolivia . . . . . 1·25 35
1972 30c. G. "Inti" Peredo and map of Bolivia . . . . . 1·50 40

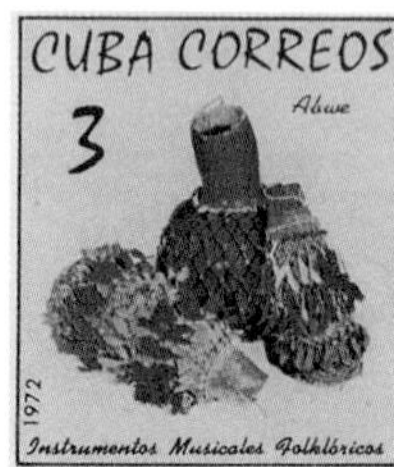

509 "Abwe" (shakers)

1972. Traditional Musical Instruments. Mult.
1973 3c. Type **509** 10 10
1974 13c. "Bonko enchemiya" (drum) . . . . 1·25 35
1975 30c. "Iya" (drum) . . . . . 1·50 40

510 Cuban 2c. Stamp of 1951

1972. National Philatelic Exhibition, Matanzas. Multicoloured.
1976 13c. Type **510** . . . . . . 1·25 35
1977 30c. Cuban 25c. airmail stamp of 1951 . . . . . 1·75 45

511 Viking Longship

1972. Maritime History. Ships Through the Ages. Multicoloured.
1978 1c. Type **511** 15 10
1979 2c. Caravel (vert) 15 10
1980 3c. Galley 15 10
1981 4c. Galleon (vert) 20 10
1982 5c. Clipper 20 10
1983 13c. Steam packet . . . . . 1·50 55
1984 30c. Atomic ice-breaker "Lenin" and Adelie penguins (55 × 29 mm) . . 5·50 1·50

512 Lion of St. Mark

1972. U.N.E.S.C.O. "Save Venice" Campaign. Multicoloured.
1985 3c. Type **512** 10 10
1986 13c. Bridge of Sighs (vert) 85 35
1987 30c. St. Mark's Cathedral 1·10 65

513 Baseball Coach (poster)

516 "Gertrude G. de Avellaneda" (A. Esquivel)

515 Bronze Medal, Women's 100 m

1972. "Cuba, World Amateur Baseball Champions of 1972".
1988 **513** 3c. violet and orange . . 50 10

1972. Sports events of 1972.
1989 – 1c. multicoloured 10 10
1990 – 2c. multicoloured 10 10
1991 **513** 3c. black, orange & grn 10 10
1992 – 4c. red, black and blue 10 10
1993 – 5c. orge, bl & lt bl . . . 10 10
1994 – 13c. multicoloured . . . 1·10 45
1995 – 30c. vio, blk & bl . . . 1·40 65
DESIGNS AND EVENTS: 1c. Various sports (10th National Schoolchildren's Games); 2c. Pole vaulting (Barrientos Memorial Athletics); 3c. As Type **513**, but inscr changed to read "XI serie nacional de beisbol aficionado" and colours changed (11th National Amateur Baseball Series); 4c. Wrestling (Cerro Pelado International Wrestling Championships); 5c. Foil (Central American and Caribbean Fencing Tournament); 13c. Boxing (Giraldo Cordova Boxing Tournament); 30c. Fishes (Ernest Hemingway National Marlin Fishing Contest).

1972. Cuban Successes in Olympic Games, Munich. Multicoloured.
1996 1c. Type **515** 10 10
1997 2c. Bronze (women's 4 × 100 m relay) 10 10
1998 3c. Gold (boxing, 54 kg) . . 10 10
1999 4c. Silver (boxing, 81 kg) . . 10 10
2000 5c. Bronze (boxing, 51 kg) 10 10
2001 13c. Gold (boxing, 67 kg) 1·25 45
2002 30c. Gold (boxing, 81 kg) and Silver Cup (boxing Teofilo Stevenons) . . . . 1·50 65

1973. Death Centenary of Gertrude Gomez de Avellaneda (poetess).
2004 **516** 13c. multicoloured . . . 95 40

1973. National Museum Paintings (6th series). As T **459**. Multicoloured.
2005 1c. "Bathers in the Lagoon" (C. Enriquez) (vert) . . . 10 10
2006 2c. "Still Life" (W. C. Heda) (vert) 10 10
2007 3c. "Scene of Gallantry" (V. de Landaluse) (vert) . . . 10 10
2008 4c. "Return at Evening" (C. Troyon) (vert) 10 10
2009 5c. "Elizabetta Mascagni" (F. X. Fabre) (vert) . . . 10 10
2010 13c. "The Picador" (E. de Lucas Padilla) . . . . . 1·25 45
2011 30c. "In the Garden" (J. A. Morell) (vert) . . . . . . 1·50 65

1973. Tropical Orchids (3rd series). As Type **480**. Multicoloured.
2012 1c. "Dendrobium" (hybrid) 10 10
2013 2c. "Cypripedium exul. O' Brien" 10 10
2014 3c. "Vanda miss. Joaquin" 10 10
2015 4c. "Phalaenopsis schilleriana Reichb" . . . 10 10
2016 5c. "Vanda gilbert tribulet" 10 10
2017 13c. "Dendrobium" (hybrid) (different) . . . . 1·25 45
2018 30c. "Arachnis catherine" 1·50 65

518 Medical Examination

520 "Soyuz" Rocket on Launch-pad

519 Children and Vaccine

1973. 25th Anniv of W.H.O.
2019 **518** 10c. multicoloured . . . 55 25

1973. Freedom from Polio Campaign.
2020 **519** 3c. multicoloured 35 20

1973. Cosmonautics Day. Russian Space Exploration. Multicoloured.
2021 1c. Type **520** 25 10
2022 2c. "Luna 1" in moon orbit (horiz) 25 10
2023 3c. "Luna 16" leaving moon 25 10
2024 4c. "Venus 7" probe (horiz) 25 10
2025 5c. "Molniya 1" communications satellite 25 10
2026 13c. "Mars 3" probe (horiz) 2·00 55
2027 30c. Research ship "Kosmonavt Yury Gargarin" (horiz) . . . . 2·75 65

521 Santiago de Cuba Postmark, 1839

1973. Stamp Day. Multicoloured.
2028 13c. Type **521** 95 35
2029 30c. "Havana" postmark, 1760 . . . . 1·10 40

522 "Ignacio Agramonte" (A. Espinosa)

1973. Death Centenary of Maj.-Gen. Ignacio Agramonte.
2030 **522** 13c. multicoloured . . . 75 35

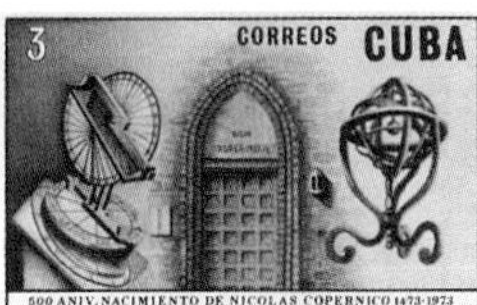

523 Copernicus' Birthplace and Instruments

1973. 500th Birth Anniv of Copernicus. Mult.
2031 3c. Type **523** 10 10
2032 13c. Copernicus and "spaceship" . . . . . . 1·00 35
2033 30c. "De Revolutionibus Orbium Celestium" and Frombork Tower . . . . 1·75 45

524 Emblem of Basic Schools

1973. Educational Development.
2035 **524** 13c. multicoloured . . . 75 20

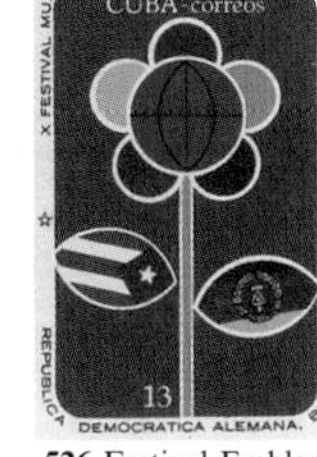

525 Jersey Breed

526 Festival Emblem

1973. Cattle Breeds. Multicoloured.
2036 1c. Type **525** 10 10
2037 2c. Charolais 10 10
2038 3c. Creole 10 10
2039 4c. Swiss 10 10
2040 5c. Holstein 10 10
2041 13c. St. Gertrude's . . . . 1·00 20
2042 30c. Brahman Cebu . . . . 1·60 40

1973. 10th World Youth and Students' Festival, East Berlin.
2043 **526** 13c. multicoloured . . . 75 20

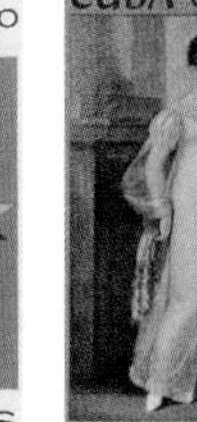

527 Siboney Farmhouse

529 "Amalia de Sajonia" (J. K. Rossler)

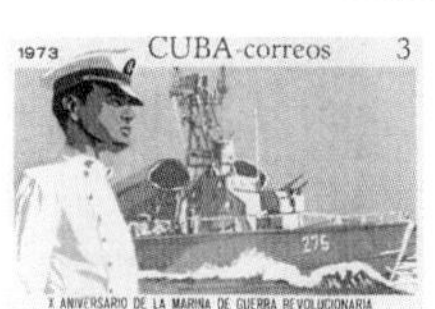

528 Midshipman and Destroyer

1973. 20th Anniv of Revolution. Mult.
2044 3c. Type **527** 20 15
2045 13c. Moncada Barracks . . 75 25
2046 30c. Revolution Square, Havana . . . . 1·10 40

1973. 10th Anniv of Revolutionary Navy.
2047 **528** 3c. multicoloured 60 20

1973. National Museum Paintings (7th series). Multicoloured.
2048 1c. Type **529** 10 10
2049 2c. "Interior" (M. Vicens) (horiz) 10 10
2050 3c. "Margaret of Austria" (J. Pantoja de la Cruz) . . 10 10
2051 4c. "Syndic of the City Hall" (anon) 10 10
2052 5c. "View of Santiago de Cuba" (J. H. Giro) (horiz) 10 10
2053 13c. "The Catalan" (J. J. Tejada) . . . . 1·10 60
2054 30c. "Guayo Alley" (J. J. Tejada) . . . . 1·50 85

530 "Spring"

1973. Centenary of World Meteorological Organization. Paintings by J. Madrazo. Mult.
2055 8c. Type **530** 30 10
2056 8c. "Summer" 30 10
2057 8c. "Autumn" 30 10
2058 8c. "Winter" 30 10

531 Weightlifting

532 "Erythrina standleyana"

1973. 27th Pan-American World Weightlifting Championships, Havana. Designs showing various stages of weightlifting exercise.
2059 **531** 1c. multicoloured 10 10
2060 – 2c. multicoloured 20 10
2061 – 3c. multicoloured 20 10
2062 – 4c. multicoloured 20 10
2063 – 5c. multicoloured 20 10
2064 – 13c. multicoloured . . . 1·25 80
2065 – 30c. multicoloured . . . 2·50 1·50

1973. Wild Flowers (1st series). Mult.
2066 1c. Type **532** 10 10
2067 2c. "Lantana camara" . . . 10 10
2068 3c. "Canavalia maritima" . . 10 10
2069 4c. "Dichromena colorata" 10 10
2070 5c. "Borrichia arborescens" 10 10
2071 13c. "Anguria pedata" . . . 85 45
2072 30c. "Cordia sebestena" . . 1·40 65
See also Nos. 2152/6.

533 Congress Emblem

1973. 8th World Trade Union Congress, Varna, Bulgaria.
2073 **533** 13c. multicoloured . . . 70 25

534 Ballet Dancers

535 True Fasciate Liguus

1973. 25th Anniv of Cuban National Ballet.
2074 **534** 13c. lt blue, bl & gold 70 25

1973. Shells. Multicoloured
2075 1c. Type **535** 20 10
2076 2c. Guitart's liguus 20 10
2077 3c. Wharton's Cuban liguus 20 10
2078 4c. Angela's Cuban liguus 30 10
2079 5c. Yellow-banded liguus . . 30 10
2080 13c. "Liguus blainianus" . . 2·00 85
2081 30c. Ribbon liguus . . . . 2·25 1·10

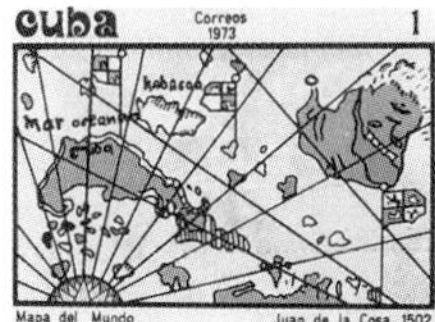

536 Juan de la Cosa's Map, 1502

1973. Maps of Cuba. Multicoloured.
2082 1c. Type **536** 10 10
2083 3c. Ortelius's map, 1572 . . 10 10
2084 13c. Bellini's map, 1762 . . 80 20
2085 40c. Cartographic survey map, 1973 . . . . 1·10 50

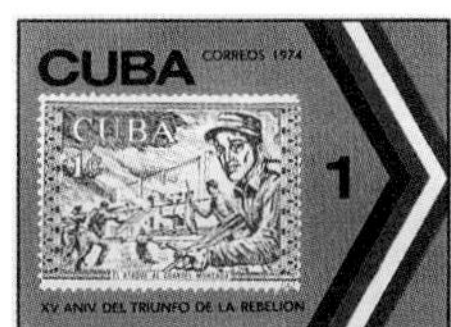

537 1c. Stamp of 1960 (No. 921)

1974. 15th Anniv of Revolution. Revolution stamps of 1960. Multicoloured.
2086 1c. Type **537** 10 10
2087 3c. 2c. stamp 20 10
2088 13c. 8c. air stamp . . . . . 1·00 60
2089 40c. 12c. air stamp . . . . 1·25 75

538 "Head of a Woman" (F. Ponce de Leon)

1974. Paintings in Camaguey Museum. Mult.
2090 1c. Type **538** 10 10
2091 3c. "Mexican Children" (J. Arche) 10 10
2092 8c. "Portrait of a Young Woman" (A. Menocal) 20 10
2093 10c. "Mulatto Woman with Coconut" (L. Romanach) 55 20
2094 13c. "Head of Old Man" (J. Arburu) 85 30

539 A. Cabral

540 "Lenin" (after J. V. Kosmin)

1974. 1st Death Anniv of Amilcar Cabral (Guinea-Bissau guerilla leader).
2095 **539** 13c. multicoloured . . . 70 20

1974. 50th Anniv of Lenin's Death.
2096 **540** 30c. multicoloured . . . 1·10 45

541 Games Emblem

542 "C. M. de Cespedes" (after F. Martinez)

1974. 12th Central American and Caribbean Games, Santo Domingo. Multicoloured.
2097 1c. Type **541** 20 10
2098 2c. Throwing the javelin . . 20 10
2199 3c. Boxing 20 10
2100 4c. Baseball player (horiz) 20 10
2101 13c. Handball player (horiz) 1·50 75
2102 30c. Volleyball (horiz) . . . 2·00 1·00

1974. Death Centenary of Carlos M. de Cespedes (patriot).
2103 **542** 13c. multicoloured . . . 70 15

543 "Portrait of a Man" (J. B. Vermay)

544 "Comecon" Headquarters Building, Moscow

1974. National Museum Paintings (8th series). Multicoloured.
2104 1c. Type **543** 10 10
2105 2c. "Nodriza" (C. A. Van Loo) 10 10
2106 3c. "Cattle by a River" (R. Morey) (46 × 32 mm) 10 10
2107 4c. "Village Landscape" (R. Morey) (46 × 32 mm) 10 10
2108 13c. "Faun and Bacchus" (Rubens) 80 40
2109 30c. "Playing Patience" (R. Madrazo) . . . . . 1·25 75

1974. 25th Anniv of Council for Mutual Economic Aid.
2110 **544** 30c. multicoloured . . . 1·00 45

545 Jose Marti and Lenin

1974. Visit of Leonid Brezhnev (General Secretary of Soviet Communist Party). Multicoloured.
2111 13c. Type **545** 65 25
2112 30c. Brezhnev with Castro 1·00 45

546 "Martian Crater"

1974. Cosmonautics Day. Science Fiction paintings by Sokolov. Multicoloured.
2113 1c. Type **546** 10 10
2114 2c. "Fiery Labyrinth" . . . 10 10
2115 3c. "Amber Wave" 10 10
2116 4c. "Space Navigators" . . 15 10
2117 13c. "Planet in the Nebula" 1·00 50
2118 30c. "The World of the Two Suns" . . . . 1·75 1·00
See also Nos. 2196/201.

547 Cuban Letter of 1874

1974. Centenary of U.P.U.
2119 **547** 30c. multicoloured . . . 1·00 45

1974. Stamp Day. Postal Markings of Pre-Stamp Exhibition. As T **521**. Multicoloured.
2120 1c. "Havana" postmark . . 10 10
2121 3c. "Matanzas" postmark 15 10
2122 13c. "Trinidad" postmark 75 15
2123 20c. "Guana Vacoa" postmark . . . . 1·10 20

548 Congress Emblem

1974. 18th Sports' Congress of "Friendly Armies".
2124 **548** 3c. multicoloured 40 10

549 "Eumaeus atala atala" (butterfly)

1974. 175th Birth Anniv of Felipe Poey (naturalist). Multicoloured.
2125 1c. Type **549** 20 10
2126 2c. "Pineria terebra" (shell) 10 10
2127 3c. Reef butterflyfish 10 10
2128 4c. "Eurema dina dina" (butterfly) 50 10
2129 13c. "Hemitrochus fuscolabiata" (shell) . . . 2·00 1·00
2130 30c. Bicoloured damsel-fish 2·50 1·25

550 A. Mompo and 'Cello

1974. 50th Anniv of Havana Philharmonic Orchestra. Leading Personalities. Multicoloured.
2132 1c. Type **550** 10 10
2133 3c. C. P. Sentenat and piano 20 10
2134 5c. P. Mercado and trumpet 25 10
2135 10c. P. Sanjuan and emblem 75 40
2136 13c. R. Ondina and flute . . 1·00 60

551 "Heliconia humilis"

552 Boxers and Global Emblem

1974. Garden Flowers. Multicoloured.
2137 1c. Type **551** 10 10
2138 2c. "Anthurium andraeanum" 10 10
2139 3c. "Canna generalis" 10 10
2140 4c. "Alpinia purpurata" . . 20 10
2141 13c. "Gladiolus grandifiorus" . . . . . . 1·10 10
2142 30c. "Amomum capitatum" 2·75 45

1974. World Amateur Boxing Championships.
2143 **552** 1c. multicoloured 15 10
2144 – 3c. multicoloured 20 10
2145 – 13c. multicoloured . . . 75 20
DESIGNS: 3c., 13c. Stages of Boxing matches similar to Type **552**.

553 Mauritius Dodo ("Dodo")

555 "Suriana maritima"

554 Salvador Allende

1974. Extinct Birds. Multicoloured.
2146 1c. Type **553** 50 25
2147 3c. Cuban macaw ("Ara de Cuba") 50 25
2148 8c. Passenger pigeon ("Paloma Migratoria") . . 1·10 40
2149 10c. Moa . . . . 3·50 70
2150 13c. Great auk ("Gran Alca") . . . . 4·50 1·00

1974. 1st Death Anniv of Pres. Allende of Chile.
2151 **554** 13c. multicoloured . . . 65 30

1974. Wild Flowers. (2nd series). Mult.
2152 1c. Type **555** 10 10
2153 3c. "Cassia ligustrina" . . . 10 10
2154 8c. "Flaveria linearis" . . . 20 15
2155 10c. "Stachytarpheta jamaicensis" . . . . . . 1·10 20
2156 13c. "Bacopa monnieri" . . 2·00 60

556 Flying Model Airplane

557 Indians playing Ball

1974. 10th Anniv of Civil Aeronautical Institute. Multicoloured.
2157 1c. Type **556** 20 10
2158 3c. Parachutist 20 10
2159 8c. Glider in flight (horiz) 30 10
2160 10c. Antonov An-2 biplane spraying crops (horiz) . . 1·00 60
2161 13c. Ilyushin Il-62M in flight (horiz) . . . . 1·60 90

1974. History of Baseball in Cuba. Mult.
2162 1c. Type **557** 10 10
2163 3c. Players of 1874 (First official game) 10 10
2164 8c. Emilio Sabourin 15 10
2165 10c. Modern players (horiz) (44 × 27 mm) 50 30
2166 13c. Latin-American Stadium, Havana (horiz) (44 × 27 mm) . . . . . . 1·00 50

558 Stamp, Cachet and Horseman

1974. Cent of "Mambi" Revolutionary Stamp.
2167 **558** 13c. multicoloured . . . 85 20

559 Comecon Headquarters Building, Moscow and Emblem

1974. 16th Socialist Countries' Customs Conference.
2168 **559** 30c. blue and gold . . . 1·00 35

560 Maj. Camilo Cienfuegos (revolutionary)

1974. 15th Anniv of Disappearance of Cienfuegos.
2169 **560** 3c. multicoloured 35 10

561 Miner's Helmet

1974. 8th World Mining Congress.
2170 **561** 13c. multicoloured . . . 1·00 20

562 Oil Refinery

1974. 15th Anniv of Cuban Petroleum Institute.
2171 **562** 3c. multicoloured 50 10

563 Earth Station

1974. Inauguration of "Inter-Sputnik" Satellite Earth Station. Multicoloured.
2172 3c. Type **563** 10 10
2173 13c. Satellite and aerial . . 55 10
2174 1p. Satellite and flags . . . 1·50 65

564 Emblems and Magnifying Glass

1974. 10th Anniv of Cuban Philatelic Federation.
2175 **564** 30c. multicoloured . . . 1·10 40

566 F. Joliot-Curie (1st president) (Picasso)

1974. 25th Anniv of World Peace Congress.
2177 **566** 30c. multicoloured . . . 1·10 40

567 R. M. Villena

1974. 75th Birth Anniv of Ruben Martinez Villena (revolutionary).
2178 **567** 3c. red and yellow . . . 30 10

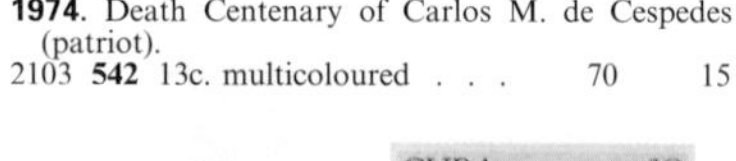

569 "The Word" (M. Pogolotti)

1975. National Museum Paintings (9th series). Multicoloured.
2180 1c. Type **569** 10 10
2181 2c. "The Silk-Cotton Tree" (H. Cleenewerk) 10 10
2182 3c. "Landscape" (G. Collazo) 10 10
2183 5c. "Still Life" (F. Peralta) 15 10
2184 13c. "Maria Wilson" (F. Martinez) (vert) . . . 70 20
2185 30c. "The Couple" (M. Fortunay) . . . . . 1·10 40

570 Bouquet and Woman's Head

1975. International Woman's Year.
2186 **570** 13c. multicoloured . . . 65 20

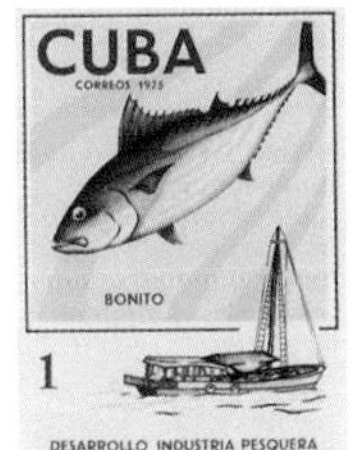

571 Skipjack Tuna and Fishing-boat

1975. Cuban Fishing Industry. Mult.
2187 1c. Type **571** 15 10
2188 2c. Blue-finned tunny . . . 15 10
2189 3c. Nassau grouper 15 10
2190 8c. Silver hake 15 15
2191 13c. Prawn . . . . 1·00 60
2192 30c. Lobster . . . . 2·25 1·00

572 Nickel

1975. Cuban Minerals. Multicoloured.
2193 3c. Type **572** 50 20
2194 13c. Copper . . . . 1·00 60
2195 30c. Chromium . . . . . . 1·50 75

1975. Cosmonautics Day. Science Fiction paintings. As T **546**. Multicoloured.
2196 1c. "Cosmodrome" 20 10
2197 2c. "Exploration craft" (vert) 25 10
2198 3c. "Earth eclipsing the Sun" 25 10
2199 5c. "On the Threshold" . . 30 10
2200 13c. "Astronauts on Mars" 1·00 50
2201 30c. "Astronauts' view of Earth" . . . . 1·50 75

573 Letter and "Correos" Postmark

1975. Stamp Day. Multicoloured.
2202 3c. Type **573** 10 10
2203 13c. Letter and steamship postmark 65 15
2204 30c. Letter and "N.A." postmark . . . . 1·00 30

574 Hoisting Red Flag over Reichstag, Berlin

1975. 30th Anniv of "Victory over Fascism".
2205 **574** 30c. multicoloured . . . 1·00 30

575 Sevres Vase

1975. National Museum Treasures. Mult.
2206 1c. Type **575** 10 10
2207 2c. Meissen "Shepherdess and Dancers" 20 10
2208 3c. Chinese Porcelain Dish—"Lady with Parasol" (horiz) 20 10
2209 5c. Chinese Bamboo Screen—"The Phoenix" 30 10
2210 13c. "Allegory of Music" (F. Boucher) . . . . . . 1·00 50
2211 30c. "Portrait of a Lady" (L. Toque) . . . . 1·10 60

576 Coloured Balls and Globe "Man"

1975. International Children's Day.
2213 **576** 3c. multicoloured 20 10

577 Cuban Vireo

1975. Birds (1st series). Multicoloured.
2214 1c. Type **577** 30 15
2215 2c. Cuban screech owl . . . 30 15
2216 3c. Cuban conure 30 15
2217 5c. Blue-headed quail dove 50 15
2218 13c. Hook-billed kite . . . 2·75 50
2219 30c. Zapata rail . . . . . . 3·00 85
See also Nos. 2301/6.

578 View of Centre

1973. 10th Anniv of National Scientific Investigation Centre.
2220 **578** 13c. multicoloured . . . 65 15

579 Commission Emblem and Drainage Equipment

1975. Int Commission on Irrigation and Drainage.
2221 **579** 13c. multicoloured . . . 65 15

580 "Cedrea mexicana"

581 Women cultivating Young Plants

1975. Reafforestation. Multicoloured.
2222 1c. Type **580** 10 10
2223 3c. "Swietonia mahagoni" 25 10
2224 5c. "Calophyllum brasiliense" 30 10
2225 13c. "Hibiscus tiliaceus" . . 75 40
2226 30c. "Pinus caribaea" . . . 1·10 70

1975. 15th Anniv of Cuban Women's Federation.
2227 **581** 3c. multicoloured 25 10

582 Conference Emblem and Broken Chains

583 Baseball

1975. International Conference on the Independence of Puerto Rico.
2228 **582** 13c. multicoloured . . . 50 15

1975. 7th Pan-American Games, Mexico. Mult.
2229 1c. Type **583** 20 10
2230 3c. Boxing 25 10
2231 5c. Handball 25 10
2232 13c. High jumping 75 40
2233 30c. Weightlifting . . . . . 1·00 50

584 Emblem and Crowd

1975. 15th Anniv of Revolutionary Defence Committees.
2235 **584** 3c. multicoloured 20 10

585 Institute Emblem

1975. 15th Anniv of Cuban "Friendship Amongst the Peoples" Institute.
2236 **585** 3c. multicoloured 15 10

586 Silver 1 Peso Coin, 1913

1975. 15th Anniv of Nationalization of Bank of Cuba. Multicoloured.
2237 13c. Type **586** 70 25
2238 13c. 1 peso banknote, 1934 70 25
2239 13c. 1 peso banknote, 1946 70 25
2240 13c. 1 peso banknote, 1964 70 25
2241 13c. 1 peso banknote, 1973 70 25

587 "La Junta", Cuba's first locomotive, 1837

1975. "Evolution of Railways". Multicoloured.
2242 1c. Type **587** 15 10
2243 3c. Steam locomotive "M. M. Prieto", 1920 . . . . 20 10
2244 5c. Russian-built Type TEM-4 diesel locomotive 20 10
2245 13c. Hungarian-built Type DVM-9 diesel locomotive . . . . 1·50 20
2246 30c. Russian-built Type M-62K diesel locomotive . . . . 1·75 35

588 Bobbins and Flag

1975. Textile Industry.
2247 **588** 13c. multicoloured . . . 55 15

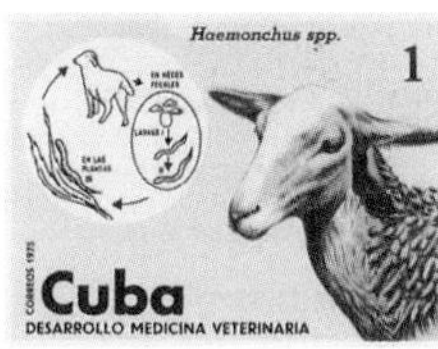

589 Sheep and Diagram

1975. Development of Veterinary Medicine. Animals and Disease Cycles. Multicoloured.
2248 1c. Type **589** 10 10
2249 2c. Dog 10 10
2250 3c. Cockerel 20 10
2251 5c. Horse 20 10
2252 13c. Pig . . . . 1·00 50
2253 30c. Ox . . . . 1·50 75

590 Manuel Ascunce Domenech

592 Communists with Flags inside Figure "1"

591 "Irrigation"

1975. Manuel Domenech Educational Detachment.
2254 **590** 3c. multicoloured 20 10

1975. Agriculture and Water-supply.
2255 **591** 13c. multicoloured . . . 65 15

1976. 1st Cuban Communist Party Congress. Multicoloured.
2256 3c. Type **592** 10 10
2257 13c. Workers with banner (horiz) 60 15
2258 30c. Jose Marti and Cuban leaders (horiz) 75 30

593 Pre-natal Exercises

1976. 8th Latin-American Obstetrics and Gynaecology Congress, Havana.
2259 **593** 3c. multicoloured 25 10

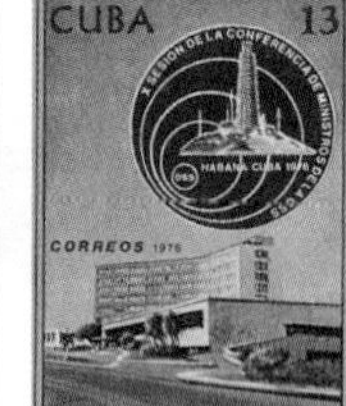

594 "Seated Woman" (V. Manuel) **595** Conference Emblem and Building

1976. National Museum Paintings (10th series). Multicoloured.
2260 1c. Type **594** 20 10
2261 2c. "Garden" (S. Rusinol) (horiz) 20 10
2262 3c. "Guadalquivir River" (M. Barron y Carrillo) (horiz) 40 10
2263 5c. "Self-portrait" (Jan Steen) 25 10
2264 13c. "Portrait of Woman" (L. M. van Loo) 85 40
2265 30c. "La Chula" (J. A. Morell) (27 × 44 mm) . . 90 50

1976. Socialist Communications Ministers' Conference, Havana.
2266 **595** 13c. multicoloured . . . 65 15

596 American Foxhound

1976. Hunting Dogs. Multicoloured.
2267 1c. Type **596** 20 10
2268 2c. Labrador retriever . . . 20 10
2269 3c. Borzoi 20 10
2270 5c. Irish setter 20 10
2271 13c. Pointer . . . . 1·25 75
2272 30c. Cocker Spaniel . . . . 1·75 1·10

597 Flags, Arms and Anthem

1976. Socialist Constitution, 1976.
2273 **597** 13c. multicoloured . . . 75 20

598 Ruy Lopez Segura

1976. History of Chess. Multicoloured.
2274 1c. Type **598** 20 10
2275 2c. Francois Philidor . . . 20 10
2276 3c. Wilhelm Steinitz 20 10
2277 13c. Emanuel Lasker . . . 85 40
2278 30c. Jose Raul Capablanca 1·00 50

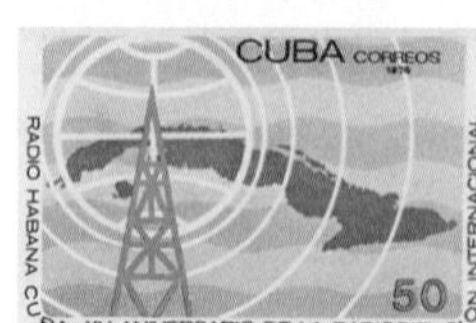

599 Radio Aerial and Map

1976. 15th Anniv of Cuban International Broadcasting Services.
2279 **599** 50c. multicoloured . . . 1·00 50

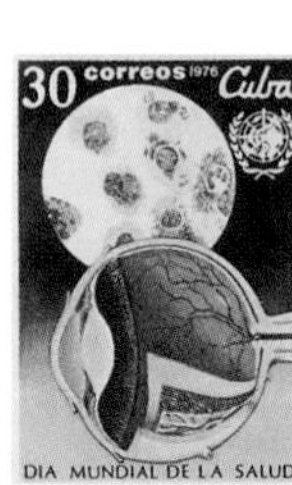

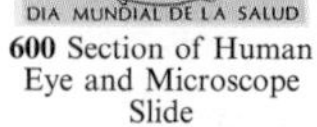

600 Section of Human Eye and Microscope Slide **601** Children in Creche

1976. World Health Day.
2280 **600** 30c. multicoloured . . . 75 30

1976. 15th Anniv of Infant Welfare Centres.
2281 **601** 3c. multicoloured 25 10

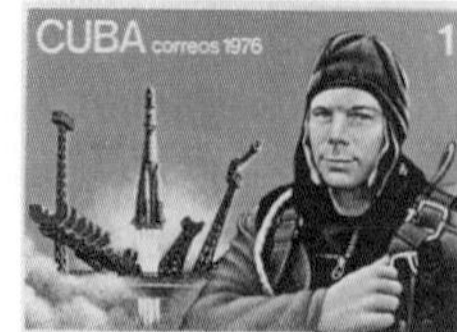

602 Y. Gagarin in Space-suit

1976. 15th Anniv of First Manned Space Flight. Multicoloured.
2282 1c. Type **602** 10 10
2283 2c. V. Tereshkova and rockets 25 10
2284 3c. Cosmonaut on "space walk" (vert) 10 10
2285 5c. Spacecraft and Moon (vert) 15 10
2286 13c. Spacecraft in manoeuvre (vert) 75 40
2287 30c. Space link 90 50

603 Cuban Machine-gunner

1976. 15th Anniv of Giron Victory. Mult.
2288 3c. Type **603** 10 10
2289 13c. Cuban pilot and Lockheed F-80 Shooting Star fighter attacking ship 70 15
2290 30c. Cuban soldier wielding rifle (vert) 85 35

604 Heads of Farmers

1976. 15th Anniv of National Association of Small Farmers (ANAP).
2291 **604** 3c. multicoloured 20 10

605 Volleyball

1976. Olympic Games, Montreal. Mult.
2292 1c. Type **605** 20 10
2293 2c. Basketball 20 10
2294 3c. Long-jumping 20 10
2295 4c. Boxing 20 10
2296 5c. Weightlifting 20 10
2297 13c. Judo 80 50
2298 30c. Swimming . . . . . . 1·50 1·00

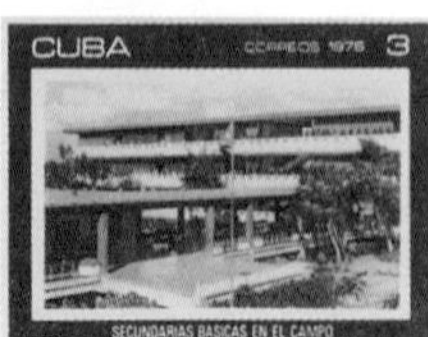

606 Modern Secondary School

1976. Rural Secondary Schools.
2300 **606** 3c. black and red 20 10

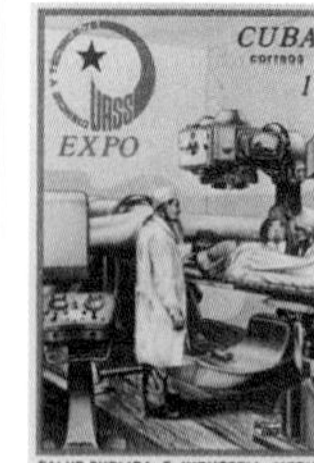

1976. Birds (2nd series). Multicoloured.
2301 1c. Type **607** 40 15
2302 2c. Cuban pygmy owl . . . 40 15
2303 3c. Fernandina's flicker . . 40 15
2304 5c. Cuban tody 75 30
2305 13c. Gundlach's hawk . . . 1·50 40
2306 30c. Cuban trogon . . . . 3·50 1·00

608 Medical Treatment **609** "El Inglesito"

1976. "Expo", Havana. Soviet Science and Technology. Multicoloured.
2307 1c. Type **608** 10 10
2308 3c. Child and deer ("Environmental Protection") 10 10
2309 10c. Cosmonauts on launch pad ("Cosmos Investigation") 25 10
2310 30c. Tupolev Tu-144 airplane ("Soviet Transport") (horiz) . . . 1·25 35

1976. Death Cent of Henry M. Reeve (patriot).
2311 **609** 13c. multicoloured . . . 35 15

610 "G. Collazo" (J. Dabour)

1976. Cuban Paintings. Multicoloured.
2312 1c. Type **610** 10 10
2313 2c. "The Art Lovers" (G. Collazo) (horiz) . . . 10 10
2314 3c. "The Patio" (G. Collazo) 10 10
2315 5c. "Cocotero" (G. Collazo) 10 10
2316 13c. "New York Studio" (G. Collazo) (horiz) . . . 60 40
2317 30c. "Emelinz Collazo" (G. Collazo) (horiz) . . . 1·25 75

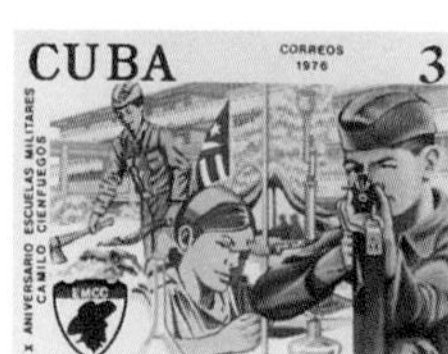

611 School Activities

1976. 10th Anniv of "Camilo Cienfuegos" Military School.
2318 **611** 3c. multicoloured 15 10

612 "Imias" (freighter)

1976. Development of Cuban Merchant Marine. Multicoloured.
2319 1c. Type **612** 25 10
2320 2c. "Comandante Camilo Cienfuegos" (freighter) . . 25 10
2321 3c. "Comandante Pinares" (cargo liner) 25 10
2322 5c. "Vietnam Heroico" (cargo liner) 40 10
2323 13c. "Presidente Allende" (ore carrier) . . . . . . 1·10 35
2324 30c. "XIII Congreso" (bulk carrier) . . . . 2·25 60

613 Emblem and part of Cine Film

1976. 8th International Cinematographic Festival of Socialist Countries, Havana.
2325 **613** 3c. multicoloured 15 10

614 Scene from "Apollo"

1976. 5th International Ballet Festival, Havana. Multicoloured.
2326 1c. Type **614** 10 10
2327 2c. "The River and the Forest" (vert) 20 10
2328 3c. "Giselle" 25 10
2329 5c. "Oedipus Rex" (vert) . . 30 10
2330 13c. "Carmen" (vert) . . . 70 45
2331 30c. "Vital Song" (vert) . . 1·25 1·00

615 Soldier and Sportsmen

1976. 3rd Military Games.
2332 **615** 3c. multicoloured 30 10

616 "Granma"

1976. 20th Anniv of "Granma" Landings.
2333 **616** 1c. multicoloured 10 10
2334 – 3c. multicoloured 10 10
2335 – 13c. multicoloured . . . 45 10
2336 – 30c. multicoloured . . . 75 35
DESIGNS: 3c. to 30c. Different scenes showing guerrillas.

618 Volleyball

1976. Cuban Victories in Montreal Olympic Games. Multicoloured.
2338 1c. Type **618** 10 10
2339 2c. Hurdling 10 10
2340 3c. Running 10 10
2341 8c. Boxing 15 10
2342 13c. Winning race 70 35
2343 30c. Judo . . . . 1·10 70

619 "Golden Cross Inn" (S. Scott)

1977. National Museum Paintings (11th series). Multicoloured.
2345 1c. Type **619** 10 10
2346 3c. "Portrait of a Man" (J. Verspronck) (vert) . . 10 10
2347 5c. "Venetian Landscape" (F. Guardi) 20 10
2348 10c. "Valley Corner" (H. Cleenewerck) (vert) 15 10
2349 13c. "F. Xaviera Paula" (anon) (vert) 70 15
2350 30c. "F. de Medici" (C. Allori) (vert) . . . . 1·00 35
The vert designs are slightly larger, 27 × 43 mm.

620 Motor Bus

1977. Rural Transport.
2351 **620** 3c. multicoloured 40 10

621 Map of Cuba

1977. Constitution of Popular Government.

2352	**621** 13c. multicoloured	35	15

622 Cuban Green Woodpecker

1977. Cuban Birds. Multicoloured.

2353	1c. Type **622**	35	20
2354	4c. Cuban grassquit	45	20
2355	10c. Cuban blackbird	80	25
2356	13c. Zapata wren	1·10	25
2357	30c. Bee hummingbird	2·25	55

623 Mechanical Scoop and Emblem

1977. Air. 6th Latin-American and Caribbean Sugar Exporters Meeting, Havana.

2358	**623** 13c. multicoloured	40	15

624 Fire-mouthed Cichlid

1997. Fish in Lenin Park Aquarium, Havana. Multicoloured.

2359	1c. Type **624**	10	10
2360	3c. Tiger barb	10	10
2361	5c. Koi carp	15	10
2362	10c. Siamese fightingfish	20	10
2363	13c. Freshwater angelfish (vert)	75	20
2364	30c. Buenos Aires tetra	1·50	40

625 "Sputnik 1" and East German Stamp

1977. 20th Anniv of 1st Artificial Satellite. Multicoloured.

2365	1c. Type **625**	10	10
2366	3c. "Luna 16" and Hungarian stamp	20	10
2367	5c. "Cosmos" and North Korean stamp	25	10
2368	10c. "Sputnik 3" and Polish stamp	40	25
2369	13c. Earth, Moon and Yugoslav stamp	85	50
2370	30c. Earth, Moon and Cuban stamp	1·10	75

626 Antonio Maria Romeu

1977. Cuban Musicians. Multicoloured.

2372	3c. Type **626** (postage)	30	15
2373	13c. Jorge Ankerman (air)	70	30

627 "Hibiscus rosa sinensis"

1977. Birth Centenary of Dr. Juan Tomas Roig (botanist). Cuban Flowers. Multicoloured.

2374	1c. Type **627** (postage)	10	10
2375	2c. "Nerium oleander"	10	10
2376	5c. "Allamanda cathartica"	20	10
2377	10c. "Pelargonium zonale"	35	10
2378	13c. "Caesalpinia pulcherrima" (air)	60	40
2379	30c. "Catharanthus roseus"	1·10	80

628 Horse-drawn Fire Engine

1977. Fire Prevention Week, Multicoloured.

2381	1c. Type **628**	10	10
2382	2c. Horse-drawn fire engine (different)	10	10
2383	6c. Early motor fire pump	10	10
2384	10c. Modern motor fire pump	25	10
2385	13c. Turntable-ladder	50	30
2386	30c. Heavy rescue vehicle	1·10	80

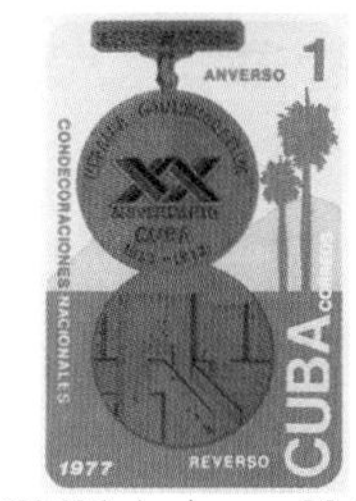

629 20th Anniversary Medal

1977. National Decorations.

2387	**629** 1c. mult (postage)	10	10
2388	– 3c. multicoloured	15	10
2389	– 13c. multicoloured (air)	35	10
2390	– 30c. multicoloured	65	30

DESIGNS: 3c. to 30c. Various medals and ribbons.

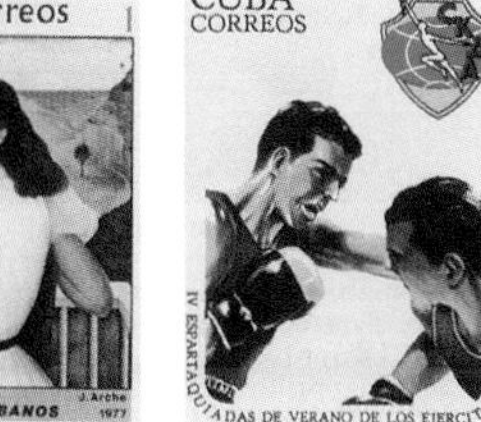

630 "Portrait of Mary" **631** Boxing

1977. Painting by Jorge Arche. Mult.

2391	1c. Type **630** (postage)	10	10
2392	3c. "Jose Marti"	10	10
2393	5c. "Portrait of Aristides"	10	10
2394	10c. "Bathers" (horiz)	25	10
2395	13c. "My Wife and I" (air)	30	10
2396	30c. "The Game of Dominoes" (horiz)	65	30

1977. Military Spartakiad. Multicoloured.

2398	1c. Type **631** (postage)	10	10
2399	3c. Volleyball	10	10
2400	5c. Parachuting	10	10
2401	10c. Running	20	10
2402	13c. Grenade-throwing (air)	30	10
2403	30c. Rifle-shooting (horiz)	65	30

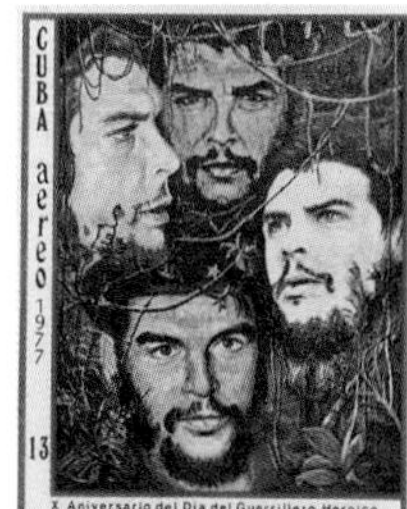

632 Che Guevara

1977. Air. 10th Anniv of Guerrilla Heroes Day.

2404	**632** 13c. multicoloured	40	10

633 Curtiss A-1 Seaplane and Parla Stamp of 1952

1977. 50th Anniv of Cuban Air Mail. Mult.

2405	1c. Type **633** (postage)	10	10
2406	2c. Ford 5-AT trimotor airplane and Havana–Key West cachet	20	10
2407	5c. Flying boat "American Clipper" and first flight cachet	25	10
2408	10c. Douglas DC-4 and Havana-Madrid cachet	40	30
2409	13c. Lockheed Super Constellation and Havana–Mexico cachet (air)	60	40
2410	30c. Ilyushin Il-18 and Havana–Prague cachet	1·00	60

634 Cruiser "Aurora"

1977. 60th Anniv of Russian Revolution.

2411	**634** 3c. black, red and gold	25	10
2412	– 13c. black, red and gold	50	25
2413	– 30c. gold, red and black	1·00	70

DESIGNS: 13c. Lenin and flags; 30c. Hammer and sickle with scenes of technology.

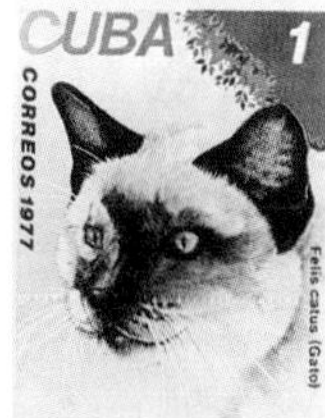

636 Cat

1977. Felines in Havana Zoo. Multicoloured.

2415	1c. Type **636** (postage)	20	10
2416	2c. Leopard (black race)	20	10
2417	8c. Puma	25	10
2418	10c. Leopard	90	50
2419	13c. Tiger (air)	1·00	60
2420	30c. Lion	1·40	1·00

637 Cienfuegos Uprising

1977. 20th Anniv of Martyrs of the Revolution. Multicoloured.

2421	3c. Type **637** (postage)	20	10
2422	20c. Attack on the Presidential Palace	45	15
2423	13c. Landing from the "Corynthia" (air)	65	35

638 Clinic, Havana

1977. 75th Anniv of Pan-American Health Organization.

2424	**638** 13c. multicoloured	10	10

639 Map of Cuba and Units of Measurement

1977. International System of Measurement.

2425	**639** 3c. multicoloured	10	10

640 University Building and Coat of Arms

1978. 250th Anniv of Havana University. Multicoloured.

2426	3c. Type **640** (postage)	10	10
2427	13c. University building and crossed sabres (air)	30	10
2428	30c. Student crowd and statue	50	30

641 "Jose Marti" (A. Menocal) **642** "Seated Woman" (R. Madrazo)

1978. Air. 125th Anniv of Jose Marti (patriot).

2429	**641** 13c. multicoloured	30	10

1978. National Museum Paintings (12th series). Multicoloured.

2430	1c. Type **642** (postage)	10	10
2431	4c. "Girl" (J. Sorolla)	10	10
2432	6c. "Landscape with Figures" (J. Pilliment) (horiz)	20	10
2433	10c. "The Cow" (E. Abela) (horiz)	35	10
2434	13c. "El Guadalquivir" (M. Barron) (horiz) (air)	75	50
2435	30c. "H. E. Ridley" (J. J. Masqueries)	75	50

643 Patrol Boat, Frontier Guard and Dog

1978. 15th Anniv of Frontier Troops.

2436	**643** 13c. multicoloured	1·00	15

644 Cuban Solitaire

1978. Cuban Birds. Multicoloured.

2437	1c. Type **644** (postage)	60	25
2438	4c. Cuban gnatcatcher	60	30
2439	10c. Oriente warbler	1·60	40
2440	13c. Zapata sparrow (air)	2·10	70
2441	30c. Cuban macaw and ivory-billed woodpecker (vert)	3·00	1·10

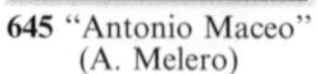
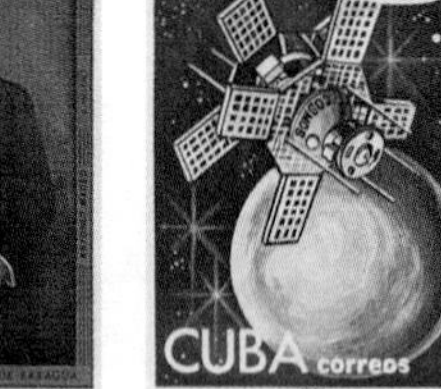

645 "Antonio Maceo" (A. Melero) **646** "Intercosmos" Satellite

1978. Air. Centenary of Baragua Protest.

2442	**645**	13c. multicoloured	30	10

1978. Cosmonautics Day. Multicoloured.

2443	1c. Type **646** (postage)	10	10
2444	2c. "Luna 24" (horiz)	10	10
2445	5c. "Venus 9"	15	10
2446	10c. "Cosmos" (horiz)	15	10
2447	13c. "Venus 10" (horiz) (air)	30	10
2448	30c. "Lunokhod 2" (36 × 46 mm)	55	30

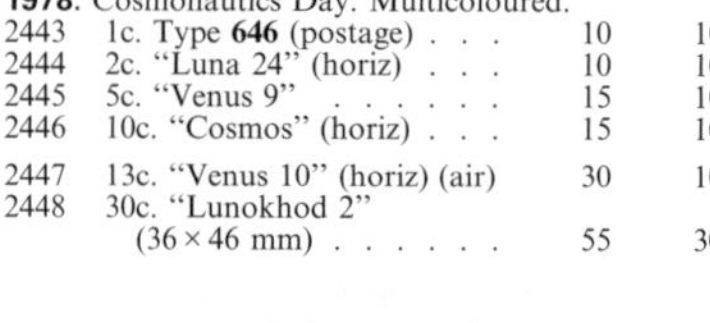

647 Smiling Worker and Emblem

1978. 9th World Federation of Trade Unions Congress, Prague.

2449	**647**	30c. red and black	45	25

648 Parliament Building, Budapest and 1919 Hungarian Stamp

1978. Air "Socifilex" Stamp Exhibition, Budapest.

2450	**648**	30c. multicoloured	55	30

649 "Melocactus guitarti"

1978. Cactus Flowers. Multicoloured.

2451	1c. Type **649** (postage)	10	10
2452	4c. "Leptocereus wrightii"	10	10
2453	6c. "Opuntia militaris"	10	10
2454	10c. "Cylindropuntia hystrix"	30	10
2455	13c. "Rhodocactus cubensis" (air)	50	30
2456	30c. "Harrisia taetra"	85	50

650 Satellite and Globe

1978. Air. World Telecommunications Day.

2457	**650**	30c. multicoloured	55	30

651 Africans and O.A.U. Emblem

1978. Air. 15th Anniv of Organization of African Unity.

2458	**651**	30c. multicoloured	50	30

653 Clown Barb

1978. Fish in Lenin Park Aquarium, Havana. Multicoloured.

2460	1c. Type **653** (postage)	10	10
2461	4c. Flame tetra	25	10
2462	6c. Guppy	30	10
2463	10c. Dwarf gourami	35	20
2464	13c. Veil-tailed goldfish (air)	70	40
2465	30c. Brown discus	1·00	70

654 Basketball **655** Moncada Fortress

1978. 13th Central American and Caribbean Games. Multicoloured.

2466	1c. Type **654** (postage)	10	10
2467	3c. Boxing	10	10
2468	5c. Weightlifting	10	10
2469	10c. Fencing (horiz)	25	10
2470	13c. Volleyball (air)	50	35
2471	30c. Running	75	45

1978. 25th Anniv of Attack on Moncada Fortress. Multicoloured.

2472	3c. Type **655** (postage)	10	10
2473	13c. Soldiers with rifles (air)	25	10
2474	30c. Dove and flags	50	25

656 Prague

1978. 11th World Youth and Students' Festival, Havana. Multicoloured.

2475	3c. Type **656** (postage)	10	10
2476	3c. Budapest	10	10
2477	3c. Berlin	10	10
2478	3c. Bucharest	10	10
2479	3c. Warsaw	10	10
2480	13c. Moscow (air)	25	15
2481	13c. Vienna	25	15
2482	13c. Helsinki	25	15
2483	13c. Sofia	25	15
2484	13c. Berlin	25	15
2485	30c. Havana (46 × 36 mm)	55	25

657 Marching Soldiers with Flag

1978. 5th Anniv of Young Workers Army.

2486	**657**	3c. multicoloured	10	10

658 "Pargo"

1978. Fishing Fleet. Multicoloured.

2487	1c. Type **658** (postage)	15	10
2488	2c. Fish-processing ship	15	10
2489	5c. Shrimp fishing boat	15	10
2490	10c. Stern trawler	35	15
2491	13c. "Mar Carbide" (air)	60	20
2492	30c. Refrigeration and processing ship	1·10	40

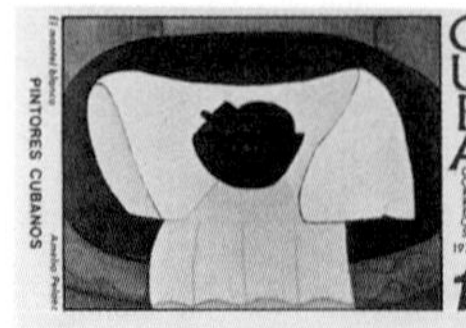

660 "The White Coat" (Pelaez del Casal)

1978. Painting by Amelia Pelaez del Casal. Multicoloured.

2494	1c. Type **660** (postage)	10	10
2495	3c. "Still Life with Flowers"	10	10
2496	6c. "Women"	20	10
2497	10c. "Fish"	30	10
2498	13c. "Flowering Almond" (air)	40	30
2499	30c. "Still Life in Blue"	80	50

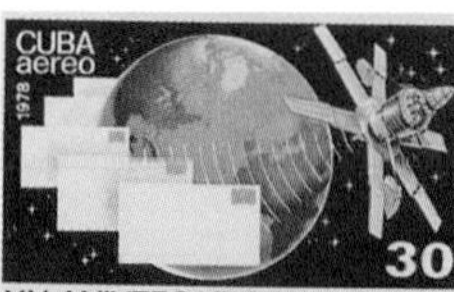

661 Letters, Satellite and Globe

1978. Air 20th Anniv of Organization for Communication Co-operation between Socialist Countries.

2501	**661**	30c. multicoloured	50	30

663 Hand

1978. Air. International Anti-Apartheid Year.

2503	**663**	13c. black, pink & mve	1·10	1·10

664 White Rhinoceros

1978. Animals in Havana Zoo. Multicoloured.

2504	1c. Type **664** (postage)	20	10
2505	4c. Okapi (vert)	20	10
2506	6c. Mandrill	20	10
2507	10c. Giraffe (vert)	40	25
2508	13c. Cheetah (air)	75	50
2509	30c. African elephant (vert)	1·25	75

665 "Grand Pas de Quatre"

1978. 30th Anniv of National Ballet Company. Multicoloured.

2510	3c. Type **665** (postage)	20	10
2511	13c. "Giselle" (air)	35	15
2512	30c. "Genesis"	75	60

666 Hibiscus **668** Fidel Castro and Soldier

667 Julius and Ethel Rosenberg

1978. Pacific Flowers.

2513	**666** 1c. mult (postage)	10	10
2514	– 4c. multicoloured	10	10
2515	– 6c. multicoloured	20	10
2516	– 10c. multicoloured	35	20
2517	– 13c. mult (air)	50	30
2518	– 30c. multicoloured	85	50

DESIGNS: 4c. to 30c. Different flowers.

1978. Air. 25th Death Anniv of Julius and Ethel Rosenberg (American Communists).

2519	**667**	13c. multicoloured	25	10

1979. 20th Anniv of Revolution. Mult.

2520	3c. Type **668**	10	10
2521	13c. Symbols of industry	30	15
2522	1p. Flag, flame and globe	1·75	95

669 Julio Mella

1979. 50th Death Anniv of J. A. Mella.

2523	**669**	13c. multicoloured	20	10

670 Blue-headed Quail Dove

1979. Doves and Pigeons. Multicoloured.

2524	1c. Type **670**	45	15
2525	3c. Key West quail dove	50	15
2526	7c. Grey-faced quail dove	50	15
2527	8c. Ruddy quail dove	60	15
2528	13c. White-crowned pigeon	1·25	40
2529	30c. Plain pigeon	2·25	1·25

671 "Genre Scene" (D. Teniers)

1979. National Museum Paintings (13th series). Multicoloured.

2530	1c. Type **671**	10	10
2531	3c. "Arrival of Spanish Troops" (J. Meissonier)	15	10
2532	6c. "A Joyful Gathering" (Sir David Wilkie)	15	10
2533	10c. "Capea" (E. de Lucas Padilla)	25	10
2534	13c. "Teatime" (R. Madrazo) (vert)	35	25
2535	30c. "Peasant in front of a Tavern" (Adriaen van Ostade)	75	40

672 "Nymphaea capensis"

673 "20" Flag and Film Frames

1979. Aquatic Flowers. Multicoloured.
2536 3c. Type **672** 20 10
2537 10c. "Nymphaea ampla" . . 25 10
2538 13c. "Nymphaea coerulea" 35 15
2539 30c. "Nymphaea rubra" . . 75 25

1979. 20th Anniv of Cuban Cinema.
2540 **673** 3c. multicoloured 10 10

674 Rocket Launch

1979. Cosmonautics Day. Multicoloured.
2541 1c. Type **674** 10 10
2542 4c. "Soyuz" 10 10
2543 6c. "Salyut" 10 10
2544 10c. "Soyuz" and "Salyut" link-up 25 10
2545 13c. "Soyuz" and "Salyut" 40 10
2546 30c. Parachute and capsule 75 30

675 Hands and Globe

1979. 6th Non-Aligned Countries Summit Conference. Multicoloured.
2548 3c. Type **675** 10 10
2549 13c. "6" ("Against Colonialism") 20 10
2550 30c. Joined coin and globe ("A New Economic Order") 50 30

676 Cuna Indian Tapestry, Panama

1979. 20th Anniv of "House of the Americas" Museum.
2551 **676** 13c. multicoloured . . . 20 10

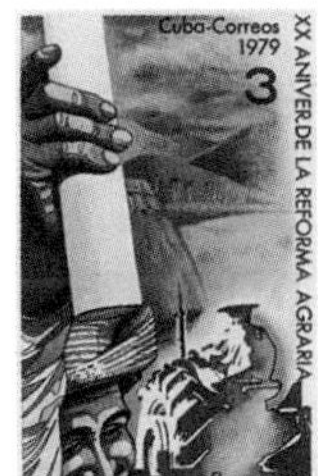
677 Farmer holding Title Deed

1979. 20th Anniv of Agrarian Reform.
2552 **677** 3c. multicoloured 10 10

679 "Eulepidotis rectimargo"

1979. Cuban Nocturnal Butterflies. Mult.
2554 1c. Type **679** 10 10
2555 4c. "Othreis materna" . . . 10 10
2556 6c. "Noropsis hieroglyphica" 25 10
2557 10c. "Heterochroma sp." . . 25 10
2558 13c. "Melanchroia regnatrix" 75 50
2559 30c. "Attera gemmata" . . 1·50 1·00

680 Children's Heads

1979. Air. International Year of the Child.
2560 **680** 13c. multicoloured . . . 20 10

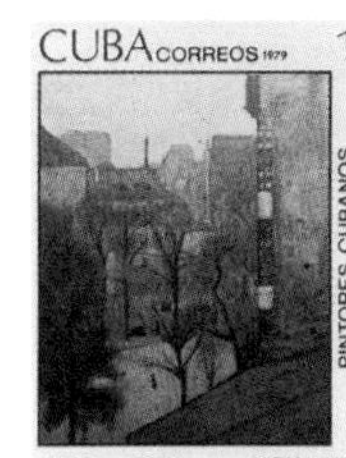
681 "Avenue du Maine, Paris"

1979. 10th Death Anniv of Victor Manuel Garcia (painter). Multicoloured.
2561 1c. Type **681** 10 10
2562 3c. "Portrait of Enmita" . . 10 10
2563 6c. "Rio San Juan, Matanzas" 20 10
2564 10c. "Landscape with Woman carrying Hay" . . 20 10
2565 13c. "Still-life with Vase" . . 30 10
2566 30c. "Street by Night" . . . 60 30

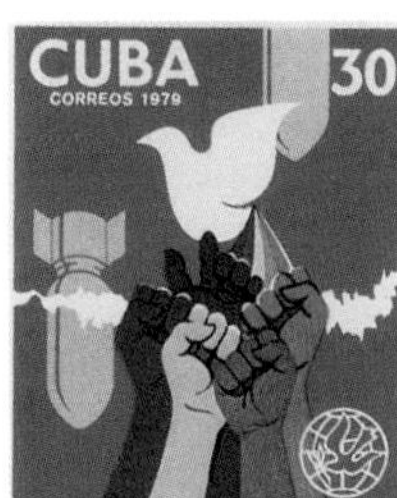
682 Clenched Fists, Dove and Bombs

1979. 30th Anniv of World Peace Council.
2568 **682** 30c. multicoloured . . . 55 25

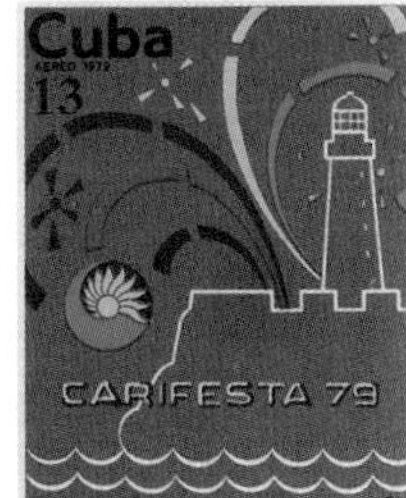
683 Lighthouse and Fireworks

1979. Air. "Carifesta 79" Festival, Havana.
2569 **683** 13c. multicoloured . . . 50 10

684 Wrestling

1979. Pre-Olympics, Moscow 1980. Mult.
2570 1c. Type **684** 10 10
2571 4c. Boxing 10 10
2572 6c. Volleyball 20 10
2573 10c. Rifle-shooting 20 10
2574 13c. Weightlifting 35 10
2575 30c. High jump 75 25

685 "Rosa eglanteria"

686 Council Emblem

1979. Roses. Multicoloured.
2576 1c. Type **685** 20 10
2577 2c. "Rosa centifolia anemonoides" 20 10
2578 3c. "Rosa indica vulgaris" 20 10
2579 5c. "Rosa eglanteria var. punicea" 20 10
2580 10c. "Rosa sulfurea" . . . 20 10
2581 13c. "Rosa muscosa alba" 40 10
2582 20c. "Rosa gallica purpurea velutina, Parva" 70 20

1979. 30th Anniv of Council of Mutual Economic Aid.
2583 **686** 13c. multicoloured . . . 20 15

687 Games Emblem and Activities

1979. Air. "Universiada 79" 10th World University Games, Mexico City.
2584 **687** 13c. green, gold & turq 25 15

688 Conventions Palace

1979. Air. 6th Non-Aligned Countries Summit Conference, Havana.
2585 **688** 50c. multicoloured . . . 80 60

689 Sir Rowland Hill and Casket containing Freedom of the City of London

1979. Air. Death Centenary of Sir Rowland Hill.
2586 **689** 30c. multicoloured . . . 75 20

690 Ford 5-AT Trimotor

1979. 50th Anniv of Cuban Airlines. Mult.
2587 1c. Type **690** 10 10
2588 2c. Sikorsky S-38 flying boat 10 10
2589 3c. Douglas DC-3 . . . . 30 10
2590 4c. Ilyushin Il-18 . . . . . 30 20
2591 13c. Yakovlev Yak-40 . . . 85 50
2592 40c. Ilyushin Il-62M . . . . 1·75 90

691 Rumanian "New Constitution" Stamp of 1948

1979. Air. "Socfilex 79" Stamp Exhibition, Bucharest.
2593 **691** 30c. multicoloured . . . 50 30

692 Camilo Cienfuegos

1979. 20th Anniv of Disappearance of Camilo Cienfuegos (revolutionary).
2594 **692** 3c. multicoloured 15 10

693 Alvaro Reinoso and Sugar Cane

1979. 15th Anniv of Sugar Cane Institute and 150th Birth Anniv of Alvaro Reinoso.
2595 **693** 13c. multicoloured . . . 30 15

694 Chimpanzees

1979. Young Zoo Animals. Multicoloured.
2596 1c. Type **694** 10 10
2597 2c. Leopards 10 10
2598 3c. Fallow deer 15 10
2599 4c. Lions 20 10
2600 5c. Brown bears 25 10
2601 13c. Eurasian red squirrels 50 25
2602 30c. Giant pandas . . . . . 1·00 50
2603 50c. Tigers . . . . 1·50 75

695 Ground Receiving Station

1979. Air. 50th Anniv of International Radio Consultative Committee.
2604 **695** 30c. multicoloured . . . 50 20

696 "Rhina oblita"

1980. Insects. Multicoloured.
2605 1c. Type **696** 10 10
2606 5c. "Odontocera josemartii" (vert) 10 10
2607 6c. "Pinthocoelium columbinum" 10 10
2608 10c. "Calosoma splendida" (vert) 30 10
2609 13c. "Homophileurus cubanus" (vert) 60 30
2610 30c. "Heterops dimidiata" (vert) . . . . 1·00 40

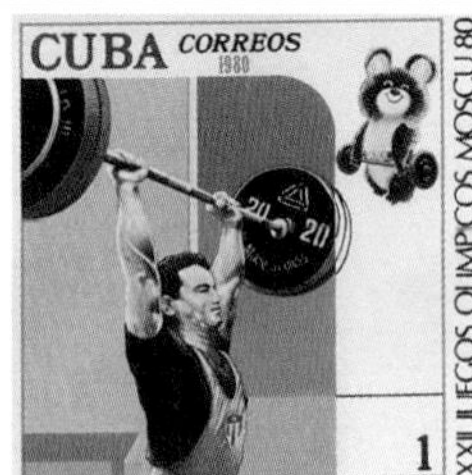

697 Weightlifting

1980. Olympic Games, Moscow. Multicoloured.
2611 1c. Type **697** 10 10
2612 2c. Shooting 10 10
2613 5c. Javelin 15 10
2614 6c. Wrestling 15 10
2615 8c. Judo 25 10
2616 10c. Running 25 10
2617 13c. Boxing 40 10
2618 30c. Volleyball 80 35

698 "Oak Trees" (Henry Joseph Harpignies)

1980. National Museum Paintings (14th series). Multicoloured.
2620 1c. Type **698** 10 10
2621 4c. "Family Reunion" (Willem van Mieris) (horiz) 10 10
2622 6c. "Poultry" (Melchior de Hondecoeter) 10 10
2623 9c. "Innocence" (Williams A. Bouguereau) 15 10
2624 13c. "Venetian Scene II" (Michele Marieschi) (horiz) 50 10
2625 30c. "Spanish Country-women" (Joaquin Dominguez Bequer) . . . 75 35

700 Intercosmos Emblem

1980. Intercosmos Programme. Mult.
2627 1c. Type **700** 10 10
2628 4c. Satellite and globe (Physics) 10 10
2629 6c. Satellite and dish aerial (Communications) 10 10
2630 10c. Satellite, grid lines and map (Meteorology) . . . 15 10
2631 13c. Staff of Aesculapius, rocket and satellites (Biology and Medicine) 25 10
2632 30c. Surveying Satellite . . . 50 35

701 Cuban Stamps of 1955 and 1959 (⅔-size illustration)

1980. 125th Anniv of Cuban Stamps.
2633 **701** 30c. blue, red & lt blue 55 30

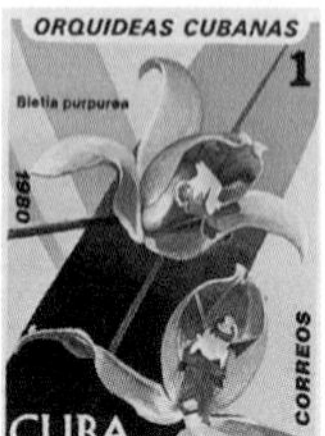

702 "Bletia purpurea"

1980. Orchids. Multicoloured.
2634 1c. Type **702** 10 10
2635 4c. "Oncidium leiboldii" . . 10 10
2636 6c. "Epidendrum cochieatum" 20 10
2637 10c. "Cattleyopsis lindenii" 25 10
2638 13c. "Encyclia fucata" . . . 40 25
2639 30c. "Encyclia phoenicea" 1·00 50

703 Bottle-nosed Dolphin

1980. Marine Mammals. Multicoloured.
2640 1c. Type **703** 25 10
2641 3c. Humpback whale (vert) 25 10
2642 13c. Cuvier's beaked whale 60 40
2643 30c. Caribbean monk seal 1·50 80

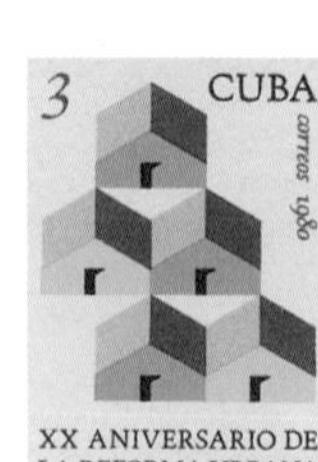

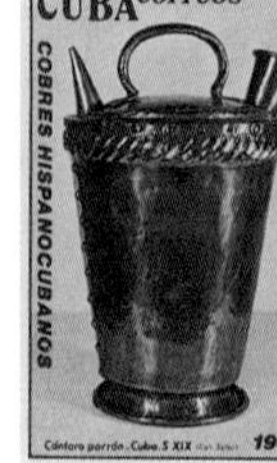

704 Houses **705** Pitcher

1980. "Moncada" Programme. Mult.
2644 3c. Type **704** 10 10
2645 13c. Refinery 20 10
ANNIVERSARIES: 3c. Urban Reform (20th Anniv). 13c. Foreign industry (20th Anniv).

1980. Copper Handicrafts. Multicoloured.
2646 3c. Type **705** 10 10
2647 13c. Wine container (38 × 26 mm) 20 15
2648 30c. Two handled pitcher 50 30

706 Emblem, Flag and Roses **708** Flags

1980. 20th Anniv of Cuban Women's Federation.
2649 **706** 3c. multicoloured 10 10

1980. 20th Anniv of 1st Havana Declaration.
2651 **708** 13c. multicoloured . . . 20 15

709 Building Galleon "Nuesta Sra. de Atocha", 1620

1980. Cuban Shipbuilding. Multicoloured.
2652 1c. Type **709** 15 10
2653 3c. Building ship of the line "El Rayo", 1749 . . . . 15 10
2654 7c. Building ship of the line "Santisima Trinidad", 1769 . . . . 15 10
2655 10c. "Santisima Trinidad" at sea, 1805 (vert) 50 30
2656 13c. Building steamships "Colon" and "Congreso", 1851 . . . . 1·00 60
2657 30c. Cardenas and Chullima shipyards . . . . 1·50 1·00

710 Arnaldo Tamayo

1980. Air. 1st Cuban–Soviet Space Flight.
2658 **710** 13c. multicoloured . . . 30 15
2659 30c. multicoloured . . . 55 30

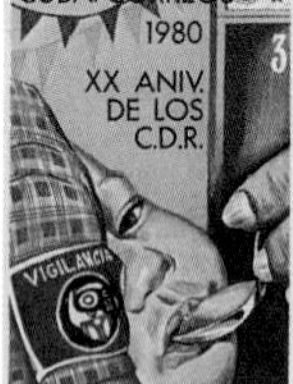

711 U.N. General Assembly **712** Child being Fed

1980. 20th Anniv of Fidel Castro's First Speech at the United Nations.
2660 **711** 13c. multicoloured . . . 20 10

1980. 20th Anniv of Revolution's Defence Committees.
2661 **712** 3c. multicoloured 15 10

714 Inspection Locomotive

1980. Early Locomotives. Multicoloured.
2663 1c. Type **714** 20 10
2664 2c. Inspection locomotive, Chaparra Sugar Company 20 10
2665 7c. Fireless locomotive, San Francisco Sugar Mill . . 30 10
2666 10c. Saddle-tank locomotive, Australia Estate 40 10
2667 13c. Steam locomotive . . . 70 10
2668 30c. Oil-fired locomotive, 1909, Smith Comas Estate 1·75 60

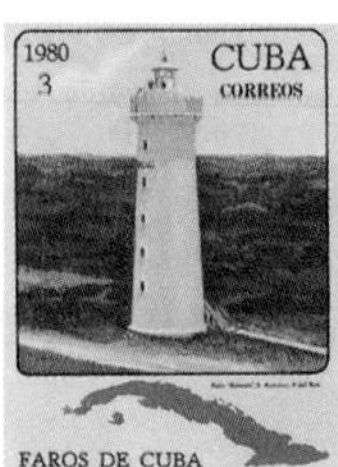

715 "Roncali" Lighthouse, San Antonio

1980. Lighthouses (1st series). Multicoloured.
2669 3c. Type **715** 20 10
2670 13c. Jagua, Cienfuegos . . . 35 20
2671 30c. Punta Maisi, Guantanamo 80 70
See also Nos. 2746/8, 2859/61 and 2920/2.

716 Bronze Medal

1980. Cuban Olympic Medal Winners. Mult.
2672 13c. Type **716** 20 15
2673 30c. Silver medal 60 20
2674 50c. Gold medal . . . . . 1·00 50

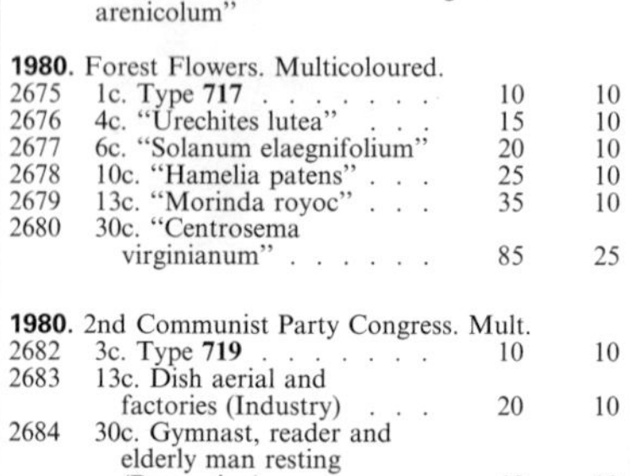

717 "Pancratium arenicolum" **719** Congress Emblem

1980. Forest Flowers. Multicoloured.
2675 1c. Type **717** 10 10
2676 4c. "Urechites lutea" . . . 15 10
2677 6c. "Solanum elaegnifolium" 20 10
2678 10c. "Hamelia patens" . . . 25 10
2679 13c. "Morinda royoc" . . . 35 10
2680 30c. "Centrosema virginianum" 85 25

1980. 2nd Communist Party Congress. Mult.
2682 3c. Type **719** 10 10
2683 13c. Dish aerial and factories (Industry) . . . 20 10
2684 30c. Gymnast, reader and elderly man resting (Recreation) 45 20

720 "Lady Mayo" (Anton van Dyck)

1981. National Museum Paintings (15th series). Multicoloured.
2685 1c. Type **720** 10 10
2686 6c. "La Hilandera" (Giovanni B. Piazzeta) . . 10 10
2687 10c. "Daniel Collyer" (Francis Cotes) 15 10
2688 13c. "Gardens of Palma de Mallorca" (Santiago Rusinol) (horiz) 20 15
2689 20c. "Landscape with Road and Houses" (Frederick W. Watts) (horiz) 30 15
2690 50c. "Landscape with Sheep" (Jean F. Millet) (horiz) 90 50

721 Short-finned Mako

1981. Fishes. Multicoloured.
2691 1c. Type **721** 15 10
2692 3c. Opah 15 10
2693 10c. Sailfish 20 15
2694 13c. Oceanic sunfish (vert) 1·50 35
2695 30c. Dolphin and flying-fish 75 30
2696 50c. White marlin . . . . . 1·40 75

722 Saving Ball

1981. World Cup Football Championship, Spain (1982). (1st issue). Multicoloured.
2697 1c. Diving for ball (horiz) 10 10
2698 2c. Passing ball (horiz) . . . 10 10
2699 3c. Running with ball (horiz) 10 10
2700 10c. Type **722** 25 10
2701 13c. Heading ball 50 10
2702 50c. Tackle (horiz) . . . . 1·25 50
See also Nos. 2775/81.

723 Mother, Child, Boots and Toy Train **724** Jules Verne, Konstantin Tsiolkovsky and Sergei Korolev

1981. 20th Anniv of Kindergartens.
2704 **723** 3c. multicoloured . . . . 1·50 10

1981. 20th Anniv of First Man in Space. Mult.
2705 1c. Type **724** 10 10
2706 2c. Yuri Gagarin (first man in space) (horiz) 10 10
2707 3c. Valentina Tereshkova (first woman in space) (horiz) 10 10
2708 5c. Aleksandr Leonov (first space walker) (horiz) . . . 10 10
2709 13c. Crew of "Voskhod I" (horiz) 20 10
2710 30c. Ryumen and Popov (horiz) 50 30
2711 50c. Tamayo and Romanenko (crew of Soviet–Cuban flight) . . . 90 40

725 Jet Fighters and Rocket

1981. 20th Anniv of Defeat of Invasion Attempt by Cuban Exiles. Multicoloured.
2712 3c. Type **725** (Defence and Air Force Day) 10 10
2713 13c. Hand waving machine-pistol (Victory at Giron) 20 15
2714 30c. Book and flags (Proclamation of Revolution's socialist character) (horiz) 45 30

726 Reynold Garcia Garcia (leader of attack), Barracks and Children

1981. 25th Anniv of Attack on Goicuria Barracks.
2715 **726** 3c. multicoloured 15 10

727 Tractor and Women planting Crops

1981. 20th Anniv of National Association of Small Farmers.
2716 **727** 3c. multicoloured 15 10

729 Canelo

1981. Fighting Cocks. Multicoloured.
2718 1c. Type **729** 10 10
2719 3c. Cenizo (horiz) 10 10
2720 7c. Blanco 15 10
2721 13c. Pinto 15 10
2722 30c. Giro (horiz) 50 30
2723 50c. Jabao 95 50

730 Anniversary Emblem

733 "House in the Country" (Maria Cardidad de la O)

732 Tram

1981. 20th Anniv of Ministry of the Interior.
2724 **730** 13c. multicoloured . . . 15 10

1981. Horse-drawn Vehicles. Multicoloured.
2726 1c. Type **732** 30 10
2727 4c. Village bus 10 10
2728 9c. Brake 15 10
2729 13c. Landau 15 10
2730 30c. Phaeton 60 30
2731 50c. Hearse . . . . 1·10 50

1981. International Year of Disabled People.
2732 **733** 30c. multicoloured . . . 55 30

734 Sandinista Guerrilla and Map of Nicaragua

1981. 20th Anniv of Sandinista National Liberation Front.
2733 **734** 13c. multicoloured . . . 20 15

735 Gymnasts

1981. 20th Anniv of State Organizations. Mult.
2734 3c. Type **735** (National Sports and Physical Recreation Institute) . . . 10 10
2735 13c. "RHC", radio waves and map (Radio Havana) 15 10
2736 30c. Arrows ("Mincex" Foreign Trade Ministry) 55 30

736 Carlos J. Finlay, Mosquito and Theory

1981. Centenary of Biological Vectors Theory.
2737 **736** 13c. multicoloured . . . 20 15

737 Arms of Non-aligned Countries, Manacled Hands and Hands releasing Dove

1981. 20th Anniv of Non-aligned Countries Movement.
2738 **737** 50c. multicoloured . . . 90 50

738 White Horse

1981. Horses. Multicoloured.
2739 1c. Type **738** 10 10
2740 3c. Brown horse 10 10
2741 8c. Bucking white horse . . 15 10
2742 13c. Horse being broken-in 15 10
2743 30c. Black horse 75 40
2744 50c. Herd of horses (horiz) 1·25 70

1981. Lighthouses (2nd series). As T **715**. Mult.
2746 3c. Piedras del Norte . . . 30 10
2747 13c. Punta Lucrecia 40 20
2748 40c. Guano del Este . . . . 1·25 60

740 "Flor de Cuba Sugar Mill"

1981. 80th Anniv of Jose Marti National Library. Lithographs by Eduardo Laplante. Multicoloured.
2749 3c. Type **740** 10 10
2750 13c. "El Progreso Sugar Mill" 25 10
2751 30c. "Santa Teresa Sugar Mill" 70 30

741 Pablo Picasso and Cuban Stamp

1981. Birth Centenary of Pablo Picasso (artist).
2752 **741** 30c. multicoloured . . . 75 35

743 "Napoleon in Coronation Regalia" (Anon.)

1981. 20th Anniv of Napoleonic Museum. Mult.
2754 1c. Type **743** 10 10
2755 3c. "Napoleon with Landscape" (J. H. Vernet) (horiz) 10 10
2756 10c. "Bonaparte in Egypt" (Eduard Detaille) 15 10
2757 13c. "Napoleon on Horseback" (Hippolyte Bellange) (horiz) 15 10
2758 30c. "Napoleon in Normandy" (Bellange) (horiz) 60 30
2759 50c. "Death of Napoleon" (Anon) . . . . 1·10 45

744 Revolutionaries

745 Cuban Emerald ("Zun-Zun")

1981. 25th Anniversaries. Multicoloured.
2760 3c. Type **744** (30th November insurrection) 10 10
2761 20c. Soldier (Revolutionary Armed Forces) 20 10
2762 1p. Launch "Granma" (disembarkation of revolutionary forces) . . . 2·25 1·00

1981. Fauna.
2763 **745** 1c. blue 75 15
2764 – 2c. green . . . . 1·10 25
2765 – 5c. brown 15 15
2766 – 20c. red 50 15
2767 – 35c. lilac . . . . 1·00 20
2768 – 40c. grey 80 35

DESIGNS: 2c. Cuban conure ("Catey"); 5c. Desmarest's hutia; 20c. Cuban solenodon; 35c. American manatee; 40c. Crocodile.

746 Ortiz (after Jorge Arche y Silva)

747 Conrado Benitez

1981. Birth Centenary of Fernando Ortiz (folklorist). Multicoloured.
2769 3c. Type **746** 10 10
2770 10c. Idol (pendant) 15 10
2771 30c. Arara drum 55 25
2772 50c. Thunder god (Chango carving) 90 45

1981. 20th Anniv of Literacy Campaign. Mult.
2773 5c. Type **747** 15 10
2774 5c. Manuel Ascunce 15 10

748 Goalkeeper

749 Lazaro Pena (trade union delegate)

1982. World Cup Football Championship, Spain (2nd issue). Multicoloured.
2775 1c. Type **748** 10 10
2776 2c. Footballers 10 10
2777 5c. Heading ball 10 10
2778 10c. Kicking ball 15 10
2779 20c. Running for ball (horiz) 35 15
2780 40c. Tackle (horiz) 60 40
2781 50c. Shooting for goal . . . 85 60

1982. 10th World Trade Unions' Congress, Havana.
2783 **749** 30c. multicoloured . . . 50 30

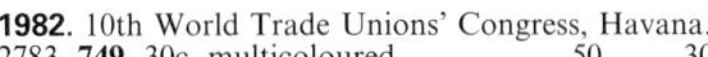

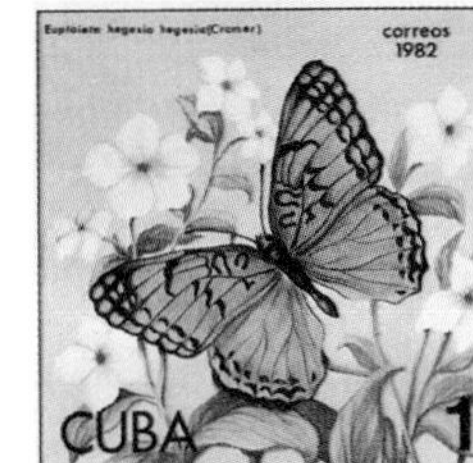

750 "Euptoieta hegesia hegesia"

1982. Butterflies. Multicoloured.
2784 1c. Type **750** 10 10
2785 4c. "Metamorpha stelenes insularis" 10 10
2786 5c. "Helicantus charithanius ramsdeni" 10 10
2787 20c. "Phoebis avellaneda" 75 25
2788 30c. "Hamadryas ferox diasia" . . . . 1·25 45
2789 50c. "Marpesia eleuchea eleuchea" . . . . 2·10 75

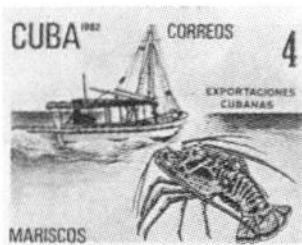

751 Lobster

1982. Exports.
2790 – 3c. green 10 10
2791 **751** 4c. red 30 10
2792 – 6c. blue 15 10
2793 – 7c. orange 15 10
2794 – 8c. lilac 15 10
2795 – 9c. grey 15 10
2796 – 10c. lilac 20 10
2797 – 30c. brown 30 15
2798 – 50c. red 85 25
2799 – 1p. brown . . . . . . 1·60 80

DESIGNS—HORIZ: 3c. Sugar; 6c. Tinned fruit; 7c. Agricultural machinery; 8c. Nickel. VERT: 9c. Rum; 10c. Coffee; 30c. Citrus fruit; 50c. Cigars; 1p. Cement.

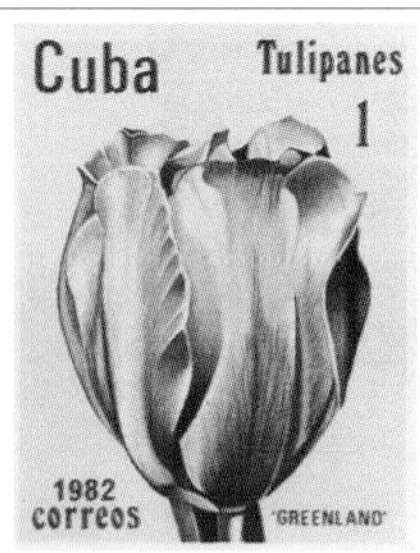

752 "Greenland" (cottage tulip)

1982. Tulips. Multicoloured.
2800 1c. Type **752** 20 10
2801 3c. "Mariette" (Lily-flowered tulip) 20 10
2802 8c. "Ringo" (triumph) . . . 25 10
2903 20c. "Black Tulip" (Darwin) 50 25
2804 30c. "Jewel of Spring" (Darwin hybrid) 80 40
2805 50c. "Orange Parrot" (parrot tulip) . . . . . . 1·40 70

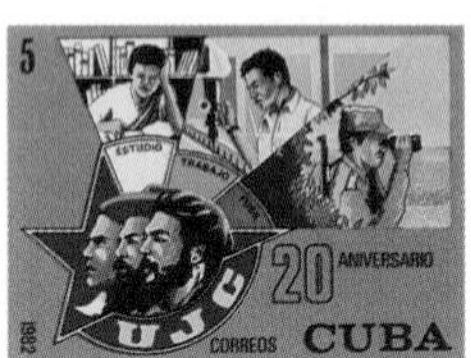

753 Youth Activities

1982. 20th Anniv of Communist Youth Union.
2806 **753** 5c. multicoloured 15 10

754 "Mars" Satellite

1982. Cosmonautics Day. Second United Nations Conference on Exploration and Peaceful Uses of Outer Space. Multicoloured.
2807 1c. Type **754** 10 10
2808 3c. "Venera" satellite . . . 10 10
2809 6c. "Salyut–Soyuz" link-up 10 10
2810 20c. "Lunokhod" moon vehicle 15 10
2811 30c. "Venera" with heatshield 50 20
2812 50c. "Kosmos" satellite . . 85 40

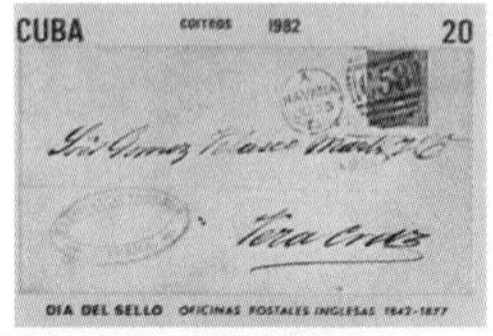

755 Letter from British Postal Agency, Havana, to Vera Cruz

1982. Stamp Day. Multicoloured.
2813 20c. Type **755** 50 15
2814 30c. Letter from French postal agency, Havana, to Tampico, Mexico 75 20

756 Map of Cuba and Wave Pattern

757 "Portrait of Young Woman" (Jean Greuze)

1982. 20th Anniv of Cuban Broadcasting and Television Institute.
2815 **756** 30c. multicoloured . . . 50 20

1982. National Museum Paintings (16th series). Multicoloured.
2816 1c. Type **757** 10 10
2817 3c. "Procession in Brittany" (Jules Breton) (46 × 36 mm) 10 10
2818 9c. "Landscape" (Jean Piliment) (horiz) 40 10
2819 20c. "Towards Evening" (William Bourgueran) . . 30 15
2820 30c. "Tiger" (Delacroix) (horiz) 50 20
2821 40c. "The Chair" (Wilfredo Lam) 60 30

759 Hurdling and 1930 Sports Stamp

1982. "Deporfilex '82" Stamp and Coin Exhibition, Havana.
2823 **759** 20c. multicoloured . . . 40 20

760 Tortoise

1982. Reptiles. Multicoloured.
2824 1c. Type **760** 10 10
2825 2c. Snake 10 10
2826 3c. Cuban crocodile 25 10
2827 20c. Iguana 70 40
2828 30c. Lizard . . . . 1·00 60
2829 50c. Snake . . . . 1·50 1·00

761 Georgi Dimitrov

763 Baseball

762 Dr. Robert Koch and Bacillus

1982. Birth Centenary of Georgi Dimitrov (Bulgarian statesman).
2830 **761** 30c. multicoloured . . . 55 20

1982. Centenary of Discovery of Tubercle Bacillus.
2831 **762** 20c. multicoloured . . . 40 20

1982. 14th Central American and Caribbean Games, Havana. Multicoloured.
2832 1c. Type **763** 10 10
2833 2c. Boxing 20 10
2834 10c. Water polo 25 10
2835 20c. Javelin 50 35
2836 35c. Weightlifting . . . . . 1·00 60
2837 50c. Volleyball . . . . . . 1·00 70

764 "Eichornia crassipes"

1982. 20th Anniv of Hydraulic Development Plan.
2838 5c. Type **764** 15 10
2839 20c. "Nymphaea alba" . . . 35 15

766 Hand holding Gun

1982. Namibia Day.
2841 **766** 50c. multicoloured . . . 80 35

767 Goal

768 "Devil" (V. P. Landaluse)

1982. World Cup Football Championship Finalists. Multicoloured.
2842 5c. Type **767** 15 10
2843 20c. Heading ball 35 20
2844 30c. Tackle 50 25
2845 50c. Saving goal 85 45

1982. 20th Anniv of National Folk Ensemble. Multicoloured.
2846 20c. Type **768** 40 20
2847 30c. "Epiphany festival" (V.P. Landaluze) (horiz) 55 30

769 Prehistoric Owl

1982. Prehistoric Animals. Multicoloured.
2848 1c. Type **769** 75 35
2849 5c. "Crocodylus rhombifer" (horiz) 20 10
2850 7c. Prehistoric eagle . . . . 3·00 45
2851 20c. "Geocapromys colombianus" (horiz) . . 50 25
2852 35c. "Megalocnus rodens" 90 50
2853 50c. "Nesophontes micrus" (horiz) . . . . 1·00 60

770 Che Guevara

1982. 15th Death Anniv of "Che" Guevara (guerrilla fighter).
2854 **770** 20c. multicoloured . . . 40 20

771 Christopher Columbus, "Santa Maria" and Map of Cuba

1982. 490th Anniv of Discovery of America by Columbus. Multicoloured.
2855 5c. Type **771** 95 35
2856 20c. "Santa Maria" (vert) 85 30
2857 35c. Caravel "Pinta" (vert) 1·40 65
2858 50c. Caravel "Nina" (vert) 1·75 80

1982. Lighthouses (3rd series). As T **715**. Multicoloured.
2859 5c. Cayo Jutias 30 10
2860 20c. Cayo Paredon Grande 75 15
2861 30c. Morro, Santiago de Cuba . . . . 1·00 30

772 George Washington (anonymous painting)

1982. 250th Birth Anniv of George Washington. Multicoloured.
2862 5c. Type **772** 15 10
2863 20c. Portrait of Washington by Daniel Huntington . . 40 15

774 Steam Locomotive (1917) and Boating Lake

1982. 10th Anniv of Lenin Park, Havana.
2865 **774** 5c. multicoloured 20 10

775 Capablanca as Child and Chess King

1982. 40th Death Anniv of Jose Capablanca (chess player). Multicoloured.
2866 5c. Type **775** 15 10
2867 20c. Capablanca and rook 40 15
2868 30c. Capablanca and knight 55 30
2869 50c. Capablanca and queen 85 45

776 Lenin, Marx, Russian Arms and Kremlin Tower

1982. 60th Anniv of U.S.S.R.
2870 **776** 30c. multicoloured . . . 55 30

777 Methods of Communications

1983. World Communications Year (1st issue).
2871 **777** 20c. multicoloured . . . 40 15
See also Nos. 2929/33.

778 Birthplace and Birth Centenary Stamp

1983. 130th Birth Anniv of Jose Marti (writer).
2872 **778** 5c. multicoloured 15 10

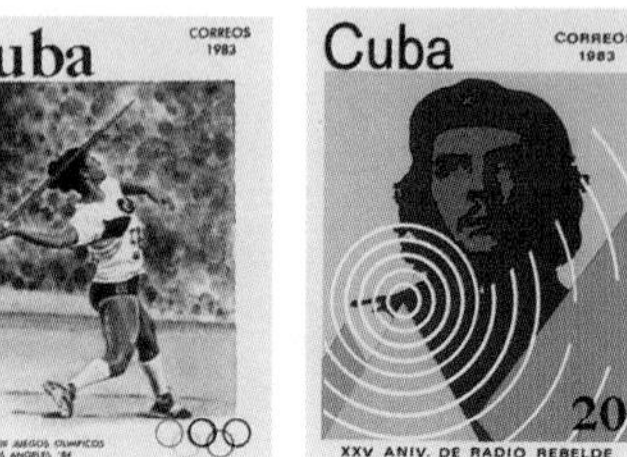

779 Throwing the Javelin

780 "Che" Guevara and Radio Waves

1983. Olympic Games, Los Angeles (1984). Multicoloured.
2873 1c. Type **779** 10 10
2874 5c. Volleyball 15 10
2875 6c. Basketball 15 10
2876 20c. Weightlifting 40 15

2877 30c. Wrestling 55 30
2878 50c. Boxing 85 45

1983. 25th Anniv of Radio Rebelde.
2880 **780** 20c. multicoloured . . . 40 15

781 Karl Marx

1983. Death Centenary of Karl Marx.
2881 **781** 30c. multicoloured . . . 55 30

782 Charles's Hydrogen Balloon **783** "Vostok 1"

1983. Bicentenary of Manned Flight. Mult.
2882 1c. Type **782** 10 10
2883 3c. Montgolfier balloon . . 10 10
2884 5c. Montgolfier balloon "Le Gustave" 15 10
2885 7c. Eugene Godard's quintuple "acrobatic" balloon 20 10
2886 30c. Montgolfier unmanned balloon . . . . 1·10 55
2887 50c. Charles Green's balloon "Royal Vauxhall" . . . . 1·10 55

1983. Cosmonautics Day. Multicoloured.
2889 1c. Type **783** 10 10
2890 4c. French "D1" satellite . . 10 10
2891 5c. "Mars 2" 15 10
2892 20c. "Soyuz" 40 15
2893 30c. Meteorological satellite 55 30
2894 50c. Intercosmos programme 85 45

784 Letter sent by First International Airmail Service

1983. Stamp Day. Multicoloured.
2895 20c. Type **784** 50 15
2896 30c. Letter sent by first Atlantic airmail service . . 75 30

786 Jose Rafael de las Heras

1983. Birth Bicentenary of Simon Bolivar. Mult.
2898 5c. Type **786** 15 10
2899 20c. Simon Bolivar 40 15

787 J. L. Tasende, Abel Santamaria and B. L. Santa Coloma

1983. 30th Anniv of Attack on Moncada Fortress. Multicoloured.
2900 5c. Jose Marti and fortress (horiz) 15 10
2901 20c. Type **787** 40 15
2902 30c. Symbol of Castro's book "History Will Absolve Me" 55 30

789 Weightlifting

1983. 9th Pan-American Games, Caracas. Mult.
2904 1c. Type **789** 15 10
2905 2c. Volleyball 20 10
2906 3c. Baseball 20 10
2907 20c. High jump 50 30
2908 30c. Basketball 75 40
2909 40c. Boxing . . . . 1·00 60

790 "Harbour" (Claude Vernet)

1983. Centenary of French Alliance (French language-teaching association).
2910 **790** 30c. multicoloured . . . 1·25 45

791 Salvador Allende and burning Presidential Palace

1983. 10th Death Anniv of Salvador Allende (President of Chile).
2911 **791** 20c. multicoloured . . . 40 15

792 Regional Peasants Committee

1983. 25th Anniv of Peasants in Arms Congress.
2912 **792** 5c. multicoloured 10 10

793 "Portrait of a Young Man"

1983. 500th Birth Anniv of Raphael. Mult.
2913 1c. "Girl with Veil" 10 10
2914 2c. "The Cardinal" 10 10
2915 5c. "Francesco M. della Rovere" 20 10
2916 20c. Type **793** 60 40
2917 30c. "Magdalena Doni" . . 75 50
2918 50c. "La Fornarina" . . . . 1·10 70

794 Quality Seal and Exports

1983. State Quality Seal.
2919 **794** 5c. multicoloured 15 10

1983. Lighthouses (4th series). As T **715**. Multicoloured.
2920 5c. Carapachibey, Isle of Youth 20 10
2921 20c. Cadiz Bay 60 35
2922 30c. Punta Gobernadora . . 75 45

795 Hawksbill Turtle

1983. Turtles. Multicoloured.
2923 1c. Type **795** 20 10
2924 2c. "Lepidochelys kempi" 25 10
2925 5c. "Chrysemys decusata" 25 10
2926 20c. Loggerhead turtle . . . 70 30
2927 30c. Green turtle 85 40
2928 50c. "Dermochelys coriacea" 1·40 1·00

796 Bell's Gallow Frame and Modern Telephones

1983. World Communications Year (2nd issue). Multicoloured.
2929 1c. Type **796** 10 10
2930 5c. Telegram and airmail envelopes and U.P.U. emblem 10 10
2931 10c. Satellite and antenna 25 10
2932 20c. Telecommunications satellite and dish aerial . . 40 15
2933 30c. Television and Radio Commemorative plaque and tower block 55 30

797 Cuban Stamps of 1933 and 1965

1983. 150th Birth Anniv of Carlos J. Finlay (malaria researcher).
2934 **797** 20c. multicoloured . . . 50 15

798 "Jatropha angustifolia" **799** Tobacco Flowers

1983. Flora and Fauna. Multicoloured. (a) Flowers.
2935 5c. Type **798** 10 10
2936 5c. "Cochlospermum vitifolium" 10 10
2937 5c. "Tabebuia lepidota" . . 10 10
2938 5c. "Kalmiella ericoides" . . 10 10
2939 5c. "Jatropha integerrima" 10 10
2940 5c. "Melocactus actinacanthus" 10 10
2941 5c. "Cordia sebestana" . . . 10 10
2942 5c. "Tabernaemontana apoda" 10 10
2943 5c. "Lantana camera" . . . 10 10
2944 5c. "Cordia gerascanthus" . . 10 10
2945 5c. "Opuntia dillenii" . . . 10 10
2946 5c. "Euphorbia podocarpifolia" 10 10
2947 5c. "Dinema cubincola" . . 10 10
2948 5c. "Guaiacum officinale" 10 10
2949 5c. "Magnolia cubensis" . . 10 10

(b) Birds.
2950 5c. Bee hummingbird . . . 60 15
2951 5c. Northern mockingbird 60 15
2952 5c. Cuban tody 60 15
2953 5c. Cuban Amazon 60 15
2954 5c. Zapata wren 60 15
2955 5c. Brown pelican . . . . . 1·00 20
2956 5c. Great red-bellied woodpecker 60 15
2957 5c. Red-legged thrush . . . 60 15
2958 5c. Cuban conure 60 15
2959 5c. Eastern meadowlark . . 60 15
2960 5c. Cuban grassquit 60 15
2961 5c. White-tailed tropic bird 60 15
2962 5c. Cuban solitaire 60 15
2963 5c. Great lizard cuckoo . . 60 15
2964 5c. Cuban gnatcatcher . . . 60 15

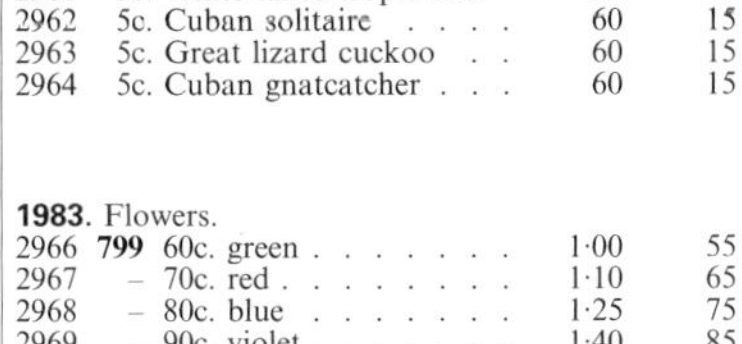

1983. Flowers.
2966 **799** 60c. green . . . . 1·00 55
2967 – 70c. red . . . . 1·10 65
2968 – 80c. blue . . . . 1·25 75
2969 – 90c. violet . . . . 1·40 85
DESIGNS: 70c. Lily; 80c. Mariposa; 90c. Orchid.

800 Flag and Plan of El Jigue Battlefield

1983. 25th Anniv of Revolution (1st issue). Multicoloured.
2970 5c. Type **800** 10 10
2971 20c. Flag and railway tracks at Santa Clara . . . . . 2·50 75

801 Flag and Revolutionaries

1983. 25th Anniv of Revolution (2nd issue). Multicoloured.
2972 20c. Type **801** 35 15
2973 20c. "25" and star 35 15
2974 20c. Workers and Cuban Communist Party emblem 35 15

802 Lazaro Gonzalez, CTC Emblem and 15th Congress Flag

1984. 45th Anniv of Revolutionary Workers' Union.
2975 **802** 5c. multicoloured 10 10

803 "Ixias balice balice"

1984. Butterflies. Multicoloured.
2976 1c. Type **803** 10 10
2977 2c. "Phoebis avellaneda avellaneda" 10 10
2978 3c. "Anthocaris sara sara" 10 10
2979 5c. "Victorina superba superba" 20 10
2980 20c. "Heliconius cydno cydnides" 70 10
2981 30c. "Parides gundlachianus calzadillae" . . . . . . 1·25 45
2982 50c. "Catagramma sorana sorana" . . . . 2·00 70

804 Clocktower and Russian Stamps of 1924–25

1984. 60th Death Anniv of Lenin.
2983 **804** 30c. multicoloured . . . 50 25

805 Risso's Dolphin

1984. Whales and Dolphins. Multicoloured.
2984 1c. Type **805** 10 10
2985 2c. Common dolphin . . . 10 10
2986 5c. Sperm whale (horiz) . . 20 10
2987 6c. Spotted dolphin 20 10
2988 10c. False killer whale (horiz) 50 30
2989 30c. Bottle-nosed dolphin 1·00 70
2990 50c. Humpback whale (horiz) . . . . 1·50 1·00

806 Sandino and Crowd holding Banner

1984. 50th Death Anniv of Augusto C. Sandino.
2991 **806** 20c. multicoloured . . . 35 15

807 Red Cross Flag and Stamp of 1946

1984. 75th Anniv of Cuban Red Cross.
2992 **807** 30c. multicoloured . . . 80 70

808 Scene from Cartoon Film

1984. 25th Anniv of Cuban Cinema.
2993 **808** 20c. multicoloured . . . 55 50

809 "Brownea grandiceps"

1984. Caribbean Flowers. Multicoloured.
2994 1c. Type **809** 10 10
2995 2c. "Couroupita guianensis" 10 10
2996 5c. "Triplaris surinamensis" 15 10
2997 20c. "Amherstia nobilis" . . 55 50
2998 30c. "Plumieria alba" . . . 80 70
2999 50c. "Delonix regia" . . . . 1·40 1·25

810 "Electron 1"

1984. Cosmonautics Day. Multicoloured.
3000 2c. Type **810** 10 10
3001 3c. "Electron 2" 10 10
3002 5c. "Intercosmos 1" 15 10
3003 10c. "Mars 5" 30 15
3004 30c. "Soyuz 1" 80 70
3005 50c. Soviet–Bulgarian space flight, 1979 . . . . 1·40 1·25

811 Mexican Mail Runner

1984. Stamp Day. Multicoloured.
3007 20c. Type **811** 55 50
3008 30c. Egyptian boatman . . 80 70
Nos. 3007/8 show details of mural by R. R. Radillo in Havana Stamp Museum.
See also Nos. 3097/8, 3170/1, 3336/7 and 3619/20.

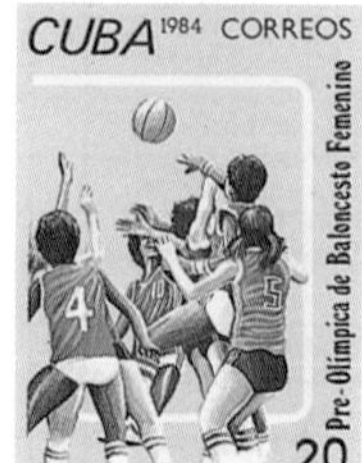

813 Basketball

1984. Pre-Olympics.
3010 **813** 20c. multicoloured . . . 55 50

814 Pink Roses

816 Saver and Pile of Coins

815 Workers in Field

1984. Mothers' Day. Multicoloured.
3011 20c. Type **814** 55 50
3012 20c. Red roses 55 50

1984. 25th Anniv of Land Reform Act.
3013 **815** 5c. multicoloured 15 10

1984. 1st Anniv of People's Saving Bank.
3014 **816** 5c. multicoloured 15 10

817 Locomotive

1984. Locomotives. Multicoloured.
3015 1c. Type **817** 15 10
3016 4c. Locomotive No. 73 . . . 20 10
3017 5c. Locomotive (different) 25 10
3018 10c. Locomotive (different) 40 10
3019 30c. Locomotive No. 350 . . 95 30
3020 50c. Locomotive No. 495 . . 1·90 55

819 Baron de Coubertin and Runner with Olympic Flame

1984. 90th Anniv of Int Olympic Committee.
3022 **819** 30c. multicoloured . . . 80 70

820 Baby with Toy Dog

1984. Children's Day.
3023 **820** 5c. multicoloured 15 10

821 Wrestling

822 Emilio Roig de Leuchsenring

1984. Olympic Games, Los Angeles. Mult.
3024 1c. Type **821** 10 10
3025 3c. Throwing the discus . . 10 10
3026 5c. Volleyball 15 10
3027 20c. Boxing 55 50
3028 30c. Basketball 80 70
3029 50c. Weightlifting . . . . . 1·40 1·25

1984. 20th Death Anniv of Emilio Roig de Leuchsenring.
3031 **822** 5c. multicoloured 15 10

824 Cow in Pasture

1984. Cattle. Multicoloured.
3033 2c. Type **824** 10 10
3034 3c. Cuban Carib 10 10
3035 5c. Charolaise (vert) 10 10
3036 30c. Cuban Cebu (vert) . . 75 40
3037 50c. White-udder cow . . . 1·00 70

825 Men's Volleyball

1984. Friendship Tournament. Mult.
3038 3c. Type **825** 10 10
3039 5c. Women's volleyball . . . 10 10
3040 8c. Water polo 30 10
3041 30c. Boxing 60 40

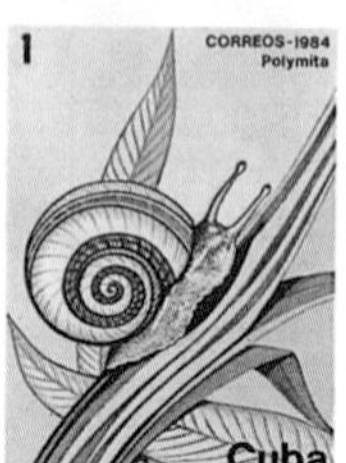

826 Polymita

1984. Cuban Wildlife. Multicoloured.
3042 1c. Type **826** 10 10
3043 2c. Cuban solenodon . . . 10 10
3044 3c. "Alsophis cantherigerus" (snake) 10 10
3045 4c. "Osteopilus septentrionalis" (frog) . . 10 10
3046 5c. Bee hummingbirds . . . 45 15
3047 10c. Bushy-tailed hutia . . . 65 25
3048 30c. Cuban tody . . . . . 2·75 1·10
3049 50c. Peach-faced lovebird . . 4·50 1·40

827 King Ferdinand and Queen Isabella

1984. "Espamer '85" International Stamp Exhibition, Havana. Multicoloured.
3050 5c. Type **827** 10 10
3051 20c. Columbus departing from Palos de Moguer . . 1·00 45
3052 30c. "Santa Maria", "Pinta" and "Nina" . . . . . . 1·40 65
3053 50c. Columbus arriving in America 75 70

829 Flag and Soldier

1984. 25th Anniv of National Militia.
3055 **829** 5c. multicoloured 10 10

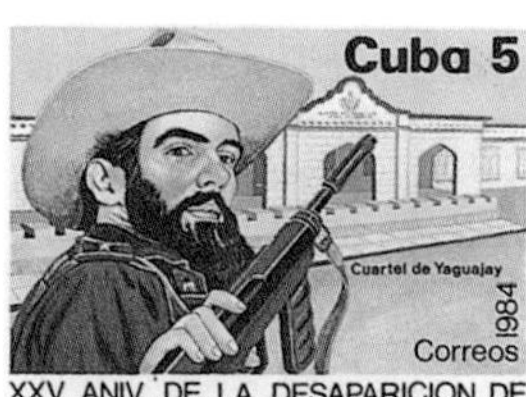

830 Camilo Cienfuegos

1984. 25th Anniv of Disappearance of Camilo Cienfuegos (revolutionary).
3056 **830** 5c. multicoloured 10 10

831 Mother breast-feeding Baby

1984. Infant Survival Campaign.
3057 **831** 5c. multicoloured 10 10

832 Morgan, 1909

1984. Cars. Multicoloured.
3058 1c. Type **832** 10 10
3059 2c. Austin, 1922 . . . . . . 10 10
3060 5c. Dion-Bouton, 1903 . . . 10 10
3061 20c. "T" Ford, 1908 . . . . 30 25
3062 30c. Karl Benz, 1885 . . . 70 40
3063 50c. Karl Benz, 1910 . . . 1·10 70

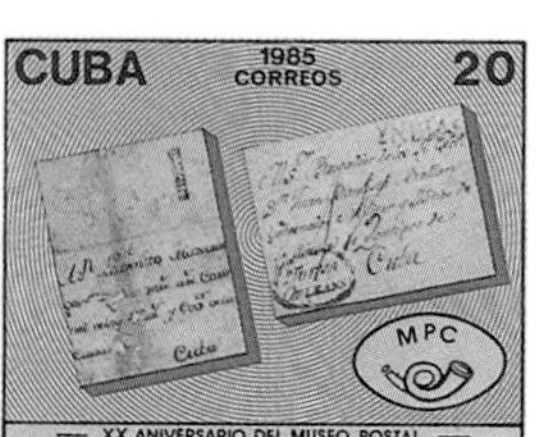

833 18th-century Letters and Museum Emblem

1985. 20th Anniv of Cuban Postal Museum.
3064 **833** 20c. multicoloured . . . 30 25

834 Celia Sanchez (after E. Escobedo)

1985. 5th Death Anniv of Celia Sanchez (revolutionary).
3065 **834** 5c. multicoloured 10 10

835 Pigeon

1985. "Porto-1985" International Pigeon Exhibition, Oporto, Portugal.
3066 **835** 20c. multicoloured . . . 30 25

836 Chile (1962)

1985. World Cup Football Championship, Mexico (1986) (1st issue). Multicoloured.
3067 1c. Type **836** 10 10
3068 2c. England (1966) 10 10
3069 3c. Mexico (1970) 10 10
3070 4c. West Germany (1974) . . 10 10
3071 5c. Argentina (1978) 10 10
3072 30c. Spain (1982) 45 40
3073 50c. Sweden (1958) 75 70
See also Nos. 3135/40.

837 Pteranodon

1985. Baconao Valley National Park. Prehistoric Animals (1st series). Multicoloured.
3075 1c. Type **837** 10 10
3076 2c. Brontosaurus 10 10
3077 4c. Iguanodontus 20 15
3078 5c. Estegosaurus 20 15
3079 8c. Monoclonius 25 20
3080 30c. Corythosaurus . . . . 1·25 80
3081 50c. Tyrannosaurus . . . . 1·25 1·00
See also Nos. 3264/9.

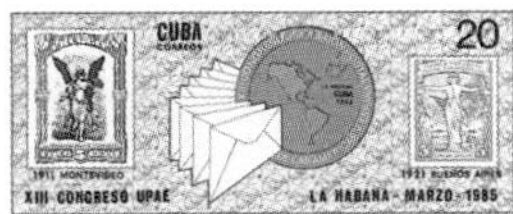

838 Uruguay 1911 and Argentina 1921 Congress Stamps and Emblem (½-size illustration)

1985. 13th Postal Union of the Americas and Spain Congress, Havana.
3082 **838** 20c. multicoloured . . . 1·75 50

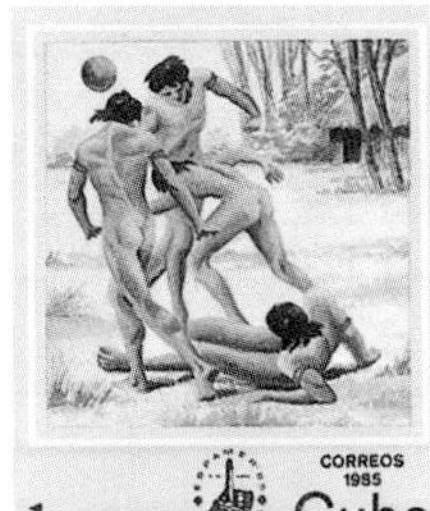

839 Indians playing Football

1985. "Espamer '85" International Stamp Exhibition, Havana. Multicoloured.
3083 1c. Type **839** 10 10
3084 2c. Indian sitting by fire . . 10 10
3085 5c. Fishing with nets and spears 30 10
3086 20c. Making pottery 30 25
3087 30c. Hunting with spears . . 45 40
3088 50c. Decorating canoe and paddle . . . . 1·90 1·10

840 Spaceship circling Moon

1985. Cosmonautics Day. Multicoloured.
3090 2c. Type **840** 10 10
3091 3c. Spaceships 10 10
3092 10c. Cosmonauts meeting in space 15 15
3093 13c. Cosmonauts soldering in space 20 15
3094 20c. "Vostok II" and Earth 30 25
3095 50c. "Lunayod I" crossing moon crater 75 70

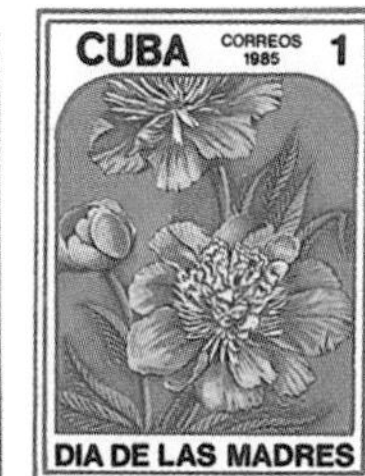

841 Lenin's Tomb **842** Peonies

1985. 12th World Youth and Students' Festival, Moscow.
3096 **841** 30c. multicoloured . . . 45 40

1985. Stamp Day. As T **811**. Multicoloured.
3097 20c. Roman soldier and chariot 30 25
3098 30c. Medieval nobleman and monks 45 40

1985. Mothers' Day. Multicoloured.
3099 1c. Type **842** 10 10
3100 4c. Carnations 15 10
3101 5c. Dahlias 20 10
3102 13c. Roses 30 15
3103 20c. Roses (different) . . . 50 25
3104 50c. Tulips . . . . 1·00 70

843 Guiteras and Aponte

1985. 50th Death Anniv of Antonio Guiteras and Carlos Aponte (revolutionaries).
3105 **843** 5c. multicoloured 10 10

844 Star, "40" and Soldier with Flag

1985. 40th Anniv of End of Second World War.
3106 **844** 5c. multicoloured 10 10
3107 – 20c. multicoloured . . . 30 25
3108 – 30c. red, yellow & violet 45 40
DESIGNS: 20c. "40" and Soviet Memorial, Berlin-Treptow; 30c. Dove within "40".

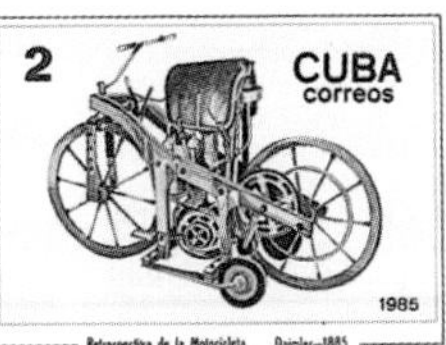

846 Daimler, 1885

1985. Centenary of the Motor Cycle. Multicoloured.
3110 2c. Type **846** 10 10
3111 5c. Kayser tricycle, 1910 . . 20 10
3112 10c. Fanomovil, 1925 . . . 25 15
3113 30c. Mars "A 20", 1926 . . 75 50
3114 50c. Simson "BSW", 1936 1·10 85

847 La Plata and Hermanos Ameijeiras Hospitals

1985. Development of Health Care since the Revolution.
3115 **847** 5c. multicoloured 10 10

848 Flowers and Soldier with Gun

1985. 25th Anniv of Federation of Cuban Women.
3116 **848** 5c. multicoloured 10 10

849 Athletes and Emblem

1985. World University Games, Kobe, Japan.
3117 **849** 50c. multicoloured . . . 90 85

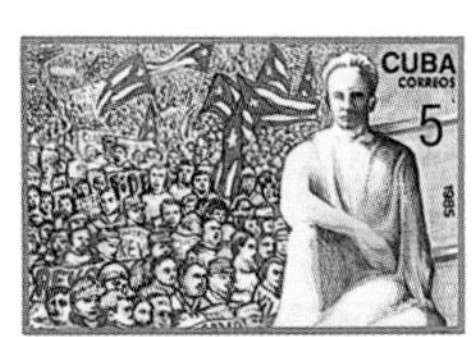

850 Crowd, Flags and Statue

1985. 25th Anniv of First Havana Declaration.
3118 **850** 5c. multicoloured 10 10

852 Emblem in "25"

1985. 25th Anniv of Committees for Defence of the Revolution.
3120 **852** 5c. multicoloured 10 10

853 Cherub Angelfish

1985. Fishes. Multicoloured.
3121 1c. Type **853** 20 15
3122 3c. Rock beauty 20 15
3123 5c. Four-eyed butterflyfish 20 15
3124 10c. Reef butterflyfish . . . 35 30
3125 20c. Spot-finned butterflyfish 85 60
3126 50c. Queen angelfish . . . . 2·10 1·75

854 Cuban and Party Flags and Central Committee Building **856** U.N. Building, New York, and Emblem

1985. 20th Anniv of Cuban Communist Party and Third Party Congress.
3127 **854** 5c. multicoloured 10 10

1985. 40th Anniv of U.N.O.
3129 **856** 20c. multicoloured . . . 35 30

857 Old Square and Arms

1985. U.N.E.S.C.O. World Heritage. Old Havana. Multicoloured.
3130 2c. Type **857** 10 10
3131 5c. Real Fuerza Castle . . . 10 10
3132 20c. Havana Cathedral . . . 35 30
3133 30c. Captain General's Palace 55 50
3134 50c. El Templete 90 85

858 Footballers **860** Ministry Emblem

859 Red Flags and Emblem

1986. World Cup Football Championship, Mexico (2nd issue).
3135 **858** 1c. multicoloured 10 10
3136 – 4c. multicoloured 10 10
3137 – 5c. multicoloured 10 10
3138 – 10c. multicoloured . . . 15 10
3139 – 30c. multicoloured . . . 55 45
3140 – 50c. multicoloured . . . 90 85
DESIGNS: 4c. to 50c. Various footballing scenes.

1986. 3rd Cuban Communist Party Congress, Havana. Multicoloured.
3142 5c. Type **859** 10 10
3143 20c. Red and national flags 35 30

1986. 25th Anniv of Ministry of Interior Trade.
3144 **860** 5c. multicoloured 10 10

861 People practising Sports **862** "Tecomaria capensis"

1986. 25th Anniv of National Sports Institute.
3145 **861** 5c. multicoloured 10 10

1986. Exotic Flowers. Multicoloured.
3146 1c. Type **862** 10 10
3147 3c. "Michelia champaca" . . 15 10
3148 5c. "Thunbergia grandiflora" 20 10
3149 8c. "Dendrobium phalaenopsis" 25 10
3150 30c. "Allamanda violacea" 75 50
3151 50c. "Rhodocactus bleo" . . 1·10 85

863 Gundlach and Red-winged Blackbird

1986. 90th Death Anniv of Juan C. Gundlach (ornithologist). Multicoloured.
3152 1c. Type **863** 40 20
3153 3c. Olive-capped warbler . . 40 20
3154 7c. La Sagra's flycatcher . . 70 50
3155 9c. Yellow warbler 90 60
3156 30c. Grey-faced quail dove 3·50 2·50
3157 50c. Common flicker . . . 5·50 4·00

864 Pioneers and "25" 865 Gomez and Statue

1986. 25th Anniv of Jose Marti Pioneers.
3158 **864** 5c. multicoloured 10 10

1986. 150th Birth Anniv of Maximo Gomez.
3159 **865** 20c. multicoloured . . . 35 30

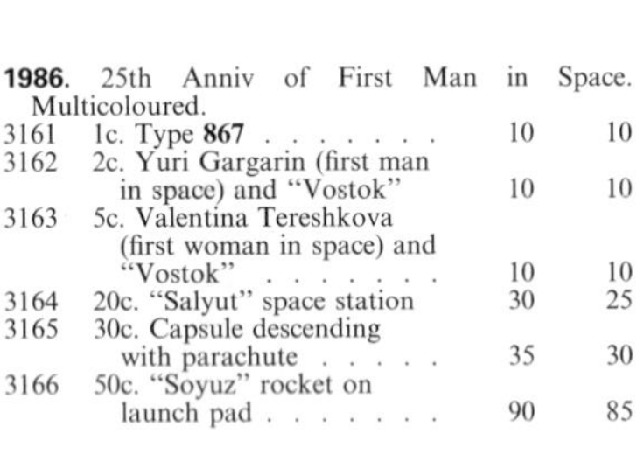

866 Nursery Nurse with Children 867 "Vostok" and Korolev (designer)

1986. 25th Anniv of Children's Day Care Centres.
3160 **866** 5c. multicoloured 10 10

1986. 25th Anniv of First Man in Space. Multicoloured.
3161 1c. Type **867** 10 10
3162 2c. Yuri Gargarin (first man in space) and "Vostok" 10 10
3163 5c. Valentina Tereshkova (first woman in space) and "Vostok" 10 10
3164 20c. "Salyut" space station 30 25
3165 30c. Capsule descending with parachute 35 30
3166 50c. "Soyuz" rocket on launch pad 90 85

868 National Flag and 1981 Stamp 869 Reels as National Flag and Globe and Tape forming "25"

1986. 25th Anniv of Socialist State (1959) and Victory at Giron. Multicoloured.
3168 5c. Type **868** 10 10
3169 20c. Flags and arms 30 25

1986. Stamp Day. As T **811** showing details of mural by R. R. Radillo in Havana Stamp Museum. Multicoloured.
3170 20c. Early mail coach . . . 30 25
3171 30c. Express rider 35 30

1986. 25th Anniv of Radio Havana Cuba.
3172 **869** 5c. multicoloured 10 10

870 "Stourbridge Lion", U.S.A., 1829

1986. "Expo '86" World's Fair, Vancouver. Railway Locomotives. Multicoloured.
3173 1c. Type **870** 15 10
3174 4c. "Rocket", Great Britain, 1829 . . . . 15 10
3175 5c. First Russian locomotive, 1845 . . . . 15 10
3176 8c. Marc Seguin's locomotive, France, 1830 25 10
3177 30c. First Canadian locomotive, 1836 . . . . 70 20
3178 50c. Steam locomotive, Belgium Grand Central Railway, 1872 . . . . . 1·90 35

871 Hand holding Machete and Farmer ploughing and driving Tractor

1986. 25th Anniv of National Association of Small Farmers.
3180 **871** 5c. multicoloured 10 10

872 Dove and Arms on Coin

1986. International Peace Year.
3181 **872** 30c. multicoloured . . . 35 30

873 Emblem

1986. 25th Anniv of Ministry of the Interior.
3182 **873** 5c. multicoloured 10 10

874 King

1986. 18th Death Anniv of Martin Luther King (human rights campaigner).
3183 **874** 20c. multicoloured . . . 30 25

875 Bonifacio Byrne

1986. 50th Death Anniv of Bonifacio Byrne (poet).
3184 **875** 5c. multicoloured 10 10

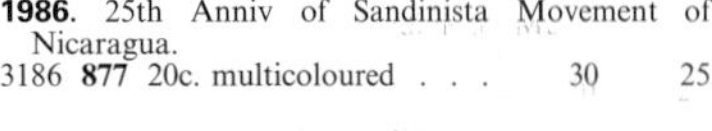
876 Dove, Pen Nib and Paint Brush 877 Sandino and Pres. Ortega of Nicaragua

1986. 25th Anniv of National Union of Cuban Writers and Artists.
3185 **876** 5c. multicoloured 10 10

1986. 25th Anniv of Sandinista Movement of Nicaragua.
3186 **877** 20c. multicoloured . . . 30 25

878 Tanker, Tupolev Tu-154 and Lorry

1986. 25th Anniv of Ministry of Transport.
3187 **878** 5c. multicoloured 30 15

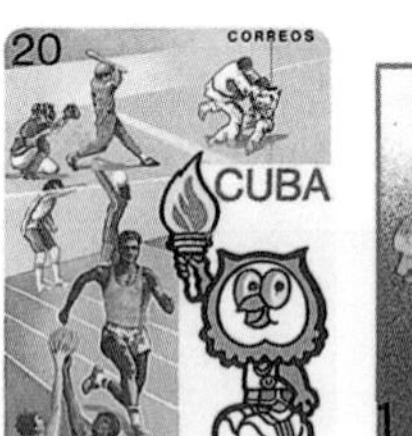

879 Sportsmen and Emblem 882 "Cattleya hardyana"

881 Map

1986. 5th Central American and Caribbean University Games, Havana.
3188 **879** 20c. multicoloured . . . 35 30

1986. 25th Anniv of Non-Aligned Countries Movement.
3190 **881** 50c. multicoloured . . . 80 75

1986. Orchids. Multicoloured.
3191 1c. Type **882** 10 10
3192 4c. "Brassolaeliocattleya" "Horizon Flight" 15 10
3193 5c. "Phalaenopsis" "Margit Moses" 20 15
3194 10c. "Laeliocattleya" "Prism Palette" 25 20
3195 30c. "Phalaenopsis violacea" 75 60
3196 50c. "Disa uniflora" . . . . 1·00 90

883 Mayan House and Jade Statue (Belize)

1986. Latin American History. Pre-Columbian Culture (1st series). Multicoloured.
3197 1c. Type **883** 10 10
3198 1c. Inca vessel and Gateway of the Sun, Tiahuanacu (Bolivia) 10 10
3199 1c. Spain 1930 1p. stamp of Columbus and 500th anniv of Columbus's discovery of America emblem 10 10
3200 1c. Diaguitan duck-shaped pitcher and ruins, Pucara de Quitor (Chile) 10 10
3201 1c. Archaeological park, San Augustin and Quimbayan statuette (Columbia) . . . 10 10
3202 5c. Moler memorial and Chorotega decorated earthenware statue (Costa Rica) 10 10
3203 5c. Tabaco idol and typical aboriginal houses (Cuba) 10 10
3204 5c. Spain 1930 40c. stamp of Martin Pinzon and anniversary emblem . . . 10 10
3205 5c. Typical houses and animal shaped seat (Dominica) 10 10
3206 5c. Tolita statue and Ingapirca fort (Ecuador) 10 10
3207 10c. Maya vase and Tikal temple (Guatemala) . . . 15 15
3208 10c. Copan ruins and Maya idol (Honduras) 15 15
3209 10c. Spain 1930 30c. stamp of Vincent Pinzon and anniversary emblem . . . 15 15
3210 10c. Chichen-Itza temple and Zapoteca urn (Mexico) 15 15
3211 10c. Punta de Zapote idols and Ometepe ceramic (Nicaragua) 15 15
3212 20c. Tonosi ceramic and Barrile monolithic sculptures (Panama) . . . 35 30
3213 20c. Machu Picchu ruin and Inca figure (Peru) 35 30
3214 20c. Spain 1930 10p. stamp of Columbus and Pinzon brothers and anniversary emblem 35 30
3215 20c. Typical aboriginal dwellings and triangular stone carving (Puerto Rico) 35 30
3216 20c. Santa Ana female figure and Santo Domingo cave (Venezuela) 35 30

See also Nos. 3276/95, 3371/90, 3458/77, 3563/82, 3666/85 and 3769/88.

884 Medal and Soldier with Rifle

1986. 50th Anniv of Formation International Brigades in Spain.
3217 **884** 30c. multicoloured . . . 50 45

885 "Two Children" (Gutierrez de la Vega)

1986. National Museum Paintings (17th series). Multicoloured.
3218 2c. Type **885** 10 10
3219 4c. "Sed" (Jean-Gorges Vibert) (horiz) 10 10
3220 6c. "Virgin and Child" (Niccolo Abbate) 20 10
3221 10c. "Bullfight" (Eugenio de Lucas Velazquez) (horiz) 25 15
3222 30c. "The Five Senses" (Anon) (horiz) 75 45
3223 50c. "Meeting at Thomops Castle" (Jean Louis Ernest) (horiz) . . . . . 1·00 75

886 People and "Granma"

1986. 30th Annivs of "Granma" Landings (5c.) and Revolutionary Armed Forces (20c.). Multicoloured.
3224 5c. Type **886** 10 10
3225 20c. Soldier, rifle and flag 35 30

887 Scholars and "Che" Guevara

1986. 25th Anniv of Scholarship Programme.
3226 **887** 5c. multicoloured 10 10

888 Man learning to write and Sanmarti 890 "Gitana" (Joaquin Sorolla)

889 Map and Revolutionaries

1986. 25th Anniv of Literacy Campaign.
3227 **888** 5c. multicoloured 10 10

1987. 30th Anniv of Attack on La Plata Garrison.
3228 **889** 5c. multicoloured 10 10

1987. National Museum Paintings (18th series). Multicoloured.
3229 3c. Type **890** 10 10
3230 5c. "Sir Walter Scott" (Sir John W. Gordon) . . . 20 10
3231 10c. "Farm Meadows" (Alfred de Breanski) (horiz) 25 15

3232 20c. "Still Life" (Isaac van Duynen) (horiz) 35 30
3233 30c. "Landscape with Figures" (Francesco Zuccarelli) (horiz) 60 45
3234 40c. "Waffle Seller" (Ignacio Zuloaga) 75 60

891 Palace, Delivery Van and Echeverria

1987. 30th Anniv of Attack on Presidential Palace.
3235 **891** 5c. multicoloured 10 10

892 Lazarus Ludwig Zamenhof (inventor) and Russia 1927 14k. Stamp

1987. Centenary of Esperanto (invented language).
3236 **892** 30c. multicoloured . . . 50 45

894 Badge and Slogan

1987. 25th Anniv and 5th Congress of Youth Communist League.
3238 **894** 5c. multicoloured 10 10

895 "Intercosmos I" Satellite
897 Dahlias

896 Cover with Postal Fiscal Stamp, 1890

1987. Cosmonautics Day. 20th Anniv of Intercosmos Programme. Multicoloured.
3239 3c. Type **895** 10 10
3240 5c. "Intercosmos II" 10 10
3241 10c. "TD" 15 15
3242 20c. "Cosmos 93" 35 30
3243 30c. "Molniya" 50 45
3244 50c. "Vostok 3" 80 75

1987. Stamp Day. Multicoloured.
3246 30c. Type **896** 75 60
3247 50c. Cover with bisect, 1869 1·00 80

1987. Mothers' Day. Multicoloured.
3248 3c. Type **897** 10 10
3249 5c. Roses 20 10
3250 10c. Roses in basket 25 15
3251 13c. Decorative dahlias . . 35 20
3252 30c. Cactus dahlias . . . 75 45
3253 50c. Roses (different) . . . 1·00 25

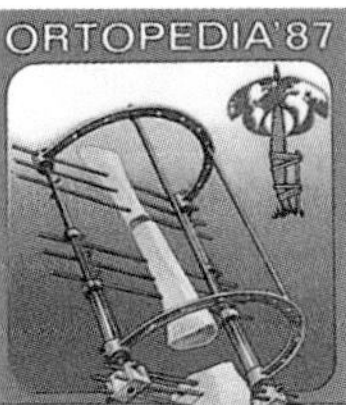

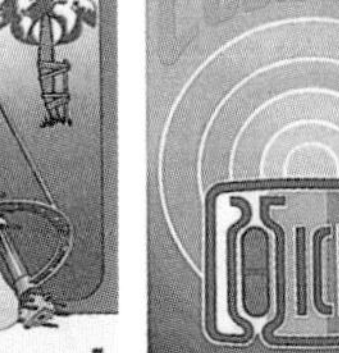

898 Fractured Femur Immobilised in Frame
899 Emblem

1987. "Orthopedia '87" Portuguese and Spanish Speaking Countries' Orthopedists Meeting, Havana.
3254 **898** 5c. multicoloured 10 10

1987. 25th Anniv of Cuban Broadcasting and Television Institute.
3255 **899** 5c. multicoloured 10 10

900 Battle Monument, Sierra Maestra Mountains

1987. 30th Anniv of Battle of El Uvero.
3256 **900** 5c. multicoloured 10 10

901 Messenger with Pack Llamas and 1868 Stamp (Bolivia)

1987. "Capex '87" International Stamp Exhibition, Toronto. 19th-century Mail Carriers as depicted on cigarette cards. Multicoloured.
3257 3c. Type **901** 10 10
3258 5c. Postman and motor car and 1900 stamp (France) 10 10
3259 10c. Messenger on elephant and 1883 stamp (Siam) . . 15 15
3260 20c. Messenger on camel and 1879 stamp (Egypt) 35 30
3261 30c. Mail troika and stamp (Russia) 50 45
3262 50c. Messenger on horseback and stamp (Indo-China) 80 75

902 Model of Prehistoric Animal

1987. Prehistoric Valley, Baconao National Park (2nd series). Designs showing various exhibits.
3264 **902** 3c. multicoloured 10 10
3265 – 5c. multicoloured 20 10
3266 – 10c. multicoloured . . . 25 15
3267 – 20c. multicoloured . . . 55 30
3268 – 35c. multicoloured . . . 75 50
3269 – 40c. multicoloured . . . 90 60

903 Pais and Rafael Maria Mendive Popular University Buildings

1987. 30th Death Anniv of Frank Pais (teacher and student leader).
3270 **903** 5c. multicoloured 10 10

904 Flags and Sportsmen

1987. 10th Pan-American Games, Indianapolis.
3271 **904** 50c. multicoloured . . . 1·00 75

905 Memorial

1987. 30th Anniv of Cienfuegos Uprising.
3272 **905** 5c. multicoloured 10 10

908 Coins and 1968 Independence War Centenary 30c. Stamp

1987. 20th Anniv of Heroic Guerilla Fighters Day.
3275 **908** 50c. multicoloured . . . 1·00 90

909 Tehuelche Man and Red-crowned Ant-tanager (Argentina)

1987. Latin American History (2nd series). Multicoloured.
3276 1c. Type **909** 20 20
3277 1c. Red-billed toucan and Tibirica man (Brazil) . . 20 20
3278 1c. Spain 1930 5c. stamp of La Rabida Monastery and 500th anniv of Columbus's discovery of America emblem 10 10
3279 1c. Andean condor and Lautaro man (Chile) . . . 20 20
3280 1c. Calarca man and hoatzin (Colombia) 20 20
3281 5c. Cuban trogon and Hatuey man (Cuba) . . . 45 20
3282 5c. Scaly-breasted ground dove and Enriquillo man (Dominican Republic) . . 45 20
3283 5c. Spain 1930 30c. stamp of departure from Palos and anniversary emblem . . . 10 10
3284 5c. Toucan barbet and Ruminahui man (Ecuador) 45 20
3285 5c. Resplendent quetzal and Tecum Uman man (Guatemala) 45 20
3286 10c. Anacaona woman and limpkin (Haiti) 75 20
3287 10c. Lempira man and slaty flowerpiercer (Honduras) 75 20
3288 10c. Spain 1930 10p. Columbus stamp and anniversary emblem . . . 15 10
3289 10c. Northern royal flycatcher and Cuauhtemoc woman (Mexico) 75 20
3290 10c. Painted redstart and Nicarao man (Nicaragua) 75 20
3291 20c. Andean cock of the rock and Atahualpa man (Peru) . . . . 1·25 30
3292 20c. Atlactl man and red-tailed hawk (El Salvador) 1·25 50
3293 20c. Spain 1930 10p. stamp of arrival in America and anniversary emblem . . . 35 50
3294 20c. Abayuba man and red-breasted plantcutter (Uruguay) . . . . 1·25 50
3295 20c. Guaycaypuro man and blue and yellow macaw (Venezuela) . . . . 1·25 50

910 1950 2c. Train Stamp

1987. 150th Anniv of Cuban Railway. Designs showing Cuban stamps.
3296 **910** 3c. red, brown & black 10 10
3297 – 5c. multicoloured 10 10
3298 – 10c. multicoloured . . . 15 10
3299 – 20c. multicoloured . . . 35 25
3300 – 35c. multicoloured . . . 65 45
3301 – 40c. multicoloured . . . 75 55
DESIGNS: 5c. 1965 7c. "BB.69,000" diesel locomotive stamp; 10c. 1975 1c. French-built "La Junta" locomotive stamp; 20c. 1975 3c. M. M. Prieto" locomotive stamp; 35c. 1980 10c. locomotive stamp; 40c. 1980 13c. locomotive stamp.

911 Satellites and Russia 1927 14k. Stamp

1987. 70th Anniv of Russian Revolution.
3303 **911** 30c. multicoloured . . . 50 45

912 "Landscape" (Domingo Ramos)

1988. 170th Anniv of San Alejandro Arts School, Havana. Multicoloured.
3304 1c. Type **912** 10 10
3305 2c. "Portrait of Rodriguez Morey" (Eugenio Gonzalez Olivera) 10 10
3306 3c. "Landscape with Malangas and Palm Trees" (Valentin Sanz Carta) 15 10
3307 5c. "Ox-carts" (Eduardo Morales) 20 15
3308 10c. "Portrait of Elena Herrera" (Armando Menocal) (vert) 25 20
3309 30c. "The Rape of Dejanira" (Miguel Melero) (vert) 75 50
3310 50c. "The Card Player" (Leopoldo Romanach) . . 1·00 85

913 "Boletus satanas"
915 Mario Munoz Santiago Monument, de Cuba

914 Radio Operator, Satellite and Caribe Ground Station

1988. Poisonous Mushrooms. Multicoloured.
3311 1c. Type **913** 10 10
3312 2c. "Amanita citrina" . . . 10 10
3313 3c. "Tylopilus felleus" . . . 10 10
3314 5c. "Paxillus involutus" . . 20 10
3315 10c. "Inocybe patouillardii" 40 15

3316 30c. "Amanita muscaria" 1·00 40
3317 50c. "Hypholoma fasciculare" 1·60 70

1988. 30th Anniv of Radio Rebelde.
3318 **914** 5c. multicoloured 10 10

1988. 30th Anniv of Mario Munoz Third Front.
3319 **915** 5c. multicoloured 10 10

916 Frank Pais Memorial and Eternal Flame

917 Red Roses

1988. 30th Anniv of Frank Pais Second Eastern Front.
3320 **916** 5c. multicoloured 10 10

1988. Mothers' Day. Multicoloured.
3321 1c. Type **917** 10 10
3322 2c. Pale pink roses 10 10
3323 3c. Daisies 10 10
3324 5c. Dahlias 10 10
3325 13c. White roses 15 15
3326 35c. Carnations 50 45
3327 40c. Pink roses 60 55

918 "Gorizont" Satellite

1988. Cosmonautics Day. Multicoloured.
3328 2c. Type **918** 10 10
3329 3c. "Mir"–"Kvant" link 10 10
3330 4c. "Signo 3" 10 10
3331 5c. Mars space probe 10 10
3332 10c. "Phobos" 15 15
3333 30c. "Vega" space probe 45 40
3334 50c. Space craft 75 70

1988. Stamp Day. As T **811**. Details of mural by R. R. Radillo in Havana Stamp Museum. Mult.
3336 30c. Telegraphist and mail coach 45 40
3337 50c. Carrier pigeon 75 70

919 Storage Tanks, Products, Sugar Cane and Laboratory Equipment

1988. 25th Anniv of ICIDCA (Cuban Institute for Research on Sugarcane Byproducts).
3338 **919** 5c. multicoloured 10 10

920 Havana–Madrid, 1948

1988. Cubana Airlines Transatlantic Flights. Mult.
3339 2c. Type **920** 10 10
3340 4c. Havana–Prague, 1961 15 10
3341 5c. Havana–Berlin, 1972 20 15
3342 10c. Havana–Luanda, 1975 30 25
3343 30c. Havana–Paris, 1983 75 50
3344 50c. Havana–Moscow, 1987 1·25 90

922 Steam Train (½-size illustration)

1988. Postal Union of the Americas and Spain Colloquium on "America" Postage Stamps, Havana.
3346 **922** 20c. multicoloured 1·25 50

923 "Megasoma elephas"

1988. Beetles. Multicoloured.
3347 1c. Type **923** 10 10
3348 3c. "Platycoelia flavoscutellata" (vert) 20 10
3349 4c. "Plusiotis argenteola" 25 15
3350 5c. "Hetersoternus oberthuri" 30 20
3351 10c. "Odontotaenius zodiacus" 40 25
3352 35c. "Chrysophora chrysochlora" (vert) 90 75
3353 40c. "Phanaeus leander" 1·10 1·00

924 Chess Pieces

1988. Birth Centenary of Jose Capablanca (chess master). Multicoloured.
3354 30c. Type **924** 45 40
3355 40c. Juan Corzo, Capablanca and flags (1901 Cuban Championship) (horiz) 60 55
3356 50c. Emanuel Lasker and Capablanca (1921 World Championship) (horiz) 75 70
3357 1p. Checkmate in 1921 game with Lasker 1·50 1·25
3358 3p. "J. R. Capablanca" (E. Valderrama) 4·00 3·50
3359 5p. Chess pieces, flag, globe and Capablanca 6·00 5·50

925 Sun and Fortress

1988. 35th Anniv of Assault on Moncada Fortress.
3361 **925** 5c. red, yellow & black 10 10

927 Camilo Cienfuegos, "Che" Guevara and Map

1988. 30th Anniv of Rebel Invasion Columns.
3363 **927** 5c. multicoloured 10 10

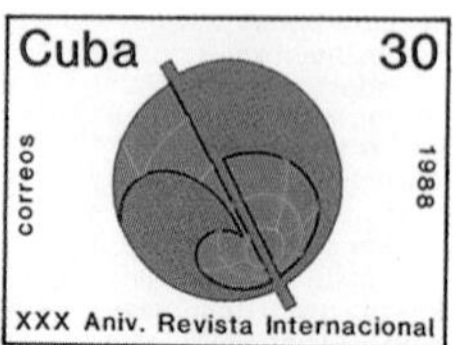

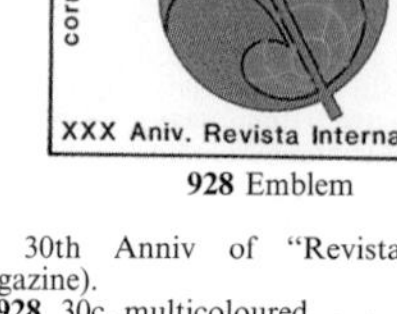

928 Emblem

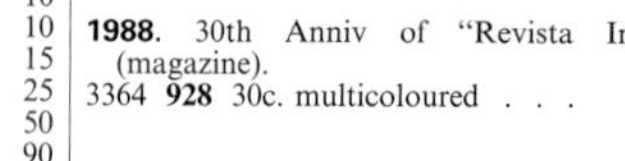

1988. 30th Anniv of "Revista Internacional" (magazine).
3364 **928** 30c. multicoloured 45 40

929 Locomotive "Northumbrian", 1831

1988. Railway Development. Multicoloured.
3365 20c. Type **929** 35 15
3366 30c. Locomotive "E. L. Miller", 1834 65 30
3367 50c. "La Junta" (Cuba's first locomotive, 1840s) 1·40 55
3368 1p. Electric railcar 2·40 80
3369 2p. Russian-built M-62K diesel locomotive 4·50 1·90
3370 5p. Diesel railcar set 10·50 5·25

930 Arms and Jose de San Martin (Argentina)

1988. Latin-American History (3rd series). Mult.
3371 1c. Type **930** 10 10
3372 1c. Arms and M. A. Padilla (Bolivia) 10 10
3373 1c. 1944 10c. Discovery of America stamp 10 10
3374 1c. Arms and A. de Silva Xavier, "Tiradentes" (Brazil) 10 10
3375 1c. Arms and Bernardo O'Higgins (Chile) 10 10
3376 5c. A. Narino and arms (Colombia) 10 10
3377 5c. Arms and Jose Marti (Cuba) 10 10
3378 5c. 1944 13c. Discovery of America stamp 10 10
3379 5c. Arms and Juan Pablo Duarte (Dominican Republic) 10 10
3380 5c. Arms and Antonio Jose de Sucre (Ecuador) 10 10
3381 10c. Manuel Jose Arce and arms (El Salvador) 15 10
3382 10c. Arms and Jean Jacques Dessalines (Haiti) 15 10
3383 10c. 1944 5c. Discovery of America airmail stamp 15 10
3384 10c. Miguel Hidalgo and arms (Mexico) 15 10
3385 10c. Arms and J. Dolores Estrada (Nicaragua) 15 10
3386 20c. Jose E. Diaz and arms (Paraguay) 30 25
3387 20c. Arms and Francisco Bolognesi (Peru) 30 25
3388 20c. 1944 10c. Discovery of America airmail stamp 30 25
3389 20c. Arms and Jose Gervasio Artigas (Uruguay) 30 25
3390 20c. Simon Bolivar and arms (Venezuela) 30 25

931 Maces and Governor's Palace

1988. 20th Anniv of Havana Museum.
3391 **931** 5c. multicoloured 10 10

932 Ballerinas and Mute Swan

1988. 40th Anniv of National Ballet (3392) and 150th Anniv of Grand Theatre, Havana (3393). Multicoloured.
3392 5c. Type **932** 40 25
3393 5c. Theatre, 1838 and 1988 10 10

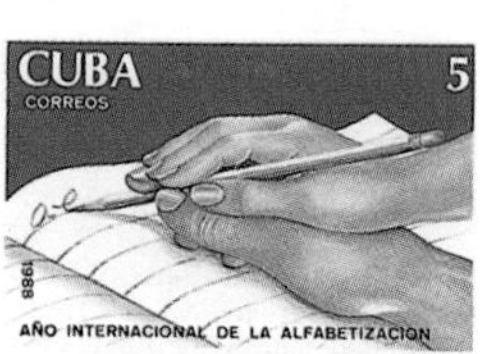

933 Practising Letters

1988. International Literacy Year.
3394 **933** 5c. multicoloured 10 10

934 Emblem

1988. 40th Anniv of Declaration of Human Rights.
3395 **934** 30c. multicoloured 50 45

935 Ernesto Che Guevara Plaza

1988. 30th Anniv of Battle of Santa Clara.
3396 **935** 30c. multicoloured 50 45

936 National Flag forming "30"

1989. 30th Anniv of Revolution.
3397 **936** 5c. multicoloured 10 10
3398 20c. multicoloured 30 25
3399 30c. gold, blue and red 50 45
3400 50c. gold, blue and red 80 75

937 "Pleurotus levis"

1989. Edible Mushrooms. Multicoloured.
3401 2c. Type **937** 10 10
3402 3c. "Pleurotus floridanus" 10 10
3403 5c. "Amanita caesarea" 15 10
3404 10c. "Lentinus cubensis" (horiz) 35 10
3405 40c. "Pleurotus ostreatus" (red) 1·25 60
3406 50c. "Pleurotus ostreatus" (brown) 1·40 75

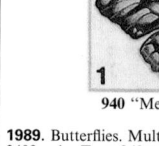

939 1982 30c. Cuban Stamp

1989. 50th Anniv of Revolutionary Workers' Union.
3408 **939** 5c. multicoloured 10 10

940 "Metamorpho dido"

1989. Butterflies. Multicoloured.
3409 1c. Type **940** 10 10
3410 3c. "Callithea saphhira" 10 10
3411 5c. "Papilio zagreus" 20 10
3412 10c. "Mynes sestia" 30 15
3413 30c. "Papilio dardanus" 1·00 70
3414 50c. "Catagranma sorana" 1·75 1·25

941 Footballer **942** "30" and Arms

1989. World Cup Football Championship, Italy (1990).
3415 **941** 1c. multicoloured 10 10
3416 – 3c. multicoloured 15 10
3417 – 5c. multicoloured 20 15
3418 – 10c. multicoloured . . . 25 20
3419 – 30c. multicoloured . . . 70 60
3420 – 50c. multicoloured . . . 1·00 90
DESIGNS: 3c to 50c. Various footballers.

1989. 30th Anniv of National Revolutionary Police.
3422 **942** 5c. multicoloured 10 10

943 "Zodiac" Rocket and 1934 Australian Cover

1989. Cosmonautics Day. Rocket Post (1st series). Multicoloured.
3423 1c. Type **943** 10 10
3424 3c. Rocket and cover from India to Poland, 1934 . . 15 10
3425 5c. Rocket and 1934 English cover 20 15
3426 10c. "Icarus" rocket and 1935 Dutch cover 35 25
3427 40c. "La Douce France" rocket and 1935 French cover 85 75
3428 50c. Rocket and 1939 Cuban cover . . . . . . 1·00 90
See also Nos. 3516/21.

1989. Stamp Day. As T **811**. Details of mural by R. R. Radillo in Havana Stamp Museum. Mult.
3429 30c. Mail coach 50 45
3430 50c. 18th-century sailing packet . . . . 3·75 1·50

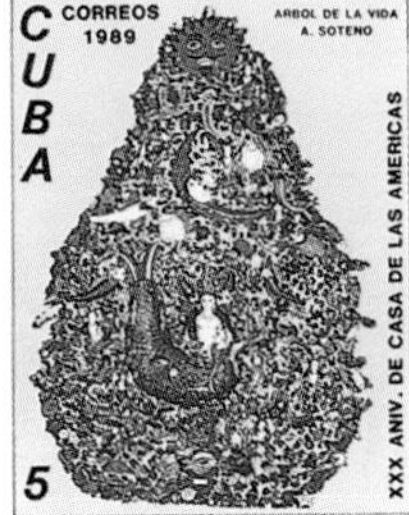

944 "Tree of Life" (A. Soteno)

1989. 30th Anniv of "House of the Americas" Museum, Havana.
3431 **944** 5c. multicoloured 10 10

946 Coded Envelope

1989. Post Codes.
3433 **946** 5c. multicoloured 10 10

947 Tobacco Flowers **948** Signing Decree

1989. Mothers' Day. Perfumes and Flowers. Mult.
3434 1c. Type **947** 10 10
3435 3c. Violets 15 15
3436 5c. Mariposa 20 20
3437 13c. Roses 30 25
3438 30c. Jasmine 75 65
3439 50c. Orange-flower . . . . 1·10 1·00

1989. 30th Anniv of Agrarian Reform Law.
3440 **948** 5c. multicoloured 10 10

949 "40" and Headquarters Building, Moscow

1989. 40th Anniv of Council for Mutual Economic Aid.
3441 **949** 30c. multicoloured . . . 50 45

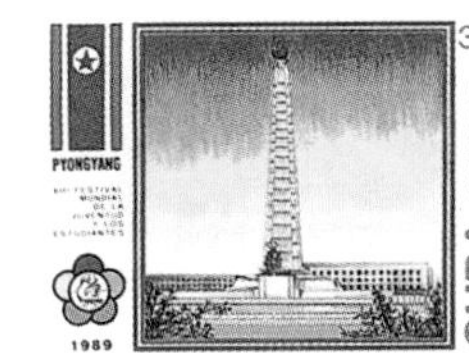

950 Tower of Juche Idea, Pyongyang

1989. 13th World Youth and Students' Festival, Pyongyang.
3442 **950** 30c. multicoloured . . . 50 45

952 Toco Toucan

1989. "Brasiliana '89" Stamp Exhibition. Rio de Janeiro. Birds. Multicoloured.
3444 1c. Type **952** 20 10
3445 3c. Chestnut-bellied heron 20 10
3446 5c. Scarlet ibis 30 10
3447 10c. White-winged trumpeter 50 15
3448 35c. Harpy eagle . . . . . 1·90 70
3449 50c. Amazonian umbrellabird . . . . . . 2·40 1·10

953 "El Fenix" (galleon)

1989. Cuban Sailing Ships. Multicoloured.
3450 1c. Type **953** 10 10
3451 3c. "Triunfo" (ship of the line) 10 10
3452 5c. "El Rayo" (ship of the line) 10 10
3453 10c. "San Carlos" (ship of the line) 25 10
3454 30c. "San Jose" (ship of the line) 85 50
3455 50c. "San Genaro" (ship of the line) . . . . 1·40 85

954 Carved Stone and Men in Dugout Canoe

1989. America. Pre-Columbian Cultures. Mult.
3456 5c. Type **954** 10 10
3457 20c. Cave painters 30 25

955 Domingo F. Sarmiento and "Govenia utriculata" (Argentina)

1989. Latin American History (4th series). Multicoloured.
3458 1c. Type **955** 10 10
3459 1c. Machado de Assis and "Laelia grandis" (Brazil) 10 10
3460 1c. El Salvador 1892 1p. Columbus stamp 10 10
3461 1c. Jorge Isaacs and "Cattleya trianae" (Colombia) 10 10
3462 1c. Alejo Carpentier and "Cochleanthes discolor" (Cuba) 10 10
3463 5c. "Oxalis adenophylla" and Pablo Neruda (Chile) 10 10
3464 5c. Pedro H. Urena and "Epidendrum fragrans" (Dominican Republic) . . 10 10
3465 5c. El Salvador 1893 2p. City of Isabela stamp . . 10 10
3466 5c. Juan Montalvo and "Miltonia vexillaria" (Ecuador) 10 10
3467 5c. "Odontoglossum rossii" and Miguel A. Asturias (Guatemala) 10 10
3468 10c. "Laelia anceps" and Jose C. del Valle (Honduras) 15 10
3469 10c. "Laelia ancepes alba" and Alfonso Reyes (Mexico) 15 10
3470 10c. El Salvador 1893 5p. Columbus Statue stamp 15 10
3471 10c. "Brassavola acaulis" and Ruben Dario (Nicaragua) 15 10
3472 10c. Belisario Porras and "Pescatorea cerina" (Panama) 15 10
3473 20c. Ricardo Palma and "Coryanthes leucocorys" (Peru) 30 25
3474 20c. Eugenio Maria de Hostos and "Guzmania berteroniana" (Puerto Rico) 30 25
3475 20c. El Salvador 1893 10p. Departure from Palos stamp 30 25
3476 20c. "Cypella herbertii" and Jose E. Rodo (Uruguay) 30 25
3477 20c. "Cattleya mossiae" and Romulo Gallegos (Venezuela) 30 25

956 Cienfuegos and Flag

1989. 30th Anniv of Disappearance of Camilo Cienfuegos (revolutionary).
3478 **956** 5c. multicoloured 10 10

957 Church Tower

1989. 475th Anniv of Trinidad City.
3479 **957** 5c. multicoloured 10 10

958 "Outskirts of Niza" (E. Boudin)

1989. Paintings in National Museum. Mult.
3480 1c. "Family Scene" (Antoine Faivre) 10 10
3481 2c. "Flowers" (Emile J. H. Vernet) 10 10
3482 5c. "Judgement of Paris" (Charles Le Brun) 10 10
3483 20c. Type **958** 35 20
3484 30c. "Portrait of Sarah Bernhardt" (G. J. V. Clairin) (36 × 46 mm) 40 35
3485 50c. "Fishermen in Harbour" (C. J. Vernet) 90 60

959 Archery

1989. 11th Pan-American Games, Havana (1st issue). Multicoloured.
3486 5c. Type **959** 20 10
3487 5c. Shooting 20 10
3488 5c. Fencing 20 10
3489 5c. Cycling 20 10
3490 5c. Water polo 20 10
3491 20c. Lawn tennis (vert) . . . 30 40
3492 30c. Swimming (vert) . . . 80 60
3493 35c. Diving (vert) 80 70
3494 40c. Hockey . . . . 1·10 85
3495 50c. Basketball (vert) . . . 1·25 1·00
See also Nos. 3584/93 and 3621/30.

960 Front Page

1989. Centenary of "Golden Age" (children's magazine compiled by Jose Marti).
3496 **960** 5c. blue, black and red 10 10

961 "Almendares" (paddle-steamer)

1990. 25th Anniv of Postal Museum. Mult.
3497 5c. Type **961** 15 10
3498 30c. Mail train . . . . . . 3·25 1·25

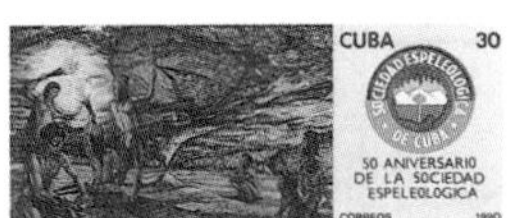

962 Cave Painters ($\frac{1}{2}$-size illustration)

1990. 50th Anniv of Speleological Society.
3499 **962** 30c. multicoloured . . . 40 35

963 Player No. 11 and Colosseum
964 Baseball

1990. World Cup Football Championship, Italy. Multicoloured.
3500 5c. Type **963** 20 10
3501 5c. Player No. 10 . . . . . 20 10
3502 5c. Player No. 8 . . . . . 20 10
3503 10c. Goalkeeper 25 10
3504 30c. Player No. 11 and arch 60 55
3505 50c. Player 85 80

1990. Olympic Games, Barcelona (1992) (1st issue). Multicoloured.
3507 1c. Type **964** 10 10
3508 4c. Running 10 10
3509 5c. Basketball 10 10
3510 10c. Volleyball 25 10
3511 30c. Wrestling (horiz) . . . 75 50
3512 50c. Boxing . . . . 1·10 85
See also Nos. 3604/9 and 3692/7.

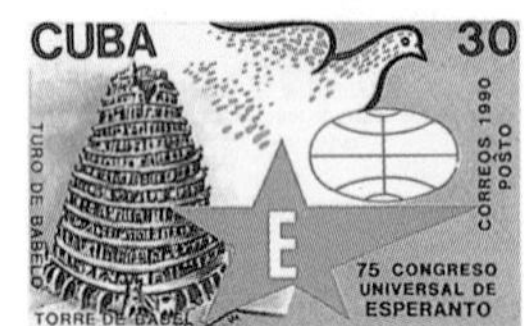

965 Tower of Babel, Dove and Globe

1990. 75th Esperanto Congress, Havana.
3514 **965** 30c. multicoloured . . . 40 35

1990. Cosmonautics Day. Rocket Post (2nd series). As T **943**. Multicoloured.
3516 1c. 1932 Austrian Cover and "U12" rocket 10 10
3517 2c. 1933 German cover, rocket and liner 10 10
3518 3c. 1934 Netherlands cover, "NRB" rocket and windmill 10 10
3519 10c. 1935 Belgian cover and rocket 15 10
3520 30c. 1935 Yugoslavian cover and "JUGI" rocket . . . 40 35
3521 50c. 1936 U.S.A. cover and rocket 65 60

1990. Stamp Day. As T **811**. Showing details of mural by R. R. Radillo in Havana Stamp Museum. Multicoloured.
3522 30c. Russian-built Type TEM-4 diesel locomotive leaving station 2·75 90
3523 50c. De Havilland Comet 1 airplane 65 60

967 Flag and Globe

1990. Centenary of Labour Day.
3524 **967** 5c. multicoloured 10 10

969 Hill and Penny Black

1990. 150th Anniv of the Penny Black. Mult.
3526 2c. Type **969** 10 10
3527 3c. Twopenny blue 10 10
3528 5c. G.B. 1855 4d. stamp . . 10 10
3529 10c. G.B. 1847 1s. embossed stamp 15 10
3530 30c. G.B. paid hand-stamp 60 50
3531 50c. Twopenny blues on cover to Malta 85 80

970 Celia Sanchez (after O. Yanes)

1990. 70th Birth Anniv of Celia Sanchez Manduley (revolutionary).
3532 **970** 5c. multicoloured 10 10

971 Flags and Ho Chi Minh

1990. Birth Centenary of Ho Chi Minh (Vietnamese leader).
3533 **971** 50c. multicoloured . . . 65 60

972 Hogfish and Sample Analysis

1990. 25th Anniv of Oceanology Institute. Mult.
3534 5c. Type **972** 15 10
3535 30c. "Arrecife coralino" and research vessel 80 35
3536 50c. Lobster and diver collecting samples 65 60

973 "Banara minutiflora"
974 Windsurfing

1990. 5th Latin American Botanical Congress. Multicoloured.
3537 3c. Type **973** 10 10
3538 5c. "Oplonia nannophylla" 20 15
3539 10c. "Jacquinia brunnescens" 25 20
3540 30c. "Rondeletia brachycarpa" 70 60
3541 50c. "Rondeletia odorata" 1·00 65

1990. Tourist Sports. Multicoloured.
3542 5c. Type **974** 20 15
3543 10c. Underwater fishing (horiz) 25 20
3544 30c. Sea fishing (horiz) . . . 70 60
3545 40c. Shooting 75 65

975 "The Flute of Pan" (detail)

1990. Paintings by A. G. Menocal in National Museum. Multicoloured.
3546 5c. Type **975** 20 20
3547 20c. "Shepherd" 40 30
3548 50c. "Ganymede" . . . . . 1·00 75
3549 1p. "Venus Anadiomena" 2·25 1·25

976 Great Crested Grebe

1990. "New Zealand 90" International Stamp Exhibition, Auckland. Birds. Multicoloured.
3551 2c. Type **976** 15 10
3552 3c. Weka rail 15 10
3553 5c. Kea 15 10
3554 10c. Bush wren 45 15
3555 30c. Grey butcher bird . . . 1·25 55
3556 50c. Parson bird . . . . . 2·10 1·00

977 Lighthouse

1990. 8th U.N.O. Congress on Crime Prevention and Treatment of Delinquents.
3558 **977** 50c. red, blue and silver 65 60

978 Caravel and Shoreline

1990. America. The Natural World. Mult.
3559 5c. Type **978** 25 20
3560 20c. Christopher Columbus and native village 75 60

979 Cameraman

1990. 40th Anniv of Cuban Television.
3561 **979** 5c. multicoloured 10 10

980 Steam Locomotive No. 1712 and Havana Railway Station

1990. 30th Anniv of Nationalization of Railways.
3562 **980** 50c. multicoloured . . . 1·50 1·10

981 Flag and Couple (Argentina)

1990. Latin-American History (5th series). Multicoloured.
3563 1c. Type **981** 10 10
3564 1c. Flag and couple (Bolivia) 10 10
3565 1c. Argentina 1892 5c. Discovery of America stamp 10 10
3566 1c. Flag and couple (Colombia) 10 10
3567 1c. Flag and couple (Costa Rica) 10 10
3568 5c. Flag and couple (Cuba) 10 10
3569 5c. Flag and couple (Chile) 10 10
3570 5c. Dominican Republic 1900 ½c. Columbus stamp 10 10
3571 5c. Flag and couple (Ecuador) 10 10
3572 5c. Flag and couple (El Salvador) 10 10
3573 10c. Flag and couple (Guatemala) 15 10
3574 10c. Flag and couple (Mexico) 15 10
3575 10c. Puerto Rico 1893 3c. Discovery of America stamp 25 10
3576 10c. Flag and couple (Nicaragua) 15 10
3577 10c. Flag and couple (Panama) 15 10
3578 20c. Flag and couple (Paraguay) 30 20
3579 20c. Flag and couple (Peru) 30 20
3580 20c. El Salvador 1894 10p. Columbus stamp 30 20
3581 20c. Flag and couple (Puerto Rico) 30 20
3582 20c. Flag and couple (Venezuela) 30 20

982 Player
983 Boxing

1990. 11th World Pelota Championship.
3583 **982** 30c. multicoloured . . . 45 30

1990. 11th Pan-American Games, Havana (1991) (2nd issue). As T **959**. Multicoloured.
3584 5c. Kayaking 20 10
3585 5c. Rowing 20 10
3586 5c. Yachting 30 10
3587 5c. Judo 20 10
3588 5c. Show jumping 20 10
3589 10c. Table tennis 25 20
3590 20c. Gymnastics (vert) . . . 45 30
3591 30c. Baseball (vert) 65 45
3592 35c. Basketball (vert) . . . 80 45
3593 50c. Football (vert) . . . . 1·25 70

1990. 16th Central American and Caribbean Games, Mexico. Multicoloured.
3594 5c. Type **983** 10 10
3595 30c. Baseball 45 30
3596 50c. Volleyball 80 45

984 "Chioides marmorosa"
986 Long Jumping

985 Guerra Aguiar and 1966 3c. Stamp

1991. Butterflies. Multicoloured.
3597 2c. Type **984** 20 10
3598 3c. "Composia fidelissima" 20 10
3599 5c. "Danaus plexippus" . . 20 10
3600 10c. "Hypolimnas misippus" 40 30
3601 30c. "Hypna iphigenia" . . 1·00 70
3602 50c. "Hemiargus ammon" 1·60 1·00

1991. 1st Death Anniv of Jose Guerra Aguiar (founder of Cuban Postal Museum).
3603 **985** 5c. multicoloured 10 10

1991. Olympic Games, Barcelona (1992) (2nd issue). Multicoloured.
3604 1c. Type **986** 10 10
3605 2c. Throwing the javelin . . 15 10
3606 3c. Hockey 20 15
3607 5c. Weightlifting 25 20
3608 40c. Cycling . . . . 1·00 70
3609 50c. Gymnastics . . . . . 1·25 80

987 Yuri Gagarin and "Vostok" **988** Statue and Flag

1991. 30th Anniv of First Man in Space. Mult.
3611 5c. Type **987** . . . 20 10
3612 10c. "Soyuz" and Y. Romanenko . . . 25 20
3613 10c. "Salyut" space station and A. Tamayo . . . 25 20
3614 30c. "Mir" space station (left half) . . . 75 60
3615 30c. "Mir" space station (right half) . . . 75 60
3616 50c. Launch of "Buran" space shuttle . . . 1·25 1·00
Nos. 3612/13 and 3614/15 respectively were issued together, se-tenant, forming composite designs.

1991. 30th Anniversaries. Multicoloured.
3617 5c. Type **988** (proclamation of Socialism) . . . 10 10
3618 50c. Playa Giron (invasion attempt by Cuban exiles) 1·25 55

1991. Stamp Day. Designs as T **811** showing details of mural by R. R. Radillo in Havana Stamp Museum. Multicoloured.
3619 30c. Rocket (vert) . . . 75 60
3620 50c. Dish aerial . . . 1·25 1·00

1991. 11th Pan-American Games, Havana (3rd series). As T **959**. Multicoloured.
3621 5c. Volleyball (vert) . . . 10 10
3622 5c. Synchronized swimming (vert) . . . 10 10
3623 5c. Weightlifting (vert) . . . 10 10
3624 5c. Baseball (vert) . . . 10 10
3625 5c. Gymnastics (vert) . . . 10 10
3626 10c. Ten-pin bowling . . . 30 20
3627 20c. Boxing (vert) . . . 60 40
3628 30c. Running . . . 85 60
3629 35c. Wrestling . . . 1·00 70
3630 50c. Judo . . . 1·40 1·10

989 Simon Bolivar and Map

1991. 165th Anniv of Panama Congress.
3631 **989** 50c. multicoloured . . . 80 45

990 Dirigible Balloon Design and Jean-Baptiste Meusnier

1991. "Espamer '91" Iberia–Latin America Stamp Exhibition, Buenos Aires. Airships. Mult.
3632 5c. Type **990** . . . 20 10
3633 10c. First steam-powered dirigible airship and Henri Giffard . . . 30 20
3634 20c. Paul Hanlein and first airship with gas-powered motor . . . 50 30
3635 30c. "Deutschland" (first airship with petrol motor) and Karl Wolfert . . . 80 60
3636 50c. David Schwarz and first rigid aluminium airship 1·25 75
3637 1p. Ferdinand von Zeppelin and airship "Graf Zeppelin" . . . 2·00 1·25
No. 3637 is inscr "Hindenburg".

992 Cayo Largo

1991. Tourism. Multicoloured.
3645 20c. Type **992** . . . 75 25
3646 20c. Varadero . . . 60 50
3647 30c. San Carlos de la Cabana Fortress (horiz) 70 60
3648 30c. Castillo de los Tres Reyes del Morro (horiz) 70 60

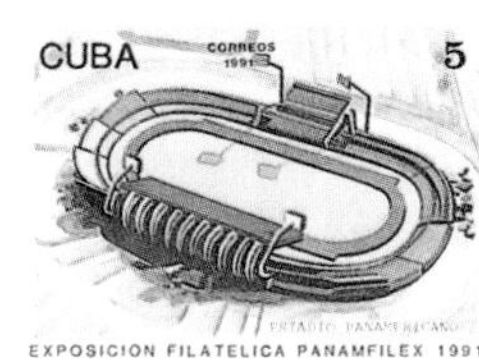

993 Stadium

1991. "Panamfilex 1991" Pan-American Stamp Exhibition. Multicoloured.
3649 5c. Type **993** . . . 20 10
3650 20c. Baragua swimming-pool complex . . . 50 40
3651 30c. Ramon Fonst hall . . . 85 50
3652 50c. Reynaldo Paseiro cycle-track . . . 1·40 1·00

994 "Kataoka Dengoemon Takafusa" (Utagawa Kuniyoshi)

1991. "Phila Nippon '91" International Stamp Exhibition, Tokyo. Multicoloured.
3654 5c. Type **994** . . . 20 10
3655 10c. "Night Walk" (Hosoda Eishi) . . . 30 20
3656 20c. "Courtesans" (Torii Kiyonaga) . . . 50 35
3657 30c. "Conversation" (Kitagawa Utamaro) . . . 70 60
3658 50c. "Inari-bashi Bridge" (Ando Hiroshige) . . . 1·75 1·25
3659 1p. "On the Terrace" (Torii Kiyonaga) . . . 2·25 1·50

996 Statue of Jose Marti

1991. 4th Cuban Communist Party Congress.
3661 **996** 5c. multicoloured . . . 10 10
3662 – 50c. black, blue and red 80 45
DESIGN: 50c. Party emblem.

997 Christopher Columbus and Pinzon Brothers

1991. America. Voyages of Discovery. Mult.
3663 5c. Type **997** . . . 10 10
3664 20c. "Santa Maria", "Nina" and "Pinta" . . . 60 20

998 Marti (after F. Martinez)

1991. Centenary of Publication of "The Simple Verses" by Jose Marti.
3665 **998** 50c. multicoloured . . . 80 45

999 Julian Aguirre and Charango (Argentina)

1991. Latin-American History (6th series). Music. Multicoloured.
3666 1c. Type **999** . . . 10 10
3667 1c. Eduardo Caba and antara (pipes) (Bolivia) . . 10 10
3668 1c. Chile 1853 10c. stamp 10 10
3669 1c. Heitor Villalobos and trumpet with gourd resonator (Brazil) . . . 10 10
3670 1c. Guillermo Uribe-Holguin and cununo macho (drum) (Colombia) . . . 10 10
3671 5c. Claves (sticks) and Miguel Failde (Cuba) . . 20 10
3672 5c. Enrique Soro and Araucanian kultrum (Chile) . . . 20 10
3673 5c. Chile 1903 10c. on 30c. stamp . . . 20 10
3674 5c. Rondador (xylophone) and Segundo L. Moreno (Ecuador) . . . 20 10
3675 5c. Marimba and Ricardo Castillo (Guatemala) . . . 20 10
3676 10c. Vihuela and Carlos Chavez (Mexico) . . . 30 25
3677 10c. Luis A. Delgadillo and maracas (Nicaragua) . . . 30 25
3678 10c. Chile 1906 2c. stamp 30 25
3679 10c. Alfredo de Saint-Malo and mejorana (Panama) 30 25
3680 10c. Jose Asuncion Flores and harp (Paraguay) . . . 30 25
3681 20c. Daniel Alomia and quena (flute) (Peru) . . . 50 30
3682 20c. Cuatro (guitar) and Juan Morell y Campos (Puerto Rico) . . . 50 30
3683 20c. Chile 1905 10c. stamp 50 30
3684 20c. Eduardo Fabini and tamboril (drums) (Uruguay) . . . 50 30
3685 20c. Cuatro (guitar) and Juan V. Lecuna (Venezuela) . . . 50 30

1000 Mascot

1991. 1st Jose Marti Pioneers Congress.
3686 **1000** 5p. multicoloured . . . 10 10

1001 Toussaint L'Ouverture (revolutionary leader)

1991. Bicentenary of Haitian Revolution.
3687 **1001** 50c. multicoloured . . . 80 45

1002 "35", Stars and Soldier

1991. 35th Anniversaries. Multicoloured.
3688 5c. Type **1002** (Revolutionary Armed Forces) . . . 10 10
3689 50c. Launch "Granma" (disembarkation of revolutionary forces) (vert) . . . 1·25 60

1003 Agramonte (after F. Martinez)

1991. 150th Birth Anniv of Ignacio Agramonte (poet).
3690 **1003** 5c. multicoloured . . . 10 10

1005 Table Tennis and Plan of Montjuic Complex

1992. Olympic Games, Barcelona (3rd issue). Mult.
3692 3c. Type **1005** . . . 20 10
3693 5c. Handball and Vall d'Hebron complex . . . 25 20
3694 10c. Shooting and Badalona complex . . . 30 25
3695 20c. Long jumping and Montjuic complex (vert) 60 50
3696 35c. Judo and Diagonal complex . . . 1·00 75
3697 50c. Fencing and Montjuic complex . . . 1·40 1·00

1006 Flooded Terraces and Dead Trees

1992. Environmental Protection. Mult.
3699 5c. Type **1006** . . . 10 10
3700 20c. Whale and dead fish in polluted sea . . . 45 20
3701 35c. Satellite picture of ozone levels over Antarctica and gas mask in polluted air . . . 60 35
3702 40c. Rainbows, globe, doves and nuclear explosion . . 70 40

1007 Blue Angelfish

1992. Fishes. Multicoloured.
3703 5c. Type **1007** . . . 15 10
3704 10c. Jackknife-fish . . . 25 15
3705 20c. Blue tang . . . 60 25
3706 30c. Sergeant-major . . . 85 45
3707 50c. Yellow-tailed damselfish 1·50 75

1008 Boxer

1992. Dogs. Multicoloured.

3708 5c. Type **1008** 20 10
3709 10c. Great dane 25 20
3710 20c. German shepherd . . . 60 40
3711 30c. Short-haired, long-haired and wire-haired dachshunds . . . . 1·00 70
3712 35c. Dobermann . . . . . 1·25 90
3713 40c. Fox terrier . . . . . . 1·40 1·00
3714 50c. Poodle . . . . 1·50 1·10

1009 Badge

1992. 30th Anniv and Sixth Congress of Youth Communist League.

3716 **1009** 5c. multicoloured . . . 10 10

1010 Jose Marti

1992. Centenary of Cuban Revolutionary Party.

3717 **1010** 5c. multicoloured . . . 10 10
3718 50c. multicoloured . . . 85 50

1011 Columbus Sighting Land

1992. America. 500th Anniv of Discovery of America by Columbus. Multicoloured.

3719 5c. Type **1011** 25 20
3720 20c. Columbus landing at San Salvador 75 50

1012 Alhambra, Sierra Nevada

1992. "Granada 92" International Philatelic Exhibition. Designs showing views of the Alhambra. Multicoloured.

3721 5c. Type **1012** 20 10
3722 10c. Sunset 30 20
3723 20c. Doorway and arches 60 40
3724 30c. Courtyard of the Lions 80 50
3725 35c. Bedroom 90 70
3726 50c. View of Albaicin from balcony . . . . 1·25 1·00

1013 Facade and Plate

1992. 50th Anniv of La Bodeguita del Medio (restaurant).

3727 **1013** 50c. multicoloured . . . 85 50

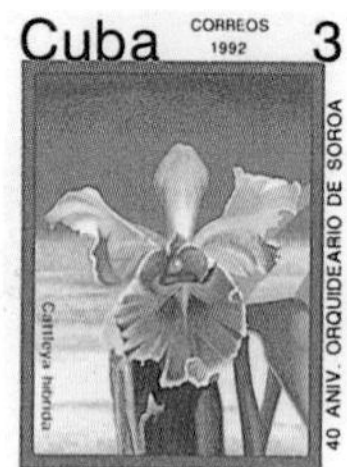

1014 "Cattleya hibrida"

1992. 40th Anniv of Soroa Orchid Garden. Mult.

3728 3c. Type **1014** 20 10
3729 5c. "Phalaenopsis sp." . . . 20 10
3730 10c. "Cattleyopsis lindenii" 30 20
3731 30c. "Bletia purpurea" . . . 1·00 75
3732 35c. "Oncidium luridum" 1·25 1·00
3733 40c. "Vanda hibrida" . . . 1·50 1·25

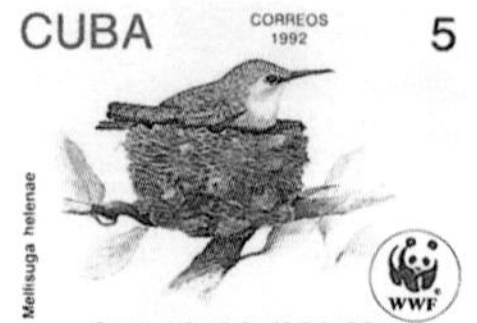

1015 Hummingbird

1992. The Bee Hummingbird. Multicoloured.

3734 5c. Type **1015** 30 15
3735 10c. Perched on twig . . . 40 20
3736 20c. Perched on twig with flowers 90 25
3737 30c. Hovering over flower 1·40 40

1016 Guardalavaca Beach

1992. Tourism. Multicoloured.

3738 10c. Type **1016** 20 10
3739 20c. Hotel Bucanero 45 25
3740 30c. View of Havana . . . 70 35
3741 50c. Varadero beach . . . . 1·10 65

1017 Eligio Sardinas

1992. "Olymphilex '92" International Olympic Stamps Exhibition, Barcelona. Designs showing Cuban sportsmen. Multicoloured.

3742 5c. Type **1017** 30 10
3743 35c. Ramon Fonst (fencer) 1·00 75
3744 40c. Sergio "Pipian" Martinez (cyclist) . . . . . 1·10 85
3745 50c. Martin Dihigo (baseball player) . . . . 1·40 1·00

1019 Alvarez Cabral

1992. "Genova '92" International Thematic Stamp Exhibition. Explorers and their ships. Multicoloured.

3747 5c. Type **1019** 10 10
3748 10c. Alonso Pinzon 20 10
3749 20c. Alonso de Ojeda . . . 45 25
3750 30c. Amerigo Vespucci . . . 65 35
3751 35c. Henry the Navigator 75 40
3752 40c. Bartolomeu Dias . . . 90 45

1020 High Jumping

1992. 6th World Athletics Cup, Havana. Mult.

3754 5c. Type **1020** 30 10
3755 20c. Throwing the javelin 60 40
3756 30c. Throwing the hammer 1·00 70
3757 40c. Long jumping (vert) . . 1·10 80
3758 50c. Hurdling (vert) . . . . 1·50 1·00

1021 Men's High Jump (Gold) and Women's Discus (Gold)

1992. Cuban Olympic Games Medal Winners. Multicoloured.

3760 5c. Type **1021** 40 20
3761 5c. Men's 4 × 400 m relay (silver) and men's discus (bronze) 40 20
3762 5c. Men's 4 × 100 m relay and women's high jump and 800 m (bronze) . . . 40 20
3763 20c. Baseball (gold) 75 60
3764 20c. Boxing (7 gold and 2 silver) 75 60
3765 20c. Women's volleyball (gold) 75 60
3766 50c. Men's judo (bronze) and women's judo (gold, silver and 2 bronze) . . . 1·50 1·00
3767 50c. Greco-roman (gold and 2 bronze) and freestyle (gold and bronze) wrestling . . . . 1·50 1·00
3768 50c. Fencing (silver, bronze) and weightlifting (silver) 1·50 1·00

1022 Christopher Columbus and Queen Isabella the Catholic

1992. Latin-American History (7th series). Multicoloured.

3769 1c. Type **1022** 10 10
3770 1c. Columbus at Rabida Monastery 10 10
3771 1c. Columbus presenting plans to King Ferdinand and Queen Isabella . . . 10 10
3772 1c. Columbus before Salamanca Council . . . 10 10
3773 1c. Departure from Palos . . 10 10
3774 5c. Fleet stopping off at Canary Islands 20 10
3775 5c. Columbus reassuring crew 20 10
3776 5c. Sighting of land 20 10
3777 5c. Columbus landing . . . 20 10
3778 5c. Columbus's encounter with Amerindians 20 10
3779 10c. "Santa Maria" grounded off Hispaniola 30 20
3780 10c. Arrival of "Nina" at Palos 30 20
3781 10c. Columbus's procession through Barcelona . . . 30 20
3782 10c. Columbus before King and Queen 30 20
3783 10c. Departure from Cadiz on second voyage 30 20
3784 20c. King and Queen welcoming Columbus . . 30 20
3785 20c. Fleet leaving on third voyage 55 60
3786 20c. Columbus's deportation in chains from Hispaniola 55 60
3787 20c. Fleet embarking on fourth voyage 55 60
3788 20c. Death of Columbus at Valladolid 55 60

1023 Chacon

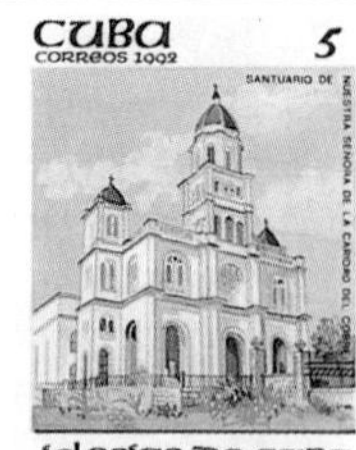

1024 Sanctuary of Our Lady of Charity, Cobre

1992. Birth Centenary of Jose Maria Chacon y Calvo (historian).

3789 **1023** 30c. multicoloured . . . 50 30

1992. Churches. Multicoloured.

3790 5c. Type **1024** 20 10
3791 20c. St. Mary's Church, Rosario 60 50
3792 30c. Church of the Holy Spirit, Havana 80 60
3793 50c. Guardian of the Holy Angel Church, Pena Pobre, Havana . . . . . 1·25 90

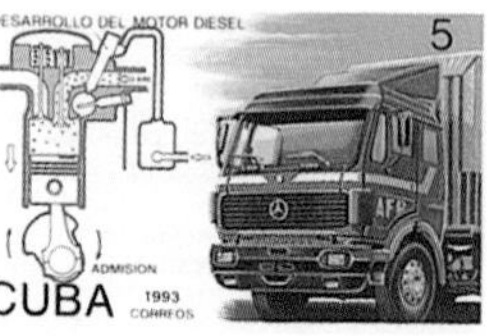

1025 Diagram of Engine and Truck

1993. Development of Diesel Engine. Each showing an engine at a different stage of cycle. Multicoloured.

3794 5c. Type **1025** 10 10
3795 10c. Motor car 15 10
3796 30c. Tug 75 30
3797 40c. Diesel locomotive . . . 2·50 1·25
3798 50c. Tractor . . . . 1·00 80

1026 Player

1993. Davis Cup Men's Team Tennis Championship. Designs showing tennis players. Multicoloured.

3800 5c. Type **1026** 25 20
3801 20c. Double-handed backhand 50 35
3802 30c. Serve 85 50
3803 35c. Stretched forehand (horiz) 90 70
3804 40c. Returning drop shot (horiz) . . . . 1·10 80

1027 Pedro Emilio Roux

1993. Scientists. Multicoloured.

3806 3c. Type **1027** (bacteriologist) 10 10
3807 5c. Carlos Finlay (biologist) 20 15
3808 10c. Ivan Petrovich Pavlov (physiologist) 30 20
3809 20c. Louis Pasteur (chemist) 60 40
3810 30c. Santiago Ramon y Cajal (histologist) 85 55
3811 35c. Sigmund Freud (psychiatrist) . . . . . . 1·00 70
3812 40c. Wilhelm Roentgen (physicist) . . . . 1·10 80
3813 50c. Joseph Lister (surgeon) 1·50 1·10

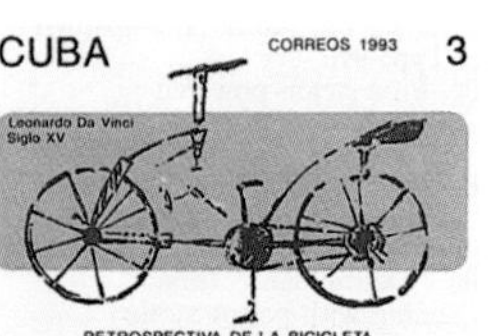

1028 Bicycle Design by Leonardo da Vinci

1993. Bicycles. Multicoloured.

3815 3c. Type **1028** 10 10
3816 5c. Draisiana hobby-horse 10 10

3817 10c. Michaux boneshaker . . . 20 10
3818 20c. Starley penny-farthing . . . 50 40
3819 30c. Lawson "Safety" bicycle . . . 65 50
3820 35c. Modern bicycle . . . 75 60

1029 "Valencian Fishwives"

1993. Paintings by Joaquin Sorolla in the National Museum. Multicoloured.
3821 3c. "Child eating Melon" (vert) . . . 10 10
3822 5c. Type **1029** . . . 10 10
3823 10c. "Regatta" . . . 20 10
3824 20c. "Peasant Girl" . . . 35 20
3825 40c. "Summertime" . . . 70 40
3826 50c. "By the Sea" . . . 90 50

1030 "Four Winds" and Statue of Barberan and Collar

1993. 60th Anniv of Seville (Spain)–Camaguey (Cuba) Flight by Mariano Barberan and Joaquin Collar.
3827 **1030** 30c. multicoloured . . . 40 20

1031 Northern Jacana

1993. "Brasiliana '93" International Stamp Exhibition, Rio de Janeiro. Water Birds. Multicoloured.
3828 3c. Type **1031** . . . 15 15
3829 5c. Great blue heron (27 × 44 mm) . . . 15 15
3830 10c. Black-necked stilt . . . 35 20
3831 20c. Black-crowned night heron . . . 60 35
3832 30c. Sandhill crane (27 × 44 mm) . . . 90 50
3833 50c. Limpkin . . . 1·50 80

1032 Fidel Castro and Text

1993. Anniversaries. Multicoloured.
3834 5c. Type **1032** (40th anniv of publication of "History Will Absolve Me") . . . 10 10
3835 5c. Jose Marti (140th birth anniv) and Rafael M. Mendive (vert) . . . 10 10
3836 5c. Carlos M. de Cespedes and broken wheel (125th anniv of Yara Proclamation) . . . 10 10
3837 5c. Moncada Barracks (40th anniv of attack on barracks) . . . 10 10

1033 "Sedum allantoides" 1034 Devillier's Swallowtail

1993. Cienfuegos Botanical Garden. Mult.
3838 3c. Type **1033** . . . 10 10
3839 5c. "Heliconia caribaea" . . . 20 10
3840 10c. "Anthurium andraeanum" . . . 35 25
3841 20c. "Pseudobombax ellipticum" . . . 55 40
3842 35c. "Ixora coccinea" . . . 90 65
3843 50c. "Callistemon specious" . . . 1·50 1·00

1993. "Bangkok 1993" International Stamp Exhibition. Butterflies. Multicoloured.
3844 3c. Type **1034** . . . 20 10
3845 5c. Giant brimstone . . . 25 15
3846 20c. Great southern white . . . 60 40
3847 30c. Buckeye . . . 85 50
3848 35c. White peacock . . . 1·10 75
3849 50c. African monarch . . . 1·50 1·10

1035 Greater Flamingo 1036 Simon Bolivar

1993. America. Endangered Animals. Mult.
3850 5c. Type **1035** . . . 50 30
3851 50c. Roseate spoonbill . . . 75 60

1993. Latin-American Integration. Mult.
3852 50c. Type **1036** . . . 70 50
3853 50c. Jose Marti . . . 70 50
3854 50c. Benito Juarez . . . 70 50
3855 50c. Che Guevara . . . 70 50
Nos. 3852/5 were issued together, se-tenant, forming a composite design.

1037 Swimming

1993. 17th Central American and Caribbean Games, Ponce, Puerto Rico. Multicoloured.
3856 5c. Type **1037** . . . 10 10
3857 10c. Pole vaulting . . . 30 20
3858 20c. Boxing . . . 50 40
3859 35c. Gymnastics (parallel bars) (vert) . . . 75 55
3860 50c. Baseball (vert) . . . 90 70

1038 Grajales 1039 Tchaikovsky

1993. Death Centenary of Mariana Grajales.
3862 **1038** 5c. multicoloured . . . 10 10

1993. Death Centenary of Pyotr Tchaikovsky (composer). Multicoloured.
3863 5c. Type **1039** . . . 50 10
3864 20c. Ballerina in "Swan Lake" . . . 50 35
3865 30c. Statue of Tchaikovsky . . . 80 50
3866 50c. Tchaikovsky Museum (horiz) . . . 1·40 1·00

1040 Flag, Dove and Broken Chains 1041 Players Challenging for Ball

1994. 35th Anniv of Revolution.
3867 **1040** 5c. multicoloured . . . 10 10

1994. World Cup Football Championship, U.S.A.
3868 **1041** 5c. multicoloured . . . 20 10
3869 – 20c. multicoloured . . . 35 20
3870 – 30c. multicoloured . . . 50 30
3871 – 35c. multicoloured . . . 70 45
3872 – 40c. multicoloured . . . 75 60
3873 – 50c. multicoloured . . . 1·00 80
DESIGNS: 20c. to 50c. Various footballing scenes.

1042 Blue Persian

1994. Cats. Multicoloured.
3875 5c. Type **1042** . . . 10 10
3876 10c. Havana . . . 20 15
3877 20c. Maine coon . . . 60 40
3878 30c. British blue shorthair . . . 90 60
3879 35c. Black and white bicolour Persian . . . 1·10 80
3880 50c. Golden Persian . . . 1·50 1·00

1043 Sage

1994. Medicinal Plants. Multicoloured.
3882 5c. Type **1043** . . . 25 15
3883 10c. Aloe . . . 25 15
3884 20c. Sunflower . . . 75 60
3885 30c. False chamomile . . . 1·00 80
3886 40c. Pot marigold . . . 1·50 1·00
3887 50c. Large-leaved lime . . . 1·75 1·25

1044 London Public Transport, 1860

1994. Carriages. Multicoloured.
3888 5c. Type **1044** . . . 20 10
3889 10c. Coach of King Fernando VII and Maria Luisa of Spain . . . 25 20
3890 30c. French Louis XV style coach . . . 80 50
3891 35c. Queen Isabel II of Spain's gala-day coach . . . 1·00 80
3892 40c. Empress Catherine II of Russia's summer carriage . . . 1·10 1·00
3893 50c. Havana cab (68 × 27 mm) . . . 1·40 1·10

1045 Caribbean Edible Oyster

1994. Aquaculture. Multicoloured.
3894 5c. Type **1045** . . . 30 20
3895 20c. "Cardisoma guanhumi" (crab) . . . 50 40
3896 30c. Red-breasted tilapia . . . 90 70
3897 35c. "Hippospongia lachne" (sponge) . . . 90 70
3898 40c. "Panulirus argus" (crustacean) . . . 1·00 80
3899 50c. Common carp . . . 1·60 1·10

1046 Ancient Greek Athletes and Olympic Flag

1994. Centenary of International Olympic Committee. Multicoloured.
3900 5c. Type **1046** . . . 40 20
3901 30c. Olympic flag and world map in Olympic colours . . . 1·00 75
3902 50c. Olympic flag and flame . . . 1·75 1·25

1047 Michael Faraday (discoverer of electricity)

1994. Scientists. Multicoloured.
3903 5c. Type **1047** . . . 20 10
3904 10c. Marie Sklodowska-Curie (co-discoverer of radium) . . . 20 15
3905 20c. Pierre Curie (co-discoverer of radium) . . . 50 35
3906 30c. Albert Einstein (formulated Theory of Relativity) . . . 75 50
3907 40c. Max Planck (physicist) . . . 1·00 75
3908 50c. Otto Hahn (chemist) . . . 1·25 1·00

1048 "Opuntia dillenii"

1994. Cacti. Multicoloured.
3909 5c. Type **1048** . . . 30 20
3910 10c. "Opuntia millspaughii" (vert) . . . 35 25
3911 30c. "Leptocereus santamarinae" . . . 1·00 70
3912 35c. "Pereskia marcanoi" . . . 1·25 85
3913 40c. "Dendrocereus nudiflorus" (vert) . . . 1·50 1·00
3914 50c. "Pilocereus robinii" . . . 1·75 1·10

1050 Rough Collies

1994. Dogs. Multicoloured.
3916 5c. Type **1050** . . . 25 15
3917 20c. American cocker spaniels . . . 60 40
3918 30c. Dalmatians . . . 90 60
3919 40c. Afghan hounds . . . 1·25 90
3920 50c. English cocker spaniels . . . 1·50 1·10

1051 "Carpilius corallinus" (crab)

1994. Cayo Largo. Multicoloured.
3921 15c. Type **1051** . . . 50 35
3922 65c. Shore and Cayman Islands ground iguana (vert) . . . 2·00 1·40
3923 75c. House and brown pelican . . . 1·90 1·10
3924 1p. Fence and common green turtle . . . 2·75 1·90

1052 Cienfuegos

1994. 35th Anniv of Disappearance of Camilo Cienfuegos (revolutionary).
3925 **1052** 15c. multicoloured . . . 50 25

1053 Yellow-edged Grouper

1994. Caribbean Animals. Multicoloured.

3926 10c. Type **1053** 50 20
3927 15c. Spotted eagle ray (vert) 60 30
3928 15c. Sailfish 60 30
3929 15c. Greater flamingoes (vert) 45 25
3930 65c. Bottle-nosed dolphin 1·75 1·00
3931 65c. Brown pelican (vert) . . 1·50 1·00

1054 Douglas DC-3

1994. 50th Anniv of I.C.A.O.

3932 **1054** 65c. multicoloured . . . 1·50 70

1055 Bronze Statues of Deer

1994. 55th Anniv of Havana Zoo. Mult.

3933 15c. Type **1055** 50 30
3934 65c. Green-winged macaw 1·50 1·00
3935 75c. Eurasian goldfinch . . 1·90 1·25

1056 Boy with Stockbook

1994. 30th Anniv of Cuban Philatelic Federation.

3936 **1056** 15c. multicoloured . . . 40 10

1057 Anole

1994. Reptiles. Multicoloured.

3937 15c. Type **1057** 45 20
3938 65c. Dwarf gecko . . . . . 1·90 1·00
3939 75c. Curly-tailed lizard . . . 2·00 1·00
3940 85c. Dwarf gecko (different) 2·25 1·10
3941 90c. Anole . . . . 2·50 1·25
3942 1p. Dwarf gecko (different) 3·00 1·40

1058 Cover and Spanish Mail Packet (18th-century sea mail)

1059 Cover of "Postal History of Cuba" by Jose Guerra Aguiar

1994. America. Postal Transport. Mult.

3943 15c. Type **1058** 40 20
3944 65c. Cover and messenger on horseback (19th-century rebel post) (horiz) . . . . 1·60 1·10

1995. 30th Anniv of Postal Museum.

3945 **1059** 15c. multicoloured . . . 50 20

1060 Jose Marti and Flag

1995. Centenary of War of Independence.

3946 **1060** 15c. multicoloured . . . 20 10

1061 Boxing

1063 1855 Cuba and Puerto Rico ½r. Stamp

1062 Siboney Cow

1995. 12th Pan-American Games, Mar del Plata, Argentina. Multicoloured.

3947 10c. Type **1061** 40 20
3948 15c. Weightlifting 55 30
3949 65c. Volleyball . . . . . . 2·50 1·00
3950 75c. Wrestling (horiz) . . . 2·50 1·00
3951 85c. Baseball (horiz) . . . . 3·00 1·50
3952 90c. High jumping (horiz) 3·00 1·50

1995. 50th Anniv of F.A.O.

3953 **1062** 75c. multicoloured . . . 1·25 50

1995. Postal Anniversaries.

3954 **1063** 15c. blue and black . . 30 10
3955 – 65c. multicoloured . . . . 1·25 1·00

DESIGNS: 15c. Type **1063** (140th anniv of first Cuban postage stamp); 65c. Colonial-style letterbox and letter (140th anniv of domestic postal service).

1064 Queen Angelfish

1995. 35th Anniv of National Aquarium. Mult.

3956 10c. Type **1064** 40 30
3957 15c. Shy hamlet 60 30
3958 65c. Porkfish . . . . 2·25 1·00
3959 75c. Red-spotted hawk-fish 2·50 1·10
3960 85c. French angelfish . . . 3·50 1·50
3961 90c. Blue tang . . . . . . 3·50 1·75

1065 Portrait of Marti and Death Scene

1995. Death Centenary of Jose Marti (revolutionary). Multicoloured.

3962 15c. Type **1065** 20 10
3963 65c. Marti and Maximo Gomez in boat 85 50
3964 75c. Marti and Montecristi Declaration 95 55
3965 85c. Marti, Antonio Maceo and Gomez . . . . 1·10 65
3966 90c. Mausoleum and casket (vert) . . . . 1·10 65

1066 Maceo

1995. Centenary of Battle of Peralejo and 150th Birth Anniv of Antonio Maceo (revolutionary).

3967 **1066** 15c. multicoloured . . . 20 10

1067 Gulf Fritillary

1995. Butterflies. Multicoloured.

3968 10c. Type **1067** 15 10
3969 15c. "Eunica tatila" 20 10
3970 65c. "Melete salacia" . . . 85 50
3971 75c. Cuban clearwing . . . 95 55
3972 85c. Palmira sulphur . . . . 1·10 65
3973 90c. Cloudless sulphur . . . 1·10 65

1068 Supermarine Spitfire (Great Britain)

1995. 2nd World War Combat Planes. Mult.

3974 10c. Type **1068** 15 10
3975 15c. Ilyushin Il-2 (Russia) 20 10
3976 65c. Curtiss P-40 (United States) 85 50
3977 75c. Messerschmitt ME-109 (Germany) 95 55
3978 85c. Morane Saulnier 406 (France) . . . . 1·10 65

1069 Lecuona

1070 Horse in Stable

1995. Birth Cent of Ernesto Lecuona (composer).

3979 **1069** 15c. multicoloured . . . 20 10

1995. "Singapore '95" International Stamp Exhibition. Arab Horses. Multicoloured.

3980 10c. Type **1070** 15 10
3981 15c. Two greys (horiz) . . . 20 10
3982 65c. Tethered horse 85 50
3983 75c. Horse in field 95 55
3984 85c. Mare and foal . . . . 1·10 65
3985 90c. Grey galloping in field 1·10 65

1072 Wrestling

1995. Olympic Games, Atlanta (1996) (1st issue). Multicoloured.

3987 10c. Type **1072** 15 10
3988 15c. Weightlifting 20 10
3989 65c. Volleyball 85 50
3990 75c. Running 95 55
3991 85c. Baseball . . . . 1·10 65
3992 90c. Judo . . . . 1·10 65

See also Nos. 4044/8.

1073 Acana Factory

1995. 400th Anniv of Sugar Production in Cuba. Paintings by Eduardo Laplante. Multicoloured.

3994 15c. Type **1073** . . . . . . 1·50 25
3995 65c. Manaca factory 85 50

1074 Flag and Anniversary Emblem

1995. 50th Anniv of U.N.O.

3996 **1074** 65c. multicoloured . . . 85 60

1075 Lion

1076 St. Clare of Assisi's Convent

1995. Animals from Havana Zoological Gardens. Multicoloured.

3997 10c. Type **1075** 15 10
3998 15c. Grevy's zebra (horiz) 20 10
3999 65c. Orang-utan 85 50
4000 75c. Indian elephant (horiz) 95 55
4001 85c. Eurasian red squirrel (horiz) . . . . 1·10 65
4002 90c. Common racoon (horiz) 1·10 65

1995. 50th Anniv of U.N.E.S.C.O. World Heritage Sites. Multicoloured.

4003 65c. Type **1076** 85 50
4004 75c. St. Francis of Assisi's Monastery church 95 55

1077 "Bletia patula"

1078 Greta Garbo

1995. Orchids. Multicoloured.

4005 40c. Type **1077** 50 30
4006 45c. "Galeandra beyrichii" 60 35
4007 50c. "Vanilla dilloniana" . . 65 35
4008 65c. "Macradenia lutescens" 85 50
4009 75c. "Oncidium luridum" 95 55
4010 85c. "Ionopsis utricularioides" . . . . . 1·10 65

1995. Centenary of Motion Pictures. Designs showing film stars (except No. 4015). Mult.

4011 15c. Type **1078** 20 10
4012 15c. Marlene Dietrich . . . 20 10
4013 15c. Marilyn Monroe . . . 20 10
4014 15c. Charlie Chaplin 20 10
4015 15c. Lumiere Brothers (inventors of cine camera) 20 10
4016 15c. Vittorio de Sica 20 10
4017 15c. Humphrey Bogart . . . 20 10
4018 15c. Rita Montaner 20 10
4019 15c. Cantinflas 20 10

1080 Great Red-bellied Woodpecker

1995. America. Environmental Protection. Mult.

4021 15c. Type **1080** 20 10
4022 65c. Cuban tody 80 45

1081 Alfonso Goulet and Francisco Crombet Ballon

1995. Death Centenaries of Generals killed during War of Independence (1st issue). Mult.

4023	15c. Type **1081**	20	10
4024	15c. Jesus Calvar, Jose Guillermo Moncada and Tomas Jordan	20	10
4025	15c. Francisco Borrero and Francisco Inchaustegui	20	10

Nos. 4023/5 were issued together, se-tenant, forming a composite design of the national flag behind the portraits.

See also Nos. 4089/91 and 4162/3.

1082 Least Tern and Aerial View

1083 Carlos de Cespedes

1995. Coco Key. Multicoloured.

4026	10c. Type **1082**	10	10
4027	15c. White ibis and beach	20	10
4028	45c. Stripe-headed tanager and villas	55	30
4029	50c. Red-legged thrush and apartments	60	35
4030	65c. Northern mocking-bird and villas around pool	80	45
4031	75c. Greater flamingo and couple in pool	95	55

1996. Independence Fighters.

4032	– 10c. orange	10	10
4033 **1083**	15c. green	20	10
4034	– 65c. blue	80	45
4035	– 75c. red	95	55
4036	– 85c. green	1·00	60
4037	– 90c. brown	1·10	65
4040	– 1p.05 mauve	1·25	75
4041	– 2p.05 brown	2·50	1·50
4042	– 3p. brown	3·75	2·25

DESIGNS: 10c. Serafin Sanchez; 65c. Jose Marti; 75c. Antonio Maceo; 85c. Juan Gualberto Gomez; 90c. Quintin Bandera; 1p.05, Ignacio Agramonte; 2p.05, Maximo Gomez; 3p. Calixto Garcia.

1084 Leonardo da Vinci

1996. Scientists. Multicoloured.

4046	10c. Type **1084**	10	10
4047	15c. Mikhail Lomonosov (aerodromic machines)	30	10
4048	65c. James Watt (steam engine)	1·10	60
4049	75c. Guglielmo Marconi (first radio transmitter)	1·25	75
4050	85c. Charles Darwin (theory of evolution)	1·50	85

1085 "Che" Guevara and Emblem

1996. 30th Anniv of Organization of Solidarity of Peoples of Africa, Asia and Latin America.

4051 **1085**	65c. multicoloured	80	45

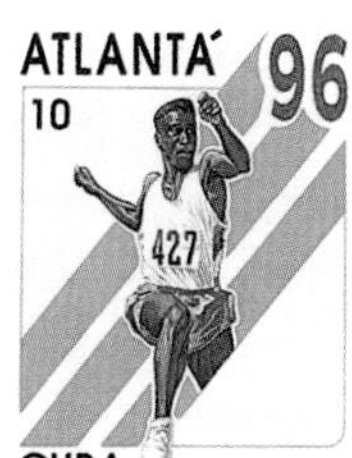

1086 Athletics

1996. Olympic Games, Atlanta (2nd issue). Multicoloured.

4052	10c. Type **1086**	10	10
4053	15c. Weightlifting	20	10
4054	65c. Judo	80	45
4055	75c. Wrestling (horiz)	95	55
4056	85c. Boxing (horiz)	1·10	65

1087 Cierva C.4 Autogyro

1996. "Espamer" Spanish–Latin American and "Aviation and Space" Stamp Exhibitions, Seville, Spain. Multicoloured.

4058	15c. Type **1087**	20	10
4059	65c.35 2-L airplane	80	45
4060	75c. C-201 Alcotan airplane	95	55
4061	85c. CASA C-212 Aviocar	1·10	65

1088 Belted Kingfisher

1996. Death Centenary of Juan Gundlach (ornithologist). Birds. Multicoloured.

4063	10c. Type **1088**	10	10
4064	15c. American redstart	20	10
4065	65c. Common yellowthroat	80	45
4066	75c. Painted bunting	95	55
4067	85c. Cedar waxwing	1·10	65

1089 Yuri Gagarin (cosmonaut)

1090 National Flag and Hand holding Gun

1996. 35th Anniv of First Man in Space. Mult.

4069	15c. Type **1089**	20	10
4070	65c. Globes and "Vostok I" (spaceship) (horiz)	80	45

1996. 35th Anniversaries. Multicoloured.

4071	15c. Type **1090** (victory at Giron)	20	10
4072	65c. Flags and "35" (Declaration of Socialist character of the Revolution)	80	45

1091 "Bahama"

1996. "CAPEX'96" International Stamp Exhibition, Toronto, Canada. 18th-century Ships of the Line built in Cuban Yards. Multicoloured.

4073	10c. Type **1091**	10	10
4074	15c. "Santissima Trinidad"	20	10
4075	65c. "Principe de Asturias"	80	45
4076	75c. "San Pedro de Alcantara"	95	55
4077	85c. "Santa Ana"	1·10	65

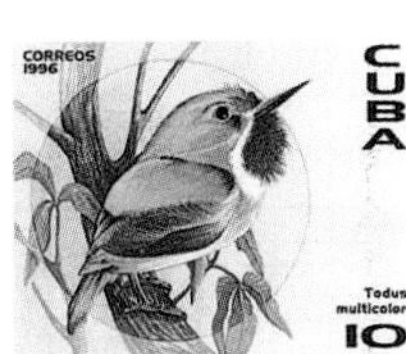

1092 Cuban Tody

1996. Caribbean Animals. Multicoloured.

4079	10c. Type **1092**	10	10
4080	15c. Purple-throated carib ("Eulampis jugularis")	20	10
4081	15c. Wood duck ("Aix sponsa")	20	10
4082	15c. Spot-finned butterflyfish	20	10
4083	65c. "Popilio cresphontes" (butterfly)	80	45
4084	65c. Indigo hamlet	80	45

1093 "Epidendrum porpax"

1996. Orchids. Multicoloured.

4085	5c. Type **1093**	10	10
4086	10c. "Cyrtopodlium punctatum"	15	10
4087	15c. "Polyrrhiza lindeni"	20	10

1094 Charging into Battle and Maceo

1996. Death Cent of General Jose Maceo.

4088 **1094**	15c. multicoloured	20	10

1996. Death Centenaries of Generals killed during War of Independence (2nd issue). As T **1081**. Multicoloured.

4089	15c. Esteban Tamayo and Angel Guerra	20	10
4090	15c. Juan Fernandez Ruz, Jose Maria Aguirre and Serafin Sanchez	20	10
4091	15c. Juan Bruno Zayas and Pedro Vargas Sotomayor	20	10

Nos. 4089/91 were issued together, se-tenant, forming a composite design.

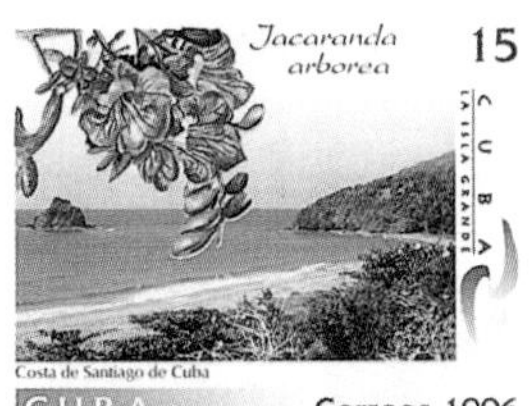

1095 "Jacaranda arborea" and Coast, Santiago de Cuba

1996. Tourism and Flowers. Multicoloured.

4092	15c. Type **1095**	20	10
4093	65c. "Begonia bissei" and San Pedro de la Roca Fort	1·25	45
4094	75c. "Byrsonima crassifolia" and Baconao Park, Santiago de Cuba (vert)	95	55
4095	85c. "Pereskia zinniiflora" and Sanctuary, Cobre (vert)	1·10	65

1096 Baldwin Locomotive No. 1112, 1878

1996. Steam Railway Locomotives. Mult.

4096	10c. Type **1096**	10	10
4097	15c. American locomotive No. 1302, 1904	20	10
4098	65c. Baldwin locomotive No. 1535, 1906	80	45
4099	75c. Rogers locomotive, 1914	95	55
4100	90c. Baldwin locomotive, 1920	1·25	75

1097 Free Negroes, 19th-century

1098 Children

1996. America. Costumes. Multicoloured.

4101	15c. Type **1097**	20	10
4102	65c. Guayabera couple, 20th-century	80	45

1996. 50th Anniv of U.N.I.C.E.F.

4103 **1098**	15c. multicoloured	20	10

1099 Capablanca and Pieces

1996. 75th Anniv of Jose Raul Capablanca's First World Championship Victory. Mult.

4104	15c. Type **1099**	20	10
4105	65c. Capablanca and tournament	80	45
4106	75c. Globe on king and Capablanca	95	55
4107	85c. Capablanca as boy playing chess	1·00	60
4108	90c. Capablanca playing in tournament	1·25	75

1100 Flag and "Granma"

1101 Monument, Santiago de Cuba

1996. 40th Anniversaries of "Granma" Landings (15c.) and Revolutionary Armed Forces (65c.). Multicoloured.

4109	15c. Type **1100**	30	10
4110	65c. "40", flag and soldier with rifle	1·25	75

1996. Death Centenary of General Antonio Maceo. Multicoloured.

4111	10c. Type **1101**	10	10
4112	15c. Maceo	25	15
4113	15c. Memorial of Maceo's disembarkation, Duaba (horiz)	25	15
4114	65c. "Fall of Antonio Maceo" (detail, A. Menocal) (horiz)	1·25	75
4115	75c. Maceo, Panchito Gomez Toro and monument, San Pedro (horiz)	1·50	90

1102 Women's Judo and Gold Medal (Driulis Gonzalez)

1996. Cuban Medal Winners at Olympic Games, Atlanta. Multicoloured.

4116	10c. Type **1102**	15	10
4117	10c. Freestyle wrestling and bronze medal	15	10
4118	15c. Weightlifting and gold medal (Pablo Lara)	25	15
4119	15c. Greco-Roman wrestling and gold medal (Feliberto Aguilera)	25	15
4120	15c. Fencing and silver medal	25	15
4121	15c. Swimming and silver medal	25	15
4122	65c. Women's volleyball and gold medal	1·25	75
4123	65c. Boxing and gold medal (Maikro Romero, Hector Vinent, Ariel Hernandez and Felix Savon)	1·25	75
4124	65c. Women's running and silver medal	1·25	75
4125	65c. Baseball and gold medal	1·25	75

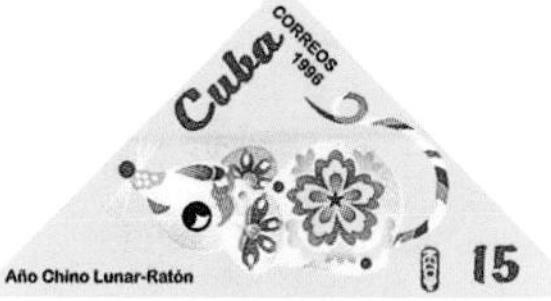

1103 Rat

1996. Chinese New Year. Year of the Rat.

4126 **1103**	15c. multicoloured	40	20

1104 Minho Douro, Portugal

1996. "Espamer '98" Spanish–Latin American Stamp Exhibition, Havana. Railway Locomotives. Multicoloured.

4127 15c. Type **1104** 25 15
4128 65c. Vulcan Iron Works, Brazil . . . . 1·25 75
4129 65c. Baldwin, Dominican Republic . . . . 1·25 75
4130 65c. Alco, Panama . . . . 1·25 75
4131 65c. Baldwin, Puerto Rico 1·25 75
4132 65c. Slaughter Gruning Co, Spain . . . . 1·25 75
4133 75c. Yorkshire Engine Co, Argentine Republic . . . 1·40 80
4134 75c. Porter, Chile . . . . . 1·40 80
4135 75c. Locomotive, Paraguay 1·40 80
4136 75c. Locomotive No. 12, Mexico . . . . 1·40 80

1105 Seal-point Siamese

1107 Dromedary

Centenario del Cine Cubano
1106 "Romance del Palmar", 1938

1997. "Hong Kong '97" International Stamp Exhibition. Cats. Multicoloured.

4138 10c. Type **1105** 10 10
4139 15c. Burmese 25 15
4140 15c. Japanese bobtail (horiz) 25 15
4141 65c. Singapura (horiz) . . . 1·25 75
4142 75c. Korat (horiz) . . . . . 1·40 80

1997. Centenary of Cuban Films. Mult.

4144 15c. Type **1106** 25 15
4145 65c. "Memorias del Subdesarrollo", 1968 (vert) . . . . 1·25 75

1997. Zoo Animals. Multicoloured.

4146 10c. Type **1107** 20 10
4147 15c. White rhinoceros . . . 40 15
4148 15c. Giant panda 40 15
4149 75c. Orang-utan . . . . . . 1·75 1·10
4150 90c. European bison . . . . 2·00 1·25

1108 Ox

1997. Chinese New Year. Year of the Ox.

4151 **1108** 15c. multicoloured . . . 60 20

1109 Menelao Mora and Palace

1997. 40th Anniv of Attack on Presidential Palace.

4152 **1109** 15c. multicoloured . . . 25 15

1110 Players

1997. World Cup Football Championship, France (1998).

4153 **1110** 10c. multicoloured . . . 20 10
4154 – 15c. multicoloured (red face value) 40 15
4155 – 15c. multicoloured (mauve face value) 40 15
4156 – 65c. multicoloured . . . 1·60 1·00
4157 – 75c. multicoloured . . . 1·75 1·10

DESIGNS: 15c. to 75c. Footballers (different).

1111 Youths with Flags and Emblem

1997. 35th Anniv of Communist Youth Union.

4159 **1111** 15c. multicoloured . . . 25 15

1112 "Caledonia"

1997. Stamp Day. Postal Services. Mult.

4160 15c. Type **1112** (170th anniv of maritime service) . . . 45 15
4161 65c. Fokker F.10A Super Trimotor airplane (70th anniv of international airmail) . . . . 1·25 75

1113 Adolfo del Castillo and Enrique del Junco Cruz-Munoz

1997. Death Centenaries of Generals killed during War of Independence (3rd issue).

4162 15c. Type **1113** 25 15
4163 15c. Alberto Rodriguez Acosta and Mariano Sanchez Vaillant 25 15

Nos. 4162/3 were issued together, se-tenant, forming a composite design.

1114 Black-bordered Orange

1997. Butterflies. Multicoloured.

4164 10c. Type **1114** 20 10
4165 15c. Bush sulphur ("Eurema dina") 40 15
4166 15c. Zebra ("Colobura dirce") 40 15
4167 65c. Red admiral . . . . . 1·50 1·00
4168 85c. "Kricogonia castalia" 1·75 1·00

1115 Luperon

1116 Royal Palms

1997. Death Cent of Gen. Gregorio Luperon.

4169 **1115** 65c. multicoloured . . . 1·25 75

1997. 150th Anniv of Chinese Presence in Cuba.

4170 **1116** 15c. multicoloured . . . 80 35

1117 National Flag and United Nations Emblem

1997. 50th Anniv of Cuban United Nations Association.

4171 **1117** 65c. multicoloured . . . 1·50 75

1118 Rainbow and Dove holding Olive Branch

1997. 14th World Youth and Students Festival, Cuba. Multicoloured.

4172 10c. Type **1118** 15 10
4173 15c. "Alma Mater" (statue) 25 15
4174 15c. Children on play apparatus (vert) 25 15
4175 65c. Che Guevara . . . . . 1·25 75
4176 75c. Statue and tower . . . 1·40 80

1119 Pharos of Alexandria

1997. Seven Wonders of the Ancient World. Mult.

4177 10c. Type **1119** 25 10
4178 15c. Egyptian pyramids . . 25 15
4179 15c. Hanging Gardens of Babylon 25 15
4180 15c. Colossus of Rhodes . . 30 15
4181 65c. Mausoleum of Halicarnassus . . . . . . 1·25 75
4182 65c. Statue of Zeus at Olympia . . . . 1·25 75
4183 75c. Temple of Artemis at Ephesus . . . . 1·40 80

1120 Pais and Testamonial of Fidel Castro

1997. 40th Death Anniv of Frank Pais (revolutionary).

4184 **1120** 15c. multicoloured . . . 25 15

1121 Mahatma Gandhi, Indian Flag and State Arms

1122 Saffron Finch ("Sicalis flaveola")

1997. 50th Anniv of Indian Independence.

4185 **1121** 15c. multicoloured . . . 25 15

1997. Birds of the Caribbean. Multicoloured.

4186 15c. Type **1122** 25 15
4187 15c. Red-headed barbet ("Eubucco bourcierii") . . 25 15
4188 15c. Cuban Amazon ("Amazona leucocephala") 25 15
4189 15c. Blue-crowned trogon ("Trogon curucui") . . . 25 15
4190 65c. Blue-throated goldentail ("Hylocharis eliciae") . . 1·25 75
4191 65c. Yellow-crowned Amazon ("Amazona ochrocephala") . . . . . 1·25 75
4192 75c. Eurasian goldfinch ("Carduelis carduelis") . . 1·40 80

1123 Franz Liszt and Memorial Stone commemorating his first Concert when Aged Nine

1997. Composers. Multicoloured.

4193 10c. Type **1123** 30 15
4194 15c. Johann Sebastian Bach and original manuscript score of Sonata in G minor for violin 35 20
4195 15c. Frederic Chopin and birthplace, Zelazowa Wola, Poland 35 20
4196 15c. Ludwig van Beethoven and Karntnerther Theatre where he presented the Ninth Symphony Mass in D major 35 20
4197 65c. Ignacio Cervantes and detail of score of "La Solitaria" (dance) . . . . 1·25 75
4198 75c. Wolfgang Amadeus Mozart and detail of score of first attempt at choral composition . . . 1·40 80

1124 Cuban Solitaire and Valle de Vinales

1997. Tourism. Multicoloured.

4199 10c. Type **1124** 30 15
4200 15c. Cuban crow and Cape Jutia 35 20
4201 65c. Olive-caped warbler and Soroa Falls (vert) . . 1·25 75
4202 75c. Giant kingbird and San Juan River (vert) . . . . 1·40 80

1125 "Hibiscus elatus" ("Majagua")

1997. Caribbean Flowers. Multicoloured.

4203 15c. Type **1125** 35 20
4204 15c. Rose periwinkle ("Vicaria") 35 20
4205 15c. Geiger tree ("Vomitel") 35 20
4206 15c. Bur marigold ("Romerillo") 35 20
4207 65c. Minnie root ("Salta perico") . . . . 1·25 75
4208 75c. Marilope . . . . 1·40 80

1126 Facade 1127 Congress Emblem

1997. 50th Anniv of Oriente University.
4209 **1126** 15c. multicoloured . . . 35 20

1997. 5th Cuban Communist Party Congress and 30th Death Anniv of Ernesto "Che" Guevara (revolutionary). Multicoloured.
4210 15c. Type **1127** 35 20
4211 65c. Che Guevara and letter from Guevara to Fidel Castro . . . . 1·25 75
4212 75c. Portrait of Che Guevara . . . . 1·40 80

1128 19th-century Post Box and Postman

1130 Soviet Flag, Lenin and "Aurora" (cruiser)

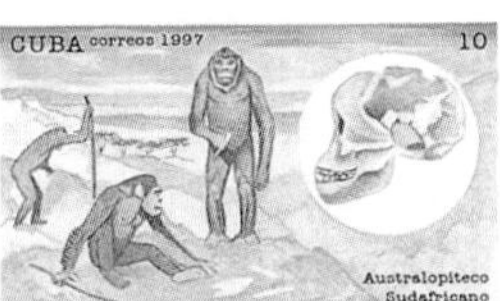

1129 Australopithecus, South Africa

1997. America. The Postman. Multicoloured.
4213 15c. Type **1128** 35 20
4214 65c. 20th-century post boxes and postman . . . . . . 1·25 75

1997. Prehistoric Man. Multicoloured.
4215 10c. Type **1129** 30 15
4216 15c. Pithecanthropus, Java 35 20
4217 15c. Sinanthropus, China . . 35 20
4218 15c. Neanderthal man . . . 35 20
4219 65c. Cro-Magnon man . . . 1·25 75
4220 75c. Oberkassel man, Germany . . . . 1·40 80

1997. 80th Anniv of Russian Revolution.
4221 **1130** 75c. multicoloured . . . 2·40 80

1131 "John Bull", 1831

1997. Railway Locomotives. Multicoloured.
4222 10c. Type **1131** 20 10
4223 15c. Baldwin steam locomotive, 1910–13 . . . 30 15
4224 15c. Locomotive "Old Ironsides", 1832, U.S.A. 30 15
4225 65c. Russian-built Type TEM-4.1 diesel locomotive, 1970 . . . . 1·25 75
4226 75c. Russian-built Type TE-114k diesel locomotive, 1975 . . . . 1·40 80
No. 4222 is inscribed "1830".

1132 National Flag and Capitol, Havana

1997. 50th Anniv of U.N. Conference on Trade and Employment, Havana.
4227 **1132** 65c. multicoloured . . . 1·25 75

1133 Garcia and 1970 30c. Stamp

1997. Birth Centenary of Victor Manuel Garcia (painter).
4228 **1133** 15c. multicoloured . . . 35 20

1134 Havana Cathedral and Pope John Paul II

1998. Papal Visit. Multicoloured.
4229 65c. Type **1134** . . . . . . 1·25 75
4230 75c. Our Lady of Charity Cathedral (vert) . . . . . 1·40 80

1135 Menendez

1136 Players

1998. 50th Death Anniv of Jesus Menendez (labour leader).
4232 **1135** 15c. multicoloured . . . 35 20

1998. World Cup Football Championship, France. Multicoloured.
4233 10c. Type **1136** 30 15
4234 15c. Player in purple shirt lying on ground and player in red and white stripes 40 30
4235 15c. Player in yellow and black strip 50 40
4236 65c. Player in blue shirt tackling player in red and white strip (horiz) . . . . 1·50 1·00
4237 65c. Player in red and blue strip fending off player in light blue strip (horiz) . . 1·50 1·00

1137 Isabel Rubio Diaz

1138 Revee

1998. Death Centenary of Captain Isabel Rubio Diaz (founder of mobile military hospital during War of Independence).
4239 **1137** 15c. multicoloured . . . 35 20

1998. Death Centenary of Brigadier General Vidal Ducasse Revee (revolutionary).
4240 **1138** 15c. multicoloured . . . 35 20

1139 Radio Operator and Che Guevara

1998. Communicators' Day. 40th Anniv of Radio Rebelde.
4241 **1139** 15c. multicoloured . . . 35 20

1140 Shand Mason & Co Horse-drawn Fire Engine, 1901 (Havana)

1998. Fire Engines. Multicoloured.
4242 10c. Type **1140** 30 15
4243 15c. Horse-drawn personnel and equipment vehicle, 1905 (Havana Municipal Service) 50 20
4244 15c. American–French Fire Engine Co vehicle, 1921 (Guanabacoa) 50 20
4245 65c. Chevrolet 6400 fire engine, 1952 (used throughout Cuba) . . . . 1·50 75
4246 75c. American-French-Foamite Co fire engine, 1956 (Havana) . . . . . 1·75 80

1141 Monument and Antonio Maceo (revolutionary)

1998. 120th Anniv of Baragua Protest (against slavery).
4247 **1141** 15c. multicoloured . . . 35 20

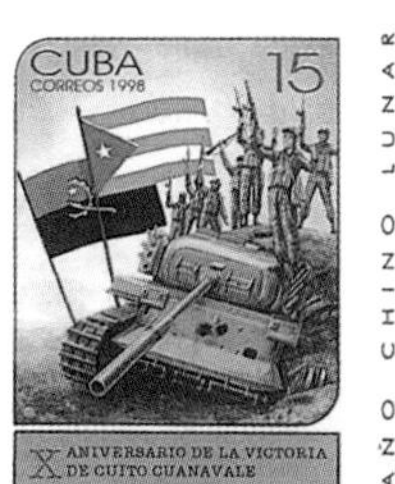

1142 Flags, Soldiers and Tank 1143 Tiger

1998. 10th Anniv of Victory of Angolan Government and Cuban Forces in Defence of Cuito Cuanavale, Angola.
4248 **1142** 15c. multicoloured . . . 35 20

1998. Chinese New Year. Year of the Tiger.
4249 **1143** 15c. multicoloured . . . 75 40

1144 Chihuahua ("Tatiana Vasti de Nino Angelo")

1998. Champion Dogs. Multicoloured.
4250 10c. Type **1144** 30 15
4251 15c. Beagle ("Danco") . . . 40 20
4252 15c. Mexican naked hound ("Xolot del Mictlan") . . 40 20
4253 65c. German spaniel ("D'Milican Nalut Aiwa") 1·40 80
4254 75c. Chow-chow ("Yoki II") 1·50 90

1145 Ancestor of Chimpanzee

1998. Evolution of the Chimpanzee. Multicoloured.
4255 10c. Type **1145** 30 15
4256 15c. Head and skull of "Pan troglodytes blumenbach" 40 20
4257 15c. Chimpanzee and hand and foot 40 20
4258 65c. Mother with infant and new-born chimp . . . . 1·40 80
4259 75c. On branch and distribution map . . . . 1·50 90

1147 Skate

1998. Deep Sea Fishes. Multicoloured.
4261 15c. Type **1147** 40 20
4262 15c. Gulper ("Eurypharynx pelecanoides") 40 20
4263 65c. "Caulophryne" sp. . . 1·50 80
4264 75c. Sloan's viperfish . . . 1·60 95

1148 Garcia Lorca

1998. Birth Cent of Federico Garcia Lorca (poet).
4265 **1148** 75c. multicoloured . . . 1·60 95

1149 Crab

1150 Diana, Princess of Wales

1998. International Year of the Ocean. Mult.
4266 65c. Type **1149** . . . . . . 1·40 80
4267 65c. Fishes . . . . 1·40 80

1998. Diana, Princess of Wales Commemoration. Multicoloured.
4268 10c. Type **1150** 30 15
4269 10c. Wearing patterned dress 30 15
4270 10c. Wearing yellow and pink jacket 30 15
4271 15c. Wearing checked jacket 40 20
4272 15c. Wearing red jacket . . 40 30
4273 65c. Wearing white jacket 1·40 80
4274 75c. Wearing purple jacket 1·50 90

1151 Abel Santamaria

1998. 45th Anniv of Attack on Moncada Barracks. Multicoloured.
4275 15c. Type **1151** 40 30
4276 65c. Jose Marti . . . . . . 1·40 80

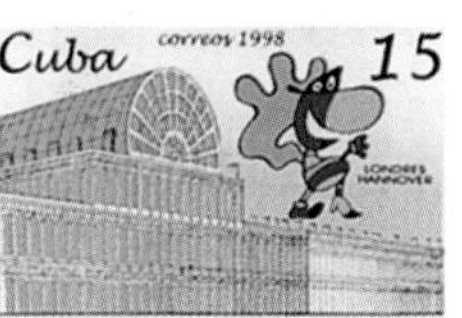

1152 The Crystal Palace, London (Great Exhbition, 1851)

1998. "Expo 2000" World's Fair, Hanover, Germany.
4277 **1152** 15c. multicoloured . . . 40 20
4278 – 15c. multicoloured . . . 40 20
4279 – 15c. multicoloured . . . 40 20
4280 – 15c. black, red & yellow 40 20
4281 – 65c. multicoloured . . . 1·40 80
4282 – 75c. multicoloured . . . 1·50 90
DESIGNS—HORIZ: No. 4277, Type **1152**; 4278, Atomium, Brussels (International Exhibition, 1958); 4280, Map and flag of Germany; 4282, Twipsy (mascot) on globe and fireworks. VERT: No. 4279, Twipsy; 4281, Eiffel Tower, Paris (Exhibition, 1889).

1153 Baseball

1998. 18th Central American and Caribbean Games, Maracaibo, Venezuela.
4283 **1153** 15c. multicoloured . . . 30 15

1154 Kim Il Sung and Pyongyang Landmarks

1998. 50th Anniv of Korean People's Democratic Republic (North Korea).
4284 **1154** 75c. multicoloured . . . 1·50 90

1155 Japanese Bust

1998. Cent of First Japanese Immigrant to Cuba.
4285 **1155** 75c. multicoloured . . . 1·50 90

1156 "Coelogyne flaccida" **1157** Buildings and Emblem

1998. 30th Anniv of National Botanical Garden. Orchids. Multicoloured.
4286 10c. Type **1156** 40 20
4287 15c. "Dendrobium fimbriatum" 40 20
4288 15c. Bamboo orchid ("Arundina graminifolia") 40 20
4289 65c. "Bletia patula" . . . . 1·40 80
4290 65c. Nun's orchid ("Phaius tankervilliaea") . . . . . 1·40 80

1998. 5th Congress of Revolution Defence Committees.
4291 **1157** 15c. multicoloured . . . 30 15

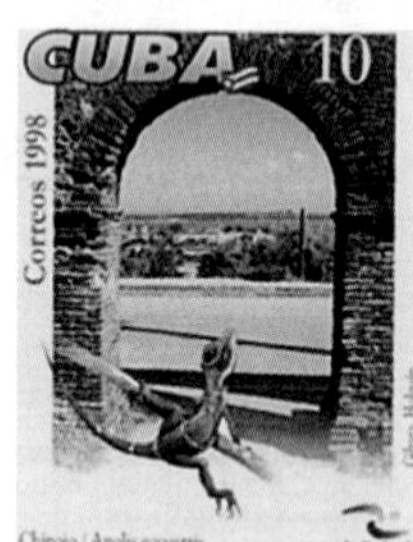

1158 Knight Anole and Archway, Gibara

1998. World Tourism Day. Views of Holguin. Multicoloured.
4292 10c. Type **1158** 30 15
4293 15c. Water lizard, Mirador de Mayabe 40 20
4294 65c. Water chameleon, Guardalavaca Beach (horiz) . . . . 1·40 80
4295 75c. Stone lizard, Pinares de Mayari (horiz) . . . . . 1·50 90

1159 Bernarda Toro (Manana) **1160** Two Conures

1998. America. Famous Women. Independence Activists. Multicoloured.
4296 65c. Type **1159** . . . . . . 1·40 80
4297 75c. Maria Cabrales . . . . 1·50 90

1998. The Cuban Conure. Multicoloured.
4298 10c. Type **1160** 30 15
4299 15c. Head of conure 40 20
4300 65c. Conure on branch . . . 1·40 80
4301 75c. Conure and leaves . . 1·50 90

1161 "Swan Lake"

1998. 50th Anniv of Cuban National Ballet.
4302 **1161** 15c. blue 40 20
4303 – 65c. multicoloured . . . 1·40 80
DESIGN: 65c. "Giselle".

1162 Apartment Building on O'Farrill and Goicuria Streets, Havana, and Victims

1998. 40th Death Anniv of Rogelia Perea, Angel Ameijeiras and Pedro Gutierrez (revolutionaries).
4304 **1162** 15c. multicoloured . . . 30 15

1163 Capt. Braulio Coroneaux (revolutionary) and Tank

1998. 40th Anniv of Battle of Guisa.
4305 **1163** 15c. multicoloured . . . 30 15

1164 Family holding Hands and United Nations Emblem **1165** Garcia Iniguez

1998. 50th Anniv of Universal Declaration of Human Rights.
4306 **1164** 65c. multicoloured . . . 1·40 80

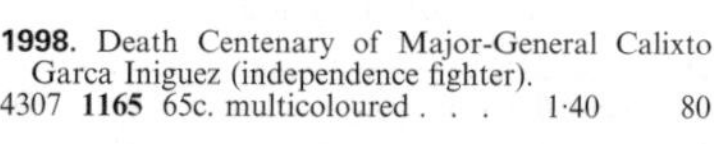
1998. Death Centenary of Major-General Calixto Garca Iniguez (independence fighter).
4307 **1165** 65c. multicoloured . . . 1·40 80

1166 Varela and San Carlos Seminary, Havana

1998. 145th Death Anniv of Felix Varela (philosopher and Vicar-General of New York).
4308 **1166** 75c. multicoloured . . . 1·50 90

1167 Carlos Manuel de Cespedes

1998. Cent of Cuban War of Independence. Mult.
4309 15c. Type **1167** 40 20
4310 15c. Ignacio Agramonte Loynaz 40 20
4311 15c. Maximo Gomez Baez 40 20
4312 15c. Jose Maceo Grajales . . 40 20
4313 15c. Salvador Cisneros Betancourt 40 20
4314 15c. Calixto Garcia Iniguez 40 20
4315 15c. Adolfo Flor Crombet 40 20
4316 15c. Serafin Sanchez Valdivia 40 20
4317 65c. Jose Marti Perez . . . 1·40 80
4318 75c. Antonio Maceo Grajales . . . . 1·50 90

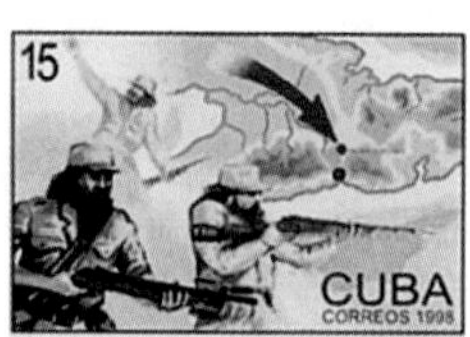

1168 Revolutionaries and Map

1998. 40th Anniv of Capture of Palma Soriano by Revolutionaries.
4319 **1168** 15c. multicoloured . . . 30 15

1169 "Granma" Landings

1999. 40th Anniv of Revolution. Multicoloured.
4320 65c. Type **1169** . . . . . . 1·40 80
4321 65c. Camilo Cienfuegos and Fidel Castro . . . . . . 1·40 80
4322 65c. Castro and white doves 1·40 80

1170 Police Car and Motor Cycle

1999. 40th Anniv of National Revolutionary Police.
4323 **1170** 15c. multicoloured . . . 30 15

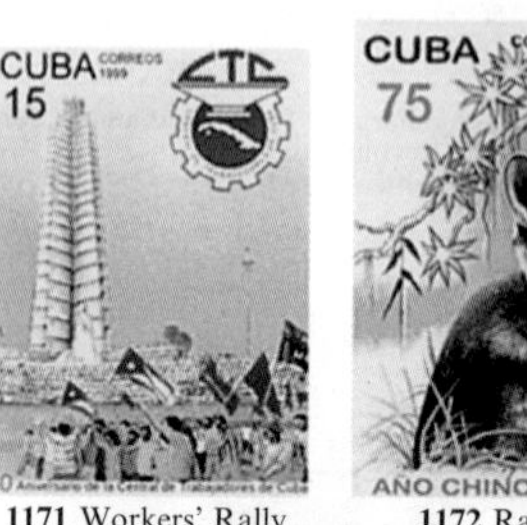

1171 Workers' Rally **1172** Rabbit

1999. 60th Anniv of Revolutionary Workers' Union.
4324 **1171** 15c. multicoloured . . . 30 15

1999. Chinese New Year. Year of the Rabbit.
4325 **1172** 75c. multicoloured . . . 1·40 80

1173 Lenin

1999. 75th Death Anniv of Vladimir Ilich Lenin (Russian statesman).
4326 **1173** 75c. multicoloured . . . 1·40 80

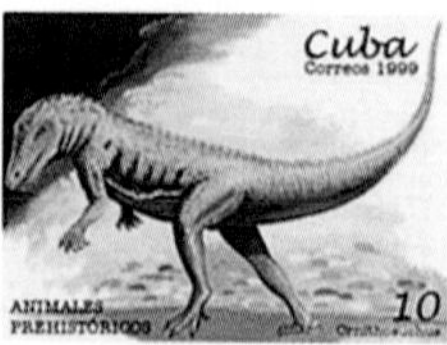

1174 Ornithosuchus

1999. Prehistoric Animals. Multicoloured.
4327 10c. Type **1174** 30 15
4328 15c. Bactrosaurus 40 20
4329 15c. Saltopus 40 20
4330 65c. Protosuchus . . . . . 1·40 80
4331 75c. Mussaurus . . . . . . 1·50 90

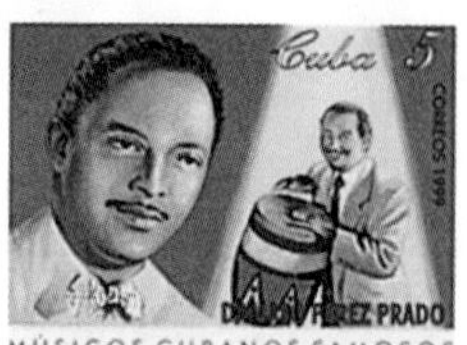

1175 Damaso Perez Prado

1999. Cuban Musicians. Multicoloured.
4332 5c. Type **1175** 15 10
4333 15c. Benny More 40 20
4334 15c. Chano Pozo 40 20
4335 35c. Miguelito Valdes . . . 70 40
4336 65c. Bola de Nieve . . . . 1·40 80
4337 75c. Rita Montaner . . . . 1·50 90

1176 Bolivar **1177** Emblem

1999. Centenary of Simon Bolivar's Visit to Cuba. Multicoloured.
4338 65c. Type **1176** . . . . . . 1·40 80
4339 65c. Simon Bolivar House and statue, Havana . . . 1·40 80

1999. 40th Anniv of State Security Department of the Ministry of the Interior.
4340 **1177** 65c. multicoloured . . . 1·40 80

1179 Postal Rocket

1999. Stamp Day.
4342 15c. Type **1179** (60th anniv) 40 20
4343 65c. Rider on horse (130th anniv of rebel postal service) . . . . 1·40 80

1180 Painting by Roberto Matta

1999. 40th Anniv of House of the Americas (cultural organization).
4344 **1180** 65c. multicoloured . . . 1·40 80

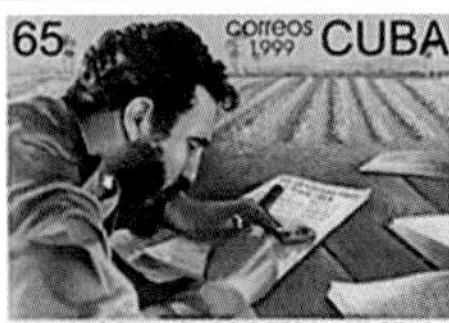

1182 Castro drafting Reform Law

1999. 40th Anniv of Agrarian Reform Law.
4346 **1182** 65c. multicoloured . . . 1·40 80

1183 Royal Gramma

1999. Birth Bicentenary of Felipe Poey (naturalist). Fishes. Multicoloured.
4347 5c. Type **1183** 15 10
4348 15c. Peppermint basslet . . 40 20
4349 65c. Golden hamlet ("Hypoplectrus gummigutta") . . . . . 1·40 80
4350 65c. Dusky damselfish ("Stegastes dorsopunicans") . . . . 1·40 80

1185 Baseball

1999. 13th Pan-American Games, Winnipeg, Canada. Multicoloured.
4353 15c. Type **1185** 40 20
4354 65c. Volleyball (vert) . . . . 1·40 80
4355 75c. Boxing . . . . 1·50 90

1186 "Victory of Wioming" (Gao Hong)

1999. 50th Anniv of People's Republic of China. Paintings. Multicoloured.
4356 5c. Type **1186** 15 10
4357 15c. "Nanchang Revolt" (Cai Lang) 40 20
4358 40c. "Red Army crossing Marsh" (Gao Quan) . . . 75 40
4359 65c. "Occupation of Presidential Palace" (Cheng Yifei and Wei Jingahan) . . . . 1·40 80
4360 75c. "Founding of the Republic Ceremony" (Dong Xiwen) . . . . . 1·50 90

1187 "Morning Glory" (Qi Baishi)

1999. "China 1999" International Stamp Exhibition, Peking. Chinese Paintings. Multicoloured.
4361 5c. Type **1187** 15 10
4362 5c. "Three Galloping Horses" (Xu Beihong) . . 15 10
4363 15c. "Hunan Woman" (Fu Baoshi) 40 20
4364 15c. "Village of Luxun" (Wu Guanzhong) 40 20
4365 15c. "Crossing" (Huangzhou) 40 20
4366 40c. "Pine Tree" (He Xiangning) 75 40
4367 65c. "Sleeping Woman" (Jin Shangyi) . . . . 1·40 80
4368 75c. "Poetic Scene in Xun Yang" (Chen Yifei) . . . 1·50 90

1188 Heinrich von Stephan (founder) and Emblem

1999. 125th Anniv of Universal Postal Union.
4369 **1188** 75c. multicoloured . . . 1·50 90

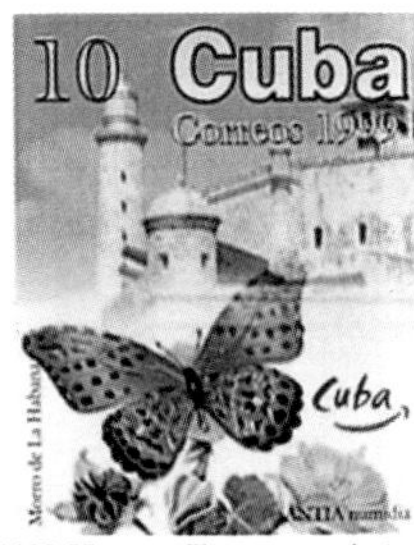

1189 Havana Fortress and *Antia numidia*

1999. World Tourism Day. Butterflies and Views of Havana. Multicoloured.
4370 10c. Type **1189** 10 10
4371 15c. Cathedral and black swallowtail 30 20
4372 65c. St. Francis of Assisi Convent and flambeau . . 1·40 80
4373 75c. National Senate and *Eueides cleobaea* . . . . 1·50 90

1190 Map of Germany on Globe

1999. "EXPO 2000" World's Fair, Hanover. Mult.
4374 5c. Type **1190** 10 10
4375 15c. Twipsy (mascot) (vert) 30 20
4376 15c. Exhibition site, Philadelphia, 1876 . . . . 30 20
4377 15c. Exhibition site, Osaka, 1970 . . . . 30 20
4378 65c. Exhibition site, Hanover . . . . 1·40 80
4379 75c. Exhibition site, Montreal, 1967 . . . . . 1·50 90

1191 Fokker F.27 Friendship

1999. 70th Anniv of Cuban Airlines. Multicoloured.
4380 15c. Type **1191** 30 20
4381 15c. Douglas DC-10 . . . . 30 20
4382 65c. Airbus Industrie A320 1·40 80
4383 75c. Douglas DC-3 . . . . 1·50 90

1192 Atomic Cloud and Feral Rock Pigeon

1194 Cienfuegos

1193 MINFAR Headquarters

1999. America. A New Millennium without Arms. Multicoloured.
4384 15c. Type **1192** 30 20
4385 65c. Globe and dove . . . . 1·40 80

1999. 40th Anniversaries. Multicoloured.
4386 15c. Type **1193** (Ministry of Revolutionary Armed Forces) 30 20
4387 65c. Militia members (National Revolutionary Militia) . . . . 1·40 80

1999. 40th Anniv of Disappearance of Major Camilo Cienfuegos (revolutionary).
4388 **1194** 15c. multicoloured . . . 30 20

1195 Vieja Plaza

1999. 9th Latin American Summit of Heads of State and Government, Havana. Multicoloured.
4389 65c. Type **1195** . . . . . . 1·40 80
4390 75c. San Francisco de Asis Plaza . . . . 1·50 90

1197 Hemingway and Fisherman

1999. Birth Cent of Ernest Hemingway (writer).
4393 **1197** 65c. multicoloured . . . 1·40 80

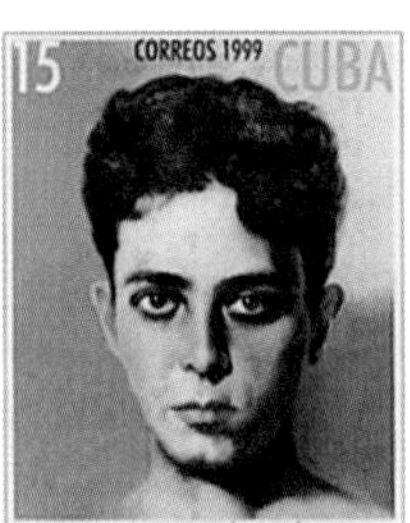

1198 Villena

1999. Birth Centenary of Ruben Martinez Villena (revolutionary).
4394 **1198** 15c. multicoloured . . . 30 20

1199 Romay Chacon

1999. 150th Death Anniv of Tomas Romay Chacon (scientist).
4395 **1199** 65c. multicoloured . . . 1·40 80

1200 Dragon

2000. Chinese New Year. "Year of the Dragon".
4396 **1200** 15c. multicoloured . . . 30 20

1201 "Hot Rumba"

2000. Paintings by Concepcion Ferrant. Mult.
4397 10c. Type **1201** 15 10
4398 15c. "Cachumba" 30 20
4399 65c. "House of the babalao" 1·40 80
4400 75c. "Tata Cunengue" . . . 1·50 90

1202 *Helcyra superba*

2000. "BANGKOK 2000" International Stamp Exhibition. Butterflies. Multicoloured.
4401 10c. Type **1202** 15 10
4402 15c. *Pantaporia punctata* . . 30 20
4403 15c. *Neptis themis* 30 20
4404 65c. *Curetis acuta* . . . . . 1·40 80
4405 75c. *Chrysozephyrus ataxus* 1·50 90

1203 World Map

2000. Group of 77 South Summit, Havana.
4406 **1203** 75c. multicoloured . . . 1·50 90

1204 Lenin

2000. 130th Birth Anniv of Vladimir Ilich Lenin.
4407 **1204** 75c. multicoloured . . . 1·50 90

1205 Cuba and Puerto Rico 1855 1r. Stamp

2000. Stamp Day. Multicoloured.
4408 65c. Type **1205** (145th anniv of first Cuba and Puerto Rico stamp) . . . . . . 1·40 80
4409 90c. Jaime Gonzalez Crocier (airmail pioneer), airplane and cover (70th anniv of the airmail service) . . . 1·75 1·10

1206 Commander Guevara and Map

2000. 35th Anniv of Visit of "Che" Guevara (guerrilla fighter) to Congo.
4410 **1206** 65c. multicoloured . . . 1·40 80

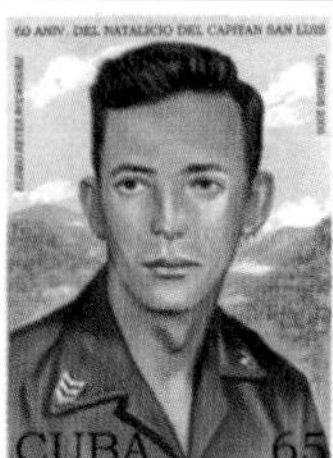

1207 Captain San Luis

2000. 60th Birth Anniv of Eliseo Reyes Rodriguez ("Captain San Luis").
4411 **1207** 65c. multicoloured . . . 1·40 80

1208 Baldwin Locomotive, 1882

2000. "Stamp Show 2000" International Stamp Exhibition, London. Steam Locomotives. Mult.
4412 5c. Type **1208** 10 10
4413 10c. Baldwin locomotive, 1895 . . . . 15 10
4414 15c. Baldwin locomotive, 1912 . . . . 30 20
4415 65c. Alco locomotive, 1919 1·40 80
4416 75c. Alco locomotive, 1925 1·50 90

1209 Henri Giffard and Steam-powered Dirigible Airship

2000. "WIPA 2000" International Stamp Exhibition, Vienna. Airship Development. Multicoloured.
4418 10c. Type **1209** 10 10
4419 15c. Albert and Gaston Tissander and airship (vert) 20 10
4420 50c. Charles Renard, Arthur Krebs and *La France* (airship) 70 40
4421 65c. Pierre and Paul Lebaudy and airship . . . 90 50
4422 75c. August von Perseval and airship . . . . 1·10 65

1210 Emblem

2000. 2nd World Meeting of "Friendship and Solidarity with Cuba", Havana.
4424 **1210** 65c. multicoloured . . . 90 50

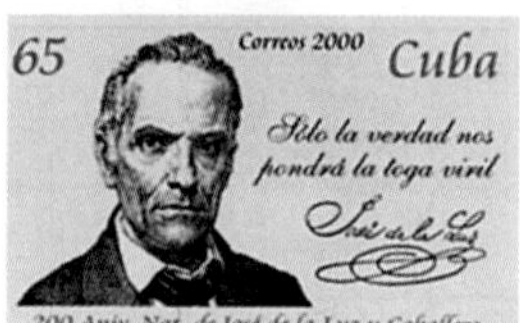

1211 Caballero

2000. Birth Bicentenary of Jose de la Luz y Caballero (educator).
4425 **1211** 65c. multicoloured . . . 90 50

1212 Music Score, Roldan and Violin

2000. Birth Centenary of Amadeo Roldan (musician and conductor).
4426 **1212** 65c. multicoloured . . . 90 50

1213 Mother holding Child ("Child of El Senor Don Pomposo")

2000. *The Golden Age* (children's magazine by Jose Marti). Designs illustrating stories featured in the magazines. Multicoloured.
4427 5c. Type **1213** 10 10
4428 10c. Child with doll ("The Black Doll") 15 10
4429 15c. Child reading ("Mischevious Child") . . 20 10
4430 50c. "The Nightingale" (Hans Christian Andersen) 70 40
4431 65c. Frontispiece 90 50
4432 75c. "The Enchanted Prawn" (Edourd R. L. Laboulaye) . . . . 1·10 65

1214 Members' Flags

2000. 20th Anniv of Latin American Association for Integration (A.L.A.D.I.).
4434 **1214** 65c. multicoloured . . . 90 50

1216 Running

2000. Olympic Games, Sydney. Multicoloured.
4436 5c. Type **1216** 10 10
4437 15c. Football 20 10
4438 65c. Baseball 90 50
4439 75c. Cycling . . . . 1·10 65

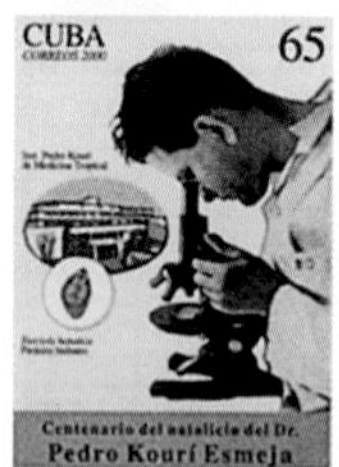

1217 Esmeja using Microscope

2000. Birth Centenary of Dr. Pedro Kouri Esmeja (tropical disease and parasitology pioneer).
4440 **1217** 65c. multicoloured . . . 90 50

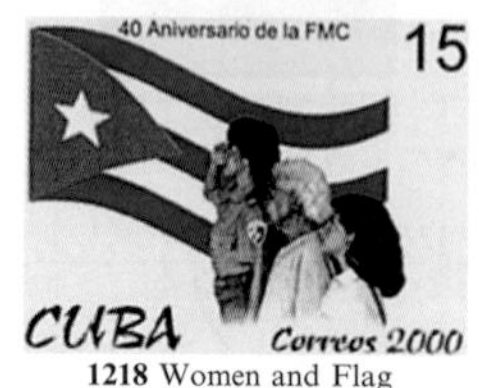

1218 Women and Flag

2000. 40th Anniv of Federation of Cuban Women.
4441 **1218** 15c. multicoloured . . . 20 10

1219 18th-century Sailing Packet

2000. "Espana 2000" World Stamp Exhibition, Madrid. Multicoloured.
4442 10c. Type **1219** 15 10
4443 15c. Statue, La Cibeles Plaza, Madrid and Spain 1850 6c. stamp 20 10
4444 15c. Crystal Palace, Madrid (venue) and 1850 cover 20 10
4445 65c. Palace of Communications, Madrid and set of Spain 1850 stamps 90 50
4446 75c. Galician Centre, Havana with Cuba and Puerto Rico 1855 ½r. stamp . . . . 1·10 65

1220 Senen Casas Reguerio Railway Station, Santiago de Cuba

2000. 20th Congress of Pan-American Railways.
4448 **1220** 65c. multicoloured . . . 90 50

1221 Coconut Forest Bay, Hainan, China

2000. 40th Anniv of Cuba–China Diplomatic Relations. Joint issue with China. Multicoloured.
4449 15c. Type **1221** 20 10
4450 15c. Varadero beach, Matanzas, Cuba 20 10
Nos. 4449/50 were issued together, se-tenant, forming a composite design.

1222 Hawksbill Turtle (*Eretmochelys imbricata*), Guardalavaca

2000. World Tourism Day. Diving Sites. Mult.
4451 10c. Type **1222** 15 10
4452 15c. Nassau grouper (*Epinephelus striatus*), El Colony 20 10
4453 65c. French angelfish (*Pomacanthus paru*), Santa Lucia (horiz) 80 45
4454 75c. Black margate (*Anisotremus surinamensis*), Maria la Gorda (horiz) 95 55

1223 House and People Gardening

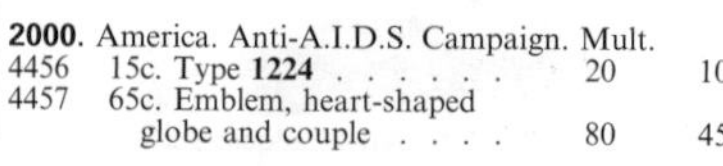

1224 Emblem, Heart-shaped Globe and Family

2000. 40th Anniv of Committees for Defense of the Revolution (CDR).
4455 **1223** 15c. multicoloured . . . 20 10

2000. America. Anti-A.I.D.S. Campaign. Mult.
4456 15c. Type **1224** 20 10
4457 65c. Emblem, heart-shaped globe and couple 80 45

1225 Soldiers carrying Flags

2000. 25th Anniv of Cuban International Mission to Angola.
4458 **1225** 75c. multicoloured . . . 95 55

1226 Humboldt and Guesthouse, Trinidad

2000. Bicentennial of Friedrich Wilhelm Heinrich Alexander von Humboldt's Visit to Cuba. Mult.
4459 15c. Type **1226** 20 10
4460 65c. Humboldt, frontispiece of *On the Island of Cuba* (political essay) and Humboldt House, Havana 80 45

1227 *Polymita picta iolimbata*

2000. New Millennium. Snails. Multicoloured.
4461 65c. Type **1227** 80 45
4462 65c. *Polymita picta roseolimbata* 80 45
4463 65c. *Polymita picta picta* . . 80 45
4464 65c. *Polymita picta nigrolimbata* 80 45
4465 65c. *Polymita versicolor* . . 80 45
Nos. 4461/4 were issued together, se-tenant, forming a composite design.

EXPRESS MAIL STAMPS

E 34

1900. As Type E **34**, but inscr "immediata".
E306 E **34** 10c. orange . . . . . 32·00 8·50

1902. Inscr "inmediata".
E307 E **34** 10c. orange . . . . . 2·00 1·00

E **39** J. B. Zayas

1910.
E320 E **39** 10c. blue and orange 4·00 1·40

E **41** Bleriot XI and Morro Castle

1914.
E352 E **41** 10c. blue . . . . . . 6·00 1·40

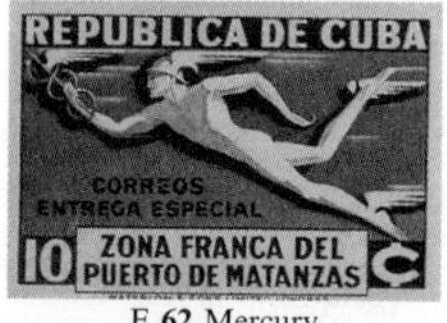

E **62** Mercury

1936. Free Port of Matanzas. Inscr as T **61**. Perf or imperf (same prices).
E409 E **62** 10c. purple (express) 3·50 3·50
E413 – 15c. blue (air express) 12·00 2·00
DESIGN: 15c. Maya Lighthouse.

E **67** "Triumph of the Revolution"

1936. Maximo Gomez Monument.
E422 E **67** 10c. orange 3·75 2·75

E **71** Temple of Quetzalcoatl (Mexico)

1937. American Writers and Artists Association.
E424v E **71** 10c. orange 3·75 2·75
E424w – 10c. orange 3·75 2·75
DESIGN: No. 424w, Ruben Dario (Nicaragua).

E **114**

1945.
E485 E **114** 10c. brown 4·25 60

E **146** Government House, Cardenas

1951. Centenary of Cuban Flag.
E559 E **146** 10c. red, blue & orge 2·75 95

E **150** Capablanca Club, Havana

1951. 30th Anniv of Jose Capablanca's Victory in World Chess Championship.
E568 E **150** 10c. purple & green 5·50 2·25

1952. As No. 549 surch **10c E. ESPECIAL**.
E595 **143** 10c. on 2c. brown 1·25 40

E **161** National Anthem and Arms E **176** Roseate Tern

1952. 50th Anniv of Republic.
E605 E **161** 10c. blue & orange 2·75 1·10

1952. Postal Employees' Retirement Fund. Inscr "ENTREGA ESPECIAL".
E627 **165** 10c. olive 1·75 85

1953.
E673 E **176** 10c. blue 4·00 2·00

1954. Postal Employees' Retirement Fund. Portrait of G. H. Saez as No. 684, inscr "ENTREGA ESPECIAL".
E686 10c. olive 1·90 95

1955. Postal Employees' Retirement Fund. Vert portrait (F. Varela) as T **191**, inscr "ENTREGA ESPECIAL".
E741 10c. lake 2·00 95

1956. Postal Employees' Retirement Fund. Vert portrait (J. J. Milanes) as T **200**, inscr "ENTREGA ESPECIAL".
E768 10c. black and red 1·90 95

1957. Postal Employees' Retirement Fund. As T **216** but inscr "ENTREGA ESPECIAL".
E812 10c. turquoise & brown 1·75 85
PAINTING: 10c. "Yesterday" (Cabrera).

1957. Postal Employees' Retirement Fund. As T **236** but inscr "ENTREGA ESPECIAL".
E856 10c. violet and brown 1·75 85
DESIGN—HORIZ: 10c. Statue of Gen. A. Maceo, Independence Park, Pinar del Rio.

E **238** Motor-cyclist in Havana

1958.
E858 E **238** 10c. blue 1·40 65
E954 10c. violet 1·40 65
E955 10c. orange 1·40 65
E859 20c. green 1·40 65

1958. Poey Commem. As Nos. 890/2 but inscr "ENTREGA ESPECIAL".
E893 10c. multicoloured 5·50 2·75
E894 20c. red, blue and black 8·50 5·50
DESIGNS—HORIZ: Fish: 10c. Black-finned snapper; 20c. Spotted mosquitofish.

1960. Surch **HABILITADO ENTREGA ESPECIAL 10c.**
E961 **55** 10c. on 20c. pink 1·10 35
E962 10c. on 50c. turquoise 1·10 35

1962. Stamp Day. As T **289** but inscr "ENTREGA ESPECIAL".
E1023 10c. brown & bl on yell 6·50 1·25
DESIGN: 10c. 18th-century sailing packet.

E **991** Great Red-bellied Woodpecker

1991. Birds. Multicoloured.
E3638 45c. Type E **991** 1·00 25
E3639 50c. Cuban solitaire 1·00 25
E3640 2p. Cuban trogon 5·00 1·25
E3641 4p. Cuban grassquit 11·00 2·50
E3642 5p. Ivory-billed woodpecker 13·00 3·00
E3643 10p. Cuban amazon (horiz) 30·00 6·00
E3644 16p.45 Bee hummingbird (horiz) 50·00 12·00

POSTAGE DUE STAMPS

D **42**

1914.
D335 D **42** 1c. red 1·25 65
D337 2c. red 1·25 65
D340 5c. red 2·75 1·10

CUNDINAMARCA Pt. 20

One of the states of the Granadine Confederation. A Department of Colombia from 1886, now uses Colombian stamps.

100 centavos = 1 peso.

1 2

1870. Imperf.
1 **1** 5c. blue 2·75 2·75
2 **2** 10c. red 10·00 10·00

3 4

1877. Imperf.
5 **3** 10c. red 1·25 1·25
6 **4** 20c. green 2·25 2·25
7 – 50c. mauve 3·00 3·00
8a – 1p. brown 5·00 5·00
The 50c. and 1p. are in larger Arms designs.

11 13

1884. Imperf.
14 **11** 5c. blue 50 60

1885. Imperf.
17 **13** 5c. blue 30 30
18 10c. red 1·50 1·50
19 10c. red on lilac 90 90
20 20c. green 1·25 1·25
21 50c. mauve 1·75 1·75
22 1p. brown 2·00 2·00

14 15

1904. Imperf or perf. Various frames.
23 **14** 1c. orange 15 15
24 2c. blue 15 15
35 2c. grey 45 45
25 **15** 3c. red 20 20
26 5c. green 20 20
27 10c. brown 20 20
28 15c. pink 25 25
29 20c. blue on green 20 20
32 20c. blue 40 40
42 40c. blue 30 30
30 50c. mauve 25 25
31 1p. green 25 25
The illustrations show the main type. The frames and position of the arms in Type **15** differ for each value.

REGISTRATION STAMP

R 17

1904. Imperf or perf.
R46 R **17** 10c. brown 75 75

CURACAO Pt. 4

A Netherlands colony consisting of two groups of islands in the Caribbean Sea, N. of Venezuela. Later part of Netherlands Antilles.

100 cents = 1 gulden.

1 2 4

1873.
13 **1** 2½c. green 5·50 8·75
7 3c. bistre 55·00 £120
14 5c. red 12·50 12·50
26 10c. blue 70·00 18·00
27 12½c. yellow £110 55·00
22 15c. brown 32·00 20·00
23 25c. brown 55·00 8·75
24 30c. grey 42·00 50·00
17 50c. lilac 2·40 3·00

1889.
37 **2** 1c. grey 1·60 1·75
38 2c. mauve 1·60 1·75
39 2½c. green 5·50 4·00
40a 3c. brown 6·25 5·50
41 5c. red 24·00 2·00

1891. Surch **25 CENT**.
42 **1** 25c. on 30c. grey 17·00 15·00

1892.
43 **4** 10c. blue 1·60 1·60
44 12½c. green 19·00 8·00
45 15c. red 3·25 3·25
46 25c. brown £110 6·50
47 30c. grey 3·25 8·00

1895. Surch **2½ cent** (No. 48) or **2½ CENT** (No. 50).
48 **1** 2½c. on 10c. blue 15·00 9·50
50 2½c. on 30c. grey £140 6·25

1899. 1898 stamps of Netherlands surch **CURACAO** and value.
51 **12** 12½c. on 12½c. blue 28·00 8·75
52 25c. on 25c. blue and red 2·40 2·25
53 **13** 1g.50 on 2½g. lilac 22·00 22·00

9 10

11

1903.
54 **9** 1c. olive 2·00 1·50
55a 2c. brown 14·50 4·00
56 2½c. green 6·00 60
57 3c. orange 9·75 6·25
58 5c. red 9·75 60
59 7½c. grey 30·00 7·25
60 **10** 10c. slate 15·00 2·50
61 12½c. blue 2·00 65
62 15c. brown 18·00 13·50
63 22½c. olive and brown 18·00 14·00
64 25c. violet 18·00 3·00
65 30c. brown 40·00 16·00
66 50c. brown 36·00 10·00
67 **11** 1½g. brown 40·00 32·00
68 2½g. blue 38·00 32·00

12 13

14

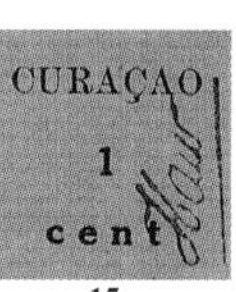

15

1915.
69 **12** ½c. lilac 1·75 1·75
70 1c. olive 30 40
71 1½c. blue 30 20
72 2c. brown 1·40 1·25
73 2½c. green 1·10 25

74 3c. yellow 2·50 1·90
75 3c. green 3·00 2·75
76 5c. red 2·10 25
77 5c. green 4·00 2·75
78 5c. mauve 2·10 25
79c 12 7½c. bistre 1·25 20
80 13 10c. red 18·00 3·50
81 12 10c. lilac 5·50 5·50
82 10c. red 4·50 1·90
83 13 12½c. blue 3·00 1·00
84 12½c. red 2·50 2·00
85 15c. olive 90 1·60
86 15c. blue 5·00 2·75
87 20c. blue 8·00 3·00
88 20c. olive 3·00 2·25
89 22½c. orange 3·00 3·00
90 25c. mauve 4·00 1·60
91 30c. slate 4·00 1·60
92 35c. slate and orange 4·00 5·75
93a 14 50c. green 5·50 40
94 1½g. violet 16·00 13·50
95 2½g. red 25·00 22·00

1918.
96 15 1c. black on buff 7·25 3·75

1919. Surch **5 CENT**.
97 13 5c. on 12½c. blue 4·50 2·50

17 Queen Wilhelmina

20

1923. Queen's Silver Jubilee.
98 17 5c. green 1·10 2·50
99 7½c. green 1·90 2·50
100 10c. red 3·00 4·50
101 20c. grey 3·00 4·50
102 1g. purple 35·00 21·00
103 2g.50 black 70·00 £180
104 5g. brown 90·00 £225

1927. Unissued Marine Insurance stamps, as Type M 22 of Netherlands, inscr "CURACAO", surch **FRANKEERZEGEL** and value.
105 3c. on 15c. green 35 35
106 10c. on 60c. red 35 35
107 12½c. on 75c. brown 35 35
108 15c. on 1g.50 blue 2·75 2·75
109 25c. on 2g.25 brown 6·00 6·00
110 30c. on 4½g. black 13·50 10·50
111 50c. on 7½g. red 7·25 7·00

1928.
112 20 6c. orange 1·50 35
113 7½c. orange 65 55
114 10c. red 1·50 55
115 12½c. brown 1·50 1·25
116 15c. blue 1·50 55
117 20c. blue 5·50 90
118 21c. green 9·00 10·00
119 25c. purple 3·50 2·25
120 27½c. black 11·50 12·50
121 30c. green 5·50 1·10
122 35c. black 2·00 1·10

1929. Air. Surch **LUCHTPOST** and value.
123 13 50c. on 12½c. red 14·00 14·00
124 1g. on 20c. blue 14·00 14·00
125 2g. on 15c. olive 40·00 42·00

1929. Surch **6 ct.** and bars.
126 20 6c. on 7½c. orange 1·60 1·25

23

24a

1931. Air.
126a 23 10c. green 20 20
126b 15c. slate 45 20
127 20c. red 1·00 25
127a 25c. olive 90 1·00
127b 30c. yellow 45 45
128 35c. blue 1·10 1·10
129 40c. green 75 55
130 45c. orange 2·10 2·10
130a 50c. red 1·00 65
131 60c. purple 75 45
132 70c. black 6·50 2·10
133 1g.40 brown 4·00 4·75
134 2g.80 bistre 4·50 5·25

1931. Surch.
134a 12 1½ on 2½c. green 3·50 3·25
135 2½ on 3c. green 1·10 95

1933. 400th Birth Anniv of William I of Orange.
136 24a 6c. orange 1·60 1·25

25 Frederik Hendrik

26 "Johannes van Walbeeck"

1934. 300th Anniv of Dutch Colonization. Inscr "1634 1934".
137 – 1c. black 1·10 1·25
138 – 1½c. mauve 85 35
139 – 2c. orange 1·10 1·25
140 25 2½c. green 90 1·40
141 5c. brown 90 1·10
142 6c. blue 85 35
143 – 10c. red 2·10 1·25
144 – 12½c. brown 6·25 6·25
145 – 15c. blue 1·90 1·50
146 26 20c. black 3·00 2·50
147 21c. brown 11·00 14·00
148 25c. green 11·50 11·50
149 – 27½c. purple 13·50 16·00
150 – 30c. red 11·50 7·00
151 – 50c. yellow 11·50 11·50
152 – 1g.50 blue 48·00 52·00
153 – 2g.50 green 50·00 55·00
PORTRAITS: 1c. to 2c. Willem Usselinx. 10c. to 15c. Jacob Binckes. 27½c. to 50c. Cornelis Evertsen, the younger. 1g.50, 2g.50, Louis Brion.

1934. Air. Surch **10 CT.**
154 23 10c. on 20c. red 21·00 16·00

27

28 Queen Wilhelmina

1936.
155A 27 1c. brown 30 20
156A 1½c. blue 30 20
157A 2c. orange 30 20
158A 2½c. green 30 20
159A 5c. red 30 20

1936.
160 28 6c. purple 75 20
161 10c. red 1·10 20
162 12½c. green 1·60 90
163 15c. blue 1·40 55
164 20c. orange 1·40 55
165 21c. black 2·50 2·75
166 25c. red 1·60 1·10
167 27½c. brown 3·25 33
168 30c. bistre 75 35
169 50c. green 3·50 35
170 1g.50 brown 23·00 12·50
171a 2g.50 red 18·00 13·00

29 Queen Wilhelmina

30 Dutch Flags and Arms

1938. 40th Anniv of Coronation.
172 29 1½c. violet 20 30
173 6c. red 85 75
174 15c. blue 1·60 1·25

1941. Air. Prince Bernhard Fund to equip Dutch Forces. Centres in red, blue and orange.
175 30 10c.+10c. red 18·00 16·00
176 15c.+25c. blue 25·00 20·00
177 20c.+25c. brown 25·00 20·00
178 25c.+25c. violet 25·00 20·00
179 30c.+50c. orange 25·00 20·00
180 35c.+50c. green 25·00 20·00
181 40c.+50c. brown 25·00 20·00
182 50c.+1g. blue 25·00 20·00

31 Queen Wilhelmina

33 Aruba

1941.
248 31 6c. violet 1·50 2·00
184a 10c. red 2·40 1·10
185 12½c. green 2·75 1·10
251 15c. blue 1·50 2·40
187 20c. orange 1·90 90
188 21c. grey 4·50 2·10
254 25c. red 20 20
255 27½c. brown 1·50 1·60
256 30c. bistre 1·75 1·10
257 50c. green 2·10 20
192 50c. green (21 × 26 mm) 16·00 55
193 1½g. brown (21 × 26 mm) 21·00 1·40
194 2½g. purple (21 × 26 mm) 21·00 1·40
See also Nos. 258/61.

1942.
195 – 1c. brown and violet 25 25
196 – 1½c. green and blue 25 25
197 – 2c. brown and black 1·25 35
198 – 2½c. yellow and green 25 25
199 33 5c. black and red 1·00 25
200 – 6c. blue and purple 60 60
DESIGNS—HORIZ: 1c. Bonaire. 2c. Saba. 2½c. St. Maarten. 6c. Curacao. VERT: 1½c. St. Eustatius.

34 Queen Wilhelmina and Douglas DC-2 over Atlantic Ocean

35 Dutch Royal Family

1942. Air.
201 34 10c. blue and green 35 35
202 – 15c. green and red 45 35
203 – 20c. green and brown 55 35
204 – 25c. brown and blue 50 35
205 – 30c. violet and red 55 55
206 34 35c. green and violet 90 55
207 – 40c. brown and green 1·10 55
208 – 45c. black and red 65 35
209 – 50c. black and violet 1·60 35
210 – 60c. blue and brown 1·60 90
211 34 70c. blue and brown 2·00 90
212 – 1g.40 green and blue 11·00 1·75
213 – 2g.80 blue & ultramarine 16·00 2·50
214 – 5g. green and purple 27·00 13·00
215 – 10g. brown and green 35·00 20·00
DESIGNS: 15, 40c., 1g.40, Fokker airplane "Zilvermeeuw" over coast. 20, 45c., 2g.80, Map of Netherlands West Indies. 25, 50c., 5g. Side view of Douglas DC-2 airplane. 30, 60c., 10g. Front view of Douglas DC-2 airplane.

1943. Birth of Princess Margriet.
216 35 1½c. orange 30 30
217 2½c. red 30 30
218 6c. black 1·00 65
219 10c. blue 1·00 80

1943. Air. Dutch Prisoners of War Relief Fund. Nos. 212/15 surch **Voor Krijgsgevangenen** and new value.
220 40c.+50c. on 1g.40 green & bl 6·25 4·75
221 45c.+50c. on 2g.80 blue & ult 4·25 4·50
222 50c.+75c. on 5g. green & pur 6·25 4·50
223 60c.+100c. on 10g. brn & grn 6·25 4·75

37 Princess Juliana

38 Map of Netherlands

1944. Air. Red Cross Fund. Cross in red; frame in red and blue.
224 37 10c.+10c. brown 2·10 1·60
225 15c.+25c. green 2·00 1·60
226 20c.+25c. black 2·00 1·75
227 25c.+25c. grey 2·00 1·75
228 30c.+50c. purple 2·00 1·75
229 35c.+50c. brown 2·00 1·75
230 40c.+50c. green 2·00 2·00
231 50c.+100c. violet 2·00 2·00

1946. Air. Netherlands Relief Fund. Value in black.
232 38 10c.+10c. orange & grey 1·10 1·25
233 15c.+25c. grey and red 1·25 1·25
234 20c.+25c. orange & grn 1·25 1·25
235 25c.+25c. grey & violet 1·25 1·25
236 30c.+50c. buff & green 1·25 1·40
237 35c.+50c. orange & red 1·25 1·40
238 40c.+75c. buff & blue 1·25 1·60
239 50c.+100c. buff & violet 1·25 1·60

1946. Air. National Relief Fund. As T **38** but showing map of Netherlands Indies and inscr "CURACAO HELPT ONZEOOST". Value in black.
240 10c.+10c. buff & violet 1·10 1·25
241 15c.+25c. buff & blue 1·25 1·25
242 20c.+25c. orange & red 1·25 1·25
243 25c.+25c. buff & green 1·25 1·25
244 30c.+50c. grey & violet 1·25 1·40
245 35c.+50c. orange & grn 1·25 1·40
246 40c.+75c. grey & red 1·25 1·60
247 50c.+100c. orange & grey 1·25 1·60

1947. Size 25 × 31½ mm.
258 31 1½g. brown 3·50 1·10
259 2½g. purple 45·00 10·75
260 5g. olive £100 £150
261 10g. orange £125 £275

40 Aeroplane and Posthorn

41 Douglas DC-2 and Waves

1947. Air.
262 40 6c. black 35 15
263 10c. red 35 15
264 12½c. purple 50 15
265 15c. blue 50 30
266 20c. green 65 35
267 25c. orange 65 20
268 30c. violet 90 35
269 35c. red 90 55
270 40c. green 90 55
271 45c. violet 1·10 80
272 50c. red 1·10 20
273 60c. blue 1·25 55
274 70c. brown 2·75 1·10
275 41 1g.50 black 2·00 80
276 2g.50 red 13·50 3·50
277 5g. green 21·00 7·00
278 7g.50 blue 65·00 55·00
279 10g. violet 50·00 17·00
280 15g. red 80·00 65·00
281 25g. brown 75·00 55·00

1947. Netherlands Indies Social Welfare Fund. Surch **NIWIN** and value.
282 28 1½c.+2½c. on 6c. purple 90 90
283 2½c.+5c. on 10c. red 90 90
284 5c.+7½c. on 15c. blue 90 90

43

45 Queen Wilhelmina

1948. Portrait of Queen Wilhelmina.
285 43 6c. purple 1·00 1·10
286 10c. red 1·00 1·50
287 12½c. green 1·00 90
288 15c. blue 1·00 1·10
289 20c. orange 1·00 2·00
290 21c. black 1·00 2·00
291 25c. mauve 35 20
292 27½c. brown 20·00 17·00
293 30c. olive 18·00 1·25
294 50c. green 16·00 20
295 1g.50c. brn (21½ × 28½ mm) 28·00 7·50

1948. Golden Jubilee.
296 45 6c. orange 65 65
297 12½c. blue 65 65

46 Queen Juliana

47

1948. Accession of Queen Juliana.
298 46 6c. red 55 55
299 12½c. green 55 55

1948. Child Welfare Fund. Inscr "VOOR HET KIND".
300 47 6c.+10c. brown 2·40 1·60
301 – 10c.+15c. red 2·40 1·60
302 – 12½c.+20c. green 2·40 1·60
303 47 15c.+25c. blue 2·40 1·75
304 – 20c.+30c. brown 2·40 1·90
305 – 25c.+35c. violet 2·40 2·00
DESIGNS—10, 20c. Native boy in straw hat. 12½, 25c. Curly-haired girl.

POSTAGE DUE STAMPS

For stamps as Nos. D42/61 and D96/105 in other colours see Postage Due stamps of Netherlands Indies and Surinam.

D 3

D 5

1889.
D42C D 3 2½c. black and green 2·40 2·75
D43C 5c. black and green 1·60 1·60
D44C 10c. black and green 24·00 21·00
D45C 12½c. black and green £275 £140
D46C 15c. black and green 16·00 14·00
D47C 20c. black and green 7·00 7·00
D48C 25c. black and green £140 £110
D49C 30c. black and green 8·50 7·25

D50C 40c. black and green 8·50 7·25
D51C 50c. black and green 30·00 23·00

1892.
D52C D 5 2½c. black and green 35 30
D53C 5c. black and green 65 55
D54C 10c. black and green 1·50 50
D55A 12½c. black and green 1·90 1·25
D56C 15c. black and green 2·40 1·25
D57A 20c. black and green 3·00 1·25
D58C 25c. black and green 1·40 95
D59A 30c. black and green 21·00 12·00
D60A 40c. black and green 25·00 12·50
D61A 50c. black and green 40·00 13·50

1915.
D 96a D 5 2½c. green 55 55
D 97a 5c. green 55 55
D 98a 10c. green 50 50
D 99a 12½c. green 1·40 1·50
D100a 15c. green 1·40 1·50
D101a 20c. green 55 1·00
D102a 25c. green 20 10
D103a 30c. green 2·10 2·40
D104 40c. green 2·50 3·00
D105a 50c. green 1·75 2·25

For later issues see **NETHERLANDS ANTILLES**.

CYPRUS Pt. 1

An island in the East Mediterranean. A British colony, which became a republic within the British Commonwealth in 1960.

1880. 12 pence = 1 shilling.
1881. 40 paras = 1 piastre; 180 piastres = 1 pound.
1955. 1000 mils = 1 pound.
1983. 100 cents = 1 pound.

1880. Stamps of Great Britain (Queen Victoria) optd **CYPRUS**.
1 **7** ½d. red £100 £100
2 **5** 1d. red 11·00 32·00
3 **41** 2½d. mauve 2·25 8·00
4 – 4d. green (No. 153) £120 £200
5 – 6d. grey (No. 161) £500 £650
6 – 1s. green (No. 150) £650 £450

1881. Stamps of Great Britain (Queen Victoria) surch with new values.
9 **5** ½d. on 1d. red 45·00 65·00
10 30 paras on 1d. red £100 80·00

7

13

1881.
31 **7** ½pi. green 4·50 70
40 ½pi. green and red 4·00 1·25
32 30pa. mauve 4·50 4·50
41 30pa. mauve and green 2·00 1·25
33 1pi. red 11·00 1·75
42 1pi. red and blue 5·50 1·25
34 2pi. blue 14·00 1·75
43 2pi. blue and purple 6·50 1·25
35a 4pi. olive 18·00 23·00
44 4pi. olive and purple 14·00 4·50
21 6pi. grey 45·00 17·00
45 6pi. brown and green 11·00 14·00
46 9pi. brown and red 15·00 17·00
22 12pi. brown £170 35·00
47 12pi. brown and black 17·00 50·00
48 18pi. grey and brown 45·00 45·00
49 45pi. purple and blue 90·00 £130

1882. Surch.
25 **7** ½pi. on ½pi. green £130 6·50
24 30pa. on 1pi. red £1400 £100

1903. As T **7** but portrait of King Edward VII.
60 5pa. brown and black 1·00 70
61 10pa. orange and green 3·00 50
50 ½pi. green and red 3·75 1·25
51 30pa. violet and green 7·00 2·75
64 1pi. red and blue 4·25 1·00
65 2pi. blue and purple 5·50 1·75
66 4pi. brown and purple 10·00 7·50
67 6pi. brown and green 12·00 15·00
68 9pi. brown and red 28·00 8·50
69 12pi. brown and black 24·00 38·00
70 18pi. black and brown 30·00 11·00
71 45pi. purple and blue 75·00 £140

1912. As T **7** but portrait of King George V.
74b 10pa. orange and green 2·25 1·25
86 10pa. grey and yellow 12·00 6·50
75 ½pi. green and red 1·75 20
76 30pa. violet and green 2·50 60
88 30pa. green 7·00 40
77 1pi. red and blue 3·75 1·75
90 1pi. violet and red 3·00 4·00
91 1½pi. yellow and black 4·00 4·50
78 2pi. blue and purple 6·50 2·00
93 2pi. red and blue 9·00 22·00
94 2¾pi. blue and purple 7·00 9·00
79 4pi. olive and purple 4·25 4·75
80 6pi. brown and green 3·50 8·50
81 9pi. brown and red 23·00 26·00
82 12pi. brown and black 13·00 32·00
83 18pi. black and brown 25·00 29·00
84 45pi. purple and blue 75·00 £120
100 10s. green and red on yellow £350 £750
101 £1 purple and black on red £1000 £1700

1924.
103 **13** ¼pi. grey and brown 1·00 15
104 ½pi. black 2·50 8·00
118 ½pi. green 2·25 95
105 ¾pi. green 2·25 90
119 ¾pi. black 2·00 10
106 1pi. purple and brown 2·00 70
107 1½pi. orange and black 2·00 6·50
120 1½pi. red 2·50 30
108 2pi. red and green 2·25 12·00
121 2pi. yellow and black 5·50 3·25
122 2½pi. blue 3·00 30
109 2¾pi. blue and purple 3·25 2·75
110 4pi. olive and purple 3·25 2·50
111 4½pi. blk & orge on green 3·50 3·50
112 6pi. brown and green 3·75 5·50
113 9pi. brown and purple 6·00 4·25
114 12pi. brown and black 9·00 55·00
115 18pi. black and orange 20·00 5·00
116 45pi. purple and blue 35·00 38·00
117 90pi. grn & red on yellow 80·00 £170
102 £1 purple & black on red £325 £650
117a £5 black on yellow £2750 £6000

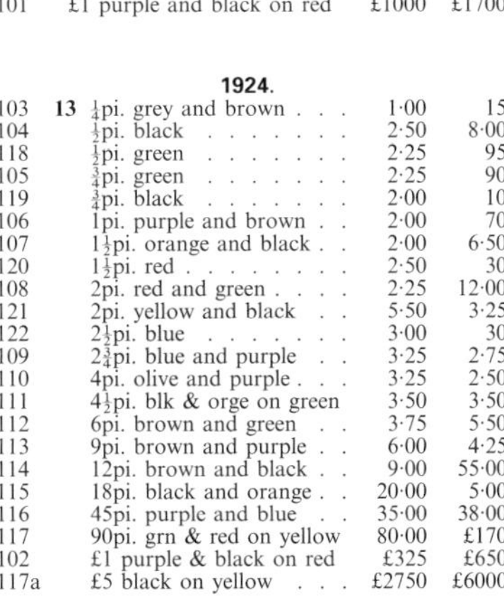

14 Silver coin of Amathus, 6th-century B.C.

1928. 50th Anniv of British Rule. Dated "1878 1928".
123 **14** ¾pi. violet 2·75 1·00
124 – 1pi. black and blue 3·00 1·50
125 – 1½pi. red 4·50 2·00
126 – 2½pi. blue 3·50 2·25
127 – 4pi. brown 5·50 6·00
128 – 6pi. blue 6·50 21·00
129 – 9pi. purple 7·50 11·00
130 – 18pi. black and brown 17·00 18·00
131 – 45pi. violet and blue 38·00 48·00
132 – £1 blue and brown £200 £300
DESIGNS—VERT: 1pi. Philosopher Zeno; 2½pi. Discovery of body of St. Barnabas; 4pi. Cloister, Abbey of Bella Paise; 9pi. Tekke of Umm Haram; 18pi. Statue of Richard I, Westminster; 45pi. St. Nicholas Cathedral, Famagusta, (now Lala Mustafa Pasha Mosque); £1 King George V. HORIZ: 1½pi. Map of Cyprus; 6pi. Badge of Cyprus.

24 Ruins of Vouni Palace

30 St. Sophia Cathedral, Nicosia (now Selimiye Mosque)

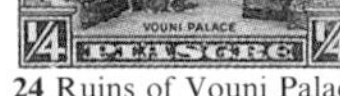

1934.
133 **24** ¼pi. blue and brown 1·00 50
134 – ½pi. green 1·25 1·00
135 – ¾pi. black and violet 1·00 10
136 – 1pi. black and brown 1·00 80
137 – 1½pi. red 1·50 55
138 – 2½pi. blue 1·75 1·75
139 **30** 4½pi. black and red 3·00 3·75
140 – 6pi. black and blue 9·00 12·00
141 – 9pi. brown and violet 6·50 4·50
142 – 18pi. black and green 40·00 28·00
143 – 45pi. green and black 65·00 48·00
DESIGNS—HORIZ: ½pi. Small Marble Forum, Salamis; ¾pi. Church of St. Barnabas and St. Hilarion, Peristerona; 1pi. Roman theatre, Soli; 1½pi. Kyrenia Harbour; 2½pi. Kolossi Castle; 45pi. Forest scene, Troodos. VERT: 6pi. Bayraktar Mosque, Nicosia; 9pi. Queen's Window, St. Hilarion Castle; 18pi. Buyuk Khan, Nicosia.
The ¼pi. to 2½pi. values have a medallion portrait of King George V.

1935. Silver Jubilee. As T **13** of Antigua.
144 ¾pi. blue and grey 1·75 40
145 1½pi. blue and red 3·50 2·50
146 2½pi. brown and blue 3·75 1·50
147 9pi. grey and purple 13·00 13·00

1937. Coronation. As T **2** of Aden.
148 ¾pi. grey 60 20
149 1½pi. red 90 80
150 2½pi. blue 2·00 1·25

36 Map of Cyprus

37 Othello's Tower, Famagusta

38 King George VI

1938.
151 – ¼pi. blue and brown 20 20
152 – ½pi. green 50 10
152a – ½pi. violet 2·25 20
153 – ¾pi. black and violet 14·00 50
154 – 1pi. orange 80 10
155 – 1½pi. red 5·50 1·50
155a – 1½pi. violet 50 30
155ab – 1½pi. green 2·75 40
155b – 2pi. black and red 70 10
156 – 2½pi. blue 24·00 2·50
156a – 3pi. blue 1·50 15
156b – 4pi. blue 3·00 30
157 **36** 4½pi. grey 70 10
158 – 6pi. black and blue 1·25 1·00
159 **37** 9pi. black and purple 2·25 20
160 – 18pi. black and olive 6·00 85
161 – 45pi. green and black 18·00 2·50
162 **38** 90pi. mauve and black 22·00 5·00
163 – £1 red and blue 48·00 24·00
DESIGNS: 2pi. Peristerona Church; 3pi., 4pi. Kolossi Castle. All other values except 4½pi., 9pi., 90pi. and £1 have designs as 1934 issue but portrait of King George VI.

1946. Victory. As T **9** of Aden.
164 1½pi. violet 15 10
165 3pi. blue 15 15

1948. Silver Wedding. As T **10/11** of Aden.
166 1½pi. violet 50 20
167 £1 blue 42·00 48·00

1949. U.P.U. As T **20/23** of Antigua.
168 1½pi. violet 40 70
169 2pi. red 1·50 1·50
170 3pi. blue 70 1·00
171 9pi. purple 1·50 1·50

1953. Coronation. As T **13** of Aden.
172 1½pi. black and green 1·25 10

39 Carobs

42 Mavrovouni Copper Pyrites Mine

49 St. Hilarion Castle

53 Arms of Byzantium, Lusignan, Ottoman Empire and Venice

1955.
173 **39** 2m. brown 10 40
174 – 3m. violet 10 15
175 – 5m. orange 70 10
176 **42** 10m. brown and green 1·00 10
177 – 15m. olive and blue 2·50 45
178 – 20m. brown and blue 1·00 15
179 – 25m. turquoise 2·00 60
180 – 30m. black and lake 1·50 10
181 – 35m. brown and turquoise 65 40
182 – 40m. green and brown 1·00 60
183 **49** 50m. blue and brown 85 30
184 – 100m. mauve and green 12·00 60
185 – 250m. blue and brown 9·00 8·50
186 – 500m. slate and purple 27·00 11·00
187 **53** £1 lake and slate 24·00 38·00
DESIGNS—As Type **39**: 3m. Grapes; 5m. Oranges. As Type **42**: 15m. Troodos Forest; 20m. Beach of Aphrodite; 25m. 5th-century B.C. coin of Paphos; 30m. Kyrenia; 35m. Harvest in Mesaoria; 40m. Famagusta harbour. As Type **49**: 100m. Hala Sultan Tekke; 250m. Kanakaria Church. As Type **53**: 500m. Coins of Salamis, Paphos, Citium and Idalium.

(**54**)

55 Map of Cyprus

1960. Nos. 173/87 optd as T **54** ("CYPRUS REPUBLIC" in Greek and Turkish).
188 **39** 2m. brown 20 75
189 – 3m. violet 20 15
190 – 5m. orange 1·00 10
191 **42** 10m. brown and green 80 10
192 – 15m. olive and blue 75 10
193 – 20m. brown and blue 50 1·50
194 – 25m. turquoise 1·25 1·50
195 – 30m. black and lake 1·75 10
196 – 35m. brown and turquoise 1·75 70
197 – 40m. green and brown 2·00 2·25
198 **49** 50m. blue and brown 2·00 60
199 – 100m. mauve and green 9·00 60
200 – 250m. blue and brown 25·00 3·75
201 – 500m. slate and purple 40·00 18·00
202 **53** £1 lake and slate 48·00 50·00

1960. Constitution of Republic.
203 **55** 10m. sepia and green 30 10
204 30m. blue and brown 65 10
205 100m. purple and slate 2·00 2·00

56 Doves

1962. Europa.
206 **56** 10m. purple and mauve 10 10
207 40m. blue and cobalt 20 15
208 100m. emerald and green 20 20

57 Campaign Emblem

1962. Malaria Eradication.
209 **57** 10m. black and green 15 15
210 30m. black and brown 30 15

63 St. Barnabas's Church

1962.
211 – 3m. brown and orange 10 30
212 – 5m. purple and green 10 10
213 – 10m. black and green 15 10
214 – 15m. black and purple 30 15
215 **63** 25m. brown and chestnut 30 20
216 – 30m. blue and light blue 20 10
217 – 35m. green and blue 35 10
218 – 40m. black and blue 1·25 1·75
219 – 50m. bronze and bistre 50 10
220 – 100m. brown and bistre 3·50 30
221 – 250m. black and brown 8·50 2·25
222 – 500m. brown and green 15·00 8·00
223 – £1 bronze and grey 16·00 28·00
DESIGNS—VERT: 3m. Iron Age jug; 5m. Grapes; 10m. Bronze head of Apollo; 15m. Selimiye Mosque, Nicosia; 35m. Head of Aphrodite; 100m. Hala Sultan Tekke; 500m. Mouflon. HORIZ: 30m. Temple of Apollo Hylates; 40m. Skiing, Troodos; 50m. Salamis Gymnasium; 250m. Bella Paise Abbey; £1 St. Hilarion Castle.

72 Europa "Tree"

1963. Europa.
224 **72** 10m. blue and black 1·50 20
225 40m. red and black 6·50 2·00
226 150m. green and black 22·00 6·00

73 Harvester

75 Wolf Cub in Camp

1963. Freedom from Hunger.
227 **73** 25c. ochre, sepia and blue . . . 30 25
228 – 75m. grey, black and lake . . . 1·75 1·00
DESIGN: 75m. Demeter, Goddess of Corn.

1963. 50th Anniv of Cyprus Scout Movement and 3rd Commonwealth Scout Conference, Platres. Multicoloured.
229 3m. Type **75** 10 20
230 20m. Sea Scout 35 10
231 150m. Scout with Mouflon . . . 1·00 2·50
MS231a 110 × 90 mm. Nos. 229/31 (sold at 250m.) Imperf . . . £100 £180

79 Children's Centre, Kyrenia

1963. Centenary of Red Cross. Multicoloured.
232 10m. Nurse tending child (vert) 50 15
233 100m. Type **79** . . . . 2·00 3·50

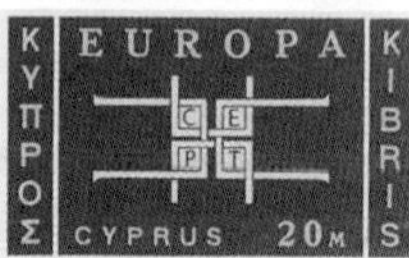

80 "Co-operation" (emblem)

1963. Europa.
234 **80** 20m. buff, blue and violet . . . 2·00 40
235 30m. grey, yellow and blue . . . 2·25 40
236 150m. buff, blue and brown . . . . 19·00 9·00

1964. U.N. Security Council's Cyprus Resolution, March 1964. Nos. 213 etc. optd with U.N. emblem and **1964**.
237 10m. black and green 15 10
238 30m. blue and light blue . . 15 10
239 40m. black and blue 15 20
240 50m. bronze and bistre . . . 15 10
241 100m. brown and bistre . . . 15 50

82 Soli Theatre

1964. 400th Birth Anniv of Shakespeare. Mult.
242 15m. Type **82** 40 15
243 35m. Curium Theatre 40 15
244 50m. Salamis Theatre 40 15
245 100m. Othello Tower, and scene from "Othello" . . . 1·00 2·25

86 Running

89 Europa "Flower"

1964. Olympic Games, Tokyo.
246 **86** 10m. brown, black & yell . . . 10 10
247 – 25m. brown, black and slate 20 10
248 – 75m. brown, black and chest 35 65
MS248a 110 × 90 mm. Nos. 246/8 (sold at 250m.) Imperf . . . 6·00 14·00
DESIGNS—HORIZ: 25m. Boxing; 75m. Charioteers.

1964. Europa.
249 **89** 20m. brown and ochre . . 1·00 10
250 30m. ultramarine and blue . . 1·25 10
251 150m. olive and green . . 13·00 5·00

90 Dionysus and Acme

1964. Cyprus Wines. Multicoloured.
252 10m. Type **90** 25 10
253 40m. Silenus (satyr) (vert) . . 55 1·25
254 50m. Commandaria wine (vert) 55 10
255 100m. Wine factory . . . . 1·50 2·00

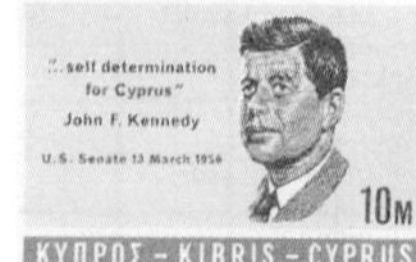

94 President Kennedy

1965. President Kennedy Commemoration.
256 **94** 10m. blue 10 10
257 40m. green 25 35
258 100m. red 30 35
MS258a 110 × 90 mm. Nos. 256/8 (sold at 250m.) Imperf . . . 3·00 7·00

95 "Old Age"

98 I.T.U. Emblem and Symbols

1965. Introduction of Social Insurance Law.
259 **95** 30m. drab and green . . . 15 10
260 – 45m. green, blue and ultramarine 20 10
261 – 75m. brown and flesh . . . 1·25 2·50
DESIGNS—(As Type **95**): 45m. "Accident". LARGER (23 × 48 mm): 75m. "Maternity".

1965. Centenary of I.T.U.
262 **98** 15m. black, brown & yell . . 75 20
263 60m. black, grn & lt grn . . 6·50 2·75
264 75m. black, indigo & bl . . 7·00 4·75

99 I.C.Y. Emblem

1965. International Co-operation Year.
265 **99** 50m. brown and green . . 75 10
266 100m. purple and green . . 1·25 50

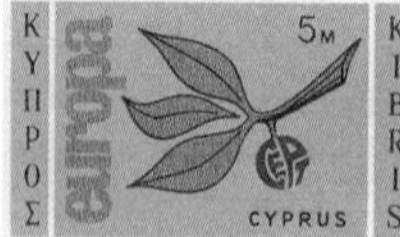

100 Europa "Sprig"

1965. Europa.
267 **100** 5m. black, brown & orge . . 25 10
268 45m. black, brown & grn . . 1·75 1·50
269 150m. black, brn & grey . . 5·50 3·75

1966. U.N. General Assembly's Cyprus Resolution. Nos. 211, 213, 216 and 221 optd **U.N. Resolution on Cyprus 18 Dec. 1965**.
270 3m. brown and orange . . . 10 30
271 10m. black and green 10 10
272 30m. blue and light blue . . 10 15
273 250m. black and brown . . . 55 2·00

102 Discovery of St. Barnabas's Body

1966. 1900th Death Anniv of St. Barnabas.
274 **102** 15m. multicoloured . . . 10 10
275 – 25m. drab, black and blue . 15 10
276 – 100m. multicoloured . . . 45 2·00
MS277 110 × 91 mm. 250m. multicoloured (imperf) . . . 3·50 13·00

DESIGNS—HORIZ: 25m. St. Barnabas's Chapel; 250m. "Privileges of Cyprus Church". VERT: 100m. St. Barnabas (icon).

1966. No. 211 surch **5M**.
278 5m. on 3m. brown & orange . . 10 10

107 General K. S. Thimayya and U.N. Emblem

1966. General Thimayya Commemoration.
279 **107** 50m. black and brown . . 30 10

108 Europa "Ship"

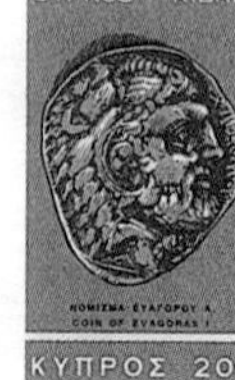

113 Silver Coin of Evagoras I

109 Stavrovouni Monastery

1966. Europa.
280 **108** 20m. green and blue . . . 25 10
281 30m. purple and blue . . 25 10
282 150m. bistre and blue . . 2·00 3·00

1966. Multicoloured.
283 3m. Type **109** 40 10
284 5m. Church of St. James, Trikomo 10 10
285 10m. Zeno of Citium (marble bust) 15 10
286 15m. Minoan wine ship of 700 B.C. (painting) 15 10
287 20m. Type **113** . . . . . . 1·25 1·00
288 25m. Sleeping Eros (marble statue) 30 10
289 30m. St. Nicholas Cathedral, Famagusta 50 20
290 35m. Gold sceptre from Curium 50 30
291 40m. Silver dish from 7th century 70 30
292 50m. Silver coin of Alexander the Great 90 10
293 100m. Vase, 7th century B.C. . . 3·75 15
294 250m. Bronze ingot-stand . . 1·00 40
295 500m. "The Rape of Ganymede" (mosaic) . . . 2·25 70
296 £1 Aphrodite (marble statue) . . 2·00 6·50
DESIGNS—VERT (As Type **109**): 5m. and 10m. HORIZ (As Type **113**): 15m., 25m. and 50m. VERT (As Type **113**): 30m., 35m., 40m. and 100m.
Nos. 294/6 are as Type **113** but larger, 28 × 40 mm.

123 Power Station, Limassol

124 Cogwheels

1967. First Development Programme. Mult.
297 10m. Type **123** 10 10
298 15m. Arghaka-Maghounda Dam (vert) 15 10
299 35m. Troodos Highway (vert) . . 20 10
300 50m. Hilton Hotel, Nicosia (vert) 20 10
301 100m. Famagusta Harbour (vert) . . . . 20 1·10

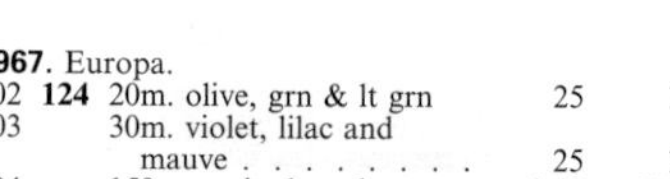

1967. Europa.
302 **124** 20m. olive, grn & lt grn . . 25 10
303 30m. violet, lilac and mauve 25 10
304 150m. sepia, brn chestnut . . 1·40 2·25

125 Throwing the Javelin

1967. Athletic Games, Nicosia. Multicoloured.
305 15m. Type **125** 20 10
306 35m. Running 20 35
307 100m. High-jumping . . . . 30 1·00
MS308 110 × 90 mm. 250m. Running (amphora) and Map of Eastern Mediterranean (imperf) . . . 1·25 6·50

127 Ancient Monuments

1967. International Tourist Year. Multicoloured.
309 10m. Type **127** 10 10
310 40m. Famagusta Beach . . . 15 90
311 50m. Hawker Siddeley Comet-4 at Nicosia Airport . . 15 10
312 100m. Skier and youth hostel . . 20 95

128 Saint Andrew Mosaic

129 "The Crucifixion" (icon)

1967. Centenary of St Andrew's Monastery.
313 **128** 25m. multicoloured . . . 10 10

1967. Cyprus Art Exhibition, Paris.
314 **129** 50m. multicoloured . . . 10 10

130 The Three Magi

131 Human Rights Emblem over Stars

1967. 20th Anniv of U.N.E.S.C.O.
315 **130** 75m. multicoloured . . . 20 20

1968. Human Rights Year. Multicoloured.
316 50m. Type **131** 10 10
317 90m. Human Rights and U.N. emblems 30 70
MS318 95 × 75½ mm. 250m. Scroll of Declaration . . . 60 4·75

134 Europa "Key"

1968. Europa.
319 **134** 20m. multicoloured . . . 15 10
320 30m. multicoloured . . . 15 10
321 150m. multicoloured . . . 80 2·25

135 U.N. Children's Fund Symbol and Boy drinking Milk

1968. 21st Anniv of U.N.I.C.E.F.
322 **135** 35m. brown, red and black 10 10

136 Aesculapius

137 Throwing the Discus

1968. 20th Anniv of W.H.O.
323 **136** 50m. black, green and olive 10 10

1968. Olympic Games, Mexico. Multicoloured.
324 10m. Type **137** 10 10
325 25m. Sprint finish 10 10
326 100m. Olympic Stadium (horiz) . . . . 20 1·25

138 I.L.O. Emblem

141 Europa Emblem

139 Mercator's Map of Cyprus, 1554

1969. 50th Anniv of I.L.O.
327 **138** 50m. brown and blue . . 15 10
328 90m. brown, black and grey 15 55

1969. 1st International Congress of Cypriot Studies.
329 **139** 35m. multicoloured . . . 20 30
330 – 50m. multicoloured . . . 20 10
DESIGN: 50m. Blaeu's map of Cyprus, 1635.

1969. Europa.
331 **141** 20m. multicoloured . . . 20 10
332 30m. multicoloured . . . 20 10
333 150m. multicoloured . . . 80 2·00

142 European Roller ("Roller")

1969. Birds of Cyprus. Multicoloured.
334 5m. Type **142** 40 15
335 15m. Audouin's gull 60 15
336 20m. Cyprus warbler 60 15
337 30m. Jay ("Cyprus Jay") (vert) 60 15
338 40m. Hoopoe (vert) 65 30
339 90m. Eleonora's falcon (vert) 1·50 5·00

143 "The Nativity" (12th-century wall painting)

1969. Christmas. Multicoloured.
340 20m. Type **143** 15 10
341 45m. "The Nativity" (14th-century wall painting) 15 20
MS342 110 × 90 mm. 250m. "Virgin and Child between Archangels Michael and Gabriel" (6th–7th-century Mosaic) (imperf) 3·00 12·00

146 Mahatma Gandhi

1970. Birth Centenary of Mahatma Gandhi.
343 **146** 25m. blue, drab and black 15 10
344 75m. brown, drab and black 20 65

147 "Flaming Sun"

1970. Europa.
345 **147** 20m. brown, yell & orge 20 10
346 30m. blue, yellow & orge 20 10
347 150m. purple, yell & orge 80 2·50

148 Gladioli

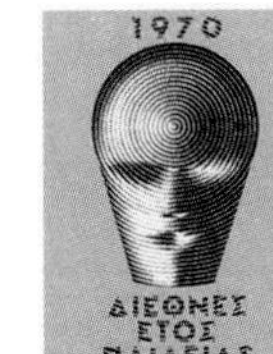
149 I.E.Y. Emblem

1970. Nature Conservation Year. Multicoloured.
348 10m. Type **148** 10 10
349 50m. Poppies 15 10
350 90m. Giant fennel . . . . . 50 1·40

1970. Anniversaries and Events.
351 **149** 5m. black and brown . . 10 10
352 – 15m. multicoloured . . . 10 10
353 – 75m. multicoloured . . . 15 75
DESIGNS AND EVENTS: 5m. International Education Year. HORIZ: 15m. Mosaic (50th General Assembly of International Vine and Wine Office); 75m. Globe, dove and U.N. emblem (25th anniv of United Nations).

152 Virgin and Child

153 Cotton Napkin

1970. Christmas. Wall-painting from Church of Panayia Podhythou, Galata. Multicoloured.
354 25m. Archangel (facing right) 15 20
355 25m. Type **152** 15 20
356 25m. Archangel (facing left) 15 20
357 75m. Virgin and Child between Archangels (42 × 30 mm) 15 30

1971. Multicoloured.
358 3m. Type **153** 30 35
359 5m. Saint George and Dragon (19th-century bas-relief) 10 10
360 10m. Woman in festival costume 15 50
361 15m. Archaic Bichrome Kylix (cup) (horiz) 20 10
362 20m. A pair of donors (Saint Mamas Church) 35 65
363 25m. "The Creation" (6th-century mosaic) . . . 30 10
364 30m. Athena and horse-drawn chariot (4th-century B.C. terracotta) (horiz) . . 30 10
365 40m. Shepherd playing pipe (14th-century fresco) . . . 1·00 1·00
366 50m. Hellenistic head (3rd-century B.C.) 80 10
367 75m. "Angel" (mosaic detail), Kanakaria Church . . . . 1·75 1·00
368 90m. Mycenaean silver bowl (horiz) . . . . 2·00 2·00
369 250m. Moufflon (detail of 3rd-century mosaic) (horiz) 1·50 30
370 500m. Ladies and sacred tree (detail 6th-century amphora) (horiz) 80 40
371 £1 Horned god from Enkomi (12th-century bronze statue) . . . . 1·50 60
SIZES: 24 × 37 mm or 37 × 24 mm 10m. to 90m., 41 × 28 mm or 28 × 41 mm 250m. to £1.

154 Europa Chain

1971. Europa.
372 **154** 20m. blue, ultram & blk 15 10
373 30m. green, myrtle & blk 15 10
374 150m. yellow, grn & blk 80 2·75

155 Archbishop Kyprianos

1971. 150th Anniv of Greek War of Independence. Multicoloured.
375 15m. Type **155** 10 10
376 30m. "Taking the Oath" (horiz) 10 10
377 100m. Bishop Germanos, flag and freedom-fighters . . . 20 50

156 Kyrenia Castle

1971. Tourism. Multicoloured.
378 15m. Type **156** 10 10
379 25m. Gourd on sunny beach (vert) 10 10
380 60m. Mountain scenery (vert) 20 60
381 100m. Church of Saint Evlalios, Lambousa . . . 20 65

157 Madonna and Child in Stable

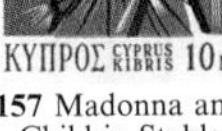
159 "Communications"

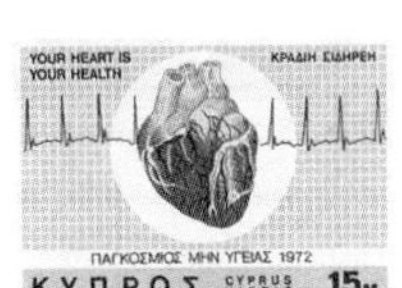
158 Heart

1971. Christmas. Multicoloured.
382 10m. Type **157** 10 10
383 50m. The Three Wise Men 15 35
384 100m. The Shepherds 20 35

1972. World Heart Month.
385 **158** 15m. multicoloured . . . 10 10
386 50m. multicoloured . . . 20 45

1972. Europa.
387 **159** 20m. orange, sepia & brn 25 15
388 30m. orange, ultram & bl 25 15
389 150m. orge, myrtle & grn 2·00 4·00

160 Archery

1972. Olympic Games, Munich. Multicoloured.
390 10m. Type **160** 25 10
391 40m. Wrestling 35 15
392 100m. Football . . . . . . 75 1·40

161 Stater of Marion

162 Bathing the Child Jesus

1972. Ancient Coins of Cyprus (1st series).
393 **161** 20m. blue, black and silver 20 10
394 – 30m. blue, black and silver 20 10
395 – 40m. brown, blk & silver 20 20
396 – 100m. pink, black and silver . . . . 60 1·00
COINS: 30m. Stater of Paphos; 40m. Stater of Lapithos; 100m. Stater of Idalion.
See also Nos. 486/9.

1972. Christmas. Detail of mural in Holy Cross Church, Agiasmati. Multicoloured.
397 10m. Type **162** 10 10
398 20m. The Magi 10 10
399 100m. The Nativity 15 30
MS400 100 × 90 mm. 250m. Showing the mural in full (imperf) 1·10 4·50

163 Mount Olympus, Troodos

1973. 29th International Ski Federation Congress. Multicoloured.
401 20m. Type **163** 10 10
402 100m. Congress emblem . . . 25 35

164 Europa "Posthorn"

1973. Europa.
403 **164** 20m. multicoloured . . . 15 10
404 30m. multicoloured . . . 15 10
405 150m. multicoloured . . . 1·10 3·00

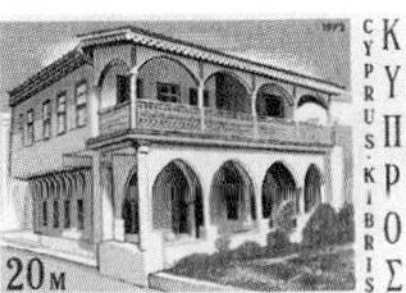
165 Archbishop's Palace, Nicosia

1973. Traditional Architecture. Multicoloured.
406 20m. Type **165** 10 10
407 30m. House of Hajigeorgajis Cornessios, Nicosia (vert) 10 10
408 50m. House at Gourri, 1850 (vert) 15 10
409 100m. House at Rizokarpaso, 1772 . . . . 40 75

1973. No. 361 surch **20M**.
410 20m. on 15m. multicoloured 15 15

167 Scout Emblem

168 Archangel Gabriel

1973. Anniversaries and Events.
411 **167** 10m. green and brown . . 20 10
412 – 25m. blue and lilac . . . 20 10
413 – 35m. olive, stone and green 20 25
414 – 50m. blue and indigo . . 20 10
415 – 100m. brown and sepia 50 80
DESIGNS AND EVENTS—VERT: 10m. (60th anniv of Cyprus Boy Scouts); 50m. Airline emblem (25th anniv of Cyprus Airways); 100m. Interpol emblem (50th anniv of Interpol). HORIZ: 25m. Outlines of Cyprus and the E.E.C. (Association of Cyprus with "Common Market"); 35m. F.A.O. emblem (10th anniv of F.A.O.).

1973. Christmas. Murals from Araka Church. Multicoloured.
416 10m. Type **168** 10 10
417 20m. Madonna and Child . . 10 10
418 100m. Araka Church (horiz) 40 75

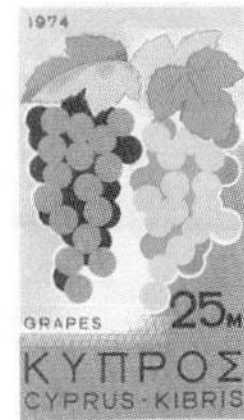
169 Grapes

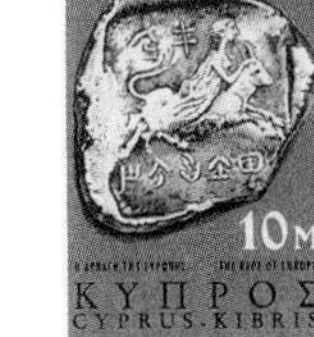
170 "The Rape of Europa" (Silver Stater of Marion)

1974. Products of Cyprus. Multicoloured.
419 25m. Type **169** 10 15
420 50m. Grapefruit 20 60
421 50m. Oranges 20 60
422 50m. Lemons 20 60

1974. Europa.
423 **170** 10m. multicoloured . . . 15 10
424 40m. multicoloured . . . 35 30
425 150m. multicoloured . . . 1·10 2·75

171 Title Page of A. Kyprianos' "History of Cyprus" (1788)

174 "Refugees"

1974. 2nd International Congress of Cypriot Studies. Multicoloured.
426 10m. Type **171** 10 10
427 25m. Solon (philosopher) in mosaic (horiz) 15 10
428 100m. "Saint Neophytos" (wall painting) 60 75
MS429 111 × 90 mm. 250m. Ortelius' map of Cyprus and Greek Islands, 1584. Imperf 1·25 5·00

1974. Obligatory Tax. Refugee Fund. No. 359 surch **REFUGEE FUND** in English, Greek and Turkish and **10M**.
430 10m. on 5m. multicoloured 10 10

1974. U.N. Security Council Resolution 353. Nos. 360, 365, 366 and 369 optd **SECURITY COUNCIL RESOLUTION 353 20 JULY 1974**.
431 10m. multicoloured 20 10
432 40m. multicoloured 25 50
433 50m. multicoloured 25 10
434 250m. multicoloured . . . . 60 2·75

1974. Obligatory Tax. Refugee Fund.
435 **174** 10m. black and grey . . . 10 10

175 "Virgin and Child between Two Angels", Stavros Church

1974. Christmas. Church Wall-paintings. Mult.
436 10m. Type **175** 10 10
437 50m. "Adoration of the Magi", Ayios Neophytos Monastery (vert) 20 10
438 100m. "Flight into Egypt", Ayios Neophytos Monastery 25 45

176 Larnaca–Nicosia Mail-coach, 1878

1975. Anniversaries and Events.
439 **176** 20m. multicoloured . . . 25 10
440 – 30m. blue and orange . . 25 60
441 **176** 50m. multicoloured . . . 25 10
442 – 100m. multicoloured . . . 40 1·40
DESIGNS AND EVENTS—HORIZ: 20m., 50m. Centenary of Universal Postal Union. VERT: 30m. "Disabled Persons" (8th European Meeting of International Society for the Rehabilitation of Disabled Persons); 100m. Council flag (25th anniv of Council of Europe).

177 "The Distaff" (M. Kashalos)

178 Red Cross Flag over Map

1975. Europa. Multicoloured.
443 20m. Type **177** 25 40
444 30m. "Nature Morte" (C. Savva) 25 50
445 150m. "Virgin and Child of Liopetri" (G. P. Georghiou) 40 80

1975. Anniversaries and Events. Multicoloured.
446 25m. Type **178** 20 10
447 30m. Nurse and lamp (horiz) 20 10
448 75m. Woman's steatite idol (horiz) 20 90
EVENTS: 25m.25th anniv of Red Cross; 30m. International Nurses' Day; 75m. International Women's Year.

179 Submarine Cable Links

181 Human-figured Vessel, 19th-century

1976. Telecommunications Achievements.
449 **179** 50m. multicoloured . . . 30 10
450 – 100m. yellow, vio & lilac 35 90
DESIGN—HORIZ: 100m. International subscriber dialling.

1976. Surch **10M**.
451 **153** 10m. on 3m. multicoloured 20 60

1976. Europa. Ceramics. Multicoloured.
452 20m. Type **181** 20 10
453 60m. Composite vessel, 2100–2000 B.C. 50 80
454 100m. Byzantine goblet . . . 90 1·75

182 Self-help Housing

1976. Economic Reactivation. Multicoloured.
455 10m. Type **182** 10 10
456 25m. Handicrafts 15 20
457 30m. Reafforestation 15 20
458 60m. Air communications . . 30 55

183 Terracotta Statue of Youth

184 Olympic Symbol

1976. Cypriot Treasures.
459 **183** 5m. multicoloured 10 60
460 – 10m. multicoloured . . . 10 40
461 – 20m. red, yellow and black 20 40
462 – 25m. multicoloured . . . 20 10
463 – 30m. multicoloured . . . 20 10
464 – 40m. green, brown & blk 30 45
465 – 50m. lt brown, brn & blk 30 10
466 – 60m. multicoloured . . . 30 20
467 – 100m. multicoloured . . . 40 40
468 – 250m. blue, grey and black . . . . 50 1·50
469 – 500m. black, brown & grn 60 2·00
470 – £1 multicoloured . . . . 1·00 2·25
DESIGNS—VERT: 10m. Limestone head (23 × 34 mm); 20m. Gold necklace from Lambousa (24 × 37 mm); 25m. Terracotta warrior (24 × 37 mm); 30m. Statue of a priest of Aphrodite (24 × 37 mm); 250m. Silver dish from Lambousa (28 × 41 mm); 500m. Bronze stand (28 × 41 mm); £1 Statue of Artemis (28 × 41 mm). HORIZ: 40m. Bronze tablet (37 × 24 mm); 50m. Mycenaean crater (37 × 24 mm); 60m. Limestone sarcophagus (37 × 24 mm); 100m. Gold bracelet from Lambousa (As Type **183**).

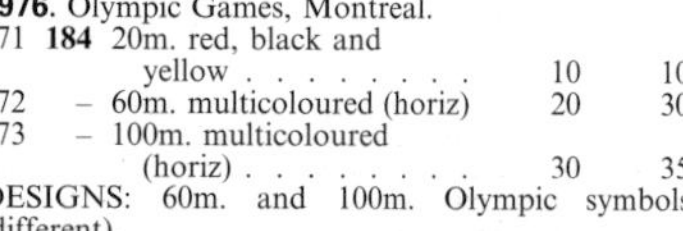

1976. Olympic Games, Montreal.
471 **184** 20m. red, black and yellow 10 10
472 – 60m. multicoloured (horiz) 20 30
473 – 100m. multicoloured (horiz) 30 35
DESIGNS: 60m. and 100m. Olympic symbols (different).

185 "George Washington" (G. Stuart)

186 Children in Library

1976. Bicentenary of American Revolution.
474 **185** 100m. multicoloured . . . 40 30

1976. Anniversaries and Events.
475 **186** 40m. multicoloured . . . 15 15
476 – 50m. brown and black . . 15 10
477 – 80m. multicoloured . . . 30 60
DESIGNS AND EVENTS: 40m. Type **186** (Promotion of Children's books); 50m. Low-cost housing (HABITAT Conference, Vancouver); 80m. Eye protected by hands (World Health Day).

187 Archangel Michael

188 "Cyprus 74" (wood engraving by A. Tassos)

1976. Christmas. Multicoloured.
478 10m. Type **187** 10 10
479 15m. Archangel Gabriel . . . 10 10
480 150m. The Nativity 45 80
Designs show icons from Ayios Neophytis Monastery.

1977. Refugee Fund.
481 **188** 10m. black 20 10
See also Nos. 634 and 892 (after No. 728).

189 "View of Prodhromos" (A. Diamantis)

1977. Europa. Paintings. Multicoloured.
482 20m. Type **189** 20 10
483 60m. "Springtime at Monagroulli" (T. Kanthos) 30 55
484 120m. "Old Port, Limassol" (V. Ioannides) . . . . . . 60 1·75

190 500m. Stamp of 1960

192 Archbishop Makarios in Ceremonial Robes

191 Bronze Coin of Emperor Trajan

1977. Silver Jubilee.
485 **190** 120m. multicoloured . . . 30 30

1977. Ancient Coins of Cyprus (2nd series).
486 **191** 10m. black, gold and blue 15 10
487 – 40m. black, silver and blue 30 30
488 – 60m. black, silver & orge 35 35
489 – 100m. black, gold and green 50 95

DESIGNS: 40m. Silver tetradrachm of Demetrios Poliorcetes; 60m. Silver tetradrachm of Ptolemy VIII; 100m. Gold octadrachm of Arsinoe II.

1977. Death of Archbishop Makarios. Mult.
490 20m Type **192** 15 10
491 60m. Archbishop in doorway 20 10
492 250m. Head and shoulders portrait . . . . 50 1·10

193 Embroidery, Pottery and Weaving

1977. Anniversaries and Events. Multicoloured.
493 20m. Type **193** 10 10
494 40m. Map of Mediterranean 15 20
495 60m. Gold medals 20 20
496 80m. Sputnik 20 85
DESIGNS COMMEMORATE: 20m. Revitalization of handicrafts; 40m. "Man and the Biosphere" Programme in the Mediterranean region; 60m. Gold medals won by Cypriot students in the Orleans Gymnasiade; 80m. 60th anniv of Russian Revolution.

194 "Nativity"

1977. Christmas. Children's Paintings Mult.
497 10m. Type **194** 10 10
498 40m. "The Three Kings" . . 10 10
499 150m. "Flight into Egypt" . . 25 80

195 Demetrios Libertis

1978. Cypriot Poets.
500 **195** 40m. brown and bistre . . 10 10
501 – 150m. grey, black and red 30 80
DESIGN: 150m. Vasilis Michaelides.

196 Chrysorrhogiatissa Monastery Courtyard

197 Archbishop of Cyprus, 1950–1977

1978. Europa. Architecture. Multicoloured.
502 25m. Type **196** 15 10
503 75m. Kolossi Castle 25 35
504 125m. Municipal Library, Paphos . . . . 45 1·50

1978. Archbishop Makarios Commem. Mult.
505 15m. Type **197** 15 20
506 25m. Exiled in Seychelles, 9 March 1956–28 March 1957 . . . . 15 20
507 50m. President of the Republic 1960–1977 . . . 20 25
508 75m. "Soldier of Christ" . . 20 30
509 100m. "Fighter for Freedom" 25 35
MS510 100 × 80 mm. 300m. "The Great Leader" (imperf) 1·00 2·50

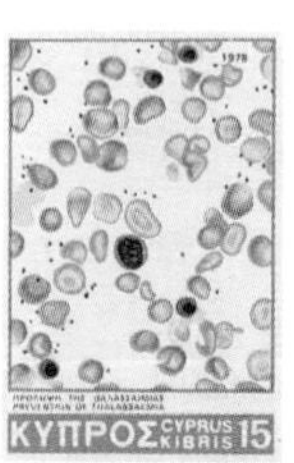
198 Affected Blood Corpuscles (Prevention of Thalassaemia)

199 Icon Stand

1978. Anniversaries and Events.
511 **198** 15m. multicoloured . . . 10 10
512 – 35m. multicoloured . . . 15 10
513 – 75m. black and grey . . . 20 30
514 – 125m. multicoloured . . . 35 80
DESIGNS—VERT: 35m. Aristotle (sculpture) (2300th death anniv). HORIZ: 75m. "Heads" (Human Rights); 125m. Wright brothers and Wright Flyer I (75th anniv of Powered Flight).

1978. Christmas.
515 **199** 15m. multicoloured . . . 10 10
516 – 35m. multicoloured . . . 15 10
517 – 150m. multicoloured . . . 40 60
DESIGNS: 35m., 150m. Different icon stands.

200 Aphrodite (statue from Soli)

1979. Goddess Aphrodite (1st issue). Multicoloured.
518 75m. Type **200** 25 10
519 125m. Aphrodite on shell (detail from Botticelli's "Birth of Venus") 35 25
See also Nos. 584/5.

201 Van, Larnaca–Nicosia Mail-coach and Envelope

1979. Europa. Communications. Multicoloured.
520 25m. Type **201** 15 10
521 75m. Radar, satellite and early telephone 30 20
522 125m. Aircraft, ship and envelopes . . . . 65 1·25

202 Peacock Wrasse

1979. Flora and Fauna. Multicoloured.
523 25m. Type **202** 15 10
524 50m. Black partridge (vert) 70 60
525 75m. Cedar (vert) 45 30
526 125m. Mule . . . . 50 1·25

203 I.B.E. and U.N.E.S.C.O. Emblems

204 "Jesus" (from Church of the Virgin Mary of Arakas, Lagoudhera)

1979. Anniversaries and Events.
527 **203** 15m. multicoloured . . . 10 10
528 – 25m. multicoloured . . . 10 10
529 – 50m. black, brown and ochre 20 15
530 – 75m. multicoloured . . . 25 10
531 – 100m. multicoloured . . . 30 20
532 – 125m. multicoloured . . . 30 75
DESIGNS AND COMMEMORATIONS—VERT: 15m. Type **203** (50th anniv of International Bureau of Education); 125m. Rotary International emblem and "75" (75th anniv). HORIZ: 25m. Graphic design of dove and stamp album (20th anniv of Cyprus Philatelic Society); 50m. Lord Kitchener and map of Cyprus (Cyprus Survey Centenary); 75m. Child's face (International Year of the Child); 100m. Graphic design of footballers (25th anniv of U.E.F.A. European Football Association).

1979. Christmas. Icons. Multicoloured.
533 15m. Type **204** 10 10
534 35m. "Nativity" (Church of St Nicholas, Famagusta District) (29 × 41 mm) . . . 10 10
535 150m. "Holy Mary" (Church of the Virgin Mary of Arakas) 25 45

205 1880 ½d. Stamp with "969" (Nicosia) Postmark

1980. Centenary of Cyprus Stamps. Multicoloured.
536 40m. Type **205** 10 10
537 125m. 1880 2½d. stamp with "974" (Kyrenia) postmark 15 15
538 175m. 1880 1s. stamp with "942" (Larnaca) postmark 15 20
MS539 105 × 85 mm. 500m. 1880 ½d., 1d., 2½d., 4d., 6d. and 1s. stamps (90 × 75 mm). Imperf 70 85

206 St. Barnabas (patron saint of Cyprus)

208 Gold Necklace, Arsos (7th-century B.C.)

207 Sailing

1980. Europa. Personalities. Multicoloured.
540 40m. Type **206** 15 10
541 125m. Zeno of Citium (founder of Stoic philosophy) 30 20

1980. Olympic Games, Moscow. Multicoloured.
542 40m. Type **207** 10 10
543 125m. Swimming 20 20
544 200m. Gymnastics 25 25

1980. Archaeological Treasures.
545 **208** 10m. multicoloured . . . 30 70
546 – 15m. multicoloured . . . 30 70
547 – 25m. multicoloured . . . 30 30
548 – 40m. multicoloured . . . 40 65
549 – 50m. multicoloured . . . 40 10
550 – 75m. multicoloured . . . 90 1·25
551 – 100m. multicoloured . . . 65 15
552 – 125m. multicoloured . . . 65 60
553 – 150m. multicoloured . . . 75 15
554 – 175m. multicoloured . . . 75 1·00
555 – 200m. multicoloured . . . 75 30
556 – 500m. multicoloured . . . 75 1·25
557 – £1 multicoloured . . . . 1·00 1·25
558 – £2 multicoloured . . . . 1·75 2·00
DESIGNS—HORIZ: 15m. Bronze cow, Vouni Palace (5th-cent B.C.); 40m. Gold finger-ring, Enkomi (13th-cent B.C.); 500m. Stone bowl, Khirokitia (6th-millennium B.C.). VERT: 25m. Amphora, Salamis (6th-cent B.C.); 50m. Bronze cauldron, Salamis (8th-cent B.C.); 75m. Funerary stele, Marion (5th-cent B.C.). 100m. Jug (15–14th-cent B.C.); 125m. Warrior (terracotta) (6th–5th-cent B.C.); 150m. Lions attacking bull (bronze relief), Vouni Palace (5th-cent B.C.); 175m. Faience rhyton, Kition (13th-cent B.C.); 200m. Bronze statue of Ingot God, Enkomi (12th-cent B.C.); £1 Ivory plaque, Salamis (7th-cent B.C.); £2 "Leda and the Swan" (mosaic), Kouklia (3rd-cent A.D.).

209 Cyprus Flag

1980. 20th Anniv of Republic of Cyprus. Multicoloured.
559 40m. Type **209** 10 10
560 125m. Signing Treaty of Establishment (41 × 29 mm) 20 15
561 175m. Archbishop Makarios 35 25

210 Head and Peace Dove

1980. International Day of Solidarity with Palestinian People.
562 **210** 40m. black and grey . . . 20 20
563 – 125m. black and grey . . 35 35
DESIGN: 125m. Head and dove with olive branch.

211 Pulpit, Tripiotis Church, Nicosia

212 Folk Dancing

1980. Christmas. Multicoloured.
564 25m. Type **211** 10 10
565 100m. Holy Doors, Panayia Church Paralimni 15 20
565 125m. Pulpit, Ayios Lazaros Church, Larnaca 15 20

1981. Europa. Folklore, showing folk-dancing from paintings by T. Photiades.
567 **212** 40m. multicoloured . . . 30 10
568 – 175m. multicoloured . . . 60 50

213 Self-portrait

214 "Ophrys kotschyi"

1981. 500th Anniv of Leonardo da Vinci's Visit. Multicoloured.
569 50m. Type **213** 40 10
570 125m. "The Last Supper" (50 × 25 mm) 70 40
571 175m. Cyprus lace and Milan Cathedral 95 60

1981. Cypriot Wild Orchids. Multicoloured.
572 25m. Type **214** 40 60
573 50m. "Orchis punctulata" . . 50 70
574 75m. "Ophrys argolica elegans" 55 80
575 150m. "Epipactis veratrifolia" 65 90

215 Heinrich von Stephan

1981. Anniversaries and Events.
576 **215** 25m. dp green, grn & bl 15 10
577 – 40m. multicoloured . . . 15 10
578 – 125m. black, red and green 30 25
579 – 150m. multicoloured . . . 35 30
580 – 200m. multicoloured . . . 40 35
DESIGNS AND COMMEMORATIONS: 25m. Type **137** (150th birth anniv of Heinrich von Stephan (founder of U.P.U.); 40m. Stylised man holding dish of food (World Food Day); 125m. Stylised hands (International Year for Disabled People); 150m. Stylised building and flower (European Campaign for Urban Renaissance); 200m. Prince Charles, Lady Diana Spencer and St. Paul's Cathedral (Royal Wedding).

216 "The Lady of the Angels" (from Church of the Transfiguration of Christ, Palekhori)

217 "Louomene" (Aphrodite bathing) (statue, 250 B.C.)

1981. Christmas. Murals from Nicosia District Churches. Multicoloured.
581 25m. Type **216** 20 10
582 100m. "Christ Pantokrator" (Church of Madonna of Arakas, Lagoudera) (vert) 60 20
583 125m. "Baptism of Christ" (Church of Our Lady of Assinou, Nikitari) 70 30

1982. Aphrodite (Greek goddess of love and beauty) Commemoration (2nd issue). Mult.
584 125m. Type **217** 55 45
585 175m. "Anadyomene" (Aphrodite emerging from the waters) (Titian) 70 65

218 Naval Battle with Greek Fire, 985 A.D.

1982. Europa. Historic Events. Multicoloured.
586 40m. Type **218** 60 10
587 175m. Conversion of Roman Proconsul Sergius Paulus to Christianity, Paphos, 45 A.D. . . . . 1·00 2·50

219 "XP" (monogram of Christ) (mosaic)

1982. World Cultural Heritage. Multicoloured.
588 50m. Type **219** 20 10
589 125m. Head of priest-king of Paphos (sculpture) (24 × 37 mm) 40 25
590 225m. Theseus (Greek god) (mosaic) 60 95

1982. No. 550 surch **100**.
591 100m. on 75m. Funerary stele, Marion (5th-century B.C.) 50 50

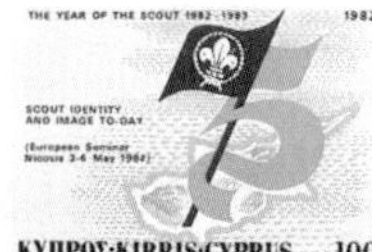

221 Cyprus and Stylised "75"

1982. 75th Anniv of Boy Scout Movement. Multicoloured.
592 100m. Type **221** 25 20
593 125m. Lord Baden-Powell . . 30 30
594 175m. Camp-site 35 55

222 Holy Communion, The Bread

1982. Christmas.
595 **222** 25m. multicoloured . . . 10 10
596 – 100m. gold and black . . 30 15
597 – 250m. multicoloured . . . 70 1·00
DESIGN—VERT: 100m. Holy Chalice. HORIZ: 250m. Holy Communion, The Wine.

223 Cyprus Forest Industries' Sawmill

1983. Commonwealth Day. Multicoloured.
598 50m. Type **223** 10 10
599 125m. "Ikarios and the Discovery of Wine" (3rd-century mosaic) . . . 20 25
600 150m. Folk-dancers, Commonwealth Film and Television Festival, 1980 25 35
601 175m. Royal Exhibition Building, Melbourne (Commonwealth Heads of Government Meeting, 1981) 25 40

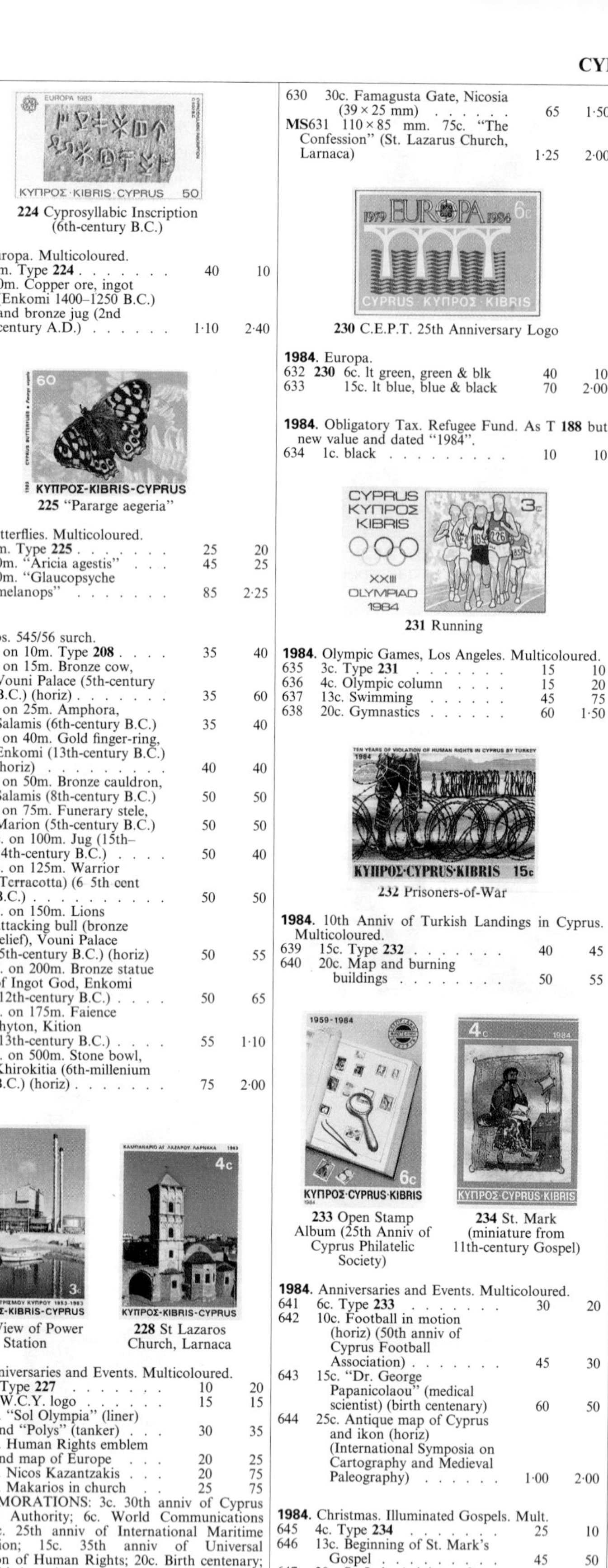

224 Cyprosyllabic Inscription (6th-century B.C.)

1983. Europa. Multicoloured.
602 50m. Type **224** 40 10
603 200m. Copper ore, ingot (Enkomi 1400–1250 B.C.) and bronze jug (2nd century A.D.) . . . . . . 1·10 2·40

225 "Pararge aegeria"

1983. Butterflies. Multicoloured.
604 60m. Type **225** 25 20
605 130m. "Aricia agestis" . . . 45 25
606 250m. "Glaucopsyche melanops" . . . . 85 2·25

1983. Nos. 545/56 surch.
607 1c. on 10m. Type **208** 35 40
608 2c. on 15m. Bronze cow, Vouni Palace (5th-century B.C.) (horiz) 35 60
609 3c. on 25m. Amphora, Salamis (6th-century B.C.) 35 40
610 4c. on 40m. Gold finger-ring, Enkomi (13th-century B.C.) (horiz) 40 40
611 5c. on 50m. Bronze cauldron, Salamis (8th-century B.C.) 50 50
612 6c. on 75m. Funerary stele, Marion (5th-century B.C.) 50 50
613 10c. on 100m. Jug (15th–14th-century B.C.) 50 40
614 13c. on 125m. Warrior (Terracotta) (6 5th cent B.C.) 50 50
615 15c. on 150m. Lions attacking bull (bronze relief), Vouni Palace (5th-century B.C.) (horiz) 50 55
616 20c. on 200m. Bronze statue of Ingot God, Enkomi (12th-century B.C.) 50 65
617 25c. on 175m. Faience rhyton, Kition (13th-century B.C.) . . . . 55 1·10
618 50c. on 500m. Stone bowl, Khirokitia (6th-millenium B.C.) (horiz) . . . . 75 2·00

227 View of Power Station

228 St Lazaros Church, Larnaca

1983. Anniversaries and Events. Multicoloured.
619 3c. Type **227** 10 20
620 6c. W.C.Y. logo 15 15
621 13c. "Sol Olympia" (liner) and "Polys" (tanker) . . . 30 35
622 15c. Human Rights emblem and map of Europe . . . 20 25
623 20c. Nicos Kazantzakis . . . 20 75
624 25c. Makarios in church . . 25 75
COMMEMORATIONS: 3c. 30th anniv of Cyprus Electricity Authority; 6c. World Communications Year; 13c. 25th anniv of International Maritime Organization; 15c. 35th anniv of Universal Declaration of Human Rights; 20c. Birth centenary; 25c. 70th birth anniv.

1983. Christmas. Church Towers. Multicoloured.
625 4c. Type **228** 15 10
626 13c. St. Varvara Church, Kaimakli, Nicosia 40 35
627 20c. St. Ioannis Church, Larnaca . . . . 70 1·50

229 Waterside Cafe, Larnaca

1984. Old Engravings. Each brown and black.
628 6c. Type **229** 15 15
629 20c. Bazaar at Larnaca (39 × 25 mm) 40 85
630 30c. Famagusta Gate, Nicosia (39 × 25 mm) . . . . . . 65 1·50
MS631 110 × 85 mm. 75c. "The Confession" (St. Lazarus Church, Larnaca) 1·25 2·00

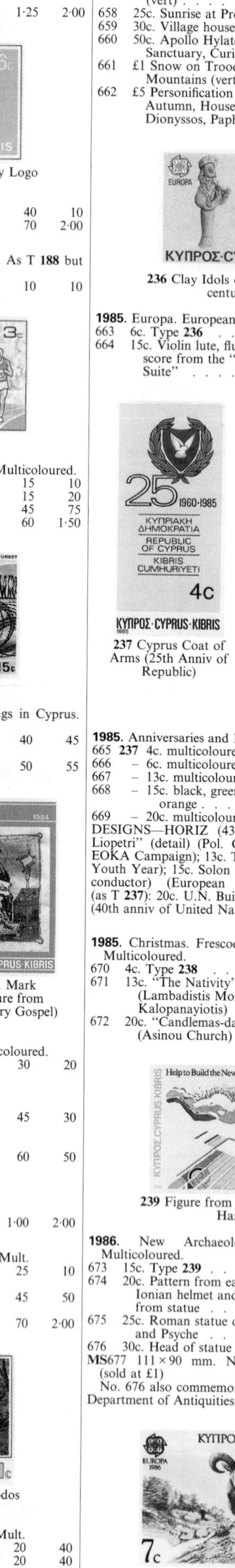

230 C.E.P.T. 25th Anniversary Logo

1984. Europa.
632 **230** 6c. lt green, green & blk 40 10
633 15c. lt blue, blue & black 70 2·00

1984. Obligatory Tax. Refugee Fund. As T **188** but new value and dated "1984".
634 1c. black 10 10

231 Running

1984. Olympic Games, Los Angeles. Multicoloured.
635 3c. Type **231** 15 10
636 4c. Olympic column 15 20
637 13c. Swimming 45 75
638 20c. Gymnastics . . . . . . 60 1·50

232 Prisoners-of-War

1984. 10th Anniv of Turkish Landings in Cyprus. Multicoloured.
639 15c. Type **232** 40 45
640 20c. Map and burning buildings 50 55

233 Open Stamp Album (25th Anniv of Cyprus Philatelic Society)

234 St. Mark (miniature from 11th-century Gospel)

1984. Anniversaries and Events. Multicoloured.
641 6c. Type **233** 30 20
642 10c. Football in motion (horiz) (50th anniv of Cyprus Football Association) 45 30
643 15c. "Dr. George Papanicolaou" (medical scientist) (birth centenary) 60 50
644 25c. Antique map of Cyprus and ikon (horiz) (International Symposia on Cartography and Medieval Paleography) . . . . . . 1·00 2·00

1984. Christmas. Illuminated Gospels. Mult.
645 4c. Type **234** 25 10
646 13c. Beginning of St. Mark's Gospel 45 50
647 20c. St. Luke (miniature from 11th-century Gospel) . . . 70 2·00

235 Autumn at Platania, Troodos Mountains

1985. Cyprus Scenes and Landscapes. Mult.
648 1c. Type **235** 20 40
649 2c. Ayia Napa Monastery . . 20 40
650 3c. Phini Village–panoramic view 20 30
651 4c. Kykko Monastery 20 30
652 5c. Beach at Makronissos, Ayia Napa 20 20
653 6c. Village street, Omodhos (vert) 30 20
654 10c. Panoramic sea view . . 45 30
655 13c. Windsurfing 55 25
656 15c. Beach at Protaras . . . 65 25
657 20c. Forestry for development (vert) 80 50
658 25c. Sunrise at Protaras (vert) 1·00 1·00
659 30c. Village house, Pera . . . 1·25 1·25
660 50c. Apollo Hylates Sanctuary, Curium . . . . 2·00 1·75
661 £1 Snow on Troodos Mountains (vert) . . . . . 3·50 3·00
662 £5 Personification of Autumn, House of Dionyssos, Paphos (vert) 13·00 15·00

236 Clay Idols of Musicians (7/6th century B.C.)

1985. Europa. European Music Year. Mult.
663 6c. Type **236** 50 35
664 15c. Violin lute, flute and score from the "Cyprus Suite" . . . . 90 2·00

237 Cyprus Coat of Arms (25th Anniv of Republic)

238 "The Visit of the Madonna to Elizabeth" (Lambadistis Monastery, Kalopanayiotis)

1985. Anniversaries and Events.
665 **237** 4c. multicoloured 15 15
666 – 6c. multicoloured 15 15
667 – 13c. multicoloured . . . . 25 1·00
668 – 15c. black, green and orange . . . . 1·00 1·25
669 – 20c. multicoloured . . . . 30 1·75
DESIGNS—HORIZ (43 × 30 mm): 6c. "Barn of Liopetri" (detail) (Pol. Georghiou) (30th anniv of EOKA Campaign); 13c. Three profiles (International Youth Year); 15c. Solon Michaelides (composer and conductor) (European Music Year). VERT—(as T **237**): 20c. U.N. Building, New York, and flags (40th anniv of United Nations Organization).

1985. Christmas. Frescoes from Cypriot Churches. Multicoloured.
670 4c. Type **238** 20 10
671 13c. "The Nativity" (Lambadistis Monastery, Kalopanayiotis) 50 65
672 20c. "Candlemas-day" (Asinou Church) . . . . . 70 2·00

239 Figure from Hellenistic Spoon Handle

1986. New Archaeological Museum Fund. Multicoloured.
673 15c. Type **239** 45 45
674 20c. Pattern from early Ionian helmet and foot from statue 60 75
675 25c. Roman statue of Eros and Psyche 65 95
676 30c. Head of statue . . . . . 75 1·10
MS677 111 × 90 mm. Nos. 673/6 (sold at £1) 12·00 16·00
No. 676 also commemorates the 50th anniv of the Department of Antiquities.

240 Cyprus Moufflon and Cedars

1986. Europa. Protection of Nature and the Environment. Multicoloured.
678 7c. Type **240** 35 30
679 17c. Greater flamingos ("Flamingos") at Larnaca Salt Lake . . . . 1·40 2·50

241 Cat's-paw Scallop

1986. Sea Shells. Multicoloured.
680 5c. Type **241** 30 15
681 7c. Atlantic trumpet triton . . 35 15
682 18c. Purple dye murex . . . 60 70
683 25c. Yellow cowrie . . . . . 1·00 2·00

1986. Nos. 653 and 655 surch.
684 7c. on 6c. Village street, Omodhos (vert) 40 30
685 18c. on 13c. Windsurfing . . 1·10 70

243 Globe Outline Map of Cyprus and Barn Swallows (Overseas Cypriots' Year)

1986. Anniversaries and Events. Multicoloured.
686 15c. Type **243** . . . . 1·00 45
687 18c. Halley's Comet over Cyprus beach (40 × 23 mm) 1·25 2·00
688 18c. Comet's tail over sea and Edmond Halley (40 × 23 mm) . . . . . . 1·25 2·00
Nos. 687/8 were printed together, se-tenant, forming a composite design.

244 Pedestrian Crossing

1986. Road Safety Campaign. Multicoloured.
689 5c. Type **244** 65 30
690 7c. Motor cycle crash helmet 70 30
691 18c. Hands fastening car seat belt . . . . 1·50 3·00

245 "The Nativity" (Church of Panayia tou Araka)

1986. Christmas. International Peace Year. Details of Nativity frescoes from Cypriot churches. Multicoloured.
692 5c. Type **245** 25 15
693 15c. Church of Panayia tou Moutoulla 65 30
694 17c. Church of St. Nicholas tis Steyis . . . . 75 2·00

246 Church of Virgin Mary, Asinou

1987. Troodos Churches on the World Heritage List. Multicoloured.
695 15c. Type **246** . . . . 70 1·10
696 15c. Fresco of Virgin Mary, Moutoulla's Church . . . 70 1·10
697 15c. Church of Virgin Mary, Podithou . . . . 70 1·10
698 15c. Fresco of Three Apostles, St. Ioannis Lampadistis Monastery . . 70 1·10
699 15c. Annunciation fresco, Church of the Holy Cross, Pelentriou . . . . 70 1·10
700 15c. Fresco of Saints, Church of the Cross, Ayiasmati . . 70 1·10
701 15c. Fresco of Archangel Michael and Donor, Pedoula's Church of St. Michael . . . . 70 1·10

702 15c. Church of St. Nicolaos, Steyis . . . . 70 1·10
703 15c. Fresco of Prophets, Church of Virgin Mary, Araka . . . . 70 1·10

247 Proposed Central Bank of Cyprus Building

1987. Europa. Modern Architecture.
704 **247** 7c. multicoloured 50 30
705 – 18c. black, grey and green 1·10 2·00
DESIGN: 18c. Headquarters complex, Cyprus Telecommunications Authority.

248 Remains of Ancient Ship and Kyrenia Castle

1987. Voyage of "Kyrenia II" (replica of ancient ship). Multicoloured.
706 2c. Type **248** 35 20
707 3c. "Kyrenia II" under construction, 1982–5 . . . 45 90
708 5c. "Kyrenia II" at Paphos, 1986 . . . . 75 20
709 17c. "Kyrenia II" at New York, 1986 . . . . 1·75 90

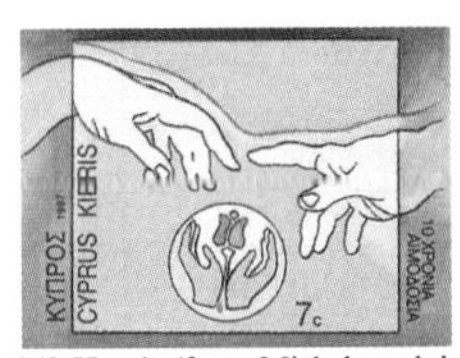

249 Hands (from Michelangelo's "Creation") and Emblem

1987. Anniversaries and Events. Multicoloured.
710 7c. Type **249** (10th anniv of Blood Donation Co-ordinating Committee) . . 50 25
711 15c. Snail with flowered shell and countryside (European Contryside Campaign) . . 1·10 40
712 20c. Symbols of ocean bed and Earth's crust ("Troodos '87" Ophiolites and Oceanic Lithosphere Symposium) . . . . 1·40 3·00

250 Nativity Crib

1987. Christmas. Traditional Customs. Mult.
713 5c. Type **250** 35 15
714 15c. Door knocker decorated with foliage . . . . 1·10 35
715 17c. Bowl of fruit and nuts 1·25 2·00

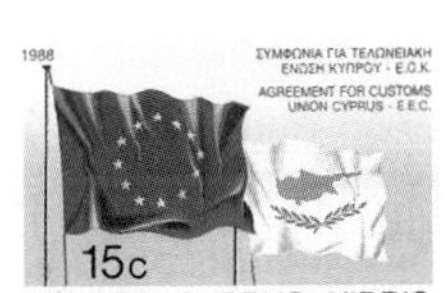

251 Flags of Cyprus and E.E.C.

1988. Cypriot–E.E.C. Customs Union. Mult.
716 15c. Type **251** . . . . 80 1·50
717 18c. Outline maps of Cyprus and E.E.C. countries . . . 80 80

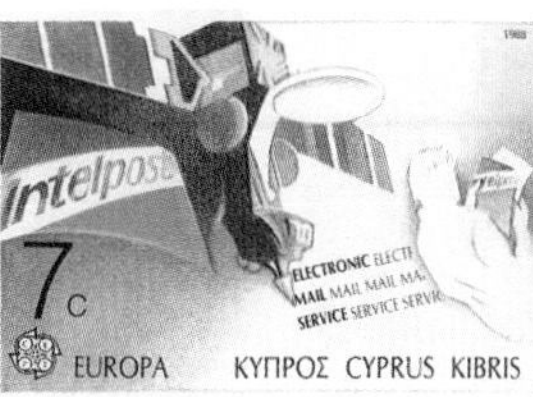

252 Intelpost Telefax Terminal

1988. Europa. Transport and Communications. Multicoloured.
718 7c. Type **252** . . . . 65 1·00
719 7c. Car driver using mobile telephone . . . . 65 1·00
720 18c. Nose of Cyprus Airways airliner and greater flamingos . . . . 2·25 2·75
721 18c. Boeing 739 airliner in flight and greater flamingos 2·25 2·75

253 Sailing

255 "Cyprus 74" (wood-engraving by A. Tassos)

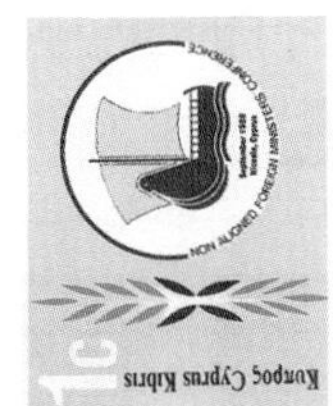

254 Conference Emblem

1988. Olympic Games, Seoul. Multicoloured.
722 5c. Type **253** 30 20
723 7c. Athletes at start 35 40
724 10c. Shooting 40 70
725 20c. Judo . . . . 90 1·50

1988. Non Aligned Foreign Ministers' Conference, Nicosia.
726 **254** 1c. black, blue and green 10 10
727 – 10c. multicoloured 45 70
728 – 50c. multicoloured . . . . 2·25 2·50
DESIGNS: 10c. Emblem of Republic of Cyprus; 50c. Nehru, Tito, Nasser and Makarios.

1988. Obligatory Tax. Refugee Fund. Variously dated.
892 **255** 1c. black and grey 10 10

1988. No. 651 surch **15c**.
730 15c. on 4c. Kykko Monastery 1·50 1·00

256 "Presentation of Christ at the Temple" (Church of Holy Cross tou Agiasmati)

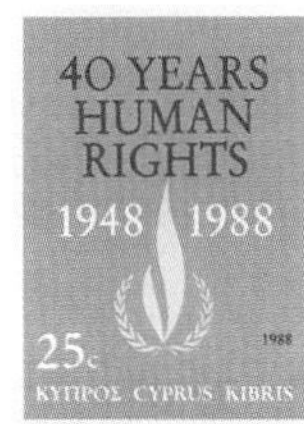

257 Human Rights Logo

1988. Christmas. Designs showing frescoes from Cypriot churches. Multicoloured.
731 5c. Type **256** 25 20
732 15c. "Virgin and Child" (St. John Lampadistis Monastery) 55 25
733 17c. "Adoration of the Magi" (St. John Lampadistis Monastery) . . . . 80 1·75

1988. 40th Anniv of Universal Declaration of Human Rights.
734 **257** 25c. lt blue, dp blue & bl 90 1·25

258 Basketball

1989. 3rd Small European States' Games, Nicosia. Multicoloured.
735 1c. Type **258** 20 15
736 5c. Javelin 30 15
737 15c. Wrestling 55 20
738 18c. Athletics . . . . 70 1·00
MS739 109 × 80 mm. £1 Angel and laurel wreath (99 × 73 mm). Imperf 5·00 6·00

259 Lingri Stick Game

1989. Europa. Children's Games. Multicoloured.
740 7c. Type **259** . . . . 1·00 1·40
741 7c. Ziziros . . . . 1·00 1·40
742 18c. Sitsia . . . . 1·10 1·50
743 18c. Leapfrog . . . . 1·10 1·50

260 "Universal Man"

1989. Bicentenary of the French Revolution.
744 **260** 18c. multicoloured 80 60

261 Stylized Human Figures

262 Worker Bees tending Larvae

1989. Centenary of Interparliamentary Union (15c.) and 9th Non-Aligned Summit Conference, Belgrade (30c.). Multicoloured.
745 15c. Type **261** 50 40
746 30c. Conference logo . . . . 1·00 1·10

1989. Bee-keeping. Multicoloured.
748 3c. Type **262** 25 25
749 10c. Bee on rock-rose flower 60 50
750 15c. Bee on lemon flower . . 85 50
751 18c. Queen and worker bees 95 1·50

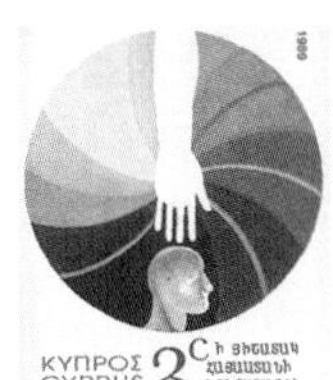

263 Outstretched Hand and Profile (aid for Armenian earthquake victims)

264 Winter (detail from "Four Seasons")

1989. Anniversaries and Events. Multicoloured.
752 3c. Type **263** 25 60
753 5c. Airmail envelope (Cyprus Philatelic Society F.I.P. membership) 40 10
754 7c. Crab symbol and daisy (European Cancer Year) 65 1·25
755 17c. Vegetables and fish (World Food Day) . . . . 1·00 1·25

1989. Roman Mosaics from Paphos. Multicoloured.
756 1c. Type **264** 25 65
757 2c. Personification of Crete (32 × 24 mm) 30 65
758 3c. Centaur and Maenad (24 × 32 mm) 35 65
759 4c. Poseidon and Amymone (32 × 24 mm) 50 70
760 5c. Leda 50 20
761 7c. Apollon 55 25
762 10c. Hermes and Dionysos (24 × 32 mm) 65 30
763 15c. Cassiopeia . . . . . . 1·25 45
764 18c. Orpheus (32 × 24 mm) 1·25 50
765 20c. Nymphs (24 × 32 mm) 1·50 75
766 25c. Amazon (24 × 32 mm) 1·50 80
767 40c. Doris (32 × 24 mm) . . . 2·25 1·50
768 50c. Heracles and the Lion (39 × 27 mm) . . . . . . 2·25 1·50
769 £1 Apollon and Daphne (39 × 27 mm) . . . . . . 3·50 3·00
770 £3 Cupid (39 × 27 mm) . . . 8·50 9·50

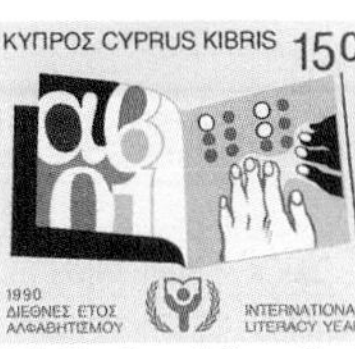

265 Hands and Open Book (International Literacy Year)

1990. Anniversaries and Events. Multicoloured.
771 15c. Type **265** 55 50
772 17c. Dove and profiles (83rd Inter-Parliamentary Conference, Nicosia) . . . 65 90
773 18c. Lions International emblem (Lions Europa Forum, Limassol) 75 90

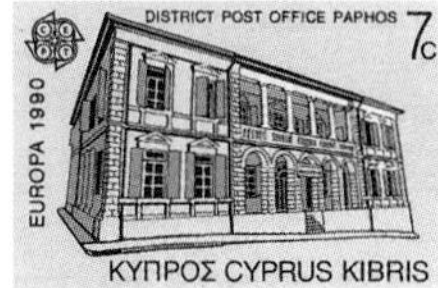

266 District Post Office, Paphos

1990. Europa. Post Office Buildings. Mult.
774 7c. Type **266** . . . . 1·25 25
775 18c. City Centre Post Office, Limassol . . . . 1·50 2·50

267 Symbolic Lips (25th anniv of Hotel and Catering Institute)

1990. European Tourism Year. Multicoloured.
776 5c. Type **267** 25 25
777 7c. Bell tower, St. Lazarus Church (1100th anniv) . . 30 25
778 15c. Butterflies and woman 1·75 45
779 18c. Birds and man . . . . . 2·25 3·50

268 Sun (wood carving)

269 "Chionodoxa lochiae"

1990. 30th Anniv of Republic. Multicoloured.
780 15c. Type **268** 65 45
781 17c. Bulls (pottery design) . . 75 60
782 18c. Fishes (pottery design) 85 70
783 40c. Tree and birds (wood carving) . . . . 2·25 3·50
MS784 89 × 89 mm. £1 30th Anniversary emblem. Imperf 3·75 5·50

1990. Endangered Wild Flowers. Book illustrations by Elektra Megaw. Multicoloured.
785 2c. Type **269** . . . . 45 1·00
786 3c. "Pancratium maritimum" 45 1·00
787 5c. "Paeonia mascula" . . . 65 20
788 7c. "Cyclamen cyprium" . . 70 25
789 15c. "Tulipa cypria" . . . . 1·40 30
790 18c. "Crocus cyprius" . . . 1·50 3·00

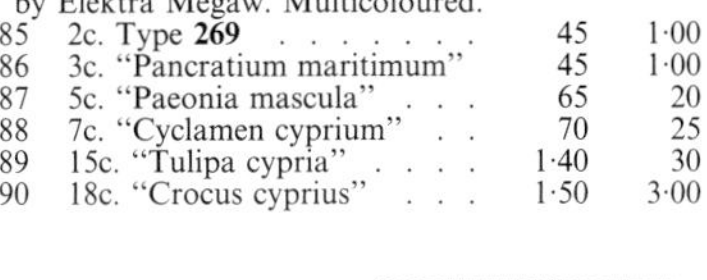

270 "Nativity"

271 Archangel

1990. Christmas. 16th-century Icons. Mult.
791 5c. Type **270** 40 20
792 15c. "Virgin Hodegetria" . . 1·25 30
793 17c. "Nativity" (different) . . 1·50 3·00

1991. 6th-century Mosaics from Kanakaria Church. Multicoloured.
794 5c. Type **271** 20 15
795 15c. Christ Child 75 20
796 17c. St. James . . . . 1·50 1·50
797 18c. St. Matthew . . . . . . 1·00 1·75

272 "Ulysses" Spacecraft

1991. Europa. Europa in Space. Multicoloured.
798 7c. Type **272** 90 20
799 18c. "Giotto" and Halley's Comet . . . . 1·60 2·50

273 Young Cyprus Wheatear

1991. Cyprus Wheatear. Multicoloured.

800 5c. Type **273** 70 40
801 7c. Adult bird in autumn plumage 75 40
802 15c. Adult male in breeding plumage . . . . 1·10 50
803 30c. Adult female in breeding plumage . . . . 1·60 2·75

274 Mother and Child with Tents

1991. 40th Anniv of U.N. Commission for Refugees. Each deep brown, brown and silver.

804 5c. Type **274** 25 15
805 15c. Three pairs of legs . . . 90 65
806 18c. Three children . . . . . 1·10 2·00

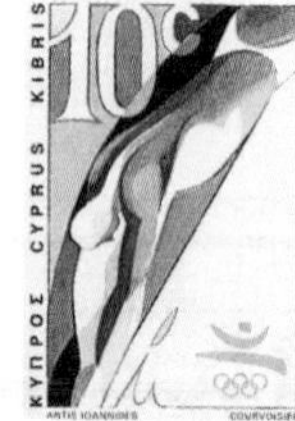

275 The Nativity

276 Swimming

1991. Christmas. Multicoloured.

808 5c. Type **275** 25 15
809 15c. Saint Basil 60 40
810 17c. Baptism of Jesus . . . . 90 1·75

1992. Olympic Games, Barcelona. Multicoloured.

811 10c. Type **276** 60 35
812 20c. Long jump . . . . . . 1·00 70
813 30c. Running . . . . 1·40 1·40
814 35c. Discus . . . . 1·60 2·50

277 World Map and Emblem ("EXPO '92" Worlds Fair, Seville)

1992. Anniversaries and Events. Multicoloured.

815 20c. Type **277** . . . . 1·40 80
816 25c. European map and football (10th under-16 European Football Championship) . . . . . 1·50 95
817 30c. Symbols of learning (inauguration of University of Cyprus) . . . . 1·50 2·75

278 Compass Rose and Map of Voyage

1992. Europa. 500th Anniv of Discovery of America by Columbus. Multicoloured.

818 10c. Type **278** . . . . 90 1·25
819 10c. "Departure from Palos" (R. Balaga) . . . . 90 1·25
820 30c. Fleet of Columbus . . . 1·40 1·75
821 30c. Christopher Columbus . . 1·40 1·75

Nos. 818/19 and 820/1 were each issued together, se-tenant, forming composite designs.

279 "Chamaeleo chamaeleon"

1992. Reptiles. Multicoloured.

822 7c. Type **279** 55 30
823 10c. "Lacerta laevis troodica" (lizard) 75 45
824 15c. "Mauremys caspica" (turtle) 90 80
825 20c. "Coluber cypriensis" (snake) . . . . 1·00 2·00

280 Minoan Wine Ship of 7th Century B.C. and Modern Tanker

1992. 7th International Maritime and Shipping Conference, Nicosia.

826 **280** 50c. multicoloured . . . . 3·00 3·00

281 "Visitation of the Virgin Mary to Elizabeth", Church of the Holy Cross, Pelendri

282 School Building and Laurel Wreath

1992. Christmas. Church Fresco Paintings. Mult.

827 7c. Type **281** 40 25
828 15c. "Virgin and Child Enthroned", Church of Panayia tou Araka 75 65
829 20c. "Virgin and Child", Ayios Nicolaos tis Stegis Church . . . . 1·10 1·90

1993. Centenary of Pancyprian Gymnasium (secondary school).

830 **282** 10c. multicoloured 60 50

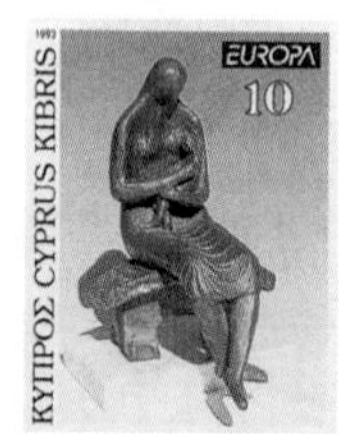

283 "Motherhood" (bronze sculpture, Nicos Dymiotis)

1993. Europa. Comtemporary Art. Multicoloured.

831 10c. Type **283** 50 40
832 30c. "Motherhood" (painting, Christoforos Savva) (horiz) 1·25 2·00

284 Women Athletes (13th European Cup for Women)

1993. Anniversaries and Events. Multicoloured.

833 7c. Type **284** 40 30
834 10c. Scout symbols (80th anniv of Scouting in Cyprus) (vert) 55 40
835 20c. Water-skier, dolphin and gull (Moufflon Encouragement Cup) (inscr "Mufflon") . . . . 10·00 10·00
835a 20c. Water-skier, dolphin and seabird (inscr "Moufflon") 95 95
836 25c. Archbishop Makarios III and monastery (80th birth anniv) . . . . . . 1·40 2·00

285 Red Squirrelfish

1993. Fishes. Multicoloured.

837 7c. Type **285** 40 25
838 15c. Red scorpionfish 65 55
839 20c. Painted comber 75 85
840 30c. Grey triggerfish . . . . 1·40 2·25

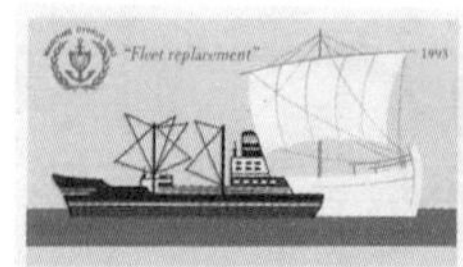

286 Conference Emblem

1993. 12th Commonwealth Summit Conference.

841 **286** 35c. brown and ochre . . 1·60 1·90
842 40c. brown and ochre . . 1·90 2·40

287 Ancient Sailing Ship and Modern Coaster

1993. "Maritime Cyprus '93" International Shipping Conference, Nicosia.

843 **287** 25c. multicoloured . . . . 1·40 1·40

288 Cross from Stavrovouni Monastery

290 Symbols of Disability (Persons with Special Needs Campaign)

289 Copper Smelting

1993. Christmas. Church Crosses. Multicoloured.

844 7c. Type **288** 30 25
845 20c. Cross from Lefkara . . 75 75
846 25c. Cross from Pedoulas (horiz) . . . . 1·00 2·00

1994. Europa. Discoveries. Ancient Copper Industry. Multicoloured.

847 10c. Type **289** 50 35
848 30c. Ingot, ancient ship and map of Cyprus . . . . . 1·25 2·00

1994. Anniversaries and Events. Multicoloured.

849 7c. Type **290** 40 25
850 15c. Olympic rings in flame (Centenary of International Olympic Committee) . . . 65 55
851 20c. Peace doves (World Gymnasiade, Nicosia) . . . 80 80
852 25c. Adults and unborn baby in tulip (International Year of the Family) . . . . . 1·10 2·00

291 Houses, Soldier and Family

1994. 20th Anniv of Turkish Landings in Cyprus. Multicoloured.

853 10c. Type **291** 50 40
854 50c. Soldier and ancient columns . . . . 2·00 3·00

292 Black Pine

1994. Trees. Multicoloured.

855 7c. Type **292** 30 25
856 15c. Cyprus cedar 55 55
857 20c. Golden oak 70 80
858 30c. Strawberry tree . . . . 1·10 2·00

293 Airliner, Route Map and Emblem

1994. 50th Anniv of I.C.A.O.

859 **293** 30c. multicoloured . . . . 1·50 1·75

294 "Virgin Mary" (detail) (Philip Goul)

295 Woman from Paphos wearing Foustani

1994. Christmas. Church Paintings. Multicoloured.

860 7c. Type **294** 50 25
861 20c. "The Nativity" (detail) (Byzantine) . . . . . . 1·25 70
862 25c. "Archangel Michael" (detail) (Goul) . . . . . . 1·50 2·50

1994. Traditional Costumes. Multicoloured.

863 1c. Type **295** 25 60
864 2c. Bride from Karpass . . . 35 60
865 3c. Woman from Paphos wearing sayia 40 60
866 5c. Woman from Messaoria wearing foustani 50 70
867 7c. Bridegroom 55 20
868 10c. Shepherd from Messaoria 70 40
869 15c. Woman from Nicosia in festive costume . . . . . . 1·25 40
870 20c. Woman from Karpass wearing festive sayia . . . 1·25 50
871 25c. Woman from Pitsillia . . 1·50 60
872 30c. Woman from Karpass wearing festive doupletti 1·60 70
873 35c. Countryman . . . . . . 1·60 1·00
874 40c. Man from Messaoria in festive costume . . . . . . 1·75 1·50
875 50c. Townsman . . . . . . 1·90 1·75
876 £1 Townswoman wearing festive sarka . . . . 2·75 2·75

296 "Hearth Room" Excavation, Alassa, and Frieze

297 Statue of Liberty, Nicosia (left detail)

1995. 3rd International Congress of Cypriot Studies, Nicosia. Multicoloured.

877 20c. Type **296** 75 75
878 30c. Hypostyle hall, Kalavasos, and Mycenaean amphora . . . . 1·00 1·75
MS879 110 × 80 mm. £1 Old Archbishop's Palace, Nicosia (107 × 71 mm). Imperf 3·50 4·50

1995. 40th Anniv of Start of E.O.K.A. Campaign. Different details of the statue. Multicoloured.

880 20c. Type **297** . . . . 90 1·10
881 20c. Centre detail (face value at top right) . . . . . . 90 1·10
882 20c. Right detail (face value at bottom right) . . . . . 90 1·10

Nos. 880/2 were printed together, se-tenant, forming a composite design.

298 Nazi Heads on Peace Dove over Map of Europe

299 Symbolic Figure holding Healthy Food

1995. Europa. Peace and Freedom. Multicoloured.
883 10c. Type **298** 75 35
884 30c. Concentration camp prisoner and peace dove 2·00 2·75

1995. Healthy Living. Multicoloured.
885 7c. Type **299** 25 25
886 10c. "AIDS" and patients (horiz) 50 50
887 15c. Drug addict (horiz) . . . 55 55
888 20c. Smoker and barbed wire 75 1·00

300 European Union Flag and European Culture Month Logo

1995. European Culture Month and "Europhilex '95" International Stamp Exhibition, Nicosia. **MS**891 blue, yellow and stone or multicoloured (others).
889 20c. Type **300** 55 60
890 25c. Map of Europe and Cypriot church . . . . . 70 1·10
MS891 95 × 86 mm. 50c. Peace dove (42 × 30 mm); 50c. European Cultural Month symbol (42 × 30 mm) 5·50 6·50

301 Peace Dove with Flags of Cyprus and United Nations

1995. Anniversaries and Events. Multicoloured.
893 10c. Type **301** (50th anniv of United Nations) 35 35
894 15c. Hand pushing ball over net (cent of volleyball) (vert) 75 50
895 20c. Safety pin on leaf (European Nature Conservation Year) (vert) 85 70
896 25c. Clay pigeon contestant (World Clay Target Shooting Championship) 95 1·75

302 Reliquary from Kykko Monastery

303 Family (25th anniv of Pancyprian Organization of Large Families)

1995. Christmas.
897 **302** 7c. multicoloured 25 25
898 – 20c. multicoloured 70 60
899 – 25c. multicoloured . . . . 85 1·60
DESIGNS: 20, 25c. Different reliquaries of Virgin and Child from Kykko Monastery.

1996. Anniversaries and Events. Multicoloured.
900 10c. Type **303** 45 35
901 20c. Film camera (centenary of cinema) 75 70
902 35c. Silhouette of parent and child in globe (50th anniv of U.N.I.C.E.F.) . . . . . 1·40 1·60
903 40c. "13" and Commonwealth emblem (13th Conference of Commonwealth Speakers and Presiding Officers) . . 1·50 2·50

304 Maria Synglitiki

306 Watermill

305 High Jump

1996. Europa. Famous Women. Multicoloured.
904 10c. Type **304** 50 30
905 30c. Queen Caterina Cornaro 1·50 2·25

1996. Centennial Olympic Games, Atlanta. Multicoloured.
906 10c. Type **305** 50 30
907 20c. Javelin 85 65
908 25c. Wrestling . . . . 95 1·00
909 30c. Swimming . . . . . . 1·25 2·00

1996. Mills. Multicoloured.
910 10c. Type **306** 60 40
911 15c. Olivemill 75 50
912 20c. Windmill 90 90
913 25c. Handmill . . . . 1·00 1·75

307 Icon of Our Lady of Iberia, Moscow

1996. Cyprus–Russia Joint Issue. Orthodox Religion. Multicoloured.
914 30c. Type **307** . . . . 1·50 1·75
915 30c. Stravrovouni Monastery, Cyprus . . . . 1·50 1·75
916 30c. Icon of St. Nicholas, Cyprus . . . . 1·50 1·75
917 30c. Voskresenskie Gate, Moscow . . . . 1·50 1·75

308 "The Nativity" (detail)

1996. Christmas. Religious Murals from Church of The Virgin of Asinou. Multicoloured.
918 7c. Type **308** 50 25
919 20c. "Virgin Mary between the Archangels Gabriel and Michael" . . . . 1·25 60
920 25c. "Christ bestowing Blessing" (vert) . . . . . 1·60 2·50

309 Basketball

1997. Final of European Basketball Cup.
921 **309** 30c. multicoloured . . . . 2·00 1·75

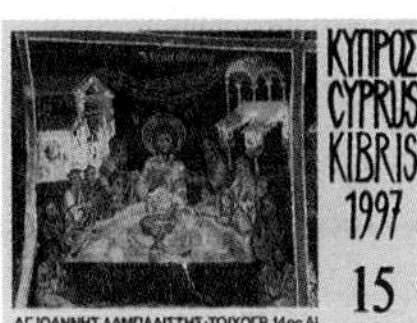

310 "The Last Supper"

1997. Easter. Religious Frescoes from Monastery of St. John Lambadestis. Multicoloured.
922 15c. Type **310** 50 50
923 25c. "The Crucifixion" . . . 75 1·25

311 Kori Kourelleni and Prince

1997. Europa. Tales and Legends. Multicoloured.
924 15c. Type **311** 75 40
925 30c. Digenis and Charon . . 1·25 2·25

312 "Oedipoda miniata" (grasshopper)

1997. Insects. Multicoloured.
926 10c. Type **312** 50 30
927 15c. "Acherontia atropos" (hawk moth) 75 40
928 25c. "Daphnis nerii" (hawk moth) . . . . 1·25 1·10
929 35c. "Ascalaphus macaronius" (owl-fly) . . . 1·40 1·75

313 Archbishop Makarios III and Chapel

1997. 20th Death Anniv of Archbishop Makarios III.
930 **313** 15c. multicoloured . . . . 1·00 50

314 The Nativity

1997. Christmas. Byzantine Frescos from the Monastery of St. John Lambadestis. Mult.
931 10c. Type **314** 40 25
932 25c. Three Kings following the star . . . . 1·40 70
933 30c. Flight into Egypt . . . 1·50 2·50

315 Green Jasper

1998. Minerals. Multicoloured.
934 10c. Type **315** 40 30
935 15c. Iron pyrite 60 45
936 25c. Gypsum 80 80
937 30c. Chalcedony . . . . . . 1·00 1·75

316 Players competing for Ball

1998. World Cup Football Championship, France.
938 **316** 35c. multicoloured . . . . 1·75 1·40

317 Cataclysmos Festival, Larnaca

1998. Europa. Festivals. Multicoloured.
939 15c. Type **317** . . . . 1·00 40
940 30c. House of Representatives, Nicosia (Declaration of Independence) . . . . . . 1·50 2·25

318 Mouflon Family Group

319 Flames and Globe Emblem

1998. Endangered Species. Cyprus Mouflon. Mult.
941 25c. Type **318** . . . . 1·00 1·25
942 25c. Mouflon herd . . . . . 1·00 1·25
943 25c. Head of ram . . . . . 1·00 1·25
944 25c. Ram on guard . . . . . 1·00 1·25

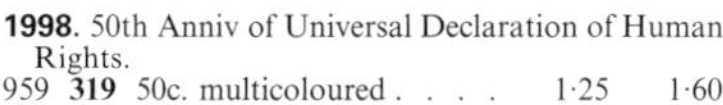

1998. 50th Anniv of Universal Declaration of Human Rights.
959 **319** 50c. multicoloured . . . . 1·25 1·60

320 World "Stamp" and Magnifying Glass

1998. World Stamp Day.
960 **320** 30c. multicoloured . . . . 1·40 1·40

321 "The Annunciation"

322 "Pleurotus eryngii"

1998. Christmas. Multicoloured.
961 10c. Type **321** 35 20
962 25c. "The Nativity" 80 65
963 30c. "The Baptism of Christ" 1·00 1·75
MS964 102 × 75 mm. Nos. 961/3 1·90 2·25

1999. Mushrooms of Cyprus. Multicoloured.
965 10c. Type **322** 30 30
966 15c. "Lactarius deliciosus" 60 40
967 25c. "Sparassis crispa" . . . 90 90
968 30c. "Morchella elata" . . . 1·00 1·60

323 Pair of Moufflons at Tripylos Reserve

1999. Europa. Parks and Gardens. Multicoloured.
969 15c. Type **323** 60 40
970 30c. Turtles on beach at Lara Reserve . . . . 1·00 1·40

324 Council of Europe Building, Emblem and Flags

1999. 50th Anniv of Council of Europe.
971 **324** 30c. multicoloured . . . . 1·10 1·25

325 Temple of Hylates Apollo, Kourion

1999. Cyprus–Greece Joint Issue. 4000 Years of Greek Culture. Multicoloured.

972 25c. Type **325** . . . . 85 1·00
973 25c. Mycenaean pot depicting warriors . . . . 85 1·00
974 25c. Mycenaean crater depicting horse . . . . . 85 1·00
975 25c. Temple of Apollo, Delphi . . . . 85 1·00

326 Paper Aeroplane Letters and U.P.U. Emblem

1999. 125th Anniv of Universal Postal Union. Multicoloured.

976 15c. Type **326** 60 40
977 35c. "125" and U.P.U. emblem . . . . 1·00 1·40

327 Container Ship and Cypriot Flag

1999. "Maritime Cyprus '99" Conference. Sheet 103 × 80 mm, containing T **327** and similar horiz designs. Multicoloured.

MS978 25c. Type **327**; 25c. Binoculars and chart; 25c. Stern of container ship; 25c. Tanker 2·75 3·25

328 Cypriot Refugee Fund Stamps and Barbed Wire

(½-size illustration)

1999. 25th Anniv of Turkish Landings in Cyprus. Sheet 110 × 75mm. Imperf.

MS979 **328** 30c. multicoloured 1·00 1·10

329 Angel

330 Woman's Silhouette with Stars and Globe

1999. Christmas. Multicoloured.

980 10c. Type **329** 35 10
981 25c. The Three Kings 80 60
982 30c. Madonna and child . . 1·10 1·75

2000. Miss Universe Beauty Contest, Cyprus. Sheet 80 × 65 mm, containing T **330** and similar vert design. Multicoloured.

MS983 15c. Type **330**; 35c. Statue of Aphrodite and apple 1·00 1·10

331 Necklace, 4500–4000 B.C.

332 "Building Europe"

2000. Jewellery. Multicoloured.

984 10c. Type **331** 20 25
985 15c. Gold earrings, 3rd-cent B.C. 35 40
986 20c. Gold earring from Lampousa, 6th–7th-cent . . 45 50
987 25c. Brooch, 19th-cent . . . 55 60
988 30c. Gold cross, 6th–7th-cent 65 70
989 35c. Necklace, 18th–19th-cent 75 80
990 40c. Gold earring, 19th-cent 85 90
991 50c. Spiral hair ring, 5th–4th-cent B.C. . . . . . . 1·10 1·25
992 75c. Gold-plated silver plaques from Gialia, 700–600 B.C. (horiz) . . . . . 1·60 1·75
993 £1 Gold frontlet from Egkomi, 14th–13th-cent B.C. (horiz) . . . . 2·25 2·40
994 £2 Gold necklace from Egkomi, 13th-cent B.C. (horiz) . . . . 4·25 4·50
995 £3 Buckles, 19th-cent (horiz) 6·50 6·75

2000. Europa.

996 **332** 30c. multicoloured . . . . 1·00 1·00

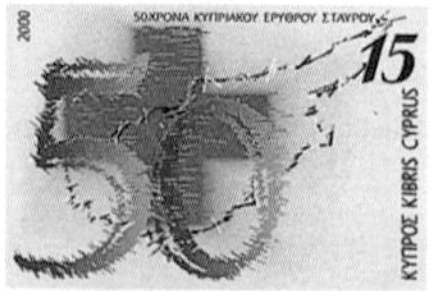

333 "50", Cross and Map of Cyprus

2000. 50th Anniv of Red Cross in Cyprus.

997 **333** 15c. multicoloured . . . . 1·00 60

334 Flame, Map of Cyprus and Broken Chain

335 Weather Balloon, Map and Satellite

2000. 45th Anniv of Struggle for Independence.

998 **334** 15c. multicoloured . . . . 1·00 60

2000. 50th Anniv of World Meteorological Organization.

999 **335** 30c. multicoloured . . . . 1·50 1·50

336 Monastery of Antifontis, Kalograia

337 Council of Europe Emblem

2000. Greek Orthodox Churches in Northern Cyprus.

1000 **336** 10c. brown and red . . . 50 25
1001 – 15c. dp green & green 70 35
1002 – 25c. dp violet & violet 1·00 70
1003 – 30c. red and grey . . . 1·10 1·40

DESIGNS—VERT: 15c. Church of St. Themonianos, Lysi. HORIZ: 25c. Church of Panagia Kanakaria, Lytrhagkomi; 30c. Church of Avgasida Monastery, Milia.

2000. 50th Anniv of European Convention of Human Rights

1004 **337** 30c. multicoloured . . . 1·10 1·25

338 Archery

339 "The Annunciation"

2000. Olympic Games, Sydney. Multicoloured.

1005 10c. Type **338** 40 25
1006 15c. Gymnastics 55 35
1007 25c. Diving 80 70
1008 35c. Trampolining . . . . . 95 1·50

2000. Christmas. Gold Gospel Covers. Multicoloured.

1009 10c. Type **339** 40 25
1010 25c. "The Nativity" 80 55
1011 30c. "The Baptism of Christ" . . . . 1·00 1·25

340 "25" and Commonwealth Symbol

2001. 25th Anniv of Commonwealth Day.

1012 **340** 30c. multicoloured . . . 1·00 1·00

341 Silhouette, Dove and Barbed Wire

2001. 50th Anniv of United Nations High Commissioner for Refugees.

1013 **341** 30c. multicoloured . . . 1·00 1·00

342 Pavlos Liasides

2001. Birth Centenary of Pavlos Liasides (poet).

1014 **342** 13c. chocolate, ochre & brown 55 35

343 Bridge over River Diarizos

2001. Europa. Cypriot Rivers. Multicoloured.

1015 20c. Type **343** 60 50
1016 30c. Mountain torrent, River Akaki . . . . . . 80 1·00

344 *Pathenope massena*

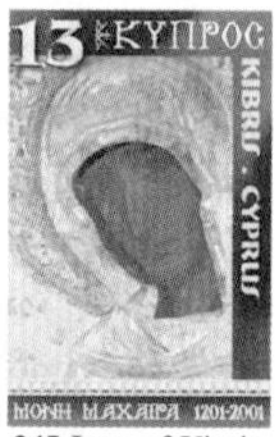

345 Icon of Virgin Mary

2001. Crabs. Multicoloured.

1017 13c. Type **344** 35 20
1018 20c. *Calappa granulata* . . . 60 50
1019 25c. *Ocypode cursor* 70 70
1020 30c. *Pagurus bernhardus* . . 80 1·00

2001. Christmas. 800th Anniv of Macheras Monastery. Multicoloured.

1021 13c. Type **345** 20 20
1022 25c. Macheras Monastery 70 60
1023 30c. Ornate gold crucifix . . 80 90

346 Loukis Akritas

2001. Loukis Akritas (writer) Commemoration.

1024 **346** 20c. green and brown . . 70 50

347 Tortoiseshell and White Cat

2002. Cats. Multicoloured.

1025 20c. Type **347** 55 60
1026 20c. British blue 55 60
1027 25c. Tortoiseshell and white 55 60
1028 25c. Red and silver tabby 55 60

348 Acrobat on Horseback

350 Mother Teresa

349 *Myrtus communis*

2002. Europa. Circus. Multicoloured.

1029 20c. Type **348** 45 50
1030 30c. Clown on high wire . . 65 70

2002. Medicinal Plants. Multicoloured.

1031 13c. Type **349** 25 30
1032 20c. *Lavandula stoechas* . . 45 50
1033 25c. *Capparis spinosa* . . . 55 60
1034 30c. *Ocimum basilicum* . . . 65 70

2002. Mother Teresa (founder of Missionaries of Charity) Commemoration.

1035 **350** 40c. multicoloured . . . 85 90

351 Blackboard on Easel

2002. International Teachers' Day. Multicoloured.

1036 13c. Type **351** 25 30
1037 30c. Computer 65 70

352 Agate Seal-stone (5th century B.C.)

2002. "Cyprus - Europhilex '02", Stamp Exhibition, Nicosia. Cypriot Antiquities showing Europa. Multicoloured.

1038 20c. Type **352** 45 50
1039 20c. Silver coin of Timochares (5th–4th century B.C.) 45 50
1040 20c. Silver coin of Stasioikos (5th century B.C.) 45 50
1041 30c. Clay lamp (green backgound) (2nd century A.D.) 65 70
1042 30c. Statuette of Europa on the Bull (7th–6th century B.C.) 65 70
1043 30c. Clay lamp (purple backgound) (1st century B.C.) 65 70

MS1044 105 × 71 mm. 50c. Statue of Aphrodite with maps of Crete and Cyprus; 50c. "Europa on the Bull" (painting by Francesco di Giogio) 2·25 2·40

353 "Nativity"

2002. Christmas. Details from "Birth of Christ" (wall painting), Church of Metamorphosis Sotiros, Palechori. Multicoloured.

1045 13c. Type **353** 25 30
1046 25c. "Three Wise Men" . . 55 60
1047 30c. "Birth of Christ" (complete painting) (38 × 38 mm) 65 70

354 Triumph Roadster 1800, 1946

2003. International Historic Car Rally. Multicoloured.

1048 20c. Type **354** 45 50
1049 25c. Ford model T, 1917 . . 55 60
1050 30c. Baby Ford Y 8hp, 1932 65 70

TURKISH CYPRIOT POSTS

After the inter-communal clashes during December 1963, a separate postal service was established on 6 January 1964, between some of the Turkish Cypriot areas, using handstamps inscribed "KIBRIS TURK POSTALARI". During 1964, however, an agreement was reached between representatives of the two communities for the restoration of postal services. This agreement to which the United Nations representatives were a party, was ratified in November 1966 by the Republic's Council of Ministers. Under the scheme postal servcies were provided for the Turkish Cypriot communities in Famagusta, Limassol, Lefka and Nicosia, staffed by Turkish Cypriot employees of the Cypriot Department of Posts.

On 8 April 1970, 5m. and 15m. locally produced labels, originally designated "Social Aid Stamps", were issued by the Turkish Cypriot community and these can be found on commercial covers. These local stamps are outside the scope of this catalogue.

On 29 October 1973 Nos. 1/7 were placed on sale, but were again used only on mail between the Turkish Cypriot areas.

Following the intervention by the Republic of Turkey in July 1974 these stamps replaced issues of the Republic of Cyprus in that part of the island, north and east of the Attila Line, controlled by the Autonomous Turkish Cypriot Administration.

1974. 1000 mils = 1 pound.
1978. 100 kurus = 1 lira.

1 50th Anniversary Emblem

1974. 50th Anniv of Republic of Turkey.
1 – 3m. multicoloured . . . . . . 30·00 30·00
2 – 5m. multicoloured 60 40
3 – 10m. multicoloured 50 20
4 **1** 15m. red and black . . . . . 2·50 1·50
5 – 20m. multicoloured 70 20
6 – 50m. multicoloured . . . . . 2·00 1·50
7 – 70m. multicoloured . . . . . 16·00 16·00
DESIGNS—VERT: 3m. Woman sentry; 10m. Man and woman with Turkish flags; 20m. Ataturk statue, Kyrenia Gate, Nicosia; 50m. "The Fallen". HORIZ: 5m. Military parade, Nicosia; 70m. Turkish flag and map of Cyprus.

1975. Proclamation of the Turkish Federated State of Cyprus. Nos. 3 and 5 surch **KIBRIS TURK FEDERE DEVLETI 13.2.1975** and value.
8 30m. on 20m. multicoloured . . 75 1·00
9 100m. on 10m. multicoloured 1·25 2·00

3 Namik Kemal's Bust, Famagusta

1975. Multicoloured.
10 3m. Type **3** 15 40
11 10m. Ataturk Statue, Nicosia 15 10
12 15m. St. Hilarion Castle . . . 25 20
13 20m. Ataturk Square, Nicosia 35 20
14 25m. Famagusta Beach . . . 35 30
15 30m. Kyrenia Harbour 45 10
16 50m. Lala Mustafa Pasha Mosque, Famagusta (vert) 50 10
17 100m. Interior, Kyrenia Castle 80 90
18 250m. Castle walls, Kyrenia 1·00 2·25
19 500m. Othello Tower, Famagusta (vert) . . . . . 1·50 4·50
See also Nos. 36/8.

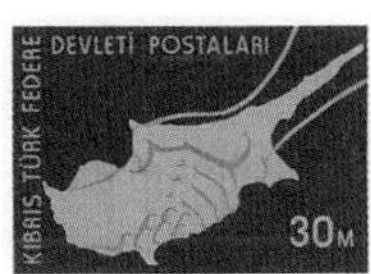
4 Map of Cyprus

1975. "Peace in Cyprus". Multicoloured.
20 30m. Type **4** 20 15
21 50m. Map, laurel and broken chain 25 20
22 150m. Map and laurel-sprig on globe (vert) . . . . 65 1·00

5 "Pomegranates" (I. V. Guney)

1975. Europa. Paintings. Multicoloured.
23 90m. Type **5** 70 90
24 100m. "Harvest Time" (F. Direkoglu) 80 90

1976. Nos. 16/17 surch.
25 10m. on 50m. multicoloured 35 70
26 30m. on 100m. multicoloured 35 80

7 "Expectation" (ceramic statuette)

9 Olympic Symbol "Flower"

8 Carob

1976. Europa. Multicoloured.
27 60m. Type **7** 40 80
28 120m. "Man in Meditation" 60 1·25

1976. Export Products. Fruits. Multicoloured.
29 10m. Type **8** 15 10
30 25m. Mandarin 20 10
31 40m. Strawberry 25 25
32 60m. Orange 35 65
33 80m. Lemon . . . . 40 1·75

1976. Olympic Games, Montreal. Multicoloured.
34 60m. Type **9** 25 20
35 100m. Olympic symbol and doves 35 25

10 Kyrenia Harbour

11 Liberation Monument, Karaeglanoglu (Ay Georghios)

1976. Multicoloured.
36 5m. Type **10** 40 15
37 15m. St. Hilarion Castle . . . 40 15
38 20m. Ataturk Square, Nicosia 40 15

1976. Liberation Monument.
47 **11** 30m. blue, pink and black 15 20
48 – 150m. red, pink and black 35 45
DESIGN: 150m. Liberation Monument (different view).

12 Hotel, Salamis Bay

1977. Europa. Multicoloured.
49 80m. Type **12** 65 80
50 100m. Kyrenia Port 75 80

13 Pottery

14 Arap Ahmet Pasha Mosque, Nicosia

1977. Handicrafts. Multicoloured.
51 15m. Type **13** 10 10
52 30m. Pottery (vert) 10 10
53 125m. Basketware 30 50

1977. Turkish Buildings in Cyprus. Multicoloured.
54 20m. Type **14** 10 10
55 40m. Paphos Castle (horiz) . . 10 10
56 70m. Bekir Pasha aqueduct (horiz) 15 20
57 80m. Sultan Mahmut library (horiz) 15 25

15 Namik Kemal (bust) and House, Famagusta

1977. Namik Kemal (patriotic poet). Multicoloured.
58 30m. Type **15** 15 15
59 140m. Namik Kemal (portrait) (vert) 35 60

16 Old Man and Woman

17 Oratory in Buyuk Han, Nicosia

1978. Social Security.
60 **16** 150k. black, yellow and blue 10 10
61 – 275k. black, orange and green 15 15
62 – 375k. black, blue and orange 25 20
DESIGNS: 275k. Injured man with crutch; 375k. Woman with family.

1978. Europa. Multicoloured.
63 225k. Type **17** 50 30
64 450k. Cistern in Selimiye Mosque, Nicosia 90 70

18 Motorway Junction

1978. Communications. Multicoloured.
65 75k. Type **18** 15 10
66 100k. Hydrofoil 15 10
67 650k. Boeing 720 at Ercan Airport 50 35

19 Dove with Laurel Branch

20 Kemal Ataturk

1978. National Oath.
68 **19** 150k. yellow, violet and black 10 10
69 – 225k. black, red and yellow 10 10
70 – 725k. black, blue and yellow 20 20
DESIGNS—VERT: 225k. "Taking the Oath". HORIZ: 725k. Symbolic dove.

1978. Ataturk Commemoration.
71 **20** 75k. turquoise & dp turq . . 10 10
72 450k. pink and brown . . . 15 15
73 650k. blue and light blue . . 20 25

1979. Nos. 30/3 surch.
74 50k. on 25k. Mandarin . . . 10 10
75 1l. on 40m. Strawberry 15 10
76 3l. on 60m. Orange 15 10
77 5l. on 80m. Lemon 35 15

22 Gun Barrel with Olive Branch and Map of Cyprus

1979. 5th Anniv of Turkish Peace Operation in Cyprus. Sheet 72 × 52 mm. Imperf.
MS78 **22** 15l. black, blue and green 80 1·25

23 Postage Stamp and Map of Cyprus

24 Microwave Antenna

1979. Europa. Communications. Multicoloured.
79 2l. Type **23** 10 10
80 3l. Postage stamps, building and map 10 10
81 8l. Telephones, Earth and satellite 20 30

1979. 50th Anniv of International Consultative Radio Committee.
82 **24** 2l. multicoloured 20 10
83 5l. multicoloured 20 10
84 6l. multicoloured 25 15

25 School Children

26 Lala Mustafa Pasha Mosque, Magusa

1979. International Year of the Child. Mult.
85 1½l. Type **25** 25 15
86 4½l. Children and globe (horiz) 40 20
87 6l. College children 60 20

1980. Islamic Commemorations. Multicoloured.
88 2½l. Type **26** 10 10
89 10l. Arap Ahmet Pasha Mosque, Lefkosa 30 15
90 20l. Mecca and Medina . . . 50 20
COMMEMORATIONS: 2½l. 1st Islamic Conference in Turkish Cyprus; 10l. General Assembly of World Islam Congress; 20l. Moslem Year 1400 AH.

27 Ebu-Su'ud Efendi (philosopher)

28 Omer's Shrine, Kyrenia

1980. Europa. Personalities. Multicoloured.
91 5l. Type **27** 20 10
92 30l. Sultan Selim II 70 40

1980. Ancient Monuments.
93 **28** 2½l. blue and stone 10 10
94 – 3½l. green and pink 10 10
95 – 5l. brown on green 15 10
96 – 10l. mauve and green . . . 20 10
97 – 20l. blue and yellow 35 25
DESIGNS: 3½l. Entrance gate, Famagusta; 5l. Funerary monuments (16th-century), Famagusta; 10l. Bella Paise Abbey, Kyrenia; 20l. Selimiye Mosque, Nicosia.

29 Cyprus 1880 6d. Stamp

30 Dome of the Rock

1980. Cyprus Stamp Centenary.
98 **29** 7½l. black, brown and green 20 10
99 – 15l. brown, dp blue & bl 25 10
100 – 50l. black, red and grey . . 65 55
DESIGNS—HORIZ: 15l. Cyprus 1960 Constitution of the Republic 30m. commemorative stamp. VERT: 50l. Social Aid local, 1970.

1980. Palestinian Solidarity. Multicoloured.
101 15l. Type **30** 30 15
102 35l. Dome of the Rock (horiz) 70 30

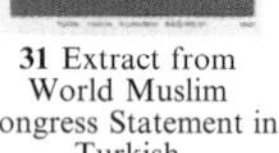

31 Extract from World Muslim Congress Statement in Turkish

32 "Ataturk" (F. Duran)

1981. Day of Solidarity with Islamic Countries.
103 **31** 1l. buff, red and brown . . 15 55
104 – 35l. light green, black green 55 85
DESIGN: 35l. Extract in English.

1981. Ataturk Stamp Exhibition, Lefkosa.
105 **32** 10l. multicoloured 25 35

33 Folk-dancing

35 Wild Convolvulus

34 "Kemal Atatürk" (I. Calli)

1981. Europa. Folklore. Multicoloured.
106 10l. Type **33** 40 15
107 30l. Folk-dancing (different) 60 35

1981. Birth Centenary of Kemal Atatürk. Sheet 70 × 95 mm. Imperf.
MS108 **34** 150l. multicoloured 1·10 1·25

1981. Flowers. Multicoloured.
109 1l. Type **35** 10 10
110 5l. Persian cyclamen (horiz) 10 10
111 10l. Spring mandrake (horiz) 10 10
112 25l. Corn poppy 15 10
113 30l. Wild arum (horiz) . . . 15 10
114 50l. Sage-leaved rock rose . . 20 20
115 100l. "Cistus salviaefolius L." 30 30
116 150l. Giant fennel (horiz) . . 50 90

36 Stylised Disabled Person in Wheelchair

1981. Commemorations. Multicoloured.
117 7½l. Type **36** 25 35
118 10l. Heads of people of different races, peace dove and barbed wire (vert) . . 35 55
119 20l. People of different races reaching out from globe, with dishes (vert) 50 85
COMMEMORATIONS: 7½l. International Year for Disabled Persons; 10l. Anti-Apartheid publicity; 20l. World Food Day.

37 Turkish Cypriot and Palestinian Flags

1981. Palestinian Solidarity.
120 **37** 10l. multicoloured 30 40

38 Prince Charles and Lady Diana Spencer

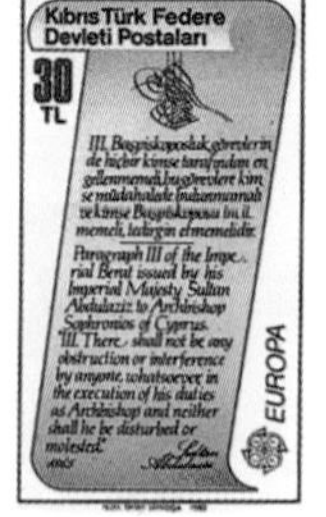

39 Charter issued by Sultan Abdul Aziz to Archbishop Sophronios

1981. Royal Wedding.
121 **38** 50l. multicoloured . . . . 1·00 85

1982. Europa (CEPT). Sheet 83 × 124 mm containing T **39** and similar vert design. Mult.
MS122 30l. × 2. Type **39**; 70l. × 2, Turkish forces landing at Tuzla, 1571 4·50 5·00

40 Buffavento Castle

42 Cross of Lorraine, Koch and Bacillus (Centenary of Koch's Discovery of Tubercle Bacillus)

41 "Wedding" (A. Orek)

1982. Tourism. Multicoloured.
123 5l. Type **40** 10 10
124 10l. Windsurfing (horiz) . . . 15 10
125 15l. Kantara Castle (horiz) 25 15
126 30l. Shipwreck (300 B.C.) (horiz) 60 40

1982. Paintings (1st series). Multicoloured.
127 30l. Type **41** 15 30
128 50l. "Carob Pickers" (O. Nazim Selenge) (vert) 30 70
See also Nos. 132/3, 157/8, 176/7, 185/6, 208/9, 225/7, 248/50, 284/5, 315/16, 328/9, 369/70 and 436/7.

1982. Anniversairies and Events. Multicoloured.
129 10l. Type **42** . . . . 1·00 40
130 30l. Spectrum on football pitch (World Cup Football Championships, Spain) . . 1·75 1·10
131 70l. "75" and Lord Baden-Powell (75th Anniv of Boy Scout movement and 125th birth anniv) (vert) . . . . 2·25 4·00

43 "Calloused Hands" (Salih Oral)

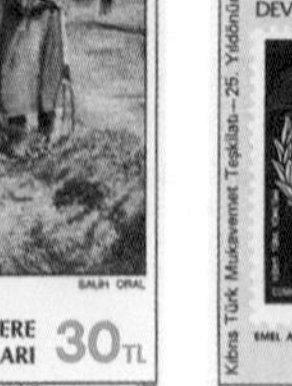

45 First Turkish Cypriot 10m. Stamp

1983. Paintings (2nd series). Multicoloured.
132 30l. Type **43** . . . . 75 1·40
133 35l. "Malya–Limassol Bus" (Emin Cizenel) . . . . . . 75 1·40

1983. Anniversaries and Events. Multicoloured.
135 15l. Type **45** 80 50
136 20l. "Turkish Achievements in Cyprus" (horiz) 80 60
137 25l. "Liberation Fighters" . . 90 80
138 30l. Dish aerial and telegraph pole (horiz) . . . . 1·10 1·25
139 50l. Dove and envelopes (horiz) . . . . 2·50 3·25
EVENTS: 15, 20, 25l. T.M.T. (25th anniv of Turkish Cypriot Resistance Organization); 30, 50l. World Communications Year.

46 European Bee Eater

1983. Birds of Cyprus. Multicoloured.
140 10l. Type **46** . . . . 80 1·25
141 15l. Eurasian goldfinch . . . 1·00 1·25
142 50l. European robin . . . . 1·25 1·50
143 65l. Golden oriole . . . . . 1·40 1·50

1983. Establishment of Republic. Nos. 109, 111/12 and 116 optd **Kuzey Kibris Turk Cumhuriyeti 15.11.1983**, or surch also.
144 10l. Spring mandrake 20 15
145 15l. on 1l. Type **35** 30 15
146 25l. Corn poppy 40 25
147 150l. Giant fennel . . . . . 2·25 3·25

48 C.E.P.T. 25th Anniversary Logo

1984. Europa.
148 **48** 50l. yellow, brown and black . . . . 2·25 3·00
149 100l. lt blue, blue & black 2·25 3·00

49 Olympic Flame

50 Ataturk Cultural Centre

1984. Olympic Games, Los Angeles. Multicoloured.
150 10l. Type **49** 15 10
151 20l. Olympic events within rings (horiz) 35 25
152 70l. Martial arts event (horiz) 60 1·75

1984. Opening of Ataturk Cultural Centre, Lefkosa.
153 **50** 120l. stone, black and brown . . . . 1·25 1·75

52 Turkish Cypriot Flag and Map

1984. 10th Anniv of Turkish Landings in Cyprus. Multicoloured.
154 20l. Type **52** 50 25
155 70l. Turkish Cypriot flag within book . . . . 1·00 2·00

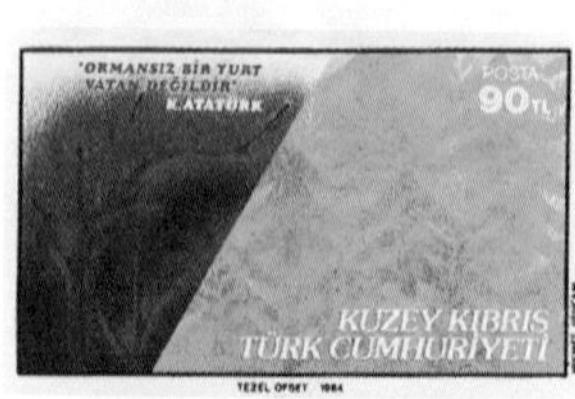

53 Burnt and Replanted Forests

1984. World Forestry Resources.
156 **53** 90l. multicoloured . . . . 1·25 1·75

54 "Old Turkish Houses, Nicosia" (Cevdet Cagdas)

1984. Paintings (3rd series). Multicoloured.
157 20l. Type **54** 50 40
158 70l. "Scenery" (Olga Rauf) 1·10 2·00
See also Nos. 176/7, 185/6, 208/9, 225/7, 248/50, 284/5, 315/16, 328/9 and 369/70.

55 Kemal Ataturk, Flag and Crowd

56 Taekwondo Bout

1984. 1st Anniv of Turkish Republic of Northern Cyprus. Multicoloured.
159 20l. Type **55** 50 40
160 70l. Legislative Assembly voting for Republic (horiz) 1·10 2·00

1984. Int Taekwondo Championship, Girne.
161 **56** 10l. black, brown and grey 40 25
162 – 70l. multicoloured . . . . 1·60 2·50
DESIGN: 70l. Emblem and flags of competing nations.

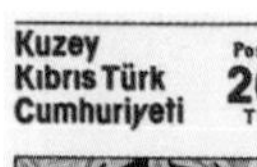

57 "Le Regard"

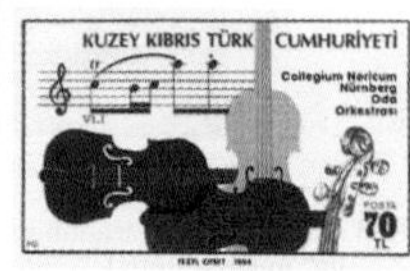

58 Musical Instruments and Music

1984. Exhibition by Saulo Mercader (artist). Multicoloured.
163 20l. Type **57** 30 25
164 70l. "L'equilibre de L'esprit" (horiz) . . . . 1·10 2·25

1984. Visit of Nurnberg Chamber Orchestra.
165 **58** 70l. multicoloured . . . . 1·50 2·25

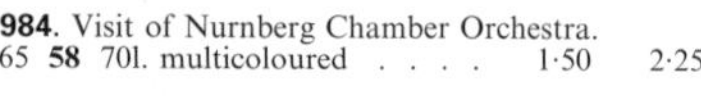

59 Dr. Fazil Kucuk (politician)

61 George Frederick Handel

60 Goat

1985. 1st Death Anniv of Dr. Fazil Kucuk (politician). Multicoloured.
166 20l. Type **59** 30 30
167 70l. Dr. Fazil Kucuk reading newspaper . . . . 95 2·00

1985. Domestic Animals. Multicoloured.
168 100l. Type **60** 55 30
169 200l. Cow and calf 90 80
170 300l. Ram . . . . 1·25 2·00
171 500l. Donkey . . . . 2·00 3·25

1985. Europa. Composers.
172 **61** 20l. purple, green & lt grn 2·00 2·50
173 – 20l. purple, brown and pink . . . . 2·00 2·50
174 – 100l. purple, blue & lt blue 2·50 3·00
175 – 100l. purple, brn & lt brn 2·50 3·00
DESIGNS: No. 173, Giuseppe Domenico Scarlatti; 174, Johann Sebastian Bach; 175, Buhurizade Mustafa Itri Efendi.

1985. Paintings (4th series). As T **54**. Mult.
176 20l. "Village Life" (Ali Atakan) 60 50
177 50l. "Woman carrying Water" (Ismet V. Guney)) 1·40 2·50

62 Heads of Three Youths

1985. International Youth Year. Multicoloured.
178 20l. Type **62** 75 40
179 100l. Dove and globe . . . . 3·50 4·00

63 Parachutist (Aviation League)

65 Karagoz Show Puppets

64 Griffon Vulture

1985. Anniversaries and Events.
180 **63** 20l. multicoloured . . . . 1·75 45
181 – 50l. black, brown and blue 2·00 1·25
182 – 100l. brown . . . . 1·75 2·75
183 – 100l. multicoloured . . . . 1·75 2·75
184 – 100l. multicoloured . . . . 2·25 2·75
DESIGNS—VERT: No. 181, Louis Pasteur (Centenary of Discovery of Rabies vaccine); 182, Ismet Inonu (Turkish statesman) (birth centenary (1984)). HORIZ: 183, "40" in figures and symbolic flower (40th anniv of United Nations Organization); 184, Patient receiving blood transfusion (Prevention of Thalassaemia).

1986. Paintings (5th series). As T **54**. Mult.
185 20l. "House with Arches" (Gonen Atakol) 50 30
186 100l. "Ataturk Square" (Yalkin Muhtaroglu) . . . 1·75 1·75

1986. Europa. Protection of Nature and the Environment. Sheet 82×76 mm, containing T **64** and similar horiz design. Multicoloured.
MS187 100l. Type **64**; 200l. Litter on Cyprus landscape 8·50 7·00

1986. Karagoz Folk Puppets.
188 **65** 100l. multicoloured . . . . 2·25 2·50

66 Old Bronze Age Composite Pottery

1986. Archaeological Artefacts. Cultural Links with Anatolia. Multicoloured.
189 10l. Type **66** 55 20
190 20l. Late Bronze Age bird jug (vert) 95 30
191 50l. Neolithic earthenware pot . . . . 1·75 2·00
192 100l. Roman statue of Artemis (vert) . . . . . . 2·25 3·50

67 Soldiers, Defence Force Badge and Ataturk (10th anniv of Defence Forces)

69 Prince Andrew and Miss Sarah Ferguson

68 Guzelyurt Dam and Power Station

1986. Anniversaries and Events. Multicoloured.
193 20l. Type **67** . . . . 1·00 30
194 50l. Woman and two children (40th anniv of F.A.O.) . . 1·40 1·40
195 100l. Football and world map (World Cup Football Championship, Mexico) (horiz) . . . . 3·00 3·75
196 100l. Orbit of Halley's Comet and "Giotto" space probe (horiz) . . . . 3·00 3·75

1986. Modern Development (1st series). Mult.
197 20l. Type **68** . . . . 1·25 30
198 50l. Low cost housing project, Lefkosa . . . . . 1·40 1·40
199 100l. Kyrenia Airport . . . . 3·25 4·25
See also Nos. 223/4 and 258/63.

1986. 60th Birthday of Queen Elizabeth II and Royal Wedding. Multicoloured.
200 100l. Queen Elizabeth II . . 2·00 2·50
201 100l. Type **69** . . . . 2·00 2·50

70 Locomotive No. 11 and Trakhoni Station

1986. Cyprus Railway. Multicoloured.
202 50l. Type **70** . . . . 3·50 2·75
203 100l. Locomotive No. 1 . . . 4·00 4·25

1987. Nos. 94, 96/7 and 113 optd **Kuzey Kibris Turk Cumhuriyeti** or surch also (No. 205).
204 10l. mauve and green 50 70
205 15l. on 3½l. green and pink 50 70
206 20l. blue and yellow 55 75
207 30l. multicoloured . . . . . 70 1·10

1987. Paintings (6th series). As T **54**. Mult.
208 50l. "Shepherd" (Feridun Isiman) . . . . 1·25 1·25
209 125l. "Pear Woman" (Mehmet Uluhan) . . . . 1·75 3·00

72 Modern House (architect A. Vural Behaeddin)

1987. Europa. Modern Architecture. Multicoloured.
210 50l. Type **72** . . . . 1·00 30
211 200l. Modern house (architect Necdet Turgay) . . . . . 1·75 3·25

73 Kneeling Folk Dancer

74 Regimental Colour (1st anniv of Infantry Regiment)

1987. Folk Dancers. Multicoloured.
212 20l. Type **73** 60 20
213 50l. Standing male dancer . . 90 40
214 200l. Standing female dancer 2·00 1·75
215 1000l. Woman's headdress . . 4·75 6·50

1987. Anniversaries and Events. Multicoloured.
216 50l. Type **74** . . . . 1·50 85
217 50l. President Denktash and Turgut Ozal (1st anniv of Turkish Prime Minister's visit) (horiz) . . . . 1·50 85
218 200l. Emblem and Crescent (5th Islamic Summit Conference, Kuwait) . . . 2·75 3·75
219 200l. Emblem and laurel leaves (Membership of Pharmaceutical Federation) (horiz) . . . . 2·75 3·75

75 Ahmet Belig Pasha (Egyptian judge)

76 Tourist Hotel, Girne

1987. Turkish Cypriot Personalities.
220 **75** 50l. brown and yellow . . 65 40
221 – 50l. multicoloured 65 40
222 – 125l. multicoloured . . . . 1·50 3·00
DESIGNS: 50l. (No. 221) Mehmet Emin Pasha (Ottoman Grand Vizier); 125l. Mehmet Kamil Pasha (Ottoman Grand Vizier).

1987. Modern Development (2nd series). Mult.
223 150l. Type **76** . . . . 1·50 1·50
224 200l. Dogu Akdeniz University . . . . 1·75 2·25

1988. Paintings (7th series). As T **54**. Mult.
225 20l. "Woman making Pastry" (Ayhan Mentes) (vert) . . 50 30
226 50l. "Chair Weaver" (Osman Guvenir) 75 75
227 150l. "Woman weaving a Rug" (Zekai Yesiladali) (vert) . . . . 1·75 3·50

77 "Piyale Pasha" (tug)

1988. Europa. Transport and Communications. Multicoloured.
228 200l. Type **77** . . . . 2·25 75
229 500l. Dish aerial and antenna tower, Selvilitepe (vert) . . 3·00 4·50
No. 229 also commemorates the 25th anniv of Bayrak Radio and Television Corporation.

78 Lefkosa

79 Bulent Ecevit

1988. Tourism. Multicoloured.
230 150l. Type **78** 80 80
231 200l. Gazi-Magusa . . . . . 90 1·00
232 300l. Girne . . . . 1·50 2·00

1988. Turkish Prime Ministers. Multicoloured.
233 50l. Type **79** 60 85
234 50l. Bulent Ulusu 60 85
235 50l. Turgut Ozal 60 85

80 Red Crescent Members on Exercise

1988. Civil Defence.
236 **80** 150l. multicoloured . . . . 1·25 1·50

81 Hodori the Tiger (Games mascot) and Fireworks

1988. Olympic Games, Seoul. Multicoloured.
237 200l. Type **81** . . . . 1·00 1·00
238 250l. Athletics . . . . 1·25 1·25
239 400l. Shot and running track with letters spelling "SEOUL" . . . . 1·75 2·00

82 Sedat Simavi (journalist)

83 "Kemal Atatürk" (I. Calli)

1988. Anniversaries and Events.
240 **82** 50l. green 25 25
241 – 100l. multicoloured 50 45
242 – 300l. multicoloured . . . . 70 1·00
243 – 400l. multicoloured . . . . 1·50 1·75
244 – 400l. multicoloured . . . . 1·00 1·75
245 – 600l. multicoloured . . . . 2·00 2·50
DESIGNS—HORIZ: No. 241, Stylised figures around table and flags of participating countries (International Girne Conferences); 244, Presidents Gorbachev and Reagan signing treaty (Summit Meeting). VERT: No. 242, Cogwheels as flowers (North Cyprus Industrial Fair); 243, Globe (125th anniv of International Red Cross); 245, "Medical Services" (40th anniv of W.H.O.).

1988. 50th Death Anniv of Kemal Atatürk. Sheet 72×102 mm, containing T **83** and similar vert designs. Multicoloured.
MS246 250l. Type **83**; 250l. "Kemal Atatürk" (N. Ismail); 250l. In army uniform; 250l. In profile 2·75 2·75

84 Abstract Design

1988. 5th Anniv of Turkish Republic of Northern Cyprus. Sheet 98×76 mm. Imperf.
MS247 **84** 500l. multicoloured 2·25 2·25

1989. Paintings (8th series). As T **54**. Mult.
248 150l. "Dervis Pasa Mansion, Lefkosa" (Inci Kansu) . . 90 60
249 400l. "Gamblers' Inn, Lefkosa" (Osman Guvenir) 1·75 2·25
250 600l. "Mosque, Paphos" (Hikmet Ulucam) (vert) . . 2·50 3·00

85 Girl with Doll

1989. Europa. Children's Games. Multicoloured.
251 600l. Type **85** . . . . 2·00 1·25
252 1000l. Boy with kite . . . . 2·25 3·50

86 Meeting of Presidents Vassiliou and Denktash

1989. Cyprus Peace Summit, Geneva, 1988.
253 **86** 500l. red and black . . . . 1·25 1·25

87 Chukar Partridge

1989. Wildlife. Multcoloured.
254 100l. Type **87** 65 25
255 200l. Cyprus hare 70 35
256 700l. Black partridge . . . . 2·50 2·00
257 2000l. Red fox . . . . 3·00 4·00

88 Road Construction

1989. Modern Development (3rd series). Mult.
258 100l. Type **88** 15 15
259 150l. Laying water pipeline (vert) 20 20
260 200l. Seedling trees (vert) . . 30 30
261 450l. Modern telephone exchange (vert) . . . . . 75 1·00
262 650l. Steam turbine power station (vert) . . . . . . 1·00 1·75
263 700l. Irrigation reservoir . . 1·25 1·75

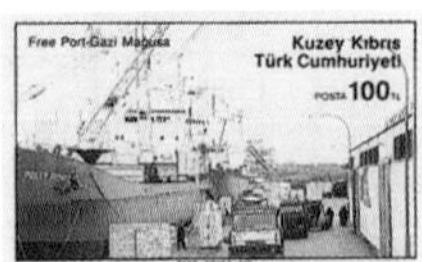

89 Unloading "Polly Pioneer" (freighter) at Quayside (15th anniv of Gazi Magusa Free Port)

1989. Anniversaries.
264 **89** 100l. multicoloured 70 20
265 – 450l. black, blue and red 80 80
266 – 500l. black, yellow and grey 80 80
267 – 600l. black, red and blue 2·00 2·25
268 – 1000l. multicoloured . . . 3·25 4·25
DESIGNS—VERT (26 × 47 mm): 450l. Airmail letter and stylized bird (25th anniv of Turkish Cypriot postal service). HORIZ (as T **89**): 500l. Newspaper and printing press (centenary of "Saded" newspaper); 600l. Statue of Aphrodite, lifebelt and seabird (30th anniv of International Maritime Organization); 1000l. Soldiers (25th anniv of Turkish Cypriot resistance).

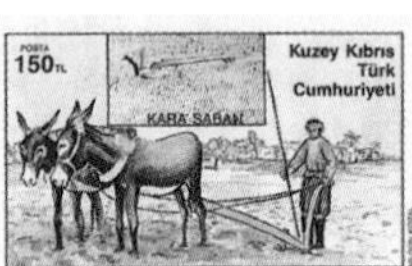

90 Erdal Inonu **91** Mule-drawn Plough

1989. Visit of Professor Erdal Inonu (Turkish politician).
269 **90** 700l. multicoloured 80 90

1989. Traditional Agricultural Implements. Mult.
270 150l. Type **91** 30 25
271 450l. Ox-drawn threshing sledge 75 85
272 550l. Olive press (vert) . . . 90 1·10

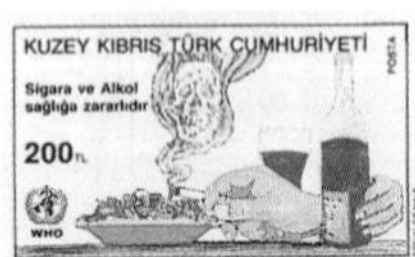

92 Smoking Ashtray and Drinks

1990. World Health Day. Multicoloured.
273 200l. Type **92** 85 40
274 700l. Smoking cigarette and heart . . . . 1·90 2·75

93 Yenierenkoy Post Office

1990. Europa. Post Office Buildings. Mult.
275 1000l. Type **93** . . . . 1·50 75
276 1500l. Ataturk Meydani Post Office . . . . 2·25 3·25
MS277 105 × 72 mm. Nos. 275/6 × 2 6·50 8·00

94 Song Thrush **96** Amphitheatre, Soli

95 Two Football Teams

1990. World Environment Day. Birds. Mult.
278 150l. Type **94** . . . . 2·00 65
279 300l. Blackcap . . . . 2·75 90
280 900l. Black redstart . . . . . 4·25 3·50
281 1000l. Chiff-chaff . . . . . 4·25 3·50

1990. World Cup Football Championship, Italy. Mult.
282 300l. Type **95** 75 50
283 1000l. Championship symbol, globe and ball . . . . . . 2·50 3·25

1990. Paintings (9th series). As T **54**. Multicoloured.
284 300l. "Abstract" (Filiz Ankacc) 25 25
285 1000l. Wooden sculpture (S. Tekman) (vert) . . . . 85 1·50

1990. Tourism. Multicoloured.
286 150l. Type **96** 40 20
287 1000l. Swan mosaic, Soli . . 1·75 2·50

97 Kenan Evren and Rauf Denktas

1990. Visit of President Kenan Evren of Turkey.
288 **97** 500l. multicoloured . . . . 1·00 1·00

98 Road Signs and Heart wearing Seat Belt

1990. Traffic Safety Campaign. Multicoloured.
289 150l. Type **98** 75 30
290 300l. Road signs, speeding car and spots of blood . . 1·00 50
291 1000l. Traffic lights and road signs . . . . 3·00 3·75

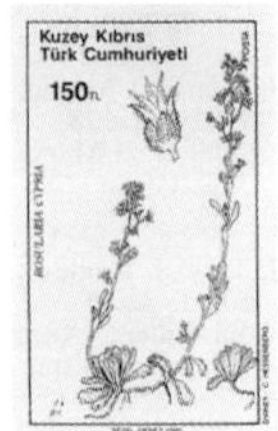

99 Yildirim Akbulut **100** "Rosularia cypria"

1990. Visit of Turkish Prime Minister Yildrim Akbulut.
292 **99** 1000l. multicoloured . . . 1·10 1·10

1990. Plants. Multicoloured.
293 150l. Type **100** 55 20
294 200l. "Silene fraudratrix" . . 65 30
295 300l. "Scutellaria sibthorpii" . . 75 35
296 600l. "Sedum lampusae" . . 1·10 85
297 1000l. "Onosma caespitosum" 1·25 1·75
298 1500l. "Arabis cypria" . . . 1·75 3·00

101 Kemal Ataturk at Easel (wood carving)

1990. International Literacy Year. Multicoloured.
299 300l. Type **101** 75 35
300 750l. Globe, letters and books 2·00 2·50

1991. Nos. 189, 212 and 293 surch.
301 **66** 250l. on 10l. multicoloured 80 80
302 **73** 250l. on 20l. multicoloured 80 80
303 **100** 500l. on 150l. multicoloured . . . . . 1·25 1·25

103 "Ophrys lapethica" **104** "Hermes" (projected shuttle)

1991. Orchids (1st series). Multicoloured.
304 250l. Type **103** . . . . 1·25 60
305 500l. "Ophrys kotschyi" . . . 2·25 2·75
See also Nos. 311/14.

1991. Europa. Europe in Space. Sheet 78 × 82 mm, containing T **104** and similar vert design. Multicoloured.
MS306 2000l. Type **104**; 2000l. "Ulysses" (satellite) 8·00 8·00

105 Kucuk Medrese Fountain, Lefkosa **106** Symbolic Roots (Year of Love to Yunus Emre)

1991. Fountains. Multicoloured.
307 250l. Type **105** 40 15
308 500l. Cafer Pasa fountain, Magusa 60 30
309 1500l. Sarayonu Square fountain, Lefkosa . . . . 1·25 1·40
310 5000l. Arabahmet Mosque fountain, Lefkosa . . . . 3·25 4·50

1991. Orchids (2nd series). As T **103**. Mult.
311 100l. "Serapias levantina" . . 70 20
312 500l. "Dactylorhiza romana" 1·75 50
313 2000l. "Orchis simia" . . . . 3·25 3·50
314 3000l. "Orchis sancta" . . . 3·50 4·25

1991. Paintings (10th series). As T **54**. Mult.
315 250l. "Hindiler" (S. Cizel) (vert) . . . . 1·50 50
316 500l. "Dusme" (A. Mene) (vert) . . . . 2·00 2·25

1991. Anniversaries and Events.
317 **106** 250l. yellow, black and mauve 25 25
318 – 500l. multicoloured . . . 45 60
319 – 500l. multicoloured . . . 45 60
320 – 1500l. multicoloured . . . 3·00 3·75
DESIGNS—VERT: No. 318, Mustafa Cagatay commemoration; 319, University building (5th anniv of Eastern Mediterranean University). HORIZ: No. 320, Mozart (death bicentenary).

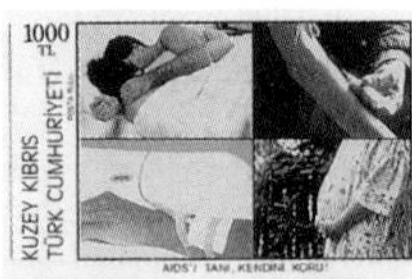

107 Four Sources of Infection

1991. "AIDS" Day.
321 **107** 1000l. multicoloured . . . 2·25 1·75

108 Lighthouse, Gazimagusa

1991. Lighthouses. Multicoloured.
322 250l. Type **108** . . . . 1·60 50
323 500l. Ancient lighthouses, Girne harbour . . . . . . 2·00 1·25
324 1500l. Modern lighthouse, Girne harbour . . . . . . 3·75 4·50

109 Elephant and Hippopotamus Fossils, Karaoglanoglu

1991. Tourism (1st series). Multicoloured.
325 250l. Type **109** . . . . 1·50 40
326 500l. Roman fish ponds, Lambusa . . . . 1·60 65
327 1500l. Roman remains, Lambusa . . . . 2·50 3·75
See also Nos. 330/3 and 351/2.

1992. Paintings (11th series). As T **54**, but 31 × 49 mm. Multicoloured.
328 500l. "Ebru" (A. Kandulu) 50 20
329 3500l. "Street in Lefkosa" (I. Tatar) . . . . 2·75 3·75

1992. Tourism (2nd series). As T **109**. Mult.
330 500l. Bugday Camii, Gazimagusa 60 60
331 500l. Clay pigeon shooting 60 60
332 1000l. Salamis Bay Hotel, Gazimagusa . . . . 1·00 1·00
333 1500l. Casino, Girne (vert) 2·00 2·75

111 Green Turtle

1992. World Environment Day. Sea Turtles. Sheet 105 × 75 mm, containing T **111** and similar horiz design. Multicoloured.
MS335 1000l. × 2, Type **111**: 1500l. × 2, Loggerhead turtle 6·50 6·50

112 Gymnastics **113** New Generating Station, Girne

1992. Olympic Games, Barcelona. Multicoloured.
336 500l. Type **112** 70 90
337 500l. Tennis 70 90
338 1000l. High jumping (horiz) 80 1·00
339 1500l. Cycling (horiz) . . . . 2·75 3·00

1992. Anniversaries and Events (1st series). Multicoloured.
340 500l. Type **113** 40 40
341 500l. Symbol of Housing Association (15th anniv) 40 40
342 1500l. Domestic animals and birds (30th anniv of Veterinary Service) . . . . 2·75 3·00
343 1500l. Cat (International Federation of Cat Societies Conference) . . . . 2·75 3·00

114 Airliner over Runway

1992. Anniversaries and Events (2nd series). Multicoloured.
344 1000l. Type **114** (17th anniv of civil aviation) . . . . . 1·60 1·60
345 1000l. Meteorological instruments and weather (18th anniv of Meteorological Service) . . 1·60 1·60
346 1200l. Surveying equipment and map (14th anniv of Survey Department) . . . 2·00 2·50

115 Zubiye

1992. International Conference on Nutrition, Rome. Turkish Cypriot Cuisine. Multicoloured.
347 2000l. Type **115** . . . . . . 1·00 1·00
348 2500l. Cicek Dolmasi . . . . 1·25 1·25
349 3000l. Tatar Boregi . . . . . 1·50 1·60
350 4000l. Seftali Kebabi . . . . 1·75 2·00

1993. Tourism (3rd series). As T **109**. Mult.
351 500l. St. Barnabas Church and Monastery, Salamis . . 30 15
352 10000l. Ancient pot . . . . . 3·50 4·50

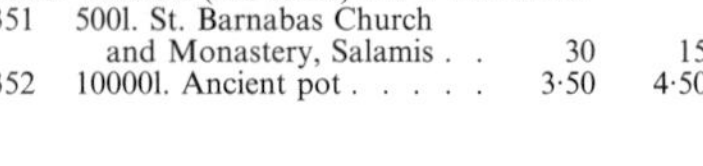

116 Painting by Turksal Ince **117** Olive Tree, Girne

1993. Europa. Contemporary Art. Sheet 79 × 69 mm, containing T **116** and similar vert design. Multicoloured.
MS353 2000l. Type **116**; 3000l. Painting by Ilkay Onsoy 1·75 2·00

1993. Ancient Trees. Multicoloured.
354 500l. Type **117** 20 15
355 1000l. River red gum, Kyrenia Gate, Lefkosa . . 30 25
356 3000l. Oriental plane, Lapta 80 1·25
357 4000l. Calabrian pine, Cinarli 90 1·60

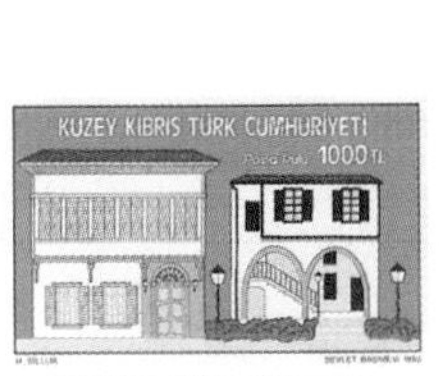

118 Traditional Houses

119 National Flags turning into Doves

1993. Arabahmet District Conservation Project, Lefkosa. Multicoloured.
358 1000l. Type **118** . . . . . . 1·00 40
359 3000l. Arabahmet street . . . 2·00 2·75

1993. 10th Anniv of Proclamation of Turkish Republic of Northern Cyprus.
360 **119** 500l. red, black and blue 20 20
361 – 500l. red and blue 20 20
362 – 1000l. red, black and blue 30 30
363 – 5000l. multicoloured . . . 1·60 2·50
DESIGNS—HORIZ: No. 361, National flag forming figure "10"; No. 362, Dove carrying national flag; No. 363, Map of Cyprus and figure "10" wreath.

120 Kemal Ataturk

121 "Soyle Falci" (Goral Ozkan)

1993. Anniversaries. Multicoloured.
364 500l. Type **120** (55th death anniv) 20 20
365 500l. Stage and emblem (30th anniv of Turkish Cypriot theatre) (horiz) 20 20
366 1500l. Branch badges (35th anniv of T.M.T. organization) (horiz) . . . 40 50
367 2000l. World map and computer (20th anniv of Turkish Cypriot news agency) (horiz) 90 90
368 5000l. Ballet dancers and Caykovski'nin (death centenary) (horiz) . . . . 3·50 3·75

1994. Art (12th series). Multicoloured.
369 1000l. Type **121** 20 20
370 6500l. "IV. Hareket" (sculpture) (Senol Ozdevrim) . . . . 1·10 1·60
See also Nos. 436/7.

122 Dr. Kucuk and Memorial

1994. 10th Death Anniv of Dr. Fazil Kucuk (politician).
371 **122** 1500l. multicoloured . . . 60 70

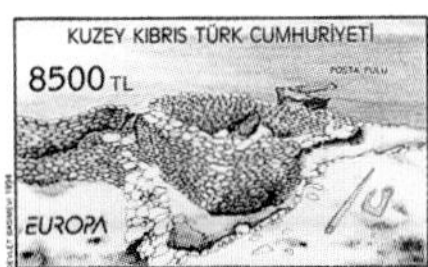

123 Neolithic Village, Girne

1994. Europa. Archaeological Discoveries. Sheet 73 × 79 mm, containing T **123** and similar horiz design. Multicoloured.
MS372 8500l. Type **123**; 8500l. Neolithic man and implements 5·50 5·50

124 Peace Doves and Letters over Pillar Box

125 World Cup Trophy

1994. 30th Anniv of Turkish Cypriot Postal Service.
373 **124** 50000l. multicoloured . . 3·00 4·50

1994. World Cup Football Championship, U.S.A. Multicoloured.
374 2500l. Type **125** 50 25
375 10000l. Footballs on map of U.S.A. (horiz) . . . . . . 1·75 2·50

126 Peace Emblem

1994. 20th Anniv of Turkish Landings in Cyprus.
376 **126** 2500l. yellow, green and black 40 30
377 – 5000l. multicoloured . . . 60 60
378 – 7000l. multicoloured . . . 80 1·00
379 – 8500l. multicoloured . . . 1·10 1·50
DESIGNS—HORIZ: 5000l. Memorial; 7000l. Sculpture; 8500l. Peace doves forming map of Cyprus and flame.

127 Cyprus 1934 4½ pi. Stamp and Karpas Postmark

1994. Postal Centenary. Multicoloured.
380 1500l. Type **127** 25 20
381 2500l. Turkish Cypriot Posts 1979 Europa 2l. and Gazimagusa postmark . . 35 30
382 5000l. Cyprus 1938 6pi. and Bey Keuy postmark . . . 60 70
383 7000l. Cyprus 1955 100m. and Aloa postmark . . . . 80 1·10
384 8500l. Cyprus 1938 18pi. and Pyla postmark . . . . . . 1·00 1·50

128 Trumpet Triton

1994. Sea Shells. Multicoloured.
385 2500l. Type **128** 45 30
386 12500l. Mole cowrie . . . . 1·25 1·75
387 12500l. Giant tun . . . . . 1·25 1·75

1994. Nos. 280, 295, 315 and 317 surch.
388 1500l. on 250l. Type **106** . . 15 10
389 2000l. on 900l. Black redstart 1·50 60
390 2500l. on 250l. "Hindiler" (Sizel) 30 30
391 3500l. on 300l. "Scutellaria sibthorpii" . . . . 1·50 1·50

130 Donkeys on Mountain

1995. European Conservation Year. Multicoloured.
392 2000l. Type **130** 30 20
393 3500l. Coastline 30 30
394 15000l. Donkeys in field . . . 1·50 2·50

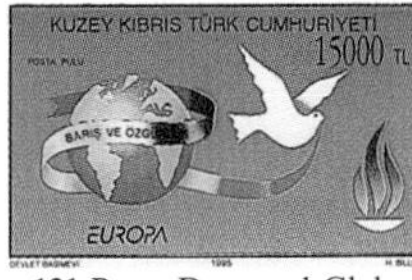

131 Peace Dove and Globe

1995. Europa. Peace and Freedom. Sheet 72 × 78 mm, containing T **131** and similar horiz design. Mult.
MS395 15000l. Type **131**; 15000l. Peace doves over map of Europe 3·25 3·50

132 Sini Katmeri

1995. Turkish Cypriot Cuisine. Multicoloured.
396 3500l. Type **132** 20 20
397 10000l. Kolokas musakka and bullez kizartma . . . 55 65
398 14000l. Enginar dolmasi . . . 90 1·60

133 "Papilio machaon"

1995. Butterflies. Multicoloured.
399 3500l. Type **133** 30 15
400 4500l. "Charaxes jasius" . . 35 20
401 15000l. "Cynthia cardui" . . 1·00 1·40
402 30000l. "Vanessa atalanta" 1·75 2·50

134 Forest

1995. Obligatory Tax. Forest Regeneration Fund.
403 **134** 1000l. green and black . . 2·25 40

135 Beach, Girne

1995. Tourism. Multicoloured.
404 3500l. Type **135** 30 20
405 7500l. Sail boards 50 45
406 15000l. Ruins of Salamis (vert) . . . . 1·00 1·25
407 20000l. St. George's Cathedral, Gazimagusa (vert) . . . . 1·00 1·25

136 Suleyman Demirel and Rauf Denktas

1995. Visit of President Suleyman Demirel of Turkey.
408 **136** 5000l. multicoloured . . . 40 40

137 Stamp Printing Press

138 Kultegin Epitaph and Sculpture

1995. Anniversaries.
409 **137** 3000l. multicoloured . . . 40 40
410 – 3000l. multicoloured . . . 40 40
411 – 5000l. multicoloured . . . 70 70
412 – 22000l. ultram, bl & blk 1·00 1·50
413 – 30000l. multicoloured . . 1·40 2·00
414 – 30000l. multicoloured . . 1·40 2·00
DESIGNS—HORIZ: No. 409, Type **137** (20th anniv of State Printing Works); 410, Map of Turkey (75th anniv of Turkish National Assembly); 411, Louis Pasteur (chemist) and microscope (death centenary); 412, United Nations anniversary emblem (50th anniv); 413, Guglielmo Marconi (radio pioneer) and dial (centenary of first radio transmissions). VERT: No. 414, Stars and reel of film (centenary of cinema).

1995. Centenary of Deciphering of Orhon Epitaphs. Multicoloured.
415 5000l. Type **138** 75 40
416 10000l. Epitaph and tombstone . . . . 1·25 1·60

139 "Bosnia" (sculpture)

140 Striped Red Mullet

1996. Support for Moslems in Bosnia and Herzegovina.
417 **139** 10000l. multicoloured . . 1·25 1·50

1996. Fishes. Multicoloured.
418 6000l. Type **140** 75 30
419 10000l. Peacock wrasse . . . 1·00 45
420 28000l. Common two-banded seabream . . . . 1·75 2·00
421 40000l. Dusky grouper . . . 2·25 2·75

141 Palm Trees

142 Beria Remzi Ozoran

1996. Tourism. Multicoloured.
422 100000l. Type **141** 75 30
423 150000l. Pomegranate . . . . 1·25 55
424 250000l. Ruins of Bella Paise Abbey (horiz) . . . . . . 1·75 2·00
425 500000l. Traditional dancers (horiz) . . . . 3·00 3·50

1996. Europa. Famous Women. Multicoloured.
426 15000l. Type **142** 75 25
427 50000l. Kadriye Hulusi Hacibulgur . . . . 2·00 2·75

143 Established Forest

1996. World Environment Day. Sheet 72 × 78 mm, containing T **143** and similar horiz design. Multicoloured.
MS428 50000l. Type **143**; 50000l. Conifer plantation 5·50 5·50

144 Basketball

1996. Olympic Games, Atlanta. Sheet 105 × 74 mm, containing T **144** and similar horiz designs. Multicoloured.
MS429 15000l. Type **144**, 15000l. Discus throwing; 50000l. Javelin throwing; 50000l. Volleyball 3·25 3·75

145 Symbolic Footballs

1996. European Football Championship, England. Multicoloured.
430 15000l. Type **145** . . . . . . 1·00 65
431 35000l. Football and flags of participating nations . . . 1·75 2·25

146 Houses on Fire (Auxiliary Fire Service)

147 "Amanita phalloides"

1996. Anniversaries and Events. Multicoloured.
432 100000l. Type **146** 75 40
433 200000l. Colour party (20th anniv of Defence Forces) (vert) 80 55
434 500000l. Children by lake (Nasreddin-Hoca Year) . . 1·10 1·25
435 750000l. Flowers (Children's Rights) . . . . 1·50 2·00

1997. Arts (13th series). As T **121**. Multicoloured.
436 250000l. "City" (Lebibe Sonuc) (horiz) . . . . . . 1·00 50
437 700000l. "Woman opening Letter" (Ruzen Atakan) (horiz) . . . . 2·00 2·75

1997. Fungi. Multicoloured.
438 150000l. Type **147** 50 30
439 250000l. "Morchella esculenta" 65 65
440 250000l. "Pleurotus eryngii" 65 65
441 700000l. "Amanita muscaria" 1·40 2·50

148 Flag on Hillside

150 Prime Minister Necmettin Erbakan of Turkey

149 Mother and Children playing Leapfrog

1997. Besparmak Mountains Flag Sculpture.
442 **148** 60000l. multicoloured . . 1·25 1·50

1997. Europa. Tales and Legends. Multicoloured.
443 25000l. Type **149** . . . . . . 1·00 30
444 70000l. Apple tree and well 2·00 2·75

1997. Visit of the President and the Prime Minister of Turkey.
445 15000l. Type **150** 30 20
446 80000l. President Suleyman Demirel of Turkey (horiz) 1·25 2·00

151 Golden Eagle

152 Coin of Sultan Abdulaziz, 1861–76

1997. Birds of Prey. Multicoloured.
447 40000l. Type **151** . . . . . . 1·00 1·00
448 40000l. Eleonora's falcon . . 1·00 1·00
449 75000l. Common kestrel . . . 1·50 1·75
450 100000l. Western honey buzzard . . . . 1·75 2·00

1997. Rare Coins. Multicoloured.
451 25000l. Type **152** 30 20
452 40000l. Coin of Sultan Mahmud II, 1808–39 . . . 40 35
453 75000l. Coin of Sultan Selim II, 1566–74 . . . . 65 1·00
454 100000l. Coin of Sultan Mehmed V, 1909–18 . . . 90 1·75

153 Open Book and Emblem

1997. Anniversaries.
455 **153** 25000l. multicoloured . . 55 20
456 – 40000l. multicoloured . . 65 30
457 – 100000l. black, red and stone . . . . 1·50 1·50
458 – 150000l. multicoloured . . 2·00 2·75
DESIGNS—HORIZ: 25000l. Type **153** (centenary of Turkish Cypriot Scouts); 40000l. Guides working in field (90th anniv of Turkish Cypriot Guides); 150000l. Rudolph Diesel and first oil engine (centenary of the diesel engine). VERT: 100000l. Couple and symbols (AIDS prevention campaign).

154 Ahmet and Ismet Sevki

1998. Ahmet and Ismet Sevki (photographers) Commemoration. Multicoloured.
459 40000l. Type **154** 50 25
460 105000l. Ahmet Sevki (vert) 1·60 2·25

155 "Agrion splendens" (dragonfly)

156 Wooden Double Door

1998. Useful Insects. Multicoloured.
461 40000l. Type **155** 55 25
462 65000l. "Ascalaphus macaronius" (owl-fly) . . . 70 40
463 125000l. "Podalonia hirsuta" 1·50 1·75
464 150000l. "Rhyssa persuasoria" . . . . 1·75 2·00

1998. Old Doors.
465 **156** 115000l. multicoloured . . 1·50 1·75
466 – 140000l. multicoloured . . 1·50 1·75
DESIGN: 140000l. Different door.

157 Legislative Assembly Building (Republic Establishment Festival)

1998. Europa. Festivals. Multicoloured.
467 40000l. Type **157** 65 25
468 150000l. Globe, flags and map (Int Children's Folk Dance Festival) (vert) . . . 2·00 2·50

158 Marine Life

1998. International Year of the Ocean.
469 **158** 40000l. multicoloured . . 75 40
470 – 90000l. multicoloured . . 1·50 1·75
DESIGN: 90000l. Different underwater scene

159 Prime Minister Mesut Yilmaz of Turkey

1998. Prime Minister Yilmaz's Visit to Northern Cyprus.
471 **159** 75000l. multicoloured . . 1·50 1·50

160 Pres. Suleyman Demirel of Turkey

162 Deputy Prime Minister Bulent Ecevit

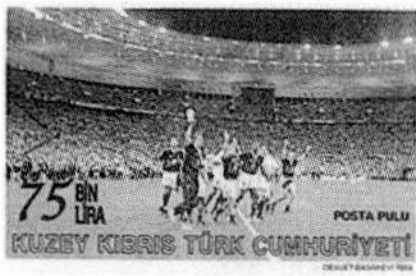

161 Victorious French Team

1998. President Demirel's "Water for Peace" Project.
472 75000l. Type **160** . . . . . . 1·00 50
473 175000l. Turkish and Turkish Cypriot leaders with inflatable water tank (horiz) . . . . 2·00 2·50

1998. World Cup Football Championship, France. Multicoloured.
474 75000l. Type **161** . . . . . . 1·00 50
475 175000l. World Cup trophy (vert) . . . . 2·00 2·50

1998. Visit of the Deputy Prime Minister of Turkey.
476 **162** 200000l. multicoloured . . 1·75 2·00

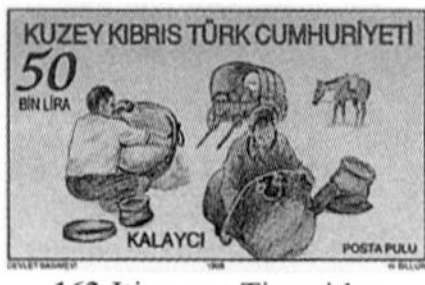

163 Itinerant Tinsmiths

1998. Local Crafts. Multicoloured.
477 50000l. Type **163** 35 25
478 75000l. Basket weaver (vert) 55 35
479 130000l. Grinder sharpening knife (vert) . . . . 95 1·10
480 400000l. Wood carver . . . . 3·00 3·75

164 Stylised Satellite Dish

165 Dr. Fazil Kucuk

1998. Anniversaries. Multicoloured (except No. 483).
481 50000l. Type **164** 70 25
482 75000l. Stylised birds and "15" 75 85
483 75000l. "75" and Turkish flag (red, black and orange) . . 75 85
484 175000l. Scroll, "50" and quill pen (vert) . . . . . . 1·25 2·00
MS485 72 × 78 mm. 75000l. As No. 482; 75000l. Map of Northern Cyprus . . . . 1·50 1·75
ANNIVERSARIES: No. 481, 35th anniv of Bayrak Radio and Television; 482, **MS**485, 15th anniv of Turkish Republic of Northern Cyprus; 483, 75th anniv of Turkish Republic; 484, 50th anniv of Universal Declaration of Human Rights.

1999. 15th Death Anniv of Dr. Fazil Kucuk (politician).
486 **165** 75000l. multicoloured . . 1·00 1·00

166 Otello

1999. Performance of Verdi's Opera Otello in Cyprus. Sheet 78 × 74 mm, containing T **166** and similar vert design. Multicoloured.
MS487 200000l. Type **166**; 200000l. Desdemona dead in front of fireplace . . . . 2·75 2·75

167 "Malpolon monspessulanus insignitus" (Montepellier)

1999. Snakes. Multicoloured.
488 50000l. Type **167** 60 30
489 75000l. "Hierophis jugularis" 80 45
490 195000l. "Vipera lebetina lebetina" (levantine viper) 1·50 1·75
491 220000l. "Natrix natrix" (grass snake) . . . . . . 1·50 1·75

168 Entrance to Cave

1999. Europa. Parks and Gardens. Incirli Cave. Multicoloured.
492 75000l. Type **168** 75 25
493 200000l. Limestone rocks inside cave (vert) . . . . . 1·50 2·00

169 Peace Dove and Map of Cyprus

1999. 25th Anniv of Turkish Landings in Cyprus. Multicoloured.
494 150000l. Type **169** . . . . . 1·25 1·00
495 250000l. Peace dove, map of Cyprus and sun . . . . . 1·50 1·75

170 Air Mail Envelope and Labels

1999. Anniversaries and Events. Multicoloured.
496 75000l. Type **170** (35th anniv of Turkish Cypriot Posts) 40 25
497 225000l. "125" and U.P.U. emblem (125th anniv of U.P.U.) 85 90
498 250000l. Total eclipse of the Sun, August 1999 . . . . 1·25 1·50

171 Turkish Gateway, Limassol

1999. Destruction of Turkish Buildings in Southern Cyprus. Each light brown and brown.
499 75000l. Type **171** 40 25
500 150000l. Mosque, Evdim . . 65 40
501 210000l. Bayraktar Mosque, Lefkosa 80 60
502 1000000l. Kebir Mosque, Baf (vert) . . . . 4·00 5·00

172 Mobile Phone

2000. New Millennium. Technology.
503 **172** 75000l. black, green and blue 35 20
504 – 150000l. black and blue 55 25
505 – 275000l. multicoloured . . 90 1·00
506 – 300000l. multicoloured . . 1·10 1·40
DESIGNS: 150000l. "Hosgeldin 2000"; 275000l. Computer and "internet" in squares; 300000l. Satellite over Earth.

173 Beach Scene

2000. Holidays. Multicoloured.
507 300000l. Type **173** . . . . . 1·25 1·40
508 340000l. Deck-chair on sea-shore . . . . 1·25 1·40

174 "Building Europe"

2000. Europa. Sheet 77 × 68 mm, containing T **174** and similar vert design. Multicoloured.
MS509 300000l. Type **174**; 300000l. Map of Europe with flower creating Council of Europe emblem and map of Cyprus 2·25 2·50

175 Bellapais Abbey
176 Pres. Ahmet Sezer of Turkey

2000. 4th International Bellapais Music Festival. Multicoloured.
510 150000l. Type **175** 65 50
511 350000l. Emblem (vert) . . . 1·25 1·50

2000. Visit of President Ahmet Sezer of Turkey.
512 **176** 150000l. multicoloured . . 1·00 1·00

177 Olympic Torch and Rings
179 Grasshopper on Cactus

2000. Olympic Games, Sydney. Multicoloured.
513 125000l. Type **177** 65 40
514 200000l. Runner (horiz) . . . 1·10 1·25

2000. No. 418 surch **50000 LIRA POSTA PULU**.
515 50000l. on 6000l. Type **140** 50 20

2000. Nature. Insects and Flowers. Multicoloured.
516 125000l. Type **179** 25 20
517 200000l. Butterfly on flower 40 30
518 275000l. Bee on flower . . . 50 45
519 600000l. Snail on flower . . . 1·00 1·25

180 Traditional Kerchief

2000. Traditional Handicrafts. Kerchiefs.
520 **180** 125000l. multicoloured . . 40 30
521 – 200000l. multicoloured . . 60 45
522 – 265000l. multicoloured . . 80 1·00
523 – 350000l. multicoloured . . 90 1·25
DESIGNS: 200000l. to 350000l. Different kerchiefs.

181 Lusignan House, Lefkosa

2001. Restoration of Historic Buildings. Mult.
524 125000l. Type **181** 40 25
525 200000l. The Eaved House, Lefkosa 60 75

182 "Cuprum Kuprum Bakir Madeni" (Inci Kansu)

2001. Modern Art. Multicoloured.
526 125000l. Type **182** 10 15
527 200000l. "Varolus" (Emel Samioglu) 15 20
528 350000l. "Ask Kuslara Ucar" (Ozden Selenge) (vert) . . 30 35
529 400000l. "Suyun Yolculugu" (Ayhatun Atesin) 30 35

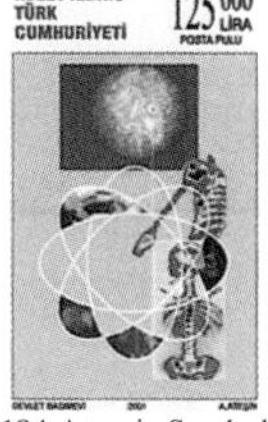

183 Degirmenlik Reservoir
184 Atomic Symbol and X-ray

2001. Europa. Water Resources. Multicoloured.
530 200000l. Type **183** 20 25
531 500000l. The Waters of Sinar 50 55

2001. World Environment Day. Radiation. Mult.
532 125000l. Type **184** 30 20
533 450000l. Radiation symbol and x-ray of hand 80 90

185 Ottoman Policeman, 1885
186 MG TF Sports Car, 1954

2001. Turkish Cypriot Police Uniforms. Multicoloured.
534 125000l. Type **185** 10 15
535 200000l. Colonial policeman, 1933 . . . . 15 20
536 500000l. Mounted policeman, 1934 . . . . 40 45
537 750000l. Policewoman, 1983 60 65

2001. Classic Cars. Multicoloured.
538 175000l. Type **186** 10 15
539 300000l. Vauxhall 14, 1948 25 30
540 475000l. Bentley, 1922 . . . 40 45
541 600000l. Jaguar XK 120, 1955 . . . . 50 55

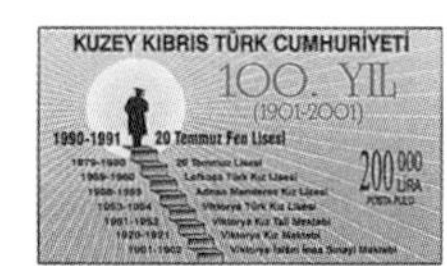

187 Graduate at Top of Steps and College Names

2001. Anniversaries.
542 **187** 200000l. multicoloured . . 15 20
543 – 200000l. black, mauve and brown 15 20
DESIGNS—HORIZ: No. 542, Type **187** (Centenary of Higher Education). VERT: No. 543, Book cover of *The Genocide Files* by Harry Scott Gibbons (anniversary of publication).

188 Chef mincing Logs into Letters (U. Karsu)
189 Turtle

2002. Caricatures. Multicoloured.
544 250000l. Type **188** 20 25
545 300000l. Overfed people drinking from inflated cow, and starving children (M. Kayra) (horiz) 25 30
546 475000l. Can of cola parachuting down to pregnant African woman (S. Gazi) 40 45
547 850000l. Artist painting trees in city (M. Tozaki) 70 75

2002. Tourism. Underwater Scenes. Multicoloured.
548 250000l. Type **189** 20 25
549 300000l. Starfish on rock . . 25 30
550 500000l. Fish in rocks . . . 40 45
551 750000l. Part of wreck . . . 60 65

190 Stilt-walker
192 Woman in White Tunic and Trousers

191 Turkish Football Team

2002. Europa. Circus. Sheet 79 × 72 mm, containing T **190** and similar vert design. Multicoloured.
MS552 600000l. Type **190**; 600000l. Child on high wire 50 55

2002. World Cup Football Championship, Japan and Korea (2002). Multicoloured.
553 300000l. Type **191** 25 30
554 1000000l. Football Stadium, World Cup Trophy and footballer 80 85

2002. Traditional Costumes. Multicoloured.
555 250000l. Type **192** 20 25
556 300000l. Man wearing grey jacket 25 30
557 425000l. Man in blue jacket and trousers 35 40
558 700000l. Woman in yellow tunic 55 60

193 "Accident by Bridge"

2002. Children's Paintings. Multicoloured.
559 300000l. Type **193** 25 30
560 600000l. "Burning House" (vert) 50 55

194 Sureyya Ayhan (athlete)
195 Oguz Karayel (footballer) (70th birth anniv)

2002. Sporting Celebrities. Multicoloured.
561 300000l. Type **194** 25 25
562 1000000l. Grand Master Park Jung-tae (taekwon-do) . . 90 95

2002. Celebrities' Anniversaries. Multicoloured.
563 100000l. Type **195** 10 10
564 175000l. Mete Adanir (footballer) (40th birth anniv) 10 10
565 300000l. M. Necati Ozkan (30th death anniv) 25 30
566 575000l. Osman Turkay (astronomer) (1st death anniv) (horiz) 55 60

CYRENAICA Pt. 8

Part of the former Italian colony of Libya, N. Africa. Allied Occupation, 1942–49. Independent Administration, 1949–52. Then part of independent Libya.

Stamps optd **BENGASI** formerly listed here will be found under Italian P.O.s in the Turkish Empire, Nos. 169/70.

100 centesimi = 1 lira.

Stamps of Italy optd **CIRENAICA**.

1923. Tercent of Propagation of the Faith.
1 **66** 20c. orange and green . . . 4·00 18·00
2 30c. orange and red . . . . 4·00 18·00
3 50c. orange and violet . . . 2·75 20·00
4 1l. orange and blue . . . . . 2·75 26·00

1923. Fascist March on Rome stamps.
5 **77** 10c. green . . . . 4·25 7·25
6 30c. violet . . . . 4·25 7·50
7 50c. red . . . . 4·25 8·25
8 **74** 1l. blue . . . . 4·25 21·00
9 2l. brown . . . . 4·25 25·00
10 **75** 5l. black and blue . . . . . 4·25 35·00

1924. Manzoni stamps (Nos. 155/60).
11 **77** 10c. black and purple . . . 5·00 20·00
12 – 15c. black and green . . . 5·00 20·00
13 – 30c. black . . . . 5·00 20·00
14 – 50c. black and brown . . . 5·00 20·00
15 – 1l. black and blue . . . . 40·00 £150
16 – 5l. black and purple £400 £1300

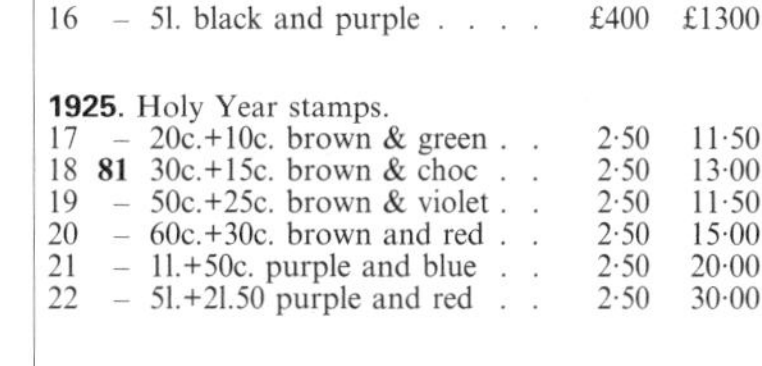

1925. Holy Year stamps.
17 – 20c.+10c. brown & green . . 2·50 11·50
18 **81** 30c.+15c. brown & choc . . 2·50 13·00
19 – 50c.+25c. brown & violet . . 2·50 11·50
20 – 60c.+30c. brown and red . . 2·50 15·00
21 – 1l.+50c. purple and blue . . 2·50 20·00
22 – 5l.+2l.50 purple and red . . 2·50 30·00

1925. Royal Jubilee stamps.
23 **82** 60c. red . . . . 30 5·25
24 1l. blue . . . . 50 5·25
24a 1l.25 blue . . . . 2·50 11·00

1926. St. Francis of Assisi stamps.
25 **83** 20c. green . . . . 1·50 6·50
26 – 40c. violet . . . . 1·50 6·50
27 – 60c. red . . . . 1·50 11·50
28 – 1l.25 blue . . . . 1·50 18·00
29 – 5l.+2l.50 olive (as No. 196) 4·25 35·00

6 8

1926. Colonial Propaganda.
30 **6** 5c.+5c. brown . . . . . . 60 4·00
31 10c.+5c. olive . . . . . . 60 4·00
32 20c.+5c. green . . . . . . 60 4·00
33 40c.+5c. red . . . . 60 4·00
34 60c.+5c. orange . . . . . 60 4·00
35 1l.+5c. blue . . . . 60 6·50

1927. 1st National Defence stamps of Italy optd **CIRENAICA**.
36 **89** 40+20c. black & brown . . 1·75 15·00
37 – 60+30c. brown and red . . 1·75 15·00
38 – 1l.25+60c. black & blue . . 1·75 30·00
39 – 5l.+2l.50 black & green . . 2·75 40·00

1927. Volta Centenary stamps of Italy optd **Cirenaica**.
40 **90** 20c. violet . . . . 5·00 18·00
41 50c. orange . . . . 6·50 11·50
42 1l.25 blue . . . . 10·00 26·00

1928. 45th Anniv of Italian–African Society.
43 **8** 20c.+5c. green . . . . . . 1·60 5·25
44 30c.+5c. red . . . . 1·60 5·25
45 50c.+10c. violet . . . . . 1·60 9·25
46 1l.25+20c. blue . . . . . 1·75 10·50

Stamps of Italy optd **CIRENAICA**. Colours changed in some instances.

1929. 2nd National Defence stamps.
47 **89** 30c.+10c. black & red . . . 3·00 10·50
48 50c.+20c. grey & lilac . . . 3·00 12·50
49 1l.25+50c. blue & brown . . 3·75 20·00
50 – 5l.+2l. black & green . . . 3·75 35·00

1929. Montecassino stamps (No. 57 optd **Cirenaica**).
51 **104** 20c. green . . . . 3·75 8·25
52 – 25c. red . . . . 3·75 8·25
53 – 50c.+10c. red . . . . . 3·75 10·00
54 – 75c.+15c. brown . . . . 3·75 10·00
55 **104** 1l.25+25c. purple . . . . . 7·25 16·00
56 – 5l.+1l. blue . . . . . . 7·25 20·00
57 – 10l.+2l. brown . . . . . 7·25 26·00

1930. Marriage of Prince Humbert and Princess Marie Jose stamps.
58 **109** 20c. green . . . . 1·00 3·00
59 50c.+10c. red . . . . . . 80 4·00
60 1l.25+25c. red . . . . . . 80 9·25

1930. Ferrucci stamps (optd **Cirenaica**).
61 **114** 20c. violet . . . . 1·60 1·60
62 – 25c. green . . . . 1·60 1·60
63 – 50c. black . . . . 1·60 3·25
64 – 1l.25 blue . . . . 1·60 6·50
65 – 5l.+2l. red . . . . 5·00 13·00

1930. 3rd National Defence stamps.
66 **89** 30c.+10c. turq & grn . . . 13·00 16·00
67 – 50c.+10c. purple & green . . 13·00 20·00
68 – 1l.25+30c. lt brown & brn . 13·00 30·00
69 – 5l.+1l.50 green and blue . . 42·00 65·00

13
17 Columns of Leptis

1930. 25th Anniv (1929) of Italian Colonial Agricultural Institute.
70 **13** 50c.+20c. brown . . . . . 2·25 10·00
71 1l.25+20c. blue . . . . . 2·25 10·00
72 1l.75+20c. green . . . . . 2·25 12·00
73 2l.55+50c. violet . . . . . 3·25 20·00
74 5l.+1l. red . . . . 3·25 28·00

1930. Virgil Bimillenary stamps optd **CIRENAICA**.
75 **118** 15c. violet . . . . 85 4·00
76 – 20c. brown . . . . 85 2·00
77 – 25c. green . . . . 85 1·60
78 – 30c. brown . . . . 85 2·00
79 – 50c. purple . . . . 85 1·60
80 – 75c. red . . . . 85 3·00
81 – 1l.25 blue . . . . 85 4·00

82 – 5l.+11.50 purple 3·00 21·00
83 – 10l.+21.50 brown 3·00 32·00

1931. St. Anthony of Padua stamps optd **Cirenaica** (75c., 5l.) or **CIRENAICA** (others).
84 **121** 20c. brown 1·25 8·25
85 – 25c. green 1·25 3·25
86 – 30c. brown 1·25 3·25
87 – 50c. purple 1·25 3·25
88 – 75c. grey (as No. 308) 1·25 8·25
89 – 11.25 blue 1·25 16·00
90 – 5l.+21.50 brn (as No. 310) 3·50 38·00

1932. Air stamps of Tripolitania optd **Cirenaica**.
91 **18** 50c. red 65 30
92 60c. orange 4·00 8·00
93 80c. purple 4·00 11·50

1932. Air stamps of Tripolitania of 1931 optd **CIRENAICA** and bars.
94 **18** 50c. red 1·00 1·00
95 80c. purple 5·25 12·00

1932. Air.
96 – 50c. violet 3·25 10
97 – 75c. red 5·00 5·00
98 – 80c. blue 5·00 10·00
99 **17** 1l. black 1·60 10
100 2l. green 2·00 5·00
101 5l. red 3·75 10·00
DESIGN—VERT: 50c. to 80c. Arab on Camel.

18 "Graf Zeppelin"

1933. Air. "Graf Zeppelin". Inscr "CROCIERA ZEPPELIN".
102 **18** 3l. brown 5·75 55·00
103 – 5l. violet 5·75 55·00
104 – 10l. green 5·75 £110
105 – 12l. blue 5·75 £120
106 **18** 15l. red 5·75 £120
107 – 20l. black 5·75 £140
DESIGNS: 5l., 12l. "Graf Zeppelin" and Roman galley, 10l., 20l. "Graf Zeppelin" and giant archer.

19 Air Squadron

1933. Air. Balbo Transatlantic Mass Formation Flight by Savoia Marchetti S-55X Flying Boats.
108 **19** 19l.75 blue and green 11·50 £300
109 44l.75 blue and red 11·50 £300

1934. Air. Rome–Buenos Aires Flight. T **17** (new colours) optd with Savoia Marchetti S-71 airplane and **1934-XII PRIMO VOLO DIRETTO ROMA = BUENOS-AYRES TRIMOTORE "LOMBARDI-MAZZOTTI"** or surch also.
110 **17** 2l. on 5l. brown 2·00 32·00
111 3l. on 5l. green 2·00 32·00
112 5l. brown 2·00 35·00
113 10l. on 5l. pink 2·25 35·00

21 Arab Horseman

1934. 2nd International Colonial Exn, Naples.
114 **21** 5c. brn & grn (postage) 2·75 9·00
115 10c. black and brown 2·75 9·00
116 20c. blue and red 2·75 7·50
117 50c. brown and violet 2·75 7·50
118 60c. blue and brown 2·75 9·75
119 1l.25 green and blue 2·75 16·00

120 – 25c. orange & blue (air) 2·75 9·00
121 – 50c. blue and green 2·75 7·50
122 – 75c. orange and brown 2·75 7·50
123 – 80c. green and brown 2·75 9·00
124 – 1l. green and red 2·75 10·00
125 – 2l. brown and blue 2·75 16·00
DESIGNS: 25 to 75c. Arrival of Caproni Ca 101 mail plane; 80c. to 2l. Caproni Ca 101 mail plane and Venus of Cyrene.

22

1934. Air. Rome–Mogadiscio Flight.
126 **22** 25c.+10c. green 3·25 5·00
127 50c.+10c. brown 3·25 5·00
128 75c.+15c. red 3·25 5·00
129 80c.+15c. black 3·25 5·00
130 1l.+20c. brown 3·25 5·00
131 2l.+20c. blue 3·25 5·00
132 3l.+25c. violet 16·00 42·00
133 5l.+25c. orange 16·00 42·00
134 10l.+30c. purple 16·00 42·00
135 25l.+2l. green 16·00 42·00

OFFICIAL AIR STAMP

1934. Optd **SERVIZIO DI STATO** and crown.
O136 **22** 25l.+2l. red £1600 £1100

For stamps of British Occupation see under British Occupation of Italian Colonies.

CZECHOSLOVAK ARMY IN SIBERIA Pt. 5

During the War of 1914–18 many Czech and Slovak soldiers in the Austro-Hungarian armies surrendered to the Russian Army. After the war many of these formed an army in Siberia and fought the Bolshevists. They issued stamps for their own postal service and these were also sold to the public on the Siberian Railway.

100 kopeks = 1 rouble.

1 Church in Irkutsk

3 Sentry

1919. Imperf.
1 **1** 25k. red 17·00 12·50
2 – 50k. green 17·00 32·00
3 **3** 1r. red 32·00 25·00
DESIGN: 50k. Armoured train "Orlik".

1920. Perf.
4 **1** 25k. red 14·00 10·00
5 – 50k. green (as No. 2) 14·00 10·00
6 **3** 1r. brown 21·00 19·00

4 Lion of Bohemia

1919.
7 **4** (25k.) red and blue 1·75

1920. No. 7 optd **1920**.
8 **4** (25k.) red and blue 8·00

1920. No. 8 surch.
9 **4** 2(k.) red and blue 35·00
10 3(k.) red and blue 35·00
11 5(k.) red and blue 35·00
12 10(k.) red and blue 35·00
13 15(k.) red and blue 35·00
14 25(k.) red and blue 35·00
15 35(k.) red and blue 35·00
16 50(k.) red and blue 35·00
17 1r. red and blue 35·00

CZECHOSLOVAKIA Pt. 5

Formed in 1918 by the Czechs of Bohemia and Moravia and the Slovaks of northern Hungary (both part of Austro-Hungarian Empire). Occupied by Germany in 1939 (see note after No. 393c); independence restored 1945.

On 31 December 1992 the Czech and Slovak Federative Republic was dissolved, the two constituent republics becoming independent as the Czech Republic and Slovakia.

100 haleru = 1 koruna.

1

2 Hradcany, Prague

1918. Roul.
1 **1** 10h. blue 13·50 15·00
2 20h. red 13·50 15·00

1918. (a) Imperf.
4 **2** 3h. mauve 10 10
9 30h. olive 25 10
10 40h. orange 25 10
12 100h. brown 65 10
14 400h. violet 1·40 25

(b) Imperf or perf.
5 **2** 5h. green 10 10
6 10h. red 10 10
7 20h. green 10 10
8 25h. blue 10 10
13 200h. blue 1·10 10

3

1919. Imperf or perf.
3 **3** 1h. brown 10 10
38 5h. green 10 10
39 10h. green 10 10
40 15h. red 10 10
41 20h. red 10 10
28 25h. purple 10 10
49 30h. mauve 35 10
11 50h. purple 25 10
30 50h. blue 25 10
50 60h. orange 25 10
32 75h. green 65 10
33 80h. green 1·10 10
34 120h. black 1·10 40
35 300h. green 3·50 40
36 500h. brown 2·10 35
37 1000h. purple 11·50 80

6

7

1919. 1st Anniv of Independence and Czechoslovak Legion Commemoration.
61 **6** 15h. green 10 10
62 25h. brown 10 10
63 50h. blue 10 10
64 **7** 75h. grey 10 10
65 100h. brown 10 10
66 120h. violet on yellow 10 10

1919. Charity. Stamps of Austria optd **POSTA CESKOSLOVENSKA 1919**. A. Postage stamp issue of 1916.
67 **49** 3h. violet 10 40
68 5h. green 10 40
69 6h. orange 50 60
70 10h. purple 60 90
71 12h. blue 60 60
72 **60** 15h. red 10 10
73 20h. green 10 10
75 25h. blue 10 25
76 30h. violet 10 25
77 **51** 40h. green 10 25
78 50h. green 10 25
79 60h. blue 10 25
80 80h. brown 10 25
81 90h. purple 45 60
82 1k. red on yellow 30 40
83aa **52** 2k. blue 1·40 2·10
85aa 3k. red 5·25 7·00
87a 4k. green 13·00 14·00
89a 10k. violet £350 £300

B. Air stamps of 1918 optd **FLUGPOST** or surch also.
91 **52** 1k.50 on 2k. mauve 90·00 80·00
92 2k.50 on 3k. yellow £120 £110
93 4k. grey £650 £500

C. Newspaper stamp of 1908. Imperf.
94 **N 43** 10h. red £1500 £1500

D. Newspaper stamps of 1916. Imperf.
95 **N 53** 2h. brown 10 25
96 4h. green 25 35
97 6h. blue 25 30
98 10h. orange 3·00 4·50
99 30h. red 1·50 1·50

E. Express Newspaper stamps of 1916.
100 **N 54** 2h. red on yellow 26·00 25·00
101 5h. green on yellow £1200 £900

F. Express Newspaper stamps of 1917.
102 **N 61** 2h. red on yellow 10 15
103 5h. green on yellow 10 15

G. Postage Due stamps of 1908.
104 **D 44** 2h. red £5000 £3500
105 4h. red 21·00 21·00
106 6h. red 11·00 8·00
108 14h. red 45·00 4·00
109 25h. red 35·00 32·00
110 30h. red £350 £275
111 50h. red £800 £700

H. Postage Due stamps of 1916.
112 **D 55** 5h. red 10 10
113 10h. red 15 20
114 15h. red 15 20
115 20h. red 1·90 2·40
116 25h. red 1·00 1·50
117 30h. red 40 80
118 40h. red 1·00 1·50
119 50h. red £400 £250
120 **D 56** 1k. blue 9·00 7·00
121 5k. blue 30·00 30·00
122 10k. blue £325 £250

I. Postage Due stamps of 1916 (optd **PORTO** or surch **15** also).
123 **36** 1h. black 21·00 17·00
124 – 15h. on 2h. violet 95·00 85·00

J. Postage Due stamps of 1917 (surch **PORTO** and value).
125 **50** 10h. on 24h. blue 70·00 75·00
126 15h. on 36h. violet 40 60
127 20h. on 54h. orange 85·00 90·00
128 50h. on 42h. brown 40 65

1919. Various stamps of Hungary optd **POSTA CESKOSLOVENSKA 1919**. A. Postage stamp issue of 1900 ("Turul" type).
129 **7** 1f. grey £2250 £1600
130 2f. yellow 3·50 5·25
131 3f. orange 38·00 25·00
132 6f. olive 4·25 5·25
133 50f. lake on blue 55 60
134 60f. green on red 40·00 35·00
135 70f. brown on green £2250 £1600

B. Postage stamp issue of 1916 ("Harvester" and "Parliament" types).
136 **18** 2f. brown (No. 245) 10 10
137 3f. red 10 10
138 5f. green 10 10
139 6f. blue 45 60
140 10f. red (No. 250) 90 1·25
141 10f. red (No. 243) £300 £200
142 15f. purple (No. 251) 10 25
143 15f. purple (No. 244) £170 £110
144 20f. brown 7·00 9·00
145 25f. blue 55 60
146 35f. brown 7·00 10·50
147 40f. green 1·90 2·00
148 **19** 50f. purple 55 65
149 75f. green 45 50
150 80f. green 90 1·10
151 1k. red 1·25 1·25
152 2k. brown 7·00 10·50
153 3k. grey and violet 35·00 35·00
154 5k. lt brown & brown 85·00 65·00
155 10k. mauve and brown £1200 £850

C. Postage stamp issue of 1918 ("Charles" and "Zita" types).
156 **27** 10f. red 10 10
157 20f. brown 25 30
158 25f. blue 1·50 1·10
159 **28** 40f. green 2·75 2·50
160 50f. purple 38·00 26·00

D. War Charity stamps of 1916.
161 **20** 10+2f. red 30 60
162 – 15+2f. lilac (No. 265) 45 90
163 **22** 40+2f. red 6·75 3·75

E. Postage stamps of 1919 ("Harvester" type inscr "MAGYAR POSTA").
164 **30** 10f. red (No. 305) 7·50 9·00
165 20f. brown £5500 £6500

F. Newspaper stamp of 1900.
166 **N 9** 2f. orange (No. N136) 10 30

G. Express Letter stamp of 1916.
167 **E 18** 2f. olive & red (No. E245) 10 30

H. Postage Due stamps of 1903 with figures in black.
170 **D 9** 1f. green (No. D170) £1300 £1000
173 2f. green £650 £550
174 5f. green £1400 £1100
168 12f. green £5000 £4000
172 50f. green £325 £225

I. Postage Due stamps of 1915 with figures in red.
176 **D 9** 1f. green (No. D190) £150 £110
177 2f. green 60 50
178 5f. green 9·00 14·00
179 6f. green 1·50 1·75
180 10f. green 30 45
181 12f. green 1·90 2·40
182 15f. green 5·25 9·00
183 20f. green 70 1·10
184 30f. green 30·00 38·00

9 President Masaryk

10

11 Allegories of Republic

12 Hussite **13**

1920.
185 **9** 125h. blue 60 20
186 500h. black 2·75 2·00
187 1,000h. brown 4·50 4·25

1920.
188 **10** 5h. blue 10 10
189 5h. violet 10 10
190 10h. green 10 10
191 10h. olive 10 10
192 15h. brown 10 10
196 **11** 20h. red 10 10

No.	Type	Description		
193b	**10**	20h. orange	10	10
197	**11**	25h. brown	10	10
194a	**10**	25h. green	10	10
198	**11**	30h. purple	10	10
195	**10**	30h. purple	10	10
199	**11**	40h. brown	4·00	10
200		50h. red	10	10
201		50h. green	10	10
202		60h. blue	10	10
203	**12**	80h. violet	10	25
204		90h. sepia	30	50
205	**13**	100h. green	40	10
206	**11**	100h. brown	45	10
227	**13**	100h. red on yellow	2·00	10
207	**11**	150h. red	3·00	70
208		185h. orange	1·25	20
209	**13**	200h. purple	70	10
228		200h. blue on yellow	6·00	10
210	**11**	250h. green	2·25	45
211	**13**	300h. red	1·50	10
229		300h. purple on yellow	5·25	10
212		400h. brown	4·25	55
213		500h. green	5·25	55
214		600h. purple	7·00	55

1920. Air. Surch with airplane and value. Imperf or perf.

No.	Type	Description		
215	**2**	14k. on 200h. blue (No. 13)	15·00	25·00
216	**3**	24k. on 500h. brn (No. 36)	38·00	38·00
220		28k. on 1000h. pur (No. 37)	38·00	32·00

1920. Red Cross Fund. Surch with new value in emblem

No.	Type	Description		
221	**2**	40h.+20h. yellow	80	95
222	**3**	60h.+20h. green	80	95
223	**9**	125h.+25h. blue	2·25	2·75

1922. Surch with airplane and value.

No.	Type	Description		
224	**13**	50 on 100h. green	1·50	2·25
225		100 on 200h. purple	3·75	3·75
226		250 on 400h. brown	6·00	8·00

18 President Masaryk, after portrait by M. Savatimsky

20

23a

1923. 5th Anniv of Republic.

No.	Type	Description		
230	**18**	50h. (+50h.) green	90	65
231		100h. (+100h.) red	1·25	1·10
232		200h. (+200h.) blue	6·25	6·50
233		300h. (+300h.) brown	7·50	8·00

1925.

No.	Type	Description		
234	**20**	40h. orange	75	20
235		50h. green	1·50	10
236		60h. purple	1·90	10
237	**18**	1k. red	90	10
238		2k. blue	3·00	30
245		3k. brown	6·75	10
240		5k. green	1·75	30

The 1, 2 and 3k. (which with the 5k. differ slightly in design from the haleru values) come in various sizes, differing in some cases in the details of the designs.

1925. International Olympic Congress. Optd **CONGRES OLYMP. INTERNAT. PRAHA 1925.**

No.	Type	Description		
246	**18**	50h. (+50h.) green	5·25	10·00
247		100h. (+100h.) red	8·25	14·00
248		200h. (+200h.) blue	50·00	90·00

1926. 8th All-Sokol Display, Prague. Optd **VIII. SLET VSESOKOLSKY PRAHA 1926.**

No.	Type	Description		
249	**18**	50h. (+50h.) green	4·25	6·00
250		100h. (+100h.) red	4·25	6·00
251		200h. (+200h.) blue	20·00	21·00
252		300h. (+300h.) brown	32·00	45·00

1926.

No.	Type	Description		
254b	**23a**	50h. green	10	10
254c		60h. purple	60	10
254d		1k. red	25	10

25 Karluv Tyn Castle

26 Strahov

27 Pernstyn Castle

28 Orava Castle

30 Hradcany, Prague

1926. Perf or imperf × perf.

No.	Type	Description		
267	**25**	20h. red	25	10
268	**27**	30h. green	10	10
258	**28**	40h. brown	50	10
259	**25**	1k.20 purple	35	45
270	**26**	1k.20 purple	35	10
271	**25**	1k.50 red	35	10
272	**27**	2k. green	25	10
263	**30**	2k. blue	75	10
273	**25**	2k.50 blue	5·25	25
273a	–	2k.50 blue	35	10
273b	**28**	3k. brown	45	10
264a	**30**	3k. red	1·75	10
265	–	4k. purple	5·25	65
277	–	5k. green	7·50	1·10

DESIGNS—As T **25/28**: 2k.50 (No. 273a), Statue of St. Wenceslas, Prague. As T **30**: 4, 5k. Upper Tatra.

32 Hradek Castle

33 Pres. Masaryk

1928. 10th Anniv of Independence.

No.	Type	Description		
278	**32**	30h. black	10	10
279	–	40h. brown	10	10
280	–	50h. green	15	15
281		60h. red	15	25
282	–	1k. red	25	20
283	–	1k.20 purple	35	65
284	–	2k. blue	40	65
285	–	2k.50 blue	1·25	1·75
286	**33**	3k. sepia	1·00	1·25
287	–	5k. violet	1·25	2·25

DESIGNS—HORIZ: 40h. Town Hall, Levoca; 50h. Telephone Exchange, Prague; 60h. Village of Jasina; 1k. Hluboka Castle; 1k.20, Pilgrim's House, Velehrad; 2k.50, The Grand Tatra. VERT: 2k. Brno Cathedral; 5k. Town Hall, Prague.

34 National Arms

35 St. Wenceslas on Horseback

1929. Perf or imperf × perf.

No.	Type	Description		
287a	**34**	5h. blue	10	10
287b		10h. brown	10	10
288		20h. red	10	10
289		25h. green	10	10
290		30h. purple	10	10
291a		40h. brown	10	10

1929. Death Millenary of St. Wenceslas.

No.	Type	Description		
293	**35**	50h. green	15	10
294	–	60h. violet	30	10
295	–	2k. blue	65	35
296	–	3k. brown	95	25
297	–	5k. purple	3·00	2·50

DESIGNS: 2k. Foundation of St. Vitus's Church; 3k., 5k. Martyrdom of St. Wenceslas.

36 Brno Cathedral

1929.

No.	Type	Description		
298	**36**	3k. brown	1·10	10
299	–	4k. blue	3·50	60
300	–	5k. green	3·00	35
301	–	10k. violet	7·50	3·00

DESIGNS: 4k. Tatra Mountains; 5k. Town Hall, Prague; 10k. St. Nicholas Church, Prague.

38

39

1930.

No.	Type	Description		
302a	**38**	50h. green	10	10
303		60h. purple	45	10
304		1k. red	10	10

See also No. 373.

1930. 80th Birthday of President Masaryk.

No.	Type	Description		
305	**39**	2k. green	70	35
306		3k. red	1·10	35
307		5k. blue	3·00	2·40
308		10k. black	6·00	4·75

40 Fokker F.IXD

41 Smolik S.19

1930. Air.

No.	Type	Description		
394	**40**	30h. violet	10	10
309		50h. green	10	20
310		1k. red	25	30
311	**41**	2k. green	45	70
312		3k. purple	1·40	95
313	–	4k. blue	85	90
314	–	5k. brown	2·75	1·90
315	–	10k. blue	4·00	5·25
316	–	20k. violet	5·00	5·00

DESIGNS—As Type **41**: 4, 5k. Smolik S.19 with tree in foreground; 10, 20k. Fokker F.IXD over Prague.

43 Krumlov

44 Dr. Miroslav Tyrs

1932. Views.

No.	Type	Description		
317	–	3k.50 purple (Krivoklat)	1·25	1·00
318	–	4k. blue (Orlik)	1·40	60
319	**43**	5k. green	2·25	60

1932. Birth Centenary of Dr. Tyrs, founder of the "Sokol" Movement.

No.	Type	Description		
320	**44**	50h. green	30	10
321		1k. red	80	10
322	–	2k. blue	5·00	40
323	–	3k. brown	8·00	50

On the 2k. and 3k. the portrait faces left.

46 Dr. M. Tyrs

47 Church and Episcopal Palace, Nitra

1933.

No.	Type	Description		
324	**46**	60h. violet	10	10

1933. 1100th Anniv of Foundation of 1st Christian Church at Nitra.

No.	Type	Description		
325	**47**	50h. green	30	10
326	–	1k. red (Church gateway)	3·25	25

49 Frederick Smetana

50 Consecrating Colours at Kiev

1934. 50th Death Anniv of Smetana.

No.	Type	Description		
327	**49**	50h. green	10	10

1934. 20th Anniv of Czechoslovak Foreign Legions.

No.	Type	Description		
328	**50**	50h. green	20	10
329	–	1k. red	25	10
330	–	2k. blue	1·75	25
331	–	3k. brown	2·25	30

DESIGNS—HORIZ: 1k. French battalion enrolling at Bayonne. VERT: 2k. Standard of the Russian Legion; 3k. French, Russian and Serbian legionaries.

52 Antonin Dvorak

53 "Where is my Fatherland?"

1934. 30th Death Anniv of Dvorak.

No.	Type	Description		
332	**52**	50h. green	10	10

1934. Centenary of Czech National Anthem.

No.	Type	Description		
333	**53**	1k. purple	30	20
334		2k. blue	80	40

54 Autograph portrait of Pres. Masaryk

55

1935. 85th Birthday of President Masaryk.

No.	Type	Description		
335	**54**	50h. green	15	10
336		1k. red	30	10
337	**55**	2k. blue	1·00	35
338		3k. brown	2·10	50

See also No. 374.

56 Czech Monument, Arras

57 Gen. M. R. Stefanik

1935. 20th Anniv of Battle of Arras.

No.	Type	Description		
339	**56**	1k. red	40	10
340		2k. blue	95	45

1935. 16th Death Anniv of Gen. Stefanik.

No.	Type	Description		
341	**57**	50h. green	10	10

58 St. Cyril and St. Methodius

59 J. A. Komensky (Comenius)

60 Dr. Edward Benes

60a Gen. M. R. Stefanik

61 Pres. Masaryk

1935. Prague Catholic Congress.

No.	Type	Description		
342	**58**	50h. green	15	10
343		1k. red	25	10
344		2k. blue	95	45

1935.

No.	Type	Description		
345	**59**	40h. blue	10	10
346	**60**	50h. green	10	10
390	**60a**	50h. green	10	10
347		60h. violet	10	10
391		60h. blue	7·00	14·00
348	**61**	1k. purple	10	10
395		1k. purple	10	10

No. 390 differs from No. 341 in having an ornament in place of the word "HALERU".

No. 348 has "l Kc" in value tablets, No. 395 "l K".

62 Symbolic of Infancy

63 K. H. Macha

1936. Child Welfare.

No.	Type	Description		
349	–	50h.+50h. green	25	35
350	**62**	1k.+50h. red	40	55
351	–	2k.+50h. blue	1·10	1·50

DESIGN: 50h., 2k. Grandfather, mother and child from centre of Type **62** (enlarged).

1936. Death Centenary of Macha (poet).

No.	Type	Description		
352	**63**	50h. green	10	10
353		1k. red	30	10

64 Banska Bystrica

65 Podebrady

1936.

No.	Type	Description		
354	–	1k.20 purple	10	10
355	**64**	1k.50 red	10	10
355a	–	1k.60 olive	10	10
356	–	2k. green	10	10
357	–	2k.50 blue	10	10
358	–	3k. brown	10	10
359	–	3k.50 violet	70	45
360	**65**	4k. violet	30	10
361	–	5k. green	30	10
362	–	10k. blue	55	45

DESIGNS—As Type **64**: 1k.20, Palanok Castle; 1k.60, St. Barbara's Church, Kutna Hora; 2k. Zvikov (Klingden Berg) Castle; 2k.50, Strecno Castle; 3k. Hruba Skala Castle (Cesky Raj); 3k.50, Slavkov Castle; 5k. Town Hall, Olomouc ($23\frac{1}{2} \times 29\frac{1}{2}$ mm). As Type **65**: 10k. Bratislava and Danube.

66 President Benes

1937.

No.	Type	Description		
363	**66**	50h. green	10	10

67 Mother and Child

68 "Lullaby"

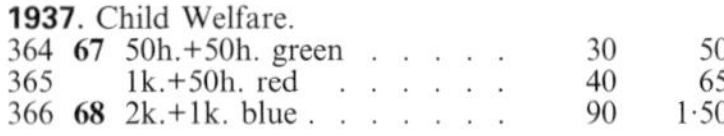

1937. Child Welfare.
364 **67** 50h.+50h. green 30 50
365 1k.+50h. red 40 65
366 **68** 2k.+1k. blue . . . . 90 1·50

69 Czech Legionaries

70 Prague

1937. 20th Anniv of Battle of Zborov.
367 **69** 50h. green 15 10
368 1k. red 15 10

1937. 16th Anniv of Founding of Little Entente.
369 **70** 2k. green 45 10
370 2k.50 blue 70 50

71 J. E. Purkyne

73 Peregrine Falcon

1937. 150th Birth Anniv of J. E. Purkyne (physiologist).
371 **71** 50h. green 10 10
372 1k. red 15 10

1937. Mourning for Pres. Masaryk. As T **38** and **55**, but panels of T **55** dated "14.IX.1937".
373 **38** 50h. black 10 10
374 **55** 2k. black 25 10

1937. Labour Congress, Prague. Optd **B.I.T. 1937**.
375 **66** 50h. green 15 30
376 **64** 1k.50 red 15 30
377 – 2k. green (No. 356) 35 60

1938. 10th International Sokol Display, Prague.
378 **73** 50h. green 15 10
379 1k. red 15 10

74 Pres. Masaryk and Slovak Girl

75 Czech Legionaries at Bachmac

1938. Child Welfare and Birthday of Late President Masaryk.
380 **74** 50h.+50h. green 30 50
381 **74** 1k.+50h. red 40 65

1938. 20th Anniv of Battles in Russia, Italy and France. Inscr "1918 1938".
382 **75** 50h. green 20 10
383 – 50h. green 10 10
384 – 50h. green 10 10
DESIGNS: Czech Legionaries at Doss Alto (No. 383) and at Vouziers (No. 384).

76 J. Fugner

77 Armament Factories, Pilsen

1938. 10th Sokol Summer Games.
385 **76** 50h. green 10 10
386 1k. red 10 10
387 2k. blue 15 10

1938. Provincial Economic Council Meeting, Pilsen.
388 **77** 50h. green 10 10

78 St. Elizabeth's Cathedral, Kosice

79 "Peace"

1938. Kosice Cultural Exhibition.
389 **78** 50h. green 10 10

1938. 20th Anniv of Czech Republic.
392 **79** 2k. blue 15 10
393 3k. brown 35 10

1939. Inauguration of Slovak Parliament. No. 362 surcharged **Otvorenie slovenskeho snemu 18.1.1939** and **300 h** between bars.
393b 300h. on 10k. blue . . . . 55 3·00
No. 393b was only issued in Slovakia but was withdrawn prior to the establishment of the Slovak state. The used price is for cancelled to order stamps.

80 Jasina

1939. Inaug of Carpatho-Ukrainian Parliament.
393c **80** 3k. blue . . . . 10·00 65·00
The used price is for cancelled-to-order.

From mid-1939 until 1945, Czechoslovakia was divided into the German Protectorate of Bohemia and Moravia and the independent state of Slovakia. Both these countries issued their own stamps. Germany had already occupied Sudetenland where a number of unauthorized local issues were made at Asch, Karlsbad, Konstantinsbad, Hiklasdorf, Reichenberg-Maffersdorf and Rumburg. Hungary occupied Carpatho-Ukraine and the stamps of Hungary were used there. In 1945, upon liberation, stamps of Czechoslovakia were once again issued.

81 Clasped Hands

82 Arms and Soldier

1945. Kosice Issue. Imperf.
396 **81** 1k.50 purple . . . . 1·50 2·00
397 **82** 2k. red 20 25
398 5k. green . . . . 2·00 1·75
399 6k. blue 45 40
400 **81** 9k. red 25 35
401 13k. brown 65 70
402 20k. blue . . . . 1·40 1·40

83 Arms and Linden Leaf

84 Linden Leaf and Buds

85 Linden Leaf and Flower

1945. Bratislava Issue. Imperf.
403 **83** 50h. green 10 10
404 1k. purple 10 10
405 1k.50 red 10 10
406 2k. blue 10 10
407 2k.40 red 30 30
408 3k. brown 10 10
409 4k. green 15 10
410 6k. violet 15 10
411 10k. brown 30 20

1945. Prague Issue.
412 **84** 10h. black 10 10
413 30h. brown 10 10
414 50h. green 10 10
415 60h. blue 10 10
416 **85** 60h. blue 10 10
417 80h. red 10 10
418 120h. red 10 10
419 300h. purple 10 10
420 500h. green 10 10

86 Pres. Masaryk

87 Staff Capt. Ridky

1945. Moscow Issue. Perf.
421 **86** 5h. violet 10 10
422 10h. yellow 10 10
423 20h. brown 10 10
424 50h. green 10 10
425 1k. red 10 10
426 2k. blue 10 10

1945. War Heroes.
427 **87** 5h. grey 10 10
428 – 10h. brown 10 10
429 – 20h. red 10 10
430 – 25h. red 10 10
431 – 30h. violet 15 10
432 – 40h. brown 10 10
433 – 50h. green 10 10
434 – 60h. violet 15 10
435 **87** 1k. red 10 10
436 – 1k.50 red 10 10
437 – 2k. blue 10 10
438 – 2k.50 violet 10 10
439 – 3k. brown 10 10
440 – 4k. mauve 10 10
441 – 5k. green 10 10
442 – 10k. blue 15 10
PORTRAITS: 10h., 1k.50, Dr. Novak. 20h., 2k. Capt. O. Jaros. 25h., 2k.50, Staff Capt. Zimprich. 30h., 3k. Lt. J. Kral. 40h., 4k. J. Gabcik (parachutist). 50h., 5k. Staff Capt. Vasatko. 60h., 10k. Fr. Adamek.

88 Allied Flags

89 Russian Soldier and Slovak Partisan

1945. 1st Anniv of Slovak Rising.
443 **88** 1k.50 red 10 10
444 – 2k. blue 10 10
445 **89** 4k. brown 20 25
446 – 4k.50 violet 20 25
447 – 5k. green 25 40
DESIGNS—VERT: 2k. Banska Bystrica. HORIZ: 4k.50, Sklabina; 5k. Strecno and partisan.

90 Pres. Masaryk

91 Pres. Benes

92

1945.
452 – 30h. purple 10 10
448 **90** 50h. brown 10 10
453 **91** 60h. blue 15 10
449 – 80h. green 10 10
454 – 1k. orange 10 10
455 **90** 1k.20 red 15 10
456 1k.20 mauve 10 10
450 **91** 1k.60 green 15 10
457 – 2k.40 red 15 10
458 **91** 3k. purple 20 10
459 **90** 4k. blue 15 10
460 5k. green 20 10
461 **91** 7k. black 25 10
462 – 10k. blue 55 10
451 **90** 15k. purple 50 10
462a – 20k. brown 85 10
PORTRAIT: 30h., 80h., 1k., 2k.40, 10k., 20k. Gen. M. R. Stefanik.

1945. Students' World Congress, Prague.
463 **92** 1k.50+1k.50 red 10 10
464 2k.50+2k.50 blue 20 20

93 J. S. Kozina Monument

94 St. George and Dragon

1945. Execution of Jan Stadky Kozina, 1695.
465 **93** 2k.40 red 15 10
466 4k. blue 20 25

1946. Victory.
467 **94** 2k.40+2k.60 red 15 15
468 4k.+6k. blue 20 15

94a Lockheed Constellation over Charles Bridge, Prague

1946. Air. 1st Prague–New York Flight.
468b **94a** 24k. blue on buff . . . 90 85
See also Nos. 475/6.

95 Capt. F. Novak and Westland Lysander

96 Lockheed Constellation over Bratislava

1946. Air.
469 **95** 1k.50 red 15 10
470 5k.50 blue 35 15
471 9k. purple 60 20
472 **96** 10k. green 50 35
473 **95** 16k. violet 80 30
474 **96** 20k. blue 80 50
475 **94a** 24k. red . . . . 1·00 75
476 50k. blue . . . . 2·00 1·25

97 K. H. Borovsky

98 Brno

1946. 90th Death Anniv of Borovsky (Independence advocate).
477 **97** 1k.20h. grey 10 10

1946.
478 **98** 2k.40 red 40 15
479 – 7k.40 violet (Hodonin) (horiz) 20 10

100 Emigrants

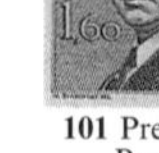
101 President Benes

1946. Repatriation Fund.
480 – 1k.60+1k.40 brown . . . 55 55
481 **100** 2k.40+2k.60 red 20 25
482 – 4k.+4k. blue 30 45
DESIGNS: 1k.60, Emigrants' departure; 4k. Emigrants' return.

1946. Independence Day.
483 **101** 60h. blue 10 10
484 1k.60 green 10 10
485 3k. purple 10 10
486 8k. purple 20 10

102 Flag and Symbols of Transport, Industry, Agriculture and Learning

103 St. Adalbert

1947. "Two Year Plan".
487 **102** 1k.20 green 10 10
488 2k.40 red 10 10
489 4k. blue 50 20

1947. 950th Death Anniv of St. Adalbert (Bishop of Prague).
490 **103** 1k.60 black 45 45
491 2k.40 red 65 60
492 5k. green . . . . 1·00 40

104 "Grief" **105** Rekindling Flame of Remembrance

1947. 5th Anniv of Destruction of Lidice.
493 **104** 1k.20 black 30 30
494 1k.60 black 45 45
495 **105** 2k.40 mauve 55 45

106 Congress Emblem **107** Pres. Masaryk

1947. Youth Festival.
496 **106** 1k.20 purple 45 25
497 4k. grey 45 15

1947. 10th Death Anniv of Pres Masaryk.
498 **107** 1k.20 black on buff . . . 15 10
499 4k. blue on cream 25 25

108 Stefan Moyses **109** "Freedom"

1947. 150th Birth Anniv of Stefan Moyses (Slavonic Society Organizer).
500 **108** 1k.20 purple 15 10
501 4k. blue 25 25

1947. 30th Anniv of Russian Revolution.
502 **109** 2k.40 red 30 15
503 4k. blue 50 15

110 Pres. Benes

1948.
504 **110** 1k.50 brown 10 10
505 2k. purple (19 × 23 mm) 10 10
506 5k. blue (19 × 23 mm) . . 15 10

111 "Athletes paying Homage to Republic" **115** Dr. J. Vanicek

1948. 11th Sokol Congress, Prague. (a) 1st issue.
507 **111** 1k.50 brown 10 10
508 3k. red 15 10
509 5k. blue 40 10

(b) 2nd issue. Inscr "XI. VSESOKOLSKY SLET V PRAZE 1948".
515 **115** 1k. green 10 10
516 – 1k.50 brown 15 10
517 – 2k. blue 15 10
518 **115** 3k. purple 20 10
PORTRAIT: 1k.50, 2k. Dr. J. Scheiner.

112 Charles IV **113** St. Wenceslas and Charles IV

1948. 600th Anniv of Charles IV University, Prague.
510 **112** 1k.50 brown on buff . . . 10 10
511 **113** 2k. brown on buff 15 10
512 3k. red on buff 15 10
513 **112** 5k. blue on buff 20 20

114 Insurgents **117** Fr. Palacky and Dr. F. L. Rieger

1948. Centenary of Abolition of Serfdom.
514 **114** 1k.50 black 10 10

1948. Cent of Constituent Assembly at Kromeriz.
519 **117** 1k.50 violet on buff . . . 10 10
520 3k. purple on buff 15 10

118 J. M. Hurban **119** President Benes

1948. Centenary of Slovak Insurrection.
521 **118** 1k.50 brown 10 10
522 – 3k. red (L. Stur) 10 10
523 – 5k. blue (M. Hodza) . . . 20 20

1948. Death of President Benes.
524 **119** 8k. black 10 10

120 "Independence" **121** President Gottwald

1948. 30th Anniv of Independence.
525 **120** 1k.50 blue 15 10
526 3k. red 20 15

1948.
772 **121** 15h. green 35 10
773 20h. brown 45 10
526a 1k. green 20 10
774 1k. lilac . . . . 1·10 10
527 1k.50 brown 20 10
528b 3k. red 30 10
775 3k. black 80 10
529 5k. blue 55 10
530 20k. violet (23 × 30 mm) 60 10
See also No. 538.

122 Czech and Russian Workers **123** Girl and Birds

1948. 5th Anniv of Russian Alliance.
531 **122** 3k. red 10 10

1948. Child Welfare.
532 – 1k.50+1k. purple 30 10
533 – 2k.+1k. blue 15 10
534 **123** 3k.+1k. red 25 10
DESIGNS: 1k.50, Boy and birds; 2k. Mother and child.

124 V. I. Lenin **125** Pres. Gottwald Addressing Rally

1949. 25th Death Anniv of Lenin.
535 **124** 1k.50 purple 30 10
536 5k. blue 30 25

1949. 1st Anniv of Gottwald Government.
537 **125** 3k. brown 10 10

1949. As T **121** (23 × 30 mm) but inscr "UNOR 1948".
538 **121** 10k. green 35 25

126 P. O. Hviezdoslav **127** Mail Coach and Steam Train

1949. Poets.
539 **126** 50h. purple 10 10
540 – 80h. red 10 10
541 – 1k. green 10 10
542 – 2k. blue 30 10
543 – 4k. purple 30 10
544 – 8k. black 45 10
PORTRAITS: 80h. V. Vancura. 1k. J. Sverma. 2k. J. Fucik. 4k. J. Wolker. 8k. A. Jirasek.

1949. 75th Anniv of U.P.U.
545 **127** 3k. red . . . . 1·00 1·00
546 – 5k. blue 60 35
547 – 13k. green . . . . . . 1·60 40
DESIGNS: 5k. Mounted postman and mail van; 13k. Sailing ship and Douglas DC-2 airliner.

128 Girl Agricultural Worker **130** Industrial Worker

1949. 9th Meeting of Czechoslovak Communist Party.
548 **128** 1k.50 green 45 50
549 – 3k. red 25 25
550 **130** 5k. blue 45 50
DESIGN—HORIZ: 3k. Workers and flag.

131 F. Smetana and National Theatre, Prague **132** A. S. Pushkin

1949. 125th Birth Anniv of Smetana (composer).
551 **131** 1k.50 green 15 10
552 5k. blue 65 30

1949. 150th Birth Anniv of A. S. Pushkin (poet).
553 **132** 2k. green 25 25

133 F. Chopin and Warsaw Conservatoire **134** Globe and Ribbon

1949. Death Centenary of Chopin (composer).
554 **133** 3k. red 45 25
555 8k. purple 45 50

1949. 50th Sample Fair, Prague.
556 **134** 1k.50 purple 25 25
557 5k. blue 80 75

135 Zvolen Castle

1949.
558 **135** 10k. lake 60 10

1949. Air. Nos. 469/76 surch.
559 **95** 1k. on 1k.50 red 15 10
560 3k. on 5k.50 blue 25 10
561 6k. on 9k. purple 40 10
562 7k.50 on 16k. violet . . . 50 25
563 **96** 8k. on 10k. green 50 55
564 12k.50 on 20k. blue . . . 90 45
565 **94a** 15k. on 24k. red . . . . 2·25 75
566 30k. on 50k. blue . . . . 1·75 75

137 Mediaeval Miners **138** Modern Miner

1949. 700th Anniv of Czechoslovak Mining Industry and 150th Anniv of Miners' Laws.
567 **137** 1k.50 violet 50 40
568 **138** 3k. red . . . . 5·25 1·90
569 – 5k. blue . . . . 4·00 1·50
DESIGN—HORIZ: 5k. Miner with cutting machine.

139 Carpenters **140** Dove and Buildings

1949. 2nd T.U.C., Prague. Inscr 1949".
570 **139** 1k. green . . . . 3·00 1·25
571 – 2k. purple (Mechanic) . . 1·90 50

1949. Red Cross Fund. Inscr "CS CERVENY KRIZ".
572 **140** 1k.50h.+50h. red . . . . 3·50 1·60
573 – 3k.+1k. red . . . . . . 3·50 1·60
DESIGN—VERT: 3k. Dove and globe.

141 Mother and Child **142** Joseph Stalin

1949. Child Welfare Fund. Inscr "DETEM 1949".
574 **141** 1k.50+50h. grey . . . . . 3·25 1·10
575 – 3k.+1k. red . . . . . . 4·75 1·75
DESIGN: 3k. Father and child.

1949. 70th Birth Anniv of Joseph Stalin.
576 **142** 1k.50 green on buff . . . 75 40
577 – 3k. purple on buff . . . . 4·00 1·50
PORTRAIT: 3k. Stalin facing left.

143 Skier **144** Efficiency Badge

1950. Tatra Cup Ski Championship.
578 **143** 1k.50 blue . . . . 2·75 1·00
579 **144** 3k. red and buff . . . . 2·75 1·00
580 **143** 5k. blue . . . . 1·90 85

145 V. Mayakovsky **146** Soviet Tank Driver and Hradcany, Prague

1950. 20th Death Anniv of Mayakovsky (poet).
581 **145** 1k.50 purple . . . . . . 2·10 1·10
582 3k. red . . . . 1·75 80

1950. 5th Anniv of Republic (1st issue).
583 **146** 1k.50 green 25 20
584 – 2k. purple 95 80
585 – 3k. red 20 10
586 – 5k. blue 40 20
DESIGNS: 2k. "Hero of Labour" medal; 3k. Workers and Town Hall; 5k. "The Kosice Programme" (part of text).

147 Factory and Workers

1950. 5th Anniv of Republic (2nd issue).
587 **147** 1k.50 green . . . . 1·40 75
588 – 2k. brown . . . . 1·75 65
589 – 3k. red 90 35
590 – 5k. blue 90 30
DESIGNS: 2k. Crane and Tatra Mts; 3k. Labourer and tractor; 5k. Three workers.

148 S. K. Neumann

1950. 75th Birth Anniv of S. K. Neumann (writer).
591 **148** 1k.50 blue 25 10
592 3k. purple . . . . 1·10 85

149 Bozena Nemcova **150** "Liberation of Colonial Nations"

1950. 130th Birth Anniv of Bozena Nemcova (authoress).
593 **149** 1k.50 blue . . . . 1·25 80
594 7k. purple 25 20

1950. 2nd International Students' World Congress, Prague. Inscr "II KONGRES MSS".
595 **150** 1k.50 green 15 10
596 – 2k. purple . . . . 1·50 1·25
597 – 3k. red 20 25
598 – 5k. blue 40 50
DESIGNS—HORIZ: 2k. Woman, globe and dove ("Fight for Peace"); 3k. Group of students ("Democratisation of Education"); 5k. Students and banner ("International Students, Solidarity").

151 Miner, Soldier and Farmer **152** Z. Fibich

1950. Army Day.
599 **151** 1k.50 blue 90 75
600 – 3k. red 25 35
DESIGN: 3k. Czechoslovak and Russian soldiers.

1950. Birth Centenary of Fibich (composer).
601 **152** 3k. red . . . . 1·40 1·40
602 8k. green 25 15

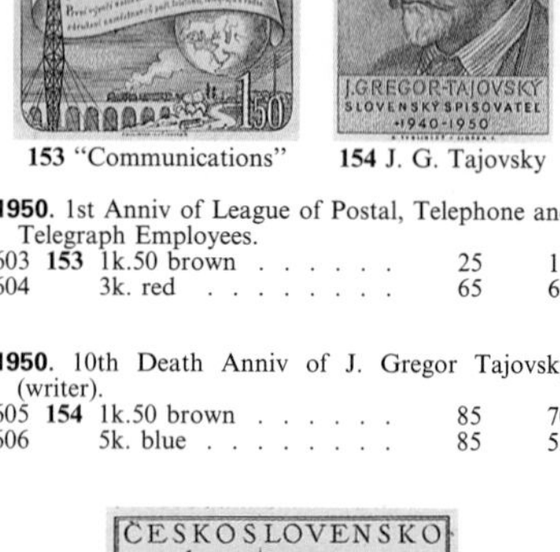

153 "Communications" **154** J. G. Tajovsky

1950. 1st Anniv of League of Postal, Telephone and Telegraph Employees.
603 **153** 1k.50 brown 25 15
604 3k. red 65 65

1950. 10th Death Anniv of J. Gregor Tajovsky (writer).
605 **154** 1k.50 brown 85 70
606 5k. blue 85 55

155 Reconstruction of Prague

1950. Philatelic Exhibition, Prague.
607 **155** 1k.50 blue 35 20
608 3k. red 60 55

156 Czech and Russian Workers

1950. Czechoslovak–Soviet Friendship.
609 **156** 1k.50 brown 55 25
610 5k. blue 75 50

157 Dove (after Picasso)

1951. Czechoslovak Peace Congress.
611 **157** 2k. blue . . . . 5·00 2·75
612 3k. red . . . . 3·00 1·60

158 Julius Fucik **159** Mechanical Hammer

1951. Peace Propaganda.
613 **158** 1k.50 grey 50 35
614 5k. blue . . . . 1·90 1·75

1951. Five Year Plan (heavy industry).
615 **159** 1k.50 black 10 10
616 – 3k. brown 15 10
617 **159** 4k. blue 65 50
DESIGN—HORIZ: 3k. Installing machinery.

160 Industrial Workers **161** Karlovy Vary

1951. International Women's Day.
618 **160** 1k.50 olive 25 10
619 – 3k. red . . . . 2·40 65
620 – 5k. blue 50 10
DESIGNS: 3k. Woman driving tractor; 5k. Korean woman and group.

1951. Air. Spas.
621 **161** 6k. green . . . . 2·25 75
622 – 10k. purple . . . . 2·25 95
623 – 15k. blue . . . . 5·50 75
624 – 20k. brown . . . . 7·00 2·25
DESIGNS—Ilyushin Il-12 airplane over: 10k. Piestany; 15k. Marianske Lazne; 20k. Silac.

162 Miners **163** Ploughing

1951. Mining Industry.
625 **162** 1k.50 black 80 60
626 3k. purple 10 15

1951. Agriculture.
627 **163** 1k.50 brown 50 65
628 – 2k. green (Woman and cows) . . . . 1·75 1·40

164 Tatra Mountains **165** Partisan and Soviet Soldier

1951. Recreation Centres. Inscr "ROH".
629 **164** 1k.50 green 20 10
630 – 2k. brown 90 70
631 – 3k. red 25 10
DESIGNS: 2k. Beskydy Mts; 3k. Krkonose Mts.

1951. 30th Anniv of Czechoslovak Communist Party. Inscr "30 LET" etc.
635 – 1k.50 grey 95 25
632 – 2k. brown 25 10
633 **165** 3k. red 30 10
636 – 5k. blue . . . . 1·90 90
634 – 8k. black 70 30
DESIGNS—HORIZ: 1k.50, 5k. Gottwald and Stalin; 8k. Marx, Engels, Lenin and Stalin. VERT: 2k. Factory militiaman.

167 Dvorak **168** Gymnast

1951. Prague Musical Festival.
637 **167** 1k. brown 25 10
638 – 1k.50 grey (Smetana) . . 1·25 55
639 **167** 2k. brown . . . . 1·25 60
640 – 3k. purple (Smetana) . . 25 15

1951. 9th Sokol Congress.
641 **168** 1k. green 55 20
642 – 1k.50 brown (Woman discus thrower) 55 25
643 – 3k. red (Footballers) . . . 1·25 25
644 – 5k. blue (Skier) . . . . . 3·25 1·25

1951. 10th Death Anniv of Bohumir Smeral. As T **154**, but portrait of Smeral.
645 1k.50 grey 45 40
646 3k. purple 45 15

170 Scene from "Fall of Berlin" **172** A. Jirasek

173 "Fables and Fates" (M. Ales)

1951. International Film Festival, Karlovy Vary. Inscr "SE SOVETSKYM FILMEM", etc.
647 **170** 80h. red 35 25
648 – 1k.50 grey 35 25
649 **170** 4k. blue . . . . 1·10 75
DESIGN: 1k.50, Scene from "The Great Citizen".

1951. 30th Death Anniv of J. Hybes (politician). As T **154**, but portrait of Hybes.
650 1k.50 brown 10 10
651 2k. red . . . . 1·00 35

1951. Birth Centenary of Jirasek (author).
652 **172** 1k.50 black 40 10
653 **173** 3k. red 40 10
654 – 4k. black 40 10
655 **172** 5k. blue . . . . 1·90 1·10
DESIGN—As Type **173**: 4k. "The Region of Tabor" (M. Ales).

174 Miner and Pithead **176** Soldiers Parading

1951. Miner's Day.
656 **174** 1k.50 brown 15 10
657 – 3k. red (miners drilling) . . 15 10
658 **174** 5k. blue . . . . 1·25 95

1951. Army Day. Inscr "DEN CS ARMADY 1951".
659 **176** 80h. brown 25 20
660 – 1k. green 25 25
661 – 1k.50 black 40 25
662 – 3k. purple 40 25
663 – 5k. blue . . . . 1·60 60
DESIGNS—VERT: 1k. Gunner and field-gun; 1k.50, Pres. Gottwald; 3k. Tank driver and tank; 5k. Two pilots and aircraft.

178 Stalin and Gottwald **179** P. Jilemnicky

1951. Czechoslovak–Soviet Friendship.
664 **178** 1k.50 black 10 10
665 – 3k. red 15 10
666 **178** 4k. blue . . . . 1·25 45
DESIGN ($23\frac{1}{2} \times 31$ mm): 3k. Lenin, Stalin and Russian soldiers.

1951. 50th Birth Anniv of Jilemnicky (writer).
667 **179** 1k.50 purple 20 15
668 2k. blue 70 35

180 L. Zapotocky **181** J. Kollar

1952. Birth Centenary of Zapotocky (socialist pioneer).
669 **180** 1k.50 red 10 15
670 4k. black . . . . 1·00 35

1952. Death Centenary of Kollar (poet).
671 **181** 3k. red 10 10
672 5k. blue . . . . 1·00 50

182 Lenin Hall, Prague **183** Dr. E. Holub and Negro

1952. 40th Anniv of 6th All-Russian Party Conference.
673 **182** 1k.50 red 10 25
674 5k. blue . . . . 1·00 60

1952. 50th Death Anniv of Dr. Holub (explorer).
675 **183** 3k. red 40 25
676 5k. blue . . . . 2·00 1·40

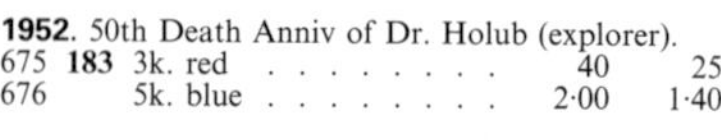

184 Electric Welding

1952. Industrial Development.
677 **184** 1k.50 black 35 15
678 – 2k. brown . . . . 1·40 50
679 – 3k. red 15 10
DESIGNS: 2k. Foundry; 3k. Chemical plant.

185 Factory-worker and Farm-girl
186 Young Workers

1952. International Women's Day.
680 **185** 1k.50 blue on cream . . . 1·00 40

1952. International Youth Week.
681 **186** 1k.50 blue 10 10
682 – 2k. green 15 10
683 **186** 3k. red . . . . 1·60 65
DESIGN: 2k. Three heads and globe.

187 O. Sevcik
188 J. A. Komensky (Comenius)

1952. Birth Centenary of Sevcik (musician).
684 **187** 2k. brown 70 45
685 3k. red 15 15

1952. 360th Birth Anniv of Komensky (educationist).
686 **188** 1k.50 brown . . . . . . 1·25 50
687 11k. blue 25 10

189 Anti-fascist
190 Woman and Children

1952. "Fighters Against Fascism" Day.
688 **189** 1k.50 brown 10 10
689 2k. blue . . . . 1·00 50

1952. Child Welfare.
690 **190** 2k. purple on cream . . . 1·25 1·10
691 3k. red on cream 15 15

191 Combine Harvester

1952. Agriculture Day.
692 **191** 1k.50 blue . . . . 1·90 1·10
693 2k. brown 25 25
694 – 3k. red (Combine drill) . . 25 25

192 May Day Parade

1952. Labour Day.
695 **192** 3k. red 30 35
696 4k. brown . . . . 1·40 80

193 Russian Tank and Crowd

1952. 7th Anniv of Liberation.
697 **193** 1k.50 red 60 50
698 5k. blue . . . . 1·75 1·40

194 Boy Pioneer and Children
195 J. V. Myslbek

1952. International Children's Day.
699 **194** 1k.50 brown 10 10
700 2k. green . . . . 1·40 70
701 – 3k. red (Pioneers and teacher) 15 10

1952. 30th Death Anniv of Myslbek (sculptor).
702 **195** 1k.50 brown 10 10
703 2k. brown . . . . 1·10 1·00
704 – 8k. green 15 10
DESIGN: 8k. "Music" (statue).

196 Beethoven
197 "Rebirth of Lidice"

1952. International Music Festival, Prague. No. 706 inscr "PRAZSKE JARO 1952", etc.
705 **196** 1k.50 brown 30 25
706 – 3k. lake 30 25
707 **196** 5k. blue . . . . 1·60 90
DESIGN—HORIZ: 3k. The House of Artists.

1952. 10th Anniv of Destruction of Lidice.
708 **197** 1k.50 black 10 10
709 5k. blue 90 55

198 Jan Hus
199 Bethlehem Chapel, Prague

1952. Renovation of Bethlehem Chapel and 550th Anniv of Installation of Hus as Preacher.
710 **198** 1k.50 brown 10 10
711 **199** 3k. brown 10 10
712 **198** 5k. black . . . . 1·10 75

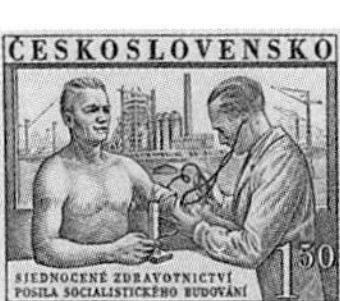

200 Testing Blood-pressure
201 Running

1952. National Health Service.
713 **200** 1k.50 brown 25 80
714 – 2k. violet 30 10
715 **200** 3k. red 70 10
DESIGN—HORIZ: 2k. Doctor examining baby.

1952. Physical Culture Propaganda.
716 **201** 1k.50 brown . . . . . . 2·00 35
717 – 2k. green (Canoeing) . . 50 85
718 – 3k. brown (Cycling) . . . 3·25 45
719 – 4k. blue (Ice hockey) . . 15 2·25

202 F. L. Celakovsky

1952. Death Centenary of Celakovsky (poet).
720 **202** 1k.50 sepia . . . . 1·60 10
721 2k. green 40 85

203 M. Ales
204 Mining in 17th Century

1952. Birth Centenary of Mikulas Ales (painter) (1st issue).
722 **203** 1k.50 green . . . . . . 2·25 20
723 6k. brown . . . . 1·25 1·75
See also Nos. 737/8.

1952. Miner's Day.
724 **204** 1k. brown 10 70
725 – 1k.50 blue . . . . 10 1·00
726 – 2k. black 10 10
727 – 3k. brown 15 10
DESIGNS: 1k.50, Mining machinery; 2k. Petr Bezruc Mine, Ostrava; 3k. Mechanical excavator.

205 Jan Zizka
206 "Fraternization" (after Pokorny)

1952. Army Day.
728 **205** 1k.50 red 15 10
729 **206** 2k. brown 15 10
730 – 3k. red 15 10
731 **205** 4k. black . . . . 1·75 70
DESIGNS: 3k. Soldiers marching with flag.

207 R. Danube, Bratislava
208 Lenin, Stalin and Revolutionaries

1952. National Philatelic Exhibition, Bratislava.
732 **207** 1k.50 brown 10 10

1952. 35th Anniv of Russian Revolution.
733 **208** 2k. brown . . . . 1·25 80
734 3k. red 10 10

209 Nurses and Red Cross Flag
211 Flags

210 Matej Louda z Chlumu (Hussite Warrior)

1952. 1st Czechoslovak Red Cross Conference.
735 **209** 2k. brown . . . . 1·25 55
736 3k. red 15 10

1952. Birth Centenary of Mikulas Ales (2nd issue).
737 **210** 2k. brown 25 10
738 – 3k. black 65 10
DESIGN: 3k. "Trutnov" (warrior fighting dragon).

1952. Peace Congress, Vienna.
739 **211** 3k. red 20 10
740 4k. blue . . . . 1·40 70

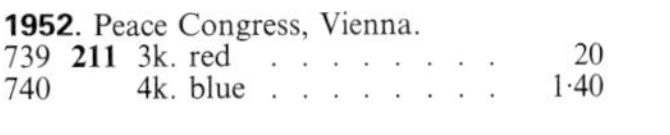

212 "Dove of Peace" (after Picasso)
213 Smetana Museum, Prague

1953. 2nd Czechoslovak Peace Congress, Prague.
741 **212** 1k.50 sepia 10 10
742 – 4k. blue 10 35
DESIGN: 4k. Workman, woman and child (after Lev Haas).

1953. 75th Birth Anniv of Prof. Z. Nejedly (museum founder).
743 **213** 1k.50 brown 10 10
744 – 4k. black . . . . 1·40 65
DESIGN: 4k. Jirasek Museum, Prague.

214 Marching Soldiers
215 M. Kukucin

1953. 5th Anniv of Communist Govt.
745 **214** 1k.50 blue 15 10
746 – 3k. red 15 10
747 – 8k. brown . . . . 2·00 80
DESIGNS—VERT: 3k. Pres. Gottwald addressing meeting. HORIZ: 8k. Stalin, Gottwald and crowd with banners.

1953. Czech Writers and Poets.
748 **215** 1k. grey 10 10
749 – 1k.50 brown 10 10
750 – 2k. lake 10 10
751 – 3k. brown 50 40
752 – 5k. blue . . . . 1·90 75
PORTRAITS—VERT: 1k.50, J. Vrchlicky. 2k. E. J. Erben. 3k. V. M. Kramerius. 5k. J. Dobrovsky.

216 Torch and Open Book
217 Woman Revolutionary

1953. 10th Death Anniv of Vaclavek (writer).
753 **216** 1k. brown . . . . 1·50 50
754 – 3k. brown (Vaclavek) . . 15 10

1953. International Women's Day.
755 – 1k.50 blue 15 10
756 **217** 2k. red . . . . 1·00 50
DESIGN—VERT: 1k.50, Mother and baby.

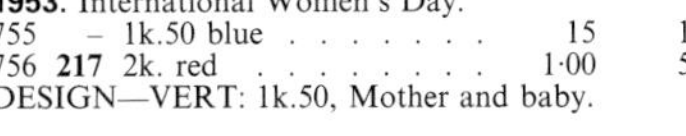

218 Stalin
219 Pres. Gottwald

1953. Death of Stalin.
757 **218** 1k.50 black 35 20

1953. Death of President Gottwald.
758 **219** 1k.50 black 20 10
759 3k. black 20 10

220 Pecka, Zapotocky and Hybes

1953. 75th Anniv of 1st Czech Social Democratic Party Congress.
760 **220** 2k. brown 25 10

221 Cyclists

1953. 6th International Cycle Race.
761 **221** 3k. blue 60 30

222 1890 May Day Medal

223 Marching Crowds

1953. Labour Day.
762 **222** 1k. brown . . . . 1·75 85
763 – 1k.50 blue 10 10
764 **223** 3k. red 20 10
765 – 8k. green 25 10
DESIGNS—As Type **222**: 1k.50, Lenin and Stalin; 8k. Marx and Engels.

224 Hydro-electric Barrage **225** Seed-drills

1953.
766 **224** 1k.50 green 95 40
767 – 2k. blue 20 10
768 – 3k. brown 20 10
DESIGNS—VERT: 2k. Welder and blast furnaces, Kuncice. HORIZ: 3k. Gottwald Foundry, Kuncice.

1953.
769 **225** 1k.50 brown 20 10
770 – 7k. green (Combine harvester) . . . . . . 1·60 1·10

226 President Zapotocky **229**

1953.
776 **226** 30h. blue 60 10
780 **229** 30h. blue 55 10
777 **226** 60h. red 30 10
781 **229** 60h. pink . . . . 1·10 10

227 J. Slavik **228** L. Janacek

1953. Prague Music Festival. (a) 120th Death Anniv of Slavik (violinist).
778 **227** 75h. blue 60 10

(b) 25th Death Anniv of Janacek (composer).
779 **228** 1k.60 brown . . . . . . 1·25 10

230 Charles Bridge, Prague

1953.
782a **230** 5k. grey . . . . 4·50 10

231 J. Fucik **232** Book, Carnation and Laurels

1953. 10th Death Anniv of Julius Fucik (writer).
783 **231** 40h. black 20 10
784 **232** 60h. mauve 50 25

233 Miner and Banner **234** Volley ball

1953. Miner's Day.
785 **233** 30h. black 20 10
786 – 60h. purple . . . . 1·25 50
DESIGN: 60h. Miners and colliery shafthead.

1953. Sports.
787 **234** 30h. red . . . . 2·10 1·40
788 – 40h. purple . . . . 3·75 70
789 – 60h. purple . . . . 3·75 70
DESIGNS—HORIZ: 40h. Motor cycling. VERT: 60h. Throwing the javelin.

235 Hussite Warrior **236** "Friendship" (after T. Bartfay)

1953. Army Day.
790 **235** 30h. sepia 25 10
791 – 60h. red 30 20
792 – 1k. red . . . . 1·75 1·25
DESIGNS: 60h. Soldier presenting arms; 1k. Czechoslovak Red Army soldiers.

1953. Czechoslovak–Korean Friendship.
793 **236** 30h. sepia . . . . 2·50 1·10

237 Hradcany, Prague and Kremlin, Moscow

1953. Czechoslovak–Soviet Friendship: Inscr "MESIC CESKOSLOVENSKO SOVETSKEHO", etc.
794 **237** 30h. black . . . . 1·00 55
795 – 60h. brown . . . . 1·25 75
796 – 1k.20 blue . . . . 2·50 1·40
DESIGNS: 60h. Lomonosov University, Moscow; 1k.20, "Stalingrad" tug, Lenin Ship-Canal.

238 Ema Destinnova (Opera Singer) **239** National Theatre, Prague

1953. 70th Anniv of National Theatre, Prague.
797 **238** 30h. black 95 80
798 **239** 60h. brown 25 10
799 – 2k. sepia . . . . 2·25 80
PORTRAIT—As Type **238**: 2k. E. Vojan (actor).

240 J. Manes (painter) **241** Vaclav Hollar (etcher)

1953.
800 **240** 60h. lake 25 10
801 1k.20 blue . . . . 1·50 95

1953. Inscr "1607 1677".
802 **241** 30h. black 25 10
803 – 1k.20 black . . . . 1·25 55
PORTRAIT: 1k.20, Hollar and engraving tools.

242 Leo Tolstoy **243** Class 498.0 Steam Locomotive

1953. 125th Birth Anniv of Tolstoy (writer).
804 **242** 60h. green 15 10
805 1k. brown . . . . 1·40 40

1953.
806 **243** 60h. blue and brown . . . 65 25
807 – 1k. blue and brown . . . 1·60 90
DESIGN: 1k. Ilyushin Il-12 (30th anniv of Czech airmail services).

244 Lenin (after J. Lauda)

245 Lenin Museum, Prague

1954. 30th Death Anniv of Lenin.
808 **244** 30h. sepia 45 10
809 **245** 1k.40 brown . . . . . . 1·75 1·25

246 Gottwald Speaking **247** Gottwald Mausoleum, Prague

248 Gottwald and Stalin (after relief by O. Spaniel)

1954. 25th Anniv of 5th Czechoslovak Communist Party Congress. Inscr "1929 1954".
810 **246** 60h. brown 30 10
811 – 2k.40 lake . . . . 3·75 1·40
DESIGN: 2k.40, Revolutionary and flag.

1954. 1st Anniv of Deaths of Stalin and Gottwald.
812 **247** 30h. sepia 25 20
813 **248** 60h. blue 30 10
814 – 1k.20h. lake . . . . . . 1·75 85
DESIGN—HORIZ: As Type **247**: 1k.20h. Lenin-Stalin Mausoleum, Moscow.

249 Girl and Sheaf of Corn **250** Athletics

1954.
815 – 15h. green 25 10
816 – 20h. lilac 30 10
817 – 40h. brown 45 10
818 – 45h. blue 45 10
819 – 50h. green 30 10
820 – 75h. blue 30 10
821 – 80h. brown 30 10
822 **249** 1k. green 65 10
823 – 1k.20 blue 30 10
824 – 1k.60 black . . . . 2·25 10
825 – 2k. brown . . . . 1·90 10
826 – 2k.40 blue . . . . 2·25 10
827 – 3k. red . . . . 1·50 10
DESIGNS: 15h. Labourer; 20h. Nurse; 40h. Postwoman; 45h. Foundry worker; 50h. Soldier; 75h. Metal worker; 80h. Mill girl; 1k.20, Scientist; 1k.60, Miner; 2k. Doctor and baby; 2k.40 Engine-driver; 3k. Chemist.

1954. Sports.
828 **250** 30h. sepia . . . . 2·25 85
829 – 80h. green . . . . 6·50 3·50
830 – 1k. blue . . . . 1·40 60
DESIGNS—HORIZ: 80h. Hiking. VERT: 1k. Girl diving.

251 Dvorak **252** Prokop Divis (physicist)

1954. Czechoslovak Musicians. Inscr as in T **251**.
831 **251** 30h. brown . . . . 1·00 25
832 – 40h. red (Janacek) . . . . 1·40 25
833 – 60h. blue (Smetana) . . . 80 15

1954. Bicentenary of Invention of Lightning Conductor by Divis.
834 **252** 30h. black 25 10
835 75h. brown . . . . 1·25 40

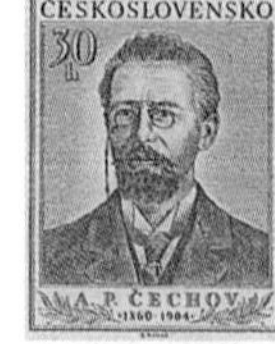

253 Partisan **254** A. P. Chekhov

1954. 10th Anniv of Slovak National Uprising. Inscr "1944–29. 8–1954".
836 **253** 30h. red 20 10
837 – 1k.20 bl (Woman partisan) . . . . 1·10 90

1954. 50th Death Anniv of Chekhov (playwright).
838 **254** 30h. green 20 10
839 45h. brown . . . . 1·25 50

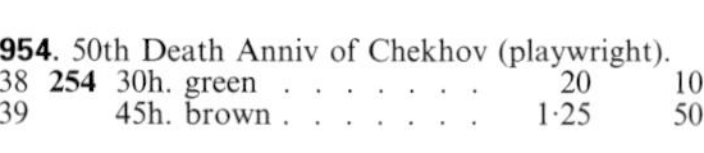

255 Soldiers in Battle **257** J. Neruda

256 Farm Workers in Cornfield

1954. Army Day. 2k. inscr "ARMADY 1954".
840 **255** 60h. green 20 10
841 – 2k. brown . . . . 1·25 1·10
DESIGN: 2k. Soldier carrying girl.

1954. Czechoslovak–Russian Friendship.
842 **256** 30h. brown 15 10
843 – 60h. blue 25 10
844 – 2k. salmon . . . . 1·75 1·40
DESIGNS: 60h. Factory workers and machinery; 2k. Group of girl folk dancers.

1954. Czechoslovak Poets.
845 **257** 30h. blue 50 15
846 – 60h. red . . . . 1·50 30
847 – 1k.60 purple 40 15
PORTRAITS—VERT: 60h. J. Jesensky. 1k.60 J. Wolker.

258 Ceske Budejovice

1954. Czechoslovak Architecture. Background in buff.
848 – 30h. black (Telc) 90 10
849 – 60h. brown (Levoca) . . . 45 10
850 **258** 3k. blue . . . . 1·75 1·40

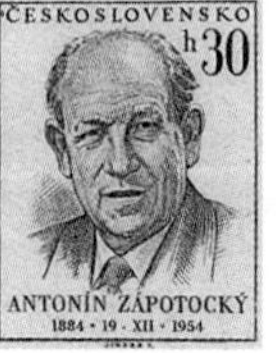

259 President Zapotocky **260** "Spirit of the Games"

1954. 70th Birthday of Zapotocky.
851 **259** 30h. sepia 45 10
852 60h. blue 70 10
See also Nos. 1006/7.

1955. 1st National Spartacist Games (1st issue). Inscr as in T **260**.
853 **260** 30h. red . . . . 1·50 40
854 – 45h. black & blue (Skier) 4·25 30
See also Nos. 880/2.

261 University Building

1955. 35th Anniv of Comenius University, Bratislava. Inscr as in T **261**.
855 **261** 60h. green 30 10
856 – 75h. brown . . . . 1·75 55
DESIGN: 75h. Comenius Medal (after O. Spaniel).

262 Cesky Krumlov

1955. Air.
857 **262** 80h. green . . . . 1·10 20
858 – 1k.55 sepia . . . . 1·50 35
859 – 2k.35 blue . . . . 1·50 15
860 – 2k.75 purple . . . . . . 2·75 30
861 – 10k. blue . . . . 5·25 1·25
DESIGNS: 1k.55, Olomouc; 2k.35, Banska Bystrica; 2k.75, Bratislava; 10k. Prague.

263 Skoda Motor Car **264** Russian Tank-driver

1955. Czechoslovak Industries.
862 **263** 45h. green 70 50
863 – 60h. blue 15 10
864 – 75h. black 25 10
DESIGNS: 60h. Shuttleless jet loom; 75h. Skoda Machine-tool.

1955. 10th Anniv of Liberation. Inscr as in T **264**.
865 – 30h. blue 25 10
866 **264** 35h. brown . . . . . . 1·25 55
867 – 60h. red 25 10
868 – 60h. black 25 10
DESIGNS—VERT: 30h. Girl and Russian soldier; No. 867, Children and Russian soldier. HORIZ: No. 868, Stalin Monument, Prague.

265 Agricultural Workers **266** "Music and Spring"

1955. 3rd Trades' Union Congress. Inscr as in T **265**.
869 – 30h. blue 15 10
870 **265** 45h. green . . . . 1·25 55
DESIGN: 30h. Foundry worker.

1955. International Music Festival, Prague. Inscr as in T **266**.
871 **266** 30h. indigo and blue . . . 35 10
872 – 1k. blue and pink . . . . 1·25 1·25
DESIGN: 1k. "Music" playing a lyre.

267 A. S. Popov (60th anniv of radio discoveries) **268** Folk Dancers

1955. Cultural Anniversaries. Portraits.
873 – 20h. brown 20 10
874 – 30h. black 20 10
875 – 40h. green 70 15
876 – 60h. black 45 10
877 **267** 75h. purple . . . . 1·40 50
878 – 1k.40 black on yellow . . 35 25
879 – 1k.60 blue 35 20
PORTRAITS: 20h. Jakub Arbes (writer). 30h. Jan Stursa (sculptor). 40h. Elena Marothy-Soltesova (writer). 60h. Josef V. Sladek (poet). 1k.40 Jan Holly (poet). 1k.60 Pavel J. Safarik (philologist).

1955. 1st National Spartacist Games (2nd issue). Inscr as in T **268**.
880 – 20h. blue 85 40
881 **268** 60h. green 25 10
882 – 1k.60 red 90 25
DESIGNS: 20h. Girl athlete; 1k.60, Male athlete.

269 "Friendship" **270** Ocova Woman, Slovakia

1955. 5th World Youth Festival, Warsaw.
883 **269** 60h. blue 35 10

1955. National Costumes (1st series).
884 **270** 60h. sepia, rose and red 10·00 7·00
885 – 75h. sepia, orange & lake 5·75 5·00
886 – 1k.60 sepia, blue & orge 10·00 5·50
887 – 2k. sepia, yellow and red 13·00 5·50
DESIGNS: 75h. Detva man, Slovakia; 1k.60, Chodsko man, Bohemia; 2k. Hana woman, Moravia.
See also Nos. 952/5 and 1008/11.

271 Swallowtail

1955. Animals and Insects.
888 – 20h. black and blue . . . 55 10
889 – 30h. brown and red . . . 55 10
890 – 35h. brown and buff . . . 1·10 15
891 **271** 1k.40 black and yellow . . 5·25 1·90
892 – 1k.50 black and green . . 55 15
DESIGNS: 20h. Common carp; 30h. Stag beetle; 35h. Grey partridge; 1k.50, Brown hare.

272 Tabor

1955. Towns of Southern Bohemia.
893 **272** 30h. purple 20 10
894 – 45h. red 75 55
895 – 60h. green 20 10
TOWNS: 45h. Prachatice; 60h. Jindrichuv Hradec.

273 Motor Cyclists and Trophy

1955. 30th Int Motor Cycle Six-Day Trial.
896 **273** 60h. purple . . . . 2·40 25

274 Soldier and Family **275** Hans Andersen

1955. Army Day. Inscr as in T **274**.
897 **274** 30h. brown 25 10
898 – 60h. grn (Tank attack) . . 1·75 1·25

1955. Famous Writers. Vert portraits.
899 **275** 30h. red 15 10
900 – 40h. blue (Schiller) . . . 2·10 80
901 – 60h. purple (Mickiewicz) 25 10
902 – 75h. blk (Walt Whitman) 50 10

276 Railway Viaduct

1955. Building Progress. Inscr "STAVBA SOCIALISMU".
903 **276** 20h. green 30 25
904 – 30h. brown 30 10
905 – 60h. blue 30 10
906 – 1k.60 red 55 10
DESIGNS: 30h. Train crossing viaduct; 60k. Train approaching tunnel; 1k.60, Housing project, Ostrava.

277 "Electricity" **278** Karlovy Vary

1956. Five Year Plan. Inscr "1956–1960".
907 **277** 5h. brown 25 10
908 – 10h. black 25 10
909 – 25h. red 25 10
910 – 30h. green 25 10
911 – 60h. blue 35 10
DESIGNS—HORIZ: 10h. "Mining"; 25h. "Building"; 30h. "Agriculture"; 60h. "Industry".

1956. Czechoslovak Spas (1st series).
912 **278** 30h. green . . . . 1·40 25
913 – 45h. brown . . . . 1·25 35
914 – 75h. purple . . . . 6·25 3·50
915 – 1k.20 blue 90 15
SPAS: 45h. Marianske Lazne; 75h. Piestany; 1k.20, Vysne Ruzbachy, Tatra Mountains.

279 Jewellery **280** "We serve our People" (after J. Cumpelik)

1956. Czechoslovak Products.
916 **279** 30h. green 25 10
917 – 45h. blue (Glassware) . . 4·75 2·75
918 – 60h. purple (Ceramics) . . 1·00 10
919 – 75h. black (Textiles) . . . 25 10

1956. Defence Exhibition.
920 **280** 30h. brown 20 10
921 – 60h. red 20 10
922 – 1k. blue . . . . 3·25 3·25
DESIGNS: 60h. Liberation Monument, Berlin; 1k. "Tank Soldier with Standard" (after T. Schor).

281 Cyclists

282 Discus Thrower, Hurdler and Runner

1956. Sports Events of 1956.
923 **281** 30h. green and blue . . . 2·75 20
924 – 45h. blue and red . . . . 1·10 20
925 – 60h. blue and buff . . . . 1·50 45
926 **282** 75h. brown and yellow . . 1·00 20
927 – 80h. purple & lavender . . 1·00 20
928 **282** 1k.20 green & orange . . 95 35
DESIGNS—As Type **281**. VERT: 30h. T **281** (9th International Cycle Race); 45h. Basketball players (5th European Women's Basketball Championship, Prague). HORIZ: 60h. Horsemen jumping (Pardubice Steeplechase); 80h. Runners (International Marathon, Kosice). T **282**: 75h., 1k.20, (16th Olympic Games, Melbourne).

283 Mozart **284**

1956. Bicentenary of Birth of Mozart and Prague Music Festival. Centres in black.
929 **283** 30h. yellow . . . . 1·00 70
930 – 45h. green . . . . 14·50 9·50
931 – 60h. purple 55 10
932 – 1k. salmon . . . . 1·60 45
933 – 1k.40 blue . . . . 2·75 90
934 – 1k.60 lemon . . . . . . 1·00 15
DESIGNS: 45h. J. Myslivecek; 60h. J. Benda; 1k. "Bertramka" (Mozart's villa); 1k.40, Mr. and Mrs. Dushek; 1k.60, Nostic Theatre.

1956. 1st National Meeting of Home Guard.
935 **284** 60h. blue 90 20

285 J. K. Tyl **286** Naval Guard

1956. Czech Writers (1st issue).
936 – 20h. purple (Stur) 70 10
937 – 30h. blue (Sramek) . . . 35 10
938 **285** 60h. black 25 10
939 – 1k.40 pur (Borovsky) . . 4·50 2·40
See also Nos. 956/9.

1956. Frontier Guards' Day.
940 **286** 30h. blue . . . . 1·10 40
941 – 60h. green 15 10
DESIGN: 60h. Military guard and watchdog.

287 Picking Grapes

1956. National Products.
942 **287** 30h. lake 25 10
943 – 35h. green 30 25
944 – 80h. blue 60 15
945 – 95h. brown . . . . 1·50 1·60
DESIGNS—VERT: 35h. Picking hops. HORIZ: 80h. Fishing; 95h. Logging.

288 "Kladno", 1855

1956. European Freight Services Timetable Conference. Railway engines.
946 – 10h. brown . . . . 1·25 10
947 **288** 30h. black 75 10
948 – 40h. green . . . . 3·50 15
949 – 45h. purple . . . . 19·00 9·50
950 – 60h. blue 75 10
951 – 1k. blue . . . . 1·25 15
DESIGNS—VERT: 10h. "Zbraslav", 1846. HORIZ: 40h. Class 534, 1945; 45h. Class 556.0, 1952; 60h. Class 477.0, 1955; 1k. Class E499.0 electric locomotive, 1954.

1956. National Costumes (2nd series). As T **270**.
952 30h. sepia, red and blue . . . 2·25 70
953 1k.20 sepia, blue and red . . 2·25 15
954 1k.40 brown, yellow & red 4·00 1·90
955 1k.60 sepia, green & red . . 2·40 30
DESIGNS: 30h. Slovacko woman; 1k.20, Blata woman; 1k.40, Cicmany woman, 1k.60, Novohradsko woman.

1957. Czech Writers (2nd issue). As T **285**. On buff paper.
956 15h. brown (Olbracht) . . . 30 10
957 20h. green (Toman) 30 10
958 30h. sepia (Salda) 30 10
959 1k.60 blue (Vansova) 55 10

289 Forestry Academy, Banska Stiavnica

1957. Towns and Monuments Anniversaries.
960 – 30h. blue 20 10
961 **289** 30h. purple 20 10
962 – 60h. red 40 10
963 – 60h. brown 40 10
964 – 60h. green 30 10
965 – 1k.25 black . . . . 3·50 1·40
DESIGNS: No. 960, Kolin; 962, Uherske Hradiste; 963, Charles Bridge, Prague; 964, Karlstejn Castle; 965, Moravska Trebova.

290 Girl Harvester

1957. 3rd Collective Farming Agricultural Congress, Prague.
966 **290** 30h. turquoise 70 10

291 Komensky's Mausoleum **292** J. A. Komensky (Comenius)

1957. 300th Anniv of Publication of Komensky's "Opera Didactica Omnia".
967 **291** 30h. brown 40 10
968 – 40h. green 40 10
969 **292** 60h. brown . . . . 1·90 1·10
970 – 60h. red 55 10
DESIGNS: As Type **291**: 40h. Komensky at work; 1k. Illustration from "Opera Didactica Omnia".

293 Racing Cyclists

1957. Sports Events of 1957.
971 **293** 30h. purple and blue . . . 35 10
972 60h. green and bistre . . 1·60 1·40
973 – 60h. violet and brown . . 35 10
974 – 60h. purple and brown . . 35 10
975 – 60h. black and green . . 35 10
976 – 60h. black and blue . . . 1·00 10
DESIGNS—HORIZ: Nos. 971/2 (10th Int Cycle Race); 973, Rescue squad (Mountain Rescue Service); 975, Archer (World Archery Championships, Prague). VERT: 974, Boxers (European Boxing Championships, Prague); 976, Motor Cyclists (32nd Int Motor Cycle Six-Day Trial).

294 J. B. Foerster

1957. Int Music Festival Jubilee. Musicians.
977 – 60h. violet (Stamic) . . . 25 10
978 – 60h. black (Laub) 25 10
979 – 60h. blue (Ondricek) . . . 25 10
980 **294** 60h. sepia 25 10
981 – 60h. brown (Novak) . . . 90 10
982 – 60h. turquoise (Suk) . . . 25 10

295 J. Bozek (founder) **296** Young Collector Blowing Posthorn

1957. 250th Anniv of Polytechnic Engineering Schools, Prague.
983 **295** 30h. black 15 10
984 – 60h. brown 35 10
985 – 1k. purple 35 15
986 – 1k.40 violet 50 15
DESIGNS—VERT: 60h. F. J. Gerstner; 1k. R. Skuhersky. HORIZ: 1k.40, Polytechnic Engineering Schools Building, Prague.

1957. Junior Philatelic Exn, Pardubice.
987 **296** 30h. orange and green . . 50 10
988 – 60h. blue and brown . . . 2·10 1·25
DESIGN: 60h. Girl sending letter by pigeon.

297 "Rose of Friendship and Peace" **298** Karel Klic and Printing Press

1957. 15th Anniv of Destruction of Lidice.
989 – 30h. black 35 10
990 **297** 60h. red and black . . . 1·00 35
DESIGN: 30h. Veiled woman.

1957. Czech Inventors.
991 **298** 30h. black 15 10
992 – 60h. blue 35 10
DESIGN: 60h. Joseph Ressel and propeller.

299 Chamois **300** Marycka Magdonova

1957. Tatra National Park.
993 **299** 20h. black and green . . 65 45
994 – 30h. brown and blue . . . 65 10
995 – 40h. blue and brown . . . 1·25 30
996 – 60h. green and yellow . . 50 10
997 – 1k.25 black and ochre . . 1·25 1·25
DESIGNS—VERT: 30h. Brown bear. HORIZ: 40h. Gentian; 60h. Edelweiss; 1k.25 (49 × 29 mm), Tatra Mountains.

1957. 90th Birthday of Petr Bezruc (poet).
998 **300** 60h. black and red . . . 50 10

301 Worker with Banner **303** Television Tower and Aerials

302 Tupolev Tu-104A and Paris–Prague–Moscow Route

1957. 4th World T.U.C., Leipzig.
999 **301** 75h. red 50 15

1957. Air. Opening of Czechoslovak Airlines.
1000 **302** 75h. blue and red . . . 80 10
1001 – 2k.35 blue and yellow . . 95 10
DESIGN: 2k.35, "Prague–Cairo–Beirut–Damascus".

1957. Television Development.
1002 **303** 40h. blue and red . . . 25 10
1003 – 60h. brown and green . . 30 10
DESIGN: 60h. Family watching television.

304 Youth, Globe and Lenin

1957. 40th Anniv of Russian Revolution.
1004 **304** 30h. red 20 10
1005 – 60h. blue 35 10
DESIGN: 60h. Lenin, refinery and Russian emblem.

1957. Death of President Zapotocky. As T **259** but dated "19 XII 1884–13 XI 1957".
1006 30h. black 10 10
1007 60h. black 25 10

1957. National Costumes (3rd series). As T **270**.
1008 45h. sepia, red and blue . . 2·75 1·25
1009 75h. sepia, red and green . . 1·90 80
1010 1k.25 sepia, red & yellow . . 2·75 65
1011 1k.95 sepia, blue and red . . 3·25 2·10
DESIGNS—VERT: 45h. Pilsen woman; 75h. Slovacko man; 1k.25, Hana woman; 1k.95, Tesin woman.

305 Artificial Satellite ("Sputnik 2") **306** Figure Skating (European Championships, Bratislava)

1957. International Geophysical Year. Showing globe and dated "1957–1958".
1012 – 30h. brown . . . . . . 1·40 45
1013 – 45h. brown and blue . . 30 25
1014 **305** 75h. red and blue . . . 2·00 65
DESIGNS—HORIZ: 30h. Radio-telescope and observatory. VERT: 45h. Lomnicky Stit meteorological station.

1958. Sports Events of 1958.
1015 **306** 30h. purple 90 20
1016 – 40h. blue 30 20
1017 – 60h. brown 30 10
1018 – 80h. violet . . . . . . 1·40 65
1019 – 1k.60 green 50 15
EVENTS: 40h. Canoeing (World Canoeing Championships, Prague); 60h. Volleyball (European Volleyball Championships, Prague); 80h. Parachuting (4th World Parachute-jumping Championship, Bratislava); 1k.60, Football (World Cup Football Championship, Stockholm).

307 Litomysl Castle (birthplace of Nejedly) **309** Jewellery

308 Soldiers guarding Shrine of "Victorious February"

1958. 80th Birthday of Nejedly (musician).
1020 **307** 30h. green 20 10
1021 – 60h. brown 20 10
DESIGN—HORIZ: 60h. Bethlehem Chapel, Prague.

1958. 10th Anniv of Communist Govt.
1022 – 30h. blue and yellow . . 25 10
1023 **308** 60h. brown and red . . 25 10
1024 – 1k.60 green and orange 35 10
DESIGNS—VERT: 30h. Giant mine-excavator. HORIZ: 1k.60, Combine-harvester.

1958. Brussels International Exhibition. Inscr "Bruxelles 1958".
1025 **309** 30h. red and blue . . . 25 10
1026 – 45h. red and lilac . . . 60 10
1027 – 60h. violet and green . . 25 10
1028 – 75h. blue and orange . . 1 10 80
1029 – 1k.20 green and red . . 60 10
1030 – 1k.95 brown and blue . . 70 15
DESIGNS—VERT: 45h. Toy dolls; 60h. Draperies; 75h. Kaplan turbine; 1k.20, Glassware. HORIZ: ($48\frac{1}{2} \times 29\frac{1}{2}$ mm), 1k.95, Czech pavilion.

310 George of Podebrady and his Seal

1958. National Exhibition of Archive Documents. Inscr as in T **310**.
1031 **310** 30h. red 35 10
1032 – 60h. violet 35 10
DESIGN: 60h. Prague, 1628 (from engraving).

311 Hammer and Sickle

1958. 11th Czech Communist Party Congress and 15th Anniv of Czech–Soviet Friendship Treaty. 45h. inscr as in T **311** and 60h. inscr "15. VYROCI UZAVRENI".
1033 **311** 30h. red 20 10
1034 – 45h. green 20 10
1035 – 60h. blue 20 10
DESIGNS: 45h. Map of Czechoslovakia, with hammer and sickle; 60h. Atomic reactor, Rez (near Prague).

312 "Towards the Stars" (after sculpture by G. Postnikov) **313** Pres. Novotny

1958. Cultural and Political Events. 45h. inscr "IV. KONGRES MEZINARODNI", etc, and 60h. inscr "I. SVETOVA ODBOROVA", etc.
1036 **312** 30h. red 70 40
1037 – 45h. purple 20 25
1038 – 60h. blue 20 10

DESIGNS—VERT: 45h. Three women of different races and globe (4th Int Democratic Women's Federation Congress, Vienna). HORIZ: 60h. Boy and girl with globes (1st World T.U. Conference of Working Youth, Prague). Type **312** represents the Society for the Dissemination of Cultural and Political Knowledge.

1958.

1039	**313**	30h. violet	45	10
1039a		30h. purple	3·50	1·00
1040		60h. red	45	10

314 Telephone Operator

316 "The Poet and the Muse" (after Max Svabinsky)

315 Karlovy Vary (600th Anniv)

1958. Communist Postal Conference, Prague. Inscr as in T **314**.

1041	**314**	30h. sepia and brown	30	10
1042	–	45h. black and green	30	30

DESIGN: 45h. Aerial mast.

1958. Czech Spas (2nd series).

1043	**315**	30h. lake	10	10
1044	–	40h. brown	10	10
1045	–	60h. green	15	10
1046	–	80h. sepia	30	10
1047	–	1k.20 blue	45	15
1048	–	1k.60 violet	1·10	65

SPAS: 40h. Podebrady; 60h. Marianske Lazne (150th Anniv); 80h. Luhacovice; 1k.20, Strbske Pleso; 1k.60, Trencianske.

1958. 85th Birthday of Dr. Max Svabinsky (artist).

1049	**316**	1k.60 black	3·25	80

317 S. Cech

319 Parasol Mushroom

318 Children's Hospital, Brno

1958. Writers' Anniversaries.

1050	–	30h. red (Julius Fucik)	25	10
1051	–	45h. violet (Gustav K. Zechenter)	95	45
1052	–	60h. blue (Karel Capek)	15	10
1053	**317**	1k.40 black	50	10

1958. National Stamp Exn, Brno. Inscr as in T **318**.

1054	**318**	30h. violet	20	10
1055	–	60h. red	20	10
1056	–	1k. sepia	45	10
1057	–	1k.60 myrtle	1·60	1·50

DESIGNS: 60h. New Town Hall, Brno; 1k. St. Thomas's Church, Red Army Square; 1k.60, (50 × 28½ mm), Brno view.

1958. Mushrooms.

1058	**319**	30h. buff, green & brown	40	20
1059	–	40h. buff, red & brown	45	20
1060	–	60h. red, buff and black	55	25
1061	–	1k.40 red, green & brn	65	35
1062	–	1k.60 red, green & blk	5·25	2·00

DESIGNS—VERT: 40h. Cep; 60h. Red cap; 1k.40, Fly agaric; 1k.60, Boot-lace fungus.

320 Children sailing

322 Garlanded Woman ("Republic") with First Czech Stamp

321 Bozek's Steam Car of 1815

1958. Inauguration of U.N.E.S.C.O. Headquarters Building, Paris. Inscr "ZE SOUTEZE PRO UNESCO".

1063	**320**	30h. red, yellow & blue	20	10
1064	–	45h. red and blue	50	10
1065	–	60h. blue, yellow & brn	20	10

DESIGNS: 45h. Mother, child and bird; 60h. Child skier.

1958. Czech Motor Industry Commemoration.

1066	**321**	30h. violet and yellow	65	10
1067	–	45h. brown and green	50	10
1068	–	60h. green and orange	65	10
1069	–	80h. red and green	50	10
1070	–	1k. brown and green	50	10
1071		1k.25 green & yellow	1·60	75

DESIGNS: 45h. "President" car of 1897; 60h. Skoda "450" car; 80h. Tatra "603" car; 1k. Skoda "706" motor coach; 1k.25, Tatra "III" and Praga "VS 3" motor trucks in Tibet.

1958. 40th Anniv of 1st Czech Postage Stamps.

1072	**322**	60h. blue	25	10

323 Ice Hockey Goalkeeper

1959. Sports Events of 1959.

1073	–	20h. brown and grey	30	10
1074	–	30h. brown & orange	30	10
1075	**323**	60h. blue and green	30	10
1076	–	1k. lake and yellow	30	10
1077	–	1k.60 violet and blue	45	10
1078	–	2k. brown and blue	1·60	1·25

DESIGNS: 20h. Ice hockey player (50th anniv of Czech Ice Hockey Association); 30h. Throwing the javelin; 60h. (Type **323**) World Ice Hockey Championships, 1959; 1k. Hurdling; 1k.60, Rowing; 2k. High jumping.

324 U.A.C. Emblem

325 "Equal Rights"

1959. 4th National Unified Agricultural Co-operatives Congress, Prague.

1079	**324**	30h. lake and blue	20	10
1080	–	60h. blue and yellow	40	10

DESIGN: 60h. Artisan shaking hand with farmer.

1959. 10th Anniv of Declaration of Human Rights.

1081	**325**	60h. green	15	10
1082	–	1k. sepia	25	10
1083	–	2k. blue	1·40	55

DESIGNS: 1k. "World Freedom" (girl with Dove of Peace); 2k. "Freedom for Colonial Peoples" (native woman with child).

326 Girl with Doll

327 F. Joliot-Curie (scientist)

1959. 10th Anniv of Young Pioneers' Movement.

1084	**326**	30h. blue and yellow	30	10
1085	–	40h. black and blue	30	25
1086	–	60h. black and purple	30	10
1087	–	80h. brown and green	30	25

DESIGNS: 40h. Boy hiker; 60h. Young radio technician; 80h. Girl planting tree.

1959. 10th Anniv of Peace Movement.

1088	**327**	60h. purple	1·40	40

328 Man in outer space and Moon Rocket

329 Pilsen Town Hall

1959. 2nd Czech Political and Cultural Knowledge Congress, Prague.

1089	**328**	30h. blue	90	35

1959. Centenary of Skoda Works and National Stamp Exhibition, Pilsen. Inscr "PLZEN 1959".

1090	**329**	30h. brown	15	10
1091	–	60h. violet and green	15	10
1092	–	1k. blue	25	20
1093	–	1k.60 black & yellow	1·25	1·00

DESIGNS: 60h. Part of steam turbine; 1k. St. Bartholomew's Church, Pilsen; 1k.60, Part of SR-1200 lathe.

330 Congress Emblem and Industrial Plant

1959. 4th Trades Union Congress, Prague.

1094	**330**	30h. red and yellow	20	10
1095	–	60h. olive and blue	20	10

DESIGN: 60h. Dam.

331 Zvolen Castle

1959. Slovak Stamp Exhibition, Zvolen.

1096	**331**	60h. olive and yellow	35	10

332 F. Benda (composer)

1959. Cultural Anniversaries.

1097	**332**	15h. blue	20	10
1098	–	30h. red	20	10
1099	–	40h. green	30	10
1100	–	60h. brown	30	10
1101	–	60h. black	55	10
1102	–	80h. violet	30	10
1103	–	1k. brown	30	10
1104	–	3k. brown	1·40	1·10

PORTRAITS: 30h. Vaclav Klicpera (dramatist); 40h. Aurel Stodola (engineer); 60h. (1100) Karel V. Rais (writer); 60h. (1101) Haydn (composer); 80h. Antonin Slavicek (painter); 1k. Petr Bezruc (poet). 3k. Charles Darwin (naturalist).

333 "Z" Pavilion

1959. Int Fair, Brno. Inscr "BRNO 6-20. IX. 1959".

1105	–	30h. purple & yellow	15	10
1106	–	60h. blue	15	10
1107	**333**	1k.60 blue & yellow	45	10

DESIGNS: 30h. View of Fair; 60h. Fair emblem and world map.

334 Revolutionary (after A. Holly)

1959. 15th Anniv of Slovak National Uprising and 40th Anniv of Republic. Inscr "1944 29.8.1959".

1108	**334**	30h. black & mauve	15	10
1109	–	60h. red	20	10
1110	–	1k.60 blue & yell	40	10

DESIGNS—VERT: 60h. Revolutionary with upraised rifle (after sculpture "Forward" by L. Snopka). HORIZ: 1k.60, Factory, sun and linden leaves.

335 Moon Rocket

1959. Landing of Russian Rocket on Moon.

1111	**335**	60h. red and blue	1·25	25

336 Lynx

1959. 10th Anniv of Tatra National Park. Inscr "1949 TATRANSKY NARODNY PARK 1959".

1112	–	30h. black and grey	65	10
1113	–	40h. brown & turquoise	65	10
1114	**336**	60h. red & yellow	90	10
1115	–	1k. brown & blue	2·00	75
1116	–	1k.60 brown	1·75	10

DESIGNS—HORIZ: 30h. Alpine marmots; 40h. European bison; 1k. Wolf; 1k.60, Red deer.

337 Stamp Printing Works, Peking

1959. 10th Anniv of Chinese People's Republic.

1117	**337**	30h. red and green	25	10

338 Bleriot XI Monoplanes at First Czech Aviation School

1959. Air. 50th Anniv of 1st Flight by Jan Kaspar.

1118	**338**	1k. black and yellow	15	10
1119	–	1k.80 black & blue	75	10

DESIGN: 1k.80, Jan Kaspar and Bleriot XI in flight.

339 Great Spotted Woodpecker

341 Exercises

340 Tesla and Electrical Apparatus

1959. Birds.
1120 **339** 20h. multicoloured . . . 85 15
1121 – 30h. multicoloured . . . 85 15
1122 – 40h. multicoloured . . . 2·10 1·10
1123 – 60h. multicoloured . . . 85 15
1124 – 80h. multicoloured . . . 85 20
1125 – 1k. red, blue & black . . 85 20
1126 – 1k.20 brn, blue & blk . . 1·10 40
BIRDS: 30h. Blue tit; 40h. Eurasian nuthatch; 60h. Golden oriole; 80h. Eurasian goldfinch; 1k. Northern bullfinch; 1k.20, River kingfisher.

1959. Radio Inventors.
1127 **340** 25h. black and red . . . 1·10 20
1128 – 30h. black and brown . . 15 10
1129 – 35h. black and lilac . . . 20 10
1130 – 60h. black and blue . . 25 10
1131 – 1k. black and green . . 20 10
1132 – 2k. black and bistre . . 80 85
INVENTORS (each with sketch of invention): 30h. Aleksandr Popov; 35h. Edouard Branly; 60h. Guglielmo Marconi; 1k. Heinrich Hertz; 2k. Edwin Armstrong.

1960. 2nd National Spartacist Games (1st issue). Inscr as in T **341**.
1133 **341** 30h. brown and red . . 1·10 10
1134 – 60h. blue & light blue . . 45 25
1135 – 1k.60 brown & bistre . . 70 30
DESIGNS: 60h. Skiing; 1k.60, Basketball.
See also Nos. 1160/2.

342 Freighter “Lidice”

1960. Czech Ships.
1136 – 30h. green and red . . . 80 15
1137 – 60h. red and turquoise 25 10
1138 – 1k. violet and yellow . . 80 25
1139 **342** 1k.20 purple and green 1·75 90
SHIPS: 30h. Dredger “Praha Liben”; 60h. Tug “Kharito Latjev”; 1k. River boat “Komarno”.

343 Ice Hockey

1960. Winter Olympic Games. Inscr as in T **343**.
1140 **343** 60h. sepia and blue . . . 45 25
1141 – 1k.80 black & green . . 3·75 2·10
DESIGN: 1k.80, Skating pair.
See also Nos. 1163/5.

344 Trencin Castle

345 Lenin

1960. Czechoslovak Castles.
1142 5h. blue (Type **344**) 15 10
1143 10h. black (Bezdez) 15 10
1144 20h. orange (Kost) 25 10
1145 30h. green (Pernstejn) . . . 25 10
1146 40h. brn (Kremnica) . . . 25 10
1146a 50h. black (Krivoklat) . . 25 10
1147 60h. red (Karestejn) . . . 45 10
1148 1k. purple (Smolenice) . . 30 10
1149 1k.60 blue (Kokorin) . . . 65 10

1960. 90th Birth Anniv of Lenin.
1150 **345** 60h. olive 85 25

346 Soldier and Child

1960. 15th Anniv of Liberation.
1151 **346** 30h. lake and blue . . . 30 10
1152 – 30h. green and lavender 25 10
1153 – 30h. red and pink . . . 25 10
1154 – 60h. blue and buff . . . 25 10
1155 – 60h. purple and green . . 25 10
DESIGNS—VERT: No. 1152, Solider with liberated political prisoner; 1153, Child eating pastry. HORIZ: No. 1154, Welder; 1155, Tractor-driver.

347 Smelter

1960. Parliamentary Elections.
1156 **347** 30h. red and grey . . . 15 10
1157 – 60h. green and blue . . 20 10
DESIGN: 60h. Country woman and child.

348 Red Cross Woman with Dove

1960. 3rd Czechoslovak Red Cross Congress.
1158 **348** 30h. red and blue . . . 10 10

349 Fire-prevention Team with Hose

1960. 2nd Firemen's Union Congress.
1159 **349** 60h. blue and pink . . . 35 10

1960. 2nd National Spartacist Games (2nd issue). As T **341**.
1160 30h. red and green 40 10
1161 60h. black and pink 40 10
1162 1k. blue and orange 60 25
DESIGNS: 30h. Ball exercises; 60h. Stick exercises; 1k. Girls with hoops.

1960. Olympic Games, Rome. As Type **343**.
1163 1k. black and orange . . . 50 25
1164 1k.80 black and red . . . 1·25 25
1165 2k. black and blue . . . . 2·00 85
DESIGNS: 1k. Sprinting; 1k.80, Gymnastics; 2k. Rowing.

350 Czech 10k. Stamp of 1936

1960. National Philatelic Exn, Bratislava (1st issue).
1166 – 60h. black and yellow . . 40 10
1167 **350** 1k. black and blue . . . 90 10
DESIGN: 60h. Hand of philatelist holding stamp Type **350**.
See also Nos. 1183/4.

351 Stalin Mine, Ostrava-Hermanice
352 V. Cornelius of Vsehra (historian)

1960. 3rd Five Year Plan (1st issue).
1168 **351** 10h. black and green . . 25 10
1169 – 20h. lake and blue . . . 25 10
1170 – 30h. blue and red . . . 25 10
1171 – 40h. green and lilac . . . 25 10
1172 – 60h. blue and yellow . . 25 10
DESIGNS: 20h. Hodonin Power Station; 30h. Klement Gottwald Iron Works, Kuncice; 40h. Excavator; 60h. Naphtha refinery.
See also Nos. 1198/1200.

1960. Cultural Anniversaries.
1173 **352** 10h. black 20 10
1174 – 20h. brown 30 10
1175 – 30h. red 40 10
1176 – 40h. green 45 10
1177 – 60h. violet 50 10
PORTRAITS: 20h. K. M. Capek Chod (writer); 30h. Hana Kvapilova (actress); 40h. Oskar Nedbal (composer); 60h. Otakar Ostricil (composer).

353 Zlin Trener 6 flying upside-down

1960. 1st World Aviation Aerobatic Championships, Bratislava.
1178 **353** 60h. violet and blue . . 90 25

354 “New Constitution”

1960. Proclamation of New Constitution.
1179 **354** 30h. blue and red . . . 25 10

355 Worker with “Rude Pravo”

1960. Czechoslovak Press Day (30h.) and 40th Anniv of Newspaper “Rude Pravo”.
1180 – 30h. blue and orange . . 10 10
1181 **355** 60h. black and red . . . 20 10
DESIGN—HORIZ: (inscr “DEN TISKU”): 30h. Steel-workers with newspaper.

356 Globes

1960. 15th Anniv of W.F.T.U.
1182 **356** 30h. blue and bistre . . 25 10

357 Mail Coach and Ilyushin Il-18B

1960. Air. National Philatelic Exhibition, Bratislava (2nd issue).
1183 **357** 1k.60 blue and grey . . 2·50 1·40
1184 – 2k.80 green & cream . . 4·00 2·00
DESIGN: 2k.80, MIL Mi-4 helicopter over Bratislava.

358 Mallard

1960. Water Birds.
1185 – 25h. black and blue . . 50 10
1186 – 30h. black and green . . 1·10 20
1187 – 40h. black and blue . . 70 20
1188 – 60h. black and pink . . 80 20
1189 – 1k. black and yellow . . 1·25 20
1190 **358** 1k.60 black and lilac . . 2·40 1·60
BIRDS—VERT: 25h. Black-crowned night heron; 30h. Great crested grebe; 40h. Northern lapwing; 60h. Grey heron. HORIZ: 1k. Greylag goose.

359 “Doronicum clusii tausch”

1960. Flowers. Inscr in black.
1191 **359** 20h. yellow, orge & grn 50 10
1192 – 30h. red and green . . . 65 20
1193 – 40h. yellow and green . . 65 20
1194 – 60h. pink and green . . 70 20
1195 – 1k. blue, violet & green 1·00 35
1196 – 2k. yellow, green & pur 2·40 1·25
FLOWERS: 30h. “Cyclamen europaeum L”; 40h. “Primula auricula L”; 60h. “Sempervivum mont L”; 1k. “Gentiana clusil perr, et song”; 2k. “Pulsatilla slavica reuss”.

360 A. Mucha (painter and stamp designer)

361 Automatic Machinery

1960. Stamp Day and Birth Centenary of Mucha.
1197 **360** 60h. blue 70 10

1961. 3rd Five Year Plan (2nd issue).
1198 **361** 20h. blue 10 10
1199 – 30h. red 20 10
1200 – 60h. green 20 10
DESIGNS: 30h. Turbo-generator and control desk; 60h. Excavator.

362 Motor Cyclists (Int Grand Prix, Brno)

1961. Sports Events of 1961.
1201 **362** 30h. blue and mauve . . 20 10
1202 – 30h. red and blue . . . 20 10
1203 – 40h. black and red . . . 35 10
1204 – 60h. purple and blue . . 35 10
1205 – 1k. blue and yellow . . . 35 10
1206 – 1k.20 green & salmon . . 35 10
1207 – 1k.60 brown and red . . 1·60 1·00
DESIGNS—VERT: 30h. (No. 1202), Athletes with banners (40th anniv of Czech Physical Culture); 60h. Figure skating (World Figure Skating Championships, Prague); 1k. Rugger (35th anniv of rugby football in Czechoslovakia); 1k.20, Football (60th anniv of football in Czechoslovakia); 1k.60, Running (65th anniv of Bechovice–Prague Marathon Race). HORIZ: 40h. Rowing (European Rowing Championships, Prague).

363 Exhibition Emblem

365 J. Mosna

364 "Sputnik 3"

1961. "PRAGA 1962" Int Stamp Exn (1st issue).
1208 **363** 2k. red and blue . . . . 2·00 20
See also Nos. 1250/6, 1267/70, 1297/1300 and 1311/15.

1961. Space Research (1st series).
1209 – 20h. red and violet . . . 50 10
1210 **364** 30h. blue and buff . . . 50 10
1211 – 40h. red and green . . . 45 15
1212 – 60h. violet and yellow 30 10
1213 – 1k.60 blue and green . . 50 10
1214 – 2k. purple and blue . . . 1·50 1·00
DESIGNS—VERT: 20h. Launching cosmic rocket; 40h. Venus rocket. HORIZ: 60h. "Lunik 1"; 1k.60, "Lunik 3" and Moon; 2k. Cosmonaut (similar to T **366**).
See also Nos. 1285/90 and 1349/54.

1961. Cultural Anniversaries.
1215 **365** 60h. green 30 10
1216 – 60h. black 40 10
1217 – 60h. blue 40 10
1218 – 60h. red 30 10
1219 – 60h. brown 30 10
PORTRAITS: No. 1216, J. Uprka (painter); 1217, P. O. Hviezdoslav (poet); 1218, A. Mrstik (writer); 1219, J. Hora (poet).

366 Man in Space

1961. World's 1st Manned Space Flight.
1220 **366** 60h. red and turquoise 55 10
1221 3k. blue and yellow . . . 2·00 50

367 Kladno Steel Mills

368 "Instrumental Music"

1961.
1222 **367** 3k. red 85 10

1961. 150th Anniv of Prague Conservatoire.
1223 **368** 30h. sepia 30 10
1224 – 30h. red 35 10
1225 – 60h. blue 30 10
DESIGNS: No. 1224, Dancer; 1225, Girl playing lyre.

369 "People's House" (Lenin Museum), Prague

1961. 40th Anniv of Czech Communist Party.
1226 **369** 30h. brown 25 10
1227 – 30h. blue 25 10
1228 – 30h. violet 25 10
1229 – 60h. red 25 10
1230 – 60h. myrtle 25 10
1231 – 60h. red 25 10
DESIGNS—HORIZ: No. 1227, Gottwald's Museum, Prague. VERT: No. 1228, Workers in Wenceslas Square, Prague; 1229, Worker, star and factory plant; 1230, Woman wielding hammer and sickle; 1231, May Day procession, Wenceslas Square.

370 Manasek Doll

371 Gagarin waving Flags

1961. Czech Puppets.
1232 **370** 30h. red and yellow . . 20 10
1233 – 40h. sepia & turquoise 20 10
1234 – 60h. blue and salmon . . 20 10
1235 – 1k. green and blue . . . 20 10
1236 – 1k.60 red and blue . . . 1·25 35
PUPPETS: 40h. "Dr. Faustus and Caspar"; 60h. "Spejbl and Hurvinek"; 1k. Scene from "Difficulties with the Moon" (Askenazy); 1k.60, "Jasanek" of Brno.

1961. Yuri Gagarin's (first man in space) Visit to Prague.
1237 **371** 60h. black and red . . . 25 10
1238 – 1k.80 black and blue . . 45 10
DESIGN: 1k.80, Yuri Gagarin in space helmet, rocket and dove.

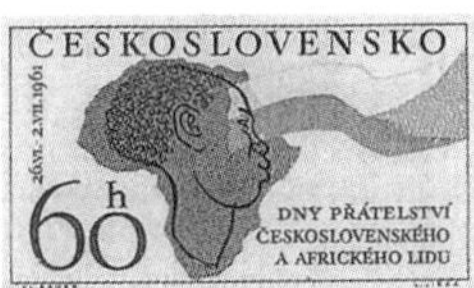

372 Woman's Head and Map of Africa

1961. Czecho-African Friendship.
1239 **372** 60h. red and blue . . . 25 10

373 Map of Europe and Fair Emblem

1961. Int Trade Fair, Brno. Inscr "M.V.B. 1961".
1240 **373** 30h. blue and green . . 15 10
1241 – 60h. green & salmon . . 25 10
1242 – 1k. brown and blue . . . 25 10
DESIGNS—VERT: 60h. Horizontal drill. HORIZ: 1k. Scientific discussion group.

374 Clover and Cow

375 Prague

1961. Agricultural Produce.
1243 – 20h. purple and blue . . 15 10
1244 **374** 30h. ochre and purple 15 10
1245 – 40h. orange and brown 15 10
1246 – 60h. bistre and green . . 20 10
1247 – 1k.40 brown & choc . . 40 10
1248 – 2k. blue and purple . . . 1·40 50
DESIGNS: 20h. Sugar beet, cup and saucer; 40h. Wheat and bread; 60h. Hops and beer; 1k.40, Maize and cattle; 2k. Potatoes and factory.

1961. 26th Session of Red Cross Societies League Governors' Council, Prague.
1249 **375** 60h. violet and red . . . 1·00 10

376 Orlik Dam

1961. "Praga 1962" International Stamp Exhibition (2nd and 3rd issues).
1250 **376** 20h. black and blue . . 75 30
1251 – 30h. blue and red . . . 45 10
1252 – 40h. blue and green . . 75 30
1253 – 60h. slate and bistre . . 75 30
1267 – 1k. purple and green . . 55 50
1254 – 1k.20 green and pink . . 90 45
1268 – 1k.60 brown and violet 95 65
1269 – 2k. black and orange . . 1·50 1·10
1255 – 3k. blue and yellow . . . 1·60 45
1256 – 4k. violet and orange . . 2·25 1·25
1270 – 5k. multicoloured . . . 22·00 17·00
DESIGNS—As Type **376**: 30h. Prague; 40h. Hluboka Castle from lake; 60h. Karlovy Vary; 1k. Pilsen; 1k.20, North Bohemian landscape; 1k.60, High Tatras; 2k. Iron-works, Ostrava-Kuncice; 3k. Brno; 4k. Bratislava. (50 × 29 mm): 5k. Prague and flags.

377 Orange-tip

1961. Butterflies and Moths. Multicoloured.
1257 15h. Type **377** 35 10
1258 20h. Southern festoon . . . 50 10
1259 30h. Apollo 90 25
1260 40h. Swallowtail 90 25
1261 60h. Peacock . . . . 1·10 25
1262 80h. Camberwell beauty . . 1·25 25
1263 1k. Clifden's nonpareil . . . 1·25 25
1264 1k.60 Red admiral . . . . 1·40 40
1265 2k. Brimstone . . . . . . 2·75 1·90

378 Congress Emblem and World Map

1961. 5th W.F.T.U. Congress, Moscow.
1266 **378** 60h. blue and red . . . 45 10

379 Racing Cyclists (Berlin–Prague–Warsaw Cycle Race)

380 K. Kovarovic (composer, centenary of birth)

1962. Sports Events of 1962.
1271 **379** 30h. black and blue . . 25 10
1272 – 40h. black and yellow . . 20 10
1273 – 60h. grey and blue . . . 30 10
1274 – 1k. black and pink . . . 30 10
1275 – 1k.20 black and green 30 10
1276 – 1k.60 black and green 1·40 55
DESIGNS: 40h. Gymnastics (15th World Gymnastics Championships, Prague); 60h. Figure Skating (World Figure Skating Championships, Prague); 1k. Bowling (World Bowling Championships, Bratislava); 1k.20, Football (World Cup Football Championship, Chile); 1k.60, Throwing the discus (7th European Athletic Championships, Belgrade).
See also No. 1306.

1962. Cultural Celebrities and Anniversaries.
1277 **380** 10h. brown 10 10
1278 – 20h. blue 10 10
1279 – 30h. brown 10 10
1280 – 40h. purple 15 10
1281 – 60h. black 15 10
1282 – 1k.60 myrtle 40 10
1283 – 1k.80 blue 50 10
DESIGNS—As Type **380**: 20h. F. Skroup (composer); 30h. Bozena Nemcova (writer); 60h. Rod of Aesculapius and Prague Castle (Czech Medical Association Cent); 1k.60, L. Celakovsky (founder, Czech Botanical Society). HORIZ: (41 × 22½ mm): 40h. F. Zaviska and K. Petr; 1k.80, M. Valouch and J. Hronec. (These two commemorate Czech Mathematics and Physics Union Cent).

381 Miner holding Lamp

1962. 30th Anniv of Miners' Strike, Most.
1284 **381** 60h. blue and red . . . 25 10

382 "Man Conquers Space"

384 Dove and Nest

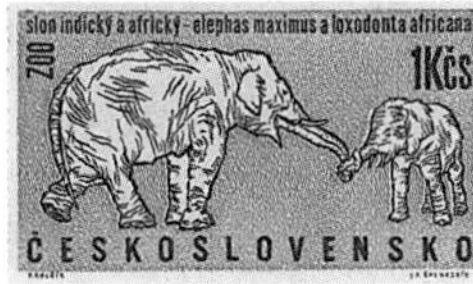

383 Indian and African Elephants

1962. Space Research (2nd series).
1285 **382** 30h. red and blue . . . 25 10
1286 – 40h. blue and orange . . 25 10
1287 – 60h. blue and pink . . . 25 10
1288 – 80h. purple and green . . 60 10
1289 – 1k. blue and yellow . . . 25 25
1290 – 1k.60 green and yellow 1·40 60
DESIGNS—VERT: 40h. Launching of Soviet rocket; 1k. Automatic station on Moon. HORIZ: 60h. "Vostok-II"; 80h. Multi-stage automatic rocket; 1k.60, Television satellite station.

1962. Animals of Prague Zoos.
1291 – 20h. black & turquoise 55 10
1292 – 30h. black and violet . . 55 10
1293 – 60h. black and yellow . . 65 10
1294 **383** 1k. black and green . . 95 10
1295 – 1k.40 black and mauve 1·00 25
1296 – 1k.60 black and brown 2·10 1·10
ANIMALS—VERT: 20h. Polar bear; 30h. Chimpanzee; 60h. Bactrian camel. HORIZ: 1k.40, Leopard; 1k.60, Wild horses.

1962. Air. "Praga 1962" International Stamp Exhibition (4th issue).
1297 **384** 80h. multicoloured . . . 50 25
1298 – 1k.40 red, blue & black 2·00 2·75
1299 – 2k.80 multicoloured . . 3·25 2·75
1300 – 4k.20 multicoloured . . 4·75 2·75
DESIGNS: 1k.40, Dove; 2k.80, Flower and bird; 4k.20, Plant and bird. All designs feature "Praga 62" emblem. The 80h. and 2k.80 are inscr in Slovakian and the others in Czech.

385 Girl of Lidice

386 Klary's Fountain, Teplice

1962. 20th Anniv of Destruction of Lidice and Lezaky.
1301 **385** 30h. black and red . . . 35 10
1302 – 60h. black and blue . . 35 10
DESIGN: 60h. Flowers and Lezaky ruins.

1962. 1200th Anniv of Discovery of Teplice Springs.
1303 **386** 60h. green and yellow . . 45 10

387 Campaign Emblem

388 Swimmer with Rifle

1962. Malaria Eradication.
1304 **387** 60h. red and black . . . 15 10
1305 – 3k. blue and black . . . 1·25 65
DESIGN: 3k. Campaign emblem and dove (different).

1962. Czechoslovakia's Participation in World Cup Football Championship Final, Chile. As No. 1275 but inscr "CSSR VE FINALE" and new value.
1306 1k.60 green and yellow . . . 1·25 20

1962. 2nd Military Spartacist Games. Inscr as in T **388**.
1307 **388** 30h. myrtle and blue . . 15 10
1308 – 40h. violet and yellow 20 10
1309 – 60h. brown and green . . 25 10
1310 – 1k. blue and red 30 10
DESIGNS: 40h. Soldier mounting obstacle; 60h. Footballer; 1k. Relay Race.

389 "Sun" and Field (Socialized Agriculture) **390** Swallow, "Praga 62" and Congress Emblems

1962. "Praga 1962" Int Stamp Exn (5th issue).
1311 **389** 30h. multicoloured . . . 3·00 1·10
1312 – 60h. multicoloured . . . 80 25
1313 – 80h. multicoloured . . . 3·50 2·40
1314 – 1k. multicoloured . . . 3·50 2·75
1315 – 1k.40 multicoloured . . 3·50 2·75
DESIGNS—VERT: 60h. Astronaut in "spaceship"; 1k.40, Children playing under "tree". HORIZ: 80h. Boy with flute, and peace doves; 1k. Workers of three races. All have "Praga 62" emblem.

1962. F.I.P. Day (Federation Internationale de Philatelie).
1316 **390** 1k.60 multicoloured . . 4·75 4·00

391 Zinkovy Sanatorium and Sailing Dinghy **392** Cruiser "Aurora"

1962. Czech Workers' Social Facilities.
1317 – 30h. black and blue . . 20 10
1318 **391** 60h. sepia and ochre . . 25 10
DESIGN—HORIZ: 30h. Children in day nursery, and factory.

1962. 45th Anniv of Russian Revolution.
1319 **392** 30h. sepia and blue . . . 10 10
1320 60h. black and pink . . 25 10

393 Astronaut and Worker

1962. 40th Anniv of U.S.S.R.
1321 **393** 30h. red and blue . . . 25 10
1322 – 60h. black and pink . . 30 10
DESIGN—VERT: 60h. Lenin.

394 Crane ("Building Construction")

1962. 12th Czech Communist Party Congress, Prague
1323 **394** 30h. red and yellow . . 25 10
1324 – 40h. blue and yellow . . 25 10
1325 – 60h. black and pink . . 25 10
DESIGNS—VERT: 40h. Produce ("Agriculture"). HORIZ: 60h. Factory plants ("Industry").

395 Stag Beetle **396** Table Tennis (World Championships, Prague)

1962. Beetles. Multicoloured.
1326 20h. Caterpillar-hunter (horiz) 25 10
1327 30h. Cardinal beetle (horiz) 25 10
1328 60h. Type **395** 25 10
1329 1k. Great dung beetle (horiz) 85 10
1330 1k.60 Alpine longhorn beetle 1·25 35
1331 2k. Blue ground beetle . . . 3·00 1·40

1963. Sports Events of 1963.
1332 **396** 30h. black and green . . 25 10
1333 – 60h. black and orange 25 10
1334 – 80h. black and blue . . 25 10
1335 – 1k. black and violet . . 30 10
1336 – 1k.20 black and brown 30 20
1337 – 1k.60 black and red . . 90 20
DESIGNS: 60h. Cycling (80th Anniv of Czech Cycling); 80h. Skiing (1st Czech Winter Games); 1k. Motor-cycle dirt track racing (15th Anniv of "Golden Helmet" Race, Pardubice); 1k.20, Weightlifting (World Championships, Prague); 1k.60, Hurdling (1st Czech Summer Games).

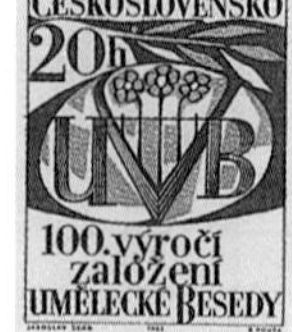

397 Industrial Plant **398** Guild Emblem

1963. 15th Anniv of "Victorious February" and 5th T.U. Congress.
1338 **397** 30h. red and blue . . . 15 10
1339 – 60h. red and black . . . 15 10
1340 – 60h. black and red . . . 15 10
DESIGNS—VERT: No. 1339, Sun and campfire. HORIZ: No. 1340, Industrial plant and annual "stepping stones".

1963. Cultural Anniversaries.
1341 **398** 20h. black and blue . . 10 10
1342 – 30h. red 10 10
1343 – 30h. red and blue . . . 10 10
1344 – 60h. black 15 10
1345 – 60h. purple and blue . . 15 10
1346 – 60h. myrtle 15 10
1347 – 1k.60 brown 45 10
DESIGNS—VERT: No. 1341 (Artist's Guild cent); 1342, E. Urx (journalist); 1343, J. Janosik (national hero); 1344, J. Palkovic (author); 1346, Woman with book, and children (cent of Slovak Cultural Society, Slovenska Matice); 1347, M. Svabinsky (artist, after self-portrait). HORIZ: 1345, Allegorical figure and National Theatre, Prague (80th anniv).

399 Young People

1963. 4th Czech Youth Federation Congress, Prague.
1348 **399** 30h. blue and red . . . 25 10

1963. Space Research (3rd series). As T **364** but inscr "1963" at foot.
1349 30h. purple, red & yellow 15 10
1350 50h. blue and turquoise . . 25 10
1351 60h. turquoise & yellow . . 25 10
1352 1k. black and brown . . . 55 10
1353 1k.60 sepia and green . . . 40 10
1354 2k. violet and yellow . . . 1·60 75
DESIGNS—HORIZ: 30h. Rocket circling Sun; 50h. Rockets and Sputniks leaving Earth; 60h. Spacecraft and Moon; 1k. "Mars 1" rocket and Mars; 1k.60, Rocket heading for Jupiter; 2k. Spacecraft returning from Saturn.

400 TV Cameras and Receiver

1963. 10th Anniv of Czech Television Service. Inscr as in T **400**.
1355 **400** 40h. blue and orange . . 20 10
1356 – 60h. red and blue . . . 20 10
DESIGN—VERT: 60h. TV transmitting aerial.

401 Broadcasting Studio and Receiver

1963. 40th Anniv of Czech Radio Service. Inscr as in T **401**.
1357 **401** 30h. purple and blue . . 15 10
1358 – 1k. purple & turquoise 25 10
DESIGN—VERT: 1k. Aerial mast, globe and doves.

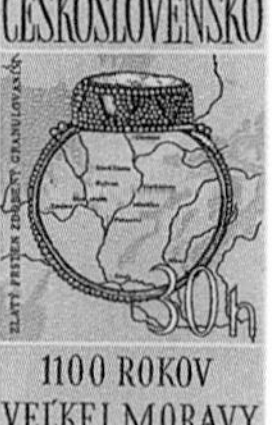

402 Ancient Ring and Moravian Settlements Map **404** Singer

403 Tupolev Tu-104A

1963. 1100th Anniv of Moravian Empire.
1359 **402** 30h. black and green . . 20 10
1360 – 1k.60 black and yellow 40 10
DESIGN: 1k.60, Ancient silver plate showing falconer with hawk.

1963. 40th Anniv of Czech Airlines.
1361 **403** 80h. violet and blue . . 80 20
1362 – 1k.80 blue and green . . 1·50 45
DESIGN: 1k.80, Ilyushin Il-18B.

1963. 60th Anniv of Moravian Teachers' Singing Club.
1363 **404** 30h. red 35 10

405 Nurse and Child **406** Wheatears and Kromeriz Castle

1963. Centenary of Red Cross.
1364 **405** 30h. blue and red . . . 35 10

1963. National Agricultural Exhibition.
1365 **406** 30h. green and yellow . . 35 10

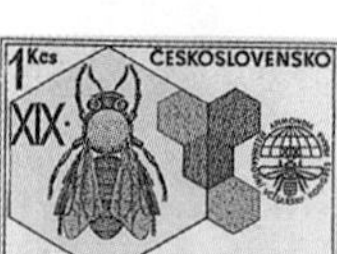

407 Honey Bee, Honeycomb and Congress Emblem **409** "Modern Fashion"

408 "Vostok 5" and Bykovsky

1963. 19th International Bee-keepers' Congress ("Apimondia '63").
1366 **407** 1k. brown and yellow . . 45 10

1963. 2nd "Team" Manned Space Flights.
1367 **408** 80h. pink and blue . . . 35 10
1368 – 2k.80 blue and purple . . 2·25 25
DESIGN: 2k.80, "Vostok 6" and Valentina Tereshkova.

1963. Liberec Consumer Goods Fair.
1369 **409** 30h. black and mauve 35 10

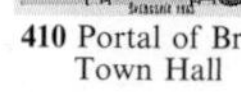

410 Portal of Brno Town Hall **411** Cave and Stalagmites

1963. Brno International Fair.
1370 **410** 30h. purple and blue . . 25 10
1371 – 60h. blue and salmon . . 30 10
DESIGN: 60h. Tower of Brno Town Hall.

1963. Czech Scenery. (a) Moravia.
1372 **411** 30h. brown and blue . . 25 10
1373 – 80h. brown and pink . . 40 10

(b) Slovakia.
1374 – 30h. blue and green . . . 30 10
1375 – 60h. blue, green & yellow 30 10
DESIGNS: No. 1373, Macocha Chasm; 1374, Pool, Hornad Valley; 1375, Waterfall, Great Hawk Gorge.

412 Mouse

1963. 2nd International Pharmacological Congress, Prague.
1376 **412** 1k. red and black . . . 45 10

413 Blast Furnace **414** "Aid for Farmers Abroad"

1963. 30th International Foundry Congress, Prague.
1377 **413** 60h. black and blue . . 25 10

1963. Freedom from Hunger.
1378 **414** 1k.60 sepia 45 10

415 Dolls **416** Canoeing

1963. U.N.E.S.C.O. Folk Art. Multicoloured.
1379 60h. Type **415** 15 10
1380 80h. Rooster 25 10
1381 1k. Vase of flowers 35 20
1382 1k.20 Detail of glass-painting "Janosik and his Men" 35 10
1383 1k.60 Stag 35 20
1384 2k. Horseman . . . . . . 2·75 1·10

1963. Olympic Games, Tokyo, 1964, and 50th Anniv of Czech Canoeing (30h.).
1385 **416** 30h. blue and green . . 30 10
1386 – 40h. brown and blue . . 30 10
1387 – 60h. lake and yellow . . 25 10
1388 – 80h. violet and red . . . 30 20
1389 – 1k. blue and red 30 20
1390 – 1k.60 ultram & blue . . 1·50 70
DESIGNS: 40h. Volleyball; 60h. Wrestling; 80h. Basketball; 1k. Boxing; 1k.60, Gymnastics.

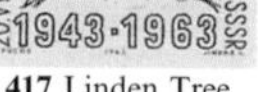

417 Linden Tree **418** "Human Reason and Technology."

1963. 20th Anniv of Czech–Soviet Treaty of Friendship.
1391 **417** 30h. brown and blue . . 15 10
1392 – 60h. red and green . . . 15 10
DESIGN: 60h. Hammer and sickle, and star.

1963. Technical and Scientific Knowledge Society Congress.
1393 **418** 60h. violet 35 10

419 Chamois **420** Figure Skating

1963. Mountain Animals.
1394 **419** 30h. multicoloured . . . 65 15
1395 – 40h. multicoloured . . . 65 30
1396 – 60h. sepia, yellow & grn 1·00 35
1397 – 1k.20 multicoloured . . 1·00 15
1398 – 1k.60 multicoloured . . 1·40 40
1399 – 2k. brown, orge & grn 4·00 2·25
ANIMALS: 40h. Ibex; 60h. Mouflon; 1k.20, Roe deer; 1k.60, Fallow deer; 2k. Red deer.

1964. Sports Events of 1964.
1400 **420** 30h. violet and yellow 15 10
1401 – 80h. blue and orange . . 15 10
1402 – 1k. brown and lilac . . . 80 20
DESIGNS—VERT: 30h. Type **420** (Czech Students' Games); 1k. Handball (World Handball Championships). HORIZ: 80h. Cross-country skiing (Students' Games).

421 Ice Hockey **423** Magura Hotel, Zdiar, High Tatra

422 Belanske Tatra Mountains, Skiers and Tree

1964. Winter Olympic Games, Innsbruck.
1403 **421** 1k. purple and turquoise 75 30
1404 – 1k.80 green & lavender 1·00 55
1405 – 2k. blue and green . . . 2·50 2·10
DESIGNS—VERT: 1k.80, Tobogganing. HORIZ: 2k. Ski jumping.

1964. Tourist Issue.
1406 **422** 30h. purple and blue . . 20 10
1407 – 60h. blue and red . . . 30 10
1408 – 1k. brown and olive . . 55 10
1409 – 1k.80 green and orange 1·00 35
DESIGNS: 60h. Telc (Moravia) and motorcamp; 1k. Spis Castle (Slovakia) and angler; 1k.80, Cesky Krumlov (Bohemia) and sailing dinghies. Each design includes a tree.

1964. Trade Union Recreation Hotels.
1410 **423** 60h. green and yellow . . 20 10
1411 – 80h. blue and pink . . . 20 10
DESIGN: 80h. "Slovak Insurrection" Hotel, Lower Tatra.

424 Statuary (after Michelangelo)

1964. U.N.E.S.C.O. Cultural Anniversaries.
1412 **424** 40h. black and green . . 20 10
1413 – 60h. black and red . . . 20 10
1414 – 1k. black and blue . . . 45 15
1415 – 1k.60 black and yellow 45 10
DESIGNS—HORIZ: 40h. Type **424** (400th death anniv of Michelangelo); 60h. Bottom, "Midsummer Night's Dream" (400th birth anniv of Shakespeare); 1k.60, King George of Podebrady (500th anniv of his mediation in Europe). VERT: 1k. Galileo Galilei (400th birth anniv).

425 Yuri Gagarin

1964. "Space Exploration". On cream paper.
1416 **425** 30h. blue and black . . 55 15
1417 – 60h. red and green . . . 30 10
1418 – 80h. violet and lake . . 55 20
1419 – 1k. violet and blue . . . 85 25
1420 – 1k.20 bronze and red . . 55 25
1421 – 1k.40 turq & black . . . 1·25 55
1422 – 1k.60 turq & violet . . . 3·75 1·25
1423 – 2k. red and blue 85 25
ASTRONAUTS—HORIZ: 60h. Titov; 80h. Glenn; 1k.20, Popovich and Nikolaev. VERT: 1k. Carpenter; 1k.40, Schirra; 1k.60, Cooper; 2k. Tereshkova and Bykovsky.

426 Campanula **427** Miner of 1764

1964. Wild Flowers.
1424 **426** 60h. purple, orge & grn 1·50 10
1425 – 80h. multicoloured . . . 1·50 10
1426 – 1k. blue, pink & green 1·50 40
1427 – 1k.20 multicoloured . . 60 30
1428 – 1k.60 violet & green . . 80 40
1429 – 2k. red, turq & violet . . 4·75 1·90
FLOWERS: 80h. Musk thistle; 1k. Chicory; 1k.20, Yellow iris; 1k.60, Marsh gentian; 2k. Common poppy.

1964. Czech Anniversaries.
1430 – 30h. black and yellow . . 25 10
1431 – 60h. red and blue . . . 50 10
1432 **427** 60h. sepia and green . . 25 10
DESIGNS—HORIZ: (30½ × 22½ mm): 30h. Silesian coat of arms (stylized) (150th Anniv of Silesian Museum, Opava). (41½ × 23 mm): 60h. (No. 1431), Skoda ASC-16 fire engine (Centenary of Voluntary Fire Brigades); 60h. (No. 1432), (Bicentenary of Banska Stiavnica Mining School).

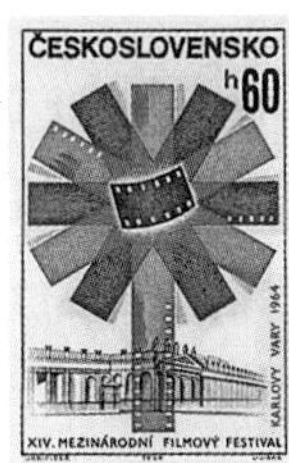

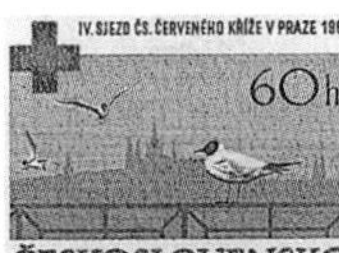

428 Cine-film "Flower" **429** Hradcany, Praque and Black-headed Gulls

1964. 14th Int Film Festival, Karlovy Vary.
1433 **428** 60h. black, blue & red 1·60 10

1964. 4th Czech Red Cross Congress, Prague.
1434 **429** 60h. violet and red . . . 45 10

430 Human Heart **431** Slovak Girl and Workers

1964. 4th European Cardiological Congress, Prague.
1435 **430** 1k.60 red and blue . . . 1·00 10

1964. 20th Anniv of Slovak Rising and Dukla Battles.
1436 **431** 30h. red and brown . . 10 10
1437 – 60h. blue and red . . . 10 10
1438 – 60h. sepia and red . . . 10 10
DESIGNS: No. 1437, Armed Slovaks; 1438, Soldiers in battle at Dukla Pass.

432 Hradcany, Prague **433** Cycling

1964. Millenary of Prague.
1439 **432** 60h. brown & mauve . . 45 10

1964. Olympic Games, Tokyo. Multicoloured.
1440 60h. Type **433** 40 20
1441 80h. Throwing the discus and pole vaulting (vert) 45 20
1442 1k. Football (vert) 45 20
1443 1k.20 Rowing (vert) 55 35
1444 1k.60 Swimming 90 35
1445 2k.80 Weightlifting . . . . 4·00 2·40

434 Common Redstart **435** Brno Engineering Works (150th Anniv)

1964. Birds. Multicoloured.
1446 30h. Type **434** 35 10
1447 60h. Green woodpecker . . 65 10
1448 80h. Hawfinch 90 25
1449 1k. Black woodpecker . . . 90 30
1450 1k.20 European robin . . . 90 35
1451 1k.60 Eurasian roller . . . 1·40 90

1964. Czech Engineering.
1452 **435** 30h. brown 10 10
1453 – 60h. green and salmon 25 10
DESIGN: 60h. Class T334.0 diesel-hydraulic shunter.

436 "Dancing Girl" **437** Mountain Rescue Service (10th Anniv)

1965. 3rd National Spartacist Games.
1454 **436** 30h. red and blue . . . 10 10
See also Nos. 1489/92.

1965. Sports Events of 1965.
1455 **437** 60h. violet and blue . . 20 10
1456 – 60h. lake and orange . . 20 10
1457 – 60h. green and red . . . 20 10
1458 – 60h. green and yellow . . 20 10
SPORTS: No. 1456, Exercising with hoop (1st World Artistic Gymnastics Championships, Prague); 1457, Cycling (World Indoor Cycling Championships, Prague); 1458, Hurdling (Czech University Championships, Brno).

438 Domazlice **439** Exploration of Mars

1965. 700th Annivs of Six Czech Towns, and 20th Anniv of Terezin Concentration Camp (No. 1465).
1459 **438** 30h. violet and yellow 20 10
1460 – 30h. violet and blue . . 20 10
1461 – 30h. blue and olive . . . 20 10
1462 – 30h. sepia and olive . . 20 10
1463 – 30h. green and buff . . . 20 10
1464 – 30h. slate and drab . . . 20 10
1465 – 30h. red and black . . . 20 10
TOWNS: No. 1460, Beroun; 1461, Zatec; 1462, Policka; 1463, Lipnik and Becvou; 1464, Frydek-Mistek; 1465, Terezin concentration camp.

1965. Int Quiet Sun Years and Space Research.
1466 – 20h. purple and red . . 25 10
1467 – 30h. yellow and red . . 25 10
1468 – 60h. blue and yellow . . 25 10
1469 – 1k. violet & turquoise . . 50 10
1470 – 1k.40 slate and salmon 50 25
1471 **439** 1k.60 black and pink . . 50 25
1472 – 2k. blue & turquoise . . 1·40 1·25
DESIGNS—HORIZ: 20h. Maximum sun-spot activity; 30h. Minimum sun-spot activity ("Quiet Sun"); 60h. Moon exploration; 1k.40, Artificial satellite and space station; 2k. Soviet "Kosmos" and U.S. "Tiros" satellites. VERT: 1k. Space-ships rendezvous.

440 Horse Jumping (Amsterdam, 1928)

1965. Czechoslovakia's Olympic Victories.
1473 **440** 20h. brown and gold . . 20 10
1474 – 30h. violet and green . . 20 10
1475 – 60h. blue and gold . . . 20 10
1476 – 1k. brown and gold . . 40 20
1477 – 1k.40 green and gold . . 85 55
1478 – 1k.60 black and gold . . 85 55
1479 – 2k. red and gold 85 25
DESIGNS (each with city feature): 30h. Throwing the discus (Paris, 1900); 60h. Marathon (Helsinki, 1952); 1k. Weightlifting (Los Angeles, 1932); 1k.40, Gymnastics (Berlin, 1936); 1k.60, Rowing (Rome, 1960); 2k. Gymnastics (Tokyo, 1964).

441 Leonov in Space

1965. Space Achievements.
1480 **441** 60h. purple and blue . . 15 20
1481 – 60h. blue and mauve . . 15 20
1482 – 3k. purple and blue . . . 1·40 1·10
1483 – 3k. blue and mauve . . 1·40 1·10
DESIGNS: No. 1481, Grissom, Young and "Gemini 3"; 1482, Leonov leaving spaceship "Voskhod 2"; 1483, "Gemini 3" on launching pad at Cape Kennedy.

442 Soldier

1965. 20th Anniv of Liberation. Inscr "20 LET CSSR".
1484 **442** 30h. olive, black & red 20 10
1485 – 30h. violet, blue & red 20 10
1486 – 60h. black, red & blue 25 10
1487 – 1k. violet, brown & orge 50 20
1488 – 1k.60 multicoloured . . 85 40
DESIGNS: 30h. (No. 1485), Workers; 60h. Mechanic; 1k. Building worker; 1k.60, Peasant.

443 Children's Exercises

1965. 3rd National Spartacist Games.
1489 **443** 30h. blue and red . . . 15 10
1490 – 60h. brown and blue . . 20 10
1491 – 1k. blue and yellow . . . 30 10
1492 – 1k.60 red and brown . . 35 25
DESIGNS: 60h. Young gymnasts; 1k. Women's exercises; 1k.60, Start of race.

444 Slovak "Kopov"

1965. Canine Events.
1493 **444** 30h. black and red . . . 40 10
1494 – 40h. black & yellow . . 40 10
1495 – 60h. black and red . . . 50 10
1496 – 1k. black and red . . . 95 10
1497 – 1k.60 black & yellow . . 60 25
1498 – 2k. black and orange . . 2·10 1·10
DOGS: 30h. Type **444**; 1k. Poodle (Int Dog-breeders' Congress, Prague); 40h. German sheepdog; 60h. Czech "fousek" (retriever), (both World Dog Exn, Brno); 1k.60, Czech terrier; 2k. Afghan hound (both Plenary Session of F.C.I.—Int Federation of Cynology, Prague).

445 U.N. Emblem

1965. U.N. Commem and Int Co-operation Year.
1499 **445** 60h. brown & yellow . . 20 10
1500 – 1k. blue and turquoise 45 10
1501 – 1k.60 red and gold . . . 45 30
DESIGNS: 60h. T **445** (The inscr reads "Twentieth Anniversary of the signing of the U.N. Charter"); 1k. U.N. Headquarters ("20th Anniv of U.N."); 1k.60, I.C.Y. emblem.

446 "SOF" and Linked Rings

1965. 20th Anniv of World Federation of Trade Unions.
1502 **446** 60h. red and blue . . . 35 10

447 Women of Three Races

448 Children's House

1965. 20th Anniv of International Democratic Women's Federation.
1503 **447** 60h. blue 35 10

1965. Prague Castle (1st series). Inscr "PRAHA HRAD".
1504 **448** 30h. green 20 10
1505 – 60h. sepia 25 10
DESIGN—VERT: 60h. Mathias Gate.
See also Nos. 1572/3, 1656/7, 1740/1, 1827/8, 1892/3, 1959/60, 2037/8, 2103/4, 2163/4, 2253/4, 2305/6, 2337/8, 2404/5, 2466/7, 2543/4, 2599/2600, 2637/8, 2685/6, 2739/40, 2803/4, 2834/5, 2878/9, 2950/1, 2977/8 and 3026/7.

449 Marx and Lenin

450 Jan Hus

1965. 6th Organization of Socialist Countries' Postal Ministers Conference, Peking.
1506 **449** 60h. red and gold . . . 25 10

1965. Various Anniversaries and Events (1st issue).
1507 **450** 60h. black and red . . . 25 10
1508 – 60h. blue and red . . . 25 10
1509 – 60h. lilac and gold . . . 25 10
1510 – 1k. blue and orange . . 30 10
DESIGNS—VERT: No. 1507, T **450** (reformer, 550th death anniv); 1508, G. J. Mendel (publication cent in Brno of his study of heredity). HORIZ: (30½ × 23 mm): No. 1509, Jewellery emblems ("Jablonec 65" Jewellery Exn); 1510, Early telegraph and telecommunications satellite (I.T.U. cent).

1965. Various Anniversaries and Events (2nd issue).
1512 30h. black and green . . . 15 10
1513 30h. black and brown . . . 15 10
1514 60h. black and red 20 10
1515 60h. brown on cream . . . 20 10
1516 1k. black and orange . . . 20 10
DESIGNS—As Type **450**. HORIZ: No. 1512, L. Stur (nationalist, 150th birth anniv); 1513, J. Navratil (painter, death cent). VERT: No. 1514, B. Martinu (composer, 75th birth anniv). LARGER—VERT: (23½ × 30½ mm): No. 1515, Allegoric figure (Academia Istropolitana, Bratislava, 500th anniv). HORIZ: (30 × 22½ mm): No. 1516, Emblem (IUPAC Macromolecular Symposium, Prague).

452 "Fourfold Aid"

454 Levoca

453 Dotterel

1965. Flood Relief.
1517 **452** 30h. blue 15 10
1518 – 2k. black and olive . . . 70 40
DESIGN—HORIZ: 2k. Rescue by boat.

1965. Mountain Birds. Multicoloured.
1519 30h. Type **453** 60 10
1520 60h. Wallcreeper (vert) . . . 60 10
1521 1k.20 Redpoll 65 30
1522 1k.40 Golden eagle (vert) . . 1·10 35
1523 1k.60 Ring ousel 90 40
1524 2k. Spotted nutcracker (vert) 2·00 1·50

1965. Czech Towns. (a) Size 23 × 19 mm.
1525 **454** 5h. black and yellow . . 10 10
1526 – 10h. blue and bistre . . 20 10
1527 – 20h. sepia and blue . . . 10 10
1528 – 30h. blue and green . . 20 10
1529 – 40h. sepia and blue . . . 20 10
1530 – 50h. black and buff . . . 25 10
1531 – 60h. red and blue . . . 30 10
1532 – 1k. violet and green . . 35 10

(b) Size 30½ × 23½ mm.
1533 – 1k.20 olive and blue . . . 30 10
1534 – 1k.60 blue and yellow . . . 55 10
1535 – 2k. bronze and green . . . 70 10
1536 – 3k. purple & yellow . . . 85 10
1537 – 5k. black and pink . . . . 1·60 10
TOWNS: 10h. Jindrichuv Hradec; 20h. Nitra; 30h. Kosice; 40h. Hradec Kralove; 50h. Telc; 60h. Ostrava; 1k. Olomouc; 1k.20, Ceske Budejovice; 1k.60, Cheb; 2k. Brno; 3k. Bratislava; 5k. Prague.

455 Coltsfoot

457 "Music"

456 Panorama of "Stamps"

1965. Medicinal Plants. Multicoloured.
1538 30h. Type **455** 25 10
1539 60h. Meadow saffron . . . 45 10
1540 80h. Common poppy . . . 50 10
1541 1k. Foxglove 60 15
1542 1k.20 Arnica . . . . 1·00 25
1543 1k.60 Cornflower 75 35
1544 2k. Dog rose . . . . 3·00 1·50

1965. Stamp Day.
1545 **456** 1k. red and green . . . 3·75 3·50

1966. 70th Anniv of Czech Philharmonic Orchestra.
1546 **457** 30h. black and gold . . 55 25

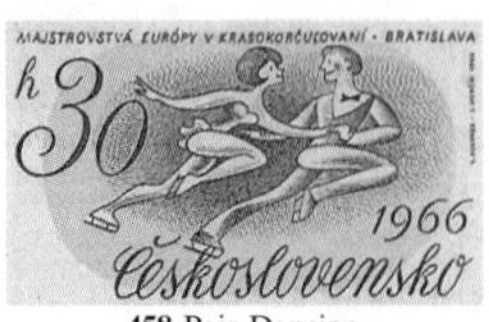

458 Pair Dancing

1966. Sports Events of 1966. (a) European Figure Skating Championships, Bratislava.
1547 **458** 30h. red and pink . . . 15 10
1548 – 60h. emerald and green 20 10
1549 – 1k.60 brown & yellow 40 20
1550 – 2k. blue and turquoise 2·50 35
DESIGNS: 60h. Male skater leaping; 1k.60, Female skater leaping; 2k. Pair-skaters taking bows.

(b) World Volleyball Championships, Prague.
1551 – 60h. red and buff 20 10
1552 – 1k. violet and blue 25 10
DESIGNS—VERT: 60h. Player leaping to ball; 1k. Player falling.

459 S. Sucharda (sculptor)

460 "Ajax", 1841, Austria

1966. Cultural Anniversaries.
1553 **459** 30h. green 15 10
1554 – 30h. blue 15 10
1555 – 60h. red 20 10
1556 – 60h. brown 20 10
PORTRAITS: No. 1553, Type **459** (birth centenary); 1554, Ignac J. Pesina (veterinary surgeon, birth bicentenary); 1555, Romain Rolland (writer, birth centenary); 1556, Donatello (sculptor, 500th death anniv).

1966. Railway Locomotives.
1557 **460** 20h. brown on cream . . 40 10
1558 – 30h. violet on cream . . 40 10
1559 – 60h. purple on cream . . 40 15
1560 – 1k. blue on cream . . . 75 15
1561 – 1k.60 blue on cream . . 80 15
1562 – 2k. red on cream . . . . 3·25 1·25
LOCOMOTIVES: 30h. "Karlstejn", 1865; 60h. Class 423.0 steam locomotive, 1946; 1k. Class 498.0 steam locomotive, 1946; 1k.60, Class S699.0 electric locomotive, 1964; 2k. Class T699.0 diesel locomotive, 1964.

462 Brown Trout

1966. World Angling Championships, Svit. Mult.
1564 30h. Type **462** 30 10
1565 60h. Eurasian perch (horiz) 50 10
1566 1k. Common (Mirror) carp (horiz) 65 10
1567 1k.20 Northern pike (horiz) 65 15
1568 1k.40 European grayling (horiz) . . . . 1·00 25
1569 1k.60 European eel (horiz) 3·00 1·00

463 "Solidarity of Mankind"
465 Belvedere Palace

464 W.H.O. Building

1966. 20th Anniv of U.N.E.S.C.O.
1570 **463** 60h. black and yellow . . 25 10

1966. Inaug of W.H.O. Headquarters, Geneva.
1571 **464** 1k. ultramarine and blue 45 10

1966. Prague Castle (2nd series).
1572 **465** 30h. blue 20 10
1573 – 60h. black and yellow . . 35 20
DESIGN: 60h. Wood triptych, "Virgin and Child" (St. George's Church).
See also Nos. 1656/7 and 1740/1.

467 Scarce Swallowtail

1966. Butterflies and Moths. Multicoloured.
1575 30h. Type **467** 40 10
1576 60h. Moorland clouded yellow 70 10
1577 80h. Lesser purple emperor 70 20
1578 1k. Apollo 70 25
1579 1k.20 Scarlet tiger moth . . 1·40 35
1580 2k. Cream-spot tiger moth 4·50 1·90

468 Flags

1966. 13th Czechoslovakian Communist Party Congress.
1581 **468** 30h. red and blue . . . 20 10
1582 – 60h. red and blue . . . 20 10
1583 – 1k.60 red and blue . . . 65 10
DESIGNS: 60h. Hammer and sickle; 1k.60, Girl.

469 Indian Village

1966. "North American Indians". Centenary of Naprstek's Ethnographic Museum, Prague.
1584 **469** 20h. blue and orange . . 20 10
1585 – 30h. black and brown . . 20 10
1586 – 40h. sepia and blue . . . 20 10
1587 – 60h. green and yellow . . 25 10
1588 – 1k. purple and green . . 35 10
1589 – 1k.20 blue and mauve 50 20
1590 – 1k.40 multicoloured . . 1·25 60
DESIGNS—VERT: 30h. Tomahawk; 40h. Haida totem poles; 60h. Katchina, "good spirit" of Hopi tribe; 1k.20, Dakote calumet (pipe of peace); 1k.40, Dakota Indian chief. HORIZ: 1k. Hunting American bison.

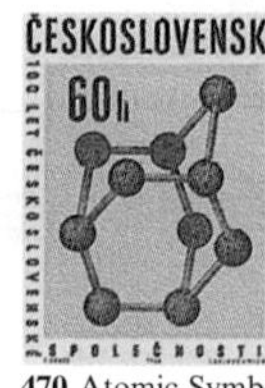

470 Atomic Symbol

1966. Centenary of Czech Chemical Society.
1591 **470** 60h. black and blue . . 35 10

471 "Guernica", after Picasso (½-size illustration)

1966. 30th Anniv of International Brigade's War Service in Spain.
1592 **471** 60h. black and blue . . 1·75 1·75

472 Pantheon, Bratislava

473 Fair Emblem

1966. Cultural Anniversaries.
1593 **472** 30h. lilac 20 10
1594 – 60h. blue 25 10
1595 – 60h. green 25 10
1596 – 60h. brown 25 10
DESIGNS: Type **472** (21st anniv of liberation of Bratislava); 1594, L. Stur (Slovak leader) and Devin Castle; 1595, Nachod (700th anniv); 1596, Arms, globe, books and view of Olomouc (400th anniv of State Science Library).

1966. Brno International Fair.
1597 **473** 60h. black and red . . . 25 10

474 "Atomic Age"

475 Olympic Coin

1966. Jachymov (source of pitch-blende).
1598 **474** 60h. black and red . . . 35 10

1966. 70th Anniv of Olympic Committee.
1599 **475** 60h. black and gold . . 20 10
1600 – 1k. blue and red 85 20
DESIGN: 1k. Olympic flame and rings.

476 Missile Carrier, Tank and Mikoyan Gurevich MiG-21D Fighter

1966. Military Manoeuvres.
1601 **476** 60h. black and yellow . . 35 10

477 Moravian Silver Thaler (reverse and obverse)

480 Eurasian badger

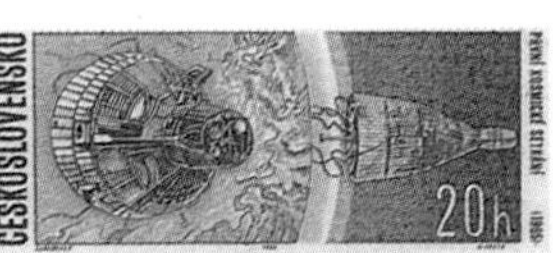

479 First Space Rendezvous

1966. Brno Stamp Exhibition.
1602 **477** 30h. black and red . . . 30 10
1603 – 60h. black and orange 30 10
1604 – 1k.60 black and green 85 30
DESIGNS—HORIZ: 60h. "Mercury"; 1k.60, Brno buildings and crest.

1966. Space Research.
1606 **479** 20h. violet and green . . 30 10
1607 – 30h. green and orange 30 10
1608 – 60h. blue and mauve . . 30 10
1609 – 80h. purple and blue . . 30 10
1610 – 1k. black and violet . . 30 10
1611 – 1k.20 red and blue . . . 1·40 55
DESIGNS: 30h. Satellite and "back" of Moon; 60h. "Mariner 4" and first pictures of Mars; 80h. Satellite making "soft" landing on Moon; 1k. Satellite, laser beam and binary code; 1k.20, "Telstar", Earth and tracking station.

1966. Game Animals. Multicoloured.
1612 30h. Type **480** 20 10
1613 40h. Red deer (vert) 25 10
1614 60h. Lynx 30 10
1615 80h. Brown hare 40 25
1616 1k. Red fox 50 25
1617 1k.20 Brown bear (vert) . . 50 30
1618 2k. Wild boar . . . . . . 3·75 1·10

481 "Spring" (V. Hollar)

1966. Art (1st series).
1619 **481** 1k. black . . . . 5·50 2·25
1620 – 1k. multicoloured . . . 3·25 2·25
1621 – 1k. multicoloured . . . 3·50 2·75
1622 – 1k. multicoloured . . . 3·25 2·25
1623 – 1k. multicoloured . . . 28·00 20·00
PAINTINGS: No. 1620, "Mrs. F. Wussin" (J. Kupecky); 1621, "Snowy Owl" (K. Purkyne); 1622, "Bouquet" (V. Spale); 1623, "Recruit" (L. Fulla).
See also Nos. 1669, 1699/1703, 1747, 1753, 1756, 1790/4, 1835/8, 1861/5, 1914/18, 1999/2003, 2067/71, 2134/9, 2194/8, 2256/60, 2313/16, 2375/9, 2495/9, 2549/53, 2601/5, 2655/9, 2702/6, 2757/61, 2810/14, 2858/62, 2904/8, 2954/6, 3000/2, 3044/7, 3077/81 and 3107/9.

482 "Carrier Pigeon"

1966. Stamp Day.
1624 **482** 1k. blue and yellow . . . 1·10 90

483 "Youth" (5th Czech Youth Federation Congress)

484 Distressed Family

1967. Czech Congresses.
1625 **483** 30h. red and blue . . . 20 10
1626 – 30h. red and yellow . . 20 10
DESIGN: No. 1626, Rose and T.U. emblem (6th Trade Union Congress).

1967. "Peace for Viet-Nam".
1627 **484** 60h. black and salmon 25 10

485 Jihlava

1967. International Tourist Year.
1628 **485** 30h. purple 15 10
1629 – 40h. red 15 10
1630 – 1k.20 blue 40 30
1631 – 1k.60 black . . . . . 1·90 50
DESIGNS—As Type **485**: 40h. Brno. (76 × 30 mm): 1k.20, Bratislava; 1k.60, Prague.

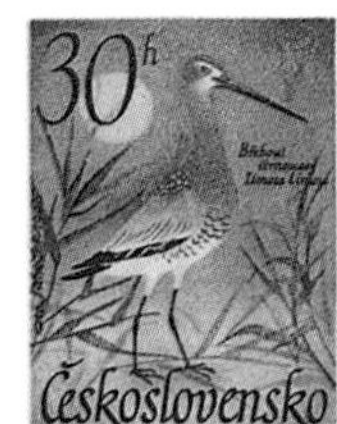

486 Black-tailed Godwit

1967. Water Birds. Multicoloured.
1632 30h. Type **486** 25 10
1633 40h. Common shoveler (horiz) 35 10
1634 60h. Purple heron 35 10
1635 80h. Penduline tit 70 25
1636 1k. Pied avocet 70 25
1637 1k.40 Black stork . . . . 1·50 40
1638 1k.60 Tufted duck (horiz) 2·75 1·75

487 Sun and Satellite

1967. Space Research.
1639 **487** 30h. red and yellow . . 15 10
1640 – 40h. blue and grey . . . 15 10
1641 – 60h. green and violet . . 25 10
1642 – 1k. blue and mauve . . 25 10
1643 – 1k.20 black and blue . . 40 25
1644 – 1k.60 lake and grey . . 1·75 45
DESIGNS: 40h. Space vehicles in orbit; 60h. "Man on the Moon" and orientation systems; 1k. "Exploration of the planets"; 1k.20, Lunar satellites; 1k.60, Lunar observatory and landscape.

488 Gothic Art (after painting by Theodoric)

1967. World Fair, Montreal. Multicoloured.
1645 30h. Type **488** 15 10
1646 40h. Jena Codex—ancient manuscript, "Burning of John Hus" 15 10
1647 60h. Lead crystal glass . . . 20 10
1648 80h. "The Shepherdess and the Chimney Sweep" (Andersen's Fairy Tales), after painting by J. Trnka 30 10
1649 1k. Atomic diagram ("Technical Progress") . . 35 25
1650 1k.20 Dolls by P. Rada ("Ceramics") . . . . . . 1·75 95

489 Bicycle Wheels and Dove

1967. Sports Events of 1967.
1652 **489** 60h. black and red . . . 20 10
1653 – 60h. black & turquoise 20 10
1654 – 60h. black and blue . . 20 10
1655 – 1k.60 black and violet 1·50 45
DESIGNS—HORIZ: Type **489** (20th Warsaw–Berlin–Prague Cycle Race): No. 1654, Canoeist in kayak (5th World Canoeing Championships). VERT: No. 1653, Basketball players (World Women's Basketball Championships); 1655, Canoeist (10th World Water-slalom Championships).

1967. Prague Castle (3rd series). As Type **465**.
1656 30h. lake 20 10
1657 60h. slate 50 10
DESIGNS: 30h. "Golden Street"; 60h. St. Wenceslas' Hall.

490 "PRAZSKE 1967"

491 Synagogue Curtain (detail)

1967. Prague Music Festival.
1659 **490** 60h. violet and green . . 25 10

1967. Jewish Culture.
1660 **491** 30h. red and blue . . . 20 10
1661 – 60h. black and green . . 25 10
1662 – 1k. blue and mauve . . 35 10
1663 – 1k.20 red and brown . . 50 10
1664 – 1k.40 black and yellow 50 10
1665 – 1k.60 green and yellow 3·75 2·75
DESIGNS: 60h. Printers' imprint (1530); 1k. Mikulov jug (1801); 1k.20, "Old-New" Synagogue, Prague (1268); 1k.40, Jewish memorial candelabra, Pinkas Synagogue (1536) (The memorial is for Czech victims of Nazi persecution); 1k.60, David Gans' tombstone (1613).

492 Lidice Rose

493 "Architecture"

1967. 25th Anniv of Destruction of Lidice.
1666 **492** 30h. black and red . . . 25 10

1967. 9th Int Architects' Union Congress, Prague.
1667 **493** 1k. black and gold . . . 35 10

494 Petr Bezruc

1967. Birth Centenary of Petr Bezruc (poet).
1668 **494** 60h. black and red . . . 25 10

1967. Publicity for "Praga 68" Stamp Exhibition. As Type **481**. Multicoloured.
1669 2k. "Henri Rousseau" (self-portrait) . . . . 2·40 1·40

495 Skalica

1967. Czech Towns.
1670 **495** 30h. blue 20 10
1671 – 30h. lake (Presov) . . . 20 10
1672 – 30h. green (Pribram) . . 20 10

496 Thermal Fountain and Colonnade, Karlovy Vary

1967. Postal Employees' Games.
1673 **496** 30h. violet and gold . . 25 10

497 Ondrejov Observatory and Universe

1967. 13th Int Astronomic Union Congress, Prague.
1674 **497** 60h. silver, blue & purple 1·75 35

498 "Miltonia spectabilis"

1967. Botanical Garden Flowers. Multicoloured.
1675 20h. Type **498** 25 10
1676 30h. Cup and saucer plant 25 10
1677 40h. "Lycaste deppei" . . . 25 15
1678 60h. "Glottiphyllum davisii" 40 10
1679 1k. Painter's palette 60 25
1680 1k.20 "Rhodocactus bleo" 60 40
1681 1k.40 "Dendrobium phalaenopsis" . . . . . 2·40 65

499 Eurasian Red Squirrel

500 Military Vehicles

1967. Fauna of Tatra National Park.
1682 **499** 30h. black, orge & yell 35 10
1683 – 60h. black and buff . . . 35 10
1684 – 1k. black and blue . . . 40 15
1685 – 1k.20 black, yell & grn 60 15
1686 – 1k.40 black, yell & pink 85 25
1687 – 1k.60 black, orge & yell 3·00 1·10
DESIGNS: 60h. Wild cat; 1k. Stoat; 1k.20, Hazel dormouse; 1k.40, West European hedgehog; 1k.60, Pine marten.

1967. Army Day.
1688 **500** 30h. green 25 10

501 Prague Castle ("PRAGA 62")

503 Pres. Novotny

1967. Air. "PRAGA 1968" Int Stamp Exhbition (1st issue).
1689 **501** 30h. multicoloured . . . 15 10
1690 – 60h. multicoloured . . . 25 20
1691 – 1k. multicoloured . . . 25 20
1692 – 1k.40 multicoloured . . 35 25
1693 – 1k.60 multicoloured . . 35 35
1694 – 2k. multicoloured . . . 55 25
1695 – 5k. multicoloured . . . 2·50 2·10
DESIGNS (Sites of previous Int Stamp Exns): 60h. Selimiye Mosque, Edirne ("ISTANBUL 1963"); 1k. Notre Dame, Paris ("PHILATEC 1964"); 1k.40, Belvedere Palace, Vienna ("WIPA 1965"); 1k.60, Capitol, Washington ("SIPEX 1965"); 2k. Amsterdam ("AMPHILEX 1967"). (40 × 55 mm): 5k. Prague ("PRAGA 1968").
See also Nos. 1718/20, 1743/8, 1749/54 and 1756.

502 Cruiser "Aurora"

1967. 50th Anniv of October Revolution.
1696 **502** 30h. red and black . . . 10 10
1697 – 60h. red and black . . . 15 10
1698 – 1k. red and black . . . 15 10
DESIGNS—VERT: 60h. Hammer and sickle emblems; 1k. "Reaching hands".

1967. Art (2nd series). As T **481**. Multicoloured.
1699 60h. "Conjurer with Cards" (F. Tichy) 25 25
1700 80h. "Don Quixote" (C. Majernik) 25 25
1701 1k. "Promenade in the Park" (N. Grund) 55 55
1702 1k.20 "Self-Portrait" (P. J. Brandl) 55 55
1703 1k.60 "Epitaph to Jan of Jeren" (Czech master) . . 4·25 4·25
All in National Gallery, Prague.

1967.
1704 **503** 2k. green . . . . 1·25 10
1705 3k. brown . . . . 1·75 10

504 Letov L-13 Glider

1967. Czech Aircraft. Multicoloured.
1706 30h. Type **504** 15 10
1707 60h. Letov L-40 Meta-Sokol 20 10
1708 80h. Letov L-200 Morava 20 10
1709 1k. Letov Z-37 Cmelak crop-sprayer 45 10
1710 1k.60 Zlin Z-526 Trener Master 55 10
1711 2k. Aero L-29 Delfin jet trainer . . . . 1·75 65

505 Czech Stamps of 1920

1967. Stamp Day.
1712 **505** 1k. lake and silver . . . 1·75 1·40

506 "CESKOSLOVENSKO 1918–1968"

1968. 50th Anniv of Republic (1st issue).
1713 **506** 30h. red, blue & ultram 70 25
See also Nos. 1780/1.

507 Skater and Stadium

1968. Winter Olympic Games, Grenoble.
1714 **507** 60h. black, yell & ochre 15 10
1715 – 1k. brown, bistre & blue 30 10
1716 – 1k.60 black, grn & lilac 55 10
1717 – 2k. black, blue & yellow 1·10 50
DESIGNS: 1k. Bobsleigh run; 1k.60, Ski jump; 2k. Ice hockey.

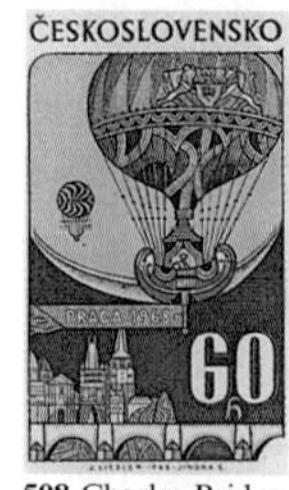

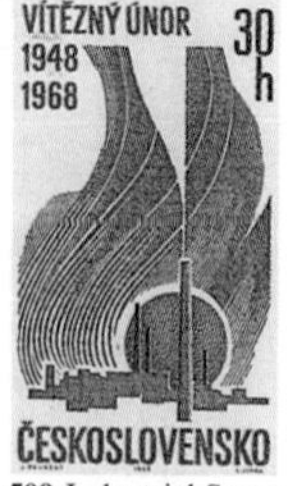

508 Charles Bridge, Prague, and Charles's Hydrogen Balloon

509 Industrial Scene and Red Sun

1968. Air. "PRAGA 1968" International Stamp Exhibition (2nd issue). Multicoloured.
1718 60h. Type **508** 45 15
1719 1k. Royal Summer-house, Belvedere, and William Henson's "Aerial Steam Carriage" 70 25
1720 2k. Prague Castle and airship 80 55

1968. 20th Anniv of "Victorious February".
1721 **509** 30h. red and blue . . . 10 10
1722 – 60h. red and blue . . . 15 10
DESIGN: 60h. Workers and banner.

510 Battle Plan

511 Human Rights Emblem

1968. 25th Anniv of Sokolovo Battles.
1723 **510** 30h. red, blue & green 45 10

1968. Human Rights Year.
1724 **511** 1k. red . . . . 1·10 30

512 Liptovsky Mikulas (town) and Janko Kral (writer)

1968. Various Commemorations.
1725 **512** 30h. green 25 10
1726 – 30h. blue and orange . . 25 10
1727 – 30h. red and gold . . . 25 10
1728 – 30h. purple 25 10
1729 – 1k. multicoloured . . . 40 10
DESIGNS—VERT: No. 1726, Allegorical figure of woman (150th anniv of Prague National Museum); 1727, Girl's head (cent of Prague National Theatre); 1728, Karl Marx (150th anniv of birth); 1729, Diagrammatic skull (20th anniv of W.H.O.).

513 "Radio" (45th anniv)

1968. Czech Radio and Television Annivs.
1730 **513** 30h. black, red and blue 20 10
1731 – 30h. black, red and blue 20 10
DESIGN: No. 1731, "Television" (15th anniv).

514 Athlete and Statuettes

515 Pres. Svoboda

1968. Olympic Games, Mexico. Multicoloured.
1732 30h. Type **514** 15 10
1733 40h. Runner and seated figure (Quetzalcoatl) . . . 20 10
1734 60h. Netball and ornaments 25 10
1735 1k. Altar and Olympic emblems 35 10
1736 1k.60 Football and ornaments 50 20
1737 2k. Prague Castle and key 70 55

1968.
1738 **515** 30h. blue 10 10
1738a 50h. green 10 10
1739 60h. red 25 10
1739a 1k. red 30 10

1968. Prague Castle (4th series). As Type **465**.
1740 30h. multicoloured 25 10
1741 60h. black, green & red . . 25 10
DESIGN: 30h. "Bretislav I" (from tomb in St. Vitus' Cathedral); 60h. Knocker on door of St. Wenceslas' Chapel.

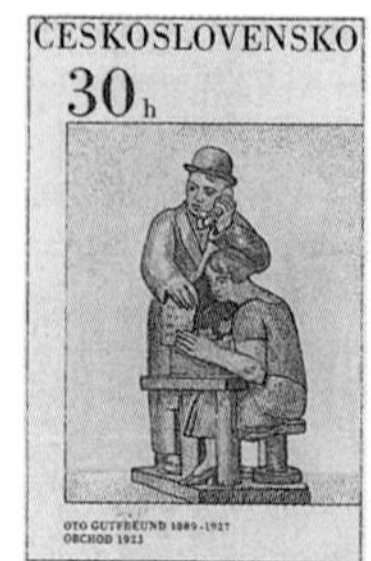

516 "Business" (sculpture by O. Gutfreund)

519 Symbolic "S"

518 Horse-drawn Coach on Rails "Hannibal" (140th Anniv of Ceske-Budejovice–Linz Railway)

1968. "PRAGA 1968" Int Stamp Exn (3rd Issue). Multicoloured.
1743 30h. Type **516** 20 10
1744 40h. Broadcasting building, Prague 20 10
1745 60h. Parliament Building . . 20 20
1746 1k.40 "Prague" (Gobelin tapestry by Jan Bauch) . . 50 25
1747 2k. "The Cabaret Artiste" (painting by F. Kupka) (size 40 × 50 mm) . . . . 1·90 1·40
1748 3k. Presidential standard . . 50 45

1969. "PRAGA 1968" Int Stamp Exn (4th issue).
1749 30h. green, yellow & grey 20 10
1750 60h. violet, gold & green . . 20 10
1751 1k. indigo, pink and blue . . 30 20
1752 1k.60 multicoloured 55 25
1753 2k. multicoloured . . . . . 1·10 90
1754 3k. black, blue, pink & yell 1·25 35
DESIGNS—As Type **516**: 30h. St. George's Basilica, Prague Castle; 60h. Renaissance fountain; 1k. Dvorak's Museum; 1k.60, "Three Violins" insignia (18th-cent house); 3k. Prague emblem of 1475. As Type **481**: 2k. "Josefina" (painting by Josef Manes, National Gallery, Prague).

1968. "PRAGA 1968" (6th issue—F.I.P. Day). As T **481**.
1756 5k. multicoloured . . . . . 4·25 3·50
DESIGN: 5k. "Madonna of the Rosary" (detail from painting by Albrecht Durer in National Gallery, Prague).

1968. Railway Anniversaries.
1757 **518** 60h. multicoloured . . . 30 15
1758 – 1k. multicoloured . . . 85 25
DESIGN: 1k. Early steam locomotive "Johann Adolf" and modern electric locomotive (centenary of Ceske-Budejovice–Pilsen Railway).

1968. 6th Int Slavonic Congress, Prague.
1759 **519** 30h. red and blue . . . 55 10

520 Adrspach Rocks and "Hypophylloceras bizonatum" (ammonite)

1968. 23rd Int Geological Congress, Prague.
1760 **520** 30h. black and yellow . . 20 10
1761 – 60h. black and mauve 20 10
1762 – 80h. black, pink & lav 25 10
1763 – 1k. black and blue . . . 35 10
1764 – 1k.60 black and yellow 1·40 55
DESIGNS: 60h. Basalt columns and fossilised frog; 80h. Bohemian "Paradise" and agate; 1k. Tatra landscape and "Chlamys gigas" shell; 1k.60, Barrandien (Bohemia) and limestone.

521 M. J. Hurban and Standard-bearer

1968. 120th Anniv of Slovak Insurrection and 25th Anniv of Slovak National Council.
1765 **521** 30h. blue 10 10
1766 – 60h. red 10 10
DESIGN: 60h. Partisans (120th anniv of Slovak Insurrection).

522 "Man and Child" (Jiri Beutler, aged 10)

1968. Munich Agreement. Drawings by children in Terezin concentration camp. Multicoloured.
1767 30h. Type **522** 20 10
1768 60h. "Butterflies" (Kitty Brunnerova, aged 11) . . 30 10
1769 1k. "The Window" (Jiri Schlessinger, aged 10) . . 45 10
The 1k. is larger (40 × 22 mm).

523 Banska Bystrica

525 Ernest Hemingway

524 National Flag

1968. Arms of Czech Regional Capitals (1st series). Multicoloured.
1770 60h. Type **523** 20 10
1771 60h. Bratislava 20 10
1772 60h. Brno 20 10
1773 60h. Ceske Budejovice . . . 20 10
1774 60h. Hradec Kralove . . . 20 10
1775 60h. Kosice 20 10
1776 60h. Ostrava 20 10
1777 60h. Pilsen 20 10
1778 60h. Usti nad Labem . . . 20 10
1779 1k. Prague (vert) 75 10
See also Nos. 1855/60, 1951/6, 2106/8 and 2214/15.

1968. 50th Anniv of Republic (2nd issue).
1780 **524** 30h. deep blue & blue 20 10
1781 – 60h. multicoloured . . . 20 10
DESIGN: 60h. Prague and Bratislava within outline "map".

1968. U.N.E.S.C.O. "Cultural Personalities of the 20th century in Caricature" (1st series).
1783 **525** 20h. black and red . . . 15 10
1784 – 30h. multicoloured . . . 15 10
1785 – 40h. red, black & lilac 15 10
1786 – 60h. black, green & bl 15 10
1787 – 1k. black, brn & yell . . 45 10
1788 – 1k.20 black, vio & red 50 20
1789 – 1k.40 black, brn & orge 1·40 45
PERSONALITIES: 30h. Karel Capek (dramatist); 40h. George Bernard Shaw; 60h. Maxim Gorky; 1k. Picasso; 1k.20, Taikan Yokoyama (painter); 1k.40, Charlie Chaplin.
See also Nos. 1829/34.

1968. Art (3rd series). As T **481**. Paintings in National Gallery, Prague. Multicoloured.
1790 60h. "Cleopatra II" (J. Zrzavy) 50 30
1791 80h. "The Black Lake" (J. Preisler) 70 50
1792 1k.20 "Giovanni Francisci as a Volunteer" (P. Bohun) . . . . 1·40 1·10
1793 1k.60 "Princess Hyacinth" (A. Mucha) 90 45
1794 3k. "Madonna and Child" (altar detail, Master Paul of Levoca) . . . . 4·00 3·50

526 "Cinder Boy"   528 Red Crosses forming Cross

527 5h. and 10h. Stamps of 1918

1968. Slovak Fairy Tales. Multicoloured.

1795	30h. Type **526**	15	10
1796	60h. "The Proud Lady"	25	10
1797	80h. "The Knight who ruled the World"	30	10
1798	1k. "Good Day, Little Bench"	40	15
1799	1k.20 "The Enchanted Castle"	45	15
1800	1k.80 "The Miraculous Hunter"	2·00	50

1968. Stamp Day and 50th Anniv of 1st Czech Stamps.

1801	**527** 1k. gold and blue	1·40	1·25

1969. 50th Anniv of Czech Red Cross and League of Red Cross Societies.

1802	**528** 60h. red, gold and sepia	25	10
1803	– 1k. red, blue and black	45	20

DESIGN: 1k. Red Cross symbols within heart-shaped "dove".

529 I.L.O. Emblem   530 Wheel-lock Pistol, c. 1580

1969. 50th Anniv of Int Labour Organization.

1804	**529** 1k. black and grey	25	10

1969. Early Pistols. Multicoloured.

1805	30h. Type **530**	15	10
1806	40h. Italian horse-pistol, c. 1600	20	10
1807	60h. Kubik wheel-lock carbine, c. 1720	20	10
1808	1k. Flint-lock pistol, c. 1760	30	10
1809	1k.40 Lebeda duelling pistols, c. 1830	50	20
1810	1k.60 Derringer pistols, c. 1865	1·60	35

531 University Emblem and Symbols (50th Anniv of Brno University)

1969. Anniversaries.

1811	**531** 60h. black, blue & gold	20	10
1812	– 60h. blue	20	10
1813	– 60h. multicoloured	20	10
1814	– 60h. black and red	20	10
1815	– 60h. red, silver & blue	20	10
1816	– 60h. black and gold	20	10

DESIGNS and ANNIVERSARIES: No. 1812, Bratislava Castle, open book and head of woman (50th Anniv Comenius University, Bratislava); 1813, Harp and symbolic eagle (50th Anniv Brno Conservatoire); 1814, Theatrical allegory (50th Anniv Slovak National Theatre (1970); 1815, Arms and floral emblems (Slovak Republican Council, 50th Anniv); 1816, Grammar school and allegories of Learning (Zniev Grammar School. Cent).

532 Veteran Cars of 1900–05

1969. Motor Vehicles. Multicoloured.

1817	30h. Type **532**	40	10
1818	1k.60 Veteran Cars of 1907	70	20
1819	1k.80 Prague Buses of 1907 and 1967	1·75	85

533 "Peace" (after L. Guderna) (½-size illustration)

1969. 20th Anniv of Peace Movement.

1820	**533** 1k.60 multicoloured	55	25

534 Engraving by H. Goltzius

1969. Horses. Works of Art.

1821	**534** 30h. sepia on cream	25	10
1822	– 80h. purple on cream	25	10
1823	– 1k.60 slate on cream	40	20
1824	– 1k.80 black on cream	40	25
1825	– 2k.40 mult on cream	2·50	65

DESIGNS—HORIZ: 80h. Engraving by M. Merian. VERT: 1k.60, Engraving by V. Hollar; 1k.80, Engraving by A. Durer; 2k.40, Painting by J. E. Ridinger.

535 Dr. M. R. Stefanik as Civilian and Soldier

1969. 50th Death Anniv of General Stefanik.

1826	**535** 60h. red	35	10

536 "St. Wenceslas" (mural detail, Master of Litomerice, 1511)

1969. Prague Castle (5th series). Multicoloured.

1827	3k. Type **536**	2·10	1·40
1828	3k. Coronation Banner of the Czech Estates, 1723	2·10	1·40

See also Nos. 1892/3, 1959/60, 2037/8, 2103/4, 2163/4, 2253/4, 2305/6, 2337/8, 2404/5, 2466/7, 2543/4, 2599/600 and 2637/8.

1969. U.N.E.S.C.O. "Cultural Personalities of the 20th Century in Caricature" (2nd series). Designs as Type **525**.

1829	30h. black, red and blue	10	10
1830	40h. black, violet & blue	15	10
1831	60h. black, red & yellow	15	10
1832	1k. multicoloured	30	10
1833	1k.80 black, blue & orge	40	10
1834	2k. black, yellow & green	2·00	60

DESIGNS: 30h. P. O. Hviezdoslav (poet); 40h. G. K. Chesterton (writer); 60h. V. Mayakovsky (poet); 1k. Henri Matisse (Painter); 1k.80, A. Hrdlicka (anthropologist); 2k. Franz Kafka (novelist).

537 "Music"

538 Astronaut, Moon and Aerial View of Manhattan

1969. "Woman and Art". Paintings by Alfons Mucha. Multicoloured.

1835	30h. Type **537**	30	10
1836	60h. "Painting"	35	10
1837	1k. "Dance"	50	10
1838	2k.40 "Ruby and Amethyst" (40 × 51 mm)	2·00	1·10

1969. Air. 1st Man on the Moon. Multicoloured.

1839	60h. Type **538**	20	10
1840	3k. "Eagle" module and aerial view of J. F. Kennedy Airport, New York	2·40	1·10

539 Soldier and Civilians

1969. 25th Anniv of Slovak Rising and Battle of Dukla.

1841	**539** 30h. bl & red on cream	10	10
1842	– 30h. grn & red on cream	10	10

DESIGN: No. 1842, General Svoboda and partisans.

540 Ganek (½-size illustration)

1969. 20th Anniv of Tatra National Park.

1843	**540** 60h. purple	15	10
1844	– 60h. blue	15	10
1845	– 60h. green	15	10
1846	– 1k.60 multicoloured	1·75	45
1847	– 1k.60 multicoloured	45	15
1848	– 1k.60 multicoloured	45	15

DESIGNS: No. 1844, Mala Valley; 1845, Bielovodska Valley. (SMALLER 40 × 23 mm): 1846, Velka Valley and gentian; 1847, Mountain stream, Mala Valley and gentian; 1848, Krivan Peak and autumn crocus.

541 Bronze Belt Fittings (8th–9th century)

1969. Archaeological Discoveries in Bohemia and Slovakia. Multicoloured.

1849	20h. Type **541**	15	10
1850	30h. Decoration showing masks (6th–8th century)	15	10
1851	1k. Gold Earrings (8th–9th century)	25	10
1852	1k.80 Metal Crucifix (obverse and reverse) (9th century)	50	25
1853	2k. Gilt ornament with figure (9th century)	1·75	50

542 "Focal Point"—Tokyo

1969. 16th U.P.U. Congress, Tokyo.

1854	**542** 3k.20 multicoloured	1·60	1·00

1969. Arms of Czech Regional Capitals (2nd series). As T **523**. Multicoloured.

1855	50h. Bardejov	20	10
1856	50h. Hranice	20	10
1857	50h. Kezmarok	20	10
1858	50h. Krnov	20	10
1859	50h. Litomerice	20	10
1860	50h. Manetin	20	10

1969. Art (4th series). As T **481**. Multicoloured.

1861	60h. "Great Requiem" (F. Muzika)	55	50
1862	1k. "Resurrection" (Master of Trebon)	55	50
1863	1k.60 "Crucifixion" (V. Hloznik)	55	50
1864	1k.80 "Girl with Doll" (J. Bencur)	55	75
1865	2k.20 "St. Jerome" (Master Theodoric)	2·75	2·10

543 Emblem and "Stamps"

1969. Stamp Day.

1866	**543** 1k. purple, gold & blue	1·50	1·10

544 Ski Jumping

1970. World Skiing Championships, High Tatras. Multicoloured.

1867	50h. Type **544**	20	10
1868	60h. Cross-country skiing	20	10
1869	1k. Ski jumper "taking off"	20	10
1870	1k.60 Woman skier	1·10	35

545 J. A. Comenius (300th Death Anniv)

1970. U.N.E.S.C.O. Anniversaries of World Figures.

1871	**545** 40h. black	15	10
1872	– 40h. grey	25	10
1873	– 40h. brown	25	10
1874	– 40h. red	15	10
1875	– 40h. red	15	10
1876	– 40h. brown	15	10

DESIGNS: No. 1872, Ludwig van Beethoven (composer, birth bicent); 1873, Tosef Manes (artist, 150th birth anniv); 1874, Lenin (birth cent); 1875, Friedrich Engels (150th birth anniv); 1876, Maximilian Hell (astronomer, 250th birth anniv).

546 Bells

1970. World Fair, Osaka, Japan. "Expo 70". Multicoloured.

1877	50h. Type **546**	15	10
1878	80h. Heavy Machinery	25	10
1879	1k. Beehives (folk sculpture)	25	10
1880	1k.60 "Angels and Saints" (17th-century icon)	45	35
1881	2k. "Orlik Castle, 1787" (F. K. Wolf)	50	35
1882	3k. "Fujiyama" (Hokusai)	2·40	80

Nos. 1880/2 are larger, 51 × 37 mm.

547 Town Hall, Kosice

549 Lenin

548 "Autumn, 1955"

1970. 25th Anniv of Kosice Reforms.

1883	**547** 60h. blue, gold & red	35	10

1970. Paintings by Joseph Lada. Multicoloured.

1884	60h. Type **548**	20	10
1885	1k. "The Magic Horse" (vert)	40	10

1886 1k.80 "The Water Demon" (vert) 45 20
1887 2k.40 "Children in Winter, 1943" . . . . 2·00 55

1970. Birth Centenary of Lenin.
1888 **549** 30h. red and gold . . . 10 10
1889 – 60h. black and gold . . 10 10
DESIGN: 60h. Lenin (bareheaded).

550 Prague Panorama and Hand giving "V" Sign

1970. 25th Anniv of Prague Rising and Liberation of Czechoslovakia.
1890 **550** 30h. purple, gold & blue 20 10
1891 – 30h. green, gold & red 20 10
DESIGN: No. 1891, Soviet tank entering Prague.

1970. Prague Castle. Art Treasures (6th series). As Type **536**. Multicoloured.
1892 3k. "Hermes and Athena" (painting by B. Spranger) 1·90 1·75
1893 3k. "St. Vitus" (bust) . . . 1·90 1·75

551 Compass and "World Capitals" (½-size illustration)

1970. 25th Anniv of United Nations.
1894 **551** 1k. multicoloured . . . 45 25

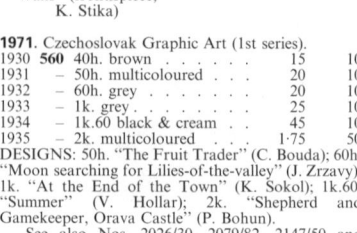

552 Thirty Years War Cannon and "Baron Munchausen"

1970. Historic Artillery. Multicoloured.
1895 30h. Type **552** 15 10
1896 60h. Hussite bombard and St. Barbara 15 10
1897 1k.20 Austro-Prussian War field-gun and Hradec Kralove 45 10
1898 1k.80 Howitzer (1911) and Verne's "Colombiad" . . 75 25
1899 2k.40 Mountain-gun (1915) and "Good Soldier Schweik" . . . . 1·50 50

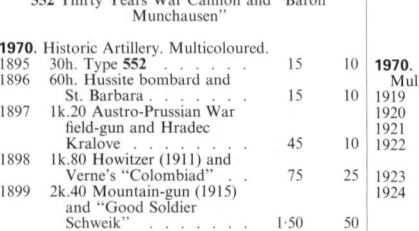

553 "Rude Pravo"

554 "Golden Sun", Bridge-tower, Prague

1970. 50th Anniv of "Rude Pravo" (newspaper).
1900 **553** 60h. red, drab & black 20 10

1970. Ancient Buildings and House-signs from Prague, Brno and Bratislava. Multicoloured.
1901 40h. Type **554** 15 10
1902 60h. "Blue Lion" and Town Hall tower, Brno 25 10
1903 1k. Gothic bolt and Town Hall tower, Bratislava . . 25 10
1904 1k.40 Coat of arms and Michael Gate, Bratislava 1·90 35
1905 1k.60 "Moravian Eagle" and Town Hall gate, Brno 40 20
1906 1k.80 "Black Sun", "Green Frog" and bridge-tower, Prague 60 20

555 World Cup Emblem and Flags

1970. World Cup Football Championship, Mexico. Multicoloured.
1907 20h. Type **555** 10 10
1908 40h. Two players and badges of Germany and Uruguay 15 10
1909 60h. Two players and badges of England and Czechoslovakia 20 10
1910 1k. Three players and badges of Rumania and Czechoslovakia 30 10
1911 1k.20 Three players and badges of Brazil and Italy 50 10
1912 1k.80 Two players and badges of Brazil and Czechoslovakia . . . . . 1·75 30

556 "S.S.M." and Flags

557 Dish Aerial

1970. 1st Congress of Czechoslovak Socialist Youth Federation.
1913 **556** 30h. multicoloured . . . 35 10

1970. Art (5th series). As T **481**. Multicoloured.
1914 1k. "Mother and Child" (M. Galanda) 25 25
1915 1k.20 "The Bridesmaid" (K. Svolinsky) 50 35
1916 1k.40 "Walk by Night" (F. Hudecek) 50 40
1917 1k.80 "Banska Bystrica Market" (detail, D. Skutecky) 65 45
1918 2k.40 "Adoration of the Kings" (Vysehrad Codex) 2·10 2·40

1970. "Intercosmos". Space Research Programme. Multicoloured.
1919 20h. Type **557** 10 10
1920 40h. Experimental satellite 15 10
1921 60h. Meteorological satellite 20 10
1922 1k. Astronaut ("medical research") 25 10
1923 1k.20 Solar research 30 10
1924 1k.60 Rocket on Launch-pad . . . . 1·25 40

558 "Adam and Eve with Archangel Michael" (16th-century)

1970. Slovak Icons. Multicoloured.
1925 60h. Type **558** 20 25
1926 1k. "Mandylon" (16th-century) (horiz) . . 30 30
1927 2k. "St. George slaying the Dragon" (18th-century) (horiz) 50 50
1928 2k.80 "St. Michael the Archangel" (18th-century) 2·50 2·10

559 Czech 5h. Stamps of 1920

1970. Stamp Day.
1929 **559** 1k. red, black & green 90 85

560 "Songs from the Walls" (frontispiece, K. Stika)

561 Saris Church

1971. Czechoslovak Graphic Art (1st series).
1930 **560** 40h. brown 15 10
1931 – 50h. multicoloured . . . 20 10
1932 – 60h. grey 20 10
1933 – 1k. grey 25 10
1934 – 1k.60 black & cream . . 45 10
1935 – 2k. multicoloured . . . 1·75 50
DESIGNS: 50h. "The Fruit Trader" (C. Bouda); 60h. "Moon searching for Lilies-of-the-valley" (J. Zrzavy); 1k. "At the End of the Town" (K. Sokol); 1k.60, "Summer" (V. Hollar); 2k. "Shepherd and Gamekeeper, Orava Castle" (P. Bohun).
See also Nos. 2026/30, 2079/82, 2147/50 and 2202/5.

1971. Regional Buildings.
1936 – 50h. multicoloured . . 10 10
1936a – 1k. black, red & blue 20 10
1937 **561** 1k.60 black, vio & grn 45 10
1938 – 2k. multicoloured . . . 55 10
1939 – 2k.40 multicoloured . . 55 10
1940 – 3k. multicoloured . . . 70 10
1941 – 3k.60 multicoloured . . 85 10
1942 – 5k. multicoloured . . . 95 10
1943 – 5k.40 multicoloured . . 95 10
1944 – 6k. multicoloured . . . 1·40 10
1945 – 9k. multicoloured . . . 2·10 10
1946 – 10k. multicoloured . . 1·75 15
1947 – 14k. multicoloured . . 2·25 10
1948 – 20k. multicoloured . . 3·00 50
DESIGNS—HORIZ: 50h., 3k.60, Church, Chrudimsko, 2k.40, House, Jicinsko, 5k.40, Southern Bohemia baroque house, Posumavi; 10k. Wooden houses, Liptov; 14k. House and belfry, Valassko; 20k. Decorated house, Cicmany. (22 × 19 mm): 3k. Half-timbered house, Melnicko; 6k. Cottages, Orava; 9k. Cottage, Turnovsko. VERT: (19 × 22 mm): 1k. Ornamental roofs, Horacko; 2k. Bell-tower, Hornsek; 5k. Watch-tower, Nachodsko.

562 "The Paris Commune" (allegory) (½-size illustration)

1971. U.N.E.S.C.O. World Annivs. Multicoloured.
1949 1k. Type **562** 30 25
1950 1k. "World Fight against Racial Discrimination" (allegory) 30 25

1971. Arms of Czech Regional Capitals (3rd series). As Type **523**. Multicoloured.
1951 60h. Ceska Trebova 15 10
1952 60h. Karlovy Vary 15 10
1953 60h. Levoca 15 10
1954 60h. Trutnov 15 10
1955 60h. Uhersky Brod 15 10
1956 60h. Zilina 15 10

563 Chorister

564 Lenin

1971. 50th Annivs. Multicoloured.
1957 30h. Type **563** (Slovak Teachers' Choir) 20 10
1958 30h. Edelweiss, ice-pick and mountain (Slovak Alpine Organisation) (19 × 48 mm) 20 10

1971. Prague Castle (7th series). Art Treasures. As Type **536**. Multicoloured.
1959 3k. brown, buff and black 2·10 1·90
1960 3k. multicoloured . . . . . 2·10 1·90
DESIGNS: No. 1959, "Music" (16th-century wall painting); 1960, Head of 16th-century crozier.

1971. 50th Anniv of Czech Communist Party.
1961 30h. Type **564** 10 10
1962 40h. Hammer and sickle emblems 10 10
1963 60h. Clenched fists 15 10
1964 1k. Emblem on pinnacle . . 20 10

565 "50" Star Emblem

1971. 14th Czech Communist Party Congress. Multicoloured.
1965 30h. Type **565** 10 10
1966 60h. Clenched fist, worker and emblems (vert) . . . 15 10

566 Common Pheasant

1971. World Hunting Exn, Budapest. Mult.
1967 20h. Type **566** 45 10
1968 60h. Rainbow trout 15 10
1969 80h. Mouflon 20 10
1970 1k. Chamois 20 10
1971 2k. Red deer 45 20
1972 2k.60 Wild boar . . . . . 3·00 65

567 Motorway Junction (diagram)

1971. World Road Congress.
1973 **567** 1k. multicoloured . . . 25 10

568 Class T478.3 Diesel Locomotive

569 Gymnasts

1971. Cent of Prague C.K.D. Locomotive Works.
1974 **568** 30h. black, red & blue 10 10

1971. 50th Anniv of Proletarian Physical Federation.
1975 **569** 30h. multicoloured . . . 10 10

570 "Procession" (from "The Miraculous Bamboo Shoot" by K. Segawa)

1971. Biennial Exhibition of Book Illustrations for Children, Bratislava. Multicoloured.
1976 60h. "Princess" (Chinese Folk Tales, E. Bednarova) (vert) 20 10
1977 1k. "Tiger" (Animal Fairy Tales, Hanak) (vert) . . . 20 10
1978 1k.60 Type **570** 55 25

571 Coltsfoot and Canisters

1971. International Pharmaceutical Congress, Prague. Medicinal Plants and Historic Pharmaceutical Utensils. Multicoloured.
1979 30h. Type **571** 10 10
1980 60h. Dog rose and glass jars 15 10
1981 1k. Yellow pheasant's-eye and hand scales 25 10
1982 1k.20 Common valerian, pestle and mortar 40 10
1983 1k.80 Chicory and crucibles 55 20
1984 2k.40 Henbane and grinder 1·40 50

573 "Co-operation in Space"

1971. "Intersputnik" Day.
1997 **573** 1k.20 multicoloured . . 35 10

574 "The Krompachy Revolt" (J. Nemcik) (½-size illustration)

1971. 50th Anniv of The Krompachy Revolt.
1998 **574** 60h. multicoloured . . . 35 10

1971. Art (6th issue). As Type **481**. Multicoloured.
1999 1k. "Waiting" (I. Weiner-Kral) 40 35
2000 1k.20 "The Resurrection" (unknown 14th century artist) 40 35
2001 1k.40 "Woman with Jug" (M. Bazovsky) 55 40
2002 1k.80 "Woman in National Costume" (J. Manes) . . 70 50
2003 2k.40 "Festival of the Rosary" (Durer) . . . . 2·40 2·50

575 Wooden Dolls and Birds

576 Ancient Greek Runners

1971. 25th Anniv of U.N.I.C.E.F. Czech and Slovak Folk Art. Multicoloured.
2004 60h. Type **575** (frame and U.N.I.C.E.F. emblem in bl) 15 10
2005 60h. Type **575** (frame and U.N.I.C.E.F. emblem in black) . . . . 2·75 1·40
2006 80h. Decorated handle . . . 20 10
2007 1k. Horse and rider 20 10
2008 1k.60 Shepherd 35 20
2009 2k. Easter eggs and rattle 50 25
2010 3k. Folk hero . . . . 2·10 60

1971. 75th Anniv of Czechoslovak Olympic Committee and 1972 Games at Sapporo and Munich. Multicoloured.
2011 30h. Type **576** 10 10
2012 40h. High Jumper 10 10
2013 1k.60 Skiers 50 10
2014 2k.60 Discus-throwers, ancient and modern . . . 1·75 65

577 Posthorns

1971. Stamp Day.
2015 **577** 1k. multicoloured . . . 35 10

578 Figure Skating

1972. Winter Olympic Games, Sapporo, Japan. Multicoloured.
2016 40h. Type **578** 10 10
2017 50h. Skiing 15 10
2018 1k. Ice hockey 50 10
2019 1k.60 Bobsleighing . . . . 1·10 45

579 Sentry

580 Book Year Emblem

1972. 30th Annivs.
2020 – 30h. black and brown . . 10 10
2021 – 30h. black, red & yellow 10 10
2022 **579** 60h. multicoloured . . . 20 10
2023 – 60h. black, red & yellow 20 10
ANNIVERSARIES: No. 2020, Child and barbed wire (Terezin Concentration Camp); 2021, Widow and buildings (Destruction of Lezaky); 2022, Type **579** (Czechoslovak Unit in Russian Army); 2023, Hand and ruined building (Destruction of Lidice).

1972. International Book Year.
2024 **580** 1k. black and red . . . 35 10

581 Steam Locomotive No. 2 and Class E499.0 Electric Locomotive

582 Cycling

1972. Centenary of Kosice–Bohumin Railway.
2025 **581** 30h. multicoloured . . . 35 10

1972. Czechoslovak Graphic Art (2nd series). As Type **560**. Multicoloured.
2026 40h. "Pasture" (V. Sedlacek) 10 10
2027 50h. "Dressage" (F. Tichy) 15 10
2028 60h. "Otakar Kubin" (V. Fiala) 20 15
2029 1k. "The Three Kings" (E. Zmetak) 30 25
2030 1k.60 "Toilet" (L. Fulla) . . 1·40 1·25

1972. Olympic Games, Munich. Multicoloured.
2031 50h. Type **582** 10 10
2032 1k.60 Diving 35 20
2033 1k.80 Kayak-canoeing . . . 40 25
2034 2k. Gymnastics . . . . . . 1·25 45

583 Players in Tackle

1972. World and European Ice Hockey Championships, Prague. Multicoloured.
2035 60h. Type **583** 25 10
2036 1k. Attacking goal 45 10

1972. Prague Castle (8th series). Roof Decorations. As T **536**. Multicoloured.
2037 3k. Bohemian Lion emblem (roof boss), Royal Palace 1·00 80
2038 3k. "Adam and Eve" (bracket), St. Vitus Cathedral . . . . 2·50 2·50

1972. Czech Victory in Ice Hockey Championships. Nos. 2035/6 optd.
2039 **583** 60h. multicoloured . . . 7·00 7·00
2040 – 1k. multicoloured . . . 7·00 7·00
OVERPRINTS: 60h. **CSSR MISTREM SVETA**. 1k. **CSSR MAJSTROM SVETA**.

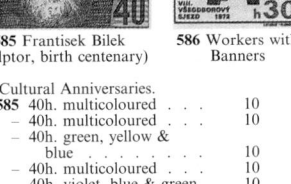

585 Frantisek Bilek (sculptor, birth centenary)

586 Workers with Banners

1972. Cultural Anniversaries.
2041 **585** 40h. multicoloured . . . 10 10
2042 – 40h. multicoloured . . . 10 10
2043 – 40h. green, yellow & blue 10 10
2044 – 40h. multicoloured . . . 10 10
2045 – 40h. violet, blue & green 10 10
2046 – 40h. green, brown & orge 10 10
DESIGNS: No. 2042, Antonin Hudecek (painter, birth cent); 2043, Janko Kral (poet, 150th birth anniv); 2044, Ludmila Podjavorinska (writer, birth cent); 2045, Andrej Sladkovic (painter, death cent); 2046, Jan Preisler (painter, birth cent).

1972. 8th Trade Union Congress, Prague.
2047 **586** 30h. violet, red & yellow 10 10

587 Wire Coil and Cockerel

1972. Slovak Wireworking. Multicoloured.
2048 20h. Type **587** 10 10
2049 60h. Aeroplane and rosette 15 10
2050 80h. Dragon and gilded ornament 20 10
2051 1k. Steam locomotive and pendant 55 10
2052 2k.60 Owl and tray 75 55

588 "Jiskra" (freighter)

1972. Czechoslovak Ocean-going Ships. Mult.
2053 50h. Type **588** 25 10
2054 60h. "Mir" (freighter) . . . 30 10
2055 80h. "Republika" (freighter) 35 10
2056 1k. "Kosice" (tanker) . . . 40 10
2057 1k.60 "Dukla" (freighter) 60 10
2058 2k. "Kladno" (freighter) . . 1·60 40
Nos. 2056/8 are size 49 × 30 mm.

589 "Hussar" (ceramic tile)

1972. "Horsemanship". Ceramics and Glass. Multicoloured.
2059 30h. Type **589** 10 10
2060 60h. "Turkish Janissary" (enamel on glass) 15 10
2061 80h. "St. Martin" (painting on glass) 25 10
2062 1k.60 "St. George" (enamel on glass) 45 10
2063 1k.80 "Nobleman's Guard, Bohemia" (enamel on glass) 55 10
2064 2k.20 "Cavalryman, c. 1800" (ceramic tile) . . . . . . 1·60 50

590 Revolutionary and Red Flag

1972. 55th Anniv of Russian October Revolution and 50th Anniv of U.S.S.R.
2065 **590** 30h. multicoloured . . . 10 10
2066 – 60h. red and gold . . . 15 10
DESIGN: 60h. Soviet star emblem.

1972. Art (7th issue). As T **481**.
2067 1k. multicoloured 70 45
2068 1k.20 multicoloured 95 55
2069 1k.40 brown and cream . . 95 65
2070 1k.80 multicoloured . . . . 1·00 1·00
2071 2k.40 multicoloured . . . . 2·10 2·25
DESIGNS: 1k. "Nosegay" (M. Svabinsky); 1k.20, "St. Ladislav fighting a Nomad" (14th century painter); 1k.40, "Lady with Fur Cap" (V. Hollar); 1k.80, "Midsummer Night's Dream" (J. Liesler); 2k.40, "Self-portrait" (P. Picasso).

591 Warbler feeding young European Cuckoo

1972. Songbirds. Multicoloured.
2072 60h. Type **591** 40 15
2073 80h. European cuckoo . . . 50 15
2074 1k. Black-billed magpie . . 50 15
2075 1k.60 Northern bullfinch (30 × 23 mm) 65 25
2076 2k. Eurasian goldfinch (30 × 23 mm) . . . . . . 1·10 35
2077 3k. Song thrush (30 × 23 mm) . . . . . . 5·00 1·40

592 "Thoughts into Letters"

1972. Stamp Day.
2078 **592** 1k. black, gold & pur . . 45 40

1973. Czechoslovak Graphic Art (3rd series). As Type **560**. Multicoloured.
2079 30h. "Flowers in the Window" (J. Grus) . . . 10 10
2080 60h. "Quest for Happiness" (J. Balaz) 15 10
2081 1k.60 "Balloon" (K. Lhotak) 45 20
2082 1k.80 "Woman with Viola" (R. Wiesner) . . . . . . 1·50 25

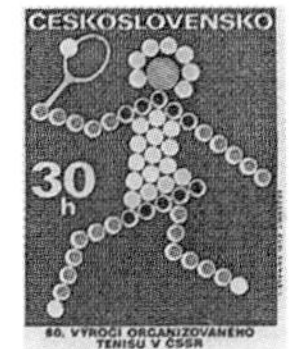

593 "Tennis Player"

594 Red Star and Factory Buildings

1973. Sports Events. Multicoloured.
2083 30h. Type **593** 35 10
2084 60h. Figure skating 20 10
2085 1k. Spartakaid emblem . . . 35 10
EVENTS: 30h. 80th anniv of lawn tennis in Czechoslovakia; 60h. World Figure Skating Championships, Bratislava; 1k. 3rd Warsaw Pact Armies Summer Spartakiad.

1973. 25th Anniv of "Victorious February" and People's Militia (60h.).
2086 **594** 30h. multicoloured . . . 10 10
2087 – 60h. blue, red & gold . . 15 10
DESIGN: 60h. Militiaman and banners.

595 Jan Nalepka and Antonin Sochar

1973. Czechoslovak Martyrs during World War II.
2088 **595** 30h. black, red and gold on cream 10 10
2089 – 40h. black, red and green on cream 15 10
2090 – 60h. black, red and gold on cream 15 10
2091 – 80h. black, red and green on cream 15 10
2092 – 1k. black, pink and green on cream . . . 20 10
2093 – 1k.60 black, red and silver on cream . . . 1·25 50
DESIGNS: 40h. Evzen Rosicky and Mirko Nespor; 60h. Vlado Clementis and Karol Smidke; 80h. Jan Osoha and Josef Molak; 1k. Marie Kuderikova and Jozka Jaburkova; 1k.60, Vaclav Sinkule and Eduard Urx.

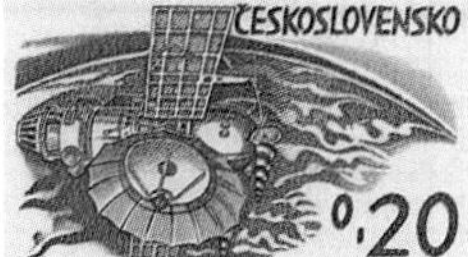

596 Russian "Venera" Space-probe

1973. Cosmonautics' Day. Multicoloured.
2094 20h. Type **596** 10 10
2095 30h. "Cosmos" satellite . . 10 10
2096 40h. "Lunokhod" on Moon 10 10
2097 3k. American astronauts Grissom, White and Chaffee . . . . 1·00 70
2098 3k.60 Russian cosmonaut Komarov, and crew of "Soyuz II" . . . . 1·10 1·40
2099 5k. Death of Yuri Gagarin (first cosmonaut) . . . . 4·25 4·00
Nos. 2094/6 are size 40 × 23 mm.

597 Radio Aerial and Receiver **598** Czechoslovak Arms

1973. Telecommunications Annivs. Multicoloured.
2100 30h. Type **597** 10 10
2101 30h. T.V. colour chart . . . 10 10
2102 30h. Map and telephone . . 10 10
ANNIVERSARIES: No. 2100, 50th anniv of Czech broadcasting; 2101, 20th anniv of Czechoslovak television service; 2102, 20th anniv of nationwide telephone system.

1973. Prague Castle (9th series). As Type **536**. Multicoloured.
2103 3k. Gold seal of Charles IV 1·75 2·00
2104 3k. Rook showing Imperial Legate (from "The Game and Playe of Chesse" by William Caxton) 90 60

1973. 25th Anniv of May 9th Constitution.
2105 **598** 60h. multicoloured . . . 10 10

1973. Arms of Czech Regional Capitals (4th series). As T **523**.
2106 60h. multicoloured (Mikulov) 20 10
2107 60h. multicoloured (Smolenice) 20 10
2108 60h. black and gold (Zlutice) 20 10

599 "Learning." **600** Tulip

1973. 400th Anniv of Olomouc University.
2109 **599** 30h. multicoloured . . . 10 10

1973. Olomouc Flower Show. Multicoloured.
2110 60h. Type **600** 95 55
2111 1k. Rose 75 25
2112 1k.60 Anthurium 35 20
2113 1k.80 Iris 40 25
2114 2k. Chrysanthemum . . . . 1·75 2·25
2115 3k.60 Boat orchid . . . . . 1·10 30
Nos. 2112/13 and 2115 are smaller, size 23 × 50 mm.

601 Irish Setter

1973. 50th Anniv of Czechoslovak Hunting Organization. Hunting Dogs. Multicoloured.
2116 20h. Type **601** 10 10
2117 30h. Czech whisker 10 10
2118 40h. Bavarian mountain bloodhound 10 10
2119 60h. German pointer . . . 15 10
2120 1k. Golden cocker spaniel 20 10
2121 1k.60 Dachshund . . . . . 2·00 60

602 "St. John the Baptist" (M. Svabinsky) **603** Congress Emblem

1973. Birth Centenary of Max Svabinsky (artist and designer).
2122 **602** 20h. black and green . . 10 10
2123 – 60h. black and yellow . . 20 10
2124 – 80h. black 25 25
2125 – 1k. green 25 25
2126 – 2k.60 multicoloured . . 2·10 1·90
DESIGNS: 60h. "August Noon"; 80h. "Marriage of True Minds"; 1k. "Paradise Sonata 1"; 2k.60, "The Last Judgement" (stained glass window).

1973. 8th World Trade Union Congress, Varna, Bulgaria.
2127 **603** 1k. multicoloured . . . 10 10

604 Tupolev Tu-104A over Bitov Castle

1973. 50th Anniv of Czechoslovak Airlines. Multicoloured.
2128 30h. Type **604** 10 10
2129 60h. Ilyushin Il-62 and Bezdez Castle 15 10
2130 1k.40 Tupolev Tu-134A and Orava Castle 40 10
2131 1k.90 Ilyushin Il-18 and Veveri Castle 55 20
2132 2k.40 Ilyshin Il-14P and Pernstejn Castle . . . . . 2·75 60
2133 3k.60 Tupolev Tu-154 and Trencin Castle 70 25

1973. Art (8th series). As Type **481**.
2134 1k. multicoloured . . . . . 1·75 1·60
2135 1k.20 multicoloured . . . . 1·75 1·60
2136 1k.80 black and buff 65 50
2137 2k. multicoloured 75 65
2138 2k.40 multicoloured 90 75
2139 3k.60 multicoloured . . . . 1·10 1·25
DESIGNS: 1k. "Boy from Martinique" (A. Pelc); 1k.20, "Fortitude" (M. Benka); 1k.80, Self-portrait (Rembrandt); 2k. "Pierrot" (B. Kubista); 2k.40, "Ilona Kubinyiova" (P. Bohun); 3k.60, Madonna and Child" (unknown artist, c. 1350).

605 Mounted Postman

1973. Stamp Day.
2140 **605** 1k. multicoloured . . . 25 25

606 "CSSR 1969–1974" **607** Bedrich Smetana (composer) (150th birth anniv)

1974. 5th Anniv of Federal Constitution.
2141 **606** 30h. red, blue and gold 10 10

1974. Celebrities' Birth Anniversaries.
2142 **607** 60h. multicoloured . . . 20 10
2143 – 60h. multicoloured . . . 20 10
2144 – 60h. brown, blue & red 20 10
DESIGNS AND ANNIVERSARIES: No. 2143, Josef Suk (composer, birth anniv); 2144, Pablo Neruda (Chilean poet, 70th birth anniv).

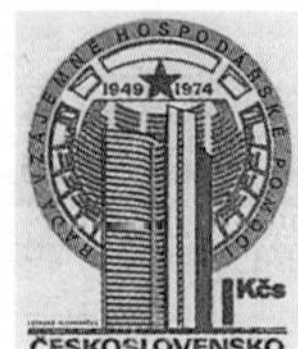

608 Council Building, Moscow

1974. 25th Anniv of Communist Bloc Council of Mutual Economic Assistance.
2145 **608** 1k. violet, red & gold . . 10 10

609 Exhibition Allegory

1974. "BRNO 74" National Stamp Exhibition (1st issue).
2146 **609** 3k.60 multicoloured . . 80 25

1974. Czechoslovak Graphic Art (4th series). As T **560**. Inscr "1974". Multicoloured.
2147 60h. "Tulips" (J. Broz) . . . 20 10
2148 1k. "Structures" (O. Dubay) 30 10
2149 1k.60 "Golden Sun-Glowing Day" (A. Zabransky) . . 55 15
2150 1k.80 "Artificial Flowers" (F. Gross) . . . . 1·50 35

610 Oskar Benes and Vaclav Prochazka

1974. Czechoslovak Partisan Heroes. Mult.
2151 30h. Type **610** 10 10
2152 40h. Milos Uher and Anton Sedlacek 10 10
2153 60h. Jan Hajecek and Marie Sedlackova 15 10
2154 80h. Jan Sverma and Albin Grznar 20 10
2155 1k. Jaroslav Neliba and Alois Hovorka 30 10
2156 1k.60 Ladislav Exnar and Ludovit Kukorelli . . . . 1·50 25

611 "Water—Source of Energy"

1974. International Hydrological Decade. Mult.
2157 60h. Type **611** 55 30
2158 1k. "Water for Agriculture" 55 30
2159 1k.20 "Study of the Oceans" 55 30
2160 1k.60 Decade emblem . . . 60 30
2161 2k. "Keeping water pure" 1·75 2·00

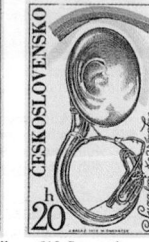

612 "Telecommunications" **613** Sousaphone

1974. Inauguration of Czechoslovak Satellite Telecommunications Earth Station.
2162 **612** 30h. multicoloured . . . 25 10

1974. Prague Castle (10th series). As Type **536**. Multicoloured.
2163 3k. "Golden Cockerel", 17th-century enamel locket . . . . 1·75 1·90
2164 3k. Bohemian glass monstrance, 1840 . . . . 1·75 1·90

1974. Musical Instruments. Multicoloured.
2165 20h. Type **613** 15 10
2166 30h. Bagpipes 15 10
2167 40h. Benka violin 20 10
2168 1k. Sauer pyramid piano . . 30 15
2169 1k.60 Hulinsky tenor quinton . . . . 1·25 30

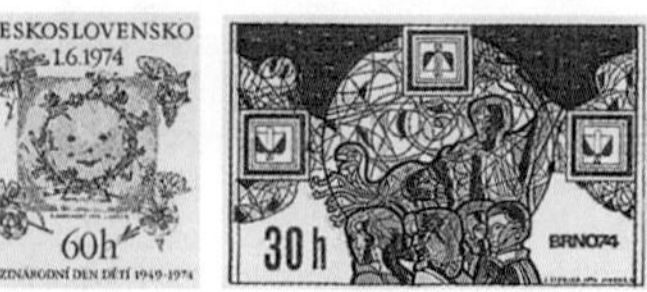

614 Child and Flowers (book illustration) **615** "Stamp Collectors"

1974. 25th International Children's Day.
2170 **614** 60h. multicoloured . . . 10 10

1974. "BRNO 74" National Stamp Exhibition (2nd issue). Multicoloured.
2171 30h. Type **615** 10 10
2172 6k. "Rocket Post" . . . . . 2·00 1·25

616 Slovak Partisan **617** "Hero and Leander"

1974. Czechoslovak Anniversaries. Multicoloured.
2173 30h. Type **616** 15 10
2174 30h. Folk-dancer 15 10
2175 30h. Actress holding masks 15 10
EVENTS: No. 2173, 30th anniv of Slovak Uprising; 2174, 25th anniv of Slovak SLUK Folk Song and Dance Ensemble; 2175, 25th anniv of Bratislava Academy of Music and Dramatic Arts.

1974. Bratislava Tapestries. "Hero and Leander" (1st series). Multicoloured.
2176 2k. Type **617** . . . . . . 1·50 1·25
2177 2k.40 "Leander Swimming across the Hellespont" . . 1·50 1·75
See also Nos. 2227/8 and 2281/2.

618 "Soldier on Guard" **620** Posthorn and Old Town Bridge Tower, Prague

619 U.P.U. Emblem and Postilion

1974. Old Shooting Targets. Multicoloured.
2178 30h. Type **618** 15 10
2179 60h. "Pierrot and Owl", 1828 . . . . 20 15
2180 1k. "Diana awarding Marksman's Crown", 1832 . . . . 30 15
2181 1k.60 "Still Life with Guitar", 1839 . . . . . 45 40
2182 2k.40 "Stag", 1834 . . . . 70 60
2183 3k. "Turk and Giraffe", 1831 . . . . 2·75 2·75

1974. Centenary of Universal Postal Union. Mult.
2184 30h. Type **619** 10 10
2185 40h. Early mail coach . . . 10 10
2186 60h. Early railway carriage 35 10

2187 80h. Modern mobile post office 25 10
2188 1k. Ilyushin Il-14 mail plane 60 10
2189 1k.60 Dish aerial, earth station . . . . 1·00 35

1974. Czechoslovak Postal Services.
2190 **620** 20h. multicoloured . . . 10 10
2191 – 30h. red, blue & brn . . 10 10
2192 – 40h. multicoloured . . . 10 10
2193 – 60h. orange, yell & bl . . 15 10
DESIGNS: 30h. P.T.T. emblem within letter; 40h. Postilion; 60h. P.T.T. emblem on dove's wing.
See also No. 2900.

1974. Art (9th series). As Type **481**. Multicoloured.
2194 1k. "Self-portrait" (L. Kuba) 80 70
2195 1k.20 "Frantisek Ondricek" (V. Brozik) 80 70
2196 1k.60 "Pitcher with Flowers" (O. Khubin) . . 80 70
2197 1k.80 "Woman with Pitcher" (J. Alexy) . . . 80 70
2198 2k.40 "Bacchanalia" (K. Skreta) . . . . 2·00 2·40

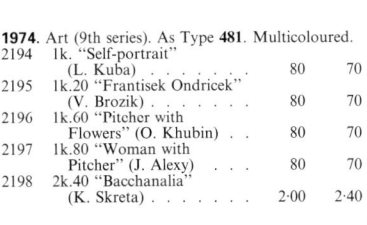

621 Stylized Posthorn

1974. Stamp Day.
2199 **621** 1k. multicoloured . . . 25 10

622 Winged Emblem

1975. Coil Stamps.
2200 **622** 30h. blue 10 10
2201 60h. red 15 10

1975. Czechoslovak Graphic Art (5th series). Engraved Hunting Scenes. As T **560**.
2202 60h. brown & cream 25 10
2203 1k. brown and cream . . . 30 15
2204 1k.60 brown & green . . . 45 25
2205 1k.80 brown & lt brown . . 1·75 50
DESIGNS: 60h. "Still Life with Hare" (V. Hollar); 1k. "The Lion and the Mouse" (V. Hollar); 1k.60, "Deer Hunt" (detail, P. Galle); 1k.80, "Grand Hunt" (detail, J. Callot).

623 "Woman"

624 Village Family

1975. International Women's Year.
2206 **623** 30h. multicoloured . . . 10 10

1975. 30th Anniv of Razing of 14 Villages. Multicoloured.
2207 60h. Type **624** 20 10
2208 1k. Women and flames . . . 25 10
2209 1k.20 Villagers and flowers 40 10

625 "Little Queens" (Moravia)

1975. Czechoslovak Folk Customs. Multicoloured.
2210 60h. Type **625** 60 60
2211 1k. Shrovetide parade, Slovakia 60 60
2212 1k.40 "Maid Dorothea" (play) 60 60
2213 2k. "Morena" effigy, Slovakia . . . . 1·40 1·40

1975. Arms of Czech Regional Capitals (5th series). As T **523**.
2214 60h. black, gold and red . . 25 10
2215 60h. multicoloured 25 10
ARMS: No. 2214, Nymburk. 2215, Znojmo.

626 Partisans at Barricade (½-size illustration)

1975. Czechoslovak Anniversaries.
2216 **626** 1k. multicoloured . . . 30 20
2217 – 1k. sepia and cream . . 30 20
2218 – 1k. multicoloured . . . 30 20
DESIGNS and ANNIVERSARIES: No. 2216, Type **626** (30th anniv of Czech Rising); 2217, Liberation celebrations (30th anniv of Liberation by Soviet Army); 2218, Czech–Soviet fraternity (5th anniv of Czech–Soviet Treaty).

627 Youth Exercises

1975. National Spartacist Games.
2219 **627** 30h. purple, bl & pink 10 10
2220 – 60h. red, lilac & yellow 15 10
2221 – 1k. violet, red & yell . . 25 20
DESIGNS: 60h. Children's exercises; 1k. Adult exercises.

628 Siamese Tigerfish and Lined Seahorse

1975. Aquarium Fishes. Multicoloured.
2222 60h. Type **628** 15 10
2223 1k. Siamese fighting fish and freshwater angelfish . . . 30 10
2224 1k.20 Veil-tailed goldfish . . 65 15
2225 1k.60 Clown anemone-fish and butterflyfish 75 25
2226 2k. Yellow-banded angelfish, palette surgeonfish and semicircle angelfish . . . 3·50 65

1975. Bratislava Tapestries. "Hero and Leander" (2nd series). As T **617**. Multicoloured.
2227 3k. "Leander's Arrival" . . 90 70
2228 3k.60 "Hermione" . . . . . 2·25 2·40

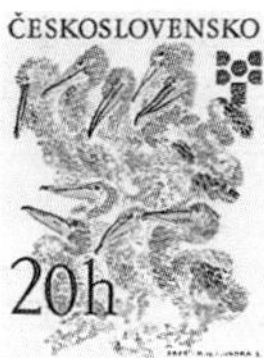
629 "Pelicans" (N. Charushin)

1975. Biennial Exhibition of Book Illustrations for Children, Bratislava. Multicoloured.
2229 20h. Type **629** 10 10
2230 30h. "Sleeping Hero" (L. Schwarz) 10 10
2231 40h. "Horseman" (V. Munteau) 15 10
2232 60h. "Peacock" (K. Ensikat) 20 10
2233 80h. "The Stone King" (R. Dubravec) 70 35

630 "CZ-150" Motor Cycle (1951)

1975. Czechoslovak Motor Cycles. Multicoloured.
2234 20h. Type **630** 15 10
2235 40h. "Jawa 250", 1945 . . . 20 10
2236 60h. "Jawa 175", 1935 . . . 25 10
2237 1k. Janatka "ITAR", 1921 30 15
2238 1k.20 Michi "Orion", 1903 25 10
2239 1k.80 Laurin and Klement, 1898 . . . . 1·60 40

631 "Solar Radiation"

632 President Gustav Husak

1975. Co-operation in Space Research.
2240 **631** 30h. violet, yellow & red 15 10
2241 – 60h. red, lilac & yellow 20 10
2242 – 1k. purple, yell & blue 25 10
2243 – 2k. multicoloured . . . 55 10
2244 – 5k. multicoloured . . . 3·00 2·75
DESIGNS—HORIZ: 60h. "Auroa Borealis"; 1k. Cosmic radiation measurement; 2k. Copernicus and solar radiation. VERT (40 × 50 mm): 5k. "Apollo–soyuz" space link.

1975.
2245 **632** 30h. blue 10 10
2246 60h. red 15 10

633 Oil Refinery

1975. 30th Anniv of Liberation. Multicoloured.
2247 30h. Type **633** 15 10
2248 60h. Atomic power complex 15 10
2249 1k. Underground Railway, Prague 40 10
2250 1k.20 Laying oil pipelines 30 15
2251 1k.40 Combine-harvesters and granary 30 20
2252 1k.60 Building construction 1·10 35

1975. Prague Castle. Art Treasures (11th series). As T **536**. Multicoloured.
2253 3k. Late 9th-century gold earring 95 75
2254 3k.60 Leather Bohemian Crown case, 1347 . . . . 1·90 2·00

1975. Art (10th series). As T **481**.
2256 1k. red, brown and black . . 75 75
2257 1k.40 multicoloured 75 75
2258 1k.80 multicoloured 75 75
2259 2k.40 multicoloured . . . . 1·10 1·25
2260 3k.40 multicoloured . . . 1·75 1·60
PAINTINGS—VERT: 1k. "May" (Z. Sklenar); 1k.40, "Girl in National Costume" (E. Nevan); 2k.40, "Fire" (J. Capek); 3k.40, "Prague, 1828" (V. Morstadt). HORIZ: 1k.80, "Liberation of Prague" (A. Cermakova).

635 Posthorn Motif

1975. Stamp Day.
2261 **635** 1k. multicoloured . . . 35 25

636 Frantisek Halas (poet)

1975. Celebrities' Anniversaries.
2262 **636** 60h. multicoloured . . . 15 10
2263 – 60h. multicoloured . . . 15 10
2264 – 60h. multicoloured . . . 30 10
2265 – 60h. blue, red & yellow 15 10
2266 – 60h. multicoloured . . . 15 10
DESIGNS AND ANNIVERSARIES—HORIZ: No. 2262, Type **636** (75th birth anniv); 2266, Ivan Krasko (poet, birth cent). VERT: No. 2263, Wilhelm Pieck (German statesman, birth cent); 2264, Frantisek Lexa (Egyptologist, birth cent); 2265, Jindrich Jindrich (ethnographer, birth cent).

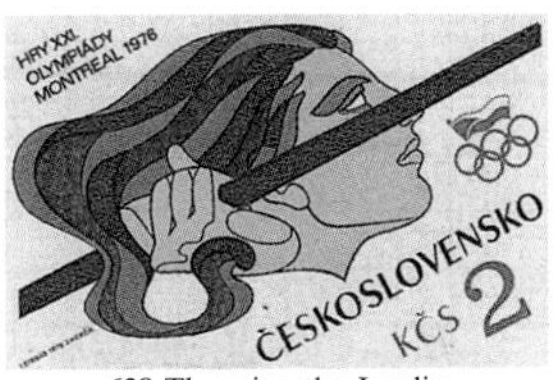
637 Ski Jumping

1976. Winter Olympic Games, Innsbruck. Mult.
2267 1k. Type **637** 20 10
2268 1k.40 Figure skating 30 20
2269 1k.60 Ice hockey . . . . . 1·25 30

638 Throwing the Javelin

1976. Olympic Games, Montreal. Multicoloured.
2270 2k. Type **638** 45 20
2271 3k. Relay-racing 80 30
2272 3k.60 Putting the shot . . . 3·00 1·10

639 Table Tennis Player

1976. European Table Tennis Championships, Prague and 50th Anniv of Organized Table Tennis in Czechoslovakia.
2273 **639** 1k. multicoloured . . . 35 10

640 Star Emblem and Workers

641 Microphone and Musical Instruments

1976. 15th Czechoslovak Communist Party Congress, Prague. Multicoloured.
2274 30h. Type **640** 10 10
2275 60h. Furnace and monolith 15 10

1976. Cultural Events and Anniversaries.
2276 **641** 20h. multicoloured . . . 10 10
2277 – 20h. multicoloured . . . 10 10
2278 – 20h. multicoloured . . . 10 10
2279 – 30h. multicoloured . . . 10 10
2280 – 30h. violet, red & blue 10 10
DESIGNS—HORIZ: No. 2276, Type **641** (50th anniv of Czechoslovak Radio Symphony Orchestra); 2278, Stage revellers (30th anniv of Nova Scena Theatre, Bratislava); 2279, Folk dancers, Wallachia (International Folk Song and Dance Festival, Straznice). VERT: No. 2277, Ballerina, violin and mask (30th anniv of Prague Academy of Music and Dramatic Art); 2280, Film "profile" (20th Film Festival, Karlovy Vary).

1976. Bratislava Tapestries. "Hero and Leander" (3rd series). As T **617**. Multicoloured.
2281 3k. "Hero with Leander's body" . . . . 2·00 1·25
2282 3k.60 "Eros grieving" . . . 85 60

642 Hammer, Sickle and Red Flags

1976. 55th Anniv of Czechoslovak Communist Party.
2283 **642** 30h. blue, gold and red 15 10
2284 – 60h. multicoloured . . . 20 10
DESIGN: 60h. Hammer and Sickle on flag.

643 Manes Hall, Czechoslovakia Artists' Union

1976. Air. "PRAGA 78" International Stamp Exhibition (1st issue). Prague Architecture. Multicoloured.
2286 60h. Type **643** 35 10
2287 1k.60 Congress Hall, Julius Fucik Park 40 20
2288 2k. Powder Tower, Old Town (vert) 70 25
2289 2k.40 Charles Bridge and Old Bridge Tower 55 25
2290 4k. Old Town Square and Town Hall (vert) 85 30
2291 6k. Prague Castle and St. Vitus Cathedral (vert) 3·50 1·00
See also 2313/16, 2326/30, 2339/42, 2349/52, 2358/62, 2389/93, 2407/12, 2413/17 and 2420/3.

644 "Warship" (Frans Huys)
645 "UNESCO" Plant

1976. Ship Engravings.
2292 **644** 40h. blk, cream & drab . . . 35 10
2293 – 60h. blk, cream & grey . . . 35 10
2294 – 1k. black, cream & grn . . . 60 10
2295 – 2k. black, cream & blue . . . 1·25 45
DESIGNS: 60h. "Dutch Merchantman" (V. Hollar); 1k. "Ship at Anchor" (N. Zeeman); 2k. "Galleon under Full Sail" (F. Chereau).

1976. 30th Anniv of U.N.E.S.C.O.
2296 **645** 2k. multicoloured . . . 95 55

647 Merino Ram
648 "Stop Smoking"

1976. "Bountiful Earth" Agricultural Exhibition, Ceske Budejovice. Multicoloured.
2298 30h. Type **647** 15 10
2299 40h. Berna-Hana Cow . . . 15 10
2300 1k.60 Kladruby stallion . . 45 10

1976. W.H.O. Campaign against Smoking.
2301 **648** 2k. multicoloured . . . 90 40

649 Postal Code Emblem
650 "Guernica 1937" (I. Weiner-Kral)

1976. Coil Stamps. Postal Code Campaign.
2302 **649** 30h. green 10 10
2303 – 60h. red 15 10
DESIGN: 60h. Postal map.

1976. 40th Anniv of International Brigades in Spanish Civil War.
2304 **650** 5k. multicoloured . . . 1·25 55

1976. Prague Castle. Art Treasures (12th series). As T **536**. Multicoloured.
2305 3k. "Prague Castle, 1572" (F. Hoogenberghe) . . . 2·00 1·90
2306 3k.60 "Satyrs" (relief from summer-house balustrade) 60 70

651 Common Zebra with Foal

1976. Dvurkralove Wildlife Park. Multicoloured.
2307 10h. Type **651** 15 10
2308 20h. African elephant, calf and cattle egret (vert) . . 50 15
2309 30h. Cheetah 15 10
2310 40h. Giraffe and calf (vert) 15 10
2311 60h. Black rhinoceros . . . 20 10
2312 3k. Bongo with offspring (vert) . . . . 2·00 65

1976. "PRAGA 1978" International Stamp Exhibition (2nd series). Art (11th series). As T **481**. Multicoloured.
2313 1k. "Flowers in Vase" (P. Matejka) 80 55
2314 1k.40 "Oleander Blossoms" (C. Bouda) . . . . 1·10 80
2315 2k. "Flowers in Vase" (J. Brueghel) . . . . . . 1·75 1·40
2316 3k.60 "Tulips and Narcissi" (J. R. Bys) 80 80

652 Postilion, Postal Emblem and Satellite

1976. Stamp Day.
2317 **652** 1k. blue, mauve & gold 25 10

653 Ice Hockey
654 Arms of Vranov

1977. 6th Winter Spartakiad of Warsaw Pact Armies. Multicoloured.
2318 60h. Type **653** 25 10
2319 1k. Rifle shooting (Biathlon) 30 10
2320 1k.60 Ski jumping . . . . . 1·40 45
2321 2k. Slalom 50 25

1977. Coats of Arms of Czechoslovak Towns (1st series). Multicoloured.
2322 60h. Type **654** 15 10
2323 60h. Kralupy and Vltavou 15 10
2324 60h. Jicin 15 10
2325 60h. Valasske Mezirici . . . 15 10
See also Nos. 2511/14, 2612/15, 2720/3, 2765/7, 2819/21 and 3017/20.

655 Window, Michna Palace
656 Children Crossing Road

1977. "PRAGA 78" International Stamp Exhibition (3rd issue). Historic Prague Windows. Multicoloured.
2326 20h. Type **655** 10 10
2327 30h. Michna Palace (different) 10 10
2328 40h. Thun Palace 10 10
2329 60h. Archbishop's Palace . . 15 10
2330 5k. Church of St. Nicholas 2·25 65

1977. 25th Anniv of Police Aides Corps.
2331 **656** 60h. multicoloured . . . 10 10

657 Cyclists at Warsaw (starting point)
658 Congress Emblem

1977. 30th Anniv of Peace Cycle Race. Mult.
2332 30h. Type **657** 15 10
2333 60h. Cyclists at Berlin . . . 20 10
2334 1k. Cyclists at Prague (finishing point) 85 25
2335 1k.40 Cyclists and modern buildings 40 15

1977. 9th Trade Unions Congress.
2336 **658** 30h. gold, red & carmine 10 10

1977. Prague Castle (13th series). As T **536**.
2337 3k. multicoloured . . . . . 1·10 1·25
2338 3k.60 green, gold & black 1·90 1·60
DESIGNS: 3k. Onyx cup, 1350 (St. Vitus Cathedral); 3k.60, Bronze horse, 1619 (A. de Vries).

659 French Postal Rider, 19th-century

1977. "PRAGA 78" International Stamp Exhibition (4th issue). Multicoloured.
2339 60h. Type **659** 15 10
2340 1k. Austrian postal rider, 1838 . . . . 30 10
2341 2k. Austrian postal rider, c. 1770 . . . . . . 50 25
2342 3k.60 German postal rider, 1700 . . . . 2·25 80

660 Coffee Pots
661 Mlada Boleslav Headdress

1977. Czechoslovak Porcelain.
2343 **660** 20h. multicoloured . . . 10 10
2344 – 30h. multicoloured . . . 10 10
2345 – 40h. multicoloured . . . 15 10
2346 – 60h. multicoloured . . . 20 10
2347 – 1k. blue, grn & violet . . 25 10
2348 – 3k. blue, gold and red 2·10 60
DESIGNS: 30h. Vase; 40h. Amphora; 60h. Jug, beaker, cup and saucer; 1k. Plate and candlestick; 3k. Coffee pot, cup and saucer.

1977. "PRAGA 78" International Stamp Exhibition (5th issue). Regional Headdresses. Multicoloured.
2349 1k. Type **661** 75 80
2350 1k.60 Vazek . . . . 3·50 3·50
2351 3k.60 Zavadka 75 80
2352 5k. Belkovice . . . . 1·25 1·10

662 V. Bombova's Illustrations of "Janko Gondashik and the Golden Lady"

1977. 6th Biennial Exhibition of Children's Book Illustrators, Bratislava. Multicoloured.
2353 40h. Type **662** 10 10
2354 60h. "Tales of Amur" (G. Pavlishin) 15 10
2355 1k. "Almgist et Wiksel" (U. Lofgren) 25 10
2356 2k. "Alice in Wonderland" and "Through the Looking Glass" (Nicole Claveloux) 75 25
2357 3k. "Eventyr" (J. Trnka) . . 2·25 65

663 Airships LZ-5 and "Graf Zeppelin"
664 U.N.E.S.C.O. Emblem, Violin and Doves

1977. Air. "PRAGA 1978" International Stamp Exhibition (6th issue). Early Aviation. Mult.
2358 60h. Type **663** 15 10
2359 1k. Clement Ader's monoplane "Eole", Etrich Holubice and Dunne D-8 30 10
2360 1k.60 Jeffries and Blanchard balloon, 1785 . . . . . . 40 15
2361 2k. Lilienthal biplane glider, 1896 . . . . 50 15
2362 4k.40 Jan Kaspar's Bleriot XI over Prague . . . . . 3·50 85

1977. Congress of U.N.E.S.C.O. International Music Council.
2363 **664** 60h. multicoloured . . . 10 10

665 "Peace"
666 Yuri Gagarin

1977. European Co-operation for Peace. Mult.
2364 60h. Type **665** 15 30
2365 1k.60 "Co-operation" . . . 40 45
2366 2k.40 "Social Progress" . . 1·50 60

1977. Space Research. Multicoloured.
2367 20h. S. P. Koroliov (space technician, launch of first satellite) 10 10
2368 30h. Type **666** (first man in space) 10 10
2369 40h. Aleksei Leonov (first space walker) 10 10
2370 1k. Neil Armstrong (first man on the Moon) . . . 25 10
2371 1k.60 "Salyut" and "Skylab" space stations 1·25 35

667 Revolutionaries and Cruiser "Aurora"
668 "Wisdom"

1977. 60th Anniv of Russian Revolution, and 55th Anniv of U.S.S.R. Multicoloured.
2372 30h. Type **667** 15 10
2373 30h. Russian woman, Kremlin, rocket and U.S.S.R. arms 15 10

1977. 25th Anniv of Czechoslovak Academy of Science.
2374 **668** 3k. multicoloured . . . 70 30

1977. Art (12th series). As Type **481**.
2375 2k. multicoloured 75 80
2376 2k.40 multicoloured . . . . 2·50 2·75
2377 2k.60 stone and black . . . 2·10 1·60
2378 3k. multicoloured . . . . . 1·00 1·00
2379 5k. multicoloured . . . . . 1·00 1·00
DESIGNS: 2k. "Fear" (J. Mudroch); 2k.40, "Portrait of Jan Francis" (P. M. Bohun); 2k.60, "Self Portrait" (V. Hollar); 3k. "Portrait of a Girl" (L. Cranach); 5k. "Cleopatra" (Rubens).

669 "Bratislava, 1574" (G. Hoefnagel)

1977. Historic Bratislava (1st series). Mult.
2380 3k. Type **669** . . . . . . 1·90 2·00
2381 3k.60 Bratislava Arms, 1436 1·10 80
See also Nos. 2402/3, 2500/1, 2545/6, 2582/3, 2642/3, 2698/9, 2736/7, 2793/4, 2842/3, 2898/9, 2952/3, 2997/8 and 3034/5.

670 Posthorn and Stamps

1977. Stamp Day.
2382 **670** 1k. multicoloured . . . 25 10

671 Z. Nejedly (historian)
674 Modern Coins

672 Civilians greeting Armed Guards

1978. Cultural Anniversaries. Multicoloured.
2383 30h. Type **671** (birth cent) 10 10
2384 40h. Karl Marx (160th birth anniv) 10 10

1978. 30th Annivs of "Victorious February" and National Front. Multicoloured.
2385 1k. Type **672** 20 10
2386 1k. Intellectual, peasant woman and steel worker 20 10

1978. Soviet–Czechoslovak Space Flight. No. 2368 optd **SPOLECNY LET SSSR*CSSR**.
2387 30h. red 20 15
2388 3k.60 blue 4·25 4·50

1978. 650th Anniv of Kremnica Mint and "PRAGA 1978" International Stamp Exhibition (7th issue). Multicoloured.
2389 20h. Type **674** 10 10
2390 40h. Culture medal, 1972 (Jan Kulich) 10 10
2391 1k.40 Charles University Medal, 1948 (O. Spaniel) 2·40 35
2392 3k. Ferdinand I medal, 1563 (L. Richter) 80 40
2393 5k. Gold florin of Charles Robert, 1335 95 50

675 Tyre Marks and Ball — **676** Hands supporting Globe

1978. Road Safety.
2394 **675** 60h. multicoloured 10 10

1978. 9th World Federation of Trade Unions Congress, Prague.
2395 **676** 1k. multicoloured 25 10

677 Putting the Shot

1978. Sports.
2396 – 30h. multicoloured 15 10
2397 **677** 40h. multicoloured 15 10
2398 – 60h. multicoloured 70 15
2399 – 1k. multicoloured 35 10
2400 – 2k. yellow, blue & red 55 25
2401 – 3k.60 multicoloured 1·75 85
DESIGNS AND EVENTS—HORIZ: 70th anniv of bandy hockey: 30h. Three hockey players, World Ice Hockey Championships; 60h. Tackle in front of goal; 2k. Goalmouth scrimmage. VERT: European Athletics Championships, Prague: 1k. Pole vault; 3k.60, Running.

1978. Historic Bratislava (2nd series). As T **669**.
2402 3k. green, violet and red 1·25 1·40
2403 3k.60 multicoloured 2·75 2·50
DESIGNS: 3k. "Bratislava" (Orest Dubay); 3k.60, "Fishpond Square, Bratislava" (Imro Weiner-Kral).

1978. Prague Castle (14th series). As T **536**.
2404 3k. yellow, black & green 95 80
2405 3k.60 multicoloured 3·25 2·50
DESIGNS: 3k. Memorial to King Premysl Otakar II, St. Vitus Cathedral; 3k.60, Portrait of King Charles IV (Jan Ocka).

678 Ministry of Posts, Prague

1978. 14th COMECON Meeting, Prague.
2406 **678** 60h. multicoloured 10 10

679 Palacky Bridge

1978. "PRAGA 78" International Stamp Exhibition (8th issue). Prague Bridges. Multicoloured.
2407 20h. Type **679** 10 10
2408 40h. Railway bridge 55 10
2409 1k. Bridge of 1st May 25 10
2410 2k. Manes Bridge 45 15
2411 3k. Svatopluk Cech Bridge 55 30
2412 5k.40 Charles Bridge 3·50 95

680 St. Peter and other Apostles — **681** Dancers

1978. "PRAGA 78" International Stamp Exhibition (9th issue). Prague Town Hall Astronomical Clock. Multicoloured.
2413 40h. Type **680** 15 10
2414 1k. Astronomical clock face 20 15
2415 2k. Centre of Manes's calendar 35 15
2416 3k. "September" (grape harvest) 2·10 70
2417 3k.60 "Libra" (sign of the Zodiac) 1·25 25

1978. 25th Vychodna Folklore Festival.
2419 **681** 30h. multicoloured 10 10

682 Gottwald Bridge

1978. "PRAGA 78" International Stamp Exhibition (10th issue). Modern Prague. Multicoloured.
2420 60h. Type **682** 65 10
2421 1k. Powder Gate Tower and Kotva department store 25 10
2422 2k. Ministry of Posts 55 25
2423 6k. Prague Castle and flats 2·10 1·10

685 Fair Buildings — **686** "Postal Newspaper Service" (25th Anniv)

1978. 20th International Engineering Fair, Brno.
2426 **685** 30h. multicoloured 10 10

1978. Press, Broadcasting and Television Days.
2427 **686** 30h. green, blue & orge 10 10
2428 – 30h. multicoloured 10 10
2429 – 30h. multicoloured 10 10
DESIGNS: No. 2428, Microphone, newspapers, camera and Ministry of Information and Broadcasting; 2429, Television screen and Television Centre, Prague (25th anniv of Czechoslovak television).

687 Horses falling at Fence

1978. Pardubice Steeplechase. Multicoloured.
2430 10h. Type **687** 10 10
2431 20h. Sulky racing 10 10
2432 30h. Racing horses 15 10
2433 40h. Passing the winning post 15 10
2434 1k.60 Jumping a fence 40 20
2435 4k.40 Jockey leading a winning horse 2·50 90

688 Woman holding Arms of Czechoslovakia

1978. 60th Anniv of Independence.
2436 **688** 60h. multicoloured 10 10

689 "Still Life with Flowers" (J. Bohdan) — **690** Violinist and Bass Player (J. Konyves)

1978. 30th Anniv of Slovak National Gallery, Bratislava. Multicoloured.
2437 2k.40 Type **689** 80 55
2438 3k. "Dream in a Shepherd's Hut" (L. Fulla) (horiz) 80 70
2439 3k.60 "Apostle with Censer" (detail, Master of the Spis Chapter) 3·75 3·50

1978. Slovak Ceramics.
2440 **690** 20h. multicoloured 10 10
2441 – 30h. blue and violet 10 10
2442 – 40h. multicoloured 10 10
2443 – 1k. multicoloured 20 10
2444 – 1k.60 multicoloured 1·60 25
DESIGNS: 30h. Horseman (J. Franko); 40h. Man in Kilt (M. Polasko); 1k. Three girl singers (I. Bizmayer); 1k.60, Miner with axe (F. Kostka).

691 Alfons Mucha and design for 1918 Hradcany Stamp

1978. Stamp Day.
2445 **691** 1k. multicoloured 25 10

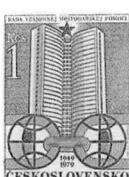

692 Council Building, Moscow

1979. Anniversaries.
2446 – 30h. brown, grn & orge 10 10
2447 – 60h. multicoloured 15 10
2448 **692** 1k. multicoloured 20 10
DESIGNS—HORIZ: 30h. Girl's head and ears of wheat (30th anniv of Unified Agricultural Co-operatives); 60h. Czechoslovakians and doves (10th anniv of Czechoslovak Federation). VERT: 1k. Type **692** (30th anniv of Council of Economic Mutual Aid).

693 "Soyuz 28"

1979. 1st Anniv of Russian–Czech Space Flight. Multicoloured.
2449 30h. Type **693** 15 10
2450 60h. A. Gubarev and V. Remek (vert) 15 10
2451 1k.60 J. Romanenko and G. Grechko 45 10
2452 2k. "Salyut 6" space laboratory 1·90 40
2453 4k. "Soyuz 28" touch down (vert) 85 40

694 "Campanula alpina" — **695** Stylized Satellite

1979. 25th Anniv of Mountain Rescue Service. Multicoloured.
2455 10h. Type **694** 10 10
2456 20h. "Crocus scepusiensis" 10 10
2457 30h. "Dianthus glacialis" 10 10
2458 40h. Alpine hawkweed 15 10
2459a 3k. "Delphinium oxysepalum" 1·25 50

1979. Anniversaries.
2460 **695** 10h. multicoloured 10 10
2461 – 20h. multicoloured 10 10
2462 – 20h. blue, orge & lt bl 10 10
2463 – 30h. blue, gold & red 10 10
2464 – 30h. red, blue & blk 10 10
2465 – 60h. multicoloured 15 10
DESIGNS AND EVENTS—HORIZ: No. 2460, Type **695** 30th anniv of Telecommunications Research. 46 × 19 mm: (No. 2461), Artist and model (30th anniv of Academy of Fine Arts, Bratislava); 2462, Student and technological equipment (40th anniv of Slovak Technical University, Bratislava); 2463, Musical instruments and Bratislava Castle (50th anniv of Radio Symphony Orchestra, Bratislava); 2464, Pioneer's scarf and I.Y.C. emblem (30th anniv of Young Pioneer Organization and International Year of the Child); 2465, Adult and child with doves (30th anniv of Peace Movement).

1979. Prague Castle (15th series). As T **536**. Multicoloured.
2466 3k. Burial crown of King Premysl Otakar II 2·40 2·40
2467 3k.60 Portrait of Miss B. Reitmayer (Karel Purkyne) 1·25 1·00

696 Arms of Vlachovo Brezi — **697** Healthy and Polluted Forests

1979. Animals in Heraldry. Multicoloured.
2468 30h. Type **696** 10 10
2469 60h. Jesenik (bear and eagle) 15 10
2470 1k.20 Vysoke Myto (St. George and the dragon) 30 10
2471 1k.80 Martin (St. Martin on horseback) 1·60 40
2472 2k. Zebrak (half bear, half lion) 40 10

1979. Man and the Biosphere. Multicoloured.
2473 60h. Type **697** 15 15
2474 1k.80 Clear and polluted water 45 30
2475 3k.60 Healthy and polluted urban environment 2·50 85
2476 4k. Healthy and polluted pasture 95 40

698 Numeral and Printed Circuit — **699** Industrial Complex

1979. Coil Stamps.
2477 – 50h. red 15 10
2478 **698** 1k. brown 20 10
2478a – 2k. green 50 25
2478b – 3k. purple 80 35
DESIGNS: Numeral and—50h. Dish aerial; 2k. Airplane; 3k. Punched tape.

1979. 35th Anniv of Slovak Uprising.
2479 **699** 30h. multicoloured 10 10

700 Illustration by Janos Kass

1979. International Year of the Child and Biennial Exhibition of Children's Book Illustrations, Bratislava. Designs showing illustrations by artists named. Multicoloured.

2480 20h. Type **700** 10 10
2481 40h. Rumen Skorcev . . . 15 10
2482 60h. Karel Svolinsky . . . 15 10
2483 1k. Otto S. Svend 30 10
2484 3k. Tatyana Mavrina . . . 1·90 45

701 Modern Bicycles

1979. Historic Bicycles. Multicoloured.

2485 20h. Type **701** 15 10
2486 40h. Bicycles, 1910 . . . . 15 10
2487 60h. "Ordinary" and tricycle, 1886 . . . . . . 15 10
2488 2k. "Bone-shakers", 1870 45 25
2489 3k.60 Drais cycles, 1820 . . 2·50 65

702 Bracket Clock (Jan Kraus)

1979. Historic Clocks. Multicoloured.

2490 40h. Type **702** 10 10
2491 60h. Rococo clock 15 10
2492 80h. Classicist clock . . . . 1·60 35
2493 1k. Rococo porcelain clock (J. Kandler) 25 10
2494 2k. Urn-shaped clock (Dufaud) 45 25

1979. Art (13th series). As T **481**.

2495 1k.60 multicoloured 65 55
2496 2k. multicoloured 75 60
2497 3k. multicoloured . . . . . 1·00 70
2498 3k.60 multicoloured . . . . 2·75 2·75
2499 5k. yellow and black . . . . 1·10 1·25

DESIGNS: 1k.60, "Sunday by the River" (Alois Moravec); 2k. "Self-portrait" (Gustav Mally); 3k. "Self-portrait" (Ilja Jefimovic Repin); 3k.60, "Horseback Rider" (Jan Bauch); 5k. "Village Dancers" (Albrecht Durer).

1979. Historic Bratislava (3rd issue). As T **669**. Multicoloured.

2500 3k. "Bratislava, 1787" (L. Janscha) . . . . . . 1·10 90
2501 3k.60 "Bratislava, 1815" (after stone engraving by Wolf) . . . . 2·50 2·40

703 Postmarks, Charles Bridge and Prague Castle

1979. Stamp Day.

2502 **703** 1k. multicoloured . . . 25 10

704 Skiing

1980. Winter Olympic Games, Lake Placid.

2503 **704** 1k. multicoloured . . . 25 10
2504 – 2k. red, pink & blue . . 1·60 40
2505 – 3k. multicoloured . . . 1·00 55

DESIGNS: 2k. Ice skating; 3k. Four-man bobsleigh.

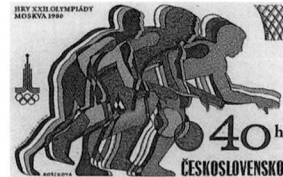

705 Basketball

1980. Olympic Games, Moscow, Multicoloured.

2506 40h. Type **705** 15 10
2507 1k. Swimming 25 10
2508 2k. Hurdles . . . . 2·40 40
2509 3k.60 Fencing 85 35

706 Marathon

1980. 50th International Peace Marathon, Kosice.

2510 **706** 50h. multicoloured . . . 10 10

1980. Arms of Czech Towns (2nd series). As T **654**.

2511 50h. blue, black and gold 15 10
2512 50h. black and silver 15 10
2513 50h. multicoloured 15 10
2514 50h. gold, black and blue 15 10

DESIGNS: No. 2511, Bystrice nad Pernstejnem; 2512, Kunstat; 2513, Rozmital pod Tremsinem; 2514, Zlata Idka.

707 Bratislava Opera House and Bakovazena as King Lear

708 Tragic Mask

1980. 60th Anniv of Slovak National Theatre, Bratislava.

2515 **707** 1k. blue, yellow & orange 25 10

1980. 50th Anniv of Theatrical Review "Jiraskuv Hronov".

2516 **708** 50h. multicoloured . . . 10 10

709 Mouse in Space **710** Police Parade Banner

1980. "Intercosmos" Space Programme.

2517 **709** 50h. blue, black and red 15 10
2518 – 1k. multicoloured . . . 30 10
2519 – 1k.60 violet, blk & red 2·25 50
2520 – 4k. multicoloured . . . 1·00 35
2521 – 5k. blue, black & purple 1·50 50

DESIGNS—VERT: 1k. Weather map and satellite; 1k.60, "Inter-sputnik" T.V. transmission; 4k. Survey satellite and camera. HORIZ: 5k. Czech-built satellite station; 10k. "Intercosmos" emblem.

1980. 35th Anniv of National Police Corps.

2523 **710** 50h. gold, red & blue . . 10 10

711 Lenin **712** Flag, Flowers and Prague Buildings

1980. 110th Birth Anniv of Lenin and 160th Birth Anniv of Engels.

2524 **711** 1k. brown, red & grey 20 10
2525 – 1k. blue and brown . . . 20 10

DESIGN: No. 2525, Engels.

1980. Anniversaries. Multicoloured.

2526 50h. Type **712** 15 10
2527 1k. Child writing "Mir" (peace) 20 10
2528 1k. Czech and Soviet arms 20 10
2529 1k. Flowers, flags and dove 20 10

ANNIVERSARIES: No. 2526, 35th anniv of May uprising; 2527, 35th anniv of Liberation; 2528, 10th anniv of Czech–Soviet Treaty; 2529, 25th anniv of Warsaw Pact.

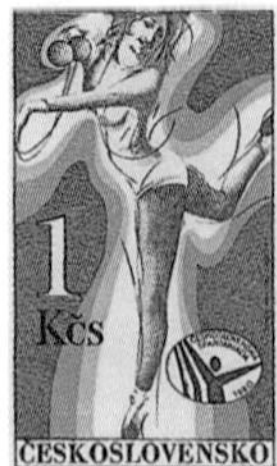

713 Gymnast

1980. National Spartakiad.

2530 – 50h. black, red & blue 10 10
2531 **713** 1k. multicoloured . . . 20 10

DESIGN: HORIZ: — 50h. Opening parade of athletes.

715 "Gerbera jamesonii" **716** "Chod Girl"

1980. Olomuc and Bratislava Flower Shows. Multicoloured.

2533 50h. Type **715** 15 15
2534 1k. "Aechmea fasciata" . . 1·75 40
2535 2k. Bird of paradise flower 35 25
2536 4k. Slipper orchid 85 40

1980. Graphic Cut-outs by Cornelia Nemeckova.

2537 **716** 50h. multicoloured . . . 15 10
2238 – 1k. mauve, brown & red 25 10
2539 – 2k. multicoloured . . . 45 25
2540 – 4k. multicoloured . . . 2·50 70
2541 – 5k. blue, mauve & lt bl 1·10 50

DESIGNS: 1k. "Punch with his dog"; 2k. "Dandy cat with Posy"; 4k. Lion and Moon ("Evening Contemplation"); 5k. Dancer and piper ("Wallacchian Dance").

717 Map of Czechoslovakia and Family **718** Heads

1980. National Census.

2542 **717** 1k. multicoloured . . . 25 10

1980. Prague Castle (16th series). As T **536**. Multicoloured.

2543 3k. Gateway of Old Palace 2·40 2·75
2544 4k. Armorial lion . . . . . 1·10 75

1980. Historic Bratislava (4th issue). As T **669**. Multicoloured.

2545 3k. "View across the Danube" (J. Eder) . . . . 2·40 2·75
2546 4k. "The Old Royal Bridge" (J. A. Lantz) . . . . . . 1·10 75

1980. 10th Anniv of Socialist Youth Federation.

2547 **718** 50h. blue, orange & red 10 10

1980. Paintings (14th series). As T **481**.

2549 1k. buff, blue and brown . . 1·25 1·00
2550 2k. multicoloured . . . . . 2·00 2·10
2551 3k. red, brown and green . . 55 45
2552 4k. multicoloured 65 55
2553 5k. green, buff and black . . 85 80

DESIGNS—VERT: 1k. "Pavel Jozef Safarik" (Jozef B. Klemens); 2k. "Peasant Revolt" (mosaic, A. Podzemma); 3k. Bust of Saint from Lucivna Church; 5k. "Labour" (sculpture, Jan Stursa). HORIZ: 4k. "Waste Heaps" (Jan Zrzavy).

719 Carrier Pigeon

1980. Stamp Day.

2554 **719** 1k. black, red & blue . . 25 10

720 Five Year Plan Emblem **721** Invalid and Half-bare Tree

1981. 7th Five Year Plan.

2555 **720** 50h. multicoloured . . . 10 10

1981. International Year of Disabled Persons.

2556 **721** 1k. multicoloured . . . 25 10

722 Landau, 1800 **723** Jan Sverma (partisan)

1981. Historic Coaches in Postal Museum.

2557 **722** 50h. yellow, black & red 20 10
2558 – 1k. yellow, black & grn 30 10
2559 – 3k.60 lt blue, blk & bl 2·00 40
2560 – 5k. stone, black & red 1·25 35
2561 – 7k. yellow, black & blue 1·50 65

DESIGNS: 1k. Mail coach, c. 1830–40; 3k.60, Postal sleigh, 1840; 5k. Mail coach and four horses, 1860; 7k. Coupe carriage, 1840.

1981. Celebrities' Anniversaries. Multicoloured.

2562 50h. Type **723** (80th birth anniv) 25 10
2563 50h. Mikulas Schneider-Trnavsky (composer) (birth cent) 35 10
2564 50h. Juraj Hronec (mathematician) (birth cent) 25 10
2565 50h. Josef Hlavka (architect) (150th birth anniv) . . . 25 10
2566 1k. Dimitri Shostakovich (composer) (75th birth anniv) 60 10
2567 1k. George Bernard Shaw (dramatist) (125th birth anniv) 60 10
2568 1k. Bernardo Bolzano (philosopher) (birth bicent) . . . . 1·50 25
2569 1k. Wolfgang Amadeus Mozart (composer) (225th birth anniv) 75 15

725 Party Member with Flag

1981. 60th Anniv of Czechoslovak Communist Party. Multicoloured.

2571 50h. Type **725** 10 15
2572 1k. Symbols of progress and hands holding flag 20 15
2573 4k. Party member holding flag bearing symbols of industry (vert) 80 40

726 Hammer and Sickle

1981. 16th Czechoslovak Communist Party Congress. Multicoloured.

2574 50h. Type **726** 10 10
2575 1k. "XVI" and Prague buildings 25 10

727 Fallow-plough **728** Man, Woman and Dove

1981. 90th Anniv of Agricultural Museum.

2577 **727** 1k. multicoloured . . . 25 10

1981. Elections to Representative Assemblies.

2578 **728** 50h. red, stone & blue 10 10

729 "Uran" (Tatra Mountains) and "Rudy Rijen" (Bohemia)

1981. Achievements of Socialist Construction (1st series). Multicoloured.
2579 80h. Type **729** (Trade Union recreational facilities) . . 25 10
2580 1k. Prague–Brno–Bratislava expressway 30 10
2581 2k. Jaslovske Bohunice nuclear plant 50 25
See also Nos. 2644/6, 2695/7, 2753/5 and 2800/2.

1981. Historic Bratislava (5th issue). As T **669**. Multicoloured.
2582 3k. "Bratislava, 1760" (G. B. Probst) . . . . . 2·75 2·75
2583 4k. "Grassalkovichov Palace, 1815" (C. Bschor) 80 70

731 Puppets

732 Map

1981. 30th National Festival of Amateur Puppetry Ensembles, Chrudim.
2585 **731** 2k. multicoloured . . . 45 30

1981. National Defence. Multicoloured.
2586 40h. Type **732** (Defence of borders) 10 10
2587 50h. Emblem of Civil Defence Organization (30th Anniv) (vert) . . . 15 10
2588 1k. Emblem of Svazarm (Organization for Co-operation with Army, 30th anniv) (28 × 23 mm) 25 10

733 Edelweiss, Climbers and Lenin

1981. 25th International Youth Climb of Rysy Peaks.
2589 **733** 3k.60 multicoloured . . 85 40

734 Illustration by Albin Brunovsky

736 Skeletal Hand removing Cigarette

735 Gorilla Family

1981. Biennial Exhibition of Book Illustrations for Children, Bratislava. Multicoloured.
2590 50h. Type **734** 15 15
2591 1k. Adolf Born 30 20
2592 2k. Vive Tolli 60 25
2593 4k. Etienne Delessert . . . 90 40
2594 10k. Suekichi Akaba . . . . 3·00 1·25

1981. 50th Anniv of Prague Zoo. Multicoloured.
2595 50h. Type **735** 30 10
2596 1k. Lion family 35 15
2597 7k. Przewalski's horses . . . 2·75 1·50

1981. Anti-smoking Campaign.
2598 **736** 4k. multicoloured . . . 1·75 85

1981. Prague Castle (17th series). As T **536**. Multicoloured.
2599 3k. Fragment of Pernstejn terracotta from Lobkovic Palace (16th century) . . 90 45
2600 4k. St. Vitus Cathedral (19th century engraving by J. Sembera and G. Dobler) . . . . 2·25 2·75

1981. Art (15th series). As T **481**.
2601 1k. multicoloured . . . . . 3·50 3·25
2602 2k. brown 60 50
2603 3k. multicoloured 80 65
2604 4k. multicoloured 90 70
2605 5k. multicoloured . . . . . 1·10 1·60
DESIGNS: 1k. "View of Prague from Petrin Hill" (V. Hollar); 2k. "Czech Academy of Arts and Sciences Medallion" (Otakar Spaniel); 3k. South Bohemian embroidery (Zdenek Sklenar); 4k. "Peonies" (A. M. Gerasimov); 5k. "Figure of a Woman Standing" (Picasso).

737 Eduard Karel (engraver)

1981. Stamp Day.
2606 **737** 1k. yellow, red and blue 25 10

738 Lenin

739 Player kicking Ball

1982. 70th Anniv of 6th Russian Workers' Party Congress, Prague.
2607 **738** 2k. red, gold and blue 55 25

1982. World Cup Football Championship, Spain. Multicoloured.
2609 1k. Type **739** 20 15
2610 3k.60 Heading ball 75 40
2611 4k. Saving goal . . . . . . 2·50 65

740 Hrob

741 Conference Emblem

1982. Arms of Czech Towns (3rd series). Multicoloured.
2612 50h. Type **740** 20 10
2613 50h. Mlada Boleslav 20 10
2614 50h. Nove Mesto and Metuji 20 10
2615 50h. Trencin 20 10
See also Nos. 2720/3, 2765/7, 2819/21 and 3017/20.

1982. Tenth World Federation of Trade Unions Congress, Havana.
2616 **741** 1k. multicoloured . . . 25 10

742 Workers and Mine

1982. 50th Anniv of Great Strike at Most (coalminers' and general strike).
2617 **742** 1k. multicoloured . . . 25 10

743 Locomotives of 1922 and 1982

1982. 60th Anniv of International Railways Union.
2618 **743** 6k. multicoloured . . . 1·75 70

744 Worker with Flag

745 Georgi Dimitrov

1982. 10th Trade Unions Congress, Prague.
2619 **744** 1k. multicoloured . . . 25 10

1982. Birth Centenary of Georgi Dimitrov (Bulgarian statesman).
2620 **745** 50h. multicoloured . . . 10 10

747 "Euterpe" (Crispin de Passe)

749 Child's Head, Rose and Barbed Wire (Lidice)

1982. Engravings with a Music Theme.
2622 **747** 40h. black, gold & brown 15 10
2623 – 50h. black, gold & red 20 10
2624 – 1k. black, gold & brown 30 15
2625 – 2k. black, gold & blue 50 25
2626 – 3k. black, gold & green 2·40 70
DESIGNS: 50h. "The Sanguine Man" (Jacob de Gheyn); 1k. "The Crossing of the Red Sea" (Adriaen Collaert); 2k. "Wandering Musicians" (Rembrandt); 3k. "Beggar with Viol" (Jacques Callot).

1982. 40th Anniv of Destruction of Lidice and Lezaky. Multicoloured.
2628 1k. Type **749** 30 10
2629 1k. Hands and barbed wire (Lezaky) 30 10

750 Memorial and Statue of Jan Zizka

1982. 50th Anniv of National Memorial, Prague.
2630 **750** 1k. multicoloured . . . 25 10

752 Krivoklat Castle

1982. Castles. Multicoloured.
2632 50h. Type **752** 20 10
2633 1k. Interior and sculptures at Krivoklat Castle . . . 35 15
2634 2k. Nitra Castle 65 30
2635 3k. Archaeological finds from Nitra Castle . . . . 1·00 40

1982. Prague Castle (18th series). As T **536**.
2637 3k. brown and green . . . . 2·40 70
2638 4k. multicoloured . . . . . 1·25 95
DESIGNS: 3k. "St. George" (statue by George and Martin of Kluz, 1372); 4k. Tomb of Prince Vratislav I, Basilica of St. George.

753 Ferry "Kamzik" in Bratislava Harbour

1982. Danube Commission. Multicoloured.
2639 3k. Type **753** 80 30
2640 3k.60 "TR 100" tug at Budapest . . . . 1·00 40

1982. Historic Bratislava (6th issue). As T **669**.
2642 3k. black and red . . . . . 1·90 85
2643 4k. multicoloured . . . . . 2·10 1·25
DESIGNS: 3k. "View of Bratislava with Steamer"; 4k. "View of Bratislava with Bridge".

754 Agriculture

1982. Achievements of Socialist Construction (2nd series). Multicoloured.
2644 20h. Type **754** 10 10
2645 1k. Industry 35 10
2646 3k. Science and technology 95 45
See also Nos. 2695/7, 2753/5 and 2800/2.

755 "Scientific Research"

1982. 30th Anniv of Academy of Sciences.
2647 **755** 6k. multicoloured . . . 1·10 55

756 Couple with Flowers and Silhouette of Rider

1982. 65th Anniv of October Revolution and 60th Anniv of U.S.S.R. Multicoloured.
2648 50h. Type **756** 15 10
2649 1k. Cosmonauts and industrial complex 20 10

757 "Jaroslav Hasek" (writer) (Jose Malejovsky)

759 President Husak

758 Jaroslav Goldschmied (engraver) and Engraving Tools

1982. Sculptures. Multicoloured.
2650 1k. Type **757** 30 10
2651 2k. "Jan Zrzavy" (patriot) (Jan Simota) 55 25
2652 4k.40 "Leos Janacek" (composer) (Milos Axman) . . . . 1·10 55
2653 6k. "Martin Kukucin" (patriot) (Jan Kulich) . . 1·50 75
2654 7k. "Peaceful Work" (detail) (Rudolf Pribis) . . . . . 3·00 1·25

1982. Art (16th series). As T **481**. Multicoloured.
2655 1k. "Revolution in Spain" (Josef Sima) . . . . . . 1·60 95
2656 2k. "Woman drying Herself" (Rudolf Kremlicka) . . . . 2·50 2·25
2657 3k. "The Girl Bride" (Dezider Milly) . . . . . 1·60 90
2658 4k. "Oil Field Workers" (Jan Zelibsky) . . . . . 1·60 1·25
2659 5k. "The Birds Lament" (Emil Filla) . . . . 1·75 1·50

1983. Stamp Day.
2660 **758** 1k. multicoloured . . . 25 10

1983. 70th Birthday of President Husak.
2661 **759** 50h. blue 10 10
See also No. 2911.

760 Jaroslav Hasek (writer)

761 Armed Workers

1983. Celebrities' Anniversaries.
2662 **760** 50h. green, blue & red 15 15
2663 – 1k. brown, blue & red 25 15
2664 – 2k. multicoloured . . . 45 25
2665 – 5k. black, blue & red . . 1·40 50
DESIGNS: Type **760** (birth centenary); 1k. Julius Fucik (journalist) (80th birth and 40th death annivs); 2k. Martin Luther (church reformist) (500th birth anniv); 5k. Johannes Brahms (composer) (150th birth anniv).

1983. Anniversaries. Multicoloured.
2666 50h. Type **761** (35th anniv of "Victorious February") 15 10
2667 1k. Family and agriculture and industrial landscapes (35th anniversary of National Front) 25 15

762 Radio Waves and Broadcasting Emblem

763 Ski Flyer

1983. Communications. Multicoloured.

2668 40h. Type **762** (60th anniv of Czech broadcasting) . . 15 10
2669 1k. Television emblem (30th anniv of Czech television) 20 10
2670 2k. W.C.Y. emblem and "1983" (World Communications Year) (40 × 23 mm) 45 25
2671 3k.60 Envelopes, Aero A-10 aircraft and mail vans (60th anniv of airmail and 75th anniv of mail transport by motor vehicles) (49 × 19 mm) . . 1·00 50

1983. 7th World Ski Flying Championships, Harrachov.

2672 **763** 1k. multicoloured . . . 25 10

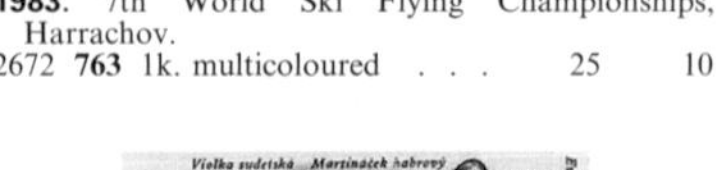

765 Emperor Moth and "Viola sudetica"

1983. Nature Protection. Multicoloured.

2674 50h. Type **765** 20 10
2675 1k. Water lilies and edible frogs 40 15
2676 2k. Red crossbill and cones 1·60 40
2677 3k.60 Grey herons . . . . 1·60 50
2678 5k. Lynx and "Gentiana asclepiadea" . . . . . . 1·50 45
2679 7k. Red deer . . . . . . 3·25 1·50

766 Ivan Stepanovich Kbnev

1983. Soviet Army Commanders. Multicoloured.

2680 50h. Type **766** 15 10
2681 1k. Andrei Ivanovich Yeremenko 25 15
2682 2k. Rodion Yakovlevich Malinovsky 55 25

767 Dove

768 "Rudolf II" (Adrian de Vries)

1983. World Peace and Life Congress, Prague.

2683 **767** 2k. multicoloured . . . 45 40

1983. Prague Castle (19th series).

2685 **768** 4k. multicoloured . . . 1·40 1·00
2686 – 5k. orange, blk & red . . 85 1·00

DESIGN: 5k. Kinetic relief with timepiece by Rudolf Svoboda.

769 Mounted Messenger (Oleg K. Zotov)

1983. 9th Biennial Exhibition of Book Illustration for Children.

2687 **769** 50h. multicoloured . . . 15 10
2688 – 1k. multicoloured . . . 25 10
2689 – 4k. multicoloured . . . 95 40
2690 – 7k. red and black . . . 1·40 55

DESIGNS: 1k. Boy looking from window at birds in tree (Zbigniew Rychlicki); 4k. "Hansel and Gretel" (Lisbeth Zwerger); 7k. Three young negroes (Antonio P. Domingues).

770 Ilyushin Il-62 and Globe

1983. World Communications Year and 60th Anniv of Czechoslovak Airlines.

2692 **770** 50h. red, purple & pink 15 10
2693 – 1k. purple, red & pink 30 10
2694 – 4k. purple, red & pink 1·90 85

DESIGNS—VERT: 1k. Ilyushin Il-62 and envelope. HORIZ: 4k. Ilyushin Il-62 and Aero A-14 biplane.

1983. Achievements of Socialist Construction (3rd series). As T **754**.

2695 50h. Surveyor 15 10
2696 1k. Refinery 30 10
2697 3k. Hospital and operating theatre 75 50

1983. Historic Bratislava (7th series). As T **669**.

2698 3k. green, red and black . . 1·75 70
2699 4k. multicoloured . . . . . 1·75 70

DESIGNS: 3k. Sculptures by Viktor Tilgner; 4k. "Mirbachov Palace" (Julius Schubert).

771 National Theatre, Prague

772 "Soldier with Sword and Shield" (Hendrik Goltzius)

1983. Czechoslovak Theatre Year.

2700 **771** 50h. brown 15 10
2701 – 2k. green 55 25

DESIGN: 2k. National Theatre and Tyl Theatre, Prague.

1983. Art (17th series), showing works from the National Theatre, Prague. As Type **481**.

2702 1k. multicoloured . . . . . 1·25 90
2703 2k. multicoloured . . . . . 2·75 90
2704 3k. yellow, black and blue 1·00 60
2705 4k. multicoloured . . . . . 1·00 60
2706 5k. multicoloured . . . . . 1·00 60

DESIGNS: 1k. "Zalov" (lunette detail by Mikolas Ales); 2k. "Genius" (stage curtain detail, Vojtech Hynais); 3k. "Music" and "Lyrics" (ceiling drawings, Frantisek Zenisek); 4k. "Prague" (detail from President's box, Vaclav Brozik); 5k. "Hradcany Castle (detail from President's box, Julius Marak).

1983. Period Costume from Old Engravings. Multicoloured.

2707 40h. Type **772** 15 10
2708 50h. "Warrior with Sword and Lance" (Jacob de Gheyn) 15 10
2709 1k. "Lady with Muff" (Jacques Callot) 30 10
2710 4k. "Lady with Flower" (Vaclav Hollar) . . . . . 1·10 40
2711 5k. "Gentleman with Cane" (Antoine Watteau) . . . 2·25 80

773 Karel Seizinger (stamp engraver)

1983. Stamp Day.

2712 **773** 1k. multicoloured . . . 25 10

774 National Flag, with Bratislava and Prague Castles

775 Council Emblem

1984. 15th Anniv of Czechoslovak Federation.

2713 **774** 50h. multicoloured . . . 10 10

1984. 35th Anniv of Council for Mutual Economic Aid.

2714 **775** 1k. multicoloured . . . 25 25

776 Cross-country Skiing

1984. Winter Olympic Games, Sarajevo. Mult.

2715 2k. Type **776** 45 25
2716 3k. Ice hockey 70 40
2717 5k. Biathlon . . . . 1·50 65

777 Olympic Flag, Ancient Greek Athletes and Olympic Flame

1984. 90th Anniv of International Olympic Committee.

2719 **777** 7k. multicoloured . . . 1·25 55

1984. Arms of Czech Towns (4th series). As T **740**. Multicoloured.

2720 50h. Turnov 30 10
2721 50h. Kutna Hora 30 10
2722 1k. Milevsko 45 25
2723 1k. Martin 45 25

778 "Soyuz" and Dish Aerials

779 Vendellin Opatrny

1984. "Interkosmos" International Space Flights. Multicoloured.

2724 50h. Type **778** 20 10
2725 1k. "Salyut"–"Soyuz" complex 35 15
2726 2k. Cross-section of orbital station 55 25
2727 4k. "Salyut" taking pictures of Earth's surface 75 50
2728 5k. "Soyuz" returning to Earth . . . . 1·00 65

1984. Anti-fascist Heroes.

2729 **779** 50h. black, red & blue 20 10
2730 – 1k. black, red & blue . . 30 10
2731 – 2k. black, red & blue . . 55 25
2732 – 4k. black, red & blue . . 1·10 40

DESIGNS: 1k. Ladislav Novomesky; 2k. Rudolf Jasiok; 4k. Jan Nalepka.

780 Musical Instruments

781 Telecommunications Building

1984. Music Year.

2733 **780** 50h. lt brown, gold & brn 20 10
2734 – 1k. multicoloured . . . 25 10

DESIGN: 1k. Organ pipes.

1984. Central Telecommunications Building, Bratislava.

2735 **781** 2k. multicoloured . . . 55 25

1984. Historic Bratislava (8th series). As T **669**. Multicoloured.

2736 3k. Arms of Vintners' Guild 1·25 85
2737 4k. Painting of 1827 Skating Festival . . . . 1·25 85

1984. Prague Castle (20th series). As T **768**. Multicoloured.

2739 3k. Weather cock, St. Vitus Cathedral 75 80
2740 4k. King David playing psaltery (initial from Roudnice Book of Psalms) . . . . 1·40 1·25

783 Jack of Spades (16th century)

1984. Playing Cards. Multicoloured.

2741 50h. Type **783** 20 10
2742 1k. Queen of Spades (17th century) 35 10
2743 2k. Nine of Hearts (18th century) 50 25
2744 3k. Jack of Clubs (18th century) 85 35
2745 5k. King of Hearts (19th century) . . . . 1·25 55

784 Family and Industrial Complex

1984. 40th Anniv of Slovak Uprising.

2746 **784** 50h. multicoloured . . . 10 10

785 Soldiers with Banner

1984. 40th Anniv of Battle of Dukla Pass.

2747 **785** 2k. multicoloured . . . 45 25

786 High Jumping

1984. Olympic Games, Los Angeles. Mult.

2748 1k. Type **786** 30 15
2749 2k. Cycling 50 25
2750 3k. Rowing 70 40
2751 5k. Weightlifting . . . . . 1·10 55

1984. Achievements of Socialist Construction (4th series). As T **754**. Multicoloured.

2753 1k. Telephone handset and letters (Communications) 40 10
2754 2k. Containers on railway trucks and river barge (Transport) 75 30
2755 3k. Map of Transgas pipeline 65 45

1984. Art (18th series). As T **481**. Multicoloured.

2757 1k. "Milevsky River" (Karel Stehlik) 40 75
2758 2k. "Under the Trees" (Viktor Barvitius) 80 90
2759 3k. "Landscape with Flowers" (Zolo Palugyay) 1·25 60
2760 4k. Illustration of king from Vysehrad Codex . . . . 1·60 80
2761 5k. "Kokorin" (Antonin Manes) . . . . 2·00 95

787 Dove and Head of Girl

788 Zapotocky

1984. 45th Anniv of International Students Day.

2762 **787** 1k. multicoloured . . . 25 10

1984. Birth Centenary of Antonin Zapotocky (politician).

2763 **788** 50h. multicoloured . . . 10 10

789 Bohumil Heinz (engraver) and Hands engraving

1984. Stamp Day.

2764 **789** 1k. multicoloured . . . 25 25

1985. Arms of Czech Towns (5th series). As T **740**. Multicoloured.

2765 50h. Kamyk nad Vltavou 30 10

2766 50h. Havirov 30 10

2767 50h. Trnava 30 10

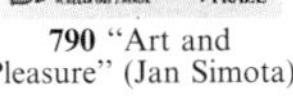

790 "Art and Pleasure" (Jan Simota)

792 Helmet, Mail Shirt and Crossbow

791 View of Trnava

1985. Centenary of Prague University of Applied Arts.

2768 **790** 3k. multicoloured . . . 60 40

1985. 350th Anniv of Trnava University.

2769 **791** 2k. multicoloured . . . 35 20

1985. Exhibits from Military Museum. Mult.

2770 50h. Type **792** 15 10

2771 1k. Cross and star of Za vitezstvi order 30 10

2772 2k. Avia B-534 airplane and "Soyuz 28" (horiz) . . . 70 25

795 State Arms and Crowd

796 State Arms and Soldiers with National Flag

1985. 40th Anniv of Kosice Reforms.

2775 **795** 4k. multicoloured . . . 70 40

1985. 40th Anniv of National Security Forces.

2776 **796** 50h. multicoloured . . . 10 10

798 Emblem and Ice Hockey Players

1985. World and European Ice Hockey Championships, Prague.

2778 **798** 1k. multicoloured . . . 25 10

799 Pieces on Chessboard

802 Tennis

1985. 80th Anniv of Czechoslovak Chess Organization.

2779 **799** 6k. multicoloured . . . 1·50 70

800 Freedom Fighters and Prague

1985. Anniversaries. Multicoloured.

2780 1k. Type **800** (40th anniv of May uprising) 20 10

2781 1k. Workers shaking hands, flags and industrial motifs (15th anniv of Czechoslovak–Soviet Treaty) 20 10

2782 1k. Girl giving flowers to soldier, Prague Castle and tank (40th anniv of liberation) 20 10

2783 1k. Soldiers and industrial motifs (30th anniv of Warsaw Pact) 20 10

1985. Czechoslovak Victory in Ice Hockey Championships. No. 2778 optd **CSSR MISTREM SVETA**.

2784 **798** 1k. multicoloured . . . 5·25 5·00

1985. National Spartakiad. Multicoloured.

2785 50h. Type **802** 15 10

2786 1k. Gymnasts performing with ribbons (48 × 19 mm) 20 10

803 Study for "Fire" and "Republic" (Josef Capek)

1985. Anti-fascist Artists. Multicoloured.

2787 50h. Type **803** 15 10

2788 2k. "Geneva Conference on Disarmament" and "Prophecy of Three Parrots" (Frantisek Bidlo) 45 25

2789 4k. "Unknown Conscript" and "The almost peaceful Dove" (Antonin Pelc) . . 70 40

805 Moscow Buildings and Young People holding Doves

1985. 12th World Youth and Students' Festival, Moscow.

2791 **805** 1k. multicoloured . . . 25 10

806 Figures on Globe

807 Rocking Horse (Kveta Pacovska)

1985. 40th Anniv of World Federation of Trade Unions.

2792 **806** 50h. multicoloured . . . 10 10

1985. Historic Bratislava (9th series). As T **669**.

2793 3k. lt brown, green & brown 70 75

2794 4k. black, green and red . . 1·00 1·10

DESIGNS: 3k. Tapestry (Elena Holeczyova); 4k. Pottery.

1985. 10th Biennial Exhibition of Book Illustrations for Children, Bratislava. Mult.

2795 1k. Type **807** 20 10

2796 2k. Elves (Gennady Spirin) 35 20

2797 3k. Girl, butterfly and flowers (Kaarina Kaila) 65 30

2798 4k. Boy shaking hands with hedgehog (Erick Ingraham) 80 40

1985. Achievements of Socialist Construction (5th series). As T **754**. Multicoloured.

2800 50h. Mechanical excavator 10 10

2801 1k. Train and map of Prague underground railway 30 15

2802 2k. Modern textile spinning equipment 35 25

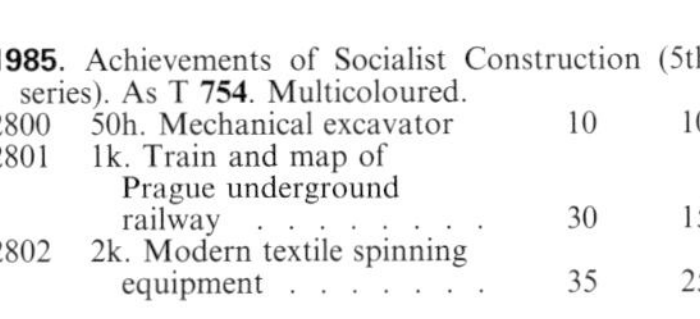

808 Gateway to First Courtyard

809 Jug (4th century)

1985. Prague Castle (21st series).

2803 **808** 2k. black, blue & red . . 50 30

2804 – 3k. multicoloured . . . 1·10 40

DESIGN: 3k. East side of Castle.

1985. Centenary of Prague Arts and Crafts Museum. Glassware. Multicoloured.

2805 50h. Type **809** 10 10

2806 1k. Venetian glass container (16th century) 20 10

2807 2k. Bohemian glass with hunting scene (18th century) 40 25

2808 4k. Bohemian vase (18th century) 65 40

2809 6k. Bohemian vase (c. 1900) 1·40 65

1985. Art (19th series). As T **481**. Multicoloured.

2810 1k. "Young Woman in Blue Dress" (Josef Ginovsky) 1·60 1·00

2811 2k. "Lenin on Charles Bridge" (Martin Sladky) 1·60 1·00

2812 3k. "Avenue of Poplars" (Vaclav Rabas) . . . . . 1·60 1·00

2813 4k. "Beheading of St. Dorothea" (Hans Baldung Grien) . . . . . 1·60 1·00

2814 5k. "Jasper Schade van Westrum" (Frans Hals) 1·60 1·00

810 Bohdan Roule (engraver) and Engraving Plate

1985. Stamp Day.

2815 **810** 1k. multicoloured . . . 25 10

811 Peace Dove and Olive Twig

1986. International Peace Year. Multicoloured.

2816 **811** 1k. multicoloured . . . 25 10

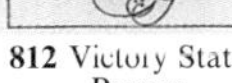

812 Victory Statue Prague

813 Zlin Z-50LS Airplane, Locomotive "Kladno" and Rock Drawing of Chariot

1986. 90th Anniv of Czech Philharmonic Orchestra.

2817 **812** 1k. black, brown & vio 25 10

1986. "Expo '86" International Transport and Communications Exhibition, Vancouver.

2818 **813** 4k. multicoloured . . . 70 40

1986. Arms of Czech Towns (6th series). As T **740**. Multicoloured.

2819 50h. Vodnany 25 10

2820 50h. Zamberk 25 10

2821 50h. Myjava 25 10

814 Banner, Industry and Hammer and Sickle

1986. 17th Communist Party Congress, Prague. Multicoloured.

2822 50h. Type **814** 10 10

2823 1k. Buildings, hammer and sickle and star 25 10

815 Couple, Banner and Star

1986. 65th Anniv of Czechoslovakian Communist Party. Multicoloured.

2824 50h. Type **815** 10 10

2825 1k. Workers, banner and hammer and sickle . . . 25 10

816 Map and Stylized Man

1986. National Front Election Programme.

2826 **816** 50h. multicoloured . . . 10 10

817 Emblem and Crest on Film

1986. 25th Int Film Festival, Karlovy Vary.

2827 **817** 1k. multicoloured . . . 25 10

818 Musical Instruments

819 Ilyushin Il-86 and Airspeed Envoy II

1986. 40th Anniv of Prague Spring Music Festival.

2828 **818** 1k. multicoloured . . . 25 10

1986. 50th Anniv of Prague–Moscow Air Service.

2829 **819** 50h. multicoloured . . . 10 10

820 Sports Pictograms

1986. 90th Anniv of Czechoslovak Olympic Committee.

2830 **820** 2k. multicoloured . . . 45 25

821 Map and Goalkeeper

1986. World Cup Football Championship, Mexico.

2831 **821** 4k. multicoloured . . . 80 55

822 Globe, Net and Ball

1986. Women's World Volleyball Championship, Prague.

2832 **822** 1k. multicoloured . . . 35 10

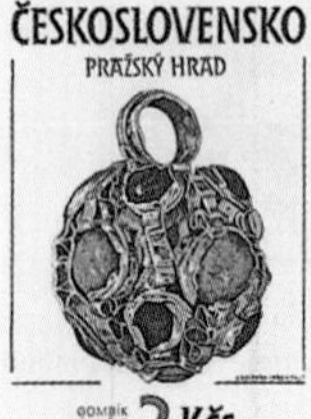

824 Funeral Pendant **825** Wooden Cock, Slovakia

1986. Prague Castle (22nd series).
2834 **824** 2k. multicoloured . . . 55 50
2835 – 3k. orange, brown & bl 65 65
DESIGN: 3k. "Allegory of Blossoms" (sculpture, Jaroslav Horejc).

1986. 40th Anniv of U.N.I.C.E.F. Toys. Mult.
2836 10h. Type **825** 10 10
2837 20h. Wooden soldier on hobby horse, Bohemia . . 10 10
2838 1k. Rag doll, Slovakia . . . 15 10
2839 2k. Doll 35 10
2840 3k. Mechanical bus 50 25

826 Registration Label and Mail Coach

1986. Centenary of Registration Label.
2841 **826** 4k. multicoloured . . . 60 30

1986. Historic Bratislava (10th series). As T **669**.
2842 3k. black, red and blue . . 60 55
2843 4k. black, red and green . . 75 70
DESIGNS: 3k. Sigismund Gate, Bratislava Castle; 4k. "St. Margaret with a Lamb" (relief from Castle).

827 Eagle Owl

1986. Owls. Multicoloured.
2844 50h. Type **827** 25 10
2845 2k. Long-eared owl 55 25
2846 3k. Tawny owl 55 40
2847 4k. Barn owl 70 50
2848 5k. Short-eared owl . . . . 1·50 60

829 Type "Kt8" Articulated Tram and 1920s' Prague Tram

1986. Rail Vehicles. Multicoloured.
2850 50h. Type **829** 20 10
2851 1k. Series E 458.1 electric shunting engine and 1882–1913 steam locomotive . . 30 10
2852 3k. Series T 466.2 diesel locomotive and 1900–24 steam locomotive 70 35
2853 5k. Series M 152.0 railcar and 1930–35 railbus . . . 95 60

830 "The Circus Rider" (Jan Bauch)

1986. Circus and Variety Acts on Paintings. Multicoloured.
2854 1k. Type **830** . . . . . . 1·25 25
2855 2k. "The Ventriloquist" (Frantisek Tichy) . . . . 1·50 35
2856 3k. "In the Circus" (Vincent Hloznik) . . . . 1·45 55
2857 6k. "Clown" (Karel Svolinsky) . . . . 1·75 1·25

1986. Art (20th series). As T **481**. Multicoloured.
2858 1k. "The Czech Lion, May 1918" (Vratislav H. Brunner) . . . . . . 1·50 65
2859 2k. "Boy with Mandolin" (Jozef Sturdik) . . . . 1·40 75
2860 3k. "The Metra Building" (Frantisek Gross) 80 80
2861 4k. "Maria Maximiliana of Sternberk" (Karel Skreta) 80 95
2862 5k. "Adam and Eve" (Lucas Cranach) . . . . 1·10 1·10

831 Brunner and Stamps of 1920

1986. Stamp Day. Birth Centenary of Vratislav Hugo Brunner (stamp designer).
2863 **831** 1k. multicoloured . . . 25 10

832 Bicyclists

1987. World Cross-country Cycling Championships, Mlada Boleslav.
2864 **832** 6k. multicoloured . . . 95 55

833 Pins and Ball

1987. 50th Anniv of Czechoslovakian Bowling Federation.
2865 **833** 2k. multicoloured . . . 35 25

834 Gold Stars of Heroes of C.S.S.R. and of Socialist Labour

1987. State Orders and Medals.
2866 **834** 50h. red, black & gold 10 10
2867 – 2k. multicoloured . . . 30 25
2868 – 3k. multicoloured . . . 55 40
2869 – 4k. multicoloured . . . 70 55
2870 – 5k. multicoloured . . . 95 60
DESIGNS: 2k. Order of Klement Gottwald; 3k. Order of the Republic; 4k. Order of Victorious February; 5k. Order of Labour.

835 Poplar Admiral

1987. Butterflies and Moths. Multicoloured.
2871 1k. Type **835** 20 10
2872 2k. Eyed hawk moth . . . 45 25
2873 3k. Large tiger moth 75 40
2874 4k. Viennese emperor moth 1·00 40

836 Emblem

1987. Nuclear Power Industry.
2875 **836** 5k. multicoloured . . . 80 55

837 Emblem **839** Stained Glass Window, St. Vitus's Cathedral (Frantisek Sequens)

1987. 11th Trades Union Congress, Prague.
2876 **837** 1k. multicoloured . . . 10 10

1987. Prague Castle (23rd series). Multicoloured.
2878 2k. Type **839** 45 40
2879 3k. Arms (mural), New Land Rolls Hall, Old Royal Palace 75 55
See also Nos. 2950/1 and 2977/8.

840 Telephone, 1894

1987. "Praga 88" Int Stamp Exhibition (1st issue). Technical Monuments. Multicoloured.
2880 3k. Type **840** 45 35
2881 3k. Mail Van, 1924 . . . . 45 35
2882 4k. Tank locomotive "Archduke Charles" 1907 90 35
2883 4k. Prague tram, 1900 . . . 90 35
2884 5k. Steam roller, 1936 . . . 90 55
See also Nos. 2900, 2923/6, 2929/32 2934/7 and 2940/3.

841 "When the Fighting Ended" (Pavel Simon) **843** Chickens in Kitchen (Asun Balzola)

842 Prague Town Hall Clock and Theory of Functions Diagram

1987. 45th Anniv of Destruction of Lidice and Lezaky. Multicoloured.
2885 1k. Type **841** 25 10
2886 1k. "The End of the Game" (Ludmila Jirincova) . . . 25 10

1987. 125th Anniv of Union of Czech Mathematicians and Physicists. Multicoloured.
2887 50h. Type **842** 10 10
2888 50h. J. M. Petzval, C. Strouhal and V. Iarnik 10 10
2889 50h. Trajectory of Brownian motion and earth fold diagram 10 10

1987. 11th Biennial Exhibition of Book Illustrations for Children, Bratislava. Designs showing illustrations by artists named. Multicoloured.
2890 50h. Type **843** 35 15
2891 1k. Cranes with egg at railway points (Frederic Clement) 45 15
2892 2k. Birds on nest (Elzbieta Gaudasinska) 35 25
2893 4k. Couple looking over rooftops (Marija Lucija Stupica) 35 30

844 Barbed Wire, Flames and Menorah

1987. 40th Anniv of Terezin Memorial.
2895 **844** 50h. multicoloured . . . 10 10

845 "OSS" and Communications Equipment

1987. 30th Anniv of Organization of Socialist Countries' Postal Administrations.
2896 **845** 4k. multicoloured . . . 70 10

846 Purkyne and Microtome

1987. Birth Bicentenary of Jan Evangelista Purkyne (physiologist).
2897 **846** 7k. multicoloured . . . 1·25 70

1987. Historic Bratislava (11th series). As T **669**.
2898 3k. buff, black and blue . . 50 50
2899 4k. black and brown . . . . 1·00 1·00
DESIGNS: 3k. Detail of projecting window by Vyzdoby; 4k. "View of Bratislava" (engraving, Hans Mayer).

848 Postilion **849** Symbols of Industry, Lenin and Red Flag

1987. "Praga '88" International Stamp Exhibition (2nd issue).
2900 **848** 1k. multicoloured . . . 25 10

1987. 70th Anniv of Russian Revolution (2901) and 65th Anniv of USSR (2902). Multicoloured.
2901 50h. Type **849** 15 10
2902 50h. Hammer and sickle . . 15 10

1987. Art (21st series). As T **481**.
2904 1k. multicoloured 70 25
2905 2k. multicoloured 90 70
2906 3k. multicoloured . . . . . 1·25 75
2907 4k. black, blue and red . . 90 90
2908 5k. multicoloured . . . . . 1·25 1·00
DESIGNS: 1k. "Enclosure of Dreams" (Kamil Lhotak); 2k. "Tulips" (Ester Simerova-Martincekova); 3k. "Bohemian Landscape" (triptych, Josef Lada); 4k. "Accordion Player" (Josef Capek); 5k. "Self-portrait" (Jiri Trnka).

850 Obrovsky and Detail of 1919 Stamp

1987. Stamp Day. 105th Birth Anniv of Jakub Obrovsky (designer).
2909 **850** 1k. multicoloured . . . 10 10

851 "Czechoslovakia", Linden Tree and Arms

1988. 70th Anniv of Czechoslovakia.
2910 **851** 1k. multicoloured . . . 10 10

1988. 75th Birthday of President Husak.
2911 **759** 1k. brown and red . . . 10 10

852 Ski Jumping and Ice Hockey

1988. Olympic Games, Calgary and Seoul. Mult.
2912 50h. Type **852** 10 10
2913 1k. Basketball and football 15 10
2914 6k. Throwing the discus and weightlifting 90 40

853 Red Flags and Klement Gottwald Monument, Pecky

1988. 40th Annivs of "Victorious February" (2915) and National Front (2916). Multicoloured.
2915 50h. Type **853** 10 10
2916 50h. Couple and detail of "Czech Constitution, 1961" (Vincent Hloznik) 10 10

854 Laurin and Klement Car, 1914

1988. Historic Motor Cars. Multicoloured.
2918 50h. Type **854** 10 10
2919 1k. Tatra "NW" type B, 1902 . . . . 15 10
2920 2k. Tatra "NW" type E, 1905 . . . . 40 20
2921 3k. Tatra "12 Normandie", 1929 . . . . 55 25
2922 4k. "Meteor", 1899 . . . . 75 40

855 Praga Post Office and Velka Javorina T.V. Transmitter

1988. "Praga '88" International Stamp Exhibition (3rd issue) and 70th Anniv of Postal Museum. Multicoloured.
2923 50h. Type **855** 10 10
2924 1k. Mlada Boleslav telecommunications centre and Carmelite Street post office, Prague 30 10
2925 2k. Prague 1 and Bratislava 56 post offices 45 25
2926 4k. Malta Square, Prague, and Prachatice post offices 90 40

856 Woman with Linden Leaves as Hair and Open Book

857 Strahov Monastery

1988. 125th Anniv of Slovak Cultural Society.
2928 **856** 50h. multicoloured . . . 10 10

1988. "Praga '88" International Stamp Exhibition (4th issue). National Literature Memorial, Strahov Monastery. Multicoloured.
2929 1k. Type **857** 15 10
2930 2k. Open book and celestial globe 35 20
2931 5k. Illuminated initial "B", scrolls and decorative binding 80 50
2932 7k. Astrological signs, Strahov, illuminated book and globe . . . . 1·50 1·10

858 Waldstein Garden Fountain

1988. "Praga '88" International Stamp Exhibition (5th issue). Prague Fountains.
2934 **858** 1k. black, lilac & blue 15 10
2935 – 2k. multicoloured . . . 35 20
2936 – 3k. black, orange & lilac 55 35
2937 – 4k. black, orange & grn 65 45
DESIGNS: 2k. Old Town Square; 3k. Charles University; 4k. Courtyard, Prague Castle.

860 Trade Unions Central Recreation Centre

1988. "Praga '88" International Stamp Exhibition (6th issue). Present-day Prague. Multicoloured.
2941 50h. Type **860** 10 10
2942 1k. Koospol foreign trade company 20 10
2943 2k. Motol teaching hospital 40 10
2944 4k. Palace of Culture . . . 75 25

1988. Prague Castle (24th series). As T **839**. Multicoloured.
2950 2k. 17 th-century pottery jug 30 35
2951 3k. "St. Catherine" (Paolo Veronese) 45 55

1988. Historic Bratislava (12th series). As T **669**. Multicoloured.
2952 3k. Hlavne Square (detail of print by R. Alt-Sandman) 45 40
2953 4k. Ferdinand House . . . 50 55

1988. Art (22nd series). As T **481**.
2954 2k. multicoloured 40 40
2955 6k. brown, black and blue 1·25 1·10
2956 7k. multicoloured . . . . . 1·75 1·50
DESIGNS: 2k. "Field Workers carrying Sacks" (Martin Benka); 6k. "Woman watching Bird" (Vojtech Preissig); 7k. "Leopard attacking Horseman" (Eugene Delacroix).

865 Benda and Drawings

1988. Stamp Day. 106th Birth Anniv of Jaroslav Benda (stamp designer).
2957 **865** 1k. multicoloured . . . 10 10

866 Emblem **867** Globe and Truck

1989. 20th Anniv of Czechoslovak Federal Socialist Republic.
2958 **866** 50h. multicoloured . . . 10 10

1989. Paris–Dakar Rally. Multicoloured.
2959 50h. Type **867** 10 10
2960 1k. Globe and view of desert on truck side . . . 15 10
2961 2k. Globe and truck (different) 30 15
2962 4k. Route map, turban and truck 50 25

868 Taras G. Shevchenko

870 Dove and Pioneers

869 "Republika" (freighter)

1989. Birth Anniversaries.
2963 **868** 50h. multicoloured . . . 15 10
2964 – 50h. multicoloured . . . 15 10
2965 – 50h. brown and green . . 15 10
2966 – 50h. brown and green . . 15 10
2967 – 50h. black, brn & dp brn 15 10
2968 – 50h. multicoloured . . . 15 10
DESIGNS: No. 2963, Type **868** (Ukrainian poet and painter, 175th anniv); 2964, Modest Petrovich Musorgsky (composer, 150th anniv); 2965, Jan Botto (poet, 160th anniv); 2966, Jawaharlal Nehru (Indian statesman, cent); 2967, Jean Cocteau (writer and painter, centenary); 2968, Charlie Chaplin (actor, centenary).

1989. Shipping.
2969 **869** 50h. grey, red and blue 15 10
2970 – 1k. multicoloured . . . 20 10
2971 – 2k. multicoloured . . . 25 10
2972 – 3k. grey, red and blue 35 20
2973 – 4k. multicoloured . . . 40 25
2974 – 5k. multicoloured . . . 45 35
DESIGNS: 1k. "Pionyr" (trawler); 2k. "Brno" (tanker); 3k. "Trinec" (container ship); 4k. "Orlik" (container ship); 5k. "Vltava" (tanker) and communications equipment.

1989. 40th Anniv of Young Pioneer Organization.
2975 **870** 50h. multicoloured . . . 10 10

1989. Prague Castle (25th series). As T **839**.
2977 2k. brown, yellow and red 20 20
2978 3k. multicoloured 40 35
DESIGNS: 2k. King Kard of Bohemia (relief by Alexandra Colin from Archduke Ferdinand I's mausoleum); 3k. "Self-portrait" (V. V. Reiner).

872 White-tailed Sea Eagle

1989. Endangered Species.
2980 **872** 1k. multicoloured . . . 15 25

873 Fire-bellied Toads

1989. Endangered Amphibians. Multicoloured.
2981 2k. Type **873** 30 25
2982 3k. Yellow-bellied toad . . 45 35
2983 4k. Alpine newts 85 55
2984 5k. Carpathian newts . . . 1·10 60

874 Dancers

1989. 40th Anniv of Slovak Folk Art Collective.
2985 **874** 50h. multicoloured . . . 10 10

875 Horsemen and Mountains

1989. 45th Anniv of Slovak Rising.
2986 **875** 1k. multicoloured . . . 10 10

876 "Going Fishing" (Hannu Taina)

877 "Nolanea verna"

1989. 12th Biennial Exhibition of Book Illustrations for Children. Multicoloured.
2987 50h. Type **876** 10 10
2988 1k. "Donkey Rider" (Aleksandur Aleksov) . . 15 10
2989 2k. "Animal Dreams" (Jurgen Spohn Zapadny) 25 15
2990 4k. "Scarecrow" (Robert Brun) 40 25

1989. Poisonous Fungi.
2992 **877** 50h. brown, deep brown and green 10 10
2993 – 1k. multicoloured . . . 20 10
2994 – 2k. green and brown . . 35 25
2995 – 3k. brown, yellow & red 45 35
2996 – 5k. multicoloured . . . 65 55
DESIGNS: 1k. Death cap; 2k. Destroying angel; 3k. "Cortinarius orellanus"; 5k. "Galerina marginata".

1989. Historic Bratislava (13th series). As T **669**.
2997 3k. multicoloured 35 40
2998 4k. black, red and green . . 55 50
DESIGNS: 3k. Devin Fortress and flower; 4k. Devin Fortress and pitcher.

878 Jan Opletal (Nazi victim)

1989. 50th Anniv of International Students Day.
2999 **878** 1k. multicoloured . . . 10 10

1989. Art (24th series). As T **481**. Multicoloured.
3000 2k. "Nirvana" (Anton Jasusch) 25 25
3001 4k. "Dusk in the Town" (Jakub Schikaneder) (horiz) 50 50
3002 5k. "Bakers" (Pravoslav Kotik) (horiz) 80 70

879 Bearded Falcon Stamp, Pens and Bouda

1989. Stamp Day. 5th Death Anniv of Cyril Bouda (stamp designer).
3003 **879** 1k. brown, yellow & red 10 10

880 Practising Alphabet **881** Tomas Masaryk (first President)

1990. International Literacy Year.
3004 **880** 1k. multicoloured . . . 10 10

1990. Birth Anniversaries. Multicoloured.
3005 50h. Type **881** (140th anniv) 10 10
3006 50h. Karel Capek (writer, centenary) 10 10
3007 1k. Vladimir Ilyich Lenin (120th anniv) 15 10
3008 2k. Emile Zola (novelist, 150th anniv) 30 15
3009 3k. Jaroslav Heyrovsky (chemist, centenary) . . . 35 20
3010 10k. Bohuslav Martinu (composer, centenary) . . 1·10 65

882 Pres. Vaclav Havel

883 Players

1990.
3011 **882** 50h. ultram, bl & red . . 10 10

1990. Men's World Handball Championship.
3012 **883** 50h. multicoloured . . . 10 10

884 Snapdragon

885 Pope John Paul II

1990. Flowers. Multicoloured.
3013 50h. Type **884** 10 10
3014 1k. "Zinnia elegans" 15 10
3015 3k. Tiger flower 35 25
3016 5k. Madonna lily 55 40

1990. Arms of Czech Towns (7th series). As T **740**. Multicoloured.
3017 50h. Bytca 10 10
3018 50h. Podebrady 10 10
3019 50h. Sobeslav 10 10
3020 50h. Prostejov 10 10

1990. Papal Visit.
3021 **885** 1k. brown, yellow & red 10 10

886 Woman holding Flags

888 Footballers

1990. 45th Anniv of Liberation.
3022 **886** 1k. multicoloured . . . 10 10

1990. World Cup Football Championship, Italy.
3024 **888** 1k. multicoloured . . . 10 10

889 Victory Signs

1990. Free General Election.
3025 **889** 1k. multicoloured . . . 10 10

1990. Prague Castle (26th series). As T **824**.
3026 2k. multicoloured 50 40
3027 3k. green, dp green & red 70 65
DESIGNS: 2k. Jewelled glove (from reliquary of St. George); 3k. Seal of King Premsyl Otakar II of Bohemia.

890 Map of Europe and Branch

1990. 15th Anniv of European Security and Co-operation Conference, Helsinki.
3028 **890** 7k. multicoloured . . . 80 55

891 Milada Horakova

1990. 40th Anniv of Execution of Milada Horakova.
3029 **891** 1k. multicoloured . . . 10 10

892 Poodles

1990. "Inter Canis" Dog Show, Brno. Mult.
3030 50h. Type **892** 10 10
3031 1k. Afghan hound, Irish wolfhound and greyhound 15 10
3032 4k. Czech terrier, bloodhound and Hanoverian bearhound 40 30
3033 7k. Cavalier King Charles, cocker and American cocker spaniels 65 50

1990. Historic Bratislava (14th series). As T **669**.
3034 3k. black and red 40 35
3035 4k. multicoloured 65 55
DESIGNS: 3k. Coin; 4k. "M. R. Stefanik" (J. Mudroch).

893 Horses jumping

1990. Centenary of Pardubice Steeplechase. Mult.
3036 50h. Type **893** 10 10
3037 4k. Horses galloping 45 35

894 Alpine Marmot

1990. Mammals. Multicoloured.
3038 50h. Type **894** 10 10
3039 1k. European wild cat . . . 10 10
3040 4k. Eurasian beaver 45 30
3041 5k. Common long-eared bat 60 40

895 European Flag

1990. Helsinki Pact Civic Gathering, Prague.
3042 **895** 3k. blue, yellow & gold 35 30

896 Snow-covered Church

1990. Christmas.
3043 **896** 50h. multicoloured . . . 10 10

1990. Art (25th series). As T **481**. Multicoloured.
3044 2k. multicoloured 40 35
3045 3k. black, brown & blue . . 50 40
3046 4k. multicoloured 60 60
3047 5k. multicoloured 70 75
DESIGNS—HORIZ: 2k. "Krucemburk" (Jan Zrzavy). VERT: 3k. "St. Agnes" (detail of sculpture, Josef Vaclav Myslbek); 4k. "Slovene in his Homeland" (detail, Alfons Mucha); 5k. "St. John the Baptist" (detail of sculpture, Auguste Rodin).

897 Karel Svolinsky (stamp designer) and "Czechoslovakia"

1990. Stamp Day.
3048 **897** 1k. purple, lilac & blue 10 10

898 Judo Throw

899 Svojsik

1991. European Judo Championships, Prague.
3049 **898** 1k. multicoloured . . . 10 10

1991. 80th Anniv of Czechoslovak Scout Movement and 115th Birth Anniv of A. B. Svojsik (founder).
3050 **899** 3k. multicoloured . . . 35 10

900 Jan Hus preaching

901 Alois Senefelder

1991. Anniversaries.
3051 **900** 50h. brown, stone & red 10 10
3052 – 1k. multicoloured . . . 10 10
3053 – 5k. multicoloured . . . 60 30
DESIGNS AND EVENTS: 50h. Type **900** (600th anniv of Bethlehem Chapel, Prague); 40 × 23 mm: 1k. Estates Theatre, Prague (re-opening) and Mozart (death bicent); 49 × 20 mm: 5k. Paddle-steamer "Bohemia" (150th anniv of boat excursions in Bohemia).

1991. Birth Anniversaries.
3054 **901** 1k. green, brown & red 20 10
3055 – 1k. black, green & red 20 10
3056 – 1k. blue, mauve & red 20 10
3057 – 1k. violet, blue and red 20 10
3058 – 1k. brown, orange & red 20 10
DESIGNS: No. 3054, Type **901** (inventor of lithography, 220th anniv); 3055, Andrej Kmet (naturalist, 150th anniv); 3056, Jan Masaryk (politician, 105th anniv); 3057, Jaroslav Seifert (composer, 90th anniv); 3058, Antonin Dvorak (composer, 150th anniv).

902 "Magion II" Satellite and Earth

903 Exhibition Pavilion, 1891

1991. Europa. Europe in Space.
3059 **902** 6k. blue, black & red . . 70 50

1991. Cent of International Exhibition, Prague.
3060 **903** 1k. blue, grey & mauve 10 10

904 Bearded Penguins, Map and Flag

1991. 30th Anniv of Antarctic Treaty.
3061 **904** 8k. multicoloured . . . 90 55

905 Blatna Castle

906 Jan Palach

1991. Castles. Multicoloured.
3062 50h. Type **905** . . . . . . 10 1·00
3063 1k. Bouzov 10 10
3064 3k. Kezmarok 40 25

1991. Jan Palach Scholarship.
3065 **906** 4k. black 35 30

907 Rip

908 "The Frog King" (Binette Schroeder)

1991. Beauty Spots.
3066 **907** 4k. red, blue & yellow 45 40
3067 – 4k. purple, green & blk 45 40
DESIGN: No. 3067, Krivan.

1991. 13th Biennial Exhibition of Book Illustrations for Children. Multicoloured.
3068 1k. Type **908** 10 10
3069 2k. "Pinocchio" (Stasys Eidrigevicius) 25 15

909 Hlinka

910 "Prague Jesus Child" (Maria-Victoria Church)

1991. 53rd Death Anniv of Father Andrej Hlinka (Slovak nationalist).
3070 **909** 10k. black . . . . 1·25 55

1991. Prague and Bratislava. Multicoloured.
3071 3k. Type **910** 45 40
3072 3k. St. Elisabeth's Church, Bratislava 45 40

911 "Gagea bohemica"

912 Boys in Costume

1991. Nature Protection. Flowers. Multicoloured.
3073 1k. Type **911** 10 10
3074 2k. "Aster alpinus" 20 20
3075 5k. "Fritillaria meleagris" 55 40
3076 11k. "Daphne eneorum" . . 1·25 75

1991. Art (26th series). As T **481**. Multicoloured.
3077 2k. "Family at Home" (Max Ernst) 20 20
3078 3k. "Milenci" (Auguste Renoir) 30 30
3079 4k. "Christ" (El Greco) . . 75 40
3080 5k. "Coincidence" (Ladislav Guderna) 85 55
3081 7k. "Two Japanese Women" (Utamaro) . . . . 1·10 80

1991. Christmas.
3082 **912** 50h. multicoloured . . . 10 10

913 Martin Benka (stamp designer) and Slovakian 1939 Stamp

1991. Stamp Day.
3083 **913** 2k. red, black & orange 35 10

914 Biathlon

916 Player

1992. Winter Olympic Games, Albertville.
3084 **914** 1k. multicoloured . . . 10 10

1992. World Ice Hockey Championship, Prague and Bratislava.
3086 **916** 3k. multicoloured . . . 35 35

917 Traffic Lights

1992. Road Safety Campaign.
3087 **917** 2k. multicoloured . . . 45 20

918 Tower, Seville Cathedral

1992. "Expo '92" World's Fair, Seville.
3088 **918** 4k. multicoloured . . . 25 25

919 Amerindian, "Santa Maria" and Columbus

1992. Europa. 500th Anniv of Discovery of America by Columbus.
3089 **919** 22k. multicoloured . . . 2·50 1·90

920 J. Kubis and J. Gabcik

1992. Free Czechoslovak Forces in World War II. Multicoloured.
3090 1k. Type **920** (50th anniv of assassination of Reinhard Heydrich) 10 10
3091 2k. Spitfires (air battles over England, 1939–45) . . . 20 10
3092 3k. Barbed wire and soldier (Tobruk, 1941) 25 15
3093 6k. Soldiers (Dunkirk, 1944–45) 90 25

921 Tennis Player

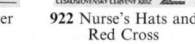

922 Nurse's Hats and Red Cross

1992. Olympic Games, Barcelona.
3094 **921** 2k. multicoloured . . . 35 10

1992. Red Cross.
3095 **922** 2k. multicoloured . . . 25 10

923 Player

924 Crawling Cockchafer

1992. European Junior Table Tennis Championships, Topolcany.
3096 **923** 1k. multicoloured . . . 10 10

1992. Beetles. Multicoloured.
3097 1k. Type **924** 10 10
3098 2k. "Ergates faber" 20 10
3099 3k. "Meloe violaceus" . . . 25 10
3100 4k. "Dytiscus latissimus" . . 30 45

925 Troja Castle

1992.
3101 **925** 6k. multicoloured . . . 60 45
3102 – 7k. black and lilac . . . 70 60
3103 – 8k. multicoloured . . . 90 75
DESIGNS—VERT: 7k. "St. Martin" (sculpture, G. R. Donner), Bratislava Cathedral. HORIZ: 8k. Lednice Castle.

926 Double Head and Posthorns

1992. Post Bank.
3104 **926** 20k. multicoloured . . . 1·75 70

927 Anton Bernolak and Georgius Fandly

1992. Bicentenary of Slovak Education Assn.
3105 **927** 5k. multicoloured . . . 55 30

928 Cesky Krumlov

929 Organ

1992.
3106 **928** 3k. brown and red . . . 35 10

1992. Art (27th series). As T **481**.
3107 6k. black and brown 50 50
3108 7k. multicoloured 65 70
3109 8k. multicoloured . . . . . 1·00 90
DESIGNS—VERT: 6k. "The Old Raftsman" (Koloman Sokol); 8k. "Abandonned" (Toyen). HORIZ: 7k. "Still Life with Grapes" (Georges Braque).

1992. Christmas.
3110 **929** 2k. multicoloured . . . 10 10

930 Jindra Schmidt (engraver)

1992. Stamp Day.
3111 **930** 2k. multicoloured . . . 10 10

NEWSPAPER STAMPS

N **4**

N **67** Dove

N **94** Messenger

1918. Imperf.
N24 N **4** 2h. green 10 10
N25 5h. green 10 10
N26 6h. red 10 10
N27 10h. lilac 10 10
N28 20h. blue 10 10
N29 30h. brown 10 10
N30 50h. orange 10 10
N31 100h. brown 45 10

1925. Surch with new value and stars.
N249 N **4** 5 on 2h. green 60 55
N250 5 on 6h. red 35 85

1926. Newspaper Express stamps optd **NOVINY** or surch also.
N251 E **4** 5h. on 2h. pur on yell 10 10
N253 5h. green on yellow . . 45 25
N254 10h. brown on yellow 10 10

1934. Optd **O.T.**
N332 N **4** 10h. lilac 10 10
N333 20h. blue 10 10
N334 30h. brown 15 10

1937. Imperf.
N364 N **67** 2h. brown 10 10
N365 5h. blue 10 10
N366 7h. orange 10 10
N367 9h. green 10 10
N368 10h. lake 10 10
N369 12h. blue 10 10
N370 20h. green 10 10
N371 50h. brown 10 10
N372 1k. olive 10 10

1946. Impert.
N467 N **94** 5h. blue 10 10
N468 10h. red 10 10
N469 15h. green 10 10
N470 20h. green 10 10
N471 25h. purple 10 10
N472 30h. brown 10 10
N473 40h. red 10 10
N474 50h. brown 10 10
N475 1k. grey 10 10
N476 5k. blue 10 10

EXPRESS NEWSPAPER STAMPS

E **4**

1918. Imperf. On yellow or white paper.
E24 E **4** 2h. purple 10 10
E25 5h. green 10 10
E26 10h. brown 45 45

OFFICIAL STAMPS

O **92**

O **103**

1945.
O463 O **92** 50h. green 10 10
O464 1k. blue 10 10
O465 1k.20 purple 15 10
O466 1k.50 red 10 10
O467 2k.50 blue 15 10
O468 5k. purple 20 30
O469 8k. red 30 45

1947.
O490 O **103** 60h. red 10 10
O491 80h. olive 10 10
O492 1k. blue 10 10
O493 1k.20 purple 10 10
O494 2k.40 red 10 10
O495 4k. blue 15 10
O496 5k. purple 15 30
O497 7k.40 violet 20 30

PERSONAL DELIVERY STAMPS

P **66**

1937. For Prepayment. "V" in each corner.
P363 P **66** 50h. blue 20 35

1937. For Payment on Delivery. "D" in each corner.
P364 P **66** 50h. red 20 35

P **95**

1946.
P469 P **95** 2k. blue 20 20

POSTAGE DUE STAMPS

D **4**

1919. Imperf.
D24 D **4** 5h. olive 10 10
D25 10h. olive 10 10
D26 15h. olive 10 10
D27 20h. olive 10 10
D28 25h. olive 10 10
D29 30h. olive 25 10
D30 40h. olive 25 25
D31 50h. olive 25 10
D32 100h. brown . . . . . . 1·25 10
D33 250h. orange . . . . . . 6·00 1·10
D34 400h. red . . . . 8·25 1·10
D35 500h. green . . . . . . 3·00 25
D36 1000h. violet . . . . . 3·00 35
D37 2000h. blue . . . . . . 16·00 75

1922. Postage stamps surch **DOPLATIT** and new value. Imperf or perf.
D229 **2** 10 on 3h. mauve 10 10
D224a 20 on 3h. mauve 10 10
D230 30 on 3h. mauve 10 10
D257 **3** 30 on 15h. red . . . . . 1·75 30
D231 **2** 40 on 3h. mauve 10 10
D258 **3** 40 on 15h. red 35 25
D225 50 on 75h. green 25 25
D262 60 on 50h. purple . . . . 3·00 1·50
D263 60 on 50h. blue . . . . 3·50 1·90
D232 60 on 75h. green 40 10
D226 60 on 80h. green 35 10
D227 100 on 80h. green . . . 30 10
D233 100 on 120h. black . . . 90 10
D264 **2** 100 on 400h. violet . . . 55 10
D265 **3** 100 on 1000h. purple . . 1·10 30
D228 **2** 200 on 400h. violet . . . 55 25

1924. Postage Due stamp surch.
D249 D **4** 10 on 5h. olive 10 10
D250 20 on 5h. olive 10 10
D251 30 on 15h. olive 10 10
D252 40 on 15h. olive 10 10
D253 50 on 250h. orange . . 60 10
D234 50 on 400h. red 55 10
D254 60 on 250h. orange . . 90 20
D235 60 on 400h. red . . . . 2·10 60
D255 100 on 250h. orange . . 1·25 25
D236 100 on 400h. red . . . 1·25 25
D256 200 on 500h. green . . 3·00 1·75

1926. Postage stamps optd **DOPLATIT** or surch also.
D266 **13** 30 on 100h. green . . . 10 10
D279 **11** 40 on 185h. orange . . . 10 10
D267 **13** 40 on 200h. purple . . . 10 10
D268 40 on 300h. red . . . . 1·10 25
D280 **11** 50 on 20h. red 10 10
D281 50 on 150h. red 25 10
D269 **13** 50 on 500h. green . . . 55 10
D282 **11** 60 on 25h. brown . . . 25 25
D283 60 on 185h. orange . . . 25 10
D270 **13** 60 on 400h. brown . . . 45 10
D278 **11** 100h. brown 55 20
D284 100 on 25h. brown . . . 60 10
D271 **13** 100 on 600h. purple . . . 1·75 35

D **34**

D **94**

1928.
D285 D **34** 5h. red 10 10
D286 10h. red 10 10
D287 20h. red 10 10
D288 30h. red 10 10
D289 40h. red 10 10
D290 50h. red 10 10
D291 60h. red 10 10
D292 1k. blue 10 10
D293 2k. blue 35 10
D294 5k. blue 60 10
D295 10k. blue . . . . . . 1·25 10
D296 20k. blue . . . . . . 2·40 10

1946.
D467 D **94** 10h. blue 10 10
D468 20h. blue 10 10
D469 50h. blue 15 10
D470 1k. red 30 10
D471 1k.20 red 35 10
D472 1k.50 red 40 10
D473 1k.60 red 45 10
D474 2k. red 60 10
D475 2k.40 red 65 10
D476 3k. red . . . . 1·00 10
D477 5k. red . . . . 1·60 10
D478 6k. red . . . . 2·25 10

D **257**

D **258**

1954.
D845 D **257** 5h. green 10 10
D846 10h. green 10 10
D860 30h. green 10 10
D861 50h. green 15 10
D849 60h. green 15 10
D850 95h. green 35 10
D863 D **258** 1k. violet 25 10
D864 1k.20 violet 30 10
D865 1k.50 violet 45 10
D854 1k.60 violet 40 10
D855 2k. violet 75 10
D866 3k. violet . . . . . . 1·50 30
D867 5k. violet . . . . . . 2·00 45

D **572** Stylized Plant

1971.
D1985 – 10h. pink and blue 10 10
D1986 – 20h. blue & purple 10 10
D1987 – 30h. pink & green 10 10
D1988 – 60h. green & pur . . 15 10
D1989 – 80h. blue & orange 20 10
D1990 – 1k. green & red . . 25 10
D1991 – 1k.20 orange & grn 30 10
D1992 – 2k. red and blue . . 55 20
D1993 – 3k. yellow & black 95 20
D1994 – 4k. blue & brown 1·10 30
D1995 D **572** 5k.40 lilac and red 1·60 35
D1996 – 6k. yellow and red 2·00 45
DESIGNS: Various stylized plants as Type D **572**.

CZECH REPUBLIC Pt. 5

Formerly part of Czechoslovakia, a federation dissolved on 31 December 1992 when the constituent republics became separate states.

100 haleru = 1 koruna.

1 State Arms

1993.
1 **1** 3k. multicoloured 25 20

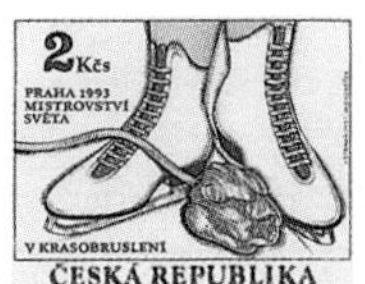

2 Skater's Boots and Tulip

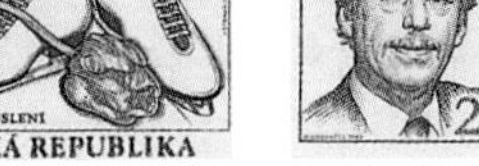

3 Pres. Vaclav Havel

1993. Ice Skating Championships, Prague.
2 **2** 2k. multicoloured 20 15

1993.
3 **3** 2k. purple, blue & mauve . . 10 15
3a 3k.60 violet, mauve & blue 30 15

4 St. John and Charles Bridge, Prague

1993. 600th Death Anniv of St. John of Nepomuk (patron saint of Bohemia).
4 **4** 8k. multicoloured 85 45

5 "Hladovy Svaty I" (Mikulas Medek)

1993. Europa. Contemporary Art.
5 **5** 14k. multicoloured . . . . . 7·50 2·40

6 Church of Sacred Heart, Prague

1993.
6 **6** 5k. multicoloured . . . . . . 1·50 45
See also No. 45.

7 Brevnov Monastery

1993. U.N.E.S.C.O. World Heritage Site. Millenary of Brevnov Monastry, Prague.
7 **7** 4k. multicoloured 40 25

8 Weightlifter — 9 Town Hall Tower and Cathedral of St. Peter and St. Paul

1993. Junior Weightlifting Championships, Cheb.
8 **8** 6k. multicoloured 55 35

1993. 750th Anniv of Brno.
9 **9** 8k. multicoloured . . . . . . 1·90 70

10 Sts. Cyril and Methodius

12 Ceske Budejovice

1993. 1130th Anniv of Arrival of Sts. Cyril and Methodius in Moravia.
10 **10** 8k. multicoloured 75 30

1993. Towns.
12 **12** 1k. brown and red 10 10
13 – 2k. red and blue 10 10
14 – 3k. blue and red 15 10
15 – 3k. blue and red 25 20
16 – 5k. green and brown 50 15
17 – 6k. green and yellow 60 30
18 – 7k. brown and green 60 35
20 – 8k. violet and yellow . . . 40 30
21 – 10k. green and red 55 35
23 – 20k. red and blue . . . . . 1·10 90
26 – 50k. brown and green . . . 30 1·60
DESIGNS—VERT: 2k. Usti nad Labem; 3k. (15) Brno; 5k. Pilsen; 6k. Slanyi; 7k. Antonin Dvorak Theatre, Ostrava; 8k. Olomouc; 10k. Hradec Kralove; 20k. Prague; 50k. Opava. HORIZ: 3k. (14) Cesky Krumlov (U.N.E.S.C.O. World Heritage Site).

13 Rower

14 August Sedlacek (historian, 150th anniv)

1993. World Rowing Championships, Racice.
27 **13** 3k. multicoloured 25 30

1993. Birth Anniversaries.
28 **14** 2k. buff, blue and green . . 15 15
29 – 3k. buff, blue and violet . . 30 20
DESIGN: 3k. Eduard Cech (mathematician, centenary).

15 Pedunculate Oak

17 St. Nicholas

16 "Composition" (Joan Miro)

1993. Trees. Multicoloured.
30 5k. Type **15** 35 20
31 7k. Hornbeam 50 30
32 9k. Scots pine 70 45

1993. Art (1st series). Multicoloured.
33 11k. Type **16** . . . . 2·10 1·25
34 14k. "Green Corn Field with Cypress" (Vincent van Gogh) . . . . 3·50 1·50
See also Nos. 62/4, 116/18, 140/2, 174/6, 200/1, 221/2, 252/4, 282/4, 312/14 and 350/2.

1993. Christmas.
35 **17** 2k. multicoloured 25 10

18 "Strahov Madonna"

1993. Christmas.
36 **18** 9k. multicoloured . . . . . 3·00 90

19 "Family" (C. Littasy-Rollier)

20 Kubelik

1994. International Year of the Family.
37 **19** 2k. multicoloured 10 10

1994. 54th Death Anniv of Jan Kublik (composer and violinist).
38 **20** 3k. yellow and black 25 10

21 Voltaire (writer, 300th anniv)

1994. Birth Anniversaries.
39 **21** 2k. purple, grey & mauve 15 25
40 – 6k. black, blue and green . . 45 25
DESIGN: 6k. Georg Agricola (mineralogist, 500th anniv).

22 Athletes

23 Marco Polo and Fantasy Animal

1994. Winter Olympic Games, Lillehammer, Norway.
41 **22** 5k. multicoloured 40 30

1994. Europa. Discoveries. Marco Polo's Journeys to the Orient. Multicoloured.
42 14k. Type **23** . . . . 1·10 1·25
43 14k. Marco Polo and woman on fantasy animals . . . . 1·10 1·25

24 Benes

26 Crayon Figures

25 Cubist Flats by Josef Chochol, Prague

1994. 110th Birth Anniv of Edvard Benes (President of Czechoslovakia 1935–38 and 1945–48).
44 **24** 5k. violet and purple . . . 40 20

1994. U.N.E.S.C.O. World Heritage Sites. Mult.
45 8k. Market place, Telc . . . . 1·10 60
46 9k. Type **25** . . . . 1·25 75
No. 45 is similar to Type **6**.

1994. For Children.
47 **26** 2k. multicoloured 10 10

27 "Stegosaurus ungulatus"

1994. Prehistoric Animals. Multicoloured.
48 2k. Type **27** 20 10
49 3k. "Apatosaurus excelsus" . . 30 10
50 5k. "Tarbosaurus bataar" (vert) 50 30

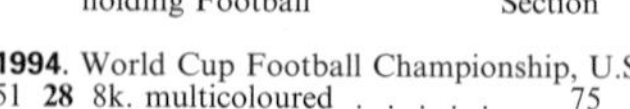
28 Statue of Liberty holding Football — 29 Flag of Prague Section

1994. World Cup Football Championship, U.S.A.
51 **28** 8k. multicoloured 75 45

1994. 12th Sokol (sports organization) Congress, Prague.
52 **29** 2k. multicoloured 10 15

30 Olympic Flag and Flame

1994. Centenary of Int Olympic Committee.
53 **30** 7k. multicoloured 60 40

31 Stylized Carrier Pigeons

1994. 120th Anniv of Universal Postal Union.
54 **31** 11k. multicoloured 90 80

32 Common Stonechat

33 NW, 1900

1994. Birds. Multicoloured.
55 3k. Type **32** 20 15
56 5k. Common rosefinch 30 25
57 14k. Bluethroat . . . . 1·25 75

1994. Racing Cars. Multicoloured.
58 2k. Type **33** 15 15
59 3k. L & K, 1908 . . . . . . 25 15
60 9k. Praga, 1912 . . . . 70 45

34 Angel

35 Emblem

1994. Christmas.
61 **34** 2k. multicoloured 10 10

1994. Art (2nd series). As T **16**.
62 7k. black and buff 48 55
63 10k. multicoloured 95 10
64 14k. multicoloured . . . . . 1·60 1·10
DESIGNS—VERT: 7k. "The Old Man and the Woman" (Lucas van Leyden); 10k. "Moulin Rouge" (Henri de Toulouse-Lautrec); 14k. "Madonna of St. Vitus".

1995. 20th Anniv of World Tourism Organization.
65 **35** 8k. blue and red 70 45

36 E.U. and Czech Republic Flags — 37 Engraver's Transposition of 1918 Czechoslovakia 2h. Newspaper Stamp

1995. Association Agreement with European Union.
66 **36** 8k. multicoloured 70 45

1995. Czech Stamp Production.
67 **37** 3k. blue, grey and red . . . 25 20

38 Johannes Marcus Marci

39 Jiri Voskovec (actor and dramatist)

1995. Birth Anniversaries.
68 **38** 2k. sepia, stone & brown . . 20 10
69 – 5k. multicoloured 35 30
70 – 7k. purple, grey & mauve 70 35

DESIGNS: 2k. Type **38** (academic, 400th anniv); 5k. Ferdinand Peroutka (journalist and dramatist, centenary); 7k. Premysl Pitter (founder of Youth Care Centre, centenary).

1995. 90th Birth Anniversaries of Members of the Liberated Theatre, Prague. Caricatures from posters by Adolf Hoffmeister.

71 **39** 3k. black, yellow & orange . . 25 10
72 – 3k. black, yellow & green . . 25 10
73 – 3k. black, yellow & blue . . 25·00 10

DESIGNS: No. 72, Jan Werich (dramatist and actor); 73, Jaroslav Jezek (composer) (anniv 1996).

40 Church and Buildings

41 Buff-tailed Bumble Bee

1995. Townscapes.

75 **40** 40h. brown and pink . . . 10 10
76 – 60h. brown and stone . . . 10 10

DESIGN: 60h. Buildings, church and archway.

1995. European Nature Conservation Year. Endangered Insects. Multicoloured.

84 3k. Type **41** 25 10
85 5k. Praying mantis 40 30
86 6k. Banded agrion 55 30

42 Sandstone Arch, Labske Piskovce

1995. Rock Formations. Multicoloured.

87 8k. Stone Organ (basalt columns), Central Bohemia 85 60
88 9k. Type **42** 85 70

43 Rose and Women's Profiles

1995. Europa. Peace and Freedom. Multicoloured.

89 9k. Type **43** 85 40
90 14k. Butterfly, girl and profiles of ageing woman . . . . . 1·10 70

44 Cat

46 Wrestlers

45 Early Steam Train leaving Chocen Tunnel

1995. For Children.

91 **44** 3k.60 multicoloured 40 25

1995. 150th Anniv of Olomouc–Prague Railway.

92 **45** 3k. black, brown & blue . . 35 10
93 – 9k.60 black, brown & red 70 40

DESIGN: 9k.60. Crowd welcoming arrival of first train at Prague.

1995. World Greco-Roman Wrestling Championship, Prague.

94 **46** 3k. brown, stone and red . . 40 10

47 Violinist and Washerwoman (Vladimir Rencin)

49 Houses around smiling Sun

1995. Cartoons. Cartoons by named artists. Multicoloured.

95 3k. Type **47** 20 10
96 3k.60 Angel and naked man (Vladimir Jiranek) 30 10
97 5k. Champagne cork flying through ringmaster's hoop (Jiri Sliva) 40 30

1995. 25th Anniv of SOS Children's Villages.

99 **49** 3k. multicoloured 25 10

50 Gothic Window

51 Rontgen and X-Ray Tube

1995. Architectural Styles.

101 **50** 2k.40 red and green . . . 10 10
102 – 3k. green and blue 25 10
103 – 3k.60 violet and green . . 35 10
104 – 4k. blue and red . . . . . 30·00 15
105 – 4k.60 mauve and green . . 40 10
107 – 9k.60 blue and mauve . . 70 45
108 – 12k.60 brown and blue . . 85 45
109 – 14k. green and mauve . . 1·25 55

DESIGNS: 3k. Secession window; 3k.60, Roman window; 4k. Classicist doorway; 4k.60, Rococo window; 9k.60, Renaissance doorway; 12k.60, Cubist window; 14k. Baroque doorway.

1995. Centenary of Discovery of X-Rays by Wilhelm Rontgen.

113 **51** 6k. buff, black & violet . . 55 25

52 Emblem

1995. 50th Anniv of U.N.O.

114 **52** 14k. multicoloured . . . . 1·25 65

53 Christmas Tree

55 Stamp Design by Jaroslav Benda

54 Allegory of Music

1995. Christmas.

115 **53** 3k. multicoloured 25 20

1995. Art (3rd series). As T **16**.

116 6k. black, blue and buff . . . 45 45
117 9k. multicoloured 75 60
118 14k. multicoloured . . . . . 1·25 90

DESIGNS: 6k. "Parisienne" (Ludek Marold); 9k. "Bouquet" (J. K. Hirschely); 14k. "Portrait of the Sculptor Josef Malinsky" (Antonin Machek).

1996. Cent of Czech Philharmonic Orchestra.

119 **54** 3k.60 multicoloured . . . 30 30

1996. Tradition of Czech Stamp Production.

120 **55** 3k.60 multicoloured . . . 30 20

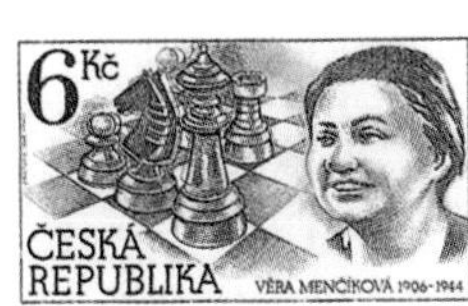

56 Mencikova and Chessmen

1996. 90th Birth Anniv of Vera Mencikova (chess champion).

121 **56** 6k. black, buff and red . . 50 30

57 Woman with Bowl of Easter Eggs

58 Sudek and Camera

1996. Easter.

122 **57** 3k. multicoloured 25 20

1996. Birth Cent of Josef Sudek (photographer).

123 **58** 9k.60 buff, black & grey 80 45

59 Jiri Guth-Jarkovsky (first President of National Olympic Committee) and Stadium

62 Ema Destinnova (singer)

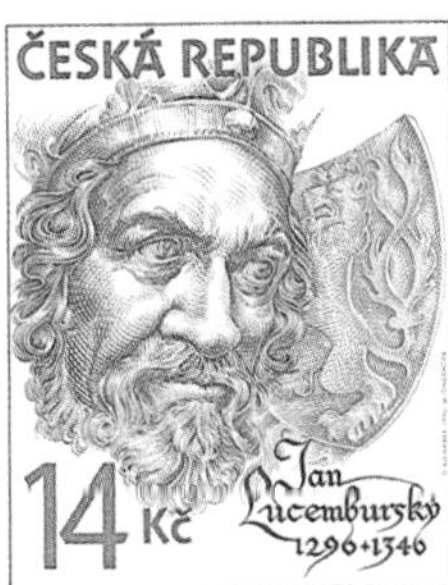

60 Jan (John the Blind)

1996. Centenary of Modern Olympic Games.

124 **59** 9k.60 multicoloured . . . 80 45

1996. Bohemian Kings of the Luxembourg Dynasty.

125 **60** 14k. blue, grey & purple 1·25 90
126 – 14k. green, grey & purple 1·25 90
127 – 14k. green, grey & purple 1·25 90
128 – 14k. blue, grey & purple 1·25 90

DESIGNS: No. 126, Karel (Charles IV, Holy Roman Emperor); 127, Vaclav IV; 128, Sigismund.

1996. Europa. Famous Women.

130 **62** 8k. lilac, black & mauve 70 50

63 Entering Stage as Pierrot

64 Throwing the Javelin

1996. Birth Bicentenary of Jean Gasparde Deburau (mime actor).

131 **63** 12k. multicoloured 90 50

1996. Olympic Games, Atlanta.

132 **64** 3k. multicoloured 25 10

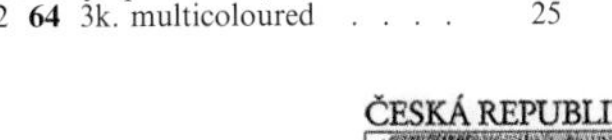

65 Boy and Girl on Cat

66 St. John of Nepomuk's Church, Zelena Hora

1996. For Children.

133 **65** 3k. multicoloured 25 10

1996. Tourist Sites. Multicoloured.

134 8k. Type **66** (U.N.E.S.C.O. World Heritage Site) . . . 65 50
135 9k. Prague Loretto 75 60

67 Boy playing Flute and Flowers forming Butterfly

1996. 50th Anniv of U.N.I.C.E.F.

136 **67** 3k. multicoloured . . . . 2·25 10

68 Black Horse

1996. Kladruby Horses. Multicoloured.

137 3k. Type **68** 25 10
138 3k. White horse 25 10

1996. Art (4th series). As T **16**. Multicoloured.

140 9k. "Eden" (Josef Vachal) . . 65 60
141 11k. "Breakfast with Egg" (Georg Flegel) (vert) . . . 90 75
142 20k. "Baroque Chair" (Endre Nemes) (vert) . . . . . . 1·50 1·10

70 Brahe

1996. 450th Birth Anniv of Tycho Brahe (astronomer).

143 **70** 5k. multicoloured 40 30

71 Letov S-1

72 Nativity

1996. Biplanes. Multicoloured.

144 7k. Type **71** 55 15
145 8k. Aero A-11 . . . . 65 20
146 10k. Avia BH-21 . . . . . . 80 35

1996. Christmas.

147 **72** 3k. multicoloured 25 10

73 Czechoslovakia 1920 Stamp Design of V. Brunner

74 Easter Symbols

1997. Czech Stamp Production.

148 **73** 3k.60 blue and red 25 10

1997. Easter.

149 **74** 3k. multicoloured 25 10

75 Dog's-tooth Violet

76 Girl and Cats ("Congratulations")

1997. Endangered Plants. Multicoloured.

150 3k.60 Type **75** 25 10
151 4k. Bog arum 35 10
152 5k. Lady's slipper 35 10
153 8k. Dwarf bearded iris . . . 70 30

1997. Greetings Stamp.

154 **76** 4k. multicoloured 30 10

77 St. Adalbert

78 Prince Bruncvik, Neomenie and Lion

1997. Death Millenary of St. Adalbert (Bishop of Prague).

155 **77** 7k. lilac 55 40

1997. Europa. Tales and Legends. Multicoloured.

156 8k. Type **78** 65 50
157 8k. King Wenceslas IV watching Zito the Magician in cart pulled by cocks . . 65 50·00

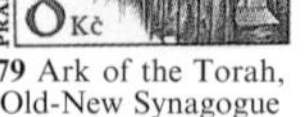

79 Ark of the Torah, Old-New Synagogue (east side)

81 Rakosnicek (cartoon character) and Rowan Berries

1997. Jewish Monuments in Prague. Each black, blue and red.

158 8k. Type **79** 70 50
159 10k. Grave of Rabbi Loew (Chief Rabbi of Prague), Old Jewish Cemetery . . . 75 60

1997. For Children.

161 **81** 4k.60 multicoloured . . . 40 10

82 Krizik and Arc Lamp

1997. 150th Birth Anniv of Frantisek Krizik (electrical engineer).

162 **82** 6k. pink, blue and red . . 45 20

83 Swimmer

1997. European Swimming and Diving Championships, Prague.

163 **83** 11k. black, buff & blue . . 75 40

84 Mrs. Muller and Svejk in Wheelchair

1997. 110th Anniv of "Fortunes of the Good Soldier Svejk" (novel by Jaroslav Hasek). Illustrations by Josef Lada. Multicoloured.

164 4k. Type **84** 35 15
165 4k.60 Lt. Lukas and Col. Kraus von Zillergut with stolen dog 35 15
166 6k. Svejk smoking pipe . . . 40 35

85 Prague Castle

1997. "Praga 1998" International Stamp Exhibition. Multicoloured.

167 15k. Type **85** . . . . . . 1·00 75
168 15k. View of Prague Old Town . . . . 1·00 75

86 Post Bus, 1928

1997. Historic Service Vehicles. Multicoloured.

170 4k. Type **86** 30 10
171 4k.60 Škoda Sentinel lorry, 1924 . . . . 30 20
172 8k. Tatra fire engine, 1933 . . 60 45

87 Carp, Candle, Fir, Apple and Nut

88 Olympic Rings and Ice Hockey Puck

1997. Christmas.

173 **87** 4k. multicoloured 30 10

1997. Art (5th series). As T **16**.

174 7k. multicoloured 35 15
175 12k. green and black . . . . 1·00 75
176 16k. multicoloured . . . . . 1·10 1·10

DESIGNS—HORIZ: 7k. "Landscape with Chateau in Chantilly" (Antonin Chittussi). VERT: 12k. "The Prophets came out of the Desert" (Frantisek Bilek); 16k. "Parisian Second-hand Booksellers" (T. F. Simon).

1998. Winter Olympic Games, Nagano, Japan.

177 **88** 7k. multicoloured 45 25

89 Jakub Obvrovsky's 1920 Design

90 Pres. Vaclav Havel

1998. Czech Stamp Production.

178 **89** 12k.60 brown and green . . 90 50

1998.

179 **90** 4k.60 green and red . . . 40 10
179a 5k.40 blue and brown . . 40 10
179b 6k.40 agate and blue . . 30 15

91 Cupid and Heart

92 Slalom

1998. St. Valentine's Day.

180 **91** 4k. multicoloured 30 10

1998. World Skibob Championships, Spindleruv Mlyn.

181 **92** 8k. multicoloured 60 30

94 Chick in Egg Shell

1998. Easter.

183 **94** 4k. multicoloured 30 10

95 Observatory Building and Telescope Dome

1998. Centenary of Ondrejov Observatory.

184 **95** 4k.60 yellow, black & red 40 30

98 Grey Partridge

99 Book and Copyright Symbol

1998. Endangered Species. Multicoloured.

187 4k.60 Type **98** 40 30
188 4k.60 Black grouse ("Lyrurus tetrix") 40 60
189 8k. White deer ("Cervus elphus") 50 30
190 8k. Elk ("Alces alces") . . . 50 45

1998. World Book and Copyright Day.

191 **99** 10k. multicoloured 75 30

100 The King's Ride, Moravia

1998. Europa. National Festivals. Multicoloured.

192 11k. Type **100** 75 55
193 15k. Carnival masks . . . . 1·10 70

101 Devil Musicians

102 Frantisek Kmoch (composer)

1998. For Children. Multicoloured.

194 4k. Type **101** 30 10
195 4k.60 Water sprite riding catfish 35 10

1998. Anniversaries. Multicoloured.

196 4k. Type **102** (150th birth anniv) 30 10
197 4k.60 Frantisek Palacky (historian, birth bicent) . . 40 30
198 6k. Rafael Kubelik (conductor, 2nd death anniv) 45 30

103 Prague Barricades, June 1848

1998. 150th Anniv of 1848 Revolutions.

199 **103** 15k. multicoloured . . . 1·10 60

1998. Art (6th series). As T **16**. Multicoloured.

200 22k. "Amorpha-Two-coloured Fugue" (Frantisek Kupka) . . . . 1·50 1·10
201 23k. "Flight" (Paul Gauguin) 1·50 1·25

104 St. Barbara's Cathedral, Kutna Hora

1998. World Heritage Sites. Multicoloured.

202 8k. Type **104** 60 30
203 11k. Chateau Valtice 90 45

105 Soldiers with Flags

106 Capricorn

1998. 80th Anniv of Founding of Czechoslovak Republic. Paintings by Vojtech Preissig. Mult.

204 4k.60 Type **105** 40 10
205 5k. Soldiers marching 40 30
206 12k.60 Flags in Mala Street, Prague . . . . 1·00 60

1998. Signs of the Zodiac.

206a – 40h green, brown & blk 10 10
207 **106** 1k. yellow, red and black 10 10
208 – 2k. black, lilac and blue 10 10
209 – 5k. red, black and yellow 40 10
210 – 5k.40 green, black & brn 40 10
211 – 8k. red, black & purple 50 30
212 – 9k. green, black & orge 60 30
213 – 10k. yellow, blue & black 75 30
214 – 12k. orange, blue & black 85 50
216 – 17k. multicoloured . . . 75 45
217 – 20k. violet, black & brn 1·40 70
218 – 26k. multicoloured . . . 1·10 65

DESIGNS: 40h. Pisces; 2k. Virgo; 5k. Taurus; 5k.40; Scorpio; 8k. Cancer; 9k. Libra; 10k. Aquarius; 12k. Leo; 17k. Gemini; 20k. Sagittarius; 26k. Aries.

107 People following Star

1998. Christmas. Multicoloured.

219 4k. Type **107** 25 15
220 6k. Angel with trumpet over village (vert) 50 90

1998. Art (7th series). As T **16**. Multicoloured.

221 15k. Section of "The Greater Cycle" (Jan Preisler) . . . 1·10 90
222 16k. "Spinner" (Josef Navratil) (vert) . . . . . 1·40 1·00

108 1929 2k.50 Prague Stamp

1999. Czech Stamp Production.

223 **108** 4k.60 multicoloured . . . 40 20

109 Cat

110 Ornate Cockerel

1999. Cats. Multicoloured.

224 4k.60 Type **109** 35 15
225 5k. Cat with kitten 35 25
226 7k. Two cats 60 30

1999. Easter.

227 **110** 3k. multicoloured 25 10

111 Hoopoe

1999. Nature Conservation. Multicoloured.

228 4k.60 Type **111** 40 25
229 4k.60 European bee eater ("Merops apiaster") . . . 40 40

230 5k. "Euphydryas maturna" 40 25
231 5k. Rosy underwing ("Catocala electa") 40 25

112 Emblem

1999. Admission of Czech Republic into North Atlantic Treaty Organization.
232 **112** 4k.60 blue and red . . . 40 20

113 Emblem and Sky

1999. 50th Anniv of Council of Europe.
233 **113** 7k. multicoloured 55 20

114 Josef Rossler-Orovsky (co-founder)

1999. Centenary of Czech Olympic Committee.
234 **114** 9k. multicoloured 65 40

115 Sumava National Park

1999. Europa. Parks and Gardens. Multicoloured.
235 11k. Type **115** 85 50
236 17k. Podyji National Park . . 1·25 75

116 "Ferda the Ant, Pytlik the Beetle and The Proud Ladybird"

117 Chain Bridge, Stadlec

1999. For Children. Birth Centenary of Ondrej Sekora (children's writer).
237 **116** 4k.60 multicoloured . . . 30 10

1999. Bridges. Multicoloured.
238 8k. Type **117** 60 40
239 11k. Wooden bridge, Cernvir (horiz) 85 55

118 King Wenceslas I handing over Grant and Miners

1999. 750th Anniv of Granting of Jihlava Mining Rights.
240 **118** 8k. multicoloured 60 30

119 "UPU", Globe and Emblem

121 Priessnitz and Treatments

1999. 125th Anniv of Universal Postal Union.
241 **119** 9k. black, blue and green 60 45

1999. Birth Bicent of Vincenc Priessnitz (folk healer).
243 **121** 4k.60 multicoloured . . . 30 10

122 Woman

123 Clown Doctor and Laughing New-born Baby

1999. Folk Art. Beehives. Multicoloured.
244 4k.60 Type **122** 20 15
245 5k. St. Joseph with Infant Jesus 35 25
246 7k. Sweeper 65 25

1999. Graphic Humour of Miroslav Bartak. Multicoloured.
247 4k.60 Type **123** 25 10
248 5k. Dog disobeying No Smoking and No Dogs sign 40 30
249 7k. Night sky seeping in under window 65 30

125 Baby Jesus with Sheep and Lamb

127 Czechoslovakia 1938 1k.+50h. Child Welfare Stamp

1999. Christmas.
251 **125** 3k. multicoloured 25 10

1999. Art (8th series). As T **16**. Multicoloured.
252 13k. "Red Orchid" (Jindrich Styrsky) (vert) 90 70
253 17k. "Landscape with Marsh" (Julius Marak) (vert) . . . . 1·25 95
254 26k. "Monument" (Frantisek Hudecek) (vert) . . . . . 1·60 1·40

2000. Czech Stamp Production.
257 **127** 5k.40 multicoloured . . . 40 25

128 Kutna Hora Coat of Arms and 14th-century Miners

130 Animal-shaped Cake and Painted Eggs

2000. 700th Anniv of Granting of Royal Mining Rights to Kutn Hora.
258 **128** 5k. multicoloured 40 25

2000. Easter.
260 **130** 5k. multicoloured 40 30

132 Vitezslav Nezval (poet) (centenary)

134 "Building Europe"

2000. Birth Anniversaries.
262 **132** 5k. blue, lilac and violet 40 25
263 – 8k. mauve, red and violet 50 35
DESIGN: 8k. Gustav Mahler (composer, 140th anniv).

2000. Europa.
265 **134** 9k. multicoloured 60 40

135 Alarm Clock and Bird

137 *Geastrum pouzarii*

136 Fermat's Great Theorem

2000. International Children's Day.
266 **135** 5k.40 multicoloured . . . 40 25

2000. World Mathematics Year.
267 **136** 7k. multicoloured 45 40

2000. Endangered Fungi. Multicoloured.
268 5k. Type **137** 20 25
269 5k. Devil's boletus (*Boletus satanas*) 20 25
270 5k.40 *Verpa bohemica* . . . 30 30
271 5k.40 *Morchella pragensis* . . 30 30

138 Old Town Bridge Tower

2000. Historic Buildings. Multicoloured.
272 9k. Type **138** 35 55
273 11k. St. Nicolas's Church . . 45 55
274 13k. Municipal Hall 55 65

139 Leaves

2000. Annual International Monetary Fund and World Bank Group Meeting, Prague.
275 **139** 7k. multicoloured 55 40

140 Chariot Racing (detail from amphora)

2000. Olympic Games, Sydney.
276 **140** 9k. red, black and green 60 50
277 – 13k. multicoloured . . . 90 65
DESIGN: 13k. Canoeing and Czech flag.

141 Northern Goshawk and Common Pheasant (Autumn)

142 Nativity

2000. Hunting and Gamekeeping. Multicoloured.
278 5k. Type **141** 20 30
279 5k. Deer (winter) 20 45
280 5k.40 Mallard and ducklings (spring) 25 30
281 5k.40 Deer (summer) 25 30

2000. Art (9th series). As T **16**. Multicoloured.
282 13k. "St. Luke the Evangelist" (Master Theodoricus) (vert) 90 65
283 17k. "Simon with the Infant Jesus" (Petr Jan Brandl) (vert) . . . . 1·10 75
284 26k. "Brunette" (Alfons Mucha) (vert) . . . . . . 1·60 1·40

2000. Christmas.
285 **142** 5k. multicoloured 40 25

143 Cat

144 Czechoslovakia 1951 5c. Stamp

2000. Old and New Millennia. Multicoloured.
286 9k. Type **143** 60 50
287 9k. Magician pulling rabbit from hat 60 50

2001. Czech Stamp Production. 150th Birth Anniv of Alois Jirasek (writer).
288 **144** 5k.40 multicoloured . . . 40 25

145 Jan Amos Komensky (Comenius) (philosopher)

146 Cockerel and Woman

2001.
289 **145** 9k. black, red and brown 60 50

2001. Easter.
290 **146** 5k.40 multicoloured . . . 40 25

149 Pond

2001. Europa. Water Resources.
293 **149** 9k. lilac and black 60 45

150 Players

151 Maxipes Fik riding Bicycle

2001. Men's European Volleyball Championship, Ostrava.
294 **150** 12k. multicoloured . . . 1·00 65

2001. International Children's Day. *Vecernicek* (cartoon created by Rudolf Cechura).
295 **151** 5k.40 multicoloured . . . 1·00 25

152 Frantisek Skroup (composer)

153 Cats

2001. Birth Anniversaries. Multicoloured.
296 5k.40 Type **152** (bicentenary) 35 25
297 16k. Frantisek Halas (poet, centenary) . . . . 1·10 60

2001. Greetings Stamp. "Congratulations".
298 **153** 5k.40 multicoloured . . . 40 25

154 West Highland White Terrier

2001. Dogs. Multicoloured.
299 5k.40 Type **154** 35 25
300 5k.40 Beagle 35 25
301 5k.40 Golden retriever . . . 35 25
302 5k.40 German shepherd . . . 35 25

155 Fennec Fox (*Fennecus zerda*)

2001. Zoo Animals. Multicoloured.
303 5k.40 Type **155** 35 25
304 5k.40 Lesser panda (*Ailurus fulgens*) 35 25
305 5k.40 Siberian tiger (*Panthera tigris altaica*) 35 25
306 5k.40 Orang-utan (*Pongo pygmaeus*) 35 25

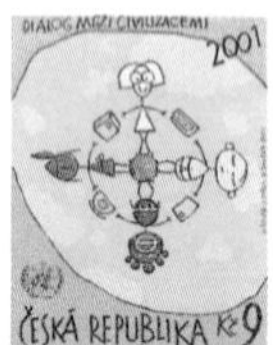

156 Emblem

157 Windmill, Kuzelov

2001. "Dialogue between Civilizations".
307 **156** 9k. multicoloured 60 40

2001. Mills. Multicoloured.
308 9k. Type **157** 50 50
309 14k.40 Water mill, Strehom 80 70

158 Kromeriz Chateau

2001. U.N.E.S.C.O. World Heritage Sites. Mult.
310 12k. Type **158** 75 60
311 14k. Holasovice village . . . 70 70

2001. Art (10th series). As T **16**.
312 12k. black, buff and blue . . 80 75
313 17k. multicoloured . . . . . 1·25 90
314 26k. multicoloured . . . . . 1·90 1·50
DESIGNS—VERT: 12k. "The Annunciation of the Virgin Mary" (Michael Jindrich Rentz); 17k. "Sans-Souci Bar in Nimes" (Cyril Bouda); 26k. "The Goose Keeper" (Vaclav Brozik).

159 Christmas Tree and Half Moon carrying Gifts

160 1938 2k. Stamp

2001. Christmas.
315 **159** 5k.40 multicoloured . . . 40 25

2002. 40th Death Anniv of Max Svabinsky (stamp designer).
316 **160** 5k.40 multicoloured . . . 40 30

161 Skier

162 Ski Jumper

2002. Winter Paralympic Games, Salt Lake City, U.S.A.
317 **161** 5k.40 multicoloured . . . 40 25

2002. Winter Olympic Games, Salt Lake City, U.S.A.
318 **162** 12k. multicoloured . . . 80 65

163 Girl with Easter Egg and Boy with Easter Sticks

2002. Easter.
319 **163** 5k.40 multicoloured . . . 25 15

164 Jaromir Vejvoda, Josef Poncar and Karel Vacek

2002. Composers' Birth Centenaries.
320 **164** 9k. black, red and violet 40 25

2002. No. 318 optd **ALES VALENTA ZLATA MEDAILE**.
321 **162** 12k. multicoloured . . . 50 30

166 "Divan" (Vlaho Bukovac)

2002.
322 **166** 17k. multicoloured . . . 70 45
A stamp in a similar design was issued by Croatia.

167 Circus Tent, Clown and Lion

2002. Europa. Circus.
323 **167** 9k. multicoloured 40 25

168 "Piano Keys–Lake" (Frantisek Kupka)

169 Mole and Butterfly

2002. Art. Sheet 148 × 105 mm, containing T **169** and similar vert design. Multicoloured.
MS324 23k. Type **168**. 31k. "Man with Broken Nose" (bust) (Auguste Rodin) 95 95

2002. For Children.
325 **169** 5k.40 multicoloured . . . 25 15

170 Pearl Oysters

171 Hus

2002. Nature Conservation.
326 **170** 9k. multicoloured 40 25

2002. Jan Hus (clergyman and preacher) Commemoration.
327 **171** 9k. multicoloured 40 25

172 *Maculinea nausithous*

2002. Endangered Species. Butterflies. Sheet 109 × 65 mm, containing T **172** and similar horiz designs. Multicoloured.
MS328 5k.40, Type **172**; 5k.40, *Maculinea alcon*; 9k. *Maculinea teleius*; 9k. *Maculinea arion* 1·25 1·25

173 Pansy

174 Zatopek

2002. Flowers.
335 **173** 6k.40 multicoloured . . . 30 15

2002. 80th Birth Anniv of Emil Zatopek (athlete).
340 **174** 9k. multicoloured 45 25

175 Chateau, Litomysl, Bohemia

2002. U.N.E.S.C.O. World Heritage Sites. Mult.
341 12k. Type **175** 50 30
342 14k. Holy Trinity Column, Olumouc, Moravia (vert) 60 35

176 Angel, St. Nicholas with Basket of Gifts, and Devil

177 Star and Christmas Tree

2002. St Nicholas.
343 **176** 6k.40 multicoloured . . . 30 15

2002. Christmas.
344 **177** 6k.40 multicoloured . . . 30 15

178 Emblem

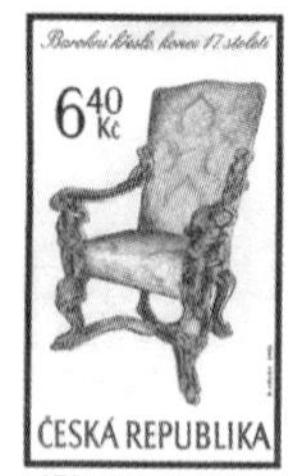

179 17th-century Armchair

2002. North Atlantic Treaty Organization Summit Meeting, Prague.
345 **178** 9k. azure, red and blue 40 25

2002. Antique Furniture. Multicoloured.
346 6k.40 Type **179** 30 15
347 9k. Sewing table, 1820 . . . 40 25
348 12k. Thonet dressing table, 1860 . . . . 50 30
349 17k. Armchair, 1923 . . . . 75 45

2002. Art (11th series). As T **16**.
350 12k. black and blue 50 30
351 20k. multicoloured 85 50
352 26k. multicoloured . . . . . 1·10 65
DESIGNS—HORIZ: 12k. "Forlorn Woman" (Jarsolav Panuska). VERT: 20k. "St. Wenceslas" (stained glass window) (Mikolas Ales); 26k. "Young Man with Lute" (Jan Peter Molitor).

180 Lion (statue, Josef Max)

2003. 10th Anniv of Czech Republic. Sheet 78 × 118 mm.
MS353 **180** 25k. brown, blue and red 1·10 1·10

181 Czechoslovakia 1937 2k.50 Stamp

182 Jaroslav Vrchlicky

2003. Czech Stamp Production. Jan C. Vondrous (stamp designer) and K. Seizinger (engraver) Commemoration.
354 **181** 6k.40 multicoloured . . . 30 15

2003. 150th Birth Anniversaries. Multicoloured.
355 6k.40 Type **182** (writer) . . . 30 15
356 8k. Josef Thomayer (physician and writer) . . . 35 20

DAHOMEY Pt. 6; Pt. 12

A French colony on the W. Coast of Africa, incorporated in French West Africa in 1944. In 1958 it became an autonomous republic within the French Community, and in 1960 was proclaimed fully independent. The area used the issues of French West Africa from 1944 until 1960.

100 centimes = 1 franc.

1899. "Tablet" key-type inscr "DAHOMEY ET DEPENDANCES".
1 D 1c. black and red on blue . . 85 90
2 2c. brown & blue on buff . . 60 70
3 4c. brown & blue on grey . . 1·40 1·50
4 5c. green and red . . . . . . 2·75 1·10
5 10c. red and blue . . . . . . 3·25 2·50
6 15c. grey and red . . . . . . 4·00 1·75
7 20c. red & blue on green . . 9·00 14·50
8 25c. black & red on pink . . 6·75 3·50
9 25c. blue and red . . . . . . 6·75 11·50
10 30c. brown & bl on drab . . 13·50 17·00
11 40c. red & blue on yellow 9·00 8·75
12 50c. brown & red on blue 10·00 21·00
13 50c. brown & blue on blue 32·00 17·00
14 75c. brown & red on orge 65·00 50·00
15 1f. green and red . . . . . . 32·00 32·00
16 2f. violet and red on pink . . 80·00 85·00
17 5f. mauve & blue on blue . . 85·00 90·00

1906. "Faidherbe", "Palms" and "Balay" key-types inscr "DAHOMEY".
18 I 1c. grey and red . . . . . . 1·40 85
19 2c. brown and red . . . . . 1·40 65
20 4c. brown & red on blue . . 1·90 1·25
21 5c. green and red . . . . . 4·75 50
22 10c. pink and blue . . . . . 19·00 55
23 J 20c. black & red on blue . . 9·50 9·00
24 25c. blue and red . . . . . 6·00 6·25
25 30c. brown & red on pink 12·50 13·00
26 35c. black & red on yellow 45·00 5·00
27 45c. brown & red on green 16·00 17·00
28 50c. violet and red . . . . . 11·50 16·00
29 75c. green & red on orange 16·00 19·00
30 K 1f. black and red on blue . . 23·00 32·00
31 2f. blue and red on pink . . 90·00 85·00
32 5f. red & blue on yellow . . £100 £110

1912. Surch in figures.
33 05 on 2c. brown & blue on buff . . . . 85 1·25
34 05 on 4c. brown & blue on grey . . . . 95 1·40
35 05 on 15c. grey and red . . . 1·10 2·00
36 05 on 20c. red & blue on green . . . . 80 2·25
37 05 on 25c. blue and red . . . 1·25 3·00
38 05 on 30c. brown & bl on drab . . . . 95 1·75
39 10c. on 40c. red & bl on yellow . . . . 85 1·00
40 10c. on 50c. brn & bl on blue 1·10 2·75
40a 10c. on 50c. brn & red on blue £850 £900
41 10c. on 75c. brown and red on orange . . . . 4·50 8·00

6 Native Climbing Palm

11 Rene Caillie

1913.
42 6 1c. black and violet 10 15
43 2c. pink and brown 10 20
44 4c. brown and black 10 45
45 5c. green and light green . . 1·40 70
60 5c. violet and purple 15 45
46 10c. pink and red . . . . . 1·75 55
61 10c. green and lt green . . . 75 1·25
75 10c. green and red 10 10
47 15c. purple and brown . . . 20 25
48 20c. brown and grey . . . . 60 1·10
76 20c. green . . . . 15 1·40
77 20c. black and mauve . . . 15 60
49 25c. blue & ultramarine . . . 2·50 1·60
62 25c. orange and purple . . . 20 20
50 30c. violet and brown . . . 3·00 4·00
63 30c. carmine and red . . . 95 4·00
78 30c. violet and yellow . . . 60 50
79 30c. green and olive 50 75
51 35c. black and brown . . . 1·10 1·75
80 35c. green and turquoise . . 85 3·25
52 40c. orange and black . . . 65 70
53 45c. blue and grey . . . . . 70 2·50
54 50c. brown & chocolate . . 4·50 6·50
64 50c. blue & ultramarine . . . 20 2·25
81 50c. blue and red 20 20
82 55c. brown and green . . . 50 2·50
83 60c. violet on pink . . . . 1·75 2·75
84 65c. green and brown 25 95
55 75c. violet and blue 35 55
85 80c. blue and brown . . . . 50 3·00
86 85c. pink and blue . . . . . 50 2·75
87 90c. red and carmine . . . . 75 1·90
87a 90c. red and brown . . . . 1·40 3·25
56 1f. black and green . . . . 65 1·00
88 1f. light blue and blue . . . 1·25 1·00
89 1f. red and brown 50 45
90 1f. red and light red . . . . 2·00 2·75
91 1f.10 brown and violet . . . 3·25 4·50
92 1f.25 brown and blue . . . 17·00 18·00
93 1f.50 light blue and blue . . 2·50 2·00
94 1f.75 orange and brown . . 3·75 3·50
94a 1f.75 ultramarine & blue . . 60 2·00
57 2f. brown and yellow . . . 1·00 65
95 3f. mauve on pink . . . . . 3·00 3·00
58 5f. blue and violet . . . . . 2·50 3·50

1915. Surch 5c and red cross.
59 6 10c.+5c. pink and red . . . . 45 2·00

1922. Surch in figures and bars.
65 6 25c. on 2f. brown & yellow 1·40 3·00
66 60 on 75c. violet on pink . . 25 2·75
67 65 on 15c. purple & brown 1·60 3·75
68 85 on 15c. purple & brown 1·75 3·75
69 90c. on 75c. red and carmine 2·00 3·50
70 1f.25 on 1f. lt blue & blue . . 45 3·00
71 1f.50 on 1f. lt blue & blue . . 1·40 1·90
72 3f. on 5f. red and green . . . 6·50 10·00
73 10f. on 5f. brown & blue . . 4·25 7·00
74 20f. on 5f. green and red . . 2·50 8·00

1931. "Colonial Exhibition" key-types inscr "DAHOMEY".
96 E 40c. green . . . . 5·00 7·50
97 F 50c. mauve . . . . 5·25 7·25
98 G 90c. red . . . . 5·50 6·75
99 H 1f.50 blue . . . . 5·50 7·00

1937. Paris Int Exn. As Nos. 110/15 of Cameroun.
100 20c. violet . . . . 1·25 3·25
101 30c. green . . . . 1·00 3·00
102 40c. red . . . . 65 3·25
103 50c. brown . . . . 1·00 2·00
104 90c. red . . . . 70 2·25
105 1f.50 blue . . . . 60 1·60

1938. Int Anti-cancer Fund. As T **19** of Cameroun.
106 1f.75+50c. blue . . . . . . 5·00 15·00

1939. Death Centenary of R. Caillie (explorer).
107 **11** 90c. orange . . . . 40 2·00
108 2f. violet . . . . 95 3·25
109 2f.25 blue . . . . 1·25 3·50

1939. New York World's Fair. As T **20** of Cameroun.
110 1f.25 red . . . . 1·90 3·00
111 2f.25 blue . . . . 2·00 2·25

1939. 150th Anniv of French Revolution. As T **25** of Cameroun.
112 45c.+25c. green . . . . . . 4·25 11·00
113 70c.+30c. brown . . . . . . 5·25 11·00
114 90c.+35c. orange . . . . . 4·50 11·00
115 1f.25+1f. red . . . . 4·50 11·00
116 2f.25+2f. blue . . . . 4·25 11·00

12 African Landscape

13 Native Poling Canoe

1940. Air.
117 **12** 1f.90 blue . . . . 1·25 2·50
118 2f.90 red . . . . 1·25 3·00
119 4f.50 green . . . . 1·40 2·75
120 4f.90 olive . . . . 1·10 2·75
121 6f.90 orange . . . . 90 3·25

1941.
122 **13** 2c. red . . . . 15 1·25
123 3c. blue . . . . 15 2·50
124 5c. violet . . . . 95 2·75
125 10c. green . . . . 25 2·50
126 15c. black . . . . 15 2·25
127 – 20c. brown . . . . 1·10 2·75
128 – 30c. violet . . . . 45 2·75
129 – 40c. red . . . . 55 2·75
130 – 50c. green . . . . 95 2·75
131 – 60c. black . . . . 65 2·75
132 – 70c. mauve . . . . 1·75 3·25
133 – 80c. black . . . . 1·10 2·75
134 – 1f. violet 30 35
135 – 1f.30 violet . . . . 1·00 3·25
136 – 1f.40 green . . . . 1·75 3·25
137 – 1f.50 red . . . . 1·25 3·00
138 – 2f. orange . . . . 95 3·50
139 – 2f.50 blue . . . . 1·90 3·25
140 – 3f. red . . . . 55 2·75
141 – 5f. green . . . . 60 2·25
142 – 10f. brown . . . . 70 4·00
143 – 20f. black . . . . 1·00 4·50
DESIGNS HORIZ: 20c. to 70c. Village on piles. VERT: 80c. to 2f. Sailing pirogue on Lake Nokoue; 2f.50 to 20f. Dahomey warrior.

1941. National Defence Fund. Surch **SECOURS NATIONAL** and value.
143a 6 +1f. on 50c. blue & red . . 3·75 5·50
143b +2f. on 80c. blue & brn . . 4·50 6·25
143c +2f. on 1f.50 lt blue & bl 6·00 9·25
143d +3f. on 2f. brown & yell 6·00 8·25

14b Village on Piles and Marshal Petain

1942. Marshal Petain Issue.
143e **14b** 1f. green . . . . 40 2·75
143f 2f.50 blue . . . . 25 3·00

14c Maternity Hospital, Dakar

1942. Air. Colonial Child Welfare Fund.
143g **14c** 1f.50+3f.50 green . . . . 20 2·50
143h – 2f.+6f. brown . . . . . 20 2·50
143i – 3f.+9f. red . . . . . . 90 2·50
DESIGNS: 2f. Dispensary, Mopti. (48½ × 27 mm): 3f. "Child welfare".

14d "Vocation"

1942. Air. "Imperial Fortnight".
143j **14d** 1f.20+1f.80 blue & red 1·10 2·50

14e Camel Caravan

1942. Air.
143k **14e** 50f. blue and green . . . 3·75 4·75

15 Ganvie Village

1960.
144 **15** 25f. brn, red & bl (postage) 75 25
145 – 100f. brown, ochre & bl (air) . . . . 3·25 2·25
146 – 500f. red, bistre & green 12·00 4·25
DESIGNS: 100f. Somba fort; 500f. Royal Court, Abomey.

1960. 10th Anniv of African Technical Co-operation Commission. As T **62** of Cameroun.
147 5f. blue and purple . . . . . 1·60 2·00

16 Conseil de l'Entente Emblem

17 Prime Minister Maga

1960. 1st Anniv of Conseil de l'Entente.
148 **16** 25f. multicoloured . . . . 1·75 1·90

1960. Independence Proclamation.
149 **17** 85f. purple and sepia . . . 90 55

18 Weaver

1961. Artisans.
150 **18** 1f. purple and orange . . . 10 10
151 – 2f. chocolate and brown 10 10
152 – 3f. orange and green . . . 10 10
153 – 4f. lake and bistre 15 15
154 **18** 6f. red and lilac 15 15
155 – 10f. myrtle and blue . . . 25 20
156 – 15f. violet and purple . . . 35 25
157 – 20f. turquoise and blue . . 45 30
DESIGNS—VERT: 2f., 10f. Wood-carver. HORIZ: 3f., 15f. Fisherman casting net; 4f., 20f. Potter.

1961. 1st Anniv of Independence. No. 149 surch **100 F President de la Republique**.
158 **17** 100f. on 85f. pur & sepia 1·50 1·50

20 Doves and U.N. Emblem

22 Wrecked Car and Fort

1961. 1st Anniv of Admission into U.N.O.
159 **20** 5f. multicoloured (postage) 25 20
160 60f. multicoloured 75 60
161 200f. multicoloured (air) 2·50 1·90

1961. Abidjan Games. Optd **JEUX SPORTIFS D'ABIDJAN 24 AU 31 DECEMBRE 1961**.
162 **15** 25f. brown, red and blue 45 30

1962. Air. Foundation of "Air Afrique" Airline. As T **69** of Cameroun.
163 25f. blue, brown & black . . 45 35

1962. Malaria Eradication. As T **70** of Cameroun.
164 25f.+5f. brown 45 45

1962. 1st Anniv of Portuguese Evacuation from Fort Ouidah.
165 **22** 30f. multicoloured 45 25
166 60f. multicoloured 70 40

1962. 1st Anniv of Union of African and Malagasy States. As No. 328 of Cameroun.
167 **72** 30f. multicoloured 50 35

23 Map, Nurses and Patients

1962. Red Cross.
168 **23** 5f. red, blue and purple . . 15 15
169 20f. red, blue and green . . 30 25
170 25f. red, blue and sepia . . 40 30
171 30f. red, blue and brown 45 40

24 Peuhl Herd-boy

25 Boxing

1963. Dahomey Tribes.
172 A 2f. violet and blue 10 10
173 B 3f. black and blue 10 10
174 **24** 5f. green, brown & black 15 10
175 C 15f. brown, chest & turq 25 15
176 D 20f. black, red & green . . 40 20
177 E 25f. turquiose, brown & bl 40 15
178 D 30f. brown, mauve & red 45 30
179 E 40f. blue, brown, & green 55 25
180 C 50f. brown, black & green 65 30
181 **24** 60f. orange, red & purple 70 45
182 B 65f. brown and red 90 50
183 A 85f. brown and blue . . . 1·50 75
DESIGNS—VERT: A, Ganvie girl in pirogue; B, Bariba chief of Nikki; C, Ouidah witch-doctor and python; D, Nessoukoue witch-doctors of Abomey. HORIZ: E, Dahomey girl.

1963. Freedom from Hunger. As T **76** of Cameroun.
184 25f.+5f. red, brown & green 50 50

1963. Dakar Games.
185 **25** 50c. black and green . . . 10 10
186 – 1f. black, bistre & brown 10 10
187 – 2f. brown, blue & bronze 10 10
188 – 5f. black, red & brown . . 15 10
189 **25** 15f. purple and violet . . . 25 20
190 – 20f. black, green & red . . 40 30
DESIGNS—HORIZ: 1f., 20f. Football. VERT: 2f., 5f. Running.

27 U.A.M. Palace

1963. Air. Meeting of Heads of State of African and Malagasy Union.
191 **27** 250f. multicoloured . . . . 3·00 1·75

28 Presidential Palace, Cotonou

1963. 3rd Anniv of Independence.
192 **28** 25f. multicoloured 35 25

1963. Air. African and Malagasy Posts and Telecommunications Union. As T **18** of Central African Republic.
193 25f. red, buff, brown & blue 40 25

29 Boeing 707 Airliner

1963. Air.
194 **29** 100f. bistre, green & violet 1·75 60
195 – 200f. violet, brown & grn 3·00 1·60
196 – 300f. purple, grn and blue 4·25 2·25
197 – 500f. purple, brown & blue 7·75 3·25
DESIGNS: 200f. Aerial views of Boeing 707; 300f. Cotonou Airport; 500f. Boeing 707 in flight.

30 Toussaint L'Ouverture

31 Flame on U.N. Emblem

1963. 150th Death Anniv of Toussaint L'Ouverture (Haitian statesman).
198 **30** 25f. multicoloured 35 20
199 30f. multicoloured 40 25
200 100f. multicoloured . . . . 1·10 65

1963. 15th Anniv of Declaration of Human Rights. Multicoloured. Background colours given.
201 **31** 4f. blue 10 10
202 6f. brown 15 15
203 25f. green 35 25

32 Sacred Boat of Isis, Philae

1964. Air. Nubian Monuments Preservation.
204 **32** 25f. brown and violet . . . 80 50

33 Somba Dance (Taneka Coco)

1964. Native Dances.
205 **33** 2f. black, red and green . . 10 10
206 – 3f. red, green and blue . . 10 10
207 – 10f. black, red & violet . . 20 15
208 – 15f. sepia, lake & green . . 25 15
209 – 25f. blue, brown and orge 40 25
210 – 30f. red, orange & brown 45 30
DANCES—HORIZ: 3f. Nago (Pobe-Ketou). 15f. Nago (Ouidah). 30f. Nessou houessi (Abomey). VERT: 10f. Baton (Paysbariba). 25f. Sakpatassi (Abomey).

34 Running

1964. Olympic Games, Tokyo.
211 **34** 60f. green and brown . . . 65 50
212 – 85f. purple and blue . . . 1·25 75
DESIGN: 85f. Cycling.

1964. French, African and Malagasy Co-operation. As T **88** of Cameroun.
213 25f. brown, violet & orange 40 25

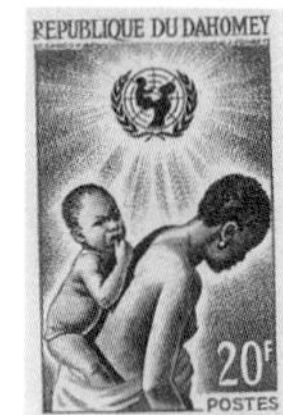

35 Mother and Child

36 Satellite and Sun

1964. 18th Anniv of U.N.I.C.E.F.
214 **35** 20f. black, green & red . . 35 25
215 – 25f. black, blue & red . . 40 25
DESIGN: 25f. Mother and child (different).

1964. International Quiet Sun Year.
216 **36** 25f. green and yellow . . . 45 20
217 – 100f. yellow and purple . . 1·25 65
DESIGN: 100f. Another satellite and Sun.

37 "Weather"

1965. Air. World Meteorological Day.
218 **37** 50f. multicoloured 65 45

38 Rug Pattern

1965. Abomey Rug-weaving. Multicoloured.
219 20f. Bull, tree, etc. (vert) . . 30 25
220 25f. Witch-doctor, etc. (vert) 45 30
221 50f. Type **38** 70 35
222 85f. Ship, tree, etc . . . . . 1·25 70

39 Baudot's Telegraph and Ader's Telephone

40 Sir Winston Churchill

1965. Centenary of I.T.U.
223 **39** 100f. black, purple & orge 1·40 1·00

1965. Air. Churchill Commemoration.
224 **40** 100f. multicoloured . . . . 1·40 1·10

41 Heads of Three Races within I.C.Y. Emblem

1965. Air. International Co-operation Year.
225 **41** 25f. lake, green & violet . . 35 20
226 85f. lake, green & blue . . 80 55

42 Lincoln

1965. Air. Death Centenary of Abraham Lincoln.
227 **42** 100f. multicoloured . . . . 1·25 95

43 Cotonou Port

1965. Inaug of Cotonou Port. Multicoloured.
228 25f. Type **43** 65 25
229 100f. Cotonou Port . . . . . 1·60 85
The two stamps joined together form a complete design and were issued se-tenant in the sheets.

44 Spanish Mackerel

45 Independence Monument

1965. Fishes.
230 **44** 10f. black, turquoise & bl 40 25
231 – 25f. orange, grey & blue 55 40
232 – 30f. blue and turquoise . . 1·00 50
233 – 50f. grey, orange & blue 1·40 80
FISHES: 25f. Sama seabream. 30f. Sailfish. 50f. Tripletail.

1965. 2nd Anniv of 28th October Revolution.
234 **45** 25f. red, grey and black . . 35 20
235 30f. red, blue and black . . 40 25

1965. No. 177 surch **1f**.
236 1f. on 25f. turq, brn & bl . . 15 10

47 Arms and Pres. Kennedy

1965. Air. 2nd Death Anniv of Pres. Kennedy.
237 **47** 100f. brown and green . . 1·50 1·00

48 Dr. Schweitzer and Hospital Scene

1966. Air. Schweitzer Commemoration.
238 **48** 100f. multicoloured . . . . 1·50 90

49 Porto-Novo Cathedral

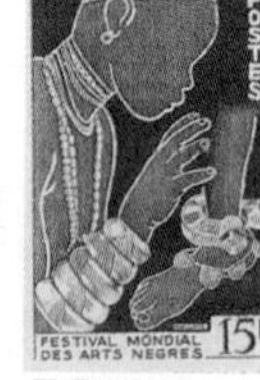

50 Beads, Bangles and Anklets

1966. Dahomey Cathedrals.
239 **49** 30f. purple, blue & green 30 20
240 – 50f. brown, blue & purple 50 30
241 – 70f. purple, blue & green 80 50
DESIGNS—VERT: 50f. Ouidah Church (old Pro-Cathedral). HORIZ: 70f. Cotonou Cathedral.

1966. World Festival of Negro Arts, Dakar.
242 **50** 15f. purple and black . . . 25 15
243 – 30f. red, purple & blue . . 35 25
244 – 50f. blue and brown . . . 60 40
245 – 70f. lake and black . . . . 1·10 65
DESIGNS: 30f. Building construction; 50f. Craftsman; 70f. Religious carvings.

1966. 5th Anniv of France–Dahomey Treaty. Nos. 228/9 surch **ACCORD DE COOPÉRATION FRANCE - DAHOMEY 5e Anniversaire - 24 Avril 1996.**
246 **43** 15f. on 25f. mult 35 25
247 – 15f. on 100f. mult 35 25

52 W.H.O. Building and Emblem

1966. Inaug of W.H.O. Headquarters, Geneva.
248 **52** 30f. multicoloured (post) 40 30
249 – 100f. multicoloured (air) 1·40 1·00
DESIGN (48 × 27 mm): 100f. W.H.O. building (different view) and emblem.

53 African Pygmy Goose

54 Industrial Emblems

1966. Air. Birds. Multicoloured.
250 50f. Type **53** . . . . 2·50 95
251 100f. Fiery-breasted bush shrike . . . . 3·50 1·40
252 500f. Iris glossy starling . . . 17·00 9·25
See also Nos. 271/2.

1966. Air. "Europafrique".
253 **54** 100f. multicoloured . . . . 1·50 85

55 Pope Paul and St. Peter's

1966. Air. Pope Paul's Visit to U.N.
254 **55** 50f. red, brown & green . . 55 35
255 – 70f. red, green and blue . . 85 45
256 – 100f. purple and blue . . . 1·25 85
DESIGNS—HORIZ: 70f. Pope Paul and New York. VERT: (36 × 48 mm); 100f. Pope Paul and U.N. General Assembly.

1966. Air. Inauguration of DC-8F Air Services. As T **54** of Central African Republic.
258 30f. grey, black and purple 50 30

56 Scout signalling with flags

1966. Scouting.
259 **56** 5f. red, ochre and brown 10 10
260 – 10f. mauve, green & black 15 10

261 – 30f. orange, red & violet 35 25
262 – 50f. brown, green & blue 70 40
DESIGNS—VERT: 10f. Tent-pole and banners; 30f. Scouts, camp-fire and map. HORIZ: 50f. Constructing bridge.

57 Scientific Emblem

1966. Air. 20th Anniv of U.N.E.S.C.O.
264 **57** 30f. plum, blue & purple 35 25
265 – 45f. lake and green 50 40
266 – 100f. blue, lake & black . . 1·25 80
DESIGNS—VERT: 45f. Cultural Emblem; HORIZ: 100f. Educational emblem.

58 "The Nativity" (15th-cent. Beaune Tapestry)

1966. Air. Christmas. Multicoloured.
268 50f. Type **58** . . . . 10·25 3·00
269 100f. "The Adoration of the Shepherds" (after Jose Ribera) . . . . 10·25 4·50
270 200f. "Madonna and Child" (after A. Baldovinetti) . . 19·00 6·75
See also Nos. 311/14, 348/51, 384/7 and 423/6.

59 African Broad-billed Roller

60 "Clappertonia ficifolia"

1967. Air. Birds. Multicoloured.
271 200f. Type **59** . . . . 9·50 3·75
272 250f. African Emerald cuckoo 12·50 5·25

1967. Flowers. Multicoloured.
273 1f. Type **60** 10 10
274 3f. "Hewittia sublobata" . . 15 10
275 5f. "Clitoria ternatea" . . . 20 15
276 10f. "Nymphaea micrantha" 35 15
277 5f. "Commelina forskalaei" 35 25
278 30f. "Eremomastax speciosa" 75 35

1967. Nos. 182/3 surch.
279 30f. on 65f. brown & red . . 40 30
280 30f. on 85f. brown & blue . . 40 30

62 Bird bearing Lions Emblem

63 "Ingres" (self-portrait)

1967. 50th Anniv of Lions International.
281 **62** 100f. blue, green & violet 1·50 80

1967. Air. Death Centenary of Ingres (painter). Multicoloured.
282 100f. Type **63** . . . . 2·10 1·25
283 100f. "Oedipus and the Sphinx" (after Ingres) . . . 2·10 1·25
See also Nos. 388/90, 429/30, 431/2 and 486/7.

64 "Suzanne" (barque)

1967. Air. French Sailing ships. Multicoloured.
284 30f. Type **64** 90 35
285 45f. "Esmeralda" (schooner) (vert) . . . . 1·25 55
286 80f. "Marie Alice" (schooner) (vert) . . . . 2·10 75
287 100f. "Antonin" (barque) . . 2·50 1·10

1967. Air. 50th Birth Anniv of Pres. Kennedy. Nos. 227 and 237 surch **29 MAI 1967 50e Anniversaire de la naissance de John F. Kennedy.**
288 **42** 125f. on 100f. mult . . . . 1·75 90
289 **47** 125f. on 100f. brn & grn 1·75 90

66 "Man in the City" Pavilion

1967. World Fair, Montreal.
290 **66** 30f. brn & grn (postage) 40 20
291 – 70f. red and green 90 50
292 – 100f. blue & brown (air) 1·10 65
DESIGNS—HORIZ: 70f. "New Africa" pavilions. VERT: (27 × 48 mm): 100f. "Man Examines the Universe".

67 Dr. Konrad Adenauer (from painting by O. Kokoschka)

68 "Economic Association"

1967. Air. Dr. Adenauer Commemoration.
294 **67** 70f. multicoloured . . . . 1·10 90

1967. Europafrique.
296 **68** 30f. multicoloured 35 25
297 – 45f. multicoloured 50 25

69 Scouts Climbing

1967. World Scout Jamboree, Idaho.
298 **69** 30f. ind, brn & bl (postage) 35 15
299 – 70f. purple, green & blue 90 55
300 – 100f. pur, grn & bl (air) . . 1·10 65
DESIGNS—HORIZ: 70f. Scouts with canoe. VERT: (27 × 48 mm): 100f. Jamboree emblem, rope and map.

1967. Air. Riccione Stamp Exhibition. No. 270 surch **RICCIONE 12-29 Aout 1967** and value.
302 150f. on 200f. mult . . . . . 2·10 1·50

71 Rhone at Grenoble

1967. Winter Olympic Games, Grenoble.
303 **71** 30f. blue, brown & green 40 25
304 – 45f. blue, green & brown 60 40
305 – 100f. purple, green & blue 1·40 90
DESIGNS—VERT: 45f. View of Grenoble. HORIZ: 100f. Rhone Bridge, Grenoble, and Pierre de Coubertin.

1967. Air. 5th Anniv of U.A.M.P.T. As T **123** of Cameroun.
307 100f. green, red & purple . . 1·10 90

72 Currency Tokens

73 Pres. de Gaulle

1967. 5th Anniv of West African Monetary Union.
308 **72** 30f. black, red & green . . 40 30

1967. Air. "Homage to General de Gaulle". President Soglo of Dahomey's visit to Paris.
309 **73** 100f. multicoloured . . . . 2·10 1·40

74 "The Adoration" (Master of St. Sebastian)

1967. Air. Christmas. Religious paintings. Mult.
311 30f. "Virgin and Child" (M. Grunewald) (vert) . . 40 35
312 50f. Type **74** 80 45
313 100f. "The Adoration of the Magi" (Ulrich Apt the Elder) (vert) . . . . . . 1·40 90
314 200f. "The Annunciation" (M. Grunewald) (vert) . . 3·00 1·40

75 Venus de Milo and "Mariner 5"

76 African Buffalo

1968. Air. "Exploration of the Planet Venus". Multicoloured.
315 70f. Type **75** . . . . 1·00 55
316 70f. Venus de Milo and "Venus 4" . . . . . . 1·00 55

1968. Fauna (1st series). Multicoloured.
318 15f. Type **76** 25 15
319 30f. Lion 45 25
320 45f. Kob 80 40
321 70f. Crocodile . . . . 1·25 45
322 100f. Hippopotamus . . . . 2·25 1·10
See also Nos. 353/7.

77 W.H.O. Emblem

1968. 20th Anniv of W.H.O.
323 **77** 30f. brown, blue & ultram 40 30
324 70f. multicoloured . . . . 3·75 1·25

78 Gutenberg Memorial, Strasbourg

79 Dr. Martin Luther King

1968. Air. 500th Death Anniv of Johann Gutenberg.
325 **78** 45f. green and orange . . . 60 35
326 – 100f. deep blue & blue . . 1·40 85
DESIGNS: 100f. Gutenberg statue, Mainz, and printing-press.

1968. Air. Martin Luther King Commemoration.
328 – 30f. black, brown & yellow 50 30
329 – 55f. multicoloured 80 45
330 **79** 100f. multicoloured . . . . 1·25 80
DESIGNS: 55f. Dr. King receiving Nobel Peace Prize. LARGER (25 × 46 mm): 30f. Inscription "We must meet hate with creative love" (also in French and German).

80 Schuman

1968. Air. 5th Anniv of Europafrique.
332 **80** 30f. multicoloured 40 25
333 – 45f. purple, olive & orge 55 35
334 – 70f. multicoloured 90 40
DESIGNS: 45f. De Gasperi; 70f. Dr. Adenauer.

81 "Battle of Montebello" (Philippoteaux)

1968. Air. Red Cross. Paintings. Multicoloured.
335 30f. Type **81** 50 35
336 45f. "2nd Zouaves at Magenta" (Riballier) . . . 65 45
337 70f. "Battle of Magenta" (Charpentier) . . . . . . 1·25 80
338 100f. "Battle of Solferino" (Charpentier) . . . . . . 1·75 1·00

82 Mail Van

1968. Air. Rural Mail Service. Multicoloured.
339 30f. Type **82** 35 25
340 45f. Rural Post Office and mail van 45 30
341 55f. Collecting mail at river-side 60 35
342 70f. Loading mail on train 3·75 1·25

83 Aztec Stadium

1968. Air. Olympic Games, Mexico.
343 **83** 30f. green and purple . . . 40 25
344 – 45f. lake and blue 65 35
345 – 70f. brown and green . . . 1·00 55
346 – 150f. brown and red . . . 1·90 1·10
DESIGNS—VERT: 45f. "Pelota-player" (Aztec figure); 70f. "Uxpanapan wrestler" (Aztec figure). HORIZ: 150f. Olympic Stadium.

1968. Air. Christmas. Paintings by Foujita. As T **74**. Multicoloured.
348 30f. "The Nativity" (horiz) 55 40
349 70f. "The Visitation" . . . . 1·10 55
350 100f. "Virgin and Child" . . 1·40 95
351 200f. "Baptism of Christ" . . 2·75 1·90

1968. Air. "Philexafrique" Stamp Exhibition, Abidjan (Ivory Coast, 1969). As T **137** of Cameroun. Multicoloured.
352 100f. "Diderot" (L. M. Vanloo) . . . . 1·75 1·75

84 Warthog

1969. Fauna (2nd series). Multicoloured.
353 5f. Type **84** 15 10
354 30f. Leopard 50 25
355 60f. Spotted hyena . . . . . 1·00 45

356 75f. Olive baboon . . . . . 1·40 55
357 90f. Hartebeest . . . . . . 2·00 90

1969. Air. "Philexafrique" Stamp Exn, Abidjan, Ivory Coast (2nd issue). As T **138** of Cameroun.
358 50f. violet, sepia and blue . . 1·10 1·10
DESIGN: 50f. Cotonou harbour and stamp of 1941.

85 Heads and Globe

1969. 50th Anniv of I.L.O.
359 **85** 30f. multicoloured 40 25
360 70f. multicoloured 95 55

86 "The Virgin of the Scales" (C. da Sesto-Da Vinci School)

1969. Air. Leonardo da Vinci Commem. Mult.
361 100f. Type **86** . . . . 1·40 75
362 100f. "The Virgin of the Rocks" (Da Vinci) . . . . 1·40 75

87 "General Bonaparte" (J. L. David)

1969. Air. Birth Bicentenary of Napoleon Bonaparte. Multicoloured.
363 30f. Type **87** . . . . 1·10 1·00
364 60f. "Napoleon I in 1809" (Lefevre) . . . . 2·00 1·25
365 75f. "Napoleon at the Battle of Eylau" (Gros) (horiz) 2·50 1·75
366 200f. "General Bonaparte at Arcola" (Gros) . . . . . 5·50 3·25

88 Arms of Dahomey

1969.
367 **88** 5f. multicoloured (postage) 15 15
368 30f. multicoloured 45 30
369 50f. multicoloured (air) . . 45 25

89 "Apollo 8" over Moon

1969. Air. Moon flight of "Apollo 8". Embossed on gold foil.
370 **89** 1,000f. gold . . . . 15·00

1969. Air. 1st Man on the Moon (1st issue). Nos. 315/6 surch **ALUNISSAGE APOLLO XI JUILLET 1969**, lunar module and value.
371 **75** 125f. on 70f. (No. 315) . . 1·75 1·40
372 – 125f. on 70f. (No. 316) . . 1·75 1·40

91 Bank Emblem and Cornucopia

93 Dahomey Rotary Emblem

92 Kenaf Plant and Mill, Bohicon

1969. 5th Anniv of African Development Bank.
373 **91** 30f. multicoloured 50 40

1969. "Europafrique". Multicoloured.
374 30f. Type **92** (postage) . . . 40 25
375 45f. Cotton plant & mill, Parakou 50 30
376 100f. Coconut and palm-oil plant, Cotonou (air) . . . 1·10 70

1969. Air. Rotary International Organization.
378 **93** 50f. multicoloured 65 40

1969. Air. No. 250 surch.
379 **53** 10f. on 50f. multicoloured 50 20

95 Sakpata Dance

96 F. D. Roosevelt

1969. Dahomey Dances. Multicoloured.
380 10f. Type **95** (postage) . . . 30 25
381 30f. Guelede dance 40 30
382 45f. Sato dance 50 35
383 70f. Teke dance (air) 80 45

1969. Air. Christmas. Paintings. As T **58**. Mult.
384 30f. "The Annunciation" (Van der Stockt) 40 30
385 45f. "The Nativity" (15th-cent. Swabian School) 60 40
386 110f. "Virgin and Child" (Masters of the Gold Brocade) . . . . 1·60 1·00
387 200f. "The Adoration of the Magi" (Antwerp School, c. 1530) . . . . . 2·50 1·90

1969. Air. Old Masters. As T **63**. Multicoloured.
388 100f. "The Painter's Studio" (G. Courbet) . . . . . . 1·40 90
389 100f. "Self-portrait with Gold Chain" (Rembrandt) . . . 1·40 90
390 150f. "Hendrickje Stoffels" (Rembrandt) . . . . . . 2·10 1·25

1970. Air. 25th Death Anniv of Franklin D. Roosevelt.
391 **96** 100f. black, green & bl . . 1·25 55

97 Rocket and Men on Moon

98 "U.N. in War and Peace"

1970. Air. 1st Man on Moon (2nd issue).
392 **97** 30f. multicoloured 40 25

The 50, 70, 110f. values were only issued in miniature sheet form.

1970. 25th Anniv of U.N.
394 **98** 30f. indigo, blue & red . . 40 25
395 40f. green, blue & brown 50 30

99 Walt Whitman and African Village

1970. Air. 150th Birth Anniv of Walt Whitman (American poet).
396 **99** 100f. brown, blue & grn . . 1·25 50

1970. Air. Space Flight of "Apollo 13". No. 392 surch **40F APOLLO 13 SOLIDARITE SPATIALE INTERNATIONALE.**
397 **97** 40f. on 30f. multicoloured 75 75

101 Footballers and Globe

1970. Air. World Cup Football Championship, Mexico. Multicoloured.
398 40f. Type **101** 50 40
399 50f. Goalkeeper saving goal 60 45
400 200f. Player kicking ball . . 2·50 1·10

1970. 10th Anniv (1969) of Aerial Navigation Security Agency for Africa and Madagascar (A.S.E.C.N.A.). As T **150** of Cameroun.
401 40f. red and purple 60 25

103 Mt. Fuji and "EXPO" Emblem

104 "La Justice" and "La Concorde" (French warships)

1970. World Fair "EXPO 70", Osaka, Japan. Multicoloured.
402 5f. Type **103** (postage) . . . 45 20
403 70f. Dahomey Pavilion (air) 70 45
404 120f. Mt. Fuji and temple . . 1·25 65

1970. 300th Anniv of Ardres Embassy to Louis XIV of France.
405 **104** 40f. brown, blue & green 1·00 35
406 – 50f. red, brown & green 60 35
407 – 70f. brown, slate & bistre 90 50
408 – 200f. brown, blue & red 2·50 1·10
DESIGNS: 50f. Matheo Lopes; 70f. King Alkemy of Ardres; 200f. Louis XIV of France.

1970. Air. Brazil's Victory in World Cup Football Championship. No. 400 surch **BRESIL–ITALIE 4 – 1** and value.
409 100f. on 200f. multicoloured 1·40 70

106 Mercury

107 Order of Independence

1970. Air. Europafrique.
410 **106** 40f. multicoloured 50 35
411 70f. multicoloured 80 45

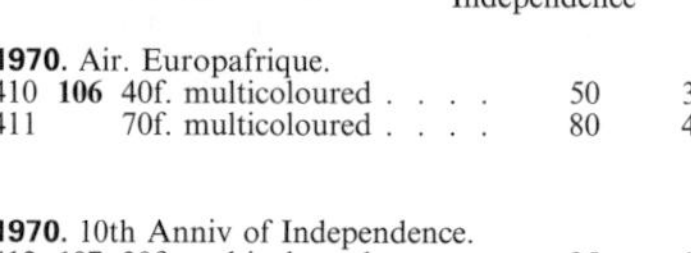

1970. 10th Anniv of Independence.
412 **107** 30f. multicoloured 25 15
413 40f. multicoloured 40 20

108 Bariba Horseman

109 Beethoven

1970. Bariba Horsemen. Multicoloured.
414 1f. Type **108** 10 10
415 2f. Two horsemen 10 10
416 10f. Horseman facing left . . 25 20
417 40f. Type **108** 50 30
418 50f. As 2f. 70 35
419 70f. As 10f. 95 60

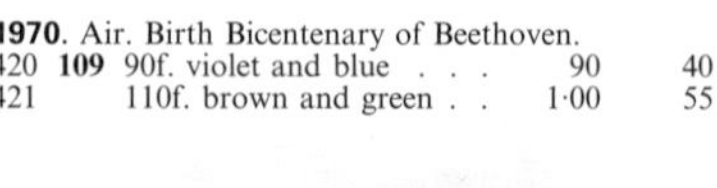

1970. Air. Birth Bicentenary of Beethoven.
420 **109** 90f. violet and blue . . . 90 40
421 110f. brown and green . . 1·00 55

110 Emblems of Learning

111 "The Annunciation"

1970. Air. Laying of Foundation Stone, Calavi University.
422 **110** 100f. multicoloured . . . 1·00 50

1970. Air. Christmas. Miniatures of the Rhenish School c. 1340. Multicoloured.
423 40f. Type **111** 40 25
424 70f. "The Nativity" 70 45
425 110f. "The Adoration of the Magi" . . . . 1·60 90
426 200f. "The Presentation in the Temple" . . . . 2·50 1·60

112 De Gaulle and Arc de Triomphe

1971. Air. 1st Death Anniv of Gen. Charles de Gaulle. Multicoloured.
427 40f. Type **112** 55 45
428 500f. De Gaulle and Notre Dame, Paris . . . . 5·00 2·50

1971. Air. 250th Death Anniv of Watteau. Paintings. As T **63**. Multicoloured.
429 100f. "The Dandy" . . . . . 1·75 1·10
430 100f. "Girl with Lute" . . . 1·75 1·10

1971. Air. 500th Birth Anniv of Durer. As T **63**. Multicoloured.
431 100f. Self-portrait, 1498 . . . 1·40 90
432 200f. Self-portrait, 1500 . . . 2·75 1·60

113 Hands supporting Heart

114 "The Twins" (wood-carving) and Lottery Ticket

1971. Racial Equality Year.
433 **113** 40f. red, brn & green . . 40 25
434 – 100f. red, blue & green . . 95 50
DESIGN—HORIZ: 100f. "Heart" on Globe.

1971. 4th Anniv of National Lottery.
435 **114** 35f. multicoloured 35 15
436 40f. multicoloured 40 25

115 Kepler, Earth and Planets

1971. Air. 400th Birth Anniv of Johannes Kepler (astronomer).
437 **115** 40f. black, pur and blue 55 40
438 – 200f. green, red & blue . . 2·25 1·25
DESIGN: 200f. Kepler, globe, satellite and rocket.

116 Boeing 747 Airliner linking Europe and Africa

1971. Air. Europafrique.
439 **116** 50f. orge, blue & black . . 75 45
440 – 100f. multicoloured . . . 2·25 80
DESIGN: 100f. "General Mangin" (liner) and maps of Europe and Africa.

117 Cockerel and Drum (King Ganyehoussou)

1971. Emblems of Dahomey Kings. Multicoloured.
441 25f. Leg, saw and hatchet (Agoliagbo) 25 15
442 35f. Type **117** 40 25
443 40f. Fish and egg (Behanzin) (vert) 40 25
444 100f. Cow, tree and birds (Guezo) (vert) . . . . . . 1·00 45
445 135f. Fish and hoe (Ouegbadja) . . . . 1·75 90
446 140f. Lion and sickle (Glele) 1·60 90

1971. Air. 10th Anniv of U.A.M.P.T. As T **184** of Cameroun. Multicoloured.
447 100f. U.A.M.P.T. H.Q., Brazzaville and Arms of Dahomey . . . . 1·00 50

119 "Adoration of the Shepherds" (Master of the Hausbuch)

1971. Air. Christmas. Paintings. Multicoloured.
448 40f. Type **119** 60 35
449 70f. "Adoration of the Magi" (Holbein) 95 45
450 100f. "Flight into Egypt" (Van Dyck) (horiz) . . . . 1·25 60
451 200f. "Birth of Christ" (Durer) (horiz) . . . . . . 2·50 1·40

120 "Prince Balthazar" (Velazquez)

1971. Air. 25th Anniv of U.N.I.C.E.F. Paintings of Children. Multicoloured.
452 40f. Type **120** 65 40
453 100f. "The Maids of Honour" (detail, Velazquez) . . . . 1·40 65

1972. No. 395 surch in figures.
454 **98** 35f. on 40f. green, bl & brn 40 25

122 Cross-country Skiing **123** Scout taking Oath

1972. Winter Olympic Games, Sapporo, Japan.
455 **122** 35f. purple, brown and green (postage) 50 30
456 – 150f. purple, blue and brown (air) . . . . . . 1·75 90
DESIGN: 150f. Ski-jumping.

1972. Air. International Scout Seminar, Cotonou. Multicoloured.
457 35f. Type **123** 25 20
458 40f. Scout playing "xylophone" 40 25
459 100f. Scouts working on the land (26 × 47 mm) . . . . 1·00 55

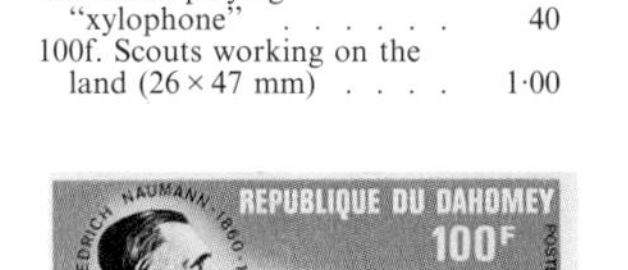
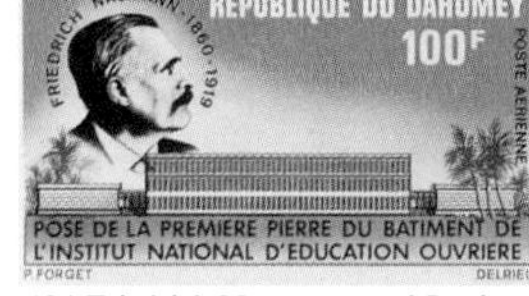

124 Friedrich Naumann and Institute Building

1972. Air. Laying of Foundation Stone for National Workers Education Institute. Multicoloured.
461 100f. Type **124** 90 50
462 250f. Pres. Heuss of West Germany and Institute . . 25 1·10

125 Stork with Serpent

1972. Air. U.N.E.S.C.O. "Save Venice" Campaign. Mosaics in St. Mark's Basilica. Multicoloured.
463 35f. Type **125** 55 35
464 40f. Cockerels carrying fox 65 45
465 65f. Noah releasing dove . . 1·10 80

126 Exhibition Emblem and Dancers

1972. Air. 12th International Philatelic Exhibition, Naples.
466 **126** 100f. multicoloured . . . 95 50

127 Running

129 Brahms, and Clara Schumann at Piano

128 Louis Bleriot and Bleriot XI

1972. Air. Olympic Games, Munich.
467 **127** 20f. brown, grn & blue . . 30 20
468 – 85f. brown, blue & green 85 45
469 – 150f. brown, blue & grn 1·75 80
DESIGNS: 85f. High-jumping; 150f. Putting the shot.

1972. Air. Birth Centenary of Louis Bleriot (pioneer airman).
471 **128** 100f. blue, violet & red 1·75 90

1972. 75th Death Anniv of Johannes Brahms (composer).
472 – 30f. black, brn & violet 40 25
473 **129** 65f. black, violet & lake 70 45
DESIGN—VERT: Brahms and opening bars of "Soir d'Ete".

130 "The Hare and the Tortoise"

1972. Fables of Jean de La Fontaine.
474 **130** 10f. grey, blue & lake . . 25 15
475 – 35f. blue, lake & purple 40 25
476 – 40f. indigo, blue & purple 55 35
DESIGNS—VERT: 35f. "The Fox and the Stork". HORIZ: 40f. "The Cat, the Weasel and the Little Rabbit".

131 "Adam" (Cranach)

1972. Air. 500th Birth Anniv of Lucas Cranach (painter). Multicoloured.
477 150f. Type **131** . . . . 1·75 1·00
478 200f. "Eve" (Cranach) . . . 2·50 1·40

132 Africans and 500f. Coin

1972. 10th Anniv of West African Monetary Union.
479 **132** 40f. brown, grey & yell 65 20

133 "Pauline Borghese" (Canova)

1972. Air. 150th Death Anniv of Antonio Canova.
480 **133** 250f. multicoloured . . . 2·75 1·40

1972. Air. Olympic Medal Winners. Nos. 467/9 optd as listed below.
481 **127** 20f. brown, blue & grn . . 30 20
482 – 85f. brown, blue & green 85 40
483 – 150f. brown, blue & grn 1·75 85
OVERPRINTS: 20f. **5.000m. – 10.000m. VIREN 2 MEDAILLES D'OR**. 85f. **HAUTEUR DAMES MEYFARTH MEDAILLE D'OR**. 150f. **POIDS KOMAR MEDAILLE D'OR**.

135 Pasteur and Apparatus

1972. Air. 150th Birth Anniv of Louis Pasteur (scientist).
485 **135** 100f. pur, violet & grn . . 1·00 50

1972. Air. Paintings by G. de la Tour. As T **63**. Multicoloured.
486 35f. "Hurdy-gurdy Player" (vert) 40 30
487 150f. "The New-born Child" 1·75 1·10

136 "The Annunciation" (School of Agnolo Gaddi)

1972. Air. Christmas. Religious Paintings. Mult.
488 35f. Type **136** 35 20
489 125f. "The Nativity" (Simone dei Crocifissi) . . . . . . 1·00 50
490 140f. "The Adoration of the Shepherds" (P. di Giovanni) . . . . 1·50 80
491 250f. "Adoration of the Magi" (Giotto) . . . . . 2·25 1·25

137 Dr. Hansen, Microscope and Bacillus

139 Arms of Dahomey

138 Statue and Basilica, Lisieux

1973. Centenary of Identification of Leprosy Bacillus by Hansen.
492 **137** 35f. brown, purple & blue 30 25
493 – 85f. brown, orange & grn 65 50
DESIGN: 85f. Dr. Gerhard Armauer Hansen.

1973. Air. Birth Centenary of St. Theresa of Lisieux. Multicoloured.
494 40f. Type **138** 45 30
495 100f. St. Theresa of Lisieux (vert) . . . . 1·20 65

1973.
496 **139** 5f. multicoloured 10 10
497 35f. multicoloured 25 15
498 40f. multicoloured 30 15

140 Scouts in Pirogue

1973. Air. 24th World Scouting Congress, Nairobi, Kenya.
499 **140** 15f. purple, green & blue 35 15
500 – 20f. blue and brown . . . 25 20
501 – 40f. blue, green & brown 40 25
DESIGNS—VERT: 20f. Lord Baden-Powell. HORIZ: 40f. Bridge-building.

141 Interpol Badge and "Communications" **142** "Education in Nutrition"

1973. 50th Anniv of International Criminal Police Organization (Interpol).
503 – 35f. brown, green & red 30 20
504 **141** 50f. green, brown & red 45 30
DESIGN—HORIZ: 35f. Interpol emblem and web.

1973. 25th Anniv of World Health Organization. Multicoloured.
505 35f. Type **142** 30 20
506 100f. Pre-natal examination 80 45

1973. Pan-African Drought Relief. No. 321 surch **SECHERESSE SOLIDARITE AFRICAINE** and value.
507 100f. on 70f. multicoloured 1·00 55

144 Copernicus, "Venera" and "Mariner" Probes and Plane of Solar System

1973. Air. 500th Birth Anniv of Copernicus.
508 **144** 65f. black, purple & yell 85 45
509 – 125f. green, blue & purple 1·40 70
DESIGN—VERT: 125f. Copernicus.

1973. U.A.M.P.T. As T **216** of Cameroun.
510 100f. violet, red & black . . 80 40

1973. Air. African Fortnight, Brussels. As T **217** of Cameroun.
511 100f. black, green & blue . . 70 40

145 White Grouper

1973. Fishes.
512 **145** 5f. dp blue and blue . . . 25 20
513 – 15f. black and blue . . . 40 20
514 – 35f. lt brn, brn & grn . . 90 40
DESIGNS: 15f. African spadefish; 35f. Blue-pointed porgy.

148 W.M.O. Emblem and World Weather Map

1973. Air. Centenary of I.M.O./W.M.O.
515 **148** 100f. brown and green . . 95 10

149 "Europafrique"

1973. Air. Europafrique.
516 **149** 35f. blue, green & yell . . 35 20
517 – 40f. brown, ultram & bl 40 25
DESIGN: 40f. Europafrique, plant and cogwheels.

150 President John F. Kennedy **152** Chameleon

151 Footballers

1973. Air. 10th Death Anniv of President Kennedy.
518 **150** 200f. grn, violet & grn . . 1·90 1·40

1973. Air. World Football Championship Cup.
520 **151** 35f. green, brn & bistre 35 20
521 – 40f. brown, blue & orange 40 25
522 – 100f. green, brown & blue 65 45
DESIGNS: 40f., 100f. Football scenes similar to Type **151**.

1973. 1st Anniv of 26th October Revolution. Multicoloured.
523 35f. Type **152** 35 20
524 40f. Arms of Dahomey (vert) 35 25

153 "The Annunciation" (Dirk Bouts) **155** "The Elephant, the Chicken and the Dog"

1973. Air. Christmas. Multicoloured.
525 35f. Type **153** 40 30
526 100f. "The Nativity" (Giotto) 70 50
527 150f. "The Adoration of the Magi" (Botticelli) . . . . 1·40 80
528 200f. "The Adoration of the Shepherds" (Bassano) (horiz) . . . . 1·75 1·25

1974. Air. "Skylab". No. 515 surch **OPERATION SKYLAB 1973-1974** and value.
529 **148** 200f. on 100f. brn & grn 1·50 95

1974. Dahomey Folk Tales. Multicoloured.
530 5f. Type **155** 15 10
531 10f. "The Sparrowhawk and the Dog" 20 10
532 25f. "The Windy Tree" (horiz) 30 20
533 40f. "The Eagle, the Snake and the Chicken" (horiz) 40 20

156 Snow Crystal and Skiers

1974. Air. 50th Anniv of Winter Olympic Games.
534 **156** 100f. blue, brn and vio . . 95 65

157 Alsatian

1974. Breeds of Dogs. Multicoloured.
535 40f. Type **157** 35 25
536 50f. Boxer 40 25
537 100f. Saluki 80 50

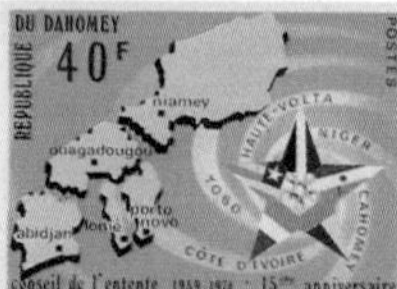

158 Map of Member Countries

1974. 15th Anniv of Council of Accord.
538 **158** 40f. multicoloured 35 15

159 Lenin (50th Death Anniv)

1974. Air. Celebrities' Anniversaries.
539 **159** 50f. purple and red . . . 50 30
540 – 125f. brn & green . . . . 1·10 65
541 – 150f. blue & purple . . . 1·60 1·10
DESIGNS AND ANNIVERSARIES: 125f. Marie Curie (40th death anniv); 150f. Sir Winston Churchill (birth cent).

160 18th-century Persian Bishop **161** Beethoven and opening bars of the "Moonlight" Sonata

1974. Air. 21st Chess Olympiad, Nice. Mult.
542 50f. Type **160** 55 35
543 200f. 19th-century Siamese queen . . . . 1·75 1·10

1974. Air. Famous Composers.
544 **161** 150f. red and black . . . 1·25 80
545 – 150f. red and black . . . 1·25 80
DESIGN: No. 545, Chopin.

162 Earth seen through Astronaut's Legs

1974. Air. 5th Anniv of 1st Manned Moon Landing.
546 **162** 150f. brn, blue & red . . 1·40 85

Sets commemorating the World Cup, U.P.U. Centenary, Treaty of Berne, Space Exploration and West Germany's World Cup Victory appeared in 1974. Their status is uncertain.

1974. Air. 11th Pan-Arab Scout Jamboree, Batroun, Lebanon. Nos. 499/500 surch **XIe JAMBOREE PANARABE DE BATROUN – LIBAN** and value.
547 **140** 100f. on 15f. purple, green and blue 65 45
548 – 140f. on 20f. bl & brn . . 1·25 65

1974. Air. West Germany's Victory in World Cup Football Championships. Nos. 521/2 surch **R F A 2 HOLLANDE 1** and value.
549 100f. on 40f. brn, bl & orge 65 45
550 150f. on 100f. grn, brn & bl 1·00 80

165 U.P.U. Emblem and Globe

1974. Air. Centenary of U.P.U.
551 **165** 35f. violet and red 35 30
552 – 65f. blue and red . . . . 1·25 60
553 – 125f. green, blue & lt bl 2·75 1·00
554 – 200f. blue, yellow & brn 1·75 1·25
DESIGNS: 65f. Concorde in flight over African village; 125f. French mobile post office, circa 1860; 200f. Drummer and mail van.

166 "Lion of Belfort"

1974. Air. 70th Death Anniv of F. Bartholdi (sculptor).
555 **166** 100f. brown . . . . . . 1·25 65

1974. Air. 30th Death Anniv of Philippe de Champaigne (painter). As T **153**. Mult.
556 250f. "Young Girl with Falcon" . . . . 2·25 1·40

167 Locomotive No. 3.1102, 1911, France

1974. Steam Locomotives.
557 **167** 35f. multicoloured 80 35
558 – 40f. grey, black & red . . 1·00 45
559 – 100f. multicoloured . . . 2·50 85
560 – 200f. multicoloured . . . 4·25 1·90
DESIGNS: 40f. Goods locomotive, 1877; 100f. Crampton Type 210 locomotive, 1849; 200f. Stephenson locomotive "Aigle", 1846, France.

168 Rhamphorhynchus

1974. Air. Prehistoric Animals. Multicoloured.
561 35f. Type **168** 35 20
562 150f. Stegosaurus . . . . . 1·00 70
563 200f. Tyrannosaurus . . . . 1·50 95

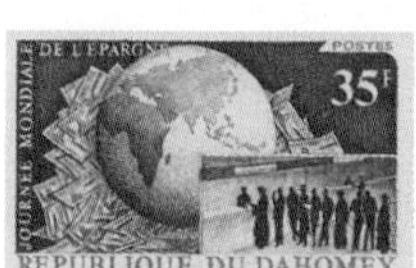

169 Globe, Notes and Savings Bank

1974. World Savings Day.
564 **169** 35f. brown, myrtle & grn 35 25

170 Europafrique Emblem on Globe

1974. Air. Europafrique.
565 **170** 250f. multicoloured . . . 1·90 1·40

1974. Air. Christmas. Paintings by Old Masters. As T **153**. Multicoloured.
566 35f. "The Annunciation" (Schongauer) 30 20
567 40f. "The Nativity" (Schongauer) 35 25
568 100f. "The Virgin of the Rose Bush" (Schongauer) . . . 80 45
569 250f. "The Virgin, Infant Jesus and St. John the Baptist" (Botticelli) . . . . 2·25 1·40

171 "Apollo" and "Soyuz" Spacecraft

1975. Air. "Apollo–Soyuz" Space Link. Mult.
570 35f. Type **171** 35 25
571 200f. Rocket launch and flags of Russia and U.S.A. . . . 1·60 90
572 500f. "Apollo" and "Soyuz" docked together . . . . . 3·50 2·25

172 Dompago Dance, Hissi **173** Flags on Map of Africa

1975. Dahomey Dances and Folklore. Mult.
573 10f. Type **172** 20 15
574 25f. Fetish dance, Vaudou-Tchinan 30 15
575 40f. Bamboo dance, Agbehoun 40 30
576 100f. Somba dance, Sandoua (horiz) 75 50

1975. "Close Co-operation with Nigeria". Multicoloured.
577 65f. Type **173** 40 30
578 100f. Arrows linking maps of Dahomey and Nigeria (horiz) 65 40

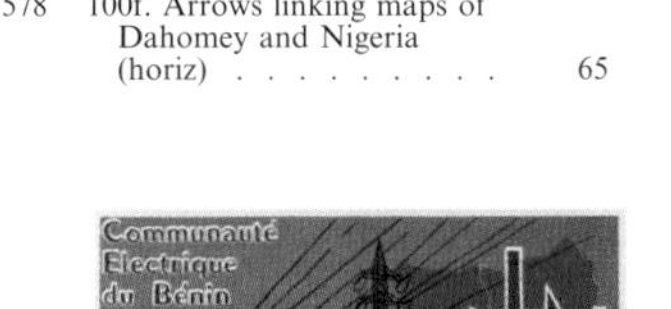

174 Community Emblem and Pylons

1975. Benin Electricity Community. Mult.
579 40f. Type **174** 35 25
580 150f. Emblem and pylon (vert) . . . . 1·10 65
C.E.B. = "Communaute Electrique du Benin".

175 Head of Ceres

1975. Air. "Arphila 75" International Stamp Exhibition, Paris.
581 **175** 100f. purple, ind & blue 90 55

176 Rays of Light and Map **178** Dr. Schweitzer

1975. "New Dahomey Society".
582 **176** 35f. multicoloured 30 20

1975. Air. "Apollo–Soyuz" Space Test Project. Nos. 570/1 surch **RENCONTRE APOLLO-SOYOUZ 17 Juil. 1975** and value.
583 **171** 100f. on 35f. mult 65 45
584 – 300f. on 200f. mult . . . 2·00 1·10

1975. Birth Centenary of Dr. Albert Schweitzer.
585 **178** 200f. olive, brown & green . . . . 1·75 90

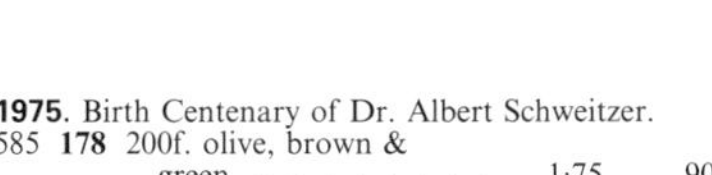

179 "The Holy Family" (Michelangelo) **180** Woman and I.W.Y. Emblem

1975. Air. Europafrique.
586 **179** 300f. multicoloured . . . 1·90 1·25

1975. International Women's Year.
587 **180** 50f. blue and violet . . . 35 25
588 – 150f. orange, brn & grn 1·10 65
DESIGN: 150f. I.W.Y. emblem within ring of bangles.

181 Continental Infantry **183** "Allamanda cathartica"

182 Diving

1975. Air. Bicent of American Revolution.
589 **181** 75f. lilac, red & green . . 55 35
590 – 135f. brown, pur & bl . . 95 70
591 – 300f. brown, red & blue 2·00 1·40
592 – 500f. brown, red & grn 3·50 1·75
DESIGNS: 135f. "Spirit of 76"; 300f. Artillery battery; 500f. Cavalry.

1975. Air. Olympic Games, Montreal.
593 **182** 40f. brown, bl and vio . . 35 25
594 – 250f. brown, grn & red 1·60 1·10
DESIGN: 250f. Football.

1975. Flowers. Multicoloured.
595 10f. Type **183** 15 10
596 35f. "Ixora coccinea" 30 15
597 45f. "Hibiscus rosa-sinensis" 45 30
598 60f. "Phaemeria magnifica" 55 40

184 "The Nativity" (Van Leyden)

1975. Air. Christmas. Multicoloured.
599 40f. Type **184** 35 25
600 85f. "Adoration of the Magi" (Rubens) (vert) 55 45
601 140f. "Adoration of the Shepherds" (Le Brun) . . . 1·00 65
602 300f. "The Virgin of the Blue Diadem" (Raphael) (vert) 2·00 1·50

For later issues see **BENIN**.

PARCEL POST STAMPS

1967. Surch **COLIS POSTAUX** and value.
P271 **18** 5f. on 1f. (postage) . . . 10 10
P272 – 10f. on 2f. (No. 151) . . 25 25
P273 **18** 20f. on 6f. 30 30
P274 – 25f. on 3f. (No. 152) . . 40 40
P275 – 30f. on 4f. (No. 153) . . 45 45
P276 – 50f. on 10f. (No. 155) . . 70 70
P277 – 100f. on 20f. (No. 157) 1·50 1·50
P278 – 200f. on 200f. (No. 195) (air) . . . . 3·00 2·25
P279 **29** 300f. on 100f. . . . . . 3·50 3·00
P280 – 500f. on 300f. (No. 196) 6·50 4·50
P281 – 1000f. on 500f. (No. 197) 14·00 11·00
P282 – 500f. on 100f. (No. 145) 55·00 55·00

POSTAGE DUE STAMPS

1906. "Natives" key-type inscr "DAHOMEY" in blue (10, 30c.) or red (others).
D33 L 5c. green . . . . 1·75 1·50
D34 10c. red . . . . 3·00 2·75
D35 15c. blue on blue . . . . . 4·00 3·00
D36 20c. black on yellow . . . 3·00 7·00
D37 30c. red on cream . . . . 3·25 8·00
D38 50c. violet . . . . 8·50 25·00
D39 60c. black on buff . . . . 6·50 21·00
D40 1f. black on pink . . . . . 30·00 55·00

1914. "Figure" key-type inscr "DAHOMEY".
D59 M 5c. green . . . . 10 2·25
D60 10c. red . . . . 15 2·00
D61 15c. grey . . . . 40 2·00
D62 20c. brown . . . . 40 2·75
D63 30c. blue . . . . 1·00 3·00
D64 50c. black . . . . 75 3·75
D65 60c. orange . . . . 1·25 2·25
D66 1f. violet . . . . 1·75 3·25

1927. Surch in figures.
D96 M 2f. on 1f. mauve . . . . . 1·75 1·75
D97 3f. on 1f. brown . . . . . 2·50 4·50

D 14 Native Head **D 26** Panther attacking African

1941.
D143 **D 14** 5c. black . . . . . . 1·10 2·75
D144 10c. red . . . . 20 2·75
D145 15c. blue . . . . . . 10 2·00
D146 20c. green . . . . . . 35 2·75
D147 30c. orange . . . . . 1·25 3·00
D148 50c. brown . . . . . 1·90 3·25
D149 60c. green . . . . . . 1·90 3·50
D150 1f. red . . . . 2·25 3·50
D151 2f. yellow . . . . . . 2·75 3·25
D152 3f. purple . . . . . . 2·75 4·25

1963.
D191 **D 26** 1f. red and green . . . 10 10
D192 2f. green & brown . . 10 10
D193 5f. blue and orange . . 10 10
D194 10f. black and purple 25 25
D195 20f. orange & blue . . 30 30

D 72 Pirogue

1967.
D308 **D 72** 1f. plum, blue & brn 10 10
D309 A 1f. brown, bl & plum 10 10
D310 B 3f. green, orge & brn 10 10
D311 C 3f. brown, orge & grn 10 10
D312 D 5f. purple, blue & brn 15 15
D313 E 5f. brown, blue & pur 35 20
D314 F 10f. green, vio & brn 30 30
D315 G 10f. brown, grn & vio 30 30
D316 H 30f. violet, red & bl 50 50
D317 I 30f. blue, red & vio . 50 50
DESIGNS: A, Heliograph; B, Old morse receiver; C, Postman on cycle; D, Old telephone; E, Renault ABH diesel railcar; F, Citroen "2-CV" mail van; G, Radio station; H, Douglas DC-8-10/50CF airliner; I, "Early Bird" satellite.

DANISH WEST INDIES Pt. 11

A group of islands in the West Indies formerly belonging to Denmark and purchased in 1917 by the United States, whose stamps they now use. Now known as the United States Virgin Islands.

1855. 100 cents = 1 dollar.
1905. 100 bit = 1 franc.

1 **2** **5**

1855. Imperf.
4 **1** 3c. red . . . . 29·00 48·00

1872. Perf.
6 **1** 3c. red . . . . 60·00 £150
7 4c. blue £150 £300

1873.
31 **2** 1c. red and green . . . . . 8·75 13·00
32 3c. red and blue . . . . . . 7·25 9·50
33 4c. blue and brown . . . . . 8·00 7·50
19 5c. brown and green . . . . 19·00 12·00
21 7c. yellow and purple . . . . 21·00 70·00
25 10c. brown and blue . . . . . 19·00 22·00
27 12c. green and purple . . . . 29·00 £100
28 14c. green and lilac £450 £800
29 50c. lilac £100 £180

1887. Handstamped **1 CENT**.
37 **2** 1c. on 7c. yellow & purple . . 45·00 £140

1895. Surch **10 CENTS 1895**.
38 **2** 10c. on 50c. lilac . . . . . . 26·00 48·00

1900.
39 **5** 1c. green . . . . 2·40 2·40
40 2c. red . . . . 6·25 18·00
41 5c. blue . . . . 12·50 18·00
42 8c. brown . . . . 22·00 40·00

1902. Surch **2** (or **8**) **CENTS 1902**.
43 **2** 2c. on 3c. red and blue . . . 6·50 17·00
47 8c. on 10c. brown & blue . . 8·00 8·25

1905. Surch **5 BIT 1905**.
48 **2** 5b. on 4c. blue & brown . . 12·00 38·00
49 **5** 5b. on 5c. blue . . . . 10·00 29·00
50 5b. on 8c. brown . . . . . . 10·00 30·00

10 King Christian IX **11** Charlotte Amalie Harbour and Training ship "Ingolf"

1905.
51 **10** 5b. green . . . . 3·75 3·00
52 10b. red . . . . 3·75 3·00
53 20b. blue and green . . . . 7·50 6·50
54 25b. blue . . . . 7·50 7·50
55 40b. grey and red . . . . . 7·50 6·00
56 50b. grey and yellow . . . . 7·50 8·25
57 **11** 1f. blue and green . . . . . 16·00 26·00
58 2f. brown and red . . . . . 26·00 38·00
59 5f. brown and yellow . . . 55·00 £180

14 King Frederik VIII **15** King Christian X

1907.
60 **14** 5b. green . . . . 2·25 1·10
61 10b. red . . . . 2·25 1·00
62 15b. brown and violet . . . 3·75 3·75
63 20b. blue and green . . . . 22·00 18·00
64 25b. blue . . . . 2·25 1·90
65 30b. black and red . . . . 40·00 38·00
66 40b. grey and red . . . . . 5·50 4·50
67 50b. brown and yellow . . . 5·25 7·00

1916.
68 **15** 5b. green . . . . 4·25 4·00
69 10b. red . . . . 4·25 42·00
70 15b. brown and lilac . . . . 4·25 42·00
71 20b. blue and green . . . . 4·25 42·00
72 25b. blue . . . . 4·25 10·00
73 30b. black and red . . . . 4·25 55·00
74 40b. grey and red . . . . . 4·25 55·00
75 50b. brown and yellow . . . 4·25 55·00

POSTAGE DUE STAMPS

D 6 **D 12**

1902.
D43 **D 6** 1c. blue . . . . 4·75 13·50
D44 4c. blue . . . . 9·00 19·00
D45 6c. blue . . . . 17·00 40·00
D46 10c. blue . . . . 16·00 45·00

1905.
D60 **D 12** 5b. grey and red . . . 4·00 5·00
D61 20b. grey and red . . . 5·75 12·00
D62 30b. grey and red . . . 5·25 12·00
D63 50b. grey and red . . . 5·00 26·00

DANZIG Pt. 7

A Baltic seaport, from 1920–1939 (with the surrounding district) a free state under the protection of the League of Nations. Later incorporated in Germany. Now part of Poland.

1920. 100 pfennige = 1 mark.
1923. 100 pfennige = 1 Danzig gulden.

Stamps of Germany inscr "DEUTSCHES REICH" optd or surch.

1920. Optd **Danzig** horiz.
1 10 5pf. green . . . 25 35
2 10pf. red . . . 25 35
3 24 15pf. brown . . . 25 35
4 10 20pf. blue . . . 25 35
5 30pf. black & orge on buff 35 35
6 40pf. red . . . 25 35
7 50pf. black & pur on buff 40 55
8 12 1m. red . . . 60 65
9 1m.25 green . . . 35 80
10 1m.50 brown . . . 80 1·10
11 13 2m. blue . . . 1·60 3·25
12 2m.50 red . . . 1·60 3·25
13 14 3m. black . . . 4·25 9·00
14 10 4m. red and black . . . 5·00 5·75
15a 15 5m. red and black . . . 1·90 2·50

1920. Surch **Danzig** horiz and large figures of value.
16 10 5 on 30pf. black and orange on buff . . . 20 20
17 10 on 20pf. blue . . . 20 20
18 25 on 30pf. black and orange on buff . . . 20 20
19 60 on 30pf. black and orange on buff . . . 65 60
20 80 on 30pf. black and orange on buff . . . 65 65

1920. Optd **Danzig** diagonally and bar.
21 24 2pf. grey . . . £100 £140
22 2½pf. grey . . . £130 £260
23 10 3pf. brown . . . 10·50 21·00
24 5pf. green . . . 35 30
25 24 7½pf. orange . . . 48·00 65·00
26 10 10pf. red . . . 3·75 8·75
27 24 15pf. violet . . . 50 50
28 10 20pf. blue . . . 50 65
29 25pf. blk & red on yell . . 70 50
30 30pf. blk & orge on buff 45·00 85·00
31 40pf. black and red . . . 1·50 2·10
32 50pf. blk & pur on buff . . £130 £260
32a 60pf. mauve . . . £900 £2250
33 75pf. black and green . . . 65 60
34 80pf. blk & red on pink . . 2·00 4·00
34a 12 1m. red . . . £900 £2100

1920. Optd **DANZIG** three times in semicircle.
34b 13 2m. blue . . . £900 £2200

1920. No. 5 of Danzig surch **MARK 1 MARK** and Types of Germany with burelage added surch with new value and **DANZIG** (36/37), **Danzig** (38, 40f) or **DANZIG** and flag (40e).
35 A 10 1m. on 30pf. black and orange on buff . . . 55 1·25
36 A 1¼m. on 3pf. brown . . 55 1·25
37 A 24 2m. on 35pf. brown . . 55 1·25
38 A 3m. on 7½pf. orange . . 55 1·25
39 A 5m. on 2pf. grey . . . 55 1·25
40AF 10m. on 7½pf. orange . . 1·00 1·90

1920. Air. No. 6 of Danzig surch with airplane or wings and value.
41 10 40 on 40pf. red . . . 1·25 2·50
42 60 on 40pf. red . . . 1·25 2·50
43 1m. on 40pf. red . . . 1·25 2·50

13 Hanse Kogge

1921. Constitution of 1920.
44 13 5pf. purple and brown . . . 25 30
45 10pf. violet and orange . . 30 25
46 25pf. red and green . . . 55 60
55 40pf. red . . . 1·10 90
48 80pf. blue . . . 55 65
49 – 1m. grey and red . . . 1·60 1·90
50 – 2m. green and blue . . . 3·25 4·25
51 – 3m. green and black . . . 1·40 2·25
52 – 5m. red and grey . . . 1·50 2·00
53 – 10m. brown and green . . . 1·90 4·50
The mark values are as Type **13**, but larger.

15 16 Sabaltnig PIII over Danzig

1921. Air.
57 15 40pf. green . . . 35 50
58 60pf. purple . . . 35 50
59 1m. red . . . 35 50
60 2m. brown . . . 35 50
116 16 5m. violet . . . 35 70
117 10m. green . . . 35 70
118 20m. brown . . . 35 60
119 15 25m. blue . . . 50 60
120 16 50m. orange . . . 50 60
121 100m. red . . . 50 60
122 250m. brown . . . 50 60
123 500m. red . . . 45 35
Nos. 120 to 123 are similar to Type **16**, but larger.

1921. No. 33 of Danzig surch **60** and bars.
63 10 60 on 75pf. black & green 45 1·00

18 19

1921.
64 18 5pf. orange . . . 25 25
65 10pf. brown . . . 20 20
66 15pf. green . . . 20 20
67 20pf. grey . . . 20 20
68 25pf. green . . . 20 20
69 30pf. red and blue . . . 25 25
70 40pf. red and green . . . 20 25
71 50pf. red and green . . . 20 25
72 60pf. red . . . 45 35
73 75pf. purple . . . 15 25
74 80pf. red and black . . . 20 40
75 80pf. green . . . 15 25
76 1m. red and orange . . . 20 40
77 1.20m. blue . . . 1·25 1·25
78 1.25m. red and purple . . 10 25
79 1.50m. grey . . . 20 25
80 2m. red and grey . . . 2·50 3·00
81 2m. red . . . 10 25
82 2.40m. red and brown . . 80 1·25
83 3m. red and purple . . . 6·50 5·75
84 3m. red . . . 15 25
106 4m. blue . . . 10 40
86 5m. green . . . 10 25
87 6m. red . . . 10 25
88 8m. blue . . . 30 85
89 10m. orange . . . 10 25
90 20m. brown . . . 10 30
110 40m. blue . . . 10 40
111 80m. red . . . 10 40

1921. Rouletted.
91 19 5m. green, black and red 1·25 2·10
91b 9m. orange and red . . . 2·50 6·25
92 10m. blue, black and red 1·25 2·10
93 20m. black and red . . . 1·25 2·10

20 21

1921. Tuberculosis Week.
93a 20 30pf.(+30pf.) grn & orge 45 40
93b 60pf.(+60pf.) red & yell . . 1·10 1·00
93c 1.20m.(+1.20m.) bl & orge (25 × 29½ mm) . . . 1·60 1·75

1922.
94b 21 50m. red and gold . . . 1·50 3·00
95a 100m. red and green . . . 2·75 5·25

1922. Surch in figures.
96 18 6 on 3m. red . . . 25 35
97 8 on 4m. blue . . . 25 65
98 20 on 8m. blue . . . 25 65

25 26

1923.
99 25 50m. red and blue . . . 10 35
136 50m. blue . . . 10 35
100 100m. red and green . . 35 35
137 100m. green . . . 10 35
101 150m. red and purple . . 10 35
138 200m. orange . . . 10 50
102 26 250m. red and purple . . 25 35
103 500m. red and grey . . . 25 35
104 1000m. pink and brown . . 25 35
105 5000m. pink and silver . . 90 4·50
139 10000m. red and orange . . 40 60
140 20000m. red and blue . . 40 90
141 50000m. red and green . . 40 90

28

1923. Poor People's Fund.
123b 28 50+20m. red . . . 20 60
123c 100+30m. purple . . . 20 60

29 35 Etrich/Rumpler Taube

1923.
124 29 250m. red and purple . . . 15 35
125 300m. red and green . . . 10 35
126 500m. red and grey . . . 15 35
127 1000m. brown . . . 15 35
128 1000m. red and brown . . 15 35
129 3000m. red and violet . . 15 35
130 5000m. pink . . . 10 35
131 20000m. blue . . . 10 35
132 50000m. green . . . 10 35
133 100000m. blue . . . 10 35
134 250000m. purple . . . 10 35
135 500000m. grey . . . 10 35

1923. Surch with figure of value and **Tausend** (T) or **Million** or **Millionen** (M).
142 25 40T. on 200m. orange . . 80 2·00
143 100T. on 200m. orange . . 80 1·90
144 250T. on 200m. orange . . 7·00 11·00
145 400T. on 100m. green . . . 40 25
146 29 500T. on 50000m. green . . 40 40
147 1M. on 10000m. orange . . 3·25 5·50
148 1M. on 10000m. red . . . 25 35
149 2M. on 10000m. red . . . 25 35
150 3M. on 10000m. red . . . 25 35
151 5M. on 10000m. red . . . 25 35
152 10M. on 10000m. lavender 35 1·00
158 26 10M. on 1000000m. orge 30 65
153 29 20M. on 10000m. lavender 25 65
154 25M. on 10000m. lavender 25 65
155 40M. on 10000m. lavender 25 65
156 50M. on 10000m. lavender 25 65
159 100M. on 10000m. lav . . 25 65
160 300M. on 10000m. lav . . 25 65
161 500M. on 10000m. lav . . 25 65

1923. Surch **100000** and bar.
157 26 100000 on 20000m. red and blue . . . 60 6·00

1923. Air.
162a 35 250,000m. red . . . 35 1·00
163a 500,000m. red . . . 35 1·00

1923. Surch in **Millionen**.
164a 35 2m. on 100,000m. red . . 35 1·00
165a 5m. on 50,000m. red . . . 35 1·00

1923. Surch with new currency, **Pfennige** or **Gulden**.
166 25 5pf. on 50m. red . . . 30 35
167 10pf. on 50m. red . . . 30 35
168 20pf. on 100m. red . . . 30 35
169 25pf. on 50m. red . . . 3·25 8·00
170 30pf. on 50m. red . . . 3·00 1·60
171 40pf. on 100m. red . . . 2·00 1·90
172 50pf. on 100m. red . . . 2·00 3·25
173 75pf. on 100m. red . . . 6·00 16·00
174 26 1g. on 1000000m. red . . . 4·00 6·50
175 2g. on 1000000m. red . . . 8·50 29·00
176 3g. on 1000000m. red . . . 21·00 50·00
177 5g. on 1000000m. red . . . 40·00 65·00

39 40 Etrich/Rumpler Taube

1924.
177b 39 3pf. brown . . . 1·25 1·25
268 5pf. orange . . . 75 1·50
178e 7pf. green . . . 1·10 2·40
178f 8pf. green . . . 1·60 4·00
270 10pf. green . . . 70 1·40
180 15pf. grey . . . 3·25 2·75
180b 15pf. red . . . 1·25 90
181 20pf. red and carmine . . 10·00 50
182 20pf. grey . . . 1·40 1·50
183 25pf. red and grey . . . 14·50 2·40
272 25pf. red . . . 3·25 6·00
185 30pf. red and green . . . 8·50 50
186 30pf. purple . . . 1·50 3·50
186a 35pf. blue . . . 1·60 1·10
187 40pf. blue and indigo . . 6·50 70
188 40pf. red and brown . . . 8·50 8·00
189 40pf. blue . . . 1·50 3·00
274 50pf. red and blue . . . 2·10 8·00
190b 55pf. red and purple . . . 5·00 11·50
191 60pf. red and green . . . 5·50 14·00
192 70pf. red and green . . . 3·25 4·50
193 75pf. red and purple . . . 8·00 6·00
194 80pf. red and brown . . . 2·10 5·50

1924. Air.
195 40 10pf. red . . . 17·00 3·75
196 20pf. mauve . . . 1·60 1·25
197 40pf. brown . . . 3·25 1·60
198 1g. green . . . 3·25 1·90
199 – 2½g. purple (22 × 40 mm) 26·00 32·00

42 Oliva 44 Fountain of Neptune

1924.
200 42 1g. black and green . . . 30·00 70·00
275 1g. black and orange . . . 4·50 14·00
201 – 2g. black and purple . . . 60·00 £100
206 – 2g. black and red . . . 4·00 4·75
202 – 3g. black and blue . . . 3·50 6·00
203 – 5g. black and lake . . . 4·00 7·50
204 – 10g. black and brown . . . 65·00 90·00
DESIGNS—HORIZ: 2g. Krantor and River Mottlau; 3g. Zoppot. VERT: 5g. St. Mary's Church; 10g. Town Hall and Langemarkt.

1929. Int Philatelic Exhibition. Various frames.
207 44 10pf.(+10pf.) blk & grn . . 2·10 3·00
208 15pf.(+15pf.) blk & red . . 2·10 3·00
209 25pf.(+25pf.) blk & bl . . 8·00 8·50

1930. 10th Anniv of Constitution of Free City of Danzig. Optd **1920 15. November 1930**.
210 39 5pf. orange . . . 3·25 3·25
211 10pf. green . . . 4·00 4·00
212 15pf. red . . . 7·00 9·00
213 20pf. red and carmine . . 3·50 5·00
214 25pf. red and grey . . . 4·50 9·00
215 30pf. red and green . . . 8·75 22·00
216 35pf. blue . . . 40·00 75·00
217 40pf. blue and indigo . . . 12·50 35·00
218 50pf. red and blue . . . 40·00 65·00
219 75pf. red and purple . . . 40·00 65·00
220 42 1g. black and orange . . . 40·00 65·00

1932. Danzig Int Air Post Exn ("Luposta"). Nos. 200/4 surch **Luftpost-Ausstellung 1932** and value.
221 42 10pf.+10pf. on 1g. black and green . . . 13·00 20·00
222 – 15pf.+15pf. on 2g. black and purple . . . 13·00 20·00
223 – 20pf.+20pf. on 3g. black and blue . . . 13·00 20·00
224 – 25pf.+25pf. on 5g. black and lake . . . 13·00 10·00
225 – 30pf.+30pf. on 10g. black and brown . . . 13·00 20·00

1934. "Winter Relief Work" Charity. Surch **5 W.H.W.** in Gothic characters.
226 39 5pf.+5pf. orange . . . 7·00 18·00
227 10pf.+5pf. green . . . 22·00 45·00
228 15pf.+5pf. red . . . 14·00 32·00

1934. Surch.
229 39 6pf. on 7pf. green . . . 1·10 1·40
230a 8pf. on 7pf. green . . . 1·60 1·60
231 30pf. on 35pf. blue . . . 11·00 20·00

50 Junkers F-13 51

1935. Air.
233 50 10pf. red . . . 1·40 70
234 15pf. yellow . . . 1·50 1·10
235 25pf. green . . . 1·50 1·60
236 50pf. blue . . . 7·25 8·00
237 51 1g. purple . . . 4·50 10·00

52 Stockturm, 1346 54 Brosen War Memorial

1935. Winter Relief Fund.
238 52 5pf.+5pf. orange . . . 60 1·25
239 – 10pf.+5pf. green . . . 90 1·75
240 – 15pf.+10pf. red . . . 1·75 3·00
DESIGNS—HORIZ: 10pf. Lege Tor. VERT: 15pf. Georgshalle, 1487.

1936. 125th Anniv of Brosen. Inscr "125 JAHRE OSTEEBAD BROSEN".
241 – 10pf. green . . . 75 70
242 – 25pf. red . . . 1·25 2·00
243 54 40pf. blue . . . 1·60 4·00
DESIGNS—HORIZ: 10pf. Brosen Beach; 25pf. Zoppot end of Brosen Beach.

55 Frauentor and Observatory **56** D(anziger) L(uftschutz) B(und) **57a** Danziger Dorf, Magdeburg

1936. Winter Relief Fund.
244 – 10pf.+5pf. blue . . . . . 1·90 2·50
245 **55** 15pf.+5pf. green . . . . . 1·90 4·00
246 – 25pf.+10pf. red . . . . . 3·25 5·25
247 – 40pf.+20pf. brn & red . . 4·50 8·25
248 – 50pf.+20pf. blue . . . . . 8·00 12·50
DESIGNS—VERT: 10pf. Milchkannenturm; 25pf. Krantor. HORIZ: 40pf. Langgartertor; 50pf. Hohestor.

1937. Air Defence League.
249 **56** 10pf. blue . . . . 35 1·40
250 15pf. purple . . . . 1·25 2·25

1937. Foundation of Danzig Community. Magdeburg.
253 **57a** 25pf. (+25pf.) red . . . . 2·50 5·25
254 – 40pf. (+40pf.) red & bl . . 2·50 5·25
DESIGN—HORIZ: 40pf. Village and Arms of Danzig and Magdeburg.

58 Madonna and Child **59** Schopenhauer

1937. Winter Relief Fund. Statues.
255 **58** 5pf.+5pf. violet . . . . . 2·25 5·25
256 – 10pf.+5pf. brown . . . . 2·25 4·25
257 – 15pf.+5pf. orange & blue 2·25 6·50
258 – 25pf.+10pf. green & blue 3·00 7·00
259 – 40pf.+25pf. blue & red . . 5·25 14·00
DESIGNS: 10pf. Mercury; 15pf. The "Golden Knight"; 25pf. Fountain of Neptune; 40pf. St. George and Dragon.

1938. 150th Birth Anniv of Schopenhauer (philosopher). Portraits inscr as in T **59**.
260 – 15pf. blue (as old man) . . 1·60 1·75
261 – 25pf. brown (as youth) . . 3·25 6·50
262 **59** 40pf. red . . . . 1·60 3·25

60 Yacht "Peter von Danzig" (1936) **61** Teutonic Knights

1938. Winter Relief Fund. Ships.
276 **60** 5pf.+5pf. green . . . . . 90 1·60
277 – 10pf.+5pf. brown . . . . 1·40 2·50
278 – 15pf.+10pf. olive . . . . . 1·50 2·50
279 – 25pf.+10pf. blue . . . . . 2·00 3·25
280 – 40pf.+15pf. purple . . . . 3·00 6·50
DESIGNS: 10pf. Dredger "Fu Shing"; 15pf. Liner "Columbus"; 25pf. Liner "Hansestadt Danzig"; 40pf. Sailing ship "Peter von Danzig" (1472).

1939. 125th Anniv of Prussian Annexation. Historical designs.
281 **61** 5pf. green . . . . 45 2·00
282 – 10pf. brown . . . . 75 2·10
283 – 15pf. blue . . . . 90 2·75
284 – 25pf. purple . . . . 1·40 3·50
DESIGNS: 10pf. Danzig–Swedish treaty of neutrality, 1630; 15pf. Danzig united to Prussia, 2.1.1814; 25pf. Stephen Batori's defeat at Weichselmunde, 1577.

62 Gregor Mendel

1939. Anti-cancer Campaign.
285 **62** 10pf. brown 45 85
286 – 15pf. black (Koch) . . . . 45 1·40
287 – 25pf. green (Rontgen) . . . 75 2·40

OFFICIAL STAMPS

1921. Stamps of Danzig optd **D M**.
O 94 **18** 5f. orange 25 35
O 95 10pf. brown 25 25
O 96 15pf. green 25 25
O 97 20pf. grey 25 25
O 98 25pf. green 25 25
O 99 30pf. red and blue . . . 55 65
O100 40pf. red and green . . 25 25
O101 50pf. red and green . . 25 25
O102 60pf. red 25 25
O103 75pf. purple 10 30
O104 80pf. red and black . . . 75 1·25
O105 80pf. green . . . . . . 10 1·00
O106 1m. orange 25 25
O107 1m.20 blue . . . . . . 1·60 1·10
O108 1m.25 red and purple . . 65 35
O109 1m.50 grey 25 45
O110 2m. red and grey . . . . 16·00 16·00
O111 2m. red 20 30
O112 2m.40 red and brown . . 1·00 2·50
O113 3m. red and purple . . . 11·00 13·00
O114 3m. red 25 45
O122 4m. blue 20 55
O116 5m. green 25 40
O117 6m. red 25 35
O118 10m. orange 25 35
O119 20m. brown 25 35

1922. Stamps of Danzig optd **D M**.
O120a **19** 5m. green, black and red (No. 91) . . . . . . 4·00 6·50
O126a **25** 50m. red and blue . . . 20 50
O142 50m. blue 25 40
O127a 100m. red and green . . 20 50
O143 100m. green 25 40
O144 200m. orange 25 40
O145 **29** 300m. red and green . . 25 50
O146 500m. red and grey . . 25 55
O147 100m. red and brown 25 40

1922. No. 96 optd **D M**.
O121 **18** 6 on 3m. red 25 65

1924. Optd **Dienst-marke**.
O195 **39** 5pf. orange . . . . . . 1·75 1·60
O196 10pf. green . . . . . . 2·50 2·50
O197 15pf. grey . . . . . . 2·60 2·10
O198 15pf. red . . . . 20·00 7·50
O199 20pf. red and carmine . . 2·00 1·60
O200 25pf. red and black . . . 20·00 22·00
O201 30pf. red and green . . . 2·50 5·00
O202 35f. blue . . . . 45·00 45·00
O203 40pf. blue and indigo . . 6·50 7·00
O204 50pf. red and blue . . . 20·00 26·00
O205 75pf. red and purple . . 40·00 85·00

POSTAGE DUE STAMPS

D 20 D 39

1921. Value in "pfennig" (figures only).
D 94 **D 20** 10pf. purple 40 35
D 95 20pf. purple 25 35
D 96 40pf. purple 25 35
D 97 60pf. purple 25 35
D 98 75pf. purple 25 35
D 99 80pf. purple 25 35
D112 100pf. purple 45 65
D100 120pf. purple 25 35
D101 200pf. purple . . . . 1·00 1·25
D102 240pf. purple . . . . 25 1·25
D114 300pf. purple . . . . 1·10 1·10
D115 400pf. purple . . . . 75 1·10
D116 500pf. purple . . . . 50 1·10
D117 800pf. purple . . . . 45 3·25

Value in "marks" ("M" after figure).
D118a **D 20** 10m. purple 45 37
D119a 20m. purple 45 65
D120a 50m. purple 45 70
D121 100m. purple 45 70
D122 500m. purple 45 70

1923. Surch with figures and bar.
D162 **D 20** 1000 on 100m. pur . . £130 £300
D163 5000 on 50m. purple 35 65
D164 10000 on 20m. pur . . 35 65
D165 50000 on 500m. pur 35 65
D166 100000 on 20m. pur 1·00 1·10

1924.
D178 **D 39** 5pf. blue and black . . 55 80
D179 10pf. blue and black 40 65
D180 15pf. blue and black 90 1·10
D181 20pf. blue and black 90 1·75
D182 30pf. blue and black 5·50 1·75
D183 40pf. blue and black 2·00 2·50
D184 50pf. blue and black 1·90 2·10
D185 60pf. blue and black 13·00 18·00
D186 100pf. blue and black 16·00 7·50
D187 3g. blue and red . . . 8·50 45·00

1932. Surch in figures over bar.
D226 **D 39** 5 on 40pf. blue & blk 2·50 7·00
D227 10 on 60pf. bl & blk 40·00 11·00
D228 20 on 100pf. bl & blk 2·50 7·25

DEDEAGATZ Pt. 6

Former French Post Office, closed in August 1914. Dedeagatz was part of Turkey to 1913, then a Bulgarian town.

25 centimes = 1 piastre.

1893. Stamps of France optd **Dedeagh** or surch also in figures and words.
59 **10** 5c. green . . . . 8·50 11·00
60 10c. black on lilac . . . . 18·00 17·00
62a 15c. blue . . . . 23·00 24·00
63 1pi. on 25c. black on red 29·00 25·00
64 2pi. on 50c. red . . . . . 55·00 45·00
65 4pi. on 1f. olive . . . . . 60·00 55·00
66 8pi. on 2f. brn on blue . . 80·00 70·00

1902. "Blanc", "Mouchon" and "Merson" key-types inscr "DEDEAGH". Some surch in figures and words.
67a A 5c. green . . . . 1·90 2·25
68 B 10c. red . . . . 1·25 1·50
70 15c. orange . . . . 2·50 2·40
71 1pi. on 25c. blue . . . . . 2·75 3·00
72 C 2pi. on 50c. brown & lav 6·00 8·00
73 4pi. on 1f. red and green 12·50 11·50
74 8pi. on 2f. lilac & yellow . . 19·00 19·00

DENMARK Pt. 11

A kingdom in N. Europe, on a peninsula between the Baltic and the North Sea.

1851. 96 rigsbank skilling = 1 rigsdaler.
1875. 100 ore = 1 krone.

1 2 4

1851. Imperf.
3 **1** 2r.b.s. blue £2500 £650
4 **2** 4r.b.s. brown . . . . £525 25·00

1854. Dotted background. Brown burelage. Imperf.
8 **4** 2sk. blue . . . . 60·00 45·00
9b 4sk. orange . . . . £275 7·00
12 8sk. green . . . . £350 50·00
13 16sk. lilac £400 £120

5 7 8

1858. Background of wavy lines. Brown burelage. Imperf.
15 **5** 4sk. brown . . . . 80·00 5·00
18 8sk. green . . . . £650 65·00

1863. Brown burelage. Roul
20 **5** 4sk. brown . . . . 95·00 11·00
21 **4** 16sk. mauve £1100 £450

1864. Perf.
22 **7** 2sk. blue . . . . 65·00 28·00
25 3sk. mauve . . . . 80·00 48·00
28 4sk. red . . . . 40·00 5·25
29 8sk. bistre . . . . £325 80·00
30a 16sk. green . . . . £500 80·00

1870. Value in "skilling".
39 **8** 2sk. blue and grey . . . . . 50·00 18·00
42 3sk. purple and grey . . . . 95·00 60·00
44 4sk. red and grey . . . . . 48·00 6·75
46 8sk. brown and grey . . . . £190 48·00
48 16sk. green and grey £250 £110
37 48sk. lilac and brown £450 £160

1875. As T **8**, but value in "ore".
80 **8** 3ore grey and blue . . . . . 2·75 3·25
81 4ore blue and grey . . . . . 4·50 20
56 5ore blue and red . . . . . 21·00 42·00
82 8ore red and grey . . . . . 4·00 20
83 12ore purple and grey . . . 4·50 1·90
84 16ore brown and grey . . . 11·50 2·40
72 20ore grey and red . . . . . £110 15·00
85 25ore green and grey . . . . 7·25 2·40
86 50ore purple and brown . . 23·00 11·00
87 100ore orange and grey . . . 23·00 8·00

10 **14** King Christian IX 15

1882.
96 **10** 1ore orange . . . . 35 40·00
97 5ore green . . . . 2·40 10
98 10ore red . . . . 2·00 10
99 15ore mauve . . . . 8·00 45
100 20ore blue . . . . 12·00 1·60
101 24ore brown . . . . 6·50 2·25

1904. No. 82 and 101 surch.
102 **8** 4ore on 8ore red & grey 1·40 1·90
103 **10** 15ore on 24ore brown . . 2·25 2·75

1904.
119 **14** 5ore green . . . . 2·50 10
104 10ore red . . . . 2·40 10
105 20ore blue . . . . 10·50 70
106 25ore brown . . . . 17·00 1·90
107 50ore lilac . . . . 45·00 35·00
108 100ore brown . . . . . . 8·50 20·00

1905. Solid background.
173 **15** 1ore orange 20 15
174 2ore red . . . . 1·50 15
175 3ore grey . . . . 3·75 30
176 4ore blue . . . . 4·00 25
177 5ore brown 50 10
178 5ore green 45 20
179 7ore green . . . . 1·90 1·50
180 7ore violet . . . . 8·75 2·50
181 8ore grey . . . . 3·00 1·50
114 10ore pink . . . . 4·00 10
182 10ore green 60 15
183 10ore brown . . . . 2·40 20
184 12ore lilac . . . . 14·00 3·25
115 15ore mauve . . . . 10·00 60
116 20ore blue . . . . 23·00 50
For stamps with lined background but without hearts, see Nos. 265/76k.

17 King Frederik VIII **20** G.P.O., Copenhagen

1907.
121 **17** 5ore green 80 10
122 10ore red . . . . 1·50 10
124 20ore blue . . . . 8·75 40
125 25ore brown . . . . 17·00 40
127 35ore orange . . . . . . 3·00 2·10
128 50ore purple . . . . 18·00 2·40
130 100ore brown . . . . . . 60·00 1·50

1912. (a) Nos. 84 and 72 surch **35 ORE**.
131 **8** 35ore on 16ore brn & grey 7·50 23·00
132 35ore on 20ore grey and red 13·00 28·00

(b) No. O98 surch **35 ORE FRIMAERKE**.
133 **O 9** 35ore on 32ore green . . 13·00 38·00

1912.
134 **20** 5k. red . . . . £150 70·00

21 King Christian X **22**

1913.
135 **21** 5ore green 60 10
136 7ore orange . . . . 1·90 50
137 8ore grey . . . . 5·75 2·75
138 10ore red 80 10
139 12ore grey . . . . 3·50 4·25
141a 15ore mauve . . . . 1·60 10
142 20ore blue . . . . 8·00 20
143 20ore brown 55 10
144 20ore red 90 10
145 25ore brown . . . . 10·50 20
146 25ore black and brown . . 40·00 2·00
147 25ore red . . . . 1·90 40
148 25ore green . . . . 1·90 30
149 27ore black and red . . . 16·00 21·00
150 30ore black and green . . 16·00 1·00
151 30ore orange . . . . 1·90 2·00
152 30ore blue 95 25
153 35ore yellow . . . . 14·00 1·75
154 35ore black and yellow . . 4·25 2·50
155 40ore black and violet . . 15·00 1·60
156 40ore blue . . . . 2·50 55
157 40ore yellow . . . . 1·10 55
158 50ore purple . . . . 26·00 1·50
159 50ore black and purple . . 35·00 65
160a 50ore grey . . . . 5·50 20
161 60ore blue and brown . . 35·00 2·00
162 60ore blue . . . . 6·75 45
163 70ore green and brown . . 16·00 1·40
164 80ore green . . . . 32·00 7·00
165 90ore red and brown . . . 9·50 1·75
166 **22** 1k. brown . . . . 70·00 50
167 **21** 1k. blue and brown . . . 23·00 95
168 **22** 2k. black . . . . 95·00 3·00
169 **21** 2k. purple and grey . . . 32·00 6·25
170 **22** 5k. violet . . . . 8·50 4·75
171 **21** 5k. brown and mauve . . 3·75 3·25
172 10k. green and red . . . £170 21·00

1915. (a) No. O94 surch **DANMARK 80 ORE POSTFRIM.**
186 **O 9** 80ore on 8ore red . . . . 22·00 60·00

(b) No. 83 surch **80 ORE**.
187 **8** 80ore on 12ore pur & grey 21·00 55·00

1918. Newspaper stamps surch **POSTFRIM. ORE 27 ORE DANMARK**.
197 **N 18** 27ore on 1ore green . . 2·75 5·25
198 27ore on 5ore blue . . . 3·50 11·50
199 27ore on 7ore red . . . 1·90 4·25
200 27ore on 8ore green . . 2·40 4·50

201 27ore on 10ore lilac . . 1·90 4·50
202 27ore on 20ore green . . 2·25 6·00
203 27ore on 29ore orge . . 2·00 4·50
204 27ore on 38ore orge . . 11·00 42·00
205 27ore on 41ore brn . . 4·75 20·00
194 27ore on 68ore brn . . 3·00 17·00
206 27ore on 1k. pur & grn 1·90 3·75
195 27ore on 5k. grn & pk 4·00 9·25
196 27ore on 10k. bl & stone 3·75 12·50

1919. No. 135 surch **2 ORE**.
207 **21** 2ore on 5ore green £1000 £300

27 Castle of Kronborg, Elsinore
29 Roskilde Cathedral

1920. Recovery of Northern Schleswig.
208 **27** 10ore red . . . . 1·75 15
209 10ore green . . . . 4·50 25
210 – 20ore slate . . . . 1·60 25
211 **29** 40ore brown . . . . 6·00 2·50
212 40ore blue . . . . 26·00 3·25
DESIGN—HORIZ: 20ore Sonderborg Castle.

1921. Nos. 136 and 139 surch **8 8**.
217 **21** 8 on 7ore orange . . . . . 1·75 1·50
213 8 on 12ore green . . . . . 1·90 3·50

1921. Red Cross. Nos. 209/10 surch with figure of value between red crosses.
214 **27** 10ore+5ore green . . . . 9·00 26·00
215 – 20ore+10ore grey . . . . 12·00 32·00

1921. No. 175 surch **8**.
216 **15** 8 on 3ore grey . . . . . . 2·00 1·75

33 King Christian IV
34 King Christian X
35

1924. 300th Anniv of Danish Post. A. Head facing to left.
218A **33** 10ore green . . . . . . 3·25 2·75
221A **34** 10ore green . . . . . . 3·25 2·75
219A **33** 15ore mauve . . . . . . 3·25 2·75
222A **34** 15ore mauve . . . . . . 3·25 2·75
220A **33** 20ore brown . . . . . . 3·25 2·75
223A **34** 20ore brown . . . . . . 3·25 2·75

B. Head facing to right.
218B **33** 10ore green . . . . . . 3·25 2·75
221B **34** 10ore green . . . . . . 3·25 2·75
219B **33** 15ore mauve . . . . . . 3·25 2·75
222B **34** 15ore mauve . . . . . . 3·25 2·75
220B **33** 20ore brown . . . . . . 3·25 2·75
223B **34** 20ore brown . . . . . . 3·25 2·75

1925. Air.
224 **35** 10ore green . . . . 12·00 16·00
225 15ore lilac . . . . 29·00 32·00
226 25ore red . . . . 18·00 25·00
227 50ore grey . . . . 60·00 85·00
228 1k. brown . . . . 60·00 85·00

1926. Surch **20 20**.
229 **21** 20 on 30ore orange . . . . 2·75 5·25
230 20 on 40ore blue . . . . . 3·25 6·25

38
39
40 Caravel

1926. 75th Anniv of First Danish stamps.
231 **38** 10ore olive 50 10
232 **39** 20ore red 85 10
233 30ore blue . . . . 3·25 50

1926. Various stamps surch.
234 **15** 7 on 8ore grey . . . . . . 1·00 2·10
235 **21** 7 on 20ore red 40 60
236 7 on 27ore black & red . . 2·40 5·75
237 12 on 15ore lilac . . . . . 1·25 3·25

1926. Official stamps surch **DANMARK 7 ORE POSTFRIM.**
238 **O 9** 7ore on 1ore orange . . . 3·00 5·25
239 7ore on 3ore grey . . . . 12·50 13·00
240 7ore on 4ore blue . . . . 2·40 5·50
241 7ore on 5ore green . . . 35·00 45·00
242 7ore on 10ore green . . . 2·40 5·25
243 7ore on 15ore lilac . . . 2·40 4·50
244 7ore on 20ore blue . . . 10·00 26·00

1927. Solid background.
246 **40** 15ore red . . . . 2·50 10
247 20ore grey . . . . 5·75 55
248 25ore blue 40 25
249 30ore yellow 55 10
250 35ore red . . . . 11·00 50
251 40ore green . . . . 9·75 10

For stamps with lined background see Nos. 277b, etc.

41
42 King Christian X
43 Numeral

1929. Danish Cancer Research Fund.
252 **41** 10ore (+5ore) green . . . 2·50 4·50
253 15ore (+5ore) red . . . . 3·75 6·50
254 25ore (+5ore) blue . . . . 13·50 27·00

1930. 60th Birthday of King Christian X.
255 **42** 5ore green . . . . 1·00 10
256 7ore violet . . . . 4·25 1·40
257 8ore grey . . . . 13·00 10·50
258 10ore brown . . . . 1·90 10
259 15ore red . . . . 6·50 10
260 20ore grey . . . . 11·50 2·75
261 25ore blue . . . . 4·25 45
262 30ore yellow . . . . 4·25 85
263 35ore red . . . . 8·25 1·50
264 40ore green . . . . 7·75 50

1933. Lined background.
265 **43** 1ore green 10 10
266 2ore red 10 10
267 4ore blue 25 25
268 5ore green 65 15
268c 5ore purple 10 10
268d 5ore orange 10 10
268e 6ore orange 10 10
269 7ore violet . . . . 1·25 25
269a 7ore green . . . . 1·00 40
269b 7ore brown 15 15
270 8ore grey 35 15
270a 8ore green 15 10
271 10ore orange . . . . . . 6·75 10
271b 10ore brown . . . . . . 5·00 20
271c 10ore violet 20 20
271d 10ore green 10 10
272 12ore green 10 10
272a 15ore green 10 10
272c 20ore blue 10 10
272e 25ore green 25 10
272f 25ore blue 10 10
273 30ore green 10 10
273a 30ore orange 10 10
273c 40ore orange 10 10
273d 40ore purple 10 10
274 50ore brown 10 10
274d 60ore green 75 35
274e 60ore grey 40 30
275 70ore red 45 10
275a 70ore green 15 15
275d 80ore green 20 10
275e 80ore brown 30 25
276 100ore green 30 10
276a 100ore blue 30 10
276b 125ore brown 35 15
276c 150ore green 35 10
276ca 150ore violet 40 15
276d 200ore green 45 10
276e 230ore green 55 25
276f 250ore green 55 25
276g 270ore green 55 35
276h 300ore green 70 25
276i 325ore green 70 30
276j 350ore green 70 40
276k 375ore green 80 60

45 King Christian X
47 Fokker FVIIa over Copenhagen
49 Hans Andersen

1933. T **40** with lined background.
277b **40** 15ore red . . . . 2·10 15
277de 15ore green . . . . . . 5·75 15
278a 20ore grey . . . . 3·25 15
278b 20ore red 40 10
279 25ore blue . . . . 40·00 12·50
279b 25ore brown 40 20
280a 30ore orange 50 15
280b 30ore blue 75 15
281 35ore violet 40 10
282 40ore green . . . . . . 3·00 10
282b 40ore blue 95 10
283 **45** 50ore grey 90 10
283a 60ore green . . . . . . 2·25 15
283b 75ore blue 45 20
284 1k. brown . . . . 3·25 20
284a 2k. red . . . . 5·00 55
284b 5k. violet . . . . 8·00 1·75

1934. Nos. 279 and 280a surch.
285 **40** 4 on 25ore blue 25 25
286 10 on 30ore orange . . . . 2·10 1·60

1934. Air.
287 **47** 10ore orange . . . . . . 75 1·00
288 15ore red . . . . 2·25 3·25
289 20ore green . . . . 2·40 3·50
290 50ore green . . . . 2·40 3·50
291 1k. brown . . . . 8·00 11·00

1935. Centenary of Hans Andersen's Fairy Tales.
292 – 5ore green . . . . 3·00 10
293 **49** 7ore violet . . . . 1·40 1·25
294 – 10ore orange . . . . . . 4·25 10
295 **49** 15ore red . . . . 9·50 10
296 20ore grey . . . . 9·25 50
297 30ore blue . . . . 1·75 15
DESIGNS: 5ore "The Ugly Duckling"; 10ore "The Little Mermaid".

51 St. Nicholas's Church, Copenhagen
52 Hans Tausen

53 Ribe Cathedral
54 Dybbol Mill

1936. 400th Anniv of Reformation.
298 **51** 5ore green 95 10
299 7ore mauve . . . . 95 1·40
300 **52** 10ore brown . . . . 1·40 10
301 15ore red . . . . 2·00 10
302 **53** 30ore blue . . . . 8·75 40

1937. H. P. Hanssen (North Schleswig patriot) Memorial Fund.
303 **54** 5ore+5ore green 40 50
304 10ore+5ore brown . . . . 2·10 3·00
305 15ore+5ore red . . . . . 2·10 3·75

56 King Christian X

1937. Silver Jubilee of King Christian X.
306 – 5ore green . . . . 1·00 10
307 **56** 10ore brown 90 15
308 – 15ore red 90 10
309 **56** 30ore blue . . . . 11·00 1·10
DESIGNS—HORIZ: 5ore Marselisborg Castle and "Rita" (King's yacht); 15ore Amalienborg Castle.

1937. Copenhagen Philatelic Club's 50th Anniv Stamp Exhibition. No. 271b optd **K.P.K. 17.-26. SEPT. 19 37** (="Kobenhavns Philatelist Klub").
310 **43** 10ore brown . . . . 95 1·25

58 Emancipation Monument
59 B. Thorvaldsen
61 Queen Alexandrine

1938. 150th Anniv of Abolition of Villeinage.
311 **58** 15ore red 50 10

1938. Centenary of Return of Sculptor Thorvaldsen to Denmark.
312 **59** 5ore purple 20 10
313 – 10ore violet 25 10
314 **59** 30ore blue . . . . 1·40 30
DESIGN: 10ore Statue of Jason.

1939. Red Cross Charity. Cross in red.
314a **61** 5ore+3ore purple 25 25
315 10ore+5ore violet 30 25
316 15ore+5ore red 30 30

1940. Stamps of 1933 (lined background) surch.
317 **43** 6 on 7ore green 15 25
318 6 on 8ore grey 15 25
319a **40** 15 on 40ore green 45 70
320 20 on 15ore red 75 10
321 40 on 30ore blue 50 20

65 Queen Ingrid (when Princess) and Princess Margrethe
66 Bering's Ship "Sv. Pyotr"

1941. Child Welfare.
322 **65** 10ore+5ore violet 20 20
323 20ore+5ore red 20 25

1941. Death Bicent of Vitus Bering (explorer).
324 **66** 10ore violet 25 10
325 20ore brown 60 10
326 40ore blue 40 25

67 King Christian X
68 Round Tower of Trinity Church

1942.
327 **67** 10ore violet 10 10
328 15ore green 10 10
329 20ore red 20 10
330 25ore brown 35 10
331 30ore orange 35 10
332 35ore purple 30 20
333 40ore blue 35 10
333a 45ore olive 35 10
334 50ore grey 50 10
335 60ore green 45 10
335a 75ore blue 45 15

1942. Tercentenary of the Round Tower.
336 **68** 10ore violet 10 10

69 Focke-Wulf Condor
70 Osterlars Church

1943. 25th Anniv of D.D.L. Danish Airlines.
337 **69** 20ore red 10 10

1944. Red Cross. No. 336 surch **5** and red cross.
338 **68** 10ore+5ore violet 10 10

1944. Danish Churches.
339 – 10ore violet 10 10
340 **70** 15ore green 15 25
341 – 20ore red 15 10
DESIGNS: 10ore Ejby Church; 20ore Hvidbjerg Church.

71 Ole Romer
72 King Christian X
73 Arms

1944. Birth Tercent of Romer (astronomer).
342 **71** 20ore brown 20 10

1945. King Christian's 75th Birthday.
343 **72** 10ore mauve 20 10
344 20ore red 25 10
345 40ore blue 50 20

1946.
346 **73** 1k. brown 60 10
346a 1k.10 purple . . . . . . 2·50 90
346b 1k.20 grey . . . . 1·00 10
346c 1k.20 blue . . . . 1·10 25
346d 1k.25 orange . . . . . . 1·75 10
346e 1k.30 green . . . . . . 3·00 90
346f 1k.50 purple 85 10
346g 2k. red . . . . 1·25 10
347 2k.20 orange . . . . . . 1·60 10
347a 2k.50 orange . . . . . . 1·00 10
347b 2k.80 grey . . . . 1·50 20
347c 2k.80 green 85 50
347d 2k.80 green 85 35
347e 2k.90 purple . . . . . . 2·50 10
347f 3k. green 85 10
347g 3k.10 purple . . . . . . 3·50 25
347h 3k.30 red 95 50
347i 3k.50 purple . . . . . . 1·10 10
347j 3k.50 blue . . . . 1·75 1·75
347k 4k. grey . . . . 1·00 10
347l 4k.10 brown . . . . . . 3·50 25
347m 4k.30 brown . . . . . . 1·90 1·60
347n 4k.30 green . . . . . . 2·50 1·90
347o 4k.50 brown . . . . . . 3·25 15
347p 4k.60 grey . . . . 1·75 1·75
347q 4k.70 purple . . . . . . 2·00 1·50
348 5k. blue . . . . 2·50 10
348a 5k.50 blue . . . . 1·90 50
348b 6k. black . . . . 1·40 10
348c 6k.50 green . . . . . . 1·60 35
348d 6k.60 green . . . . . . 2·00 1·40
348e 7k. mauve . . . . 1·60 10
348f 7k.10 purple . . . . . . 1·50 80
348g 7k.30 green . . . . . . 2·00 1·75
348h 7k.50 green . . . . . . 2·10 1·60
348i 7k.70 purple . . . . . . 1·90 70
348j 8k. orange . . . . 1·90 10
348k 9k. brown . . . . 1·75 10

348l 10k. yellow 1·90 10
348la 10k.50 blue 1·75 10
348m 11k. brown 2·50 1·75
348n 12k. brown 3·00 35
348o 14k. brown 3·50 35
348p 16k. red 4·00 50
348q 17k. red 4·50 55
348r 18k. brown 4·75 50
348s 20k. blue 4·25 40
348t 22k. red 4·75 70
348u 23k. green 5·00 1·00
348v 24k. green 5·00 75
348w 25k. green 5·50 30
348x 26k. green 6·00 90
348z 50k. red 11·00 1·40

74 Tycho Brahe
75 Symbols of Freedom

1946. 400th Birth Anniv of Tycho Brahe (astronomer).
349 **74** 20ore red 30 10

1947. Liberation Fund.
350 **75** 15ore+5ore green 20 30
351 – 20ore+5ore red (Bombed railways) 70 45
352 – 40ore+5ore blue (Flag) 45 70

77 Class H Steam Goods Train
79 I. C. Jacobsen

1947. Centenary of Danish Railways.
353 – 15ore green 35 10
354 **77** 20ore red 50 10
355 – 40ore blue 2·50 1·25
DESIGNS—HORIZ: 15ore First Danish locomotive "Odin"; 40ore Diesel-electric train "Lyntog" and train ferry "Fyn".

1947. 60th Death Anniv of Jacobsen and Centenary of Carlsberg Foundation for Promotion of Scientific Research.
356 **79** 20ore red 25 10

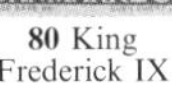
80 King Frederick IX
81 "The Constituent Assembly of the Kingdom" (after Constantin Hansen)

1948.
357a **80** 15ore green 75 20
358 15ore violet 45 10
359a 20ore red 45 10
360 20ore brown 20 10
361 25ore brown 85 20
362 25ore red 2·40 10
362a 25ore blue 50 10
362b 25ore violet 20 10
363 30ore orange 8·50 30
363b 30ore red 30 15
364 35ore green 20 15
365 40ore blue 3·00 40
366 40ore grey 70 10
367 45ore bistre 95 10
368 50ore grey 1·10 20
369 50ore blue 1·90 10
369a 50ore green 20 10
370 55ore brown 17·00 1·00
371a 60ore blue 45 10
371b 65ore grey 45 15
372 70ore green 1·25 10
373 75ore purple 75 15
373a 80ore orange 45 10
373b 90ore bistre 1·60 10
373c 95ore orange 50 25

1949. Centenary of Danish Constitution.
374 **81** 20ore brown 30 10

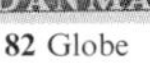
82 Globe

83 Kalundborg Transmitter

1949. 75th Anniv of U.P.U.
375 **82** 40ore blue 50 30

1950. 25th Anniv of State Broadcasting.
376 **83** 20ore brown 30 10

84 Princess Anne-Marie
85 "Fredericus Quartus" (warship)
86 H. C. Oersted (after C. A. Jensen)

1950. National Children's Welfare Assn.
377 **84** 25ore+5ore red 35 35

1951. 250th Anniv of Naval Officers' College.
378 **85** 25ore red 50 20
379 50ore blue 2·75 60

1951. Death Centenary of Oersted (physicist).
380 **86** 50ore blue 1·00 40

87 Mail Coach
88 Hospital Ship "Jutlandia"

1951. Danish Stamp Centenary.
381 **87** 15ore violet 50 15
382 25ore red 50 15

1951. Danish Red Cross Fund.
383 **88** 25ore +5ore red 55 55

89 "Life-Saving" (relief, H. Solomon)
91 Memorial Stone, Skamlings-banken
92 Runic Stone at Jelling

1952. Centenary of Danish Life-Saving Service.
384 **89** 25ore red 35 15

1953. Netherlands Flood Relief Fund. Surch **NL+10**.
385 **80** 30ore+10ore red 95 80

1953. Danish Border Union Fund.
386 **91** 30ore+5ore red 95 80

1953. 1,000 years of Danish Kingdom. Inscr "KONGERIGE i 1000 AR". (a) 1st series.
387 **92** 10ore green 20 15
388 – 15ore lilac 20 15
389 – 20ore brown 20 15
390 – 30ore red 20 15
391 – 60ore blue 35 15
DESIGNS: 15ore Vikings' camp, Trelleborg; 20ore Kalundborg Church; 30ore Nyborg Castle; 60ore Goose Tower, Vordinborg.

(b) 2nd series.
392 – 10ore green 15 15
393 – 15ore lilac 15 15
394 – 20ore brown 15 15
395 – 30ore red 15 15
396 – 60ore blue 50 15
DESIGNS: 10ore Spottrup Castle; 15ore Hammershus Castle; 20ore Copenhagen Stock Exchange; 30ore King Frederik V statue; 60ore Soldier's Statue (H. V. Bissen).

93 Telegraph Table, 1854

94 Head of Statue of King Frederik V at Amalienborg

1954. Telecommunications Centenary.
397 **93** 30ore brown 30 20

1954. Bicent of Royal Academy of Fine Arts.
398 **94** 30ore red 45 15

1955. Liberty Fund. Nos. 350/1 surch.
399 **75** 20+5 on 15ore +5ore grn 85 70
400 – 30+5 on 20ore +5ore red 85 75

1955. Nos. 268e, 269b, 359a and 362 surch.
401 **43** 5ore on 6ore orange 20 15
402 5ore on 7ore brown 20 15
403 **80** 30ore on 20ore red 15 15
404 30ore on 25ore red 50 25

98 S. Kierkegaard (philosopher)
99 Ellehammer's Aircraft

1955. Death Centenary of Kierkegaard.
405 **98** 30ore red 30 10

1956. 50th Anniv of 1st Flight by J. C. H. Ellehammer.
406 **99** 30ore red 45 10

100 Whooper Swans

102 National Museum

1956. Northern Countries' Day.
407 **100** 30ore red 1·00 10
408 60ore blue 1·00 55

1957. Danish Red Cross Hungarian Relief Fund. No. 373c surch **Ungarns-hjaelpen 30 + 5**.
409 **80** 30ore+5ore on 95ore orange 50 40

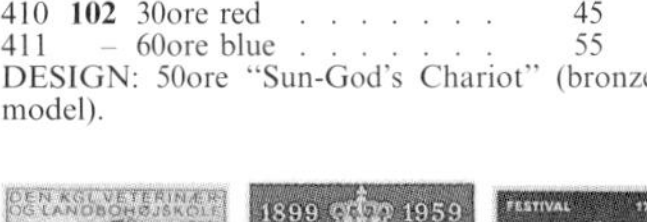
1957. 150th Anniv of National Museum.
410 **102** 30ore red 45 10
411 – 60ore blue 55 50
DESIGN: 50ore "Sun-God's Chariot" (bronze age model).

103 Harvester

105 King Frederik IX

106 Margrethe Schanne in "La Sylphide"

1958. Centenary of Danish Royal Veterinary and Agricultural College.
412 **103** 30ore red 20 10

1959. Greenland Fund. No. 363b surch **Gronlands-fonden + 10**.
413 **80** 30ore+10ore red 65 60
The Greenland Fund was devoted to the relatives of the crew and passengers of the "Hans Hedtoft", the Greenland vessel lost at sea on 30 January 1959.

1959. 60th Birthday of King Frederik IX.
414 **105** 30ore red 15 10
415 35ore purple 35 20
416 60ore blue 35 10

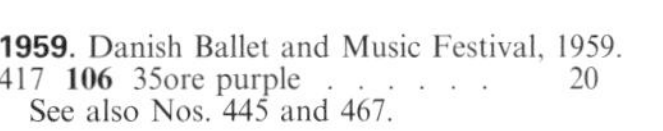
1959. Danish Ballet and Music Festival, 1959.
417 **106** 35ore purple 20 10
See also Nos. 445 and 467.

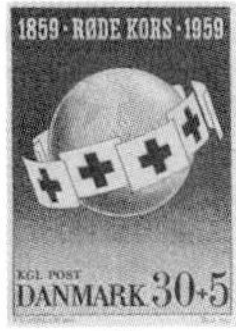
107

109 Sowing Machine

1959. Centenary of Red Cross.
418 **107** 30ore+5ore red 35 35
419 60ore+5ore red & blue 50 50

1960. World Refugee Year. Surch 30 **Verdensflygtninge-aret 1959-60** and uprooted tree.
420 **80** 30ore on 15ore violet 20 10

1960. 1st Danish Food Fair.
421 **109** 12ore green 15 10
422 – 30ore red 15 10
423 – 60ore blue 50 30
DESIGNS: 30ore Combine-harvester; 60ore Plough.

110 King Frederik and Queen Ingrid

111 Ancient Bascule Light

1960. Royal Silver Wedding.
424 **110** 30ore red 30 10
425 60ore blue 45 40

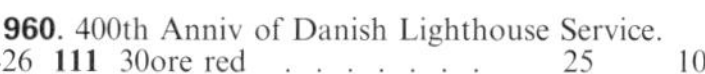
1960. 400th Anniv of Danish Lighthouse Service.
426 **111** 30ore red 25 10

112 N. Finsen

113 Mother and Child

1960. Birth Cent of Niels R. Finsen (physician).
427 **112** 30ore red 15 15

1960. W.H.O. 10th European Regional Committee Meeting.
428 **113** 60ore blue 45 35

113a Conference Emblem

114 Queen Ingrid

1960. Europa.
429 **113a** 60ore blue 35 35

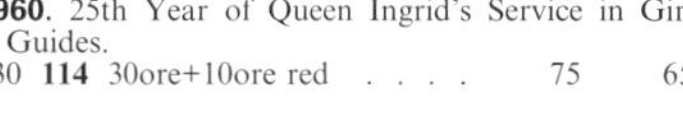
1960. 25th Year of Queen Ingrid's Service in Girl Guides.
430 **114** 30ore+10ore red 75 65

115 Douglas DC-8

116 Coastal Scene

1961. 10th Anniv of Scandinavian Airlines System (SAS).
431 **115** 60ore blue 45 15

1961. 50th Anniv of Society for Preservation of Danish National Amenities.
432 **116** 30ore red 15 10

117 King Frederik IX

118 Borkop Watermill

119 African Mother and Child

1961.
433 **117** 20ore brown 15 10
434 25ore brown 15 10
435 30ore red 15 10
436 35ore green 50 40
437 35ore red 15 10
438 40ore grey 60 10
438a 40ore brown 15 10
439 50ore turquoise 35 10
439a 50ore red 20 10
439b 50ore brown 35 10
440 60ore blue 45 10
440a 60ore red 70 10
441 70ore green 70 20
442 80ore orange 85 10
442a 80ore blue 80 30
442b 80ore green 40 10
443 90ore olive 2·50 30

443a 90ore blue 55 15
444 95ore purple 80 50

1962. Danish Ballet and Music Festival, 1962. As T **106** but inscr "15–31 MAJ".
445 60ore blue 20 20

1962. "Dansk Fredning" (Preservation of Danish Natural Amenities and Ancient Monuments) and Centenary of Abolition of Mill Monopolies.
446 **118** 10ore brown 15 15

1962. Aid for Under-developed Countries.
447 **119** 30ore+10ore red 60 55

120 "Selandia"

1962. 50th Anniv of Freighter "Selandia".
448 **120** 60ore blue . . . . 1·40 80

121 "Tivoli"

1962. 150th Birth Anniv of George Carstensen (founder of Tivoli Pleasure Gardens, Copenhagen).
449 **121** 35ore purple 15 20

122 Cliffs, Island of Mon
123 Wheat

1962. "Dansk Fredning" (Preservation of Danish Natural Amenities and Ancient Monuments).
450 **122** 20ore brown 15 15

1963. Freedom from Hunger.
451 **123** 35ore red 15 15

124 Rail and Sea Symbols
125 19th-century Mail Transport

1963. Opening of Denmark–Germany Railway ("Bird-flight Line").
452 **124** 15ore green 25 15

1963. Centenary of Paris Postal Conference.
453 **125** 60ore blue 25 35

126 Hands
127 Prof. Niels Bohr

1963. Danish Cripples Foundation Fund.
454 **126** 35ore+10ore red 65 55

1963. 50th Anniv of Bohr's Atomic Theory.
455 **127** 35ore red 30 20
456 60ore blue 40 35

128 Ancient Bridge, Immervad
129 "Going to School" (child's slate)

1964. Danish Border Union Fund.
457 **128** 35ore+10ore red 45 45

1964. 150th Anniv of Institution of Primary Schools.
458 **129** 35ore brown 25 10

130 Princesses Margrethe, Benedikte and Anne-Marie
131 "Exploration of the Sea"

1964. Danish Red Cross Fund.
459 **130** 35ore+10ore red 40 40
460 60ore+10ore blue & red 1·00 60

1964. International Council for the Exploration of the Sea Conference, Copenhagen.
461 **131** 60ore blue 45 45

132 Danish Stamp "Watermarks, Perforations and Varieties"
133 Landscape, R. Karup

1964. 25th Anniv of Stamp Day.
462 **132** 35ore pink 20 10

1964. "Dansk Fredning" (Preservation of Danish Natural Amenities and Ancient Monuments).
463 **133** 25ore brown 15 20

134 Office Equipment
135 Morse Key, Teleprinter Tape and I.T.U. Emblem

1965. Centenary of 1st Commercial School.
464 **134** 15ore green 15 15

1965. Centenary of I.T.U.
465 **135** 80ore blue 35 10

136 C. Nielsen
137 Child in Meadow

1965. Birth Centenary of Carl Nielsen (composer).
466 **136** 50ore red 15 10

1965. Danish Ballet and Music Festival, 1965. As T **106** but inscr "15-31 MAJ".
467 50ore red 15 10

1965. Child Welfare.
468 **137** 50ore+10ore red 45 35

138 Bogo Windmill
139 Titles of International Red Cross Organizations

1965. "Dansk Fredning" (Preservation of Danish Natural Amenities and Ancient Monuments).
469 **138** 40ore brown 10 10

1966. Danish Red Cross Fund.
470 **139** 50ore+10ore red . . . 25 35
471 80ore+10ore bl & red . . 45 55

140 Heathland
141 C. Kold

1966. Centenary of Danish Heath Society.
472 **140** 25ore green 10 20

1966. 150th Birth Anniv of Christen Kold (educationist).
473 **141** 50ore red 10 10

142 Almshouses, Copenhagen
143 Trees at Bregentved

1966. "Dansk Fredning" (Preservation of Danish Natural Amenities and Ancient Monuments).
474 **142** 50ore red 15 10
475 **143** 80ore blue 45 25

144 G. Jensen
145 Fund Emblem

1966. Birth Cent of Georg Jensen (silversmith).
476 **144** 80ore blue 40 25

1966. "Refugee 66" Fund.
477 **145** 40ore+10ore brown . . . 40 40
478 50ore+10ore red 40 40
479 80ore+10ore blue 75 70

146 Barrow in Jutland
147 Musical Instruments

1966. "Dansk Fredning" (Preservation of Danish Natural Amenities and Ancient Monuments).
480 **146** 1k.50 green 55 10

1967. Cent of Royal Danish Academy of Music.
481 **147** 50ore red 10 10

148 Cogwheels
149 Old City and Windmill

1967. European Free Trade Assn.
482 **148** 80ore blue 40 10

1967. 800th Anniv of Copenhagen.
483 **149** 25ore green 10 10
484 – 40ore brown 20 10
485 – 50ore brown 30 10
486 – 80ore blue 65 50
DESIGNS: 40ore Old bank and ship's masts; 50ore Church steeple and burgher's house; 80ore Building construction.

150 Princess Margrethe and Prince Henri de Monpezat
151 H. C. Sonne

1967. Royal Wedding.
487 **150** 50ore red 20 10

1967. 150th Anniv of Hans Sonne (founder of Danish Co-operative Movement).
488 **151** 60ore red 20 10

152 "Rose"
153 Porpoise and Cross-anchor

1967. The Salvation Army.
489 **152** 60ore+10ore red 40 35

1967. Centenary of Danish Seamen's Church in Foreign Ports.
490 **153** 90ore blue 35 25

154 Esbjerg Harbour
155 Koldinghus Castle

1968. Cent of Esbjerg Harbour Construction Act.
491 **154** 30ore green 20 10

1968. 700th Anniv of Koldinghus Castle.
492 **155** 60ore red 20 10

156 "The Children in the Round Tower" (Greenlandic legend)
157 Shipbuilding

1968. Greenlandic Child Welfare.
493 **156** 60ore+10ore red 45 45

1968. Danish Industries.
494 **157** 30ore green 10 10
495 – 50ore brown 10 10
496 – 60ore red 10 10
497 – 90ore blue 65 70
INDUSTRIES: 50ore Chemicals, 60ore Electric power, 90ore Engineering.

158 "The Sower"
159 Viking Ships (from old Swedish coin)

1969. Bicentenary of Danish Royal Agricultural Society.
498 **158** 30ore green 15 10

1969. 50th Anniv of Northern Countries' Union.
499 **159** 60ore red 40 10
500 90ore blue 85 95

160 King Frederik IX
161 Colonnade

1969. King Frederik's 70th Birthday.
501 **160** 50ore brown 25 25
502 60ore red 25 25

1969. Europa.
503 **161** 90ore blue 60 45

162 Kronborg Castle
163 Fall of Danish Flag

1969. 50th Anniv of "Danes Living Abroad" Association.
504 **162** 50ore brown 15 10

1969. 750th Anniv of "Danish Flag Falling from Heaven".
505 **163** 60ore red, blue & black 20 10

164 M. A. Nexo

165 Niels Stensen (geologist)

1969. Birth Cent of Martin Andersen Nexo (poet).
506 **164** 80ore green 40 10

1969. 300th Anniv of Stensen's "On Solid Bodies".
507 **165** 1k. sepia 40 10

166 "Abstract"

167 Symbolic "P"

1969. "Non-figurative" stamp.
508 **166** 60ore red, rose and blue 20 10

1969. Birth Cent of Valdemar Poulsen (inventor).
509 **167** 30ore green 15 10

168 Princess Margrethe, Prince Henri and Prince Frederik (baby)

169 "Postgiro"

1969. Danish Red Cross.
510 **168** 50ore+10ore brn & red 45 35
511 60ore+10ore brn & red 45 35

1970. 50th Anniv of Danish Postal Giro Service.
512 **169** 60ore and orange 15 10

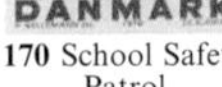

170 School Safety Patrol

171 Child appealing for Help

1970. Road Safety.
513 **170** 50ore brown 20 10

1970. 25th Anniv of Save the Children Fund.
514 **171** 60ore+10ore red 45 45

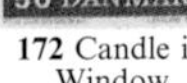

172 Candle in Window

173 Red Deer in Park

1970. 25th Anniv of Liberation.
515 **172** 50ore black, yellow & bl 20 10

1970. 300th Anniv of Jaegersborg Deer Park.
516 **173** 60ore brown, red & grn 10 10

174 Ship's Figurehead ("Elephanten")

175 "The Reunion"

1970. 300th Anniv of "Royal Majesty's Model Chamber" (Danish Naval Museum).
517 **174** 30ore multicoloured . . . 10 10

1970. 50th Anniv of North Schleswig's Reunion with Denmark.
518 **175** 60ore violet, yellow & grn 10 10

176 Electromagnetic Apparatus

1970. 150th Anniv of Oersted's Discovery of Electromagnetism.
519 **176** 80ore green 35 10

177 Bronze-age Ship (from engraving on razor)

1970. Danish Shipping.
520 **177** 30ore purple and brown 20 10
521 – 50ore brn and purple . . 20 10
522 – 60ore brown and green 20 10
523 – 90ore blue and green . . 60 55
DESIGNS: 50ore Viking shipbuilders (Bayeux Tapestry); 60ore "Emanuel" (schooner); 90ore "A. P. Moller" (tanker).

178 Strands of Rope

179 B. Thorvaldsen from self-portrait

1970. 25th Anniv of United Nations.
524 **178** 90ore red, green & blue 65 55

1970. Birth Bicentenary of Bertel Thorvaldsen (sculptor).
525 **179** 2k. blue 70 45

180 Mathilde Fibiger (suffragette)

181 Refugees

1971. Centenary of Danish Women's Association ("Kvindesamfund").
526 **180** 80ore green 35 10

1971. Aid for Refugees.
527 **181** 50ore brown 25 15
528 60ore red 25 15

182 Danish Child

183 Hans Egede

1971. National Children's Welfare Association.
529 **182** 60ore+10ore red 45 45

1971. 25th Anniv of Hans Egede's Arrival in Greenland.
530 **183** 1k. brown 40 10

184 Swimming

185 Georg Brandes

1971. Sports.
531 **184** 30ore green and blue . . 15 10
532 – 50ore dp brown & brown 15 10
533 – 60ore yellow, blue & grey 45 10
534 – 90ore violet, green & bl 70 60
DESIGNS: 50ore Hurdling; 60ore Football; 90ore Yachting.

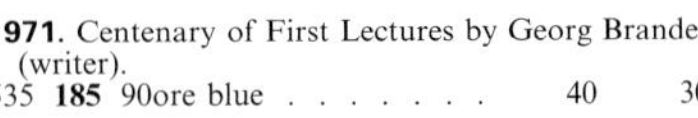

1971. Centenary of First Lectures by Georg Brandes (writer).
535 **185** 90ore blue 40 30

186 Beet Harvester

1972. Centenary of Danish Sugar Production.
536 **186** 80ore green 35 20

187 Meteorological Symbols

1972. Cent of Danish Meteorological Office.
537 **187** 1k.20 brown, blue & pur 50 40

188 King Frederik IX

189 "N. F. S. Grundtvig" (pencil sketch, P. Skovgaard)

1972. King Frederik IX-In Memoriam.
538 **188** 60ore red 20 10

1972. Death Centenary of N. F. S. Grundtvig (poet and clergyman).
539 **189** 1k. brown 40 25

190 Locomotive "Odin", Ship and Passengers

191 Rebild Hills

1972. 125th Anniv of Danish State Railways.
540 **190** 70ore red 30 10

1972. Nature Protection.
541 **191** 1k. green, brown & blue 40 10

192 Marsh Marigold

193 "The Tinker" (from Holberg's satire)

1972. Centenary of "Vanforehjemmet" (Home for the Disabled).
542 **192** 70ore+10ore yellow & bl 45 40

1972. 250th Anniv of Theatre in Denmark and of Holberg's Comedies.
543 **193** 70ore red 20 10

194 W.H.O. Building, Copenhagen

195 Little Belt Bridge

1972. Inauguration of World Health Organization Building, Copenhagen.
544 **194** 2k. black, blue and red 60 45

1972. Danish Construction Projects.
545 **195** 40ore green 10 10
546 – 60ore brown 25 10
547 – 70ore red 25 10
548 – 90ore green 40 35
DESIGNS: 60ore Hanstholm port; 70ore Limfjord Tunnel; 90ore Knudshoved port.

196 House, Aeroskobing

197 Johannes Jensen

1972. Danish Architecture.
549 **196** 40ore black, brown & red 10 10
550 – 60ore blue, green & brn 10 10
551 – 70ore brown, red & verm 25 10
552 – 1k.20 grn, brn & dp brn 80 65
DESIGNS—28 × 21 mm: 60ore Farmhouse, East Bornholm; 37 × 21 mm: 1k.20, Farmhouse, Hvide Sande; 21 × 37 mm: 70ore House, Christanshavn.

1973. Birth Cent of Johannes Jensen (writer).
553 **197** 90ore green 40 10

198 Cogwheels and Guardrails

199 P. C. Abildgaard (founder)

1973. Centenary of 1st Danish Factory Act.
554 **198** 50ore brown 10 10

1973. Bicentenary of Royal Veterinary College, Christianshavn.
555 **199** 1k. blue 40 30

200 "Rhododendron impeditum"

201 Nordic House, Reykjavik

1973. Cent of Jutland Horticultural Society.
556 **200** 60ore violet, green & brn 40 20
557 – 70ore pink, green & red 40 20
DESIGN: 70ore "Queen of Denmark" rose.

1973. Nordic Countries' Postal Co-operation.
558 **201** 70ore multicoloured . . . 30 10
559 1k. multicoloured 95 75

202 Stella Nova and Sextant

203 "St. Mark the Evangelist" (Book of Dalby)

1973. 400th Anniv of Tycho Brahe's "De Nove Stella" (book on astronomy).
560 **202** 2k. blue 60 25

1973. 300th Anniv of Royal Library.
561 **203** 1k.20 multicoloured . . . 50 40

204 Heimaey Eruption

205 "Devil and Scandalmongers" (Fanefjord Church)

1973. Aid for Victims of Heimaey Eruption, Iceland.
562 **204** 70ore+20ore red and blue 50 40

1973. Church Frescoes. Each red, turquoise and yellow on cream.
563 70ore Type **205** 75 25
564 70ore "Queen Esther and King Xerxes" (Tirsted Church) 75 25
565 70ore "The Harvest Miracle" (Jetsmark Church) 95 25
566 70ore "The Crowning with Thorns" (Biersted Church) 80 25
567 70ore "Creation of Eve" (Fanefjord Church) 80 25

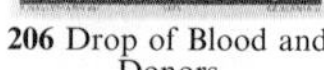

206 Drop of Blood and Donors   **207** Queen Margrethe

1974. Blood Donors Campaign.
568 **206** 90ore red and violet . . . 30 10

1974.
569 **207** 60ore brown 30 25
570 60ore orange 30 20
571 70ore red 15 10
572 70ore brown 15 20
573 80ore green 40 20
574 80ore brown 30 10
575 90ore purple 40 10
576 90ore red 55 20
577 90ore olive 45 15
577a 90ore grey . . . . . 1·40 1·00
578 100ore blue 50 30
579 100ore grey 40 20
580 100ore red 40 10
580a 100ore brown 40 10
580b 110ore orange 55 25
580c 110ore brown 40 20
581 120ore grey 45 30
581b 120ore red 45 10
582 130ore blue 90 65
582a 130ore red 45 10
582b 130ore brown 45 30
582c 140ore orange 95 85
582d 150ore blue 60 45
582e 150ore red 55 40
582f 160ore blue 75 50
582g 160ore red 50 10
582h 180ore green 55 15
582i 180ore blue 75 55
582j 200ore blue 65 55
582k 210ore grey . . . . . 1·10 1·00
582l 230ore green 75 25
582m 250ore green 85 45

208 Theatre Facade   **209** Hverringe

1974. Centenary of Tivoli Pantomime Theatre, Copenhagen.
583 **208** 100ore blue 35 10

1974. Provincial Series.
584 **209** 50ore multicoloured . . . 20 15
585 – 60ore grn, dp grn & mve 35 35
586 – 70ore multicoloured . . . 35 45
587 – 90ore multicoloured . . . 35 15
588 – 120ore grn, red & orge . . 35 45
DESIGNS—HORIZ: 60ore Carl Nielsen's birthplace, Norre Lyndelse; 70ore Hans Christian Andersen's birthplace, Odense; 1k.20, Hindsholm. VERT: 90ore Hessselagergaard.

210 Orienteering   **211** "Iris spuria"

1974. World Orienteering Championships.
589 **210** 70ore brown and blue . . 50 40
590 – 80ore blue and brown . . 25 10
DESIGN: 80ore Compass.

1974. Cent of Botanical Gardens, Copenhagen.
591 **211** 90ore blue, green & brn 35 10
592 – 120ore red, green and blue 45 40
DESIGN: 120ore "Dactylorhiza purpurella" (orchid).

212 Mail-carriers of 1624 and 1780   **213** Pigeon with Letter

1974. 350th Anniv of Danish Post Office.
593 **212** 70ore bistre and purple 30 20
594 – 90ore green and purple 35 10
DESIGN: 90ore Johan Colding's postal balloon (1808) H.M.S. "Edgar" and H.M.S. "Dictator".

1974. Centenary of U.P.U.
595 **213** 120ore blue 40 10

215 Radio Equipment of 1925   **216** Queen Margrethe and I.W.Y. Emblem

1975. 50th Anniv of Danish Broadcasting.
597 **215** 90ore pink 35 10

1975. International Women's Year.
598 **216** 90ore+20ore red 55 50

217 Floral Decorated Plate   **218** Moravian Brethren Church Christiansfeld

1975. Danish Porcelain.
599 **217** 50ore green 10 10
600 – 90ore red 40 10
601 – 130ore blue 65 75
DESIGNS: 90ore Floral decorated tureen; 130ore Floral decorated vase and tea-caddy.

1975. European Architectural Heritage Year.
602 **218** 70ore brown 35 35
603 – 120ore green 40 35
604 – 150ore blue 35 20
DESIGNS—HORIZ: 120ore Farmhouse, Lejre. VERT: 150ore Anna Queenstraede (street), Helsingore.

219 "Numskull Jack" (V. Pedersen)   **220** Watchman's Square, Aabenraa

1975. 170th Birth Anniv of Hans Christian Andersen.
605 **219** 70ore grey and brown . . 45 45
606 – 90ore brown and red . . 45 10
607 – 130ore brown and blue 1·10 90
DESIGNS: 90ore Hans Andersen (from photograph by G. E. Hansen); 130ore "The Marshking's Daughter" (L. Frolich).

1975. Provincial series. South Jutland.
608 **220** 70ore multicoloured . . . 30 35
609 – 90ore brown, red & blue 30 10
610 – 100ore multicoloured . . 40 20
611 – 120ore blue, black & grn 45 35
DESIGNS—VERT: 90ore, Haderslev Cathedral. HORIZ: 100ore, Mogeltonder Polder; 120ore, Estuary of Vidaaen at Hojer floodgates.

221 River Kingfisher

1975. Danish Endangered Animals.
612 **221** 50ore blue 35 20
613 – 70ore brown 35 30
614 – 90ore brown 35 10
615 – 130ore blue 80 65
616 – 200ore black 45 10
DESIGNS: 70ore West European hedgehog; 90ore Cats; 130ore Pied avocets; 200ore European otter.
The 90ore also commemorates the centenary of the Danish Society for the Prevention of Cruelty to Animals.

222 Viking Longship

1976. Bicentenary of American Revolution.
618 **222** 70ore+20ore brown . . . 55 50
619 – 90ore+20ore red . . . 55 50
620 – 100ore+20ore green . . . 55 50
621 – 130ore+20ore blue . . . 55 50
DESIGNS: 90ore Freighter "Thingvalla"; 100ore Liner "Frederik VIII"; 130ore Cadet full-rigged ship "Danmark".

223 "Humanity"   **224** Old Copenhagen

1976. Centenary of Danish Red Cross.
622 **223** 100ore+20ore black and red 40 35
623 130ore+20ore black, red and blue 55 45

1976. Provincial Series. Copenhagen.
624 **224** 60ore multicoloured . . . 20 25
625 – 80ore multicoloured . . . 20 25
626 – 100ore red & vermilion 45 25
627 – 130ore grn, dp brn & brn 85 90
DESIGNS—VERT: 80ore View from the Round Tower; 100ore Interior of the Central Railway Station. HORIZ: 130ore Harbour buildings.

225 Handicapped Person in Wheelchair   **226** Mail Coach Driver (detail from "A String of Horses outside an Inn" (O. Bache))

1976. Danish Foundation for the Disabled.
628 **225** 100ore+20ore black and red 50 40

1976. "Hafnia 76" Stamp Exhibition.
629 **226** 130ore multicoloured . . 70 65

227 Prof. Emil Hansen   **228** Moulding Glass

1976. Centenary of Carlsberg Foundation.
631 **227** 100ore red 40 10

1976. Danish Glass Industry.
632 **228** 60ore green 15 25
633 – 80ore brown 30 10
634 – 130ore blue 45 65
635 – 150ore red 30 10
DESIGNS: 80ore Removing glass from pipe; 130ore Cutting glass; 150ore Blowing glass.

229 Five Water Lilies   **230** "Give Way"

1977. Northern Countries Co-operation in Nature Conservation and Environment Protection.
636 **229** 100ore multicoloured . . 30 10
637 130ore multicoloured . . 70 95

1977. Road Safety.
638 **230** 100ore brown 50 10

231 Mother and Child   **232** Allinge

1977. 25th Anniv of Danish Society for the Mentally Handicapped.
639 **231** 100ore+20ore green, blue and brown 30 45

1977. Europa.
640 **232** 1k. brown 40 10
641 – 1k.30 blue . . . . 2·40 2·10
DESIGN: 1k.30, Farm near Ringsted.

233 Kongeaen   **234** Hammers and Horseshoes

1977. Provincial Series. South Jutland.
642 **233** 60ore green and blue . . 70 50
643 – 90ore multicoloured . . . 40 30
644 – 150ore multicoloured . . 40 30
645 – 200ore grn, pur & emer 50 35
DESIGNS: 90ore Skallingen; 150ore Torskind; 200ore Jelling.

1977. Danish Crafts.
646 **234** 80ore brown 30 10
647 – 1k. red 30 10
648 – 1k.30 blue 55 45
DESIGNS: 1k. Chisel, square and plane; 1k.30, Trowel, ceiling brush and folding rule.

235 Globe Flower   **236** Handball Player and Emblem

1977. Endangered Flora.
649 **235** 1k. green, yellow & brn 35 10
650 – 1k.50 green, ol & brn . . 70 50
DESIGN: 1k.50, "Cnidium dubium".

1978. Men's Handball World Championship.
651 **236** 1k.20 red 40 10

237 Christian IV on Horseback   **238** Jens Bang's House, Aalborg

1978. Centenary of National History Museum, Frederiksborg.
652 **237** 1k.20 brown 40 10
653 – 1k.80 black 55 25
DESIGN: 1k.80, North-west aspect of Frederiksborg Castle.

1978. Europa.
654 **238** 1k.20 brown 35 10
655 – 1k.50 blue and dp blue 80 60
DESIGN: 1k.50, Plan and front elevation of Frederiksborg Castle, Copenhagen.

239 Kongenshus Memorial Park   **240** Boats in Harbour

1978. Provincial Series. Central Jutland.
656 **239** 70ore multicoloured . . . 30 30
657 – 1k.20 multicoloured . . . 40 10
658 – 1k.50 multicoloured . . . 75 55
659 – 1k.80 blue, brn & grn . . 45 40
DESIGNS: 1k.20, Post office, Aarhus Old Town; 1k.50, Lignite fields, Soby; 1k.80, Church wall, Stadil Church.

1978. Fishing Industry.
660 **240** 70ore green 30 25
661 – 1k. brown 30 25
662 – 1k.80 black 40 25
663 – 2k.50 brown 55 25
DESIGNS: 1k. Eel traps; 1k.80, Fishing boats on the slipway; 2k.50, Drying ground.

241 Campaign Emblem

1978. 50th Anniv of Danish Cancer Campaign.
664 **241** 120ore+20ore red 50 40

242 Common Morel **243** Early and Modern Telephones

1978. Mushrooms.
665 **242** 1k. brown 55 40
666 – 1k.20 red 55 10
DESIGN: 1k.20, Satan's mushroom.

1979. Centenary of Danish Telephone System.
667 **243** 1k.20 red 50 10

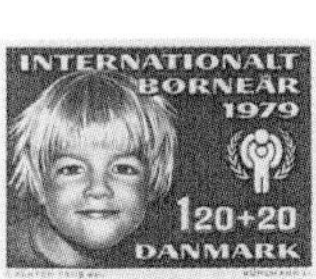

244 Child **245** University Seal

1979. International Year of the Child.
668 **244** 1k.20+20ore red & brn . . 40 40

1979. 500th Anniv of Copenhagen University.
669 **245** 1k.30 red 40 10
670 – 1k.60 black 45 40
DESIGN: 1k.60, Pentagram representing the five faculties.

246 Letter Mail Cariole **247** Pendant

1979. Europa.
671 **246** 1k.30 red 75 10
672 – 1k.60 blue . . . . 1·10 65
DESIGN: 1k.60, Morse key and sounder.

1979. Viking "Gripping Beast" Decorations.
673 **247** 1k.10 brown 35 10
674 – 2k. green 60 35
DESIGN: 2k. Key.

248 Mols Bjerge **249** Silhouette of Oehlenschlager

1979. Provincial Series. North Jutland.
675 **248** 80ore green, ultram & brown 30 25
676 – 90ore multicoloured . . . 90 90
677 – 200ore grn, orge & red . . 50 20
678 – 280ore slate, sepia & brn 60 60
DESIGNS. 90ore Orslev Kloster; 200ore Trans; 280ore Bovbjerg.

1979. Birth Bicentenary of Adam Oehlenschlager (poet).
679 **249** 1k.30 red 40 15

250 Music, Violin and Dancers (birth cent of Jacob Gade (composer)) **251** Royal Mail Guards' Office, Copenhagen (drawing, Peter Klaestrup)

1979. Anniversaries.
680 **250** 1k.10 brown 40 25
681 – 1k.60 blue 45 30
DESIGN: 1k.60, Dancer at bar (death centenary of August Bournonville (ballet master)).

1980. Bicentenary of National Postal Service.
682 **251** 1k.30 red 40 10

252 Stylized Wheelchair **253** Karen Blixen (writer)

1980. 25th Anniv of Foundation for the Disabled.
683 **252** 130ore+20ore red 50 40

1980. Europa.
684 **253** 1k.30 red 40 10
685 – 1k.60 blue 70 50
DESIGN: 1k.60, August Krogh (physiologist).

254 Symbols of Employment, Health and Education **255** Lindholme Hoje

1980. U.N. Decade for Women World Conference.
686 **254** 1k.60 blue 50 35

1980. Provincial Series. Jutland North of Limfjorden. Multicoloured.
687 80ore Type **255** 30 25
688 110ore Skagen lighthouse (vert) 35 25
689 200ore Borglum 50 15
690 280ore Fishing boats at Vorupor 90 75

256 Silver Pitcher, c. 1641

1980. Nordic Countries Postal Co-operation.
691 **256** 1k.30 black and red . . . 35 10
692 – 1k.80 blue & dp blue . . 70 60
DESIGN: 1k.80, Bishop's bowl.

257 Earliest Danish Coin, Hedeby (c. 800)

1980. Coins from the Royal Collection.
693 **257** 1k.30 red and brown . . 35 25
694 – 1k.40 olive and green . . 70 60
695 – 1k.80 blue and grey . . . 70 60
DESIGNS: 1k.40, Silver coin of Valdemar the Great and Bishop Absalon (1152–82); 1k.80, Christian VII gold current ducat (1781).

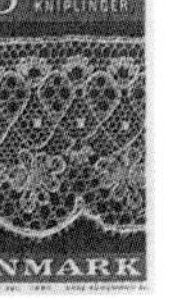

258 Lace Pattern **259** Children Playing in Yard

1980. Lace Patterns. Various designs showing lace.
696 **258** 1k.10 brown 35 40
697 – 1k.30 red 35 10
698 – 2k. green 55 10

1981. National Children's Welfare Association.
699 **259** 1k.60+20ore red 55 45

260 Original Houses, 1631 **261** Tilting at a Barrel (Shrovetide custom)

1981. 350th Anniv of Nyboder (Naval Barracks), Copenhagen.
700 **260** 1k.30 red and yellow . . 45 50
701 – 1k.60 red and yellow . . 35 10
DESIGN: 1k.60, 18th-century terraced houses.

1981. Europa.
702 **261** 1k.60 red 50 20
703 – 2k. blue 70 35
DESIGN: 2k. Midsummer bonfire.

262 Soro **263** Rigensgade District, Copenhagen

1981. Provincial Series. Zealand and Surrounding Islands.
704 **262** 100ore blue and brown 35 30
705 – 150ore black and green 35 35
706 – 160ore brown and green 40 10
707 – 200ore multicoloured . . 55 45
708 – 230ore blue and brown 60 40
DESIGNS: 150ore N. F. S. Grundtvig's childhood home, Udby; 160ore Kaj Munk's childhood home, Opager; 200ore Gronsund; 230ore Bornholm.

1981. European Urban Renaissance Year.
709 **263** 1k.60 red 40 15

264 Decaying Tree **265** Ellehammer at Lindholm, 1906

1981. International Year for Disabled Persons.
710 **264** 2k.+20ore blue 70 75

1981. History of Aviation.
711 **265** 1k. green and black . . . 25 40
712 – 1k.30 brown & dp brn . . 35 40
713 – 1k.60 vermilion & red . . 25 10
714 – 2k.30 blue & dp blue . . 1·00 40
DESIGNS: 1k.30, A. T. Botved's Fokker biplane "R-1" (Copenhagen–Tokyo, 1926); 1k.60, Hojriis Hillig's Bellanca Special "Liberty" (U.S.A.–Denmark, 1931); 2k.30, Douglas DC-7C "Seven Seas" (first Polar flight, 1957).

266 Queen Margrethe II **267** Revenue Cutter "Argus"

1982.
715 **266** 1k.60 red 45 10
716 1k.60 green . . . . . . 1·75 1·40
717 1k.80 brown 60 35
718 2k. red 60 15
719 2k.20 green . . . . . . 1·50 70
720 2k.30 violet 65 55
721 2k.50 red 65 10
722 2k.70 blue 85 50
723 2k.70 red . . . . 1·00 10
724 2k.80 red 85 10
725 3k. violet 85 15
726 3k. red 85 10
727 3k.20 violet 90 25
727a 3k.20 red 95 10
728 3k.30 black . . . . . . 1·00 45
729 3k.40 green . . . . . . 1·60 1·25
730 3k.50 blue . . . . . . 1·00 25
730a 3k.50 purple . . . . . 1·00 35
730b 3k.50 red . . . . 1·00 10
731 3k.70 blue . . . . . . 1·00 55
732 3k.75 green . . . . . . 1·10 85
733 3k.80 blue . . . . . . 1·00 25
734 3k.80 purple . . . . . . 1·10 1·00
735 4k.10 blue . . . . . . 1·25 15
736 4k.20 violet 90 65
737 4k.40 blue . . . . . . 1·25 90
738 4k.50 purple . . . . . . 1·10 1·60
739 4k.75 blue . . . . . . 1·10 70

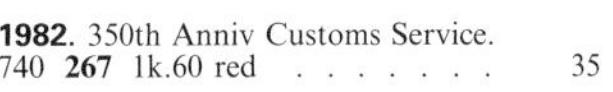

1982. 350th Anniv Customs Service.
740 **267** 1k.60 red 35 10

268 Skater **269** Villein (Abolition of adscription, 1788)

1982. World Figure Skating Championships, Copenhagen.
741 **268** 2k. blue 55 30

1982. Europa.
742 **269** 2k. brown 75 10
743 – 2k.70 blue 95 70
DESIGN: 2k.70, Procession of women (Enfranchisement of women, 1915).

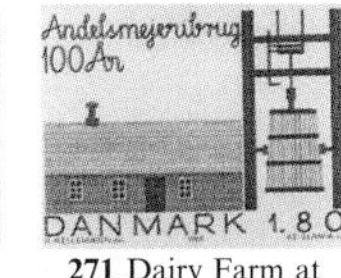

270 Distorted Plant **271** Dairy Farm at Hjedding and Butter Churn

1982. 25th Anniv of Danish Multiple Sclerosis Society.
744 **270** 2k.+40ore red . . . . . 1·10 70

1982. Centenary of Co-operative Dairy Farming.
745 **271** 1k.80 brown 60 35

272 Hand holding Quill Pen **273** Blicher (after J. V. Gertner)

1982. 400th Anniv of Record Office.
746 **272** 2k.70 green 75 25

1982. Birth Bicent of Steen Steensen Blicher (poet).
747 **273** 2k. red 65 15

274 Odense Printing Press, 1482 **275** Petersen and the Number Men

1982. 500th Anniv of Printing in Denmark.
748 **274** 1k.80 brown 60 40

1982. Birth Centenary of Robert Storm Petersen (cartoonist).
749 **275** 1k.50 red and blue . . . 45 40
750 – 2k. green and red 60 40
DESIGN—HORIZ: 2k. Peter and Ping with dog.

276 Library Seal

1982. 500th Anniv University Library.
751 **276** 2k.70 brown and black . . 80 25

277 "Interglobal Communications" **278** Nurse tending Patient

1983. World Communications Year.
752 **277** 2k. orange, red & blue . . 85 25

1983. Red Cross.
753 **278** 2k.+40ore blue & red . . 80 75

279 Clown and Girl with Balloon **280** Lene Koppen

1983. 400th Anniv of Dyrehavsbakken Amusement Park.
754 **279** 2k. multicoloured 60 15

1983. World Badminton Championships.
755 **280** 2k.70 blue 85 30

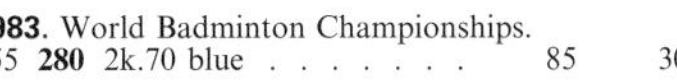

281 Burin and Engraving of lore Numeral Stamp **282** Egeskov Castle

1983. 50th Anniv of Danish Recess-printed Stamps.
756 **281** 2k.50 red 65 15

1983. Nordic Countries Postal Co-operation. "Visit the North".
757 **282** 2k.50 dp brown & brn . . 60 25
758 – 3k.50 dp blue & blue . . 90 35
DESIGN: 3k.50, Troldkirken long barrow, North Jutland.

283 Kildeskovshallen Recreation Centre, Copenhagen

284 Weights and Measures

1983. Europa.
759 **283** 2k.50 red and brown . . 85 10
760 – 3k.50 dp blue & blue . . 1·10 55
DESIGN: 3k.50, Sallingsund Bridge.

1983. 300th Anniv of Weights and Measures Ordinance.
761 **284** 2k.50 red 65 10

285 Title Page of Law

286 Crashed Car and Hand with Eye (Police)

1983. 300th Anniv of King Christian V's Danish Law (code of laws for Norway).
762 **285** 5k. dp brown & brown 1·40 45

1983. Life-saving Services.
763 **286** 1k. brown 20 20
764 – 2k.50 red 35 30
765 – 3k.50 blue . . . . 1·50 35
DESIGNS: 2k.50 Ladder, stretcher and fire-hose (ambulance and fire services); 3k.50 Lifebelt and lifeboat (sea-rescue services).

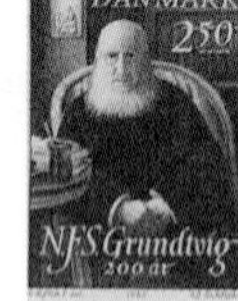

287 Family Group

288 Grundtvig (after Constantin Hansen)

1983. The Elderly in Society.
766 **287** 2k. green 60 40
767 – 2k.50 red 65 10
DESIGN: 2k.50 Elderly people in train.

1983. Birth Bicentenary of Nicolai Frederik Severin Grundtvig (writer).
768 **288** 2k.50 brown 65 25

289 Perspective Painting

1983. Birth Bicentenary of Christoffer Wilhelm Eckersberg (painter).
769 **289** 2k.50 red 65 25

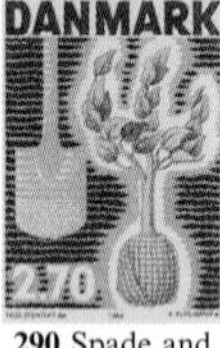
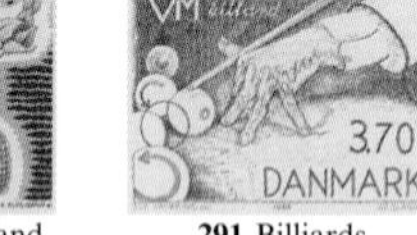

290 Spade and Sapling

291 Billiards

1984. Plant a Tree Campaign.
770 **290** 2k.70 yellow, red and green 75 25

1984. World Billiards Championships.
771 **291** 3k.70 green 95 30

292 Athletes

293 Compass Rose

1984. Olympic Games, Los Angeles.
772 **292** 2k.70+40ore mult . . . . 1·10 90

1984. Bicentenary of Hydrographic Department (2k.30) and 300th Anniv of Pilotage Service (2k.70).
773 **293** 2k.30 green 65 55
774 – 2k.70 red 80 10
DESIGN: 2k.70, Pilot boat.

294 Parliament Emblem

295 Girl Guides

1984. 2nd Direct Elections to European Parliament.
775 **294** 2k.70 yellow and blue . . 75 25

1984. Scout Movement.
776 **295** 2k.70 multicoloured . . . 75 15

296 Bridge

297 Anchor (memorial to Danish Sailors)

1984. Europa. 25th Anniv of European Post and Telecommunications Conference.
777 **296** 2k.70 red 95 10
778 3k.70 blue . . . . 1·40 80

1984. 40th Anniv of Normandy Invasion.
779 **297** 2k.70 purple 80 15

298 Prince Henrik

299 Old Danish Inn

1984. 50th Birthday of Prince Henrik.
780 **298** 2k.70 brown 80 15

1984.
781 **299** 3k. multicoloured . . . . 90 1·00

300 Shoal of Fish (research)

1984. Danish Fisheries and Shipping.
782 **300** 2k.30 blue and green . . 95 70
783 – 2k.70 blue and red . . . 75 20
784 – 3k.30 blue and violet . . 1·00 70
785 – 3k.70 blue & ultramarine 1·00 65
DESIGNS: 2k.70, Ships (sea transport); 3k.30, "Bettina" (deep sea fishing boat); 3k.70, Deck of trawler "Jonna Tornby".

301 Heart and Cardiograph

302 Bird with Letter

1984. Heart Foundation.
786 **301** 2k.70+40ore red 85 75

1984.
787 **302** 1k. multicoloured 35 15

303 "Holberg meeting Officer and Dandy" (Wilhelm Marstrand)

304 Woman and Sabbath Candles

1984. 300th Birth Anniv of Ludvig Holberg (historian and playwright).
788 **303** 2k.70 black, stone & red 80 15

1984. 300th Anniv of Jewish Community.
789 **304** 3k.70 multicoloured . . . 95 70

305 "Ymer sucking Milk from the Cow Odhumble" (Nicolai Abildgaard)

1984. Paintings. Multicoloured.
790 5k. "Carnival in Rome" (Christoffer Wilhelm Eckersberg) (horiz) . . . . 1·90 1·40
791 10k. Type **305** . . . . . . 3·25 2·25

306 Gothersgade Reformed Church, Copenhagen

1985. 300th Anniv of French and German Reformed Church in Denmark.
792 **306** 2k.80 red 80 10

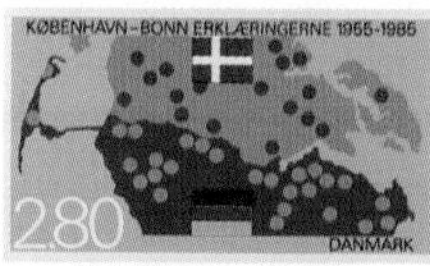

307 Flags and Border

1985. 30th Anniv of Copenhagen–Bonn Declarations.
793 **307** 2k.80 multicoloured . . . 95 40

308 Flag, Girl and Boy

310 Music Score

1985. International Youth Year.
794 **308** 3k.80 multicoloured . . . 95 40

1985. Europa. Music Year.
796 **310** 2k.80 yell, red & verm . . 1·00 40
797 – 3k.80 black, bl & grn . . 1·50 1·10
DESIGN: 3k.80, Music score (different).

311 Flames and Houses

312 Queen Ingrid and "Chrysanthemum frutescens" "Sofieri"

1985. 40th Anniv of Liberation.
798 **311** 2k.80+50ore mult . . . . 1·10 1·25
The surtax was for the benefit of Resistance veterans.

1985. 50th Anniv of Queen Ingrid's Arrival in Denmark.
799 **312** 2k.80 multicoloured . . . 80 25

313 Faro Bridges

314 St. Canute and Lund Cathedral

1985. Inauguration of Faro Bridges.
800 **313** 2k.80 multicoloured . . . 80 10

1985. 900th Anniv of St. Canute's Deed of Gift to Lund.
801 **314** 2k.80 black and red . . . 70 15
802 – 3k. black and red . . . . 1·10 70
DESIGN: 3k. St. Canute and Helsingborg.

315 Gymnastics

316 Woman Cyclist

1985. Sports. Multicoloured.
803 2k.80 Type **315** 90 10
804 3k.80 Canoeing . . . . . . 1·10 45
805 6k. Cycling . . . . 1·50 80

1985. United Nations Women's Decade.
806 **316** 3k.80 multicoloured . . . 95 45

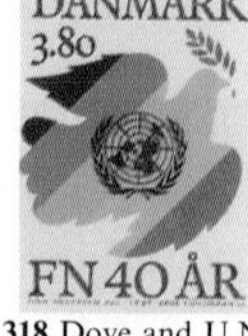

317 Kronborg Castle

318 Dove and U.N. Emblem

1985. 400th Anniv of Kronborg Castle, Elsinore.
807 **317** 2k.80 multicoloured . . . 80 15

1985. 40th Anniv of U.N.O.
808 **318** 3k.80 multicoloured . . . 90 60

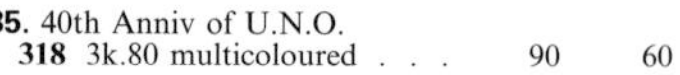

319 Niels and Margrethe Bohr

320 Tapestry (detail) by Caroline Ebbesen

1985. Birth Centenary of Niels Bohr (nuclear physicist).
809 **319** 2k.80 multicoloured . . . 95 85

1985. 25th Anniv of National Society for Welfare of the Mentally Ill.
810 **320** 2k.80+40ore mult . . . . 1·00 85

321 "D" in Sign Language

322 Stern of Boat

1985. 50th Anniv of Danish Association of the Deaf.
811 **321** 2k.80 brown & black . . 80 25

1985.
812 **322** 2k.80 multicoloured . . . 80 25

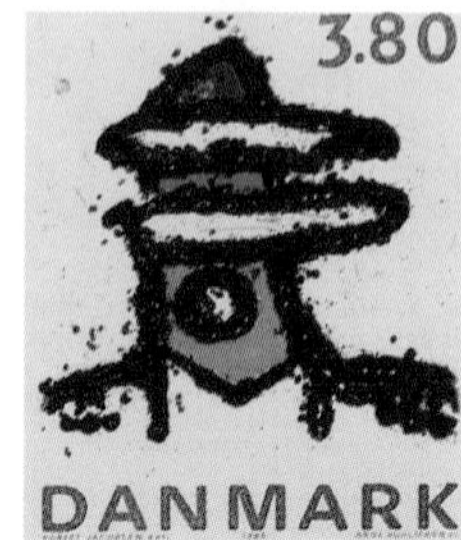

323 "Head"

1985.
813 **323** 3k.80 multicoloured . . . 1·75 1·25

324 Leaves and Barbed Wire

1986. 25th Anniv of Amnesty International.
814 **324** 2k.80 multicoloured . . . 80 10

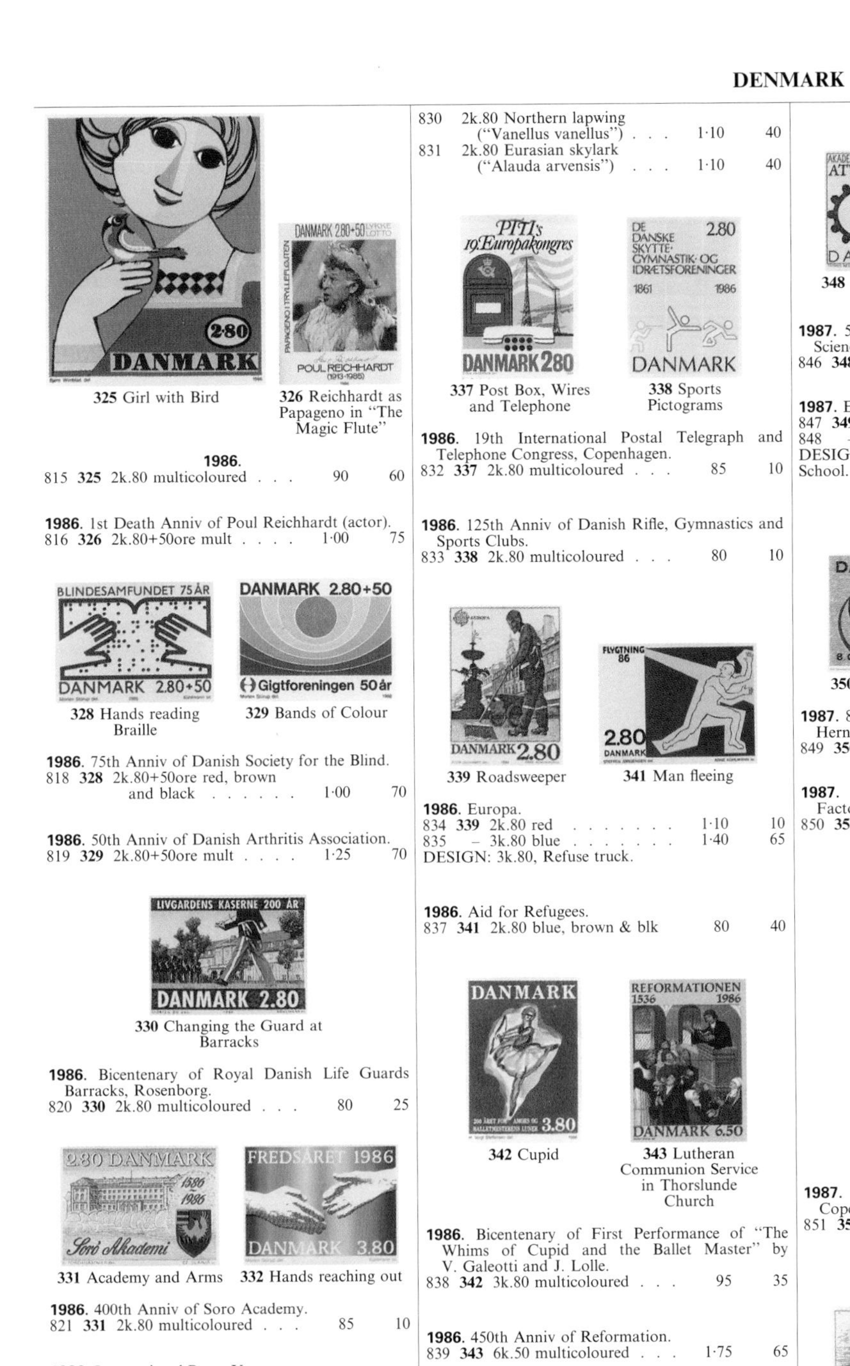

325 Girl with Bird

326 Reichhardt as Papageno in "The Magic Flute"

1986.
815 **325** 2k.80 multicoloured . . . 90 60

1986. 1st Death Anniv of Poul Reichhardt (actor).
816 **326** 2k.80+50ore mult . . . . 1·00 75

328 Hands reading Braille

329 Bands of Colour

1986. 75th Anniv of Danish Society for the Blind.
818 **328** 2k.80+50ore red, brown and black . . . . 1·00 70

1986. 50th Anniv of Danish Arthritis Association.
819 **329** 2k.80+50ore mult . . . . 1·25 70

330 Changing the Guard at Barracks

1986. Bicentenary of Royal Danish Life Guards Barracks, Rosenborg.
820 **330** 2k.80 multicoloured . . . 80 25

331 Academy and Arms

332 Hands reaching out

1986. 400th Anniv of Soro Academy.
821 **331** 2k.80 multicoloured . . . 85 10

1986. International Peace Year.
822 **332** 3k.80 multicoloured . . . 1·10 40

333 Prince Frederik

334 Station

1986. 18th Birthday of Crown Prince Frederik.
823 **333** 2k.80 black and red . . . 1·00 10

1986. Inaug of Hoje Tastrup Railway Station.
824 **334** 2k.80 black, bl & red . . 85 10

335 Aalborg

336 Common Raven

1986. Nordic Countries Postal Co-operation. Twinned Towns.
825 **335** 2k.80 black 90 10
826 – 3k.80 blue and red . . . 1·10 40
DESIGN: 3k.80, Thisted.

1986. Birds. Multicoloured.
827 2k.80 Type **336** . . . . . . 1·10 40
828 2k.80 Common starling ("Sturnus vulgaris") . . . 1·10 40
829 2k.80 Mute swan ("Cygnus olor") . . . . 1·10 40
830 2k.80 Northern lapwing ("Vanellus vanellus") . . . 1·10 40
831 2k.80 Eurasian skylark ("Alauda arvensis") . . . 1·10 40

337 Post Box, Wires and Telephone

338 Sports Pictograms

1986. 19th International Postal Telegraph and Telephone Congress, Copenhagen.
832 **337** 2k.80 multicoloured . . . 85 10

1986. 125th Anniv of Danish Rifle, Gymnastics and Sports Clubs.
833 **338** 2k.80 multicoloured . . . 80 10

339 Roadsweeper

341 Man fleeing

1986. Europa.
834 **339** 2k.80 red . . . . 1·10 10
835 – 3k.80 blue . . . . 1·40 65
DESIGN: 3k.80, Refuse truck.

1986. Aid for Refugees.
837 **341** 2k.80 blue, brown & blk 80 40

342 Cupid

343 Lutheran Communion Service in Thorslunde Church

1986. Bicentenary of First Performance of "The Whims of Cupid and the Ballet Master" by V. Galeotti and J. Lolle.
838 **342** 3k.80 multicoloured . . . 95 35

1986. 450th Anniv of Reformation.
839 **343** 6k.50 multicoloured . . . 1·75 65

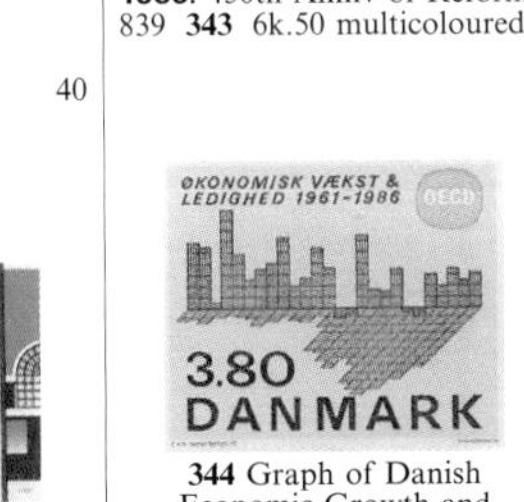

344 Graph of Danish Economic Growth and Unemployment Rate

345 Abstract

1986. 25th Anniv of Organization of Economic Co-operation and Development.
840 **344** 3k.80 multicoloured . . . 1·25 10

1987.
841 **345** 2k.80 multicoloured . . . 80 10

346 Price Label through Magnifying Glass

347 Fresco

1987. 40th Anniv of Danish Consumer Council.
842 **346** 2k.80 black and red . . . 85 10

1987. Ribe Cathedral. Multicoloured.
843 3k. Type **347** 85 40
844 3k.80 Stained glass window (detail) . . . . 1·25 70
845 6k.50 Mosaic (detail) . . . . 1·90 1·10

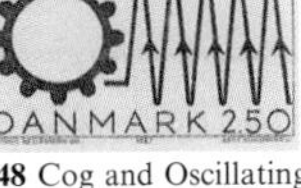

348 Cog and Oscillating Waves

349 Gentofte Central Library

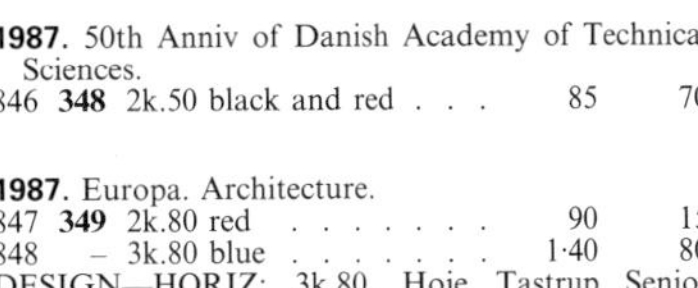

1987. 50th Anniv of Danish Academy of Technical Sciences.
846 **348** 2k.50 black and red . . . 85 70

1987. Europa. Architecture.
847 **349** 2k.80 red 90 15
848 – 3k.80 blue . . . . 1·40 80
DESIGN—HORIZ: 3k.80, Hoje Tastrup Senior School.

350 Ball and Ribbons

351 Pigs

1987. 8th Gymnaestrada (World Gymnastics Show), Herning.
849 **350** 2k.80 multicoloured . . . 80 10

1987. Centenary of First Co-operative Bacon Factory, Horsens.
850 **351** 3k.80 multicoloured . . . 95 55

352 1912 5k. Stamp, Steam Locomotive and Mail Wagon

1987. "Hafnia 87" International Stamp Exhibition, Copenhagen.
851 **352** 280ore multicoloured . . 1·10 1·00

353 Single Scull

354 Abstract

1987. World Rowing Championships, Bagsvaerd Lake.
853 **353** 3k.80 indigo and blue . . 1·10 40

1987.
854 **354** 2k.80 multicoloured . . . 85 10

355 Waves

1987. 25th Anniv of Danish Epileptics Association.
855 **355** 2k.80+50ore blue, red and green . . . . 1·10 80

356 Rask

357 Association Badge

1987. Birth Bicentenary of Rasmus Kristjan Rask (philologist).
856 **356** 2k.80 red and brown . . 80 10

1987. 125th Anniv of Clerical Association for Home Mission in Denmark.
857 **357** 3k. brown 80 10

358 Lions supporting Monogram

1988. 400th Anniv of Accession of King Christian IV.
858 **358** 3k. gold and blue 85 10
859 – 4k.10 multicoloured . . . 1·25 35
DESIGN: 4k.10, Portrait of Christian IV by P. Isaacsz.

359 Worm and Artefacts

360 St. Canute's Church

1988. 400th Birth Anniv of Ole Worm (antiquarian).
860 **359** 7k.10 brown . . . . . . 2·00 1·10

1988. Millenary of Odense.
861 **360** 3k. brown, black & green 1·10 10

361 African Mother and Child

362 Sirens, Workers and Emblem

1988. Danish Church Aid.
862 **361** 3k.+50ore mult . . . . . 1·10 70

1988. 50th Anniv of Civil Defence Administration.
863 **362** 2k.70 blue and orange . . 80 50

363 Blood Circulation of Heart

364 Postwoman on Bicycle

1988. 40th Anniv of W.H.O.
864 **363** 4k.10 red, blue and black 1·10 45

1988. Europa. Transport and Communications. Multicoloured.
865 3k. Type **364** 95 10
866 4k.10 Mobile telephone . . . 1·40 45

365 "King Christian VII riding past Liberty Monument" (C. W. Eckersberg)

366 "Men of Industry" (detail, P. S. Kroyer)

1988. Bicentenary of Abolition of Villeinage.
867 **365** 3k.20 multicoloured . . . 95 55

1988. 150th Anniv of Federation of Danish Industries.
868 **366** 3k. multicoloured 85 25

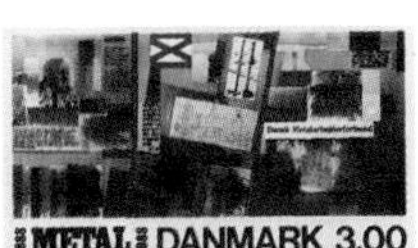

367 Speedway Riders

368 Glass Mosaic (Niels Winkel)

1988. World Speedway Championships.
869 **367** 4k.10 multicoloured . . . 1·10 40

1988. Centenary of Danish Metalworkers' Union.
870 **368** 3k. multicoloured 85 10

369 College

1988. Bicent of Tonder Teacher Training College.
871 **369** 3k. brown 85 10

370 "Tribute to Leon Degand" (Robert Jacobsen)

1988. Franco-Danish Cultural Co-operation.
872 **370** 4k.10 red and black 1·60 1·10

371 Emblem **372** Lumby Windmill

1988. 5th Anniv of National Council for the Unmarried Mother and Her Child.
873 **371** 3k.+50ore red 1·10 70

1988. Mills.
874 **372** 3k. black, red & orange 90 10
875 – 7k.10 black, ultramarine and blue 2·10 1·00
DESIGN: 7k.10, Veistrup water mill.

373 "Bathing Boys 1902" (Peter Hansen)

1988. Paintings. Multicoloured.
876 4k.10 Type **373** 1·60 1·40
877 10k. "Hill at Overkoerby. Winter 1917" (Fritz Syberg) 3·25 2·75

374 "The Little Mermaid" (statue, Edvard Eriksen), Copenhagen **375** Army Members in Public House

1989. Centenary of Danish Tourist Association.
878 **374** 3k.20 green 95 10

1989. 102nd Anniv of Salvation Army in Denmark.
879 **375** 3k.20+50ore mult 1·40 70

376 Footballer **377** Emblem

1989. Centenary of Danish Football Association.
880 **376** 3k.20 red, blk & lt red 95 10

1989. 40th Anniv of N.A.T.O.
881 **377** 4k.40 bl, cobalt & gold 1·25 45

378 "Valby Woman" **379** "Parliament Flag"

1989. Nordic Countries' Postal Co-operation. Traditional Costumes. Engravings by Christoffer Wilhelm Eckersberg. Multicoloured.
882 3k.20 Type **378** 85 10
883 4k.40 "Pork Butcher" 1·40 55

1989. 3rd Direct Elections to European Parliament.
884 **379** 3k. blue and yellow 90 55

380 Lego Bricks **381** Tractor, 1917

1989. Europa. Children's Toys. Multicoloured.
885 3k.20 Type **380** 1·00 10
886 4k.40 Wooden guardsmen by Kay Bojesen 1·60 55

1989. Centenary of Danish Agricultural Museum.
887 **381** 3k.20 red 95 10

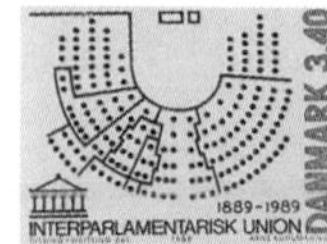

382 Diagram of Folketing (Parliament) Chamber

1989. Centenary of Interparliamentary Union.
888 **382** 3k.40 red and black 1·40 80

383 Chart and Boat Identity Number

1989. Centenary of Danish Fishery and Marine Research Institute.
889 **383** 3k.20 multicoloured 95 10

384 "Ingemann" (after J. V. Gertner) **385** Scene from "They Caught the Ferry" (50th anniv of Danish Government Film Office)

1989. Birth Bicentenary of Bernhard Severin Ingemann (poet)
890 **384** 7k.70 green 2·10 85

1989. Danish Film Industry.
891 **385** 3k. blue, black & orge 90 40
892 – 3k.20 pink, blk & orge 90 10
893 – 4k.40 brown, blk & orge 1·25 45
DESIGNS: 3k.20, Scene from "The Golden Smile" (birth cent of Bodil Ipsen, actress); 4k.40, Carl Th. Dreyer (director, birth cent).

386 Stamps

1989. 50th Stamp Day.
894 **386** 3k.20 salmon, orge & brn 95 10

387 "Part of Northern Citadel Bridge" (Christen Kobke)

1989. Paintings. Multicoloured.
895 4k.40 Type **387** 1·60 1·40
896 10k. "A Little Girl, Elise Kobke, with Cup" (Constantin Hansen) 2·75 2·50

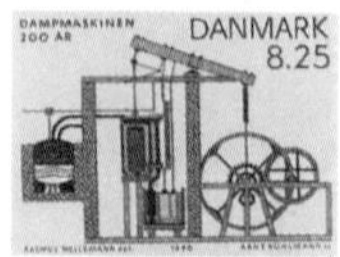

388 Silver Coffee Pot (Axel Johannes Kroyer, 1726) **389** Andrew Mitchell's Steam Engine

1990. Centenary of Museum of Decorative Art, Copenhagen.
897 **388** 3k.50 black and blue 1·00 10

1990. Bicent of Denmark's First Steam Engine.
898 **389** 8k.25 brown 2·25 90

390 Queen Margrethe II **391** Royal Monogram over Door of Haderslev Post Office

1990.
910 **390** 3k.50 red 1·00 10
911 3k.75 green 1·25 1·25
912 3k.75 red 1·00 10
913 4k. brown 1·00 30
914 4k.50 violet 1·25 80
915 4k.75 blue 1·25 35
916 4k.75 violet 1·25 60
917 5k. blue 1·25 35
918 5k.25 black 1·40 1·10
919 5k.50 green 1·25 1·25

1990. Europa. Post Office Buildings.
930 **391** 3k.50 yellow, red & blk 1·10 10
931 – 4k.75 multicoloured 1·50 45
DESIGN: 4k.75, Odense Post Office.

392 Main Guardhouse, Rigging Crane and Ships (after C. O. Willars)

1990. 300th Anniv of Nyholm.
932 **392** 4k.75 black 1·25 35

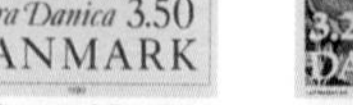

393 Covered Ice Dish **394** Marsh Mallow

1990. Bicentenary of Flora Danica Banquet Service. Multicoloured.
933 3k.50 Type **393** 1·10 70
934 3k.50 Sauce boat 1·10 70
935 3k.50 Lidded ice pot 1·10 70
936 3k.50 Serving dish 1·10 70

1990. Endangered Flowers. Multicoloured.
937 3k.25 Type **394** 90 45
938 3k.50 Red helleborine 1·50 10
939 3k.75 Purple orchis 1·25 70
940 4k.75 Lady's slipper 1·25 45

395 Insulin Crystals **396** Gjellerup Church

1990. 50th Anniv of Danish Diabetes Association.
941 **395** 3k.50+50ore mult 1·50 1·25

1990. Jutland Churches. Each brown.
942 3k.50 Type **396** 1·00 10
943 4k.75 Veng Church 1·10 40
944 8k.25 Bredsten Church (vert) 2·50 80

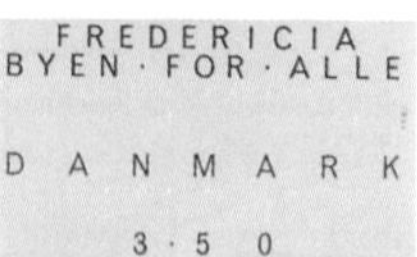

397 Slogan and Braille

1990. Fredericia: "Town for Everybody" (access for the handicapped project).
945 **397** 3k.50 red and black 1·00 30

398 "Tordenskiold and Karlsten's Commandant" (Otto Bache) **399** Bicycle (Bicycle stealing)

1990. 300th Birth Anniv of Admiral Tordenskiold (Peter Wessel).
946 **398** 3k.50 multicoloured 1·00 25

1990. Campaigns.
947 **399** 3k.25 multicoloured 1·10 55
948 – 3k.50 black, bl & mve 1·25 15
DESIGN: 3k.50, Glass and car (Drunken driving).

400 IC3 Diesel Passenger Train, 1990

1991. Railway Locomotives.
949 **400** 3k.25 blue, red & green 1·10 80
950 – 3k.50 black and red 1·10 15
951 – 3k.75 brown & dp brn 1·10 65
952 – 4k.75 black and red 1·25 45
DESIGNS: 3k.50, Class A steam locomotive, 1882; 3k.75, Class MY diesel-electric locomotive, 1954; 4k.75, Class P steam locomotive, 1907.

401 Satellite Picture of Denmark's Water Temperatures **402** First Page of 1280s Manuscript

1991. Europa. Europe in Space. Mult.
953 3k.50 Type **401** 1·25 15
954 4k.75 Denmark's land temperatures 1·50 50

1991. 750th Anniv of Jutland Law.
955 **402** 8k.25 multicoloured 2·40 1·10

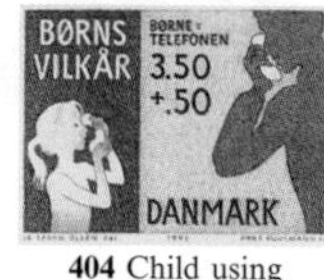

403 Fano **404** Child using Emergency Helpline

1991. Nordic Countries' Postal Co-operation. Tourism. Multicoloured.
956 3k.50 Type **403** 1·10 25
957 4k.75 Christianso 1·25 45

1991. 15th Anniv of Living Conditions of Children (child welfare organization).
958 **404** 3k.50+50ore blue 1·40 1·00

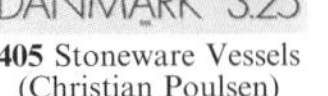

405 Stoneware Vessels (Christian Poulsen)

406 Man cleaning up after Dog

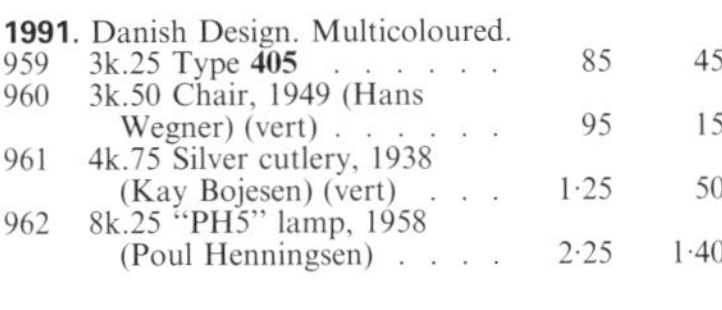

1991. Danish Design. Multicoloured.
959 3k.25 Type **405** 85 45
960 3k.50 Chair, 1949 (Hans Wegner) (vert) 95 15
961 4k.75 Silver cutlery, 1938 (Kay Bojesen) (vert) . . . 1·25 50
962 8k.25 "PH5" lamp, 1958 (Poul Henningsen) . . . . 2·25 1·40

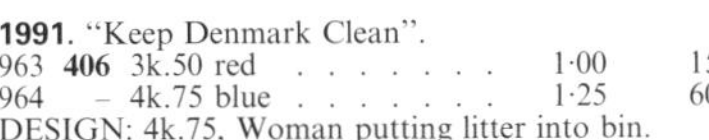

1991. "Keep Denmark Clean".
963 **406** 3k.50 red . . . . 1·00 15
964 – 4k.75 blue . . . . 1·25 60
DESIGN: 4k.75, Woman putting litter into bin.

407 Nordic Advertising Congress 1947 (Arne Ungermann)

1991. Posters. Multicoloured.
965 3k.50 Type **407** . . . . . . 1·00 25
966 4k.50 Poster Exhibition, Copenhagen Zoo, 1907 (Valdemar Andersen) . . . 1·75 1·25
967 4k.75 D.D.L. (Danish Airlines, 1945) (Ib Andersen) . . . . 1·25 55
968 12k. Casino's "The Sinner", 1925 (Sven Brasch) . . . . 3·00 2·40

408 "Lady at Her Toilet" (Harald Giersing)

409 Skarpsalling Earthenware Bowl

1991. Paintings. Multicoloured.
969 4k.75 Type **408** . . . . . . 1·50 1·40
970 14k. "Road through Wood" (Edvard Weie) . . . . . . 3·50 3·50

1992. Re-opening of National Museum, Copenhagen. Exhibits from Prehistoric Denmark Collection.
971 **409** 3k.50 brown and lilac . . 1·00 15
972 – 4k.50 green and blue . . 1·50 85
973 – 4k.75 black & brown . . 1·40 55
974 – 8k.25 purple & green . . 2·25 1·50
DESIGNS: 4k.50, Grevensvaenge bronze figure of dancer; 4k.75, Bottom plate of Gundestrup Cauldron; 8k.25, Hindsgavl flint knife.

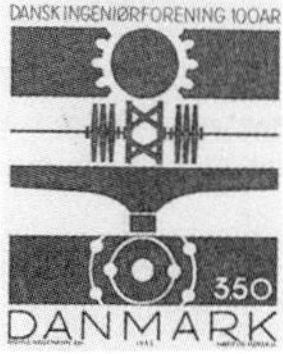

410 Aspects of Engineering

412 Potato Plant

1992. Centenary of Danish Society of Chemical, Civil, Electrical and Mechanical Engineers.
975 **410** 3k.50 red . . . . 1·00 30

1992. Europa. 500th Anniv of Discovery of America by Columbus.
977 **412** 3k.50 green & brown . . 1·00 15
978 – 4k.75 green & yellow . . 1·75 95
DESIGN: 4k.75, Head of maize.

413 Royal Couple in 1992 and in Official Wedding Photograph

1992. Silver Wedding of Queen Margrethe and Prince Henrik.
979 **413** 3k.75 multicoloured . . . 1·10 65

414 Hare, Eurasian Sky Lark and Cars

1992. Environmental Protection. Multicoloured.
980 3k.75 Type **414** 95 15
981 5k. Atlantic herrings and sea pollution . . . . 1·25 50
982 8k.75 Felled trees and saplings (vert) . . . . . . 2·10 1·25

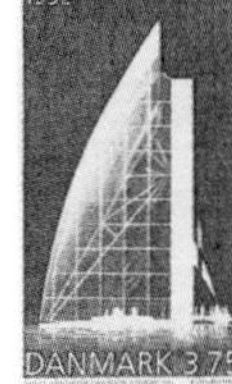

415 Celebrating Crowd

416 Danish Pavilion

1992. Denmark, European Football Champion.
983 **415** 3k.75 multicoloured . . . 1·10 15

1992. "Expo '92" World's Fair, Seville.
984 **416** 3k.75 blue . . . . 1·00 25

417 "Word"

418 "A Hug"

1992. 50th Anniv of Danish Dyslexia Association.
985 **417** 3k.75+50ore mult . . . . 1·40 1·10

1992. Danish Cartoon Characters.
986 **418** 3k.50 purple, red & gold 95 45
987 – 3k.75 violet and red . . . 95 15
988 – 4k.75 black and red . . . 1·25 1·25
989 – 5k. blue and red . . . . 1·25 35
DESIGNS: 3k.75, "Love Letter"; 4k.75, "Domestic Triangle"; 5k. "The Poet and his Little Wife".

419 Abstract

420 "Jacob's Fight with the Angel" (bible illustration by Bodil Kaalund)

1992. European Single Market.
990 **419** 3k.75 blue and yellow . . 1·00 75

1992. Publication of New Danish Bible.
991 **420** 3k.75 multicoloured . . . 1·00 40

421 "Landscape from Vejby, 1843" (Johan Thomas Lundbye)

1992. Paintings. Multicoloured.
992 5k. Type **421** . . . . 1·50 1·10
993 10k. "Motif from Halleby Brook, 1847" (Peter Christian Skovgaard) . . . 2·75 2·25

422 Funen Guldgubber

423 Small Tortoiseshell

1993. Danish Treasure Trove. Guldgubber (anthropomorphic gold foil figures). Mult.
994 3k.75 Type **422** . . . . . . 1·00 15
995 5k. Bornholm guldgubber (vert) . . . . 1·40 35

1993. Butterflies. Multicoloured.
996 3k.75 Type **423** . . . . . . 1·00 30
997 5k. Large blue . . . . 1·40 40
998 8k.75 Marsh fritillary . . . . 2·75 1·60
999 12k. Red admiral . . . . . 3·25 2·50

424 Untitled Painting (Troels Worsel)

1993. Europa. Contemporary Art. Mult.
1000 3k.75 Type **424** . . . . . 1·10 35
1001 5k. "The 7 Corners of the Earth" (Stig Brogger) (vert) . . . . 1·60 65

425 "Pierrot" (Thor Bogelund, 1947)

426 "Danmark"

1993. Nordic Countries' Postal Co-operation. Tourism. Publicity posters for Tivoli Gardens, Copenhagen. Multicoloured.
1002 3k.75 Type **425** . . . . . . 1·00 15
1003 5k. Child holding balloons (Wilhelm Freddie, 1987) (vert) . . . . 1·50 40

1993. Training Ships. Multicoloured.
1004 3k.75 Type **426** . . . . . 1·25 40
1005 4k.75 "Jens Krogh" (25 × 30 mm) . . . . . . 1·25 90
1006 5k. "Georg Stage" . . . . 1·60 70
1007 9k.50 "Marilyn Anne" (36 × 26 mm) . . . . . . 2·40 1·60

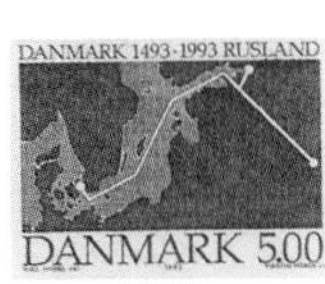

427 Map

428 Prow of Viking Ship

1993. Inauguration of Denmark–Russia Submarine Cable and 500th Anniv of Friendship Treaty.
1008 **427** 5k. green . . . . 1·50 45

1993. Children's Stamp Design Competition.
1009 **428** 3k.75 multicoloured . . 1·00 15

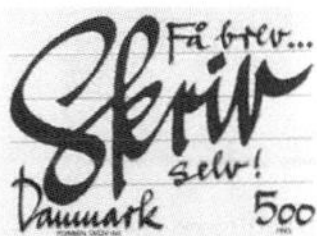

429 Emblem

430 "If you want a Letter...Write one Yourself"

1993. 75th Anniv of Social Work of Young Men's Christian Association.
1010 **429** 3k.75+50ore green, red and black . . . . . . 1·40 1·00

1993. Letter-writing Campaign.
1011 **430** 5k. ultram, bl & blk . . 1·40 50

431 Silver Brooch and Chain, North Falster

1993. Traditional Jewellery. Multicoloured.
1012 3k.50 Type **431** . . . . . 1·00 55
1013 3k.75 Gilt-silver brooch with owner's monogram, Amager . . . . 1·00 15
1014 5k. Silver buttons and brooches, Laeso . . . . . 1·50 35
1015 8k.75 Silver buttons, Romo 2·40 2·25

432 "Assemblage" (Vilhelm Lundstrom)

433 Duck

1993. Paintings. Multicoloured.
1016 5k. Type **432** . . . . . . 1·50 1·40
1017 15k. "Composition" (Franciska Clausen) . . . 4·00 3·25

1994. Save Water and Energy Campaign.
1018 **433** 3k.75 multicoloured . . 1·00 15
1019 – 5k. green, red & black 1·25 35
DESIGN: 5k. Spade (in Danish "spar" = save) and "CO2".

434 Marselisborg Castle, Aarhus

1994. Royal Residences.
1020 **434** 3k.50 dp brn, grn & brn 1·00 55
1021 – 3k.75 multicoloured . . 1·00 15
1022 – 5k. grn, dp brn & brn 1·40 40
1023 – 8k.75 dp brn, grn & brn 2·40 1·25
DESIGNS: 3k.75, Amalienborg Castle, Copenhagen; 5k. Fredensborg Castle, North Zealand; 8k.75, Graasten Castle, South Jutland.

435 "Danmark" and Wegener's Weather Balloon, Danmarkshavn

436 Copenhagen Tram No. 2, 1911

1994. Europa. Discoveries. "Danmark" Expedition to North-East Greenland, 1906–08.
1024 **435** 3k.75 purple . . . . . . 1·10 15
1025 – 5k. black . . . . 1·50 45
DESIGN: 5k. Johan Peter Koch and theodolite.

1994. Trams. Multicoloured.
1026 3k.75 Type **436** 95 15
1027 4k.75 Aarhus tram, 1928 . . 1·25 1·10
1028 5k. Odense tram, 1911 (vert) 1·25 70
1029 12k. Copenhagen horse tram "Honen", 1880 (37 × 21 mm) . . . . . . 3·00 2·75

437 Prince Henrik

438 Kite

1994. Danish Red Cross Fund. 60th Birthday of Prince Henrik, the Prince Consort.
1030 **437** 3k.75+50ore mult . . . 1·25 1·00

1994. Children's Stamp Design Competition.
1031 **438** 3k.75 multicoloured . . 1·00 45

439 Emblem

440 House Sparrows

1994. 75th Anniv of I.L.O.
1032 **439** 5k. multicoloured . . . 1·25 45

1994. Protected Animals. Multicoloured.
1033 3k.75 Type **440** 90 15
1034 4k.75 Badger . . . . 1·10 95
1035 5k. Red squirrel (vert) . . . 1·25 50
1036 9k.50 Pair of black grouse 2·40 2·10
1037 12k. Black grass snake (36 × 26 mm) . . . . . . 3·00 2·75

441 Teacher

1994. 150th Anniv of Folk High Schools.
1038 **441** 3k.75 multicoloured . . 1·00 15

442 Study for "Italian Woman with Sleeping Child" (Wilhelm Marstrand)

1994. Paintings. Multicoloured.
1039 5k. Type **442** . . . . . . 1·40 1·25
1040 15k. "Interior from Amaliegade with the Artist's Brothers" (Wilhelm Bendz) . . . . 3·75 3·50

443 The Red Building (architect's drawing, Hack Kampmann)

444 Anniversary Emblem

1995. 800th Anniv of Aarhus Cathedral School.
1041 **443** 3k.75 multicoloured . . 1·00 25

1995. 50th Anniv of United Nations Organization. U.N. World Summit for Social Development, Copenhagen.
1042 **444** 5k. multicoloured . . . 1·25 50

445 Avernako

446 Field-Marshal Montgomery and Copenhagen Town Hall

1995. Danish Islands. Each brown, blue and red.
1043 3k.75 Type **445** . . . . . 1·00 15
1044 4k.75 Fejo . . . . 1·25 85
1045 5k. Fur . . . . 1·25 50
1046 9k.50 Endelave . . . . . . 2·50 1·50

1995. Europa. Peace and Freedom. Mult.
1047 3k.75 Type **446** . . . . . 1·10 15
1048 5k. White coaches (repatriation of Danes from German concentration camps) (horiz) . . . . 1·60 50
1049 8k.75 Dropping of supplies from Allied aircraft (horiz) . . . . 2·25 1·40
1050 12k. Jews escaping by boat to Sweden (horiz) . . . . 3·00 2·50

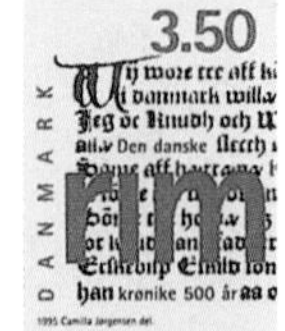

447 Detail of Page

448 Stage

1995. 500th Anniv of "The Rhymed Chronicle" by Friar Niels (first book printed in Danish).
1051 **447** 3k.50 multicoloured . . 1·00 45

1995. Nordic Countries' Postal Co-operation. Music Festivals. Multicoloured.
1052 3k.75 Type **448** (25th anniv of Roskilde Festival) . . . 95 15
1053 5k. Violinist (21st anniv of Tonder Festival) (20 × 38 mm) . . . . . . 1·25 40

449 Broken Feather

1995. 50th Anniv of National Society of Polio and Accident Victims.
1054 **449** 3k.75+50ore red . . . . 1·25 1·10

450 "Midsummer Eve" (Jens Sondergaard)

1995. Paintings. Multicoloured.
1055 10k. Type **450** . . . . . . 2·50 2·00
1056 15k. "Landscape at Gudhjem" (Niels Lergaard) . . . . 4·00 3·25

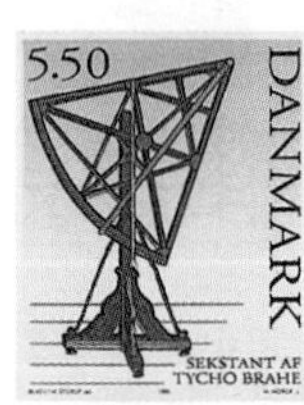

451 Sextant

453 The Round Tower

452 TEKNO Model Vehicles

1995. 450th Birth Anniv of Tycho Brahe (astronomer). Multicoloured.
1057 3k.75 Uraniborg (Palace Observatory) . . . . . . 1·00 35
1058 5k.50 Type **451** . . . . . 1·40 1·00

1995. Danish Toys. Multicoloured.
1059 3k.75 Type **452** 95 15
1060 5k. Edna (celluloid doll), Kirstine (china doll) and Holstebro teddy bear . . 1·25 40
1061 8k.75 Toy bin-plate locomotives and rolling stock . . . . 2·25 1·50
1062 12k. Glud & Marstrand horse-drawn fire engine and carriage . . . . . . 3·00 2·40

1996. Copenhagen, European Cultural Capital. Multicoloured.
1063 3k.75 Type **453** 95 25
1064 5k. Christiansborg . . . . . 1·25 40
1065 8k.75 Dome of Marble Church as hot-air balloon 2·25 1·50
1066 12k. "The Little Mermaid" on stage . . . . 3·00 2·50

454 Disabled Basketball Player

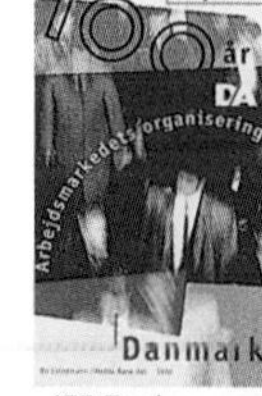

455 Businessmen

1996. Sport. Multicoloured.
1067 3k.75 Type **454** . . . . . 1·00 15
1068 4k.75 Swimming . . . . . 1·25 90
1069 5k. Yachting . . . . 1·25 45
1070 9k.50 Cycling . . . . 2·40 1·75

1996. Cent of Danish Employers' Confederation.
1071 **455** 3k.75 multicoloured . . 1·00 15

456 Asta Nielsen (actress)

457 Roskilde Fjord Boat

1996. Europa. Famous Women.
1072 – 3k.75 brown & dp brn 1·10 15
1073 **456** 5k. grey and blue . . . 1·25 45
DESIGN: 3k.75, Karin Blixen (writer).

1996. Wooden Sailing Boats.
1074 **457** 3k.50 brn, bl & red . . . 1·00 70
1075 – 3k.75 lilac, grn & red . . 1·00 15
1076 – 12k.25 blk, brn & red . . 3·25 2·50
DESIGNS—As T **457**: 12k.25, South Funen Archipelago smack; 20 × 38 mm: 3k.75, Limfjorden skiff.

458 Fornaes

459 Ribbons forming Hearts within Star

1996. Lighthouses. Multicoloured.
1077 3k.75 Type **458** . . . . . 1·00 15
1078 5k. Blavandshuk . . . . . 1·25 40
1079 5k.25 Bovbjerg . . . . . . 1·50 1·10
1080 8k.75 Mon . . . . 2·40 1·50

1996. AIDS Foundation.
1081 **459** 3k.75+50ore red & blk 1·25 1·00

460 Vase

1996. 150th Birth Anniv of Thorvald Bindesboll (ceramic artist). Multicoloured.
1082 3k.75 Type **460** 95 15
1083 4k. Portfolio cover . . . . 1·10 75

461 "At Lunch" (Peder Kroyer)

1996. Paintings. Multicoloured.
1084 10k. Type **461** . . . . . . 2·50 2·25
1085 15k. "Girl with Sunflowers" (Michael Ancher) . . . . 3·75 3·00

462 Queen Margrethe waving to Children

463 Queen Margrethe

1997. Silver Jubilee of Queen Margrethe. Mult.
1086 3k.50 Queen Margrethe and Prince Henrik 95 55
1087 3k.75 Queen Margrethe and Crown Prince Frederik . . 1·00 15
1088 4k. Queen Margrethe at desk . . . . 1·10 80
1089 5k.25 Type **462** . . . . . 1·25 1·10

1997.
1092 **463** 3k.75 red . . . . 1·00 10
1093 4k. green . . . . 1·10 70
1094 4k. red . . . . 1·10 35
1095 4k.25 brown . . . . . . 1·25 90
1096 4k.50 blue . . . . 1·25 60
1097 4k.75 brown . . . . . . 1·25 1·10
1098 5k. violet . . . . 1·25 35
1099 5k.25 blue . . . . 1·40 75
1100 5k.50 red . . . . 1·40 1·10
1101 5k.75 blue . . . . 1·40 75
1104 6k.75 green . . . . . . 1·60 1·50

464 Karlstrup Post Mill, Zealand

465 The East Tunnel

1997. Centenary of Open Air Museum, Lyngby. Construction Drawings by B. Ehrhardt.
1111 **464** 3k.50 brown & purple 90 50
1112 – 3k.75 lilac and green . . 95 15
1113 – 5k. green and lilac . . . 1·10 45
1114 – 8k.75 green & brown . . 2·50 1·40
DESIGNS: 3k.75, Ellested water mill, Funen; 5k. Fjellerup Manor Barn, Djursland; 8k.75, Toftum farm, Romo.

1997. Inauguration of Railway Section of the Great Belt Link. Multicoloured.
1115 3k.75 Type **465** . . . . . 1·00 15
1116 4k.75 The West Bridge . . . 1·25 90

466 Sneezing

468 King Erik and Queen Margrete I

467 Electric Trains under New Carlsberg Bridge

1997. Asthma Allergy Association.
1117 **466** 3k.75+50ore mult . . . 1·25 1·00

1997. 150th Anniv of Copenhagen–Roskilde Railway. Multicoloured.
1118 3k.75 Type **467** 95 15
1119 8k.75 Steam train under original Carlsberg bridge (after H. Holm) . . . . . 2·25 1·10

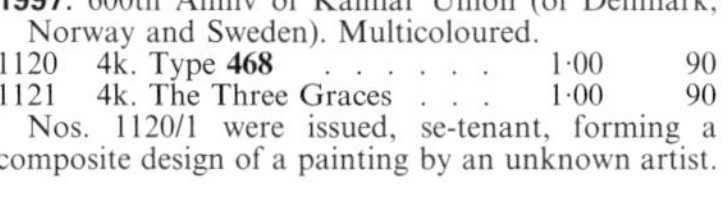
1997. 600th Anniv of Kalmar Union (of Denmark, Norway and Sweden). Multicoloured.
1120 4k. Type **468** . . . . . . 1·00 90
1121 4k. The Three Graces . . . 1·00 90
Nos. 1120/1 were issued, se-tenant, forming a composite design of a painting by an unknown artist.

469 Post Office Cars on Great Belt Ferry

1997. Closure of Travelling Post Offices.
1122 **469** 5k. multicoloured . . . 1·25 50

470 "The Tinder-box"

1997. Europa. Tales and Legends by Hans Christian Andersen.
1123 **470** 3k.75 dp brn & brn . . 1·10 35
1124 – 5k.25 red, dp grn & grn 1·40 1·00
DESIGN: 5k.25, "Thumbelina".

471 "Dust dancing in the Sun" (Vilheim Hammershoi)

472 Faaborg Chair (Kaare Klint)

1997. Paintings. Multicoloured.
1125 9k.75 Type **471** . . . . . 2·50 2·25
1126 13k. "Woman Mountaineer" (Jens Willumsen) . . . . 3·00 2·75

1997. Danish Design. Multicoloured.
1127 3k.75 Type **472** 95 30
1128 4k. Margrethe bowls (Sigvard Bernadotte and Acton Bjorn) . . . . . . 1·00 75
1129 5k. The Ant chairs (Arne Jacobsen) (horiz) . . . . 1·25 35
1130 12k.25 Silver bowl (Georg Jensen) . . . . 3·00 3·00

473 Workers

474 Roskilde Cathedral and Viking Longship

1998. Centenary of Danish Confederation of Trade Unions. Multicoloured.
1131 3k.50 Type **473** (General Workers' Union in Denmark) 95 65
1132 3k.75 Crowd at meeting (Danish Confederation of Trade Unions) . . . . . 1·00 15
1133 4k.75 Nurse (Danish Nurses' Organization) . . . . . . 1·25 90
1134 5k. Woman using telephone (Union of Commercial and Clerical Employees in Denmark) . . . . 1·25 30

1998. Millenary of Roskilde.
1135 **474** 3k.75 multicoloured . . 1·00 15

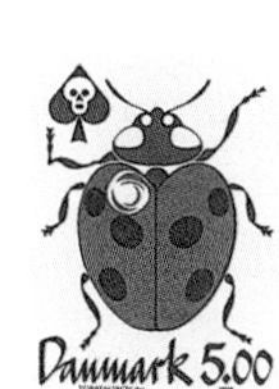
475 Seven-spotted Ladybird

476 Postman, 1922

1998. Environmental Issues. Gardening Without Chemicals.
1136 **475** 5k. red and black . . . 1·25 30

1998. Post and Tele Museum, Copenhagen. Mult.
1137 3k.75 Type **476** . . . . . 1·00 30
1138 4k.50 Morse operator, 1910 1·25 85
1139 5k.50 Telephonist, 1910 . . 1·50 1·10
1140 8k.75 Postman, 1998 . . . . 2·50 1·75

477 The West Bridge

1998. Inauguration of Road Section of the Great Belt Link. Each blue, black and red.
1141 5k. Type **477** . . . . . . 1·75 65
1142 5k. The East Bridge . . . . 1·75 65

478 Harbour Master

479 Horse (Agriculture Show)

1998. Nordic Countries' Postal Co-operation. Shipping. Multicoloured.
1143 6k.50 Type **478** . . . . . 1·60 1·40
1144 6k.50 Sextant and radar image of Copenhagen harbour . . . . 1·60 1·40
Nos. 1143/4 were issued together, se-tenant, forming a composite design.

1998. Europa. National Festivals. Mult.
1146 3k.75 Type **479** 80 30
1147 4k.50 Aarhus Festival Week 1·00 75

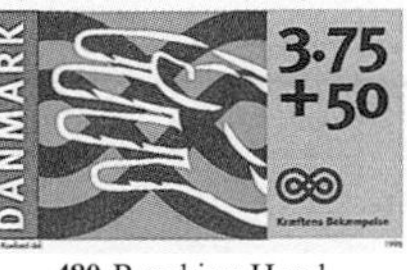
480 Reaching Hand

1998. Anti-cancer Campaign.
1148 **480** 3k.75+50ore red, orange and black . . . . . . 1·00 1·00

481 "Danish Autumn" (Per Kirkeby)

1998. Philatelic Creations. Multicoloured.
1149 3k.75 Type **481** . . . . . 1·10 85
1150 5k. "Alpha" (Mogens Andersen) (vert) . . . . 1·25 1·00
1151 8k.75 "Imagery" (Ejler Bille) (vert) . . . . 2·40 1·90
1152 19k. "Celestial Horse" (Carl-Henning Pedersen) 5·00 4·50

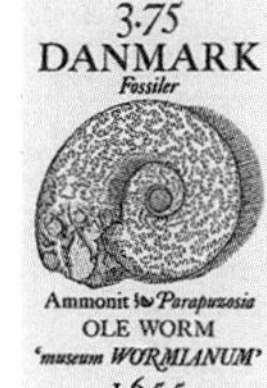
482 Ammonite (from "Museum Wormianum" by Ole Worm)

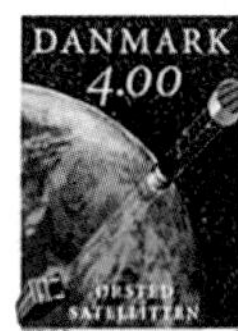
483 Satellite and Earth

1998. Fossils. Designs reproducing engravings from geological works. Each black and red on cream.
1153 3k.75 Type **482** 95 25
1154 4k.50 Shark's teeth (from "De Solido" by Niels Stensen) . . . . 1·25 1·00
1155 5k.50 Sea urchin (from "Stevens Klint" by Soren Abildgaard) . . . . . . 1·40 1·00
1156 15k. Pleurotomariida (from "Den Danske Atlas" by Erich Pontoppidan) . . . 3·50 3·00

1999. Launch of "Orsted" Satellite (Danish research satellite).
1158 **483** 4k. multicoloured . . . 1·00 80

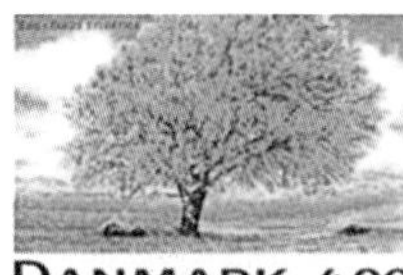
484 Beech

1999. Deciduous Trees. Multicoloured.
1159 4k. Type **484** . . . . . . 1·00 30
1160 5k. Ash (vert) . . . . . . 1·25 75
1161 5k.25 Small-leaved lime (vert) . . . . 1·40 55
1162 9k.25 Pendunculate oak . . 2·25 1·60

485 Home Guard

1999. 50th Anniv of Home Guard.
1163 **485** 3k.75 multicoloured . . 1·10 80

486 Northern Lapwing and Eggs

1999. Harbingers of Spring. Multicoloured.
1164 4k. Type **486** . . . . . . 1·00 15
1165 5k.25 Greylag goose with chicks . . . . 1·25 60

487 Emblem and Jet Fighters

488 Vejlerne

1999. 50th Anniv of North Atlantic Treaty Organization.
1167 **487** 4k.25 multicoloured . . 1·10 90

1999. Europa. Parks and Gardens. Multicoloured.
1168 4k.50 Type **488** . . . . . 1·10 70
1169 5k.50 Langli Island . . . . 1·25 75

489 Anniversary Emblem

490 "g" and Paragraph Sign

1999. 50th Anniv of Council of Europe.
1170 **489** 9k.75 blue . . . . 2·25 1·60

1999. 150th Anniv of Danish Constitution.
1171 **490** 4k. red and black . . . 1·00 15

491 Kjeld Petersen and Dirch Passer

1999. 150th Anniv of Danish Revue.
1172 **491** 4k. red . . . . 1·10 15
1173 – 4k.50 black . . . . . . 1·10 55
1174 – 5k.25 blue . . . . 1·25 1·00
1175 – 6k.75 mauve . . . . . . 1·40 1·10
DESIGNS: 4k.50, Osvald Helmuth; 5k.25, Preben Kaas and Jorgen Ryg; 6k.75, Liva Weel.

492 Emblem

493 The "Black Diamond"

1999. Alzheimer's Disease Association.
1176 **492** 4k.+50ore. red and blue 80 1·00

1999. Inauguration of Royal Library Extension, Copenhagen.
1177 **493** 8k.75 black . . . . . . 2·00 1·50

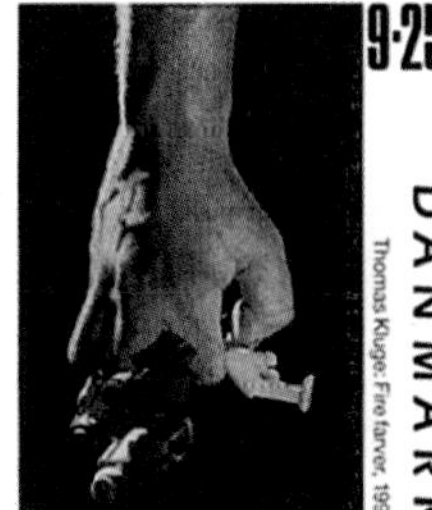
494 "Four Colours" (Thomas Kluge)

1999. Paintings. Multicoloured.
1178 9k.25 Type **494** . . . . . 2·00 1·75
1179 16k. "Boy" (Lise Malinovsky) . . . . . . 3·75 3·00

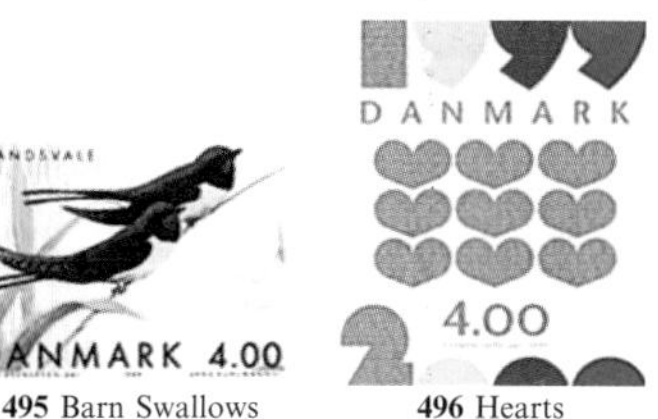
495 Barn Swallows

496 Hearts

1999. Migratory Birds. Multicoloured.
1180 4k. Type **495** . . . . . . 1·00 30
1181 5k.25 Greylag geese with goslings . . . . 1·25 30
1182 5k.50 Eiders . . . . 1·25 95
1183 12k.25 Arctic tern feeding chick . . . . 2·75 2·40

1999. New Millennium. Multicoloured.
1185 4k. Type **496** 95 25
1186 4k. Horizontal wavy lines 95 25

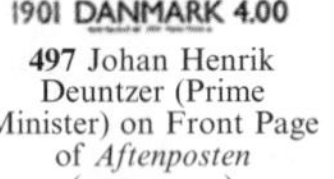
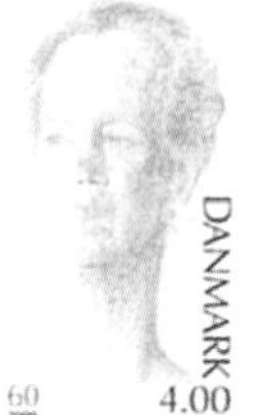

497 Johan Henrik Deuntzer (Prime Minister) on Front Page of *Aftenposten* (newspaper)

498 Queen Margrethe II (Pia Schutzmann)

2000. The Twentieth Century (1st series).

1187	**497**	4k. black and cream	1·00	25
1188	–	4k.50 multicoloured	1·00	70
1189	–	5k.25 multicoloured	1·10	55
1190	–	5k.75 multicoloured	1·40	65

DESIGNS—4k. Type **497** (Venstre (workers') party victory in election, 1901); 4k.50, Caricature of Frederik Borgbjerg (party member, Alfred Schmidt) (first Social Democrat Lord Mayor in Denmark, 1903); 5k.25, Asta Nielson and Poul Reumert (actors) in scene from *The Abyss* (film), 1910; 5k.75, Telephone advertising poster, 1914.

See also Nos. 1207/10, 1212/15 and 1221/4.

2000. 60th Birthday of Queen Margrethe II.

1191	**498**	4k. black and red	90	25
1192		5k.25 black and blue	1·25	55

499 Queen Margrethe II

2000.

1194	**499**	4k. red	95	10
1195		4k.25 blue	1·00	60
1196		4k.50 red	1·10	70
1196b		4k.75 brown	80	1·00
1197		5k. green	1·10	75
1198		5k.25 blue	1·25	45
1199		5k.50 violet	1·25	45
1200		5k.75 green	1·40	60
1201		6k. brown	1·50	1·00
1201a		6k.50 green	1·50	1·25
1202		6k.75 red	1·50	1·40
1203		7k. purple	1·60	1·50

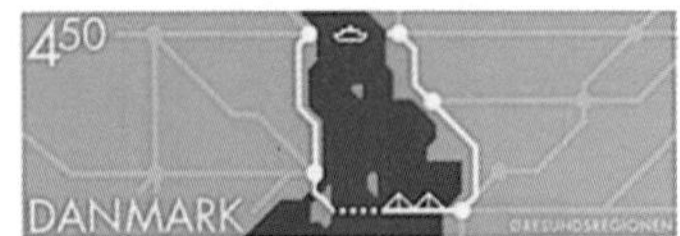

500 Map of Oresund Region

2000. Inauguration of Oresund Link (Denmark–Sweden road and rail system).

1205	**500**	4k.50 blue, white & blk	1·00	90
1206	–	4k.50 blue, green & blk	1·00	90

DESIGN: No. 1206, Oresund Bridge.

501 Suffragette on Front Page of *Politiken* (newspaper)

502 "Building Europe"

2000. The Twentieth Century (2nd series).

1207	**501**	4k. red, blk & cream	90	25
1208	–	5k. multicoloured	1·00	90
1209	–	5k.50 multicoloured	1·10	1·00
1210	–	6k.75 multicoloured	1·50	1·25

DESIGNS—4k. Type **501** (women's suffrage, 1915); 5k. Caricature of Thorvald Stauning (Prime Minister 1924–26 and 1929–42) (Herluf Jensenius) (The Kanslergade Agreement (economic and social reforms)), 1933; 5k.50, Poster for *The Wheel of Fortune* (film), 1927; 6k.75, Front page of *Radio Weekly Review* (magazine), 1925.

2000. Europa.

1211	**502**	9k.75 multicoloured	2·10	1·90

503 Front Page of *Kristeligt Dagblad* (newspaper), 5 May 1945

504 Linked Hands

2000. The Twentieth Century (3rd series).

1212	**503**	4k. black and cream	90	25
1213	–	5k.75 multicoloured	1·10	65
1214	–	6k.75 multicoloured	1·40	1·25
1215	–	12k.25 multicoloured	2·75	2·40

DESIGNS—4k. Type **503** (Liberation of Denmark); 5k.75, Caricature of Princess Margrethe (Herlif Jenserius) (adoption of new constitution, 1953); 6k.75, Ib Schonberg and Hvid Moller (actors) in a scene from *Cafe Paradise* (film), 1950; 12k.25, Front cover of brochure for Danish Arena televisions, 1957.

2000. Cerebral Palsy Association.

1216	**504**	4k.+50ore blue and red	1·10	1·00

505 Lockheed C-130 Hercules Transport Plane

2000. 50th Anniv of Royal Danish Air Force.

1217	**505**	9k.75 black and red	2·10	1·75

506 "Pegasus" (Kurt Trampedach)

2000. Paintings. Multicoloured.

1219	4k. Type **506**	60	1·00
1220	5k.25 "Untitled" (Nina Sten-Knudsen)	1·60	1·25

507 Front Page of *Berlingske Tidende* (newspaper), 3 October 1972

2000. The Twentieth Century (4th series).

1221	**507**	4k. red, blk & cream	90	30
1222	–	4k.50 multicoloured	1·00	75
1223	–	5k.25 blk, red & cream	1·25	70
1224	–	5k.50 multicoloured	1·25	70

DESIGNS: 4k. Type **507** (referendum on entry to European Economic Community); 4k.50, Caricature from *Blaekspruttén* (magazine), 1969 (The Youth Revolt); 5k.25, Poster for *The Olsen Gang* (film, 1968); 5k.50, Web page (development of the internet).

508 Kite

2001. 40th Anniv of Amnesty International.

1225	**508**	4k.+50 ore blk & red	1·00	95

509 Palm House

2001. 400th Anniv of Copenhagen University Botanical Gardens. Multicoloured.

1226	4k. Type **509**	85	35
1227	6k. Lake (28 × 21 mm)	1·25	95
1228	12k.25 Giant lily-pad (28 × 21 mm)	2·50	2·40

510 "a", Text and Flowers

2001. Reading. Danish Children's Book "ABC" (first reader) by Halfdan Rasmussen. Multicoloured.

1229	4k. Type **510**	90	30
1230	7k. "Z" and text	1·40	1·10

511 Martinus William Ferslew (designer and engraver)

512 Hands catching Water

2001. 150th Anniv of First Danish Stamp. Each black, red and brown.

1231	4k. Type **511**	85	35
1232	5k.50 Andreas Thiele (printer)	1·10	90
1233	6k. Frantz Christopher von Jessen (Copenhagen postmaster)	1·25	1·00
1234	10k.25 Magrius Otto Sophus (Postmaster-General)	2·10	1·75

2001. Europa. Water Resources. Multicoloured.

1235	4k.50 Type **512**	1·00	30
1236	9k.75 Woman in shower	2·00	1·75

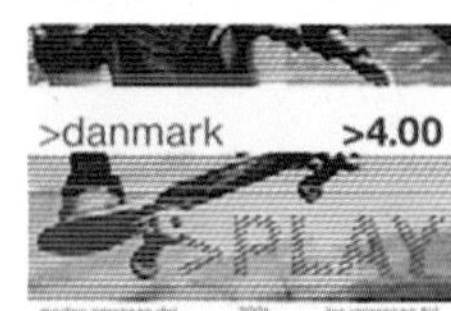

513 Skateboarder

2001. Youth Culture. Multicoloured.

1237	4k. Type **513**	85	35
1238	5k.50 Couple kissing	1·10	90
1239	6k. Mixing records	1·25	1·00
1240	10k.25 Pierced tongue	1·75	1·75

514 "Missus" (Jorn Larsen)

2001. Paintings.

1242	**514**	18k. black and red	4·00	4·00
1243	–	22k. multicoloured	5·25	5·25

DESIGN: 22k. "Postbillede" (Henning Damgaard-Sorensen).

515 Queen Margrethe II with 1984 Prince Henrik and 1994 Marselisborg Castle Stamps

517 Rasmus Klump (Vilhelm Hansen)

516 *Bukken-Bruse*

2001. "HAFNIA '01" International Stamp Exhibition, Copenhagen. Multicoloured.

1244	4k. Type **515**	70	30
1245	4k.50 King Frederik IX with 1985 Queen Ingrid and 1994 Graasten Castle stamps	75	30
1246	5k.50 King Christian X with 1994 Amalienborg Castle and 1939 Queen Alexandrine stamps	90	90
1247	7k. King Christian IX with 1994 Fredensborg Castle and 1907 King Frederick VIII stamps	1·10	1·10

2001. Ferries.

1249	**516**	3k.75 black, green and emerald	65	20
1250	–	4k. black, brown and green	70	30
1251	–	4k.25 black, green and blue	75	30
1252	–	6k. grey, black and red	1·00	10

DESIGNS: 4k. *Ouro*; 4k.25, *Hjarno*; 6k. *Barsofargen*.

2002. Danish Cartoons. Multicoloured.

1253	4k. Type **517**	70	30
1254	5k.50 Valhalla (Peter Madsen)	90	90
1255	6k.50 Jungo and Rita (Flemming Quist Moller)	1·10	1·00
1256	10k.50 Cirkleen (Hanne and Jannik Hastrup)	1·90	1·75

518 Back View

2002. Nordic Countries' Postal Co-operation. Modern Art. Showing "The Girls in the Airport" (sculpture, Hanne Varming). Each black, bronze on cream.

1258	4k. Type **518**	75	45
1259	5k. Front view	90	55

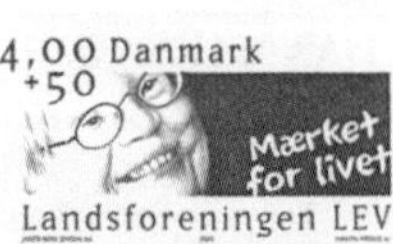

519 Face

2002. L.E.V. National Association (mental health foundation).

1260	**519**	4k. +50ore brown, agate on cream	85	85

520 Clown (Luna Ostergard)

521 Jon's Chapel, Bornholm

2002. Europa. Circus. Winning Entries in Stamp Design Competition. Multicoloured.

1261	4k. Type **520**	75	45
1262	5k. Clown (different) (Camille Wagner Larsen)	90	55

2002. Landscape Photographs by Kirsten Klein.

1263	**521**	4k. black and brown	75	45
1264	–	6k. black	1·10	65
1265	–	6k.50 deep green and green	1·25	70
1266	–	12k.50 black and blue	2·30	1·40

DESIGNS: 6k. Trees, Vestervig; 6k.50, Woods, Karskov, Langeland; 12k.50, Cliffs and beach, Stenbjerg, West Jutland.

522 1953 Nimbus Motorcycle and Sidecar

2002. Postal Vehicles. Multicoloured.

1267	4k. Type **522**	75	45
1268	5k.50 1962 Bedford CA van	1·00	60
1269	10k. 1984 Renault 4 van	1·80	1·10
1270	19k. 1998 Volvo FH12 lorry	3·50	2·10

523 *Dana* (marine research ship) and Atlantic Cod

2002. Centenary of International Council for the Exploration of the Sea. Multicoloured.
1271 4k. Type **523** 75 45
1272 10k. Hirtshals lighthouse and atlantic cod . . . . . 1·80 1·10
MS1273 186 × 61 mm. 4k. Type **523**; 10k.50 Lighthouse and atlantic cod 2·75 2·75
Stamps of a similar design were issued by Faroe Islands and Greenland.

524 "Children's Corner" (Jens Birkemose)

2002. Paintings.
1274 **524** 5k. red and blue 90 55
1275 – 6k.50 multicoloured . . 1·20 70
DESIGN: 6k.50 "Maleren og modellen" (Frans Kannik).

525 Underground Train

2002. Inauguration of Copenhagen Metro.
1276 **525** 5k.50 black, green and brown on cream . . . 1·00 60

526 Dianas Have, Horsholm (Vandkunsten Design Studio)

2002. Modern Housing. Multicoloured.
1277 4k. Type **526** 75 45
1278 4k.25 Bapistry, Long House and Gate (Poul Ingemann) Blangstedgard, Odense 80 45
1279 5k.50 Dansk Folkeferie, Karrebaeksminde (Stephan Kappel) . . . . 1·00 60
1280 6k.50 Terrasser, Fredensborg (Jorn Utzon) 1·20 70
1281 9k. Soholm, Klampenborg (Arne Jacobsen) . . . . . 1·70 1·00

MILITARY FRANK STAMPS

1917. Nos. 135 and 138 optd **S F** (= "Soldater Frimaerke").
M188 **21** 5ore green . . . . . . 11·00 17·00
M189 10ore red . . . . 9·75 14·00

NEWSPAPER STAMPS

N 18

1901.
N185 **N 18** 1ore green . . . . . 11·00 95
N186 5ore blue . . . . . . 27·00 6·25
N133 7ore red . . . . . . 14·00 60
N188 8ore green . . . . . . 28·00 1·10
N189 10ore lilac . . . . . . 27·00 1·40
N135 20ore green . . . . . . 23·00 85
N191 29ore orange . . . . 40·00 2·10
N136 38ore orange . . . . 32·00 85
N193 41ore brown . . . . . 45·00 1·60
N137 68ore brown . . . . . 80·00 15·00
N138 1k. purple & green . . 23·00 1·25
N139 5k. green and pink . . £140 16·00
N140 10k. blue and stone . . £150 29·00

OFFICIAL STAMPS

O 9

1871. Value in "skilling".
O51a **O 9** 2sk. blue . . . . £110 60·00
O52 4sk. red . . . . 40·00 9·25
O53 16sk. green £375 £130

1875. Value in "ore".
O185 **O 9** 1ore orange 70 70
O100 3ore lilac 70 70
O186 3ore grey . . . . 2·25 4·25
O101 4ore blue . . . . 1·10 1·10
O188 5ore green 50 35
O189 5ore brown . . . . . . 1·40 10·00
O 94 8ore red . . . . 7·25 1·25
O104 10ore red . . . . 1·25 90
O191 10ore green . . . . . . 2·25 2·25
O192 20ore lilac . . . . . . 12·00 19·00
O193 20ore blue . . . . . . 12·50 £705
O 98 32ore green . . . . . . 17·00 15·00

PARCEL POST STAMPS

1919. Various types optd **POSTFAERGE**.
P208 **21** 10ore red . . . . . . 27·00 35·00
P209 **15** 10ore green . . . . . . 9·50 7·15
P210 10ore brown . . . . . 11·00 3·75
P211 **21** 15ore lilac . . . . . . 13·50 17·00
P212 30ore orange . . . . . 12·50 13·00
P213 30ore blue . . . . . . 1·90 3·50
P214 50ore black & purple . . £140 £150
P215a 50ore grey . . . . . . 18·00 9·00
P216 **22** 1k. brown . . . . . . 80·00 £100
P217 **21** 1k. blue and brown . . 40·00 18·00
P218 5k. brown & mauve . . 70 1·25
P219 10k. green and red . . . 35·00 48·00

1927. Stamps of 1927 (solid background) optd **POSTFAERGE**.
P252 **40** 15ore red . . . . 11·50 5·75
P253 30ore yellow . . . . . . 10·50 8·00
P254 40ore green . . . . . . 16·00 7·00

1936. Stamps of 1933 (lined background) optd **POSTFAERGE**.
P491 **43** 5ore purple 20 30
P299 10ore orange . . . . . 14·50 11·50
P300 10ore brown 90 90
P301 10ore violet 20 25
P302 10ore green 90 60
P303a **40** 15ore red 30 80
P304 30ore blue . . . . . . 3·75 3·00
P305 30ore orange 20 55
P306 40ore green . . . . . 2·40 2·25
P307 40ore blue 20 60
P308 **45** 50ore grey 45 85
P309 1k. brown 70 70

1945. Stamps of 1942 optd **POSTFAERGE**.
P346 **67** 30ore orange . . . . . 1·25 1·00
P347 40ore blue 60 85
P348 50ore grey 70 85

1949. Stamps of 1946 and 1948 optd **POSTFAERGE**.
P376 **80** 30ore orange . . . . . 2·25 1·00
P377 30ore red . . . . . . 90 1·00
P378 40ore blue . . . . . . 1·75 1·00
P379 40ore grey . . . . . . 90 1·00
P380 50ore grey . . . . . . 9·25 2·00
P381 50ore green . . . . . 75 1·00
P382 70ore green . . . . . 75 1·00
P383 **73** 1k. brown . . . . . . 1·00 1·25
P384 1k.25 orange . . . . . 3·75 5·00
P495 2k. red . . . . 1·75 1·90
P496 5k. blue . . . . 4·00 4·00

1967. Optd **POSTFAERGE**.
P488 **117** 40ore brown 60 60
P492 50ore brown 60 45
P489 80ore blue 60 60
P493 90ore blue . . . . . . 1·10 80

1975. Optd **POSTFAERGE**.
P597 **207** 100ore blue . . . . . . 1·10 1·10

POSTAGE DUE STAMPS

1921. Stamps of 1905 and 1913 optd **PORTO**.
D214 **15** 1ore orange . . . . . . 1·40 1·40
D215 **21** 5ore green . . . . . . 3·75 1·60
D216 7ore orange . . . . . . 2·25 1·25
D217 10ore red . . . . 14·00 6·25
D218 20ore blue . . . . . . 10·50 5·75
D219 25ore black and brown 18·00 1·60
D220 50ore black & purple . . 6·00 2·25

D 32

1921. Solid background.
D221 **D 32** 1ore orange 40 60
D222 4ore blue . . . . . . 1·90 1·75
D223 5ore brown . . . . . 1·90 60
D224 5ore green . . . . . 1·40 35
D225 7ore green . . . . . 11·00 12·00
D226 7ore violet . . . . . 20·00 24·00
D227 10ore green . . . . . 1·90 45
D228 10ore brown . . . . . 1·40 35
D229 20ore blue 90 50
D230 20ore grey . . . . . 1·90 1·25
D231 25ore red . . . . . . 3·25 1·00
D232 25ore lilac . . . . . . 2·25 1·75
D233 25ore blue . . . . . 3·25 3·50
D234 1k. blue . . . . 42·00 5·25
D235 1k. blue and brown . . 6·50 3·50
D236 5k. violet . . . . . . 9·50 5·50
For stamps with lined background see Nos. D285/97.

1921. Military Frank stamp optd **PORTO**.
D237 **21** 10ore red (No. M189) . . 6·75 5·00

1934. Lined background.
D285 **D 32** 1ore green 10 10
D286 2ore red 10 10
D287 5ore green 10 10
D288 6ore green 25 20
D289 8ore mauve . . . . . 1·75 1·60
D290 10ore orange 10 10
D291 12ore blue 30 40
D292 15ore violet 25 25
D293 20ore grey 15 10
D294 25ore blue 20 15
D295 30ore green 40 15
D296 40ore purple 60 35
D297 1k. brown 45 10

1934. Surch **PORTO 15**.
D298 **15** 15 on 12ore lilac . . . . 3·25 2·50

SPECIAL FEE STAMPS

1923. No. D227 optd **GEBYR GEBYR**.
S218 **D 32** 10ore green . . . . . 9·25 1·75

S 36

1926. Solid background.
S229 **S 36** 10ore green . . . . . . 4·75 65
S230 10ore brown . . . . . 5·25 55

1934. Lined background.
S285 **S 36** 5ore green 10 10
S286 10ore orange 10 10

DHAR Pt. 1

A state of Central India. Now uses Indian stamps.

4 pice = 1 anna.

1

2

1897. Imperf.
1 **1** ½pice black on red . . . . . 2·25 2·75
3 ¼a. black on orange . . . . 2·50 3·50
4 ½a. black on mauve . . . . 3·75 4·50
5 1a. black on green . . . . . 7·50 12·00
6 2a. black on yellow . . . . . 25·00 40·00

1898. Perf.
7b **2** ½a. red . . . . 3·00 5·50
8 1a. purple . . . . 3·25 6·50
10 2a. green . . . . 6·00 21·00

DIEGO-SUAREZ Pt. 6

A port in N. Madagascar. A separate colony till 1896, when it was incorporated with Madagascar.

100 centimes = 1 franc.

1890. Stamps of French Colonies (Type J Commerce), surch **15** sideways.
1 J 15 on 1c. black on blue . . . £170 70·00
2 15 on 5c. green . . . . £450 70·00
3 15 on 10c. black on lilac . . . £180 55·00
4 15 on 20c. red on green . . . £450 70·00
5 15 on 25c. black on red . . . 85·00 21·00

2

3

1890. Various designs.
6 **2** 1c. black . . . . £350 85·00
7 5c. black . . . . £325 75·00
8 15c. black . . . . 85·00 32·00
9 25c. black . . . . £110 35·00

1891.
10 **3** 5c. black . . . . £120 70·00

1891. Stamps of French Colonies. (Type J Commerce) surch **1891 DIEGO-SUAREZ 5 c.**
13 J 5c. on 10c. black on lilac . . £160 80·00
14 5c. on 20c. red on green . . . £140 65·00

1892. Stamps of French Colonies (Type J Commerce) optd **DIEGO-SUAREZ**.
15 J 1c. black on blue . . . . . . 24·00 12·50
16 2c. brown on buff . . . . . 28·00 13·50
17 4c. brown on grey . . . . . 28·00 22·00
18 5c. green on green . . . . . 85·00 55·00
19 10c. black on lilac . . . . . 23·00 23·00
20 15c. blue on blue . . . . . . 18·00 12·50
21 20c. red on green . . . . . . 26·00 21·00
22 25c. black on pink . . . . . 16·00 13·50
23 30c. brown on drab £850 £600
24 35c. black on orange £850 £600
25 75c. red on pink . . . . . . 65·00 26·00
26 1f. green . . . . 60·00 40·00

1892. "Tablet" key-type inscr "DIEGO-SUAREZ ET DEPENDANCES".
38 D 1c. black on blue . . . . . 1·75 3·75
39 2c. brown on buff . . . . . 2·25 1·25
40 4c. brown on grey . . . . . 85 4·00
41 5c. green on green . . . . . 1·60 4·75
42 10c. black on lilac . . . . . 5·75 6·50
43 15c. blue . . . . 4·25 11·00
44 20c. red on green . . . . . 8·75 10·00
45 25c. black on pink . . . . . 6·50 8·75
46 30c. brown on drab . . . . 9·00 22·00
47 40c. red on yellow . . . . . 15·00 13·50
48 50c. red on pink . . . . . . 19·00 13·00
49 75c. brown on yellow . . . 42·00 26·00
50 1f. green . . . . 60·00 35·00

1894. "Tablet" key-type inscr "DIEGO-SUAREZ".
51 D 1c. black on blue . . . . . 50 2·75
52 2c. brown on buff . . . . . 1·25 3·50
53 4c. brown on grey . . . . . 1·75 3·50
54 5c. green on green . . . . . 2·25 5·25
55 10c. black on lilac . . . . . 5·75 6·25
56 15c. blue . . . . 3·50 5·50
57 20c. red on green . . . . . 8·00 14·50
58 25c. black on pink . . . . . 4·25 4·00
59 30c. brown on drab . . . . 9·00 6·25
60 40c. red on yellow . . . . . 7·75 5·00
61 50c. red on pink . . . . . . 6·00 8·00
62 75c. brown on yellow . . . 2·75 6·00
63 1f. green . . . . 8·25 12·00

POSTAGE DUE STAMPS

D 4

1891.
D11 **D 4** 5c. violet . . . . 65·00 24·00
D12 50c. black on yellow . . 65·00 35·00

1892. Postage Due stamps of French Colonies overprinted **DIEGO-SUAREZ**.
D27 **D 4** 1c. black . . . . £100 50·00
D28 2c. black . . . . £110 45·00
D29 3c. black . . . . £110 50·00
D30 4c. black . . . . £100 60·00
D31 5c. black . . . . £110 60·00
D32 10c. black . . . . 27·00 25·00
D33 15c. black . . . . 27·00 27·00
D34 20c. black £160 £110
D35 30c. black . . . . 90·00 60·00
D36 60c. black £850 £600
D37 1f. brown £1600 £850

DJIBOUTI Pt. 6

A port in French Somaliland S. of the Red Sea, later capital of French Territory of the Afars and the Issas.

100 centimes = 1 franc.

1893. "Tablet" key-type stamp of Obock optd **DJ**.
83 D 5c. green & red on green . . £110 £120

1894. Same type surch in figures and **DJIBOUTI**.
85 D 25 on 2c. brn & bl on buff £275 £180
86 50 on 1c. blk & red on blue £325 £225

1894. Triangular stamp of Obock optd **DJIBOUTI** or surch **1** also.
87 **5** 1f. on 5f. red £600 £400
88 5f. red £1400 £1100

12 Djibouti (The apparent perforation is part of the design.)

13 "Pingouin" (French gunboat)

14 Crossing the Desert

1894. Imperf.
89 **12** 1c. red and black . . . . 1·10 1·25
90 2c. black and red 45 45
91 4c. blue and brown . . . 3·00 1·90
92 5c. red and green . . . . 2·25 1·60
93 5c. green . . . . 2·50 3·50
94 – 10c. green and brown . . . 3·75 1·00
95 – 15c. green and lilac . . . 3·25 1·75
96 – 25c. blue and red . . . . 5·00 2·00
97 – 30c. red and brown . . . 3·75 3·75
98 – 40c. blue and yellow . . . 55·00 48·00
99 – 50c. red and blue . . . . 18·00 12·00
100 – 75c. orange and mauve . . 35·00 29·00
101 – 1f. black and olive . . . . 21·00 21·00
102 – 2f. red and brown . . . . 85·00 70·00
103 **13** 5f. blue and red £190 £120
104 **14** 25f. blue and red £850 £850
105 50f. red and blue £650 £650
DESIGNS— As Type **12**: 10 to 75c. Different views of Djibouti; 1, 2f. Port of Djibouti.

1899. As last, surch.
108 – 0.05 on 75c. orge & mve 55·00 32·00
109 – 0.10 on 1f. blk & olive . . 70·00 60·00
106 **12** 0.40 on 4c. blue & brown £2750 19·00
110 – 0.40 on 2f. red & brown £550 £350
111 **13** 0.75 on 5f. blue and red . . £450 £375

1902. Rectangular stamp of Obock surch **0.05**.
107 **6** 0.05 on 75c. lilac & orange £1200 £900

1902. Triangular stamps of Obock surch.
112 **7** 5c. on 25f. blue and brown 55·00 60·00
113 10c. on 50f. green & red . . 75·00 60·00

1902. Nos. 98/9 surch.
114 5c. on 40c. blue and yellow 2·25 2·00
115 10c. on 50c. red and blue . . 15·00 20·00

1902. Stamps of Obock surch **DJIBOUTI** and value.
120 **6** 5c. on 30c. yellow & grn . . 5·50 12·50
116 10c. on 25c. black & blue 4·50 7·75
118 **7** 10c. on 2f. orange & lilac 35·00 50·00
119 10c. on 10f. lake and red . . 30·00 30·00

For later issues see **FRENCH SOMALI COAST**, **FRENCH TERRITORY OF THE AFARS AND THE ISSAS** and **DJIBOUTI REPUBLIC**.

DJIBOUTI REPUBLIC Pt. 12

Formerly French Territory of the Afars and the Issas.

112 Map and Flag

115 Head Rest

1977. Independence. Multicoloured.
685 45f. Type **112** . . . . 1·50 80
686 65f. Map of Djibouti (horiz) 2·25 95

1977. Various stamps of the French Territory of the Afars and the Issas optd **REPUBLIQUE DE DJIBOUTI** or surch also. (a) Sea Shells.
687 **81** 1f. on 4f. mult 20 20
688 – 2f. on 5f. brown, mauve and violet (629) 20 20
689 – 20f. brown & grn (633) . . 55 55
690 – 30f. brn, pur & grn (634) 65 65
691 – 40f. brown & grn (635) . . 90 90
692 – 45f. brn, grn & bl (636) . . 1·00 1·00
693 – 60f. black & brn (638) . . 1·40 1·40
694 – 70f. brn, bl & blk (639) . . 1·90 1·90

(b) Flora and Fauna.
695 **103** 5f. on 20f. multicoloured 20 20
696 **106** 45f. multicoloured 90 90
697 – 50f. multicoloured (675) 1·40 1·40
698 **107** 70f. multicoloured . . . . 1·60 1·60
699 – 100f. multicoloured (653) 2·50 2·50
700 – 150f. multicoloured (676) 3·00 3·00
701 – 300f. multicoloured (654) 7·50 7·50

(c) Buildings.
702 **99** 8f. grey, red & bl (postage) 30 30
703 **109** 500f. mult (air) . . . . . 9·75 8·25

(d) Celebrities.
704 **111** 55f. red, grey & grn (air) 1·40 1·10
705 – 75f. red, brn & grn (682) 2·50 2·50
706 **104** 200f. blue, green and orange (postage) . . . 3·75 3·75

(e) Sport.
707 **108** 200f. multicoloured . . . 4·50 4·50

1977. Local Art. Multicoloured.
708 10f. Type **115** 20 10
709 20f. Water cask (vert) 45 15
710 25f. Washing jar (vert) . . . 65 20

116 Ostrich

117 "Glossodoris"

1977. Birds. Multicoloured.
711 90f. Type **116** . . . . 2·75 1·00
712 100f. Vitelline masked weaver 3·75 1·75

1977. Sea Life. Multicoloured.
713 45f. Type **117** . . . . 1·00 90
714 70f. Turtle . . . . 1·10 45
715 80f. Catalufa . . . . 1·60 65

118 Map, Dove and U.N. Emblem

1977. Air. Admission to the United Nations.
716 **118** 300f. multicoloured . . . 4·50 2·75

119 Crabs "Uca lactea"

1977. Fauna. Multicoloured.
717 15f. Type **119** 45 15
718 50f. Klipspringer . . . . . . 1·25 40
719 150f. Dolphin (fish) . . . . . 3·25 2·00

120 President Hassan Gouled Aptidon and Flag

1978.
720 **120** 65f. multicoloured 90 45

121 Marcel Brochet MB 101

1978. Air. Djibouti Aero Club. Multicoloured.
721 60f. Type **121** 95 60
722 85f. De Havilland Tiger Moth . . . . 1·25 80
723 200f. Morane Saulnier Rallye Commodore . . . . 2·75 1·60

122 "Charaxes hansali"

123 "Head of an Old Man"

1978. Butterflies. Multicoloured.
724 5f. Type **122** 10 10
725 20f. "Colias electo" 55 20
726 25f. "Acraea chilo" 80 40
727 150f. "Junonia hierta" . . . 3·00 1·50

1978. Air. 400th Birth Anniv of Rubens. Mult.
728 50f. Type **123** 85 35
729 500f. "The Hippopotamus Hunt" (detail) . . . . . . 8·00 3·25

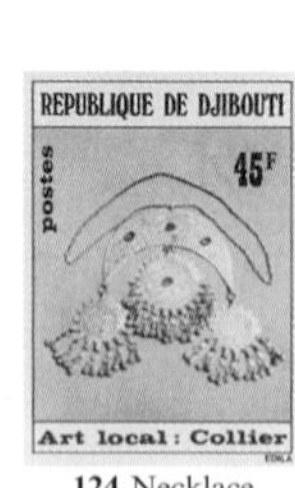

124 Necklace

125 Player with Cup

1978. Native Handicrafts. Multicoloured.
730 45f. Type **124** 85 40
731 55f. Necklace . . . . 1·10 45

1978. Air. World Cup Football Championship, Argentina. Multicoloured.
732 100f. Type **125** . . . . 1·40 45
733 300f. World Cup, footballer and map of Argentina . . 4·25 1·25

126 "Bougainvillea glabra"

1978. Flowers. Multicoloured.
734 15f. Type **126** 40 10
735 35f. "Hibiscus schizopetalus" 70 20
736 250f. "Caesalpinia pulcherrima" . . . . . . 4·50 85

1978. Air. Argentina's Victory in World Cup Football Championship. Nos. 722/3 optd.
737 100f. Type **125** . . . . 1·60 45
738 300f. World Cup, footballer and map of Argentina . . 4·50 1·50
OVERPRINTS: 100f. **ARGENTINE CHAMPION 1978**; 300f. **ARGENTINE HOLLANDE 3–1**.

128 "The Hare" (Albrecht Durer)

1978. Air. Paintings. Multicoloured.
739 100f. "Tahitian Women" (Paul Gauguin) (horiz) . . 1·90 55
740 250f. Type **128** . . . . 4·75 1·90

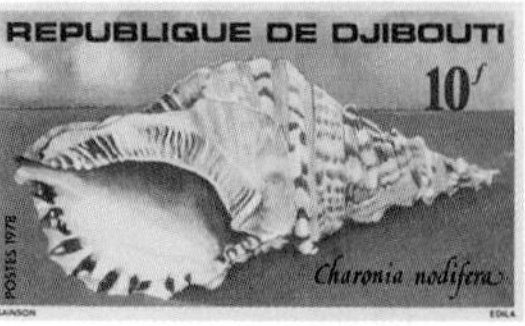

129 Knobbed Triton

1978. Sea Shells. Multicoloured
741 10f. Type **129** 75 35
742 80f. Trumpet triton . . . . . 2·50 90

130 Copper-banded Butterflyfish

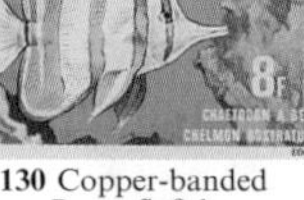

131 Dove and U.P.U. Emblem

1978. Fishes. Multicoloured.
743 8f. Type **130** 40 15
744 30f. Yellow tang 85 25
745 40f. Harlequin sweetlips . . . 1·60 45

1978. Air. "Philexafrique" Exhibition, Libreville, Gabon (1st issue) and Int. Stamp Fair, Essen, W. Germany. As T **237** of Benin. Multicoloured.
746 90f. Jay and Brunswick 1852 3sqr. stamp . . . . 1·90 1·40
747 90f. African spoonbill and Djibouti 1977 optd 300f. stamp . . . . 1·90 1·40

1978. Air. Centenary of Paris U.P.U. Congress.
748 **131** 200f. green, brn & turq 2·75 1·40

132 Alsthom BB 1201 Diesel Locomotive

1979. Djibouti–Addis Ababa Railway. Mult.
749 40f. Type **132** 90 40
750 55f. Pacific locomotive No. 231 . . . . 80 30
751 60f. Steam locomotive No. 130 . . . . 1·00 35
752 75f. Alsthom CC 2001 diesel-electric locomotive . . . . 1·40 60

133 Children learning to Count

1979. International Year of the Child. Multicoloured.
753 20f. Type **133** 35 10
754 200f. Mother and child . . . 3·00 1·25

134 De Havilland Twin Otter over Crater

1979. Ardoukoba Volcano. Multicoloured.
755 30f. Sud Aviation Alouette II helicopter over crater . . . 65 40
756 90f. Type **134** . . . . 1·90 70

135 Sir Rowland Hill and 300f. Stamp, 1977

1979. Death Centenary of Sir Rowland Hill. Multicoloured.
757 25f. Type **135** 35 10
758 100f. Letters with 1894 50f. and 1977 45f. stamps . . . 2·25 60
759 150f. Loading mail on ship 2·25 80

136 Junkers Ju 52/3m and Dewoitine D-338 Trimotor

1979. Air. 75th Anniv of Powered Flight. Multicoloured.
760 140f. Type **136** . . . . 2·25 95
761 250f. Potez 63-11 bomber and Supermarine Spitfire Mk. VII . . . . 3·25 1·90
762 500f. Concorde and Sikorsky S-40 flying boat "American Clipper" . . . . 7·25 3·25

137 Djibouti, Local Woman and Namaqua Dove

1979. "Philexafrique 2" Exhibition, Gabon (2nd issue). Multicoloured.
763 55f. Type **137** . . . . 2·25 1·40
764 80f. U.P.U. emblem, map, Douglas DC-8-60 "Super Sixty", Alsthom diesel-electric train and postal runner . . . . 2·75 1·25

138 "Opuntia"

1979. Flowers. Multicoloured.
765 2f. Type **138** 10 10
766 8f. "Solanacea" (horiz) . . . 20 10
767 15f. "Trichodesma" (horiz) . . 35 10
768 45f. "Acacia etbaica" (horiz) 65 15
769 50f. "Thunbergia alata" . . . 90 15

139 "The Washerwoman"

1979. Air. Death Centenary of Honore Daumier (painter).
770 **139** 500f. multicoloured . . . 8·25 2·75

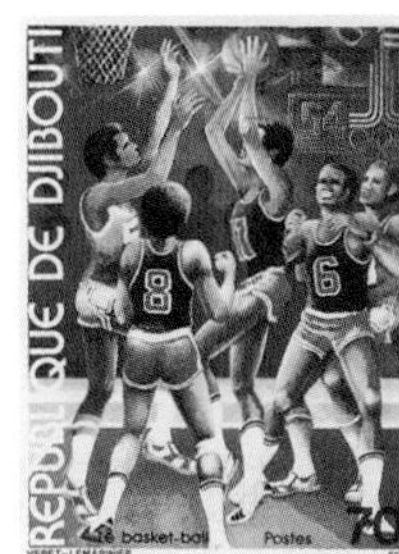

140 Basketball

1979. Pre-Olympic Year. Multicoloured.
771 70f. Type **140** . . . . 1·10 30
772 120f. Running . . . . 1·60 55
773 300f. Football . . . . 2·75 85

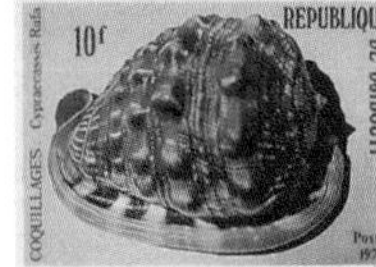

141 Bull-mouth Helmet

1979. Shells. Multicoloured.
774 10f. Type **141** 20 15
775 40f. Arthritic spider conch . . 1·00 20
776 300f. Ventral harp . . . . . 5·50 1·60

142 Winter Sports Equipment and Mosque

1980. Air. Winter Olympic Games, Lake Placid.
777 **142** 150f. multicoloured . . . 2·25 65

143 Lions Club Banner and Steam Locomotive

1980. Djibouti Clubs. Multicoloured.
778 90f. Rotary Club banner and Morane Saulnier MS 892 (75th anniv of Rotary International) . . . . . . 1·75 70
779 100f. Type **143** . . . . 2·50 50

144 "Colotis danae" **147** Basketball

145 Boeing 737

1980. Butterflies. Multicoloured.
780 5f. Type **144** 20 20
781 55f. "Danaus chrysippus" . . 1·00 65

1980. Air. Foundation of "Air Djibouti".
782 **145** 400f. multicoloured . . . 6·00 2·25

1980. Air. Winter Olympic Games. No. 777 surch with names of Medal Winners.
783 **142** 80f. on 150f. . . . . . . 1·10 45
784 200f. on 150f. . . . . . 2·75 1·25
OVERPRINTS: 80f. **A.M. MOSER-PROEL AUTRICHE DESCENT DAMES MEDAILLE D'OR**. 200f. **HEIDEN USA 5 MEDAILLES D'OR PATINAGE DE VITESSE**.

1980. Olympic Games, Moscow. Multicoloured.
785 60f. Type **147** 90 20
786 120f. Football . . . . 1·60 45
787 250f. Running . . . . 3·00 1·00

148 "Apollo XI" Moon Landing

1980. Air. Conquest of Space. Multicoloured.
788 200f. Type **148** . . . . 2·75 65
789 300f. "Apollo-Soyuz" link-up 4·50 1·00

149 Samisch v Romanovsky Game, Moscow, 1925

1980. Founding of International Chess Federation, 1924. Multicoloured.
790 20f. Type **149** 70 15
791 75f. "Royal Chess Party" (15th-century Italian book illustration) . . . . 1·90 40

150 Satellite and Earth Station

1980. Air. Inauguration of Satellite Earth Station.
792 **150** 500f. multicoloured . . . 7·25 1·90

151 Sieve Cowrie

1980. Shells. Multicoloured.
793 15f. Type **151** 50 20
794 85f. Chambered nautilus . . 1·90 65

152 Sir Alexander Fleming and Penicillin

1980. Anniversaries. Multicoloured.
795 20f. Type **152** 50 20
796 130f. Jules Verne and space capsules . . . . 2·25 65
ANNIVERSARIES: 20f. Discovery of penicillin, 25th anniv. 130f. Jules Verne, 75th death anniv.

153 "Graf Zeppelin" and Sphinx

1980. Air. 80th Anniv of First Zeppelin Flight. Multicoloured.
797 100f. Type **153** . . . . 2·00 60
798 150f. Ferdinand von Zeppelin 2·50 90

154 Capt. Cook and H.M.S. "Endeavour"

1980. Death Bicentenary (1979) of Captain James Cook. Multicoloured.
799 55f. Type **154** 90 80
800 90f. Cook's ships and map of voyages . . . . 1·60 1·10

155 "Voyager" and Saturn

1980. Air. Space Exploration.
801 **155** 250f. multicoloured . . . 4·00 1·10

156 Saving a Goal

1981. Air. World Cup Football Eliminators. Multicoloured.
802 80f. Type **156** . . . . 1·10 35
803 200f. Tackle . . . . 2·75 80

157 Transport **158** Yuri Gagarin and "Vostok 1"

1981. Air European–African Economic Convention.
804 **157** 100f. multicoloured . . . 3·00 90

1981. Air. Space Anniversaries and Events. Multicoloured.
805 75f. Type **158** (20th anniv of first man in space) . . . . 1·10 35
806 120f. "Viking" exploration of Mars (horiz) . . . . 1·60 50
807 150f. Alan Shepard and "Freedom 7" (20th anniv of first American in space) 2·25 65

159 Arabian Angelfish

1981. Djibouti Tropical Aquarium. Mult.
808 25f. Type **159** 60 15
809 55f. Moorish idol . . . . . 1·40 35
810 70f. Golden trevally . . . . 1·60 90

160 Caduceus, Satellite and Rocket

1981. World Telecommunications Day.
811 **160** 140f. multicoloured . . . 1·90 55

161 German 231 and American RC4 Diesel Locomotives

1981. Locomotives. Multicoloured.
812 40f. Type **161** 85 30
813 55f. George Stephenson, "Rocket" (1829) and Djibouti locomotive . . . 1·25 40
814 65f. French TGV and Japanese "Hikari" high speed trains . . . . 1·75 40

162 Antenna on Globe and Morse Key

1981. Djibouti Amateur Radio Club.
815 **162** 250f. multicoloured . . . 3·50 1·10

163 Prince Charles and Lady Diana Spencer

1981. Royal Wedding. Multicoloured.
816 180f. Type **163** . . . . 2·75 85
817 200f. Prince Charles and Lady Diana in wedding dress . . . . 3·00 1·10

164 Admiral Nelson and H.M.S. "Victory"

1981. Admiral Nelson Commemoration. Mult.
818 100f. Type **164** . . . . 1·60 1·00
819 175f. Nelson and stern view of H.M.S. "Victory" . . . 2·75 1·50

165 Tree Hyrax and Scout tending Campfire

1981. 28th World Scouting Congress, Dakar, and Fourth Panafrican Scouting Conference, Abidjan. Multicoloured.
820 60f. Type **165** . . . . 1·25 40
821 105f. Scouts saluting, map reading and greater kudu 1·60 50

166 "Football Players" (Picasso)

1981. Air. Paintings. Multicoloured.
822 300f. Type **166** . . . . 5·00 1·40
823 400f. "Portrait of a Man in a Turban" (Rembrandt) . . 5·50 1·90

167 Launch

168 19th-century Chinese Pawn and Knight

1981. Air. Space Shuttle. Multicoloured.
824 90f. Type **167** . . . . 1·40 45
825 120f. Space Shuttle landing 1·75 65

1981. Chess Pieces. Multicoloured.
826 50f. 13th-century Swedish pawn and queen (horiz) . . 1·10 35
827 130f. Type **168** . . . . 2·25 80

169 Aerial View

1981. Inauguration of Djibouti Sheraton Hotel.
828 **169** 75f. multicoloured . . . . 1·10 40

1981. 2nd Flight of Space Shuttle "Columbia". Nos. 824/5 optd.
829 90f. Type **167** . . . . 1·40 55
830 120f. Space Shuttle landing 1·75 85
OPTS: 90f. **COLUMBIA 2eme VOL SPATIAL 12 NOVEMBRE 1981**. 120f. **JOE ENGLE et RICHARD TRULY 2eme VOL SPATIAL—12 Nov. 1981**.

171 "Clitoria ternatea"

1981. Flowers. Multicoloured.
831 10f. Type **171** 20 10
832 30f. "Acacia mellifera" (horiz) 45 15
833 35f. "Punica granatum" (horiz) 70 20
834 45f. Malvacee 85 20

1981. World Chess Championship, Merano (1st issue). Nos. 826/7 optd.
835 50f. multicoloured 95 35
836 130f. multicoloured . . . . . 2·25 80
OPTS: 50f. **Octobre-Novembre 1981 ANATOLI KARPOV VICTOR KORTCHNOI MERANO (ITALIE)**. 130f. **ANATOLI KARPOV Champion du Monde 1981**.
See also Nos. 843/4.

173 Saving Goal

1982. Air. World Cup Football Championship, Spain. Multicoloured.
837 110f. Type **173** . . . . 1·60 55
838 220f. Footballers . . . . . . 3·25 1·10

174 John H. Glenn

175 Dr. Robert Koch, Bacillus and Microscope

1982. Air. Space Anniversaries. Mult.
839 40f. "Luna 9" (15th anniv of first unmanned moon landing) 55 20
840 60f. Type **174** (20th anniv of flight) 90 35
841 180f. "Viking 1" (5th anniv of first Mars landing) (horiz) . . . . 2·40 85

1982. Centenary of Robert Koch's Discovery of Tubercle Bacillus.
842 **175** 305f. multicoloured . . . 4·75 1·60

176 14th-century German Bishop and 18th-century Marie de Medici Bishop

177 Princess of Wales

1982. World Chess Championship, Merano (2nd issue). Multicoloured.
843 125f. Type **176** . . . . 2·50 75
844 175f. Late 19th-century queen and pawn from Nuremberg 3·00 95

1982. Air. 21st Birthday of Princess of Wales. Multicoloured.
845 120f. Type **177** . . . . 1·60 85
846 180f. Princess of Wales (different) . . . . 2·50 1·00

178 I.Y.C. Stamp, Collector, Greater Flamingoes and Emblems

1982. "Philexfrance" International Stamp Exhibition, Paris. Multicoloured.
847 80f. Type **178** . . . . 2·50 1·25
848 140f. Rowland Hill stamp Exhibition Centre and U.P.U. emblem . . . . . 2·25 95

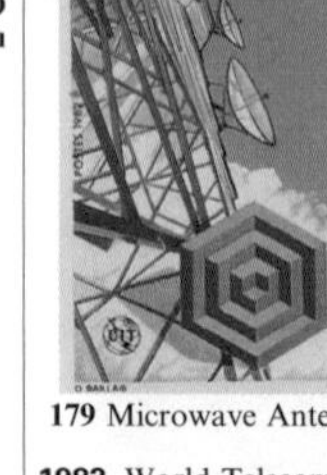

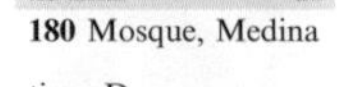

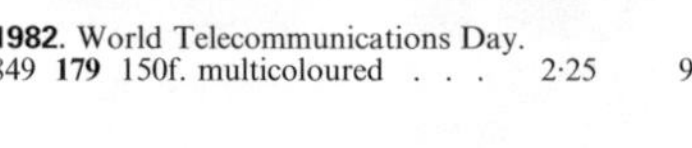

179 Microwave Antenna

180 Mosque, Medina

1982. World Telecommunications Day.
849 **179** 150f. multicoloured . . . 2·25 90

1982. Air. 1350th Death Anniv of Mohammed.
850 **180** 500f. multicoloured . . . 6·75 2·50

181 Lord Baden-Powell

1982. Air. 125th Birth Anniv of Lord Baden-Powell. Multicoloured.
851 95f. Type **181** . . . . 1·25 55
852 200f. Saluting Scout and camp . . . . 2·75 1·10

182 Bus and Jeep

1982. Transport. Multicoloured.
853 20f. Type **182** 35 15
854 25f. Ferry and dhow 65 35
855 55f. Boeing 727-100 airliner and Alsthom Series BB 500 diesel locomotive and train 3·75 55

1982. Air. World Cup Football Championship winners. Nos. 837/8 optd.
856 110f. Type **173** . . . . 1·60 65
857 220f. Footballers . . . . . . 3·00 1·40
OPTS: 110f. **ITALIE RFA 3-1 POLOGNE FRANCE 3-2**. 220f. **ITALIE RFA 3-1 2 RFA 3 POLOGNE**.

1982. Air. Birth of Prince William of Wales. Nos. 845/6 optd.
858 120f. Type **177** . . . . 1·60 85
859 180f. Princess of Wales (different) . . . . 2·50 1·10
OPTS: 120f. **21 JUIN 1982 WILLIAM-ARTHUR-PHILIPPE-LOUIS PRINCE DES GALLES**. 180f. **21ST JUNE 1982 WILLIAM-ARTHUR-PHILIP-LOUIS PRINCE OF WALES**.

185 Satellite, Dish Aerial and Conference

1982. Air. Second U.N. Conference on the Exploration and Peaceful Uses of Outer Space, Vienna.
860 **185** 350f. multicoloured . . . 5·00 1·60

186 Franklin D. Roosevelt

187 Red Sea Cowrie

1982. Air. 250th Birth Anniv of George Washington and Birth Centenary of Franklin D. Roosevelt. Multicoloured.
861 115f. Type **186** . . . . 1·60 55
862 250f. George Washington . . 3·25 1·10

1982. Shells. Multicoloured.
863 10f. Type **187** 25 15
864 15f. Sumatran cone 40 20
865 25f. Lovely cowrie 55 25
866 30f. Engraved cone 75 40
867 70f. Heavy bonnet . . . . . 1·75 75
868 150f. Burnt cowrie . . . . . 3·50 1·25

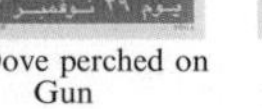

188 Dove perched on Gun

189 Montgolfier's Balloon, 1783

1982. Palestinian Solidarity Day.
869 **188** 40f. multicoloured 55 25

1983. Air. Bicentenary of Manned Flight. Mult.
870 35f. Type **189** 60 75
871 45f. Henri Giffard's balloon "Le Grand Ballon Captif", 1878 . . . . 90 45
872 120f. Balloon "Double Eagle II", 1978 . . . . 2·25 1·10

190 Volleyball

192 Martin Luther King

191 Bloch 220 Gascogne

1983. Air. Olympic Games, Los Angeles (1984). Multicoloured.
873 75f. Type **190** . . . . 1·10 45
874 125f. Wind-surfing . . . . . 2·25 1·25

1983. Air. 50th Anniv of Air France. Mult.
875 25f. Type **191** 40 25
876 100f. Douglas DC-4 . . . . 1·40 1·00
877 175f. Boeing 747-200 . . . . 2·50 1·25

1983. Flowers. As T **171**. Multicoloured.
878 5f. Ipomoea 10 10
879 50f. Moringa (horiz) 85 35
880 55f. Cotton flower . . . . . 1·00 40

1983. Air. Celebrities. Multicoloured.
881 180f. Type **192** (15th death anniv) . . . . 2·25 90
882 250f. Alfred Nobel (150th birth anniv) . . . . 3·25 1·40

193 W.C.Y. Emblem

194 Yacht and Rotary Club Emblem

1983. World Communications Year.
883 **193** 500f. multicoloured . . . 6·75 2·75

1983. Air. International Club Meetings. Mult.
884 90f. Type **194** . . . . 2·00 1·50
885 150f. Minaret and Lions Club emblem . . . . 2·00 90

195 Renault, 1904

1983. Air. Early Motor Cars. Multicoloured.
886 60f. Type **195** . . . . 1·25 40
887 80f. Mercedes Knight, 1910 (vert) . . . . 1·90 50
888 100f. Lorraine-Dietrich, 1912 2·25 80

197 "Vostok VI"

1983. Air. Conquest of Space. Multicoloured.
890 120f. Type **197** . . . . 1·60 65
891 200f. "Explorer I" . . . . . 2·75 1·10

198 Development Projects

1983. Donors Conference.
892 **198** 75f. multicoloured . . . . 1·10 55

199 Red Sea Marginella

1983. Shells. Multicoloured.
893 15f. Type **199** 40 15
894 30f. Jickeli's cone 85 25
895 55f. MacAndrew's cowrie . . 1·40 60
896 80f. Cuvier's cone . . . . . 1·90 75
897 100f. Tapestry turban . . . . 2·10 1·00

200 "Colotis chrysonome"

1984. Butterflies.
898 5f. Type **200** 10 10
899 20f. "Colias erate" 25 20
900 30f. "Junonia orithyia" . . . 45 30
901 75f. "Acraea doubledayi" . . 1·40 90
902 110f. "Byblia ilithya" . . . . 1·75 1·40

201 Speed Skating

1984. Air. Winter Olympic Games, Sarajevo. Mult.
903 70f. Type **201** . . . . 1·10 40
904 130f. Ice dancing . . . . . . 1·90 70

203 Microlight

1984. Air. Microlight Aircraft. Multicoloured.
906 65f. Type **203** . . . . 1·00 80
907 85f. Powered hang-glider "Jules" . . . . 1·25 1·00
908 100f. Microlight (different) 1·50 1·25

1984. Air. Winter Olympic Games Medal Winners. Nos. 903/4 optd.
909 70f. **1000 METRES HOMMES OR: BOUCHER (CANADA) ARGENT: KHLEBNIKOV (URSS) BRONZE: ENGELSTADT (NORV.)** 1·10 55
910 130f. **DANSE OR: TORVILL-DEAN (G.B.) ARGENT: BESTEMIANOVA-BUKIN (URSS) BRONZE: KLIMOVA-PONOMARENKO (URSS)** . . . . 1·90 85

205 "Marguerite Matisse with Cat"

1984. Air. 30th Death Anniv of Matisse and Birth Centenary of Modigliani. Multicoloured.
911 150f. Type **205** . . . . 2·50 90
912 200f. "Mario Varvogli" (Modigliani) . . . . 3·50 1·40

206 Randa

1984. Landscapes. Multicoloured.
913 2f. Type **206** 10 10
914 8f. Ali Sabieh 10 10
915 10f. Lake Assal 15 10
916 15f. Tadjoura 20 10
917 40f. Alaili Dada (vert) . . . 55 20
918 45f. Lake Abbe 60 25
919 55f. Obock . . . . 1·50 85
920 125f. Presidential Palace . . . 3·00 1·60

207 Marathon

1984. Air. Olympic Games, Los Angeles. Mult.
921 50f. Type **207** 65 30
922 60f. High jump 85 35
923 80f. Swimming . . . . 1·10 45

208 Battle of Solferino

1984. Air. 125th Anniv of Battle of Solferino and 120th Anniv of Red Cross.
924 **208** 300f. multicoloured . . . 4·50 1·60

209 Bleriot and Diagram of Bleriot XI

1984. Air. 75th Anniv of Louis Bleriot's Cross-Channel Flight. Multicoloured.
925 40f. Type **209** 65 50
926 75f. Bleriot and Bleriot XI and Britten Norman Islander aircraft . . . . . 1·10 90
927 90f. Bleriot and Boeing 727 airliner . . . . 1·25 1·10

210 Marathon

212 Men on Moon, Telescope and Planets

211 U.S.A. Attack-pumper Fire Engine

1984. Membership of International Olympic Committee.
928 **210** 45f. multicoloured 65 30

1984. Fire Fighting. Multicoloured.
929 25f. Type **211** 70 20
930 95f. French P.P.M. rescue crane . . . . 2·10 65
931 100f. Canadair CL-215 fire-fighting amphibian . . . . 2·25 1·25

1984. Air. 375th Anniv of Galileo's Telescope. Multicoloured.
932 120f. Type **212** . . . . 1·60 65
933 180f. Galileo, telescope and planets . . . . 2·50 1·00

213 Football Teams (Europa Cup)

1984. Air. European Football Championship and Olympic Games, Los Angeles. Multicoloured.
934 80f. Type **213** . . . . 1·25 55
935 80f. Football teams (Olympic Games) . . . . 1·25 55

214 Motor Carriage, 1886

1984. 150th Birth Anniv of Gottlieb Daimler (automobile designer). Multicoloured.
936 35f. Type **214** 55 20
937 65f. Cannstatt-Daimler cabriolet, 1896 . . . . . . 1·00 35
938 90f. Daimler "Phoenix", 1900 1·50 55

215 Pierre Curie

1985. Pierre and Marie Curie (physicists). Mult.
939 150f. Type **215** (150th birth anniv) . . . . 2·25 85
940 150f. Marie Curie (50th death anniv) . . . . 2·25 85

216 White-throated Bee Eater

1985. Birth Bicentenary of John J. Audubon. Multicoloured.
941 5f. Type **216** 25 15
942 15f. Chestnut-bellied sand-grouse . . . . 1·10 45
943 20f. Yellow-breasted barbet 1·25 50
944 25f. European roller . . . . 1·50 55

217 Dr. Hansen, Bacilli, Lepers and Lions Emblem
218 Globe and Pictograms

1985. Air. International Organizations. Mult.
946 50f. Type **217** (World Leprosy Day) 80 40
947 60f. Rotary International emblem and pieces on chessboard . . . . 1·40 65

1985. International Youth Year.
948 **218** 10f. multicoloured 80 25
949 30f. multicoloured . . . . 2·25 50
950 40f. multicoloured . . . . 3·00 90

219 Steam Locomotive No. 29, Addis Ababa–Djibouti Railway

1985. Railway Locomotives. Multicoloured.
951 55f. Type **219** . . . . 1·50 65
952 75f. "Adler", 1835 (150th anniv of German railways) 2·25 85

220 Planting Sapling
221 Victor Hugo (novelist)

1985. Foundation of Djibouti Scouting Association. Multicoloured.
953 35f. Type **220** 65 30
954 65f. Childcare . . . . 1·40 45

1985. Writers. Multicoloured.
955 80f. Type **221** . . . . 1·10 50
956 100f. Arthur Rimbaud (poet) 1·40 60

222 Dish Aerials, Off-shore Oil Rigs and Building

1985. Air. "Philexafrique" Stamp Exhibition, Lome (1st issue). Multicoloured.
957 80f. Type **222** . . . . 2·25 1·50
958 80f. Carpenter, girl at microscope and man at visual display unit . . . . 1·60 1·10
See also Nos. 969/70.

1985. Shells. As T **199**. Multicoloured.
959 10f. Twin-blotch cowrie . . . 25 15
960 15f. Thrush cowrie 35 20
961 30f. Vice-Admiral cowrie . . 95 25
962 40f. Giraffe cone . . . . . . 1·10 55
963 55f. Terebra cone . . . . . 1·75 75

223 Team Winners on Rostrum

1985. 1st Marathon World Cup, Hiroshima. Multicoloured.
964 75f. Type **223** . . . . 1·00 45
965 100f. Finishing line and officials . . . . 1·50 65

224 Launch of "Ariane"

1985. Air. Telecommunications Development. Mult.
966 50f. International Transmission Centre . . . 65 30
967 90f. Type **224** . . . . 1·25 50
968 120f. "Arabsat" satellite . . . 1·60 65

225 Windsurfing and Tennis

1985. Air. "Philexafrique" Stamp Exhibition, Lome, Togo (2nd issue). Multicoloured.
969 100f. Type **225** . . . . 2·00 1·25
970 100f. Construction of Tadjoura road . . . . . . 1·60 1·10

226 Edmond Halley, Bayeux Tapestry and Comet

1986. Appearance of Halley's Comet. Multicoloured.
971 85f. Type **226** . . . . 1·10 45
972 90f. Solar system, comet trajectory and space probes "Giotto" and "Vega 1" . . 1·40 55

227 Footballers

1986. Air. World Cup Football Championship, Mexico. Multicoloured.
973 75f. Type **227** . . . . 1·00 45
974 100f. Players and stadium . . 1·40 65

228 Runners on Shore

1986. "ISERST" Solar Energy Project. Mult.
975 50f. Type **228** 65 30
976 150f. "ISERST" building . . 2·00 85

229 "Santa Maria"

1986. Historic Ships of Columbus, 1492. Multicoloured.
977 60f. Type **229** . . . . 1·90 1·25
978 90f. "Nina" and "Pinta" . . 2·50 2·00

230 Statue of Liberty, Eiffel Tower and French and U.S. Flags

1986. Air. Centenary of Statue of Liberty.
979 **230** 250f. multicoloured . . . 3·25 1·40

231 Rainbow Runner

1986. Red Sea Fish. Multicoloured.
980 20f. Type **231** 80 50
981 25f. Sehel's grey mullet . . . 1·00 50
982 55f. Blubber-lipped snapper 2·40 1·25

232 People's Palace

1986. Public Buildings. Multicoloured.
983 105f. Type **232** . . . . 1·40 55
984 115f. Ministry of the Interior, Posts and Telecommunications . . . 1·60 65

233 Transmission Building and Keyboard

1986. Inauguration of Sea-Me-We Submarine Communications Cable.
985 **233** 100f. multicoloured . . . 1·40 65

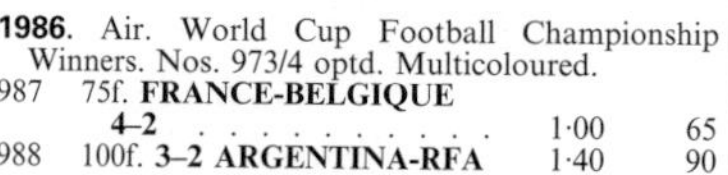

1986. Air. World Cup Football Championship Winners. Nos. 973/4 optd. Multicoloured.
987 75f. **FRANCE-BELGIQUE 4–2** . . . . 1·00 65
988 100f. **3–2 ARGENTINA-RFA** 1·40 90

235 Javanese Bishop, Knight and Queen

1986. Air. World Chess Championship, London and Leningrad. Multicoloured.
989 80f. Type **235** . . . . 1·40 65
990 120f. German rook, pawn and king . . . . 2·25 1·00

1986. 5th Anniv of Inaug of Djibouti Sheraton Hotel. No. 828 surch **5e ANNIVERSAIRE**.
991 **169** 55f. on 75f. mult 90 55

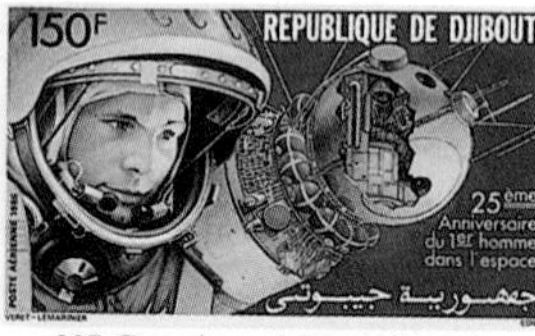

237 Gagarin and Space Capsule

1986. Air. 25th Anniv of First Man in Space and 20th Anniv of "Gemini 8"–"Agena" Link-up. Multicoloured.
992 150f. Type **237** . . . . 2·25 65
993 200f. "Gemini 8" and "Agena" craft over Earth 3·00 1·00

238 Amiot 370

1987. Air. Flight Anniversaries and Events. Multicoloured.
994 55f. Type **238** (45th anniv of first Istres-Djibouti flight) 90 60
995 80f. "Spirit of St Louis" and Charles Lindbergh (60th anniv of first solo flight across North Atlantic) . . 1·10 95
996 120f. Dick Rutan, Jeana Yeager and "Voyager" (first non-stop flight around the world) . . . . 1·75 1·25

239 Louis Pasteur and Vaccination Session

1987. Centenary of Pasteur Institute. National Vaccination Campaign in Djibouti.
997 **239** 220f. multicoloured . . . 3·25 1·10

241 "Macrolepiota imbricata"
242 Hare

1987. Fungi. Multicoloured.
999 35f. Type **241** . . . . 1·25 65
1000 50f. "Lentinus squarrosulus" 2·00 95
1001 95f. "Terfezia boudieri" . . 3·50 1·50

1987. Wild Animals. Multicoloured.
1002 5f. Type **242** 10 10
1003 30f. Young dromedary with mother 45 20
1004 140f. Cheetah . . . . 2·25 80

243 President Hassan Gouled Aptidon, Map, Flag and Crest

1987. Air. 10th Anniv of Independence.
1005 **243** 250f. multicoloured . . . 3·25 1·40

244 Pierre de Coubertin (founder of modern Games) and Athlete lighting Flame

1987. Olympic Games, Calgary and Seoul (1st issue) (1988). Multicoloured.
1006 85f. Type **244** . . . . 1·10 45
1007 135f. Ski-jumper . . . . . 1·60 65
1008 140f. Runners and spectators . . . . 1·90 80
See also No. 1021.

245 "Telstar" Satellite

1987. Air. Telecommunications Anniversaries. Multicoloured.
1009 190f. Type **245** (25th anniv) 2·50 90
1010 250f. Samuel Morse and morse key (150th anniv of morse telegraph) . . . . 3·25 1·40

246 Djibouti Creek and Quay, 1887

1987. Air. Centenary of Djibouti City.
1011 **246** 100f. agate and stone . . 2·00 1·40
1012 – 150f. multicoloured . . . 2·25 80
DESIGN: 150f. Aerial view of Djibouti, 1987.

247 Comb **249** Anniversary Emblem

1988. Traditional Djibouti Art. Multicoloured.
1014 30f. Type **247** 45 20
1015 70f. Water pitcher 95 45

1988. Air. 125th Anniv of Red Cross.
1017 **249** 300f. multicoloured . . . 4·25 1·60

250 Rabat and Footballers

1988. 16th African Nations Cup Football Championship, Morocco.
1018 **250** 55f. multicoloured . . . 85 35

251 Ski Jumping **252** Doctor examining Child

1988. Winter Olympic Games, Calgary.
1019 **251** 45f. multicoloured . . . 65 30

1988. U.N.I.C.E.F. "Universal Vaccinations by 1990" Campaign.
1020 **252** 125f. multicoloured . . . 1·75 65

253 Runners and Stadium

1988. Air. Olympic Games, Seoul (2nd issue).
1021 **253** 105f. multicoloured . . . 1·40 55

1988. Air. Paris–Djibouti–St. Denis (Reunion) Roland Garros Air Race. No. 994 surch **PARIS-DJIBOUTI-ST DENIS LA REUNION RALLYE ROLAND GARROS 70 F**.
1022 **238** 70f. on 55f. mult . . . . 1·25 65

255 Animals at Water Trough

1988. Anti-drought Campaign.
1023 **255** 50f. multicoloured . . . 85 35

256 Djibouti Post Offices of 1890 and 1977

1988. Air. World Post Day.
1024 **256** 1000f. multicoloured . . 13·50 4·00

257 Combine Harvester, Tractor and Ploughman with Camel

1988. 10th Anniv of International Agricultural Development Fund.
1025 **257** 135f. multicoloured . . . 1·75 65

258 De Havilland Tiger Moth, 1948, and Socata Tobago, 1988

1988. 40th Anniv of Michel Lafoux Air Club.
1026 **258** 145f. multicoloured . . . 2·00 95

1988. 1st Djibouti Olympic Medal Winner. No. 1021 optd **AHMED SALAH 1re MEDAILLE OLYMPIQUE**.
1027 **253** 105f. multicoloured . . . 1·40 90

260 "Lobophyllia costata"

1989. Underwater Animals. Multicoloured.
1028 90f. Type **260** . . . . 1·40 35
1029 160f. Giant spider conch . . 3·25 1·40

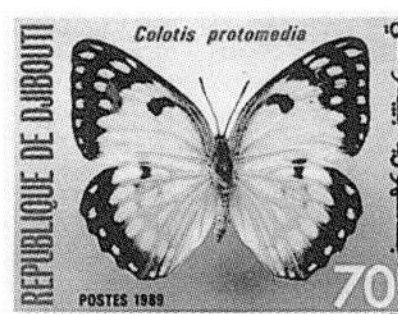

261 "Colotis protomedia"

1989.
1030 **261** 70f. multicoloured . . . 90 60

1989. Nos. 849 and 913 surch **70f.**
1031 **206** 70f. on 2f. mult 95 45
1032 **179** 70f. on 150f. mult . . . 95 45

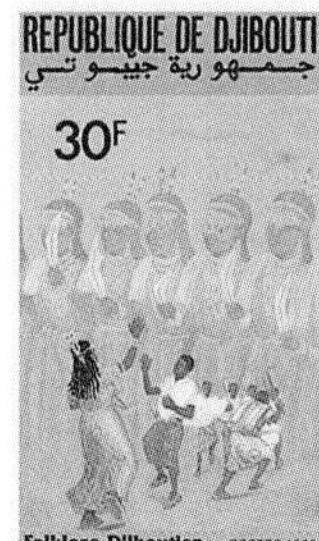

263 Dancers **264** Pale-bellied Francolin ("Francolin de Djibouti")

1989. Folklore. Multicoloured.
1033 30f. Type **263** 40 20
1034 70f. Dancers with parasol 1·00 45

1989.
1035 **264** 35f. multicoloured . . . 75 35

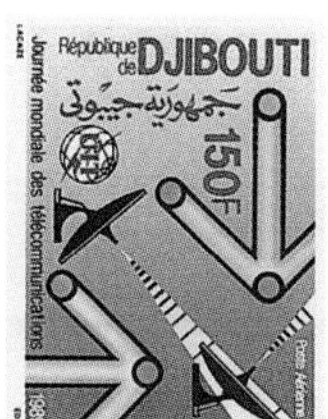

265 Arrows and Dish Aerials

1989. Air. World Telecommunications Day.
1036 **265** 150f. multicoloured . . . 1·90 65

266 "Calotropis procera"

1989.
1037 **266** 25f. multicoloured . . . 35 15

267 Emblem, Declaration and People

1989. Air. "Philexfrance 89" International Stamp Exhibition, Paris, and Bicentenary of Declaration of Rights of Man.
1038 **267** 120f. multicoloured . . . 1·60 65

268 Emblem and State Arms **270** Child going to School

269 Collecting Salt

1989. Cent of Interparliamentary Union.
1039 **268** 70f. multicoloured . . . 95 35

1989. Air. Lake Assal.
1040 **269** 300f. multicoloured . . . 4·00 1·10

1989. International Literacy Year.
1041 **270** 145f. multicoloured . . . 1·90 65

271 Tourka Maddw Cave Painting

1989.
1042 **271** 5f. multicoloured 10 10

272 Traditional Ornaments

1989.
1043 **272** 55f. multicoloured . . . 80 35

1990. Nos. 914 and 916/17 surch.
1044 30f. on 8f. multicoloured . . 40 15
1045 50f. on 40f. mult 65 30
1046 120f. on 15f. mult . . . . . 1·60 45

274 Water-storage Drums and Arid Landscape

1990. Anti-drought Campaign.
1047 **274** 120f. multicoloured . . . 1·60 55

275 Basketry

1990. Traditional Crafts. Multicoloured.
1048 30f. Type **275** 40 20
1049 70f. Jewellery (vert) 95 35

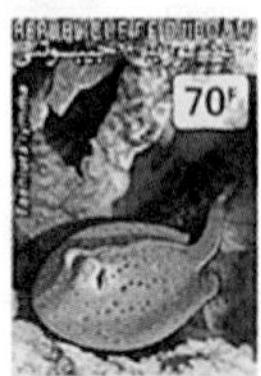

275a Blue-spotted Stingray

1990. Multicoloured, colour of face-value box given.
1049b **275a** 70f. yellow . . . . .
1049c 100f. green . . . . .

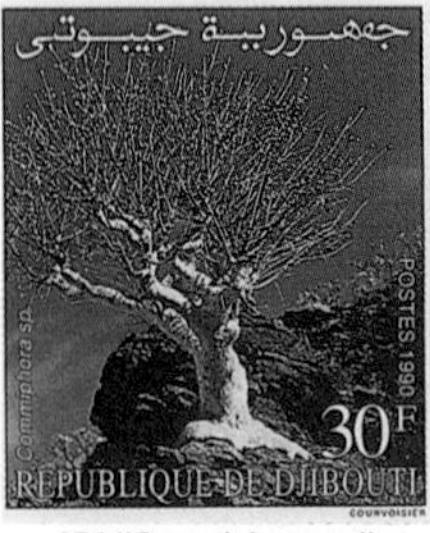

276 "Commiphora sp." **277** Footballers

1990.
1050 **276** 30f. multicoloured . . . 45 30

1990. World Cup Football Championship, Italy.
1051 **277** 100f. multicoloured . . . 1·40 55

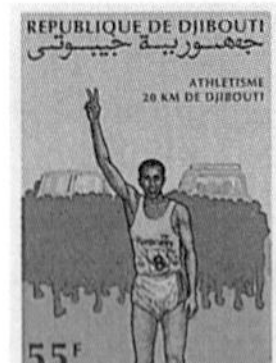

278 Athlete **279** Queue of Patients

1990. Djibouti 20 km Race.
1052 **278** 55f. multicoloured . . . 80 35

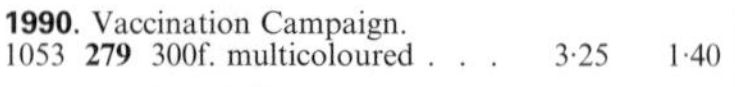

1990. Vaccination Campaign.
1053 **279** 300f. multicoloured . . . 3·25 1·40

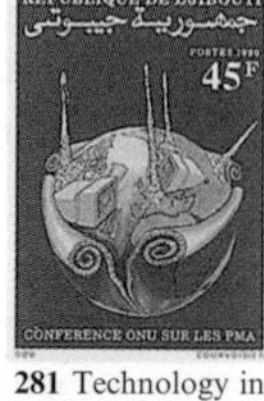

280 De Gaulle **281** Technology in Developed Countries

1990. Birth Centenary of Charles de Gaulle (French statesman).
1054 **280** 200f. multicoloured . . . 2·50 1·25

1990. United Nations Conference on Less Developed Countries.
1055 **281** 45f. multicoloured . . . 60 35

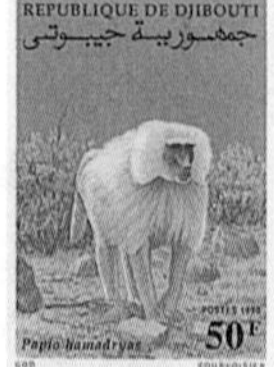

282 Mammoth and Fossilized Remains **283** Hamadryas Baboon

1990.
1056 **282** 90f. multicoloured . . . 1·40 65

1990.
1057 **283** 50f. multicoloured . . . 65 35

284 Emblem and Map **285** "Acropora"

1991. African Tourism Year.
1058 **284** 115f. multicoloured . . . 1·50 85

1991. Corals. Multicoloured.
1059 40f. Type **285** 55 35
1060 45f. "Seriatopora hytrise" 65 35

286 Pink-backed Pelican

1991. Birds. Multicoloured.
1061 10f. Type **286** 35 15
1062 15f. Western reef heron . . 50 25
1063 20f. Goliath heron (horiz) 75 30
1064 25f. White spoonbill (horiz) 90 40

287 Osprey

1991.
1065 **287** 200f. multicoloured . . . 4·00 2·50

288 Traditional Game

1991.
1066 **288** 250f. multicoloured . . . 3·25 1·40

289 Diesel Locomotive

1991. Djibouti–Ethiopia Railway (1st issue).
1067 **289** 85f. multicoloured . . . 2·25 75
See also No. 1076.

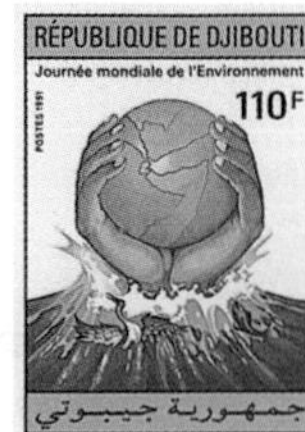

290 Hands holding Earth above Polluted Sea

1991. World Environment Day.
1068 **290** 110f. multicoloured . . . 1·50 55

291 Windsurfers and Islets

1991. "Philexafrique" Stamp Exhibition.
1069 **291** 120f. multicoloured . . . 90 45

292 Handball **293** Harvesting Crops

1991. Olympic Games, Barcelona (1992) (1st issue).
1070 **292** 175f. multicoloured . . . 1·40 70
See also No. 1079.

1991. World Food Day.
1071 **293** 105f. multicoloured . . . 80 40

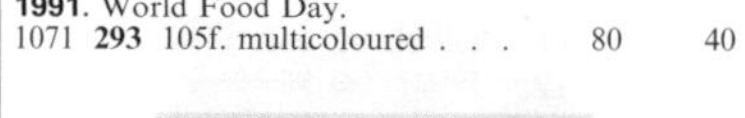

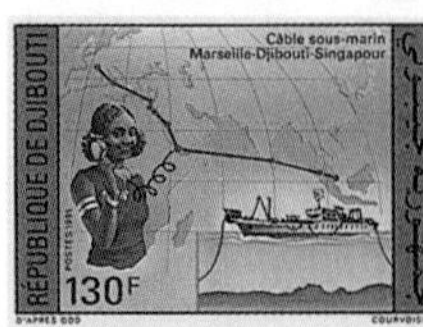

294 Route-map, Woman using Telephone and Cable-laying Ship

1991. Inauguration of Marseilles–Djibouti–Singapore Submarine Cable.
1072 **294** 130f. multicoloured . . . 1·50 70

295 Columbus and Ships

1991. 500th Anniv (1992) of Discovery of America by Columbus (1st issue).
1073 **295** 145f. multicoloured . . . 1·60 80
See also No. 1080.

296 Rimbaud, Ship and Serpent

1991. Death Centenary of Arthur Rimbaud (poet). Multicoloured.
1074 90f. Type **296** . . . . 1·10 50
1075 150f. Rimbaud, camel train and map . . . . 1·10 55

297 Camel Driver and Diesel Train

1992. Djibouti–Ethiopia Railway (2nd issue).
1076 **297** 70f. multicoloured . . . 1·50 45

298 Boys Playing Game

1992. Traditional Games.
1078 **298** 100f. multicoloured . . . 80 40

299 Athlete and Globe **301** Crushing Grain

300 Caravel crossing Atlantic

1992. Olympic Games, Barcelona (2nd issue).
1079 **299** 80f. multicoloured . . . 60 30

1992. 500th Anniv of Discovery of America by Columbus (2nd issue).
1080 **300** 125f. multicoloured . . . 1·40 65

1992. Traditional Methods of Preparing Food. Multicoloured.
1081 30f. Type **301** 25 10
1082 70f. Winnowing 55 25

302 Players, Map of Africa and Final Result **303** "Ariane" Rocket and Satellite

1992. 18th African Nations Cup Football Championship, Senegal.
1083 **302** 15f. multicoloured . . . 10 10

1992. International Space Year. Multicoloured.
1084 120f. Type **303** 90 45
1085 135f. Satellite and astronaut (horiz) . . . . 1·00 50

304 Salt's Dik-dik

1992.
1086 **304** 5f. multicoloured 10 10

305 Loggerhead Turtle

1992.
1087 **305** 200f. multicoloured . . . 1·50 75

306 Preparing Mofo

1992. Mofo. Multicoloured.
1088 45f. Type **306** . . . .
1089 75f. Cooking mofo . . . .

307 Nomadic Girl

1993. Traditional Costumes. Multicoloured.
1090 70f. Type **307** 55 25
1091 120f. Nomadic girl with headband 90 45

308 White-eyed Gull ("Geoland a Iris Blanc")

1993.
1092 **308** 300f. multicoloured . . . 3·50 1·40

309 Amin Salman Mosque

1993.
1093 **309** 500f. multicoloured . . .

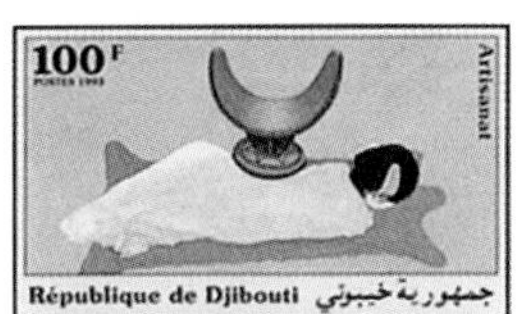
310 Headrest

1993. Crafts. Multicoloured.
1094 100f. Type **310** . . . . . .
1095 125f. Flask . . . .

311 Savanna Monkey

1993.
1096 **311** 150f. multicoloured . . .

312 Flags of Member Countries

1993. 30th Anniv of Organization of African Unity.
1097 **312** 200f. multicoloured . . .

313 Woman carrying Water on Back

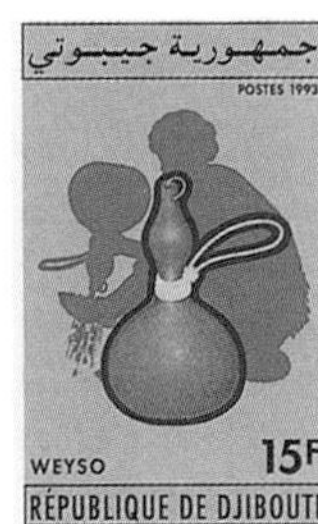
314 Plants and Spacecraft

1993. Water Carriers. Multicoloured.
1098 30f. Type **313** . . . .
1099 50f. Man carrying water on yoke . . . .

1993. Space.
1100 **314** 90f. multicoloured . . .

315 Water Jar

316 Pipes

1993. Utensils. Multicoloured.
1101 15f. Type **315** 10 10
1102 20f. Hangol (agricultural tool) 15 10
1103 25f. Comb 20 10
1104 30f. Water-skin 25 10

1993. Musical Instruments. Multicoloured.
1105 5f. Type **316** 10 10
1106 10f. Hand-held drum and lines of women 10 10

318 Runners and Route Map

319 Mother with Children

1994. Djibouti 20 km Race.
1108 **318** 50f. multicoloured . . . 40 20

1994. U.N.I.C.E.F. Breast-feeding Campaign. Multicoloured.
1109 40f. Type **319** 30 15
1110 45f. Woman breast-feeding baby 35 15

320 Stadium

1994. Hassan Gouled Aptidon Stadium.
1111 **320** 70f. multicoloured . . . 55 25

321 Spinner Dolphins

1994.
1112 **321** 120f. multicoloured . . .

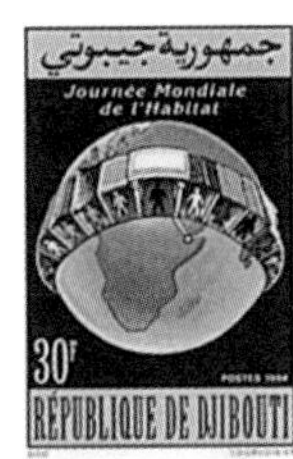
322 Houses encircling Globe

1994. World Housing Day.
1113 **322** 30f. multicoloured . . .

323 White-bellied Bustards

1994.
1114 **323** 10f. multicoloured . . .

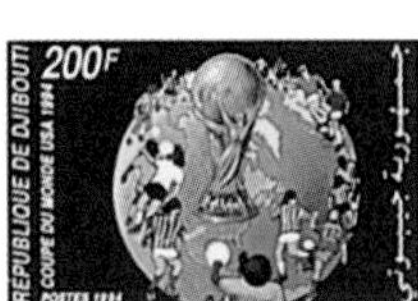
324 Trophy, Globe and Players

1994. World Cup Football Championship, U.S.A.
1115 **324** 200f. multicoloured . . .

325 Nomadic Man

1994. Traditional Costumes. Multicoloured.
1116 100f. Type **325** . . . . . .
1117 150f. Town dress . . . . .

326 Golden Jackals

1994.
1118 **326** 400f. multicoloured . . .

327 Walkers

1994. World Walking Day.
1119 **327** 75f. multicoloured . . .

328 Book Rests

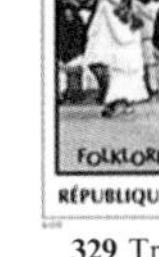
329 Traditional Dancers

1994. Traditional Crafts.
1120 **328** 55f. multicoloured . . .

1994. Folklore.
1121 **329** 35f. multicoloured . . .

330 Camel, Ostrich and Net

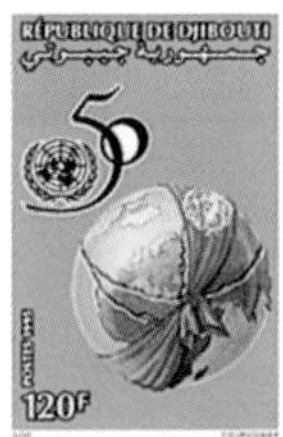
331 U.N. Flag tied around Cracked Globe

1995. Centenary of Volleyball.
1122 **330** 70f. multicoloured . . .

1995. 50th Anniv of U.N.O.
1123 **331** 120f. multicoloured . . .

332 Drawing Water from Well

1995. Drought Relief Campaign.
1124 **332** 100f. multicoloured . . .

333 Greater Flamingo

1995. Birds. Multicoloured.
1125 30f. Type **333** . . . .
1126 50f. Sacred ibis . . . . . .

334 Camel Rider

1995. Telecommunications Day.
1127 **334** 125f. multicoloured . . .

335 Spotted Hyena

1995.
1128 **335** 200f. multicoloured . . .

336 Council held under Tree

337 Nomads

1995.
1129 **336** 150f. multicoloured . . .

1995. Nomadic Life.
1130 **337** 45f. multicoloured . . .

338 Palm Tree, Map and Emblem

1995. 50th Anniv of F.A.O.
1131 **338** 250f. multicoloured . . .

339 Development Project and Emblem

340 Traditional Costume

1995. 30th Anniv of African Development Bank.
1132 **339** 300f. multicoloured . . .

1995.
1133 **340** 90f. multicoloured . . .

341 Trophy on Map and Football

342 Leopard

1996. Africa Cup Football Championship.
1134 **341** 70f. multicoloured . . .

1996. Wildlife. Multicoloured.
1135 70f. Type **342** . . . .
1136 120f. Ostrich (vert) . . . .

343 Woman wearing Amber Necklace

344 Olympic Flag

1996. Traditional Crafts.
1137 **343** 30f. multicoloured . . .

1996. Olympic Games, Atlanta.
1138 **344** 105f. multicoloured . . .

345 "Commicarpus grandiflorus"

346 Women's Rite

1996.
1139 **345** 350f. multicoloured . . .

1996. Folklore.
1140 **346** 95f. multicoloured . . .

347 The Lion and the Three Bullocks

1996. Stories and Legends.
1141 **347** 95f. multicoloured . . .

348 Children with Flags

1996. National Children's Day.
1142 **348** 130f. multicoloured . . .

349 Fox and Tortoise

350 Mother and Child

1997. Stories and Legends. The Tortoise and the Fox. Multicoloured.
1143 60f. Type **349** . . . .
1144 60f. Fox running away from tortoise . . . .
1145 60f. Tortoise winning race

1997. 50th Anniv of U.N.I.C.E.F. Multicoloured.
1146 80f. Type **350** . . . .
1147 90f. Arms cradling globe of children . . . .

351 Dancers

352 Using Necklace as Pendulum

1997. Folklore.
1148 **351** 70f. multicoloured . . .

1997. Local Fortune Telling. Multicoloured.
1149 200f. Type **352** . . . . . .
1150 300f. Using pebbles . . . .

353 Woman weaving Basket

355 Arta Post Office

354 Writing Board

1997. Women's Day.
1151 **353** 250f. multicoloured . . .

1997. Traditional Implements. Multicoloured.
1152 30f. Type **354** . . . .
1153 400f. Bowl and spoon (vert)

1997. 20th Anniv of Independence. Multicoloured.
1154 30f. Type **355** . . . .
1155 100f. Telecommunications station . . . .
1156 120f. Undersea cable, route map and cable ship (horiz) . . . .

356 Goats in Tree

1997.
1157 **356** 120f. multicoloured . . .

357 Diana, Princess of Wales

1998. Diana, Princess of Wales Commemoration.

1158	**357**	125f. multicoloured . . .	95	45
1159		130f. multicoloured . . .	1·00	50
1160		150f. multicoloured . . .	1·25	60

358 Paradise Tanager

1998. International Year of the Ocean. Mult.
1161 75c. Type **358** . . . . . .
1162 75c. Red-eyed tree frog ("Agalychnis callidryas")
1163 75c. Common dolphin ("Delphinus delphis") and humpback whale ("Megaptera novaeangliae") . . . . .
1164 75c. Savanna monkey ("Cercopithecus aethiops") . . . .
1165 75c. Great hammerhead ("Sphyrna mokarran") and yellow-lipped sea snakes ("Laticaudia colubrina") . . . .
1166 75c. Long-horned cowfish ("Lactoria cornuta") and common dolphin ("Delphinus delphis") . .
1167 75c. Common dolphins ("Delphinus delphis") . .
1168 75c. Striped mimic blenny ("Aspidontus taeniatus") and foxface ("Lovulpinus") . . . . .
1169 75c. Big-fin reef squid ("Sepioteuthis lessoniana)
1170 75c. Ornate butterflyfish ("Chaetodon ornatissimus) and blue shark ("Prionace glauca")
1171 75c. Hermit crab ("Eupagurus bernherdus")
1172 75c. Common octopus ("Octopus vulgaris") . . .

Nos. 1161/72 were issued together, se-tenant, forming a composite design.

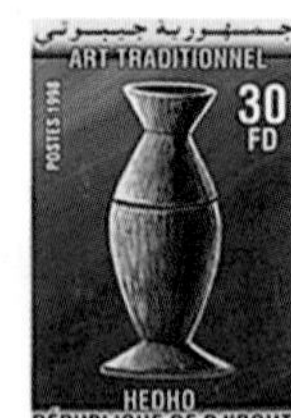

359 Gandhi

360 Vase

1998. 50th Death Anniv of Mahatma Gandhi (Indian patriot).
1173 **359** 250f. multicoloured . . .

1998. Traditional Art.
1174 **360** 30f. multicoloured . . .

361 Woman carrying Basket on Back and Road-crossing Officer

1998. Women's Rights and International Peace.
1175 **361** 70f. multicoloured . . .

362 Water Pump and Donkey carrying Water Containers

1998. World Water Day.
1176 **362** 45f. multicoloured . . .

363 Football, Trophy and Eiffel Tower

364 Octopus

1998. World Cup Football Championship, France.
1177 **363** 200f. multicoloured . . .

1998. Marine Life. Multicoloured.
1178 20f. Type **364** . . . .
1179 25f. Shark (horiz) . . . . .

365 Catmint and Cats

366 Globe using Mobile Phone and Computer

1998.
1180 **365** 120f. multicoloured . . .

1998. World Telecommunications Day.
1181 **366** 150f. multicoloured . . .

367 National Bank

368 Flags of Member States and Emblem

1998. Public Buildings.
1182 **367** 100f. multicoloured . . .

1998. Inter-Governmental Authority on Development.
1183 **368** 85f. multicoloured . . .

369 Boys playing Goos

1998. Traditional Games.
1184 **369** 110f. multicoloured . . .

370 Fishing Harbour

1998. Public Buildings.
1185 **370** 100f. multicoloured . . .

371 Gulls sp. and Maskali Island

1998. Tourist Sites.
1186 **371** 500f. multicoloured . . .

372 Mother Teresa

1998. Mother Teresa (founder of Missionaries of Charity) Commemoration.
1187 **372** 130f. multicoloured . . . 90 45

POSTAGE DUE STAMP

D 248 Milking Bowl

1988. Traditional Djibouti Art.
D1016 D **248** 60f. multicoloured 90 65

DODECANESE ISLANDS Pt. 8

A group of islands off the coast of Asia Minor occupied by Italy in May 1912 and ceded to her by Turkey in 1920. The islands concerned are now known as Kalimnos, Kasos, Kos, Khalki, Leros, Lipsoi, Nisiros, Patmos, Tilos (Piskopi), Rhodes (Rodos), Karpathos, Simi and Astipalaia. Castelrosso came under the same administration in 1921.

In 1944 the Dodecanese Islands were occupied by British forces (see **BRITISH OCCUPATION OF ITALIAN COLONIES**). In 1947 they were transferred to Greek administration, since when Greek stamps have been used.

A. ITALIAN OCCUPATION

100 centesimi = 1 lira.

1912. Stamps of Italy optd **EGEO**.
1 **39** 25c. blue . . . . 30·00 17·00
2 – 50c. violet . . . . 30·00 17·00

1912. Stamps of Italy optd, or surch also, for the individual islands (all in capitals on Nos. 6 and 10, in upper and lower case on others). A. Calimno
3A **31** 2c. brown 4·50 4·25
4A **37** 5c. green 1·40 4·25
5A 10c. red 40 4·25
6A **41** 15c. grey 19·00 8·25
7A **37** 15c. grey 2·75 25·00
8A **41** 20c. on 15c. grey 10·00 17·00
10A 20c. orange 2·75 25·00
11A **39** 25c. blue 4·00 4·25
12A 40c. brown 40 4·25
13A 50c. violet 40 4·25

B. Caso
3B **31** 2c. brown 4·75 4·25
4B **37** 5c. green 1·60 4·25
5B 10c. red 40 4·25
6B **41** 15c. grey 22·00 8·25
7B **37** 15c. grey 2·75 25·00
8B **41** 20c. on 15c. grey 65 12·00
10B 20c. orange 2·10 20·00
11B **39** 25c. blue 40 4·25
12B 40c. brown 40 4·25
13B 50c. violet 40 7·50

C. Cos
3C **31** 2c. brown 4·75 4·25
4C **37** 5c. green 45·00 4·25
5C 10c. red 2·25 4·25
6C **41** 15c. grey 22·00 8·25
7C **37** 15c. grey 2·75 35·00
8C **41** 20c. on 15c. grey 10·00 21·00
10C 20c. orange 2·10 21·00
11C **39** 25c. blue 19·00 4·25
12C 40c. brown 40 4·25
13C 50c. violet 40 7·50

D. Karki
3D **31** 2c. brown 4·75 4·25
4D **37** 5c. green 1·60 4·25
5D 10c. red 1·60 4·25
6D **41** 15c. grey 22·00 8·25
7D **37** 15c. grey 2·75 26·00
8D **41** 20c. on 15c. grey 1·25 15·00
10D 20c. orange 2·75 24·00
11D **39** 25c. blue 40 4·25
12D 40c. brown 40 4·25
13D 50c. violet 40 7·50

E. Leros
3E **31** 2c. brown 4·75 4·25
4E **37** 5c. green 3·50 4·25
5E 10c. red 70 4·25
6E **41** 15c. grey 35·00 8·25
7E **37** 15c. grey 2·75 22·00
8E **41** 20c. on 15c. grey 10·00 16·50
9E 20c. orange 27·00 85·00
11E **39** 25c. blue 21·00 4·25
12E 40c. brown 2·75 4·25
13E 50c. violet 40 7·50

F. Lipso
3F **31** 2c. brown 4·75 4·25
4F **37** 5c. green 1·90 4·25
5F 10c. red 85 4·25
6F **41** 15c. grey 21·00 8·25
7F **37** 15c. grey 2·75 22·00
8F **41** 20c. on 15c. grey 80 15·00
10F 20c. orange 2·75 25·00
11F **39** 25c. blue 40 4·25
12F 40c. brown 1·25 4·25
13F 50c. violet 40 7·50

G. Nisiros
3G **31** 2c. brown 4·75 4·25
4G **37** 5c. green 1·60 4·25
5G 10c. red 40 4·25
6G **41** 15c. grey 19·00 8·25
7G **37** 15c. grey 13·50 23·00
8G **41** 20c. on 15c. grey 80 15·00
10G 20c. orange 55·00 65·00
11G **39** 25c. blue 1·40 4·25
12G 40c. brown 40 4·25
13G 50c. violet 2·75 7·50

H. Patmos
3H **31** 2c. brown 4·75 4·25
4H **37** 5c. green 1·60 4·25
5H 10c. red 1·40 4·25
6H **41** 15c. grey 19·00 8·25
7H **37** 15c. grey 2·75 25·00
8H **41** 20c. on 15c. grey 10·00 20·00
9H 20c. orange 45·00 85·00
11H **39** 25c. blue 55 4·25
12H 40c. brown 2·50 4·25
13H 50c. violet 40 7·50

I. Piscopi
3I **31** 2c. brown 4·75 4·25
4I **37** 5c. green 1·50 4·25
5I 10c. red 40 4·25
6I **41** 15c. grey 22·00 8·25
7I **37** 15c. grey 10·00 25·00
8I **41** 20c. on 15c. grey 80 15·00
10I 20c. orange 27·00 38·00
11I **39** 25c. blue 40 4·25
12I 40c. brown 40 4·25
13I 50c. violet 40 7·50

J. Rodi
3J **31** 2c. brown 40 4·25
4J **37** 5c. green 1·40 4·25
5J 10c. red 40 4·25
6J **41** 15c. grey 23·00 8·25
7J **37** 15c. grey 85·00 38·00
8J **41** 20c. on 15c. grey 75·00 80·00
10J 20c. orange 4·25 10·00
11J **39** 25c. blue 1·40 4·25
12J 40c. brown 2·25 4·25
13J 50c. violet 40 7·50

K. Scarpanto
3K **31** 2c. brown 4·75 4·25
4K **37** 5c. green 1·40 4·25
5K 10c. red 40 4·25
6K **41** 15c. grey 17·00 8·25
7K **37** 15c. grey 10·00 19·00
8K **41** 20c. on 15c. grey 80 17·00
10K 20c. orange 27·00 27·00
11K **39** 25c. blue 4·50 4·25
12K 40c. brown 40 4·25
13K 50c. violet 1·40 7·50

L. Simi
3L **31** 2c. brown 4·75 4·25
4L **37** 5c. green 14·50 4·25
5L 10c. red 40 4·25
6L **41** 15c. grey 28·00 28·00
7L **37** 15c. grey 75·00 75·00
8L **41** 20c. on 15c. grey 5·75 5·75
10L 20c. orange 38·00 38·00
11L **39** 25c. blue 1·90 4·25
12L 40c. brown 40 4·25
13L 50c. violet 40 7·50

M. Stampalia
3M **31** 2c. brown 4·75 4·25
4M **37** 5c. green 40 4·25
5M 10c. red 40 4·25
6M **41** 15c. grey 21·00 8·25
7M **37** 15c. grey 6·75 19·00
8M **41** 20c. on 15c. grey 65 12·00
10M 20c. orange 25·00 27·00
11M **39** 25c. blue 55 4·25
12M 40c. brown 2·25 4·25
13M 50c. violet 40 7·50

1916. Optd **Rodi**.
14 **33** 20c. orange 2·00 4·25
15 **39** 85c. brown 40·00 60·00
16 **34** 1l. brown & green 2·00

1 Rhodian Windmill
2 Knight kneeling before the Holy City

1929. King of Italy's Visit.
17 **1** 5c. purple 85 20
18 – 10c. brown 85 20
19 – 20c. red 85 20
20 – 25c. green 85 20
21 **2** 30c. blue 85 20
22 – 50c. brown 85 20
23 – 1l.25 blue 85 1·00
24 **2** 5l. purple 85 1·25
25 – 10l. green 1·75 2·75
DESIGNS—As Type **1**: 10c. Galley of Knights of St. John; 20c., 25c. Knight defending Christianity; 50c., 1l.25, Knight's tomb.

1930. 21st Hydrological Congress. Nos. 17/25 optd **XXI Congresso Idrologico**.
26 5c. purple 13·50 11·50
27 10c. brown 15·00 11·50
28 20c. red 23·00 10·00
29 25c. green 30·00 10·00
30 30c. blue 15·00 12·00
31 50c. brown £375 30·00
32 1l.25 blue £300 50·00
33 5l. purple £160 £250
34 10l. green £160 £275

1930. Ferrucci issue of Italy (colours changed) optd for each individual island, in capitals. A. CALINO; B. CASO; C. COO; D. CALCHI; E. LERO; F. LISSO; G. NISIRO; H. PATMO; I. PISCOPI; J. RODI; K. SCARPANTO; L. SIMI; M. STAMPALIA.
35 **114** 20c. violet 1·90 3·00
36 – 25c. green 1·90 3·00
37 – 50c. black 1·90 5·75
38 – 1l.25 blue 1·90 5·75
39 – 5l.+2l. red 2·75 10·00
Same prices for each of the 13 islands.

1930. Air. Ferrucci air stamps of Italy (colours changed) optd **ISOLE ITALIANE DELL'EGEO**.
40 **117** 50c. purple 5·75 11·50
41 1l. blue 5·75 11·50
42 5l.+2l. red 12·00 32·00

1930. Virgil stamps of Italy optd **ISOLE ITALIANE DELL'EGEO**.
43 – 15c. violet (postage) 1·00 5·75
44 – 20c. brown 1·00 5·75
45 – 25c. green 1·00 2·50
46 – 30c. brown 1·00 2·50
47 – 50c. purple 1·00 2·50
48 – 75c. red 1·00 5·75
49 – 1l.25 blue 1·00 8·25
50 – 5l+1l.50 purple 2·40 17·00
51 – 10l.+2l.50 brown 2·40 17·00
52 **119** 50c. green (air) 1·40 12·00
53 1l. red 1·40 13·50
54 7l.70+1l.30 brown 3·00 24·00
55 9l.+2l. grey 3·00 25·00

1931. Italian Eucharistic Congress. Nos. 17/25 optd **1931 CONGRESSO EUCARISTICO ITALIANO.**
56 5c. red 4·00 5·75
57 10c. brown 4·00 5·75
58 20c. red 4·00 10·00
59 25c. green 4·00 10·00
60 30c. blue 4·00 10·00
61 50c. brown 30·00 24·00
62 1l.25 blue 23·00 42·00

1932. St. Antony of Padua stamps of Italy optd **ISOLE ITALIANE DELL'EGEO.**
63 **121** 20c. purple 15·00 9·00
64 – 25c. green 15·00 9·00
65 – 30c. brown 15·00 11·00
66 – 50c. purple 15·00 7·50
67 – 75c. red 15·00 12·50
68 – 1l.25 blue 15·00 14·50
69 – 5l.+2l.50 orange 15·00 55·00

1932. Dante stamps of Italy optd **ISOLE ITALIANE DELL'EGEO.**
70 – 10c. green (postage) 95 2·40
71 – 15c. violet 95 2·40
72 – 20c. brown 95 2·40
73 – 25c. green 95 2·40
74 – 30c. red 95 2·40
75 – 50c. purple 95 1·00
76 – 75c. red 95 3·00
77 – 1l.25 blue 95 2·40
78 – 1l.75 sepia 1·10 3·00
79 – 2l.75 red 1·10 3·00
80 – 5l.+2l. violet 1·40 9·25
81 **124** 10l.+2l.50 brown 1·40 13·50
82 **125** 50c. red (air) 1·00 2·40
83 – 1l. green 1·00 2·40
84 – 3l. purple 1·00 2·75
85 – 5l. red 1·00 2·75
86 **125** 7l.70+2l. sepia 1·40 6·75
87 – 10l.+2l.50 blue 1·40 12·00
88 **127** 100l. olive and blue 15·00 70·00
No. 88 is inscribed instead of optd.

1932. Garibaldi issue of Italy (colours changed) optd for each individual island in capital letters. A. CALINO; B. CASO; C. COO; D. CARCHI; E. LERO; F. LIBO; G. NISIRO; H. PATMO; I. PISCOPI; J. RODI; K. SCARPANTO; L. SIMI; M. STAMPALIA.
89 – 10c. sepia 8·00 12·00
90 **128** 20c. brown 8·00 12·00
91 – 25c. green 8·00 12·00
92 **128** 30c. black 8·00 12·00
93 – 50c. lilac 8·00 12·00
94 – 75c. red 8·00 12·00
95 – 1l.25 blue 8·00 12·00
96 – 1l.75+25c. sepia 8·00 12·00
97 – 2l.55+50c. red 8·00 12·00
98 – 5l.+1l. violet 8·00 12·00
Same prices for each of the 13 islands.

1932. Air. Garibaldi air stamps of Italy optd **ISOLE ITALIANE DELL'EGEO.**
99 **130** 50c. green 30·00 55·00
100 – 80c. red 30·00 55·00
101 **130** 1l.+25c. blue 30·00 55·00
102 – 2l.+50c. brown 30·00 55·00
103 – 5l.+1l. black 30·00 55·00

8

1932. 20th Anniv of Italian Occupation of Dodecanese Islands.
106 **8** 5c. red, black and green 5·00 8·25
107 10c. red, black and blue 5·00 5·00
108 20c. red, black and yellow 5·00 5·00
109 25c. red, black and violet 5·00 5·00
110 30c. red, black and red 5·00 5·00
111 – 50c. red, black and blue 5·00 5·00
112 – 1l.25 red, purple & blue 5·00 12·00
113 – 5l. red and blue 15·00 35·00
114 – 10l. red, green and blue 42·00 55·00
115 – 25l. red, brown and blue £275 £600
DESIGN—VERT: 50c. to 25l. Arms on map of Rhodes.

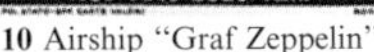
10 Airship "Graf Zeppelin"

11 Wing from Arms of Francesco Sans

1933. Air. "Graf Zeppelin".
116 **10** 3l. brown 32·00 90·00
117 5l. purple 32·00 £110
118 10l. green 32·00 £180
119 12l. blue 32·00 £225
120 15l. red 32·00 £225
121 20l. black 32·00 £225

1933. Air. Balbo Mass Formation Flight issue of Italy optd **ISOLE ITALIANE DELL'EGEO.**
122 **135** 5l.25+19l.75 red, green and blue 27·00 75·00
123 **136** 5l.25+44l.75 red, green and blue 27·00 75·00

1934. Air.
124 **11** 50c. black and yellow 20 20
125 80c. black and red 3·00 2·75
126 1l. black and green 1·75 20
127 5l. black and mauve 5·25 7·25

1934. World Football Championship stamps of Italy (some colours changed) optd **ISOLE ITALIANE DELL'EGEO.**
128 **142** 20c. red (postage) 40·00 40·00
129 – 25c. green 40·00 40·00
130 – 50c. violet £140 20·00
131 – 1l.25 blue 40·00 70·00
132 – 5l.+2l.50 blue 40·00 £170
133 – 50c. brown (air) 4·25 25·00
134 – 75c. red 4·25 25·00
135 – 5l.+2l.50 orange 12·50 50·00
136 – 10l.+5l. green 12·50 70·00

1934. Military Medal Centenary stamps of Italy (some colours changed) optd **ISOLE ITALIANE DELL'EGEO.**
157 **146** 10c. grey (postage) 30·00 40·00
158 – 15c. brown 30·00 40·00
159 – 20c. orange 30·00 40·00
160 – 25c. green 30·00 40·00
161 – 30c. red 30·00 40·00
162 – 50c. green 30·00 40·00
163 – 75c. red 30·00 40·00
164 – 1l.25 blue 30·00 40·00
165 – 1l.75+1l. violet 19·00 40·00
166 – 2l.55+2l. red 19·00 40·00
167 – 2l.75+2l. brown 19·00 40·00
168 – 25c. green (air) 38·00 50·00
169 – 50c. grey 38·00 50·00
170 – 75c. red 38·00 50·00
171 – 80c. brown 38·00 50·00
172 – 1l.+50c. green 29·00 50·00
173 – 2l.+1l. blue 29·00 50·00
174 – 3l.+2l. violet 29·00 50·00

16

19 Dante House, Rhodes

1935. Holy Year.
177 **16** 5c. orange 8·25 11·50
178 10c. brown 8·25 11·50
179 20c. red 8·25 13·50
180 25c. green 8·25 13·50
181 30c. purple 8·25 15·00
182 50c. brown 8·25 15·00
183 1l.25 blue 8·25 38·00

1938. Augustus the Great stamps of Italy (colours changed) optd **ISOLE ITALIANE DELL'EGEO.**
186 **163** 10c. brown (postage) 2·25 4·50
187 – 15c. violet 2·25 4·50
188 – 20c. brown 2·25 4·50
189 – 25c. green 2·25 4·50
190 – 30c. purple 2·25 4·50
191 – 50c. green 2·25 4·50
192 – 75c. red 2·25 4·50
193 – 1l.25 blue 2·25 4·50
194 – 1l.75+1l. orange 3·00 10·00
195 – 2l.55+2l. brown 3·00 10·00
196 – 25c. violet (air) 2·40 2·75
197 – 50c. green 2·40 2·75
198 – 80c. blue 2·40 8·00

199	–	1l.+1l. purple	3·75	12·00
200	164	5l.+1l. red	6·00	25·00

1938. Giotto stamps of Italy optd **ITALIANE ISOLE DELL'EGEO.**

201	1l.25 blue (No. 527)	95	1·75
202	2l.75+2l. brown (530)	1·10	6·75

1940. Colonial Exhibition. Inscr as in T **19**.

203	–	5c. brown (postage)	30	65
204	–	10c. orange	30	65
205	19	25c. green	65	1·25
206	–	50c. violet	65	1·25
207	–	75c. red	65	1·60
208	19	1l.25 blue	65	1·90
209	–	2l.+75c. red	65	10·00

DESIGNS—VERT: 5c., 50c. Roman Wolf statue; 10c., 75c., 2l. Crown and Maltese Cross.

210	50c. brown (air)	85	1·90
211	1l. violet	85	1·90
212	2l.+75c. blue	85	3·75
213	5l.+2l.50 brown	85	6·00

DESIGNS—HORIZ: Savoia Marchetti S.M.75 airplane over: 50c., 2l. statues, Rhodes Harbour; 1, 5l. Government House, Rhodes.

1943. Aegean Relief Fund. Nos. 17/25 surch **PRO ASSISTENZA EGEO** and value.

214	1	5c.+5c. purple	70	70
215	–	10c.+10c. brown	70	70
216	–	20c.+20c. red	70	70
217	–	25c.+25c. green	70	70
218	2	30c.+30c. blue	1·40	1·10
219	–	50c.+50c. brown	1·40	1·40
220	–	1l.25+1l.25 blue	1·75	1·75
221	2	5l.+5l. purple	70·00	70·00

1944. War Victims' Relief. Nos. 17/20 and 22/23 surch **PRO SINISTRATI DI GUERRA**, value and stag symbol.

224	1	5c.+3l. purple	1·40	2·40
225	–	10c.+3l. brown	1·40	2·40
226	–	20c.+3l. red	1·40	2·40
227	–	25c.+3l. green	1·40	2·40
228	–	50c.+3l. brown	1·40	2·40
229	–	1l.25+5l. blue	21·00	25·00

1944. Air. War Victims Relief. Surch **PRO SINISTRATI DI GUERRA** and value.

232	11	50c.+2l. blk & yellow	6·75	2·50
233		80c.+2l. black and red	8·25	5·00
234		1l.+2l. black & green	10·00	5·75
235		5l.+2l. black & mauve	50·00	55·00

1945. Red Cross Fund. Nos. 24/5 surch **FEBBRAIO 1945 + 10** and Cross.

236	+10l. on 5l. purple	6·75	10·00
237	+10l. on 10l. green	6·75	10·00

EXPRESS STAMPS

1932. Air. Garibaldi Air Express stamps of Italy optd **ISOLE ITALIANE DELL'EGEO.**

E104	E 3	2l.25+1l. red & blue	38·00	70·00
E105		4l.50+1l.50 grey and yellow	38·00	70·00

1934. Air. As Nos. E442/3 of Italy, but colours changed, optd **ISOLE ITALIANE DELL'EGEO.**

E175	2l.+1l.25 blue	30·00	48·00
E176	4l.50+2l. green	30·00	48·00

E 17

1935.

E184	E 17	1l.25 green	1·75	1·40
E185		2l.50 orange	2·50	3·00

1943. Aegean Relief Fund. Surch **PRO ASSISTENZA EGEO** and value.

E222	E 17	1l.25+1l.25 green	35·00	20·00
E223		2l.50+2l.50 orge	40·00	27·00

1944. Nos. 19/20 surch **ESPRESSO** and value.

E230	1l.25 on 25c. green	40	1·25
E231	2l.50 on 50c. red	40	1·25

PARCEL POST STAMPS

P 12

1934.

P137	P 12	5c. orange	1·75	1·75
P138		10c. red	1·75	1·75
P139		20c. green	1·75	1·75
P140		25c. violet	1·75	1·75
P141		50c. blue	1·75	1·75
P142		60c. black	1·75	1·75
P143	–	1l. orange	1·75	1·75
P144	–	2l. red	1·75	1·75
P145	–	3l. green	1·75	1·75
P146	–	4l. violet	1·75	1·75
P147	–	10l. blue	1·75	1·75

DESIGN: 1l. to 10l. Left half: Stag as in Type E 17; Right half: Castle.

POSTAGE DUE STAMPS

D 14 Badge of the Knights of St. John

D 15 Immortelle

1934.

D148	D 14	5c. orange	1·10	1·40
D149		10c. red	1·10	1·40
D150		20c. green	1·10	70
D151		30c. violet	1·10	1·00
D152		40c. blue	1·10	2·40
D153	D 15	50c. orange	1·10	70
D154		60c. red	1·10	3·75
D155		1l. green	1·10	3·75
D156		2l. violet	1·10	2·40

B. GREEK MILITARY ADMINISTRATION

100 lepta = 1 drachma.

1947. Stamps of Greece optd with characters as in Type G 1.

G1	–	10d. on 2000d. blue (No. 623)	55	55
G3	89	50d. on 1d. grn (No. 642)	1·10	1·10
G4		250d. on 3d. brn (No. 643)	1·10	1·10

Σ. Δ. Δ.
ΔΡΧ.
50

(G 1)

1947. Stamps of Greece surch as Type G 1.

G 5	–	20d. on 500d. brown (No. 582)	55	55
G 6	–	30d. on 5d. green (No. 574)	55	55
G 7	106	50d. on 2d. brown	70	70
G 8	–	250d. on 10d. brown (No. 510)	1·10	1·10
G 9	–	400d. on 15d. green (No. 511)	1·60	1·60
G10	–	1000d. on 200d. blue (No. 581)	1·10	1·10

DOMINICA Pt. 1

Until 31 December 1939 one of the Leeward Islands, but then transferred to the Windward Islands. Used Leeward Island stamps concurrently with Dominican issues from 1903 to above date.

1874. 12 pence = 1 shilling;
20 shillings = 1 pound.
1949. 100 cents = 1 West Indian dollar.

1

1874.

13	1	½d. yellow	2·50	10·00
20		½d. green	1·50	5·50
5		1d. lilac	5·50	2·00
22a		1d. red	2·75	6·00
15		2½d. brown	£140	2·00
23		2½d. blue	3·75	5·00
7		4d. blue	£110	2·50
24		4d. grey	3·00	4·50
8		6d. green	£150	20·00
25		6d. orange	8·00	45·00
9		1s. mauve	£120	50·00

1882. No. 5 bisected and surch with a small ½.

10	1	½(d.) on half 1d. lilac	£160	40·00

1882. No. 5 bisected and surch with large ½.

11	1	½(d.) on half 1d. lilac	29·00	16·00

1883. No. 5 bisected and surch **HALF PENNY** vert.

12	1	½d. on half 1d. lilac	65·00	20·00

1886. Nos. 8 and 9 surch in words and bar.

17	1	½d. on 6d. green	4·25	3·50
18		1d. on 6d. green	£20000	£10000
19		1d. on 1s. mauve	14·00	16·00

9 "Roseau from the Sea" (Lt. Caddy)

10

1903.

37	9	½d. green	3·50	3·25
38		1d. grey and red	2·00	40
29		2d. green and brown	2·50	4·50
30		2½d. grey and blue	5·00	4·00
31		3d. purple and black	8·00	3·25
32		6d. grey and brown	4·50	18·00
43		1s. mauve and green	3·75	55·00
34		2s. black and purple	26·00	29·00
45		2s.6d. green and orange	22·00	60·00
46	10	5s. black and brown	60·00	60·00

1908.

48bw	9	1d. red	1·00	50
64		1½d. orange	3·00	11·00
65		2d. grey	2·75	3·25
66		2½d. blue	2·00	8·50
51		3d. purple on yellow	3·00	4·25
52a		6d. purple	3·50	18·00
53		1s. black on green	3·00	2·75
53b		2s. purple and blue on blue	25·00	85·00
70		2s.6d. black and red on blue	32·00	90·00

1914. As T **10**, but portrait of King George V.

54	5s. red and green on yellow	55·00	80·00

1916. No. 37 surch **WAR TAX ONE HALFPENNY.**

55	9	½d. on ½d. green	75	75

1918. Optd **WAR TAX.**

57	9	½d. green	15	50
58		3d. purple on yellow	1·50	4·00

1919. Surch **WAR TAX 1½D.**

59	9	1½d. on 2½d. orange	15	55

1920. Surch **1½D.**

60	9	1½d. on 2½d. orange	2·50	4·50

16

1923.

71	16	½d. black and green	1·75	60
72		1d. black and violet	2·00	1·75
73		1d. black and red	9·00	1·00
74		1½d. black and red	2·75	65
75		1½d. black and brown	9·00	70
76		2d. black and grey	1·75	50
77		2½d. black and yellow	1·50	9·00
78		2½d. black and blue	4·25	2·00
79		3d. black and blue	1·50	12·00
80		3d. black and red on yellow	1·50	1·00
81		4d. black and brown	2·50	5·50
82		6d. black and mauve	3·50	7·00
83		1s. black on green	2·25	2·75
84		2s. black and blue on blue	10·00	18·00
85		2s.6d. black and red on blue	18·00	19·00
86		3s. black and purple on yellow	3·25	12·00
87		4s. black and red on green	11·00	21·00
90		5s. black and green on yellow	9·00	50·00
91		£1 black and purple on red	£225	£350

1935. Silver Jubilee. As T **13** of Antigua.

92	1d. blue and red	75	20
93	1½d. blue and grey	1·50	1·00
94	2½d. brown and blue	1·50	2·50
95	1s. grey and purple	1·50	3·50

1937. Coronation. As T **2** of Aden.

96	1d. red	40	10
97	1½d. brown	40	10
98	2½d. blue	60	1·25

17 Fresh Water Lake

21 King George VI

1938.

99	17	½d. brown and green	10	15
100	–	1d. black and red	20	20
101	–	1½d. green and purple	30	70
102	–	2d. red and black	50	1·25
103a	–	2½d. purple and blue	20	1·25
104	–	3d. olive and brown	30	50
104a	–	3½d. blue and mauve	2·00	2·00
105	17	6d. green and violet	1·75	1·50
105a		7d. green and brown	1·75	1·50
106	–	1s. violet and olive	3·00	1·50
106a	–	2s. grey and purple	5·50	8·00
107	17	2s.6d. black and red	12·00	4·75
108	–	5s. blue and brown	7·50	8·00
108a	–	10s. black and orange	12·00	15·00

DESIGNS—As Type **17**: 1d., 3d., 2s., 5s. Layou River; 1½d., 2½d., 3½d. Picking Limes; 2d., 1s., 10s. Boiling Lake.

1940.

109a	21	¼d. brown	10	10

1946. Victory. As T **9** of Aden.

110	1d. red	20	10
111	3½d. blue	20	10

1948. Silver Wedding. As T **10/11** of Aden.

112	1d. red	15	10
113	10s. brown	11·00	23·00

1949. U.P.U. As T **20/23** of Antigua.

114	5c. blue	15	15
115	6c. brown	1·00	2·00
116	12c. purple	45	1·00
117	24c. olive	30	30

1951. Inauguration of B.W.I. University College. As T **24/25** of Antigua.

118	3c. green and violet	50	85
119	12c. green and red	75	30

23 Drying Cocoa

1951. New Currency.

120	–	½c. brown	10	30
121	23	1c. black and red	10	30
122	–	2c. brown and green	10	30
123	–	3c. green and purple	15	1·50
124	–	4c. orange and sepia	70	1·60
125	–	5c. black and red	85	30
126	–	6c. olive and brown	90	30
127	–	8c. green and blue	90	70
128	–	12c. black and green	60	1·25
129	–	14c. blue and purple	95	1·50
130	–	24c. purple and red	75	30
131	–	48c. green and orange	3·75	8·00
132	–	60c. red and black	3·75	6·00
133	–	$1.20 green and black	4·50	6·00
134	–	$2.40 orange and black	23·00	35·00

DESIGNS: ½c. As Type **21**, but with portrait as Type **23**. HORIZ (as Type **23**): 2c., 60c. Carib baskets; 3c., 48c. Lime plantation; 4c. Picking oranges; 5c. Bananas; 6c. Botanical Gardens; 8c. Drying vanilla beans; 12c., $1.20, Fresh Water Lake; 14c. Layou River, 24c. Boiling Lake. VERT: $2.40, Picking oranges.

1951. New Constitution. Stamps of 1951 optd **NEW CONSTITUTION 1951.**

135	3c. green and violet	15	70
136	5c. black and red	15	80
137	8c. green and blue	15	15
138	14c. blue and violet	50	20

1953. Coronation. As T **13** of Aden.

139	2c. black and green	20	10

1954. As Nos 120/34 but with portrait of Queen Elizabeth II.

140	½c. brown	10	30
141	1c. black and red	10	10
142	2c. brown and green	55	1·50
143	3c. green and purple	1·25	30
144	3c. black and red	3·25	2·25
145	4c. orange and brown	20	10
146	5c. black and red	1·50	50
147	5c. blue and brown	10·00	1·00
148	6c. green and brown	40	10
149	8c. green and blue	80	10
150	10c. green and brown	5·00	2·25
151	12c. black and green	50	10
152	14c. blue and purple	30	10
153	24c. purple and red	40	10
154	48c. green and orange	1·75	8·00
155	48c. brown and violet	1·25	80
156	60c. red and black	1·00	1·00
157	$1.20 green and black	16·00	7·00
158	$2.40 orange and black	16·00	14·00

DESIGNS (New)—HORIZ: Nos. 144, 155, Mat making; 147, Canoe making; 150, Bananas.

1958. British Caribbean Federation. As T **25** of Antigua.

159	3c. green	40	10
160	6c. blue	60	1·25
161	12c. red	70	15

40 Seashore at Rosalie

1963.

162	40	1c. green, blue and sepia	10	85
163	–	2c. blue	30	30
164	–	3c. brown and blue	1·00	1·00
165	–	4c. green, sepia and violet	10	10
166	–	5c. mauve	30	20
167	–	6c. green, bistre and violet	10	60
168	–	8c. green, sepia and black	30	20
169	–	10c. sepia and pink	10	10
170	–	12c. green, blue and sepia	70	10
171	–	14c. multicoloured	70	10
204	–	15c. yellow, green and brown	70	10

173 – 24c. multicoloured . . . . 8·50 20
174 – 48c. green, blue and black 75 70
175 – 60c. orange, green and black . . . . 1·00 70
176 – $1.20 multicoloured . . . 6·50 1·00
177 – $2.40 blue, turq & brn . . 3·25 2·50
178 – $4.80 green, blue and brown . . . . 9·00 20·00
DESIGNS—VERT. 2c., 5c. Queen Elizabeth II (after Annigoni); 14c. Traditional costume; 24c. Imperial amazon ("Sisserou Parrot"); $2.40, Trafalgar Falls; $4.80, Coconut palm. HORIZ: 3c. Sailing canoe; 4c. Sulphur springs; 6c. Road making; 8c. Dug-out canoe; 10c. Crapaud (frog); 12c. Scott's Head; 15c. Bananas; 48c. Goodwill; 60c. Cocoa tree; $1.20, Coat of Arms.

1963. Freedom from Hunger. As T **28** of Aden.
179 15c. violet 15 10

1963. Centenary of Red Cross. As T **33** of Antigua.
180 5c. red and black 20 40
181 15c. red and blue 40 60

1964. 400th Birth Anniv of Shakespeare. As T **34** of Antigua.
182 15c. purple 20 10

1965. Centenary of I.T.U. As T **36** of Antigua.
183 2c. green and blue 10 10
184 48c. turquoise and grey . . . 45 20

1965. I.C.Y. As T **37** of Antigua.
185 1c. purple and turquoise . . 10 20
186 15c. green and lavender . . . 35 10

1966. Churchill Commemoration. As T **38** of Antigua.
187 1c. blue 10 75
188 5c. green 20 10
189 15c. brown 40 10
190 24c. violet 50 20

1966. Royal Visit. As T **39** of Antigua.
191 5c. black and blue 75 30
192 15c. black and mauve . . . . 1·00 30

1966. World Cup Football Championship. As T **40** of Antigua.
193 5c. multicoloured 25 15
194 24c. multicoloured 85 15

1966. Inauguration of W.H.O. Headquarters, Geneva. As T **41** of Antigua.
195 5c. black, green and blue . . 15 15
196 24c. black, purple and ochre 30 15

1966. 20th Anniv of U.N.E.S.C.O. As T **54/6** of Antigua.
197 5c. red, yellow and orange . . 20 15
198 15c. yellow, violet and olive 50 10
199 24c. black, purple and orange 60 15

56 Children of Three Races

1967. National Day. Multicoloured.
205 5c. Type **56** 10 10
206 10c. The "Santa Maria" and motto 40 15
207 15c. Hands holding motto ribbon 15 15
208 24c. Belaire dancing 15 20

57 John F. Kennedy

1968. Human Rights Year. Multicoloured.
209 1c. Type **57** 10 10
210 10c. Cecil E. A. Rawle . . . 10 10
211 12c. Pope John XXIII . . . 50 15
212 48c. Florence Nightingale . . 20 25
213 60c. Albert Schweitzer . . . 20 25

1968. Associated Statehood. Nos. 162 etc, optd **ASSOCIATED STATEHOOD**.
214 1c. green, blue and sepia . . 10 10
215 2c. blue 10 10
216 3c. brown and blue 10 10
217 4c. green, sepia and violet . . 10 10
218 5c. mauve 10 10
219 6c. green, bistre and violet . . 10 10
220 8c. green, sepia and black . . 10 10
221 10c. sepia and pink 55 10
222 12c. green, blue and brown 10 10
224 14c. multicoloured 10 10
225 15c. yellow, green and brown 10 10
226 24c. multicoloured . . . . . 4·00 10
227 48c. green, blue and black . . 55 1·50
228 60c. orange, green and black 90 1·00
229 $1.20 multicoloured . . . . 1·00 3·25
230 $2.40 blue, turquoise and brown . . . . 1·00 2·50
231 $4.80 green, blue and brown 1·25 6·00

1968. National Day. Nos. 162/4, 171 and 176 optd **NATIONAL DAY 3 NOVEMBER 1968**.
232 1c. green, blue and sepia . . 10 10
233 2c. blue 10 10
234 3c. brown and blue 10 10
235 14c. multicoloured 10 10
236 $1.20 multicoloured 55 40

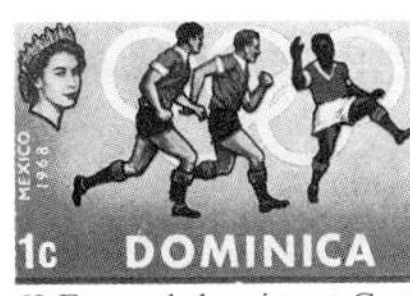

60 Forward shooting at Goal

1968. Olympic Games, Mexico. Multicoloured.
237 1c. Type **60** 10 10
238 1c. Goalkeeper attempting to save ball 10 10
239 5c. Swimmers preparing to dive 10 10
240 5c. Swimmers diving 10 10
241 48c. Javelin-throwing 15 15
242 48c. Hurdling 15 15
243 60c. Basketball 90 25
244 60c. Basketball players . . . 90 25

61 "The Small Cowper Madonna" (Raphael)
62 "Venus and Adonis" (Rubens)

1968. Christmas.
245 **61** 5c. multicoloured 10 10

1969. 20th Anniv of World Health Organization.
246 **62** 5c. multicoloured 20 10
247 – 15c. multicoloured 30 10
248 – 24c. multicoloured 30 10
249 – 50c. multicoloured 50 40
DESIGNS: 15c. "The Death of Socrates" (J.-L. David); 24c. "Christ and the Pilgrims of Emmaus" (Velasquez); 50c. "Pilate washing his Hands" (Rembrandt).

66 Picking Oranges

71 "Spinning" (J. Millet)

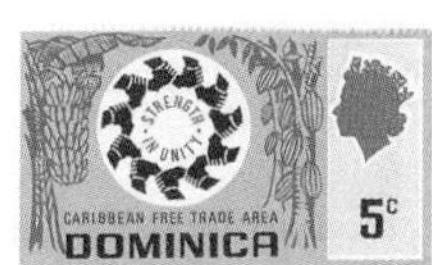

67 "Strength in Unity" Emblem and Fruit Trees

1969. Tourism. Multicoloured.
250 10c. Type **66** 15 10
251 10c. Woman, child and ocean scene 15 10
252 12c. Fort Yeoung Hotel . . . 50 10
253 12c. Red-necked amazon . . . 50 10
254 24c. Calypso band 30 10
255 24c. Women dancing 30 15
256 48c. Underwater life 30 25
257 48c. Skin-diver and turtle . . 30 25

1969. 1st Anniv of C.A.R.I.F.T.A. (Caribbean Free Trade Area). Multicoloured.
258 5c. Type **67** 10 10
259 8c. Hawker Siddeley H.S.748 aircraft, emblem and island 30 20
260 12c. Chart of Caribbean Sea and emblem 30 25
261 24c. Steamship unloading, tug and emblem 40 25

1969. 50th Anniv of International Labour Organization. Multicoloured.
262 15c. Type **71** 10 10
263 30c. "Threshing" (J. Millet) 15 15
264 38c. "Flax-pulling" (J. Millet) 15 15

72 Mahatma Gandhi weaving and Clock Tower, Westminster

1969. Birth Cent of Mahatma Gandhi. Mult.
265 6c. Type **72** 25 10
266 38c. Gandhi, Nehru and Mausoleum 40 15
267 $1.20 Gandhi and Taj Mahal 45 1·25
All stamps are incorrectly inscribed "Ghandi".

75 "Saint Joseph"

1969. National Day. Multicoloured.
268 6c. Type **75** 10 10
269 8c. "Saint John" 10 10
270 12c. "Saint Peter" 10 10
271 60c. "Saint Paul" 30 50

79 Queen Elizabeth II

99 "Virgin and Child with St. John" (Perugino)

80 Purple-throated Carib ("Humming Bird") and Flower

1969. Centres multicoloured; colours of "D" given.
272a **79** ½c. black and silver . . 30 1·50
273 **80** 1c. black and yellow . . . 30 1·75
274 – 2c. black and yellow . . . 15 10
275a – 3c. black and yellow . . . 2·75 1·50
276a – 4c. black and yellow . . . 2·75 1·50
277a – 5c. black and yellow . . . 2·00 1·75
278a – 6c. black and brown . . . 2·50 2·75
279 – 8c. black and brown . . . 20 10
280 – 10c. black and yellow . . 20 10
281 – 12c. black and yellow . . 20 10
282 – 15c. black and blue . . . 20 10
283 – 25c. black and red 30 10
284a – 30c. black and olive . . 1·50 70
285 – 38c. black and purple . . 8·00 1·75
286 – 50c. black and brown . . 50 45
287 – 60c. black and yellow . . 55 1·50
288 – $1.20 black and yellow . . 1·00 1·75
289 – $2.40 black and gold . . 1·00 4·00
290 – $4.80 black and gold . . 1·25 7·00
DESIGNS—HORIZ (As Type **80**): 2c. Poinsettia; 3c. Redneck pigeon ("Ramier"); 4c. Imperial amazon ("Sisserou"); 5c. "Battus polydamas" (butterfly); 6c. "Dryas julia" (butterfly); 8c. Shipping bananas; 10c. Portsmouth Harbour; 12c. Copra processing plant; 15c. Straw workers; 25c. Timber plant; 30c. Pumice mine; 38c. Grammar school and playing fields; 50c. Roseau Cathedral. (38 × 26½ mm): 60c. Government Headquarters. (40 × 27 mm): $1.20, Melville Hall airport. (39½ × 26 mm): $2.40, Coat of arms. VERT: (26 × 39 mm): $4.80, As Type **79**, but larger.

1969. Christmas. Paintings. Multicoloured.
291 6c. "Virgin and Child with St. John" (Lippi) 10 10
292 10c. "Holy Family with Lamb" (Raphael) 10 10
293 15c. Type **99** 10 10
294 $1.20 "Madonna of the Rose Hedge" (Botticelli) 35 40
MS295 89 × 76 mm. Nos. 293/4. Imperf 75 1·00

101 Astronaut's First Step onto the Moon

1970. Moon Landing. Multicoloured.
296 ½c. Type **101** 10 10
297 5c. Scientific experiment on the Moon and flag 15 10
298 8c. Astronauts collecting rocks 15 10
299 30c. Module over Moon . . 30 15
300 50c. Moon plague 40 25
301 60c. Astronauts 40 30
MS302 116 × 112 mm. Nos. 298/301. Imperf 2·00 2·00

107 Giant Green Turtle

1970. Flora and Fauna. Multicoloured.
303 6c. Type **107** 30 20
304 24c. Atlantic flyingfish . . . 40 45
305 38c. Anthurium lily 50 65
306 60c. Imperial and red-necked amazons . . . . 2·75 5·50
MS307 160 × 111 mm. Nos. 303/6 5·50 6·50

108 18th-century National Costume

1970. National Day. Multicoloured.
308 5c. Type **108** 10 10
309 8c. Carib basketry 10 10
310 $1 Flag and chart of Dominica 30 40
MS311 150 × 85 mm. Nos. 308/10 50 1·40

109 Scrooge and Marley's Ghost

1970. Christmas and Death Centenary of Charles Dickens. Scenes from "A Christmas Carol". Multicoloured.
312 2c. Type **109** 10 10
313 15c. Fezziwig's Ball 20 10
314 24c. Scrooge and his Nephew's Party 20 10
315 $1.20 Scrooge and the Ghost of Christmas Present . . . 65 90
MS316 142 × 87 mm. Nos. 312/15 1·00 3·50

110 "The Doctor" (Sir Luke Fildes)

1970. Centenary of British Red Cross. Multicoloured.
317 8c. Type **110** 10 10
318 10c. Hands and Red Cross . . 10 10
319 15c. Flag of Dominica and Red Cross emblem 15 10
320 50c. "The Sick Child" (E. Munch) 50 45
MS321 108 × 76 mm. Nos. 317/20 85 2·75

111 Marigot School

1971. International Education Year. Multicoloured.
322 5c. Type **111** 10 10
323 8c. Goodwill Junior High School 10 10
324 14c. University of West Indies (Jamaica) 10 10
325 $1 Trinity College, Cambridge 35 30
MS326 85 × 85 mm. Nos. 324/5 50 1·25

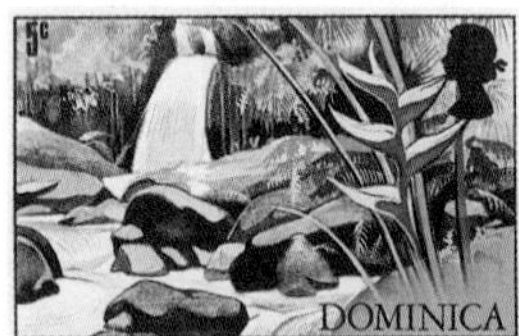

112 Waterfall

1971. Tourism. Multicoloured.
327 5c. Type **112** 15 10
328 10c. Boat-building 15 10
329 30c. Sailing 25 10
330 50c. Yacht and motor launch 40 30
MS331 130 × 86 mm. Nos. 327/30 85 1·00

113 U.N.I.C.E.F. Symbol in "D"

1971. 25th Anniv of U.N.I.C.E.F.
332 **113** 5c. violet, black and gold 10 10
333 10c. yellow, blk & gold 10 10
334 38c. green, blk & gold . . 10 10
335 $1.20 orange, blk & gold 30 45
MS336 84 × 79 mm. Nos. 333 and 335 50 1·40

114 German Boy Scout

1971. World Scout Jamboree, Asagiri, Japan. Various designs showing Boy Scouts from the nations listed. Multicoloured.
337 20c. Type **114** 15 15
338 24c. Great Britain 20 15
339 30c. Japan 25 20
340 $1 Dominica . . . . 50 2·00
MS341 114 × 102 mm. Nos. 339/40 1·00 2·25

Both No. 340 and the $1 value from the miniature sheet show the national flag of the Dominican Republic in error.

"Dominica" on the scout's shirt pocket is omitted on the $1 value from the miniature sheet.

115 Groine at Portsmouth

1971. National Day. Multicoloured.
342 8c. Type **115** 10 10
343 15c. Carnival scene 10 10
344 20c. Carifta Queen (vert) . . 10 10
345 50c. Rock of Atkinson (vert) 20 25
MS346 63 × 89 mm. $1.20, As 20c. 50 70

116 Eight Reals Piece, 1761

1972. Coins.
347 **116** 10c. black, silver and violet 10 10
348 – 30c. black, silver and green 15 15
349 – 35c. black, silver and blue 15 20
350 – 50c. black, silver and red 25 1·75
MS351 86 × 90 mm. Nos. 349/50 50 1·25

DESIGNS—HORIZ: 30c. Eleven and three bitt pieces, 1798. VERT: 35c. Two reals and two bitt pieces, 1770; 50c. Mocos, pieces-of-eight and eight reals-eleven bitts piece, 1798.

117 Common Opossum

1972. U.N. Conference on the Human Enviroment, Stockholm. Multicoloured.
352 ½c. Type **117** 10 10
353 35c. Brazilian agouti (rodent) 30 15
354 60c. Orchid . . . . 2·00 50
355 $1.20 Hibiscus . . . . 1·25 1·60
MS356 139 × 94 mm. Nos. 352/5 5·00 9·00

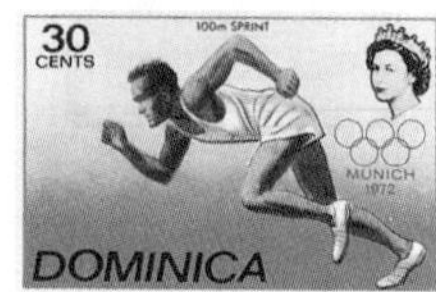

118 Sprinter

1972. Olympic Games, Munich. Multicoloured.
357 30c. Type **118** 10 10
358 35c. Hurdler 15 15
359 58c. Hammer-thrower (vert) 20 20
360 72c. Long-jumper (vert) . . . 40 40
MS361 98 × 96 mm. Nos. 359/60 75 1·00

119 General Post Office

1972. National Day. Multicoloured.
362 10c. Type **119** 10 10
363 20c. Morne Diablotin 10 10
364 30c. Rodney's Rock 15 15
MS365 83 × 96 mm. Nos. 363/4 50 70

1972. Royal Silver Wedding. As T **52** of Ascension, but with Bananas and Imperial Parrot in background.
366 5c. green 20 10
367 $1 green 60 40

121 "The Adoration of the Shepherds" (Caravaggio)

122 Launching of Weather Satellite

1972. Christmas. Multicoloured.
368 8c. Type **121** 10 10
369 14c. "The Myosotis Virgin" (Rubens) 10 10
370 30c. "Madonna and Child with St Francesca Romana" (Gentileschi) . . 15 10
371 $1 "Adoration of the Kings" (Mostaert) . . . . 50 1·25
MS372 102 × 79 mm. Nos. 370/1. Imperf 60 80

1973. Centenary of I.M.O./W.M.O. Multicoloured.
373 ½c. Type **122** 10 10
374 1c. Nimbus satellite 10 10
375 2c. Radiosonde balloon . . . 10 10
376 30c. Radarscope (horiz) . . . 15 15
377 35c. Diagram of pressure zones (horiz) 20 20
378 50c. Hurricane shown by satellite (horiz) 30 35
379 $1 Computer weather-map (horiz) 60 65
MS380 90 × 105 mm. Nos. 378/9 70 1·75

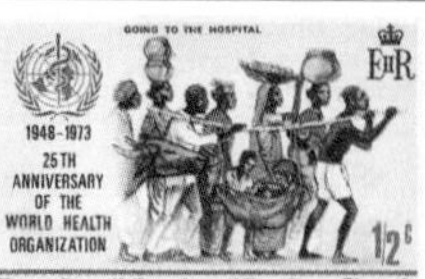

123 Going to Hospital

1973. 25th Anniv of W.H.O. Multicoloured.
381 ½c. Type **123** 10 10
382 1c. Maternity care 10 10
383 2c. Smallpox inoculation . . 10 10
384 30c. Emergency service . . . 30 15
385 35c. Waiting for the doctor 30 15
386 50c. Medical examination . . 30 25
387 $1 Travelling doctor 40 60
MS388 112 × 110 mm. Nos. 386/7 75 1·25

124 Cyrique Crab

1973. Flora and Fauna. Multicoloured.
389 ½c. Type **124** 10 10
390 22c. Blue land-crab 30 10
391 25c. Bread fruit 30 15
392 $1.20 Sunflower . . . . . . 55 2·00
MS393 91 × 127 mm. Nos. 389/2 1·50 4·00

125 Princess Anne and Captain Mark Phillips

1973. Royal Wedding.
394 **125** 25c. multicoloured 10 10
395 – $2 multicoloured 30 30
MS396 79 × 100 mm. 75c. as 25c. and $1.20 as $2 40 30

DESIGN: $2 As Type **125**, but with different frame.

126 "Adoration of the Kings" (Brueghel)

1973. Christmas. Religious Paintings. Multicoloured.
397 ½c. Type **126** 10 10
398 1c. "Adoration of the Magi" (Botticelli) 10 10
399 2c. "Adoration of the Magi" (Durer) 10 10
400 12c. "Mystic Nativity" (Botticelli) 20 10
401 22c. "Adoration of the Magi" (Rubens) 25 10
402 35c. "The Nativity" (Durer) 25 10
403 $1 "Adoration of the Shepherds" (Giorgione) . . 60 55
MS404 122 × 98 mm. Nos. 402/3 85 1·10

127 Carib Basket-weaving

1973. National Day. Multicoloured.
405 5c. Type **127** 10 10
406 10c. Staircase of the Snake 10 10
407 50c. Miss Caribbean Queen (vert) 15 15
408 60c. Miss Carifta Queen (vert) 15 15
409 $1 Dance group (vert) 25 30
MS410 95 × 127 mm. Nos. 405/6 and 409 40 65

128 University Centre, Dominica

1973. 25th Anniv of West Indies University. Multicoloured.
411 12c. Type **128** 10 10
412 30c. Graduation ceremony . . 10 10
413 $1 University coat of arms 25 35
MS414 97 × 131 mm. Nos. 411/13 30 55

129 Dominica 1d. Stamp of 1874 and Map

1974. Stamp Centenary. Multicoloured.
415 ½c. Type **129** 10 10
416 1c. 6d. stamp of 1874 and posthorn 10 10
417 2c. 1d. stamp of 1874 and arms 10 10
418 10c. Type **129** 20 10
419 50c. As 1c. 40 30
420 $1.20 As 2c. 50 70
MS421 105 × 121 mm. Nos. 418/20 1·00 1·50

130 Footballer and Flag of Brazil

1974. World Cup Football Championship, West Germany. Multicoloured.
422 ½c. Type **130** 10 10
423 1c. West Germany 10 10
424 2c. Italy 10 10
425 30c. Scotland 50 10
426 40c. Sweden 50 10
427 50c. Netherlands 55 35
428 $1 Yugoslavia 90 90
MS429 89 × 87 mm. Nos. 427/8 70 80

131 Indian Hole

1974. National Day. Multicoloured.
430 10c. Type **131** 10 10
431 40c. Teachers' Training College 10 10
432 $1 Bay Oil distillery plant, Petite Savanne 50 45
MS433 96 × 143 mm. Nos. 430/2 60 65

132 Churchill with "Colonist"

1974. Birth Centenary of Sir Winston Churchill. Multicoloured.
434 ½c. Type **132** 10 10
435 1c. Churchill and Eisenhower 10 10
436 2c. Churchill and Roosevelt 10 10
437 20c. Churchill and troops on assault-course 15 10
438 45c. Painting at Marrakesh 20 10
439 $2 Giving the "V" sign . . . 50 1·00
MS440 126 × 100 mm. Nos. 438/9 70 1·50

133 Mailboats "Orinoco" (1851) and "Geesthaven" (1974)

1974. Centenary of U.P.U. Multicoloured.
441 10c. Type **133** 20 10
442 $2 De Haviland D.H.4 (1918) and Boeing 747-100 (1974) 80 1·00
MS443 107 × 93 mm. $1.20 as 10c. and $2.40 as $2 1·00 1·40
Nos. 442 and **MS**443 are inscr "De Havilland".

134 "The Virgin and Child" (Tiso)

1974. Christmas. Multicoloured.
444 ½c. Type **134** 10 10
445 1c. "Madonna and Child with Saints" (Costa) 10 10
446 2c. "The Nativity" (school of Rimini, 14th-century) 10 10
447 10c. "The Rest on the Flight into Egypt" (Romanelli) 20 10
448 25c. "The Adoration of the Shepherds" (da Sermoneta) 35 10
449 45c. "The Nativity" (Guido Reni) 45 10
450 $1 "The Adoration of the Magi" (Caselli) 65 40
MS451 114 × 78 mm. Nos. 449/50 60 1·00

135 Queen Triggerfish

1975. Fishes. Multicoloured.
452 ½c. Type **135** 10 10
453 1c. Porkfish 10 10
454 2c. Sailfish 10 10
455 3c. Swordfish 10 10
456 20c. Great barracuda 75 50
457 $2 Nassau grouper 1·75 2·75
MS458 104 × 80 mm. No. 457 2·25 6·00

136 "Myscelia antholia"

1975. Dominican Butterflies. Multicoloured.
459 ½c. Type **136** 10 40
460 1c. "Lycorea ceres" 10 40
461 2c. "Anaea marthesia" ("Siderone nemesis") 15 40
462 6c. "Battus polydamas" 50 55
463 30c. "Anartia lytrea" 1·00 70
464 40c. "Morpho peleides" 1·00 75
465 $2 "Dryas julia" 1·40 7·50
MS466 108 × 80 mm. No. 465 1·50 4·75

137 "Yare" (cargo liner)

1975. "Ships tied to Dominica's History". Mult.
467 ½c. Type **137** 20 35
468 1c. "Thames II" (liner), 1890 20 35
469 2c. "Lady Nelson" (cargo liner) 20 35
470 20c. "Lady Rodney" (cargo liner) 60 35
471 45c. "Statesman" (freighter) 80 55
472 50c. "Geestcape" (freighter) 80 80
473 $2 "Geeststar" (freighter) 1·50 4·50
MS474 78 × 103 mm. Nos. 472/3 2·00 5·00

138 "Women in Agriculture"

1975. International Women's Year. Multicoloured.
475 10c. Type **138** 10 10
476 $2 "Women in Industry and Commerce" 40 60

139 Miss Caribbean Queen, 1975
140 "Virgin and Child" (Mantegna)

1975. National Day. Multicoloured.
477 5c. Type **139** 10 10
478 10c. Public library (horiz) 10 10
479 30c. Citrus factory (horiz) 10 10
480 $1 National Day Trophy 25 50
MS481 130 × 98 mm. Nos. 478/80. Imperf 50 1·40

1975. Christmas. "Virgin and Child" paintings by artists named. Multicoloured.
482 ½c. Type **140** 10 10
483 1c. Fra Filippo Lippi 10 10
484 2c. Bellini 10 10
485 10c. Botticelli 15 10
486 25c. Bellini 25 10
487 45c. Correggio 30 10
488 $1 Durer 55 50
MS489 139 × 85 mm. Nos. 487/88 1·00 1·50

141 Hibiscus

1975. Multicoloured.
490 ½c. Type **141** 10 70
491 1c. African tulip 15 70
492 2c. Castor-oil tree 15 70
493 3c. White cedar flower 15 70
494 4c. Egg plant 15 70
495 5c. Needlefish ("Gare") 20 70
496 6c. Ochro 20 80
497 8c. Zenaida dove ("Mountain Dove") 2·75 80
498 10c. Screw pine 20 15
499 20c. Mango longue 30 15
500 25c. Crayfish 35 15
501 30c. Common opossum 90 80
502 40c. Bay leaf groves 90 80
503 50c. Tomatoes 40 50
504 $1 Lime factory 55 65
505 $2 Rum distillery 1·00 3·50
506 $5 Bay Oil distillery 1·25 5·00
507 $10 Queen Elizabeth II (vert) 1·75 15·00
Nos. 502/7 are larger, 28 × 44 mm ($10) or 44 × 28 (others).

142 American Infantry
143 Rowing

1976. Bicentenary of American Revolution. Mult.
508 ½c. Type **142** 10 10
509 1c. British three-decker, 1782 10 10
510 2c. George Washington 10 10
511 45c. British sailors 30 10
512 75c. British ensign 40 40
513 $2 Admiral Hood 60 1·25
MS514 105 × 92 mm. Nos. 512/13 1·00 3·00

1976. Olympic Games, Montreal. Multicoloured.
515 ½c. Type **143** 10 10
516 1c. Shot putting 10 10
517 2c. Swimming 10 10
518 40c. Relay 15 10
519 45c. Gymnastics 15 10
520 60c. Sailing 20 20
521 $2 Archery 55 80
MS522 90 × 140 mm. Nos. 520/1 85 75

144 Ringed Kingfisher

1976. Wild Birds. Multicoloured.
523 ½c. Type **144** 10 75
524 1c. Mourning dove 15 75
525 2c. Green-backed heron ("Green Heron") 15 75
526 15c. Blue-winged hawk (vert) 75 35
527 30c. Blue-headed hummingbird (vert) 1·00 55
528 45c. Bananaquit (vert) 1·10 60
529 $2 Imperial amazon ("Imperial Parrot") (vert) 2·25 12·00
MS530 133 × 101 mm. Nos. 527/9 3·75 14·00

1976. West Indian Victory in World Cricket Cup. As Nos. 559/60 of Barbados.
531 15c. Map of the Caribbean 75 1·25
532 25c. Prudential Cup 75 1·75

145 Viking Spacecraft System
146 "Virgin and Child with Saints Anthony of Padua and Roch" (Giorgione)

1976. Viking Space Mission. Multicoloured.
533 ½c. Type **145** 10 10
534 1c. Landing pad (horiz) 10 10
535 2c. Titan IIID and Centaur DII 10 10
536 3c. Orbiter and lander capsule 10 10
537 45c. Capsule, parachute unopened 20 15
538 75c. Capsule, parachute opened 30 70
539 $1 Lander descending (horiz) 35 75
540 $2 Space vehicle on Mars (horiz) 50 2·00
MS541 104 × 78 mm. Nos. 539/40 1·10 2·25

1976. Christmas. "Virgin and Child" paintings by artists named. Multicoloured.
542 ½c. Type **146** 10 10
543 1c. Bellini 10 10
544 2c. Mantegna 10 10
545 6c. Mantegna (different) 10 10
546 25c. Memling 15 10
547 45c. Correggio 20 10
548 $3 Raphael 1·00 1·00
MS549 104 × 85 mm. 50c. as No. 547 and $1 as No. 548 1·00 1·10

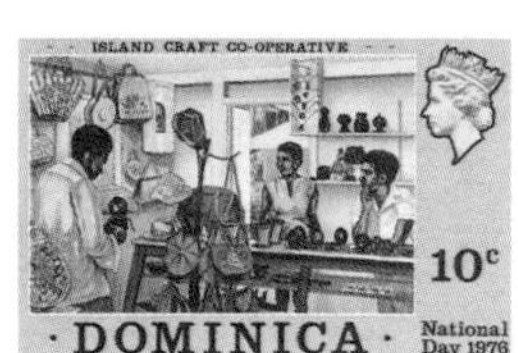

147 Island Craft Co-operative

1976. National Day. Multicoloured.
550 10c. Type **147** 10 10
551 50c. Harvesting bananas 15 10
552 $1 Boxing plant 30 35
MS553 96 × 122 mm. Nos. 550/2 50 90

148 American Giant Sundial
150 Joseph Haydn

149 The Queen Crowned and Enthroned

1976. Shells. Multicoloured.
554 ½c. Type **148** 10 10
555 1c. Flame helmet 10 10
556 2c. Mouse cone 10 10
557 20c. Caribbean vase 35 10
558 40c. West Indian fighting conch 55 25
559 50c. Short coral shell 55 25
560 $3 Apple murex 2·00 3·25
MS561 101 × 55 mm. $2 Long-spined star shell 1·10 1·40

1977. Silver Jubilee. Multicoloured.
562 ½c. Type **149** 10 10
563 1c. Imperial State Crown 10 10
564 45c. The Queen and Princess Anne 15 10
565 $2 Coronation Ring 25 30
566 $2.50 Ampulla and Spoon 30 40
MS567 104 × 97 mm. $5 Queen Elizabeth and Prince Philip 75 1·25

1977. 150th Death Anniv of Ludwig van Beethoven. Multicoloured.
568 ½c. Type **150** 10 10
569 1c. Scene from "Fidelio" 10 10
570 2c. Maria Casentini (dancer) 10 10
571 15c. Beethoven and pastoral scene 30 10
572 30c. "Wellington's Victory" 30 10
573 40c. Henriette Sontag (singer) 30 10
574 $2 The young Beethoven 75 2·00
MS575 138 × 93 mm. Nos. 572/4 1·10 3·25

151 Hiking

1977. Caribbean Scout Jamboree, Jamaica. Mult.
576 ½c. Type **151** 10 10
577 1c. First-aid 10 10
578 2c. Camping 10 10
579 45c. Rock climbing 25 15
580 50c. Canoeing 30 20
581 $3 Sailing 1·40 1·75
MS582 111 × 113 mm. 75c. Map-reading; $2 Campfire sing-song 1·00 1·25

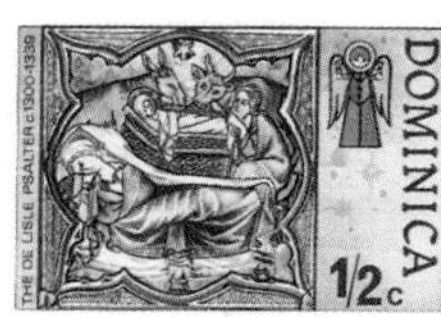

152 Holy Family

1977. Christmas. Multicoloured.
583 ½c. Type **152** 10 10
584 1c. Angel and Shepherds 10 10
585 2c. Holy Baptism 10 10
586 6c. Flight into Egypt 15 10
587 15c. Three Kings with gifts 15 10
588 45c. Holy Family in the Temple 30 10
589 $3 Flight into Egypt (different) 80 1·10
MS590 113 × 85 mm. 50c. Virgin and Child; $2 Flight into Egypt (different) 60 75

1977. Royal Visit. Nos. 562/66 optd **ROYAL VISIT W.I. 1977**.
591 ½c. Type **149** 10 10
592 1c. Imperial State Crown 10 10
593 45c. The Queen and Princess Anne 15 10
594a $2 Coronation Ring 30 30
595a $2.50 Ampulla and Spoon 35 35
MS596 104 × 79 mm. $5 Queen Elizabeth and Prince Philip 1·00 1·50

154 "Sousouelle Souris"

1978. "History of Carnival". Multicoloured.
597 ½c. Type **154** 10 10
598 1c. Sensay costume 10 10
599 2c. Street musicians 10 10
600 45c. Douiette band 15 10
601 50c. Pappy Show wedding 15 10
602 $2 Masquerade band 45 60
MS603 104 × 88 mm. $2.50, No. 602 60 65

155 Colonel Charles Lindbergh and "Spirit of St. Louis"

1978. Aviation Anniversaries. Multicoloured.
604 6c. Type **155** 20 40
605 10c. "Spirit of St. Louis", New York, 20 May, 1927 25 10
606 15c. Lindbergh and map of Atlantic 35 10
607 20c. Lindbergh reaches Paris, 21 May, 1927 45 10
608 40c. Airship LZ-1, Lake Constance, 1900 55 20

609 60c. Count F. von Zeppelin and Airship LZ-2, 1906 . . 65 30
610 $3 Airship "Graf Zeppelin", 1928 . . . . 1·40 2·00
MS611 139 × 108 mm. 50c. Ryan NYP Special "Spirit of St. Louis" in mid-Atlantic; $2 Airship LZ-127 "Graf Zeppelin", 1928 1·40 1·10

The 6, 10, 15, 20 and 50c. values commemorate the 50th anniversary of first solo transatlantic flight by Col. Charles Lindbergh; the other values commemorate anniversaries of various Zeppelin airships.

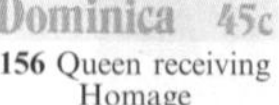

156 Queen receiving Homage

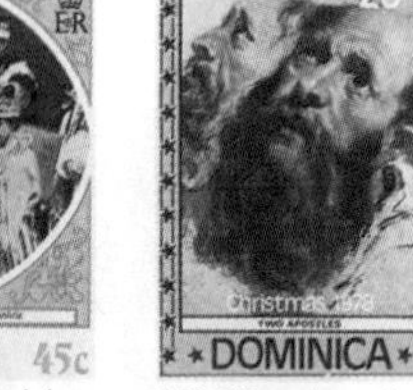

158 "Two Apostles"

157 Wright Flyer III

1978. 25th Anniv of Coronation. Multicoloured.
612 45c. Type **156** 15 10
613 $2 Balcony scene 30 30
614 $2.50 Queen and Prince Philip 40 40
MS615 76 × 107 mm. $5 Queen Elizabeth II 75 75

1978. 75th Anniv of First Powered Flight. Mult.
616 30c. Type **157** 15 15
617 40c. Wright Type A, 1908 . . 20 20
618 60c. Wright Flyer I 25 30
619 $2 Wright Flyer I (different) 85 1·10
MS620 116 × 89 mm. $3 Wilbur and Orville Wright 1·00 1·00

1978. Christmas. Paintings by Rubens. Mult.
621 20c. Type **158** 10 10
622 45c. "Descent from the Cross" 15 10
623 50c. "St Ildefonso receiving the Chasuble" 15 10
624 $3 "Assumption of the Virgin" 35 80
MS625 113 × 83 mm. $2 "The Holy Family" (Sebastiano del Piombo*) 75 75

*This painting was incorrectly attributed to Rubens on the stamp.

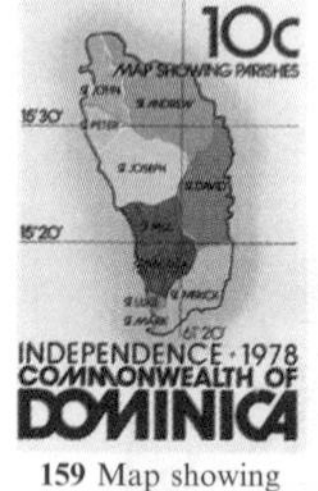

159 Map showing Parishes

161 Sir Rowland Hill

1978. Independence. Multicoloured.
626 10c. Type **159** 60 15
627 25c. "Sabinea carinalis" (national flower) 55 15
628 45c. New National flag . . . 70 15
629 50c. Coat of arms 60 30
630 $2 Prime Minister Patrick John . . . . 70 2·50
MS631 113 × 90 mm. $2.50, Type **159** 1·00 1·25

1978. Nos. 490/507 optd **INDEPENDENCE 3rd NOVEMBER 1978**.
632 ½c. Type **57** 40 10
633 1c. African tulip 45 10
634 2c. Castor-oil tree 45 10
635 3c. White cedar flower . . . 50 15
636 4c. Egg plant 50 15
637 5c. Needlefish ("Gare") . . . 50 15
638 6c. Ochro 50 15
639 8c. Zenaida dove . . . . . . 2·50 20
640 10c. Screw pine 50 15
641 20c. Mango longue 60 15
642 25c. Crayfish 70 20
643 30c. Common opossum . . . 70 20
644 40c. Bay leaf groves 70 25
645 50c. Tomatoes 80 30
646 $1 Lime factory 80 65
647 $2 Rum distillery . . . . . . 1·00 1·00
648 $5 Bay Oil distillery . . . . 1·25 2·25
649 $10 Queen Elizabeth II . . . 1·75 4·50

1979. Death Centenary of Sir Rowland Hill.
650 **161** 25c. multicoloured 10 10
651 – 45c. multicoloured 15 10
652 – 50c. black, violet and mauve 15 10
653 – $2 black, mauve and yellow 35 65
MS654 186 × 96 mm. $5 black and red 1·00 1·25

DESIGNS: 45c. Great Britain 1840 2d. blue; 50c. 1874 1d. stamp; $2 Maltese Cross cancellations; $5 Penny Black.

162 Children and Canoe

1979. International Year of the Child. Multicoloured.
655 30c. Type **162** 25 15
656 40c. Children with bananas 25 15
657 50c. Children playing cricket 1·25 80
658 $3 Child feeding rabbits . . . 1·75 2·00
MS659 117 × 85 mm. $5 Child with catch of fish 1·00 1·50

163 Nassau Grouper

1979. Marine Wildlife. Multicoloured.
660 10c. Type **163** 40 15
661 30c. Striped dolphin 70 35
662 50c. White-tailed tropic-bird 2·25 65
663 60c. Brown pelican . . . . . 2·25 1·50
664 $1 Long-finned pilot whale 2·50 1·75
665 $2 Brown booby . . . . . . 3·00 4·50
MS666 120 × 94 mm. $3 Elkhorn coral 1·50 1·40

No. 661 is inscr "SPOTTED DOLPHIN" in error.

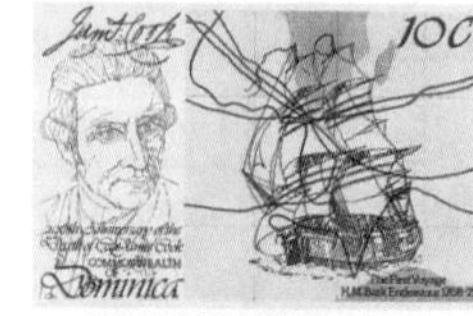

164 H.M.S. "Endeavour"

1979. Death Bicent of Captain Cook. Mult.
667 10c. Type **164** 65 30
668 50c. H.M.S. "Resolution" (Second Voyage) . . . . 1·10 1·00
669 60c. H.M.S. "Discovery" (Third Voyage) . . . . . 1·25 1·50
670 $2 Detail of Cook's chart of New Zealand, 1770 . . . . 1·60 2·50
MS671 97 × 90 mm. Captain Cook and signature 1·25 2·00

165 Cooking at Campfire

1979. 50th Anniv of Girl Guide Movement in Dominica. Multicoloured.
672 10c. Type **165** 20 10
673 20c. Pitching emergency rain tent 25 10
674 50c. Raising Dominican flag 35 10
675 $2.50 Singing and dancing to accordion 90 80
MS676 110 × 86 mm. $3 Guides of different age-groups 75 1·25

166 Colvillea

169 Mickey Mouse and Octopus playing Xylophone

167 Cathedral of the Assumption, Roseau

1979. Flowering Trees. Multicoloured.
677 20c. Type **166** 15 10
678 40c. "Lignum vitae" 20 15
679 60c. Dwarf poinciana 25 15
680 $2 Fern tree 50 75
MS681 114 × 89 mm. $3 Perfume tree 75 1·10

1979. Christmas. Cathedrals. Multicoloured.
682 6c. Type **167** 10 10
683 45c. St. Paul's, London (vert) 15 10
684 60c. St. Peter's, Rome . . . 15 10
685 $3 Notre Dame, Paris (vert) 55 60
MS686 113 × 85 mm. 40c. St. Patrick's, New York; $2 Cologne Cathedral (both vert) 50 80

1979. Hurricane Relief. Nos. 495, 502 and 506/7 optd **HURRICANE RELIEF**.
687 5c. Gare 10 10
688 40c. Bay leaf groves 10 10
689 $5 Bay Oil distillery . . . . 1·00 1·25
690 $10 Queen Elizabeth II . . . 1·25 1·75

1979. International Year of the Child. Walt Disney Cartoon Characters. Multicoloured.
691 ½c. Type **169** 10 10
692 1c. Goofy playing guitar on rocking-horse 10 10
693 2c. Mickey Mouse playing violin and Goofy on bagpipes 10 10
694 3c. Donald Duck playing drum with a pneumatic drill 10 10
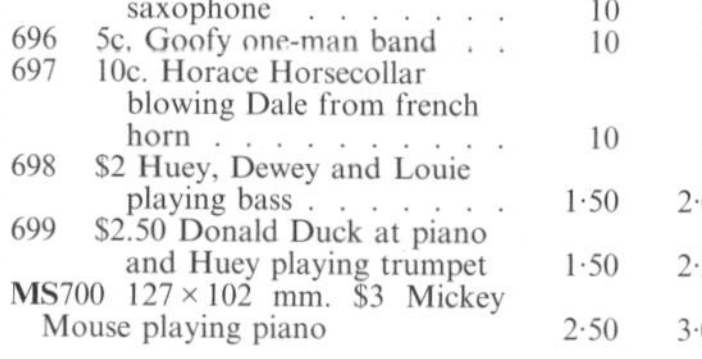
695 4c. Minnie Mouse playing saxophone 10 10
696 5c. Goofy one-man band . . 10 10
697 10c. Horace Horsecollar blowing Dale from french horn 10 10
698 $2 Huey, Dewey and Louie playing bass . . . . . . 1·50 2·00
699 $2.50 Donald Duck at piano and Huey playing trumpet 1·50 2·25
MS700 127 × 102 mm. $3 Mickey Mouse playing piano 2·50 3·00

170 Hospital Ward

1980. 75th Anniv of Rotary International. Mult.
701 10c. Type **170** 10 10
702 20c. Electro-cardiogram . . . 15 10
703 40c. Mental hospital site . . 20 15
704 $2.50 Paul Harris (founder) 55 90
MS705 128 × 113 mm. $3 Interlocking cogs of Rotary emblem and globe 60 80

1980. "London 1980" International Stamp Exhibition. Optd **LONDON 1980**.
706 **161** 25c. multicoloured 25 10
707 – 45c. multicoloured 30 15
708 – 50c. brown, blue and red 30 15
709 – $2 brown, red and yellow 80 60

171 Shot Putting

1980. Olympic Games, Moscow. Multicoloured.
710 30c. Type **171** 15 10
711 40c. Basketball 60 15
712 60c. Swimming 35 20
713 $2 Gymnastics 60 65
MS714 114 × 86 mm. $3 The marathon 70 90

172 "Supper at Emmaus" (Caravaggio)

1980. Famous Paintings. Multicoloured.
715 20c. Type **172** 20 10
716 25c. "Portrait of Charles I Hunting" (Van Dyck) (vert) 20 10
717 30c. "The Maids of Honour" (Velasquez) (vert) 25 10
718 45c. "The Rape of the Sabine Women" (Poussin) 25 10
719 $1 "Embarkation for Cythera" (Watteau) . . . 35 35
720 $5 "Girl before a Mirror" (Picasso) (vert) . . . . . . 1·00 1·50
MS721 114 × 111 mm. $3 "The Holy Family" (Rembrandt) (vert) 60 80

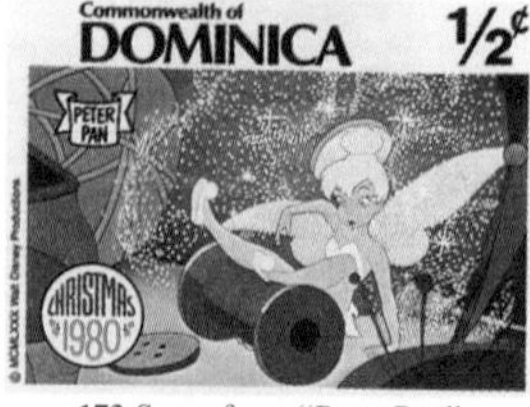

173 Scene from "Peter Pan"

1980. Christmas. Scenes from "Peter Pan". Multicoloured.
722 ½c. Type **173** (Tinker Bell) . . 10 10
723 1c. Wendy sewing back Peter's shadow 10 10
724 2c. Peter introduces the mermaids 10 10
725 3c. Wendy and Peter with lost boys 10 10
726 4c. Captain Hook, Pirate Smee and Tiger Lily . . . 10 10
727 5c. Peter with Tiger Lily and her father 10 10
728 10c. Captain Hook captures Peter and Wendy 10 10
729 $2 Peter fights Captain Hook 2·25 1·50
730 $2.50 Captain Hook in crocodile's jaws . . . . . 2·25 1·75
MS731 124 × 98 mm. $4 Peter Pan 4·00 3·50

174 Queen Elizabeth the Queen Mother in Doorway

1980. 80th Birthday of the Queen Mother.
732a **174** 40c. multicoloured . . . 15 15
733a $2.50 multicoloured . . 45 60
MS734 85 × 66 mm. $3 multicoloured 75 2·00

175 Douglas Bay

1981. "Dominica Safari". Multicoloured.
735 20c. Type **175** 10 10
736 30c. Valley of Desolation . . 10 10
737 40c. Emerald Pool (vert) . . 10 10
738 $3 Indian River (vert) . . . . 75 1·10
MS739 84 × 104 mm. $4 Trafalgar Falls (vert) 1·10 1·40

1981. Walt Disney's Cartoon Character, Pluto. As T **169**. Multicoloured.
740 $2 Pluto and Fifi . . . . . . 80 1·50
MS741 128 × 102 mm. $4 Pluto in scene from film "Pluto's Blue Note" 1·25 1·50

176 Forest Thrush

1981. Birds. Multicoloured.
742 20c. Type **176** 55 30
743 30c. Wied's crested flycatcher 65 35
744 40c. Blue-hooded euphonia 75 45
745 $5 Lesser Antillean pewee . . 3·50 4·75
MS746 121 × 95 mm. $3 Imperial Amazon 2·75 1·75

177 Windsor Castle **178** Lady Diana Spencer

1981. Royal Wedding. Multicoloured.
747 40c. Prince Charles and Lady Diana Spencer . . . 10 10
748 60c. Type **177** 15 15
749a $4 Prince Charles flying helicopter 30 50
MS750 96 × 82 mm. $5 Westland HU Mk 5 Wessex helicopter of Queen's Flight 85 90

1981. Royal Wedding. Multicoloured.
751 25c. Type **178** 20 35
752 $2 Prince Charles . . . . . 50 1·00
753 $5 Prince Charles and Lady Diana Spencer . . . . . . 1·75 2·50

1981. Christmas. Scenes from Walt Disney's cartoon film "Santa's Workshop". As T **169**.
754 ½c. multicoloured 10 10
755 1c. multicoloured 10 10
756 2c. multicoloured 10 10
757 3c. multicoloured 10 10
758 4c. multicoloured 15 10
759 5c. multicoloured 15 10
760 10c. multicoloured 20 10
761 45c. multicoloured . . . . . 1·50 30
762 $5 multicoloured . . . . . . 4·25 5·50
MS763 129 × 103 mm. $4 multicoloured 4·00 3·50

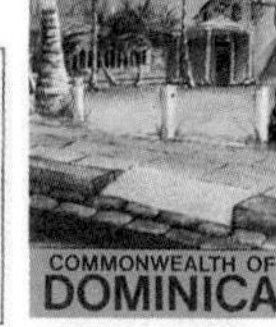

179 Ixora **180** Curb Slope for Wheelchairs

1981. Plant Life. Multicoloured.
764A 1c. Type **179** 10 50
765A 2c. Flamboyant 10 70
766A 4c. Poinsettia 15 70
767A 5c. Bois caribe (national flower of Dominica) . . . 15 50
768A 8c. Annatto or roucou . . 20 50
769A 10c. Passion fruit 30 20
770A 15c. Breadfruit or yampain 55 20
771A 20c. Allamanda or buttercup 40 20
772A 25c. Cashew nut 40 20
773A 35c. Soursop or couassol 45 30
774A 40c. Bougainvillea 45 30
775A 45c. Anthurium 50 35
776A 60c. Cacao or cocoa . . . 1·25 70
777A 90c. Pawpaw tree or papay 70 1·25
778A $1 Coconut palm . . . . . 1·50 1·25
779A $2 Coffee tree or cafe . . . 1·00 3·00
780B $5 Heliconia or lobster claw 3·25 5·50
781A $10 Banana fig . . . . . . 2·25 11·00
Nos. 769, 770, 776, 778, 780 and 781 come with or without imprint date.

1981. International Year for Disabled People. Multicoloured.
782 45c. Type **180** 40 15
783 60c. Bus with invalid step . . 50 20
784 75c. Motor car controls adapted for handicapped 60 30
785 $4 Bus with wheelchair ramp 1·00 2·50
MS786 82 × 96 mm. $5 Specially designed elevator control panel 4·25 3·00

181 "Olga Picasso in an Armchair" **182** "Gone Fishing"

1981. Birth Centenary of Picasso. Multicoloured.
787 45c. Type **181** 35 15
788 60c. "Bathers" 40 15
789 75c. "Woman in Spanish Costume" 40 25
790 $4 "Detail of Dog and Cock" 1·00 2·25
MS791 140 × 115 mm. $5 "Sleeping Peasants" (detail) 2·50 3·50

1982. World Cup Football Championship, Spain. Walt Disney Cartoon Characters. As T **169**. Mult.
792 ½c. Goofy chasing ball with butterfly net 10 10
793 1c. Donald Duck with ball in beak 10 10
794 2c. Goofy as goalkeeper . . . 10 10
795 3c. Goofy looking for ball . . 10 10
796 4c. Goofy as park attendant puncturing ball with litter spike 10 10
797 5c. Pete and Donald Duck playing 10 10
798 10c. Donald Duck after kicking rock instead of ball 15 10
799 60c. Donald Duck feeling effects of a hard game and Daisy Duck dusting ball 1·50 1·25
800 $5 Goofy hiding ball under his jersey from Mickey Mouse . . . . 5·50 6·50
MS801 132 × 105 mm. $4 Dale making off with ball 4·00 3·25

1982. Norman Rockwell (painter) Commemoration. Multicoloured.
802 10c. Type **182** 10 10
803 25c. "Breakfast" 20 10
804 45c. "The Marbles Champ" 30 30
805 $1 "Speeding Along" 55 65
No. 802 is inscribed "Golden Days" and No. 803 " The Morning News".

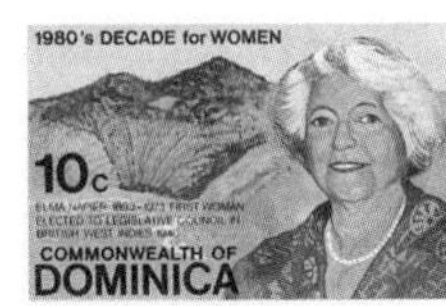

183 Elma Napier (first woman elected to B.W.I. Legislative Council)

1982. Decade for Women. Multicoloured.
806 10c. Type **183** 10 10
807 45c. Margaret Mead (anthropologist) 30 30
808 $1 Mabel (Cissy) Caudeiron (folk song composer and historian) 55 55
809 $4 Eleanor Roosevelt . . . . 2·25 2·25
MS810 92 × 83 mm. $3 Florence Nightingale 2·00 3·00

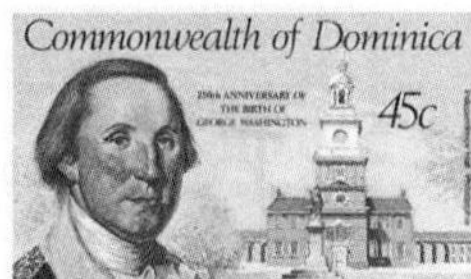

184 George Washington and Independence Hall, Philadelphia

1982. 250th Birth Anniv of George Washington and Birth Centenary of Franklin D. Roosevelt. Multicoloured.
811 45c. Type **184** 25 25
812 60c. Franklin D. Roosevelt and Capitol, Washington D.C. 30 35
813 90c. Washington at Yorktown (detail "The Surrender of Cornwallis" by Trumbull) 40 55
814 $2 Construction of dam (from W. Groppers' mural commemorating Roosevelt's) "New Deal" 70 1·60
MS815 115 × 90 mm. $5 Washington and Roosevelt with U.S.A. flags of 1777 and 1933 2·00 3·25

185 "Anaea dominicana" **186** Prince and Princess of Wales

1982. Butterflies. Multicoloured.
816 15c. Type **185** . . . . 1·50 35
817 45c. "Heliconius charithonia" 2·50 65
818 60c. "Hypolimnas misippus" 2·75 1·75
819 $3 "Biblis hyperia" . . . . . 5·50 6·00
MS820 77 × 105 mm. $5 "Marpesia petreus" 7·00 5·00

1982. 21st Birthday of Princess of Wales. Multicoloured.
821 45c. Buckingham Palace . . . 20 10
822 $2 Type **186** 50 70
823 $4 Princess of Wales . . . . 1·10 1·25
MS824 103 × 75 mm. $5 Princess Diana (different) 2·50 2·25

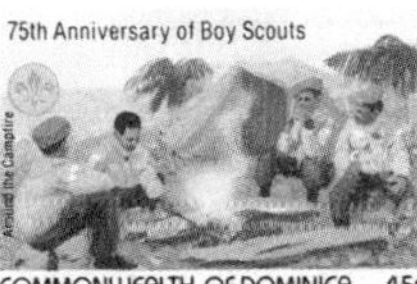

187 Scouts around Campfire

1982. 75th Anniv of Boy Scouts Movement. Mult.
825 45c. Type **187** . . . . 1·25 50
826 60c. Temperature study, Valley of Desolation . . . 1·75 1·25
827 75c. Learning about native birds . . . . 2·25 1·50
828 $3 Canoe trip along Indian River . . . . 4·25 5·50
MS829 99 × 70 mm. Dominican scouts saluting the flag (vert) 1·50 3·25

1982. Birth of Prince William of Wales. Nos. 821/3 optd **ROYAL BABY 21.6.82**.
830 45c. Buckingham Palace . . . 30 30
831 $2 Type **186** . . . . 80 1·10
832 $4 Princess of Wales . . . . 1·40 1·90
MS833 103 × 75 mm. $5 Princess Diana (different) 2·00 2·75

188 "Holy Family of Francis I" **189** Cuvier's Beaked Whale

1982. Christmas. Raphael Paintings. Multicoloured.
834 25c. Type **188** 15 10
835 30c. "Holy Family of the Pearl" 15 10
836 90c. "Canigiani Holy Family" 30 35
837 $4 "Holy Family of the Oak Tree" . . . . 1·25 1·50
MS838 95 × 125 mm. $5 "Holy Family of the Lamp" 1·50 2·00

1983. Save the Whales. Multicoloured.
839 45c. Type **189** . . . . 2·00 65
840 60c. Humpback whale . . . 2·25 1·75
841 75c. Black right whale . . . 2·25 2·25
842 $3 Melon-headed whale . . . 4·50 6·50
MS843 99 × 72 mm. $5 Pygmy sperm whale 4·00 4·00

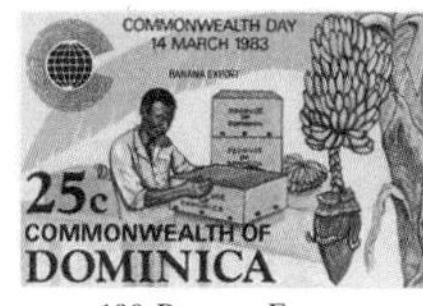

190 Banana Export

1983. Commonwealth Day. Multicoloured.
844 25c. Type **190** 15 15
845 30c. Road building 15 20
846 90c. Community nursing . . 30 45
847 $3 Tourism-handicrafts . . . 75 1·50

191 Map and Satellite Picture of Hurricane

1983. World Communications Year. Multicoloured.
848 45c. Type **191** 20 25
849 60c. Aircraft-to-ship transmission 25 35
850 90c. Satellite communications 30 45
851 $2 Shortwave radio . . . . . 75 1·00
MS852 110 × 85 mm. $5 Communications satellite 1·50 2·75

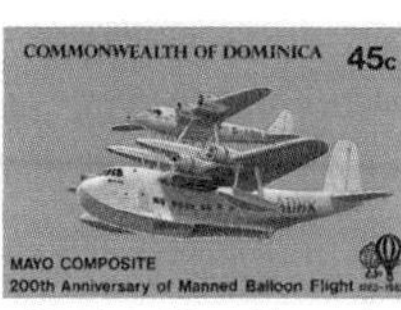

192 Short-Mayo Composite

1983. Bicentenary of Manned Flight. Mult.
853 45c. Type **192** 50 30
854 60c. Macchi M.39 Schneider Trophy seaplane 60 65
855 90c. Fairey Swordfish torpedo bomber . . . . . 70 1·50
856 $4 Airship LZ-3 . . . . . . 1·25 4·75
MS857 105 × 79 mm. $5 "Double Eagle II" (balloon) 1·50 2·75

193 Duesenberg "SJ", 1935

1983. Classic Motor Cars. Multicoloured.
858 10c. Type **193** 25 15
859 45c. Studebaker "Avanti", 1962 . . . . 35 25
860 60c. Cord "812" 40 35
861 75c. MG "TC", 1945 . . . . 45 50
862 90c. Camaro "350 SS", 1967 50 60
863 $3 Porsch "356", 1948 . . . 1·00 1·60
MS864 110 × 75 mm. $5 Ferrari "312 T", 1975 1·50 2·75

194 "Charity"

1983. Christmas. 500th Birth Anniv of Raphael. Multicoloured.
865 45c. Type **194** 30 30
866 60c. "Hope" 30 30
867 90c. "Faith" 40 60
868 $4 "The Cardinal Virtues" 1·00 3·25
MS869 101 × 127 mm. $5 "Justice" 1·25 2·75

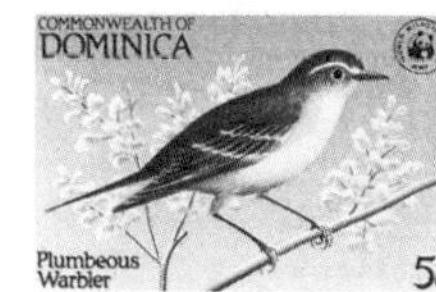

195 Plumbeous Warbler

1984. Birds. Multicoloured.
870 5c. Type **195** . . . . 2·25 1·10
871 45c. Imperial amazon ("Imperial Parrot") . . . . 4·50 75
872 60c. Blue-headed hummingbird . . . . . . 5·00 3·25
873 90c. Red-necked amazon ("Red-necked Parrot") . . 6·00 6·00
MS874 72 × 72 mm. $5 Greater flamingos 4·00 4·50

196 Donald Duck **197** Gymnastics

1984. Easter. Multicoloured.
875 ½c. Type **196** 10 10
876 1c. Mickey Mouse 10 10
877 2c. Tortoise and Hare . . . 10 10
878 3c. Brer Rabbit and Brer Bear 10 10
879 4c. Donald Duck (different) 10 10
880 5c. White Rabbit 10 10
881 10c. Thumper 10 10
882 $2 Pluto . . . . 3·25 2·75
883 $4 Pluto (different) . . . . . 4·50 4·00
MS884 126 × 100 mm. $5 Chip and Dale 3·50 4·00

1984. Olympic Games, Los Angeles. Multicoloured.
885 30c. Type **197** 20 25
886 45c. Javelin-throwing 30 35
887 60c. High diving 40 45
888 $4 Fencing . . . . 2·00 2·50
MS889 104 × 85 mm. $5 Equestrian event 3·25 3·25

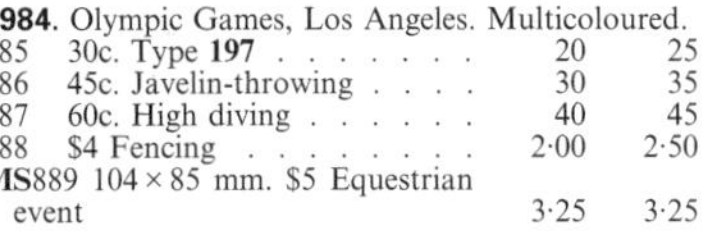

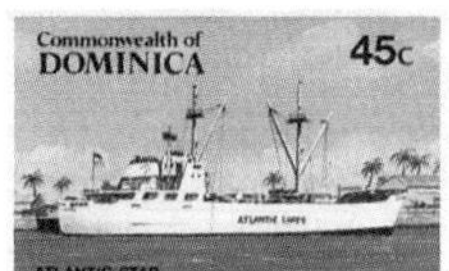

198 "Atlantic Star"

1984. Shipping. Multicoloured.
890 45c. Type **198** . . . . 1·75 75
891 60c. "Atlantic" (liner) . . . . 2·00 1·25
892 90c. Carib fishing boat . . . 2·50 2·50
893 $4 "Norway" (liner) . . . . 6·00 8·50
MS894 106 × 79 mm. $5 "Santa Maria", 1492 3·75 5·50

1984. U.P.U. Congress, Hamburg. Nos. 769 and 780 optd **19th UPU CONGRESS HAMBURG**.
895 10c. Passion fruit 10 10
896 $5 Heliconia or lobster claw 2·75 3·75

200 "Guzmania lingulata"
201 "The Virgin and Child with Young St. John" (Correggio)

1984. "Ausipex" International Stamp Exhibition, Melbourne. Bromeliads. Multicoloured.
897 45c. Type **200** 30 35
898 60c. "Pitcairnia angustifolia" 40 55
899 75c. "Tillandsia fasciculata" 50 75
900 $3 "Aechmea smithiorum" 2·00 3·25
MS901 75 × 105 mm. $5 "Tillandsia utriculata" 2·75 4·25

1984. 450th Death Anniv of Correggio (painter). Multicoloured.
902 25c. Type **201** 30 20
903 60c. "Christ bids Farewell to the Virgin Mary" 40 40
904 90c. "Do not Touch Me" . . 50 80
905 $4 "The Mystical Marriage of St Catherine" . . . . . 80 3·25
MS906 89 × 60 mm. $5 "The Adoration of the Magi" 1·75 3·50

202 "Before the Start" (Edgar Degas)

1984. 150th Birth Anniv of Edgar Degas (painter). Multicoloured.
907 30c. Type **202** 30 25
908 45c. "Race on the Racecourse" 35 35
909 $1 "Jockeys at the Flagpole" 55 1·10
910 $3 "Racehorses at Longchamp" . . . . . . 80 3·50
MS911 89 × 60 mm. $5 "Self-portrait" (vert) 2·00 3·75

203 Tabby

1984. Cats. Multicoloured.
912 10c. Type **203** 20 15
913 15c. Calico shorthair 25 15
914 20c. Siamese 35 15
915 25c. Manx 40 20
916 45c. Abyssinian 65 30
917 60c. Tortoise-shell longhair 70 65
918 $1 Cornish rex . . . . 80 1·00
919 $2 Persian . . . . 1·00 3·00
920 $3 Himalayan . . . . 1·25 4·00
921 $5 Burmese . . . . 1·50 7·00
MS922 105 × 75 mm. $5 Grey Burmese, Persian and American shorthair 3·50 7·00

204 Hawker Siddeley H.S.748
205 Donald Duck, Mickey Mouse and Goofy with Father Christmas

1984. 40th Anniv of International Civil Aviation Organisation. Multicoloured.
923 30c. Type **204** . . . . 1·00 50
924 60c. De Havilland Twin Otter 100 . . . . 1·75 50
925 $1 Britten Norman Islander 2·00 1·60
926 $3 De Havilland Twin Otter 100 (different) . . . . . . 3·00 6·00
MS927 102 × 75 mm. $5 Boeing 747-200 2·50 3·50

1984. Christmas. Walt Disney Cartoon Characters. Multicoloured.
928 45c. Type **205** . . . . 1·25 30
929 60c. Donald Duck as Father Christmas with toy train 1·50 70
930 90c. Donald Duck as Father Christmas in sleigh . . . . 2·00 1·75
931 $2 Donald Duck and nephews in sledge . . . . 3·25 3·75
932 $4 Donald Duck in snow with Christmas tree . . . . 4·25 5·50
MS933 127 × 102 mm. $5 Donald Duck and nephews opening present 3·50 4·00

206 Mrs. M. Bascom presenting Trefoil to Chief Guide Lady Baden-Powell

1985. 75th Anniv of Girl Guide Movement. Mult.
934 35c. Type **206** 60 30
935 45c. Lady Baden-Powell inspecting Dominican brownies 80 35
936 60c. Lady Baden-Powell with Mrs. M. Bascom and Mrs. A. Robinson (guide leaders) . . . . 1·00 65
937 $3 Lord and Lady Baden-Powell (vert) . . . . 2·50 3·50
MS938 77 × 105 mm. $5 Flags of Dominica and Girl Guide Movement 3·50 4·00

1985. Birth Bicentenary of John J Audubon (ornithologist) (1st issue). As T **198** of Antigua. Multicoloured.
939 45c. Clapper rail ("King Rail") . . . . 1·10 30
940 $1 Black and white warbler (vert) . . . . 2·00 1·25
941 $2 Broad-winged hawk (vert) 2·75 2·75
942 $3 Ring-necked duck . . . . 3·50 3·25
MS943 101 × 73 mm. $5 Reddish egret 3·50 3·75
See also Nos. 1013/16.

207 Student with Computer
208 The Queen Mother visiting Sadlers Wells Opera

1985. Duke of Edinburgh's Award Scheme. Multicoloured.
944 45c. Type **207** 40 30
945 60c. Assisting doctor in hospital . . . . 1·50 40
946 90c. Two youths hiking . . . 1·60 80
947 $4 Family jogging . . . . . 3·25 5·50
MS948 100 × 98 mm. $5 Duke of Edinburgh 2·75 3·00

1985. Life and Times of Queen Elizabeth the Queen Mother. Multicoloured.
949 60c. Type **208** . . . . 1·50 50
950 $1 Fishing in Scotland . . . 1·50 60
951 $3 On her 84th birthday . . 2·25 3·00
MS952 56 × 85 mm. $5 Attending Garter ceremony, Windsor Castle 3·25 3·00

209 Cricket Match ("Sports")

1985. International Youth Year. Multicoloured.
953 45c. Type **209** . . . . 3·50 1·50
954 60c. Bird-watching ("Environmental Study") 3·75 2·25
955 $1 Stamp collecting ("Education") . . . . . . 4·00 3·25
956 $3 Boating ("Leisure") . . . 5·50 7·50
MS957 96 × 65 mm. $5 Young people linking hands 2·75 4·00

1985. 300th Birth Anniv of Johann Sebastian Bach (composer). As T **206** of Antigua. Antique musical instruments.
958 45c. multicoloured . . . . . 1·50 40
959 60c. multicoloured . . . . . 1·75 60
960 $1 multicoloured . . . . . . 2·25 1·00
961 $3 multicoloured . . . . . . 4·00 3·50
MS962 199 × 75 mm. $5 black 3·00 4·50
DESIGNS: 45c. Cornett; 60c. Coiled trumpet; $1 Piccolo; $3 Violoncello piccolo; $5 Johann Sebastian Bach.

1985. Royal Visit. As T **207** of Antigua. Mult.
963 60c. Flags of Great Britain and Dominica 75 50
964 $1 Queen Elizabeth II (vert) 75 1·25
965 $4 Royal Yacht "Britannia" 1·75 5·50
MS966 111 × 83 mm. $5 Map of Dominica 3·50 4·00

1985. 150th Birth Anniv of Mark Twain (author). As T **118** of Anguilla showing Walt Disney cartoon characters in scenes from "Tom Sawyer". Multicoloured.
967 20c. "The glorius white-washer" 75 30
968 60c. "Aunt Polly's home dentistry" . . . . 1·50 75
969 $1 "Aunt Polly's pain killer" 2·00 1·25
970 $1.50 Mickey Mouse balancing on fence . . . . 2·50 3·00
971 $2 "Lost in the cave with Becky" . . . . 2·75 3·50
MS972 126 × 101 mm. $5 Mickey Mouse as pirate 5·50 7·00

1985. Birth Bicentenaries of Grimm Brothers (folklorists). Designs as T **119** of Anguilla showing Walt Disney cartoon characters in scenes from "Little Red Cap". Multicoloured.
973 10c. Little Red Cap (Daisy Duck) meeting the Wolf . . 30 20
974 45c. The Wolf at the door . . 85 30
975 90c. The Wolf in Grandmother's bed . . . . 1·75 1·75
976 $1 The Wolf lunging at Little Red Cap . . . . 2·00 1·75
977 $3 The Woodsman (Donald Duck) chasing the Wolf . . 3·75 5·00
MS978 126 × 101 mm. $5 The Wolf falling into cooking pot 5·00 5·50

1985. 40th Anniv of United Nations Organization. Designs as T **208** of Antigua showing United Nations (New York) stamps. Multicoloured.
979 45c. Lord Baden-Powell and 1984 International Youth Year 35c. 70 50
980 $2 Maimonides (physician) and 1966 W.H.O. Building 11c. . . . . 1·50 3·25
981 $3 Sir Rowland Hill (postal reformer) and 1976 25th anniv of U.N. Postal Administration 13c. . . . 1·50 3·50
MS982 110 × 85 mm. $5 "Apollo" spacecraft 2·75 3·25

210 Two Players competing for Ball

1986. World Cup Football Championship, Mexico. Multicoloured.
983 45c. Type **210** . . . . 1·75 40
984 60c. Player heading ball . . . 2·00 1·50
985 $1 Two players competing for ball (different) . . . . . . 2·25 1·75
986 $3 Player with ball . . . . . 4·50 6·00
MS987 114 × 84 mm. $5 Three players 8·00 10·00

211 Police in Rowing Boat pursuing River Pirates, 1890

1986. Centenary of Statue of Liberty. Mult.
988 15c. Type **211** . . . . 2·50 65
989 25c. Police patrol launch, 1986 . . . . 2·50 85
990 45c. Hoboken Ferry Terminal c. 1890 . . . . . 2·25 85
991 $4 Holland Tunnel entrance and staff, 1986 . . . . . 4·75 6·50
MS992 104 × 76 mm. $5 Statue of Liberty (vert) 4·00 5·00

1986. Appearance of Halley's Comet (1st issue). As T **123** of Anguilla. Multicoloured.
993 5c. Nasir al Din al Tusi (Persian astronomer) and Jantal Mantar Observatory, Delhi 30 30
994 10c. Bell XS-1 Rocket Plane breaking sound barrier for first time, 1947 . . . . . . 35 30
995 45c. Halley's Comet of 1531 (from "Astronomicum Caesareum", 1540) 80 30
996 $4 Mark Twain and quotation, 1910 . . . . . 3·50 4·00
MS997 104 × 71 mm. $5 Halley's Comet over Dominica 3·00 3·50
See also Nos. 1032/6.

1986. 60th Birthday of Queen Elizabeth II. As T **125** of Anguilla.
998 2c. multicoloured 10 15
999 $1 multicoloured 70 80
1000 $4 multicoloured . . . . . 2·00 3·00
MS1001 120 × 85 mm. $5 black and brown 3·50 4·00
DESIGNS: 2c. Wedding photograph, 1947; $1 Queen meeting Pope John Paul II, 1982; $4 Queen on royal visit, 1982; $5 Princess Elizabeth with corgis, 1936.

212 Mickey Mouse and Pluto mounting Stamps in Album

1986. "Ameripex" International Stamp Exhibition, Chicago. Showing Walt Disney cartoon characters. Multicoloured.
1002 25c. Type **212** 60 40
1003 45c. Donald Duck examining stamp under magnifying glass 80 65
1004 60c. Chip n' Dale soaking and drying stamps . . . . 1·10 1·50
1005 $4 Donald Duck as scoutmaster awarding merit badges to Nephews 3·50 6·00
MS1006 127 × 101 mm. $5 Uncle Scrooge conducting stamp auction 4·00 8·00

213 William I
214 "Virgin at Prayer"

1986. 500th Anniv (1985) of Succession of House of Tudor to English Throne. Multicoloured.
1007 10c. Type **213** 40 40
1008 40c. Richard II 80 80
1009 50c. Henry VIII 90 90
1010 $1 Charles II . . . . 1·00 1·75
1011 $2 Queen Anne . . . . . . 1·50 3·00
1012 $4 Queen Victoria . . . . . 2·00 4·50

1986. Birth Bicentenary (1985) of John J. Audubon (ornithologist) (2nd issue). As T **198** of Antigua showing original paintings. Multicoloured.
1013 25c. Black-throated diver . . 1·50 50
1014 60c. Great blue heron (vert) 2·00 1·50
1015 90c. Yellow-crowned night heron (vert) . . . . . . 2·00 2·25
1016 $4 Common shoveler ("Shoveler Duck") . . . 4·50 6·50
MS1017 73 × 103 mm. $5 Canada goose ("Goose") 10·00 12·00

1986. Royal Wedding. As T **213** of Antigua. Multicoloured.
1018 45c. Prince Andrew and Miss Sarah Ferguson . . 35 30
1019 50c. Prince Andrew 45 45
1020 $4 Prince Andrew climbing aboard aircraft . . . . . 2·00 3·00
MS1021 88 × 88 mm. $5 Prince Andrew and Miss Sarah Ferguson (different) 4·00 4·75

1986. World Cup Football Championship Winners, Mexico. Nos. 983/6 optd **WINNERS Argentina 3 W. Germany 2**.
1022 45c. Type **210** . . . . . 1·50 55
1023 60c. Player heading ball . . 1·75 1·50
1024 $1 Two players competing for ball . . . . 2·25 2·50
1025 $3 Player with ball . . . . 5·00 7·00
MS1026 114 × 84 mm. $5 Three players 8·50 11·00

1986. Christmas. Paintings by Durer. Multicoloured.
1027 45c. Type **214** . . . . . . 1·00 35
1028 60c. "Madonna and Child" 1·50 1·25

1029 $1 "Madonna of the Pear" 2·00 2·25
1030 $3 "Madonna and Child with St. Anne" 5·50 8·50
MS1031 76×102 mm. $5 "The Nativity" 8·00 11·00

1986. Appearance of Halley's Comet (2nd issue). Nos. 993/6 optd as T **218** of Antigua.
1032 5c. Nasir al Din al Tusi (Persian astronomer) and Jantal Mantar Observatory, Delhi 15 15
1033 10c. Bell XS-1 Rocket Plane breaking sound barrier for first time, 1947 20 15
1034 45c. Halley's Comet of 1531 (from "Astronomicum Caesareum", 1540) 55 30
1035 $4 Mark Twain and quotation, 1910 2·50 3·50
MS1036 104×71 mm. $5 Halley's Comet over Dominica 3·25 3·50

215 Broad-winged Hawk

216 Poulsen's Triton

1987. Birds of Dominica. Multicoloured.
1037 1c. Type **215** 20 60
1038 2c. Ruddy quail dove 20 60
1039 5c. Red-necked pigeon 30 60
1040 10c. Green-backed heron ("Green Heron") 30 20
1041 15c. Moorhen ("Common Gallinule") 40 20
1042 20c. Ringed kingfisher 40 20
1043 25c. Brown pelican 40 20
1044 35c. White-tailed tropic bird 40 30
1045 45c. Red-legged thrush 50 30
1046 60c. Purple-throated carib 65 45
1047 90c. Magnificent frigate bird 70 70
1048 $1 Brown trembler ("Trembler") 80 80
1049 $2 Black-capped petrel 1·25 4·25
1050 $5 Barn owl 3·00 6·00
1051 $10 Imperial amazon ("Imperial Parrot") 5·00 11·00

1987. America's Cup Yachting Championships. As T **222** of Antigua. Multicoloured.
1052 45c. "Reliance", 1903 60 30
1053 60c. "Freedom", 1980 70 55
1054 $1 "Mischief", 1881 80 90
1055 $3 "Australia", 1977 1·25 3·00
MS1056 113×83 mm. $5 "Courageous", 1977 (horiz) 3·00 3·50

1987. Birth Centenary of Marc Chagall (artist). As T **225** of Antigua. Multicoloured.
1057 25c. "Artist and His Model" 30 20
1058 35c. "Midsummer Night's Dream" 35 20
1059 45c. "Joseph the Shepherd" 40 25
1060 60c. "The Cellist" 45 30
1061 90c. "Woman with Pigs" 60 45
1062 $1 "The Blue Circus" 65 50
1063 $3 "For Vava" 1·25 1·60
1064 $4 "The Rider" 1·50 1·60
MS1065 Two sheets, each 110×95 mm. (a) $5 "Purim" (104×89 mm). (b) $5 "Firebird" (stage design) (104×89 mm) Set of 2 sheets 3·75 5·00

1987. Sea Shells.
1066 **216** 35c. multicoloured 20 20
1067 – 45c. violet, black and red 25 25
1068 – 60c. multicoloured 30 40
1069 – $5 multicoloured 2·40 4·25
MS1070 109×75 mm. $5 multicoloured 3·25 5·50
DESIGNS—VERT: 45c. Elongate janthina; 60c. Banded tulip; $5 Deltoid rock shell. HORIZ: $5 (MS1070) Junonia volute.
No. 1066 is inscribed "TIRITON" in error.

217 "Cantharellus cinnabarinus"

1987. "Capex '87" International Stamp Exhibition, Toronto. Mushrooms of Dominica. Multicoloured.
1071 45c. Type **217** 1·50 50
1072 60c. "Boletellus cubensis" 2·00 1·25
1073 $2 "Eccilia cystiophorus" 4·25 4·50
1074 $3 "Xerocomus guadelupae" 4·50 5·00
MS1075 85×85 mm. $5 "Gymnopilus chrysopellus" 10·00 11·00

218 Discovery of Dominica, 1493

1987. 500th Anniv (1992) of Discovery of America by Columbus (1st issue). Multicoloured.
1076 10c. Type **218** 40 25
1077 15c. Caribs greeting Columbus's fleet 50 30
1078 45c. Claiming the New World for Spain 65 35
1079 60c. Wreck of "Santa Maria" 80 60
1080 90c. Fleet leaving Spain 1·00 1·00
1081 $1 Sighting the New World 1·10 1·25
1082 $3 Trading with Indians 2·25 3·00
1083 $5 Building settlement 3·25 4·00
MS1084 Two sheets, each 109×79 mm. (a) $5 Fleet off Dominica, 1493. (b) $5 Map showing Columbus's route, 1493 Set of 2 sheets 7·00 9·00
See also Nos. 1221/5, 1355/63, 1406/14, 1547/53 and 1612/13.

1987. Milestones of Transportation. As T **226** of Antigua. Multicoloured.
1085 10c. H.M.S. "Warrior" (first ironclad warship, 1860) 50 50
1086 15c. "MAGLEV-MLU 001" (fastest train), 1979 60 60
1087 25c. "Flying Cloud" (fastest clipper passage New York–San Francisco) (vert) 70 70
1088 35c. First elevated railway, New York, 1868 (vert) 80 80
1089 45c. Peter Cooper's locomotive "Tom Thumb" (first U.S. passenger locomotive), 1829 80 80
1090 60c. "Spray" (Slocum's solo, circumnavigation), 1895–98 (vert) 90 90
1091 90c. "Sea-Land Commerce" (fastest Pacific passage), 1973 (vert) 1·25 1·25
1092 $1 First cable cars, San Francisco, 1873 1·40 1·40
1093 $3 "Orient Express", 1883 3·00 3·50
1094 $4 "Clermont" (first commercial paddle-steamer), 1807 3·25 3·75

219 "Virgin and Child with St. Anne" (Durer)

220 Three Little Pigs in People Mover, Walt Disney World

1987. Christmas. Religious Paintings. Mult.
1095 20c. Type **219** 30 15
1096 25c. "Virgin and Child" (Murillo) 30 15
1097 $2 "Madonna and Child" (Foppa) 1·50 2·25
1098 $4 "Madonna and Child" (Da Verona) 2·75 4·25
MS1099 100×78 mm. $5 "Angel of the Annunciation" (anon, Renaissance period) 2·50 3·75

1987. 60th Anniv of Mickey Mouse (Walt Disney cartoon character). Cartoon characters in trains. Multicoloured.
1100 20c. Type **220** 45 35
1101 25c. Goofy driving horse tram, Disneyland 45 35
1102 45c. Donald Duck in "Roger E. Broggie", Walt Disney World 75 65
1103 60c. Goofy, Mickey Mouse, Donald Duck and Chip 'n Dale aboard "Big Thunder Mountain" train, Disneyland 85 75
1104 90c. Mickey Mouse in "Walter E. Disney", Disneyland 1·40 1·25
1105 $1 Mickey and Minnie Mouse, Goofy, Donald and Daisy Duck in monorail, Walt Disney World 1·50 1·40
1106 $3 Dumbo flying over "Casey Jr" 3·25 3·75
1107 $4 Daisy Duck and Minnie Mouse in "Lilly Belle", Walt Disney World 3·75 4·50
MS1108 Two sheets, each 127×101 mm. (a) $5 Seven Dwarfs in Rainbow Caverns Mine train, Disneyland (horiz). (b) $5 Donald Duck and Chip n'Dale on toy train (from film "Out of Scale") (horiz) Set of 2 sheets 5·50 7·00

1988. Royal Ruby Wedding. As T **234** of Antigua.
1109 45c. multicoloured 70 30
1110 60c. brown, black and green 80 50
1111 $1 multicoloured 1·00 1·00
1112 $3 multicoloured 2·00 3·75
MS1113 102×76 mm. $5 multicoloured 3·00 3·75
DESIGNS: 45c. Wedding portrait with attendants, 1947; 60c. Princess Elizabeth with Prince Charles, c. 1950; $1 Princess Elizabeth and Prince Philip with Prince Charles and Princess Anne, 1950; $3 Queen Elizabeth; $5 Princess Elizabeth in wedding dress, 1947.

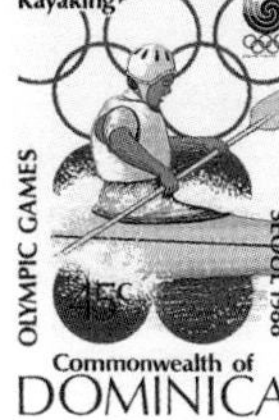

221 Kayak Canoeing

222 Carib Indian

1988. Olympic Games, Seoul. Multicoloured.
1114 45c. Type **221** 60 25
1115 60c. Taekwon-do 80 60
1116 $1 High diving 85 1·00
1117 $3 Gymnastics on bars 1·75 3·75
MS1118 81×110 mm. $5 Football 2·50 3·50

1988. "Reunion '88" Tourism Programme. Mult.
1119 10c. Type **222** 10 10
1120 25c. Mountainous interior (horiz) 10 15
1121 35c. Indian River 10 15
1122 60c. Belaire dancer and tourists 15 30
1123 90c. Boiling Lake 20 60
1124 $3 Coral reef (horiz) 60 2·00
MS1125 112×82 mm. $5 Belaire dancer 1·75 2·00

1988. Stamp Exhibitions. Nos. 1092/3 optd.
1126 $1 First cable cars, San Francisco, 1873 (optd **FINLANDIA 88**, Helsinki) 1·00 75
1127 $3 "Orient Express", 1883 (optd **INDEPENDENCE 40**, Israel) 2·75 2·75
MS1128 Two sheets, each 109×79 mm. (a) $5 Fleet off Dominica, 1493 (optd **OLYMPHILEX '88, Seoul**). (b) $5 Map showing Columbus's route, 1493 (optd **Praga '88, Prague**) Set of 2 sheets 4·25 5·50

223 White-tailed Tropic Bird

225 Gary Cooper

224 Battery Hens

1988. Dominica Rain Forest Flora and Fauna. Multicoloured.
1129 45c. Type **223** 50 50
1130 45c. Blue-hooded euphonia ("Blue-throated Euphonia") 50 50
1131 45c. Smooth-billed ani 50 50
1132 45c. Scaly-breasted thrasher 50 50
1133 45c. Purple-throated carib 50 50
1134 45c. "Marpesia petreus" and "Strymon maesites" (butterflies) 50 50
1135 45c. Brown trembler ("Trembler") 50 50
1136 45c. Imperial amazon ("Imperial Parrot") 50 50
1137 45c. Mangrove cuckoo 50 50
1138 45c. "Dynastes hercules" (beetle) 50 50
1139 45c. "Historis odius" (butterfly) 50 50
1140 45c. Red-necked amazon ("Red-necked Parrot") 50 50
1141 45c. Tillandsia (plant) 50 50
1142 45c. Bananaquit and "Polystacha luteola" (plant) 50 50
1143 45c. False chameleon 50 50
1144 45c. Iguana 50 50
1145 45c. "Hypolimnas misippus" (butterfly) 50 50
1146 45c. Green-throated carib 50 50
1147 45c. Heliconia (plant) 50 50
1148 45c. Agouti 50 50
Nos. 1129/48 were printed together, se-tenant, forming a composite design.

1988. 10th Anniv of International Fund for Agricultural Development. Multicoloured.
1149 45c. Type **224** 50 30
1150 60c. Pig 70 65
1151 90c. Cattle 95 1·25
1152 $3 Black belly sheep 2·25 4·00
MS1153 95×68 mm. $5 Tropical fruits (vert) 2·25 3·50

1988. Entertainers. Multicoloured.
1154 10c. Type **225** 25 25
1155 35c. Josephine Baker 30 25
1156 45c. Maurice Chevalier 35 25
1157 60c. James Cagney 45 30
1158 $1 Clark Gable 65 50
1159 $2 Louis Armstrong 1·25 1·00
1160 $3 Liberace 1·50 1·75
1161 $4 Spencer Tracy 2·00 2·25
MS1162 Two sheets, each 105×75 mm. (a) $5 Humphrey Bogart. (b) $5 Elvis Presley Set of 2 sheets 7·00 6·00

1988. Flowering Trees. As T **242** of Antigua. Multicoloured.
1163 15c. Sapodilla 10 10
1164 20c. Tangerine 10 10
1165 25c. Avocado pear 10 10
1166 45c. Amherstia 20 25
1167 90c. Lipstick tree 40 55
1168 $1 Cannonball tree 45 55
1169 $3 Saman 1·25 1·75
1170 $4 Pineapple 1·60 2·00
MS1171 Two sheets, each 96×66 mm. (a) $5 Lignum vitae. (b) $5 Sea grape Set of 2 sheets 4·50 6·00

1988. 500th Birth Anniv of Titian (artist). As T **238** of Antigua. Multicoloured.
1172 25c. "Jacopo Strada" 15 15
1173 35c. "Titian's Daughter Lavinia" 20 15
1174 45c. "Andrea Navagero" 20 15
1175 60c. "Judith with Head of Holoferenes" 25 15
1176 $1 "Emilia di Spilimbergo" 40 50
1177 $2 "Martyrdom of St. Lawrence" 70 1·25
1178 $3 "Salome" 1·00 2·00
1179 $4 "St. John the Baptist" 1·25 2·25
MS1180 Two sheets, each 110×95 mm. (a) $5 "Self Portrait". (b) $5 "Sisyphus" Set of 2 sheets 5·00 6·50

226 Imperial Amazon

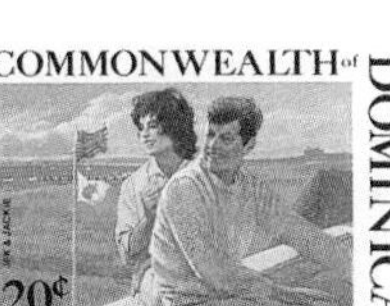

227 President and Mrs. Kennedy

1988. 10th Anniv of Independence. Multicoloured.
1181 20c. Type **226** 1·50 40
1182 45c. Dominica 1874 1d. stamp and landscape (horiz) 90 30
1183 $2 1978 Independence 10c. stamp and landscape (horiz) 1·50 2·75
1184 $3 Carib wood (national flower) 1·75 3·25
MS1185 116×85 mm. $5 Government Band (horiz) 2·25 3·50

1988. 25th Death Anniv of John F. Kennedy (American statesman). Multicoloured.
1186 20c. Type **227** 10 10
1187 25c. Kennedy sailing 10 10
1188 $2 Outside Hyannis Port house 80 1·50
1189 $4 Speaking in Berlin (vert) 1·60 2·50
MS1190 100×71 mm. $5 President Kennedy (vert) 2·10 3·50

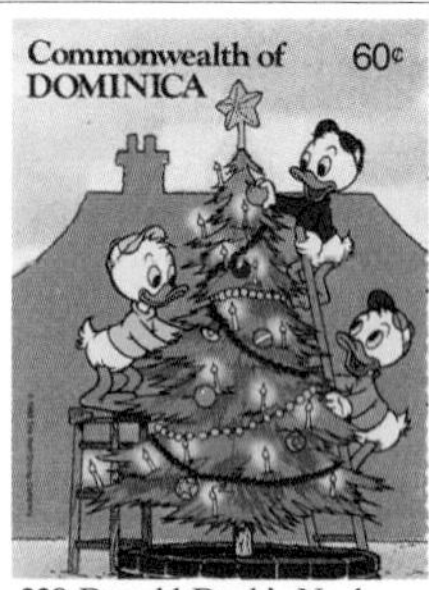

228 Donald Duck's Nephews decorating Christmas Tree

1988. Christmas. "Mickey's Christmas Mall". Walt Disney Cartoon Characters. Multicoloured.
1191 60c. Type **228** 55 65
1192 60c. Daisy Duck outside clothes shop 55 65
1193 60c. Winnie the Pooh in shop window 55 65
1194 60c. Goofy with parcels . . 55 65
1195 60c. Donald Duck as Father Christmas 55 65
1196 60c. Mickey Mouse contributing to collection 55 65
1197 60c. Minnie Mouse 55 65
1198 60c. Chip n' Dale with peanut 55 65
MS1199 Two sheets, each 127 × 102 mm. (a) $6 Mordie Mouse with Father Christmas. (b) $6 Mickey Mouse at West Indian market Set of 2 sheets 6·50 8·00
Nos. 1191/8 were printed together, se-tenant, forming a composite design.

229 Raoul Wallenberg (diplomat) and Swedish Flag

1988. 40th Anniv of Universal Declaration of Human Rights. Multicoloured.
1200 $3 Type **229** . . . . 2·00 2·50
MS1201 92 × 62 mm. $5 Human Rights Day logo (vert) 2·75 3·25

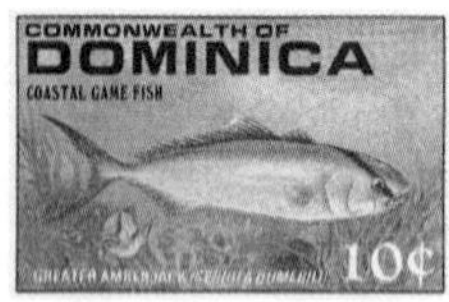

230 Greater Amberjack

1988. Game Fishes. Multicoloured.
1202 10c. Type **230** 20 15
1203 15c. Blue marlin 20 15
1204 35c. Cobia 35 30
1205 45c. Dolphin (fish) 45 30
1206 60c. Cero 60 55
1207 90c. Mahogany snapper . . 85 95
1208 $3 Yellow-finned tuna . . . 2·50 3·25
1209 $4 Rainbow parrotfish . . . 3·00 3·75
MS1210 Two sheets, each 104 × 74 mm. (a) $5 Manta. (b) $5 Tarpon Set of 2 sheets 9·00 10·00

231 Leatherback Turtle

1988. Insects and Reptiles. Multicoloured.
1211 10c. Type **231** 45 35
1212 25c. "Danaus plexippus" (butterfly) . . . . 1·25 75
1213 60c. Green anole (lizard) . . 1·60 1·25
1214 $3 "Mantis religiosa" (mantid) . . . . 4·00 6·50
MS1215 119 × 90 mm. $5 "Dynastes hercules" (beetle) 3·00 4·50

1989. Olympic Medal Winners, Seoul. Nos. 1114/17 optd.
1216 45c. Type 221 (optd **Men's C-1, 500m O. Heukrodt DDR**) 20 25
1217 60c. Taekwon-do (optd **Women's Flyweight N. Y. Choo S. Korea**) 25 35
1218 $1 High diving (optd **Women's Platform Y. Xu China**) 40 60
1219 $3 Gymnastics on bars (optd **V. Artemov USSR**) 1·25 2·25
MS1220 81 × 110 mm. $5 Football (optd **USSR defeated Brazil 3–2 on penalty kicks after a 1–1 tie**) 3·50 4·00

1989. 500th Anniv (1992) of Discovery of America by Columbus (2nd issue). Pre-Columbian Carib Society. As T **247** of Antigua but horiz. Mult.
1221 20c. Carib canoe 20 20
1222 35c. Hunting with bows and arrows 30 20
1223 $1 Dugout canoe making . . 70 90
1224 $3 Shield contest . . . . . 1·75 3·00
MS1225 87 × 71 mm. $6 Ceremonial dress 2·75 4·00

233 Map of Dominica, 1766

235 "Oncidium pusillum"

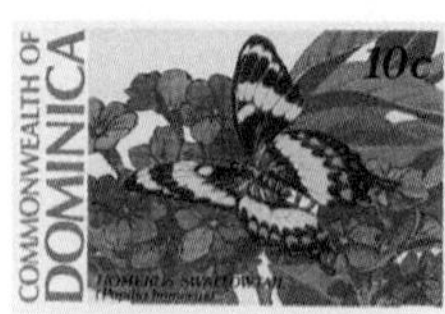

234 "Papilio homerus"

1989. "Philexfrance '89" International Stamp Exhibition, Paris. Multicoloured.
1226 10c. Type **233** 45 30
1227 35c. French coin of 1653 (horiz) 65 40
1228 $1 French warship, 1720 (horiz) . . . . 1·40 1·25
1229 $4 Coffee plant (horiz) . . . 2·00 3·25
MS1230 98 × 98 mm. $5 Exhibition inscription (horiz) (black, grey and yellow) 3·00 4·00

1989. Japanese Art. Paintings by Taikan. As T **250** of Antigua but vert. Multicoloured.
1231 10c. "Lao-tzu" (detail) . . . 10 10
1232 20c. "Red Maple Leaves" (panels 1 and 2) 10 10
1233 45c. "King Wen Hui learns a Lesson from his Cook" (detail) 20 25
1234 60c. "Red Maple Leaves" (panels 3 and 4) 25 35
1235 $1 "Wild Flowers" (detail) 45 50
1236 $2 "Red Maple Leaves" (panels 5 and 6) . . . . . 85 1·10
1237 $3 "Red Maple Leaves" (panels 7 and 8) . . . . . 1·00 1·60
1238 $4 "Indian Ceremony of Floating Lamps on the River" (detail) . . . . . 1·25 2·00
MS1239 Two sheets. (a) 78 × 102 mm. $5 "Innocence" (detail). (b) 101 × 77 mm. $5 "Red Maple Leaves" (detail) Set of 2 sheets 4·75 5·75

1989. Butterflies. Multicoloured.
1255 10c. Type **234** 40 30
1256 15c. "Morpho peleides" . . 45 30
1257 25c. "Dryas julia" 65 30
1258 35c. "Parides gundlachianus" 70 30
1259 60c. "Danaus plexippus" . . 1·00 75
1260 $1 "Agraulis vanillae" . . . 1·25 1·25
1261 $3 "Phoebis avellaneda" . . 2·75 3·25
1262 $5 "Papilio andraemon" . . 3·75 5·00
MS1263 Two sheets. (a) 105 × 74 mm. $6 "Adelpha cytherea". (b) 105 × 79 mm. $6 "Adelpha iphicala" Set of 2 sheets 8·00 9·00

1989. Orchids. Multicoloured.
1264 10c. Type **235** 35 30
1265 35c. "Epidendrum cochleata" 70 30
1266 45c. "Epidendrum ciliare" 75 40
1267 60c. "Cyrtopodium andersonii" . . . . 1·00 80
1268 $1 "Habenaria pauciflora" 1·25 1·25
1269 $2 "Maxillaria alba" . . . 2·00 2·25
1270 $3 "Selenipedium palmifolium" . . . . 2·50 2·75
1271 $4 "Brassavola cucullata" 3·25 3·75
MS1272 Two sheets, each 108 × 77 mm. (a) $5 "Oncidium lanceanum". (b) $5 "Comparettia falcata" Set of 2 sheets 8·00 9·00

236 "Apollo 11" Command Module in Lunar Orbit

1989. 20th Anniv of First Manned Landing on Moon. Multicoloured.
1273 10c. Type **236** 30 30
1274 60c. Neil Armstrong leaving lunar module 70 70
1275 $2 Edwin Aldrin at Sea of Tranquility . . . . 1·60 2·00
1276 $3 Astronauts Armstrong and Aldrin with U.S. flag 2·00 2·50
MS1277 62 × 77 mm. $6 Launch of "Apollo 11" (vert) 4·50 6·00

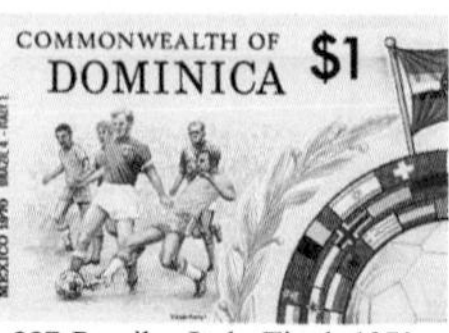

237 Brazil v Italy Final, 1970

1989. World Cup Football Championship, Italy (1st issue). Multicoloured.
1278 $1 Type **237** . . . . 1·75 2·00
1279 $1 England v West Germany, 1966 . . . . . 1·75 2·00
1280 $1 West Germany v Holland, 1974 . . . . . 1·75 2·00
1281 $1 Italy v West Germany, 1982 . . . . 1·75 2·00
MS1282 106 × 86 mm. $6 Two players competing for ball 4·00 4·75
Nos. 1278/81 were printed together, se-tenant, forming a composite central design of a football surrounded by flags of competing nations.
See also Nos. 1383/7.

238 George Washington and Inauguration, 1789

1989. "World Stamp Expo '89" International Stamp Exhibition, Washington. Bicentenary of U.S. Presidency. Multicoloured.
1283 60c. Type **238** 80 80
1284 60c. John Adams and Presidential Mansion, 1800 . . . . 80 80
1285 60c. Thomas Jefferson, Graff House, Philadelphia and Declaration of Independence 80 80
1286 60c. James Madison and U.S.S. "Constitution" defeating H.M.S. "Guerriere", 1812 . . . . 80 80
1287 60c. James Monroe and freed slaves landing in Liberia 80 80
1288 60c. John Quincy Adams and barge on Erie Canal 80 80
1289 60c. Millard Fillmore and Perry's fleet off Japan . . 80 80
1290 60c. Franklin Pierce, Jefferson Davis and San Xavier Mission, Tucson 80 80
1291 60c. James Buchanan, "Buffalo Bill" Cody carrying mail and Wells Fargo Pony Express stamp 80 80
1292 60c. Abraham Lincoln and U.P.U. Monument, Berne 80 80
1293 60c. Andrew Johnson, polar bear and Mount McKinley, Alaska 80 80
1294 60c. Ulysses S. Grant and Golden Spike Ceremony, 1869 . . . . 80 80
1295 60c. Theodore Roosevelt and steam shovel excavating Panama Canal 80 80
1296 60c. William H. Taft and Admiral Peary at North Pole 80 80
1297 60c. Woodrow Wilson and Curtis "Jenny" on first scheduled airmail flight, 1918 . . . . 80 80
1298 60c. Warren G. Harding and airship U.S.S. "Shenandoah" at Lakehurst 80 80
1299 60c. Calvin Coolidge and Lindbergh's "Spirit of St Louis" on trans-Atlantic flight 80 80
1300 60c. Mount Rushmore National Monument . . . 80 80
1301 60c. Lyndon B. Johnson and Earth from Moon as seen by "Apollo 8" crew . . . 80 80
1302 60c. Richard Nixon and visit to Great Wall of China 80 80
1303 60c. Gerald Ford and "Gorch Fock" (German cadet barque) at Bicentenary of Revolution celebrations 80 80
1304 60c. Jimmy Carter and President Sadat of Egypt with Prime Minister Begin of Israel 80 80
1305 60c. Ronald Reagan and space shuttle "Columbia" 80 80
1306 60c. George Bush and Grumman TBF Avenger (fighter-bomber) 80 80

1989. "Expo '89" International Stamp Exhibition, Washington (2nd issue). Landmarks of Washington. Sheet 77 × 62 mm, containing horiz design as T **257** of Antigua. Multicoloured.
MS1307 $4 The Capitol 2·50 3·25

1989. Mickey Mouse in Hollywood (Walt Disney cartoon character). As T **267** of Antigua. Mult.
1308 20c. Mickey Mouse reading script 40 40
1309 35c. Mickey Mouse giving interview 55 55
1310 45c. Mickey and Minnie Mouse with newspaper and magazines 65 65
1311 60c. Mickey Mouse signing autographs 75 75
1312 $1 Trapped in dressing room . . . . 1·25 1·25
1313 $2 Mickey and Minnie Mouse with Pluto in limousine . . . . 2·00 2·50
1314 $3 Arriving at Awards ceremony . . . . 2·25 2·75
1315 $4 Mickey Mouse accepting award . . . . 2·40 2·75
MS1316 Two sheets, each 127 × 102 mm. (a) $5 Mickey Mouse leaving footprints at cinema. (b) $5 Goofy interviewing Set of 2 sheets 7·50 8·50

1989. Christmas. Paintings by Botticelli. As T **259** of Antigua. Multicoloured.
1317 20c. "Madonna in Glory with Seraphim" 40 30
1318 25c. "The Annunciation" . . 40 30
1319 35c. "Madonna of the Pomegranate" 55 40
1320 45c. "Madonna of the Rosegarden" 65 45
1321 60c. "Madonna of the Book" 80 60
1322 $1 "Madonna under a Baldachin" . . . . 1·00 90
1323 $4 "Madonna and Child with Angels" . . . . . . 3·00 4·50
1324 $5 "Bardi Madonna" . . . 3·50 4·75
MS1325 Two sheets, each 71 × 96 mm. (a) $5 "The Mystic Nativity". (b) $5 "The Adoration of the Magi" Set of 2 sheets 7·00 9·00

240 Lady Olave Baden-Powell and Agatha Robinson (Guide leaders)

241 Jawaharal Nehru

1989. 60th Anniv of Girl Guides in Dominica. Multicoloured.
1326 60c. Type **240** . . . . . . 1·00 1·00
MS1327 70 × 99 mm. $5 Doris Stockmann and Judith Pestaina (horiz) 3·50 4·00

1989. Birth Centenary of Jawaharal Nehru (Indian statesman). Multicoloured.
1328 60c. Type **241** . . . . . . 1·50 1·25
MS1329 101 × 72 mm. $5 Parliament House, New Delhi (horiz) 3·50 4·00

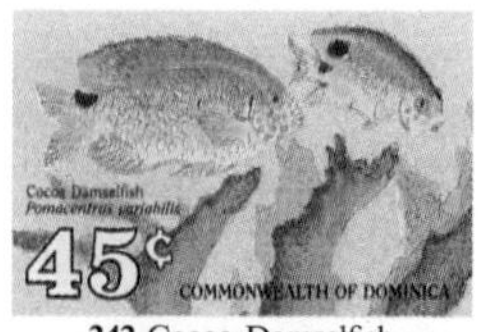

242 Cocoa Damselfish

1990. Tropical Fishes. Multicoloured.
1330 45c. Type **242** 45 55
1331 45c. Stinging jellyfish . . . 45 55
1332 45c. Dolphin (fish) 45 55
1333 45c. Atlantic spadefish and queen angelfish 45 55
1334 45c. French angelfish . . . 45 55
1335 45c. Blue-striped grunt . . . 45 55

1336 45c. Porkfish 45 55
1337 45c. Great hammerhead 45 55
1338 45c. Atlantic spadefish 45 55
1339 45c. Great barracuda 45 55
1340 45c. Southern stingray 45 55
1341 45c. Black grunt 45 55
1342 45c. Spot-finned butterflyfish 45 55
1343 45c. Dog snapper 45 55
1344 45c. Band-tailed puffer 45 55
1345 45c. Four-eyed butterflyfish 45 55
1346 45c. Lane snapper 45 55
1347 45c. Green moray 45 55
Nos. 1330/47 were printed together, se-tenant, forming a composite design.

243 St. Paul's Cathedral, London, c. 1840 **244** Blue-headed Hummingbird

1990. 150th Anniv of the Penny Black and "Stamp World London 90" International Stamp Exhibition.
1348 **243** 45c. green and black 50 25
1349 – 50c. blue and black 65 35
1350 – 60c. blue and black 65 45
1351 – 90c. green and black 1·10 85
1352 – $3 blue and black 2·75 3·50
1353 – $4 blue and black 2·75 3·50
MS1354 Two sheets. (a) 103 × 79 mm. $5 ochre and black. (b) 85 × 86 mm. $5 red and brown Set of 2 sheets 6·50 7·50
DESIGNS: 50c. British Post Office "accelerator" carriage, 1830; 60c. St. Paul's and City of London; 90c. Travelling post office, 1838; $3 "Hen and chickens" delivery cycle, 1883; $4 London skyline; $5 (a) Type **243**; (b) Motor mail van, 1899.

1990. 500th Anniv (1992) of Discovery of America by Columbus (3rd issue). New World Natural History—Seashells. As T **260** of Antigua. Mult.
1355 10c. Reticulated cowrie-helmet 30 30
1356 20c. West Indian chank 40 40
1357 35c. West Indian fighting conch 50 35
1358 60c. True tulip 75 60
1359 $1 Sunrise tellin 1·00 1·00
1360 $2 Crown cone 1·75 2·75
1361 $3 Common dove shell 2·50 3·50
1362 $4 Common or Atlantic fig shell 2·75 3·50
MS1363 Two sheets, each 103 × 70 mm. (a) $5 King helmet. (b) $6 Giant tun Set of 2 sheets 6·50 8·00

1990. Birds. Multicoloured.
1364 10c. Type **244** 35 35
1365 20c. Black-capped petrel 45 45
1366 45c. Red-necked amazon ("Red-necked Parrot") 65 40
1367 60c. Black swift 80 70
1368 $1 Troupial 1·25 1·25
1369 $2 Common noddy ("Brown Noddy") 2·00 2·50
1370 $4 Lesser Antillean pewee 3·25 3·50
1371 $5 Little blue heron 3·75 4·25
MS1372 Two sheets, each 103 × 70 mm. (a) $6 Imperial amazon. (b) $6 House wren Set of 2 sheets 7·00 8·00

1990. 90th Birthday of Queen Elizabeth the Queen Mother. As T **266** of Antigua.
1373 20c. multicoloured 20 15
1374 45c. multicoloured 35 25
1375 60c. multicoloured 60 60
1376 $3 multicoloured 2·25 3·00
MS1377 80 × 90 mm. $5 multicoloured 2·75 3·50
DESIGNS: 20c. to $5, Recent photographs of Queen Mother.

1990. Olympic Games, Barcelona (1992) (1st issue). As T **268** of Antigua. Multicoloured.
1378 45c. Tennis 1·25 40
1379 60c. Fencing 1·25 50
1380 $2 Swimming 2·00 3·25
1381 $3 Yachting 2·50 3·75
MS1382 100 × 70 mm. $5 Boxing 4·25 5·50
See also Nos. 1603/11.

245 Barnes, England

1990. World Cup Football Championship, Italy (2nd issue). Multicoloured.
1383 15c. Type **245** 40 30
1384 45c. Romario, Brazil 70 30
1385 60c. Franz Beckenbauer, West Germany manager 85 70
1386 $4 Lindenberger, Austria 3·25 5·00
MS1387 Two sheets, each 105 × 90 mm. (a) $6 McGrath, Ireland (vert). (b) $6 Litovchenko, Soviet Union (vert) Set of 2 sheets 7·50 9·00

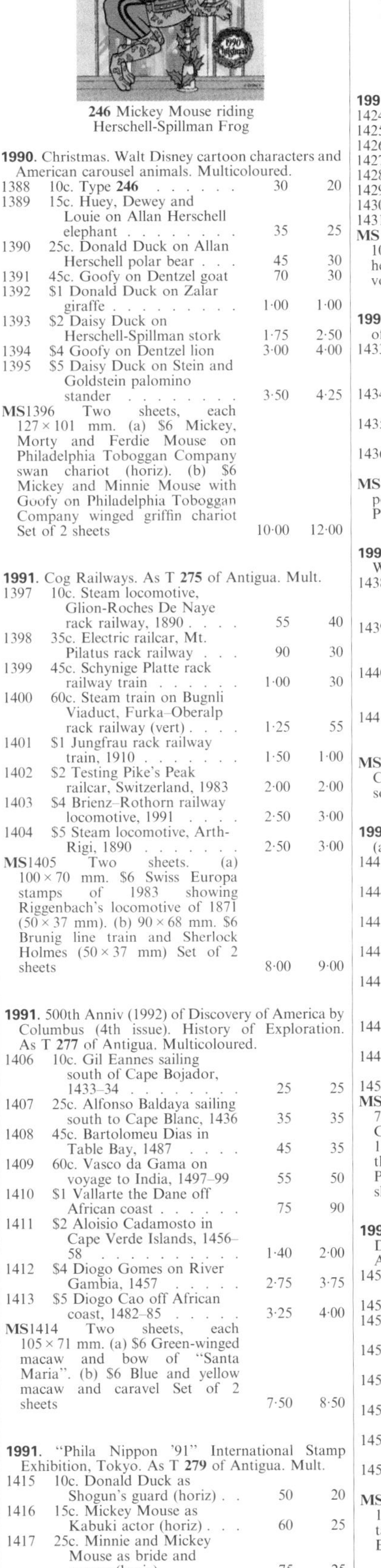

246 Mickey Mouse riding Herschell-Spillman Frog

1990. Christmas. Walt Disney cartoon characters and American carousel animals. Multicoloured.
1388 10c. Type **246** 30 20
1389 15c. Huey, Dewey and Louie on Allan Herschell elephant 35 25
1390 25c. Donald Duck on Allan Herschell polar bear 45 30
1391 45c. Goofy on Dentzel goat 70 30
1392 $1 Donald Duck on Zalar giraffe 1·00 1·00
1393 $2 Daisy Duck on Herschell-Spillman stork 1·75 2·50
1394 $4 Goofy on Dentzel lion 3·00 4·00
1395 $5 Daisy Duck on Stein and Goldstein palomino stander 3·50 4·25
MS1396 Two sheets, each 127 × 101 mm. (a) $6 Mickey, Morty and Ferdie Mouse on Philadelphia Toboggan Company swan chariot (horiz). (b) $6 Mickey and Minnie Mouse with Goofy on Philadelphia Toboggan Company winged griffin chariot Set of 2 sheets 10·00 12·00

1991. Cog Railways. As T **275** of Antigua. Mult.
1397 10c. Steam locomotive, Glion-Roches De Naye rack railway, 1890 55 40
1398 35c. Electric railcar, Mt. Pilatus rack railway 90 30
1399 45c. Schynige Platte rack railway train 1·00 30
1400 60c. Steam train on Bugnli Viaduct, Furka–Oberalp rack railway (vert) 1·25 55
1401 $1 Jungfrau rack railway train, 1910 1·50 1·00
1402 $2 Testing Pike's Peak railcar, Switzerland, 1983 2·00 2·00
1403 $4 Brienz–Rothorn railway locomotive, 1991 2·50 3·00
1404 $5 Steam locomotive, Arth-Rigi, 1890 2·50 3·00
MS1405 Two sheets. (a) 100 × 70 mm. $6 Swiss Europa stamps of 1983 showing Riggenbach's locomotive of 1871 (50 × 37 mm). (b) 90 × 68 mm. $6 Brunig line train and Sherlock Holmes (50 × 37 mm) Set of 2 sheets 8·00 9·00

1991. 500th Anniv (1992) of Discovery of America by Columbus (4th issue). History of Exploration. As T **277** of Antigua. Multicoloured.
1406 10c. Gil Eannes sailing south of Cape Bojador, 1433–34 25 25
1407 25c. Alfonso Baldaya sailing south to Cape Blanc, 1436 35 35
1408 45c. Bartolomeu Dias in Table Bay, 1487 45 35
1409 60c. Vasco da Gama on voyage to India, 1497–99 55 50
1410 $1 Vallarte the Dane off African coast 75 90
1411 $2 Aloisio Cadamosto in Cape Verde Islands, 1456–58 1·40 2·00
1412 $4 Diogo Gomes on River Gambia, 1457 2·75 3·75
1413 $5 Diogo Cao off African coast, 1482–85 3·25 4·00
MS1414 Two sheets, each 105 × 71 mm. (a) $6 Green-winged macaw and bow of "Santa Maria". (b) $6 Blue and yellow macaw and caravel Set of 2 sheets 7·50 8·50

1991. "Phila Nippon '91" International Stamp Exhibition, Tokyo. As T **279** of Antigua. Mult.
1415 10c. Donald Duck as Shogun's guard (horiz) 50 20
1416 15c. Mickey Mouse as Kabuki actor (horiz) 60 25
1417 25c. Minnie and Mickey Mouse as bride and groom (horiz) 75 25
1418 45c. Daisy Duck as geisha 90 25
1419 $1 Mickey Mouse in Sokutai court dress 1·50 90
1420 $2 Goofy as Mino farmer 2·00 2·25
1421 $4 Pete as Shogun 3·25 3·75
1422 $5 Donald Duck as Samurai (horiz) 3·50 4·00
MS1423 Two sheets, each 127 × 112 mm. (a) $6 Mickey Mouse as Noh actor. (b) $6 Goofy as Kabubei-jishi dancer Set of 2 sheets 11·00 12·00

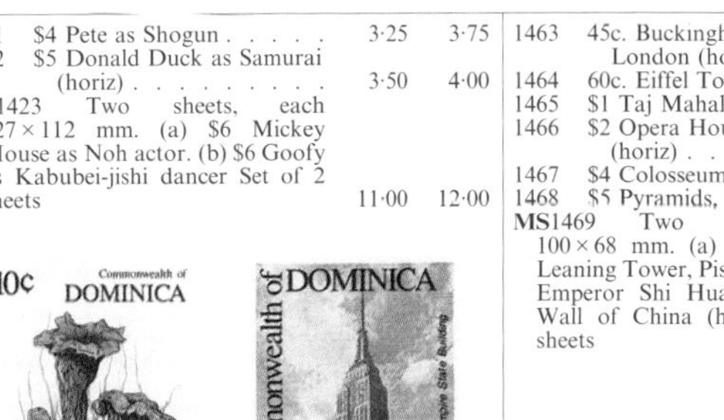

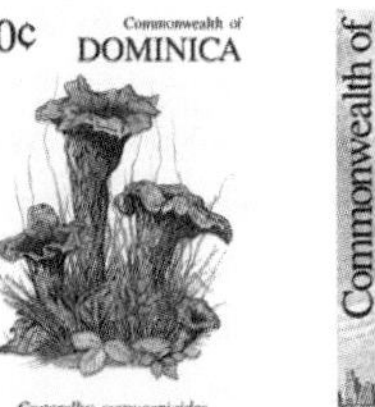

247 "Craterellus cornucopioides"

248 Empire State Building, New York

1991. Fungi. Multicoloured.
1424 10c. Type **247** 25 25
1425 15c. "Coprinus comatus" 50 25
1426 45c. "Morchella esculenta" 50 25
1427 60c. "Cantharellus cibarius" 60 30
1428 $1 "Lepista nuda" 80 70
1429 $2 "Suillus luteus" 1·40 1·75
1430 $4 "Russula emetica" 2·25 2·75
1431 $5 "Armillaria mellea" 2·25 2·75
MS1432 Two sheets, each 100 × 70 mm. (a) $6 "Fistulina hepatica". (b) $6 "Lactarius volemus" Set of 2 sheets 8·00 8·50

1991. 65th Birthday of Queen Elizabeth II. As T **280** of Antigua. Multicoloured.
1433 10c. Queen and Prince William on Buckingham Palace Balcony, 1990 40 20
1434 60c. The Queen at Westminster Abbey, 1988 75 50
1435 $2 The Queen and Prince Philip in Italy, 1990 1·60 2·00
1436 $5 The Queen at Ascot, 1986 2·75 3·00
MS1437 68 × 90 mm. $5 Separate portraits of Queen and Prince Philip 4·25 4·50

1991. 10th Wedding Anniv of Prince and Princess of Wales. As T **280** of Antigua. Multicoloured.
1438 15c. Prince and Princess of Wales in West Germany, 1987 85 25
1439 40c. Separate photographs of Prince, Princess and sons 1·50 25
1440 $1 Separate photographs of Prince William and Prince Henry 1·50 95
1441 $4 Prince Charles at Caister and Princess Diana in Thailand 4·00 4·50
MS1442 68 × 90 mm. $5 Prince Charles, and Princess Diana with sons on holiday 4·50 4·50

1991. Death Centenary (1990) of Vincent van Gogh (artist). As T **278** of Antigua. Multicoloured.
1443 10c. "Thatched Cottages" (horiz) 50 30
1444 25c. "The House of Pere Eloi" (horiz) 70 30
1445 45c. "The Midday Siesta" (horiz) 85 30
1446 60c. "Portrait of a Young Peasant" 1·10 35
1447 $1 "Still Life: Vase with Irises against Yellow Background" 1·50 85
1448 $2 "Still Life: Vase with Irises" (horiz) 2·00 2·00
1449 $4 "Blossoming Almond Tree" (horiz) 2·75 3·00
1450 $5 "Irises" (horiz) 2·75 3·00
MS1451 Two sheets. (a) 77 × 102 mm. $6 "Doctor Gachet's Garden in Auvers". (b) 102 × 77 mm. $6 "A Meadow in the Mountains: Le Mas de Saint-Paul" (horiz). Imperf Set of 2 sheets 8·00 8·50

1991. International Literacy Year (1990). Scenes from Disney cartoon film "The Little Mermaid". As T **269** of Antigua. Multicoloured.
1452 10c. Ariel, Flounder and Sebastian (horiz) 30 25
1453 25c. King Triton (horiz) 45 30
1454 45c. Sebastian playing drums (horiz) 60 30
1455 60c. Flotsam and Jetsam taunting Ariel (horiz) 85 55
1456 $1 Scuttle, Flounder and Ariel with pipe (horiz) 1·25 1·00
1457 $2 Ariel and Flounder discovering book (horiz) 2·00 2·00
1458 $4 Prince Eric and crew (horiz) 3·25 3·50
1459 $5 Ursula the Sea Witch (horiz) 3·50 4·00
MS1460 Two sheets, each 127 × 102 mm. $6 Ariel without tail (horiz). (b) $6 Ariel and Prince Eric dancing Set of 2 sheets 8·50 10·00

1991. World Landmarks. Multicoloured.
1461 10c. Type **248** 40 30
1462 25c. Kremlin, Moscow (horiz) 40 30
1463 45c. Buckingham Palace, London (horiz) 70 30
1464 60c. Eiffel Tower, Paris 85 60
1465 $1 Taj Mahal, Agra (horiz) 3·00 1·50
1466 $2 Opera House, Sydney (horiz) 3·75 3·00
1467 $4 Colosseum, Rome (horiz) 3·50 4·00
1468 $5 Pyramids, Giza (horiz) 4·00 4·50
MS1469 Two sheets, each 100 × 68 mm. (a) $6 Galileo on Leaning Tower, Pisa (horiz). (b) $6 Emperor Shi Huang and Great Wall of China (horiz) Set of 2 sheets 12·00 13·00

249 Japanese Aircraft leaving Carrier "Akagi"

1991. 50th Anniv of Japanese Attack on Pearl Harbor. Multicoloured.
1470 10c. Type **249** 25 25
1471 15c. U.S.S. "Ward" (destroyer) and Consolidated Catalina flying boat attacking midget submarine 30 25
1472 45c. Second wave of Mitsubishi A6M Zero-Sen aircraft leaving carriers 50 25
1473 60c. Japanese Mitsubishi M6M Zero-Sen aircraft attacking Kaneche naval airfield 60 30
1474 $1 U.S.S. "Breeze", "Medusa" and "Curtiss" (destroyers) sinking midget submarine 80 70
1475 $2 U.S.S. "Nevada" (battleship) under attack 1·40 1·50
1476 $4 U.S.S. "Arizona" (battleship) sinking 2·25 2·50
1477 $5 Mitsubishi A6M Zero-Sen aircraft 2·25 2·50
MS1478 Two sheets, each 118 × 78 mm. (a) $6 Mitsubishi A6M Zero-Sen over anchorage. (b) $6 Mitsubishi A6M Zero-Sen attacking Hickam airfield Set of 2 sheets 7·50 8·00

250 "Eurema venusta"

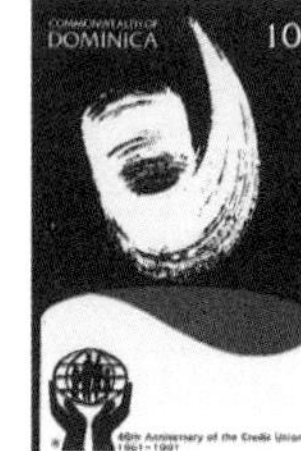

251 Symbolic Cheque

1991. Butterflies. Multicoloured.
1479 1c. Type **250** 30 60
1480 2c. "Agraulis vanillae" 30 60
1481 5c. "Danaus plexippus" 40 60
1482 10c. "Biblis hyperia" 40 15
1483 15c. "Dryas julia" 50 15
1484 20c. "Phoebis agarithe" 50 20
1485 25c. "Junonia genoveva" 50 20
1486 35c. "Battus polydamas" 60 30
1487 45c. "Leptotes cassius" 60 30
1487a 55c. "Ascia monuste" 75 55
1488 60c. "Anaea dominicana" 70 35
1488a 65c. "Hemiargus hanno" 75 55
1489 90c. "Hypolimnas misippus" 80 55
1490 $1 "Urbanus proteus" 80 60
1490a $1.20 "Historis odius" 1·00 1·50
1491 $2 "Phoebis sennae" 1·50 2·00
1492 $5 "Cynthia cardui" ("Vanessa cardui") 2·50 4·00
1493 $10 "Marpesia petreus" 4·75 6·50
1494 $20 "Anartia jatrophae" 9·50 12·00

1991. Birth Centenary (1990) of Charles De Gaulle (French statesman). As T **283** of Antigua.
1495 45c. brown 1·50 75
MS1496 70 × 100 mm. $5 brown and blue 4·25 4·75
DESIGN—VERT: 45c. De Gaulle in uniform.

1992. 40th Anniv of Credit Union Bank.
1497 **251** 10c. grey and black 30 20
1498 – 60c. multicoloured 1·25 80
DESIGN—HORIZ: 60c. Credit Union symbol.

252 "18th-Century Creole Dress" (detail) (Agostino Brunias)

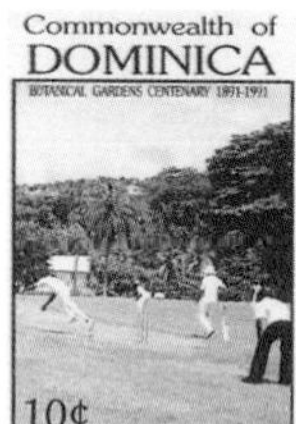

254 Cricket Match

253 Island Beach

1991. Creole Week. Multicoloured.
1499 45c. Type **252** 70 25
1500 60c. Jing Ping band 90 60
1501 $1 Creole dancers . . . . . 1·25 1·75
MS1502 100 × 70 mm. $5 "18th-century Stick-fighting Match" (detail) (Agostino Brunias) (horiz) 4·25 5·50

1991. Year of Environment and Shelter. Mult.
1503 15c. Type **253** 15 15
1504 60c. Imperial amazon . . . 2·50 1·25
MS1505 Two sheets. (a) 100 × 70 mm. $5 River estuary. (b) 70 × 100 mm. $5 As 60c. Set of 2 sheets 12·00 13·00

1991. Christmas. Religious Paintings by Jan van Eyck. As T **287** of Antigua. Multicoloured.
1506 10c. "Virgin Enthroned with Child" (detail) 60 30
1507 20c. "Madonna at the Fountain" 75 30
1508 35c. "Virgin in a Church" 90 30
1509 45c. "Madonna with Canon van der Paele" . . . . . 1·00 30
1510 60c. "Madonna with Canon van der Paele" (detail) . . 1·50 60
1511 $1 "Madonna in an Interior" . . . . 1·75 1·00
1512 $3 "The Annunciation" . . 3·00 4·00
1513 $5 "The Annunciation" (different) . . . . 4·00 6·50
MS1514 Two sheets, each 102 × 127 mm. (a) $5 "Virgin and Child with Saints and Donor". (b) $5 "Madonna with Chancellor Rolin" Set of 2 sheets 10·00 12·00

1992. 40th Anniv of Queen Elizabeth II's Accession. As T **288** of Antigua. Multicoloured.
1515 10c. Coastline 10 10
1516 15c. Mountains overlooking small village 10 10
1517 $1 River estuary 55 60
1518 $5 Waterfall . . . . 3·25 3·50
MS1519 Two sheets, each 74 × 97 mm. (a) $6 Roseau. (b) $6 Mountain stream Set of 2 sheets 7·00 8·00

1992. Centenary (1991) of Botanical Gardens. Multicoloured.
1520 10c. Type **254** . . . . . . 1·25 60
1521 15c. Scenic entrance 40 20
1522 45c. Traveller's tree 40 25
1523 60c. Bamboo House 55 30
1524 $1 The Old Pavilion 80 70
1525 $2 "Ficus benjamina" . . . 1·40 2·00
1526 $4 Cricket match (different) 4·00 3·50
1527 $5 Thirty-five Steps . . . . 3·00 3·50
MS1528 Two sheets, each 104 × 71 mm. (a) $6 Past and present members of national cricket team. (b) $6 The Fountain Set of 2 sheets 7·00 8·00

1992. Easter. Religious Paintings. As T **291** of Antigua. Multicoloured.
1529 10c. "The Supper at Emmaus" (Van Honthorst) 20 20
1530 15c. "Christ before Caiaphas" (Van Honthorst) (vert) 25 25
1531 45c. "The Taking of Christ" (De Boulogne) 40 30
1532 60c. "Pilate washing his Hands" (Preti) (vert) . . . 55 45
1533 $1 "The Last Supper" (detail) (Master of the Church of S. Francisco d'Evora) 75 75
1534 $2 "The Three Marys at the Tomb" (detail) (Bouguereau) (vert) . . . 1·50 2·00
1535 $3 "Denial of St. Peter" (Terbrugghen) . . . . . 1·75 2·50
1536 $5 "Doubting Thomas" (Strozzi) . . . . 2·75 3·75
MS1537 Two sheets, each 72 × 102 mm. (a) $6 "The Crucifixion" (detail) (Grünewald) (vert). (b) $6 "The Resurrection" (detail) (Caravaggio) (vert) Set of 2 sheets 7·00 8·50

1992. "Granada '92" International Stamp Exhibition, Spain. Art of Diego Rodriguez Velasquez. As T **292** of Antigua. Mult.
1538 10c. "Pope Innocent X" (detail) 15 10
1539 15c. "The Forge of Vulcan" (detail) 20 10
1540 45c. "The Forge of Vulcan" (different detail) 40 25
1541 60c. "Queen Mariana of Austria" (detail) 50 30
1542 $1 "Pablo de Valladolid" . . 80 70
1543 $2 "Sebastian de Morra" . . 1·25 1·60
1544 $3 "King Felipe IV" (detail) 1·60 2·25
1545 $4 "King Felipe IV" . . . . 1·75 2·40
MS1546 Two sheets, each 120 × 95 mm. (a) $6 "The Drunkards" (110 × 81 mm). (b) $6 "Surrender of Breda" (110 × 81 mm). Imperf Set of 2 sheets 6·50 7·00

255 Columbus and "Dynastes hercules" (beetle)

1992. 500th Anniv of Discovery of America by Columbus (5th issue). World Columbian Stamp "Expo '92", Chicago. Multicoloured.
1547 10c. Type **255** 50 30
1548 25c. Columbus and "Leptodactylus fallax" (frog) 90 25
1549 75c. Columbus and red-necked amazon (bird) . . 2·50 1·00
1550 $2 Columbus and "Ameiva fuscata" (lizard) . . . . . 2·25 2·25
1551 $4 Columbus and royal gramma (fish) . . . . . 2·50 3·25
1552 $5 Columbus and "Rosa sinensis" (flower) . . . . 2·50 3·25
MS1553 Two sheets, each 100 × 67 mm. (a) $6 Ships of Columbus (horiz). (b) $6 "Mastophyllum scabricolle" (katydid) (horiz) Set of 2 sheets 6·50 7·50

1992. "Genova '92" International Thematic Stamp Exhibition. Hummingbirds. As T **295** of Antigua. Multicoloured.
1554 10c. Female purple-throated carib 60 25
1555 15c. Female rufous-breasted hermit 60 25
1556 45c. Male Puerto Rican emerald 85 30
1557 60c. Female Antillean mango . . . . 1·10 45
1558 $1 Male green-throated carib . . . . 1·50 85
1559 $2 Male blue-headed hummingbird . . . . . . 2·00 2·00
1560 $4 Female eastern streamertail . . . . . . 2·50 2·75
1561 $5 Female Antillean crested hummingbird . . . . . . 2·75 3·00
MS1562 Two sheets, each 105 × 72 mm. (a) $6 Jamaican Mango ("Green Mango"). (b) $6 Vervain hummingbird Set of 2 sheets 10·00 11·00

1992. Prehistoric Animals. As T **290** of Antigua, but horiz. Multicoloured.
1563 10c. Head of Camptosaurus 60 25
1564 15c. Edmontosaurus 65 25
1565 25c. Corythosaurus 75 25
1566 60c. Stegosaurus . . . . . 1·25 30
1567 $1 Torosaurus . . . . . . 1·50 70
1568 $3 Euoplocephalus . . . . 2·25 2·25
1569 $4 Tyrannosaurus . . . . . 2·25 2·50
1570 $5 Parasaurolophus . . . . 2·50 2·75
MS1571 Two sheets, each 100 × 70 mm. (a) $6 As 25c. (b) $6 As $1 Set of 2 sheets 7·50 7·50

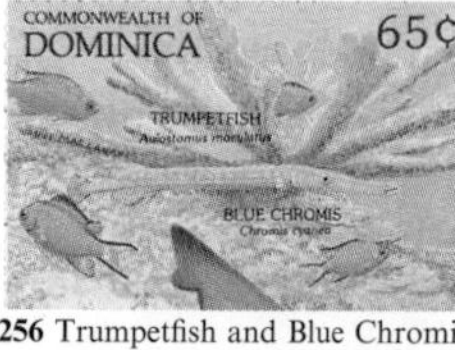

256 Trumpetfish and Blue Chromis

1992. Marine Life. Multicoloured.
1572/1601 65c. × 30. As Type **256** 12·00 13·00
MS1602 Two sheets, each 73 × 105 mm. (a) $6 multicoloured (Harlequin bass). (b) $6 multicoloured (Flamefish) Set of 2 sheets 9·00 10·00

1992. Olympic Games, Barcelona (2nd issue). As T **268** of Antigua. Multicoloured.
1603 10c. Archery 30 25
1604 15c. Two-man canoeing . . 35 25
1605 25c. Men's 110 m hurdles 40 25
1606 60c. Men's high jump . . . 70 30
1607 $1 Greco-Roman wrestling 1·00 65
1608 $2 Men's gymnastics—rings 1·50 2·00
1609 $4 Men's gymnastics—parallel bars . . . . . . 2·75 3·25
1610 $5 Equestrian dressage . . . 3·50 3·50
MS1611 Two sheets, each 100 × 70 mm. (a) $6 Women's platform diving. (b) $6 Men's hockey Set of 2 sheets 7·50 9·00

1992. 500th Anniv of Discovery of America by Columbus (6th issue). Organization of East Caribbean States. As Nos. 1670/1 of Antigua. Multicoloured.
1612 $1 Columbus meeting Amerindians 65 65
1613 $2 Ships approaching island 1·10 1·25

1992. Hummel Figurines. As T **302** of Antigua. Multicoloured.
1614 20c. Angel playing violin . . 30 15
1615 25c. Angel playing recorder 30 15
1616 55c. Angel playing lute . . . 50 30
1617 65c. Seated angel playing trumpet 60 35
1618 90c. Angel on cloud with lantern 75 65
1619 $1 Angel with candle . . . 80 70
1620 $1.20 Flying angel with Christmas tree . . . . . 90 1·25
1621 $6 Angel on cloud with candle . . . . 3·25 5·00
MS1622 Two sheets, each 97 × 127 mm. (a) Nos. 1614/17. (b) Nos. 1618/21 Set of 2 sheets 6·50 7·50

257 Brass "Reno" Locomotive, Japan (1963)

1992. Toy Trains from Far Eastern Manufacturers. Multicoloured.
1623 15c. Type **257** 55 25
1624 25c. Union Pacific "Golden Classic" locomotive, China (1992) 65 25
1625 55c. L.M.S. third class brake carriage, Hong Kong (1970s) 90 30
1626 65c. Brass Wabash locomotive, Japan (1958) 1·00 35
1627 75c. Pennsylvania "Duplex" type locomotive, Korea (1991) . . . . 1·10 75
1628 $1 Streamlined locomotive, Japan (post 1945) . . . . 1·25 80
1629 $3 Japanese National Railways Class "C62" locomotive, Japan (1960) 2·25 2·50
1630 $5 Tinplate friction driven trains, Japan (1960s) . . . 2·50 3·25
MS1631 Two sheets, each 119 × 87 mm. (a) $6 "Rocket's" tender, Japan (1972) (multicoloured) (51½ × 40 mm). (b) $6 American model steam train presented to Emperor of Japan, 1854 (black, blackish olive and flesh) (40 × 51½ mm). Set of 2 sheets 8·00 8·00

258 Goofy in "Two Weeks Vacation", 1952

1992. 60th Anniv of Goofy (Disney cartoon character). Designs showing sports from cartoon films. Multicoloured.
1632 10c. Type **258** 60 20
1633 15c. "Aquamania", 1961 . . 70 20
1634 25c. "Goofy Gymnastics", 1949 . . . . 85 20
1635 45c. "How to Ride a Horse", 1941 . . . . . 1·10 25
1636 $1 "Foul Hunting", 1947 . . 1·75 75
1637 $2 "For Whom the Bulls Toil", 1953 . . . . 2·50 2·75
1638 $4 "Tennis Racquet", 1949 3·25 3·75
1639 $5 "Double Dribble", 1946 3·25 3·75
MS1640 Two sheets, each 128 × 102 mm. (a) $6 "The Goofy Sports Story", 1956 (vert). (b) $6 "Aquamania", 1961 (different) (vert) Set of 2 sheets 10·00 11·00

259 "Graf Zeppelin", 1929

260 Elvis Presley

1992. Anniversaries and Events. Multicoloured.
1641 25c. Type **259** 60 30
1642 45c. Elderly man on bike . . 60 30
1643 45c. Elderly man with seedling 40 30
1644 45c. Elderly man and young boy fishing 40 30
1645 90c. Space Shuttle "Atlantis" . . . . 1·00 60
1646 90c. Konrad Adenauer (German statesman) . . . 60 60
1647 $1.20 Sir Thomas Lipton and "Shamrock N" (yacht) . . . . 1·50 1·25
1648 $1.20 Snowy egret (bird) . . 1·50 1·25
1649 $1.20 Wolfgang Amadeus Mozart . . . . 2·00 1·25
1650 $2 Pulling fishing net ashore 1·50 1·75
1651 $3 Helen Keller (lecturer) . . 2·00 2·50
1652 $4 Eland (antelope) . . . . 3·25 3·50
1653 $4 Map of Allied Zones of Occupation, Germany, 1949 . . . . 3·25 3·50
1654 $4 Earth resources satellite 3·25 3·50
1655 $5 Count von Zeppelin . . 3·50 3·50
MS1656 Five sheets. (a) 100 × 70 mm. $6 Airship propeller. (b) 100 × 70 mm. $6 "Mir" Russian space station with "Soyuz". (c) 70 × 100 mm. $6 Cologne Cathedral. (d) 100 × 70 mm. $6 Rhinoceros hornbill (bird). (e) 100 × 70 mm. $6 Monostatos from "The Magic Flute" Set of 5 sheets 17·00 18·00
ANNIVERSARIES AND EVENTS: Nos. 1641, 1655, **MS**1656a, 75th death anniv of Count Ferdinand von Zeppelin; 1642/4, International Day of the Elderly; 1645, 1654, **MS**1656b, International Space Year; 1646, 1653, **MS**1656c, 25th death anniv of Konrad Adenauer; 1647, Americas Cup Yachting Championship; 1648, 1652, **MS**1656d, Earth Summit '92, Rio; 1649, **MS**1656e, Death bicent of Mozart; 1650, International Conference on Nutrition, Rome; 1651, 75th anniv of International Association of Lions Clubs.
No. **MS**1656b is inscribed "M.I.R." and No. **MS**1656d "Rhinocerus Hornbill", both in error.

1993. Bicentenary of the Louvre, Paris. As T **305** of Antigua. Multicoloured.
1657 $1 "Madonna and Child with St. Catherine and a Rabbit" (left detail) (Titian) 70 70
1658 $1 "Madonna and Child with St. Catherine and a Rabbit" (right detail) (Titian) 70 70
1659 $1 "Woman at her Toilet" (Titian) 70 70
1660 $1 "The Supper at Emmaus" (left detail) (Titian) 70 70
1661 $1 "The Supper at Emmaus" (right detail) (Titian) 70 70
1662 $1 "The Pastoral Concert" (Titian) 70 70
1663 $1 "An Allegory, perhaps of Marriage" (detail) (Titian) 70 70
1664 $1 "An Allegory, perhaps of Marriage" (different detail) (Titian) 70 70
MS1665 70 × 100 mm. $6 "The Ship of Fools" (Bosch) (52 × 85 mm) 4·00 4·50

1993. 15th Death Anniv of Elvis Presley (singer). Multicoloured.
1666 $1 Type **260** 90 80
1667 $1 Elvis with guitar 90 80
1668 $1 Elvis with microphone 90 80

261 Plumbeous Warbler

1993. Birds. Multicoloured.
1669 90c. Type **261** . . . . . . 1·00 1·00
1670 90c. Black swift . . . . . . 1·00 1·00
1671 90c. Blue-hooded euphonia 1·00 1·00
1672 90c. Rufous-throated solitaire . . . . 1·00 1·00
1673 90c. Ringed kingfisher . . . 1·00 1·00
1674 90c. Blue-headed hummingbird . . . . . . 1·00 1·00
1675 90c. Bananaquit . . . . . 1·00 1·00

1676 90c. Brown trembler (“Trembler”) . . . . . . 1·00 1·00
1677 90c. Forest thrush . . . . . 1·00 1·00
1678 90c. Purple-throated carib 1·00 1·00
1679 90c. Ruddy quail dove . . . 1·00 1·00
1680 90c. Least bittern . . . . . 1·00 1·00
MS1681 Two sheets, each 100 × 70 mm. (a) $6 Imperial amazon. (b) $6 Red-necked amazon Set of 2 sheets 8·50 8·50

Nos. 1669/80 were printed together, se-tenant, forming a composite design.

262 School Crest

1993. Cent of Dominica Grammar School. Mult.
1682 25c. Type **262** 20 15
1683 30c. V. Archer (first West Indian headmaster) . . . 25 20
1684 65c. Hubert Charles (first Dominican headmaster) 45 50
1685 90c. Present school buildings 65 80

263 Leatherback Turtle on Beach

1993. Turtles. Multicoloured.
1686 25c. Type **263** 50 15
1687 55c. Hawksbill turtle swimming 70 40
1688 65c. Atlantic ridley turtle . . 80 50
1689 90c. Green turtle laying eggs 1·00 70
1690 $1 Green turtle swimming 1·00 70
1691 $2 Hawksbill turtle swimming (different) . . . 1·50 2·00
1692 $4 Loggerhead turtle . . . 2·25 3·00
1693 $5 Leatherback turtle swimming . . . . 2·25 3·00
MS1694 Two sheets, each 99 × 70 mm. (a) $6 Green turtle hatchling. (b) $6 Head of hawksbill turtle Set of 2 sheets 8·00 9·00

264 Ford “Model A”, 1928

1993. Centenaries of Henry Ford's First Petrol Engine (90c., $5) and Karl Benz's First Four-wheeled Car (others). Multicoloured.
1695 90c. Type **264** 65 45
1696 $1.20 Mercedes Benz car winning Swiss Grand Prix, 1936 . . . . 85 55
1697 $4 Mercedes Benz car winning German Grand Prix, 1935 . . . . 2·25 2·75
1698 $5 Ford “Model T”, 1915 2·25 2·75
MS1699 Two sheets, each 99 × 70 mm. (a) $3 Benz “Viktoria”, 1893; $3 Mercedes Benz sports coupe, 1993. (b) $6 Ford “G.T.40”, Le Mans, 1966 (57½ × 48 mm) Set of 2 sheets 7·00 7·50

1993. 40th Anniv of Coronation. As T **307** of Antigua.
1700 20c. multicoloured 60 75
1701 25c. brown and black . . . 60 75
1702 65c. multicoloured . . . . . 85 1·00
1703 $5 multicoloured . . . . . 4·25 4·50
MS1704 71 × 101 mm. $6 multicoloured 5·50 6·50

DESIGNS: 20c. Queen Elizabeth II at Coronation (photograph by Cecil Beaton); 25c. Queen wearing King Edward's Crown during Coronation ceremony; 65c. Coronation coach; $5 Queen and Queen Mother in carriage. (28½ × 42½ mm)—$6 “Queen Elizabeth II, 1969” (detail) (Norman Hutchinson).

265 New G.P.O. and Duke of Edinburgh

1993. Anniversaries and Events. Each brown, deep brown and black (Nos. 1707, 1717) or multicoloured (others).
1705 25c. Type **265** 30 25
1706 25c. “Bather with Beach Ball” (Picasso) (vert) . . . 30 25
1707 65c. Willy Brandt and Pres. Eisenhower, 1959 . . . . 35 35
1708 90c. As Type **265** but portrait of Queen Elizabeth II 60 45
1709 90c. “Portrait of Leo Stein” (Picasso) (vert) 60 45
1710 90c. Monika Holzner (Germany) (speed skating) (vert) 60 45
1711 90c. “Self-portrait” (Marian Szczyrbula) (vert) 60 45
1712 90c. Prince Naruhito and engagement photographs 60 45
1713 $1.20 16th-century telescope (vert) 85 70
1714 $3 “Bruno Jasienski” (Tytus Czyzewski) (vert) . . . . 1·75 2·25
1715 $3 Modern observatory (vert) . . . . 2·00 2·25
1716 $4 Ray Leblanc and Tim Sweeney (U.S.A.) (ice hockey) (vert) . . . . . . 2·50 2·75
1717 $5 “Wilhelm Unde” (Picasso) (vert) . . . . . 2·25 3·00
1718 $5 Willy Brandt and N. K. Winston at World's Fair, 1964 . . . . 2·25 3·00
1719 $5 Masako Owada and engagement photographs 2·25 3·00
1720 $5 Pres. Clinton and wife applauding . . . . 2·25 3·00
MS1721 Seven sheets, each 105 × 75 mm (a, c and f) or 75 × 105 mm (others). (a) $5 Copernicus (vert). (b) $6 “Man with Pipe” (detail) (Picasso) (vert). (c) $6 Willy Brandt, 1972. (d) $6 Toni Nieminen (FInland) (120 metre ski jump) (vert). (e) $6 “Miser” (detail) (Tadeusz Makowski) (vert). (f) $6 Masako Owada (vert). (g) $6 Pres. W. Clinton (vert) Set of 7 sheets 20·00 23·00

ANNIVERSARIES AND EVENTS: Nos. 1705, 1708, Opening of New General Post Office Building; 1706, 1709, 1717, **MS**1721b, 20th death anniv of Picasso (artist); 1707, 1718, **MS**1721c, 80th birth anniv of Willy Brandt (German politician); 1710, 1716, **MS**1721d, Winter Olympic Games '94, Lillehammer; 1711, 1714, **MS**1721e, “Polska '93” International Stamp Exhibition, Poznan; 1712, 1719, **MS**1721f, Marriage of Crown Prince Naruhito of Japan; 1713, 1715, **MS**1721a, 450th death anniv of Copernicus (astronomer); 1720, **MS**1721g, Inauguration of U.S. President William Clinton.

No. 1714 is inscribed “Tyrus” in error.

266 Hugo Eckener in New York Parade, 1928

1993. Aviation Anniversaries. Multicoloured.
1722 25c. Type **266** 80 30
1723 55c. English Electric Lightning F.2 (fighter) . . 1·50 40
1724 65c. Airship “Graf Zeppelin” over Egypt, 1929 . . . . 1·50 55
1725 $1 Boeing 314A (flying boat) on transatlantic mail flight . . . . 1·60 85
1726 $2 Astronaut carrying mail to the Moon . . . . . . 2·25 2·50
1727 $4 Airship “Viktoria Luise” over Kiel harbour, 1912 3·25 3·75
1728 $5 Supermarine Spitfire (vert) . . . . 3·25 3·75
MS1729 Three sheets, each 99 × 70 mm. (a) $6 Hugo Eckener (42½ × 57 mm). (b) $6 Royal Air Force crest (42½ × 57 mm). (c) $6 Jean-Pierre Blanchard's hot air balloon, 1793 (vert) Set of 3 sheets 11·00 11·00

ANNIVERSARIES: Nos. 1722, 1724, 1727, **MS**1729a, 125th birth anniv of Hugo Eckener (airship commander); 1723, 1728, **MS**1729b, 75th anniv of Royal Air Force; 1725/6, **MS**1729c, Bicentenary of first airmail flight.

267 Maradona (Argentina) and Buchwald (Germany)

268 Ornate Chedi, Wat Phra Boromathat Chaiya

1993. World Cup Football Championship, U.S.A. (1994) (1st issue). Multicoloured.
1730 25c. Type **267** 70 20
1731 55c. Ruud Gullit (Netherlands) 95 40
1732 65c. Chavarria (Costa Rica) and Bliss (U.S.A.) 95 45
1733 90c. Diego Maradona (Argentina) . . . . 1·40 75
1734 90c. Leonel Alvares (Colombia) . . . . 1·40 75
1735 $1 Altobelli (Italy) and Yong-hwang (South Korea) . . . . 1·40 80
1736 $2 Stopyra (France) . . . . 2·25 2·25
1737 $5 Renquin (Belgium) and Yaremtchuk (Russia) . . 3·25 4·00
MS1738 Two sheets. (a) 73 × 103 mm. $6 Nestor Fabbri (Argentina). (b) 103 × 73 mm. $6 Andreas Brehme (Germany) Set of 2 sheets 7·50 8·00

See also Nos. 1849/56.

1993. Asian International Stamp Exhibitions. Multicoloured. (a) “Indopex '93”, Surabaya, Indonesia.
1739 25c. Type **268** 30 30
1740 55c. Temple ruins, Sukhothai 50 30
1741 90c. Prasat Hin Phimai, Thailand 70 45
1742 $1.65 Arjuna and Prabu Gilling Wesi puppets . . 1·00 1·00
1743 $1.65 Loro Blonyo puppet 1·00 1·00
1744 $1.65 Yogyanese puppets . . 1·00 1·00
1745 $1.65 Wayang gedog puppet, Ng Setro . . . . 1·00 1·00
1746 $1.65 Wayang golek puppet 1·00 1·00
1747 $1.65 Wayang gedog puppet, Raden Damar Wulan . . . . 1·00 1·00
1748 $5 Main sanctuary, Prasat Phanom Rung, Thailand 2·25 2·50
MS1749 105 × 136 mm. $6 Sculpture of Majaphit noble, Pura Sada 3·25 3·75

(b) “Taipei '93”, Taiwan.
1750 25c. Aw Boon Haw Gardens, Causeway Bay 30 30
1751 65c. Observation building, Kenting Park 50 30
1752 90c. Tzu-en pagoda on lakeshore, Taiwan 70 45
1753 $1.65 Chang E kite . . . . 1·00 1·00
1754 $1.65 Red Phoenix and Rising Sun kite . . . . . 1·00 1·00
1755 $1.65 Heavenly Judge kite 1·00 1·00
1756 $1.65 Monkey King kite . . 1·00 1·00
1757 $1.65 Goddess of Luo River kite . . . . 1·00 1·00
1758 $1.65 Heavenly Maiden kite 1·00 1·00
1759 $5 Villa, Lantau Island . . 2·25 2·50
MS1760 105 × 136 mm. $6 Jade sculpture of girl, Liao Dynasty 3·25 3·75

(c) “Bangkok '93”, Thailand.
1761 25c. Tugu Monument, Java 30 30
1762 55c. Candi Cangkuang mon, West Java 50 30
1763 90c. Merus, Pura Taman Ayun, Mengwi 70 45
1764 $1.65 Hun Lek puppets of Rama and Sita . . . . . 1·00 1·00
1765 $1.65 Burmese puppet . . . 1·00 1·00
1766 $1.65 Burmese puppets . . . 1·00 1·00
1767 $1.65 Demon puppet at Wat Phra Kaew . . . . 1·00 1·00
1768 $1.65 Hun Lek puppet performing Khun Chang 1·00 1·00
1769 $1.65 Hun Lek puppets performing Ramakien . . 1·00 1·00
1770 $5 Stone mosaic, Ceto . . . 2·25 2·50
MS1771 105 × 136 mm. $6 Thai stone carving 3·25 3·75

No. 1753 is inscribed “Chang E Rising Up th the Moon” in error.

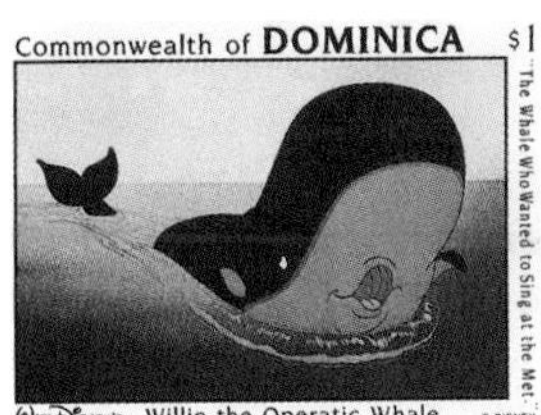

269 Willie

1993. “Willie the Operatic Whale”. Scenes from Walt Disney's cartoon film. Multicoloured.
1772 $1 Type **269** . . . . . . 1·10 1·10
1773 $1 Willie's pelican friend . . 1·10 1·10
1774 $1 Willie singing to seals . . 1·10 1·10
1775 $1 Willie singing “Lucia” 1·10 1·10
1776 $1 Willie in “Pagliacci” . . 1·10 1·10
1777 $1 Willie as Mephistopheles 1·10 1·10
1778 $1 Tetti Tatti searching for Willie . . . . 1·10 1·10
1779 $1 Whalers listening to Willie . . . . 1·10 1·10
1780 $1 Tetti Tatti with harpoon gun . . . . 1·10 1·10
MS1781 Two sheets. (a) 130 × 102 mm. $6 Seals listening to Willie. (b) 97 × 118 mm. $6 Willie in Heaven (vert) Set of 2 sheets 7·00 8·00

270 “Adoration of the Magi” (detail) (Durer)

1993. Christmas. Religious Paintings. Each black, yellow and red (Nos. 1782/5) or multicoloured (others).
1782 25c. Type **270** 35 20
1783 55c. “Adoration of the Magi” (different detail) (Durer) 55 30
1784 65c. “Adoration of the Magi” (different detail) (Durer) 65 35
1785 90c. “Adoration of the Magi” (different detail) (Durer) 80 65
1786 90c. “Madonna of Foligno” (detail) (Raphael) 80 65
1787 $1 “Madonna of Foligno” (different detail) (Raphael) 90 70
1788 $3 “Madonna of Foligno” (different detail) (Raphael) 2·00 3·00
1789 $5 “Madonna of Foligno” (different detail) (Raphael) 2·75 4·00
MS1790 Two sheets, each 105 × 130 mm. (a) $6 “Adoration of the Magi” (different detail) (Dürer) (horiz). (b) $6 “Madonna of Foligno” (different detail) (Raphael) Set of 2 sheets 7·00 8·00

1994. “Hong Kong '94” International Stamp Exhibition (1st issue). As T **317** of Antigua. Multicoloured.
1791 65c. Hong Kong 1988 Peak Tramway 50c. stamp and skyscrapers . . . . 85 1·00
1792 65c. Dominica 1991 Cog Railways $5 stamp and Hong Kong Peak tram . . 85 1·00

Nos. 1791/2 were printed together, se-tenant, forming a composite design.

See also Nos. 1793/8.

1994. “Hong Kong '94” International Stamp Exhibition (2nd issue). Tang Dynasty Jade. As T **318** of Antigua, but vert. Multicoloured.
1793 65c. Horse 65 70
1794 65c. Cup with handle . . . 65 70
1795 65c. Vase with birthday peaches 65 70
1796 65c. Vase 65 70
1797 65c. Fu Dog with puppy . . 65 70
1798 65c. Drinking cup 65 70

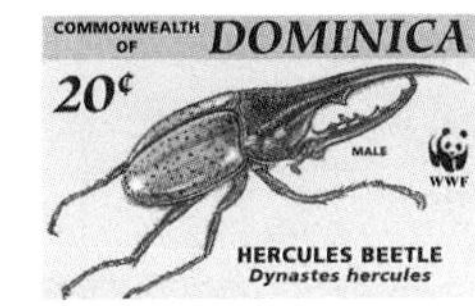

271 Male “Dynastes hercules” (beetle)

1994. Endangered Species. Birds and Insects. Multicoloured.
1799 20c. Type **271** 20 15
1800 25c. Male “Dynastes hercules” (different) . . . 20 15
1801 65c. Male “Dynastes hercules” (different) . . . 45 35
1802 90c. Female “Dynastes hercules” 60 55
1803 $1 Imperial Amazon (“Imperial Parrot”) . . . 90 75
1804 $2 “Marpesia petreus” (butterfly) . . . . 1·50 2·00
1805 $3 “Hypolimnus misippus” (butterfly) . . . . 2·00 2·50
1806 $5 Purple-throated carib . . 2·75 3·50
MS1807 Two sheets, each 98 × 70 mm. (a) $6 Blue-headed hummingbird. (b) $6 “Libytheana fulvescens” (butterfly) Set of 2 sheets 7·50 8·50

Nos. 1803/7 do not carry the W.W.F. Panda emblem.

272 “Laelio-cattleya”

273 “Russula matoubenis”

1994. Orchids. Multicoloured.
1808 20c. Type **272** 35 15
1809 25c. "Sophrolaelio cattleya" 35 15
1810 65c. "Odontocidium" . . . 70 45
1811 90c. "Laelio-cattleya" (different) 90 75
1812 $1 "Cattleya" . . . . . . 1·00 75
1813 $2 "Odontocidium" (different) . . . . . . 1·50 2·00
1814 $3 "Epiphronitis" . . . . 2·00 2·75
1815 $4 "Oncidium" . . . . . 2·00 2·75
MS1816 Two sheets, each 100 × 70 mm. (a) $6 "Cattleya" (different). (b) $6 "Schombo cattleya" Set of 2 sheets 7·50 8·00

1994. Fungi. Multicoloured.
1817 20c. Type **273** 40 25
1818 25c. "Leptonia caeruleocapitata" 40 25
1819 65c. "Inocybe littoralis" . . 60 35
1820 90c. "Russula hygrophytica" 70 55
1821 $1 "Pyrrhoglossum lilaceipes" 80 70
1822 $2 "Hygrocybe konradii" . 1·25 1·75
1823 $3 "Inopilus magnificus" . . 1·75 2·25
1824 $5 "Boletellus cubensis" . . 2·25 2·75
MS1825 Two sheets, each 110 × 85 mm. (a) $6 "Lentinus strigosus". (b) $6 "Gerronema citrinum" Set of 2 sheets 7·50 7·50

274 "Appias drusilla"

1994. Butterflies. Multicoloured.
1826 20c. Type **274** 35 15
1827 25c. "Didonis biblis" . . . 35 15
1828 55c. "Eurema daira" . . . 70 45
1829 65c. "Hypolimnas misippus" 75 45
1830 $1 "Phoebis agarithe" . . . 1·00 75
1831 $2 "Marpesia petreus" . . 1·50 2·00
1832 $3 "Libytheana fulvescens" 1·75 2·75
1833 $5 "Precis evarete" . . . . 2·50 3·50
MS1834 Two sheets, each 100 × 70 mm. (a) $6 "Chlorostrymon maesites". (b) $6 "Vanessa cardui" Set of 2 sheets 9·00 9·50

275 Dachshund

1994. Chinese New Year ("Year of the Dog"). Multicoloured.
1835 20c. Type **275** 30 25
1836 25c. Beagle 30 25
1837 55c. Greyhound 50 30
1838 90c. Jack Russell terrier . . 70 55
1839 $1 Pekingese 80 70
1840 $2 Wire fox terrier . . . . 1·25 1·50
1841 $4 English toy spaniel . . . 2·25 2·75
1842 $5 Irish setter . . . . 2·25 2·75
MS1843 Two sheets, each 102 × 72 mm. (a) $6 Welsh corgi. (b) $6 Labrador retriever Set of 2 sheets 7·50 7·50

1994. Royal Visit. Nos. 1700/4 optd **ROYAL VISIT FEBRUARY 19, 1994.**
1844 20c. multicoloured . . . . . 90 1·00
1845 25c. brown and black . . . 90 1·00
1846 65c. multicoloured . . . . . 1·50 1·75
1847 $5 multicoloured . . . . . 3·25 3·75
MS1848 71 × 101 mm. $6 multicoloured 6·00 6·50

277 Des Armstrong (U.S.A.)

1994. World Cup Football Championship, U.S.A. (2nd issue). Multicoloured.
1849 25c. Jefferey Edmund (Dominica) 50 25
1850 $1 Type **277** 75 80
1851 $1 Dennis Bergkamp (Netherlands) 75 80
1852 $1 Roberto Baggio (Italy) 75 80
1853 $1 Rai (Brazil) 75 80
1854 $1 Cafu (Brazil) 75 80
1855 $1 Marco van Basten (Netherlands) 75 80
MS1856 Two sheets. (a) 70 × 100 mm. $6 Roberto Mancini (Italy). (b) 100 × 70 mm. $6 Player and Stanford Stadium, San Francisco Set of 2 sheets 8·00 9·00

278 Scout Backpacking

1994. 10th Caribbean Scout Jamboree. Multicoloured.
1857 20c. Type **278** 35 15
1858 25c. Cooking over campfire 35 15
1859 55c. Erecting tent 60 30
1860 65c. Serving soup 70 45
1861 $1 Corps of drums . . . . 1·00 75
1862 $2 Planting tree . . . . . . 1·50 2·00
1863 $4 Sailing dinghy . . . . . 2·25 2·75
1864 $5 Saluting . . . . 2·25 2·75
MS1865 Two sheets, each 100 × 70 mm. (a) $6 Early scout troop. (b) $6 Pres. Crispin Sorhaindo (chief scout) (vert) Set of 2 sheets 8·50 9·00

1994. 25th Anniv of First Manned Moon Landing. As T **326** of Antigua. Multicoloured.
1866 $1 Crew of "Apollo 14" . . 80 85
1867 $1 "Apollo 14" mission logo 80 85
1868 $1 Lunar module "Antares" on Moon 80 85
1869 $1 Crew of "Apollo 15" . . 80 85
1870 $1 "Apollo 15" mission logo 80 85
1871 $1 Lunar crater on Mt. Hadley 80 85
MS1872 99 × 106 mm. $6 "Apollo 11" logo and surface of Moon 4·00 4·25

1994. Centenary of International Olympic Committee. Gold Medal Winners. As T **327** of Antigua. Multicoloured.
1873 55c. Ulrike Meyfarth (Germany) (high jump), 1984 . . . . 60 40
1874 $1.45 Dieter Baumann (Germany) (5000 m), 1992 1·40 1·75
MS1875 106 × 76 mm. $6 Ji Hoon Chae (South Korea) (500 metres speed skating), 1994 3·25 3·50

1994. Centenary (1995) of First English Cricket Tour to the West Indies. As T **329** of Antigua. Multicoloured.
1876 55c. David Gower (England) (vert) 40 30
1877 90c. Curtly Ambrose (West Indies) and Wisden Trophy 60 60
1878 $1 Graham Gooch (England) (vert) 70 80
MS1879 76 × 96 mm. $3 First English touring team, 1895 2·75 2·40

1994. 50th Anniv of D-Day. As T **331** of Antigua. Multicoloured.
1880 65c. American Waco gliders 60 45
1881 $2 British Horsa glider . . . 1·25 1·40
1882 $3 British glider and troops attacking Pegasus Bridge 1·50 1·75
MS1883 107 × 77 mm. $6 British Hadrian glider 3·25 3·50

279 Pink Bird and Red Flowers Screen Painting

280 Dippy Dawg

1994. "Philakorea '94" International Stamp Exhibition, Seoul. Multicoloured.
1884 55c. Type **279** 25 30
1885 55c. Bird with yellow, pink and red flowers 25 30
1886 55c. Pair of birds and yellow flowers 25 30
1887 55c. Chickens and flowers . 25 30
1888 55c. Pair of birds and pink flowers 25 30
1889 55c. Ducks and flowers . . 25 30
1890 55c. Blue bird and red flowers 25 30
1891 55c. Common pheasant and flowers 25 30
1892 55c. Stork and flowers . . . 25 30
1893 55c. Deer and flowers . . . 25 30
1894 65c. P'alsang-jon Hall (38 × 24 mm) 30 35
1895 90c. Popchu-sa Temple (38 × 24 mm) 35 40
1896 $2 Uhwajong Pavillion (38 × 24 mm) 85 90
MS1897 100 × 70 mm. $4 Spirit Post Guardian (38 × 24 mm) 1·75 2·25

1994. 65th Anniv (1993) of Mickey Mouse. Walt Disney Cartoon Characters. Multicoloured.
1898 20c. Type **280** 45 20
1899 25c. Clarabelle Cow 45 20
1900 55c. Horace Horsecollar . . 70 35
1901 65c. Mortimer Mouse . . . 80 45
1902 $1 Joe Piper . . . . 1·25 85
1903 $3 Mr. Casey . . . . 2·25 2·50
1904 $4 Chief O'Hara . . . . . 2·50 3·00
1905 $5 Mickey and The Blot . . 2·50 3·00
MS1906 Two sheets, each 127 × 102 mm. (a) $6 Minnie Mouse with Tanglefoot. (b) $6 Minnie and Pluto (horiz) Set of 2 sheets 10·00 11·00

281 Marilyn Monroe

284 Pig's Head facing Right

283 Wood Duck

1994. Entertainers. Multicoloured.
1907 20c. Sonia Lloyd (folk singer) 30 20
1908 25c. Ophelia Marie (singer) 30 20
1909 55c. Edney Francis (accordion player) 50 30
1910 65c. Norman Letang (saxophonist) 60 35
1911 90c. Edie Andre (steel-band player) 70 55
1912 90c. Type **281** 95 95
1913 90c. Marilyn Monroe wearing necklace 95 95
1914 90c. In yellow frilled dress 95 95
1915 90c. In purple dress 95 95
1916 90c. Looking over left shoulder 95 95
1917 90c. Laughing 95 95
1918 90c. In red dress 95 95
1919 90c. Wearing gold cluster earrings 95 95
1920 90c. In yellow dress 95 95
MS1921 Two sheets, each 106 × 76 mm. (a) $6 Marilyn Monroe with top hat. (b) $6 With arms above head Set of 2 sheets 7·50 7·50
No. 1907 is inscribed "Llyod" in error.

1994. Christmas. Religious Paintings. As T **336** of Antigua. Multicoloured.
1922 20c. "Madonna and Child" (Luis de Morales) 25 10
1923 25c. "Madonna and Child with Yarn Winder" (De Morales) 25 10
1924 55c. "Our Lady of the Rosary" (detail) (Zurbaran) 40 30
1925 65c. "Dream of the Patrician" (detail) (Murillo) 50 55
1926 90c. "Madonna of Charity" (El Greco) 70 45
1927 $1 "The Annunciation" (Zurbaran) 75 50
1928 $2 "Mystical Marriage of St. Catherine" (Jusepe de Ribera) . . . . 1·25 2·00
1929 $3 "The Holy Family with St. Bruno and Other Saints" (detail) (De Ribera) . . . . 1·50 2·50
MS1930 Two sheets. (a) 136 × 97 mm. $6 "Adoration of the Shepherds" (detail) (Murillo). (b) 99 × 118 mm. $6 "Vision of the Virgin to St. Bernard" (detail) (Murillo) Set of 2 sheets 7·50 8·50

1994. First Recipients of Order of the Caribbean Community. As Nos. 2046/8 of Antigua. Mult.
1931 25c. Sir Shridath Ramphal 20 10
1932 65c. William Demas 50 50
1933 90c. Derek Walcott 70 80

1995. 18th World Scout Jamboree, Netherlands. Nos. 1860 and 1863/4 optd **18th World Scout Jamboree Mondial, Holland, May 6, 1995.**
1934 65c. Serving soup 60 35
1935 $4 Sailing dinghy . . . . . 2·25 2·75
1936 $5 Saluting . . . . 2·25 2·75
MS1937 Two sheets, each 100 × 70 mm. (a) $6 Early scout troop. (b) $6 Pres. Crispin Sorhaindo (chief scout) (vert) Set of 2 sheets 7·50 8·00

1995. Water Birds. Multicoloured.
1938 25c. Type **283** 70 30
1939 55c. Mallard 80 40
1940 65c. Blue-winged teal . . . 85 55
1941 65c. Cattle egret (vert) . . . 85 90
1942 65c. Snow goose (vert) . . . 85 90
1943 65c. Peregrine falcon (vert) 85 90
1944 65c. Barn owl (vert) 85 90
1945 65c. Black-crowned night heron (vert) 85 90
1946 65c. Common grackle (vert) 85 90
1947 65c. Brown pelican (vert) . . 85 90
1948 65c. Great egret (vert) . . . 85 90
1949 65c. Ruby-throated hummingbird (vert) . . . 85 90
1950 65c. Laughing gull (vert) . . 85 90
1951 65c. Greater flamingo (vert) 85 90
1952 65c. Moorhen ("Common Morehen") (vert) 85 90
1953 $5 Red-eared conure ("Blood eared parakeet") 3·00 3·75
MS1954 Two sheets, each 105 × 75 mm. (a) $5 Trumpeter swan (vert). (b) $6 White-eyed vireo Set of 2 sheets 7·00 7·50
Nos. 1941/5 were printed together, se-tenant, forming a composite design.
No. 1946 is inscribed "Common Gralkle" in error.

1995. Chinese New Year ("Year of the Pig"). Multicoloured.
1955 25c. Type **284** 40 40
1956 65c. Pig facing to the front 45 45
1957 $1 Pig facing left 50 50
MS1958 101 × 50 mm. Nos. 1955/7 1·25 1·50
MS1959 105 × 77 mm. Two pigs (horiz) 1·25 1·50

1995. 50th Anniv of End of Second World War in Europe. As T **340** of Antigua. Multicoloured.
1960 $2 German Panther tank in the Ardennes . . . . . . 1·25 1·25
1961 $2 American fighter-bomber 1·25 1·25
1962 $2 American mechanized column crossing the Rhine 1·25 1·25
1963 $2 Messerschmitt Me 163B Komet and Allied bombers . . . . 1·25 1·25
1964 $2 V2 rocket on launcher 1·25 1·25
1965 $2 German U-boat surrendering . . . . . . 1·25 1·25
1966 $2 Heavy artillery in action 1·25 1·25
1967 $2 Soviet infantry in Berlin 1·25 1·25
MS1968 106 × 76 mm. $6 Statue and devastated Dresden ($56\frac{1}{2} \times 42\frac{1}{2}$ mm) 3·50 3·75

285 Paul Harris (founder) and Emblem

1995. 90th Anniv of Rotary International.
1969 **285** $1 brown, purple & blk 75 75
MS1970 70 × 100 mm. $6 red and black 2·75 2·25
DESIGN: $6 Rotary emblems.

1995. 50th Anniv of End of Second World War in the Pacific. As T **340** of Antigua. Multicoloured.
1971 $2 Mitsubishi A6M Zero-Sen torpedo-bomber . . . 1·25 1·25
1972 $2 Aichi D3A "Val" dive bomber . . . . 1·25 1·25
1973 $2 Nakajima B5N "Kate" bomber . . . . 1·25 1·25
1974 $2 "Zuikaku" (Japanese aircraft carrier) . . . . . 1·25 1·25
1975 $2 "Akagi" (Japanese aircraft carrier) . . . . . 1·25 1·25
1976 $2 "Ryuho" (Japanese aircraft carrier) . . . . . 1·25 1·25
MS1977 108 × 76 mm. $6 Japanese torpedo-bomber at Pearl Harbor 4·00 4·00

286 Boxing

1995. Olympic Games, Atlanta (1996). (1st Issue). Multicoloured.
1978 15c. Type **286** 30 25
1979 20c. Wrestling 35 25
1980 25c. Judo 45 25
1981 55c. Fencing 50 30
1982 65c. Swimming 60 35
1983 $1 Gymnastics (vert) 80 70

1984 $2 Cycling (vert) . . . . . 2·00 1·75
1985 $5 Volleyball . . . . 2·75 3·25
MS1986 Two sheets, each 104 × 74 mm. (a) $6 Show jumping. (b) $6 Football (vert) Set of 2 sheets 7·00 7·50
See also Nos. 2122/45 and 2213.

1995. 50th Anniv of United Nations. As T **341** of Antigua. Multicoloured.
1987 65c. Signatures and U.S. delegate 40 45
1988 $1 U.S. delegate 55 60
1989 $2 Governor Stassen (U.S. delegate) . . . . 85 1·25
MS1990 100 × 71 mm. $6 Winston Churchill 3·25 3·50
Nos. 1987/9 were printed together, se-tenant, forming a composite design.

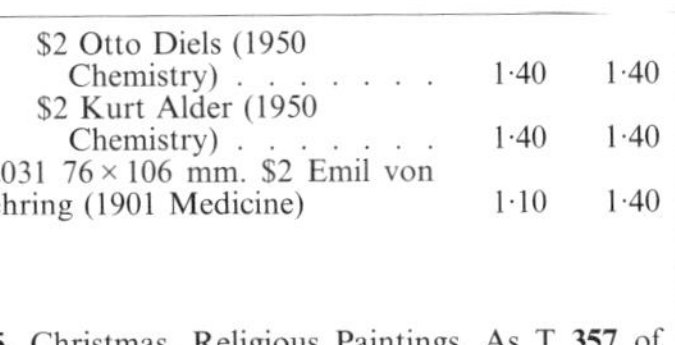

287 Market Customers

289 Oscar Sanchez (1987 Peace)

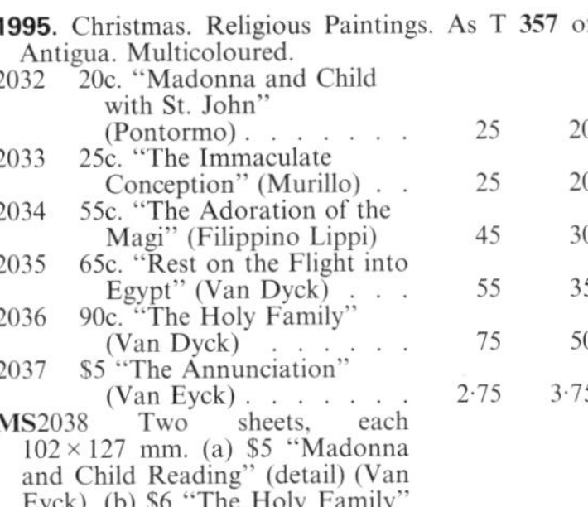

288 Monoclonius

1995. 50th Anniv of Food and Agriculture Organization. T **287** and similar multicoloured designs.
MS1991 110 × 74 mm. 90c., $1, $2 Panorama of Dominican market 1·60 1·75
MS1992 101 × 71 mm. $6 Women irrigating crops (horiz) 2·50 2·75

1995. 95th Birthday of Queen Elizabeth the Queen Mother. As T **344** of Antigua.
1993 $1.65 brown, lt brown & blk 90 1·10
1994 $1.65 multicoloured . . . . 90 1·10
1995 $1.65 multicoloured . . . . 90 1·10
1996 $1.65 multicoloured . . . . 90 1·10
MS1997 103 × 126 mm. $6 multicoloured 3·50 3·75
DESIGNS: No. 1993, Queen Elizabeth the Queen Mother (pastel drawing); 1994, Holding bouquet of flowers; 1995, At desk (oil painting); 1996, Wearing blue dress; **MS**1997, Wearing ruby and diamond tiara and necklace.

1995. "Singapore '95" International Stamp Exhibition. Prehistoric Animals. Multicoloured.
1998 20c. Type **288** 50 30
1999 25c. Euoplocephalus 50 30
2000 55c. Head of coelophysis . . 60 30
2001 65c. Head of compsognathus 65 35
2002 90c. Dimorphodon 75 75
2003 90c. Ramphorynchus . . . 75 75
2004 90c. Head of giant alligator 75 75
2005 90c. Pentaceratops 75 75
2006 $1 Ceratosaurus (vert) . . . 75 75
2007 $1 Comptosaurus (vert) . . 75 75
2008 $1 Stegosaur (vert) 75 75
2009 $1 Camarasaurs (vert) . . . 75 75
2010 $1 Baronyx (vert) 75 75
2011 $1 Dilophosaurus (vert) . . 75 75
2012 $1 Dromaeosaurids (vert) 75 75
2013 $1 Deinonychus (vert) . . . 75 75
2014 $1 Dinicthys (terror fish) (vert) 75 75
2015 $1 Head of carcharodon (Giant-toothed shark) (vert) 75 75
2016 $1 Nautiloid (vert) 75 75
2017 $1 Trilobite (vert) 75 75
MS2018 Two sheets. (a) 95 × 65 mm. $5 Sauropelta. (b) 65 × 95 mm. $6 Triceratops (vert) Set of 2 sheets 6·50 7·50
Nos. 2002/5 and 2006/17 were respectively printed together, se-tenant, forming composite designs.
Nos. 2002/5 do not carry the "Singapore '95" exhibition logo.

1995. Centenary of Nobel Prize Trust Fund. Mult.
2019 $2 Type **289** . . . . . . 1·40 1·40
2020 $2 Ernst Chain (1945 Medicine) . . . . 1·40 1·40
2021 $2 Aage Bohr (1975 Physics) 1·40 1·40
2022 $2 Jaroslav Seifert (1984 Literature) . . . . . . 1·40 1·40
2023 $2 Joseph Murray (1990 Medicine) . . . . 1·40 1·40
2024 $2 Jaroslav Heyrovsky (1959 Chemistry) . . . . 1·40 1·40
2025 $2 Adolf von Baeyer (1905 Chemistry) . . . . 1·40 1·40
2026 $2 Eduard Buchner (1907 Chemistry) . . . . 1·40 1·40
2027 $2 Carl Bosch (1931 Chemistry) . . . . 1·40 1·40
2028 $2 Otto Hahn (1944 Chemistry) . . . . 1·40 1·40
2029 $2 Otto Diels (1950 Chemistry) . . . . 1·40 1·40
2030 $2 Kurt Alder (1950 Chemistry) . . . . 1·40 1·40
MS2031 76 × 106 mm. $2 Emil von Behring (1901 Medicine) 1·10 1·40

1995. Christmas. Religious Paintings. As T **357** of Antigua. Multicoloured.
2032 20c. "Madonna and Child with St. John" (Pontormo) 25 20
2033 25c. "The Immaculate Conception" (Murillo) . . 25 20
2034 55c. "The Adoration of the Magi" (Filippino Lippi) 45 30
2035 65c. "Rest on the Flight into Egypt" (Van Dyck) . . . 55 35
2036 90c. "The Holy Family" (Van Dyck) 75 50
2037 $5 "The Annunciation" (Van Eyck) . . . . 2·75 3·75
MS2038 Two sheets, each 102 × 127 mm. (a) $5 "Madonna and Child Reading" (detail) (Van Eyck). (b) $6 "The Holy Family" (detail) (Ribera) Set of 2 sheets 6·50 7·00

1995. Centenary (1992) of Sierra Club (environmental protection society). Endangered Species. As T **320** of Antigua. Multicoloured.
2039 $1 Florida panther 50 50
2040 $1 Manatee 50 50
2041 $1 Sockeye salmon 50 50
2042 $1 Key deer facing left . . . 50 50
2043 $1 Key deer doe 50 50
2044 $1 Key deer stag 50 50
2045 $1 Wallaby with young in pouch 50 50
2046 $1 Wallaby feeding young 50 50
2047 $1 Wallaby and young feeding 50 50
2048 $1 Florida panther showing teeth (horiz) 50 50
2049 $1 Head of Florida panther (horiz) 50 50
2050 $1 Manatee (horiz) 50 50
2051 $1 Pair of manatees (horiz) 50 50
2052 $1 Pair of sockeye salmon (horiz) 50 50
2053 $1 Sockeye salmon spawning (horiz) 50 50
2054 $1 Pair of southern sea otters (horiz) 50 50
2055 $1 Southern sea otter with front paws together (horiz) 50 50
2056 $1 Southern sea otter with front paws apart (horiz) 50 50

290 Street Scene

1995. "A City of Cathay" (Chinese scroll painting). Multicoloured.
2057 90c. Type **290** 55 60
2058 90c. Street scene and city wall 55 60
2059 90c. City gate and bridge . . 55 60
2060 90c. Landing stage and junk 55 60
2061 90c. River bridge 55 60
2062 90c. Moored junks 55 60
2063 90c. Two rafts on river . . 55 60
2064 90c. Two junks on river . . 55 60
2065 90c. Roadside tea house . . 55 60
2066 90c. Wedding party on the road 55 60
MS2067 Two sheets, each 106 × 77 mm. (a) $2 City street and sampan; $2 Footbridge. (b) $2 Stern of sampan (vert); $2 Bow of sampan (vert) Set of 2 sheets 3·75 4·25

291 "Bindo Altoviti" (Raphael)

1995. Paintings by Raphael. Multicoloured.
2068 $2 Type **291** . . . . 1·60 1·60
2069 $2 "Pope Leo with Nephews" . . . . 1·60 1·60
2070 $2 "Agony in the Garden" 1·60 1·60
MS2071 110 × 80 mm. $6 "Pope Leo X with Cardinals Giulio de Medici and Luigi dei Rossi" (detail) 3·50 4·25

292 Rat

1996. Chinese New Year ("Year of the Rat").
2072 **292** 25c. black, violet and brown 25 35
2073 – 65c. black, red and green 45 55
2074 – $1 black, mauve and blue 55 65
MS2075 100 × 50 mm. Nos. 2072/4 1·25 1·50
MS2076 105 × 77 mm. $2 black, green and violet (two rats) 1·25 1·50
DESIGNS: 65c., $1, $2, Rats and Chinese symbols (different).

293 Mickey and Minnie Mouse (Year of the Rat)

1996. Chinese Lunar Calendar. Walt Disney Cartoon Characters. Multicoloured.
2077 55c. Type **293** 65 70
2078 55c. Casey Jones (Year of the Ox) 65 70
2079 55c. Tigger, Pooh and Piglet (Year of the Tiger) . . . 65 70
2080 55c. White Rabbit (Year of the Rabbit) 65 70
2081 55c. Dragon playing flute (Year of the Dragon) . . 65 70
2082 55c. Snake looking in mirror (Year of the Snake) . . . 65 70
2083 55c. Horace Horsecollar and Clarabelle Cow (Year of the Horse) 65 70
2084 55c. Black Lamb and blue birds (Year of the Ram) 65 70
2085 55c. King Louis reading book (Year of the Monkey) 65 70
2086 55c. Cock playing lute (Year of the Cock) 65 70
2087 55c. Mickey and Pluto (Year of the Dog) 65 70
2088 55c. Pig building bridge (Year of the Pig) 65 70
MS2089 Two sheets. (a) 127 × 102 mm. $3 Basil the Great Mouse Detective (Year of the Rat). (b) 102 × 127 mm. $6 Emblems for 1996, 1997 and 2007 Set of 2 sheets 7·00 8·00

294 Steam Locomotive "Dragon", Hawaii

1996. Trains of the World. Multicoloured.
2090 $2 Type **294** . . . . 1·10 1·25
2091 $2 Class 685 steam locomotive "Regina", Italy . . . . 1·10 1·25
2092 $2 Class 745 steam locomotive, Calazo to Padua line, Italy . . . . 1·10 1·25
2093 $2 Mogul steam locomotive, Philippines . . . . 1·10 1·25
2094 $2 Class 23 and 24 steam locomotives, Germany . . 1·10 1·25
2095 $2 Class BB-15000 electric locomotive "Stanislaus", France . . . . 1·10 1·25
2096 $2 Class "Black Five" steam locomotive, Scotland . . 1·10 1·25
2097 $2 Diesel-electric locomotive, France . . . . 1·10 1·25
2098 $2 LNER class A4 steam locomotive "Sir Nigel Gresley", England . . . . 1·10 1·25
2099 $2 Class 9600 steam locomotive, Japan . . . 1·10 1·25
2100 $2 "Peloponnese Express" train, Greece . . . . . 1·10 1·25
2101 $2 Porter type steam locomotive, Hawaii . . . . . 1·10 1·25
2102 $2 Steam locomotive "Holand", Norway . . . 1·10 1·25
2103 $2 Class 220 diesel-hydraulic locomotive, Germany . . 1·10 1·25
2104 $2 Steam locomotive, India 1·10 1·25
2105 $2 East African Railways Class 29 steam locomotive 1·10 1·25
2106 $2 Electric trains, Russia . . 1·10 1·25
2107 $2 Steam locomotive, Austria . . . . 1·10 1·25
MS2108 Two sheets, each 103 × 73 mm. (a) $5 L.M.S. steam locomotive "Duchess of Hamilton", England. (b) $6 Diesel locomotives, China Set of 2 sheets 6·50 7·00

295 Horse-drawn Gig, 1965

1996. Traditional Island Transport. Multicoloured.
2109 65c. Type **295** 70 35
2110 90c. Early automobile, 1910 85 55
2111 $2 Lorry, 1950 . . . . . . 1·50 1·75
2112 $3 Bus, 1955 . . . . 1·75 2·25

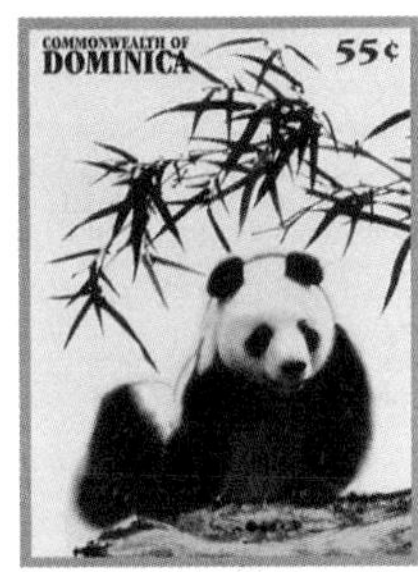

296 Giant Panda

1996. "CHINA '96" 9th Asian International Stamp Exhibition, Peking. Giant Pandas. Multicoloured.
2113 55c. Type **296** 60 60
2114 55c. Panda on rock 60 60
2115 55c. Panda eating bamboo shoots 60 60
2116 55c. Panda on all fours . . 60 60
MS2117 Two sheets. (a) 90 × 125 mm. $2 Huangshan Mountain, China (50 × 75 mm). (b) 160 × 125 mm. $3 Panda sitting (50 × 37 mm) Set of 2 sheets 3·25 3·25

1996. 70th Birthday of Queen Elizabeth II. As T **364** of Antigua. Multicoloured.
2118 $2 As Type **364** of Antigua 1·10 1·25
2119 $2 Queen in robes of Order of St. Michael and St. George . . . . . . 1·10 1·25
2120 $2 Queen in blue dress with floral brooch . . . . . . 1·10 1·25
MS2121 103 × 125 mm. $6 Queen at Trooping the Colour 3·75 3·75

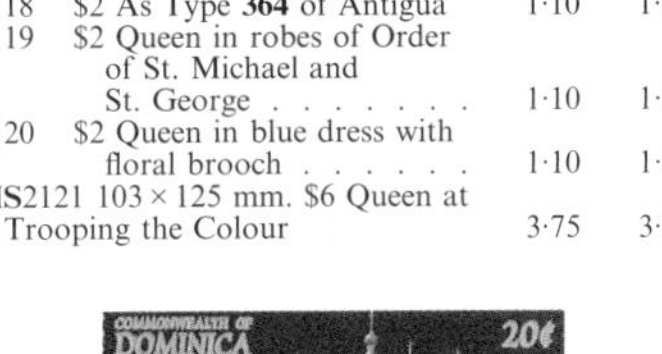

297 Moscow Stadium, 1980

1996. Olympic Games, Atlanta (2nd issue). Multicoloured.
2122 20c. Type **297** 25 25
2123 25c. Hermine Joseph (running) (vert) 30 25
2124 55c. Zimbabwe women's hockey team, 1980 . . . 60 40
2125 90c. Jerome Romain (long jump) (vert) 55 60
2126 90c. Sammy Lee (diving), 1948 and 1952 (vert) . . . 55 60
2127 90c. Bruce Jenner (decathalon), 1976 (vert) 55 60
2128 90c. Olga Korbut (gymnastics), 1972 (vert) 55 60
2129 90c. Steffi Graf (tennis), 1988 (vert) 55 60
2130 90c. Florence Griffith-Joyner (track and field), 1988 (vert) 55 60
2131 90c. Mark Spitz (swimming), 1968 and 1972 (vert) . . . 55 60
2132 90c. Li Ning (gymnastics), 1984 (vert) 55 60
2133 90c. Erika Salumae (cycling), 1988 (vert) . . . 55 60
2134 90c. Abebe Bikila (marathon), 1960 and 1964 (vert) 55 60
2135 90c. Ulrike Meyfarth (high jump), 1972 and 1984 (vert) 55 60
2136 90c. Pat McCormick (diving), 1952 and 1956 (vert) 55 60
2137 90c. Takeichi Nishi (equestrian), 1932 (vert) 55 60
2138 90c. Peter Farkas (Greco-Roman wrestling), 1992 (vert) 55 60
2139 90c. Carl Lewis (track and field), 1984, 1988 and 1992 (vert) 55 60

2140	90c. Agnes Keleti (gymnastics), 1952 and 1956 (vert)	55	60
2141	90c. Yasuhiro Yamashita (judo), 1984 (vert)	55	60
2142	90c. John Kelly (single sculls), 1920 (vert)	55	60
2143	90c. Naim Suleymanoglu (weightlifting), 1988 and 1992 (vert)	55	60
2144	$1 Polo (vert)	70	70
2145	$2 Greg Louganis (diving), 1976, 1984 and 1988	1·25	1·40
MS2146	Two sheets, each 105×75 mm. (a) $5 Joan Benoit (marathon), 1984 (vert). (b) $5 Milt Campbell (discus) Set of 2 sheets	5·50	6·50

Nos. 2126/34 and 2135/43 respectively were printed together, se-tenant, the backgrounds forming composite designs.

1996. 50th Anniv of U.N.I.C.E.F. As T **366** of Antigua. Multicoloured.

2147	20c. Child and globe (horiz)	25	15
2148	55c. Child with syringe and stethoscope (horiz)	45	35
2149	$5 Doctor and child (horiz)	2·75	3·50
MS2150	74×104 mm. $5 African child	2·75	3·25

1996. 3000th Anniv of Jerusalem. Vert designs as T **367** of Antigua. Multicoloured.

MS2151	114×95 mm. 90c. Shrine of the Book, Israel Museum; $1 Church of All Nations; $2 The Great Synagogue	2·25	2·25
MS2152	104×74 mm. $5 Hebrew University, Mount Scopus	3·25	3·25

1996. Centenary of Radio. Entertainers. As T **368** of Antigua. Multicoloured.

2153	90c. Artie Shaw	60	50
2154	$1 Benny Goodman	65	55
2155	$2 Duke Ellington	1·25	1·40
2156	$4 Harry James	2·25	2·50
MS2157	70×99 mm. $6 Tommy and Jimmy Dorsey (horiz)	3·50	4·00

298 Irene Peltier in National Dress

1996. Local Entertainers. Multicoloured.

2158	25c. Type **298**	25	20
2159	55c. Rupert Bartley (steel-band player)	40	35
2160	65c. Rosemary Cools-Lartigue (pianist)	50	40
2161	90c. Celestine 'Orion' Theophile (singer)	65	65
2162	$1 Cecil Bellot (band master)	70	80

299 Humphrey Bogart as Sam Spade

1996. Centenary of Cinema. Screen Detectives. Multicoloured.

2163	$1 Type **299**	65	70
2164	$1 Sean Connery as James Bond	65	70
2165	$1 Warren Beatty as Dick Tracy	65	70
2166	$1 Basil Rathbone as Sherlock Holmes	65	70
2167	$1 William Powell as the Thin Man	65	70
2168	$1 Sidney Toler as Charlie Chan	65	70
2169	$1 Peter Sellers as Inspector Clouseau	65	70
2170	$1 Robert Mitchum as Philip Marlowe	65	70
2171	$1 Peter Ustinov as Hercule Poirot	65	70
MS2172	105×75 mm. $6 Margaret Rutherford as Miss Marple	3·25	3·75

300 Scribbled Filefish

301 Anthony Trollope and Postal Scenes

1996. Fishes. Multicoloured.

2173	1c. Type **300**	15	30
2174	2c. Lionfish	15	30
2175	5c. Porcupinefish	25	30
2176	10c. Powder-blue surgeon fish	30	30
2177	15c. Red hind	40	30
2178	20c. Golden butterflyfish	45	20
2179	25c. Copper-banded butterflyfish	45	20
2180	35c. Pennant coralfish	50	25
2181	45c. Spotted drum	50	30
2182	55c. Blue-girdled angelfish	60	35
2183	60c. Scorpionfish	60	35
2184	65c. Harlequin sweetlips	60	40
2185	90c. Flame angelfish	80	60
2186	$1 Queen triggerfish	90	75
2187	$1.20 Spotlight parrotfish	1·00	1·00
2188	$1.45 Black durgon	1·25	1·50
2189	$2 Glass-eyed snapper	1·75	2·00
2190	$5 Balloonfish	3·50	3·75
2191	$10 Creole wrasse	6·00	7·00
2192	$20 Sea bass	11·00	12·00

For these designs size 24×21 mm, see Nos. 2374/91.

1996. World Post Day. Multicoloured.

2193	10c. Type **301**	15	15
2194	25c. Anthony Trollope and Dominican postmen	20	20
2195	55c. "Yare" (mail streamer)	45	35
2196	65c. Rural post office	50	40
2197	90c. Postmen carrying mail	65	50
2198	$1 Grumman Goose (seaplane) and 1958 Caribbean Federation 12c. stamp	70	60
2199	$2 Old and new post offices and 1978 Independence 10c. stamp	1·25	1·50
MS2200	74×104 mm. $5 18th-century naval officer	2·75	3·00

302 "Enthroned Madonna and Child" (S. Veneziano)

303 "Herdboy playing the Flute" (Li Keran)

1996. Christmas. Religious Paintings. Mult.

2201	25c. Type **302**	25	20
2202	55c. "Noli Me Tangere" (Fra Angelico)	45	35
2203	65c. "Madonna and Child Enthroned" (Angelico)	50	40
2204	90c. "Madonna of Corneto Tarquinia" (F. Lippi)	65	50
2205	$2 "The Annunciation" and "The Adoration of the Magi" (School of Angelico)	1·25	1·50
2206	$5 "Madonna and Child of the Shade" (Angelico)	2·75	3·25
MS2207	Two sheets. (a) 76×106 mm. $6 "Coronation of the Virgin" (Angelico). (b) 106×76 mm. $6 "Holy Family with St. Barbara" (Veronese) (horiz) Set of 2 sheets	7·00	7·50

1997. Lunar New Year ("Year of the Ox"). Paintings by Li Keran. Multicoloured.

2208	90c. Type **303**	60	60
2209	90c. "Playing Cricket in the Autumn"	60	60
2210	90c. "Listening to the Summer Cicada"	60	60
2211	90c. "Grazing in the Spring"	60	60
MS2212	76×106 mm. $2 "Return in Wind and Rain" (34×51 mm).	1·00	1·10
MS2212a	135×80 mm. 55c. × 4. Designs as Nos. 2208/11	1·00	1·10

304 Lee Lai-shan (Gold Medal – Windsurfing, 1996)

1997. Olympic Games, Atlanta (3rd issue). Mult.

2213	$2 Type **304**	1·25	1·50
MS2214	97×67 mm. $5 Lee Lai-shan wearing Gold medal (37×50 mm)	2·75	3·25

305 "Meticella metis"

1997. Butterflies. Multicoloured.

2215	55c. Type **305**	50	55
2216	55c. "Coeliades forestan"	50	55
2217	55c. "Papilio dardanus"	50	55
2218	55c. "Mylothris chloris"	50	55
2219	55c. "Poecilmitis thysbe"	50	55
2220	55c. "Myrina silenus"	50	55
2221	55c. "Bematistes aganice"	50	55
2222	55c. "Euphaedra neophron"	50	55
2223	55c. "Precis hierta"	50	55
2224	90c. "Coeliadas forestan" (vert)	60	65
2225	90c. "Spialia spio" (vert)	60	65
2226	90c. "Belenois aurota" (vert)	60	65
2227	90c. "Dingana bowkom" (vert)	60	65
2228	90c. "Charaxes jasius" (vert)	60	65
2229	90c. "Catacroptera cloanthe" (vert)	60	65
2230	90c. "Colias electo" (vert)	60	65
2231	90c. "Junonia archesia" (vert)	60	65
MS2232	Two sheets, each 102×71 mm. (a) $6 "Eurytela dryope". (b) "Acraea natalica" Set of 2 sheets	7·00	7·50

No. 2230 is inscribed "Collas electo" in error.

Nos. 2215/23 and 2224/31 respectively were printed together, se-tenant, with the backgrounds forming a composite design.

1997. 50th Anniv of U.N.E.S.C.O. As T **374** of Antigua. Multicoloured.

2233	55c. Temple roof, China	50	35
2234	65c. The Palace of Diocletian, Split, Croatia	55	40
2235	90c. St. Mary's Cathedral, Hildesheim, Germany	60	50
2236	$1 The Monastery of Rossanou, Mount Athos, Greece	65	65
2237	$1 Carved face, Copan, Honduras (vert)	65	70
2238	$1 Cuzco Cathedral, Peru (vert)	65	70
2239	$1 Church, Olinda, Brazil (vert)	65	70
2240	$1 Canaima National Park, Venezuela (vert)	65	70
2241	$1 Galapagos Islands National Park, Ecuador (vert)	65	70
2242	$1 Church ruins, La Santisima Jesuit Missions, Paraguay (vert)	65	70
2243	$1 San Lorenzo Fortress, Panama (vert)	65	70
2244	$1 Fortress, National Park, Haiti (vert)	65	70
2245	$2 Scandola Nature Reserve, France	1·25	1·50
2246	$4 Church of San Antao, Portugal	2·25	2·75
MS2247	Two sheets, each 127×102 mm. (a) $6 Chengde Lakes, China. (b) $6 Pavilion, Kyoto, Japan Set of 2 sheets	6·50	7·50

No. 2234 is inscr "DICELECIAN" in error.

306 Tanglefoot and Minnie

1997. Disney Sweethearts. Multicoloured.

2248	25c. Type **306**	35	20
2249	35c. Mickey and Minnie kissing on ship's wheel	45	20
2250	55c. Pluto and kitten	60	30
2251	65c. Clarabelle Cow kissing Horace Horsecollar	60	35
2252	90c. Elmer Elephant and tiger	75	55
2253	$1 Minnie kissing Mickey in period costume	80	70
2254	$2 Donald Duck and nephew	1·40	1·60
2255	$4 Dog kissing Pluto	2·00	2·75
MS2256	Three sheets. (a) 126×100 mm. $5 Simba and Nala in "The Lion King". (b) 133×104 mm. $6 Mickey covered in lipstick and Minnie (horiz). (c) 104×124 mm. $6 Mickey and Pluto Set of 3 sheets	8·50	9·00

307 Afghan Hound

308 "Oncidium altissimum"

1997. Cats and Dogs. Multicoloured.

2257	20c. Type **307**	35	25
2258	25c. Cream Burmese	35	25
2259	55c. Cocker spaniel	45	35
2260	65c. Smooth fox terrier	50	40
2261	90c. West highland white terrier	60	65
2262	90c. St. Bernard puppies	60	65
2263	90c. Boy with grand basset	60	65
2264	90c. Rough collie	60	65
2265	90c. Golden retriever	60	65
2266	90c. Golden retriever, Tibetan spaniel and smooth fox terrier	60	65
2267	90c. Smooth fox terrier	60	65
2268	$1 Snowshoe	65	70
2269	$2 Sorrell Abyssinian	1·10	1·25
2270	$2 British bicolour shorthair	1·10	1·25
2271	$2 Maine coon and Somali kittens	1·10	1·25
2272	$2 Maine coon kitten	1·10	1·25
2273	$2 Lynx point Siamese	1·10	1·25
2274	$2 Blue Burmese kitten and white Persian	1·10	1·25
2275	$2 Persian kitten	1·10	1·25
2276	$5 Torbie Persian	2·75	3·25
MS2277	Two sheets, each 106×76 mm. (a) $6 Silver tabby. (b) $6 Shetland sheepdog Set of 2 sheets	7·00	8·00

Nos. 2262/7 and 2270/5 respectively were printed together, se-tenant, with the backgrounds forming composite designs.

1997. Orchids of the Caribbean. Multicoloured.

2278	20c. Type **308**	40	25
2279	25c. "Oncidium papilio"	40	25
2280	55c. "Epidendrum fragrans"	45	35
2281	65c. "Oncidium lanceanum"	50	40
2282	90c. "Campylocentrum micranthum'	60	50
2283	$1 "Brassavola cucculata" (horiz)	65	70
2284	$1 "Epidendrum ibaguense" (horiz)	65	70
2285	$1 "Ionopsis utricularioides" (horiz)	65	70
2286	$1 "Rodriguezia lanceolata" (horiz)	65	70
2287	$1 "Oncidium cebolleta" (horiz)	65	70
2288	$1 "Epidendrum ciliare" (horiz)	65	70
2289	$4 "Pogonia rosea"	2·25	2·50
MS2290	Two sheets, each 106×76 mm. (a) $5 "Oncidium ampliatum" (horiz). (b) $5 "Starhopea grandiflora" (horiz) Set of 2 sheets	6·00	6·50

Nos. 2283/8 were printed together, se-tenant, with the backgrounds forming a composite design.

309 "Mary, Mary Quite Contrary"

1997. 300th Anniv of Mother Goose Nursery Rhymes. Sheet 72×102 mm.

MS2291	**309** $6 multicoloured	3·25	3·50

1997. 10th Anniv of Chernobyl Nuclear Disaster. As T **376** of Antigua. Multicoloured.

2292	$2 As Type **376** of Antigua	1·25	1·40
2293	$2 As Type **376** of Antigua but inscribed "CHABAD'S CHILDREN OF CHERNOBYL" at foot	1·25	1·40

1997. 50th Death Anniv of Paul Harris (founder of Rotary International). As T **377** of Antigua. Multicoloured.

2294	$2 Paul Harris and irrigation project, Honduras	1·25	1·50
MS2295	78×107 mm. $6 Paul Harris with Rotary and World Community Service emblems	3·25	3·50

1997. Golden Wedding of Queen Elizabeth and Prince Philip. As T **378** of Antigua. Multicoloured.

2296	$1 Queen Elizabeth II	70	75
2297	$1 Royal Coat of Arms	70	75
2298	$1 Queen Elizabeth and Prince Philip in shirt sleeves	70	75
2299	$1 Queen Elizabeth and Prince Philip in naval uniform	70	75

2300 $1 Buckingham Palace . . . 70 75
2301 $1 Prince Philip . . . 70 75
MS2302 100×71 mm. $6 Queen Elizabeth and Prince Philip with flower arrangement 3·50 3·75

1997. "Pacific '97" International Stamp Exhibition, San Francisco. Death Centenary of Heinrich von Stephan (founder of the U.P.U.). As T **379** of Antigua.
2303 $2 violet . . . 1·25 1·40
2304 $2 brown . . . 1·25 1·40
2305 $2 brown . . . 1·25 1·40
MS2306 82×119 mm. $6 blue and grey 3·50 3·75
DESIGNS: No. 2303, Kaiser Wilhelm II and Heinrich von Stephan; 2304, Heinrich von Stephan and Mercury; 2305, Early Japanese postal messenger; MS2306, Heinrich von Stephan and Russian postal dog team, 1895.

310 "Ichigaya Hachiman Shrine"

1997. Birth Centenary of Hiroshige (Japanese painter). "One Hundred Famous Views of Edo". Multicoloured.
2307 $1.55 Type **310** . . . 1·25 1·25
2308 $1.55 "Blossoms on the Tama River Embankment" . . . 1·25 1·25
2309 $1.55 "Kumano Junisha Shrine, Tsunohazu" . . . 1·25 1·25
2310 $1.55 "Benkei Moat from Soto-Sakurada to Kojimachi" . . . 1·25 1·25
2311 $1.55 "Kinokuni Hill and View of Akasak Tameike" 1·25 1·25
2312 $1.55 "Naito Shinjuku, Yotsuya" . . . 1·25 1·25
MS2313 Two sheets, each 102×127 mm. (a) $6 "Sanno Festival Procession at Kojimachi l-chome". (b) $6 "Kasumigaseki" Set of 2 sheets 7·50 8·00

1997. 175th Anniv of Brothers Grimm's Third Collection of Fairy Tales. The Goose Girl. As T **380** of Antigua. Multicoloured.
2314 $2 Goose girl with horse . . 1·25 1·40
2315 $2 Geese in front of castle . . 1·25 1·40
2316 $2 Goose girl . . . 1·25 1·40
MS2317 124×96 mm. $6 Goose girl (horiz) 3·25 3·50

311 Hong Kong Skyline at Dusk

312 Yukto Kasaya (Japan) (ski jump), 1972

1997. Return of Hong Kong to China. Multicoloured.
2318 65c. Type **311** . . . 60 70
2319 90c. Type **311** . . . 70 80
2320 $1 Type **311** . . . 75 85
2321 $1 Hong Kong at night . . 75 85
2322 $1.45 Hong Kong by day 1·00 1·25
2323 $2 Hong Kong at night (different) . . . 1·25 1·50
2324 $3 Type **311** . . . 1·50 1·75

1997. Winter Olympic Games, Nagano, Japan (1998). Multicoloured.
2325 20c. Type **312** . . . 40 25
2326 25c. Jens Weissflog (Germany) (ski jump), 1994 . . . 40 25
2327 55c. Anton Maier (Norway) (100 m men's speed skating), 1968 . . . 50 45
2328 55c. Ljubov Egorova (Russia) (women's 5 km cross-country skiing), 1994 50 45
2329 65c. Swedish ice hockey, 1994 . . . 60 45
2330 90c. Bernhard Glass (Germany) (men's single luge), 1980 . . . 65 60
2331 $1 Type **312** . . . 70 80
2332 $1 As No. 2326 . . . 70 80
2333 $1 As No. 2327 . . . 70 80
2334 $1 Christa Rethenburger (Germany) (women's 100 m speed skating), 1988 . . . 70 80
2335 $4 Frank-Peter Roetsch (Germany) (men's biathlon), 1988 . . . 2·25 2·50
MS2336 Two sheets, each 106×76 mm. (a) $5 Charles Jewtraw (U.S.A.) (men's 500 m speed skating), 1924. (b) $5 Jacob Tullin Thams (Norway) (ski jumping), 1924 Set of 2 sheets 5·50 6·50

1997. World Cup Football Championship, France (1998). As T **383** of Antigua. Multicoloured (except Nos. 2343/4, 2348, 2350, 2353/4).
2337 20c. Klinsmann, Germany (vert) . . . 40 25
2338 55c. Bergkamp, Holland (vert) . . . 60 35
2339 65c. Ravanelli, Italy (vert) 60 65
2340 65c. Wembley Stadium, England . . . 60 65
2341 65c. Bernabeu Stadium, Spain . . . 60 65
2342 65c. Maracana Stadium, Brazil . . . 60 65
2343 65c. Stadio Torino, Italy (black) . . . 60 65
2344 65c. Centenary Stadium, Uruguay (black) . . . 60 65
2345 65c. Olympiastadion, Germany . . . 60 65
2346 65c. Rose Bowl, U.S.A. . . 60 65
2347 65c. Azteca Stadium, Mexico . . . 60 65
2348 65c. Meazza, Italy (black) 60 65
2349 65c. Matthaus, Germany . . 60 65
2350 65c. Walter, West Germany (black) . . . 60 65
2351 65c. Maradona, Argentina 60 65
2352 65c. Beckenbaur, Germany 60 65
2353 65c. Moore, England (black) 60 65
2354 65c. Dunga, Brazil (black) 60 65
2355 65c. Zoff, Italy . . . 60 65
2356 90c. Klinkladze, Georgia . . 70 60
2357 $2 Shearer, England (vert) 1·25 1·40
2358 $4 Dani, Portugal (vert) . . 2·25 2·50
MS2359 Two sheets. (a) 102×126 mm. $5 Mario Kempes, Argentina (vert). (b) 126×102 mm. $6 Ally McCoist, Scotland (vert) Set of 2 sheets 6·50 7·00

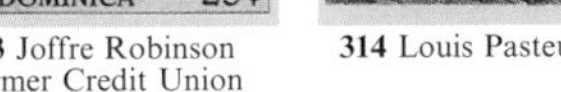

313 Joffre Robinson (former Credit Union President)

314 Louis Pasteur

1997. 40th Anniv of Co-operative Credit Union League.
2360 **313** 25c. blue and black . . . 25 20
2361 – 55c. green and black . . 45 40
2362 – 65c. purple and black . . 55 55
2363 – 90c. multicoloured . . . 65 70
MS2364 94×106 mm. $5 multicoloured 2·50 2·75
DESIGNS—As T **313**: 55c. Sister Alicia (founder); 65c. Lorrel Bruce (first Credit Union President). 30×60 mm: $5 Sister Alicia, Joffre Robinson and Lorrel Bruce.

1997. Medical Pioneers.
2365 **314** 20c. brown . . . 40 25
2366 – 25c. pink and red . . . 40 25
2367 – 55c. violet . . . 50 35
2368 – 65c. red and brown . . . 55 45
2369 – 90c. yellow and olive . . 65 55
2370 – $1 blue and ultramarine 70 70
2371 – $2 black . . . 1·25 1·40
2372 – $3 red and brown . . . 1·50 1·75
MS2373 Two sheets, each 70×100 mm. (a) $5 multicoloured. (b) $6 multicoloured Set of 2 sheets 6·50 7·00
DESIGNS: 25c. Christiaan Barnard (first heart transplant); 55c. Sir Alexander Fleming (discovery of penicillin); 65c. Camillo Golgi (neurologist); 90c. Jonas Salk (discovery of polio vaccine); $1 Har Gobind Khorana (genetics); $2 Elizabeth Black (first woman doctor); $3 Sir Frank MacFarlane Burnet (immunologist); $5 (**MS**2373a), Sir Alexander Fleming (different); $6 (**MS**2373b), Louis Pasteur (different).

1997. Fishes. As Nos. 2175/92, but smaller, 24×21mm.
2374 5c. Porcupinefish . . . 15 30
2375 10c. Powder-blue surgeonfish . . . 15 30
2376 15c. Red hind . . . 25 30
2377 20c. Golden butterflyfish . . 30 30
2378 25c. Copper-banded butterflyfish . . . 35 30
2379 35c. Pennant coralfish . . . 50 35
2380 45c. Spotted drum . . . 50 30
2381 55c. Blue-girdled angelfish 60 40
2382 60c. Scorpionfish . . . 60 40
2383 65c. Harlequin sweetlips . . 60 40
2384 90c. Flame angelfish . . . 80 60
2385 $1 Queen triggerfish . . . 90 75
2386 $1.20 Spotlight parrotfish 1·00 1·00
2387 $1.45 Black durgon . . . 1·25 1·50
2388 $2 Glass-eyed snapper . . . 1·75 2·00
2389 $5 Balloonfish . . . 3·50 3·75
2390 $10 Creole wrasse . . . 6·00 7·00
2391 $20 Seabass . . . 11·00 12·00

315 Diana, Princess of Wales

316 "Echo et Narcisse" (Toile)

1997. Diana, Princess of Wales Commemoration. Multicoloured.
2392 $2 Type **315** . . . 1·25 1·40
2393 $2 Wearing diamond-drop earrings . . . 1·25 1·40
2394 $2 Resting head on hand . . 1·25 1·40
2395 $2 Wearing tiara . . . 1·25 1·40
MS2396 76×106 mm. $5 Diana, Princess of Wales 3·50 3·50

1997. Christmas. Paintings.
2397 20c. Type **316** . . . 25 15
2398 55c. "The Archangel Raphael leaving the Family of Tobias" (Rembrandt) . . . 45 35
2399 65c. "Seated Nymphs with Flute" (Francois Boucher) 50 40
2400 90c. "Angel" (Rembrandt) 65 50
2401 $2 "Dispute" (Raphael) . . 1·25 1·40
2402 $4 "Holy Trinity" (Raphael) 2·25 2·50
MS2403 Two sheets, each 114×104 mm. (a) $6 "The Annunciation" (Botticelli) (horiz). (b) $6 "Christ on the Mount of Olives" (El Greco) (horiz) Set of 2 sheets 7·00 8·00
No. MS2403a is inscribed "Study (of the) Muse" in error.

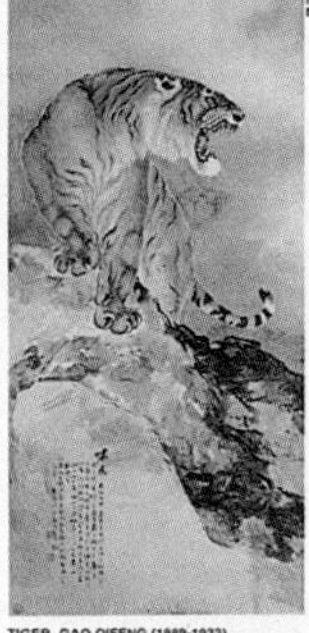

317 "Tiger" (Gao Qifeng)

318 Akira Kurosawa

1998. Chinese New Year ("Year of the Tiger"). Multicoloured.
2404 55c. Type **317** . . . 25 30
2405 65c. "Tiger" (Zhao Shao'ang) . . . 35 40
2406 90c. "Tiger" (Gao Jianfu) 45 50
2407 $1.20 "Tiger" (different) (Gao Jianfu) . . . 55 60
MS2408 95×65 mm. $3 "Spirit of Kingship" (Gao Jianfu) (48×40 mm) 1·40 1·50

1998. Millennium Series. Famous People of the Twentieth Century. Multicoloured (except Nos. 2411, 2414/15 and **MS**2417). (a) Japanese Cinema Stars.
2409 $1 Type **318** . . . 50 55
2410 $1 "Rashomon" directed by Kursawa (56×42 mm) . . 50 55
2411 $1 Toshiro Mifune in "Seven Samurai" (black and grey) (56×42 mm) 50 55
2412 $1 Toshiro Mifune . . . 50 55
2413 $1 Yasujiro Ozu . . . 50 55
2414 $1 "Late Spring" directed by Ozu (black and grey) (56×42 mm) . . . 50 55
2415 $1 Sessue Hayakawa in "Bridge on the River Kwai" (brown, deep brown and black) (56×42 mm) . . . 50 55
2416 $1 Sessue Hayakawa . . . 50 55
MS2417 110×80 mm. $6 Akira Kurosawa (brown, red and black) 3·00 3·25

(b) Sporting Record Holders. Multicoloured.
2418 $1 Jesse Owens (winner of four Olympic gold medals, Berlin, 1936) . . . 65 70
2419 $1 Owens competing at Berlin (56×42 mm) . . . 65 70
2420 $1 Isaac Berger competing (56×42 mm) . . . 65 70
2421 $1 Isaac Berger (weightlifter) 65 70
2422 $1 Boris Becker (Wimbledon champion) . . . 65 70
2423 $1 Boris Becker on court (56×42 mm) . . . 65 70
2424 $1 Ashe with Wimbledon trophy (56×42 mm) . . . 65 70
2425 $1 Arthur Ashe (1st African-American Wimbledon singles champion, 1975) . . . 65 70
MS2426 $6 Franz Beckenbauer (captain of German football team) (horiz) 3·25 3·50

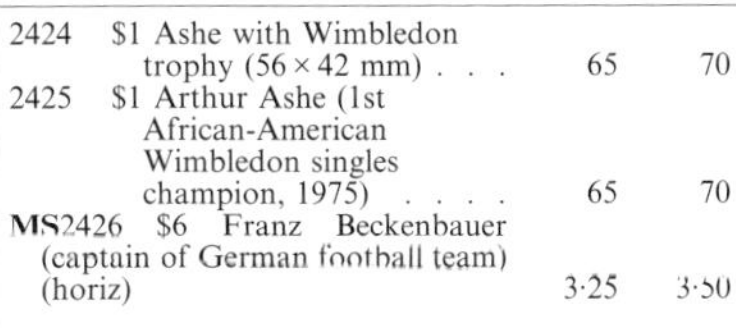

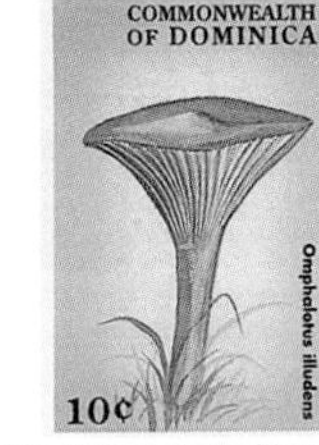

319 "Omphalotus illudens"

1998. Fungi of the World. Multicoloured.
2427 10c. Type **319** . . . 10 10
2428 15c. "Inocybe fastigiata" . . 10 10
2429 20c. "Marasmius plicatulus" 10 15
2430 50c. "Mycena lilacifolia" . . 25 30
2431 55c. "Armillaria straminea" and "Calastrina argiolus" (butterfly) . . . 25 30
2432 90c. "Tricholomopsis rutilans" and "Melitaea didyma" (butterfly) . . . 45 50
2433 $1 "Lepiota naucina" . . . 50 55
2434 $1 "Cortinarius violaceus" 50 55
2435 $1 "Boletus aereus" . . . 50 55
2436 $1 "Tricholoma aurantium" 50 55
2437 $1 "Lepiota procera" . . . 50 55
2438 $1 "Clitocybe geotropa" . . 50 55
2439 $1 "Lepiota acutesquamosa" 50 55
2440 $1 "Tricholoma saponaceum" . . . 50 55
2441 $1 "Lycoperdon gemmatum" . . . 50 55
2442 $1 "Boletus ornatipes" . . . 50 55
2443 $1 "Russula xerampelina" . . 50 55
2444 $1 "Cortinarius collinitus" 50 55
2445 $1 "Agaricus meleagris" . . 50 55
2446 $1 "Coprinus comatus" . . 50 55
2447 $1 "Amanita caesarea" . . 50 55
2448 $1 "Amanita brunnescens" 50 55
2449 $1 "Amanita muscaria" . . 50 55
2450 $1 "Morchella esculenta" . . 50 55
MS2451 76×106 mm. $6 "Cortinarius violaceus" 3·00 3·25
Nos. 2433/41 and 2442/50 respectively were printed together, se-tenant, with the backgrounds forming composite designs.

320 Topsail Schooner

1998. History of Sailing Ships. Multicoloured.
2452 55c. Type **320** . . . 25 30
2453 55c. "Golden Hind" (Drake) 25 30
2454 55c. "Moshulu" (barque) . . 25 30
2455 55c. "Bluenose" (schooner) 25 30
2456 55c. Roman merchant ship 25 30
2457 55c. "Gazela Primiero" (barquentine) . . . 25 30
2458 65c. Greek war galley . . . 35 40
2459 90c. Egyptian felucca . . . 45 50
2460 $1 Viking longship . . . 50 55
2461 $2 Chinese junk . . . 95 1·00
MS2462 Two sheets, each 106×76 mm. (a) $5 "Pinta" (Columbus). (b) $5 Chesapeake Bay skipjack Set of 2 sheets 4·75 5·00
No. 2457 is inscribed "GAZELA PRIMERIRO", and both Nos. 2458/9 "EGYPTIAN FELUCCA", all in error.

321 "Steamboat Willie", 1928

1998. 70th Anniv of Mickey and Minnie Mouse. Multicoloured.
2463 25c. Type **321** . . . 70 75
2464 55c. "The Brave Little Tailor", 1938 . . . 85 90
2465 65c. "Nifty Nineties", 1941 90 95
2466 90c. "Mickey Mouse Club", 1955 . . . 1·10 1·25
2467 $1 Mickey and Minnie at opening of Walt Disney World, 1971 . . . 1·10 1·25

2468 $1.45 "Mousercise Mickey and Minnie", 1980 . . . 1·25 1·40
2469 $5 "Runaway Brain", 1995 (97 × 110 mm) . . . . 2·50 2·75
MS2470 Two sheets, each 130 × 104 mm. (a) $5 Walt Disney with Mickey and Minnie Mouse. (b) $5 Mickey and Minnie at 70th birthday party with Donald and Daisy Duck, Goofy and Pluto. Imperf Set of 2 sheets 7·50 8·00

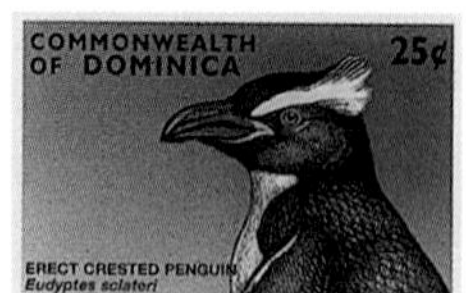

322 Big-crested Penguin ("Erect Crested Penguin")

1998. Sea Birds. Multicoloured.
2471 25c. Type **322** 10 15
2472 65c. Humboldt penguin . . 35 40
2473 90c. Red knot 45 50
2474 90c. Greater crested tern . . 45 50
2475 90c. Franklin's gull 45 50
2476 90c. Australian pelican . . . 45 50
2477 90c. Fairy prion 45 50
2478 90c. Andean gull 45 50
2479 90c. Blue-eyed cormorant ("Imperial Shag") 45 50
2480 90c. Grey phalarope ("Red Phalarope") 45 50
2481 90c. Hooded grebe 45 50
2482 90c. Least aucklet 45 50
2483 90c. Little grebe 45 50
2484 90c. Pintado petrel ("Cape Petrel") 45 50
2485 90c. Slavonian grebe ("Horned Grebe") 45 50
2486 $1 Audubon's shearwater 50 55
MS2487 Two sheets, each 100 × 70 mm. (a) $5 Blue-footed booby. (b) $5 Fulmar Set of 2 sheets 4·75 5·00
Nos. 2474/85 were printed together, se-tenant, with the backgrounds forming a composite design.

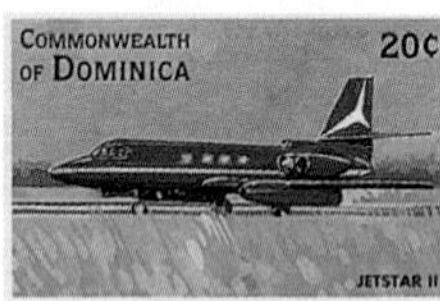

323 Jetstar II

1998. Modern Aircraft. Multicoloured.
2488 20c. Type **323** 10 15
2489 25c. AN 225 . . . . 10 15
2490 55c. L.I.A.T. Dash-8 . . . 25 30
2491 65c. Cardinal Airlines, Beech-99 . . . . 35 40
2492 90c. American Airlines Eagle 45 50
2493 $1 SR 71 "Blackbird" spy plane 50 55
2494 $1 Stealth Bomber 50 55
2495 $1 Northrop YF23 . . . . 50 55
2496 $1 F-14A Tomcat 50 55
2497 $1 F-15 Eagle S 50 55
2498 $1 MiG 29 Fulcrum 50 55
2499 $1 Europa X5 . . . . 50 55
2500 $1 Camion 50 55
2501 $1 E 400 . . . . 50 55
2502 $1 CL-215 C-GKDN amphibian 50 55
2503 $1 Piper Jet 50 55
2504 $1 Beech Hawker 50 55
2505 $1 Lockheed YF22 . . . . 50 55
2506 $1 Piper Seneca V 50 55
2507 $1 CL-215 amphibian . . . 50 55
2508 $1 Vantase 50 55
2509 $2 Itansa HFB 320 . . . . 95 1·00
MS2510 Two sheets. (a) 88 × 69 mm. $6 F1 Fighter. (b) 69 × 88 mm. $6 Sea Hopper seaplane Set of 2 sheets 6·00 6·50

1998. 50th Anniv of Organization of American States. As T **399** of Antigua. Multicoloured.
2511 $1 Stylised Americas 50 55

1998. 25th Death Anniv of Pablo Picasso (painter). As T **400** of Antigua. Multicoloured.
2512 90c. "The Painter and his Model" 45 50
2513 $1 "The Crucifixion" . . . 50 55
2514 $2 "Nude with Raised Arms" (vert) . . . . . . 95 1·00
MS2515 122 × 102 mm. $6 "Cafe at Royan" 3·00 3·25

1998. Birth Centenary of Enzo Ferrari (car manufacturer). As T **401** of Antigua. Mult.
2516 55c. 365 GT 2+2 . . . . . 60 40
2517 90c. Boano/Ellena 250 GT 80 80
2518 $1 375 MM coupe 90 90
MS2519 104 × 70 mm. $5 212 (91 × 34 mm) 2·75 3·00

1998. 19th World Scout Jamboree, Chile. As T **402** of Antigua. Multicoloured.
2520 65c. Scout saluting 35 40
2521 $1 Scout handshake 50 55
2522 $2 International scout flag 95 1·00
MS2523 76 × 106 mm. $5 Lord Baden-Powell 2·40 2·50

324 Mahatma Gandhi

327 Common Cardinal ("Northern Cardinal")

325 Fridman Fish

1998. 50th Death Anniv of Mahatma Gandhi. Multicoloured.
2524 90c. Type **324** 45 50
MS2525 106 × 75 mm. $6 Gandhi spinning thread 3·00 3·25

1998. 80th Anniv of Royal Air Force. As T **404** of Antigua. Multicoloured.
2526 $2 H.S. 801 Nimrod MR2P (reconnaissance) . . . . . 95 1·00
2527 $2 Lockheed C-130 Hercules (transport) . . . . 95 1·00
2528 $2 Panavia Tornado GR1 95 1·00
2529 $2 Lockheed C-130 Hercules landing . . . . 95 1·00
MS2530 Two sheets, each 90 × 68 mm. (a) $5 Bristol F2B fighter and Golden eagle (bird). (b) $6 Hawker Hart and EF-2000 Euro-fighter Set of 2 sheets 5·50 5·75
No. 2529 is inscribed "Panavia Tornado GR1" in error.

1998. International Year of the Ocean. Multicoloured.
2531 25c. Type **325** 10 15
2532 55c. Hydrocoral 25 30
2533 65c. Feather-star 35 40
2534 90c. Royal angelfish 45 50
2535 $1 Monk seal 50 55
2536 $1 Galapagos penguin . . . 50 55
2537 $1 Manta ray 50 55
2538 $1 Hawksbill turtle 50 55
2539 $1 Moorish idols 50 55
2540 $1 Nautilus 50 55
2541 $1 Giant clam 50 55
2542 $1 Tubeworms 50 55
2543 $1 Nudibranch 50 55
2544 $1 Spotted dolphins 50 55
2545 $1 Atlantic sailfish 50 55
2546 $1 Sailfin flying fish 50 55
2547 $1 Fairy basslet 50 55
2548 $1 Atlantic spadefish . . . 50 55
2549 $1 Leatherback turtle . . . 50 55
2550 $1 Blue tang 50 55
2551 $1 Coral-banded shrimp . . 50 55
2552 $1 Rock beauty 50 55
MS2553 Two sheets, each 110 × 85 mm. (a) $5 Humpback whale and calf (56 × 41 mm). (b) $6 Leafy sea-dragon (56 × 41 mm) Set of 2 sheets 5·50 5·75
Nos. 2535/43 and 2544/52 respectively were printed together, se-tenant, with the backgrounds forming composite designs.

1998. Save the Turtles Campaign. Nos. 1686/7, 1689/90 and 1692 optd **Save the Turtles.**
2554 25c. Type **263** 10 15
2555 55c. Hawksbill turtle swimming 25 30
2556 90c. Green turtle laying eggs 45 50
2557 $1 Green turtle swimming 50 55
2558 $4 Loggerhead turtle . . . 1·90 2·00

1998. Christmas. Birds. Multicoloured.
2559 25c. Type **327** 10 15
2560 55c. Eastern bluebird . . . 25 30
2561 65c. Carolina wren 35 40
2562 90c. Blue jay 45 50
2563 $1 Evening grosbeak 50 55
2564 $2 Bohemian waxwing . . . 95 1·00
MS2565 Two sheets, each 70 × 97 mm. (a) $5 Northern Parula. (b) $6 Painted bunting Set of 2 sheets 5·50 5·75

328 "Magpies and Hare" (Ts'ui Pai)

1999. Chinese New Year ("Year of the Rabbit").
2566 **328** $1.50 multicoloured . . 70 75

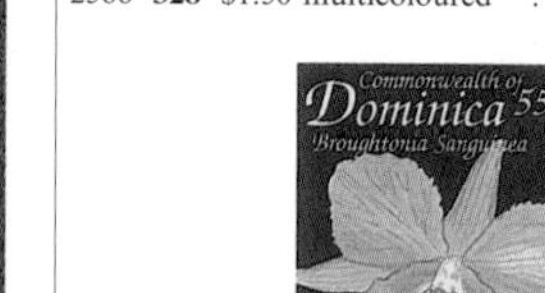

329 "Broughtonia sanguinea"

1999. Orchids of the Caribbean. Multicoloured.
2567 55c. Type **329** 25 30
2568 65c. "Cattleyonia Keith Roth" "Roma" 35 40
2569 90c. "Comparettia falcata" 45 50
2570 $1 "Dracula erythiochaete" 50 55
2571 $1 "Lycasle aromatica" . . 50 55
2572 $1 "Masdevallia marguerile" 50 55
2573 $1 "Encyclia marlae" . . . 50 55
2574 $1 "Laelia gouldiana" . . . 50 55
2575 $1 "Huntleya meleagris" . . 50 55
2576 $1 "Galeandria baueri" . . 50 55
2577 $1 "Lycale deppei" 50 55
2578 $1 "Anguloa clowesii" . . . 50 55
2579 $1 "Lemboglossum cervantesii" 50 55
2580 $1 "Oncidium cebolleta" . . 50 55
2581 $1 "Millonia" 50 55
2582 $1 "Pescatorea lehmannll" 50 55
2583 $1 "Sophronitis coccinea" 50 55
2584 $1 "Pescatorea cerina" . . . 50 55
2585 $1 "Encyclia vitellina" . . . 50 55
2586 $2 "Cochleanthes discolor" 95 1·00
MS2587 Two sheets, each 76 × 89 mm. (a) $5 "Lepanthes ovalis". (b) $5 "Encyclia cochleata" Set of 2 sheets 4·75 5·00

330 County Donegal Petrol Rail Car No. 10, Ireland

1999. "Australia '99" International Stamp Exhibition, Melbourne. Diesel and Electric Trains. Multicoloured.
2588 $1 Type **330** 50 55
2589 $1 Canadian Pacific rail car, Canada 50 55
2590 $1 Class WDM locomotive, India 50 55
2591 $1 Bi-polar locomotive, No. E-2, U.S.A. 50 55
2592 $1 Class X locomotive, Australia 50 55
2593 $1 Class "Beijing" locomotive, China 50 55
2594 $1 Class E428 locomotive, Italy 50 55
2595 $1 Class 581 twelve-car train, Japan 50 55
2596 $1 Class 103.1 locomotive, West Germany 50 55
2597 $1 Class 24 Trans-Pennine train, Great Britain . . . 50 55
2598 $1 Amtrak Class GG1, No. 902, U.S.A. 50 55
2599 $1 Class LRC train, Canada 50 55
2600 $1 Class EW train, New Zealand 50 55
2601 $1 Class SS1 Shao-Shani, China 50 55
2602 $1 Gulf, Mobile and Ohio train, U.S.A. 50 55
2603 $1 Class 9100 locomotive, France 50 55
MS2604 Two sheets, each 106 × 76 mm. (a) $5 X-2000 tilting express train, Sweden (vert). (b) $6 Class 87 locomotive, Great Britain (vert) Set of 2 sheets 5·50 5·75
No. 2589 is inscribed "USA - RDC Single Rail Car" in error.

331 Hypacrosaurus

1999. Prehistoric Animals. Multicoloured.
2605 25c. Tyrannosaurus (vert) 10 15
2606 65c. Type **331** 35 40
2607 90c. Sauropelta 45 50
2608 $1 Barosaurus 50 55
2609 $1 Rhamphorhynchus . . . 50 55
2610 $1 Apatosaurus 50 55
2611 $1 Archaeopteryx 50 55
2612 $1 Diplodocus 50 55
2613 $1 Ceratosaurus 50 55
2614 $1 Stegosaurus 50 55
2615 $1 Elaphrosaurus 50 55
2616 $1 Vulcanodon 50 55
2617 $1 Psittacosaurus 50 55
2618 $1 Pteranodon 50 55
2619 $1 Ichthyornis 50 55
2620 $1 Spinosaurus 50 55
2621 $1 Parasaurolophus 50 55
2622 $1 Ornithomimus 50 55
2623 $1 Anatosaurus 50 55
2624 $1 Triceratops 50 55
2625 $1 Baryonx 50 55
2626 $2 Zalambdalestes . . . . . 95 1·00
MS2627 Two sheets, each 106 × 80 mm. (a) $5 Yangchuanosaurus. (b) $6 Brachiosaurus (vert) Set of 2 sheets 5·50 5·75
Nos. 2608/16 and 2617/25 respectively were each printed together, se-tenant, with the backgrounds forming composite designs.

332 Miss Sophie Rhys-Jones

1999. Royal Wedding.
2628 **332** $3 blue and black . . . 1·40 1·50
2629 – $3 multicoloured . . . 1·40 1·50
2630 – $3 blue and black . . . 1·40 1·50
MS2631 78 × 108 mm. $6 multicoloured 3·00 3·25
DESIGNS: No. 2629 and **MS**2631, Miss Sophie Rhys-Jones and Prince Edward; 2630, Prince Edward.

1999. "iBRA '99" International Stamp Exhibition, Nuremberg. As T **416** of Antigua. Multicoloured.
2632 65c. "Eendracht" (Dirk Hartog) with Cameroons Expeditionary Force 1915 2d. and 3d. surcharges . . 35 40
2633 90c. "Eendracht" with Kamerun 1900 10pf. and 25pf. stamps 45 50
2634 $1 Early German railway locomotive with Kamerun 1900 5m. stamp 50 55
2635 $2 Early German railway locomotive with Kamerun 1890 overprinted 50pf. stamp . . . . 95 1·00
MS2636 138 × 109 mm. $6 Exhibition emblem and Kamerun 5m. stamp postmarked 1913 3·00 3·25

1999. 150th Death Anniv of Katsushika Hokusai (Japanese artist). As T **417** of Antigua, but vert. Multicoloured.
2637 $2 "Pilgrims at Kirifuri Waterfall" . . . . 95 1·00
2638 $2 "Kakura-Sato" (rats pulling on rope) . . . . . 95 1·00
2639 $2 "Travellers on the Bridge by Ono Waterfall" . . . 95 1·00
2640 $2 "Fast Cargo Boat battling the Waves" . . . 95 1·00
2641 $2 "Kakura-Sato" (rats with barrels) . . . . 95 1·00
2642 $2 "Buufinfinh and Weeping Cherry" . . . . 95 1·00
2643 $2 "Cuckoo and Azalea" . . 95 1·00
2644 $2 "Soldiers" (with lamp) 95 1·00
2645 $2 "Lovers in the Snow" . . 95 1·00
2646 $2 "Ghost of Koheiji" . . . 95 1·00
2647 $2 "Soldiers" (with hand on hip) . . . . 95 1·00
2648 $2 "Chinese Poet in Snow" 95 1·00
MS2649 Two sheets, each 101 × 72 mm. (a) $5 "Empress Jito". (b) $6 "One Hundred Poems by One Hundred Poets" Set of 2 sheets 5·50 5·75

1999. 10th Anniv of United Nations Rights of the Child Convention. As T **419** of Antigua. Multicoloured.
2650 $3 Small girl (vert) . . . . 1·40 1·50
2651 $3 Small boy (vert) . . . . 1·40 1·50
2652 $3 Small boy and girl (vert) 1·40 1·50
MS2653 85 × 110 mm. $6 Peace dove 3·00 3·25
Nos. 2650/2 were printed together, se-tenant, forming a composite design which continues onto the sheet margins.

1999. "PhilexFrance '99" International Stamp Exhibition, Paris. Railway Locomotives. Two sheets, each containing horiz designs as T **420** of Antigua. Multicoloured.
MS2654 Two sheets, each 106 × 81 mm. (a) $5 Steam locomotive "L'Aigle", 1855. (b) $6 Mainline diesel locomotive, 1963 Set of 2 sheets 5·50 5·75

1999. 250th Birth Anniv of Johann von Goethe (German writer). As T **421** of Antigua.
2655 $2 multicoloured . . . . . 95 1·00
2656 $2 blue, purple and black 95 1·00
2657 $2 multicoloured . . . . . 95 1·00
MS2658 76 × 100 mm. $6 grey, black and brown 3·00 3·25
DESIGNS—HORIZ: No. 2655, Faust and astrological sign; 2656, Von Goethe and Von Schiller; 2657, Faust tempted by Mephistopheles. VERT: No. **MS**2658, Johann von Goethe.

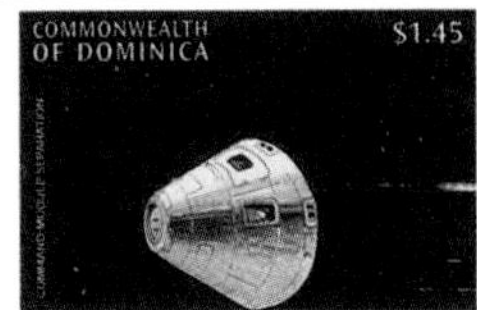

333 Command Module

1999. 30th Anniv of First Manned Landing on Moon. Multicoloured.
2659 $1.45 Type **333** 70 75
2660 $1.45 Service module . . . 70 75
2661 $1.45 Booster separation . . 70 75
2662 $1.45 Lunar and command modules 70 75
2663 $1.45 Tracking telescope . . 70 75
2664 $1.45 Goldstone radio telescope 70 75
MS2665 106 × 76 mm. $6 "Apollo 11" after splashdown 3·00 3·25

1999. "Queen Elizabeth the Queen Mother's Century". As T **444** of Antigua.
2666 $2 black and gold . . . . . 95 1·00
2667 $2 black and gold . . . . . 95 1·00
2668 $2 multicoloured . . . . . 95 1·00
2669 $2 multicoloured . . . . . 95 1·00
MS2670 153 × 157 mm. $6 multicoloured 3·00 3·25
DESIGNS: No. 2666, Queen Elizabeth, 1939; 2667, Queen Mother in Australia, 1958; 2668, Queen Mother in blue hat and coat, 1982; 2669, Queen Mother laughing, 1982. (37 × 50 mm)—No. **MS**2670, Queen Mother in 1953.

334 Female Dancer and "DOMFESTA"   335 Family

1999. 21st Anniv of Dominica Festivals Commission. Multicoloured.
2671 25c. Type **334** 10 15
2672 55c. "21st BIRTHDAY" logo 25 30
2673 65c. Carnival Development Committee emblem . . . 35 40
2674 90c. World Creole music emblem 45 50
MS2675 90 × 90 mm. $5 "21st BIRTHDAY" logo (different) (33 × 48 mm) 2·40 2·50

1999. International Year of the Elderly. Sheet 90 × 50 mm, containing T **335** and similar vert designs. Multicoloured.
MS2676 25c. Type **335**; 65c. Parents and grandparents; 90c. Family around elderly woman in chair 85 90

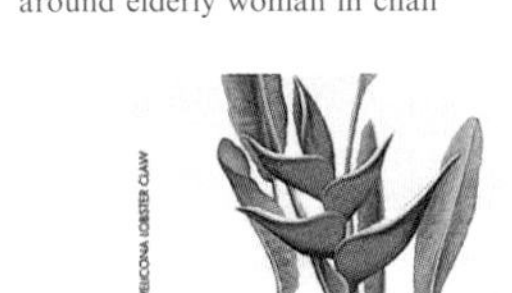

336 Helicona Lobster Claw

1999. Flora and Fauna. Multicoloured.
2677 25c. Type **336** 10 15
2678 65c. Broad-winged hawk . . 35 40
2679 90c. White-throated sparrow 45 50
2680 90c. Blue-winged teal . . . 45 50
2681 90c. Racoon 45 50
2682 90c. Alfalfa butterfly 45 50
2683 90c. Foot bridge 45 50
2684 90c. Whitetail deer 45 50
2685 90c. Grey squirrel 45 50
2686 90c. Banded-purple butterfly 45 50
2687 90c. Snowdrops 45 50
2688 90c. Bullfrog 45 50
2689 90c. Mushrooms 45 50
2690 90c. Large-blotched ensatina 45 50
2691 $1 Anthurium 50 55
2692 $1.55 Blue-headed hummingbird 75 80
2693 $2 Bananaquit . . . . . . 95 1·00
2694 $4 Agouti . . . . 1·90 2·00
MS2695 Two sheets, each 100 × 70 mm. (a) $5 Eastern chipmunk. (b) $6 Black-footed ferret Set of 2 sheets 5·50 5·75
Nos. 2679/90 were printed together, se-tenant, with the backgrounds forming a composite design.

337 Yellow-crowned Parrot   338 Bombing of Pearl Harbor, 1941

1999. Christmas. Birds. Multicoloured.
2696 25c. Type **337** 10 15
2697 55c. Red bishop 25 30
2698 65c. Troupial 35 40
2699 90c. Puerto Rican woodpecker 45 50
2700 $2 Mangrove cuckoo . . . 95 1·00
2701 $3 American robin . . . . 1·40 1·50
MS2702 76 × 98 mm. $6 "Mary with Child beside the Wall" (Dürer) (drab, black and cream) 3·00 3·25
No. 2699 is inscribed "PUERTO RECAN WOODPECKER" and No. **MS**2702 "MARYWITH", both in error.

1999. New Millennium. People and Events of Thirteenth Century (1200–50). As T **445** of Antigua. Multicoloured.
2703 55c. Leonardo Fibonacci (mathematician, 1202) . . 25 30
2704 55c. St. Francis of Assisi (founder of Franciscan Order, 1207) 25 30
2705 55c. Mongol horsemen (Conquest of China, 1211) 25 30
2706 55c. Children with banner (Children's Crusade, 1212) 25 30
2707 55c. King John signing Magna Carta, 1215 . . . 25 30
2708 55c. University class (foundation of Salamanca University, 1218) 25 30
2709 55c. Snorre Sturlusson (author of the "Edda", 1222) 25 30
2710 55c. Ma Yuan (Chinese painter) in garden (died 1224) 25 30
2711 55c. Genghis Khan (Mongol Emperor) (died 1227) . . 25 30
2712 55c. Student and Buddha (establishment of Zen Buddhism in Japan, 1227) 25 30
2713 55c. Galleys (The Sixth Crusade, 1228) 25 30
2714 55c. Seals (Lubeck–Hamburg Treaty, 1230) 25 30
2715 55c. Cardinal and angel (Holy Inquisition, 1231) 25 30
2716 55c. Palace interior (conquest of Cordoba, 1236) 25 30
2717 55c. San Marino (town founded, 1243) 25 30
2718 55c. Maimonides (Jewish philosopher) (died 1204) (59 × 39 mm) 25 30
2719 55c. Notre Dame Cathedral, Paris (completed 1250) . . 25 30

1999. New Millennium. People and Events of Twentieth Century (1940–49). Multicoloured.
2720 55c. Type **338** 25 30
2721 55c. Sir Winston Churchill (British Prime Minister, 1940) 25 30
2722 55c. Children in front of set (start of television broadcasting in U.S.A., 1940) 25 30
2723 55c. Anne Frank (Holocaust, 1942) 25 30
2724 55c. Troops wading ashore (D-Day, 1944) 25 30
2725 55c. Churchill, Roosevelt and Stalin (Yalta Conference, 1945) 25 30
2726 55c. U.N. Headquarters, New York (United Nations Organization, 1945) 25 30
2727 55c. American G.I. and concentration camp (Surrender of Germany, 1945) 25 30
2728 55c. Hoisting the Red Flag on the Reichstag (Fall of Berlin, 1945) 25 30
2729 55c. "Eniac" (first operational computer, 1946) 25 30
2730 55c. Indian with flag (Independence of India, 1947) 25 30
2731 55c. Early transistor, 1947 25 30
2732 55c. Mahatma Gandhi assassinated, 1948 . . . . 25 30
2733 55c. Israelis with flag (Establishment of Israel, 1948) 25 30
2734 55c. Aircraft and children (Berlin Airlift, 1948) . . . 25 30
2735 55c. Atomic bomb test, New Mexico, 1948 (59 × 39 mm) 25 30
2736 55c. Great Wall of China (People's Republic established, 1949) 25 30
No. 2732 is inscribed "Ghandi" in error.

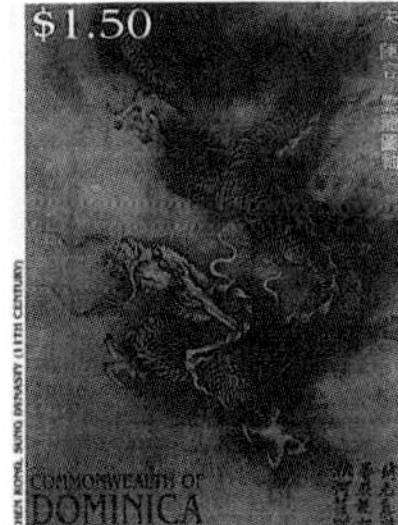

339 "Dragon flying in the Mist" (Chen Rong)

2000. Chinese New Year ("Year of the Dragon"). Multicoloured.
2737 $1.50 Type **339** 70 75
MS2738 80 × 60 mm. $4 Red dragon (horiz) 1·90 2·00

340 European Shorthair

2000. Cats and Dogs of the World. Multicoloured.
2739 $1 Type **340** 50 55
2740 $1 Devon rex 50 55
2741 $1 Chartreux 50 50
2742 $1 Bengal 50 55
2743 $1 American wirehair . . . 50 55
2744 $1 Siberian 50 55
2745 $1 Burmese 50 55
2746 $1 American shorthair . . . 50 55
2747 $1 Asian longhair 50 55
2748 $1 Burmilla 50 55
2749 $1 Snowshoe 50 55
2750 $1 Pekeface Persian 50 55
2751 $1 Himalayan Persian . . . 50 55
2752 $1 Japanese bobtail 50 55
2753 $1 Seychelles longhair . . . 50 55
2754 $1 Exotic shorthair 50 55
2755 $1 Jack Russell puppy (vert) 50 55
2756 $1 Shar pei puppies (vert) 50 55
2757 $1 Basset hound puppy (vert) 50 55
2758 $1 Boxer puppies (vert) . . 50 55
2759 $1 Wire-haired terrier (cross) puppy (vert) 50 55
2760 $1 Golden retriever puppies (vert) 50 55
MS2761 Three sheets, each 101 × 81 mm. (a) $6 Sleeping cat. (b) Grey cat with yellow eyes. (c) $6 Beagle puppy (vert) Set of 3 sheets 9·00 9·25

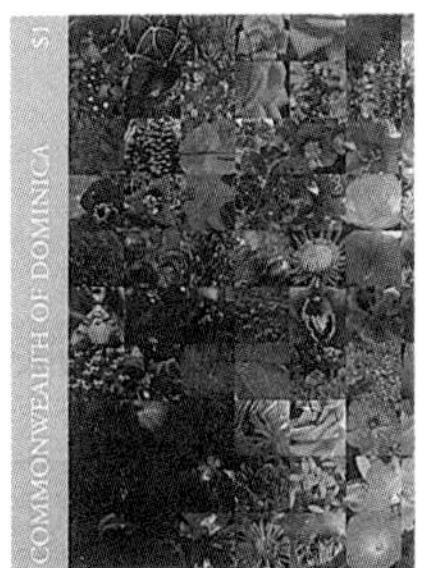

341 Flowers forming Top of Head

2000. Faces of the Millennium: Diana, Princess of Wales. Designs showing collage of miniature flower photographs. Multicoloured.
2762 $1 Type **341** (face value at left) 50 55
2763 $1 Top of head (face value at right) 50 55
2764 $1 Ear (face value at left) 50 55
2765 $1 Eye and temple (face value at right) 50 55
2766 $1 Cheek (face value at left) 50 50
2767 $1 Cheek (face value at right) 50 55
2768 $1 Blue background (face value at left) 50 55
2769 $1 Chin (face value at right) 50 55
Nos. 2762/9 were printed together, se-tenant, in sheetlets of 8 with the stamps arranged in two vertical columns separated by a gutter also containing miniature photographs. When viewed as a whole, the sheetlet forms a portrait of Diana, Princess of Wales.

342 Giant Swallowtail

2000. Butterflies. Multicoloured.
2770 $1.50 Type **342** 70 75
2771 $1.50 Tiger pierid 70 75
2772 $1.50 Orange theope butterfly 70 75
2773 $1.50 White peacock 70 75
2774 $1.50 Blue tharops 70 75
2775 $1.50 Mosaic 70 75
2776 $1.50 Banded king shoemaker 70 75
2777 $1.50 Figure-of-eight butterfly 70 75
2778 $1.50 Grecian shoemaker . . 70 75
2779 $1.50 Blue night butterfly 70 75
2780 $1.50 Monarch 70 75
2781 $1.50 Common morpho . . . 70 75
2782 $1.50 Orange-barred sulphur 70 75
2783 $1.50 Clorinde 70 75
2784 $1.50 Small flambeau . . . 70 75
2785 $1.50 Small lace-wing . . . 70 75
2786 $1.50 Polydamas swallowtail 70 75
2787 $1.50 The atala 70 75
MS2788 Three sheets, each 100 × 70 mm. (a) $6 Polydamas swallowtail (vert). (b) $6 Blue-green reflector (vert). (c) $6 Sloane's urania (vert) Set of 3 sheets 9·00 9·25

343 Passion Flower

2000. Flowers. Multicoloured. (a) Size 28 × 42 mm.
2789 65c. Type **343** 35 40
2790 90c. Spray orchid 45 50
2791 $1 Peach angels trumpet . . 50 55
2792 $4 Allamanda . . . . . . 1·90 2·00

(b) Size 32 × 48 mm.
2793 $1.65 Bird of paradise . . . 80 85
2794 $1.65 Lobster claw heliconia 80 85
2795 $1.65 Candle bush 80 85
2796 $1.65 Flor de San Miguel 80 85
2797 $1.65 Hibiscus 80 85
2798 $1.65 Oleander 80 85
2799 $1.65 Anthurium 80 85
2800 $1.65 Fire ginger 80 85
2801 $1.65 Shrimp plant 80 85
2802 $1.65 Sky vine thumbergia 80 85
2803 $1.65 Ceriman 80 85
2804 $1.65 Morning glory 80 85
MS2805 Two sheets, each 76 × 106 mm. (a) $6 Bird of Paradise and butterfly (38 × 50 mm). (b) $6 Hibiscus and hummingbird (38 × 50 mm) Set of 2 sheets 6·00 6·25
Nos. 2793/8 and 2799/804 were each printed together, se-tenant, with the backgrounds forming composite designs.

2000. 400th Birth Anniv of Sir Anthony Van Dyck (Flemish painter). As T **429** of Antigua. Multicoloured.
2806 $1.65 "The Ages of Man" (horiz) 80 85
2807 $1.65 "Portrait of a Girl as Ermina accompanied by Cupid" (horiz) 80 85
2808 $1.65 "Cupid and Psyche" (horiz) 80 85
2809 $1.65 "Vertumnus and Pomona" (horiz) 80 85
2810 $1.65 "The Continence of Scipio" (horiz) 80 85
2811 $1.65 "Diana and Endymion surprised by a Satyr" (horiz) 80 85
2812 $1.65 "Ladies-in-Waiting" (horiz) 80 85
2813 $1.65 "Thomas Wentworth, Earl of Strafford, with Sir Philip Mainwaring" (horiz) 80 85
2814 $1.65 "Dorothy Rivers Savage, Viscountess Andover, and her sister Lady Elizabeth Thimbleby" (horiz) . . . 80 85
2815 $1.65 "Mountjoy Blount, Earl of Newport, and Lord George Goring with a Page" (horiz) 80 85
2816 $1.65 "Thomas Killigrew and an Unidentified Man" (horiz) 80 85
2817 $1.65 "Elizabeth Villiers, Lady Dalkeith, and Cecilia Killigrew" (horiz) 80 85
2818 $1.65 "Lady Jane Goodwin (Mrs. Arthur)" 80 85
2819 $1.65 "Philip Herbert, Earl of Pembroke" 80 85
2820 $1.65 "Philip, Lord Wharton" 80 85
2821 $1.65 "Sir Thomas Hammer" 80 85

2822 $1.65 "Olivia Porter" . . . 80 85
2823 $1.65 "Sir Thomas Chaloner" 80 85
MS2824 Three sheets, each 128×103 mm. (a) $5 "Archilles and the Daughters of Lycomedes" (vert). (b) $5 "Amaryllis and Mirtilo" (vert). (c) $6 "Aletheia, Countess of Arundel" (vert) Set of 3 sheets 8·00 8·25
No. 2813 is inscribed "Wenthworth" in error.

2000. 18th Birthday of Prince William. As T **433** of Antigua. Multicoloured.
2825 $1.65 In skiing gear 80 85
2826 $1.65 In red jumper 80 85
2827 $1.65 Holding order of service 80 85
2828 $1.65 Prince William laughing 80 85
MS2829 100×80 mm. $6 Prince William with Prince Harry (37×50 mm) 3·00 3·25

2000. "EXPO 2000" World Stamp Exhibition, Anaheim. Space Satellites. As T **434** of Antigua. Multicoloured.
2830 $1.65 "Essa 8" 80 85
2831 $1.65 "Echo 1" 80 85
2832 $1.65 "Topex Poseidon" . . 80 85
2833 $1.65 "Diademe" 80 85
2834 $1.65 "Early Bird" 80 85
2835 $1.65 "Molyna" 80 85
2836 $1.65 "Explorer 14" 80 85
2837 $1.65 "Luna 16" 80 85
2838 $1.65 "Copernicus" 80 85
2839 $1.65 "Explorer 16" 80 85
2840 $1.65 "Luna 10" 80 85
2841 $1.65 "Arybhattan" 80 85
MS2842 Two sheets, each 106×76 mm. (a) $6 "Eole". (b) $6 "Hipparcos" 6·00 6·25
Nos. 2830/5 and 2836/41 were printed together, se-tenant, with the backgrounds forming composite designs.

2000. 25th Anniv of "Apollo–Soyuz" Joint Project. As T **435** of Antigua. Multicoloured.
2843 $3 Saturn 1B ("Apollo" launch vehicle) . . . . . 1·40 1·50
2844 $3 "Apollo 18" command module . . . . 1·40 1·50
2845 $3 Donald Slayton ("Apollo 18" crew) . . . 1·40 1·50
MS2846 88×71 mm. $6 Spacecraft about to dock (horiz) 3·00 3·25
No. 2843 is inscribed "Vechicle" in error.

2000. 50th Anniv of Berlin Film Festival. As T **436** of Antigua. Multicoloured.
2847 $1.65 Satyajit Ray (director of Ashani Sanket) 80 85
2848 $1.65 *Mahanagar*, 1964 . . 80 85
2849 $1.65 *La Tulipe*, 1952 . . . 80 85
2850 $1.65 *Le Salaire de la Peur*, 1953 . . . . 80 85
2851 $1.65 *Les Cousins*, 1959 . . 80 85
2852 $1.65 *Hon Dansade en Sommar*, 1952 . . . . . 80 85
MS2853 97×103 mm. $6 *Buffalo Bill and the Indians*, 1976 3·00 3·25

2000. 175th Anniv of Stockton and Darlington Line (first public railway). As T **437** of Antigua. Multicoloued.
2854 $3 George Stephenson and *Locomotion No. 1*, 1875 1·40 1·50
2855 $3 John B. Jervis's *Brother Jonathan*, 1832 . . . . . 1·40 1·50
No. 2855 is inscribed "Jonathon" in error.

2000. 250th Death Anniv of Johann Sebastian Bach (German composer). Sheet 77×88 mm, containing vert portrait as T **438** of Antigua.
MS2856 $6 brown and black 3·00 3·25

2000. Election of Albert Einstein (mathematical physicist) as *Time Magazine* "Man of the Century". Sheet 117×91 mm, containing vert portrait as T **439** of Antigua.
MS2857 $6 multicoloured 3·00 3·25

344 Count Ferdinand von Zeppelin

2000. Centenary of First Zeppelin Flight. Mult.
2858 $1.65 Type **344** 80 85
2859 $1.65 LZ-1 at Lake Constance, 1900 . . . . 80 85
2860 $1.65 LZ-10 *Schwaben*, over flock of sheep, 1911 . . . 80 85
2861 $1.65 LZ-6 and LZ-7 *Deutschland* in hangar, Friedrichshafen 80 85
2862 $1.65 LZ-4 at Luneville, 1913 . . . . 80 85
2863 $1.65 LZ-11 *Viktoria-Luise* over Kiel Harbour . . . 80 85
MS2864 93×115 mm. $6 As No. 2859 3·00 3·25
No. 2861 is inscribed "Friedrichshrfed" in error.

2000. Olympic Games, Sydney. As T **441** of Antigua. Multicoloured.
2865 $2 Jesse Owens (athletics), Berlin (1936) . . . . . . 95 1·00
2866 $2 Pole-vaulting . . . . . . 95 1·00
2867 $2 Lenin Stadium, Moscow (1980) and U.S.S.R. flag 95 1·00
2868 $2 Ancient Greek discus-thrower . . . . 95 1·00

2000. West Indies Cricket Tour and 100th Test Match at Lord's. As T **442** of Antigua. Multicoloured.
2869 $4 Norbert Phillip . . . . . 1·90 2·00
MS2870 121×104 mm. $6 Lord's Cricket Ground (horiz) 3·00 3·25
No. 2869 is inscribed "Phillp" in error.

2000. 80th Birthday of Pope John Paul II. As T **341**, showing collage of miniature religious photographs. Multicoloured.
2871 $1 Top of head (face value at left) 50 55
2872 $1 Top of head (face value at right) 50 55
2873 $1 Ear (face value at left) 50 55
2874 $1 Forehead (face value at right) 50 55
2875 $1 Neck (face value at left) 50 55
2876 $1 Cheek (face value at right) 50 55
2877 $1 Shoulder (face value at left) 50 55
2878 $1 Hands (face value at right) 50 55
Nos. 2871/8 were printed together, se-tenant, in sheetlets of 8 with the stamps arranged in two vertical columns separated by a gutter also containing miniature photographs. When viewed as a whole, the sheetlet forms a portrait of Pope John Paul.

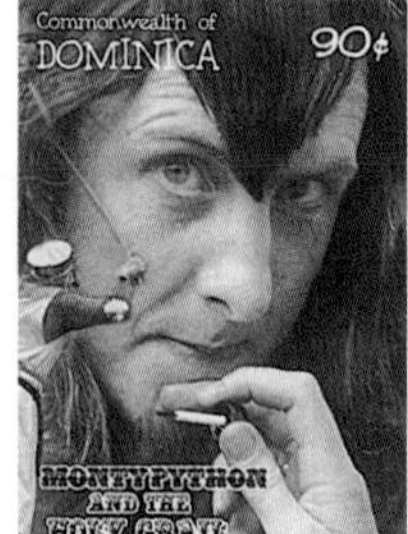

345 Roger the Shrubber

2000. *Monty Python and the Holy Grail* (comedy film). Multicoloured.
2879 90c. Type **345** 45 50
2880 90c. Three-headed giant . . 45 50
2881 90c. Attacking the castle . . 45 50
2882 90c. King Arthur and knight 45 50
2883 90c. Headless knight 45 50
2884 90c. Limbless Black Knight 45 50

346 Member of The Crystals

347 Bob Hope singing

2000. Famous Girl Pop Groups. The Crystals. Mult.
2885 90c. Type **346** 45 50
2886 90c. Group member with long hair (blue background in top right corner) 45 50
2887 90c. Group member with long hair (yellow background in top right corner) 45 50
2888 90c. Group member with short hair 45 50
Nos. 2885/8 were printed together, se-tenant, forming a composite design.

2000. Bob Hope (American entertainer).
2889 **347** $1.65 black, blue and lilac 80 85
2890 – $1.65 multicoloured . . 80 85
2891 – $1.65 black, blue and lilac 80 85
2892 – $1.65 multicoloured . . 80 85
2893 – $1.65 black, blue and lilac 80 85
2894 – $1.65 multicoloured . . 80 85
DESIGNS: No. 2890, Entertaining troops; 2891, As English comic character; 2892, In 50th birthday cake; 2893, Making radio broadcast; 2894, With Man in the Moon.

348 David Copperfield

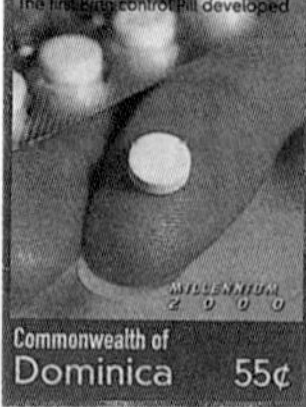

349 First Birth-control Pill, 1961

2000. David Copperfield (conjurer).
2895 **348** $2 multicoloured . . . . 95 1·00

2000. Monarchs of the Millennium. As T **447** of Antigua.
2896 $1.65 multicoloured 80 85
2897 $1.65 black, stone and brown 80 85
2898 $1.65 multicoloured 80 85
2899 $1.65 black, stone and brown 80 85
2900 $1.65 multicoloured 80 85
2901 $1.65 black, stone and brown 80 85
MS2902 115×135 mm. $6 multicoloured 3·00 3·25
DESIGNS: No. 2896, King Edward IV of England; 2897, Tsar Peter the Great of Russia; 2898, King Henry VI of England; 2899, King Henry III of England; 2900, King Richard III of England; 2901, King Edward I of England; **MS**2902, King Henry VIII of England.

2000. Popes of the Millennium. As T **447** of Antigua. Each black, yellow and green.
2903 $1.65 Clement X 80 85
2904 $1.65 Innocent X 80 85
2905 $1.65 Nicholas V 80 85
2906 $1.65 Martin V 80 85
2907 $1.65 Julius III 80 85
2908 $1.65 Innocent XII 80 85
MS2909 115×135 mm. $6 Clement XIV (brown, yellow and black) 3·00 3·25

2000. Christmas and Holy Year. As T **452** of Antigua. Multicoloured.
2910 25c. Angel in blue robe . . 10 15
2911 65c. Young angel 35 40
2912 90c. Angel with drapery . . 45 50
2913 $1.90 As 25c. 90 95
2914 $1.90 As 65c. 90 95
2915 $1.90 As 90c. 90 95
2916 $1.90 As $5 . . . . 90 95
2917 $5 Head and shoulders of angel . . . . 2·40 2·50
MS2918 110×120 mm. $6 Angel's face (as 25c.) 3·00 3·25

2000. New Millennium. People and Events of the Fourteenth Century (1350–1400). As T **445** of Antigua. Multicoloured.
2919 65c. Couple with hawk (Minnesangers in Germany, 1350) 35 40
2920 65c. Acamapitzin, first King of the Aztecs, 1352 . . . 35 40
2921 65c. Rat (end of Black Death, 1353) 35 40
2922 65c. Giotto's *Campanile* (completed by Francesco Talenti, 1355) 35 40
2923 65c. First French franc, 1360 . . . . 35 40
2924 65c. Emperor Hung-wu (foundation of Ming Dynasty, 1360) 35 40
2925 65c. Tamerlane (foundation of Timurid Empire, 1369) 35 40
2926 65c. "Triumph of Death" (Francis Traini), 1370 . . 35 40
2927 65c. Robin Hood (first appearance in English legends, 1375) 35 40
2928 65c. "The Knight" (The Canterbury Tales by Geoffrey Chaucer, 1387) 35 40
2929 65c. Mounted samurai (disputed succession in Japan, 1392) 35 40
2930 65c. Refugees (Jews expelled from France, 1394) . . . 35 40
2931 65c. Temple of the Golden Pavilion, Kyoto (constructed, 1394) . . . 35 40
2932 65c. Carving, Strasbourg Cathedral (completed, 1399) 35 40
2933 65c. Alhambra Palace, Granada (completed, 1390) (60×40 mm) . . . 35 40
2934 65c. Ife Bronzes produced in Nigeria, 1400 . . . . . 35 40
No. 2929 is inscribed "SUDDESSION" in error.

2000. New Millennium. Two Thousand Years of Chinese Paintings. As T **446** of Antigua. Mult.
2935 55c. "Eight Prize Steeds" (Guiseppe Castiglione) . . 25 30
2936 55c. "Oleanders" (Wu Hsi Tsai) 25 30
2937 55c. "Mynah and Autumn Flowers" (Chang Hsiung) 25 30
2938 55c. "Hen and Chicks beneath Chrysanthemums," (Chu Ch'ao) 25 30
2939 55c. "Long Living Pine and Crane" (Xugu) 25 30
2940 55c. "Flowers and Fruits" (Chu Lien) 25 30
2941 55c. "Lotus and Willow" (Pu Hua) 25 30
2942 55c. "Kuan-Yin" (Ch'ien Hui-an) 25 30
2943 55c. "Human Figures" (Jen Hsun) 25 30
2944 55c. "Han-Shan and Shih-Te" (Ren Yi) 25 30
2945 55c. "Landscape and Human Figure" (Jen Yu) 25 30
2946 55c. "Poetic Thoughts while Walking with a Staff" (Wangchen) 25 30
2947 55c. "Peony" (Chen Heng-ko) 25 30
2948 55c. "Plum and Orchid" (Wu Chang-shih) 25 30
2949 55c. "Monkey" (Kao Chi-feng) 25 30
2950 55c. "Grapes and Locust" (Chi Pai-shih); and "Galloping Horse" (Xu Beihong) (60×40 mm) . . 25 30
2951 55c. "The Beauty" (Lin Fengmian) 25 30
No. 2937 is inscribed "YNAH" and No. 2948 "ORCHIS", both in error.

2000. New Millennium. People and Events of Twentieth Century (1960–69). Multicoloured.
2952 55c. Type **349** 25 30
2953 55c. Yuri Gagarin (first man in Space), 1961 . . . . . 25 30
2954 55c. Fans with The Beatles tickets, 1962 . . . . . . 25 30
2955 55c. Funeral of President John F. Kennedy, 1963 25 30
2956 55c. Martin Luther King's "I Have a Dream" speech, 1963 . . . . . . 25 30
2957 55c. Betty Friedan (author of *The Feminist Mystique*), 1963 . . . . 25 30
2958 55c. Duke of Edinburgh and Jomo Kenyatta (independence of Kenya), 1963 . . . . 25 30
2959 55c. Anti-smoking poster, 1964 . . . . 25 30
2960 55c. Civil Rights demonstrators (U.S. Civil Rights Act), 1964 . . . . 25 30
2961 55c. Troops outside Saigon (U.S. involvement in Vietnam), 1965 . . . . . 25 30
2962 55c. Ernesto "Che" Guevara (Cuban revolutionary) killed in Peru, 1965 . . . 25 30
2963 55c. Dr. Christiaan Barnard (first heart transplant operation), 1967 . . . . 25 30
2964 55c. General Moshe Dayan addressing Arabs ("Six-Day" War), 1967 . . . . 25 30
2965 55c. Death of Ho Chi Minh (North Vietnamese leader), 1969 . . . . . . 25 30
2966 55c. Neil Armstrong on the Moon, 1969 . . . . . . 25 30
2967 55c. Couple at Berlin Wall, 1961 (60×40 mm) 25 30
2968 55c. Woodstock Festival, 1969 . . . . 25 30

350 Ancient Star Signs

2000. New Millennium. Inventions. Multicoloured.
2969 55c. Type **350** 25 30
2970 55c. Precision tools 25 30
2971 55c. Astral chart 25 30
2972 55c. Growth of medicine . . 25 30
2973 55c. Exchange of medical information 25 30
2974 55c. Monastic chapterhouse 25 30
2975 55c. Water alarm clock . . 25 30
2976 55c. Weighted clock 25 30
2977 55c. Spring-loaded miniature clock movement 25 30
2978 55c. Glass blowing 25 30
2979 55c. Early screws 25 30
2980 55c. Wood lathe 25 30
2981 55c. Ship building 25 30
2982 55c. Interchangeable rifle parts 25 30
2983 55c. Study of movement . . 25 30
2984 55c. The Industrial Revolution (60×40 mm) 25 30
2985 55c. Concept of efficiency 25 30

351 "Snake in the Wilderness" (Hwa Yan)

2001. Chinese New Year. "Year of the Snake".
2986 **351** $1.20 multicoloured . . 55 60

352 Female Green-throated Carib

2001. Hummingbirds. Multicoloured.
2987 $1.25 Type **352** 60 65
2988 $1.25 Male bee hummingbird ("Mellisuga helenae") 60 65
2989 $1.25 Male bee hummingbird ("Russelia eqoisetiformis") 60 65
2990 $1.25 Female bahama woodstar 60 65
2991 $1.25 Antillean mango . . . 60 65
2992 $1.25 Female blue-headed hummingbird 60 65
2993 $1.65 Male streamertail . . 80 85
2994 $1.65 Purple-throated carib 80 85
2995 $1.65 Vervain hummingbird 80 85
2996 $1.65 Bahama woodstar . . 80 85
2997 $1.65 Puerto Rican emerald 80 85
2998 $1.65 Antillean crested hummingbird 80 85
MS2999 Two sheets. (a) $5 Unidentified hummingbird. (b) $6 Hispaniolan emerald Set of 2 sheets 5·50 5·75

Nos. 2987/92 and 2993/8 were each printed together, se-tenant, with the backgrounds forming composite designs.

No. 2987 is inscribed "Fehale Greentriroated Carib", No. 2990 "Tenale", No. 2994 "Triroated", No. 2998 "Cresteo" and No. **MS**2999b "Hispaniolian", all in error.

No. 2989 carries the inscription "Russelia eqoisetiformis". This should read "Russelia equisetiformis", and refers to the plant (commonly known as a Firecracker Plant) at the bottom of the stamp, not the hummingbird.

353 Puerto Rican Crested Toad

2001. Caribbean and Latin-American Fauna. Mult.
3000 15c. Type **353** 10 10
3001 20c. Axolotl 10 15
3002 $1.45 St. Vincent amazon ("St. Vincent Parrot") . . 70 75
3003 $1.45 Indigo macaw 70 75
3004 $1.45 Guianian cock of the rock ("Cock of the Rock") 70 75
3005 $1.45 Cuban solenodon . . 70 75
3006 $1.45 Cuban hutia 70 75
3007 $1.45 Chinchilla 70 75
3008 $1.45 Chilian flamingo ("South American Flamingo") 70 75
3009 $1.45 Golden conure . . . 70 75
3010 $1.45 Ocelot 70 75
3011 $1.45 Giant armadillo . . . 70 75
3012 $1.45 Margay 70 75
3013 $1.45 Maned wolf 70 75
3014 $1.90 Panamanian golden frog 90 95
3015 $2.20 Manatee . . . . . . 1·00 1·10
MS3016 Two sheets, each 106 × 71 mm. (a) $6 Hawksbill turtle. (b) $6 Anteater Set of 2 sheets 6·00 6·25

Nos. 3002/7 and 3008/13 were each printed together, se-tenant, with the backgrounds forming composite designs.

2001. Characters from "Pokemon" (children's cartoon series). As T **454** of Antigua. Multicoloured.
3017 $1.65 "Butterfree No. 12" 80 85
3018 $1.65 "Bulbasaur No. 01" 80 85
3019 $1.65 "Caterpie No. 10" . . 80 85
3020 $1.65 "Charmander No. 04" 80 85
3021 $1.65 "Squirtle No. 07" . . 80 85
3022 $1.65 "Pidgeotto No. 17" 80 85
MS3023 75 × 105 mm. $6 "Nidoking No. 34" 3·00 3·25

354 Large Blue and Green Fish

2001. Diving in the Caribbean. Depicting marine life. Multicoloured.
3024 15c. Type **354** 10 10
3025 65c. Ray 35 40
3026 90c. Octopus 45 50
3027 $2 Shark . . . . 95 1·00
3028 $2 Starfish . . . . 95 1·00
3029 $2 Seahorse . . . . . . 95 1·00
3030 $2 Pink anemonefish . . . . 95 1·00
3031 $2 Crab . . . . 95 1·00
3032 $2 Moray eel . . . . . . 95 1·00
3033 $3 Pink anemonefish . . . . 1·40 1·50
MS3034 78 × 57 mm. $5 Young turtle 2·40 2·50

355 Banded Sea-snake

2001. Caribbean Marine Life. Multicoloured.
3035 15c. Type **355** 10 10
3036 25c. Soldierfish 10 15
3037 55c. False moorish idol ("Banner Fish") 25 30
3038 90c. Crown of Thorns starfish 45 50
3039 $1.65 Red sponge and shoal of anthias 80 85
3040 $1.65 Undulate triggerfish ("Orange-Striped Trigger Fish") 80 85
3041 $1.65 Coral hind ("Coral Grouper") and soft tree coral 80 85
3042 $1.65 Peacock fan-worms and Gorgonian sea fan . . 80 85
3043 $1.65 Sweetlips and sea fan 80 85
3044 $1.65 Giant clam and golden cup coral 80 85
3045 $1.65 White-tipped reef shark, lionfish and sergeant majors 80 85
3046 $1.65 Blue-striped snappers 80 85
3047 $1.65 Great hammerhead shark, stovepipe sponge and pink vase sponge . . 80 85
3048 $1.65 Hawaiian monk seal and bluetube coral . . . 80 85
3049 $1.65 False clown anemonefish ("Common Clown Fish"), chilka seahorse and red feather star coral 80 85
3050 $1.65 Bat starfish and brown octopus 80 85
MS3051 Two sheets, each 88 × 83 mm. (a) $5 Regal anglefish. (b) $5 Pink anenomefish Set of 2 sheets 5·00 5·50

Nos. 3039/44 and 3045/50 were each printed together, se-tenant, with the backgrounds forming composite designs.

No. 3045 is inscribed "Sargent" and 3049 "Cconn", both in error.

356 Prince Albert in Military Uniform

357 Mao Tse-tung in 1945

2001. Death Centenary of Queen Victoria. Multicoloured.
3052 $2 Type **356** . . . . 95 1·00
3053 $2 Young Queen Victoria wearing crown . . . . . 95 1·00
3054 $2 Young Queen Victoria wearing tiara . . . . . . 95 1·00
3055 $2 Prince Albert in evening dress . . . . 95 1·00
MS3056 106 × 122 mm. $6 Queen Victoria in 1897 (38 × 50 mm) 3·00 3·25

2001. 25th Death Anniv of Mao Tse-tung (Chinese leader). Portraits. Multicoloured.
3057 $2 Type **357** . . . . 95 1·00
3058 $2 Mao in 1926 . . . . . . 95 1·00
3059 $2 Mao in 1949 . . . . . . 95 1·00
MS3060 135 × 110 mm. $3 Mao Tse-tung with farm workers in 1930 1·40 1·50

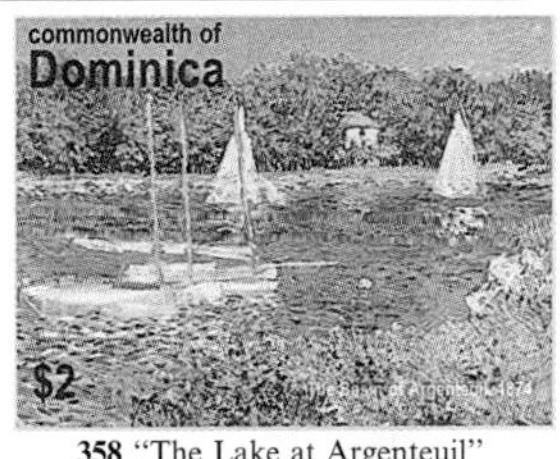

358 "The Lake at Argenteuil"

2001. 75th Death Anniv of Claude-Oscar Monet (French painter). Multicoloured.
3061 $2 Type **358** . . . . 95 1·00
3062 $2 "Bridge at Argenteuil" 95 1·00
3063 $2 "Railway bridge at Argenteuil" . . . . . . 95 1·00
3064 $2 "Seine bridge at Argenteuil" . . . . . . 95 1·00
MS3065 139 × 111 mm. $6 "Woman with Parasol – Madame Monet and her Son" (vert) 3·00 3·25

359 Queen Elizabeth at Coronation

360 Verdi as a Young Man

2001. 75th Birthday of Queen Elizabeth II. Multicoloured.
3066 $1.20 Type **359** 55 60
3067 $1.20 Queen Elizabeth wearing yellow hat . . . 55 60
3068 $1.20 Bare-headed portrait after Annigoni 55 60
3069 $1.20 Queen Elizabeth wearing fur hat 55 60
3070 $1.20 With Prince Andrew as a baby 55 60
3071 $1.20 Wearing white hat and pearl necklace 55 60
MS3072 78 × 102 mm. $6 Queen Elizabeth in Guards uniform taking salute at Trooping the Colour 3·00 3·25

2001. Death Centenary of Giuseppe Verdi (Italian composer). Multicoloured.
3073 $2 Type **360** . . . . 95 1·00
3074 $2 "Lady Macbeth" . . . . 95 1·00
3075 $2 Orchestra . . . . 95 1·00
3076 $2 Score for Verdi's *Macbeth* (opera) . . . . 95 1·00
MS3077 76 × 105 mm. $6 Verdi as an old man 3·00 3·25

Nos. 3073/6 were printed together, se-tenant, with the backgrounds forming a composite design.

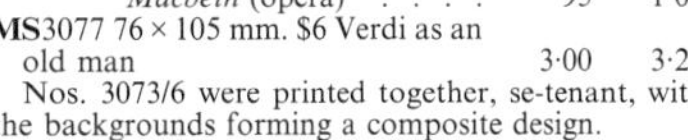

361 "Daruma" (Tsuji Kako)

363 *Cantharellus cibarius*

362 "Two Women Waltzing"

2001. "Philanippon '01" International Stamp Exhibition, Tokyo. Japanese Paintings. Multicoloured.
3078 25c. Type **361** 10 15
3079 55c. "Village by Bamboo Grove" (Takeuchi Seiho) 25 30
3080 65c. "Mountain Village in Spring" (Suzuki Hyakunen) 35 40
3081 90c. "Gentleman amusing Himself" (Domoto Insho) 45 50
3082 $1 "Calmness of Spring Light" (Takeuchi Seiho) 50 55
3083 $1.65 "Thatched Cottages in Willows" (Tsuji Kako) . . 80 85
3084 $1.65 "Joy in the Garden" (Tsuji Kako) 80 85
3085 $1.65 "Azalea and Butterfly" (Kikuchi Hobun) 80 85
3086 $1.65 "Pine Grove" (Tsuji Kako) 80 85
3087 $1.65 "Woodcutters talking in an Autumn Valley" (Kubota Beisen) 80 85
3088 $1.65 "Waterfowl in Snow" (Tsuji Kako) 80 85
3089 $1.65 "Heron and Willow" (Tsuji Kako) 80 85
3090 $1.65 "Crow and Cherry Blossoms" (Kikuchi Hobun) 80 85
3091 $1.65 "Chrysanthemum Immortal" (Yamamoto Shunkyo) 80 85
3092 $1.65 "Cranes of Immortality" (Tsuji Kako) 80 85
3093 $2 "Su's Embankment on a Spring Morning" (Tomioka Tessai) . . . . 95 1·00
MS3094 Three sheets. (a) 95 × 118 mm. $6 "Girl" (Suzuki Harunobu) (38 × 50 mm). (b) 105 × 90 mm. $6 "Kamo Riverbank in the Misty Rain" (Tsuji Kak) (38 × 50 mm). (c) 125 × 91 mm. $6 "Diamond Gate" (Tsuji Kak) (38 × 50 mm) Set of 3 sheets 9·00 9·25

No. **MS**3094c is inscribed "DIAMON GATE" in error.

2001. Death Centenary of Henri de Toulouse-Lautrec (French painter). Multicoloured.
3095 $2 Type **362** . . . . 95 1·00
3096 $2 "The Medical Inspection" . . . . 95 1·00
3097 $2 "Two Girlfriends" . . . 95 1·00
3098 $2 "Woman pulling up her Stockings" . . . . 95 1·00
MS3099 66 × 86 mm. $6 "Self-portrait" 3·00 3·25

2001. Fungi of the World. Multicoloured.
3100 15c. Type **363** 10 10
3101 25c. *Hygrocybe pratensis* . . 10 15
3102 55c. *Leccinum aurantiacum* 25 30
3103 90c. *Caesar's amanita* (horiz) 45 50
3104 90c. *Agaricus augustus* (horiz) 45 50
3105 90c. *Clitocybe nuda* (horiz) 45 50
3106 90c. *Hygrocybe plavescens* (horiz) 45 50
3107 90c. *Stropharia kaufmanii* (horiz) 45 50
3108 90c. *Hygrophorus speciosus* (horiz) 45 50
3109 $2 *Marasmiellus candidus* . . 95 1·00
3110 $2 *Calostoma cinnabarina* . . 95 1·00
3111 $2 *Cantharellus infundibuliformis* . . . . 95 1·00
3112 $2 *Hygrocybe punicea* . . . 95 1·00
3113 $2 *Dictyophora indusiata* . . 95 1·00
3114 $2 *Agrocybe praecox* . . . . 95 1·00
3115 $3 *Mycena haematopus* . . . 1·40 1·50
MS3116 Two sheets. (a) 76 × 54 mm. $5 Gymnophilus spectabilis (horiz). (b) 54 × 76 mm. $5 Amanita muscaria (horiz) Set of 2 sheets 5·00 5·25

364 St. Vincent Amazon ("St. Vincent Parrot")

365 Yellow Warbler

2001. Caribbean Fauna. Multicoloured.
3117 $1.45 Type **364** 70 75
3118 $1.45 Painted bunting . . . 70 75
3119 $1.45 Jamaican giant anole 70 75
3120 $1.45 White-fronted capuchin monkey 70 75
3121 $1.45 Strand racerunner . . 70 75
3122 $1.45 Agouti 70 75
3123 $2 Cook's tree boa . . . . 95 1·00
3124 $2 Tamandua . . . . 95 1·00

3125 $2 Common iguana . . . . 95 1·00
3126 $2 Solenodon . . . . 95 1·00
MS3127 Four sheets. (a) 63×92 mm. $5 American purple gallinule. (b) 63×92 mm. $5 Rufous-tailed jaramar. (c) 92×63 mm. $5 Ruby-throated hummingbird (horiz). (d) 73×52 mm. $5 Bottlenose dolphins (horiz) Set of 4 sheets 9·50 9·75

2001. Birds. Multicoloured.
3128 5c. Type **365** 10 10
3129 10c. Palm chat 10 10
3130 15c. Snowy cotinga 10 10
3131 20c. Blue-grey gnatcatcher 10 15
3132 25c. Belted kingfisher . . . 10 15
3133 55c. Red-legged thrush . . . 25 30
3134 65c. Bananaquit 35 40
3135 90c. Yellow-bellied sapsucker 45 50
3136 $1 White-tailed tropicbird 50 55
3137 $1.45 Ruby-throated hummingbird 70 75
3138 $1.90 Painted bunting . . . 90 95
3139 $2 Great frigate bird . . . . 95 1·00
3140 $5 Brown trembler . . . . 2·40 2·50
3141 $10 Red-footed booby . . . 4·75 5·00
3142 $20 Sooty tern . . . . . . 9·50 9·75

367 Larry, Moe and Curly in Overalls

2001. Scenes from *The Three Stooges* (American T.V. comedy series). Multicoloured.
3144 $1 Type **367** 70 75
3145 $1 Larry, Moe and Curly with woman in floral dress 70 75
3146 $1 Larry, Moe and Curly under table 70 75
3147 $1 Larry, Moe and Curly attacking singer in red dress 70 75
3148 $1 Larry, Moe and Curly with pony in cot 70 75
3149 $1 Larry in naval uniform, being arrested 70 75
3150 $1 Larry in evening dress (face value at top left) . . 70 75
3151 $1 Curly in green shirt . . . 70 75
3152 $1 Moe in evening dress (face value at top right) 70 75
MS3153 Two sheets. (a) 126×95 mm. $5 Larry with pony in cot. (b) 95×126 mm. $5 Moe and Larry in radio studio Set of 2 sheets 5·00 5·25

368 Queen Elizabeth II

369 United States Team, Brazil, 1950

2001. Golden Jubilee.
3154 $1 multicoloured 50 55
No. 3154 was printed in sheetlets of 8, containing two vertical rows of four, separated by a large illustrated central gutter. Both the stamp and the illustration on the central gutter are made up of a collage of miniature flower photographs.

2001. World Cup Football Championship, Japan and Korea (2002). Multicoloured.
3155 $2 Type **369** . . . . 95 1·00
3156 $2 Publicity poster, Switzerland, 1954 . . . . 95 1·00
3157 $2 Publicity poster, Sweden, 1958 . . . . 95 1·00
3158 $2 Zozimo (Brazil), Chile, 1962 . . . . 95 1·00
3159 $2 Gordon Banks (England), England, 1966 95 1·00
3160 $2 Pele (Brazil), Mexico, 1970 . . . . 95 1·00
3161 $2 Daniel Passarella (Argentina), Argentina, 1978 . . . . 95 1·00
3162 $2 Paolo Rossi (Italy), Spain, 1982 . . . . . . 95 1·00
3163 $2 Diego Maradona (Argentina), Mexico, 1986 95 1·00
3164 $2 Publicity poster, Italy, 1990 . . . . 95 1·00
3165 $2 Seo Jungulon (South Korea), U.S.A., 1994 . . 95 1·00
3166 $2 Jürgen Klinsmann (Germany), France, 1998 95 1·00
MS3167 Two sheets, each 88×75 mm. (a) $5 Detail of Jules Rimet Trophy, Uruguay, 1930. (b) $5 Detail of World Cup Trophy, Japan/Korea, 2002 Set of 2 sheets 5·00 5·25

370 "Madonna and Child" (Giovanni Bellini)

2001. Christmas. Paintings by Giovanni Bellini. Multicoloured.
3168 25c. Type **370** 10 15
3169 65c. "Madonna with Child" 35 40
3170 90c. "Baptism of Christ" . . 45 50
3171 $1.20 "Madonna with Child" (different) 55 60
3172 $4 "Madonna with Child" (different) . . . . 1·90 2·00
MS3173 136×76 mm. $6 "Madonna with Child and Sts. Catherine and Mary Magdalene" 3·00 3·25

371 Horse and Groom

2001. Chinese New Year ("Year of the Horse"). Paintings by Lum Mei. Multicoloured.
3174 $1.65 Type **371** 80 85
3175 $1.65 Two horses grazing 80 85
3176 $1.65 Groom with sick horse 80 85
3177 $1.65 Two horses galloping 80 85

2002. Golden Jubilee (2nd issue). As T **473** of Antigua. Multicoloured.
3178 $2 Queen Elizabeth in blue hat and coat . . . . . 95 1·00
3179 $2 Queen Elizabeth presenting Prince Philip with polo trophy . . . . 95 1·00
3180 $2 Queen Elizabeth in evening dress . . . . . . 95 1·00
3181 $2 Queen Elizabeth in pink hat and coat . . . . . . 95 1·00
MS3182 76×108 mm. $6 Princess Elizabeth and Duke of Edinburgh, 1948. 3·00 3·25

2002. "United We Stand". Support for Victims of 11 September 2001 Terrorist Attacks. As T **474** of Antigua.
3183 $2 U.S. Flag as Statue of Liberty and Dominica flag 95 1·00

2002. Shirley Temple in *Just Around the Corner*. As T **469** of Antigua showing film scenes. Mult.
3184 $1.90 With maid and dogs (horiz) 90 95
3185 $1.90 Penny (Shirley Temple) with father and Lola (horiz) 90 95
3186 $1.90 With father in study (horiz) 90 95
3187 $1.90 Carving turkey (horiz) 90 95
3188 $1.90 Talking to S. G. Henshaw (horiz) 90 95
3189 $1.90 Collecting money from crowd (horiz) 90 95
3190 $2 Frowning at boy 90 95
3191 $2 Pretending to shoot with Gus the chauffeur 90 95
3192 $2 Penny wearing apron and talking to father 90 95
3193 $2 Cutting boy's hair . . . 90 95
MS3194 106×75 mm. $6 Dancing in the rain 3·00 3·25

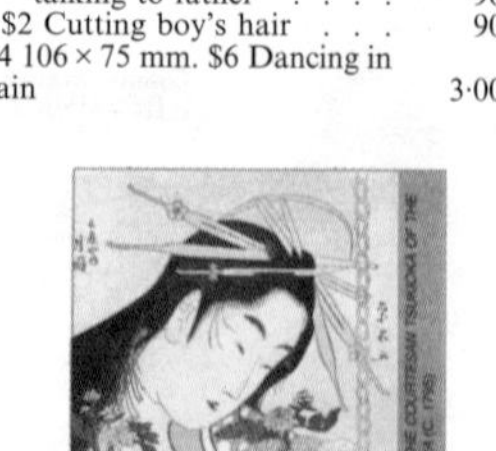

372 "Courtesan Tsukioka" (Ichirakutei Eisui)

2002. Japanese Art. Multicoloured.
3195 $1.20 Type **372** 55 60
3196 $1.20 "Woman and Servant in the Snow" (Eishosai Choki) 55 60
3197 $1.20 "Courtesan Shiratsuyu" (Chokosai Eisho) 55 60
3198 $1.20 "Ohisa of the Takashima-Ya" (Utagawa Toyokuni) 55 60
3199 $1.20 "Woman and Cat" (Utagawa Kunimasa) . . 55 60
3200 $1.20 "Genre Scenes of Beauties" (detail) (Keisai Eisen) 55 60
3201 $1.65 "Women inside and outside a Mosquito Net" (Suzuki Harushige) . . . 80 85
3202 $1.65 "Komachi at Shimizu" (Suzuki Harushige) 80 85
3203 $1.65 "Women viewing Plum Blossoms" (Suzuki Harunobu) 80 85
3204 $1.65 "Women cooling themselves at Shijogawara in Kyoto" (Utagawa Toyohiro) 80 85
3205 $1.65 "Women reading a Letter" (Kitagawa Utamaro) 80 85
3206 $1.65 "Women dressed for Kashima Dance at Niwaka Festival" (Kitagawa UTamaro) . . 80 85
3207 $1.90 "Iwai Kiyotaro" (Kunimasa) 90 95
3208 $1.90 "Otani Hiriji III and Arashi Ryuzo" (Toshusai Sharaku) 90 95
3209 $1.90 "Ichikawa Komazo II" (Katsukawa Shunko) 90 95
3210 $1.90 "Ichikawa Yaozo III and Sakata Hangoro III" (Sharaku) 90 95
3211 $1.90 "Tanimura Torazo" (Sharaku) 90 95
3212 $1.90 "Iwai Kiyotaro as Oishi" (Toyokuni) 90 95
MS3213 Three sheets. (a) 85×125 mm. $5 "Iwai Hanshiro IV and Sawamura Sojuro III" (Torii Kyonaga) (horiz). (b) 85×110 mm. $5 "Actor Nakamura Riko" (Katsukawa Shunsho). (c) $6 "Daughter of the Motoyanagi-Ya" (Suzuki Harunobu) 7·75 8·00

2002. International Year of Mountains. Vert designs as T **481** of Antigua. Multicoloured.
3214 $2 Mount Everest . . . . . 95 1·00
3215 $2 Mount Kilimanjaro . . . 95 1·00
3216 $2 Mount McKinley . . . . 95 1·00

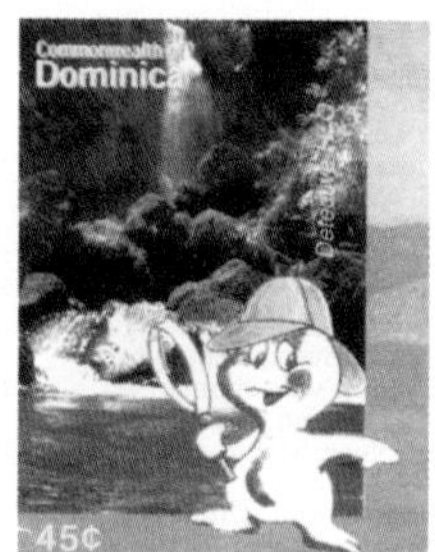

373 Waterfall and "Detective H²O"

2002. U.N. Year of Ecotourism. Each including a member of the Eco Squad (cartoon characters). Multicoloured.
3217 45c. Type **373** 20 25
3218 50c. Waterfall and "Factman" 25 20
3219 55c. River and "B.B." . . . 25 20
3220 60c. Sea cliffs and "Stanley the Starfish" 30 35
3221 90c. River and "Toxi" . . . 45 50
3222 $1.20 Forest and "Adopt" 55 60
MS3223 117× 96 mm. $6 Park and "Litterbit" 3·00 3·25

2002. Winter Olympic Games, Salt Lake City. As T **482** of Antigua but horiz. Multicoloured.
3224 $2 Downhill skiing . . . . 95 1·00
3225 $2 Two man bobsleigh . . . 95 1·00
MS3226 84×114 mm. Nos. 3218/19 1·90 2·00

374 Colonel Baden-Powell in Military Uniform

375 Olive Oyl in Rowing Boat

2002. 20th World Scout Jamboree, Thailand. Mult.
3227 $3 Type **374** . . . . 1·40 1·50
3228 $3 Agnes Baden-Powell (founder of Girl Guides) 1·40 1·50
3229 $3 Maceo Johnson . . . . 1·40 1·50
MS3230 80×99 mm. $6 Lord Baden-Powell in Scout uniform 3·00 3·00

2002. 75th Anniv of First Solo Transatlantic Flight. As T **484** of Antigua but vert. Multicoloured.
3231 $3 Charles Lindbergh and the *Spirit of St. Louis* (aircraft) . . . . 1·40 1·50
3232 $3 Charles and Anne Lindbergh in flying kit . . 1·40 1·50
MS3233 117×83 mm. $6 Charles Lindbergh and the *Spirit of St. Louis* 3·00 3·00

2002. "Popeye " (cartoon character) in New York. Multicoloured.
3234 $1 Type **375** 50 55
3235 $1 Brutus with oar 50 55
3236 $1 Sweet Pea 50 55
3237 $1 Wimpy 50 55
3238 $1 Jeep 50 55
3239 $1 Popeye with telescope . . 50 55
3240 $1.90 Popeye and Olive Oyl at Bronx Zoo 90 95
3241 $1.90 Popeye and Olive Oyl on ferry passing Statue of Liberty 90 95
3242 $1.90 Popeye and Olive Oyl by Empire State Building 90 95
3243 $1.90 Popeye skating at Rockefeller Centre . . . 90 95
3244 $1.90 Popeye pitching at baseball game 90 95
3245 $1.90 Popeye holding hose 90 95
MS3246 Two sheets, each 83×114 mm. (a) $6 Popeye and Olive Oyl dancing (horiz). (b) $6 Popeye flexing muscles 6·00 6·25
No. 3243 is inscribed "ROCKERFELLER" in error

376 Brown Trembler

377 Willem Einthoven (Medicine, 1924)

2002. Fauna. Multicoloured designs.
3247 $1.50 Type **376** 70 75
3248 $1.50 Snowy cotinga 70 75
3249 $1.50 Bananaquit 70 75
3250 $1.50 Painted bunting . . . 70 75
3251 $1.50 Belted kingfisher . . . 70 75
3252 $1.50 Ruby-throated hummingbird 70 75
3253 $1.50 Field cricket 70 75
3254 $1.50 Migratory grasshopper 70 75
3255 $1.50 Honey bee 70 75
3256 $1.50 Hercules beetle . . . 70 75
3257 $1.50 Black ant 70 75
3258 $1.50 Cicada 70 75
3259 $1.50 Carolina sphinx . . . 70 75
3260 $1.50 White-lined sphinx . . 70 75
3261 $1.50 Orizaba silkmoth . . 70 75
3262 $1.50 Hieroglyphic moth . . 70 75
3263 $1.50 Hickory tussock moth 70 75
3264 $1.50 Diva moth 70 75
3265 $1.50 Sei whale 70 75
3266 $1.50 Killer whale 70 75
3267 $1.50 Blue whale 70 75
3268 $1.50 White whale 70 75
3269 $1.50 Pygmy whale 70 75
3270 $1.50 Sperm whale 70 75
MS3271 Four sheets, each 100×70 mm. (a) $6 Yellow-bellied sapsucker (horiz). (b) $6 Bumble bee (horiz). (c) $6 Ornate moth (horiz). (d) $6 Grey whale (horiz) 11·50 12·00
Nos. 3241/6 (birds), 3247/52 (insects), 3253/8 (moths) and 3259/64 (whales) were each printed together, se-tenant, with the backgrounds forming composite designs.
Nos. 3248 and 3259 are inscribed "Ctinga" or "Carilina", both in error.

2002. "Amphilex '02", International Stamp Exhibition, Amsterdam. (a) Dutch Nobel Prize Winners.
3272 **377** $1.50 black and green . . 70 75
3273 – $1.50 black and orange 70 75
3274 – $1.50 black and violet 70 75
3275 – $1.50 black and salmon 70 75
3276 – $1.50 black and sepia . . 70 75
3277 – $1.50 black and green . . 70 75
DESIGNS: No. 3273, Economics Prize medal; 3274, Peter Debye (Chemistry, 1935); 3275, Frits Zernike (Physics, 1953); 3276, Jan Tinbergen (Economics, 1969); 3277, Simon van de Meer (Physics, 1984).

(b) Dutch Lighthouses. Multicoloured.
3278 $1.50 Marken lighthouse . . 70 75
3279 $1.50 Harlingen lighthouse 70 75
3280 $1.50 Den Oever lighthouse 70 75
3281 $1.50 De Ven lighthouse . . 70 75

3282 $1.50 Urk lighthouse . . . 70 75
3283 $1.50 Oosterleek lighthouse 70 75

(c) Dutch Women's Traditional Costumes. Multicoloured. Each 37 × 51 mm.
3284 $3 Lace cap from Zuid Holland . . . .
3285 $3 Winged headdress from Zeeland . . . . 1·40 1·50
3286 $3 Scarf and shawl from Limburg . . . . 1·40 1·50

2002. 25th Death Anniv of Elvis Presley (American entertainer). As T **488** of Antigua showing Elvis with microphone.
3287 $1.50 black 70 75

378 Compass

2002. 550th Birth Anniv of Amerigo Vespucci (explorer). Multicoloured.
3288 $3 Type **378** . . . . 1·40 1·50
3289 $3 Studying chart . . . . . 1·40 1·50
3290 $3 Rolled chart . . . . . . 1·40 1·50
MS3291 98 × 78 mm. $5 Amerigo Vespucci and Spanish soldier (30 × 42mm) 2·40 2·50

379 Princess Diana **380** John F. Kennedy in Navy Uniform

2002. 5th Death Anniv of Diana, Princess of Wales. Multicoloured.
3292 $1.90 Type **379** 90 95
3293 $1.90 Princess Diana carrying rose spray . . . 90 95
3294 $1.90 Wearing white yoked dress 90 95
3295 $1.90 In lace top 90 95
MS3296 98 × 66 mm. $5 Princess Diana wearing tiara fur coat 2·40 2·50

2002. Presidents John F. Kennedy and Ronald Reagan Commemoration. Multocoloured.
3297 $1.90 Type **380** 90 95
3298 $1.90 Wearing brown suit (face value in red) 90 95
3299 $1.90 Wearing brown suit (face value in blue) . . . 90 95
3300 $1.90 In fawn suit 90 95
3301 $1.90 John F. Kennedy smiling 90 95
3302 $1.90 John F. Kennedy frowning 90 95
3303 $1.90 Looking up 90 95
3304 $1.90 With hand on chin . . 90 95
3305 $1.90 Ronald Reagan in film role as deputy marshal . . 90 95
3306 $1.90 Wearing green T-shirt 90 95
3307 $1.90 In red pullover . . . 90 95
3308 $1.90 Wearing blue T-shirt 90 95
3309 $1.90 Nancy and Ronald Reagan (wearing blue shirt) (horiz) 90 95
3310 $1.90 Nancy Reagan (horiz) 90 95
3311 $1.90 Ronald Reagan (horiz) 90 95
3312 $1.90 Nancy and Ronald Reagan (wearing pink shirt) (horiz) 90 95

381 Rams

2003. Chinese New Year ("Year of the Ram").
3313 **381** $1.65 multicoloured . . 80 85

382 Confucius (Chinese philosopher)

2003. Science Fiction. Six sheets, each 145 × 100 mm, containing T **382** and similar vert designs. Multicoloured.
MS3314 Six sheets. (a) $6 Type **382**. (b) $6 Nazca Lines, Peru. (c) $6 Atlas carrying Globe. (d) $6 Zoroaster. (e) $6 Mayan calendar. (f) $6 Presidents Franklin D. Roosevelt and John F. Kennedy (both deaths predicted by Edgar Casey) 18·00 19·00
No. **MS**3314(e) is inscribed "Calender" in error.

APPENDIX

The following stamps have either been issued in excess of postal needs, or have not been made available to the public in reasonable quantities at face value.

1978.

History of Aviation. $16 × 30, each embossed on gold foil.

DOMINICAN REPUBLIC Pt. 15

The Eastern portion of the island of Hispaniola in the W. Indies finally became independent of Spain in 1865.

1865. 8 reales = 1 peso.
1880. 100 centavos = 1 peso.
1883. 100 centimos = 1 franco.
1885. 100 centavos = 1 peso.

1

3

1865. Imperf.
1 **1** ½r. black on red £225 £200
3 ½r. black on green £350 £350
2 1r. black on green £600 £550
4 1r. black on yellow £1100 £950

1865. Imperf.
5 **3** ½r. black on buff £125 £100
7 ½r. black on red . . . . . . 40·00 40·00
12 ½r. black on grey £120 £120
18 ½r. black and blue on red . . 50·00 30·00
19 ½r. black on yellow . . . . . 25·00 25·00
20 1r. black on green . . . . . 50·00 50·00
9 1r. black on blue . . . . . . 35·00 35·00
15 1r. black on flesh £100 £100
21 1r. black on lilac £200 £200

4 **5** **15**

1879. Perf.
22 **4** ½r. violet . . . . 1·50 1·50
24 1r. red . . . . 1·50 1·50

1880. Rouletted.
35 **5** 1c. green 60 60
36 2c. red 60 60
28 5c. blue 85 70
38 10c. pink 60 60
39 20c. bistre 70 70
40 25c. mauve . . . . 1·25 1·00
32 50c. orange . . . . 1·50 1·10
33 75c. blue . . . . 3·25 3·25
34 1p. gold . . . . 4·00 4·00

1883. Surch.
44 **5** 5c. on 1c. green . . . . . . 1·10 1·00
73 10c. on 2c. red . . . . . . 2·00 2·00
46 25c. on 5c. blue . . . . . . 4·00 3·50
47 50c. on 10c. pink . . . . . 12·00 6·00
58 1f. on 20c. bistre . . . . . . 7·00 7·00
51 1f.25 on 25c. mauve . . . . 11·00 11·00
52 2f.50 on 50c. orange . . . . 14·00 14·00
53 3f.75 on 75c. blue . . . . . 16·00 16·00
64 5f. on 1p. gold . . . . 50·00 50·00

1885. Figures in lower corners only.
77 **15** 1c. green 30 15
78 2c. red 30 15
79 5c. blue 50 20
80 10c. orange 80 30
81 20c. brown 85 50
82 50c. violet . . . . 4·50 3·00
83 1p. red . . . . 10·00 10·00
84 2p. brown . . . . 12·00 10·00

1895. As T **15** but figures in four corners.
85 1c. green 60 30
86 2c. red 60 30
87 5c. blue 70 30
88 10c. orange 75 30

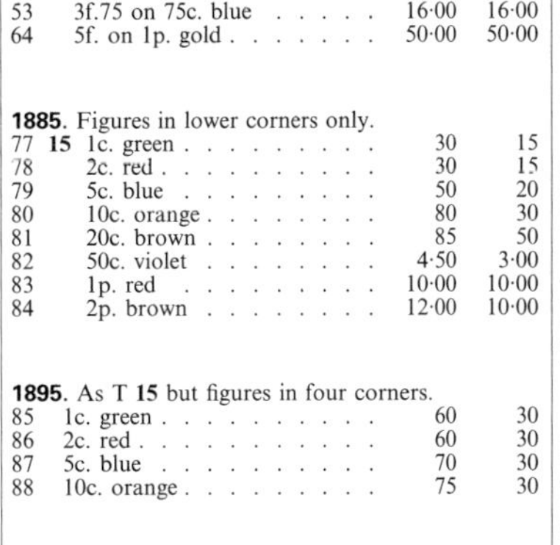

18 Voyage of Mendez from Jamaica to Santo Domingo **19** Sarcophagus of Columbus

1899. Columbus Mausoleum Fund.
98 **19** ½c. black . . . . 1·00 1·00
99 – ½c. black . . . . 1·00 1·00
89 **18** 1c. purple . . . . 4·50 3·50
90 1c. green . . . . 1·00 40
91 – 2c. red 50 50
92 **19** 5c. blue 75 55
93 – 10c. orange . . . . 2·00 1·00
94 – 20c. brown . . . . 4·00 4·00
95 – 50c. green . . . . 4·00 4·00
96 – 1p. black on blue . . . . . 12·00 10·00
97 – 2p. brown on cream . . . . 25·00 25·00
DESIGNS—AS TYPE **18**: ½c. (No. 99), 1p. Columbus at Salamanca Assembly; 2c. Enriquillo's Rebellion; 20c. Toscanelli replying to Columbus; 50c. Las Casas defending Indians. As Type **19**: 10c. Hispaniola guarding remains of Columbus; 2p. Columbus Mausoleum, Santo Domingo Cathedral.

20 Island of Hispaniola

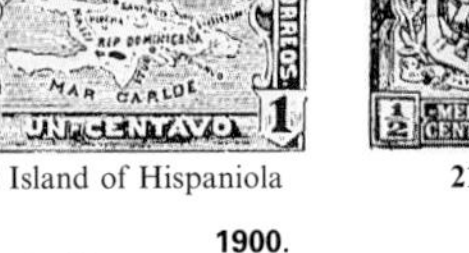

21

1900.
100 **20** ½c. blue 45 40
101 ½c. red 45 40
102 1c. olive 45 35
103 2c. green 45 35
104 5c. brown 45 35
105 10c. orange 35 35
106 20c. purple . . . . 1·50 1·50
107 50c. black . . . . 1·40 1·25
108 1p. brown . . . . 1·40 1·25

1901.
109 **21** ½c. lilac and red 25 25
110 1c. lilac and olive 35 20
111 2c. lilac and green 35 20
112 5c. lilac and brown 35 25
113 10c. lilac and orange . . . 75 30
114 20c. lilac and brown . . . 1·50 80
115 50c. lilac and black . . . . 4·50 2·50
116 1p. lilac and brown . . . . 9·50 7·00

24 Sanchez **25** Fortress of Santo Domingo

1902. 400th Anniv of Santo Domingo.
125 **24** 1c. black & green 25 25
126 2c. black & red (Duarte) 25 25
127 5c. blk & blue (Duarte) . . 25 25
128 10c. blk & orge (Sanchez) 25 25
129 12c. blk & violet (Mella) 25 25
130 20c. black & red (Mella) 25 25
131 **25** 50c. black and brown . . . 1·60 1·75

1904. Surch with new value.
132 **21** 2c. on 50c. lilac & black 5·50 4·25
133 2c. on 1p. lilac & brown 7·50 4·50
134 5c. on 50c. lilac & black 2·00 1·60
135 5c. on 1p. lilac and brown 3·00 2·40
136 10c. on 50c. lilac & black 4·75 4·00
137 10c. on 1p. lilac & brown 4·75 4·00

1904. Official stamps optd **16 de Agosto 1904** or surch **1** also.
138 **O 23** 1c. on 20c. blk & yell . . 3·25 2·75
139 2c. black and red . . . 5·00 3·00
140 5c. black and blue . . . . 3·00 2·25
141 10c. black and green . . 4·75 3·25

1904. Postage Due stamps optd **REPUBLICA DOMINICANA CENTAVOS CORREOS** or surch **1** also.
142 **D 22** 1c. on 2c. sepia . . . . 1·75 85
143 1c. on 4c. sepia 70 50
145 2c. sepia 70 35

1905. Surch **1905** and new value.
146 **15** 2c. on 20c. brown . . . . 5·00 4·00
147 5c. on 20c. brown . . . . 2·25 1·40
148 10c. on 20c. brown . . . . 5·00 4·00

1905.
149 **21** ½c. orange and black . . . 1·00 55
150 1c. blue and black . . . . 1·25 50
151 2c. mauve and black . . . 1·25 40
152 5c. red and black . . . . 1·50 70
153 10c. green and black . . . 2·75 1·40
154 20c. olive and black . . . 8·50 4·75
155 50c. brown and black . . . 27·00 15·00
156 1p. grey and black £150 £150

1906. Postage Due stamps surch **REPUBLICA DOMINICANA.** and new value.
157 **D 22** 1c. on 4c. sepia 70 40
158 1c. on 10c. sepia 85 40
159 2c. on 5c. sepia 85 40

1907.
168 **21** ½c. black and green 55 15
169 1c. black and red 55 15
170 2c. black and brown . . . 55 15
171 5c. black and blue 60 20
164 10c. black and purple . . . 85 35
165 20c. black and olive . . . 4·75 2·40
166 50c. black and brown . . . 4·75 4·00
167 1p. black and violet . . . 12·00 6·50

1911. No. O178 optd **HABILITADO. 1911**.
182 **O 23** 2c. black and red . . . 1·00 50

34

35 Jaun Pablo Duarte

1911.
183 **34** ½c. black and orange . . . 25 15
184 1c. black and green 25 10
185 2c. black and red 25 10
186 5c. black and blue 50 15
187 10c. black and purple . . . 1·00 40
188 20c. black and olive . . . 5·50 3·25
189 50c. black and brown . . . 2·40 2·00
190 1p. black and violet . . . 4·00 2·40
For stamps in other colours see Nos. 235/8 and for stamps in similar type see No. 240/6.

1914. Birth Centenary of Duarte. Background in red, white and blue.
195 **35** ½c. black and orange . . . 45 35
196 1c. black and green 45 35
197 2c. black and red 45 35
198 5c. black and grey 55 40
199 10c. black and mauve . . . 85 50
200 20c. black and olive . . . 2·00 1·40
201 50c. black and brown . . . 2·75 2·40
202 1p. black and lilac . . . . 4·00 3·00

1915. Nos. O177/181 optd **Habilitado 1915** or surch **MEDIO CENTAVO** also.
203 **O 23** ½c. on 20c. blk & yell . . 50 35
204 1c. black and green . . 70 25
205 2c. black and red . . . 70 35
206 5c. black and blue . . . 85 35
207 10c. black and green . . 2·00 1·60
208 20c. black and yellow . . 6·50 5·50

1915. Optd **1915**.
209 **34** ½c. black and mauve . . . 55 15
210 1c. black and brown . . . 55 10
211 2c. black and olive . . . . 2·00 25
213 5c. black and red . . . . 2·00 25
214 10c. black and blue . . . . 2·00 35
215 20c. black and red . . . . 5·50 1·25
216 50c. black and green . . . 6·00 2·75
217 1p. black and orange . . . 12·00 5·50

1916. Optd **1916**.
218 **34** ½c. black and mauve . . . 70 10
219 1c. black and green . . . . 1·40 10

1917. Optd **1917**.
220 **34** ½c. black and mauve . . . 1·00 25
221 1c. black and green . . . . 1·00 10
222 2c. black and olive 85 10
223 5c. black and red . . . . 7·50 70

1919. Optd **1919**.
224 **34** 2c. black and olive . . . . 4·00 10

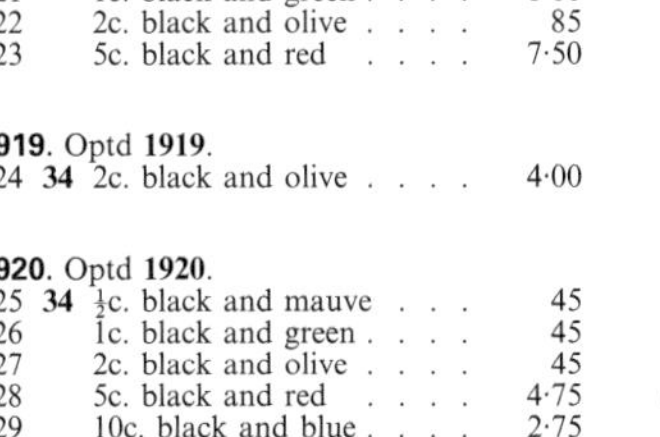

1920. Optd **1920**.
225 **34** ½c. black and mauve . . . 45 20
226 1c. black and green 45 10
227 2c. black and olive 45 10
228 5c. black and red . . . . 4·75 45
229 10c. black and blue . . . . 2·75 20

No.	Type	Description	Mint	Used
230		20c. black and red	4·75	45
231		50c. black and green	40·00	10·00

1921. Optd **1921**.

No.	Type	Description	Mint	Used
233	34	1c. black and green	1·25	25
234		2c. black and olive	2·40	30

1922.

No.	Type	Description	Mint	Used
235	34	½c. black and red	25	10
236		1c. green	70	10
237		2c. red	1·00	10
238		5c. blue	2·00	25

41

43 Exhibition Pavilion

1924. Straight top to shield.

No.	Type	Description	Mint	Used
240	41	1c. green	40	10
241		2c. red	55	10
242		5c. blue	55	10
243		10c. black and blue	6·50	1·40
245		50c. black and green	35·00	2·00
246		1p. black and orange	12·00	8·50

1927. National and West Indian Exn, Santiago.

No.	Type	Description	Mint	Used
248	43	2c. red	70	45
249		5c. blue	85	45

45 Air Mail Routes

1928. Air.

No.	Type	Description	Mint	Used
256	45	10c. deep blue	5·75	3·00
280		10c. pale blue	1·90	75
271		10c. yellow	4·00	3·00
272		15c. red	7·75	4·00
281		15c. turquoise	4·00	1·10
273		20c. green	3·75	60
282		20c. brown	4·50	55
274		30c. violet	7·75	4·50
283		30c. brown	7·25	1·75

46 Ruins of Fortress of Columbus

47 Horacio Vasquez

1928.

No.	Type	Description	Mint	Used
258	46	½c. red	45	25
259		1c. green	40	10
260		2c. red	40	10
261		5c. blue	1·00	25
262		10c. blue	1·00	25
263		20c. red	1·50	40
264		50c. green	8·50	4·75
265		1p. yellow	15·00	10·00

1929. Frontier Agreement with Haiti.

No.	Type	Description	Mint	Used
266	47	½c. red	40	20
267		1c. green	40	15
268		2c. red	45	15
269		5c. blue	85	25
270		10c. blue	3·00	55

48 Jesuit Convent of San Ignacio de Loyola

49 After the Hurricane

1930.

No.	Type	Description	Mint	Used
275	48	½c. brown	50	40
276		1c. green	45	10
277		2c. red	45	10
278		5c. blue	1·25	35
279		10c. blue	2·40	85

1930. Hurricane Relief.

No.	Type	Description	Mint	Used
284	–	1c. green and red	15	35
285	–	2c. red	20	25
286	49	5c. blue and red	35	50
287		10c. yellow and red	40	70

DESIGN: 1c., 2c. Riverside.

1931. Air. Hurricane Relief. Surch with airplane, **HABILITADO PARA CORREO AEREO** and premium. Imperf or perf.

No.	Type	Description	Mint	Used
288	49	5c.+5c. blue and red	6·50	6·50
289		5c.+5c. black and red	15·00	15·00
290		10c.+10c. yellow & red	5·00	6·50
291		10c.+10c. black & red	15·00	15·00

52 Cathedral of Santo Domingo

1931.

No.	Type	Description	Mint	Used
294	52	1c. green	50	15
295		2c. red	50	15
296		3c. purple	55	10
297		7c. blue	1·40	20
298		8c. brown	2·40	70
299		10c. blue	3·00	85

53 Old Sun Dial, 1754

1931. Air.

No.	Type	Description	Mint	Used
300	53	10c. red	5·00	60
301		10c. blue	2·00	55
302		10c. green	8·00	2·75
303		15c. mauve	3·75	55
304		20c. blue	7·25	1·60
306		30c. green	3·25	40
307		50c. brown	8·00	80
308		1p. orange	13·00	2·75

54 Fort Ozama

1932.

No.	Type	Description	Mint	Used
309	54	1c. green	50	40
310		1c. green	25	10
311		3c. violet	35	10

No. 310 is inscribed "CORREOS".

1932. Red Cross stamps inscr "CRUZ ROJA DOMINICANA", with cross in red and optd **HABILITADO Dic. 20-1932 En. 5-1933 CORREOS** or surch also.

No.	Type	Description	Mint	Used
312		1c. green	20	15
313		3c. on 2c. violet	30	15
314		5c. blue	70	60
315		7c. on 10c. blue	1·10	85

56 F. A. de Merino

57 Cathedral of Santo Domingo

1933. Birth Centenary of F. A. de Merino.

No.	Type	Description	Mint	Used
316	–	½c. violet	25	15
317	56	1c. green	25	15
318	–	2c. red	70	55
319	56	3c. violet	35	15
320	–	5c. blue	45	20
321	–	7c. blue	90	35
322	–	8c. green	1·25	70
323	56	10c. orange	1·00	25
324	–	20c. red	2·25	1·40
325	57	50c. olive	9·00	5·50
326		1p. sepia	22·00	13·00

DESIGNS—VERT: ½c., 5c., 8c. Merino's Tomb; 2c., 7c., 20c. Merino in uniform.

1933. Portraits as T **56**.

No.	Type	Description	Mint	Used
327		1c. black and green	50	25
328		3c. black and violet	55	15
329		7c. black and blue	1·60	55

DESIGNS: 1c., 7c. Pres. Trujillo in uniform; 3c. Pres. Trujillo in evening dress.

1933. Air. Optd **CORREO AEREO INTERNO**.

No.	Type	Description	Mint	Used
330	52	2c. red	40	30

60 Fokker Super Universal over Fort Ozama

1933. Air.

No.	Type	Description	Mint	Used
331	60	10c. blue	3·50	50

61 San Rafael Suspension Bridge

1934.

No.	Type	Description	Mint	Used
332	61	½c. mauve	55	25
333		1c. green	80	15
334		3c. violet	1·25	10

62 Trujillo Bridge

1934. (a) Postage. As T **62** but without airplane and inscr "CORREOS".

No.	Type	Description	Mint	Used
335	–	½c. brown	50	15
336	–	1c. green	80	10
337	–	3c. violet	1·00	10

(b) Air.

No.	Type	Description	Mint	Used
338	62	10c. blue	3·25	50

64 National Palace

1935. For obligatory use on mail addressed to the President.

No.	Type	Description	Mint	Used
346	64	25c. orange	2·00	15

1935. Opening of Ramfis Bridge. As T **62** but view of Ramfis Suspension Bridge.

No.	Type	Description	Mint	Used
347		1c. green	45	10
348		3c. brown	45	10
349		5c. purple	1·00	50
350		10c. pink	2·00	1·00

66 Airplane and Carrier Pigeon

1935. Air.

No.	Type	Description	Mint	Used
351	66	10c. light blue and blue	2·50	45

67 President Trujillo

1935. Frontier Agreement.

No.	Type	Description	Mint	Used
352	67	3c. brown and yellow	30	15
353	–	5c. brown and orange	35	10
354	–	7c. brown and blue	55	10
355	–	10c. brown and purple	85	10

RECTANGULAR DESIGNS: Portrait as Type **67**. Red, white and blue ribbons in side panels on 7c. or diagonally across 5c. and 10c.

69 Post Office, Santiago de los Caballeros

1936.

No.	Type	Description	Mint	Used
356	69	½c. violet	30	20
357		1c. green	30	10

70

1936. Air.

No.	Type	Description	Mint	Used
358	70	10c. blue	2·75	45

71 George Washington Avenue, Ciudad Trujillo

1936. Dedication of George Washington Avenue.

No.	Type	Description	Mint	Used
359	71	½c. brown	35	25
360		2c. brown and red	60	20
361		3c. brown and yellow	60	15
362		7c. brown and blue	85	50

72 Gen. A. Duverge

74 "Flight"

1936. National Archives and Library Fund. Inscr "PRO ARCHIVO Y BIBLIOTECA NACIONALES".

No.	Type	Description	Mint	Used
363	–	½c. lilac	25	15
364	–	1c. green	20	10
365	–	2c. red	20	10
366	–	3c. violet	25	10
367	–	5c. blue	40	25
368	72	7c. blue	70	50
369	–	10c. orange	85	30
370	–	20c. olive	3·25	1·90
371	–	25c. purple	3·25	2·00
372	–	30c. red	5·00	2·75
373	–	50c. brown	6·00	2·75
374	–	1p. black	15·00	12·00
375	–	2p. brown	40·00	35·00

DESIGNS—As Type **72**: ½c. J. N. de Caceres; 1c. Gen. G. Luperon; 2c. E. Tejera; 3c. Pres. Trujillo; 5c. Jose Reyes; 10c. Felix M. Del Monte; 25c. F. J. Peynado; 30c. Salome Urena; 50c. Gen. Jose Ma. Cabral; 1p. Manuel Js. Galvan; 2p. Gaston F. Deligne. TRIANGULAR: 20c. National Library.

1936. Air.

No.	Type	Description	Mint	Used
376	74	10c. blue	2·10	35

75 Obelisk in Ciudad Trujillo

1937. 1st Anniv of Naming of Ciudad Trujillo (formerly Santo Domingo).

No.	Type	Description	Mint	Used
377	75	1c. green	20	10
378		3c. violet	40	10
379		7c. blue	1·25	60

76 Discus Thrower and National Flag

1937. 1st National Olympic Games, Ciudad Trujillo. Flag blue, white and red.

No.	Type	Description	Mint	Used
380	76	1c. green	6·50	70
381		3c. violet	8·50	50
382		7c. blue	15·00	2·75

77 "Peace, Labour and Progress"

1937. 8th Year of Trujillo Presidency.

No.	Type	Description	Mint	Used
383	77	3c. violet	35	10

78 San Pedro de Macoris Airport

1937. Air.

No.	Type	Description	Mint	Used
384	78	10c. green	1·25	10

79 Fleet of Columbus

1937. Air. Pan-American Goodwill Flight.
385 **79** 10c. red . . . . 3·75 1·25
386 A 15c. violet . . . . 1·75 70
387 B 20c. blue . . . . 1·75 70
388 A 25c. purple . . . . . . 2·50 85
389 B 30c. green . . . . . . 2·25 70
390 A 50c. brown . . . . . . 4·25 1·00
391 B 75c. olive . . . . 11·00 11·00
392 **79** 1p. red . . . . 12·00 2·75
DESIGNS—A, Junkers F-13 aircraft in Goodwill Flight; B, Junkers F-13 aircraft over Columbus Lighthouse.

83 Father Billini **84** Globe and Torch of Liberty

1938. Birth Centenary of Father Billini.
396 **83** ½c. orange 15 10
397 5c. violet 45 15

1938. 150th Anniv of U.S. Constitution.
398 **84** 1c. green 30 10
399 3c. violet 45 10
400 10c. orange 85 20

85 Bastion, Trinitarian Oath and National Flag

1938. Centenary of Trinitarian Rebellion.
401 **85** 1c. green 40 20
402 3c. violet 50 15
403 10c. orange . . . . 1·00 45

86 Martin M-130 Flying Boat over Obelisk **87** Arms of University

1938. Air.
404 **86** 10c. green . . . . 1·40 15

1938. 400th Anniv of Santo Domingo University.
405 **87** ½c. orange 25 15
406 1c. green 35 10
407 3c. violet 40 10
408 7c. blue 85 40

89 N.Y. Fair Symbol, Lighthouse, Flag and Cornucopia

1939. New York World's Fair. (a) Postage. Flag in blue, white and red.
418 **89** ½c. orange 35 15
419 1c. green 40 15
420 3c. violet 40 15
421 10c. yellow . . . . 1·25 45

(b) Air. Flag, etc, replaced by airplane.
422 10c. green . . . . 1·50 55

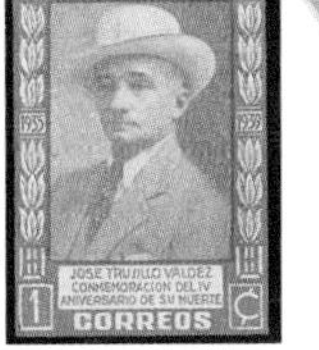

90 Jose Trujillo Valdez **91**

1939. 4th Death Anniv of Jose Trujillo Valdez. Black borders.
423 **90** ½c. grey 25 15
424 1c. green 35 10
425 3c. brown 40 10
426 7c. blue 85 50
427 10c. violet . . . . 1·50 40

1939. Air.
428 **91** 10c. green . . . . 1·40 20

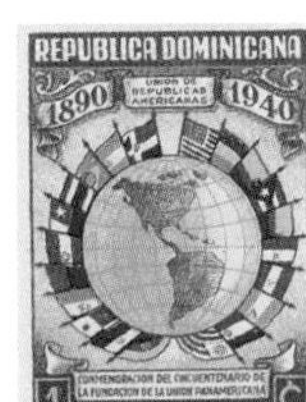

92 Western Hemisphere and Union Flags **93** Sir Rowland Hill

1940. 50th Anniv of Pan-American Union. Flags in national colours.
429 **92** 1c. green 25 10
430 2c. red 35 15
431 3c. violet 55 10
432 10c. orange . . . . 1·10 20
433 1p. brown . . . . 15·00 10·00

1940. Centenary of 1st Adhesive Postage Stamps.
434 **93** 3c. mauve . . . . 6·50 40
435 7c. blue . . . . 12·00 1·50

94 Julia Molina de Trujillo

1940. Mothers' Day.
436 **94** 1c. green 30 10
437 2c. red 40 10
438 3c. orange 50 10
439 7c. blue . . . . 1·25 45

95 Central America and Arms of Dominican Republic

1940. 2nd Caribbean Conference, Trujillo City.
440 **95** 3c. red 40 10
441 7c. blue 85 15
442 1p. green . . . . 8·50 4·25

96 Lighthouse, Aeroplane and Caravels

1940. Air. Discovery of America and Columbus Memorial Lighthouse. Inscr "PRO FARO DE COLON".
443 **96** 10c. blue . . . . 1·40 50
444 – 15c. brown 80 70
445 – 20c. red 80 70
446 – 25c. mauve 80 35
447 – 50c. green . . . . 4·00 1·60
DESIGNS: 15c. Columbus and lighthouse; 20c. Lighthouse; 25c. Columbus; 50c. Caravel and wings.

99 Marion Military Hospital **100** Post Office, San Cristobal

1940.
457 **99** ½c. brown 25 20

1941. Air.
458 **100** 10c. mauve 65 15

101 Trujillo Fortress

1941.
460 **101** 1c. green 15 10
461 – 2c. red 15 10
462 – 10c. brown 55 10
DESIGN—VERT: 2, 10c. Statue of Columbus, Ciudad Trujillo.

103 Sanchez, Duarte, Mella and Trujillo

1941. Trujillo-Hull Treaty.
463 **103** 3c. mauve 25 10
464 4c. red 30 10
465 13c. blue 70 20
466 15c. brown . . . . 2·00 85
467 17c. blue . . . . 2·00 90
468 1p. orange . . . . 7·50 3·25
469 2p. grey . . . . 15·00 7·50

104 Bastion of 27 February

1941.
470 **104** 5c. blue 55 20

105 Rural School, Torch of Knowledge and Pres. Trujillo

1941. Popular Education Campaign.
471 **105** ½c. brown 20 10
472 1c. green 25 10

106 Globe and Winged Envelope

1941. Air.
473 **106** 10c. brown 55 10
474 75c. orange . . . . 3·25 2·00

107 National Reserve Bank

1942.
475 **107** 5c. brown 40 10
476 17c. blue . . . . 1·00 40

108 Symbolic of Communications **109** Our Lady of Highest Grace

1942. 8th Anniv of Postal and Telegraph Services Day.
477 **108** 3c. multicoloured . . . . 4·00 1·00
478 15c. multicoloured . . . . 8·00 4·00

1942. 20th Anniv of Our Lady of Highest Grace.
479 **109** ½c. grey 85 10
480 1c. green . . . . 1·60 10
481 3c. mauve . . . . 7·50 10
482 5c. purple . . . . 2·40 10
483 10c. red . . . . 6·50 25
484 15c. blue . . . . 7·50 35

111 Banana Tree **112** Cows

1942.
494 **111** 3c. green and brown . . . 45 10
495 4c. black and red 50 20
496 **112** 5c. brown and blue . . . 45 10
497 15c. green and purple . . 85 35

113 Party Emblems and Votes

1943. Re-election of Gen. Trujillo to Presidency.
498 **113** 3c. orange 40 10
499 4c. red 50 15
500 13c. purple . . . . 1·10 20
501 1p. blue . . . . 5·00 1·90

114 Trujillo Market

1943.
502 **114** 2c. brown 15 10

115 Douglas DC-3

1943. Air.
503 **115** 10c. mauve 50 10
504 20c. blue 55 15
505 25c. olive . . . . 6·75 2·75

116 Bastion of 27 February **117** Monument and Dates

1944. Centenary of Independence. (a) Postage. Flag in blue and red.
506 **116** ½c. ochre 10 10
507 1c. green 10 10
508 2c. red 15 10
509 3c. purple 15 10
510 5c. orange 20 10
511 7c. blue 25 10
512 10c. brown 40 30
513 20c. olive 70 45
514 50c. blue . . . . 2·00 1·40

(b) Air. Flag in grey, blue and red.
515 **117** 10c. multicoloured 40 10
516 20c. multicoloured 50 15
517 1p. multicoloured . . . . 2·40 1·60

118 Dr. Martos Sanatorium

1944. Tuberculosis Relief Fund.
518 **118** 1c. blue and red 15 10

119 Nurse and Battlefield

1944. 80th Anniv of International Red Cross.
519 **119** 1c. green, red and yellow 15 10
520 2c. brown, red and yellow 35 10
521 3c. blue, red and yellow 35 10
522 10c. red and yellow . . . 70 15

120 Communications Building, Ciudad Trujillo

1944. Air.
523 **120** 9c. blue and green 25 10
524 13c. red and brown . . . 35 10
525 25c. red and orange . . . 50 10
526 30c. blue and black . . . 1·10 80

121 Municipal Building, San Cristobal
122 Emblem of Communications

1945. Centenary of 1st Constitution of Dominican Republic.
527 **121** ½c. blue 10 10
528 1c. green 10 10
529 2c. orange 10 10
530 3c. brown 15 10
531 10c. blue 45 15

1945. Centres in blue and red.
532 **122** 3c. orange (postage) . . . 15 10
533 20c. green 80 20
534 50c. blue . . . . 1·60 60
535 7c. green (air) 20 25
536 12c. orange 25 15
537 13c. blue 30 15
538 25c. brown 60 20

124 Flags and National Anthem
125 Law Courts, Ciudad Trujillo

1946. Air. National Anthem.
540 **124** 10c. red 45 40
541 15c. blue . . . . 1·00 70
542 20c. brown . . . . 1·25 70
543 35c. orange . . . . 1·40 70
544 – 1p. green . . . . 13·00 10·00
DESIGN: 1p. As Type **124**, but horiz.

1946.
545 **125** 3c. brown and buff . . . 20 10

126 Caribbean Air Routes

1946. 450th Anniv of Santo Domingo.
546 **126** 10c. mult (postage) . . . 40 15
547 10c. multicoloured (air) 35 15
548 13c. multicoloured 55 15

127 Jimenoa Waterfall
128 Nurse and Child

1947. Centres multicoloured, frame colours given.
549 **127** 1c. green (postage) . . . 15 10
550 2c. red 15 10
551 3c. blue 15 10
552 13c. purple 45 25
553 20c. brown . . . . 1·00 25
554 50c. yellow . . . . 1·90 1·00
555 18c. blue (air) 50 50
556 23c. red 70 55
557 50c. violet . . . . 1·00 45
558 75c. brown . . . . 1·40 1·00

1947. Obligatory Tax. Tuberculosis Relief Fund.
559 **128** 1c. blue and red 15 10

129 State Building, Ciudad Trujillo

1948.
560 **129** 1c. green (postage) . . . 10 10
561 3c. blue 15 10
562 37c. brown (air) . . . . . 1·00 70
563 1p. orange . . . . 2·75 1·60

130 Ruins of San Francisco Church, Ciudad Trujillo
131 El Santo Socorro Sanatorium

1949.
564 **130** 1c. green (postage) . . . 10 10
565 3c. blue 15 10
566 7c. olive (air) 15 10
567 10c. brown 15 10
568 15c. red 50 25
569 20c. green 70 45

1949. Tuberculosis Relief Fund.
570 **131** 1c. blue and red 15 10

132 General Pedro Santana
133 Monument

1949. Centenary of Battle of Las Carreras.
571 **132** 3c. blue (postage) 15 10
572 **133** 10c. red (air) 25 10

134 Bird and Globe
136 Hotel Jimani

135 Youth Holding Banner
138 Ruins of Church and Hospital of St. Nicholas of Bari

1949. 75th Anniv of U.P.U.
573 **134** 1c. brown and green . . . 15 10
574 2c. brown and yellow . . 15 10
575 5c. brown and blue . . . 20 10
576 7c. brown and blue . . . 45 15

1950. Tuberculosis Relief Fund.
584 **135** 1c. blue and red 20 10

1950. Various Hotels.
585 **136** ½c. brown (postage) . . . 10 10
586 – 1c. green (Hamaca) . . . 10 10
587 – 2c. orange (Hamaca) . . 10 10
588 – 5c. blue (Montana) . . . 20 10
589 – 15c. orge (San Cristobal) 45 10
590 – 20c. lilac (Maguana) . . . 85 15
591 **136** $1 yellow and brown . . 3·25 1·40
592 – 12c. bl (Montana) (air) . . 25 10
593 – 37c. red (San Cristobal) 1·90 1·50

1950. 13th Pan-American Sanitary Congress. Inscr as T **138**.
595 **138** 2c. brown & green (postage) 20 10
596 – 5c. brown and blue . . . 25 10
597 – 12c. orange & brn (air) 55 10
DESIGNS—VERT: 5c. Medical school; 12c. Map and aeroplane.

139 "Suffer Little Children to Come Unto Me"
148
148a
148b

1950. Child Welfare. (a) Child at left with light hair.
598 **139** 1c. blue 25 10

(b) Child at left with dark hair.
599 **139** 1c. blue 85 15

(c) Child at left with dark hair.
626 **148** 1c. blue 20 10

(d) Child at left with light hair.
627 **148a** 1c. blue 15 10

(e) Dark hair, smaller figures and square value tablet.
628 **148b** 1c. blue 15 10
There are two versions of No. 628, differing in size.
See also Nos. 835 and 907.

140 Isabella the Catholic

1951. 500th Birth Anniv of Isabella the Catholic.
600 **140** 5c. brown and blue . . . 25 10

141 Santiago Tuberculosis Sanatorium

1952. Tuberculosis Relief Fund.
601 **141** 1c. blue and red 15 10

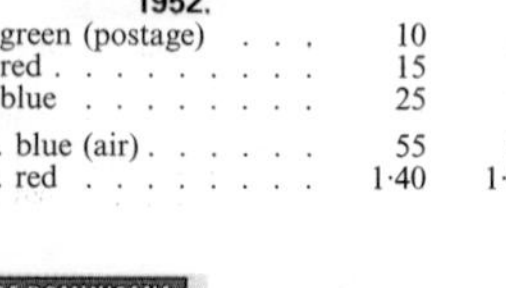

142 Dr. S. B. Gautier Hospital

1952.
602 **142** 1c. green (postage) . . . 10 10
603 2c. red 15 10
604 5c. blue 25 10
605 23c. blue (air) 55 55
606 29c. red . . . . 1·40 1·00

143 Columbus Lighthouse and Flags

144

1953. 460th Anniv of Columbus's Discovery of Santo Domingo. (a) Postage.
607 **143** 2c. green 15 10
608 5c. blue 20 10
609 10c. red 35 20

(b) Air. Similar design inscr "S./S.A.S./XMY", etc.
610 12c. brown 35 15
611 14c. blue 35 20
612 20c. sepia 65 40
613 23c. purple 70 45
614 25c. blue 70 45
615 29c. green 90 45
616 1p. brown . . . . 3·25 2·00
DESIGN: Nos. 610/16, Douglas DC-6 airplane over Columbus Lighthouse.

1953. Anti-cancer Fund. No. 619 has "1 c" larger with line through "c" and no stop. No. 620 is as 619 but with smaller "c".
618 **144** 1c. red 20 10
619 1c. red 35 10
620 1c. red 15 10
See also Nos. 1029/30, 1066/7, 1171a, 1196a, 1237a, 1270a and 1338a.

145 T.B. Children's Dispensary

1953. Obligatory Tax. Tuberculosis Relief Fund.
621 **145** 1c. blue and red 15 10
There are two versions of this design.

146 Treasury
149 Jose Marti

150 Monument to Trujillo Peace
147 Rio Haina Sugar Factory

1953.
622 **146** ½c. brown 10 10
623 2c. blue 10 10
624 **147** 5c. brown and blue . . . 15 10
625 **146** 15c. orange 50 15

1953. Birth Cent of Marti (Cuban revolutionary).
629 **149** 10c. sepia and blue . . . 30 15

1954.
630 **150** 2c. green 10 10
631 7c. blue 15 10
632 20c. orange 55 10
There are two versions of No. 631.

151
152 Rotary Emblem

1954. Air. Marian Year.
633 **151** 8c. purple 15 10
634 11c. blue 25 10
635 33c. orange 70 45

1955. 50th Anniv of Rotary International.
636 **152** 7c. blue (postage) 30 10
637 11c. red (air) 25 15

153

154 Pres. R. Trujillo

1955. Obligatory Tax. Tuberculosis Relief Fund.
638 **153** 1c. black, red & yellow 15 10

1955. 25th Year of Trujillo Era.
639 **154** 2c. red (postage) 10 10
640 – 4c. green 15 10
641 – 7c. blue 15 10
642 – 10c. brown 35 15
643 – 11c. red, yell & bl (air) . . 30 10
644 – 25c. purple 45 25
645 – 33c. brown 70 40
DESIGNS: 4c. Pres. R. Trujillo in civilian clothes; 7c. Equestrian statue; 10c. Allegory of Prosperity; 11c. National flags; 25c. Gen. Hector B. Trujillo in evening clothes; 33c. Gen. Hector B. Trujillo in uniform.

156 Angelita Trujillo

1955. Child Welfare.
654 **156** 1c. violet 15 10

157 Angelita Trujillo

158 Gen. R. Trujillo

1955. Peace and Brotherhood Fair, Ciudad Trujillo.
656 **158** 7c. purple (postage) . . . 25 10
657 10c. green 35 15
655 **157** 10c. blue and ultramarine 35 15
658 **158** 11c. red (air) 25 10

159 "B.C.G." = "Bacillus" Calmette-Guerin

160 Punta Caucedo Airport

1956. Obligatory Tax. Tuberculosis Relief Fund.
659 **159** 1c. multicoloured 15 10

1956. 3rd Caribbean Region Aerial Navigation Conference.
660 **160** 1c. brown (postage) . . . 10 10
661 2c. orange 20 10
662 11c. blue (air) 35 10

161 Cedar Tree

162 Fanny Blankers-Koen and Dutch Flag

1956. Re-afforestation. Inscr "REPOBLACION FORESTAL".
664 **161** 5c. green, brown and red (postage) 20 10
665 – 6c. green and purple . . . 25 10
666 – 13c. green & orge (air) . . 35 10
DESIGNS: 6c. Pine tree; 13c. Mahogany tree.

1957. Olympic Games (1st issue). Famous Athletes. Flags in national colours.
667 **162** 1c. mult (postage) 10 10
668 – 2c. sepia, purple & blue . . 10 10
669 – 3c. purple and red 15 15
670 – 5c. orange, pur & blue . . 25 15
671 – 7c. green and purple . . . 35 25
673 – 11c. blue and red (air) . . 20 20
674 – 16c. red and green 30 30
675 – 17c. black and purple . . 40 40
DESIGNS—(each with national flag of athlete): 2c. Jesse Owens; 3c. Kee Chung Sohn; 5c. Lord Burghley; 7c. Bob Mathias; 11c. Paavo Nurmi; 16c. Ugo Frigerio; 17c. Mildred Didrickson.
See also Nos. 689/96, 713/21, 748/56 and 784/91.

163 Horse's Head and Globe

165

1957. 2nd Int Livestock Fair, Ciudad Trujillo.
677 **163** 7c. blue, brown & red . . 25 10

1957. Hungarian Refugees Fund. Nos. 667/75 surch with red cross in circle surrounded by **ASISTENCIA REFUGIADOS HUNGAROS 1957** and **+2c**.
678 **162** 1c.+2c. (postage) 10 10
679 – 2c.+2c. 10 10
680 – 3c.+2c. 10 10
681 – 5c.+2c. 15 15
682 – 7c.+2c. 25 25
684 – 11c.+2c. (air) 40 40
685 – 16c.+2c. 40 40
686 – 17c.+2c. . . . . 1·50 1·50

1957. Obligatory Tax. Tuberculosis Relief Fund.
688 **165** 1c. multicoloured 15 10

166 Chris Brasher and Union Jack (steeplechase)

1957. Olympic Games (2nd issue). Winning Athletes. Inscr "MELBOURNE 1956". Flags in national colours.
689 – 1c. brown & bl (postage) 10 10
690 – 2c. red and blue 10 10
691 – 3c. blue 10 10
692 – 5c. olive and blue . . . 15 10
693 – 7c. red and blue 25 15
694 – 11c. green & blue (air) . . 20 20
695 **166** 16c. purple and blue . . . 25 25
696 – 17c. sepia and green . . . 30 30
DESIGNS—(each with national flag of athlete): 1c. Lars Hall (Sweden, pentathlon); 2c. Betty Cuthbert (Australia, 100 and 200 m); 3c. Egil Danielson (Norway, javelin-throwing); 5c. Alain Mimoum (France, marathon); 7c. Norman Read (New Zealand, 50 km walk); 11c. Robert Morrow (U.S.A.; 100 and 200 m); 17c. A. Ferreira da Silva (Brazil; hop, step and jump).

1957. 50th Anniv of Boy Scout Movement, and Birth Cent of Lord Baden-Powell. Nos 689/96 surch **CENTENARIO LORD BADEN-POWELL, 1857-1957 +2c**. surrounding Scout badge.
699 1c.+2c. brn & bl (postage) . . 15 15
700 2c.+2c. red and blue 20 15
701 3c.+2c. blue 25 25
702 5c.+2c. olive and blue . . . 35 25
703 7c.+2c. red and blue 40 30
704 11c.+2c. grn & blue (air) . . 40 35
705 16c.+2c. purple and blue . . 50 50
706 17c.+2c. sepia and green . . 55 55

168 Mahogany Flower

1957.
709 **168** 2c. red and green 10 10
710 4c. red and mauve 10 10
711 7c. green and blue 25 10
712 25c. orange and brown . . 55 25

169 Gerald Ouellette and Canadian Flag (rifle-shooting)

1957. Olympic Games (3rd issue). More winning athletes. Flags in national colours.
713 **169** 1c. brown (postage) . . . 10 10
714 – 2c. sepia 10 10
715 – 3c. violet 10 10
716 – 5c. orange 15 15
717 – 7c. slate 20 20
719 – 11c. blue (air) 20 15
720 – 16c. red 30 30
721 – 17c. purple 35 35
DESIGNS—(each with national flag of athlete): 2c. Ron Delaney (Ireland, 1500 m); 3c. Tenley Albright (U.S.A., figure-skating); 5c. J. Capilla (Mexico, high-diving); 7c. Ercole Baldini (Italy, cycle-racing); 11c. Hans Winkler (Germany, horse-jumping); 16c. Alfred Oerter (U.S.A., discus-throwing); 17c. Shirley Strickland (Australia, 80 m hurdles).
The designs of Nos. 714, 716 and 720 are arranged with the long side of the triangular format uppermost.

170

171 Cervantes, Open Book, Marker and Globe

1958. Tuberculosis Relief Fund.
723 **170** 1c. red and claret 10 10
See also No. 763.

1958. 4th Latin-American Book Fair.
724 **171** 4c. green 10 10
725 7c. mauve 15 10
726 10c. bistre 25 10

1958. U.N. Relief and Works Agency for Palestine Refugees. Nos. 713/21 surch. A. For Jewish Refugees. Star of David and **REFUGIADOS**.
727 1c.+2c. brown (postage) . . . 15 15
728 2c.+2c. brown 20 20
729 3c.+2c. violet 20 20
730 5c.+2c. orange 25 25
731 7c.+2c. blue 35 35
732 11c.+2c. blue (air) 25 25
733 16c.+2c. red 35 35
734 17c.+2c. purple 40 40

B. For Arab Refugees. Red Crescent and **REFUGIADOS**.
735 1c.+2c. brown (postage) . . . 15 15
736 2c.+2c. brown 20 20
737 3c.+2c. violet 20 20
738 5c.+2c. orange 25 25
739 7c.+2c. blue 35 35
740 11c.+2c. blue (air) 25 25
741 16c.+2c. red 35 35
742 17c.+2c. purple 40 40

172 Gen. R. Trujillo and Arms of Republic

173 "Rhadames" (freighter)

1958. 25th Anniv of Gen Trujillo's designation as "Benefactor of the Country".
743 **172** 2c. mauve and yellow . . 10 10
744 4c. green and yellow . . . 10 10
745 7c. sepia and yellow . . . 15 10

1958. Merchant Marine Day.
747 **173** 7c. blue . . . . 1·25 30

174 Gillian Sheen and Union Jack (fencing)

175

176 Dominican Republic Pavilion

1958. Olympic Games (4th issue). More winning athletes. Flags in national colours.
748 **174** 1c. slate, blue and red (postage) 10 10
749 – 2c. brown and blue . . . 10 10
750 – 3c. multicoloured 15 15
751 – 5c. multicoloured 20 20
752 – 7c. multicoloured 25 25
754 – 11c. sepia, olive and blue (air) 25 25
755 – 16c. blue, orge & grn . . 30 30
756 – 17c. blue, yell and red . . 1·00 50
DESIGNS (each with national flag of athlete)— VERT: 2c. Milton Campbell (U.S.A., decathlon). HORIZ: 3c. Shozo Sasahara (Japan, featherweight wrestling); 5c. Madeleine Berthod (Switzerland, skiing); 7c. Murray Rose (Australia, 400 m and 1,500 m free-style); 11c. Charles Jenkins and Thomas Courtney (U.S.A., 400 m and 800 m, and 1600 m relay); 16c. Indian team in play (India, hockey); 17c. Swedish dinghies (Sweden, sailing).

1958. Inauguration of U.N.E.S.C.O. Headquarters Building, Paris.
758 **175** 7c. blue and red 15 10

1958. Brussels International Exhibition.
759 **176** 7c. green (postage) . . . 20 15
760 9c. grey (air) 20 15
761 25c. violet 50 30

1959. Obligatory Tax. Tuberculosis Relief Fund. As T **170** but inscr "1959".
763 **170** 1c. red and lake 15 10

1959. I.G.Y. Nos. 748/56 surch with globe and **ANO GEOFISICO INTERNACIONAL 1957-1958 +2c**.
764 1c.+2c. (postage) 25 25
765 2c.+2c. 30 30
766 3c.+2c. 35 35
767 5c.+2c. 40 40
768 7c.+2c. 45 45
770 11c.+2c. (air) 50 50
771 16c.+2c. 70 70
772 17c.+2c. . . . . 1·00 1·00

178 Leonidas R. Trujillo (Team Captain)

179 Gen. Trujillo before National Shrine

1959. Jamaica–Dominican Republic Polo Match, Trujillo City. Inscr as in T **178**.
774 **178** 2c. violet (postage) . . . 15 10
775 – 7c. brown 30 15
776 – 10c. green 35 25
777 – 11c. orange (air) 30 25
DESIGNS—HORIZ: 7c. Jamaican team; 10c. Dominican Republic team's captain on horseback; 11c. Dominican Republic team.

1959. 29th Year of Trujillo Era.
778 **179** 9c. multicoloured 20 10

180 Gen. Trujillo and Cornucopia

1959. National Census of 1960. Centres in black, red and blue. Frame colours given.
780 **180** 1c. pale blue 15 10
781 9c. green 30 15
782 13c. orange 35 25

181 Trujillo Stadium

1959. 3rd Pan-American Games, Chicago.
783 **181** 9c. black and green . . . 35 20

1959. 3rd Pan-American Games, Chicago. Nos. 667/71 and 673/5, surch **III JUEGOS DEPORTIVOS PANAMERICANOS + 2** and runner.
784 **162** 1c.+2c. mult (postage) . . 15 15
785 – 3c.+2c. multicoloured . . 15 15
786 – 3c.+2c. pur & red 15 15
787 – 5c.+2c. multicoloured . . 15 15
788 – 7c.+2c. multicoloured . . 20 20

789 – 11c.+2c. blue, red and orange (air) 20 20
790 – 16c.+2c. red, green and carmine 30 30
791 – 17c.+2c. multicoloured . . 30 30

182 Emperor Charles V

183 Rhadames Bridge

1959. 4th Death Centenary of Emperor Charles V.

792 **182** 5c. mauve 15 10
793 9c. blue 15 10

1959. Opening of Rhadames Bridge.

794 – 1c. black and green . . . 10 10
795 **183** 2c. black and blue 15 10
796 – 2c. black and red 15 10
797 **183** 5c. brown and bistre . . . 20 15

DESIGN—Nos. 794, 796, Close-up view of Rhadames Bridge.

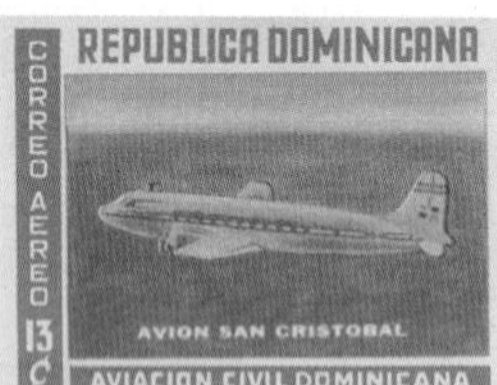

184 Douglas DC-4 Airliner, "San Cristobal"

1960. Air. Dominican Civil Aviation.

798 **184** 13c. multicoloured 45 15

185

1960. Obligatory Tax. Tuberculosis Relief Fund.

779 **185** 1c. red, blue and cream 20 15

186 Sosua Refugee Colony

1960. World Refugee Year. Inscr "ANO MUNDIAL DE LOS REFUGIADOS". Centres in black.

800 **186** 5c. green & brn (postage) 10 10
801 9c. blue, purple & red . . 20 10
802 13c. green, brn & orge . . 25 15

803 – 10c. green, mauve and purple (air) 35 30
804 – 13c. green and grey . . 45 35

DESIGN: Nos. 802/803, Refugee children.

1960. World Refugee Year Fund. Nos. 800/4 surch +5 with c below.

805 **186** 5c.+5c. green and brown (postage) 15 15
806 9c.+5c. bl, pur & red . . 20 20
807 13c.+5c. green, brown and orange 40 40

808 – 10c.+5c. green, mauve and purple (air) 25 25
809 – 13c.+5c. green & grey . . 30 30

188 General Post Office, Ciudad Trujillo

1960.

811 **188** 2c. black and blue 10 10

189 Cattle in Street

1960. Agricultural and Industrial Fair, San Juan de la Maguana.

812 **189** 9c. black and red 25 15

190 Gholam Takhti (Iran, lightweight wrestling)

192

1960. Olympic Games, 1960. More Winning Athletes of Olympic Games, Melbourne, 1956. Flags in national colours.

813 **190** 1c. black, grn & red (postage) 10 10
814 – 2c. brown, turq & orge 10 10
815 – 3c. blue and red 10 10
816 – 5c. brown and blue . . . 15 15
817 – 7c. brn, blue & green . . 15 15

819 – 11c. brown, grey & bl (air) 20 20
820 – 16c. green, brown & red 25 25
821 – 17c. ochre, blue & black 30 30

DESIGNS (each with national flag of athlete): 2c. Mauru Furukawa (Japan, 200 m breast-stroke swimming); 3c. Mildred McDaniel (U.S.A., high jump); 5c. Terence Spinks (spelt "Terrence" on stamp) (Great Britain, featherweight boxing); 7c. Carlo Pavesi (Italy, fencing); 11c. Pat McCormick (U.S.A., high diving); 16c. Mithat Bayrack (Turkey, Greco-Roman welterweight wrestling); 17c. Ursula Happe (Germany, women's 200 m breaststroke swimming).

1961. Surch **HABILITADO PARA** and value.

823 – 2c. on 1c. black and green (No. 794) 15 10
824 **168** 9c. on 4c. red & mauve 45 10
825 9c. on 7c. green & blue 45 15
826 **146** 36c. on ½c. brown . . . . 1·50 70
827 **127** 1p. on 50c. yellow . . . . 3·25 1·90

1961. Obligatory Tax. Tuberculosis Relief Fund.

828 **192** 1c. red and blue 10 10

See also No. 876.

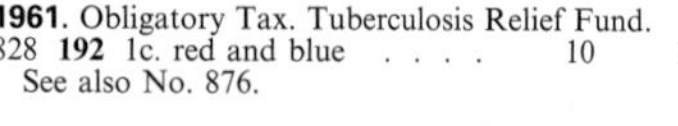

193 Madame Trujillo and Houses

1961. Welfare Fund.

829 **193** 1c. red 20 10

194

195 Coffee Plant and Cocoa Beans

1961.

830 **194** 1c. brown 10 10
831 2c. myrtle 10 10
832 4c. purple 40 35
833 5c. blue 25 10
834 9c. orange 30 20

1961. Obligatory Tax. Child Welfare. As Nos. 627/8 but with "ERA DE TRUJILLO" omitted. (a) Size 23½ × 32 mm.

835 **148a** 1c. blue 15 10

(b) Size 21¾ × 32 mm.

907 **148b** 1c. blue 15 10

1961.

836 **195** 1c. green (postage) . . . 10 10
837 2c. brown 10 10
838 4c. violet 10 10
839 5c. blue 10 10
840 9c. grey 25 10

841 13c. red (air) 25 25
842 33c. yellow 55 55

1961. 15th Anniv of U.N.E.S.C.O. Nos. 813/21 surch **XV ANIVERSARIO DE LA UNESCO +2c**.

843 1c.+2c. (postage) 10 10
844 2c.+2c. 10 10
845 3c.+2c. 10 10
846 5c.+2c. 15 15
847 7c.+2c. 15 15

849 11c.+2c. (air) 25 25
850 16c.+2c. 35 35
851 17c.+2c. 35 35

197 Mosquito and Dagger

198 Plantation

1962. Malaria Eradication.

853 **197** 10c. mauve (postage) . . 15 10
854 10c.+2c. mauve 20 15
855 20c. sepia 35 30
856 20c.+2c. sepia 35 25
857 25c. green 45 55

858 13c. red (air) 25 20
859 13c.+2c. red 25 25
860 33c. orange 50 50
861 33c.+2c. orange 60 60

1962. Farming and Industrial Development. Flag in red and blue.

863 **198** 1c. green and blue 10 10
864 2c. red and blue 10 10
865 3c. brown and blue . . . 10 10
866 5c. blue 15 10
867 15c. orange and blue . . 25 15

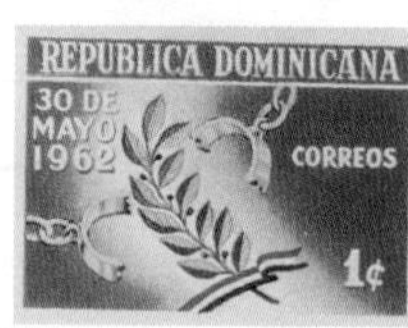

199 Laurel Sprig and Broken Link

1962. 1st Anniv of Assassination of Pres. Trujillo.

868 **199** 1c. mult (postage) 10 10
869 – 9c. red, blue and ochre . . 25 15
870 – 20c. red, blue & turq . . 45 25
871 – 1p. red, blue & violet . . 2·75 1·60

873 **199** 13c. multicoloured (air) 25 20
874 – 50c. red, blue & mauve 1·00 70

DESIGNS—VERT: 9c., 1p. "Justice" on map. HORIZ: 20c., 50c. Flag and flaming torch.

200 Map and Laurel

201 U.P.A.E. Emblem

1962. Martyrs of June 1959 Revolution.

875 **200** 1c. black 25 15

1962. Tuberculosis Relief Fund. As No. 828 but inscr "1962".

876 **192** 1c. red and blue 10 10

1962. 50th Anniv of Postal Union of the Americas and Spain.

877 **201** 2c. red (postage) 10 10
878 9c. orange 25 15
879 14c. turquoise 25 20

880 13c. blue (air) 35 20
881 22c. brown 45 40

202 Archbishop Nouel

203 Globe, Riband and Campaign Emblem

1962. Birth Cent of Archbishop Adolfo Nouel.

882 **202** 2c. myrtle & green (postage) 10 10
883 9c. brown and orange . . 25 15
884 13c. purple and brown . . 30 20

885 – 12c. blue (air) 35 20
886 – 25c. violet 50 40

DESIGN: Air stamps as Type **202** but different frame.

1963. Freedom from Hunger. Riband in red and blue.

888 **203** 2c. green 10 10
891 2c.+1c. green 10 10
889 5c. mauve 15 10
892 5c.+2c. mauve 20 20
890 9c. orange 25 15
893 9c.+2c. orange 20 20

204 Duarte

1963. 120th Anniv of Separation from Haiti.

895 **204** 2c. blue (postage) 10 10
896 – 7c. green (Sanchez) . . . 15 15
897 – 9c. purple (Mella) 15 15

898 – 15c. salmon (air) 20 15

DESIGN—HORIZ: 15c. Sanchez, Duarte and Mella.

205 Espaillat, de Rojas and Bono

1963. "Centenary of the Restoration".

899 **205** 2c. green 10 10
900 – 4c. red 10 10
901 – 5c. brown 10 10
902 – 9c. blue 15 15

DESIGNS: 4c. Rodriguez, Cabrera and Moncion; 5c. Capotillo Monument; 9c. Polanco, Luperon and Salcedo.

206 Nurse tending Patient

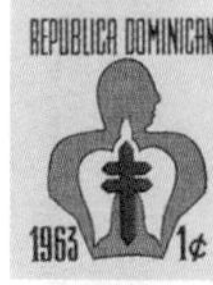

207

1963. Centenary of Red Cross. Cross in red.

904 **206** 3c. grey (postage) 10 10
905 6c. green 15 10

906 – 10c. grey (air) 25 20

DESIGN—HORIZ: 10c. Map of continents bordering Atlantic.

1963. Obligatory Tax. T.B. Relief Fund.

908 **207** 1c. red and blue 15 10

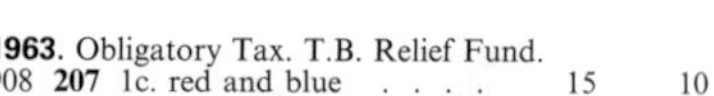

208 Scales of Justice and Globe

1963. 15th Anniv of Declaration of Human Rights.

911 **208** 6c. red (postage) 15 10
912 50c. green 80 55

913 7c. brown (air) 20 15
914 10c. blue 25 15

209 Rameses II in War Chariot, Abu Simbel

1964. Nubian Monuments Preservation. Designs as T **209**, also surch **2c** in circle.

915 **209** 3c. red (postage) 10 10
916 3c.+2c. red 15 15
917 – 6c. blue 15 10
918 – 6c.+2c. blue 15 15
919 **209** 9c. brown 20 15
920 9c.+2c. brown 25 25

921 – 10c. violet (air) 25 20
922 – 10c.+2c. violet 20 20
923 – 13c. yellow 25 20
924 – 13c.+2c. yellow 25 25

DESIGNS—HORIZ: 6c. Heads of Rameses II. VERT: 10c., 13c. As Type **209**.

211 M. Gomez (founder) **212** Palm Chat

1964. Bicentenary of Bani Foundation.

925	**211**	2c. blue & light blue	10	10
926		6c. purple and brown	15	10

1964. Dominican Birds. Multicoloured.

927	1c. Narrow-billed tody (postage)	1·75	15
928	2c. Hispaniolan emerald	1·75	15
929	3c. Type **212**	1·75	15
930	6c. Hispaniolan amazon	2·10	15
931	6c. Hispaniolan trogons	2·50	15
932	10c. Hispaniolan woodpecker (air)	3·75	20

The 1c., 2c. and 6c. (No. 931) are smaller (26 × 37½ mm); the 10c. is horiz (43½ × 27½ mm).

213 Rocket

1964. "Conquest of Space".

933	–	1c. blue (postage)	10	10
934	**213**	2c. green	10	10
935	–	3c. blue	15	10
936	**213**	6c. blue	25	15
937	**213**	7c. green (air)	25	25
938		10c. blue	35	70

DESIGNS—VERT: 1c. Rocket launching. HORIZ: 3c., 10c. Capsule in orbit.

214 Pres. Kennedy

1964. Air. Pres. Kennedy Commemoration.

940	**214**	10c. brown and buff	35	25

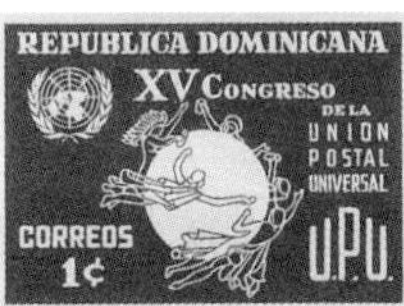

215 U.P.U. Monument, Berne

1964. 15th U.P.U. Congress, Vienna.

941	**215**	1c. red (postage)	10	10
942		4c. green	15	10
943		5c. orange	15	10
944		7c. blue (air)	15	10

216 I.C.Y. Emblem **217** Hands and Lily

1965. International Co-operation Year.

945	**216**	2c. blue and light-blue (postage)	10	10
946		3c. green and emerald	10	10
947		6c. red and pink	15	10
948		10c. violet & lilac (air)	25	20

1965. 4th Mariological and 11th Int Marian Congresses. Multicoloured.

949	2c. Type **217** (postage)	10	10
950	6c. Virgin of the Altagracia	35	25
951	10c. Douglas DC-8 airliner over Basilica of Virgin of Altagracia (39½ × 31½ mm) (air)	30	15

218 Flags Emblem **219** Lincoln

1965. 75th Anniv of Organization of American States.

952	**218**	2c. multicoloured	10	10
953		6c. multicoloured	15	10

1965. Air. Death Centenary of Abraham Lincoln.

954	**219**	17c. grey and blue	35	25

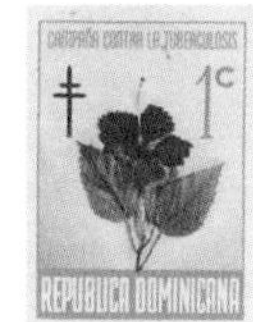

220 ½r. Stamp of 1865 **221** Hibiscus

1965. Stamp Centenary.

955	**220**	1c. multicoloured (post)	10	10
956		2c. multicoloured	10	10
957		6c. multicoloured	15	10
958	–	7c. multicoloured (air)	25	20
959	–	10c. multicoloured	25	25

DESIGN: 7c., 10c. As Type **220**, but showing 1r. stamp of 1865.

1966. Obligatory Tax. Tuberculosis Relief Fund.

963	**221**	1c. red and green	15	10
999	–	1c. mauve, lilac & red	10	10
1015	–	1c. multicoloured	10	10
1016	–	1c. multicoloured	10	10
1017	–	1c. multicoloured	10	10

DESIGN (21½ × 30 mm): No. 999, Orchid. (20 × 28 mm): No. 1015, Dogbane; 1016, Violets; 1017, "Eeanthus capitatus".

222 I.T.U. Emblem and Symbols **223** W.H.O. Building

1966. Air. Centenary (1965) of I.T.U.

964	**222**	28c. red and pink	55	40
965		45c. green and emerald	55	70

1965. Inaug of W.H.O. Headquarters, Geneva.

966	**223**	6c. blue	15	10
967		10c. purple	20	15

224 Man supporting "Republic" **225** "Ascia monuste"

1966. General Elections.

968	**224**	2c. black and green	10	10
969		6c. black and red	15	10

1966. Butterflies. Multicoloured.

970	1c. Type **225** (postage)	10	10
971	2c. "Heliconius charitonius"	10	10
972	3c. "Phoebis sennae sennae"	15	15
973	6c. "Anteos clorinde clorinde"	25	25
974	8c. "Siderone hemesis"	35	35
975	10c. "Eurema gundlachia" (air)	45	25
976	50c. "Clothilda pantherata pantherata"	2·10	1·00
977	75c. "Papilio androgeus epidaurus"	3·00	1·50

Nos. 975/7 are larger, 35 × 24½ mm.

1966. Hurricane Inez Relief. Nos. 970/77 surch **PRO DAMNIFICADOS CICLON INES** and value.

978	**225**	1c.+2c. mult (postage)	15	10
979	–	2c.+2c. multicoloured	15	10
980	–	3c.+2c. multicoloured	15	10
981	–	6c.+4c. multicoloured	30	25
982	–	8c.+4c. multicoloured	40	30
983	–	10c.+5c. mult (air)	40	35
984	–	50c.+10c. mult	1·40	1·40
985	–	75c.+10c. mult	1·75	1·75

227 National Shrine **228** Emblem and Map

1967. (a) Postage.

986	**227**	1c. blue	10	10
987		2c. red	10	10
988		3c. green	10	10
989		4c. grey	10	10
990		5c. yellow	10	10
991		6c. orange	10	10

(b) Air. Size 20½ × 25 mm.

992	**227**	7c. olive	15	10
993		10c. lilac	15	15
994		20c. brown	30	25

1967. Development Year. Emblem and map in black and blue.

996	**228**	2c. orange and yellow	10	10
997		6c. orange	15	10
998		10c. green	25	15

229 Rook and Knight **230** Civil Defence Emblem

1967. 5th Central American Chess Championship, Santo Domingo.

1000	**229**	25c. mult (postage)	55	40
1001	–	10c. black & grn (air)	35	25

DESIGN: 10c. Bishop and pawn.

1967. Obligatory Tax. Civil Defence Fund.

1003	**230**	1c. multicoloured	15	15

231 Alliance Emblem **232** Institute Emblem

1967. 6th Anniv of "Alliance for Progress".

1004	**231**	1c. green (postage)	10	10
1005		8c. grey (air)	15	10
1006		10c. blue	20	15

1967. 25th Anniv of Inter-American Agricultural Institute.

1007	**232**	3c. green (postage)	10	10
1008		6c. pink	15	10
1009	–	12c. mult (air)	20	15

DESIGN: 12c. Emblem and cornucopia.

233 Child and Children's Home **234** Hand Holding Invalid

1967. Obligatory Tax. Child Welfare.

1010	**233**	1c. red	25	10
1010a		1c. orange	15	10
1011		1c. violet	10	10
1011a		1c. brown	15	10
1037		1c. green	10	10

See also No. 1278a.

1968. Obligatory Tax. Rehabilitation of the Handicapped.

1012	**234**	1c. yellow and green	10	10
1013		1c. blue	10	10
1014		1c. bright purple	10	10
1015		1c. brown	10	10

236 W.M.O. Emblem

1968. World Meteorological Day.

1019	**236**	6c. mult (postage)	20	15
1020		10c. multicoloured (air)	25	20
1021		15c. multicoloured	35	25

237 Ortiz v. Cruz **238** "Lions" Emblem

1968. World Lightweight Boxing Championship. Designs showing similar scenes of the contest.

1024	**237**	6c. pur & red (postage)	15	15
1025	–	7c. green & yellow (air)	15	10
1026	–	10c. blue and brown	25	15

1968. Lions International.

1027	**238**	6c. mult (postage)	15	10
1028		10c. multicoloured (air)	25	15

1968. Obligatory Tax. Anti-cancer Fund.

1029	**144**	1c. green	10	10
1030		1c. orange	10	10

239 Wrestling

1968. Olympic Games, Mexico. Multicoloured.

1031	1c. Type **239** (postage)	10	10
1032	6c. Running	15	10
1033	25c. Boxing	70	35
1034	10c. Weightlifting (air)	25	25
1035	33c. Pistol-shooting	80	70

240 Map of Americas and House **241** Carved Stool

1969. 7th Inter-American Savings and Loans Congress, Santo Domingo. Multicoloured.

1038	6c. Type **240** (postage)	15	10
1039	10c. Latin-American flags (air)	25	15

1969. Taino Art. Multicoloured.

1040	1c. Type **241** (postage)	10	10
1041	2c. Female idol (vert)	10	10
1042	3c. Three-cornered footstone	10	10
1043	4c. Stone axe (vert)	15	10
1044	5c. Clay pot	15	15
1045	7c. Spatula and carved handles (vert) (air)	25	10
1046	10c. Breast-shaped vessel	35	25
1047	20c. Figured vase (vert)	35	75

242 School Playground and Torch **243** Community Emblem

1969. Obligatory Tax. Education Year.

1048	**242**	1c. blue	10	10

1969. Community Development Day.

1049	**243**	6c. gold and green	15	10

244 C.O.T.A.L. Emblem
245 I.L.O. Emblem

1969. 12th C.O.T.A.L. (Confederation of Latin American Tourist Organizations) Congress, Santo Domingo.
1050 **244** 1c. blue, red and light blue (postage) 10 10
1051 – 2c. lt green & green 10 10
1052 – 6c. red 15 10
1053 – 10c. brown (air) 30 10
DESIGNS—VERT: 2c. Boy with flags. HORIZ: (39 × 31 mm): 6c. C.O.T.A.L. Building and emblem; 10c. "Airport of the Americas", Santo Domingo.

1969. 50th Anniv of I.L.O.
1054 **245** 6c. blk & turq (postage) 25 10
1055 10c. black and red (air) 15 15

246 Taking a Catch
247 Las Damas Hydro-electric Scheme

1969. World Baseball Championships, Santo Domingo.
1056 **246** 1c. grey and green (postage) 10 10
1057 – 2c. green 10 10
1058 – 3c. brown and violet 10 10
1059 – 7c. orange and purple (air) 20 15
1060 – 10c. red 25 15
1061 – 1p. brown and blue 2·00 1·40
DESIGNS—VERT: 3c. Making for base; 10c. Player making strike. HORIZ: (43 × 30½ mm): 2c. Cibao Stadium; 7c. Tetelo Vargas Stadium; 1p. Quisqueya Stadium.

1969. National Electrification Plan.
1062 **247** 2c. mult (postage) 10 10
1063 – 3c. multicoloured 10 10
1064 – 6c. purple 15 10
1065 – 10c. red (air) 20 10
DESIGNS—HORIZ: 3c. Las Damas Dam; 6c. Arroyo Hondo substation; 10c. Haina River power station.

1969. Obligatory Tax. Anti-cancer Fund. T **144** redrawn in larger format and inscriptions.
1066 **144** 1c. purple 10 10
1067 1c. green 15 10

248 Tavera Dam

1969. Completion of Dam Projects. Mult.
1068 6c. Type **248** (postage) 15 10
1069 10c. Valdesia Dam (air) 20 10

249 Juan Pablo Duarte
250 Outline Map, Arms of Census Office and Family

1970. Juan Pablo Duarte (patriot) Commem.
1070 **249** 1c. green (postage) 10 10
1071 2c. red 10 10
1072 3c. purple 10 10
1073 6c. blue 15 10
1074 10c. brown (air) 20 15

1970. National Census.
1075 **250** 5c. blk & grn (postage) 10 10
1076 – 6c. ultram and blue 15 10
1077 – 10c. multicoloured (air) 25 15
DESIGNS: 6c. Arms and quotation; 10c. Arms and buildings.

251 Open Book and Emblem
252 Abelardo Urdaneta

1970. Obligatory Tax. Int Education Year.
1078 **251** 1c. purple 10 10

1970. Birth Cent of A. R. Urdaneta (sculptor).
1079 **252** 3c. blue (postage) 10 10
1080 – 6c. green 15 10
1081 – 10c. blue (air) 20 15
DESIGNS—HORIZ: (39½ × 27 mm): 6c. "One of Many" (sculpture). VERT: (25 × 39 mm): 10c. Prisoner (statue).

253 Masonic Symbols
255 New U.P.U. Building

254 Telecommunications Satellite

1970. 8th Inter-American Masonic Conference, Santo Domingo.
1082 **253** 6c. green (postage) 15 10
1083 10c. brown (air) 20 10

1970. World Telecommunications Day.
1084 **254** 20c. grey & grn (postage) 50 30
1085 7c. grey and blue (air) 15 10

1970. New U.P.U. Headquarters Building, Berne.
1086 **255** 6c. brn & grey (postage) 15 10
1087 10c. brown & yell (air) 15 10

256 I.E.Y. Emblem
257 Pedro Alejandrino Pina

1970. International Education Year.
1088 **256** 4c. purple (postage) 10 10
1089 15c. mauve (air) 20 15

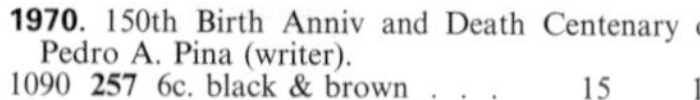

1970. 150th Birth Anniv and Death Centenary of Pedro A. Pina (writer).
1090 **257** 6c. black & brown 15 10

258 Children with Book
259 Emblem and Stamp Album

1970. 1st World Book Exhibition, and Cultural Festival, Santo Domingo.
1091 **258** 5c. green (postage) 10 10
1092 – 7c. multicoloured (air) 15 10
1093 – 10c. multicoloured 20 15
DESIGNS: 7c. Dancers; 10c. U.N. emblem within "wheel".

1970. Air. "EXFILICA 70" Inter-American Philatelic Exhibition, Caracas, Venezuela.
1094 **259** 10c. multicoloured 20 15

260 Communications Emblems
261 Virgin of Altagracia

1971. Obligatory Tax. Postal and Telecommunications School. (a) Size 18 × 20½ mm.
1095 **260** 1c. blue and red (white background) 15 10

(b) Size 19 × 22 mm.
1095a **260** 1c. blue and red (red background) 15 10
1095b 1c. blue, red and green 15 10
1095c 1c. blue, red and yellow 15 10
1095d 1c. blue, red and mauve 15 10
1095e 1c. blue, red and light blue 10 10
1096 1c. blue and red (blue background) 10 10

1971. Inauguration of Our Lady of Altagracia Basilica. Multicoloured.
1097 3c. Type **261** (postage) 10 10
1098 17c. Basilica (22½ × 36 mm) (air) 35 25

262 Parcel, Emblem and Map
263 Manuel Objio

1971. Air. 25th Anniv of C.A.R.E. (Cooperative for American Relief Everywhere).
1099 **262** 10c. green and blue 15 15

1971. Death Cent of Manuel Rodriguez Objio (poet).
1100 **263** 6c. blue 15 10

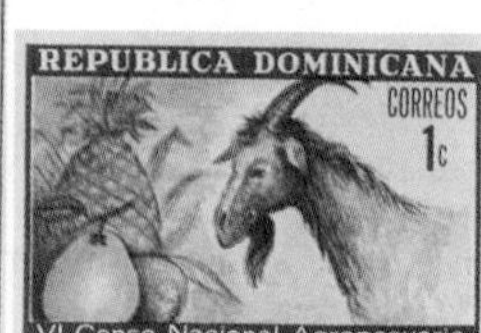

264 Boxing and Canoeing
265 Goat and Fruit

1971. 2nd National Games.
1101 **264** 2c. brown and orange (postage) 10 10
1102 – 5c. brown and green 15 10
1103 – 7c. purple & grey (air) 15 10
DESIGNS: 5c. Basketball; 7c. Volleyball.

1971. 6th National Agricultural Census. Mult.
1104 1c. Type **265** (postage) 10 10
1105 2c. Cow and goose 10 10
1106 3c. Cocoa pods and horse 10 10
1107 6c. Bananas, coffee beans and pig 15 10
1108 25c. Cockerel and grain (air) 40 30

266 Jose Nunez de Caceres
267 Shepherds and Star

1971. 150th Anniv of 1st Declaration of Independence.
1109 **266** 6c. blue, violet and light blue (postage) 15 10
1110 – 10c. bl, red & yell (air) 25 20
DESIGN: 10c. Flag of the Santo Domingo–Colombia Union.

1971. Christmas.
1111 **267** 6c. brn, yell & bl (post) 15 10
1112 – 10c. red, blk & yell (air) 15 15
DESIGN: 10c. Spanish bell of 1493.

268 Child on Beach
269 Book Year Emblem

1971. 25th Anniv of U.N.I.C.E.F.
1113 **268** 6c. mult (postage) 15 10
1114 15c. multicoloured (air) 25 20

1971. International Book Year.
1115 **269** 1c. green, red and blue (postage) 10 10
1116 2c. brown, red and blue 10 10
1117 12c. purple, red and blue (air) 20 15

270 Magnifier on Map
271 Orchid

1972. Air. "Exfilima 71" Inter American Philatelic Exhibition, Lima, Peru.
1118 **270** 10c. multicoloured 25 15

1972. Obligatory Tax. Tuberculosis Relief Fund.
1119 **271** 1c. multicoloured 10 10

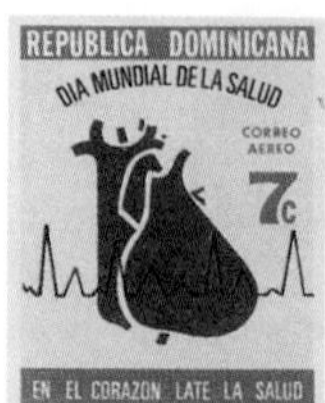

272 Heart Emblem
273 Mask

1972. Air. World Health Day.
1120 **272** 7c. multicoloured 15 10

1972. Taino Arts and Crafts. Multicoloured.
1121 2c. Type **273** (postage) 10 10
1122 4c. Spoon and amulet 10 10
1123 6c. Nasal aspirator (horiz) 10 10
1124 8c. Ritual vase (horiz) (air) 15 10
1125 10c. Atlantic trumpet triton (horiz) 30 10
1126 25c. Ritual spatulas 45 25

274 Globe

1972. World Telecommunications Day.
1127 **274** 6c. mult (postage) 15 10
1128 21c. multicoloured (air) 35 20

275 Map and "Stamps"

1972. 1st National Stamp Exn, Santo Domingo.
1129 **275** 2c. mult (postage) 10 10
1130 33c. mult (air) 60 35

276 Basketball

1972. Olympic Games, Munich. Mult.
1131 2c. Type **276** (postage) . . . 10 10
1132 33c. Running (air) 70 40

277 Club Badge

1972. 50th Anniv of Int Activo 20–30 Club.
1133 **277** 1c. mult (postage) . . . 10 10
1134 20c. mult (air) 35 20

278 Emilio Morel and Quotation

1972. Morel (poet and journalist). Commem.
1135 **278** 6c. mult (postage) . . . 15 10
1136 10c. mult (air) 15 10

279 Bank Building

1972. 25th Anniv of Central Bank. Mult.
1137 1c. Type **279** 10 10
1138 5c. One-peso banknote . . . 10 10
1139 25c. 1947 50c. coin and mint 40 25

280 Nativity Scene 281 Student and Letter-box

1972. Christmas. Multicoloured.
1140 2c. Type **280** (postage) . . . 10 10
1141 6c. Poinsettia (horiz) 15 10
1142 10c. "La Navidad" Fort, 1492 (horiz) (air) 15 10

1972. Publicity for Correspondence Schools.
1143 **281** 2c. red and pink 10 10
1144 6c. blue and light blue 15 10
1145 10c. green and yellow . . 20 10

282 View of Dam 283 Invalid in Wheel-chair

1973. Inauguration of Tavera Dam.
1146 **282** 10c. multicoloured . . . 20 10

1973. Obligatory Tax. Rehabilitation of the Handicapped.
1147 **283** 1c. green 10 10

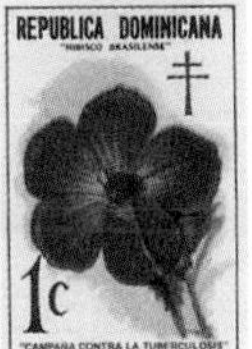
284 Long-jumping, Diving, Running, Cycling and Weightlifting 285 Hibiscus

1973. 12th Central American and Caribbean Games, Santo Domingo. Multicoloured.
1148 2c. Type **284** (postage) . . . 10 10
1149 2c. Boxing, football, wrestling and shooting . . 10 10
1150 2c. Fencing, tennis, high-jumping and sprinting . . 10 10
1151 2c. Putting the shot, throwing the javelin and show-jumping 10 10
1152 25c. Type **284** 55 25
1153 25c. As No. 1149 . . . . . 55 25
1154 25c. As No. 1150 . . . . . 55 25
1155 25c. As No. 1151 . . . . . 55 25
1156 8c. Type **284** (air) 15 10
1157 8c. As No. 1149 . . . . . 15 10
1158 8c. As No. 1150 . . . . . 15 10
1159 8c. As No. 1151 . . . . . 15 10
1160 10c. Type **284** 25 15
1161 10c. As No. 1149 . . . . . 25 15
1162 10c. As No. 1150 . . . . . 25 15
1163 10c. As No. 1151 . . . . . 25 15

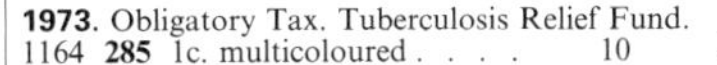

1973. Obligatory Tax. Tuberculosis Relief Fund.
1164 **285** 1c. multicoloured 10 10

286 Christ carrying the Cross 287 Global Emblem

1973. Easter. Multicoloured.
1165 2c. Type **286** (postage) . . . 10 10
1166 6c. Belfry, Church of Our Lady of Carmen (vert) . . 15 10
1167 10c. Belfry, Chapel of Our Lady of Succour (vert) (air) 20 10

1973. Air. 70th Anniv of Pan-American Health Organization.
1168 **287** 7c. multicoloured 15 10

288 Weather Zones

1973. Cent of World Meteorological Organization.
1169 **288** 6c. mult (postage) . . . 15 10
1170 7c. multicoloured (air) 15 10

289 Forensic Scientist

1973. Air. 50th Anniv of International Criminal Police Organization (Interpol).
1171 **289** 10c. blue, green and light blue 20 15

1973. Obligatory Tax. Anti-cancer Fund. As T **144** but dated "1973".
1171a **144** 1c. olive 15 10
See also Nos. 1270a and 1338a.

290 Maguey Drum

1973. Opening of Museum of Dominican Man, Santo Domingo. Multicoloured.
1172 1c. Type **290** (postage) . . . 10 10
1173 2c. Amber carvings 10 10
1174 4c. Cibao mask (vert) . . . 10 10
1175 6c. Pottery (vert) 15 10
1176 7c. Model ship in mosaic (vert) (air) 15 10
1177 10c. Maracas rattles 20 15

291 Nativity Scene

1973. Christmas. Multicoloured.
1178 2c. Type **291** (postage) . . . 10 10
1179 6c. "Prayer" (stained-glass window) (vert) 15 10
1180 10c. Angels beside crib (air) 20 15

292 Scout Badge

1973. 50th Anniv of Dominican Boy Scouts. Multicoloured.
1181 1c. Type **292** (postage) . . . 10 10
1182 5c. Scouts and flag 10 10
1183 21c. Scouts cooking, and Lord Baden Powell (air) 40 30
No. 1182 is smaller, size 26 × 36 mm.

293 Stadium and Basketball Players 294 Belfry, Santo Domingo Cathedral

1974. 12th Central American and Caribbean Games, Santo Domingo. Multicoloured.
1184 2c. Type **293** (postage) . . . 10 10
1185 6c. Arena and cyclist . . . 15 10
1186 10c. Swimming pool and diver (air) 20 15
1187 25c. Stadium, soccer players and discus-thrower . . . 50 35

1974. Obligatory Tax. Rehabilitation of the Handicapped. As T **283** but larger, 22 × 27 mm.
1187a **283** 1c. blue 15 15

1974. Holy Week.
1188 **294** 2c. mult (postage) . . . 10 10
1189 – 6c. purple, green & ol . . 15 10
1190 – 10c. multicoloured (air) 20 15
DESIGN—VERT: 6c. "Sorrowful Mother" (D. Bouts). HORIZ: 10c. "The Last Supper" (R. M. Budi).

295 Francisco del Rosario Sanchez Bridge

1974. Dominican Bridges. Multicoloured.
1191 6c. Type **295** (postage) . . . 15 10
1192 10c. Higuamo Bridge (air) 20 15

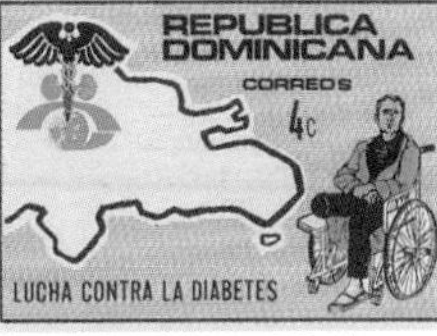
296 Emblem and Patient

1974. Anti-diabetes Campaign. Mult.
1193 4c. Type **296** (postage) . . . 10 10
1194 5c. Emblem and pancreas 10 10
1195 7c. Emblem and Kidney (air) 15 10
1196 33c. Emblem, eye and heart 70 45

1974. Obligatory Tax. Anti-cancer Fund. As T **144** but dated "1974".
1196a **144** 1c. orange 15 10

297 Steam Train

1974. Centenary of Universal Postal Union. Mult.
1197 2c. Type **297** (postage) . . . 45 55
1198 6c. Stage-coach 15 10
1199 7c. "Eider" mail steamer (air) 60 15
1200 33c. Boeing 727-200 of Dominicana Airways . . 95 30

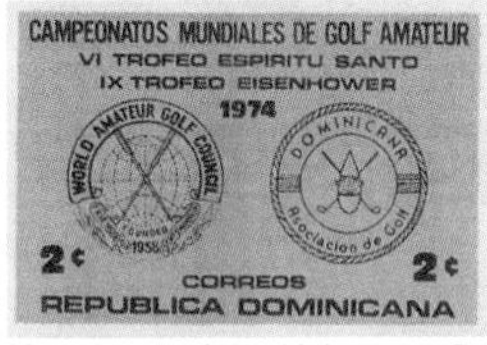
298 Emblems of World Amateur Golf Council and of Dominican Golf Association

1974. World Amateur Golf Championships.
1202 **298** 2c. black and yellow (postage) 10 10
1203 – 6c. multicoloured 10 10
1204 – 10c. multicoloured (air) 25 15
1205 – 20c. multicoloured . . . 45 30
DESIGNS—VERT: 6c. Golfers teeing-off. HORIZ: 10c. Council emblem and golfers; 20c. Dominican Golf Association emblem, golfer and hand with ball and tee.

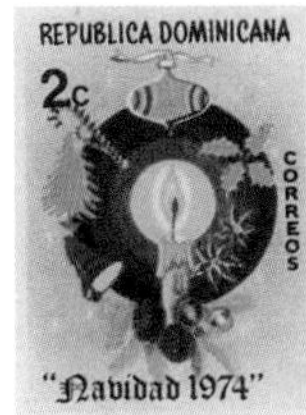

299 Christmas Decorations 301 Dr. Defillo

300 Tomatoes

1974. Christmas. Multicoloured.
1206 2c. Type **299** (postage) . . . 10 10
1207 6c. Virgin and Child 15 10
1208 10c. Hand holding dove (horiz) (air) 20 15

1974. 10th Anniv of World Food Programme. Multicoloured.
1209 2c. Type **300** (postage) . . . 10 10
1210 3c. Avocado pears 10 10
1211 5c. Coconuts 10 10
1212 10c. Bee, hive and cask of honey (air) 20 15

1975. Birth Centenary of Dr. Fernando Defillo (medical scientist).
1213 **301** 1c. brown 10 10
1214 6c. green 15 10

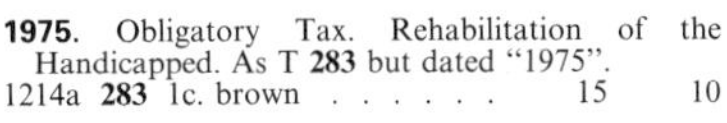

1975. Obligatory Tax. Rehabilitation of the Handicapped. As T **283** but dated "1975".
1214a **283** 1c. brown 15 10

302 "I am the Resurrection and the Life" 303 Spanish 6c. Stamp of 1850

1975. Holy Week. Multicoloured.
1215 2c. Type **302** (postage) . . . 10 10
1216 6c. Bell tower, Nuestra Senora del Rosario convent 15 10
1217 10c. Catholic emblems (air) 20 15

1975. Obligatory Tax. Tuberculosis Relief Fund. As T **221** but dated "1975".
1217a **221** 1c. multicoloured . . . 15 10
DESIGN: 1c. "Catteeyopsis rosea".

1975. Air. "Espana 75" International Stamp Exhibition, Madrid.
1218 **303** 12c. black, red & yell . . 25 15

304 Hands supporting "Agriculture" and Industry

305 Earth Station

1975. 16th Meeting of Industrial Development Bank Governors, Santo Domingo.
1219 **304** 6c. mult (postage) . . . 15 10
1220 10c. mult (air) 20 15

1975. Opening of Satellite Earth Station. Multicoloured.
1221 5c. Type **305** (postage) . . . 10 10
1222 15c. Hemispheres and satellites (horiz) (air) . . . 30 20

306 "Apollo" Spacecraft with Docking Tunnel

307 Father Castellanos

1975. "Apollo–Soyuz" Space Link. Mult.
1223 1c. Type **306** (postage) . . . 10 10
1224 4c. "Soyuz" spacecraft . . . 10 10
1225 2p. Docking manoeuvre (air) 3·25 2·00
The 2p. is larger, 42 × 28 mm.

1975. Birth Cent of Father Rafael C. Castellanos.
1226 **307** 6c. brown and buff . . . 15 10

308 Women encircling I.W.Y. Emblem

1975. International Women's Year.
1227 **308** 3c. multicoloured 10 10

309 Guacanagarix

310 Basketball

1975. Indian Chiefs. Multicoloured.
1228 1c. Type **309** (postage) . . . 10 10
1229 2c. Guarionex 10 10
1230 3c. Caonabo 10 10
1231 4c. Bohechio 10 10
1232 5c. Cayacoa 10 10
1233 6c. Anacaona 15 10
1234 9c. Hatuey 20 15
1235 7c. Mayobanex (air) 15 10
1236 8c. Cotubanama with Juan de Esquivel 15 10
1237 10c. Enriquillo and wife, Mencia 20 15

1975. Obligatory Tax. Anti-cancer Fund. As T **144** but dated "1975".
1237a **144** 1c. violet 15 10

1975. 7th Pan-American Games, Mexico City. Multicoloured.
1238 2c. Type **310** (postage) . . . 10 10
1239 6c. Baseball 15 10
1240 7c. Volleyball (horiz) (air) 15 15
1241 10c. Weightlifting (horiz) . . 25 15

311 Carol-singers

1975. Christmas. Multicoloured.
1242 2c. Type **311** (postage) . . . 10 10
1243 6c. "Dominican" Nativity 15 10
1244 10c. Dove and Peace message (air) 20 15

312 Pearl Sergeant Major ("Abudefdul marginatus")

1976. Fishes. Multicoloured.
1245 10c. Type **312** 35 25
1246 10c. Puddingwife ("Halichoeres radiata") 35 25
1247 10c. Squirrelfish ("Holocentrus ascensionis") 35 25
1248 10c. Queen angelfish ("Angelochthys ciliaris") 35 25
1249 10c. Aya snapper ("Lutianus aya") 35 25

313 Valdesia Dam

1976. Air. Inauguration of Valdesia Dam.
1250 **313** 10c. multicoloured . . . 15 15

1976. Obligatory Tax. Rehabilitation of the Disabled. As T **283** but dated "1976".
1250a **283** 1c. blue 15 10

314 Orchid

1976. Obligatory Tax. Tuberculosis Relief Fund.
1251 **314** 1c. multicoloured 10 10

315 "Magdalene" (E. Godoy)

316 Schooner "Separacion Dominicana"

1976. Holy Week. Multicoloured.
1252 2c. Type **315** (postage) . . . 10 10
1253 6c. "The Ascension" (V. Priego) 10 10
1254 10c. "Mount Calvary" (E. Castillo) (air) 20 15

1976. Navy Day.
1255 **316** 20c. multicoloured . . . 1·75 40

317 National Flower and Maps

1976. Bicentenary of American Revolution, and "Interphil '76" Int Stamp Exn, Philadelphia.
1256 **317** 6c. mult (postage) . . . 15 10
1257 – 9c. multicoloured 20 10
1258 – 10c. multicoloured (air) 50 15
1259 – 75c. black and orange 1·50 1·00
DESIGNS—HORIZ: 9c. Maps within cogwheels; 10c. Maps within hands. VERT: 75c. George Washington and Philadelphia buildings.

318 Flags of Spain and Dominican Republic

1976. Visit of King and Queen of Spain. Multicoloured.
1260 6c. Type **318** (postage) . . . 35 10
1261 21c. King Juan Carlos I and Queen Sophia (air) . . . 1·00 35

319 Various Telephones

1976. Telephone Centenary. Multicoloured.
1262 6c. Type **319** (postage) . . . 15 10
1263 10c. A. Graham Bell (horiz) (air) 20 15

320 "Duarte's Vision" (L. Desangles)

1976. Death Centenary of Juan Duarte (patriot). Multicoloured.
1264 2c. Type **320** (postage) . . . 10 10
1265 6c. "Juan Duarte" (R. Mejia) (vert) 15 10
1266 10c. Text of Duarte's Declaration (vert) (air) . . 20 15
1267 33c. "Duarte Sailing to Exile" (E. Godoy) 70 45

321 Fire Hydrant

322 Commemorative Text and Emblem

1976. Dominican Fire Service. Multicoloured.
1268 4c. Type **321** (postage) . . . 10 10
1269 6c. Fire Service emblem . . 15 10
1270 10c. Fire engine (horiz) (air) 20 15

1976. Obligatory Tax. Anti-cancer Fund. As T **144** but dated "1976".
1270a **144** 1c. green 15 10

1976. 50th Anniv of Dominican Radio Club.
1271 **322** 6c. black & red (postage) 15 10
1272 10c. black & blue (air) 20 15

323 Map and Caravel

325 Virgin and Child

324 Boxing

1976. "Hispanidad 1976". Multicoloured.
1273 6c. Type **323** (postage) . . . 60 15
1274 21c. Heads of Spaniard and Dominicans (air) 45 30

1976. Olympic Games, Montreal. Mult.
1275 2c. Type **324** (postage) . . . 10 10
1276 3c. Weightlifting 10 10
1277 10c. Running (air) 20 15
1278 25c. Basketball 50 35

1976. Obligatory Tax. Child Welfare. As T **233** but dated "1976".
1278a **233** 1c. mauve 15 10

1976. Christmas. Multicoloured.
1279 2c. Type **325** (postage) . . . 10 10
1280 6c. The Three Kings (22 × 32 mm) 15 10
1281 10c. Angel with bells (22 × 32 mm) (air) 20 15

326 Cable-car and Beach Scenes

1977. Tourism. Multicoloured.
1282 6c. Type **326** (postage) . . . 15 10
1283 10c. Tourist activities (air) 20 15
1284 12c. Fishing and hotel . . . 25 15
1285 25c. Horse-riding and waterfall 50 35
No. 1283 measures 36 × 36 mm, No. 1284 35 × 26 mm and No. 1285 26 × 35 mm.

327 Championships Emblem

1977. 10th Central American and Caribbean Children's Swimming Championships, Santo Domingo.
1286 **327** 3c. mult (postage) . . . 10 10
1287 5c. multicoloured 10 10
1288 10c. multicoloured (air) 20 15
1289 25c. multicoloured . . . 30 35

1977. Obligatory Tax. Rehabilitation of the Disabled. As T **283** but dated "1977".
1289a **283** 1c. blue 15 10

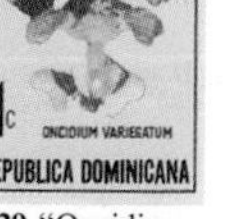

328 Allegory of Holy Week

329 "Oncidium variegatum" (orchid)

1977. Holy Week.
1290 **328** 2c. mult (postage) 10 10
1291 – 6c. black and mauve 10 10
1292 – 10c. blk, red & bl (air) 20 10
DESIGNS: 6c. Christ crowned with thorns; 10c. Church and book.

1977. Obligatory Tax. Tuberculosis Relief Fund.
1293 **329** 1c. multicoloured 10 10

330 Gulls in Flight

1977. 12th Annual Lions Clubs Convention, Santo Domingo.
1294 **330** 2c. mult (postage) 10 10
1295 6c. multicoloured 15 10
1296 7c. multicoloured (air) 15 10

331 "Battle of Tortuguero" (G. Fernandez)

1977. Navy Day.
1297 **331** 20c. multicoloured 90 30

332 "Miss Universe" Emblem

333 "Nymphaea ampla" ("Nymphea" on stamp)

1977. Air. "Miss Universe" Competition.
1298 **332** 10c. multicoloured 20 15

1977. Dominican Flora. Plants in the Dr. Rafael M. Moscoso National Botanical Gardens. Mult.
1299 2c. Type **333** (postage) 10 10
1300 4c. "Broughtonia domingensis" 10 10
1301 6c. "Cordia sebestena" 15 10
1302 7c. "Melocatus lemairei" (cactus) (air) 15 10
1303 33c. "Coccothrinax argentea" (tree) 70 45

334 Computers and Graph

1977. Seventh Inter-American Statistic Conference. Multicoloured.
1304 6c. Type **334** (postage) 15 10
1305 28c. Factories and graph (27 × 37 mm) (air) 55 35

335 Haitian Solenodon

1977. 8th Inter-American Veterinary Congress. Multicoloured.
1306 6c. Type **335** (postage) 15 10
1307 20c. Iguana 40 25
1308 10c. "Red Roman" stud bull (air) 20 15
1309 25c. Greater Flamingo (vert) 3·00 45

336 Main Gateway of Casa del Cordon

337 Tools and Crown of Thorns at Foot of Cross

1978. "Hispanidad 1977". Multicoloured.
1310 6c. Type **336** (postage) 15 10
1311 21c. Gothic-style window, Casa del Tostado (28 × 41 mm) (air) 45 30

1978. Holy Week.
1312 **337** 2c. mult (postage) 10 10
1313 – 6c. green 15 10
1314 – 7c. multicoloured (air) 15 10
1315 – 10c. multicoloured 20 15
DESIGNS—(22 × 33 mm): 6c. Christ wearing Crown of Thorns. (27 × 37 mm): 7c. Facade of Santo Domingo Cathedral; 10c. Facade of Dominican Convent.

338 Schooner "Duarte"

339 Cardinal Octavio A. Beras Rojas

1978. Air. Navy Day.
1316 **338** 7c. multicoloured 75 15

1978. Consecration of First Cardinal from Dominican Republic.
1317 **339** 6c. mult (postage) 15 10
1318 10c. multicoloured (air) 20 15

340 Microwave Antenna

1978. Air. 10th World Telecommunications Day.
1319 **340** 25c. multicoloured 50 35

341 First Dominican Airmail Stamp and Map of First Airmail Service

342 Pres. Manuel de Troncoso

1978. Air. 50th Anniv of First Dominican Airmail Stamp.
1320 **341** 10c. multicoloured 20 15

1978. Birth Centenary of President Troncoso.
1321 **342** 2c. brown, mauve & blk 10 10
1322 6c. brown, grey & black 15 10

343 Globe, Football and Emblem

344 Father Juan N. Zegri y Moreno (founder)

1978. Air. World Cup Football Championship, Argentina. Multicoloured.
1323 12c. Type **343** 25 15
1324 33c. Emblem and map on football pitch 75 45

1978. Centenary of Merciful Sisters of Charity. Multicoloured.
1325 6c. Type **344** (postage) 15 10
1326 21c. Symbol of the Order (air) 40 30

345 Boxing

1978. 13th Central American and Caribbean Games, Medellin, Colombia. Multicoloured.
1327 2c. Type **345** (postage) 10 10
1328 6c. Weightlifting 15 10
1329 7c. Baseball (vert) (air) 15 10
1330 10c. Football (vert) 20 15

346 Douglas DC-6, Boeing 707 and Wright Flyer I

347 Sun over Landscape

1978. Air. 75th Anniv of First Powered Flight.
1331 **346** 7c. multicoloured 15 15
1332 – 10c. brown, yellow & red 35 15
1333 – 13c. blue & dp blue 45 20
1334 – 45c. multicoloured 1·25 75
DESIGNS: 10c. Wright brothers and Wright Glider No. I; 13c. Diagram of airflow over wing; 45c. Wright Flyer I and world map.

1978. Tourism. Multicoloured.
1335 2c. Type **347** (postage) 10 10
1336 6c. Sun over beach 15 10
1337 7c. Sun and musical instruments (air) 15 10
1338 10c. Sun over Santo Domingo 20 15

1978. Obligatory Tax. Anti-cancer Fund. As T **144** but dated "1977".
1338a **144** 1c. purple 15 10

348 Galleons

349 Flags of Dominican Republic and United Nations

1978. "Hispanidad 1978". Multicoloured.
1339 2c. Type **348** (postage) 10 10
1340 21c. Figures holding hands in front of globe (air) 45 25

1978. Air. 33rd Anniv of United Nations.
1341 **349** 33c. multicoloured 70 25

350 Mother and Child

351 Dove, Lamp and Poinsettia

1978. Obligatory Tax. Child Welfare.
1342 **350** 1c. green 10 10

1978. Christmas. Multicoloured.
1343 2c. Type **351** (postage) 10 10
1344 6c. Dominican family and star 15 10
1345 10c. Statue of the Virgin (vert) (22 × 33 mm) (air) 20 15

352 Pope John Paul II

353 Map of Island, Iguana and Radio Transmitter

1979. Air. Visit of Pope John Paul II.
1346 **352** 10c. multicoloured 70 20

1979. Air. 1st Expedition of Radio Amateurs to Beata Island.
1347 **353** 10c. multicoloured 20 15

354 University Seal

355 Starving Child

1979. Obligatory Tax. 440th Anniv of Santo Domingo University.
1348 **354** 2c. blue 10 10

1979. International Year of the Child.
1349 **355** 2c. orge & blk (postage) 10 10
1350 – 7c. multicoloured (air) 15 10
1351 – 10c. multicoloured 20 15
1352 – 33c. multicoloured 70 45
DESIGNS: 7c. Children reading book; 10c. Head and protective hands; 33c. Hands and vases.

1979. Obligatory Tax. Rehabilitation of the Disabled. As T **283** but dated "1979".
1353 **283** 1c. green 15 10

356 Crucifixion

357 "Turnera ulmifolia"

1979. Holy Week. Multicoloured.
1354 2c. Type **356** (postage) 10 10
1355 3c. Christ carrying cross (horiz) 10 10
1356 10c. Pope John Paul II with Crucifix (air) 20 15

1978. Obligatory Tax. Tuberculosis Relief Fund. Dated "1978".
1357 **357** 1c. multicoloured 10 10

358 Admiral J. Cambiaso

359 Map, Stamp Album and Philatelic Equipment

1979. Air. 135th Anniv of Battle of Tortuguero.
1358 **358** 10c. multicoloured 20 15

1979. Air. "Exfilna" Third National Stamp Exhibition.
1359 **359** 33c. blue, green and black 70 45

360 "Stigmaphyllon periplocifolium"

1979. Flowers from National Botanical Gardens.
1360 **360** 50c. grey, yellow and black (postage) 1·00 70
1361 – 7c. multicoloured (air) 15 10

1362 – 10c. multicoloured . . . 20 15
1363 – 13c. blue, mauve & blk 25 15
DESIGNS: 7c. "Passiflora foetida"; 10c. "Isidorea pungens"; 13c. "Calotropis procera".

362 Heart and Section through Artery

1979. Dominican Cardiology Institute.
1364 **362** 3c. mult (postage) 10 10
1365 – 1p. black, red & blue . . 2·00 1·40
1366 – 10c. multicoloured (air) 20 15
DESIGNS: VERT: 10c. Human figure showing blood circulation. HORIZ: 1p. Cardiology Institute and heart.

363 Baseball

1979. 8th Pan-American Games, Puerto Rico. Multicoloured.
1367 2c. Type **363** (postage) . . . 10 10
1368 3c. Cycling (vert) 10 10
1369 7c. Running (vert) (air) . . 15 10

364 Football

365 Sir Rowland Hill and First Dominican Republic Stamp

1979. 3rd National Games. Multicoloured.
1370 2c. Type **364** (postage) . . . 10 10
1371 25c. Swimming (horiz) . . . 55 35
1372 10c. Tennis (air) 20 15

1979. Air. Death Centenary of Sir Rowland Hill.
1373 **365** 2p. multicoloured . . . 4·25 1·10

366 Thomas Edison (inventor)

367 Hand removing Electric Plug

1979. Centenary of Electric Light-bulb. Mult.
1374 25c. Type **366** (postage) . . 55 30
1375 10c. "100" forming lightbulb (horiz) (air) 20 15

1979. "Save Energy". Multicoloured.
1376 2c. Type **367** 10 10
1377 6c. Car being refuelled . . . 15 10

368 Hispaniolan Conure

369 Lions Emblem

1979. Birds. Multicoloured.
1378 2c. Type **368** (postage) . . . 1·00 25
1379 6c. Hispaniolan trogon . . . 1·10 25
1380 7c. Black-crowned palm tanager (air) . . . . . . 1·60 35
1381 10c. Chat-tanager . . . . . . 2·40 35
1382 45c. Black-cowled oriole . . 7·00 1·25

1979. 15th Anniv of Dominican Republic Lions Club. Multicoloured.
1383 20c. Type **369** (postage) . . 45 20
1384 10c. Melvin Jones (founder) (air) 20 10

371 Holy Family

372 Christ carrying Cross

1979. Christmas. Multicoloured.
1386 2c. Type **371** (postage) . . . 10 10
1387 10c. Three Kings (air) . . . 20 15

1980. Holy Week.
1388 **372** 3c. black, red and lilac (postage) 10 10
1389 – 7c. blk, red & yell (air) 15 10
1390 – 10c. black, red & bistre 20 15
DESIGNS: 7c. Crucifixion; 10c. Resurrection.

1980. Obligatory Tax. Rehabilitation of the Disabled. As T **283** but dated "1980".
1391 **283** 1c. olive and green . . . 10 10

374 Navy Crest

376 Cocoa Harvest

375 "Stamp"

1980. Air. Navy Day.
1392 **374** 21c. multicoloured . . . 45 30

1980. Air. 25th Anniv of Dominican Philatelic Society.
1393 **375** 10c. multicoloured . . . 20 15

1980. Agricultural Year. Multicoloured.
1394 1c. Type **376** 10 10
1395 2c. Coffee 10 10
1396 3c. Plantain 10 10
1397 4c. Sugar cane 10 10
1398 5c. Maize 10 10

377 Cotuf Gold Mine, Pueblo Viejob

379 "Tourism"

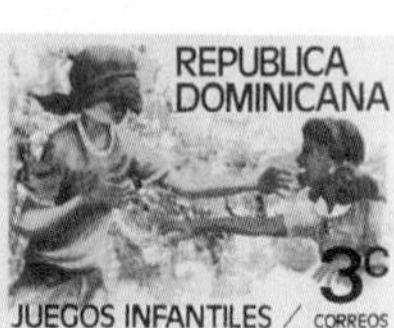

378 Blind Man's Buff

1980. Nationalization of Gold Mines. Mult.
1399 6c. Type **377** (postage) . . . 15 10
1400 10c. Drag line mining (air) 20 15
1401 33c. General view of location of gold mines . . 70 45

1980. Children's Games. Multicoloured.
1402 3c. Type **378** 10 10
1403 4c. Marbles 10 10
1404 5c. Spinning top 10 10
1405 6c. Hopscotch 15 10

1980. Air. World Tourism Conference, Manila, Philippines. Multicoloured.
1406 10c. Type **379** 20 15
1407 33c. Conference emblem . . 70 45

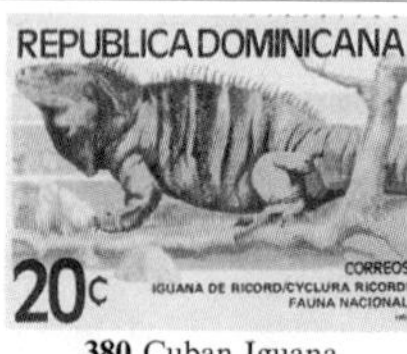

380 Cuban Iguana

1980. Animals. Multicoloured.
1408 20c. Type **380** (postage) . . 45 30
1409 7c. American crocodile (air) 15 10
1410 10c. Hispaniolan hutia . . . 25 15
1411 25c. American manatee . . . 65 35
1412 45c. Hawksbill turtle 95 60

381 "El Merengue" (Jaime Colson)

1980. Paintings. Multicoloured.
1413 3c. Type **381** (postage) . . . 10 10
1414 50c. "The Mirror" (G. H. Ortega) . . . . 1·10 70
1415 10c. "Genesis de un Ganga" (Paul Guidicelli) (air) . . 20 15
1416 17c. "The Countryman" (Yoryi Morel) 35 25

1980. Obligatory Tax. Anti-cancer Fund. As T **144** but dated "1980".
1417 **144** 1c. blue and violet . . . 10 10

383 Map of Catalina Island

384 Rotary Emblem on Globe

1980. Air. Visit of Radio Amateurs to Catalina Island.
1418 **383** 7c. green, blue & black 15 10

1980. Air. 75th Anniv of Rotary International. Multicoloured.
1419 10c. Type **384** 20 15
1420 33c. Rotary emblem in "75" 70 45

385 Carrier Pigeons with Letters

1980. Centenary of U.P.U. Membership. Mult.
1421 33c. Type **385** 70 45
1422 45c. Row of stylized pigeons and letter 95 60
1423 50c. Carrier pigeon with letter and letter . . . . . 1·10 70

1980. Obligatory tax. Child Welfare. As T **350** but dated "1980".
1425 **350** 1c. blue 10 10

386 The Three Kings

387 Arms of Salcedo

1980. Christmas. Multicoloured.
1426 3c. Type **386** (postage) . . . 10 10
1427 6c. Carol singers 15 10
1428 10c. The Holy Family (air) 20 15

1981. Centenary of Salcedo Province. Mult.
1429 6c. Type **387** (postage) . . . 15 10
1430 10c. Arms and map of Salcedo (air) 20 15

388 Juan Pablo Duarte

389 Industrial Symbols

1981. Juan Pablo Duarte (patriot). Commemoration.
1431 **388** 2c. brown and ochre . . 10 10

1981. Air. Chemical Engineering Seminar.
1432 **389** 10c. multicoloured . . . 20 15
1433 – 33c. gold and black . . . 70 45
DESIGN: 33c. Emblem of Dominican College of Engineering and Architecture (CODIA).

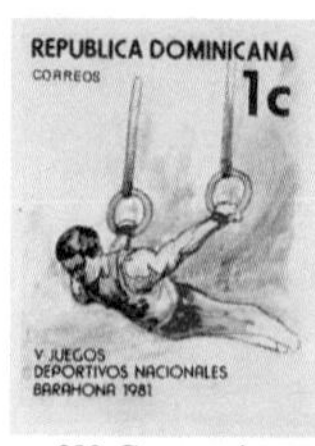

390 Gymnastics

391 Mother Mazzarello

1981. Fifth National Games (1st issue). Mult.
1434 1c. Type **390** (postage) . . . 10 10
1435 2c. Running 10 10
1436 3c. Pole-vaulting 10 10
1437 6c. Boxing 15 10
1438 10c. Baseball (air) 20 15
See also Nos. 1463/4.

1981. Death Centenary of Mother Mazarello (founder of Daughters of Mary).
1439 **391** 6c. brown and black . . 15 10

392 Admiral Juan Alejandro Acosta

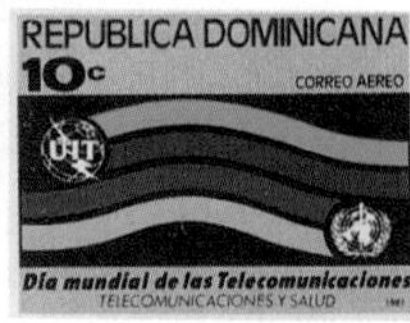

393 Radio Waves

1981. Air. 137th Anniv of Battle of Tortuguero.
1440 **392** 10c. multicoloured . . . 20 15

1981. Obligatory Tax. Tuberculosis Relief Fund. Dated "1981".
1441 **357** 1c. multicoloured 10 10

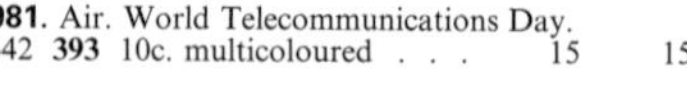

1981. Air. World Telecommunications Day.
1442 **393** 10c. multicoloured . . . 15 15

394 Pedro Henriquez Urena

395 Forest

1981. 35th Death Anniv of Pedro Henriquez Urena.
1443 **394** 6c. pale grey and grey 15 10

1981. Forest Conservation. Multicoloured.
1444 2c. Type **395** 10 10
1445 6c. Forest river 15 10

396 Heinrich von Stephan

397 "Disabled People"

1981. Air. 150th Birth Anniv of Heinrich von Stephan (founder of U.P.U.).
1446 **396** 33c. brown and yellow 70 45

1981. Air. International Year of Disabled Persons. Multicoloured.
1447 7c. Type **397** 15 10
1448 33c. Cobbler in wheelchair 70 45

398 Exhibition Emblem

1981. Air. "Expuridom '81" International Stamp Exhibition, Santo Domingo.
1149 **398** 7c. black, blue and red 15 10

399 Target

1981. Air. 2nd World Air Gun Shooting Championship. Multicoloured.
1450 10c. Type **399** 20 15
1451 15c. Stylized riflemen . . . 30 20
1452 25c. Stylized pistol shooters 55 55

400 Family and House

1981. National Census. Multicoloured.
1453 3c. Type **400** 10 10
1454 6c. Farmer with cow and agricultural produce . . . 15 10

1981. Obligatory Tax. Anti-cancer Fund. As T **144** but dated "1981".
1455 **144** 1c. blue and deep blue 10 10

401 Fruit

1981. Air. World Food Day. Multicoloured.
1456 10c. Type **401** 20 15
1457 50c. Fish, eggs and vegetables . . . . 1·10 70

402 Gem Stones and Jewellery

403 Javelin-throwing

1981. Air. Exports. Multicoloured.
1458 7c. Type **402** 15 10
1459 10c. Handicrafts 20 15
1460 11c. Fruit 25 15
1461 17c. Cocoa, coffee, tobacco and sugar 35 25

1981. Obligatory Tax. Child Welfare. As T **350** but dated "1981".
1462 **350** 1c. green 10 10

1981. Air. 5th National Games, Barahona (2nd issue). Multicoloured.
1463 10c. Type **403** 20 15
1464 50c. Cycling . . . . 1·10 70

404 "Encyclia cochleata"

1981. Air. Orchids. Multicoloured.
1465 7c. Type **404** 10 15
1466 10c. "Broughtonia domingensis" 15 20
1467 25c. "Encyclia truncata" . . 55 35
1468 65c. "Elleanthus capitatus" 1·60 1·10

405 Bells **406** Juan Pablo Duarte

1981. Christmas. Multicoloured.
1469 2c. Type **405** (postage) . . . 10 10
1470 3c. Holly 10 10
1471 10c. Dove and moon (air) 20 15

1982. Juan Pablo Duarte (patriot) Commemoration.
1472 **406** 2c. light blue and blue 10 10

407 Citizens arriving at Polling Station

1982. National Elections. Multicoloured.
1473 2c. Type **407** 10 10
1474 3c. Entering polling booth (vert) 10 10
1475 6c. Casting vote 15 10

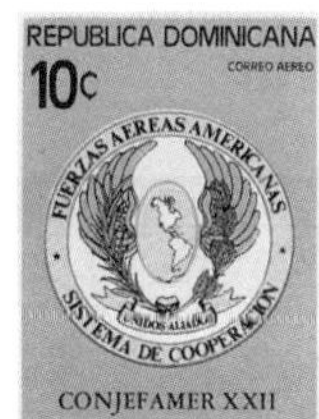

408 American Air Forces Co-operation Emblem

1982. Air. 22nd American Air Force's Commanders Conference, Buenos Aires.
1476 **408** 10c. multicoloured . . . 20 15

409 Naval Cadet Parade

1982. Air. Battle of Tortuguero Commem.
1477 **409** 10c. multicoloured . . . 20 15

410 Tackling **411** Lord Baden-Powell (statue)

1982. Air. World Cup Football Championship, Spain. Multicoloured.
1478 10c. Type **410** 20 15
1479 21c. Dribbling 45 30
1480 33c. Heading ball into goal 70 45

1982. Air. 75th Anniv of Boy Scout Movement. Multicoloured.
1481 10c. Type **411** 20 15
1482 15c. Scouting emblems (horiz) 30 20
1483 25c. Baden-Powell and scout at camp fire 55 35

412 "Study of Daylight" **413** Cathedral and House

1982. Energy Conservation. Multicoloured.
1484 1c. Type **412** 10 10
1485 2c. "Save rural electricity" . 10 10
1486 3c. "Use wind power" . . . 10 10
1487 4c. "Switch off lights" . . . 10 10
1488 5c. "Conserve fuel" 15 10
1489 6c. "Use solar energy" . . . 15 10

1982. Air. 25th Congress of Latin-American Tourist Organizations Confederation, Santo Domingo. Multicoloured.
1490 7c. Congress emblem . . . 15 10
1491 10c. Type **413** 20 15
1492 33c. Dancers and beach scene 70 45

414 Exhibition Emblem

1982. Air. "Espamer '82" Stamp Exhibition, Puerto Rico. Multicoloured.
1493 7c. Stamp bearing map of Puerto Rico (horiz) . . . 15 10
1494 13c. Stylized postage stamps (horiz) 30 20
1495 50c. Type **414** . . . . . . 1·10 70

415 Emilio Prud'Homme and Score of Dominican National Anthem **416** President Guzman

1982. 50th Death Anniv of Emilio Prud'Homme (composer).
1496 **415** 6c. multicoloured 15 10

1982. President Antonio Guzman Commemoration.
1497 **416** 6c. multicoloured 15 10

417 Baseball

1982. Central American and Caribbean Games, Cuba. Multicoloured.
1498 3c. Type **417** (postage) . . . 10 10
1499 10c. Basketball (air) 20 15
1500 13c. Boxing 30 20
1501 25c. Gymnastics 55 30

418 "Harbour" (Alejandro Bonilla)

1982. Air. Paintings. Multicoloured.
1502 7c. Type **418** 15 10
1503 10c. "Portrait of a Woman" (Leopoldo Navarro) . . . 20 15
1504 45c. "Portrait of Amelia Francasci" (Luis Desangles) 95 65
1505 2p. "Portrait" (Abelardo Rodriguez Urdaneta) . . 4·25 2·75

419 Horse-drawn Carriage

1982. Centenary of San Pedro de Macoris Province. Multicoloured.
1506 1c. Type **419** (postage) . . . 10 10
1507 2c. Stained-glass window, San Pedro Apostle Church (25 × 34½ mm) . . 10 10
1508 5c. Centenary emblem . . . 15 10
1509 7c. View of San Pedro de Macoris City (air) 45 20

420 "Santa Maria" and Map of Voyage

1982. Air. 490th Anniv of Discovery of America by Columbus. Multicoloured.
1510 7c. Type **420** . . . . 1·00 30
1511 10c. "Santa Maria" . . . . 1·25 35
1512 21c. Statue of Columbus, Santo Domingo 45 30

421 Central Bank

1982 35th Anniv of Central Bank.
1513 **421** 10c. multicoloured . . . 20 15

422 St. Theresa of Avila **423** Christmas Tree Decorations

1982. 400th Death Anniv of St. Theresa of Avila.
1514 **422** 6c. multicoloured 15 10

1982. Christmas. Multicoloured.
1515 6c. Type **423** (postage) . . . 10 10
1516 10c. Tree decorations (different) (air) 20 15

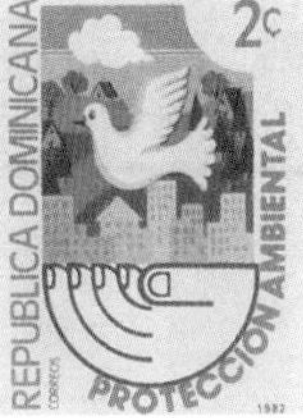

424 Hand holding Rural and Urban Environments

1982. Environmental Protection. Mult.
1517 2c. Type **424** 10 10
1518 3c. Hand holding river in the country 10 10
1519 6c. Hand holding forest . . 10 10
1520 20c. Hand holding swimming fish 35 25

425 Adults writing

1983. National Literacy Campaign. Mult.
1521 2c. Girl and boy writing on blackboard 10 10
1522 3c. Type **425** 10 10
1523 6c. Children, rainbow and pencil 10 10

426 Clasped Hands and Eiffel Tower

1983. Air. Centenary of French Alliance (French language-teaching association).
1524 **426** 33c. multicoloured . . . 50 30

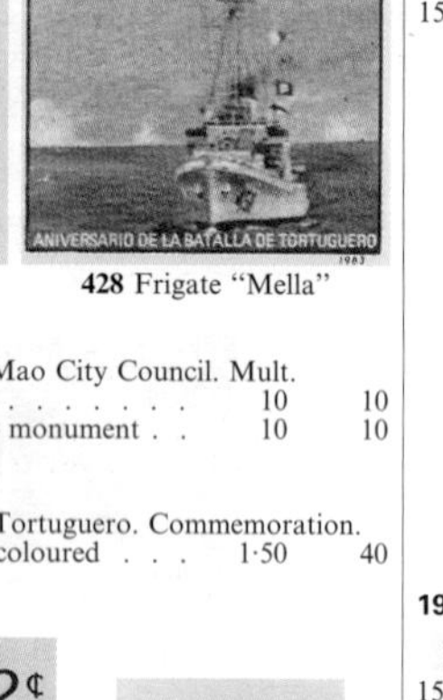

427 Arms of Mao City Council **428** Frigate "Mella"

1983. Centenary of Mao City Council. Mult.
1525 1c. Type **427** 10 10
1526 5c. Centenary monument . . 10 10

1983. Air. Battle of Tortuguero. Commemoration.
1527 **428** 15c. multicoloured . . . 1·50 40

429 Antonio del Monte y Tejada **430** Red Cross

1983. Dominican Historians.
1528 **429** 2c. red & brn (postage) 10 10
1529 – 3c. pink and brown . . . 10 10
1530 – 5c. blue and brown . . . 15 10
1531 – 6c. lt brown & brown . . 15 10
1532 – 7c. pink & brown (air) 15 10
1533 – 10c. grey and brown . . 20 15
DESIGNS: 3c. Manuel Ubaldo Gomez; 5c. Emiliano Tejera; 6c. Bernardo Pichardo; 7c. Americo Lugo; 10c. Jose Gabriel Garcia.

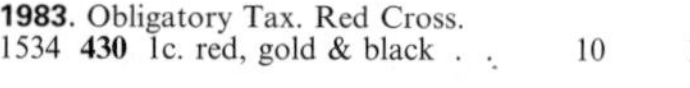
1983. Obligatory Tax. Red Cross.
1534 **430** 1c. red, gold & black . . 10 10

431 Dish Aerial and W.C.Y. Emblem **432** "Simon Bolivar" (Plutarco Andujar)

1983. Air. World Communications Year.
1535 **431** 10c. light blue & blue . . 20 15

1983. Air. Birth Bicentenary of Simon Bolivar.
1536 **432** 9c. multicoloured 15 10

433 Pictogram of Rehabilitation **434** Basketball and Gymnastics

1983. Obligatory Tax. Rehabilitation of the Disabled.
1537 **433** 1c. blue 10 10

1983. Air. Pan-American Games, Venezuela. Multicoloured.
1538 7c. Type **434** 15 10
1539 10c. Boxing and pole vaulting 20 15
1540 15c. Baseball, weightlifting and cycling 25 15

435 Emilio Prud'Homme and Jose Reyes (composers)

1983. Cent of Dominican National Anthem.
1541 **435** 6c. multicoloured 10 10

1983. Obligatory Tax. Anti-cancer Fund. As T **144** but dated "1983".
1542 **144** 1c. turquoise & green . . 10 10

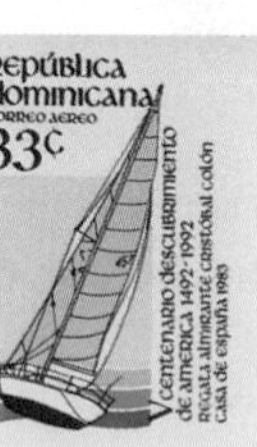

436 "Sotavento" (winner of 1982 regatta) **437** Arms

1983. Air. Christopher Columbus Regatta and 500th Anniv (1992) of Discovery of America by Columbus (1st issue).
1543 – 10c. stone, brn & blk . . 1·00 45
1544 – 21c. multicoloured . . . 1·25 60
1545 **436** 33c. multicoloured . . . 1·90 65
DESIGNS—HORIZ: 10c. Old map of Greater Antilles; 21c. Christopher Columbus Regatta trophy.
See also Nos. 1583/5, 1617/20, 1649/52, 1683/6, 1717/20, 1754/7, 1777/80, 1791/4 and 1805/8.

1983. 125th Anniv of Dominican Freemasons.
1547 **437** 4c. multicoloured 10 10

438 Our Lady of Regla Church **439** Clocktower

1983. 300th Anniv of Our Lady of Regla Church.
1548 **438** 3c. deep blue & blue . . 10 10
1549 – 6c. red and deep red . . 10 10
DESIGN: 6c. Statue of Our Lady of Regla.

1983. 450th Anniv of Monte Cristi Province.
1550 **439** 1c. green and black . . . 10 10
1551 – 2c. multicoloured 10 10
1552 – 5c. grey 10 10
1553 – 7c. grey and blue 15 10
DESIGNS—VERT: 2c. Provincial coat of arms. HORIZ: 5c. Wooden building in which independence of Cuba was signed; 7c. Men digging out salt crystals.

1983. Obligatory Tax. Child Welfare. As T **350** but dated "1983".
1554 **350** 1c. green 10 10

440 Commission Emblem

1983. Air. 10th Anniv of Latin American Civil Aviation Commission.
1555 **440** 10c. blue 15 10

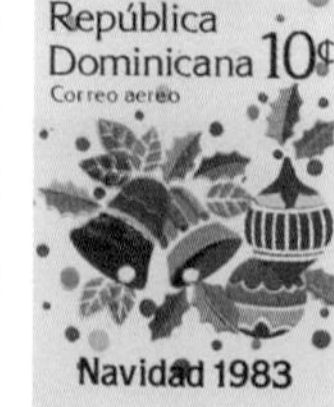

441 Baseball, Boxing and Cycling **442** Bells and Christmas Tree Decorations

1983. 6th National Games, San Pedro de Macoris. Multicoloured.
1556 6c. Type **441** (postage) . . . 10 10
1557 10c. Weightlifting, running and swimming (air) . . . 15 10

1983. Air. Christmas.
1558 **442** 10c. multicoloured . . . 15 10

443 "Portrait of a Girl" (Adriana Billini)

1983. Air. Paintings. Multicoloured.
1559 10c. "The Litter" (Juan Bautista Gomez) (horiz) 15 10
1560 15c. "The Meeting between Maximo Gomez and Jose Marti at Guayubin" (Enrique Garcia Godoy) (horiz) 20 15
1561 21c. "St. Francis" (Angel Perdomo) 30 20
1562 33c. Type **443** 45 30

444 Monument to Heroes of Capotillo

1983. 120th Anniv of Restoration of the Republic.
1563 **444** 1c. purple and blue . . . 10 10

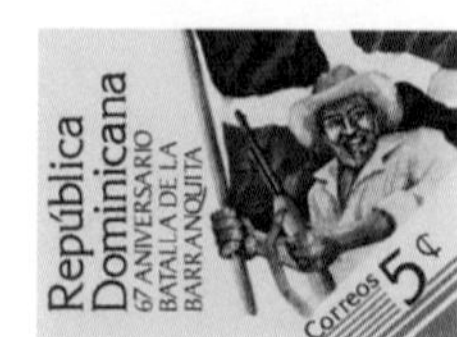

445 Man holding Dominican Flag and Rifle

1983. 67th Anniv of Battle of Barranquita.
1564 **445** 5c. multicoloured 10 10

446 Matias Ramon Mella and Dominican Flag

1984. 140th Anniv of Independence. Mult.
1565 6c. Type **446** 10 10
1566 25c. Puerta de la Misericordia and Mella's rifle 15 15

447 Dr. Heriberto Pieter

1984. Birth Centenary of Dr. Heriberto Pieter.
1567 **447** 3c. multicoloured 10 10

448 Jose Maria Imbert, Fernando Valerio, Cannon and National Flag

1984. 140th Anniv of Battle of Santiago.
1568 **448** 7c. multicoloured 10 10

449 Coastguard Patrol Boat

1984. 140th Anniv of Battle of Tortuguero.
1569 **449** 10c. multicoloured . . . 1·00 20

450 Monument to the Heroes of June 1959

1984. 25th Anniv of Expedition to Constanza, Maimon and Estero Hondo.
1570 **450** 6c. multicoloured 10 10

451 Salome Urena

1984. Birth Centenary of Pedro Henriquez Urena (poet).
1571 **451** 7c. pink and brown . . . 10 10
1572 – 10c. yellow and brown 10 10
1573 – 22c. yellow and brown 15 15
DESIGNS: 10c. Lines from poem "Mi Pedro"; 22c. Pedro H. Urena.

452 Running

1984. Olympic Games, Los Angeles. Each in blue, red and black.
1574 1p. Type **452** 55 50
1575 1p. Weightlifting 55 50
1576 1p. Boxing 55 50
1577 1p. Baseball 55 50

453 Stygian Owl

455 Pope John Paul II

454 Christopher Columbus landing in Hispaniola

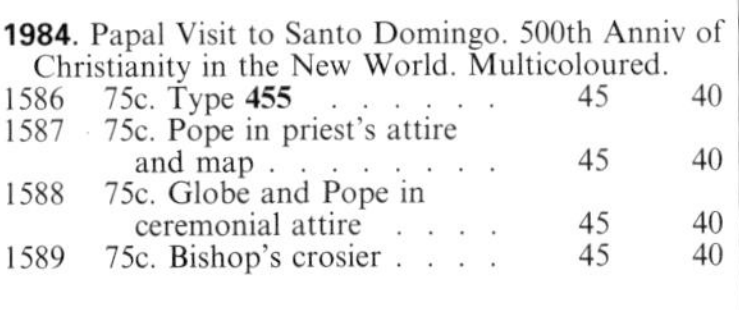

1984. Protection of Wildlife. Multicoloured.

1578	10c. Type **453**	1·50	30
1579	15c. Greater flamingo	2·00	40
1580	25c. White-lipped peccary	15	10
1581	35c. Haitian solenodon	25	20

1984. 500th Anniv (1992) of Discovery of America by Columbus (2nd issue).

1582 **454**	10c. multicoloured	10	10
1583 –	35c. multicoloured	25	20
1584 –	65c. brown, yell & blk	40	35
1585 –	1p. multicoloured	55	50

DESIGNS: 35c. Destruction of Fort La Navidad; 65c. First mass in America; 1p. Battle of Santo Cerro.

1984. Papal Visit to Santo Domingo. 500th Anniv of Christianity in the New World. Multicoloured.

1586	75c. Type **455**	45	40
1587	75c. Pope in priest's attire and map	45	40
1588	75c. Globe and Pope in ceremonial attire	45	40
1589	75c. Bishop's crosier	45	40

456 Gomez on Horseback

1984. 150th Birth Anniv (1986) of Maximo Gomez (leader of Cuban Revolution). Multicoloured.

1590	10c. Type **456**	10	10
1591	20c. Maximo Gomez	15	10

457 "Navidad 1984"

1984. Christmas.

1592 **457**	5c. mauve, blue and gold	10	10
1593 –	10c. blue, gold & mauve	10	10

DESIGN: 10c. "Navidad 1984" (different).

458 "The Sacrifice of the Kid" (Eligio Pichardo)

1984. Art. Multicoloured.

1594	5c. Type **458**	10	10
1595	10c. "Pumpkin Sellers" (statuette, Gaspar Mario Cruz) (vert)	10	10
1596	25c. "The Market" (Celeste Woss y Gil)	15	15
1597	50c. "Horses in a Storm" (Dario Suro)	30	25

459 Old Church, Higuey

1985. Our Lady of Altagracia's Day. Mult.

1598	5c. Type **459**	10	10
1599	10c. "Our Lady of Altagracia" (1514 painting)	15	10
1600	25c. Basilica of Our Lady of Altagracia, Higuey	35	30

460 Sanchez, Durate and Mella

1985. 141st Anniv of Independence.

1601 **460**	5c. multicoloured	10	10
1602	10c. multicoloured	15	10
1603	25c. multicoloured	35	30

461 Gen. Antonia Duverge

1985. 141st Anniv of Azua Battle.

1604 **461**	10c. cream, red & brown	15	10

462 Santo Domingo Lighthouse, 1853

463 Flags and Emblem

1985. 141st Anniv of Battle of Tortuguero.

1605 **462**	25c. multicoloured	35	30

1985. 25th Anniv of American Airforces Co-operation System.

1606 **463**	35c. multicoloured	50	45

464 Carlos Maria Rojas (first Governor)

465 Table Tennis Player

1985. Centenary of Espaillat Province.

1607 **464**	10c. multicoloured	10	10

1985. "MOCA 85" (Seventh National Games). Multicoloured.

1608	5c. Type **465**	10	10
1609	10c. Walking race	10	10

466 Young People of Different Races

1985. International Youth Year. Mult.

1610	5c. Type **466**	10	10
1611	25c. The Haitises	15	10
1612	35c. Mt. Duarte summit	20	15
1613	2p. Mt. Duarte	90	85

467 Evangelina Rodriguez (first Dominican woman doctor)

468 Emblem

1985. International Decade for Women.

1614 **467**	10c. multicoloured	10	10

1985. 15th Central American and Caribbean Games, Santiago.

1615 **468**	5c. multicoloured	10	10
1616	25c. multicoloured	15	10

469 Fourth Christopher Columbus Regatta

1985. 500th Anniv (1992) of Discovery of America by Columbus (3rd issue). Multicoloured.

1617	35c. Type **469**	1·00	30
1618	50c. Foundation of Santo Domingo, 1496	25	20
1619	65c. Chapel of Our Lady of the Rosary, 1496	35	30
1620	1p. Christopher Columbus's arrival in New World	45	40

470 Bust of Enriquillo

471 Arturo de Merino

1985. 450th Death Anniv of Enriquillo (Indian chief). Multicoloured.

1621	5c. Enriquillo in Bahoruco mountains (mural) (46 × 32 mm)	10	10
1622	10c. Type **470**	10	10

1985. Centenary of Ordination of Fernando Arturo de Merino (former President).

1623 **471**	25c. multicoloured	15	10

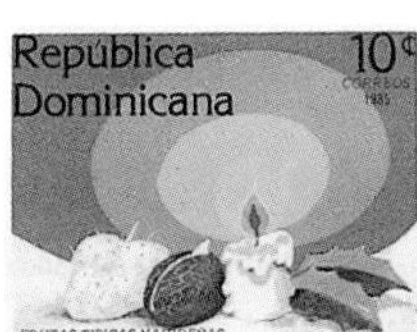

472 Fruit, Candle and Holly

1985. Christmas.

1624 **472**	10c. multicoloured	15	10
1625	25c. multicoloured	15	10

473 Haina Harbour

1985. 25th Anniv of Inter-American Development Bank. Multicoloured.

1626	10c. Type **473**	55	15
1627	25c. Map and ratio diagram of development activities	15	10
1628	1p. Tavera-Bao-Lopez hydro-electric complex	45	40

474 Mirabal Sisters

1985. 25th Death Anniv of Minerva, Patria and Maria Mirabal.

1629 **474**	10c. multicoloured	10	10

475 Tomb of Duarte, Sanchez and Mella

1986. National Independence Day.

1630 **475**	5c. multicoloured	10	10
1631	10c. multicoloured	10	10

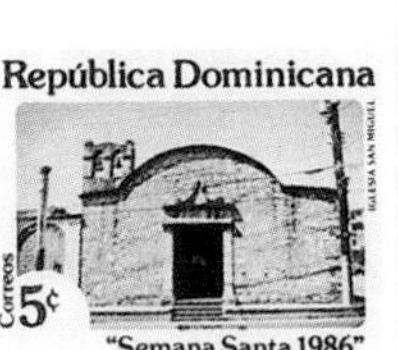

476 St. Michael's Church

478 Voters, Ballot Box and Map

477 "Leonor" (schooner) and Dominican Navy Founders

1986. Holy Week. Santo Domingo Churches. Multicoloured.

1632	5c. Type **476**	10	10
1633	5c. St. Andrew's Church	10	10
1634	10c. St. Lazarus's Church	10	10
1635	10c. St. Charles's Church	10	10
1636	10c. St. Barbara's Church	10	10

1986. Navy Day.

1637 **477**	10c. multicoloured	80	20

1986. National Elections. Multicoloured.

1638	5c. Type **478**	10	10
1639	10c. Hand dropping voting slip into ballot box	30	10

479 Emblem

480 Weightlifting

1986. Creation of "Inposdom" (Dominican Postal Institute).

1640 **479**	10c. blue, red and gold	10	10
1641	25c. blue, red and silver	15	10
1642	50c. blue, red and black	25	20

1986. 15th Central American and Caribbean Games, Santiago. Multicoloured.

1643	10c. Type **480**	10	10
1644	25c. Gymnast on rings	15	10
1645	35c. Diving	20	15
1646	50c. Show-jumping	25	20

481 Ercilia Pepin

482 Fifth Christopher Columbus Regatta

1986. Writers' Birth Centenaries. Each brown and silver.
1647 5c. Type **481** 10 10
1648 10c. Ramon Emilio Jiminez and Victor Garrido . . . 10 10

1986. 500th Anniv (1992) of Discovery of America by Columbus (4th issue). Multicoloured.
1649 25c. Type **482** 30 10
1650 50c. Foundation of Isabela city 25 20
1651 65c. Spanish soldiers 35 30
1652 1p. Columbus before King of Spain 45 40

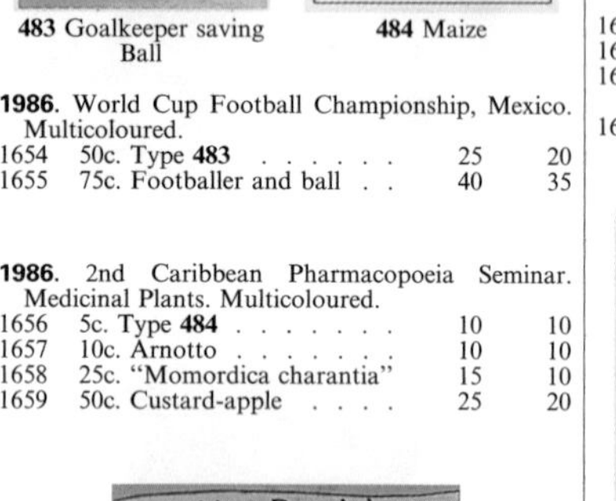

483 Goalkeeper saving Ball
484 Maize

1986. World Cup Football Championship, Mexico. Multicoloured.
1654 50c. Type **483** 25 20
1655 75c. Footballer and ball . . 40 35

1986. 2nd Caribbean Pharmacopoeia Seminar. Medicinal Plants. Multicoloured.
1656 5c. Type **484** 10 10
1657 10c. Arnotto 10 10
1658 25c. "Momordica charantia" 15 10
1659 50c. Custard-apple 25 20

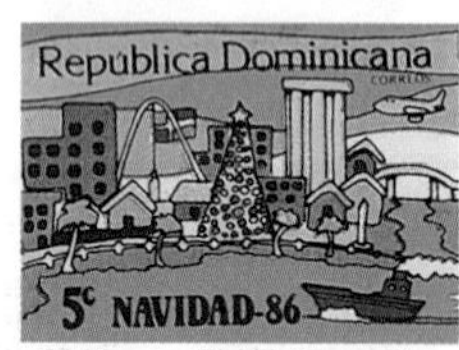

485 Town with Christmas Tree

1986. Christmas. Multicoloured.
1660 5c. Type **485** 15 10
1661 25c. Village 15 10

486 Gomez on Horseback
488 Emblem

1986. 150th Birth Anniv of Maximo Gomez.
1662 **486** 10c. black and mauve . . 10 10
1663 – 25c. black and brown . . 15 10
DESIGN: 25c. Head of Gomez.

1987. 16th Pan-American Ophthalmology Congress, Santo Domingo.
1676 **488** 50c. red, blue & black 20 15

489 "Ascension of Jesus Christ" (stained glass window, St. John Bosco Church)
490 "Sorghum bicolor"

1987. Ascension Day.
1677 **489** 35c. multicoloured . . . 10 10

1987. Edible Plants. Multicoloured.
1678 5c. Type **490** 10 10
1679 25c. "Maranta arundinacea" 10 10
1680 65c. "Calathea allouia" . . 20 15
1681 1p. "Voandzeia subterranea" 35 30

491 Emblem and People on Map

1987. 25th Anniv of Club Activo 20–30 in Dominican Republic.
1682 **491** 35c. multicoloured . . . 10 10

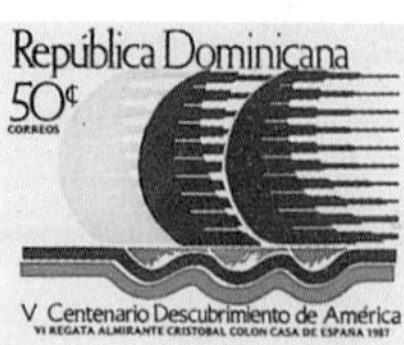

492 Sixth Christopher Columbus Regatta

1987. 500th Anniv (1992) of Discovery of America by Columbus (5th issue). Multicoloured.
1683 50c. Type **492** 10 10
1684 75c. Columbus writing diary 15 10
1685 1p. Foundation of city of Santiago 20 15
1686 1p.50 Columbus and Bobadilla 30 25

493 Games Emblem
494 Jose Antonio Hungria

1987. 50th Anniv of La Vega Province Games.
1688 **493** 40c. multicoloured . . . 10 10

1987. Writers' Birth Anniversaries.
1689 **494** 10c. brown & lt brown 10 10
1690 – 25c. dp green & green 10 10
DESIGN: 25c. Joaquin Sergio Inchaustegui.

495 Baseball
496 Statue

1987. 8th National Games, San Cristobal. Multicoloured.
1691 5c. Type **495** 10 10
1692 10c. Boxing 10 10
1693 50c. Karate 10 10

1987. 150th Birth Anniv of Fr. Francisco Xavier Billini.
1694 **496** 10c. deep blue and blue 10 10
1695 – 25c. green and olive . . 10 10
1696 – 75c. brown and pink . . 15 10
DESIGNS: 25c. Fr. Billini; 75c. Ana Hernandez de Billini (mother).

497 Maj. Frank Feliz and Airplane

1987. 50th Anniv of Pan-American Flight for Columbus Lighthouse Fund.
1697 **497** 25c. multicoloured . . . 20 10

498 Spit-roasting Pig

1987. Christmas. Multicoloured.
1699 10c. Type **498** 10 10
1700 50c. Passengers disembarking from airplane 20 10

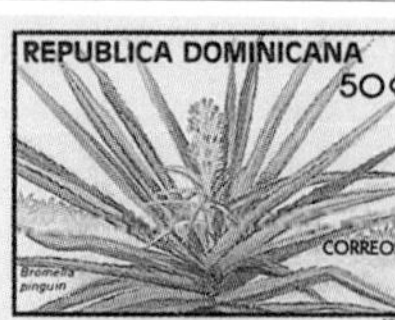

499 "Bromelia pinguin"

1988. Flowers. Multicoloured.
1701 50c. Type **499** 10 10
1702 50c. "Tillandsia compacta" (vert) 10 10
1703 50c. "Tillandsia fasciculata" 10 10
1704 50c. "Tillandsia hotteana" (vert) 10 10

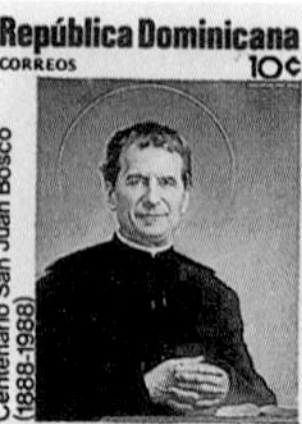

500 St. John Bosco

1988. Death Centenary of St. John Bosco (founder of Salesian Brothers). Multicoloured.
1705 10c. Type **500** 10 10
1706 70c. Stained glass window 15 10

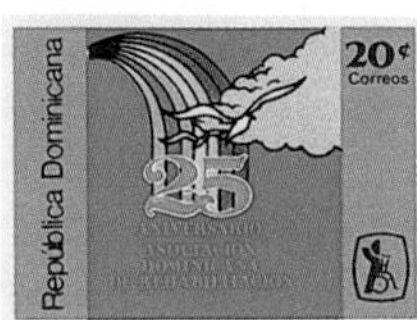

501 Rainbow, Doves and Cloud

1988. 25th Anniv of Dominican Rehabilitation Association.
1707 **501** 20c. multicoloured . . . 10 10

502 Perdomo
503 Emblem

1988. Birth Centenary of Dr. Manuel Emilio Perdomo.
1708 **502** 20c. brown and flesh . . 10 10

1988. 25th Anniv of Dominican College of Engineering and Architecture (CODIA).
1709 **503** 20c. multicoloured . . . 10 10

504 Church and Madonna and Child
505 Flags and Juan Pablo Duarte (Dominican patriot)

1988. Centenary of Parish Church of Our Lady of the Carmelites, Duverge.
1710 **504** 50c. multicoloured . . . 10 10

1988. Mexican Independence Day. Mult.
1711 50c. Type **505** 10 10
1712 50c. Flags and Miguel Hidalgo (Mexican patriot) 10 10

506 Athletics
507 Seventh Christopher Columbus Regatta

1988. Olympic Games, Seoul. Multicoloured.
1713 50c. Type **506** 10 10
1714 70c. Table tennis 15 10
1715 1p. Judo 20 15
1716 1p.50 "Ying Yang symbol and Balls" (Tete Marella) (horiz) 30 25

1988. 500th Anniv of Discovery of America by Columbus (6th issue). Multicoloured.
1717 50c. Type **507** 10 10
1718 70c. Building fort at La Vega Real, 1494 . . . . 15 10
1719 1p.50 Bonao Fort 30 25
1720 2p. Nicolas de Ovando (Governor of Hispaniola) 40 35

508 Duarte, Mella and Sanchez
509 Parchment, Knife and Pestle and Mortar

1988. 150th Anniv of Trinitarian Rebellion.
1722 **508** 10c. silver, red and blue 10 10
1723 – 1p. multicoloured . . . 20 15
1724 – 5p. multicoloured . . . 95 90
DESIGNS: 1p. Plaza La Trinitaria; 5p. Plaza de la Independencia.

1988. 13th Pan-American and 16th Central American Congresses of Pharmacy and Biochemistry.
1725 **509** 1p. multicoloured . . . 20 15

510 "Doni Tondo" (Michelangelo)
511 Emblem

1988. Christmas. Multicoloured.
1726 10c. Type **510** 10 10
1727 20c. Stained glass window 10 10

1988. 50th Anniv of Dominican Municipal Association.
1728 **511** 20c. multicoloured . . . 10 10

512 Ana Teresa Paradas

1988. 28th Death Anniv of Ana Teresa Paradas (lawyer).
1729 **512** 20c. red 10 10

513 Birds

1989. Bicentenary of French Revolution.
1730 **513** 3p. red, blue and black 30 25

516 Battle Scene

1989. 145th Anniv of Battle of Tortuguero.
1737 **516** 40c. multicoloured . . . 70 25

517 Drug Addict

1989. Anti-drugs Campaign.

1738 **517** 10c. multicoloured . . . 10 10
1739 20c. multicoloured . . . 10 10
1740 50c. multicoloured . . . 10 10
1741 70c. multicoloured . . . 10 10
1742 1p. multicoloured . . . 10 10
1743 1p.50 multicoloured . . 15 15
1744 2p. multicoloured . . . 20 15
1745 5p. multicoloured . . . 50 45
1746 10p. multicoloured . . . 1·00 95

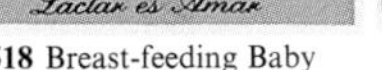

518 Breast-feeding Baby

519 Eugenio Maria de Hostos

1989. Mothers' Day.

1747 **518** 20c. multicoloured . . . 10 10

1989. 150th Birth Anniversaries. Mult.

1748 20c. Type **519** 10 10
1749 20c. Gen. Gregorio Luperon 10 10

520 Baseball

1989. 50th Anniv of Baseball Minor League.

1750 **520** 1p. multicoloured . . . 10 10

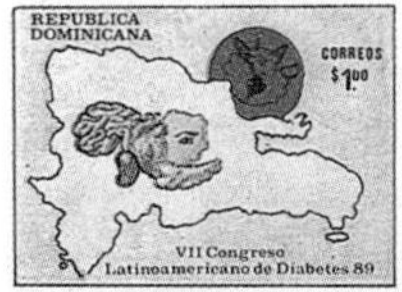

521 Map and Human Organs

1989. 7th Latin American Diabetes Association Congress.

1751 **521** 1p. multicoloured . . . 10 10

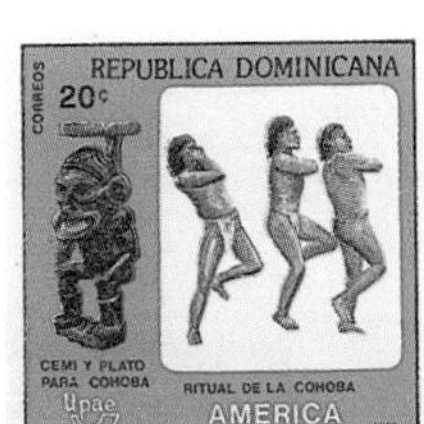

522 Cohoba Artefact and Ritual Dance

1989. America. Pre-Columbian Culture. Mult.

1752 20c. Type **522** 10 10
1753 1p. Taina vessel, pounding instrument and Indians preparing manioc cake . . 10 10

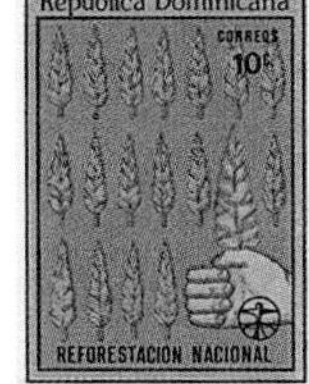

523 Eighth Christopher Columbus Regatta

524 Dead and Living Leaves

1989. 500th Anniv (1992) of Discovery of America by Columbus (7th issue). Multicoloured.

1754 50c. Type **523** 10 10
1755 70c. Brother Pedro de Cordoba preaching to Indians (horiz) 10 10
1756 1p. Columbus dividing Indian lands (horiz) . . . 10 10
1757 3p. Brother Antonio Montesinos giving sermon (horiz) 30 25

1989. National Reafforestation Campaign. Mult.

1758 10c. Type **524** 10 10
1759 20c. Forest 10 10
1760 50c. Forest and lake 10 10
1761 1p. Living tree and avenue of dead trees 10 10

525 Map and Cyclist

526 Mary and Body of Jesus

1990. 9th National Games, La Vega. Mult.

1762 10c. Type **525** 10 10
1763 20c. Map and runner . . . 10 10
1764 50c. Map and handball player 10 10

1990. Holy Week. Multicoloured.

1765 20c. Type **526** 10 10
1766 50c. Jesus carrying cross . . 10 10

527 Cogwheel and Workers

1990. International Labour Day.

1767 **527** 1p. multicoloured . . . 10 10

528 Avenida Mexico

1990. Urban Development. Multicoloured.

1768 10c. Type **528** 10 10
1769 20c. Avenida Nunez de Caceres road tunnel . . . 10 10
1770 50c. National Library . . . 10 10
1771 1p. V Centenario Motorway 10 10

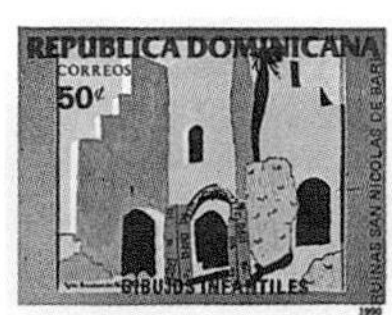

529 Penny Black

530 "Ruins of St. Nicholas's Church, Bari"

1990. 150th Anniv of the Penny Black. Mult.

1772 **529** 1p. multicoloured . . . 10 10

1990. Children's Drawings. Multicoloured.

1774 50c. Type **530** 10 10
1775 50c. "House, Tostado" . . . 10 10

531 Members' Flags

532 Yachts (Ninth Christopher Columbus Regatta)

1990. Centenary of Organization of American States.

1776 **531** 2p. multicoloured . . . 20 15

1990. 500th Anniv (1992) of Discovery of America by Columbus (8th issue). Multicoloured.

1777 50c. Type **532** 40 10
1778 1p. Confrontation between natives and sailors (horiz) 10 10
1779 2p. Meeting of Columbus and Guacanagari (horiz) 20 15
1780 5p. Caonabo imprisoned by Columbus (horiz) 45 30

533 Amerindians in Canoe

534 Perez Rancier

1990. America. Multicoloured.

1781 50c. Type **533** 30 10
1782 3p. Amerindian in hammock 25 15

1991. Birth Centenary of Dr. Tomas Eudoro Perez Rancier (physician).

1783 **534** 2p. black and yellow . . 20 10

535 First Official Mass in America

536 Boxing

1991. Spanish America. Multicoloured.

1784 50c. Type **535** 10 10
1785 1p. Arms (first religious orders) 10 10
1786 3p. Map of Hispaniola (first European settlement) (horiz) 30 20
1787 4p. Christopher Columbus (first viceroy and governor) 45 30

1991. 11th Pan-American Games, Havana. Multicoloured.

1788 30c. Type **536** 10 10
1789 50c. Cycling 10 10
1790 1p. Putting the shot 10 10

537 Yachts (10th Christopher Columbus Regatta)

538 Eye and Hands

1991. 500th Anniv (1992) of Discovery of America by Columbus (9th issue). Multicoloured.

1791 30c. Type **537** 10 10
1792 50c. Meeting of three cultures (horiz) 10 10
1793 3p. Columbus and Doctor Alvarez Chanco (horiz) 30 20
1794 4p. Enriquillo's war (horiz) 45 30

1991. Cornea Bank.

1795 **538** 3p. black and red . . . 30 20

539 "Santa Maria"

540 Meeting Emblem

1991. America. Voyages of Discovery. Mult.

1796 1p. Type **539** 20 15
1797 3p. Columbus and fleet . . 40 25

1992. 33rd Annual Meeting of Governors of Inter-American Development Bank, Santo Domingo.

1798 **540** 1p. multicoloured . . . 10 10

541 Valentin Salinero (founder)

542 Flags of Cuba, Dominican Republic and Puerto Rica, and Magnifying Glass

1992. Centenary (1991) of Order of the Apostles.

1799 **541** 1p. brown, black & blue 10 10

1992. "Espanola 92" Stamp Exhibition.

1800 **542** 3p. black, violet & red 30 20

543 First Monastery in Americas

1992. Ruins. Multicoloured.

1801 50c. Type **543** 10 10
1802 3p. First hospital in Americas 30 20

544 La Vega Cathedral and Pope

545 Yacht (11th Christopher Columbus Regatta)

1992. Visit of Pope John Paul II. Mult.

1803 50c. Type **544** 10 10
1804 3p. Santo Domingo Cathedral and Pope . . . 30 20

1992. 500th Anniv of Discovery of America by Columbus (10th issue). Multicoloured.

1805 50c. Type **545** 10 10
1806 1p. Amerindian women preparing food and Columbus (horiz) 10 10
1807 2p. Amerindians demonstrating use of tobacco to Columbus (horiz) 20 10
1808 3p. Amerindian woman and Columbus by maize field (horiz) 30 20

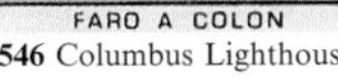

546 Columbus Lighthouse

547 Convention Emblem

1992.

1809 **546** 30c. multicoloured . . . 10 10
1810 1p. multicoloured . . . 10 10

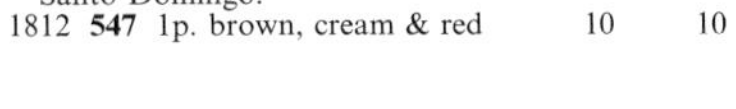

1992. 23rd Pan-American Round Table Convention, Santo Domingo.

1812 **547** 1p. brown, cream & red 10 10

548 First Royal Palace in Americas, Santo Domingo

549 Torch Bearer

1992. America. Multicoloured.
1813 50c. Type **548** 10 10
1814 3p. First Vice-regal residence in Americas, Colon . . . 30 20

1992. 10th National Games, San Juan.
1815 **549** 30c. multicoloured . . . 10 10
1816 – 1p. multicoloured . . . 10 10
1817 – 4p. black and blue . . . 40 25
DESIGNS: 1p. Emblem of Secretary of State for Sports Education and Recreation; 4p. Judo.

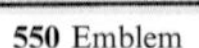

550 Emblem **551** Ema Balaguer

1993. 7th Population and Housing Census.
1818 **550** 50c. blue, black & pink 10 10
1819 1p. blue, black & brown 10 10
1820 3p. blue, black & grey 30 20
1821 4p. blue, black & green 40 25

1993. Ema Balaguer (humanitarian worker) Commemoration.
1822 **551** 30c. multicoloured . . . 10 10
1823 50c. multicoloured . . . 10 10
1824 1p. multicoloured . . . 10 10

552 Emblem and Stylized Figures

1993. 50th Anniv of Santo Domingo Rotary Club. Multicoloured.
1825 30c. Type **552** 10 10
1826 1p. National flags and rotary emblem 10 10

553 Institute

1993. Inauguration of New Dominican Postal Institute Building.
1827 **553** 1p. multicoloured . . . 10 10
1828 3p. multicoloured . . . 30 20
1829 4p. multicoloured . . . 40 25
1830 5p. multicoloured . . . 50 30
1831 10p. multicoloured . . . 95 60

554 Palm Chat and Books **556** Chest (first university)

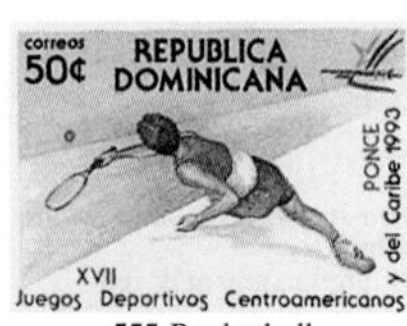

555 Racketball

1993. Ten Year Education Plan.
1833 **554** 1p.50 multicoloured . . 1·40 1·40

1993. 17th Central American and Caribbean Games, Ponce (Puerto Rico). Multicoloured.
1834 50c. Type **555** 10 10
1835 4p. Swimming 40 25

1993. American Firsts in Hispaniola (1st series). Multicoloured.
1836 50c. Type **556** 10 10
1837 3p. First arms conferred on American city 30 20
See also Nos. 1840 and 1882/3.

557 Hispaniolan Conure

1993. America. Endangered Animals. Mult.
1838 1p. Type **557** . . . . 1·25 95
1839 3p. Rhinoceros iguana . . . 30 20

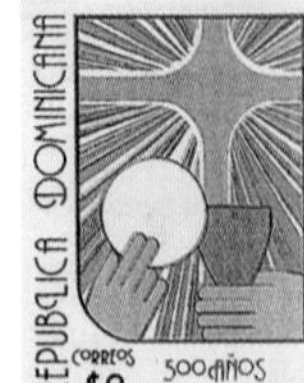

558 Cross and Eucharist (500th anniv of first Mass)

1994. American Firsts in Hispaniola (2nd series).
1840 **558** 2p. multicoloured . . . 20 10

559 State Flag, 1946 15c. and 1944 3c. Stamps

1994. 5th National Stamp Exhibition.
1841 **559** 3p. multicoloured . . . 30 20

560 Signing of Independence Treaty (left-hand detail)

1994. 150th Anniv of Independence. Mult.
1842 2p. Type **560** 20 10
1843 2p. Signing of Independence Treaty (right-hand detail) 20 10
1844 2p. State flag 20 10
1845 2p. Soldier with young woman 20 10
1846 2p. Boy helping woman make flag 20 10
1847 3p. Revolutionaries (back view of left-hand man) . . 30 20
1848 3p. Revolutionaries (window behind men) 30 20
1849 3p. State arms 30 20
1850 3p. Revolutionaries (all turned away from door) 30 20
1851 3p. Revolutionaries with flag 30 20
Stamps of the same value were issued together, se-tenant, Nos. 1842/3, 1845/6, 1847/8 and 1850/1 forming composite designs.

561 Solenodon on Dead Wood

1994. The Haitian Solenodon. Multicoloured.
1853 1p. Type **561** 10 10
1854 1p. Solenodon amongst leaves 10 10
1855 1p. Solenodon on stony ground 10 10
1856 1p. Solenodon eating insect 10 10

562 Fusiliers behind Barricade (19 March) **563** Ballot Boxes

1994. 150th Anniversaries of Battles of 19 and 30 March. Multicoloured.
1857 2p. Type **562** 20 10
1858 2p. Battle at fort (30 March) 20 10

1994. National Elections.
1859 **563** 2p. multicoloured . . . 20 10

564 "Virgin of Amparo" **565** Goalkeeper

1994. 150th Anniv of Naval Battle of Puerto Tortuguero.
1860 **564** 3p. multicoloured . . . 30 20

1994. World Cup Football Championship, U.S.A. Multicoloured.
1861 4p. Type **565** 40 25
1862 6p. Players contesting possession of ball 60 40

566 Figures in Houses

1994. Ema Balguer Children's City.
1863 **566** 1p. mauve and brown . . 10 10

567 1866 Medio Real Stamp and Cancellation

1994. Stamp Day.
1864 **567** 5p. red, black & yellow 45 30

568 Postal Carrier on Horseback **571** Writing Desk and Constitution

1994. America. Postal Vehicles. Multicoloured.
1865 2p. Type **568** 20 10
1866 6p. Schooner 50 35

1994. 150th Anniv of First Constitution of Dominican Republic.
1876 **571** 3p. multicoloured . . . 25 15

572 Flight into Egypt

1994. Christmas. International Year of the Family. Multicoloured.
1877 2p. Type **572** 20 10
1878 3p. Family 25 15

573 Ruins of St. Francis's Monastery

1994. 500th Anniv of Concepcion de la Vega.
1879 **573** 3p. multicoloured . . . 25 15

574 Wall of La Isabela Church

1994. 500th Anniv of First Church in Dominican Republic. Multicoloured.
1880 3p. Type **574** 25 15
1881 3p. Temple of the Americas 25 15
Nos. 1880/1 were issued together, se-tenant, forming a composite design.

1994. American Firsts in Hispaniola (3rd series). As T **556**. Multicoloured.
1882 2p. First coins, 1505 . . . . 20 10
1883 5p. Antonio Montesino (first plea for justice (in Advent sermon), 1511) 45 30

575 "Hypsirhynchus ferox"

1994. National Natural History Museum. Snakes. Multicoloured.
1884 2p. Type **575** 20 10
1885 2p. "Antillophis parvifrons" 20 10
1886 2p. "Uromacer catesbyi" . . 20 10
1887 2p. Bahama boa ("Epicrates striatus") 20 10
Nos. 1884/5 and 1886/7 respectively were issued together, se-tenant, each pair forming a composite design of a tree and the snakes.

576 Taekwondo

1995. Pan-American Games, Mar del Plata, Argentine Republic.
1888 **576** 4p. blue, red & black . . 35 20
1889 – 13p. green, black & yell 1·25 80
DESIGN: 13p. Tennis.

577 Allegory of Dominican Agriculture

1995. 50th Anniv of F.A.O.
1890 **577** 4p. multicoloured . . . 35 20

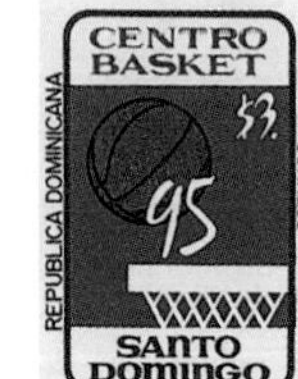

578 Jose Marti, Maximo Gomez and Monte Cristi Clock Tower **579** Emblem

1995. Centenaries.
1891 **578** 2p. brown, pink & black 20 10
1892 – 3p. pink, black & blue 25 15
1893 – 4p. black and pink . . . 35 20
DESIGNS: 3p. Jose Marti on Cuban national flag (death centenary); 4p. Gomez and Marti signing Monte Cristi manifesto.

1995. "Centrobasket" Basketball Championship, Santo Domingo.
1894 **579** 3p. blue, red & black . . 25 15

580 "Pimenta ozua"  **581** San Souci Port

1995. Medicinal Plants. Multicoloured.
1895 2p. Type **580** 20 10
1896 2p. "Melocactus communis" 20 10
1897 3p. "Smilax sp." 25 15
1898 3p. "Zamia sp." 25 15

1995. Tourism. Multicoloured.
1899 4p. Type **581** 35 20
1900 5p. Barahona airport . . . 45 30
1901 6p. G. Luperon airport . . 55 35
1902 13p. Las Americas airport 1·25 80

582 Ruins of Jacagua Church

1995. 500th Anniv of Santiago de los Caballeros.
1903 **582** 3p. multicoloured . . . 25 15

583 Sei Whale ("Balaenoptera borealis")

1995. Natural History Museum. Whales. Mult.
1904 3p. Type **583** 25 15
1905 3p. Humpback whales ("Megaptera novaeangliae") 25 15
1906 3p. Sperm whales ("Physeter macrocephalus") 25 15
1907 3p. Cuvier's beaked whales ("Ziphius cavirostris") . . 25 15

584 Rafael Colon  **585** Cancelled 1880 2c. Stamp

1995. Singers. Multicoloured.
1908 2p. Type **584** 20 10
1909 3p. Casandra Damiron . . . 25 15

1995. Stamp Day.
1910 **585** 4p. multicoloured . . . 35 20

586 Player  **587** Anniversary Emblem

1995. Centenary of Volleyball.
1911 **586** 6p. multicoloured . . . 55 35

1995. 50th Anniv of U.N.O.
1913 **587** 2p. blue and gold . . . 20 10
1914 – 6p. multicoloured . . . 55 35
DESIGN—33 × 55 mm: 6p. Allegorical design.

588 Allegory  **589** Columbus Lighthouse

1995. 4th World Conference on Women, Peking.
1915 **588** 2p. multicoloured . . . 20 10

1995.
1916 **589** 10p. ultram, blue & blk 90 60
1994 10p. green and silver . . 85 55
2025 10p. mauve and silver . . 75 50
2089 10p. yellow and black . . 75 50

590 Enriquillo Lake  **591** Antonio Mesa (tenor)

1995. America. Environmental Protection. Mult.
1917 2p. Type **590** 20 10
1918 6p. Mangrove plantation . . 55 35

1995. Singers. Each red and brown.
1919 2p. Type **591** 20 10
1920 2p. Susano Polanco (tenor) 20 10
1921 2p. Julieta Otero (soprano) 20 10

592 Cathedral

1995. Centenary of Santiago Cathedral.
1922 **592** 3p. multicoloured . . . 25 15

593 Corsair Fighter

1995. 50th Anniv of Dominican Air Force (1st issue). Multicoloured.
1923 2p. Type **593** 20 10
1924 2p. Stearman Pt-17 Kaydett bomber 20 10
1925 2p. North American T-6 Texan trainer 20 10
1926 2p. Consolidated PBY-5A Catalina amphibian . . . 20 10
1927 2p. Bristol Beaufighter fighter 20 10
1928 2p. De Havilland Mosquito bomber 20 10
1929 2p. Lockheed P-38 Lightning fighter 20 10
1930 2p. North American P-51 Mustang fighter 20 10
1931 2p. Boeing B-17 Flying Fortress bomber 20 10
1932 2p. Republic P-47 Thunderbolt fighter . . . 20 10
1933 2p. De Havilland Vampire jet fighter 20 10
1934 2p. Curtiss C-46 Commander 20 10
1935 2p. Boeing B-26 Invader . . 20 10
1936 2p. Douglas C-47 Skytrain transport 20 10
1937 2p. T-28D Trojan 20 10
1938 2p. T-33A Silverstar 20 10
1939 2p. Cessna T-41D 20 10
1940 2p. T-34 Mentor 20 10
1941 2p. Cessna O-2A 20 10
1942 2p. Cessna A-37B Dragonfly fighter 20 10
See also Nos. 1958/63, 2026/31 and 2040/4.

594 Brito  **596** Children

595 Yachts

1996. 50th Death Anniv of Eduardo Brito (singer).
1943 **594** 1p. multicoloured . . . 10 10
1944 – 2p. multicoloured . . . 20 10
1945 – 3p. black and pink . . . 25 15
DESIGNS—55 × 35 mm: 2p. Brito playing maracas. As T **594**: 3p. Brito (different).

1996. Hispaniola Cup Yachting Championship.
1946 **595** 5p. multicoloured . . . 45 30

1996. 50th Anniv of U.N.I.C.E.F.
1947 **596** 2p. black and green . . 20 10
1948 – 4p. black and green . . 35 20
DESIGN—4p. As T **596** but motif reversed.

597 Arturo Pallerano, Freddy Gaton and Rafael Herrera

1996. National Journalists' Day.
1949 **597** 5p. multicoloured . . . 45 30

598 Emblem, Astronaut and Biplane

1996. "Espamer" Spanish–Latin American and "Aviation and Space" Stamp Exhibitions, Seville, Spain.
1950 **598** 15p. multicoloured . . . 1·40 90

599 Judo

1996. Olympic Games, Atlanta. Each black, blue and red.
1951 5p. Type **599** 45 30
1952 15p. Torchbearer . . . . . 1·40 90

600 Greek 1896 2l. Olympic Stamp

1996. Centenary of Modern Olympic Games.
1953 **600** 6p. green, red & black 55 35
1954 – 15p. multicoloured . . . 1·40 90
DESIGN: 15p. Dominican Republic 1937 7c. Olympic stamp.

601 "Girl at Postbox"

1996. "The Post is your Friend". Winning Entries in Children's Stamp Design Competition. Mult.
1955 3p. Type **601** 20 10
1956 3p. Representations of world post 20 10
1957 3p. Postal carrier on horseback delivering letter (vert) 20 10

602 Sikorsky S-55

1996. 50th Anniv of Air Force (2nd issue). Helicopters. Multicoloured.
1958 3p. Type **602** 20 10
1959 3p. Sud Aviation Alouette II 20 10
1960 3p. Sud Aviation Alouette III 20 10
1961 3p. OH-6A Cayuse 20 10
1962 3p. Bell 205 A-1 . . . . . 20 10
1963 3p. Aerospatiale SA.365 Dauphin 2 . . . . 20 10

603 Workers and Children  **604** Man

1996. United Nations Decade against Drug Trafficking.
1964 **603** 15p. multicoloured . . . 1·40 90

1996. America. Costumes. Multicoloured.
1965 2p. Type **604** 15 10
1966 6p. Woman 50 30

605 Stylized Dinghy

1996. 26th International "Sunfish" Dinghy Sailing Championships. Multicoloured.
1967 6p. Type **605** 50 30
1968 10p. Sailor in dinghy (horiz) 85 55

606 1905 1p. Stamp

1996. Stamp Day.
1969 **606** 5p. stone and black . . . 40 25

607 Ridgway's Hawk ("Buteo ridgwayi")  **608** Mirabal Sisters

1996. Birds. Multicoloured.
1970 2p. Type **607** 15 10
1971 2p. Hispaniolan conure ("Aratinga chloroptera") 15 10
1972 2p. Hispaniolan amazon ("Amazona ventralis") . . 15 10
1973 2p. Rufous-breasted cuckoo ("Hyetornis rufigularis") 15 10
1974 2p. Hispaniolan lizard cuckoo ("Saurothera longirostris") 15 10
1975 2p. Least pauraque ("Siphonorhis brewsteri") 15 10
1976 2p. Hispaniolan emerald ("Chlorostilbon swainsonii") 15 10
1977 2p. Narrow-billed tody ("Todus angustirostris") 15 10
1978 2p. Broad-billed tody ("Todus subulatus") . . . 15 10
1979 2p. Hispaniolan trogon ("Temnotrogon roseigaster") 15 10
1980 2p. Antillean piculet ("Nesoctites micromegas") 15 10
1981 2p. Hispaniolan woodpecker ("Melanerpes striatus") 15 10
1982 2p. La Selle thrush ("Turdus swalesi") 15 10
1983 2p. Antillean siskin ("Carduelis dominicensis") 15 10
1984 2p. Palm chat ("Dulus dominicus") 15 10
1985 2p. Green-tailed ground warbler ("Microligea palustris") 15 10
1986 2p. Flat-billed vireo ("Vireo nanus") 15 10
1987 2p. White-winged ground warbler ("Xenoligea montana") 15 10
1988 2p. La Selle thrush ("Turdus swalesi dodae") 15 10
1989 2p. Chat-tanager ("Calyptophilus frugivorus tertius") . . . 15 10
1990 2p. White-necked crow ("Corvus leucognaphalus") 15 10
1991 2p. Chat-tanager ("Calyptophilus frugivorus neibae") . . . 15 10

1996. International Day of No Violence against Women.
1992 **608** 5p. multicoloured . . . 40 25
1993 10p. multicoloured . . . 85 55

609 Leatherback Turtles ("Dermochelys coriacea")

1996. Turtles. Multicoloured.
1995 5p. Type **609** 40 25
1996 5p. Loggerhead turtles ("Caretta caretta") . . . 40 25
1997 5p. Indian Ocean green turtles ("Chelonia mydas") 40 25
1998 5p. Hawksbill turtles ("Eretmochelys imbricata") 40 25
Nos. 1995/8 were issued together, se-tenant, forming a composite design.

610 Youths leaping for Sun

611 Flag and Lyrics by Emilio Prudhomne

1997. National Youth Day.
1999 **610** 3p. multicoloured . . . 25 15

1997. National Anthem. Each black, blue and red.
2000 2p. Type **611** 15 10
2001 3p. Flag and score by Jose Reyes 25 15

612 Salome Urena

613 Comet, Palm Tree and House

1997. Death Cent of Salome Urena (educationist).
2002 **612** 3p. multicoloured . . . 25 15

1997. Hale-Bopp Comet.
2003 **613** 5p. multicoloured . . . 40 25

614 Mascot with Torch and Emblem

1997. 11th National Games. Multicoloured.
2005 2p. Type **614** 15 10
2006 3p. Mascot with baseball bat (26 × 36 mm) 25 15
2007 5p. Athlete breasting tape (36 × 26 mm) 40 25

615 Von Stephan

616 Blood Vessel

1997. Death Centenary of Heinrich von Stephan (founder of U.P.U).
2008 **615** 10p. violet, blk & red . . 85 55

1997. 15th International Haemostasis and Thrombosis Congress.
2010 **616** 10p. multicoloured . . . 85 55

617 Helmet, Flowers and Epaulettes

618 Emblem

1997. Death Cent of General Gregorio Luperon.
2011 **617** 3p. multicoloured . . . 25 15

1997. 80th Anniv of Spanish House in Santo Domingo.
2012 **618** 5p. multicoloured . . . 40 25

619 First Minting

1997. Centenary of the Peso.
2013 **619** 2p. multicoloured . . . 15 10

620 Icon

1997. 75th Anniv of Coronation of "Our Lady of Altagracia" (icon). Multicoloured.
2014 3p. Type **620** 25 15
2015 5p. Icon and church 40 25

621 Dog attacking Postman on Motor Cycle

1997. America. The Postman. Multicoloured.
2016 2p. Type **621** 15 10
2017 6p. Dog attacking postman delivering letter (35½ × 37 mm) 45 30

622 Weeping Child, Mother Teresa and Man on Donkey

1997. Int Fight against Poverty Day.
2018 **622** 5p. multicoloured . . . 40 25

623 1936 and 1899 2p. Stamps

1997. Stamp Day.
2019 **623** 5p. brown and black . . 40 25

624 Buildings

1997. 50th Anniv of Central Bank.
2020 **624** 10p. multicoloured . . . 75 50

625 "Erophyllus bombifrons"

1997. Bats. Multicoloured.
2021 5p. Type **625** 40 25
2022 5p. Cuban fruit-eating bat ("Brachyphylla nana") . . 40 25
2023 5p. Kerr's mastiff bat ("Molossus molossus") . . 40 25
2024 5p. Red bat ("Lasiurus borealis") 40 25

626 Air Force Badge

1997. 50th Anniv of Air Force (3rd issue). Division Badges, Multicoloured.
2026 3p. Type **626** 25 15
2027 3p. Air Command North . . 25 15
2028 3p. Air Command 25 15
2029 3p. Rescue 25 15
2030 3p. Maintenance Command 25 15
2031 3p. Combat Squadron . . . 25 15

627 Facade

1997. 50th Anniv of National Palace.
2032 **627** 10p. multicoloured . . . 75 50

628 Painting

1998. 1st Regional Symposium on Influence of Pre-Columbian Culture on Contemporary Caribbean Art.
2033 **628** 6p. multicoloured . . . 45 30

629 Emblem

630 Open Book

1998. 75th Anniv of American Chamber of Commerce of Dominican Republic.
2034 **629** 10p. blue, red and gold 75 50

1998. 25th Anniv of National Book Fair and First International Book Fair, Santo Domingo.
2035 **630** 3p. blue, red and black 25 15
2036 – 5p. blue, red and black 40 25
DESIGN—40 × 40 mm: 5p. Book Fair emblem.

631 Emblem

1998. 50th Anniv of Organization of American States. Multicoloured.
2037 5p. Type **631** 40 25
2038 5p. As Type **631** but inscr for the 50th anniv of signing of the Organization charter . . . 40 25

632 Olive Branches, Menorah and Star of David

1998. 50th Anniv of State of Israel.
2039 **632** 10p. ultram, bl & mve 75 50

633 General Frank Felix Miranda

1998. 50th Anniv of Air Force (4th issue). Mult.
2040 3p. Type **633** 25 15
2041 3p. Curtiss-Wright R-19 . . 25 15
2042 3p. Coronel Ernesto Tejeda (portrait at right) 25 15
2043 3p. As No. 2042, but portrait at left 25 15
2044 3p. As Type **633**, but portrait at right 25 15

634 Sundial

1998. 500th Anniv of Santo Domingo. Mult.

2045 2p. Type **634** 15 10
2046 3p. St. Lazarus's Church and Hospital (horiz) . . . 25 15
2047 4p. First cathedral in the Americas (horiz) 30 20
2048 5p. Fortress (horiz) 40 25
2049 6p. Tower of Honour (horiz) 45 30
2050 10p. St. Nicholas of Bari's Church and Hospital . . 75 50

635 Theatre

1998. 25th Anniv of National Theatre.

2051 **635** 10p. multicoloured . . . 75 50

636 Latin Inscription

1998. 44th Anniv of Latin Union.

2052 **636** 10p. gold, grey & black 75 50

637 Cocoa Beans and Route Map of First American–Europe Shipment, 1502

1998. 25th Anniv of Int Cocoa Organization.

2053 **637** 10p. multicoloured . . . 75 50

638 Nino Ferrua (stamp designer)

1998. Stamp Day.

2054 **638** 5p. multicoloured . . . 40 25

639 Pope John Paul II venerating Portrait of Virgin Mary

1998. 20th Anniv of Pontificate of Pope John Paul II. Multicoloured.

2055 5p. Type **639** 40 25
2056 10p. Pope John Paul II . . 75 50

640 Bay Rum

1998. Medicinal Plants. Multicoloured.

2057 3p. Type **640** 20 10
2058 3p. "Pimenta haitiensis" . . 20 10
2059 3p. "Cymbopogon citratus" 20 10
2060 3p. Seville orange ("Citrus aurantium") 20 10

641 Juana Saltitopa (Independence fighter)

1998. America. Famous Women. Multicoloured.

2061 2p. Type **641** 15 10
2062 6p. Anacaona (Indian chief) 45 30

642 Earth and Emblem

643 Statue of Columbus

1998. International Year of the Ocean.

2063 **642** 5p. multicoloured . . . 35 25

1998. "Expofila 98" Stamp Exhibition, Santo Domingo. 500th Anniv of Santo Domingo.

2064 **643** 5p. multicoloured . . . 35 25

644 Fernando Valerio

1998. Military Heroes. Each brown and green.

2065 3p. Type **644** 20 10
2066 3p. Benito Moncion 20 10
2067 3p. Jose Maria Cabral . . . 20 10
2068 3p. Antonio Duverge . . . 20 10
2069 3p. Gregorio Luperon . . . 20 10
2070 3p. Jose Salcedo 20 10
2071 3p. Fco. Salcedo 20 10
2072 3p. Gaspar Polanco 20 10
2073 3p. Santiago Rodriguez . . 20 10
2074 3p. Admiral Juan Cambiaso 20 10
2075 3p. Jose Puello 20 10
2076 3p. Jose Imbert 20 10
2077 3p. Admiral Juan Acosta . . 20 10
2078 3p. Marcos Adon 20 10
2079 3p. Matias Mella 20 10
2080 3p. Francisco Sanchez . . . 20 10
2081 3p. Juan Pablo Duarte . . . 20 10
2082 3p. Olegario Tenares . . . 20 10
2083 3p. General Pedro Santana 20 10
2084 3p. Juan Sanchez Ramirez 20 10

645 Banknotes

1998. 150th Anniv of Paper Money.

2085 **645** 10p. multicoloured . . . 75 50

646 Spit-roasting Pig

1998. Christmas. Multicoloured.

2086 2p. Type **646** 15 10
2087 5p. Three Wise Men on camels 35 25

647 Couple and Human Rights Emblem

1998. 50th Anniv of Universal Declaration of Human Rights.

2088 **647** 10p. multicoloured . . . 75 50

648 Vega's Lyria

1998. Shells. Multicoloured.

2090 5p. Type **648** 35 25
2091 5p. Queen conch ("Strombus gigas") . . . 35 25
2092 5p. West Indian top shell ("Cittarium pica") 35 25
2093 5p. Bleeding tooth ("Nerita peloronta") 35 25

649 Hernandez

1998. Birth Bicentenary of Gaspar Hernandez (priest and Independence fighter).

2094 **649** 3p. multicoloured . . . 20 10

650 Earth

1999. 10th National Congress, First International Postgraduate Lectures and 25th Anniv of Dominican Society for Endocrinology and Nutrition.

2095 **650** 10p. multicoloured . . . 75 50

652 Cigar and Tobacco Leaf

1999. Exports. Multicoloured.

2097 6p. Type **652** 45 30
2098 10p. Woman sewing (textiles) (vert) 75 50

653 Magnifying Glass over Map of Dominican Republic

1999. 155th Anniv of Office of Comptroller-General.

2099 **653** 2p. multicoloured . . . 15 10

654 Bosch, "The Seagull" (poem) and Main Tower, Santo Domingo

1999. Contemporary Writers. 90th Birthday of Pres. Juan Bosch (poet). Multicoloured.

2100 2p. Type **654** 15 10
2101 10p. Portrait of Bosch (vert) 75 50

655 "Pseudophoenix ekmanii"

657 Baseball

656 Gen. Juan Pablo Duarte (revolutionary)

1999. Flowers and their Fruit. Multicoloured.

2102 5p. Type **655** 35 25
2103 5p. "Murtigia colabura" . . 35 25
2104 5p. "Pouteria dominguensis" 35 25
2105 5p. "Rubus dominguensis" 35 25

1999.

2106 **656** 3p. multicoloured . . . 20 15

1999. 13th Pan-American Games, Winnipeg, Canada. Multicoloured.

2107 5p. Type **657** 35 25
2108 6p. Weightlifting 45 30

658 Tomas Bobadilla y Briones

1999. Leaders of the Dominican Republic. Mult.

2109 3p. Type **658** 20 15
2110 3p. Pedro Santana (President, 1844–48, 1853–56 and 1859–61) 20 15
2111 3p. Manuel Jimenez (President, 1848–49) . . . 20 15
2112 3p. Buenaventura Baez (President, 1849–53, 1856–58, 1865–66, 1868–74 and 1876–78) 20 15
2113 3p. Manuel de Regla Motta (President, June–October 1856) 20 15
2114 3p. Jose Desiderio Valverde (President, 1858–59) . . . 20 15
2115 3p. Jose Antonio Salcedo . . 20 15
2116 3p. Gaspar Polanco 20 15

659 "St. Christopher"

1999. Jose Vela Zanetti (Spanish artist) Commemoration. Multicoloured

2117 2p. Type **659** 15 10
2118 3p. "Bride and Groom" . . 20 15
2119 5p. "Burial of Christ" (horiz) 35 20
2120 6p. "Cock-fighting" 45 30
2121 10p. "Self-portrait" 75 50

660 "Strataegus quadrifoveatus"

1999. Insects. Multicoloured.
2122 5p. Type **660** 35 20
2123 5p. "Anetia jaegeri" (butterfly) 35 20
2124 5p. "Polyancistroydes tettigonidae" 35 20
2125 5p. Stick insect ("Phasmidae aploppus") 35 20

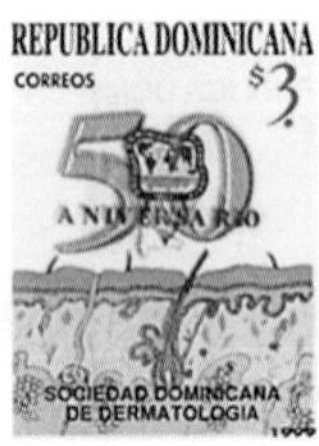

661 Emblem and Cross-section of Skin

1999. 50th Anniv of Dominican Dermatological Society.
2126 **661** 3p. multicoloured . . . 20 15

662 Maternity Clinic, Santo Domingo

1999. 900th Anniv of Sovereign Military Order of Malta. Multicoloured.
2127 2p. Type **662** 15 10
2128 10p. Maltese Cross and anniversary emblem ($36\frac{1}{2} \times 38$ mm) 75 50

663 Children

1999. 50th Anniv of S.O.S. Children's Villages.
2129 **663** 10p. multicoloured . . . 85 55

1999. International Year of the Elderly.
2130 **664** 2p. black and blue . . . 20 10
2131 – 5p. black and red . . . 45 30
DESIGN: 5p. Woman.

665 Teacher and Students

666 Dove, Skull and Crossbones, Gun, Emblem and Mines

1999. Teachers' Day.
2132 **665** 5p. multicoloured . . . 45 30

1999. America. A New Millennium without Arms. Multicoloured.
2133 2p. Type **666** 20 10
2134 6p. Atomic cloud and emblem 50 30

667 Luis F. Thomen (philatelist and author)

669 Map of Caribbean and Whale

664 Man

668 Globe and Forests

1999. Stamp Day.
2135 **667** 5p. drab, black and green 45 30

1999. New Millennium. Multicoloured.
2136 3p. Type **668** 25 10
2137 5p. Astronaut, satellite, computer and man . . . 45 30

1999. 2nd Summit of African, Caribbean and Pacific Heads of State. Multicoloured.
2138 5p. Type **669** 45 30
2139 6p. Moai Statues, Easter Island 50 30
2140 10p. Map of Africa and lion 85 55

670 Means of Communication

1999. 125th Anniv of Universal Postal Union.
2141 **670** 6p. multicoloured . . . 50 30

671 Globe and "50"

1999. 50th Anniv of Union of Latin American Universities.
2143 **671** 6p. multicoloured . . . 50 30

1999. As No. 1916 but colours changed.
2144 **589** 10p. brown and silver . . 85 55

672 Juan Garcia (trumpeter)

1999. Classical Musicians.
2145 **672** 5p. blue and black . . . 45 30
2146 – 5p. mauve and black . . 45 30
2147 – 5p. green and black . . 45 30
DESIGNS: 2146, Manuel Simo (saxophonist); 2147, Jose Ravelo (clarinettist).

673 Santiago and Cotui Banknotes

1999. Centenary of Banknotes. Multicoloured.
2148 2p. Type **673** 20 10
2149 2p. San Francisco de Macoris and La Vega banknotes 20 10
2150 2p. San Cristobal and Samana banknotes . . . 20 10
2151 2p. Santo Domingo and San Pedro de Macoris banknotes (horiz) 20 10
2152 2p. Puerto Plata and Moca banknotes (horiz) 20 10

674 Emblem

1999. 75th Anniv of Spanish Chamber of Trade and Industry.
2154 **674** 10p. multicoloured . . . 85 55

675 Emblem

2000. 25th Anniv of Anti-Drugs Campaign.
2155 **675** 5p. multicoloured . . . 45 30

676 Institute Facade

2000. Duartiano Institute.
2156 **676** 2p. multicoloured . . . 20 10

677 Child's Head and Emblem

2000. Prevention of Child Abuse Programme.
2157 **677** 2p. multicoloured . . . 20 10

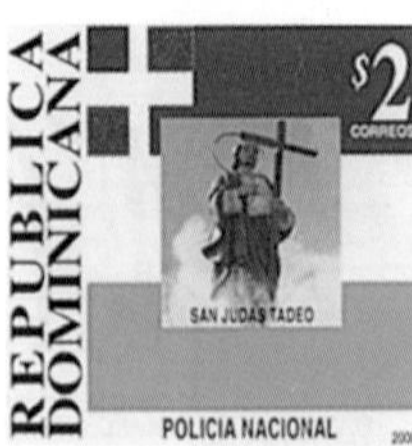

678 Flag and San Judas Tadeo (statue)

2000. National Police Force. Multicoloured.
2158 2p. Type **678** 20 10
2159 5p. Flag and Police emblem (37×28 mm) 45 30

679 Institute Building and Emblem

2000. 25th Anniv of Industry and Technology Institute.
2160 **679** 2p. multicoloured . . . 20 10

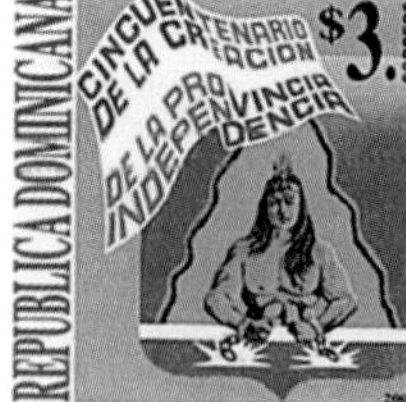

680 Emblem

2000. 50th Anniv of Independence.
2161 **680** 3p. multicoloured . . . 25 10

681 Baseball Glove and Ball

2000. 12th National Youth Games, La Romana. Multicoloured.
2162 2p. Type **681** 20 15
2163 3p. Boxing gloves 25 15
2164 5p. Emblem and mascot (35×36 mm) 45 30

682 Violinist (Dario Suro)

683 Building, Scales of Justice and Hand posting Ballot Paper

2000. Art. Multicoloured.
2165 5p. Type **682** 45 30
2166 10p. Portrait of man (Theodore Chasseriau) . . 85 55

2000. Presidential Elections.
2167 **683** 2p. multicoloured . . . 20 15

684 Enrique de Marchena Dujarric (pianist)

2000. Classical Musicians. Each black, orange and brown.
2168 5p. Type **684** 45 30
2169 5p. Julio Alberto Hernandez Camejo (pianist) 45 30
2170 5p. Ramon Diaz (flautist) 45 30

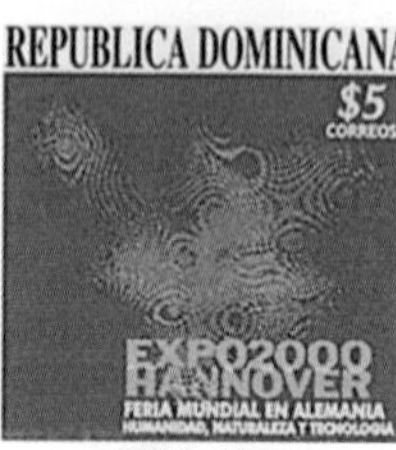

685 Emblem

2000. "EXPO 2000" World's Fair, Hanover. Multicoloured.
2171 5p. Type **685** 45 30
2172 10p. Emblem 85 55

EXPRESS DELIVERY STAMPS

E 40 Biplane

1920.
E232 E **40** 10c. blue . . . . . . 5·50 1·00

E 42

1925. Inscr "ENTREGA ESPECIAL".
E247 E **42** 10c. blue 10·00 2·00

1927. Inscr "EXPRESO".
E250 E **42** 10c. brown 5·00 1·00
E459 10c. green 2·00 70

E **123**

1945.
E539 E **123** 10c. blue, red & carm 45 20

E **137** Shield, Hand and Letter

1950.
E594 E **137** 10c. red, grn & blue 45 20

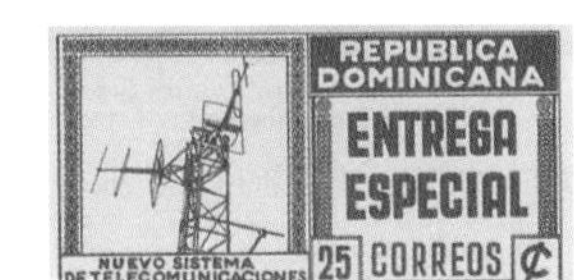
E **161**

1956.
E663 E **161** 25c. green 70 30

E **228** Pigeon and Letter

1967.
E995 E **228** 25c. blue 65 25

E **345** Globe, and Pigeon carrying Letter
E **370** Motorcycle Messenger and Airplane

1978.
E1330 E **345** 25c. multicoloured 55 30

1979.
E1385 E **370** 25c. ultram, bl & red 55 35

E **514** Motor Cyclist

1989. Special Delivery.
E1731 E **514** 1p. multicoloured 10 10

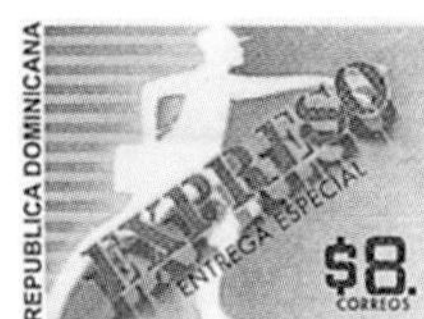
E **651** Postman

1999.
E2096 E **651** 8p. multicoloured 60 30

OFFICIAL STAMPS

O **23** Bastion of 27 Febuary
O **44** Columbus Lighthouse

1902.
O121 O **23** 2c. black and red 25 15
O122 5c. black and blue 40 15
O123 10c. black and green 45 20
O124 20c. black and yellow 55 35

1910. As Type O 23, but inscr "27 DE FEBRERO 1844" and "10 DE AGOSTO 1865" at sides.
O177 O **23** 1c. black and green 15 15
O178 2c. black and red 15 15
O179 5c. black and blue 25 20
O180 10c. black and green 55 40
O181 20c. black and yellow 1·00 55

1928.
O251 O **44** 1c. green 10 10
O252 2c. red 10 10
O253 5c. blue 15 15
O254 10c. blue 25 25
O255 20c. yellow 35 35

1931. Air. Optd **CORREO AEREO**.
O292 O **44** 10c. blue 12·00 10·00
O293 20c. yellow 12·00 10·00

O **82** Columbus Lighthouse

1937. White letters and figures.
O393 O **82** 3c. violet 25 10
O394 7c. blue 35 25
O395 10c. yellow 45 35

O **88** Columbus Lighthouse

1939. Coloured letters and figures.
O409 O **88** 1c. green 10 10
O410 2c. red 10 10
O411 3c. violet 10 10
O412 5c. blue 25 15
O414 7c. blue 55 15
O415 10c. orange 40 15
O416 20c. brown 1·00 25
O577 50c. mauve 1·25 70
O417 50c. red 2·00 85
No. O417 has smaller figures of value than No. O577.

1950. Values inscr "CENTAVOS ORO".
O578 O **88** 5c. blue 15 10
O581 7c. blue 15 10
O579 10c. yellow 35 15
O582 20c. brown 35 25
O583 50c. purple 85 55

POSTAGE DUE STAMPS

D **22**

D **110**

1901.
D117 D **22** 2c. sepia 40 10
D118 4c. sepia 50 15
D119 5c. sepia 1·00 20
D175 6c. sepia 1·40 50
D120 10c. sepia 1·60 20

1913.
D239 D **22** 1c. olive 40 35
D191 2c. olive 35 20
D192 4c. olive 40 15
D193 6c. olive 50 15
D194 10c. olive 70 30

1942. Size 20½ × 25½ mm.
D485 D **110** 1c. red 15 10
D486 2c. blue 15 10
D487 2c. blue 70 50
D488 4c. green 15 15
D489 6c. brown and buff 20 20
D490 8c. orange & yellow 25 20
D491 10c. mauve and pink 35 30

1966. Size 21 × 25½ mm. Inscr larger and in white.
D492 D **110** 1c. red 70 70
D493 2c. blue 70 70
D494 4c. green 1·75 1·75

REGISTRATION STAMPS

1935. De Merino stamps of 1933 surch **PRIMA VALORES DECLARADOS SERVICIO INTERIOR** and value in figures and words.
R339 – 8c. on ½c. (No. 316) 1·40 1·00
R340 – 8c. on 7c. blue 35 15
R342 **56** 15c. on 10c. orange 35 15
R343 – 30c. on 8c. green 1·40 50
R344 – 45c. on 20c. red 2·00 70
R345 **57** 70c. on 50c. olive 4·75 1·00

R **97** National Coat of Arms
R **98** National Coat of Arms

1940.
R448 R **97** 8c. black and red 45 20
R449 15c. black & orange 85 30
R450 30c. black and green 1·40 15
R451 70c. black & purple 3·25 1·00

1944. Redrawn. Larger figures of value and "c" as in Type R **98**.
R452 R **98** 45c. black and blue 1·60 35
R453 70c. black and green 2·00 30

1953.
R454 R **98** 8c. black and red 45 20
R455 10c. black and red 50 15
R456 15c. black & orange 9·50 2·40

R **155**
R **221**

1955. Redrawn. Arms and "c" smaller.
R646 R **155** 10c. black and red 35 10
R647 10c. black and lilac 70 25
R648 15c. black & orange 1·40 1·10
R649 20c. black & orange 60 35
R650 20c. black and red 70 45
R651 30c. black and green 90 20
R652a 40c. black and green 1·25 55
R653 45c. black and blue 2·50 1·10
R654 60c. black & yellow 1·60 1·10
R655 70c. black & brown 2·50 1·40

1963. Redrawn as Type R **97**.
R909 10c. black and orange 40 25
R910 20c. black and orange 55 45

1965.
R961 R **221** 10c. black & lilac 35 20
R962 40c. black & yellow 1·40 85

R **282a**

R **487**

1973.
R1335 R **282a** 10c. black & violet 35 15
R1148 20c. black & orge 70 55
R1149 40c. black & green 85 45
R1150 70c. black and blue 1·60 1·10

1986. Redrawn with figures of value and "c" smaller. Inscribed "PRIMA DE VALORES DECLARADOS". Arms in black.
R1664 R **487** 20c. mauve 10 10
R1665 60c. orange 20 15
R1666 1p. blue 35 30
R1667 1p.25 pink 40 35
R1668 1p.50 red 50 45
R1669 3p. green 1·00 95
R1670 3p.50 bistre 1·25 1·10
R1671 4p. yellow 1·40 1·25
R1672 4p.50 green 1·50 1·40
R1673 5p. brown 1·75 1·50
R1674 6p. grey 2·00 1·75
R1675 6p.50 blue 2·25 2·00

R **515**

1989. Inscr "PRIMA VALORES DECLARADOS". Arms in black.
R1732 R **515** 20c. purple 10 10
R1733 60c. orange 10 10
R1734 1p. blue 10 10
R1735 1p.25 pink 15 10
R1736 1p.50 red 15 15

R **569**

R **570**

1994. Arms in black.
R1867 R **569** 50c. mauve 10 10
R1868 R **570** 1p. blue 10 10
R1869 1p.50 red 15 10
R1870 2p. pink 20 10
R1871 3p. blue 25 15
R1872 5p. yellow 45 30
R1873 6p. green 55 35
R1874 8p. green 70 45
R1875 10p. silver 90 60

DUBAI Pt. 19

One of the Trucial States in the Persian Gulf. Formerly used the stamps of Muscat. British control of the postal services ceased in 1963.

On 2 December 1971, Dubai and six other Gulf Sheikhdoms formed the State of the United Arab Emirates. U.A.E. issues commenced in 1973.

1963. 100 naye paise = 1 rupee.
1966. 100 dirhams = 1 riyal.

IMPERF STAMPS. Some of the following issues exist imperf from limited printings.

1 Hermit Crab

2 Shaikh Rashid bin Said

1963.
1 **1** 1n.p. red & blue (postage) 10 10
2 A 2n.p. brown and blue 10 10
3 B 3n.p. sepia and green 10 10
4 C 4n.p. orange and purple 10 10
5 D 5n.p. black and violet 15 10
6 E 10n.p. black and brown 15 15
7 **1** 15n.p. red and drab 20 15
8 A 20n.p. orange and red 30 20
9 B 25n.p. brown and green 30 20
10 C 30n.p. red and grey 30 25
11 D 35n.p. deep blue and lilac 40 25
12 E 50n.p. sepia and orange 65 35
13 F 1r. salmon and blue 1·40 60
14 G 2r. brown and bistre 3·00 1·40
15 H 3r. black and red 6·00 3·00
16 **1** 5r. brown and turquoise 10·00 4·75
17 **2** 10r. black, turq & purple 22·00 10·00
18 J 20n.p. blue & brown (air) 25 15
19 K 25n.p. purple and yellow 1·60 30
20 J 30n.p. black and red 40 15
21 K 40n.p. purple and brown 2·10 45
22 J 50n.p. red and green 75 25
23 K 60n.p. black and brown 2·00 1·00
24 J 75n.p. green and violet 3·25 60
25 K 1r. brown and yellow 5·75 90

DESIGNS (Postage)—HORIZ: A, Common cuttlefish; B, Edible snail; C, Crab; D, Turban sea urchin; E, Radish murex; F, Mosque; G, Buildings; H, Ancient wall and tower; I, Dubai view. (Air)—HORIZ: J, Peregrine falcon in flight over bridge. VERT: K, Peregrine falcon.

3 Dhows

4 Mosquito

1963. Centenary of Red Cross.
26 **3** 1n.p. bl, yell & red (postage) 25 25
27 – 2n.p. brown, yellow & red 25 25
28 – 3n.p. brown, orange & red 25 25
29 – 4n.p. brown, red & green 30 25
30 **3** 20n.p. brn, yell & red (air) 70 40
31 – 30n.p. blue, orange & red 75 50

32 – 40n.p. black, yellow & red . . 95 95
33 – 50n.p. violet, red & turq . . 2·75 1·25
DESIGNS: 2, 30n.p. First aid field post; 3, 40n.p. Camel train; 4, 50n.p. March moth.

1963. Malaria Eradication.
34 **4** 1n.p. brown & red (postage) 10 10
35 1n.p. brown and green . . . 10 10
36 1n.p. red and blue 10 10
37 – 2n.p. blue and red 10 10
38 – 2n.p. red and brown 10 10
39 – 3n.p. blue and brown 10 10
40 **4** 30n.p. green & purple (air) 25 15
41 – 40n.p. grey and red 35 25
42 – 70n.p. yellow and purple . . 70 40
DESIGNS: 2, 40n.p. Mosquito and snake emblem; 3, 70n.p. Mosquitoes and swamp.

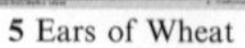

5 Ears of Wheat **7** Scout Gymnastics

6 U.S. Seal and Pres. Kennedy

1963. Air. Freedom from Hunger.
43 **5** 30n.p. brown and violet . . . 25 10
44 – 40n.p. olive and red 35 15
45 – 70n.p. orange and green . . . 70 65
46 – 1r. blue and brown 95 50
DESIGNS: 40n.p. Palm and campaign emblem; 70n.p. Emblem within hands; 1r. Woman bearing basket of fruit.

1964. Air. Pres. Kennedy Memorial Issue.
47 **6** 75n.p. black & green on grn 75 50
48 1r. black & brown on buff 1·10 75
49 1¼r. black & red on grey . . 1·60 95

1964. World Scout Jamboree, Marathon (1963).
50 **7** 1n.p. bistre & brown (postage) 10 10
51 – 2n.p. brown and red 10 10
52 – 3n.p. brown and blue 10 10
53 – 4n.p. blue and mauve 10 10
54 – 5n.p. turquoise and blue . . 10 10
55 **7** 20n.p. brown & green (air) 25 15
56 – 30n.p. brown and violet . . . 35 20
57 – 40n.p. green and blue 55 25
58 – 70n.p. grey and green 70 40
59 – 1r. red and blue . . . . . . 1·25 65
DESIGNS: 2, 30n.p. Bugler; 3, 40n.p. Wolf cubs; 4, 70n.p. Scouts on parade; 5n.p., 1r. Scouts with standard.

1964. Nos. 27/8 surch.
59b 20n.p. on 2n.p. brown, yellow and red . . . . 18·00
59c 30n.p. on 3n.p. brown, orange and red . . . . . 18·00

8 Spacecraft

1964. Air. "Honouring Astronauts". Multicoloured.
60 1n.p. "Atlas" rocket (vert) . . 10 10
61 2n.p. "Mercury" capsule (vert) 10 10
62 3n.p. Type **8** 10 10
63 4n.p. Two spacecraft 10 10
64 5n.p. As No. 60 . . . . 10 10
65 1r. As No. 61 . . . . 65 45
66 1½r. Type **8** 95 60
67 2r. As No. 63 . . . . 1·60 95

9 Globe, New York and Dubai Harbours

1964. New York World's Fair.
68 **9** 1n.p. red & blue (postage) . . 25 10
69 – 2n.p. blue, red and mauve . . 10 10
70 **9** 3n.p. green and brown . . . 25 10
71 – 4n.p. red, green & turquoise 10 10
72 **9** 5n.p. violet, olive & green . . 25 10
73 – 10n.p. black, brown & red . . 10 10
74 – 75n.p. black, grn & bl (air) 90 45
75 – 2r. ochre, turquoise & brn . . 1·75 90
76 – 3r. orange, turquoise & green 2·25 1·25

DESIGNS: 2, 4, 10n.p. New York skyline and Dubai hotel; 75n.p., 2, 3r. Statue of Liberty, New York, and "Rigorous" (tug), Dubai.

10 Flame of Freedom and Scales of Justice

1964. Air. 15th Anniv of Human Rights Declaration. Flame in red.
77 **10** 35n.p. brown and blue . . . 25 10
78 50n.p. green and blue . . . 45 25
79 1r. black and turquoise . . 85 40
80 3r. ultramarine and blue . . 2·25 90

11 Shaikh Rashid bin Said and View of Dubai

1964.
81 **11** 10n.p. olive, red & brown (postage) 20 10
82 A 20n.p. brown, red & green 35 10
83 **11** 30n.p. black, red & blue . . 35 15
84 A 40n.p. blue, red & cerise . . 45 25
85 B 1r. olive, red & brn (air) . . 1·00 45
86 C 2r. brown, red & green . . . 2·25 95
87 B 3r. black, red and blue . . . 3·50 1·60
88 C 5r. blue, red and cerise . . . 5·50 3·75
SCENES: A, Waterfront; B, Waterside buildings; C, Harbour.

1964. Air. Winter Olympic Games, Innsbruck. Nos. 55/9 optd with Olympic Rings, Games Emblem and **INNSBRUCK 1964**.
89 **7** 20n.p. brown and green . . . 40 40
90 – 30n.p. brown and violet . . . 55 50
91 – 40n.p. green and blue 75 65
92 – 70n.p. grey and green . . . . 1·10 1·00
93 – 1r. red and blue . . . . . . 2·25 1·75

1964. Air. 48th Birth Anniv of Pres. Kennedy. Optd **MAY 29** (late President's birthday).
94 **6** 75n.p. blk & grn on grn . . . 1·25 1·25
95 1r. black & brown on buff 2·25 1·90
96 1¼r. black and red on grey 2·75 2·50

1964. Air. Anti-T.B. Campaign. Optd **ANTI TUBERCULOSE** in English and Arabic, and Cross of Lorraine. Perf or roul.
101 **3** 20n.p. brown, yell & red . . 3·25 3·25
102 – 30n.p. blue, orange & red 3·25 3·25
103 – 40n.p. black, yellow & red 3·25 3·25
104 – 50n.p. violet, red & turq . . 3·25 3·25

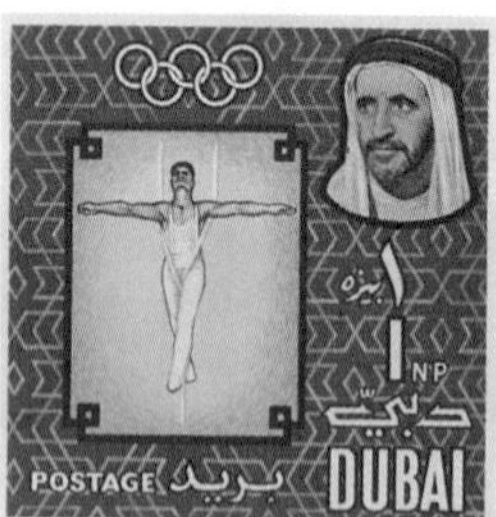

15 Gymnastics

1964. Olympic Games, Tokyo.
105 **15** 1n.p. brown and olive . . 10 10
106 – 2n.p. sepia & turquoise . . 10 10
107 – 3n.p. blue and brown . . . 10 10
108 – 4n.p. violet and yellow . . 10 10
109 – 5n.p. ochre and slate . . . 10 10
110 – 10n.p. blue and buff . . . 15 15
111 – 20n.p. olive and red . . . 25 15
112 – 30n.p. blue and yellow . . 50 25
113 – 40n.p. green and buff . . . 85 50
114 – 1r. purple and blue . . . . 2·25 1·25
DESIGNS: 2n.p. to 1r. Various gymnastic exercises as Type 12, each with portrait of Ruler.

1964. Air. 19th Anniv of U.N. Nos. 43/6 optd **UNO 19th ANNIVERSARY** in English and Arabic.
115 **5** 30n.p. brown and violet . . 65 40
116 – 40n.p. olive and red . . . . 1·25 80
117 – 70n.p. orange and green . . 1·75 1·25
118 – 1r. blue and brown . . . . 3·00 1·90

17 Shaikh Rashid and Shaikh Ahmad of Qatar

1964. "Educational Progress". Portraits in black; torch orange.
119 **17** 5n.p. purple (postage) . . . 15 10
120 10n.p. red 15 10
121 15n.p. blue 20 10
122 – 20n.p. olive 25 15
123 – 30n.p. red (air) 90 45
124 – 40n.p. brown . . . . 2·00 75
125 – 50n.p. blue . . . . 2·75 90
126 – 1r. green . . . . 3·75 1·50
DESIGNS: 20, 30, 40n.p. Shaikh Rashid and Shaikh Abdullah of Kuwait; 50n.p., 1r. Shaikh Rashid and Pres. Nasser of Egypt.

1964. Air. Outer Space Achievements, 1964. Optd **OUTER SPACE ACHIEVEMENTS 1964** in English and Arabic, **RANGER 7** and space capsule motif.
127 1r. multicoloured (No. 65) . . 2·50 2·50
128 1½r. multicoloured (No. 66) 2·50 2·50
129 2r. multicoloured (No. 67) . . 2·50 2·50

19 Globe and Rockets

1964. Space Achievements. Unissued stamps surch as T **19**. Multicoloured.
130 10n.p. on 75n.p. "Man on Moon" (25 × 78 mm) . . . 2·50 2·50
131 20n.p. on 1r.50 Type **19** . . . 3·25 3·25
132 30n.p. on 2r. "Universe" (25 × 78 mm) . . . . . . 3·25 3·25

1964. Air. 1st Death Anniv of Pres. J. Kennedy. As No. 47 with colours changed, optd **22 NOVEMBER**.
133 **6** 75n.p. black and green . . . 8·50 6·25

21 Telephone Handset

1966. Opening of Dubai Automatic Telephone Exchange.
134 **21** 10n.p. brn & grn (postage) 10 10
135 15n.p. red and plum . . . 20 10
136 25n.p. green and blue . . . 25 10
137 – 40n.p. blue & grn (air) . . 35 20
138 – 60n.p. orange and sepia . . 80 35
139 – 75n.p. violet and black . . 90 55
140 – 2r. green and red . . . . . 3·25 2·10
DESIGN: Nos. 137/40, As Type **21** but showing telephone dial.

22 Sir Winston Churchill and Catafalque

1966. Churchill Commemoration. (a) Postage.
142 **22** 1r. black and violet 40 30
143 1r.50 black and olive . . . 65 30
144 3r. black and blue . . . . 1·50 1·10
145 4r. black and red . . . . . 2·50 1·90

(b) Air. Nos. 142/5 optd **AIR MAIL** in English and Arabic and with black borders.
147 **22** 1r. black and violet 40 30
148 1r.50 black and olive . . . 65 50
149 3r. black and blue . . . . 1·50 1·10
150 4r. black and red . . . . . 2·50 1·90

23 Ruler's Palace **24** Bridge

1966.
152 **23** 5n.p. brown and blue . . . 10 10
153 10n.p. black and orange . . 10 10
154 15n.p. blue and brown . . 15 10
155 A 20n.p. blue and brown . . 20 15
156 25n.p. red and blue 20 15
157 B 35n.p. violet and green . . 30 20
158 40n.p. turquoise & blue . . 45 25
159 **24** 60n.p. green and red . . . 60 25
160 1r. ultramarine and blue 95 50
161 C 1r.25 brown and black . . 1·25 85
162 D 1r.50 purple and green . . 2·10 1·10
163 3r. brown and violet . . . 4·00 2·10
164 E 5r. red . . . . 6·75 5·25
165 10r. blue . . . . 15·00 11·00
DESIGNS—HORIZ: (28 × 21 mm): A, Waterfront, Dubai; B, Bridge and dhow. As Type **24**: C, Minaret (Ruler's portrait on right); D, Fort Dubai. VERT: (32½ × 42½ mm): E, Shaikh Rashid bin Said.

25 Oil Rig **26** "Tasman" (oil rig)

1966. Air. Oil Exploration. (a) "Land" series as T **25**.
166 – 5n.p. black and lilac . . . 20 10
167 – 15n.p. black and bistre . . 35 15
168 – 25n.p. black and blue . . . 55 30
169 – 35n.p. black and red . . . 70 35
170 – 50n.p. black and brown . . 1·00 50
171 **25** 70n.p. black and red . . . 2·25 1·10
DESIGNS—HORIZ: 5n.p. Map of Dubai; 15n.p. Surveying; 25n.p. Dubai Petroleum Company building; 35n.p. Oil drilling. VERT: 50n.p. Surveying with level.

(b) "Sea" series as T **26**.
173 **26** 10n.p. purple and blue . . 20 10
174 – 20n.p. mauve and green . . 30 10
175 **26** 30n.p. brown and green . . 55 10
176 – 40n.p. lilac and agate . . . 55 15
177 **26** 50n.p. blue and olive . . . 85 20
178 – 60n.p. blue and violet . . . 95 35
179 **26** 75n.p. green and brown . . 1·50 50
180 – 1r. green and blue . . . . 1·75 70
DESIGN: 20, 40, 60n.p. and 1r. Ocean well-head.

27 Rulers of Gulf Arab States (⅗-size illustration)

1966. Gulf Arab States Summit Conference.
182 **27** 35p. multicoloured 85 50
183 60p. multicoloured . . . . 2·25 1·40
184 150p. multicoloured . . . 4·50 3·50

28 Jules Rimet Cup

1966. World Cup Football Championship. Multicoloured.
185 40d. Type **28** 35 15
186 60d. Various football scenes 45 25
187 1r. Various football scenes . . 70 35
188 1r.25 Various football scenes 90 45
189 3r. Wembley Stadium, London . . . . 1·40 1·10

1966. England's World Cup Victory. Nos. 185/9 optd **ENGLAND WINNERS**.
191 **28** 40d. multicoloured 35 15
192 – 60d. multicoloured 45 25
193 – 1r. multicoloured 70 35
194 – 1r.25 multicoloured 90 45
195 – 3r. multicoloured . . . . . 1·40 1·10

29 Rulers of Dubai and Kuwait, and I.C.Y. Emblem

1966. International Co-operation Year (1965). Currency expressed in rupees.
197 **29** 1r. brown and green . . . 1·00 50
198 A 1r. green and brown . . . 1·00 50
199 B 1r. blue and violet . . . . 1·00 50
200 C 1r. blue and violet . . . . 1·00 50
201 D 1r. turquoise and red . . . 1·00 50
202 E 1r. turquoise and red . . . 1·00 50
203 F 1r. violet and blue . . . . 1·00 50
204 G 1r. violet and blue . . . . 1·00 50
205 H 1r. red and turquoise . . . 1·00 50
206 I 1r. red and turquoise . . . 1·00 50
HEADS OF STATE and POLITICAL LEADERS (Ruler of Dubai and): A, Pres. John F. Kennedy. B, Prime Minister Harold Wilson; C, Pres. Helou of the Lebanon; D, Pres. De Gaulle; E, Pres. Nasser; F, Pope Paul VI; G, Ruler of Bahrain; H, Pres. Lyndon Johnson; I, Ruler of Qatar.

30 "Gemini" Capsules manoeuvring

1966. "Gemini" Space Rendezvous. Mult.
208 35d. Type **30** 40 15
209 40d. "Gemini" capsules linked 40 15
210 60d. "Gemini" capsules separating 50 25
211 1r. Schirra and Stafford in "Gemini 6" 90 40
212 1r.25 "Gemini" orbits . . . 1·25 65
213 3r. Borman and Lovell in "Gemini 7" . . . . 2·00 1·25

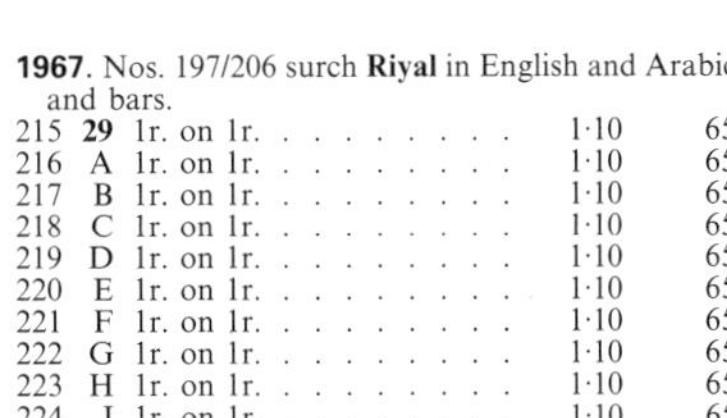

1967. Nos. 197/206 surch **Riyal** in English and Arabic and bars.
215 **29** 1r. on 1r. . . . . 1·10 65
216 A 1r. on 1r. . . . . 1·10 65
217 B 1r. on 1r. . . . . 1·10 65
218 C 1r. on 1r. . . . . 1·10 65
219 D 1r. on 1r. . . . . 1·10 65
220 E 1r. on 1r. . . . . 1·10 65
221 F 1r. on 1r. . . . . 1·10 65
222 G 1r. on 1r. . . . . 1·10 65
223 H 1r. on 1r. . . . . 1·10 65
224 I 1r. on 1r. . . . . 1·10 65

1967. Gemini Flight Success. Nos. 208/13 optd **SUCCESSFUL END OF GEMINI FLIGHT**.
226 **30** 35d. multicoloured 45 20
227 – 40d. multicoloured 45 20
228 – 60d. multicoloured 50 25
229 – 1r. multicoloured 90 40
230 – 1r.25 multicoloured . . . . 1·25 65
231 – 3r. multicoloured . . . . . 2·00 1·25

1967. Nos. 152/61, 163/5 with currency names changed by overprinting in English and Arabic (except Nos. 244/5 which have the currency name in Arabic only).
233 **23** 5d. on 5n.p. 20 10
234 10d. on 10n.p. 20 10
235 15d. on 15n.p. 30 15
236 A 20d. on 20n.p. 45 20
237 25d. on 25n.p. 50 20
238 B 35d. on 35n.p. 60 20
239 40d. on 40n.p. 80 25
240 **24** 60d. on 60n.p. . . . . . 1·25 30
241 1r. on 1r. . . . . 1·90 45
242 C 1r.25 on 1r.25 . . . . . . 3·50 90
243 D 3r. on 3r. . . . . 6·00 2·50
244 E 5r. on 5r. . . . . 11·00 5·00
245 10r. on 10r. . . . . 17·00 10·00

37 "The Moving Finger writes..."

1967. Rubaiyat of Omar Khayyam. Mult.
246 60d. Type **37** . . . . 1·10 40
247 60d. "Here with a Loaf of Bread..." . . . . 1·10 40
248 60d. "So, while the Vessels..." 1·10 40
249 60d. "Myself when young..." 1·10 40
250 60d. "One Moment in Annihilation's Waste..." . . 1·10 40
251 60d. "And strange to tell..." 1·10 40

38 "The Straw Hat" (Rubens)

1967. Paintings. Multicoloured.
253 1r. Type **38** . . . . 1·60 40
254 1r. "Thomas, Earl of Arundel" (Rubens) . . . . 1·60 40
255 1r. "A peasant boy leaning on a sill" (Murillo) . . . . 1·60 40
See also Nos. 273/5.

39 Ruler and Lanner Falcon

40 "Bayan" (dhow)

1967.
257 **39** 5d. red and orange 60 30
258 10d. sepia and green . . . 60 25
259 20d. purple and blue . . . 75 25
260 35d. turquoise & mauve . . 1·00 35
261 60d. blue and green . . . 2·00 55
262 1r. green and purple . . . 2·75 1·10
263 **40** 1r.25 purple and blue . . . 2·75 55
264 3r. purple and blue . . . . 3·25 1·60
265 5r. violet and green . . . . 6·75 3·25
266 10r. green and mauve . . . 10·00 6·00

41 Globe and Scout Badge

1967. World Scout Jamboree, Idaho. Mult.
267 10d. Type **41** 35 15
268 20d. Dubai scout and dromedaries 70 20
269 35d. Bugler 90 25
270 60d. Jamboree emblem and U.S. flags . . . . 1·60 30
271 1r. Lord Baden-Powell . . . 2·25 60
272 1r.25 Idaho on U.S. Map . . 3·00 1·25

1967. Goya's Paintings in National Gallery, London. As T **38**. Multicoloured.
273 1r. "Dr. Peral" . . . . . . 1·60 45
274 1r. "Dona Isabel Cobos de Porcel" . . . . 1·60 45
275 1r. "Duke of Wellington" . . 1·60 45

42 Kaiser-i-Hind ("Teinopalpus imperialis")

1968. Butterflies and Moths. Multicoloured.
277 60d. Type **42** . . . . 1·60 25
278 60d. "Erasmia pulchella" . . 1·60 25
279 60d. Gaudy baron ("Euthalia indica") . . . . 1·60 25
280 60d. Atlas moth ("Attacus atlas") . . . . 1·60 25
281 60d. "Dysphania militaris" 1·60 25
282 60d. "Neochera butleri" . . 1·60 25
283 60d. African monarch ("Danaus chrysippus") . . 1·60 25
284 60d. Chestnut tiger ("Danaus tytia") . . . . 1·60 25

43 "Madonna and Child" (Ferruzi)

1968. Arab Mothers' Day. Multicoloured.
285 60d. "Games in the Park" (Zandomeneghi) 40 25
286 1r. Type **43** 65 35
287 1r.25 "Mrs Cockburn and Children" (Reynolds) (wrongly inscr "Cookburn") . . . . . . 1·25 60
288 3r. "Self-portrait with Daughter" (Vigee-Lebrun) 1·90 1·10

44 "Althea rosea"

1968. Flowers. Multicoloured.
289 60d. Type **44** . . . . 1·60 25
290 60d. "Geranium lancastriense" . . . . . . 1·60 25
291 60d. "Catharanthus roseus" 1·60 25
292 60d. "Convolvulus minor" 1·60 25
293 60d. "Opuntia" . . . . . . 1·60 25
294 60d. "Gaillardia aristata" . . 1·60 25
295 60d. "Heliopsis" . . . . . . 1·60 25
296 60d. "Centaurea moschata" 1·60 25

45 Running

1968. Olympic Games, Mexico. Multicoloured.
297 15d. Type **45** 70 10
298 20d. Swimming 75 10
299 25d. Boxing . . . . 1·25 15
300 35d. Water-polo . . . . . . 1·40 20
301 40d. High jump . . . . . . 1·75 20
302 60d. Gymnastics . . . . . . 2·50 30
303 1r. Football . . . . 3·50 40
304 1r.25 Fencing . . . . 4·75 50

46 "Young Girl with Kitten" (Perronneau)

1968. Children's Day. Multicoloured.
306 60d. "Two Boys with Mastiff" (Goya) 50 15
307 1r. Type **46** 80 30
308 1r.25 "Soap Bubbles" (Manet) . . . . 1·25 35
309 3r. "The Fluyder Boys" (Lawrence) . . . . 2·00 60

47 Common Pheasant

1968. Arabian Gulf Birds. Multicoloured.
310 60d. Type **47** . . . . 1·90 20
311 60d. Red-collared dove ("Turtle Dove") . . . . . . 1·90 20
312 60d. Western red-footed falcon ("Red-footed flaca") 1·90 20
313 60d. European bee eater ("Bee-eater") . . . . . . 1·90 20
314 60d. Hoopoe . . . . 1·90 20
315 60d. Great egret ("Common Egret") . . . . 1·90 20
316 60d. Little terns . . . . . . 1·90 20
317 60d. Lesser black-backed gulls . . . . 1·90 20

48 "Bamora" (freighter), 1914

1969. 60th Anniv of Dubai Postal Service. Multicoloured.
318 25d. Type **48** 30 10
319 35d. De Havilland D.H.66 Hercules airplane, 1930 . . 40 10
320 60d. "Sirdhana" (liner), 1947 80 20
321 1r. Armstrong Whitworth Atalanta airplane, 1938 . . 80 45
322 1r.25 "Chandpara" (freighter), 1949 . . . . . 1·25 60
323 3r. Short Sunderland flying boat, 1943 . . . . 1·50 80

49 "Madonna and Child" (Bartolome Murillo)

1969. Arab Mothers' Day. Multicoloured.
325 60d. Type **49** 60 20
326 1r. "Madonna with Rose" (Francesco Mozzola (Parmigianino)) . . . . . 1·10 30
327 1r.25 "Mother and Children" (Peter Paul Rubens) . . . 1·50 60
328 3r. "Campori Madonna" (Antonio Correggio) . . . 3·50 90
No. 326 wrongly inscribed "Mazzuoli".

50 Porkfish

1969. Fishes. Multicoloured.
329 60d. Type **50** . . . . 1·25 25
330 60d. Greasy ("Spotted") grouper . . . . 1·25 25
331 60d. Diamond fingerfish ("Moonfish") . . . . . 1·25 25
332 60d. Striped sweetlips . . . . 1·25 25
333 60d. Blue-ringed angelfish ("Blue angel") . . . . . 1·25 25
334 60d. Roundel ("Texas") skate 1·25 25
335 60d. Black-backed ("Striped") butterflyfish . . . . . . 1·25 25
336 60d. Emperor ("Imperial") angelfish . . . . 1·25 25

51 Burton, Doughty, Burckhardt, Thesiger and Map

1969. Explorers of Arabia.
337 **51** 25d. brown and green . . . 70 20
338 60d. blue and brown . . . 1·25 35
339 1r. green and blue . . . . 2·50 50
340 1r.25 black and red . . . . 3·25 1·25

52 Underwater Storage Tank Construction

1969. Oil Industry. Multicoloured.
341 5d. Type **52** 20 15
342 20d. Floating-out storage tank 45 15
343 35d. Underwater tank in operation 85 45
344 60d. Ruler, oil rig and monument . . . . 1·75 60
345 1r. Fateh marine oilfield . . . 2·40 90

53 Astronauts on Moon

1969. 1st Man on the Moon. Multicoloured.

346		60d. Type **53** (postage)	50	25
347		1r. Astronaut and ladder	65	25
348		1r.25 Astronauts planting U.S. flag on Moon (horiz) (62 × 38 mm) (air)	85	35

54 "Weather Reporter" launching Radio-Sonde and Handley Page Hastings Weather Reconnaissance Airplane

1970. World Meteorological Day. Mult.

349		60d. Type **54**	45	15
350		1r. Kew-type radio-sonde and dish aerial	65	30
351		1r.25 "Tiros" satellite and rocket	80	40
352		3r. "Ariel" satellite and rocket	1·50	90

55 New Headquarters Building

1970. New U.P.U. Headquarters Building, Berne. Multicoloured.

353		5d. Type **55**	25	10
354		60d. U.P.U. Monument, Berne	1·00	25

56 Charles Dickens

1970. Death Cent of Charles Dickens. Mult.

355		60d. Type **56**	35	15
356		1r. Signature, quill and London sky-line (horiz)	70	35
357		1r.25 Dickens and Victorian street	90	70
358		3r. Dickens and books (horiz)	1·75	1·40

57 "The Graham Children" (Hogarth)

1970. Children's Day. Multicoloured.

359		35d. Type **57**	25	10
360		60d. "Caroline Murat and Children" (Gerard) (vert)	55	20
361		1r. "Napoleon as Uncle" (Ducis)	1·00	40

58 Shaikh Rashid

1970. Multicoloured.

362		5d. Type **58**	15	15
363		10d. Dhow building (horiz)	25	10
364		20d. Al Maktum Bridge (horiz)	45	15
365		35d. Great Mosque	50	10
366		60d. Dubai National Bank (horiz)	85	15
367		1r. International airport (horiz)	1·75	25
368		1r.25 Harbour project (horiz)	2·50	65
369		3r. Hospital (horiz)	3·50	1·40
370		5r. Trade school (horiz)	5·25	2·75
371		10r. Television and "Intelsat 4"	9·00	5·00

The riyal values are larger, 40 × 25 or 25 × 40 mm.

59 Terminal Building and Control Tower

1971. Opening of Dubai International Airport. Multicoloured.

372		1r. Type **59**	1·90	1·25
373		1r.25 Airport entrance	2·40	1·50

60 Telecommunications Map and Satellites

1971. Outer Space Telecommunications Congress, Paris. Multicoloured.

374		60d. Type **60** (postage)	40	15
375		1r. Rocket and "Intelsat 4" (air)	55	30
376		5r. Eiffel Tower and Goonhilly aerial	2·00	1·75

61 Scout Badge, Fan and Map

62 Albrecht Durer

1971. 13th World Scout Jamboree, Asagiri (Japan). Multicoloured.

377		60d. Type **61**	35	15
378		1r. Canoeing	60	30
379		1r.25 Rock-climbing	75	55
380		3r. Scouts around camp-fire (horiz)	1·50	1·25

1971. Famous People (1st issue). Mult.

381		60d. Type **62** (postage)	25	10
382		1r. Sir Isaac Newton (air)	65	30
383		1r.25 Avicenna	90	45
384		3r. Voltaire	1·40	75

See also Nos. 388/91.

63 Boy in Meadow

1971. 25th Anniv of U.N.I.C.E.F. Mult.

385		60d. Type **63** (postage)	25	15
386		5r. Children with toys (horiz)	1·75	75
387		1r. Mother and children (air)	35	15

1972. Famous People (2nd issue). As T **62**. Multicoloured.

388		10d. Leonardo da Vinci (postage)	10	10
389		35d. Beethoven	30	15
390		75d. Khalil Gibran (poet) (air)	30	20
391		5r. Charles de Gaulle	2·75	2·00

65 Nurse supervising children

1972. Air. World Health Day. Multicoloured.

392		75d. Type **65**	70	20
393		1r.25 Doctor treating baby (horiz)	1·50	70

67 Gymnastics

1972. Olympic Games, Munich. Multicoloured.

399		35d. Type **67** (postage)	25	10
400		40d. Fencing	45	10
401		65d. Hockey	65	20
402		75d. Water-polo (air)	90	25
403		1r. Horse-jumping	1·10	35
404		1r.25 Athletics	1·50	60

POSTAGE DUE STAMPS

1963. Designs as T **1** but inscr "DUE".

D26	L	1n.p. red and grey	20	20
D27	M	2n.p. blue and bistre	20	20
D28	N	3n.p. green and red	20	20
D29	L	4n.p. red and green	20	20
D30	M	5n.p. black and red	20	20
D31	N	10n.p. violet and olive	25	25
D32	L	15n.p. red and blue	85	55
D33	M	25n.p. green & brown	1·90	1·40
D34	N	35n.p. orange and blue	4·25	2·75

DESIGNS—HORIZ: L, Common European cockle; M, Common blue mussel; N, Portuguese oyster.

D 66 Shaikh Rashid

1972.

D394	**D 66**	5d. grey, blue & brn	55	60
D395		10d. brn, ochre & bl	80	90
D396		20d. brn, red and blue	1·50	1·60
D397		30d. violet, lilac & blk	2·00	2·25
D398		50d. brn, ochre & pur	4·25	4·50

DUNGARPUR Pt. 1

A state of Rajasthan. Now uses Indian stamps.

12 pies = 1 anna; 16 annas = 1 rupee.

1 State Arms

2 Maharawal Lakshman Singh

1933.

1	**1**	¼a. yellow	—	£160
2		¼a. red	—	£450
3		¼a. brown	—	£300
4		1a. blue	—	£130
5		1a. red	—	£1500
6		1a.3p. mauve	—	£190
7		2a. green	—	£275
8		4a. red	—	£475

1932. T **2** (various frames).

9	**2**	¼a. orange	£800	65·00
10		½a. red	£225	48·00
11		1a. blue	£225	40·00
12		1a.3p. mauve	£800	£180
13		1¼a. violet	£850	£180
14		2a. green	£1000	£350
15		4a. brown	£800	£150

DUTTIA (DATIA) Pt. 1

A state of Central India. Now uses Indian stamps.

12 pies = 1 anna; 16 annas = 1 rupee.

2 (½a.) Ganesh

3 (4a.) Ganesh

1894?. Imperf.

1	**2**	½a. black on green	£8000	
2a		2a. blue on yellow	£2500	

Nos. 1/2a are as Type **2**, but have rosettes in lower corners.

1896. Imperf.

4	**3**	¼a. black on orange	£3250	
5		½a. black on green	£4500	
6		2a. black on yellow	£1900	
7		4a. black on red	£1300	

Stamps of Type **3** come with the circular handstamp as shown on Type **2**. Examples of Nos. 4/5 without handstamp are worth slightly less than the prices quoted.

1896. Imperf.

8b	**2**	½a. black on green	19·00	£190
3		1a. red	£2500	£3000
9		1a. black	75·00	£225
10		2a. black on yellow	25·00	£200
11		4a. black on red	21·00	£170

4 (½a.)

5 (¼a.)

1897. Imperf.

12	**4**	½a. black on green	70·00	£425
13		1a. black	£140	
14		2a. black on yellow	85·00	
15		4a. black on red	80·00	

1899. Imperf, roul or perf.

16c	**5**	¼a. red	3·75	16·00
38		¼a. blue	2·75	10·00
37		¼a. black	4·25	20·00
17		½a. black on green	2·50	16·00
30		½a. green	5·50	22·00
35		½a. blue	3·25	14·00
39		½a. pink	3·00	15·00
18		1a. black	2·75	16·00
31		1a. purple	5·00	23·00
36		1a. pink	3·00	16·00
19b		2a. black on yellow	2·50	18·00
32		2a. brown	13·00	26·00
33		2a. lilac	5·50	26·00
20		4a. black on red	3·00	17·00
34		4a. brown	75·00	

INDEX